WHO'S WHO
IN ASIA
AND THE PACIFIC NATIONS

WHO'S WHO
IN ASIA
AND THE PACIFIC NATIONS

(Formerly Who's Who in Australasia and the Pacific Nations)

Publisher:
Nicholas S. Law

Compiling Editors:
Benjamin Kay
Cara Bootman

Editor in Chief:
Jon Gifford

Senior Editor/Production Manager:
Jocelyn Timothy

Assistant Editors:
Barbara Cooper
Ann Dewison
Gillian George

All communications to: International Biographical Centre,
Cambridge CB2 3QP, England

WHO'S WHO
IN ASIA
AND THE PACIFIC NATIONS

FOURTH EDITION

1999

International Biographical Centre
Cambridge, England

©1999 by Melrose Press Ltd, Cambridge, England

First Edition   1989

Second Edition   1991

Third Edition   1997

Fourth Edition   1999

ISBN: 0 948875 63 1

Printed and bound in Great Britain by
MPG Books Ltd, Bodmin, Cornwall

CONTENTS

Foreword by the Director General   VII

Table of Abbreviations   VIII - XX

Biographies Section   1 - 487

Appendix A   491 - 504

Appendix B   505-508

Appendix C   509-511

Appendix D   512-523

INTERNATIONAL BIOGRAPHICAL CENTRE
RANGE OF REFERENCE TITLES

From one of the widest ranges of contemporary biographical reference works published under any one imprint, some IBC titles date back to the 1930's. Each edition is compiled from information supplied by those listed, who include leading personalities of particular countries or professions. Information offered usually includes date and place of birth; family details; qualifications; career histories; awards and honours received; books published or other creative work; other relevant information including postal address. Naturally there is no charge or fee for inclusion.

New editions are freshly compiled and contain on average 80-90% new information. New titles are regularly added to the IBC reference library.

Titles include:

Dictionary of International Biography

Who's Who in Asia and the Pacific Nations

International Authors and Writers Who's Who

International Who's Who in Community Service

International Who's Who in Education

International Who's Who in Medicine

International Who's Who in Music and Musicians' Directory, Volume One, Classical and Light Classical

International Who's Who in Music, Volume Two, Popular Music

Men of Achievement

The World Who's Who of Women

International Who's Who in Poetry and Poets' Encyclopaedia

Outstanding People of the 20th Century

2000 Outstanding Scientists of the 20th Century

2000 Outstanding Artists and Designers of the 20th Century

2000 Outstanding Scholars of the 20th Century

Enquiries to:

International Biographical Centre
Cambridge CB2 3QP
England

FOREWORD BY THE EDITORIAL DIRECTOR

The Fourth Edition of Who's Who in Asia and the Pacific Nations (formerly Who's Who in Australasia and the Pacific Nations) has undergone an expansive overhaul in response to the development of its target region. This edition, which contains some 8000 entries, has had to live up to the huge success of the previous volumes and it has taken a great deal of time and hard work to fully revise, edit, compile and print a fitting successor to the previous editions.

The target coverage has been expanded to over 70 countries and territories in the Asian Pacific area including many areas that have received little or no recognition in a reference work before. *Who's Who in Asia and the Pacific Nations* includes men and women of significant social standing and influence in a variety of fields and professions in this perpetually evolving and developing region. Every attempt has also been made to cover important governmental, civic, diplomatic and royal individuals who occupy these areas.

Due to the successful response to the last edition, the Fourth Edition will also include a useful appendix, listing organizations and societies from a wide variety of fields and professions. Indeed, the demand for general information on this geographical area has seen the inclusion of three more appendices to this edition which cover details such as currencies, capital cities, embassies and Chambers of Commerce.

We at the IBC are proud once more to bring together details of the lives of men and women of many professions, interests and nationalities so that *Who's Who in Asia and the Pacific Nations* will be useful to general readers as well as to libraries and researchers throughout the world.

It cannot be emphasized too strongly that there has been no charge or fee of any kind for inclusion of any biographee; entry has been made based on personal merit.

We are grateful to the countless organizations and associations throughout the region which have made recommendations to our editors and researchers. We must also thank readers of previous editions who have assisted in the same way. To all involved, including the researchers and editors of the IBC, many thanks.

While every care has been taken to eliminate errors and to ensure accuracy and relevance when compiling a work of this magnitude, it is always possible that an occasional error may be made. If this is the case here, my apologies in advance.

Nicholas S Law

International Biographical Centre
Cambridge CB2 3QP, England

September 1999

TABLE OF ABBREVIATIONS

The following abbreviations are frequently used in the compilation of biographical sketches

A

AA	Associate of Arts
AAAS	American Association for the Advancement of Science
AAUP	American Association of University Professors
AAUW	American Association of University Women
ABC	American Broadcasting Company
	Australian Broadcasting Commission
ABI	American Biographical Institute
AC	Companion of the Order of Australia
Acad	Academic
Acady	Academy
Acct	Accountant
Acctcy	Accountancy
Acctng	Accounting
Ach(mnt)	Achieve(ment)
ACP	American College of Physicians
ACS	American College of Surgeons
ACT	Australian Capital Territory
Adj	Adjunct
Admin	Administration
Admnstr	Administrator
Admnstv	Administrative
Adv(d)	Advance(d)
Advmnt	Advancement
Advsr(s)	Advisor(s)
Advsry	Advisory
Advt	Advertisement
Advtng	Advertising
AFB	Air Force Base
Agcy	Agency
Agric	Agriculture
Agricl	Agricultural
Agt	Agent
AIA	American Institute of Architects
AIM	American Institute of Management
AK	Alaska
AL	Alabama
ALA	American Library Association
Alban	Albania
Alta	Alberta
AM	Member of the Order of Australia
Am(n)	America(n)
AMA	American Medical/Management/ Marketing/Missionary Association
AMA	Assistant Masters' Association
	Associate of the Museums Association
	Auckland Mathematical Association
	Australian Medical Association
Amb	Ambassador
AO	Officer of the Order of Australia
Appt	Appointment
Apr	April
Apt	Apartment
AR	Arkansas
Arch	Architecture
Archt(l)	Architect(ural)
ASCAP	American Society of Composers, Authors & Publishers
Assn	Association
Assoc(d)	Associate(d)
Asst	Assistant
Astron	Astronomy
Att-Gen	Attorney-General
Attd('d)	Attend(ed)
Attn	Attention

Attng	Attending
Atty	Attorney
Aug	August
AUS	Army of the United States
Aust	Australia; Austria
Austl	Australian
Austn	Austrian
Auth	Author; Authoress; Authentic; Authorize
Authy	Authority
Auto	Automatic; Automobile; Automotive
Autobiog	Autobiography
Autobiogl	Autobiographical
AUT(S)	Association of University Teachers (Scotland)
Aux	Auxiliary
AVA	Audio Visual Aids
	Alberta Veterinary Association (Can)
	Associate of Valuers' Association
	Australian Veterinary Association
AVC	American Veterans' Committee
	Army Veterinary Corps
Av Cert	Aviator's Certificate
AVD	Army Veterinary Department
Ave	Avenue
AVI	Association of Veterinary Inspectors
AVLA	Audio Visual Language Association
AVM	Air Vice-Marshal
AVR	Army Volunteer Reserve
AVRI	Animal Virus Research Institute
AVS	Anti-Vivisection Society
AWAS	Australian Women's Army Service
Awd('d)	Award(ed)
AWeldI	Associate of the Welding Institute
AWG	Art Workers' Guild
AZ	Arizona

B

b	born
BA	Bachelor of Arts
BAA	Bachelor of Art and Architecture
BAAdmin	Bachelor of Arts in Administration
BACAH	British Association of Consultants in Agriculture and Horticulture
BAcc	Bachelor of Accountancy
BAChem	Bachelor of Arts in Chemistry
BAdmin	Bachelor of Administration
BA(Econ)	Bachelor of Arts in Economics
BA(Ed)	Bachelor of Arts in Education
BAgEc	Bachelor of Agricultural Economics
BAgr(Hort)	Bachelor of Agriculture (Horticulture)
BAgrSc	Bachelor of Agricultural Science
BA(J)	Bachelor of Arts in Journalism
Balt	Baltimore
BA(Mus)	Bachelor of Arts in Music
BAN	British Association of Neurologists
BAO	Bachelor of Obstetrics
Bapt	Baptist
BA(PE)	Bachelor of Arts in Physical Education
BAPM	British Association of Physical Medicine
BAPS	British Association of Paediatric/Plastic Surgeons
Bar	Barrister
BArch	Bachelor of Architecture
BAS	Bachelor of Agricultural Science
BA(SS)	Bachelor of Arts in Social Science
bat	Battalion
BA(Theol)	Bachelor of Arts in Theology

BBA	Bachelor of Business Administration
BBC	British Broadcasting Corporation
BC	British Columbia (Canada)
BCE	Bachelor of Civil Engineering
BCL	Bachelor of Civil Law
BCS	Bachelor of Commercial Science
Bd	Board
BD	Bachelor of Divinity
BDentSc	Bachelor in Dental Science
BDS	Bachelor of Dental Surgery
BEChem	Bachelor of Chemical Engineering
BEcon	Bachelor of Economics
BEd	Bachelor of Education
BEE	Bachelor of Electrical Engineering
bef	before
beg	beginning
BEM	British Empire Medal
BEng	Bachelor of Engineering
BEngTech	Bachelor of Engineering in Technology
BFA	Bachelor of Fine Arts
BFor	Bachelor of Forestry
BForSc	Bachelor of Forestry Science
bibliog	bibliographer
BIM	British Institute of Management
biochem	biochemistry
biog	biograph; biographer; biographic; biographical; biography
biogeog	biogeography
bio	biology
biol	biological
biolst	biologist
bish	bishop
BJ	Bachelor of Journalism
BJuris	Bachelor of Jurisprudence
bkg	banking; booking; book-keeping
Bklyn	Brooklyn (USA)
bldg	building
BldgE	Building Engineer
BLett	Bachelor of Letters
BLibSc	Bachelor of Library Science
BLitt	Bachelor of Literature
BLL	Bachelor of Laws
blvd	boulevard
BMA	British Medical Association
BMath	Bachelor of Mathematics
BMed	Bachelor of Medicine
BMedBiol	Bachelor of Medical Biology
BMedSc	Bachelor of Medical Science
BMus	Bachelor of Music
BN	Bachelor of Nursing
BNSc	Bachelor of Nursing Science
BOptom	Bachelor of Optometry
BoT	Board of Trade
bot(l)	botanic(al)
botst	botanist
BPaed	Bachelor of Paediatrics
BPharm	Bachelor of Pharmacy
BPhil	Bachelor of Philosophy
BPhysEd	Bachelor of Physical Education
br	branch
brdcst(ng)	broadcast(ing)
Brig	Brigade; Brigadier
Brig-Gen	Brigadier-General
Brisb	Brisbane
Brit	British; Britain; Britannia; Briton
BRurSc	Bachelor of Rural Science
BS	Bachelor of Science
BScApp	Bachelor of Applied Science
BSLitt	Bachelor of Sacred Letters
BSTh	Bachelor of Sacred Theology
BT	Bachelor of Teaching
BTech	Bachelor of Technology
BTechEd	Bachelor of Technical Education
BTh	Bachelor of Theology
bur	bureau
bus	business
Bus Mngr	Business Manager
BVM	Bachelor of Veterinary Medicine
BVSc	Bachelor of Veterinary Science
BVMS	Bachelor of Veterinary Medicine and Surgery
BVS	Bachelor of Veterinary Surgery

C

CA	California
CAA	Canadian Authors' Association
	Civil Aviation Authority
CAB	Canadian Association of Broadcasters
	Citizens' Advice Bureau
CAD	Civil Air Defense (USA)
CAG	Composers'-Authors Guild
Calg	Calgary (Can)
Can(ad)	Canada(ian)
cand	candidate
Cantab	Cantabrigian (Cambridge University Degrees)
Cap	Captain
CAPAC	Composers' Authors' and Publishers' Association of Canada
Cartog	Cartographer; cartography
cas	casual; casualty
cath	cathedral; catholic
CB	Companion of the Most Honourable Order of the Bath
CBC	Children's Book Council (USA)
	Canadian Broadcasting Corporation
CBE	Commander of the Order of the British Empire
CBS	Columbia Broadcasting System (USA)
CCNY	City College of the City University of New York
CDA	Canadian Dental Association
	Civil Defence Act
	Colonial Dames of America
CDAS	Civil Defence Ambulance Service
CDipFA	Certified Diploma in Finance and Accounting
CdO	Commissioned Officer
Cdre	Commodore
C&E	Customs & Excise
CEA	Canadian Electrical Association
	Council for Educational Advance
	Council for Economic Advisers (USA)
CEng	Chartered Engineer
CEO	Chief Education Officer
cert	certificate; certified; certify
CFA	Chartered Financial Analyst (USA)
	Council of Foreign Affairs
CFM	Cadet Forces Medal
	Council of Foreign Ministers
CGI	City and Guild Institute
CGM	Conspicuous Gallantry Medal
Ch	Church
Chan	Chancellor
Chanc	Chancery
chap	chapel; chaplain
chapt	chapter
Ch Clk	Chief Clerk
Ch Coll	Christ's College, Cambridge
chem	chemical; chemist; chemistry
chf	chief
chgph	choreographer; choreographic; choreography
Ch Hist	Church Hist
Chgo	Chicago
Chmbr(s)	Chamber(s)
Chmbr of Comm	Chamber of Commerce
Chmn	Chairman

CIA	Central Intelligence Agency
	Corporation of Insurance Agents
CIB	Central Intelligence Board
CIC	Chemical Institute of Canada
CIEE	Companion of the Institution of Electrical Engineers
CIIA	Canadian Institute of International Affairs
CIMarE	Companion of the Institute of Marine Engineers
CIMechE	Companion of the Institution of Mechanical Engineers
CIS	Catholic Information Society
	Chartered Institute of Secretaries
CISPM	International Confederation of Popular Music Societies
CIT	California Institute of Technology
	Carnegie Institute of Technology
civ(n)	civil(ian)
clin(l)	clinic(al)
clk	clerk
cmdng	commanding
Cmdr	Commander
Cmdr in Chf	Commander in Chief
Cmdt	Commandant
CMH	Congressional Medal of Honor (USA)
cmnty(ies)	community(ies)
CMO	Chief Medical Officer
Cncl	Council
Cnclr	Councillor
Cnslr	Counsellor
cnslt(ng)	consultant(ing)
cntr	centre; center
cntrl	central
co	county; company
CO	Colorado; Commanding Officer
C of E	Church of England
Col	Colonel
coll	college
collect	collection
com	commerce
coml	commercial
comm(s)	communication(s)
commdty	commodity
commdties	commodities
commn(s)	commission(s)
commng	commissioning
commnr	commissioner
comp	Comparative
conf(s)	conference(s)
confedn	confederation
congl	congregational
Cons	Conservative
conserv	conservation
const(l)	constitution(al)
constrn	construction
contbn(s)	contribution(s)
contbr(s)	contributor(s)
contemp	contemporary
conv	convention
co-op	co-operative; co-operation
co-ord(ng)	co-ordinate; co-ordinator; co-ordinating
co-ptnr	co-partner
corp	corporation
corresp	correspondent; corresponding
Corr Mbr	Corresponding Member
CPA	Certified Public Accountant
CPH	Certificate in Public Health
cres	crescent
crt	court
CStJ	Commander of the Order of St John of Jerusalem
CT	Connecticut

D

ctf	certificate; certify
cttee	committee
cty	city
CUNY	City University of New York
cur	current
curric	curriculum
CWA	Crime Writers' Association
C'wlth	Commonwealth
CWL	Catholic Women's League
Czech	Czechoslovakia

d	daughter(s)
DA	Doctor of Arts
	District Attorney (USA)
DAgri	Doctor of Agriculture
DAgriSc	Doctor of Agricultural Science
DAppSc	Doctor of Applied Science
DAR	Daughters of the American Revolution
DArch	Doctor of Architecture
DBA	Doctor of Business Administration
DBE	Dame Commander of the Order of the British Empire
DBM	Diploma in Business Management
DC	District of Columbia
	Deputy Chief/Commissioner/ Consul/Counsel
DCB	Dame Commander of the Most Honourable Order of the Bath
DCE	Doctor of Civil Engineering
	Diploma in Chemical Engineering
DCh	Doctor of Surgery
DCH	Diploma in Child Health
DCL	Doctor of Civil Law
DCM	Distinguished Conduct Medal
DCMG	Dame Commander of the Most Distinguished Order of St Michael and St George
DCnL	Doctor of Canon Law
DComL	Doctor of Commercial Law
DComm	Doctor of Commerce
DCompL	Doctor of Comparative Law
DC of S	Deputy Chief of Staff
DCSc	Doctor of Commercial Science
DCVO	Dame Commander of the Royal Victorian Cross
DD	Doctor of Divinity
	Department of Defense (USA)
DDG	Deputy Director General
DDH	Diploma in Dental Health
DDPH	Diploma in Dental Public Health
DDS	Doctor of Dental Surgery
DDSc	Doctor of Dental Science
DE	Delaware
Dec	December
decd	deceased
DEcon	Doctor of Economics
DEconSc	Doctor of Economic Science
ded	dedicate(d); dedication
DEd	Doctor of Education
Def	Defence; Defense; defendent
deg	degree
Deleg	Delegate
Dem	Democratic; Democrat
DEn	Doctor of English
DEng	Doctor of Engineering
Dep Dir	Deputy Director
Dept	Department
des(ig)	Designer; Design(ate)
det	detach; detachment; detail; determine
Dev	Development
DFA	Department of Foreign Affairs

	Diploma in Foreign Affairs
	Doctor of Fine Arts
DFC	Distinguished Flying Cross
DFM	Distinguished Flying Medal
DH	Doctor of Humanities
DHL	Doctor of Humane Letters
Dip(l)	Diploma(te)
Dir	Director
Dir Gen	Director General
Dist	District
Distbn	Distribution
Distbr	Distributor
Disting	Distinguished
Div	Division
div	divorced
DJur	Doctor of Jurisprudence
DJurSc	Doctor of Juristic Science
DL	Doctor of Laws
DLit	Doctor of Letters
DLitt	Doctor of Literature
DLittS	Doctor of Sacred Letters
DLSc	Doctor of Library Science
DMath	Doctor of Mathematics
DMD	Doctor of Dental Medicine
DMed	Doctor of Medicine
DMedSc	Doctor of Medical Science
DMus	Doctor of Music
Doct	Doctorate; Doctoral
DPharm	Doctor of Pharmacy
DPol Sc	Doctor of Political Science
DPsy	Doctor of Psychology
Dpty	Deputy
Dr	Doctor; Drive
DrChem	Doctor of Chemistry
Drhc	Honorary Doctor
DrNatSci	Doctor of Natural Science
DrPH	Doctor of Public Health/Hygiene
DSc	Doctor of Science
DSC	Distinguished Service Cross
DSM	Distinguished Service Medal
DSO	Distinguished Service Order
DSocS	Doctor of Social Sciences
DSTh	Doctor of Sacred Theology
DStJ	Dame of Justice of the Order of St John of Jerusalem
DTech	Doctor of Technology
DTh	Doctor of Theology
DUniv	Doctor of the University
DVM	Doctor of Veterinary Medicine
DVS	Doctor of Veterinary Science
DZool	Doctor of Zoology

E

e	east
ea	each
east	eastern
ecol	ecology
econ(s)	economic(s)
ed	editor; edition
Ed in Ch	Editor in Chief
edit	edited
editl	editorial
educ	education
educl	educational
educr	educator
EEC	European Economic Community
eg	for example
E in Ch	Engineer in Chief
elec(l)	electric(al)
electn	electrician
electr engin	electrical engineering
electron(s)	electronic(s)

elem	elementary
em	eminent
Em	Eminence
Emb	Embassy
emer	emergency
Emer	Emeritus
empld	employed
ency	encyclopaedia
Eng	England
Engl	English
engr	engineer
engrng	engineering
ent	entrance
ENT	Ear, Nose & Throat
environ(l)	environment(al)
epid	epidemic
Episc	Episcopal; Episcopalian
equip	equipment
equiv	equivalent
ergon	ergonomics
esn(tl)	essence; essential
esp	especially
est(ab)	establish(ment)
etc	et cetera
Eur(n)	Europe(an)
eV	registered association (Germany)
evac(n)	evacuate; evacuation
eval	evaluate; evaluation
Evang	Evangelical; Evangelist
evid	evidence
ex	excellent; except; excess; exchange;
exam	examination
exch	exchange
exec	executive
exhib(n)	exhibit(ion)
exhibnr	exhibitioner
exp	experience
expdn	expedition
expmt(l)	experiment(al)
ex-Pres	ex-President
ext	extend
extn	extension

F

fab	fabric; fabricate; fabulous
fac	Faculty
FACA	Fellow, American College of Anaesthetists
FAIA	Fellow, Association of International Accountants
	Fellow, American Institute of Architects
FAIC	Fellow, American Institute of Chemists
FAIS	Fellow, Amalgamated Institute of Secretaries
FALPA	Fellow, Incorporated Society of Auctioneers and Landed Property Agents
FAO	Food and Agriculture Organization
FAPHI	Fellow, Association of Public Health Inspectors
FAS	Faculty of Architects and Surveyors
FBA	Federal Bar Association
FBI	Federal Bureau of Investigation (USA)
FCA	Fellow, Institute of Chartered Accountants
FCH	Fellow, Chartered Insurance Institute
FCIS	Fellow, Chartered Institute of Secretaries
FDA	Food and Drug Administration (USA)
Feb	February
fed	federal
fedn	federation

Fell(shp)	Fellow(ship)
fem	female
fest	festival
FGS	Fellow, Geological Society
fgt	freight
FIA	Fellow, Institute of Actuaries
FIArb	Fellow, Institute of Arbitrators
FIB	Fellow, Institute of Bankers
fic(t)	fiction(al)
FIC	Fellow, Institute of Chemistry
FIChemE	Fellow, Institution Chemical Engineers
fig	figure
FIInst	Fellow, Imperial Institute
FIITech	Fellow, Institute of Industrial Technicians
FILE	Fellow, Institute of Legal Executives
fin(l)	finance; financial
Fin Sec	Financial Secretary
FJI	Fellow, Institute of Journalists
FL	Florida
FLA	Fellow, Library Association
Flt Cmndr	Flight Commander
Flt Lt	Flight Lieutenant
Flt Sgt	Flight Sergeant
fmd	formed
fmr(ly)	former(ly)
fndn	foundation
fndng	founding
fndr	founder
fndry	foundry
fol(ng)	follow(ing)
for	foreign
formn	formation
FPA	Family Planning Association
FPS	Fellow, Pharmaceutical Society
FRAM	Fellow, Royal Academy of Music
frat	college fraternity
FRCP	Fellow, Royal College of Physicians
FRCS	Fellow, Royal College of Surgeons
FRGS	Fellow, Royal Geographical Society
FRIBA	Fellow, Royal Institute of British Architects
FRIC	Fellow, Royal Institute of Chemistry
FRICS	Fellow, Royal Institute of Chartered Surveyors
FRS	Fellow, Royal Society
FRSA	Fellow, Royal Society of Arts
FRSL	Fellow, Royal Society of Literature
FSA	Fellow, Society of Antiquaries Fellow, Society of Arts
FSE	Fellow, Society of Engineers
Ft	Fort
fund	fundamental
fwd(ng)	forward(ing)
FWeldI	Fellow, Welding Institute
FZS	Fellow, Zoological Society

G

GA	Georgia
gall	gallery
GATT	General Agreement of Tariffs and Trade
gaz	gazette
GB	Great Britain
GBE	Knight (or Dame), Grand Cross Order of the British Empire
GC	George Cross
GCB	Knight, Grand Cross of the Bath
GCMG	Knight Grand Cross of the Most Distinguished Order of St Michael and St George
GCSI	Knight Grand Commander of the Most Exalted Order of the Star of India
GCStJ	Dame Grand Cross of the Order of St Johnof Jerusalem
GCVO	Dame Grand Cross of the Royal Victorian Order
gdn(s)	garden(s)
Gen	General
geog	geography; geographer
geogl	geographical
geol	geology; geologist; geologic
geom	geometry; geometer; geometric
geophy	geophysics
geopol	geopolitics
Geo Wash Univ	George Washington University
GIMechE	Grad, Institution of Mechanical Engineers
GINucE	Grad, Institution of Nuclear Engineers
GM	George Medal
GMB	Grand Master of the Order of the Bath
GMBE	Grand Master of the Order of the British Empire
GmbH	limited liability co
GMC	General Medical Council
GMIE	Grand Master of the Order of the Indian Empire
GMKP	Grand Master of the Knights of St Patrick
GMMG	Grand Master of the Order of St Michael and St George
Gov	Governor
Gov Gen	Governor General
govng	governing
govt(l)	government(al)
grad	graduate
grp	group
Grp Capt	Group Captain
Grp Cmdr	Group Commander
gt(r)	great(er)
gtee	guarantee
gynae	gynaecology
gynaecol	gynaecological

H

Hal Orch	Hallé Orchestra
Harv L S	Harvard Law School
Harv Univ	Harvard University
hb	haemoglobin
h'cap(d)	handicap(ped)
Hd	Head
hdng	heading
hem	heamorrage
HEW	Dept of Health, Educational and Welfare
HI	Hawaii
hist	history
histl	historical
histn	historian
hlth	health
HM	Her/His Majesty
HM	Headmaster; Headmistress
HMA	Headmasters' Association
HNC	Higher National Certificate
HND	Higher National Diploma
hndbk	handbook
HO	Head Office Home Office
HoC	House of Commons
HoD	head of department
HoL	House of Lords
HoR	House of Representatives
hon(s)	honorary; honour(s); honor(s); honourable

pnl	panel		rada	radioactive
pnt	point		RAF	Royal Air Force
pol(s)	politic(s)		rat	rate
Pol Ad	political adviser		ratn	ration
polit	political		ratng	rating
Pol Sc	Political Science		RC	Roman Catholic
pop	popular; population		RCAF	Royal Canadian Air Force
pop mus	popular music		RC Ch	Roman Catholic Church
pops	popular concerts		RCN	Royal Canadian Navy
pos	positive			Royal College of Nursing
posn	position		rcpt	receipt
poss	possible		rd	road
postgrad	postgraduate		rdr	reader
pot	potential		re	with reference to
ppr	paper		Rear Adm	Rear Admiral
ppty	property		rec	record
PR	public relations		rcd	received
prac	practice		recdng	recording
prcs	process		recip	recipient
prej	prejudice		recog	recognition
prelim	preliminary		recom	recommend
Pres(dtl)	President(ial)		Rec SEc	Recording Secretary
Presby	Presbyterian		ref	reference
prev	previous		reg(l)	region(al)
prf	proof		regd	registered
pri	priority		regt	regiment
Prin	principal		rehab	rehabilitation
pro	proceed; procedure		relig	religion; religious
prod(r)	produce(r)		rels	relations
prodn	production		rep	represent
Prof	Professor		repr	representative
profl	professional		repro	reproduce
profn	profession		repub(n)	republic(an)
prog	programme; progam		res	resident
progng	programming		resn	residence
proj(n)	project(ion)		resc(s)	resource(s)
prom	promote		resp	responsible
prop	property		retd	retired
prov	province		Rev	Reverend
provcl	provincial		rfrd	referred
pseud	pseudonym		RI	Rhode Island
psych	psychiatrist; psychiatric; psychiatry		rl est	real estate
psychol	psychologist; psychologic; psychology		RN	Royal Navy
pt	part			Registered Nurse (USA)
PTA	Parent-Teacher Association		RNA	Romantic Novelists' Association
ptnr	partner		rot	rotary
pt-time	part-time		rout	routine
pt ex	part exchange		Roy	Royal
pub	public		R Phil S	Royal Philharmonic Society
publng	publishing		rprt(d)	report(ed)
publr	publisher		rpt(d)	repeat(ed)
publs	publications		rqr	require
publshd	published		rqmt	requirement
pur	purchase		R S Arts	Royal Society of Arts
pvte	private		rsch(r)	research(er)
			rsn	reason
			rsq	rescue
			rtd	return(ed)
			rte	route
			rtg	rating
			rtn	retain
			Rt Hon	Right Honourable
			Rt Rev	Right Reverend

Q

QC	Queen's Counsel
QFSM	Queen's Fire Service Medal
Qld	Queensland
qlty	quality
QM	Quartermaster
QMG	Quartermaster General
qnty	quantity
qtly	quarterly
qual	qualification

S

S	South
s	son
SA	Société Anonyme
	South Australia
S Afr	South Africa
S Am	South America

R

RAA	Royal Academy of Arts
RAAF	Royal Australian Air Force

San Fran	San Francisco
SAR	Sons of the American Revolution
Sask	Saskatchewan (Canada)
S At	South Atlantic
SC	South Carolina
sch	school
sched	schedule(d)
sci	science; scientific
sci-fi	science fiction
schl(shp)	scholar(ship)
S Coll	Staff College
s con	self contained
Sc & T	Science and Technology
sculp	sculptor; sculptress; sculptural; sculpture
SD	South Dakota
SEATO	Southeast Asia Treaty Organization
Sec	Secretary
Sec-Gen	Secretary-General
Sec of St	Secretary of State
secnd	secondary
sect	section
sel	select; selected; selection
sem	seminary
Sen	Senator
SEN	State Enrolled Nurse
sen clk	senior clerk
S Eng Off	Senior Engineer Officer
sent	sentence
sep	separate
Sept	September
seq	sequel; sequence
ser	series; serial
serv(s)	service(s)
sess	session
sev	several
sfgd	safeguard
sgd	signed
sgl	single
Sgt	Sergeant
Sgt Maj	Sergeant Major
SHAEF	Supreme Headquarters, Allied Expeditionary Forces
SHAPE	Supreme Headquarters, Allied Powers in Europe
shd	should
shtg	shortage
sig	signal
sign	signature
sim(l)	similar(ly)
sing	singular
sis	sister
sit	situation
Smith Inst	Smithsonian Institute (USA)
sml	small
SML	Science Museum Library
snd	sound
Snr	senior
soc	society
socl	social; socialist
sociol	sociology
sociolgcl	sociological
sociolgst	sociologist
soc sci	social science
Sol(-Gen)	Solicitor(-General)
soln	solution
solv	solvent
soph	sophomore
Sov	Soviet
sov	sovereign
spec	special; specially; specific; specimen; spectrum; speculation
spec appt	special appointment
special	specialized
specif	specifically; specification
spp	species

spt	support
sptng	supporting
sq	square
sqdn	squadron
Sqdn Ldr	Squadron Leader
SRN	State Register
S/Sgt	Staff Sergeant
St	street
	Saint
stand	standard
stat(s)	statistic(s)
statn	statistician
stdy	study
sten	stenographer
stenog	strenography
stn	station
stndng	standing
stud	student
subd	subdivision
subsq(ly)	subsequent(ly)
subj	subject
subs	subsidiary
subst	substitute
suc	succeed
succ	successor
suff	sufficient
sug(gn)	suggest(ion)
sum	summary
sums	summons
SUNY	State University of New York
super	superior
supp(l)	supplement(ary)
Supt	Superintendent
suptng	superintending
supvsr	supervisor
surg	surgeon; surgical; surgery
surv	survey; surveyor
swbd	switchboard
syl	syllable
syll	syllabus
sym	symbol; symbolic
symm	symmetry; symmetrical
symp	symposium
symph	symphony
synth	synthetic
syst	system

T

tab	table
tar	tariff
Tas	Tasmania
T Aviv	Tel Aviv
taxn	taxation
tchng	teaching
tchr	teacher
tctl	tactical
TD	Teaching Diploma
tech	technical
techn	technician
technol	technology
tecn	technique
tel	telephone
telecomms	telecommunications
teleg	telegraphic
telg	telegraphist
teleph	telephony
temp	temperature
ten	tenant
tency	tenancy
term	terminology
tert	tertiary

test	testimony
testm	testimonial
text	textile
Th	Theology
th	theatre
theat	theatrical
theo	theology
theol	theological
theor	theory
theort	theoretical
therap	therapeutic
therm	thermal
thermochm	thermochemistry
thermodyn	thermodynamics
thes	thesis
TILS	Technical Information and Library Service
TIS	technical information service
tkt	ticket
t'ment	tournament
tmpry	temporary
TN	Tennessee
togr	together
tour	tourism
tox	toxicology
toxi	toxicologist
toxicol	toxicological
tpk	turnpike
trad	tradition
tradl	traditional
trag	tragedy
trans	translate
transf(d)	transfer(red)
transl	translation
transp(n)	transport(ation)
transpl(n)	transplant(ation)
trav	travel
Trb	Tribune
Tr Co	trust company
Tr Coll	training college
treas	treasurer; treasury
trml	terminal
trnee	trainee
trng	training
trp	troop
tstee	trustee
tstr	tester
TTD	Teachers Training Diploma
turb	turbine
turboprop	turbine propelled
tv	television
TVA	Tennessee Valley Authority
TX	Texas
typ	type; typical
typog	typography
ty	territory

U

UC	University College
UCL	University College, London
UCLA	University of California at Los Angeles
UGC	University Grants Committee
UK	United Kingdom
UN	United Nations
unab	unabridged
unaccomp	unaccompanied
unan	unanimous
unasgd	unassigned
unatt	unattached
unauthd	unauthorized
unbd	unbound

unc	uncertain
UNC	United Nations Command
uncir	uncirculated
unclass	unclassified
uncond	unconditioned
uncor	uncorrected
undergrad	undergraduate
undsgd	undersigned
undtk	undertake
UNESCO	United Nations Educational, Scientific and Cultural Organization
unexpl	unexplained
UNFAO	United Nations Food and Agricultural Organization
UNGA	United Nations General Assembly
UNHQ	United Nations Headquarters
UNIC	United Nations Information Centre
UNICEF	United Nations International Children's Emergency Fund
unif	uniform
unis	unison
univ	university
unkn	unknown
unop	unopposed
unpub	unpublished
U of A	University of Alaska
U of NC	University of North Carolina
UPI	United Press International (USA)
URA	University Research Associates
urg	urgent
urol	urology
USA	United States of America
USAAF	United States Army Air Force
USAF	United States Air Force
USAr	United States Army Reserve
USCorps	United Services Corps
USDA	United States Department of Agriculture
u/sec	under secretary
USN	United States Navy
USNR	United States Naval Reserve
USSAF	United States Strategic Air Force
USSR	Union of Soviet Socialist Republics
usu(ly)	usual(lly)
USV	United States Volunteers
UT	Utah
UTC	University Training Corps
utd	united
UV	ultra-violet
UVL	ultra-violet light

V

VA	Virginia
	Veterans' Administration
V Adm	Vice Admiral
vac	vacant; vacancy
vacc	vaccine; vaccination
val	value; valley
valn	valuation
valid	validate; validation
var	various
varn	variation
vasc	vascular
vch	vehicle
vcm	vacuum
vcnty	vicinity
vd	void
veg	vegetation
veh	vehicular
Ven	Venerable
vent	ventilate
vern	version

vet	veterinary
VFW	Veterans of Foreign Wars
vfy	verify
VI	Virgin Islands
Vic	Victoria
vis	visitor
visng	visiting
vltg	voltage
vlv	valve
voc	vocational
vocab	vocabulary
voctl	vocational
vol	volume
volun	volunteer
voly	voluntary
vou	voucher
VP	Vice President
	Vice Principal
Vry	Viceroy
vsn	vision
VT	Vermont
Vte	Viscount
Vtess	Viscountess
vtd	voted
vtng	voting
vy	very

Y

YC	Yale College
YEA	Yale Engineering Association
YEO	Youth Employment Officer
YES	Youth Employment Service
YMCA	Young Men's Christian Association
yng	young
yr(ly)	year(ly)
yth	youth
YUL	Yale University Library
Y Univ	Yale University
YWCA	Young Women's Christian Association

Z

Zag	Zagreb
Zam	Zambia
ZC	Zionist Congress
ZG	Zoological Gardens
zoochem	zoochemistry
zoogeog	zoogeography
zool	zoology; zoologist; zoological
ZS	Zoological Society
Zur	Zürich

W

W	west
w	with
WA	Washington State
	Western Australia
war	warrant
warn	warning
warr	warranty
Wash DC	Washington DC
wea	weather
weap	weapon
Wel Adm	welfare administration
weld	welding
Wel Dept	welfare department
west	western
Westmr	Westminster
Wes Univ	Wesleyan University
WGA	Writers' Guild of America
WHO	World Health Organization
whse	warehouse
whlse	wholesale
WI	Wisconsin
Wind I	Windward Islands
wit	witness
withdrl	withdrawal
witht	without
wk	week
Wm & Mary Coll	William and Mary College
wrk	work
wrkng	working
wt	weight
WTAA	World Trade Alliance Association
WV	West Virginia
WWF	World Wildlife Fund
WWI	World War I
WWII	World War II
WY	Wyoming

Biographies

Biographies

A

ABALKHAIL Sheikh Mohamed Ali, b. 1935, Buraida. m. 1966, 2 s, 2 d. Education: BA, Cairo Univ. Appointments: Asst Dir of Off of Min of Comm, later Dir; Dir Gen of Inst of Pub Admin; Dep Min of Fin Nat Econ, then Vice-Min; Min of State; Min for Fin Nat Econ 1975-95; Chmn Bd Saudi Int Bank London; Chmn Ctr for Econ and Mngmt Studies. Honours: Belgium, Egypt, France, Niger, Pakistan, Saudia Arabia, Sudan, Germany, Morocco, Spain. Membership: JP Morgan Int Cncl. Hobbies: Reading, some sports. Address: P O Box 287, Riyadh 11411, Saudi Arabia.

ABANI M C, b. 18 Dec 1942, Jodhpur, India. Scientist. m. Mrs Kamal Abani, 2 d. Education: MSc, Phys, Univ of Jodhpur, India; PhD, Phys, Gujarat Univ, 1991. Appointment: Sci Offr, AEET, India (now Bhabha Atomic Rsch Cntr, Mumbai), 1965-. Publications: Published many pprs in sci jrnls. Membership: Sec, IARP, 1991-93; Life Mbr, IARP, INS and NAARRI. Hobbies: Social work; Teaching; Watching Movies and History. Address: Head, RM&CA Section, RSS Division BARC, Mumbai 400 085, India.

ABBOTT Russell Joseph, b. 1 Mar 1942, Brooklyn, USA. Professor. 2 s, 1 d. Education: BA, Columbia Univ, 1962; MA, Harvard Univ, 1963; PhD, Univ of S CA, 1973. Appointment: Prof, CA Univ, Los Angeles. Publication: Software Engineering, 1986. Membership: ACM. Address: Department of Mathematics & Computer Science, California University, Los Angeles, CA 90032, USA.

ABD GAZEE Mohd Yusoff, b. 16 July 1949, Gemas, N Sembilan. Oil Company Executive. m. Suhainy, 12 Nov 1974, 4 d. Education: BS, Mechs Engrng, Sek Men Than Ku Abdul Rahman, Gemas, 1967. Appointments: Steet Maker, Malayawata Penai, 1968-75; Mechl Techn, Esso Refinary, 1975-82; Senior Exec, Mngr, Pefronas Penapisan, 1982-. Memberships: Inst Diagnostic Engrs, UK; Amn Soc Mechl Engrng; Amn Welding Soc; Boy Scout Assoc. Hobbies: Computers; Comm Electrons; Aviation. Address: 18 Jalan 59 Rantau Petronas, Kerteh Terengganu 24300, Malaysia.

ABDEL JABER Tayseer, b. 1 June 1940, Jerusalem. Economist. m. Hind, 27 Feb 1970, 2 s, 2 d. Education: BSc, Econs, Cairo Univ; MSc, PhD, Econs, Univ S CA. Appointments: Cmmnr, UN Under Sec-Gen, Min of Labour and Socl Devel. Publications: Economic Integration in Developing Countries, 1970; Arab Economy Integration, 1972. Honours: Independence & Starr Decoration, Jordan, 1975, 1994. Memberships: Chmn, Inst of Mngmt Cnslts, 1995-97; Jordan Bus Assn; Sec-Gen, World Affairs Cncl, Bd Mbr, 1998-. Hobbies: Gardening; Table tennis; Travel. Address: PO Box 926550, Amman 11110, Jordan.

ABDOULLAEV Kamoloudin, (Kamoul Abdullo), b. 21 Feb 1950, Gharm, Tajikistan. Historian. m. Lola Makhmoudova, 5 Mar 1983, 1 s, 1 d. Education: Tajik State Univ; Grad, Dushanbe Inst of Hist of USSR, Moscow. Appointments: Rsch Fell, Inst of Hist of Acady of Sci of Tajikistan, 1975; Hd, Dept Polit Rsch, Inst of Polit Rsch, 1989; Asst Prof, Tajik State Univ, Hist, 1991; Proj Offr, Aga Khan Hum Proj for Cntrl Asia, 1997. Publications: With the Weapon of a Printed Word, 1999; series of articles. Honours: Fulbright Schlshp, Wash DC, 1994; Kennan Inst for Advd Russian Studies, Regl Exchange Schl, 1995; Brit Acady Visng Schlr, 1996. Memberships: Cntrl Asia Rsch and Dev Cntr, USA, repr in Tajikistan. Hobbies: Travel; Tennis. Address: a/ia 92, 734025, Dushanbe, Tajikistan.

ABDOULMANOV Khoussain, b. 11 June 1927. Lecturer. m. Evgeniy Gulevich, 1 s, 1 d. Education: Refrigerating Engr, Astrakhan Inst of Fishing Fleet & Econ w hons, 1953; Cand Tech Scis, Cncl of Moscow Engrng Bldg Inst, 1965; Awd'd rank Prof, Cttee of Russian Fedn of Higher Educ, 1993. Appointments: Asst

Lectr, -1960; Snr Lectr, 1960-90; Prof, 1990-; currently, Hd, Refrigerating Dept, Petropavlovsk-Kamchatsky State Acady of Fishing Fleet. Honour: Veteran of Labour. Address: Prospect Rybakov 13/1, Flat 78, Petroparlovsk-kamchatsky 683024, Russia.

ABDUL AL AZIZ BASHIR Munir, b. 28 Sept 1930, Mosul. m. Gecsy Iren 1961, 2 s. Education: Fine Arts Inst, Baghdad. Appointments: Instr, Fine Arts Acady, 1946-60; Dir Cmnty Arts Acady, 1950-56; Hd, Music Dept, Baghdad Radio and TV, 1949-60; Art Advsr and Gen Dir, Music Dept, Iraqi Min of Culture and Info 1973-93; Gen Dir, Babylon Intl Fest, 1986-91; Vice-Pres, Intl Music Cncl, UNESCO, 1986-91; Sec-Gen, Arab Acady of Music, 1974-; Creative Works: Has perfd solo in more than 50 countries sine 1954; Num recordings. Honours: Num hons and awds inclng: Tchaikovsky Medal-USSR; Chopin Medal, Poland; UNESCO Intl Prize; Decorations from France, Spain Poland, Italy, Jordan, Cuba. Hobby: Reading. Address: Arab Academy of Music, Al-Mansour, P O Box 1650, Baghdad, Iraq.

ABDUL LATIF Haji Jaya bin, b. 1939. m. 6 children. Education: Manchester Univ. Appointments: Pres, Brunei State Yth Cncl 1977-80; Govt Dep Agt, London, 1981-82; Cmdr to Malaysia 1982-84; High-Commnr 1984-86; Amb, Philippines, 1986-87; Perm Repr of Brunei Darussalam to UN, 1987-93. Membership: Fmr Mbr, World Assembly of Yth; World Assembly of Muslim Yth and Asian Yth Cncl. c/o Ministry of Foreign Affairs, Jalan Subok, Bandar Seri Begawan 1120, Brunei.

ABDUL-GHANI Abdulaziz, b. 4 July 1939, Haifan, Taiz. m. Aseya Hamza 1966, 4 s, 1 d. Education: Tchr High Schl, Aden Coll, Colorando Coll, Colorado Univ. Appointments: Tchr, Balquis Coll, Aden, 1964-67; Min, Hlth Sana'a, 1967-68; Dir, Yemen Bank for Reconstrn and Dev, 1968; Min Econs, 1968-69; Chmn, Tech Off Bd Plng, 1969-71; Yemen Oil Co, 1971; Gov, Centrl Bank Yemen, 1971-75; Lectr, Univ Sana'a, 1972-74; Supreme Cncl for Reconstrn of Earthquake Affected Areas, 1983; PM, 1975-80, 1983-90, 1994-97. Honours: Phd, Mareb Sash, First Class, 1987. Membership: Cmd Cncl, 1975-78; Vice-Pres, 1980-83; Perm Cttee, Presdtl Advsry Cncl, Yemeni Econ Soc, 1983; Presdtl Cncl, 1990-94; Gen People's Congress. Hobbies: Swimming, Hiking. Address: c/o Office of the Prime Minister, Sana'a, Yemen.

ABDULGANI Roeslan, b. 1914, Surabaya, East Java. m. Sihwati Nawangwulan 1938, 2 s, 3 d. Education: Tchr Trng Coll, Surabaya; Active in Nat Yth Mvmt seeking indep from Dutch; Active in anti-Japanese underground during Japanese occ. Appointments: Ed bakti, East Java 1945; Sec-Gen min of Info 1947-53; Sec-Gen min For Affrs 1953-56; Deleg to UN 1951, 1956, 1966; Sec-Gen Afro-Asian Conf, Bandung 1955; head deleg to Suez Conf 1956; Min For Affrs 1956-56; Vice-Chmn Nat Cncl 1957--59; Vice-Chmn Supreme Advsry Cncl 1959-62; Co-ordng Min and Min of Info 1963-65; Dep PM for Polit Instns 1966; Perm Repr to UN 1967-71; Lectr Monash Univ and other Austrl Univs 1972; Rsch Fell Prince Bernhard Fund, Netherlands, UK 1973; Vice-Pres 24th UN Gen Asst 1969; Cnslt Natl Def and Scrty Cncl of Indonesia; Cnslt on probs of mass media UNESCO Paris 1977; Chmn Team of Advsrs to Pres on State Ideology Pancasila 1978. Publications: In Search of Indonesian Identity, The Bandung Spirit, Indonesian and Asian-African Nationalism, Pantjasila: The Prime Mover of the Indonesian Revolution, Hero's Day: In Memory of the Fighting in Surabaya on 10 November 1945, The Hundred Days in Surabaya that Shook Indonesia, Impact of Utopian-Scientific and Religious Socialism on Indonesian Socialism, 25 Years: Indonesia in the UN, Personal Experiences During the Japanese Occupation, and others. Honours: Several honours degrees; Indonesian medals. Membership: Const Assbly 1957; PNI-Indonesian Natl Pty. Hobbies: Walking; Reading; Classical music. Address: 11 Jalan Diponegoro, Jakarta, Indonesia.

ABDULKASAN Meriam, b. 9 Nov 1959, Poblacion Buluan, India. Social Worker. m. H Abusama, 29 Dec

1979, 3 s, 1 d. Education: BS, Socl Wrk; Grad, MPA. Appointments: Socl Wrkr, 1981-88; SWO III, 1988-. Memberships: Philippine Assn of Socl Wrkrs. Hobbies: Reading; Cooking; TV Programmes. Address: 29 Int B Donothio Compound, Sinsuat Ave, Catototo City, Philippines.

ABDULLAH Al Naser, b. 31 Dec 1957, Dhaka, Bangladesh. Journalist. m. Nazma Hossain, 21 Nov 1986, 3 s. Education: MSS; LLB. Appointments: Chmn, Bd of Eds, Dainik Birol, The Daily Evening News, Islamic News Soc. Memberships: Bangladesh Jrnlsts Assn; Bangladesh Supreme Crt Bar Assn. Hobby: Reading Religious Books. Address: 55/7 Paikpara, Mirpur-1, Dhaka 1216, Bangladesh.

ABDULLAH Yousuf bin Al-Alawi bin. Appointment: Minister of State for Foreign Affairs, Oman. Address: Ministry of Foreign Affairs, POB 252, Muscat 113, Oman.

ABDULLAH BIN MOHD SALLEH Tan Sri, b. 24 June 1926, Malacca. m. Mahani Abdul Razak, 2 s, 1 d. Education: Malay Coll, Kuala Kangsar; Univ Malaya, Singapore. Appointments: Posts in Admin and Dip Serv, 1955-71; Sec-Gen, Min of Agric and Fisheries, 1972; Dir-Gen, Pub Serv Dept, 1974; Chf Sec to Govt of Malaysia, Sec to Cabinet, Hd of Civ Serv, 1976-78; Chmn and Chf Exec, PETRONAS Natl Pet Co, Malaysia, 1979-83, Pres, 1984-87. Hobby: Golf. Address: 21 Jalan Setiajaya, Damansara Heights, Kuala Lumpur, Malaysia.

ABDULLAH IBN ADBUL AZIA AL-SAUDHRH (Crown Prince), Saudi Arabia. Appointments: Cmdr, Natl Guard, 1962-; Second Dep, PM, 1975-82; First Dep, PM and Cmdr, Natl Guard, June 1982-; Became Crown Prince, June 1982. Hobbies: Hunting; Horse riding. Address: 21 Jalan Setiajaya, Damansara Heights, Kuala Lumpur, Malaysia.

ABDULLOJANOV Abdumalik, b. 6 Jan 1949, Khodzent. Education: Odessa Inst of Technol. Appointments: Dep Chf Engr, Dep Dir Kaizakum Mill 1971-73; Dep Dir, Dir Nauss Mill 1973-80; First Dep Min of Purchases Tajik SSR 1980-86; First Dep, Min of Bread Production, 1986-87; Min, 1987-92; Chmn NON Corp, Sept-Nov 1992; PM, Tajikistan, 1992-93; Amb to Russia 1993-95; Unsuccessful Presdtl Cand, Nov 1994. Membership: Acady of Ind fmr USSR Cncl of Mins.

ABE Tohru, b. 30 Nov 1930, Tokyo, Japan. President, Japan Rheumatism Association; Professor of Medicine. m. Haruko Abe, 2 d. Education: Department of Medicine, Keio University, Tokyo, Japan. Appointment: Dir, Saitama Medl Cntr/Sch Kawagoe, Japan. Membership: Pres, Japan Rheumatism Assn, 1993-99. Hobbies: Collection of China wear; Classical music. Address: 7-3-2 Minami Aoyama, Minato-ku, Tokyo 107-0062, Japan.

ABEL Rajaratnam, b. 11 Sept 1945, Prakasapuram. Physician. m. Jolly, 25 June 1975, 1 s, 1 d. Education: MB; Bach of Surg; MBBS; MPH. Appointments: Physn, Scheer Mem Hosp, Banepa; Nepal, 1971-72; Physn, Seventh Day Adventist Hosp, Ranchi, India, 1972-77; Nuzvid, India, 1977-78. Honours: Delta Omega, Alpha Chapt. Hobbies: Reading; Following major sports; Travel. Address: A-1 Ruhsa Campus, PO Vellore District, KV Kuppam 632209, India.

ABEYSEKERA Irangani Manel, b. 14 Aug 1933. Former Diplomat and Ambassador of Sri Lanka; Consultant on Gender Development. m. Mr Hector Abeysekera. Education: MA (Oxon); Mbr, New Hall, Cambridge. Appointments: 1st Woman in Sri Lanka For Serv, 1958; Chf of Protocol, 1974-80; Amb to Thailand and Permanent Repr to ESCAP, 1980-84; Amb to Germany, Austria and Switz, 1988-92; Dir, Gen (Polit Affairs), Min of For Affairs, 1992-93. Honours: Zonta Woman of Achievement, 1985; Hon Fell, Somerville Coll, Oxford, 1996. Memberships: Current Pres, Sri Lanka Women's Conf; Cnslt of 104 affiliates countrywide); Chairperson, Natl Cttee on Women for Sri Lanka, 1999-2000; Coord, Intl Rels, SAARC Fedn of Univ Women, 1998-2001; Mbr of Bd of Colombo YWCA,

1998-. Hobbies: Music; Reading; Theatre; Gardening. Address: 23/3 Rosmead Place, Colombo 00700, Sri Lanka.

ABIDI Saiyed Asif Husain, b. 4 Apr 1940, Baragaon, India. Scientist; Educator. m. Sayeeda Tasneem, 30 Jan 1967, 1 s, 2 d. Education: PhD; MPhil; MSc. Appointments: Snr Fisheries Insp, Govt of Uttar Pradesh, 1962-63; Lectr, St Thomas Coll, 1963-65; Scientist, Intl Indian Ocean Expedition Prog, 1965-66; Scientist, Natl Inst of Oceanography, 1966-70; Fisheries Offr, Dir of Fisheries, Govt of Tanzania, 1970-76; Snr Scientist, Natl Inst of Oceanography, 1976-78; Dir of Fisheries, Govt of India, Andaman and Nicobar Is, 1978-80; Snr Scientist, Offr in Charge, Natl Inst of Oceanography, 1980-83; Prin Sci Offr, Govt of India, Dept of Ocean Dev, 1983-87; Dir, 1987-95; Advsr, 1995-96; Dir and Vice Chan, Cntrl Inst of Fisheries Educ, Seemed Univ 1996-. Creative Works: 90 Sci Rsch Publs; 100 Pop Sci Articles; 18 Books. Honours: Gold Medal, Zool Soc of India; Great Son of the Soil Awd; Dr Norman H Dill mem Gold medal, Indian Soc of Biosci. Memberships: Fell, Natl Acady of Sci; Fell, Zool Soc of India; Fell, Zool Soc of London; Fell, Soc of Biosci; Fell, Ultrasonic Soc of India; Fell, Indian Fisheries Assn. Hobbies: Badminton; Fishing; Reading; Writing. Address: Central Inst of Fisheries Education, Seven Bungalows, Versova, Andheri, Yari Road, Mumbai 400061, Inida.

ABNER Kunar Luckner, b. 1939. Government Official. m. Betty Knisha, 1962, 3 children. Education: AA. Appointments: US Armed Forces, 1962-64; Clk, Cong Nitijela, 1966-69; Mbr, 1970-; Mbr, Legislature, 1979-; Min of Jus, Govt of Marshall Is, Majuro. Memberships: Vice Chmn, Marshalls Electric Co; Marshall Is Sewer and Water Co; Marshall Is Fishing Inc, appropriation cttee; Copra Stabilization Bd, Mbr, Advsry Bd; Marshall Is Dev Bd; Marshall Is Tennis Club. Address: Ministry of Justice, PO Box 2, Majuro, MH 96960, Marshall Islands.

ABRAHAM Plammoottil, b. 19 July 1936, Kerala, India. Scientist; Editor. m. Lily, 4 Jan 1963, 5 s, 1 d. Education: MSc. Appointments: Health Phys Div, BARC; CIRUS Reactor, Plutonium Plant, Trombay; Health Phys, Tarapur Atomic Power Stat, 1967-72. Publications include: Light of Life, mng ed; How's Your Life?, auth; num mag articles; How's Your Family?, ed; How Do You Write?. Honours: Awd, Pentecostal Press Assn of India, 1994. Memberships include: IAEA Tech Cttee; Sec, Indian Assn for Radiation Protection; Chief Ed, SCAVENGER; Min of Environment's Expert Cttee for nuclr facilities, 1989-; Chmn, Light of Life Soc of India, 1987-; VP, Asia Evangelistic Fellowship, 1996-. Address: Christian Digest Society, India PO Box 4576, 21 YMCA Road, Bombay 40008, India.

ABU-ARAB Mahmoud, b. 3 Sept 1953, Acre, Israel. Psychologist. m. Zlatica Minichova, 21 Mar 1981, div, Apr 1993, 2 d. Education: MA, Comenius Univ, Bratislava, Slovakia, 1981; PhD, 1985. Psychol, Bratislava City Cncl, 1982-83; Psych Hosp, Pezenok, Slovakia, 1984; Lectr, Ibrahimeih Coll, Jerusalem, 1986-88; Rsch Offr, Arab Studies Soc, Jerusalem, 1987-88; Cnslr Granville Tafe Coll, Sydney, NSW, Aust, 1988-; Hd, Dept of Psychol, Al-Amal Hosp, Jeddah, Saudi Arabia, 1993-94; Pvt Prac, 1994-; Speaker, Presenter in field. Creative Works: Standardization Psychology Screening Inventory on Slovak Population, 1984; Psychological Test on Palestinian Population, 1988; Contbr, Articles to Profl Jrnls. Memberships: Austl Psychol Soc; NSW Cnslrs Assn; Natl Accupuncture Detoxification Assn; Psychols Austl Assn for Applied Psychophysiology and Biofeedback; Austl Pain Soc. Hobbies: Bushwalking; Skiing; Travelling; Reading. Address: P O Box 391, Granville, Sydney, NSW, 2142, Aust.

ABU-RUKAH Yousef Habous, b. 20 May 1960, Jordan. Assistant Professor. Education: BSc, Geol, MS Univ of Baroda, India, 1983; MSc, Geol, AM Univ of Aligarh, India, 1986; PhD, Environ Geol, MS Univ of Baroda, India, 1990. Appointment: Asst Prof, Dept of Earth and Environ Scis, Yarmouk Univ, Jordan, 1991-. Publications include: Pyrite Nodules in Early Cretaceous

Sandstone from Wadi Zerka North Jordan, 1993; Various Variables Migration in Landfill Site Using Statistical Explanation. A Case Study - Elakader Landfill Site, North Jordan, 1997; Factor Analysis Determination of Trace Element Contamination in Urban Soils of North Jordan. Memberships: Sev. Address: Department of Earth & Environmental Sciences, Yarmouk University, Irbid, Jordan.

ABU-ZIDAN Fikri Mahmoud, b. 19 May 1957, Libya. Surgeon; Researcher. m. I Raad, 27 Mar 1989, 3 s. Education: MD; FRCS, Glasgow; PhD. Appointments: Demonstrator of Anatomy, 1981-83; Surgn, 1983-93; Rschr, 1993-. Publications: Num articles in profl med jrnls. Honour: Grant, Auckland Med Rsch Fndn, 1998. Membership: Fell, Roy Coll of Physns and Surgs, Glasgow, 1987. Hobbies: Swimming; Football; Learning Languages; Reading. Address: Department of Surgery, Auckland Hospital, Faculty of Medicine, Auckland University, Auckland, New Zealand.

ABUELMA'ATTI Muhammad Taher, b. 15 Oct 1942, Cairo, Egypt. Educator; Researcher. m. Saher R Ahmad, 12 Aug 1973, 4 s, 2 d. Education: BSc, Elec Engrng, Univ Cairo; PhD, Elec Engrng, Univ Bradford, England. Appointments: Asst Prof, Assoc Prof, Univ Bahrain; Prof, King Fahd Univ of Petroleum & Minerals, Saudi Arabia, 1991-. Publications: Over 400 articles in profl jrnls. Honours: Ex Tchng Awd, 1995, Ex Rsch Awd, 1996, King Fahd Univ of Petroleum & Minerals. Hobbies: Reading; Travel. Address: King Fahd University of Petroleum & Minerals, Box 203, Dhahran 31261, Saudi Arabia.

ABYKAYEV Nurtai Abykayevich, b. 15 May 1947, Dzhambul, Almaty Region. m. 3 children. Education: Ural Polytech Inst, Almaty Higher CP Sch. Appointments: Engr Almaty fctry of hvy mach constrn, 1972-76; CP functionary, 1976-88; Asst to Chmn Cncl of Mins of Kazakh SSR, 1988-89; Asst to First Sec Cen Cttee CP of Kazakhstan, 1989-90; Hd, Adm of Pres and PM Repub of Kazakhstan; Amb to UK-also accred to Denmark, Norway and Sweden, 1995-96; First Asst to Pres of Kazakhstan, Sept 1996-. Membership: Security Cncl, 1990-95. Address: Residence of the President, Square of the Republic, 480091 Almaty, Republic of Kazakhstan.

ACHARJYO L N, b. 1 June 1936, Orissa, India. Veterinarian; Wildlife Conservationist. m. Mrs P K Acharjya, 19 Nov 1961, 1 s, 2 d. Education: BVSc & AH, Bihar Univ, 1955-59; MVSc, Path, Orissa Univ of Agric & Technol, 1983-85. Appointments include: Zoo Veterinarian, Nandankanan Zool Park, 1960-92; Expert Zoo Veterinarian, Arignar Anna Zool Park, Chennai, 1992, Tata Steel Zool Park, Jamshedpur, 1994, 1997; Resource person, Small Population Dynamics and Tools of Recovery w Lion-tailed Macaque as a case study, 1996. Publications include: Directory of Indian Zoos, 1989; Research and Popular Papers/Notes on Wildlife Numbering over 200, Vol I, 1996; Indian Zoo Year Book, vol II, 1997. Honours include: Univ Gold Medal, 1985; C M Singh Awd, 1996. Memberships include: Nature and Wildlife Conservation Soc of Orissa; Bombay Nat Hist Soc; Zoo Outreach Org; Orissa Veterinary Assn; Zool Soc of Orissa; Orissa Livestock Dev Soc. Hobby: Conservation of Wildlife. Address: House No M-71, Housing Board Colony, Baramunda, Bhubaneswar, 751003, Orissa, India.

ACHARUPARAMBIL Daniel, b. 12 May 1939, Palliport, Kerala, S India. Archbishop of Verapoly. Education: L Ph, Poona; MA in Indian Philos and relig, BHu Banaras; PhD, Pont Univ di S Thomaso Aquino, Rome. Appointments: Dean of Fac of Missiology, PUU, Rome, 1986-88; Vice Chan, PUU, 1988-94. Publications: Books: The Destiny of Man; Spiritualita e mistica indu; La Spiritualita dell' Induismo. Membership: Consultor of Pontifical Cnsl for Interrelig dialogue, 1990-95. Hobby: Reading. Address: Latin Archbishop's House, PB No 2581, Cochin 682031, Kerala State, S India.

ACHARYA Santosh S, b. 1 June 1971, Dubalgunde. Assistant Teacher. Education: BA; VLI; MA; KAS; IPS; Dip in Paint. Appointments: Asst Tchr, Govt Hr Primary

Sch, Bolegaon 58416, Bhalke, Bidar. Publications: Essay, Stories, 1996; Fine Arts, 1997; Small Songs Writing, 1998. Honours: Best Tchrs in Dist & State; Best Artist in Div; Best Poet in Dist. Memberships: Tchr Assn; Vet Inspector Assn Mbr. Hobbies: Pen friends; Singing; Writing; Arts; Sports; Cinema. Address: Dubalgunde 585418, Bidar, India.

ACHUTHAN Mavelikara, b. 19 Dec 1926, Kerala, India. Professor. m. G Indira Devi, 1 s, 1 d. Education: MA, Sanskrit; MA, Malayalam; MA, Hindi; MA, Vedanta; MEd; PhD, Sanskrit. Appointments: Tchr; Lectur; Prof; Prin; Chmn, Bd of Studies, Univ of Kerala. Publications: Jagannatha Pandita on Alankaras; Educational Practices in Manu, Panini and Kautilya. Honour: Snr Fellship, Dept of Culture, Govt of India. Memberships: Prof of Sanskrit; Educ Offr; Trng Coll Prin. Hobbies: Literature; Public Speaking; Research in Indology. Address: Saijyotsna, Jawahar Nagar, Trivandrum, Kerala, India.

ADACHI Yukihiko, b. 22 Sept 1943, Nagaokakyo City, Kyoto, Japan. Director, Professor of Medicine. m. Miwa, 13 Mar 1971, 2 d. Education: MD; PhD. Appointments: Asst Prof, 1975-91, Assoc Prof, 1991-97, Kinki Univ; Dir, Prof of Med, Mie Univ Sch of Med, 1997-. Publications: Num articles in profl jrnls. Honours: Mitsukoshi Awd, Yng Med Rschrs, 1974; Awd of Encouragement, Japan Soc of Gastroentol, 1988. Memberships: Amn Assn of the Study of Liver Disease; Eurn Assn for the Study of the Liver; Intl Assn for the Study of the Liver. Hobbies: Museums; Gardening. Address: 604-282 Kannonji-cho, Tsu City, Mie 514 0062, Japan.

ADAMS Jeanie, b. 8 Sept 1945, Hamilton, Victoria, Australia. Writer; Illustrator. m. John H, 9 May 1970, 3 s. Education: BA, Anthropol and Sociol, Hons, Monash Univ, 1970; BEd, Art and Craft, Melbourne CAE, 1989. Appointments: Var tchng posts; Curator, Made W Meaning Crafts of Aboriginal Far N Qld, 1995. Publications: Pigs & Honey, 1989; Going for Oysters, 1991; Mangrover Alive, 1992. Honours: Austl Childrens Book Cncl Book of the Yr Jnr Fiction Awd. Hobbies: Textile Arts; Printmaking. Address: 7 Swales Street, Mundinburra, Queensland 4812, Australia.

ADAMS Kenneth Menzies, b. 28 Oct 1922, Melbourne, Aust. Retired Schoolteacher. m. Verna, 22 May 1948, 3 children. Appointments: Tchr, Kewell E Primary, 1948; Box Hill High, 1949-51; Wangaratu High, 1952-61; Mitcham High, 1962-67; Nunawading High, 1968-73; Dpty Prin, Hallam High, 1974-76; Prin, Doveton High, 1977-82. Publications: Seeing History, vols 1-4, 1968-72. Address: 20 Ledni Avenue, Heathmont 3135, Vic, Australia.

ADAMS Maxim, b. 21 Apr 1947. Meteorologist. m. Jeanne Sabelberg, 13 Sept 1975, 1 s, 1 d. Education: BSc Eng 1968, BSc 1977, London; MSc, Monash Univ, 1989. Appointment: Bur of Meteor, Aust, 1977-. Publications: Sev pprs and 4 vols of stud notes, 1981-96. Honours: Siemens Mem Schlsp, 1965; Maths Prize, 1976. Hobbies: Keeping Fit; Cycling; Bushwalking. Address: Bureau of Meteorology, GPO Box 1289K, Melbourne, Vic 3001, Australia.

ADAMS Phillip Andrew, b. 12 July 1939, Aust. Film Maker; Author; Broadcaster. m. (1) diss, 3 d. (2) ptnr Patrice Newell, 1d. Career: Columnist and Critic, 1956-; Fndn Chmn, Film Bd, Aust Cncl, 1972-75; Victorian Govt Rep, Aust Children's TV Fndn, 1981-; Pres, Victorian Cncl of the Arts, 1982-86; Chmn, Aust Film Commn, 1983-90; Chmn, Commn for the Future, 1985-90; Presenter, Late Night Live, Radio Natl netwrk. Creative Works: Feature films incl: Jack And Jill: A Postscript, 1970; The Naked Bunyip, 1971; The Adventures of Barry McKenzie, 1972; Don's Party, 1975; The Getting of Wisdom, 1976; Grendel Grendel Grendel, 1980; We of the Never Never, 1982; Lonely Hearts, 1982; Fighting Back, 1983; Abra Cadabra, 1983; Kitty and the Bagman; A Personal History of the Australian Surf; Publications: Adams With Added Enzymes, 1970; The Unspeakable Adams, 1977; More Unspeakable Adams, 1979; Un-Censored Adams, 1981; The Inflammable Adams,

1983; Adams Versus God, 1985; The Penguin Book of Australian Jokes, 1995; The Penguin Book of jokes from Cyperspace, 1995; The Penguin Book of More Australian Jokes, 1996; Classic Columns; The Big Questions, 1996; Emperors of the Air, 1997; Retreat from Tolerance, 1997; More Big Questions, 1998; The Penguin Book of Schoolyard Jokes, 1998; A Billion Voices, 1999. Honours: Longford Awd, Outstndng Servs to Aust Film Ind, 1982; Gold Lion, Cannes Fest, for Break Down The Barriers, Intl Yr Disabled Person; Snr ANZAC Fell, 1985; Henry Lawson Arts Awd, 1987; Aust Humanist Of Yr, 1987; AM, 1987; AO, 1992; 14 AFI Awds; DUniv (Griffith); FRSA. Hobbies: Collecting antiquities. Address: Elmswood, via Grundy, NSW 2337, Australia.

ADAMSON Mary Anne, b. 25 June 1954, Berkeley, California, USA. Geographer. m. Richard Harrington, 20 Sept 1974. Education: BA, 1974, MA, 1975, PhD Cand, 1978, Univ CA, Berkeley. Appointments: Tchng & Rsch Asst, Univ CA, Berkeley; Sci, Cnslt, LLNL; ESL Inc, PG&E Corp, 1990-. Memberships: Assn of Am Geogs; Assn of Pacific Coast Geogs; Nature Conservancy. Hobbies: Folk Dancing; Reading; Spelunking; Travel. Address: 245 Market Street, San Francisco, CA 94105, USA.

ADCOCK Warren David, b. 10 Sept 1928, Aust. Managing Director. m. Margaret Munnoch, 5 Sept 1952, 5 d. Education: E Sydney Tech Coll. Appointments: Mngng Dir, King Gee Clothing Co Pty Ltd, 1958-71; Mngng Dir, Bradmill Garment Divsn, 1972-83; Dir, Bradmill Ltd, 1979-83; Mngng Dir, Cobolt Clothing Co Pty Ltd, 1983-. Honour: OBE, 1977. Memberships: Life Mbr, Apparel Mfrs Assn, NSW, Pres, 1961-65; Life Mbr, Chmbr of Mfrs, Pres, Austl Clothing Mfrs Cncl, 1966-68; Cncl Mbr, Ctrl Indl Secretariat, Natl Clothing Ind Trng Cttee, Consumer Affairs Cncl, NSW, 1968-74, NSW VP, 1972; Chmn, Meridan Sch Cncl, 1974-79, Pres, 1975-77; Fndn Mbr, Mfng Ind Advsry Cncl, NSW, 1976; Univ Cncl, 1977-81; Pres, Austl Confedn of Apparel Mfrs, 1980, Fndn Pres, 1970-72; Chmn, Confedn of Austl Indl Trade Cncl, 1980-83; Roy Sydney Yacht Sqdn; Eleanora Country Club. Hobbies: Boating; Golf. Address: 5 Hallstrom Close, Northbridge, NSW 2063, Australia.

ADDALA Narayana Swamy, b. 12 Nov 1949, Visakhapatnam, India. Associate Professor. m. Indira, 24 Aug 1981, 1 s, 1 d. Education: PhD, Geophysics, Hydrology; Msc (Tech), Geophys; P G Dip, Applied Stats; BS, P G Dip, Hydrology (Hungary); P G Certs in Remote Sensing and Image Processing (ITC, Netherlands). Appointments: Univ Rsch Fell; Jnr Rsch Fell; Postdoct Fell (CSIR); Rsch Assoc (UGC); Asst Prof, Assoc Prof. Publications: 60 sci publs, 1980-98. Honours: Intl Soc for Photogrammetry and Remote Sensing. Memberships: Chmn, Jrnl Cttee, 3rd World Assn for Remote Sensing; Amn Geophysical Union; Intl Assn for Hydrological Scis; Life Mbr, Assn for Exploration Geophysicists; Fndr Mbr, Assn of Hydrologists of India; Life Mbr, Indian Remote Sensing Soc; Life Mbr, Indian Assn of Hydroogists; Life Mbr, India Meteorological Soc. Hobbies: Sports; Games. Address: H No 53-34-12, KRM Colony, Nr Sangam Paka, Visakhaptnam 530013, India.

ADE Wolfgang Roland, b. 15 Jan 1947, Stuttgart, Germany. Research and Scientific Officer. m. Shizuko Okawa, 22 Nov, 1 d. Education: Appl Managerial Econs, 1972-74; Med Sch, Univs of Hohenheim, Heidelberg and Tübingen. Appointments: Rsch Fell, Tokyo Womens Med Coll, 1982-87; Lectr, Tokyo Womens Med Coll, 1987-89; Med Advsr, Nippon Roussel/Hoechst Marion Rsch, 1983-; Rsch and Sci Offr, Juro Wada Commemorative Heart and Lungs Inst, 1987-. Publication: One Hundred Years after Ludwig Rehn's Cardiorrhaphy - History and State of the Art of Cardio-Thoracic Surgery, 1998. Memberships: World Soc of Cardio-Thoracic Surgns, Sec-Gen; World Artificial Organ, Immunol and Transp Soc, Sec. Hobbies: Poetry; History. Address: 20-7, Aoto 3-chome, Katsushika-ku, Tokyo, Japan.

ADGAONKAR Chandrashekhar, b. 18 Dec 1940, Umred, India. Post Graduate Teacher. m. Vijaya, 25 Feb 1969, 1 s, 1 d. Education: MSc, Phys, Electrons; PhD,

Solid State. Appointments: Lectr, 1963-86; Deputation to Univ of Baghdad, 1981-83; Rdr, 1986-91; Hd Dept of Electrons, 1991-; Univ of Baghdad, Iraq, 1981-83. Publications: Innovative Expmts in Phys; 7 PhD Publshd pprs in Intl Jrnls. Honours: Govt Daxina Fell; UGC Rsch Grant. Memberships: Fell, Instn of Electrons and Telecomm Engrs; Fell, Ultrasonic Soc of India. Hobbies: Classical Music; Painting. Address: Inst of Science, RT Road, Nagpur 440 001, India.

ADHIKARI Man Mohan, b. June 1920, Kathmandu. Education: Banares Hindu Univ, India. Appointments: Gen-Sec, Nepal Communist Pty, 1953; Chmn, Communist Pty of Nepal, Unified Marxist-Leninist, 1991-; PM, Nepal, 1994-95; Membership: joined Quit India Mvt 1942; imprisoned in India for polit activities for 18 mths; returned to Nepal, 1947; Imprisoned in Nepal for polit activities for 3 yrs; Imprisoned for involvement in attempt to overthrow monarchy, 1960-69. Address: Communist Party of Nepal, Madan Nagar Balkhu, P O Box 5471, Kathmandu, Nepal.

ADIKARAM Matilda, b. 6 July 1951, Ragama. Teacher. m. 8 Jan 1977, 1 s, 2 d. Education: BA. Appointments: Pres, Cath Tchrs Team. Creative Works: Composing Peace Songs; Short Stories; Poems. Memberships: Samasgweye. Hobbies: Music; Socl Serv. Address: Sri Lanka.

ADIREKSARN Pongpol, b. 23 Mar 1942. Minister of Agriculture and Co-operatives. Education: BA, MA, Intl Rels, USA. Appointments: Asst Sec, Min of Transp and Comm, 1981; Mbr of Parl, 1983, 1991-92, 1995, 1996; Min of For Affairs, 1992; Sec, Ldr of Opposition, 1993; Min to Prime Min's Off, 1995; Min of Agric and Co-ops. Honour: Kt Grand Cross, 1st Class, Most Noble Order of Crown of Thailand. Address: 19 Soi Aree, Phaholyotin Road, Phayathai, Bangkok, Thailand.

ADIREKSARN Pramara, b. 6 Jan 1914. Education: Chulachomklao Royal Mil Acady. Appointments: Mil career until 1951; Dep Comms Min, 1951; MP for Saraburi, 1956-; Ind Min, 1956; Dep Premier, 1975-76; Min Def, 1975; Min Agric, 1976; Fndr Chat Thai Pty, 1976; Pty Leader, 1976-86; Fmr Interior Min, Fmr Ind Min; Min Ind, Sept-Dec 1990; Fmr Min Interior 1990-91. Address: c/o Ministry of the Interior, Bangkok 10200, Thailand.

ADNAN Etel, b. 24 Feb 1925, Beirut, Lebanon. Writer; Painter. Education: Licence es Lettres; Diplome d'Etudes Sup, Univ Paris; Postgrad, Univ CA, Berkeley and Harvard. Appointment: Prof of Philos, Dominican Coll, San Rafael, CA, USA, 1958-72. Publications: Sitt Marie Rose; Spring Flowers Own; The Arab Apocalypse; Journey to Mount Tamalpaïs; The Spring Flowers Own and The Manifestations of the Voyage; Paris, When It's Naked; Of Cities and Women; There. Honour: Prix France, Pays Arabes, Paris, 1977. Address: 35 Marie Street, Sausalito, CA 94965, USA.

ADNI Daniel, b. 6 Dec 1951, Haifa. Education: Conservatoire of Music in Paris. Appointments: 1st Recital in Haifa, 1963; Profl debut, London, 1970; New York Debut, 1976; Played at most musical centres in the world incl UK, Germany, Israel, USA, Japan, S Afr, Switz, Norway, Netherlands, Romania, Aust, NZ, Finland, Austria. Creative Works: over 20 records. Honours: 1st Prize, Paris Conservatoir; 1st Prize, Young Concert Artists' Auditions, NY. Hobbies: Cinema; Theatre; Bridge; Walks; Sightseeing. Address: c/o 64A Menelik Road, London NW2 3RH, England.

ADOOR Gopalakrishnan, b. 3 July 1941, Adoor, Kerala. m. R Sunanda, 1972, 1 d. Appointments: Dir, Natnl Film Dev Corp, 1980-83; Chmn Film and TV Inst India, 1987-89 and 1993-96; Chmn 7th Intl Children's Film Fest of India, 1991; Chmn Jury Singapore Intl Film Fest. Creative Works include: Swayamvaram, 1972; Kodiyettam, 1977; Elippathayam, 1981 - British Film Inst Award -; Mukhamukham, 1984 - Intl Film Critics' Prize, New Dehli -; Anantaram, 1987; Mathilukal, 1989; Vidheyan, 1993; Kathapurushan, 1995; more than 24

short and documentary films. Publications: Plays: Vaiki vanna velicham, 1961; Ninte rajyam varunnu, 1963; The World of Cinema, 1983; collects essays. Honours: Num intl film awds; Awd'd title of Padmashir, 1984. Memberships: Working Group on Natl Film Plcy, 1979-80; Facs of Fine Arts, Univ of Kerala, Calicut and Mahatma Ghandi Univs, 1985-89; Advsry Cttee, Natl Film Archive of India, 1988-90; Jury, Intl Film Fest of India, 1983; Venice Intl Film Fest, 1988; Bombay Intl Film Fest, 1990; Hawaii Intl Film Fest; Sochi Intl Film Fest; Alexandria Intl Film Fest. Address: Darsanam, Trivandrum, 695 017, Kerala, India.

ADVANI Chanderban Ghanshamdas, b. 23 July 1924, Hyserbad Sind. Businessman. m. Vena Devi, 30 Nov 1958, 1 s, 1 d. Education: BA. Appointments: Mngr, Narain Advani & Co, Karachi; Proprietor, Nephews Coml Corp, Karachi; Mngr, L L Mohnani, Yokohama; CEO, Nephews Intl Inc, Yokohama. Publications: Articles to var mags, NGO's socl and welfare assns. Honours: Medals, Citations, Mayors of Mumbai (India), Yokohama (Japan), Key to both countries. Memberships: Indian Chmbr of Com, Japan; Indian Merchants Assn of Yokohama; Yokohama Chmbr of Com-Ind, Yokohama; Sinim Lodge, Shriners Club, Tokyo. Hobbies: Stamps; Coin collection; Having friends all over the world in all spheres. Address: 502, New Port Building, 25 Yamashita Cho, Naka Ku, Yokohama 231-86-91, Jpan.

ADVANI Lal K, b. 8 Nov 1927, Karachi. m. Kamala Jagtiani, 1965, 1 s, 1 d. Education: St Patrick's High Schl, Karachi; DG Natl Coll, Hyderabad, Sind; Govt Law Coll, Bombay. Appointments: joined Rashtriya Swayam Sevak Sangh - RSS social work org -, 1942; Sec of Karachi branch, 1947; joined Bharatiya Jana Sangh - BJS -, 1951; pty work in Rajasthan until 1958; Sec Delhi State Jana Sangh, 1958-63; Vice-Pres, 1965-67; Joint Ed of BJS paper Organizer, 1960-67; ldr of Jana Sangh Gp, 1966; Chmn Metrop Cncl, 1967; Hd of Jana Sangh Parl Grp, 1970; Pres Bhartatiya Jana Sangh, 1973-77 - incorp in Janata; detained during emergency 1975-77; Gen Sec Janata Pty, Jan-May 1977; Min Info and Broadcasting, 1977-79; Min Home Affairs, 1998-; Gen Sec Bharatiya Janata Pty, 1980-86; Pres, 1986-90 and June 1993-; Ldr of Opposition Lok Sabha, Dec 1990 - March 1991 and 1991-1996. Publications: A Prisoner's Scrap-Book, The People Betrayed. Memberships: Cen Exec of BJS, 1966; Interim Metrop Cncl Delhi, 1966; Rajya Sabha, 1970; Hobbies: Theatre; Cinema; Books. Address: Bharatiya Janata Pty, 11 Ashok Road, New Delhi 110 001, India.

AFFANDI Achmad, b. 27 Oct 1927, Kuningan, W Java. Education: Univ Indonesia, Bogor, Army Staff and Command Coll, Bandung and Univ Kentucky. Appointments: Tchr Snr High Sch and Tchrs' Coll Bogo, 1953-57; Asst Fac of Agric Bogor, 1957-58; Asst Lectr, 1959-60; Jr Lectr Inst Agric Bogo, 1960-62; Lectr, 1962-64; Hd Bur for Equip and Campus Dev Dept of Higher Educ and Sci, 1962-64; Snr Offic, Dept of Def and Security, 1965-67; Dir of Animal Husbandry Bimas - Mass Guidance - poultry farming, 1968-69; Agric Attache The Hague, 1969-71; Sec Bimas Supvsry Body Dept of Agric, 1971-73; Insp-Gen Dept of Agric, 1973-74; Dir-Gen Food Crops Dept of Agric, 1974; Jr Min for Food Prodn, 1978-83; Min of Agric, 1983-88.

AGARWAL M B S, b. 26 Aug 1957, Jaipur, India. Engineer. m. Raj, 23 Apr 1983, 1 s, 1 d. Education: BEng. Memberships: IEEE; Snr Mbr, ISA; Chartered Engr, ASTM. Hobbies: Reading; Writing; Internet surfing. Address: 109-A, Adarsh Nagar, Ajmer 305008, India.

AGARWAL Umesh Kumar, b. 24 Jan 1951. Librarian; Teacher. m. Purnima Agarwal, 18 June 1979, 1 s, 3 d. Education: BSc 1975, BLibSc 1977, Univ of Udaipur; MLibSc and Doc, Univ of Rajasthan, 1978; MA, Sociol, 1985, PhD, M L Sukhadia Univ, Udaipur. Appointments: Univ of Jabalpur, 1978-79; Gujarat Ayurved, Jamnagar, 1979-83; M L Sukhadia Univ, 1983-. Publications: Pushtakalaya Vargikaran: Dewi Bindu Padhati; Dewi Bindu Vargikaran; Pushtakalaya Prashashan; Public Library Services in India; Library Legislation in India; 20th Century Library Legislation in India; Contbr of sev pprs to profl natl and intl level confs. Honours: Professionally recognised; Enthusiast for Libs and Libnshp. Memberships: Life Mbr: ILA; IASLIC; IATLIS; AALDI; RLA; BLA; GGSS; KLA; MALA; MLAI; Univ Libns Assn of India. Hobbies: Study; Teaching. Address: 55 Gayatri Marg, Amal Ka Kanta, Udaipur 313001, India.

AGASIMUNDIN Mahantesh Adappa, b. 1 June 1958, Benakanadoni, India. Social Worker. m. Shakuntala, 22 Apr 1985, 1 s, 1 d. Education: BA, V M Coll, Hungund, 1980; MA, Sociology, Karnataka Univ, Dharwad, 1982. Appointments: Field Worker, Khadi Gramodhyog Sanghs (KGS), 1981-; Field Worker, BIRDS Vol Orgn, Naganur, Gokak Taluk, Belgaum Dist, 1982-; Environ Asst Proj Offr in India Dev Serv (I), Dharwad, 1983-90; Estab Vol Orgn, Bijapur Integrated Rural Dev Soc (BIRDS), Hungund, Bagalkot Dist, 1990; Currently, Dir, BIRDS. Publications: Press articles; Self-Help Group Guideline. Hobbies: Social work (Social change through people's participation); Population innovation; Networking; Federations; Article writing; Research; Reading; Working in non-formal education; Group songs (issue-based); Street drama, magic show & puppetry show; Sports (carram, volleyball, roleplays, rural games). Address: V K Koutal, Negilayogi Nilaya, Gadag, Karnataka, India.

AGPALO Remigio E, b. 10 June 1928, Mamburao, Occidental, Mindoro, Philippines. Professor of Political Science. Education: BA (Govt), w Highest Hons, Univ of Maine, USA, 1952; MA (Govt), IN Univ, USA, 1956; PhD, IN Univ, 1958. Appointments: Instr, Polit Sci, 1953, Full Prof of Polit Sci, 1969, Prof Emer 1988, Univ of the Philippines; Natl Socl Scientist (Polit Sci), Awd'd by the Philippines Socl Sci Cncl, 1990. Publications: The Political Process in the Philippines, 1962; A Study of Politics in Occidental Mindoro, 1972; Jose P Laurel, 1992; Adventures in Political Science, 1996. Honours: Phi Beta Kappa; Phi Kappa Phi, Univ of ME, USA, 1953; Snr Specialist, E-W Cntr, Honolulu, HI, 1966-67; Natl Socl Scientist (Polit Sci), awd'd by Phil Socl Sci Cncl, 1990; One of Pillars of Coll of Socl Scis and Philos, 1999. Memberships: Philippine Polit Sci Assn, 1962-; Nigerian Polit Sci Assn, 1977-78; Natl Rsch Cncl of the Philippines, 1977-. Hobby: Tennis. Address: Department of Political Science, University of the Philippines, Diliman, Quezon City, Philippines 1101.

AGRAWAL Surendra Prasad, b. 23 May 1929, Gowan, India. Education: BSc, 1949, BA, 1952, Agra Univ; Ctf, Lib Sci, 1952, MA, 1954, Aligarh Muslim Univ. Appointments: Mbr, Hindi Advsry Cttee, Min of Coal, Govt of India; Mbr, Bd of Stdies, Sch of Archival Studies, Natl Archives of India. Publications include: Educational Planning in India: With a Slant to Educational Financing and Administration; Integrated Library System: Two Case Studies; Development/Discussion Diary of India, 1990-91. Honours: PhD, Honoris causa, Intl Univ Fndn, 1988; D R Kalia Awd, Assn of Govt Libns & Info Scis; Freedom Fighters Samman Pension. Memberships include: Indian Soc of Agricl Econs, Bombay; Delhi Artists Assn; Intl Fedn of Lib Assns and Insrtns; Indian Cncl for Child Educ. Hobbies: Reading; Writing; Cooking. Address: B-5/73 Azad Apartments, Sri Aurobindo Marg, New Delhi 110016, India.

AGUAS Primo Bautista, b. 6 Feb 1956, Manila, Philippines. Banker. m. Mariles, 22 Jan 1983, 1 s, 3 d. Education: BA, Econs. Appointments: Prin, SGV Cnsltng, 1988-90; Ptnr, Andersen Cnsltng, 1990-92. Membership: Philippine Computer Soc. Hobbies: Golf; Photography; Gym; Reading. Address: 195-B F Manalo Street, Metro Manila, Philippines.

AHANKARI Saroj, b. 11 Mar 1926. Teacher. m. Srinivas, 7 May 1940, 1 s, 1 d. Education: BA; BEd; MEd. Appointments: Hd Mistress, Govt Primary Sch, Omerga, 1954-55; Hd Mistress, Govt HS, Udgir, 1955-57; Hd Mistress, ZP HS, Latur, 1957-65; Hd Mistress, ZP HS, Kalam, 1965-70; Hd Mistress, ZP HS, Latur, 1970-84. Publications: Poems: Pushpanjali, 1987; Kavya Sugandh, 1993; Phulrani, 1997; Poems for Children: Khau Ghya Khau, 1987; Chiu Cha Ghas, 1991; Kulfi Malai, 1993; Stories: Chandane Phulale, 1988; Chandrama, 1993;

Tarangan, 1993; Essays: Leehu Mee Pustak, 1991; Dramas: Teen Ekankika, 1991; Autobiography: Shura Mee Vandile, 1997. Honours: Sahitya Sharda Awd, Cultural Awd, Govt of Maharashtra, 1993; Bal Kumar Sahitya Gaurav, Lit Awd by Panchayati Raj, 1994; Adhya Kavi Mukund Raj Awd, 1996; Felicitated by: Pres and Ex-Mins Inst, Govt of Maharashtra, Chmn Najura Sugar Factory, Mngmt of Shri Marwads Rajasthan Vidyalaya, Shri Shivrav Patil, Hon Speaker of the Parl of Indian Repub; Hon Chf Min of Maharashtra Govt; Invited to recite poems and lect in All India Marathi Confs at Ambajogai, Nander, Sholapur, Pune, Kolhapur, Satara Parli Vaijnath. Memberships: Freedom Fighter's Assn, India; Nariprobodhan Manch; Andhashradhan Manch; Andhashradha Nirmulan Samiti; Jagruti Mahila Mandal; Seva Muktigram; Pensioners Assn, Maharashtra; Life Mbr, Tilak Nagar Housing Soc, Latur. Hobbies: Social, Cultural and Literary drive for women; Upliftment of downtrodden women; Critical Literary Reading. Address: Saroj Kunj, Tilak Nagar, Latur 413 512, MS, India.

AHIR Durga Dass, b. 5 June 1939, Bath-Kalan, Punjab, India. Community Adviser. m. 27 July 1957, 2 s, 2 d. Education: Inter Exam, Arts Fac, Punjab Univ, 1957; Deg Coll, Camp Coll, New Delhi, 1958-60. Appointments: Clerical, NDMC, New Delhi, 1959-62; Checker, Messenger, COD Donnington, Telford, 1962-63; Welder, GKN Sankey, Telford, 1963-83; Volun Advice Wrkr, Asian Cultural Soc, Telford Dev Corp, 1985-86; Proj Supvsr, Asian Cultural Proj, Telford, 1986-87; Community Advsr, Wrekin Dist Cncl, Telford, 1987-; JP, Shropshire Commn of the Peace, Telford Crt, 1991; Parish Cnclr, Hadley Parish, Telford, 1991-95. Honours: Educ Ind Ptnrshp Awd, Cntr for the Stdy of Comprehensive Schs, 1992; Spec Awd, Servs to Community, W Mercia Constabulary Silver Jubilee Anniversary, Droitwich, 1992; Cert of Appreciation, Dr Ambedkar Buddhist Soc, Frankfurt, Germany, 1994; Invitation from HRH Prince of Wales for wrk on behalf of ethnic minority grps, St James's Palace, London, 1994; Awd for Excellence, Wrekin Cncl AGM Servs to Ethnic Minorities, 1994-95; Invitation from Ld Chan and Speaker to 50th Independence Celebration of India and Pakistan, 1997; Invitation to Gdn Pty at Buckingham Palace, 1997. Memberships: Police & Community Consultative Grp, 1985-; GMB's Race Advsry Cttee, W Midlands, 1987-; Victim Support Scheme of Telford, 1991; SACRE, 1991; BICA, 1994; Race Equality Forum of Telford & Shropshire, 1994-; Bd of Gov, 2 Shropshire Schs; Advsry Panel, Telford Coll Arts and Technol; Review Cttee, Shropshire Probation Servs. Hobbies: Political Lobbying; Attending Social Functions. Address: 1 Wheatley Crescent, Hadley, Telford TF1 4PZ, England.

AHMAD Awang Mohammed Yussof, b. 1944, Brunei. m. 2 c. Education: West Aust and Manchester Univs. Appointments: Admin Offr, Brunei Educ Dept, 1972-75; Acting Dist Offr of Belait Dist and Chmn Belait and Seria Municipal Bd, 1975-76; Acting Sec Pub Serv Comm and Dep Controller Customs and Excise, 1976; Sr Admin Offr, Off of Gen Advsr to Sultan of Brunei Darussalam, 1980-81; Dep Dir of Estab Dept 1981; Dist Offr, Tutong Dist, 1983-84; Amb to Philippines, 1984-86; Perm Rep to UN 1986-87. Address: c/o Ministry of Foreign Affairs, Bandar Seri Begawan, Brunei.

AHMAD Datuk Abdul Ajib bin, b. 13 Sept 1947, Segamat, Johore. Education: Malay Coll Kuala Kangsar, Perak, Mara Inst of Technol and Univ of Malay. Appointments: served with min of For Affairs; later Exec Shell Oil Co, Kuala Lumpur; Press Sec to Dato Musa Hitam - Min of Primary Inds later Dep PM - 1975-82; Menteri Besar Johor, 1982; MP, 1986; Min PM Dept, 1986-87. Membership: UMNO Supreme Cncl, 1984-. Hobbies: Sport, reading. Address: c/o UMNO Baru, Menara Dato' Onn, 38th Floor, Jalan Tun Dr, Ismail, 50480 Kuala Lumpur, Malaysia.

AHMAD Sultan Hashim. Minister of Defence. Appointment: Min of Def, Iraq, 1995-. Address: Ministry of Defence, North Gate, Baghdad, Iraq.

AHMAD Wasim, b. 10 Apr 1957, Chapra, Bihar, India. Reader. m. Aiysha, 26 Dec 1986, 1 s, 2 d. Education: MSc; MPhil; PhD; DSc. Appointments: Jnr Rsch Fell, 1978; Snr Rsch Fell, 1980; Postdoct Fell, 1982; Pool Sci, 1983; Lectr, 1988; Snr Lectr, 1992; Rdr, 1997-. Publications: 2 books, over 80 rsch pprs, sev chaps in books. Honours: YMSA, 1993; Roy Soc Vis Fellshp, 1995. Memberships: Fell, Linnean Soc of London, Zoological Soc of India; Indian Soc of Parasitols; Nematologic Soc of India. Hobbies: Studying Books; Exploring. Address: c/o Department of Zoology, Aligarh Muslim University, Aligarh 202002, India.

AHMAD NADZERI Abo Hanan, b. Perak, Malaysia. Geophysicist. m. Noraini, 5 Nov 1990, 2 d. Education: BApplSci, Geol. Appointments: Mineralogist for Ashton Mining, 1994-96; Geophysicist for Fugro Geodetic, 1997-. Memberships: Geological Soc of Malaysia; Inst of Geol, Malaysia. Hobbies: Writing; Jungle trekiing; Reading. Address: No 7 Jalan 9C/6, Taman Setapak Indah, 53100 Kuala Lumpur, Malaysia.

AHMADIEH Hamid, b. 28 June 1953, Tehran, Iran. Professor of Ophthalmology. m. Gisoo, 15 Spet 1977, 1 s, 1 d. Education: MD, Tehran Univ of Med Scis, 1971-78. Appointments: Instr, Ophthalmol, Tehran Univ of Med Scis, 1982-84; Asst Prof, Ophthalmol, Shahid Beheshti Univ of Med Scis, 1986-93; Dir, Vitreoretinal Serv-Labbafinejad Med Cntr, 1986-; Dir, Res Trng, Labbafinejad Med Cntr and Shahid Beheshti Univ of Med Scis, 1989-; Assoc Prof, Ophthalmol, 1986-93, Prof, 1999-, Shahid Beheshti Univ of Med Scis. Publications incl: Posterior segment triple surgery after traumatic eye injuries, 1995; Surgical management of cataract and posterior chamber intraocular lens implantation in Fuchs' heterochromic iridocyclitis, 1997; Primary Capsulectomy and Anterior Vitrectomy Combined with Lensectomy and PC IOL Implantation in Children: Limbal vs Pars Plana Approach. Memberships: Amn Acady of Ophthalmol; Iranian Soc of Ophthalmol; Iranian Retina Soc; Club Jules Gonin. Hobby: Sport. Address: Labbafinejad Medical Center, Pasdaran Avenue, Boostan 9th Street, Tehran 16666, Iran.

AHMED Fakhruddin, b. 1 Apr 1931. m. (1) Helen Ahmed, 1963 (dec 1984), (2) Masuda Khan, 1989, 1 s, 1 d. Education: Dhaka Univ, Fletcher Sch of Law and Diplomacy, Boston, USA. Appointments: For Serv of Pakistan, 1954-71; Junior Diplomatist, Saudi Arabia, 1957-59; Vice-Consul, USA 1959-63; Second Sec Iran, 1963-65; First Sec then Acting High Commnr Ghana, 1967-68; Served Min of For Affairs, 1968-71; Dir 1968-70; Dir-Gen, 1971; with For Serv of Bangladesh, 1972; Additional Sec the For Sec Min of For Affairs, 1972-76; Amb to Italy - also accred to Switzerland; Perm Rep to FAO, 1976-78; Amb to Yugoslavia - also accred to Greece, Albania - 1978-82; High Commnr in UK, 1982-86; Amb to Portugal, 1983-86; For Sec, Min of For Affairs, June 1986 - May 1987; Advsr for For Affairs with Cabinet rank, 1990-91. Memberships: Observer Grp for Sri Lanka Presdtl Election, 1988; Int Observer Grp, Feb 1989; SAARC Non-Govtl Observer Mission to Parly Elections in Pakistan, Oct 1990. Hobbies: Reading; Writing; Photography. Address: c/o Ministry of Foreign Affairs, 23/6 Mirpur Road, Topkhana Road, Dhaka, Bangladesh.

AHMED Haroon, b. 2 Mar 1936, Calcutta, India. Professor of Microelectronics. m. Evelyn Anne Travers Goodrich, 4 July 1969, 1 s, 2 d. Education: BSc, 1958; PhD, 1963; ScD, 1996. Appointments: GEC, 1958-59; Rsch Fell, 1962, Demonstrator in Engrng, 1963, Lectr Engrng, 1967, Rdr in Microelectronics, 1992, Cambridge Univ. Publications: Introduction to Physical Electronics (w A H W Beck), 1968; Electronics for Engineers (w P J Spreadbury), 1973, 1984. Honour: Fell, Roy Acady of Engrng. Memberships: FIEE; FInst Phys. Hobbies: Golf; Tennis. Address: Microelectronics Research Centre, Cavendish Laboratory, Madingley Road, Cambridge, CB3 OHE, UK.

AHMED Kazi Zafar, b. 1 July 1940, Cheora. Politician. m. 3 d. Education: Dhaka Univ. Appointments: Sec East

Pakistan Students Union Cen Cttee, 1957; Off Sec, 1957-62; Gen Sec, 1962-63; imprisoned several times for politcal activities between 1963 and 1965; Pres Bangla Sramik Fed, 1967; actively participated in struggle for independence, 1971; Sec-Gen Cen Cttee Natl Awami Pty, 1972-74; United People's Party 1974; Sec-Gen, 1974; Chmn Cen Cttee, 1979-; Min of Educ, 1978; Dpty PM also in charge of Ports, Shipping and River Transport, 1986-87; Pol Advsr to the Pres and Min of Info, 1988-91; PM, 1989-91. Memberships: Nationalist Front, 1978; Ed Nayajug. Address: c/o Office of the Prime Minister, Dhaka, Bangladesh.

AHMED Moudud, b. 1940, Noakhali. m. Hasna Jasimuddin, 2 s. Education: Dhaka Univ. Appointments: fmr Gen-Sec East Pakistan House, England; took an active part in struggle for independence, organising External Publicity Div of Bangladesh Gov in exile; Ed Bangladesh - weekly; Lawyer, Bangladesh Supreme Court, 1972-74; Gen Sec Cttee for Civil Liberties Legal Aid, 1974; imprisoned during State of Emergency, 1974; Hd, Bangladesh delegation to 32nd Session UN Gen Ass, 1977; Advsr to Pres, 1977; Min of Comms, 1985-86; Dep PM in charge of Min of Inds, July 1986-1988; PM and Min of Ind, 1988-89; Vice-Pres, 1989-90; under house arrest, 1990-91; imprisoned Dec 1991-. Publications: Bangladesh Contemporary Events and Documents; Bangladesh Constitutional Quest for Autonomy, 1974. Honours: Fell South Asian Inst of Heidelberg Univ, Harvard Univ Centre for Intl Affairs.

AHMED Nasim, b. Oct 1927, New Delhi, India. m. 1 d. Education: Union of Forman Christian Coll, Lahore, Punjab; St Stephen's Coll, Delhi; London Sch of Econs. Appointments: mbr of staff Pakistani newspaper Dawn, 1949-72; Chf Overseas Corresp, 1961-72; Sec Fed Min of Info and Broadcasting, Islamabad; Chmn Pakistani Broadcasting Corp and Pakistan Tv Corp, 1972-76; Amb to Denmark, 1976-78; Mngng Dir of a publishing co, London, 1978-81; Advsr to Dir-Gen Inter-Govtl Bur for Informatics, Rome, 1982-89; Perm Rep of Pakistan to UN, 1989-91; fmr Pres C'wlth Corresps Assn; For Press Assn, London. Honours: Fell Pakistan Soc UK, 1950. Memberships: Royal Inst Intl Affairs, Intl Inst for Strategic Studies, London. Address: c/o Ministry of Foreign Affairs, Constitution Avenue, Islamabad, Pakistan.

AHMED Shahabuddin, b. 1930, Pemal of Kendua, Greater Mymensingh Dist. 2 s, 3 d. Education: Dhaka Univ, Lahore Civil Serv Acady, Univ of Oxford. Appointments: Sub-Div Offr Civil Serv of Pakistan, 1954; later Additional Dep Commnr; transferred to Judicial Br, 1960; Fmr Additional Dist and Sess Judge, Dhaka; Fmr Dist and Sess Judge, Comilla and Chittagong; Fmr Registrar High Court of East Pakistan; elevated to High Court Bench, 1972; mbr Labour Appellate Tribunal, 1973-74; Judge of Appellate Div Supreme Court of Bangladesh, 1980; Chf Justice, 1990, 1991-95; Chmn Commn of Enquiry into police shootinngs of studs, 1983; Natl Pay Commn, 1984; Bangladesh Red Cross Soc, 1978-82; Acting Pres of Bangladesh, 1990-91; Pres of Bangladesh, Oct 1996-. Address: Office of the President, Dhaka, Bangladesh.

AHN Chung-Si, b. 7 May 1944, Kyungbuk, Korea. Professor of Political Science. m. Bong-Sook Sohn (Ahn), 20 Nov 1969, 2 d. Education: BA, 1967, MA, 1971, Polit Sci, Seoul Natl Univ; PhD, Polit Sci, Univ of HI, 1977. Appointments include: Visng Prof, (Politics Dept) & Fell (Cntr of Intl Studies), Princeton Univ, 1988-89; Prof, Dept of Pol Sc, Seoul Natl Univ, 1979-; Adj Prof, Grad Inst for Intl & Area Studies, Seoul Natl Univ; Chmn, Dept of Pol Sc, Seoul Natl Univ, 1991-93; Dir, Inst of Socl Scis, Seoul Natl Univ, 194-96; Pres, Korean Assn of Se Asian Studies, 1995-97; VP, Study Grp, Politics of Local-Global Rels, Intl Polit Sci Assn, 1995-; Mbr of Bd, 1995-, VP, 1996-97, Pres, 1997-98, Jacob Intl Soc for Collaborative Studies; Visng Fell, Inst of SE Asian Studies, Singapore, 1996-97; Visng Prof, Dept of Pol Sc, Natl Univ of Singapore, 1996-97. Publications: 9 books in Korean; 5 books in Engl inclng: (co-ed) Southeast Asia and Korea: Economic Development and Policy Reform, 1996; Koreans and Korean Business Interests in Central Europe and CIS Countires, 1998. Memberships include: Intl Pol Sc Assn; Amn Pol Sc Assn; Policy Advsry Cncl, Min of For Affairs, Repub of Korea, 1995-; Mbr & Sec Gen, Korea-ASEAN 21st Century Forum, Min of For Affairs & Trade, 1996-98; Founding & Bd Mbr, EBS (Korea Educl Brdcstng System), 1997-. Address: Department of Political Science, Seoul National University, Seoul, Korea 151-742.

AHN Jinho, b. 6 Sept 1963, Seoul, Korea. Professor. m. K Park, 8 May 1988, 1 s. 1 d. Education: BS, MS, Seoul Natl Univ; PhD, Univ TX at Austin. Appointments: Microelectronics Rsch Ctr, UT, 1989-92; NEC Microelectronics Rsch Labs, 1992-95; Hanyang Univ, 1995-. Publications: 40 refereed tech jrnl pprs; Co-auth, Handbook of Thin Film Technology. Memberships: Materials Rsch Soc; Japan Soc Applied Phys; IEEE; NY Acady Scis; MRS-Korea; Korean Inst Metals and Materials; IMAPS-Korea. Hobby: Golf. Address: Dept Materials Engineering, Hanyang University, Seoul 133-791, Korea.

AI Yunjun, b. 23 May 1929, Xinshao, Hunan, China. Teacher. m. Long Yueying, 16 Feb 1949, 1 s, 2 d. Education: Grad, Wuhan Univ. Appointments: Chinese People's Liberation Army, 1949; Probational Staff Offr, Chenghou Mil Sub-Command, Hunan, 1951-52; Tchr, Wuhan Inst of Water Conservancy, 1954-78; Tchr, Changsha Railway Univ, 1978-; Hd of Tchng and Rsch, 1986-96. Publications include: The Soviet Union Thesis Collection: Method of Descriptive Geometry and its Applications (translation), 1959 Analytical Guide of Engineering Graphics, 1984; Projective Transformation of Conics; The Key Point of Engineering Drawing Course Must Be Computer Graphics Processing. Honours: 3rd prize, Sci Rsch Accomplishments, Prov Educl Commn of Hunan, 1988; 3rd Prize, Ex Rsch Ppr, Hunan Sci and Technol Soc, 1988; 2nd Awd, Ex Tchng, Changsha Railway Univ, 1989; 1st Prize, Ex Tchng, Changsha Railway Univ, 1991; Spec Subsidy, Govt of China, 1992; 1st Awd, Ex Tchng, Changsha Railway Univ, 1992; 2nd Awd, Ex Tchng, Prov Educl Commn, 1993; 2000 Millennium Medal of Honour, ABI, 1998. Memberships: CEGS, 1981-93; Assoc Chmn, Hunan Engrng Graphics Soc, 1984-96. Hobby: Literature. Address: Department of Machine and Electric, Changsha Railway University, 154 Shaoshan Road, Changsha, Hunan 410075, China.

AIK Chong Tek, b. 2 Dec 1961, Singapore. International Timber Trader. m. Elly, 26 Aug 1993, 2 s. Education: BS, Gen Bus (Mngmt And Stats), NY Univ, Sch of Bus Admin, 1985; MBA, Fin, Cty Univ of NY, Baruch Coll, Grad Sch, 1986. Appointments: Rsch Analyst, Strategic Plng Assocs Pte Ltd, 1986-87; Mktng Dir, Kong Hwa Enterprises Pte Ltd, 1987-; Chf Advsr cum Gen Mngr, PT Royindo Karyalestari, 1988-. Honour: Fndrs Day Awd for Outstndng Schlshp, NY Univ, Sch of Bus Admin; Best Exporter Awd, S Kalimantan, Indonesia, 1994. Hobbies: Tennis; Table tennis. Address: PT Royindo, Karya Lestari, Jalan K S Tubun No 176, Banjarmasin 70241, South Kalimatan, Indonesia.

AIKMAN Colin Campbell, b. 24 Feb 1919, Picton, NZ. Consultant. m. Betty Alicia James, 14 Jan 1952, 3 d. Education: LLM, Vic Univ Coll, 1941; PhD, London Sch of Econs, Eng, 1948. Appointments: Bar, Sol, High Crt of NZ, 1940-41; Staff 1943-45, Legal Advsr 1948-55, Dept External Affairs; Prof of Juris and Constl Law, 1955-68, Dean of Law Fac, 1957-59, 1962-67, Vic Univ of Wellington; Vice Chan, Univ of the S Pacific, 1968-74; NZ High Commnr to India and Bangladesh, Amb to Nepal, 1975-78; Dir, NZ Inst of Intl Affairs, 1978-85; Cnslt, 1986-; Advsr on Constl Dev, Cook Is, W Samoa and Niue, 1962-67. Publications: 3 reports on constitutional devs in Cook Islands; Contbns to periodicals and other publs particularly Vic Univ Law Review and NZ Intl Review. Honours: NZ Travelling Schl in Law, 1941; Silver Jubilee Medal, 1977; CBE, 1990; Tstee, Norman Kirk Mem Trust, 1979, Chmn 1994-99; NZ Appointee to Cncl of Natl Univ of Samoa, 1985-98; Hon Dr, Univ of S Pacific, 1992; Hon LLD, Vic Univ of Wellington, 1992; West Samoa Order of Tiafau, 1993; Hon Dr of the Univ, Natl Univ of Samoa, 1996. Memberships: Wellington Club; Wellington Golf Club; Wellington Cricket Assn; Cntrl Dists Cricket Assn. Hobbies: Cricket; Golf; Carpentry. Address: 28 Korokoro Road, Petone, New Zealand.

AINO Koichiro, b. 1928. Appointments: Fmr Vice-Min of For Affairs; Min of State and Dir-Gen of the Econ Plng Agcy, Jan - Aug 1989. Memberships: HoR. Address: House of Representatives, 1-7-1 Nagato-cho, Chiyoda-ku, Tokyo 100, Japan.

AITKEN Bruce Alexander, b. 28 Oct 1950, Invercargill, NZ. Master of Knox College, University of Otago; Barrister; Solicitor. m. Wendy Alison Elizabeth McKean, 11 Dec 1976, 1 s, 3 d. Education: Grad LLB, Univ of Otago, 1976. Appointments: Pres, Knox Coll Studs' Club, Univ of Otago, 1971; Deacon, 1972, Elder, 1975, Convenor, Theol Hall Cttee, 1993-, Presby Ch; Admitted as Bar an Sol, H Crt, NZ, 1975; Asst Master, Knox Coll, 1976; Admitted to Ptnrshp, Rutherford McKinnon & Neil, 1979; Pres, Univ of Otago Crt of Convocation and Grads' Assn, 1981-84; Organist and Choirmaster, Knox Ch, Dunedin, 1988-; Ptnr, McKinnon Aitken Martin, law firm, 1988-; Master of Knox Coll, 1995-. Memberships: Otago Dist Law Soc, 1975-; NZ Law Soc, 1975-; Fell, Knox Coll, Dunedin, 1977-95; Roy Sch of Ch Music (Otago and Southland Br Chmn), 1991-; Pres, Dunedin Sinfonia, 1993-. Mbr of Cncl, Knox Coll and Salmond Hall Inc; Mbr, Otago Fndn Trust Bd; Mbr of Cncl, Univ of Otago; Chmn, Univ of Otago Dev Soc; Dunedin Sinfonia Bd. Hobbies: Snow skiing; Jogging; Walking; Watching rugby; Reading; Gardening. Address: The Master's Lodge, Knox College, Knox Street, Opoho, Dunedin, New Zealand.

AITMATOV Chingiz Torekulovich, b. 12 Dec 1928, Sheker Village, Kirghizia. Diplomat; Writer. m. Maria Urmatova, 3 s, 1 d. Education: Kirghiz Agric Inst. Appointments: Fmrly Corresp for Pravda; First Sec of Cinema Union of Kirghiz SSR, 1964-69; Chmn, 1969-86; Chmn Union of Writers of Kyrgyzstan, 1986-; Cand mbr Cen Cttee of CP of Kirghiz SSR, 1969-71; People's Writer of Kirghiz SSR, 1968; Vice-Chmn Cttee of Solidarity with Peoples of Asian and African Countries, 1974-89; Dep to USSR Supreme Soviet, 1966-89; Chmn Issyk-Kul Forum, 1986-; Chf Ed Innostrannaya Literatura, 1988-90; Peoples Dep of the USSR, 1989-91; USSR - now Russian - Amb to Luxembourg, 1990-92; Amb to Belgium and Luxembourg, 1992-96. Publications: inclng stories: Face to Face; Short Stories; Melody 1961; Tales of the Hills and the Steppes 1963; Stories 1967; Mother Earth and Other Stories 1989; novels: Djamilya, 1959; My Poplar in a Red Kerchief, 1960; Camel's Eye; The First Teacher; Farewell Gulsary; Mother Earth, 1963; The White Steamship; The Lament of the Migrating Bird; The Ascent of Mount Fuji, 1973; co-auth of Earth and Water, 1978; Works - 3 vols - 1978; Early Storks, 1979; Stories 1979; Piebald Dog; Running Along the Sea Shore; The Day Lasts More Than a Hundred Years; The White Cloud of Chingiz Khan, 1991; A Conversation at the Foothill of Fudjyama Mountain - with Daisaku Ikeda - 1992; The Brand of Cassandra, 1994. Honours: Lenin Prize Tales of the Hills and the Steppes, 1963; Austrian State Prize for Eurn Lit, 1994; Hero Socialist Labour, 1978; State Prize in Lit, 1968, 1977, 1983 and other decorations and prizes from Germany, India, Turkey and USA. Memberships: CPSU, 1959-91; Prestl Cncl 1990-91; Kirghiz Acady Sci, 1974; Eurn Acady Arts Sci and Hum, 1983; World Acady of Art Sci,1987; Hobby: Skiing. Address: Embassy of the Kyrgyz Republic, rue Tenbosch, 1050 Brussels, Belgium.

AJI Muhammade Rouzi, b. 27 Dec 1934, Kashgar, China. Physician. m. Hamragul, 15 Oct 1952, 1 s, 1 d. Education: Bach Med. Appointments: Res, Internal Med, 1962, Snr Reg, 1978, Cnslt of Cardiol, 1980, Snr Cnslt of Cardiol, 1990. Publications include: The Handbook of Emergency Medicine, 1978; Cardiac Disease, 1982. Honour: Specl Stipend, Ctrl Govt, 1993-. Memberships: Standing Mbr, Xinjiang Med Assn, Gerentol Assn; Vice Chmn, Cardiol Assn. Hobbies: Music; Writing. Address: No 2 Geriatric Department, 1st Affiliated Hospital, Xinjaing Medical University, Urumqi 830054, China.

AKAMATSU Ryoko, b. 24 Aug 1929, Osaka. 1 s. Education: Tsuda Coll and Univ of Tokyo. Appointments: Min of Labour, 1953; Dir Women Workers' Div, 1972-75; Dir-Gen Yamanashi Labour Stand Bur, 1975-78; Cnslr in charge of Women's Affairs, PMs Off, 1978-79; Min Perm Miss to UN, 1979-82; Dir-Gen Women's Bur, Min of Labour, 1982-85; Amb to Uruguay, 1986-89; Pres Japan Inst of Workers' Evolution, 1989-93; Prof Bunkyo Women's Coll, 1992-93; Min of Educ, Sci, Culture and Sports, 1993-94; Prof, Grad Course of Bunkyo Women's Univ; Exec Dir, Biuako Hall, Cntr for the Perfng Arts, Shiga. Publications: Girls Be Ambitious (autobiog), 1990; Beautiful Uruguay, 1990. Hobbies: Reading; Swimming; Listening to classical music. Address: 5-11-22-309, Roppongi, Minato-ku, Tokyo 106-0032, Japan.

AKAY Adnan, b. 13 Oct 1948, Samsun, Turkey. Professor. Education: PhD, Mech Engrng. Appointments include: Prof, Dept of Mech Engrng, Wayne State Univ, 1986-89; Guest Prof, Mech Engrng, Univ of Rome, La Sapienza, Rome, Italy, 1992; De Vlieg Prof, Mech Engrng, Wayne State Univ, 1989-92; Prof and Hd, Dept of Mech Engrng, Carnegie Mellon Univ, 1992-. Memberships: Fell, ASME; Fell, Acoustic Soc Am; Chair, 1997-98, United Engrng Fndn. Address: Mechanical Engineering Department, Carnegie Mellon University, Pittsburgh, PA 15213, USA.

AKAYEV Askar, b. 10 Nov 1944. President of the Kyrgyz Republic. m. Professor Mayram Duyshenovna Akayeva, 2 s, 2 d. Education: Grad, Leningrad Inst of Precise Mech & Optics (w distinction), 1967; Cand of Scis degree, 972; DSc, 1976. Appointments: Engr, Asst, Lectr, Snr Lectr, Hd of Dept, Politechnical Inst in Frunze, 1972-; Prepared 20 cands of Scis and 3 Drs of Scis; Hd, Sci Dept, USSr Cntrl Cttee of Communist Party of Khrghyzia, 1986-87; Elected Pres, Kyrgyz Repub by Parl, 1990, re-elected 1991, confirmed by referendum, 1994; Elected Pres of Kyrgyz Repub by nat suffrage, in accordance with Constn of Kyrgyz Repub, 1995-. Honours include: Grand Cross for Freedom & Unity, by Assn for Unity of Latin Am, 1991; Hon Prof, Moscow State Univ, 1992; Awd, Intl Unity Fndn, estab by Dj Neru, 1995; Hon Academician, Intl Engrng Acady, Moscow, 1996; Hon Academician of Int Acady of Creations, 1996; Hon Dr, Natl Acady of Azerbaijan & Natl Acady of Armenian Repub, 1997; Awd for Outstndng Leadership, Assn for Study of Nationalities (USA), 1997; Academician, Intl Informatization Acady, Can, 1997; Intl Personal Acady of Ukraine awd'd Order For the Dev of Sci & Educ, 1998; Hon docts, dips, citizenships. Memberships include: Pres, Kurgyz Acady of Scis, 1989; NY Acady of Scis; IAS.

AKBULUT Yildirim, b. 1935, Erzincan. Politician. m. 3 c. Education: Univ of Istanbul. Appointments: fmr practising lawyer; Dep for Erzincan, 1983-; PM of Turkey, 1989-91; fmr Dep Speaker of Parl, Speaker, 1987-89; Min of Interior, 1986-87. Memberships: Motherland Party. Address: c/o Office of the Prime Minister, Basbakanlik, Bakanliklar, Ankara, Turkey.

AKELLA Jagannadham, b. 13 Sept 1937, Kakinada, India. Scientist; Geochemist. m. Lalita, 1967, 3 d. Education: MSc, BSc, hons, Andhra Univ; PhD, Indian Inst of Technol, Kharagpur. Appointments: Snr Lectr, Rajastan Univ, 1962-63; German Acad Exchange Schl, 1963-66; Rsch Assoc, Univ CA, Los Angeles, 1967-72; Snr Sci, Lawrence Livermore Natl Labs, Livermore 1977-. Publications: Over 100 sci articles in profl jrnls. Honours: Natl Rsch Cncl and Natl Acady of Scis Rsch Fell at NASA, 1974-77; Awd of Ex, Dept of Energy, LLNL, USA, 1994. Memberships: Fell, Mineralogical Soc of India, Amn Mineralogical Soc; Mbr, Amn Geophysl Union. Hobbies: Reading; Theatre; Travel; Gardening. Address: L-201 Lawrence Livermore National Laboratory, University of California, Livermore, CA 94550, USA.

AKERS-JONES David (Sir), b. 14 Apr 1927, UK. Retired Civil Servant. m. Jane Spickernell, 8 Sept 1951, 1 d. Education: MA, Oxford Univ, 1952. Appointments: Brit India Steam Navig Co, 1944-49; Malayan Civ Serv, 1953-57; Hong Kong Govt, 1957-87; Chmn, Natl Mutual

Ins Co Ltd, Hong Kong, Global Asset Mngmt (HK) Ltd, Dir, Hysan Dev Co Ltd, Sime Darby Hong Kong Ltd; Dep Chmn, CNT Group Ltd; Dir, China Everbright Intl; Dir K Wah Intl Holdings Ltd; Dir, Shui On Property Co Ltd. Honours: CMG, 1977; KBE, 1985; Hon DCL, Kent; Hon LLD, Chinese Univ of Hong Kong; Hon DSSc, Cty Univ, Hong Kong. Memberships: Hon Mbr RICS, 1991; Cncl Govs Austl Natl Gall, 1992. Hobbies: Gardening; Painting; Walking; Music. Address: Dragon View, Tsing Lung Tau, 14 Miles Castle Peak Road, New Territories, Hong Kong.

AKIHITO. b. 23 Dec 1933, Tokyo. Emperor of Japan. m. Michiko Shoda, 1959, 2 s, 1 d. Education: Gakushuin Schls and Fac of Pols and Econs Gakushuin Univ. Appointments: Offic investiture as Crown Prince, 1952; succeeded, 7 Jan 1989; crowned, 12 Nov 1990; undertaken visits to some 37 countries and travelled widely throughout Japan. Publications: 25 papers in jrnl of Ichthyological Soc of Japan. Honours: Hon Pres or Patron Asian Games, 1958; Intl Sports Games for the Disabled, 1964; Eleventh Pacific Sci Congress, 1966; Japan World Exposition, 1970; Intl Skill Contest for the Disabled, 1981; Hon Sec Intl Conf on Indo-Pacific Fish, 1985. Memberships: Ichthyological Soc of Japan; Hon Mbr Linnean Soc London. Hobbies: Taxonomic study of gobiid fish; Natural history and conservation; History; Tennis. Address: The Imperial Palace, 1-1 Chiyoda, Chiyoda-ku, Tokyo 100, Japan.

AKIMOTO Tatsuru, b. 26 Oct 1941, Tokyo, Japan. Professor. m. Katsuko, 30 June 1970, 2 s. Education: LLB, Tokyo Metro Univ; Master of Socl Work, Wayne State Univ; Dr of Socl Welfare, City Univ of NY, Hunter Coll. Appointments: Labour Analyst, Tokyo Metro Govt Bur of Labour; Assoc Prof, Josai Univ; Employment Promotion Specialist, ILO; Prof, Japan Women's Univ. Publications: Detroit - The Necessity of Social Unionism, 1981; Japan in the Passing Lane, 1982; A New Tide of US Labor Movement - Seen From 80s, 1992; Shrinkage of Urban Slums in Asia and their Employment Aspects, 1998. Memberships: Japan Assn for Labour Sociol; Japan Assn for Socl Welfare Studies; Japan Assn for Socl Policy Studies; JIRA; NASW, USA. Hobbies: Travel; Tennis. Address: 1-1-1 Nishiikuta, Tama-ku, Kawasaki-shi, Kanagawa 214-8565, Japan.

AKINE Yasuyuki, b. 19 May 1943, Shanghai, China. Physician. m. Masako Kuroda, 17 May 1970, 1 s, 1 d. Education: MD, Kyushu Univ, 1968. Appointments: Prof, Univ of Tsukuba, 1995; Dir, Proton Med Rsch Cntr, Univ of Tsukuba, 1996. Membership: Japanese Soc of Radiation Oncologists. Address: 3-650 Namiki, Tsukuba, 305-0044, Japan.

AKRAM Dure-Samin, b. 27 May 1947, Physician (Pediatrician). m. Fareed, 7 Aug 1984, 1 d. Education: MBBS, MD MPH, Dipl, Amn Bds in Pediats. Appointments: Asst Prof, Assoc Physn, Pediats, Jinnah Postgrad Med Cntr, Karachi, Pakistan, 1976-80; Asst Prof, 1982-85, Assoc Prof, 1985-91, Prof of Pediats, 1991-95, Regularised as Prof of Pediats, 1995-, Dow Med Coll, Karachi, Pakistan. Publications: Nutrition Curriculum for Doctors & Health Workers for Nutrition Support Programme, auth; National Nutrition Curriculum, co-auth; National Lactation Management Curriculum, co-auth; Curriculum for Community-Oriented Teaching for Medical Students, Dow Medical College, Karachi, co-auth; Curriculum for Under-graduates in Reproductive Health, co-auth. Memberships include: Pakistan Med Assn; Pakistan Pediat Assn; APHA; AAP; Intl MCH Assn; Natl Acady of Med Scis; Pakistan Med Rsch Soc. Hobbies: Writing; Reading. Address: 12-A/1 North Avenue, DHA PH I, Karachi, Pakistan.

AL AHMAD Sabah (Sheikh), b. 1929. First Deputy Premier and Foreign Minister, Kuwait. Appointments: Acting Fin and Oil Min, 1965-67; For Min, Acting Info Min, 1971-75; Dpty Premier and Acting Interior Min, Dpty Premier and For Min, 1978; Dpty Premier and For Min, Acting Info Min, 1981-82; For Min, 1963-91. Address: Ministry of Foreign Affairs, PO Box 3-Safat 13001, Kuwait.

AL HADI Mohammed Sharif, b. 11 Oct 1943, Dubai, United Arab Emirates. Businessman. m. Fatma Abdul Rahim Al Mulla, 3 s, 4 d. Education: Dip, Banking. Appointments: Hd, Currency and Banking Dept, UAE Ctrl Bank, 1973 Sec to Bd, Secs Dept, 1973-74, Br Mngr, Dubai, 1974-84, 1st BranchMngnr, 1984, 1st Expert, UAE Brs, 1994; Proprietor, Hadison Grp; Dir, Al Razouki Intl Exchange Co. Honours: Sev Merit Ctfs, UAE Ctrl Bank. Memberships: Amn Mngmt Bur, NY; Instn of Bankers, London. Hobbies: Reading; Travel. Address: PO Box 51666, Dubai, United Arab Emirates.

AL ROUDHAN Nasser Abdallah, b. 11 Feb 1950. Minister of State for Cabinet Affairs. Education: BBA, Univ of Kuwait. Appointments: Hd, Shareholding Co's Sect, Min of Com and Ind, 1975-78; Insurance Co's Supvsr, 1978-85; MP, 1985; Min of State for Housing Affairs, 19; Min of Com and Ind, 1990; Min of Plng, 1992; Dpty Prime Min and Fin Min, 1996; Min of State for Cabinet Affairs. Address: Council of Ministers, General Secretariat, PO Box 1397, Safat 13014, Kuwait.

AL RQOBAH Hmoud, b. 1951. Minister of Electricity and Water; Minister of Public Works. Education: BS, Cheml Engrng; MS, USA, 1977. Appointments: Dir Gen, KISR, 1988; Min of Electricity and Water, 1990; Min of Oil, 1992; Min of Electricity and Water, Min of Pub Wrks. Address: Ministry of Public Works, PO Box 8, Safat 13001, Kuwait.

AL SABAH Salem (Sheikh). Minister of Defence. Appointments: Dir. Legal and Pol Depts, For Ministry, 1963-65; Amb, London, 1963-65 (Sweden, Norway and Denmark); Amb, WA, 1971-75 (Canada, Venezuela); Min of Socl Affairs and Labour, 1975; Def Min, 1978-86; Dpty Premier and Def Min, 1978-86, 1986-88; Chf, Natl POWs and Affairs Cttee. Address: Ministry of Defence. PO Box 1170, Safat 13012, Kuwait.

AL SALEH Ali Saleh Abdulla, b. 28 Dec 1942, Bahrain. Minister of Commerce. m. Afaf Radhi S Al-Mousawi, 1970, 1 s, 2 d. Education: BCom. Appointments: Min of Com, State of Bahrain; Chmn, Bahrain Stock Exchange; Chmn, Bahrain Promotion & Mktng Bd, Bahrain Intl Exhibns Cntr, Standards & Metrology Cttee; Bd of Trustees, Bahrain Cntr for Studies Rsch. Hobbies: Reading; Music; Travel. Address: c/o Ministry of Commerce, PO Box 5479, Manama, Bahrain.

AL-ALI Ali Salem (Sheikh). Minister of Finance and Communications. Appointments: Engr, Kuwait Oil Co; Finl Analyst, Mngmt Dept, Finl Market; Advsr, Ministry of Electricity; Min of Fin and Comms. Address: Ministry of Communications, PO Box 318, Safat 13004, Kuwait.

AL-ARRAYED Jalil E, b. 26 Jan 1933, Manama, Bahrain. Professor Emeritus. m. Jalila, 28 Nov 1958, 2 s, 1 d. Education: BA, Chem, Am Univ of Beirut, 1954; MEd, Sci Educn, Leicester Univ, England, 1964; PhD, Comparative Sci Educn, Bath Univ, England, 1974. Appointments: Sci and Math Tchr, Bahrain Second Sch, 1954-59; Sci Inspector, 1959-62; Prin, Men's Tchr Trng Coll, 1964-72; Under-Sec, Min of Educ, 1974-82; Rector, Bahrain Univ Coll of Arts, Sci and Educ, 1982-87; VP for Acad Affairs, 1987-91, Acting Pres, 1990, Univ Bahrain. Publications: A Critical Analysis of School Science Teaching in Arab Countries; Some Aspects of Contemporary Management Thought; Development and Evaluation of University Faculty in Arab Gulf States. Honours: Bahrain Govt Dept of Educn Gold Medal, 1969; Bahrain Min of Educn Prize, Acad Achievement, 1975; ABI Commemorative Medal of Hon, 1988; ABI World Decoration of Ex, 1989; Bahrain Govt State Awd, Outstndng Profl Servs, 1992; Outstndng Contbrn Ctf, Intl Assn of Univ Pres, 1996. Memberships include: Fndng Cttee, Arabian Gulf Univ, 1980-85; Cncl for Higher Educ, Arab Bur of Educ for the Gulf States, Riyadh, Saudi Arabia, 1976-82; IIEP Cncl of Cnslt Fells, 1984-92. Hobbies: Reading; Music; Stamp Collecting; Drawing; Painting. Address: PO Box 26165, Manama, Bahrain.

AL-ASHAIK Abdullah Ibn Mohammed Ibn Ibrahim, b. 1949. Education: BA, Shariah Coll, 1975, PhD, 1987,

Imam Mohammed Ibn Saud Univ; MA, Al-Azhar Univ, Cairo, 1980. Appointments: Dean, Imam Mohammed Ibn Saud Univ, 1975; Asst Prof, 1988; Min of Jus, 1992. Address: Ministry of Justice, University Street, Riyadh 11137, Saudi Arabia.

AL-ASSAF Ibrahim Ibn Abdulaziz Ibn Abdullah, b. 1949. Minister of Finance and National Economy. Education: BA, Econs and Pol Sci, King Saud Univ, Riyadh; MA, Econs, Denver Univ, CO, USA; PhD, Econs, CO State Univ, Fort Collins, USA. Appointments: Lectr, Principles of Econ, 1971-82, Assoc Prof, Econ, Hd, Dept of Administrative Scis, 1982-86, King Abdulaziz Mil Coll, Riyadh; Guest Lectr, Coll of Command and Staff, 1982-83; Pt-time Advsr, Saudi Dev Fund, 1982-86; Alternate Saudi Exec Dir, Intl Monetary Fund, 1986-89; Exec Dir, Exec Bd, World Bank Grp, 1989-95; Vice-Gov, Saudi Monetary Agy, 1995; Min of State and Mbr of Cncl of Mins, 1995-96; Min of Fin and Natl Econ, 1996-. Address: Min of Finance and National Economy, Airport Road, Riyadh 11177, Saudi Arabia.

AL-BASSAM Moayed, b. 23 Aug 1955, Saudi Arabia. Oil Export Executive. m. Susan L Al-Bassam, 17 Jan 1993, 1 s. Education: BS, Chem Engrng, Kuwait Univ, 1980; BS, Pet Engrng, 1982, MS, Pet Engrng, 1984, Univ of South CA, Los Angeles, USA; Dip Pet Engrng, Cert Pet Engr, Intl Pet Inst, OK, USA, 1986. Appointments: Saudi Arabian Texaco Inc. Publications: Co-auth, books: Surface Operations in Petroleum I, 1986; Surface Operations in Petroleum II, 1986; 6 pprs in prfl jrnls, 1982-92. Honours: Pi Epsilon Tau (Natl Pet Engrng Hon Soc); Pi Kappa Phi (Natl All Univ Hon Soc); PhD, Pepperdine Univ, Malibu, 1983; Intl Hall of Fame, 1984. Memberships: Chm GAOCMAO (Gulf Area Oil Co Mutual Aid Orgn); Amn Soc of Pet Engrs; Amn Inst of Chem Engrs; Natl Assn of Corrosion Engrs. Hobbies: Playing tennis; Spending time with his family. Address: Saudi Arabian Texaco Inc, PO Box 88, Al-Khafji 31971, Kingdom of Saudi Arabia.

AL-DAKHIL AbdulAziz. Minister of Commerce and Industry. Appointments: Sev snr posts in pub prosecution; Dir, Pub Prosecution, 1984; Jus Undersec, 1987; Min of State for Cabinet Affairs, 1992, 1996; Min of Com and Ind. Address: Ministry of Commerce and Industry, PO Box 2944, Safat 13030, Kuwait.

AL-JISHI Majid Jawad, b. 1931. Government Official. m. Education: BS, Civ Engrng, Amn Univ of Beirut, 1955. Appointments: Engr, Pub Wrks Directorate, Bahrain, 1955-56; Constrn Engr, contracting co, Qatar, 1957-61; Proj Engr, Roads Div, Min of Pub Wrks, Govt of Kuwait, 1961-64; Engrng Cnslt, bahrain, 1964-68; Asst Dir, Dir, Dept of Pub Wrks and Dev, Govt of Abu Dhabi, 1968-70; Dir, Plng, Min of Dev and Engrng Servs, Govt of Bahrain, 1970-72; Undersec, Min of Plng, 1973-75; Min of Wrks, Power and Water, 1975-94; Min Wrks and Agric, 1995-. Address: Ministry of Works and Agriculture, POB 1000, 1000 Government House, Government Road, Manama, Bahrain.

AL-KHALIFA Isa Ibn Salman (Sheikh), b. 3 July 1933. Amir of Bahrain. m. 5 children. Career: Appointed Heir Apparent, 1958; Ruler of Bahrain, 1961-; Amir, 1971-. Honours: KCMG, Eng; KG, Eng. Address: Office of the Amir, Rifa's Palace, POB 555, Manama, Bahrain.

AL-KHALIFA Khalifa bin Sulman (Sheikh), b. 1935, Bahrain. Prime Minister of Bahrain. m. 2 s, 1 d. Appointments: Pres, Educ Cncl, 1957-60; Sec of Govt, 1959-60; Hd of Fin, 1960-66; Dir, 1961; Pres, Elec Bd, 1961; Pres, Admin Cncl, 1966-70; State Cncl, 1970-73; Chair, Bahrain Monetary Agcy; Prime Minister, 1973-75, 1978-. Address: Office of the Prime Minister, POB 1000, Government House, Government Road, Manama, Bahrain.

AL-KULAIB Ahmad, b. 1953, Qibla. Minister of Justice; Minister of Awqaf and Islamic Affairs. Education: BA, Socl Servs, Cairo Univ, 1976. Appointments: Dir, Ahmadi and Jahra Governorates, 1984-89; Bd Mbr, Pub Socl Affairs Inst, 1988; MP, 1992; Min of Socl Affairs and

Labour, 1994; Min of Jus, Min of Awqaf and Islamic Affairs. Address: Ministry of Justice and Legal Affairs, PO Box 6, Safat 13001, Kuwait.

AL-MAHAYNI Mohamad Khaled, b. 30 May 1943, Damascus, Syria. Minister of Finance. m. Falak Sakkal, 1966, 2 s, 2 d. Education: PhD, Econs, Damascus, Univ, 1991. Appointments: Fin Dir, var pub estabs, 1961-76; Auditor, 1970-; Var snr positions Min of Fin, 1977-87; Min of Fin, 1987-; Prof Econs, Damascus Univ, 1992-. Publications: Methodology of the General State Budget in the Syrian Arab Republic, 1994; Financial Planning Policies (Expositional and Analysis), 1994; Government Accounting, 1995. Memberships: Var econ and ministerial cttees, Gov of Syria to IBRD in Wash. Hobbies: Reading; Computers. Address: Ministry of Finance, Jule Jammal Street, PO Box 13136, Damascus, Syria.

AL-MALIKI Shabib Lazim, b. 1 July 1936, Baghdad, Iraq. Government Official. m. 6 children. Education: BSc, Law, Baghdad Univ; Dip in Intl Law. Appointments: gov, Karbala Govt, Iraq, 1968-73; Gov, Nineveh, 1972-73; Dpty Min, Min, Agric, 1973-75; Min Jus, 1991-. Publications: The Law as a Tool for the Arab World; The Unified Arab Parliament. Memberships: Sec Gen, Arab Jurists Union, 1975-; Perm Commn, Human Rights and Pol Freedom in Arab World, 1979; Consultative Commn, Intl Org, Anti-Racial Discrimination, 1979; Intl Lawyers' Union, Dpty Chmn, 1976; Iraqi Hunting Club; Arab Ba'ath Socialist Party. Address: Ministry of Justice, Baghdad, Iraq.

AL-MOUSSA Ali. Planning Minister; State Minister for Administrative Development. Education: Grad, Pub Admin, Amn Univ, Beirut, 1970. Appointments: Asst Undersec, Plng Ministry; Dpty Gov, Cntrl Bank; Mbr, Supreme Cncl of Plng, 1995-98; Plng Min, State Min for Adminstv Dev. Address: Ministry of Planning, PO Box 15, Safat 13001, Kuwait.

AL-OMAR Ahmad Faisal, b. 1 July 1939, Kazo, Hama, Syria. University Professor. m. Hiam Al Wani, 9 Sept 1965, 2 s, 2 d. Education: MSc, Univ of Birmingham, 1968; PhD, 1968. Appointments: Dean, Fac Engrng, Aleppo Univ 1975-77; Dean, Fac Mechl Engrng, 1984-86, 1995-97; Dean, Fac Engrng, Sana's Univ 1989-91. Publications: 5 Books, Thermo and Internal Combustion Engines; 12 Pprs; Many Articles. Honours: Min of Ind for Undergrad Univ of Aleppo for Postgrad Stdy. Memberships: Engrng Syndicate; Tchrs Union. Hobbies: Swimming; Reading; Travel. Address: P O Box 370, 21 Acasia St, New Shabba Aleppo, Syria.

AL-OUN Jassem, b. 1946. Minister of Social Affairs and Labour; Minister of Housing. Appointments: MP, 1981, 1985, 1992; Min of Socl Affairs and Labour, 1992; Min of Electricity, Water and Comms, 1996; Min of Socl AFfairs and Labour, Min of Housing. Address: Ministry of Social Affairs and Labour, PO Box 563, Safat 13006, Kuwait.

AL-RAHMAH Abdullah Nasser, b. 20 Dec 1943, Al-Rass-Qassim, Saudi Arabia. University Staff. m. 25 June 1968, 3 s, 5 d. Education: BS, King Saud Univ, 1969; PhD, Mycology, Glasgow Univ, 1975. Appointments: Demonstrator, 1969-71, Asst Prof, 1975-77, Assoc Prof, 1977-86, Prof, 1986, Hd, 1985-87, Botany & Microbiology Dept, Coll of Sci, King Saud Univ; Mbr Editl Bd, Jrnl of Coll of Sci, KSU, 1983-85; Vice Dean, Univ Lib, King Saud Univ; Mbr Coll of Sci, 1985-87; Mbr, Cntr for Desert Studies Cncl, KSU, 1987-93. Publications: Over 40 rch pprs on Mycology and Plant Pathology, in Arab and intl sci jrnls; Auth, books on Mycology in Arabic. Memberships: Brit Mycological Soc; Arabian Plant Protection Soc; Saudi Biol Soc; 2nd Conf on Mycology, FL; 3rd Conf on Plant Path, Geneva. Hobbies: Reading; Excursions; Photography. Address: Botany and Microbiology Department, College of Science, King Saud University, PO Box 2455, Riyadh 11451, Saudi Arabia.

AL-RASHEED Mohammed Ibn Ahmed, b. 1944. Education: BA, Arabic Lang, Al-Imam Mohammed Ibn Saud Islamic Univ, 1964; MSc, Personnel Mngmt, Univ of IN, USA, 1969; PhD, Higher Educ Mngmt, Univ of OK, USA, 1972. Appointments: Tchng Asst, Fac of Sharia and Islamic Stdies, King Saud Univ, 1964-65, Asst Prof, 1972-79, Assoc Prof, 1979-89, Assoc Dean, Fac of Educ, 1974-76, Dean, 1976-79; Gen Dir, Arab Educ Off, Gulf Co-op Cncl, 1979-88; Fndr, Gulf Univ, Bahrain, 1979-88; Min of Educ, 1995-. Address: Ministry of Education, Airport Road, Riyadh 11148, Saudi Arabia.

AL-SABAH Mohammed (Sheikh). Interior Minister. Appointments: Dir Gen of Gen Directorate of Nationality and Visa Dept; Gov, Al-Ahmadi, 1991-; Interior Min. Address: Ministry of Interior, PO Box 11, Safat 101, Kuwait.

AL-SABAH Saud Nasser (Sheikh), b. 3 Oct 1944. Minister of Oil. Education: Univ Degree, Law, London Univ, Eng. Appointments: Legal Dept, For Ministry, 1969; Amb to UK, 1975-80; Non-res Amb to Sweden, 1975-80; Amb to USA; Info Min, 1996-98; Min of Oil. Address: Ministry of Oil, PO Box 5077, Safat 13051, Kuwait.

AL-SABIH Adel, b. 1953. Health Minister; Acting Education and Higher Education Minister. Education: Doct, Mechl Engrng, NC State Univ, 1983. Appointments: Num posts, Kuwait Univ; Ed-in-Chf, local mag; Mbr, Supreme Pet Cncl, 1993-; Min of Hlth, Acting Educ and Higher Educ Min, 1997-. Address: Ministry of Education, PO Box 7, Safat 13001, Kuwait.

AL-SALEH Ali Saleh Abdallah, b. 28 Dec 1942. Minister of Commerce. m. 3 children. Education: BCom, Ain Shams Univ, Cairo, 1966. Appointments: Min Com, Govt of Bahrain, 1995-; Chmn, Bahrain Stock Exch, Bahrain Promotion and Mktng Bd, Bahrain Intl Exhbn Conf Bd, Stds and Metrology Commn, Bd Tstees, Bahrain Cntr Stdies and Rsch; Dpty Chmn, Shurs (Consultative Cncl); Tstee, Univ Bahrain. Membership: Bahrin Cncl of Com and Ind. Address: Ministry of Commerce, POB 5479, Diplomatic Area, Manama, Bahrain.

AL-SAUD Naif Ibn Abdulaziz (HRH), b. 1934. Education: Religion, Diplomacy and Security Affairs. Appointments: Gov of Riyadh, 1953-54; Dpty Min of Interior; Min of State for Internal Affairs, 1970; Pres, Supreme Cncl for Info; Min of Interior, 1975-. Address: Ministry of the Interior, PO Box 2933, Riyadh 11134, Saudi Arabia.

AL-SHAKAR Karim Ebrahim, b. 23 Dec 1945, Bahrain. Diplomat. m. Fatima Al-Mansouri, 1979. Education: BA, Polit Sci, Delhi Univ, 1970. Appointments: Attaché, Min of For Affairs, Bahrain, 1970; Mbr, Permanent Mission to UN, later Min For Affairs, 1972-76; 1st Sec, Min of For Affairs, Bahrain, 1981; Cnsllr, Min of For Affairs, Bahrain, 1981; Amb, Permanent Repr to UN, Geneva, Other intl orgns in Switz, Consul-Gen to Swiss Fedn (also non-res Amb to Germany, Austria, Permanent Repr to UN/UNIDO, Vienna), 1982-87; Amb, Permanent Repr to UN, NY, 1987-90; Amb to Uk (non-res Amb to Repub of Ireland, Netherlands, Denmark), 1990-95; Dir, Intl Directorate, Min of For Affairs, Bahrain, 1995-. Address: Ministry of Foreign Affairs, PO Box 547, Manama, State of Bahrain.

AL-SULTAN Yousef Yacoub, b. 1947. Assistant Director General. m. 5 children. Education: BSc, Chem, BSc, Maths, Toledo Univ, 1971; MSc, Chem, Univ of Manchester Inst of Sci and Technol, UK, 1977; PhD, Sci & Technol Policy, Univ of Aston, Birmingham, UK, 1984; Post Doct Prog in Sci and Technol Policies, Sci Policy Rsch Unit, Univ of Brighton, Sussex, UK, 1986, 1995. Appointments: Tutor, Chem Dept, Kuwait Univ, 1971-74; Profl, Cntrl Analytical Lab, Kuwait Inst for Sci Rsch (KISR), 1974-76; Hd, Spectroscopy Sect, Cntrl Analaytical Lab, KISR, 1977-80; Assoc Rsch Techno-Econs Div, KISR, 1984-88; Asst Dir Gen, KISR, 1988-. Publications: Pprs, reviews, conf pprs, books inclng: (co-auth) Nutritive Values of Kuwaiti Food, 1980;

The Meat of Sacrificed Animals in Islamic Religion, 1980; (auth) Iraqi Aggression on Kuwait: Claims and Consequences from Islamic Perspectives, 1994; Ed-in-Chf, contbr, to Chemistry Dictionaries and The Kuwait Scientific Encyclopedia: Chemistry, Volumes 1-9. Honours include: Top of 1997 Sci Personality in Kuwait, Al-Wajaha (Prestige) Magazine, No 14, Jan 1998. Memberships include: Fndr, Kuwaiti Chem Soc, 1980; Fell, Roy Soc Chem, UK, 1984; Amn Inst of Chem; Brit Inst of Chem; Roy Inst of Chem in Brit; Amn Pharm Assn; Chromatography-Spectroscopy Inst, Can; Environ Protection Soc, Kuwait; Chem Inst of Can; Chartered Mbr, Intl Technol Inst, 1984; Mbr, Bd of Dirs, Kuwaiti Chem Soc, 1988-90, 1990-92, 1992-94, 1994-96. Address: PO Box 14089, 72851 Al-Fayha, Kuwait.

AL-THANI Abdulla bin Khalifa (Sheikh). Government Official. Appointments: Min of Interior, Doha, Qatar, 1989; Acting Min of Fin and Pet; Prime Min. Address: Office of the Prime Minister, Doha, Qatar.

ALAGAPPA Muthiah. Researcher. Education: PhD Intl Affairs, Fletcher Sch Law and Diplomacy, Tufts Univ. Appointments: Adj fac, Univ Malayav and Natl Univ Malaysia; Sr Fellow, Inst Strategic and Intl Studies, Malaysia; Vstg Prof, Columbia Univ; Dir of Studies, East-West Ctr. Publications: Articles in profl journals in field of intl politics and security;Auth-Ed, Political Legitimacy in Southeast Asia: The Quest for Moral Authority, 1995; Auth-Ed, Asian Security Practice: Material and Ideational Influences, 1998. Memberships: Editl Bd, The Pacific Review, and The Australian Journal of International Affairs; Intl Advsry Bd, Cambridge Asia-Pacific Studies; Rsch Cncl of the Intl Forum for Democratic Stdies; Editl Cttee, Contemporary Issues of the Asia-Pacific. Address: Director of Studies, Research Program, East-West Centre, 1601 East-West Road, Honolulu, HI 96848, USA.

ALAINI Mohsen Ahmed al-, b. 20 Oct 1932, Bani Bahloul, N Yemen. m. Aziza Abulaham, 1962, 2 s, 2 d. Education: Fac of Law, Cairo Univ and the Sorbonne, Paris. Appointments: Sch tchr Aden, 1958-60; Intl Confedn of Arab Trade Unions, 1960-62; Min of For Affairs Yemeni Repub, Sept-Dec 1962, 1974-80; Perm Rep to UN, 1962-65, 1965-66, 1967-69; Min of For Affairs May-July 1965; PM, Nov-Dec 1967; Amb to USSR, 1968-70; PM, Min of For Affairs, Feb 1971 - Sept 1971 - Dec 1972, June 1974 - Jan 1975; Amb to France Aug-Sept 1974 - 1965-76; Amb to UK 1973-74; Amb to Fed Repub of Germany, 1981-84; Amb to USA, 1984-; Perm Rep to UN, 1980-81. Address: Embassy of the Yemen Republic, 2600 Virginia Avenue, NW, Suite 705, Washington, DC 20037, USA.

ALARCON Fabian. Politician. Appointments: Fmrly Speaker of Congress; Acting Pres of Ecuador, 6-10 Feb 1997; Pres of Ecuador, 11 Feb 1997-. Address: Office of the President, Palacio Nacional, Garcia Moreno 1043, Quito, Ecuador.

ALATAS Ali, b. 4 Nov 1932, Jakarta. Politician. m. Yunisa Alatas, 1956, 3 d. Education: Acady for For Affairs and Sch of Law, Univ of Indonesia. Appointments: Financial and Econ Ed PIA Nat news Agency Jakarta; joined Min of For Affairs, 1954; Second Sec - later first Sec - Bangkok Thailand, 1956-69; Dir Info and Cultural Affairs Jakarta, 1960-65; Dir 1965-66, 1970-72; Cnslr - later Min Cnslr - Washington DC, 1966-70; Sec Directorate Gen for Polit Affairs Jakarta, Chef de Cabinet to Min of For Affairs, 1972-75; Perm Rep to UN 1976-78, 1982-84, 1985-87; Sec to Vice-Pres of Indonesia, 1978-82; Chmn First Cttee 40th UN Gen Ass, 1985; Min of For Affairs, May 1988. Honours: Indonesian Order of Merit. Hobbies: Golf; Reading; Music; Swimming. Address: Ministry of Foreign Affairs, ul Taman, Pejambon No 6, Jakarta, Indonesia.

ALBAKRI Dhia, b. 27 Sept 1949, Baghdad, Iraq. Environmental Geologist. m. Taghred, 13 Aug 1982, 2 d. Education: BSc; MSc; PhD. Appointments: Univ of Sydney, 1994-; Univ of New Eng, Aust, 1992-94; Kuwait Inst for Sci Rsch, 1980-91. Publications: 90 publs &

presentations inclng monographs, rsch reports, chapts in books, jrnl articles & conf pprs. Honours: Postgrad Schlsp, Univ of Iraq, 1973-75; Postgrad Schlsp, Iraq Min of Higher Educ, 1976-80. Memberships: Austl Geol Soc; AAAS; Intl Assn of Sedimentologist. Hobbies: Reading; Walking; Swimming. Address: PO Box 883, University of Sydney, Orange, NSW 2800, Australia.

ALBUQUERQUE Olav Gregory, b. 9 May 1963, Mumbai, India. Legal Correspondent (Journalism). Education: MSc, LLM, PhD, Univ of Bombay, Mumbai, Maharashtra, India. Appointments: Sub-Ed, The Daily, 1983-84; Snr Sub-Ed, Mid-Day, 1984-85; Snr Sub-Ed, Evening News of India, 1986; Snr Sub-Ed, Times of India News Serv, 1987; Law Reporter, Times of India, 1995. Publications: Over 100 articles in var newspapers; over 200 rsch pprs in acad jrnls. Honours: Maharashtra Govt Awd, Devl Jrnlsm, 1988; Bombay Univ Silver Medal, 1990; Selected for Indal Rsch Fellowship, 1993; Best Christian Jrnlst in India, 1994. Hobbies: Swimming; Table-Tennis; Reading; Badminton. Address: Sea-Lord, B 7/5, Cuffe-Parade, Mumbai 400005, India.

ALBUQUERQUE Roy, b. 21 June 1950, Bombay. Image Specialist. m. Lisette, 7 Dec 1987, 2 s, 1 d. Education: BS; LLB; DPR. Appointments: Sales Exec, Roy Typewiters, Bombay, 1973-77; Pub Rels Asst, Pegel und Sohn, Saudi Arabia; Sales Repr, Shaldmair Paints, 1978-79; Pub Rels, Indian Express, Bombay, 1979-81; Mngr, Hindustan Diamond Co, 1981-89; Chf of Pub Rels and Advtng, TACA Intnl Ltd, 1989-. Publications: Golden Book of Manners and Etiquette, 1987; Writen for Var Publs. Honours: Anchorperson for Image Enhancement, Televised by Star TV. Memberships: Advtng Club of Bombay; Brit Cncl; WIAA; Assoc of Bus Comm; Cath Gymkhana. Hobbies: Books; Numismatics; Philately; Music. Address: Usha Sadan A-5A, Colaba, Bombay 400005, India.

ALDER Keith Frederick, b. 4 Sept 1921, Melbourne, Aust. Metallurgist. m. Pauline Robertson, 16 Jan 1947, 3 s. Education: BSc, 1942, MSc, 1944, Univ Melbourne, Osmond Coll. Appointments: Metallurgist, Annumition Factory, Vic, 1946; Lectr, Metallurgy, Newcastle Tech Coll, NSW, 1946-51; Snr Lectr, Metallurgy, Univ Melbourne, 1952-53; Snr Sci Offr, UK Min of supply; Ldr, Metallurgy, Austl Atomic Energy Cmmn, 1954-61, Harwell, UK, 1954-57; Dir, AAEC Rsch Estab, Lucas Heights, 1961-71; Commnr, AAEC, 1968-82, Gen Mngr, 1976-82. Publications: Australia's Uranium Opportunities, 1997; Sev profl articles in jrnls; Honour: AM, 1983. Memberships: Fell, Austl Acady of Technol and Engrng; Fell, Inst of Radio and Electron Engrs, Aust. Hobbies: Sailing; Electronics; Amateur Radio. Address: 2 Eulbertie Avenue, Warrawee, NSW 2074, Australia.

ALDERTON Eileen Joan (Lynch-Gardner), b. 20 Sept 1928. Journalist; Author. m. Hugh Lynch-Gardner, dec 1992, 29 Oct 1949, 2 s. Education: Trained as jrnlst, Daily Express and Odhams Press, London. Career: Features & Fiction Ed, Everywoman, Odhams Press and Fleetway Publns; Sub-ed, sev IPC mags; Freelance Features Writer, Melbourne, 1974-; Consolidated Press, Sydney, 1975-; Gen Feature Writer, Sub-ed, Medl Corresp, Austl Women's Weekly; Sub-ed The Bulletin (spec music mag for bicentennial); Book Reviewer, Feature Writer for This Aust; Fiction Ed, Austl Women's Weekly, -1991; Lectr, Creative Writing, Austl Soc Auths; Soc Women Writers; Fellshp of Aust Writers, Coll Further Educ, S Coast (workshops); Readings at workshops; ABC interview, reading of short story, Oriel Bookshop, Paddington, for Femimist Week. Publications: Novels: A Month Of Sundays; Eventide; Historical features, press releases for local papers; Short stories: In IPC Mags, UK and US; Cosmopolitan US and UK; Sun Herald; Australian Women's Weekly, Cleo; This Australia; Published in anthology: Speaking To The Sun; Stories read on radio. Honours: 2 Medl Awds, Aust Women's Weekly. Membership: Aust Soc Auths. Hobbies: Reading; Music; Opera; Visiting art galleries; Theatre. Address: 18/23 Baden St, Coogee, NSW 2034, Australia.

ALDRAIHEM Osama Jasem, b. 15 Oct 1966, Riyadh, Saudi Arabia. Professor. m. Seeren, 10 June 1993, 1 s, 1 d. Education: BS, Mech Engrng, 1990; MS, Mech Engrng, 1994; PhD, Mech Engrng, 1997. Appointments: Hosp Engr, 1990-91; Tchng Asst, 1991-92; Asst Prof, 1997-. Publication: Device for Combined Bending and Twisting Actuation, 1996. Honours: Prince Bander Bin Sultan Awd, 1994, 1997. Membership: ASME, assoc mbr. Hobby: Reading. Address: PO Box 800, Riyadh 11421, Saudi Arabia.

ALDRED Michael John, b. 18 June 1954. Oral Pathologist. m. Susan Elizabeth Smith, 9 Aug 1976, 1 s, 2 d. Education: BDS, 1977; FDSRCS, 1981; PhD, 1986; MRCPath, 1987; Grad Cert Educ, 1995; FFOP (RCPA), 1996; FRCPath, 1997. Appointments: Lectr in Oral Path, Univ Wales, 1978-91; Rsch Fell, Medl Rsch Cncl, 1989-92; Snr Lectr, Univ of Wales, 1991-92; Snr Lectr, Rdr, Oral Bio, Univ Queensland; Prof of Dental Med, Univ Melbourne. Publications: Over 60 pprs in refereed jrnls. Memberships: IAOP; IADR; ANZAOP; AASD; SEEADE; OMSANZ; RCPath; RCPA; RCSEng; PROBLARC; Sec, ANZ Div of IADR, 1993-95; Sec/Treas, ANZAOP, 1993-98; Pres, AASD, 1996-. Address: School of Dental Science, The University of Melbourne, 711 Elizabeth Street, Melbourne, Victoria 3000, Australia.

ALEBUA Ezekiel. Appointments: Fmr Dep PM; PM of the Solomon Is, 1986-89. Memberships: Solomon Is Utd Party - SIUPA. Address: c/o Office of the Prime Minister, Honiara, Solomon Islands.

ALEMAN LACAYO Arnoldo. President of Nicaragua. Appointments: Fmr Ldr, pro-Somoza Liberal Stud Yth Org, 1960s; Imprisoned, 1980; House Arrest, 1989; Mayor of Managua, 1990; Ldr, Liberal Party Alliance, 1996. Address: Office of the President, Casa de Gobierno, Apdo 2398, Managua, Nicaragua.

ALESANA Tofilau Eti. Appointments: PM of West Samoa - now Samoa - July 1988-; also in charge of For Affairs, Labour, Brdcstng, Justice, Police and Prisons, Atty Gen; Ldr Human Rights Protection Party - HRPP. Address:

ALEXANDER (Padinjarethalakal) Cherian, b. 20 Mar 1921, Kerala. m. Ackama Alexander, 1942, 2 s, 2 d. Education: India MA, MLitt, DLitt. Appointments: Indian Admin Serv Kerala Cadre, 1948; Dev Commnr Small Scale Inds, 1960-63; Sr Advsr Centre for Indl Dev UN NY, 1963-66; Chf UN Project on Small Inds and Chf Advsr to Govt of Iran, 1970-73; Dev Commnr Small Scale Inds, 1973-75; Sec, For Trade later Com Sec, 1975-78; Snr Advsr later Exec Dir and Asst Sec-Gen Intl Trade Centre UNCTAD-GATT Geneva, 1978-81; Prin Sec to PM of India, 1981-85; High Cmmnr in UK, 1985-88; Gov Tamil Nadu, 1988-89; Maharashtra, 1993-. Publications: The Dutch in Malabar; Buddhism in Kerala; Industrial Estates in India; My Years With Indira Ghandi; Perils of Democracy. Hobby: Reading. Address: c/o Raj Bhavan, Mumbai, Maharashtra, India.

ALEXANDER Christine Anne, b. 9 July 1949, Hastings, NZ. University Lecturer. m. Peter Fraser Alexander, 18 June 1977, 1 s, 1 d. Education: BA, 1970, MA, 1971, Univ of Canterbury; PhD, Univ of Cambridge, 1978. Appointments: Asst Lectshp, Univ of Canterbury, 1972; Tutor, 1978-83, Lectr, 1986-88, Snr Lectr, 1988-92, Assoc Prof, 1993-98, Prof, Sch of English, 1998- Univ of NSW, Aust; Fell Inst Arts and Hum, Univ N Carolina, 1996; Visng Fellshp Dept of English Duke Univ, 1996, Princeton Univ, 1996; Lib Fellshp, Dept of English, Princeton Univ, 1996. Publications: Something About Arthur by Charlotte Brontë, 1981; Bibliography of the Manuscripts of Charlotte Brontë, 1982; The Early Writings of Charlotte Brontë, 1983; Edn, Early Writings of Charlotte Brontë, 3 vols, 1987-; The Art of the Brontës, 1994; High Life in Verdopolis: A Tale from the Glasstown by Charlotte Brontë, 1995; Contbr to books: Charlotte Brontë at Roe Head; Search After Love; William Shenstone; Imagining Africa; Lord Brotherton; Articles, reviews in var jrnls; Authorial Voice, 1990. Honours: NZ Postgrad Schlshps; NZ Univ Womens Fellshp; Travel

Grants; Spec Rsch Grants; Brit Acady Rose Mary Crawshay Prize, 1984; Austl Rsch Cncl Snr Rsch Fellshp; Fell, Austl Acady Hums, 1995. Memberships: Brontë Soc; Austl Lang and Lit Assoc; Austl Victorian Stdies Assoc; Austl and S Pacific Assoc for Comparative Lit Stdies; Cambridge Soc; Jane Austen Soc; Assoc for Stdy of Austl Lit; Bibliographical Soc of Aust and NZ; Soc for Textual Schlshp; Soc for Hist of Authshp, Reading and Publng; Sydney Soc of Lit and Ethics. Address: School of English, University of New South Wales, PO Box 1, Kensington, NSW 2033, Australia.

ALEXANDER Munro Scott, b. 2 Dec 1915, Aust. Surgeon. m. Joan Hastie, 10 Feb 1943, 1 s, 2 d. Education: MB, MS, Univ of Sydney; FRACS. Appointments: Served Citizen Mil Forces, 1933-39; Austl Army Med Corps, 1940-45; Hon Cnsltng Surg, Roy Hosp for Women, Sydney, NSW, 1976-; Cnsltng Surg Emer, Balmain Hosp; Hon Col (retd), Austl Army Med Corps. Honours: OBE; Twice mentioned in dispatches, WII. Memberships: Fell, Austl Med Assn, Fed Cncl Mbr 1967-70, Cncl Mbr, NSW Br 1950-70, Pres NSW Br 1959-60; Fmr Mbr, Invest Cttee, under NSW Med Prac Act. Hobbies: Sailing; Gardening. Address: Unit 97, Cutler Village. Colooli Road, Narrabeen, NSW 2101, Australia.

ALEXANDER Peter Fraser, b. 24 July 1949, S Africa. University Lecturer. m. Christine, 18 June 1997, 1 s, 1 d. Education: BA, Hons, Witwatersrand; MA, Leeds; PhD, Cambridge. Appointments: Lectr, Snr Lectr, Assoc Prof, Prof, Univ NSW. Publications include: Roy Campbell: A Critical Biography, 1982; William Plomer, 1989; Leonard and Virginia Woolf, 1992; Alan Paton:A Biography, 1994; Les Murray: A Life in Progress, 1999. Memberships: Fell, Austl Acady of the Humanities; Austl Univs Lang and Lit Assn; Assn for the Study of Austl Lit; African Studies Assn of Aust and the Pacific; UNSW Staff Assn; Kipling Soc; Cambridge Soc. Hobbies: Reading; Writing; Cycling. Address: Department of English, University of New South Wales, Sydney 2052, Australia.

ALGOSAIBI Ghazi A, b. 2 Mar 1940, Al Hasa, Saudi Arabia. m. 1968, 3 s, 1 d. Education: LLB, Law, Univ of Cairo, 1961; MA, Intl Rels, Univ of Southern CA, 1964; PhD, Intl Rels, Univ of London, 1970. Appointments: Lectr, Fac of Com, 1965-70, Asst Prof, 1970-74, Dean, Fac of Com, Hd, Pol Sci Dept, 1971-73, King Saud Univ, Riyadh; Dir Gen, Rail Road Org, Dammam, 1974-75; Min of Ind and Elec, 1975-82; Min of Hlth, 1982-84; Saudi Amb to Bahrain, 1984-92; Saudi Amb to Brit, 1992-. Publications: Num collects of poetry and literary miscellanies; Novels: An Apartment Called Freedom; The Mental House; Seven; Plays: The Golden Cage; He-She; Social Science: Development: Face to Face; Development: The Big Questions; Cultural Invasion and other Issues; The Gulf Crisis: An Attempt to Understand; Transl, International Relations by Joseph Frankel; A Poet's Story (autobiog); Life in Administration (autobiog). Honours: Decorations from Saudi Arabia, Kuwait, Qatar, Bahrain, Morocco, France, Spain, Germany, Sweden, Finland, Venezuela, Indonesia. Memberships include: Sec, Supreme Oil Cncl, 1974-75; Vice Chmn, Dammam's Munic Cncl, 1974-75; Supreme Yth and Sports Cncl, 1974-75; Bd Dirs, Indl Rsch Cntr, Sadaf Pet Co, Jubail, Yenpet Pet Co, Yanbu; Supreme Labour Cncl; Bd Dirs, Saudi Pub Invstmt Fund; Cttee, State Prize in Lit. Address: Royal Embassy of Saudi Arabia, 30 Charles Street. London W1, England.

ALHEGELAN Sheikh Faisal Abdul Aziz al-, b. 7 Oct 1929, Jeddah. Diplomat. m. Nouha Tarazi, 1961, 3 s. Education: Fac of Law, Fouad Univ, Cairo. Appointments: Min of For Affairs 1952-54; servd Emb in Washington DC, 1954-58; Chf of Protocol in Min, 1958-60; Polit Advsr to HM King Sa'ud, 1960-61; Amb to Spain, 1961-68; Amb to Venezuela and Argentina, 1968-75; Amb to Denmark, 1975-76, Amb to UK, 1976-79; Amb to USA, 1979-83; Amb to France, 1996-; Min of State, Apr-Sept 1984; Min of Hlth, 1984-96; Amb to Paris 1996-; Chmn Bd of Dirs, Saudi Red Cres Soc, 1984; Saudi Anti-Smoking Soc, 1985; Chmn Bd of Trustees, Saudi Cncl for Hlth Specialities, 1992-. Honours: Order of King Abdulaziz; Gran Cruz Cordon of King Abdul Aziz; Order of Isabela la Catolica - Spain; Gran Cordon; Orden del Libertador -Venezuela; Grande Oficial; Orden Riobranco - Brazil; May Grand Decoration - Argentina; Hon KBE. Memberships: Cncl of Mins - Saudi Arabia. Hobbies: Bridge; Golf. Address: Embassy of Saudi Arabia, 5 av Hoche, 75008 Paris, France.

ALI Sadiq, b. 1910, Udaipur, Rajasthan. m. Shrimati Shanti Sadiq Ali, 1951. Education: Allahabad Univ. Appointments: Assocd with Indian freedom movement, 1930; Perm Sec All-India Congress Cttee, 1938-47; Gen Sec Indian Natl Congress, 1958-64, 1966-69; Chf Ed AICC Econ Review, 1960-69; Chmn Gandhi Natl Mus and Library New Delhi, 1965-; Pres Opposition Congress Party, 1971-73; Gov of Maharashtra, 1977-80; Gov Tamil Nadu, 1980-82; Cen Gandhi Smarak Nidhi, 1991-. Publications: Know Your Country; Congress Ideology and Programme; Culture of India; General Election 1957; Towards Socialist Thinking in Congress; Campaign Against Nuclear Arms. Memberships: Lok Sabha, 1951-52; Rajya Sabha, 1958-70. Address: A-23.139 Lodhi Colony, New Delhi 110003, India.

ALI Sardar Asif Ahmad, b. 21 Oct 1940. m. 3 c. Education: Lawrence Coll Murree; Govt Coll Lahore; St John's Coll Oxford; Middle Temple London; MA. Appointments: Lectr FC Coll Lahore, 1966-68; Advsr on agric and polit affairs to Govt of W Pakistan, 1969-70; Pres Punjab Kissan Tanzeem - org of peasants and small farmers - 1976-79; Snr Vice-Pres Majlis-i-Quaid-e-Azam, 1978-81; Dir Punjab Co-op Union Lahore, 1982-84; Vice-Pres Punjab Provincial Co-op Bank Ltd Lahore, 1984-87; Chmn Parl Budget Cttee, 1991-92; fmr Min of State for Econ Affairs; Min of For Affairs, 1993-. Publications: articles in newspapers and journals. Memberships: Fed Advsry Cncl, 1981-83; indep Natl Assn, 1985-88, 1990-; Taxation Reform Cttee, 1985-87; Public Accts Cttee, 1991-93. Hobby: Mountain-trekking. Address: Ministry of Foreign Affairs, Constitution Avenue, Islamabad, Pakistan.

ALI Zaheer Sayyid, b. 5 Nov 1953, Karachi, Pakistan. Secretary; Bank Executive. m. Maharah, 11 Dec 1982, 3 s, 1 d. Education: MA, Intl Rels; Master Commerce; Dip Mercantile Law. Appointments: Sec; Cnslt; Mng Dir; Snr Mngr. Publications: Var pprs and articles on fin, intl trade. Memberships: Inst of Bankers, UK, Zimbabwe, S Africa, Pakistan. Hobbies: Camera hunting only; Wildlife; Nature. Address: Apt #14, Hassan Plaza, Patel Bagh, Quetta, Pakistan.

ALINGTON Margaret Hilda, b. 30 Sept 1920. Librarian; Author. m. William Hildebrand Alington, 29 Dec 1955, 1 s, 2 d. Education: BA, Univ of NZ. Appointments: Canterbury Univ Coll Lib, 1942-43; St Margaret's Coll Lib, Christchurch, 1945-48; Leeds Univ Lib, 1949-51; Auckland Univ Coll Lib, 1952; Alexander Turnbull Lib, Wellington, 1953-56; Univ of IL Lib, 1957-59; Pt time Lectr, Sch of Arch, Vic Univ of Wellington, 1979-. Publications: Frederick Thatcher and St Paul's: An Ecclesiological Study, 1965; Unquiet Earth: A History of the Bolton Street Cemetery, 1978; Old St Paul's and Bishopscourt in Historic Buildings of New Zealand: North Island, 1979; Goodly Stones and Timbers: A History of St Mary's Church, New Plymouth, 1988; Life After Death: An Old Cemetery Becomes a Memorial Park in The Making of Wellington 1800-1914, 1990; High Point: St Mary's Church, Karori, Wellington, 1866-1991, 1998; Contbr: New Zealand Historic Places, 1983-; The Dictionary of New Zealand Biography, 1990-. Honours: Civic Awd, 1997; ONZM, 1999. Memberships: Old St Paul's Advsry Cttee, 1967-94; Friends of Old St Paul's Cttee, 1967-80; Friends of Bolton St Cemetery, Cttee 1977-87; Friends of the Turnbull Lib, Cttee 1989-92; Mbr of sev environmental grps. Hobbies: Music; Reading; Walking. Address: 60 Homewood Crescent, Karori, Wellington, New Zealand.

ALLAN Percy, b. 24 July 1946, London, UK. Consultant. Education: BEcon; MEcon. Appointments: Snr Economist, Westpar, 1971-75; Asst Chf Economist, NSW Treasury, 1976-80; Snr Policy Advsr to Treas and Premier, 1981-85; Sec, NSW Treasury, Chmn, NSW Treasury Corp, 1985-94; Fin Dir, Borce Ltd, 1994-96; Dir, The Allan Cnsltng Grp, 1996-98; Prin, Percy Allan & Assocs Ltd, 1999-. Honours: Visng Prof, Macquerie Grad Sch of Mngmt, 1996-; AM, Gen Div, 1996. Memberships: Fell, Soc of CPAs; Austl Inst of Mngmt and Aust Inst of Co Dirs. Hobbies: Reading (Social sciences); Movies; Art; Travel. Address: 10 St Marys Street, Balmain, NSW, Australia 2041.

ALLARS Margaret Nita, b. 30 Aug 1953, Sydney, Australia. University Academic and Lawyer. m. George Verghese Kurien, 6 Aug 1983, 1 s, 1 d. Education: BA, hons; LLB, hons; DPhil. Appointment: Prof of Pub Law, Fac of Law, Univ Sydney. Publications: Introduction to Australian Administrative Law, 1990; Administrative Law: Cases and Commentary, 1997; Administrative Law Title in Halsbury's Laws of Australia, 1991, 1999. Honours: C'wlth Schlsp and Fellshp Plan Awd, 1981; Leverhulme Fell, 1997; Fell, Acady of Socl Scis in Aust, 1998. Hobby: Swimming. Address: Faculty of Law, University of Sydney, 173-175 Phillip Street, Sydney 2000, Australia.

ALLEN Barry John, b. 10 June 1940, Melbourne, Aust. Medical Scientist. m. Cynthia, 27 Feb 1969, 2 d. Education: BSc, 1961, MSc, 1963, Melbourne; PhD, Wollongong, 1977; DSc, Melbourne, 1984. Appointments: Rsch Scientist (AAEC), SRS, PRS, SPRS, 1984; CRS, ANSTO, 1992; Prin Hosp Scientist, SGH, 1994; Prof UW, US, 1992; UNSW, 1997. Publications: Over 230 publs in neutron phys, stellar nucleosynthesis, boron neutron capture therapy, in vivo body composition, experimental radiation oncology. Honours: Fell, AIP, 1972; APS, 1981; ACPSEM, 1992. Memberships: Pres, ISNCT, 1988-90; Pres, ACPSEM, 1998-99. Hobbies: Weightlifting; Sailing; Hiking. Address: St George Cancer Care Centre, Gray Street, Kogarah, 2217 NSW, Australia.

ALLEN David Edmund, b. 1 Aug 1948. Professor. 11 Oct 1975, 3 d. Education: MA Econs, St Andrews Univ, 1970; MPhil Econs, 1976; Leicester Univ, PhD, Univ of WA, 1996. Appointments: Lectr, 1975-79, Leicester Poly; Lectr, Edinburgh Univ, 1979-86; Lectr, Snr Lectr, Univ of WA, 1986-92; Challenge Bank Prof of Fin, Curtin Univ, 1992-96; Prof of Fin, Edith Cowan Univ, 1996-. Publications: Finance a Theoretical Introduction, 1983; The Economics of Modern Business, w W D Reekie. Memberships: Amn Fin Assn; Acctng Assn of Aust & NZ. Hobbies: Reading; Sailing; Surfing; Karate; Jogging. Address: 37 Roche Road, Duncraig, WA 6027, Australia.

ALLEN Geoffrey David, b. 9 Dec 1941, Hopetown, Aust. Management Consultant. m. Catherine, 18 Dec 1965, 1 s, 1 d. Education: BA, Hons; MBA, Melbourne. Appointments: Press Sec, Ldr Opposition, 1972-73 to Fed Treas, 1971-72, Pvte Sec to Min for Labour and Natl Serv, 1969-71, Fed Pub Serv, 1966-69; Lectr, Snr Res Fell, Univ Melbourne Grad Sch of Bus Admin, 1974-79; Exec Dir, Austl Ind Dev Assn, 1978-83; Fndn Exec Dir, Bus Cl Aust, 1983-88; Snr Assoc, Prin Assoc, Melbourne Bus Sch, 1980-; Dir, World Comp Pracs Pty Ltd, 1990-, Pasminco Ltd, 1994-, Melbourne Bus Sch Ltd, 1996-. Memberships include: Chmn, Austl Govt's Trade Plcy Advsry Cncl; Melbourne Club; Athenaeum Club. Hobbies: Reading; Theatre; Films; Gardening. Address: 4th Floor, 128 Exhibitions Street, Melbourne, Victoria 3000, Australia.

ALLEN James Albert, b. 4 May 1924, Aust. Emeritus Professor. m. Daphne Burling, 7 Aug 1948, 1 s, 1 d. Education: MSc; PhD; Univ of Qld; Univ of Bristol; FRACI; FTSE; FACE; FAIM. Appointments: Served RAAF, 1943-45; Snr Sci Offr, Chem Rsch Lab, Dept of Sci and Indl Rsch, 1950-52; Snr Lectr, Phys Chem, Univ of Tas, 1952-55; Sect Ldr, Cntrl Rsch Labs, ICI (Aust) Ltd, Melbourne, Vic, 1955-59; Assoc Prof, 1959-61, Prof of Chem, 1961-71; Dpty Vice Chan, 1969-71, Emer Prof 1971-, Univ of Newcastle, NSW; Simon Snr Rsch Fell, Univ of Manchester, Eng, 1965; Exec Offr, CSIRO, 1971-76; Pres, Roy Austl Chem Inst, 1976; Chmn, Cncl of Austl Inst for Marine Scis, 1977-82; Pres, Austl Cncl of Professions, 1979-81; Exec Dir, Austl Railway Rsch and

Dev Org, 1985-86. Publications: Scientific Innovation and Industrial Prosperity; Studies in Innovation in the Steel and Chemical Industries; Energy Changes in Chemistry; Outline of Polymer Chemistry. Honours: Leighton Medallist, 1978; AO, 1982; Hon LLD, Univ of Qld, 1984; Hon DSc, Univ of Newcastle, NSW, 1988. Address: 8 Urangan Court, Helensvale, Qld 4212, Australia.

ALLENDE Isabel, b. 8 Aug 1942, Lima. m. (1) Miguel Frias 1962, 1 s, 1 d; (2) William Gordon 1988. Appointments: Jrnlst Paula Mag, 1967-74; Jrnlst Mampato Mag, 1969-74; Channel 13 World Hunger Campaign, 1964; Channel 7 var humorous progs, 1970-74; Maga-Cine-Ellas, 1973; Admin Marroco Sch Caracas, 1978-82; Freelance jrnlst El Nacional newspaper Caracas, 1976-83; Visng Tchr Montclair State Coll NJ, 1985; Writer, 1981-. Publications: Novels - The House of the Spirits, 1982; Of Love and Shadows, 1984; Eva Luna, 1981; Aphrodite, 1998; Short stories - Tales of Eva Luna, 1990; The Infinite Plan, 1992, Paula - memoir - 1995; children's story - La Gorda de Porcelana, 1984. Honours: Novel of the Yr Panorama Literario - Chile - 1983; Point de Mire - Belgium - 1985; Auth of the Yr and Book of the Yr - Germany, 1984; Grand Prix d'Evasion - France - 1984; Colima for Best Novel - Mexico - 1985; Auth of Yr - Germany - 1986; Mulheres Best Novel - Portugal - 1987. Address: 15 Nightingale Lane, San Rafael, CA 94901, USA.

ALLGROVE John Michael, b. 24 Oct 1932, Malaysia. Consultant. m. Maureen Ireland, 24 Jan 1966, 3 s, 1 d. Education: BAgSc, Reading Univ, Berkshire, Eng, 1957. Appointments: Swift and Co, Sydney, Aust, 1957-61; Asst Trade Commnr, Calcutta, India, 1962-63; Asst Trade Commnr, Cairo, Egypt, 1963-64; Trade Commnr, Hong Kong, 1966-67; Trade Commnr, Taipei, 1967-69; Snr Trade Commnr, Bangkok, 1970-73; Min Coml, Paris, France, 1974-79; Min, Coml, Jakarta, 1979-83; Min, Coml, Seoul, 1983-87; Consul Gen, Frankfurt, Germany, 1988-91; Exec Gen Mngr, SE Asia, Singapore, 1991-95; Ret'd from Aust Trade Commn Serv, Oct 1995; Cnslt, JA Intl; Dir, Guide Dogs Assn of SA and NT. Hobbies: Painting; Gardening; Swimming. Address: 32 Hackett Terrace, Marryatville, SA 5068, Australia.

ALLISON Michael John, b. 30 June 1940, Ipswich, Suffolk, Eng. Consultant. m. Janette Eaves Morse, 10 Mar 1967, 2 s. Education: Higher Natl Dip (HND), Mechl Engrng, N E Essex Tech Coll, Colchester Essex, Eng, 1961. Fellshp Dip, Mechl Engrng, RMIT, 1974-76; Grad Dip in Quality Technol (AOQ Prize), 1976-79. Appointments: Des Draughtsman, Ransomes & Rapier Ltd, Eng, 1961-63; Contract Draughtsman, Ford Motor Co, Eng, 1963-64; Proj Engr, Ford Motor Co, Geelong, 1964-67; Mfrng Rsch Engr, Boeing Co Seattle, USA, 1967-70; Mfrng Engr, Aeronca Inc, OH, USA, 1970-71; Mngr of Prod Engrng and Quality Control, Fexdrive Inds Pty Ltd, Melbourne, 1971-78; Class 2, through to Prin Engr, 1978-88, Supvsng Engr, 1988-90, Austl Telecomms Corp, Melbourne, Aust; Cnslt, Stockdals Pty Ltd, 1990-. Publications: Profl jrnls; Seminar presentations; Audio tape and book: Productivity Improvement Through Quality Planning, 1992. Honour: Shilkin Prize, Lit in the Field of Quality, 1994. Hobby: Computer progamming. Address: 8 Brixton Avenue, Eltham, Vic 3095, Australia.

ALLSOP John Leslie, b. 12 Apr 1924, Sydney, Australia. Neurologist. m. Philippa Gordon Bain, 30 Aug 1947, 2 s, 1 d. Education: MB BS, 1946; MD, honoris causa, 1992; FRACP. Appointments: Asst Physn, 1953-63, Hon Physn, 1963-70, Visng Neurol, 1970-89, Chmn, Bd of Dirs, 1973-84, Cnslt Neurol, 1989-, Roy Prince Alfred Hosp. Publications: Sev articles in profl jrnls. Honours: Chevalier of Ordre Natl du Mérite, France, 1978; AM, 1991. Memberships include: Austl Assn of Neurols. Hobbies: Woodwork; Golf. Address: 57 Ocean Street, Woollahra, NSW 2025, Australia.

ALMAZAN Anselmo, b. 4 Nov 1933, Lupao, Nueva Ecija, Philippines. Civil Engineer; Geodetic Engineer; Civil Engineering Educator; Real Estate Broker. m. Cecilia P Alalan, 4 s. Education: Assoc in Surveying, 1955, MS, Civil Engrng (Structure), 1972, Univ of Philippines, Diliman; BS, Civil Engrng, Natl Univ, Manila, 1957; MS Math (Pure/Applied Math), Far Eastern Univ, Manila, 1964; PhD Maths Educ, Centro Escolar Univ, Manila, Philippines, 1977. Appointments: Coll Pres, St Louis Coll of Tuguegarao, Cagayan, 1976-80; Pres, Almazan Cnstrn and Engrng Servs, QC, 1978-88; Professorial Lectr, Col of Engrng, Univ of the Philippines, Diliman, 1986-88; Chmn, Dept of Geodetic Engrng, Coll of Engrng, Diliman, Quezon Cty, 1988-92; Dir, Trng Cntr for Applied Geodesy and Photogrammetry Natl Engrng Cntr, Quezon Cty, 1989-92; Prof, Coll of Engrng, Quezon Cty, 1986-. Publications: 14 pprs publd & presented. Honours include: Ctfs of merit or recog; Plaque of Recog, Outsndng Geodetic Engr for the Academe, NCR GEP Awd, 1993; Plaque of Presdtl Awd for Ldrshp, NCR, GEP, DAP, Tagaytay Cty, 1998; Professorial Chair, Geodesy, as Ceaser Nuguid Professorial Chair of Geodesy, Jan 1998 to Dec 1999. Address: 24 Mahabagin Street, Teachers Village West, Diliman, Quezon City, Philippines.

ALMIRANTE Corazon Yabes, b. 13 Mar 1939, Baguio Cty, Philippines. Physician. m. Johnny, 12 Dec 1964, 4 s. Education: MD; MSc; PhD. Appointments: Proj Dir, Perinatal Cntr, 1986; Hd, Dept of Perinatology, Perinatal Cntr, Philippine Children's Medl Cntr, 1988-. Publications: Primer on Women's Health, 1993; Increasingly Safe and Successful Pregnancies, 1996. Honours: Outstndng Perf on Women's Hlth, 1997; Hamis Awd on Perinatal Cncl, 1997. Memberships: Pres, Patient Inst Philippines, 1989-; Philippine Medl Womens' Assn, 1992-93; Pres, Orgn Gustosis, 1994-95. Hobbies include: Reading. Address: 8 Dr Lazcano Street, Quezon City 1103, Philippines.

ALONI Shulamit, b. 1929, Tel Aviv. 3 s. Appointments: partd in the def of Jerusalem during the War of Independence; wrkd as tchr; columnist for sev newspapers; prodr of radio progs dealing with legis and legal procs; Chmn Israel Consumers' Cncl; Civil Rights Movement Min Witht Portfolio, June-Oct 1974; CRM ldr and MK, 1974-; servd on num Cttees; Min of Educ, representing the Meretz coalition, 1992; Min of Comms, Sci and Tech, 1993-96. Publications: Inclng books on legal and polit subjects. Honours: Fell Israel Consumers' Cncl; Fell Civil Rights Movement. Memberships: Mapai, 1959; Knesset, Labour, 1965-69; Meretz, coalition party. Address: Ministry of Communications, 23 Yaffo Street, Jerusalem 91999, Israel.

ALSEHRI Mohammad Yahra, b. 11 Mar 1959, Taif. Surgeon. m. Sara Mohammad, 3 s, 4 d. Education: FRCSC; FACS. Appointments: Asst Prof, Cnslt Surg, Coll of Cntrl Hosp, Abha, 1990-; Chmn, Dept of Surg, Assir Cntrl Hosp, 1991-92; Assoc Prof, Coll of Med, Abha, King Saud Univ, 1993; Dean, Coll of Med, King Saud Univ, Abha. Honours: Awd of Excellence, Saudi Cntrl Attaché in Ottowa; Tchr of Yr Awd, Coll of Med, Abha, 1991. Memberships: Fell, Roy Coll of Surgs, Can; Fell, Amn Coll of Surg; NY Academy of Scis. Address: Dean, College of Medicine, King Saud Univ, PO Box 641, Abha, Saudi Arabia.

ALSTON Richard Kenneth Robert. Education: Xavier Coll Melbourne; Melbourne and Monash Univs; LLM, BCom. Appointments: Fed Pres UNA of Aust, 1977-79; Natl Chmn Austl Cncl for Overseas Aid, 1978-83; State Pres Liberal Party Vic Div, 1979-82; Sen for Vic, 1986-; Dep Chmn Senate Stndng Cttee on Legal and Constl Affairs, 1986; Jt Parl Cttee on Natl Crime Authy, 1987; Senate Stndng Cttee on Fin and Pub Admin, 1987; Chmn Afghan-Austl Cncl, 1987-; Shadow Min for Comms, 1989-90; Shadow Min for Socl Security, Child Care and Retirement Incomes, 1990-92; Shadow Min for Socl Security, Child Care and Superannuation, 1992; Shadow Min for Superannuation and Child Care and Shadow Min Asstng Ldr on Socl Policy, 1992-93; Dep Ldr of Opposition in Senate, 1993-96; Dep Ldr of Gov in Senate, March 1996; Shadow Min for Comms and the Arts, 1994-96; Min for Comms and the Arts, March 1996-. Honours: Fell Inst of Dirs, 1983-88. Memberships: Amnesty Intl Parl Grp. Hobbies: Aboriginal art, modern literature, Oriental Rugs, jogging, reading, pumping iron. Address: Parliament House, Canberra, ACT 2600, Australia.

ALSTON Robert, b. 10 Feb 1938. British High Commissioner to New Zealand and Western Samoa; Governor, Pitcairn, Henderson, Oeno & Ducie Islands (Retired). m. Patricia Claire Essex, 8 Mar 1969, 1 s, 1 d. Education: BA, Mod Hist, Ardingly Coll, Sussex New Coll, Oxford. Appointments: 3rd Sec, Kabul, 1963; Eastern Dept, FO, 1966; Hd, Computer Stdy Team, FCO, 1969; 1st Sec, (Econ), Paris, 1971; 1st Sec, Hd of Chancery, Tehran, 1974; Asst Hd, Energy, Sci & Space Dept, FCO, 1977; Hd, Jnt Nuc Unit, FCO, 1978; Polit Cnslr, UK Deleg to NATO, 1981; Hd, Def Dept, FCO, 1984; Amb to Oman, 1986; 2nd to Home Civ Serv, 1990; Asst Under-Sec of State (Pub Depts), FCO, 1992. Honour: CMG, 1987. Hobbies: Gardening; Travel; Music. Address: c/o Foreign and Commonwealth Office (Wellington), King Charles Street, London SW1A 2AH, England.

ALTURKI Abdulrazaq Ali, b. 10 June 1960, Al-Khobar. Director of Marketing. m. Khadija Saeed Al-Hilali, 31 Jan 1986. Education: Bachelor, Intl Studies & Sociol (Hons), Univ OR, Eugene, 1986; Master, Spec Educ, Univ of WA, Seattle, USA, 1988; Educ for Global Citizenship, Amn Univ, Wash DC, 1991; MA, Intl Affairs, Amn Univ, Wash DC, 1992. Appointments: Pres Muslim Students Assn, NW Coast, 1980s; Polit Analyst, Saudi Arabian Emb, Wash DC, 1991, 1992; Hum Resources Dev Mngr, AATCO, 1988-90; Dir, Mktng, Namma Cargo Servs Co Ltd, 1992-; Chmn, Info Cttee, Dir, Pub Rels, East Prov Rehab Soc for Disabled Persons, 1992-. Publications: Num books and rschs incl: Saudi Arabian-Japan Relationship; Closing the Gap Between Rich and Poor Nations; Indonesia: Politics, Economy and Culture; Die But With Dignity; Capital Punishment in the Islamic Religion; Women's Right in Islam; The Art of Diplomatic Lying; Meeting Saudi Arabian Manpower Needs; Expatriate Education and Training; The Art of Marketing; Sev articles on mktng and handicapped. Honours: Golden Key Natl Hon Soc Awd from Univ of OR, Eugene, USA; Di Damma Mu, Natl Hon Soc in Socl Sci. Memberships include: Saudi Arabian Spec Educl Bd; Mbr of Bd, Cnsltng Grp of Media for Natl Protection of Handicapped Rights System; Handicapped Sports Club, Al-Hassa, Saudi Arabia; Inst of Sales & Mktng Mngmt, London; Exec Bd, Arabian Handicapped Orgn.

ALTYNBAYEV Mukhtar. Appointments: Lt-Gen; Min of Def, Kazakstan, 1997-. Address: Ministry of Defence, Almaty, Kazakstan.

ALVA Dinker Shanker, b. 2 July 1933, Mangalore, Karnataka. Businessman. m. Shashikala Alva, 1960, 1 s, 1 d. Education: Madras Univ; BSc, BSc-Tech. Appointments: Asst Weaving Master Delhi Cloth and Gen Mills Ltd, 1954-58; Indl Consultant IBCON Pvt Ltd, 1958-60; Sales Exec Bombay Dyeing and Mfng Co Ltd, 1960-66; Gen Man Anglo-French Textiles Ltd, 1966-69; Gen Man - Sales - Bombay Dyeing and Mfng Co Ltd, 1969-74; Sales Dir, 1974-75; Dir, 1976-79; Pres, 1979-88; Man Dir, 1988-; Dir Archway Invmnt Co Ltd Sanghi Polyesters Ltd, Natl Peroxide Ltd, Britannia Inds Ltd, Wadia BSN India Ltd, Indian Cotton Mills Fedn; Dep Chmn Cttee of Admin Cotton Textiles Export Promotion Cncl. Memberships: Govrng Cttee Bombay Textile Rsch Assn; Mngmt Cttee All India Exporters' Chamber; The Bombay Millowners' Assn. Hobbies: Music; Reading; Tennis. Address: Neville House, Ballard Estate, Bombay 400038, India.

ALVA CASTRO Luis, b. Trujilo. Education: Univ Nacional de Trujillo. Appointments: Fmr Dir Corporacion de Desarrollo Economico y Social de la Libertade; Dep for Libertad; has held var posts in Partido Aprista Peruano inclng Sec-Gen of North Regl Org; ; Chmn Natl Planning Comm of Partido Aprista Peruano; Second Vice-Pres of Repub; Pres Cncl of Mins - PM - and Min of Econ and Fin, 1985-87. Publications: La Necesidad del Cambio; Manejo Presupuestal del Peru; En Defensa del Pueblo; Endeudamiento Externo del Peru; Deuda Externa: Un reto para los Latinoamericanos and other books and essays. Memberships: Polit Comm and Natl

Sec for Electoral Matters. Address: c/o Ministry of Economy and Finance, Cuadra Avenida Abancay 5, Lima, Peru.

ALWIS Jayasena, b. 31 Mar 1939, Galle, Sri Lanka. Agriculture Program Officer, Asian Productivity Organization. m. Ratna, 15 Aug 1972, 1 s. Education: BA (Hons), Sri Lanka, Postgrad Dip in Dev Studies, Cambridge. Appointments: Asst Commnr of Election, 1966; Asst Dir of Agricl Dev, 1970; Dir, Land Reform, 1974; Dir of Water Resources Dev and Irrigation Mngmt, 1985; Dir, Agrarian Rsch Inst, 1987; Additional Sec of Agric Min, 1989; State Sec, Min of Coconut Inds and Crop Diversification, 1990; Agric Prog Offr, Asian Productivity Orgn,, 1992. Honours: D B Jayathilake Schlshp on results of the Univ Entrance Exam, 1959. Memberships: Asia Pacific Assn in Agric and Environ, 1997; World Assn of Soil and Water Conservation, 1998. Hobbies: Insight meditation; Cricket; Sumo wrestling. Address: Asian Productivity Organization, 8-4-14, Akasaka, Minato-ku, Tokyo 107-0052, Japan.

AMANO Kosei, b. 1905. Appointments: Prev posts incl Dir-Gen Natl Land Agcy; Chmn Cttee on Constrn; Chmn Cttee on Discipline; Chmn Cttee on Budget, HoR; Chmn Liberal Dem Party - LDP - Comm on Highways; Min of Constrn, 1986-87; Memberships: Liberal Dem Party. Address: c/o Ministry of Construction, 1-3 Kasumigaseki 2-chome, Chiyoda-ku, Tokyo, Japan.

AMARJIT SINGH Tateja, b. 30 June 1953, Shimla. Teacher. m. Kirpal Kaun, 8 Aug 1982, 2 s, 3 d. Education: Five yr Dip, Coml Art, Art Coll, Chandigarh. Appointments: Lectr, Coml Art, Govt Arts and Crafts Inst, Nabha, 1977. Creative Works: 61 Paintings, Compositions; Collect of 50 Pieces of Stone Sculpture. Honours: Awd, Govt Coll of Educ; 1st Prize in Poster; Awd, Art Coll; Lalit Shri Awd; Awd, Shri-Sanman; Many Hons. Memberships: Mehram Grp of Publs; Punjab Pardesh Sanskrit Acady; Lalit Kaka Acady; CHD Rotary. Hobbies: Photography; Painting; Writing. Address: Lectr in Coml Art, Govt of Arts and Crafts, Teachers Training Inst, Nabha Pin Code 147201, India.

AMARSANAA Jugnee, b. 1953, Ulan Bator, Mongolia. Government Executive. m. Education: Stud, Mongolian State Univ, 1975; Engl Trng, 1978; PhD, Law, Moscow, 1988. Appointments: Lectr, Mongolian State Univ, 1975-81; Hd Dept, Min of Jus, 1981-85; Hd, Bd, Min of Jus and Arbitrage, 1985-89; Hd, Dept Inst Pol, 1989-90; Min Jus, 1990-92; Dpty Dir, Acady of State and Socl Stdy, 1992-93; Hd Dept, Law Inst Admin and Mngmt Dev, 1994-. Memberships: Pres, Mongolian Advsrs Union, 1993-; Gen Cncl, Crts for Mongolia. Address: Ministry of Justice, Sumbuugiin St, Ulan Bator 38, Mongolia.

AMBIKAPATHY Patmalar, b. 25 Aug 1944. Barrister; Solicitor. m. A Ambikapathy, 1 s, 1 d. Education: BA; Bar-at-Law, Lincolns Inn, London; MPhil, Cambridge. Honours: Intl Peace Schlsp, 1967, 1968. Memberships: Emily's List, Victoria; Family Violence Prevention Cmmn. Hobbies: Walking; Yoga; Music; Theatre. Address: PO Box 136, West Ballarat, West Victoria 3350, Australia.

AMEER Makhoul, b. 19 June 1958. Director. m. Janan, 2 d. Education: 2nd Deg, Sociol, Univ of Haifa, Israel. Appointments: Freelance Jrnlst, Haifa, 1987-89; Coord, Unit of Educ for Democracy in Arab Schs, Intl Cntr for Peace, Tel Aviv, 1989-91; Coord, Prog for Advancement of Arab Studs, 1990-92; Dir of Partnership, 1992-96; Dir, Ittijah, Haifa, 1995-; Union of Arab NGO's. Address: PO Box 9577, Haifa 31095, Israel.

AMERASINGHE Chittharanjan Felix, b. 2 Mar 1933, Colombo. m. Wimala Nalini Pieris, 1964, 1 s, 2 d. Education: Roy Coll Colombo; Trinity Hall Camb Univ; Harvard Univ Law Sch. Appointments: Supvsr in Law Trinity Hall Camb Univ, 1955-57; Jnr exec Caltex Oil Co Colombo, 1959-61; Lectr in Law Univ Ceylon, 1962-65; Consultant Law Govt Ceylon, 1963-70; Snr lectr, 1965-68; Rdr, 1968-69; Prof of Law, 1969-71; Cnsel World Bank, 1970-75; Snr Cnsl, 1975-81; Exec Sec-Dir World Bank Admin Tribunal, 1981-96; Judge UN Tribunal NY, 1997-; Consultant in Intl Law Govt Ceylon, 1963-70; Adj Prof Intl Law Sch of Law Am Univ, 1991-93. Publications: Some Aspects of the Actio Iniuriarum in Roman-Dutch Law, 1966; State Responsibility for Injuries to Aliens, 1967; Defamation and Other Injuries in Roman-Dutch Law, 1968; Studies in International Law, 1969; The Doctrines of Sovereignty and Separation of Powers in the Law of Ceylon, 1970; The Law of the International Civil Service - 2 vols - 1988; Documents on International Administrative Tribunals, 1989; Case Law of the World Bank Administrative Tribunal, 1989; Local Remedies in International Law, 1990; Principles of the Institutional Law of International Organizations, 1996; arcticles in leading and intl law jrnls. Honours: Henry Arthur Thomas Classical Award Camb Univ, 1953; Angus Classical Prize, 1953; Clement Davies Prize for Law, 1955; Major Schl and Prize Trinity Hall Camb, 1953-56; Trinity Hall Law Studship, 1956-59; Yorke Prize, 1964; Rsch Fellshp Harvard Univ Law Sch, 1957; Cert of Merit Am Soc of Intl Law, 1988-89; Hon Prof of Intl Law Univ of Colombo, 1991-94. Hobbies: Religious reflection; Classical and jazz music; Art; Artifacts; Philately; Photography; Walking. Address: The World Bank, 1818 H St NW, Washington, DC 20433, USA.

AMERASINGHE Desha-Priya C, b. 2 Aug 1939, Colombo, Sri Lanka. Lawyer. m. Gloria Shirin, 12 Dec 1970, 2 s. Education: LLM (Hons) (Cantab); DIL (Cantab); LLB (Hons) (Ceylon); Atty-at_law. Appointments: Sec, Asian Dev Bank, 1994-97; Dir, N Amn Repr Off, 1997-. Hobbies: Tennis; Photography. Address: 1730 Pennsylvania Avenue NW, Suite 975, Washington DC 20006, USA.

AMERASINGHE-GANENDRA Shalini, b. 14 Oct 1965, Colombo, Sri Lanka. Principal, Art Gallery Owner. m. Dr Dennis Ganendra, 2 July 1993, 2 s. Education: Maths, Stanford Univ, 1982-84; LLB (Hons), MA, Cambridge Univ, 1984-87; LLM Masters Prog, Columbia Univ Law Sch (postgrad), 1988-89; UK, Barrister, 1988; NY, Atty-at-Law, 1989. Appointments: Snr Assoc, Corp Fin and Merchant banking Prac Grp, Shearman & Sterling, 1989-93; Grp Legal Advsr (based in Kuala Lumpur), Crosby Grp of Cos, 1993-95; Owner, The Private Gallery (emphasis on Asian Art), 1995-. Honours include: Dr Cooper's Law Studentship, Cambridge Univ, 1987; Natl Cum Laude Schl, USA, 1982. Memberships: Exec Cttee, Oxford and Cambridge Soc (Malaysia); Exec Cttee, Kuala Lumpur Speakers' Club; Roy Asiatic Soc (Malaysian Branch); Book Grp; Bankers' Club; Roy Selangor Golf Club; Roy Selangor Club; Lake Club; Subang Jaya Golf Club. Hobbies: Collecting art; Music; Photography; Travel. Address: 20 Jalan 16/6, 46350 Petaling Jaya, Selangor, Malaysia.

AMIN Navin, b. 13 Sept 1937, Varnama, India. Doctor of Medicine. m. Saroj, 24 Mar 1978, 1 s, 1 d. Education: MD; FRCP; FACP; FAAFP; DTM and H. Appointments: Chmn, Prog Dir, Pediats, Prof of Family Med, U C Irvine; Prof of Med, UCLA; Prof of Family Med, UC Stanford. Creative Works: 3 Book Chapts; 730 Lects and Seminars; 12 Rsch Pprs. Honours: Alan Milan Gold Medal; Tchr of the Year, 1982, 1983, 1991, 1999; Physn of the Year, 1998. Memberships: Amn Coll of Physns; Roy Coll of Physns and Surgs of UK; Infectious Diseases Soc of Am. Hobbies: Music; Reading; Watching TV. Address: Kern Medical Cntr, 1830 Flower St, Bakersfield, CA 93305, USA.

AMIRI Shabnam, b. 26 May 1972, Tehran, Iran. Speech Pathologist. m. Sh M Mirzaie, 13 Sept 1996. Education: BS. Appointments: Working on treatment of stuttering in 2 grps of schls and adults; Clin studying on delayed speech and lang disorders in preschoolers. Publications: Thesis: Voice disorders and their management, 1996; Translation a book in terms of Reading, Writing and Dyslexia (by Andrew W Ellis). Memberships: Iran Speech Therapy Assn, 1993-. Hobbies: Reading; Speech Pathology; Watching Football matches; English; Music. Address: 2nd Floor, No 26, Ally 146, South Rashid Street, Tehranpars, Tehran, Iran.

AMIT Meir, b. 17 Mar 1921, Tiberias. m. Yona Kelman, 1942, 3 d. Education: Columbia Univ, NY. Appointments: Served in Israeli Def Forces, 1948-68; Fmr Hd of Mil Intell and Hd of Israeli Security Serv; Pres Koor Inds, 1968-77; Min of Transport and Comm, 1977; Mgmnt Consultant, 1982; Chmn MA'OF, 1982-85; Dir Zim Lines, Israel Corp, 1985-99; Yachin, DSI Teva Pharm Lapidot Oil Drilling; Chmn Gen Satellite Corp Spacecom Satellite Comms; Chmn, Spacecom; Dir, Mobilcom. Memberships: Kibbutz Alonim, 1939; Knesset, 1977-81. Hobbies: Photography; Collecting dolls and educational games. Address: 11 Hibat Zion Street, Ramat-Gan 52391, Israel.

AMITAL Yehuda, b. 1925, Transylvania. m. 5 children. Education: Yeshiva studies in Jerusalem; ordained in Jerusalem. Appointments: Migrated to Israel, 1944; joined Haganah during war of independence; Hd Yeshivat Har Etzion, 1968-; fndr Meimad the Movement for Relig Zionist Renewal, 1993; Min without Portfolio, 1995-96; Rank of Cap in army reserve. Address: The Knesset, Jerusalem, Israel.

AMORNVIVAT Sompong, b. 3 July 1941, Bangkok, Thailand. Minister of Labour and Social Welfare. m. Pecharee Amornvivat. Education: Bach of Bus Admin, Curry Coll, Milton, MA, USA; Master, Pol Sci, Chiang Mai Univ, Thailand. Appointments: Mngng Dir, Thai Amarit Brewery Co Ltd; Dpty Min of Agric and Co-ops, 1990-91; Min of INd, 1992-93; Min of Labour and Socl Welfare, 1994-95; Pres Min, Prime Min's Off, 1996-; Dpty Min, Transp and Comms, 1997. Honour: Kt Grand Cordon, Spec Class, Most Exalted Order of the White Elephant, 1995. Address: Government House, Bangkok 10300, Thailand.

AMOUZEGAR Jamshid, b. 25 June 1923. Politician. m. Ulrike Amouzegar, 1951. Education: Univs of Teheran, Cornell, Washington. Appointments: UN Expert Mission to Iran, 1951; Chf Engring Dept, 1952-55; Dep Min of Hlth, 1955-58; Min of Labour, 1958-59; Min of Agric, 1959-60; Consulting Engr, 1960-64; Chmn Intl Civil Serv Advsry Bd of UN, 1962-67; Min of Hlth, 1964-65;; Min of Fin, 1965-74; Min of Interior and Employment, 1974-76; Min of State, 1976-77; Sec-Gen Rastakhiz Party, 1976-77, Jan-Aug 1978; PM of Iran, 1977-78; Pres OPEC, 1974; Fmr Chf Oil Negotiator to Shah. Honours: First Order of the Taj. Hobbies: Listening to music; Reading; Poetry.

AMUDUN Niyaz, b. 1932. Government Official. Appointments: joined CPP, 1953; First Sec Urumqi Municipality CCP, 1977-79; Vice-Chmn Govt of Xinjiang Uygur Autonomous Region, 1979-83; Chmn Standing Cttee of Xinjiang Uygur Autonomous Region People's Congress, 1985-; Dep Sec Xinjiang Uygur Autonomous Region Cttee CCP, 1985-; Standing Cttee of 7th Xinjiang PC, 1989-. Address: Standing Committee of Xinjiang Uygur Autonomous Region People's Congress, Urumqi, People's Republic of China.

AN Ou, b. 29 Apr, 1932, Liaoyang, Liaoning Prov, China. Scientific Researcher. m. 23 Sept 1959, 3 s. Education: Grad, Phys Dept, Beijing Normal Univ, 1956; Adv Stdy of X-Rays Phys, Crystal Plasticity, Optical Mineralogy, Inst Phys, Inst Geol, Chinese Acady Scis, 1956-59. Appointments: Rschr, Geodynamics, Inst of Geomechs, Min Geol and Inst of Crustal Dynamics, State Seismological Bur; currently Rsch Prof, Dir, Dept, Evaluating ctteeman of learning, degree and Snr Title, Editing Ctteeman of 3 jrnls; Rsch Bd of Advsrs, American Biographical Inst. Publications: 103 pieces of treatises; Prin publs incl: Time-Space Distribution of Maximum Horizontal Shearing Strain in Soils Before the 1976 Tangshan Earthquake, Seismology and Geology, 1983; Analysis of Observing Data for Seismic Source Dynamic from Earth's Roatation in East Asia Continent, Seismology and Geology, 1987; Forecast of Risk Area and Risk Time of Strong Earthquakes in Honghe Faults by Superposition Method of Residual and Present Stress Field, 1996; Measurement of Paleotectonic Residual Stress Field in Xinshuihe Fault Zone and Its Control on Large Earthquakes, Seismology and Geology, 1993;

Systematic Monograph: Tectonic Stress Field, 1992; Oil Pool in Hidden Mountain, 1999. Honours: Natl Sci Meeting Awd, 1978; Sci and Technol 2nd Awd of Provl Ministerial Grade, 1981; Natl Earthquake Sci Fndn Awd, 1997. Memberships: Chinese Phys Soc, 1957; Beijing Geol Soc, 1962; Beijing Mech Soc, 1985; Dir, Chinese Seismological Soc, 1990. Hobbies: Music; Growing flowers; Travel. Address: POB 2855, Beijing 100085, China.

AN Peijian, b. 10 Dec 1939, Weinan Shaanxi, China. Senior Engineer. m. Wang Shufen, 30 Apr 1965, 1 s, 1 d. Education: Grad, Shaanxi Norm Univ, China, 1962. Appointments: Grp Ldr, Xian Inst Applied Optics, 1962-80; Proj Engr, 1981-86; Snr Engr, 1986-; Lectr, Beijing Univ Tech, 1977; Tchr, Masters, Xian Inst Applied Optics, 1988-94. Creative Works: Articles to profl jrnls. Honours: 2nd Order Awd of Sci and Technol Progress; 3rd Order Awd of Sci and Tech Progress; Hon Cert, Cncl of Sci and Technol. Memberships: Chinese Optical Soc; Soc Chinese Ordnance Inds. Hobbies: Mountain Climbing; Bicycling; Reading; Walking; Watching TV. Address: 1 Middle Electron West St, P O Box 123, Xian 710065, China.

AN Zhendong, b. 5 Sept 1930. Government Official; Engineer. Education: Hebei Ind Coll, 1951. Appointments: Engr Qiqihar Admin Railroad, 1952-58; Engr Heilongjiang Sillicon Rectifier Factory, 1963-67; Engr dep factory dir Harbin Rectifier Equip Factory,m 1967-81; Chf Engr 2nd Light Ind Bur, 1981-82; Vice-Gov Heilongjiang, 1983-90; Vice-Chmn Standing Cttee Heilongjiang PCC, 1990-; Vice-Chmn 6th, 7th, 8th, 9th and 10th Cen Cttee Jiusan Soc; 6th 7th, 8th dep to Natl People's Congress; Mbr, Stndng Cttee 5th CCPCC, 1998-; VP Chinese Package Soc; Dir Chinese Ind Econ Soc. Creative Works: inclng: Signal and Radio Telephone in Railroad Cars, 1958; Fire-fighting Automatic System in Cities, 1963; Explosion proof Rectifier Equipment in Coal Mines, 1973; Power Factor Electricity Regulator, 1976. Honours: Named Model Worker of special grade of Harbin; the Model Worker of Heilongjiang Prov. Address: People's Congress Standing Committees of Heilonjiang, Nangang District, Harbin 150001, People's Republic of China.

AN Zijie (T K Ann), b. 1212, Dinghai Co, Zhejiang Prov. Appointments: Vice-Chmn Commn for Drafting Basic Law of Projected Hong Kong Spec Admin Reg, 1985-; Vice-Chmn 8th Natl Cttee, 1993-; Chmn Preparatory Cttee Hong Kong Spec Admin Reg. Memberships: Perm Mbr, 7th Natl Cttee CPPCC, 1988-92. Address: National Committee of Chinese People's Consultative Political Committee, 23 Taiping Qiao Street, Beijing, People's Republic of China.

ANAND Bal Krishnan, b. 19 Sept 1917, Lahore, India. Medical Teacher and Administrator. m. Kamila Parsi, 13 Sept 1942 (decd), 1 s, 2 d. Education: MB BS; MD; DSc (hc); Postdoct Fell, Yale Univ, USA, 1950-51. Appointments: Prof, Physiology, Lady Hardinge Medl Coll, New Delhi, 1949-57; Prof, All India Inst of Medl Scis, New Delhi, 1957-74; Prof Emeritus, 1977-; Advsr, Armed Forces Medl Servs, 1963-74; Vice-Dean, later on Dean ASSM, 1964-74; Pres, XXVI Intl Congress of Physiological Scis, New Delhi, 1974; Asst Dir, WHO (SE Asia), 1974-77; Pres, Indian Natl Bd of Exams, 1979-82; Vice-Chan, BH Univ, Varanesi, 1978; Dir, Inst of Medl Scis, Srinagar, 1982-85. Publications: Over 200 sci pprs in Indian & intl jrnls on neurophysiology and endocrinology & yoga. Honours: Rockefeller Fndn Fell, Yale Univ Sch of Med, 1950-51; Watamull Fndn Awd in Med, 1961; ICMR Snr Rsch Awd, 1962; Sir Shanti Swaroop Bhatnagar Mem Awd for Sci Rsch in Med, 1963; Padma Shri, Pres of India, 1969; Medl Cncl of India Silver Jubilee Rsch Awd, 1969; Dr B C Roy Eminent Medl Man Awd, 1984. Hobbies: Reading Sports. Address: B9/21 Vasant Vihar, New Delhi 110057, India.

ANAND PANYARACHUN. Politician; Business Executive. Education: Univ of Cambridge. Appointments: Fmr Amb to Canada, USA, UN and Germany, 1970s; Later Hd Min of For Affairs; Fmr Exec Chmn Saha Union

- indl conglomerate; Chmn Fedn of Inds; PM of Thailand, 1991-92. Address: c/o Office of the Prime Minister, Government House, Thanon Nakhon Pathom Road, Bangkok 10300, Thailand.

ANBARI Abdul-Amir al-, b. 10 Oct 1934. Diplomat. m. 1 s, 2 d. Education: Univ of Baghdad and Harvard Univ. Appointments: Fmrly held posts in Iraq Natl Oil Co, OPEC and Iraqi Min of Oil; High Commn for Mktng; Arab Pet Invmnt Corp; Exec Bd of Org of Arab Pet Exporting Countries - OAPEC; Fmr Judge Judicial Tribunal of Arab Pet Exporting Countries; Exec Chmn and Pres Iraqi Fund for External Dev; Gov Islamic Dev Bank; Dir-Gen Multilateral Econ Rels Dept Min of for Affairs, 1984-85; Amb to UK, 1984-86; Amb to USA, 1986-88; Perm Rep to UN NY, 1988-92; Amb to UNESCO Paris, 1992-. Memberships: Fmr mbr Bd State Org for Oil Refineries; fndng mbr Bd of Trustees of Inst of Intl Dev Law, Rome; Mbr Bd of Govs OAPEC Fund for Intl Dev. Address: Permanent Delegation of Iraq to UNESCO, 1 rue Miollis, 75015 Paris, France.

ANDERSEN John Everard, b. 19 Dec 1934, Melbourne, Aust. Environmental Engineer. m. Hedda, 13 Jan 1962, 2 s, 2 d. Education: BE; PhD. Appointments: Shift Engr, Gas and Fuel Corp of Vic, 1960-65; Rsch Chem Engr, CRA Ltd, 1965-71; Prof of Sci, Dir, Broken Hill Div, Univ NSW, 1972-82; Environ Educ Cnslt, 1983-. Publications: 28 pprs in profl jrnls. Honour: Adj Prof of Environ Systems Engrng, Univ SA, 1996-. Memberships: FIEAust; FAusIMM; MEIA; FRACI. Hobby: Amateur radio. Address: 230 Young Street, Unley, SA 5061, Australia.

ANDERSEN René, b. 21 July 1959, Copenhagen, Denmark. Banker. m. Annette, 15 Aug 1987, 1 d. Education: Bach of Sci and Econs, 1984; Master's Deg, Econs and For Trade, 1986. Appointments: Treas, Sales Mngr, SEB, London. 1989-92; Hd of Sales, SEB, Frankfurt, 1993-94, London, 1994-98, SEB Hong Kong, Treas, Hd of Trading and Capital Mkt; Hd of Sales, Standard Chartered Bank, London, 1999. Membership: Ind FOREX Assn. Hobbies: Tennis; Squash; Swimming. Address: 9 Rectory Orchard, Wimbledon, London SW19 5AS, London.

ANDERSON Barbara, b. 14 Apr 1926, NZ. Writer; Playwright. m. Neil Anderson, 1951, 2 s. Education: BSc, Univ Otago, 1946; BA, Vic Univ, Wellington, 1983. Creative works: Published: I Think We Should Go Into The Jungle, (short stories), 1989; Girls High, 1990; Portrait of the Artist's Wife, 1992; All The Nice Girls, 1993; The House Guest, 1995; Proud Garments, 1996; The Peacocks and Other Stories (short stories), 1997 Sev radio plays. Honours: John Cowie Reid Mem Awd for Play, 1986; Ansett/Sunday Star Short Story Awd, 1988; Timaru Herald/Aorak Short Story Awd, 1990; Vic Univ Fellshp, 1991; Goodman Fielder Wattie Awd, 1992; Schlshp of Letters, 1994. Membership: Cttee Mbr, PEN (NZ), 1992-94. Listed in: International Authors and Writers Who's Who. Address: c/o Victoria University Press, Victoria University, PO Box 600, Wellington, New Zealand.

ANDERSON Campbell McCheyne, b. 17 Sept 1941, Sydney, Australia. Managing Director. m. Sandra McLean Harper, 23 Mar 1965, 2 s, 1 d. Education: BEcon, Univ of Sydney, 1963. Appointments: Audit Clk, Priestley & Morris, 1958; Grad Trainee, Boral Ltd, 1962-68; Mngng Dir, Gen Mngr, Reef Oil NL, 1969-71; The Burmah Oil Co Plc, 1972-85; Renison Goldfields Consolidated Ltd, 1985-93; Mngng Dir, N Ltd. Memberships: Minerals Cncl of Aust; Aust Japan Soc of Vic; Bus Cncl of Aust. Hobbies: Golf; Swimming; Horse Racing. Address: 193 Domain Road, South Yarra, Victoria 3041, Australia.

ANDERSON Christopher John, b. 9 Dec 1947. Television Executive. m. Gabriella Elizabeth Douglas, 13 Sept 1969, 1 s, 1 d. Education: BEcons, Sydney Uiv, 1968; Postgrad Dip, Sch of Bus, Columbia Univ, NY, 1982. Appointments: Jrnlst, 1966-67, Corresp, 1967-70, The Times, London; Polit Corresp, 1972-75, Asst

Ed/Dpty Ed, 1976-79, Sunday Herald, Sydney; Ed, Sun-Herald, 1979-81; Ed, 1981-83, Ed-in-Chf, 1983-87, Sydney Morning Herald; Mngng Dir, Grp Editl Dir, 1987-91; John Fairfax Ltd, 1966-91; Hd of News, Current Affairs and Info Servs, 1991-93, Mngng Ed, 1993-95, Austl Brdcstng Corp; Dir: TVNZ Thailand, TVNZ Malaysia, TVNZ Aust Pty Ltd, S Pacific Pictures, Sky TV, Clear Comms, 1995-, Grp Chf Exec, 1995-97, TVNZ; Chf Exec Offr, Optus Communications, Australia, 1997-. Memberships: Intl Press Inst; Radio and TV News Dirs Assn of N Am; Natl Publrs Assn of Aust; Fmr Bd Mbr, 1981-87, Austl Press Cncl. Hobbies: Reading; Cricket. Address: c/o Cable and Wireless Optus, 101 Miller Street, North Sydney, New South Wales 2060, Australia.

ANDERSON David Charles, b. 27 Apr 1931, Oakland, California, USA. Librarian; Writer; Editor; Publisher. m. Jean Lynn Hess, 8 June 1957, 4 s, 1 d. Education: BA, 1952, BLS, 1953, Univ CA, Berkeley. Appointments: Libn, CA State Off of Local Planning, 1957-62; CA State Dept of Fin, 1960-62; Serials Cataloger, Gen Lib, Univ CA, Davis, 1962-71; Hd, Tech Servs, Carlson Hlth Scis Lib, 1971-91; Info Specl, UC Cntr for Animal Alternatives, 1992-98; Publr Humans and Other Species, 1990-. Publications include: From Solomon's Songbook: The Odes, 1984. Memberships: Med Lib Assn; Chair, Publrs & Info Ind Rels Cttee, 1981-85; Vet Med Lib Sect; Northern CA Nevada Med Lib Grp; Nature in Legend and Story, bd mbr. Hobbies: Piano; Classical Music; Gardening. Address: 8732 Rock Springs Road, Penryn, CA 95663-9622, USA.

ANDERSON John Duncan, b. 14 Nov 1956. Politician. m. Julia Gillian Robertson, 1987, 1 s, 2 d. Education: St Paul's Coll Univ of Sydney. Appointments: Fmr Farmer and grazier; MP for Gwydir NSW; Dep Ldr NPA; Shadow Min for Primary Ind, 1993-96; Min for Primary Inds and Energy, Mar 1996-. Memberships: Natl Party of Aust. Hobby: Farming. Address: Parliament House, Canberra, ACT 2600, Australia.

ANDERSON John Muir (Sir), b. 14 Sept 1914, Aust. State Bank Commissioner. m. Audrey Jamieson, 19 Mar 1949, 1 s, 1 d. Education: Melbourne Univ. Appointments: Served w 2nd AIF, SE Asia; Pres, 2/6 Indep Coy, 1st Austl Para Bn, 1952-56; Treas, 1956-61, Liberal and Country Party; Tree, 1960-67, Chmn, 1967, Melbourne Exhbn; Cmmnr, 1962-, Chmn, 1967, State Bank of Vic; Cmmnr, Melbourne Harbor Trust, 1972-; Treas, Liberal Party, 1978-79; Dir, Vic Ins Co Ltd; Dir, NZ Insurance Co Ltd; Mngng Dir, King Oscar Fine Foods Pty Ltd; Proprietor, John M Anderson & Co Pty Ltd. Honours: CMG, 1957; Created Kt, 1969. Hobbies: Politics; Swimming. Address: 25 Cosham Street, Brighton, Vic 3186, Australia.

ANDERSON Kym, b. 26 Feb 1950, Adelaide, S Aust. Economist. m. Bronwyn Margaret (née Nankivell), 12 Jan 1974, 3 d. Education: BAgEc (Hons), UNE, 1971; MEc, Univ of Adelaide, 1974; MA, Univ of Chgo, 1975; MA, 1976, PhD, 1977, Stanford Univ. Appointments: Rsch Fell, ANU, 1977-83; Prof, Univ of Adelaide, 1984-; On leave as Cnslr, GATT, Secretariat, Geneva, 1990-92. Publications: 14 books; 160 articles in jrnls or as chapts in other books. Honour: Apptd Rsch Fell, Eur's London-based Cntr for Econs Policy Rsch, 1992-. Memberships: Fell, Acady of Socl Scis in Aust, 1994-; Pres, Austl Agric and Resc Econs Soc, 1996-97. Hobbies: Farming; Sail boarding; Skiing; Church; Tennis. Address: School of Economics, University of Adelaide, Adelaide, SA 5005, Australia.

ANDERSON Michelle, b. 19 July 1945, Melbourne, Aust. Book Publisher. m. 1967, dissolved 1997, 2 s. Education: Loreto Convent, Mandeville Hall, Toorak, Melbourne. Appointments: Dir, Hill of Content Publng Pty Ltd, 1991-; Cttee mbr, Small Publr Assn, 1997-. Publications: Publd bestselling and awd-winning titles in areas of gen hlth and childrens' books inclng You Can Conquer Cancer; Baby Massage (now in 12 langs); Peacetimes; Lifetimes. Hobbies: Music; Reading; Tennis; Painting. Address: 89 Alexandra Avenue, South Yarra, Vic 3141, Australia.

ANDERSONS Andrew, b. 5 July 1942, Aust. Architect. m. Sara Bennett, 26 Feb 1972, 2 d. Education BArch, hons, Sydney Univ; MArch, Yale Univ, USA. Appointments: NSW Pub Wrks Dept, 1964-65; Ove Arup Assocs, London, 1966-67; Prin Arch, Spec Proj Sect, NSW Pub Wrks Dept, 1967-88; Visng Prof of Arch, Univ NSW, 1981 Asst Govt Arch, Spec Projs Sect, 1984; Joined Peddle Thorp, 1988; Pt-time Prof of Arch, Univ NSW, 1989; Dir, Peddle Thorp Archs, 1989. Honours: Cty of Sydney Awd, 1973; RAIA Merit Awds, 1975, 1980, 1988, 1994, 1996; Merit Awd, Concrete Inst of Aust, 1981; AO, 1983; Pres Awd, Roy Austl Inst of Archs, 1988; Lloyd Rees Awd for Civic Design, 1988; RAIA Natl Design Awd for Civic Des, 1988; Sir John Sulman Awd, 1973, 1989. Hobbies: Opera; Theatre; Classical Music; Swimming; History of Art and Architecture in Latvia. Address: 10 Alexander Street, Paddington, NSW 2021, Australia.

ANDERTON James Patrick, b. 21 Jan 1938, Auckland. Politician. m. twice, 3 s, 1 d. Education: Seddon Memorial Tech Coll; Auckland Tchrs Trng Coll. Appointments: Tchr for two years; Child Welfare Offr Educ Dept Wanganui; Cath Yth Movement Orgr, 1960-65; Cty Cnclr Manukau, 1965-68; Sec Cath Diocesan Off Auckland, 1967-69; Export Mngr UEB Textiles, 1969-70; Mngng Dir Anderton Holdings, 1971-; Cty Cnclr Auckland, 1974-77; Cnclr Auckland Regl Authy, 1977-80; joined Labour Party, 1963; held posts at Electorate, Regl and Exec levels; Pres NZ Labour Party, 1979-84; MP for Sydenham, 1984; resigned from Labour Party, 1989 and fmd the New Labour Party; re-elected MP for Sydenham - now Wigram - 1990 a NLP Candidate; Elected First Ldr of Alliance Party - fmd 1991. Memberships: Policy Cncl, 1979-89. Hobbies: Chess, cricket and classical guitar. Address: Parliament Buildings, Wellington, New Zealand.

ANDREWS John Thomas, b. 20 Mar 1927, Brighton, Eng. Nuclear Medicine Physician. m. Iris Mary Groves, 1957, 4 s. Education: HMS Conway, 1942-43, 2nd Mate's Cert 1946; Queen Mary Coll, 1949; London Hosp Med Coll, 1950-55; LRCP (Lond), MRCS (Eng), 1955; MBBS (Lond), 1955; DObst RCOG, 1958; Roy Australasian Coll of Phyns, MRACP, 1969, FRACP, 1970, Roy Australasian Coll of Radiologists, MRACR, 1963; FRACR, 1977, Dip ABNM, 1973, MD, 1980. Appointments: Cadet to 2nd Offr, Brit Merchant Nav, 1943-48; House Offr and Jnr Registrar, London Hosp, 1955-59; Registrar, Launceston Gen Hosp, Tas, 1959-60; Gen Practitioner, Launceton, 1960-61; Trainee Radiotherapist and Radiotherapist, Cancer Inst, Melbourne, 1961-66; Dir of Nucl Med, Roy Melbourne Hosp, 1966-92; Dir. Nuc Med, 1992-98, Part-Time Physn, Nucl Med, 1998-, Monash Medl Cntr. Publications: Nuclear Medicine: Clinical and Technological Bases (co-auth w M J Milne), 1977; Scientific pprs: Auth or Co-auth of 95 pprs mostly concerning Nuc Med. Honours: Baker Fell, Roy Australasian Coll of Radiologists, 1969; As Intl Cnclr for Aust, Intl Physns for Prevention of Nucl War, 1985; Mbr, deleg, attending Oslo when the above body received the 1985 Nobel Peace Prize. Memberships: Austl and NZ Soc of Nuc Med, Past Pres and Former Chairperson, Accreditation Bd; Austl and NZ Assn of Phyns in Nuc Med; Roy Australasian Colls of Physns and Radiologists; AMA; Med Assn for Prevention of War, Aust, Past VP. Address: 400 New Street, Brighton, Melbourne, Vic 3186, Australia.

ANDRIESSEN Edward, b. 2 Feb 1947, Netherlands. Veterinary Surgeon. m. Lynnette, 20 Dec 1970. Education: BVSc. Publication: Meat Safety, Quality & Veterinary Public Health, 1998. Membership: Austl Vet Assn. Hobbies: Sailing; Fishing; Writing. Address: Australian Quarantine & Inspection Service, 8 Butler Street, Port Adelaide, SA 5015, Australia.

ANEMA Durlynn Carol, b. 23 Dec 1935, San Diego, CA, USA. Author; Educator; Counselor. m. Vernon Garten, 30 July 1988, 2 s, 1 d. Education: BA; MA; EdD; PhD. Appointments: Dir, Lifelong Learning, Univ of Pacific, 1980-84; Prof, Comm, Univ of Pacific, 1984-89; VP, Educ, Women's Mins Inst, 1992-98; Cnslr, Covenant Ch, 1993-98. Publications: Don't Get Fired, 1979; Get Hired, 1980; California Yesterday and Today, 1984; Late Life, 1989; Options, 1992; Harriet Chalmers Adams, 1997. Honours: Phi Kappa Phi; Susan B Anthony Awd, 1989. Memberships: Soc of Profl Jrnlsts; Amn Assn Christian Cnslrs; Soc of Christian Therapists. Hobbies: Travel; Hiking; Bicycling; Reading. Address: 401 Oak Ridge Ct, Valley Spurges, CA 95252, USA.

ANG Hooi Hoon, b. 11 Jan 1964, Ipoh Peark, Malysia. Lecturer; Researcher. Education: BPharm (Hons), 1988, Conversion of status from MSc to PhD, 1990, PhD, 1993, Univ of Sci, Malaysia; Registration w Pharm Bd, Malaysia, 1992; Admitted to PHP Inst of Asia, Japan, awd Gold Medal "Doct Fell of the Inst", 1995. Appointments: Grad Asst, Sch of Pharm Scis, Univ of Sci, Malaysia, 1988-90; Asst Quality Control Mngr, Ho Yan Hor Sdn Bhd, Ipoh Perak, 1992-93; Lectr, Sch of Pharm Scis, Univ of Sci, Malaysia, 1994-. Publications: 26 in refereed jrnls; 2 invited lects; 29 abstracts and proceeedings. Honours include: Malaysian Pharm Soc (MPS) Gold Medal Awd, Malaysian Pharm Soc, 1988; Young Scientist Awardee, China, Indonesia, Japan, Malaysia; Gold Medal-Doct Fell PHP Inst of Asia, Japan, 1995; Sole recip, 1996 ASAIHL (Assn of the SE Asia Inst of Higher Learning), Visng Fellshp, Visng Professorship, Fac of Med, Natl Univ of Singapore. Memberships: Malaysian Pharm Soc; Malaysian Soc of Parasitology and Tropical Med; Malaysian Microbiology Soc; Japanese Soc of Parasitology; Korean Soc of Parasitology; Third World Acady Sci, Italy; Malaysian Nat Prod Soc; Malaysian Technol Forum; Malaysian Invention and Des Soc; Vice Chmn, 1994-95, Hon Sec, 1995-, Malaysian Pharm Soc, Penang. Hobbies: Listening to Songs and music; Reading; Sight-seeing; Hiking; Shopping. Address: School of Pharmaceutical Sciences, University Science Malaysia; Minden 11800, Penang, Malaysia.

ANG Lee, b. 1954, Taipei. Film Direstor. m. Jane Lin. Education: NY Univ; Moved to USA, 1978. Creative Works: Films: Pushing Hands, 1992; The Wedding Banquet, 1993; Eat Drink Man Woman, 1995; Sense and Sensibility, 1996; The Ice Storm, 1998. Honours: Winner of natl script-writing contest - Taiwanese Govt, 1990.

ANGEL James Robert, b. 20 Sept 1935, Sydney, Aust. Academic. Education: BA 1959, MA 1965, DipEd 1966, Univ of Sydney; PhD, Austl Natl Univ, 1970. Appointments: Colombo Plan Expert, N Borneo, 1959-65; Off of Educ, Sydney, 1965; Rsch Schl, Austl Natl Univ, 1966-70; Lectr Hist 1970-75, Snr Lectr 1975-94, Univ of Sydney; Ed, Current Affairs Bulletin, Univ of Sydney, 1982-85; Vice Prin, Snr Fell, St Andrews Coll 1982-87; Snr Tutor, St Pauls Coll 1990-97. Publications include: Independence and Alliance: Australia in World Affairs 1975-80 (co-ed), 1982; The Australian Club: The First 50 Years 1938-88, 1987; Diplomacy in the Market Place: Australia in World Affairs, 1981-90 (co-ed), 1992. Memberships include: Pres, Univ Sydney Arts Assn, 1972-75; Pres 1975-79, NSW Br Austl Inst of Intl Affairs; Rsch Chmn, Austl Inst of Intl Affairs, 1985-87; Patron, Savoy Arts Co, 1985. Honour: OBE, 1979. Hobby: Music. Address: PO Box 815, Narrabeen, New South Wales 2101, Australia.

ANGLE Roger Roy, b. 2 Aug 1938, USA. Writer. m. 1960, 1 s. Education: MFA. Appointments: Pt-time Coll Tchr, 1973-81; Copy Ed, The Beacon, Wichita, KS, 1964-67; Investigative Reporter, Photographer, The Gazette & Daily, York, PA, 1967-69; Regl Coord, S CA Poetry in Schs, 1973-76; Reporter, 1979-82, Ed, 1983-85, The Newport Ensign, Newport Beach, CA, 1979-85; PR Cnslt, Freelance Writer, 1986-; PR Dir, The Schraff Grp, Costa Mesa, CA, 1995-96. Publications: Poetry, short fiction and sev articles in profl jrnls and mags. Honours: Nominated, Pulitzer Prize, 1967, Heywood Broun Awd, 1967; Hon Mention, Thomas L Stokes Awd, 1967; Fell, Squaw Valley Cmty of Writers, 1974; Second Best Feature Story, CNPA, 1980; Second Best Front Page, CNPA, 1983; Best Edl Page, CA Newspprs Publrs Assn, 1983; 1st Place, Orange County Fair, 1985; Top Schlsp, Squaw Valley Cmty of Writers, 1992. Address: 3837½ Midway Avenue, Culver City, CA 90232, USA.

ANGOVE Thomas William Carlyon, b. 8 Aug 1917, Renmark, S A, Aust. Vigneron. m. (1) Jean Primrose (née Sawers), 1942, 2 s, 1 d, (2) Beverley Robertson, 1958, 2 d. Education: St Peter's Coll, Adelaide; Grad, Oenology, Roseworthy Agricl Coll. Career: Flight Lt, Roy Austl Air Force, SW Pacific, 1941-44; Vigneron and Distiller; Chmn, Dirs, Angove's Pty Ltd (Mngng Dir, 1947-82. Honours: 1939-45 Star; Pacific Star; 1939-45 War Medal; Austl Serv Medal; JP, 1948; Queen's Silver Jubilee Medal, 1977; Patron Austl Wine Industry, 1993; AM, 1994. Memberships: Austl Wine and Brandy Prodrs Assn, 1945-; Roy Agricl and Horticultural Soc (SA), 1954-; Austl Wine Rsch Inst, 1967-77; Assn Austl Agricl Technologists; Chmn, SA local Bd Guardian Roy Exchange Ins Ltd; Hobbies: Flying; Boating; Hunting; Fishing. Address: Renmark, South Australia.

ANGUS-LEPPAN Pamela Edith, b. Zambia. Director; Manager; Accountant. m. Emeritus Professor Peter Vincent Angus-Leppan, 11 July 1953, 1 s, 2 d. Education: BSc, Chem and Phys (1s Class Distinction), Witwatersrand Univ, S Africa, 1952; BCom (Hons), 1975, MCom (Hons), 1985, Univ NSW; CPA (AASA, Mgmt Acctbg) Advd Spec Accreditaion; PhD Coursework Prog completed AGSM, 1983. Appointments include: Lectr, Phys, Univ Natal, Durban, S Africa, 1954; Rsch Chem, Paint Ind Rsch Inst, S Africa, 1954-59; Mngmt Acct, CSR Ltd, Sydney, Aust, 1976-77; Lectr, Acctng and Fin Systems, Univ NSW, 1977-83; Mngng Dir, Tamsin Pty Ltd, Aust, 1979-; Cnslt, Dept Energy, Mines and Resources, Ottawa, Can, 1982; Snr Lectr, Mngmt Acctcy, Univ of NSW, 1983-87; Dir, Fin and Control, Singer Thailand Ltd, 1987-90; Dir, Bd of Dirs, Singer Thailand Ltd, 1988-90; Dir and Prin Cnslt, PAL Cnslts, 1990-; Dpty Warden, Intl House, Univ NSW, 1993. Publications: (book) Financial Modelling, 1986; 65 publs in bus, profl and acad jrnls; 10 commissioned reports; Chapt in intl textbook, Financial Reporting in the Pacific Asia Region (ed Ronald Ma), 1997. Honours include: UNSW Awds, 1973, 1974, 1985, UNSW Medal for Acad Achievement, 1976; UNSW Grants, 1980, 1983, 1984, 1984, 1985; Rsch Grant, Univ of Adelaide, 1984-85; Pen Intl Short Story Competition, 1st Prize, 1992. Memberships include: Cncl Mbr UNSW Cncl 1981-85, 1992-98; Dir, Exec Dir, UNSW Intl House, 1983-98; Soc, Women Writers, NSW, Treas, 1995-97; Fellshp Austl Writers; Dir, Kensington Colls, UNSW, 1996-98; Bd Mbr, VP, Pres, UNSW Alumni Assn. Address: PO Box 51, Coogee, NSW 2034, Australia.

ANGYAL Stephen John, b. 21 Nov 1914, Hungary. Emeritus Professor. m. Helga Steininger, 28 Feb 1941, 1 s, 1 d. Education: Univ of Sci, Budapest; PhD, DSc, Univ of NSW. Appointments: Rsch Chem, Nicholas Pty Ltd, Melbourne, Vic, Aust, 1941-46; Lectr in Chem, Univ of Sydney, 1946-52; Assoc Prof 1953, Prof of Organic Chem 1960-79, Dean, Fac of Sci 1977-79, Emer Prof 1980-, Univ of NSW; Visng Prof, Univ of CA, USA, 1957; Visng Prof, Oxford Univ, Eng, 1968; Professeur Associe, Univ of Grenoble, France, 1976. Publications: About 200 orig pprs in sci jrnls in organic chem; Part auth of book, Conformational Analysis, 1966. Honours: Nuffield Dominion Travelling Fellshp to Cambridge Univ, Eng, 1952; Carnegie Grant to USA, 1953; H G Smith, Mem Medal, Roy Austl Chem Inst, 1958; OBE, 1977; Haworth Mem Medal and Lectshp, Chem Soc, London, 1980; Hudson Awd, Amn Chem Soc, 1987. Memberships: Fell, Roy Austl Chem Inst; Fell, Austl Acady of Sci; Hungarian Acady of Sci. Hobbies: Skiing; Swimming; Piano. Address: 304 Sailors Bay Road, Northbridge, NSW 2063, Australia.

ANH NGOC (Nguyen Dúc Ngoc), b. 1 Aug 1943, Nghê An, Vietnam. Poet. m. Vuthihang, 1970, 1 s, 1 d. Education: BA, Lit. Appointments: Ed, For Lit Sect, Lit & Art Mag of the Armed Forces, 1979-. Publications: Books of verse: The Scent of the Land and the Colour of the Flag, 1977; A Thousand Miles and a Footstep, 1984; The Four-Faced Mekong, 1986. Honours: Runner-up, Lit & Arts Weekly's Poetry Competition, 1973; Winner, same competition, 1975. Memberships: Vietnam Writers' Union, 1980-. Hobby: Soccer. Address: 4 Ly Nam De Street, Hanoi, Vietnam.

ANI R S, b. 20 May 1976, Trivandrum, India. Social Worker. Education: BCom; Specialised Course, Mkt Mngmt; Engl Typewriting. Hobbies: Reading; Travelling. Address: M/S Sree Kamaraj Service Society, H O Pravachambalam, Nemom POst, Thiruvananthapuram 695020, India.

ANIL KUMAR Swami Rajan, b. 17 June 1954, Mysore, India. Medical Doctor; Businessman. m. Reena Renganathan, 16 June 1984, 1 s, 1 d. Education: BSc; MBBS; MACF; DICAC. Honours: Gold Medal, Accupuncture, Sri Lanka, 1981; Awd, Ex in Arch, The Village Hlth Club, 1994. Membership: Korean Accupuncture Fndn. Hobbies: Horse Riding; Landscaping; Music; Cricket; Cartoonist; Collecting Antiques; Designing Houses. Address: The Village Naturopathy #106, Nanjangud Road, Mysore 570 004, India.

ANJARD Ronald P, b. 31 July 1935, Chgo, IL, USA. Consultant; Professor; Author. m. Marie B Anjard, 3 s, 1 d. Education: BS, Metallurgical Engrng, Carnegie Mellon Univ/CIT, 1957; Masters, Indl Admin, Purdue Univ/Krannert, 1968; AS, Supervision, IN Univ, 1973; PhD Hums (hon), London Inst for Applied Rsch, 1976; BS, Bus Admin, USNY, 1978; BA, Hums, T A Edison, 1979; PhDE, Engrng, Univ WI, 1979; PhD, Educ, Univ WI, 1981; PhD, Metallurgical/Materials Engr, CPU, 1982; masters Computer Resource Mngmt, Webster Univ, 1992; Additional studies: Law (25% JD earned) & Electrons, IN Univ, Bus at LSU, Univ of CA, Butler Univ. Publications: Over 1000 intl presentations, publs, workshops. Honours include: Fitzgerald Awd, Nat; Assn of Diocesan Ecumenical Offrs, 1994, 1997; Fitzgerald Awd for Ecumenical Achievement, 1994; IEPS Electrons Packaging Achievement Awd, 1994; Outstndng Profl Achievement, T A Edison Coll 1994; John A Wagnon Tech Achievement (ISHM), 1994; ASQC Ishikawa Medal, 1995. Hobbies: Writing; Travel; Sports; Photography. Address: BX420950/SD, CA 92142, USA.

ANSARI Gholamreza, b. 22 Nov 1955, Shahrood. Diplomat. m. Shahih Shirazi, 4 d. Education: Allameh Tabatabaee Univ Tehran. Appointments: Gov-Gen Piranshahr Cty; Dep Gov-Gen Azarbayejan Prov; Supt of Gov-Gen of Azarbayejan Prov; Dept Gen Dir of For Natls and Refugees Dept, 1980-88; Charge D'Affaires London Emb, 1992-. Hobbies: Reading; Jogging; Swimming. Address: Embassy of Iran, 16 Prince's Gate, London, SW7 1PT, England.

ANSARI Mohammad Hamid, b. 1 Apr 1937, Calcutta. Diplomat. m. Salma Kazmi, 1964, 2 s, 1 d. Education: Aligarh Muslim Univ. Appointments: Joined Indian For Serv, 1961; Served Iraq, Morocco, Saudi Arabia, 1962-69; Min of For Affairs, 1969-72; First Sec Cnslr Indian Mission to EEC, 1972-75; Charge d'Affaires Jeddah, 1975-76; Amb to UAE, 1976-80; Chf of Protocol to Govt of India, 1980-85; High Commnr in Aust, 1985-89; Amb to Afghanistan, 1989-90; Amb to Iran, 1990-92; Perm Rep to UN, 1992-93; Pres UNDP Exec Bd, 1994-95; Padma Shree. Hobbies: Reading; Golf.

ANSELL Graham Keith, b. 2 Mar 1931 Lower Hutt, New Zealand. Diplomat. m. Mary Diana Wilson, 1953, 3 s, 1 d. Education: Horowhenua Coll, Palmerston North Boys' Sch and Vic Univ, Wellington. Appointments: Dept of Inds and Com, 1948-51; Dept of External Affairs, 1951-56; Second Sec High Commn to Ottawa, 1956-59; Asst then Acting Hd, Econ and Socl Affairs Div Dept External Affairs, 1959-62; Dep High Commnr Apia, 1962-64; Dep High Commnr Canberra, 1964-68; Hd Econ Div Min of For Affairs, 1968-71; Min NZ Emb Tokyo, 1971-73; High Commnr in Fiji, 1973-76; High Commnr in Nauru, 1974-76; Amb to Belgium, Luxembourg and the Eurn Communities - also accred to Denmark, 1977-81; Dir NZ Plng Cncl, 1981-82; Amb to Japan, 1983-84; Dep Sec Min of For Affairs, 1984-85; High Commnr in Aust, 1985-89; Chf Exec Min of For

Affairs and Trade, 1989-91; Dir Natl Bank of NZ, 1991-; Dir Asian NZ Meat Co, 1991-98; NZ Meat Prodrs Bd, 1990-96. Membership: Bd Asia 2000 Fndn, 1994-97. Hobbies: Music; Walking; Gardening. Address: 13 Tainui Street, Raumati Beach, New Zealand.

ANUKRITI, b. 23 Oct 1981, Hisar, India. Publications: Phulwari Ke Phool (book of songs for children), 1999. Honours: Awds in debates, quiz and painting competitions. Hobbies: Reading; Writing; Cricket; Tennis; Football. Address: D/O Dr R N Manav, 706, Sector-13, Hisar - 125005, Haryana, India.

ANUMAKONDA Jagadeesh, b. 13 Aug 1947, Nellore, India. Renewable Energy Expert. m. Vaiderbhi, 1 Oct 1979, 1 s, 2 d. Education: BSc, VR Coll, Nellore, 1961-62; MSc, Sri Venkateswara Univ, 1974-76; PhD, Univ Roorkee, 1980-85. Appointments: Tchr, Phys, VR Coll, Nellore, 1968-89; Rschr, Danish Folkcentre for Renewable Energy, Denmark, 1989-90; Rschr, Wind Energy, ENEA CRE CASACCIA, Rome, 1990-92; Dir, Murugappa Chettiar Rsch Cntr, Chennai, 1993-95; VP, Adv Radio Masts Ltd, Hyderabad, 1995-96; Dir, Infrastructure Cnsltng & Engrs Pvt Ltd, Bangalore, 1996-97; Freelance Wind Energy Cnslt, 1997-. Publications: Over 100 rsch pprs in profl jrnls. Honours: Margaret Nobel Fndn Awd in Energy Technol, 1994; Intl Man of the Yr, IBC, 1997; Golden Jubilee of Independence of India Awd, 1997; United Writers Assn Lifetime Achievement Awd, 1998; CBR Awd in Sci & Technol, Hyderabad, 1998. Memberships: Sigma Xi; Fell, Roy Meteorol Soc; CEU, Rome; Solar Energy Soc of India; IPV Prima Viri, Rome; Energy Environ Grp, New Delhi. Hobbies: Inventing; Creative Writing; Social Service. Address: 2/210 First Floor, Nawabpet, Nellore 524 002, India.

ANWAR Sheikh Muhammad, b. 25 Mar 1943, Amritsar, India. Television Controller. m. 4 d. Education: Fairfield Univ, Conn and Pakistan Admin Staff Coll. Appointments: Contract Prodr-Dir and script-writer Pakistan TV - PTV - Lahore, 1964-66; Prog prodr, 1966-72; Exec Prodr News and Cur Affairs, 1972-79; Dep Controller O'seas Div PTV HQ Islamabad, 1979-90; Prog Mngr PTV Rawalpindi-Islamabad, 1980-81; Comms Consultant to the min of Info and Brdstng Islamabad, 1981-83; Dep Controller of Progs PTV HQ Islamabad, 1983-85; Prodr Grp-8 PTV Lahore, 1985-86; Gen Mngr PTV Peshawar, 1986-87; Controller Prog Plng PTV HQ Islamabad, 1988; Educl TV, 1988; Progs Trng Acady, 1989-90; Prgs Admin, 1990-92; Intl Rels, 1990-93; Controller Progs Admin Sport Archives, 1994-96; Gen Mngr PTV Cntr, Lahore, 1992-94; Controller PTV Acady PTV HQ Islamabad; Exec Prodr Local Area Transmission PTV Lahore, 1996-97; Visng Prof of Comms Quaid-e-Azam Univ of Pakistan Info Servs Acady, 1983-90; Examiner Fed Pub Serv Comm - Info Grp; Visng Prof Fine Arts Dept Punjab Univ, 1993. Memberships: Intl Inst of Comm London, 1981; Roy TV Soc London, 1983-. Address: PTV-Centre, Lahore, Pakistan.

AOKI Shinji. Politician. Appointments: Fmr Chmn Cttee on Constrn; Fmr Vice-Chmn Soc Dem Party of Japan - SDPJ - Diet Affairs Cttee for House of Cnclrs; Fmr Min of Labour. Memberships: House of Cnclrs; SDPJ. Address: Ministry of Labour, 1-2-2, Kasumigaseki, Chiyoda-ku, Tokyo 100, Japan.

AOKI Torao, b. 16 Jan 1926, Tokyo, Japan. University Professor. m. 17 Feb 1955, 1 s, 1 d. Education: BA, Law, Fac of Law, Tokyo Univ, 1950; MA, Econs, Univ of S CA, 1952-54. Appointments: Asisn Dept IMF, 1965-69; Exec Dir, Inter Amn Dev Bank, 1978-79; Cnslr, Fin Min of Japan, 1977-79; Dir, Small Bus Credit Guaranty Corp, 1979-83; Visng Prof, LaSalle Univ, 1984; Prof of Econ, Niigata Univ, 1983-91; Cnslt, Econ Dev Inst World Bank, 1986-96; Var Positions in the Min of Fin. Creative Works: Japan's Public Sector: How is the Go; Varnment Financed. Honours: The Third Order of the Sacred Treasure, 1998. Memberships: Japan Fiscal Sci Assn; Japan Chapt of the Intl Fiscal Assn; Soc of Rsch and

Info. Address: 5-1-7 Shin-machi, Hoya-shi, Tokyo, 202-0023, Japan.

AOYAGI Machiko, b. Yokohama, Japan. Professor. m. Kiyotaka, b. 2 Oct 1960, 2 s. Education: PhD, Grad Sch of Tokyo, Metrop Univ. Appointments: Asst Prof, Seisen Women's Univ, 1972-76; Prof, Rikkyo Univ, 1976-96; Prof, Ibaraki Christian Coll, 1997-. Publications: Modekngei: A New Religion in Palau, Micronesia, 1986; Culture and Society in Tonga, 1991. Memberships: Japanese Soc of Ethnology, cttee mbr, 1976-; Japanese Soc for Oceanic Studies, 1980-; Japanese Soc for NZ Studies, 1997-. Address: 6-3-36 Osawa, Mitaka, Tokyo 181-0015, Japan.

AOYAMA Seiko, b. 20 Dec 1931. Professor. m. Yoshiobu Aoyama, 12 Nov 1954, 1 s, 1 d. Education: BA, Engl Lit, Univ of Nagoya; MA, Engl Lit, Univ of Tokyo. Appointments: Prof, Kyoritsu Women's Jnr Coll, Tokyo; Prof, Ferris Women's Univ, Yokohama; Prof, Aoyama Gakuin Univ, Tokyo. Publications: Shakespeare's Women, 1981; Charlotte Brontë's Pilgrimage, 1984; Shakespearean Tragedy and Its Transformation, 1985; Shakespeare and London, 1986; Shakespeare's Popular World, 1991; Brontë Sisters, 1995. Memberships: English Lit Soc of Japan, Gen Meeting Cttee, 1983-86, Cnclr, 1990-92, editl cttee, 1991-93; Shakespeare Soc of Japan, exec cttee, 1993-97; Intl Shakespeare Conf, deleg from Japan, 1980-; Intl Shakespeare Assn; The Brontë Soc; The Renaissance Inst. Listed in: The World Who's Who of Women. Hobby: Theatregoing. Address: 1-16-15 Ryoke, Urawa, Saitama-Ken 336-0901, Japan.

AOYAMA Yoshinobu, b. 20 Aug 1923, Hiroshima, Japan. Emeritus Professor. m. Seiko Aoyama, 12 Nov 1954, 1 s, 1 d. Education: BA, Tokyo Univ. Appointments: Toyo Univ, Japan, 1956; Japan Women's Univ, 1960; Josai Intl Univ, 1992. Publications: Studies on Anglo-Saxon Society, 1974; Fendal Monarchy of England, 1978; Arthurian Legends, 1985; Glastonbury Abbey, 1992. Memberships: Histl Soc of Japan; Société Internationale Arturienne. Address: 1-16-15 Ryoke, Urawa, Saitama 336-0901, Japan.

APPLE Raymond, b. 27 Dec 1935, Melbourne, Aust. Senior Rabbi. m. Marian, 27 Dec 1960, 2 s, 2 d. Education: Melbourne hs; Melbourne Univ; Univ of New Eng; London Sch of Jewish Stdies. Appointments: Headmaster, Utd Jewish Educ Bd, Melbourne, 1955-58; Relig Dir, Assn for Jewish Yth, London, 1960-65; Rabbi, Hampstead Synagogue, London, 1965-72; Snr Rabbi, Grt Synagogue, Sydney, 1972-; Lectr, Judaic Studies, Sydney Univ, 1975-; Judge and Registrar, Sydney Beth Din (Jewish Ecclesiastical Ct), 1975-; Snr Rabbi, Austl Def Force, 1988-. Publications: Making Australian Society: The Jews, 1981; The Hampstead Synagogue, 1892-1967, 1967; Pprs on relig, educ and hist. Honours include: Mbr, Order of Aust; Reserve Force Decoration; Queen's Silver Jubilee Medal, 1971. Memberships: Hon VP, NSW Bd of Jewish Educ, 1973-; Past Grand Chaplain Utd Grand Lodge, NSW, 1985-; Pres, Assn of Rabbis of Aust and NZ, 1980-84, 1988-92; Pres, Aust Jewish Histl Soc, 1985-89. Address: The Great Synagogue, 166 Castlereagh Street, Sydney, NSW 2000, Australia.

APPLEBY Richard Franklin, b. 17 Nov 1940, Essendon, Vic, Aust. Anglican Bishop of the Northern Territory. m. Elizabeth Appleby, 10 Dec 1966, 2 d. Education: BSc (Melbourne); ThL (Hons), Austl Coll of Theol. Appointments: Curate Glenroy, 1967-67; Curate of Nth Balwyn and Chap to Apprentices and Probation Hostels, 1969-70; Chap to Christ Church Grammar Sch, 1970-71; Warden, Wollaston Coll and Chap to Archbish Perth, 1972-75; Rector, Belmont (Perth), 1975-80; Dean Bathhurst and Examining Chap to Bish Bathhurst, 1980-83; Pres, NSW Ecumenical Cl, 1987-89; Aux Bish Newcastle, 1983-92. Address: Bishop's Lodge, 131 Playford Street, Parap, NT 0820, Australia.

APPLEYARD Ronald George, b. 26 Nov 1920, Aust. Former Art Gallery Administrator. m. Janet Appleyard, 1950, dec 1987, 3 s. Appointments: Joined, 1937, Asst

Keeper, 1948, Keeper of Prints, 1951-73, Asst to the Dir, 1960, Asst Dir, 1962-76, Dpty Dir, 1976-82, Art Gall of SA; Served AIF, 1941-45. Publication: S T Gill - The South Australian Years 1839-1852, (jntly), 1986. Honours Co-recip, Overseas Stdy Grant, Calouste Gulbenkian Fndn, Brit Cncl & US State Depts, 1964; Overseas Grant, Visual Arts Bd, 1975; OAM, 1981. Memberships: Fell, Art Mus Assn of Aust, Fndn Sec, 1963-75, VP, 1975-76, Pres, 1976-78; Hon Life Mbr, SA Br, Arts Cncl of Aust, Cnclr, 1965-80, Pres, 1974-77 Cncl Mbbr, Art Gall of SA Fndn, 1982-93; Austl Natl Cttee, Intl Cncl of Mus, 1970-77; Fell, Mus Assn UK, 1968; Visual Arts Cttee, Austl Natl Advsry Cttee for UNESCO, 1965-71.Address: 4 Wenlock Street, Brighton, SA 5048, Australia.

ARAI Toshihiko, b. 12 Sept 1937, Niigata, Japan. Retired Professor. m. Hatsue Aoki, 1 Dec 1963, 1 s, 2 d. Education: MD, Keio Univ Sch of Med, 1962; PhD, Medl Microbio, Grad Sch, Keio Univ, 1968. Appointments: Rsch Assoc, Div of Bio, Univ of TX, Dallas, 1970-72; Asst Prof, 1973-85, Assoc Prof, 1985, Dept of Microbio, Keio Univ Sch of Med; Prof, Dept of Microbio, Meiji Coll of Pharm, 1985-97. Publications: 15 books in Japanese; 140 Orig acad papers; 80 Pprs in coml jrnls; 300 Abstracts for acad meetings. Honour: Sanshikai Awd, Keio Univ Sch of Med, 1968. Memberships: Japan Soc of Bacteriology; Amn Soc for Microbio; Japan Soc of Chemotherapy; Japan Assn of Infectious Diseases; Japan Antibiotic Rsch Assn; Pharm Soc of Japan. Address: 5-1-23 Yatsu, Narashino-shi, Chiba-ken 275-0026, Japan.

ARAKI Kenji, b. 12 Oct 1934, Yokohama, Japan. University Professor. m. Kaneko, 1 s, 2 d. Education: BEng, Yokohama Natl Univ, Japan, 1958; DEng, Univ Tokyo, 1970. Appointments: Prof, 1984-, Hd of Dr Course of Prodn Scis Maj, 1994-96, Hd of Info Processing Cntr, 1995-97, Saitama Univ; Invited Prof, Natl Tsing Hua Univ, Taiwan, 1975. Publication: Ed, Proceedings of the 3rd JHPS International Symposium on Fluid Power, Japan, 1996. Honours: Prizes, Best Ppr, Fluid Power Technol Promotion Fndn, 1984, Japan Hydraulics and Pneumatics Soc, 1996, Soc of Instrument and Control Engrs, 1998. Memberships: Japan-China Sci and Technol Exchange Assn; Japan-Italy Sci and Technol Coop Proj (Artificial Intelligence); Dir, Japan Hydraulics and Pneumatic Soc, 1990, 1992-98. Address: Saitama University, Faculty of Engineering, 255 Shimo okubo, Satana Urawa 358, Japan.

ARANUI-FAED Julia Anne, b. 8 Jan 1945, Blenheim, NZ. Psychiatrist. m. (1) James Matheson Faed, (2) Whetu-o-te-Ata Aranui, 4 s, 1 d. Education: BMedSci, Otago, 1968; MBCMB, 1969; DPN, 1973; DipChild Psych, 1982; DMA (Massey), 1985. Appointments: House Surg, Dunedin Hosp, 1970-71; Registrar in Psychol Med, Univ Otago, Dunedin, 1972-73; Medl Offr, Chery Farm Hosp, Dunedin, 1974-78; Cnslt, Psych, Northside Clin, Sydney, Aust, 1978-79; Registrar, Child Psych Servs, W Lothian, Edinburgh, Scot, 1979-81; Cnslt Psych, Otago Hosp Bd, Dunedin, 1981-84, 1989-93, Dir Forensic Servs, 1981-88; Snr Lectr, Psychol Med, Otago Medl Sch, Dunedin, 1984-88; Cnslt Psych, Star of the Morning Ltd, Wanganui, 1993-. Creative works: Poetry, painting, carving, 1963-; Miscellaneous wrks publd and exhibtd. Memberships: Schizophrenia Fellshp, NZ; Fell, Roy Austl and NZ Coll Psychs; Australasian Inst Psych; Intl Hosp Fedn; NZ Fedn Univ Women. Hobbies: Computer studies; Virtual reality; Creative writing; Art; Photography; Music; Spirituality. Address: Star of the Morning Ltd, PO Box 4044, Wanganui, New Zealand.

ARASHI Qadi Abdul Karim al-. Politician. Appointments: Fmr Min for Local Govt and the Treas; Speaker of the Constituent People's Assembly, 1978; Chmn Provisional Presl Cncl, June-July 1978; Vice-Pres Yemen Arab Rep, 1978-90. Memberships: Presl Cncl of Yemen, May 1990-. Address: Constituent People's Assemby, Sana'a, Yemen.

ARBULU GALLIANI Guillermo, b. Trujillo. Government Official. m. Bertha Tanaka de Azcarate, 1 s, 2 d. Education: Chorillos Mil Acady. Appointments: Sub-Lt Eng Corps, 1943; Lt, 1946; Cap, 1949; Maj, 1955; Lt-Col, 1959; Col, 1964; Brig-Gen, 1971; Div Gen, 1975-; Fmr Chf of Staff 1st Light Div; Fmr Dir of Logistics; Fmr Chf of Ops Armed Forces Gen Staff; Fmr Dir of Mil Eng Coll; Fmr Instr Higher War Coll; Fmr Advsr to Mins of Mining and Fisheries; Fmr Pres Empresa Publica de Servicios Pesqueros - State Fishing Corp; Pres Joint Armed Forces Command; PM and Min of Def, 1976-78; Amb to Chile, 1978-79; Amb to Spain, 1979-80; Deleg to Latin Am Conf of Mins of Labour; Rep of Min of For Affairs to negotiations for Andean Pact; Rep to 11th Am Mil Congress. Honours: Cmmdr Mil Order of Ayacucho; Jorge Chavez Award; Grand Offr of Peruvian Crosses of Aeronautical Merit; Naval Merit; Grand Cross Peruvian Order of Mil Merit; Grand Offr Mayo Cross of Mil Merit - Argentina. Address: c/o Ministry of Foreign Affairs, Lima, Peru.

ARCHER John William, b. 29 Jan 1950, Sydney, Australia. Microwave Engineer. m. Joan, 27 Jan 1973, 2 s. Education: BS, Bach of Elecr Engin, 1st Class Hons, Dr Philos, Sydney Univ. Appointments: Snr Electns Engr, NRAO, VA, USA, 1977-84; Chf Rsch Scientist, CSIRO, Sydney, 1984-99. Publications: Book Chapts: Infrared and MM-Waves, Vol 15, 1986; Handbook on Microwave and Optical Components, Vol 2, 1989; More than 90 jrnl and conf pprs. Memberships: Fell, Inst of Elecl and Electn Engrs. Hobbies: Tennis; Golf; Fishing. Address: CSIRO-TIP, P O Box 76, Epping, NSW 1710, Australia.

ARDEN Felix Wilfrid, b. 20 Apr 1910, Singapore. Consultant Paediatrician (Retired). m. (1) Dorothy Ray, 29 Dec 1936, dec 1979, (2) Florence Joy Richards, 15 Dec 1980, 1 s, 1 d. Education: MBBS 1931, MD 1934, Univ of Adelaide; MRCP, London, 1936; FRCP, London, 1974; FRACP, 1972 (elect); MD Hon, Univ of Qld, 1986. Appointments: Med Supt, Adelaide Children's Hosp, 1936-38; Med Supt, 1938-46; Roy Children's Hosp, Brisbane; Snr Visng Physn, 1946-70, Visng Paediatn, Roy Women's Hosp, Brisbane, 1946-56; Visng Paediatn, Dept of Children's Servs 1968-91; Pvte Cnsltng Prac, Paediats, 1946-91. Publications: Auth of many sci pprs, mainly in Med Jrnl of Aust, 1934-, inclng The Jackson Lecture (Brisbane); The Swift Lectures (Adelaide); The Helen Mayo Oration. Honours: CBE, 1984; Qld Father of the Yr, 1983. Memberships: Brit Med Assn, later Austl Med Assn, 1932-75, Pres 1956; Austl Paediat Assn, later Austl Col of Paediats, 1950, Pres 1974, Hon Mbr 1987-; Paediat Soc of Qld, Pres 1970. Address: 26 Christian Street, Clayfield, Qld 4011, Australia.

ARDITO-BARLETTA Nicolas, b. 21 Aug 1938, Aquadulce, Cocle. Economist. m. Maria C Rivera Ardito-Barletta, 2 s, 1 d. Education: PhD, Econs, Univ of Chgo; MS, Agricl Econs, NC State Univ. Appointments: Cabinet Mbr and Dir Plng, 1968-70; Min of Plng and Econ Policy, 1973-78; Pres, Latin Amn Econ System (SELA) Constituent Assembly, 1975; Negotiator of Econ Aspects of Panama Canal Treaties, 1976-77; VP, World Bank for Latin Am & the Caribbean, 1978-84; Fndr, 1st Pres, Latin Amn Export Bank, 1978; Pres of Panama, 1984-85; Gen Dir of the Intl Cntr for Econ Growth, 1986-95; Admnstr Gen, Interoceanic Reg Authority (ARI), 1995-. Creative works: Num Latin Amn and Panamian Dev Studies. Honours: Decorated by sev Latin Amn nations. Memberships: Bds of Dirs of sev corps, banks and policy instns. Hobbies: Tennis; Music. Address: PO Box 7737, Panama 9, Republic of Panama.

AREND Robert Lee, b. 30 Aug 1944, Bridgeman, MI, USA. Professor. m. Evelyn Arend, 2 s, 1 d. Education: BA, Moody Bible Inst, 1968; BA, W Mich Univ, 1968; MA, Trinity Evangelical Divinity Sch, 1970; MA, Northwestern Univ, 1971; Postgrad, Purdue Univ (PhD Cand), 1973-76; CA Community Colls, life instr credits in Engl, Supvsn, Humanities, Speech. Appointments: Asst Prof, Grace Coll, Winona Lake, IN, 1971-76; Prof, Dpty Chair, Christian Heritage Coll, El Cajon, CA, 1977-90; Asst Prof, Engl, Sd Miramar Coll and Cuyamaca Coll and Palomar Coml Coll, -1981; Full Prf, Engl, Miramar Coll, San Diego, 1990-; Publications: Fundamentals of Speech Communication, 1988; Poetry in the Key of David, English Exercises for Christian Students, 1990; num articles in var schl jrnls in Engl. Honours: Tchng Awd, Yrbook dedication, Christian Heritage Coll, 1990; Outstndng Fac of Yr, Miramar Coll, 1998; Sigma Tau Hon Soc. Memberships: Shakespeare Assn; Natl Cncl of Tchrs of Engl; MLA; CCCC. Hobbies: Reading; Tennis; Hiking; Jogging; Tennis. Address: Miramar College, 10440 Black Mountain Road, San Diego, CA 92126, USA. .

ARENS Moshe, b. 7 Dec 1925, Lithuania. Politician. Education: MA and CA Insts of Technol USA. Appointments: Assoc Prof of Aeronautical Engrng Technion - Israel Inst of Technol - Haifa; Dep Dir Israel Aircraft Inds Lod; Amb to USA, 1982-83; Min of Def, 1983-84; Min without Portfolio, -1987; Min of For Affairs, 1988-90; Min of Def, 1990-92; Elected to Knesset. Publications: Broken Covenant, 1994; sev books on propulsion and flight mechanics. Honours: Israel Def Prize, 1971; Assoc Fell, AIAA. Memberships: Knesset Fin Cttee, 1973. Address: c/o Ministry of Defence, Rehov Kaplan, Hakirya, Tel-Avia 67659, Israel.

ARIAS Ricardo Alberto, b. 11 Sept 1939, Panama Cty, Panama. Minister of Foreign Affairs. m. 4 children. Education: Georgetown Univ, Wash DC, USA; Univ of Puerto Rico; Yale Univ, CT, USA. Appointments: Fndr and Pres, Panamanian Stock Exchange; Fndr and Pres, Bd of Dirs, La Prensa Newsppr; Assoc, Fabrega, López and Pedreschi law firm, 1967-68; Ptnr, Galindo, Arias adn López, 1968; Prof of Fiscal and Admin Law, Univ Santa María La Antigua, Panama, 1973-78; Amb to USA, 1994-95; Min of For Affairs. Address: Ministry of Foreign Affairs, Panamá 4, Panama.

ARIAS STELLA Javier, b. 2 Aug 1924, Lima. Politician; Pathologist. m. Nancy Castillo, 4 c. Education: San Luis Sch Univ Natl Mayor de San Marcos and San Fernando Medl Sch. Appointments: Lectr in univs in England, USA, Argentina, Mexico and Brazil; work on path now known as the 'Arias Stella Reaction or Phenomenon'published, 1954; Natl Sec Gen Accion Popular - polit party - 1959; Min of Pub Hlth, 1963-65, 1967-68; in exile Argentina, 1973, Venezuela, 1974; Min for For Affairs, 1980-83; Perm Rep to the UN, 1984-86. Publications: Nearly 100 works on path. Honours: Hipolito Unanue, Peru; Premio Roussel Peru and num decorations. Address: Ministry of Foreign Affairs, Ucayali 363, Lima, Peru.

ARIDOR Yoram, b. 24 Oct 1933, Tel-Aviv. m. 3 c. Education: Hebrew Univ of Jerusalem. Appointments: Cttee for Legislation and Justice, 1969-81; Chmn Herut - Freedom - Movement in Histradrut - Gen Fed of Labour, 1972-77; Chmn Cttee for Interior and Environmental Affairs, 1975-77; Chmn Sub-Cttee for Constl Law, 1975-77; Dep Min in PMs off, 1977-81; Chmn Sec, 1979-87 Herut Movements; Min of Fin, 1981-83; Min of Comms, Jan-July 1981; Amb to UN, 1990-92; Fmr Gov IMF. Memberships: Knesset, 1969-88; Cntrl Cttee Herut Movement, 1961-90. Address: 38 Haoranim Street, Ramat-Efal, Israel.

ARIMA Eitoku, b. 20 Feb 1933, Kanoya, Japan. Surgeon; Director of Geriatric Health Services Facility. m. Naoko, 19 May 1964, 1 s, 2 d. Education: DMedSc. Appointments: Dir, Heim Berg, Geriatric Hlth Servs Facility; Cnslt Dr, Keiaikai Incorporated Hosps, Miyama Hosp, Miki Hosp and Hohyoh Hosp, 1998-; Visng Prof, Electron Microscopy, Histology, Embryology and Gastroenterological Surg, 1st Medl Coll of PLA, Guang Zhou, 1995-; Visng Prof, Surg, Jinzhou Medl Coll, Jinzhou, China, 1997-. Publications: Guide Book on Pediatric Surgery for Citizens, 1969; Co-auth, 16 books on Surgical, Pediatric or Electron Microscopic Region, 1978-; Contbr, articles to medl and electron microscope jrnls, 1959-. Honours: Haraldria Soc (Sihopu (Soberana Instituicao Helaldica Ordem da Paz Universal, Sao Paulo, Brazil; Order of Peace Universal, 1997. Memberships: Spec Mbr, Japanese Soc, Gastroenterological Surg; Overseas Mbr, Brit Assn of Pediat Surgs; Pacific Assn of Pediat Surgs. Hobbies: Touring; Fishing; Mountain climbing; Judo (5th) Dan;

Golf. Address: 6-33-19 Murasakibaru Kagosihma 890-0082, Japan.

ARIMA Masataka, b. 2 Mar 1929, Kagoshima, Japan. Medical Doctor. m. 7 Dec 1958, 2 d. Education: DMedSc. Appointments: Dir, Tokyo Metrop Medl Cntr for Severely Disabled; Pres, Japan League on Intellectual Disabilities. Creative Works: Advance in Developmental Disorder Medicine; Health Problems in Mental Retardation. Honours: PM's Awd of Achvmnt, Servs to Persons with Disability. Memberships: Japanese Soc of Child Neurology; Intl Assn for Sci Stdy Disabilities. Hobbies: Travel; Sightseeing. Address: 3-44-10 Sakuragaoka, Higashiyamato, Tokyo, Japan.

ARIMA-NISHIDA Takashi, b. 17 Dec 1931, Kyoto, Japan. m. Oota Yoshiko, 15 Nov 1957, 1 s, 1 d. Education: Econs, Doshisha Univ, 1954. Appointments: Tchr, Osaka Coll Lit, 1968-; Mngr, Kyoto Bank Branch, 1974-78; Cnslt Ed, Mag Shito Shiso (Poetry and Thought), 1989-; Pres, Pegasus Learning Co Ltd, 1989; Vice Chmn, Takbune Corp 1989-; Tchr, Kyoto Coll Art, 1991-. Publications: Poetry incl: North South East and West, 1991; Selected Poems, 1992; The Memory of India, 1992; Song of Little Odysseus, 1994; Children's Songs; Criticism; Transls; Recdngs: Little Planet, Suginami Children's Choir, 1985; Sounds Of Asia (music by Kei Ogula), 1990; Owl's Lullaby, 1990; Contbns to anthols. Honours: 29th Sankei Prize for Children's Publ, 1981; Intl Eminent Poet Dip, Intl Poet's Acady, 1993. Memberships: Rep, Kyoto Contemporary Poetry Assn; Japan Writers Assn; Japan PEN Club; World Acady Art and Culture (USA), L'Etrave, (France). Hobby: Travel. Address: 1-29-103 Izumikawa-cho, Shimogamo, Sakyo-ku, Kyoto 606-0807, Japan.

ARIYASU Laurence, b. 9 Nov 1957, San Fernando, CA, USA. Physician. Education:BA/BA, Bio/Chem; MD. Appointments: Chf Hd and Neck Surg, Vallejo Kaiser, 1991, Cnslt Chf HNS NorRon CA Kaiser, 1996; Chmn SPORT Cttee, 1996; Bd of Dirs Solano County Medl Soc, Chair, Formulary Cttee, 1997; Mbr, Natl Prods Cncl, 1997. Publications: 3-D Reconstruction of Re Cochlea, 1989; Beneficial Effects if Methylprednosoline in Acute Vestibular Vertigo, 1990; Uvulectomy in Re Office Setting, 1995. Honour: 4th Place Bay Area Res Rsch Symposium, 1988. Memberships: CA Medl Assn Alternate Deleg, 1997-; Solano County Medl Soc, Bd of Dirs, 1997-; Amn Acady of Otolarygology, Hd and Neck Surg. Hobbies: Oil painting; Stained glass; Photography; Skiing; Travel. Address: 975 Sereno Drive, Vallejo, CA 94589, USA.

ARIYOSHI George Ryoichi, b. 3 Dec 1926, Honolulu, Hawaii, USA. Consultant. m. Jean M, 2 May 1955, 2 s, 1 d. Education: BA, MI Univ, 1949; JD, Univ MI Law Sch, 1952. Appointments: Pres Advsry Cttee on Trade Policy & Negotiations. Publiction: With Obligation to All, (book). Honours include: Hon Doct in Law, Univ of the Philippines, Univ of Guam, MI Univ, 1975; Hon Doct in Humanities, Univ of the Visayas, 1977, Sokka Univ, Japan, 1984, Univ HI, 1986; Disting Alumni Awd, MI Univ, Univ HI, 1975; Grand Cordon of the Sacred Treasure, Japanese Govt, 1985; Emperor's Silver Cup, Japan, 1987. Memberships include: Bd Dir, Pub Broadcasting Serv; Japan-HI Econ Cncl; Bd Trustee, Japan-Am Soc of HI, The Nature Conservancy of HI; Natl Ctteeman, Democratic Party of HI; Bd of Gov, Japanese Cultural Cntr of HI. Hobbies: Golf; Swimming; Spectator Sports. Address: 999 Bishop Street, 23rd Floor, Honolulu, HI 96813, USA.

ARMINANA Ruben, b. 15 May 1947, Santa Clara, Cuba. University President; Professor. m. Marne Olson, 17 Dec 1988, 1 s. 1 d. Education: AA, 1966; Hill Jnr Coll; BA, 1968, MA, 1970, Univ TX at Austin; PhD, 1983, Univ New Orleans. Appointments: VP, Fin and Dev, CA State Poly Univ, Pomona, 1988-92; Pres, Sonoma State Univ, 1992-. Publications: Co-author, Hemisphere West - El futuro, 1968; Co-ed, Colloquim on Central America: a Time for Understanding, Background Readings, 1985. Honours: Kiwanis Schl, 1966; Books Schl, 1966; Outstndng Ldr Awd, United Citizens of Louisiana, 1979;

Disting Alum, Hill Coll, 1991. Memberships: Pres, Western Coll Assn, 1994-96; WASC; Bd Dirs, CSU Inst, 1997-. Hobby: Mask collecting. Address: Sonoma State University, 1801 East Cotati Avenue, Rohnert Park, CA 94928-3609, USA.

ARMSTRONG Gillian May, b. 18 Dec 1950. Film Director. 2 d. Education: Grad, Dip Film and TV, Swinburne College Advd Educ. Creative works include: Smokes and Lollies, documentary, 1975; Feature films: My Brilliant Career, 1979; Starstruck, 1982; Mrs Soffel, 1984; High Tide, 1987; Fires Within, 1990; The Last Days of Chez Nous, 1991; Little Women, 1995; Not Fourteen Again, 1996; Oscar and Lucinda, 1996-97; Feature documentaries incl: Bingo; Bridesmaids and Braces; Bob Dylan; Tom Petty Concert Movie for HBO. Honours include: Brit Film Critics Awd (Best First Feature), My Brilliant Career, 1979; AM, 1984; Christopher (Hum) Awd, Little Women, 1995; Best Film High Tide Houston Film Fest; The Last Days of Chez Nous and Mrs Soffel selected for Berlin Film Fest; Best Film, Best Dir, My Brilliant Career Selected for Offic Competition Cannes Film Fest and NY Film Fest; Dorothy Arzner Directing Awd from US Women in Film, 1995; Best Documentary, AFI Awds, 1996 Address: c/o Hilary Lindstead Association, PO Box 1536, Strawberry Hills, NSW 2012, Australia.

ARMSTRONG Patrick Hamilton, b. 10 Oct 1941, Leeds, Yorkshire, UK. University Teacher. m. Moyra Elizabeth Jane Irvine, 8 Aug 1964, 2 s. Education: BSc (Hons), 1963, MA, 1966, Univ Coll, Univ of Durham; PhD, CNAA, 1970. Appointments: Lectr, Coll of Arts and Technol, Cambridge, 1964-75; Snr Lectr, Univ of West Aust, 1975-; Hd of Dept, 1980-82; Dpty Chf Examiner Intl Baccalaureate, 1996-. Publications: The Changing Landscape, 1975; Charles Darwin in Western Australia, 1986; A Naturalist in the Falklands, 1992. Honours: Var intl fellshps inclng: Open Univ; Darwin Coll, Cambridge; South CT State Univ; Univ Coll, Durham; St Deniol's Lib, Hawarden, N Wales. Memberships: Brit Ecological Soc; Inst of Brit Geographers; Inst of Austl Geographers. Hobbies: Photography; Bird watching; Old books. Address: Department of Geography, University of Western Australia, Nedlands, West Australia 6907, Australia.

ARNDT Bettina Mary, b. 1 Aug 1949, Penrith, Eng. Journalist. m. (1) Dennis Minogue, 1977, dec 1981, (2) Warren Scott, 21 June 1986, 1 s, 1 d. Education: BSc, Austl Natl Univ; MPsych, Univ NSW. Appointments: Ed, Co-Publr, Forum Mag, 1973-81; Mbr, Cncl, Austl Natl Univ, 1975-84; Syndicated Column, The Age, 1981-85; Feature Writer, Austl Consolidated Press, 1981-95; Feature Writer, The Austl, 1991-95; Feature Writer, Sydney Morning Herald and The Age, 1995-; Regular Guest, ABC Radio; Lectr on Sexuality to Medl Studs, Univ NSW, Univ Sydney, and num profl community grps and orgs. Publications: Private Lives, 1986; All About Us, 1989; Taking Sides, 1995. Listed in: Who's Who in Australia. Hobby: Reading.

ARNDT Heinz Wolfgang, b. 26 Feb 1915, Breslau, Germany. Emeritus Professor of Economics. m. Ruth Strohsahl, 12 July 1941, 2 s, 1 d. Education: BA, 1936, MA, 1938, BLitt, 1938, Oxford Univ, Eng. Appointments: Leverhulme Rsch Fell, London Sch of Econs, 1938-41; Rsch Asst, Roy Inst of Intl Affairs, 1941-43; Asst Lectr, Econs, Univ of Manchester, 1943-46; Snr Lectr, Econs, Univ of Sydney, NSW, Aust, 1946-50; Prof of Econs, Sch of Gen Studies, 1951-63; Rsch Sch of Pacific Studies, 1963-80, Dean, Fac of Econs, 1959-60, Dpty Bd Chmn, Inst of Adv Studies, 1976-78, 1978-80, Visng Fell, Devel Studies Cntr, 1981-, Austl Natl Univ, Canberra, ACT; Visng Prof, Univ of SC, USA, 1954; Indian Stats Inst, Indian Plng Cmmn, 1958-59; Cnslt: UN Confs, 1966, 1967, UNIDO, 1983, 1984, 1985; Dpty Dir, Country Studies Divsn, OECD, Paris, 1972, ADB, 1982-88. Publications include: The Economic Lessons of the Nineteen-Thirties, 1944; The Australian Trading Banks, 1957; A Small Rich Industrial Country, 1969; Australia and Asia, 1972; The Rise and Fall of Economic Growth, 1978; The Indonesian Economy, 1984; A Course

Through Life, 1985; Economic Development: The History of an Idea, 1987; Asian Diaries, 1987; Pembangunan Ekonomi Indonesia: Pandangan Seorang Tetangga, 1991; Fifty Years of Development Studies, 1993; Essays in International Economics 1944-1994, 1996; South East Asia's Economic Crisis, 1998; Ed, Bulletin of Indonesian Econ Stdies, 1965-1; Asian-Pacific Econ Lit, 1987-; Num articles in learned jrnls. Honours: Disting Fell, Econ Soc of Aust, 1994; Disting Serv Star, Indonesia, 1995. Memberships: Econ Soc of Aust & NZ, Pres 1957-59; Austl Assn for Cultural Freedom, Pres, 1979-86; Var commns, expert grps. Hobbies: Music; Chess. Address: Australian National University, PO Box 4, Canberra, ACT 0200, Australia.

ARNOLD Roslyn Mary, b. 25 Jan 1945, Sydney, Aust. Professor of Education. 1 d. Education: BA; DipEd; MA; MEd; PhD. Appointments: Lectr; Snr Lectr; Prof; Hd of Dept. Publications: Writing Development - Magic in the Brain, 1991; Mirror the Wind, 1997; Num articles and poems in jrnls and newspapers. Honour: Univ of Sydney Tchng Excellence Awd, 1994. Memberships: Editl Bd, Engl Educ, UASA, 1993-; Rsch Bd, Natl Assn Drama in Educ, 1993-; Natl Tchrs Assn Tchrs of Engl, USA; Cncl Loreto Coll Normanhurst. Hobbies: Writing poetry and fiction; Gardening; Classical music; Reading; Entertainment. Address: 5/322 Edgecliff Road, Woollahra 2025, Australia.

ARORA Jagdish, b. 15 Jan 1956. Library and Information Scientist. m. Anita Arora, 8 Feb 1983, 1 s. Education: BSc, Biol Scis; MA, Pol Sci; BLlbSc; MLISc; PhD, Lib Sci. Appointments: Asst Documentation Offr, ICRISAT, 1980-83; Documentation Offr, Natl Inst of Immunology (N11), 1983-91; Dpty Libn and Hd, Computer Applications, Indian Inst of Technol, Delhi, 1991-. Publications: Sev rsch articles and bibliographies. Honours: Need-cum-Merit Schlshp, 1971-75; Govt of Rajasthan, 3rd in BLibSc Exam, Univ of Rajasthan, 1975; CSIR Travel Fellowship, 1992, 1995; DST Travel Fellowship, 1995; Vistorshp Scheme of Brit Cncl, 1993; Fulbright Fellshp in Lib and Info Sci, USA, 1997-98. Memberships: Life Mbr, Indian Lib Assn; Life Mbr, Medl Lib Assn of India (MLAI); Life Mbr, Soc for Info Sci. Hobbies: Indoor games; Reading. Address: Deputy Librarian, Indian Institute of Technology, Hauz Khas, New Delhi 110 016, India.

ARTEAGA Rosalía, b. 1956. Politician. Appointments: Jrnlst, Tchr and Lawyer; Prov Gov, 1986; Vice Min of Culture, 1992; Min of Educ, 1994; VP, 1996-; Interim Pres (1st woman), 1997; Fndr, Ind Movt for Authentic Repub, 1996. Address: Office of the Vice President, Manuel Larrea y Arenas, Edif Consejo Provincial de Pichincha 21, Quito, Ecuador.

ARTHUR Paul Felix, b. 26 June 1953. Agricultural Scientist. m. Alberta Eshun, 23 Jan 1983, 2 s, 1 d. Education: BSc Hons, Univ of Ghana, Legon, Ghana, 1977; MSc, 1982, PhD, 1990, Univ of Alta, Edmonton, Can. Appointments: Rsch Offr, 1982-89, Rsch Assoc, 1989-91, Rsch Sci, 1991-95, Snr Rsch Sci, 1995-, NSW Agric, Aust. Honours: Univ of Ghana, Legon Hall Schl, 1975-76; Univ of Alta Postdoc Fellshp, 1989-91. Memberships: Assn for Advmnt of Animal Breeding and Genetics, Ed 1995-; Amn Soc of Animal Sci; Austl Soc of Animal Prodn. Hobbies: Football; Gardening; Reading. Address: New South Wales Agriculture, Agricultural Research Centre, Trangie, NSW 2823, Australia.

ARUNANONDCHAI Surat, b 28 Sept 1954, Bangkok, Thailand. Businessman. m. Rossukon, 14 May 1980, 4s. Education: BSc, MSc, PhD, Electr Eng, Thailand and Abroad. Appointments: Dir, Siam Comms; Mngng Dir, Siam Sino Tech Co; Chmn, Unique Place Co. Publications: Auth of books, articles reflecting Thailand's soc from 1988-. Honours: Writing Awds, 1983-; Mngmt Awds, 1983-; Bus Awds, 1985-. Memberships: YMCA; NYAS; IBC; ABI. Listed in: Dictionary of International Biography; Who's Who in the World. Hobbies: Reading; Writing; Collecting Stamps; Playing tennis. Address: Siam Communications, 286/6-7 Surawongse Road, Bangkok, Thailand 10500.

ARYAL Krishna Raj, b. Dec 1928, Kathmandu. Politician. m. Shanta Laxmi, 1956, 1 s. Education: Tri-Chandra Coll; Allahabad Univ, India; OR Univ, USA. Appointments: Lectr Natl Tchrs Trng Cntr, 1954-56; Prof Coll of Educ; Dir Publs Govt Educ Dev Proj, 1956-59; Ed Educ Quarterly, 1956-59; Ed Nabin Shikshya, 1956-59; Fndr Admin and Prin Shri Ratna Rajya Laxmi Girls Coll, 1961-71; Asst Min for Educ, 1971-72; Min of State, 1972-73; Min, 1973-75; Min of For Affairs, 1975-79; Amb to France also accred to Spain, Italy, Portugal and Israel and Perm Dec to UNESCO, 1980-84; Chmn Asian Grp UNESCO, 1982-83; Fmr Sec Cricket Assn of Nepal; Chmn Brahmacharya Ashram. Publications: incl: Monarchy in the Making of Nepal - in English; Education for the Development of Nepal - in English; The Science of Education - Nepali. Honours: Gorakha Dakhinbahu - 1st Class Grand Cordon of Yugoslav Star; Order of the Rising Sun 1st Class - Japan; Grand Officier Order Nat du Merite -France; Order of Civil Merit 1st Class - Spain; and other decorations. Memberships: Bur Grp 77 UNESCO, 1982-83; Hon mbr Raj Sabha, 1985-90; Rastriya Panchayat - unicameral legis - 1986-90; Exec mbr World Hindu Fedn. Address: 17/93 Gaihiri Dhara, Kathmandu, Nepal.

AS-SAHAF Muhammad Saeed, b. 1940, Hillay Cty, Babylon. Diplomat. Education: BA, Univ of Baghdad. Appointments: Dir Gen, Baghdad Brdcstng and TV, 1968-74; Amb to India, 1974; Non-Res Amb to Nepal and Myanmar; Perm Rep to UN, 1977; Tchr, 1978-80; Dpty Min of For Affairs, 1983-84; Min of State for For Affairs, 1990; Amb to Italy, Sweden. Address: Ministry of Foreign Affairs, Opposite State Org for Roads and Bridges, Karradat Mariam, Baghdad, Iraq.

AS-SAID Fahar Bin Taimour, b. 1925. Minister of Defence. m. 1 s, 3 d. Education: Indian Mil Acady; Pakistan Mil Acady (Kakhl). Appointments: Served, Pakistan Army; Spec Liaison Offr, Dept of Def, 1970-73; Dpty Min of Def, 1973-79; Min of Interior, 1974-76, Yth Affairs, 1976-79; Dpty Prime Min for Security and Def, 1979-. Address: Ministry of Defence, POB 113, Muscat 113, Oman.

ASANBAYEV Erik Magzumovich, b. 1936, Baygabul, Turgai Dist. Politician. m. 2 c. Education: Kazak Univ. Appointments: Economist Min of Fin, 1958-59; Lectr Kazak Univ, 1959-63; Hd of Dept Inst of Econs, 1963-67; Hd of Dept Dep Min of Fin, 1967-75; Snr psts in CP and Gov, 1975-88; Dep Chmn Cncl of Mins, 1988-89; Sec Cntr Cttee Kazakh CP, 1989-90; Chmn Kazak SSR Supreme Soviet, 1991; VP Kazakstan, 1991-96; Amb to Germany, 1996-. Memberships: CPSU, 1967-91; Joined Socl Party of Kazakstan, Aug 1991. Address: House of the Government, Square of the Republic 64, 48001 Almaty, Kazakstan.

ASH-SHARA Farouk, b. 1938, Dara'a, Syria. Minister of Foreign Affairs. m. 2 children. Education: Univs of Damascus and London. Appointments: Amb to Italy, 1976-80; Min of State for For Affairs, Acting Min of Jus, Min of Info, 1980-84. Address: Ministry of Foreign Affairs, Damascus, Syria.

ASHER Mukul G, b. 17 Dec 1943, Mumbai. Academic Economist. m. Pragnya, 25 Aug 1969, 1 d. Education: BA, hons; MA; PhD. Appointments: Assoc Prof, Natl Univ of Singapore, 1990-; Vis Asst Prof, Marquette Univ. Publications: Social Security in Malaysia and Singapore, 1994; The Macroeconomics of Financing Government Expenditure (co-auth), 1997; Environment and the Developing World (co-auth), 1998. Memberships: Indian Econ Assn; Econ Soc of Singapore; Am Econ Assn. Hobbies: Cricket; Music. Address: Department of Economics, National University of Singapore, 10 Kent Ridge Crescent, Singapore 119260, Singapore.

ASHIDA Jun, b. 21 Aug 1930, Kyoto. Fashion Designer. m. Tomoko Tomita, 1960, 2 d. Education: Studied under Jun-ichi Nakahara, 1948-52. Appointments: Consultant Des to Takashimaya Dept Store, 1960; Est Jun Ashida Co Ltd and Jun Ashida label, 1963; Exclusive Des to HIH - now Empress - Crown Princess Michiko, 1966-76; Des for sev mbrs Imperial family; Presented first collection in Paris, 1977; Launched Miss Ashida and Jun Ashida for Men labels, 1985-86; Opened shop Paris, 1989; Des uniforms for Japanese Pavilion Expo World Fair Seville, 1992; All Nippon Airways, Fuji, Xerox, Imperial Hotel, Nomura Securities, Idemitsu Kosan, Tokyo Kaijo, Japanese team at Olympic Games Atlanta, 1996. Publications: Young Man - essays - 1986; Jun Ashida, 30 Years of Design, 1993; Articles on fashion and lifestyle in daily newspapers. Honours: FEC Award, 1972; Purple Ribbon Medal, Cavaliere, Ordine al Merito - Italy. Memberships: Postal Serv Cncl of Min of Posts and Telecomms. Hobbies: Tennis; Golf. Address: 1-3-3 Aobadai, Meguro-ku, Tokyo 153, Japan.

ASHIHARA Yoshinobu, b. 7 July 1918, Tokyo, Japan. Architect. m. Hatsuko Takahashi, 1944, 1 s, 1 d. Education: B Arch, DEng in Arch, Univ of Tokyo; M Arch, Harvard Univ Grad Sch, USA. Appointments: Archl Firms, Tokyo, 1946-52, Marcel Breuer's, New York City, USA, 1953; Hd, Yoshinobu Ashihara Archt & Assocs, Tokyo, 1955-; Lectr in Arch, 1955-59, Prof of Arch, 1959-65, Hosei Univ, Tokyo; Prof of Arch, Musashino Art Univ, Tokyo, 1964-70; Visng Prof, Sch of Arch and Bldg, Univ NSW, Aust, 1966, Dept of Arch, Univ of HI, USA, 1969; Prof of Arch, Univ of Tokyo, 1970-79; Prof Emer, Univ of Tokyo, Musashino Art Univ. Creative Works include: Chuo-Koron Bldg; Sony Bldg; Komazawa Olympic Gymnasium, 1965; Japanese Pavilion, Expo 67, Montreal; Fuji Film Bldg, 1969; Natl Mus of Japanese Hist, 1980; Daiichi Kangyo Bank Hd Off, 1981; Tokyo Metropolitan Art Space, 1990. Publications include: Exterior Design in Architecture, 1970; The Aesthetic Townscape, 1983; The Hidden Order, 1989; The Aesthetics of Tokyo, 1998. Honours: Rockefeller Travel Grant to Eur, 1954; Awd for Chuo-Koron Bldg, 1960, Spec Awd for Komazawa Olympic Gymnasium, 1965, Archl Inst of Japan; Min of Educn Awd for Japan Pavilion, Expo 1967, Montreal; Golden Triangle Awd, NSID, USA, 1970; Commendatore, Ordine al Merito, Italy, 1970; Hon FAIA, 1979; Hon Fell, Am Inst of Archs, 1979; Cmdr, Order of the Lion, Finland, 1985; Japan Art Acady Awd, 1984; Hon Fell, Roy Austl Inst of Archs, 1987; Person of Cultural Merits Awd, 1991; Order of Culture, 1998. Memberships: Pres, Japan Arch Assn, 1980-82; Archl Inst of Japan, 1985-87. Hobbies: Sauna; Travel. Address: Sumitomo-Seimei Building, 31-15 Sakuragaoka-cho, Shibuya-Ku, Tokyo, 150-0031.

ASHMAN Gerald Barry, b. 27 Nov 1941. Member of Victorian State Parliament. m. June, 1968, 1 s, 1 d. Education: Asst Dir, State Chmbr of Comm & Ind & Exec Dir, Small Bus Assn of Vic, 1983-88; State MP for Boronia Prov, 1988-96; State MP for Koonung Prov, 1996. Memberships: Bd Vic Health Promotion Fndn; Bd Univ Cncl RMIT; Dir, Technisearch & Resources RMIT; Hon Justices of the Peace; Rotary; RACV. Hobbies: Politics; MG cars; Gardening. Address: Unit 1, 426-430 Burwood Highway, Wantirna South, Vic 3152, Australia.

ASHMOLE (Harold) David, b. 31 Oct 1949. Senior Principal Dancer, Australian Ballet (Retired). Education: Sandye Place, Beds; Roy Ballet Sch, Solo Seal; Roy Acady of Dancing; ARAD. Appointments: Joined Roy Ballet Co, 1968, Soloist, 1972, Prin, 1975; Transferred to Sadler's Wells Roy Ballet, 1976, Snr Prin, 1978-84; Appeared in: Dame Alicia Markova's Master Classes, BBC TV, 1980; Maina Gielgud's Steps, Notes & Squeaks, Aberdeen Intl Fest, 1981; Guest appearances w Scottish Ballet, 1981, Bolshoi (for UNESCO Gala), 1986, Sadlers Wells Roy Ballet at Roy Opera House, 1986 (season) and in Japan, Germany, S Africa & France; Classical Ballets incl: La Bayadere, Coppelia, Daphins & Chloe, Giselle, Nutcracker, Raymonda, The Seasons, Sleeping Beauty, Swan Lake, La Sylphide; Other Ballets incl (choregraphy by Ashton): Cinderella, The Two Pigeons, La Fille Mal Gardée, Les Rendezvous, The Dream, Lament of the Waves, Symphonic Variations, Birthday Offering; (Balanchine): Apollo, Prodigal Son, Serenade, The Four Temperaments, Agon, Tchaikovsky Pas de Deux; (Bejart): Gafte Parisiènne, Webern Opus 5, Songs of a Wayfarer, Le Concours; (Bintley): Night Moves, Homage to Chopin, The Swan of Tuonela; (Cranko): Brouillards, Pineapple Poll, The Taming of the Shrew, Onegin; (Darrell): The Tales of Hoffmann (de Valois): Checkmate, The Rake's Progress; (Fokine): Les Sylphides, Petrushka (Hynd): Papillon; (Lander): Etudes; (Lifar): Suite en Blanc; (Macmillan): Concerto, Elite Syncopations, Romeo & Juliet, Quartet, Song of the Earth, Symphony; (Massine): La Boutique Fantasque; (Miller-Ashmole): Snugglepot-and-Cuddlepie; (Nijinska): Les Biches; (Nureyev): Don Quixote; (Robins): Dances at a Gathering, Requiem Canticles, In the Night, Concert; (Seymour): Intimate Letters, Rashamond; (Samsova): Paquita; (Tetley): Gemini, Laborintus, Orpheus; (van Manen): Grosse Fugue, 5 Tangos; (Wright): Summertide; (Prokovsky): The Three Musketeers; Retd from dancing, 1993; Elected, bd, Austl Ballet Co, 1994-; Dir Austl Ballet Fndn, 1995-; Lectr, Classical Dance, Victorian Coll of the Arts, Univ Melbourne. Honour: 98 Grad Dip Ed VP Arts. Hobbies: Moorcroft Pottery Collecting; Gardening; Fishing. Address: c/o Australian Ballet, 2 Kavanagh Street, South Melbourne, Vic 3205, Australia.

ASOK Suyambu Pandian, b. 15 Apr 1965, Rajavinkoil. Teacher. m. Mrs A Geetha, 30 Aug 1992, 1 s, 2 d. Education: BE, Mech Engrng; ME, Thermal Scis. Appointments: Instr, 1986, Assoc Lectr, 1987, Lectr, 1988, Snr Lectr, 1995, Asst Prof, 1998. Publication: Engineering Drawing Textbook, manuscript preparation. Honours: Best Natl Serv Scheme Offr, MK Univ Awd, 1998; Best Natl Serv Scheme Offr, Tamil Nadu State Awd, 1998. Memberships: Indian Soc of Tech Educ; Solar Energy Soc of India; Inst of Engrs, India; ISHRAE. Hobbies: Reading books; Playing cricket; Solar Energy Research. Address: Department of Mechanical Engineering, Mepco Schlenk Engineering College, Sivakasi, 626 005, India.

ASTOLFI Ivo Ernesto, b. 18 July 1938, Varese, Italy. Public Servant. m. (1) Susan M Marshall, 1965, div, 2 s, 2 d, (2) Eleanor Laing, 1997. Education: BA, 1966; LLB Hons, 1962, Univ of Melbourne. Appointments: Articled Clk, Aleck Sacks and Son, 1962-63; Ptnr, A J Lopes and Astolfi, Sols, 1963-66; C'wlth Atty Gens Dept, Legal Offr, 1969-72; Snr Legal Offr, 1972-76, Prin Legal Offr 1975-90; Commnr for Corp Affairs, 1981-86; Snr Asst Sec, 1986-88; Off of Austl Capit Terr; Asst Legis Parly Cnsl, 1989-; Snr Asst, Parly Cnsl, 1990; Prin Asst Parly Cnsl, 1991-. Honours: Vic Snr Govt Schlsp, 1956; C'wlth Schlsp, 1956. Memberships: Law Soc of ACT; VP, 1990-94, Competition Sec, 1996, 1999, ACT Table Tennis Assn. Hobbies: History; Current Affairs; Sport. Address: 4 Bolliger Place, Florey, ACT 2615, Australia.

ASTON Harold George (Sir), b. 13 Mar 1923, Aust. Company Chairman; Chief Executive. m. Joyce Smith, 25 Mar 1947, 1 s, 1 d. Appointments: Served AIF, 1941-45 Gen Mngr, 1963-67, Mngng Dir, 1967-70, Bond's Inds Ltd; Dpty Chmn, 1970-80, Chmn, Chf Exec, Bonds Coats Patons Ltd, 1980-; Chmn, Maryborough Holdings Ltd, 1982-; Dir, Mfrs Mutual Ins Ltd, 1982- Dir (non-exec), Downard-Pickfords Pty Ltd, 1983-; Dir, Austl Mfrs Life Assurance Ltd, 1984-; Dir, Austl Guarantee Corp Ltd, 1984-; Gov, Aesop Fndn, 1988-. Honours: CBE, 1976; Created Knight, 1983. Memberships: Dpty Chmn, Austl Mfng Cncl, 1981-82; Pres, Confed of Austl Inds, 1980-82, Dir, 1978, VP, NSW Chamber of Mfrs, 1979; Chmn, Natl Trades & Inds Cncl, 1978-80; Fed Cncl of Assn Chambers of Mfrs of Aust, Natl Gen Cncl, Fndn Mbr, Textile Cncl of Aust. Hobbies: Walking; Gardening; Travelling. Address: 58/129 Surf Parade, Broadbeach, Qld 4218, Australia.

ASTON Warren Peter, b. 21 Aug 1951, New Plymouth, NZ. Managing Director and Founder, Bountiful Travel & Tours. 2 s, 4 d. Education: Nelson Coll, Ch Coll, NZ. Appointment: Vice-Chmn, Mil Mus of the Pacific, Brisbane. Publications: In the Footsteps of Lehi, Salt Lake City: Deseret, 1994; Some Notes on the Tribal Origins of NHM, seminar for Arabian Studies, Cambridge, 1995; Discvering the Alien Agenda, Mufon Grand Rapids Michigan Symposium, 1997. Honours: Assoc Fell, Austl Inst of Travel and Tours. Hobbies: Travel; Arabian culture and archaeology; Theology; Comparative religion;

Astronautics. Address: PO Box 133, Stones Corner, Qld 4120, Australia.

ASUGAR Henry C, b. 5 Mar 1948, Namoluk, Chuuk State, FSM. Chief Clerk, FSM Congress. m. Maggie Maipi, 30 Oct 1979, 1 s, 3 d. Education: IPU Austl Chapt Fellshp, Canberra, Aust, 1991; Humphrey Inst for Legis Mngmt, Univ of MN, 1993-. Appointments: Mnging Ed, Met Poraus Newspaper, Chuuk State; Dpty Exec, Dir, TOCA, Chuuk State; Adnvstv Asst, Chuuk Congressional Deleg, CFSM; Chf Clk, CFSM. Memberships: Amn Soc of Legis Clks and Secs, 1987-. Hobbies: Fishing; Gardening; Sports; Basketball; Tennis. Address: Po Box 1078, Kolonia, Pohnpei State, FSM 96941.

ATH-THANI Hamad bin Jasim bin Jaber (Sheikh), b. 1959, Doha. Appointments: Dir of Off and Min of Munic Affairs; Min of Agric and Munic Affairs; Acting Min of Elec and Water. Address: Min of For Affairs, POB 250, Doha, Qatar.

ATH-THANI Muhammad bin Khalifa (Sheikh), b. 1965, Doha. Minister of Finance, Economy and Trade. m. Education: BSc, George Washington Univ, Wash Dc, USA. Appointments: Rep, OPEC, OAPEC, Ministerial Cttees for Fin, Econ, Stndng Cttee for Econ and Coml Co-op, OIC; Sec of State, Min of Fin and Pet, 1989-92; Under-Sec of State, Min of Fin, Econ and Trade. Address: Ministry of Finance, Economy and Trade, POB 83, Doha, Qatar.

ATKINS William Theodore, b. 14 May 1918, Lebanon, PA, USA. Retired Insurance Executive; Attorney. m. Katherine Shank; 25 Apr 1942, Elena Garcia Ramsey, 27 Sept 1974, 1 s, 2 d. Education: BS Com, Cntrl YMCA Coll, 1945; JD, De Paul Univ, 1949; Bar IL, 1950, CA, 1960. Surety claim adjuster Continental Casualty Co, Chgo, 1940-52; Mngr, Surety Claims Mfrs Casualty/Pacific Natl Fire Ins Cos, Philadelphia and San Fran, 1952-59; W Utd Pacific/Reliance Ins Cos/Utd Pacific Life Ins, Tacoma, Wash, 1959-81; VP, Assoc Counsel, 1981; VP, Reliance Ins Co, Tacoma, 1975-81; Retired, 1981; Pres, Nuhou Corp, 1995-. Memberships include: Bd Dirs, Kauai (HI) Concert Assn, 1982-, Pres, 1983-85, Treas, 1986-; Bd Dirs, HI Assn Music Socs, Honolulu, 1983-90, Treas, 1985-87, Pres, 1987-89; Sec Na Lima Kokua, THe Vols of Nat Tropical Bot Gdn, Kauai, 1987-91, Treas, 1991-95; Bd Dirs, HI Utd Meth Union, Honolulu, 1993-, Fin Cttee, 1994-, Treas, Interfaith Cncl, 1994-; Trustee, Waioli Corp-Grove Farm Homestead Mus, Hanalei Mission House Mus, Lihue, 1985-, Mbr Fin Cttee, 1985-90, Mbr Exec Cttee, 1987-90, Pres, 1990-95; Treas, Kauai Interfaith Iniki Recovery Effort, Lihue, 1992-; Vice-Chmn, Bd Trustees, Lihue Utd Ch, 1996-; ABA; Kauai Orchid Soc. Address: 5867 Haaheo Pl Kapaa, HI 96746-9646, USA.

ATUKORELE Dayananda, b. 10 Apr 1947, Colombo, Sri Lanka. Medical Doctor. m. Mrs G C Atukorele, 10 Dec 1989, 2 s, 1 d. Education: MBBS (Cey); Dip Family Med (Col); MCGP (Sri Lanka); Ctfs, Hosp Admin, Psychol, Ind Med Family Physn; Trained as Team Physn Sports Med, 2 ctfs, FIMS approved and NSW. Appointments: Med Offr, Dept Health, Sri Lanka; Family Physn, Colombo; Emergency Accidents and ENT, Univ of Ileife, Nigeria; Ind Physn, Saudi Arabia, Bangladesh and Sri Lanka. Publications: Health for Better Performance and Stress Management, in progress; Articles on sports related sunjects. Honours: Mercantile Sector Quiz Comp (Lions Club), 1994, 1996; Honoured for Treating Rugby Players in 14 tournaments,(7yrs rugby doctor), 1998. Memberships: Coll of Gen Practitioners; Fac of Occupational Med, Sri Lanka; Sri Lanka Sports Med Assn; Indep Med Practitioners Assn. Hobbies: Sports; Current Affairs; Social Services (Lions Clubs); Travelling. Address: No 34 Mahamega Gardens, Mahamegarama Road, Maharagama, Sri Lanka.

AU Lanard Choi King, b. 8 Apr 1943, Hong Kong, China. Managing consultant. m. Eva Ho, 7 Apr 1993, 1 s. Education: PhD, Management. Appointments: Dpty Prin Trng Mngr, Grp trng; Mngr, Dir of Hrd Cnslt; Mngng Cnslt. Publications: Handbook for Managers; Team

Building (Chinese). Memberships: Fell, Inst Personnel Dev, UK; Chmn Inst of Trng Profls, Hong Kong, 1996-97. Hobbies: Reading; Fishing; Playing Mahjong; Tennis.

AU Peter Chak Tong, b. 26 May 1953, Hong Kong. University Professor. m. Sophia Yee Wan Liu, 2 June 1979, 1 s, 1 d. Education: BSc, hons, Univ Liverpool 1977; PhD, Univ Bradford, 1981. Appointments: Postdoct, Univ Coll Cardiff, 1980-86; Assoc Prof, Prof, Xiamen Univ, 1986-90; Lectr, Assoc Prof, Hong Kong Bapt Univ, 1990-. Publications: Over 60 rsch pprs in profl jrnls. Honour: Nan Qiang Prize, Xiamen Univ, 1988. Membership: Fell, Roy Soc of Chem, England, 1992-. Hobby: Research on Ageing. Address: Department of Chemistry, Hong Kong Baptist University, Kowloon Tong, Hong Kong.

AU YEUNG Anthony Yan Ling, b. 27 July 1962, Hong Kong. Accountant. m. Monica Lee Yee Man, 12 Jan 1997. Education: BBA, (1st Class Hons), Chinese Univ of Hong Kong. Appointments: Corp Mngmt Acct, Kowloon-Canton Railway Corp, 1986-88; Snr Bus Analyst, Standard Chartered Bank, 1988-92; Treas Plng Mngr, Kowloon-Canton Railway Corp, 1992-98; Supvsng Cnslt, PricewaterhouseCoopers, 1998-. Memberships: Assoc Mbr, Hong Kong Inst of Co Secs; Assoc Mbr, Inst of Chartered Secs and Admin; Fell, Hong Kong Soc of Accts; Fell, Assn of Chartered Cert Accts. Hobbies: Swimming; Reading; Cantonese popular music. Address: Flat C, 30/F, Block 1, Jubilee Garden, Fo Tan, New Territories, Hong Kong.

AUBERT Eric Louis, b. 3 May 1921, Bellingen, NSW, Aust. Pianist; Music Educator. m. Jane Eleanor Mary McDiarmid, 15 Feb 1958, 1 s, 1 d. Education: DSCM, Piano, State Conservatorium Music, NSW, 1948.Appointments: Pianist, pub concerts, perfs for ABC Radio and TV; Accompanist to Sydney Symph Orch, playing piano, celeste, harpsichord, 1950-56; Recd sev piano wrks by Austl composers, 1955; Educr: Snr Lectr, Dpty Prin, NSW Conservatorium Music, Newcastle Br, 1956-83. Hobbies: Electrical and automotive repair work; Tennis. Address: 5 Edison Street, Adamstown Heights, NSW 2289, Australia.

AUGUSTEYN Robert Cornelis, b. 31 May 1941, Amsterdam, The Netherlands. Director of the National Vision Research Institute of Australia and Scientist. m. M E Whitfield, 16 May 1964, 2 d. Education: BS; BS (Hons); PhD (Queensland); DipEd (Melbourne). Appointments: Harkness Fell, Columbia Univ, 1969-71; Lectr, 1972-79, Snr Lectr, 1980-88, Rdr Biochem, 1989-91, Univ Melbourne; Editl Bd, Current Eye Rsch, 1986-; Jess Cox Rsch Fell, MIT, 1987. Publications: The Eye, Vols 1 and 2 (co-auth); Var sci articles on biochem of the lens and causes of cataracts & presbyopia; Reviewer, Experimental Eye Research and other jrnls, 1991-. Honours: Half Blue Qld Univ, table tennis; Qualified tennis umpire. Memberships include: Fin Cttee, Vic Lions Fndn Inc; Cncl Vic Coll Optometry; Austl Rsch Cncl, 1974-. Hobby: Table tennis. Address: National Vision Research, Institute of Australia, 386 Cardigan Street, Carlton, Victoria 3053, Australia.

AULD Bruce Archibald, b. 26 Sept 1945. Agricultural Scientist. m. Roslyn Helene Campbell, 15 May 1971, 1 s. Education: BSc Agr; MSc Agr; PhD. Appointments: Rsch Agronomist, NSW Agric, 1967-70; Rsch Fell, Sydney Univ, 1971-74; Postdoc Fell, Reading Univ, Eng, 1975; Prin Rsch Sci, NSW Agric, Orange, 1976-. Publications: Weeds: An Illustrated Botanical Guide to the Weeds of Australia, 1987; Weed Control Economics, 1987; Weed Control in Rice, 1997; Inventor: Mycoherbicide, Australian Patent, 1988. Honours: Churchill Fell, 1983; Acady of Sci Travel Fellshp, 1994. Memberships: Fell, Austl Inst of Agric Sci; Cttee Mbr, Weed Sci Soc of Am; Chmn, Intl Bioherbicide Grp; Chmn, Food and Agric Org of UN Weed Cttee, Asia/Pacific. Hobbies: Music; Gardening; Reading. Address: Agricultural Institute, Forest Road, Orange, NSW 2800, Australia.

AUSTIN Anthony Russell, b. 6 Apr 1943, Melbourne, Aust. Academic and Education Consultant. m. Cecilia, 14

July 1981, 3 s. Education: BA; BEd; MA; Med; PhD. Appointments: Tchr/Lectr, Vic Educ Dept, 1965-68; Lectr, Snr Lectr, Hd of Dept, Comm Skills, Admnstv Coll of Papua New Guinea, 1969-75; Snr Curric Offr Engl, 1976-77, Supt Curric, 1978-79, Papua New Guinea Dept of Educ; Dir, Solomon Islands Cntr, Univ of S Pacific, 1980; Prin Educ Offr Socl and Cultural Educ, North Territory Dept of Educ, 1981-85; Snr, Lectr, Socl Educ, Fac of Educ, Darwin Inst of Educ, 1986-88; Snr Lectr, Socl Educ, North Territory Univ, 1989-90; Team Ldr, West Samoa Second Tchrs Profl Dev Proj, 1991-94; Assoc Prof, Fac of Educ, North Territory Univ, 1991-95, 1997-99; Prin Lectr Educl Studies, Hong Kong Inst of Educ, 1995-97; Austl Team Ldr Vanuatu, Austl Secnd Educ Proj, 1999-. Publications: Pprs and books inclng: Technical Training and Development in Papua 1874-1941, 1978; Simply the Survival of the Fittest: Aboriginal Policy in South Australia's Northern Territory, 1992; I Can Picture the Old Home So Clearly: The Commonwealth and "Half-Caste" Youth 1911-1939, 1993; Never Trust a Government Man: The Commonwealth and Aboriginal Policy Development 1911-1939, 1997; Connection and Disconnection: Encounters Between Settles and Indigenous People in the Northern Territory (ed w S Parry), 1999. Honours: North Territory Inst of Educ Awd for Small Scale Rsch, 1986; North Territory Hist Awd, 1987. Memberships: Austl Coll of Educ; Histl Soc of North Territory; Natl Trust (Aust); North Territory Inst of Educl Rsch; Oral Hist Assn of Aust; Intl Oral Hist Assn; Socl Educ Assn of Aust. Hobby: Gardening. Address: Vanuatu Teachers college, Private Mail Bag 076, Port Vila, Vanuatu.

AUSTIN Margaret Elizabeth, b. 1 Apr 1933, Dunedin, New Zealand. Educator; Politician. m. John Maurice, 7 May 1955, 1 s, 2 d. Education: BS, Bot, Zool, Univ of Canterbury, 1953; Dip Tchng, Coll of Educ, Christchurch, 1954; MIBiol, Inst of Bio, London, 1970; AIE Assoc of Inst of Educ, London, 1981. Appointments: Sci Tchr, 1954-84; Admnstr, 1977-84; MP, 1984-96; Snr Govt Whip, -1990; Min Internal Affairs, Rsch Sci and Technol, Arts and Culture, 1990; Educl Cnslt, 1997-. Honours: Roy Soc Silver Medal, 1994; MNZM, 1997; Tchng Fell, Univ of Canterbury, 1970; Commonweath Fell, Inst of Educ, London, 1980-81. Memberships: Ed, Admin Soc, Chair (Canterbury), 1978-80; (Sec) NZ Sci Tchrs Assn, 1974-80; Osteoporosis (Canterbury), 1993-; Chair, Cntr for NZ Music, 1997-; Chair, Osteoporosis NZ, 1998-. Hobbies: Classical music; Theatre; NZ botany. Address: 11A St Clio Street, Christchurch 8004, New Zealand.

AUSTRIA Benjamin Suarez, b. 29 Jan 1946, Manila, Philippines. Professor of Geology. m. Cristina, 23 Apr 1977, 2 s, 3 d. Education: BS, Geol, Univ of the Philippines, 1965; MA, Geol, 1968, PhD, 1975, Harv Univ, USA. Appointments: Prof, Geol, Univ of Philippines, 1981-; Dir, Natl Inst of Geol Scis, 1987-93; Snr VP, 1988-, Dir, 1990-, Trans Asia Oil and Energy Dev Corp. Publication: Geochemical Implications of Iron in Sphalerite (PhD dissertation), 1975. Honours: Phi Kappa Phi, 1966; UN Fell, Ore Mineralogy, 1966-68; Lepanto Chair in Geol, Univ of Philippines, 1973; Disting Geologist, Soc of Philippines, 1989; 1992 Achievement Awd, Natl Rsch Cncl of the Philippines; Fell, Soc of Econ Geologists, 1993. Memberships: Pres, Geol Soc of Philippines, 1987; Chmn, AIME-SME (Philippine Sect), 1996-97; Exec Dir, Energy Dev and Utilization Fndn Inc, 1997-. Hobby: Collecting minerals. Address: National Institute of Geological Sciences, University of the Philippines, Diliman, Quezon City 1101, Philippines.

AVDIEV Rita. Managing Director. Education: BArch; FRAIA; FAIB; FVLE (Econ). Appointments: Mngng Dir, The Avdiev Grp, 1981-; Chmn, VICTEC Grp Trng Ltd, 1996-. Publications: Pprs on property and bus issues. Membership: Pres, Urban Land Inst of Aust, 1982-84. Listed in: Who's Who of Australia, 1997. Hobbies: All the arts; Rock music; Kite flying. Address: The Avdiev Group, Level 37, Australia Square, 264 George Street, Sydney, NSW 2000, Australia.

AVE Joop, b. 5 Dec 1934. Government Official. Education: Stud, For Serv Acady, 1957; Deg, Pol Sci,

Univ Philippines, Manila. Appointments: Dpty Dir, Protocol, Ministry of For Affairs, 1965-67; Consul, NY, 1967-71; Exec Asst to Pres, UN Gen Assembly, 1971-72; Chf of Protocol, Presdtl Palace, 1972-78; Dir Gen, Protocol and Consular Affairs, Chf, State Protocol, Ministry of For Affairs, 1978-82; Dir Gen, Tourism, 1982-93, Min, 1993-, Ministry of Tourism, Post and Telecomm, Govt Indonesia. Address: Ministry of Tourism, Jalan Keban Sirith 36, Jakarta, Indonesia.

AVINASH Khare, b. 23 July 1957, Satna, India. Scientist. m. Varsha, 15 June 1982, 1 s, 1 d. Education: MSc, Phys; PhD, Plasma Phys. Appointments: Rsch Assoc, 1984-86; Sci Offr, Oxon Univ, Eng, 1986-88; Fell, 1988-92; Assoc Prof, 1992-97; Snr Assoc Prof, 1997-. Publications: About 100 articles in intl sci jrnls. Honour: Homi Bhabha Young Sci Awd, 1993. Membership: Ed, Bd Mbr, Indian Jrnl of Physics, 1997-. Hobbies: Music; Football; Martial Arts. Address: A/201 Manila Towers, Opp Rajpath Club Satellite, Ahmedabad, Gujrat, India.

AVINASH Shyam, b. 10 Aug 1949, Purulia. Agriculturalist. m. Padma, 12 May 1968, 2 s. Appointment: Hon Ed, Sarokar Mag. Publications: Books in Hindi: Hafte Ka Din (short stories), 1988; Sabke Jeevan Mein (poems), 1996; Roshni Ke Andhere Mein (drama), 1998. Hobbies: Reading; Writing. Address: PN Ghosh Street, Purulia 723101, India.

AVISON Francis Aaron Ezekiel (Sir) (Baron Emery IV), b. 12 Apr 1934. Director; Diamond Trader. m. Joyce Ashby, dec 1977, 2 s, 1 d. Education: PhD, Psych, Thomas Edison; St Olavs; DSocSc, Trinity; Dr Sc, Santi Pauli; DO, Intl Univ; DD, Harmony; Prof, Educ, ICCI. Appointments: In prac as Psychol, 1960-94; Rsch Dir, Socl Rsch Fndn, 1976; Pres, Emery Diamonds Intl; World Pres, New Spirituality Movement, 1989; Chmn, Diamond Bank of Switzerland, 1994. Publications: Books: How You Can Use Hypnosis, 1965; Study Technique, 1972; One Good Woman, 1985; Anthology of Poetry, 1985. Honours: Kt Order of St John of Jerusalem, 1974; Inherited family title, Baron Emery de Beauveax (IV), 1996. Memberships: Amn Bd Certified Specialst in Psychotherapy, 1972; Fell, Acady of Behavioural Sci, 1973; Amn Bd Examiners in Psychotherapy, 1974. Listed in: Who's Who In Australia. Hobbies: Investigating Paranormal Phenomena; Reading; Writing; Poetry; Music; Movies. Address: PO Box 634, Parramatta, NSW 2124, Australia.

AVNER Yehuda, b. 30 Dec 1928, Manchester, Eng. Diplomat. m. Miriam Avner, 1952, 1 s, 3 d. Education: Manchester High Sch; London Sch of Jrnlsm. Appointments: Emigrated to Israel; Ed of Publs: The Jewish Agency Jerusalem, 1956-64; Min of For Affairs, 1964-67; Ed of Polit Publs, 1964-67; Dir of For Press Bur, 1972-74; Asst to PM, 1964-67; First Sec then Cnslr Emb WA DC, 1968-72; Asst to PM, 1972-74; Seconded to PMs Bur, 1974-77; Advsr to PM, 1974-77, 1977-83; Amb to UK, 1983-88; Dir-Gen Clore Fndn, 1989-90; Insp-Gen Israel For Serv, 1991-92; Amb to Aust, 1992-96. Publications: "The Young Inheritors": A Portrait of Israeli Youth. Hobbies: Music; Writing. Address: c/o Ministry of Foreign Affairs, Hakirya, Romena, Jerusalem 91950, Israel.

AVRICK David Bancroft, b. 10 Jan 1938, NY, NY, USA. Consultant. 1 s. Education: BS, Mktng. Appointments: Cnlt, JFAX Corp, Craftmatic Org Ltd, Craftmatic UK Ltd, Shrink Trax; Pres, A Moving Experience Ltd, Speakers and Seminars Inc; Serial Event Ed, Inspirator mag. Honours: Hon Citizen, New Orleans; Hon Citizen, City of Knoxville; Hon Citizen, Atlanta; Kentucky Col, Hon by US Congress. Address: 999 Andante Road, Santa Barbara, CA 93105, USA.

AWAD Muhammad Hadi, b. 5 May 1934. Diplomat. m. Adelah Moh'd Hadi Awad, 1956, 1 s, 3 d. Education: Murray House Coll of Educ. Appointments: Tchr, 1953-59; Educ Offr, 1960-62; Chf Insp of Schs, 1963-65; VP As-Shaab Coll, 1965-67; Perm Rep to Arab League, 1968-70, concurrently Amb to UAR, also accred to Sudan, Lebanon, Libya and Iraq; Perm Sec Min for For

Affairs, 1970-73; Amb to UK, 1973-80, concurrently to Spain and Sweden, 1974-80; Amb to Denmark, Portugal, the Netherlands, 1975-80; Amb to Tunisia and Perm Rep to the Arab League, 1980-91; Dir West Eur Dept Min of For Affairs, 1990-. Hobbies: Photography. Address: c/o Ministry of Foreign Affairs, P O Box 19262, Sana'a, Yemen.

AWAL Abdul. Service (Police Department). m. Panna, 6 May 1983, 2 s. Education: Master, Polit Sci, Chittagong Univ, Chittagong, Bangladesh, session 1982. Appointments: Radio Banglsdesh & Bangladesh TV - as a Lerick composure. Creative works: About 500 recorded songs. Honours: UN Peace Medal (UNPM), 1989; Pres Police Medal (PPM), 1992. Hobbies: Book reading; Social work. Address: Vill & Post, Paniarup, PS, Kasba Dist: B, Baria, Bangladesh.

AYAKANNU Mathialagan, b. 15 Mar 1939, Tamil Nadu, India. Professor. m. Vasuki, 7 Apr 1965, 3 s. Education: PhD, Computer Engrng; ME, Electrons Engrng; BE, Tele comms Engrng. Appointments: Assoc Lectr, Anna Univ; Lectr; Asst Prof; Prof; Dean; Dir, Acads, Tamil Nadu Inst of Info Technol. Creative Works: Three Transl Works in Tamil. Honours: Best Rsch Thesis Awd, Indian Inst of Sci. Memberships: IE; IETE; ISE; Telematics Forum of India. Hobbies: Writing Verses in Tamil; Transl in Tamil. Address: 6 Mahadevan Street, Chromepet, Chennai 600 044, Tamil Nadu, India.

AYALA-LASSO Jose, b. 29 Jan 1932, Quito. Diplomat. m. 4 c. Education: Pontificia Univ Catolica del Ecuador; Univ Cen del Ecuador; Univ Catholique de Louvain Belgium. Appointments: Sev For Affairs posts at embs in Japan, Repub of Korea, China, Italy; Min of For Affairs, 1977; Fmr Amb to Belgium, Luxembourg, Peru, EEC; Lectr Intl Law Inst Univ Cen del Ecuador; Dep Legal Sec Perm Commn for the South Operation; Perm Rep to UN, 1989-94; Chmn Security Cncl Cttee concerning fmr Yugoslavia, 1991; Chmn wrkng grp to est post of High Commnr for Human Rights, 1993; UN High Cmmnr for Human Rights, 1994-97; Min of For Affairs, 1997-. Honours: Grand Cross Natl Order of Merit - Ecuador; Num decorations from Japan, Belgium, Brazil, etc. Address: Ministry of Foreign Affairs, Avenida 10 de Agosto y Carrion, Quito, Ecuador.

AYKUT Imren, b. 1941, Adana. Politician. Education: Istanbul Univ and Oxford Univ. Appointments: Fmr Mngr of trades unions; Indl rels expert in Turkish glass inds; Fmr Sec-Gen Paper Ind Employers' Union; Dep Natl Assembly, 1983-; Min of Labour and Socl Security, Dec 1987-91; Gov Spokesperson, 1991; Pres Turkish Inter-Parl Grp, 1991-. Publications: Over 40 articles and rsch papers. Memberships: Constl Assembly, 1981; Motherland Party. Hobbies: Hand-made carpets; Antiquities. Address: Turkiye Buyuk Millet Meclisi, Parlamentolararasi Birlik Turk Grubu, Baskanigi, Ankara, Turkey.

AYLWIN AZOCAR Patricio, b. 26 Nov 1918. Lawyer; Politician. m. Leonor Oyarzun Ivanovic, 1948, 5 c. Appointments: Senator, 1965-73; Pres Christian Dem Party - PDC, 1965-67, 1973-76, 1987-88; Ldr opposition coalition rejecting Gen Pinochet in natl plebiscite, Oct 1988; Opposition coalition cand, 1989; PDC cand for Pres, 1989. Pres of Chil, 1990-94; Pres Corporacion Justicia y Democracia. Publications: El Juicio Arbitral, 1943; La Transicion Chilena; Discursos escogidos Marzo, 1990-92; Crecimiento con Equidad; Discursos escogidos, 1992-94; Justicia, Democracia y Desarrollo; Conferencias y discursos, 1994-95; El Reencuentro de los Demócratas. Del Golpe Militar al Triunfo del No, 1998. Address: Teresa Salas Noo 786, Providencia, Santiago, Chile.

AYOUB Fouad, b. 1944, Amman, Jordan. Ambassador. m. 2 s, 1 d. Education: BA, MA, Philos, CA Univ, San Fran. Appointments: Press Sec, His Majesty King Hussein, 1977; Mbr, Jordanian Delegation to Madrid Peace Conf, 1991; Amb of the Hashemite Kingdom of Jordan to the Crt of St James's, 1991; Non-Res Amb of the Hashemite Kingdom of Jordan to Iceland and Ireland,

1992. Honours: Awds from Jordan, Germany, France, Greece, Italy, Spain, Indonesia, Finland, Austria, Sweden. Membership: Fell, Harvard Univ, Cntr for Intl Affairs, 1983-84. Hobby: Reading. Address: Embassy of the Hashemite Kingdom of Jordan, 6 Upper Phillimore Gardens, London W8 7HB, England.

AYUB KHAN Gohar. Appointment: Minister of Foreign Affairs, Pakistan, 1997-. Address: Ministry of Foreign Affairs, Constitution Avenue, Islamabad, Pakistan.

AYYALASOMAYAJULA Vajreswari, b. 30 Dec 1952, Vizianagaram. Scientist. m. Mr A Satyanandam, 6 May 1992, 1 d. Education: MSc; PhD. Appointments: Rsch Asst, 1980-82; Asst Rsch Offr, 1982-86; Rsch Offr, 1986-91; Snr Rsch Offr, 1991-96; Asst Dir, 1996. Honours: Venkata Krishnaiah Choudhury Mem Prize, 1969-70; State Merit Schlshp, 1969-72; Venkatakrishnaia Cowdary Mem Prize, 1970-71; Pasumarti Venkata Ratnam Schlshp, 1971-72; Angara Somaskhara Rao Mem Prize, 1971-72; Bd of Studies, Andhra Univ, 1972-73. Memberships: Amn Oil Chemists Soc; Oil Technologists Assn of India; Indian Women Scientists Assn. Hobbies: Counseling; Indian music; Reading; Travelling. Address: National Institute of Nutrition (ICMR), JamaiOsmania PO Hyderabad 500007, India.

AYYOUBI Mahmoud Ben Saleh al-, b. 1932. Politician. Appointments: Fmr Dir-Gen for Admin Affairs Euphrates Dept; Min of Educ, 1969-71; Dep Premier, 1970-71; VP, 1971-75; PM, 1972-76. Memberships: Baath Party Regl Command, 1971-75, Jan 1980-. Address: c/o Office of the Prime Minister, Damascus, Syria.

AZER Samy Aziz, b. 28 Mar 1953, Cairo, Egypt. Gastroentrologist; Educator. m. 9 Oct 1984, 2 d. Education: B, Med and Surg, 1977; M, Med, 1983, MEd, 1993; PhD, Univ of Sydney, 1995. Appointments: Postdoctoral Fell, Univ of KS Medl Cntr, 1994-; Tutor, Path, Univ of Sydney, 1996-98; Snr Lectr, Fac of Med, Univ of Sydney, 1998-. Creative Works: Writer, Medl Column, El-Telegraph, Aust, 1996-97; Contbr to books, articles to profl jrnls. Honours: Schl, Min of Educ, 1968-71; Undergrad Schl, 1972-77; Postgrad Schl, Univ of Sydney, 1993-94. Memberships: Amn Coll of Gastroenterology; Amn Assn for Stdy of Liver Diseases; Univ of NSW Union. Hobbies: History of medicine; Egyptology; Soccer. Address: P O Box 794, Fairfield, NSW 2165, Australia.

AZHAR Mohd Zain, b. 22 June 1956, Penang, Malaysia. Psychiatrist; Psychotherapist. m. Linda Kamal, 15 Dec 1985, 2 d. Education: MD, Natl Univ Malaysia, 1982; MPM, Univ Malaya, 1988; Dip.Cog.Th, Oxford, 1994. Appointments: Med Offr, Penang Hosp, 1982-85; Res Psych, 1988-94; Cnslt Psych & Psychotherapist, 1994-, Prof of Psych, 1994-, Univ Hosp Med Sch. Publications: Over 50 articles in prof sci jrnls. Honours: ASEAN Fellshp, 1994. Memberships: Malaysian Med Assn; Malaysian Psych Assn; IACP; BABCP; WFMH; APAP; PERSIKOL. Hobbies: Cooking; Gardening. Address: c/o Psychotherapy Clinic, University Hospital Medical School, Kubang Kerian, 16150 Kota Bhara, Malaysia.

AZIMOV Yakhe Nuriddinovich, b. 4 Dec 1947, Khodjend, Tajikistan. Politician. m. 1 s, 2 d. Education: Tashkent Inst of Textile Ind. Appointments: Worked Ura-Tubin Tricot Factory, 1971-75; Engr Hd of rug prodn ; Dir Kairak-Kum rug factory, 1975-82; Dep Chf Engr, Chf Engr, Dir-Gen of rug prodns, 1982-96; Pres Jt Stock Co Kolinkho, Kairakum, Jan 1996-; Chmn Cncl of Mins, PM of Tajikistan, Feb 1996-. Address: Council of Ministers, Rudaki prosp 42, 743051 Dushanbe, Tajikistan.

AZIZ Abdul Malim, b. 30 Apr 1930. Publishing Company Executive. m. 17 Apr 1954, 5 s, 4 d. Education: Malay, Engl & Arabic. Appointments: Corres, Melayu Raya (newsppr), Singapore, 1952-53; Ed, Info Offr, Brunei Shell, Seria, 1953-69; Dpty Dir, Publns Gov Info Servs, Kuala Lumpur, Malaysia, 1970-84; Admin Mngr,

(ABE) Britain, Kuala Lumpur, 1985-86; Exec Ed, Sarawak Tribune, Utusan Sarawak, Jiwa Bakti, 1987, 1993, 1994-; Dir, Sarawak Press, 1993-. Honours: AMN, 1980; PJK, 1983. Memberships: Exec Cncl Mbr, Scouts, Brunei, 1961-69; Welfare Cncl, 1962-69; Dir, Rotary Club, Brunei, 1964-69. Listed in: Who's Who in the World. Hobbies: Adventure; Stamp Collecting. Address: 103, Jalan USJ 12/2A, UEP Subang Jaya, 47600 Petaling Jaya, Selangor, Malaysia.

AZIZ Dato' Seri Paduka Rafidah, b. 4 Nov 1943, Selama Perak. Politician. m. Mohammed Basir bin Ahmad, 3 c. Education: Univ of Malaya. Appointments: Tutor Asst Lectr, Lectr and Chmn Rural Dev Div Fac of Econs Univ of Malaya, 1966-76; Mbr Parl, 1978-; Dep Min of Fin, 1977-80; Min of Pub Enterprise, 1980-88; Min of Intl Trade and Ind, March 1988-; Holder of many other pub appts and deleg to num intl confs. Memberships: UMNO Supreme Cncl, 1975-; Ahli Mangku Negara; Datuk Paduka Mahkota Selangor. Hobbies: Reading; Decoration; Music; Squash. Address: Ministry of International Trade and Industry, Block 10, Kompleks Rejabat Kerajaan, Jalan Duta, 50622 Kuala Lumpur, Malaysia.

AZIZ Tariq, b. 1936, Mosul. Politician. Education: Baghdad Univ. Appointments: Mbr Staff Al-Jumhuriyah, 1958; Chf Ed Al-Jamahiir, 1963; Baath press, Syria, 1963-1966; Chf Ed Al-Thawra publsng house; Dep PM, 1981; Min of For Affairs, 1983; Dep PM, 1991-. Memberships: Revolutionary Command Cncl Gen Affairs Bur, 1972; Reserve mbr Arab Baath Socl Party Ldrship, 1974-77; Elected mbr Baath Regl Ldrship, 1977. Address: Offices of the Deputy Prime Ministers, Karradat Mariam, Baghdad, Iraq.

AZKOUI Karim, b. 15 July 1915, Raschaya. Diplomat. m. Eva Corey, 1947, 1 s, 1 d. Education: Jesuit Univ of St Joseph Beirut and Univ of Paris, Berlin, Bonn and Munich. Appointments: Prof of Hist, Arab and French Lit and Philos in var colls in Lebanon, 1939-46; Dir of Arabic publsng house and monthly Arabic review The Arab World Beirut, 1943-45; Hd Rapporteur Cttee on Genocide, 1948; Mbr Lebanese Deleg to UN NY, 1947-50; Acting Perm Deleg to UN, 1950-53; Hum Cultural and Socl Cttee of Gen Assembly, 1951; Cttee on Freedom of Info, 1951; Hd of UN Affairs Dep Min of For Affairs, 1953-57; Chmn Negotiating Cttee for Extra Budgetary Funds, 1952-54; Hd Perm Deleg to UN, 1957-59; First Vice-Chmn Human Rights Commn, 1958; Consul-Gen in Aust and NZ, 1959-61; Amb to Ghana, Guinea and Mali, 1961-64; Amb to Iran and Afghanistan, 1964-66; Jrnlst, 1966-68; Prof of Philos Beirut Coll for Women, 1968-72; Prof Lebanese Univ, 1970-72; Chf Ed The Joy of Knowledge Arabic Encyclopedia - 10 vols - 1978-; Vice-Chmn Cttee for Def of Human Rights in Lebanon. Publications: Reason and Faith in Islam - in German - 1938; Reason in Islam - in Arabic - 1946; Freedom - co-author - 1956; Freedom of Association - UN - 1968; Trans into Arabic Consciencism - Nkrumah - 1964; Arab Thought in the Liberal Age - Albert Hourani - 1969. Honours: Order of Cedar - Lebanon; Order of Holy Sepulchre - Jerusalem; Order of St Marc - Alexandria; Order of the Brillain Star - Repub of China; Order of Southern Star - Brazil; Order of St Peter and Paul - Damascus. Memberships: PEN Emer World Cncl Hague, 1971-; Mbr Bd of Trustees Bd of Mngmnt of Theol Sch of Balamand Lebanon. Hobbies: Reading; Writing.

B

BA Jin (Li Yaotang), b. 25 Nov 1904, Chengdu, Sichuan Prov. Writer; Journalist m. Xiao Shan, 1944 - dec 1972, 1 s, 1 d. Education: For Lang Sch Chengdu; Studied in France and adopted name Ba Jin - taken from first syllable of Bakunin and the last of Kropotkin, 1926. Appointments: Ed fortnightly provincial Ban Yue, 1928; Writer and Translator Shanghai, 1929; Visited Japan, 1934; Chf Ed Shanghai Cultural Life Publsng House 1935; Joined Lu Xun's China Lit Work Soc, 1936; Co-Ed - with Mao Dun - Shouting Weekly and Bonfire Weekly, 1937; Vice-Chmn Union of Chinese Writers, 1953 - now Chmn; Dep to NPC, 1954; Chf Ed People's Lit, 1957-58; Vice-Chmn China Fedn of Lit and Art Circles, 1960; Chf Ed Shanghai Lit, 1961; in disgrace, 1968-77; Vice-Chmn 5th Municipal CPPCC Cttee Shanghai, 1977-83; Exec Cncl China Welfare Inst, 1978-; Vice-Chmn China Fed of Lit and Art Circles, 1978-; Pres China PEN Cntr, 1980-; Pres Chinese Writers' Assc, 1981-; Pres China Lit Fndn, 1986-; Vice-Chmn 7th Natl Cttee CPPCC, 1988-93; Vice Chmn 8th Natl Cttee, 1993-. Publications: Extinction, 1928; The Family, 1931; Trilogy of Love, 1932-33; The History of the Nihilist Movement, 1936; Spring, 1937; Autom, 1940; Festival Day of Warsaw, 1950; Living Among Heroes, 1953; Three Comrades, 1962; Essays by the Sickbed, 1984. Honours: Hon Pres Fiction Soc, 1984-; Hon Chmn China Shakespeare Rsch Fndn, 1984-; Hon Mbr AAAS, 1985; Medal of Intl Friendship USSR, 1990. Memberships: Mbr Presidium 6th Natl CPPCC Cttee, 1983-88. Address: c/o China PEN, Shatan Beijie 2, Beijing, Peole's Republic of China.

BA Monghke, b. 1 Oct 1954, Inner Mongolia, China. Teacher. m. Narangere, 1 Aug 1979, 1 s, 1 d. Education: Postgrad AM. Appointments: Tchr, Monglian Lang Tech, Inner Mongolia, 1975-78; Tchr, Inner Mongolian Tchrs Univ, 1982-98. Publications: History of the Mergen Sume, A Study on Lobsandanbijalsan Lama Oegegen Sume; Essays; Over 50 pprs. Honours: Inner Mongolian Excellent Intellectual, 1976; Min or Prov Level Sci Rsch Prize (4 x). Memberships: Dpty Dir, Mongolian Lit Assn of China; Soc of China Minority Lit. Hobby: Music. Address: Department of Mongolian Language and Literature, Inner Mongolian Teacher's University, Huhhot, China.

BABA Encik Abdul Ghafa Bin, b. 18 Feb 1925, Kuala Pilah, Negrei Sembilan. Politician. Education: Sultan Idris Tchrs Trng Coll, Tanjong Malim. Appointments: Sch Tchr, 1949-55; Chf Min of Malacca, 1955-67; Chmn MARA, 1967; Sen and Min without Portfolio, 1967; Min of Natl and Rural Dev, 1974; Chmn Kompleks Kewangan Bd, Pegi Malaysia Bhd, Dunlop Estates Bhd, 1976-86; Dep PM and Min of Natl and Rural Dev, 1986-93; Acting PM, Jan 1989; VP UMNO, 1974; Left UMNO, Nov 1993; Rejoined, March 1995. Memberships: Mbr Fedn Legis Cncl, 1955. Hobby: Golf. Address: c/o Ministry of National and Rural Development, Kewangar Complex, 5th Floor, Jalan Raja Laut, 50606 Kuala Lumpur, Malaysia.

BABA Takanobu, b. 4 Nov 1947, Japan. Computer Scientist. m. Hideko, 15 Sept 1976, 1 s, 2 d. Education: BE, Kyoto Univ, 1970; MEng, 1972; DEng, 1978. Appointments: Rsch Assoc, Univ of Electro-Commns, 1975-78, Lectr, 1978-79; Lectr, Utsunomiya Univ, 1979-82, Assoc Prof, 1982-90, Prof of Computer Sci, 1990-; Vis Prof, Univ MD, Coll Park, USA, 1982-83; Vis Rsch Assoc, 1985. Publications include: Microprogrammable Parallel Computer, 1987; Computer Architecture, 1994. Memberships: IEEE; Info Processing Soc of Japan; Inst of Electrons, Info & Commn Engrs. Hobby: Tennis. Address: Utsunomiya University, Department of Information Science, Ishii-machi 2753, Utsunomiya 321, Japan.

BABADJHAN Ramz, b. 1921, Uzbekistan. Poet; Playwright. m. 1947, 1 s, 2 d. Education: Pedagogical Inst Tashkent. Appointments: Dep Chmn Uzbek Writers' Union; Chmn Uzbek Repub Cttee on Rels with African and Asian Writers; Pres, Soc on Cultural Rels with Compatriots Living Abroad "Vatan", 1990-94. Publications: First works publshd, 1935; publs incl: New Rubais; For You, My Love; The Heart Never Sleeps; Selected Poetry; A Poet Lives Twice; Living Water; Yusuf and Zuleyha; 1001 Crane; Sides; Uncle and Nephew; You Cannot Deceive a Gipsy. Honour: USSR State Prize, 1972. Membership: Mbr CPSU, 1951-91. Hobbies: Photography; Travelling. Address: Levanevsky Str 34, 700070 Tashkent, Uzbekistan.

BABAR Abdul Hakim, b. 5 Apr 1945, Lahore, Pakistan. Plastic Surgeon. m. Mumtaz, 6 Apr 1973, 2 s, 2 d. Education: Dipl, Amn Bd of Surg, Amn Bd of Plastic Surg; Fell, Amn Coll of Surgs. Appointments: Clin Asst Prof, Plastic Surg, Hahneman Med Coll, 1978-89; Cnslt, Hd, Dept of Plastic Surg, Mayo Hosp, 1989-. Memberships: Amn Coll of Surns; Amn Soc of Plastic & Reconstructive Surgns; Intl Soc of Burn Injuries; Islamic Med Assn of N Am. Hobbies: Photography; Travel. Address: 8-C Model Town, Lahore 54700, Pakistan.

BABAR Mumtaz Jabeen, b. 15 Jan 1950, Pakistan. Psychiatrist. m. Abdul Hakim Babar, 6 Apr 1973, 2 s, 2 d. Education: Dipl, Amn Bd of Physl Med and Rehab, 1982; Fell, Am Acady of Physl Med and Rehab. Appointments: Cnslt, St Lawrence Rehab Cntr, NJ, USA, 1982-87; Asst Prof, Hd, Dept of Physl Med and Rehab, Sh-Zayed Hosp, Lahore, 1988-95; Childrens Hosp and Inst of Child Hlth, Lahore, 1995-. Membership: Acady of Physl Med and Rehab. Hobbies: Travel; Reading. Address: 8-C Model Town, Lahore 54700, Pakistan.

BABIKIAN Khatchik Diran, b. 1924, Cyprus. m. 1956, 5 d. Education: Coll Italien Beirut; Fac Francaise de Droit Beirut; Fac de Paris; Univ of London. Appointments: Bar; Dep for Beirut, 1957, 1960, 1964, 1968, 1972, 1992, 1996; Min for Admin Reform, 1960-61; Min of Pub Hlth, 1968-69; Min of Tourism, 1969-70; Min of Info, 1972-73; Mbr Parl Commn on Justice; Pres Traffic Commn, Parl Commn on Plng Lebanese Mngmnt Assc, 1972, 1992, 1995; Min of Plng, 1973, 1990-95; Min of Justice, 1980-82, 1990-92; Pres Armenian Natl Assembly, 1972, 1976; Pres Exec Cncl Armenian Ch of Cilicia, 1983-99. Memberships: Assc Libanaise contre la Drogue; Assc Libanaise pour la Diabete; Assc Libanaise pour l'Habitat; VP World Assc of French-Speaking Parliamentarians, 1982, 1999; Personal Rep of Pres of Repub at Conseil Perm de la Francophonie, 1992-97. Honours: Officier Legion d'honneur; Ufficiale Ordine del Merito - Italy. Hobbies: Violin; Languages. Address: Place de l'Etoile, Beirut, Lebanon.

BABU Kunwar Seth Ganesh, b. 17 June 1933, Lucknow, India. Service (retired). m. Krishna Kamini, 7 June 1959, 3 s. Education: BS, 1950; LLB, 1958. Appointments: Gen Mngr, Ordnance Clothing Factory Shahjahanpur, 1979; Ordnance Parachute Factory, Kanpur, 1979-91; Ordnance Equipment Factory Hazratpur, 1983-85. Creative works: Prodn of new def clothing, parachutes, rubberised equipment, 1979-91. Honours: Best Ordnance Factory Efficiency Trophy, 1983-84, 1988-89; Shantu Shahaney Mem Shield Best Prodn Engr, 1985. Memberships: Def Dress Implementation Team, 1985-88; Aerial Rsch and Dev Panel, 1979-91; Chmn, Made-up Textiles Cttee Bur of Indian Stands, 1988-91. Hobbies: Reading; Tennis; Badminton. Address: 384-D, Shyamnagar, Kanpur 208013, India.

BABULA William, b. 19 May 1943, Stamford, CT, USA. University Dean; Author. m. Karen L Gemi, 19 June 1965, 2 s. Education: BA, Rutgers Univ, 1965; MA, Univ of CA at Berkeley, 1967; PhD, 1969. Appointments: Asst Prof, Engl, Univ Miami, Coral Gables, FL, USA, 1969-75; Assoc Prof, 1975-77, Prof, 1977-81, Chmn Dept Engl, 1976-81, Dean of Arts and Humanities, Sonoma St Univ, Rohnert Park, 1981-. Publications include: The Last Jogger in Virginia, 1983; The Orthodontist and the Rock Star, 1984; Greenearth, 1984; Football and Other Seasons, The Great American Basketball Shoot, 1984; Ms Skywriter Inc, 1987; Plays: The Fragging of Lt Jones, 1987; The Winter of Mrs Levy, 1988; Productions: West Coast Ensemble, 1992; Mark Twain Masquers, 1994; Novels: The Bombing of Berkeley and Other Pranks,

1984; St John's Baptism, 1988; According to St John, 1989; St John and the Seven Veils, 1990; St John's Bestiary, 1994; Contbr, articles to var jrnls, short stories in lit mags. Honours: 1st Prize, Gualala Arts Comp; Phi Beta Kappa; FL Endowment Hum Grantee, 1980-81. Memberships: Dramatists Guild; Auths League Am; Associated Writing Progs; Mystery Writers Am. Address: School of Arts and Humanities, Sonoma State University, Rohnert Park, 94928, USA.

BACHMAN William David, b. 30 July 1952, Phila, PA, USA. Photographer; Writer. m. Sally Rodd, 25 Feb 1984. Education: BA, Asian Studies, Austl Natl Univ, 1974. Publications: (books) Off The Road Again, 1989; Local Colour: Travels in the Other Australia, 1994; Australian Colours, 1998. Hundreds of mag and book contbns and exhibns, Detours, 1988; Animal Vegetable Mineral, 1996; Local Colour, 1997. Honours: Austl Ski Fedn Photogr of the Yr, 1988; Austl Geog Photog of the Yr, 1997. Memberships: ACMP (Soc of Advtng Coml and Mag Photogrs); AIPP (Austl Inst of Profl Photog). Hobbies: Skiing; Golf; Fly Fishing. Address: 55 Mayston St, East Hawthorn, Vic 3123, Australia.

BADAL Sukhbir Singh, b. 9 July 1962, Badal, Faridkot Dist, Punjab, India. Member of Parliament. m. Harsimrat Badal, 21 Nov 1991, 1 d. Education: BA, HOns, Econs, MA, Econs, Panjab Univ, Chandigarh; MBA, CA State Univ, USA. Appointments: Elected, 11th Lok Sabha, 1996; Mbr, Cttee on Com, 1996-97; Mbr Consultative Cttees, Min of External Affairs, Min of Com; Re-elected, 12th Lok Sabha, 1998; Union Min of State, Ind, 1998-. Honour: North Zone Clay Modelling Comp, Chandigarh. Memberships: Mngr, Sch at Gidder Baha, Punjab; Golf Club, Chandigarh; Pres's Polo Club, New Delhi. Hobbies: Travelling; Skeet and trap shooting; Making sculptures. Address: 12 Safdarjang Road, New Delhi, India.

BADAWI Datuk Abdullah Bin Haj, b. 26 Nov 1939, Pulau Pinang. Politician. m. Datin Endon bint Datuk Mahmud. Education: Univ of Malaya. Appointments: Asst Sec Pub Serv Dept, 1964; Asst Sec MAGERAN, 1969; Asst Sec Natl Security Cncl, 1971; Dir - Yth - Min of Sport; Dir Min of Yth and Culture, 1971-74; Dep Sec-Gen, 1974-78; Min without Portfolio, PM Dept, 1982; Min of Educ, 1984-86; Min of Def, 1986-87; VP UMNO Supreme Cncl, 1984; Many other pub appts. Honours: Recipient of 4 awards. Memberships: Mbr UMNO Supreme Cncl, 1982-. Address: Dewan Rakyat, Parliament Buiding, 50680 Kuala Lumpur, Malaysia.

BADDAMS Violet Thenie, b. 13 May 1917, Fremantle, WA, Aust. Retired Headmistress. Education: BA, Adelaide Univ, 1938; Dip of Secnd Educ, Adelaide Tchrs Coll (now Adelaide Coll of Adv Educ), 1940. Appointments: Stud Tchr, Vine Vale Prim Sch, 1935; Asst Mistress, Mt Barker HS, SA, 1939-43; Snr Mistress, Whyalla Tech HS, SA, 1943-44; Hdmistress, Sydney SCEGGS, Moss Vale, NSW, 1945-52; Hdmistress, Shelford CEGGS, Vic, 1953-63; Hdmistress, Woodlands CEGGS, Glenelg, SA, 1964-80, now retd. Honours: AM, 1938; D Univ, Adelaide, 1988. Memberships include: Austl Coll of Educ, VP, 1972-81; Assn of Hds of Indep Girls' Schs of Aust, 1945-, Pres, 1978-79; Hon Life Mbr, Utd Assns of Hds of Girls' and Boys' Indep Schs; Assn of Hds of Indep Girls' Schs in SA, Pres, 1969-71, 1976-77; Incorp Assn of Registered Tchrs in Vic, Pres, 1962-63, Hon Life Mbr, 1964-; Indep Schs Bd of SA, 1964-; Educ Cttee, Cncl of the Univ of Adelaide, 1968-87; Arts Fac, Chmn of the 4C Cttee, 1981-87; Cncl, Sturt Coll of Adv Educ; Pub Exams Bd, 1966, 1967, 1969, 1971, 1976-79; Educ Bd, Dept of Veterans' Affairs, 1979-; Volun Tutor, Adult Lit Scheme, 1979-; Austl Fedn of Univ Women, 1938-. Hobbies: Golf; Croquet; Reading; Music; Arts and Crafts. Address: Unit 58, Mason Towers, 13 Moseley Street, Glenelg, SA 5045, Australia.

BADGER Geoffrey Malcolm, b. 10 Oct 1916, Port Augusta, SA, Aust. Retired Scientist and Educator. m. Edith Maud Chevis, 27 Apr 1941. Education: Dip, Indl Chem, Gordon Inst of Technol, MSc, Univ of Melbourne, 1938; PhD, Univ of London, 1941; DSc, Univ of Glasgow,

1949. Appointments: Rsch Chem, ICI (Manchester), 1941-43; Instr Lt, RN, 1943-46; Rsch Fell, Glasgow, 1946-49; Snr Lectr, 1949-50, Rdr, 1951-54, Prof of Organic Chem, 1955-64, Emer Prof, 1965, Dpty Vice Chan, 1966-67, Vice Chan, 1967-77, Univ of Adelaide; Mbr, Exec CSIRO, 1965; Chmn, ASTEC, Advising PM, 1977-82. Publications: Over 200 pprs publd in sci jrnls in Eng and Aust (some as co-auth); Four books on sci subjects, two on explorers. Honours: AO, 1975; KB, 1979; HG Smith Medal, Roy Austl Chem Inst, 1951; A E Leighton Medal, Roy Austl Chem Inst, 1971; W D Chapman Medal, Inst of Engrs, 1974; ANZAAS Medal, 1981; DUniv, Univ of Adelaide. Memberships: Fell, Austl Acady of Sci, Pres, 1974-78; Fell, Roy Soc of Chem; Fell, Roy Austl Chem Inst, Pres, 1964-65; Fell, Austl and NZ Assn for the Advmnt of Sci, Pres, 1979-80; Fell, Austl Acady of Technol Scis and Engrng. Hobbies: Reading; Writing; Walking; Travel. Address: 1 Anna Court, Delfin Island, West Lakes, SA 5021, Australia.

BADRAN Ibrahim, b. 19 July 1939. m. 4 c. Director. Education: Univs of Cairo and London. Appointments: Lectr in Electr Engng, Univ of Libya Tripoli, 1970-74; Chf Engr and Hd Electricity Section, Consultancy and Arch, Min of Plng Baghdad, 1974-76; Dir of Plng and Dir of Standards and Specif Jordan Electricity Authy, 1978-80; Dir of Energy Min of Trade and Ind, 1980-84; Gov for Jordan IAEA, 1982-90; Sec-Gen - Under Sec - Min of Ind and Trade, 1984-85; Chmn Bd Dirs Coml Cntrs Co-op Jordan, 1984-85; Chmn Bd Dirs Jordan Glass Co, 1985-87; Sec-Gen Min of Energy and Nat Rescs, 1985-90; Sec-Gen - Under Sec - Min of Ind and Trade, 1990-91; Chmn Bd Dirs Coml Cntrs Co-op Jordan, 1990-91; Advsr to PM, 1991-94; Co-ord-Gen of Peace Process Min of For Affairs, 1994-95; Exec Dir Noor Al-Hussein Fndn, 1995-; Fmr Dir Jordanian Pet Refinery, Jordanian Phosphate Co, Jordan Valley Authy, Jordan Water Authy, Jordan Elecricity Authy, Jordan Nat Rescs Authy, Ind Bank of Jordan, etc; Num other profl and acad appts and affiliations. Publications: Aut or co-auth of 13 books on aspects of sci, technol, nuclear energy, nat rescs and dev in the Arab world; two theort plays. Address: Noor Al-Hussein Foundation, P O Box 926687, Amman 11110, Jordan.

BADRAN Mudar, b. 1934, Jerash. Education: Univ of Damascus, Syria. Appointments: Lt and Legal Cnslt Jordanian armed forces, 1957; Maj and Legal Advsr to the Armed Forces Treas, 1962; Asst Chf Jordanian For Intell, 1965; Dep Chf of Gen Intell, 1966; Chf, 1968; Retd Maj-Gen, 1970; Chf Chamberlain of the Roy Court, 1970; Sec-Gen Natl Security Advsr to HM King Hussein - qv - 1970; Min in the Roy Court, 1972; Natl Security Advsr to King Hussein, 1973; Min of Educ, 1973-74; Chf of the Roy Court, 1974-76; Min of Def and of For Affair, 1976-79; PM, 1976-79, 1980-84; Min of Def, 1980-84, 1989. Honours: Hon LL.D - Leicester - 1991. Memberships: Natl Consultative Cncl, 1979-; Fmr mbr Exec Cncl of the Arab Natl Union.

BADWAL Sukhvinder P S, b. 28 Feb 1951. Chief Research Scientist. m.(1) Janet Mary, 26 Feb 1977, 3 s, 1 d, (2) Kulvir Badwal, Mar 1999. Education: BSc Hons; MSc Hons; PhD. Appointments: Rsch Sci, 1981-84, Snr Rsch Sci, 1984-88, Prin Rsch Sci 1988-92, Snr Prin Rsch Sci 1992-97, Chf Rsch Sci, 1997-, CSIRO; Dir R and D, 1992-97, Gen Mngr Technol Strategy, 1997-99, Ceramic Fuel Cells Ltd. Publications: Over 155 articles in intl jrnls, book chapts, 113 conf presentations, over 30 pats; Ed of 2 books; Assoc Ed, Solid State Ionic Jrnl, 1991-; Co-ed: Intl Jrnl of Ionics, 1997-. Membership: Intl Soc for Solid State Ionics; Mbr Intl Energy Agcy Exec Cttee on Advd Fuel Cells. Listed in: Who's Who in the World; Australian Men and Women of Science and Engineering. Hobbies: Photography; Bush Walking. Address: CSIRO, Manufacturing Science and Technology, Normanby Road, Gate 4, Clayton, Vic 3168, Australia.

BAGABANDU Natsagiyn, b. 22 Apr 1959, Zavkhan Prov, Mongolia. Politician. Appointments: Ed, Food Technol Inst of USSR; Ulan Bator Brewery and Distillery, 1972-75; Chf of Dept, Mongolian People's Revolutionary Party, Cttee of Cntrl Prov, 1980-84; Chf of Div, Advsr,

Cntrl Cttee, MPRP, 1978-90; Sec, Dpty Chair, Cntrl Cttee, 1990-92; Chair, 1997; Mbr of State, Great Hural, Chair, 1992-96; Pres of Mongolia, 1997-. Address: State Palace, Ulan Bator 12, Mongolia.

BAGGS Sydney Allison, b. 15 July 1930. Architect; Environmental Scientist; Landscape Architect. m. Joan Constance Mendham, 2 Feb 1952, 1 s, 2 d. Education: Dip Arch, Sydney Tech Coll, 1952; BArch, Arch Univ, Univ NSW, 1968; Grad Dip, Landscape Arch Univ NSW, 1970; MArch, Univ NSW, 1975; PhD, Univ NSW, 1982; Bldg Biol and Ecology Dip, BBE Inst NZ, 1994. Career: 25 yrs in priv archtl and landscape consultancy prac; 11 yrs Snr Lectr, Fac Arch, Univ NSW; Ptnr, Roberts & Baggs; Snr Lectr, Univ NSW; Jt Mngng Dir, ECA Space Des Pty Ltd; Mngng Dir, PEOPL Grp; Mbr, Intl Bd Advsrs, Environic Fndn Intl, 1992-. Publications: Over 70 inclng 6 books, published in Eur, Eng, USSR, China, Thailand, Japan, USA, Aust; Prin auth, illustrator, Australian Earth-covered Building, 1985, revised 2nd ed, 1991; The Healthy House, 1996; The Underworld of Myth, Mystery and Religion, forthcoming; Articles in Nature and Health; Ed-in-Chf, contbr articles, journal, Geotecture, 10 yrs. Honours: (with D W Baggs): Natl Energy Mngmt Merit Awd, for Energy Efficient Home, 1986; HIA Top Home Awd: Energy-Efficient Home, 1989-90; 4 HIA Top Home Awds for Innovative Des, 1989-93; Blackett Awd, Royal Inst Archts (w NSW Govt Archt), Bldg Outstndng Arch Merit, Brewarrina Aboriginal Cultural Mus, 1990; Merit Awd, Bradford CSR Energy Conquest Des Awd, Com Bldgs, 1992-93; Fell, Roy Soc Arts, 1995. Memberships: FRAIA; FRSA, London; RIBA; EIA; NELA; Fndng Pres, Geotecture Intl Assn; Fndng Mbr, Intl Des Extreme Environments Assn, 1992. Listed in: Who's Who of Australian Writers; International Authors and Writers Who's Who; Five Hundred Leaders of Influence; Dictionary Of International Biography; The International Directory Of Distinguished Leadership; Five Thousand Personalities Of The World; Who's Who In Australia. Address: 39 Cheryl Crecent, Newport Beach, NSW 2106, Australia.

BAHADORI Iran, b. 20 Apr 1955, Tehran, Iran. Deaf Studies. m. Abbas S Tehrani, 24 July 1975, 1 s, 1 d. Education: BA, Spec Educ. Appointments: Farsi Sign Lang Study and Rsch Off, 1975; Exec of Deaf Studies and Rsch, 1981; Executor, Deaf News, IRIB, 1987. Publications: Collection of Deaf Signs, book, 1989; Executor, Intl Off in Welfare Org of Iran, 1990; Auditory Training of Deaf Children, 1994; Farsi Sign Language (2), 1997; A Guide to Deaf Children's Parents, 1997; Language Training to the Deaf Children, 1998; Farsi Sign Language (3), 1998. Memberships: Iranian Natl Cntr for the Deaf, 1975; Khorasan Deaf Cntr, 1983; Soc of Deaf Family, 1975. Hobbies: Driving; Football; Art. Address: No 3 Siyavash Alley, Sabt St, Tajrish Square, Tehran 19898, Iran.

BAHADUR Raj, b. 21 Aug 1912. Politician. m. Vidyawati Srivastava, 1936, 4 s, 1 d; Education: Maharaja's Coll Jaipur, Agra Coll and St John's Coll, Agra. Appointments: Imprisoned for participation in freedom struggle, 1945 and 1947; Sec Assembly Praja Parishad Party, 1943-48; Gen Sec Matsya Union Congress Cttee, 1948-49; Pres Bharatpur Bar Assn, 1948-51; Elected to Constituent Assembly of India, 1948-50; Sec Congress Party in Parl, 1950-52; Dep Min later Min of State for Comms, 1951-56; Led Indian Deleg to 10th Sess of Intl Civ Aviation Org Caracas; Min of Comms, 1956-57; Min of State for Transp and Comms, 1957-62; Min of State for Transp, 1962-63; Min of Transp, 1963-65; Min of Civ Aviation, 1965; Min of Info and Brdcstng, 1966-67; Advocate Supreme Court of India, 1967; Amb to Nepal, 1968-71, Min of Parl Affairs Shipping and Transp, 1971-73; Min of Comms, 1973-74; Min of Tourism and Civ Aviation, 1973-76; Ldr Congress - S - grp. Honours: Awd'd Tamrapatra, 1974. Memberships: Cntr Advsry Cttee Bharatpur State, 1939-42; Municipal Commn, 1941-42; Resigned from posts in connection with "Quit India" Movement; Rep Assembly, 1943; Union Parl, 1950-67, 1971-77; Rajasthan PCC and All-India Congress Cttee, 1956-82; Rajasthan State Legis Assembly, June 1980-; Upper

House of Raj Sabha. Hobby: Collecting books. Address: 3 Hospital Road, Jaipur, Rajasthan, N-33 Panchshila Park, New Delhi 110017, India.

BAHADUR KC Kaisher, b. 28 Jan 1907, Kathmandu. Diplomat. m. Home Kumari, 1923, 1 s 1 d. Education: St Paul's Miss Sch, St Xavier's Coll Calcutta and Univ Coll Calcutta. Appointments: Translr and Lectr Tri-Chandra Coll, 1930-32; Rsch in MSS inscriptions and sculputre Nepal, 1932-45; Nepalese Res in Tibet, 1946-49; Sec Min of Educ Hlth and Local Self Govt, 1956-61; Deleg to UN, 1956-57; Deleg UNESCO, 1960; Amb to People's Repub of China concurrently to Mongolian People's Repub and Burma, 1961-65; Amb to Repub of Indonesia and Kingdom of Laos, 1962-65; Chmn Nepal Pub Serv Commn, 1966-70; Chf Ed Civ Serv Jrnl of Nepal. Publications: Countries of the World, 1935; Ancient and Modern Nepal, 1953; Judicial Customs of Nepal Part I, 1958, Part II 1965; Eroticism in Nepalese Art, 1960; Introduction to Kathmandu and Patan, 1961; Universal Value of Nepalese Aesthetics Parts I and II, 1961-62; Transl of Kirataruniye Nepal and her Neighbours, 1974; Nepal after the Revolution of 1950, 1975; Memoirs of My Four Years and Three Months in the People's Republic of China and South-East Asia; Transl of Nepalese inscriptions; Ensemble of the Stone Sculpture and Licchavi Inscriptions of Nepal, 1980-85. Honours: Awd'd Italian Order of Merit, 1953; Order of the Gurkhas - 1st Class - of King Mahendra, 1962; Recipient of Coral Casket and Bowl, Govt of People's Repub of China on Nepal-China work, 1974. Hobbie: Researching.

BAHARNA Husain Mohammad al-, b. 5 Dec 1932, Manama. International Legal Advisor. m. 3 s, 2 d. Education: Baghdad Law Coll Iraq, London Univ and Cambridge Univ. Appointments: Legal Advsr Min of For Affairs Kuwait, 1962-64; Legal Advsr and Analyst Arab Gulf Affairs Arabian-Am Oil Co Saudi Arabia, 1965-68; Legal Advsr Dept of For Affairs Bahrain, 1969-70; Legal Advsr to the State and mbr Cncl of State Pres Legal Cttee, 1970-71; Min of State for Legal Affairs, 1971; Chmn Deleg of Bahrain to UN Preparatory Commn for Intl Sea Bed Authy and Intl Tribunal for Law of the Sea, 1983; Mbr Deleg of Bahrain to Sixth - Legal - Cttee UN Gen Assembly, 1986; UN Intl Law Commn Geneva, 1987; Deleg of Bahrain to Summit of Hds of State of Gulf Co-op Cncl, 1991; Fmr legal advsr and deleg num intl confs and summit meetings. Publications: The Legal Status of the Arab Gulf States, 1968; Legal and Constitutional Systems of the Arabian Gulf States - in Arabic - 1975; The Arabian Gulf States - Their Legal and Political Status and their International Problems, 1975; articles in learned jrnls. Honours: Hon Mbr Euro-Arab Forum for Arbitration and Bus Law Paris; Arab Hist Medal - Union of Arab Historians - 1986. Memberships: Mbr Cttee of Experts on Control of Transnational and Intl Criminality and for the estab of the Intl Criminal Court Siracusa Italy, June 1990; Cncl mbr Cntr for Islamic and Middle East Law; SOAS London Univ; Editl Bd Arab Law Quarterly; Brit Inst of Intl and Comp Law; Amn Soc of Intl Law; Intl Law Assn; Egyptian Soc of Intl Law; Assc Mbr Intl Commn of Jurists; English Bar, Lincon's Inn and Bahraini Bar. Hobby: Reading. Address: P O Box 790, Manama, Bahrain.

BAI Bibo, b. 15 May 1955. Linguist. m. Xu Xianming, 1 Jan 1983, 1 s. Education: Studied BA in Engl, Yunnan Normal Univ, 1977-80; Studied MA, Lings, Postgrad Sch of the Chinese Acady of Socl Scis, Beijing, China, 1985-88; Lings, Univ of OR, 1997; Theol, Southern Evangelical Seminary, 1997-98. Appointments: Tchr, Middle Sch, 1973-76; Engl Tchr, Luchun Co, 1980-85; Served w Inst of Nationality Studies of Honghe Prefecture, 1988-92, 1994-96; Yunnun Nationalities Coll, Kunming, China, 1992-94; Tchr, Chinese and Rsch Ethnic Langs, Adam Mickiewcz Univ, 1996-97. Publications: Hani Proverbs, co-auth w Bai Zu'e, 1991; Hani Textbook, co-auth w Bai Zu'e, 1994; Hani-English English-Hani Dictionary, co-compiler w Dr Paul Lewis, 1996; Theses: Namimg System of the Hani, 1989; On the Existential Verbs of the Hani Language, 1991; An Analysis of the Difficult Points When the Hani People Learn Mandarin, 1991; Other bilingual books and papers. Memberships: Chinese Minority Nationality Studies Assn.

Hobbies: Touring; Special interest in different Hani dialects and translating. Address: Insitute of Nationality Studies of Honghe Prefecture, Jianshui County 654300, Yunnan, China.

BAI Chunli, b. 26 Sept 1953, Liaoning Prov, China. Professor. Education: Grad, Dept of Chem, Peking Univ, 1978; MS, 1981, PhD, 1985, Chem, Inst of Chem, Chinese Acady of Scis (CAS); Appointments: Rsch Assoc, in field of scanning probe microscopy, CA Inst Technol, 1985-87; Inst of Chem of CAS; Visng Prof, Inst for Materials Rsch at Tohoku Univ of Japan, 1991-92; Dev var of microscopes in China, study wide var of materials w combination of scanning probe microscopes and other techniques. Publications: 9 books; Sev book chapts (two China Book Awd winners, 1993, 1995, 1997, 1998); Ed-in-Chf, 15 books under title of Doctoral books. Honours: 16 awds and prizes for contbn to sci community. Memberships: VP, CAS; Academician, CAS; Fell, Third World Acady of Scis; VP, All-Cina Yth Fedn; VP, West Returned Schls Assn; Pres, Chinese Chem Soc; Exec Cncl Mbr, Chinese Material Rsch Soc; Chinese Electron Microscopy Soc. Address: Chinese Academy of Sciences, 52 Sanlihe Road, Beijing 100864, China.

BAI Jiefu, b. 1929, Suide Co, Shaanxi Prov. Appointments: Joined CCP, 1948; Dep to 5th NPC, 1983-87; Dep to 6th NPC, 1988-92; Vice-Pres China Assn for Intl Friendship, 1985-; Chmn 6th Beijing CPPCC Municipal Cttee, 1986-; Chmn 7th, 1991-94; Deleg to CCP 13th Congress, 1991; Exec Pres Soc for Study of Anti-Japanese Agression War, 1991-. Address: Beijing Chinese People's Political Consultative Council, 279 Dongsi Beidaji Street, Dongcheng District, Beijing 100007, People's Republic of China.

BAI Jing, b. 9 Oct 1956, Changchun, China. Professor. m. Xian Wu, 14 Dec 1983, 1 d. Education: PhD. Appointments: Tchng Asst, 1981, Rsch Asst, 1982, Rsch Assoc, 1985, Asst Prof, 1987, Assoc Prof, 1988, Prof, 1991. Publications: Modelling and Simulation of Physiological Systems, 1994; Simulation of Circulation System, 1995; Mechanisms of Ultrasonic Imaging, 1998. Honours: Young Sci Awd, 1990; Prog of Sci and Technol Awd, 1996. Membership: Snr Mbr, IEEE, 1993. Hobby: Reading. Address: Department of Electrical Engineering, Tsinghua University, Beijing, China.

BAI Jinian, b. 1926, Shaanxi Prov. Appointments: Joined CCP, 1942; Sec CCP Cttee Shaanxi, 1984-. Memberships: Mbr 12th Cntr Cttee CCP, 1985-87; Mbr Standing and Econ Cttee 7th CPPCC, 1988-92, 8th 1993-. Address: Shaanxi Provincial Chinese Communist Party, Xian, Shaanxi, People's Republic of China.

BAI Qincai, b. 1932, Qutai Co, Shanxi Prov. Appointments: Joined CCP, 1955; Vice-Gov of Shanxi Prov, 1983-93; Gov Shaanxi Prov, 1993-94; Vice Chmn All-China Fedn of Supply and Mktng Co-op; Dep Sec CCP Shaanxi Prov Cttee. Memberships: Mbr Shanxi Standing Commn CCP, 1985-93; Mbr 14th CCP Cntr Cttee, 1992-. Address: c/o Office of Governor, Xi'an City, Shaanxi Provine, People's Republic of China.

BAI Shangwu, b. 1928, Xing Co, Shanxi Prov. Chinese Party Official. Appointments: Joined CCP, 1945; Chmn Sichuan Prov Polit Sci and Law Cttee, 1983-; Polit Commisar Sichuan Prov People's Govt, 1983-88; Vice-Chmn Standing Commn, Sichuan Prov People's Congress, 1988-. Memberships: Mbr Standing Cttee CCP Prov Cttee Sichuan, 1983-; Mbr 8th NPC, 1993-. Address: Sichuan Provincial People's Government, Chengdu, People's Republic of China.

BAI Shixian, b. 26 Jan 1926. Professor of Mechanical Engineering. Education: BE, Northwestern Coll of Engrng, Shansi, China, 1947. Appointments: Lectr, Beijing Inst of Aeronautics, 1952-61; Assoc Prof 1961-83, Prof 1983-, Beijing Polytech Univ. Publications: Advanced Mechanisms, book, 1988; Over 50 pprs in Theory of Machines; Over 20 pprs in jrnls. Honours: May 1st Medal, 1987; Labour's Medal of Beijing, 1987; Sci Progress

Prize, Beijing, 1992. Memberships: Chinese Mech Engrng Soc; Chinese People's Polit Consultative Conf. Hobby: Photography. Address: Beijing Polytechnic University, Beijing 100022, China.

BAI Shuxiang, b. 1939. Ballet Dancer. Education: Beijing Coll of Dancing. Appointments: Prin Dancer Cntr Ballet Co, 1958-; Dir, 1984-90. Performances incl: Swan Lake; Giselle; The Fountain of Bakhchisarai; The Emerald; Sylvia; Red Women Army; Song of Yimeng; Song of Jiaoyang. Honours: First Grade Dancer of the Nat - awd. Memberships: Mbr 5th Natl Cttee CPPCC, 1978-82; Mbr 6th Natl Cttee CPPCC, 1983-87; Mbr 7th Natl Cttee CPPCC, 1988-92; Mbr 8th Natl Cttee CPPCC, 1993-; Perm Mbr China Dancers Assn, now Chmn. Address: Chinese Dancers' Association, Di An Men Dong Daji, Beijing 100009, People's Republic of China.

BAI Yu Hai, b. 25 Apr 1941, Siping, China. Scientific Researcher. m. Zhao Yu Zhen, 31 Oct 1969, 1 s, 1 d. Education: Grad, Dept of Phys, Jilin Univ. Appointments: Inst of Acoustics Academia Sinica, 1965; Inst of Phys, 1971; Inst of Solids Mex Planck, 1980; Hong Kong City Polytechnic, 1990; Inst of Acoustics, 1991. Creative Works: More than 50 articles in profl jrnls. Memberships: Acoustics Soc of China; Phys Soc of China; NY Acady of Sci. Hobbies: Lit; Art; Music. Address: Inst of Acoustics, Academia Sinica, 17 Zhong Guan Cun Rd, Beijing 100080, China.

BAI Yuxing, b. 1 Dec 1938, Anyang City, China. Microelectronics Research Technology. m. Li Duhua, Jan 1970, 1 s, 1 d. Education: Prof, Moscow Energy Univ. Publications: Sev articles in profl jrnls. Honour: Aerospace Progress Awd, 1994. Memberships: HIC Assn of China; Shaanxi Prov Electron Assn. Hobbies: Reading; World Knowledge. Address: Xian Microelectronics Research Institute Aerospace Corporation of Chna, 8 Taiyi Road, Xian Shaanxi 710054, China.

BAI-ENPEI, b. Sept 1946, Qingjian Co, Shaanxi Province. Acting Governor. Education: Northwest Technol Univ, 1965. Appointments: Joined CCP, 1973; Vice-Sec CPP Ya'nan Prefectural Cttee, 1983; Sec CPP Yan'an Prefectural Cttee, 1985; Alt Mbr 13th CCP Cntr Cttee, 1987; Vice-Sec CPP Inner Mongolia Autonomous Regl Cttee, 1990; Alt Mbr 14th CCP Cntr Cttee, 1992; Vice-Sec CPP Qinghai Provincial Cttee Acting Gov Qinghai Prov, 1997-. Memberships: 15th CCP Cntr Cttee, 1997-. Address: Office of the Governor, Qinghai Provincial Government, Xining City, Qinghai Province, People's Republic of China.

BAILEY Keels Dale, b. 5 Oct 1936, Belvedere, SC, USA. Psychologist. m. Phyllis Bekemeyer, 23 June 1984, 1 s, 3 d. Education: BA, Coll of Wooster; STB, Harvard Univ; ThD, Sch of Theol at Claremont; Ordained Presby Minister-San Fran Presby. Appointments: Chair-8th Annual Intl Conference of the Assn for Imago Relationship Therapy, 1999. Publications: Imago Relationship Therapy As A Spiritual Path. Honours: Serv Recog Awd, Assn for Imago Relationship Therapy, 1998. Memberships: Amn Psych Assn, California; Assn of Marriage and Family Therapists; Inst for Imago Relationship Therapy; Assn for Imago Relationship Therapy-Pres-SF Chapt, 1994-99. Hobbies: Travel; Communication Remodeling. Address: 1250 Washington Avenue, Albany, CA 94706, USA.

BAILEY Peter Hamilton, b. 3 Sept 1927, Melbourne, Aust. Adjunct Professor. m. Leila May Giles, 10 Dec 1955, 3 s, 1 d. Education: LLM, Melbourne Univ, 1950; MA, Corpus Christi Coll, Oxford, Eng, 1953; Bar, High Crt of Aust, 1979; Bar, Solicitor, ACT Supreme Crt, 1980. Appointments: C'wlth Treas, 1946; Sec, Pub Accts Cttee, 1955-57; Asst Sec, Loans and Investment Br, Treas, 1962-65; 1st Asst Sec, PM's Dept, 1965-68; Dept of Cabinet Off, 1968-71; Dpty Sec, Dept of PM and Cabinet, 1972-76; Mbr, Roy Cmmn on Austl Govt Admin, 1974-76; Ldr, Task Force, Co-ord in Welfare and Hlth, 1976-78; Spec Advsr on Human Rights, Atty Gen and Dept, 1978-81; Dpty Chmn, Human Rights Cmmn, 1981-86; Visng Fell, 1987-98, Adjunct Prof, 1991-, Fac of Law,

Austl Natl Univ. Publications: Human Rights: Australia in an International Context, 1990; Bringing Human Rights to Life, 1993; Human Rights, The Laws of Australia, title ed, 1996; Civil and Political Rights, Halsbury's Laws of Australia, 1998. Contbrns to sev profl jrnls. Honours: Rhodes Schl for Vic, 1950; OBE, 1972; AM, 1998. Memberships: Inst of Pub Admin Austl; Econ Soc of Aust; Austl Inst of Intl Affairs; Intl Cmmn of Jurists (Austl Chapt), Pres, Canberra BA. Hobbies: Music; Sailing; Motorcycling; Squash; Gardening. Address 12/14 Currie Crescent, Kingston, ACT 2604, Australia.

BAILLIE Peter William, b. 31 Oct 1949, Hobart, Tasmania. Geologist. m. Denise, 22 Feb 1975, 1 s, 1 d. Education: BS, Tasmania; MSc (Hons), Dip Geoscience, Macquarie Univ. Appointments: Tasmania Dept Mines, 1970-93; WA Dept Minerals & Energy, 1993-97; Nopec Intl Pty Ltd, 1997-. Honours: Hon Rsch Assoc, Univ of Tasmania, 1993; Hon Rsch Fell, UWA, 1994-; Dpty Mbr, MERIWA, 1996-. Memberships: Geol Soc of Aust, Sec, 1990-92; Convenor 10th Aust Geol Convention, 1990. Hobbies: Photography; The arts. Address: 21 Allerton Way, Booragoon, WA 6154, USA.

BAIN James Keith, b. 1 Oct 1929, Sydney, Aust. Company Director; Farmer. m. Janette Isabelle Grace King, 11 Feb 1958, 1 s, 1 d. Education: Fell, Certified Practicing Accts; Fell, Securities Inst of Aust; Fell, Austl Inst of Mngmt; Fell, Inst of Dirs in Aust. Appointments: Joined L P Bain & Sons (now Deutsche Bank Ltd), 1947, Jnr Ptnr, 1955, Chmn of Ptnr, 1972-86; Cttee Mbr, Sydney Stock Exch, 1976-86, Chmn, 1983-87; Chmn, Austl Assoc Stock Exchs, 1984, 1986 (now Austl Stock Exch); Chmn, Natwest Aust Bank Ltd, 1985-91; Chmn, Centenary Inst of Cancer Rsch and Cell Biol, 1990-93; Dir, State Lib Fndn, 1989-96, (Chmn, 1989-95); Pres, Lib Cncl of NSW, 1990-96; Chmn, Intl Air Servs Cmmn, 1994-99; Chmn Cncl, Natl Lib of Aust, 1998-. Publications: Auth of num articles; Num speeches on de-regulation of Stockbroking Ind; Prime mover in intro of SEATS computerised tradng syst, 1987. Honour: AM, 1986. Memberships include: State Lib of NSW Fndn, 1989-96; Bd Mbr, Natl Portrait Gall Bd, 1998-; Patron, Sydney Inst; Natl Cncl Mbr, Austl Opera. Listed in: Who's Who in Australia; Who's Who in Business in Australia. Hobbies: Golf; Bridge. Address: Apartment 3, 124 Wolseley Road, Point Piper, NSW 2027, Australia.

BAINES Peter George, b. 23 May 1941, Melbourne, Australia. Scientist. m. Gail Sylvia Coote, 23 July 1969, div 1989, 2 s. Education: BA (Hons), 1964, BSc, 1965, Melbourne Univ; PhD, Cambridge Univ, 1969. Appointments: Experimental Offr, Aero Rsch Labs, Melbourne, 1964-66; Rsch Assoc, MIT, MA, USA, 1969-71; Queens Fell in Marine Sci, 1971-73; Rsch Scientist, CSIRO Atmos Rsch, Melboure, 1973-77; Prin Rsch Scientist, 1977-88; Snr Prin Rsch Scientist, 1988-98; Chf Rsch Scientist, 1998-. Publications: Topographic Effects in Stratified Flows, 1995; 62 pprs in refereed jrnls. Honours: Queen's Fellshp in Marine Sci, C'wlth of Aust, 1971-73; Priestley Medal, Aust Met Oceanog Soc, 1997. Memberships: Fell, Roy Met Soc; Amn Geophys Union; Roy Soc Vic; Aust Oceanog Soc, Pres, 1988-90. Hobbies: Tennis; History; Music; The arts. Address: CSIRO Atmospheric Research, Aspendale 3195, Australia.

BAIZAGI Bhanudas, b. 1 June 1969, India. Service. m. Nanda, 8 May 1990, 1 s, 1 d. Education: BA, 1995. Publications: Sev articles in profl jrnls. Membership: Mehousashtsa Sanskreetic Kala Abhiyan, Nasik, 1997. Hobbies: Music; Drama. Address: Bharud Smarat, Kolelwasti, Yesjaon, Ta Khopeergaan District A Nagar, India.

BAIS Ramesh, b. 2 Aug 1948, Raipur, Madhya Pradesh, India. Member of Parliament. m. Rambai Bais, 23 May 1969, 1 s, 2 d. Education: BSE, Bhopal, Madhya Pradesh. Appointments: Cncly, Munic Copt, Raipur, 1978-83; Mbr, Madhya Pradesh Legislative Assembly, 1980-85; Mbr, Estimates cttee, Madhya Pradesh Legislative Assembly, 1980-82, Lib Cttee, 1982-85; Pradesh Mantri, Bharatiya Janata Pty, Madhya Pradesh,

1982-88; Elected, 9th Lok Sabha, 1989; VP, BJP, Madhya Pradesh, 1989-90, 1994-96; Mbr, Pub Accounts Cttee, Mbr Consultative Cttee, Min of Steel and Mines, 1990-91; Mbr, Natl Exec, BJP, 1993-, Mbr, Exec Cttee, 1994-; Re-elected 11th Lok Sabha, 1996; Mbr, Cttee on Agric, Cttee on Petitions, Consultative Cttee, Min of Ind, 1996-97; Re-elected, 12th Lok Sabha, 1998; Union Min of State, Steel and Mines, 1998-. Membership: Chmn, Madhya Pradesh Seeds and Farm Dev Corp, 1992-93. Hobbies: Woodcraft; Painting; Interior decorating; Gardening. Address: Ravi Nagar, Raipur 492001, Madhya Pradesh, India.

BAJAMAL Abdulkader Abdulrahman, b. 18 Feb 1946, Seiyun-Hadhramout. Minister of Planning. m. 1976, 2 s, 2 d. Education: Cairo Univ. Appointments: First Dep Min of Plng and Dev People's Dem Repub of Yemen, 1978; Lectr in Econs Aden Univ, 1978-80; Min of Ind, Chmn Bd Oil, Mineral and Electricity Authy, 1980-85; Min of Energy and Minerals, 1985; MP Repub of Yemen - following union of fmr People's Dem Repub of Yemen and fmr Yemen Arab Repub - 1990-91; Chmn Bd Pub Free Zone Authy, 1991-94; Dep PM, 1994-97; Min of Plng and Dev, Oct 1994-. Publications: New Administration Accountancy, 1978; The Patterns of Development in the Arab Countries, 1981 - jtly; Policies and Guidelines for Privatizaton in the Republic of Yemen, 1994. Honours: Awd'd Medal of Yemeni Unity; Medal of Yemeni Revolution; Medal of Yemeni Indep. Hobbies: Sports; Table tennis. Address: Ministry of Planning and Development, P O Box 175, Sana'a, Republic of Yemen.

BAJRACHARYA Subarna K, b. 17 Dec 1944, Nepal. Chief Librarian. Education: Master in Libnshp, West MI Univ, MI, USA, 1981. Lib Cnslt (pt-time), Water and Energy Commn HMG/N, Kathmandu, 1982-84; Profl Staff Mbr, Intl Cntr for Integrated Mtn Dev (ICIMOD), Kathmandu, Nepal, 1984-86; Instl Strengthening for Environmental Mngmt Proj, Natl Plng Commn, IUCN/Nepal Kathmandu, 1990-91; Chf Libn, APROSC, Natl Socio-Econ Documentation Cntr (previously Natl Agricl Documentation Cntr, 1977-88), 1991-. Publications: Inter Library Loan Cooperation Among Agricultural Libraries in Nepal, 1983; Information Dissemination in Nepal with Special Reference from Agricultural Sciences and Technology, 1989; Status of Information Network in Nepal Volun Ppr, presented in Expert Grp Mtng of Hindu Kush - Himalayan Reg, Beijing, China, 1992; Exploitation and Utilization of Scientific and Technical Information Country Paper, presented in ISTIC, Beijing, China, 1993; Lifetime Dpty Gov, ABIRA, 1997. Memberships: Life Mbr, Nepal Lib Assn, 1981; IAALD, 1982-89; Life Mbr, Nepal Vipasana Cntr, 1988; Life Mbr, Baudha Bridhashram, 1994; Life Mbr, CDS/ISIS Soc, Nepal, 1994; Life Mbr, ABIRA, 1997. Address: Ward No 1, Kupondel, Lalitpur District, Bagmati Zone, Nepal.

BAKAR Baki Bin, b. 27 Dec 1952, Kuching, Malaysia. Lecturer. m. Maria, 10 Apr 1977, 2 s, 2 d. Education: BAgric.Sc; MSc; PhD; CBiol; MBiol. Appointments: Snr Rsch Offr, Mardi, 1976-93; Prof, Univ of Malaya, 1993-. Publications: 70 articles in profl jrnls. Memberships: WSSA; Brit Ecol Soc; IOB. Hobbies: Worlds History; Classical Music. Address: Institute of Biological Sciences, University of Malaya, 50603 Kuala Lumpur, Malaysia.

BAKER Alan Anthony, b. 19 Aug 1938, London, UK. Scientist. m. Sandy, 26 Mar 1958, 2 s. Education: PhD, Nottingham Univ, 1967. Appointments: Rsch Asst, Brit Iron and Steel Rsch Assn, UK; Rsch Scientist, Rolls Royce Rsch Ldr Def Sci and Technol Rsch Orgn, Aust. Publications: Composite Materials for Aircraft Structures; Bonded Repair of Aircraft Structures. Honours: Engrng Excellence Awd, 1979; Mins Awd for Def Sci, 1990. Memberships: Fell, Inst of Engrs, Aust; Fell, Acady of Technological Sci and Engrng. Hobbies: Tennis; Antique clocks. Address: 8 Gould Street, Frankston, Vic 3199, Australia.

BAKER Arthur Barrington (Barry), b. 24 June 1939, Brisbane, Australia. Anaesthetist. m. Jane, 2 s, 1 d. Education: MBBS (Qld); DPhil (Oxon); FANZCA; FRCA; FFICANZCA. Appointments: Rdr in Anaesthesia (Queensland Univ), 1972-75; Fndn Prof of Anaesthesia and of Intensive Care, Otage Univ, 1975-92; Nuffield Prof of Anaesthetics, Sydney Univ, 1992-. Publications: Physiology of Artificial Ventilation. Honours: Crt of Hon, RACS, 1992; Orton Medal, ANZCA, 1993; Joseph Professorship, ANZCA, 1997. Memberships: Dean, Fac of Anaesthetics, Roy Australasian Coll of Surgs, 1987-90. Hobbies: Chess; Mountaineering; Reading. Address: 45 Llewellyn Street, Rhodes, NSW, Australia 2138.

BAKER Dorothy Maskell, b. 9 Sept 1914, Mundoona, Aust. Artist; Writer. m. John Y Baker, Sept 1936, 2 s. Education: Melbourne Tech Coll; George Bell Art Sch. Appointments: Spec Guest, Cttee of Inaugural Arts Fest, China, 1988. Publications: Contbrns to Weekly Times; Newspprs; Illus articles in Art. Honours: Fell, Vic Artists Soc; Highest Awd for Serv to Art, VAS, 1983; Hon Life Mbr, VAS, Malvern Artists Soc, Sesame Artists Soc; Med of Hon, Lifelong Achievement, ABI; Med of Hon, Accademia Eur, Italy. Memberships: Pres, Vic Artists Soc, 1980-83, Dpty Pres, 1979-80; Malvern Artists Soc; Realists Guild of Aust; Vic Gall Soc; Womens Art Gall. Listed in: World Who's Who of Women; Who's Who in the World; Who's Who in Australia; Dictionary of International Biography. Hobbies: Travel; Sketching; Painting. Address: 90 Pakington Street, Kew, Vic 3101, Australia.

BAKER Robert John, b. 29 July 1939, Armidale, NSW, Aust. University Lecturer. m. (1) Vicki Patricia Stuart, 5 Aug 1963, dec, 5 s, 1 d, (2) Barbara Ann Trehy, 16 Aug 1986, 2 step children. Education: BA Hons, 1960, MA Hons, 1963, Univ New Eng; MA Hons, Edinburgh Univ, Scotland, 1965. Appointments: Tutor, Classics, 1963, Lectr, Snr Lectr, Classics, Ancient Hist, 1971-90, Assoc Prof, Classics, Ancient Hist, 1991-, Univ New Eng, Armidale, NSW; Lectr, Snr Lectr, Classics, Univ Tas, 1965-71. Publications: Propertius I: Translated With an Introduction, Literary Commentary and Latin Text, 1990; Num articles in profl jrnls. Honours: Austl C'wlth Postgrad Rsch Awd, 1961-63; Brit C'wlth Schlshp, UK, 1963-65; C'wlth Stdy Awd, Inst Classical Stdys, London, 1974-75; Visng Rsch Fell, Dept Hum, Glasgow Univ, Scotland, 1974. Memberships: Austl Soc Classical Stdies, Exec Cttee Mbr, 1975-, Jnt Ed, jrnl Antichthon, 1990-92. Hobbies: Gardening; Camping; Listening to classical music; Reading. Address: School of Classics History and Religion, University of New England, Armidale, NSW 2351, Australia.

BAKHT Sikander, b. 24 Aug 1918, Delhi. Politician. m. Raj Sharma, 1952, 2 s. Education: Delhi Univ. Appointments: Detained for 18 months during emergency, 1975-76; Min of Works Hsg Supply and Rehab, 1977-79; Gen Sec Janata Party, 1977; Gen Sec Bharatiya Janata Party - BJP - 1980-82; Vice-Pres, 1982-93; Min for Urban Affairs Employment and External Affairs, May 1996; Min of Ind, 1998-; Ldr of Opposition in Rajya Sabha, 1992-96, 1996-98. Memberships: Mbr of Indian Natl Congress until 1969; Mbr All-India Congress Cttee - Org; Mbr Working Cttee, 1969-77; Mbr Delhi Metrop Cncl for 10 yrs; Mbr for Chandni Chowk, Lok Sabha, 1977; Mbr Janata Party, 1977; Mbr for Madhya Pradesh Rajya Sabha, 1990-96, Apr 1996-. Hobbies: Sports; Music. Address: 25 Tughlak Road, New Delhi 110011, India.

BAKIR Sherif, b. Cairo, Egypt. Consultant Cardiologist. m. 1981, 2 s, 1 d. Education: MD, Cardiology, Ain Shams Univ, 1992; MSc, Cardiology, Ain Shams Univ Egypt; MBBCh, Cairo Univ, 1980. Appointments: Heat of Cardiology Dept, Kalba & Khafakkan Hosps; Chmn, Sci Cttee, Kalbu Hosp. Publication: Spotlight on Congestive Heart Failure, 1989. Honour: Dr Ali Essu Awd for Master's deg, 1st place. Memberships: ACC; Egyptian Dr Syndicate; Egypt Heart Soc. Hobbies: Reading; Swimming. Address: Kalba, Sharjah, UAE, PO 11195, United Arab Emirates.

BAKLIEN Asbjorn, b. 6 June 1929. Emeritus Profesor of Chemistry. m. Eva Marianne Hanich, 3 Nov 1952, 3 s. Education: Cand Mag; Cand Real, Oslo; PhD. Appointments: Rsch Mngr, ICI Aust, 1973-86; Prof, Monash Univ, 1986-94. Honour: Rsch Medal, Roy Soc of Vic, 1971. Memberships: Fell, Austl Acady of Technological Scis and Engrng. Hobby: Golf. Address: 28 Scarlet Ash Drive, Lower Templestowe, Vic 3107, Australia.

BAKUS Gerald Joseph, b. 5 Dec 1934, Thorp, Wisconsin, USA. Biologist. m. Grace E, 26 Dec 1953, 1 s, 1 d. Education: PhD, Zoology, Univ WA, Seattle. Appointments: Asst Prof, 1962-67, Assoc Prof, 1967-85, Prof, 1985-, Univ S CA. Publications: The Spanish Guitar, 1977; Quantitative Ecology and Marine Biology, 1990; Coral Reef Ecosystems, 1993. CD-Roms: Sponges, 1997; Natural History of Santa Catalina Island, 1998; Statistics and Modeling for Beginners, 1998; Natural History of Southern California, 1999. Honours: Fulbright Fell, Lectrshp, Chile, 1987, Disting Lectrshp, Thailand, Malaysia, Philippines, Indonesia, 1996. Memberships: Fell, Great Barrier Reef Cttee of Aust, 1976, Amn Assn for the Adv of Sci, 1981; AAAS; Intl Soc of Chem Ecol; Pacific Sci Assn; S CA Acady of Scis. Hobbies: Hiking; Multimedia Development. Address: Department of Biological Sciences, University of Southern California, Los Angeles, CA 90089-0371, USA.

BALAKRISHNAN Uckath Variyath, b. 3 May 1953, Kerala, India. Researcher. m. Sudha, 18 Jan 1989, 1 s. Education: MSc, PhD. Appointments: Rsch Asst, Tata Inst, Tifr, Bombay; Rsch Assoc; Lectr, Tutor, Open Univ, Singapore, Inst of Mngmnt. Creative Works: 18 publs, On the Sum of Divisor Functions; Asymptotic Estimates for a Class of Summatory Functions; Articles to profl jrnls. Honours: Endowment gold medal, 1976; Grant, Swiss Natl Rsch Fund, 1994, 1996. Memberships: Sch of Maths, Tata Inst, 1976-93. Hobbies: Maths; Reading; Thinking; Yoga; Music. Address: 19 Jalan Gembira, Singapore 369125, Singapore.

BALASUBRAMANIAN Mayuram S, b. 13 Dec 1959, New Delhi, India. Chemical Engineer. m. Vidya, 13 July 1983, 1 s, 1 d. Education: BTech, Chem Engrng, Indian Inst of Technol, New Delhi. Appointments: Mngmt Trainee, 1981-82, Jnr Engr, 1982-83, Asst Engr, 1983-86, Snr Engr, 1986-90, Dpty Mngr, 1990-, Mngr, 1990-, Process Design & Devel Divsn, Engrs India Ltd, New Delhi. Publications: Sev articles in profl jrnls. Honours: Technol Prize, Devel. Memberships: Indian Inst of Chem Engrs. Hobbies: Reading; Music; Travel. Address: D-77 City Apts, Plot 21, Vasundhara Enclave, New Delhi, India.

BALASURIYA Stanislaus Tissa, b. 29 Aug 1924, Kahatagasdigiliya. Cleric. Education: Univ of Ceylon; Gregorian Univ Rome; Oxford Univ; Maris Stella Coll Negombo; St Patrick's Coll Jaffna; St Joseph's Coll Colombo. Appointments: Helped fnd Aquinas Univ with Fr Peter Pillai Jan, 1954; Rector, 1964-71; Fndr Cntr for Soc and Relig Colombo, Aug 1971; Dir, 1971-; Citizens Cttee for Natl Harmony in Sri Lanka, 1977-91; Vis Prof of Faith and Socl Justice Fac of Theol Univ of Ottawa, 1993-94; Ed Logos, Quest, Voices of the Third World, Social Justice, Sadharanaya. Publications: Jesus Christ and Human Liberation; Eucharist and Human Liberation; Catastrophe July '83; Planetary Theology; Mary and Human Liberation; Liberation of the Affluent; Humanization Europe; Indicators of Social Justice; Third World Theology of Religious Life; Right Relationships; Re-rooting of Christian Theology, 1991; Doing Marian Theology in Sri Lanka. Honours: Khan Memorial Gold Medal for Econs. Hobbies: Writing; Organic farming. Address: Centre for Society and Religion, 281 Deans Road, Colombo 10, Sri Lanka.

BALDWIN Peter, b. 12 Apr 1951. Politician. Education: Univ of Sydney Macquarie Univ. Appointments: Fmr Engr and computer progr; Min for Higher Educ and Employment Servs and Min Asstng Treas, 1990-93; Min for Socl Security, 1993-96; Shadow Min for Fin, 1997-. Memberships: Mbr NSW State Parl - Upper House - 1976-82; Austl Labor Party Mbr for Sydney HoR, 1983-; Mbr Parly Cttee on For Affairs Def and Trade, 1987-90; HoR Standing Cttee on Ind Sci and Technol, 1987-90. Address: Level 3, 10 Mallet Street, Camperdown, NSW 2050, Australia.

BALE William Christopher, b. 7 May 1941, Hobart, Tas, Aust. Legal Practitioner. m. Jillian, 29 Aug 1964, 2 s, 1 d. Education: LLB Hons, Univ of Tas, 1964. Appointments: Ptnr, Piggott, Wood and Barker, Bars and Sols, 1967-86; Sol-Gen, Tas, 1986-; Crown Sol, Tas, 1988-90, 1996-. Honours: Queens Cncl, 1986; Memberships: Rotary Intl; Tas Law Soc; Tas and Austl Bar Assn, Hobbies: Lawn Bowles; Yachting; Photography; Gardening. Address: Level 8, Executive Bldg, 15 Murray St, Hobart, Tas 7005, Australia.

BALES Peter, b. 8 May 1953, Sydney, Aust. Music and Management Consultant. Education: Dip, Mngmt Ldrshp Ctf IV. Appointments: Mngr, Marvel Records, 1970-80; CEO, Makeshift Music, 1980-. Publications: Music and book products from Makeshift Music. Memberships: Austl Record Ind Assn (ARIA); AIR. Hobby: Music. Address: 13 Nowra Street, Marayong, NSW 2148, Australia.

BALKS Megan Ruby, b. 18 Sept 1960. Lecturer in Earth Sciences. m. Errol Mitchel Balks, 16 Dec 1978, 1 s. Education: BSc Hons I, Massey Univ, NZ; DPhil, Waikato Univ, NZ. Appointments: Soil Sci, DSIR Dunedin, NZ, 1984-88; Asst Lectr, Univ of Waikato, Hamilton, NZ, 1988-90; Lectr, Univ of Waikato, Hamilton, NZ, 1990-. Publications: A range of sci pprs related to soils, effluent irrigation, Antarctic soils and permafrost. Memberships: Cncl Mbr, NZ Soc of Soil Sci, 1992-98; Waikato Conserv Bd, 1996-. Hobbies: Soil Science; Environmental Science; Antarctica; Tramping; Photography. Address: c/o Department of Earth Sciences, University of Waikato, Private Bag 3105, Hamilton, New Zealand.

BALLINGER Charles Edwin, b. 3 June 1935, West Mansfield, Ohio, USA. Education. m. Venita R, 12 June 1982. Education: BA, DePaw Univ; MA, PhD, OH Univ. Appointment: Exec Dir, Natl Assn for Yr-Round Educn, 1980-. Publication: The Year-Round School: Where Learning Never Stops, 1987. Memberships: Phi Delta Kappa; Am Educl Rsch Assn; Assn for Supervision & Curriculum Devel; Natl Assn for Yr-Round Educn. Address: PO Box 711386, San Diego, CA 92171-1386, USA.

BALNAVE Derick, b. 17 June 1941, Lisburn, N Ireland. Academic. m. Maureen, 2 Aug 1968, 1 s, 1 d. Education: BSc, 1963, PhD, 1966, DSc, 1983, Queen's Univ, Belfast, N Ireland. Appointments: Sci Offr, Snr Sci Offr, Prin Sci Offr, Dept of Agric, N Ireland, 1966-77; Lectr, Snr Lectr, Rdr, Queen's Univ, Belfast, 1967-77; Snr Lectr, Assoc Prof, Rsch Dir, Poultry Rsch Fndn, Univ Sydney, 1978-; Adj Prof, NC State Univ, USA, 1995-. Publications: Over 135 sci pprs in profl jrnls. Memberships: Fell, Roy Soc of Chem, 1974-; World's Poultry Sci Assn; Poultry Sci Assn; NY Acady of Scis. Hobbies: Sport; Music; Genealogy. Address: Department of Animal Science, University of Sydney, Camden, NSW 2570, Australia.

BALU Venkatraman, b. 6 Dec 1928, Guntur, Andhra Pradesh, India. Artist; Creative Communicator; Senior Government of India Executive; Global Peace Activist since 1982. m. Shakuntala, 3 May 1957, 3 s. Education: BS (Hons); MA; Dip in Eurn Langs. Appointments: Coll Tchr, Tamil Nadu, 1950; Snr Sci Offr (Tech), Cncl of Sci and Indl Rsch, New Delhi, 1951-64; Dir and Hd of Mktng and Promotion, Coffee Bd, Min of Com, 1964-86; Indian Corresp, F O Licht & Co, Germany; Currently on his One Man Global Peace Mission through Art. Publications: Day Dreams; Glory of Puttaparthi; Divine Glory; Shristi - The Fine Art of Balu: Shanti - Peace Collages of V Balu; Stories for children; Peace + Children = Peaceful Children. Honours: Key of the Cty, OJAI, CA; Rajyothsava Awd (highest awd, Govt of Karnataka) for excellence in art, 1990-; Bronze memento, Pres, Exec Cncl of UNESCO (for outstndng contbn to promotion of peace), 1992; Silver Memento, Johannestifts in Berlin '92; Medallion of the Cty by Mayor of Dilbeek, Belgium, 1993; Ugadi Puraskhar, 1995; Awd'd Snr Fellshp (as outstndng artist) by Indian Govt. Membership: Chmn, Pub Rels Soc of India. Address: Gitalaya, No 1, South Cross Road, Basavangudi, Bangalore 56004, South India.

BAMBRICK Susan Caroline, b. 20 Oct 1941, Brisbane, Australia. Economist. m. Hugh, 24 Apr 1965, 2 s, 1 d. Education: BEcon, hons, Univ Qld; PhD, Austl Natl Univ, 1970. Appointments: Dean of Students, Master, Univ House, Austl Natl Univ; Dir, Univ New England Coffs Harbour Cntr, 1991-92; PVC, LaTrobe Univ, 1993-. Publication: Ed, Cambridge Encyclopedia of Aust, 1994. Honour: OBE, 1983. Hobby: Music. Address: 332 Antill Street, Hackett, ACT 2602, Australia.

BANAGAR Rudrappa, b. Koppal. Businessman. Education: BA. Appointment: Kannda Sahitya Sammelana. Publications: Poems. Honour: Cert for Poems, 1996. Hobby: Writing poetry. Address: Mahalakshimi Electricals, Nr Bus Stand, Koppal 583231, Karnataka, India.

BANASHANKARAIAH C S, b. 14 May 1944, Chikkanayakanahalli. Teacher. m. Sarojamma K R, 6 Apr 1975, 2 d. Education: Rastra Bhasha Praveen, 1970; BA, 1971; TCH, 1973; MA, 1974; BEd, 1976. Appointments: Govt Instns, 1964-76; Natl hs Basavanagvd, Bangalore, 1976-. Creative Works: Kannada Grammar and Composition; Kannada Text Books for Vi Std to X Std; More than 20 Progs; Thesis; Articles; Poems. Honours: Best Tchr Awd, 1996; Best Tchr Awd, 1998; Shikshana Ratna Title. Memberships: Gandhi Peace Fndn; Kannada Sahitya Parishat. Hobbies: Composing poems; Research; Cricket. Address: Kannada Pandit, National High School, Basavanagudi, Bangalore 4, Karnataka State 560004, India.

BANDAR IBN SULTAN IBN ABDULAZIZ AL-SAUD, b. 2 Mar 1949, Taif. Diplomat. m. HRH Princess Haifa bint Faisal ibn Abdulaziz al-Saud, 2 s, 3 d. Educaton: RAF Coll Cranwell USAF; Advd Prog and Johns Hopkins Univ. Appointments: Fighter pilot Roy Saudi Air Force, 1969-82; In charge of spec Saudi Arabian liaison miss to USA for pur of AWACS and other def equip, 1981; Def and Mil Att Saudi Arabian Mil Miss to USA, 1982-83; Amb to USA, 1983-. Hobbies: Flying; Racquetball; Reading. Address: Royal Embassy of Saudi Arabia, 601 New Hampshire Avenue, NW, Washington, DC 20037, USA.

BANDARANAIKE Sirimavo Ratwatte Dias, b. 17 Apr 1916, Ratnapura, Sri Lanka. Politician. m. S W R D Bandaranaike, 1940, 1 s, 2 d. Appointments: Pres, Sri Lanka Freedom Party, 1960-; Prime Min, Min of Def and Internal Affairs, 1960-65; Mbr, Senate, -1965; Ldr of Opposition, 1965-70, 1988-; Prime Min, Min of Def and For Affairs, Plng, Econ Affairs and Plan Implementation, 1970-77; Prime Min of Sri Lanka, 1994-. Hobbies: Gardening; Reading; Cooking. Address: Prime Minister's Office, 150 R A de Me, Mawatha, Colombo 3, Sri Lanka.

BANDARANAYAKE Raja Christie, b. 4 Apr 1935, Kandy, Sri Lanka. Doctor. m. Chandrani, 12 Aug 1964, 1 s. 2 d. Education: MBBS, Ceylon; PhD, London; MSEd, So Cal; FRACS, Melbourne. Appointments: Snr Lectr and Hd, Dept Anatomy, Univ Sri Lanka; Assoc Prof and Dir (Acad), Sch of Medl Educ, Univ NSW, Sydney, Aust; Prof and Chmn, Dept Anatomy, Arabian Gulf Univ, Bahrain. Publications: Co-author, Multiple Choice Questions in Basic Surgical Sciences, 1991; Reorientation of Medical Education: Introducing Problem-based Learning, 1992. Honours: ANZAME Fred Katz Memorial Medal, 1991; Fell, Roy Australasian Coll of Surgs, elected, 1991. Memberships: Australasian and NZ Assn for Medl Educ, various posts; Anatomy Cttee, Roy Austalasian Coll of Surgs, Melbourne, various posts; Aust Medl Cncl, Bd of Examiners, 1989-95. Hobbies: History; Snooker; Travel. Address: Dept of Anatomy, Arabian Gulf University, PO Box 22979, Manama, Bahrain.

BANERJI Arun Kumar, b. 14 Aug 1944, Calcutta, India. Teacher. m. S Banerji, May 1974, 1 d. Education: BA, Hons; MA, Polit Sci; PhD, 1972. Appointments: Asst Prof, Polit Sci, Presidency Coll, 1974-78; Rdr, Intl Rels, Jadavpur Univ, 1978-86; Prof, Intl Rels, 1986-, Dean, Fac of Arts, 1998-. Publications: 6 books as auth and contrb ed, over 45 articles in profl jrnls. Honours: State Schlshp, 1967-71; Fulbright-ACLS Grantee, 1983-84; Exchange Vis, Egypt and Israel, 1989, 1998. Memberships: W

Bengal Polit Sci Assn; IDSA, New Delhi; Fulbright Assn. Hobbies: Poetry reading; Music. Address: Sonali, 81A New Santoshpur Main Road, Calcutta 700075, West Bengal, India.

BANERJI Asoka Nath, b. 19 Dec 1917, Banaras. Politician. Education: Patna and Calcutta Univs. Appointments: Servd in army, 1941-46; Joined Indian Admin Serv, 1947; Var posts, 1947-56; Dep Gen Mngr Durgapur Steel Project, 1956-61; Iron and Steel Controller for India, 1961-63; Gen Mngr Rourkela Steel Plant, 1964-67; Dep Chmn Hindustn Steel Ltd, 1967-69; Dir-Gen Bur of Pub Enterprises, 1969-73; Spec Sec Min of Indl Dev, 1973-74; Sec Min of Works and Hsng, 1974-76; Advsr to Gov of Gujarat, Chmn Pub Enterprises Sel Bd, Chmn Bnkg Serv Commn, 1976; Started legal practice in Supreme Court and Delhi High Court, 1977-81; Gov Himachal Pradesh, 1981-83; Gov Karnataka, 1983-88.

BANERJI Shishir Kumar, b. 21 Oct 1913, Uttarpara. Former Administrator and Diplomat. m. Gauri Chatterjee, 2 s, 2 d. Education: Allahabad Univ, New Coll, Oxford, UK. Appointments: Joined ICS, 1937; Dpty Commnr, ICS, 1937-46; Sec, Civ Supplies, Cntrl Prov Govt, 1946-47; 1st Sec, Charge d'Affaires, Tehran, Iran, 1947-49; Dpty Sec, Min of External Affairs, 1949-51; Dpty High Commnr, Lahore, 1951-54; Cnslt-Gen, San Fran, USA, 1954-56; Chmn, UN Visng Miss, Brit and French Togoland, 1955; Envoy to Syria, 1956; Amb, 1957-58; High Commnr, Malaya; Commnr, Singapore, Sarawak, Brunei, N Borneo, 1958-59; Jnt Sec, Min of External Affairs, 1960-61; Chf of Protocol, 1961-64; Chf Inspector, Indian Miss Abroad, 1964; Amb, Fed Repub of Germany, 1964-67; Japan, 1967-70; Sec, Min of External Affairs, 1970-72; Lt-Gov, Goa, Daman and Diu, 1972-77. Publications: From Dependence to Non-alignment; Experiences of an Indian Administrator and Diplomat; Forty Years After Independence; The Change in India. Memberships: Assn of Indian Dipls; Indian Intl Cntr; Indian Natl Trust for Art and Cultural Heritage. Address: 3 Vasant Marg, Vasant Vihar, New Delhi, India.

BANGS John Wesley III, b. 26 Dec 1941, Philadelphia, PA. Law Enforcement Executive. m. Donna L, 1 June 1963, 2 s, 1 d. Education: AA, Summa Cum Laude, E Los Angeles Coll, 1976. Appointments: Los Angeles Police Dept Offr, 1964-70; Sgt, 1970-74; Lt, 1974-84; Los Angeles Intl Airport Police Bur, 1988-97; Acting Chf of Police, 1997-. Publications: Psychological Evaluation of Police Officer Candidates, 1968; co-Auth, NIMH, Narcotics Overview. Honours: CA Commn on Peace Offr Stands Trng: Basic, Inter, Advd, Supervisory, Mngmt. Memberships: CA Narcotics Offr Assn; CA Peace Offr Assn; Intl Assn of Chf of Police; Intl Assn Airport, Seaport Police; Airport Law Enforcement Agcy Network. Hobbies: Shooting; Fishing; Hunting; Youth Activities; Sports. Address: #1 World Way, CA 90045, USA.

BANHARN SILPAARCHA Nai, b. 20 July 1932, Suphan Buri. m. Nang Jamsai, 1 s, 2 d. Education: Bangkok Bus Coll. Appointments: Dep Sec-Gen Chat Thai Party; MP for Suphan Buri, 1976-; Dep Min of Ind, 1976-86; Min of Comms, 1986-88; Min of the Interior, 1988-90. Memberships: Mbr Municipal Assn Suphan Buri, 1974; Subsequently Mbr Natl Legis Assn; Mbr Senate, 1975. Address: c/o Ministry of the Interior, Atsadang Road, Bangkok 10200, Thailand.

BANISTER Judith, b. 10 Sept 1943, Wash DC, USA. Demographer; Educator. m. Dr Kim Woodard, 17 Dec 1966, 1 s, 1 d. Education: BA, Hist, Swarthmore Coll, 1965; PhD, Demography, Stanford Univ, 1978; Postdoct Rsch Fell, E-W Population Inst, Honlulu, 1978-80; Appointments: Statistician-Demographer, US Bur of Census, Wash, 1980-82; Chf China Br Cntr for Intl Rsch, 1982-92; Cntr for Intl Rsch, Wash, 1992-94; Intl Progs Cntr, Wash, 1994-97; Pt-time Prof, Geo Wash Univ, 1981-92; Prof Demography, Socl Scis Div, Hong Kong Univ Sci and Technol, 1997-. Publications: China's Changing Population, 1987; Vietnam Population Dynamics and Prospects, 1993; Co-auth: The Population of North Korea, 1992; Human Dimensions of Asian

Security, 1996; Articles in profl jrnls. Memberships: Population Assn Am; Intl Union for Sci Study of Population; Assn Asian Studies; Natl Cttee on US-China Rels; Asia Soc Hong Kong; Amn Chmbr of Com, Hong Kong; Hong Kong Sociol Assn. Address: Hong Kong University of Science & Technology, Rm 3385 Academic Building, Clear Water Bay, Kowloon, Hong Kong.

BANKA Baldeo Prasad, b. 2 June 1948, Calcutta, India. Director. m. Manju Devi, 11 June 1973, 1 d. Education: LLB; MCom. Appointments: Pt Ispat Indo, Indonesia; Jay Engrng Works Ltd, Calcutta; Sahoo Jain Servs Ltd, Calcutta. Honour: Best Intl Exec Awd, Asean Programma Cnslts, Jakarta, 1996. Memberships: Iron and Steel Soc; Bur of Intl Recycling. Hobbies: New Developments; Science. Address: Pt Ispat Indo, Sepanjang Sidoarjo, PO Box 1083, Surabaya, Indonesia.

BANKS John, b 2 Dec 1946. Member of Parliament. m. 3s. Education: Heretaunga Coll; Avondale Coll. Appointments: Coml Prop Developer; Ptnr, Grp of Auckland Licd Restaurants; Chmn, NZ Licd Restaurants, Cabaret Assn; Mbr, Natl Pty, 1972-; Cnclr, Birkenhead Borough; Min of Tour; Min of Sport, Fitness and Leisure; 1993-96; Radio Host, Radio Pacific, 1990-93; Min of local govt, 1993-96; MP, Whangarel. Address: c/o Parliament Bldgs, Wellington, New Zealand.

BANNISTER Barry John, b. 17 May 1947, Brisbane, Qld, Aust. Educational Administrator. m. Susan Mary Russell, 2 Jan 1971, 2 s, 1 dec, 2 d. Education: Tchrs Dip, 1971; BA, 1973; BLitt, 1977; Grad Dip Curric, 1979; MEd, 1980; PhD, 1987. Career: Dir, Cntr for Applied Rsch in Mngmt, North Terretory Univ, 1985-90; Hd and Postgrad Coordr, Hong Kong Polytech Univ Dept Mngmt, 1990-93; Exec Dir, Grad Sch, RMIT Univ, Melbourne, 1993-96; Assoc VP, Lingnan Univ, 1996-99; Mngng Dir, TAFE Intl, W Aust Dept of Trng, 1999-. Publications: Over 60 in intl acad and profl jrnls as well as books and rsch reports; Specialist: Policy Evaluation, Management Education and Training. Honours: C'wlth Acad Schlshps, 1971, 1972; Lions Intl Awd Community Serv, 1980; Excellence in Publ, 1991. Memberships: Advsry Bd, Intl Bus Ethics Inst; Fndng Educ Bd Chmn, Aust Evaluation Soc; Amn Evaluation Soc; Intl Cttee. Hobbies: Golf; Theatre; Classical music. Address: Western Australian Department of Training, Royal Street, Perth, WA, Australia.

BANNON John Charles, b. 7 May 1943. Politician. m. (1) Robyn Layton, 1968, div, 1 d, (2) Angela Bannon, 1982. Education: BA, LLB, Univ Adelaide. Appointments: Indl Advocate, Austl Workers Union, 1969-73; Advsr to C'wlth Min Labour and Immigration, 1973-75; Asst Dir, SA Dept Labour and Ind, 1975-77; Mbr, House Assembly, 1977-93; Min Community, Min Local Govt, Min Recreation and Sport, 1978-79; Ldr Opposition, 1979-82; Premier, Treas, SA, 1982-92; Min, State Dev, 1982-85; Min Arts, 1982-89; Natl Pres, Austl Labour Party, 1988-91; Dir, Austl Brdcstng Corp, 1994-; Mbr, Cncl, Constl Centenary Fndn, 1995-; Dir, Adelaide Symphony Orch, 1997-; Co-Ed, New Federalist, 1998-. Publications: The Crucial Colony, 1994; Articles, monographs on Fed/State rels. Listed in: International Who's Who. Hobbies: Running; Treeplanting; The Arts. Address: PO Box 323, Rundle Mall, Adelaide, SA 5000, Australia.

BANSAL Manu, b. 12 Oct 1974, Udaipur (Rajasthan), India. Dentist. m. Dr Richa, 11 Feb 1999. Education: BDS. Publications: Chf Ed, Coll mag, publd for 2nd time in 40 yrs of prestigious coll of dental surg, Manipal. Honours: 23 prizes for educl exams inclng: GB Jayant Kumar Gold Medal, Best BDS student, 1997; Dr Sunder J Vazirani Mem Gold Medal, Best Outgoing BDS Student, 1997; Also, Prithvi Raval Merit Awd,, Natl Level Conf at Jaipur (Raj), Intl Coll of Dentists (India and Sri Lanka Sect), 1998. Memberships: India Dental Assn (IDA); Fell, All India Gen Educ; Var students cncls at the coll level; Ed-in-Chf of the coll mag; Lions Club Intl 7 var other NGOs. Hobbies: Painting; Helping the needy. Address: 53, Moti Magri Scheme, Udaipur 313001, Rajasthan, India.

BANWELL Martin Gerhardt, b. 24 Nov 1954, Lower Hutt, NZ. Organic Chemist. m. Catherine, 2 s. Education: BSc; BSc (Hons); PhD. Appointments: Lectr, Dept of Chem, Univ of Auckland; Lectr, Snr Lectr, Assoc Prof, Rdr, Univ of Melbourne; Snr Fell, IAS. Honours: Rennie Medal of the Rpy Austl Chem Inst, 1986; Grimwade Pize for Indl Chem, 1992. Memberships: Fell, Roy Austl Chem Inst; Amn Chem Soc; Roy Soc of Chem. Hobbies: Music; Hiking; Skiing; Surfing. Address: 6 Marawa Place, Aranda, ACT 0200, Australia.

BAO Bin, b. 1928, Jilin, China. Business Executive. Education: Shanghai Univ. Appointments: Joined CCP, 1949; Vice Min of Machine Bldng, 1960-82; Gen Mngr, China Natl Automotive Ind Corp, 1993-. Address: China National Automotive Industry Corporation, 12 Fuxing Menwai Street, Beijing 100860, China.

BAO Hui-qiao, b. 27 July 1940, Sishuang, China. Musician. 1 s, 1 d. Education: Master Deg. Appointments: Solo Pianist, Natl Philharmonic Soc of China, 1970; VP, Socl Conservatory of Music. Creative Works: Over 30 CD's, VCD's, Tapes & Disks. Honours: 5th Prize of 2nd Intl George Enescu Comp; 1st Prize, Natl Comp, 1964; 1st Prize, Natl Comp of Chopin, 1965. Membership: Musicians Assn of China. Hobbies: Painting; Writing; Swimming. Address: Guang Xi Man Bei Li 4-1804, Beijing 100028, China.

BARA Mauricio Ricardo, b. 26 Apr 1961, El Salvador. Veterinarian. m. Luz de Maria, 23 Feb 1985, 3 s. Education: DVM, 1982, Post Dip Vet St, 1990; PhD, Animal Health and Prodn, 1998. Appointments: Veterinary Offr, El Salvador, 1983-85; Veterinary Cnslt, Dairy and Pigs, El Salvador, 1985-89; Tutorial Fell, Univ of Qld, Aust, 1992-95; Veterinary Intern, Univ of Qld, 1995-96; Veterinary Registar, Cnslt, Univ of Qld, 1996-. Memberships: Austl Veterinary Assn; Austl Coll of Veterinary Scis; Australasian Pig Sci Assn. Hobbies: Art; Bonsai; Martial Arts (Karate). Address: 6 Karen Street, Camira, Qld 4300, Australia.

BARABAS Janos, b. 13 Mar 1940, Szeged. Diplomat. m. Bacskai Etelka, 21 Nov 1972, 1 s. Education: Moscow State Inst of Intl Rels, 1965; hs of Polit Scis, Hungary, 1982. Appointments: New Delhi, 1968-71; Saigon (Intl Commn for Control and Supvsn, ICCS, 1973-74; Asst Ed, 1st Hungarian-Hindi Dictionary, 1974; Ulan-Bator, DCM, 1975-80; Moscow DCM, 1983-90; Amb, Islamabad, 1996-. Honours: 3 Hungarian orders of merit; 3 for medals for merit. Hobbies: International relations; History of South-Asia. Address: Ministry of Foreign Affairs, Budapest, Hungary.

BARAK Ehud, b. 2 Feb 1942, Israel. Government Minister; Former Army Officer. m. Nava Cohen, 3 d. Education: Hebrew Univ Jerusalem; Stanford Univ CA. Appointments: Enlisted in Israeli Def Force, 1959; Grad Infantry Offrs course, 1962; Commando course France, 1963; Armoured Corps Co Cmdrs course, 1968; Var command roles; Also served in operations branch of Gen Staff; Active serv in Six Day War 1967 and Yom Kippur War 1973; Cmdr Tank Cmdrs course, 1974; Hd Gen Staff Plng Dept, 1982-83; Dir IDF Mil Intell, 1983-86; Cmdr Cntr Command, 1986-87; Dep Chf of Gen Staff Israeli Def Force, 1987-91; Chf of Gen Staff, 1991-94; Min of Interior, 1995; Min of For Affairs, 1995-1996; Chmn Labour Party, 1997-. Memberships: Knesset; Parl Security and For Affairs Cttee, 1996. Hobbies: Playing the piano. Address: Knesset, Jerusalem, Israel.

BARAM Uzi, b. 1937, Jerusalem. Politician. Appointments: Co-fndr Labour Party's Young Guard Sec, 1966-70; Chmn Young Ldrship Dept World Zionist Org, 1972-75; Chmn Labour Party, Jerusalem branch, 1975-81; Sec-Gen Labour Party, Jerusalem branch, 1984-88; Chmn Immigration and Absorption Cttee, 1984-92; Min of Tourism, 1992-96 fmrly of Relig Affairs. Memberships: Knesset, 1977-; For Affairs and Def Cttee, 1984-92. Address: c/o Ministry of Tourism, P O Box 1018, 24 Rehov King George, Jerusalem 91000, Israel.

BARCHHA Sailesh, b. 26 Aug 1962. Investment Banker. m. Alka S Barchha, 2 May 1987, 2 s. Education: BA Hons Bus Studies; Reg'd w Nasad, NY, SFA in Eng. Appointments: Hd of NRI Unit, Merrill Lynch Intl Bank Ltd, resp for Afr, Mid E, India and Eur; Credit Suisse First Boston, Zurich, 1996-97; VP, Credit Agricole Indosuez, resp for Africa, US, UK, Eur and India. Honour: Hon by Asian Age as Most Up-Coming Prominent Banker. Memberships: E W Charity Cttee, Hunger ProjCharity, Young Asians Grp, Local Chmbr of Comm; Invited onto Banking Cttee. Hobbies: Sports; Travel; Classic Cars; Being involved with care of older people. Address: 21 Milburn Close, Bramingham Park, Luton, Bedfordshire LU3 4EH, England.

BARENBOIM Daniel, b. 15 Nov 1942, Buenos Aires, Argentina. Concert Pianist and Conductor. m. (1) Jacqueline du Pre 1967, dec 1987. (2) Elena Bashkirova 1988, 2 s. Education: Santa Cecilia Acady Rome; Studied piano with his father and other musical subjs with Nadia Boulanger, Edwin Fischer and Igor Markevitch; Debut in Buenos Aires at age of seven; Played Bach D Minor Concerto with orch at Salzburg Mozarteum at age of nine; Has played in Eur regularly, 1954-; Yrly tours of USA, 1957-; Has toured Japan, Aust and S Am; Has played with or conducted London Phil, Philharmonia Orch, London Symphy Orch, Royal Phil, Chicago Symphony Orch, NY Phil, Philadelphia Orch, Israel Orch, Vienna Phil, Berlin Phil; Frequently tours with English Chamber Orch and with them recds for EMI - incl complete Mozart Piano Concertos and late Symphonies; Other recdng projs incl complete Beethoven Sonatas and Beethoven Concertos with New Philharmonia Orch conducted by Klempere; Has appeared in series of Master-classes on BBC tv; Presented Fest of Summer Music on South Bank London, 1968, 1969; Ldng role in Brighton Fest, 1967-69; Appears regularly at Edinburgh Fest; Conductor Edinburgh Fest Opera, 1973; Musical Dir Orchestre de Paris, 1975-89; Chicago Symphony Orch, 1991-; Musical and Artistic Dir Deutsche Staatsoper Berlin, 1992-. Publications: A Life In Music, jntly, 1991. Honours: Beethoven Medal, 1958; Paderewski Medal, 1963; Beethoven Soc Medal, 1982; Hon DMus - Manchester, 1997. Address: c/o Daniel Barenboim Secretariat, 29 rue de la Coulouvreniere, 1204 Geneve, Switzerland.

BARKER Alwyn (Bowman) (Sir), b. 5 Aug 1900, Adelaide, SA, Aust. Chartered Engineer; Grazier. m. Isabel Lucas, 17 June 1926, 1 s, dec, 1 d. Education: Univ Adelaide, 1919-1922, 1929-32; BE; BSc. Appointments: Prodn Mngr, Holden's Motor Body Builders, SA, 1925-30; Lectr, Indl Engrng, 1929-63, Mbr, Fac Engrng, 1937-67, Univ Adelaide; Wrks Mngr, 1931-40, Mngng Dir, 1952-67, Chmn, 1967-80, Kelvinator Aust Ltd, SA; Gen Mngr, Richards Inds Ltd, fmrly Chrysler Aust Ltd, now Mitsubishi Motors Aust Ltd, SA, 1940-52; Fedl Pres, 1952-53, 1959-61, Pres, Adelaide Division, 1952-53, Austl Inst Mngmt; Chmn, Municipal Tramways Trust, SA, 1953-68; Dir, 11 pub cos; Mbr, Mfng Inds Advsry Cncl, 1958-72; Mbr, Advsry Cttee Rsch and Dev, 1967-72; Pres, Instn Prodn Engrs, Aust, 1970-72. Honours: Companion, Order St Michael and St George, 1961; Kt, 1969; Fell, Inst Engrs Aust; CEng; Fell, Instn Elecl Engrs; Fell, Inst Engrs Aust; FIAM; Hon FAIM. Listed in: Who's Who in Australia; Debrett's; The International Year Book; Others. Address: 51 Hackney Road, Hackney, SA 5069, Australia.

BARKER James Stuart Flinton, b. 6 July 1931. Emeritus Professor. m. Maureen Elizabeth Ferguson, 30 Apr 1955, 2 s, 2 d. Education: BAgrSc, Hons I, Univ of Qld, 1955; PhD, Univ of Sydney, 1962. Appointments: Prof of Animal Sci and Hd of Dept, UNE, 1979-93; FAO/UNEP Expert Panel on Animal Genetic Resources, 1983-90; Visng Prof, Univ of CA, Davis, 1991; ARC Snr Rsch Fell, 1993-98. Publications: 150 refereed jrnls and book chapts, 6 books joint ed, 79 conf proceedings and non-refereed jrnls. Honours: Fell, Austl Acady of Technological Sci and Engrng, 1983; Fell, Assn for the Advmnt of Animal Breeding and Genetics, 1997; Helen Newton Turner Medal, 1998. Memberships: Austl Assn of Animal Breeding and Genetics, Fndn Pres 1979-81; Austl Soc of Animal Prod; Genetics Soc of Aust, Pres 1981-82;

Soc for Advancment of Breeding Researches in Asia and Oceania, Chmn, Farm Animals Sect 1976-, VP 1989-93, Pres 1993-97. Hobbies: Reading; Bushwalking. Address: Department of Animal Science, University of New England, Armidale, NSW 2351, Australia.

BARKL Michael Laurence Gordon, b. 9 Aug 1958, Sydney, Australia. Musician. m. Sharyn, 25 Jan 1986, 1 d. Education: BMus, NSW Cons; MMus, Hons, UNE; PhD, Deakin; Grad DipEd, SCAE, FTCL. Appointments: Hd Tchr, Music, Illawarra Inst of Technol, 1987-. Publications: Compositions: Voce di Testa for Orchestra, 1981; Ballade for 6 instruments, 1984; The Laird of Drumblair for 7 instruments, 1987; Red for recorder, 1996. Honour: Intl Valentino Bucchi Composition Competition, 1981. Memberships: Writer Full Mbr, Australasian Performing Right Assn; Austl Coll of Educ, 1997-. Hobby: Visual art. Address: Illawarra Institute of Technology Goulburn College, View Street, Goulburn, NSW 2580, Australia.

BARLOW George Edgerton, b. 22 Nov 1924, Melbourne, Aust. Retired Scientist m. Helen June Heidenreich, 2 Aug 1952, 2 s, 1 d. Education: BSc, Phys, 1944; MSc, Phys, 1947, Melbourne Univ. Appointments: Roy Aircraft Est, Farnborough, Eng, 1948-50; Sect Ldr, 1950-57, Prin Rsch Sci, 1960-65, Weapons Res Est, Aust; Austl Emb, Wash DC, USA, 1957-60; Dpty Chf Def Sci, Austl Dept of Def, 1980-87. Publications: Var tech pprs on computers and data processing. Honour: AM, 1987. Membership: MAIP. Hobbies: Tennis; Golf; Skiing; Collecting vintage jazz recordings. Address: 11 Whitham Place, Pearce, ACT 2607, Australia.

BARMAN Bhaskar Roy, b. 19 Feb 1950, Comilla, Badurtala, Bangladesh. Teacher (Grade I). m. Shyamali, 19 Nov 1985, 1 s. Education: BA (Hons) Engl, MBB Coll (then affiliated to Calcutta Univ); MA, Engl, Calcutta Univ; BEd, Tripura Univ. Appointment: Apptd tchr at a Govt Higher Secnd Sch. Publications: Modern Short Stories: The Trap & Other Stories; Melange: An Anthology of Short Stories Translated into English from Bengali; Folktales of Tripura; Bouquet: an anthology of short stories translated into English from Bengali; The Rhymester, a novel translated into English from Bengali; Engl novel: A Gateway to Heaven (in prog). Honours include: Man-of-Yr 1997 Awds, ABI; 20th Century Awd for Achievement in lit, IBC; UWA Life-Time Achievement Awd, Utd Writers Assn, Chennai, India. Memberships: Writers Forum, Ranchi, Chennai, India; Utd Writers Assn, Chennai, India; Rsch Bd of Advsrs, ABI Inc; Tripura Repr of Poets Fndn, Calcutta, W Bengal, India. Hobbies: Directing plays; The supernatural and preternatural. Address: South Bank of Girls Bodhjung Dighi, Itakhola Road, Banamalipur, Agartala 799 001, West Tripura, India.

BARNALA Surjit Singh, b. 21 Oct 1925, Ateli, Gurgaon Dist - now in Haryana. Politician; Lawyer. m. Surjit Kaur 1954, 3 s, 1 d. Education: Lucknow Univ. Appointments: Shiromani Akali Dal MP for Barnala, 1967-77; Educ Min of Punjab, 1969-71; MP from Sangrur, 1977; Union Agric Irrigation and Food Min in Janata Govt, 1977-80; Elected Pres Shiromani Akali Dal, 1985; Chf Min of Punjab, 1985-87; Gov Tamil Nadu, 1990. Hobbies: Painting; Reading; Ecology. Address: Barnala Sangrur Dist, Punjab, India.

BARNARD Peter Deane, b. 25 Apr 1932. Dentist. 1 s, 1 d. Education: BDS, 1954, MDS, 1967, DDSc, 1991, Univ of Sydney, NSW, Aust; MPH, Univ of MI, USA, 1956; FRACDS, 1965; FAPHA, 1966; FICD, 1972. Appointments: Snr Lectr in Preventive Dentistry 1961-69, Assoc Prof of Preventive Dentistry 1970-97, Univ of Sydney, NSW, Aust; Dir, Preventive Dentistry, Westmead Hosp, 1984-97; Cnslt, World Health Org, India 1972, Indonesia 1974-75, Malaysia 1984; Lt-Col (retired), Austl Army; Retd, 1997. Publications: Num publs in dental jrnls and monographs, Austl Dental Assn and Univ of Sydney. Honours: Meritorious Serv Awd, Austl Dental Assn, 1985; Alan Docking Sci Awd, Intl Assn for Dental Rsch, ANZ Div, 1993. Memberships: Mbr 19 Austl, USA and Intl Orgs; Vice Chmn, Comm of Pub Hlth Servs, Federation

Dentaire Internationale, 1970-76. Address: Westmead Hospital, Westmead, NSW 2145, Australia.

BARNARD Trevor (John), b. 3 Jan 1938, London, Eng. Concert Pianist; Lecturer in Music. m. Helen Richmond, 28 Aug 1974. Education: Roy Acady of Music, London; Roy Coll of Music, London; Herbert Fryer; Harold Craxton; Inst of Musical Instrument Technol, London, 1946-60; ARCM, 1954; Grad, MIMIT, 1960. Appointments: Pianist-in-Res, Boston Univ Radio, 1967-71; Fac, New Eng Conservatory of Music, MA, USA, 1968-72; Piano Tutor, Monash Univ, Aust, 1972-74; Lectr in Music, Melbourne Coll of Advd Educn, 1974-88; Lectr in Music, Univ of Melbourne, 1989-; Many appearances as pianist, BBC and ABC; Music-in-the-Round chmbr music fests; Many orchs, music socs. Creative Works: Recordings: An Introduction to Piano Music; Bliss Piano Concerto; J S Bach Transciptions and Modern Australian Piano Music. Publications: Pedalling and Other Reflections on Piano Teaching, 1990; A Guide to the Study of Solo Piano Repertoire at Tertiary Level, 1995; Basic Pedalling Techniques (article, Clavier Jrnl), 1998. Honour: Full Schlsp, Roy Coll of Music, 1955. Memberships: Hon Sec, Austl Musicians Guild, 1982-93; Pres, Camberwell Music Soc, 1990-. Listed in: International Who's Who in Music. Hobbies: Golf; Swimming; Yoga. Address: 10 Grosvenor Road, Glen Iris, Vic 3146, Australia.

BARNES Jimmy, b. Scotland. Guitarist; Vocalist. Appointments: Ld singer, Austl grp, Cold Chisel, 1979-83; Solo artiste, 1984-. Creative works: Recdngs w Cold Chisel: Breakfast at Sweethearts, 1979; East, 1980; Circus Animals, 1982; Solo albums: Body Swerve, 1984; Jimmy Barnes, 1985; Freight Train Heart, 1987; Barnestorming, 1988; Two Fires, 1990; Heat, 1993; Psychlone, 1995. Listed in: International Who's Who in Music - Volume 2, Popular Music. Address: c/o Michael Long Management, PO Box 494, Double Bay, NSW 2028, Australia.

BARNES Richard John, b. 10 Dec 1931, Yallourn, Australia. University Teacher; Writer. m. Josephine, 2 children, 1 dec. Education: MA, Melbourne; MA, Cantab. Appointments: Snr Clk Directorate Educn, Navy Off, 1952-53; Snr Tutor, Engl, Univ Melbourne, 1953-55; Lectr, Engl, RAAF Coll, Pt Cook, 1956-58; Lectr, 1963-64, Snr Lectr, Engl, Univ WA, 1965-70; Snr Lectr, 1970-71, Rdr, Engl, LaTrobe Univ, 1972-91; Retd, 1996; Emer Prof, 1996-. Publications: Joseph Furphy, 1963; The Writer in Australia, 1969; Henry Kingsley, 1971; Henry Lawson's Short Stories, 1985; The Order of Things, 1990; Bushman and Bookworm (w L Hoffmann), 1995; Made in Shepparton, 1998. Address: 222 Research Road, Warrandyte, Victoria 3113, Australia.

BARNETT Alfred John, b. 27 Mar 1915, Dunolly, Aust. Medical Practitioner. m. Hazel Virgie Evans, 1 Aug 1942, 3 s, 2 decd. Education Wesley Coll, Melbourne; MD, Univ of Melbourne, 1947; FRACP; FRCP. Appointments: Served in AIF, 1941-46; Assoc, Acting Physn to Out Patients, Roy Melbourne Hosp, 1946-48; RSL Travelling Schl, Asst to Med Unit, St Mary's Hosp, London, Eng, 1948-49; Assoc Dir, Clin Rsch Unit, Physn, Alfred Hosp, Melbourne, Aust, 1950-80. Publications: Book: Peripheral Vascular Disease (w J R F Fraser), 1956; Scleroderma (Progressive Systemic Sclerosis), 1974; Chapt in Systematic Sclerosis (co-auth); About 80 sci pprs. Honour: BMA Stawell Prize in Med, 1954. Memberships: Austl Med Assn; Roy Coll of Physns, London; Roy Australasian Coll of Physns; Vic Soc for Pathol and Expmntl Med; Cardiac Soc of Aust and NZ. Listed in: Who's Who in Australia. Hobby: Home Gardening. Address: 6 Talbot Street South, Ballarat, Vic 3350, Australia.

BARNETT Paul William, b. 23 Sept 1935, Narromine, NSW, Australia. Anglican Clergyman; Bishop. m. Anita, 30 Nov 1965, 2 s, 2 d. Education: MA (hons) Univ of Sydney; PhD, London. Appointments: Rector, St Barnabas, Sydney; Holy Trinity, Adelaide; Master, Robert Menzies Coll; Bish, N Sydney, Visng Fell, Hist, Macquarie Univ, 1987-. Publications: Is the New Testament History,

1986; Bethlehem to Patmos, 1989; The Two Faces of Jesus, 1990; The Truth About Jesus, 1994; New International Commentary on Second Corinthians, 1997; Jesus and the Logic of History, 1997. Hobbies: Classical music; Rugby watching; Beach fishing. Address: 229 Fullers Road, Chatswood, NSW 2067, Australia.

BARNETT Peter Leonard, b. 21 July 1930. Journalist; Broadcaster; Administrator. m. Siti Nuraini Jatim 1970, 1 s. Education: Univ of WA. Appointments: Canberra Reporter and Columnist The West Austl, 1953-57; South-East Asia Corresp Austl Brdcstng Commn, 1963, 1964; Jakarta Reporter, 1962; NY and UN Corresp, 1964-67; WA Corresp, 1967-70; News Ed Radio Aust Melbourne, 1971-72; WA Corresp, 1972-80; Controller Melbourne, 1980-84; Dir, 1984-89; Exec Dir Austl Brdcstng Corp, 1984-89; Vice-Chmn Operating Cttee Cncl for Econ Dev of Aust; VP Austl Inst of Intl Affairs. Honours: Australia Award, 1988. Hobbies: Swimming; Gardening; Literature; Musical composition. Address: CEDA House, 123 Lonsdale Street, Melbourne 3000, Australia.

BAROT Navinchandra Motilal, b. 1924. Trade Union President. 3 s, 1 d. Education: BA; LLB. Appointments: pres, Textile Labour Assn; Pres, Natl Labour Orgn, VP, Twaro. Publication: (book) Gandhian Path in Trade Unionism. Memberships: Visng Fac Mbr, Indian Inst of Mngmt, Ahmedabad. Address: No 8, Upasana, Shaktinagar Soc, Near Sharda Society, Paldi, Ahmedabad 38007, India.

BARR Hugh, b. 7 Sept 1941. Research Scientist; Recreationist. Education: BSc, 1962, MSc, 1964, PhD, 1968 Henderson HS Univ of Auckland; Univ of Toronto. Appointments: Rsch Sci, Dept of Sci and Indl Rsch, DSIR, 1968-92; Snr Sci, Indl Rsch Ltd, 1992-96; Bus Cnslt, InfoSmart Ltd, 1996-. Honour: NZ Commemoration Medal, 1990. Memberships: Fed Mtn Clubs of NZ Exec, 1976-97, Pres 1981-84, 1993-96; Environment and Conserv Orgs of NZ, 1978-81; 1997-99; Pres, Operational Rsch Soc of NZ, 1976-81; Co-Chmn, NZ Cncl of Outdoor Recreation Assns, 1997-. Hobbies: Tramping; Mountaineering; Photography. Address: 12 Versailles Street, Wellington 5, New Zealand.

BARRATT-BOYES Brian Gerald (Sir), b. 13 Jan 1924, Wellington, NZ. Cardiothoracic and Vascular Surgeon. m. (1) diss, 1986, (2) Sara Rose Monester, 1986, 5 children. Education: MB, ChB, 1946, ChM, 1962, Univ of Otago Med Sch; Fell, Roy Australasian Coll of Surgs, 1952, Amn Coll of Surgs, 1959, Roy Soc of NZ, 1970, Am Coll of Surgs, Hon, 1977, Roy Coll of Surgs (UK), Hon, 1985; DSc, (Hon), CO Univ, USA, 1985. Appointments include: Fellshp, Cardiac Thoracic Surg, Mayo Clin, USA, 1953-55; Nuffield Travelling Fellshp, Univ of Bristol, Eng, 1956; Snr Thoracic Surgn, 1957-65, Surg-i/c, CTS Unit, 1965-89, Green Lane Hosp, Auckland, NZ; Pvte Prac, Mater Misericordiae CTS Unit, 1966-90. Publications include: 144 sci pprs in med jrnls, 1956-98; Original work, homograft aortic valve surgery & profound hypothermia-circulatory arrest techniques for correction of congenital heart disease in infancy. Books: Heart Disease in Infancy: Diagnosis & Surgical Treatment (ed w J M Neutze, E A Harris), 1973; Cardiac Surgery (w Dr J W Kirklin, NY, USA), 1985; Cardiac Surgery (w J W Kirklin), 1993. Honours include: R T Hall Prize, orig wrk, homograft surg, Austl & NZ Cardiac Soc, 1966; Humanitarian Awd, 50th Anniversary Lions Intl, 1968; CBE, 1966; KBE, 1971; Rene Leriche Prize and medal, 1987; Hon Fell, Amn Coll of Cardiol, 1989; Awd for Ex in Surg, Roy Australasia Coll of Surgns, 1994; Hon Fell Roy Australasian Coll of Physns, 1995; Famous New Zealanders Stamp Issue, NZ Post (Sci Med and Educ Sect), 1995. Memberships: Pres, Cardiac Soc of Aust and NZ; Brit Cardiac Soc Med Assn of NZ; Fell, Roy Soc of NZ James IV Assn of Surgs, USA; Hon Fell, Assn of Surgs of GB and Ireland; Amn Surg Assn. Hobbies: Farming; Fishing; Tennis; Golf. Address: Greenhills, Box 51, Waiwera, New Zealand.

BARRETT Donald Steele, b. 25 Sept 1929, Adelaide, Australia. Classical Scholar; Educator. m. Karen, 9 July

1976, 2 d. Education: BA, Hons, MA, Univ Qld; Ctf Tchr, Kelvin Grove Tchrs Coll. Appointments: Second Tchr, Qld Educn Dept, 1951-59; Lectr in Classics and Ancient Hist, Univ Qld, 1960-65; Snr Lectr, 1966-72, Rdr, 1973-94, Dean, Fac of Arts, 1983-94, Rsch Cnslt, 1994-, Mbr, Senate, 1990-94, Univ Qld. Publications: Sev articles in profl jrnls. Honours: C'wlth Study Grant, Univ London, 1966; Hon Life Mbr, Univ Qld Acad Staff Assn; Hon Mbr, Assn for Tertiary Educn Mngmt. Membership: Austl Soc for Classical Studies. Hobbies: Classical Music; Running; Surfing; Cooking; Collecting Reference Books. Address: Department of Classics & Ancient History, University of Queensland, Qld 4072, Australia.

BARRETT Paul Robert, b. 28 Apr 1936. Applied Physicist. Education: BSc, Phys; MSc, Reactor Technol; PhD, Phys, Univ of Birmingham. Appointments: Rsch Physicist, Atomic Power Div, Engl Elec Co Ltd, 1960-62; Asst Prof of Engrng, UCLA, CA, 1962-66; Snr Lectr, Nuc Engrng, Univ NSW, Aust, 1966-78; Assoc Prof of Mechl Engrng, UNSW, Aust, retd 1989. Publications: Sev sci pprs on stochastic methods in nuc engrng. Memberships: UK Inst of Phys; Fell, Austl Inst of Phys. Hobbies: Operatic symphonic music; Spanish American literature; Propagation methods in horticulture; Duplicate contract bridge. Address: 20 Ranch Avenue, Glenbrook, NSW 2773, Australia.

BARROS D'SA Aires Agnelo Barnabe, b. 9 June 1939, Nairobi. Consultant Vascular Surgeon; Honorary Lecturer. m. 12 May 1972, 4 d. Education: MB, BCh, BAO, 1965; MD, hons, 1975, Queen's Univ of Belfast; FRCS, Edinburgh, 1969; FRCS, Eng, 1969; ECFMG Cert USA, 1965. Appointments: Vascular Surg, Reconstrn Cardiovascular Rsch Cntr Intl Providence Med Cntr, Seattle, USA, 1977-78; Cnslt Vascular Surg, Roy Vic Hosp, Belfast, 1978; Examiner, FRCS, Roy Coll of Surgs, Edinburgh, 1984; Examiner of theses for higher degs, UK and Eur, 1984-99; Exec Cncl, Vascular Surgl Soc, 1986; Regl Advsr, Roy Coll of Surgs of Eng, 1988; Fac of Med, Queen's Univ of Belfast, 1989; Roy Coll Surgs rep, Northern Ireland Cncl of Postgrad Med & Dental Educ, 1989; Advsry Cttee, Brit Vascular Fndn, 1994; Hon Mbr, Vascular Sect, Roy Australasian Coll of Surgns, 1994. Publications: Over 200 articles and over 250 comms and invited lectrs; Co-Ed, Book, Vascular Surgery: Current Questions, 1991; Emergency Vascular Practice, co-ed; Film: Carotid Endarterectomy, Merit Awd for Surgl Educ. Edl Bd Mbr, Eurn Jrnl of Vascular and Endovascular Surg. Honours: Hunterian Profshp, Roy Coll of Surgns, England, 1979; James IV Surgl Traveller to N Am, Aust, S E Asia, 1983; Rovsing and Tcherning Lectr, Denmark, 1987; Jnt Lectrshp, Roy Coll of Surgs of Edinburgh and Acady of Med, Singapore, 1989; Gore Visitor, Roy Australasian Coll of Surgs, 1994. Memberships include: Fell, Roy Soc of Med; Assn Surgs of GB and Ireland, 1978; Eurn Soc of Surgl Rsch; Surg Res Soc; Eurn Soc Cardiovascular Surg; Fndr Mbr, Eurn Soc of Vascular Surg, Roy Soc of Med, Venous Forum and Forum of Angiology; Intl Soc of Pathophysiol, 1992; Intl Soc of Surg, 1995; Intl Coll of Surgs, 1995. Listed in: Debrett's People of Today; American Physicians' Who's Who. Hobbies: The Environment (Environmental Inverstigation Agency, Greenpeace, Earthlife Association, Friends of the Earth); Music; Books; Painting; Travel. Address: Vascular Surgery Unit, Royal Victoria Hospital, Belfast, Northern Ireland.

BARRY David Andrew, b. 19 Apr 1958, Brisbane, Australia. Academic. m. Suellen Jill de Waard, 16 May 1986, 1 s, 1 d. Education: BA, BSc, Bach Applied Sci; DPhil. Appointments: Lectr, Subsurface Hydrology, 1989, Snr Lectr, 1991, Assoc Prof, 1994, Univ of West Austl. Publications: More than 100 publson ground water contamination in profl jrnls and books. Honours: Visng Assoc Prof, Univ of N Carolina, 1994; Visng Sci, Massachussetts Inst of Technol, 1996. Memberships: Amn Geophys Union, 1986-; Intl Soil Sci Soc, 1994-; Editl Bd, Advances in Water Research, jrnl, 1998-. Hobby: Swimming. Address: Department of Environmental Engineering, University of Western Australia, Nedlands, WA 6907, Australia.

BARTHOLOMEUSZ Hugh, b. 20 July 1953. Doctor. m. Helga, 3 children. Education: Grad, Med, Univ Qld; Grad, Princess Alexandra Hosp & Greenslopes Repatriation Hosp. Appointments: Registrar, Gen Surg, Greenslopes Hosp; Adv Trng, Plastic Surg, Princess Alexandra Hosp, Roy Brisbane Hosp, Queen Elizabeth Hosp; Pvte Prac, Plastic Surg, Ipswich; Ret CO, Queensland Air Trng Corps; Grp Cap, RAAF Specialist Reserve; Cnslt, Plastic Surg to the Dir Gen Air Force Hlth Servs. Memberships: Chmn, St Paul's Natl Trust Restoration Cttee; Chmn, Med Exec Cttee, Bd Mbr, St Andrews Hosp; Chmn, Cncl of W Moreton Anglican Coll, 1993-'; World Pres, Intl Air Cadet Exchange Assn, 1996-; Sec, Air Trng Corps Natl Cncl, 1996-; VP, Australasian Day Surg Assn, 1998-. Hobbies: Golf; Cricket; Tennis. Address: Tri Rhosen House, 1 Court Street, Ipswich 4305, Australia.

BARTLE Graham Alfred Reginald, b. 6 Nov 1928, Ballarat, Vic, Aust. Lecturer in Music. m. Ruth Marian Walker, 11 May 1963, 1 s, 3 d. Education: FTCL (Organ), 1949, BA, Dip in Educ, 1953, BMus, 1964, MMus, 1971, Univ of Melbourne. Appointments: Tchr, Yallourn HS, Vic, 1954-57; Tchr, Univ HS, Vic, 1958-61; Lectr, Secnd Tchrs Coll, Vic, 1962-65; Lectr, 1966-72, Snr Lectr, 1972-78, Dpty Dean, 1978-93, Retd, 1993, Fac of Music, Univ of Melbourne. Publications: Music in Australian Schools, 1968; The Teachers Role in Curriculum Design (chap), 1974; International Directory of Music Education, 1992, 2nd ed, 1996; Australian Yearbook of Music and Music Education, 1998. Contbr to num profl jrnls. Honours: Ormond Exhbn, 1958; Composition Prize, Fac of Music, Univ of Melbourne, 1960. Memberships: Fndr Mbr, Chmn, 1972-73, Vic Chap, Austl Soc of Music Educ; Chmn, 1978-83, Music Subj Cttee, Vic Inst of Secnd Educn; Music Educrs Natl Conf; Incorp Soc of Musicians; Intl Kodaly Soc; Kodaly Music Educ Inst of Aust; VP, Vic Music Tchrs Assn; Natl Plng Cttee, Intl Soc for Music Educ Conf, Canberra, 1988; Bd Mbr, 1996-2000, Intl Soc of Music Educ; Trinity Coll Guild. Bd Mbr, Inst of the Arts, Austl Natl Univ, 1994-97; Stndng Cttee of Convocation, Univ of Melbourne. Listed in: International Who's Who in Music and Musicians' Directory, Volume I. Hobby: Gardening. Address: 10 Chaucer Crescent, Canterbury, Vic 3126, Australia.

BARTLETT Henry Francis, b. 8 Mar 1916, London, Eng. Painter. m. Amanda Roy, 25 July 1940. Education: MA, Queen's Coll, Oxford, 1938; Ruskin Sch of Drawing, Oxford, 1934-38; Univ of CA at Berkeley (Harkness Fell), 1938-40. Appointments: Brit Dipl Serv, 1940-75, incl: Consul, Khorramshahr, 1964-67; Consul Gen, Brisbane, 1967-69; Cnslr, Manila, 1969-72; Amb to Paraguay, 1972-75; Exec Offr, Utah Fndn, Brisbane, 1976-89. Creative Works: One Man Shows of Painting: Galerie Chartentier, Paris, 1947; London Gall, 1950; Galeria Karger, Caracas, 1957, 1959; Galeria Arte de Coleccionistas, Mexico Cty, 1962; Des Arts Cntr, Brisbane, 1969; Town Gall, Brisbane, 1978, 1981, 1983, 1985, 1988, 1990, 1992, 1994, 1996. Honours: CMG, 1975; OBE, 1964. Memberships: Tree, Qld Art Gall, 1977-87; Tree, Qld Cultural Cntr Trust, 1980-87; Hon Prof, Universidad Nacional de Asuncion, Paraguay, 1975. Listed in: Who's Who in Australia. Hobby: Painting. Address: 14/341 Bowen Terrace, New Farm, Brisbane, Qld 4005, Australia.

BARTLETT DIAZ Manuel, b. Feb 1936, Puebla. Politician. Education: Natl Univ of Mexico; Univs of Paris and Manchester. Appointments: Advsr Cntr Off of Credit Min of Fin, 1962-64; Asst to Sec-Gen Natl Fedn of Rural Workers, 1963-64; Asst Sec PRI - Institutional Revolutionary Party - 1964-68; Prof of Gen Theory of the State Natl Univ of Mexico, 1968; Var posts at Min of Interior, 1969-76; Sec Fedn Electoral Commn, 1970-76; Sec Admin Bd Natl Bank of Co-op Dev and Dir of Polit Affairs Min of For Affairs, 1976-79; Advsr to Min of Progng and Budget, 1979; Sec-Gen Natl Exec Cttee of PRI, 1981; Min of the Interior, 1982-88; Min of Pub Educ, 1988-92. Address: c/o Secretariat of State for Public Education, Republica de Argentina y Gonzalez Obregon 28, 06029, Mexico, DF, Mexico.

BARTON Allan Douglas, b. 3 Mar 1933, Melbourne, Aust. University Professor. 2 children. Education: BCom (Melb); PhD (Cantab). Appointments: Prof of Acctng, 1975-98; Pro Vice Chancellor, (Fin and Dev) Austl Natl Univ, Canberra, 1984-96. Publications: The Anatomy of Accounting, 3rd ed, 1984; Jt ed, Readings in Advanced Accounting Theory, 1983. Memberships: Austl Soc of CPA's, Pres, 1983, ACT Div, 1983-84; Acctng Assn of Aust & NZ, Pres, 1968; Fll, Roy Econ Soc. Hobbies: Sailing; Gardening; Bush walking. Address: 21 Dugdale Street, Cook, ACT 2614, Australia.

BARTON Charles Edward, b. 17 July 1943. Geophysicist. widower, 1 s, 1 d. Education: BSc; Dip.Ed; PhD. Appointments: Hd, Phys Dept, Kangaru Sch, Kenya; Tchng Asst, Ray Geophysl, Libya; Rsch Assoc, Univ of Edinburgh; Asst Rsch Prof, Univ RI; Hd of Geomagnetism, Austl Geol Survey. Memberships: Sub-Cttee, Seismol and Phys of the Earths Interior; IAGA Working Grp V-8; Regl Advsry Cttee, Aust and NZ Am Geophysl Union; Vice Chmn, Chmn, IAGA Working Grp V-8; Chmn, Sub-Cttee, Geomagnetism and Aeronomy, Natl Cttee for Solar-Terrestrial and Space Phys, Austl Acady of Scis; Chmn of Advsry Bd, Intl Serv for Geomagnetic Indices; Exec, Intl Assn of Geomagnetism and Aeronomy. Hobbies: Climbing; Walking; Skiing; Painting. Address: c/o Australian Geological Survey Organization, GPO Box 278, Canberra, ACT 2601, Australia.

BARTUREN Duenas, b. 5 Nov 1936, Lima. Politician; Civil Servant. Education: Univ Natl Mayor de San Marcos. Appointments: Taught at Grad Bus Admin Sch, 1965-66; Subsequently at Pub Admin Sch; Specialist in preparation and eval of invmnt projs Interamerican Dev Bank, 1972-73; Hd Plng Off Natl Fisheries Co, 1970-73; Dep Fin Dir Centromin Peru, 1979-84; Min of Agric, 1985-86. Address: Avenida Salaverry s/n, Edificio M de Trabajo, Lima, Peru.

BARUAH Tultul, b. 5 Apr 1947, Golaghat, Assam, India. Teacher. m. B Baruah, 28 Apr 1974, 1 d. Education: MA; PhD; LLB. Appointment: Lectr, DHSK Coll, Dibrugarh. Publications: Book on med anthropol. Memberships: Inst of Socl Rsch of Appl Anthropol, Kharagpur. Hobbies: Reading; Travel; Research. Address: Zig Zag Road, Central Chowkidinghee, Dibrugarh 786001, Assam, India.

BARZEL Amnon, b. 5 July 1935, Tel Aviv. Art Writer; Critic; Consultant; Music Director. m. Shafrira Glikson, 1956, 1 s, 1 d. Education: Hebrew Univ Jerusalem; Sorbonne Paris. Appointments: Art Consultant for Cty of Tel Aviv, 1975-76; Curator Biennale of Venice Italy, 1976-78, 1980; 'Two Environments' Forte Belvedere Florence and Castle of Prato Italy, 1978; Sao Paulo Biennale Brazil, 1985; Fndng Curator 'Contemp Art Meetings' Tel Hai Israel, 1980-83; Villa Celle Art Spaces Collect Giuliano Gori Prato Italy, 1981-82; Fndng Dir Cntr of Contemp Art Luigi Pecci Prato Italy, 1986-; Consultant for creation of Mus of Contemp Art Florence, Italy, 1989; Dir Sch for Curators, 1991-. Publications: Isaac Frenel, 1973; Dani Karavan, 1978; Art in Israel, 1986; Europe Now, 1988; Julian Schnable, 1989; Enzo Cucchi, 1989; Contemporary Russian Artists - jnt Ed, 1990. Memberships: Mbr Curatorial Cttee for Intl Sculpture Cntr - ISC - WA DC USA. Hobbies: Poetry; Holy contemporary philosophy. Address: Centro per l'Art Contemporanea Luigi Pecci, Viale della Repubblica 277, 50047 Prato, Italy.

BASAK Aditya, b. 14 Mar 1953, Calcutta, India. Freelance Artist. m. Mamta, 20 July 1980, 2 d. Education: Govt Coll of Art & Craft, 1977. Publications: Album, 1960-91; Expression in Bronze. Honours: Natl Awd, 1986; State Govt Awd, 1989; Snr Fellowship, Min of Human Resource Dev. Hobbies: Literature; Films. Address: 19A Brindaban Basak St, Calcutta, 700005, India.

BASAK Nanda Dulal, b. 2 July 1955. Library Scientist. m. Sulekha Basak, 20 May 1986, 1 d. Education: BSc, MLibSc, Calcutta Univ; BLibSc, Jadavpur Univ.

Appointment: Indian Stats Inst Lib, 1977. Publications; Over 36 tech articles in profl jrnls. Memberships: Bengal Lib Assn; Indian Lib Assn; Indian Assn of Special Libns and Info Cntrs; Assn of Govt Libns and Info Cntrs; Banqiya Bijnan Parishad. Hobbies: Reading newspapers and journals; D-Xing. Address: 305/6 Roy Bahadur Road, New Alipore, Calcutta 700 053, India.

BASAK Subal C, b. 3 Jan 1959, Dhupguri (WB), India. Faculty Member. m. Saswati, 9 Dec 1990, 1 d. Education: Dpharm, B Pharm (Hons), M Pharm, Jadavpur University, Calcutta, India. Appointments: Lectr, SCS Coll of Pharm, Harapanahalli, 1985-86; Snr Lectr, Inst of Pharm Technol, Annamalai Univ, 1986-. Publications: 11 rsch pprs. Honours: Silver Medals, First Mark in 6 subjs of D Pharm Exam, 1976-77; BADC Schlshp, Belgium, Aug-Sept, 1989. Memberships: Assoc, Inst of Chemists; LM, Indian Soc for Tech Educ, ISTE; ISCA. Hobbies: Travelling; Correspondence. Address: Department of Pharm Technology, Annamalai University, Annamalainagar 608002, India.

BASANG, b. 1937, Lang, Tibet. Party Official. Education: Tibetan Minorities Inst, 1956. Appointments: Served as a slave to the Landlord of Chika, 1947-56; Jnd the CCP, 1959; Vice-Chmn Tibet Autonomous Region Revolutionary Cttee, 1968-79; Sec Secr CCP Cttee Tibet, 1971-77; Chmn Women's Fedn of Tibet, 1973; Chmn Langxian Co Revolutionary Cttee, 1974; Dep Hd Ldng Grp for Party Consolidation CCP Cttee Tibet, 1977; Sec CPC 4th Tibet Autonomous Regl Cttee, 1977; Dep Sec 5th Autonomous Regl Cttee, 1977-; Dep for Tibet to 5th NPC, 1978; Vice-Chmn People's Govt of Tibet, 1979-83; Vice-Chmn CPPCC 6th Tibet Regl Cttee, Jan 1993-. Memberships: Mbr 10th CCP Cntr Cttee, 1973; Mbr Standing Cttee 4th NPC, 1975; Mbr CCP 11th Cntr Cttee, 1977; 5th NPC, 1978; Mbr Pres, 1979; Mbr 12th CCP Cntr Cttee, 1982-86; Mbr Cntr Discipline Inspection Commn CCPCC. Address: Chinese Communist Party Tibet Autonomous Region, Lhasa, People's Republic of China.

BASFORD Kaye Enid, b. 10 Aug 1952. University Reader. m. Geoffrey Alan Basford, 15 Feb 1974, 1 s, 1 d. Education: AMusA; BSc Hons; MLitSt; PhD. Appointments: Technologist B, Stat Cnslt, 1974-80, Technologist A, Stat Cnslt, 1981-84, Snr Profl Offr 1985-87, Snr Lectr in Biometry 1988-93, Rdr in Biometry 1994-, Dpty Dean, Fac of Agric Sci 1993-96, Sch of Land and Food, Univ of Qld, Aust. Publication: Mixture Models: Inference and Applications to Clustering, 1988; Graphical Analysis of Multiresponse Data: Illustrated with a Plant Breeding Trial. Honours include: Bronze, Silver and Gold Standard, Duke of Edinburgh's Awd Scheme, Aust, 1968-73; Univ of Qld Intl Collab Rsch Awd, Princeton Univ, 1990; Dept of Ind, Technol and Commerce Awd in Bilateral Sci and Technol Prog, Leiden Univ, 1992; Univ of Qld Intl Collaborative Rsch Awd to Princeton Univ, 1994. Memberships: Inst of Maths Stats, Roy Stat Soc; Stat Soc of Aust; Qld Br Sec 1987-88, Pres 1989-90; Intl Biometric Soc, Australasian Reg Pres, 1997-98; Intl Stat Assn for Educ; Classification Soc of N Am; Austl Inst of Agric Sci and Technol; Austl Fulbright Assn; Qld Chapt Pres 1995-. Hobbies: Basketball; Reading; Camping. Address: School of Land and Food, The University of Queensland, Brisbane, Qld 4072, Australia.

BASHARMAL Khodaidad, b. 15 July 1945, Laghman. Public Servant; Physician. m. 4 children. Education: Univ of Nangrahar Med Sch Univ of TX USA. Appointments: Fmrly Physn Good Samaritan Hosp OH; Lctr then Chf Physiology Dept Jalalabad Med Sch; Chf Admin East Zone, 1980-83; Dep For Min, 1983-84; Pres Dept of Scis and Pub Hlth Watan Party of Afghanistan, 1984-87; Min of Educ, 1987-90; Amb to Poland, 1990-91; Perm Rep of Afghanistan to UN, 1991-92. Address: c/o Ministry of Foreign Affairs, Shah Mahmud Ghazi Street, Shar-i-Nau, Kabul, Afghanistan.

BASIR Ismail, b. 1927, Taiping Perak State. Banker. Education: Serdang Agricl Coll; Durham Univ. Appointments: Lectr Univ Pertanian Malaysia; Asst Agricl Offr Serdang Agricl Coll; Dir Agricl Dept; Dir-Gen Agric later Exec Dir Johore State Dev Corpn; Chmn Natl Padi and Rice Authy, 1981-; Food Inds Malaysia, 1981-; Dir Bank Negara, 1981-; Exec Chmn Bank Bumiputra Malaysia Bhd, 1985; Hd BMF Kewangan Bumiputra; Bumiputra Merchant Bankers, 1985; and sev other cos. Address: Bank Bumiputra Malaysia Berhad, Menara Bumiputra, Jalan Melaka, Kuala Lumpur 01-18, Malaysia.

BASNET Ral Bahadur, b. 1 May 1952, Chinang, Bhutan. President, Bhutan National Democratic Party. m. Marikala, 5 Feb 1976, 3 d. Education: Bach of Com and Admin, Victoria Univ, NZ. Appointment: President, Bhutan Natl Dem Party. Hobbies: Soccer; Tennis; Reading. Address: Bhutan National Democratic Party, POB 3334, Kathmandu, Nepal.

BASSETT George William, b. 26 Mar 1910, NSW, Aust. Retired University Professor. m. Phyllis, 29 Dec 1934, 2 d. Education: BA, 1929, Dip Ed, 1930, MA, 1932, Sydney Univ; PhD, Univ London, Eng, 1940. Appointments: Tchr, NSW, 1931-41; Lectr, Sydney Tchrs Coll, 1942-47; Prin, Armidale Tchrs Coll, 1948-60; Prof, Univ Qld, 1961-80. Publications: Num articles in profl jrnls; Auth, co-auth, 11 books on educ. Honours: AM, 1979; Aust and NZ Assn Advmnt Sci Medal, 1980; Austl Coll Educ Medal, 1982. Memberships: Fell, Austl Coll Educ, Natl Pres, 1967-68; Fell, Qld Inst Educl Admin; Fellshp, Austl Cncl of Educl Admin. Listed in: Notable Australians, 1978. Address: Unit 20, Helpman Court, Cypress Gardens Retirement Community, Gooding Drive, Clear Island Waters, Qld 4226, Australia.

BASTIAAN Ross Jan, b. 24 Jan 1951, Melbourne, Vic, Aust. Peridontist. m. Deborah deCourcey, 17 Sept 1988, 2 s. Education: LDS, Vic; MDS, Melbourne Univ, 1975; MSc, Univ London, 1977; FRACDS, 1979; FICD, 1986; FADI; FPFA. Appointments: Num hosp appts, 1974-; Pt-time Lectr, Univ Melbourne Dental Sch, 1974-; Peridontist, pvte specialist prac, 1979-; Forensic Dentist, Vic Police Force and State Coroner, 1981-90; Col, Royal Austl Army Dental Corps Reserve, 1989-; Dir, Odyssey House Drug Rehab Cntr, Melbourne, 1990-; Hon Dental Surg to Gov-Gen Aust, 1992-; Mbr, Cncl, Austl War Mem, Canberra, ACT, 1995-. Creative Works: Co-auth: Images of Gallipoli, 1988; Co-auth, Gallipoli Plaques - A Guide to the ANZAC Battlefields, 1990, 2nd ed, 1991; Chapts in 3 dental textbooks; 25 sci papers; 4 mil hist papers; 103 bronze sculpted plaques, 1990-95, commemorating Austl and NZ involvement in WWI, Spanish Civil War and WWII, sited in 15 countries inclng at House of Commons, Austl War Mem, Italian Natl War Mem El Alamein, Imperial War Mus UK, Shrine of Remembrance Melbourne, Sir Edward 'Weary' Dunlop Mem Melbourne, Papua New Guinea Parl House; Melbourne Cricket Ground; War Cabinet Rooms, Melbourne; Historial Peronne, France. Honours: Intl Assn Dental Rsch Awd, 1974; Paul Harris Fell'ship, Rotary Intl, 1990; OAM, 1991; ANZAC of Yr, Returned Serviceman's League Aust, 1991; Adv Aust Awd, Austl Hist, 1992; Commendation, Gen Peter Gration, Chf Def Force Aust; Honorary Treas, Roy Austl Coll of Dental Surgs, 1996-; Reserve Force Decoration, 1996. Memberships: Roy Australasian Coll Dental Surgs, Vic, Chmn, 1988; Austl Soc Peridontology, Vic, Chmn, 1988; Austl Dental Assn, Vic, Chmn, Postgrad Cttee, 1985; Dir, Austl War Memorial Fndn, Canberra. Listed in: Who's Who in Australia; Writers of Australia. Hobbies: Military historian; Tennis; Sculpting. Address: 22 Carpenter Street, Brighton, Vic 3186, Australia.

BASU Aparna (née Mehta), b. 31 Oct 1931, Ahmedabad, India. Professor. m. Prahlad Basu, 10 May 1959, 2 d. Education: BA, Tripos, Cambridge, UK; MA, Geo Wash Univ, Wash DC, USA; PhD, Univ of Cambridge, UK. Appointments: Prof of Hist, Univ of Delhi, India. Publications: Growth of Education and Poltical Development in India, 1974; Essays in the History of Education, 1982; Women's Struggle: History of All India Women's Conference 1927-1990, 1990; Mridula Sarabhai: Rebel With a Cause, 1996; History of Delhi University, 1998; From Freedom to Independence, 1998. Memberships: Sec Gen, All India Women's Conf, 1990-95; Snr VP, All India Women's Conf, 1995-; Editl Advsry Board, Indian Econ and Socl Hist Review; Indian Jrnl of Gender Studies, Gender and Hist, Women's Hist; SNDT Univ Sen, Convenor, Univ Grants Commn Natl Subj Panel on Hist and Archaeology; Board of Indian Cncl of Histl Rsch; India Intl Cntr; Indian Assn of Women's Studies; Cntr for Women's Dev Studies; Indian Hist Congress. Address: The Retreat, 460, Sector 15-A, NOIDA, 201301, India.

BASU Jyoti, b. 1914. Politician; Lawyer. Education: St Xavier's Coll. Appointments: Went to Eng; Called to Middle Temple Bar; During stay in Eng actively assocd with India League and Fedn of Indian Students in Eng; Sec of London Majlis; Came in contact with CP of GB; Returned to Calcutta, 1940; A ldr of fmr East Bengal Railroad Workers' Union; Elected to Bengal Legis Cncl, 1946; After Partition remained a mbr of W Bengal Legis Assn; Arrested for mbrship of CP after party was banned, 1948; Released on orders of High Court; Became Chmn Edl Bd Swadhinata; Fmr Sec Prov Cttee of CP; Imprisoned, 1948, 1949, 1953, 1955, 1963, 1965; Dep Chf Min and Min in charge of Fin in first United Front Govt, 1967; Dep Chf Min in second United Front Govt; MP for Satgachia, 1977; Ldr of Left Front Legislature Party; Chf Min of W Bengal, 1977-. Memberships: Mbr W Bengal Legis Ass, 1952-72; Mbr Natl Cncl Cntr Exec Cttee and Natl Secr until CP split, 1963; Mbr Politbureau CP of India - Marxist. Address: Chief Minister's Secretariat, Writers' Bldg, Calcutta, India.

BASU Kaushik, b. 9 Jan 1952, Calcutta, India. Economist. m. Alaka Basu, 21 July 1977, 1 s, 1 d. Education: BA (Hons) Delhi Univ; MSc (Econ), PhD, London Sch of Econs. Appointments: Prof of Econs, Delhi Sch of Econs, 1985; Visng Prof, Princeton Univ, 1989-91; C Marks Prof, Cornell Univ, 1996-. Publications: Lectures in Industrial Organization Theory, 1992; Analytical Develpment Economics, 1997. Honours; Fell, Econometric Socl Recip, Mahalanobis Mem Awd; Disting Vis, London Sch of Econs, 1993. Address: Department of Economics, Cornell University, Ithaca, NY 14853, USA.

BASU Tarun Tapin, b. 5 Dec 1939, Khulna. State Government Officer. m. Namita, 10 Aug 1967, 2 s, 1 d. Education: Intermediate Com and Tech Trng. Appointments: Spvsr, Ind Trng Inst, Suri, Birbhum, Bengal. Creative Works: Auth, 2 Poetry Books; Ed, Half Yearly Lit Mag. Honours: Hon by Bangladesh Kavita Club, Pabna, Kavi Bande Ali Mia Padak, 1993. Memberships: Birbhum Sahitya Parisad; Njkhil Bharat Sahityasammelan. Hobbies: Letter Writing. Address: S P More Post Suri Dist, Birbhum, West Bengal, 731101, India.

BASUKI Hari Satriyo, b. 10 Nov 1948, Malang. Manager; Researcher. m. Rochanda Jati, 8 Mar 1980, 2 s. Education: S1 (IR). Appointments: Hd of Microwave Lab, 1981-82, Hd of Telephone Lab, 1982-83, Hd of Antenna Lab, 1983-84; Mngr of Control, 1990-. Publications: ED: Bulletin LEN, 1983; Bulletin IPT, 1990. Honour: SCUPS, 1997. Memberships: IEEE; AAAS; NYAS; ORARI; IKNI; ICA. Hobbies: Radio communications; Photography; Camping; Correspondence. Address: Puslitbang inkom-lipi, Jl Cisitu 21/154D, Bandung 40135, Indonesia.

BATRA Ranjit, b. 18 Mar 1943, Bombay, India. Director. m. Neelam, 2 May 1974, 1 s, 2 d. Education: BCom, Sydenham Coll of Commerce and Econs, Bombay. Appointment: Client Serv Exec Dir. Memberships: Indo Amn Soc; Advtng Club; Intl Advtng Assn of India Chapt. Hobbies: Swimming; Table Tennis; Hiking. Address: Ratan Batra Pvt Ltd, Gul Manor, 8 Strand Road, Colaba, Mumbai 400 005, India.

BATT Neil Leonard Charles, b. 14 June 1937, Hobart, Tas, Aust. Company Director. m. Karen Green, 14 June 1986, 1 s, 5 d. Education: BA, Hons, Univ Tas, 1963. Appointments: Elected, House of Assembly, 1969, Min of Transp, Chf Sec, 1972-74, Min for Natl Parks, 1974-77, Min for Educ, Recreation and Arts, 1974-77, Min for Econ Plng, Min for Forests, 1977-80, Dpty Premier, Treas, 1977-80, Tas Parly; Chf Exec, UNICEF, Bangladesh, 1979-80; Chmn of Airlines, WA, 1980-82, Res Dir, WA,

1980-82, Res Dir, Vic and Tas, 1982-86, TNT/Ansett Grp of Cos; Ldr of Opposition, Tas Parly, 1986-89; Ombudsman for Tas, 1989-91; Chmn, Hlth Care Corp of Aust Pty Ltd, 1994-; Chmn, Audit Cttee, Port Phillip Cncl; Chmn of Dirs, Heine Mngmt Ltd, 1994-; Exec Dir, Hlth Benefits Cncl of Vic, 1991-. Honour: AO, 1991. Hobbies: Sailing; Swimming. Address: 16 Kooyong Road, North Caulfield, Victoria, Australia.

BATTEN Jonathan Andrew, b. 25 Apr 1958, Melbourne, Aust. University Lecturer. Education: Bach Deg, Bus; MBA; PhD. Appointments: AIDC, 1984; BOT, 1986; Credit Lyonnais, 1987; IBM, 1995; UWS, 1996. Publication: International Finance, 1993. Honour: Austrade in Intl Mktng, 1985. Membership: Fell, Austl Inst of Banking and Fin. Hobby: Collecting tribal art. Address: 129 Reservoir Street, Surry Hills, NSW 2010, Australia.

BATTERHAM Robin John, b. 3 Apr 1941, Melbourne, Aust. Technologist. 3 s. Education: BE, 1965; PhD, 1969; AMusA Organ, 1986. Appointments: Dpty Dir Music, Scots Ch, Melbourne; Chf CSIRO Div Mineral Engrng, 1984-88; VP, Rsch and Tech Comalco Ltd, Resource and Proc Devs CRA Ltd, 1988-94; CR Acady Tech Sch, 1988-93; Pres, Int Mineral Processing Congress, 1989-93; Co-Chmn Phys Schs Panel Co-op Rsch Cntrs, 1992-; G K Williams Co-op Rsch Cntr, 1993-; Chmn, Aust Inst Mining and Metall Proceeding Commn, 1994-; VP, Rsch and Tech RTZ-CRA, 1994-97; Mngng Dir, Rsch and Technol Dev Rio Trito, 1997-. Honours: Esso Awd for Excellence in Chem Engrng, 1992; Disting Lectr Univ BC and CA, Kernot Medal (Univ of Melbourne), 1996. Memberships: FTSE; CE; FAUSIMM; FISS, FIChemE. Hobbies: Skiing; Cycling; Trekking; Music. Address: 99 Coventry Street, South Melbourne, Vic 3205, Australia.

BATTLES Lara, b. 13 Oct 1949, San Pedro, CA, USA. Marriage, Family, Child Therapist. 1 s. Education: BS, Psychol, Montana St Univ, 1971; MA, Cnslng Psychol, Loyola-Marymount Univ, 1975. Honour: Natl Merit Schl, 1967. Membership: CA Assn of Marriage and Family Therapists, 1983-. Hobbies: Space Travel; Gardening; Music; Fostering world peace. Address: 210 S Mason Street, Arrayo Grande, CA 93420, USA.

BATU Bagen, b. 1924, Zhenlai Co, Jilin Prov. Government Official. m. 1950, 3 d. Appointments: Joined CCP, 1946; Vice-Chmn Autonomous Regl Govt Inner Mongolia, 1979-83; 1st 2nd, 4th, 5th, 6th and 7th Inner Mongolia Autonomous Regl People's Congress, Chmn, 1983-93; Dep for Inner Mongolia 4th, 5th, 6th and 7th NPC; Ldr 8th Prov Spoken and Written Mongolian Language Co-ordination Grp, 1983-; Vice-Chmn China Sports Assn for the Elderly, 1992; VP China Yellow River Culture Econs and Dev Rsch Inst, 1995; Pres Inner Mongolia Yellow River Culture Econs and Dev Rsch Inst, 1995. Memberships: Mbr Presidium 4th, 5th, 6th and 7th Autonomous Regl People's Congress; Mbr Presidium 6th, 7th NPC; Alt mbr Cntr Cttee CCP, 1982-92; Mbr Standing Cttee 8th CPPCC and Vice-Chmn Ethnic Affairs Cttee CPPCC, 1993-. Hobbies: Tennis; Calligraphy. Address: Bldg 4, Inner Yard, 1 Qingcheng Lane, Huhhot 010015, People's Republic of China.

BATYGIN Yuri, b. 25 Sept 1954, Moscow, Russia. Accelerator Physicist. m. G Batygina, 6 Oct 1979, 1 s, 1 d. Education: PhD, Moscow Engrng Phys Inst, 1984. Appointments: Snr Rschr, MEPHI, 1984-94; Contract Rschr, RIKEN, Japan, 1994-. Publications: Sev articles in profl jrnls. Honours: Awd, Best Sci Presentation, CERN Accelerator Sch, Rhodes, Greece, 1993. Memberships: Am Physl Soc; NY Acady of Scis. Hobbies: Sport; Music. Address: RIKEN 2-1, Hirosawa, Wako-shi, Saitama 351-01, Japan.

BAUER Gaston Egon, b. 7 May 1923, Vienna, Austria. Consulant Cardiologist. m. Phyllis Smith, 7 Jan 1949, 3 s. Education: MB, BS, Sydney, Aust, 1946; MRCP, 1951, FRCP, 1972, London, Eng; MRACP, 1952; FRACP, 1968; FACC, 1992; Fell of Senate, Univ of Sydney, 1982-93; MD, hon causa, Univ of Sydney, 1995. Appointments: Hon Physn, Sydney Hosp, 1956-76; Hon Cnsltng Physn, Hornsby Dist Hosp, 1964-81; Hon Cnslt

Physn, Manly Dist Hosp, 1964-; Warden, Clin Sch, Roy N Shore Hosp, 1979-85. Publications: Contbr of over 130 pprs in jrnls and 9 chapts in medl books. Honours: Univ Medal, Univ of Sydney, 1946; Arthur E Milles Grad Prize, 1946; Clayton Mem Prize in Med, 1946; Archie Telfer Prize, Sydney Hospitallers, 1963; AM, 1988. Memberships: Cardiac Soc of Aust and NZ; Austl Med Assn; Corresp Mbr, Roy Soc of Med, London. Hobbies: Music; Football. Address: 115 Shirley Road, Roseville, NSW 2069, Australia.

BAUER Margaret Susan, b. 15 Nov 1956, Sydney, Australia. Secondary Science Teacher. Education: BSc, Sydney Univ; Dip. Educn, Sydney Tchrs Coll. Appointment: Exec, Hd Tchr, Ashfield Boys HS, 1993-. Publication: Dynamic Science. Memberships: Sci Tchrs Assn, 1978-; NSW Sci Tchrs Assn, Cnclr, 1994-96. Hobbies: Photography; Beach Coming; Bush Walking. Address: Ashfield Boys High School, Liverpool Road, Ashfield, NSW 2131, Australia.

BAUER Steven M, b. 8 Nov 1949, Hemet, CA, USA. Engineer. m. Myung-Hee, 10 Sept 1983, 2 d. Education: BA; BS. Appointments: Cost Containment Engr; Assoc Nuclear, Engr; Asst Nuclear Engr. Publications: 1000 Tech Letters, 1995-98. Honours: Outsndng Serules (KC), 1989; Vol of the Yr Awd (ARC), 1990-91. Memberships: AAAS. Hobbies: Personal computer; Working out; Garden. Address: 131 Monroe Court, San Bernardino, CA 92408-4137, USA.

BAUME Peter Erne (The Hon), b. 30 Jan 1935, Sydney, NSW, Aust. Senator; University Chancellor. m. Jennifer Broughton Tuson, 15 Dec 1958, 1 s, 1 d. Education: MB, BS, 1959; MD, 1969, Univ Sydney; MRACP, 1962; FRACP, 1971. Appointments: Hon Asst Physn, Roy N Shore Hosp, 1966-74; Cnslt Physn, 1967-80; Senator for NSW; Chmn, Senate Stndng Cttee Socl Welfare, 1976-80; Govt Whip, Senate, 1978-80; Min Aboriginal Affairs, 1980-82; Min Hlth, 1982; Min Educ, 1982-83; Shadow Min Educ and Yth Affairs, 1983-84; Shadow Min, Community Servs and Status of Women, 1985-87; Prof, Hd, Sch Community Med, Univ NSW; Chair, Austl Sports Drug Agcy, 1991-99; Dpty Chair, Austl Natl Cncl AIDS, 1993-94; Pt-time Commnr, Austl Law Reform Commn, 1993-97; Chan, Austl Natl Univ, ACT, 1994-. Publications: Contbns to 39 books and reports, 67 contbns to other medl pubs. Honours: Norton Manning Prize, Univ Sydney; Offr of the Order of Aust, 1992. Memberships include: NSW Cncl Civil Liberties; Austl Parl Grp, Amnesty Intl; Chmn Trees, Roy Austl Coll Ophthalmologists Benevolent Fund; Life Mbr, Soc St Vincent de Paul; Many other orgs. Address: University of New South Wales, PO Box 1, Kensington, NSW 2033, Australia.

BAUMGARTNER Paul August, b. 28 Jan 1934, Campbelltown, Australia. Food Technologist. m. Marlene, 3 Jan 1970, 2 d. Education: BScAgr, Univ Sydney; Dip, Tertiary Educn, Univ New England. Appointments: Dean, Fac of Sci Technol & Agricl, 1996, Prov Chancellor, Rsch & Cnslty, Univ W Sydney, 1998. Honour: Awd of Merit, Austl Inst of Food Sci & Technol, 1983. Memberships: Fell, Austl Inst of Food Sci & Technol; Catering Inst of Aust; Am Meat Sci Assn; Inst of Food Technols. Hobbies: Theatre; Reading; Gardening; Sports Spectator. Address: University of Western Sydney, Hawkesbury, Richmond, NSW 2753, Australia.

BAVADRA Adi Kuini Teimumu Vuikaba, b. 23 Dec 1949. Politician. m. (1) Dr Timoci Bavadra fmr PM of Fiji, dec 1989, (2) Clive Speed 1991, 2 s, 2 d, 8 step-children. Education: Univ of the South Pacific; Austl Natl Univ. Appointments: Repr Fiji Pub Service Assn women at world conf org by Pub Service Intl, 1984; Pres Fiji Labour Party, 1989-91; Lived in Aust, 1991-94; Stood as All Natls Congress cand in gen elections, 1994; Pres ANC, now merged with Fijian Assn, FA, 1994; Hd offic Fiji deleg to World Conf on UN End of Decade for Women Nairobi; Past Pres Fiji Pub Servants Assn, women's wing; Univ of S Pacific Alumni Assn. Hobbies: Reading; Bible Study; Political Debates; Biographies of world leaders and

literary figures. Address: General Post Office 633, Suva, Fiji.

BAY Yew Chuan, b. 12 June 1943, Singapore. Director. m. Phoa Keng Wa, 18 Mar 1967, 1 s, 1 d. Education: BCh, Electr Engrng, MBA, Melbourne Univ. Appointments: Var positions with Mobil in Aust, Malysia, Singapore, NY, inclng: Plng Mngr, Admin Dir, Regl Planner, Supply Ops Mngr and Mktng; Grp Gen Mngr, Exec Dir and COO and Coo-Amcol Holdings Ltd; Dir, Amcol Subsidiaries and affiliates; Vice Chmn, Impact Holdings and subsidiaries. Honours: Past Pres, Rotary Club of Singapore W, 1993-94; Chmn, Sch Advsry Cttee, 1998; Vice Chmn, Singapore Mfrs Assn, Jurong Br, 1995-. Memberships: Assoc Mbr, Inst of Engrs; Fell, Inst of Dirs; Cttee Mbr, Rotary Family Serv Cntr; Hobbies: Golf; Reading; Tennis. Address: 94 Westlake Avenue, Singapore 574279.

BAYKAM Bedri, b. 26 Apr 1957. Painter; Writer; Politician. Education: French Lycee Istanbul Univ of Paris I, Pantheon-Sorbonne,France; CA Coll of Arts and Crafts Oakland CA USA. Appointments: 70 solo exhibns Paris, Brussels, Rome, NY, Istanbul, Munich, Stockholm, Helsinki, London, San Francisco, Havana, Ankara. Publications Incl: The Brain of Paint - Boyanin Beyni, 1990; Monkey's Right to Paint, 1994; Secular Turkey Without Concession, 1995; Fleeting Moments, Enduring Delights, 1996; The Color of the Era, 2997; His Eyes Rest Upon Us, 1997; The Years of 69, 1998. Honours: Painter of the Year, Nokta magazine, 1987, 1989, 1990, 1996, 1998; Toison d'Or Awd, Cannes, 1994. Memberships: Cntr Bd CHP, Repubn Party of the People, 1995-98. Hobbies: Tennis; Football; Rock music. Address: Palanga Cad 33/23, Ortakoy, Istanbul 80840, Turkey.

BAYLY Ian Albert Edgar, b. 3 Aug 1934. Zoologist; Limnologist. div, 3 s. Education: MSc, NZ; PhD, Qld; DSc, Monash. Appointments: Lectr in Zool, Univ of Qld, 1959-64; Snr Lectr in Zool, Monash Univ, 1965-70; Rdr in Zool, Monash Univ, 1971-95; Rsch Assoc, Yale Univ, USA, 1967. Publications: Inland Waters and Their Ecology, book, w W D Williams, 1973; Rock of Ages, 1999; 90 sci pprs in periodicals. Honour: Jolly Awd, Austl Soc of Limnology, 1975. Memberships: VP, Austl Conserv Fndn, 1973-75; Pres, Austl Soc for Limnology, 1978-79. Hobby: Classical Music. Listed in: Who's Who in the World. Address: 501 Killiecrankie Road, Flinders Island, TAS 7255, Australia.

BEACHAM Arthur, b. 27 July 1913, Wales. Emeritus Professor; Economist. m. Margaret Beacham, 10 Sept 1938, dec, 1 s, 1 d. Education: BA, Wales; MA, Liverpool; PhD, Belfast; Univ Coll, Wales; Jevons Rsch Stud, Univ Liverpool, 1935-36; Leon Rsch Fell, Univ London, 1942-43. Appointments: Lectr, Econs, Queen's Univ, Belfast, Northern Ireland, 1938-45; Snr Lectr, 1945-47, Prof, Econs, 1951-63, Univ Coll Wales; Prof, Indl Rels, Univ Coll, Cardiff, 1947-51; Vice-Chan, Univ Otago, NZ, 1964-66; Gonner Prof, Applied Econs, Liverpool Univ, Eng, 1966-75; Dpty Vice-Chan, Acting Vice-Chan, 1975-79, Emer Prof, 1980-, Murdoch Univ, WA. Publications: Economics of Industrial Organisation. Honours: Hon LLD, Univ Otago, 1969; Hon DUniv, Murdoch Univ, 1982; OBE. Membership: Cnclr, Roy Econs Soc, 1972-75. Hobbies: Golf; Gardening. Address: 10 Mannersley Street, Carindale, Qld 4152, Australia.

BEAR Isabel Joy, b. 4 Jan 1927, Aust. Research Scientist. Education: DAppSc; FRMIT; AMTC. Appointments: Expmtl Scientist, Atomic Energy Rsch Estab, Harwell, Eng, 1950-51; Rsch Asst, Birmingham Univ, 1951-53; Expmtl Offr, 1953-67, Snr Rsch Scientist, 1967, Prin Rsch Scientist, 1972, Snr Prin Rsch Scientist, Div Mineral Chem/Products, 1979-92, Hon Fell, 1992-97, C'wlth Sci and Indl Rsch Org, Aust; Pt-time Commnr, Victorian Post-Secnd Educ Commn, 1986-90. Honours: Leighton Medallist, Roy Austl Chem Inst, 1988; AM, 1986. Memberships: Fell, Roy Austl Chem Inst, Mbr Profl Assessment Cttee, Hist and Archives Cttee, Women in Chem Sub-Cttee; MAusIMM; Chmn, Advsry Cttee Technological Rsch and Dev in Colls Advd Educ, 1987-90. Listed in: Who's Who in Australia. Address:

2/750 Waverley Road, Glen Waverley, Vic 3150, Australia.

BEATH Betty, b. 19 Nov 1932, Bundaberg, Qld, Aust. Composer; Lecturer; Pianist; Examiner. m. David Cox, 1 s, 1 d. Education: Music Dip, Queensland Conservatorium Music; TMusA; AMusA; LTCL; AMusA, Singing; Regd Tchr. Appointments: Hd, Music Dept, St Margaret's Girls Sch; Lectr, Composition, Queensland Conservatorium Music; Ed, ASMUSE, music publng, Qld Chapt, Austl Soc Music Educ; Examiner; Austl Music Exams Bd. Creative Works: Num compositions inclng: Piccolo Victory, instrumental ensemble, performed Brisbane Baroque Trio; Brisbane Waters, solo, bass clarinet, tape; Yunggamurra and The Ninya, prose and verse settings, voice, instrumental ensemble; 3 Psalms, voice, instrumental ensemble; Indonesian Triptych, solo voice, piano; Sermon to the Birds, 2-pt vocal, instrumental ensemble; River Songs, Cycle for soprano and orch, 1992; Journeys: An Indonesian Triptych, orchl, 1994; Asmaradana, orchl, 1994; Golden Hours, orchl, 1995; Dreams and Visions, orchl, 1995; Encounters with Violin and Cello, 1999; Music dramas for children; Pieces recd Austl Brdcstng Commn; Publications: The Raja Who Married an Angel, 1979; Reflections from Bali, 1981; Walking in Sunshine, 1981; Francis, 1983; Spice and Magic, 1983; Contbns, Libretto mag, newsletters and other publs. Honours: Spec Travel and Rsch Grant for Indonesia, 1974; Intl Cncl Women's Conf, Can, 1975; Deleg to 3rd Intl Congress Women in Music, Mexico, 1984; Exec Bd, Intl League Women Composers, 1984-85, 1986-87, 1988-89; Asmaradana included in Music of Aust Prog, Trade and Cultural Miss, Jakarta, Aust Today Indonesia, 1994. Memberships: Musicology Soc Aust; Aust-Indonesia Assn; Greek Community St George; Intl League Women Composers. Listed in: Women Composers, Conductors and Musicians of the 20th Century, 1988; Contemporary Composers, 1992. Listed in: Five Hundred Notable Women; World Who's Who of Women; International Encyclopaedia of Women Composers; Oxford Companion to Australian Music; Contemporary Composers. Hobbies: Indonesian, Greek and Chinese culture; Nature study; Walking; Gardening. Address: 8 St James Street, Highgate Hill, Queensland 4101, Australia.

BEATTIE David Stuart (Honorable Sir), b. 29 Feb 1924, Sydney, Aust. Lawyer; Administrator. m. Norma Macdonald, 1950, 3 s, 4 d. Education: Dilworth Sch; Univ of Auckland; GCMG; GCVO; QSO; QC; LLD. Appointments: Naval Offr, WWII; Bar, Solicitor, Judge of Supreme Crt, 1969-80; Gov-Gen, NZ, 1980-85; Pres, Auckland Dist Law Soc, 1964; NZ Servs Rugby, 1944-45; Chmn, Roy Cmmn on Crts, 1977-79; Winston Churchill Trust, 1976-80; Admiralty Reform Cttee, 1973; Chmn, Ministerial Wrkng Party on Sci and Technol, 1986; Pres, NZ Intl Fest of Arts, 1987-; Pres, NZ Olympic and C'wlth Games Assn. Memberships: Chmn, Trustees, NZ Sports Fndn, 1977-80; Patron, NZ Rugby Football Union, NZ Squash Racquets Assn. Address: 18 Golf Road, Heretaunga, Upper Hutt, New Zealand.

BEATTIE Peter Douglas, b. 18 Nov 1952, Sydney, Aust. Premier of Queensland; Member of Parliament. m. Heather, 2 s, 1 d. Education: BA, LLB Univ Qld; MA, QUT. Appointments: Co Sec and Dir, var Labour Co's; Solicitor, Supreme Crt, Qld, admitted 1978; Qld State Campaign Dir, 16 different elections, 1981-88; Ex-Official Mbr, Natl Exec, 1981-88; State Sec, Qld Br, 1981-88; Atty-Gen's Cttee, 1989-92; Family Servs and Aboriginal and Islander Affairs Cttee, 1992-; Local Govt Housing and Plng, 1989-; Mbr, Ministerial Legislative Cttee, Emergency Servs, Rural Cmnties and Consumer Affairs, 1992-; Chmn, Criminal Justice Cttee, 1990-92; Mbr, Parly Pub Wrks Cttee, 1992-; Min Hlth, 1995-96, Ind and Small Bus, 1996-97; Shadow Min for Econs and Trade Dev, 1996-98; Qld Ldr of the Opposition, 1996-98; Premier, Qld, 1998-. Publications: In the Arena, 1990; The Year of the Dangerous Ones. Memberships include: Qld Law Soc; Chinese Bus Assn; Soc of St Andrew of Scotland; Qld Assn Mental Hlth; Media Entertainment and Arts Alliance; Australasian Stdy of Parly Grp, formation of Brisbane. Hobbies: Squash; Jogging; Swimming; Reading; Writing. Address: 49 Dalrymple Street, Wilston, Qld 4051, Australia.

BEAUMONT Bryan Alan, b. 29 Dec 1938. Judge. m. Jeanette A Wilkie, 10 Jan 1967, 2 s, 3 d. Education: LLB. Appointments: QC, 1978; Judge, Fed Crt of Aust, 1983; Judge, Sup Crt, ACT, 1983; Judge, Sup Crt of Norfolk Is, 1989-93; Chf Jus, Sup Crt of Norfolk Is, 1993-; Presdtl Mbr, Admnstv Appeals Tribunal, 1983-; Actng Judge, Sup Crt of Vanuatu, 1993-; Judge, Tongan Crt of Appeal, 1997-. Memberships: Chmn, Austl Inst of Judicial Admin, 1990-92; Amn Law Inst, 1995-. Hobbies: Tennis; Music; Theatre. Address: Federal Court of Australia, Law Courts Building, Queen's Square, Sydney, NSW, Australia.

BEAUREPAIRE Beryl Edith (Dame), b. 24 Sept 1923. Aust. m. Ian Beaurepaire, 26 Mar 1946, dec 24 June 1996, 2 s. Education: Univ Melbourne. Appointments: Served Women's Austl Aux Air Force, 1942-45; Commissioned ASO, 1945; Mbr, Natl Exec, YWCA, Aust, 1969-77; VP, Citizens Welfare Serv, Vic, 1970-86; Chmn, Bd Mngmt, Fintona Girls Sch, 1973-87; Chmn, Vic Women's Sect, 1973-76, Chmn, Fed Women's Cttee, 1974-76, VP, 1976-86, Victorian Division, Liberal Party; Mbr, Fed Women's Advsry Cttee Wrkng Party, 1977; Convener, Natl Women's Advsry Cncl, 1978-82; Mbr, Austl Children's TV Fndn Bd, 1982-88; Bd Mbr, Victorian 150th Authy, 1982-87; Mbr, 1982-93, Chmn, 1985-93, Cncl Austl War Mem; Pres, Victorian Assn The Most Ex Order of Brit Empire, 1987-91; Mbrm, Austl Bi-Centennial Multicultural Fndn, 1989-91; Patron, Portsea Childrens Camp, 1996-; Peninsula Hlth Care Network Fndn, 1996-; Epilepsy Fndn of Vic Inc, 1999. Honours: OBE, 1975; Silver Jubilee Medal, 1977; DBE, 1981; AC, 1991. Address: 18 Barton Drive, Mt Eliza, Vic 3930, Australia.

BEAZLEY Kim Christian, b. 14 Dec 1948, Perth. Politician. m. (1) Mary Beazley, 1974 - Div 1989, 2 d; (2) Susannah Beazley, 1990, 1 d. Education: Univ of WA; Oxford Univ. Appointments: Fmr lectr in Socl and Polit Theor Murdoch Univ Perth; MP fo Swan, 1980-; Min for Aviation, 1983-84; Specl Min for State, 1983-84; Min for Def, Dec 1984-90; Ldr of the House, 1988-96; Min for Transp and Comms, 1990-91; Min of Fin, 1991; Min of Employment Educ and Trng, 1991-93; Min of Fin, 1993-96; Dep PM, 1995-96; Specl Min for State, 1993-96; Ldr of Labor Party, March 1996-. Address: c/o ALP, Centenary House, 19 National Circuit, Barton, ACT 2600, Australia.

BEBY Jayaram, b. 14 May 1953. Researcher. m. Shakunthala, 1 d. Education: BS, Chem, Phys and Maths, 1974, MSc, Chem, 1976, Univ of Mysore, India; PhD, Medicinal/Pharm Chem, Bangalore Univ, Indian Inst of Sci, Bangalore, 1980-84. Appointments: Chemist, Mysore Acetate and Chems Ltd, Asst Mandya, India, 1976-78; (Lectr)/Assoc (Rdr) Prof, Dept of Chem, V V Pura Col of Sci, Bangalore Univ, 1978-89; Snr Post Doc/Rsch Asst Prof, Dept of Biochem, Molecular Bio, Coll of Pharm, Univ KY Med Cntr, Lexington, 1991-94; Snr Scientist, Transduction Labs, Prodn Mngr, Molecular Bio, Peptide Div, Lexington, KY, 1995-. Publications: 23 in refereed jrnls; 9 rsch pprs. Honours include: Schlshps, Univ of Mysore, 1972-76, 1974-76; Tchr Rsch fellshp, Univ Grants Commn, Govt of India, New Delhi, 1981-84; Univ Grants Commn Rsch Awd, Govt of India, New Delhi, India, 1988-89; Robert A Welch Postdoct Fellshp, 1989-90; NIH Rsch Associateship, 1990-95; Cited, Most Disting Scientist in USA and Can by Amn Men and Women of Sci, 1994. Hobbies: Playing music; Working in garden. Address: 2705 Southview Drive, Lexington, KY 40503, USA.

BECK Felix, b. 13 Dec 1931, Opava, Czech Republic. Medical Scientist. m. Anne, 14 Oct 1961, 2 d. Education: MBChB, MD, DSc. Appointments: Prof, Univ London, 1971-72, Univ Leicester, 1972-89; Profl Fell, Univ Melbourne, Cnslt, Howard Florey Inst of Ex Physiol and Med, Univ Fell, Univ Leicester, 1990-. Publications: Pprs, articles and books on devel biol. Honour: Fulbright Fell, 1963-64. Memberships: Past Pres, Eurn Teratol Soc, Anatomical Soc of GB and Ireland. Hobbies: Travel; Talking. Address: Howard Florey Institute for Experimental Physiology & Medicine, University of Melbourne, Parkville, Victoria 3052, Australia.

BECKER Carl Bradley, b. 27 Apr 1951, Chgo, IL, USA. Japanologist; Philosopher. Education: Univ HI: BA Philos summa, 1971; MA, Buddhist Philos summa, 1973; PhD Comparative Philos summa 1981, E-W Cntr; DLitt Comparative Relig UC Hon, Intl Univ Bombay, 1992. Appointments: Rschr, Kyoto Univ, 1976-79; E-W Cntr, Honolulu, 1979-81; Prof, Philos and Relig, South IL Univ, 1981-83; Osaka Univ, Japan, 1983-86; Univ HI, 1986-88; Tsukuba Univ, Japan, 1988-92; Kyoto Univ, Japan, 1992-. Publications: Kanji Finder Index, 1980; Christianity: History and Philosophy, 1985; Communication East and West, 1988; Paranormal Experiences and Survival of Death, 1992; Breaking the Circle, 1993. Memberships: Assn Asian Studies; Soc Asian and Comparative Philos; Intl Assn of Near-Death Studies; Intl Inst For Study of Death; Jintai Kagaku Rsch Assn; Dir, Japan Holistic Medl Assn; Japan Assn Relig Studies; Japan Comm Assn; Soc For Values in Higher Educ; Biotechnol Assn; NY Acady Scis; World Comm Assn. Honours: USA-NSF Grants in Archaeology, 1969-70; E-W Cntr Comm Schls, 1972-81; Danforth Fndn Grad Fellowship, 1972-81; Crown Prince Akihito Fellowship, 1974-75; Japan Min Educ Fellowship, 1976-78; Imai Dissertation Fellowship, 1980-81; Ashby Awd, Best Paper on Relig, Acady of Relig and PR, 1982; Fulbright Grants: Japan, 1983; China, 1987; SIETAR Awd, Best Paper on Intercultural Comms, IJIR, 1986; Phi Kappa Phi. Hobbies: Photography; Cycling; Psychic research. Address: Integrated Hum Sciences, Kyoto University, Yoshida Nihon Matsu-cho, Sakyo-ku, Kyoto, 60601, Japan.

BECKWITH Athelstan Laurence Johnson, b. 20 Feb 1930, Perth, WA, Aust. Professor of Organic Chemistry. m. Phyllis Kaye Marshall, 10 Jan 1953, 1 s, 2 d. Education: BSc, Univ of WA, 1951; DPhil, Balliol Coll, Oxford Univ, Eng, 1956. Appointments: Rsch Sci, CSIRO, Melbourne, 1957-58; Lectr in Chem, Univ of Adelaide, 1958; Visng Lectr, Imperial Coll, London, Eng, 1962; Prof of Organic Chem, Univ of Adelaide, 1965; Visng Prof, Univ of York, 1968; Currently, Prof of Organic Chem, Rsch Sch of Chem, Austl Natl Univ, Prof Emer, 1996-. Publications: Num sci pprs and reviews in profl jrnls. Honours: Rennie Mem Medal, 1960; H G Smith Mem Medal, 1980; Austl Acady of Sci, 1973, VP, 1985-86, Treas, 1997-; Carnegie Fell, 1968; Von Humboldt Snr Awd, 1995; Centenary Medal, 1992; Birch Medal, 1992; Leighton Meml Medal, 1997; Memberships: Fell, Roy Soc of Chem; Am Chem Soc; Roy Austl Chem Inst, Fell, Fed Pres, 1984. Listed in: International Who's Who; Who's Who in Australia. Hobbies: Reading; Performing Music; Model Making; Golf. Address: Department of Chemistry, Australian National University, GPO Box 4, Canberra, ACT 2601, Australia.

BEDDAL David, b. 27 Nov 1948. Politician. m. Helen Beddall, 1 d; 2 s from previous marriage. Appointments: Mbr of Staff C'Wlth Banking Corp, 1967-78; Loans Offr Austl Guarantee Corp Ltd, 1978-83; Coml fin consultant, 1979-83; Chmn Jnt Standing Cttee Min on For Affairs and Def, 1984-87; Chmn HoR Standing Cttee on Ind Sci and Technol, 1987-93; Min for Small Bus and Customs, 1990-93; Min for Comms, 1993; Min for Rescs, 1993-96. Memberships: HoR for Fadden, Queensland, 1983; HoR for Rankin, 1984-. Address: House of Representatives, Canberra, ACT 2600, Australia.

BEDFORD Richard Dodgshun, b. 3 Jan 1945. Professor of Geography. m. Janet Sholto Douglas, 20 Aug 1969, 1 s, 1 d. Education: BA, Univ of Auckland; MA 1st Class Hons, Univ of Auckland; PhD, Aust Natl Univ. Appointments: Lectr in Geog, Univ of Canterbury, Christchurch, 1972-76; Snr Lectr in Geog, Univ of Canterbury, 1976-89; Prof of Geog, Univ of Waikato, Hamilton, 1989-. Publications: 8 books and monographs; 120 jrnl articles, chapts in books and conf papers. Honour: 1990 NZ Commemorative Medal. Memberships: Mbr of Cncl, NZ Geographical Soc, 1974-99; NZ Natl Commn for UNESCO, 1995-99; IGBP Cttee, Roy Soc of NZ, 1995-99. Listed in: Who's Who in New Zealand.

Hobbies: Gardening; Reading. Address: Department of Geography, University of Waikato, PB 3105, Hamilton, New Zealand.

BEDI Bishan Singh, b. 25 Sept 1946. Cricketer. m. (1) Glenith Jill Bedi 1969, 1 s, 1 d; (2) Inderjit Bedi 1980. Education: Punjab Univ. Appointments: Empld by Steel Authy of India New Delhi; Slow left-arm bowler; played for Northern Punjab, 1961-62 to 1966-67, Delhi 1968-69 to 1980-81, Northamptonshire 1972-77; Played in 67 Tests for India - 1967-68 to 1979 - 22 as cap taking 266 wickets - average 28.7; Took 1560 first-class wickets; Toured Eng 1971, 1974, 1975 - World Cup, 1976. Honours: Hon Life mbr MCC, 1981, natl selector; Padma Shri, 1969; Arjuna Award, 1971. Hobbies: Reading; Photography; Swimming; Letter writing. Address: Ispat Bhawan, Lodhi Rd, New Delhi 3, India.

BEDNARIK Robert Gerhard, b. 6 Apr 1944, Baden, Vienna, Austria. Publisher; Author. m. Elfriede, 8 Feb 1971, 1 s, 1 d. Appointments: Mngng Dir, Archaeological Publs, Inc, 1983-; Gen Ed and Convenor, Intl Fedn of Rock Art Orgns, 1988-. Publcations: About 1000 articles and books, 400 in refereed sci jrnls. Honours: Hon Dip for servs to world rock art, Turin, 5 Sept, 1995. Memberships: Austl Rock Art Rsch Assn, Sec, Ed; Archaeological and Anthropological Soc of Vic, Ed. Address: 3 Buxton Street, Elsternwick 3185, Australia.

BEECH Allan Montgomery, b. 17 Jan 1921, Newcastle, NSW, Aust. Surgeon. m. Lorna Joan Bromilow, 17 Aug 1951, 1 s, 2 d. Education: MBBS, Melbourne Univ, Aust, 1944; FRACS, 1953; FRCS (Eng), 1954. Appointments: Brit C'wlth Occupation Force, RAAF, Japan, 1947; Gen Surg, Prince Henry's Hosp, Melbourne, 1956-80; Surg, 1st Austl Field Hosp, Vietnam, 1970; Asst Police Med Offr, 1967-79; Police Med Offr, Vic, 1979-88; Lectr in Anatomy, Melbourne Univ; Lectr in Surg, Monash Univ; Cnslt Surg, RAAF (Grp Capt), 1973-80. Publication: Management Chronic Ulceration. Honours: Mbr, Gen Div Order of Aust, AM, 1991; Kt of Venerable Order of St John of Jerusalem, KStJ, 1984; Hon Surg to HM RAAF, 1973-80; Reserve Force Decoration. Memberships: RACS, Road Trauma Cttee Vic; Chmn, Red Cross Blood Bank, 1973-83. Address: 7 Crowther Place, Brighton, Vic 3186, Australia.

BEEKE James William, b. 18 Jan 1950, Michigan, USA. Educator. m. Ruth, 1 May 1970, 3 s, 2 d. Education: BA, cum laude, Educn; MA, Educl Admin. Appointments: Tchr, Prin, Asst Inspector, Inspector of Independent Schs for BC. Publications: 7 books and num articles in profl jrnls. Honours: Ctf of Regoc, Min of Educn, 1991. Memberships: Soc of Christians in BC, bd mbr, 1993-96; Christian Principals Assn of BC, bd mbr, 1992-96. Hobbies: Camping; Bird Watching; Hiking. Address: 10435 McGrath Road, Rosedale, British Columbia V0X 1X0, Canada.

BEEMAN Josiah Horton, b. 8 Oct 1935. Diplomat. m. Susan Louise Sturman, 28 Oct 1995, 1 d. Education: BA, CA Univ at San Fran. Appointment: US Amb to NZ and Western Samoa, 1994-. Publication: Northern Ireland and the Politics of Reconciliation. Memberships: Hon Patron, Amn Chmbr of Com, NZ; Patron, NZ-Am Assn. Listed in: Who's Who in America; Who's Who in Politics. Hobbies: Travel; Music; Piano; Reading; Croquet. Address: American Embassy, 29 Fitzherbert Terrace, Throndon, Wellington, New Zealand.

BEETHAM William Ronald, b. 3 June 1925, Melbourne, Vic, Aust. Consultant Orthopaedic Surgeon. m. Mary Beetham, 17 Mar 1950, 2 s. Education: MBBS, Melbourne, 1949; FRACS, 1961; FACS, 1974; FACRM, Fndn Fell; FASMF, 1978. Appointments: Gen Surg, Warranambool, Vic, 1954-61; Cnslt Orthopaedic Surg, Ballarat and Melbourne, Vic, 1961-; Lectr, Sports Med, Ballarat Univ Coll, 1975-82. Publications: Orthopaedic Training in Developing Countries; Epidural Venography of the Lumbar Spine; Lumbar Discography; Clinical and Pathological Correlation and Surgical Evaluation; The Lumbar Facet Joint and Low Back Pain. Honours: Paul Harris Fell, Rotary Intl, 1978; ACROD Presdtl Awd, 1978.

Memberships: Chmn, CARE-Medico Orthopaedic Trng Prog, Indonesia, 1969-79; Fell, Brit Orthopaedic Assn; Fell, Austl Orthopaedic Assn; Fndn Mbr, Intl Soc Stdy of Lumbar Spine; Corresp Fell, Indonesian Orthopaedic Assn; Life Mbr, Spine Soc Aust, 1990; Fell, Roy Soc Med, 1991; Hon Fell, West Pacific Orthopaedic Assn, 1992. Hobbies: Gardening and plant propagation; Woodwork. Address: Cedar Court, PO Box 35, Miners Rest, Vic 3352, Australia.

BEFU Harumi, b. 20 Mar 1930, Los Angeles, California, USA. College Professor. m. Kei, 23 Aug 1959, 1 s, 1 d. Education: PhD, Anthropol. Appointments: Univ NE, 1961-62; Univ MO, 1962-64; Univ MI, 1964-65; Stanford Univ, 1965-95; Kyoto Bunkyo Univ, 1996-. Publications: Japan: An Anthropological Introduction, 1970; The Challenge of Japan's Internationalization, 1984. Honours: Guggenheim Fellshp, 1971; Fulbright Fellshp, 1978; Natl Endowment for the Hum, 1983. Memberships: Amn Anthropol Assn; Assn for Asian Stdies; Eurn Assn for Japanese Stdies. Hobbies: Reading; Classical Music. Address: Department of Cultural Anthropology, Kyoto Bunkyo University, Makishima-cho Senzoku 80, Uji-Shi 611-00411, Japan.

BEGG Heather, b. 1 Dec 1932, Nelson, NZ. Opera Singer (Mezzo Soprano). Education: St Mary's Music Coll, Auckland, 1949-53; Sydney Conservatorium of Music, 1954-56; Natl Sch of Opera, London, 1957-59; Pupil of Florence Wiese-Norberg, London. Appointments: Debut, Auckland, NZ, as Azucena in Il Trovatore, 1954; Natl Opera of Aust, 1954-56; Carl Rosa Co, London, 1960; Sadler's Wells Opera, 1961-64; NZ Opera Co, 1964-66; Roy Opera, Covent Garden, Guest Artist, 1959-99, res, 1972-76; Engl Natl Opera, Guest, 1968-72; Austl Opera, 1976-; Guest artist in Edinburgh, Salzburg and Orange Fests, Strasbourg, Bordeaux, Milan, Vancouver, Chgo, San Fran, San Diego, Barcelona; Concert artist and recitalist for radio and TV in Eng, NZ, Aust. Creative works: Recordings include: Unitel film of Le Nozze di Figaro; Les Troyens, conducted by Colin Davis; Mefistofele; I Puritani; The Little Sweep; Southern Voices; Die Fledermaus; Adriana Lecouvreur; Dialogues of the Carmelites; La Fille du Régiment; The Mikado; Patience; Voss; Gipsy Princess. Honours: Sydney Sun Aria Winner, 1955; Recip, NZ Govt Music Bursary, 1956; Countess of Munster Schl, 1959; OBE, 1978. Hobbies: Tapestry; Photography; Painting; Gardening. Address: c/o Opera Australia, 480 Elizabeth Street, Surry Hills, NSW 2010, Australia.

BEGG Leanne Mary, b. 12 Sept 1965, Brisbane, Aust. Veterinary Surgeon. m. Martin, 17 Nov 1996, 1 d. Education: BVSc; Dip Vet Clin Stdy; MS; MACVSc; Dip ACVIM. Appointments: Internship, Univ of Sydney, 1988; Assoc, Randwick Equine Cntr, 1989-91; Residency, MI State Univ, USA, 1991-94; Ptnr, Randwick Equine Cntr, 1994-. Memberships: Austl Vet Assn; Austl Jockey Club. Hobbies: Horse Riding; Horse Racing. Address: Randwick Equine Centre, P O Box 195, Randwick, NSW 2031, Australia.

BEISCHER David Albert, b. 11 July 1962, Ballmoney, N Ireland. Veterinary Surgeon. m. Caroline, 2 s. Education: BV Sc Hons, Univ QLD; BAgSc Hons, Univ Melbourne; MAgSc, Univ QLD. Appointments: Tutorial Fells, Dept of Animal Prodn, Univ QLD, 1984-86; Vet Surg, Mt Eliza Vet Clinic, 1991-92; Deniliquin Vet Clinic, 1992-96; Wonthaggi Vet Clinic, 1996-. Creative Works: Masters Thesis. Honours: Microbiol Exhibition, Univ of Melbourne, 1982. Memberships: Austl Vet Assn; Austl Assn of Cattle Vets. Hobbies: Tennis; Squash; Running; Cycling; Bush Walking; Snow Skiing. Address: 50 Watt St, Wonthaggi, Vic 3995, Australia.

BELAUNDE TERRY Fernando, b. 7 Oct 1913. Politician; Architect. Education: France; USA. Appointments: Dean in Sch of Arch Lima, 1948-56; Ldr Accion Popular - AP - 1956-; Presl Cand, 1956, 1962; Pres of Peru, 1963-68 - deposed by mil coup; Fled to NY, Oct 1968; Lectng at Harvard Univ, Nov 1968; Returned to Peru briefly, Dec 1970; Deported, returned, Jan 1976;

Pres Peru, July 1980-85. Publications: Peru's Own Conquest - autobiog.

BELAVADI Prabhakar, b. 17 Nov 1946, Hassan, Karnataka, India. Teacher; Researcher. m. B P Gayathridev, 9 May 1974, 2 s. Education: BS, Karnatak Univ, Dharwar, 1966; MSc, Chem, Karnatak Univ, Dharwar, 1968; PhD, Chem, Karnatak Univ, Dharwar, 1984. Appointments: Demonstrator, 1970; Lectr, 1976; Rdr, 1984; Prof, 1993; Dir, Physl Educ, 1989; Students Welfare Offr, 1992; Dir, Inst of Sugar Technol, 1995. Publications: Kannada Poems, 1969-90; 1 poem in Karnataka Sahitya Acady book, 1994. Honours: Best District Gov Awd, Y's Men Intl, 1992; Talents Awd, 2nd Ins for Tal Sea, 1998. Memberships: Life Mbr, Servas Intl; Charter Sec, Pres, Disrict Gov, Y's men Intl, 1990-94. Hobbies: Teaching; Sports; Writing; Receiving guests. Address: 1-867/22A, Chiranjeevi, mahaveer Nagar, Gulbarga 585102, Karnataka, India.

BELINO Manuel, b. 15 May 1957, Pasay City, Philippines. Mechanical Engineer. Education: BSME, Mapua Inst of Technol, Manila; MEng Educ, De La Salle Univ, Manila; MTheol Studies, Harvard Univ, USA. Appointments: Asst Prof, 1990-; Chair, ME Dept, 1995-96; Assoc Dean, 1992-95. Honours: Mapua Inst of Technol, ME Dept Awd, Outstndng Mech Engr, 1994. Memberships: Am Soc of Mech Engrs; Philippine Inst Mech Engrng Educrs, VP. Hobbies: Traveling; Cooking; Reading; Gardening. Address: 31 Grasshopper Street, St Mary's Village, Talon II, Las Pinas City, 1701, Philippines.

BELL John Anthony, b. 1 Nov 1940, Newcastle, NSW, Aust. Actor. m. Ann Volska, 29 Aug 1965, 2 d. Education: BA, Hons, Sydney. Appointments: Hd of Acting (NIDA), Co Dir, Nimrod Th, 1970-84; Artistic Dir, Bell Shakespeare Co, 1990-. Honours: OBE, 1974; AM, 1986; DLitt (Hon), Newcastle, 1994; DLitt (Hon), Sydney, 1997. Address: c/o Bell Shakespeare Company, PO Box 10, Millers Point, NSW 2000, Australia.

BELL Kenneth Wellesley, b. 29 Mar 1928, Sydney, Aust. Optometrist. m. Gay, 14 Dec 1963. Education: Optometry Dip, ASTC, 1952; The Use of Drugs in Refraction and Examination of the Eyes, Univ NSW, 1973. Appointments: Sec, The Contact Lens Society of Australia, 1966-; Mbr, Optometrists Registration Bd, NSW, 1973-76, 1979-82; Chmn, Optometrists Registration Board, 1982-88. Memberships: Optometrists Assn Aust; The Contact Lens Soc of Aust, Sec, 1966-; Past Pres, Optometrists Assn of NSW. Hobbies: Golf; Gardening. Address: 818 Australia Square Tower, 264 George Street, Sydney, NSW 2000, Australia.

BELLAIR John Mitchell, b. 22 May 1909. Author. m. (1) Alison Joan Macrae, 10 Dec 1935, dec, 1 d, (2) Margaret McCullagh Mitchell. Education: Scotch Coll; Ormond Coll; 2 yrs agricl sci, Melbourne Univ. Appointments: Commanded a Machine Gun Co, WWII, 2nd AIF, 1939-45; Pres, Shire of Romsey, Vic, 1951, 1958. Publications: Amateur Soldier, 1984; From Snow to Jungle, 1988; The School That Was, 1992; In Hearn's Footsteps, 1993; Yesterday's Man and Other Verse, 1995. Memberships: Aust Soc of Auths; Natl Book Cncl; Vic Writers' Cntr. Listed in: Who's Who of Australian Writers. Hobbies: Gardening; Painting; Travelling; Legacy. Address: Applecross, St Georges Road, Upper Beaconsfield, Vic 3808, Australia.

BELLIN Howard, b. 30 Oct 1933, NYC, USA. Chairman. m. Barbara Ann Box, 12 May 1962, 1 s, 1 d. Education: BSc, Carnegie-Mellon Univ, Pittsburgh, PA, USA, 1955. Appointments: Mfng Mngmt, Gillette Co; Mfng Mngmt, Allied Corp; Mngng Dir, Avin Plating; Fndr, Chmn, I-F Cnsltng Grp; Editl Bd, Jrnl of Marketing Channels. Publications: Contbr articles to profl jrnls. Membership: Am Club, Sydney, NSW. Hobbies: Running; Photography; History; Travel. Address: 17 Moule Avenue, Brighton, Vic 3186, Australia.

BELTON Charles Humphrey, b. 12 Sept 1919. Medical Officer. m. (1) Aileen Cosby Johnston, 1942, (2) Margaret Miriam Fanselow Hart, 1968, 7 s, 6 d.

Education: BSc 1942, MB 1952, Univ of NZ. Appointments: Pt Anaesthetist, Nelson Hosp; Pt Med Offr, Addiction Clinic, Nelson Hosp. Publications: 5: Articles on medl topics publs in NZ Med Jrnl. Honours: Elect Fell, Roy NZ Coll of Gen Prac. Membership: NZ Med Assn. Hobbies: Trout fishing; Fly making; Gardening; Rock wall construction. Address: Maranui, Maitai Valley, Nelson, New Zealand.

BEN Kunlong, b. 23 Feb 1941, Jiangsu, China. Immunologist. m. Xiaomei Cao, 1 d. Education: DVM. Appointments: Rsch Asst, 1968-78, Rsch Assoc, 1978-88, Assoc Prof, 1988-92, Prof, 1992-, Kunming Inst of Zoology, CAS. Publications: Disease of Laboratory Macaques, 1978; More than 80 other pprs. Memberships: AAAS; Intl Soc of Primatol; Intl Soc of Reproductive Immunol; Chinese Soc of Immunol. Hobbies: Sports; History. Address: Kunming Institute of Zoology, Chinese Academy of Sciences, Kunming, Yunnan 650223, China.

BEN ELISSAR Eliahu, b. 2 Aug 1932, Radom, Poland. Politician; Diplomat. m. Nitza Efrony, 1979, 1 s. Education: Sorbonne Paris; Univ of Geneva. Appointments: Escaped from Poland to Palestine, 1942; Returned to Eur as student, 1950; Govt serv Israel and abroad until 1965; Corresp for L'Aurore and Le Journal de Geneve in Israel; Active mbr of Herut Movement; Elected to Ctr Cttee of Herut, 1970; Party Spokesman, 1971; Herut Exec Cttee, 1972; Deleg to World Zionist Congress, 1972, 1987, 1992; Herut Directorate, 1978; In charge of Info Dept during Likud natl election campaigns, 1973, 1977; Chmn Herut World Exec, 1988-91; Hd of Israel's first deleg to Cairo Mena House talks, 1977; Dir-Gen PMs Off, 1977-80; Israel's First Amb to Egypt, 1980-81; Mbr, Knesset, 1981-96; Mbr, 1981-82, 1984-89, 1993-96, Chmn, 1982-84, 1989-92, For Affairs and Def Cttee; Mbr Knesset Faction Exec, 1984-92; Mbr, Bd of Govs Jewish Agcy, 1989-92; Mbr deleg to Madrid Conf, 1991; Mbr deleg to UN Gen Assembly, 1992; Amb of Israel to US, 1996-98; Amb of Israel to France, 1996-. Publications: La Politique Etrangere du IIIeme Reich et les Juifs; La Guerre israeloarabe; No More War. Honours: Grand Officier Ordre de l'Ethiopie, 1964; Grand Cruz Extraordinaria Orden de la Democracia - Colombia - 1980. Memberships: Mbr Advsry Cttee Israeli Cncl on For Rels; Mbr Pub Cncl Eibshitz Inst of Holocaust Studies; Fndng Mbr Cttee Menachem Begin Heritage Fndn. Address: The Israeli Embassy, Paris, France

BEN-DAVID Zadok, b. 1949, Bayhan, Yemen. Sculptor. m. Dana Pugach, 1991. Education: Acady of Art and Design Jerusalem; Reading Univ, 1974-75; St Martin's Sch of Art London, 1975-76. Appointments: Sculp tchr at St Martin's Sch of Art, 1977-82; Sculp tchr at Ravensbourne Coll of Art and Design Bromley, 1982-85; First one man show at Air Gall London, 1980; Exhibns - solo and grp - in Antwerp, London, NY, Jerusalem, Melbourne, Munich, Glasgow, Tel Aviv, 1984-; Repd Israel in the Biennale di Venezia Italy, 1988; Recent solo exhbns: San Fran Art Inst, San Fran, 1998; Museum beelden ann zee, Scheveningen, Holland, 1999; Mercedes Benz Forum, Stuttgart, Germany; Grp exhbn, Influences on British Sculpture in the 20th Century, Salisbury Cath, Salisbury, Eng, 1999. Publications: - catalogues - Zadok Ben-David, 1987; The Israeli Pavilion-The Venice Biennale, 1988. Address: 65 Warwick Avenue, London, W9 2PP, England.

BEN-ELIEZER Benjamin, b. 1936, Iraq. Politician; Army Officer. Appointments: Emigrated to Israel, 1949; Career Offr Israel Def Forces; Cmdr Six Day War, 1967; Served on IDF Mil Mission to Singapore, 1970-73; Cmdr Yom Kippur War, 1973; Fist CO South Lebanon, 1977-78; Cmdr Judea and Samaria, 1978-81; Govt Co-ord of Activities in the Administered Areas, 1983-84; Min of Housing and Constrn, 1992-96; Served on For Affairs Cttee, 1988-92. Memberships: Knesset, 1984-; Labour. Address: Ministry of Construction and Housing, P O Box 18110, Kiryat Hamemshala (East), Jerusalem 91180, Israel.

BEN-NATA Asher, b. 15 Feb 1921, Vienna. Diplomat. m. Erika - Rut - Frudt, 1940, 1 s, 1 d. Education: ZP

Hayut Hebrew Coll Vienna; Inst des Hautes Etudes Intls Geneva. Appointments: Co-fndr and mbr Kibbutz Mederot-Zeraim, 1938-44; Latterly Sec and Treas; Polit Dept Jewish Agcy, 1944-45; On miss to Eur to org rescue of Jews and illegal immigration to Palestine; Attached to HO of Jewish Agcy, 1945-47; Min of For Affairs, 1948-51; Studies in Geneva, 1951-53; Govt Rep on Bd of Red Sea Inkodeh Co, 1953-56; Gen Mgr, 1955-56; Rep of Min of Def in Eur, 1956-58; Dir-Gen Min of Def, 1959-65; Amb to Fedl Repub of Germany, 1965-70; Amb to France, 1970-75; Pres Israel-German Assn, 1973-; Pol Ad to Min of Def, 1975-78; Chmn Ben-Gurion Fndn, 1983-; Advsr to PM on Spec Affairs, 1985-; Amb on Spec Miss, 1993. Publications: Briefe an den Botschafter, 1970; Dialogue avec des Allemands, 1973. Honours: Dr hc - Gen Gurion Univ, 1990; Officier Legion d'honneur; Cmdr ordre natl - Ivory Coast; Cmdr ordre de l'Etoile equatoriale - Gabon; Louis Waiss Peace Prize, 1974. Address: 89 Haim Levanon Street, Tel-Aviv 69345, Israel.

BENAUD Richard, b. 6 Oct 1930. Cricket; Commentator. m. (1) 2 s, (2) Daphne Elizabeth Surfleet, 1967, 2 s. Appointments: Right-hand middle-order batsman and right-arm leg-break and googly bowler; Played for NSW, 1948-49 to 1963-64 - cap 1958-59 to 1962-63; Played in 63 Tests for Aust, 1951-52 to 1963-64, 28 as cap scoring 2201 runs - average 24.4 - inclng 3 hundreds, taking 248 wickets - average 27.0; First to score 2000 runs and take 200 wickets in Tests; Scored 11719 runs - 23 hundreds - and took 945 wickets in first-class cricket; Toured Eng 1953, 1956, 1961; Intl sports consultant; TV Commentator BBC 1960-99, Channel 4, 1999-, Channel Nine 1977-. Publications: Way of Cricket, 1960; Tale of Two Tests, 1962; Spin Me a Spinner, 1963; The New Champions, 1965; Willow Patterns, 1972; Benaud on Reflection, 1984; The Appeal of Cricket, 1995; Anything But...: An Autobiography, 1998. Hobby: Golf. Address: 19/178 Beach Street, Coogee, New South Wales 2034, Australia.

BENAWA Abdul Raouf, b. 1913. Writer; Administrator. Education: Ganj Pub Sch Kandahar. Appointments: Mbr Words Dept Afghan Acady and Asst Info Dept, 1940; Dir Publ Dept Afghan Acad, 1941; Gen Dir Pushtu Tolana; Sec Afghan Acady and Dir Kabul mag; Proprietor weekly mag Hewad; Mbr Hist Dept, 1950; Dir Internal Publ Dept, 1951; Gen Dir, 1952; Press Attache India, 1953-56; Pres Radio Kabul, 1956-63; Press and Cultural Cnslr Cairo, 1963. Publications: Women in Afghanistan; Mir Wiess Neeka; Literary Sciences; Pushtu Songs; De Ghanamo Wazhai; Pushtoonistan; A Survey of Pushtoonistan; Rahman Baba; Pir mohammad Kakar; Khosh-hal Khan se Wai; Pushtoo Killi, Vol 4; Kazim Khan-e-Shaida; Transls: Mosa-fir Iqbal; Geetan-Jali Tagoor; Da Darmistatar Pushtoo Seerane; Leaders of Pashtoonistan; History of Hootaki; Preshana afkar - poem; Da zra khwala; Pashto writers today - 2 vols; Pashto reader for schools; Pachakhan - A leader of Pashtoni; Landei - public poems; plays: I-Zoor gonahgar - Old criminal; Ishtebah - confusion; Kari bar asal; Aashyanae aqab; Zarang Chaoki der khater; Hakoomat baidar.

BENITEZ Rene B, b. 18 Jan 1962, Manila, Philippines. Investment Banker. m. Bettina, 1 May 1993, 1 s. Education: MA, Econs, Yale Univ. Appointments: Pres, Amalgamated Investment Bank Corp; Former Pres, Makati Fin Corp; Former CEO, DBS Securities. Publications: Sev articles in profl jrnls. Honours: Intl Mngmt Hons, Yale, 1985; Hon Mention, HS, 1980; 2nd Hons, Grave Sch. Memberships: Dir, Makati Rotary Club; Fndng Mbr, Philippines Stock Exchange; Philippines Econ Soc. Address: 6805 Ayala Avenue, Makati, Philippines.

BENNETT Sir Charles Moihi To Arawaka, b. 1913. Retired Diplomat. Education: Univ of NZ; Exeter Coll Oxford. Appointments: Schoolmaster, 1937; Staff mbr NZ Brdcstng Serv, 1938-39; Serv with NZ Army in UK, Greece, Crete, N Africa, cmdng Maori Battalion from Alamein to Tunis, 1939-46; Staff mbr War Hists Sect Internal Affairs Dept; Asst Controller Maori Welfare Div Maori Affairs Dept, 1951-57; Dir, 1957-58; NZ High

Commnr to Malaya, the first Maori to ld an overseas Miss, 1959-63; Asst Sec Dept of Maori Affairs Wellington, 1963-69; VP NZ Labour Party, 1970-72; Pres, 1973-76; Dir Bank of NZ, 1976-78. Honours: Hon LLD, Univ Canterbury NZ. Memberships: Mbr Ngarimu Scholarship Fund Bd, 1947-50; Mbr State Lit Advsry Cttee NZ Parole Bd, 1951. Address: 72 Boucher Avenue, Te Puke 3071, New Zealand.

BENNETT Isobel Ida, b. 9 July 1909, Brisbane, Qld, Aust. Marine Biologist; Author. Education: Somerville House, Brisbane, 1923-25. Appointments: Sec, Libn; Demonstrator; Rsch Asst, Univ Sydney, 1933-71; Auth. Publications: On The Seashore, 1969; Shores Of Macquerie Island, 1971; The Fringe Of The Sea, 1974; On The Australian Seashore, 1974; Lord Howe Island (with Jean Edgecombe), 1980; Norfolk Island (with Jean Edgecombe), 1983; The Great Barrier Reef, 7th edition, 1988; Australian Seashores (with W J Dakin), 1952, completely revised version with over 500 new colour photographs, 1987; Collins Eyewitness Handbook, Australian Seashores, 1992; Co-ed, A Coral Reef Handbook, 1993. Honours: 1st recip, Hon MSc, Univ Sydney, 1962; Whitley Mem Awd, Best Illustrated Book on Aust Natural Hist, 1982, Best Text Book, Aust Natural Hist, 1988, Roy Zool Soc NSW; Mueller Medallist, ANZAAS, 1982; Hon Life Mbr, Aust Coral Reef Soc, 1984; Offr Order Aust, 1984; DSc (hons causa) Univ NSW, 1995. Memberships: Rsch Assoc, The Aust Mus, Sydney; Aust Marine Sci Assn; Linnean Soc NSW; Aust Coral Reef Soc; Aust Fedn Univ Women; Roy Zool Soc NSW. Listed in: Who's Who In Australia, 1962-95; Who's Who of Australian Writers; The World Who's Who of Women; Five Thousand Personalities of the World; International Who's Who of Professional and Business Women; Who's Who in Australasia and the Far East. Hobbies: Orchid growing; Beachcombing; Photography; Travel. Address: 30 Myola Rd, Newport, NSW 2106, Australia.

BENNETT Phillip Harvey (General Sir), b. 27 Dec 1928, Perth, WA, Aust. m. Margaret Heywood, 18 May 1955, 2 s, 1 d. Education: RMC, Duntroon; JSSC (UK); RCDS (UK); PSC (AUST); PH (Aust); Hon LLD (NSW), 1987; Hon LLD (Tas), 1992. Appointments: Served 1950 and 1952: 3rd Bn, Korea (despatches), Sch of Infantry (Instr), 25 Cdn Bde, Korea, Pacific Is Regt, PNG, 16th Bn Cameron Highlanders of WA; Commando Trng, Roy Marines, Eng, Malta and Cyprus, 1957-58; OC 2 Commando Co, Melbourne, 1958-61; Austl Staff Coll, 1961-62; Snr Instr, Chf Instr, Offr, Cadet Sch, Portsea, 1962-65; AAG Directorate of Personal Servs, AHQ, 1965-67; Co 1 RAR, 1967-69 (served Vietnam, DSO); Exch Instr, Jnt Servs Staff Coll, Eng, 1969-71; COL, Directorate of Co-ord and Org, AHQ, 1971-74; COS, HQ Fd Force Cmnd, 1974-75; RCDS, Eng, 1976; Cmdr, 1st Divsn, 1977-79; Asst Chf of Def Force Staff, 1979-82; Chf of the Gen Staff, 1982-84; Chf of the Def Force, Aust, 1984-87; Hon Col, Roy Tas Regt, 1987-95; Gov of Tas, 1987-95; Chmn, Austl War Memorial Fndn, 1996-; Natl Pres, Order of Aust Assn, 1997-. Honours: Companion of the Disting Serv Order, 1969; AO, 1981; KBE, 1983; AC, 1985; Kt of the Order of St John of Jerusalem, 1988. Hobbies: Golf; Reading. Address: c/o Commonwealth Club, 25 Forster Crescent, Yarralumla, ACT 2600, Australia.

BENSON James B Jr, b. 8 May 1930, Phila, PA, USA. Police Science Instructor. m. Hiroko, 14 Apr 1955. Education: Bach, Police Sci. Appointments: Fell, Amn Assn of Criminology; Fell, Amn Assn of Profl Hypnotherapists. Creative Works: Devotion in Blue, 1973; Lawmans Lament, 1974; num Law Enforcement mag Articles. Honours: Hon Dr of Law, 1968; Hon PhD, Clinl Hypnotherapy, 1992; J Edgar Hoover Disting Pub Serv Awd. Memberships: Mil Police Cnslt; Amn Assoc of Criminology. Hobbies: Criminology; Photography. Address: 1400 S Sunkist St Space 199, Anaheim, CA 92806-5624, USA.

BENTLEY John Clive, b. 22 Mar 1944, Weston-Super-Mare, England. Retired. m. Christine, 28 Dec 1968, 1 s, 1 d. Education: BA; Grad Dip, Spec Educ.

Publications: The Mark of the Swastika, 1985; Heads They Win Tales We Lose: The Rampage of Rampo, 1985; I Love You Danny Rocco, 1992. Hobbies: Tennis; Skiing. Address: PO Box 17, Ridgley, Tas 7321, Australia.

BERAN Harry, b. 23 May 1935, Vienna, Austria. Senior Lecturer; Philosopher. m. Clare Harding. Education: BA (Syd); PhD (Syd). Appointments: Mngr, Nestlé Co of Aust, 1960-64; Lectr, Univ of New Eng, 1971-76; Snr Lectr, Univ Wollongong, 1977-. Publications: Massim Art, 1980; The Consent Theory of Political Obligation, 1987; Mutuaga A 19th C New Guinea Master Craver, 1996. Honours: Commonwealth Undergrad Schlshp Austl Govt, 1964-67; Commonwealth Postgrad Schlshp Austl Govt, 1968-70. Memberships: Australasian Assn of Philos; Pacific Arts Assn; Oceanic Art Soc, Pres, 1996-98. Hobbies: Oceanic Art (collecting & researching). Address: 17 Neil Street, Epping, NSW 2121, Australia.

BERAN Roy Gary, b. 6 Mar 1950, Sydney, Aust. Neurologist. m. Maureen Riley, 13 Oct 1974, 1 s, 3 d. Education: MBBS, 1972; FRACGP, 1978; FRACP, 1981; Grad Dip, Further Educ, Adelaide CAE, 1982; Grad Dip, Tertiary Educ, NEU, 1982; MD, 1984; FAFPHM, 1990; B Leg S, 1992; FACLM, 1997. Appointments: Roy Rehab Hosp, 1981-; RAN Cnslt Neurol, 1982-; Neurol, Fairfield Hosp, 1983-; Neurol, Macquarie Hosp & Liverpool Hosp, 1984; Visng Fell, Sch of Community Med & St Lukes Hosp, 1993-. Publications include: Learning About Epilepsy; Epidemiological Studies of Epilepsy in Sydney, Australia; Cost of Epilepsy; Epilepsy and the Law; Epilepsy: Facts About Fits; Economic Evaluation of Epilepsy Management. Honours: UNSW Pub Hlth Prize, 1972; Francis Hardy Faulding em Rsch Fellshp Prize, 1981; Winston Churchill Mem Trust Fellshp, 1982; Employer of the Yr, NSW, 1990; Gov World Assn Med Law, 1996; Bd Mbr, Austl Inst Hlth Law and Ethics, 1996; Francis Hardy Faulding Memorial Rsch Fellshp; VP, Austl Coll Legal Med, 1998. Memberships: RACP; RACGP; AFPHM; ACLM; AAN; Aust Mil Med Assn; ASA; ESA; NEAA Med Panel; ACROD; ILAE Commn Econ Aspects Epilepsy; WAML; AIHLE. Hobbies: Skiing; Surfing; Travelling; Writing; Law; Human Nature. Address: Suite 5, 6th Floor, 12 Thomas Street, Chatswood, NSW 2067, Australia.

BEREDER Frederic Laurent, b. 18 May 1960, Oran, Algeria. Architect. m. Jin, 10 Oct 1991, 1 s, 1 d. Education: MArch. Appointments: Duct Sarl; Dumez Japan; SEC; Nichisutsu Sekkei. Publication: Sanno estate, archt work, 1998. Memberships: ACCJ, 1996; Ordre des Architectes; Col des Experts Archts. Hobby: Art work. Address: Gyosai, Building #706, 5-27-5 Okusawa, Setagaya-Ku, Tokyo 158-0083, Japan.

BERESFORD Bruce, b. 16 Aug 1940. Film Director. m. (1) Rhoisin Beresford 1965, 2 s, 1 d; (2) Virginia Duigan 1989, 1 d. Education: Univ of Sydney. Appointments: Worked in advtng; Worked for Austl Brdcstng Commn; Went to Eng, 1961; Odd jobs inclng tchng; Film ed Nigeria, 1964-66; Sec to British Film Insts Prodn Bd, 1966; Feature film dir, 1971-; Dird many short films, 1960-75. Creative Works: Dird feature films - The Adventures of Barry Mackenzie, 1972; Barry Macknezie Holds His Own, 1974; Side by Side, 1975; Don's Party, 1976; The Getting of Wisdom, 1977; Money Movers, 1979; Breaker Morant, 1980; Puberty Blues, 1981; The Club, 1981; Tender Mercies, 1983; King David, 1984; Crimes of the Heart, 1986; Fringe Dwellers, 1986; Aria - segment - 1987; Her Alibi, 1988; Driving Miss Daisy, 1989 - Acady Award Best Film 1990; Mr Johnson, 1990; Black Robe, 1990; Rich in Love, 1993; A Good Man in Africa, 1993; Silent Fall, 1994; The Last Dance, 1995; Paradise Road, 1996. Address: c/o Anthony A Williams, 50 Oxford Street, Paddington, NSW 2021, Australia.

BERGERSEN Fraser John, b. 26 May 1929, Hamilton, NZ. Research Scientist. m. Gladys Irene Heather, 5 July 1952, 2 s, 1 d. Education: BSc, MSc, Hons, Univ of Otago, NZ; DSc, Univ NZ. Appointments: Assoc, Bacteriol Dept, Univ Otago, 1951-54; Rsch Sci,

Div of Plant Ind, CSIRO, Canberra, 1954-94; Visng Fell, Austl Natl Univ, 1994-99. Publications: Methods for Evaluating Biblogical Nitrogen Firation, 1980; Root Modules of Legumes - Structure and Functions, 1982. Honours: Rivett Medal, CSIRO, 1968; FRS, London, 1981; FAA, 1985. Membership: Cncl, Austl Acady of Sci, 1987-93, For Sec, 1989-93. Hobbies: Music; Gardening. Address: 13 Ferdinand Street, Campbell, ACT 2612, Australia.

BERGQUIST Patricia Rose, b. 10 Mar 1933, Auckland, New Zealand. Scientist; University Professor. m. Peter L, 5 July 1958, 1 d. Education: BS, 1954, MSc, 1956, PhD, 1961, DSc, 179, Univ of Auckland, NZ. Appointments: Lectr, Zool, 1958; Snr Lectr, Assoc Prof, Personal Rsch Chair, Zool, 1979; Bd of Fndn for Rsch Sci & Technol, 1989-93; Asst Vice Chan Acad, 1989-96; Prime Min's Spec Cttee on Nuclear Propulsion, 1991-92; Dpty Vice Chan, 1993. Publications: 128 sci publs; 1 book, 1978. Honours: FRSNZ, 1981; Hector Medalist RSNZ, 1989; NZ Marine Scis Prize, for dictinguished contbn to Marine Bio, 1994; Dame Cmdr, Brit Empire, 1994. Memberships: NZ Marine Scis Soc; Systematics Assn of NZ; Roy Soc f NZ. Hobbies include: Gardening; Music. Address: 3A Pakerangi Crescent, Ellerslie, Auckland 5, New Zealand.

BERI Rajiv, b. 22 Sept 1952, India. Managing Director, Macmillan India Ltd. m. Nutan, 11 Dec 1981, 2 d. Education: BA (Engl Hons); LLB; PG Dip Personnel Mngmt. Appointments: Chmn, Trng and Seminars, Fedn of Indian Publrs; Chmn, Trng Cttee, Fedn of Publrs Booksellers Assn. Memberships: F I P (India); FPBAI (India). Address: Macmillan India Ltd, 315-316, Raheja Chambers, 12 Museum Road, Bangalore 560 001, India.

BERKMAN Donald Alexander, b. 20 Jan 1934. Geologist. m. (1) Margaret Lees, 1959, (2) Lesley Vincent, 1984; 2 s, 3 d. Appointments: Geol, Reynolds Metals, 1957-59; CRA Exploration, 1960-68; Exploration Mngr, AOG Minerals, 1968-80; Mobil Energy Minerals, 1981-83; Cnsltng Geol, 1983-. Publications: Field Geologists Manual, 1976; Making the Mount Isa Mine 1923-32, 1996. Memberships: Geol Soc of Aust, 1970; Australasian Inst of Mining and Metall, 1956; Mineral Ind Cnslts Assn, 1984. Hobbies: Reading; Gardening. Address: 391 Annerley Road, Annerley, Qld 4103, Australia.

BERKOVIC Samuel Frank, b. 13 Oct 1953. Neurologist; Clinical Researcher. m. Helena Makowski, 6 Dec 1977, 1 s, 2 d. Education: MBBS; BMedSci; MD; FRACP. Appointments: Assoc Prof, Dept Med Univ Melb, 1995-98; Snr Lectr Med, 1989-94; Dir, Comprehensive Epilepsy Prog, Austin Hosp, 1994-; Hon Neurologist, Roy Children's Hosp, Melb, 1992-; Adj Prof, Dept Neurology and Neurosurgery, Fac Med, McGill Univ, Montreal, Can, 1989-; Hamilton Fairley Fell NHMRC Univ, Melb, 1985-88. Publications: Over 150 peer reviewed jrnl publs relating to epilepsy. Honours: Amn Epilepsy Soc Res Recog Awd, Clinl Investigator, 1995; Eric Susman Prize RACP, 1993; Selwyn Smith Medl Rsch Prize, Univ of Melbourne, 1997. Memberships: Chmn, Commn on Neuroimaging, 1994-; Chmn, Sci Cttee 21st Intl Epilepsy Congress, 1994-95; Chmn, Vic Stat Cttee Aust Assn Neurologists, 1992-95; Med Adv Panel on Driving and Epilepsy, Vic, 1991-. Hobbies: Tennis; Cycling. Address: Epilepsy Research Institute, Austin and Repatriation Medical Centre, Heidelberg, Vic 3084, Australia.

BERMAN Yitzhak, b. 1913, Russia. Lawyer; Politician. Education: Tchr Trng Coll, Jerusalem; Univ Coll London; Inner Temple London. Appointments: Settled in Palestine, 1921; Served in British Army, 1942-45; Gen Mgr, Willis Overland Kaizer Assembly Plant, Haifa, 1950-54; Pvte Law prac Tel-Aviv, 1954-; Speaker, March 1980-81; Min of Energy, 1981-82. Memberships: Irgun Zevayi Leumi, later Maj, Israeli Def Force, 1948-50; Fmr mbr, Liberal Party; Knesset, 1977-84. Hobbies: Reading; Theatre; Hiking. Address: 9 Bavli St, P O Box 32351, Tel-Aviv 61322, Israel.

BERNAD Miguel Anselmo, b. 8 May 1917, Misamis, Philippines. Catholic Priest; Professor. Education: STL, Woodstock Coll, MD, USA, 1947; MA, Yale Univ, New Haven, CT, USA, 1950; PhD, Yale, 1951. Appointments: Classics Tchr, Ateneo de Manila hs, 1939-41; Prof of Lit, Ateneo de Manila Univ, 1952-77; Ed, Philippine Studies (quarterly), Manila, 1955-59; Visng Prof of Lit, Natl Taiwan Univ, Taipei, 1971; Tam Kang Coll of Arts and Scis, Taipei, 1971; Prof of Lit, Xavier Univ, 1977-93, retired 1993; Fndng Ed, Kinaadman, a jrnl of South Philippines, 1977-; Columnist, The Philippine Star, 1987-. Publications include: Bamboo and the Greenwood Tree, 1961; History Against the Landscape, 1968; The Christianization of the Philippines, 1972; Adventure in Vietnam, 1974; Filipinos in Laos, 1974; The Lights of Broadway and Other Essays, 1980; Tradition and Discontinuity, 1983; Rizal and Spain: An Essay in Biographical Context, 1986; The February Revolution and Other Reflections, 1986; The Inverted Pyramid and Other Political Reflections, 1991; Five Great Missionary Experiments and Cultural Issues in Asia, 1991. Address: Xavier University, Cagayan de Oro, Cagayan de Oro 9000, The Philippines.

BERRETT Rebecca, b. 30 Oct 1960, Canberra, Australia. Author; Illustrator; Artist. 3 s. Education: Distinction in Lettering, Showcard & Ticketwriting, 1981, Childrens Book Illustration, 1984, Adelaide Coll of TAFE; Lino-Print Illustration, McGregor Summer Sch, 1986; Cartooning, Adelaide Coll of TAFE, 1989. Appointments: Tchr, Lectr, Vis Auth, Illustrator, SE Qld Primary & Second Schs & Libs. Creative Works: Sev exhbns. Publications: The Junk Drawer, 1988; What I Really Think, 1989; Bits and Pieces; Going Nowhere, 1995. Hobbies: Art; Literature; Travel; Photography. Address: Mail Service 191, Cambooya, Qld 4358, Australia.

BERTHELEMY Eric, b. 13 July 1962, Orléans, France. Banker. m. Dupuy, 26 June 1993, 2 s. Education: High Coml Stdies; Master's degree in Law; IEP Econ Stdies, Paris. Appointments: SG M&A, SG Asian Dept, SG Seoul.

BERTRAM Christopher David, b. 22 Jan 1950. Lecturer; Researcher. Education: BA (Oxon), Dept Engrng Sci, 1968-71; DPhil, 1972-75; MA (Oxon), 1977. Appointments: Tech Mngmt Apprentice, Brit Aircraft Corp, Bristol, 1968-72; Postdoct Fell, 1976, Rsch Asst, 1977, Physiology, Johns Hopkins Univ, Baltimore; Rsch Assoc, Cambridge Univ Dept Appl Maths and Theort Phys, 1977-80; Lectr, 1980-85, Snr Lectr, 1985-90, Assoc Prof, 1991-, Grad Sch Biomed Engrng, Univ of NSW, Sydney, Aust. Publications: The Dynamics of Collapsible Tubes, chapt in book: Biological Fluid Dynamics, 1995; Over 50 papers in profl jrnls. Honours: Editl Bd, Med and Biol Engrng and Computers (biomed engrng jrnl), 1987-; World Cncl for Biomechanics, 1993-; Fell, Instn of Engrs, Aust, 1995-. Listed in; Who's Who in the World. Hobbies: Music (orchestral player); Tennis; Rollerblading. Address: Graduate School of Biomedical Engineering, University of New South Wales, Sydney, NSW 2052, Australia.

BESLEY Morrish Alexander (Tim), b. 14 Mar 1927, New Plymouth, NZ. Company Chairman; Director. m. Nancy Cave, 15 Jan 1952, 3 s. Education: BE, Civ, Univ NZ; Bachelor Legal Stdys, Macquarie Univ; Fell, Inst Engrs Aust; Bar at Law. Appointments: Engr, Min Wrks, NZ, 1950; Snowy Mtns Hydro-Electric Authy, Aust, 1950-67; 1st Asst Sec, Dept External Territories, 1967; 1st Asst Sec, Dept Treas, 1973-76; Exec Mbr, For Invmnt Review Bd, 1975-76; Sec, C'wlth Dept Bus and Consumer Affairs, and Comptroller Gen Customs, 1976-81; Mngng Dir, 1982-87, Chmn, Chf Exec, 1987, Monier Ltd; Dir, Amcor Ltd, 1985-97; Chmn, Monier Redland Ltd, 1988; Chmn, Redland Aust, 1988-95; Chmn, The CIG Grp, 1988-93; Chmn, C'wlth Banking Corp, 1988-91; Chmn, Leighton Holdings Ltd, 1990-; Chmn, C'wlth Bank Aust, 1991-; Other cur Dir'ships: O'Connell St Assocs Pty Ltd; Chan, Macquarie Univ, 1994-; Pres, Austl Acady of Techological Scis and Engrng, 1998-. Honour: AO, 1992. Memberships: Tstee, Roy Bot Gdns Sydney Fndn; Gov, Cncl Govs, Austl Natl Gall Fndn; Legacy Torch Bearers Cttee; Metal Trades Ind

Assn, NSW Cncl, Natl Exec; Salvation Army, Sydney Advsry Bd, Red Shield Appeal Cttee; World Vision Aust Bd Ref; FTSE. Listed in: Who's Who in Australia. Hobbies: Golf; Fishing. Address: PO Box 71, Chatswood, NSW 2057, Australia.

BESSELL Justin Raymond, b. 10 Jan 1964, Adelaide, South Australia. Surgeon. m. Sara, 31 Mar 1990, 1 s, 2 d. Education: MBBS, Adelaide, 1987; MD, Adelaide, 1996; FRACS, 1998.

BESWICK Richard John, b. 7 Dec 1937, Derby, Tasmania. Member of Parliament. m. Dorothy, 19 Sept 1959, 5 s, 1 d. Education: Tasmanian Coll of Advd Educ (external). Appointments: Electorate of Bass, 1979; Re-elected, State Elections, 1982, 1986, 1989, 1992, 1996; Min of: Primary Ind, Forestries, Sea Fisheries & Water Resources, 1982-84; Education, Lands and Natl Pks & Wildlife, 1984-86; Housing & Consumer Affairs, Employment & Trng Labour & Ind, 1986-89; Dpty Premier, 1992-96; Min for: Educ & Arts, 1992-96; Employment Indl Res & trng, 1992-94; Pub Sect Mngmt, 1994-95; Indl Rels & Trng, 1994-96; Primary Ind & Fisheries, 1995-96; Currently Min for: Police and Pub Safety, Forests, Mines, 1996-. Memberships: Roy Soc of Tasmania; Commonwealth Parly Assn; Tas farmers & Graziers Assn; Austl Forest Growers. Hobbies: Farming; Church; Reading; Sport. Address: 6 Arthur Street, Scottsdale, Tasmania, Australia.

BETHUNE (Walter) Angus (Hon Sir), b. 10 Sept 1908, Tas, Aust. Retired Pastoralist. m. Alexandra Perronet Pritchard, 30 Jan 1936, 1 s, 1 d. Appointments: Mbr, Hamilton Municipal Cncl, 1936-56; MHA Wilmot (Tas), 1946-75, Dpty Warden, 1955-56; (Ret), Ldr Parly Liberal Party, 1960-72, Ldr of the Opposition, 1960-69, Premier and Treas, 1969-72, Pres, Clarendon Children's Home, 1977-82, St John's Ambulance, 1979-86, RAAF (Air Crew), 1940-43. Honours: KB, 1979; Offr of St John, 1983. Address: 1 Quinn Court, Sandy Bay Tasmania 7005, Australia.

BETTERIDGE Maurice Stanley, b. 19 Feb 1927, NZ. Canon; Educator. m. Jacqueline Prime, 28 June 1952, 1 s, 1 d. Education: MA; BD; LTh; STM; Canterbury Univ, NZ; Gen Seminary, NY, USA. Appointments: Schmaster, Nelson Coll, NZ, 1950-52; Curate, Nelson Cath, NZ, 1952-53; Vicar, Lincoln, 1954-57; Vicar, St Matthews, Dunedin, NZ, 1959-65; Chaplain, Univ of New Eng, Aust, 1965-72; Archdeacon, Armidale, 1970-72; Fed Sec, CMS, 1973-78; Lectr in Ecclesiastical Hist, Univ of Sydney, 1976-78; Prin, Ridley Coll, Univ of Melbourne, 1979-92; Canon, St Paul's Cath, 1987-. Honour: Fulbright Schl, 1957-58. Hobbies: Golf; Book Collecting. Address: 355 Upper Heidelberg Road, Ivanhoe, Melbourne, Vic 3079, Australia.

BETTS Geoffrey James, b. 10 May 1920, Aust. Building Society Chairman. m. Betty Campbell, 7 Nov 1942, 3 s. Appointments include: Served Austl Imperial Forces, 1940-45; Mngng Dir, Target Aust Pty Ltd, 1968-76; Dir, The Myer Emporium Ltd, 1972-76; Chmn, Army and Air Force Canteen Serv, 1977-82; Dir, 1977-86, Chmn, 1982-86, Pyramid Bldg Soc. Honours: MBE, 1982; AM, 1995. Memberships: FAMI; Snr VP, Geelong Hosp Gen Cttee, 1980-83; Pres, Cncl, Gordon Tech Coll, 1981-84; Pres, TAFE Coll Cncls Assn, 1981-85. Listed in: Who's Who in Australia. Address: 42 Aphrasia Street, Newtown, Geelong, Vic 3220, Australia.

BEZBORUAH Dhirendra Nath, b. 1 Dec 1933, Boloma, India. Journalist. m. Kalpana, 4 Feb 1958, 1 s, 2 d. Education: MA, Engl Lit; Postgrad Dip, Appl Lings. Appointments: Lectr, Cotton Coll; Educn Offr, Bd of Second Educn, Assam; Rdr, Engl, NCERT; Ed, The Sentinel. Publications: Translation of Mrityunjay, 1983; Num articles in profl jrnls. Honours: Harmony Awd, New Delhi, 1991; B D Goeenka Awd, Ex in Jrnlsm, 1997. Memberships: Pres, Mysore Film Soc, 1978; Pres, Eds Guild of India, 1995-97. Hobbies: Photography; Carpentry; Music. Address: Shanti, Maniram Dewan Road, Chandmari, Guwahati 781 003, Assam, India.

BEZIAN Mohammad Saeid, b. 1 July 1966, Ahwaz, Iran. Mechanical Engineer. m. 11 Oct 1998. Education: BS, Mech Engrng. Appointment: Transfer of Know-How Course, Japan, 1991. Membership: Iranian Soc of Mech Engrs. Hobbies: Basketball; Climbing. Address: Hafez Street No 440, Ahwaz 61956, Iran.

BHAGAT Bali Ram, b. 1 Oct 1922. Politician. Education: Patna Coll. Appointments: Sec Bihar Provl Congress Cttee, 1949; Parl Sec Min of Fin, 1952-55; Dep Min for Fin, 1955-63; Min of State for Plng, 1963-67; Min of State for Def, March-Nov 1967; Min of State for External Affairs, 1967-69; Min in charge of For Trade and Supply, 1969-70; Min for Steel and Heavy Ind, 1970-71; Speaker Lok Sabha, 1976-77; Min of External Affairs, 1985-86. Memberships: Mbr Provisional Parl, 1950-52; Mbr Lok Sabha, 1952-77. Address: B-7, Maharani Bagh, New Delhi 110065, India.

BHAGWAT Arun Moreshwar, b. 11 July 1939, Seoni, India. Operational Radiation Protection (Health Physics). m. Ms Sandhya, 29 Nov 1968, 1 s, 1 d. Education: BSc, Nagpur Univ, 1959; MSc, Phys Chem, Vikram Univ, 1961; One Yr Training, Operational Radiation Protection, Chalk River Nuclr Lab, Can, 1966-67; PhD, Phys, Gujarat Univ, 1985. Appointments: Sci Offr, BARC, 1961; Hd, RHC Sect, RSSD, BARC, 1994; HD, Radiation Safety Systems Div, BARC, 1998. Publications: Solid State Nuclear Track Detection: It's Theory and Applications, 1993; Radiation Protection: Its Evolution and the Trends for the Future, 1996. Honours: Elect Fell, Maharashtra Acady of Scis, 1996; IAEA Cnslt, Working Grp, Nuclr and Radiation Safety in SE Asia, 1996. Memberships: Indian Assn for Radiation Protection; Nuclr Track Soc of India, Sec, 1996-98; Indian Nuclr Soc; Indian Soc for Radiation Physics. Hobbies: Teaching; Cooking. Address: Block No 9/C, Kamet, Anushaktinagar, Mumbai 400 094, India.

BHAJAN LAL Chaudhri, b. 6 Oct 1930. Politician. Education: Bahwal Nagar W Pakistan. Appointments: Min in Haryana Cabinet, 1970-75; Min for Co-op Dairy Dev, Animal Husbandry, Labour and Employment, 1978-79; Chf Min of Haryana, 1979-86, 1991-96; Union Min of Environment and Forests, Oct 1986-88; Union Min of Agric and Rural Dev, 1988-89. Hobbies: Nature; Wildlife. Memberships: Haryana Legis Ass, 1968-. Address: Chief Ministers Secretariat, Chadigarh, India.

BHAKARE Niranjan M, b. 10 June 1965, Rahimabad, India. Social Worker. m. Shanta, 10 Mar 1993, 1 s, 3 d. Appointment: Socl Worker. Publications: A Street Play in Marathi, Tufan Sutlay Wara. Honours: Over 30 awds. Memberships: Sev. Hobbies: Music; Social Service. Address: Rahimabad Paluke Sillod, District Aurangabad 43112, India.

BHAKAT Sandeep Kumar, b. 29 Apr 1964, Bolbur, India. Teacher. m. Susmita Bhakat, 8 July 1997, 1 s. Education: BSc, hons, 1984; MSc, Maths, 1986; PhD, Maths, 1996. Appointments: Educn Offr, Govt of W Bengal, 1987-89; Tchr, Visva Bharati; Student Welfare Offr, Coord, Maths, Siksha-Satra, Visra-Bharati; Exec Mbr, Visra-Bharati Alumni Assn; Asst Sec, Visra-Bharati Tchrs Cncl. Publications: Sev articles in profl jrnls. Memberships: Indian Sci Congress Assn; NY Acady of Scis; Assn for Improvement of Maths Tchng; Calcutta Maths Soc; Indian Soc for Fuzzy Maths and Info Processing. Address: Sukhnogarh, Bhubandanga, Bolpur 731204, Birbhum, India.

BHAKTA Mansingh, b. 3 Dec 1931. Advocate; Solicitor. m. Ramila, 30 Dec 1958. Education: BA, hons; LLB. Appointments: Snr Ptnr, Kanga & Co Advocates & Sols; Dir, sev large cos. Publications: Sev pprs in profl jrnls. Honour: 1st Prize, Bombay Incorp Law Soc, 1960. Memberships: Income Tax Appellate Tribunal Bar Assn; Chmn, Law Cttee, Indian Merchants Chamber. Hobbies: Reading; Coin Collecting. Address: Readymoney Mansion, 43 Veer Nariman Road, Bombay 400 001, India.

BHAN Suraj, b. 1 Oct 1928, Vill Mehlanwali, Jagradhri, Haryana. Governor of Uttar Pradesh. m. Chameli Devi,

1935, 3 s, 4 d. Education: MA; LLB. Appointment: In Govt Serv, Off of Postmaster Gen, Punjab Circle, 1950-67. Memberships include: Formed Punjab Scheduled Castes Welfare Assn, 1950, Pres, 1950-66; Associated w Bhartiya Jan Sangh, 1967-; Associated w P&T Trade Union in var capacities, 1952-67; Gen Sec, Bhartiya Depressed League, 1978-; Served as State Pres, Bhartiya Janata Party (BJP) of Haryana; Served as All India Gen Sec & VP, BJP; Jailed for polit reasons sev times inclng, 1975-77; Elected to Seventh Lok Sabha, 1980-84; Elected to Haryana Legis Assembly, 987-91; Ldr of Opposition, Haryana Legis Assembly, 1989-90; Dpty Speaker, Lok Sabha, 1979-98; Gov, Uttar Pradesh, 1998-; Fought continuously against casteism and worked for the benefit of Schedule Caste & Schedule Tribes labourers & farmers. Hobbies: Reading; Gardening; Volleyball; Hockey. Address: Governor, UP, Raj Bhavan, Lucknow 227132, India.

BHARADWAJ Narmada Shanker, b. 20 Aug 1956, Khandwa, India. Government Official. m. Seema Bharadwaj, 21 Nov 1981, 1 s, 1 d. Education: BSc, Botany, Zoology, Chem, 1975-76, MBA, 1977-78, MA, Polit Sci, 1979-80, Univ of Sagar. Appointments: Area Organiser, Block Devel Offr,, AOTW Hargone, BDO Gogawa, BDO Dharampuri, 1981-86; Dist Organiser, Asst Project Admnstr, DOTW Rewa, APA Puspgarh, APA Khargone, 1986-92; Asst Cmmnr, ACTW Surguja, PA (ITDP, Pushpgarh, ACTW Shahdol, ACTW Dhar, 1992-. Publications: Effective Teaching in Small Schools; Notes on Margin; Study and Field Testing on Multigrade Teaching; Study and Field Testing on Teaching-Learning Through Comics. Honours: Natl Awd, All India Comp of Innovative Experiments & Practices in Sch Educn, 1996-97; Hon, Indian Jaycees. Memberships: SARTHAK; Natl Cncl of Educn; All India Primary Tchrs Fedn. Hobbies: Writing; Reading; Painting; Acting; Cricket; Collecting Antiques; Fossils; Literature. Address: Assistant Commissioner, Tribal Development, Dhar (Madhya Pradesh) 454 001, India.

BHARGAVA Veena, b. 15 Sept 1938, Shimla, India. Artist. m. K P Bhargava, 10 May 1958, dec, 1 s, 1 d. Education: Initially Med Student, Calcutta; Dip in Fine Art, Drawing and Painting, Govt Coll of Art, Calcutta, 1962; Art Students League of NY, 1959-60. Career: Freelance Artist. Creative Works: Cityscapes, 1970; Victim Series, 1971; Pavement Series, 1976; Angst Series, 1984; Bull Series, 1984-86; Bandwalla Series, 1985-86; Performer Series, 1992-95; Goat Series, 1992-94; Deva Dwar Series, 1994-98. Honours: Birla Acady of Art and Culture, Calcutta, 1972, 1973, 1974, 1981; Natl Awd, Lalit Kala Akademi, New Delhi, 1986. Membership: Lalit Kala Akademi, Artists Constituency. Hobbies: Music; Theatre; Film; Literature; Photography; Tennis. Address: 5C Ballygunge Court, 12/2ABC Ballygunge Park Road, Calcutta 700019, India.

BHATIA Harbhajan Singh, b. 3 Nov 1928, Lahore, Pakistan. Airport Engineer. m. Dharam, 1 s, 1 d. Education: BSc, hons; DIC; PGDM. Appointments: Chf Cnslt, EMAS Techno Cnslt Ltd; Bd Mbr, Intl Airports Authy of India; Prin Engr, Ghana Acady of Scis & PWD; Snr Sci Offr, Centra Rd Rsch Inst. Publications: 46 pprs in profl jrnls. Honours: Gold Medal, IRC, Imperial Coll, Pakistan. Memberships: Fell, Brit Cncl; VP, CIT-India; VP, Assn of Cnsltng Engrs, India; Fell, Inst of Civil Engrs, India; Fell, Inst of Transp & Highways, CIT, Inst of Engrs, India, Indian Geol Soc. Hobbies: Writing; Poetry; Social Work. Address: EMA Technoconsultants Pvt Ltd, 3/6 Kalkaji Ext, New Delhi 110019, India.

BHATIA S K, b. 26 Apr 1941. Publisher. m. Durgesh Bhatia, 21 June 1965, 1 s, 1 d. Education: BA; BAMS; Dip LibSc; Dip Bus Mngmt. Appointments: Libn, PGDAV Coll, New Dehi, 1958-68; Asst Mngr, M/S Lalvani Bros (Wholesalers), New Delhi, 1969-75; gen Mngr, D K Publr's Distributors, 1975-85; Proprietor, Reliance Publishing House, Nagar, New Delhi, 1985-. Publications: Directory of Universities and Colleges of India; Directory of Libraries in Delhi, 1986, 2nd ed, 1999; Dictionary of Library and Information Science, 1997; Directory of Business Management Institutions in India, 1999;

Directory of Book Trade in India. 1999. Honours: Best Dist Chmn, Book Bank, 1994-95; Best Regl Chmn; Best Zone Chmn. Memberships: Hon Sec, Fedn of Publr's and Booksellers Assns in India, 1996-97, 1995-96; VP, Delhi State Booksellers and Publrs Assn, 1994-95, 1995-96, Pres, 1997-98, 1998-99, 1999-2000 Dist P R O Lions Clubs Intl Dist 321 A1, 1996-97; Life mbr, Indian Soc of Authors; Fedn of Educ Publrs in India; UPSC; Dist Cabinet Treas, Lions Clubs Intl, 1997-98; Indian Lib Assn; Pres, Delhi State Booksellers' and Publr's Assn; Life Mbr, Hindu Writers' Forum. Listed in: Who's Who in India; Who's Who in the World. Address: Lion Dr S K Bhatia, Reliance Publishing House, 3026/7H Ranjit Nagar, N Delhi 110008, India.

BHATNAGAR Dharmendra, b. 30 Sept 1955, Ajmer, India. Civil Servant. m. Abha Bhatnagar, 28 Oct 1982, 1 s, 1 d. Education: MA, Hist; LLB. Appointments: Asst Collector, Exec Magistrate, City Magistrate Kota; Addl Dist Magistrate, Ajmer. Honours: Gibson Gold Medal, 1978; State Awd, Govt of Rajasthan, 1997. Membership: Gen Sec, Dist Offrs Club, Kota. Address: B-326 Trivenimars, Gopal Pura By Pass, Jaipur, India.

BHATNAGAR Shashi Prakash, b. 28 Nov 1962, Lucknow, India. Civil Engineer. Education: BE (Civil); LLB. Appointments: Engr Trainee to Snr Asst Engr, Tata Cnsltng Engrs, Mumbai, India, 1983-91; Dir, SPB Engrng Servs, Lucknow, 1991-; Dir, GPB Computer Servs, Lucknow, 1991-. Publications: Introductory Computer Science, 1996; Programming With Basic, 1996. Memberships: Instn of Engrs (India); Amn Soc of Civil Engrs; Assn of Cnsltng Civil Engrs (India); Indian Geotech Soc; Indian Soc of Earthquake Technol; Assoc Mbr, Computer Soc of India. Hobbies: Ham radio; Helping the blind; Planting Trees. Address: 557/9, Omnagar, Alambagh, Lucknow 226005, UP, India.

BHATT Chit Ranjan, b. 19 Feb 1998, India. Company President, KK UTI Group. m. Indira, 30 Sept 1979, 1 s. Education: MSC. Appointments: Univ Prof, 1968; Mushroom expert, 1970; Ikebana, from Japan, 1970; Sci Offr Incharge, UKSN, Travel/Tourism, 1976; Estab UKSN UKSS, Estab KK UTI Grp of Cos for Tourism. Honour: MSc, Botany, Mushroom expertise, travel trade, Jata, 1968. Hobbies: Travelling; Nature; Rock climbing; Internet; Mushrooms. Address: K K United Travel Service International # 302, Dai Ichi Arai Place, Nishi-Kasai 6-15-8, Edogawa-ku, Tokyo, Japan.

BHATTACHARJEE Madhab, b. 7 Jan 1933, Calcutta, India. Sculptor. m. Sefali, 2 s, 1 d. Education: Dip, Govt Coll of Arts & Crafts, Calcutta, 1956; Govt of India Cultural Schl, MS Univ Baroda, 1958-60. Appointments: Birla Indl & Technol Mus, Calcutta, 1963-93. Publications: Sev articles in profl jrnls. Honours: Natl Awd, 1961; Gov Gold Medal, Acady of Fine Arts, Calcutta, 1961; K D Ghon Medal, Oriental Art Soc, Calcutta, 1984; Ctf of Merit, 1972; Awd, All India Fine Arts & Crafts Soc, 1996. Membership: Calcutta Arts Fair, 1967-81. Address: 18/D Baghbazar Street, Calcutta 700003, India.

BHATTACHARYA Debesh, b. 15 Mar 1940, Calcutta, India. Professor; Researcher. m. Ellen, 15 Nov 1980, 2 d. Education: BA, hons, MA, Calcutta Univ; Dip, Adv Econ Devel, PhD, Manchester. Appointments: Prof of Econs, Univ Sydney, 1990-; Dir, Cntr for S Asian Studies, 1996-. Publications: Sev books and num articles in profl jrnls. Memberships: Gen Sec, Manchester Univ Indian Students, 1965-68; Acting Gen Sec, Calcutta Univ Students Union, 1958. Hobbies: Swimming; Cricket. Address: 17 Cheltenham Road, Croydon, NSW 2132, Australia.

BHATTACHARYA Dureaprasad, b. 1 Jan 1927. Professor; Reseacher. m. 8 May 1959, 2 s. Education: Grad, Econs. Appointments: Sub-Ed, Daily Paschim Banga Patika, Calcutta, 1948; Coml Ed, Daily Satyayng (Times of India Grp), Calcutta, 1949-53; Field Publicity Offr, Govt of India, 1954-56; Fac Mbr, Hd, Pre-Census Population Studies Unit, Indian Stats Inst, Calcutta, 1956-86; Dir, Pre-Census Population Project of India, 1961-; Dir, Bibliography of Bengali Writings on Socl Scis

1800-1948, Indian Cncl of Socl Scis Rsch, 1981-; Dir, Rsch Project, Econ Hist of India, Indian Cncl of Histl Rsch, 1993-. Publications include: Ramjanmabhumi Babri Masjid O'Bharatvarsha, 2nd ed, 1993; Report on the Population Estimates of India, Vol V 1831-1840, 1994; Archival Records for Population Studies in the Indian Sub-Continent 1850-1900, 1996. Memberships: Intl Union for Sci Studies of Population; Asiatic Soc of Bengal; Indian Stats Inst; Indian Histl Records Cmmn; Socio-Econ Rsch Inst; Indian Assn for the Study of Population; Indian Hist Congress; Regl Records Survey Cttee, Govt of W Bengal; Bangiya Sahitya Parishad. Hobbies: Quantitative Study of Social and Economic History; Socio-Economic Conditions. Address: P14 Meghnad Abasan, PO Pratulla Kanan, Calcutta 59, India.

BHATTACHARYA Sati Nath, b. 20 Jan 1942. Academic; Researcher. m. 4 July 1973, 1 s, 1 d. Education: BChem Engrng; MEng; PhD. Appointments: Lectr, 1966-69, 1975-80, Snr Lectr, 1980-88, Prin Lectr, 1988-90, Assoc Prof, 1991-93, Prof, 1994-, Dir, 1988-, Rheology and Materials Processing Cntr, RMIT, Aust. Publications: Auth, about 160 sci publs in jrnls and conf proceedings. Honour: Chemcon 1990 Medal in India. Memberships: Fell, Inst of Chem Engrs, Eng; Sec, VP and Pres, Austl Soc of Rheology, 1979-85. Hobbies: Reading; Music; Gardening; Travelling. Address: Rheology and Materials Processing Centre, Royal Melbourne Institute of Technology, La Trobe St, Melbourne, Vic 3000, Australia.

BHATTACHARYYA Kakali, b. 23 July 1957. Librarian. Education: MA, Sanskrit; BLIS; LLB; MLIS (IGNOU). Appointments: Evening Asst Libn, IASLIC, 1987-89; Cataloguer and Classifier, TTTI, Calcutta, 1988; Libn, Hindi HS, 1989-90; Libn, ABB, Calcutta, 1991-98; Advocate, Calcutta High Crt, 1999-. Publications: Bibliog and Proj Asst, M N Roy; Compiled 2 bibliographies on ESP and Fabric Filter, 1991. Honour: Three Star Merit Ctf, Govt of India, 1973. Memberships: IASLIC, 1987; BLA, 1988; BCL, 1991; DESIDOC, 1996. Hobbies: Travel; Reading; Music; Friendship. Address: Manasbahar, P-27A Manasbag, Flat No 20, PO Belghoria, Calcutta 700056, India.

BHATTACHARYYA Prodipeswar, b. 1 May 1941, Jorhat, Assam, India. Professor of Mathematics. m. Lakshmi, 5 Nov 1975, 1 d. Education: DIC; MS; PhD, Imperial Coll, London. Appointments: Univ MN, USA; Univ Hamburg, Germany; IIT Madras; Dean, IIT Guwahati; Univ of Peradenyia Fed Univ of Abeokuta; Vice-Chan, Tezpur Univ (Cntrl Govt of India). Publications: Over 60 rsch pprs. Honours: Univ Gold Medal, Guwahati Univ, 1963. Memberships: Indian Maths Soc; Calcutta Maths Soc; Indian Sci Congress; Am Maths Soc. Hobbies: Reading; Writing; Music; Travel. Address: Vice-Chancellor, Tezpur University, Tezpur-784025, Assam, India.

BHATTAR Vasudeva, b. 3 May 1966, Bangalore, India. Priest. m. Gwathi, 12 May 1992, 1 s, 1 d. Appointments: Sri Byala Anjaneya Temple, Ganganagar, Bangalore, 12 yrs; Pooja, Sri Kodandarama Temple, Ganganagar, Bangalore, 5 yrs. Memberships: Fndr Pres, Karnataka State Archak & Agamik Welfare Soc, Bangalore; Fndr, Srikar Agama-Veda Pathashala, Bangalore; Kannada Sahitya Parishat; Amala's Vacation Club. Address: 29 5 Main 5 Cross, Kodandarama Temple, Ganganagar, Bangalore 4, India.

BHATTAR Venkatarama, b. 22 May 1966, Mysore. Sanskrit Pandit. m. Lakshmi, 24 Aug 1986, 1 s, 2 d. Education: MA; MEd; AGAMA; VEDA; SAHITYA PANDIT. Appointments: Priest, 1985; Sanskrit Pandit, 1991. Creative Works: 5 Sanskrit Books, 1995-98; 3 Hindi Books, 1996-98. Honours: Outstndng Personality Hon, 1998; Many more hons. Memberships: State Archax and Agamik Assn. Hobbies: To serve the soc; Music. Address: Sabha Qts, APS Road, V V Puram, Bangalore 4, India.

BHATTARAI Krishna Prasad, b. 24 Dec 1924. Politician. Appointments: Served 14 yrs imprisonment for

opposition to absolute monarchy in Nepal; Pres Nepali Congress Party - banned for 29 yrs until 1990; PM of Nepal - presiding over interim multiparty govt - 1990-91. Address: Nepali Congress Central Office, Baneshwar, Kathmandu, Nepal.

BHATTI Muhammad Ishtar, b. 26 Sept 1957, Multan. University Lecturer. m. Asma, 1 May 1985, 1 s, 1 d. Education: PhD, Monash Univ, Aust; MSc, Univ of Alberta, Can. Appointments: Lectr, Sch of Intl Bus, Griffith Univ, Queensland, 1992-. Publications: Recent Development in Hypothesis Testing (spec issue of Pakistan J of Stats, w M L King), 1994; (book) Testing Regression Models, 1995. Membership: MIS (UK), 1986; Intl Stats Inst, 1996. Hobbies: Squash playing; Walking; Tracking. Address: School of International Business, IBP, Griffith University, Nathan, Queensland 4111, Australia.

BHICHAI RATTAKUL Nai, b. 16 Sept 1926. Politician. m. Nang Charoye, 2 s, 1 d. Education: St Peter's Sch Bangkok; St Stephen's Coll Hong Kong. Appointments: Fmr Mgng Dir Jawarad Co Ltd; Pres Thai Phar Mfng Assn; VP Druggists Assn of Thailand; Dir Thai Chamber of Com; Dir Bd of Trade; Dir Assn of Thai Inds; Rep of Thai Employers to Gen Confs of ILO Geneva; Joined Dem Party, 1958; MP for Bangkok Metropolis, 1969-71, 1975-; Min of For Affairs, 1975-86; Dep PM, 1986-90; Dep Ldr Dem Party. Memberships: Dep mbr Asian Advsry Cttee of ILO; Mbr Natl Convention; Mbr Natl Legis Assn; Mbr Const Scrutiny Cttee, 1973. Address: Government House, Nakhan Pathan Road, Bangkok 10300, Thailand.

BHOJENDRA S B, b. 13 Apr 1945, Mysore, India. Director. m. S B Manorama, 10 July 1975, 1 child. Education: BEng, Natl Inst of Engrng, Mysore, 1971; Univ Mysore. Appointments: Asst Dir, Shimoga, Raichur, 1974-78; Dpty Dir, Small Scale Inds, Bangalore, 1978-82; Joint Dir, Gen Mngr, Dist Inds Cntr, Gulbarga, 1982-84; Offr of Specl Duty, Karnataka State Electron Dept Corp, Bangalore, 1984-87; Chf Mngr, Ex-Officio Joint Dir, Indl Estate, Karnataka State Small Inds Devel Corp, Bangalore, 1987-93; Gen Mngr, Dist Inds Cntr, Tumkur, 1989-91; Chmn, Mngng Dir, Mysore Crome Tanning Co, Bangalore, 1991-94; Gen Mngr, Inds & Trng, Karnataka State SC/ST Devel Corp, Bangalore, 1994-95; Mngng Dir, Mysore Paints & Varnishes Ltd, 1995-98; Joint Dir, Trng Prog. Honours include: Priyadarshini Indira Gandhi Awd, 1995. Address: c/o District Industries Centre, Kohinoor Road, Madikeri, Coorg District, Karnataka, India.

BHOTIWIHOK Savit, b. 19 Aug 1945. Minister to Prime Minister's Office. Education: BSc, MA Inst of Technol, USA, 1967; MS, 1968, PhD, 1972, Harv Univ; Natl Def Coll, Thailand, Class 33, 1991. Appointments: Advsr to Prime Min, 1976; Sec to Min of Ind, 1977-79; Dir, Off of Natl Water Rescs Cttee, 1983-87; Dir, Cntr for Integrated Plan of Ops, 1983-89; Dir, Off of Eastern Seaboard Cttee, 1985-92, Southern Seaboard Cttee, 1989-92; Snr Plng Expert, Off of the Prime Min, 1988-91; Advsr, Prime Min's Off, 1991-92; Mbr of Parl, Bangkok Constituency 4, 1992-95; Min to Prime Min's Pff, 1992-95; Mbr of Parl, Bangkok Constituency 3, 1996-; Min to Prime Min's Off, 1997-. Honour: Kt Grand Cordon, Spec Class, Most Exalted Order of the White Elephant.

BHOWN Abhoyjit S, b. 29 Mar 1962, Bikaner, India. Engineering; Business Management. m. Nivedita, 1 s. Education: MS, Maths; BS, MS, PhD, Chem Engrng. Appointments: Dpty Dir, Chem Engrng, SRI Intl, 1993-98; Pres, Facilichem Inc, 1998-. Honours include: Rsch Project of Yr, 1997. Memberships: AICHE; ACS. Hobby: Racquetball. Address: 333 Ravenswood Avenue, Menlo Park, CA 94025, USA.

BHUIYAN Md Shoaib, b. 13 Apr 1964, Chandpur, Bangladesh. Engineering Faculty. m. Runa Lisa, 13 Mar 1996, 1 d. Education: DEng, Nagoya Inst of Technol, Nagoya, Japan 1996. Appointments: Sci Offr, Bangladesh Atomic Energy Cmmn, 1990; Lectr, Univ Grants Cmmn of Bangladesh, 1990-92; Rsch Assoc, Nagoya Inst of Technol, Nagoya, Japan, 1996-.

Publications: 13 peer-reviewed articles in profl neorocomputing and computer vision jrnls. Honours: Postgrad Rsch Schlsp, Japanese Govt Min of Educn, 1992-96; Talent-Pool Merit Schlsp, Univ Dhaka, Bangladesh, 1987-89. Memberships: IEEE; IEEE-CS; IEEE-CS-TPAMI; IEICE, Japan. Hobbies: Reading; Travel; Gourmet Food. Address: Meijo Jutaku 2-508, 3-1 Meijo, Kita, Nagoya 462-0846, Japan.

BHUMIBOL ADULYADEJ (King of Thailand), b. 5 Dec 1927 Cambridge MA USA. m. Her Majesty the present Queen Sirikit, 1950, 1 s, 3 d. Education: Bangkok; Lausanne Switzerland. Succeeded his brother the late King Ananda Mahidol, June 1946. Address: Chitralada Villa, Bangkok, Thailand.

BHUTTO Benazir, b. 21 June 1953. Politician. m. Asif Ali Zardari, 1987, 1 s, 2 d. Education: Harvard Univ; Lady Margaret Hall Oxford. Appointments: Under house arrest, 1977-84; Ldr in exile of Pakistan People's Party with her mother Nusrat and involved in the Movement for the Restoration of Democracy in Pakistan, 1984-; Returned to Pakistan, 1986; PM of Pakistan, 1988-90, 1993-96; Also fmr Min of Fin and Econ Affairs; Removed from position by Presdl decree and charged with corruption and abuse of power, Aug 1990; Co-Chmn Pakistan People's Party, Chmn, 1993-; Opposition ldr, 1990-93; Hd Parly For Affairs Cttee, 1993-96; Dismissed by Presdl decree, Nov 1996; Dismissal upheld by Supreme Court, Jan 1997. Publication: Daughter of The East - autobiog - 1988. Honours: Dr hc, Harvard, 1989; Lady Margaret Hall Oxford, 1989. Address: Pakistan People's Party, 70 Clifton, Karachi 75600, Pakistan.

BICKERSTAFF Robert, b. 26 July 1932, Sydney, Aust. Opera Singer (Baritone); Teacher, Voice. m. Ann Howard. Education: Studied at the NSW Conservatorium w Lyndon Jones; Melbourne Conservatorium w Henri Portnoj; Paris w Dominique Modesti. Career: Debut: Thoas in Iphigénie en Tauride, Marseilles, 1962; Sang in Nice, Bordeaux, Marseilles; Prin Baritone, Sadler's Wells and Engl Natl Opera, 1964-70; Roles included: Amonasro, Escamillo, MacBeth, Boccanegra, Scarpia, Wotan, Mozart's Count Almaviva and Eugene Onegin; Guest appearances w Pittsburgh Opera, Welsh Natl Opera and at Covent Gdn; Over 60 roles in Opera; Other roles include Wagner's Flying Dutchman, Ezio in Attila, Luna in Il Trovatore, Renato in Un Ballo in Maschera, Enrico in Lucia di Lammermoor and Massenet's Herode; Boris in Lady MacBeth of Mtsensk by Shostakovich, Adelaide Festl; Oratorio and recital perfs; Appearances on BBC radio and TV; Previously Prof of Singing, Roy Acady of Music, London, and Tutor of Singing, King's Coll, Cambridge. Creative works: Recordings include: La Juive. Honour: Hon ARAM, 1978. Membership: Soc of Musicians, London. Listed in: International Who's Who in Music; Who's Who in the World. Hobbies: Reading; Golf; Outdoor activities. Address: 8 William Street, North Sydney, NSW 2060, Australia.

BIDDLE Donald Sidney, b. 12 Mar 1923, Burwood, Australia. Education Consultant. m. Eileen Mary Newton, 20 Mar 1943, 2 d. Education: Tchr Ctf, Primary Educ, Sydney Tchrs Coll, 1941; BA, Hons, Geog, 1950, MEd, 1964, Univ Sydney; PhD, Univ of London, Inst of Educ, 1974. Appointments: One-Tchr Sch, Walliston via Deniliquin, 1942; War Serv, RAAF, 1942-45; One-Tchr Sch, Collingullie via Wagga Wagga, 1945-46; CRT Schlsp, Univ Sydney, 1947-50; Geog Tchr, Griffith HS, 1951-54; Tchr-in-Charge, Geog, N Sydney Boys HS, 1955-56; Com Master, Glen Innes HS, 1957; Lectr, Geog, 1958-62; Snr Lectr, 1963-65; Hd, Dept of Geog, 1966-68; Asst Prin, 1969-72; Dpty Prin, 1974-75; Dpty Prin, Hd, Div of Postgrad Dips and Degs, 1975-76; Vice Prin, 1976-79; Prin, 1980-82, Sydney Tchrs Coll; Study Leave, Univ of London, Inst of Educ, 1972-74; Educ Cnslt, 1983-96. Publications: 52 articles in profl jrnls; 10 books and monographs. Honours: Slade Prize in Geog, Univ Sydney, 1947; Geog Soc of NSW Prize, Univ Sydney, 1948; Thomas and Ethel Mary Ewing Schlsp, Univ Sydney, 1972-74; Austl Imperial Rels Trust Fellshp, 1973-74; FACE, 1978; Macdonald Holmes Medal, 1979; FNGTA, 1988; FNGS, 1988; Profl Servs Cmmdn, Austl

Inst of Geogs, 1989; Thomson Medal, RGS, Qld, 1996. Memberships: Austl Coll of Educ; Austl Geog Tchrs Assn; Geog Assn, Sheffield, England; Geog Soc of NSW; Geog Tchrs Assn of NSW; Hong Kong Geog Assn; Inst of Austl Geogs; Intl Geog Union Cmmn on Geog Educn; Roy Geog Soc, Qld. Hobbies: Golf; Lawn Bowls; Travel; Reading. Address: 27 Plateau Road, Collaroy Plateau, NSW 2097, Australia.

BIDWELL Dafne, b. Stockbridge, England. Writer. m. Peter Jones, 3 s, 2 d. Appointments: Freelance Lectr, Tutor, Creative Writing, Schs & Cmty Grps, 1978-. Publications: The Tiger Gang and the Hijackers, 1976; The Tiger Gang and the Car Thieves, 1977; Seeker Seven, 1984. Honour: Austl Cncl Lit Bd Rsch Grant, 1979. Memberships: Fell, Austl Writers, Soc of Women Writers. Hobbies: Painting; Tennis. Address: 11 Galway Grove, Waterford, WA 6152, Australia.

BIGELOW Robert Sidney, b. 26 Apr 1918. University Lecturer; Reader. m. Moyra Frances Hale, 15 Jan 1946, 4 s. Education: BSc, 1950; PhD, 1954. Appointments: McGill Univ, 1953; Univ Canterbury, NZ, 1962. Publications: The Grasshoppers of New Zealand, 1967; The Dawn Warriors, 1969; The Stubborn Bear, 1970. Listed in: Who's Who in New Zealand. Hobbies: Tramping; Mountaineering; Astronomy; Woodworking. Address: 24 Beckford Road, St Martins, Christchurch 2, New Zealand.

BILLINGSLEY John, b. 14 Aug 1939. Professor of Engineering. m. Rosalind Elisabeth Wilson, 18 May 1964, 2 s, 1 d. Appointments: Engr, Smiths Aviation Div, 1962; Univ Demonstrator, ADR Cambridge Univ, 1967; Fell, Sudney Sussex Coll, Cambridge, 1968; Rdr, Prof, Portsmouth Polytech, 1976; Prof Engrng, Univ of Southern Qld, 1992. Publications: DIY Robotics, 1986; Controlling with Computers, 1989. Memberships: Fell, IEE; IEAust; Snr Mbr, IEEE; CEng; CPEng. Listed in: Who's Who in Australia; Who's Who in the World. Hobby: Feeding kookaburras. Address: Faculty of Engineering and Surveying, University of Southern Queensland, Toowoomba, Qld 4350, Australia.

BILIMORIA Karan Faridoon, b. 26 Nov 1961, Hyderabad, India (arrived in Brit, 1981). Managing Director. m. Heather, 11 Dec 1993, 1 s. Education: BCom (Hons); ACA (Eng & Wales); MA (Law) Cambridge. Memberships: Carlton Club, Delhi; Gymkhana Club; Uni Pitt Club, Cambridge; Uni Polo Club; Asian Conservative Club in House of Lords; VP, Cambridge Union, 1988; Cambridge Blue in Polo, 1988. Hobbies: Squash; Polo; Current affairs; Sports. Address: Cobra Beer Ltd, The Plaza, 535 King Road, Chelsea, London, SW10 0SZ, England.

BILNEY Gordon, b. 21 June 1939, Renmark S Aust. Politician; Former Diplomat. m. (1) Elizabeth Gunton, 1967, div 1995, 2 d. Education: Univ of Adelaide. Appointments: Joined Dip Serv Dept of For Affairs, 1966; Mbr personal staff successive Mins for For Affairs, 1973-75; Served in Jakarta, Manila, Geneva, Paris, then High Commnr in West Indies, 1980-82; Hd OECD, EC and Energy Br Dept of For Affairs Econ Div, 1982-83; Chmn Parly Jt Cttee on For Affairs, Def and Trade, 1987; Min for Def Sci and Personnel, 1990-93; Min for Dev Co-op and for Pacific Island Affairs, 1993-96. Memberships: HoR for Kingston, 1983-96; Labor Party. Hobbies: Gardening; Reading; Fishing; Tennis; Chess. Address: 2 Jervois Terrace, Marino, SA 5049, Australia.

BINDU Binduji Maharaj, b. 7 Feb 1958, Allahabad, UP, India. Journalist. Education: Ayurved Ratna, Master of Indian Med. Appointments: Currently, Dir, Kavita Maha Vidyalaya. Publications: Leek Se Hatkar (poems); Num articles and poems in mags of repute. Honours: Bhagawan Dhanwantary Sadbhavana Awd; Dr Ambedkar Fellshp; Mahaveer Vishva Sadbhava Awd; Sraswat Samman; Dakshin Keasari. Memberships: JCI of India; Pres, Gemini Sahitya Acady, Haryana; A B Swatantra Lekhak Munch, Delhi, Regl Pres. Hobbies: Helping depressed people; Writing; Journalism; Travelling. Address: Udaseen, 13-3-391, Nirvan Akhada, Purana

Pul, Hyderabad (AP) India Pin 500 006.

BINGHAM Richard Eardley, b. 4 June 1955, Windlesham, Eng. Public Servant. m. Sharon, 24 Jan 1981, 2 s, 1 d. Education: BLL, 1976, Dip of Welfare Law, 1985, Univ of Tasmania. Appointments: Dir (Legis & Policy) Law Dept, 1986-90; Dir of Policy, Dept of Environ & Land Mngmt, 1990-94; Sec, Dept of Justice, 1994-. Address: Department of Justice, 15 Murray Street, Hobart, Tasmania 7000, Australia.

BIPUL ACHARYA, b. 23 Dec 1969, Dinhata. Businessman; Writer. Education: MA, Econs; BEd. Appointments: Ed, Sahitya Akash Mag, 1989; Book publishing; Editing; Writing; Literary composition. Honours: Sahitya Awd of 14th Century, Kabita Club, Bangladesh, 1994; Nazrul Awd, S S Pathagar Bagura, 1995; Marrichika Sahitya Awd, 1996; Sahitya, Jagat, Awd, 1996. Hobbies: Literacy; Listening to music; Organising; Travelling. Address: C/o Jyotish Bhawan, PO Dinhata, DT Cooch Behar, PIN-736 135, WB, India.

BIRCH David Ian, b. 3 Dec 1950, Nottingham, UK (settled Aust, 1985). Professor. Education: York Univ, UK. Appointments: Lectr, Engl Lang and Linguistics, Natl Univ Singapore, 1981-85; Snr Lectr, Engl and Comparative Lit, Murdoch Univ, WA, 1985-94; Prof and Hd, Dept Comms and Media Studies Cntrl Qld Univ, 1993-96; Pro-Vice Chancellor (Acad), Cntrl Qld Univ, 1996-97; Prof and Hd Lit and Comm Stdies, Deakin Univ, Melbourne. Publications: Auth: Early Reformation English Polemics, 1983; Language, Literature and Critical Practice, 1991; Singapore Media: Communication Strategies and Practices, 1993: Ed of sev wrks inclng: Cultural Studies in the Asia Pacific, 1994; Language in Context: A Functional Linguistic Theory of Register, 1995; Teaching the Postmodern, 1995; Framing (Postcolonial) Culture, 1996; Gen Ed, book series, Culture and Communication in Asia, 1995-98; Ed, Social Semiotics, 1993-; Mbr, editl bds for natl and intl jrnls. Memberships: Austl Linguistics Assn Aust; Australasian Lang and Lit Assn; Australasian and S Pacific Assn for Comparative Lit Studies; Aust Cultural Studies Assn; Poetics and Linguistics Assn; Austl Comms Assn. Hobbies: Theatre; Food, Cooking. Address: 24/32 Porter Street, Prahran, Vic 3181, Australia.

BIRCH Louis Charles, b. 8 Feb 1918. Emeritus Professor, University of Sydney. Education: BAgrSc, 1939; DSc, 1948. Appointments: Rsch Offr, Waite Agric Rsch Ind, 1939-46; CSIRO Overseas Rsch Schlsp, Oxford & Chgo, 1946-47; Snr Lectr Zool, Univ Sydney, 1948-54; Rdr, 1954-58; Challis Prof Bio, Univ Sydney, 1958-83; Emer Prof, 1983-. Publications include: The Liberation of Life: From the Cell to the Community, 1981; The Ecological Web: and the Distribution and Abundance of Animals, 1984; On Purpose, 1990; Liberating Life: Contemporary Approaches to Ecological Theology, 1990; Regaining Compassion: For Humanity and Nature, 1993; Feelings, 1995; Living with the Animals, 1997 Honour: Gold Medal, Ecol Soc Aust, 1988; Templeton Prize, 1990. Memberships: Fell, Aust Acady Sci, 1961; Fell, AAAS; Hon Life Mbr, Brit Econ Soc; Hon Life Mbr, Econ Soc Am. Hobbies: Surfing; Organ; Music. Address: 5A/73 Yarranabbe Road, Darling Point, NSW 2027, Australia.

BIRCH William Francis (The Right Honourable Sir), b. 1934, Hastings, NZ. Politician. m. Rosa Birch, 4 c. Education: Hamilton Tech Coll, NZ; Wellington Tech Corresp Sch. Appointments: Cnslt, Surveying, Engrng, Pukekohe, NZ, 1957; Dpty Mayor, Pukekohe, 6 yrs; MP for Franklin, Natl Party, 1972-; Jnr Govt Whip, 1974; Snr Govt Whip, 1975; Min Energy, Min Natl Dev, Min Regl Dev, 1978-84; Opposition Spokesman Fin, 1985-86; Min Labour, State Servs, Min Immigration and Pacific Is Affairs, 1990-93; Min Employment, 1991-93; Min Hlth, 1993; Min Fin, 1993-; Min of Revenue, 1996-98, 1999-; Treas, 1998-99. Address: c/o Parliament Buildings, Wellington, New Zealand.

BIRCHALL Nicholas John Wardlaw (His Honour Judge), b. 25 July 1933, Aust. District Court Judge. m. Suzan Dercsenyi, 4 Feb 1958, 1 s, 1 d. Education: LLB,

Univ of Adelaide; Admitted to SA Bar, 1955. Appointments include: Ptnr, Mohr Birchall & Co, 1961-66; Judge, Dist Crt of SA, 1979-. Memberships: Life Mbr, Adelaide Univ Cricket Club, Pres, 1974-86; Pres, Studs Rep Cncl, Univ of Adelaide, 1953-54; Mbr of Cncl, Law Soc of SA, 1959-61; Fmr Mbr, SA Bar Assn; Fmr Chmn, St Peter's Old Collegians Cricket Club; Chmn, Motor Fuel Licensing Bd, 1974-79; Chmn, Tchrs Registration Bd, 1976-79; SA Cricket Assn, Assn Cttee, 1974-86, Ground & Fin Cttee, 1977-86. Hobbies: Cricket; Reading. Address: 27 Craighill Road, St Georges, SA 5064, Australia.

BIRCHAM Deric Neale (Sir), b. 16 Dec 1934, Wellington, NZ. University President. m. Patricia Simkin, 18 Apr 1960, 1 s, 2 d. Education: Ba, Visual Comm, CA Univ, San Fran, 1985; MBA, Psychol Mngmt, Univ CA, San Fran, 1987; PhD, Relig Lit, Intl Univ, Harmony Coll of Applied Sci, 1994. Appointments: NZ Govt, Visual Comm, Publicity and PR, 1952-78; Hd of Medl Photog and Hd, Medl Illustrations Dept, Univ of Otago and All Hosps in prov of Otago, 1979-89; Dir Gen, Chair, Bd of Dirs and Pres, Intl Inst of Nat Med Inc, 1989-; CEO, Pres, Chair, Bd of Dirs, Intl Medl, Sci and Educ Cnslts, 1994-; Apptd Univ Pres, Cnsltng Prof to Asian Deleg, Acad Bd Mbr, Oxford Intl Univ (Spain), 1998-2004. Publications: (auth) 13 inclng: Deric's Photo Notes Vol 1, Vol 2 (Ltd Ed), 1994; Photography from the Basic's Upwards (Ltd Ed), 1996; Nerve Stimulation, 1998; Nerve Stimulation Therapeutics, 1998; Aspects of Photography, 1998; Aspects of Management, 1998; 3 as co-auth incl: Radiation Therapy (Video Production), 1995; 7 as major contbr incl: Discover the Way of Survival, 1997. Honours: Very num incl: Gold Medal of Merit, Imperial Order of St Germon, 1998; Oxford Intl Univ, for Rsch and Writing 2 Textbooks for this Univ, 1998; Presdtl Distinguished Visng VIP Awd, Pres Lee of Taiwan, 1998; Albert Schweitzer Gold Medal of Hum, Polish Acady of Med, 1999; The titles: Hon Arch Deacon, Amn Fellshp of Christian Chs, 1997; Baron of Kingston, 1998; Count Palatine, 1998; Knighthoods incl: Kt Grand Cross, CJ St S, 1998; Kts Gold Cross of Merit GCM.ST.S, 1998; KGC, Sov Mil Order of St John of Jeruslem, 1998. Memberships include: Fell Roy Photog Soc of GB, 1969-; FRSA (Eng), 1969; NZ Profl Photogs Assn, 1970. Address: 131 Tirohanga Road, Lower Hutt, Wellington, New Zealand.

BIRD Eric Charles Frederick, b. 2 Sept 1930, Tunbridge Wells, Eng. Geomorphologist. m. Juliet Frances Wain, 30 June 1962, 3 d. Education: MSc, London, 1955, Melbourne, 1975; PhD, ANU, 1960. Appointments: Lectr, Environl Sci, Univ Coll, London, 1960-63; Snr Lectr, Geog, ANU Canberra, 1963-66; Assoc Prof, Geomorphology, Univ of Melbourne, 1966-92; Scientific Dir, Geostdies P/l, 1977-. Publications: Coasts, 1968, 3rd edn, 1984; Coastive Changes, 1985; The World's Coastline, 1985; Sumberging Coasts, 1993; The Coast of Victoria, 1994; Geology and Scenery of Dorset, 1995; Beach Management, 1996; Shaping the Isle of Wight, 1997; The Coasts of Cornwall, 1998. Hobbies: Coastal research; Landscape literature. Address: 242 Beach Road, Black Rock, Vic 3193, Australia.

BIRD John Roger, b. 26 Aug 1927. Physicist. m. Betty Isabel Rowntree, 6 Dec 1952, 2 d. Education: MSc; PhD. Appointments: Rsch Sci, Atomic Energy Rsch Estab, Eng; Rsch Sci, Lucas Heights Rsch Labs, NSW, Aust. Publications: Co Auth: Ion Beam Analysis in Archaeology and the Arts, 1983; Ion Beam Techniques for Materials Analysis, 1989; Pacific Obsidian Studies, 1998; Accelerator Mass Spectrometry, 1998; About 150 articles in sci jrnls. Membership: Fell, Austl Inst of Phys. Address: 24 Cumbee Lane, Caringbah, NSW 2229, Australia.

BIRD Trevor Stanley, b. 27 Aug 1949. Electronics Engineer. m. Valerie Irene Grant, 17 May 1975, 1 s, 2 d. Education: BApplSci, Univ Melbourne, 1971; MApplSci, Univ Melbourne, 1973; PhD, Univ Melbourne, 1977. Appointments: Postdoc Rsch Fell, Queen Mary Coll, Univ London, 1976-78; Lectr, James Cook Univ, 1978-83; Cnslt, Plessey Radar Plc, 1982-83; Rsch Sci, CSIRO Aust, 1984-; Chief Rsch Sci, currently; Hon Professorial Fell in Electronics, Macquarie Univ, 1997-. Publications: Over 100 rsch pprs and articles. Honours: IREE Fisk Prize, 1970; John Madsen Medal, Inst of Engrs, Aust, 1988, 1992, 1995, 1996; CSIRO Medal, 1990, 1998. Memberships: Fell, Inst of Engrs, Aust; Fell, IEE; Fell, IEEE; Fell Austl Acady of Technol, Sci and Engrng. Hobbies: Cricket; Tennis; Reading; German Language. Address: CSIRO Telecommunications & Industrial Physics, PO Box 76, Epping, NSW 1710, Australia.

BIRD-WALTON Nancy, b. 16 Oct 1915, Aust. Aviatrix. m. 16 Dec 1938, 1 s, 1 d. Appointments: Learned to fly, 1933; Coml Pilot, 1935; Owner, Pilot, Far W Children's Hlth Scheme; Fndr and Patron, Austl Women Pilot Assn. Publications: Born to Fly, 1961; My God it's A Woman, 1990. Honours: Coronation Medal, 1936, 1955; OBE, 1966; Hon MEng, Sydney Univ, 1987; AM, 1990; Hon DSc, Newcastle Univ, 1995. Membership: Guild of Air Pilots and Air Navigators. Listed in: Who's Who in Australia; American Who's Who of Women. Hobby: Public speaking. Address: 22 Adderstone Avenue, North Sydney, NSW 2060, Australia.

BIRENDRA Bir Bikram Shah Dev (King of Nepal), b. 28 Dec 1945, Kathmandu. m. Queen Aishwarya Rajya Laxmi Devi Shah, 1970, 2 s, 1 d. Educaiton: St Joseph's Coll Darjeeling; Eton Coll Eng; Univ of Tokyo; Harvard Univ. Appointments: Has travelled extensively throughout Eur, North and South Am, USSR, Iran, Japan, China and several African countries; Grand Master of all medals and decorations of the Kingdom of Nepal; Supreme Cmdr-in-Chf Roy Nepalese Army; Patron Roy Nepal Acady of Sci and Technol; Patron King Mahendra Trust for Nat Conserv; Patron Lumbini Dev Trust; Patron Pashupati Area Dev Trust; Chan Tribhuvan Univ; Chan Mahendra Sanskrit Univ; Came to the throne 31 Jan 1972, coronation24 Feb 1975. Honours: Hon Field-Marshal - UK - 1980; Numerous other decorations. Hobbies: Nature conservation; Riding; Painting. Address: Narayanhity Royal Palace, Kathmandu, Nepal.

BIRLA Ganga Prasad, b. 2 Aug 1922, Calcutta. Industrialist. m. Nimala Devi Birla, 1952, 1 s, 1 d. Education: Calcutta Univ. Appointments: Pres Indian Paper Mills Assn Calcutta, 1947-48, 1954-55, 1955-56; Chmn Hindustan Motors Ltd, Orient Paper & Inds Ltd, 1957-; Pres Employers' Assn Calcutta, 1962-63, 1964-65; Mngng Dir Birla Brothers Pvt Ltd, 1982-; Chmn Bd of Govs Birla Inst of Technol Ranchi; Chmn Bd of Govs Birla Inst of Sci Rsch; Pres Bd of Govs Calcutta Med Rsch Inst; Pres Mngmt Cttee BM Birla Heart Rsch Cntr Calcutta. Memberships: Red Cross Soc. Hobbies: Music; Art; Literature; Archaeology; Sport; Travel. Address: Birla House, 8/9 Alipore Road, Calcutta 700 027, India.

BIRON Cemal, b. 15 Jan 1919, Istanbul, Turkey. Professor. m. Meela, 5 Sept 1947, 1 s, 1 d. Education: BS, MT Sch of Mines, USA, 1943; BS, Univ UT, USA, 1944; PhD, Univ Durham, England, 1955. Appointments: Eregli Coal Mines Agency, Turkey, 1944-64; Tech Univ of Istanbul, Turkey, 1964-. Publications: Undersea Coal Mining; Supports in Mines; Design of Supports; Introduction to Mining Engineering. Honours: Sev. Memberships: Cham of Mining Engnrg, Turkey; AIME, USA; World Mining Congress; Mining Inst, England. Hobbies: Photography; Hiking; Reading. Address: Istanbul Technical University, Maslak, Istanbul 80626, Turkey.

BIRRELL James Peter, b. 24 Oct 1928, Melbourne, Aust. Architect; Town Planner. m. Franki Clegg, 4 s, 2 d. Education: BArch, Univ of Melbourne, 1952; Fell, Roy Melbourne Inst of Technol in Arch, 1953. Appointments: Arch, C'wlth Dept of Works, Melbourne, Canberra and Darwin, 1947-55; Chf Arch, Brisbane Cty Cncl, 1954-60; Univ Arch, Univ of Qld, 1961-66; Prin, James Birral & Ptnrs Pty Ltd, 1966-99; Dir, Natl Capital Authy of Aust, 1997-. Publications: Biography of Walter Burley Griffin, 1964; Water From the Moon, 1989. Honours: High Commendation, Univ of Qld, 1967; Citation, Meritorious Arch, 1970. Memberships include: Life Fell, Roy Austl Inst of Archs; Fell, Roy Town Planning Inst, London; Fell, Roy Soc of Hlth; Life fell, Roy Austl Plng Inst. Hobbies: Classical Music; Food; Wine; Fishing. Address: 104 Duporth Avenue, Maroochydore, Qld 4558, Australia.

BIRRELL Mark Alexander, b. 7 Feb 1958, Melbourne, Vic, Aust. Member of Parliament. m. Jennifer Anne Thomas, 2 Feb 1985, 2 d. Education: BEcon; LLB. Appointments: State Pres, Liberal Studs Union, 1977; State Pres, 1980, Fed Pres, 1982, Young Liberal Movement; State Exec, Fed Exec, Liberal Party, 1980-82; Elected to Parl, 1983; Shadow Min, 1985-92; Govt Ldr, Legis Cncl, 1992-; Min Maj Projs, Min Conserv and Environment, 1992-96; Min Ind, Sci and Technol, 1996-. Publication: Ed, Australian States - Towards a Renaissance, 1987. Memberships: Dir, Austl Inst Pol Sc, 1982-88; Natl Trust Aust; Dir, Federation Cncl, 1997-. Listed in: Who's Who in Australia. Hobbies: Cycling; Photography. Address: 173 Canterbury Road, Canterbury, Vic 3126, Australia.

BIRTLES Terence Grant, b. 21 Apr 1938, Wellington, New Zealand. Geographer. m. Grace, 11 Sept 1971, 1 s, 3 d. Education: BA; BEd; MA; Dip Crim; Dip Intl Law. Appointments: HS Tchr, 1962-63; Dmnstr, Geod, Townsville Univ Coll, 1964; Geog Tchr, Newington Coll, 1965; Tchng Fell, Dept Geog, Univ of Sydney, 1966-67; Assoc Prof Geog, West Washington State Coll, 1967; Lectr, Geog, Macquarie Univ, Sydney, 1967-; Lectr, Geog, Macquarie Univ, Sydney, 1968-69; Prin Lectr, App Geog, Canberra Coll Advd Educ, 1970-89; Assoc Prof, App Geog, Univ of Canberra, 1989-99; Visng Fell Univ of Leicester, 1999. Honour: Univ Medal, Univ of Sydney, 1968. Membership: Elect Life Mbr, Natl Tertiary Educ Union, 1996. Hobbies: Beef Breeding; Miniature Pony Breeding. Address: 217 Osburn Drive, MacGregor, ACT 2615, Australia.

BISHOP Anthony Ralph, b. 14 Jan 1936, Adelaide, SA, Aust. Judge. m. (1) 1 s, 1 d, (2). Education: LLB, Univ of Adelaide, 1961; Admitted to the Bar, 1962. Appointments: Marshal to Jus of the Engl High Crt, 1964; Asst Crown Prosecutor, 1968-70; Asst Crown Solicitor, 1978-85. Memberships: Pengiun Book Collectors Soc (UK); Book Collectors Soc (SA). Hobbies: Vintage motoring; Book collecting. Address: c/o Judges Chambers, District Court of South Australia, Adelaide, SA 5000, Australia.

BISHOP George David, b. 30 May 1949, MI, USA. University Professor. m. Jane Andrew, 9 June 1973, 1 s, 1 d. Education: BA; MS; PhD. Appointments: Rsch Psychol, Dept of Psych, Walter Reed Army Inst of Rsch, Washington, DC, USA, 1975-79; Visng Asst Prof, Dept of Sociol, Anthropol and Psychol, Amn Univ in Cairo, Egypt, 1979-81; Assoc Prof, Div of Behavioral and Cultural Scis, Univ of TX at San Antonio, USA, 1981-93; Assoc Prof, Dept of Socl Work and Psychol, Natl Univ of Singapore, 1991-. Publications include: El Desafio Del SIDA, in Spanish, auth, 1996; Psicologia Sociale Della Salute, in Italian, auth, 1996; Progress in Asian Social Psychology, vol 1, co-auth, 1997; Psychologia, co-auth, 1997; Psychology and Health, auth, 1998; AIDS Care, co-auth, 1998; Personality and Individual Differences, co-auth, 1998; Applied Psychology: An International Review, auth, 1998; Journal of Health Psychology, co-auth, 1999. Honours include: Rsch Grant: Action for AIDS, Singapore, 1996; Natl Univ of Singapore, 1996, 1997; Disting Visng Prof, Amn Univ in Cairo, 1998. Memberships: Singapore Psychol Soc, 1992-; Soc for Behavioral Med, 1990-; Amn Psychol Assn, 1977-; Amn Psychol Soc, 1993-; Soc for Personality and Socl Psychol, 1977-; Soc for Psychol Study of Socl Issues, 1975-; Eurn Health Psychol Soc, 1996-. Hobbies: Music; Cycling; Swimming; Travel. Address: Department of Social Work and Psychology, National University of Singapore, 10 Kent Ridge Crescent, Singapore 119260.

BISHOP John Barrington, b. 22 Apr 1937, Sans Souci, NSW, Aust. Barrister. Education: BA (Syd); LLM (Syd); PhD (London). Appointments: Legal Clrk, Solicitor, Att-Gen's Dept, NSW, 1969-78; Lectr, Snr Lectr, Macquarie Univ Law Sch, 1978-87; Barrister, 1978-. Publications: Criminal Procedure (2nd ed), 1998.

Memberships: NSW Bar Assn; Lay Canon, St Andrew's Cath Ch, Sydney. Address: St James' Hall, 13/169 Phillip St, Sydney, Australia.

BISHOP Peter Orlebar, b. 14 June 1917, Tamworth, NSW, Aust. Academic. m. Hilare Louise Holmes, 20 Feb 1942, 1 s, 2 d. Education: MB, BS, Univ Sydney; DSc; Res Medl Offr, Neurol Registrar, Roy Prince Alfred Hosp, 1941-42; Postgrad Fell, Natl Hosp Nervous Diseases, London, 1946-47, Dept Anatomy, UCL, 1947-50. Appointments: Surg Lt, Roy Austl Naval Reserve, 1942-46; Prince Alfred Hosp, Sydney, 1946; Dept Anatomy, UCL, Eng, 1947-50; Fell, Dept Surg, 1950-51, Snr Lectr, 1951-54, Rdr, 1954-55, Prof, Hd Dept Physiology, 1955-67, Hon Rsch Assoc, Dept Anatomy and Histology, 1987-, Univ Sydney, NSW; Prof, Hd, Dept Physiology, John Curtin Sch Medl Rsch, 1967-82, Prof Emer, 1983-, Visng Fell, Dept Behavioural Bio, Rsh Sch Biol Scis, 1983-87, Austl Natl Univ, Canberra, ACT; Japan Soc Promotion Sci Visng Prof, Osaka Univ Medl Sch, 1974; Keio Univ Medl Sch, Tokyo, 1982; Guest Prof, Neuro and Psychophysiology Lab, Cath Univ, Leuven, Belgium, 1984-85; Visng Prof, Univ Zurich, Switzerland, 1985; Fell, St John's Coll, Cambridge, Eng, 1986. Honours: Hon MD, Univ Sydney, 1983; AO, 1985; Co-recip, Aust Prize, 1993; Sev fellshps. Memberships include: FAA; FRS; Hon Mbr, Austl Physiological and Pharmacological Soc; Hon Mbr, Austl Neurosci Soc; Physiological Soc GB; Cncl, Intl Brain Org; Fell, Natl Vision Rsch Inst, Aust; Hon Mbr, Ophthalmological Soc, NZ; Commn Neurophysiology; Cncl, Intl Union Physiological Scis, 1968-77; Hon Mbr, Neurosurg Soc Aust, 1970; Hon Mbr, Austl Assn Neurologists, 1977. Listed in: Num biog vols. Hobby: Bushwalking. Address: 139 Cape Three Points Road, Avoca Beach, NSW 2251, Australia.

BISHOP Rosalinda, b. 18 Oct 1950, Philippines. Information Manager; Choreographer. m. Roy Bishop (div), 1 s. Education: BS Educ, Univ of Nueva Caceres, Philippines, 1969; MA Educ, Univ of Nueva Caceres, Philippines, 1974; MBA, Ortanez Univ, Philippines, 1979; Assoc Dip, lib Prac, Sydney Tech Coll, Aust, 1990; Master Lib & Info Mngmt, Charles Sturt Univ, Aust, 1998. Appointments: Tchr, Dept of Educ, Philippines, 1969-74; Rsch/Analyst, Armed Forces of the Philippines, 1974-75; For Exchange Offr, Cntrl Bank of Philippines, 1975-80; Lib Offr, Parl House, Canberra, Aust, 1981-82; Admnstv Serv Offr, Austl Bur of Stats, Canberra, Aust, 1982-86; Circulation Offr, Univ of West Sydney, Aust, 1986-88; Acquisitions Offr, Austl Cath Univ, Sydney, Aust, 1988-94; Snr Lib Supvsr, State Lib, Sydney, NSW, 1995-. Honours: Recip, Outstndng Migrant Awd, 1984; Best Cultural Perf Awd, 1991; Mrs Philippines Aust Beauty Pageant, 1993. Memberships: Dir/Choreographer, Philippine Dance Ensemble, 1985-; Sec, Philippine Austl Country Club, 1986-89; Pub Rel Offr, Filipino Women's Assn, 1987-91; Treas, Philippine Austl Entertainment Network, 1997-; An Lib Assn, 1997-; Austl Lib & Info Assn, 1997-; Assn for Lib Collections & Tech Servs, 1998; Protocol Mngr & Choreographer, Mrs Philippines Aust Beauty Quest, 1994-; Sydney Morning Herald Lit Club, 1996-.

BISSETT Sally Ann, b. 7 Oct 1969, Leongatha, Aust. Veterinarian. Education: VCE, 1987; BUSc, 1992; MUSc, 1997. Appointments: Vet, Small Animal Assn, 1992; Master Stud, Massey Univ, NZ, 1995; Res, Univ of Pennsylvania, 1997. Creative Works: 5 Sci Publs, Amn Jrnl of Vet Rsch. Memberships: Austl Small Animal Vet Assn. Hobbies: Swimming; Body Surfing; Water Polo; Film. Address: c/o VHUP 3850 Spruce St, Philadelphia, PA 19104, USA.

BISTA Kirti Nidhi, b. 1927. Politician. Education: Tri-Chandra Coll Kathmandu; Lucknow Univ. Appointments: Asst Min for Educ, 1961-62; Min for Educ, 1962-64; Ldr Nepalese delegs to UN Gen Assemblies, 1964, 1965, 1966 and to UNESCO Gen Confs, 1962, 1964, 1966 and to var otherconfs; Min for For Affairs and Educ, 1964-66; Vice-Chmn Cncl of Mins and Min for For Affairs and Econ Plng, 1966-67; Dep PM and Min for For Affairs and Educ, 1967-68; Perm Rep to UN, 1968-69;

PM, 1969-70, 1971-73, 1977-79; Min of Fin Gen Admin and Palace Affairs, 1969-73; Min of Fin Palace Affairs and Def, 1978-79; Accompanied HM the King on many State Visits. Honours: Order of the Right Hand of Gurkhas - First Class; Fed German Order of Merit; Legion d'honneur. Memberships: Mbr Roy Advsry Cttee, 1979-70. Address: Gyaneshwor, Kathmandu, Nepal.

BISWAS Abdul Rahman. Politician. Appointments: Fmr Speaker House of Ass; Pres of Bangladesh, 1991-96. Address: c/o Office of the President, Dhaka, Bangladesh.

BITARAF Hibibollah, b. 1956, Yazd. Government Official. m. Zahra Mansurie, 1981, 3 d. Education: Tehran Univ. Appointments: Gov-Gen, 1987-90; Dep Min for Energy, 1991-95; Exec Mngr of Karon 3 and 4 - dam and energy plant - proj, 1995-97; Min for Energy, 1997-. Publication: Fluid Mechanics. Hobbies: Studying; Mountaineering; Table Tennis; ;Pilgrimage; Travelling. Address: Ministry of Energy, No 81, Felestin Shoumali Ave, Tehran 14154, Iran.

BLACK Eric Ries Edward, b. 30 Apr 1909. Retired Army Officer; Life Vice-President, Melbourne Branch, RAF Assn. Education: RMC Sandhurst. Career: Cmsnd Roy Warwickshire Regt, 1932; Seconded RAF, 1937-46; Wing Cmdr 26 & 208 Sqdns, Middle E; Liaison Off, Siege of Tobruk, 1941; Haifa, 1942; MID twice, Grp Capt, 1942; CO 213 Grp RAF, 1943; SOA Levant Cmd, 1944; Lt-Col, Roy Warwickshire Regt Egypt, 1946; Col RAR 1952; Good Neighbour Club, Yth Cncl of Vic, 1959-74; Mbr, Brit Cwlth Day Movement, Lord Mayor's Childrens Camp Cttee, 1959-79; Sec, Boy Scout Pan Pacific Jamboree, 1955-56; Gen Sec, Vic Scout Assn of Aust, 1959-70; Pres, Melbourne Br, RAF Assn, 1977-94; Cnslt Boy Scouts Assn, Vic, 1971-74; Assoc, Trinity Coll, Univ Melbourne, 1979-84; Chmn, Trees & Tree, Vic Br, Rats of Tobruk Assn, Pastoral Wrkr, 1985. Honours: OBE for serv in Tobruk, 1942; Presdtl Cert, RAF HQ, London, 1994. Memberships: RACV. Listed in: Who's Who In Australia, 1995. Hobbies: Sailing; Reading; Opera; Ballet. Address: 2-25 Rockley Road, South Yarra, Vic 3141, Australia.

BLACK James Walter, b. 8 Feb 1941, Glasgow, Scotland. Queen's Counsel. 2 s, 2 d. Education: Trinity Coll, Glenalmond, Perthshire, Scotland, 1954-59; St Catharines Coll, Cambridge, Eng, 1960-63; BA, 1963, MA, 1967, Cantab. Appointments: Admitted to the Bar of Eng and Wales, 1964; Appointed a Recorder, 1976; Queen's Cnsl, Eng and Wales, 1979; Admitted to the Bar of NSW, 1986; Queen's Cnsl, NSW, 1987; Admitted to Bar of ACT, 1990. Honour: Exhibitioner in Classics, St Catharine's Coll, Cambridge, Eng, 1959. Memberships: Mid Temple, London; Law Cncl of Aust. Hobbies: Fishing; Sailing; Golf; Travel. Address: Edmund Barton Chambers, 44 MLC Building, Martin Place, Sydney, NSW 2000, Australia.

BLACK Shirley Temple, b. 23 Apr 1928, Santa Monica, CA. Actress; Diplomat. m. (1) John Agar Jr, 1945, dissolved 1949, 1 d; m. (2) Charles A Black, 1950, 1 s, 1 d. Education: Privately and Westlake Sch for Girls. Appointments: Career as film actress commenced at 3 1/2 yrs; First full-length film was Stand Up and Cheer; Narrator/actress in TV series Shirley Temple Storybook, 1958; Hostess/Actress Shirley Temple Show, 1960; Deleg to UN NY, 1969-70; Amb to Ghana, 1974-76; White House Chf of Protocol, 1976-77; Amb to Czechoslovakia, 1989-92; Dir Natl Multiple Sclerosis Soc. Publication: Child Star, 1988. Films Include: Little Miss Marker; Baby Take a Bow; Bright Eyes; Our Little Girl; The Little Colonel; Curly Top; The Littlest Rebel; Captain January; Poor Little Rich Girl; Dimples; Stowaway; Wee Willie Winkie; Heidi; Rebecca of Sunnybrook Farm; Little Miss Broadway; Just Around the Corner; The Little Princess; Susannah of the Mounties; The Blue Bird; Kathleen; Miss Annie Rooney; Since You Went Away; Kiss and Tell; That Hagen Girl; War Party; The Bachelor and the Bobby-Soxer; Honeymoon. Honours: Dame Order of Knights of Malta - Paris - 1968; Am Exemplar Medal, 1979; Gandhi Memorial Intl Fndn Award, 1988;

Numerous state decorations. Memberships: Mbr US Commn for UNESCO, 1973-; Mbr US Deleg on African Refugee Problems Geneva, 1981. Address: c/o Academy of Motion Picture Arts and Sciences, 8949 Wilshire Blvd, Beverly Hills, CA 90211, USA.

BLACKMORE Sheila Margaret, b. 26 Nov 1922, Aust. Educational Administrator. Education: Stotts Bus Coll, NSW. Appointments: Sgt, WAAAF, 1941-45; Chmn of Dirs, S M Blackmore Pty Ltd, 1946-99; Dir, Dunmore Lang Coll, Macquarie Univ, 1979-95; Fndr, Nadow Aust (Off and Computer Trng for the Disabled), NSW, 1965-; Wound Care Patient Advsr, Sydney Adventist Hosp, NSW, 1997. Publications: The Parallel Handicap, 1978; The Peopleware Handicap, 1979; The Peopleware Handicap - The NOW Problem - The NADOW NOW Solution, 1979; A Computer Training Scheme for the Disabled, 1980; Blackmore Back to Work Programme, 1984; The Australian Insurance Institute Insurance of Liabilities: Claims Practice Rehabilitation, 1985. Honours: MBE, 1971; Hon Fell, Dunmore Lang Coll, Macquarie Univ, 1995. Memberships: FAIM; Girl Guides Assn, State Cncl. Hobbies: Reading; Music; Polo; Gardening; Sports. Address: 8 Sydney Road, East Lindfield, NSW 2070, Australia.

BLACKWELL Susan Barbara, b. 24 May 1957, Sydney, Australia. Book Publisher. ptnr R J Fryda. Education: BA, Sydney Univ; LLB, Univ of Technol, Sydney. Appointments: Asst Dir, 1986-88, Exec Dir, 1988-, Austl Publrs Assn Ltd; Dir, Austl Copyright Cncl, 1989-. Memberships: Austl Copyright Cncl, 1983-; Copyright Soc, 1985-99; Dante Alighieri Soc, 1988-90; Natl Schl Commns Forum, 1996-; Copyright Law Review Cttee, 1999. Hobbies: Sailing; Music; Travel; Tennis; Reading. Address: c/o Australian Publishers Association Ltd, 60-89 Jones Street, Ultimo, NSW 2007, Australia.

BLAINEY Ann Warriner, b. 22 June 1935. Biographer. m. Professor Geoff Blainey, 15 Feb 1957, 1 d. Education: BA (Hons), Melbourne. Publications: The Farthing Poet, 1968; Immortal Boy: A Portrait of Leigh Hunt, 1985; If God Prospers Me: A Portrait of Frederick John Cato, 1991. Memberships: Pres, Lyceum Club, Melbourne, 1980-82; Advsry Cncl of Opera Aust. Address: PO Box 257, East Melbourne, Victoria 3002, Australia.

BLAINEY Geoffrey Norman, b. 1930, Aust. Writer. Appointments: Prof of Econs Hist and Hist, Melbourne Univ, 1968-88; Chan, Univ Ballarat, 1994-98; Cnclr, Austl War Memorial, 1997-. Publications: The Peaks of Lyell, 1954; A Centenary History of the University of Melbourne, 1957; Gold and Paper, 1958; Mines in the Spinifex, 1960; The Rush That Never Ended, 1963; A History of Camberwell, 1965; If I Remember Rightly: The Memoirs of W S Robinson, 1966; Co-Auth and Ed, Wesley College: The First Hundred Years, 1967; The Tyranny of Distance, 1966; Across a Red World, 1968; The Rise of Broken Hill, 1968; The Steel Master, 1971; The Causes of War, 1973; Triumph of the Nomads, 1975; A Land Half Won, 1980; The Blainey View, 1982; Our Side of the Country, 1984; All for Australia, 1984; The Great Seesaw, 1988; A Game of Our Own: The Origins of Australian Football, 1990; Eye on Australia, 1991; Jumping Over the Wheel, 1993; A Shorter History of Australia, 1994; White Gold, 1997; A History of the AMP, 1999. Memberships: Chmn, C'wlth Lit Fund, 1971-73; Aust Cncl, 1977-81; Chmn, Aust-China Cncl, 1979-84. Listed in: International Authors and Writers Who's Who. Address: PO Box 257, East Melbourne, Vic 3002, Australia.

BLAKE Anthony John Dyson, b. 1 July 1942, Melbourne, Australia. Vice Chancellor. m. Marjorie, 9 Jan 1965, 1 s, 1 d. Education: BSc, Melbourne; MSc, Melbourne; BEd, Melbourne; PhD, Purdue, Indiana. Appointments: Dean, Sch of Educ, Riverina-Murray JHE, 1980-85; Dpty Prin, Sydney CAE, 1985-88; Prin Kuring-Gai CAE, 1988-90; Dpty Vice Chan, UB, 1990-96; Vice Chan, UB, 1996-. Memberships: Austl Assn for Rsch in Educ; Austl Vice Chan Cttee, Quality Network for Univs. Hobbies: Reading; Walking; Gardening; Fishing; Travel. Address: University of Technology, Sydney Broadway, NSW 2007, Australia.

BLAKE George Raymond, b. 12 Oct 1959, Encino, CA, USA. Project Engineer. Education: Coll Credit toward BSEE; W Coast Univ, Los Angeles, CA, USA. Publications: High-Speed Digital Fiber-Optic Links, ppr in proceedings, Intl Telemetry Conf, Las Vegas, NV, USA, 1993. Hobbies: Music; Theatre; Fishing; Hunting; Camping; Travel; Wine. Address: 2294, Caldwell Avenue, Simi Valley, CA, USA.

BLAKE Sir Peter, b. 1948, Auckland. Yachtsman. m. Pippa Blake, 1979, 1 s, 1 d. Education: Takapuna Grammar Sch; Auckland Technol Inst. Appointments: Began sailing at age eight; Aged 18 built own 23ft keelboat in which he won NZ championships; Moved to Eng, 1971; Winner Fastnet Race, 1979, 1989; Winner Sydney-Hobart Race, 1980, 1984; Winner Round Aust Two-Handed Race, 1988; Whitbread Round the World Race, 1989-90; CEO Team NZ Ltd; Ams Cup Def 2000, 1994-. Honours: NZ Yachtsman of the Year, 1982, 1989-90; NZ Sports Personality of the Year, 1989; NZ Sportsman of the Year, 1990; Numerous other awards. Address: Longshore, 3 Western Pa-ade, Emsworth, Hants, P010 7HS, England.

BLAKEMORE John Stewart, b. 24 Nov 1939, Newcastle, NSW, Aust. Management Consultant. m. Deirdre June Flynn, 10 Apr 1965, 2s. Education: BSc, Univ of NSW, Sydney, 2964; MSc Univ of Newcastle, NSW, 1966; PhD, 1969; Postgrad, Austl Sch of Nuclear Technol, 1970. Appointments: Rsch Sci, AAEC, Lucas Heights, NSW, 1969-70; Chf Metallurgist, John Lysaght, Newcastle, 1970-77, Tubemakers, Newcastle, 1977-79; Engrng Mngr, Wormald Machinery Grp, 1979-82; Gen Mngr, Pyrotek, Sydney, 1982-84; Mktng Dir, John Morris, Sydney, 1983-84; Div Gen Mngr, GEC, Sydney 1984-85; Mngng Dir, Blakemore Cnslts, Sydney, 1985-; Dir, MASC P/L NSW. Publications: The Quality Solution, 1989; The Quality Solution for the Plastics Industry, 1995; Quality Habits of Best Business Practice, 1995; Strategic Planning for Business, 1998. Honours: C'wlth Schl, 1957; Intl Nickel Fell, 1966-69; PhD, 1968. Memberships: Dir, Fell, Austl Inst of Mngmt; Mbr, Inst of Engrs; Mbr, Inst Materials; Fell, Austl Org Qlty; Fell, Qlty Soc, Aust; Mbr Inst Mngmt Cnslts; CP Eng (UK); C Eng; Fell, Austl Inst Co Dirs; Pres, 1970-73, 1978-79, Liberal Pty, Newcastle; Pres, Citizens Grp, 1980-81. Listed in: Who's Who in the World. Hobbies: Piano; Sailing; Politics; Mathematics. Address: 31A Macmasters Parade, Macmasters Beach, NSW 2251, Australia.

BLAKEMORE Michael Howard, b. 18 June 1928, Sydney, NSW, Aust. Theatre and Film Director. m. (1) Shirley Bush, 1960, 1 s, (2) Tanya McCallin, 1986, 2 d. Education: Sydney Univ; Royal Acady Dramatic Art, Eng. Appointments: Actor w Birmingham Repertory Th, Shakespeare Mem Th, others, 1952-66; Co-Dir, Glasgow Citizens' Th, 1966-68, 1st prodn The Investigation; Assoc Artistic Dir, Natl Th London, 1971-76; Dir, Players, NY, USA, 1978; Res Dir, Lyric Th, Hammersmith, London, 1980. Creative works: Prodns inclng: A Day in the Death of Joe Egg, 1967; Arturo Ui, 1969; The National Health Day, 1969; Long Day's Journey into Night, 1971; The Front Page, 1972; Macbeth, 1972; The Cherry Orchard, 1973; Design for Living, 1973; Separate Tables, 1976; Plunder, 1976; Privates on Parade, 1977; Candida, 1977; Make and Break, 1980; Travelling North, 1980; The Wild Duck, 1980; All My Sons, 1981; Noises Off, NY, 1983-84; Benefactors, 1984; Lettice and Lovage, 1987; Uncle Vanya, 1988; Tosca, Welsh Natl Opera, 1992; The Sisters Rosensweig, 1994; Films: A Personal History of the Australian Surf, 1981; Privates on Parade, 1983; City of Angels, 1989; Lettice and Lovage, 1990; After the Fall, 1990; The Ride Down Mount Morgan, 1991; Country Life, writer, dir, 1994; Death Defying Acts, 1995; Now You Know, 1995; Novel: Next Season, published 1969. Honours: Best Dir, London Critics, 1972; Drama Desk Awd, Noises Off, NY; Evening Standard Film Awd, 1982; Hollywood Dramalogue Awd, 1984; NY Outer Critics Circle Awd, 1983, 1989, 1990; Film Critics of Aust Screenplay Awd, 1994; 5 Tony Noms. Listed in: International Who's Who; Who'w Who in Theatre; Who's Who in America. Hobby: Surfing. Address: 18 Upper Park Road, London NW3 2UP, England.

BLANCHFIELD BROWN Janene, b. 17 Apr 1949, Wangaratta, Aust. International Consultant to Philanthropy; Keynote Speaker; Author. 2 s. Appointments: Intl Corp Cnslt, Strategic Plng and Devl Bd Advsry and Evaluation for Not for Profit Orgs and NGO's; Trust Devl and Advsry Servs; CEO, ITHAA, Info Technol Hlth Awareness; Chmn, Martyn-Cuthbertson Ldrshp Awd. Memberships: Cntr for Not for Profit Bds, Wash; Past Pres, Sec, Bus and Profl Women's Club of Melbourne; Austl Bus in Eur; Aust Day Cncl Vic. Hobbies: Travel; Languages; Cross Cultural Negotiations; Music. Address: PO Box 369, Toorak, Vic 3142, Australia.

BLANDY Richard John, b. 8 Dec 1938. Economist. m. Roslyn Anne, 9 Mar 1963, 3 d. Education: 1st Class Hons Deg, Econs, Adelaide Univ, 1961; MA Deg, Econs and Educ, 1967; PhD, Columbia Univ, New York, USA, 1969. Appointments: Tutor in Econs, Univ of Adelaide, 1962; Mbr of Econ Div, Intl Labour Off, Geneva, Switzerland, 1963-66; Rsch Assoc, Intl Inst for Labour Studies, Geneva, Switzerland, 1968; Snr Lectr, Econs, Flinders Univ of SA, 1969-73; Proj Mngr, Population and Employment Project, World Employment Prog, ILO, Geneva, 1972; Dir, Inst of Labour Studies, Flinders Univ of SA, 1972-75; Reader, Econs, Flinders Univ of SA, 1974-75; Prof of Econs, Flinders Univ of SA, 1975-97; Dir, Natl Inst of Labour Studies, Flinders Univ of SA, 1980-92; Assoc Commnr, Inds Asst Commn, Ind Commn, Canberra, 1984; Dir, Inst of Applied Econ and Socl Rsch, Univ of Melbourne and Ronald F Henderson Prof of Applied Econ and Socl Rsch, 1992-94; Chief Exec Offr, SA Dev Cncl, Adelaide, 1995-97; Exec Dir, AustralAsia Econs Pty Ltd, 1997-; Adjunct Prof of Econs, Northern Territory Univ, 1997-; Adjunct Prof, Inst for Rsch into Intl Competitiveness, Curtin Univ, 1994-; Emer Prof, Flinders Univ of SA, 1998-. Publications include: Australia at the Cross Roads: Our Choices to the Year 2000, 1980; How Labour Markets Work, 1982; Structured Chaos: The Process of Productivity Advance, 1985; Data Processing in Australia: A Profile and Forward Perspective of Skills and Usage, 1986; Industry Assistance and the Labour Market: The New Zealand Experience, 1987; Reforming Tertiary Education in New Zealand, 1988; Budgetary Stress: The South Australian Experience, 1989; Labour Productivity and Living Standards, 1990; Study of the Labour Market for Academics, 1990; Where the Jobs Are 1993, 1993; The Population Growth Prospects of the Darwin Region, 1997. Honours: Fell, Acady of Socl Scis in Aust, 1981-; Bur of Ind Econs Small Bus Rsch Awd, 1993. Memberships: Austl Cncl on Population and Ethnic Affairs, 1981-84; SA Cncl on Technological Change, 1980-82; SA Dev Cncl, 1980-86; SA Tripartite Working Party/Advsry Cttee on Manpower Forecasting, 1979-82; Seymour Coll Cncl of Govs, 1981-88; Austl Stats Advsry Cncl, 1983-89; Southern Dev Bd Adelaide, Chmn, 1987-90; Flinders Univ Cncl, 1989-92; Natl Inst of Labour Studies Bd of Govs, Dpty Chmn, 1992-94, Chmn, 1995-98; Munic Assn of Vic, Strengthening Local Econ Capacity Prog, State Advsry Bd, 1993-94; SA Multicultural Forum, 1995-; SA Bus Vision 2010, 1997-. Listed in: Who's Who in Australia; Who's Who in the World. Hobbies: Tennis; Golf; Bridge; Gardening. Address: 88B Queen Street, Norwood, SA 5067, Australia.

BLASHKI Pamela Ruth, b. 28 Aug 1956. Author; Public Relations Consultant. m. Josef Hompas, 22 Mar 1991, 2 s, 1 d. Publications: Chai the Kangaroo, 1985; A Sometimes River, 1986; The Legend, 1987; A Kingdom Lost, 1989. Honour: Variety Club, Gold Heart Awd, 1989. Memberships: Variety Club; Aust Soc of Auths. Hobbies: The Restoration of Wynyard in the Adelaide Hills. Address: Wynyard, PO Box 352, Littlehampton, SA 5250, Australia.

BLEWETT Neal (The Honourable), b. 24 Oct 1933. Australian High Commissioner. m. (1) Jill, 10 Sept 1962, dec 1988, 1 s, 1 d. Education: Univ Tas, Oxford Univ. Appointments: Snr Schl, Tas Rhodes Sch, 1957; Snr Schl, St Antony's Coll, Oxford, 1959-61; Lectr, St Edmund Hall, Oxford Univ, 1961-63; Lectr, Pols, 1964-69; Mbr, Cl Univ Adelaide, 1972-74; Prof, Dept Pol Theor and Insts, Flinders Univ, SA, 1974-77; Pres, SA Cl Civil Liberties, 1975-76; MHR (ALP) Bonython SA, 1977-94; Mbr, Jt House Cttee on For Affairs and Def, 1977-80; Deleg to Aust Constitutional Convention, 1978; Opposition Spokesman Hlth & Tas Affairs, 1980-83, Min Hlth, 1983-87, Min Cmnty Servs and Hlth, 1987-90; Min Socl Security, 1991-93; Chmn, Procedures Cttee, House of Reps, 1993-94; Austl High Comnr to UK, 1994-; Mbr, Exec Bd, Min Trade and Dev, WHO, 1995-98. Publications: The Peers, The Parties and the People, 1972, Playford to Dunstan: The Politics of Transition (Jointly), 1971. Honour: AC, 1995. Membership: Trades Hall. Hobbies: Bushwalking; Reading; Cinema. Address: Australia House, Strand, London WC2B 4LA, England.

BLIUC Radu Cristian, b. 19 Nov 1969, Iasi, Romania. Lecturer. m. Dana 23 Apr 1993, 1 s, 1 d. Education: BS, Gh Asachi, Tech Univ, Iasi; MSc, Civil Engrng, Gh Asachi Tech Univ, Iasi. Appointments: Alex Ltd, Iasi; Gh Asachi, Tech Univ, Iasi. Honours: Univ Coll Postgrad Rsch Schlshp, Austl Def Force Acady, 1997. Address: ADFA University College, University of New South Wales, School of Civil Engineering, Canberra, ACT 2600, Australia.

BLOOM Walter Russell, b. 2 Dec 1948. Professor of Mathematics. m. Lynette Myra Butler, 3 Nov 1971, 2 d. Education: BSc, Univ Tas, Hons I; PhD, ANU; DSc, Univ Tas. Appointments: Lectr in Maths, Univ Tas, 1974; Lectr in Maths, Murdoch Univ, 1975, Snr Lectr 1982, Assoc Prof 1988, Personal Chair, 1995; Dean, Sch Physl Scis, Engrng and Technol, Murdoch Univ, 1991-96; Hon Assoc, W Aust Maritime Mus, 1998-; Ed, Perth Numismatic Jrnl. Publications: Harmonic Analysis of Probability Measures on Hypergroups, book, w Herbert Heyer, 1995; 60 jrnl publs. Honours: Fulbright Fellshp, 1976; Goethe Inst Lang Schlsp, 1979; Alexander von Humboldt Rsch Fellshp, 1987, 1991, 1998-99; Fell, Austl Math Soc; Hon Life Mbr, Austl Math Soc; Fell, Roy Numismatic Soc. Membership: Pres, Perth Numismatic Soc, 1988-91. Listed in: Who's Who in Australia. Hobbies: Numismatics; Classical Music. Address: Murdoch University, Perth, WA 6150, Australia.

BLUCHER William Arthur (The Honorable), b. 12 Dec 1931, Norfolk Is, S Pacific. Company Director. m. (1) Joan Marion Davis, 10 July 1954, div 1993, 3 s, 2 d, (2) Yvonne Isobel Vaja, 22 Sept 1993. Education: Sydney Tech Coll. Appointments: Min, Norfolk Is Legis Assembly to 1991; Regl Mngr, E W Airlines Ltd, 1983-89; Dir, Sev Cos, inclng Chmn, Dir, Bruchel Ltd, 1980-; Dir, Sec, Norfolk Is Shipping Line; Mngng Dir, Martins Agcies Ltd, Norfolk Is, 1971-. Memberships include: Rotary Intl. Listed in: Who's Who in Business Australasia. Hobbies: Tennis; Swimming; Horseriding; Reading; Community Affairs. Address: Middle Gate Road, Norfolk Island, South Pacific.

BLUM Yehuda Zvi, b. 2 Oct 1931, Bratislava. Professor of International Law. m. Moriah, 30 June 1966, 2 s, 1 d. Education: MJur, Jerusalem; PhD, London; Dr Jur hc, Yeshiva Univ. Appointments: Snr Asst Legal Advsr, Israel Min of For Affairs, 1962-65; Prof, Intl Law, Hebrew Univ, Jerusalem, 1965-; Amb, Perm Repr of Israel to Un, NY, 1978-84. Publications: Historic Titles in International Law, 1965; Secure Boundaries and Middle East Peace, 1971; For Zion's Sake, 1987; Eroding the United Nations Charter, 1993. Memberships: Amn Soc of Intl Law; Intl Law Assn. Address: Faculty of Law, Hebrew University, Mount Scopus, Jerusalem, Israel.

BLUNT Charles William, b. Sydney, Australia. Economist. Education: BCom; CPA. Hobbies: Golf; Tennis; Fishing. Address: PO Box 66, Wahroonga, New South Wales, Sydney, Australia.

BLYTON Josie Voon Chin, b. 12 Nov 1941, Penang, Malaysia. Administrative Officer for Australian Government. m (2) Neville Manning Blyton, 14 Oct 1990, 1 s, 1 d. Appointments: Averling Barford Ltd, Eng, 1967-69; KA Vereingte Verlagauslietrung (VTG Tanktainers), Germany, 1977-78; Volun Wrker, Raf Volounteer Community, Cyprus, 1977-78; Task Force Grp (Boat People), Eng, 1979-81; Swallow Mfng Co Ltd,

Eng, 1979-81; Interpreter/Translator, Uniting Ch Aust, N Melbourne, 1982-84; Mandarin Lang, Pilot Proj, Richmond, 1982-84; N Melbourne Sch Cncl, 1982-89; Co-ord, N Melbourne Primary Sch, (Mandarin Lang), 1982-90; Ethnic Affairs Commn, Melbourne, 1983-85; Sec, Bright Moon Buddhist Soc, Melbourne, 1983-91; Ethnic Welfare Offr, Melbourne Cty Cncl, 1982-84; Skill Exch Grp, Essendon, Aust, 1984-85; Home Tutor Scheme (Migrants), Melbourne, 1983-86; Dept Community Welfare Serv, Melbourne, 1984-85; UN Assn, Melbourne, 1986; Asian-Aust Consultative Cncl (Fndn Mbr), 1988-93; Dept Def, 1987-; Pub Offr/Sec, Ming De Chinese Saturday Assn, 1992-. Honours: World Fndn Successful Women, 1991; Intl Woman of Yr, 1991-92; Intl Order of Merit (IOM), 1993; Disting Ldrship Awd, 1993. Memberships: Aust-Asian Assn Vic, 1992-; Hong Kong Club Vic, 1992-; Aust-Indian Soc Melbourne, 1992-; Fndn Mbr and Pres Buddhist Community Assn Inc, Melbourne, 1992-; Chinese Chmbr Comm, Vic, 1992-96; Chinese Profl and Bus Assn Vic, 1993-. Membership: Fellow, ABI, 1993. Hobbies: Travel; Reading; Music; Theatre; Organising Community and Ethnic activities. Address: 2 Mullum Dr, Donvale, Vic 3111, Australia.

BLYTON Neville Manning, b. 12 Sept 1922, Sydney. Aust. Company Director; Consul. m (1) Eunice Phyllis Mossman, dec 1989, (2) Josie V C Liew, 1990. Appointments include: Dir: H C Sleigh Ltd, 1970-81; Golden Fleece Petroleum Ltd, 1970-81; White Inds Ltd, 1976-79; Warkworth Mining Ltd, 1976-81; H C Sleigh Resources Lts, 1976-81; Warkworth Coal Sales Ltd, 1978-81; Tasmanian Bd Mills Ltd, 1980-81; Country & Western Enterprises Pty Ltd, 1980-81; Tassi Timber Products Pty Ltd, 1980-81; Tasboard Export Promotions Pty Ltd, 1980-81; Tasboard Southern Timbers Pty Ltd, 1980-81; TBM Properties Pty Ltd, 1980-81; Westwood Homes Pty Ltd, 1980-81; Exec Dir, H C Sleigh Ltd, 1970-81; Consul for Belgium, 1973-88; Chmn, North Woodchips Pty Ltd, 1972-81; Portion Control Foods Pty Ltd, 1978-81; Neville M Blyton & Assocs, 1981-; Chf Exec, JNO McCall Coal Co, 1987-90; Vp, Aust Free China Assn, 1990-; Natl Pres, Aust Inst of Export, 1991-92; Dpty Pres, Aust Inst of Export, Victorian Div, 1992-94; Chmn, Coll of Intl Bus (Vic) Ltd, 1993-97; Collingwood Masonic Cntr Ltd, 1993-; Mbr, Aust-Asian Assn Victoria Inc, 1992-; Pres, 1994-. Honours: OBE, 1967; KOC (Kt in Order of Crown of Belgium), 1988; Fell, Aust Mktng Inst; Fell, Aust Inst Co Dirs; Fell, Aust Inst Export; Dpty Gov, ABI Rsch Assn. Memberships: Dir, 1959-78, Pres, 1967-69, Melbourne Chmbr of Com; Dir, 1967-75, Natl Pres, 1971-73, Austl Chmbr of Com; Mbr 1962-64, Exec Mbr, 1965-69, C'wlth Govt Export Dev Cncl; Victorian Gov Export Adv Cttee, 1979-84; Victorian Gov China Adv Cttee, 1980-93. Hobbies: Reading; Music; Photography; Theatre. Address: 2 Mullum Dr, Donvale, Vic 3111, Australia.

BOARDMAN Camron, b. 10 Dec 1970. Member of Victorian Legislative Council. Education: VCE; Austl Army Reserve Offr Trng Course. Appointments: Natl Aust Bank; Vic Police Force; Austl Army Reserve; Mbr, Vic Legislative Cncl, Prof of Chelsea. Memberships: Parly Environ & Natural Resources Cttee; Chart Inst of Transp; Lib Party of Aust; C'wlth Parly Assn; Natl Trust; McLelland Gallery Socl Monash Syme Bus Assocs; Frankston Chamber of Com; Roy Childrens Hosp Ski Club; Skiing Aust. Address: 445 Nepean Highway, Frankston, PO Box 1132, Victoria 3199, Australia.

BOASHASH Boualem, b. 21 June 1953, Nezlioua, Algeria. Professor. m. 4 June 1983, 2 s. Education: Baccalaureat, Maths & Scis, Grenoble, France, 1973; Dip D'Ingenieur Physique-Electronique ICPI, Lyon, France, 1978; Dip D'Etudes Approfondies in Signal Processing, Grenoble, 1979; Dip de Docteur Ingenieur INPG, Grenoble, 1982. Appointments: Rsch Engr, Elf Aquitaine Geophysl Rsch Cntr, Pau, France, 1979-82; Snr Lectr, Inst Natl des Scis Appliquees, Lyon, France, 1982-83; Assoc Prof, Univ Qld, 1984-91; Prof, Signal Processing, Bond Univ, Aust, 1989-91, Qld Univ of Technol, 1991-. Publications: 2 books, 10 book chapts, num articles in profl jrnls. Memberships: IEEE. Hobbies: Soccer; International Affairs; Social Studies; History of Sciences; Development of Human Thoughts. Address: Signal Processing Research Centre, School of Electrical & Electronic Systems Engineering, Queensland University of Technology, GPO Box 2434, Brisbane, Qld 4001, Australia.

BOBRYSHEV Yuri, b. 12 Feb 1956. Scientist. m. Irine, 1 s, 1 d. Education: PhD. Appointments: Sci, 1978-91, Snr Sci, 1992-, St Vincent's Hosp, Sydney, Aust. Publications: 48 sci pprs, 1978-98. Honours: Grants, 1991, 1992, 1994, 1995, 1996, 1997. Memberships: NYAS; AAAS. Hobbies: Art; Music. Address: 1/8 Pitt Street, Randwick, NSW 2031, Australia.

BODI Leslie, b. 1 Sept 1922, Budapest, Hungary. University Professor. m. Marianne Marton, 10 June 1950, 1 d. Education: DPhil 1948, DipEd 1949, Univ of Budapest. Appointments: Tutor and Lectr, Univ of Budapest, 1946-57; HS Tchr, Melbourne CEGS, Aust, 1957-58; Lectr in German, Newcastle Univ Coll, 1958-60; Snr Lectr in German 1961-63, Prof of German and Chmn of Dept, 1963-87, Em Prof 1988-, Assoc of Fac 1989-, Monash Univ; Visng Prof, Vienna Univ, 1991; Visng Prof, Graz Univ, 1991; Budapest Univ, 1994; Cntrl Eurn Univ, Budapest, 1994-; Visng Fell, Intl Rsch Cntr for Cultural Rsch, Vienna, 1994, Tübingen, 1999. Publications: Heinrich Heine, 1951; Therese Huber, Adventures on a Journey to New Holland, Ed, 1966; German Culture in the Libraries of Melbourne, co-auth, 1967; Tauwetter in Wien, 1977, revised ed 1995; The Austrian Problem, co-ed, 1982; The German Connection, co-ed, 1985; Image of a Continent, co-auth, 1991; Num articles on German and Aust Lit; Weltbürger-Textwelten: Festschrift H Kreuzer, co-ed, 1995; Paul Weidmann: Der Eroberer (co-ed), 1997. Honours: Offr's Cross, Order of Merit, Fed Repub of Germany, 1973; Offr's Cross, Order for Arts and Lit, Repub of Aust, 1976; Antipodean Enlightments Festschrift für Leslie Bodi, ed W Veit et al, 1987; Friedrich Gundolf Prize for German Studies Abroad, German Acady for Lang and Lit, 1989; DLitt Hon, Monash Univ, 1990; Goethe Medal, Goethe-Inst, 1991; Hon Mbr, Hungarian Acady of Scis, 1995; Alexander von Humboldt Rsch Awd, 1997; Hon Dr and Prof, ELTE, Budapest, 1997. Memberships: Intl Assn of Germanists; Australasian Lang and Lit Assn; Aust and Pacific Assn of Comparative Lit; Internationale Heinrich Heine Gess ellschaft; 18th Century Aust Histl Soc; Intl PEN Club; Aust Assn of Germanists; Inst for Aust & Intl Lit Rsch, Vienna, 1994-. Listed in: Who's Who in Australia; Ki Kicsoda, Budapest; Kürschners Gelehrten-Kalender. Address: 25 Beddoe Avenue, Clayton, Vic 3168, Australia.

BOELEN Meeuwis K, b. 25 Aug 1956, Netherlands. Senior Lecturer. m. Mary, 14 May 1981, 1 s, 1 d. Education: BSc,, MSc, Ultrecht; PhD, Austl Natl Univ. Appointments: Rsch Offr, 1986-89, Lectr, 1989-92, Snr Lectr, 1993-; Vis Assoc Prof, 1995; Hd, Divsn of Biol Sci, 1996-. Publications: Sev articles in profl jrnls. Memberships: Austl Neurosci Soc; Intl Brain Rsch Org; Intl Soc of Neurochem; Assn of Rsch Vision and Ophthalmol. Address: LaTrobe University, PO Box 199, Bendigo, Victoria 3552, Australia.

BOGER David Vernon. Professor of Chemical Engineering. m. 7 Oct 1967, 1 s, 2 d. Education: BS Chem Engrng; MS Chem Engrng; PhD Chem Engrng. Appointments: Lectr, Snr Lectr, Rdr, Monash Univ; Prof Chem Engrng, Univ of Melbourne; Dpty Dean Engrng; Assoc Dean (Rsch) Engrng; Dpty Dir, Advd Mineral Prods Rsch Ctr; Rsch Prog Ldr, Co-op Rsch Cntr for Indl Plant Biopolymers; Hd, Dept of Cheml Engrng, 1997-. Creative Works: 200 Jrnl articles; Conf pprs; Book chapts; Books. Honours: Ann Awd, Brit Soc Rheol, 1983; Roy Soc of Vic Rsch Medal, 1985; Esso Awd for Excellence, Chem Engrng, 1991; Pol Eureka Prize, Environment Rsch, 1993; Aust Soc Rheol Medal, 1994; Walter Ahlström Environment Prize, 1995; Alcoa Environment Excellence Awd, 1995; CSIRO External Medal for Rsch Ex, 1998. Memberships: I Chem E (UK), 1968, Fell, 1986; Brit Soc Rheol; Austl Soc Rheol; Amn Soc Rheol; Fell, Austl Acady of Tech Scis & Engrng; Fell, Austl Acady Scis. Listed in: Australia Engineering; Contemporary Achievement; Science & Engineering; The World. Hobbies: Farming; Fishing. Address: Department of Chemical Engineering, University of Melbourne, Parkville, Vic 3052, Australia.

BOGGS George R, b. 4 Sept 1944, Conneaut, OH, USA. Educator. m. Ann, 8 Aug 1969, 3 s. Education: BS, OH State Univ; MA, Univ of CA at Santa Barbara; PhD, Univ TX, Austin. Appointments: Tchng Asst, OH State Univ, 1965-66; Tchng Asst, Univ CA, Santa Barbara, 1966-68; Guest Lectr, CA State Univ at Chico Cmnty Coll as an Instn, 1970, 1983, 1984; Instr Chem, Butte Coll, 1968-85; Chmn, Div of Nat Sci and Allied Hlth, Butte Coll, 1972-81; Assoc Dean of Instrn, Butte Coll, 1981-85; Adj Instr, Austin Cmnty Coll, Effective Interviewing, 1982; Supt/Pres, Palomar Cmnty Coll District, 1985-; Guest Lectr, Univ of TX at Austin, 1989, 1990, 1996; Guest Lectr, San Diego State Univ, 1996. Publications: Num articles to profl jrnls. Honours: Schlshps, fellshps, hons incl: Upsilon Pi Upsilon, 1964, Pres, 1965-66; Phi Kappa Phi, 1983; Hon Elder, Natl Cncl on Black Amn Affairs, 1993; Profl of Yr Awd, The Ldrshp Alliance, La Jolla, CA, 1994; Marie Y Martin Chf Exec Offr Awd, Assn of Cmnty Coll Tstees, Miami Beach, FL, 1996; Natl Cncl for Rsch and Plng Mngmt Recog Awd, Natl Cncl for Rsch and Plng, Anaheim, CA, 1997. Memberships include: Assn of CA Cmnty Coll Admnstrs, 1980-. Hobbies: Writing; Photography; Woodworking. Address: 1140 West Mission Road, San Marcos, CA 92069-1487, USA.

BOHAN Edmund, b. 5 Oct 1935, Christchurch, NZ. Singer (Tenor); Writer. m. Gillian Margaret Neason, 18 Nov 1968, 1 s, 1 d. Education: MA, Hons, Univ of Canterbry, NZ; Studies singing w Godfrey Stirling (Sydney), Eric Green and Gustave Sacker (London). Appointments: Debut, Oratorio, 1956, Opera, 1962, NZ; Repertoire of over 170 operas and major wrks incl Opera, Oratorio Concerts in Eng, Eur, Australasia, Brazil; Opera Engl Opera Grp, Dublin Grand Opera; London Chmbr Opera; State Opera of S Aust, Canterbury Opera NZ; Wellington Cty Opera; Wexford Fest, NZ Intl Fest of the Arts, Aldeburgh Fest, Norwich Triennial, Adelaide Fest; TV/radio incl Austl Brdcstng, BBC proms, ABC, NZ Radio; Film, Barber of Seville; Venues incl Royal Fest Hall, Queen Elizabeth Hall and other major halls w RPO, London Concert, BBC Concert and Ulster Orchs; Oratorio Soloist w Brit, Austl and NZ Choral Socs. Creative works: Recdngs include: A Gilbert and Sullivan Spectacular; When Song is Sweet; Sweet and Low; Gilbert and Sullivan w Band and Voice; The Olympians. Publications include: The Writ of Green Wax, 1971; The Buckler, 1972; Edward Stafford: NZ's First Statesman, 1994; The Opawa Affair, 1996; Contbns to New Zealand Dictionary of Biography, 1991, 1993, 1996, 1998; New Zealand: The Story So Far - A Short History, 1997; The Dancing Man, 1997; Blest Madman: Fitzgerald of Canterbury, 1998; To Be a Hero: A Life of Sir George Grey, 1998; The Matter of Parihaka, 1999; Var articles and reviews. Memberships: NZ Soc of Auths. Listed in: New Zealand Who's Who in Aoteora. Hobbies: Gardening; Reading. Address: 5 Vincent Place, Opawa, Christchurch, New Zealand.

BOLAND Roy Charles, b. 28 July 1950, USA. University Professor. Education: Conf Interpreters Dip, Sydney, 1971; BA Hons, Sydney Univ, 1973; MA, 1976; DipEd, Adelaide Univ, 1977; PhD, Flinders Univ, 1986. Appointments: Tutor, Spanish Dept, Monash Univ, Vic, Aust, 1978-80; Lectr, 1981-85, Snr Lectr, 1986-90, Auckland Univ, NZ; Prof, Univ La Trobe, Melbourne, Vic, Aust, 1991-; Dir, Cntr Galician Stdys Aust NZ, 1995. Publications include: Books; Articles in var profl jrnls; Gen Ed, Voz Hispanica; Ed, Antipodas, Journal of Hispanic Studies. Honours: Instituto Vox Awd, 1986; Schlshp, Spanish Min For Affairs, 1987; Intl Grant, Universidad Menendez y Pelayo, 1991; Intl Grant, Universidad Complutense, 1992; Rsch Grant, Xunta de Galicia, 1993. Memberships include: Intl Assn Hispanists; Eurn Assn Eurn Tchrs; Amn Assn Tchrs Spanish and Portuguese; Editl Bd, var learned jrnls. Listed in: Who's Who in Australia. Hobbies include: Tennis; Wine tasting; Rugby; Cricket. Address: Department of Spanish, La Trobe University, Bandoura, Vic 3083, Australia.

BOLE Filipe, b. 23 Aug 1936. Education: BA, Univ of NZ, Wellington; Dip in Secnd Sch Tchng, Auckland Tchrs Coll; MA, Hist, Victoria Univ, NZ. Appointments: Ministry of Educ, var posts, incl Perm Sec for Educ, 1962-80; Perm Rep to UN w Amb to USA and High Commnr to Can, 1980-83; Min, Dpty Prime Min, Min for For Affairs and External Trade, 1983; Spec Advsr, Review of Constn of Repub of Fiji, 1994; Min for For Affairs w Spec Responsibility on Constn Review and ALTA, 1994; Min for For Affairs, Tourism and Civil Aviation, 1995. Address: National Planning, PO Box 2351, Government Buildings, Suva, Fiji.

BOLITHO Elaine Elizabeth, b. 12 Dec 1940, Christchurch, NZ. Researcher; Writer. m. Ian James Bolitho, 14 Dec 1963, 2 s, 1 dec, 2 d. Education: BA, 1988, BA Hons, 1989, PhD, World Religions, 1993, Vic Univ of Wellington, NZ. Appointments: Ins Offr, 1957-63, Full-time mother, 1964-85, Univ Stdies, 1985-92, Full-time Rschr and Writer, 1993-. Publications: Meet The Baptists - Postwar Personalities and Perspectives, 1993; Meet the Baptists - Postwar Personalities and Perspectives, 1994; Reefton School of Mines: Stories of Jim Bolityo, 1999; Contbns to num books and jrnls. Honours: Eileen Duggan Prize for NZ lit, 1986; Sarah Ann Rhodes Rsch Fellshp, 1990; Helen Stewart Royle Schlshp, 1991-93; Meet the Bapts, Epworth Book of the Month, 1993. Memberships: Christian Rsch Assn, 1994-; Soc of Auths (PEN), 1997-; Wesley Histl Soc, Honoured Mbr, 1996-. Hobbies: Stamp collecting; Reading historical novels; Spending time with friends and family. Address: 33 Kandy Crescent, Ngaio, Wellington 6004, New Zealand.

BOLKIAH Mohamed, b. 27 Aug 1947, Bandar Seri Begawan. Minister of Foreign Affairs. m. Pengiran Anak Isteri Pengiran Anak Hajah Zariah, 10 children. Education: Vic Inst, Kuala Lumpur; Sultan Omar Ali Saifuddin Coll, Brunei Darussalam; Roy Mil Acad, Sandhurst, England, 1965-67; Mbrm Privy Cncl, 1965-. Appointments: Min of For Affairs, 1984-; Chmn, Brunei Darussalam's Cncl of Succession, 1985-. Honours: Title, Yang Teramat Mulia Paduka Seri Pengiran Temanggong, 1967; Title, Duli Yang Teramat Mulia Paduka Seri Pengiran Perdana Wazir, 1970. Memberships: Brunei Darussalam's Privy Cncl, 1968-; Brunei Darussalam's Cncl of Mins, 1970-; Chmn, Constl Review Cttee, 1992-; Chmn, Ministerial Econ Cncl, 1998-. Hobbies: Martial arts; Badminton. Address: High Commission of Brunei Darussalam, 19 Belgrave Square, London SW1X 8PG, England.

BOLLARD Edward George, b. 21 Jan 1920, Ireland. Research Scientist. m. (1) Constance Mary Esmond, 1947, dec 1971, 2 s, 1 d, (2) Joy Elizabeth Cook, 1972. Education: BSc, Univ NZ, 1941; PhD, Cambridge Univ, Eng, 1948. Appointments: Rsch Scientist, 1948-74, Divisional Dir, 1974-80, Dept Sci and Indl Rsch, NZ; Hon Prof, 1973-85, Pro-Chan, 1989-91, Univ Auckland. Publications include: Prospects for Horticulture in New Zealand, 1981; Science and Technology in New Zealand, 1986; Further Prospects for Horticulture: The Continuing Importance of Research, 1996; Num profl papers. Honours: Rsch Medal, NZ Assn Scientists, 1958; C'wlth Fell'ship, Cornell Univ, 1956-57; Hector Medal, 1972; CBE, 1983; DSc honoris causa, 1983. Memberships: FRSNZ, Pres, 1981-85; Fell, NZ Inst Chem, 1967. Listed in: Who's Who in New Zealand. Hobbies: Keel yacht sailing; Classical music. Address: 22 Dunkerron Avenue, Epsom, Auckland 3, New Zealand.

BOLLIG John, b. 30 Mar 1933, Euskirchen, Germany. Architect; Urban Planner. m. Yolanda, 3 s, 1 d. Education: BArch; BSc; Postgrad Dip, Town and Reg Plng; MA, Environ, Sci and Town Plng; PhD, Environ, Sci and Town Plng. Appointments: Var Govt and Ministerial Advsry Bds and Cttees. Honours: Advd Aust Awd, 1987; Austl Design Awd, 1989; Citizen of the Yr Awd, 1998; OAM, 1999. Memberships: Roy Austl Inst of Archs; Roy Inst Brit Archs; Roy Austl Plng Inst. Hobbies: Jogging; Swimming; Tennis. Address: 8 Cook Street, West Perth, WA 6005 Australia.

BOLOTIN Herbert Howard, b. 11 Jan 1930, NYC, USA. Professor of Nuclear Physics. m. Charlotte Marilyn Pearlman, 11 Feb 1951, 1 s, 1 d. Education: BSc, CCNY, 1950; MSc, 1952, PhD, 1955, IN Univ; DSc, Univ Melbourne, Aust, 1980. Appointments: Physicist, US Naval Radiological Def Lab, 1955-58; Physicist, Brookhaven Natl Lab, 1958-61; Asst Prof, MI State Univ, 1961-62; Physicist, Argonne Natl Lab, 1962-71; Prof, Phys, Univ Melbourne, Vic, Aust, 1971-96; Prof Emer, 1996-. Publications: Over 100 sci publs; Auth, textbook Intermediate Level Electromagnetism; Auth, many lay-oriented sci articles in mags and newspapers. Honours: Rsch Medal, Roy Soc Vic, 1989; Fndn Fell, Roy Soc Vic, 1995. Memberships: Fell, Austl Inst Phys, Chmn, Victorian Bch; Pres, Roy Soc Vic, 1997-. Listed in: American Men and Women of Science; Pictorial Who's Who; Who's Who in Australia; Who's Who in the Commonwealth; Men of Achievement; Who's Who in the World. Address: School of Physics, University of Melbourne, Parkville, Vic 3052, Australia.

BOLZ George Michael, b. 22 Mar 1948, Vienna, Austria. Consulting Electronic Systems Engineer. m. Glenda Jean Johnstone, 30 Aug 1998. Education: BEng, Univ of Melbourne, Aust, 1970; Bachelor of Com, 1977. Appointments: Engr, Dept of Civ Aviation, Melbourne, 1970; Snr Engr, Dept of Transp, Melbourne, 1978; Prin Engr, Civ Aviation Authy, Melbourne, 1987; Snr Systs Engr, Avtel Pty Ltd, Brunei Darussalam, 1989; Snr Cnslt, 1990; Comms Engrng Cnslt, Intl Civ Aviation Org, Pakistan, 1991; Cnslt Engr, Melbourne, 1992; Exec Dir, Mayer Bolz Pty Ltd, Melbourne, 1996-. Honours: Fellshp, French Agcy for Tech Ind and Econ Co-op, Paris, France, 1978. Memberships: Inst of Engrs, Aust; Inst of Elecl and Electrons Engrs; Air Traffic Control Assn; Austl Inst of Mngmnt; Natl Trust of Aust; Natl Gall Soc of Vic. Hobbies: Opera; Ballet; Fine Arts; Heritage. Address: Mayer Bolz Pty Ltd, P O Box 578, Kew, Vic 3101, Australia.

BOMBALL Richard John (Air Vice-Marshal), b. 13 Oct 1937, Aust. Retired Air Force Officer. m. Aileen Clarke, 5 Apr 1958, 2 s, 1 d. Education: Roy Coll of Def Studies. Appointments include: Squadron Ldr, RAAF, 1968; Cmndng Offr, No 3 (Mirage) Squadron, 1973-74, Wing Cmndr, 1973; Dir, Staff, RAAF Staff Coll, 1975-78; Grp Cap, 1978; Dir, Operational Requirements, 1982; Air Commodore, 1984; Offr Cmndng, RAAF, Williamtown, 1984-86; Air Vice-Marshal, 1988, Chf of Air Force Devel, Cmdt, Austl Def Force Acady, 1990-93; Chmn, Newcastle Airport Ltd, 1993-; Chmn, Environmental Trade Dev Zone, ACT, 1997-98. Publications: A Fair Go (jointly), 1994; Trade Development? A Capital Idea!, 1998. Honours: AFC, 1956; AO, 1990. Membership: FAICD, 1993. Listed in: Who's Who in Australia. Hobbies: Golf; Skiing. Address: 11 Parker Street, Curtin, ACT 2605, Australia.

BOMMER William, b. 4 June 1946, Batavia, NY, USA. Professor of Medicine. m. Marla, 26 July 1977, 2 s, 1 d. Education: AB; MD. Appointments: Prof of Med, Univ of CA, Davis, CA; Dir, Non-Invasive Cardiol, Univ of CA, Davis Medl Cntr. Membership: Fell, Amn Coll of Cardiol. Address: School of Medicine, Division of Cardiovascular, 4860 Y Street, Suite 2800, Sacramento, CA 95817, USA.

BOND Alan Maxwell, b. 17 Aug 1946, Cobden, Vic, Aust. Professor of Chemistry. m. 19 Dec 1969, 2 s. Education: BSc, 1966; PhD, 1971; DSc, 1977. Appointments include: Fndn Prof Chem, Div Chem & Physl Scis, Deakin Univ, Aust, 1978-1990; Hartung Lectr, 1981; Snr Rsch Fell, Dept Chem, Univ Southampton, Eng, 1983; Visng Prof, Inorganic Chem Lab, Oxford Univ, Eng, 1988; Lectr, Roy Soc Chem, Aust, 1990; Prof Chem, Sch Chem, La Trobe Univ, Aust, 1990-1995; Prof Chem, Dept Chem, Monash Univ, Aust, 1995-. Publications: Modern Polarographic Methods in Analytical Chemistry, 1980; Critical Survey of Stability Constants and Related Thermodynamic Data of Fluoride Complexes in Aqueous Solution, 1980; Electrochemistry: The Interfacing Science, 1984; 500 Research papers. Creative works include: Patents: The Determination of Electrochemically Active Components in a Process Stream Using Stripping Voltammetry, 1987; Apparatus and Method for Amperometric Detection at the Trace or Subpicomole Level in a Flow-Jet Cell, 1988; Electrochemical Method for Determination of Solid-Phase Components, 1991; Electrochemical Detector for Determination of Solid-Phase Components, 1991. Honours include: Stokes Medal, 1992; Liversidge Awd, 1992; Erskine Fellshp, 1993; Fndn Lectureship Awd, Fedn Asian Chem Socs, 1993; Roy Soc of Chem Awd for Electrochem, 1997 Austl Rsch Cncl Spec Investigator Awd, 1997-99; Hinshelwood Lectureship, Univ of Oxford, 1998-; Christensen Fellshp, St Catherine's Coll, Oxford, 1998; H G Smith Medal, Roy Austl Chem Inst, 1998; Inaugural Gutman Lectr, Roy Austl Chem Inst, Electrochem Div, 1999; Pasminco Lectr, Univ of Tas, 1999. Memberships: Fell, Roy Austl Chem Inst; Amn Chem Soc; USA Electrocheml Soc; Fell, Austl Acad of Sci; Fell, Roy Soc Chem. Hobby: Cricket. Address: Department of Chemistry, Monash University, Clayton, Vic 3168, Australia.

BOND Eric Ernest, b. 9 Feb 1918, Aust. Chemist. m. Patricia Carter, 16 Apr 1952, 2 d. Education: AMTC, Melbourne Tech Coll. Appointments: Cereal Chem, Dept Agric, Vic, 1939; Chf Chem, Brunton & Co, 1940-47; Dir, Bread Rsch Inst Aust, 1947-83; Offr i/c, Cncl Sci and Indl Rsch Org Wheat Rsch Unit, 1957-83; Chmn, Natl Assn Testing Authys, 1979-82; Pres, 1985-92, Hon Gov, Nutr Rsch Fndn, Univ Sydney. Honours: MBE, 1971; Farrer Mem Medal, 1971; F B Guthrie Medal, 1979. Memberships: Fell, Roy Austl Chem Inst, Chmn, Cereal Chem Grp, 1951, 1962; Fell, Austl Inst Food Sci and Technol; Hon Pres, Intl Assn Cereal Chem; Life Mbr, Amn Assn Cereal Chems; Life Mbr, Amn Soc Bakery Engrs. Listed in: International Year Book and Statesmen's Who's Who; Who's Who in Australia. Hobby: Golf. Address: 2 Mycumbene Avenue, East Lindfield, NSW 2070, Australia.

BOND Malcolm James, b. 11 Jan 1959, Clare, Aust. Senior Lecturer in Psychology. m. Carolyn, 30 Apr 1994, 1 s. 1 d. Education: BA Hons; PhD. Appointments: Snr Tutor, 1987-90; Lectr, 1991-97; Snr Lectr, 1998-, Flinders Univ of SA. Publications: Numerous rsch articles in Medl and Psychol jrnls. Memberships: Aust Psychol Soc; Aust Coll of Educ. Hobbies: Gardening; Music; Sports. Address: School of Medicine, Flinders University of South Australia, GPO Box 2100, Adelaide 5001, Australia.

BONYTHON Charles Warren, b. 11 Sept 1916, Adelaide, SA, Aust. Former Chemical Engineer and Company Director. m. Cynthia Eyres Young, 12 Apr 1941, 1 s, 2 d. Education: St Peter's Coll, Adelaide; St Mark's Coll, Univ of Adelaide; BSc, 1938. Appointments: Rsch and Mngmt, ICI Aust Ltd, 1940-66; Dir, Dampier Salt Ltd, 1968-79; Active in heritage and conservation, 1957-; Mbr, SA Mus Bd, 1952-82; Pres, Conservation Cncl of SA, 1971-75; Pres, Natl Trust of SA, 1971-76; Pres, Natl Parks Fndn of SA, 1985-89. Publications: Books: Walking the Flinders Ranges; Conservation in Australia; Walking the Simpson Desert; I'm No Lady: The Reminiscences of Constance Jean, Lady Bonython, OBE, ed; The Great Filling of Lake Eyre in 1974 (co-ed). Honours: AO, 1980; John Lewis Gold Medal for Exploration, Roy Geog Soc of Australasia, SA Br, 1984. Memberships: Fell, Roy Austl Chem Inst; Fell, Roy Geog Soc. Hobbies: Bushwalking in Outback Australia (and other countries); Traversed on foot the Flinders Ranges, 1967-68, the Simpson Desert, 1973, the MacDonnell Ranges, 1976, round Lake Eyre, 1982, Eyre's Horseshoe of Lakes, 1990. Address: Romalo House, 24 Romalo Avenue, Magill, South Australia 5072, Australia.

BONYTHON Hugh Reskymer (Kym), b. 15 Sept 1920, Adelaide, Aust. Art Collector; Radio Broadcaster; Writer; Critic. m. (1) Jean Paine, 23 Dec 1942, 1 s, 1 d, (2) Julianne McClure, 28 Oct 1957, 2 s, 1 d. Education: Queens Coll, Adelaide, 1927-29; St Peters Coll, Adelaide, 1930-38. Appointments: Served RAAF, 1940-45; Farmer, Jersey Cattle Stud Breeder, Mt Pleasant, SA, 1946-55; Art Collector, 1945-; Radio Brdcstr, Austl Brdcstng Commn, 1937-75; Regular Writer, Critic on Jazz and Art im mags and newspprs; Convenor, Australians for Constl Monarchy, 1993. Publications: Modern Australian Painting and Sculpture, 1960; The Australian Painters,

1964-66; 1950-75, Modern Australian Painting; 1960-70, Modern Australian Painting; 1970-75, Modern Australian Painting; 1975-80, Modern Australian Painting; Autobiog: Ladies Legs and Lemonade, 1979. Honours include: Outstndng Contbrn by an Individual, Austl Natl Tourism Awd, 1987; Companion, AC, 1987; Offr, AO, 1981; DFC, 1946; Air Force Cross, 1944; Unit US Presl Citation, 1942. Memberships include: Bd Mbr, Arts Rsch Trng and Support Arts Ltd, 1977-81; Fndn Bd Mbr, Austereo Ltd, 1979-91; Bd and Cncl, Adelaide Intl Film Fest, 1978-79; Cnclr, Adelaide City Cncl, 1978-81; Gov, Adelaide Fest of Arts, 1978-82; Bd, Aust-Japan Fndn, 1981-86; Chmn, SA Jubilee Bd, 1980-87; Mbr, SA Cncl, Aust Bicentennial Authy, 1981-88; Patron, Specific Learning Difficulties Assn, SA, 1979-94; Patron, Muscular Dystrophy Assn, SA, 1987-95; Cncl, Art Gallery of SA Fndn, 1989-90; Am Friends of the Austl Natl Gall Fndn Inc, 1990-; Pres, RAAF Beaufort Sqdns Assn, 1981-; Patron, Classic Motorcycle Owners Assn; Ulysses Motor Cycle Club; Naval, Mil and Air Force Club. Address: 107 Brougham Place, North Adelaide, SA 5006, Australia.

BOOTH Charles David, b. 19 Mar 1959, Paterson, New Jersey, USA. Academic. m. Carol J Petersen, 22 Mar 1989, 1 s. Education: BA, Yale Univ, 1977-81; JD, Harvard Law Sch, 1981-84. Appointments: Assoc, Cleary Gottlieb Steen & Hamilton, 1984-86; Asst Prof, William S Richardson Sch of Law, Univ HI, Manoa, 1986-89; Counsel, Gelber & Gelber, 1987-88; Lectr, Fac of Law, Univ Hong Kong, 1989-97; Assoc Prof, Fac of Law, Univ Hong Kong, 1997-; Assoc Dean, 1996-99, Acting Dean, 1999-, Fac of Law, Univ Hong Kong. Publications: Ed, Hong Kong Commercial Law: Current Issues and Development, 1996; Living in Uncertain Times: The Need to Strengthen Hong Kong Transnational Insolvency Law, 1996. Memberships: NY Bar; Am Bar Assn; NJ Bar; Intl Bar Assn; INSOL; Am Bankruptcy Inst; Inter-Pacific Bar Assn. Hobbies: Tennis; Hiking; Travel. Address: Faculty of Law, University of Hong Kong, Pok Fu Lam Road, Hong Kong.

BOOTH David Ross, b. 19 Mar 1952, Melbourne, Aust. Economist. Education: BEcon, Monash Univ, 1974; MEcon, La Trobe Univ, 1980; Dip Ed, Melbourne Univ, 1983; PhD, Monash (to be completed). Appointments: Tutor, Regl-Urban Econs, Melbourne Univ, 1977-80; Master, Melbourne Grammar Sch, 1981-87; Snr Tutor, Asst Lectr, Temporary Lectr, Econs, Monash Univ, 1988-99. Hobbies: Economics of sport; Sports broadcasting; Australian Rules Football. Address: Bundara, Mornington Road, Flinders, Vic 3929, Australia.

BOOTH Edward Allan, b. 17 Aug 1915, NSW, Aust. Medical Practitioner. m. Diana Florence Kay, 28 Feb 1948, 1 s, 2 d. Education: MB, BS, DDR, FRACR, FRSM, Sydney Univ, 1935-40. Appointments: Med Fac, Sydney Univ, 1935-40; Med Residency, Roy Prince Alfred Hosp, 1940-42; Lt Col, retd, RAAMC, 1942-47; Radiologist, Pvte Prac, 1947-86; Pres, NSW AMA Cncl, 1966-67; Coll of Radiologists, 1964. Publications: Radiology in Obstetrics, 1958; Hiatal Hernia, 1955. Honours: Queens Jubilee Medal; AM, 1979; Gold Medal, Roy Austl Coll of Radiologists, 1979; Fell, Austl Med Assn; VP, NSW Br, AMA, 1980. Memberships: AMA; RACR; RSM. Hobbies: Reading; Music; Gardening; Cricket. Address: 3 Lynwood Avenue, Killara, NSW 2071, Australia.

BOOTH KIRBY Frances Marjorie, b. 13 Nov 1943, Sydney, NSW, Aust. Medical Practitioner; Ophthalmic Surgeon. m. 3 June 1980. Education: MB BS, Univ of Sydney, 1976; Dip in Ophthalmol, London, England, 1971; FRACS, 1977; FRACO, 1991. Appointments: Jnr Res, Sutherland Dist Hosp, 1967; St Bartholomew's Hosp, London, Eng, 1968; SHO, Western Ophthalmic Hosp, 1969; Clin Asst, Western Ophthalmic Hosp, Moorfields Hosp, Sheffield Hosp, 1971-72; Concord Hosp, Sydney, Aust, 1976-77; Roy Prince Alfred Hosp, 1978; Visng Med Offr, Young Hosp, 1981-85, Balmain Hosp, Sydney, 1980-90, Concord Hosp, Sydney, 1980-, Metro Eye Hosp, Ashfield, 1986-94, Hunters Hill Hosp, 1994-; Mbr, Care Aust Eye Team, Bosnia, 1993; Fndng Mbr, Papua New Guinea Eye Care Proj, 1995-. Publications: Contbr of articles in jrnls, seminars and sci meetings. Memberships: Exec Cttee, Med Staff Assn, Concord Hosp, 1988-90, 1998-; Cnclr, NSW Br of Austl Coll of Ophthalmologists, 1995-; Austl Med Assn; Plan Foster Parents; Synod Mbr, Diocese of Sydney, 1981-83; Vice Chmn, Hunters Hill Club (Pres, Tennis Club), 1995-96; Dir, Ophthalmology Concord Hosp, 1998-. Listed in: Worlds Who's Who of Women; Who's Who of Intellectuals; Debretts Handbook of Australia. Hobbies: Reading; Gardening; Travel. Address: 8 Johnson Street, Hunters Hill, Sydney, NSW 2110, Australia.

BORBIDGE Robert Edward (The Hon), b. 12 Aug 1954, Vic, Aust. Member of Legislative Assembly. m. Jennifer Gooding, 5 May 1984, 1 s, 1 d. Appointments: Mbr for Surfers Paradise, Legis Assembly Qld, 1980-; Min Ind, Small Bus, Technol, Comms, 1987-Jan 1989; Min Ind, Small Bus, Technol, Tourism, 1989; Min Police, Emergency Servs, Tourism, 1989; Dpty Ldr Opposition, 1989-91; Shadow Min Ind, Small Bus, 1989-; Ldr Opposition, 1991-96, 1998-; Premier, 1996-98; Ldr, Qld Nat Party-Lib Party Coalition, 1992-. Membership: Surfers Paradise Rotary Club. Hobbies: Reading; Travel; Swimming. Address: Parliament House, Brisbane, Australia.

BORG Sonia, b. 20 Feb 1931, Vienna, Austria. Scriptwriter. Appointments: Actor, Scriptwriter, Ed, Assoc Prodr, Austl TV Drama. Publications: Num. Honours: AWGIE, Best Screenplay, 1977, 1983; AO, 1985. Hobbies: Aboriginal culture and history; Animal welfare; Protection of the Environment. Address: 10 Mt McKenzie Track, Wyelangta 3238, Victoria, Australia.

BORGO BUSTAMENTE Enrique, b. 22 Aug 1928. Government Official. m. 4 children. Education: Grad, Natl Univ of El Salvador, 1952; Postgrad, Univ Rome, 1955-57, Univ El Salvador, 1967. Appointments: Judge, Penal of San Vicente, 1955; Lawyer, Salvadoran Socl Ins Inst, 1957-60; Lawyer, Advsr, Cntrl Bank, 1961-70; Pvte Prac, 1970-; Prof, Univ of El Salvador, 1957-82; VP, Govt of El Salvador. Address: Office of the President, Avenida Cuba Calle Dario Gonzalez 806, Barrio San Jacinto, San Salvador, El Salvador.

BORN Peter, b. 27 July 1959, Cologne, Germany. Banker. m. Erika Born, 1986, 1 d. Education: MBA, Univ of Passau, Germany, 1980-86. Appointments: Regl Dir, Indo-German Chamber of Com, New Delhi, 1987-92; Asst VP, Commerzbank HQ Frankfurt Intl Banking Dept, 1998-; Chf Rep, Commerzbank AG Soul Rep Off. Honours: Paul Harris Rotary Fndn, 1990. Memberships: Roary Club; Bilateral Cmmn for the Promotion of German Investment in India. Hobby: Travel. Address: Commerzbank AG Seoul Representative Office, 8th Floor, Hanway Building, 70 Da-dong, Chung-ku, Seoul, Korea.

BORRELL Jerry, b. 23 May 1952, Texas, USA. Journalist. 2 s. Education: MSc. Appointments: Rschr, Lib of Congress, 1979-81; Snr Ed, Computer Graphics World, 1980-81; Ed in Chf, Digital Des, 1982-1983; Snr Ed, Mini Microsystems, 1983-85; Ed iin Chief, Macworld, 1985-92; Pres and Fndr, Sumeria Inc; Auth and Ed of 25 CD Roms. Publications: Over 300 Articles, Interviews, Columns; Var Acad, Trade, Consumer Press. Honours: Best Columnist, 1990; Best Magazine, 1992. Address: 100 Eucalyptus Drive, San Francisco, CA 94132, USA.

BORSARU Mihai, b. 19 Mar 1941. Scientist. m. Ruxandra, 3 Aug 1968, 2 s. Education: MSc; Dip in Educ; PhD. Appointments: Rsch Physicist, Inst Atomic Phys, Bucharest, Romania, 1963-69; Rsch Physicist, Niels Bohr Inst, Univ Copenhagen, Denmark, 1969-70; PhD stud, Austl Natl Univ, Austl, 1970-74; Snr Prin Rsch Scientist, C'wlth Sci & Indl Rsch Org, Austl, 1975-. Creative work: Contbr to book, Nuclear Geophysics in Modern Society, in progress. Honour: Excellence in Coal Rsch, Austl Coal Assn, 1995. Hobbies: Tennis; Walking; Classical Music; Gardening. Address: 59 Moordale St, Chapel Hill, Brisbane, Qld 4069, Australia

BOSE Anand Bose, b. 14 Mar 1970, Madras, India. Educationist. m. Susan, 4 May 1995, 1 d. Education: MEcon; MEd; MEngl. Publication: Requiem for a Squirrel, 1998. Honour: Hon Mbrship, Paradoxicist Lit Movement for Contbns, Arizona, USA, 1998. Membership: Anthroposophical Soc Switzerland, 1998. Hobbies: Poetry; Aesthetics; Fiction; Parapsychology. Address: Vadaketh Kurianoor, Kerala, 689550, India.

BOSE Haradhan, b. 26 Aug 1926, Chapra, India. Information Scientist. m. Amita Bose, 6 Feb 1954, 1 s. Education: BSc, Calcutta Univ; Postgrad Dip, Lib Sci, BHU; MLISc, Delhi Univ. Appointments: Libn, Bihar Inst of Technol, Sindri, 1958-62; Snr Libn, Ctrl Mining Rsch Inst, Dhanbad, 1962-64; Snr Documentation Asst, INSDOC, Delhi, 1964-68; Sci B, 1968-74, Sci C, 1974-82, Lib Offr E1, 1982-86, Publications and Info Directorate, CSIR, Delhi. Publications: Information Science: Principles and Practice; Universal Decimal Classification: Theory and Practice. Membership: Indian Assn of Specl Libs and Info Cntrs, Calcutta. Hobby: Photography. Address: Flat No A16, Cluster No 13, Purbachal Housing Estate, Salt Lake City, Calcutta 700 097, India.

BOSE Isimeli, b. 11 Mar 1945. Government Minister Education: Prelim Engrng Stdy, Canterbury Univ; BA, Engl, Admin, Univ of S Pacific; Dip, Prof, Shipping, Norwegian Shipping Acady. Appointments: Asst Field Offr, Asst Chemist, Pacific Sugar Mills, 1965-66; Tchr, DAV HS, Ba, 1968-71; Stud, Lectr, Univ of S Pacific, 1972-74; Asst Sec, Marine and PAF, Ministry of Tourism, Transp and Civil Aviation, 1975-77; Ports Authy of Fiji, Asst Wharf Mngr, Spec Projs Offr, Offr i/c Transp and Equipment, Mngr, Labour Sec and Internal Audit, 1977-79, Mngr, Ops, 1982; Dir Ops, PAF, 1983, Dpty Dir-Gen, 1984, Dir-Gen and Chf Exec, 1984; Min for Com, Ind, Trade and Pub Enterprises, 1996-. Address: PO Box 2118, Government Buildings, Suva, Fiji.

BOSE Suprabhat Kumar, b. 22 Dec 1948. Librarian. m. 27 Apr 1980, 2 s. Education: BSc; BLibSc; MLIS; DFL, Russian. Appointments: Libn in Cntrl Rsch Inst for Jute and Allied Fibres, Barrackpore, ICAR, 1971-. Memberships: Life Mbr, Indian Assn of Spec Libs Info Cntrs, Calcutta; Life Mbr, Assn of Agric Libn & Documentalists of India, UAS Dharwad. Hobbies: Reading Sacred books; Social work. Address: Vill Ilsoba, PO Ilsoba Mondlai, Hooghly, WB 712 146, India.

BOSLER Nancy Deloi, b. 24 Jan 1935, Strathfield, NSW, Aust. Writer; Historian. m. Wilfred (Bill) Bosler, 1 s, 2 d. Education: BEd, Fac Adult Educ, Univ of Technol, Sydney, 1992; Master, Local Govt Mngmt, Fac of Engrng, Univ of Technol, Sydney, 1996. Appointments: Commonwealth Bank, 1950-57; Creative Leisure Movement, 1971-96; Freelance Jrnlst/Writer, 1973-; Dept of Educ, 1979-84; Histn, 1983-; Warringah Shire Cncl, 1984-92; Pittwater Cncl, 1992-96. Publications include: Australian Macramé Animals and Flowers, 1983; Christmas Decorations in Australia, 1983; Australian Patchwork and Appliqué, 1984; Anzac, Something to be Proud Of, 1986; Narrabeen, 1989; Manly Warringah: People, Places & Pastimes; Contbng auth, Warringah History, Textile Crafts for Beginners; Ed, What Does Peace Mean to me?; The World in the Year 2000; Articles in newspapers, mag jrnls, conf pprs. Honours: Relig Press Awd, 1975; Outstdng Citizen Awd, Warringah Shire Cncl, 1975; Frank McAskill Trophy, 1983; Anzac of the Yr, 1984; Philip Geeves Mem Hist Awd, 1986; Adv Aust Awd, 1987; Fellshp, Fellshp of Austl Writers, 1989; NSW Govt Community Serv Awd, 1990; Medal, Order of Aust, 1992; Children's Week Awd, 1992. Memberships include: JP; Soc of Austl Genealogists; Austl Soc of Auths; Fellshp Austl Auths; Dir, Local Hist Resource Unit; Cttee on Ageing. Address: 107 Claudare Street, Collaroy Plateau, NSW 2097, Australia.

BOSTOCK Thomas Edward, b. 3 May 1939, Melbourne, Aust. Solicitor. m. Jennifer, 16 Jan 1965, 3 s (1 decd), 1 d. Education: LLB (hons), Univ of Melbourne. Appointments: Solicitor, Ashurst Morris Crisp (London), 1963-64; Solicitor, Mallesons, 1964-70; Ptnr, Mallesons, 1970-86, Ptnr, Mallesons Stephen Jacques, 1987-. Publications; Num articles on corp, banking and taxation law. Honours: Cavagliere Ufficiale (Italy), 1982.

Memberships: Banking Law Assn, Pres, 1986-88. Hobbies: Literature; Music; Gardening; Golf. Address: 19 Robinson Road, Hawthorn, Victoria 3122, Australia.

BOSTOK Janice Mae, b. 9 Apr 1942. Editor. m. Silvester Bostok, 6 Sep 1964, 2 s, 1 d. Education: BA w double maj in Engl Lit & some Women's Studies, Univ of Qld, 1986. Appointments: Fmr Ed and Publr, Tweed, Haiku mag, 1972-79; Ed, Paper Wasp Haiku Jrnl, 1994-; Haiku Ed, Hobo Mag, 1995-; Judge, Scope Haiku Contest, 1995; Read Warana's Writer's Week, 1995; Asia-Pacific Ed, Red Moon Anthology. Publications: Banana Leaves, 1972; Walking into the Sun, 1974; Hearing the Wind, 1976; On Sparse Brush, 1978; Silver Path of Moon, 1996; Still Waters, 1997; The Farmer Tends His Land, 1997; Shadow-Patches, 1998; Poetry published in var anthologies inclng: International Haiku Festival Anthology, Romania, 1992; HSA Member's Anthology, 1995; Sumi-E Artwrk published privately & in Tweed, Paper Wasp & Social Alternatives. Honours: Book Awd for, Walking into the Sun, Haiku Soc of Am, 1974; Var monthly & qtly mag awds for Best of Issue. Memberships: Haiku Soc of Am; Paper Wasp Haiku Grp, Brisbane; Haiku Soc of Brit; Fellshp of Austl Writers Qld; Poetry Soc of NZ. Listed in: Who's Who in the World; Who's Who of Women; Dictionary of International Biography; Who's Who of Australian Writers. Hobby: Sumi-E Painting. Address: Campbell's Road, Dungay, NSW 2484, Australia.

BOSWELL David Ross, b. 22 June 1950, Hamilton, NZ. Medical Practitioner. m. Rosheen, 17 July 1974, 3 s, 1 d. Education: BS, 1971, MBChB, 1974, Auckland; PhD, Otago, 1982; FRACP, 983; FRCPA, 1985. Appointments: Chem Pathologist, Clinl Dir, Middlemore Hosp, 1997. Publications: Num sci and medl pprs and articles. Memberships: Roy Coll of Pathologists of Australasia, Chf Examiner, 1994-; Roy Australasian Coll of Physns. Hobbies: Reading; Walking; Skiing. Address: 42 St Andrews Road, Epsom, Auckland, New Zealand.

BOSWORTH Michal Gwyn, b. 5 Feb 1944, Auckland, NZ. Writer; Researcher. m. Richard, 23 Sept 1965, 1 s, 1 d. Education: BA; DipEd. Appointments: Rschr, Austl Dictionary of Biog, 1971-87; Self-employed w var employers, 1971-97. Publications: (w Emma Ciccotosto) Emma: A Recipe For Life, 1995; Emma: A Translated Life, 1990; (w R Bosworth) Fremantles' Italy, 1990; Australian Lives, 1987; Environment Australia, 1981. Honour: Premier's Prize for Non-Fiction, West Aust, 1991. Memberships: Heritage Cncl West Aust, 1996-97; Profl Histns and Rschrs Assoc, WA Inc, 1989-. Hobbies: Tennis; Theatre; Opera. Address: PO Box 320, South Fremantle, Western Australia 6162, Australia.

BOUBLIK Jaroslav Haman, b. 1 May 1959. Scientific Director. m. Sharyn Reidy, 11 Dec 1992. Education: BSc Hons, PhD, Monash Univ; MRACI, CChem. Appointments: Fulbright Fell, 1985; Neil Hamilton Fairley Fell, 1986; Visng Rsch Fell, Salk Inst, 1988; Head, Peptide Chem Lab, Baker Inst, 1989; Hon Lectr, Dept Chem, Monash Univ, 1991; Sci Dir, Aquaconnexions Pty Ltd, 1993-. Publications: PhD Thesis, 1984; Over 30 publns in sci lit, 1981-. Honours: Fulbright Fellshp, 1985; Austl Acady Sci, Academia Sinica Exch Fell, 1984. Memberships: Roy Austl Chem Inst, 1990; Charter mbr, Amn Peptide Soc, 1990. Listed in: Who's Who in the World. Hobbies: Sailboarding; Cycling. Address: Unit 2, 33 Scott Street, Elwood, Vic 3184, Australia.

BOUEZ Faris, b. 15 jan 1955, Beirut, Lebanon. Minister of Foreign Affairs. m. Zalfa Hraoui, 1985, 3 children. Education: Mission Laique Française; Antoura Coll; John Moulin Univ, France. Appointments: Lawyer, pvte prav, 1978-; Pol Advsr to Pres, 1989-90; Envoy of Pres, France, Holy See, Syria, 1990; Min of For Affairs. Address: Ministry of Foreign Affairs, sur Sursock, Achrafiyé, Beirut, Lebanon.

BOUMELHA Penelope Ann, b. 10 May 1950, London, Eng. University Professor. 1 d. Education: BA, 1972; MA, 1981, DPhil, 1981, Univ of Oxford. Appointments: Rschr/Compiler, Mansell Publng, 1981-84; Lectr, Univ of West Aust, 1985-90; Jury Prof, Univ of Adelaide, 1990; Hd, Div of Hums and Socl Scis, Univ of Adelaide, 1996; Dpty Vice Chan, Educ, Univ of Adelaide, 1999. Honour: Fell, Acady of Hums of Aust, 1997. Address: University of Adelaide, Adelaide, South Australia 5005, Australia.

BOURAS Gillian, b. 18 Aug 1945, Melbourne, Australia. Writer; Teacher. m. George Bouras, 4 Jan 1969, 3 s. Education: BA, MEd, Univ Melbourne. Publications: A Foreign Wife, 1986; A Fair Exchange, 1991; Aphrodite and the Others, 1994; A Stranger Here, 1996. Honours: Felix Meyer Schlsp, Univ Melbourne, 1988; Hawthornden Fellshp, Scotland, 1992; NSW State Lit Awd, 1994; Category A Fellshp, Aust Cncl, 1996. Hobbies: Reading; Travel; Walking; Modern Greek. Address: c/o Curtis Brown, PO Box 19, Paddington, NSW 2021, Australia.

BOURKE Colin John, b. 15 Sept 1936, Sunshine, Australia. Professor. m. Eleanor, 8 Nov 1980, 3 s, 1 d, 1 step-d. Education: BCom; BEd; LLB; MEd; TPTC. Appointments: Gen Mngr, Aboriginal Dev Cmmn, 1981-82; Asst Dec, Dept of Aboriginal Affairs, 1983-84, Austl Inst of Aboriginal Studies, 1984-87; Hd, Sch of Aboriginal and Islander Stdies, Univ SA, 1987-91. Publications: Before the Invasion, 1980; Aboriginal Australia. Honour: MBE, 1978; Memberships: Austl Press Cncl, 1981-91; Austl Coll of Educ. Hobbies: Gardening; Walking. Address: 128 Reio Avenue, McGill, SA 5072, Australia.

BOWEN Lionel Frost, b. 28 Dec 1922, Sydney, NSW, Aust. Politician. m. Claire Bowen, 1953, 5 s, 3 d. Education: Univ Sydney. Appointments: Fmrly practised as Solicitor; Mbr, NSW Parl, 1962-69; Mbr, House Reps, 1969-90; Postmaster-Gen, Spec Min State, Min Mfng Ind, 1972-75; Dpty Ldr Opposition, 1977-83; Dpty PM, Min Trade, Min assisting PM in C'wlth-State Affairs, 1983-84; Dpty PM, Atty-Gen, 1984-90; Min assisting PM, 1984-88; VP, Exec Cncl, 1984-87; Dpty Chmn, Advtng Standards Cttee, 1990; Chmn, Natl Gall, Canberra, ACT, 1991-94; Austl Labor Party. Honour: AC. Listed in: International Who's Who. Address: 24 Mooramie Avenue, Kensington, NSW 2033, Australia.

BOWRING Aubrey Charles, b. 10 Jan 1924, Sydney, Aust. Paediatric Surgeon. m. Patricia Elizabeth Stoney, 6 Sept 1950, 3 s, 3 d. Education: Univ of Sydney, 1942-48; Roy Coll of Surgns, 1954; MBBS, FRCS, FRCS (Edinburgh), 1956; FRACS, 1968. Appointments: Cnslt Practice in Paediat Surg, Macquarie, Sydney, Hon Surgn, Roy Alexandra Hosp for Children, 1956-64; Hd, Dept of Surg, 1964-89, Cnslt Paediat Surgn, 1989-, Prince of Wales Childrens Hosp; Assoc Prof, Paediat Surg, Univ of NSW, 1964-89. Publications: Auth of sev articles in Med and Surg Jrnls and sev pprs presented at meetings of Med and Surg Socs. Honours: Blue for Boxing, Univ of Sydney, 1944; Visng Lectr, Univ Cty of Nagoya, 1980; AM, 1984; Swift Mem Lectr, Adelaide Childrens Hosp, 1986; Visng Lectr, Univ of Papua New Guinea, 1988. Memberships: Austl Assn of Paediat Surgns; Austl Coll of Paediats; Brit Assn of Paediat Surgns; Pacific Assn of Paediat Surgns. Hobbies: Clay Target Shooting; Surf Fishing. Address: 39 Kendall Road, Castlecove 2069, Australia.

BOX Mervyn Steve, b. 29 Nov 1929, Aust. RAAF Chaplain. m. Gwenda Eastman, 12 Mar 1955, 2 s, 3 d. Education: BA, Univ of Melbourne; BD, Melbourne Coll of Divinity; Grad Dip, Relig Educn; Ordained Min, Meth Ch, 1957. Appointments: Home Missions Trng Coll, 1950; Prahran Meth Mission, 1951, Meth Parishes, 1955-67; Chaplain, Geelong Trng Prison, 1960-64; Commnd Offr, RAAF, 1963; Laverton, 1963-67; Chaplain, RAAF Uniting Ch, 1967-87; PFA, var postings, 1967-80, Support Cmnd Unit, Melbourne, 1980-83, Vic Barracks, E Sale, 1984-85, Cmnd Chaplain, Support Cmnd, Melbourne, Prin Air Chaplain, 1985-87, Uniting Ch, Ballarat, S Parish, 1989-94; Dir, Western Community Savings Credit Union, 1978-80; Min, Karingal Uniting Ch, Frankston, 1996-. Honour: AM, 1981. Membership: Hon Chaplain, RAAF Assn, Vic Br. Hobbies: Football; Tennis; Cricket. Address: 15 McRae Street, Seaford, Vic 3198, Australia.

BOYAPATI Manoranjan Choudary, b. 10 Aug 1946, Mustabad, Gannavaram, Krishna, AP, India. Scientist. m. Dhanalakshmi, 1973, 1 s, 1 d. Education: PhD. Appointments include: Sci B, RRL, Hyderabad, 1981-86; Sci C, 1986-90, Sci E1, 1990-95, Sci EII, 1995-98, Sci F, 1998-, IICT, Hyderabad. Publications include: An Economical Industrial Method for the Manufacture of Colloidal Sulphur Chemistry and Industry, 1986; Synthesis of New Aryl Naphthoquinones by Using Palladium Acetate in Acetic Acid, 1986; A New Alkyl Peroxovandium Catalyst for Selective Oxidation of Benzyl Cyanides, 1996; Acylation of Aromatic Ethers with Acid Anhydrides in the Presence of Cation-Exchanged Clays, 1998. Honours include: Shanti Swarup Bhatnagar Awd, 1990. Address: Indian Institute of Chemical Technology, Tarnaka Uppal Road, Hyderabad 500 007, Andhra Pradesh, India.

BOYCE Peter John, b. 20 Feb 1935, Aust. University Vice-Chancellor; Political Scientist. m. Lorinne Peet, 3 Jan 1962, 1 s, 2 d. Education: MA, Univ WA; PhD, Duke Univ, USA. Appointments: Rsch Fell, then Fell, Dept Intl Rels, Austl Natl Univ, 1964-66; Nuffield Fell, St Antony's Coll, Oxford, Eng, 1966-67; Snr Lectr, then Rdr, Pol Sc, Tas Univ, 1967-75; Prof, Hd, Dept Govt, Queensland Univ, 1976-79; Prof, Pols, Univ WA, 1980-84; Mbr, Consultative Cttee Rels w Japan, 1981-83; Mbr, Hum Rights Commn, 1981-85; Vice-Chan, Murdoch Univ, WA, 1985-96; Visng Prof, Univ Tas, Hobart, 1996-; Visng Rsch Fell, Merton Coll, Oxford, Eng, Hilary Term 1996; Fowler Hamilton Fell, Christchurch Coll, Oxford, Hilary Term, 1997. Publications: Malaysia and Singapore in International Diplomacy, 1968; Foreign Affairs for New States, 1977. Honour: AO, 1995. Listed in: Who's Who; Who's Who in Australia. Address: Department of Political Science, University of Tasmania, Box 252 C, Hobart, Tas 7001, Australia.

BOYD Brian David, b. 30 July 1952, Belfast, Northern Ireland. University Teacher. m. (1) Janet Bower Eden, 1974, div 1980, (2) Bronwen Mary Nicholson, 1983, 3 stepd. Education: BA, 1972, MA w Hons, 1974, Univ of Canterbury, Christchurch, NZ; PhD, Univ of Toronto, Can, 1979; Postdoct Fell, Univ of Auckland, 1979. Appointments: Lectr, 1980, Snr Lectr, 1985, Assoc Prof, 1992-, Prof, 1998-, Univ of Auckland, NZ; Editl Bd, Nabokov Studies; Visng Prof, Univ of Nice-Sophia Antipolis, 1994-95. Publications: Nabokov's Ada: The Place of Consciousness, 1985; Vladimir Nabokov: The Russian Years, 1990; Vladimir Nabokov: The American Years, 1991; Ed, Nabokov: Novels and Memoirs 1941-1951, 1996; Ed, Nabokov's Novels, 1955-1962, 1996; Ed, Nabokov: Novels 1969-1974, 1996; The Presents of the Past: Literature in English Before 1900, 1998; Nabokov's Pale Fire: The Magic of Artistic Discovery; Co-Ed, Nabokov's Butterflies, 1999. Honour: James Cook Fell, Roy Soc of NZ, 1997-99. Listed in: International Authors and Writers Who's Who; Who's Who in the World; People of Today; Contemporary Authors; Dictionary of International Biography. Address: Department of English, University of Auckland, Private Bag 92019, Auckland, New Zealand.

BOYLE Gregory John, b. 20 Feb 1950, Melbourne, Australia. Professor of Psychology. m. 7 Mar 1970, 2 s, 2 d. Education: BSc, hons; Dip.Ed; MEd; PhD, Melbourne; MA; PhD, DE, USA. Appointments: Maths and Sci Tchr, Stated Educn Dept, Vic, 1974-75; Lectr, Psychol, Inst Cath Educn, 1976-85; Lectr, Educl Psychol, Univ Melbourne, 1985-89; Snr Lectr, Psychol, Univ Qld, 1990-92; Assoc Prof, 1993-95, Prof, 1995-, Bond Univ. Publications include: Schizotypal Personality Traits: Entension of Previous Psychometric Investigations, 1997; Personality and Employee Selection: Credibility Regained, 1997; Six Month Prevalence of Phobic Symptoms in Iceland: An Epidemiological Postal Survey, 1998; Static Five-Factor Models of Personality: A Reply to Engvik, 1998; Affective and Evaluative Descriptors in the McGill Pain Questionnaire: Category Variations and Intensity Invariance, 1998. Membership: Austl Psychol Soc. Hobbies: Music; Motorbike Riding; International Travel. Address: Dept of Psychology, Bond University, Qld 4229, Australia.

BRABHAM John Arthur (Jack) (Sir), b. 2 Apr 1926. Racing Driver. Education: Hurstville and Kogarah Tech. Career: World Champion Racing Driver, 1959, 1960, 1966; Ferodo World Trophy for Motor Sport, 1966; Won Austl Grand Prix 3 times; Constructors Champion of the World, 1966, 1967. Publications: When The Flag Drops (jointly) 1971. Honours: Kt, 1979; OBE. Memberships: RAC(Lon); BRDC(Lon); ARDC(Aust). Hobbies: Flying; Water skiing; Scuba diving. Address: 5 Ruxley Lane, Ewell, Surrey KT19 0JB, England.

BRADFORD Max R, b. 1942. Government Minister. m. Rosemary, 2 step-children. Appointments: Chf Exec, NZ Bankers Assn; Dir, Advocacy, NZ Employers Fedn; Econ and Fin Cnslt; NZ Treasury; IMF, Wash DC, USA; Elected to Parl, Tarawera, 1990; Min of Labour, Energy, Immigration and Bus Dev, 1996; Chair, Parly Fin and Expenditure and Labour Select Cttee; Chf Exec, Natl Party; Min for Enterprise and Com, Min for Tertiary Educ, Min of Def. Address: 13 Amohia Street, PO Box 2481, Rotorua 3201, New Zealand.

BRADLEY Donald Edward, b. 26 Sept 1943, Santa Rosa, CA, USA. Law. m. 2 s, 1 d. Education: AB, Dartmouth Coll; JD, Hastings Coll of Law, Univ of California; LLM (Tax), New York Univ Sch of Law. Appointments: Mbr, Wilson Sonsini Goodrich & Rosati, 1984-; Ptnr, Pillsbury Madison Sutro, 1978-84. Memberships: Chmn, CEO, Attys Ins Mutual Risk Retention Grp Inc. Address: Wilson Sonsini Goodrich & Rosati, 650 Page Mill Road, Palo Alto, California, USA.

BRADLEY John, b. 9 July 1933, Bangor, Wales. Sandoz Professor of Clinical Immunology. m. Brenda Mary Whitehouse, 27 Apr 1961, 2 s, 1 dec, 2 d. Education: BS, MB ChB, 1957, MD, 1967, Fac of Med, Birmingham Univ, Eng; FRCP Ed, 1973; FRCP, 1975; FRACP, 1977; FRCPA, 1977. Appointments: Hlth Scis Cntr, Univ TX, Dallas, TX, USA, 1967-68; Lectr, Dept of Med, 1969-71; Snr Lectr and Cnslt Physn, 1971-73; Dir, Immun Dept, Univ Liverpool, Eng, 1973-75; Sandoz Prof of Clin Immun, Flinders Univ of S Aust; Prof and Hd, Dept of Immunology, Allergy and Arthritis, Flinders Univ and Medl Cntr. Publications: Clinical Immunology, 1997; Cntbr of articles in scientific and medl jrnls. Honours: Hon Prof in Immunology, Shanghai, 1991-; Hon Prof and Advsry, Min of Hlth, Vietnam; US Pub Hlth Fellshp, 1967, 1968; Wellcome Travelling Fellshp, 1971. Memberships: Austl Soc of Immun; Brit Soc of Immunology; Fell, Mbr of Cncl, Australasian Coll of Tropical Med, 1997-. Listed in: Who's Who in Australia; Who's Who in the World; Who's Who in Science and Engineering; Men of Achievement; Australian Directory of Academics; 5000 Personalities of the World. Hobbies: Music; Walking. Address: Department of Immunology Allergy and Arthritis, Flinders Medical Centre and University, Bedford Park, Adelaide, SA 5042, Australia.

BRADLEY Paul William, b. 26 Jan 1961, Walnut Creek, CA, USA. Logistics Compnay General Manager. Education: BA Polit Sci (cum laude), 1980-83; Parly Govt prog, Cath Univ of Am, 1984; Master, Intl Mngmt, Amn Grad Sch of Mngmt (Thunderbird), 1986-87; Asian Securities Prog, Asian Inst of Mngmt Wharton Sch, 1996. Appointments: Congl Asst to Sen Paul Laxalt, US Sen, 1981; Spec Asst to Geoff Lawler, MP, Brit House of Commons, 1984; Mngr, Amn Pres Cos, 1987-90; District Mngr, N Y K Line, 1991-92; Regl Mngr, Asia Mktng, NYK Line, 1992-95; Gen Mngr, ASEAN Reg, BDP Asia-Pacific (Singapore), Singapore, 1995-. Honours: Presdtl Gold Cert of Appreciation, Pres Ronald Reagan, 1980; Mbr, Presdtl Inaugural Cttee, 1980, 1989; Chmn, Coll Repubns of NV, 1982; Outstndng Young Man of Am, 1985. Memberships: Mbr, Amn Assn of Polit Cnslts, 1992-84; Amn Chmbr of Com, Hong Kong, Exec Cttee, Hong Kong Liner Shipping Assn, 1992-95; Alumni Educ Cnslr, Amn Grad Sch of Intl Mngmt, 1992-. Address: BDP, Asia-Pacific (Singapore), Block 511, Kampong, Bahru Road, #02-03, Keppel Districpark, Singapore 099447 (65), 370-4200.

BRADSHAW John Lockyer, b. 23 Feb 1940. Experimental Neuropsychologist. m. Judith Anne Taylor, 10 Sept 1966, 1 d. Education: MA (Oxon); PhD (Sheffield); DSc (Monash). Appointments: Systs Analyst, Imperial Chem Inds, 1962-64; Lectr in Psychol, Univ of Otago, 1967-68; Lectr to Prof, Personal Chair, Monash Univ, Aust, 1968-99. Publications: Human Cerebral Asymmetry, 1983; Hemispheric Specialization and Psychological Function, 1989; The Evolution of Lateral Asymmetries, 1993; Clinical Neuropsychology, Behavioral and Brain Sciences, 1995; Human Evolution: A Neuropsychological Perspective, 1997. Memberships: Fell, Brit Psychol Soc; Fell, Acady of Socl Scis in Aust. Listed in: Who's Who in Australia. Hobbies: Photography; Languages; Archaeology; Travel. Address: Neuropsychology Research Unit, Monash University, Clayton, Vic 3168, Australia.

BRADSTOCK E Margaret, b. 18 May 1942, Melbourne, Australia. Senior Lecturer. 3 s, 2 d. Education: BA, hons; Dip.Ed; MA, hons; PhD. Appointments: Grad Asst, Maths, HS; Grad Asst, Engl, HS; Tutor, Engl, Macquarie; Tutor, Engl, Lectr, Engl, Snr Lectr, Univ NSW. Publications include: Rattling the Orthodoxies: A Life of Ada Cambridge; Small Rebellions; Beyond Blood; Words From the Same Heart; Edge City on Two Different Plans. Honours: Henry Lawson Awd for Verse, 1984; Runner-up, Premiers Poetry Awd, Qld, 1994; 1st, NSW Writers Cntr Gleebooks, 1997. Memberships: NSW Writers Assn; Poets Union; Round Table. Hobbies: Writing; Swimming; Drinking Champagne. Address: c/o School of English, University of New South Wales, Sydney 2052, Australia.

BRADY Ross Thomas, b. 20 July 1943, Adelaide, South Australia. Senior Lecturer. m. Pompa, 5 Jan 1973, 1 s, 2 d. Education: BSc, 1st class hons and Univ Medal, Univ of Sydney, 1966; MA, 1st class hons, Univ of New England, 1967; PhD, Univ of St Andrews, 1971. Appointments: Lectr, Maths, Univ WA, 1971; Lectr, Philos, 1972-76, Snr Lectr, 1977-, LaTrobe Univ. Publications: 34 acad pprs in profl jrnls; Co-Auth, Relevant Logics and Their Rivals. Honours: LaTrobe Ctrl Starter Grant, 1993; ARC Large Grant, 1998-99. Memberships: Austl Assn of Logic, Pres, 1998-; Austl Assn for Philos, Treas, 1989-97, Asst Treas, 1998-. Hobby: Walking. Address: c/o School of Philosophy, LaTrobe University, Bundoora, Victoria 3083, Australia.

BRAENDLER Michael Paul, b. 2 Apr 1962, Australia. Music Teacher; Musician. m. Lynne, 14 July 1990. Education: Bach of Educ, Sec Music Tchng; AMusA, Piano (Assoc Dip in Pianoforte). Appointments: Kimba Area Sch; Portland Tech Sch; Portland Sec Coll; Wangaratta Tafe; Goulburn Ovens Tafe. Membership: ISME, 1988-. Hobbies: Music Programming; Travel; Dining; Entertaining Friends. Address: PO Box 955, Wangaratta, Vic 3676, Australia.

BRAILLARD Frank, b. 28 Aug 1970, Versailles, France. Marketing Manager. Education: Grad, The Ecole Superieure de Commerce de Reims, France; MBA, Grad, GA Coll and State Univ. Appointments: Salesman, Evian Mineral Waters, France, 1991-; Product Mngr, L'Oreal Cosmetics, Germany, 1992; Prodn, Finl Controller, Seita Philippines, 1994; Mktng Mngr, Louis Vuitton Moet Hennessy, Philippines, 1998; Mktng Mngr, Hong Kong, 1998. Honours: Hon for Acad Ex, GA Coll, State Univ, GA, USA. Hobbies: Violin; Soccer; Tennis; Skiing. Address: Riche Monde Ltd, 15/F Dorset House, Taikoo Place, 979 King's Road, Quarry Bay, Hong Kong.

BRALL H B, b. 12 Jan 1942, Pakistan. Musician. m. Prabha, 7 May 1971, 1 s, 2 d. Education: BA, LTCL; LMME, India. Appointments: Music Instr, AEC, Pachmarhi, 1972-79; Music Instr, Afghanistan, 1979-81; Music Instr, AEC, 1981-85; IOAB, 1985-94; Dir of Music, 1994-97; AEC, Pachmarhi, India. Creative Works: Vijay Ghosh, 1984; Abhinandan, 1986; Shubh Prabhat, 1988; Ekta, 1992; Sorathi, 1993; Dare Devils, 1994; Godhuli, 1995; Arranged Many Indian Mil Music. Honours: COAS, Commendation Card, Jan 1998. Memberships: Rajendra Sinhji Inst. Hobbies: Reading Books; Listening, Composing Music. Address: A-10 Ganga Terrace, Mundhwa Road, Pune 411036, India.

BRANCHFLOWER Marion Rita, b. 20 Dec 1956, Melbourne, Aust. Music Teacher. m. Wesley Charles Branchflower, 9 Dec 1983, 3 s, 2 d. Education: BMusEd, Melbourne Univ, 1977; Inst of Early Childhood Devel, Suzuki Tchrs Ctf, 1979; Suzuki Talent Educn Assn Tchrs Ctf, 1980; Master of Educl Studies, Monash Univ, 1984. Appointments: Tchr of Violin, Lauriston Girls Sch, 1976-85, Tutor, Conductor, Malvern Youth Orch, 1976-85, Tutor, Margaret Sutherland Strings, 1976-78, Taught two retarded children violin, 1981-82; Taught blind piano students, 1983-87; Music Co-ord, St Clares, Box Hill, conducting two childrens orchs, 1985-94, St Patricks, Murrumbeena, 1994-96, Lauriston, 1995-. Publications: The Application of the Suzuki Method in the Teaching of Music to Blind and Handicapped Children, 1983 (published under maiden name Plumstead for Masters Thesis); Poem published in Mattoid, 1977; Other poems published in assorted mags. Memberships: Austl String Tchrs Assn; Suzuki Talent Educn Assn of Aust; Monash Univ Grad Assn; Melbourne Univ Grad Assn. Hobbies: Writing Poems and Stories; Crocheting; Embroidery; Reading; Collecting Crime Novels. Address: Yendon Road, Glenhuntly, Vic 3163, Australia.

BRAND John Anthony Guy, b. 23 June 1932, Malaysia. Architect. m. 16 Apr 1955, 1 s, 1 d. Education: Associateship in Arch, Perth Tech Coll, Aust; Life Fell, Roy Austl Inst of Archs; Assoc, Inst of Arb, Aust. Appointments: Practised as Anthony Brand, 1957-59, Brand Ferguson & Solarski, 1960-63; Dir, Forbes & Fitzhardinge, 1964-80; Dir, Brand Deykin & Hay, 1981-92; Anthony Brand Cnslt Archs, 1992-; Min, Town Planning Cttee. Honours: Bronze Medal, bldng Roy Inst of Brit Archs, 1961; Bronze Medal, bldng Roy Inst of Archs, WA Chapt, 1978; Archs Bd Awd, WA, 1988; Mbr, AO, 1990; About 12 other archl design awds. Memberships include: Past Pres, Rotary Club of Perth; Past Chmn, Wearne Hostel for the Aged; Chmn, St George's Charitable Trust; Past Commodore, Intl Yachting Fellshp of Rotarians, WA Fleet. Hobbies: Boating; Fishing; Photography; Travel. Address: 15 Mann Street, Cottesloe, WA 6011, Australia.

BRANDLE Maximilian, b. 25 July 1937, Winterthur, Switzerland. Director. m. Lorraine, July 1987, 2 s, 1 d. Education: MA, PHD, Qld. Appointments: Lectr, German, 1968; Dir, Inst of Mod Langs, 1970; Dpty Dir, Cntr for Langs Tchng & Rsch, IML Dir, 1995; Assoc Prof, 1996. Publications: Multicultural Queensland, 1988; Fanning the Winds of Change, 1990; The Queensland Experience, 1991; The Pre-war Migrants, 1995; Lettres of Australie, 1995; Languages in Continuing Education, 1996. Honour: Qld Migrant Serv Awd, 1987. Memberships: MACE; Rotary. Hobbies: Music; Fine Arts. Address: 14 Tenth Avenue, St Lucia, Qld 4067, Australia.

BRANSON Colin William, b. 26 June 1913, Aust. Executive. m. Gwen Peek, 7 Jan 1939, 1 s, 4 d. Education: BEc, DipCom, Univ of Adelaide; Univ of Melbourne; FAIM; AASA (SEWR); FSSE. Appointments: Jnr Master, 1932-35; Dir, King's Coll, SA, 1940-74; Regl Dir, Dept of Natl Devel, 1953-55; Chmn, SA Bap Theol Coll, 1954-69; Gen Mngr, SA Chmbr of Mfrs, 1956-72; Mbr, Des Cncl of Aust, 1965-75; Mbr, State Plng Authy, 1967-78; Cnclr, 1967-73, Alderman, 1973-77, Cty of Burnside; Pres, Adelaide Benevolent & Strangers Friend Soc, 1967-92; Pres, Gen, Bapt Union of Aust, 1968-71; Gen Mngr, chmbr of Com & Ind, SA Inc, 1973-78 Mbr, Immigration Review Panel, Dept of Immigration & Ethnic Affairs. Honour: AM. Memberships: Fell, Austl Inst of Mngmt, Cnclr, SA Divsn, 1950-75; Fmr Chmn, SA Inds Advsry Cttee; Past Pres, SA Br, Econs Soc of Austl & NZ; Inaugural Chmn, SA Chapt, Soc of Snr Execs, 1976-92; Cncl Chmn, Bible Soc in Aust, 1980-82. Hobby: Bowls. Address: 4 Verdelho Court, Auldana, SA 5072, Australia.

BRASCH Rudolph, b. 6 Nov 1912, Berlin, Germany. Author; Lecturer; Rabbi; Broadcaster; Telecaster. m. 16 Feb 1952. Education: PhD summa cum laude, 1936; Rabbi summa cum laude, 1938. Appointments include: Rabbi, N London Synagogue, 1938-48; Chap, London Civ Def, 1939-45; Fndr, Rabbi, Southgate and Enfield Liberal Synagogue, London, 1944-48; Fndr, Rabbi,

Dublin Progressive Synagogue, Ireland, 1946-47; Chf Min, Temple Emanuel, Sydney, NSW, Aust; Chmn, Ecclesiastical Bd, Australasian Union Progressive Judaism, 1949-79; Visng Prof, Sydney Univ, 1953; Fndr, N Shore Temple Emanuel, Sydney, 1960; Visng Prof, Natl Univ, Canberra, ACT, 1979; Rabbi, Temple Etz Ahayem, USA, 1980; Visng Prof, Univ AL, USA, 1980; Visng Prof, Univ HI, USA, 1981; Civ Marriage Celebrant, 1981-. Publications include: The Midrash Shir Hashirim Zuta, 1936; The Irish and the Jews, 1947; How Did It Begin?, 1965; The Judaic Heritage, 1969; How Did Sports Begin?, 1970; How Did Sex Begin?, 1973; Strange Customs, 1976; The Supernatural and You!, 1976; Australian Jews of Today, 1977; There's a Reason for Everything, 1982; Mistakes, Misnomers and Misconceptions, 1983; Thank God I'm an Atheist, 1987; Permanent Addresses - Australians Down Under, 1987; Even More Permanent Addresses, 1989; The Book of the Year, 1991; A Book of Comfort, 1991; A Book of Good Advice, 1993; A Book of Friendship, 1994; That Takes the Cake, 1994; A Book of Forgiveness, 1995; A Book of Anniversaries, 1996; Circles of Love, 1996; The Cat's Pyjamas, 1997; Reminiscences of a Roving Rabbi, 1998; The Star of David, 1999. Honours: Coronation Medal, 1952; JP, 1955; Hon DD, 1959; OBE, 1967; Silver Jubilee Medal, 1977; AM, 1979; Peace Prize, 1979; Hon Lt Col, AL Militia, 1980. Memberships include: Cntrl Conf Amn Rabbis; Austl Soc Auths; Austl Soc Civ Marriage Celebrants. Hobbies: Walking; Reading; Travel. Address: 14 Derby Street, Vaucluse, NSW 2030, Australia.

BRASH Alan Anderson, b. 5 June 1913, Wellington, NZ. Minister of Religion. m. Eljean Ivory Hill, 23 Nov 1938, 1 s, 1 d. Education: MA, Otago Univ, 1930-34; BD, New Coll, Edinburgh, 1934-38. Appointments: Min, St Andrews Ch, Wanganus, 1938-46; Gen Sec, Natl Cncl of Chs, 1947-52, 1950-64; St Giles Ch, Christchurch, 1952-56; Sec for Mission & Serv, E Asia Xian Conf, Pt-time, 1957-64, Full, 1964-68; Dir, Christian Aid, London, 1968-70; Dir, Interch Aid, WCC Geneva, 1970-73; Dpty Gen, Sec World Cncl of Chs, Geneva, 1974-78; Moderator, Presby Ch of NZ, 1978-79. Honours: OBE, 1968; DD, 1972. Address: 8 Gatonby Place, Avonhead, Christchurch 4, New Zealand.

BRAY Allan Victor, b. 9 Dec 1944, Melbourne, Australia. Parliamentary Officer. m. Judith L Hosking, 2 Feb 1968, 1 s, 1 d. Education: BBus, Roy Melbourne Inst of Technol, 1984. Appointments: Parly Offr, 1964-; Usher of The Black Rod, 1978-83; Clk-Asst, Legislative Cncl, 1983-88; Clk, Legislative Cncl, 1988-; Clk of the Parliaments, 1991-. Memberships: Sec, C'wlth Parly Assn, Vic Br, 1991-. Hobbies: Tennis; Music. Address: c/o Parliament House, Melbourne, Victoria 3002, Australia.

BRAY Denis Campbell, b. 24 Jan 1926, Hong Kong. Company Director. m. Marjorie Elizabeth Bottomley, 19 Feb 1952, 4 d. Education: MA 1955, Jesus Coll, Cambridge; BSc Econs, London Univ external degree. Appointments: Roy Navy, 1947-49; Hong Kong Civil Govt Serv, 1950-85; District Commnr, New Territories, 1971; Sec for Home Affairs, 1973-74, 1980-85; Hong Kong Commnr, London, 1977-80. Honours: CVO 1975; CMG, 1977; JP, 1960-75, 1987-. Hobbies: Sailing; Scuba diving. Address: 8A-7 Barrett Mansions, 8-9, Bowen Road, Hong Kong.

BRAZIER John, b. 11 March 1940, Olean, NY, USA. Physician; Attorney. div. 1 s. 1 d. Education: AAS, 1960; BS, 1963; MD, 1969; JD, 1989. Memberships: AMA; Amn Coll Surgs; Amn Coll Chest Phys; NY Acady Sci; CA Bar Assn. Hobby: Flying. Address: 1401 36th St, Sacramento, CA 95816, USA.

BREBNER John Main Thomson, b. 17 May 1935, Torry, Aberdeenshire, Scot. Psychologist. m. Jill Fawkes, 1 s, 3 d. Education: MA (Hons), Aberdeen, 1957; PhD, Exeter, 1965. Appointments: Visng Schl, Wolfson Coll, Oxford, 1991; Nuffield Rsch Asst, Univ of Exeter, 1959-62; Rsch Fell, Univ of St Andrews, 1962-64; Lectr, Univ of Dundee, 1965-69; Lectr, 1969, Snr Lectr, 1972, Assoc Prof, 1983, Univ of Adelaide. Publications:

Environmental Psychology in Building Design, 1982; Co-ed, Vols 13, 15, 16 of Stress Emotions, 1989, 1995, 1996. Honour: UK Ergonomics Soc's Rsch Awd, 1994. Memberships: Bd of Dirs, Intl Soc for Study of Individual Differences, 1993-99; Exec Bd, Div 2, Intl Assn Applied Psychol, 1990-. Hobbies: Family genealogy; Winemaking. Address: Department of Psychology, University of Adelaide, Adelaide, SA, Australia 5005.

BREED William Godfrey, b. 27 June 1941, Redruth, Cornwall, UK. University Associate Professor. m. Esther, Aug 1972, 3 s. Education: BSc (Hons), Zool, Aberdeen Univ; DPhil Oxford Univ. Appointments: Rsch Fell, Birmingham Univ, 1969-73; Lectr, Snr Lectr, Assoc Prof, Adelaide, 1973-. Membership: Pres, Austl Mammal Soc, 1997-. Hobbies: Natural History; Conservation of flora and fauna. Address: 69 Harrow Road, St Peters, South Australia, Australia.

BREEN Myles Patrick, b. 6 June 1939, Ayr, Queensland, Aust. Media Educator. m. Lorraine, 25 Mar 1969, 2 s, 5 d. Education: BAgrSc, Univ of Queensland, Aust, 1962; MS, Syracuse Univ, NY, 1965; PhD, Wayne State, Univ Detroit, MI, 1968. Appointments: Broadcaster, Austl Brdcst Cp, 1962-65; Instr, Wayne State Univ, 1968-84; Asst to Full Prof, North IL, 1968-84; Prof, Charles Sturt Univ, 1984-. Publications: Entry on Austl programming in Encyclopedia of Television, 1997; Schl jrnl entries, 1968-97. Honours: Grants: HOSO Bunka, 1984; Gannett Ldrshp, NYC, 1990; SMPTE Serv Awd, Chgo, 1981; Leaves: NIU, 1979, CSU, 1990. Memberships: Sec, Intl Inst of Comm, Austl branch, 1996-97; Aust Jrnl Assn; NCA; ICA; JEA. Hobbies: Swimming; Bushwalking. Address: 44 Osborne Avenue, Bathhurst 2795, Australia.

BREMNER John B, b. 16 Apr 1943. Professor of Organic Chemistry. m. Susan L Crawley, 13 Dec 1965, 2 s. Education: BSc; PhD; DipChem Pharmacol. Appointments: Rsch Fell Chem, Harvard Univ, 1967-68; Lectr, 1968-73, Snr Lectr, 1974-80, Rdr, 1981-91, Univ Tas; Prof Organic Chem, 1991-, Hd Dept Chem, 1994-, Univ Woll. Creative works: Many contrb articles w co-auths to profl jrnls. Memberships: Fell, Roy Austl Chem Inst, 1980; Fell Roy Soc of Chem, 1991; Amn Chem Soc. Listed in: Who's Who in Australia. Hobbies: Bushwalking; Stamp collecting. Address: 38 The Parkway, Balgownie, NSW 2519, Australia.

BRENNAN (Francis) Gerard (The Honourable Sir), b. 22 May 1928, Rockhampton, Qld, Aust. Judge. m. Dr Patricia, 26 May 1953, 3 s, 4 d. Education: Downlands Coll (Toowoomba); Univ Qld, BA, LLB. Appointments: Admitted Bar, 1951; QC, 1965; Pres, Nat; Union Aust Univ Studs, 1949; Mbr, Exec Law Cl Aust, 1974-76; Pres, Bar Assn, Qld, 1974-76; Pres, Austl Bar Assn, 1975-76; Mbr Austl Law Reform Commn, 1975-77; Pres, Admin Review Cl, 1976-79; Pres, Admin Appeals Tribunal, 1976-79; Additional Judge Supreme Crt, ACT and NT, 1976-81; Judge Fed Crt Aust, 1977-81; Justice High Crt, Aust, 1981-95; Chf Jus of Aust, 1995-98; Fndr, Scientia Prof Law, Univ NSW, Chan, Univ Technol Sydney, 1998; External Judge, Supreme Crt, Fiji, 1999. Honours: KBE, 1981; AC, 1988; Hon LLD, Trinity Coll, Dublin, 1988, Univ Qld, 1996, Univ Melbourne, 1998, Univ of Technol, Sydney, 1998. Hon DLitt, Cntrl Qld Univ, 1996, Austl Natl Univ, 1996; Hon DUniv, Griffith Univ, Qld, 1996, Memberships: C'wlth (Canb). Hobby: Reading. Address: Suite 2604, Piccadilly Tower, 133 Castlereagh Street, Sydney, NSW 2000, Australia.

BRENNAN Harold Geoffrey, b. 15 Sept 1944, Sydney, Aust. Economics Professor. m. Margaret Gytha, 14 Dec 1968, 2 s, 2 d. Education: BEcons (Hons), ANU, 1966. Appointments: Lectr, Snr Lectr Rdr, ANU, 1968-78; Prof, VPI, 1978-83; Prof, ANU, 1984-91; Dir, R888, 1981-96; Prof, R888, 1987-. Publications: Power to Tax, 1980; Reason of Rules (w Nobel Laureate James Buchanon), 1985; Democracy and Decision, 1993. Honour: Fell, Acady of Socl Scis, 1986. Membership: Amn Polit Sci Assn. Hobbies: Golf; Singing; Gardening. Address: 65 Springvale Drive, Weetaneera, ACT 2614, Australia.

BRENNAN William John (The Most Reverend), b. 16 Feb 1938. Catholic Bishop. Education: BA; MLitt; STL DipEd, Univ of Sydney; Univ of New Eng; Pontifical Urban Universita de Propaganda Fide, Rome. Appointments: Dir of Cath Educ Off, Diocese of Wilcannia-Forbes, 1966-74; Parish Priest, Nyngan, NSW, 1974-80; Parish Priest, Wentworth, NSW, 1980-83; Admnstr, Sacred Heart Cath, Broken Hill, NSW, 1983; Bish, Wagga Wagga, 1984. Address: PO Box 473, Wagga Wagga, NSW 2650, Australia.

BRERETON Paul Le Gay, b. 27 Aug 1957, N Sydney, NSW. Senior Counsel (Barrister). m. Sue, 10 Jan 1998, 1 s. Education: Univ of Sydney, 1976-81; BA (Hons), Sydney, 1990; LLB, Sydney, 1992. Appointments: Solicitor, 1982; Barrister, 1987; Snr Cnsl, 1998. Honours: Dux, Knox Grammar Sch, 1975; RFD (Res Forces Decoration), 1995. Memberships: Second-in-Cmd, Sydney Univ Regiment, 1994-96; Cmdng Offr, 4th/3rd Battalion, Roy NSW Regt, 1997-. Address: 3/180 Phillip Street, Sydney, NSW 2000, Australia.

BREURE Cornelis Jan, b. 5 Nov 1938, Aalsmeer. Oil Palm Consultant. m. Ellen Konstapel, 29 June 1971, 2 d. Education: MS, Agric, Univ Wageningen, The Netherlands, 1967; PhD, 1987. Appointments: Asst Expert, Dutch Intl Assistance Prog, Agarian Univ, La Molina, Lima, Peru, 1968-70; Agronomist-in-Charge, Dami Oil Palm Rsch Stn, Kimbe, Papua New Guinea, 1971-77; Hd, Oil Palm Agronomy Dept, Utd Brands Intl, San José, Costa Rica, 1977-79; Cnslt, Harrisons Fleing Adv Servs, London, 1979-91; PT Tania Selatan, Palembang, Indonesia, 1992-; PT Asian Agro Abadi Grp, Medan, Indonesia, 1992-; ASD De Indonesia, 1998. Publications: Articles, mainly on the oil palm, to profl jrnls. Membership: NY Acady of Scis. Hobbies: Piano playing; Golf; Sailing; Ice-skating. Address: Jl Belito No 3 Bukit Besar, Palembang, Sumatra, Selatan, Indonesia.

BREWARD Ian, b. 31 Mar 1934, Tauranga, NZ. Professor of Church History. m. Judith Marie Griffiths, 19 Nov 1960, 2 s, 1 d. Education: DipAg, 1953; MA, 1957; BD, 1960; PhD, 1963. Appointments: Farm Worker, 1950-53; Divinity Stud, 1954-60; Asst Min, Knox Ch, Dunedin, 1963-65; Prof, Ch Hist, Theol Hall, Knox Coll, 1965-81; Prof, Ch Hist, Ormond Coll, Univ of Melbourne, Aust, 1982-99. Publications: Godless Schools?, 1967; Grace and Truth, 1975; The Work of William Perkins, 1970; Australia. The Most Godless Place Under Heaven?, 1988; A History of Australian Churches, 1993. Honour: C'wlth Schl, 1960-63. Memberships: Chmn, Uniting Ch Histl Soc, Vic; Austl Histl Assn; Intl Assn for Miss Studies. Address: Ormond College, Parkville, Vic 3052, Australia.

BREWER Leo, b. 13 June 1919, St Louis, USA. Physical Chemist. m. Rose Strugo, 22 Aug 1945, 1 s, 2 d. Education: BS, 1940; PhD, 1943. Appointments: Rsch Assoc, Manhattan Dist Project, Univ CA, Radiation Lab, Berkeley, 1943-46; Asst Prof, 1946, Assoc Prof, 1950, Prof, 1955, Emer Prof, 1989, Dept of Chem, Univ of CA, Berkeley. Publications: Num articles in profl jrnls. Honours include: Lawrence Awd, Atomic Energy Cmmn; Palladium Metal, Electrochem Soc; Hume-Rothery Awd, Metallurgical Soc, Am Inst of Mining; Linford Awd, Disting Tchng, Electrochem Soc. Memberships include: Am Acady of Arts & Sci; Am Assn of Univ Profs; Am Chem Soc; Am Soc for Metals; CA Assn of Chem Tchrs; CA Native Plant Soc; Coblentz Soc; Electrochem Soc; Intl Plansee Soc for Powder Metallurgy; Materials Rsch Soc; Natl Acady of Scis; Roy Soc of Chem; Tau Beta Pi. Hobby: Growth of California Native Plants. Address: Department of Chemistry, MC 1460, University of California, Berkeley, CA 94720, USA.

BREWSTER Rudi Milton, US District Court Judge. m. Gloria J Nanson, 27 June 1954, 1 s, 2 d. Appointments: US Dist Judge, 1984. Memberships: Intl Assn of Ins Cnsl; Assoc, Am Bd of Trial Advocates, sec, 1981; Judicial Fell, Am Coll of Trial Lawyers, 1979-84; Legal Aid Soc, 1966-71; San Diego Rotary Club, pres, 1980-81, bd dir, 1977-82. Hobbies: Skiing; Hunting; Fishing; Gardening.

Address: Edward J Schwartz US Courthouse, 940 Front Street, Suite 4165, San Diego, CA 92101-8902, USA.

BRIAN Robert Francis, b. 11 Nov 1938, Utrecht, Netherlands. Parliamentary Librarian. m. Maureen Callachor, 9 May 1968, 1 s, 2 d. Education: BA, Austl Natl Univ, 1964; Dip Lib, Univ NSW, 1966. Appointments: Libn, Natl Lib of Aust, 1965-67; Libn, High Crt of Aust, 1967-70; Law Libn, Univ NSW, 1970-91; Parly Libn, NSW Parl, 1992-. Publications: Librarians and Australian Copyright Law: An Exposition of the Law in Simplified Form, 1980. Memberships: Austl Lib & Info Assn; Austl Law Libns Grp; Assn of Parly Libns of Aust; Assn of Parly Libns of Asia and the Pacific. Hobbies: Copyright; Ecclesiastical Matters. Address: 28 Lancaster Road, Dover Heights, NSW 2030, Australia.

BRIDGE Dorothy, b. 10 Feb 1938, Sydney, NSW, Aust. m. Robert (decd), 13 Feb 1990, 2 s, 1 d. Education: Jrnlsm Course, 1988; Creative Writing Advd Course, 1973-75. Appointments: Writer, Jrnlst, songwriter, 1976-; Creative Writing Tchr, Cairns Coll of TAFE, 1994-; Secretarial positions; Community activities: Naval Res cadets; Meals on Wheels; Pregnancy Help; Women's Shelter; Brownie-Guide Ldr; Red Cross; Family Grp Home; Snr Citizen's Hosps (visitor/entertainer); Cancer Support Vis (Cancer Fund). Publications: 10 books inclng: (Film script) Gold, 1984; Cassette of 4 songs, Songs From Cairns, 1987; Tips to Ensure Life Begins at Forty, 1989; Life Can Get Better at Fifty!, 1992; The Complete Guide to Creative Writing, 1994; Death - The Final Challenge, 1996; Stories, articles, poems, songs, book reviews. Honours include: Prizes for stories; Queensland Day Poetry Awd, 1983; Cert and Gold Bicentennial Medallion, Austl Consolidated Press, 1988; Nom, Cairns Businesswoman of Yr, 1989; Winner, The Examiner/Pacific Intl Competition, 1990; Prize Winner, Bush Ballad Competition, 1994; Cultural Awd, Mulgrave Shire Cncl, 1994; Winner, Independence Day Story Writing Competition, 1996. Address: 21 Blue Hills Crescent, Freshwater, Cairns, Queensland 4870, Australia.

BRIDGES-WEBB Charles, b. 15 Oct 1934, Castlemaine, Vic, Aust. Emeritus Professor. m. Anne Bridges-Webb, 3 s, 1 d. Education: MB, BS, Melbourne, 1957; MD, Monash Univ, 1971; FRACGP, 1971. Appointments include: Jnr Medl Offr, Roy Melbourne Hosp, 1958; Gen Practitioner Locums, Brit and Aust, 1959; Gen Practitioner, Deakin St Clin, Traralong, 1960-75; Visng Medl Offr, Cntrl Gippsland Hosp, 1960-75; Hon Clinl Asst, Roy Children's Hosp, Melbourne, 1965; Prof, Gen Prac, 1975-94, Emer Prof, 1995-, Univ Sydney; Gen Practitioner, Croydon Gen Prac Unit, Dept Community Med, 1976-90; Medl Offr, Infants Home, Ashfield, 1978-90; Medl Advsr, Woodfield Lodge Retirement Hostel, Haberfield, 1979-90; Num medl rsch posns inclng Austl Rep, Intl Primary Care Network, 1985-90; Chmn, Classification ttee, World Org of Family Drs (WONCA), 1991-; Dir (pt-time), RACGP NSW Rsch Unit, 1997-. Honours: Stirling Prize, Surg, Roy Melbourne Hosp, 1957; Faulding Prize, Rsch in Gen Prac, Roy Austl Coll Gen Practitioners, 1967; Rose Hunt Medal, Roy Austl Coll Gen Practitioners, 1993; Life Gov, Traralgon Community Hlth Serv. Memberships: Austl Medl Assn; Austl Assn Acad Gen Prac; Cncl Mbr, Utd Theol Coll, Sydney, 1980-87; Mbr, 1980-92, Chmn, 1986-92, Profl Stands Cttee, Unifam Marriage and Family Counselling Serv, Sydney. Hobbies: Reading; Literature; Gardening; Cricket; Football; Australian history; Food. Address: 9 Appian Way, Burwood, NSW 2134, Australia.

BRIER Eric Blyth, b. 21 May 1921. Civil Engineer. m. 21 May 1949, 3 s. Education: BEng, Univ of Qld. Appointments: Chmn Bld Ind, Adv Cncl Qld, 1970-72; Pres, Assn of Cnslt Engrs, Aust, 1980-82; Chmn, Qld Div IE Aust, 1983; Mbr Bd Prof Engrs, Qld, 1986-92. Creative works: More than 15 profl pprs publd, 1963-1994. Memberships: Fell, IE Aust; Fell, ICE; Life Mbr ACEA; Fndn Mbr and Life Fell, I Arb A. Hobbies: Golf; Gardening; Drama. Address: 18 Gunnin Street, Fig Tree Pocket, Qld 4069, Australia.

BRIGGS Dora Kathleen, b. 28 Mar 1929, Eng. University Educator; Dean. Education: BA, hons; DipEd; MEd; PhD; Westfield Coll, London Univ; Oxford Univ; Univ of Calgary, Can; Flinders Univ. Appointments: Hist Mistress, Harrogate Coll, Eng, 1953-55; Hist Mistress, Heathfield Sch, 1955-62; Prin, St Hilda's Coll, Buenos Aires, Argentina, 1962-66; Prin, Belgrano Day Sch, Buenos Aires, 1967-69; Snr Tutor, Macquarie Univ, Sydney, NSW, Aust, 1972-74; Lectr, then Snr Lectr, 1975-, Dean, Sch of Educ, 1983-89, Flinders Univ; Prin, Whyalla Campus, Univ of SA, 1989-94. Address: 175 Main Road, Blackwood, SA 5051, Australia.

BRIGGS Freda, b. 1 Dec 1930, Huddersfield, Eng. Professor of Child Development. m. 24 Dec 1952, 1 s. Education: MA, Adv Dip Educ; BEd; Fell, Coll Preceptors. Appointments: Dir, Early Childhood Studies, State Coll Vic, Coburg, Melbourne, Vic, 1976-80; Fndn Dean, De Lisa Inst of Early Childhood and Family Studies, Hartley Coll of Adv Ed, 1980-83; Prin Lectr, S Aust Coll Adv Educ, 1984-91; Assoc Prof, Univ S Aust, 1991-94; Prof, Univ S Aust, Magill, 1995-. Publications: Books: Child Sexual Abuse: Confronting The Problem, 1986; Keep Children Safe: A Personal Safety Curriculum For Children Aged 5-8 Years, 1988; Why My Child, 1993; Children And Families - Australian Perspectives, 1994; Teaching Children In The First Three Years Of School, 1995; From Victim To Offender, 1995; Developing Personal Safety Skills in Children with Disabilities, 1995; Child Protection: A Guide for Teachers and Child Care Professionals (1st auth), 1997; The Early Years of School: Teaching and Learning (1st auth), 1998; Num articles in Australian and for profl jrnls. Honours: Creswick Fellshp, 1987; ANZAC Fellshp for Rsch, 1997; Inaugural Austl Humanitarian Awd, 1998. Memberships: Save The Children Fund: Overseas Project Advsry Cttee, Educ Advsr; Intl Soc Prevention Of Child Abuse & Neglect; Brit Assn for the Study and Prevention of Child Abuse & Neglect. Listed in: International Authors. Address: University of South Australia, St Bernards Road, Magill, SA 5073, Australia.

BRINSDEN Peter Frederick (The Hon), b. 16 Oct 1922, Aust. Queen's Counsel; Former Judge. m. (1) 1 s, 1 d, (2) Margaret Brinsden, 10 Apr 1983. Education: LLB, Univ WA. Appointments: Admitted as Legal Practitioner, 1949; Sol, Qld, 1952; Mbr, 1962-73, Pres, 1970-72, Cncl Law Soc WA; QC, 1971; Bar, 1971; Pres, Law Cncl Aust, 1972-74; Mbr, Medl Bd, WA, 1972-75; Judge, Supreme Crt WA, 1976-90; Mbr, King's Pk Bd, 1978-84. Honours: AM, 1996; Hon Doct of Technol, Curtin Univ, 1998. Hobby: Orchardist. Address: Unit 7, 21/23 Hammond Road, Claremont, WA 6010, Australia.

BRISCOE Gordon, b. 18 Nov 1938, Alice Springs, Australia. Researcher. m. Norma, 2 s, 1 d. Education: BA, Hons, Hist; MA; PhD. Appointments: Pub Serv, NSW Local Govt, 1965-69; Liaison Offr, Aboriginal Legal System, 1970-71; Austl Pub Serv, 1972-92. Publications: Disease, Health & Healing: Aspects of Indigenous Health 1900-1940; Brandy and Dry: A History of Human Rights & Aboriginies 1900-1998; Sev pprs in profl jrnls. Honours: C'wlth Schlsp. Hobbies: Football; Tennis; Fishing; Cycling; Children. Address: History Program, Australian National University, Canberra, ACT 0200, Australia.

BRISK Michael Louis, b. 15 June 1939, Shanghai, China. Chemical Engineer. m. Jennifer, 6 Jan 1962, 3 s, 1 d. Education: BE Chem (Hons I and Univ Medal), Sydney, 1960; PhD, Sydney, 1965. Lectr, Chem Engrng, Univ of Sydney, 1961-65; ICI Cntrl Instrument Labs, Reading, UK (R&D), 1965-70; Snr Lectr, Chem Engrng, Univ of Sydney, 1971-82; ICI Aust Rsch Applied R&D Mngr, 1983-87; ICI Aust Engrng Advd Process Control Team Ldr, 1988-91; ICI Engrng, Intl Technol Ldr, Adv Process Control, 1992-95; Dean of Engrng, Monash Univ, Melbourne, 1995-. Honours: IEAust, IChemE, RACI, Tripartite Awd for Disting Contbns to Applied Chem Engrng In Process Control, 1993; Fell, Austl Acady of Technol Sci and Engrng, 1994. Memberships: FIE Aust; FIChemE; FTSE; Chmn, IChem (NSW Grp), 1984-86; Fndn Chmn, IEAust Process Control Soc, 1988-91. Address: Faculty of Engineering, Monash University, Clayton, Vic 3168, Australia.

BRISSENDEN Alan Theo, b. 13 Oct 1932, Griffith, NSW, Aust. Dance Critic; Writer; Academic. m. Elizabeth King, 15 Oct 1960, 2 s, 1 d. Education: BA Hons, DipEd, Sydney Univ; PhD, UCL. Appointments: Dance Critic, Sydney Morning Herald, 1952-55; Appointed Lectr, Engl, 1963, Rdr, Engl, 1982-94, Chmn, Dept Engl, 1984-86, Hon Visng Rsch Fell, Engl Dept, 1994-, Adelaide Univ, SA, 1963; Mbr, Prog Plng Cttee, 1972-84, Bd Govs, 1981-94, Adelaide Fest Arts; Dance Critic, Advertiser, 1976-84; Res Fell, Huntington Lib, CA, USA, 1979; Contbr, Dance Aust, 1980-; Dance Critic, ABC, 1984-87; Visng Fell, Wolfson Coll, Oxford, Eng, 1987, 1992; Dance Critic, The Austl, 1990-. Publications: Auth: Rolf Boldrewood, 1972; Shakespeare and The Dance, 1981; Ed: They Came To Australia, 1961; Aspects of Australian Fiction, 1990; As You Like It, 1993. Honour: AM, 1996. Memberships: SA Advsry Cttee, ABC, 1972-78, Chmn, 1977-78; Bibliographical Soc Aust and NZ, Pres, 1983-85; Arts Cncl Aust SA Div, Cttee Mbr, 1969-75, VP, Chmn, 1972-75; Natl Lit Bd Review, 1971-75; Engl Assn SA Bch, Chmn 1970-74; Austl and NZ Shakespeare Assn, Fndng VP, 1990-92, Pres, 1992-94, Hon Life Mbr, 1998; Pres, Friends State Lib SA, 1994-. Listed in: Who's Who in Australia; Who's Who of Australian Writers; Contemporary Authors. Hobbies: Family life; Music; Theatre; Walking; Conversation. Address: 71 Lockwood Road, Burnside, SA 5066, Australia.

BRITTEN-JONES Robert, b. 9 June 1928, Aust. Surgeon. m. Lucille Jost, 12 Aug 1961, 3 s, 1 d. Education: MB, BS; FRCS (Eng); FRACS. Appointments: Snr Lectr in Surg, Univ of Adelaide, 1960-63; Chmn, St Johns Ambulance Assn, SA Cntr, 1970-84; Snr Visng Surg, Roy Adelaide Hosp, 1972-95; Mbr, Crt of Examiners, 1976-86, Chmn, SA State Cttee, 1978-79, Roy Australasian Coll of Surgeons; Chmn, SA Regl Surg Trng Cttee, 1980-87; Clin Snr Lectr, Surgery, Univ of Adelaide, 1990-98. Honours: CStJ; AO, 1988-. Memberships: Austl Med Assn, SA, Hon Med Sec, 1961-63; Bd, Calvary Hosp. Address: 47a Church Terrace, Walkerville, SA 5081, Australia.

BRITTON Peter Leslie, b. 12 May 1943, London, England. Mathematics Teacher. m. Hazel Ann, 23 Feb 1963, 2 s. Education: BSc, Maths, Birmingham; Postgrad Ctf, Educn, Univ London. Appointments: Hd of Maths, Sawagongo Sch, Kenya; Snr Acad Master and Hd of Maths, Shimo-la-Tewa Sch, Kenya; Hd of Maths and Sci, All Souls' & St Gabriel's Sch, Aust. Publications: Birds of East Africa, 1980; Gulls & Terms in Birds of Africa, vol 2, 1986; Ed, The Sunbird, 1989-. Membership: Brit Ornithols Union, 1964-. Hobbies: Birds; Natural Environment. Address: All Souls' & St Gabriel's School, Charters Towers, Qld 4820, Australia.

BROADBRIDGE Philip, b. 7 Sept 1954, Adelaide, Australia. Professor of Applied Mathematics. m. Alice, 17 Jan 1976, 2 s. Education: BSc Hons, Adelaide; Dip Educ, Tasmania; PhD, Adelaide. Appointments: Snr Tutor, West Austl Inst Technol, 1982-83; Rsch Sci, C'Wlth Sci and Ind Rsch Org, 1983-87; Snr Lectr, La Trobe Univ, 1987-90; Prof, Univ Wollongong, 1991-; Hd, Dept Maths, 1993-97. Publications: Many sci publs in jrnls. Honour: Youngest Maths Prof in Aust (at time of appt). Memberships: Austl Math Soc; Austl Inst Phys; Intl Assn Math Phys; NYAS. Hobbies: Fishing; Travel; General Sport; Amnesty International. Address: School of Mathematics Applied Statistics, University of Wollongong, NSW 2522, Australia.

BROCKWELL John, b. 10 June 1929, Tongala, Victoria, Australia. Research Scientist. m. Valerie, 17 Oct 1979, 1 s, 1 d. Education: DDA, 1949. Appointments: Rsch Asst, 1949, Snr Rsch Sci, 1972, Prin Rsch Sci, 1977, Snr Prin Rsch Sci, 1989, Hon Rsch Fell, 1994, CSIRO, Aust. Publications: 220 sci pprs, chapts in books and extension articles, 1952-98. Honours: FAIAS, 1987; Clunies Ross Natl Sci and Technol Awd, 1994. Memberships: Austl Nitrogen Fixation Soc; NSW Grassland Soc. Hobbies: Bridge (President, Australian Bridge Federation, 1990-94, Winner, National Championship); Outback Touring; Gardening; Philately.

Address: 45 Bailey Place, Yarralumla Bay, ACT 2600, Australia.

BRODARTY Henry, b. 4 July 1947, Germany. Old Age Psychiatrist. m. Karoline, 13 Sept 1970, 1 s, 1 d. Education: MB BS; MD; FRACP; FRANZCP. Dir, Med Supt Psych Unit, Prince Henry Hosp, Sydney, Aust, 1980-90; Dir, Acad Dept Psychogeriatrics, 1990-; Clin Dir, Prog of Aged Care Servs, East Sydney Area Hlth Serv, Sydney, Aust, 1990-96; Prof, Psychogeriatrics, Univ NSW, Sydney, 1990-. Publications: Over 100 sci pprs and book chapts. Memberships: Dir, Intl Psychogeriatric Assn, 1994-; Chmn, Medl and Sci Panel Alzheimer's Disease Intl, 1993-; Vice Chmn Alzheimer's Disease Intl, 1998-. Address: Academic Department for Old Age Psychiatry, Prince of Wales Hospital, Randwick, NSW 2031, Australia.

BRODERICK Damien (Francis), b. 22 Apr 1944, Aust. Writer. Education: BA, Monash Univ, 1966; PhD, Deakin Univ, 1990. Appointments: Writer-in-Resn, Deakin Univ, 1986; Fell, Dept Engl and Cultural Stdies, Univ Melbourne. Publications: A Man Returned, stories, 1965; Ed, The Zeitgeist Machine, 1977; The Dreaming Dragons, 1980; The Judas Mandala, 1982, revised ed, 1990; Valencies (w Rory Barnes), 1983; Transmitters, 1984; Ed, Strange Attractors, 1985; The Black Grail, 1986; Striped Holes, 1988; Ed, Matilda at the Speed of Light, 1988; The Dark Between the Stars, stories, 1991; The Sea's Furthest End, 1993; The Architecture of Babel (theory, criticism), 1994; Reading by Starlight (theory, criticism), 1995; Theory and Its Discontents, 1997; The White Abacus, 1997; Zones (co-auth), 1997; YA (novel), 1997; The Spike: Accelerating into the Unimaginable Future (popular science), 1997; Not the Only Planet (anthology), 1998; Centaurus (ed w David D Hartwell), 1999; Stuck in Fast Forward (w Rory Barnes), 1999; The Book of Revalation (w Rory Barnes), 1999; Contbr to var periodicals. Honours: Austl SF Achmt Awds, 1981, 1985, 1989. Listed in: International Authors and Writers Who's Who.

BRODZIAK Kenn, b. 31 May 1913. Theatrical Entrepreneur. Appointments: Playwright and Th Prodr, 1936-41; Flt Lt, RAF and RAAF, 1941-45; Asst Prodr, Tivoli Circuit (Aust) Pty Ltd, 1945-46; Mngng Dir, Aztec Servs Pty Ltd, 1946-79; Mngng Dir, 1976-80, Dpty Chmn, Chmn, 1976-84, J C Williamson Prodns Ltd. Honour: OBE, 1978. Membership: Pres, Th Proprietors and Entrepreneurs Assn, 1971-73. Hobbies: Casino gambling; Swimming; Reading; Travel; Theatre. Address: 197 Canterbury Road, West St Kilda, Vic 3182, Australia.

BRONSON Charles Buchinsky, Actor. b. 3 Nov 1922, Ehrenfield PA. m. (1) Harriet Fendler, div, 2 c, (2) Jill Ireland, 1969, dec, 1 d, 2 step-c. Appointments: Played small parts in Hollywood films in the 1950s before coming into prominence in The Magnificent Seven, 1960; Other films incl: A Thunder of Drums, 1961; Lonely Are the Brave, 1962; The Great Escape, 1963; The Sandpiper, 1965; Battle of the Bulge, 1965; This Property is Condemned, 1966; The Dirty Dozen, 1967; Guns for San Sebastian, 1969; Rider in the Rain, 1969; Twinky, 1969; You Can't Win Them All, 1970; Cold Sweat, 1971; The Family, 1971; Chato's Land, 1972; The Mechanic, 1972; The Valachi Papers, 1972; Wild Horses, 1973; The Stone Killer, 1973; Mr Majestyck, 1974; Death Wish, 1974; Breakout, 1975; Hard Times, 1975; Breakheart Pass, 1976; From Noon till Three, 1976; St Ives, 1976; The White Buffalo, 1976; Telefon, 1977; Love and Bullets, 1979; Cabo Blanco, Death Wish II, 1981; Murphy's Law, 1986; Assassination, 1987; Messenger of Death, 1988; Kinjite, 1989; The Indian Runner, 1991; Death Wish V, 1993; Tv incls: Raid on Entebbe, 1976; The Legend of Jesse James; Act of Vengeance, 1986; Also appeared on many Am series during 1950s and 1960s. Address:c/o William Morris Agency, 1515 S El Camino Drive, Beverly Hills, CA 90212, USA.

BROOKS Jean Marjorie, b. 26 Mar 1924, Sussex, Eng. Novelist; English Tutor. m. William Brooks, 10 Aug 1948, 1 s, 1 d. Publications: (books) Opal Witch, 1967; Other Side of the Moon, 1968; (play) Opal Witch, 1967; (radio play) Opal Witch, 1967; (radio series) Gregory of the Outback, 1968. Hobbies: Writing novels; Coordinator of group: Novels in progress; Cinema; Theatre; Discussion groups. Address: 22 Nellie Street, Camp Hill 4152, Queensland, Australia.

BROOKS Michelle Simone, b. 30 Sept 1971, Mordialloc, Vic, Aust. Veterinary Surgeon. Education: BVSc (Hons). Hobbies: Emergency Medicine and Critical Care; Basketball; Tennis; Kickboxing; Golf. Address: C/o Animal Emergency Centre, 37 Blackburn Road. Mt Waverley, Vic 3149, Australia.

BROOME Peter John, b. 22 Feb 1930, Sydney, NSW, Aust. Company Director. m. Stella Mary Arlom, 19 Apr 1952, 2 s, 1 d. Appointments include: Co VP, 1978-; Co Dir, 1979-; Musical Dir, 1993-; Negotiated 1st Netwrk Contract w CCTV, China; Instigated Plan to Preserve Aust's Newsreel Heritage & Hist (1901-1976) by Donating All Movietone & Cinesound Extant Footage to Natl Film & Sound Archive. Memberships: Pres, 1973-89, Cncl Mbr, TV Prog Distributors Assn; Austl Cinema Pioneers Assn; Pres, Roseville Music Club; Pres, Combined Northside Music Club, N Shore, Sydney; Amn Chmbr of Com; NSW State Chmbr of Com; Co Dirs Assn. Hobby: Music: Musical Director, Ku-ring-gai Chamber Orchestra, 1958-77 and Ars Nova Chamber Orchestra, 1984-; Musical Dir, Orpheus Strings, 1992-. Address: 1/5 Closeburn Drive, Mt Victoria, NSW 2786, Australia.

BROTCHIE Phillip Edgar, b. 21 May 1939, Bendigo, Victoria, Australia. Assistant Executive Officer (Management), Bureau Meteorology. m. (1)Rebe Turner, 8 Feb 1964, div 1976, 2 s. (1 dec), 1 d. (2)Gina Owen, 3 Sept 1982, 2 s. 2 d. (1 dec). Education: BA; Assoc Dip Pers Admin; Grad Dip Pers Admin; Dip Family History Studies; MBus (Org Behav); PhD candidate, Deakin Univ. Appointments: Defence Dept, Govt Statist's Off; Defence Signals Div; Dept Labour and Nat Serv; Dept PM and Cabinet; Pub Serv Bd; Prices Justification Tribunal; Industrial Rels Bureau; Dept Employment and Industrial Rels; Bureau of Meteorol. Publications: Articles in profl jrnls on genealogy, poetry, bushwalking and the environment. Honours: Jnr Govt Schlshp, 1952; Univ Free Place, 1956; Deakin Univ Travel Schshp, 1996. Memberships: Genealog Soc of Victoria; Aust Inst of Genealog Studies; Australasian Assn Genealogists and Record Agents. Hobbies: Genealogy; Bushwalking; Travel; Music; Reading; Sport. Address: Bureau of Meteorology, 150 Lonsdale Street, Melbourne, VIC 3000, Australia.

BROUGHTON Robert Leonard, b. 15 Jan 1955, Hobart, Tasmania. Library Manager. m. Mary Ruth, 1 ss. Education: BA, Socl Scis, Pacific Hist/Legal Studies, La Trobe Univ. Appointments include: Asst Record Offr (Deputizing Archivist), Monash Univ, Clayton, 1979-81; Info Servs Supvsr, Cntrl Land Cncl, Alice Springs, 1988-90; Admnstv Offr (Mus) Ethnography Lib, Brit Mus, London, Uk, 1991; Acting Univ Archivist, Univ of Tasmania, Hobart, Aust, 1995-; Librarianship Tchr, TAFE Tasmania (pt-time), 1997-99; Rare book valuer and preservation, consultancy ongoing (pt-time), Broughton Archival Consultancy; Lib Mngr, Dept of Hlth and Hum Servs, Corp & Strategic Servs, Lib & Records Off, 1998. Publications: 6 pprs inclng: Aboriginal genealogies, the University of Tasmania experience, Austl Archivists Conf, Univs & Colls SIG Seminar, Alice Springs, NT (electron format), 1996. Memberships include: Pres, ALIA, Cntrl Aust Sect, 1990; Pres, Hamilton Downs Yth Camp (Apex), 1990; RMAA Tasmanian Branch Cncl, RMAA Loc Gov SIG Pres, 1994; Sec, AICCM Tas Inc, 1996. Hobbies: Caving; Collecting cameras; Rare books. Address: 20 Jenkins Street, Taroona 7053, Australia.

BROUN Malcolm David, b. 25 Apr 1935. Barrister. m. Wendy Sue Hannelly, 22 Dec 1972, 2 s, 3 d. Education: Sydney Univ. Appointments: Fndr, 1955, Dir, 1955-79, Chmn, Univ Co-op Bookshop Ltd, 1969-79, QC, 1982; Hd, Edmund Barton Chmbers, 1983-, Assoc Judge Dist Ct NSW, 1989-90; Chmn, Gen Prac Sect, LAWASIA. Publication: Australian Family Laws Practice, 1975-. Honours: Cyfaill y Celtaidd (CyC) - (Friend of the Celt), Hon awarded by Celtic Cncl of Aust, 1984. Memberships: Chmn Family Law Conf Law Cl Aust, 1986; Chmn, Austl Inst Family Law Arbitrators and Mediators, 1990; Chmn, Gen Prac Sect Lawasia, 1994-98. Listed in: Who's Who in Australia. Hobbies: History; Chess; Scots Gaelic. Address: Edmund Barton Chambers, 44/MLC Centre, Sydney, NSW 2000, Australia.

BROWN Alan Gordon John, b. 25 May 1931, Hillston, New South Wales, Australia. Scientist. m. (1) Betty Rix dec, 24 Apr 1954, 2 s, 2 d, (2) Erika Leslie, 29 Jan 1994. Education: BSc, 1952; MSc, 1966; Dip AFS, 1952. Appointments: Asst Chf, CSIRO Divsn of Forest Rsch, 1975-87; Dpty Chf, CSIRO Divsn of Forestry and Forest Products, 1988-90; Chf, CSIRO Divsn of Forestry, 1991-92; Hon Rsch Fell, CSIRO Forestry and Forest Products. Publications: Eucalypts for Wood Production, 1978; Management of Soil, Nutrients and Water in Tropical Plantation Forests, 1997. Honours: N W Jolly Mem Medal, Inst of Foresters and Aust, 1986; IUFRO Disting Serv Awd, 1992; Gen Divsn, AO, 1998. Memberships: Fell, Austl Acady of Technol Sci and Engrng, Inst of Foresters of Aust; C'wlth Forestry Assn. Listed in: Who's Who in Australia. Address: 3 Carmichael Street, Deakin, ACT 2600, Australia.

BROWN Bruce Macdonald, b. 24 Jan 1930. Director. m. (1) Edith Irene Raynor, 3 Jan 1953, dec, 1989, 2 s, 1 d, (2) Françoise Rousseau, 29 Sept 1990, dec 1995. Education: MA, hons, Vic Univ, Wellington. Appointments: NZ Amb to Iran, 1975-78; Asst Sec, Min of For Affairs, Wellington, 1978-81; Dpty High Commnr, London, 1981-85; Amb to Thailand, 1985-88; High Commnr to Can, 1988-92; Retd, 1992; Dir, NZ Inst of Intl Affairs, 1969-71, 1993-97; Chmn, NZIIA Rsch Cttee, 1993-. Publications: The Rise of New Zealand Labour, 1962; The United Nations, 1966; Asia and The Pacific in the 1970's, 1971; Num articles and reviews. Honours: NZ Commemoration Medal, 1990; Queen's Service Order, 1998. Memberships: RIIA, London, 1982-. Listed in: Who's Who in New Zealand; International Yearbook and Statesman's Who's Who. Hobbies: Reading; Watching Rugby and Cricket; Golf. Address: New Zealand Institute of International Affairs, Victoria University at Wellington, PO Box 600, Wellington, New Zealand.

BROWN Desmond Joseph, b. 16 Dec 1920, Sydney, NSW, Aust. Retired Medicinal Research Chemist. m. Beatrice Caroline Harrison, 19 Aug 1947, 2 s, 1 d. Education: BSc, 1941, MSc, 1947, Sydney; PhD, 1949, DIC, 1949, DSc, 1961, London, Eng. Appointments: Rsch Asst, Sydney Univ, NSW, 1943-46; Fell, Medl Chem, 1949-56, Snr Fell, Medl Chem, 1965-61, Rdr, Medl Chem, 1961-72, Hd, Medl Chem Grp, 1973-85, Visng Fell, Rsch Sch Chem, 1985-, Austl Natl Univ, Canberra, ACT. Publications: The Pyrimidines, 1962, supp I, 1970, supp II, 1985, 2nd edn, 1994; The Pteridines, 1988; The Quinazolines, 1996; Contbr, over 200 rsch papers in chem jrnls. Honour: H G Smith Mem Medallist, Roy Austl Chem Inst, 1964; Ollé Prize for Cheml Lit, Roy Austl Cheml Inst, 1997. Memberships: Roy Soc Chem; Fell, Roy Soc NSW; Intl Soc Heterocyclic Chem; Fell, Roy Austl Chem Inst. Hobbies: Gardening; Geological fossicking; Music. Address: 2 Hobbs Street, O'Connor, ACT 2602, Australia.

BROWN Gavin, b. 27 Feb 1942, Scotland. Professor. m. Barbara Routh, 1 s, 1 d. Education: MA, St Andrews; PhD, Newcastle-upon-Tyne; Hon LLD, St Andrews. Appointments: Lectr, Snr Lectr, Univ Liverpool; Prof, Dean of Sci, Univ NSW; Vice Chan, Univ Adelaide, Univ Sydney. Publications: Over 100 pprs in maths jrnls. Honours: Whittaker Prize, 1977; Austl Maths Soc Medal, 1982. Memberships: FAA; VP, Austl Acady of Scis, 1993-94. Hobby: Horse Racing. Address: 77 Wallaroy Road, Woollahra, NSW 2025, Australia.

BROWN George Stephen, b. 28 June 1945, Santa Monica, California, USA. Professor of Physics. m. Julie Dryden, 22 Mar 1997, 1 d. Education: BS, CA Inst of Technol, 1967; PhD, Cornell Univ, 1973. Appointments: Tech Staff, Bell Labs, 1973-77; Rsch Prof, Stanford Univ, 1977-91; Prof, Phys Dept, Univ CA, Santa Cruz, Chair,

1996-. Publications: Over 100 sci publns. Honour: Fell, Amn Physl Soc, 1985. Memberships: Amn Physl Soc; Amn Assn of Univ Profs; AAAS. Address: 404 Village Circle, Santa Cruz, CA 95060, USA.

BROWN James, b. 15 Aug 1925, Christchurch, NZ. Retired. m. Patricia Sutton, 6 Dec 1952, 2 d. Education: Roy Mil Coll, Duntroon, 1945-47, grad, 1947; Var Cmnd and Staff courses, NZ and Aust. Appointments: NZ Regular Army, 1948-71, attaining rank of Col; Active serv, Korea, 1951-52; Seconded as Comptroller Household, Govt House, NZ, 1961-62; Regl Commnr Civ Def, 1971-77; Offic Sec to Gov Gen NZ, 1977-85; Gen Sec, Duke of Edinburgh Awd NZ, 1986-94. Honour: Cmdr, Roy Victorian Order, 1985. Memberships: Col Cmdt, RNNZAC, 1982-86; Pres, NZ Army Assn, 1986-94; Wellington Club, NZ. Hobbies: Fly fishing; Wing shooting; Rifle shooting. Address: 7 Matenga Street, Waikanae, New Zealand.

BROWN Laurence Binet, b. 13 Aug 1927. Psychologist. m. Dorothy Fay Wood, 16 Dec 1950, 3 s, 1 d. Education: MA (NZ); Dip Ed, PhD, (London). Appointments: NZ Def Sci Corps, Lectr Univ of Adelaide; Prof, Massey Univ, Vic Univ of Wellington; Univ of NSW, Sydney; Dir, Relig Experience Rsch Cntr, Westminster Coll, Oxford. Publications: Ed, International Journal for the Psychology of Religion, Vol 1, 1990; The Human Side of Prayer, 1994; The Psychology of Religious Belief, 1996. Honour: Emeritus Prof, Univ NSW. Memberships: Fell, NZ Psychol Soc; Fell, Brit Psychol Soc. Address: 6 Easdale St, Wellington 1, New Zealand.

BROWN Leslie John, b. 21 Oct 1956, Wellington, New Zealand. Lawyer. m. Mary Self, 18 Aug 1984, 1 s, 1 d. Education: LLB, hons, Vic Univ of Wellington, 1980; Admitted as Barrister & Solicitor, High Crt of NZ, 1981. Appointments: Law Clk, Solicitor, Bell Gully & Co, Wellington, NZ, 1977-83; Asst Lectr, Lectr, Snr Lectr, Vic Univ of Wellington, 1984-. Publication: Brooker's Aviation Law, 1996. Honours: Mbr, Inaugural NZ Team to Intl Semi-Finals Philip C Jessup Intl Law Moot Crt Comp, WA DC, USA, 1979. Memberships: Fed Cncl Mbr, Offr, Aviation Law Assn of Aust & NZ Inc, 1990-. Address: c/o Victoria University of Wellington, PO Box 600, Wellington, New Zealand.

BROWN Robert, b. 2 Dec 1933, Pelaw Main, Hunter Valley, NSW. Retired Politician m. Joy Hirschausen, 1 s, 1 d. Education: Maitland Boys' High Sch; Univ of Sydney. Appointments: Active in local govt polits Greater Cessnock, 1969-80; Min for Land Transp and Shipping Support, 1988-90; Min for Land Transp, 1990-93. Publications incl: Student Economics Parts 1 and 2, 1982; The Australian Economy, 1989. Memberships: Mbr for Cessnock, NSW Legis Ass, 1978-80; Mbr for Hunter HoR, 1980-84; Mbr for Charlton, 1984-98. Hobbies: Collecting; Photography; Music; Theatre. Address: Suite 4, Level 3, Harbour Park Centre, 251 Wharf Road, Newcastle, NSW 2300, Australia.

BROWN Robert Darwin Bruce, b. 9 Oct 1955, Adelaide, SA, Aust. Flute Teacher; Flautist. Education: Cert Advd Music, Adelaide Coll TAFE Sch Music, 1980; Dip Music, 1993; Mbr, Inst Music Tchrs. Appointments: Tchr, Flute, var schs; Freelance/Pvte Tchr. Publications: Pastoral Symphony from Handel's Messiah arranged for 3 flutes and alto flute, 1982; Trill Chart for Flute, 1983; Register of Historic Flutes, 1994; Contbr, Ed, South Australian Flute News; Contbr: Pan, Brit Flute Soc; Flutist Quarterly, USA. Honours: Life Mbr, Flute Soc SA, 1986; Vice-Patron, Flute Soc of SA, 1997. Memberships: VP, Flute Soc SA; Pres, 1996-, Austl Flute Soc; Adelaide Eisteddfod Soc; Music Tchr Assn SA; Natl Flute Assn, USA; Brit Flute Soc. Hobbies: Collecting old flutes; Hiking; Tennis; Snooker; Writing and editing; Arranging music; Flute history and promotion. Address: PO Box 3228, Norwood, SA 5067, Australia.

BROWNBILL David Scott Barrington, b. 15 Nov 1938. Consultant Neurosurgeon. m. Lee Anne Wilson, 17 Mar 1988. Education: MB; BS; FRACS; FACTM; MACLM. Appointments: Mbr, Austl Surg Team, Vietnam, 1966-67; Snr Registrar, Professorial Dept of Neurosurg, Natl Hosp, London, 1973; Registrar in Neur, Natl Hosp, London, 1973; Locum Cnslt Neurologist, Roy Devon and Exeter Hosp, 1973; Neurosurg, Roy Melbourne Hosp, 1975-95 (Hd of Unit, 1975-92); Cnslt Neurosurg, Roy Womens Hosp, 1975-95; Final Yr Examiner in Surg, Melbourne Univ, 1986-; Dir, Higginbotham Neurosci Rsch Inst, 1988-93; VP, Austl Stroke and Neurosci Inst, 1993-97; Chmn, Trinity Coll Fndn, Univ of Melbourne, 1988-95; Dir, Austl Stroke and Neurosci Inst, 1993-97; Cnslt Neurosurg, Roy Melbourne Hosp, 1995-. Honours: Advd Aust Awd for med, 1991; Mbr of the Order of Aust, 1994. Memberships: Austl Medl Assn; Neurosurg Soc of Aust; Assn of Melbourne Neurosurgs, Pres, 1989-91; Amn Congress Neurol Surgs; Pres, Medico-Legal Soc of Vic, 1995-96; Mbr of Cncl, 1993-95, 1999-, Mbr Bd of Mngmt, 1999-, Trinity Coll, Univ of Melbourne; Mbr, Cttee of Convocation, Univ of Melbourne, 1999. Bd Mbr, Ballet Vic, 1974-77. Listed in: Who's Who in Australia. Hobbies: Music; Marine Biology; Underwater Photography. Address: 62 Erin Street, Richmond, Vic 3121, Australia.

BROWNBILL George Metcalfe, b. 24 May 1935, Aust. Consultant. m. Molly, 30 Nov 1957, 3 s, 1 d. Education: BA, Hons, Melbourne Univ, 1957. Appointments: Pub Serv, var appts, 1958-88; ACIL Cnsltng P/L, 1988. Publications: Num offl pprs. Hobbies: Viticulture; Horticulture; Music; Swimming. Address: 106 Brooks Road, Bywong, NSW 2621, Australia.

BROWNING Glenn Francis, b. 21 June 1961, Bathurst, Australia. Veterinary Scientist. m. Janet Elizabeth Browning, 2 s, 1 d. Education: BVSc, hons, Dip, Vet Clin Studies, Sydney; PhD, Melbourne. Appointments: Vet Rsch Offr, Moredun Inst, Edinburgh, 1988-91; Lectr, 1991-92, Snr Lectr, 1993-97, Assoc Prof, Rdr, 1998-, Univ Melbourne. Publications: Over 60 sci articles in profl jrnls. Honours: Univ Medal, 1983; Meritorious Serv Awd, Austl Vet Assn, 1997; Alexander von Humboldt Fellshp, 1998. Memberships: Edl Bd, Microbiol, 1995-; Edl Cttee, Austl Vet Jrnl, 1994-; Ed, Avidn Pathol, 1997-. Address: Veterinary Preclinical Centre, University of Melbourne, Parkville, Victoria 3052, Australia.

BRUCE Michael Ian, b. 17 Nov 1938. Research Chemist. 2 s, 1 d. Education: PhD, 1967, DSc, 1977, Univ Bristol; MA, Univ Oxford, 1976. Appointments: Lectr, Inorganic Chem, Univ Bristol, 1967-73; Prof, Inorganic Chem, 1973-82; Angas Prof of Chem, 1982-; Dean of Sci, 1988-90, Univ of Adelaide; Visng Prof, Cambridge, 1977-78; Vancouver, 1983, 1990; Toulouse, 1987; Université Louis Pasteur, Strasbourg, 1991, 1996; Visng Prof, Université de Neuchâtel, Switzerland, 1997; Université de Rennes, France, 1998. Creative works: Over 500 rsch pprs on var aspects of Organometallic Chemistry, 1996-; three books; numerous reviews. Honours: HG Smith Medal, 1986; Fell, Aust Acady of Sci, 1989; Burrows Awd, 1989. Memberships: Roy Soc of Chem, 1957-; Am Chem Soc, 1973-; Fell, Roy Austl Chem Inst, 1973-; Pres, South Austl Branch, 1979-80. Listed in: South Australia; Australia; Men & Women of Science. Hobbies: Photography; Bushwalking; Music. Address: Department of Chemistry, University of Adelaide, Adelaide 5005, SA, Australia.

BRUDERHANS Zdenek, b. 29 July 1934, Prague, Czech. Flautist; University Reader. m. Eva Holubarova, 19 Apr 1962, 1 s, 1 d. Education: Baccalaureat, Akademicke Gymnasium, Prague; Distinct Dip, Prague Conservatorium of Music; MMus, Prague Acady of Music; Debut, Prague, 1957. Appointments: Asst Prin Flutist, Prague Natl Th, 1955-59; Prin Flutist, Prague Radio Symph Orch, 1960-68; Flute Prof, Sweden, 1969-73; Lectr, Snr Lectr, Rdr, Dean of Music, 1987-89, Adelaide Univ, SA, 1973-97; Flute Soloist in Czech and Eurn Countries, USA, Eng, Aust and Asia on Radio and in Fests. Creative Works: Recordings: 10 recordings inclng 6 LP and 6 CD recitals released by Supraphon, Philips, Panton, Columbia-Nippon, Connoisseur Records, World Record Club and Aquitaine of works by Bach, Mozart, Haydn, Hindermith, Martinu, Messiaen, Berio, Debussy, Varese, Ravel, Vieru, Klusak, Rychlik and Feld; Music, Tectonics and Flute Playing, book; Cntbr to sev profl jrnls and mags. Honour: Grand Prize, Instl Competition of Wind Instruments, Prague Spring Fest, 1959. Hobby: Swimming. Address: 2 McLaughlan Avenue, Brighton, SA 5048, Australia.

BRUMBY Colin James, b. 18 June 1933, Melbourne, Vic, Aust. Composer; Lecturer; Conductor. Education: BMus, 1957; DMus, 1972; Conservatorium of Music, Univ of Melbourne. Appointments: Lectr in Music, Kelvin Grove Tchrs Coll, 1960-62; Hd of Music Dept, Greenford Grammar Sch, Middlesex, 1962-64; Lectr in Music, 1964-65, Snr Lectr, 1966-71, Assoc Prof of Music, 1976-88, Univ of Queensland. Publications: A Service of Rounds, 1985; Christmas Bells, 1986; Harlequinade, 1987; Oh Come and Worship, 1990; Missa Canonica, 1991. Creative works: Compositions: Flute Concerto; The Phoenix and the Turtle; Festival Overture on Australian Themes; Charlie Bubbles Book of Hours; Three Italian Songs for High Voice and String Quartet; Guitar Concerto; Violin Concerto 1 and 2; Piano Concerto; South Bank Overture; Symphony No 1 (The Sun); The Vision and the Gap (Cantata); Bassoon Concerto; Bassoon Sonata; Clarinet Sonatina; Flute Sonatina; Haydn Down Under (Bassoon Quintet); Victimae Paschali (SATB and Strings); Three Baroque Angels (SATB and orch); Piano Quartet; Four Australian Christmas Carols, 1986; Operas: Summer Carol; Lorenzaccio, 1986; The Heretic, 1998-99; Borromeo Suite for Flute and Guitar; Viola Concerto, Tre aspetti di Roma; Trumpet Concerto. Honour: Adv Aust Awd for Music, 1981. Memberships: Univ Qld Staff Assn; Austl Perfoming Rights Assn. Hobbies: Reading; Travel; Eating. Address: 9 Teague Street, Indooroopilly, Qld 4068, Australia.

BRUSKIN Leoniol Gregory, b. 24 May 1962, Irkutsk, Russia. Physicist. m. I Brusko, 15 June 1985, 1 d. Education: PhD, Phys & Maths, Acady of Sci, Russia, 1989. Appointments: Rsch Assoc, Inst of Applied Phys, Irkutsk, Russia, 1984; Asst Prof, 1990, Assoc Prof, 1990, Dept of Maths, Irkutsk Polytechnic; Rschr, Univ of TSukuta, Japan, 1996. Publications: Over 40 pprs in sci jrnls. Honours: Pub Commendation Awd, Min of Educ, Japan, 1997. Membership: Plasma Physics and Controlled Fusion Society, Japan, 1993-. Hobbies: Karate; Tennis; Computers. Address: Plasma Research Center, University of Tsukuba, 305 Tsukuba, Tennodai 1-1-1, Japan.

BRUTON Dean, b. 24 Dec 951, Adelaide, Aust. Artist; Educator. m. Judith, 1 s. Education: PhD (Arch), Univ of Adelaide; MA (Hums), Flinders Univ of SA; Advd Dip T (Art) Terrans CAE. Appointments: Lectr, S Austl Sch of Art; Lectr, S Austl Sch of Des. Publication: Recollections: The Contemporary Art Soc of SA, 1943-86, 1986. Membership: Des Inst of Aust; ANAT (Austl Network for Art & Technol); EAF Experimental Art Fndn. Address: University of South Australia, City West Campus 70, North Terrace, Adelaide 5001, Australia.

BRYANT Allyn Gordon, b. 5 Jan 1913, NSW, Aust. Retired Bank Manager. m. (1) 1940, (2) Nellie Walter, 1960, 3 s. Appointments include: Joined Union Bank Aust Ltd, 1929, now Aust and NZ Banking Grp Ltd, w promotion from Jnr Clk through to Mngr, Subiaco Bch, WA; Retd on superannuation, 1973-. Honours: JP, 1951; MBE, 1972. Memberships include: Life Mbr, Austl Inst Bankers; Life Gov, Hon Life Mbr, Vice Patron, Past Pres, ACTIV Fndn Inc; Hon Life Mbr, Austl Legion Ex-Serv'men and Women, WA Bch; 1st Life Mbr, Lions Club Intl, WA; Roy Assn Justices; Rsch Bd Advsrs, ABI; Life Fell, Natl Cncl on Intellectual Disability, 1975-. Hobbies: Philately; Photography; Gardening; Community service; Wines; Sport. Address: 6B Stocker Court, Craigie, WA 6025, Australia.

BRYCE Malcolm John (Hon), b. 10 Apr 1943. Company Director; Consultant; Former Member of Parliament. Education: BA. Appointments: Elected Mbr for Ascot, 1971, re-elected, 1974, 1977, 1980, 1983, 1986; Opposition Spokesman, Lands, Forest, Fed Affairs, 1974-76; Opposition Spokesman, Educ, Fed Affairs, 1976-77; Opposition Spokesman, Indl Dev, Fed Affairs,

1977-80; Elected Dpty Ldr Opposition, 1977-80, 1981-83; Dpty Premier, Min Econ Dev and Technol, 1983; Dpty Premier, Min Indl Dev, Technol, Small Bus, Def Liaison, 1984; Dpty Premier, Min Ind and Technol, Comms, Def Liaison, Min Parly and Electoral Reform, 1986-87; Resigned, Parl and Min, 1988; Chmn, WA Technol and Ind Advsry Cncl, 1988; Co Dir, Cnslt, Snr Assoc, Deloitte Ross Tohmatsu, 1990; Corporate Mngr, Dev, Invmnt, Cty of Ipswich, 1993-95; Proj Chmn, Global Info Links, 1993-95; Chmn, Austl Cntr for Innovation and Intl Competitiveness, 1996-99. Honours: Recip, US Govt Ldrs Grant, Stdy Tour USA, 1978; Represented Aust, 6th Duke of Edinburgh Stdy Conf, 1980; AO, 1989; Hon DTech, Curtin Univ, 1994. Membership: PMs Sci and Engrng Cncl, 1992-95. Address: No 6 McCullock Rise, Bullcreek, WA 6149, Australia.

BRYCE Paul, b. 8 Jul 1944. Engineer. m. 4 June 1965, 2 s, 1 d. Education: BSc, Hons 1; DPhil. Appointments: Rsch Fell, Nat Rsch Cncl, Canada, 1971; Lectr, NSW Inst of Technol, Aust, 1973; Visng Prof, Univ of Alberta, 1979; Chief Tech Advsr, UN Dev Org, 1983; Hon staff mbr, Univ Brawijaya, Indonesia, 1985; Assoc Prof, Univ of Technol, Sydney, 1989; short term Proj Mngr, Intl Expert for renewable energy schemes in Pacific & SE Asia. Creative works: Many rprts, acad pprs inclg, Rural Electrification in the Pacific; Engineers in Sustainable Development; Multi-Disciplinary Engineering Transactions, vol GE19. Honours: Set of Solomon Island postage stamps depicting work completed in the country, 1987; Cert of Achievement, PM of Solomon Islands, 1989; Fred Hollows Awd, 1994. Memberships: Fell, Inst of Engrng, Aust; Fell, Inst of Radio & Electronics Engrs, Aust; Pres, Appropriate Technol for Community & Environment. Listed in: Australian Men & Women of Science, Engineering and Technology. Address: c/o APACE Centre, PO Box 123, Broadway, NSW 2007, Australia.

BRYNER Peter, b. 16 Dec 1955, Auckland, New Zealand. Chiropractic. m. Janice, 1 Sept 1978. Education: BApplSci, Chiropractic; Postgrad Dip, Human Serv Rsch; Master Chiropractic Sci, 1999. Appointments: Lectr, RMIT, 1983-94; Chiropractic, Pvte Prac, Perth, 1994-98; Rsch Assoc, Macquarie Univ, 1997-. Honours: Pvte Prac Rsch Prize, World Chiropractic Centennial Conf, WA, 1995; Chiropractic Sci Awd, RMIT, 1981. Memberships: Chiropractors Assn of Aust; Intl Assn for the Study of Pain; Austl Pain Soc. Address: 21 Harvey Street, Burswood, Western Australia 6100, Australia.

BU Enyun, b. 20 Jan 1934. Researcher. m. Ji Yuechan, 28 May 1960, 1 s, 1 d. Education: Grad, Harbin Indl Univ, China. Appointmemts: Engr in Charge, 1985; Vice Chf Engr, 1986; Chf Engr, 1987. Publications: New Technology in Water and Wastewater Engineering, 1988; Purification Polluted Groundwater by Biochemical Method, 1989; New Process in Water and Wastewater Engineering, 1990; Treatment of Surface Water with Special Quality, 1991; New Technology in Environment Pollution Control, 1993. Honours: State Sci & Techl 2nd Grade Awd, 1977; Sci & Technol 3rd Grade Awd of Shenyang Cty, 1988; State Sci & Technol 2nd Grade Awd, 1990; Sci & Technol 2nd Grade Awd of Min of Construction, 1991; 2nd Grade Awd of Sci & Technol Assn in Jilin Province, 1990. Memberships; Editl staff of natl Water & Wastewater, 1988; Natl Appraisal Cttee on Filtration Material, 1990; Sec, Natl Rsch Assn of Lake Water Treatment on Low Temperature and Low Turbidity, 1987; Standing Cttee of Jilin Environment Sci Acady, 1988; Changchun Environment Sci Acady, 1988; Natl Rsch Assn on Adv Water Treatment, 1990. Hobby: Reading. Address: China Northeast Municipal Engineering Design & Research Institute, 8 Gongnong Avenue, Changchun, Jilin 130021, China.

BU HE - Yun Shuguang, Party and Govt Offic. b. 24 Mar 1926, Inner Mongolia. m. Zhulanqiqige, 1947, 1 s, 2 d. Education: Yan'an Inst for Nationalities and Nationalities Coll of Yan'an Univ. Appointments: Joined CCP, 1942; Lectr and Dep Dir Polit Dept of Nei Mongol Autonomous Coll in Chifeng, 1946; CCP Br Sec and Dir of Nei Mongol Art Troup, 1947-53; Ldng Party Grp Sec and Dep Dir Nei Mongol Cultural Bur, 1954-64; Chmn

Regl Fedn of Lit and Art Circles, 1954-65; Acting mbr Standing Cttee of CCP Cttee Nei Mongol and Sec and Dir of CCP Cttee of Cultural and Educ Commn Nei Mongol, 1966; Sec Municipal Party Cttee of Baotou, 1974-77; Dir Propaganda Dept of CCP Cttee Nei Mongol, 1978; Dep Dir State Nationalities Affairs Commn, 1978-81; Sec CCP Cttee and Mayor of Huhhot Cty, 1978-81; Dep Sec CCP Cttee Nei Mongol, 1981-82; Selected as mbr of CCP Cntrl Cttee, 1982; Dep Sec CCP Cttee and Chmn Provincial Govt Nei Mongol, 1983-; Presidium of 14th CCP Natl Congress, 1992-; Vice-Chmn 8th NPC Standing Cttee, 1993-. Publications: The Basic Knowledge of Autonomy in the Nationalities Region; The Nationalities Theory of Marxism and the Party's Nationalities Policies; The Animal Husbandry in Inner Mongolia Today; In the Sea of Poems - poetry coll; Bu He's Collection of Theses in Literature and Art. Memberships: Mbr 2nd 3rd, th Cncl of Chinese Fedn of Lit and Art Circles. Hobbies: Calligraphy; Lit; Art-Writing. Address: Office of the Regional Governor, Hohhot, Nei Mongol, People's Republic of China.

BUALLAY Kassim Muhammad, b. 15 Mar 1942, Muharraq. Diplomat. m. Satia Buallay, 1969, 2 s, 2 d. Education: Am Univ of Beirut. Appointments: Supvsr Bursaries Sect Min of Educ, 1963-69; Intl Civ Serv UNESCO Paris, 1970-74; Dir of Econ Affairs Min of For Affairs Bahrain, 1979-87; Amb to France, 1974-79; Amb to Tunisia, 1987-94; Perm Rep to UN NY, 1994-. Honours: Ordre nat du Merite France; Decorations of Morocco - Alawite - and Tunisia. Hobbies: Reading; Th; Music; Tennis; Gastronomy. Address: 2 UN Plaza, 25th Floor, New York, NY 10017, USA.

BUCARAM ORTIZ Abdala Jaime, b. 20 Feb 1952. Politician. m. Maria Rosa Pulley Vergara, 3 s, 1 d. Education: Colegio Salesiano 'Cristobal Colon'; Univ Estatal de Guayaquil. Appointments: Rep Ecuador Olympic Games Munich, 1972; Holder of nal Jnr 100m record - 10.5 seconds; A fndr of Ecuador's Naval Sports Fndn; Has been responsible for codes of conduct for sporting orgs etc; Taught at Colegio San Jose La Salle; Taught at trng colls for marines, navy, etc; Gov-Gen of Police Guayas, 1979-80; Advsr to natl Superintendency; Prov Cnclr for Guayas, 1980; Chf Exec Partido Roldosista Ecuatoriano, 1983-85, 1991-93; Mayor of Guayaquil, 1984; Pres Fondo de Desarrollo Urbano de Guayaquil - FODUR - 1984-85; Presdl cand - Partido Roldosista - 1988, 1992; Pres of Ecuador, 1996-; Dir var agricl coml and media cos. Publications: Ideario Politico del Partido Roldosista Ecuatoriano con sus antecedentes historicos: Principios y Estatutos; Principios de Liberacion Nacional; Principios de Justicia Social; Principios de Democracia; Principios de Politica Humanistica; Principios de Libertad; Desarrollo Economico; Principios de Politica Internacional; Las verdades de Abdala; Roldos y Abdala: Epopeya del pensamiento ecuatoriano. Honours: Fell Partido Roldosista Ecuatoriano, 1982; Num sporting awds at natl and regl level inclng Vicecampeon Sudamericano de Atletismo. Hobbies: Football; Athletics; Basketball. Address: Presidential Palace, Guayaquil, Ecuador.

BUCHANAN Ian B, b. 12 Apr 1947, Newcastle-Upon-Tyne, Eng. Vice President, Partner - Management Consultant. m. Siena Dune, 4 Sept 1982, 3 s. Education: MA, Magdalen Coll, Oxford, Eng; MBA, Wharton, Phila, 1972. Appointments: Exec Dir, ASEAN Dev Fin Co Ltd, 1972-84; Regl VP, SRI Intl, 1984-94; Booz Allen & Hamilton, 1994-. Honours: Jex-Blake Awd, Oxford Univ, 1968; Thouron Awd, Thouron Fellshp, PHila, 1970. Memberships: Asian Strategy & Leadership Inst, Malaysia; South Bank Ventures; Computer Power Grp, Aust; GE, Singapore; Natl Computer Bd. Hobies: Scuba diving; Sailing; Flying. Address: 10 Collyer Quay #05-01 Ocean Building, Singapore 049315.

BUCKLEY Jonathan David, b. 4 Dec 1963, Manchester, Eng. Physiologist. Div, 1 s. Education: BAppSc, Exercise and Sports Sci; BS (Hons); PhD. Appointments: Lectr in Physiology/Biochemistry, Univ of S Aust. Publications: Lactate Disposal in Resting Trained and Untrained Forearm Skeletal Muscle During High

Intensity Leg Exercise, 1993; Reduced Performance in Male and Female Athletes at 580 Altitude, 1997; Effect of an Oral Bovine Colostrum Supplement (Intact TM) on Running Performance, 1998. Honours: Austl Postgrad Rsch Awd, 1992-95; Astra Prize, Austl Physiological and Pharmacological Soc, 1993. Hobbies: Golf; Sports performance. Address: c/o School of Physical Education, Exercise and Sport Studies, University of South Australia, Holbrooks Road, Underdale, South Australia, 5032.

BUCKLEY Neil John (Hon Justice), b. 30 Dec 1944, Toowoomba, Qld, Aust. Judge. m. Helen Ann Carew, 13 Jan 1968, 2 s, 1 d. Appointments: Admitted as Solicitor, 1968; Ptnr, MG Lyons & Co, 1969-83; Justice of the Family Crt of Aust, 1983; Judge Admnstr of the Northern Region (Qld, NT), 1988-96; Judge Admnstr of the Northern Area (Qld, NT, NSW), 1996-99; Snr Admnstv Judge (Natl), 1999-. Publication: Report of the Working Party on the Review of the Family Court, 1990. Memberships: Family Law Cttee, Qld Law Soc, 1974-83; Family Law Cncl, 1977-83; Family Law Cttee, Law Cncl of Aust, 1978-83; Cncl Mbr, 1989; Bd Mngmt Mbr, 1992, Pres, 1996-98; Austl Inst of Judicial Admin; Mbr, Qld Domestic Violence Cncl, 1994-97. Hobbies: Rugby Union; Golf. Address: Family Court of Australia, GPO Box 9991, Brisbane, Qld 4001, Australia.

BUDDLE J Ross, b. 4 June 1942, Wellington, NZ. Veterinary Surgeon. m. Glenda Lawn, 14 May 1966, 1 s. 2 d. Education: BSc; BVSc; DVPH; FACVSc. Appointments: Vet Surg; Vet Advry Offr, Pigs; Vet Investigation Offr; Snr Lectr. Publications: Books: Animal Health in Australia, Vol 6, Bacterial and Fungal Diseases of Pigs, 1985; The Diagnosis of the Diseases of the Pigs, 1987, 1999. Memberships: Fell, Aust Coll of Vet Scientists, 1986; Austl Vet Assn. Hobbies: Landscape painting; Tennis; Jazz; Scuba diving. Address: School of Veterinary Clinical Science, Division of Veterinary and Biomedical Sciences, Murdoch University, Murdoch, WA 6150, Australia.

BUFFETT Alice Inez, b. 6 Mar 1931, Norfolk Island. Author; Specialist Linguist; Artist. Education: Undergrad Arts II, Sydney Univ. Appointments: Mbr, First Norfolk Island Legis Assembly, 1981-82; Mbr, 2nd Norfolk Island Legis Assembly, 1982-83; Mbr, 3rd Norfolk Island Legis Assembly, 1983-86; Min, 5th Norfolk Island Legis Assembly, 1989-91. Publications: Speak Norfolk Today, 1988; Annual Histl Illustrated Bi-Lingual Calendars, 14 consecutive yrs; Sev articles, paintings, 2 books: From Coconuts to Computers, 1998; Simple Spelling System for A Universal Auxiliary Language, 1998. Honours: Queen Vic Schlshp, 1945; Winston Churchill Fellshp, 1986; WOY, ABI, 1994-95; WPY, ABI, 1997; MOIF, IBC, 1995; Medal, Order of Aust, 1998. Memberships: Commonwealth Parly Assn, 1981-98; Churchill Fell, 1986; Order of Aust Assn, 1998. Hobbies: World Peace Strategies; Human relationships and intercultural communication. Address: PO Box 338, Norfolk Isand 2899, Via Australia.

BUI Khanh The, b. 18 June 1936, Binh Thuan. Professor of Linguistics. m. Ng T Mao, 20 Sept 1967, 1 s, 1 d. Education: Dr I of Arts (Philology), Natl Univ of Hanoi, DRVN Min of Higher Educ & Voctl Trng, 1981. Appointments: Tchr, Lit & Philology Dept of Univ of Hanoi; Sec, Lit & Philology Dept of Univ of Hanoi; Mbr, Bd of Vietnam-Soviet Eds, compiling books on langs of minorities in Vietnam, 1978-83; VP, Univ of Ho Chi Minh Cty; Ldr, Higher Educl Experts in Campuchea; Dirm Univ Cntr for Vietnam & SE Asia Studies, Prof I; Dean, Fac of Oriental Studies; Publications: 12 in Vietnamese or Russian inclng; The Cham Language (co-auth, Russian); The Ksing Mul Language (co-auth, Russian), 1990; Vietnamese for Foreigners, Reading and Comprehension (Selected Text and Notes), 1994; Mnong-Vietnam Dictionary (co-ed), 1994; The Mnong Langauge - An Applied Grammar, 1994; Cham-Vietnamese Dictionary (co-auth), 1995; Vietnamese-Cham Dictionary (co-auth), 1996; A Cham Grammar, 1997; Over 50 articles in Vietnamese. Honours include: Friendship of the 3rd Order, Govt of Kampuchea; 1st Order Medal "First Resistance for National Liberation, Govyt of Vietnam;

Congratulatory Certificate "Ten Years of Peace Construction, Chmn of Mins Cncl; Title: Front-Rank Tchr, successive yrs, Univ of Hanoi. Membership: Exec Cttee, Linguistics Soc of Vietnam; Folklore Soc of Vietnam. Hobbies: Swimming; Table tennis. Address: 57/ 33-34, Pham Ngoc Thach Dist 3, Ho Chi Minh City, Vietnam.

BUI Van Ba, (Phong Luu), b. 27 June 1936, Vietnam. Professor of Literary Theory. m. Phuong Thi, 23 Jan 1965, 1 s, 1 d. Education: LLD. Appointments: Hd, Lit Theory Section, 1980, Dir, Sinology Cntr, 1992, Hanoi Pedagogic Univ. Publications include: Principles of National Characters in Literature, 1983; Make and Research of the Modern Western Literary Theory, 1995; Chinese Culture and Literature with some Relations in Vietnam, 1996; Broadening the Flow of Theory, 1997; Literary Theory (ed), 3 vols, 1986-88. Honour: SRV's Eminent Tchr, 1992. Membership: Chmn, Theoretical and Critical Cncl, Vietnam Writers Assn, 1995. Hobbies: Eastern and Western poetic art. Address: 21 T1 Quanhoa, Caugiay, Hanoi, Vietnam.

BULL Brian, b. 25 Sept 1933, Subiaco, Australia. Retired Commissioner of Police. m. Patricia Cox, 3 July 1954, 1 s. Education: Dip, Legal Studies, Perth Coll. Appointment: Cmmnr, WA Police Force, 1985-94. Honours: AO, 1999; APM; Paul Harris Fell. Memberships: State VP, Soc of St Vincent de Paul, WA; Pres, Police Histl Soc, WA; Patron, Safety House of WA; Patron, Police Pipe Band; Rotary Clb. Hobby: Military History. Address: 10 Eldwick Loop, Swan View, WA 6056, Australia.

BULLOCK Brian, b. 26 Sept 1934, Sydney, NSW. Aust. Barrister and Solicitor; Company Manager. m. Janice Claire (née Whaling), 23 Aug 1967, 1 s, 1 d. Education: Admitted as Solicitor of Supreme Crt of NSW, 1957; Mbr, Austl Inst of Co Dirs; Fell, Inst of Copr Mngrs, Secs and Admnstrs; Fell, Inst of Chartered Secs. Appointments include: Prac as Sol, Sydney, 1957-70; Co Sec, Arnotts Ltd, 1970-74; Sec and Coml Dir, Leyland Aust Ltd, 1974-80; Co Sec and Mngr Coml and Legal Affairs, Aust Oil and Gas Corp Ltd, Sydney, 1980-. Memberships: Law Soc of NSW; Austl Col Law Assn; Austl Mining and Pet Law Assn; Law Cncl of Aust; Inst of Chartered Secs and Admnstrs; Inst of Corp Mngrs, Secs and Admnstrs; Austl Inst of Co Dirs; Austl Mines and Metals Assn, mbr Bd Advsry Grp, 1990-; Intl Assn of Drilling Contractors, Dir, 1989-; Austl Drilling Ind Cttee, Dir, 1995-98, Chmn, 1998-. Address: C/o Australian Oil & Gas Corporation Limited, 74 Castlereagh Street, Sydney, NSW 2000, Australia.

BULLOCK Sandra, b. 22 July 1966. Actress. Education: East Carolina Univ. Appointments: Grew up in Germany and Wash DC; Frequent appearances on Eurn stage with opera-singer mother; Appeared in off-Bradway prodns inclng No Time Flat - WPA Th; TV roles in The Preppy Murder - film; Lucky Chances - mini-series; Working Girl - NBC series. Films: Love Potion 9; The Vanishing; The Thing Called Love; When The Party's Over; Demolition Man; Wrestling Ernest Hemingway; Speed; While You Were Sleeping; Two If By Sea; Moll Flanders; A Time to Kill; In Love and War; Dir Making Sandwiches, 1996; Speed 2. Address: UTA, 9560 Wilshire Blvd, Fl 5, Beverly Hills, CA 90212, USA.

BUNCE Pauline Daphne, b. 22 Sept 1949, Eng. Lecturer; Teacher. Education: BA (UWA); MEd (UWA); MA (Deakin). Appointments: second sch tchng in WA, 1971-81; Overseas tchng and lecturing, India, Sri Lanka, Brunei, Malaysia, Hong Kong, 1982-99. Publications: Cocos Malay Culture, 1987; The Cocos (Keeling) Islands - Australian Atolls in the Indian Ocean, 1988. Honour: Citizenship Awd, Cocos (Keeling) Islands, 1988. Memberships: MACE; FRGS; FRAI. Hobbies: Travel; Photography; Outdoor adventure sports. Address: PO Box 267, Claremont, Western Australia 6010, Australia.

BUNE Poseci Waqalevu, b. 9 Sept 1946, Suva, Fiji. Diplomat. Education: Admnstv course, Roy Inst Pub Admin, London, Eng, 1970; For Serv course, Canberra, Aust, 1973; French Lang trng. Dakar Univ, Senegal, 1975. Appointments: Admnstv Cadet, 1966, Admnstv Offr, 1971, Snr Admnstv Offr, 1972, Fiji Pub Serv Dept; Under Sec Home Affairs, Suva, Fiji, 1972-73; Attached Austl Emb, Bangkok, Thailand, July-Aug 1973; 2nd Sec, 1973-74, 1st Sec, 1974-75, Fiji Miss, UN, NYC, 1973-74; Mbr Fiji Delegation, 28th Session, UN Gen Assembly, 1973, Intl Conv Elimination of All Forms Racial Discrimination, NYC, Jan 1974, 56th Session, ECOSOC, Apr 1974, World Conf Pop, Bucharest, Rumania, Aug 1974, 29th Session UN, Sept 1974; Under-Sec For Affairs, Suva, Feb-Mar 1975; Cnslr, Fiji Miss. EEC, 1976-80; Mbr, Fiji Delegation to Annual ACP Ministerial Confs, to ACP-EEC Ministerial Negotiations on 2nd Lome Conv, to Annual ACP-EEC Sugar Negotiations; Fiji's Deleg, World Conf to Combat Racism and Racial Discrimination, Geneva, Aug 1978; Mbr, Fiji Delegation, Biennial Session, FAO Conf, Rome, July-Aug 1979; Dir Indl Rels, Fiji Pub Serv Commn, 1980-81; Attended Conf Integrated Rural Dev, Shanghai-Peking, China, Aug 1983; Divisional Commnr, West Div, Min Rural Dev, Fiji, 1981-85; Fiji's Amb to Eurn Communities, Amb to Belgium, Luxembourg, Netherlands, France, Italy, 1985-87; Perm Sec Pub Serv, 1987-89; Mbr, Fiji Delegation, ESCAP Annual Sessions, 1988-90; Perm Sec to Govt and Pub Serv, 1990; Perm Sec Tourism, 1992; Perm Sec Hlth, 1993; Perm Sec Tour and Civil Aviation, 1994; Sec Pub Serv, 1994; Perm Rep Fiji to UN, NYC, 1995-. Address: 630 Third Avenue, 7th Floor, New York, NY 10017, USA.

BUNGER Debra, b. 12 Apr 1959, KY, USA. Psychiatrist. m. Christopher Cherpas, 2 d. Education: MD, Univ Louisville Sch of Med; Internshp, Cabrini Medl Cntr; Res, Boston Univ. Appointments: Pres of Medl Staff, Fremont Hosp; Medl Dir, St Lukes, 1992-97; Dir, 1997-. Memberships: Amn Psych Assn; Northern CA Psych Assn. Address: 39007 Sundale Dr, Fremont, CA 94538, USA.

BUNKLE Phillida, b. 28 Feb 1944, Sussex, England. Member of Parliament; Tertiary Teacher; Community Activist. m. 14 June 1971, separated 1992, 1 s, 1 d. Education: BA, Hons, Keele Univ, 1967; MA, Hons, Smith Coll, 1969; Kennedy Fellshp, Harvard Grad Sch of Arts and Scis, 1969-71. Appointments: Lectr, Women's Stdies, Univ MA, 1971-72; Lectr, US Hist, 1973-75, Snr Lectr, Women's Stdies, 1975-, Vic Univ; Alliance Spokeswomen for Hlth; MP, Alliance, 1996. Publications: Across the Counter: The Lives of the Working Poor in New Zealand, 1990; Second Opinion: The Politics of Women's Health in New Zealand, 1987; New Zealand Women 1985-1995: Markets and Inequality, 1996. Honours: Kennedy Fellshp, 1969-71; Human Rights Awd, NZ Humanist Soc, 1989; Spec Awd, Sir David Beattie Prize in Jrnlsm, 1987; Hodge Fellshp, 1990. Memberships: Chair, NZ Second Sweating Cmmn (Cmmnd by the Distribution Unions), 1990; Life Mbr, NZ Distribution Wrker's Union, 1991. Hobbies: Women's Health Activist; Advocate for Patients' Rights. Address: c/o Parliament House, Wellington, New Zealand.

BUNNAG Marut, b. 21 Aug 1925, Bangkok. Politician. m. Phantipha Bunnag, 2 c. Education: Thammasat Univ. Appointments: With Min of Jus until 1952; Law prac, 1952-; Min of Jus, 1979; MP, 1983; Min of Pub Hlth, 1983-86, Sept-Dec 1990; Min of Educ, 1988; Dep Ldr Dem Party. Address: c/o Ministry of Public Health, Devavesm Palace, Samsen Road, Bangkok 10200, Thailand.

BUNYAN Ruth Elizabeth, b. 16 July 1940. Educator. m. Dr Peter James Bunyan, 4 Jan 1963, 1 s, 2 d. Education: BSc, Dip Ed, Univ Melbourne; MACE; MACEA. Appointments: Maths Tchr, Geelong hs, Vic, 1962; Haematologist, Mater Hosp, Newcastle, NSW, 1964; Maths Lectr, Vic Coll of Pharm, 1966; Maths Tchr, Mitcham hs, 1973; Chf of Staff, Presby Ladies' Coll, Melbourne, 1977; Dpty Prin, St Margaret's Sch, Berwick, 1987; Prin, Strathcona BGGS, 1990-. Publications: Reg contrbs to educ jrnls. Memberships: Invergowrie Fndn; Austl Coll Educ; Univ Coll Cncl; RACV Club; Assn of Hds of Indep Schs of Aust. Hobbies: Travel; Reading; Music;

Theatre; Tennis. Address: 34 Scott Street, Canterbury, Vic 3126, Australia.

BUR Dominique, b. 28 Dec 1947, Monswiller, Bas-Rhin. High Commissioner. m. 3 children. Education: Degree in Law, Strasbourg; Inst of Pol Stdies, Strasbourg; Dip, Higher Stdies, Pub Law, Paris; Natl Sch of Admin. Appointments: Stud, Natl Sch of Admin, 1973-75; Dir, Cabinet of Prefecture, Main-et-Loire, 1975-78; Dir of Cabinet, Prefecture Seine-Saint-Denis, 1978-81; Auditor, State Cncl (Mobility), 1981-83; Min of Interior, Gen Directive of Local Cmnty, 1983-90; Dir of Cabinet of the Dir Gen, Local Cmnty; Dpty Dir, Local Fin and Econ, 1985-90; Dir, Intl Migrations Off, 1990-93; Dir, Pol Affairs, Admin and Fin, Overseas, High Offl of Def, Min of Depts and Outside Territories, 1993-95; Prefect, Govt Deleg, New Caledonia and the Wallis Isles and Futune, High Commnr, Repub of New Caledonia, 1995-.

BURBAN Bob, b. 11 Aug 1947, Germany. Geologist; Exploration Manager. Education: Associate Ballarat Sch of Mines, ABSM (Geol). Appointments: Chf Geologist (Houston Oil & Minerals); Mngr, Corp Plng & Exploration (Queensland Metals Corp); Dir, Exploration (Barramindi Gold Ltd); Discovered the Kunwarara Magnesite Deposit in Queensland, 1985. Memberships: FAustIMM; MGSA; MASEG. Address: 45 Lachlan Road, West Sunshine, Vic 3121, Australia.

BURG Josef, b. 31 Jan 1909 Dresden Germany. Politician. m. Rivka Slonim, 1943, 1 s, 2 d. Education: Univs of Berlin and Leipzig; Pedagogical Inst Leipzig; Rabbinical Seminary Berlin; Hebrew Univ Jerusalem. Appointments: Dir Palestine Off Berlin, 1936; Natl Exec Mizrachi; Zionist Gen Cncl, 1939-51; Dep Speaker First Knesset - Israel Parl - 1949-51; Min of Hlth Govt of Israel, 1951-52; Min of Posts and Telegraphs, Dec 1952-58; Min of Socl Welfare, 1959-70; Min of the Interior, 1970-76; Min of Interior and Police, 1977-84; Chmn Israeli Cabinet Cttee on Autonomy Negotiations with Egypt, 1978-82; Min of Relig Affairs, 1985-86; Intl Cttee Yad Vashem; Pres Natl Relig World Movement; Chmn Ministerial Cttees on Jerusalem; Dev of the Galilee; Crime Prevention and Cabinet procedures; Natl Relig Party. Memberships: Mbr Exec Hapoel Hamizrachi, 1944-. Address: Yad Vashem, Jerusalem, Israel.

BURGESS Marion Anne, b. 4 Apr 1948. Acoustician. m. Michael Burgess, 2 Oct 1971. Education: BSc, hons, Sydney; MSc, Acoustics, Univ NSW. Appointments: Physt, Expmtl Bldng Station, 1969; Lectr, Sch Arch, Univ NSW, 1974-85; Rsch Offr, Acoustics and Vibration Unit, Austl Def Force Acady, 1986-. Publications: Num publns on Acoustics. Memberships: Austl Acoustical Soc; Ed, Acoustics Aust. Hobbies: Walking; Gardening; Reading. Address: Acoustics and Vibration Unit, Australian Defence Force Academy, Canberra, ACT 2600, Australia.

BURKE Brian Thomas, b. 25 Feb 1947, Perth. Politician; Diplomat. m. Susanne May Nevill, 1965, 4 s, 2 d. Education: Marist Brothers Coll; Univ of WA. Appointments: Jrnlst WA Newspapers, 6 PM and TVW CHannel 7, 1965-70; Opposition Shadow Min, 1976-83; Ldr, 1981-83; Premier of WA State Treasr; Min for Women's Interests, 1983-88; Min of Tourism and Forests, 1983-85; Min Co-ordng Econ and Socl Dev, 1983-87; Amb to Ireland and the Holy See, 1988-91; Bus consultant; Labor. Memberships: Mbr Legis Ass for Balcatta - now Balga - 1973-83. Hobbies: Stamp-collecting; Swimming; Fishing; Reading; Writing poetry. Address: P O Box 668, Scarborough, WA 6019, Australia.

BURKE Colleen Zeita, b. 3 Feb 1943, Sydney, Aust. Poet; Author. m. Declan, dec, 1 s, 1 d. Education: BA, Sydney Univ, 1974. Appointments: Shorthand Typist, GIO, 1959-67; Brit Film and TV Union, 1972; Rsch Asst, 1974-75, Cmty Worker, 1975-87, Roy Prince Alfred Hosp; Writer-in-Cmty, Lit Bd, Aust Cncl, 1985-94; Tutor, Adult and Cmnty Educ, Poetry and Creative Writing, 1981-. Publications: Poetry: Go Down Singing; Hags, Rags and Scripture; The Incurable Romantic; She Moves Mountains; The Edge of It; Wildlife in Newtown; Home

Brewed and Lethal - New and Selected Poems, 1997. Biography: Doherty's Corner - Life and Work of Marie E J Pitt. Honours: 3 Grants, Austl Cncl; Shortlist, NSW Lit Awds, 1993. Memberships: Austl Soc of Auths; Poets Union Inc; NSW Writers' Cntr. Hobbies: Reading; Walking; Irish folk music. Address: 126 Lennox Street, Newtown, Sydney, NSW 2042, Australia.

BURKE Eleanor, b. 29 Mar 1943, Hamilton, Victoria, Australia. Research Director. m. Colin, 2 d. Education: Dip.Arts, Jrnlsm, RMT; MEd, Univ Adelaide. Appointments: Austl Natl Univ Cncl of Family Law & Cncl of Aust. Honour: Fell, Austl Coll of Educn, 1986-. Memberships: Austl Inst of Aboriginal & Island Studies, 1978-. Address: Aboriginal Research Institute, University of South Australia, Holbrooks Road, Underdale, SA 5032, Australia.

BURKE John Brian, b. 6 Feb 1946, Invercargiull, NZ. Mayor. m. Linda Christina Horton, 6 June 1967, 2 s. Appointments: Porirua Cty Cnclr, 1971-83; Mayor of Poriua, 1983-; Mbr, Hutt Val Energy Bd, 1974-90; Chmn, HVEB, 1986-90; Mbr, Wellington Harbour Bd, 1980-83; Mbr, Porirua Licensing Trust Bd, 1989-; Chmn, Energy Direct Community Trust, 1990-; Dir, Energy Direct Corp, 1993-96; VP, NZ Elec Supply Assn, 1989-90; Pres, Sister Cities NZ, 1996; Dir, Transalta NZ, 1996-. Honours: JP, 1983; QSO, 1989; NZ Commemoration Medal, 1990. Membership: Assoc Fell, NZ Inst Mngmt, 1989. Hobbies: Gardening; Jogging; Fitness; Music. Listed in: Who's Who in New Zealand; New Zealand Who's Who in Aotearoa. Address: 12 Bay Drive, Titahi Bay, New Zealand.

BURKE Thomas Kerry (Sir), b. 24 Mar 1942, Christchurch. politician m. 2nd Helen Paske, 1984, dec 1989, 1 s - 2 s from 1st m. Education: Univ of Canterbury; Christchurch Tchrs Coll. Appointments: Gen labourer in Auckland, 1965-66; Factory deleg Auckland Labourers' Union; Tchr Rangiora High Sch, 1967; Chmn Rangiora Post-Primary Tchrs Assn, 1969-71; MP for Rangiora, 1972-75; Tchr for Greymouth High Sch, 1975-78; MP for West Coast, 1978-; Min of Regl Dev and of Employment and Immigration, 1984-87; Speaker NZ Parl, 1987-91; Labour. Hobbies: Skiing; Swimming. Address: Karntnerstrasse 4/17, 1010 Vienna, Austria.

BURNEY Sayed Muzaffir Hussain, b. 14 Aug 1923, Bulandshahr, Uttar Pradesh. Politician. Appointments: Entered Indian Admin Serv; Var posts inclng Jnt Sec Min of Agric, 1965-72; Additional Sec in Min of Pet and Chems, 1973-75; Sec Min of Info and Brdcstng, 1975-77; Served Orissa Govt as Div Commnr and Chf Sec, 1979-80; Sec Min of Home Affairs, 1980-81; Gov of Nagaland Manipur and Tripura then Haryana, 1984-88. Publications: Many articles in English and Urdu on lit subjs and pub admin. Address: F-3/17, Vasant Vihar, New Delhi 110057, India.

BURNS Gillian Mary, b. 16 May 1963, Tamworth, Aust. Veterinarian. m. G J Haste, 1 s. Education: BS, Agric; DVM. Memberships: Amn Vet Medl Assn; Austl Vet Assn; Austl Equine Vet Assn; Amn Assn of Equine Practitioners. Hobbies: Dressage Riding; Jrnlsm; Photog; Scuba Diving. Address: PO Box 676E, Earlville, QLD 4870, Australia.

BURR Daryl, b. 24 Feb 1939, Geelong. Radio Programs Manager. m. Anne, 11 May 1968, 2 d. Education: Master of Educl Stdies; Bach of Educ. Appointments: Presenter, ECB FM, 1991; Programming Offl Appts, 1991-98; Convenor, Mngr, Presenter, Satellite, Sat FM, 1998. Memberships: East FM Radio, Cttee of Mngmt, 1991-; Prog Convenor. Hobbies: Music; Movies; Collectables. Address: PO Box 6054, North Croydon, Vic 3136, Australia.

BURRELL Christopher John, b. 8 Nov 1941. Medical Virologist. m. Margaret Eileen Cobb, 23 Dec 1970, 2 s. Education: BS, Med, 1964; MBBS, 1965, Univ Sydney; PhD, ANU, 1971; MRCPath, 1977; FRCPA, 1980; FRCPath, 1989. Appointments: Lectr, Bacterial Edinburgh Univ, 1971-79; Med Specialist, IMVS, Adelaide, 1979-85; Hd, Div of Med and Virol, IMVS,

1985-; Hd, Dept Microbiol and Immunol, Univ of Adelaide, 1990-. Publications: Over 100 sci articles on medl virology and related topics, 1970-. Honours: Wellcom Aust Medal and Awd, 1984. Memberships: Austl Soc of Microbiol (virol Convenor), 1988-91; Amn Soc Microbiol; Soc Gen Microbiol (UK). Hobbies: Sailing; Music. Address: Department of Microbiology & Immunology, University of Adelaide, Adelaide, SA 5000, Australia.

BURRELL Thomas Ross, b. 22 Sept 1927, Aust. Stockbroker. m. Margaret Thatcher, 28 Nov 1952, 3 s. Education: Assoc Acctcy , Univ Qld. Appointments: Mbr, 1957-, Cttee Mbr, 1968-80, Chmn, 1973-75, Stock Exchange, Brisbane; Pres, Brisbane Jnr Chmbr of Comm, 1958; Sen, Jnr Chmbr Intl, 1959-; Prin, Burrell & Co, 1959-; Fndn Cnclr, 1966-77, Pres, Queensland Div, 1970-73; Securities Inst of Aust; Cnclr, 1968-80, Pres, 1975-77, Brisbane Chmbr of Com; Cnclr, Aust Assocd Stock Exchs, 1973-75; Pres, Aust Cmbr of Com, 1977-79; Hon Treas, 1978-80, Cnclr, 1978-82, Vp, 1980-82, Confedn of Asian-Pacific Chmbrs of Com and Ind; Mbr, Natl Small Bus Advsry Cncl, 1978-83; Mbr, Com and Econs Fac Bd, Univ Queensland, 1978-80; Treas, 1978-87, Hon Exec Cnclr, 1981-87, World Wildlife Fund, Aust; Chmn, Assembly Bus Orgs, 1979-81; Mbr, Advsry Cncl, Raine Island Corp. Honours: OBE 1980; KCSJ; Paul Harris Fell, 1994. Memberships: FASA; FSIA; Cnclr, Sovereign Order of St John of Jerusalem; Rotary Club Brisbane W, Pres, 1993-94. Hobbies: Swimming; Tennis. Address: Unit 504, Mariners Reach, 57 Newstead Terrace, Newstead, Qld 4006, Australia.

BURROWS Steven Mark, b. 29 Apr 1955, Brisbane, Australia. Magazine Editor. m. Sharlene, 30 Sept 1995, 2 s. Education: Bach Deg, Civil Engrng, Univ NSW, 1978. Appointments: Project Mngr, Aust Post, Sydney, 1980-91; Ed, 1992-, Mngng Dir, 1996-, Skills Publng. Publications: Ed, The Australian Woodworker; House & Home. Membership: Treas, Lawson Chmbr of Comm, 1996-. Hobby: Model Railroading. Address: Skills Publishing Pty Ltd, 8 Livingstone Street, Lawson, New South Wales, Australia.

BURSTON Samuel Gerald Wood (Sir), b. 24 Apr 1915, Adelaide, SA, Aust. Grazier. m. (1) Verna Helen Peebles, 1940, dec 1980, 1 s, 1 d, (2) Phyllis Elaine Irwin, 1995. Appointments: Grazier, 1937-; Maj, MID, Austl Imperial Force, 1940-45; Pres, Victorian Rural Fire Brigs Assn, 1960-64; Chmn, Country Fire Authy, Vic, 1964-65; Pres, Graziers Assn Vic, 1973-76; Pres, Austl Woolgrowers and Graziers Cncl, 1976-79; VP, Fedn Austl Ind, 1977; Dir, Reserve Bank Aust, 1977-87; Mbr, Austl Sci and Technological Cncl, 1977-87; Chmn, Perpetual Trees and Executors, Melbourne, 1980-87; Chmn, Austl Pastoral Rsch Trust, 1988-94; Mbr, Austl Mfng Cncl; Mbr, Austl Trade Dev Cncl. Honours: OBE, 1966; Kt, 1977. Hobbies: Golf; Tennis. Address: 112 Brougham Place, North Adelaide, SA 5006, Australia.

BURTON Gregory Keith, b. 12 Feb 1956. Barrister; Arbitrator; Mediator; Author. m. Suzanne Brandstater, 19 Dec 1984, 1 s, 1 d. Education: BCL (Oxon), 1984; BA (Hons) (Syd), 1978; LLB (Hons) (Syd), 1980; Admitted to prac in NSW, High Crt and Fed Crts, Vic, ACT, WA, NT, Qld, Ireland. Appointments: Solicitor, 1980-83; Assoc to High Crt Justice, Sir William Deane, 1984-85; Priv Sec/Legal Advsr, Fed Shadow Att-Gen, 1986; Lectr, 1987-88; Priv prac, 1989-. Publications: Ed or auth, var books, jrnls, legal encyclopedias, articles, conf pprs. Honours: Univ Medal in Hist, 1978; Ed Cttee, Sydney Law Review, 1977, 1979. Memberships: Assn Inst Arts and Meds, Aust; Dir, Austl Eliz Th Trust Mbr, Dir, var fndns and charities; NSW Bar Assn; Banking Law Assn; Com Law Assn; CIS; IPA. Hobbies: Sports; Drama; Opera and performing arts; Travel. Address: 5th Floor, Wentworth Chambers, 180 Phillips Street, Sydney, NSW 2000, Australia.

BURTON Tim, b. Burbank, CA. Film Director. Education: CA Arts Inst. Appointments: Began career as animator Walt Disney Studios - projs incld The Fox and the Hound and The Black Cauldron; Animator and dir Vincent - short-length film, awds incl two from Chgo Film

Fest. Films directed: Frankenweenie - short for Disney - 1984; Aladdin; Pee-wee's Big Adventure, 1985; Beetlejuice, 1988; Batman, 1989; Edward Scissorhands, 1991; Batman Returns, 1992; Producer The Nightmare Before Christmas, 1993; Dir Ed Wood, 1994; Dir Batman Forever, 1996; Producer Cabin Boy, 1994; Dir Mars Attacks!, 1996; Producer James and the Giant Peach, 1996. Publication: My Art and Films, 1993. Address: Chapman, Bird & Grey, 1990 South Buny Drive, Suite 200, Los Angeles, CA 90025, USA.

BURTON STOCKER Bertha, b. 19 Apr 1949, Columbia, SC, USA. Case Management Specialist. m. Herbert, 24 Nov 1994. Education: BA, 1971, MSW, 1974, Johnson C Smith Univ Charlotte, NC, USA; Univ of SC, 1974. Publications: Is There Hospitality in the House?; Family and Corrections Network, 1989. Honour: Cum Laude, 1971. Membership: Delta Sigma Theta Sorority. Hobbies: Reading; Jogging; Swimming; Personal Development. Address: Friends Outside CTF; PO Box 686, Soledad, CA 93960-0686, USA.

BUSHBY Michael Bruce, b. 6 Jan 1959, Launceston, Australia. Civil Engineer. m. Janine, 23 Aug 1983, 1 s, 1 d. Education: BEng; MEng; Bach of Bus. Memberships: Instn of Engrs, Aust; Assn of Profl Engrs, Scis & Mngrs, Aust; Austl Inst of Co Dirs. Hobby: Water Skiing. Address: PO Box 386, Rosny Park, Tasmania 7018, Australia.

BUSYE Motinggo, b. 21 Nov 1937, Lampung, Indonesia. Novelist. m. Lashmi Bactiar, 24 July 1962, 4 s, 3 d. Education: 1st Cand Law Fac, Gadjah Maua Univ, Yog Yakarta, Indonesia, 1958. Appointments: Freelance Writer, 1950s; Corresp for Petangi mag, Medan, 1955; Corresp for Aneka, film & sport mag, Jakarta, 1957-64; ed, Budaya, Govt lit mag, 1959-61; Ed, Kartini, mag for women, Jakarta, 1974-; Publications: 204 books; Contbr to such mags as Budaya, Siasat, Indonesia, Sastra, Anthology of: Asian Poets, 1986, Seoul, 1995, Asian Poets Taipei; Metaphor Beyond Time: Contemporary World Poets, 1998. Honours: 1st Prize for Playwriting for Malam Jahanam, Dept of Educ & Culture, Indonesia, 1959; 2nd Prize for Short Story for, Nasehat Uniuk Anakku, Majalah Sastra, 1962; Awd for short story, Horison Magazine, 1997. Hobbies: Paintings; Film and Stage directing. Address: Jalan I-36, Utan Kayu Selatan, Jakarta Timur, Indonesia.

BUTALA Dineshchandra Mohanlal, b. 27 July 1948, Himmatnagar, Gujarat, India. Engineer; Executive. m. Aruna, 26 Nov 1976, 2 s. Education: BE Chem Engrng, MSU, Baroda, India, 1970; Dip German, 1973. Appointments: Dpty Gen Mngr, Gujarat State Fertilizers & Chems Ltd, Baroda, 1970-; Cnslt Chem Engr, Shri Ambuja Petrochem, Hyderabad, 1980-81; Process Mngr, Gujarat Nylons Ltd, Kosamba, 1988-89; Expert on Deputation to Uhde GmbH, Dortmund, Germany, 1989; Cora Engrng, Chur, Switzerland, 1978. Publications: Contbr, articles to profl jrnls. Honours: Intl Soc for Ion Ex, Poland, 1978; 2nd Best Ppr Prize, 1994. Memberships: AICHE; Indian Inst of Chem Engrs; Natl Geo Soc; Exec Mbr, Baroda Jaycees; Fertilizer Assn of India. Hobbies: Trekking; Swimming; Photography; Reading. Address: Gujarat State Fertilizers & Chemicals Ltd, Fertilizernagar, 391750, India.

BUTCHER David John, b. 19 Sept 1948, Brighton, Eng. Economist. m. Mary Georgina Hall, 20 Dec 1980, 2 d. Education: BA Hons. Appointments: Economist, Dept Labour, 1972-74; Field Offr, Clerical Workers Union, NZ Labourers Union, 1976-79; Elected MP, NZ Parl, 1978; Parly Under-Sec, Agric, Lands and Forests, NZ, 1978-87; Min Energy, Com, Regl Dev, Fin, 1987-90; Mngng Dir, David Butcher & Assocs, 1991-98. Publication: The Forum Island Countries and the Single European Market, 1993; Num rprts and articles publshd. Honours: Title of Hon, 1987; Commemorative Medal, 1990. Memberships: NZ Assn Economists; NZ Inst Pub Admin; NZ Inst of Mngmt; NZ Soc for Strategic Mngmt. Hobbies: Tramping; Reading; Music; Computers; Genealogy. Address: 13-15 Manewa Road, Hataitai, Wellington, New Zealand.

BUTCHER Elizabeth Ann, b. 19 May 1938, NSW, Aust. Administrator. Education: Leaving Ctf; SCEGGS, Darlinghurst. Appointments: Sec, Butcher & Heaton Accts, 1959; Admin Sec, Intl Convention of Archs, 1962; Sec to Dir, Inst of Dental Rsch & Clin Rsch Supvsr to Dean, Univ of Sydney, 1963-67; Rsch Co-ord, Proctor & Gamble, OH, USA, 1968-69; Admnstr, Natl Inst of Dramatic Art, Kensington, NSW, 1969-; Seconded as Asst Dir, Divsn of Cultural Activities, 1978; Interim Admnstr, Sydney Th Co, 1979. Honour: AO, 1984. Memberships: Aust Cncl, 1982-84; Chmn, Th Bd of Aust Cncl, 1982-85; Seymour Cntr Mngmt Bd, 1984-; Sydney Opera House Trust, 1986-89; Chmn, Sydney Opera House Trust, 1989-. Hobbies: Theatre; Opera; Ballet; Lace-making; Gardening. Address: c/o NIDA, Kensington, NSW 2033, Australia.

BUTLER Dorothy, b. 12 Sept 1911, Australia. Physiotherapist. 2 s, 2 d. Education: Dip, Physiotherapy. Appointments include: Roy Alexander Hosp for Children, 1935, 1937-39; Melbourne Womens Hosp, 1942. Publication: The Barefoot Bushwalker. Memberships: Sydney Bushwalkers Soc. Hobbies: Bushwalking; Mountaineering; Skiing. Address: 7 Terrigal Avenue, Turramurra 2074, Australia.

BUTLER James Keith, b. 31 Oct 1961, Memphis, Tennessee, USA. Chemist. m. Suzanne, 22 Oct 1983. Education: BS, Chem, Union Univ, Jackson, TN, 1983; MS, Inorganic Chem, Memphis Univ, 1987. Appointments: Formulations Chem, Delta Foremost, 1987; Chem, 1987, Snr Chem, 1988, Chf Chem, 1993, Am Osdnana, Publications: Sev articles in profl jrnls. Membership: Am Chem Soc. Hobby: Golf. Address: 8079 Denney Drive, Milan, TN 38358, USA.

BUTLER William Henry, b. 25 Mar 1930, Subiaco, Aust. Conservation Consultant. m. Margaret Alice Elliott, 10 Sept 1967, 2 s, 1 d. Education: Western State Coll, USA, 1966. Appointments: Vermin Hunter, 1942-45; Apprentice Fitter, Turner, 1946-51; Trainee, Advsry Tchr, WA Educn Dept, 1952-63; Self Employed, 1963-; Chmn, NT Pks and Wildlife Commn, 1996-; Chmn, Pilbarn Dev Commn, 1996-. Publications include: Num articles in sci jrnls and many books inclng: In the Wild; Looking at the Wild; Dear Harry. Honours: Hon Field Assn AMNH, 1969; MBE, 1970; Assoc, WAM, 1973; Gold Sammy, 1977; Logie Documentary Awd, 1977; Sammy Documentary Awd, 1977; Penguin Documentary Awd, 1977; Henry Lawson Awd, 1977; Childrens Austl of the Decade, 1980; Austl of the Yr, 1979; Citizen of the Yr, 1980; CBE, 1980; Whitley Awd, 1981; Hon Citizen, Tennant Creek, 1985; Patron, WANPARA, 1979; Spirit of Aust Awd, 1993; AMEEF Individual Awd for Ex, 1993; Friends of the Mus WA, 1995; Golden Gecko Individual Ex Awd, 1995; Butler Medal for Natural Hist. Memberships include: Explorers Club, USA; WA Gould League; Assn of Order of Brit Empire; Can Natl Wildlife Assn. Listed in: Who's Who in Australia; Community Leaders of the World; International Who's Who in Preservation of the Environment; Eye to Eye; International Directory of Distinguished Leadership; 5,000 Personalities of the World; Who's Who in Australasia and the Far East; Infoterra International Directory of Sources; Debrett's Handbook of Australia. Hobbies: Reading; Gardening; Woodwork. Address: GPO Box S1580, Perth, WA, Australia.

BUTROS Albert Jamil, b. 25 Mar 1934 Jerusalem. Diplomatist; Professor of English. m. Ida Maria Albina, 1962, 4 d. Education: London Univ; Univ of Exeter, Eng; Columbia Univ, USA. Appointments: Taught Engl and Maths in two pvte schs, Amman, 1950-55; Instr Tchrs Coll Amman, 1958-60; Lectr in Eng, Hunter Coll, Cty Univ of NY, 1961; Instr Miami Univ, Oxford, OH, 1962-63; Asst Prof of Engl, Univ of Jordan, 1963-65; Assoc Prof, 1965-67; Prof, 1967-69; Acting Chmn Dept of Eng, 1964-67; Chmn, 1967-73, 1974-76; Visng Prof of Eng, OH Wesleyan Univ, Delaware, OH, 1971-72; Dean, Rsch and Grad Stdies, 1973-76; Dir-Gen and Pres, Roy Sci Soc, Amman, 1976-84; Snr Rsch Fell, Intl Dev Rsch Cntr, Ottawa, Can, 1983-84; Spec Advsr to HRH, then Crown Prince, El-Hassan of Jordan, 1984-85; Prof of Engl, 1985-; Gov Intl Dev Rsch Cntr, Ottawa, Can, 1986-; Amb

to UK, 1987-91 - also accred to Ireland 1988-91, Iceland, 1990-91; Visng Prof of Engl, Jordan Univ for Women, Amman, 1995-96. Publications: Leaders of Arab Thought, 1969; Sev articles in learned jrnls; Sev transls. Honours: Istiqlal Order First Class, 1987; Order of Merit, Grande Ufficiale, Italy, 1983; K St J, 1991. Memberships: Bd of Tstees, Philadelphia Univ, Amman, 1995-. Hobbies: Reading; Writing; Translating; Art; World affairs; Walking. Address: P O Box 309, Jubeiha, Amman 11941, Jordan.

BUTT Charles Roy Morton, b. 29 Feb 1944, Wellington, Eng. Exploration Geochemist. m. Fay Margaret Helen Springall, 5 July 1969, 1 s, 2 d. Education: BA, Hons, Geol and Chem, Keele, 1967; DIC, PhD, Applied Geochem, Imperial Coll, London, 1971. Appointments: Div of Mineralogy, CSIRO, 1971; Chf Rsch Scientist, CSIRO Exploration and Mining, 1994; Prog Ldr and Dpty Dir, Coop Rsch Cntr for Landscape Evolution and Mineral Exploration (CRC LEME), 1995; Co-Ed, Jrnl of Geochemical Exploration. Publications: Over 150 pprs, rprts, chapts on exploration geochem and regolith geology; Co-ed, Regolith exploration geochemistry in tropical and sub-tropical terrains, 1992. Honours: Gold Medal, Assn of Exploration Geochemists, 1995; Disting Lectr, AEG, 1996-97; Sci and Technol Awd, Assn of Mining and Exploration Co's, 1997. Memberships: Fell, Assn of Exploration Geochems; Geol Soc of Aust. Address: 14 Orrel Avenue, Floreat Park, WA 6014, Australia.

BUTT Muhammad Amin, b. 14 Feb 1952, Gujrat, Pakistan. Government Official. m. 3 Nov 1980, 1 d. Education: Grad. Appointments: Compositor, Proof Rdr, Asst Controller (Forms), Asst Mngr (publs), Asst Controller (Admin) (HQ), Mngr of Publs. Publications: Compilation of Estacode (acts, ordinances, Pres orders, martial law regulations). Honours: Honorarium during serv, Attended courses of NIPA (Natl Inst of Pub Admin) as well as PIM (Pakistan Inst of Mngmt). Memberships: Lifetime Chmn, Dayyar-E-Habib Trust (Regd) consisting of Mosque and Madrassah. Hobbies: Study of religions; Current affairs; Literature; Playing cricket and tennis. Address: A-15/8 Jouhar Complex, Main University Road, Karachi, Pakistan.

BUTTERFIELD Rex Milton, b. 22 Dec 1921, Adelaide, SA, Aust. Consultant Veterinarian. m. Margaret Caldicot, 10 Jan 1948, 1 s, 1 d. Education: Roseworthy Dip of Agricl, 1941; BVSc, 1950; PhD, 1963; DVSc, 1968. Appointments: Pvte Prac, Vet Surgn, 1950-60; Rsch Stud, 1960-63; Prof of Vet Anatomy, 1966-86; Cnslt, 1987-. Publications: Auth of 3 books; Contbr of 80 sci articles. Honours: Roseworthy Awd of Merit; Urrbrae Prize, Angus Chevalier Awd; Hon DSc, 1996. Memberships: Austl Vet Scis; Amn Meat Sci Assn. Hobbies: Horse racing; Whittling. Address: 93 Lower Valley Road, Hazelbrook, NSW 2779, Australia.

BUTTERLEY Nigel Henry, b. 13 May 1935, Sydney, NSW, Aust. Composer; Pianist; Lecturer. Appointments: Lectr, Contemp Music, Newcastle Conservatorium, 1973-90; Snr Lectr, Newcastle Univ, 1990-91. Creative Works: Recd compositions: Laudes, 1963; In the Head the Fire, 1966; Meditations of Thomas Traherne, orchl, 1968; Violin Concerto, 1970; Explorations for Piano and Orch, 1970; Letter from Hardy's Bay, 1971; First Day Covers (w Barry Humphries), 1973; Fire in the heavens, 1973; Sometimes With One I Love (Whitman), 1976; String Quartet No 3, 1979; Uttering Joyous Leaves for piano, 1981; Goldengrove for orch, 1982; The Owl, vocal, 1983; From Sorrowing Earth for orch, 1991; The Wind stirs gently for flute and cello, 1992; Of Wood, cello, 1995; Other compositions inclng String Quartets No 1, 1965, No 2, 1974, No 4, 1995; Trio for clarinet, cello and piano, 1979; Watershore, radiophonic, 1978; Symphony, 1980; Lawrence Hargrave Flying Alone for piano, 1981; In Passing, orchl, 1982; Il Gubbo for piano, 1987; There Came a Wind Like a Bugle (Emily Dickinson), vocal, 1987; Lawrence Hargrave Flying Alone, opera, 1988; Forest I for viola and piano, 1990; The Woven Light (Kathleen Raine) for soprano and orch, 1994; Spring's Ending (Du Fu), choir, 1997. Honours: Italia Prize for Radiophonic Composition, In the Head the Fire, 1966;

AM, 1991; Austl Artists Creative Fellshp, 1991-95; Hon DMus, Newcasrle, 1996. Address: 57 Temple Street, Stanmore, NSW 2048, Australia.

BUZO Alexander John, b. 23 July 1944, Sydney, Australia. Writer. m. Merelyn, 21 Dec 1968, 3 d. Education: BA, Univ NSW, 1966. Appointments: Res Dramatist, Melbourne Th Co, 1972-73; Res Writer, James Cook Univ, 1985, Univ of Indonesia, 1995. Publications: Books: Tautology, 1980; Kiwese, 1994; Pacific Union, 1995; A Dictionary of the Almost Obvious, 1998. Honours: Gold Medal, Austl Lit Soc, 1973; Alumnae Awd, Univ NSW, 1998. Membership: Deans Cncl, Univ NSW, 1998. Hobbies: Cricket; Swimming; Tennis. Address: 14 Rawson Avenue, Queens Park, NSW 2022, Sydney, Australia.

BYRNE Donald Glenn, b. 21 July 1948. Academic. m. Anne Elizabeth, 1 s. Education: BA (Hons); PhD, Univ of Adelaide. Appointments: Rsch Fell, 1975-79, Snr Lectr, Rdr in Psychol, 1979-95, Prof of Psychol, 1995-, ANU. Publications: 9 books; Over 100 sci pprs in psychol and med, 1975-. Honours: Hon Fell, Polish Acady of Med, 1995. Memberships: Fell, Acady of the Socl Scis in Aust; Fell, Austl Psychol Soc; Fell, Intl Coll of Psychosomatic Med, Pres, 1997-99. Address: Division of Psychology, The Australian National University, Canberra, ACT 0200, Australia.

BYRNE Murray Lewis, b. 29 Aug 1928, Aust. Barrister and Solicitor. m. Adele Byrne, 2 s, 6 d. Education: St Patrick's Coll, Ballarat, Vic; LLB, Univ of Melbourne. Appointments: Bar and Sol, 1952; Mbr, Legis Cncl, Ballarat Prov, 1958-76; Min for Pub Wrks, 1970-73; Dpty Ldr, Upper House, 1971; Ldr, Upper House, 1973-76; Min for State Dev and Decentralization, Tourism and Immigration, 1973-76; Snr Ptnr, Byrne Jones & Torney, Ballarat, 1976-. Honours: Companion of the Most Disting Order of St Michael and St George, 1977; Total Community Devel Awd, 1975; Queen's Medal, 1978; Kt of the Sovereign Mil Order of Malta, 1978; Polonia Restituta, 5th Class, 1980. Memberships: Law Inst of Vic; Fndn Mbr, Assn of Sols Mortgagee Invmnt Cos; Inst of Dirs; Ballarat Club. Hobbies: Tennis; Swimming; Motor Cruiser. Address: 20 Alfred Street, Ballarat, Vic 3350, Australia.

BYRON Julie, b. Sydney, Aust. Author. Publications: Amazing Psychic Experience of the Famous, 1993, Japanese trans, 1995, Portuguese trans, 1998; Articles. Hobbies: Research; Writing. Address: PO Box 3068, Weston Creek, Canberra, ACT 2611, Australia.

BYRON Kenneth William, b. 11 July 1927, Temora, NSW, Aust. Accountant. m. Stella Mavis, 22 Jan 1957, 1 s, 1 d. Appointments: Var positions in pvte enterprise; NSW and Austl Govt Pub Serv. Publications: Lost Treasures in Australia and New Zealand, 1964; Guilty Wretch That I Am, 1984; Treasure Ships and Tropic Isles, 1985; The World's Best Fish Stories, 1994. Membership: Austl Soc of CPA's, fell mbr. Hobbies: Research; Writing; Fossicking for gold and gemstones. Address: 6 Lazar Place, Chapman, ACT 2011, Australia.

C

CAAN James, b. 26 Mar 1940 Bronx NY. Actor; Director. m. (1) DeeJay Mathis 1961, div 1966, 1 d; (2) Sheila Ryan 1976, div 1977, 1 s; (3) Linda O'Gara 1995. Appointments: Made th debut in off-Bradway prodn of La Ronde, 1960; Broadway debut in Blood Sweat and Stanley Poole, 1961; Starred in tv movie Brian's Song, 1971. Films incl: Irma La Douce, 1963; Lady in a Cage, 1964; The Glory Guys, 1965; Countdown, 1967; Games, 1967; Eldorado, 1967; Journey to Shiloh, 1968; Submarine XI, 1968; Man Without Mercy, 1969; The Rain People, 1969; Rabbit Run, 1970; T R Baskin, 1971; The Godfather, 1972; Slither, 1973; Cinderella Liberty, 1975; Freebie and the Bean, 1975; The Gamble, 1975; Funny Lady, 1975; Rollerball, 1975; The Killer Elite, 1975; Harry and Walter Go to New York, 1976; Silent Movie, 1976; A Bridge Too Far, 1977; Another Man, Another Chance, 1977; Comes a Horseman, 1978; Chapter Two, 1980; Thief, 1982; Kiss Me Goodbye, 1983; Bolero, 1983; Gardens of Stone, 1988; Alien Nation, 1989; Dad, 1989; Dick Tracy, 1990; Misery, 1991; For the Boys, 1991; Dark Backward, 1991; Honeymoon in Vegas, 1992; Flesh and Bone, 1993; The Program, 1994; North Star, 1995; Boy Called Hate, 1995; Eraser, 1996; Bulletproof, 1996; Bottle Rocket, 1996; This Is My Father, 1997; Poodle Springs, 1997; Dir and actor: Hide in Plain Sight, 1980; Dir Violent Streets, 1981; Num tv appearances. Address: Licker and Ozurquich, 2029 Century Park E # 500, Los Angeles, CA 90067, USA.

CACERES CONTRERAS Carlos, b. 7 Oct 1940, Valparaiso. Politician. m. Ines Consuelo Salarzano, 3 c. Education: Colegio de los Sagrados Corazones Valparaiso; Univ Catolica de Chile Valparaiso; Cornell Univ Ithaca NY. Appointments: Lectr Dep of Econs and Fin Univ Catolica de Valparaiso Sch of Bus Studs, 1964; Hd Firms and Fins Dept, 1973; Visng Lectr OH State Univ, 1971; Pres Banco Central de Chile, 1982; Fndr Inst of Econ Studs of Paris, 1983; Min of Fin, 1983-84; Min of the Interior, 1988-90. Memberships: Mbr Cncl of State, 1976; Mbr Mont Pelerin Soc, 1981; Mbr Inst of Econ Studs of Paris, 1983.

CADMAN Alan Glyndwr, b. 26 July 1937, Sydney, Australia. Member, House of Representatives; Parliamentary Secretary; Orchidist; Company Director. m. Vera Judith Cadman, 1 Apr 1961, 3 s. Education: Ctf of Agricl, Univ NSW. Appointments include: Elected for Mitchell, 1974, Re-elected, 1975, 1977, 1980, 1983, 1984, 1987, 1990, 1993, 1996, 1998-; Parly Sec to PM, 1981-83; Mbr, Advsry Cncl for Inter-Govt Rels, 1983-85; Shadow Min for Immigration and Ethnic Affairs, 1985-89; Acting Shadow Min for Commns, 1990, Aviation and Tourism, 1991, Snr Citizens and Aged Care, 1994, Immigration and Ethnic Affairs, 1994, Fin, 1994, Small Bus, 1995; Chf Govt Whip, 1996-97; Parly Sec for Workplace Rels and Small Bus, 1997-98. Publications: Sev articles in profl jrnls. Memberships: Lions Club of Baulkham Hills; Rotary Club of Galston and Winston Hills; Offrs Mess, RAAF Base Richmond. Address: Suite 8, 23 Terminus Street, Castle Hill, NSW 2154, Australia.

CAESAR Vance, b. 22 Dec 1944, Newkensington, PA, USA. Executive Coach. m. Carol Ann, 22 Apr 1967, 1 s. Education: BS, The Citadel; MBA, Florida Atlantic Univ; Exec MBA, Stanford Univ; PhD, Waldon Univ. Appointments: Chair, The Profl Coachers & Mentors Assn; CEO, The Vance Caesar Grp; Pres, PEH Publng Jnr. Publications: Run Easy, Run Hard How to Be a High Achiever and Still Like Yourself, 1998; Success is Not Normal, A Guide to Joy Fullness For Successful People, 1998. Honour: Lifetime Hon, Mem Med Cntr, Long Bch, CA, 1998. Hobbies: Mountaineering; Writing and Coaching. Address: 3020 Old Ranch Parkway, 3rd Floor, Seal Beach, CA 90740, USA.

CAFFREY Bradford A, b. 4 June 1938, USA. Lecturer in Law; Barrister. m. 23 Aug 1975. Education: BA, Johns Hopkins Univ, 1957; LLB, La Salle Univ, 1959; LLM, Univ Sydney, Aust, 1969; DipEd, Univ WA, Aust, 1974; PhD,

Intl Inst Advd Stdys, 1983; Dr Jur, Univ Tübingen, Germany, 1984. Appointments: Legal Offr, IBM, 1967-69; Lectr, Law, Mitchell Coll Advd Educ, 1970-71; Lectr, Law, WA Inst Technol, 1972-74; Lectr, Law, Univ NSW, 1974-80; Legal Cnslt, Purchasing Intl Pty Ltd, 1980-83; Lectr, Law, Darling Downs Inst Adult Educ, 1984-87; Legal Offr, Supply 2000 Pty Ltd, NSW, 1987-; Bar at Law, 1991-. Publications include: Many articles; Books inclng: Enforcement of Foreign Judgments, Guidebook to contract law in Australia. Memberships: Austl Soc Legal Philos; Intl Bar Assn; NSW Bar Assn. Address: 8 Eden Place, Caringbah, NSW 2229, Australia.

CAGE Nicholas, (Nicholas Coppola),b. 7 Jan 1964 Long Beach CA. Actor. Films incl: Valley Girl, 1983; Rumble Fish; Racing with the Moon; The Cotton Club; Birdy; The Boy in Blue; Raising Arizona; Peggy Sue Got Married; Moonstruck; Vampire's Kiss; Killing Time; The Short Cut; Queen Logic; Wild of Heart; Wings of the Apache; Zandalee; Red Rock Wes; Guarding Tess; Honeymoon in Vegas; It Could Happen to You; Kiss of Death; Leaving Las Vegas, 1996; The Rock, 1996; The Funeral, 1996; Con Air, 1997; Face Off, 1997. Honours: Golden Globe Awd for Best Actor, 1996; Acady Awd for Best Actor, 1996. Address: c/o 8942 Wilshire Blvd, Beverly Hills, CA 90211, USA.

CAGIMAIVEI Vilisoni, b. 19 Jan 1943. Government Minister. Education: Fiji Sch of Med, Theor and Prac of Pub Hlth, Dip in Pub Hlth Inspection for Gen Overseas Appt. Appointments: Joined Civil Serv, Clerical Offr, 1963; Asst Hlth Insp, Labasa, Taveuni, Lautoka, 1966-70; Hlth Insp, Sec to Vadi Rural Local Authy, 1973-77; Hlth Insp and Bldg Surveyor, Ba Town Cncl, 1975-95. Address: PO Box 2131, Government Buildings, Suva, Fiji.

CAGLAYANGIL Ihsan Sabri, b. 1908 Istanbul. Politician. m. Furuzende Caglayangil, 1933, 1 s, 1 d. Education: Sch of Law Istanbul. Appointments: Fmrly with Min of Interior; Gov of Antalya, 1948-53; Gov of Cannakale, 1953-54; Gov of Sivas, 1954; Gov of Bursa, 1954-60; Sen for Bursa, 1961; Min of Labour, Feb-Oct 1965; Min of For Affairs, 1965-71; Pres Senate For Affairs Cttee, 1972-79; Min of For Affairs, 1975-77; Min of For Affairs, July-Dec 1977; Pres of the Senate, 1979; Acting Pres of Turkey, Apr-Sept 1980; Detained, June-Sept 1983; Released, 1983; Jus Party. Address: Sehit Ersan Caddesi 30/15, Cankaya, Ankara, Turkey.

CAGLE Thomas M, b. 26 Apr 1927, Chillicothe, TX, USA. Electronics Engineer. m. Jane E De Bute, 16 May 1964, 2 s. Education: BS, Univ of Southern CA, LA, 1968. Appointments: US Navy, 1945-46. Engr, N Am Rockwell Corp, Los Angeles, 1950-71; Engrng Cnslt, Scottsdale, AZ, 1971-77; Eletronics Engr, Dept of Def, LA, 1977-. Publications: Copyright held for calculator -nuclear weapon, 1962; Num pprs in tech jrnls, 1954-76. Memberships: IEEE; VFW; Amn Legion; Inglewood Jaycees, Past Pres, Past Dir; YMCA, Inglewood, Past Pres; Inglewood Yth Cnslng Orgn, Past Pres; Ch of Foothills. Address: 10461 Greenbrier Road, Santa Ana, 92705, USA.

CAHALAN Peter James, b. 13 July 1947, Port Pirie, SA, Aust. Museum Director. m. Penelope Anne Baker, 3 Nov 1979, 1 s, 3 d. Education: BA, Hons, 1968, DipEd, 1970, Univ Adelaide; PhD, McMaster Univ, Can, 1977. Appointments: Tutor, Hist, Univ Adelaide, 1969-71, 1978; Tutor, Hist, La Trobe Univ, 1977; Dir, Constl Mus, 1978-82; Actng Dir, 1981-82, Dir, 1982-, Hist Trust SA. Publication: Belgian Refugee Relief in England during the Great War, 1982. Memberships: Assn Profl Histns, SA; Cncl Austl Mus Dirs; Mus's Aust, Pres, SA Bch, 1994-95, Chairperson, Stndng Cttee on Regl, Local Specialist and Mus's and Galls, 1994-; Natl Trust SA; Equipes Notre Dame. Hobbies: Swimming; Reading; Church activities. Address: 3 Christine Avenue, Belair, SA 5052, Australia.

CAHILL Desmond Philip, b. 2 July 1945. Professor of Intercultural Studies. m. Maria Minto, 5 Jan 1978, 2 d. Education: BA, Melbourne; STL, Rome; MEd, Monash; PhD, Monash. Appointments: Rsch Fell, Monash Univ, 1977; Lectr, Coburg State Coll, 1980; Prin Lectr, Phillip

Inst of Technol, 1986; Assoc Prof, 1992, Prof, 1993, RMIT University. Publications: Initial Adjustment To Schooling Of Immigrant Families (w R Taft), 1978; Review of the Commonwealth Multicultural Education Program, 1984; Intermarriages in International Contexts, 1990; Immigration and Schooling in the 1990s, 1996. Memberships: Aust Psychol Soc. Hobbies: Walking; Tourism; Reading theology. Address: RMIT UNiversity, Box 2476V, Melbourne, Vic 3001, Australia.

CAI Boling, b. 21 Sept 1946, Fuzhou, Fujian, China. Physicist. m. Huang Xueming, 15 Jan 1976, 1 s. Education: Dip, Peking Univ, 1968; MSc, Macquarie Univ, 1984. Appointments: Engr, Fujian Ctrl Inspection Inst, 1976-79; Engr, Fujian Inst of Testing Technol, 1979-81; Asst Prof, 1983-91, Dpty Dir, Asst Prof, 1991-92, Dpty Dir, Assoc Prof, 1992-. Publications: Sev pprs in profl jrls. Honours: 3rd Class Awd, Progress of Sci & Technol, Fujian Prov Govt, 1995. Memberships: IEEE; Fujian Inst of Phys; Fujian Inst of Laser Med; Fujian Inst of Optics; Cncl, Fujian Inst of Phys, 1987-; Fujian Inst of Optics, 1991-; Fujian Inst of Laser Med, 1994-. Hobbies: Classical Music; Sightseeing. Address: Fujian Institute of Testing Technology, 61 Middle Beihuan Road, Fuzhou, Fujian 350003, China.

CAI Caijun, b. 5 Oct 1925, Guangdong, China. Teacher. m. Wu Zhuqing, 30 June 1956, 2 s, 2 d. Education: MGeog. Appointments: Tchr, Hebei Normal Univ, 1954-. Publications: Index of Place Name Quadrant; The Application of Spherical Triangle Instrument in Teaching; Xihu Lake Or Lagoon. Honour: Model Tchr Awd. Memberships: Hebei Climate Assn. Hobbies: Walking; Chess; Swimming. Address: Department of Geography, Hebei Teachers University, Shijiazhuang, Hebei 050016, China.

CAI Datong, b. 6 Jan 1929, Guanzhou, Fujian Prov, China. Teacher. 1 s, 1 d. Education: Grad, Agrochemistry Sect, Nanjing Agric Coll. Creative works: Study of Labelled N-transformation in Soil-Plant-Animal System; First successfully used isotope 15N to tag the organic faeces manure of rabbit and chicken, also experimentation on crops. Memberships: Shi Ruihe; Shen Qirong; Lu Xuelan; Wu Yiwen; Wu Shanmei; Li Jingkui; Ni Miaojuan; Wang Yan. Address: Resources and Environmental Science College, Nanjing Agricultural University, Nanjing Jiangsu Province, PC 210095, China.

CAI Hongbin, b. 18 Nov 1941, Jilin Cty, China. Professor; Senior Engineer. m. Tiemei Wang, 26 Dec 1968, 1 s, 1 d. Education: Master's degree, Phys, Harbin Inst of Technol. Appointments: Welding Engr, 1983-85, Snr Engr, Hd of Lab, 1985-87, Hd of Rsch & Sci Div, 1987-91, Dpty Dir, HRIW, 1992, Dir of HRIN, 1994-98. Publications: Num in Welding Transactions and Weldings and Joinings, China, 1995-99. Honours: Outstndng Mater w excllent achievements in the wrk, State Cncl, 1986; 2nd Prize, Natl Sci & Technol Prog, State Cncl, 1987. Memberships: VP, China Welding Soc; Snr Mbr, Cncl of Chinese Mechl Engrng Soc. Hobbies: Stamp collection; Coin collection; Fishing. Address: No 111, He Xing Road, Harbin, China 150080.

CAI Jin-Xing, b. 11 Oct 1967, Gaocheng, China. Research Scientist. m. Yi Yang, 12 June 1995, 1 s. Education: BS, 1988, MS, 1994, Tsinghua Univ, Beijing, China; PhD, Univ SC, Los Angeles. Appointments: Xian, China, 1988-90; Tsinghua Univ, Beijing, 1990-94; Beijing, China, 1994-95; Univ SC, 1995-. Publications: Over 30 in tech jrnls and proceedings. Honours: Sci and Tech Progress Awd, 1st Prize, Beijing, 1994; Outstndng Rsch Paper Awd, USC, 1998. Memberships: Optical Soc of Am; IEEE Communication Soc; IEEE Leos Soc. Hobbies: Music; Chess. Address: Dept of EE Systems, EEB500, University of Southern California, Los Angeles, CA 90089-2565, USA.

CAI Jun Shi, b. 24 Feb 1932, Shanghai, China. Insurance Company Executive. m. Wei Li Zhang, 12 Apr 1959, 1 d. Education: BS, Jiao Tong Univ, Shanghai, 1951. Appointments: Engr, Shanghai Transit Co; Dir, Shanghai Pub Utilities Bur; Chmn, Shanghai Raw Water

Ltd; Chmn, Dazhong Ins Co Ltd, China. Publications: Electric Traction Motor, 1964; Chopper Control of Public Transit Vehicles, 1982; Articles to profl publs. Honours: Natl Sci and Technol Achievement Awd, Natl Sci and Technol Commn of China, 1978; PhD, Bus and Admin, honoris causa, SCUPS, 1995. Memberships: Memberships: Chmn, Pub Transport Soc of China, 1987-95; Bd Dir, China Civil Engrng Soc, 1988-97; Effective Mbr, UITP, 1989-; Barons Fell, 1997. Hobby: Classical music. Address: Dazhong Insurance Co Ltd of China, 860 Beijing Road (W), Shanghai 200041, China.

CAI Ruixian, b. 5 Feb 1934, Santou, China. Academic; Research Professor; Director. m. Lei Wanyan, 5 Aug 1961, 2 s. Education: Studied at Tsinghua Univ, Beijing Inst of Aeronautics, Jiaotong Univ, 1951-56; BSc, Jiaotong Univ, 1956. Appointments: Asst then Lectr, Tsinghua Univ, 1956-72; Engr, Changchun Locomotive Works, 1972-78; Rsch Assoc Prof, Inst of Mechanics, Academia Sinica, Beijing, 1978-80; Rsch Assoc Prof then Dir & Rsch Prof, Inst of Engrng Thermophys, Academia Sinica, Beijing, 1980-; Academician, 1991-, Mbr, Chinese Poeple's Polit Consultative Conf, 1993-; Dir, Dept of Engrng and Material Sci, NSF of China, 1994-. VP, Chinese Assn for Promoting Democracy, 1997-. Publications: Contbr of over 100 sci pprs to jrnls and confs, inclng: Constraint on Design Parameters and Twist of S1 Surfaces in Turbomachines, 1983; A Summary of Developments of the Mean-Stream-Line Method in China, 1984; Some Analytical Solutions Applicable to Verify 3-D Numerical Methods in Turbomachines, 1984; Thermodynamic Analysis and Improvement of Energy Systems, 1989. Honours: Best Student, Jiaotong Univ, Shanghai, 1955; 2nd Class Sci Ppr Awd, Jilin Prov, 1981; 2nd Class Natl Sci and Tech Improvement Awd, Academia Sinica, 1986; ist and 2nd Class Awds, Academia Sinica, 1986 and 1991. Memberships: Jrnl Ed Bd, Vice Ed-in-Chf, Chinese Soc of Engrng Thermophys, 1980-; Appraisal Cttee, Chinese Natl Natural Sci Fndn, 1984-86; Acad Deg Cttee, Academia Sinica, 1984-88; Ed Bd of Scientia Sinica and Sci Bulletin, 1984-88; VP, Chinese Soc of Engrng Thermophys, 1993-. Hobbies: Football; Table Tennis; Reading History and Novels. Address: PO Box 2706, Beijing 100080, China.

CAI Yan Wei, b. 9 Jan 1966, Tianjin, China (res in Singapore, 1993-). Education: Tianjin Art Inst, China; Nanyang Acady of Fine Arts, Singapore. Artist; Master Sculptor. Career: Paintings merged techniques of realism and Chinese Palace art of the 18th century; Used valuable metals to create outstndng wrks; Wrk displayed in Hong Kong, Singapore, Japan, Italy, USA; Commns from Cntrl Govt of China; Collected by famous collectors, natl mus, well-known personages, state ldrs of var countries, inclng: Wan Li, Chmn Stndng Cttee, Chinese Natl People's Congress; the Sultan of Brunei; Sheikh Fahad Al-Ahmad Al-Sabah, Prince of Kuwait; Travelled in many parts of SE Asia, 1993-; Now developing new oriental style. Address: Blk 9 Jalan Batu, #08-45, Singapore 431009.

CAI Yumin, b. 16 Dec 1960, Huiyang, Guangdong, China. Enterprise Administrator. m. Ye Xiaohong, 8 Feb 1986, 1 s. Education: Master, Mngmt Engrng, China Textile Univ, 1996; Dr Textile Enrng (Studying), China Textile Univ, 1998. Appointments: Gen Mngr, Huizhou Trade Dev Gen Co, 1989, 1991; Dir Gen, Huizhou Textile Enterprise (Grp), Corp. Publications: The Strategy of Development of Huizhou Textile Industry, 1997; To Promote Textile Industry Rely on Technology Advancement, 1997. Honours: Prominent Youth of China, 1993; Hon Cit of the Cty of Albany, NY, USA. Memberships: The Utd Assns of Chinese Yth, 1993; Assn of Chinese Young Enterprise, 1994. Hobby: Sport. Address: 23 Zixiling, Huizhou, Guangdong, China.

CAI Zhong-De, b. 26 Feb 1937, Shaoxing, Zhejiang Prov, China. Professor. m. 17 Sept 1969, 1 d. Education: BA, Clina East Normal Univ, 1960. Publication: The History of Chinese Music Aesthetics. Honour: China Natl Book Awds, 1996. Membership: Dir, China Assn of Music Aesthetics, 1991-. Hobby: Beijing Opera. Address: 57 Yan Nan Yuan, Beijing University, Beijing 100871, China.

CAI Zi-Xing, b. 2 Mar 1938. Scientist; Teacher. m. Huan Wen, 15 July 1942, 2 s. Education: Dips, Dept EE, Jiao Tong Univ, Xi'an, China, 1962. Appointments: Tchng Asst, Asst Prof, Dept Automation, Cntrl S Inst of Mining and Metall, Changsha, 1962-78; Snr Lectr, Dept Automation, CSIMM, 1978-83; Visng Schl, Cntr of Robotics, Dept EE and Computer Sci, Univ NV at Reno, USA, 1983; Exchange Sci, Adv Automation Rsch Lab, Dept EE, Purdue Univ, W Lafayette, IN, USA, 1984-85; Assoc Prof, Dept Automatic Control Engrng, Cntrl S Univ of Technol, Changsha, 1985-88; Edtl Bd, Robot Mag, 1987-; Snr Rsch Sci, Natl Lab of Pattern Recog, Inst Automation, Chinese Acady Scis, Beijing, 1988-89; UN Expert, granted by UN Ind Dev Org, 1989-; Visng Rsch Prof, Natl Lab Mach Perception, Cntr Info Sci, Beijing Univ, 1989-90; Prof, Dept Automatic Control Engrng, CSUT, Changsha, 1990-92; Visng Prof, Cntr for Intelligent Robotic Systems for Space Exploration, CIRSSE, Dept Elect, Computer and System Engrng, Rensselaer Poly Inst, Troy, NY, 1992-93; Prof, Supvsr for PhD Studs, Dir, Rsch Cntr for Intelligent Control, Coll Info Engrng, CSUT, Changsha, 1993-; Vice Chmn, Hunan Provincial Cttee Chinese Peoples Political Consultative Conf, 1998; Mbr Natl Cttee CPPCC, 1998; Editl Bd, Jrnl Computer Technology and Automation, 1996-; Editl Bd Jrnl Control Theory and Applications, 1998-; Mbr of Evaluation Grp in Automation, Natl Nat Sci Fndn of China, 1998-. Publications include: 16 books, textbooks; Over 300 pprs, 1986-: Intelligent Control: Principles, Techniques and Applications, 1997; Intelligent Control, 1990; Artificial Intelligence: Principles and Applications, 1987, 2nd ed, 1996; Robotics: Principles and Applications, 1988. Honours: Significant Achievement of S&T, 3rd Prize, 1981; Ex Ppr, 1st Prize, Hunan, 1986, 1997; Ex Ppr, 2nd Prize, Hunan, 1987; Ex Ppr, 1st Prize, 1988; Theort Rsch Achievement, 1st Prize, CSUT, 1989; Theort Rsch Achievement, 2nd Prize, CSUT, 1990; Chinese Ex Book of S&T, 1990; State Ex Textbook in Electrons Area, 1st Prize, 1996. Memberships include: Bd Stndng Dirs, Chinese Assn Artificial Intelligence, 1986-; Pres, Soc Intelligent Robots, 1993-; Bd Dirs, Soc Intelligent Automation, CAA, 1994-; Bd Dirs, Chinese Soc Computer Vision and Intelligent Control, CAAI, 1986-; Bd, Stndng Dirs, Soc Process Control, CAA, 1992-; Bd Dirs Soc AI and Pattern Recog, CFC, 1992-; Snr Mbr, Chinese Inst Elects, 1991-; Chinese Assn Sci Popular Writers, Hunan, China, 1991-; Intl Soc Intelligent Automation, 1992-93; Intl Soc Mini and Microcomputers, 1988-; Intl Fed Chinese Computers, 1987-; IASTED; UN Expert, UNIDO, 1998-; Snr Mbr, IEEE, 1998- Mbr NY Acady of Scis, 1998-. Hobbies: Sports; Photography. Address: Centre for Intelligent Control, College of Information Engineering, Central South University of Technology, Changsha, Hunan 410083, China.

CAI Zimin, b. 1926 Zhanghua Cty Taiwan Prov. Politician. Education: In Japan. Appointments: Chmn of Taiwan Dem Self-Govt League, 1988-; Advsr Assn for Rels across the Taiwan Straits - ARATS - 1991-. Memberships: Perm mbr 8th Standing Cttee NPC, 1993-; Mbr For Affairs Cttee. Address: National People's Congress, Tian An Men Square, Beijing 100805, People's Republic of China.

CAIN John (The Hon), b. 26 Apr 1931, Aust. Former Member of Legislative Assembly. m. Nancye Williams, 6 July 1955, 2 s, 1 d. Education: LLB, Melbourne Univ. Appointments: Mbr, Cncl, 1967-76, Treas, 1969-70, Chmn, Cncl, 1971-72, Pres, 1972-73, Law Inst Vic; Vice-Chmn, Victorian Bch, Austl Labor Party, 1973-75; Mbr, Exec Law Cncl Aust, 1973-76; Mbr, Law Reform Commn Aust, 1975-77; Mbr for Bundoora, Vic, Legis Assembly, 1976-92; Ldr Opposition, 1981-82; Min Fed Affairs, 1982-83; Atty-Gen, 1982-83; Min Resp Women's Affairs, 1982-90; Premier, 1982-90; Professorial Assoc, Pols Dept, Univ Melbourne, 1991-. Publication: John Cain's Years - Power Parties and Politics, 1995; On With the Show, 1998. Membership: Tstee, Melbourne Cricket Ground, 1982-98. Hobbies: Tennis; Swimming; Jogging. Address: 9 Magnolia Road, Ivanhoe, Vic 3079, Australia.

CALDWELL John Charles, b. 8 Dec 1928, Sydney, NSW, Aust. Demographer. m. Pat Rosie Clara Barrett, 7

Feb 1948, 4 s. Education: BA, New Eng; PhD, Austl Natl Univ. Appointments: Asst Prof, Univ of Ghana, 1962-64; Rsch Fell, ANU, 1964-67; Regl Dir, Population Cncl, 1967-70; Prof, Austl Natl Univ, 1970-. Publications: 20 books incl: Population Growth and Family Change in Africa, 1967; African Rural-Urban Migration, 1969; Theory of Fertility Decline, 1982. Honours: Hon DSc, Southampton, 1992, Austl Natl Univ, 1995; AO, 1994. Address: 23 Belconnen Way, Weetangera, ACT 2614, Australia.

CALDWELL William Roy, b. 29 Aug 1935. m. Mamie Rock, 25 Mar 1960, 1 s, 1 d. Education: ACII; FCIS; FICD; FICM. Appointments: Perm Hd and Dir of Compensation, Accident Compensation Commn, NZ, 1972; Asst Gen Mngr, Natl Ins Co of NZ Ltd, 1979; Chf Exec, RAC Ins Pty Ltd, 1982; Grp Chf Exec, RAC Grp, 1995. Publication: Aspects of No Fault Compensation, 1976. Memberships: Tree, Cttee for Econ Dev of Aust; Chmn of Dirs, Crimestoppers WA Ltd. Hobbies: Golf; Yachting; Motor racing. Address: 228 Adelaide Terrace Perth, WA 6000, Australia.

CALLAWAY Frank (Adams) (Sir), b. 16 May 1919. Emeritus Professor; Foundation Professor; Head, Department of Music. m. Kathleen Jessie Allan, 1942, 2 s, 2 d. Education: W Christchurch HS; Dunedin Tchrs Coll, NZ; MusB, Univ of Otago, NZ; Roy Acady of Music FRAM, ARCM, FTCL, FACE. Appointments: Hd, Dept of Music, King Edward Tech Coll, Dunedin, NZ, 1942-53; Reader in Music, Univ of WA, 1953-59; Mbr, RNZAF, Band, 1940-42; Conductor, King Edward Tech Coll Symph Orch, 1945-53; Univ of WA Orchestral Soc, 1953-54, Univ of WA Choral Soc, 1953-79; Guest Conductor, WA Symph Orch, SA Symph Orch, Manila Symph Orch, Adelaide Phil Choir, Orpheus Choir, Wellington, NZ; Mbr, Austl Music Examin Bd 1955-84 (Chmn 1964-66 and 1977-79); Advsry Bd, C'wlth Assistance to Austl Composers, 1966-72; Austl Natl Commn for UNESCO, 1968-82; Exec Bd, Intl Music Cncl of UNESCO, 1976-82 (Pres 1980-81, Indiv Mbr 1982-85, Life Mbr of Hon 1986); Music Bd, Aust Cncl 1969-74; Chmn, WA Arts Advsry Bd 1970-73, WA Arts Cncl, 1973-79; Chmn, Organising Cttees; Austl Natl Eisteddfod, 1979; Indian Ocean Fest, 1979, 1984; External Examiner (Music), Kenyatta Univ, Nairobi, 1985-87; Fndng Ed, Austl Jrnl of Music Educ, 1967-82; Studies in Music 1967-84, Intl Jrnl of Music Educ, 1983-85. Publications: (Gen Ed) Challenges in Music Education, 1975 (w D E Tunley); Australian Composition in the Twentieth Century, 1978. Honours: OBE, 1970; CMG, 1975; WA Citizen of the Yr, 1975; Hon MusD, Univ of WA, 1975; Melbourne Univ, 1982; Austl Natl Critics' Circle Awd for Music, 1977; KB, 1981; Sir Bernard Heinze Awd for Servs to Austl Music, 1988; Compiler, Essays in Hon of David Evatt Tunley, 1995; AO, 1995; Compiler Grainger Symposium, 1997; UNESCO INtl Music Cncl, Music Prize, 1997; Hon FMusA, 1997. Memberships: Bd of Dirs, Intl Soc for Music Educ, 1958-, Pres, 1968-72, Treas, 1972-88, Hon Pres, 1988-; Fndng Pres and Life Mbr, Austl Soc for Music Educ, 1966-71; Indian Ocean Arts Assn, 1980-85, Pres 1985-; Intl Percy Grainger Medal, 1991; Advsr, Callaway Intl Resource Cntr for Music Educ. Hobbies: Reading; Gardening. Cricket. Address: 1 Sambell Close, Churchlands, WA 6018, Australia.

CALVERT George Dennis, b. 4 Jan 1942, NZ. University Professor, Medicine and Public Health. m. Christine Ewan, 4 Nov 1988, 1 s, 2 d. Education: BMedSci, MBChB, MD, Otago, NZ; MCB, Roy Inst Chem, London; FRACP, Austl Coll of Physns; FRCPA, Coll of Pathologists of Australasia; FRCPath, Coll of Pathologists, UK; FAFPHM, Australasian Fac of Pub Hlth Med; FACHSE, Austl Coll of Hlth Serv Execs. Appointments: Intern, Res Medl Offr, Auckland Hosp, 1967-71; Snr Registrar, W Midlands Grp, Birmingham, 1972-76; Medl Specialist, Flinders Medl Cntr, Bedford Pk, S Aust, 1976-86; Prof, currently Prof Med & Pub Hlth, Univ Wollongong, Aust, 1986-; Univ NSW (conjoint), 1993-. Publications: Num sci articles. Address: University of Wollongong, Wollongong, NSW 2522, Australia.

CAM Nguyen Manh, b. 15 June 1929, Nghe An, Vietnam, Minister of Foreign Affairs. m. 4 s. Appointments: Joined Revolutionary Movt, 1945; Joined For Serv, 1952; Specialist, Soviet and E Eurn Affairs; Amb to Hungary and Austria, 1973-77, Germany, Austria and Switz, 1977-80, USSR, 1987=-91; Vice Min of For Econ Rels, 1981-87; Mbr, CPCC, 1986-; Mbr, Natl Def and Security cttee, CP Politburo, 1994. Address: Ministry of Foreign Affairs, 1 Ton That Dam, Hanoi, Vietnam.

CAMERON Clyde Robert, b. 11 Feb 1913 Murray Bridge. Retired Politician. m. (1) Ruby Helen Krahe 1939, div 1966, 2 s, 1 d; (2) Doris Maud Bradbury, 1967. Education: Gawler High Sch SA. Appointments: Worked in shearing sheds, 1928-38; Organizer SAustl Branch Austl Workers' Union, 1939; Sec AWU, 1941-49; Pres SA Branch Austl Labor Party, 1946-49, 1958, 1962; Pres AWU, 1956; Fed VP AWU, 1942-50; Indl Offr, 1944-48; Min for Labor, 1972-74; Min for Labor and Immigration, 1974-75; Chmn S Pacific Labour Mins Conf, 1973; Vice-Chmn Asian Labour Mins Conf, 1973; Chmn, 1975; Min of Sci and Consumer Affairs, June-Nov 1975; Parly deleg to UN Gen Assembly, 1976; Parl Retiring Allowances Trust Fund, 1978. Publications: Grappling with the Giants, 1974; China Communism and Coca Cola, 1980; Unions in Crisis, 1982; Oral History - 650 hrs, 6 million words; The Cameron Diaries, 1990; The Confessions of Clyde Cameron, 1990. Memberships: Mbr HoR for Hindmarsh, 1949-80; Mbr Fed Parly Labor Party Exec, 1953-75; Mbr SA Brdcstng Advsry Cttee, 1945-49, 1964-75; Mbr HoR Privileges Cttee, 1959-75, 1977. Hobbies: Rsch and recording oral hist. Address: 19 Sunlake Place, Tennyson, SA 5022, Australia.

CAMERON Donald Milner, b. 6 Feb 1940, Aust. Membership and Network Development Manager; Former Politician. m. Lila Duthie, 3 May 1980, 4 d. Education: Qld Agricl HS and Coll; Univ Qld. Appointments: BP Aust Ltd, 1958-64; Indl Offr, Assn Employees Waterside Labour, 1964-66; Mbr, Liberal, House of Reps, for Griffith, 1966-77, for Fadden, 1977-83, for Moreton, Qld, 1983-90; Dpty Govt Whip, 1975-78; Currently Membership and Netwrk Dev Mngr, Qld Chmbr of Com and Ind. Memberships: Pres, Young Liberals, Qld Div; Pres, Yth Hostels Assn, Qld; Immed Past Pres, Qld Fndn Blind People; Pres, Brisbane S Area Scouts, Natl Fndn; Pres, Fedn Austl Karate-do Orgs; Life Mbr Qld Div Lib Party of Aust, 1996. Listed in: Who's Who in Australia. Hobbies: Fishing; Rugby League Football. Address: 21 Jordan Street, Greenslopes, Qld 4120, Australia.

CAMERON Donald William, b. 11 Sept 1935. Professor of Organic Chemistry. m. Lynette Marjorie Weeks, 9 Aug 1958, 2 s, 1 d. Education: MA, 1961; ScD, Cambridge, 1969; MSc, QLD, 1958; BSc Hons, 1958; PhD, Manchester, 1960. Appointments: Salters' Fell, 1960-61; Univ Demonstrator, 1961-66; Univ Lectr, 1966-68, Cambridge; Prof of Organic Chem, Melbourne, 1968-. Publications: Num pprs in cheml lit. Honours: Univ Medal, 1958; Corday-Morgan Medal and Prize of Chem Soc, London, 1970; Citation, RACI, 1994; Leighton Memorial Medal, RACI, 1998. Memberships: Fell, Roy Austl Chem Inst, 1968; Pres, RACI, Vic br, 1974; Chmn, RACI Div of Organic Chem, 1979-80; Chmn, RACI Quals Cttee, 1992-96. Address: School of Chemistry, University of Melbourne, Parkville, Vic 3052, Australia.

CAMERON Rod(ney) MacArthur, b. 26 Feb 1948, Sydney, Australia. Market Researcher. Education: BA, Hons, Sydney Univ. Appointments: Mng Dir, ANOP Rsch Servs Pty Ltd, 1974-; Dir of Bd, ABC, 1991-96; Dir of Bd, Aust Post, 1996-; Chmn, Postal Servs Cnslt Cncl. Memberships: Fell, Market Rsch Soc; Austl Population Assn; World Assn of Pub Opinion Rsch. Hobbies: Politics; Media; Books; Music; Rugby; Cooking; Child Development. Address: PO Box 595, North Sydney, NSW 2059, Australia.

CAMERON Roy James, b. 11 Mar 1923, SA, Aust. Government Official. m. Dorothy Olive Lober, 31 Mar 1951, 2 s, 1 d. Education: MEc, Adelaide Univ; PhD, Harvard Univ, USA. Appointments: Served Austl Imperial Force, 1943-46; Lectr, Econs, Canberra Univ Coll,

1949-51; Economist, World Bank, Wash DC, USA, 1954-56; Gen, Finl and Econ Polit Div, 1956-66, Snr Treas Rep, Aust House, London, 1966, 1st Asst Sec, Transp and Ind Div, 1966-73; C'wlth Treas; Amb, Perm Rep to OCED, 1973-77; Austl Statn, 1977-85; Pres, Austl Inst Pub Admin, ACT, 1983; Commnr, Austl Electoral Commn, 1984-85; Chmn, Cttee Inquiry Into Distbn Fed Rd Grants, 1986; Mbr, Cncl, Canberra Coll Advd Educ, 1985-89; Mbr Ind Assistance Commn, 1988-92. Honour: CB, 1982. Address: 10 Mair Place, Curtin, ACT 2605, Australia.

CAMPBELL Alistair Te Ariki, b. 25 June 1925, Rarotonga. Poet; Novelist. m. Meg, 29 Feb 1958, 3 s, 2 d. Education: BA; Dip of Tchng. Ed, School Publs Branch, Dept of Educ; Snr Ed, NZ Cncl for Educl Rsch. Publications: Verse: Mine Eyes Dazzle; Kapiti: Selected Poems; Collected Poems; Stone Rain: The Polynesian Strain; Pocket Collected Poems; Fiction: The Sidewinder Trilogy; Fantasy With Witches. Honours: NZ Book Awd for Poetry, for Collected Poems, 1982; Gold Medal for TV documentary, Island of Spirits, La Spezia Intl Film Fest, 1974; NZ Arts Cncl Schlshp in Letters, 1989; Writer-in-Residence, Victoria Univ of Wellington, 1992; Pacific Islands Artists Awd, 1998; Hon DLitt, Univ Wellington 1999. Membership: Pres, PEN Intl, NZ Cntr, 1977-79. Hobbies: Reading; Classical music; Gardening. Address: 4B Rawhiti Road, Pukerua Bay, 6450, New Zealand.

CAMPBELL Angus John Dugald, b. 11 Nov 1970, Traralgon, Vic, Australia. Veterinary Surgeon. Education: Bach of Animal Sci; BVSc Hons. Honour: ASAVA Practitioner Educ Schlsp, 1998. Memberships: Melbourne Univ Mountaineering Club; Austl Small Animal Veterinary Assn; Austl Veterinary Assn; Oxley Climbing Posse. Hobbies: Rockclimbing; Mountaineering; Photography; Choral Music; Theatre. Address: Traralgon Park, Traralgon, Victoria 3844, Australia.

CAMPBELL Archibald Duncan, b. 8 Sept 1933, Victor Harbour, S Aust, Aust. Writer; Former Diplomat. m. Barbara J, 25 Feb 1967, 1 s, 4 d. Education: BA, Hons, Adelaide, 1954. Appointments: Austl Dipl Serv, 1955; Amb to Aust and Hungary, 1980-84; Dpty Sec, For Affairs and Trade, 1985-88; Amb to Italy, 1988-93. Publications: Num articles in Austl Press, 1994-. Honour: AM, 1999. Membership: Dir, Natl Gall of Aust Fndn. Hobbies: Art; Music; Golf. Address: 20/300 Riley St, Surry Hills, NSW 2010, Australia.

CAMPBELL Arthur Derek, b. 27 May 1925, Waimate, New Zealand. Chemist and Microchemical Analyst. m. Ruth F Smith, 18 Jan 1950, 2 s, 1 d. Education: MSc, 1948, PhD, 1952, Univ Otago. Appointments: Asst Lectr, 1948-50, Lectr in Chem, In Charge, Microchem Lab, 1951-59, Snr Lectr, 1960-63, Rdr, 1964-70, Personal Chair in Chem, 1971-82, Dean, Fac of Sci, 1980-82, Mellor Prof of Chem, Chmn, Dept of Chem, 1983-87, Emer Prof, 1988-, Univ Otago. Publications: Num articles in profl jrnls. Honours: Corday Morgan C'wlth Fellshp, Chem Soc, London, 1953; Morcam Green Edwards Prize, 1955; Easterfield Medal and Prize, 1959; Nuffield C'wlth Rsch Fellshp, 1961; Hon Fell, NZ Inst of Chem, 1988; OBE, 1989. Memberships: Sev. Hobbies: Gardening; Lawn Bowls; Travel. Address: 4 Dudley Place, Dunedin, New Zealand.

CAMPBELL John Duncan, b. 4 July 1940, Melbourne, Vic, Aust. Medical Practitioner. m. (1) Mary Veronica Comerford, 19 Jan 1964, dec 1991, 1 s, 4 d, (2) Patricia Gweneth Von Tiedimann, 26 Oct 1996. Education: MB BS, Univ Adelaide, 1964; DTM&H, 1970, LLM, 1985, Univ Sydney; M Hlth Admin, 1975, LLB, 1976, Univ NSW; Fell, Roy Austl Coll Medl Admnstrs. Appointments: Roy Austl Army Medl Corp, 1962-80; Intern, Roy Adelaide Hosp, 1964; RMO IRAR, S Vietnam, 1965; OC, 7 Camp Hosp, Kapooka, NSW, 1966; SMO, HQ PNG Cond, 1967-70; ADGMS, Army HQ, Canberra, 1971-72; CO, 2 Mil Hosp, 1975; Dir Medl Servs, Prince of Wales, Prince Henry and East Sub Hosps, 1976-80; Dir, Pub Hlth Servs, 1980, Dir, Medl and Allied Servs, 1981-82, Hlth Commn MSW; Dir, N Metrop Hlth Reg, 1983-85; Dir, S Metrop Hlth Reg,

1985-; Admnstr, St George Area Hlth Servs, 1988; Chf Exec Offr, Southern Sydney Area Hlth Serv, 1988-; Visng Prof, Sch Mngmt, Univ Technol, Sydney, 1988-; Chf Exec Offr, Cntrl Sydney Area Hlth Serv, 1991; Part-Time Mbr Admnstv Appeals Tribunal, 1991-; Acting Chf Exec Offr, S East Sydney Area Hlth Serv, 1995-96; Mngng Dir, Austl Hlth Intl Pty Ltd, 1996-97; Dir, Mercy Family Life Ctr, 1996-; Dir, NRMA, 1997-. Publications include: Medical, Legal and Social Aspects of After Hours Medical Services, 1979; Review of Hospital Services, 1979; Hospital Ethics Committees, 1981; Num other papers. Honour: C'wlth Schlshp, 1956. Memberships: Bar-at-Law, Supreme Crt NSW; Coll Medl Admnstrs; Fell, Austl Inst Mngmt, 1992; Fell, Austl Inst of Co Dirs; Censor in Chf, Roy Austl Coll Medl Admnstrs, 1995.Hobbies: Golf; Fishing; Squash; Reading. Address: 12 Morella Rd, Clifton Gardens, NSW 2088, Australia.

CAMPBELL Keith Oliver, b. 15 May 1920, NSW, Aust. Agricultural Economist. m. Christiana McFadyen, 17 Sept 1949, 1 s, 2 d. Education: BScAgr, Sydney, 1943; AM, 1948; PhD, Chgo, 1949; MPA, Harvard, 1949; Appointments: Econ Rsch Offr, Dept of Agricl, Sydney, 1943-49; Prin Econs Rsch Offr, 1950-51; Rdr, Agricl Econs, Univ Sydney, 1951-56; Prof, Agricl Econs, 1956-82, Dean, Fac of Agricl, 1968-70, Emer Prof, 1982-. Publications include: Agricultural Marketing and Prices, 1973; Food for the Future, 1979. Honours include: Fulbright-Hayes Schlshp, 1968; Leonard Elmhirst Meml Medal; DEc, Hon, Univ New England, 1993; DScAgr Econ, 1993. Memberships: Fell, Acady of Socl Scis, Aust; Austl Inst of Agricl Sci; Disting Life Mbr, Austl Agricl Econs Soc; Life Mbr, Intl Assn of Agricl Econs. Hobbies: Gardening; Growing camellias. Address: 188 Beecroft Road, Cheltenham, NSW 2119, Australia.

CAMPBELL Kim - Avril Phaedra. b. 10 Mar 1947. Politician; Lawyer. Education: Univ of British Columbia. Appointments: Lectr in Sci and Hist Vancouver Community Coll; Lectr in Polit Sci Univ of BC; Elected Progressive Cons HoC, 1988; Min of State Affairs and North Dev, 1989-90; Min of Jus and Att-Gen of Canada, 1990-93; Min of Def, 1993; PM of Canada, June-Nov, 1993; Progressive Cons ldr, June-Nov 1993. Publication: Time and Chance: A Political Memoir of Canada's First Woman Prime Minister, 1996. Honours: Hon Dir Volunteer Grandparents Assn; Hon Fell LSE, 1994. Memberships: Mbr BC Legis; Mbr Advsry Bd Yth Option Prog Visng Cttee Cntr for Intl Affairs Harvard Univ, 1995-. Address: 963 West 8th Avenue, Vancouver, BC, V5Z 1E4, Canada.

CAMPBELL Lynn Pamela, b. 11 Jan 1955, Bristol, England. Conservator. m. H Campbell, 5 July 1985. Education: BA, hons; Postgrad Ctf in Educ; Dip in the Conservation of Fine Art. Appointments: Roy Scottish Mus, Edinburgh, Scotland, 1984-86; Robert McDougall Art Gall, Christchurch, NZ, 1986-99. Memberships: NZ Profl Conservators Grp, VP; ICCOM; AIC; AICCM; IPC; ICCM. Hobbies: Reading; Theatre; Cinema; Tramping. Address: 2 Westby Street, Christchurch 2, New Zealand.

CAMPBELL Richard James, b. 18 Jan 1939, Sydney, Aust. Academic. m. (1) 2 s, (2) Petronella, 25 June 1989. Education: BA, BD, MA, Sydney; DPhil, Oxford. Appointments: Min, Glebe Presby Ch, 1961-65; Lectr, 1967-72, Snr Lectr, 1972-78, Rdr, 1979-93, Prof of Philos, Austl Natl Univ. Publications: Secondary Education for Canberra, 1973; From Belief to Understanding, 1976; Truth and Historicity, 1992. Honour: AM. Membership: (FACE) Fell, Austl Coll of Educ. Address: 12 Morphett Street, Dickson, ACT 2602, Australia.

CAMPBELL Roderick Samuel Fisher, b. 5 June 1924, Glasgow, Scotland. International Veterinary Consultant. m. Barbara Monica Morris, 29 June 1956, 3 s. Education: MRCVS, Glasgow Vet Coll, 1941-46; PhD, Glasgow Univ, 1964. Appointments: Lectr, Snr Lectr, Univ Glasgow Vet Sch, 1946-69; Visng Prof, Univ Khartoum, 1964-65; Visng Prof, Purdue Univ, USA, 1967-68; Fndn Prof, Tropical Vet Sci, James Cook Univ, Aust, 1969-87. Publications: Num papers. Honours: Pegasus Medal, N

Qld Bch, Austl Vet Assn, 1987; DSc honoris causa, James Cook Univ, 1988; Kesteven Medal, Austl Vet Assn, 1988; AM, 1996; Aust Coll of Vet Scis Medal, 1997; DVMS honoris causa, Galasgow Univ, 1999. Memberships: FRS Edinburgh; Fell, Austl Coll Vet Scientists; Fell, Roy Coll Pathologists; Fell, Austl Coll Tropical Med; Austl Vet Assn; Brit Vet Assn. Listed in: Who's Who of Australia; International Who's Who. Hobbies: Music; History; Golf. Address: c/o Australian Institute for Tropical Veterinary and Animal Science, James Cook University, Townsville, Queensland 4811, Australia.

CAMPBELL Walter Benjamin (Sir), b. 4 Mar 1921, NSW, Aust. Former Queensland Governor and Chief Justice (retired). m. Georgina, 18 June 1942, 1 s, 1 d. Education: MA, LLB (1st Hons), Univ of Queensland; Hon LLB, Univ of Queensland. Appointments: Barrister, 1948; QC, 1960; Supreme Crt Judge, 1967-81; Chf Justice of Queensland, 1982-85; Gov of Queensland, 1985-92. Publications: Several articles in legal and profl jrnls, 1950-96. Honours: Kt, 1979; AC, 1988; K St G, 1985. Memberships include Bar Assn of Queensland, 1965-69; Pres, Austl Bar Assn, 1966-67; Chan, Univ Queensland, 1977-82. Address: 6 Dennison Street, Ascot, Brisbane, Queensland, Australia 4007.

CAMPESE David Ian, b. 21 Oct 1962, Queanbeyan, NSW, Aust. Rugby Union Footballer. Appointments: 101 Tests for Aust, Record; 315 Test Points (64 test tries, World Record, 8 conv, 7 penalty goals, 2 field goals); Rep Aust Rugby Team (Wallabies) in World Cup, S Africa, 1995; Mbr, World Cup Winning Team (UK), 1991 (6 tries in 6 games); Aust debut 1982 v All Blacks (NZ); Plays for Randwick Club, NSW, 1987-. Address: c/o Campo's Sport & Leisure, St Ives Shopping Village, St Ives, NSW 2075, Australia.

CAMPION Jane, b. Wellington, NZ. Film Director; Screenwriter. Education: BA in Anthropology, Victoria Univ; Dip of Fine Arts, Chelsea Sch of Arts, London; Dip in Direction, Austl Film, TV and Radio Sch. Creative works: Films: Peel: An Exercise in Discipline, 1982; A Girl's Own Story, 1983; Passionless Moments, 1984; After Hours, 1984; Two Friends (for tv), 1986; Sweetie (also as co-writer), 1988; An Angel at My Table, 1990; The Piano, 1993; Portrait of a Lady, 1997; Holy Smoke, 1999. Honours include: Dip of Merit, Melbourne Film Fest, 1983; Unique Artist of Merit, Melbourne Film Fest, 1984; Rouben Mamoulian Awd for Best Overall Short Film, Sydney Film Fest, 1984; 3 Austl Film Inst Awds, 1984, 1987; 1st Prize, Amsterdam Film Fest, 1985; XL Elders Awd for Best Short Fiction, Melbourne Intl Film Fest, 1985; Palme d'Or for Best Short Film, Cannes Intl Film Fest, 1986; Golden Plaque, Chgo Intl Film Fest, 1987; 3 Austl Critics Awds, 1990; Los Angeles Critics New Generation Awd, 1990; Best For Film, Spirit of Independence Awd, USA, 1990; Best Woman Dir, Best Film, Venice Film Fest, 1990; Palme d'Or, Cannes Intl Film Fest, 1993; Acady Awd, Best Orig Screenplay, 1994; Francesco Pasinetti Awd, Venice Film Fest, Natl Union Film Jrnlsts, 1996; I A Critics Awd, 1997. Address: c/o Hilary Linstead, Hilary Linstead and Associates, PO Box 1536, Strawberry Hills, NSW 2012, Australia.

CAMRASS Joan, b. 27 Apr 1926, Harrogate, Eng. Archivist. m. Rex Camrass, 5 Jan 1960. Education: MA, Univ of Oxford. Appointments: Hd, Geog Dept, Roundhay hs, Leeds, 1948-60; Burnie hs, Tas, 1960; Ulverstone hs, Tasmania, 1961; Bah'a'í Natl Archives Offr, NZ, 1978-. Publications: Aust, Five Geographic Studies, Curriculum Resource Book Series, Univ of BC, 1972; Arohanui - Letters from Shoghi Effendi to New Zealand, 1981; Archives Systems, 1987. Memberships: FRGS (Fell Roy Geog Soc); Assn for Bah'a'í Studies, NZ. Hobbies: Dental epidemiology; Biostatistics; Survey design; Archives; Research writing; Swimming. Address: PO Box 51-422 Pakuranga, Auckland, New Zealand.

CANNON Russell David, b. 1 Mar 1942, Liverpool, Eng. Astronomer. m. Maria Fernanda Soares Barbosa, 19 Sept 1968, 1 s, 2 d. Education: BA, 1st Class Hons, 1963, MA, 1968, PhD, 1968, Trinity Coll, Cambridge Univ. Appointments: Jnr Rsch Fell, Roy Greenwich Observatory, 1965-69; Rsch Fell, Mt Stromlo Observatory, Austl Natl Univ, Canberra, ACT, Aust, 1969-72; Dpty Proj Offr, Astronomer i/c, UK Schmidt Telescope, Coonabarabran, 1973-75; Hd, UK Schmidt Telescope Unit, 1975-86, Dpty Dir, 1981-86, Roy Observatory, Edinburgh, Scotland; Dir, 1986-96, Snr Rsch Astronomer, 1996-, Anglo-Austl Observatory, Epping, NSW, Aust; Adjunct Prof, Univ of Sydney, 1996-.; Chair, Austl Telescope Natl Facilty Steering Cttee 1999-. Publications: Contbr, over 150 sci papers; The Steller Content of Local Group Galaxies, co-editor, 1998; Conference Proceedings. Memberships: Fell, Roy Astronomical Soc, Cncl, 1974-77, Editl Bd, Monthly Notices, 1982-86; Astronomical Soc Aust; Fell, Austl Inst Phys. Hobbies: Classical music; Reading; Bushwalking; Home workshop. Listed in: Who's Who in Australia. Address: Anglo-Australian Observatory, PO Box 296, Epping, NSW 2121, Australia.

CANOVA-DAVIS Eleanor, b. 18 Jan 1938, San Fran, CA. Protein Biochemist; Biotechnologist. m. Kenneth Roy, 10 Feb 1957, 2 s. Education: BA, San Fran State Univ, 1968; MS, San Fran State Univ, 1971; PhD, Univ of CA Medl Cntr, San Fran, 1977. Appointments: Lab Asst, Frederick Burk Fndn for Educ, 1969-71; Tchng Asst, Univ of CA Medl Cntr, 1971-73; Rsch Asst, Univ of CA Medl Cntr, 1972-77; NIH Postdoctoral Fell, Univ of CA, 1977-80; Asst Rsch Biochem, Univ of CA Medl Cntr, 1980-84; Snr Scientist, Liposome Technol, Menlo Park, CA, 1984-85; Snr Scientist, Genentech, 1985-. Creative Works: Auth of num profl articles; Development of a Photoaffinity Probe for ACTH Receptors; A Semisynthesis of Insulin, 1981; The Lipid Composition of Human Liver Microsomes; Many ors. Honours: Natl Inst of Arthritis, Metabolism and Digestive Diseases, 1977-80; Trav Allowance Awd; Chans Pats Fund Awd; Earl C Anthony Trust Awd; Grad Div Fellshp; Hons Convocation Awd. Memberships: Amn Chem Soc; Amn Peptide Soc; CA Schlshp Fedn; St Elizabeths Club; Tiny Tots; St Veronica's Womens Club; Foxridge Parent/Tearcher Assn; Westborough Parent/Teacher Assn; St Patrick's Circle. Hobbies: Sewing; Knitting; Reading; Bridge; Stamp Collecting. Address: 1203 Edgewood Road, Redwood City, CA 94062, USA.

CANTENOT Nicolas Hervé Marie, b. 27 Oct 1967, France. General Manager. m. Alexandra Grodzki, 22 July 1995, 1 s, 1d. Education: Graduated, Ecole Supérieure de Com, Lyon, 1989; MBA, INSEAD, 1996. Appointments: Cnslt, Bossard Cnslts, Paris, 1991-92; Regl Sales Mngr, Parfums Christian Dior, Paris, 1992-95; Gen Mngr, Christian Dior Korea, Seoul, 1996-. Membership: Conseiller du Commerce Extérieur de la France, 1998-. Hobbies: Yachting; Skiing; Opera; Classical music. Address: Parfums Christian Dior Korea, 12th Fl, Youwha Bldg, 1305-2 Seocho-dong, Seocho-ku, Seoul 137-070, Korea.

CAO Bochun, b. Nov 1941 Zhuzhou Cty Hunan Prov. Politician. Education: Zhuzhou Aeronautical Indl Trng Sch. Appointments: Joined CCP, 1966; Vice-Sec CCP Zhuzhou Cty Cttee, 1983; Sec, 1984; Sec CCP Xiangtan Cty Cttee, 1990; Vice-Gov Hunan Prov, 1991; Vice-Sec CCP Liaoning Prov Cttee, Sec Dalian Cty Cttee, 1992; Sec CCP Guangxi Zhuang Autonomous Regl Cttee, 1997-. Memberships: Alt Mbr 14th CCP Cntr Cttee, 1992; Mbr 15th CCP Cntr Cttee, 1997-. Address: Chinese Communist Party Guangxi Zhuang Autonomous Regional Committee, Naning City, Guangxi Zhuang Autonomous Region, People's Republic of China.

CAO Jia-Ding, b. 14 Sept 1940, Shanghai, China. Mathematician. Education: Grad, Dept of Math, Fudan Univ, Shanghai, 1962. Appointments: Asst, 1962-85, Lectr, 1985-88, Prof, 1988-, Dept of Math, Fudan Univ, Shanghai; Invited Conf Participant, TX, Siam, Memphis, USA. Publications: 121, of which 74 in intl jrnls, 43 in Chinese jrnls, inclng: On Linear Approximation Methods, 1964; The Solution for J Favard's Approximate Problem, 1978; On Generalized Polynomials of L V Kantorovitch and Their Asymptotic Behaviors, 1981; Properties of L-approximation by Kantorovic Type Operators Satisfying Micchelli Conditions (in Engl), 1982; On Some Results of Integral Schoenberg Splines, 1983; Generalized Integral Logarithms and Two Examples of Summation of Fourier Series, 1984; Generalizations of Timan Theorem, Lehnhoff Theorem and Telyakovskii's Theorem, 1986; Approximation by Boolean Sums of Positive Linear Operators I-VII, (w H H Gonska), 198696; Pointwise Estimates for Modified Positive Linear Operators (w H H Gonska), 1988; On Sikkema-Kantorovic Polynomials of Order k, 1989; Computation of Devore-Gopengauz Type Approximants (w Heinz H Gonska), 1989; Pointwise Estimates of Groetsch-Shisha Type, 1989; Synthetical Investigations of Texts of Approximation Theory of Functions of USA, 1990; On Butzer's Problem Converning Approximation by Algebraic Polynomials, 1992. Memberships: Amn Math Soc; Chinese Math Soc; CSIAM; NY Acady of Sci. Listed in: Men of Achievement; Who's Who in the World; International Directory of Distinguished Leadership; 5,000 Personalities of the World; Who's Who in Science and Engineering; Dictionary of International Biography; Most Admired Men and Women of the Year. Address: Department of Mathematics, Fudan University, Shanghai, China.

CAO Jie, b. 8 Dec 1931. Book Designer; Artist. m. Liu Cheng-yin, 1950, 2 s, 1 d. Education: Chinese Tradl Painting Dept, Suzhou Fine Arts Spec Sch, 1949; Bachelor. Rsch Course in China Cntrl Arts and Crafts Coll. Appointments: Suzhou Fine Arts Spec Sch, 1949; Ed and Snr Ed, People's Fine Arts Press, 1951-; Exhibn of the 10 book designers, 1985; Artistical vis to Czechoslovakia, 1984; Lectures on sci books des, 1985; Hon Pres, Heze Painting and Calligraphy Rsch Inst, Shandong Province, 1996-. Creative Works: Inspirations from Dufu's Poems, 1988; Rosy Dawn, 1988; White-Flower Azalea, 1990; Chinese Wisteria, 1990; Lotus in Sunshine and Others, 1991; Buddha in Heart, 1992; Spring Birds, 1992; Golden Autumn, 1993. Honours: Gold Medal, book design, Leipzig Intl Exhibn, 1959; Gold Medal, for design of Leipzig Intl Exhibn, 1989; Natl Integral Des Prize, 1979; 2nd Prize for Bookcover Des of the III Natl Book Exhibn, 1986; 1st Natl Prize, 1990; 2 spec prizes, 2 gold medals, 1 silver medal, 1 bronze medal, 1980-90; Premier Zhou Enlai's Prize for Bookcover Des; State Cncl's Special Allowance for Outstanding Contribution, 1995. Memberships: Chinese Artists Assn; Dir, Book Des Rsch Soc; Chinese Publrs Assn; Sino-South Korean Cultural and Artistical Experts Cttee, Intl Artists Fedn, 1999. Hobbies: Opera; Ballad singing in Suzhou dialect; Travel. Address: Room 405, Side Door, People's Fine Arts Publishing House, 32, Beizongbu Hutong, Beijing, China.

CAO Jinan, b. 18 Oct 1955, Changzhou, China. Scientist. Education: BEng, China Textile Univ, Shanghai, 1978-82; Postgrad, Dept of Japanese Lang, Dailian Inst of Fgn Langs, 1982; MEng, 1982-85, PhD, 1985-88, Tokyo Inst of Technol. Appointments: Apprentice, Mechanic, Changzhou Factory of Packaging Materials, Changzhou, 1973-78; Postdoct Rsch Fell, Univ Qld, 1989-90; Rsch Sci, Div of Coal and Energy Technol, 1990-92, Snr Rsch Sci, Div of Wool Technol, CSIRO. Publications include: A Novel Application of a Polarization Microscope for the Study of Microbiological Specimens, 1990; Studies on the Mechanism of Draw Resonance in Melt Spinning, 1991. Honours: Sev. Memberships: NY Acady of Scis; Intl Confed for Thermal Analysis and Calorimetry; Austl Thermal Analysis Soc; Austl X-Ray Analytical Assn; Austl Hair and Wool Rsch Soc. Hobbies: Go; Swimming; Movies. Address: CSIRO Division of Wool Technology, PO Box 21, Belmont, Victoria 3216, Australia.

CAO Jinde, b. 8 Nov 1963. Teacher. m. 8 Sept 1988, 1 s. Education: BS, Maths Dept, Anhui Normal Univ, Wuhu, China, 1986; MSc, Yunnan Univ, Kunming, China, 1989; PhD Sichuan Univ, Chengdu, China, 1998. Appointments: Prof, Adult Educ Coll, Yunnan Univ, China, 1996-; Rsch interests incl: Dynamical System, Stability, Periodic Soloution, Oscillation for Differential Equations and Neural Network. Publications: 4 books; 60 articles. Honours: 3rd Awd and 1st Awd of 3rd and 4th Achmnt in Sci Rsch of Colls and Univs in Yunnan Prov,

China, 1993, 1995; 2nd Awd, 1st Nat Sci Prize, Yunnan, China, 1996; 2nd Awd, 2nd Nat Sci Prize, Yunnan, 1997. Membership: IEEE Computer Soc, China. Address: Adult Education College of Yunnan University, Yunnan 650091, China.

CAO Ke-Fei, b. 14 Nov 1963, Kunming, Yunnan Prov, China. Teacher; Researcher. Education: BS, Theort Phys, Dept Phys, 1979-83, MSc, High Energy Phys (Particle Phys), Dept of Phys, 1985-88, Yunnan Univ, China. Appointments: Tchng Asst, 1983-90, Lectr, 1990-92, Assoc Prof, 1992-96, Prof, 1996-97, Dept Phys, Yunnan Inst of the Nationalities, China; Visng Schl, Cntr for Nonlinear Studies and Dept Physiology, Univ Leeds, UK, 1993-95; Prof of Phys, Dept of Phys, Yunnan Univ, 1997-; Rsch in: Chaotic Phenomena, Nonlinear Dynamics, Fractals, Complex Systems; Tchng Experience: Symbolic Dynamics, Thermodynamics and Statistical Phys, Advd Maths, Computer Prog Des, Applications of Microcomputer Softwares, Gen Phys Lab Wrk, Tchng Prac. Publications: Contbr of sci pprs in profl jrnls incl: Physical Review E (USA), Journal of Physics A (UK), Physics Letters A (The Netherlands). Creative Works: 5 main discoveries w collaborators: (1) The Global Feigenbaum Super-Universality, 1988-92; (2) The Devil's Staircase of Topological Entropy, 1994-96; (3) Global Scaling Behaviours and the Universality for the Positions of Superstable Points in all the Periodic Windows for the Quadratic Map, 1996; (4) Metric Universality of Dual Star Products in Symbolic Dynamics of Three Letters, 1997-98; (5) Complexity of Routes to Chaos and Global Regularity of Fractal Dimensions in Bimodal Maps, 1998-99. Honours: 1st Prize, 1st Tchng Skill Contest for Jnr Tchrs of Yunnan Inst of the Nationalities, 1990; 1st Prize, 2nd Sci Rsch Accomplishments, Yunnan Inst Nationalities, 1992; Excellent Tchr of Yunnan Inst Nationalities, 1992; 3rd Prize, 1st Tchng Skill Contest for Jnr Tchrs of Higher Educl Insts of Yunnan Province, 1993; Govt Spec Allowance Awd, by State Cncl of China, 1993-; 1st Prize, 1st Nat Sci Awds of Yunnan Prov, 1996. Membership: Assoc Mbr, China Cntr of Adv Sci and Technol (World Lab). Hobbies: Philately; Watching sport; Calligraphy; Classical music; Photography; Collecting and reading maps; Travel. Address: Centre for Nonlinear Complex Systems, Department of Physics, Yunnan Univ, Kunming, Yunnan 650091, China.

CAO Kejiang, b. 20 Nov 1949, Anhui, China. Cardiologist. m. Quaying Han, 4 July 1976, 1 s. Education: Bach Deg, Med, Anhui Med Univ, 1970-73; Master Deg, Med, Tongji Med Univ, 1982-84; MD, Georg-August Universitat, Germany, 1987-91. Appointments: Res, 1973, Chf Res, 1984, 1st Affiliated Hosp, Anhui Med Univ; Master Cand, Tongji Med Univ, 1982-84; Dr Cand, 1987-91, Postdoct Rsch, 1991-93, Georg-August Universitat, Germany; Assoc Prof, 1994, Dir, Cardiac Interventional Cntr, 1996-97, Prof, 1997-, 1st Affiliated Hosp, Nanjing Med Univ. Publications: Arrhythmia, 1993; Clinical Cardiology, 1994; Interventional Cardiology, 1998; Cardiomyopathy. Honours: New Med Technol Awd, Jiangsu Prov Hosp, 1995; Govt Awd, Jiangsu Prov, 1997; Nanjing Med Univ Awd, 1997; Ex Dissertation Awd, Med Assn of Jiangsu, 1997; Nanjing Model Worker, 1997; Ex Dissertation Awd, Chinese Assn of Med, 1998; Most Outstndng Dr in China, 1998. Memberships: Chinese Assn of Med. Hobbies: Table Tennis; Chess; Music. Address: Cardiology Department, 1st Affiliated Hospital, Nanjing Medical University, 300 Guangzhou Road, Nanjing 210029, China.

CAO Qingze, b. 1932 Lixian Co Hunan Prov. Government and Party Official. Appointments: Joined CCP, 1952; Sec Commn for Discipline Insp of CCP Sichuan Provincial Ctte, 1986-93, now Dep Sec; Min of Supervision, 1993-98; Dep Sec Standing Cttee CCP Cntr Commn for Inspng Discipline, 1997. Honours: Hon Pres Soc of Supervision. Address: c/o Ministry of Supervision, 35 Huayuanbei Lu, Haidan Qu, Beijing 100083, China.

CAO Shuangming, b. 1929 Linxian Co, Henan Prov. Army Officer; Party Official. Appointments: Joined CCP

1946; Dep Cmdr PLA Shengyang Mil Area Cmd, 1987-92; Cmdr, 1992-; Rank of Lt Gen, 1988. Memberships: 14th CCP Cttee, 1992-. Address: Shengyang Military Area Command, People's Liberation Army, Shengyang City, Liaoning Province, People's Republic of China.

CAO Zheng Kang, b. 19 Feb 1940, Hangzhou, China. Engineering Design. m. Shi Cong, 1 Jan 1967, 1 s, 1 d. Education: BSc, Hohai Univ. Appointments: Snr Engr, 1986, Vice Chf Engr, 1991, Shanghai Municipal Engrng Design Inst. Publication: Engineering Application Manual of Soil Treatment, 1998. Honour: China Natl Golden Awd, Ex Design, 1994. Memberships: Acad Cttee, Shanghai Civil Engrng Assn; Dir, China Rock & Soil Anchorage Engrng Assn. Hobbies: Music; Baseball. Address: Shanghai Municipal Engineering Design Institute, 3 Guo Kang Road, Shanghai 200092, China.

CAO Zhigang, b. 31 July 1939, Shanghai, China. Professor. m. Xu ZhiZhi, 1 Oct 1967, 2 s. Education: Tsinghua Univ, China. Appointments: Asst Prof, Lectr, Tsinghua Univ, 1962-83; Visng Schl, Stamford Univ, 1984-86; Assoc Prof, Prof, Tsinghua Univ, 1987-. Publications: 5 books incl: Principles of Modern Communications, 1992; Digital Processing of Speech Signal, 1995. Honours: 1st Prize, Natl Ex Engrng Textbook, 1996; 7 awds from Natl Sci Congress; Min of Electron Ind; Min of Educ. Memberships: Snr Mbr, IEEE, 1985-; Snr Fell, Chinese Inst of Comms, 1994-; NY Acady Scis, 1996-; Mbr, Bd of Dirs, Beijing, Telecomms Inst, 1997-. Hobby: Classical music. Address: Department of Engineering, Tsinghua Univ, Beijing 100084, China.

CAPE Timothy Frederick, b. 5 Aug 1915. Retired Major-General; Representative; Consultant. m. Elizabeth Rabett, 31 Aug 1961, dec 1985, 1 d. Education: Grad, Roy Mil Coll, Dontoon, 1937. Appointments: 1st Hy Brig, Roy Austl Artillery, Sydney, 1938; 13th Hy Battery, Roy Austl Artillery, Port Moresby, 1939-40; Chf Instr, Sch Artillery, 1941; Brigade Maj, Sparrow Force Timor, 1942; GSO 1 Air, 1st Austl Corps, New Guinea Force, 1942-43; GSO 1 Ops, LHQ, Melbourne, 1944; GSO 1 Air, Adv LHQ, Morotai, 1945; 1945; GSO 1 Ops, BCOF, Japan, 1946-47; GSO Plans, Army HQ, Melbourne, 1948-49; Instr, Sch Combined Ops, UK, 1950; Staff Coll, Camberly, Eng, 1951-52; Cmdt, Offr Cadet Sch, Portsea, 1954-56; Cmdt, Staff Coll, Queenscliffe, 1956-57; Dpty Master, Gen Ordnance, Army HQ, Melbourne, 1957-59; Chf of Staff, N Command, Brisbane, 1961; Dir, Staff Duties, Army HQ, Canberra, 1962-63; Cmdr, C Command, Adelaide, 1964; Gen Offr Cmdng, N Command, Brisbane, 1965-68; Master Gen Ordnance, 1968-72; Retd; Mbr, Natl Cncl, Red Cross; Chmn, Natl Disaster Relief Cttee, 1975-85; Natl Pres, Roy Utd Servs Inst Aust, 1980-83. Honours include: US Bronze Star, 1945; DSO, 1945; CBE, 1966; CB, 1972. Memberships: Melbourne Union; Roy Sydney Golf Club; C'wlth Club. Address: PO Box 4285, Manuka, ACT 2603, Australia.

CAPPELLO Eve, b. 12 Apr, Sydney, Aust. Training Specialist; Consultant. 1 s, 1 d. Education: MA, Psychol, 1976; BA, Art Hist, 1974; PhD, Psychology, 1978. Appointments: Trng Specl, Kaiser Permanente, 1997-; Commnr, Affirmative Action, Diversity Commn, Pasa Dena, 1997-; Cnslt, Govt Corps and Univs, Intl. Creative Works: Act Don't React; Perfectionist Syndrome; New Professional Touch; Why Aren't More Women Running the Show; Great Sex After 50. Honours: Life Mbrshp, Alpha Gamma Hon Soc; Bus Profl, Women, Hall of Fame; Best Speaker Awds; Natl Hall of Fame. Memberships: Chmbr of Comm; Bus and Profl Women Commnr Affirm Action Commn; ACT Intl. Hobbies: Travel; Music; Reading; Public Speaking; Writing. Address: 578 S El Molino Ave #303, Pasadena, CA 91101, USA.

CARDEN Joan Maralyn, b. Melbourne. Opera Singer. m. William Coyne 1962, div 1980, 2 d. Education: Schs in Melbourne; Lang studies in London; Trinity Coll of Music London; London Opera Cntr; Voice studies with Thea Phillips and Henry Portnoj Melbourne and Vida Harford London. Appointments: First opera engagement world

premiere of Williamson's Our Man in Havana Sadler's Wells; Joined The Austl Opera, 1971; Covent Garden debut as Gilda - Rigoletto - 1974; Glyndebourne debut as Anna - Don Giovanni - 1977; US debut at Houston as Amenaide - Tancredi - 1977; Metrop Opera Tour as Anna - Giovanni - 1978; Perf'd regularly in concert repertoire of Sydney Symph Orch and Austl Brdcstng Corp. Honours: Dame Joan Hammond Awd for Outstanding Service to Opera in Aust, 1987; Aust Creative Fellowship, 1993. Hobbies: Gardening; Theatre; Reading. Address: c/o The Australian Opera, P O Box 291, Strawberry Hills, NSW 2012, Australia.

CAREY Alan Lawrence, b. 30 Dec 1949, Sydney, Aust. Mathematician. m. Cristene Elizabeth, 20 May 1972, 2 d. Education: BSc, Hons, Sydney, 1972; MSc, Adelaide, 1973; DPhil, Oxford, 1975. Appointments: Rothmans Fell, Queen Elizabeth II Fell, Snr Tchng Fell, Adelaide Univ; Rsch Fell, Austl Natl Univ; Lectr, Snr Lectr, Assoc Prof, Prof, Adelaide Univ. Publications: 100 rsch pprs, 3 ed books. Memberships: Dean, Sch of Math Scis; Amn Math Soc; Austl Maths Soc, VP, 1995-97. Hobby: Cycling. Address: School of Mathematical Sciences, University of Adelaide, Adelaide 5005, Australia.

CARLESS Ronald, b. 26 Jan 1927. Primary School Teacher. Education: Matriculation Cert, Victorian Educ Dept; Trained Primary Tchr's Cert, Ballarat Tchrs' Coll, Vic. Appointments: Avoca, 1944-45; Rathscar N, 1945-46; Werrap, 1946; Ballarat Tchrs' Coll, 1947; Newfield, 1948; Timboon Consolidated Sch, 1948-50; Mirboo East, Moliagul, Knowsley, 1951; Rochester HES, 1952-54; Rocklyn, Beaufort HES, Youanmite N, 1954; Bromley, 1955-58; Castlemaine, 1958-62; Maryborough E, 1963-65; Concongella, 1966-68; Redan, 1969-74; Sovereign Hill Histl Park, 1975-78; Mount Pleasant, 1979; Retd 1981. Publications: Church of St Michael & All Angels, Moliagul, Victoria, 1865-1965, 1865-1980; Welcome Stranger Centenary, Moliagul, Victoria, 1969; Church of St John, Dunolly, Victoria, 1969; Rheola, Victoria, 1870-1970, 1870-1985; Church of St Mary, Dunolly, Victoria, 1971; Redan Primary School (Ballarat), Victoria, 1874-1974; Son the Mount (Moliagul), Victoria, 1980; Eddington Reflections, Victoria, 1983; Castlemaine District Schools' Sports 1959-62. Memberships: John Flynn Mem Cttee, Moliagul, Vic, Sec 1955-58; Moyston Dist Schs' Sports, Sec 1967; Welcome Stranger Centenary Cttee, Moliagul, Vic, Sec 1968-69; Goldfields' Histl and Arts Soc Inc, Dunolly, Vic, Sec 1966-84, Asst Sec, 1985-2000; W Victorian Assn of Histl Socs, Cttee Mbr 1989-91, Pres 1991-95; Lower Homebush Sch Assn, Vic, Cttee Mbr 1989-93, Pres 1994-2000. Hobbies: Local and Australian History; Antiques; Art; Music. Address: Moliagul via Dunolly, Vic 3472, Australia.

CARLSEN John Richard, b. 16 June 1970, Palo Alto, CA, USA. Engineer. Education: San Jose State Univ, 1988-91; Austin Community Coll, 1995; De Anza Coll, 1991-93, 1997-; Degrees in Gen Studies, 1997; Multidisciplinary Studies, 1998; Techl Comms, 1999. Appointments: Engrng Contractor, Nolan K Bushnell, Mountain View, CA, 1988-89; Pres, Carlsen Electron Rsch, Sunnyvale, 1988-93; Engrng Contractor, Iguana Entertainment Inc, Sunnyvale, CA, 1991-93; Snr Hardware Engr, 1993-96; Engrng Contractor, AAPPS Corp, Sunnyvale, CA, 1989; Media Vision Inc, Fremont, CA, 1991-92; Advd Layout Engr, Altera Corp, San Jose, 1996-. Creative works: Des of interfaces and software tools for dev of video games on Sony Playstation, Sega Saturn, Super Nintendo and Atari Jaguar; Contbr des for PC & Macintosh multimedia cards. Membership: IEEE. Address: 1592 Heatherdale Avenue, San Jose, CA 95126-1308.

CARLSON Rosalind, b. 13 Mar 1937, Sydney, Aust. Teacher. m. David Philip John Carlson, 18 Aug 1959, 1 s, 1 d. Education: Dip Mus Ed, NSW State Conservatorium of Music, 1958; TCert, 1959; AMusA, Theory, AMusTCL, ATCL (P) Singing Dip, 1988; Trinity Coll, London, Eng. Appointments: Tchng 1959-87, Music Mistress 1987-, Dpty Prin 1979-, Cheltenham Girls' HS; Dept of Educ, NSW; Music Examiner, 1979-; Mbr,

Secondary Music Equip Advsry Cttee, 1972-75, Convenor for recommendations to Sch Lib Serv for Music ref books, 1972-73 (later revised music lib list, 1973); Music Resource Lectr in Curric Dev on the use of Austl Broadcasting Commn (ABC) Prog, 1979; Schs Cert Appeals Cttee-Chmn for Music Moderator, 1974-75; Coord, Evaluative Prog, The Talented Child Survey, NSW Dept of Educ; Fndr, Dir, Conductor, The Carlson Chorale all-female choir, 1973-; Choir appeared in Notes on a Landscape: 10 Austl Composers (documentary film), 1980; Roy Charity Concert before HM Queen Elizabeth II, Sydney Opera House, 1980; Currently, performing standard vocal repertoire as a lyric soprano; Guest Lctr, Austl Intl Conservatorium of Music, 1997-. Publications: Choral Reviews for the American Choral Directors Association Journal; Flexi-Fingers for Beginning Pianists, 1992; Flexi-Fingers Work Book, 1993; Five Concert Pieces, 1993; Three Australian Landscapes, 1996; Psalms of Joy, 1997; Waterfall in Spring, for flute and piano, 1997. Honours: The Last of His Tribe (choral a cappella composition by Anne Boyd) dedicated to her 1979; Medal of Israel, 1980; 10 trees planted in Jerusalem Peace Forest in her hon, 1980; Composer's Awd of the Yr, Gold Coast Composition Competition, 1998. Membership: Austl Soc for Music Educ; Inst of Music Tchrs, 1979; Music Tchrs Assn, NSW, 1993, Cncl Mbr, 1998; Austl Fellshp of Composers, 1996; Choral Adsry Panel, Cty of Sydney Cultural Cncl for McDonalds Cty of Sydney Perfng Arts Challenge, 1995; Adjudicator, Eisteddfod in composition, NSW. Hobbies: Needlework and embroidery; Crochet; Reading; Composing Music; Conducting; Choral Training of Students from specialised acappella ensemble to massed choirs with orchestra. Address: Box 55 PO, Pennant Hills, NSW 2120, Australia.

CARLTON James Joseph (Jim), b. 13 May 1935, Sydney, Australia. Secretary General, Australian Red Cross. m. Diane Mary Wilson, 9 May 1964, 1 s. 2 d. Education: BSc (Syd). Appointments: Pres, Studs Rep Cncl, Univ Sydney, 1956-57; Mgr, Dexion Ltd, London, 1957-66; Cnslt, McKinsey & Co Inc, 1966-71; Gen Sec, NSW Liberal Party, 1971-77; Sec, Friends of Australian Opera, 1974-78; Mbr, Austl House of Reps, 1977-94; Mbr, Myer Cttee on Cntrs of Excellence in Austl Univs, 1981; Hlth Min, 1982-83; Min assisting in Natl Dev and Energy, 1982-83; Var Shadow Mins, 1983-93; VP, Intl Cttee for Community of Democracies, 1989-91; C'wlth Observer Team Zambian Elections, 1991; Sec Gen, Austl Red Cross, 1994-; Chairperson, Natl Archives of Austl Advsry Cncl, 1998-. Hobbies: Opera; Music; Reading; Bush walking; Cooking. Address: 155 Pelham Street, Carlton, VIC 3053, Australia.

CARMAN Raymond Maurice, b. 16 Apr 1935. University Lecturer; Scientist. m. Linda Cartmill, 11 July 1982, 1 s, 4 d. Education: MSc, PhD, DSc, Victoria Univ of Wellington and Univ of NZ. Appointments: Scientist, DSIR, Wellington, 1958-60; Visng Fell, Univ Rochester, NY, 1958-59; Reader, Univ of QLD, 1961-; Visng Fell: Univ of MI, 1967; ICI Pharms, Cheshire, 1974, 1978; Univ of Stirling, 1981; Univ of Sussex, 1986; Univ of Otago, 1990; Univ of York, 1995. Creative works: Over 150 publications in the Australian J Chemistry on natural product chemistry, possums, sterochemistry, synthesis. Hobbies: Motor Cycling; Wine; Cricket; Rugby; Bushwalking. Address: 85 Ludlow Street, Chapel Hill, Brisbane, Qld 4069, Australia.

CARMICHAEL Alexander, b. 4 July 1937, Aust. Company Director. m. Lindsey Rieper, 12 Dec 1959, 1 s, 1 d. Education: BSc, Univ Melbourne. Appointments: Cnslt, Malaysian Govt, 1966-68; Exec Dir, 1971-73, Chmn, 1978-82, Seatainer Terminals Ltd; Dpty Grp Gen Mngr, TNT Ltd, 1972-73; Mngng Dir, 1975-79, then Dir, Bulkships Ltd; Dir, R W Miller and Co, 1975-78; Dir, Sebel Ltd, 1977-80; Dpty Chmn, NSW State Dockyard, 1977-80; Chmn, NSW Lotto Bd Control, 1979-86; Chmn, Grain Handling Inquiry, 1980-81; Chmn, State Rail Authy, NSW, 1980-85; Dir, Midland Credit Ltd, 1980-83; Dir, 1980-85, Chmn, 1981-85, Santos Ltd; Dir, 1981-92, Dpty Chmn, 1987-92, Ansett Transp Inds Ltd; Chmn, Darling Harbour Authy, 1984-88; Dir, Peko Wallsend Ltd, 1986-88; Dir, North Ltd, 1988-; Dir, Energy Rescs Aust Ltd, 1992-; Dir, Price Waterhouse Australasian Ptnrshp, 1993-; Commnr, Austl Natl Railways, 1994-96. Honours: CBE, 1977; AO, 1986. Hobbies: Tennis; Travel. Address: 9 Kardinia Road, Clifton Gardens, NSW 2088, Australia.

CARNEGIE David, b. 21 June 1943, Edinburgh, Scotland. University Lecturer. m. Pauline Reynolds Neale, 21 July 1973, 1 s, 1 d. Education: BA, hons, 1965; PhD, 1967. Appointments: Asst Prof, Engl, Univ Guelph, 1967-69; Snr Lectr, Drama, Univ Otago; Asst Prof, Drama, Univ McGill, 1976-77; Snr Lectr, Drama, 1978-96, Assoc Prof, 1997-, Vic Univ. Publications: Play Writing and Playing It Right, 1980; Works of John Webster, 1995. Memberships: Shakespeare Globe Cntr, NZ, vp 1993-; NZ Th Archive, tstee, 1996-; Aust and NZ Shakespeare Assn; Malone Soc; Southern Regl Arts Cncl, 1975-76; Summer Shakespeare Trust, 1987-. Address: School of English, Film & Theatre, Victoria University of Wellington, PO Box 600, Wellington, New Zealand.

CARNLEY Peter Frederick (The Most Revd Dr), b. 17 Oct 1937, New Lambton, New South Wales, Australia. Anglican Archbishop of Perth. m. Carol Ann Dunstan, 15 Jan 1966, 1 s, 1 d. Education: Licentiate, Theol, 1st Class Hons, Austl Coll of Theol 1962; BA, 1st Class Hons, Univ of Melbourne, 1966; PhD, Univ of Cambridge, 1970. Appointments: Deacon, 1962; Priest, 1964; Lic to Officiate Diocese Melbourne, 1963-65; Lic to Officiate Diocese Ely, 1966-69; Chap, Mitchell Coll of Adv Educ, 1970; Rsch Fell, St John's Coll, Cambridge, 1971-72; Warden, St John's Coll, Univ of Qld, 1972-81; Res Canon, Brisbane, 1975-81; Examining Chap to Archbish of Brisbane, 1975-81; Anglican Archbish of Perth, 1981-. Publications: The Poverty of Historical Scepticism, 1972; The Structure of Resurrection Belief, 1987. Honours: Lucas Tooth Schlsp, 1966; Univ Prize, Biblical Archaeol, Univ Melbourne, 1962, 1963; AO, 1998. Memberships: Sev. Hobbies: Gardening; Reading; Address: c/o Anglican Church Office, GPO Box W2067, Perth, WA 6846, Australia.

CARO David Edmund, b. 29 June 1922, Melbourne, Vic, Aust. Education Consultant; University Chancellor. m. Fiona Macleod, 18 Feb 1954, 1 s, 1 d. Education: MSc, Univ Melbourne; PhD, Univ Birmingham, 1951. Appointments: 1851 Overseas Rsch Schl, Univ Birmingham, 1949-51; Lectr, 1952, Rdr, 1958, Prof, Expmtl Phys, 1961-72, Dpty Vice-Chan, 1972-77, Vice-Chan, 1982-87, Univ Melbourne; Mbr, 1962-72, Pres, 1969-70, Austl Inst Nuc Sci and Engrng; Mbr, St Catherine's Sch Cncl, 1974-77; Vice-Chan, Univ Tas, 1978-82; Mbr, Tasmanian State Cttee, Cncl Sci and Indl Rsch, 1979-82; Mbr, Tasmanian Th Co Bd, 1979-82; Chmn, Antarctic Rsch Plcy Advsry Cttee, 1979-84; Chmn, Austl Vice-Chans Cttee, 1982-83; Mbr, Bd Mngmt, Walter and Eliza Hall Inst, 1982-87; Mbr, Mngmt Cttee, 1982-92, VP, 1987-92, Roy Melbourne Hosp; Chmn, UniSuper Ltd, 1984-94; Mbr, 1985-87, Chmn, 1990-, Ludwig Inst Bd; Chmn, Austl Univs Indl Assn, 1986-87; Interim Vice-Chan, NT Univ, 1988-89; Chmn, Exec Cttee, Williamson Community Ldrship Prog, 1989-94; Chmn, Bd, Monash Surg Pvte Hosp, 1991-; Chan, Univ Ballarat, 1998-. Honours: OBE, 1977; Hon LLD, Melbourne, 1978; Hon LLD, Tas, 1982; AO, 1986; Hon DSc, Melbourne, 1988. Memberships: Fell, Inst Phys, London; Fell, Austl Inst Phys; Fell, Austl Coll Educ. Hobbies: Theatre; Gardening; Skiing. Address: 17 Fairbairn Road, Toorak, Vic 3142, Australia.

CARPENTER David Arthur, b. 22 Aug 1944. Research Scientist. m. Lynette Yeats, 4 Dec 1971, 2 s. Education: BE, Elecl; MEng Sci; PhD Biomedl Engrng, Univ NSW. Appointments: Engr, Austl Dept of Hlth, 1969-89; Physicist, Inst of Cancer Rsch, London, 1972-73; Prin Rsch Scientist, Ultrasonics Lab, CSIRO, 1989-1996. Creative works: 80 research papers on medical ultrasound, 1969-1996, 3 book chapters, 7 patents. Honours: Pres, ASUM, 1981-82; Fell, IREE, 1986-96; Hon Fell, AIUM, 1996-97; Hon Assoc, RACR. Memberships: Austl Soc for Ultrasound in Med, 1970-96, Pres, 1981-82; IREE; IE Aust; AIUM. Listed in: Who's Who in Medicine. Hobbies: Astronomy; Acoustics. Address: 44 Bellambi Street, Northbridge, NSW 2063, Australia.

CARR Earl Alexander, b. 18 Mar 1941, Jamaica. Ambassador of Jamaica to Japan. m. Hiromi Carr, 2 s, 1 d. Education: BA, Econs; MA, Polit Sci; PhD, Polit Sci. Appointments: Asst Dir, Polit Divsn, Min of For Affairs, 1977-79; Min-Cnslr, Permanent Mission of Jamaica to the UN, NY, 1979-84; Min, Dpty Chf of Mission, Emb of Jamaica, WA, DC, 1984-90; Dir, Far Eastern Divsn, Min of For Affairs and For Trade, 1990-91; Dir, Jamaica Coml and Trade Off, Taipei, 1991-93; Amb Extraordinary and Plenipotentiary, Emb of Jamaica, Tokyo, Japan, 1994, China, 1994, Korea, 1995, Indonesia, 1996; High Cmmnr to Singapore, 1995, Malaysia, 1995. Hobbies: Reading; Music. Address: Embassy of Jamaica, Toranomon Yatsuka Building 2F, 1-1-11 Atago, Minato-ku, Tokyo 102-0002, Japan.

CARR Robert John, b. 28 Sept 1947. Premier of New South Wales; Minister for the Arts and Ethnic Affairs. m. Helena John, 1973. Education: BA, Hons, Univ of NSW. Appointments: Jrnlst, ABC Current Affairs Radio, 1969-72; Educ Offr, Labour Cncl, NSW, 1972-78; Jrnlst, Bulletin, 1978-83; Min for Plng and Environt, 1984-88, Consumer Affairs, 1986, Heritage, 1986-88; Ldr of Opposition, NSW, 1988-95. Address: Macquarie Tower, 1 Farrer Place, Sydney, NSW 2000, Australia.

CARR-BOYD Ann Kirsten, b. 13 July 1938, Sydney, Aust. Composer. 3 d. Education: BMUs, 1st Class Hons, 1960, MA, 1st Class Hons, 1963, Univ of Sydney. Appointments include: Piano Tchr, 1969-99; Composition and Piano Tchr, St Ignatius Coll, Sydney, 1986-89; Austl music histn and radio presenter on Austl composition; Fndn Tchr/Lectr in composition and Austl music, Austl Intl Conservatorium of Music, Sydney, Aust, 1993-98. Creative Works: Six Piano Pictures; Lullaby for Nuck; Fanfare for Aunty in FM; Look at the Stars (all Alberts AE Edition); The Bicentennial Piano Album, 1988; Concerto for Piano and Orchestra, 1991; Undara: Dawn for solo cello and orchestra, 1995; Images for orchestra, 1995; Fantasy for harp and orchestra, 1996; Bendooley Variations for Mandolin Quintet, 1997; Shoalhaven Suite, for solo piano, 1999; Works for clarinet, flute, violin, piano, harpsichord. Honour: Nom, APRA Awds, Most Performed Classical Contemp Composition, FANDANGO, 1999. Memberships: Austl Performing Right Assn; Fellowship of Austl Composers. Honours: Sydney Moss Schlsp, Sydney Univ, 1963; Maggs Awd, Composition, Melbourne, 1975; Finalist, Aliena Intl Harpsichord Composition Awd, USA, 1986. Listed in: Grove's Dictionary of Women Composers; Who's Who of Australian Women; Chambers Musical Dictionary; Who's Who in the World; Oxford Companion to Australian Music. Hobbies: Travel; Cooking. Address: 6 Miro Crescent, Bowral NSW 2576, Australia.

CARR-RUFFINO Norma, b. 15 Dec 1932, Fort Worth, Texas, USA. Professor of Management; Author; Management Consultant. m. Alfred Ruffino, 2 s, 1 d. Education: BBA, TX Wesleyan Univ, 1968; PhD, 1969, MBA, 1973, Univ N TX. Appointments: VP, Randy's Inc, Ft Worth, TX, 1965-70; Vocational Off Educn Tchr-Coord, Ft Worth Pub Schs, 1970-73; Prof of Mngmt, San Fran Univ, 1973-. Publications: Women in Management Review, 1991; Woman Power, 1991; Business Students Guide, 1991; The Promotable Woman: 10 Essential Skills for the New Millennium, 1997; Managing Diversity: People Skills for a Multicultural Workplace, 1998; Diversity Success Strategies, 1999. Honours include: Meritorious Performance & Profl Promise Awd, 1986, 1989; Ldrshp Recog Awd, Bus Womens Ldrshp Assn, 1991, 1992; Alumna of the Ur, 1988, Outstndng Alumna, 1991, TX Wesleyan Univ. Memberships: Acady of Mngmt; World Future Assn; Natl Org for Women. Hobbies: Antiques; Travel; Metaphysics; Dancing. Address: College of Business, San Francisco State University, 1600 Holloway, San Francisco, CA 94132, USA.

CARREY Jim, b. 17 Jan 1962 Newmarket, Ont. Actor. m. Melissa Worner 1986, div, 1 d. Appointments: Began

Perfng in comedy clubs in Toronto aged 17 before moving to Hollywood; TV appearances incl: In Living Colour - sit-com. Films incl: Peggy Sue Got Married, 1986; The Dead Pool, 1988; Earth Girls Are Easy, 1989; Ace Ventura! Pet Detective; The Mask; Dumb and Dumber; Batman Forever; The Cable Guy. Address: UTA, 9560 Wilshire Boulevard, 5th Floor, Beverly Hills, CA 90212, USA.

CARRICK John Leslie (Sir), b. 4 Sept 1918, Sydney, NSW, Aust. Senator. m. 2 June 1951, 3 d. Education: BEcon, Univ of Sydney. Appointments include: Gen Sec, NSW Div, Liberal Party, 1948-71; Mbr, Senate, 1971-87; Mbr, Lib Cttee, 1971-73; Senate Stndng Cttee Educ Sci and Arts, 1971-75; Var posns, other Senate Cttees, 1971-87; Opposition Spokesman, Federalism and Intergovt Rels, 1975; Min Hsg and Constrn, 1975; Min Educ, 1975-79; Min asstng PM in Fed Affairs, 1975-78; Ldr Govt in Senate, 1978-83; VP, Exec Cncl, 1978-82; Min Natl Dev and Energy, 1979-83; Chmn, NSW Govt Cttee Review of Schs, 1988-89; Pres, Univ Sydney Dermatology Rsch Fndn, 1988-; Chmn, Gas Cncl NSW, 1990-95; Mbr, Advsry Cncl, Inst of Early Childhood, Macquarie Univ, 1990-; Chmn, Advsry Cttee GERRIC (Gifted and Talented), Univ of NSW. Honours: KCMG, 1982; Hon DLitt, Sydney Univ, 1988; Hon Fell, Austl Coll Educ, 1994. Memberships: Austl Club, Sydney; C'wlth Club, Canberra. Hobbies: Reading; Jogging; Swimming. Address: Apartment 21, 162E Burwood Road, Concord, NSW 2173, Australia.

CARRICK Roger John (Sir), b. 13 Oct 1937. British Diplomat (Retired); Consultant. m. Hilary Elizabeth Blinman, 1 Sept 1962, 2 s. Education: Jt Servs Sch for Linguists, London Univ, Sch for Slavonic and E Eurn Stdies. Appointments: Royal Navy, 1956-58; Diplomatic Serv, 1956-97; For Off, 1958-61; Third Sec Brit Legation (later Embassy), Sofia, Bulgaria, 1962-65; FO, 1965-67; Second, later First Sec (Econ), Brit Embassy, Paris, 1967-71; Hd of Chancery, Brit High Commn, Singapore, 1971-74; FCO, 1974-77; Visng Fell, Univ of CA, Berkeley, 1977-78; Cnslr, BE Wash, 1978-82; Hd of Dept, FCO, 1982-85; HM Consul-Gen, Chgo, 1985-88; Asst Under-Sec of State, FCO, 1988-90; HM Amb to Indonesia, 1990-94; Brit High Commn to Aust, 1994-97; Mbr, Bd of Tstees, Chevening Est; Jt Fndr, Worldwide Advice on Diplomatic Estates; Consultant, KPMG (Australia), 1998-. Publications: East-West Technology Transfer in perspective, 1978; Rolleround Oz, 1998. Honours: Lt of the Royal Victorian Order, 1972; Companion, Order of St Michael and St George (CMG), 1983; Kt Cmdr (KCMG), 1995. Memberships: Royal Overseas League; Cook Soc; Pilgrims; Roy Soc for Asian Affairs; Anglo-Indonesian Soc; Primary Club; Dpty Chmn and Dir, Bd of Mngmnt, Britain-Aust Soc, 1998-; Churchill Fell, Westminster Coll, Fulton, MO. Listed in: Who's Who (UK); International Who's Who. Hobbies: Sailing; Music; Reading; Travel; Avoiding gardening. Address: 43 Dornden Drive, Langton Green, Tunbridge Wells, Kent TN3 0AE, England.

CARRINGTON Cedric Gerald, b. 16 Oct 1943, Oamaru, New Zealand. Engineering Physicist. m. Janet, 7 Aug 1967, 1 s, 2 d. Education: BSc, hons; MSc, Otago; DPhil, Phys, Oxford. Appointments: Jnr Rsch Fell, Merton Coll, Oxford, 1970-72; Rsch Assoc, Univ CO, USA, 1972-73; Lectr, Snr Lectr, Prof, Phys, Otago Univ. Publication: Basic Thermodynamics, 1994. Honours: Rutherford Mem Schl, Roy Soc, London, 1967; Vis Fell, Keble Coll, Oxford, 1987; Visng Rsch Fell, Univ Melbourne, 1994. Memberships: VP, Cmmn E2, Intl Inst of Refrigeration; ASHRAE; Inst of Profl Engrs, NZ. Address: Department of Physics, University of Otago, PO Box 56, Dunedin, New Zealand.

CARROLL Diana, b. 13 Nov 1959. Business Entrepreneur. 1 d. Education: Univ SA. Appointment: Mngng Dir, Warburton Media Monitoring; Lctr, Pub Rels Univ of SA; State Cnclr, PRIA-SA. Creative works: Radio commentator; Newspaper columnist. Honor: Austl Day Cncl Bus Achmnt Awd, 1996. Memberships: Pres, Austl Assn of Brdcst Monitors; Intl Assn of Brdcst Monitors; Soc of Bus Communicators; Adelaide Bus and Profl Liberal Party; Enterprising Women; Mbr Pub Rels Inst of Aust; Tstee, Women's and Children's Hosp Fndn. Hobbies: Travel; Politics; Contemporary art; Wine. Address: c/o Warburton Media Monitoring, 68 North Terrace, Kent Town, SA 5067, Australia.

CARROLL Francis Patrick (Most Reverend), b. 9 Sept 1930, Aust. Roman Catholic Archbishop. Education: DD; DCL; De La Salle Coll, Marrickville; St Columba's Coll, Springwood; St Patrick's Coll, Manly; Pontifical Urban Univ de Propaganda Fide, Rome. Appointments: Ordained Priest, 1954; Asst Priest, Griffith, NSW, 1955-58; Asst Insp, Cath Schs, Diocese Wagga Wagga, 1957-61; Asst Priest, Albury, 1958-61; Bish's Sec, Diocesan Chan, Diocesan Dir Cath Educ, 1965-67; Consecrated Co-Adjutor Bish, 1967; Bish Wagga Wagga, 1968-83; Chmn, Natl Cath Educ Commn, 1974-78; Archbish Canberra and Goulburn, 1983. Publication: The Development of Episcopal Conferences, 1965. Honour: Hon DLit, Charles Sturt Univ, Wagga Wagga, 1994. Memberships: Intl Catechetical Commn, 1974-92; Chmn, Bish's Cttee Educ, 1980-88. Address: Archbishop's House, GPO Box 89, Canberra, ACT 2601, Australia.

CARSON Susan Dueball, b. 19 Nov 1949. Forest Scientist. m. Michael John Carson, 27 July 1981, 2 s, 1 d. Education: BS, Nat Resources, w distinction, Univ of MI, 1972; MSc, Forestry, Univ of MI, 1978; Grad studies, Plant Path, Univ of MN, 1974-76; PhD, Forestry, Minors in Genetics and Plant Path, NC State Univ, 1984. Appointments: Rsch Asst/Tchng Asst, Univ of MI, Sch of Nat Resources, Ann Arbor, MI, 1973-74; Rsch Asst/Tchng Asst, Univ of MN, Dept of Plant Path, St Paul, MN, 1974-76; Trng Instr, Environmental Educ (GS-7), USDA Forest Serv, Ottowa Natl Forest, Ironwood, MI, 1976; Techn, Systems Analyst (GS-5), USDA Forest Serv, Nast Forest Experiment Stn, Hampden, CT, 1976-77; Resistance Screening Cntr Mngr (Plant Path) (GS-11) USDA Forest Serv, 1977-81; Scientist, Genetics and Tree Improvement, Forest Rsch Inst Rotorua NZ, 1982-87; Rsch Coop Mngr, Forest Rsch Inst, Rotorua, NZ, 1987-89; Scientist, Forest Mensuration and Mngmt Systems, 1989-99; Prog Mngr, Gene Mapping and Fingerprinting, Forest Rsch Inst, 1992-97; Prog Mngr, Molecular Breeding, Forest Rsch Inst, 1997-99; Marker Applications Mngr, Fletcher Challenge Forests Biotech Ctre, NZ, 1999-. Publications: 35 refereed publs, 120 others. Honours: Alpha Lamda Delta, 1968; Tau Sigma, 1971; Gen Univ Schlshp, Univ of MI, Xi Sigma Pi and Carleton-McCarron Forestry Schlshp, 1973; Garfield Schlshp Awd, 1975; Sigma Delta Epsilon, 1975; Grad Tuition Schlshp, Univ of MI, 1976; US Dept of Agric Cert of Merit, 1978; Sigma Xi Sci Rsch Soc (full mbr), 1982; NZ/UK/Aust Tripartite STC Agreement Travel Grant, 1994; NZ/USA Collaborative Sci Prog Rsch Grant, 1996. Memberships: Amn Phytopathological Soc; NZ Genetical Soc; NZ Inst of Foresters; NZ Royal Soc; NZ Statistical Assn; Sigma Xi Sci Rsch Soc; NY Acady of Scis; Amn Assn for the Advancement of Sci. Hobbies: Reading; Swimming; Walking; Travel; Computers. Address: Fletcher Challenge Forests Biotechnology Centre, RDZ, Whakatane, New Zealand.

CARSON Wesley George, b. 15 Feb 1940, Belfast, N Ireland. Educational Consultant. m. Ruth, 10 Sept 1967, 1 s, 1 d. Education: MA; Dip.Crim; LLD. Appointments: Lectr, Univ of London; Lectr, Snr Lectr, Law, Univ of Edinburgh; Prof, Legal Stdies, Dpty Vice Chan, La Trobe Univ; Vice Chan, Univ of Auckland. Publications: 1 book; Num articles in profl jrnls. Hobbies: Fly fishing; Rugby Union. Address: PO Box 32, Foster, Vic 3960, Australia.

CARTER Darcy Cyril, b. 31 Oct 1921, Fairfield, NSW, Aust. Investor; Grazier. m. Audrey Ethel Sedgman, 7 Feb 1944, 2 s, 1 d. Education: Metro Bus Coll, 1937. Appointments: Mngr, Bank of Adelaide, 1937-80; Commissioned Offr, 2nd Austl Imperial Force (AIF), Reserve Offr (Army), 1945-68. Honours: Africa Star; Pacific Star; Austl Army Efficiency Medal, 1952; OAM, 1980; Indonesian For Min Letter of Appreciation Awd, 1975; 50 Yr Awd, Queenscliff Surf Life Saving Club. Memberships: Life Gov, Aust-China Chamber of Com and Ind of NSW; Life Mbr, Austl Bank Employees' Union. Hobbies: Surf Life Saving; Interior Decorating; Landscape Gardening; Carpentry. Address: 16 Bendemeer Road, Kingstown, NSW 2358, Australia.

CARTER John Norman, b. 28 Dec 1944, Melbourne, Aust. Endocrinologist. m. Merren, 3 May 1975, 1 s, 3 d. Education: BSc (Med); MB BS; MD; FRACP. Appointments: Cnslt Endocrinologist, Concord Hosp and Hornsby Hosp; Chmn, Commonwealth Ministerial Advsry Cttee on Diabetes; Natl Diabetes Task Force; Clinl Assoc Prof, Univ of Sydney. Memberships: Pres, Austl Diabetes Soc, 1992-94; Endocrine Soc of Aust; Austl Medl Assn. Hobbies: Golf; Tennis; Reading; Theatre; Softball. Address: 46 Lord Street, Roseville, NSW, Australia 2069.

CARTER Norman Lindsay, b. 2 Mar 1932. Research Scientist. m. Janet Catherine Cunningham, 27 Nov 1968, 2 s. Education: BA (Hons); MA (Hons, 1st Class); PhD; Assoc in Music, Aust (Violin, performing). Appointments: Rsch Psychol, Commonwealth Acoustic Labs, Sydney, 1956-60; Rsch Assoc, Bolt, Beranek & Newman Inc, Boston, MA, 1960-62; Rsch Psychol, Commonwealth Acoustic Labs, 1962-66; Hd, Effects of Noise on People Rsch, Natl Acoustic Labs, 1966-96; Hon Rsch Assoc, Univ of Sydney, 1985-86, 1996-. Publications: Numerous research reports, and scientific papers on the effects of noise, published in the proceedings of Australian and International Conferences, including: International Congress on Acoustics, 1980, 1983, 1995; Internoise, 1991; 1996; International Congresses on Noise as a Public Health Problem, 1983, 1988, 1993; Numerous scientific papers published in scientific journals including: Journal of Sound and Vibration; Journal of the Acoustical Society of America; Sleep; Hypertension; Medical Journal of Australia; Military Medicine; Australian Journal of Audiology; Acoustics Australia; Psychophysiology. Memberships: Austl Acoustical Soc, 1971-; Mbr, Cttee AV/3 (Hum Effects) & Subcttees, Stands Assn of Aust, 1966-; Fndn Mbr, Australasian Sleep Assn, 1989-; Fndn Mbr, Australasian Sleep Technols Assn, 1989-; Invited Mbr, Noise Team 3 (Physiol Effects), Noise Team 5 (Effects on Sleep), Intl Commn on Biol Effects of Noise, 1993-; Chmn, Sydney Airport Studies of Aircraft Noise and Hlth, 1992-; Pres, Chmn, Organising Cttee, 7th Intl Congress on Noise as a Pub Hlth Problem, Sydney, 1998; Amateur Chmbr Music Soc Inc, 1995-. Hobbies: Environmental issues, especially land use and coastal protection; Playing violin in chamber music ensembles and semi-professional orchestras; Kayaking; Swimming; Reading; Theatre. Address: 25 Calga Street, East Roseville, NSW 2069, Australia.

CARTER Wilfred (Air Vice-Marshal), b. 5 Nov 1912, Ratcliffe, Eng. International Disaster Consultant. m. Margaret Enid Bray, 15 Apr 1950, 1 s, dec, 1 d. Education: RAF Staff Coll; Jnt Servs Coll; Mid E Cntr Arab Stdys. Appointments: RAF: Pilot, served WWII, Bomber Cmnd; Var Cmnd and Staff appts, inclng 2 yrs on Cabinet Secretariat, 1967-69; Dir, Austl Counter Disaster Coll, 1969-79; Intl Disaster Cnslt, 1979-. Publications: Books: Disaster Preparedness and Response; Disaster Management, 1992. Honours: DFC, 1943; Mentioned in Despatches, 1943; Winner, Gordon Shephard Mem Prize, Strategic Stdys, 1955, 1956, 1957, 1961, 1965, 1967; CB, 1963. Membership: Patron, Austl Inst Emer Servs. Hobbies: Walking; Swimming. Address: Blue Range, Macedon, Vic 3440, Australia.

CARY Tristram Ogilvie, b. 14 May 1925, Oxford, Eng. Composer; Writer; Teacher. m. Doris E Jukes, 7 July 1951, div 1978, 2 s, 1 d. Education: Christ Church, Oxford (Exhbnr), 1942-43, 1946-47, interrupted by serv in RN, BA, MA; Trinity Coll of Music, AMus, TCL, LMus, TCL, 1949-51. Appointments: Debut, Wigmore Hall, London, 1949; Composing from age of 14; Record Shop Asst, 1951-54; 1st Electron Music Studiom, 1952; Self-Employed, 1955-; Music for concerts, films, radio, TV, th, musical directories, etc; Fndr, Electron Studio at Roy Coll of Music, 1967; Snr Lectr, 1974-, Rdr, Dean of Music, 1982, Univ of Adelaide; Self-Employed as Composer, Tchr, Writer, Computer Music Cnslt. Creative Works: Compositions: 345 Narcissus Trios Sonata for Guitar Alone; Three Threes and One Make Ten;

Arrangement of Bach's 6-part Ricercar, Continuum, Contours and Densities at First Hill; Peccata Mundi; Divertimento; The Songs Inside; Romantic Interiors; Steam Music; Two Songs From the Piae Cantiones; Nonet; Soft Walls; I Am Here Family Conference; Seeds; Trellises; Strands; String Quartet II; Sevens; The Dancing Girls; Strange Places; Inside Stories; Black, White and Rose; Messages; The Impossible Piano; Suite: The Ladykillers; Through Glass. Recordings Num for TV, Radio and Films. CDs: Quatermass and the Pit- Film Music by Tristram Cary Voll; The Ladykillers - Music from Ealing Films. Publications: Synthesised Music (chapt 15 of Sound Recording Practice), 1976; Illustrated Compendium of Musical Technology, 1992; Contr to sev profl jrnls and mags. Honours: Best Experimental Film of the Yr, Venice, 1958; BFA Awd 1959, 1962; Hon RCM Awd, 1971; OAM, 1991. Membership: Inst of Elec Engrs. Listed in: International Who's Who in Music. Hobbies: Swimming; Sailing; Cycling; Snooker; Cookery; Wine; Good Conversation. Address: 30 Fowlers Road, Glen Osmond, SA 5064, Australia.

CASH Pat, b. 27 May 1965. Tennis Player. m. Emily Cash, 1 s, 2 d. Education: Whitefriars Coll; Coached by Ian Barclay; Trnr Anne Quinn. Appointments: Winner US Open Jnr, 1982; Winner Austl Davis Cup team, 1983; In quarter-finals Wimbledon, 1985; Finalist Austl Open, 1987; Wimbledon Champion, 1987. Address: c/o National Tennis Centre, Flinders Park, Batman Avenue, Melbourne, VIC 3000, Australia.

CASH Samuel George Ernest, b. 12 Sept 1946, Subiaco, WA, Aust. Member of Parliament. 1 s, 3 d. Education: Scotch Coll, WA; Assoc'ship, Valuation, 1975, BBus, 1978, W Austl Inst Technol; LLB (Hons), Univ of London, 1999. Appointments: JP, 1979; Cnclr, 1980-86, Dpty Mayor, 1983-84, City of Stirling; Mbr, Legis Assembly, 1984-89, Shadow Min Police, Emer Servs, Correctives Servs, 1985-93, Mbr, Legis Cncl, 1989-, Ldr Opposition, 1989-93, Min Mines, Lands, 1993-96, Min assisting Min Rescs Dev, 1993-95, Ldr Govt, 1993-96, Min assisting Min Pub Sector Mngmt, 1994-96, Chmn Austl and NZ Mins and Energy Cncl, 1994-95, Parl WA; Pres Legislative Cncl, 1997-. Membership: Assoc, Inst Chartered Secs and Admnstrs. Hobbies: Sailing; Tennis. Address: Parliament House, Harvest Terrace, Perth, WA 6000, Australia.

CASSAB Judy, b. 15 Aug 1920, Vienna, Austria. Painter. m. John Kampfner, 1939, 2 s. Education: Budapest; Prague. Appointments: 64 individual exhibns, galls throughout Aust, London, Paris, 1953-99; Wrks in num Austl galls inclng Natl Gall, Canberra, UK galls inclng Natl Portrait Gall, London, US galls, Natl Gall Budapest; Mbr, Cncl of the Order of Aust, 1975-79; Tstee, Art Gall NSW, 1979-87. Publications: Ten Australian Portraits, lithographs; Judy Cassab, Places, Faces and Fantasies, 1985; Artists and Friends, 1988; Judy Cassab Diaries, 1995; Portraits of Artists and Friends, 1998. Honours: AO; CBE; Sev prizes inclng: Sir Charles Lloyd Jones Mem Prize, 4 times; The Trees Watercolour Prize, 1994; Pring Prize, 1994, 1997. Listed in: Who's Who in Australia; International Who's Who. Address: 16C Ocean Avenue, Double Bay, Sydney, NSW 2028, Australia.

CASSADY John Michael, b. 29 Jan 1937, Los Angeles, CA, USA. Neuroscientist; Behaviourist. m. Constance Lue Burrus, 28 Aug 1962, 3 children (1 decd). Education: BA, Psychol, Univ of CA, Los Angeles, 1955-62; MA, Psychol, Ca State Univ, Long Beach, Dept of Psychol, 1962-64; PhD, Psychol & Biological Scis, Univ of CA at Irvine, 1968-72; NIMH Postdoct Fellshp, Univ of CA at Irvine, 1973-75. Appointments include: Pacific State Hosp & Univ of CA at Los Angeles, 1964-73; Rsch Asst, Sch of Socl Scis, 1968-72, NIMH Postdoct Fell, 1973-75, Lectr, 1975-79, Dept of Psychol, Rsch Spec, Dept of Anatomy, 1978-81, Univ of CA at Irvine; Cnslt on spec occasions usually concerning the application of computers to the particular proj under discussion: UCLA Hlth Scis, other orgs, State & County reprs, 1967-81; Cnslt Servs, Sole Proprietor, Contract Servs Neurobahvioral, Sociobehavioral & Biomedical Cnslt Computer Programming, Computer Applications & Tech/Sci Writing, Los Angeles, 1981-; Computer Analyst, Carmel Rsch Cntr, Santa Monica, 1992-94; Instr, W Coast Univ, Los Angeles, CA, Bio Dept, 1992. Publications: 17 in var jrnls. Honour: NIMH Post-doct Appt, 1973-75. Memberships: Intl Behavioral Neuroscience Soc; Treasurer, hs Writer Class, 1955; Johnston Club; Brain Rsch Org. Hobbies: Recording and record keeping of reptiles found in field (field biology); Singing; Hiking and exploration; Sports. Address: Consultant Services, PO Box 641612, Los Angeles, CA 90064-6612, USA.

CASSEL Susie, b. 30 Sept 1966, Liberia, Africa. Professor of Literature. Education: BA Comm Arts and Scis, 1986, BA Psychol, Rel (Hons) and Eng (Hons), 1987, Univ S CA, LA; MA Eng and Amn Lit and Lang, 1988, Harvard Univ at Cambridge; PhD Eng, 1996, Univ CA at Riverside. Appointments: Asst to Ed, Project Innovation, 1994-; Editl Bd, Coll Student Jrnl, 1994-; Referee Rdr, Melus, 1996-97; Asst Prof, Lit and Writing Stdies, CA State San Marcos, 1996-. Publications: Faye Myenne Ng's Bone and the Structure of Cultural Nationalism; Eliza Ruhamah Scidmore, Sara Estela Ramirez, Octavia Celeste W LeVert, 1999, Am Natl Biog; And the View of the War, 1998; Pitfalls in Protocols: The Persistence of Race in the Interview Process, 1997; Need Gratification and Brain Dominance Serve as Nucleus for Transpersonal Psychology and Biofeedback Use; Computer BASIC Programs for use by Teachers to put CAI-Type Learning Modules on Computer;8 conference papers. Honours: Acad hons and profiled in Star News and Asian Community Times; and others. Memberships: Mod Lang Assn; MELUS; Assn of Asian Amn Stdies; San Diego Chinese Hist Soc. Hobbies: Classical piano; Jogging. Address: California State University Literature and Writing Studies, San Marcos, CA 92096-0001, USA.

CASSELL Russell, b. 18 Dec 1911, Harrisburg, PA, USA. Senior Research Psychologist. m. Lan Mieu Dam, 5 Oct, 2 s, 5 d. Education: EDD; ABPP; FAPSP. Appointments: Col, US Air Force, Retd; Grad Air War Coll. Publications: Nearly 12 books; Over 500 articles in var of jrnls. Honours: Hon Doct, Univ of Moscow; Ed, Natl jrnls for 29 yrs; Phi Delta Kappa; Phi Kappa Phi; Phi Sigma Pi. Memberships: Amn Psychol Assn; Freemason; Shriners. Hobbies: Piloting airplanes; Tennis. Address: 1362 Santa Cruz, Chu la Vista, CA 91910, USA.

CASSIDY John Joseph, b. 21 June 1930, Gebo, Wyoming, USA. Civil Engineer. m. Alice, 15 Mar 1953, 2 s, 1 d. Education: BSCE, 1952, MSCE, 1960, MT Univ; PhD, UnivIA, 1964. Appointments: Design Engr, MT Water Conservation Bd, 1955-58; Prof, Chmn, Civil Engrng, Univ MO, 1963-74; Chf Hydrologic Engr, Bechtel Corp, San Fran, 1974-85, Mngr, 1985-95. Publications: Hydraulic Engineering, 1984; Hydrology for Engineers and Planners, 1974; 45 tech pprs. Honours: Bechtel Fell, 1984. Memberships: ASCE; Natl Acady of Engrng; Chi Epsilon. Hobbies: Woodwork; Fly Fishing. Address: 4400 Capitol Court, Concord, CA 94518, USA.

CASTLES Alexander Cuthbert, b. 7 Mar 1933, Melbourne, Australia. Emeritus Professor of Law. m. Florence (separated), 1 s, 4 d. Education: LLB (Hons) (Melbourne); JD (Chgo). Appointments: Asst Lectr, Univ of PA; Snr Lectr, Rdr, Prof, Bonython Prof, Law Sch, Univ of Adelaide. Publications: Australia and the UN, 1974; Introduction to Australian Legal History, 1971; Chronology of Australia (co-auth), 1978; Source Book of Australian Legal History, 1979; Australian Legal History, 1982; Lawson North Terrace, 1983; Law Makers and Wayward Whigs, 1987; Annotated Bibliography of Australian Law, 1994; Shark Arm Murders, 1995. Honour: Visng Fell, UN Inst for Trng and Rsch, 1970. Memberships: Pres, UN Assn of Aust, 1967-70; Commnr (pt-time), Austl Law Reform Commn, 1975-82. Hobby: Collecting newspapers. Address: 2/112 Beulah Road, Norwood, South Australia, Australia 5067.

CASTRO Amado Alejandro, b. 29 Jun 1924 Manila. Economist. Education: Univ of the Philippines; Harvard Univ USA. Appointments: Instr in Econs Univ of Philippines, 1948-53; Asst Prof, 1954-56; Assoc Prof, 1956-62; Hd of Econs Dept, 1956-58; Acting Dean Coll of Bus Admin, Jan-Sept, 1958; Dir Inst of Econ Dev and Rsch, 1958-66; Prof of Econs,1962-; Gov and Acting Chmn Dev Bank of Philippines, 1962-66; Dean Sch of Econs, 1965-73; Prof of Monetary Econs, 1972; Econ Bur ASEAN Sec, 1977-80. Address: School of Economics, University of the Philippines, Quezon City, Philippines 3041.

CASTRO JIJON Ramon, b. 1915. Politician; Naval Officer. Education: Studied naval engrng in USA. Appointments: Fmr Naval Attache London; Cmdr in Chf of Navy, Ecuador; Pres Mil Junta, 1963-66; In exile 1966-. Address: Rio de Janeiro, RJ, Brazil.

CASTRO SALAZAR René, b. 25 Aug 1957. Minister of Natural Resources. Education: BCs, Civ Engrng, Univ Costa Rica, 1980; MA, Pub Admin, Harv Univ, 1990; Postgrad, 1993-94. Appointments: civ Engr, Snr Cnslt, Caribbean Cntrl Amn Confed Co-ops; Exec Dir, Costa Rican Natl Fedn Co-ops, 1986-89; External Cnslt, Interamerican Dev Bank, 1992; Ptnr, Estudios Profesionales, 1992-93; Vice Min, Internal Affairs, 1982-86; Undersec, Transp, 1982-86; Prof, Cntrl Mngmt Inst, 1992-93; Min, Natural Rescs, Energy, Mines, Govt Costa Rica, 1994-. Publications: Author, 2 books; Contbr, articles to profl jrnls. Memberships: Sec, Intl Rels, Natl Liberation Party Yth Org, Overseer, San José, 1981; Pres, San José Cty Cncl, 1982-86. Address: Apartado 10104, Avenida 8-10 Calle 25, 1000 San José, Costa Rica.

CASWELL Patricia Joy, b. 22 Aug 1948, Brisbane, Aust. National Executive Director. Education: Univ of Qld; La Trobe Univ. Appointments include: Tchr, Preston Coll, TAFE, 1975-76; Gen Sec, Tech Tchrs Union, Vic, 1981-84; Ind Off, Vic Trades Hall Cl, 1984-92; Exec Dir, Aust Conservation Fndn, 1992-95; Natl Exec Dir, Plan Intl Aust, 1995-. Publications: Num pprs on ind rels, women in the workforce, power ind, pub transport, lit in the workforce, conservation and the environ, economy, mngmt and equity. Honour: Pres Awd, Austl Med Assn, 1996. Address: Plan International Australia, GPO Box 2818AA, Melbourne, Vic 3001, Australia.

CATERSON Reece Vera, b. 13 Feb 1907, Sydney, Aust. Retired Journalist. m. Harold J L Caterson (decd), 29 Dec 1929, 1 s, 3 d. Publications: Collected poems: Span of Living, 1st & 2nd eds. Honours; Gold Bi-centennial Medallion for 1st ed, 26 Aug 1988, Melbourne Poetry Soc. Memberships: Vic Fellshp of Austl Writers; Austl Conservation Fndn. Hobbies: Creative writing; Painting; Pottery; Conservation. Address: C/o G K Tucker Settlement, 5 William Road, Carrum Downs, Victoria, Australia 3201.

CATO Douglas Herrod, b. 2 Dec 1940. Rsch Scientist. Education: BSc, 1961, MSc, 1978, PhD, 1986, Univ of Sydney. Appointments: Experimental Offr, Royal Austl Navy Rsch Lab, Sydney, 1961, 1973; Higher Sci Offr, Bldg Rsch Estab, UK, 1972; Snr Rsch Scientist, 1988, Prin Rsch Scientist, 1991, Def Sci & Technol Org, Sydney; Hon Assoc, Univ of Sydney, 1993. Publications: Scientific papers in Journal of Acoustical Society of America, 1976, 1978, 1980, 1981, 1991; Journal of Sound Vibration, 1976; Acoustics Australia, 1976, 1978, 1992; Memoirs Queensland Museum, 1991; Marine Mammal Science, 1992, 1995, 1996. Memberships: Fell, Acoustical Soc of Am; Austl Acoustical Soc; Austl Marine Scis Assn. Hobbies: Art; Music. Address: Defence Science & Technology Organisation, PO Box 44, Pyrmont, NSW 2009, Australia.

CATO Kenneth Willis, b. 30 Dec 1946, Brisbane, Qld, Aust. Graphic Designer. 1 d. Education: Dip Art, Roy Melbourne Inst Technol. Appointments: Dir, Cato Hibberd Des Pty Ltd, 1970; Dir, Ken Cato Des Co Pty Ltd, 1982; Chmn, Cato Des Inc Pty Ltd, 1987-98; Chmn Cato Partners Pty, Ltd, 1999-. Creative Works: Articles in num intl publs; Ed, A view from Australia; Design for Business; First Choice, 1st and 2nd editions; Hindsight; Design by Thinking; Exhibns: 6th, 7th, 8th, 9th, 10th, 13th, 14th

Biennale Graphic Des, Brno, Czechoslovakia; Die Neue Sammlung perm collect, Munich Mus; The World's Most Memorable Posters, Paris, 1986-, 1987; Danish Mus Decorative Art; NY Art Dirs Club 2nd Exhibn, 1988; Israel Mus Self Image Exhibn; Munich Pillar Art Exhibn, 1989. Honours: Awds, Aust, USA, Czechoslovakia, Germany, Singapore, Japan, inclng: Gold CLIO, Packaging Des, 1980; Gold Awd, Packaging, Packaging Cncl Aust, 1980; Critics Prize, 8th Biennale Graphic Des, Bronze Awds, 10th and 13th Biennale Graphic Des, Brno; Intl Buchkunst-Ausstellung, Leipzig; Hon Acknowledgement Awds and Bronze Medal for Book Desigs and Typographers, Packaging Cncl Aust; Gold Star Awd, ANPAC Natl Packaging Competition, 1988; Creative Dir, 1996 Melbourne Olympic Candidature; Hall of Fame Awd, Des Inst of Aust, 1995; Hon DDesign, Swinburne Univ, 1995. Memberships: Pres, Alliance Graphique Internationale; Icograda; Diseño Grafico Argentina; Amn Inst Graphic Art; Des Inst Aust; Austl Graphic Des Assn; Indl Des Cncl Aust; Austl Writers and Art Dirs Assn. Listed in: Who's Who in Graphic Design; Who's Who in Business in Australia; Who's Who in Australia. Hobbies: Golf; Theatre; Cinema; Music; Art; Football. Address: 254 Swan Street, Richmond, Vic 3121, Australia.

CAWLEY Evonne Fay, b. 31 July 1951 Griffith, NSW. Lawn Tennis Player. m. Roger Cawley 1975, 1 s, 1 d. Education: Willoughby High Sch Sydney. Appointments: Profl player since 1970; Wimbledon Champion, 1971, 1980 - singles - 1974 - doubles; Austl Champion, 1974, 1975, 1976, 1977; French Champion, 1971; Italian Champion, 1973; SA Champion, 1972; Virginia Slims Circuit Champion, 1975, 1976; Played Fedn Cup for Aust, 1971, 1972, 1973, 1974, 1975, 1976; Helping to fund wildlife sanctuary Noola Heads Queensland; Coaching children. Publications: Evonne Goolagong - with Bud Collins - 1975; Home: The Evonne Goolagong Story - with Phil Jarratt - 1993. Address: c/o IMG, 281 Clarence Street, Sydney, NSW 2000, Australia.

CAYGILL David Francis, b. 15 Nov 1948 Christchurch. Politician; Lawyer. m. Eileen E Boyd, 1974, 1 s, 3 d. Education: Univ of Canterbury. Appointments: Prac'd law in Christchurch legal firm, 1974-78; Min of Trade and Ind, Min of Natl Dev, Assoc Min of Fin, 1984-87; Min of Hlth Trade and Ind, 1987-88; Dep Min of Fin, 1988; Min of Revenue, 1988-89; Min of Fin, 1988-90; Dep Ldr of the Opposition, 1994-. Memberships: Mbr Christchurch Cty Cncl, 1971-80; Mbr HoR, 1978-; Mbr Canterbury Regl Plng Auth, 1977-80; Labor Party. Hobbies: Collecting classical music records; Sci-Fi; Following Am Pols. Address: Parliament House, Wellington, New Zealand.

CAYREL Laurent, Government Official. Appointment: Sec Gen, Govt New Caledonia. Address: Haut-Commissariat, Rep Nouvelle-Caledonie, BP C5, 98848 Noumea, New Caledonia.

CEM Ismail, Government Official. Appointment: Min For Affairs, Govt of Turkey, Ankara, 1997-. Address: Disisleri Bakanligi, Yeni Hizmet Binast, 16520 Balgat, Ankara, Turkey.

CERVANTES AGUIRRE Enrique, b. 1935, Puebla, Mexico. Secretary of National Defence. m. Martha Estela Martinez Flores. Education: 1st Place, Ecuela Superior de Guerra, Cmnd and Jt Chfs of Staff. Appointments: Lt, Lt Col, Gol; Brigadier Gen, 1980; Brigade Gen, Div Gen, 1982; Hd, 3rd Sect of Chfs of Staff, Natl Def, Hd, Chf of Staff of 27th Mil Zone, Acapulco; Guerrero and Hd, 1st Sector, Chfs of Staff of 16th Mil Zone, Irapuato, Guanajuato; Pvte Sec, Sec of Natl Def; Dir, Heróico Colegio Militar; Cmndr, var mil zones and regs; Gen Dir, Natl Def Factories, -1994; Mil and Air Attaché, Mexican Emb, Wash DC. Honour: Decorated for Mil Merit, 1976. Address: Office of the President, Mexico.

CHA Jin Soon, b. 26 Dec 1945, Seoul, Korea. Professor of Linguistics. Education: PhD, McGill Univ, 1983. Appointments: Prof, Sookmyung Women's Univ; Korean Coord, Univ of S CO. Publications: Linguistic Cohesion in Texts: Theory and Description, 1993; Current

Papers of MAK Halliday, 1994; Current Papers of Noam Chomsky, 1993; Before and Towards Communication Linguistics: Essays by Michael Gregory and Associates, 1995. Memberships: LACUS, 1996; LAGB, 1996; LSA, 1996; MLA, 1996; Rep, IFTB, Sookmyung Women's Univ, Korea, 1996. Hobbies: Fishing; Calligraphy; Sports; Photography; Music; Mountaineering. Address: Daeho A-201, 654-41 Deungchon-dong, Gangseo-gu, Seoul, Korea 157-031.

CHA Soo-Myung, b. 20 Aug 1940, Sungnam-(I)dong, Ulsan, Cty. Member of Nation Party. m. 2 s. 2 d. Education: Grad, Sch of Law, Seuol Natl Univ, 1963; Grad, Grad Sch of Judicatory, Seoul Natl Univ, 1970. Appointments: Asst Dir, Off of Plng & Coord, Min of Trade & Ind (MTI), 1963; Asst Dir, Small & Medium Ind Div 1st Bur Ind MTU, 1964; Asst Dir, Overseas Mkt Div, Trade Bur, MTI, 1968; Dir, Guidance Div, Small & Medium Ind Bur, MTI, 1970; Sec to Pres, for Econ Matters, 1972; Com Attaché, Permanent Mission of Repub of Korea, Geneva, 1973; Dir Gen, Heavy Ind Bur, MTI, 1978; Asst Min for Ind, MTI, 1980; Commnr of Korea Indl Prpty Off, 1985; Prac Law, Atty at Law (Kim & Chang), 1988-; Mbr, 14th Natl Assembly, 1992; Mbr 15th Natl Assembly, 1996-; Chmn, Fin Cttee, Hannata Party, 1996-; Exec Mbr, Fin & Econ Cttee, Ntl Assembly, 1996-. Honours: Cheon Su Medal, Natl Security Merit; Hong Jo Keunjeong Medal for Natl Security merit. Hobbies: Reading; Mountain climbing. Address: Woosung Village 106, 153-1, Nonhyun-dong, Kangam-ku, Seoul, Korea.

CHAHL Loris Avril, b. 8 Aug 1940, Queensland, Aust. University Associate Professor (Education). m. Jaswant, 7 Jan 1966, 1 s, 1 d. Education: BSc, 1960, MSc, 1966, PhD, 1970, DSc, 1990, Univ of Queensland. Appointments: Tutor/Snr Tutor, Physiol and Pharmacol, Univ of Queensland, Aust, 1960-70, 1974-79; Postdoct Fell, Univ Edinburgh, 1971-72; Lectr, Snr Lectr, Assoc Prof, Univ Newcastle, 1979-. Publications: Sci articles to profl jrnls. Memberships: Austl Physiol and Pharm Soc; Australasian Soc Chem Exper Pharmacols and Toxicols; Aust Neuroscience Soc; Intl Assoc Study of Pain; Intl Neuropeptide Soc. Address: C/o Faculty of Medicine & Health, Sciences, University of Newcastle, NSW 2308, Australia.

CHAI Songyue, b. Nov 1941 Putuo Co, Zhejian Prov. Politician. Appointments: Joined CCP 1961; Vice-Gov mbr CCP Zheijian Provincial Cttee; Dir Zhejiang Provincial Plng Commn, 1988; Vice-Gov Zhejiang Prov, 1993; Gov, 1997-. Memberships: Alt Mbr 14th CCP Cntr Cttee, 1992; Mbr 15th CCP Cntr Cttee, 1997-. Address: Office of the Govenor, Zhejiang Provincial Government, Hangzhou City, Zhejiang Province, People's Republic of China.

CHAICHAREON Pariyada, b. 26 May 1954. Business Director. m. Dr Pitak Chaichareon, 10 Feb 1985, 2 s. Education: Dip in Master of Management. Appointments: Asst to Proj Mngr, USA Trade Ctr, 1975-76; Mngng Dir, Lightning Internation Corp, 1988-90; For Div Mngr, Interconnex (Thailand) Co Ltd, 1989-90; Bus Dir, Bangkok Patana Intl Sch, 1990-. Memberships: Bd Mbr, Bangkok Patana Sch Fndn; Vice Pres, Intl Schs Assn, Thailand; Bd Mbr, Fndn for the Betterment of Moral Integrity; Min of Educ for Monitoring and Evaluating Intl Schs in Thailand; Old Eng Studs Assn; Fedn of Priv Schs in Thailand. Hobbies: Reading; Travelling; Gardening; Meditation. Address: 274/4 Soi Mahadthai 1, Ladprao 122, Bankok 10310, Thailand.

CHAIYASAN Prachuab, b. 20 Aug, Udonthani Prov, Thailand. Minister of University Affairs. m. Taptim Chaiyasan. Education: BA, Pol Sci, Thammasat Univ. Appointments: Administrator, Planned Parenthood Assn of Thailand, 1972-73; Dist Offr, Udonthani, 1974-75; Proj Administrator, ILO, UNDP, 1976; Chmn, Slot Intl Co Ltd, 1977-83; Dpty Min of Com, 1986-88; Min of Sci, Technol and Energy, 1988-90; Min of Public Hlth, 1991; Min of Agric and Co-op, 1994; Min of For Affairs, 1996. Honours: Kt Grand Cordon, Spec Class, Most Noble Order of the Crown of Thailand; Kt Grand Cordon, Spec Class, Most Exalted Order of the White Elephant. Address: Ministry of

Foreign Affairs, Saranrom Palace, Bangkok 10200, Thailand.

CHAKRABARTI Arunaloke, b. 27 Nov 1956, Chinsurah, India. Medical Mycologist. m. Sushmita, 14 Oct 1984, 1 s, 1 d. Education: MBBS; MD, Microbiol; DNB, Microbiol. Appointment: Additional Prof and Incharge, Mycol Divsn, Dept of Med Microbiol, Pgimer, Chandigarh, India. Publications: Sev articles in profl jrnls. Honours: Snr Prosector, Med Coll, Calcutta, 1974; Silver Medal, PGI, 1985; Intl Schlsp Awd, Intl Fedn of Infection Control, 1994; WHO Rsch Sci Awd, 1995. Memberships: Intl Soc for Human and Animal Mycol; Soc for Indian Human and Animal Mycols. Hobbies: Travel; Mountaineering. Address: Department of Medical Microbiology, Pgimer, Chandigarh 160012, India.

CHAKRABARTI Parthasarathi, b. 18 Jan 1958, Dakshin Barasat (WB). Teacher of Electronics Engineering. m. Runa, 22 Jan 1987, 1 d. Education: BS (Hons), Phys; BTech; MTech; PhD, Electrons Engrng. Appointments: Asst Prof, 1986-88; Assoc Prof, 1988-97; Prof, 1997-. Publications: Rsch pprs/articles in leading tech jrnls; Textbook: Analog Communication Systems. Honours: Gold Medal, Natl Schlshp, Govt of India; Indian Natl Sci Acady Visng Fellshp; SERC Visng Fellshp. Memberships: Life Mbr, Instn of Engrs, India; Life Mbr, Indian Soc for Tech Educ; Fell, Optical Soc, India. Hobby: Music. Address: P-5, New Medical Enclave, BHU, Varanasi 221005, India.

CHAKRABARTI Radharaman, b. 9 Dec 1939, Hooghly, W Bengal, India. Teacher; Administrator. m. Krishna, 1963, 1 s, 1 d. Education: BA Hons, Econ and Polit Sci, Presidency Coll, Calcutta, 1960; MA, Polit Sci, Calcutta Univ, 1962; PhD, Intl Relations, London Sch of Econs, 1969; Postdoctoral, Univ of WA, USA, 1978-79. Appointments: Asst Prof, Polit Sci, Presidency Coll, Calcutta, 1963-71; Rdr, Hd, Polit Sci, Burdwan Univ, 1971; Prof, Polit Sci, 1972; Dir, Netaji Inst of Asian Stdies, Calcutta, 1981; Vice Chan, Netaji Subhas Open Univ, Calcutta, 1997. Creative Works: Four Books; Several Articles in learned jrns. Honours: Gold Medalist, 1962; S N Banerji Prize Holder; C'wlth Schlshp; London Sch of Econ Schlshp. Memberships: Ex Cttee, Indian Polit Sci Assn; Alumnus, Hague Acady of Intl Law. Hobbies: Gardening; Dramatic Performances; Listening to Indian Music. Address: 1 Woodburn Park, Calcutta 700020, India.

CHAKRABORTI Debabrata, b. 1 Jan 1937, Hooghly, India. Psychiatrist. m. Monika, 10 July 1966, 1 s, 1 d. Education: MBBS (Calcutta); DPM (Calcutta and Eng); MRC Psych (Eng), 1975; FRCPPsych (Eng), 1992. Appointments: Cnslt Psych, King's Lynn, Norfolk, 1976-97; Retd, 1997-. Publications: Contraception and the Mentally Handicapped (co-auth), 1984, Sterilisation and the mentally handicapped, 1987, Brit Medl Jrnl. Honour: MBE, 1997. Hobbies: Writing articles; Reviewing books and films; Listening to music; Reading books. Address: 4 Binham Road, South Wootton, Kings Lynn, Norfolk PE 30 3TB, England.

CHAKRABORTY Arun Kumar, b. 25 Dec 1964. Information Librarian. m. 10 Mar 1992, 1 s. Education: BSc, Calcutta Univ, 1983; Ctf, Lib Info and Sci, BLA, 1984; Bach of Lib and Info Sci, Jadavpur Univ, 1986; Assocshp in Documentation, DRTC, ISI, Bangalore, 1987. Appointments: Lib Trainee, USIS Lib, Calcutta, 1987; Lib Trainee, Brit Cncl Lib, Calcutta, 1987; Tchng Asst, ISI, DRTC, 1989; Proj Asst, Indian Stats Inst, 1989; Documentation Offr, Wildlife Inst of India, 1989-92; Sci Libn, Cntr for Environ Educ, 1992-94; Dy Mngr, FITT, Indian Inst of Technol, 1994-. Honour: Hon Mbr Rsch Bd, ABI. Memberships: Indian Assn of Spec Libs and Intl Cntr; ILA; BLA. Hobbies: Writing; Reading; Gardening. Address: Foundation for Innovation and Technology, Transfer (FITT), Indian Institute of Technology, Hauz Khas, New Delhi 110016, India.

CHAKRABORTY Keshablal, b. 29 Sept 1950, Fulia, Nadia, W Bengal, India. Librarian. m. Namita, 1 d. Education: MLib and Information Science. Appointments:

Libn, Kritiibas Mem Community Hall cum Mus, Fulia Boyra, Nadia, WB, India. Publications: Compiler, bibliography on poet Krittibas (Bengali Ramayankar); Poet Nabin Chandra Sen, Bib on the Ramayana (thesis and articles). Memberships: Life Mbr, Indian Lib Assn; Bengal Lib Assn; Indian Assn of Spec Libs and Info Cntrs, WBPLE Assn. Hobby: Collecting documents on the Ramayana. Address: Fulia Township, PO Fulia Colony, District NADIA, West Bengal, India.

CHAKRABORTY Reema, b. 29 Dec 1975, Tinsukia, India. Education: BFA; Dip, Light Music. Creative Works: Compositions and Indian Trad Paintings, 1994-98; Sev Indian Exhbns. Honour: All India Youth Fest, Baroda, Jugrat, 1995-96. Hobbies: Singing; Dancing. Address: c/o Mr N K Chakraborty, QR No Bl/87, MCP Colony, Malanjkhand, Balaghat 481116, India.

CHAKRAVARTY Indrani, b. 27 May 1954, Calcutta, India. Gerontologist. m. Samar Chakravarty, 17 Jan 1977, 1 s, 1 d. Education: PhD. Appointments: Rsch Schl, Indian Statistical Inst, 1979-87; Fndr Pres, Calcutta Metrop Inst of Gerontology, 1988; Ashoka Fell, 1992-94; Guest Schls, Netaji Inst for Asian Studies, 1989-91. Publications: Ed, Jrl, Ageing and Society, the Indian Journal of Gerontology, 1993-; Book: Life in the Twilight Years, 1997. Honours include: Awd for ppr, Retirement in India Perspective, 4th Asia/Oceania Regl Confs of Gerontology, Yokohama, Japan, 1991; Delivered Key Speech, Chmn, Natl Level Seminar of Direction of Physical Educ and Sports Scis in the 21st Century, Kalyani Univ, W Bengal, 1994. Memberships: Hon Mbr, Soroptimist Intl; Fndr, Pres, Life Mbr, Calcutta Metrop Inst of Gerontology. Hobby: Passing time with Senior Citizens. Address: Calcutta Metropolitan Institute of Gerontology, E/1 Sopan Kutir, 53 B, Dr S C Banerjee Rd, Calcutta 700 010, India.

CHALLEN Donald William, b. 22 Dec 1949, Perth, W A, Aust. Economist. m. Anne Klein, 14 Aug 1971, 2 s. Education: BEcons (Hons 1st Class), 1970, MEcon, 1976, Univ of Tasmania. Appointments: lectr, Econs, Univ of Tasmania, 1972-78; Dir, Cntr for Regl Econ Analysis, 1980-1984; Snr Lectr, Econs, 1978-83; Rdr in Econs, 1984-, Univ of Tasmania; Chf Economist, 1984-96, Dir (Acting), 1986, Off of EPAC, Canberra; dpty Sec (Econ and Finl Policy) Dept of Treas and Fin Tasmania, 1986-91; Mngng Dir, Tasmanian Dev Authority, 1991-93; Chmn, Tasmanian Pub Fin Corp, 1993-; Chmn, Cntr for Regl Econ Analysis, 1993-; Chmn, Tasmanian Gaming Commn, 1993-; Dir, Trust Bank, 1993-; Hydro-Elec Corp, 1993-; HEC Enterprises Corp, 1993-98. Publications: (co-auth) 6 books inclng: Macroeconomic Systems: Construction, Validation and Applications, 1983; Unemployment and Inflation in the United Kingdom, 1984; Principles of Economics: Income, Wealth and Welfare in Australia, 1985; 2 monographs; Pprs in profl jrnls, conf proceedings. Membership: Fell, Austl Inst of Co Dirs. Hobbies: Golf; Bush walking; Photography; Music (listening); Writing. Address: The Treasury Building, 21 Murray Street, Hobart, Tasmania 7000, Australia.

CHALLEN Michael, b. 27 May 1932, Melbourne, Australia. Cleric. m. Judy, 2 d. Education: BSc, Melbourne; Lic of Theol, Hons. Appointments: Asst Curate, N Essendon, 1957-59; Anglican Inner City Min, 1959-71; Dir, 1963-71, Dir, Home Mission, Perth, 1971-77; Asst Bishop, 1978-91; Exec Dir, Brotherhood of St Laurence, 1991-. Honour: AM, 1988. Hobbies: Carpentry; Arts; Tennis. Address: 15 Gore Street, Fitzroy 3065, Australia.

CHAMBERLAIN Bruce Anthony (The Hon), b. 9 Aug 1939, Brighton, Vic, Aust. President of Legislative Council in the Victorian Parliament. m. Paula Swan, 6 Feb 1965, 2 s, 2 d. Education: BA, LLB, Melbourne Univ. Appointments: Bar and Sol; Mbr, Legis Assembly Vic, 1973-76; Mbr, Legis Cncl, 1976-; Shadow Atty-Gen, 1985-88; Ldr Opposition, Legis Cncl, 1986-88; Shadow Min Local Govt Plng State Growth; Shadow Min Ind, Technol and Rescs, 1988-89; Pres, Legis Cncl, Parl Vic, Oct 1992-. Memberships: Law Inst Vic; Liberal Party

Aust; Amnesty Intl; Dir, Greening Aust (Vic). Hobby: Chinese ceramics. Listed in: Who's Who in Australia. Address: 19 Martin Street, Hamilton, Vic 3300, Australia.

CHAMBERS Raymond John, b. 16 Nov 1917, Newcastle, New South Wales, Australia. Teacher; Author; Accountant. m. Margaret, 9 Sept 1939, 1 s, 2 d. Education: BEc; DSc, Econ. Appointments: Lectr, Prof, Acctng, Sydney, 1953-82; Emer Prof, 1983; Vis Prof, Univs in USA, Can, NZ, Japan, S Africa; Aust. Publications: Financial Management, 1947; Accounting and Action, 1957; Securities and Obscurities, 1973; Foundations of Accounting, 1991; An Accounting Thesaurus, 1998; Chambers on Accounting (5 vols of articles). Honours: AO, 1978; Hon DSc, Newcastle, 1990, Wollongong, 1993; Hon LLD, 1993. Memberships: Aust Soc of Cert Practising Acctns; Am Acctng Assn. Hobbies: Reading; Writing. Address: 18 Amy Street, Blakehurst, NSW 2271, Australia.

CHAMBERS Robert Stanley (Hon Justice), b. 23 Aug 1953, Auckland, NZ. High Court Judge. m. Claire Marion Taylor, 3 Sept 1977, 2 s. Education: LLB Hons, Auckland Univ, 1975; Called to NZ Bar, 1975; DPhil, Oxford Univ, Eng, 1978; Assoc, 1987, Fell, 1991, Arbitrators and Mediators Inst NZ. Appointments: Clk to Judges, Supreme Crt NZ, 1974-75; Salvesen Fell, New Coll Oxford, 1976-78; Sol, 1979-80; Lectr, Auckland Univ, 1979-83; Bar, 1981-99; Mbr, 1991-97, Chair, 1994-97, Hlth Rsch Cncl; QC, 1992-; Judge, High Crt of NZ, 1999-. Publications include: Books inclng: Co-ed, Salmond & Heuston's Law of Torts; Co-auth, The Law of Torts in New Zealand, 1991, 1997; Num articles in law jrnls. Honours: Inter Alia, Univ Jnr Schlshp, 1970; Snr Schl, 1974; Auckland Dist Law Prize, 1974; NZ Law Soc Schl, 1975; C'wlth Schl, 1975. Memberships include: Arbitrators Inst NZ; Northern Club, Auckland. Hobbies: Jogging; Skiing; Tennis; Crosswords. Listed in: New Zealand Who's Who; Debrett's Handbook of Australia and New Zealand. Address: 61 Seaview Road, Remuera, Auckland 5, New Zealand.

CHAMBERS William Bruce, b. 5 June 1933, Rutherglen, Victoria, Australia. Wine-maker; Vigneron; Farmer. m. (1)Catherine McMillan, dec, (2)Wendy Moyle, 2 s. (1 dec), 2 d. Education: Dip Oenol, Roseworthy Coll, SA. Appointments: Wine-maker, Stanley Wine, Co Clare; Wine-maker, Mngr, Chambers Rosewood Winery, Rutherglen. Memberships: Wine Judge, all Capital City Wine Shows 1960-; Chmn of Judges, Royal Melbourne Hort Soc Wine Show. Hobbies: Horses; Reading. Address: Barkley St, Rutherglen, VIC 3685, Australia.

CHAN Chiu-Po Joseph, b. 2 May 1953, Hong Kong. Periodontist. m. Man-Ching Cheng, 2 d. Education: DDS, Natl Taiwan Univ, 1972-78; Ctf, Periodontics, LA Univ, USA, 1983-85. Appointments: Res, Chf Res, Dental Dept, Chmn, Periodontics Dept, Chmn, Dental Dept. Publications: 110 articles and abstracts to profl jrnls. Membership: Dir of Bd, Acady of Periodontol, Taiwan, 1986-. Hobbies: Swimming; Music. Address: 131 4/F Roosevelt Road, Taipei, Taiwan.

CHAN Cho Chak John, b. 8 Apr 1943, Hong Kong. Company Director. m. Agnes, 19 June 1965, 1 s, 1 d. Education: BA, Hons, 1964, Dip, Mngmt Studies, 1971, Univ Hong Kong; DBA, Honoris Causa, Intl Mngmt Cntrs, 1997. Appointments: Hong Kong Govt, 1964-78, 1980-83; Sun Hung Kai Fin Co Ltd, 1978-80; Kowloon Motor Bus Co Ltd, 1993-. Honour: JP, 1993. Memberships: Fell, Chart Inst of Transport; Inst of Mngmt. Hobbies: Singing; Ten-Pin Bowling; Horse Racing. Address: No 1 Po Lun Street, Lai Chi Kok, Kowloon, Hong Kong.

CHAN Sir Julius, b. 29 Aug 1939 Tanga, New Ireland. Politician. m. Stella Ahmat, 1966, 3 s, 1 d. Education: Maurist Brothers Coll, Ashgrove, Qld; Univ of Queensland, Aust. Appointments: Co-op Offr, Papua New Guinea Admin, 1960-62; Mngng Dir, Coastal Shipping Co Pty Ltd; Dep Speaker, Vice-Chmn, Pub Accounts Cttee, 1968-72; Parl ldr People's Progress Party, 1970-97; Min of Fin and Parly Ldr of Govt Bus, 1972-77; Gov for Papua New Guinea and Vice-Chmn Asian Dev Bank, 1975-77;

Dep PM and Min for Primary Ind, 1977-78; PM, 1980-82; Dpty PM and Min of Trade and Ind, 1986-88; Dep PM, 1992-94; Min for Fin and Plng, 1992-94; Gov IBRD/IMF 1992-; Min for For Affairs and Trade, 1994-96; PM, 1994-96. Honours: Hon Dr honoris causa, Econs, Dankook Univ, Seoul, 1978; Hon Dr Technol, Papua New Guinea, 1983. Memberships: Mbr, House of Asembly, 1968-75, 1982-. Address: P O Box 6030, Boroto, Papua New Guinea.

CHAN Ka Ching, b. 27 Jan 1965, Kowloon, Hong Kong. Senior Lecturer. m. Miranda Wong, 12 June 1990, 2 s. Education: BASc, Toronto, Can, 1987; MASc, Toronto, 1989; PhD, Univ of NSW, Aust, 1995. Appointments: Lectr, Univ of NSW, 1991-97; Visng Asst Prof, Hong Kong Univ of Sci & Technol, 1997; Snr Lectr, Univ of NSW, 1997-. Publications: num articles in profl jrnls. Honours: Univ Toronto Open Master's Fell, 1988, 1989; McAllister Summer Rsch Fellshp, 1986. Memberships: ASME; SME; Inst of Indl Engrs; Chartered Profl Engr (CPEng); IEAST. Hobbies: Music; Photography. Address: 49 Jervis Drive, Illawong, NSW 2234, Australia.

CHAN Kar Ming Henry, b. 15 July 1958, Hong Kong, China. Company Director. Education: BSc, Hon, Chinese Univ of Hong Kong; Grad Dip, Bus Admin. Appointments: Mngr, HK Roy Publ, 1981-82; Analyst/Programmer, HKSAR, 1982-94; Mng Dir, Intelligent Off Co, 1994-; Mng Dir, Intelligent IT Personnel, 1998-. Memberships: China Software Ind Assn, China; HKCS; IMIS, UK; CDP, USA; HKSPIN; Exec Cncl Mbr, HKITF; Organiser, Hong Kong Chapt, Knowledge Mngmt Consortium Int, USA. Hobbies: Volleyball; Badminton; Squash; Reading. Address: 115A Kau Pui Long Road, 2/F Tokwawan, Kowloon, Hong Kong.

CHAN Monnie Yuet-Hung, b. 14 July 1966, Hong Kong. Philanthropist; Music Educator. m. Fai-Lun Lam, 6 Dec 1987, 1 s. Education: PhD Candidate, Hull; MA, Econ in Music Educ, Inst of Educ, London Univ; LTCL, Trinity Coll of Music. Appointments: Fndr, Voluntary Chairperson, Schooling Fndn For China; Pres, Hong Kong Outstndng Tchrs Assn. Creative Work: Auth, Music Educ Series, Hong Kong. Honours: ISM, Incorporated Soc of Musicians, UK. Hobbies: Reading; Swimming. Address: No 4, Pai Tau Village, Shantin, NT, Hong Kong.

CHAN Shu-Park, b. 10 Oct 1929, Canton, China. Founder and President of a University. m. Stella Lam, 26 Dec 1956, 1 s, 1 d. Education: BS, Electr Engin, VA Mil Inst, 1955; MSc, Electr Engin, 1957, PhD, 1963, Electr Engin, Univ of Il, USA. Appointments: Instr in Electr Engin and Maths, 1957-58, Instr in Maths, 1958-61, Asst Prof of Maths (on leave), 1961-63, VA Mil Inst; Rsch Assoc, Coord Sci Lab, Univ of Il, Urbana, 1962-63; Assoc Prof, Electr Engin, 1963-68; Prof and Chmn, Dept of EECS, 1969-84, Santa Clara Univ; Sabbatical to estab China Experimental Univ in China, 1984-86; Prof, Electr Engin, 1986-92, Nicholson Family Chair Prof, 1987-92, Acting Dean, Sch of Engrng, 1988-89, Prof Emeritus of Electr Engin, 1992-, Santa Clara Univ; Bd of Trustees, W Valley Mission Community Coll Dist, 1988; Fndr and Pres, Intl Technol Univ, Santa Clara, 1994-. Publications: Auth or co-auth: 6 books, 60 jrnl articles, 130 conf and symposium pprs, num tech reports; Ed 10 conf proceedings. Honours include: Eta Kappa Nu; Tau Beta Pi; Sigma Xi; Pi Mu Epsilon; Phi Kappa Phi; Hon Prof, Anhuei Univ, China, 19082-; Disting EE Alumnus Awd, Univ of IL, Urbana, 1983; Hon Prof, S China Univ of Technol, 1985-; Gen Chmn, 1986 IEEE Intl Symposium of Circuits and Systems, San Jose, CA; Wilmot J Nicholson Family Prof, 1987-92; Rschr of Yr, Sch of Engrng, Santa Clara Univ, 1991; AIAA 1994 Engr of Yr Awd, Apollo 11 25th Anniversary Banquets in San Fran, 1994; Courvoisier Leadership Awd (Educ), San Fran, 1994; Pioneer of Yr Awd (Educ) Orgn of Chinese Amns, 18th Annual Natl Convention, San Fran, 1996. Memberships: FIEEE; Amn Soc Engrng Educ. Address: International Technological University, 1650 Warburton Avenue, Santa Clara, CA 95050, USA.

CHAN Yiu Kei, b. 17 May 1960, Singapore. Director. Education: BEng, hons, Liverpool (Eng) John Moores, 1988; MSc, Imperial Coll, London, 1989. Appointments: Maintenance Supvr, Far E Org, Singapore, 1984; Engrng Asst, YP Chee & Assocs, Singapore, 1984-85; Trainee Engr, Serv Elec Lausanne, Switz, 1990-91; Project Ops Engr, The Environ Techs Intl, Singapore, 1992; Snr Engr, Eastman Automation & Robotics, Singapore, 1992-95; Dir, US-Asia Environ Ptnrshp, Singapore, 1995-. Honours: Meritorious Hon Awd, Am Emb, 1996. Memberships: Inst of Mech Engrs; Singapore Indsl Automation Assn; Fgn Servs Nats Assn. Hobbies: Travel; Back-Packing; Hiking. Address: US-AEP/Singapore, 27 Napier Road, Singapore 258508, Singapore.

CHAN Yuk Kau, b. 21 Mar 1947, Canton, China. Manager. m. Ho Ling Chan, 8 Aug 1971, 3 s. Education: MSc, DEng Cand. Appointments: Chmn Qlty Mngmt Assn; Assoc Prof, Intl Mngmt Cntr, UK; Qlty and Standards Mngr. Publications: 21 rsch pprs in intl confs and jrnls. Memberships: MBIM, 1977; NCEA, 1978; MIEE, 1979; MIBSE, 1980; CEng, 1980; MIMarE, 1980; MHKIE, 1980; SMCME, 1998; SMCQCA. Hobbies: Reading; Swimming; Stamp collecting; Music. Address: c/o MTR Corporation, 11/F MTR Tower, Telford Plaza, Kowloon Bay, Hong Kong.

CHAN FANG ON SANG Anson, b. Shanghai China. Government Official. Education: Hong Kong. Appointments: Fmr appts incl Dir Socl Welfare Dept, 1984; Sec for Econ Servs, 1987; Hd - Sec - Hong Kong Civ Serv until 1993; Chf Sec of Hong Kong, Nov 1993-; named to continue in admin after transition. Address: Office of the Chief Secrtary, Central Government Offices, Lower Albert Road, Hong Kong Special Administrative Region, People's Republic of China.

CHANCE Mary Ann, b. 6 Oct 1937, Iowa, USA. Chiropractic Physician; Editor. m. (1) 3 s, 1 d, (2) Rolf E Peters, 23 Apr 1983. Education: Dr Chiropractic, Palmer Coll Chiropractic, 1959; Grad Cert, Intl Coll Chiropractic, Preston Inst Technol, 1981. Appointments: Pvte prac, 1959-; Exec Sec, Austl Chiropractors' Assn, 1975-82; Lectr, Intl Coll Chiropractic, Melbourne, Vic, 1977-82; Ed, Chiropractic Jrnl Aust, 1983-. Publications: Num papers to govt, sev articles, num editls in profl jrnls, var conf papers; Chapts on Aust in Principles and Practice of Modern Chiropractic, and Chiropractic: An Illustrated History. Honours: Chiropractor of Yr, 1980; Meritorious Serv Awd, Aust Chiropractors Assn, 1982, 1988, 1998; Fell, Intl Coll Chiropractors, 1993. Memberships: Chiropractors' Assn Aust; Chiropractic Rsch Jrnl Eds' Cncl; Cncl Bio Eds; Austl Spinal Rsch Fndn; Assn Hist Chiropractic Aust; Soc Schly Publng. Listed in: Who's Who in Chiropractic International; World Who's Who of Women; International Who's Who of Business and Professional Women; Who's Who of Writers, Authors and Publishers; International Book of Honor; Others. Hobbies: Travel; Language; Music; Horticulture; Parapsychology; Photography. Address: 84 Peter St, PO Box 748, Wagga Wagga, NSW 2650, Australia.

CHAND Khub, b. 16 Dec 1911, Khurd, Dist Jhelum, Pre-partition India. Diplomat. m. Nirmal Singh. Education: BA (Hons) (w 2 Gold Medals), Univ of Delhi; Oriel Coll, Oxford. Appointments: Joined Indian Civil Serv, 1935-; Assigned to the Utd Provs as Jt Magistrate, Shahjahanpur, Moradabad, Jt and Additional District Magistrate, Cawnpore, Asst Commnr, Lucknow, 1935-39; Under Sec to Govt of India, Dept of Def, later, Asst Finl Advsr, Mil Fin, 1939-43, 1947; District Magistrate, Azangarh, 1943-45; Regl Food Contrller, Utd Provs, 1945-47; Hd of Indian Mil Mission to Allied Control for Germany, w rank of Maj Gen in Indian Army, 1948-50; Hd of Indian Mission to Allied High Commn for Germany, w diplomatic rank of Min Plenipotentiary and Envoy Extraordinary, 1949; Dpty and later Acting High Commnr for India in Pakistan, 1950-52; Min of India to Iraq, 1952-55 (Jordan, 1954); Jt Sec, Min of External Affairs, 1955-57; Amb of India to Italy (and Albania), 1957-60; High Commnr for India in Ghana, Sierra Leone, Commnr in Nigeria, Amb to Liberia, Guinea, Mali, led Indian Delegs on indep of Ivory Coast and Upper Volta,

1960-62; Amb to Sweden (and Finland), 1962-66; Amb to Lebanon, Jordan and Kuwait, High Commnr in Cyprus, 1966-67; Amb to Fedl Repub of Germany, 1967-70; Retd, 1971; Cnslt, Intl Dev and Bus Rels, 1972-; Prof, Intl Geopolits, Intl Mngmt Inst, India, 1984-88. Publications: Contbns to sev jrnls; (co-auth) books inclng: Memoirs of Old Mandarins of India, 1984; Peace and Conflict Resolution in the World Community, 1991; Germany in the Nineties, 1998. Honours include: Grand Cross of the Order of Merit, Germany, 1978. Memberships include: Indian Cncl of World Affairs, VP 1974-82; Oxford and cambridge Soc, New Delhi, Pres, 1979-82; Kiwanis Club, VP, 1986-90; Fedn of Indo-German Socs in India, Pres, 1976-88, Pres Emeritus, 1988. Hobbies: Travel; Oil-painting; Reading; Writing. Address: 1/8A Shanti Niketan, New Delhi 110 021, India.

CHAND Lokendra Bahadur, b. Feb 1940, Kurkutiya, Baitadi. Prime Minister of Nepal. m. Subhadra Chand, 1960, 4 s, 3 d. Education: BA, BLL, Agra Univ, India. Appointments: Mbr, Del of Nepal, UN Gen Assn, 1982; Mbr, House of Representatives, 1995; Ldr, Rastriya Prajatantra Party, 1995; Rep'd Nepal as Hd of Govt, 9th SAARC Summit, Maldives, 1997. Publications: Barshaun Kheladi (satirical essays); Hiun Ko Tanna (short stories); Netaka Saathi (one-act plays). Honours: Subikhyat Trishkati Patta; Prasiddha Prabal Goradha Dakshin Bahu; Kt Grand Cross, UK. Hobbies: Literature; Sports. Address: Office of the Prime Minister, Cen Secr, Singha Durbar, Kathmandu, Nepal.

CHANDA Nayan Ranjan, b. 8 Jan 1946, Mahadevpur, India. Editor. m. Geetanjali, Oct 1974, 2 s. Education: MA Deg. Appointments: Writer, 1970, Corresp, 1974, Dipl Corresp, 1980, WA Corresp, 1984-89, Dpty Ed, 1992, Ed, 1996, Far Eastern Econ Review; Snr Fell, Carnegie Endowment for Intl Peace, WA, USA, 1989-90; Ed, Asian Wall Street Jrnl Weekly, NY, USA, 1990-92. Publications include: Brother Enemy: The War After the War, 1986; After the Wars: Reconstruction in Afghanistan, Indochina, Central America, Southern Africa and the Horn of Africa, 1990; China, Japan and India in Southeast Asia, 1993; The Challenge of Reform in Indochina, 1993. Membership: Advsry Bd, Cntr for Intl Devel, Harvard Univ. Hobbies: Painting; Reading. Address: 25/F Citicorp Centre, 18 Whitfield Road, Causeway Bay, Hong Kong.

CHANDA Sarah, b. 11 Aug 1935, Mumbai, India. Social Activist. m. B V Chanda, 25 Jan 1970, 1 s, 2 d. Education: BA, Hist, Madras Univ; Dip, Pub Rels. Appointments: Pres, Students Union, Queen Mary's Coll, Madras; Ldr, Women's N C Contingent to the Repub Day Parade, Delhi, 1956; VP, 1978-90, Chairperson, Nominating Cttee, 1994-98, YWCA of India; Pres, 1979-83, Fndr, Chairperson, Sahodri Project, YWCA Madras; Fndr Sec, Spastics Soc of Tamil Nadu; Chairperson, Prajwala, Chittoor; UNHCR Cnslt, 1997; Hon Sec, St Mary's Ch, Chennai; Trustee, Satyamurti Cntr for Democratic Studies; Bd Mbr, Prepare, Indian Inst of Cmty Hlth; Fndr Mbr, Pravaham; Mbr, Carebola. Honour: Cadet Trophy & Baton, Pt Jawarhlal Nehru. Hobby: Making Friends. Address: YWCA of Madras, 1086 Poonamallee High Road, Chennai 600884, India.

CHANDANI Aluthge Dona Lalitha, b. 13 Sept 1957. Senior Lecturer. m. T Anura Perera, 25 July 1994, 1 d. Education: BSc, hons, MSc; PhD. Appointment: Snr Lectr. Publication: Antiferroelectric Chiral Smectic Liquid Crystals. Honours: Tejima Kinen Awd, 1990; TWAS/NARESA Awd for Yng Scis, 1995. Memberships: Sri Lanka Assn for the Adv of Sci; Inst of Chem, Ceylon. Hobby: Reading. Address: Department of Chemistry, University of Peradeniya, Peradeniya, Sri Lanka.

CHANDARASEKARA E M, b. 21 Apr 1949, Bandarawela. Farmer. m. 1 d. Memberships: Kingigawa Vegetable and Fruit Prodng and Mktng Assn. Address: Kufpma, Monaraditiya Watte, Kinigiama, Bandarawela 90100, Sri Lanka.

CHANDER Ramesh, b. 6 Sept 1939, Lahore. Teacher; Researcher. m. Neera, 18 July 1971, 1 s, 1 d. Education: BSc, Banaras Hindu Univ, 1958; MSc, Geophys, 1960;

PhD, Seismol, Lamont Doherty Geol Observ, NY, 1970.Appointments: Snr Geophys Asst, Oil and Gas Commn, 1960-62; Rsch Asst, Lamont Doherty Geol Observ, 1964-70; Rsch Assoc, Univ of MI, 1970-71; Lectr, Univ of Zambia, 1971-76; Snr Lectr, 1977; Lectr, Roorkee Univ, 1977-78; Rdr, 1978-81; Prof, 1981-. Creative Works: 69 Publs in Intl and Indian Jrnls; 10 Rsch Wrks; 11 or Rprts, Articles in jrnls. Honours: Sigma Xi, Hon Soc; Fell, Indian Acady of Scis; Fell, Indian, Geophys Union; Fell, Assn of Exploration Geophys. Hobbies: Books; Movies; Travelling. Address: Dept of Earth Sciences, University of Roorkee, Roorkee 247 667, India.

CHANDRAN Natteri V, b. 13 Aug 1946, Madras, India. Psychotherapist; Hypnotherapist; Educator. m. Chitra Ganapathy, 11 Nov 1973, 2 children. Education: BMed and Surg, Madras Univ, 1969; Dip, Clin Hypnosis, Melbourne (Aust), 1975; Dipl, Amn Bd of Medl Psychotherapists; Medl Dipl. Appointments: Res, Madras Medl Coll, 1969-71; Medl Offr, Mental Hlth Authy, Vic, Aust, 1971-77; Tchng Assoc Dept Psych, Univ of Melbourne, 1976-78; Clin Dir, Hlth Servs, Roy Melbourne Inst of Technol, 1978-83; Medl Cnslt, Roy Melbourne Inst Technol, 1979-83; Pvte Prac, Psychotherapy & Hypnosis, Vic, 1983-; Mbr, Tchng Fac, Austl Soc Hypnosis, Vic 1986-; Bd of Govs, Schizophrenia Rsch Fndn, India, 1993; Fndr: The E W Cntr, The E W Fndn of Aust, Melbourne, 1992; The E W Fndn of India, Madras, 1993; The E W Fndn of Papua New Guinea, 1995. Honours: Dux, St Joseph's Coll, Coonooor, 1961; Prizes, Debating; Sec, Pondicherry Studs Assn and Pondicherry Studs Welfare Soc, 1963-64; Sir C P Ramaswami Iyer Trophy, 1964; 1995 Man of the Yr Commemorative Medal. Memberships: Fell, Amn Bd Medl Psychotherapists; Austl Medl Assn; Intl Soc Hypnosis; Roy Austl Coll GPs; Austl Soc of Hypnosis. Address: Druid's House, 6th Floor, 407-409 Swanston Street, Melbourne, 3000, Australia.

CHANDRAN Sathish, b. 28 Mar 1962, Malaysia. Network Technology Manager. m. Education: BTech, Electrons and Comm Engnrg, Univ of Kerala, 1984; MSc, Radio Frequency Comms Engrng, Univ of Bradford, W Yorks, UK, 1988-89; PhD, Antennas and Microwave Engrng, Loughborough Univ, UK (pt-time), 1993. Appointments: Lectr, Comm Engrng, Fedl Coll Technol, Malaysia, 1985-86, 1988; Testing, Plng and Commissioning Engr, Stand Elektrik Lorenz AG, Malaysia, 1987-88; Sci and Engrng Rsch Cncl, UK, sponsored Rsch Asst, 1989-91, Rsch Assoc, 1991-93, Dept Electrons and Elecl Engrng, Loughborough Univ of Technol; Engrng and Phys Sci Rsch Cncl, UK, sponsored Snr Rsch Assoc, Dept of Elecl and Electron Engrng, Univ of Nottingham, 1994-96; Radio Networking and Des Mngr, Pewira Ericsson in Malaysia, 1996-97; Network Technol Mngr, Radio Network Plng and Transmission Network Plng, Amn Stands Div, 1988-. Publications: 11 pprs to jrnls; 15 conf pprs. Honours: Sigma XI, USA. Ivar Ahlgren Rsch Awd, Ericsson Radio Systems, Sweden. Memberships include: FRSA, UK; Fell, Remote Sensing Soc, UK; Snr Mbr, IEEE; Instn Elecl Engrs, UK; Roy Soc NZ; Mensa; Instn Engrs, Malaysia; Chartered Engr, Engrng Cncl, UK; Fndr, Pres, Intl Union of Radio Sci, Malaysia; Fndr, Chmn, IEEE Antennas and Propagation Soc, Malaysia. Hobbies: Cricket; Football; Videos; Cinemas. Address: Ericsson Malaysia, Wisma Ericsson, Jalan SS 7/19, Kelana Jaya, 47301 Petaling Jaya, Selangor D E, Malaysia.

CHANDRAPRABHA Jayaram, b. 29 June 1979, Bangalore, India. Bharatha Natyam Classical Dancer. Education: Passed Snr Bharatha Natyam Exam conducted by Govt; Undergoing Vdvat higher trng in this field of art. Publications: Auth, small hist about birth and growth of Bharatha Natyam classical dance in India. Honours: Many awds and hons for the perf of Bharatha Natyam Classical Dance. Memberships: Indian Inst for Talent Serach, Mysore, India (headed by Dr S Ramananda). Hobbies: Music; Sports. Address: No 31 8th Cross, Agrahara Dasahalli, Magadi Road, Bangalore 560079, India.

CHANDRASEKHAR Bhagwat Subramanya, b. 17 May 1945 Mysore. Cricketer; Bank Executive. m. Sandhya Rajarao, 1975, 1 s. Education: Natl Educ Soc Bangalore. Appointments: Right-arm leg-spin googly bowler; bowling arm withered by attack of polio at age of 6; Played for Mysore/Karnataka, 1963-64 to 1979-80; Played in 58 Tests for India, 1963-64 to 1979; Took 242 wickets - average 29.7; Toured Eng, 1967, 1971, 1974 and 1979. Honours: Arjuna Awd; Padma Shri, 1972. Memberships: Hon Life mbr MCC, 1981-. Hobbies: Badminton; Indian classical music. Address: 571 31st Cross, 4th Block, Jayanagar, Bangalore 560011, India.

CHANDRASEKHAR Sivaramakrishna, b. 6 Aug 1930, Calcutta, India. Physicist. m. Ila, 9 Sept 1954, 1 s, 1 d. Education: BSc, hons, 1950, MSc, 1951, Nagpur Univ; PhD, Cantab; DSc, Cantab; Hon DSc, Mysore. Appointments: Rsch Schl, Raman Rsch Inst, 1950-54; 1851 Exhbn Schl, Cavendish Lab, Cambridge, 1954-57; DSIR Fell, Acad Staff, Dept of Crystallography, Univ Coll, London, 1957-59; Rsch Fell, Davy Faraday Rsch Lab, Roy Instn, London, 1959-61; Prof, Hd, Dept of Phys, 1961-71, Snr Prof, 1966-71, Univ of Mysore; Prof, Hd, Liquid Crystal Lab, Raman Rsch Inst, 1971-90; Nehru Vis Prof, Fell, Pembroke Coll, Univ of Cambridge, 1986-87; Bhatnagar Fell, CSIR, 1990-95; Dir, Cntr for Liquid Crystal Rsch, Bangalore, Hon Prof, Jawaharlal Nehru Cntr for Adv Sci Rsch, Bangalore, 1991-. Publications: Liquid Crystals, 1992; Sev sci pprs in profl jrnls. Honours include: R D Birla Awd, Indian Phys Assn, 1992; C V Raman Birth Centenary Awd, Indian Sci Congress Assn, 1993; Roy Medal, Roy Soc, 1994; Niels Bohr UNESCO Gold Medal, 1998. Memberships: Fell, Roy Soc of London, Inst of Phys, London, Indian Natl Sci Acady, Indian Acady of Scis; Fndng Fell, Third World Acady of Scis, Trieste; Hon Fell, Natl Acady of Scis, India; Fndng Mbr, Indian Phys Assn; Hon Mbr, Intl Liquid Crystal Soc. Hobby: Painting. Address: Centre for Liquid Crystal Research, PB No 1329, Jalahalli, Bangalore 560 013, India.

CHANEY Frederick Michael (Hon), b. 28 Oct 1941, Aust. Politician. m. 19 Apr 1964, 3 s. Education: LLB. Appointments: Pub Serv, Papua New Guinea, 1964-66; Pvte law prac, 1966-74; Sen, Liberal, for WA, 1974-90; Opposition Whip, 1975; Govt Whip, 1976-78; Min Admnstv Servs, 1978; Min assisting Min Educ, 1978-79; Min Aboriginal Affairs, 1978-80; Min assisting Min Natl Dev and Energy, 1979-80; Min Socl Security, 1980-83; 1983-84; Ldr Opposition, Senate, 1983-90; Shadow Min Rescs and Energy, 1983-84; Shadow Min Ind, Technol and Com, 1984-87, 1988-89; Shadow Min Indl Rels, 1987-88, 1989-90; Dpty Ldr Opposition, 1989-90; Shadow Min Environment, 1990-93; Mbr (Liberal) House Reps for Pearce, WA, 1990-93; Rsch Fell, Grad Sch Mngmt, Univ WA, 1993-95; Mbr, Natl Native Title Tribunal, 1994-; Chan, Murdoch Univ, 1995-. Honour: AO, 1997. Hobbies: Swimming; Reading. Listed in: Who's Who in Australia; Who's Who in Business; International Who's Who. Address: 5 Melville Street, Claremont, WA 6010, Australia.

CHANG Anne Bernadette, b. Malaysia. Paediatrician. Education: MBBS; FRACP; PhD. Appointments: Intern, St Vincents Hosp, Melbourne; Reg, Mater Hosp; Fell, Roy Childrens Hosp; Paediat Respiratory Physn, Mater M Sericordiae Childrens Hosp, S Brisbane. Publications: Sev articles in profl med jrnls. Honours: St Vincents Grad Awd, 1987; Queens Coll Exhbn, 1987; Natl Hlth and Med Rsch Cncl Postgrad Schlsp, 1995-97; Viertel Clin Investigatorship, 1998. Memberships: Roy Austl Coll of Physns; Thoracic Soc of Aust and NZ. Hobbies: Bushwalking; Environmental Issues. Address: Department of Respiratory Medicine, Mater M Sericordiae Childrens Hospital, South Brisbane, Queensland 4101, Australia.

CHANG Chi-Tso, b. 8 Sept 1942. Engineer; Professor. m. Fu-Ying Huang, 10 June 1970, 1 s, 3 d. Education: PhD, Univ Wales. Appointments: Dir 1984, Sinotech Geotech Rsch Cntr; Mngr 1990, Sinotech Geotech Engrng Dept; VP 1990, Sinotech Engrng Cnslts Inc, 1992; Part time Prof, Inst of Applied Geo, Natl Cntrl Univ, 1991-. Membership: Tech Cttee 28, Geotech aspects of underground cnstrn in soft ground, ISSMFE, 1994-. Hobbies: Fishing; Swimming; Cycling. Address: No 8 Lane 261, Fu-Yuan St, Taipei 105, Taiwan, China.

CHANG Fakuan, b. 27 Oct 1924, Ying Shang County, Anhui Prov, China. Professor of Chinese Classical Literature. m. Wang Xiuchun, 2 s, 1 d. Education: University Grad, Lit. Appointments: Prof, beijing Educ Coll, 1978-; Prof, E Japanese Lang and Fin Univ, 1987-; Dir, China Rhizome Art Soc, 1993-. Publications: (auth) Handbook of Chinese Teaching in Midle School; Dictionary of Chinese Poems Appreciate; Dictionary of Chinese Traditional Drama Classics; 100 Cases of Technique of China Tang and Song CI (poetry); San-Tszy-Tszin (Three character classic) of Chinese Traditional Culture; Dictionary of the Twenty-four Histories Anecdotes; Transls of wrk by auths inclng Li Ruzhen, Zuo Zhuan, Han Fei Zi, Guan Zi, Liu Ji, Hou Fangyu, Wei Xi, Qian Qianyi, Lin Zexu, Ling Qichao; Ed, Chinese Poets Praised Beijing Through the Past Ages; Chinese Poets Praised Haidan Through the Past Ages, Selected Poems of Chinese Mountains and Waters; Red Lily (poems) by Chang Renxia, 1904-1996. Honours: Record in Dictionary of Chinese Writers. Memberships: Beijing Poems Society; Sec-gen, Xiang Shan Poems Society. Address: 24/1/501, Zhi Chun Li, Shuang Yu Shu Street, Beijing 100086, China.

CHANG Frederic P N, b. 10 Jan 1942, Taiwan. Civil Servant. m. Huang Chi-chung, 27 Sept 1969, 2 s, 1 d. Education: BA, For Langs & Lits, Natl Taiwan Univ, 1964. Appointments: Admnstv Asst, Jt Commn on Rural Reconstruction (JCRR), 1973-79; Asst, Cncl for Agricl Plang & Dev (CAPD), 1979-81; Spec Asst, CAPD, 1981-84; Sec, CAPD, 1984; Sect Chf, Cncl of Agric (COA), 1984-87; Snr Spec Asst, COA, 1987-92; Cnslr, COA, 1992-93; Dpty Dir-Gen, 1st Bur, Off of the Pres, 1993-96; Dir-Gen, Dept of Spec Affairs, Off of the Pres, 1996-97; Dpty Dir-Gen, Govt Info Off (GIO), 1997-. Publications: Solzhenitsyn: A Documentary Record (transl), 1974; Practical English (ed), 1975; A Passage to India (transl), 1975; The Open and Closed Minds (transl), 1978; Mimesis: The Representation of Reality in Western Literature (transl), 1980. Hobbies: Reading; Golf. Address: 2 Tientsin Street, Taipei 100, Taiwan, China.

CHANG H K, b. 9 July 1940, China. President and University Professor; Biomedical Engineer and Educator. m. Min-min Chou, 5 Sept 1965, 1 s, 1 d. Education: BS, Civ Engrng, Natl Taiwan Univ, 1962; MS, Structural Engrng, Stanford Univ, 1964; PhD, Fluid Mechs and Biomed Engrng, Northwestern Univ, 1969. Appointments: Asst Prof, 1969-75, Assoc Prof, 1975-76, Civ Engrng, Coll of Engrng and Appl Scis, State Univ of NY, Buffalo; Assoc Prof, Biomed Engrng and Physiol, 1976-80, Prof, 1980-84, Fac of Med, McGill Univ, Montreal, Can; Vis Prof, Facultè de Mèdecine, Univ Paris-Val de Marne, France, 1981-82; Prof, Biomed Engrng, Sch of Engrng, Prof of Physiol and Biophys, Sch of Med, 1984-90, Chmn, Dept of Biomed Engrng, Sch of Engrng 1985-90, Sch of Med, Univ S CA, LA; Fndng Dean, Prof, Chem Engrng, Sch of Engrng, Hong Kong Univ of Sci and Technol, 1990-94; Dean, Sch of Engrng, Univ Pitts, 1994-96; Pres, Univ Prof, City Univ of Hong Kong, 1996-. Publications: Respiratory Physiology: An Analytical Approach, 1989; Fluid and Solute Transport in the Airspaces of the Lungs, 1993; Over 100 sci articles in profl jrnls. Honours: Hon Prof, Peking Union Med Coll, Chinese Acady of Med Scis, 1987-; Pres, Biomed Engrng Soc, 1989-90; Fndng Fell, Amn Inst of Med and Biol Engrng, 1992-. Memberships: Fell, Hong Kong Acady of Engrng Scis, Hong Kong Instn of Engrs; Fndng Mbr, Hong Kong Inst of Sci; Fndng Fell, Amn Inst of Med and Biol Engrng; Amn Inst of Chem Engrs; Mbr, Amn Physiol Soc; Snr Mbr, Amn Soc of Civil Engrs, Biomed Engrng Soc. Hobbies: Music; Reading. Address: City University of Hong Kong, Tat Chee Avenue, Kowloon, Hong Kong.

CHANG Jen-Hsiang, b. 27 June 1953, Taiwan. Member of the Legislative Yuan, Taiwan. Education: Master deg, Agric, Chinese Wen Hua Univ, Taiwan. Appointments: Mbr, Cntrl Stndng Cttee of KMT; Mbr, Natl Unification Cncl, Taiwan. Memberships: Educl Rsch Cttee, Educ Dept, Taiwan; Visng Rschr, Cntrl Rsch Inst's Agricl Rsch Dept; Lectr, Chinese Wen Hua Univ. Hobbies: Travelling; Reading. Address: Room 515, 3-1, Section 1, Chi Nan Road, Taipei 100, Taiwan.

CHANG Johnson Ching Ming, b. 15 Mar 1942, Kaohsiung, Taiwan, China. Bank Manager. m. Mrs Yen, 4 Dec 1970, 1 s, 1 d. Education: Bachelor's Degree on the Art of Mngmnt, Natl Taiwan Univ. Appointments: Asst Mngr, The Farmers Bank of China; Dpty Mngr, Bus Dept, Bank of Kaohsiung (BOK); Pres, Info and Automation Dept (BOK); Pres, Auditors and Investigation Dept (BOK); Pres, Savings Dept (BOK). Publications: An Approach to the Strategies of Computerization For All the Inter-Banks Business Processing in Taiwan; An Evolution of 2000's Taiwan; Poetry. Honours: 1st Natl Prize for Composition: An Evaluation of 2000's Taiwan, 1995; 2nd Natl Prize for An Approach to the Strategies. Memberships: Asia-Pacific and Management Assn; Chinese Classic Poetry Assn. Hobbies: Creative Composition; Political, social and economic affairs; Poetry.

CHANG Jui-Te, b. 23 Mar 1953, Taipei. Researcher. m. Lin Hsiu-Ling, 1 d. Education: BA, Natl Cheng Kung Univ, 1976; PhD, Natl Taiwan Norm Univ, 1986. Appointments: Rsch Fell, Inst of mod Hist, Academia Sinica, 1993-; Prof, Grad Inst of Hist, Natl Taiwan norm Univ, 1998-. Creative Works: The Peiking-Hankow Railroad and Economic Development on North China 1805-1837; Railroads in Modern China; Anatomy of the Nationalist Army. Memberships: Soc for Mil Hist Studies; Soc of mod Hist. Hobbies: Reading. Address: Inst of Modern History, Academia Sinica, Nankang, Taipei, Taiwan.

CHANG King-Yuh, b. 27 Apr 1937 Hsiangtan County Hunan. Government Official. m. Grace Yu, 1964, 2 s. Education: Natl Taiwan Univ; Natl Chengchi Univ; Columbia Univ. Appointments: Lectr Hofstra Univ USA, 1968-69; Asst Prof West II Univ, 1972; Assoc Prof Natl Chengchi Univ, 1972-75; Chmn Dept of Diplomacy, 1974-77; Dir Grad Sch of Intl Law and Diplomacy, 1975-77; Prof, 1975-; Visng Fell John Hopkins Univ, 1976-77; Dep Dir Inst of Intl Rels, 1977-81; Dir, 1981-84; Ditsing Visng Schl Inst of E Asian Studies Univ of CA Berkeley, 1983; Dir-Gen Govt Info Off, 1984-87; Dir Inst of Intl Rels, 1987-90; Pres Natl Chengchi Univ, 1989-94; Min of State Exec Yuan, 1994-96. Hobbies: Reading; Mountain climbing; Sports. Address: 1 Chung Hsiao East Road, Sec 1, Taipei, Taiwan.

CHANG Peng Bei, b. Sept 1937. Professor. m. Wu Guifang, 10 Jan 1962, 2 s. Education: BSc, Jiaotong Univ, China, 1960. Appointments: Tchr, Rsch Fell, Kunming Univ of Sci and Technol, 1960; Lectr, Dir, Electro-slag Metallurgy Rsch Sect, 1978; Vice Prof, 1985; Prof, Kunming Univ of Sci and Technol, 1986; Hon Prof, Jiaotong Univ, 1988. Creative Works: Invented: Method of the Electro-slag Welding for Thick Plate, 1963; The Electro-slag Metallurgical Furnace of Two-electrode in Series, 1967; A New Method of Extraction and Remelting of Tin, 1975; The Plasma Furnace with Graphite Gun, 1980; Production of Ultrafine SnO_2 Powders using a Special Arc Atomisation Method, 1983; Production Method of Ultrafine Sb_2O_3 Powders, 1984; New Extraction and Smelting Methods of Tin, 1995. Publications: The electro-slag metallurgy for furnace with a special inner lining, 1979; Plasma Metallurgy; 30 pprs in Chinese Sci jrnls and confs. Honours: 2 Awds for Natl Invention, 1982, 1987; 2 Awds, China Innovation Assn. Memberships: Cttee, China Plasma Chem Soc; Cttee, China Assn for Ultrafine Powders Prod; Yunnan Soc of Mech and Engrng. Hobbies: Reading; Swimming. Address: 101 Building (Teacher's House), Apartment 303, Kunming University of Science and Technology, 670053 Kunming, Yunnan, China.

CHANG Sheng-Fuh, b. 23 May 1960, Tainan, Taiwan. University Professor. m. H S Lin, 25 Dec 1994. Education: PhD, Elec Engrng. Appointments: Assoc Rschr, CPTC, USA, 1991-92; R&D Mngr, Hyton Corp, 1992-94; Prof, Natl Chung Cheng Univ, 1994-.

Publication: Sev articles in profl jrnls. Honour: Disting Rschr, NSF, Taiwan, 1998. Memberships: Phi Tau Phi, 1984; IEEE, 1986; Sigma Xi, 1991. Hobbies: Chinese Classical Music Performances; Softball. Address: Department of Electrical Engineering, National Chung Cheng University, Chiayi 621, Taiwan.

CHANG Wan-hsi (Mo Jen), b. 6 June 1920, Kiukiang, Kiangsi, China. Professor; Writer. m. Li-chung Tsung, 1 Mar 1941, 2 s, 3 d. Education: Grad, Dept Pols, Mil Acady, 1939. Appointments: Gen Ed, Gen Mngr, Kung Li Pao newsppr, 1943-44; Staff, Sec to Cmdr, Chf Off, Navy Gen HQ, 1949-53; Dpty Stn Chf, Mil Brdcstng Netwrk, Tsoying, Taiwan, 1953-56; Chf, Morgue, Mil News Agcy, Min Natl Def, 1959-60; Snr Offr, Secretariat, 1967-74, Selected Rank Compiler, Secretariat, 1974-81, Dir, Lib, 1981-85, Natl Assembly Taiwan; Assoc Prof, Soochow Univ, 1961-80; Visng Prof, Chinese Inst, Kwang Ta Coll, Hong Kong. Publications: As Mo Jen, 55 wrks on lit theories, novels, poems, travel jrnls, inclng The Writing Technique of the Dream of the Red Chamber, 1966; Mo Jen's Works, 5 vols, 1972; (One Selection of Mo Jen's Short Stories and Poems); The Hermit, prose, 1980; A Collection of Mo Jen's Prose, 1980; A Praise to Mountains, poems, 1980; Mountaineer's Remarks, prose, 1983; My Candle Burns at Both Ends, prose, 1985; Flower Market, prose, 1985; Remarks on All Poems of the Tang Dynasty, 1987; Remarks on All Tsyr (prose poem) of the Tang and Sung Dynasties, 1989; A Mundane World, novel, 1991, supp 1993; A Literary Trip to Mainland China, 1992; Selection of Dr Mo Jen's Poems, 1942-1994, 1995. Honours: Novel Awd, China Lit Awd Cttee, 1955; 2 short stories in Best Short Story Selections, Paul Neff Verlag, Vienna; Golden Tripod Prize, The Mundane World, Gov Info Off, Repub China, and Chia Hsin Lit Fndn, 1991. Hon DLitt, Intl Univ Fndn; Hon DHL, Albert Einstein Intl Acady Fndn; Hon DLitt, World Univ Roundtable. Membership: Stndng Tree, China Mod Poetry Assn. Listed in: International Who's Who in Poetry; Who's Who in the World; International Authors and Writers Who's Who; Dictionary of International Biography; International Book of Honor; Book of Dedications; Many others. Address: 14 Alley 7, Lane 502, Chung Ho Street, Paitou, Taipei, Taiwan, China.

CHANG William S C, b. 4 Apr 1931, Nantong, Jiangsu, China. Engineering Educator. m. Margaret, 26 Nov 1955, 1 s, 2 d. Education: BSE, 1952, MSE, 1953, Univ MI; PhD, Brown Univ, 1957. Appointments: Lectr, Rsch Assoc, Stanford Univ, 1957-59; Asst Prof, 1959-62, Assoc Prof, 1962-65, OH State Univ, Columbus; Dir, Lab for Applied Electronics, 1965-71, Samuel Sachs Chair Prof, 1971-79, Prof, WA Univ, St Louis, MO, 1976-79; Prof, 1979-, Chair, Dept of Elec and Computer Engrng, 1993-96, Univ CA. Publications: 5 books, 150 rsch pprs. Honours: Samuel Sachs Chair, WA Univ, 1976; Disting Profl Achievement Awd, Univ MI, 1978. Hobbies: Travel; Dance. Address: Department of Electrical & Computer Engineering, MS #0407, University of California at San Diego, La Jolla, CA 92093-0407, USA.

CHANG Yih, b. 12 July 1958, Tainan, Taiwan. Materials Researcher; Educator. m. Shine Lu, 16 Dec 1984, 1 s, 1 d. Education: PhD, Stanford Univ, USA. Appointments: Cnslt, Chung Sheng Inst f Sci & Engrng, 1992; Supvsr, Dept of Hlth, Exec Yuan, China, 1993; Supvsr, Automotve Rsch & Testing Cntr, 1994; Prof, Chung Cheng Inst of Technol, 1996-98; Cnst, Pres Off, RiTEK Co, 1998; Dir, Flat Panel Display Div, RiTEK Co, 1999. Publications: Total of 20 pprs in profl jrnls; Contbr, 58 pprs on metals, semiconductors and polymers, intl & doemstic conf proceedings; Holder of 2 patents. Honours include: 2nd, 1980, 1st, 1991, Grad Awds, Dept of Def, Taipei, China; Rsch Awd, Natl Sci Cncl, Taipei, China, 1994; Best Tchng Awd, Chung Cheng Inst of Technol, Taoyun, China, 1994. Memberships: IEEE; TMS (Minerals, Metals Materials); ASM Intl; AAAS; Natl Geog Soc; Abrasive Machining Soc; Chinese Soc of Def Sci & Technol; Chinese Crystal Growth Soc; Chinese Soc of Mechl Engrs; Materials Rsch Soc; Amn Phys Soc (APS); Amn Soc of Mechl Engrs. Hobbies: Sports: basketball, golf, music, computer. Address: 14F No1, Jung-Jeng Road, Chung-Ho City, Taiwan 235, China.

CHAO Shou-po, b. 1 Mar 1941, Chunghua County, Taiwan. Governor. m. Lu Miao Shen, 2 s, 1 d. Education: LLB, Cntrl Police Coll, Taiwan; Master, Comparative Law, MCL, Univ of IL, USA; Dr, Juridical Scis. Appointments: Prof of Law, 1972-76; Commnr, Taiwan Provincial Govt, 1976-79; Prof of Law, Tunghai Univ, Natl Chunghsing Univ, Natl Chingshi Univ, 1977-. Dpty Dir Gen, Kuomintang KMT, 1979-83; Comnr, Taiwan Provincial Govt Cncl, 1979-81; Commnr, 1981-87; Dir Gen, Kuomintang, KMT, 1987-89; Chmn, Cncl of Labor Affairs, Executive Yuan, 1989-94; Sec Gen, 1994-97; Gov, 1998-. Creative Works: Getting Involved; A Comparative Study of the Choice of Law in Domestiv Relations; Law and Innovation; Social Policy, Family Welfare and Community Development; Social Problems and Social Welfare, 1990; Labor Policy and Labor Problems, 1992. Honours: Ten Outstndng Yng Persons, 1979; Eminent Alumni, IL Univ. Memberships: Sch Yth Servs; Intl Assn for Cmty Dev; Intl Cncl for Socl Welfare; Fndn for the Promotion of Socl Harmony; Mem Fndn of the Feb 28th Incident; Natl Water Lafe Saving Assn; The Assn of Chao's Family. Hobbies: Golf; Art. Address: Taiwan Provincial Government, #1 Sheng-fu Road, Chung-shing Village, Nantou County, Taiwan, China.

CHAPMAN Colin Burton, b. 30 Apr 1948, Melbourne, Aust. Pharmacist; Veterinary Surgeon. m. Margaret Helen Turnbull, 1 s, 3 d. Education: BPharm, Vic Coll of Pharm; BVSc (Hons); PhD, Unv of Melbourne. Publications: 50 publs in Aust and intl jrnls. Appointments: Lt, Roy Austl Army Medl Corps, 1971-72; Pharmacist, Darwin, Melbourne, 1972; Vet Surg, Melbourne, 1976-86; Prof of Pharmaceutics, Vic Coll of Pharm, 1987-90; Prof of Pharm, Dean, Vic Coll of Pharm, 1991-. Honour: Fell, Pharm Soc of Aust (FPS), 1990. Memberships: Pharm Soc of Aust; Aust Vet Assn. Hobbies: Landscape gardening; Farming; Philately. Address: 13 Mt Robertson Road, New Gisborne 3438, Australia.

CHAPMAN Hedley Grant Pearson, b. 27 Apr 1949, Adelaide, S Aust. Senator for South Australia, Australian Parliament. m. Sally Ringwood, 18 Apr 1981, 1 s, 1 d. Education: BA (Hons), Univ of Adelaide; Bus Innovations and Entrepeneurship Cert, Univ of S Aust. Appointments include: Mktng Exec, oil ind, 1971-75; Elected Fedl Mbr for Kingston, House of Reprs, 1975-83; Mbr, var Parly and Govt Cttees, 1975-83; Ldr, Austl deleg, Commonwealth countries conf on govt policy on yth affairs, 1979; Self-employed mngmt cnslt, 1983-87; Elected Sen, S Aust, 1987, re-elected 1990, 1996; Acting Shadow Min for var portfolios, 1989-95; Ldr, inaugural Young Polit Ldrs deleg to Japan, 1992; Temporary Chmn of Cttees (i e Acting Dpty Pres), in Sen, 1993-; Chmn, Jnt Parly Statutory Cttee on Corps and Securities, 1996-; Chmn, Govt Ind, Sci, Rescs, Sport and Tourism Cttee, 1996-; Mbr, Senate Econs Cttees; Ldr, Austl Space Ind deleg to Taiwan, 1995-. Honour: Queen's Silver Jubilee Medal, 1977. Memberships include: S Austl Farmers' Fedn, Pres, Adelaide Branch; Hon Treas, Austl Inst of Intl Affairs; Pilot Offr, RAAF Res; Mbr, Past Parish Cnclr, St Matthew's Anglican Ch, Kensington; Bd of Reference, Living Hope Cnsllng Serv; Advsry Panel, Parents Without Partners; VP, Glenelg Football Club. Hobby: Cricket. Address: 10 Northumberland Street, Heathpool, South Australia, Australia.

CHAPPELL Gregory Stephen, b. 7 Aug 1948 Adelaide. Cricketer; Business Executive. m. Judith Elizabeth Donaldson, 1971, 2 s, 1 d. Education: Plympton High Sch Adelaide; Prince Alfred Coll Adelaide. Appointments: Grandson of V Y Richardson - Austl Cricket Cap, 1935-36; Brother of I M Chappell - Austl Cricket Cap, 1971-75; Teams SA, 1966-73; Somerset, 1968-69; Queensland, 1973-84 - Cap, 1973-77, 1979-80; 87 Tests for Aust, 1970-84; 48 as Cap scoring 7100 runs - average 53.8 - inclng 24 hundreds and holding 122 catches; Scored 108 on Test debut v Eng Perth, 1970; Only Cap to have scored a century in each innings of 1st test as cap - v West Indies Brisbane, 1975; Holds record for most catches in a test match - 7 v Eng Perth, 1975; Scored 24535 first-class runs - 74 hundreds; Toured Eng, 1972, 1975, 1977, 1980; Mngng Dir AD Sports Technols - fmrly Fundamental Golf and Leisure Ltd - 1993; Dir,

1992-; Dir Greg Chappell Sports Mktng, 1995-; State Mngr of Cricket, S Austl Cricket Assn, 1998-. Honours: Austl Sportsman of the Yr, 1976; MBE for Servs to Cricket, 1979. Memberships: Hon Life Mbr MCC, 1985. Hobbies: Golf; Reading; Listening to music. Address: c/o South Australian Cricket Association, Adelaide Oval, North Adelaide, SA 5006, Australia.

CHAPRA M Umer, b. 1 Feb 1933, Bombay, India. Senior Economic Adviser. m. Khairunnisa Jamal Mundia, 11 May 1962, 2 s, 2 d. Education: BCom, 1954, MCom, 1956, Univ of Karachi; PhD, Univ MN, USA, 1961. Appointments include: Tchng and Rsch Asst, Univ MN, 1957-60; Asst Prof, Econs, Univ WI, 1960-61; Snr Econ, Assoc Ed, The Pakistan Devel Review, Pakistan Inst of Devel Econs, Karachi, 1961-62; Rdr, Econs, Ctrl Inst of Islamic Rsch, Karachi, 1962-63; Assoc Prof, Econs, Univ WI, Plattville, 1963-64; Assoc Prof, Econs, Univ KY, Lexington, 1964-65; Econ Advsr, Snr Econ Advsr, Saudi Arabian Monetary Agency, 1995-. Publications: 9 books and monographs, 50 pprs, 8 book reviews. Honours include: King Faisal Intl Awd, Islamic Studies, 1989; Islamic Devel Bank Awd, Islamic Econs, 1989. Hobbies: Reading; Writing. Address: c/o Saudi Arabian Monetary Agency, PO Box 2992, Riyadh 11169, Saudi Arabia.

CHARLES Ray, b. 23 Sep 1930. Jazz Musician. m. div, 9 children. Education: St Augustine's Sch Orlando FL. Appointments: Taught himself to play and write for every bass and wind instrument in orch specialng in piano organ and saxophone; Composes and arranges; Played at Rockin' Chair Club Seattle, Elks Club Seattle; Joined Lowell Fulsom's Blues Band; Toured for a yr; Played at Apollo Harlem; Fmd grp to accompany singer Ruth Brown; Ldr of Maxim Trio; With Atlantic Records, 1954-59; ABC Records, 1959-62; Fmd own cos Tangerine, 1962-73; Crossover Records Co, 1973-; Columbia Records, 1982-; Tours with Ray Charles Revue. Major albums incl: Ray Charles' Greatest Hits; Modern Sounds in Country and Western Music - Vols 1 and 2; Message from the People; Volcanic Action of my Soul; Through the Eyes of Love; Would You Believe; My World; Blue and Jazz. Honours:Songwriters Hall of Fame; Rock and Roll Hall of Fame, 1986; Cmdr des Artes et des Lettres, 1986; Kennedy Cntr Honor, 1986; Natl Medal of Arts, 1993; Polar Munc Prize, 1998. Address: c/o Ray Charles Entertainment, 2107 West Washington Boulevard, Los Angeles, CA 90018, USA.

CHARNOCK John Stewart, b. 29 Dec 1930. Scientist. m. Barbara Joan Schubert, 1 Nov 1957, 1 s, 1 d. Education: BSc, 1956; PhD, 1961; DSc, 1979. Appointments: Prof, Chmn, Dept of Pharmacology, Univ of Alberta, Can, 1970-1980; Chf Rsch Scientist, CSIRO, Aust, 1980-1993; Cnslt, John Charnock & Assocs, 1993-. Creative works: 18 books; 135 scientific pprs; 5 reviews. Honours: Nuffield Fellshp, Oxford Univ, 1974-75; Natl Hlth Med Rsch Fellshp, Can and USA, 1961-63. Memberships: NY Acady of Scis, 1972-; Amn Oil Chem Soc, 1976-. Hobbies: Reading; Walking; Swimming. Listed in: Who's Who in America; Who's Who in the World. Address: PO Box 2060, Normanville, SA 5204, Australia.

CHARTERIS Richard, b. 24 June 1948, Chatham Is, NZ. Musicologist; Writer; Editor. Education: BA, Vic Univ, Wellington, 1970, MA 1st Class Hons, 1972, PhD, 1976, Univs Canterbury and London. Appointments: Rothmans Rsch Fell, Univ Sydney, 1976-78; Rsch Fellshp, Univ Qld, 1979-80; Austl Rsch Cncl Chf Investigator, Music Dept, 1981-90; Austl Rsch Cncl Snr Rsch Fell (Rdr), Music Dept, 1991-94; Prof, Histl Musicology, Austl Rsch Cncl Snr Rsch Fell, Music Dept, 1995-, Univ Sydney.Publications: Auth, over 100 books and eds devoted to music of Johann Christian Bach, John Coprario, Alfonso Ferrabosco the Elder, Domenico Maria Ferrabosco, Giovanni Gabrieli, Adam Gumpelzhaimer, Hans Leo Hassler, Thomas Lupo, Claudio Monteverdi and others, mostly in series Corpus Mensurabilis Musicae, Musica Britannica, Recent Researches in the Music of the Baroque Era, Boethius Editions, Fretwork Editions King's Music Editions, Baroque and Classical Music Series, and books on composers, music and early sources in series Boethius Editions, Thematic Catalogues Series, Musicological Studies and Documents and Altro Polo; Contbr, num articles to musicological jrnls. Honours: Snr Schlshp, 1970-71; NZ UGC Travelling Schlshp, 1973-75; Louise Dyer Awd, 1975; Mary Duncan Schlshp, 1975; Austl Acady Hums Travelling Rsch Fell to UK, USA, Eur, 1979; Austl Rsch Cncl Travelling Rsch Fell to UK, USA, Eur, 1981-82, 1986; Elected Fell, Austl Acady Hums, 1990. Memberships include: Intl Musicological Soc; Roy Musical Assn; Amn Musicological Soc; Musicological Soc Aust; Viola da Gamba Socs GB and Am; Dolmetsch Fndn; Natl Early Music Assn GB; Hist Brass Soc; Early Music Assn NSW; London House Fellshp. Address: Music Department, University of Sydney, NSW 2006, Australia.

CHARUSATHIRA Prapas, b. 25 Nov 1912 Udorn Prov. Politician; Army Officer. m. Khunying Sawai, 1 s, 4 d. Education: Chulachomklao Roy Mil Acady; Natl Def Coll. Appointments: Army serv, 1933; Rose through infantry to Gen, 1960; Min of Interior, 1957-71; VP and Rector Chulalongkorn Univ, 1961-69; Dep PM, 1963-71; Army Dep Cmdr and Dep Supreme Cmdr, 1963-64; Supreme Cmdr, 1964; Dir of Security Cncl - Def and Interior - 1971-72; Dep PM Min of Interior, 1972-73; In exile, 1973-77; Returned to Thailand, Jan 1977. Publications: The Role of the Ministry of Interior in the Development of National Security; The Role of the Ministry of Interior in Maintenance of National Peace and Order. Honours: Num decorations. Memberships: Mbr Natl Exec Cncl, 1971-72. Hobbies: Sport; Boxing; Soccer; Golf; Hunting; Amateur ranching; Arms collecting. Address: 132-5 Suan Puttan Residence, Bangkok, Thailand.

CHATTERJEE Amar, b. 1 Sept 1938, Calcutta, India. Professor. m. Rita, 6 Sept 1970, 1 s, 1 d. Education: MSc; PhD; DSc; FOG. Appointments: Lectr, RPM Coll, Calcutta, 1962-69; Assoc Prof, 1969-76, Prof, 1976-79, Lusaka, Zambia, Univ Khartoum, Sudan, 1979-90; Prof, Chmn, A1 A Med Coll, India, 1990-91; Prof, Univ Sains, Malaysia, 1991-. Publications: Over 125 articles in profl jrnls. Honour: Rsch Carrier Dev Awd, Family Plng Fndn, 1976. Memberships: Soc for Study of Reproduction; Soc for Study of Fertility; Physiol Soc of India and Malaysia. Hobby: Photography. Address: Department of Physiology, School of Medical Sciences, University Sains Malaysia, 16150 Kubang Kerian, Kelantan, Malaysia.

CHATTERJEE Ashis, b. 8 Sept 1954. Librarian. m. Kakoli, 9 Dec 1983, 1 s. Education: BCom; MA (Pub Adm); BLibsc; MLIS; LLB; DBM; Dip Trg & Div; Cert in Supervision; Cert in Cons of Books; DDEd. Appointments: Asst Libn, 1982-94; Libn, 1994-, Ramarkrishna Mission Vidyamandira, Belurmath, Howrah, WB, India. Publications: 15 pprs in different LIS jrnls in India; Book: Management Courses in India, 1989; Courses and Careers for Graduates, Educational Directory, Events of 1900, forthcoming; Contbns to Intl Def Directory, USA, Worldwide Government Directory (USA). Memberships: ILA (Del); IASLIC (Cal); SIS (Del); AGLIS (Del); BLA (Cal); WBCLA (Cal); UPLA (Luck); KLA (Trvan); MLA; LAB (Dhaka); STBS (USA). Listed in: Indo-Europeans Who's Who; Indo American Who's Who; Indo-Arab; Biography International; Ref-Asia; American Biographical Inst; World Who's Who of Men and Women of Distinction. Hobbies: Prospectus collection; Travel and mix with people. Address: 1 Jnanendra Avenue, Po Uttarpara, Dt Hooghly, WB, 712258 India.

CHATTERJEE Rana Pratap, b. 24 Feb 1953. Supervisor. m. Kasturi Chatterjee, 7 June 1986, 1 d. Education: BSc; MLibSc; Assocshp, Info Sci. Appointments: Asst, Cntrl Lib, Calcutta Univ, 1981-; Libn, DC Indl Plant Servs Ltd, Calcutta, 1991; Hon Lectr, Bengal Lib Assn, 1994-; Guest Lctr, Dept of Lib Sci, Univ of Calcutta; Pt-time Lctr, Dept of Lib and info Sci, Rabindrabharati Univ, Calcutta. Publications: Microform Management in Indian Libraries: A Survey; A Brief History of Origin and Development of Scientific Journals; Inflibnet: Problems and prospects. Memberships: Bengal Lib Assn, 1981-; Indian Assn of Special Libs & Info Cntr, 1988-. Hobbies: Stamp and Coin Collecting; Trekking.

Address: c/o R K Guha, 7/68 Netajinagar, Calcutta 700 092, India.

CHATTERJEE Sunil K, b. 21 Jan 1961. Teacher. m. Anulekha Mukhopadhyay, 2 Aug 1993. Education: MSc, Chem; MLib & Inf Sc; A Inf Sc (INSDOC). Appointments: Pt-time Lectr, Dept of Lib & Inf Sc, Rabindra Bharati Univ, Calcutta, 1992-93; Lectr, Dept of Lib & Inf Sc, Jadavpur University, Calcutta 700 032, 1993-. Publications: Rsch articles (two), IASLIC Bulletin, 1990; Papers accepted in intl confs, INFORMETRICS, 1991, 1995, 1997; SCIENTOMETRICS, 1998. Honour: Univ Gold Medals, 1988, 1990. Memberships: BLA, 1993; IASLIC, 1995; Calcutta ILA, 1996; Delhi. Hobbies: Book reading; Gardening; Music. Address: Village and PO Sonaplalsi, Dist Burdwan, West Bengal 713 407, India.

CHATURKAR Shankar Kisanrao, b. 29 June 1932, Daryapur. Retired Head Accountant. m. Vimlabai, 25 May 1953, 1 s, 1 d. Education: MA, Marathi; PhD. Publications: Books: Philosophical Thoughts of Marathi Saints (Mukundaraj to Ramdas), 1979; Shri Dhyyaneshwar Maharajanchi Vicahr Sampada (Adwait Dhnyan Majiri), 1986; Dhnya Tukoba Samarth (Sadeha Vaikuntha Gaman), 1993; Vth Vaid, Shri Tukaram Gatha, 1996; Short stories: Kaivalyacha Putala, 1995; Tuka Akasha Yewadha, 1996; Ed, 5 books; essays. Honour: Hari Bhakta Parayan. Hobby: To find out philosophical thoughts of Marathi saints. Address: Daryapur Dist, Amravati (Maharashtra), India 44803.

CHAU Thoai Hong, b. 15 Nov 1954, Vietnam. Architect. m. Nov 1979, 2 s, 1 d. Education: Univ Grad; Arch Deg. Appointments: Assoc, Dai Hung Cnstrn Co Ltd, 1994-; Dir, Cnstrn & Garment Co Ltd, Ho Chi Minh City, Vietnam, 1994-. Address: 7/6F Xo Viet Nghe Tinh Street, Dist Binh Thanh Ho Chi Minh City, Vietnam.

CHAUDHARY Bansh Raj, b. 24 Aug 1947. Teacher; Researcher. m. Sandhya Chaudhary, June 1970, 2 d. Education: MSc, PhD, Botany. Appointments: Temp Lectr, 1976-79, Lectr, 1979-87, Reader, 1987-97, Prof, 1997-, Banaras Hindu Univ, 1987. Publication: Cytology, Genetics and Molecular Biology of Algae, 1996. Creative works: More than 12 contributed articles in books. Honours: Gift Mbrshp, Intl Phycol Soc, 1980-92; Visng Fell, INSA, 1991-92; Nom, INSA Exchange Prog, 1996-97; YSRK Sarma Gold Medal, 1997. Memberships: Life mbr, 6 scientific socs; Ed Bd & Exec Mbr to num Natl & Intl Socs. Hobbies: Gardening; House & Laboratory. Address: Centre of.Advanced Study in Botany, Banaras Hindu University, Varanasi 221005, India.

CHAUDHURI Amit, b. 15 May 1962, Calcutta, India. Writer; Research Fellow. m. Rosinka, 12 Dec 1991. Education: BA, hons, Univ Coll, London; DPhil, Univ Oxford. Appointments: Creative Arts Fell, Wolfson Coll, Oxford, 1992-95; Leverhulme Specl Rsch Fell, Univ Cambridge, 1997-. Publications: A Strange and Sublime Address, 1991; Afternoon Raag, 1993; Freedom Songs, 1998. Honours: Betty Trask Awd, 1991; C'wlth Writers Prize, 1992; Encore Prize, 1993; Southern Arts Lit Prize, 1993. Address: c/o Derek Johns, A P Watt, 20 John Street, London WC1 2DR, England.

CHAUDHURI Pradip, b. 6 Nov 1939, Chittagong, India. Librarian. m. Niyati, 9 May 1968, 1 s. Education: MA; Ctf, Lib Sci; PG Dip, Lib Sci. Appointments: Lib Asst, 1960, Asst Libn, 1966, Assoc Libn, 1984, Libn, 1997, Jadavpur Univ; Ed, Granthagae, 1977-80; Guest Lectr, Vidyasagar Univ, 1993. Publications: Calcutta: People and Empire, 1975; Calcutta - A Quest for 1986; Calutta Stusies: a select list of documents, 1999. Honour: Silver Plaque, 50th Anniversary of Libnshp, Calcutta Univ, 1996. Memberships: Mbr, State Book Bd, Govt of W Bengal; Mbr, Rabindra Bhavan Advsry Cttee, Santiniketan; Hon Sec, 1994-98, VP, 1999- Bangiya Sahitya Parisad; Exec Mbr, paschim Banga Bangla Acady; Asiatic Soc; ILA; IASLIC; BLA. Hobbies: Reading; Writing Poetry and Articles in Bengali. Address: F/16 Jadavpur Super Market Complex, Calcutta 700 032, West Bengal, India.

CHAVALIT Yongchaiyut. Politician; General. Appointments: Fmr Dep PM and Min of Def; Ldr New Aspiration Party; PM Min of Def, Nov 1996-. Address: Office of the Prime Minister, Government House, Thanon Nakhon Pathom, Bangkok 10300, Thailand.

CHAWLA Baldev Raj, b. 1 Oct 1942, Lyalpur, Pakistan. Publisher. m. Sudesh Chawla, 9 May 1970, 1 s, 1 d. Education: MBA; DBM; Prabhakar. Appointments: Pres, DSPBA; Proprietor, Heritage Publrs. Honours: Trophy, Best Past Pres, DSPBA; Natl Awd for a Book. Memberships: India Intl Cntr; Rotary Club Intl; VP, FPBA India. Hobbies: Reading; Writing. Address: Heritage Publishers, 32 Prakash Apts, 5 Ansari Road, New Delhi 110002, India.

CHAWLA Shanti Lal, b. 26 Oct 1936, Lahore, India. Medical Doctor. m. Kamlesh, 12 May 1967, 2 d. Education: BSc; LSMF; MBBS; DMRT (London; FFR (RCSi), Dublin. House Surg, Dayanand Medl Hosp, India, 1963-64; Asst Surg, Govt Dispensary Gurgoan, India, 1964; Rsch MO in Med & Surg, Tirath Ram Hosp, Delhi, 1966-67; Asst Surg, Govt Dispensary, Delhi, 1967-69; Snr House Offr, 1969-71, Registrar in Radiotherapy, 1974-80, Cookridge Hosp, Cheshire; Registrar in Radiotherapy, 1972-74, Snr Registrar, Catteridge Hosp Cheshire; Cnslt in Radiotherapy and Oncology, 1980-, Hd of Dept, 1980-91, Clin Dir, 1991-94, S Cleveland Hosp; Hon Clin Lectr in Radiotherapy, Univ of Newcastle-Upon-Tyne, 1980-. Publications: Num in medl jrnls. Honours: Gold Awd, North Regl Hlth Authy, Newcastle, 1990; Bronze Meallion ABI Medl Comunity Awd, Newcastle upon Tyne, 1991. Memberships: Indian Assn of Cleveland (Pres, 1987-89); Treas, Hindi Cultural Soc, 1990-; Indian Drs of Cleveland; Chmn, Local Negotiating Cttee SCH, 1996-. Hobbies: Music; Dancing; Badminton. Address: South Cleveland Hospital, Marton Road, Middlesborough, Cleveland, England.

CHEN Bangzhu, b. Sep 1934 Jiujiang City Jiangxi Prov. Politician. Education: Fac of Civ Engrng; Chonqing Constrn Engrng Coll. Appointments: Engr at Jilin Chem Indl Dist Constrn Co, 1954-65; Joined CCP, 1975; Chf Engr and Dept Mngmt No 4 and 9 Chem Indl Constrn Co Min of Chem Ind, 1966-80; Chf Engr Mngmt Jiuhua Bldg Co, 1980-84; Mayor of Yueyang and Dep Sec CCP Yueyang Cty Cttee, 1983-; Vice-Gov Hunan Prov, 1984-86; Gov, 1989-95; Dep Sec CPC 6th Hunan Provincial Cttee, 1989-; A Dep of Hunan Prov 8th NPC, 1993-; Gov Hunan Prov, 1993-; Hd Natl Ldng Grp for Placement of Demobilised Army Offrs, 1995-. Min of Internal Trade, 1995-98. Memberships: Alt mbr CCP Cntr Cttee, 1987-92; Mbr 14th Cntr Cttee CCP, 1992-; Mbr 14th CCP Cntr Cttee, 1992-97; Mbr 15th CCP Cntr Cttee, 1997-; Address: c/o Ministry of Internal Trade, 25 Yuetanbei Jie, Xicheng Qu, Beijing, People's Republic of China.

CHEN Bingqing, b. 9 Jan 1940, Wuxi, Jiangsu, China. Senior Engineer. m. Wang Wenhui, 3 Jan 1970, 1 s, 1 d. Education: Ferrous Metallurgy Dept, Beijing Univ of Sci and Technol, 1959-64; Stdied in Thermal Energy Engrng Dept Qinghua Univ, China. Appointments: Anshan Iron and Steel Corp, China, 1964-85; Employed as Snr Engr, Iron and Steel Rsch Inst, Baosteel; Over 20 pprs published on Iron and Steel and other jrnls. Honours: A patent, A Coal Gassification-Based DRI Prdn Process Based on Shaft Furnace, awd'd Gold Prize, 6th New Technol and New Prodn Conf, China. Memberships: China Metallic Soc; Bowsteel Automatic Soc. Hobbies: Sports; Reading historical novels.

CHEN Chi-Yao, b. 19 Nov 1930, Taiwan. Professor. m. Hsu-Huey Chou, 3 s, 1 d. Education: BA, Natl Taiwan Univ, 1953; Visng Schl, Wharton Sch Doct Prog, Univ PA, USA, 1976. Appointments: Assoc Prof, Grad Sch Ins, Natl Cheng-chi Univ; Assoc Prof, Univ; Hon Prof, Funan Univ of Fin and Econs, 1994-; Mngng Dir, Bd, Exec VP, Cathay Ins Co; Chmn, Fire Ins Cttee, Chmn, Fire and Allied Perils Cttee, Taipei Non-Life Ins Assn; Chmn, Engrng Ins Assn; Chmn, Non-Life Underwriters Soc, Repub China, 1990-; Dir of Bd, Guarantee Fund Compulsory Auto Ins, 1997-; Chmn, Chi-Yung Ins Fund

Taipei, 1998-. Publications: Studies on Re-insurance, 7 eds, 1986; Re-insurance - Current Research and Types of Re-insurance, 5 eds, 1990; Risk Management and Insurance, 1993; Automobile Insurance Claims - Theory and Practice, 1995; Reinsurance: Principle and Practice, 1996; Auto Insurance: Principle and Practice. Honours: Outstndng Person Awd, Min Fin, 1973; Outstndng Person of Yr Awd, Taipei Chmbr of Comm, 1974; Most Outstndng and Successful Pres, HQ Intl Young Men's Clubs, Geneva. 1979-80; Prize, Soc Ins, Repub China, 1982; Prize, Outstndng Book of Yr, Natl Cncl Sci, 1993; Acady Prize, Japan Risk Mngmt Soc, 1994. Memberships: Japan Risk Mngmt Soc; Dir, Soc Ins, Repub China; Hon Chmn Soc of Underwriters, Taipei, 1996; Pres, Risk Mngmt Soc, Taipei, 1998; Taipei SE Rotary Club. Listed in: Who's Who in the World; International Book of Honour; Dictionary of International Biography. Hobbies: Reading; Walking. Address: 2nd Floor, No 5, Alley 5, Lane 5, Section 3, Jen-Ai Road, Taipei, Taiwan.

CHEN Chih-Hsin (Zhi-Xin), b. 8 Feb 1931, Shaoxing, Zhejiang, China. Retired Professor; Private Researcher and Consultant. m. Xiu-Hua He, 27 Dec 1965, 1 s, 1 d. Education: BS, Mech Engrng, Qinghua Univ, 1952. Appointments: Engr, Changchun First Auto-Manufactory, 1952-55; Lectr, Harbin Mil Engrng Inst, 1955-60; Assoc Prof, Xian Armor Engrng Inst, 1961-70; Snr Rschr, Beijing Armor Technol Rsch Inst, 1970-80; Prof, Shanghai Univ of Technol, 1980-93; Retd Prof, Pvte Rschr, Cnslt, 1994-. Publications: Theory of Conjugate Surfaces, Vol I, 1974, Vol II, 1977; Fundamentals of the Theory of Conjugate Surfaces, 1985; Over 50 articles to profl jrnls. Honours: 1st Class Merit Awd, China Armor Cmd, 1978; Natl Natural Sci Awd, China Natl Sci and Technol Cmmn, 1987; Sci and Technol Adv Awd, China Natl Educn Cmmn, 1986. Memberships: Delegate, China Natl Peoples Congress, Beijing, 1978-83, Shanghai Peoples Congress, 1983-88. Hobbies: Reading; Travel; Cooking. Address: Lane 200, House 23, Room 401, Wu-Ninglu, Shanghai 200063, China.

CHEN Da, b, 8 Nov 1923, Leging, Zhejiang, China. Painter. m. Ci-Fang Chang, 8 Aug 1961, 2 s, 2 d. Education: BS, Trad Chinese Painting Dept, China Inst, 1956. Creative works: Painting: Song of Sheep Tender, 1958; Girl of Silkworm Tender, 1960; A Letter, 1960. Honour: Awd for Song of Sheep Tender, Art Exhbn of the Yth Get-together Holiday for the World, 1958. Hobby: A system of deep breathing exercises. Address: Jiangsu Traditional Chinese Paintings Studio, Nanjing, China 210002.

CHEN Dao-han, b. 23 Nov 1937, Shanghai, China. Astronomer. m. Zheng Hui-jun, 22 Sept 1962, 1 s, 1 d. Education: Grad, Nanjing Univ, 1958. Appointments include: Rsch Prof, Astron, Purple Mtn Observatory, Academia Sinica, Nanjing; Rsch Scientist, McDonald Observatory and Univ TX, USA, 1985; Team Ldr, Overseas Observation Team for Halley's Comet, Academia Sinica, 1986; Visng Prof, Intl Cntr Theort Phys, Italy, 1990. Publications: Over 30 papers inclng 1 on observation of Uranian Ring, 1978; Monograph, Modern Planetary Physics, 1988. Honours: China Sci Congress Awd, 1978; 3rd Class Nat Sci Awd, Academia Sinica, 1980; 2nd Class Sci Progress Awd, Academia Sinica, 1988; 1st Class Sci Progress Awd, Academia Sinica, 1989. Memberships: Org Cttee, Commn 16, Intl Astronomical Union, 1985-91; Planetary Atmosphere Commn, IUGG, 1987-91. Hobbies: Chinese local opera; Classical music. Address: Purple Mountain Observatory, Nanjing 210008, China.

CHEN De Tong, b. 3 Jan 1939, Fujian, China. Doctor. m. Bau Nai-Zhuan, 20 Jan 1968, 1 d. Education: Beijing Coll of Med. Appointments: Dir, 3rd Dept 302 Hospital, Beijing, Dir Chf Physn, 1994. Publications: 30 in profl jrnls incl: Ultrastructural observation of Resin 812 activated charcoal hollow fibrous membrane by SEM, 1998. Honours: 1 x 2nd grade, 3 x 3rd grade, 1 x 4 grade, Sci & Technol Army Awds. Memberships: Standing Cttee Mbr, Mil Digestive Internal Med Grp; Chinese & west Med Cttee of Beijing branch Vice-Dir; Chinese jrnl of

integrated tradl & west med on liver disease ed; Hong Kong intl Chinese & West Cttee of Dir. Hobby: Collecting postage-stamps. Address: 26 Feng-Tai Road, Beijing, China 202.

CHEN Dean, b. 21 Feb 1935, Fujian, China. Professor. m. Y Q Huang, Nov 1961, 1 s, 2 d. Education: Grad, Chem Dept, 1957, Postgrad, 1961, Xiamen Univ. Appointments: Lectr, 1978, Assoc Prof, 1983, Prof, 1994, Chem Dept, Xiamen Univ; Visng Schl, Chem Dept, Univ AL, USA, 1980-82; Snr Visng Schl, Dept of Chem Engrng, MS Univ, USA, 1990-92. Publications: Over 50 pprs in profl jrnls. Honours: 2 Ctf of Merits, Rsch Achvmnt, Natl Sci Meeting of China, Fujian Prov Sci Meeting, 1978, 1979; 2nd Class Awd, 1981, 1st Class Awd, 1994, Sci and Technol Adv, Natl Educ Commn, China; 3rd Class Awd, 1982 and 1995, Natl Nature Sci, Natl Commn of Sci and Technol, China. Memberships: Chinese Chem Soc; Chinese Chem Engrng Soc. Hobby: Classical Music. Address: 28-201 Haibin, Xiamen University, Xiamen 361005, China.

CHEN Dezun, b. 22 Aug 1927, Hangzhou Cty, Zhejiang Prov, China. Acupuncturist and Traditional Herbalist. m. Fang Wenjie, 25 Oct 1949, 1 s, 1 d. Education: Grad, Chinese Medl Coll w Dip, 1945. Appointments: Set up own clin, Dpty Chf, Acupuncture and Moxibustion Rsch Inst, 1951; Advsr, Brain Surg and Cardiology Dept, Huashan Hosp, 1965-75; Advsr, Dept of Opth, Shanghai Opthal Hosp, 1971; Advsr, Opth Hosp, 1972-. Creative works: 1st acupuncturist to introduce acupuncture and moxibustion into the surg to replace anesthetics. Publications: Over 12 essays inclng: Lung Surgery Using Acupuncture as Anesthetic. Honour: Advd Technol Achiever, 1977. Memberships: 3rd, 6th, 7th, 8th Chinese People's Polit Consultative Conf of Shanghai Cttee, 1980-98; Dir, Chinese Pharm Promotion Assn; Dir, Natl Anesthetic Acupuncture Assn; Tech Advsr, Shanghai Acupuncture and Moxibustion Rsch Inst, 1990-. Hobbies: Chinese Calligraphy; Ballroom dancing; Chess; Billards; Beijing Opera. Address: Suite 15, #43 Anting Road, Shanghai, China, Post Code 200031, China.

CHEN Fu-Qun, b. 2 Oct 1925, Guangdong, China. Professor; Tutor for Doctoral Candidates. m. Zheng Chuhua, 1 July 1951, 1 s, 2 d. Education: Bachelor's deg, Aeronautical Engrng Dept, Zhejiang Univ, Hangzhou, 1948. Appointments: Asst, Zhejiang Univ, 1948-52; Asst, Lectr, East China Aeronautic Inst, 1952-56; Lectr, Assoc Prof, Prof, Tutor Doct Studs, Aeroengine Dept, NWest Polytech Univ, Xian, 1956-. Publications: Co-translator, 2 textbooks: Theory of Jet Engines, 1961, 1977; Over 50 theses concerning engine/inlet compatibility, response and frequency response of turbojet engines to inlet distortion, prediction of Maximun Instantaneous Distortion (profile) by statistical methods, and numerical analysis of aerodynamics instability for engines w inlet distortion. Honours: Prizes, Sci and Technol Advancement or Achievements: 2nd Prize, Shaanxi Prov, 1978, 1986; 1st Prize, 1979, 2nd Prize, 1981, Chinese Aeronautic Acady; 3rd Prize, 1983, 2nd Prize, 1985, Min Aviation Ind; 2nd Prize, 1987, 3rd Prize, 1994, State Educ Cttee; 2nd Prize, Min Aeronautic and Astronautic Ind, 1989; 2nd Prize, Aeronautic Fndn, 1996; Titles for Contbns: Outstndng Contbn Expert, 1992, Ex Tutor Grad Stud, 1993, Min Aviation Ind. Memberships: Chinese Soc Aeronautics and Astronautics, Vice-Chf, Propulsion Aero-Thermodynamics Cttee, 1983-; Chinese Soc Engrng Thermophys; Chinese Soc Mechl Engrs; VP, 1985-93, Mbr, 1993-, Editl Cttee, Jrnl Aerospace Power; Cncl Mbr, Chinese Soc Mechl Engrs, Shaanxi Bch, 1985-89. Hobby: Tai Ji Quan boxing. Address: North 2-5-1, Northwestern Polytechnic University, Xian, Shaanxi, China.

CHEN Gang, b. 20 June 1964, Nanzhang, Hubei, China. Educator. m. Guohong Cai, 1 s. Education: BS, Huazhong Univ of Sci and Technol, China, 1984; MS, 1987; PhD, UC Berkeley, 1993. Appointments: Asst Prof, Duke Univ, 1993-97; Assoc Prof, Univ of CA, Los Angeles, 1997-. Publications: Over 50 Publs, In Microsrale Heat Transfer and Thermoelectrics. Honours: NSF Yng Investigator Awd. Memberships: ASME; MRS;

MAS. Address: UCLA Dept Mech and Aerospace Engrng, Los Angeles, CA 90095, USA.

CHEN Han-Kuei (Hankui), b. 8 Nov 1918, Jiangsu, China. Electronic Physicist. Education: BS, Natl Cntrl Univ, China, 1939; MS, Univ MI, USA, 1947; PhD, Univ IL, 1950. Appointments: Spec Rsch Asst, 1948-49, Rsch Assoc, 1950-51, Univ IL, USA; Prof, Electronics, many Chinese instns; Mbr, VP, Natl Review Cttee Coll Books on Electronics, 1963-91; Mbr, Natl Cttee, Chinese People's Polit Consultative Conf, 1964-97; Dir, Microwave Rsch Lab, 1979-; VP, Univ Acad Cttee, 1979-91, Hd, Dept Phys, 1980-84, Hon Hd, 1984-, E China Normal Univ; Mbr, Review Bd, Authorization Conferring Degs, State Cncl China, 1983-91; Hon Dir, Rsch Inst Applied Electronics, 1984-. Publications: Num papers; Co-auth, 2 books on Electronics. Honours include: Disting Serv Sci and Technol, City of Shanghai, 1977; Prize, Promotion Sci and Technol, 1988. Memberships include: Sigma Xi; Chinese Inst Electronics. Listed in: Dictionary of International Biography; Men of Achievement. Address: No 458, Lane 3671, North Zhong Shan Road, Shanghai 200062, China.

CHEN Hongben, b. 21 Oct 1928, Zhejiang, China. Professor of Physics. m. Guojun Chen, 1 Jan 1962, 1 s, 1 d. Education: Grad, Phys, Dept Sci, Natl Zhejiang Univ, 1952. Appointments: Asst, Nanjing Univ Technol, 1952-53; Asst, Qinghua (Tsinghoua) Univ, 1954-55; Asst, 1955-56, Lectr, 1956-78, Assoc Prof, 1978-88, Hd, Dept Basic Scis, 1983-87, Prof, 1988-, Hohai Univ. Publications: Selected Lecturer on Physics, 1988; An Introduction to Physics, 1991. Memberships: Cncl Mbr, Chinese Physl Soc, 1991-95; VP, Jiangsu Phys Soc, 1990-94. Listed in: Who's Who in the World. Hobbies: Photography; Classical music appreciation. Address: Department of Mathematics and Physics, Hohai University, 1 Xikang Road, Nanjing 210024, China.

CHEN Jeng-Tzong, b. 23 Aug 1962, Taiwan. Professor. m. Leu, 12 Nov 1997, 1 d. Education: PhD. Memberships: ISBE; Phi Tau Phi. Hobbies: Table Tennis; Swimming. Address: PO Box 23-36, Taipei, Taiwan.

CHEN Jiaming, b. 6 Mar 1952, Xiamen, China. Professor. m. Huang Lufeng, 26 June 1982, 1 s. Education: Master of Philos, Wuhan Univ, 1985; PhD, Grad Sch, Chinese Acady of Socl Scis, 1989. Appointments: Asst Prof, 1985, Lectr, 1986, Assoc Prof, 1991, Prof, 1994-, Dept of Philos, Xiamen Univ. Publications: L Stevenson's Seven Theories of Human Nature, 1988; S Hampshire's The Age of Reason, 1989; Contemporary Methodology of Western Philosophy and Social Sciences, 1991; Constitutive and Regulative Principles: Kant's Methodology of Philosophy, 1992; Trends of Modern Social Thoughts (ed), 1992. Honour: Brit Acady K C Wong Fell, 1995. Memberships: Cncl, Chinese Soc for Mod Fgn Philos Rsch, 1996-; Pres, Soc for Fgn Philos Rsch, Fujian Prov, 1996-; Chf Ed, Jrnl of Xiamen Univ, 1998-. Hobbies: Chinese Calligraphy; Music. Address: Room 102, Beicun Building 10, Xiamen University, Xiamen 361005, China.

CHEN Jiann-Chu, b. 17 Feb 1946, Kaobsiung, Taiwan. Professor. m. Su-Ching, 24 Sept 1978, 1 s, 1 d. Education: DAgric, Natl Kyushu Univ, Fukuoka, Japan. Appointments: Asst Prof, 1976; Prof, 1979; Prof & Dept Chmn, 1980. Publication: Analysis of Water Quality, Management of Water Quality, 1983. Honours: Rsch Awd, Educn Bur, 1984; Outstndng Rsch Awd, 1992-94, 1994-96, 1997-99. Memberships: World Agricl Soc; Asian Fisheries Soc. Address: Department of Aquaculture, National Taiwan Ocean University, 2 Pei-Ning Road, Keelung 20224, Taiwan.

CHEN Jinhua, b. 1931. Government Official; Business Executive. Appointments: Gen Mngr, China Petrochem Corp, 1990-93; Min in Charge of State Plng Commn, 1993-98; Hd, Co-ord Grp for Tertiary Inds, 1993-; Mbr, 14th Cntrl Cttee, CPC, 1992-; Cntrl Finl and Econ Ldng Grp; Hd, Co-ordination Grp for Survey of Tertiary Inds. Address: c/o State Planning Commission, 38 Yuetannan Jie, Xicheng Qu, Beijing, China.

CHEN Jinn-Shiun, b. 20 Nov 1952. Attending Doctor. m. Huang Yueh-Hwa, 2 Feb 1980, 1 s, 2 d. Education: BMed, Kaohsiung Medl Coll, Taiwan. Appointments: Sec, Soc of Colo-Rectal Surgs, China; Pharm Cttee, Chang Gung Mem Hosp; Tissue Cttee, Chang Gung Mem Hosp; Ward Mngmt Cttee, Chang Gung Mem Hosp; Surg Educ Cttee, Chang Gung Mem Hosp. Publications: Pelvic Peritoneal Reconstruction To Prevent Radiation Enteritis In Reactal Carcinoma, Dis Colon Rectum, 1992. Honour: Fell Amn Coll Surgs. Memberships: Assn Surg SE Asia; Amn Soc Colon and Rectal Surg; Surg Soc, China; Soc Colon and Rectal Surg, China. Hobby: Golf. Address: Chang Gung Memorial Hospital, 199 Tun Hwa North Road, Taipei, Taiwan, China.

CHEN Ju-Chin, b. 3 Mar 1940, Honan, China. Professor. m. Pi-Hsiu Huang, 25 Sept 1965, 2 s. Education: BS, Natl Taiwan Univ, 1962; MA, Rice Univ, 1965; PhD, Rice Univ, 1967. Appointments: rsch Scientist, Sw Cntr for Advd Studies, 1967-70; Assoc Prof, Natl Taiwan Univ, 1970-74; Prof, NTU, 1974-. Publications: Over 100 sci pprs in natl and intl jrnls. Honours: Dr Sun Yat-Sen's Awd on Rsch Publ, 1973; Natl Sci Cncl Awd on Outstndng Rsch, 1985-87; Min of Educ Awd on Excellence in Tchng, 1989. Memberships: Geological Soc of China; Geol Soc of Am; Amn Geophysical Union, Geochemical Soc. Address: Institute of Oceanography, Natl Taiwan University, Taipei, Taiwan, China.

CHEN Junsheng, b. 1927 Huanan Co Helongjiang Prov. Government Officer. Appointments: Sec-Gen Standing Cttee of Heilongjiang Prov, 1979-80; Sec Qigihar Cty CP, 1980-82; Dep Sec, 1983-84; Sec of the Fedn of TU Dep Chmn Exec Cttee, 1984-85; VP Fedn TU, 1985; Sec-Gen State Cncl, 1985-88; Sec CCP Cttee of Cntr State Organs, 1986-; Hd Ldng Grp for Econ Dev in Poor Areas - now Ldng Grp for Helping the Poor through Dev - 1986-; Hd Ldng Grp for Comprehensive Agricl Dev; Hd Ldng Grp for Housing System Reform; State Cnclr, 1988-98; Hd Govt deleg to Nepal, 1990-; Hd State Flood Control and Drought Relief HQ; Chmn Natl Green Cttee; Chmn Natl Afforestation Cttee; Bd of Dirs All-China Fedn of Supply and Mktng Co-ops; Dir Natl Co-op Soc of Supply and Sales, May 1995-. Memberships: Mbr Standing Cttee of Heilongjiang Prov CP; Mbr 13th CCP Cntr Cttee, 1987-92; Mbr 14th CCP Cntr Cttee, 1992-. Address: State Council, Beijing, China.

CHEN Li, b. 7 May 1929, Shanghai, China. Journalist. m. Zhang Yanping, 7 Feb 1953, 2 s. Education: Bach Deg, Beijing Univ, 1950; Dip, Snr Ed Trng Course, Thomson Fndn, London, 1983. Appointment: Hd, var depts, Tianjin Daily, 1953-56; Chf, Edl Dept, Tianjin Peoples Publng House, 1962; Vice Mngng Dir, Mngng Dir, Tianjin Peoples Publng House, 1979-81; Dpty Ed, Ed, China Daily, 1981-86. Publications: Sev trans. Memberships: 8th & 9th Natl Cttee of CPPCC; Standing Vice Chmn, China Soc of PR; Cncl Mbr, China Soc for Asian-African Studies. Hobby: Reading. Address: China Daily, 15 Huixin Dongjie, Chaoyang District, Beijing, China.

CHEN Li-An, b. 22 June 1937 Chingtien Co Chekiang. Government Official. m. 4 s, 1 d. Education: MA Inst of Technol; NY Univ. Appointments: Engr Honeywell Co USA, 1960-63; Prof Cty Univ of NY, 1968-70; Pres Ming Chi Inst of Technol, 1970-72; Dir Dep of Technol and Vocational Educ Min of Educ, 1972-74; Pres Natl Taiwan Inst of Technol, 1974-77; Vice-Min Min of Educ, 1977-78; Dir Dep of Org Affairs Cntr Cttee Kuomintang, 1979-80; Dep Sec-Gen Cntr Cttee Kuomintang, 1980-84; Chmn Natl Sci Cncl Exec Yuan, 1984-88; Min Min of Econ Affairs, 1988-90; Min of Natl Def, 1990; Sec Shaoxing Cty, 1991-; Left Natl Party, 1995. Address: c/o Ministry of National Defence, Chieshou Hall, Chung-King S Road, Taipei, Taiwan.

CHEN Li-rong, b. 20 Jan 1941, Shanghai, China. Professor of Solid State Physics. m. Liang-ling Fan, Sept 1968, 1 s. Education: Stud, Phys, Shanghai Univ Sci and Technol, transferring to Fudan Univ, 1958-60; Stud, Solid State Phys, 1960-63, grad, 1963, Shanghai Univ Sci and

Technol. Appointments: Tchr, Phys Dept, Rschr, Condensed State Phys, 1979-, currently Prof, Solid State Phys, Tutor, Postgrad Studs, Provost, Anhui Normal Univ, Wuhu; Mbr, 8th Anhui Province Cttee, Chinese People's Political Consultative Conf. Creative Works: Rsch in fields of statistical thermodynamic props of 2-dimensional syst, phase diagram of a binary syst and the isothermal equation of state of a solid; 52 pprs published in disting jrnls, China, Eng, Germany. Honours: 1st Prize, ppr The Collins Model and the Phase Diagram of the Two-Dimensional Alternative Binary System, Anhui Provincial Soc Sci and Technol, 1986; Prize for Advancement Sci and Technol, 3 sci rsch projs, The Statistical Thermodynamic Theory of the Two-Dimensional System, On the Melting Law at High Pressure, and The Research for the Typical Phase Diagrams of a Binary System Using the Quasiregular Model and Subregular Model, Anhui Provincial Commn Sci and Technol, 1988-1991. Address: Anhui Normal University, Wuhu, Anhui 24100 China.

CHEN Liqi, b. 22 Apr 1945, Jinjiang of Fujian, China. Chemist; Oceanographer; Polar Scientist. m. Liang Feiqing, 8 Feb 1971, 1 s, 1 d. Education: Nankai Univ, Tianjing, China; Grad Sch of Oceanography, URI, USA. Appointment: Dpty Dir, Third Inst of Oceanography, SOA; Dir, Chinese Arctic and Antarctice Admin. Publications: Antarctic Gazeteer, 1997; Collection of Papers from Phase 3, Chinese Antarctic Research, 1998. Honours: Reprs to SCAR, IASC, ATCM; Advsr on Sci and Tech Propagation for CPPR, 1997; Awds from Adv for Sci and Tech from SOA, 1995, 1996. Hobbies: Arts; Sports; Photos; Polar expeditions. Address: 1 Fuxingmenwai Avenue, Beijing 100860, China.

CHEN Lubai, b. 27 Nov 1925. Poet; Writer; Senior Editor. m. Qiu Guangrong, 15 Sept 1962, 1 d. Education: Grad, Dept of Econ, Xiamen Univ. Appointments: Profl Writer, Fujian Cultural Troupe, 1949-; Dir, Fuzhou Lit Assn, 1953-; Profl Writer, Fujian Fedn of Lit and Art Circles, 1954-; Mbr, Edl Cttee; Ed of Editl Dept of lit mag, Garden and Hot Wind, 1956-; Profl Writer, Fujian Writers' Assn, 1981-; Sec-Gen, Fujian Writers Assn, 1984-; Snr Ed, Book Editl Dept, Fujian Fedn of Lit and Art Circles, 1986-92. Creative Works: People Planting Oranges, play, 1954; Red Oranges Ripe on the Banks of the Min River, feature film, 1956; Selection of Famous Folk Choruses of Taiwan Gaoshan Nationality, words of songs, 1984. Poetry: Roses Dripping with Blood, 1987; Forgotten Dreams of the South, 1988; My Tree of Dreams, 1993; Words of Symphonic Cantata: Search for Lin Zexu's Footsteps - Sorrow and Happiness of Humen, 1997. Honours: More than 50 Natl or Fujian Provincial Awds. Memberships: China Musicians' Assn, 1981-; China Writers' Assn, 1984-; China Musical Lit Inst, 1985-; Pres, Fujian Musical Lit Inst, 1985-; Chinese Classical Poetry Inst, 1989-. Hobby: Stamp collecting. Address: Fujian Federation of Literary and Art Circles, Fenghuang Chi, Fuzhou, Fujian 350002, China.

CHEN Maureen, b. 1 July 1955, Sydney, Australia. Teacher. Appointment: Dir, Brahma Kumaris Raja Yoga Cntr, 1981-98. Honour: JP, NSW, Aust. Memberships: Chairperson, Unity for Peace, 1984-88, Million Minutes of Peace Appeal, 1986, Global Coop for a Better World, 1988-91; Moderator, Hong Kong Network on Relig and Peace, 1996-98. Address: Raja Yoga Centre, 17 Dragon Road, Tin Hau, Hong Kong.

CHEN Mei-dong, b. 19 Feb 1942, Fujian, China. Professor; Institute Director. m. Li-shang Yu, 4 Feb 1970, 1 d. Education: Dept Astronomical Surv, Wuhan Inst Surv and Drawing, Hubei Prov, 1959-64; Grad studies, Hist Astron, Inst Hist Sci, Academia Sinica, Beijing, 1964-67. Appointments: Asst Chf, Hist Astron Grp, 1965-76, Lectr, 1978, Chf, Gen Hist Sci Grp, 1979-84, Assoc Prof, 1986, Vice-Dir, 1987, Dir, 1988-93, Inst Hist Sci, Academia Sinica, Beijing. Publications: Chf ed, contbr, Scientific Achievements in Ancient China, 1978; History of Astronomy in China, 1981; Draft of History of Science and Technology in China, 1982; Short Historical Story of Science in China, 1990; A Biography of Scientists in Ancient China, 1993; A New Research on Ancient

Chinese Calendar, 1996; Star Charts in Ancient China, editor-in chief; More than 70 publd pprs on hist astron and calendars in China, and gen hist sci in China. Honours: 2nd Prize, Chinese Ex Sci Publs, Scientific Achievements in Ancient China, 1980; 2nd Prize, Chinese Ex Sci Publs, Draft of Hist of Sci and Technol in China, 1983; 1st Prize, Ex Publs on Hist Sci, Draft of Hist of Sci and Technol in China, and Hist of Astron in China, 1989. Memberships: China Soc Astron; Dpty Pres, China Soc Hist Sci and Technol; Dpty Chmn, Intl Soc Hist E Asian Sci, Technol and Med; Cncl Mbr, Intl Union Hist and Philos Sci. Hobbies: Reading; Listening to music. Address: Institute of History of Natural Science, Academia Sinica, 137 Chaonei Street, Beijing 100010, China.

CHEN Minzhang, b. 1931 Hangzhou Zhejiang. Government Official. Education: Shanghai No 2 Medl Coll. Appointments: Joined CCP, 1954; Worked a Dr at Guangci Hosp, 1955-56; Dep Dir of Internal Med and Rschr Peking Union Medl Coll Hosp, 1956-80; VP Chinese Union Medl Univ, 1980-83; Pres Union Medl Coll Hosp, 1983-84; Vice-Min of Pub Hlth, 1984-87; Min, 1987-98; Vice-Chmn China Assn for Sci and Technol; VP Chinese Medl Assn, 1984-89; Pres Chinese Red Cross Soc, 1990-94; Dep Hd Natl Disaster Relief and Disease Control Grp, 1991-. Honours: Hon Pres China Venereal Disease and AIDS Prevention Assn, 1993-; Hon Vice-Chmn Chinese Red Cross Soc, 1994-. Memberships: Alt Mbr 13th CCP Cntr Cttee, 1987092; Mbr 14th CCP Cntr Cttee, 1992-. Address: c/o Ministry of Public Health, Beijing, China.

CHEN Muhua, b. 1921 Qingtian Co Zhenjiang Prov. Politician. Education: Yanan Mil Sch. Appointments: Joined CCP 1938; Min for Econ Rels with For Cos, 1977-82; Vice-Premier, 1978-82; Hd Pop Census Ldng Grp, 1979-; Chmn Cntr Patriotic Sanitation Campaign Cttee Cntr Cttee, 1981-; In charge of the State Family Plng Commn, 1981-82; State Cnclr, 1982-; Min of For Trade, 1982-85; Pres People's Bank of China, 1985-88; Dir State Treas, Aug 1985-; Chmn Cncl People's Bank of China, June 1985; Pres China Greening Fndn; Chinese Gov World Bank, 1985-88; Asian Dev Bank, 1986-; Pres China Women Dev Fund, 1988-; Pres All-China Women's Fedn, 1988-; Vice-Chmn NPC 7th Standing Cttee, 1988-93;; Vice-Chmn 8th Standing Cttee, 1993-; Advsr Natl Co-ordn Grp for Anti-Illiteracy Work, 1994-; Advsr Chinese Assn for Promotion of the Pop Culture. Honours: Hon Chmn Bd of Dir People's Bank of China, Nov 1985-; Hon Pres China Assn of Women Judges, 1994-; Hon Pres China Assn of Women Drs; Hon Pres Assn for Import and Export Commodity Insp. Memberships: Mbr 10th Cntr Cttee of CCP, 1973; Alt Mbr Politburo 11th Cntr Cttee, 1977-87; Mbr 12th CCP Cntr Cttee, 1982-87; Mbr 13th CCP Cntr Cttee, 1987-92; Mbr 14th CCP Cntr Cttee, 1992-. Address: Standing Committee, National People's Congress, Tian An Men Square, Beijing, China.

CHEN Nian, b. 31 Oct 1948, Shanghai, China. Toxicologist. m. Naili, 6 Dec 1976, 1 s, 1 d. Education: PhD, Med, Univ Qld. Appointments: Exec Offr, Natl Occupational Hlth & Safety Cmmn; Snr Sci Offr, NICNAS; Natl Gene Technol Task Force. Publications: Sev articles in profl jrnls. Honours: Sanhao Schl, 1978-83; Ernest Singer Schl, 1985-89; NHMRC Rsch Schl, 1989. Memberships: Austl Soc of Biochems and Molecular Biols; Austl Soc of Clin and Ex Pharmacols and Toxicols. Hobbies: Reading; Experimenting. Address: PO Box 346, Merrylands, NSW 2160, Australia.

CHEN Pang-Chi, b. 8 Sept 1947, Taiwan, China. Gastroenterologist; Endoscopist. m. Ying-Erl Lin, 24 Dec 1976, 2 s. Education: MD, Taiwan Kaohsiung Medl Coll. Appointments: Assoc Prof, Medl Coll of Chang Gung Univ; Dir, Digestive Endoscopy Unit, Lin Kou Medl Cntr, Chang Gung Mem Hosp; Ed-in-Chf, Gastroenterological Jrnl of Taiwan. Publications: Over 100 articles on digestive endoscopy and digestive med in medl jrnls, 1977-98. Honours: Taiwn Medl Assn Awd, 1979, 1984; 20th Century Achievement Awd and ABI, 1995; World Lifetime Achievement Awd, 1996; Hon Citizen of Taipei Cty, 1996. Memberships: Gastroenterological Soc of

Taiwan (GEST); Digestive Endoscopy Soc of Taiwan (DEST); Amn Soc for Gastrointestinal Endoscopy (ASGE); Intl Gastro-Surg Club (IGSC); Eurn Soc of Gastroenterology and Endoscopy (EAGE). Hobbies: Art; Photography; Magazine writing. Address: Chang Gung Memorial Hospital, 199 Tun Hwa N Road, Taipei 105, Taiwan, China.

CHEN Qi Hang, b. 7 Nov 1961, Chao Zhou, Guangdong, China. Diagnostic Radiologist. m. Jingjing Yin, 25 Aug 1987, 1 s. Education: MD. Appointments: Vis Fell, Dept of Radiol, Univ CA, San Fran, 1987-88; Asst Prof, 1988-94, Assoc Prof, 1995-, Dept of Radiol, Beijing Hosp, China. Publications: Diagnosis of Clinical Computer Tomography, 1994; High Resolution CT of Lung, 1995; Computed Tomography - State of the Art and Future Application, 1995. Membership: Chinese Med Assn, Beijing. Hobbies: Sport; Music. Address: Department of Radiology, Beijing Hospital, No 1 Da Hua Road, Beijing 100730, China.

CHEN Qingru, b. 3 Dec 1926, Hangzhou Cty, Zhejiang Prov, China. Professor of Mineral Processing and Utilization. m. Zhong Yuiying, 30 Sept 1955, 2 s, 1 d. Education: Undergrad course. Appointments: Chmn, Dept of Coal Preparation & Utilization, 1961-64, Chmn, Dept of Mining Machinery, 1964-66, Beijing Inst of Mining, China; Prof, 1983-, Supvsr for doct grad, 1986-, Mineral Processing and Utilization, Dir, Mineral Processing Rsch Cntr, 1986-, CUMT, China. Publications: 9 monographs; 103 pprs. Honours: Outstndng Tutor Awd, Jiangsu Prov Educ Cttee, 1988; Oustndng Educr Awd, Jiangsu Prov, 1989; Natl Outstndng Educr Awd, All-China Fedn of Trade Unions, 1990; May 1st Model Awd, All-China Fedn of Trade Unions, 1990; Xhinese Govt Spec Allownace, 1991; 1st Class Awds, Natl Educ Cttee, 1992, 1997; 3rd Class Invention Awd, Govt of China. Memberships; Chinese Acady of Engrng; China Coal Soc; Coal Acad Jrnl Editl Bd, China Coal Soc; Particularate Sci & Technol, Amn Intl Jrnl Editl Bd USA; Standing Mbr: China Particularate Soc, China Coal Processing & Utilization Soc. Hobby: Penmanship. Address: China University of Mining and Technology, Xuhou, Jinagsu, China, 221008.

CHEN Renzhe, b. 18 June 1921, Shanghai, China. Teacher. m. Jie Wang, 24 Oct 1954, 1 s, 1 d. Education: BSc, Jiaotong Univ, 1945; MSc.Tech, Manchester Univ, England, 1949. Appointments: Design Engr, China Rehab Machine Works, Shanghai, 1950; Proj Engr, Chang Jian Jute Mill, 1951; Assoc Prof, Jiaotong Univ, 1952; Prof, Hua Dong Textile Inst, China Textile Univ, 1953. Publications: Elements of Textile Machinery Design, 1982; Yarn Mechanics, 1989. Honours: State Council Award, 1991. Membership: Shanghai Textile Soc, Hd of Textile Machinery Grp, 1980. Hobby: Chinese Beijing Opera. Address: Mechanical Engineering Department, China Textile University, 1882 West Yan-An Road, Shanghai 200051, China.

CHEN Rong-Jye, b. 19 Sept 1943, Taiwan. Diplomat. m. Y H Chang, 1970, 2 d. Education: LLB, Natl Taiwan Univ; MCL, Southern Meth Univ, USA; JD, Southern Meth Univ. Appointments: Spec, Treaty and Legal Affairs Dept, Min of For Affairs, later Sect Ch and Dpty Dir Gen; 3rd Sec, Emby in Saudi Arabia; Cnsl, Emb in S Afr; Rep, Observer's Mission of Repub of China, Namibia; Adj Prof Law, Soochow Univ, Cntrl Police Coll; Dpty Sec-Gen/Sec-Gen, SEF; Advsr, MAC; Pres, Indep News Grp; Dpty Rep to US; Dir-Gen, Treaty and Legal Affairs, MOFA. Publications: The Theory & Practice of Extradition, 1986. Honours: Fulbright Schlr, 1973-74; Disting Pub Rels Awd, 1991. Memberships: Exec Bd, Chinese Soc of Intl Law, 1997-; Taiwan Bar Assn. Hobbies: Arts; Antiques. Address: 4th Floor, 2 Ke-Chiang Road, Shihlin, Taipei, Taiwan, China.

CHEN Shi Cai, b. 1 May 1942, Chongqing, China. Professor; Interdisciplinary Science Researcher. m. Miss Li, 6 Oct 1980, 2s. Education: Double Bachelor (BS and BA). Appointment: Prof, Inst of Geol, Academia Sinica, 1997-. Publications: Tourist Research on Natural Landscapes, 1993; Tourist Speleology, 1999. Honours: 2 Silver Awds, Chinese Tourist Earthsci Assn, 1996, 1999. Membership: Intl Assn of Sci Experts in Tourism. Hobbies: Studying; Travel. Address: Institute of Geology, Chinese Academy of Sciences, PO Box 364, Beijing 100029, China.

CHEN Shisong, b. 14 Mar 1940, Sichuan. History Researcher. m. Tang Hong, 31 Aug 1967, 2 d. Education: Master, Hist Dept, Sichuan Univ. Appointments: VP, Inst of Sichuan Prov Acady of Socl Servs. Creative Works: The Life of Yu Jie, 1982; Draft History of Mongol Conquest of Sichuan Luzhou in the Song-Yuan Transition, 1985; An Outline History of Sichuan, 1986; Studies on Song-Zheyuan, 1987; A History of the Song-Yuan War, 1988; The Life of Song Zheyuan, 1992; A Whole History of Sichuan, 1993; The Rise and Fall of Dynasties in China, 1996; About 50 Articles. Honours: The Ex Awd of Hist, 1984; The Ex Awd of Hist, 1986; The Ex Awd of Hist, 1988; The Ex Awd of Hist, 1994. Memberships: Hist Assn of Sichuan Prov, 1988-; Assn for the Stdy of pop Culture in Sichuan, 1990-; All China Assn for the Stdy of Chinese Nationalities; Natl Assn for the Stdy of Yuan Dynasty, 1990-. Hobbies: Reading; Travng. Address: Inst of History, Sichuan Province Academy of Social Services, Chengdu, China.

CHEN Shu-lan, b. 2 Dec 1931, Chang Chun, China. Chief Physician; Professor. m. Liu Shan-Li, 4 May 1953, 1 s, 1 d. Education: Grad, Zhongguo Medl Univ, 1952. Appointments: Res, Attng Physn, Chf, Dept Med, Affiliated Hosp, 1953-70, Assoc Prof, Chf Physn, 1979-, Ningxia Medl Coll; Chf, Dept Internal Med, Yinchuan Munic Hosp, 1972-79; Hon Pres, Ningxia Medl Coll; Dir, Cardiology Dis Inst, NMC; Ed, Natl Medl Jrnl of China. Publications: Sinus Node Electrogram and the Measurement of Sinoatrial Conduction Time, 1986; Sinus Node Electrogram Studies in Patients with Sick Sinus Syndrome, 1986; An Epidemiological Survey of Hypertension in Wu Zhong, 1986; Diagnostic Evaluation of Sinus Node Electrogram in Sinus Brady-Arrhythmias, 1988; Epidemiological Survey on Rheumatic Heart Disease Among Urban and Rural Population, 1990; Study of Silent Myocardial Ischemia with DCG, 1992; Clinical Study of Ventricular Premature Beats by Dynamic Electrocardiogram, 1995. Memberships: Bd Mbr, Chinese Medl Assn; Bd Mbr, Assn Cardiology; Bd Mbr, Assn Medl Educ. Listed in: Dictionary of International Biography. Hobbies: Music; Literature. Address: Ningxia Medical College, Yinchuan, Ningxia 750004, China.

CHEN Shuxuan, b. 30 Mar 1936, Fuzhou, Fujian, China. Physicist. m. Shuxia Chen, 1 Jan 1968, 1 s, 1 d. Education: BSc. Appointments: Tech Personnel, 1959, Asst, 1962, Lectr, 1978, Assoc Prof, 1988. Publications: Materiality Theory - Base of Crossing Theory in Natural Subjects; Thinking Engineering - Man's Brain Intelligent Action and Thinking Model. Honours: 3rd Prize, Natl Mechanism-Electron Indl Dept, 1989; 3rd Prize, Fujian Sci Technol Assn, 1991. Memberships: Chinese Thinking Sci Rsch Inst, Fujian Inst; Fujian Instrument and Appearance Assn. Address: No 502 White Town 19, Xiamen University, Fujing, China.

CHEN Sinn-Wen, b. 24 June 1961, Tainan, Taiwan. Professor. m. Wenyuh Shieh, 6 June 1987, 1 s, 2 d. Education: BS, Chem Engrng, Natl Taiwan Univ, 1979-83; MS, Materials Sci, 1985-87, PhD, 1987-90, Univ WI, Madison, USA. Appointments: Rsch Assoc, Univ WI, Madison, 1990-91; Snr Sci, Alcoa Tech Cntr, Molten Metal Processing Divsn, 1991-92; Assoc Prof, 1992-97, Prof, 1997-, Natl Tsinghua Univ, Dept of Chem Engrng. Publications include: Microstructure, Density and Microhardness of the As-Se-Tl Chalcogenide Glass, 1997; Determination of the Melting and Solidification Characteristics of Solders by Using DSC, 1998; Ni and Cu Deposition on Fine Alumina Particles by Using the Chemical Vapor Deposition-Circulation Fluidized Bed Reactor, 1998. Honours: Yng Investigators Achievement Awd, Chinese Inst of Chem Engrs, 1996; NSC Rsch Awd, 1993, 1994, 1995, 1996, 1997; Invited Speech, Austl Pacific Forum on Intelligent Processing and Mfng of Materials. Address: Department of Chemical Engineering, National Tsinghua University, #101 Sec 2, Kuang-Fuh Road, Hsin-Chu, 30043 Taiwan.

CHEN Sun, b. 8 Nov 1934 Pingtu Co Shantung. Politician; Economist. m. 2 s. Education: Natl Taiwan Univ; Univ of OK. Appointments: Assoc Prof of Econs Natl Taiwan Univ, 1968-; Vice-Chmn Econ Plng Cncl Exec Yuan, 1973-77; Vice-Chmn Cncl for Con Plng and Dev Exec Yuan, 1977-84; Pres Natl Taiwan Univ, 1984-93; Pres Chinese Econ Assn, 1985-86; Cnclr Academia Sinica Taiwan, 1987-; Chmn Bd of Reviewers on Hum and Socl Scis Natl Sci Cncl Exec Yuan, 1990-; Min of Natl Def, 1993-96. Memberships: Mbr Bd of Reviewers on Hum and Socl Scis Natl Sci Cncl Exec Yuan, 1974-93. Address: Ministry of National Defence, 2nd Floor, 164 Poi Ai Road, Taipei, Taiwan.

CHEN Tai-Chu, b. 2 Jan 1912, Shanghai, China. Diplomat; Professor. m. Shulan, 6 Oct 1941, 1 s. Education: MA, Columbia Univ; PhD, London Univ. Appointments: Cnslr, Chinese Emb, USSR, 1946; Chf, Am Dept, Min of Fgn Affairs, Min to Aust, 1952; Amb to Liberia, 1966; Min to USA, 1972; Advsr, Min of Fgn Affairs, 1982-; Prof, var univs. Publication: Inside Russia. Essays on International Relations. Honours: Order of the Brilliant Star, 1966; Decorations From Aust & Liberia. Memberships: Dir, Sino-Am Assn, 1988-; Commentator, WA & Taipei. Hobbies: Calligraphy; Writing; Tennis. Address: PO Box 1367, Taipei, Taiwan.

CHEN Tao, b. 17 Oct 1963, Hubei, China. Teacher. m. Huang Li, 2 s. Education: BEcon, Bus Econ, 1984; MEcon, 1993. Appointments: Asst, Lectr, Wuhan Grain Ind Coll, 1984-93; Lectr, Assoc Prof, Wuhan Univ of Sci and Technol, 1994-. Publications include: Market Investigation and Prediction and Decision, 1996; Tariff Policy and China's Iron and Steel Import and Export Stragies, 1997; Optimal Decision on the Marketing Channel System of Chinese Enterprises, 1999. Memberships: China Mkt Assn; China Univ Mktng Assn. Address: c/o Department of Management Engineering, Wuhan University of Science & Technology, Wuhan, Hubei 430081, China.

CHEN Tie-Yun, b. 5 December 1918, Shanghai. Professor. m. Shou-Shiu Zheng, 22 Sept 1951, 2 s, 1 d. Education: BS, SHanghai Jiao Tong Univ, 1941; MEng, Univ of MI, 1949. Appointments: Assoc Rschr, China Rsch Inst Aeronautics, Chengdu, 1943-47; Prof, Dalian Inst Technol, 1952-54; Prof, Chair, Div Ship Structural Mechs, Shanghai, Jiao Tong Univ, 1955-. Publications: Ship Vibrations; Theory of Thin Walled Structures; Theory of Thin Shells; Ocean Engineering Structural Mechanics; 6 other publshd books. Honours: First, Second, Third, Class Awd of China Natl Progress of Sci and Technol; Disting Intellectual of O'seas, 1989. Memberships: ISSC; OMAE; ISOPE. Hobbies: Tab Tennis; Music; Ball Dancing. Address: Shanghai Jin Tong Univ, 1954 Huan Shan Rd, Shanghai 200030, China.

CHEN Ting-An, b. 8 Oct 1933, Wu-Chin. Member of Examination Yuan (Ministerial Rank). m. Chung-Ao, 30 June 1972, 2 s. Education: Dr rer pol, Econs. Appointments: Dean, Law and Com, Natl Chung-Hsing Univ; Dean, Grad Inst of Pub Fin, Natl Cheng-Chi Univ, 1973-80; Mbr Exam Yuan, 1997-; Chmn, Tax Reform Commn, 1987-89. Publications: New Trend of Economic Regulation Toward the 21st Century, 1995; Tax Policy and Foreign Sector, Taiwan Experience, FAIR, Tokyo, Japan, 1993; Fiscal Policy in a Maturing Economy, Taipei. Honours: Chung-san Fellshp, 1963; Snr Rsch Fellshp, 1976-78, 1991. Memberships: Gen Sec, Chinese Econ Assn, 1975-76; Mont Pelerin Soc, 1987-. Hobbies: Classical music and opera. Address: 12 Chao-Yi Road, Taipei Small City, An-Kang, Shing-Tien, Taipei County, Taiwan, China.

CHEN Xianzu, b. 5 Apr 1930, Xiangyang, Hubei, China. Director; Professor. m. Tian Qiong-Fang, 28 Sept 1964, 1 s, 2 d. Education: BS, Soil Sci, SW China Agric Univ, China, 1956. Appointments: SW China Agric Exp Stn, 1956-76; Yunnan Acady of Agric Sci, 1976; Dir, Soil and Fertilizer Inst, 1985. Creative Works: The Characters ofPaddy Soil and It's Improvement and Utilization in Yunnan; The Improvement of Low Productive Land. Honours: Natl Sci and Technol Prize, 1978; Yunnan Sci and Technol Finding Prize, 1978. Memberships: Soil Soc of Yunnan. Hobby: Fishing. Address: Yunnan Academy of Agricultural Sciences, Xiamacun, Kunming, Yunnan 650221, China.

CHEN Xiaohong, b. 6 Feb 1967, Tianjin, China. Researcher. Education: BS, 1989, MS, 1992, PhD, 1996, Mechs and Engrng Sci, Peking Univ. Appointments: Postdoct Rsch Fell, Univ Sydney, 1996-99; Tech Reviewer, ICCM-11 and ICFSS-3, 1997; Consultative Ed, Chinese Figures Dictionary, 1997; Rsch Assoc, Univ of Houston, TX, 1999-. Publications: Sev book chapts and articles in profl jrnls. Honours: Awd for Moral, Acad and Physl Ex, Peking Univ, 1988; Guanghua Awd, Peking Univ, 1991, 1993; Premier Ppr Awd, ACCM-1, Japan, 1998; Overseas Conf and Travel Grant, Univ Sydney, 1998. Memberships: Am Assn for the Adv of Sci; Austl Composite Structures Soc; Chinese Asutl Acads Soc. Hobbies: Travel; Music; Novels; Badminton; Volleyball; Swimming. Address: Composities Engineering and Applications Center, University of Houston, Houston, TX 77204-0903, USA.

CHEN Xiurong, b. 20 Sept 1942, Bandung, Indonesia. Researcher. m. Zhong Xiongying, 1 s, 1 d. Education: MSc, Grad Sch of Sci and Technol, Univ of China, 1981; PhD, Dept of Geog, Univ of Hong Kong, 1991. Appointments: A mid sch tchr, 1965-78; Rsch Assoc, Chinese Acady of Sci, 1982-85; Pt-time demonstrator in HKV, 1985-90; Rsch Assoc, CAS, 1990-91; Assoc Prof, CAS, 1992-. Publication: Regional Imbalance in Exploitation of Natural Resources for Crop Farming in Indonesia, 1998. Membership: Geog Soc of China, 1991. Hobbies: Badminton; Swimming. Address: Institute of Geography, Chinese Academy of Sciences, Building 917, Datun Road, Anwai 100101, Beijing, China.

CHEN Yanqing, b. 16 June 1938, Xinhua, Hunan, China. Philosopher; Educator. m. Xiaoping E, 12 Jan 1968, 2 s. Education: Dipl, China Peoples Univ. Appointments: Asst Prof, 1962-78, Lectr, 1978-81, Assoc Prof, 1981-86, Prof, 1986-, Nankai Univ. Publications: On the Initiative Consciousness, 1983; An Introduction to Contemporary Materialism, 1996; Social Philosophy of Contemporary China, 1990. Honours: Book Awd, Tianjin Govt, 1993. Memberships: China's Dialectical Materialism Assn; Assn of Philos, Tianjin; Communist Pty of China. Hobby: Walking. Address: Department of Philosophy, Nankai University, Tianjin 300071, China.

CHEN Yin Qing, b. 20 Feb 1938, China. Professor of Computing and Automation. m. Pan Jia Chan, 23 Aug 1969, 1 s, 1 d. Education: Grad, Shanghai Jiaotong Univ, 1961. Appointments: Prof; Inventor. Creative Works: Invented Fluidically Controlled Vitrous-Infusion-Cutter, 1979. Honours: Invention Medal, 1987; 3rd Awd of China Invention, 1987; Outstndng Contbrn Ctf, State Cncl of China. Address: Project 2112 Office, Shanghai University, Shanghai, China.

CHEN Yi Xin, b. 21 Nov 1926, Wuhan, China. Professor of Music Conducting. m. Gong Qi, 7 Jan 1950, 3 s, 1 d. Education: Music Dept, Yu Tsai Sch. Appointments: Tchr, Dir, Yu Tsai Sch of Arts, 1946-54; Cellist, Cultural Orch, Beijing, 1954-58; Chf Conductor, Tianjin Opera & Ballet Th, 1958-80; Prof, Conservatory of Beijing, 1980-. Publications: Chorus for Children, 1941-49; Sev orch works. Honours: Prize, China Broadcast Co, Taiwan, 1990; Specl Subsidy, State Cncl of China. Memberships: All China Musicians Soc; VP Tao Xing Zhi Study, China, 1984-. Hobbies: Fine Arts; Films. Address: 43 Bao Jia Street, Central Conservatory of Music, Beijing 100031, China.

CHEN Yuanfu, b. 22 Oct 1927, Jiangsu, Wujin, China. Teacher. m. Jingfan Hua, 27 July 1957, 2 s. Education: PhD, Moscow Textile Inst. Appointments: Assoc Hd, Lectr, 1959-64, Hd of Dept, Hd of Rsch Section, 1964-67, Preparation and Weaving Dept, Prin Lectr, 1967-77, Hd, Preparation and Weaving Dept, Hd of Rsch Section, Prin Lectr, 1977-84, E China Inst of Textile Sci and Technol; Dir, Prof, Chmn, Acad Cttee, Sch of Textile Engrng and Sci; Dir, Educ Cttee, China Textile Ind; Ctteemn, Acad Degs, Textile Rsch Inst, 1984-87; Prof, Chmn, Sch Acad Cttee, 1987-92; Prof, Coll of Textile Technol, China Textile Univ, 1992-96. Publications include: Preparation and Weaving Technology and Machinery, Part 1, 1982, Part 2, 1984; Modern Rapier Weaving Machine, 1994; Preparation and Weaving Engineering, 1996. Honours: Sci Payoffs Prize, Shanghai 1977; Natl Sci Conf Prize, Natl Sci and Technol Cttee, Beijing, 1978; Top Grade Prize, Shanghai Higher Educn Bur, 1989; Govt Specl Subsidy Prize, 1992. Memberships include: Shanghai Textile Engrng Soc. Hobby: Music. Address: c/o College Office, Textile Building, China Textile University, 1882 Yan An Road (West), Shanghai 200051, China.

CHEN Zhi Qiang, b. 21 Aug 1952, Tianjin, China. Professor. m. Liu Ge-li, 1 d. Education: PhD, Hist and Archaeol, Aristotelian Univ, Greece. Appointments: Lectr, Hist Sci, 1986, Prof, Medieval World Hist, 1994, Nankai Univ; Dpty Dir, Hist Dept, 1994, Cntr of Eurn Stdies, 1996. Publications include: Fall of Constantinople, 1996; Brief History of the Byzantine Empire, 1997; Byzantine Civilization, 1998. Memberships: VP, Chinese Assn of Ancient and Medieval World Hist, 1998; Sec Gen, Chinese Assn of Byzantine Stdies, 1995. Hobbies: Reading; Driving; Swimming. Address: History Department, Nankai University, 94 Weijin Road, Tianjin 300071, China.

CHEN Zhong-Mou, b. 23 Oct 1937, Wuxi. Electronics Device Engineer. m. Hai-Hong Qian, 1 Apr 1974, 1 s, 2 d. Education: MB, Moscow Engrng Inst, 1962; Postdoctoral Fell, Norwegian Univ of Sci and Technol, 1991. Appointments: Rsch, grp ldr, Beijing Vcm Tubes Inst, 1962-71; Chf Engrng, Offr of Rear Territory, 1968-69; Dept Hd, Xin Xiang 824 Factory, Honan, China, 1972-75; Vice Dir, Div of Microwave Propagation Xin Xiang, Chinese Electromagnetic Wave propagation Inst, 1976-78; Vice Dir, Div of Night Vsn Tubes, Nanjing Electrons Devices Inst, 1979-83; Visng Rschr, Applied Optics Grp Div of Phys, Norweigian Univ of Sci and Technol, 1983-. Creative Works: Inv, A Si Wide Barrier Photodetector and Application in Colour Sensor; Contbn to Develop and new theory of regenerative amplifier in microwave bands and design of a magnetron regenerative amplifier; Contbns to improve EBS-CCD Characteristics; Inv, Prin for colormetric measmts; Inv, New Thermionic Photodetector. Honours: World Cultural Celebrity Achmnt Prize, 1998; Man of the Yr, 1998; Intl Man of the Yr; 20th Century Awd for Achmnt. Memberships: Chinese Inst of Electrons. Address: 524 Zhong Shan E Road, Nanjing Electronic Devices Inst, 210016 Nanjing Jiangsu, China.

CHEN Zi-Li, b. 15 Mar 1935. Professor; Chief Physician. m. Zha Yang-E, 12 Feb 1970, 1 s, 1 d. Education: MB, Tongji Med Univ, Wuhan, 1956-61; Clinl Fell, NICU, McMaster Univ Med Cntr, Can, 1981-82. Appointments: Pediatn and Instr, Dept Pediats, Huanggang Med Sch Affiliated Hosp, 1961-77; Chmn, Attng Physn, 1978-86, Chmn, Prof, Chf Physn, 1987-98, Dept Neonatology, Hubei Maternal and Child Hlth Cntr. Publications: Chf Ed or Contrb to 18 books; Num rsch articles and papers. Honours: 8 Awds for med rsch, 1986-98; 2 Rsch Awds, Intl League of Somatic Scientists, 1995; Citation of Natl Advd Worker, Cntrl Hlth Min, 1986; Citation, Natl Outstndng Contrbn Specialist, Cntrl Govt, 1992. Memberships: Natl Ldng Grp of Neonatology, Chinese Med Assn, 1983-; Vice Chmn, Natl Specialist Cttee of Neonatal-Perinatal Med Rsch, 1994-; Dir, Chinese Med Assn, Hubei br, 1985-; Supvsr, Natl Neonatologist Trng Base, Cntrl Hlth min, 1983; Ctteeman, Natl Specialist Consultative Cttee, Maternal and Child Hygiene, Cntrl Hlth Min, 1989; Bd Mbr, 4 pediat jrnls. Hobbies: Literature; Music; Painting; Poetry. Address: Department of Neonatology, Maternal and Child Health Centre, 745 Wuluo Road, Wuhan, Hubei 430070, China.

CHEN Zili, b. 8 Aug 1964, Shanghai, China. Manager. m. Kan Yue, 1 s. Education: Bachelor Phys, 1986, Master, Material Sci, 1993, Shanghai Univ. Appointments: Vice Dir, Vice Chf Engr, Shanghai Permanent Mngmt Factory, 1994-96; Mngr Asst, Shanghai Instrumentation Co, Grp Ltd, Dev Plng Dept, 1996-98. Publications: Researh of SMCO material, 1986; Research of NDFEB material, 1993. Honours: Cert gainer, Shanghai Cty Govt achievement, July 1990; Cert gainer, State Achievement, Jan 1992. Hobby: reading. Address: 699 Chen Tai Rd, California Gardens No 105, Baoshan, Shanghai 200436, China.

CHEN Zu Fan, b. 31 Dec 1926, Shanghai, China. Research Professor. m. 1954, 2 s, 1 d. Appointments: Rsch Fell, Shanghai Municipal Arts and Hist Rsch Inst, 1992; Cnclr, Shanghai Municipal Political Consultative Cncl, 1993; Hon Prof, Calligraphy and Painting Rsch Inst, 1994; Creative Cnclr, China Natl Arts Inst, 1995; Snr Fell, China Natl Scl of Famous Artists, 1996; Cnsltng Ed, China Intl Cultural Exch Press, 1996; Dpty Chmn, Worldwide Buddhist Culture Soc, 1997; Artistic Dir, World Famous Artisits Assn, 1998; Hon Snr Fell, Xin Shenzhou Gall, 1998. Creative Works: Calligraphy Artists of the Modern Era, 1992; Self Practice Manual of Calligraphy, 1993; Auto Biography, Survival Against All Odds, 1999. Honours: First Class Awd, Intl Lit and Arts Expo, Beijing, China, 1994; Spec Awd, Intl Lit and Arts Expo, 1996; Gold Awd, Red Lantern Expo of Arts from Chinese Univs, 1997; Spec Awd, Lion Cup, Singapore Arts Club, 1998. Memberships: Soc of Famous Calligraphy and Painting Artists, 1994; Cross Country Artists, China Natl TV Brdcst Corp, 1995; Intl Salon of Modern Artisits, 1998. Hobbies: Classical Literatue; Chinese Arts Collecting.Address: Hall of the Humanities Research of Shanghai, 41 Sinan Road, Shanghai 200020, China.

CHEN Zuohuang, b. 2 Apr 1947, Shanghai. Orchestral Conductor. m. Zaiyi Wang, 1969, 1 c. Education: BA, Cntr Conservatory of Beijing; MM, DMA, Univ of MI, USA; Conductor China Film Phil, 1974-76; Assoc Prof Univ of KS USA, 1985-87; Prin Conductor Cntr Phil Orch of China, 1987-96; Dir Wichita Symph Orch, 1990-; Dir RI Phil Orch, 1992-96; Artistic Dir, China Natl Symph Orch, 1996-. Address: Wichita Symphony Orchestra, Century II Concert Hall, 225 W Douglas Ave, Suite 207, Wichita, KS 67202, USA.

CHENG Chung-Ying, b. 29 Sept 1935, China. Professor of Philosophy. m. Teresa Chan, June 1963, 2 s, 2 d. Education: BA, Natl Taiwan Univ, 1956; MA, Univ WA, 1958; PhD, Harvard Univ, 1963. Appointments: Asst Prof, 1963-67, Assoc Prof, 1967-72, Prof, 1972-88, Philos, Univ HI; Natl Vis Prof, Philos, Natl Taiwan Univ, 1968-70; Vis Assoc Prof, Philos, Yale Univ, 1968-70; Vis Prof, Philos, Queens Coll, City Univ NY, 1972-73, 1974; Vis Prof, Logic & Mngmt, Natl Cheng Kung Univ, 1976-77; Vis Rsch Prof, Philos, Academia Sinica Rsch Inst of Socl Scis, 1982-83; Vis Prof, Philos, Beijing Univ, 1985, E China Normal Univ, Shanghai, 1987; Vis Prof of Philos & Educn, Intl Christian Univ, Tokyo, 1992-93; Vis Schl, Inst of Far E Studies, Russian Acady of Scis, Moscow, 1994. Publications: Num articles in profl jrnls. Honours: Sev schlsps, grants & fellshps. Memberships: Am Philos Assn; Assn for Asian Studies; Am Oriental Soc; Soc for Asian & Comparative Philos; Columbia Univ Colloquium on Oriental Thought & Relig; Columbia Univ Neo-Confucian Seminar; Chinese Soc for Strategic Studies; Intl Consortium of Yijing Studies; Intl Fedn of Confucian Studies. Hobbies: Swimming; Tennis. Address: Department of Philosophy, University of Hawaii at Manoa, Honolulu, HI 96822, USA.

CHENG De-Lin, b. 17 Sept 1931, Nanjing, JiangSu, China. Researcher; Educator of Solid Mechanics. m. Zhang Xi-Ning, Oct 1969, 1 s, 1 d. Education: BS, Shandong Univ of Technol, 1951-55; PhD, The Former Soviet Union Acady of Sci, 1959-63. Appointments: Asst Prof, 1956-77; Lectr, 1978-80; Assoc Prof, 1980-85; Prof, Shandong Univ of Technol, 1985-. Publications: About 80 pprs publ in jrnls & conf proceedings; 8 projects. Honour: 1st Advd Sci & Technol Achievement Awd, Shandong Educl Cttee, 1997. Memberships: Chief Cncl, Shandong Soc of Vibration Engrng, 1989-93; Cncl of Chinese Soc of Vibration Engrng, 1991-; Hon Chmn, Shandong Soc of Vibration Engrng. Hobby: Photography. Address: Institute of Engineering Mechanics, College of Material Science and Engineering, Shandong University of Technology, 250061, Jinan, Shandong, China.

CHENG Dong, b. 11 Feb 1945. Physician. m. 19 May 1973, 1 s, 1 d. Appointments: Dr House Physn, 1967-86; Attending Physn, 1986-92; Dir, Physn, Chief, 1992-96. Creative works: The experiment study of Garlicfoetor and Norcantharidinum and Gambgicacia of Coursein, 1981-85; The research of local chemical treatment of liver cancer and clinical practice, 1991. Honours include: Over 10 awds, 1983-95. Memberships: Chinese natl Sci and Tech Assn; Anticancer Assn, Yingtan Jiangxi Province. Listed in: Dictionary of International Biography 23rd Edition. Hobbies: Visiting Factories, Cultural Installations, Research Institutes; Chess. Address: 184 Hosp of Yingtan City, Jiangxi Province, China.

CHENG Erlin, b. 1 Aug 1941, Yancheng Cty, Jiangsu Prov, China. Specialist in Seismicity, Seismic Zonation, Earthquake Mechanism, Prediction. m. Zhang meifang, 1 June 1969, 1 s, 1 d. Education: Grad, Geophysical Dept of the Univ of Sci and Technol of China, 1965. Appointments: Rsch Worker on Probation; Asst Rsch Fell; Snr Engr; Snr Engr (Prof grade). Publications: Seismic Intensity Zonation for the Marginal Region of the Qinghai-Tibet Plateau - A Case Study of the Xicheng Prefecture, 1985. Honours: Natl Sci Session Awd, 1978; 2nd-Class Awd of Seismological Bur of China. Membership: Charter Mbr, Chinese Seismological Inst. Hobbies: Music; Sports. Address: Bureau of Yancheng City, Jiangsu Province, China, 224001.

CHENG Fai Chut, b. 15 July 1933, Shanghai, China. Electrical Engineering Researcher. Education: BS, Electr Engin, Tsing Hua Univ, Beijing, China, 1957; MPhil, Electr Engin, Univ of Hong Kong, 1990. Appointments: Engr, NE Power Admin, Cntrl Lab, Harbin, 1957-73; Techn, Tomoe Electrons Co, Hong Kong, 1973-76; Lectr, Sch of Sci and Technol, Hong Kong, 1976-80; Pt-time Demonstrator, Univ of Hong Kong, 1980-88; Temp Tchr, Haking Wong Tech Inst, Hong Kong, 1987-88; Evening Visng Lectr, 1988-89, 1990-93, Rsch Asst, 1989-92, Tchng Asst, 1992-93, Hon Rsch Assoc, 1993-94, Hong Kong Polytechnic; Pt-time Rsch Asst, 1994-97, Hon Rsch Fell, 1998-99, Hong Kong Polytechnic University (renamed University in 1995). Publications: Pprs in profl jrnls. Creative works: A formula, an analytical expression of closed form, to dimension the insulation of polymeric power cables, having sufficient accuracy for engineering purposes. Honours: Outstndng Achievement Medal, Gold Star Awd, Silver Medal, MOIF, IBC, 1997; Disting Leadership Awd, 20th Century Achievement Awd, Most Admired Man of Deacde, 1997 Man of Yr Commemorative Medal, ABI, 1997; 2000 Millennium Medal of Hon, ABI, 1998. Memberships: Snr Mbr, IEEE; Assoc Mbr, IEE; Assoc Mbr, HKIE; Mbr, NY Acady Scis; Dpty Dir Gen, IBC; Dpty Gov, ABI; Mbr Rsch Bd Advsrs, ABI; Life Fell, IBC; Life Patron, ABI. Hobbies: Philosophy; Traditional Chinese Medicine; Literature; Qigong; Walking. Address: Hong Kong Polytechnic University, Department of Electrical Engineering, Hung Hom, Kowloon, Hong Kong.

CHENG Fuzhen, b. 15 Mar 1942, Wuhan, China. Astrophysicist. m. Liu Jing, 23 Jan 1971, 2 s. Education: BA, Univ Sci and Technol China, 1965; PhD, Intl Sch Advd Stdys, Italy, 1984. Appointments: Mbr, Assoc Dir, Astrophys Rsch Div, 1978-80, Lectr, 1979-86, Assoc Prof, 1986-90, Dpty Dir, Cntr Astrophys, 1986-91, Prof, 1990-, Vice-Dean Stdys, 1993-, Vice Dean, Grad Sch, 1995-98, Univ Sci and Technol China; Visng Schl, Harvard Univ, USA, 1985; Visng Scientist, STScI, USA, 1992-93; Visng Astronomer, Padova Observatory, Irtaly, 1997. Publications: 5 books; Over 100 pprs in profl jrnls. Honours: Natl Sci Meeting Awd, 1978; 2nd Class Prize, Imp Sci Achievement, Academia Sinica, 1982; 2nd Class Prize, Nat Scis, Academia Sinica, 1991; 3rd Class Prize, Nat Scis, Academia Sinica, 1992; 2nd Class Prize, Outstndng Tchng, Chinese Educ Cttee, 1993. Memberships: Intl Astronomical Union; Gen Sec, Astronomical Soc Anhui, 1989-92; VP, Chinese Astronomical Soc, 1989-92. Hobbies: Sports; Literature; Philosophy. Address: Centre for Astrophysics, University of Science and Technology of China, Hefei, Anhui, China.

CHENG Jing-Yun, b. 30 Nov 1941. Professor; Director of CAD Institute; Editor, CAE of China. m. 10 Sept 1967, Zhu Xiu-Zhen, 1 d. Education: BS, Dept Maths, Nanjing Univ, 1959-64. Appointments: Engr, Aircraft Rsch & Des Inst, 1964-83; Lectr, Assoc Prof, Prof, Shanghai Maritime Univ, 1983-. Publications: Books: Advances in CAD/CAM of China; Human-Computer Interface Design & Its Development Tools; Formal Methods in Human-Computer Interface; More than 60 Papers. Honours: Sc & T Dev Awds of Min of Aeronautics, 1981; Sci and Tech Dec Awds, Shanghai, 1996; Sci and Technol Dev Awds, Min of Comms, 1996. Memberships: Vice Dir, Human-Computer Interaction Grp of Chinese Computer Fedn. Listed in: 21st Century, 1995. Address: Department of Computer Science, Shanghai Maritime University of China, 1550 Pudong Dadao, Shanghai 200135, China.

CHENG Joseph Yu-Shek, 11 Nov 1949, Hong Kong, China. University Professor. m. Grace Yin-Ting Cheng, 18 Feb 1973, 1 s, 1 d. Education: BSocl Scis (Hons), Univ of Hong Kong, 1972; BA (Hons), Vic Univ of Wellington, NZ, 1973; PhD, Flinders Univ of S Aust, 1979. Appointments: Dean, Sch of Arts and Hums, Open Univ of HK, 1989-90; Mbr, Cntr Policy Unit, Govt of HK, 1991-92; Chair Prof of Polit Sci, Cty Univ of HK, 1992-; Publications: 20 books and 80 articles in Engl; 25 books and 85 articles in Chinese; Mainly dealing w Chinese pols, Chinese for policy and polit dev in Hong Kong. Honours: JP, 1992-; Outstndng Austl Alumnus of Hk AWd, 1993. Memberships: Guest Prof, Beijing Univ, People's Univ, Wuhan Univ, Zhongshan Univ; Fndng Ed, HK Jrnl of Socl Scis. Hobbies: Reading; Travelling. Address: Contemporary China Research Centre, City University of Hong Kong, Tat Chee Avenue, Kowloon, Hong Kong Special Admin Region, China.

CHENG Ping, b. Canton, China. Educator. m. Sabrina, 1 s, 1 d. Education: BS, OK Univ, USA, 1958; MS, MA Inst of Technol, USA, 1960; PhD, Stanford Univ, USA, 1965. Appointments: Prof, 1974-94, Chmn, 1989-94, Mech Engrng, Univ HI, USA; Prof, Hd, Mech Engrng Dept, Hong Kong Univ of Sci & Technol, 1995-. Publications: Over 140 pprs in profl jrnls. Honours: Fell, ASME, 1986-; ASME Heat Transfer Meml Awd, 1996. Memberships: ASME; AIAA; Sev edl bds. Address: Hong Kong University of Science & Technology, Department of Mechanical Engineering, Clearwater Bay, Kowloon, Hong Kong.

CHENG Pingdong, b. 18 Oct 1938, Changcha, Hunan, China. Scientist; Engineer. m. Huang Jinhua, 14 Sept 1967, 1 s, 1 d. Education: Grad Dip, Tsinghua Univ. Appointments: Vice Dir, Core Nuclear & Thermal-Hydraulic Dept, 1985, Dir, Quality Assurance Dept, 1992, Vice Chmn, Sci & Technol Cttee, 1996, Shanghai Nuclear Engrng Rsch & Design Inst. Publications: Sev pprs in profl jrnls. Honours: 7 Ministerial Sci & Tech Progress Prizes; 1 Natl Invention Prize, 1980-88; Govt Specl Subsidy, 1993-. Memberships: Dir, Chinese Computational Phys Soc, 1986-; Dir, Shanghai Nuclear Soc, 1995-. Hobbies: Literature; Chinese Classical Poems. Address: Shanghai Nuclear Engineering Research & Design Institute, No 29 Hong Cao Road, Shanghai 200233, China.

CHENG Stephen Kin Kwok, b. 21 May 1947, Hong Kong. Consultant. m. Wilai, 2 Aug 1980, 2 s, 1 d. Education: BA, hons, Hong Kong Univ, 1971; ThL, Austl Coll of Theol, 1975; BD, Melbourne Coll of Divinity, 1978; BSW, Univ W Aust, 1978; PhD, Murdoch Univ, 1998. Appointments: Tchr, Kowloon Tech Sch, 1971-73; Ord Deacon, Anglican Ch, WA, 1976; Socl Worker, Graylands Hosp, WA, 1979-84; Snr Socl Worker, Multicultural Psych Cntr, Perth, 1984-95; Dir, E Asia Access, 1995-. Memberships: Am Psychol Assn; Assoc Mbr, Intl Cncl of Psychols. Hobbies: Swimming; Reading. Address: 10 Broadhurst Crescent, Bateman, WA 6150, Australia.

CHENG Xiang Sheng, b. 16 Apr 1932, Shanghai, China. Teacher. m. Miss Cui, 28 Jan 1963, 2 s. Education: Dip, Beijing Poly Inst, 1956. Appointment: Cttee of Lib, Tong Ji Univ, 1987-. Publications: Applied Theory of Plates and Shells, 1989; Science Articles: About the Theory of Plates and Shells, 1978-93; On Some Problems for Unsymmetrical Lateral Bukling of Rectangular Plates, 1989; On Some Problems in Dynamic Computation for Thin-Walled Structures, 1990; A Free Rectangular Plate on Elastic Foundation, 1992; The Applications of Generalized Variational Principles in Nonlinear Structural Analysis, 1993. Honour: Ex Student, Beijing Poly Inst, 1956. Membership: Mechs Assn of China, 1964-. Hobbies: Various sports including gymnastics, weight lifting and China Gong Fu.

CHENG Yin Cheong, b. Hong Kong, China. Centre Director, Centre for Research and International Collaboration, Hong Kong Institute of Education. m. Chan Kwok Ping, 3 d. Education: BSc; DipEd; MA (CHUK); EdM; EdD (Harvard). Appointments: Tchng Cnslt, Univ of Hong Kong; Lectr, Snr Lectr, Prof, Chinese Univ of Hong Kong; Prof, Dir of Cntr for Rsch Intl Collaboration, Hong Kong Inst of Educ. Publications: 6 books, Over 120 articles in jrnls, inclng: School Effectiveness and School-based Management: A Mechanism for Development, 1996. Honours: Outsndng Ppr Awd, 1994; Highly Commended Ppr Awds, 1996, 1997. Memberships: Intl Congress for Sch Effectiveness and Improvement Bd, 1995; Hong Kong Univ Grants Cttee, 1998; Hong Kong Quality Educ Fund, 1998; Chf Ed, Asia Pacific Jrnl of Tchr Educ and Dev; Advsry Bds of 3 Intl Jrnls. Hobbies: Painting; Writing. Address: Centre for Research and International Collaboration, Hong Kong Institute of Education, Lo Ping Road, Tai Po, NT, Hong Kong, China.

CHENG Yumin, b. 15 July 1926, Shanghai, China. Professor. m. Hu Meizhen, 16 Aug 1945, 2 s, 1 d. Education: BA, Fudan Univ, 1947; Visng Schl, Columbia Univ, NYC, USA, 1980-81. Appointments: Asst, 1949, Lectr, 1954, Assoc Prof, 1978, Vice-Chmn, 1978-80, Chmn, 1983-85, Prof, 1985-94, Supvsr, Doct Prog Engl and Engl Lit, 1986-98, Dept For Langs and Lits, Fudan Univ, Shanghai; Ed, Contemp Engl Stdys, 1982-83. Publications: The Imperative Mood of the Russian Verb, 1957; Chf Ed, Readings in Stylistics, 1988; Linguostylistic Study of English, 1989; Logical Inference Involved in Interpreting Direct Message Sentences, in Meaning as Explanation: Advances in Sign-Based Linguistics, 1995. Honour: State Cncl Awd, Outstndng Contbns to Higher Educ, 1992; Linguistic System and its Operation, 1997. Memberships: Chinese Soc For Lang Tchng and Rsch; Writers Assn Shanghai; Shanghai Assn Lit Translators. Listed in: Five Thousand Personalities of the World; Dictionary of International Biography; Men of Achievement. Hobby: Western literature and culture. Address: Department of Foreign Languages and Literatures, Fudan University, 220 Handan Lu, Shanghai 200433, China.

CHENG-ABDULLAH Nadzariah Bing-Ying. Veterinary Surgeon. Education: 1st Degree DVM, Univ Pertanian Malaysia; 2nd Degree, PostGrad Dip in Small Animal Med and Surg, Guelph, Ont Vet Coll, Can. Appointments; Tutor, UPM, 1979-80; Lectr in Small Animal Med and Surg, UPM, 1980-. Publications: Papers in Cat Diseases (Sporothricosis, Cat AIDS, Cat Leukemia, Coronavirus of Cats, Viral Cat Diseases); Dog Diseases (Distemper, Surgical Techniques (Bone and Soft Tissue), Pancreatic Cancer, Venereal Tumor, Ovarian Cancer), Cat Parasitic Trials (Flukes, Fleas), Wildlife Surgery, Anatomy, Dog Spinal Cord, Flea Trials, Hair Scanning Electron Microscopy, Tendon Transposition, Flukes, Retinal Detatchment and Ehrlichiosis, Pulmonary Disease in Cats, Feline Semen Evaluation, Tickcide Trials. Memberships: VAM (Vet Assn Malaysia); MSAB (Malaysian Soc for Applied Biology); MSPTM (Malaysian Soc for Parasitology and Tropical Medicine); Life Mbr, PAWS (PJ Animal Welfare Soc); Life Mbr, SPCA (Soc for Prevention of Cruelty to Animals). Hobbies: Cats; Gardening; Cooking; Dog Grooming; Ophthalmology and Neurology; Snakes and Iguanas. Address: c/o Department of Clinical Studies, Faculty of Veterinary Medicine and Animal Science, University Putra Malaysia, 43400 Serdang, Selangor, Malaysia.

CHENG-HSIUNG CHIU Paul, b. 19 Feb 1942, Hwalien Co. Minister of Finance. m. 2 s. Education: Natl Taiwan Univ; OH Univ, USA. Appointments: Assoc Prof of Monetary Econ, Natl Taiwan Univ, 1973-75; Adjunct Assoc Prof, 1975-81; Pres, Hwa Nan Coml Bank, 1988; Dpty Dir Gen, Banking Dept, Cntrl Bank of China, 1975-76; Dpty Dir Gen, For Exchange Dept, 1976-81; Dir Gen, Banking Dept, 1981-88; Dpty Gov, 1988-96; Dir Gen, Econ Rsch Dept, 1989-90; Min of Fin, Taiwan. Address: Ministry of Fin, 2 Ai Kuo West Road, Taipei, Taiwan.

CHENNUPATI K Ramaiah, b. 12 Nov 1957, Katrapadu. Research. m. Lakshmi, 19 May 1991. Education: BSc, Chem, Botany, Zool, Sri Venkateswara Univ, Tirupati, 1979; MSC Chem, Meerut Univ, UP, 1982; BLISc, Info Studies, 1983, Dip in Hindi, 1983, MLISc, Computer Applications in Libs, 1984, Univ of Delhi; PhD, Hypertext, Loughborough Univ of Technol, Eng, 1993. Appointments: Trainee Libn, Inst for Def Studies & Analysis Lib, New Delhi, 1983-84; Scientist B, Def Sci Info & Documentation Cntr (DESIDOC) DR & DO, Min of Def, 1984-89; PhD Rsch, Hypertext/Hypermedia, Univ of Technol, Loughborough, Eng, 1989-93; Scientist C, Multimedia Div in DESIDOC, 1993-95; Scientist D & Incharge, Multimedia Lab, DESIDOC, 1995-; Visng Fell, Sri Venkateswara Univ, Tirupati, Univ of Madras, 1995. Publications: 23 pprs in profl jrnls; Ppr presented intl and natl confs, seminars. Honours: Vergheeze Prize, ILA Bulletin, Best Ppr, 1988; Commonwealth Schlshp, 1989. Memberships include: Assn of Computing Machinery (ACM), USA; Amn Soc for Info Sci (USA); IEEE Computer Soc; Inst of Info Scientists (UK); Lib Assn (UK); Life Mbr: Soc for Info Sci (India); Micrographics Congress of India; Indian lib Assn; Intl Wild Waterfowl Assn Inc (USA); Intl Freelance Photogrs Orgn, 1986. Hobbies: Photography; Mountaineering. Address: Defence Scientific Information & Documentation Centre (DESIDOC), Defence R & D Organisation, Ministry of Defence, Metcalfe House, Delhi, India. 110054.

CHEONG Simplicius, b. 2 Mar 1942, Singapore. Lecturer in Music. m. Cheng-Yin, 17 Jan 1987, 1 d. Education: BMus, Univ WA, Aust, 1969; MMus, 1977, MEd, 1980, Univ Sydney, NSW; MA, Aesthetics, Macquarie Univ, 1989. Appointments: Ldr, Pianist, Baroque Jazz Ensemble, EMI recdng grp, 1965-68; Prodr, Composer, Radio, TV, Singapore, 1969-74; Lectr, Music, 1975-; Currently Lectr, Jazz Stdys and Composition, Sch Music, Univ NSW, Aust. Creative Works: 3 jazz compositions, 1965, Blue Bach, Spiritual Blues, Bossa Nova Digs Bach, recorded Baroque Jazz Ensemble; Symphony No 1, 1975, recorded W Australian Symph Orch, conducted David Measham; Movement for 5 Instruments, 1982, premiered Aust Ensemble, USA, May 1982, also recorded MN Pub Radio; Divertimento for Strings and Percussion, 1982, premiered Aust Chmbr Orch, Sydney, May 1986; Jazz Fantasy for Piano, 1984, premiered David Bollard, Alice Springs, 1984, also ABC Brdcst; Contrasts for 4 Cellos, 1985, premiered Bachianas Ensemble, Sydney Opera House, Aug 1985, also ABC Brdcst; Variations for Orchestra, 1990, Natl Univ Singapore commn; Fanfare for the Chancellor, Univ NSW, 1993; Fanfare for the Vice-Chancellor, Univ NSW, 1993; Sanctus for Soprano, Alto, Tenor and Bass, 1996; Variations for Piano on a Theme by Gershwin, 1997; Rhapsody for Violin and Piano, 1998; Publd article, Art and Reality: A Critique of Marxist Aesthetics, 1982. Honour: J Hodges Prize for Musical Composition, Univ WA, 1968. Listed in Austral-Asian Who's Who. Hobbies: Swimming; Zen meditation; Jazz improvisation with trio at various jazz venues, Sydney. Address: School of Music, University of New South Wales, Kensington, NSW 2033, Australia.

CHER (Cherilyn Lapierre Sarkisian), . b. 20 May 1946, El Centro, CA. Singer; Actress. m. (1) Sonny Bono - div 1975, dec 1998 - 1 d, (2) Gregg Allman, div, 1 s. Appointments: Half of singing duo Sonny and Cher; Sonny and Cher Comedy Hour - tv - 1971-75; Own TV var series and night club act. Recdngs incl: I Got You Babe; The Beat Goes On; Bang Bang; You Better Sit Down Kids; We all Sleep Alone; Black Rose - album -

1980; Cher, 1987; Heart of Stone, 1989; It's a Man's World, 1996; The Casablanca Years, 1996; Acted in play Come Back to the Five and Dime, Jimmy Dean, Jimmy Dean. Films Incl: Good Times; Chastity; Come Back to the Five and Dime, Jimmy Dean, Jimmy Dean; Silkwood; Mask; Witches of Eastwick; Moonstruck; Suspect; Mermaids; Love and Understanding; Faithful. Honours: Has won 11 gold and 3 platinum records; Best Actress Awd Cannes Film Fest for Mask; Acady Awd for Moonstruck, 1987. Address: c/o Bill Sammeth Organisation, P O Box 960, Beverly Hills, CA 90213, USA.

CHERRY Brian Wilson, b. 10 July 1935. Professor of Engineering. m. Miriam Hatfield, 31 Dec 1960, 1 s, 1 d. Education: MA; PhD (Cantab). Appointments: Goldsmith's Rsch Fell, Churchill Coll, Cambridge; Rsch Assoc, W R Grace & Co; Snr Lectr, Prof, Monash Univ. Publications: Polymer Surfaces, 1981; Over 100 pprs in sci and technol jrnls. Honour: FTSE, 1992. Memberships: Vice-chmn, Corrosion Prevention Cntr; Vice-chmn, Coop Rsch Cntr for Adv Composites; Austl Cnclr, Intl Corrosion Cncl; FIE, Aust. Hobbies: Sailing; Opera. Address: 7 Lurnea Road, Glen Iris, Vic 3146, Australia.

CHEUNG Water C W, b. 30 May 1958, Hong Kong. Investment Banker. m. Ranina Kan, 17 Aug 1987, 1 s. Education: BASc, Civ Engrng; MBA. Appointments: MD, CIBC Singapore; VP, Chase Manhattan Bank, Hong Kong; VP, Burns Fry Ltd, Toronto. Creative Works: Pricing the Convents; Thai d and test Rd. Honours: Derivative Superstar, Global Finance. Memberships: Chartered Fin Analyst. Address: #14-10 Block 3, 132 Tanjong Rhu Rd, Singapore 436919, Singapore.

CHHOKAR Jagdeep Singh, b. 25 Nov 1944, Kharar, India. Professor. m. Kiran, 7 May 1975. Education: PhD, LA State Univ, USA; MBA, Delhi Univ; Grad, Engrng, England. Appointments: Engr, Mngr, Indian Railways, 1967-77; Intl Mktng Mngr, 1977-80; Prof, 1985-. Publications: Sev articles in profl jrnls. Honours: Phi Kappa Phi; Beta Gamma Sigma. Memberships: Acady of Mngmt, USA; Inst of Mech and Prod Engrs, England; Natl Safety Cncl, India. Hobbies: World Affairs; Reading; Travel. Address: Indian Institute of Management, Ahmedabad 380 015, India.

CHIA Swee-Ping, b. 12 Nov 1945, Pantai Remis, Malaysia. College Vice President. m. Ming-Chu Wu, 1 s, 3 d. Education: BSc, Hons, Univ of Malaya, 1967; MS, 1968, PhD, 1972, Univ IL. Appointments: Lectr, 1972-80, Assoc Prof, 1980-92, Prof, 1992-99, Univ of Malaya; Vice Pres, Inti Coll, Malaysia, 1999-; Visng Sci, Intl Cntr for Theoretical Phys, Trieste, Italy, 1974, 1975, 1978, 1986, 1988, 1989, 1996, 1998; Visng Prof, Cntr for Particle Theory, Univ TX, Austin, 1981-82; Visng Expert Sci, 1983, Visng Sci, 1995, Inst of Phys, Academia Sinica, Taiwan; Hon Acad Advsr, Inti Coll, 1987-99; Dir of Rsch on Sci and Technol, Huazi Resource and Rsch Cntr, 1987-; Intl Planning Cttee, 1993-96, Gen Cncl, 1996-; Asia Pacific Cntr for Theort Phys; Cncl Mbr, Acady of Scis, Malaysia, 1999-; Selection Cttee for Sci and Technol Awd, Malaysian Toray Sci Fndn, 1993-; Exec Ed, Malaysian Jrnl of Sci B, 1994-; Exec Ed, Malaysian Jrnl of Sci B, 1994-. Publications: Over 50 pprs in profl jrnls. Honours: Fulbright-Hayes Schlsp, 1967; Univ IL Fellshp, 1967, 1968, 1969, 1970; Sigma Xi, 1972; Fell, Malaysian Inst of Phys, 1983; Assoc, Intl Cntr of Theoretical Phys, 1985; Snr Assoc, Intl Cntr of Theoretical Phys, 1991; Fell, Acady of Scis, Malaysia, 1997. Memberships: Malaysian Inst of Phys, pres, 1991-; ASEAN Inst of Phys, Chmn, 1991-94, vp, 1995-; Am Physl Soc; SE Asia Theoretical Phys Assn. Hobbies: Chinese Chess; International Chess; Bridge; Tai-ji. Address: Inti College Malaysia, Jalan BBN 12/1, Bandar Baru Nilai, 71800 Nilai, Negeri Sembilan, Malaysia.

CHIANG Chung-Ling, b. 21 Sept 1922, Chekiang. Minister of National Defence. m. 4 s, 1 d. Education: Chinese Mil Acady, Army Cmnd and Gen Staff Coll, War Coll; Armed Forces Univ. Apppointments: Cmndr in Chf, Army, 1981-88; Exec Vice-Chf of Gen Staff, Min of Natl Def, 1988-89; Personal Chf of Staff to Pres, 1989-92; Natl

Plcy Advsry, Pres, 1992-94; Min of Natl Def. Membership: Kuomintang Cntrl Cttee, 1993-. Address: Ministry of National Defence, POB 9001, Taipei, Taiwan, China.

CHIBA Masakatsu, b. 28 Jan 1957, Ishinomaki, Miyagi, Japan. Professor. m. Yumiko, 5 July 1987, 1 s, 1 d. Education: DEng. Appointment: Prof, Dept of Mech Engrng, Fac of Engrng, Iwate Univ. Publications: Sev pprs in profl jrnls. Memberships: Japan Soc of Mech Engrng; Japan Soc of Aern and Space Sci; Japan Soc of Microgravity Appl. Hobbies: Travel; Hot Spas. Address: 1-4-1 Kita-Matsuzono, Morioka 020-0105, Japan.

CHIBA Shuji, b. 25 Apr 1942, Takefu, Japan. Professor. m. Hisae Hayashi, 23 Mar 1969, 2 d. Education: MA, Tokyo Univ of Educ, 1968. Appointments: Lectr, Otsuma Womens Univ, Tokyo, 1970-72; Lectr, 1972-73, Assoc Prof, 1973-84, Prof, 1984-, Tsuda Coll, Tokyo. Publications: Present Subjunctives in Present Day English, 1987. Honour: Ichikawa Awd, 1987. Memberships: Engl Ling Soc of Japan, dir, 1997-; Japanese Cognitive Sci Soc; Engl Lit Soc of Japan; Ling Soc of Am; NY Acady of Scis. Address: 3-13-19 Minamisawa, Higashi-Kurume-shi, Tokyo 203-0023, Japan.

CHIHARA Goro, b. 20 July 1927, Tokyo. Scientist. m. Suzuko, 27 May 1960, 1 s, 1 d. Education: Dept Pharm Sci, Tokyo Univ, 1952. Appointments: Sci Advsr, Ajinomoto Co. Creative Works: Immunopotention Ciba Found Symp; Immunomodulation Agents; Immunomodulatory Agents from Plants. Honours: Asahi Sci Awd; Princes Takamatsu Cancer Rsch Awd; Intl Awd of Future Trend on Chemotherapy. Memberships: Intl Soc Preventive Oncology; Intl Assn Immunopharmacology. Hobbies: Mountain Climbing; Drinking; Hot Springs. Address: Tanacho 49-15, Aobaku, Yokohama 227-0064, Japan.

CHIK Dato' Sabbaruddin, b. 11 Dec 1941 Temerloh Penang. Politician. Education: Abu Bakar Sec Sch Temerloh; Malay Coll Kuala Kangser Perak; Univ of Malay Inst of Socl Studies The Hague. Appointments: Asst State Sec Negeri Sembilan; Prin Asst Sec JPM; Dir Plng GPU/SERU; Dir Intl Trade Min of Trade and Ind; Dep State Sec Salangor, 1966-81; Gen Mngr Pernes Trading Sdn Bhd, 1981-82; Dep Min of Fin, 1982; Min of Culture, Arts and Tourism, 1987. Memberships: Mbr Parl for Temerloh, 1982-; Mbr UMNO Supreme Cncl, 1984-. Address: Ministry of Culture, Arts and Tourism, 34th-36th Floor, POB 5-7, Menaro Dato'Onn, Putra World Trade Centre, 50694 Kuala Lumpur, Malaysia.

CHIKAOKA Riichiro, Politician. Appointments: Fmr Parl Vice-Min of Hlth and Welfare; Dir-Gen Sci and Technol Agcy, 1996. Memberships: Mbr HoR. Address: Science and Technology Agency, 2-2-1 Kasumigaseki, Chiyoda-ku, Tokyo 100, Japan.

CHILTON Frederick Oliver (Sir), b. 23 July 1905, Aust. Former Army Officer and Government Official. Education: BA, LLB, Sydney Univ. Appointments: Commissioned, 1926; Maj, 1937; GSO 2, 1st Division, 1938-39; Seconded Austl Imperial Force, 1939; Lt-Col, 1941; Cmdr 2, 2nd Infantry Bat, 1st Libyan and Greek Campaigns, 1942; Col, GSO 1, HQ, 1st Army New Guinea Force and Milne Bay Force, 1943; Cmdt, Land HQ Tactical Sch, Brig, Cmdr, 18th Brig, Austl Imperial Force, Ramu Valley and Balikpapan Campaigns, 1943-45; Cmdr, Macassar Force, 1945-46; R of O, 1946; Controller, Jnt Intell, 1946-48; Asst Sec, 1948-50, Dpty Sec, 1950-58, Dept Def; Chmn, Repatriation Commn; Currently VP, NSW Div, Austl Red Cross Soc. Honours: DSO and Bar; CBE, 1963; Created Kt, 1969. Address: Box 129, Avalon Beach, NSW 2107, Australia.

CHIN Yoong Kheong, b. 13 Apr 1958. Chartered Accountant. m. Yap Siew Pin, 8 Aug 1988, 2 s. Education: BA Hons, Econs/Acctng; DBA. Appointments: Ptnr, KPMG Peat Marwick; Dir, KPMG Tax Servs SDN BHD; Dir, KPMG Cnsltng SDN BHD, and KPMG Peat Marwick Ltd, Vietnam, 1994-97. Publications: Malaysian Taxation, 4th ed; Malaysian Taxation Practice and Getting It Together. Honours: 1st Class Hons in BA Econs/Acctng; Crabtree Prize for Top Econs; Awd'd Gerald Veale Prize for Top Acctng. Memberships: Fell, Inst of Chartered Accts in Eng and Wales; Fell, Malaysian Inst of Accts; Malaysian Inst of Taxation; Malaysian Assn of Cert Pub Accts. Hobbies: Swimming; Golf. Address: Wisma KPMG, Jalan Dungun, Damansara Heights, 50490 Kuala Lumpur, Malaysia.

CHINERY William Addo, Ghanaian. b. 5 Apr 1934, Ghana. Biomedical Scientist; University Professor. m. Bertha Chatherine Laing, 3 Sept 1966, 4 s. Education: BSc, Hons, 1959; DAP&E, 1961; PhD, London, England, 1963. Appointments: Govt Med Entomologist, Min of Hlth, Ghana, 1959; Rsch Offr, Nat Inst of Hlth and Med Rsch, 1964; Lectr, Sr Lectr, Assoc Prof, Ghana Med Sch, 1968-80; Visng Assoc Prof, Harvard Sch Pub Hlth, USA, w ranking as Full Prof when tchng at Harv Med Sch, 1976-77; Prof, Ghana Med Sch, 1980-; Hd, Microbio Dept, 1986-94; Mbr, Expert Advsry Pannel, Vector Biol WHO, 1976-85; Mbr, Ed Bd, Ghana Jrnl of Sci, 1973-76. Publications: Auth, over 72 scientific communications in Med Entomol and Parasitol, Trop Med and Pub Hlth; Auth, some 15 lit papers; Mbr, UNESCO's Special Comm on Pollution of Environment, Ghana Br, 1976-. Honours: Listing as Disting Student, London Sch Hyg and Trop Med, 1974; 1 of 3 Ldng Mosquito Vector Workers in Africa, WHO, 1985; Life Dpty Gov, ABIRA (ABI), 1989; Mbr, Advsry Coun, IBA (IBC), 1990; KCMSS, 1990; Kt of Humanity KH, 1990; Intl Order of Merit (IOM, IBC), 1991; Fell, Inst Biol (UK), 1993; Fell, World Lit Acad (FWLA-IBC), 1993; Medals and Plaques (IBC), 1985. Memberships: Fell, Roy Soc Trop Med and Hyg; Ghana Sci Assn; Inst of Bio UK; Mbr and Exec Coun Mbr, Ghana Inst Lab Med, 1994. Hobbies: Reading; Music appreciation; Analytical thinking; Piano. Address: PO Box MP 994, Mamprobi, Accra, Ghana.

CHING Chiao-Liang Juliana, b. 23 Feb 1955, Hong Kong. Physician; Businesswoman. Education: BS (Summa cum laude) Hons in Bio, Yale Univ, 1977; MD, Univ of CA, Davis, Sch of Med, 1981. Appointments: Res Dr, UCLA Hosps and Clins, 1981-83; Res Dr, Harvard Univ Hosps, 1983-85; Mngng Dir, Ideal Choice Dev Ltd, 1987-; Mngng Dir, Chi King Dev Ltd, 1991-. Honours: Woman of the Yr, ABI, 1991-98; Order of Intl Fellshp; Intl Order of Merit. Memberships: AAAS; NY Acady of Scis; Oxford Club. Hobbies: Music; Art; Reading. Address: 4 Mount Butler Drive, Jardine's Lookout, Hong Kong, China.

CHINN Menzie David, b. 4 June 1961, Richland, Washington, USA. Economist. m. Laura Schwendinger, 2 Sept 1991. Education: BA, Harvard Univ, 1984; MA, 1988, PhD, 1991, Univ CA, Berkeley. Appointments: Asst Prof, 1991-97, Assoc Prof, 1997-, Univ CA, Santa Cruz. Publications: The Usual Suspects? Productivity and Demand Shocks and Asia-Pacific Real Exchange Rates; On the Won and Other East Asian Currencies; Whither the Yen? Implications of an Intertemporal Model of the Yen/Dollar Rate; Who Drives Real Interest Rates Around the Pacific Rim: The US or Japan?; Banking on Currency Forecasts: Is Change in Money Predictable. Honour: Amex Bank Review Yng Econ Prize, 1988. Memberships: Am Econ Assn; Eco Metric Soc. Address: Department of Economics, University of California, Santa Cruz, CA 95064, USA.

CHIOU Andrew, b. 10 Mar 1965, Kulai, Malaysia. Software Engineer. m. N C Lye, 28 Oct 1993, 1 s. Education: Bach Deg, Computing, hons; Bach Deg, Appl Sci; High Dip, Computing Studies; Dip, Computing Studies. Appointments: Systems Cnslt, 1986-91; Rsch Asst, 1995-97; Software Engr, 1997-99; Rschr, 1999-. Publications: Var pprs in profl jrnls. Honours: Fac of Appl Sci Awd, 1994; CQU Intl Educn Awd, 1995; Univ Postgrad Rsch Awd, 1995; CQU Meritorious Awd, 1996; Austl Postgrad Awd (Ind), 1999. Memberships: Austl Computer Soc; Assn of Computing Machinery; Inst of Elec and Electron Engrs. Hobbies: Classical Guitar; Plastic Modelling. Address: Faculty of Informatics & Communications, Central Queensland University, Rockhampton, Qld 4702, Australia.

CHIPP Donald Leslie, b. 21 Aug 1925 Melbourne Vic. Politician. m. (1) Monica Lalor, div 1979, 2 s, 2 d, (2) Idun G Welz, 1979, 2 d. Education: Northcote High Sch; Univ of Melbourne. Appointments: Served in RAAF, 1943-45; Registrar C'wlth Inst of Accts and Austl Soc of Accs, 1950-55; Chf Exec Offr Olympic Civic Cttee, 1955-56; Cnclr Cty of Kew, 1955-61; Sen, 1977-86; Min for Navy and Min in charge of Tourist Activities, 1966-68; Min for Customs and Excise, 1969-72; Min asstng Min for Natl Dev, 1971-72; Min for Socl Security Hlth Repatriation and Compensation, Nov-Dec 1975; Liberal to March 1977; Ldr Austl Dem Party, 1977-87. Publications: Don Chipp: The Third Man, (with J Larkin), 1978; "Chip", 1987; Num articles. Memberships: HoR, 1960-77. Address: 8 Patrick Court, Wheelers Hill, Vic 3150, Australia.

CHIRATHIVAT Supatra, b. 29 Feb 1957. 1 s, 1 d. Education: MBA. Memberships: PATA; SITE; TICA; Italian-Thai Chmbr of Com. Hobbies: Swimming; Tennis; Reading. Address: c/o The Central Plaza Hotel, 1695 Phaholyothin Road, Chatuchak, Bangkok 10900, Thailand.

CHITVIRA Thongyod, b. Suphanburi. Politician. Appointments: Mayor Suphanburi; Com Min, 1975; Pub Hlth Min, 1980; Dep PM, 1981-82, Sep-Dec 1990. Memberships: Mbr municipality Suphanburi, 1949; Mbr Provincial Cncl; Mbr Natl Ass; Mbr Socl Action Party.

CHIU Cheng-Hsiung (Paul), b. 19 Feb 1942, Hualien Co, Taiwan. Minister of Finance. m. 2 s. Education: BA, Econ, Natl Taiwan Univ, 1964; MA, Econ, 1971, PhD, Econ, 1978, OH State Univ, USA. Appointments: Assoc Prof, Dept and Grad Inst of Econs, Natl Taiwan Univ, 1973-75; Dpty Dir Gen, Banking Dept, Cntrl Bank of China, 1975-76; Adj Assoc Prof, Dept and Grad Inst of Econs, Natl Taiwan Univ, 1975-81; Dpty Dir gen, For Exchange Dept, Cntrl Bank of China, 1976-81; Dir Gen, Banking Dept, 1981-88; Adj Prof, Dept and Grad Inst of Econ, Natl Taiwan Univ, 1982-; Pres, Hua Nan Coml Bank, 1988; Dpty Gov, Cntrl Bank of China, 1988-96; Dir gen, Econ Rsch Dept, Cntrl Bank of China, 1989-90; Min of Fin, 1996-.

CHIU Chuang-Huan, b. 25 July 1925 Changhua Co. Politician. Education: Sch of Polit Sci Natl Chengchi Univ. Appointments: Dir 3rd Dep Min of Personnel Taiwan, 1965-67; Dept Dir 5th Section Cntr Cttee Kuomintang, 1967-68; Commnr Dept of Socl Affairs Taiwan Prov Govt, 1969-72; Dir Dept Socl Affairs Cntr Cttee Kuomintang, 1972-78; Min without Portfolio, 1976-78; Dep Sec-Gen Cntr Cttee Kuomintang, 1978; Min of the Interior, 1978-81; Vice-Premier Exec Yuan Repub China - Taiwan - 1981-84. Publications: Thought Regarding Social Welfare in the Three Principles of the People; A Summary of the Chinese Social Welfare System. Honours: Hon PhD, Youngnam Univ Repub of Korea. Address: Taiwan Provincial Government, Foreign Affairs Dept, 9th Floor, 15 Hangchow South Rd, Section 1, Taipei 10044, Taiwan.

CHIU Nan-Chang, b. 8 Aug 1959, Kaohsiung, Taiwan. Physician. m. M P Su, 21 Jan 1987, 2 s, 1 d. Education: MD. Appointment: Attending Physn, Dept of Pediats, Mackay Mem Hosp, 1990-. Memberships: Pediat Specialist of Taiwan, 1990; Infectious Diseases Specialist of Taiwan, 1991; Pediat Neurol Specialist of Taiwan, 1992. Address: Mackay Memorial Hospital, 92 2nd Sec Chung San North Road, Taipei 104, Taiwan.

CHIU Ren-Jong, b. 28 Nov 1922, Fukien Province, China. Professor. m. Yu Chu, 11 July 1940, 1 s, 1 d. Education: BS, Fukien Provincial Coll Agric, 1948; MS, 1958, PhD, 1961, KS State Univ, USA. Appointments include: Snr Plant Path, Sino-US Commn on Rural Reconstrn, 1961-79; Rsch Fell, Academia Sinica, 1975-87; Cncl of Agric, 1979-87; Prof, Plant Virology, Natl Chung Hsing Univ, Taichung, 1961-65, 1968-85, 1987-93. Creative Works include: Auth, co-auth, 80 sci pprs; Discoverer, Rice Transitory Yellowing Virus RTYV. Honours: Sci Achievement Awd, Agricl Assn China, 1968; Disting Serv Awd, Exec Yuan, 1983; Disting Rsch Awd, Natl Sci Cncl, 1989. Memberships: Amn Phytopathol Soc; Agricl Assn China; Pres, Plant Protection Soc Taiwan; Plant Pathol Soc Taiwan. Hobby; Photography. Address: 22 Lane 160, Ta-An Road Sec 2, Taipei City, Taiwan, China.

CHIVAS Allan Ross, b. 14 May 1950, Sydney, Australia. University Professor. Education: BSc, Hons, 1972, PhD, 1977, Univ of Sydney. Appointments: Snr Fell, Ldr, Environ Geochem Grp, Rsch Sch of Earth Scis, Austl Natl Univ, 1979-95; Prof of Geoscis, Hd, Sch of Geoscis, Univ of Wollongong, NSW, 1995-. Publications: Over 120 in profl jrnls. Honours: Edgeworth David Travelling Schlsp, Univ Sydney, 1976. Memberships: Sev geol socs. Hobbies: Travel; Fieldwork; Photography. Address: c/o School of Geosciences, University of Wollongong, NSW 2522, Australia.

CHO Hae Kyoung, b. 9 Sept 1949, S Korea. Director of Research Institute. m. Su Cho, 12 Aug 1980, 1 s, 1 d. Education: PhD, Polit Sci, Univ of TN, Knoxville, USA. Appointments: Dir, Polit Studies, Korea Inst of Socl Studies, 1989-94; Dir, Korea Inst for Policy Dev, 1994-. Publications: Sartre's Phenomenological Philosophy, 1996; Western Political Thought, 1997; North-South Relations in East Asia. Memberships: APSA (Amn Polit Sci Assn); KPSA (Korean Polit Sci Assn). Hobby: Art collections. Address: 1612-51 Bong Chun-dong, Kwanak-ku, Seoul, Korea.

CHO Hai-Hyung, b. 26 July 1934, Seoul, Korea. Corporate Chairman; Chief Executive Officer. 2 s, 1 d. Education: BS, Sloan Sch Mngmt, MIT, USA, 1958. Appointments include: Dir, Orient Press, 1971; Chf Exec Offr, Sangyong Bus Grp, 1972-82; Chmn, Korea-NZ Bus Cncl, 1978-; Mbr, Econ Plng Bd Plcy Advsry Cttee, 1980-84; Chmn, Minteq Korea Inc, 1980-; Chmn, Kookmin Univ Fndn, 1982; Chmn, Chf Exec Offr, Nara Holdings Corp, Seoul, 1986-. Honours: Order of Indl Serv Merit, Korea, 1980; Kt, Order of Falcon, Iceland, 1988; MBE, 1990; Memberships: Korea Employers Fedn, Vice-Chmn, 1980-84; Korea PR Assn, Chmn, 1988-90; Korea Operation Rsch and Mngmt Sci, Pres, 1977-79; Korea Mktng Assn, Chmn, 1994-97; Korean Acady Arbitration, Vice-Chmn, 1991-. Hobbies: Mountain hiking; Golf; Reading; Address: 1-102 Dongbinggo-dong, Yongsan-ku, Seoul, Korea.

CHO Jun-Dong, b. 21 July 1957, Seoul, Korea. Professor. m. Keum-Ju, 6 Aug 1988, 2 s. Education: PhD, Electr Engin & Computer Sci. Appointments: Snr Rschr, Samsung Electronics Co, 1993; Asst Prof, Dept of Electron Engrng, Sung Kyun Kwan Univ, 1995. Publication: High Performance Design Automation for Multi-Chip Modules, 1996. Honour: Best Pprs Awd, Des Automation Conf, Dallas, TX 1993. Membership: Snr Mbr, IEEE. Hobbies: Climbing; Tennis. Address: Department of Electrical Engineering and Computer Science, Sung Kyun Kwan University, 300 Chunchun-Dong, Suwon, Korea.

CHO Srinivasan Ramaswamy, b. 5 Oct 1934, Chennai, Tamilnadu, India. Journalist. m. Soundara, 10 June 1966, 1 s, 1 d. Education: BS; BL; Dip in Acting. Appointments: Advocate, Madras High Ct, 1957-62; Legal Advsr, TTK Grp Cos, 1962-75; Ed, Thuglak, 1970-. Creative Works: 23 Plays; 7 TV Serials; 14 Film Scripts; Dir, 4 Films; 13 Novels. Honours: Maharana Jaipur Awd, Natl Serv for Jrnlsm; B D Goeka Awd; Veerakesari Awd. Memberships: Peoples Union of Civ Liberties. Address: 46 Greenways Road, Chennai 600028, India.

CHO Yuk Kei Carlos, b. 15 July 1940, Hong Kong. Chartered Architect. m. Ruby Myao-Che Chang, 1968, 2 s. Education: BArch. Memberships: Hong Kong Jockey Club; Hong Kong Golf Club; Chinese Gen Chmbr of Com. Hobbies: Golfing; Reading; Swimming. Address: 16/F Caltex House, 258 Hennessy Road, Wanchai, Hong Kong.

CHOI Sing Ki (Xavier), b. 13 Dec 1953. Research Scientist. m. Anne Mui Chin Ng, 3 May 1984, 1 d. Education: BEng Hons I 1980, Grad Dip 1989, PhD 1984, Monash Univ, Melbourne, Vic, Aust. Appointments: Rsch

Sci 1984, Snr Rsch Sci 1990, Prin Rsch Sci 1994, C'wlth Sci and Indl Rsch Org. Publications: More than 100 pprs in jrnls, conf proceedings and tech rprts. Champion - Hong Kong School Musical Festival, 1971, 1972. Honours: Bish Bianco Schlsp, 1964-66; Monash Grad Schlsp, 1980-83. Memberships: NY Acady of Scis, 1994-99; Soc of Petrol Engrs, 1997-99; Intl Soc for Rock Mechs, Austl Geomechs Soc, 1989-99. Listed in: Who's Who in the World. Hobbies: Table-Tennis; Music; Swimming; Reading. Address: 1 Genoa Street, Dandenong North, Melbourne, Vic 3175, Australia.

CHOI Young Chul, b. 16 Oct 1943, Seoul, Korea. Diplomat. m. Chun Young Yee, 12 June 1976, 1 s, 1 d. Education: BA, Liberal Arts and Sci Coll, Seoul Natl Univ. Appointments: 3rd Sec, Can, 1977; 2nd Sec, Suriname, 1980; Cnslr, Indonesia, 1984; Cnslr, UK, 1991; Consul Gen, Frankfurt, Germany, 1997-99; Amb to Mongolia, 1999-. Address: Parktown Apt 103-1406, Sunaedong, Bundangku, Sungnamsi, Kyunggido, Rep of Korea.

CHOI Young Deuk, b. 12 May 1961, Seoul, Korea. Medical Doctor; Professor. m. K H Baek, 19, Oct 1986, 2 d. Education: MD, PhD, Yonsei Univ, Coll of Med, Dept of Urology, Seoul, Korea. Appointments: MD; PhD, Prof. Memberships: Amn Urological Assn, 1998; Soc for the Impotence Study (SSI), 1997. Hobby: Golf. Address: Department of Urlogy, Youngdong Severance Hospital, Yonsei University College of Medicine, 146-P2, Dogok-Dong, Kangnam-Ku, Seoul 135-270, Korea (Youngdong, PO Box 1217, Seoul, Korea).

CHONG Robert Foo Hee, b. 15 Oct 1940, Ipoh, Malaysia. Chemist. m. Mee Sim, 23 Mar 1973, 2 d. Education: Dip, Applied Chem. Appointments: Rsch Asst, Sect Ldr, Monsanto Chems (Aust), 1966-71; Profl Offr, 1971-82, Snr Profl Offr, Second-in-Charge Aeronautical Engrng Support Facility (RAAF) Dept of Def 1982-97; Cnclr, Cty of White Horse, 1997-. Honours: OAM, 1991. Memberships: Roy Aust Chem Inst; Pres, Communities Cncl on Ethnic Issues (East Reg), 1993-; Pres, Chinese Community Socl Servs Cntr (Fndr), 1992. Hobbies: Reading; Walking; Tai Chi; Multiculturalism and the communities. Address: 7 Leeann St, Blackburn Sth Vic 3130, Australia.

CHOONG Tung Pow Iain, b. 2 Nov 1953. Consultant. Education: Offrs Qualifying Exam - Police Force Exams Bd, Sinagpore, 1972; DJur (Law), City Univ LA, USA, 1993; MBA (Fin), Irish Bus Sch, Eire, 1994; PhD (Jurisp), Bernadean Univ, USA, 1994. Appointments: Police Off, Internal Security Dept, Min Home Affairs, Repub Singapore, 1972-74; Snr Narcotics Offr (Hd of Unit), Collation and Interrogations Unit, Cntrl Narcotics Bur, Min Home Affairs, Repub of Singapore, 1974-81; Mngr, (Hd of Div), Ops Div, Shaw Computer and Mngmt Servs, Malaysia, 1981-85; Grp Mngr (Hd Div), Legal and Admin Div, Mt Pleasure Corp, Malaysia, 1985-88; Mngng Dir/Chf Exec Offr, EduTech Resources Cntr, 1988-; Exec Dir, Country Edtns, 1994-; The Sun Edtns, 1994-96; Magnanimous Heritage, 1994-96; Mngng Dir/Chf Exec Offr, Bedrock Holdings, 1996-; Mngng Dir/Chf Exec Offr, Event Plng Servs, 1996-; Spec Advsr, Intl Progs for Gordon Inst of TAFE (Vic, Aust), 1998-. Publications: Num articles to profl jrnls incl: Systematic Selection and General Interviewing Procedures, Business Executive (UK), 1991; The Right to Strike and Lock-out, Berita Personnel (Malaysia), Oct 1991; Part Time Workers: A Need for Clearer Definition, Research taken by the International Labour Organisation (ILO) with a view to a Convention/Recommendation on Part Time Labour, 1994. Honours: Awd of Merit, Life Saving Soc of Malaysia, 1970; Paul Harris fell, Rotary Fndn of Rotary Intl, 1992; Appt as Arbritrator, Employers Panel, Indl Ct of Malaysia, Min Hum Resources, 1988-89, 1995-97. Memberships include: Pres, Xaverian Club (Sch alumni), 1995-97; Rep for Selangor, Inst of Profl Fin Mngr (UK), 1993-; Malaysian Intl Chmbrs of Comm and Ind; Fedn of Malaysian Mfrs; Malaysian Anti-Narcotics Assn. Address: 1A (1st Floor) Jalan 3/108C, Taman Sungei Besi, 57100 Kuala Lumpur, Malaysia.

CHOU Jyh-Horng, b. 6 Dec 1957, Kaohsiung, Taiwan. Professor of Mechanical Engineering. m. Mei-Lei Chao, 15 Oct 1984, 1 s, 1 d. Education: PhD, Natl Sun Yat-Sen Univ, 1989. Appointments: Instr, Natl Sun Yat-Sen Univ, 1983-86; Assoc Prof, Dir, Cntr for Automation Technol, Natl Kaohsiung Inst of Technol, Taiwan, 1986-91; Assoc Prof, 1991-92, Prof, 1993-, Chmn, 1998-, Natl Yunlin Univ of Sci and Technol. Publications: 1 book, num articles in profl jrnls. Honours: Ex Schlsp, Rotary Club, Taiwan, 1989; Ex Rsch Awd, Natl Sci Cncl, Taiwan, 1992. Memberships: Snr and Perm Mbr, Chinese Soc of Mech Engrs; Chinese Automatic Control Soc; Chinese Automation Technol Soc. Hobbies: Classical Music; Softball. Address: c/o Department of Mechanical Engineering, National Yunlin University of Science & Technology, Yunlin 640, Taiwan.

CHOU Loke-Ming, b. 4 Nov 1946, Singapore. University Academic. m. Renee Lim, 7 Sept 1976, 1 d. Education: PhD, Zool. Appointments: Sci Offr, Singapore Sci Cntr, 1972-77; Lectr, 1977-82, Snr Lectr, 1982-88, Assoc Prof, 1988-98, Prof, 1998-, Natl Univ of Singapore. Publications: (co-auth) Underwater Guide to The South China Sea, 1992-; (co-auth) Marine Parks of Thailand, 1998. Honours: Outstndng Sci Lectr, Natl Univ of Singapore, 1992; Green Leaf Awd, Min of Environ, 1994; Champion Blood Donor, Min of Hlth, 1994; Univ Tchng Excellence Awd, 1998. Memberships: Sci & Techl Advsry Cttee, Global Coral Reef Monitoring Network, 1996-; VP, Singapore Inst of Bio, 1996-. Hobby: Scuba diving. Address: Department of Biological Sciences, National University of Singapore, 10 Kent Ridge Crescent, Singapore 119260, Singapore.

CHOU Siaw Meng, b. 20 May 1961, Singapore. Senior Lecturer. m. 24 July 1987, 2 s, 1 d. Education: PhD, BEng, Dip in Mech Engrng. Appointments: Lectr, 1992; Snr Lectr, 1998. Publications: Contbr, articles in num jrnls. Honours: Overseas Rsch Students Awd, John Anderson Postgrad Studentship; Dean's List of Meritorious Standard; Prof Mellaby Prize. Memberships: Mng Ed, Automedia, Intl Jrnl of Biomed Engrng, 1988-90. Address: School of Mechanical and Production Engineering, Nanyang Technological University, Nanyang Avenue, Singapore 639798, Singapore.

CHOUDHARY Suresh Veersangappa, b. 25 Jan 1950, Parli Vaijnath, India. Medical Pratitioner. m. Saroj, 6 Feb 1976, 2 s, 2 d. Education: MBBS. Honour: Mr. Medico. Memberships: Sarvv Dharma Parishad. Hobbies: Horse Riding; Swimming; Wrestling; Preaching. Address: Vaidynath Clinic, Ganeshpar Parli, Vaijnath, Beed, India.

CHOUDHURY Atique, b. 5 May 1963, St Albans, Herts, Eng. Restauranteur; Property developer. m. Sirirat, 24 Aug 1992, 1 s. Education: NVQ Level 4 Restaurant Mngmt. Appointments: Chmn, Stoke Newington Rest Watch; Chmn, Hotel and Catering Trng Fndn (Asian Proj). Honours: Oriental Chef of the Yr, Egon Ronay's Guide, 1996; Best Prac in Bus, Hackney Chmbr of Comm. Memberships: Fndr, Thai Restaurant Eurs Assn; Ex-Gov, Sir Thomas Abney Sch. Hobbies: Badminton; Football. Address: 30 Stoke Newington Church Street, London N16 OLU, England.

CHOUDHURY Sounak Kumar, b. 30 Apr 1956, India. Mechanical Engineering Educator. m. Ludmila, 23 Mar 1985, 1 s. Education: PhD, Mechl Engrng; MSc, Engrng Sci. Appointments: Assoc Prof; Asst Prof; Visng Fac. Publications: 22 Rsch Pprs in Jrnls, 1987-99; 1 pat. Honour: Best Rsch Ppr Awd, 1994. Memberships: Inst of Engrs, 1994-. Hobbies: Reading; Music; Swimming. Address: House No 4097, PO IIT Kanpur, UP Kanpur 208 016, India.

CHOW Esther Oi-Wah, b. Hong Kong. Social Work Educator. m. 8 June 1986, 1 s. Education: BA, Hons, Sociol, Concordia Univ, Can, 1979; MSW, Socl Work, 1982, PhD Cand, Hlth and Aging, Univ of Hong Kong. Appointments: Snr Rsch Asst, Univ of Hong Kong, 1980-81; Exec Sec, Hong Kong Bapt Hosp, Au Shue Hung Hlth Cntr, 1982-89; Exec Dir, Chinese Info, 1989-92, Snr Lectr, Assoc Prof, City Univ of Hong Kong,

1992-. Publications include: A Critical Evaluation of the Senior Citizen Card Scheme in Hong Kong: From the Social Welfare and Business Perspective, 1998; Correlates of Subjective Well-being in Chinese Elderly in Hong Kong, 1998; Empowering Through Self-Help/Mutual-Aid Network, 1997. Honours: Postgrad Studshp, Univ Hong Kong, 1981-82; 2 Outstndng Socl Affairs Awds, Hong Kong Harbor Jaycees Ltd, Hong Kong Radio and TV, 1985; Coll Qlty Awds, Cty Univ Hong Kong, 1994; Schlsp, Cty Univ Hong Kong, 1994, 1995, 1996, 1997, 1998; Hong Kong Govt Dist Bd, 1995. Memberships: Amn Soc on Aging; Hong Kong Socl Workers Assn; Hong Kong Socl Welfare Personnel Reg Cncl; Hong Kong Assn of Gerontol; Hong Kong Profl Tchrs Union; Hong Kong Cncl of Socl Servs; Ontario Self-Help Rsch Network. Hobbies: Swimming; Photography; Reading; Travel; Calligraphy. Address: Division of Social Studies, City University of Hong Kong, Tat Chee Avenue, Kowloon, Hong Kong.

CHOW Gregory Chi-Chong, b. 25 Dec 1929, Macau, S China (came to USA, 1948, naturalized, 1963). Economist; Educator. m. Paula K Chen, 27 Aug 1955, 2 s, 1 d. Education: BA, Cornell Univ, 1951; MA, Univ Chgo, 1952; PhD, 1955; LLD, Lingnan Coll, 1994. Appointments: Asst Prof, MIT, 1955-59; Assoc Prof, Cornell Univ, 1959-62; Visng Prof, 1964-65; Staff Mbr, Mngr, Econ Models, IBM Rsch Cntr, Yorktown Heights, NY, 1962-70; Adj Prof, Columbia Univ, 1965-70; Visng Prof, Harvard Univ, 1967, Rutgers Univ, 1969; Prof, Dir, Econ Rsch Prog, 1970-97; Class of 1913 Prof Polit Econ, Princeton Univ, 1979-; Advsr, Chinese Nat Sci Fndn; Econ Advsr, Shandong Provcl Govt. Publications: (auth) books inclng: Econometric Analysis by Control Methods, 1981; Econometrics, 1983; The Chinese Economy, 1985; Understanding China's Economy, 1994; Dynamic Economics: Optimization by the Lagrange Method, 1997; (co-ed) Evaluating the Reliabilty of Macro-Economic Models, 1982; Asia in the 21st Century, 1997; Articles to profl jrnls. Honour: Hon Dr, Zhongshan Univ; LLD Lingnan Coll; Named Hon Prof, Fudan Univ, The Peoples Univ, Zhongshan Univ, Shandong Univ; Hon Pres, Lingnan Univ. Memberships: Fell, Econometric Soc; Amn Stats Assn; Academia Sinica; Amn Philos Soc; Amn Econ Assn; Soc for Econ Dynamics & Control. Address: 30 Hardy Drive, Princeton, NJ 08540-1211, USA.

CHOW King Lau, b. 27 Feb 1964, Hong Kong. Assistant Professor. m. L L Wong, 25 June 1995. Education: BSc, Biol, Chinese Univ of Hong Kong; PhD, Cell Biol, Baylor Coll of Med. Appointments: Rsch Assoc, Albert Einstein Coll of Med, 1990-94; Asst Prof, Hong Kong Univ of Sci & Technol, 1994-. Publications: Sev articles in profl jrnls. Honours: Belfer Fell, 1990-94; Martin Fndn Fell, 1990-92; Ralph Fox Fndn Fell, 1994-96. Memberships: AAAS; Genetics Soc Am; Am Microbiol Soc; SCBA; NY Acady of Scis; Intl Soc of Devel Biol; Soc of Devel Biol. Hobby: Classical Music. Address: c/o Department of Biology, Hong Kong University of Science & Technology, Clear Water Bay, Kowloon, Hong Kong.

CHOW Kit Boey, b. 23 Jan 1944, Singapore. Economist. Education: BSc, magna cum laude, Econs, Utah State Univ, USA, 1973; MSc, Econs, Utah State Univ, 1974. Appointment: Dir, Cntr for Bus Rsch & Dev, Fac of Bus Admin, NUS. Memberships: Ad hoc Cttee on Shipping, NOL, 1975-77; Ind Cttee, Singapore Chinese Chamber of Commerce & Ind, 1983-85; CIRET, Munich, 1985-.

CHOW Wah Soon, b. 1 Sept 1949. Research Scientist. m. Pui San Chow, 27 Oct 1977, 1 s, 2 d. Education: BSc, hons, BSc, Univ of Tasmania; PhD, Flinders Univ, S Aust. Appointments: Rsch Sci, CSIRO Div of Plant Ind, Canberra, 1977-78; Rsch Asst, Imperial Coll, London, 1979-81; Snr Sci Offr, Glasshouse Crops Rsch Inst; Snr Rsch Sci, 1985-89, Prin Rsch Sci, 1989-95, Snr Prin Rsch Sci, 1995-96, CSIRO Div of Plant Ind; Snr Fell, Rsch Sch of Biol Scis, Austl Natl Univ, 1996-. Publications: 106 sci publns on photosynthesis rsch in profl jrnls, 1974-. Memberships: Austl Soc of Plant Physiol; Austl Soc for Biophys; Japanese Soc of Plant Physiol; Scandinavian Soc for Plant Physiol; Intl Soc of

Photosynthesis. Hobby: Table Tennis. Address: Research School of Biological Sciences, Australian National University; GPO Box 475, Canberra, ACT 2601, Australia.

CHOW Yuk Tak, b. 9 Jan 1960, Hong Kong. Academic. m. Linda Hon, 12 Nov 1993. Education: BSc, Heriot Watt Univ, Edinburgh, Scotland, 1982; MSc, Univ of St Andrews, Scotland, 1983; PhD, Heriot Watt Univ, Scotland, 1988. Appointments: Rsch Assoc, Dept of Phys, Heriot Watt Univ, 1986-88; Rsch Fell, Optoelectronics Rsch Cntr, Univ of Southampton, 1989-91; Asst Prof, Dept of Elec Engrng, Cty Univ of Hong Kong, 1992-. Creative Works: 63 Publs. Memberships: Inst of Phys; Optical Soc of Am; Amn Inst of Phys; Hong Kong Instn of Engrs; Inst of Elecl Engrs; Inst of Elecl and Electron Engrs. Hobbies: Golf; Mode Helicopter; Reading; Chinese Calligraphy; Tai ChiChuan. Address: City University of Hong Kong, Dept of Electronie Engineering, Tat Chee Avenue, Kowloon, Hong Kong.

CHOWDHURY Abdul Mannan, b. 30 Dec 1950, Bangladesh. Teacher. m. 12 Apr 1976, 2 s, 1 d. Education: BA, hons; MA; MEcon; PhD. Appointments: Lectr, Asst Prof, Assoc Prof, Prof, Econs, Chittagong Univ. Publications: 8 text books, 1 rsch book, over 100 articles in profl jrnls. Honours: IRC Awd, 1973-74; DPI Awd, 1966-74; Vice Chan Awd, 1974; Rockefeller Awd, 1976-78; UMTA Awd, 1981-82; ICSSR Awd, 1991-92; ALIF Awd, 1996. Memberships include: BEO; IIIPE; AMGM; HBMD; HBPC; ALIF; SPP. Hobbies: Sightseeing; Singing; Writing. Address: Department of Economics, Chittagong University, Chittagong, Bangladesh.

CHOWDHURY Anis, b. 10 Jan 1954, Chittagong, Bangladesh. University Teacher. m. Joyce, 31 Aug 1979, 2 s, 2 d. Education: BSc, hons; MSc; MA; PhD. Appointments: Tchng Asst, Univ of Manitoba; Lectr, Univ Manitoba, Univ Singapore, Univ New England; Snr Lectr, Univ New England, Univ Western Sydney-Macarthur; Assoc Prof, Univ Western Sydney-Macarthur. Publications: The New Industrialization Ecomics of Asia, 1993; Asia-Pacific Economy - A Survey, 1997. Hoours: Univ Schlsp, 1976-78; Grad Fellshp, Univ of Manitoba, 1979-83. Memberships: Econ Soc of Aust. Hobbies: Reading; Cricket. Address: Department of Economics & Finance, University of Western Sydney-Macarthur, PO Box 555, Campbelltown, NSW 2560, Australia.

CHOWDHURY Bakul C, b. 8 Oct 1942, Comilla, Bangladesh. Teacher and Researcher. m. Sankari, 11 May 1976, 1 s. Education: MSc, Anthropology; MA, Linguistics; PhD, Ethnolinguistics. Appointments: Jnr Rsch Fell, CSIR; Field Investigator, ORG; Proj Asst of CIII; rsch Asst of ERLC; Lectr, CIIL Min of HRD Govt of India. Publications: An Introduction to Modern Linguistics; Foundation Course in Bengali; Bengali State School Reader; An Advanced Reader in Bengali. Hobby: Study of human societies and cultures. Address: Eastern Regional Language Centre, Laxmisagar, Bhubaneswar, 751006, India.

CHOWDHURY Mizanur Rahman, b. 19 Oct 1928 Chandpur. Politician. m. 1955. Education: Feni Coll. Appointments: Hdmaster Bamoni High Sch, 1952; Tchr Chandpur Nuria High Sch, 1956; Vice-Chmn Chandpur Municipality, 1959; Organising Sec East Pakistan Wing Awami League, 1966; Acting Gen-Sec, 1966, 1967; Organized Awami League election campaign, 1970; Jnt Convenor, 1976; Min of Info and Brdcstng, 1972-73; Min of Relief and Rehabilitation, 1973; Snr Vice-Chmn Jatiya Dal Party, 1984; Gen-Sec, 1985-86; Min of Posts and Telecomms, 1985-88; PM of Bangladesh, 1986-88. Memberships: Elected mbr Natl Ass of Pakistan, 1962, 1965, 1970. Hobbies: Reading. Address: c/o Jatiya Dal, Dhaka, Bangladesh.

CHOWDHURY Sougata Roy, b. 28 Dec 1973. Musician. Education: Deg, Indian Classical Music, 1996; Master Deg, Ancient Indian Hist Culture & Archaeol, 1997. Appointments: Performs in Calcutta, 1994, 1995, Bangaldesh, 1996. Creative Works: Composed Light Classical Orch for the Org MEDHA, 1997. Honour: Dover Lane Music Conf Awd, 1995. Membership: Ali Akbar Coll of Music. Hobbies: Music; Travel. Address: 12 Deshapriya Park Road, Calcutta 700026, West Bengal, India.

CHRISTENSEN Halvor Niels, b. 24 Oct 1915, Cozad, NE, USA. Biochemical Educator; Professor. m. Mary Matthews, 28 Aug 1939, 2 s, 1 d. Education: BS, Univ of NE, 1931; MSc, Purdue Univ, Lafayette, IN, 1937; PhD, Harvard Univ, Cambridge, MA, 1940. Appointments: Asst Chem, Purdue, 1935-37; Assoc Chem, Harvard, 1939-40; Biochemist Lederle Labs, 1940-42; Inst Biochem, Harvard Medl Sch, 1942-47; Prof, 1947-49; Dir, Rsch, Children's Hosp, Boston, 1947-49; Univ MI Medl Sch, 1955, Hd, Dept, 1955-70. Publications: 274 articles. Honours: Guggenheim Fell, Carlsberg Laby, Copenhagen, 1952; Nobel Guest Prof, Uppsala, Sweden, 1968-69; Amn Acady Arts and Scis; Amn Inst Nutrition. Memberships: Unitarian Serv Ctee, Medl Mission to Germany, 1950; Soc Biol Chems; Biophys Soc. Hobbies: Stamp collector; Skiing; Elementary linguistics. Address: Apt 204, 7450 Olivetas La Jolla, CA 92037, USA.

CHRISTIAN John Hinton Bassett, b. 26 Mar 1925, Gosford, Aust. Microbiologist. m. Helen Bertram, 28 Feb 1958, 2 s, 3 d. Education: BSc Hons Class I, Agric, 1951; PhD, Cambridge Univ, Eng, 1958. Appointments: Rsch Scientist, 1951-79, Chf, 1979-86, Div Food Rsch, 1979-86, Rsch Fell, Div Food Sci and Technol, 1990-, C'wlth Sci and Indl Rsch Org. Publications: Sci pprs on food microbio; Co-auth, Water Activity and Food, 1978. Honours: Awd of Merit, Austl Inst Food Sci and Technol, 1984; AO, 1987; Hon Mbr, Soc Applied Bacteriology, UK, 1987; Hon Mbr, Austl Soc Microbio, 1988. Memberships: Fndn Fell, Austl Acady Technological Scis and Engrng; Fell, Austl Inst Food Sci and Technol. Listed in: Who's Who in Australia. Hobbies: Photography; Gardening; Food standards; Food hygiene. Address: Food Science Australia, PO Box 52, North Ryde, NSW 2113, Australia.

CHRISTIANSEN Wilbur Norman (Chris), b. 9 Aug 1913. Radio Astronomer. m. Elsie Mary Hill, 5 Jan 1938, 3 s, 1 dec. Education: DSc (Melb), 1953; Hon degrees: DScEng, Sydney, DEng, Melbourne, DSc, W Sydney. Appointments: Almagamated Wireless, 1937-48; CSIRO, 1948-60; Univ of Leiden, 1960-61; Prof of Elec Engrng, Univ of Sydney, 1961-78; Visng Fell, Austl Natl Univ, 1979-84; Shorter appointments: Comm X-Ray and Radium Lab, 1935-37; Inst d'Astrophysique, 1954-55, Paris; Peking Astron Obs, 1966-67; Ootacamund, India, UNESCO Cnslt, 1978; Paris Observatory, 1979. Publications: Radiotelescopes (with Högbom, 1969, 1985, 1987; Many pprs in astron, phys and engrng jrnls. Honours: Fell, Austl Acady of Sci, 1959; P N Russel Medal, Inst of Engrs, 1970; Adion Medal, France, 1976; Hon Fellowship, Inst of Engrs, 1981; For Mbr, Chinese Acady of Scis, 1996. Memberships: InterUnion of Radio Sci, Pres, 1978-81; Life Hon Pres, 1984; Intl Astron Union, VP, 1979-81; Astron Soc Aust, Pres, 1975-79; Austl Acady of Sci For Sec, 1981-85. Hobbies: Music; Reading; Drawing. Address: 42, The Grange, 67 MacGregor Street, Deakin, ACT, Australia.

CHRISTOFFEL David Alec, b. 7 June 1929. Geophysicist. m. Marie Geraldine, 14 Dec 1957, 2 s, 1 d. Education: BSc, NZ, 1949; MSc, Phys, Canty Univ Coll, 1952; PhD, Univ of Nottingham, Phys, 1957. Appointments: NZ Def Sci Corps (Commn in RNZ Navy), 1952-59; Rsch Fell, Geophys, Univ of Brit Columbia, 1959-62; Snr Lectr, Phys, Vic Univ, Wellington, 1962-66; Assoc Prof, Phys & Geophys, VUW, 1966-93. Publications: 86 refereed papers in sci jrnls, topics: Plate Tectonics; Volcanology; Geomagnetism; Hydrology; Seismology; Physics. Honours: NZ Geophys Prize; Elected Fell, Royal Soc of NZ, 1984. Memberships: Geophys Soc Am, 1962-; Fndng VP, NZ Geophys, 1981; Geol and Geophys Royal Soc of NZ; Pres, mbr Rotary Intl, 1996; Pres Elect, Otaki Rotary Club, 2000-2001; Otaki Citizens' Advice Bur Cttee. Listed in: Who's Who in New Zealand. Hobbies: Small farming; Skiing; Tramping; Lawn Bowls. Address: 62, Old Coach Road North, Otaki, New Zealand.

CHU Eugene Poh Hwye, b. 15 Apr 1931. Surgeon. m. Lily Lee Soei Boan, 5 Jan 1958, 1 s, 2 d. Education: MBBS (Melbourne); FRCS (Edinburgh); FRCS (Eng); FACS; FHKAM(Surg). Appointments: Surg Offr in Charge; Surg Specialist, Kwong Wah Hosp, 1962-67; Hon Lectr, Surg, Hong Kong Univ, 1964-1966; Surg Cnslt, Bapt Hosp, 1967-. Memberships: Life Mbr, Hong Kong Medl Assn; Hon Sec, Hong Kong Chinese Medl Assn, 1966; Hong Kong Golf Club; Hong Kong Jockey Club. Hobbies: Golf; Numismatics. Address: Rm 316 Tung Ying Bldg, 100 Nathan Rd, Kowloon, Hong Kong.

CHU Hsun-Chih, b. 6 Sept 1930, Wuxi City, Jiangsu Prov, China. Professor of Chemistry. m. Sai-Yan Feng, 23 Aug 1958, 2 s. 1 d. Education: BS, E China Normal Univ, 1952; MSc, Fujian Normal Univ, 1957. Appointments: Assoc prof, 1978, Chmn, Chem Dept, 1980-85; Vice-Chmn, Coll Acad Degree Cttee, 1980-85, Yangzhou Univ; Prof of Chem, 1986, Dir of Univ Experimental Cntr, 1989-92, Shanghai Normal Univ. Publications: Main wrk in electro and electroanalytical field, especially for Cadmium Sulfate Standard Cell Study; 54 acad pprs. Honours: Cert of Merit for High Precision Stand Cell Study on 1st Whole Nation Acad Conf, Beijing, 1978. Memberships: Cnclr, Chinese Chem Soc, Yangzhou Cty branch, 1976-85; Chinese Chem Engrng Soc; Chmn, Chinese Corrosive & Corrosion Protective Soc, Yangzhou branch, 1979-85; Cnclr, Chinese Metrology Soc, Jiangsu prov Branch, 1980-86. Address: Department of Chemistry, Shanghai Normal Univ, 100 Guilin Road, Shanghai 200234, China.

CHU Huaizhi, b. 25 Dec 1933, China. Professor of Law. m. Shu Yan Zhang, 3 May 1963, 1 s, 1 d. Education: LLB. Appointments: Prof of Law, Peking Univ; Cnslt, Suprme Procuratorate of China. Publications: American Criminal Law, 1st ed, 1987, 2nd ed, 1996; Selected Works of Chu Huaizhi, 1997. Memberships: Revision Grp of Pena; Law of Standing Cttee of Natl People's Congress of China, 1989-97. Hobbies: Reading novels; Watching movies; Tours; Fishing. Address: Law Department, Peking University, Beijing 100871, China.

CHU Kao-Cheng, Politician. Appointments: Ldr New Party. Memberships: Mbr for Kao-hsiung Legis Cncl, 1995-. Address: New Party, 6th Floor, 7 Ching Tao East Road, Taipei, Taiwan.

CHU Meng-chow, b. 14 Aug 1933, China. Professor; Department Chairman. m. Huichu Chow, 20 Dec 1961, 1 s, 1 d. Education: Grad, Tianjin Univ, 1955. Appointments: Asst Prof, 1955-59, Lectr, 1962, Assoc Prof, 1981, Prof, Chmn, Mechl Engrng Dept, 1988-, Tianjin Univ; Assoc Rschr, Inst Mach Tool and Mfng Technol, Univ Berlin, Germany, 1981-82; Visng Prof, MI Univ, USA, Feb-June 1995. Publications include: Machine Tool Design; Machinery Noise Control; Num conf papers. Honours: Outstndng Tchr Awd, 1987; Sci and Tecn Adv Awd, Natl Educ Cttee, 1991. Memberships: Snr Mbr, Chinese Prodn Engrng Assn; Steering Cttee, Mfng Specialities Univs China; Chinese Acoustic Acad Assn. Hobbies: Music; Photography. Address: Department of Mechanical Engineering, Tianjin University, Tianjin 300072, China.

CHU Zhong-Lu, b. 2 Mar 1927, China. Professor of Biochemistry. m. Dong-Fang Zhang, 27 June 1952, 2 s, 1 d. Education: Dip, Suzhou Snr Mid Sch, 1945; Dip, Bachelor's deg, Jiangsu Medl Coll, 1952. Appointments: Rsch areas: Haematology, 1950-51, Vitaminology, Nutriology, 1952-61, Blood Coagulation, Atherosclerosis, 1962-76, Hereditary Diseases, 1977-79, Blood Platelets, chfly Antiplatelet Drugs, 1980-; Currently Prof, Biochem, 2nd Mil Medl Univ, Shanghai; Vice-Chf Engr, Shanghai Long March-Trace Medl Sci Co Ltd. Publications include: Books: Hepatic Surgery, 1982; Physiological Chemistry, 1991; Extensive published rsch wrk. Honours include: Merit, Estab of 2 Rapid Methods for Blood Smear Staining in Large Amount of Samples, Chinese People's Liberation Army, 1951; Disting Tchr, 2nd Mil Medl Univ, 1962, 1976, 1984; Chinese People's Liberation Army Sci and Technol Progress Awds: Discoveries of Antiplatelet Effects of Pilocarpine and Al3+, 1988, Discovery of

Antiplatelet Effect of Berberine, 1990, Rsch Achievement of Mechanism of Antiplatelet Effect of Berberine, 1993, Exploration and Basic Rsch on New Antiplatelet Drugs, 1995; Chinese People's Liberation Army Air Force, Sci and Technol Progress Awd, Rsch Achievement of Mechanism of Antiplatelet Effect of Chuan-xiong Injection, 1997. Memberships: Chinese Medl Soc; Chinese Biochem Soc; Intl Biochem Soc; Shanghai Informational Soc Sci and Technol. Listed in: Many including: Men of Achievement; Five Thousand Personalities of the World; Famous Doctors in the Mainland of China; Who's Who of China. Address: Department of Biochemistry, Second Military Medical University, 800 Xiang Yin Road, Shanghai 200433, China.

CHUA Nam Hai, b. 8 Apr 1944, Singapore. Professor. m. Pearl, 2 d. Education: AM, 1967, PhD, 1969, Harvard Univ; BSc, Univ Singapore, 1995. Appointments: Asst Prof, 1973-77, Assoc Prof, 1977-81, Prof, 1981-, Rockefeller Univ. Publications: Over 270 in profl sci jrnls. Honours: Fell, Academia Sinica, Taiwan, 1988, Roy Soc, UK, 1998. Hobbies: Skiing; Squash; Chinese Antique Collecting. Address: Laboratory of Plant Molecular Biology, Rockefeller University, 1230 York Avenue, NY 10021, USA.

CHUA Patrick Soon keong, b. 25 Nov 1954, Singapore. m. Susan geok-Eng Lee, 7 July 1979, 2 s, 1 d. M. Susan Geok-Eng Lee, 7 July 1979, 2 s, 1 d. Education: BEng (Hons), Univ of Liverpool, UK; PhD, Univ of Liverpool. Appointments: Pt-time tchng Asst, Univ of Liverpool, 1978-82; Asst Tech Mngr, Schmiidtmann Pte Ltd, Singapore, 1983-84; Lead Rsch and Dev Engr, 1984-85, Rsch and Dev Mngr, 1985-86, Natl Semiconductor Pte Ltd; Lectr, 1986-88, Snr Lectr, 1989-98; Assoc Prof, 1999-, Nanying Technol Univ, Singapore. Honours: Brit Gas Corp Schlshp, to pursue PhD rsch, 1979-82; Memberships: CEng; MIMechE; MIES; SrMSME; MASME; MI Mngmt. Hobbies: Jogging; Swimming. Address: 42 Fulton Avenue, Singapore 579005.

CHUA Soo-Jin, b. 7 Apr 1998, Johore, Malaysia. Professor. m. Foong Chin, Apr 1978, 1 s, 2 d. Education: BEng (1st Class Hons), Electr Engin, University of Singapore; PhD, Electr Engin, Univ of Wales, UK. Appointments: Snr Offr, Dev Bank of Singapore, 1974; Rsch Engr, Stand Telecomms Labs, Harlow, UK, 1978; Prof, Dept of Electr Engin, NUS, 1997. Publications: Mathematical Physics (co-auth w A K Ghatak), 1996. Memberships: Sr MIEEE; MIEE; MInstP. Hobbies: Reading; Badminton. Address: Department of Electrical Engineering, National University of Singapore, Kent Ridge, Singapore 119260.

CHUA Su Yin, b. 18 Sept 1954, Muar, Johore, Malaysia. Lawyer. Education: LLB, Hons, Univ of Malaysia; LLM, Harv Univ. Appointment: Notary Public. Publications: Commercial Laws of Malaysia; Franchising in Malaysia. Memberships: Intl Bar Assn; Intl Bus Law Consortium and Digest of Coml Laws of the World. Hobbies: Swimming; Antique Collecting. Listed in: Who's Who in the World. Address: 18 Jalan Parit Haji Baki, 84000 Muar, Johore, Malaysia.

CHUA Wai Fong, b. 1 Mar 1955. Professor of Accounting. m. E Chua, 14 Aug 1979, 2 d. Education: BA w Hons, 1st Class; PhD. Appointments: Prof of Acctng: Sheffield Univ, 1979-82; Sydney Univ, 1983-85; Univ of NSW, 1985-. Memberships: AAA; ICAA; ASCPA; AAANZ Exec, 1994-. Hobbies: Reading; Films. Address: School of Accounting, University of New South Wales, Sydney, NSW 2052, Australia.

CHUAN Leekpai, b. 28 July 1938, Muang District, Trang Prov, Thailand. Politician. Education: Cert in painting & Sculpture, Silpakorn Pre-Univ; LLB, Thammsat Univ, 1962; Barrister at Law, Thai Bar Assn. Appointments: Lawyer; Mbr, House of Reprs fro Trang Prov, 1969, 1975, 1976, 1979, 1983, 1986, 1988, Mar 1992, Sept 1992, 1995, 1996; Dpty Min of Justice, 1975; Min to Prime Min's Off, 1976; Min of Justice, 1980; Min of Com, 1980-81; Min of Agric & Coops, 1981-83; Min of Educ, 1983-86; Speaker of the House of Reprs, 1986-88; Min of Pub Hlth, 1988-89; Dpty Prime Min, 1990; Min of Agric and Coops, 1990; Prime Min, 1992-95; Ldr of Dem Party; Mbr, House of Reprs for Trang Prov; VP, Prince of Songkhla Univ Cncl; Mbr, Kasetsart, Srinakharinwirot and Thammasat Univ Cncls; Visng Lectr, Forensic Med Dept; Fac of Med, Chulalongkorn Univ. Honours: Kt Grand Cross (1st Class), Most Noble Order of Crown of Thailand, 1979; Kt Grand Cross (1st Class), Most Exalted Order of White Elephant, 1980; Kt, Grand Cordon of Most Noble Order of Crown of Thailand, 1981; Kt Grand Cordon (Spec Class) Most Exalted Order of White Elephant, 1982; Order of Sukatuna Spec Class Raja, Philippines, 1993; Grand Companion (3rd Class higher grade), Most Illustrious Order of Chula Chom Klao, 1996. Address: Office of the Prime Minister, Government House, Bangkok 10300, Thailand.

CHUANG Thomas Tsoi-Hung, b. 22 Mar 1944, China. (Canadian citizen). Managing Director. m. Katija F Kitchell, 19 Dec 1969, 1 s, 1 d. Education: Dip Ing, Fach Hochschule Reutlingen, W Germany, 1969. Appointments: Sales Engr, Tri-Union Indl Supplies, 1969; Mngr, Exquisite Knitwear Ltd, 1971-. Honour: Paul Harris Fell'ship, Rotary Intl. Memberships: TTV Textilia, W Germany; Pres, Rotary Club Peninsula, Hong Kong, 1988-89. Address: c/o K & E Co Ltd, Room 1507, Tower A, Silvercord, 30 Canton Road, Tsimshatsui, Kowloon, Hong Kong.

CHUI Heng Tak, b. 16 Oct 1950, Singapore. Consultant. m. P C Wong, 6 Apr 1980, 1 s. Education: MSc. Appointment: Dir. Memberships: Inst of Acoustics, UK; MIOE; Inst of Engrs, Singapore; Cncl, Environ Engrs of Singapore; MASME. Hobbies: Stamp Collecting; Reading. Address: 166 Tamarind Road, Singapore 806120, Singapore.

CHUN Celia Ann Wun Kong, b. 29 July 1963, Honlulu, HI, USA. Dancer; Teacher. m. Matthew J Wright, 24 Feb 1993, 1 d. Education: BFA, Dance, Univ of Hawaii, USA. Honours: Hawaii State Dance Cncl, contbn to arts in Hawaii, 1996; Individual Artist Performing Fellowship, State Fndn on Culture & Arts, 1999. Address: 3041 Manoa Road, Honolulu, HI 96822, USA.

CHUN Hon Wai, b. 1 Oct 1959, Hong Kong. Associate Professor. m. Yvonne Ng, 18 Oct 1993, 1 s, 2 d. Education: BA, IL Inst of Technol, 1981; MA, Univ of IL, 1983; PhD, 1987. Appointments: Snr Sci, Ascent Technol, 1993-94; Assoc Prof, City Univ og Hong Kong, 1994-. Honours: EDN Asia Innovator Awd, 1998. Memberships: AAAI; IEEE; IEE; ACNI. Address: P O B 30911, Causeway Bay, Hong Kong.

CHUNG Hae Lin, b. 19 May 1939, Korea. President; Chief Executive Officer. m. 3 s. Education: BA, Econs, Kyung Hee Univ. Appointments: Pres, CEO, Sung Chang Enterprise Co Ltd. Honour: Hon Deg, Pusan Natl Univ. Address: PO Box 27, Pusan, Korea.

CHUNG Haechang, b. 4 Nov 1939, Tae-Gu, Kyungbur Prov, India. Attorney-at-Law. m. Chang Inhee, 3 s. Education: LLB, Coll of Law, Seoul Natl Univ, 1967; MCL, Sch of Law, South Meth Univ. Appointments: Prosecutor, Taegu Dist Prosecutors' Off (DPO), 1962; Prosecutor, Daejun DPO, 1966; Prosecutor, Seoul DPO, 1968; Prosecutor, Youngdeungpo Branch Off, Seoul DPO, 1970; Prosecutor, Prosecution Div, Min of Jus, 1971; Dir, Prosecution Div, Min of Jus, 1973; Snr Prosecutor, Seoul DPO, 1976; Dpty Chf Prosecutor, Pusan DPO, 1979, Seoul DPO, 1980; Dir, Prosecution Bur, Min of Jus, 1981; Chf Prosecutor, Seoul DPO, 1981; Dpty Min of Jus, 1982; Dir, Inst of Legal Rsch & Trng, 1985; Dpty Prosecutor Gen, Supreme Prosecutors' off, 1986; Min of Jus, 1987; Dir, Korean Inst of Criminology, 1989; Chf of Staffs, Off of the Pres of the Repub of Korea, 1990; Self-employed Atty at Law, Chmn, Korean UNAFEI Alumni Assn, 1993; Chmn, Korea Crime Prevention Fndn, 1994-. Honours: Red Stripes Order of Serv, 1973; Yellow Stripes Order of Serv, 1987; Blue Stripes Order of Serv, 1990. Address: 352 17 Sokyo dong, Mapogu, Seoul 121-210, Korea.

CHUNG Hung-Yuan, b. 10 Aug 1952, Ping-Tung, Taiwan, China. Professor of NCU Electrical Engineering. m. M Y Liu, 28 Feb 1982, 2 s, 1 d. Education: PhD, Elec Engrng, NCKU, Tainan, Taiwan, China. Memberships: IEEE; Life Mbr, CIE. Hobbies: Jogging; Swimming. Address: No 52, Chung-Da, Hsing Tsung, Chung Li, 320, Taiwan, China.

CHUNG Jae Ho, b. 27 June 1960, Pusan, Korea. University Professor. m. 9 July 1988. Ma, Brown Univ, 1985; PhD, Univ of MI, 1993. Appointments: Div of Socl Sci, Hong Kong Univ of Sci & Technol, 1993-96; Dept of Intl Rels, Seoul Natl Univ, 1996-. Publications: Provinicial Strategies of Economic Reform in Post-Mao China, 1998; Cities in China, 1999; Interpreting Implementation. Honours: Hon Rsch Fell, USC, Chinese Univ of Hong Kong; Fndn Fell, Cntr for Rsch on Provcl China, Sydney. Hobby: Movies. Address: Department of International Relations, Seoul National University, Seoul, 151-742, Korea.

CHUNG Ling, b. 26 Apr 1945, Chungking, China. Professor. Education: PhD, Univ WI, 1972; Postdoct, Inst of Admin Adv for Acad Women, Univ MI, 1974. Appointments: Prof, Dir, Grad Inst of Fgn Lang & Lit, 1991-94, Prof, Chairperson, Dept of Fgn Lang & Lit, 1994-97, Prof, Dean, Coll of Liberal Arts, 1997-. Publications: Bare Foot on the Meadow, 1970; Orchid Boat: Women Poets of China, 1972; Li Ch'ing-chao, Complete Poems, 1979; Wheel of Life, 1983; Beautiful Mistake, 1983; Collection of Literary Criticism, 1984; Karma of Jade: Antique Jade, 1993; American Poetry and Chinese Dream: Chinese Cultural Modes in Modern American Verse, 1996. Honours: Natl Lit & Arts Awd, Admin Yuan, 1991; Category A Awd & Ex Awd, Natl Sci Cncl, 1991; Outstndng Rsch Awd, Sun Yat-Sen Univ, 1991; NSC Rsch Project, 1992, 1993, 1994; NSc's Category A Awd, 1994, 1995, 1996, 1997; Ex Rsch Awd, Sun Yat-Sen Univ, 1994. Memberships: Cttee, Natl Sun Yat-Sen Univ; Search Cttee, Tunghai Univ; Dir of Engl & Am Lit Assn; Pres, Tunghai Alumna, Dist of Kaohsiung & Pingtung. Hobby: Antiques. Address: 8F Pu-yuan 302, Cheng-Te Road, Tzoying District, Kaohsiung City, Taiwan.

CHUNG Won Shik, Politician. Appointments: Former Minister of Education; PM of South Korea, 1991-92. Memberships: Mbr Dem Liberal Party - DLP. Address: c/o Office of the Prime Minister, 77 Sejong-no, Chongno-ku, Seoul, Republic of Korea.

CHURCHMAN David, b. 20 July 1938, USA. Professor. Education: BA, MA, Univ of MI, 1960, 1964; Doct, UCLA, 1972. Publications: Negotiation: Process, Tactics, Theory, 1993, 1995; Num profl pprs. Honour: Malone Fellshp, Saudi Arabia, 1993. Memberships: Repub Party (Cntrl Cttee); Wednesday Morning Club; Rotary Intl; Intl Assn Conflict Mngmt; Aquaria & Zool Assn; Natl Assn of Schls. Hobbies: Rifle marksmanship; Chess; Cooking; Travel; Photography. Address: BSGP, California State University, Dominguez Hills, CA 90747, USA.

CHYNGYSHEV Tursunbek, b. 15 Oct 1942 Naryn Dist. Politician; Economist. m. Ludmila V Chyngysheva, 1968, 1 s, 1 d. Education: Kyrgyz Univ Acady of Socl Scis. Appointments: Functionary of CP of Kyrgyzstan; Hd Div of Econs Cntr Cttee of CP of Kirgizia; Mayor of Osh; Participated in dem movement since late 1980s; State Sec Kyrgyz SSR, 1991-92; PM of Kyrgyzstan, 1992-93; Gen Mngr HENFEN Ltd; VP Kyrgyz Natl Oil Co. Memberships: Mbr USSR Cttee on Operative Mngmt of Natl Econ, Aug-Dec 1991; Mbr Parl Kyrgyz Repub. Address: 194 Moskovskaya Str, Bishkek 72010, Kyrgyzstan.

CHYNOWETH Raymond, b. 18 Dec 1930. Specialist Psychiatrist. m. Daphne June Drake Kinch, 22 Feb 1956, 1 s, 1 d. Education: MB BS, London; DPM; FRCP; FRANZCP; FRC PSYCH. Appointments: House Surg, St George's Hosp, London; House Physn, Mayday Hosp, Croydon; Surg Lt, RN; Res Med Off, St George's Hosp; Med Registrar, Epsom Dist Hosp; Med Registrar,

Addenbrooke's Hosp, Cambridge; Psych Registrar, Graylingwell Hosp, Chichester; Snr Lectr, Psych, Qld Univ, Aust; Rdr in Psych, Univ of Adelaide, South Aust; Snr Cnslt Psych, Glenside Hosp, Adelaide; Assoc Prof Psych, Flinders Univ, Adelaide; Cnslt in Psychogeriatrics, WHO, Indonesia, 1993, Vietnam, 1995, NT Australia, 1997-. Memberships: Roy Soc Med; Aust Soc of Psych Rsch; Austl Assn of Geriatric Med; Austl Med Assn; Brit Med Assn; Austl Soc Geriatric Med. Hobbies: Music; Travel; Reading; Sport. Address: 15 Trevorten Avenue, Glenunga, SA 5064, Australia.

CIANI Peter, b. 16 Feb 1940, Messina, Italy. Recording Artist. m. Marta, 21 Aug 1971, 2 s. Education: Dip, Academia Della Canzone, Rome. Appointments: Films in Cinecitta Rome; Concerts, Austl and Italy; Radio and TV. Publications: 16 albums in Aust, 5 in Italy, inclng In My Own Way; In Love Again; Latin Fever; Canto All'Italiana. CDs: Australia This Beautiful Country, 1992; Caruso Napoli, 1994; Marilena, 1996, Love Is All, 1997; Italian Favourites, 3 vols, 1998. Compositions include: This Beautiful Country, 1992; Banbina Mia, 1994, In St Peter's Square, 1998; Beato Padre Pio, 1999. Honours: Gold Record from Radio 2KY, Sydney, 1975; Gold Record from EMI Aust, 1980; Knight of Grace, Sov Order of St J of J, Kts of Malta, 1994. Memberships: Austl Perf Rights Assn; Actors Equity of Aust. Hobbies: Reading; Tennis; Gardening; Music. Address: PO Box L 86, South Maroubra, NSW 2035, Australia.

CILENTO Diane, b. 1934, Aust. Actress. m. (1) diss, 1 d, (2) diss, 1 s. Education: Amn Acady Dramatic Art, NY; Roy Acady Dramatic Art, London. Career: Var state and film roles, 1953-; Films incl The Admirable Crichton, Rattle of a Simple Man, The Agony and the Ecstasy, Zero Population Growth, The Wicker Man, Hombre, Tom Jones; Plays, London and NYC incl Tiger at the Gates, Arms and the Man, Castle in Sweden, Altona, Heartbreak House, Lysistrata, Orpheus Descending, Naked (also translated Pirandello's play), Miss Julie, The Father, The Idiot; Plays, Aust, The Cherry Orchard; Starred, The Taming of the Shrew, Aust; Directed Turning, 1976, The Human Race, 1978; Built Karnak Playhouse, th in the Rainforest, 1992; Adapted Thea Astley's It's Raining in Mango, 1995; Innovated Creation, laser drama amalgamating voice, sound effects, animated laser image and effects, 1995. Publications: The Manipulator, 1968; The Hybrid, 1970. Address: Karnak, PO Box 167, Mossman, Qld 4873, Australia.

CILLER Tansu, b. 1945 Istanbul. Politician. m. 2 children. Education: Robert Coll Bogazici Univ; Univ of CT; Yale Univ. Appointments: Assoc Prof, 1978; Prof 1983; Served on acad Bds of var univs mainly in Dep of Econs Bogazici Univ; Joined True Path Party - DYP - 1990; Ldr, 1993-; Mbr of Parl, 1991; Min of State for the Econ, 1991; PM, 1993-96; Dep PM and Min of For Affairs, 1996-97. Publications: Nine publs on econs. Address: c/o True Path Party, Selanik Cod 40, Kizilay, Ankara, Turkey.

CLANCY Edward Bede (His Eminence the Cardinal Archbishop of Sydney), b. 13 Dec 1923. Roman Catholic Archbishop; Cardinal. Education: Marist Bros Coll, Parramatta; St Patrick's Coll, Manly; LSS, Biblical Inst, Rome; DD, Propaganda Fide Univ, Rome. Appointments: Ordained to Priesthood, 1949; Parish Min, Belmore, NSW, 1950-51; Parish Min, Liverpool, NSW, 1955; Sem Staff, Springwood, NSW, 1958; Sem Staff, Manly, NSW, 1966-73; Ordained Bish, Aux to His Eminence Sir James Cardinal Freeman, 1974; Appointed Archbish Canberra/Goulburn, 1979; Archbish Sydney, NSW, 1983-; Proclaimed Cardinal Priest Holy Roman Ch, title of S Maria in Vallicella; Elevated to Sacred Coll Cardinals by His Holiness Pope John Paul II, 1988; Fndn Chan, Austl Cath Univ, 1992-. Publication: The Bible: The Church's Book, 1974. Honours: AO, 1984; AC, 1992. Listed in: Who's Who in Australia. Hobbies: St Mary's Cathedral, St Mary's Road, Sydney, NSW 2000, Australia.

CLARK Bryan James, b. 11 Dec 1951, Victoria, Australia. Sports Bookmaker. Appointments include:

Fndr, Oz Sportsbetting. Hobbies: Sports; Fishing; Nightlife; Parties. Address: PO Box 43030, Casuarina, NT 0811.

CLARK Colin James, b. 3 Jan 1953. Professor; Deputy Dean. m. 1 s. Education: BBus, Acct FIT; DipEd, Vic State Coll; MBA, Monash; FCPA; ACA. Appointments: FIT Lectr, 1984-86; WI Snr Lectr, 1987-89; Dean, Fac Bus, 1989-91; Dpty Dean, Fac Bus, Vic Univ of Technol. Publications: Reforming the Public Sector (co-editor), 1999; Articles and conference pprs on pub sector acctng. Memberships: Victorian Div Cncl Austl Soc of CPAs; Chair, Pub Sector Accts Cttee, Austl Soc CPA'S, Vic, 1994-96; Chair, Egg Ind Licensing Cttee and Mbr Egg Prices Review Panel, 1989-93; Mayor, Cty of Essendon, 1981-82. Listed in: Who's Who in Australia. Address: Faculty of Business, Victoria University of Technology, PO Box 14428, Melbourne City Mail Centre, Vic 8001, Australia.

CLARK David Vickers, b. 24 Apr 1950, Harrogate, Yorks, UK. Graphic Designer. m. Robin, 1994, 3 children. Education: BA (Hons), UK; Dip of Bus (Mktng), NZ. Appointments: Hd, large NZ Graphic Des Cnsltncy Dave Clark Des; Des, many NZ large-scale projs. Publications: All Black Logo, 1986; Air New Zealand (var brands) NZ Dairy Bd, 1998. Honours: Fell, Roy Soc of Arts (UK); Pres, NZ Des Inst. Membership: Fell, Roy Soc of Arts, London. Hobbies: Judo; Rugby; Sporting administration; Design education. Address: 11 Salisbury Street, Herne Bay, Auckland, New Zealand.

CLARK Diddo, b. 20 Jan 1950, Oakland, CA, USA. Attorney; Mediator. Education: BA, Univ CA, San Diego, 1973; JD, Georgetown Univ, 1976. Appointments: Crt Appointed Mediator, 1976-; Superior Crt Judge Pro Tem, 1992-; Specl Master, 1996-. Publications: Change in the Criminal Justice System in Contra Costa Co, CA, 1972. Honour: Moot Crt Natl Champion, 1975. Memberships: Alameda Co Bar Assn; Del, CA State Bar Conf of Delegs, 1998, 1999. Hobby: Art. Address: 6 Blackthorn Road, Lafayette, CA 94549-3307, USA.

CLARK Grame Milbourne, b. 16 Aug 1935, Camden, NSW, Aust. Otolaryngologist. m. Margaret, 1 s, 4 d. MB BS (Hons) Univ of Sydney, 1957; FRCS, Edinburgh (FRCS), Otolaryngology, 1962; Fell, Roy Australasian Coll of Surgs (FRACS), 1966; MS (Master of Surgery), 1968, PhD, 1969, Univ of Sydney. Appointments include: Snr House Surg, Roy Natl Throat, Nose and Ear Hosp, Bristol, 1962; Snr Asst ENT Surg, Roy Vic Eye and Ear Hosp, Melbourne, 1963-66; 1st Asst ENT Surg, Alfred Hosp, Melbourne, 1964-66; Snr Visng ENT Surg, Repatriation Gen Hosp, 1966-71; Snr Hon ENT Surg, Roy Vic Eye and Ear Hosp, 1966-; Lectr, Dept of Physiology, Univ of Sydney, 1967-68; Cnslt Otolaryngologist, Commonwealth Acoustic Labs of Aust, 1968-73; Snr Rsch Offr, Natl Hlth and Medl Rsch Cncl of Aust, Dept of Physiology, Univ of Sydney, 1969; Prof of Otoloaryngology, Univ of Melbourne, 1970-; Cnslt Otolaryngologist to Roy Melbourne and Roy Women's Hosps, Melbourne, 1971-; Surg-in-Charge, Cochlear Implant Clin, Roy Vic Eye and Ear Hosp, 1985-. Publications: Cochlear Prostheses (co-ed), 1990; Cochlear Implantation for Infants and Children (Co-Ed), 1997. Honours include: AO, 1983; Adv Aust Awd, 1986; James Cook Medal, Roy Sc of NSW, 1992; Elected Hon Mbr, Sect of Otology, Roy Soc of Med, London, 1994; Cttee, Melbourne Achievement Awd, 1995; Sir William Upjohn Medal, Univ of Melbourne, 1997. Address: Department of Otolarygology, 384 Albert Street, East Melbourne, Vic 3002, Australia.

CLARK Helen Elizabeth, b. 26 Feb 1950, NZ. Member of Parliament. Education: BA; MA (Hons). Appointments: MP for Mt Albert, 1981-96; MP for Owairaka, 1996-; Min of Housing and Conservation, 1987-89; Min of Hlth and of Labour and Dpty Prime Min, 1989-90; Dpty Ldr of the Opposition, 1990-93; Ldr of the Opposition, 1993-. Address: Parliament House, Wellington, New Zealand.

CLARK Jane E Lindesay, b. 26 Sept 1955. Art Historian; Curator. m. David Mark Maclean, 10 Dec 1994, 1 s, 1d. Education: BA w Hons, Melbourne; MA, London. Appointments: Curator, major spec exhibns, Natl Gall of Vic, Melbourne, 1982-90; Curator of Austl Art, 1990-94; Dir of Paintings, Sotheby's Aust, 1994-. Publications: The Great 18th Century Exhibition, 1983; Golden Summers: Heidelberg and Beyond, 1985; Sidney Nolan: Landscapes and Legends, 1987; Violet Teague, 1999. Honour: Harkness Fellowship, 1988-90. Hobbies: Gardening; Reading; Travel; Lecturing. Address: c/o Sotheby's Australia, 926 High St, Armadale, Vic 3143, Australia.

CLARK John Richard James, b. 30 Oct 1932, Tas, Aust. Director, National Institute of Dramatic Art. m. Henrietta Hartley, 28 Mar 1958, 1 s, 2 d. Education: BA Hons, Univ Tas; MA, Univ Tas, 1956; MA, UCLA, USA, 1966. Appointments: Schtchr, London and Hobart, Tas, 1956-59; Lectr, Th Hist, 1960-69, Dir, 1969-, Natl Inst Dramatic Art, NSW. Creative Works include: Play prodns for Natl Inst Dramatic Art, Jane St, Sydney Th Co, Northside Th Co, Natl Sch Drama New Delhi, and Univ CA, San Diego. Honours: Harkness Fell'ship, C'wlth Fund, 1965-66; AM, 1981. Memberships include: Bd, Marian St Th Dirs, 1981-; Bd, NT Th Co Dirs, 1986-87; Chmn, Cultural Grants Advsry Govt, 1976-80. Hobby: Boating. Address: National Institute of Dramatic Art, Sydney, NSW 2052, Australia.

CLARK Linden Margaret, b. 15 June 1962, Auckland, NZ. Radio Manager. Education: BA, Hist & Music, Music Performance Dip, Auckland Univ. Appointment: Mngr, Radio NZ Intl, 1994-. Honours: Winston Churchill Fell, 1991; C'wlth Brdcstng Assn Awd for Innovation Mngmt, RNZI, 1998. Memberships: UNESCO Sub-Cmmn for Comms; Pacific Islands Broadcasting Assn. Hobbies: Music; Food; Wine. Address: Radio New Zealand International, PO Box 123, Wellington, New Zealand.

CLARK Robert William, b. 11 Mar 1957, Footscray, Melbourne, Australia. Member of Parliament. m. Karin, 1986, 1 s, 1 d. Education: BCom, Hons, 1980, LLB, 1982, BA, 1986, Melbourne Univ. Appointments: Solicitor, 1983-88; MP for Bawyn, 1988-92; MP for Box Hill, 1992-; Parly Sec to the Treas, 1992-96; Parly Sec, Treas and Multimedia, 1996-. Membership: Econ and Budget Review Cttee, Vic Parly, 1992-96. Address: 24 Rutland Road, Box Hill, Victoria 3128, Australia.

CLARKE Adrienne Elizabeth, b. 6 Jan 1938. Biochemist. 1 s, 2 d. Education: PhD; FTSE; FAA. Appointments: Dir, Plant Cell Bio Rsch Cntr, Univ of Melbourne, 1982-; Prof, Personal Chair, Univ of Melbourne, 1985-; Lt-Gov of Vic, 1997-; Chmn, Cwlth Sci and Indl Rsch Orgn (CSIRO), 1991-96; Directorships on Bds of AMP Ltd, Woolworths Ltd, WMC Ltd, AMRAD Ltd. Publications: Carbohydrate-Protein Recognition in Current Topics in Microbiology and Immunology (co-auth w I Wilson); Chemistry and Biology of (1-3)-ß-gluc, 1992. Honour: Offr, Order of Aust, 1991. Memberships: Intl Soc for Plant Molecular Bio, Pres; Friedrich Miescher-Inst, Basel, Switz, advsry bd mbr; NAS, USA, for mbr; Amn Acady of Arts and Sci; Austl Acady of Arts and Sci; Austl Acady of Technological Scis and Engnrng. Listed in: Who's Who in Australia. Hobbies: Skiing; Swimming; Bushwalking. Address: School of Botany, University of Melbourne, Parkville, Vic 3052, Australia.

CLARKE David Murray, b. 1 Sept 1952, Melbourne, Aust. Psychiatrist. m. Denise, 19 Oct 1974, 1 s, 2 d. Education: MBBS, Melbourne, 1977; MPM, Monash, 1989; PhD, Monash, 1996; FRAGCP; FRANZCP. Appointments: Res Medl Offr, St Vincents Hosp, Melbourne, 1978-79; Roy Children Hosp, 1980; Medl Offr, Spastic Soc, 1981-83; Psych Registrar, St Vincents Hosp, 1984-87; Psych, Prince Henry's Hosp and Monash Medl Cntr, 1988-; Lectr, Snr Lectr, Monash Univ, 1989-98; Assoc Prof, Monash Univ, 1999-. Memberships: Aust Medl Assn; Fell, Roy Austl and NZ Coll of Psych; Acady Psychosomatic Med; Intl Coll of Psychosomatic Med. Address: Monash University, Department of Psychological Medicine, 246 Clayton Road, Clayton, Vic

3168, Australia.

CLARKE Gary Norman, b. 10 Sept 1951, Ouyen. Medical Scientist. m. Susan, 4 Dec 1976, 1 s, 1 d. Education: BSc, Hons; MSc, Monash. Appointments: Rsch w Prof R Yanagimachi, Univ of Hawaii, USA, 1977-79; Andrology Sci, 1976-85, Snr Sci in Andrology, 1985-95, Unit Mngr, Andrology, 1995-, Roy Women's Hosp, Melbourne, Aust. Publications include: A Simplified Quantitative Cervical Mucus Penetration Test, 1997; Delivery of Normal Twins Following the Intracytoplasmic Injection of Sperm from a Patient with 47,XXY Klinefelter's Syndrome, 1997; A Simple Monthly Means Chart System for Monitoring Sperm Concentration, 1997; Quantitative Mucus Penetration: A Modified Formula for Calculating Penetration Efficiency, 1998; A Single Step Freezing/Storage Procedure for Human Semen Which Minimizes the Risk of Cross-Contamination During Storage, 1998. Honours include: Invited Fac Mbr, Andrology Workshop, Univ of Calgary, Can, 1991. Memberships: Fertility Soc of Aust, Natl Govng Cncl, 1991-96. Hobbies: Birdwatching; Chess; Reading; Billiards. Address: Andrology Unit, Royal Women's Hospital, Carlton, 3053, Australia.

CLARKE Kenneth Henry, b. 17 May 1923. Biomedical Physicist. m. Vivienne Edith Williams, 29 Jan 1959, 1 s, 2 d. Education: BSc, London; MSc, Melbourne; ARCS; F Inst P; FAIP; FACPSEM; CPhys. Appointments: Radar Off, Royal Navy, 1943-47; Physicist, Middlesex Hosp, London, 1947-49; Physicist, Austl Radiation Lab, 1950-54; Dpty Hd, Dept of Physl Scis, 1954-60, Hd, 1960-88, Peter MacCallum Cancer Inst, Melbourne; Cnslt Physicist: Prince Henry's Hosp, Melbourne, 1961-88; Alfred Hosp, Melbourne, 1965-79; Roy Women's Hosp, Melbourne, 1976-88; Retd, 1988. Publications: 25 scientific publications; Editor and Publisher, Journal, Australasian Physical and Engineering Sciences in Medicine. Honours: AO, 1991; Life Mbr, Australasian Coll of Physl Scis and Engrng in Med, 1987. Memberships: Natl Cttee for Biophysics, Austl Acad of Sci, 1969-78; Phys Advsry Cttee, Swinburne Inst of Technol, 1973-88, Chmn, 1977-87; Fndn Pres, Australasian Coll of Physl Scis and Engrng in Med; Mbr of Cncl, Swinburne Inst of Technol, 1980-87; Med Phys and Radiography Course Cttee, QLD Inst of Technol, 1983-88. Listed in: Who's Who in the Commonwealth, 1982; Men of Achievement, 1982; International Register of Profiles, 6th Edition; Who's Who in the World, 1980-81; Who's Who in Australia, 1992; International Book of Honour, 1985. Hobbies: History; French language and culture; Classical music; Concerts; Theatre; Travel. Address: 19 Marlborough Avenue, Camberwell, VIC 3124, Australia.

CLARKE Magnus, b. 10 July 1946, Reading, Berkshire, England. Broadcaster; Columnist. m. Susan Mary Hedger, 3 Apr 1976, 1 s, 1 d. Education: BA, Hons; MA, Intl Rels; PhD, Nuclear Warfare. Appointments: Off Boy, Lord Mayor of London, 1966-69; Wilkinson Sword Mktng, 1969-70; Mngmt, Ford Motor Co, 1973; Lectr, Snr Lectr, Dir, Def Studies, Deakin Univ, 1978-95; Profl Chat Show Guest, 1983-; Radio 3AW Melbourne, 1988-; ABC TV Univ Challenge, 1988-91; Columnist, Sunday Herald Sun, Melbourne, 1994-; World Affairs Analyst, Corp Speaker. Publications: Nudism in Australia, 1982; The Nuclear Destruction of Britain, 1982. Honour: Freeman, City of London, 1969. Membership: Intl Inst for Strategic Studies. Hobbies: Nudism; Jet Skiing; Antiques; Antique Restoration. Address: South Hollick House, 2 Tara Court, Torquay, Victoria 3228, Australia.

CLARKE Roger Edward, b. 24 Mar 1941, Eng. (Aust citizen) Veterinary Surgeon. m. Jackie, 1965. Education: BVSL (Qld); MRCVS; FACVSC; Regd Spec Small Animal Surg (Vic & Qld). Appointments: Priv dairy cattle, Korumburra, S Gippsland, Vic, 1965-66; Equine prac, Warwickshire, UK, 1967-68; Mixed prac, Bundoora, Vic, 1969-; Self-employed priv spec, surg prac, Melbourne. Memberships include: Advsry Cttee, Vet Nursing, 1978-; Austl Nal Repr to the World Small Animal Vet Assn, 1980-; External examiner, Snr Acad Assoc , Univ of Melbourne, Fac of Vet Sci, 1981-; Vet Bd, Vic, 1983-; Fndn Trustee & Chmn of Bd of Trustees of the Austl Companion Animal Hlth Fndn, 1988-; Fell, Austl Coll of Vet Scientists, 1991; Austl Intl Liason Offr, Amn Animal Hosps Assn (AAHA), 1995-; Pres, Austl Vet Assn , 1996-97, 1997-98; Pres, Austl Small Animal Vet Assn; Fell, AVA. Honours: ASAVA Disting Serv Awd, 1985-; AVA Meritorious Serv Awd, 1985-; ASAVA Practitioner of Yr Awd, 1988-; Elected Fell, AVA, 1995. Address: 17-19 Plenty Road, Bundoora, Australia 3083.

CLARKE Stephen Roy, b. 9 Sept 1945. Academic. m. Kaye Beverley Dyring, 13 Apr 1968, 1 s, 2 d. Education: MA, Opl Rsch, Lancaster Univ; BSc Hons, DipEd, Melbourne Univ; PhD Swinburne Univ. Appointments: Melbourne State Coll, 1967; Lectr, 1971, Snr Lectr, 1984, Assoc Prof, 1992, Swinburne Univ of Technol. Creative works: Over 50 pprs and articles in conf proceedings and intl jrnls. Honour: Pres's Medal, Opl Rsch Soc, UK. Memberships: Opl Rsch Soc; Austl Soc Opl Rsch; Amn Statistical Assn. Hobbies: Mathematical modelling in sport; Computer forecasting of sport. Address: School of Mathematical Sciences, Swinburne University, John Street, Hawthorn, Vic 3122, Australia.

CLARKO James George (Hon), b. 21 July 1932, Cottesloe, WA, Aust. Former Speaker; Former Member Legislative Assembly. m. Edith Laurel Loudon, 25 Aug 1958, 3 d. Education: BA, Univ WA; Dip Educ, Claremont Tchrs Coll. Appointments: Fmr Lectr, Hist, Pols, WA Coll Advd Educ; Mbr for Karrinyup, 1974-89, for Marmion, 1989-96; Govt Whip, 1975-77; Mbr, Chmn, Parly Accounts Cttee, 1975-77; Chmn Cttees, Dpty Speaker, 1977-82; Min Educ, 1982-83; Shadow Min, var portfolios 1983-93, inclng Shadow Min Local Govt, Racing and Gaming, Parly and Electoral Matters, Planning; Fmr Opposition Ldr of House, Legis Assembly; Speaker, Legis Assembly, 1993-96; Cnslt and Political Lobbyist, 1996-. Honours: Air Efficiency Awd, 1970; JP, 1972; Queen's Silver Jubilee Medal, 1977. Membership: Austl Coll Educ. Hobbies: Spectator Cricket and football; Snorkelling; Reading. Address: 14 Lynn Street, Trigg, WA 6029, Australia.

CLARKSON Gresley Drummond (Hon), b. 3 Mar 1916, WA, Aust. Retired Supreme Court Judge. m. Mary McConnal Wallace, 28 May 1941, 2 s, 1 d. Education: LLB, Univ WA, 1937. Appointments: Austl Imperial Force, 1941-45 MID; QC, 1965; Judge, Supreme Crt Papua New Guinea, 1966-75; Snr Tchng Fell, Law Sch, Univ WA, 1975-81; Snr Mbr, Admnstv Appeals Tribunal, 1979-86; Pres, WA Indl Commn, 1980; Pres, Medl Servs Review Tribunal, 1983-89. Publications: Co-auth, Civil Procedure in Western Australia, 1976-1992; Auth, The Tranby Clarksons, 1995. Honour: AM, 1991. Memberships: WA Bar Assn; Law Soc WA. Listed in: Who's Who in Australia. Hobbies: Reading; Fishing. Address: 3/30 Victoria Avenue, Claremont WA 6010, Australia.

CLARO Francisco, b. 14 Jan 1942, Santiago, Chile. Physicist. m. Isabel, 16 Aug 1967, 1 s, 2 d. Education: MSc, Phys, 1969, PhD, Phys, 1972, Univ OR. Appointments: Prof of Phys, Pontificia Universidad, 1966-; Snr Assoc, Intl Cntr for Theoretical Phys, Trieste, Italy, 1989-. Publications: Over 150 sci pprs, 1 book. Honours: Premio Edl Andes, 1993; Premio Explora Conicyt, 1997. Memberships: Fell, Amn Physl Soc; Sociedad Chilena de Fisica; Dir, F Chopin Soc. Address: P Universidad Catolica de Chile, DIPUC, Casilla 114-D, Santiago, Chile.

CLAUDON Jean-Louis René, b. 28 Sept 1950, Nancy, France. Aerospace Executive. m. Haru, 19 July 1977. Education: Ingénieur ENSAM, Paris, France, 1972; MSc, Brown Univ, Providence, RI, USA, 1974; DEng, Tokyo Univ, 1981. Appointments: Dev Engr, Automobiles Peugeot, France, 1974; Coml Attaché, French Emb in Japan, 1981; Hd of Arianespace's Tokyo Off, 1986. Honour: Kt, French Natl Order of Merit. Memberships: Eurn Bus Community in Japan (EBC); Chmn, Aeronautics Space and Def Cttee, 1987-92, 1997-. Address: Seijo 5-18-15, Setagaya-ku, Tokyo 157-0066, Japan.

CLAYTON Peter Robert, b. 24 Nov 1947, Australia. Library Educator. m. (1) Rosanne Walker, (2) Adela Love, 2 s, 1 d. Education: BA, Sydney, 1968; Dip, Libnshp, NSW, 1969; MA, Canberra, 1990; PhD, NSW, 1993. Appointments: Libn, Austl Natl Univ, 1970-74; Documentation Offr, Roy Cmmn on Austl Govt Admin, 1974-75; Rdr Servs Libn, Assoc Libn, Canberra Coll of Adv Educn, 1975-89; Snr Lectr, 1989-98, Assoc Prof, Info Mngmt, 1999-, Univ Canberra; Dir, Lib and Info Studies, 1991-95; Dir, Cntr for Commn Policy and Info Mngmt Rsch, 1996-; Ed, Austl Academic and Rsch Libs, 1997-. Publications: Implementation of Organizational Innovation, 1997; Qualitative Research for the Information Professional, 1997; Sev articles in profl jrnls. Honour: Fell, Cntr for Info Studies, 1995. Memberships: Assoc Fell, Austl Inst of Mngmt; Assoc, Austl Lib and Info Assn; Austl Coll of Educn. Hobbies: Music; Opera; Photography; Films; Walking. Address: Faculty of Communication, University of Canberra, Canberra, ACT 2601, Australia.

CLEMENS Warren Frederick Martin, b. 17 Apr 1915, Aberdeen, Scotland. Supervisor. m. Anne Turnbull, 1948, 1 s, 3 d. Education MA, hons, Agricl Dip, Christs Coll, Cambridge, England, 1933-37. Appointments: Colonial Admin Serv; Posted to Brit Solomon Islands, 1938; Cadet on Malaita, 1938-41, DO, San Christoval Dist, 1941; Dist Offr, Coastwatcher, Guadalcanal, 1942; Brit Liaison Offr, First US Marine Divsn, 1942, to XIV Corps, US Army for invasion of Western Solomons, 1943-44; Solomon Island Def Force, 1942; CO, Spec Serv Battalion, SIDF, 1943, (Maj); Dist Cmmnr, Western Solomons, 1943-45; Liaison Offr, II Austl Corps, Bougainville, 1944-45; Dpty Dist Cmmnr, Samaria, Palestine, 1946 Dist Cmmnr, Gaza, 1946-48; Nicosia and Kyrenia, Cyprus, 1948-49, 1954-57; Attended Imperial Def Coll, 1958; Def Sec, 1959-60; Dir, Lansdowne Pastoral Co, 1962-70; Dir, Squatting Investments, 1965-72; Dir, Lawn Hill Pty Ltd, Dir, GTV9, 1970-83. Honours: Mil Cross, 1942; Am Legion of Merit, 1943; OBE, 1956 CBE, 1960; AM, 1993; Tribute, City of Philadelphia, USA, 1968; Hon Companion, Naval Order of US, 1983. Memberships include: Cambridge C'wlth Trust, 1979-; Chmn, Nicosia Race Club, 1952-58; Commodore, Cyprus Yacht Club, 1954-58; Chmn Cyprus Saddle Club, 1955-59; Red Cross Exec, 1969-84; Intl Socl Serv, 1970-87, Former Chmn and Cncl Mbr; Supporters of Law and Order, Vic, 1975-92; Aust-Britain Soc, Cncl Mbr and Chmn, 1977-. Listed in: Who's Who in Australia; Who's Who in the Commonwealth; Who's Who in Australasia and the Far East. Address: Dunraven, 55 Clendon Road, Toorak, Victoria 3142, Australia.

CLEMENT John Gerald, b. 14 Nov 1948. Dental Scientist. m. Pauline Rosser, 2 Nov 1973, 1 s, 2 d. Education: PhD, BDS, Univ of London; LDS, RCS, Eng; Dip Forensic Odontology (LHMC). Appointments: Prof and Fndn Chair in Forensic Odontology, Univ of Melbourne; Hon Assoc Prof, Dept of Forensic Med, Monash Univ; Cnslt, Forensic Med, Monash Univ; Cnslt, Forensic Odontologist to Victorian Inst of Forensic Med. Publications: Cranio Facial Identification in Forensic Medicine (editor/author), 1997; Approximately 50 sci articles and book chapts on anatomical and forensic topics. Honour: Austl Soc of Forensic Dentistry, 1995-. Sci Fell, Zool Soc of London, 1984-; Pres, Brit Assn for Forensic Odontology, 1986-88; Pres, Austl Soc of Forensic Dentistry, 1995-. Hobbies: Fly fishing; Restoration of old cars/motorcycles; Rugby football. Address: Oral Anatomy, Medicine and Surgery Unit, School Dental Science, University of Melbourne, 711 Elizabeth Street, Melbourne, Vic 3000, Australia.

CLIFT Kenneth Rochester, b. 7 Jan 1916, Sydney, Aust. Writer; Film Producer. m. Valerie, Oct 1943, 2 s, 2 d. Appointments: Draftsman Soldier-Salesman (Mil); Writer; Film Prodr (Advsr). Appointments: Saga of a Sig; Yes I Remember; Soldier Who Never Grew Up; Dougherty; War Dance; Maury of Sth Arm; Magic Land (film script). Honours: DCM. Memberships: N Bondi RSh & Surf Club (Life Mbr); Bondi Icebergs. Hobbies: Surf; Swimming; Writing; Films; Walking. Address: Unit 1/5 Carlisle Street, Tamaramama, NSW, Australia 2026.

CLINGAN Judith Ann, b. 19 Jan 1945, Sydney, Australia. Music Director, Composer and Educator;

Theatre Director and Designer. 1 d. Eduction: BA, Austl Natl Univ; Dip, Music Educn, Hungary. Appointments: Dir, Canberra Childrens Choir, 1967-69; Dir, Yng Music Soc, 1969-84; Dir, Gaudeamus, 1983-93; Dir of Music, Mt Barker Waldorf Sch, 1994-96; Dir, Voicebox Youth Opera, 1995-; Dir of Music, Orana Sch, ACT, 1997-. Publications include: The Complete Chorister, 1971; So Good a Thing, 1980; Music is For Everyone, 1984; Francis (opera), 1986; A Pocketful of Rye, 1985; Nganbra, 1988; Kakadu, 1990; The Grandfather Clock (opera), 1992; Songs of the Tree of Life, 1996. Honours: Aust Cncl Composition Fell, 1991; Canberra Times Artist of the Yr, 1991; Sounds Austl Awd, 1991; Churchill Fell, 1998-99. Memberships: Austl Music Cntr; Austl Natl Choral Assn; Austl Soc for Music Educn. Hobbies: Visual Arts; Writing; Reading. Address: 11 Mirbelia Crescent, Rivett, ACT 2611, Australia.

CLODUMAR Kinza. Appointment: Prime Min, Govt of Nauru, 1997-. Address: Office of the President, Yaren, Nauru.

CLONEY Edwin John, b. 18 Dec 1940, Australia. Company Director. m. Loretta, 23 Apr 1964, 1 s, 2 d. Education: Fell, Austl Ins Inst, Austl Inst of Mngmt, Austl Inst of Co Dirs. Hobbies: Golf; Reading. Address: Kurraba Road, Neutral Bay, NSW 2089, Australia.

CLOONEY George, b. 1962. Actor. m. Talia Blasam, div. Appointments: TV series: ER, 1984-85; The Facts of Life, 1985-86; Roseanne, 1988-89; Sunset Beat, 1990; Baby Talk, 1991; Sister, 1992-94; ER, 1994-. Films: Return of the Killer Tomatoes, 1988; Red Surf, 1990; Unbecoming Age, 1993; From Dusk Till Dawn, Batman and Robin. Address: William Morris Agency, 151 El Camino, Beverly Hills, CA 90212, USA.

CLOSE Glenn, b. 19 Mar 1947. Actress. m. (1) Cabot Wade, div, (2) James Marlas, 1984, div, 1 d by John Starke. Education: William and Mary Coll. Appointments: Joined New Phoenix Repertory Co, 1974; Co-owner The Leaf and Bean Coffee House, Bozeman, 1991-. Stage appearances incl: Love for Love; The Rules of the Game; The Singular Life of Albert Nobbs; Childhood; Real Thing; A Streetcar Named Desire; King Lear; The Rose Tattoo; Benefactors; Death and the Maiden; Sunset Boulevard. Films incl: The World According to Garp, 1982; The Big Chill, 1983; The Natural, 1984; The Stone Boy, 1984; Maxie, 1985; Jagged Edge, 1985; Fatal Attraction, 1987; Dangerous Liaisons, 1989; Hamlet, 1989; Reversal of Fortune, 1989; The House of Spirits, 1990; Meeting Venus, 1990; Hamlet, 1990; Immediate Family, 1991; The Paper, 1994; Mary Reilly, 1994; Serving in Silence: The Margaret Cammermeyer Story, 1995; 101 Dalmatians, 1996; Mars Attacks!, 1996; Air Force One, 1997; Paradise Road, 1997; num tv film appearances. Address: c/o CAA 9830 Wilshire Boulevard, Beverly Hills, CA 90212, USA.

CLUNIES-ROSS Adrian (Major-General), b. 10 Oct 1933, Sydney, NSW, Aust. Soldier. m. Julienne Honora Anthony, 25 Aug 1961, 2 s, 1 d. Education: Grad, Roy Mil Coll, 1955; Grad, Austl Staff Coll, 1967; Grad, US Command and Gen Staff Coll, 1972; Jnt Servs Staff Coll, 1975; Grad, Qld Univ. Appointments: Cmdr, 8th Bat, RAR, 1972-74; Cmdr, 4th Mil Dist, 1980-82; Cmdr, 1st Div, 1984-85; Chf Ops, 1985-90. Publication: The Grey Eight in Vietnam, 1969-70. Honours: MBE, 1971; AO, 1986. Memberships: Mbr of Cncl and Dpty Chmn, Austl War Memorial; Pres, Roy Austl Regt Fndn; Immediate Past Pres, Regular Def Force Welfare Assn; Chmn, Natl Def Cttee, Returned Servs League; Cttee Mbr, Austl Decorative and Fine Arts Soc, ACT Branch. Listed in: Who's Who in Australia. Hobbies: Military history; Current affairs; Jogging; Tennis. Address: 13 Birdwood Street, Hughes, ACT 2605, Australia.

CLYNE Densey, b. 4 Dec 1926, Eng. Writer; Naturalist; Photographer; Film Maker. m. Peter Clyne, 21 Jan 1950, div 1975. Appointment: Co-Dir, Mantis Wildlife Films Pty Ltd, 1975-. Creative Works: Books incl: How to Keep Insects as Pets, 1978; Garden Jungle, 1979, repr, 1996; Cicadas, 1979; Spiders, 1981; Wildlife in the Suburbs, 1982; Nature City series containing Moths, Birds, Lizards, Night Animals, 1982; Silkworms, 1984; More Wildlife in the Suburbs, 1984; Densey Clyne's Wildlife of Australia, 1988; Rainforest, 1989; How to Attract Butterflies to Your Garden, 1990, repr, 1996;; Catch Me If You Can!, 1992; Plants of Prey, 1992; Cicada Sing-song, 1992; Flutter By, Butterfly, 1994; Spotlight on Spiders, 1995; It's A Frog's Life, 1995. Documentary film scripts incl: Garden Jungle; Aliens Among Us; Now You See Me; Blueprint for Survival; Every Care But No Responsibility; Come Into My Parlour; Butterfly Farming in Papua New Guinea; To Be A Butterfly; Webs of Intrigue; Regular wildlife segments written and presented over 8 yrs for TV; Num sci pprs to profl jrnls and mags. Honours include: Book Awds: C J Dennis Awd for Garden Jungle, Wildlife in the Suburbs, Roy Zoological Soc, NSW, 1982; Best Children's Series, Nature City; Roy Zoological Soc, NSW, Gilbert Whitley Awd for Garden Jungle; Wilderness Soc Environ Awd for Children's Lit, 1996; Film Awds: TV Soc, Penguin, Best Documentary Dir, 1977; Shell Awd $2000 TV Soc, 1977; Austl Geographic Soc Awd for Ex, 1996; Many other film awds shared w Jim Frazier FRPS ACS as cameraman/dir. Memberships: Fell, Roy Photographic Soc; Fell, Roy Entomological Soc. Hobbies: Listening to Music; Cloud Watching; Walking on Deserted Beaches; Cats; Reading; Gardening; Exploring the Countryside. Address: 14 Taylor Road, Dural, NSW 2158, Australia.

CLYNE Michael George, b. 12 Oct 1939, Melbourne, Aust. University Professor. m. Irene (Donohoue Clyne), 1 d. Education: BA, Hons (Melb), 1960; MA (Melb), 1962; PhD (Monash), 1965. Appointments: Tchng Fell to Snr Lectr in German, Monash Univ, 1962-72; Assoc Prof, German, Monash Univ, 1972-88; Prof of Linguistics, Monash Univ, 1988-; Rsch Dir, Lang and Soc Cntr, Natl Langs and Lit Inst of Aust, 1990-; Visng Prof, Stuttgart, 1972-73, Heidelberg, 1997. Honours: AM, 1993; Austrian Cross of Hon for Sci and the Arts (1st Class), 1996; Hon Life Mbr, Applied Linguistics Assn of Aust, 1988; Hon Dr, Philos, Univ of Munich, 1997; Grimm Prize, 1999. Memberships: Fell, Acady of Soc Scis in Aust, 1982; Fell, Austl Acady of the Hums, 1983; Austl Linguistic Soc, Pres, 1986-88. Hobbies: Reading; Music. Address: Department of Linguistics, Monash University, 3168, Australia.

COADY Cecil Anthony John (Tony), b. 18 Apr 1936, Sydney, Aust. Philosophy Educator. m. Margaret, 1 Sept 1962, 2 s. Education: BA, Sydney Univ, 1960; MA, Univ of Melbourne, 1962; BPhil, Oxford Univ, 1965; MA, Cambridge Univ, 1973. Appointments: Lectr, Corpus Christi Coll, Oxford, 1965-66; Lectr, Univ of Melbourne, 1966-69; SnrLectr, 1969-77; Rdr, 1977-90; Boyce Gibson Prof of Philos, Univ of Melbourne, 1990-. Publication: Testimony: A Philosophical Study, 1992. Honours: Commonwealth Fell, St Johns Coll, Cambridge, 1973; Schl in Res, Rockefeller Fndn, Bellagio, 1992; Lawrence Rockfeller Fell, Ethics & Pub Affairs, Cntr for Hum Values, Princeton Univ, 1993-94. Membership: Austl Acady of Hums. Hobbies: Reviewing; Reading; Cultivating chillies. Address: Philosophy Department, University of Melbourne, Parkville, Victoria, Australia 3052.

COATES Henry John, b. 28 Dec 1932, Aust. Army Officer; Chief of General Staff. m. Diana Begg, 23 Nov 1957, 2 s, 1 d. Education: Roy Mil Coll, Duntroon; BA Hons, Univ WA; MA, Austl Natl Univ; psc, Aust, 1968; jssc, Aust 1974; rcds, Aust, 1981. Appointments: Served 1st Armoured Regt, 1956-57, 1961-62; Cap, 1958; Adjutant, 10th Light Horse, 1958-60; Cap Instr, Roy Mil Coll, 1963; Maj, 1964; Exch Armoured Offr, Brit Army of Rhine, 1965-66; Cmdr, Cavalry Sqdn, 3rd Cavalry Regt, South Vietnam, 1970-71; Lt-Col, 1971; CO, Roy Mil Coll, Duntroon, 1971-73; Staff Offr, Army HQ, 1973-74; Served US Army, Ft Hood, TX, USA, 1975-76; Col, 1977; Col, Ops, HQ Field Force Command, 1977-78; Brig, 1979; Dir-Gen, Ops and Plans, 1979-80; Dpty Chf Ops, Ops Br, Canberra, 1982-83; Maj-Gen, 1983; Cmdt, Roy Mil Coll, Duntroon, 1983-84; Hd, Austl Def Staff, Wash DC, 1984-87; Chf Gen Staff, Austl Army, Canberra, 1990; Lt-Gen, 1990. Publications: Suppressing Insurgency,

1992; Bravery Above Blunder, 1999. Honours: MBE, 1971; AO, 1987; AC, 1992. Memberships: C'wlth Club; Austl Club, 1994. Listed in: Who's Who in Australia. Hobbies: Military history; Jogging; Tennis. Address: 14 Durville Crescent, Griffith, ACT 2603, Australia.

COATES Peter Cunliff, b. 11 June 1928. Managing Director. m. (1) 1955, dec 1974, (2) Margaret Anthony, 7 Mar 1979, 2 d. Education: Constantine Tech Coll; King's Coll; Durham Univ. Appointments include: Proj Mngr, Power Gas Corp, UK, 1957-62; Mngr, Power Gas Corp, Bombay, India, 1962-66; Mngng Dir, 1967-90, Chmn, 1990-95, Davy McKee Pacific Pty Ltd (fmrly Davy Pacific Pty Ltd); Chmn, Ceramic Fuel Cells Ltd, 1992-; Dir, Ausmelt Ltd, 1996-; Chmn, Heat Exchangers Intl Ltd, 1993-96; Dir, Gascor (Gas and Fuel), 1995-97. Honour: CBE, 1977. Memberships: Past Victorian Chmn, Fed Pres, Austl Brit Trade Assn; Hon Vice Vhmn, Aust-Brit Soc; Tree, CEDA; Chartered Engr; Fell, Instn Mechl Engrs; Fell, Instn Energy, UK; Fell, Austl Inst Energy. Listed in: Who's Who in Australia; Notable Australians - The Pictorial Who's Who. Address: 1 Sowter Court, Donvale, Vic 3111, Australia.

COBURN John, b. 23 Sept 1925, Ingham, Queensland, Aust. Artist (Painter). m. Doreen Gadsby, 5 Jan 1991. Education: Natl Art Sch, Sydney, ASTC Dip Painting, 1950. Appointments: Tchr, Natl Art Sch, Sydney, 1959-68; Trustee, Art Gall of NSW, 1976-80; Hd, Natl Art Sch, Sydney, 1972-74. Creative works: Paintings collected in Natl Gall of Aust; All Austl State Galls; Sydney Opera House; Vatican Mus, Rome; Kennedy Cntr for Performing Arts, Wash. Honours: AM, 1980; DLitt (James Cook), 1992. Membership: Blake Soc for Relig Art. Hobby: Reading. Address: 4/425 Pacific Highway, Lindfield, NSW 2070, Australia.

COCHRAN Robert Graeme, b. 18 Mar 1925, Maryborough, Vic, Aust. Management Consultant. m. 30 May 1958, 1 s, 1 d. Education: BComm, Melbourne Univ, 1949. Appointments: Mbr, 1957-84, Chmn, 1972-84, Harness Racing Bd, 1957-84; Ptnr, Brightford Cochran and Assocs, 1961-74; Dir, Sci Methods (Aust) Pty Ltd, 1966-; Mngng Dir, BCA Mngmt Servs Pty Ltd, 1970-; Pres, Austl Harness Racing Cncl, 1976-84; Pres, Interdominion Trotting Cncl, 1978-84; Pres, World Trotting Assn, 1979-81. Honours: OBE; J P Stratton Awd, Ausl Harness Racing Cncl, 1984. Membership: Fell, Austl Soc Cert Practising Accts. Hobby: Breeding of Standardbred Horses. Address: 14 Isabella Street, Moorabbin, Vic 3189, Australia.

COCKROFT Bruce, b. 21 Oct 1929, Swan Hill, Vic, Aust. Agricultural Scientist. m. Ruth E, 10 June 1953, 3 s, 1 d. Education: BAgric.Sci, 1953; MAgric.Sci, 1956; PhD, 1968. Appointments: Rsch Sci, Dept of Agric, 1953; Dir, Rsch Inst, Tatura, 1968; Dir, Rsch Inst, Kyabram, 1978, Cnslt, 1987. Publications: Over 80 pprs in profl jrnls. Honours: Fell, Austl Inst of Agricl Sci, 1984; Hon Life Mbr, Soil Sci Soc, Aust, 1988. Memberships: Austl Inst of Agricl Sci; Soil Sci Soc, Aust. Hobbies: Music; Gardening; Art. Address: 22 Arcadia Downs Drive, Kialla, Victoria 3631, Australia.

CODRINGTON Stephen Bruce, b. 27 July 1953, Sydney, Aust. Author; School Chief Executive. m. Dianne, 11 Dec 1976, 3 s, 1 d. Education: BA, Dip Ed, 1975; BA, Hons I, 1976; PhD, 1983. Appointments include: Res Tutor, Robert Menzies Coll, 1976; Hd, Geog, St Igatius Coll, Riverview, Aust, 1977-88; Pt-time Lectr, Univ of West Sydney (Macarthur), 1986, 1989; Geog Tchr, Stonyhurst Coll, Lancs, UK, 1987; Prin, St Paul's Grammar Sch, Penrith, Aust, 1989-97; Fndn Prin, St Paul's Open Acady, Aust, 1990-97; Mngng Dir, St Paul's Overseas Schs Mngmt Corp, 1995-97; Co-Fndr, Light of the World Intl Sch, Harbin, China, 1995; Chf Exec, Kristin Sch, Auckland, NZ, 1997-. Publications: Books incl: Gold From Gold, 1979; People's China, 1982; Australia and its Neighbours: A Student Source Book, 1985; The Geography Skills Book, 1989; (Co-auth) Appreciating Australia, 1994; World of Contrasts (4th ed), 1994; Understanding Environments, 1995; Investigating Our World, 1996; Changing Communities, 1996; Pprs to jrnls;

Monographs and chapts in books. Honours: FRGS, 1990: FNGTA (Fell, Geog Tchrs Assn of NSW), 1991; FACE (Fell, Austl Coll of Educ), 1992; MOIF, 1996; FIBA, 1996; Named Intl Man of the Yr (Educ), IBC, 1995-96; Intl Cultural Dip of Hon, ABI, 1996. Memberships include: Assn of Hds of Indep Schs of NZ; Indep Schs Cncl of NZ; Educ Forum of Round Table of Bus Cncl of NZ; Assn of Australasian Intl Baccalaureate Schs. Hobbies: Family; Long-distance running; Writing books; Travel; Photography; Reading; Listening to classical music. Address: Kristin School, PO Box 87, Albany, Auckland 1331, New Zealand.

COEN Ethan, b. 1958 St Louis Park Minn. Producer; Screenwriter. m. Education: Princeton Univ. Appointments: Screenwriter, with Joel Coen, Crime Wave, fmrly XYZ Murders; Prodr, screenplay, ed, Blood Simple, 1984. Other films with Joel Coen: Raising Arizona, 1987; Miller's Crossing, 1990; Barton Fink, 1991; The Hudsucker Proxy, 1994; Fargo, 1996. Honours: Palme d'Or Cannes Fest for Barton Fink. Address: c/o UTA, 9560 Wilshire Boulevard, Beverly Hills, CA 90212, USA.

COEN Joel, b. 1955 St Louis Park Minn. Film Director; Screenwriter. m. div. Education: Simon's Rock Coll; NY Univ. Appointments: Asst Ed Fear No Evil and Evil Dead; Worked with rock video crews; Screenwrite, with Ethan Coen, Crime Wave, fmrly XYZ Murders. Other films with Ethan Coen: Blood Simple, 1984; Raising Arizona, 1987; Miller's Crossing, 1990; Barton Fink, 1991; The Hudsucker Proxy, 1994; Fargo, 1996. Honours: Palme d'Or Cannes Fest for Barton Fink; Best Dir Awd Cannes Intl Film Fest, 1996. Address: c/o UTA, 9560 Wilshire Boulevard, Beverly Hills, CA 90212, USA.

COGSWELL Richard Dominic, b. 4 Aug 1951, Hobart, Tas, Aust. Barrister. m. Elizabeth Anne Collier, 28 Apr 1979, 1 s, 1 d. Education St Virgil's Coll, Hobart; LLB, Univ of Tas, 1974; Rhodes Schlsp, Tas, 1974; BA, 1976, MA, 1988, Univ of Oxford, Eng. Appointments: Assoc, Mr Jus Jacobs, High Crt of Aust, 1976-77; Solicitor, Sydney, NSW, 1978-80; Bar, Sydney, 1981-; Crown Prosecutor, NSW, 1991-; Dpty Snr Crown Prosecutor, NSW, 1997-; Snr Counsel, NSW, 1997; Queen's Counsel, Tasmania, 1998-; Memberships: NSW Bar Assn; Bd, SCEGGS Darlinghurst Ltd, 1997-; Melbourne Cricket Club; Sydney Cricket Ground; Sydney Real Tennis Club; Hobart Tennis Club. Hobbies: Real tennis; Cinema; Music; Spirituality; Cooking. Address: Crown Prosecutors' Chambers, 265 Castlereagh Street, Sydney, NSW 2000, Australia.

COHEN Alexander Kevin, b. 22 Sept 1926, Perth, WA, Aust. Physician. m. Adele Shillman, 24 Mar 1957, 1 s, 2 d. Education: MB BS, MD, 1969, Univ Adelaide; FRACP, 1970. Appointments: Res Medl Offr, Roy Adelaide Hosp, SA, 1951-52; Lectr, Path, 1953, Rsch Fell, Med, 1954, Adelaide Univ; Res Medl Offr, Postgrad Medl Sch, London, Eng, 1953; Rsch Fell, Kings Coll Hosp, London, 1954; Physn, Endocrinologist, Roy Perth Hosp, WA, 1957-; Rsch Fell, Harv Medl Sch, USA, 1962-63; Clinl Prof, 1991-, Pro-Chan, 1995-98, Chan, 1998-, Univ WA; Pres, Roy Australasian Coll Physns, 1992-94; Chmn, Cttee Pres's Medl Colls, 1993-95; Chan, Univ of Western Aust, 1998-; Pres, Diabetes Rsch Fndn, 1998-. Publications: Alcohol Hyperglycemia, 1969; Contbr, num pprs. Honours: Nortlock Rsch Fellshp, 1953; Roy Perth Travelling Fellshp, 1962; Pharm Mfrs Fellshp, 1969; Fell, Austl Medl Assn, 1975; Life Mbr, Austl Endocrine Soc, 1982; AO, 1995. Memberships include: Censor, 1980-86, Cnclr, 1985-, VP, 1990, Roy Australasian Coll Physns; Endocrine Soc Aust; Diabetic Assn Aust; Senate, Univ WA, 1981-; FRCP; FRCP Edinburgh; FRCP Ireland; Hon FACP; AM Malaysia; FCCP, Ceylon; FCPS, Pakistan. Listed in: Who's Who in Australia. Address: 4 Crawley Avenue, Crawley, WA 6009, Australia.

COHEN Edward (Sir), b. 9 Nov 1912, Melbourne, Australia. Consultant; Company Director. m. Meryl D, 1939, 1 s. Education: Scotch Coll; Univ Melbourne. Appointments: Ptnr, Pavey Wilson Cohen & Carter, 1945-76; Pres, 1965-66, Mbr, Cl Law Inst, Vic, Aust, 1959-68; former Mbr, Fac Law Univ Melbourne, Cl Legal Educ & Bd Examiners, Commnsr Affidavits, Partly Agent, Twelfth Leonard Ball Orator formerly Mbr, Intl House Cl Univ Melbourne; Mbr, Pensions Cttee, Melbourne Legacy, 1955-84, Chmn, 1961-84, Chmn Roy Women's Hosp, 1968, Million Dollar Building Appeal, Eileen Patricia Goulding Mem Fund Appeal, 1983, Life Govr Roy Children's, Roy Melbourne, Roy Women's, Austin, Prince Henry's Hosps, Adult Deaf and Dumb Soc, Vic, Corps Commissionaire, Hon Solr Queens Fund, 1951-94, Dir EZ Inds, 1956-84, Chmn, 1960-84, Pres, 1984-, Dir Electrolytic Zinc Co A'asia, 1951-84, Chmn 1960-84, Chmn Emu Bay Railway Co, 1967-84, Derwent Metals, 1957-84, Dir, Carlton & United Breweries, 1947-84, Chmn, 1967-84, CUB Fibre Containers, 1963-84, Manufs Bottle Co Vic, 1967-84, Dir Swan Brewery, 1947-57, Dir Qld Brewery (later CUB Qld), 1968-84, Chmn, Nthn Aust Breweries (CUB Nth Qld), 1967-84, Local Advr Union Assurance Soc, 1951-60, Dir Union Assurance Soc Aust, 1960-75, Comm Union Assurance, 1960-82, Chmn, 1964-82, Natl Comm Unon, 1982-84, Dir Assoc, Pulp & Paper Mills Ltd, 1951-83, Dpty Chmn, 1981-83, Dir Herald & Weekly Times Ltd, 1974-77, V Chmn, 1976-77, Dir Pelaco Ltd, 1959-68, Glazebrooks Paints and Chems Ltd, 1951-64 and other cos; Exhibitioner Greek and Roman History, Ormond Coll Univ Melbourne, Aust. Address: 1/722 Orrong Road, Toorak, Vic 3142, Australia.

COHEN Emmanuel Benjamin, b. 2 May 1941. Director. m. Patricia Marjorie Naughton, 20 Nov 1967, 2 s, 1 d. Education: BComm, hons, Univ NSW; FCPA. Appointments: Controller, ICI Plastics Grp, Aust, 1984-87; Mngr, ICI Aust Corp Distbn, 1986-87; Dir, Elders Fin Ltd, 1987-89; Fin and Admin Dir, Potter Warburg Ltd, 1989-94; Mngng Dir, Quantum Change Cnslts, 1994-; Dir, Austl Continuous Improvement Grp, 1994-; Bd Mbr, Australasia Bur Veritas Quality Intl, 1994-. Memberships: Pres, Cnclr, Austl Soc of CPA'S, 1979-80; Natl Cnclr, Austl Soc of CPA'S, 1980-82; Dir, Meth Ladies Coll, Melbourne, 1989-. Listed in: Who's Who in Australia; Who's Who in Finance and Industry. Hobbies: Art; Theatre; Literature; Tennis; Swimming. Address: 8/350 Colins Street, Melbourne, Vic 300, Australia.

COHEN Geoffrey Arthur, b. 26 Jan 1934. Chartered Accountant. m. Ola Robinson, 11 Dec 1957, 2 s, 1 d. Education: Dip, Com Law; Dip Tax Law; Chartered Acct. Appointments: Acct, Morris J Cohen, Chartered Accts, 1951-56; Ptnr, Arthur Andersen, 1965-90, Mngng Ptnr, Melbourne Off, 1973-78, Acctng and Audit prac dir, Aust, 1978-82; Dir, Foster's Brewing Grp Ltd, 1991-; Chmn, Dirs HIH Insurance, 1992-; Dir, Diversified Utd Investments Ltd, 1991-; Dir, Australian Premiun Wines Ltd, 1991-. Memberships: Inst of Chartered Accts in Aust, pres, 1986-87; Inst of Dirs Vic State Chmn, 1990-91. Hobbies: Fishing; Philately. Address: 25 Hume Street, Armadale, Vic 3143, Australia.

COHEN Judith Jacqueline, b. 7 Feb 1926, Sydney, NSW, Aust. Retired. m. Senator S H Cohen, 1953, dec, 2 d. Education: BA, LLB, Univ Sydney, 1950; Dip Ed, Univ Melbourne, 1967. Appointments: Admitted, practised as Sol, Supreme Crt NSW, 1950-53; Admitted as Bar and Sol, Supreme Crt Vic, 1953; Practised as Sol, Melbourne, 1953-55, 1962-66, 1970-75; Mbr, Victorian Advsry Cttee, ABC, 1973-76; Commnr, 1975-80, Dpty Pres, 1980-89, Austl Conciliation and Arbitration Commn; Mbr, Advsry Cttee, Socl Scis Natl Lib, 1982-84; Mbr, Cncl, Natl Lib, 1984-90; Dpty Pres, Austl Indl Rels Commn, 1989-91; Chairperson, Fed Costs Advsry Cttee, 1990-91; Mbr, Cncl, Victorian Univ Technol, 1990-93; Chairperson, Gen Ins Claims Review Panel, 1991-96. Honour: AO, 1992. Memberships: Victorian Women Lawyers Assn, 1953-; Lyceum Club Melbourne, 1984-. Address: 7 Victor Avenue, Kew, Vic 3101, Australia.

COHEN (Stephen) Marshall, b. 27 Sept 1929, New York, USA. Professor. m. Margaret Dennes, 15 Feb 1964, 1 s, 1 d. Education: BA, Dartmouth Coll, 1951; MA, 1953, Fell, Soc of Fells, 1955-58, Harvard Univ; MA, Oxon, 1977. Appointments include: Fac, Harvard Univ, 1958-62, Univ Chgo, 1962-67, Rockefeller Univ, 1967-70, City Univ of NY, 1970-83; Exec Offr, Prog in Philos, Grad Sch, City Univ of NY, 1975-83; Prof Emer of Philos and Law, Univ Prof Emer, Dean Emer, Coll of Letters, Arts and Scis, Univ of S CA, 1998. Publications include: Ed: The Philosophy of John Stuart Mill, 1961. Co-Ed: Film Theory and Criticism, 1974; What is Dance?, 1983; War and Moral Responsibility, 1974; The Rights and Wrongs of Abortion, 1974; Equality and Preferential Treatment, 1977; Marx, Justice and History, 1980; Medicine and Moral Philosophy, 1982; International Ethics, 1985; Punishment, 1995. Honours include: Guggenheim Fellshp, 1976-77; Rockefeller Fndn Humanities Fellshp, 1977. Memberships: Sev. Address: 10218 Autumn Leaf Circle, Los Angeles, CA 90077, USA.

COHEN Marvin L, b. 3 Mar 1935, Montreal, Quebec, Can (naturalized US Citizen, 1953). Professor of Physics. Education: AB, UNiv CA, Berkeley, 1957; MSc, Univ Chgo, 1958; PhD, Univ Chgo, 1964; Appointments: Mbr, Techl Staff, Bell Telephone Labs, Murray Hill, NJ, 1963-64; Snr Scientist, Lawrence Berkeley Lab, 1965-; Asst Prof, Phys, 1964-66, Assoc Prof, Phys, 1966-69; Prof of Phys, 1969-95; Univ Prof, 1995-, Univ of CA, Berkeley; Visng Prof: Cambridge Univ, Eng, 1966; Univ of Paris, France, 1972-73, summers, 1968, 1975, 1987, 1988, Univ of HI, 1978-79; Techion, Haifa, Israel, 1987-88. Honours: Alfred P Sloan Fell, 1965-67; Prof, Miller Inst for Basic Rsch in Sci, 1969-70, 1976-77, 1988; Elected Fell, Amn Phys Soc, 1969; Guggenheim Fell, 1978-79, 1990-91; Oliver E Buckley Prize for Solid State Phys, 1979; Elected, Natl Acady fo Sci, 1980; US Dept of Energy Awd for Outstndng Accomplishments in Solid Strate Phys, 1981; US Dept of Energy Awd for Sustained Outstndng Rsch in Solid State Phys, 1990; Lawrence Berkeley Lab Cert of Merit, 1991; Elected to Amn Acady Arts & Sci, 1993; Julius Edgar Lilienfeld Prize, Amn Phys Soc, 1994; Outstndng Perf Awd, Lawrence Berkeley Lab, 1995; Elected Fell, AAAS, 1997. Address: Department of Physics, University of California at Berkeley, Berkeley, CA 94720, USA.

COHEN Renée Shell, b. 2 July 1945, Paris, TX, USA. Education. 1 s. Education: (Asian Art Study Schlshp) Univ of BC, Vancouver, Can, 1977; (Grad Rsch Schlshp Grant), Univ of BC, Vancouver, Can, 1978. Appointments: Dept of Intl Studies, Ogaki Women's Coll, Ogaki-shi, Gifu-ken, Japan; Treas and Mbrshp Chair, Elected Off, Japan Assn for Lang Tchng Bilingualism Natl Interest Grp, 1996-. Publications: (book) The Story of Chiune Sugihara (Engl cnslt for textbook), 1992; (translations) Appreciating Emily Dickinson, 1994; Appreciating English Haiku, 1995; A Selection of Haiku by Francine Porad, 1996; Selected Haiku from the Writing of Anne Mckey, 1997; Translations of poetry w Ikuyo Yoshimura; Rsch articles; Contbns to jrnls. Honours: Educl grants, schlshps. Memberships: Japan Assn for Lang Tchng (JALT) 1989-; Mbr, Engl Cnslt, Evergreen Haiku Soc, 1992-; Elected Offr, Treas and Mbrshp Chair, JALT Bilingualism Natl Interest Grp, 1996-; Lic Tchr, Japanese 13-stringed Zither, Japan Todo Musical Assn, 1996-; NY Acady of Scis, 1996-. Hobbies: Reading; Swimming; Music; Poetry. Address: Azuma-cho 1-17-1, Ogaki-shi, Gifu-ken, Japan 503-0802.

COHEN Stanley Norman, b. 17 Feb 1935, Perth Amboy, NJ, USA. Geneticist; Educator. m. Joanna Lucy Wolter, 27 June 1961, 1 s, 1 d. Education: BA, Rutgers Univ, 1956; MD, 1960, ScD (hon), Univ of PA; ScD (hon) Rutgers Univ, 1994; Appointments: Intern, Mt Sinai Hosp, NYC, 1960-61; Res, Univ Hosp, Ann Arbor, MI, 1961-62; Clin Assoc Arthritis & Rheumatism br, Natl Inst Arthritis and Metabolic Diseases, Bethseda, MD, 1962-64; Snr Res in Med, Duke Univ Hosp, Durham, NC, 1964-65; Amn Cancer Soc, postdoct rsch fell, Albert Einstein Coll Med, Bronx, 1965-67, Asst Prof, Dev Bio & Cancer, 1967-68; Mbr, Fac Stanford (CA) Univ, 1968-, Prof, Med, 1975-, Prof Genetics, 1977, Chmn, Dept Genetics, 1978-86, K-T Li Prof, 1993-. Honours include: Sigma Xi; Phi Beta Kappa; Alpha Omega Alpha; Mattia Awd, Roche Inst Molecular Bio, 1977; Albert Lasker basic Medl Rsch Awd, 1980; Wolf Prize, 1981; Marvin J Johnson Awd, 1981; Disting Serv Awd, Miami Winter Symposium, 1986; LVMH Inst de la Vie Prize, 1988; Natl Medal Sci, 1988;

Cty of Med Awd, 1988; Natl Biotech Awd, 1989; Amn Chem Soc Spec Awd, 1992; Helmut Horten Rsch Awd, 1993; Lemelson/MIT Prize, 1996. Memberships include: Fell, AAAS; Amn Acady Microbiology; Amn Soc Biol Chemists; Genetics Soc Am; Amn Soc Microbiology; Assn Amn Physns; Inst Med; Mbr, Editl Bd, Jrnl Bacteriology, 1973-79, Molecular Microbio, 1986-; Proc, Natl Acady of Sci, 1996-; Assoc Ed, Plasmid, 1977-86; NAS, Chmn, Genetics Sect, 1988-91; Amn Soc Pharm & Experimental Therapeutics; Amn Soc Clin Investigation. Address: Stanford University, School of Medicine, Department of Genetics #M-320, Stanford, CA 94305, USA.

COHEN-ALMAGOR Raphael, b. 24 Oct 1961, Israel. Lecturer; Researcher. m. Zehavit, 22 Jan 1985, 1 s, 1 d. Education: BA, MA, Te Aviv Univ; DPhil, Oxford. Appointments: Lectr, Fac of Law, The Hebrew Univ, 1992-95; Snr Lectr, Dept of Comm, Univ of Haifa, 1995-. Publications: Middle Eastern Shores (poetry), 1993; The Boundaries of Liberty and Tolerance, 1994; Ed, Basic Issues in Israeli Democracy, 1994. Honours: St Catherine's Coll, Oxford, 1987-90; Fell, The Van Leer Jerusalem Inst, 1991-98; The Yigal Alon Schlshp, 1995-98; Brit Cncl, 1997; Israeli Min of Sci, 1998; Fulbright-Yitzhak Rabin Awd, 1999-2000. Memberships: Dir, Think-tank on Medl Ethics, Jerusalem, 1995-98; Fell, 21st Century Trust; Israeli Press Cncl. Hobbies: Politics; Sport; Poetry, Music; Theatre, Cinema; Stamps; Travelling. Address: Department of Communication, University of Haifa, Mount Carmel, Haifa 31905, Israel.

COLDITZ Paul Bernard, b. 30 Dec 1951, Newcastle, Aust. Medical Researcher. m. Rhonda, 30 Dec 1972, 2 s, 1 d. Education: DPhil, Oxford; MBiomedE; MBBS; FRACP; FRCPCH. Appointments: Dir, Neonatal Intensive Care Unit, King George VI Hosp, 1991; Prof, Perinatal Med, Univ of Qld, 1992-. Publication: Obstetrics and the Newborn, 1997. Memberships: Pres, 1995-97, Paediat Rsch Soc of Aust; Perinatal Soc of Aust, NZ; World Assn of Perinatal Med. Hobby: Running. Address: Perinatal Research Centre, Royal Womens Hospital, Brisbane 4029, Australia.

COLE Andrew Reginald Howard, b. 21 Apr 1924. Academic Chemist. m. Eileen Ursula Hagan, 5 Mar 1955, 1 s, 2 d. Education: BSc, Univ of WA, 1945; DPhil, 1949, DSc, 1983, Oxford Univ. Appointments: Post-Doc Fell, Natl Rsch Cncl of Canada, 1949-51; Nuffield Rsch Fell, 1952-55, Snr Lectr, Rdr in Chem, 1955-68, Prof of Physl Chem, 1969-89, Univ of WA. Publications: Chemical Properties and Reactions, 1976; Tables of Wavenumbers for the Calibration of Infrared Spectrometers, 1977. Honours: Archibald Olle Prize, Roy Austl Chem Inst, 1978; Leighton Medal, Roy Aust Chem Inst, 1984; Hon DSc, Univ of W Aust, 1992; Paul Harris Fell, Rotary Intl, 1994. Memberships: Fell, Roy Austl Chem Inst, Pres, 1982; Fell, Austl Acad of Sci, VP, 1981-82. Hobby: Golf. Address: 61 Haldane Street, Mount Claremont, WA 6010, Australia.

COLE Edmund Keith, b. 16 Oct 1919, Aust. Canon Emeritus; Author; Publisher. m. Grace Newell, 19 Aug 1944, 1 s, 2 d. Education: MA; BD Hons; ThSchol Hons; ThD. Appointments: Lectr, Moore Theol Coll, Sydney, 1944-50; Prin, St Paul's Utd Theol Coll, Kenya, 1953-60; Archdeacon, Cntrl Kenya, 1961-63; Vice-Prin, Ridley Coll, Univ Melbourne, 1964-73; Prin, Nungalinya Coll, Darwin, 1973-78; Dir, Theol Educ, Diocese Bendigo, 1978-84; Publr, Keith Cole Publns; Diocesan Archevist and Lib. Publications: Num books inclng: Mau Mau Mission, 1954; Oenpelli Pioneer, 1972; Groote Eylandt, 1975, 1983; The Aborigines of Arnhem Land, 1979; Seafarers of the Groote Archipelago, 1980; A History of Numbulwar, 1982; The Aborigines of Victoria, 1982; Fred Gray of Umbakumba, 1984; The Aborigines of Western Australia, 1985; Pethy, Lee and Mary, 1986; The Benolas, 1987; Crusade Hymns, 1987; Groote Eylandt Aborigines and Mining, 1988; Robert Hardness: the Bendigo hymnwriter, 1988; But I will be with You (autobiog), 1988; Fred P Morris and other Bendigo Hymnwriters, 1989; Men of Faith and Vision: Archdeacon A Crawford and Dean J C MacCullagh, 1989; A History of All Saints' Church, Bendigo: the rise and demise of a Cathedral, 1990; A History of Holy Trinity Church, Bendigo, 1990; A History of Christ Church, Echuca, 1990; A History of Christ Church, East Bendigo, 1990; The Bendigo Crusade Choir, 1990; A History of the Diocese of Bendigo: an Anglican diocese in rural Victoria, 1991; Sharing in Mission: The centenary history of the Victorian Branch of the Church Missionary Society, 1892-1992, 1992; Servants for Jesus' Sake: long-serving Victorian CMS missionaries, 1993; The Anglican Mission to the Chinese in Bendigo and Central Victoria 1857-1918, 1994; Ed: Molly Williams: The Rich Tapestry of my Persian Years - memoirs of Maud Hannah (Molly) Williams, a missionary nurse, 1937-1974; A Taste of Salt: A selection of sermons and articles by Bishop Oliver Heyward, 1991; Co-ed: St Paul's: a Portrait, 1995; A History of the Diocese of St Arnaud, 1998; A History of St Paul's Cathedral Church, Bendigo, 1999. Hobby: Carpentry. Address: 28 Woodbury Street, Bendigo, Vic 3550, Australia.

COLE Keith David, b. 2 Mar 1929, Cairns, Aust. Physicist. m. Valerie, 8 June 1989. Education: BSc (Hons); MSc; DipEd; DSc, Univ of Queensland. Appointments: Theoretical Physicist, Antarctic Div, 1957-63; Rsch Assoc, Univ of Chgo and CO, 1963-66; Fndn Prof of Phys, La Trobe Univ, 1966-94. Publications: Over 150 pprs in refereed sci lit on space and plasma phys. Honours: Assoc of RAS, 1983; Fell, Austl Acady of Sci 1983; Appleton Prize, Roy Soc of London, 1984. Memberships: Hon Mbr and Fmr Pres of Intl Assn of Geomagnetism and Aeronomy, 1979-83; Fmr Pres, Sci Cttee in Solar Terrestrial Phys, 1977-86. Hobby: Bush gardening. Address: School of Physics, La Trobe University, Bundoora, Vic, Australia 3083.

COLE Kris (Kristine Louise), b. 21 July 1952, Massachusetts, USA. Author; Management Consultant. m. Don Cole, 3 Mar 1973. Education: BSc (Hons), Bath Univ, 1974; Post Grad Dip (Mfng Technol), NE Essex Tech Inst, 1975; Cert Adult Trng (CTO), Huddersfield Tech Inst, 1976. Appointment: Mngng Dir, Bax Assocs Pty Ltd; Cnslt to major pub and priv sect orgns across Aust, NZ, SE Asia. Publications: How to Succeed at a Job Interview, 1991; Office Administration and Supervision, 1992; Crystal Clear Communication: Skills for Understanding and Being Understood, 1993; Supervision: Management in Action, 1998. Memberships: FAICD, Fell, Austl Inst Co Dirs; ASM, Accredited Speaking Mbr, Natl Speakers Assn; AHRI, Assoc Fell, Austl Hum Resources Inst Cnslr for S Aust, 1987-93; MAITD, Mbr, Austl Inst of Trng & Dev. Hobbies: Bushwalking; Reading; Gardening. Address: 5 Hillcrest Avenue, Crafers West, SA 5152, Australia.

COLE Michael William Henry, b. 16 Aug 1949, Keresley, England. Sales Director. m. Giuliana L Ditlatteo, 5 June 1974, 1 s, 1 d. Education: BSc, Phys, Maths, Univ of Sussex, Eng, 1970. Appointments: SISTEL, Rome, 1970-76; Siai Harchetti, Sesto Calende, Italy, 1976-80; Rep Asia Siai Marchetti, Singapore, 1980-85; Rep NE Asia Agusta, Hong Kong, 1985-88; Reg Sales Mngr, Shorts, Hong Kong, 1988-94; Reg Dir, SMS, Kuala Lumpur, 1994-95; Dir Sales, Bombardier Aerospace, 1995-. Hobbies: Scuba Diving; Swimming; Motorcycling; Boating. Address: Box 113, 31st Floor, UBN Tower, Jalan P Ramlee, 50250, Kuala Lumpur, Malaysia.

COLEMAN William Oliver, b. 6 Nov 1959, Sydney, Australia. University Lecturer. m. Anna, 10 Dec 1994, 2 s. Education: BEcon, hons, Univ Sydney, 1981; MSc, LSE, 1985; PhD, LSE, 1989. Appointments: Reserve Bank of Aust, 1982; Univ of Wellington, 1988; Univ of Tas, 1991. Publications: Money & Finance in Australia, 1995. Honour: Hist of Econs Soc Prize, Best Article, 1996. Address: School of Economics, University of Tasmania, GPO Box 252-85, Hobart 7001, Australia.

COLES David John (The Right Reverend), b. 23 Mar 1943, Auckland, NZ. Anglican Bishop. m. Ceridwen Mary Parr, 17 Jan 1970, 1 s, 1 d. Education: BA, 1965, MA Hons, 1967, Univ Auckland; BD, 1969, MTh, 1971, Univ Otago; Dip Relig Educ, Melbourne Coll Divinity, Aust, 1971; PhD, Univ Manchester, Eng, 1974. Appointments: Vicar, Glenfield, Auckland, 1974-76; Vicar, Takapuna, Auckland, 1976-84; Dean, St John's Cath, Napier, 1980-84; Dean, Christchurch Cath, 1984-90; Bish, Christchurch, 1990-. Hobbies: Skiing; Tramping; Music. Listed in: Who's Who. Address: 12 Idris Road, Christchurch 8001, New Zealand.

COLES Gerald Vivian, b. 5 Apr 1924. Occupational Hygenist. m. (1) Ruth Mary Crowe, 18 July 1953, (2) Ingrid Hildegard Engel Rutishauser, 19 July, 1976, 1 s, 1 d. Education: BS (Hons) Chem, Univ Coll, Cardiff, Wales; Grad Dip in Occupational Hygiene, London Sch of Hyg and Tropical Med. Appointments include: Chem, Anglo-Iranian Oil Co (BP), 1944-52; Rsch Asst Organic Chem, Long Ashton Rsch Stn, Univ of Bristol, 1952-55; Factories Inspector, H Overseas Civil Serv, Uganda, 1955-71; Occupational Hygenist, Brit Railways Bd, 1971-74; Snr Lectr, Occupational Hyg, 1974-76; Sci Offr, W Aust Govt Occupational Hlth Div, 1976-78; Occupational Hyg Advsr, Shell Grp of Cos, Aust, 1978-84; Retd, 1984; Pt-time cnslt, 1984-; Mbr Editl Review Bd, ACGIH Jrnl, Applied Occupational and Environmental Hyg, 1987-; Visng Fell, Occupational Hlth and Safety Unit, Austl Natl Univ, Canberra, 1994-96; Currently, Visng Lectr (Hon Snr Acad Assoc), Deakin Univ. Honour: Uganda Indep Medal, 1962. Memberships include: Fell, Royal Inst of Chem (now Royal Soc of Chem); UK Soc of Chem Ind, 1950-; Instn Indl Safety Offrs (now Inst Occupational Safety and Hlth), 1960-; Brit Occupational Hyg Soc, 1960-; Fell, Inst Pet, 1964-; Amn Conf of Governmental Indl Hygienists, 1967-; Fell, Inst Occupational Hygienists; Austl Acoustical Soc, 1976-; Royal Austl Chem Inst, 1977-, Fndn chmn Hazardous Substances Cttee, 1980-82; Occupational Hlth Soc of Aust, 1977-, Fndn pres, W Austl Branch, 1977-78; Austl Inst of Occupational Hygieneists, 1980-, Fell, 1989. Hobbies: Sailing; Yacht racing; Swimming; Mountain walking; Cross-Country Skiing. Address: 14 Tanilba Street, Werribee, Victoria 3030, Australia.

COLES Philip Walter, b. 20 July 1931. Sports Executive; Former Canoeist. Appointments: Dual Intl Rep, Aust, surf life saving and canoeing; Represented Aust, Canoeing World Championships, 1958, 1974, Olympic Games, Rome, 1960, Tokyo, 1964, Mexico, 1968; Winner, 26 Natl Canoe Titles; Mbr, Exec Bd, 1973-, Dir, Intl Rels, 1993-, Austl Olympic Cttee; Mbr, NSW Sports House Advsry Cttee, 1978-; Gen Mngr, Austl Olympic Team, Moscow, 1980; Mbr, Intl Olympic Cttee in Aust, 1982-; Dir, Exec and Full Bds, Sydney 2000 Olympic Bid Cttee, Austl Sports Commn, 1984-86, 1989-91; Sec Gen, Exec, Austl Olympic Fedn, 1985-93; Dir, Sydney Organising Cttee for Olympic Games, 1993-; Sec Gen, Intl Triathlon Union, 1994; Chmn, NSW Inst Sport, 1995; Bd Mbr, Austl Sports Drug Agcy, 1996. Honours: AM, 1983; Inducted, Austl Sporting Hall of Fame, 1993; Inducted, NSW Hall of Champions. Memberships: Patron, Triathlon Aust; N Bondi Surf Lifesaving Club; Carbine Cruising Yacht (Aust). Hobbies: Skin diving; Fishing; Surfing. Address: Level 27, The Chifley Tower, 2 Chifley Square, Sydney, NSW 2000, Australia.

COLL John Charles, b. 24 July 1944. University Administrator. m. Frances Maria Quiggin, 24 May 1968, 2 s. Education: BSc, 1st Class Hons, 1966, PhD, 1969, DSc, 1987, Univ Sydney. Appointments: Rsch Assoc, Univ IL, Urbana, 1969-71; Lectr, Imperial Coll, London, 1971-72; Lectr/Reader, James Cook Univ, Townsville, Aust, 1972-90; Pro Vice Chancellor, Cntrl Qld Univ, Rockhampton, 1991-96; Pro Vice Chancellor, and Prof in Chem, Austl Cath Univ, Sydney, 1996-. Honour: Fulbright Travelling Fell, 1969-71. Membership: Fell, Roy Ausl Chem Inst. Hobbies: Scuba diving; Underwater photography; Swimming; Travel; Singing. Address: Australian Catholic University, 40 Edward Street, North Sydney, NSW 2060, Australia.

COLLACO Iona Marie, b. 16 Feb 1954, Bombay, India. Doctor. Education: MB, BS, Bombay. Honour: Dr Shantabai Vora Prize in Gynaecol & Obs, 1977. Hobbies:

Reading; Sewing. Address: 71 Kambekar Street, Mumbai 400003, India.

COLLEY Alexander Gerald, b. 1 Aug 1909, Aust. Economist. m. Hilma, 1 d. Education: HDA; BEcon. Appointments: Admin Reg, Univ Sydney, 1936; Rsch Offr, 1948; Planning Offr, 1965. Publications: Sev articles. Honours: OAM, 1984; Disting Awd, Ma-Rung-Gai Cncl, 1978; Hon Mbr, Sydney Bush Walkers; Hon Sec, Colong Fndn for Wilderness. Hobbies: Bush Walking; Tennis; Gardening. Address: 7 Terrigal Avenue, Turramurra, NSW 2074, Australia.

COLLIER Helen Louisa, b. 17 Nov 1929, NZ. Musician; Pianist. m. Ronald Claris Gordon, 17 Nov 1962, 3 s. Education: ATCL, 1946; LRSM, 1947; Dip, NSW Conservatory of Music, Sydney, 1953; Dip, Vienna Conservatory of Music, 1960. Appointments: Piano Tchr, Samuel Marsden Sch, 1953-57; Perf as concert pianist in many cos, on radio, TV; Pvte Piano Tchr; Tutor Summer Sch, Wanganui Regl Cmnty Coll, 1985-90; Fndr, Musical Dir, Arcadian Singers, Taihape. Creative works: Num solo recitals; perf w NZ Symph and other Orchs. Honours: Bursary, NZ Govt, 1949; Travel Grant, Cntrl Reg Arts Cncl, NZ, 1989; Outstndng Achvmnt in the Arts, Taihape Rotary Club of NZ, 1996. Memberships: Inst of Regd Music Tchrs of NZ; Composers Assn of NZ; Chmn, Taihape and Dist Comm Arts Cncl; Fndrs Soc of NZ. Hobbies: Reading; Photography; Family interest. Address: Rongoiti Garden, Taihape, RDI, New Zealand.

COLLIER Henry W, b. 13 Sept 1940, Jackson, USA. Professor. Education: MBA, MA, MI Univ; BBA, Saginaw Valley State Univ; CPA (FL); CMA. Appointments: FL Atlantic Univ, 1980-87; San Remardines, 1987-91. Publications: Sev profl citations, Acctng Educn. Memberships: GLRL; ACON; PRIDE. Hobby: Philately. Address: 29/1 Sparta Street, Warilla, NSW 2528, Australia.

COLLIER James Erskine, b. 19 Mar 1926. Retired Consulting Engineer. m. Judith Farr, 18 Apr 1958, 2 s, 1 d. Education: BEng, Univ of Tas, 1950. Appointments: Engr, Shell Grp; Engr, Cnsltng Engrs Macdonald Wagner & Priddle; Engr, Pvte Prac; Retd, 1994. Memberships: Hon Fell, Instn of Engrs, Papua New Guinea, Fndn VP, 1969; Pres, Rotary Club of Hobart, 1986; Fell, Instn of Engrs Aust, Tasmanian Div Chmn, 1991, Fed Cncl Mbr, 1991-92. Hobbies: Golf; Olive groves; Maritime museums. Address: 21 McAulay Road, Sandy Bay, Tasmania 7005, Australia.

COLLIER John Donald, b. 28 Mar 1950, New Brunswick. Philosopher. Education: PhD, Philos of Sci, Univ of W Ontario; MA, UCLA; SB, Mit. Appointments: Asst Prof, Rice Univ, 1986-87; Asst Prof, Univ of Calgary, 1988-91; Snr Lectr, Univ of Melbourne, 1991-94; Rsch Assoc, Univ of Newcastle, 1994-. Honours: MIT Natl Schl, 1967; Can Rsch Fell, 1988-91. Memberships: Intl Soc for the Study of Symmetry Sci Advy Bd. Address: 365 Coal Point Road, Coal Point, NSW 2283, Australia.

COLLINGWOOD Ian, b. 5 May 1970, Christchurch, NZ. Company Director. m. Claudine, 1 s, 1 d. Education: B Com; IATA Airline Mktng; ZDU Bldng an Internet Community. Appointments: Natl Millenium Cttee, Fiji. Honours: Global Ldrshp Awd. Memberships: Tour Assn of N; Fiji Eco Tour Assn. Hobbies: Fine Arts; Extreme Sports; Meditation. Address: P O Box 9452, Nadi Airport, Fiji.

COLLINS Albert George Edward (Bert), b. 3 Oct 1918, Aust. Real Estate Valuer; Consultant. m. Mavis Daphne Dyson, 12 Apr 1941, 3 s, 1 d. Education: Commercial Course, Fell, Austl Inst of Valuers; Fell, Real Estate Inst of Aust; Fell, Austl Inst of Mngmt. Appointments: Real Estate Valuer, Valuation Prac, 1936-82; Cnslt Valuer, Austl Rep, Intl Real Estate Fedns Valuation Cttee, 1978-81; Statues Cttee, Intl Real Estate Fedn, 1981-85. Honours: Paul Harris Fell; Commnr for Declarations, Qld; Hon Admiral, TX Navy, 1982; Intl Commodore, Intl Yachting Fellshp of Rotarians, 1981-82-83. Hobbies: Physical Fitness; Football;

Yachting; Cruising. Address: 14 Vue Mirage. 200 Marine Parade, Gold Coast City, Queensland 4215, Australia.

COLLINS Bob, b. Newcastle, NSW. Politician. m. 3 children. Appointments: Worked as extension offr NT Dep of Agric; Mkt gardener Arnhem Land; Tech Offr Wildlife Rsch Div CSIRO, 1967-77; Elected as mbr for Arnhem HoR, 1977; Subsequently mbr for Arafura; Parl Ldr Austl Labor Party, 1981-86; Elected Sen for NT 1987; Min for Shipping Aviation Support and Min Asstng the PM for North Aust, 1990-92; Min for Trans and Comms, 1992-93; Min for Primary Inds and Energy, 1993-96; Shadow Min for Primary Inds and for North Aust and Territories, 1996-97. Address: 7th Floor, Hooker Bldg, Mitchell Street, Darwin, NT 0800, Australia.

COLLINS George Henry, b. 27 Mar 1935, Bristol, UK. Veterinarian. m. Michele Veness, 3 Oct 1997, 2 d. Education: BVSc; PhD; MRCVS. Appointments: Snr Lectr, Vet Parasitology; Sub Dean Student Welfare. Publications: Shedding the Blinkers - a Perception of Veterinary Education. 1997. Membership: Austl Vet Assn. Hobbies: Music; Wildlife; Writing; Education. Address: 17 Keston Avenue, Mosman, NSW 2088, Australia.

COLLIS Brian Williams, b. 8 Oct 1943. Barrister at Law. m. Margaret Virginia, 3 Nov 1972, 1 s, 1 d. Education: LLB. Appointment: Queens Cnsl, 1992; Austl Football League Tribunal, 1996-97, Chmn, 1998. Publications: Passive Smoking, 1991; Hearsay, 1993; Exemplary Damages, 1996. Membership: Victorian Football Assn, Chmn Tribunal 1979-93. Listed in: Who's Who in Australia. Hobbies: Tennis; Football; Walking; Reading. Address: Seabrook Chambers, 573 Lonsdale St, Melbourne, Vic, Australia.

COLLIS Kevin Francis, b. 18 Feb 1930, Halifax, Qld, Aust. Professor of Education. m. Beryl O'Shea, 5 May 1951, 2 s, 2 d. Education: BA, 1956, BEd, 1964, MEd, 1967, Univ Queensland; PhD, Univ Newcastle, NSW, 1972. Appointments: Tchr, elem schs, 1950-55, Tchr, Maths, Sci, secnd schs, 1956-60, Tchr, Maths, Logic, pvte sch, 1961-63, Queensland; Rsch Tchr, Expmtl Tchr, pvte sch, Queensland, 1964-67; Lectr, Snr Lectr, Assoc Prof, Fac Educ, Univ Newcastle, NSW, 1967-76; Prof, Educ, Hd, Dept Educl Stdys, Univ Tas, 1977-95; Prof Emer, Univ of Tas, 1995-; Hon Prof Educ, Univ Newcastle, NSW, 1996-. Publications: A Study of Concrete and Formal Operations in School Mathematics: A Piagetian Viewpoint, 1975; On Children's Reasoning, 1978; Co-auth, Cognitive Development - Research Based on a Neo-Piagetian Approach, 1978; Co-auth, Evaluating the Quality of Learning: The SOLO Taxonomy, 1982; Language Development and Intellectual Functioning, 1982; Co-auth, Learning to Add and Subtract, 1987; Co-auth, Mathematical Problem Solving Profiles, 1992. Honours include: Fell, Austl Coll Educ, 1983; VP, Austl Psychol Soc, Tas, 1983-89; VP, Inst Educl Rsch, Tas, 1984-90; Pres, Bd Developmental and Educl Psychols, Tas, 1986-93; Fell, Austl Psychol Soc, 1990. Memberships include: Fndn Mbr, Austl Assn Rsch Educ; Austl Assn Maths Tchrs; Intl Mbr, Amn Educl Rsch Assn; Intl Grp Stdy Psychol in Maths Educ. Listed in: Many including: Who's Who in Australia; Who's Who in Education; Who's Who in the World. Hobbies: Reading; Sport; Sailing; Camping; Gardening; Flying. Address: Centre for Special Education, Faculty of Education, University of Newcastle, University Drive, Callaghan, NSW 2308, Australia.

COLSTON Malcolm Arthur, b. 5 Apr 1938, Brisbane, Qld, Aust. Psychologist; Senator. 2 s. Education: AEd, 1964, BEd, 1966; BEd Hons, 1967, PhD, 1970, BA, 1983, Univ Qld. Appointments: Tchr, primary and secnd schs, 1957-64; Mbr, 1964-79, Maj's rank, 1970-79, granted mil title Maj, 1993, Army Reserve; Educl Guidance Offr, 1965-66; Cnslt Psychol, 1966-71; Pub Serv Rsch Offr, 1971-75; Sen, Austl Labor Party, Austl Parl, 1975-96; Indep, 1996-99. Publication: The Odd One Out, 1975. Honours: Prize, Educl Rsch, Qld Inst Educl Rsch, 1967; Queen's Silver Jubilee Medal, 1978; Austl Natl Medal, 1979; Reserve Force Medal, 1985; Parly Deleg to Cncl, Austl Natl Univ, 1986-97; Dpty Pres, Chmn Cttees, Austl

Senate, 1990-93, 1996-97. Memberships: Austl Psychol Soc; Austl Labor Party, 1958-96. Hobby: Computer programming. Address: PO Box 537, Chapel Hill, Queensland 4069, Australia.

COLVIN John Llewellyn. Education: AM, RFD, MBBS, Qld Univ, 1953; DO, London, 1959; FRCS, Edinburgh, 1960; FRACS, Aust, 1961; FRACO, Aust, 1978. Appointments: Snr Lectr, RACGP, Aust; Reg, Leeds, 1959-61; Staff Supvsr, Opth, Roy Victoria Eye and Ear Hosp, Melbourne, 1961-; Grp Capt, RAAF Reserve, Aust, 1975; Sr Assoc, Med Educ, Univ Melbourne, 1975; Dr, RAAF CANB, 1975. Honours: Hon Sp Ophth, Roy Flying Dr Serv, Aust, 1976-82; Hon Com Ophth, Hawthorn Football Club, Hawthorn, 1960. Memberships: Chmn, Vic Sect RACOphth, Vic, 1987-88; John Colvin Clinl Sch, Roy Victoria Eye and Ear Hosp, 1985; ActroMA; AMAL; RACO; RACS; RCSE. Address: Royal Victoria Eye and Ear Hospital, 32 Gisborne Street, East Melbourne, Vic 3002, Australia.

COMBE Gordon Desmond, b. 12 June 1917, South Australia, Australia. Retired. m. Margaret Eley, 28 Nov 1940, 1 s, 4 d. Education: ASA; ACIS. Appointments: Offr, State Bank of SA, 1934-39; Offr, Parly of SA, 1940-72; Ombudsman, SA, 1972-80. Publications: Responsible Government in South Australia, 1957; Parliament of South Australia, 1961. Honours: MC, 1944; CMG, 1980. Memberships: Legacy Club of Adelaide Inc; Masonic Lodge of SA. Address: 98 Penang Avenue, Melrose Park, SA 5039, Australia.

COMBE Peter Charles, b. 20 Oct 1948, Australia. Children's Composer/Entertainer. m. Carol, 7 May 1970, 1 s, 3 d. Education: Dip of Tchng. Creative works: 11 CDs, approx 180 songs; 1 book, released 1982-96; 6 videos. Honours: 3 Aria awds, 5 noms; 7 gold albums (2 platinum). Membership: Austl Performing Rights Assn. Hobbies: Family; Tennis; Reading; Music. Address: PO Box 146, Glenside, SA 5064, Australia.

COMPOMIZZO Uril Edwin, b. 15 Sept 1923, Hartford, Ark. Retired. m. Anna, 12 Jan 1947, 2 s, 1 d. Appointments: Line Mech, Stand Pacific Gas Liners Inc, Antioch, 1946-79; Instr, Safety Class, 1 yr, 1979; Outdoorsman, Fisherman; Writer, Camping and Fishing Column for Newspaper; Rprtr, Local Fishing News; Radio Interviewer; Speaker, Issues concerning Delta, Wildlife and Saving the outdoors; Pres, Citizens for safe Drinking Water, 1995-96; Ldr of successful campaign to raise funds to clean up fishing waters in Antioch, CA, 1999. Creative Works: Many articles for newspapers; Youth seminars, Get Hooked on Fishing not on Drugs; Many demonstrations; Videos. Honours: John A Britton Gold Medal; Citizen of the yr; Humanitarian of the yr; Cert of Appreciation; Many or hons. Memberships: CA Striped Bass Assn; Antioch Historical Soc; Delta Drifters Square Dance Club. Hobbies: Gdng; Fishing; Outdoor Writing; Fishing Seminars; Camping; Civic Special Events. Address: 2712 Bautista St, Antioch, CA 94509, USA.

CONDREN Conal Stratford, b. 1 Apr 1944, Greenwich, London, Eng. Academic. m. Dec 1967, 2 d. Education: BSc, MSc, PhD, London. Appointments: Asst Lectr, London Univ, 1967; Lectr, Polit Sci, 1970, Snr Lectr, 1977, Assoc Prof, 1985, Prof, 1990, Dir, Humanities Rsch Prog, 1997-, Univ NSW. Publications include: The Status and Appraisal of Classic Texts: An Essay on Political Theory, its Inheritance and on The History of Ideas; George Lawson's Politica and the English Revolution; The Language of Politics in Seventeenth-Century England; Satire, Lies and Politics: The Case of John Arbuthnot. Honours include: 2 Austl Rsch Cncl Awds, 1982, 1984. Memberships: VP, Austl and NZ Assn for Medieval and Renaissance Stdies, 1984-86, 1988-89; Visng Fell, Mbr, Clare Hall, Cambridge, 1990, Churchill Coll, Cambridge, 1996-97; Fell, Austl Acady of the Hums, 1990-. Address: 17 Tenth Avenue, Oyster Bay, Sydney 2225, Australia.

CONN Neil Raymond, b. 17 Aug 1936, Sydney, Aust. Administrator, Northern Territories. m. Lesley Jennifer, 1 s, 2 d. Education: BEc, 1st Class Hons, MEc, Univ

Sydney; PhD, Duke Univ, NC, USA. Appointments: C'wlth Bank and Reserve Bank, 1954-; Snr Lectr, Econs, Univ Sydney, 1961-75; Prin Administrator, OECD, Paris, 1975-77; Dpty Sec, NSW Treasury, 1977-81; Under Treas, NT Govt, 1981-83, 1986-96; Exec Dir, Corp Fin, CIBC, Aust, 1983-86; Administrator, NT, 1997-. Honour: James B Duke Fell, Duke Univ, 1967-68. Memberships: Territory Ins Office, 1981-83; Investnorth Mngmt Pty Ltd, 1987-95; Austl Statistics Advsry Cncl, 1987-96; NT Univ Cncl, 1987-96; Dir, Railnorth Pty Ltd, 1988-96; Chmn, Territory Loans Mngmt Corp, 1988-93; Treas and Chmn, Lords Taverners, NT, 1990-96; Gaming Control Commn, 1991-93; Dir, Darwin Perfng Arts Cntr, 1993; Chmn, NT Treas Corp, 1994-96; Chmn, Darwin Symphony Orch, 1996-; Econ Soc Aust and NZ; Phi Beta Kappa, USA. Hobbies: Golf; Tennis. Address: Government House, GPO Box 497, Darwin, NT 0801, Australia.

CONNARD Geoffrey Phillip (Hon), b. 13 Oct 1925, Melbourne, Aust. Retired Pharmaceutical Chemist. m. Judith Wills, June 1957, 2 s, 1 d. Education: MCEGrS, PhC, MPS, Victorian Coll of Pharm, 1947. Appointments: Political: Mbr Parl of Vic, 1982-96; Mbr Jt Parly Econ and Budget Review Cttee, 1982-88; Dpty Chmn, Jt Parly Socl Dev Cttee, 1988-92; Mbr, Jt Parly Econ Dev Cttee, 1992-96; Sec, Parly Liberal Party, 1988-96; Mbr, Parly Lib Cttee, 1985-96; Mbr, Intl Exec Cttee of C'wlth Parly Assn, 1993-96; Ldr delegs to Lithuania, Latvia and Estonia, 1994; Pakistan, Uzbekistan, Kazakhstan, Kyrgyzstan, 1995; Zimbawe, Botswana, Swaziland, 1996; Other: Mbr Bd Mngmt, After Care Hosp, 1974-91, Chmn, 1985-87; Fairfield Hosp, 1982-96, Chmn, 1987-90; St Georges Hosp, Inner East Geriatric Cntr, 1991-96, Vice-Chmn, 1994-96; Fndng Chmn, Macfarlane Burnett Cntr for Medl Rsch, 1987-90; Mbr Bd Mngmt, 1987-96, Mbr Macfarlane Burnett Centenary Celebration Committee; Intl Diabetes Inst, 1994-99, Chmn, 1997-99. Honour: Disting Serv Medal, Pharm Guild of Aust, 1996; Tstee, Brighton Hist Soc, Victoria Day Cncl, Leon Mow Charitable Tst. Memberships: Victorian Hosp Assn Vol Bd, chmn, Div 1 Cncl; Exec Mbr, Aust Day Cncl, 1974-97; Chmn, Travellers Aid Soc, 1994-97; Vice-Chmn, Aust Free China Assn, 1985-97; Chmn, Indep Review Panel on Supported Residential Services; Pharm Soc of Aust, 1947-97; Pharm Guild of Aust, 1951-97. Hobbies: Skiing; Reading; Politics. Address: 10 Olive Grove, Parkdale, Vic 3194, Australia.

CONNELL Desley William, b. 31 July 1938, Monto, Queensland, Aust. University Professor. m. Patricia, 27 Feb 1960, 1 s, 1 d. Education: BSc, MSc, PhD, Univ Queensland; DSc (Grif Univ). Appointments: Prof, Environmental Chem, Griffith Univ; Dir, Govt Chem Lab Queensland Hlth; Dean, Fac of Environ Scis, Griffith Univ. Publications: Bioaccumulation of Xenobiotoc Chems, 1990; Basic Concepts of Environ Chem, 1997. Honours: Rsch Prize, Austl Inst for Food Sci and Technol, 1970; Fell, Roy Austl Chem Inst, 1986; Inaugural Environ Medal, Roy Austl Chem Inst, 1990. Memberships: Pres, Australasian Soc for Ecotoxicology, 1996-99. Hobbies: Photography; Birdwatching. Address: 82, Roderick Street, Cornubia, Qld 4130, Australia.

CONOLLY Richard, b. 22 Dec 1920, Aust. Management Consultant. m. Norma Humphries, 18 May 1943, 2 d. Education: Sydney Tech Coll, Inst Admin, Univ NSW. Appointments: Served RAAF, 1943-46; Dpty Town Clk, 1946-49, Town Clk, 1949-58, Yass Municipality; Co Clk, Gen Mngr, SW Slopes Co Cncl, Electricity Supply, 1959-65; Town Clk, Willoughby Municipal Cncl, 1965-71; Fndn Dir and Chmn, NSW Metrop Waste Disposal Authy, 1971-85; Mbr, 1972-82, Chmn, 1980-82, Bd Dirs, Chatswood Dist Hosp; Dir, Bd, 1977-87, Chmn, Bd Dirs, 1987-95, Mercy Family Cntr, Waitara, NSW; State Chmn, NSW, Roy Inst Pub Admin Aust, 1983-86; Admor, Warringah Shire, NSW 1986-87; Mngmt Cnslt, 1987-; Gen Mngr, Baulkham Hills Shire Cncl, NSW, 1991-92. Publications: Pprs presented to natl and intl confs on waste mngmt. Honour: AM, 1986. Memberships: Life Fell, Inst Municipal Mngmt; Fell, Inst Pub Admin Aust; Fell, Austl Inst Mngmt. Hobbies: Golf; Tennis; Reading. Address: 145 Deepwater Road, Castle Cove, NSW 2069, Australia.

CONRAD John, b. 3 Aug 1935, USA. College Professor. m. Barbara J Daugherty, 15 June 1963, 1 s, 1 d. Education: BA, Art Educ, IN Univ of PA, 1958; MFA, Ceramics, Carnegie-Mellon Univ, 1963; PhD, Ceramic Rsch, Univ of Pittsburgh, 1970. Appointments: Art Instr, 1959-64; Adjust Instr, 1961-64; Prof of Fine Arts, 1966-; Chmn of Dept, 1980-82, 1985-88. Lectr, Demonstrator, 1992; Cnslt, Mexican Govt; Lectr, Cnslt, Factories and Educl Insts, China, 1995, 1998; Ceramic Demonstrator, San Diego Dist High Sch's Ceramic Prog, 1997-98. Creative Works: Ceramic Formulas; Contemporary Ceramic Techniques; Contemporary Ceramic Formulas; Ceramic Windchimes; Advanced Ceramic Manuals; Studio Potters Dictionary; Cone Six Ceramics; Ceramic Extruder for the Studio Potter; Sev mag articles. Honours: Disting Alumnus Awd; Tchng Ex Awd; 51 Ceramic Exhibits. Memberships: Allied Artists; Three Rivers Art Assn; Natl cncl of Educ Ceramic Arts; Allied Craftsmen of San Diego; Amn Ceramic Soc. Address: 770 Cole Ranch Road, Encinitas, CA 92024, USA.

COOGAN Clive Keith, b. 21 Apr 1925, Eastwood, New South Wales, Australia. Scientist. Education: BSc, Hons, Sydney; MSc, Sydney; PhD, Bristol; FAIP; FTSE; FRS, Vic; FRSA. Appointments: CSIRO Rsch Sci to Asst Chf; Chmn, Aust Ind Assn, 1971-75. Publications include: Magnetic Resonance (ed), 1969. Honour: Hartnett Medal, Roy Soc of Arts, 1994. Memberships: Sec, Austl Inst of Phys; CSIRO Off Assn. Hobbies: Science History; Tennis. Address: 2/37 Yongala Street, Balwyn, Victoria 3103, Australia.

COOK David Ian, b. 2 Apr 1958, London, England. Medical Practitioner; Medical Research Scientist. m. Audrey Mary Fisk, 2 s, 1 d. Education: BSc, Med, 1979, MB BS, 1983, MSc, 1984, MD, 1995, Sydney Univ. Appointments: Jnr Res Med Offr, Roy N Shore Hosp, Sydney, 1984; Temp Lectr, Physiol, Sydney Univ, 1986; Lectr in Physiol, 1987-89, Snr Lectr, 1990-91, Assoc Prof 1991-97, Assoc Dean, Fac of Med, 1995-96, Prof of Cellular Physiol, 1998-, Univ of Sydney; Vis Med Practitioner, Clin Pharm, Roy Prince Alfred Hosp, Sydney, 1991-; Fell, Med Fndn, Univ of Sydney, 1997; APPS Visiting Lectr, 1999. Publications: 103 sci articles in prof med jrnls. Honours: Gottschalk Medal, Austl Acady of Scis, 1996; John and Yvonne Almgren Rsch Awd, Natl Heart Fndn, NSW Branch. Memberships: Austl Physiol and Pharm Soc, treas, 1991-95; Intl Union of Physiol Scis, dpty chmn of gastrointestinal cmmn, 1993-, sci prog cttee of the 2001 congress, 1998-; Austl Club, Sydney; Fndn for Classical Archaeol, cncl, 1993-; Soc of Friends of the Nicholson Mus, cncl, 1998-. Hobbies: Archaeology; Renaissance Art and architecture. Address: c/o Department of Physiology, F13, University of Sydney, NSW 2006, Australia.

COOK Geoffrey Page, b. 21 Mar 1928. Engineer. m. Geraldine Valerie Turner, 16 Apr 1955, 1 s, 1 d. Education: BCE Hons. Appointments: Past MD, John Holland Grp, Past Chmn, State Electricity Commn of Vic; Chmn, Snowy Mountains Engrng Corp; Past Chmn, Telstra Super Pty Ltd; Currently Dir, Transurban City Link Ltd. Honour: AM, 1990. Memberships: Fell, Inst of Engrs, Aust; Fell, The Acady of Technological Scis & Engrs. Hobby: Tennis. Address: 6 Hamilton Close, 1 Hamilton Road, Malvern, Vic 3144, Australia.

COOK Martyn Gregory, b. 7 Sept 1958, Sydney, Aust. Antique Dealer. Career: Martyn Cook Antiques Pty Ltd, Woollahra, Sydney, Aust. Membership: Austl Antique Dealers's Assn. Hobbies: Fine arts; Travel; Swimming; Picnics. Address: 104 Queen Street, Woollahra, Sydney, NSW 2025, Australia.

COOKE Kevin George (Maj Gen), b. 21 Apr 1931, Melbourne, Australia. Company Director. m. Anne, 4 Mar 1978. Education: Law, Melbourne Univ. Appointments: Legal: Ptnr of Cooke & Cussen Sols, Melbourne, 1953-75; Snr Ptnr, 1975-87; Snr Cnslt, 1987-91; Corporate: Dir, num natl and intl cos; Government: Snr Advsr for Joint Ventures, Tourism and Trade, to Beihai Govt, China, 1994-; Mbr, Austl Defence Reserves Support Cncl, 1993-; Mbr Gold Coast Cty Cncl Intl Rels

Advsry Cttee, 1996; Military: Chief of Army Reserve, 1985-88; Hon Col, The Roy Vic Regiment, 1988-94. Honours: Off of Order of Aust; Reserve Force Decoration w 2 clasps; Efficiency Decoration w 2 clasps; Austl Active Serv Medal, 1945-75; Vietnam Logistic and Support Medal; Field Marshall Sir Thomas Blamey Medal; Sir Edmund Herring Meml Awd; Corps of Commissionaires Awd of Merit. Memberships: Fell, Austl Inst of Co Dirs; Fell, Soc of Snr Execs; Intl Bar Assn; Law Inst of Vic; Pres, Roy United Serv Inst of Qld, 1998-. Address: 47 Admiralty Drive, Paradise Waters, Qld 4217, Australia.

COOKE Robin Brunskill, (Rt Hon, Lord Cooke of Thorndon, Baron), b. 9 May 1926. Life Peer, Wellington, NZ & Cambridge in the County of Cambridgeshire; Lord of Appeal and Mbr of Judicial Cttee of Privy Cncl. m. Phyllis Annette Miller, 1952, 3 s. Education: Wanganui Collegiate Sch; LLM, 1st class hons, Vic Univ Coll, Wellington; Trav Schlshp in Law, NZ, 1950; Clare Coll. Cambridge; PhD, Cambridge, 1955. Appointments: Rsh Fell, Gonville and Caius Coll, Cambridge, 1952-56; Called to Bar, Inner Temple, 1954; Hon Bencher; Practised at NZ Bar, 1955-72, QC 1964; Judge, Supreme Crt, 1972-76; Judge, Crt of Appeal, 1976-86; Pres, Crt of Appeal, 1986-96; Western Samoa, 1982, 1994-, Cook Islands, 1981, 1982; Judge, Supreme Crt of Fiji, 1995-; Chmn, Commn of Inquiry into Housing, 1970-71; Visng Fell, All Souls Coll, Oxford, 1990; Sultan Azlan Shah Law Lectr, Malaysia, 1990; Peter Allan Mem Lectr, Hong Kong, 1994; Hamlyn Lectr, England, 1996; Commn Mbr, Intl Commn of Jurists, 1993-; Spec Status Mbr, The Am Law Inst, 1993-; Life Mbr, Lawasia. Hon LLD; Vic Univ of Wellington, 1989; Cambridge 1990; Hon DCL Oxford, 1991; Non Perm Judge Hong Kong Court of Final Appeal, 1997-. Publications: (ed) Portrait of a Profession, 1969; Ed-in-Chf, The Laws of N.Z.; Articles in law reviews and pprs at intl law confs. Honours: Kt, 1977; PC, 1977; KBE, 1986; Hon Fell, NZ Legal Rsch Fndn, 1993. Hobbies: Theatre; The Times Crossword; Watching Cricket. Listed in: Who's Who. Address: 4 Homewood Crescent, Karori, Wellington, New Zealand.

COOKSLEY William Graham Earnshaw, b. 30 May 1940. Medical Practitioner. m. Enid Vivienne Tindale, 28 Mar 1964, 1 s, 1 d. Education: MBBS 1963, MD 1978, Univ of Qld; FRACP, 1974. Appointments: Medl Offr, Roy Brisbane Hosp, 1964-68; Lectr, 1969-70, NHMRC Schl, 1971-73, Snr Lectr and Assoc Prof, 1975-88, Univ of Qld; Nuffield Fell, Harrow, Eng, 1973-74; Visng Scientist, Natl Insts of Hlth, USA, 1981; Prof, Dir, Clinl Rsch Cntr, Roy Brisbane Hosp Fndn, Brisbane, Aust, 1988-. Publications: Over 100 articles in sci lit. Honours: Univ Open Schlshp, Univ of Qld, 1958-63; Schlshp, Natl Hlth and Medl Rsch Cncl, 1971-72; Nuffield Travelling Fellshp for Aust, 1973-74. Memberships: Var Liver Orgs: Amn, Eurn; Austl; Intl; Hon Sec, Asian Pacific Assn for Stdy of the Liver, 1982-86. Hobbies: Medieval history; Gardens and trees; Art; Antiques. Address: Clinical Research Centre, Royal Brisbane Hosp, Brisbane, Qld 4029, Australia.

COOLAHAN Cathrine Anne, b. 2 Nov 1929. Artist; Designer. m. Maxwell Dominic Coolahan, 5 Mar 1951. Education: Assoc, Sydney Tech Coll, 1950. Appointments: Advtng and Publicity Des, Farmer & Co, Sydney, 1950-52; Advtng and Publicity Des, J Inglis Wright, NZ Ltd, 1952-53; Advtng and Publicity Des, Carlton Carruthers du Chateau & King, 1954-57; Asst Educ Offr, Dominion Mus, 1957-58; Fashion Illustrator, James Smith Ltd, 1959-60; Publicity Des, Carlton Carruthers, 1960-62; James Smith & Tutor, Wgtn Polytech Sch of Des, 1962-64; Self-Employed Graphic Des, Fine Arts, Curric Dev and Tchng for Sch of Des, 1964-66; Wgtn Polytech, 1966-71, 1972-83, 1984, 1985, 1995; Travelling Schlshp, QE II Arts Cncl, 1971-72. Creative Works include: Flight, Fabric Sculpture, 1984; Predater, Predator, Paper Wood, Flax Ties, Sculpture, 1984; Hunter, Paper Sculpture, 1984; Appropriations, Aquatint, 1986; Lifeguard, 3 Dimensional Etching and Hand Made Paper, 1987; Map of the Sounds, Etching, 1988; Isis & Rangi, Lithograph, 1988; Art Sees, Etching, 1989; NZ Portraits, 1990; Winged Victories and Clipped Wings, 1992; Anima, Etching, 1994. Honours include: Rep NZ at 36th Venice Bienalle, 1972; Japanese cultural ex as Printmaker to learn papermaking, 1977; QE II Purchase Grant for Retrospective Exhibn at Dowse Art Mus, 1984; QE II Grant to attend Natl Paper Conf, Tasmanian Univ Rsch Co, Hobart, Aust, 1987; Appointed Life Mbr, NZ Crafts Cncl for work on Educ Cttee with Craft Des Courses, 1989; Funding Support/Sufferage Centennial Yr Trust and QE II Arts Cnsl, Dowse Art Mus, 1992. Memberships: Bd, NZ print Cncl, 1968-76; Bd, NZ Design Cncl, 1977-84; Bd, Queen Elizabeth II Arts Cncl, 1979; Bd, Wellington Community Arts Cncl, 1981; Bd, Cntrl Reg Arts Cncl, 1982-85; Design Cncl Rep, NZ Ind Design Cncl, 1984; Bd, NZ Craft Cncl, 1984-85; Bd, Humanz, NZ Soc of the Hum, 1995-99; Chair Intl Cttee, Zonta Intl Wellington Club, 1998-99. Listed in: Artists and Galleries of Australia and New Zealand, 1979; Who's Who in New Zealand, 1978, 1991; Encyclopaedia of New Zealand, 1986. Hobbies: Gardening; Observation of Plant Responses to changing UV Light Levels and Climate Change. Address: 57 Sefton St, Wadestown, Wellington, New Zealand.

COOMBS Janet Viola, b. 16 Aug 1932, London, Eng. Barrister. Education, BA, 1961; LLB 1960. Appointments: Admitted to prac as Bar, 1959; Honours: Awd'd Papal Cross Pro Ecclesiae et Pontifice, 1994; AM, 1997. Memberships: St Thomas More Soc; NSW Bar Assn; Women Lawyers Assn; Canon Law Soc of Aust and NZ. Address: Unit 13, 174 Spit Rd, Mosman 2088, NSW, Australia.

COOMBS Robert Holman, b. 16 Sept 1934, Salt Lake City, Utah, USA. Professor. m. Carol Jean Cook, 29 May 1958, 2 s, 5 d. Education: BS, 1958, MS, 1959, Univ UT; PhD, WA Univ, 1964. Appointments: Asst Prof, Sociol, IA Univ, 1963-66; Postdoct Fell, Behavioral Sci Cntr, Bowman Gray Sch of Med, 1966, Asst Prof, 1966-68, Assoc Prof, 1968-70, Wake Forest Univ; Career Rsch Specialist, CA Dept of Mental Hygiene, Camarillo, 1970-73; Assoc Rsch Sociologist, 1970-77, Assoc Prof, Biobehavioral Scis, Sch of Med, 1977-78, Prof, 1978-, Univ CA, Los Angeles; Chf, Camarillo Neuropsychiat Inst, 1970-78; Asst Dir, Rsch, Univ CA, Los Angeles, Neuropsychiat, Inst Cntr for Hlth scis, 1978-81; Dir, Off Educn of Neuropsychiat Inst, 1980-90, Univ CA Los Angeles Family Learning Cntr, Oxnard, CA, 1977-84, Univ CA Los Angeles Grief and Bereavement Prog, 1993-; Cnslt, World Fedn for Med Educ, 1990-. Publications: Num books, chapts and articles in profl jrnls. Honours: Sev. Memberships include: Intl Sociol Assn; Intl Family Therapy Assn; World Fedn of Mental Hlth. Address: University of California at Los Angeles, School of Medicine, 760 Westwood Plaza, Los Angeles, CA 90024-1759, USA.

COOPER Martin, b. 7 Mar 1934, London, UK. Professor. m. Lois, 1 June 1966, 1 d. Education: BSc, Manchester; DipEd, Sydney; MA, Dalhousie; PhD, Ottawa. Appointments: Knox Grammar Sch, Wahroonga; Univ of Ottawa; Univ of NSW, Sydney. Publications: Textbooks on phys, stats. Memberships: Pres, Sydney Mozart Soc; Past-Commodore Trimaran Yacht Club of Aust; Past Pres, Montessori Assn of NSW. Address: 56 Charles Street, Killara, NSW, Australia 2071.

COOPER Robert Fitzgerald, b. 25 Apr 1936, Melbourne, Aust. Member of Parliament. m. Jennifer Shinnick, 5 Jan 1959, 1 s, 2 d. Education: Xavier Coll; Melbourne Inst of Technol. Appointments: Elected to Parl, 1985; Shadow Min for Local Govt, 1985-87; Shadow Min for Pol and Emerg Servs, 1987-89; Shadow Min for Local Govt and Tourism, 1989-90; Shadow Min for Pub Transp, 1990-91; Chmn, Pub Bodies Review Cttee, 1992-96; Parly Sec for Transp, Rds and Ports, 1996; Min for Transp, 1997-. Membership: Chart Inst of Transp. Hobbies: Golf; Reading; Politics; Walking. Address: 80 Collins Street, Melbourne 3000, Australia.

COPEMAN Herbert Arthur, b. 24 Sept 1923, Brisbane, Qld, Aust. Medical Practitioner. m. Peggy, 29 Nov 1947, 3 s, 1 d. Education: MBBS (UQ); FRACP. Appointments: Cnslt, Physn and Endocrinologist, Roy Brisbane Hosp, 1957-74; Dir, Postgrad Medl Educ, Univ of West Aust, Perth, 1975-88. Publications: Rsch pprs on the Endocrinology of Arterial Disease; Meditation, a chapt in Ways of Healing, 1987; Book: Let Us Not Forget to Remember - Memories of a Typhoon Pilot, 1995. Memberships: FRACP; Past Pres, Fell, Patron, Postgrad Medl Educ Fedn of Aust. Hobbies: Gardening; Walking; Fishing; Reading about religions. Address: 36 Mermaid Avenue, Emu Point, Albany, Western Australia, Australia.

COPPERMAN William H, b. 4 Dec 1932, Cleveland, USA. Value Engineer; Consultant. m. Rena June Dorn, 26 Dec 1954, 2 s. Education: BS, Duquesne Univ, 1954; MBA, Univ S CA, Los Angeles, 1962; JD, Univ San Fernando, 1977. Appointments: Corp Mngr, Value Engr, Hughes Aircraft Co, Los Angeles, 1957-89; Pres, Copperman Assocs in Value Engrng Inc, Los Angeles, 1983-; Bd Dir, Miles Value Fndn, WA. Publications: Many articles in profl jrnls. Honours: Outstndng Achievement Awd, US Army, 1986; Value Engrng Awd, Purchasing Mag, WA, 1987; Achievement in Value Engrng, US Army, 1977-82. Memberships: SAVE Intl; Value Soc. Hobbies: Computer Programming; Tennis; Golf. Address: Copperman Assocs Vanue Engineering, 32 Lincoln Place, Rancho Mirage, CA 92270-1970, USA.

COPPOLA Francis Ford, b. 7 Apr 1939 Detroit MI. Film Director; Writer. m. Eleanor Neil, 2 s - 1 dec, 1 d. Education: Hofstr Univ; Univ of CA. Appointments: Artistic Dir Zoetrope Studios, 1969-; Owner Niebaum-Coppola Estate Napa Valley. Films incl: Dementia 13, 1963; This Property is Condemned, 1965; Is Paris Burning?, 1966; You're A Big Boy Now, 1967; Finian's Rainbow, 1968; The Rain People, 1969; Patton, 1971; The Godfather, 1972; American Grafitti, 1973; The Conversation, 1974; The Godfather Part II, 1975; The Great Gatsbuy, 1974; The Black Stallion - prodr - 1977; Apocalypse Now, 1979; One from the Heart, 1982; Hammett - prodr - 1982; The Escape Artist, 1982; The Return of the Black Stallion, 1982; Rumble Fish, 1983; The Outsiders, 1983; The Cotton Club, 1984; Peggy Sue Got Married, 1986; Gardens of Stone, 1986; Life without Zoe, 1988; Tucker: The Man and His Dream 1988; The Godfather Part III, 1990; Dracula, 1991; My Family/Mi Familia, 1995; Don Juan De Marco, 1995; Jack, 1996; The Rainmaker, 1997; Exec Prodr The Secret Garden, 1993; Mary Shelley's Frankenstein, 1994; Buddy, 1997. Th Directions incl: Private Lives; The Visit of the Old Lady; San Francisco Opera Co, 1972. Honours: Cannes Film Awd for The Conversation, 1974; Dirs Guild Awd for The Godfather; Acady Awd for Best Screenply for Patton; Golden Palm - Cannes - 1979 for Apocalypse Now; Also awd'd Best Screenbplay Best Dir and Best Picture Oscars for The Godfather Part II; US Army Civ Serv Awd; Commandeur Ordre des Arts et des Lettres. Address: Zoetrope Studios, 916 Kearny Street, San Francisco, CA 94133, USA.

CORDOVEZ Diego, b. 3 Nov 1935 Quito. Diplomatist. m. Maria Teresa Somavia, 1960, 1 s. Education: Univ of Chile. Appointments: Admitted to bar, 1962; For Serv of Ecuador until 1963; Joined UN as Econ Affairs Offr, 1963; Polit Offr on spec missions to Dominican Repub, 1965, Pakistan, 1971; Dir UN Econ and Socl Cncl Sec, 1973-78; Asst Sec-Gen for Econ and Socl Matters UN, 1978-81; Spec Rep of UN Sec-Gen on Libya-Malta dispute, 1980-82; Sec-Gen rep on UN Commn of Inquiry on hostage crisis in Teheran, 1980; Snr Offr responsible for efforts to resolve Iran/Iraq war, 1980-88; Under Sec-Gen for Spec Polit Affairs, 1981-88; Spec Envoy to Grenada, 1983; UN Mediator Afghanistan, 1982-88; Rep for implementation of Geneva Accords, 1988-89; Spec Advsr to UN Sec-Gen for Cyprus; Min for For Affairs, 1988-92; Pres World Trade Cntr - Ecuador - 1993-; Spec Cnsl Le Boeuf Lamb Greene and Macrae, 1993-. Publications: UNCTAD and Development Diplomacy, 1971; Out of Afghanistan: The Inside Story of the Soviet Withdrawal - jntly - 1995. Honours: Order of Merit - Ecuador; Legion d'honneur; Grand Cross - Spain, Portugal, Brazil, Argentina, Chile, Peru, Colombia, Venezuela. Memberships: Mbr Am Soc of Intl Law. Hobbies: Reading; Carpentry. Address: Calle Afganistan 1988, El Bosque, Quito, Ecuador.

CORNELIUS Stella, b. 4 Dec 1919, Sydney, Aust. Convenor of the Conflict Resolution Network. m. Max Cornelius, 24 Oct 1943, dec Apr 1978, 1 s, 1 d. Education: Dip of Bus Admin. Appointments: Mngmt posns, 1943-78; Convenor and initiator of Peace Prog of the UN Assn of Aust, 1973-; Dir, Intl Yr of Peace (Austl Govt), 1986; Mbr, Natl Consultative Cttee on Peace and Disarmament; Mbr Natl Cttee on Human Rights Educ; Convenor and Initator, The Conflict Resolution Netwrk, 1986-; Convenor, Initiator, Media Peace Awds: Convenor and Initiator, Austl Campaign for a Min for Peace, Convenor and Initiator of the Bilateral Peace Treaties Proposal. Honours: OBE; 1978 for Com and comm serv; AO for Intl relations and peace; Hon DLitt, Macquarie Univ. Memberships: Peace Messenger of UN; FAIM. Hobby: Music. Address: PO Box 1016, Chatswood, NSW 2057, Australia.

CORNER Lynette, b. 27 Nov 1921. Art Consultant; Former Arts Administrator. m. 29 Dec 1943, Frank Henry Corner, 2 d. Education: MA (1st Class Hons), Latin, French, Vic Univ of Wellington, NZ, 1943; Cordon Bleu (Paris) Cooking Sch Cert, 1951; Wellington Tchrs Trng Coll, 1943. Appointments: Tchr, Wellington Coll, 1944; Cataloguer, Natl Lib, 1944-48; Translator-Interpreter, NZ Deleg, Paris Peace Conf, 1946; Active as Diplomatic Wife through career of Husband, 1943-80; Tstee, Natl Art Gallery, Natl Mus, Natl War Mus, 1974-85; Mbr, Natl Art Gallery Cncl, 1974-85; Dpty Chmn, Art Selection Cttee, 1976-79, Chmn, 1979-85; Art Advsr to ECNZ on formation Rutherford Trust Collection of 20th Century NZ Art, 1989-. Publications: Contbr to: An Eye, an Ear and a Voice, 1993; Contributor of numerous film and book reviews; Portrait photos in collection of HM Queen Elizabeth II and in NASA Apollo Lunar Surface Jrnl. Memberships: Cncl Mbr, NZ Acady of Fine Arts, 1974-79; Women's Cuxtes Symph, Opera, Ballet, Corcoran Art Gallery, 1968-72; Soc of Arts and Letters, Wash DC, 1969-72. Listed in: Who's Who in New Zealand; New Zealand Who's Who Aotearoa. Hobbies: The Arts; Practical Photography; Friends; Cats. Address: 26 Burnell Avenue, Wellington 6001, New Zealand.

CORNISH Richard, b. 18 Dec 1942, Summer Hill, Sydney, Aust. Artist; Writer; Lecturer; Teacher. 1 s, 2 d. Education: Dip Fine Arts (AESTC); Masters Degree in Art Hist, Flinders Univ; Dip Ed, ITATE, Sydney, CAE. Appointments: Pt time TAFE, Newcastle Sch Arts and Media, 1969-75; Newcastle Univ, 1984-86; Newcastle Tafe, 1987-89; Tamworth Tafe, 1989-91; South Cross Univ, 1992-94; Lismore, Grafton McLean Tafe, 1994-97; Tchr, Art Hist, Art Theor, drawing. Publications: The Woman Lilith, 1975; In Search of Mahgudi, 1988; The Ninth Immortal, 1988; Conceits of Unfulfilment, 1983; Across Cultural Lines, 1997. Honours: Newcastle Univ Prize for Painting, 1966; Le Gay Breton Prize for Draughtmanship AGNSW, 1967; Readers Digest Prize, Natl Art Sch, 1967; May Day Prize for Protest Painting on Vietnam War, 1969; Film Lesson in Degree Kodak Prize, 1972. Memberships; NAVA, Green/Left, Greenpeace. Hobbies: Asian and Mediterranean gourmet cooking; Growing Asian vegetables; Wit and humour.

CORNISH Robert Francis, b. 18 May 1942, England. Diplomat. m. Jane, 1964, 3 d. Appointments: British High Commn to Brunei, 1983-86; For Off Spokesman, 1990-93; Snr Trade Commnr to Hong Kong, 1993-97; British Consul Gen to Hong Kong, 1997; British Amb to Israel, 1998-. Honours: LVO, 1978; CMG, 1994. Address: British Embassy, Tel Aviv, Israel.

CORNISH Ronald, b. 21 Mar 1944, Burnie, Tas, Aust. Parliamentarian. m. Rosemary Jane Elliston, 22 Aug 1970, 3 d. Appointments: Tasmanian Police Force, 1961; Austl Police Contingent seconded UN Forces, Cyprus, 1965-66; Insp, 1976; Elected Mbr, Tasmanian House of Assembly, 1976, re-elected 1979, 1982, 1986, 1989; Opposition Spokesman, Transp, Educ, Police and Emer Servs; Appointed Opposition Whip, 1979; Tasmanian Del to C'wlth Parly Assn S Pacific Conf, Rarotonga, Cook Is's, 1981; Appointed Sec to Cabinet, Parly Sec to Premier and Govt Whip, 1982; Austl Del, USA visit, 1983; Appointed Speaker, House of Assembly, 1986; Attended

17th Conf, Presiding Offrs and Clks, Melbourne, 1986, 18th Conf, Rarotonga, 1987; Appointed Min Police and Emer Servs, Sea Fisheries, Licensing, Gaming, Rd Safety and Min Assisting Premier, 1988; Shadow Min Police and Emer Servs, Sea Fisheries, Licensing, Gaming, Rd Safety, 1989; Atty Gen, Min Justice, Min Fin and Budget Mngmt, Ldr of Govt in House of Assembly, 1992; Atty Gen, Min Justice, Min Assisting Treas, Ldr of Govt in House of Assembly, 1993. Honours: Represented Tas, Austl Rules Football, 1964; Tasmanian Profl Sprint Champion, 1971-72, 1973-74; Cur Holder, Tasmanian Veterans Athletic Recs, 100 and 400 metres. Membership: C'wlth Parly Assn. Hobbies: Travel; Athletics; Australian Rules Football; Lawn bowls; Photography. Address: 17 West Street, Burnie, Tas 7320, Australia.

CORRIGAN (Margaret) Anne, b. 9 Mar 1936, Oberon, NSW, Aust. Author; Specialist Floral Designer; Lecturer. m. Alwyn John Corrigan, 1 s, 2 d. Education: Gen and Midwifery Nursing (RN-CM), 1954-60; Coml Art, 1957; Jrnlsm, 1969; Floral Art, 1990-93; Unique rsch and writing and on the dev of educ progs, concerning multiple birth families and their children, world and Austl firsts, 1974-99. Appointments: Nurse Educ Gen (PH Hosp Sy), 1958-59; Midwifery and Midwifery Nurse Educator, Canberra, 1959-65; Pub Rels, Denmark Coph Univ and Hosps, 1965; Redfern Day Nursery Matron, 1966; Mudge Dist Hosp , Matron, 1967; Fndr, Aust Multiple Birth Assn; Natl Dir Family and Community Educ Prog, 1973-80; Lit Review Commn,and Advsry Bd, 1980-98; Jnlst, St Ives hs, NSW, 1985-90. Publications: Books: Twice as Nice, 1978, 1982; Twins and You, 1983; Potty Poems, 1980; Parenting Twins, 1991, 1995; 50 pprs on multiple birth, 1973-99; 25 years history of St Ives High School, 1989; 25 yrs history of Austl Multiple Birth Assn, 1996. Honours: Spec Awd, NSW Multiple Birth Assn, 1989; Life Mbr: East Subs Multiple Birth Assn, 1989, Austl Multiple Birth Assn, 1996; Spec Awd for Dedication, Serv and Jrmlsm, St Ives HS, 1995. Memberships: Austl Soc of Auths; Copyright Cnsl Aust; Sydney Symph Orch; Nurses Reg Bd; Roy Soc of Ag - Floral Art; Hon Mbr, St Ives hs, NSW; Life Mbr, Austl Multiple Birth Assn. Hobbies: Literature; Reading; Playing music; Travel worldwide; Excellent food; Opera House concerts; Art; Flowers and creative art; Water sport and water travel. Address: 14 Mudies Road, St Ives, NSW 2075, Australia.

CORRIGAN Robert Anthony, b. 21 Apr 1935. Educator. m. Joyce Mobley Corrigan, 2 s, 2 d. Education: AB, Brown Univ, 1957; MA, 1959, PhD, 1967, Univ PA. Appointments: Rschr, PA Histl Cmmn, 1957-59; Lectr, Amn Lit and Culture, Univ Gothenburg, Sweden, 1959-62; Lectr, Engl Lit, Bryn Mawr Coll, 1962-63; Instr, Amn Civilization, Univ PA, Visng Lectr, PA Mus Coll of Art, 1963-64; Instr, Engl, 1964-66, Asst Prof of Engl, Asst Prof of Amn Civilization, 1966-69, Assoc Prof of Engl, Assoc Prof of Amn Civilization, 1969-73, Univ IA; Visng Prof, Amn Stdies, Grinnell Coll, 1970; Dean, Coll of Arts and Scis, Prof of Engl, Univ MO, Kansas Cty, 1973-74; Provost for Arts and Hums, Prof of Engl, Univ MD, Coll Park, 1974-79; Chan, Prof of Engl, Univ MA, Boston, 1979-88; Pres, Prof of Engl and Hums, San Fran Univ, 1988-. Publications: Sev articles in profl jrnls. Honours include: Schlshp, Brown Univ, 1953-57; PA Colonial Soc Essay Awd, 1958, 1959; Corrigan Schlshp, 1989; Disting Urban Fell, Assn of Urban Univs, 1992. Memberships: Sev. Address: 1600 Holloway Avenue, San Francisco, CA 94132, USA.

CORSER Troy, b. 27 Nov 1971, Wollongong, Aust. Professional Motorcycle Racer. Career: First road race meeting, Sydney's Oran Pk, 1989; Won the NSW Lightweight Superstreet Series, 1990; Youngest rider promoted to "A" Grade, Aug 14 1990; First factory sponsored ride w Peter Jackson Yamamha team on a TZ250B, contested Austl Road Race Chamionship, also overseas debut in Malaysian round, Pan Pacific Championship, 1991; Won first Austl Superbike Championship, 1993; Contract to ride w Fast By Ferrari Ducati team, won Amn Superbike Championship, 1994; Contracted to ride factory Ducatis for Austrian Promotor Team in Superbike World Chamionship, 1994. W Promotor Power Ducati team won first World Superbike Championship (first Austl and youngest rider to do so), 1996; Moved to 500cc (GP-1) class w Yamaha, 1997; Returned to Superbikes, w Ducati AD-VF Team, 1998. Hobbies: Golf; Surfing; Motorcross; Jet ski-ing; Karting; Fitness Training.

COSBY Bill, b. 12 Jul 1937 Philadelphia. Actor. m. Camille Hanks, 1964, 5 children, one s dec. Education: Temple Univ; Univ of MA. Appointments: Served USNR, 1956-60; Pres Rhythm and Blues Hall of Fame, 1968-; Tv appearances incl: The Bill Cosby Show, 1969, 1972-73; I Spy; The Cosby Show, 1984-92; Cosby Mystery Series, 1994-; Recitals incl: Revenge, To Russell, My Brother, With Whom I Slept; Top Secret; 200 MPH; Why Is There Air; Wonderfulness; It's True, It's True, Bill Cosby is a Very Funny Fellow: Right, I Started Out as a Child; 8:15, 12:15; Hungry; Reunion, 1982; Bill Cosby...Himself, 1983; Those of You With or Without Children, You'll Understand; Num night club appearances; Exec Prodr A Different Kind of World, TV series, 1987-. Films Incl: Hickey and Boggs, 1972; Man and Boy, 1972; Uptown Saturday Night, 1974; Let's Do It Again, 1975; Mother, Jugs and Speed, 1976; Aesop's Fables; A Piece of Action, 1977; California Suite, 1978; Devil and Max Devlin, 1979; Leonard: Part VI, 1987; Ghost Dad, 1990. Publications: The Wit and Wisdom of Fat Albert, 1973; Bill Cosby's Personal Guide to Power Tennis, Fatherhood, 1986; Time Flies, 1988; Love and Marriage, 1989; Childhood, 1991. Honours: Recipient of four Emmy Awds and eight Grammy Awds. Address: c/o The Brokaw CO, 9255 Sunset Boulevard, Los Angeles, CA 90069, USA.

COSTELLO Peter Howard, b. 14 Aug 1957. Politician. m. Tanya Costello, 1982, 1 s, 2 d. Education: Monash Univ. Appointments: Solicitor, Mallesons Melbourne, 1981-84; Tutor, pt-time, Monash Univ, 1984-86; MP for Higgins, Vic, 1990-; Shadow Min for Corp Law Reform and Consumer Affairs, 1990-92; Shadow Atty-Gen and Shadow Min for Jus, 1992-93; Shadow Min for Fin, 1993-94; Dep Ldr of the Opposition and Shadow Treas, 1994-96; Dep Ldr, Liberal Party, 1996-; Treas, Mar 1996-. Publication: Arbitration in Contempt - jntly - 1986. Memberships: Mbr, Victorian Bar, 1984-90; Liberal Party. Hobbies: Swimming; Football; Reading. Address: Parliament House, Canberra, ACT 2600, Australia.

COSTNER Kevin, b. 1955. Actor. m. (1) Cindy Silva, div, 1 s, 2 d, 1 s by Bridget Rooney. Education: CA State Univ Fullerton. Appointments: Directing debut in Dances with Wolves, 1990. Films incl: Frances, 1982; The Big Chill, 1983; Testament, 1983; Silverado, 1985; The Untouchables, 1987; No Way Out, 1987; Bull Durham, 1988; Field of Dreams, 1989; Revenge, 1989; Robin Hood: Prince of Thieves, 1990; JFK, 1991; The Bodyguard, 1992; A Perfect World, 1993; Wyatt Earp, 1994; Waterworld, 1995; Tin Cup, 1996; Message in a Bottle, 1998; Co-prodr Rapa Nui; Co-prodr China Moon. Honours: Acady Awd for Best Picture with Dances with Wolves, 1991. Hobby: Golf. Address: c/o 151 El Camino Drive, Beverly Hills, CA 90212, USA.

COTHER Eric John, b. 28 Apr 1948, Ayr, Australia. Plant Pathologist. m. Norma, 1 Dec 1973, 2 d. Education: BSc, Agr, hons, Sydney; PhD, Austl Natl Univ. Appointments: Plant Pathol, NSW Agricl, Yanco, 1973-75; Rsch Sci, 1975-87, Snr Rsch Sci, 1989-95, NSW Agricl, Orange; Supbsr of Rsch, Orange, 1993-97; Key Rschr, Coop Rsch Cntr for Weed Mngmt Systems; Sub-Prog Ldr, Coop Rsch Cntr for Sustainable Rice Prodn; Prin Rsch Sci, 1995-; Ed-in-Chf, Australasian Plant Pathol, 1999-. Publications: 40 sci pprs in rsch jrnls, 60 conf contbrns, 2 book chapts. Honour: Netherlands Govt Fellshp, 1979. Memberships: Australasian Plant Pathol Soc; Amn Phytopathol Soc; Intl Soc for Plant Pathol; Austl Inst of Agricl Sci and Technol; Austl Conservation Fndn; Weed Soc of NSW; Rotary Club of Orange Daybreak. Address: "Jannannie", Hewitt Close, Orange 2800, Australia.

COTTON Sir Robert Carrington, b. 29 Nov 1915 Broken Hill NSW. Politician. m. Eve MacDougall, 1937, 1 s, 2 d. Education: St Peter's Coll Adelaide. Appointments: Fmr Fed VP Liberal Party of Aust; State Pres NSW, 1957-60; Acting Pres, 1965; Sen for NSW, 1965-78; Ldr Deleg of Fed Parl to meetings of IPU in Majorca and Geneva, 1967; Min of State for Civ Aviation, 1969-72; Min of Mfng Ind Sci and Consumer Affairs, Nov-Dec 1975; Min of Ind and Com, 1975-77; Consul-Gen NY, 1978-81; Dir Reserve Bank of Aust, 1981-82; Amb to USA, 1982-85; Chmn Kleinwort Benson Austl Income Fund - NY - 1986-; Chmn Austl Med Assn Enquiry, 1986-87; Chmn Austl Taiwan Bus Cncl, 1987-89; Dep Chmn Allders Intl Pty Ltd; Dir Hill and Knowlton Inc, 1986-91; Chmn Austl Photonics Co-op Rsch Cntr, Natl Gall of Aust Fndn, 1991-94; Dir Capital TV Holdings Ltd, Thomson-CSF Pacific Holdings Pty Ltd, 1996-. Hobbies: Photography; Writing. Address: Apartment 47, Southern Cross Gardens, 2 Spruson Street, Neutral Bay, NSW 2089, Australia.

COUGHLAN James Eric, b. 23 Oct 1955, Creswick, Australia. Academic. Education: BS, Austl Natl Univ; BA; PhD, Griffith. Appointments: Rsch Offr, Austl Bur of Statistical, 1980-87; Rsch Cnslt, Griffith Univ, 1987-89; Rsch Assoc, Griffith Univ, 1990-93; Lectr, Fac of Socl Scis, James Cook Univ, 1993-98; Snr Lectr, Sch of Psychol and Sociol, James Cook Univ, 1999-. Publications: Ed, Asians in Australia, Patterns of Migration and Settlement; The Diverse Asians, A Profile of Six Asian Communitites In Australia; Many Rprts, Monographs, Book Chapts, Articles. Honours: Departmental Merit Rsch Awd, Sociol, James Cook Univ, 1995. Memberships: Asian Studies Assn of Aust; Asian Am Studies Assn; Assn of S E Asian Studies, UK; Austl Inst of Intl Affairs; Austl Pop Assn; Chinse Studies Assn of Aust; Eurn Assn for S E Asian Studies; Intl Cntr for Asian Studies; Intl Sociolgcl Assn; Japanese Studies Assn of Aust; Natl Assn for the Educ and Advmnt of Cambodia, Laotian and Vietnamese Amns; Philippine Studies Assn of Aust; Refugee Rsch Network of Oxford Univ; Siam Soc; Vietnam Studies Assn of Aust. Hobbies: Reading; Gardening; Diving; Swimming; Music. Address: Department of Psychology and Sociology, School of Behavioural Science; James Cook University of North Queensland, Townsville, QLD 4811, Australia.

COURT Charles (Walter Michael) (Hon Sir), b. 29 Sept 1911, Crawley, Sussex, Eng. Premier, Western Australia; Politician. m. (1) Rita M, dec 1992, 5 s, (2) Judith Butt, 1997. Appointments: Chartered Acct, 1933; Fndng Ptnr, Hendry, Rae & Court, 1938-70; Served, Austl Air Force, 1940-46, Lt Col; State Registrar, Inst Chartered Accts, Aust, 1946-52, Mbr State Cncl, 1952-55; Dpty Ldr, 1957-59, 1971-72, Ldr, 1972-74, Opposition, Western Aust; Min, Western Aust, Indl dev and the NW, 1959-71, Railways, 1959-67, Transp, 1965-66; Chmn, Advsry Cttee under WA Prices Control Act, 1948-52, Taiwan Trade Assn, 1984-87; Pres, WA Band Assn, 1954-59. Publications: Num profl pprs on acctcy and econ resc dev. Honours: OBE, 1946; Hon LLD, Univ WA, 1969; Manufacturers Export Cncl Awd, 1969; James Kirby Awd, Inst of Production Engrs, 1971; Kt, 1972; KCMG, 1979; AK, 1982; Hon DTech, WA Inst of Technol, 1982; Austl Chartered Acct of Yr, 1983; Order of Brilliant Star w Grand Cordon, Taiwan, 1991; Order of the Sacred Treasure, 1st Class, Japan, 1983; Hon Dr, Murdoch Univ, 1995. Memberships include: Life Mbr, Musicians' Union, 1953; ASA, 1979; Returned Servs League, 1981; Inst of Chartered Accts of Aust, 1982; Warden WA State War Meml, 1991-92; Chmn, Advsry Cncl, Asia Res Cncl, Murdoch Univ; Patron, WA Div, PGA; WA Yth Orch; WA Opera Co; Hon Col, WA Univ Regt, SAS Regt. Hobbies: Music; Other sporting and cultural interests. Address: Unit 53, St Louis Estate, 14 Albert Street, Claremont, WA 6010. Australia.

COURT Charles Walter Michael (Hon Sir), b. 29 Sept 1911. Former Politician; Chartered Accountant. m. (1) Rita Steffanoni, 1936, dec 1992, 5 s, (2) Miss J M Butt, 1997. Education: FCA; FCIS; FASA. Appointments: Practising Chartered Acct, 1933-; Fndng Ptnr, Hendry Rae & Court, now Grant Thornton, 1938-70; Mbr, Legis Assembly, for Nedlands, 1953-82; Dpty Ldr Opposition, 1956-59, 1971-72; Min Indl Dev and NW, 1959-71; Min

Railways, 1959-67; Min Transp, 1965-66; Ldr Opposition, 1972-74; Premier Treas, Min Co-ordng Econ and Regl Dev, 1974-82; Chmn, Asia Rsch Cntr Advsry Cncl, Murdoch Univ. Honours: OBE, 1946; Mfrs Export Cncl Awd, 1969; Hon Col, Univ WA Regiment, 1969-74; Kirby Awd, Inst Prodn Engrs, 1971; Kt, 1972; Intl Presdtl Medal, Lions Intl, Perth, 1974; Hon Col, Spec Air Servs Regiment, Austl Mil Forces, 1976-80; Indl Des Cncl Aust Awd, 1978; KCMG, 1979; AK, 1982; Freeman, City of Nedlands, 1982; WA Citizen of Yr, Ind and Com WA Wk Cncl, 1982; Hon Life Mbr, Calabrese Assn WA, 1982 1st Class Order of Sacred Treasure, Japan, 1983; Chartered Acct of Yr, Inst Chartered Accts Aust, 1983; Freeman, Shire Derby/W Kimberley, 1985; Field Marshal Sir Thomas Blaney Fndn Mem Oration Medal, 1988; Order of Brilliant Star w Grand Cordon, Rep China in Taiwan, 1991; Kt Cmdr, Order of Merit, Italy, 1991; Hon LLD, Hon DUniv, Univ WA; Hon DTech, WA Inst Technol; Hon DUniv, Univ Murdoch; Hon LMASA; Hon FAMI; Hon LFAIEX. Memberships: Life Mbr, Liberal Party Aust, WA Div; Patron, Austl Spec Air Serv Assn; Pres, WA Band Assn 1954-59; Gov, Ian Clunies Ross Mem Fndn, 1985-92; Order of Aust Assn, Pres, 1986-89; Life Mbr, Inst Chartered Accts Aust; Life Mbr, RSL; Life Mbr, Musicians Union; Rotarian. Listed in: Who's Who in Australia. Hobbies: Music; Sport; Cultural interests. Address: 18 Peel Parade Coodanup, WA 6210, Australia.

COURTENAY Percy Philip, b. 20 Nov 1931, Birmingham, UK. Retired University Rector. m. Pamela, 27 July 1957, 2 d. Education: BA (Hons), London; PhD, London; Cert Ed, Cantab. Appointments: Hd, Dept of Geog, Sultan Abdul Hamid Coll, Alor Star, Malaya, 1957-60; Lectr, Snr Lectr in Geog, Coll of Educ, Southampton, UK, 1960-65; Snr Lectr, Assoc Prof, James Cook Univ of N Queensland, 1965-89; Prof, Rector, Cairns Campus, James Cook Univ of N Queensland, 1990-96. Publications: Plantation Agriculture, 1965, 1969, 1970, revised 2nd ed, 1980; A Geography of Trade and Development in Malaya, 1972; Northern Australia: Patterns and Problems of Tropical Development in an Advanced Country, 1982; The Rice Sector of Peninisular Malaysia - A Rural Paradox, 1995. Honours: Kedah (Malaya) Commemoration Medal, 1958; Kedah Installation Medal, 1961; J P Thomson Bronze Fndn Medal, Roy Geogl Soc of Australasia, 1989. Memberships: Inst of Austl Geog, Cncl Mbr, 1970-71; Malaysia Soc of Asian Stdies Assn of Aust, Chairperson, 1980-92; Commonwealth Geogl Bur, Australasian Repr, 1984-92, Elected Sec, 1984; Perc Tucker Regl Gall Advsry Cttee Townsville, 1987-90; Far North Queensland Regl Art Gall Inc, Pres, 1991-94; Cairns Gall, Fine Art Mngmt Cttee, Chmn, 1991-93. Hobbies: Southeast Asian Ceramics; Classical music; Travel and writing. Address: 28 Barron View Drive, Freshwater, Queensland 4870, Australia..

COUTTIE Peter Michael, b. 18 May 1930, Edinburgh, Scotland. Veterinary Surgeon; Nutritional Therapist; Lecturer. m. Margaret, 8 Nov 1958, 5 d. Education: BSc; MRCVS; Hon MAVA; AAC Nut E Med. Appointment: Pvte Prac. Honours: World Athletics, Steeple Chase; World Triatholon, twice. Memberships: Austl Veteran Athletic Assn; Austl Triathlon Team, 5 times. Hobbies: Farming; Athletics; Human Nutrition and Disease. Address: Cobboboonee Farm, RMB 2369, Portland, Victoria 3305, Australia.

COWAN Henry Jacob, b. 21 Aug 1919, Glogow, Germany/Poland. Professor Emeritus of Architectural Science. m. Renate Proskauer, 23 June 1952, 2 d. Education: BSc Hons, Civ and Mechl Engrng, 1939, MSc, Univ Manchester, Eng, 1940; PhD, 1952, DEng, 1963, Univ Sheffield; MArch, Univ Sydney, Aust, 1984. Appointments: Prof, Hd, Dept Archtl Sci, 1953-84, Dean, Fac Arch, 1966-67, Prof Emer, 1984-, Univ Sydney, NSW; Ed, Archtl Sci Review, 1958-; Visng Prof, Cornell Univ, USA, 1962; Ed, Vestes Mag, Fedn Austl Univ Staff Assn, 1965-78; Visng Prof, Kumasi Univ, Ghana, 1973; Visng Prof, Trabzon Univ, Turkey, 1976. Publications: Over 200 pprs and 25 books inclng: The Master Builders, 1985; Design of Reinforced Concrete, 1988; Encyclopedia of Building Technology, 1988; Handbook of Architectural Technology, 1991; A Contradiction in Terms, 1993; Structural Systems, 1995. Honours: Chapman Medal, 1956; Hon Life Mbr, Austl and NZ Archtl Sci Assn, 1977; Hon Fell, Roy Austl Inst Archts, 1979; AO, 1987; Hon DArch, Univ Sydney, 1987; Spec Serv Awd, Instn Structural Engrs, 1988; Monash Medal, 1994; Hartnett Medal, Roy Soc of Arts, 1999. Memberships include: Fell, Instn Structural Engrs; Fell, Instn Engrs Aust; Fell, Amn Soc Civ Engrs; FRSA. Hobbies: Collecting books, stamps and wines. Address: 57/6 Hale Road, Mosman, NSW 2088, Australia.

COWEN Zelman (Rt Hon Sir), b. 7 Oct 1919, Melbourne, Vic, Aust. Academic; Administrator. m. Anna Wittner, 7 June 1945, 3 s, 1 d. Education: Univ Melbourne; Univ Oxford. Appointments include: Prof, Pub Law, Dean, Fac Law, 1951-66, Emer Prof, 1967-, Profl Assoc, 1990-, Univ Melbourne; Vice-Chan, Univ New Eng, 1967-70; Vice-Chan, Univ Qld, 1970-77; Gov Gen of Aust, 1977-82; Bd Govs, Hebrew Univ, Jerusalem, 1982-; Provost, Oriel Coll, Oxford, 1982-90; Chmn, Sir Robert Menzies Cntr Austl Stdies, London, 1982-90; Bd Govs, Univ Tel Aviv, 1984-; Pro-Vice-Chan, Univ Oxford, 1988-90; Bd Govs, Weizmann Inst, 1990-; Hon Prof, Griffith Univ, 1991-; Dir, Sir Robert Menzies Mem Fndn Aust Ltd, 1991-97; Bd, Everald Compton Intl Pty Ltd, 1991-95; Chmn, 1992-94, Non-Exec Dir, 1994-96, John Fairfax Holdings Ltd; Disting Visng Prof, Vic Univ Technol, 1994-; Chmn, Austl Natl Acad Music, 1995-; QC, Qld, 1971. Publications: Ed, Dicey; Conflict of Laws, 1949; Australia and the United States: Some Legal Comparisons, 1954; Essays on the Law of Evidence, 1956; American-Australian Private International Law, 1957; Federal Jurisdiction in Australia, 1959, 2nd ed (jnt), 1978; Matrimonial Causes Jurisdiction (jnt), 1961; The British Commonwealth of Nations in a Changing World, 1964; Sir John Latham and Other Papers, 1965; Sir Isaac Isaacs, 1967, 2nd ed, 1993; Introduction to 2nd ed, Evatt: The King and His Dominion Governors, 1967; The Private Man (ABC Boyer Lectures), 1967; Individual Liberty and the Law (Tagore Law Lectures), 1975; The Virginia Lectures, 1983; Reflections on Medicine, Biotechnology and the Law (Roscoe Pound Lectures), 1986; A Touch of Healing, 1986. Honours: Num inclng: Kt, 1976; KStJ, 1977; AK, 1977; GCMG, 1977; GCVO, 1980; PC, 1981; GCOMRI, 1990; Hon Drs and Fellshps. Memberships include: Order Aust Assn, Pres, 1992-95; Aust-Brit Soc, Natl Pres, 1993-95. Hobbies: Music; Performing and visual arts. Address: 4 Treasury Place, East Melbourne, Vic 3002, Australia.

COWLING Sidney John, b. 30 July 1937, Frankston, Vic, Aust. Wildlife Biologist. m. (2) Georgina, 2 s, 3 d. Education: ADipFor, Vic Sch of Forestry, 1958; BS Forestry, Univ of Melbourne, 1962. Appointments include: Reserves Mngr, Fisheries and Wildlife Dept (FWD) of Vic, 1964-68; Offr-in-Charge, Wildlife Mngmt, FWD, Vic, 1968-75; Asst Dir (Wildlife) FWD, Vic, 1975-81; Asst Dir (Field Mngmt), FWD, Vic, 1981-84; Regl Mngr, Warragul, Dept of Conservation, Forests and Lands, 1984-87; Regl Mngr (policy Projects), 1987; Regl Mngr (Spec Ops) attached to Div of Regl Mngmt, 1987-88; Auth, Lectr, Cnslt, Wetlands and Wildlife, 1989-; Organic Herb Grower, Outtrim, S Gippsland, 1997-. Publications: Books incl: Wetlands Wildlife, 1990; Handbook of Australian, New Zealand and Antarctic Birds, Vols 1-4, 1990, 1993, 1996, 1999; Explore Melbourne's Wetlands, 1991; Mallee Country Wildlife, 1993; The Living Desert, 1995; Num pprs in profl jrnls. Memberships: Trustee, M A Ingram Trust; Hon Auditor (Past Ed, Fndn Bd Mbr and Treas), Vic Wetlands Trust; Hon Auditor, Vic Entomological Soc; Roy Australasian Ornithologists Union, Past Sec and VP; Organic Herb Growers of Aust. Hobbies: Music (clarinet and saxophone). Address: PO Box 22, Glenhuntly, Victoria, Australia 3163.

COWPERTHWAITE John James, b. 20 Nov 1944, Freetown, Sierra Leone. Architect. m. (1) Rosemary Inkson, 5 July 1969, 2 s, (2) Au Miu Po, 6 May 1992. Education: MA, Hons, Dip Arch, Cambridge Univ. Memberships: Roy Inst of Brit Archs; Assoc, Roy Incorp of Archts, Scotland; Hong Kong Inst of Archts. Hobby: Golf. Address: c/o The Architectural Practice Ltd, 15/F Success Commercial Building, 245-251 Hennessy Road, Wanchai, Hong Kong.

COX Barbara Douglas, b. 10 May 1947, Hamilton, NZ. Sociologist. m. Roy, 4 Jan 1969, 2 d. Education: ATCL, London; BA; MA, Hons. Appointments: NZ Soccer Rep, 1975-87; Auckland Women's FA Youth Coach, 1982-92. Publications: Multiple Bodies: Sportswomen, Soccer and Sexuality. Honours: Inductee, NZ Soccer Hall of Fame, 1995; MBE, Servs to Soccer, 1995; Coach of Yr, Auckland Soccer, 1991. Memberships: Sec, Auckland Women's FA, 1978-92; Exec Mbr, NZ Women's FA, 1998. Hobbies: Soccer; Stamp Collecting; Handcrafts. Address: 38 Disraeli St, Mt Eden, Auckland 3, New Zealand.

COX Brian Rothwell (The Hon Justice), b. 24 Jan 1930, Aust. Supreme Court Judge. m. Anna Morrison, 1966, 1 s, 2 d. Education: LLB, Univ Adelaide; Admitted as Bar and Sol, 1952. Appointments: QC, 1970; Sol-Gen, SA, 1970-78; Judge, Supreme Crt SA, 1978-. Address: Supreme Court, Victoria Square, Adelaide, SA 5000, Australia.

COX Christopher, b. 16 Oct 1952, St Paul, MN, USA. US Representative. m. Rebecca, 29 Aug 1993, 2 s, 1 d. Education: JD, Harvard Law Sch; MBA, Harvard Bus Sch; BA, Univ South CA. Appointments include: Law Clk, US Court of Appeals Judge Herbert Choy, 1977-78; Ptnr, Latham & Watkins, 1978-86; Tchr, fedl income tax, Harvard Bus Sch, 1982-83; Co-Fndr, co to provide Engl transl of Soviet newpaper, Pravda, 1984-; Snr Assoc Cnsl to Pres Reagan, 1986-88; Repr, CA in Congress; Chmn, Select Cttee on US Natl Security & Mil/Coml Concerns w People's Repub of China; House Ldrshp Steering Cttee; Mbr, Com Cttee, Subcttee on Oversight & Investigations; Mbr, Com Cttee, Subcttee on Telcomms, Trade & Consumer Protection; Mbr, Com Cttee, Subcttee on Fin & Hazardous Materials; Apptd by Pres Clinton to Bipartisan Commn on Entitlement & Tax Reform, 1994. Honours: Annual or regular awds: Golden Bulldog Awd, Watchdogs of the Treasury; Hero to the Taxpayer, Citizens Against Government Waste; Taxpayers Friend Awd, Natl Taxpayers Union; Friend of Small Business Awd, Natl Fedn of Indep Bus; Friend of the Consumer Awd, Consumer Alert grp, 1996; Also the Baltic nation's highest awd for living a foreign ldr from Lithuanian Pres Valdas Adamkus, 1998; Intl recog for efforts to assist Baltic indep; Observer of elections in Lithuania, Poland and Russia and El Salvador, deleg of Helsinki Commn to Estonia, Latvia & Lithuania; Met w ldrs of Israel, Jordan, Syria & Lebanon. Address: Newport Beach, CA, USA.

COX Geoffrey Arnold, b. 22 Aug 1951, Brisbane, Qld, Aust. Organist; Musicologist; Choral Conductor. Education: BA, BMus, Univ Qld, 1974; MPhil, 1977, DPhil, 1985, Univ Oxford, Eng; FTCL; ARCO. Appointments: Organ Schl, New Coll, Oxford, Eng, 1975-78; Lectr, Music, Univ Melbourne, Vic, 1979-84; Organist, Dir Music, St Peter's East Hill, Melbourne, 1980-94; Lectr, Music, 1985-90, Snr Lectr, 1990-94, Assoc Prof, 1994-, Austl Cath Univ, Mercy Campus, Ascot Vale, Vic; Asst Organist-Choirmaster, 1995-, Acting Dir of Music, 1999-, St Patrick's Cath, Melbourne. Publications: Gazetteer of Queensland Pipe Organs, 1976; Faber Early Organ Series, Vols 1-3, 1986; Organ Music in Restoration: A Study of Sources, Styles and Influences, 1989; Contbr to BIOS Jrnl, Organ Yrbook, One Voice; The Oxford Companion to Australian Music; The Cambridge Companion to the Organ. Honours: Univ Qld Medal, 1974; FRSCM, Australia, 1993. Membership: Pres, RSCM Australia, 1995-. Address: 96 Gore Street, Fitzroy, Vic 3065, Australia.

COX Laurence Grimes, b. 9 Dec 1938, Benalla, Vic, Aust. Investment Banker. m. Julie Ann Cox, 3 children. Education: BCom, Melbourne Univ; FCPA; FSIA. Appointments: Former Chmn, Austl Stock Exch Ltd; Former Exec Chmn, Potter Warburg Ltd; Chmn: Macquarie Corp Fin, Fortis Aust Lts, Transurban Cty Link Ltd, Argosy Asset Mngmnt Ltd, Murdoch Rsch Inst; Dir, Macquarie Bank Ltd, NASD Advsry Bd (USA). Honours: John Storey Medal, Mngmt, 1995; AO, 1996. Listed in: Who's Who in Australia. Hobbies: Tennis; Golf. Address:

Macquarie Bank Limited, Level 23, 101 Collins Street, Melbourne, Victoria 3000, Australia.

COX Paul, b. 16 Apr 1940, Venlo, Netherlands. Author; Film Director. 2 s, 1 d. Appointments: Films incl: Illuminations; Inside Looking Out; Lonely Hearts; Man of Flowers; My First Wife; Cactus; Vincent: The Life and Death of Vincent Van Gogh; Island; Golden Braid; A Woman's Tale; The Nun and the Bandit Exile; Lust and Revenge; The Hidden Dimension. Publications: Home of Man, co-auth; Human Still Lives of Nepal; Mirka, co-auth; I Am, co-auth w Wim Cox. Address: c/o Illumination Films, 1 Victoria Avenue, Albert Park, Vic 3208, Australia.

COX Philip Sutton, b. 1 Oct 1939, Sydney, NSW, Aust. Architect. m. Virginia Louise Gowing, 2 d. Education: BArch (Hons), 1962; Dip, Town and Country Planning, Sydney Univ, 1966. Appointments include: Priv prac: Ian McKay and Philip Cox, Archts, 1963-67; Philip Cox and Assocs, Archts, 1967-; Prof Archt, NSW Univ, 1989-. Publications: Rude Timber Buildings in Australia (w J M Freeland and W Stacey), 1972; Historic Towns of Australia (w Wesley Stacey), 1973; Building Norfolk Island, 1974; Restoring Old Australian Houses And Building, an Architectural Guide (w Howard Tanner and Peter Bridges), 1975; Architects Of Australia (Hardy Wilson), 1987; Philip Cox Architect, 1982; The Functional Tradition (w David Moore), 1987; A Place on the Coast (w W J Hawley); Painting Exhibn, Shearman Gall, 1995. Honours: Silver Medal, 1963; Gold Medal, 1984; Royal Aust Inst Arch, 1963; Sulman Prize, 1964, 1966; Blacket Prize, 1966; Wilkinson Prize, 1970; Sir Zelman Cowan Awd, 1985; Sir Robert Matthew Prize, 1986; Tracey Awd; Off Order of Aust (OA), 1988; Intl Olympic Medal, Contbn to Sports Arch; FAHA; Fell, Aust Acady Hums, 1993; Intl Olympic Medal for Contrbn to Sports Arch. Memberships: Life Fell, Roy Aust Inst Archts, Chmn, Educ Bd, Fed Chapt; Past Chmn of Hist Bldgs Cttee & Past VP of Environment Bd, NSW Chapt; Hon Fell, Amn Inst Archts, Fndng Mbr, Aust Acady Des, 1990. Hobbies: Walking; Gardening; Writing; Painting. Address: 204 Clarence Street, Sydney, NSW 2000, Australia.

COX William John Ellis (The Hon Mr Justice), b. 1 Apr 1936, Aust. Chief Justice of Tasmania. m. Jocelyn Wallace, 11 Sept 1970, 2 s, 1 d. Education: BA, LLB, Univ Tas. Appointments: Ptnr, Dobson Mitchell and Allport, Tas, 1961-76; Hon Mil ADC to Gov Tas, 1965-71; Lt-Col, Army Reserve, CO 6 Field Regt, Roy Austl Artillery, 1973-75; Magistrate, Hobart, 1976-77; Crown Advocate, 1977-82; QC, 1978; Judge, Supreme Crt Tas, 1982-95; Dpty Pres, Def Force Discipline Appeal Tribunal, 1988-95; Chf Jus, Tas, 1995-; Lt Gov of Tas, 1996-. Honours: AC; RFD; ED; Col Cmdt, Roy Austl Artillery, Tas Def Reg, 1992-97. Memberships: Past Pres, Bar Assn Tas; Past Pres, Medico Legal Soc, Tas. Hobbies: Bushwalking; Gardening. Address: Ryhope, 214 Davey Street, Hobart, Tas 7000, Australia.

COYLE Marie Bridget, b. 13 May 1935, Chgo, IL, USA. Clinical Microbiologist. m. Dr Zheng Chen, 30 Oct 1995, 1 ss. Education: BA, Mundelein Coll, 1957; BS, St Luois Univ, 1963; PhD, KS State Univ, 1965. Appointments: Sci Instr, Columbus Hosp Sch of Nursing, Chgo, IL, 1957-59; Rsch Assoc, Dept of Microbiology, Univ of Chgo, IL, 1967-70; Instr, Dept of Microbiology, Univ of IL Medl Sch, Chgo, IL, 1973-80; Assoc Dir, Microbiology Lab, Univ Hosp, Seattle, 1973-76; Dir, Microbiology Lab, Harborview Medl Cntr, Seattle, 1976-; Asst Prof, 1973-80, Assoc Prof, 1980-94, Prof, 1994-, Departments of Laboratory Med & Microbiology, Univ of WA, Seattle, WA; Acting Hd, Clin Microbiology Div, Univ Hosps, Seattle, 1997-98. Publications: 56 articles in peer-reviewed jrnls and 7 book chapts. Honours: Kappa Gamma Pi, 1957; Fell, Amn Acady Microbiology, 1982; bioMérieux Vitek Sonnenwirth Awd for Leadership in Clin Microbiology, 1994; Distinguished Mbr, Lectureship for East PA Branch of ASM, 1997; Pasteur Awd, IL Soc for Microbiology, 1997; Sigma Xi. Memberships: Amn Soc of Microbiology, 1971-; Amn Assn Univ Profs, 1973-; Conf of Pub Hlth Lab Dirs, 1975-97; Medl Mycological Soc of Ams, 1983-. Hobbies: Hiking; Biking; Skiing; Travel; Reading. Address: Department of Laboratory Medicine,

University of Washington, Box 359743, Harborview Medical Center, 325 Ninth Avenue, Seattle, WA 98104, USA.

CRAIG David Parker, b. 23 Dec 1919, NSW, Aust. Professor of Chemistry. m. Veronica Bryden-Brown, 25 Aug 1948, 3 s, 1 d. Education: BSc Hons, Univ Sydney, 1940; PhD, 1948, DSc, 1955, Univ London, Eng. Appointments: Lectr, 1944-46, Prof, 1952-56, Univ Sydney; Turner and Newall Rsch Fell, 1946-49, Lectr, 1949-52, Prof, 1956-67, Visng Prof, 1967-, UCL, Eng; Prof, Chem, 1967-84, Dean, Rsch Sch Chem, 1970-73, 1977-81, Austl Natl Univ; Firth Visng Prof, Univ Sheffield, Eng, 1973; Univ Coll, Cardiff, Wales, 1975-; Univ Bologna, Italy, 1984-89; Pt-time Mbr, Exec, Cncl Sci and Indl Rsch Org, 1980-85; Pres, Austl Acady Sci, 1990-94. Publications include: Num papers in sci jrnls; Books inclng: Co-auth, Excitons in Molecular Crystals - Theory and Applications. Honours: FRS, 1968; FAA, 1969; AO, 1985; Hon DSc, Sydney, 1985; Hon Dr Chem, Bologna, 1985. Memberships: Roy Soc Chem; Roy Austl Chem Inst; Intl Acady Quantum Molecular Sci. Hobbies: Music; Tennis. Address: 199 Dryanda Street, O'Connor, ACT, Australia.

CRAIK Duncan Robert Steele, b. 17 Feb 1916, NZ. Civil Servant. m. Audrey Mavis Ion, 17 Feb 1943, 4 d. Education: BEcon, Sydney Univ, 1940. Appointments: C'wlth Bank Aust, 1933-40; Taxation Bch, 1940-60, Asst Sec, 1960-66, 1st Asst Sec, 1966-69, Dpty Sec, 1969-73, C'wlth Treas; Auditor-Gen Aust, 1973-81; Pt-time Mbr, Admnstv Appeals Tribunal, 1981-86. Honours: OBE, 1971; CB, 1979. Memberships: Fell, fmr Pres, Roy Austl Inst Pub Admin; Fell, Austl Soc Accts, 1981-86. Address: Horton House, Castor Street, Yass, NSW, Australia.

CRAMMER Bernard, b. 30 Apr 1939, Leicester, Eng. Organic Chemist. m. Rachel Feldman, 12 Jan 1998, 2 s, 1 d. Education: BS, Univ of London, 1963; MSc, Organic Chem, Univ of Jerusalem, 1975; PhD, Organic Chem, Bar Ilan Univ, 1985. Appointments: Snr Rsch Chem, 1964-68; Pat Examiner, 1968-87; Supvsr, Lab Course, Natl Product Chem, 1977-80, 1985-86; Snr Pat Examiner, 1987-91; Hd Pat Examiner, 1991-96; Dpty Supt, Pat Examiners, Hd of Chem, Biotechnology Div, 1996-. Publications: 25 Publs; 3 Pats Publs. Honours: Awd, Min Jus for Spec Servs and Econ Savings; Awd, Rsch Fund, Soc of Chem; Israel Civ Serv Awd. Memberships: Roy Soc of Chem; Roy Soc of Hlth; Roy Stats Soc; Israel Chem Soc; Israel Assn of Engrs and Archts; Sci Rsch Soc; NY Acady Sci; Eurn Chem. Hobbies: Bridge; Photography; Classical Music; Philately; Reading; Foreign Affairs. Address: 7 Rehov Yam Sof, Ramot Eshcol, Jerusalem 97701, Israel.

CRAMOND William Alexander, b. 2 Oct 1920, Scotland. Medical Practitioner; Emeritus Professor. m. Bertine J C Mackintosh, 19 July 1949, 1 s, 1 d. Education: MB, ChB, 1947, MD, 1954, Aberdeen; DPM, London, 1952; MD aeg, Adelaide, 1964. Appointments: Dir, Mental Hlth, SA, Aust, 1961-65; Fndn Prof, Mental Hlth, Adelaide Univ, 1963-71; Fndn Dean, Med, Leicester Univ, Eng, 1971-75; Prin, Vice-Chan, Stirling Univ, Scotland, 1975-80; Dir, Mental Hlth, NSW Hlth Commn, Aust, 1980-83; Prof, Clin Psych, 1984-93, Emer Prof, 1993-, Flinders Univ, SA; Chmn, Bd Dirs, S Austl Mental Hlth Servs, 1993-95. Publications: Num articles in medl jrnls. Honours: OBE, 1960; Hon DUniv, Stirling Univ, 1984; AO, 1994. Memberships: FRCPsych; FRANZCP; FRACP; FRSE. Hobbies: Walking; Theatre; Music. Listed in: Who's Who in Australia, 1995; Who's Who. Address: 28 Tynte Street, North Adelaide, SA 5006, Australia.

CRAW James Gilbert, b. 4 Apr 1930, Launceston, Tas. Sharebroker; Financial Consultant. m. Britt, 2 Oct 1957, 3 s, 1 d. Education: MComm; MEd. Appointments: Tchng, 1951-64; Merchant Banking, 1964-75; Sharebroker, 1976-; Mbr, NZ Stock Exchange. Publications: Contbr articles to profl jrnls (education and psychology). Membership: Fndn Mbr, Psychol Soc MAPS. Hobbies: Tennis; Golf; Restoring old houses (heritage society). Address: 43/130 Great South Road, Remuera, Auckland, New Zealand.

CRAWFORD Cindy, b. 1966. Fashion Model. m. (1) Richard Gere - qv - 1991, div. Appointments: Promotes Revlon - cosmetics - and Pepsi Cola; Presents own fashion show own MTV - cable and satellite; Has appeared on num covers for mags; Model for num fashion des; Has released sev exercise videos. Film: Fair Game, 1995. Publication: Cindy Crawford's Basic Face, 1996. Address: c/o Wolf-Kassteler, 132 S Rodeo Drive, Suite 300, Beverly Hills, CA 90212, USA.

CRAWFORD Ian McLean, b. 30 Dec 1931, Sydney, NSW, Aust. Executive Consultant; Retired Rear-Admiral. m. 9 Nov 1963, 1 s, 1 d. Education: Jnt Servs Staff Coll, Latimer, 1969; Dip, Co Dir, 1989. Appointments: Roy Austl Navy, 1949-89; Austl Def and Naval Attaché, Paris, 1978-81; Dir, Gen Supply, Navy, 1981-84; Chf Supply, Dept Def, 1984-88; Hd, Naval Logistics Implementation, 1988-89; Dpty Chmn, ACT Govt Priorities Review Bd, 1990; Exec Dir, VFT Progress Grp, 1990-96; Mbr Cncl Austl War Memorial, 1998-. Publications: Num articles on VFT and logistics. Honours: Peter Mitchell Open Essay Prize, 1971; AM, Mil Div, 1985. Memberships: Austl Naval Inst; Utd Servs Inst; Tstee, NRMA-ACT Rd Safety Trust, 1991-; Pres, Austl-French Assn Profl and Tech Specialists, 1993-99; Chmn, Korean War Mem Cttee, 1993-; Canberra Bus Cncl Exec, 1992-98. Hobbies: Australiana; History; Logistics; French language and culture; Skiing; Sailing; Fishing. Address: 87 Endeavour Street, Red Hill, ACT 2603, Australia.

CRAWFORD Patricia Marcia, b. 31 Jan 1941, Sydney, Australia. Historian. m. Ian, 1 s. Education: BA, hons, Melbourne Univ; MA, PhD, Univ WA. Publications: Women and Religion in England 1500-1720, 1993; Women in the Early Mod England 1550-1720, 1998. Memberships: Fell, Roy Hist Soc, England, Austl Acady of Socl Sci. Address: History Department, University of Western Australia, Nedlands, WA 6907, Australia.

CREAGH Dudley Cecil, b. 18 Feb 1935, Brisbane, Queensland, Aust. Physicist. m. Helen (née Williams), 1 Jan 1962, 1 s, 1 d. Education: BS (1st Hons); DipEd (Qld); MSc (UNE); MSc (Brist); PhD (NSW); CPhys; CEng; FInstP; FAIP. Appointments: Tchr, Queensland, 1958-59; Lectr, Univ of New Eng, 1959-62; Lectr, Roy Mil Coll, Duntroon, 1962-65; Snr Lectr, Roy Mil Coll, Duntroon, 1965-68; Snr Lectr, Fac of Mil Studies, 1968-86, Assoc Prof, Univ Coll, 1986-96, Univ NSW; Prof of Phys, Univ of Canberra, 1996-. Memberships: Fell and Chartered Physicist, Inst of Phys; Fell, Austl Inst of Phys; Chartered Engr, Inst of Elec Engrs; Chmn, Commn on Crystallographic Apparatus, Intl Union of Crystallography, 1983-93; Cnclr, Asian Crystallographic Assn, 1990-; Pres, Soc of Crystallography in Aust, 1991-93; Mbr, Natl Cttee of Crystallography, Austl Acady of Scis, 1990-97; Chmn, Techl Cttee Austl Natl Beamline Facility, 1989-96; VP, Austl X-Ray Analytical Assn, 1991-1993; Cnclr, Intl Radiation Phys Soc, 1991-; Bd Mbr, Austl Synchrotron Rsch Prog, 1996-; Chmn, Photon Factory Cttee, Austl Synchroton Rsch Prog, 1996-; Editl Bd, Radiation Phys and Chem, 1998-. Hobbies: Music; Walking; Cricket; Rugby. Address: 2 Throsby Crescent, Griffith ACT 2603, Australia.

CREECH Wyatt B, b. 1946, Oceanside, California, USA. Government Minister. m. 3 children. Education: Dip, Sheep Farming, Massey Univ; BA, Pol Sci and Intl Pol, Victoria Univ. Appointments: Acct; Vineyard Developer; Martinborough Cnclr, 1980-86; Elected to Parl, 1988; Min of Revenue, Min of Customs, Min in Charge of Pub Trust Off and Min Responsible for Govt Superannuation Fund, 1990; Min of Snr Citizens, Assoc Min, Fin and Socl Welfare, 1991; Min, State-Owned Enterprises, 1993; Min of Revenue, of Employment, Dpty Min of Fin, 1993; Min of Educ, Ldr of the House, 1996; Dpty Prime Min, Min of Hlth. Address: 129 Main Street, Pahiatua, New Zealand.

CREEDY John, b. 17 Mar 1949, Eng. Professor of Economics. m. Kath, 23 Sept 1978. Education: BSc, Bristol; BPhil, Oxford. Appointments: Lectr in Econ, Univ of Reading; Rsch Offr, NIESR, London; Prof of Econ, Durham; Prof of Econ, Univ of Melbourne. Honour: FASSA, 1988. Publications: Many books and jrnl articles.

Address: Department of Economics, University of Melbourne, Parkville, Victoria 3052, Australia.

CREW Gary David, b. 23 Sept 1947, Brisbane, Australia. Consultant. m. Christine Joy Willis, 4 Apr 1970, 1 s, 2 d. Education: Ctf, Engrng Drafting, Qld Inst of Technol, 1970; BA, 1979, MA, 1985, Univ of Qld. Appointments: Civil and Mech Engrng Design Draftsman, 1963-73; HS Engl and Socl Sci Tchr, 1973-82; Seconded to Secondary Transition Educn Project (STEP) as Sch to Work Project Advsr, Hd of Engl, Aspley and Albany Creek Schs, 1984-89; Freelance Writer; Lectr, Qld Univ of Technol and Univ of Sunshine Coart; Contract Lit and Literacy Cnslt, Primary Schs and HS, Aust; Childrens Book Ed, Reed Books, Qld Univ Press, Lothian Books; Series Ed, After Dark Children's Series; Cnslt, Designer to Bd of Snr Second Students on Common Scaling Test Writing Task, 1989-. Publications include: The Inner Circle 1986; The House of Tommorrow, 1988; Strange Objects, 1990; No Such Country, 1992; Angel's Gate, 1993; Inventing Anthony West, 1994; The Blue Feather, 1997; Mama's Babies, 1998. Honours include: Austl Children's Book of the Year Winner, 1990, 1993, 1996; Bilby Awd, Childrens Book Choice, 1995; USA Childrens Book of Distinction, 1996; Ned Kelly Awd for Crime Writing, 1997; Short-Listed, W A PRemier's Awd, 1998. Address: PO Box 440, Maleny 4552, Australia.

CREYTON Barry, b. 29 Dec 1939. Actor; Playwright; Composer. Creative Works: Plays: Double Act, 1988; Lady Audley's Secret, 1962; How the West Was Lost, 1964; Living Together, 1982; Follow That Husband, 1973. Honour: Norman Kessell Awd (Gluggs Awd) for Outstndng Contbns to Aust Theatre, 1988. Memberships: Societe Des Auteurs et Compositeurs Dramatiques, France; Writers Guild of Am; Aust Writers Guild; Brit Actors Equity; Aust Actors Equity. Address: c/o Anthony A Williams Mgt, 50 Oxford St, Level 1, NSW 2021, Australia.

CRIBB Julian Hillary James, b. 28 Dec 1950, Halton, Bucks, Eng. Director, CSIRO National Awareness. m. Maureen, 25 Aug 1979, 1 s, 2 d. Education: BA, Classics, Univ of West Aust. Media Offr, Curtin Univ of Technol, Pub Rels Mngr, West Aust Th Co, 1970-73; Snr Jrnlst, West Farmer, 1973-77; Chf, Austl Agricl News Bur, 1975-77; Ed, Natl Farmer, 1977-83, 1984-85; Ed, The Sunday Indep, 1983-84; Agric and Rural Affairs Corresp, The Austl, 1985-88; Ed-in-Chf, Austl Rural Times, 1988-89; Sci Corresp and Sci Ed, The Austl newspaper, 1989-96. Publications: The Forgotten Country, 1983; The White Death, 1996. Memberships: Asst Sci Communicators (Inaug Pres), 1995. Honours: 32 awds for newspaper jrnlsm. Hobbies: Trout fishing; Ship modelling; Paleontology; Gardening. Address: 104 Hodgson Crescent, Pearce, ACT, Australia.

CRICHTON John Michael, (Jeffrey Hudson, John Lange, jnt pseudonym with Douglas Crichton as Michael Douglas), b. 23 Oct 1942 Chicago. Writer; Film Dir; Physician. m (4) Anne-Marie Martin, 1987, 1 d. Education: Harvard Med Sch. Appointments: Lectr in anthropology Cambridge Univ, 1965; Post-Doctoral Fellow Salk Inst La Jolla, 1969-70; Visng Writer MIT, 1988. Films Directed: The Great Train Robbery; Coma; Runaway. Publications incl: - as Michael Douglas - Dealing: or, The Berkeley to Boston Forty-Brick Lost-Bag Blues, 1972; - as Jeffrey Hudson - A Case of Need, 1968; The Andromeda Strain, 1969; - as John Lange - Odds on, 1966; Scratch One, 1967; Easy Go, 1968; Zero Cool, 1969; The Venom Business, 1969; Drug of Choice, 1970; Grave Descend, 1970; Five Patients: The Hospital Explained, 1970; Binary, 1972; The Terminal Man, 1972; Westworld - screenplay - 1973; The Great Train Robbery, 1975; Eaters of the Dead, 1976; Jasper Johns, 1977; Congo, 1980; Looker - screenplay - 1981; Electronic Life: How to Think About Computers, 1983; Runaway - screenplay - 1984; Sphere, 1987; Travels, 1988; Jurassic Park, 1990; Rising Sun, 1992; Disclosure, 1994; The Lost World, 1995; The Terminal Man, 1995; Airframe, 1996. Address: c/o Jenkins Financial Services, 433 N Camden Drive, Suite 500, Beverly Hills, CA 90210, USA.

CROCOMBE Ron, b. 8 Oct 1929, New Zealand. Academic. m. Marjorie, 7 Apr 1959, 3 s, 1 d. Education: PhD, Austl Natl Univ. Appointments: Dir, New Guinea Rsch Inst, 1965-69; Prof, Univ of S Pacific, 1969-88; Prof Em, 1989-. Publications: The Pacific Islands and the USA, 1995; The South Pacific, 1989; Pacific Neighbours, 1992; Post Secondary Education in the South Pacific, 1994. Honours: Austl Vice Chan's Awd, 1983; Ohira Rsch Awd, 1988; Woodrow Wilson Intl Cntr Awd, 1989. Memberships: Pacific Hist Assn, Pres, 1983-95; S Pacific Socl Scis Assn, Pres, 1972-74. Address: PO Box 309, Rarotonga, Cook Islands.

CROPP Glynnis Marjory, b. 23 Mar 1938, Christchurch, New Zealand. University Professor. Education: MA, NZ; Lèsl DU, Paris; Univ Canterbury, 1956-60; Univ de Paris, 1960-62, 1969-70. Appointments: Lectr in French, 1963-70, Snr Lectr, 1971-78, Rdr, 1979-84, Prof of French, 1985-, Hd, Dept of Mod Langs, 1985-92, Hd Dept of Eurn Langs, 1993-97; Hd, Sch Lang Stdies, 1998-; Dean Fac of Humanities, 1987-97, Massey Univ. Publications: 1 book; Sev scholarly articles in profl jrnls. Honour: Chevalier dans l'Ordre des Palmes académiques. Memberships: Intl Courtly Lit Soc; NZ Assn of Lang Tchrs; Intl Boethius Soc; AULLA. Hobbies: Gardening; Music. Address: 8 Moana Street, Palmerston North, New Zealand.

CROSSETT Jerry Wayne, b. 19 May 1938, Wellman, IA, USA. Export Company Owner. m. Mary Lou, 10 June 1961, 1 s, 1 d. Education: BSME, IA State Univ; MSME, CA Inst of Technol, Postgrad Certs in Bus & Engrng, UCLA. Publication: US Pat for Rocket Staging Device. Membership: Orange County Intl Mktng Assn. Hooby: Clay Target Shooting. Address: PO Box 1294, Huntington Beach, CA 92647, USA.

CROUCHER Paul Harold, b. 19 Feb 1960, Sydney, Aust. Education: BSc, 1983; Bachelor of Optometry, 1984; Fell, Australasian Coll of Behavioural Optometrics; Fell, Col of Optometrists of Vision Dev. Appointments: Clin Instr, Univ Melbourne, 1994-98; Lectr, Univ Melbourne, 1994-; Lectr, Univ NSW, 1995-; Natl Sec, ACBO, 1994-98; Pres, ACBO, 1998-. Memberships: AOA; ACBO; VCO; COVD. Hobby: Cycling. Address: 10 Nalinga Court, Warranwood, Australia 3134.

CROWE Bruce John, b. 30 May 1943. Psychologist; Management Consultant. Education: BA, Sydney, 1963; MA Hons I, Univ NSW, Aust, 1971. Appointments: Psychol Trnee, Voc Guidance Offr; RAAF Psychol; Cnslt Psychol; MBS Rsch Asst; Mngr, Assessment Servs, ITT Europe; Mngr, Staffing and Dev, STC, Sydney; Prin Cnslt, AY Servs; Indep Psychol and Mngmt Cnslt. Publication: The Effects of Subordinate Behaviour on Managerial Style, 1971. Memberships: Brit Psychol Soc, Chartered Occupational Psychol; Fell, Austl Psychol Soc, Pres 1996-2000; Fell, Inst of Mngmt Cnslts, Jnr VP 1994-96, Snr VP 1996-2000; Chartered Mbr, Austl Human Resources Inst. Hobbies: Photography; Music; Travel. Address: GPO Box 3007, Sydney, NSW 2001, Australia.

CROWE Martin David, b. 22 Sep 1962 Auckland. Cricketer. m. Simone Curtice, 1991, sep 1996. Appointments: Right-hand batsman slip fielder; Played for Auckland, 1979-80 to 1982-83; Cntr Dists, 1983-84 to 1989-90, Capt 1984-85 to 1989-90; Somerset, 1984-88; Wellington 1990-91 to 1994-95, Capt 1993-94; Played in 77 Tests for NZ, 1981-82 to 1995-96; 16 as Capt scoring 5444 runs, average 45.36, with 17 hundreds inclng NZ record 299 v Sri Lanka Wellington, Feb 1991; Scored 19608 first-class runs, 71 hundreds; Toured Eng, 1983, 1986, 1990 and 1994; 143 limited-overs intls. Publication: Out on a Limb, 1996. Honours: NZ Sportsman of the Year, 1991; Selected World Cup Champion Cricketer, 1992. Hobbies: Tennis; Golf; Wine. Address: P O Box 109302, Newmarket, Auckland, New Zealand.

CROWL Linda Sue, b. 16 Sept 1960. Editor. Education: BA, Govt (Hons) & French, 1982; MA, Intl Rels, Sch of Adv Intl Studies, Johns Hopkins Univ, 1987. Appointments: Ed, Johns Hopkins Univ, 1986-87; Ed, Ctr for Strategic & Intl Studies, 1987-89; Tchr, Peace Corps, 1989-91; Ed, Univ of the S Pacific, 1991-. Publications include: Television and Video in the Pacific Islands (ed), 1993; Science of Pacific Island Peoples (ed), 4 vols, 1994; New Politics in the South Pacific (ed), 1994; Power technology and rights: Exploring the crossroads for Pacific Islands (review), 1994; Neither Cargo nor Cult: Ritual Politics and the Colonial Imagination in Fiji, 1996; Corresp, ABD: Asian/Pacific Book Development Quarterly, 1994-; Abstracts for The Impact and Future Challenges of New Communication Technologies; Futures are Multicultural; Creative Writing by Solomon Islanders (ed); Book Publishing in the Pacific Islands, 1996. Memberships: Pacific Hist Assn; Pacific Islands Polit Sci Assn; Pacific Sci Assn; S Pacific Creative Arts Soc; S Pacific Socl Sci Assn. Hobbies: Running; Swimming; Paddling Outrigger Canoes; Sailing. Address: Institute of Pacific Studies, University of the South Pacific, PO Box 1168, Suva, Fiji.

CROWLEY Rosemary Anne, b. 30 July 1938, Melbourne, Vic, Aust. Senator for South Australia, Australian Federal Parliament. 3 s. Education: MBBS, Melbourne Univ, Vic, 1961. Appointments: Jnr RMO, 1962; Snr RMO, St Vincent' Hosp, Melbourne, 1963; Pathol Registrar, Roy Children's Hosp, Melbourne, 1964; Jnr Clin Asst Pediats Medl Dept, Adelaide Children's Hosp, 1970-71; Asst Clin Haematology Inst Med and Vet Sci, SA, 1972-74; Fndn Mbr, SA Mental Hlth Review Tribunal, 1979-83; Sen, (ALP) SA elected 1983; Min Assisting the Prime Min for the Status of Women, 1993-94; Min for Family Servs, 1993-96; Current Chair of Cmnty Affairs Refs Cttee; Fmrly Employment Educ and Trng Sen Refs Cttee, 1996-; Num cttees. Memberships: APHEDA (Austl People for Hlth Educ and Dev Abroad) Bd Mbr (previously Vice-Chair); ANZSEARCH/APHA Inc; Drs Reform Soc; Austl Fedn of Univ Women; SA Medl Womens Soc; Medl Practitioners Against War; Amnesty Intl, Parl Grp; Campaign Against Racial Exploitation; Course Advsry Cttee, Primary Hlth Care; Flinders Univ of SA; The Parks Community Cntr Yth Sports Fund; Serv to Yth Cncl - Vice Patron; Contax Netball Club Inc; Patron, Austl Womens Netball; Patron, Austl Women's Basketball. Hobbies: Jogging; Theatre; Gardening.

CROXSON Morva Olwyn, b. 10 Mar 1934, Wyndham, NZ. Music Therapist; Lecturer. m. Lawrence James Croxson, 13 Dec 1957, 2 d. Education: Piano, FTCL, 1957, LRSM Tchrs, 1959 and Perfs, 1950; Violin, ATCL, 1950; MusBac, Auckland Univ, 1966; Dip Tchng, 1982; Music Therapy, LGSM, 1983; MPhil, 1988. Appointments: Brdcstr, personality progs, NZ Brdcstng Corp, 1956-61; Home, children, community wrk, 1961-72; Snr Lectr, Music, Music Therapy, Palmerston N Tchrs Coll (now Massey Univ Coll Educ), Palmerston, 1972-97; Ed, NZ Soc Music Therapy Jrnl, 1978-82; Mbr, Massey Univ Cncl, 1991-; Mbr, Intl Sci Cttee, World Fedn Music Therapy, 1994-; Mbr, Music Advsry Grp, NZ Quals Authy, 1996-; Chan, Massey Univ, 1998-. Publications: Contbr to profl jrnls; Weekly Arts Column, newspaper, 1978-82; Fortnightly Radio Arts Prog. Honours: Schlshp, McKenzie Educ Fndn, 1981-82; Cty London/Guildhall Disablement Prize, Stud of Yr, 1983; CBE for servs to arts and the community, 1995. Memberships: Chmn, Cntrl Regl Arts Cncl, 1978-82; Queen Elizabeth II Arts Cncl NZ, 1978-82; Chmn, Queen Elizabeth II Music Adjudication Panel, 1979-82; Chmn, NZ Soc Music Therapy, 1979-81, 1984-88, Pres, 1998-; Chmn, Palmerston N Socl Plng Cttee, 1978-82; Chmn, Palmerston N Community Arts Cncl, 1971-74; Chmn, Roy McKenzie Fndn; Num natl and local community and arts portfolios and mbrships. Hobbies: Music performance; Gardening; Volunteer work with handicapped children and psychiatric patients. Address: 175 Amberley Avenue, Palmerston North, New Zealand.

CRUICKSHANK Michael James, b. 9 July 1929, Glasgow, Scotland. Marine Mining Engineer. m. (1) Beatrix I Collick, 11 July 1953, (2) Phyllis Jean Lommasson, 11 Apr 1963, (3)Victoria J White, 28 Dec 1978, 4 s. 3 d. Education: 1st Class Pass, 1953, Assoc Camborne Sch Mines; MSc Mining Engrng, 1963, CO Sch Mines; PhD Oceanography and Limnol, Univ WI,

Madison, 1978; Sloan Fell, Stanford Grad Sch Bus, 1976-77. Appointments: 11 yrs mineral ind; 19 yrs univ tchng; 14 yrs US Govt; UN Tech Cnslt; Mbr Grad Fac Ocean Engrng, Univ Hawaii, 1989-; Rschr, Tech Dir, Hawaii Nat Energy Inst, Ctr for Ocean Resources Tech, 1988-; Dir, State HI Mining and Mineral Resources Inst, 1993-; Dir, Univ HI, Marine Minerals Tech Cntr, 1994-. Publications: Author or co-author, over 200 articles and book chapts on marine engrng. Honours: Prin Investigator, 6 major projs. Memberships: Team Ldr, chair, cnslt or mbr 14, intl grps, 13 US Govt task forces, 8 non-govt grps, offr and fndng mbr sev profl socs incl Marine Tech Soc, World Dredging Assn, Intl Marine Soc and PACON Intl. Hobbies: Historic restoration. Address: 2179 Makiki Heights Drive, Honolulu, HI 96822, USA.

CRYER Rodger Earl, b. 2 Apr 1998, Detroit, MI, USA. Professor; Teacher (Psychology). m. Bellaflor B, 22 June 1985, 2 s. Education: OH Wesleyan Univ, 2 yrs; AB, San Diego State Univ, 1965; AM, Trenton State Coll, Stanford Univ, 1972; PhD, Columbia, Pacific Univ, 1984; Pt I Postdoct, Columbia-Pacific Univ. Appointments include: Voting Deleg, Guadalupe River Pk Task Force; Bd Mbr (at large) CA State Pk & Rec Bd of Din - Our Cty Forest Inc Bd; Mbr, Commonwealth Cntrl Credit Union of San Jose. Publications: Articles to jrnls. Honours: Spec Proclamation and Resolution from Cty of San Jose, 1988; Spec Merit for Outstndng Serv to the Hun Rels Cttee of Santa Clara Co, 1990. Memberships include: Chmn, Schlshp Cttee of Asian Amn Educ Assn of Santa Clara Co; Pub Rels Chmn for Filipino-Amn Movement in Educ, S Bay Chapt. Hobbies: Music; Painting; Writing; Civic activities. Address: PO Box 21917, San Jose, CA 95151-1917, USA.

CRYSTAL Billy, b. 14 Mar 1947 Long Beach NY. Actor; Comedian. m. Janice Goldfinger, 2 d. Education: Marshall Univ; Nassau Community Coll NY Univ. Appointments: Mbr of the group 3's Co; Solo appearances as a stand-up comedian; Tv appearances incl: Soap, 1977-81; The Billy Crystal Hour, 1982; Saturday Night Live, 1984-85; The Love Boat; The Tonight Show; Tv films incl: Breaking up is Hard to do, 1979; Enola Gay: The Men, The Mission, The Atomic Bomb, 1980; Death Flight; Feature Films incl: The Rabbit Test, 1978; This is Spinal Tap, 1984; Running Scared, 1986; The Princess Bride, 1987; Throw Momma from the Train, 1987; When Harry Met Sally ..., 1989; City Slickers, 1991; Mr Saturday Night (also Dir, Prodr, co-screen play-writer), 1993; Forget Paris, 1995. Publication: Absolutely Mah-velous, 1986. Address: c/o International Creative Management, 8942 Wilshire Boulevard, Beverly Hills, CA 90211, USA.

CSICSERY Sigmund M, b. 3 Feb 1929. Chemist. m. Gabrielle M Szemere, 1 Dec 1956. Education: MS, Chem Engrng, Budapest, Hungary, 1947-51; PhD, Organic Chem, Northwestern Univ, Evanston, IL, USA, 1959-61. Appointments: Rsch Chem, Monsanto Rsch and Dev Lab, Dayton, OH, USA, 1957-59; Snr Rsch Assoc, Chevron Rsch Co, Richmond, CA, USA, 1961-86; Cnslt, Unido Chf Tech Advsr in Chem, Catalysis and Zeolites, 1986-. Publications: Over 40; 26 pats in catalysis, shape selective catalysis, zeolites and related subjs. Memberships: Pres, CA Catalysis Soc, 1973-74; Dir, N Amn Catalysis Soc, 1976-80. Hobbies: Hiking; Mountain climbing; Windsurfing; Skiing; Bicycling. Address: PO Box 843, Lafayette, CA 94549, USA.

CUAYZON Delia, b. 9 Jan 1954, Tabonton, Leyte. Social Worker. Education: BSc, Socl Wrk. Appointments: Socl Wrker, 1978-98; Supervising Socl Welfare Offr, 1988-89; Sci Welfare Offr III, 1989-94; MSWDD, 1994-. Memberships: Philippine Assn of Socl Wrkrs Inc (PASWI); Intl Fedn of Socl Wrkrs (IFSW). Hobbies: Reading; Collecting Stamps.

CUBA Ivan, b. 15 Sept 1920, Nottingham. Eng. Academy President. m. Marie Irving. Education: Pupil, Kenneth Turtill, Univ of AK (Poetry); Pupil, Ida G Eise, Univ of AK (Art); DLit, World Acady of Arts and Culture, USA, 1988. Career: Exponent of the nude in oil painting (style similar to Toulouse Lautrec); Artist executor of war sketches; Composite Art Writer and painter of historic reconstructions; World War II: Survived mutiny on Troopship Aquitania, crossing Indian Ocean, 1940; Ordered to be shot; Escaped Grecian Suicide Squad to Egypt; Captured by and escaped from Gen Rommel's Army in Libya. Publications: Bhagavad Gita of Sri Lrsna; Poetry in 75 Canto; The Science of Painting; Madness in Art. Honours: Greek Gold Medal, for defence of Khalkis Swing Bridge, Greece, 1941; Poet Laureate Gold Medal, Rome, 1979; Elected Life Fell, Acady Leonardo da Vinci, Rome; Intl acad celebrity for psych writing on Art (Madness in Art); Intl Poet Laureate Awd, Intl Poets Acady, India, 1995; Intl Man of Yr, w Silver Medal, IBC, 1996; Hall of Fame, USA, 1998; Hon Repr, Centro Studi E Scambi Intl, Italy; Hon Repr, Temple of Arts Mus, USA.

CUEVAS Jose Luis, b. 26 Feb 1934, Mexico DF. Painter. m. Bertha Riestra, 1961, 3 d. Education: Univ de Mexico; Sch of Painting and Sculpture "La Esmeralda" Mexico. Appointments: Over forty one-man exhibns in NY, Paris, Milan, Mexico, Buenos Aires, Toronto, LA, WA, etc; Group Exhibns all over N and S Am, Eur, India and Japan; Works are in Mus of Modern Art, Solomon R Guggenheim Mus, Brooklyn Mus - NY -, Art Inst Chgo, Phillips Collect WADC, Muss of Albi and Lyons France, etc; Has illustrated following books: The Worlds of Kafka and Cuevas, 1959; The Ends of Legends String; Recollections of Childhood, 1962; Cuevas por Cuevas - autobiog - 1964; Cuevas Charenton, 1965; Crime by Cuevas, 1968; Homage to Quevedo, 1969; El Mundo de Jose Luis Cuevas, 1970; Cuaderno de Paris, 1977; Zarathustra, 1979; Les Obsessions Noirs, 1982; Letters to Tasenda, 1982. Publications: Cuevas by Cuevas, 1964; Cuevario, 1973; Confesiones de Jose Luis Cuevas, 1975; Cuevas por Daisy Ascher, 1979. Honours: First Intl Awd for Drawing Sao Paulo Bienal, 1959; First Intl Awd Mostra Internazionale di Bianco e Nero de Lugano Zurich, 1962; First Prize Bienal de Grabado Santiago Chile, 1964; First Intl Prize for engraving; First Biennial of New Delhi India, 1968; Natl Fine Arts Awd Mexico, 1981. Address: c/o Tasende Gallery, 820 Prospect Street, La Jolla, CA 92037, USA.

CUI Ping Yuan, b. 24 Nov 1961, Qingdao, China. Teacher. m. Chongming Xiu, 6 Aug 1986, 1 s. Education: Bachelor, 1983, Master, 1986, PhD, 1990, Harbin Inst of Technol. Appointments: Assoc Prof, 1991-93, Prof, 1993-, Harbin Inst of Technol; Currently, Dir, Aerospace Dynamic and Control Major Sect. Publications: System Identification for Aircraft, 1995; Num pprs in technol mag. Honours: Yth Sci and Technol Awd, Heilongjiang Prov, 1994. Memberships: Snr Mbr, Simulation Assn, 1991-; Snr Mbr, Aeronautics Assn, 1993-. Hobbies: Singing; Dancing; Swimming; Playing Ping Pa ball; Bridge. Address: Po Box 137, Department of Aerospace Engineering & Mechanics, Harbin Institute of Technology, Harbin 150001, China.

CUI Yun Wu, b. 23 Dec 1959. Professor of the History of Chinese Politics and Civilization. m. Xu Lin, 11 Feb 1989, 1 d. Education: BPed, 1984, MEd, 1987, Dr Hist, 1993, E China Normal Univ of Shanghai, China. Appointments: Asst, 1987-89, Lectr, 1989-93, Coll of Pedagogical Scis of E China Normal Univ; Asst Prof, 1993-96, Prof, 1996-, Pols Dept of Yunnan. Publications: books: On Yan Fu's Educational Thought, 1993; On Shuxincheng's Educational Thought, 1994; The Provincial Governors in Chinese Modernization Movement, 1995; Liangchumin's Biography, 1996; the History of Chinese Normal Education, 1996; The History of the Political System in Modern China, 1998; 8 books, (in collab) 1989-96; 35 acad theses, 1987-96. Honours: 1st Rate Awd of Shanghai's Excellent Coll Stud, 1984; 1st Rate Awd, China's YanXianjian Rsch Assn, 1987; 2nd Rate Awd of Shanghai BaoGan Awd, 1990; 2nd Rate Awd, Shanghai's Socl Sci, 1994; 1st Awd of Japanese SYLFF, Yunnan Univ, 1995; 1st Rate Awd, Excellent Coll Textbook of China Educl Cttee, 1995; 2nd Rate Awd, Yannan's Socl Sci, 1995; 2nd Rate Awd, Shanghai's Socl Sci, 1996; 1st rate Awd, Yannan's Sci Achievement, 1996. Address: Department of Politics, Yunnan University, No 52 Cuihu North Road, Kunming, Yunnan Province 650091, China.

CULLEN Michael John, b. 1945 London Eng. Politician. m. Anne Lowson Collins, 2 d. Education: Christchurch Canterbury Univ; Univ of Edinburgh. Appointments: Asst Lectr Canterbury Univ; Tutor Univ of Stirling; Snr Lectr in Hist Univ of Otago - Dunedin - and vising fell Austl Natl Univ, 1968-81; Mbr Parl, 1981-; Min of Socl Welfare, 1987-90; Assoc Min of Fin, 1987-88; Assoc Min of Hlth, 1988-90; Assoc Min of Labour, 1989-90; Opposition Spokesperson on Fin, 1991-; Dep Ldr of Opposition, 1996-; Labour Party. Hobbies: Music; Reading; House renovation; Golf. Address: Parliament House, Wellington, New Zealand.

CULVENOR Claude Charles, b. 15 May 1925, Castlemaine. Organic Chemist. m. Mary Gertrude Nicholls, 25 Oct 1947, 1 s, 2 d. Education: PhD (Melbourne), 1948; DPhil (Oxford), 1950; DSc (Melbourne), 1964. Appointments: Postdoct Rsch, Melbourne Univ, 1948, Univ Oxford, 1949, Univ CA, 1959; Rsch Scientist, Div Ind Chem, C'wlth Sci Ind Rsch Org, 1950; Ldr Rsch Grp, Pasture Toxins, Div Animal Hlth, 1971; Hon Visng Prof, Chem Dept, La Trobe Univ, 1989. Publications: Co-auth: The Pyrrolizidine Alkaloids, 1968; Plants for Medicine, 1990; Suth, books on local hist: The Boundaries of the Mount Franklin Aboriginal Reserve, 1992; Thomas Smith of Sandon, Miner, Farmer, Geologist, 1994; The Settlement of Yandoit Creek and the Gervasonis, 1995; 200 publs and reviews in sci lit. Honour: H G Smith Mem Medal of RACI, 1971. Memberships: Fell, Roy Austl Chem Inst, Pres, Vic Branch, 1976; Mbr, WHO, Working Parties, Evaluation of Carcinogenic Risk to Humans, 1975, 1982; Hazard to Humans of Pyrrolizidine Alkaloids, 1986. Hobbies: Landcare; Cattle breeding; Local history. Address: 52, Rostrevor Parade, Mont Albert North, Vic 3129, Australia.

CUMES James William Crawford, b. 23 Aug 1922, Rosewood, Aust. Diplomat; Economist; Writer. m. Heide Schulte Von Bäuminghaus, 29 May 1981, 1 d. Education: BA, Econs, Queensland; Grad of Sch of Diplomatic Studies, Canberra; PhD, Econs, London Sch of Econs and Polit Sci, UK. Appointments: Austl Army, Papua New Guinea, 1942-44; Austl Diplomatic Serv, 1944-85; Chargé d'Affaires, Bonn, 1955-56, Brussels, 1961-65; Hd, Austl Mil Miss, Berlin, 1956-58; Austl High Commnr to Nigeria, 1965-68; Austl Amb to Belgium, Luxembourg and Eurn Union, 1975-77, Austria and Hungary, 1977-80, The Netherlands, 1980-84; Served as Asst Sec, 1st Asst Sec and Dpty Sec, Austl Dept of For Affairs, 1958-85; Ldr, Dpty Ldr, Repr or Advsr to Gen Assembly of the UN, Commonwealth Prime Mins and Trade Mins Meetings, ANZUS, Colombo Plan Confs, UNIDO, IAEA, UN Econ and Socl Cncl, Orgn for Econ Coop and Dev; Gov, Bd, Intl Atomic Energy Agcy; Chmn, Countess Crt Investments Pty Ltd; Co-Chmn, Countess Crt Intl Ltd. Publications: The Indigent Rich, 1971; Inflation, 1974; Their Chastity was not too Rigid, 1979; The Reconstruction of the World Economy, 1984; Operation Equaliser, 1987; A Bunch of Amateurs, 1988; How to Become a Millionaire - without really working, 1990; Haverleigh, 1995. Hobbies: Tennis; Golf; Writing; Computer/Internet. Address: 91 La Croisette, 06400 Cannes, France.

CUMMINS James Micahel, b. 3 June 1943, Abbotta Bad, India. University Lecturer. m. Erlenè, 10 Dec 1973, 2 s. Education: BSc (London); PhD (Liverpool); FAIBiol. Appointments: Lectr, Vic Univ of Wellington, 1974-77; Assoc Prof, Queensland Univ, 1977-88; Murdoch Univ, currently. Publications: 157 rsch & tchng publs. Memberships: SSF; SSR; ASRB; AIBIOL; ESA: Sec, Austl Soc Reproductive Bio, 1982-84. Hobby: Swimming. Address: Division of Veterinary & Biomedical Sciences, Murdoch University, Murdoch, Western Australia, 6150, Australia.

CUMPSTON Ina Mary, b. Melbourne, Aust. Professor. Education: BA, Hons; MA, Hons; DPhil. Appointments: Tutor, 1942-44, Lectr, 1944-47, New Eng Univ Coll, Univ Sydney; Cabinet Off, London, 1950-55; Lectr, Roy Holloway Coll, Univ of London, 1955-57; Lectr, Birkbeck Coll, Univ of London, 1957-65; Rdr in C'wlth Hist, Birkbeck Coll, 1965-84; Visng Rdr, Univ of Ibadan, 1975;

Visng Prof, Univ of Benin, 1978. Publications: Indians Overseas in British Territories 1834-1854, 1953; The Growth of the British Commonwealth 1880-1932, 1973; Lord Bruce of Melbourne, 1989; History of Australian Foreign Policy 1901-1991, 1995; The Evolution of the Commonwealth of Nations 1900-1980, 1997. Memberships: Cttee, Inst of C'wlth Studies, London, 1980-84; Panel of Experts, Intl Fedn of Univ Women; Fell Roy Histl Soc, Roy Soc of Arts. Hobby: Walking. Address: 18 Fuller Street, Deakin, Canberra 2600, Australia.

CUNHA Abdon Longinus Da, b. 30 July 1945, Boawae, Flores, Indonesia. Archbishop of Ende. Education: Master of Civil Law, Univ of Indonesia, Jakarta. Appointments: Vicar Gen, 1987; Archbishop of Ende, 1996. Address: Katedral no 5, Ende 86312, Flores, Indonesia.

CUOMO Mark Donato, b. 22 Dec 1961, Perth, Aust. Lawyer. Education: BA, Univ of WA, 1982; BJuris, WWA, 1998; LLB, UNA, 1990. Appointments: State Sec, ALp WA Branch, 1997; Formerly Pres ACP, WA Branch, 1993-99. Address: 2nd Floor, 82 Beaufort St, Perth, WA 6000, Australia.

CUPIT Lloyd Anthony, b. 9 Dec 1937, Sydney, NSW, Aust. Minister of Religion. m. Margaret Joy Norgate, 13 Dec 1963, 2 s, 1 d. Education: Ordination Dip, 1963; BD, London, 1964; MTheol, MCD, 1976. Appointments: Exec Trainee, BP Aust, 1955-59; Pastoral Min and Theol Trainee, 1960-64; Field Linguist, Austl Bapt Miss Soc, Papua New Guinea, 1965-71; Overseas Sec, Austl Bapt Miss Soc, 1972-788; Gen Supt, Bapt Union Vic, 1978-90; Dir Evangelism and Educ, Dir Stdy and Rsch, Bapt World Alliance, 1990-. Publications: Kyaka Enga New Testament proj, 1983; Above Reproach, 1980; Peace I Leave With You, 1986; Ed, Five Till Midnight, 1994; Co-ed, Baptist Faith and Witness, 1995; Hallowed Be Your Name, 1998. Honour: Cleugh Black Mem Prize, 1963; Membership: Vic Bapt Histl Soc. Hobbies: Sport; Music; Genealogies. Address: c/- Baptist World Alliance, Curran Street, McLean, VA 22101, USA.

CURNOW (Thomas) Allen (Monro), b. 17 June 1911. Author. m. (1) Elizabeth Jaumaud LeCren, 1936, 2 s, 1 d, (2) Jenifer Mary Tole, 1965. Education: BA, DLitt, Univ Auckland, 1966. Appointments: Reporter, Sub-Ed, The Press, Christchurch, 1935-48; News Chronicle, London, 1949; Lectr in Engl 1951-67, Assoc Prof 1968-76, Univ of Auckland. Publications: 17 vols of poetry inclng: Island and Time, 1941; Sailing or Drowning, 1943; A Small Room with Large Windows, 1962; Trees, Effigies, Moving Objects, 1972; Collected Poems, 1974; An Incorrigible Music, 1979; You Will Know When You Get There, 1982; The Loop in Lone Kauri Road, 1986; Continuum: New and Later Poems, 1988; Selected Poems 1940-1989, 1990; Early Days Yet: New and Collected Poems 1941-1997, 1997. Plays: The Axe; The Overseas Expert; The Duke's Miracle; Resident of Nowhere. Criticism: Look Back Harder: selected critical writings 1935-1984. Honours: ONZ; CBE, 1986; NZ Book Awd for Poetry, 5 times; The Queen's Gold Medal for Poetry, 1989; C'wlth Poetry Prize, 1989; Cholmondeley Awd for Poetry, 1992. Listed in: The International Who's Who. Address: 62 Tohunga Crescent, Parnell, Auckland 1, New Zealand.

CURTIS Jamie Lee, b. 22 Nov 1958 Los Angeles CA. Actress. m. Christopher Guest, 1 child. Education: Choate Sch CT; Univ of the Pacific CA. Films incl: Halloween; The Fog; Terror Train; Halloween II; Road Games; Prom Night; Love Letters; Trading Places; The Adventures of Buckaroo Banzai: Across the 8th Dimension; Grandview; USA; Perfect; 8 Million Ways to Die; Amazing Grace and Chuck; A Man in Love; Dominick and Eugene; A Fish Called Wanda; Blue Steel; My Girl; Forever Young; My Girl 2. Tv: She's In The Army Now; Dorothy Stratten: Death of a Centrefold; Operation Petticoat; The Love Boat; Columbo; Quincy; Chalie's Angels; Anything but Love; Money on the Side; As Summers Die; Mother's Boys; True Lies; My Girl 2; True Lies, 1994; House Arrest, 1996; Fierce Creatures, 1996. Publication: When I was Little, 1993. Honours: Golden Globe Awd for Best Actress in a musical or comedy.

Address: c/o CAA, 9830 Wilshire Blvd, Beverly Hills, CA 90212, USA.

CURTIS Peter John, b. 6 Nov 1924. Mineralogist; Petrologist. m. 31 July 1954, 2 s, 1 d. Education: BSc, London, Spec Hons Geol (Mineralogy and Petrology); MSc, London, Geol/Geochemical Rsch; DIC, Dip of the Imperial Coll of Sci and Technol, London. Appointments: Rsch Asst (Chem), Geochemical Sect of the Geol Dept of the Royal Sch of Mines, London, 1954-58; Rsch and Field Geol, Bird & Co (P) Ltd, Rsch Dept, Calcutta, India, 1958-60; Mineralogist, Rhoanglo Mine Servs Ltd, North Rhodesia, 1960-61; Rsch Asst (Chem), Geol Dept, Univ of London, King's Coll, 1961-62; Snr Mineralogist, Rhoanglo Mine Servs Ltd, Zambia, 1962-65; Minerals Chem, Chem Div, NZ Dept of Sci and Indl Rsch, Gracefield, 1965-66; Proj Metallurgist, Geochemist, Mineralogist, Petrologist, Mt Isa Ltd, Techl Servs Lab, Mt Isa, 1966-69; Rsch Geol (Party Ldr), Carpentaria Exploration Co Ltd, Mc Arthur River Camp, 1970-71; Snr Rsch Geol, CSR Ltd (Minerals Div), 1971-79; Cnslt Mineralogist and Petrologist to mineral and pet exploration cos, furnace refractories and cement mfrs, 1979-. Memberships: Fell, Austl Inst of Mining and Metallurgy, 1979-; Amn Assn of Pet Geols, 1985-. Address: 68 Banksia Avenue, Andergrove, Mackay, Qld 4740, Australia.

CURTIS Peter John Campbell, b. 8 Sept 1929, Sydney, NSW, Aust. Diplomat. m. Chantal Courant, 1955, 5 s, 1 d. Education: BA, Sydney Univ, 1950; MA, Jurisprudence, Oxford Univ, Eng, 1954; Hon DHL, Pace Univ, NY, 1994. Appointments: Intl Labour Off, Geneva, Switzerland, 1955-57; Joined Dept For Affairs, Canberra, Aust, 1957; S and SE Asia Bch, Dept For Affairs, 1958-59; 3rd Sec, 2nd Sec, Acting 1st Sec, Austl Miss to UN, NYC, USA, 1959-63; 1st Sec, Dpty Hd Miss, Singapore, 1963-65; Hd, SE Asia Bch, Dept For Affairs, Canberra, 1965-67; Cnslr, Dpty Hd Miss, Austl Miss to UN, Geneva, Switz, 1967-69; Amb to Laos, 1969-72; Asst Sec, Personnel Bch, 1972-74; Asst Sec, Exec Bch, 1974, 1st Asst Sec, Pub Affairs and Cultural Rels Div, 1974-75, 1st Asst Sec, Def and Nuclear Div, 1980, Acting Dpty Sec, 1981-82, Dept For Affairs, Canberra; Amb to Lebanon, also Syria, Iraq, Jordan, 1975-76; High Commnr, India, Amb to Nepal, 1976-80; Amb to France, also Morocco, 1982-87; Amb to Belgium, Luxembourg and Eurn Communities, 1987-91; Consul Gen, NYC, 1991-94; Pres, Fed of Alliances Françaises of Aust, 1999. Listed in: Who's Who in Australia; International Year Book and Statesmen's Who's Who; Some others. Address: 25 Garsia St, Campbell, Canberra, ACT, Australia.

CURTIS Tony, (Bernard Schwarz), b. 3 June 1925, NY. Actor. m. (1) Janet Leigh, 1951, div 1962, 2 d; (2) Christine Kaufmann, 1963, div 1967, 2 d; (3) Leslie Allen, 1968, 2 s. Education: New Sch of Socl Rsch. Appointments: Served in US Navy. Films incl: Houdini, 1953; Black Shield of Falworth, 1954; So This is Paris?, 1954; Six Bridges to Cross, 1955; Trapeze, 1956; The Vikings, 1958; Defiant Ones, 1958; Perfect Furlough, 1958; Some Like It Hot, 1959; Spartacus, 1960; The Great Imposter, 1960; Pepe, 1960; The Outsider, 1961; Taras Bulba, 1962; Forty Pounds of Trouble, 1962; The List of Adrian Messenger, 1963; Captain Newman, 1963; Paris When It Sizzles, 1964; Wild and Wonderful, 1964; Sex and the Single Girl, 1964; Goodbye Charlie, 1964; The Great Race, 1965; Boeing, boeing, 1965; Arriverderci, Baby, 1966; Not with My Wife You Don't, 1966; Don't Make Waves, 1967; Boston Strangler, 1968; Lepke, 1975; Casanova, 1976; The Last Tycoon, 1976; The Manitou, 1978; Sextette, 1978; The Mirror Crack'd, 1980; Venom, 1982; Balboa; Midnight; Lobster Man from Mars; The High-Flying Mermaid; Prime Target; Center of the Web; Naked in New York; The Reptile Man; The Immortals; The Celluloid Closet. Tv incls: Third Girl from the Left, 1973; The Persuaders, 1971-72; The Count of Monte Cristo, 1976; Vegas, 1978; Mafia Princess, 1986; Christmas in Connecticut, 1992; A Perry Mason Mystery: The Case of the Grimacing Governor. Publications: Kid Andrew Cody and Julie Sparrow, 1977; The Autobiography, 1993. Hobbies: Painting. Address: c/o

The Blake Agency, 415 N Camden Drive, Suite 121, Beverly Hills, CA 90210, USA.

D

D'ARCY Joseph Eric, b. 25 Apr 1924. Archbishop of Hobart. Education: BA, Hons; MA; PhD; DPhil, Oxon. Appointments: Asst Priest, Oakleigh, 1950-55; Chap, Natl Civic Cl, 1955-59; Lectr, Snr Lectr, Rdr in Philos, Melbourne Univ, 1962-81; Episisc Vicar Tertiary Educ in Cath Archdiocese, Melbourne, 1969-81; Bish of Sale, Vic, 1981-88; Archbish of Hobart, Tas, 1988-. Publications: Conscience and Its Rights to Freedom, 1961, 1962, 1963, 1964, 1980; Human Acts, 1963, 1966; The Emotions, 1967; Pleasure, 1975. Memberships: Pontifical Cncl for Non-Believers, 1982-92; Pontifical Cong for Cath Educ, 1989-94; Pontifical Cong for Bishs, 1993-98; Pontifical Commn for Cultural Heritage of the Ch, 1994-99. Hobbies: Walking; Reading; Conversation. Address: Mt St Canice, GPO Box 62A, Hobart, Tas 7001, Australia.

D'ASSUMPCAO Henrique Antonio, b. 9 Aug 1934, Macau, China. Professor; Director. m. Colleen Marie, 18 Dec 1971, 2 s, 2 d. Education: BE, 1st Class hons; ME; CEng; FTSE; Hon FIEAust; FIEE; MIEEE. Appointments: Prof, Signal Processing, Dir, Collaborative Rsch Devel, Univ of SA; Dir, Coop Rsch Cntr for Sensor Signal and Info Processing; Cnclr, Austl Acady of Technol Scis and Engrng; Dir, Inst for Magnetic Resonance Rsch; Chf Def Sci and Hd Def Sci and Technol Org, 1987-90. Publications: Num pprs on signal processing and underwater acoustics; Co-inventor, Barra Sonobuoy syst. Honour: AM, 1992. Hobby: Genealogy. Address: 39 Stanley Street, Leabrook, SA 5068, Australia.

D'COSTA Maria Augusta, b. 5 May 1966, Goa. Public Servant. m. Bernard, 27 Dec 1994, 1 s, 1 d. Education: HSC (Com); Dip in Secretarial Course. Appointments: PA to Prin, Panchgani, 1986-; PA to Prin, Delhi, 1996-. Creative works: Paintings, Aug 1995. Honours: Narula Awd, Best in Academia (12th Class); Standing First in Panchgani Coll, 1985. Membership: Goan Gymkhana. Hobbies: Reading; Watching news; Games. Address: 11-A DDA (J) Flats, Vijay Mandal Enclave Behind Essex Farms, New Delhi 16, India.

D'NETTO Brian, b. 16 Sept 1957, Chennai, India. Academic. m. Elisa Marleny Cardona, 17 Aug 1991. Education: BCom, Madras Univ, India, 1978; PG, IRandPM, XLRI, Jamshedpur, 1980; BGL, Maduari, India, 1982; MBA, Univ of AR, USA, 1987; PhD, SUNY at Buffalo, 1994. Appointments: Personnel Offr, Tube Invmnt of India, 1980-82; Snr Personnel Offr, Kothari Indl Corp, 1982-86; Admnstv Offr, Confedn of Austl Ind, Jan-Aug, 1989; Lectr, Monash Univ, 1993-98; Snr Lectr, Monash, Mt Eliza Bus Sch, 1998-. Honours: Outstndng MBA Student Awd, Univ of AR; Best New Rschr Awd, Dept of Mngmt, Monash Univ, 1994; Elected Mbr, Beta Gamma; Natl Scholastic Hon Soc of Am for Outstndng Scholastic Rec. Memberships: Amn Acady of Mngmt; Cttee Mbr, Old Bedeans Assn. Hobbies: Music; Reading; Travelling; Dancing. Address: 4/26 Wright Street, Calyton, Vic 3168, Australia.

D'OTTAVIANO Itala Maria Loffredo, b. 18 July 1944, Campinas, Brazil. Mathematician; Logician. m. Carlos Roberto D'Ottaviano, 29 Apr 1968, 1 s, 2 d. Education: BSc Maths 1966, BA Music 1960, Grad Course in Music 1962, MSc Maths, State Univ of Campinas (UNICAMP), Brazil, 1974; Dr of Maths, UNICAMP, 1982; Livre Docente Maths in the area of Logic and Fndns of Maths, 1987. Appointments: Concert Pianist before becoming Mathn; HS Maths Tchr, 1967, 1968; Prof, Cath Univ of Campinas (PUCC), undergrad course, Brazil, 1967, 1968; Asst Prof, State Univ of Campinas (UNICAMP), undergrad and grad courses, Dept of Maths, 1969-86; Dir of Educ, Cty of Campinas, Brazil, 1977, 1978; Visng Schl, Univ of CA, Berkeley, 1984-85; Visng Schl, Stanford Univ, Inst of Applied Maths for Socl Scis, USA, 1984-85; Prof, UNICAMP, Dept of Maths, 1986-; Dir of Cntr for Logic Epistemology and the Hist of Sci, UNICAMP, 1986-92; Visng Schl, Wolfson Coll, Oxford Univ, Eng, 1988; Visng Tchr, Univ of Torino, Italy, 1990; Full Prof of Logic, Unicamp, 1998-. Publications: Sev pprs in Proceedings of Brazilian and International Sci Meetings, papers in sci jrnls. Honours include: Natl Schl, Brazilian Natl Rsch Cncl, 1987-; Ed of The Jrnl of Non Classical Logic, 1990; Invited Speaker, Brazilian and Intl sci meetings; Mbr, Organizing Cttees, Brazilian and Intl confs on Logic and Epistemology. Memberships: Fndng Mbr, Cntr for Logic, Epistemology and Hist of Sci, UNICAMP; Vice Sec 1981-82, Sec 1983-84, Pres, 1993-96, 1996-99, Brazilian Logic Soc; Brazilian Soc on Hist of Sci; Assn of Symbolic Logic, Ctte Mbr, Cttee Pres, 1993-95, 1995-98, Logic in Latin Am. Hobbies: Music; Dance; Opera; Reading; History; Politics; Animals (especially dogs and horses); Riding. Address: Centro de Logica, Epistemologia e História de Ciencia, Universidade Estadual de Campinas CP 6133, 13 081, Campinas, Sao Paulo, SP, Brazil.

D'SOUZA Mary Augusta, b. 26 Mar 1938, Poona, India. Teacher. Education: Masters in Engl Lit, Bombay Univ, India, 1979. Appointments: Tchr, 1962-99; Prin, HS, 1990-93. Creative Works: Cardmaking, painting, collage and crafts; Culinary Art; Vegetable Carving; Crochet. Honours: Natl Awd for Best Tchr, 1990; Lions Club Awd, 1990; Rotary Club, 1991. Membership: Sisters of the Cross of Chavanod. Hobbies: All Arts; Stitching; Embroidery; Flower making; Waxwork. Address: Holy Cross Convent, Bastora, Bardez Goa, 403507, India.

DA Huang, b. 22 Feb 1925, Tianjin, China. Professor of Economics. m. Shuzhen Luo, 20 June 1952, 2 s. Education: MA, Northern China United Univ, 1947. Appointments: Mbr, Acad Deg Cttee, State Cncl of China; Mbr, Monetary Policy Commn of the People's Bank of China, 1997. Publications: Socialist Fiscal and Financial Problems, 1981; Economics of Money and Banking, 1992; Macroeconomic Control and Money Supply, 1997. Honours: Awd, Econ Scis, Sun Yefang Fndn, 1986; Awd, Ex Textbook, State Educ Commn, 1987. Memberships: Chair, Chinese Soc for Pub Fin; Dir, Expert Advsry Cttee on the Humanities and Socl Scis Studies, Min of Educ. Hobbies: Calligraphy; Running. Address: Office of the President, Renmin University of China, Beijing 100872, China.

DA Wan Ming, b. 6 Feb 1946, Lanzhou, China. Hematologist. m. Liu Yuan, 18 Oct 1971, 1 s. Education: MD, Beijing Medl Univ. Appointments: Dir, Hematologic Dept, 1987; Dir, Lanzhou Inst of Hematology, 1992; Dir, Cntr of Hematology, PLA, 1996. Publications: Autologous Hermatopoietics Stem Cell Transplantation (ed in chf), 1996; Therapy of Leukemia (auth); Contbr articles to profl jrnls. Honours: Outstndng Achievements in the Field of Sci, IBC, Chinese Govt. Memberships: Intl Soc Hematology; China Exp Hematology; Chmn, Hematology Soc, PLA and Gansu Soc, Hematology; Vice Chmn, China Soc Sci & Technol. Hobby: Travelling. Address: Department of Hematology, Lanzhou General Hospital, 58 Xiaoxihuxjie, Qilihe, Lanzhou, Gansu, China 730050.

DA Zhenyi, b. 26 Oct 1937, Gushi, He Nan, China. College Professor. m. Liu Shuying, 27 Jan 1968, 2 s. Education: He Nan Univ, Kai Feng City. Appointments: Coll Tchr, 1959; Vice Dean of Hist Dept, 1980; Dean, Ethnology Dept; Hd, Ethnology Inst, 1988-97. Publications: Hui People in Hubei, 1993; Hui People's History in South Central China, 1995. Honours: Spec Allowance, Cntrl Govt, 1994; Spec Contbn to Nationalities' Unity, 1990. Hobby: Physical Education. Address: Ethnology Institute South Central College for Nationalities, Wu Han, Hubei, 430074, China.

DAALDER Joost, b. 28 Sept 1939. Professor of English. m. Geertruida H Broekman, 15 Jan 1966, 1 s, 1 d. Education: Cand Lit, 1960, Drs, 1965, Univ of Amsterdam. Appointments: Lectr, 1966, Snr Lectr, 1971, Univ of Otago, Dunedin, NZ; Lectr, 1976-77, Snr Lectr, 1977, Rdr in Engl, 1983-98; Prof of Engl, 1998-, Flinders Univ of S Aust. Publications include: Scholarly eds of Wyatt, Thyestes, The Changeling; About 70 scholarly articles in learned jrnls. Memberships: NY Acady Scis; Austl Lang and Lit Assn; Austl and NZ Shakespeare Assn. Listed in: Who's Who in the World; Men of Achievement. Hobbies: Studying tribal and ethnic artefacts. Address: Sch of Humanities, Flinders Univ, GPO Box 2100, Adelaide, SA 5001, Australia.

DABBARANSI Korn, b. 14 Sept 1945, Bangkok, Thailand. Deputy Prime Minister; Minister of Public Health. m. Rapeephan, 2 children. Education: Wilbraham Acady, MA, USA, 1962-64; BSc, Bus Admin, Clark Univ, MA, 1968. Appointments: Asst, Coml Cnslr, Canad Emb, 1969-74; Sec, Min of For Affairs, 1974-76; Sec, Min of Ind, 1976; Asst, Min of Ind, 1980-83; Pres Mbr, House of Representatives for Nakhon Ratchasima Prov, 1983-; Dpty Min of Ind, 1986-88; Min to Prime Min's Off, 1988-91; Chmn, House Cttee on Ind, 1992-94; Min to Prime Min's Off, 1994; Chmn, House Cttee on Energy, 1995; Dpty Prime Min, Min of INd, 1996-. Honour: Kt Grand Cordon, Spec Class, Most Exalted Order of the White Elephant. Address: 111/1 Phaholyothin Soi 5, Phaholyothin Road, Bangkok 10400, Thailand.

DADAWA Zhu Zheqin, b. 15 July 1968, Guangzhou, China. Singer. Education: BA, Chinese Lit, 1990. Creative works: (recordings) Yellow Children, 1992; Sister Drum, 1995; Voice From the Sky, 1997; (soundtrack) The King of Nanning, 1996; Chinese Box, 1997; (songs) The Story of a Red-Crowned Crane, 1990; The Tear Lake, with The Chieftains, 1996. Honours: 2nd Prize, Natl 4th Grand Prize Young Singers TV Contest, 1990; "Q" the Yr in World Music, 1995; Best Album of Yr, 20th Taiwan Jinding Phonograph Awd, 1995; Best Sound Track of Venice Film Fest Prize, 1997; Best Female Artist in YMC, 1997. Membership: ASCAP, 1998. Hobbies: Reading; Swimming; Travelling.

DAGA Satya Narayan, b. 16 Dec 1948, Dewas, India. Engineer. m. Padma Daga, 6 Mar 1974, 1 s. Education: BSc, hons, Vikram Univ, 1966; BESc, hons, Mech, Jabalpur Univ, 1969. Appointments: Dpty Gen Mngr, 1994, Snr Dpty Gen Mngr, 1995, Additional Gen Mngr, 1995-, BHEL, Bhopal. Publications: 35 tech pprs in var natl and intl confs. Honours: Gold and Silver Medals, Vikram Univ, 1966; Gold Medal, Jabalpur Univ, 1969; Title, Man of the Yr, ABI, 1998. Memberships: Fell, Instn of Engrs, India; Indian Inst of Indl Engrng; Am Soc of Mech Engrs. Hobbies: Reading; Technical Writing; Lecturing. Address: M/S Bharat Heavy Electricals Ltd, Bhopal, India.

DAHLSTROM Jane Esther, b. 12 Apr 1961, Parramatta, Aust. Medicine. m. Mark Bassett, 29 Apr 1992, 3 s, 3 d. Education: MBBS (Hons), Univ Sydney, Aust, 1985; Cert in fam plng, 1987; PhD, Austl Natl Univ, Canberra, 1992. Appointments: Anatomical Path Registrar ACT Hlth, Canberra, 1992; Visng Fell, JCSMR, Austl Natl Univ, 1992. Publications: Articles, var sci and medl jrnls. Memberships: Roy Coll of Pathologists of Australasia; Austl Soc of Cytology; Austl Vascular Soc; Canberra Medico-Legal Soc; Medl Women's Soc of ACT. Honours: Austl Natl Univ Schl, 1988-91; David Nelson Mem Trainee Awd, 1995. Hobbies: Music; Sewing. Address: PO Box 45, Garran ACT 2605, Australia.

DAI Bingguo, b. 1941 Yinjian Co Guizhou Prov. Diplomatist. Education: Sichuan Univ. Appointments: Joined CCP, 1973; Dir Dep of USSR and East Eurn Affairs min of For Affairs; Vice-Min of For Affairs; Dir Intl Liaison Dept of CCP Cntr Cttee, 1997-. Memberships: Mbr 15th CCP Cntr Cttee, 1997-. Address: International Liaison Department of Chinese Communist Party Central Committee, Beijing, People's Republic of China.

DAI Youwei, b. 3 Oct 1943, Shanghai, China. Professor. m. Jiafeng Zhao, 22 Apr 1971, 1 s. Education: PhD, Univ of CA, Berkeley, USA, 1983. Appointments: Lectr, 1984, Assoc Prof, 1987, Sect Ldr, 1989, Dept Chmn, 1994, Nanjing Univ of Sci & Technol. Publications: Turbulence Modelling and Numerical Computation, 1989; Modern Propulsion Techniques, 1990; Advanced Heat Transfer, 1992. Honours: Scientific Achievement Awds, Jaingsu Prov & Cntrl Govt, 1988, 1991, 1992, 1994. Membership: Jiangsu Fluid Mech Assn; Fell, Dpty Chmn, 1994-. Hobbies: Sports; Touring. Address: Department of

Thermal Engineering #803, Nanjing University of Science & Technology, Nanjing 210094, China.

DAI Zhiqiang, b. 3 June 1944, Shanghai, China. Government Official; Professor. m. Ruiqin Chang, 9 July 1972, 2 s. Education: Bach Deg, Hist, Fudan Univ, 1961-66. Appointments: Dpty Dir, Anyang Mus, Henan, 1979-83; Dir, Anyang Cultural Bur, 1983-84; Gen Sec, China Numismatic Soc, 1984-; Prof, Grad Sch of Peoples Bank of China, 1988-; Dpty Dir, Peoples Bank of China, 1991-94; Chf Ed, Jrnl of China Numismatics, 1991-; Dir, China Numismatic Mus, 1994-. Honours: Gold Coin and Prize for Ex Acad Achievements, 1993, 1998; Expert, Exchange of Cultural Relics, Natl Cultural Relics Bur, 1993-. Memberships: Natl Cultural Relics Appraisal Commn; Exec Chmn, Gen Sec, China Numismatic Soc; ICOM; ICOMON. Hobby: Collecting coins. Address: 22 Xijiaominxiang, Beijing 100031, China.

DAIBATA Masanori, b. 13 Mar 1961, Tokushima, Japan. Physician; Researcher. Education: MD; PhD. Appointment: Instr, Kochi Med Sch. Address: Department of Medicine, Kochi Medical School, Kochi 783-8505, Japan.

DALAI LAMA, b. 6 Jul 1935 Taktser Amdo Prov NE Tibet. Temporal and Spiritual Hedd of Tibet: Fourteenth Incarnation. Appointments: Born of Tibetan peasant family in Amdo Prov; Enthroned at Lhasa, 1940; Rights exercised by regency, 1934-50; Assumed polit power, 1950; Fled to Chumbi in S Tibet after abortive resistance to Chinese, 1950; Negotiated agreement with China, 1951; Vice-Chmn Standing Cttee Natl Cttee CPPCC, 1951-59; Hon Chmn Chinese Buddhist Assn, 1953-59; Deleg to Natl People's Congress, 1954-59; Chmn Preparatory Cttee for the "Autonomous Reg of Tibet", 1955-59; Fled Tibet to India after suppression of Tibetan natl uprising, 1959; Dr of Buddhist Philosphy - Monasteries of Sera Drepung and Gaden Lhasa, 1959; Supreme Hd of all Buddhist sects in Tibet - Xizang. Publications: My Land and Peple, 1962; The Opening of the Wisdom Eye, 1963; The Buddhism of Tibet and the Key to the Middle Way, 1975; Kindness, Clarity and Insight, 1984; A Human Approach to World Peace, 1984; Freedom in Exile - autobiog - 1990; The Good Heart, 1996. Honours: Memory Prize, 1989; Congressional Human Rights Awd, 1989; Nobel Peace Prize, 1989; Freedom Awd - USA - 1991. Memberships: Mbr Natl Cttee CPPCC, 1951-59. Hobbies: Gardening; Mechanics. Address: Thekchen Choeling, McLeod Ganj 176219, Dharamsala, Himachal Pradesh, India.

DALRYMPLE Frederick Rawdon, b. 6 Nov 1930, Sydney, NSW, Aust. Foreign Service; Diplomat. m. Ross Elizabeth Williams, 27 Feb 1957, 1 s, 1 d. Education: BA hons, Univ of Sydney, 1952; MA, 1960, Univ of Oxford, England. Appointments: Lectr in Philos, Univ of Sydney, NSW, 1955-56; Joined Austl Dept of External Affairs, 1957; Austl Amb to Israel, 1971; Promoted First Asst Sec; Austl Amb to Indonesia, 1981-85; Promoted Dpty Sec, 1985; Austl Amb to USA, 1985-89; Austl Amb to Japan, 1989-93; Chmn, ASEAN Focus Grp, 1994-; Visng Prof, Univ of Sydney, 1994-. Publications: Articles on intl devs in var jrnls including: Austl Jrnl of Intl Affairs; Columnist, Mainichi Shimbun Newsppr, Japan. Honour: AO, 1987. Listed in: Who's Who in Australia. Hobby: Golf. Address: ASEAN Focus Group Pty Ltd, GPO Box 3271, Sydney, NSW 2001, Australia.

DALY John Alfred, b. 7 Aug 1936. Educator. 2 d. Education: BA; MSc; PhD; Dip Phys Ed; DipT (Sec). Appointments: Dir, 1996-, Professor, Cntr for Olympic Studies. Publications: Books: Elysian Fields: Sport, Class and Community, 1982; Ours Were the Hearts to Dare, 1982; The Adelaide Hunt, 1986; Quest for Excellence, 1991; Feminae Ludens, 1994. Honours: Order of Aust, 1991. Memberships: Fell, ACHPER; Fell, AAPE (USA); Aust Soc of Sport Hist; Assn of Prof Histns. Hobbies: Reading; Oil Painting; Research and Writing. Address: University of South Australia, Holbrooks Road, Underdale, SA 5032, Australia.

DALY Peter Eugene, b. 21 July 1935. Company Director. m. Daphne Lilian, 8 Feb 1958, 1 s, 1 d. Appointments: Chmn, Ins Enquiries and Complaints Ltd; Chmn, Life Ins Complaints Serv Ltd; Chmn, Seal Rocks Vic Aust Pty Ltd; Chmn, Aldersgale Fin Pty Ltd; Chmn, Aegis Underwriting Agcy Pty Ltd; Dpty Chmn, Gerling Aust Ins Co Pty Ltd; Dpty Chmn, Zool Pks and Gdns Bd of Vic, 1991-99. Hobbies: Tennis; Cricket; Rugby Union. Address: Norwin, 2 Jacov Gardens, Templestowe, Vic 3106, Australia.

DALY Thomas Joseph (Lieut Gen, Sir), b. 19 Mar 1913, Ballarat, Vic, Aust. Regular Army Officer (retired). m. Heather Fitzgerald, 19 Feb 1946, 3 d. Education: St Patrick's Coll, Sale, Vic; Xavier Coll, Kew, Vic, RMC Duntroon, Imperial Def Coll, Eng, 1956; Jt Servs Staff Coll, Eng, 1949. Appointments: Dir, Jennings Inds, 1974-85; Chmn, Cncl of Austl War Mem, 1974-82; Cnclr 1966-82, Cnclr, Roy Agricl Soc, NSW, 1972-; Dir, Assoc Securities, 1971-76; Mbr, Natl Cncl of Austl Red Cross Soc, 1971-74; Col Cmdt, Roy Aust Regt, 1971-75; Chf of Gen Staff, Aust, 1966-71; GOC E Cmnd, 1963; Adjutant Gen, 1961; GOC N Cmnd, 1957; Dir, Ops and Plans, 1953; Cmndr, 28 Brit C'wlth Infantry Brig, Korea, 1952; Dir, Infantry, 1951; Dir of Mil Art, RMC Duntroon, 1949; Instr, Staff Coll, Camberly, 1946-49; CO 2-10th Battalion AIF, 1944; GSO 1 5 Div, 1942; G502 6 Austl Div, 1941; Brigade Maj 18 Infantry Brig, 1940; Adjutant 2-10th Battalion, 1939; Attached 16th-5th Lancers, India, 1938; Adjutant Third Light Horse, 1934. Publications: Articles in Press and Service jrnls. Honours include: Sword of Hon, Roy Mil Coll, Duntroon; Despatches, Mid East, 1941; Despatches, New Guinea, 1943; OBE, New Guinea, 1944; DSO Borneo, 1945; CBE, Korea, 1952; CB, 1963; KBE, 1967; Offr, Legion of Merit, USA, 1953. Hobbies: Gardening; Reading; Golf; Watching cricket and football. Address: 16 Victoria Road, Bellevue Hill, NSW 2023, Australia.

DANA Hani Osman El, b. 1 Mar 1952, Beirut, Lebanon. Banker. m. Susan Serbey, June 1995, 3 d. Education: MBA (Fin), NY Univ; BA (Econ), Amn Univ of Beirut. Appointments: VP, Chase Manhattan Bank, 1977-88; Gen Mngr, Qatar Natl Bank, 1988-93; Exec Dir, Mbr Bd of Dirs, Banque de la Mediteranée, Lebanon, 1993-. Address: Banque de la Mediteranée, PO Box 11 348, Beirut, Lebanon.

DANIEL Jeyarus Mysia, b. 13 Mar 1946, Nagercoil, India. Lecturer; Poet. m. P Daniel, 6 Sept 1973, 1 s, 1 d. Education: BSc, Chem; MA, Engl Lit; MLitt, Thesis on Emily Dickinson. Appointments: Lectr, Holy Cross Coll, Nagercoil, 1970; Lectr, St Mary's Coll, Tuticorin, 1973; Lectr, Women's Christian Coll, Nagercoil, 1975-. Publications: Poems: publ in Quest and Wanderlust, anthology, 1998; Rhapsodic Rivers, collection of poems. Memberships: Writers Forum, Ranchi, India. Hobbies: Acting and Directing - English Drama; Music; Dogs. Address: No 4 Arul Nagar, Nagercoil 629001, Tamil Nadu, India.

DANS Desmond Keith, b. Aust. MLC (ALP) for South Metropolitan, WA. m. Rikki Trenaman, 4 Nov 1961, 1 s, 1 d. Appointments: Sec, WA Br of Seaman's Union of Aust, 1969-71; Mbr, State Exec ALP, Fed Conf Deleg, 1971; MLC (ALP) for S Metro, WA, 1971; Leader of Opposition in LEG Cncl, 1976-83; Min for Indl Relations, 1983-84; Min for Tourism, Racing and Gaming, 1985-86; Min for Wrks and Servs, 1986-87; Spec Responsibilities for Ams Cup, 1984-87; Ldr of Govt in Leg Cncl, 1983-87. Hobbies: Golf; Water sports. Address: 15 Haig Road, Attadale, WA 6156, Australia.

DAO Chi Sao, b. 15 July 1940, Vietnam. Electrical Engineer. m. Tran Thi Luyen, 1 Jan 1968, 2 s, 1 d. Education: Grad, Hanoi Tech Univ; Trng in Russia, 1968-71; Mngmt Course, 1986-87. Appointments include: Electr Engr, 1963-65; Chf of Tech Dept, 1965-68; Dpty Dir, 1971-74, Dpty Gen Dir, 1975-82, Gen Dir, 1983-95, Chmn, BD Dirs, 1996-, LILAMA. Honours: 3 Labour Orders; 7 Creatives Labour Certs. Membership: Vietnam Communist Party. Address: 124 Minh Khai Street, Hai Ba Trung Dist, Hanoi, Vietnam.

DARBY Frank William, b. 20 July 1948, Brenchley, Kent, Eng. Ergonomist. m. Anne, 8 Dec 1978, 2 d. Education: MSc; CNZErg. Apppointments: Scientist, Dept of Hlth, 1978-90; Snr Occ Hlth Scientist, Deaprtment of Labour, 1990-96; Cnslt in Ergonomics, 1996-. Publications: On overuse disorders and " stress"; (Co-auth) The Pocket Shiftworker. Memberships: NZ Ergonomics Soc, Pres, 1993-95; Ergonomics Soc (UK); Comm Rsch Inst, Aust; Convenor, Bd for Cert of NZ Ergonomists. Hobbies: To make a wooden clock. Address: 467 Broadway, Miramar, Wellington, New Zealand.

DARBY Ian Andrew, b. 11 Nov 1959, Bendigo, Australia. Research Scientist. Education: BSc, hons, 1982, PhD, 1987, Univ Melbourne. Appointments: Rsch Fell, INSERM Unité 36, Paris, France, 1986-88, Dept of Pathol, Univ Geneva, Switz, 1988-90; Snr Rsch Offr, Howard Florey Inst, Univ Melbourne, 1991-94; Snr Sci, Wound Fndn of Aust, Melbourne, 1994-98; Snr Lectr, RMIT Univ, Melbourne, 1998-. Publications: Num sci publns in profl jrnls and conf presentations. Honour: Austl Soc for Med Rsch Awd, 1985. Memberships: Austl Soc for Med Rsch; Austl Wound Mngmt Assn; Eurn Tissuie Repair Soc. Hobbies: Tennis; Travel; Piano Music. Address: PO Box 71, Bundoora, Victoria 3083, Australia.

DARGIE William Alexander (Sir), b. 4 June 1912. Artist. m. Kathleen Howitt, 1 s, 1 d. Appointments: Offic War Artist, Cap, AIF; Offic War Artist, RAAF and RAN; Hd, Natl Gall Vic Art Sch, 1946-53, Mbr, 1952-73, Chmn, 1969-73, C'wlth Art Advsry Bd; Mbr, Interim Cncl, Natl Gall, Canberra, 1968-72; Mbr, Natl Capital Plng Advsry Cttee, 1969-71; Tree, Native Cultural Reserve, Port Moresby, 1970-74; Tree, Mus and Art Gall, TPNG, 1970-74; Mbr, Cncl, Natl Mus, Vic, 1978-83; Chmn, Bd Trees, McClelland Gall, 1981-87. Creative works: Num portraits inclng: HM Queen Elizabeth II for C'wlth Assn, 1954, exhibited Royal Acady and Royal Soc Portrait Painters; Sir George Pearce PC for King's Hall, Parl House, Canberra; Duke of Gloucester for C'wlth Govt; Auth: On Painting a Portrait, 1956. Honours: McPhillimy Awd, 1940; Woodward Awd, 1940; Mackay Prize, 1942; Winner, Archibald Prizes for portraits, Sir James Elder, 1941, Corporal Jim Gordon VC, 1942, Lt-Gen Sir Edmund Herring, 1945, L C Robson, 1946, Sir Marcus Clark, 1947, Sir Leslie McConnan, 1950, Essington Lewis CH, 1952, Albert Namatjira, 1956; OBE, 1959; CBE, 1969; Kt, 1970; MA honoris causa. Memberships: FRSA, London; FRAS. Listed in: Who's Who in Australia. Hobbies: Tennis; Folklore; Anthropology. Address: 19 Irilbarra Road, Canterbury, Vic 3126, Australia.

DARLING Marina Santini, b. 19 July 1959. Company Director. m. Anthony Darling, 1 s, 1 d. Education: LLB, Univ of Melbourne; BA Hons, Univ of Melbourne. Appointments: Articled Clk, Sol, Snr Assoc, Corrs Chmbrs Westgarth, 1983-87; Snr Exec, Corp Adv, Potter Warburg & Co Pty Ltd, 1987-89; Mngng Dir, CapoNero Grp, 1989-; Dir, GIO Aust Holdings Ltd, 1995-; Dir, Southern Hydro Ltd, 1995-98; Dir, Property Cncl of Aust, Vic; Dir, Pub Transp Corp, 1996; Dir, Natl Aust Tstees Ltd, 1996; Mbr Cncl of Mngmt, Austl Ballet Sch, 1997-; Mbr Sch Cncl, Melbourne Grammar Sch, 1998-; Dir, Southern Cross Broadcasting (Aust) Ltd, 1999-. Honours: William Smith Exhib, 1979; Wyselaskie Schlsp, 1980. Memberships: VP Victorian Bd of Mngmt, Property Cncl of Aust, 1996-98; Mbr Victorian Cncl, Austl Inst of Co Dirs; Roy S Yarra Law Tennis Club; Alexandra Club. Listed in: Who's Who in Australia. Hobbies: Travel; Walking; Golf; Tennis. Address: c/o CapoNero Group, PO Box 546, Toorak, Vic 3142, Australia.

DARRACOTT Stehen Lynne, b. 17 June 1943, Kingardy, Queensland, Aust. Editor. m. Eunice Joan, 23 Mar 1967, 1 s. Appointments: Cadet, Kingaroy Herald, 1960; Jrnlst, Cumberand, 1964; News Ed, Kingaloy, 1965; Jrnlst, Courier Mail, 1971; Ed, Warwick Daily News, 1973; Ed, Mngr, West Publs, 1989; Ed/Ed Mngr, Star Newspprs, 1992. Membership: Media, Entertainment and Arts Alliance. Hobbies: Reading; Teddy Bears. Address: 24 Ronland Street, Warwick 4370, Queensland, Australia.

DART John Rowland, b. 6 Sept 1931. Chief Executive. m. Anne Reed, 17 Dec 1954, 3 s, 1 d. Education: RFD, ED, BSc, DipEd, New England Univ Coll. Appointments: CMF, 1950-; Joined 1955, Prod Mngr, 1956, Natl Sales Mngr, 1960, Gen Mngr, 1965, Scott & Bowne (Asia) Pty Ltd, 1969-79; St Ives Jaycees, 1965; CO, Sydney Univ Regiment, 1967-70; Natl Sec, CMF Assn of Aust, 1969-71; Pres, Cosmetic and Toiletries Mfrs Assn of Aust, 1969-71 Chf Instr, OCTU, 1970-73; Asst Area Cmmnr, Boy Scouts Assn, Nth Metro Area, 1972-73; Chf of Staff, 2nd Divsn, 1974-76; Pres, Imperial Serv Club, 1977-80; Cmdr, 2 Trng Gr, 1978-80; Hon Aide de Camp to Gov Gen of Aust, 1979-81; Mngng Dir, Simmons Bedding Co Pty Ltd, 1979-82; Roy NSW Regiment, 1980-81; Gen Mngr, Confectionary Divsn, Lifesavers (Asia) Ltd, 1982-83; Gen Mngr, Playbill (Aust) Pty Ltd, 1984-85; Chf Exec, Austl Fedn of Travel Agents, 1985-96; Sec Gen, Universal Fedn Travel Agents Assns, Asia-Pacific Alliance, 1997. Honour: OBE, 1980. Hobbies: Sailing; Football. Address: Suite 1701, 44 Market Street, Sydney, NSW 2000, Australia.

DART Rowland Stanley James, b. 20 Dec 1906, Sydney, NSW, Aust. Retired Inspector of Schools, NSW. m. Clarice Williams, 27 Dec 1929, dec 1980, 2 s. Education: Sydney Tchrs' Coll, 1926-27; BA, Sydney Univ, 1943 (evening stud). Appointments: Irrigation Commn Offr, Accts, 1923-26; Tchr, Merungle Hill, Leeton Tchr in Charge, 1927-36; Dpty Hd, Auburn N, 1937, Newtown, 1941; Granville Secondary, 1943; Prin, Bourke Inter High, 1948; Inspector of Schs, 1950-71. Publications: Var short articles for Educ and Scouting mags. Memberships: NSW Inst of Inspectors of Schs, 1950-71, Pres 1963, Life Mbr 1972, Hon Exec Offr 1972-90; Australasian Inst of Snr Educ Admnstrs, 1956-; Life Mbr 1984, Hon Info Offr 1987; Austl Coll of Educ, 1962-; Austl Scout Assn, 1916-, holder of Leader warrants, 1925-, Commissioner, 1939-, NSW Commissioner for Leader Trng, 1942-66, Aust & New Guinea, 1966-71, NSW Commissioner for Relationships, 1972-74, Hon Commissioner, 1975-; Rotary Intl var positions, 1950-; Pres, St Ives Club, 1967-68, Hon Natl Publs Co-ord, 1976-98; Leader, Austl Scout Delegation to World Scout Conf, 1961; Patron, NSW Baden Powell Scout Guild, 1987-. Honours: OAM, 1980; Awds, Scout Assn of Aust: Medal of Merit, 1942; Silver Acorn, 1964; Silver Kangaroo (Scouting's highest Austl Awd), 1970; Rotary Intl, Paul Harris Fell Awd, 1980. Listed in: Men of Achievement; Who's Who in Australia; Who's Who in Australia and the Pacific Nations. Address: 4 Tobruk Avenue, St Ives 2075, Sydney, NSW, Australia.

DARTNALL Terence Haig, b. 4 Sept 1943, Whitstable, Kent, Eng. Philosopher; Educator. m. (1) Susan, 22 Dec 1975, (2) Wendy, 30 Feb 1982, 1 s, 1 d. Education: BA Hons, Bristol, 1967; MLitt, Edinburgh, 1969; Dip Gen Ling, Edinburgh, 1970; PhD, Otago, 1979; MSc, Sussex, 1987. Appointments: Fell, Otago Univ, 1972-75; Hd Dept, Philos, Univ of Tonga, 1976; Fell, Austl Natl Univ, 1977-78; Lectr, Adelaide Univ, 1979-81; Lectr, Natl Univ of Singapore, 1981-85; Snr Lectr, Dir of Artificial Intell, Griffith Univ, 1988-. Creative Works: Ed, Artificial Intelligence and Creativity, 1994; Perspectives on Cognitive Science, 1999; Num articles in profl jrnls. Memberships: Behavioral and Brain Scis; Editl Bd, Metascience, 1996-; Editl Bd, Dialogues in Psychol, 1997-; Editl Bd, Artificial Intell Review, 1997-; Amn Asia Artificial Intell; Austl Soc for the Hist and Philos of Sci. Hobbies: Rock climbing; Scuba; Poetry; Wine. Address: Faculty Info And Computing, Griffith University, Nathan 4111, Australia.

DAS Josyula Satyanarayana, b. 19 Apr 1955, Visakhapatnam, India. Mechanical Engineer. m. 4 June 1979, 1 s, 1 d. Education: BEng, Mech. Appointments: Sci Offr, Engr, 1977; Sci Offr, Engrs (SD), 1980; Sci Offr, Engrs (SE), 1985; Asst Mngr, Maintenance, 1986; Maintenance Mngr, 1990; Hd, Planning Sect, 1995; Maintenance Mngr, 1997. Membership: Inst of Engrs, India. Hobbies: Reading; Astrology; Meditation. Address: PO Box 80079, 87010 Labuan, Malaysia.

DAS Nimai, b. West Bengal, India. Poet. Publications: Poems: Arun Alor Abarta Theke, 1976; Archid Kichu Kaktas Kichu, 1979; Prem O Priya Sanglap, 1979; Kabita Ek Ujjwal Aushukh, 1985; Sankhamala Tumie Putul, 1986; Jagrata Manusher Kantha, 1995; Mekhechi Chander Kalanka, 1996; Nijer Kachei Artand, 1998; Suchismitake Ghire, 1998. Short Stories: Misti Madhur, 1988; Sei Tapati, 1996. Novels: Sudhu Tomari, 1992; Shilpi Beauty Basu, 1994; Singdha Anubhab, 1997. Honours include: Awd, Tarun Sadhana Samiti, Howrah, 1990; Ctf, Samanvaya Shree, Akhil Bharatiya Bhasha Sahitya Sammelan, Bhopal, 1994. Address: 56/16 Ram Mohan Mukherjee Lane, Sibpur, Howrah 711-102, West Bengal, India.

DAS Radha Raman, b. 23 Aug 1936, Varanasi, India. Vice Chancellor. m. Late Smt Annapurna, June 1958, 1 s, 1 d. Education: BSc, hons; MSc; PhD. Appointments: Lectr, BHU; Lectr, Rdr, Vikram Univ; Rdr, Prof, Vice Chan, Jiwaji Univ. Publications: 100 rsch pprs, 3 books. Honours: Gold Medal, var hons and awds. Memberships include: WLF; IIPA; IIETM; AVPB; DNAC; DACTLP; Akashwani. Hobbies: Music; Literature; Religion; Adhyatma. Address: Jiwaji University, Gwalior MP, India.

DAS Ramkrishna, b. 31 Oct 1961, Contai, West Bengal, India. Cryogenic Engineer. m. Supriya Das, 1 d. Education: BTech; MTech; PhD. Appointments: Jnr Engrng Offr, Lutheran World Serv; Jnr Project Offr, ARDB; Rsch Assoc, CSIR; Sci Off, BARC, Inida. Memberships: Assoc, The Inst of Engrs, India. Address: Bhabba Atomic Research Centre, Condensed Matter Physics Division, Trombay, Mumbai 400085, India.

DAS Rina, b. 17 May 1947, Bangladesh. Teacher; Administrator. m. Nathaniel Das, 22 Oct 1973, 1 s, 1 d. Education: BSc, hons, Botany; MSc, Taxonomy; Personal Mngmt Deg, Method of Educn; Dips in Children & Women Devel. Appointments: Lang Tchr, Biol Lectr, Asst Prof in Botany, Vice Prin, Hd, Dept of Sci, Holy Cross Coll. Publications: Sev sci articles in profl jrnls. Honours: Asa Pres, Dhaka YWCA; Tchr Trng Conf, A G Educn Instn. Memberships: Natl YWCA of Bangladesh; Pres, Treas, Dhaka YWCA; Chairperson, sev YWCA cttees. Hobbies: Reading; Writing; Volunteer Work; Tagore Songs. Address: Holy Cross College, Tejgaon, Dhaka 1215, Bangladesh.

DAS Sachchidanand, b. 5 July 1947, India. Librarian. m. Manju Das, 4 June 1969, 1 s, 1 d. Education: MA; MLib and Info Sci; PhD; Trng in Computer Application in Lib & Info Activities, INSDOC, New Delhi. Appointments: Libn, Dept Geol, Patna Univ, 1974-; Pt-time Tchr, Inst of Lib and Info Sci, Patna Univ; Acad Cnslr, Lib and Info Sci, IGNOU, New Delhi. Publications: Library Cataloguing Practice (AACR-II); Library Cataloguing Practice (CCC). Honours: Merit Ctf, Patna Univ; Gold Medal, BHU. Membership: Indian Lib Assn. Hobbies: Music; Painting. Address: L2/74 P.I.T. Colony, Kankarbagh, Patna 800020, India.

DAS Sumit Ranjan, b. 11 Dec 1955, Calcutta, India. Physicist. Education: MSc, Calcutta Univ, 1979; PhD, Univ of Chgo, USA, 1984. Appointments: Rsch Fell, Fermilab, USA, 1983-85; Rsch Fell, Caltech, USA, 1985-87; Fac, TIFR (now Assoc Prof). Publications: More than 50 pprs in intl jrnls; More than 20 invited talks in intl confs. Honours: Valentine Telegdi Awd, Univ of Chgo, 1980; S S Bhatnagar Awd, 1998. Membership: Fell, Indian Acady of Scis. Hobbies: Music; Movies. Address: Department of Theoretical Physics, Tata Institute of Fundamental Research, Mumbai 400 005, India.

DAS Syamales, b. 6 Dec 1938, Calcutta, India. College Teacher; Professor. m. 11 May 1967, 1 s, 1 d. Education: MA, Pol Sci, Calcutta Univ; Dip, Distance Educ, IGNOU, New Delhi, India. Appointments: Lectr, Pol Sci, FC Coll, W Bengal, India. Publications: Written & publ 8 books in Bengali. Memberships: Life Mbr, Indian Soc of Blood Transfusion & Immunohaematology. Hobbies: Reading; Touring. Address: Na-Para Old Kalibari Road, PO Barasat, 743101 North 24 Parganas, West Bengal, India.

DASH-YONDON Budragchaagiin, b. 17 Feb 1946 Huvsgul. Politician. m. Choijamts Batjargal, 1 s, 2 d. Education: Mongolian State Univ; State Univ of Kiev USSR. Appointments: Prof Mongolian State Univ, 1968-74; Offr at Sci and Educl Dept MPRP Cntr Cttee, 1978-79; Vice-Chan Higher Party Sch MPRP Cntr Cttee, 1979-85; Dep Hd and Hd of Dep MPRP Cntr Cttee, 1985-90; First Sec-Gen MPRP Ulan Bator Cty Party Cttee, 1990-91; MPRP Sec-Gen, 1991-96. Hobbies: Reading; Chess. Address: Mongolian People's Revolutionary Party, Central Building of the MPRP, Baga toiruu 37/1, Ulaanbaatar-11, Mongolia.

DASHKEVICH Mykhailo, b. 22 Feb 1940, Tchernigiv, Ukraine. Diplomat. m. A Fedotova, 29 Nov 1962, 1 s, 1 d. Education: Dip w Ex, Kiev's State Ling Univ. Appointments: Dipl Serv, 1973, Sec, First Sec, Min of For Affairs, Ukraine, 1973-82; Dpty Dir Gen, Dir Gen, 1992-94, Min of For Affairs, Ukraine; Amb, Ukraine to Japan. , 1995. Honour: Presdtl Order of Merits, 1997. Hobbies: Volleyball; Chess; Hunting. Address: 2-32-12, Minemi-Senzoku, Ota-ku, Tokyo.

DAT Luu Van, b. 1 Jan 1921, Vietnam. Professor. m. Hoa, 1943, 1 s, 4 d. Education: LLM, Pvt Law; MA, Econ, Indc China Univ. Appointments: Legal Advsr to the Govt; VP; Sec Gen, VLA. Creative Works: Improvement and Reform of Policy and Mechanism of the management For External Econl Rels. Honours: Order of the Resistance; Order of the Labour. Memberships: Intl Dem Lawyers Assn. Hobbies: Reading; Listening to Music; Fishing. Address: Vietnam Lawyers Assn, VLA, 4 Nguyen Thiong Hien St, Hanoi, Vietnam.

DATTA Rajat Kumar, b. 3 May 1943, Naihati, W Bengal, India. Scientist. m. Mrs Kanika Datta, 22 July 1973, 1 s, 1 d. Education: BSc, 1962, MSc, 1964, PhD, Genetics, 1969, Univ of Calcutta. Appointments: Lectr, Hooghly Mohsin Coll, Mysore, 1965-66; Jnr Rsch Fell, Univ Calcutta, 1966-69; Lectr, Rishi Bankim Coll, 1961-71; Dpty Dir, 1971-80, Jt Dir, 1980-85, Dir, 1985-, Cntrl Silk Bd, Mysore; Bd Dirs, CSR & TI, Mysore; Cnslt, FAO Iran, 1990, Govt of Malaysia, 1992-94; Exec Ed, Indian Journal of Sericulture, 1990; Wrk evolving many bivoltine and polyvoltine silkworm breeds for detection of virus diseases of silkworm. Publication: (auth) Manual on Silkworm Rearing, 1996. Honour: Seth Baldeodas Shah Natl Awd, 1990-91, 1994-95. Hobbies: Reading researches in science; Playing lawn tennis. Address: Director, Central Sericultural Research and Training Institute, Manandavadi Road, Srirampura, Mysore 570 008, India.

DATTA MUNSHI Jyoti Swarup, b. 8 Feb 1930. Teacher; Researcher. m. 19 Nov 1961, 2 d. Education: BS, Hons, MSc, Patna Univ; PhD, Banaras Hindu Univ. Appointments: Lectr, 1952-62; Rdr, 1962-70; Prof and Hd, 1970-92; CSIR Emer Scientist, 1992-95; INSA Snr Scientist, 1996-. Publications: 250 rsch publs and 6 books incl: (co-auth) Ecology of Heteropneustes Fossilis (Bloch) - An Air-Breathing Catfish of South East Asia, Memoir No 2, pp 1-174; Freshwater Biological Association of India, 1994; Fundamental of Freshwater Biology, 1995; Fish Morphology, Horizon of New Research 1-300, 1996. Honours: S L Hora Gold Medal, Ichthyological Soc of India; Chandra Kala Hora Awd of INSA; Pres, Indian Sci Congress Zool Sect. Memberships: Fell, Indian Natl Sci Acady, New Delhi; Fell, Natl Acady of Scis. Hobby: Stamp collecting. Address: University Department of Zoology, Bhagalpur University, Bhagalpur 812007, Bihar, India.

DATTAGUPTA Arghya Kusum, b. 1 Feb 1933, Dhaka, Bangladesh. Social Service and Publication. m. Sipra, 16 May 1962, 1 s, 1 d. Education: BCom; BA (Spl). Appointments: Fndr Sec, Samatt Sanstha; Pres, Soc for the Visually Handicapped. Publications: Fndr, Ed, Publr (quarterly) Samatat Prakashan, 1969, Kishore Samatat, 1991; Contbr to anthology of essays. Honours: Nehru Yth Awd, Nehru Childrens Museum, Calcutta, 1995; Eminent Ed Awd, W Bengal Bangla Acady, Govt of W Bengal, 1998. Memberships: Life Mbr, The Convention of The Teachers of the Deaf in India, 1957, Cricket Assn of

Bengal, 1978, The Junglees, 1989. Hobbies: Travelling; Social service; World news. Address: 172, Rash Behari Avenue, Nandana 302, Calcutta 29, Pin Code 700 029, India.

DATTATREYA ARALIKATTE, b. 23 Feb 1953, Arali Katte. Traditional Puppeteer. m. Ramaa, 23 June 1980, 2 s. Education: MA; MEd. Fndr, Putthali Kalaranga, a troupe of puppeteers specialising in Rod Puppetry, known as the Mudrika Sch of Puppetry. Publications: My Experiments with Puppets; Puppetry as an Educational Aid. Honours: DSERT (Directorate of State Educl Rsch and Trng) State Awd, 1996; Karmataka State Janpada Acady Awd, 1997; CCRT Natl Awd, 1998. Memberships: Unima, Vasanth Kunj, New Delhi; Crafts Cncl of Karnataka, Malleswaram, Bangalore, India. Hobby: Friendship. Address: Putthali Kalaranga, 27/14 I Cross, Obalappa Garden, Tata Silk Farm, Bangalore 560 082, India.

DAUBULU Livia, b. 2 Mar 1949, Nadroga, Fiji Islands. Teacher. 1 d. Appointments: Sch Tchr; Treas, Cagimaira Devel Assn, Fiji. Hobbies: Sewing; Reading; Playing Net Ball. Address: c/o Cagimaira Development Association, PO Box 1038 BA, Fiji.

DAUD Datuk Dr Sulaiman bin Haj, b. 4 Mar 1933 Kuching Sarawak. Politican. m. 4 c. Education: Otago Univ NZ; Univ of Toronto. Appointments: Tchr, 1954-56; Dental Offr State Govt of Sarawak, 1963-68; State Dental Offr Brunei, 1971; Polit Sec min of Primary Inds, 1972; Min for Land and Mineral Rescs Sarawak, 1973-74; Mbr Parl, 1974-; Dep Min of Land Dev, 1974-75; Dep Min of Land and Mines, 1975-76; Dep Min of Land and Regl Dev, 1976-77; Dep Min of Hlth, 1978-81; Min of Fed Territory, Mar 1981; Min of Educ, Jul 1981; Min of Sport Yth and Culture, 1984-86; Min of Land and Regl Dev, 1986-89; Min in the PMs Dept, 1989-90; VP Party Pesaka Bumiputra Bersatu, Sarawak; Other pub appts and ldr of Malaysian delegs to intl confs; Johan Bintag Sarawak; Panglima Negara Nintang Sarawak.

DAVE Makarand, b. 13 Nov 1922, Gondal, Gujarat, India. Poet; Writer. m. Kundanika, 30 Apr 1968. Appointments: Ed, Sangam, Pagdandi; Sub-Ed, Kumar, monthly, Urmi-Navrachana, monthly; Jai Hind, daily; Columnist, Janmabhoomi. Publications: 38 books, poetry, novel, essays; Studies in ancient scriptures. Honours: Many awds inclng: Meghani Awd, Sahitya, 1996; Satya Gaurav Puraskar, 1997. Membership: Chmn, Nandigram Trust. Hobbies: Anthropology, Cosmogony; Mythology; Comparative Religion. Address: Nandigram, Post Vankal, Varsad, 396007, India.

DAVERNE Gary Michiel, b. 26 Jan 1939, Auckland, NZ. Conductor; Composer. Education: Auckland Univ; Dip Tchng, Auckland Tchrs Coll, 1959; LRSM, 1965; FTCL (Composition), Trinity Coll of Music, London, 1969. Appointments: Secnd Sch Tchr, Econ(s), Acctcy, 1962-77; Musical Dir, Auckland Symph Orch, 1975-; Dir of Music, Waitangi Day Celebrations, attended by HM Queen Elizabeth II, 1975; Composer in Schs, 1978-79; Currently self-employed intl conductor, composer, arranger, record prodr, over 40 albums, 1 platinum, 2 gold; Conductor, music for TV, film and radio. Creative Works: Compositions inclng over 100 pop songs, many operettes and songs for children, piano music, 3 rock operas, extensive selection of concert accordion; Many wrks for orch recd by NZ Symph Orch inclng Rhapsody for Accordion and Orchestra (over 200 concert perfs); Over 600 TV and radio jingles; Film music. Honour: Queen's Birthday Hons, NZ Govt, ONZM, Serv to Music. Hobbies: Chess; Bridge; Fishing; Films; Playing various musical instruments including clarinet, saxophone, piano and percussion. Address: 48 Shelly Beach Road, Herne Bay, Auckland 1002, New Zealand.

DAVEY Ian Elliott, b. 22 Mar 1945, Bendigo, Vic, Aust. Pro Vice Chancellor (Research) and Vice President (International University of South Australia). Div, 1 s. Education; BA (Hons), Univ Melbourne, 1963-66; DipEd, Univ Melbourne, 1967; MA, Univ Toronto, 1971-72; PhD, Univ Toronto, 1972-75. Appointments: Lectr, Dept Educ,

Univ Adelaide, 1976-80; Dean of Grd Studies, Univ of Adelaide, 1991-94; Rdr, Dept Educ, Univ Adelaide, 1994; Pro Vice Chancellor (Rsch) and VP (Intl), Univ of S Aust, 1994-. Publications: Num articles on 19th Century schooling and socl hist of childhood. Hobbies: Reading; Cryptic crosswords. Address: University of South Australia, City West Campus, GPO Box 2471, Adelaide, South Australia 50001, Australia.

DAVID Bruno, b. 12 Mar 1962, Paris, France. Archaeologist. Education: BA (Hons); MA; PhD. Appointments: Archaeologist for Kuku Djungan Aboriginal Corp, 1994; Postdoct Fell Univ of Queensland, 1995-96; Logan Fell, Monash Univ, 1997-. Publications: In sci jrnls and popular mags; Over 100 on archaeol, inclng monographs, 1983-. Honours: Antiquity Prize, 1995; Awd'd Logan Fellship, 1997. Memberships: Austl Inst Aboriginal & Torres Strait Islander Studies, 1986; Austl Archaeological Assn; Austl Rock Art Rsch Assn. Hobbies: Bushwalking; Reading. Address: Department of Geography and Environmental Science, Monash University, Clayton 3168, Victoria, Australia.

DAVID Eduardo Lerma, b. 9 Feb 1949, Manila. Private Equity Manager. m. Lina Barretto, 19 May 1971, 4 s, 2 d. Education: AB, Hons, Econs, Ateneo de Manila; MBM, Distinction, Asian Inst of Mngmt. Appointments: Pres, H&Q Philippines Inc, 1987; Regl Mngng Dir, H&Q Asia Pacific Ltd, 1997; Bd of Trustees, Asian Inst of Mngmt, 1998. Memberships: Mngnt Assn of the Philippines; Fin Execs Inst of the Philippines. Address: 4 Corregidor Street, Ayala Heights, Quezon City, Philippines.

DAVIES George Neville, b. 20 Sept 1921. Educator. m. Valerie Todd, 9 Nov 1948, 2 s, 1 d. Education: BDS (NZ); DDS (NU); FRACDS; FDSRCS (Eng); Hon DSc (Qld). Appointments: Dental Offr, 2 NZEF, 1944-46; Hd, Dept of Preventive Dentistry, Otago Univ, 1948-63; Travelling Schl, Univ of NZ; WHO Expert Advsry Panel on Dental Health, 1957-; Commissioner 1957-82, Chmn 1976-79, Oral Stats Fedn Dentaire Intl; Mbr, Res Cl, NZ, 1960-63; Prof, Socl and Preventive Dentistry, Dean of Fac, 1964-70, Dental Univ of Qld; Mbr, Qld Dental Bd, 1969-75; Pres, Profl Bd, 1973-74; Mbr, S Brisbane Hosps Bd, 1976-79; Dpty Vice Chan (Acad) 1976-86; Acting Vice Chan, Univ of Qld, 1977-78. Honour: CBE, 1982; Cmndr, Most Noble Order of Crown of Thailand, 1991. Hobbies: Reading; Writing; Croquet; Bowls. Address: 10 Roedean Street, Fig Tree Pocket, Qld 4069, Australia.

DAVIES Helen Margaret Sarah, b. 9 July 1955, Adelaide, SA, Aust. University Lecturer. Education: BAgSc (Hons), Leeds, 1977; MAgrSc (Qld), 1985; BVSc (Qld), 1986; PhD (Melb), 1995. Appointment: Lectr, Vet Anatomy, Univ of Melbourne, 1996. Memberships: AVA; AEVA; ANZBMS; ASBMR; EFA; CRC. Hobbies: Dressage and horse sports in general; The response of tissues to exercise. Address: Faculty of Veterinary Science, University of Melbourne, Parkville, Vic 3052, Australia.

DAVIES Hugh Lucius, b. 8 Apr 1935, Perth, Western Australia. Geologist. m. Aug 1964. Education: BSc; MSc; PhD. Appointments: Geol, Austl and PNG Govts, 1956-89; Prof of Geol, Univ PNG, 1989-. Publications: Var geol pprs. Memberships: Fell, Geol Soc of Am; Geol Soc of Aust; Am Geophysl Union; Fell, Austl Inst of Mining and Metallurgy. Address: PO Box 412, University NCD, Papua New Guinea.

DAVIES John Charles, b. 16 Mar 1922, Sydney, Australia. Retired University Professor. m. Ludmilla, 23 July 1949, 2 s, 1 d. Education: BA, 1942, Dip.Ed, 1946, Sydney Univ; Docteur de l'Université de Paris, 1953. Appointments: Lectr in French, Queens Univ, Belfast, 1953; Prof of French, Univ of New England, Aust, 1959; Prof of French, Adelaide Univ, Aust, 1971. Publications: Books, essays and articles in profl jrnls. Honour: Ordre des Palmes Académiques. Memberships: Alliance Francaise of SA; L'Association des Amis d'André Gide. Hobbies: Music; Theatre; Films. Address: 33 Jarvis Street, Erindale, SA 5066, Australia.

DAVIES Robert Paul, b. 1 Nov 1936, Horsham, Vic, Aust. Consultant. m. Mary Lou Davies, 27 Feb 1960, 4 s, 3 d. Education: Dip of Pharm, Vic Coll of Pharm; BEc, Austl Natl Univ. Appointments: Comm Pharm, 1954-73; Austl Natl Univ, 1974-76; Rsch Offr, 1977; Dir, Hlth Econs Div, 1978-84; Exec Dir, 1984-91; Pharm Guild of Aust, 1977; Cnslt, 1991-. Memberships: Fell, Austl Inst of Co Dirs; Fell, Austl Inst of Mngmt; Fell, Aust Assn CPA's. Honours: Fell, honoris causa, Pharm Soc of Aust; Hon Life Mbrshp, Pharm Guild of Aust, 1989. Hobbies: Tennis; Skiing; Golf; Reading; Classical Music; Jazz. Address: 41 Endeavour St, Red Hill, ACT 2603, Australia.

DAVIES Ronald Wallace, b. 23 Dec 1940. University Dean. m. Mary M E Harries, 20 July 1962, 2 s, 1 d. Education: BSc Botany; BSc Hons, Zool; Dip in Educ, Hons; PhD, Ecol; DSc, Ecol. Appointments: Asst Lectr, Dept of Zool, Univ of Wales, 1967-68; Rsch Sci, Univ of BC, Can, 1968-69; Asst Prof of Bio, 1969-71, Assoc Prof of Bio, 1971-80, Hd of Dept of Bio, 1983-88, Hd of Dept of Biological Scis, 1989-94, Univ Calgary; Dean, Fac of Sci, Monash Univ, Melbourne, Aust, 1996-. Publications: Over 150 articles in refereed jrnls. Memberships: Brit Ecological Soc; Ecological Soc of Am; Canad Soc of Zoologists; Freshwater Biol Assn; Amn Soc for Limnology & Oceanography; N Amn Benthological Soc; Alta Assn of Profl Biolsts; Societas Internatinalis Limnologiae; Sigma Xi; Roy C'wlth Soc. Address: Faculty of Science, Monash University, Wellington Road, Clayton, Vic 3168, Australia.

DAVIES Stephen John James Frank, b. 26 Apr 1935, Sydney, NSW Aust. Ornithologist; Adjunct Professor. m. Wendy Elizabeth Adams, 1 Aug 1964, 4 d. Education: BA, 1956, MA, 1961, PhD, 1966, ScD, 1988, Univ Cambridge, Eng. Appointments: CSIRO, Div of Wildlife and Ecology, 1956-84; Dir, Roy Australasian Ornithologists Union, 1984-89; Adj Prof, Sch of Environl Bio, Curtin Univ of Technol, Perth. Publications: Australian Birds, 1984; Handbook of Australia, New Zealand and Antarctic Birds, vol 3 (co-auth), 1996. Honours: Fell, Roy Australasian Ornithologists Union; Corresp Mbr, Brit Ornithologists Union, 1987. Memberships: RAOU, pres, 1975-78, chmn, rsch cttee, 1975-85; Roy Soc of WA, pres, 1984-85. Hobby: Sheep breeding. Address: School of Biology, Curtin University of Technology, GPO Box 987U, Perth, WA 6001, Australia.

DAVIS Geena, b. 21 Jan 1957 Wareham MA. Actress. m. (1) Jeff Goldblum - qv; (2) Renny Harlin, 1993. Education: Boston Univ. Appointments: Worked as a model. Tv appearances incl: Buffalo Bill, 1983; Sara, 1985; The Hit List; Family Ties; Remington Steele. Films incl: Tootsie, 1982; Fletch, 1984; Transylvania 6-5000, 1985; The Fly, 1986; The Accidental Tourist, 1988; Earth Girls are Easy, 1989; Quick Change; The Grifters; Thelma and Louise; A League of Their Own; Hero; Angie; Speechless - also prodr; Cutthroat Island; The Long Kiss Goodnight. Honours: Acady Awd for Best Supporting Actress for The Accidental Tourist, 1988. Memberships: Mbr Mount WA Repertory The Co. Address: c/o CAA, 9830 Wilshire Boulevard, Beverly Hills, CA 90212, USA.

DAVIS Judy, b. 23 Apr 1956, Perth, WA, Aust. Actress. m. Colin Friels, 1 s, 1d. Films incl: My Brilliant Career; High Tide; Kangaroo; A Woman Called Golda; A Passage to India; Impromptu; Alice; Barton Fink; Where Angels Fear to Tread; The Naked Lunch; Husbands and Wives; The Ref; The New Age; Absolute Power, Deconstructing Harry, Celebrity. Honours: Many awds and nominations include: Best Supporting Actress, Aust Film Inst, 1993; Spec Achievement Awd, Film Critics Circle of Aust, 1994; Emmy Awd Nominations, 1995, 1997; Golden Globe nomination, 1996; Best Performance by Leading Actress Awd, AFI, 1996. Listed in: Who's Who in Australia. Address: c/o Shanahan Management Pty Ltd, PO Box 478, Kings Cross, NSW 2011, Australia.

DAVIS L Faye, b. 6 June 1937, Perth, West Aust. Writer. m. V E R Davis, 27 Sept 1958, 3 s, 1 d. Education: BA, Creative Writing and Lit. Appointments: Freelance, most recently touring wheatbelt schs in West Aust, jt FAW and Educ Dept isolated schs prog.

Publication: Paisley Print (short fiction), 1984. Memberships: Fellshp, Austl Writers; Katherine Susannah Prichard Fndn. Hobbies: Writing; Fabrics. Address: 147 Gooseberry Hill Road, Gooseberry Hill 6076, Australia.

DAVIS Richard Perceval, b. 22 Feb 1935, Nasik, India. Academic. m. Marianne Alexia (Née Williamson), 1 s, 1 d. Education: BA (Hons), Hist & Polit Sci, 1956, MLitt, 1958, MA, 1959, HDip Ed, 1960-, Univ of Dublin; PhD, Otago Univ, NZ, 1968. Appointments: Lectr in Hist, Otago Univ, 1964-66; Lectr in Hist, 1967, Snr Lectr, 1971, Rdr, 1976, Prof, 1993, Emeritus Prof, Univ of Tas. Membership: FAHA (Fell, Austl Hum Acady), 1997. Hobbies: Walking; Cricket; Rugby Union. Address: 33 Willowdene Avenue, Sandy Bay, Hobart, Tasmania 7005, Australia.

DAVIS Robert H, b. 26 Mar 1943. Arbitrator; Advocate; Lecturer; Author. m. Patricia, 10 Sept 1995, 1 s. Education: MBA, Stanford Univ Grad Sch of Bus, 1980. Appointments: Pres and CEO, Davis, Keller and Davis, Intl Arbitrators; Lectr: US Small Bus Admin, US Dept of Com, World Trade Inst; Dir, Credid/Legal Review, Jones Business Systems, Inc, 1998-; Bd Dirs, Natl Assn Credit Mngmt; Chair, Govt Affairs and Educ Cttees. Publications: Resolving International Payment Conflicts and Alternative Dispute Resolution and Contract Clauses, 1994; International Risk Management for Small Business, 1994; Canada-US-Mexico, Charting Your Business Practices; US Casino's in the International Marketplace, Managing the Risks, 1992; Transnational Arbitration As a Means of Managing Foreign Corporate Risks, 1992; Consultants Show Way in Foreign Deals, 1993; The Benefits of the NAFTA, 1993; How Business Can Enjoy the Benefits - And Avoid the Pitfalls of International Trade, 1992; Leasing as a Secondary Source of Financing in the Heavy Equipment Industry. Memberships: WA Export Cncl; Amn Arbitration Assn; Singapore Arbitration Cntr; Acady of Pol Sc; USA/NAFTA Natl Cttee, Wash DC; Natl Cttee Alliance for GATT; State of Wyoming Rep to the Natl Assn of Credit Mngmnt, 1978-82; US Dept of Com, Intl Trade Admins, Ind Consultation Prog; Special Cnslt, US Small Bus Admin on Intl Affairs; Intl and Practicing Law Insts; Intl Platform Assn; Order of DeMolay's. Listed in: Who's Who in the World; Who's Who in the West; Who's Who in Business and Finance. Hobbies: Sports; Pipe collecting and tobacco; Art. Address: PO Box 1982, Stafford, Texas 77497, USA.

DAVIS Stephen Drake, b. 17 Jan 1957, Texas, USA. Attorney. m. Susan, 4 May 1984, 2 s, 1 d. Education: JD, Univ TX, 1981. Appointments: Assoc, 1982-89, Ptnr, 1990-95, Ptnr, Admnstr Hd, Singapore Off, 1995-, Vinson & Elkins LLP. Publications: Sev articles and reviews in profl jrnls. Honours: Schlsp, Soc of Petroleum Engrs, 1975-76; LSU Top 100 Schls, 1975-78; Natl Merit Schl, 1975-79; Outstndng Cttee Ldr, Houston Yng Lawyers Assn, 1987. Memberships: Off-Shore Lawyers Liaison Cttee, Singapore; State Bar of TX; Am Bar Assn; Intl Pacific Bar Assn. Address: c/o Vinson & Elkins LLP, 16 Collyer Quay, 33-01 Hitachi Towers, Singapore 049318, Singapore.

DAVIS Thomas, b. 11 June 1917. Physician; Politician. Education: MBChB, Otago Med Sch, NZ, 1945; DTM&H, Trop Med, Univ Sydney, 1948; MD, 1955; MPH, Harvard Sch of Pub Hlth, 1954; Space Surgn, NASA, 1960. Intern, Seacliffe Mental Hosp, Auckland Pub Hosp, Greenlane Hosp, Rotorua Hosp, 1943-45; Med Offr, 1945-48, Chf Med Offr, 1948-52, Cook Islands; Rsch Assoc, Dept of Nutrition, Harvard Sch of Pub Hlth, 1953-58; Dir, Arctic Med Rsch, Arctic Aeromed Lab, 1955-56; Dir, Environ Med Divsn, US Army Med Rsch Labs, Ft Knox, KY, 1956-61; Dir, Environ Med Divsn, US Army Inst of Environ Med, Natick, MA, 1961-63; Rsch & Cnsltng Physn, Arthur D Little Inc, Cambridge, MA, 1963-71; Ldr, Majesty's Opposition, Cook Islands Parly, 1972-78; Pvte Med Pract, 1974-; PM for Cook Islands, 1978-87; Physn, Auth, 1987-; Designer, Takitumu, 1991-92, Te Au o Tonga, 1994-95. Publications: 4 books, over 150 sci and popular publns. Honours include: Knight

Cmdr of Brit Empire, 1980; Papua New Guinea Independence Medal, 1985; Cook Islander Man of the Yr, 1996. Memberships: NZ Med Assn; Cook Islands Lib & Mus Soc; Roy Soc of Trop Med & Hygiene; Roy Socof Med; Cook Islands Med & Dental Assn; Cook Islands Voyaging Soc; Cook Islands Yachting Fedn; Pacific Islands Voyaging Soc. Address: PO Box 116, Avarua, Rarotonga, Cook Islands.

DAVY John Laurence, b. 14 Mar 1949. Scientist. m. Elizabeth Anne Currer, 18 Sept 1975, 2 d. Education: BSc Hons, La Trobe Univ, 1971; PhD, Austl Natl Univ, 1974. Appointments: C'wlth Sci and Indl Rsch Org, 1974-; Prin Rsch Sci. Publications: 20 sci articles in refereed learned jrnls; 14 sci articles in conf proceedings; 14 other articles. Honours: D M Myers Univ Medal, 1971; BHP Matriculation Prize, 1966; Sibyl Mand Care Prize, 1966; GMH Rsch Fellshp, 1971-74. Memberships: ASHRAE, Acoustical Soc of Am; Austl Acoustical Soc; Austl Math Soc. Hobbies: Bicycling; Hiking; Surfing; Sailboarding; Opera. Address: CSIRO BCE, PO Box 56 Highett, Vic 3190, Australia.

DAWAGIV Luvsandorj, b. 15 May 1943, Uburkhangai, Mongolia. Diplomatist. m. Jagdal Maya, July 1971, 1 s, 2 d. Education: Moscow State Inst of Itl Rels, Diplomatic Acady, Moscow. Appointments: Joined For Serv of Monglia, 1971; Attaché, Dpty Hd, Hd of Dept, 1984-90; Hd, Eurn and Amn Dept, 1990-91; Amb in USA, 1991-95; Dir of Dept, 1995-. Honours: Recip, Order, Polar Star. Hobbies: Hunting; Travelling. Address: Peace Avenue 7a, Ulan Bator 13, Mongolia.

DAWKINS John Sydney, b. 2 Mar 1947, Perth, W Aust. Business Advisor. m. Maggie, 2 Mar 1987, 2 s, 1 d. Education: Roseworthy Dip of Agric (RDA); BEcon, Univ of West Aust; DUniv (Hon), Univ of South Aust and QUT. Appointments: Ch John Dawkins & Co; Dir, Sealcorp Holdings; Ch, Medl Corp of Alasia; Chmn, Elders Rural Servs Ltd; Mbr, House of Reps, 1974-94, Min for Fin, 1983-84, Min for Trade, 1985-87, Min for Employment Educ and Trng, 1987-92, Treas, 1992-93. Honours: Hon Decorations from Univ of SA, 1996; Qld Univ of Technol, 1997. Hobbies: Farming; Vineyard. Address: Level 25, 91 King William Street, Adelaide, S Australia 5000, Australia.

DAWSON Daryl Michael (Hon Sir), b. 12 Dec 1933. Retired Justice, High Court of Australia. m. Marylou Thomas, 12 Feb 1971. Education: LLB hons, Melbourne Univ; LLM, Yale Univ. Appointments: Lt Cmdr, RANVR; Fulbright Schl, 1955; Sterling Fell, Yale Univ, 1955-56; Mbr, Vic Bar, 1957-; Lectr in Intro to Legal Method Cl of Legal Educ, 1962-74; Ormond Coll Cl, 1965-73, Chmn 1991-92; Mbr, 1974-86, Chmn, 1987, Austl Motor Sport Appeal Cl; Vic Bar Cl, 1971-74; QC, 1971; Tas Bar, 1972-; Cl Roy Auto Club, Vic, 1972-74; Mbr, Stndng Cttee of Convocation, Univ of Melbourne, 1973-74; Sol-Gen, Vic, 1974-82; Mbr, Cl, Univ of Melbourne, 1976-86; Jus, High Crt of Aust, 1982-97; Non Perm Judge, Hong Kong Crt of Final Appeal, 1997; Adj Prof, Monash Univ, 1998; Professorial Fell, Univ Melbourne, 1998. Honours: CB, 1980; KBE, 1982; AC, 1988. Memberships: Austl Motor Sport Appeal Cl, 1970-86; Chmn, Ormond Coll, 1991-92; Gov, Ian Potter Fndn, 1998; Chmn Menzies Fndn, 1998. Listed in: Who's Who in Australia; International Who's Who. Hobby: Gardening. Address: PO Box 147, East Melbourne, Victoria 3002, Australia.

DAWSON Raymond Murray, b. 23 Sept 1943. Research Scientist. m. Rosemary Joy Ackland, 11 Dec 1971, 2 d. Education: BSc (Hons), Univ of WA; PhD, Univ of West Aust. Appointments: Cadet (Def Sci), Austl Dept Supply, 1962-; Sci Offr, Def Stands Labs (later re-named Materials Rsch Labs, then Aeronautical and Maritime Rsch Lab, run by Austl Dept Def), 1970-; At these Labs: Rsch Scientist, 1972-; Snr Rsch Scientist, 1979-; Prin Rsch Scientist, 1988-. Publications: 50 in sci jrnls: Chemistry, Biochemistry, Pharmacology. Honours: MRL Awd for Excellence (Best Rsch), Materials Rsch Lab, 1990. Memberships: Roy Austl Chem Inst; Austl Neurosci Soc; Australasian Soc of Clin and Expmtl Pharmacologists and Toxicologists; Intl Soc on

Toxinology; Austl Mil Med Assn. Hobbies: Philately; Gardening. Address: AMRL, GPO Box 4331, Melbourne, Vic 3001, Australia.

DAWSON Steven Marsh, b. 7 Sept 1942, USA. Professor of Finance. Education: PhD, Univ of MI. Appointments: Univ of HI; Visng Appts at Copenhagen Bus Sch, Univ of Intl Bus and Econ, Beijing, Natl Univ of Singapore, Chinese Univ of Hong Kong, Univ of Michigan. Honur: Regents Medal for Tchng Excellence, 1990. Memberships: Finl Mngmt Assn; Amn Fin Assn; Fin Exec Inst. Address: 2404 Maile Way, Honolulu, HI 96822, USA.

DAX Eric Cunningham, b. 18 May 1908, Nottingham, Eng. Psychiatrist. m. K Thompson, 22 Oct 1935, 1 s, 3 d. Education: BSc, MBBS, London; LMSSA; DPM; FRACP; FRANZCP; Hon MD, Melb; Hon FRC Psych, Eng. Appointments: Supt, Netherne Hosp, Eng; Chmn, Mental Hlth Authority, Aust; Coordr, Tasmania; Medl Hist, Snr Assoc Melbourne. Publications: Experimental Studies in Psychiatric Art, 1953; Asylum to Community, 1961; Cunningham Dax Collection of Psychiatric Art, 1998. Honour: AO, 1985. Membership: Pres, Austl and NZ Coll of Psychs, 1965. Address: 2/51 Maud Street, North Balwyn, Vic 3104, Australia.

DAY Richard Osborne, Clinical Pharmacologist. m. Barbara Robin Sippe, 6 Jan 1973, 1 s, 2 d. Education: MB BS (Hons) Sydney; MD, NSW; FRACP. Appointments: Medl Registrar, St Vincent's Hosp, Sydney, 1973-75; Postgrad Medl Fell, 1975-77, NHMRC Fell, 1977-80, Clin Pharm, KS Univ, 1978-80; Staff Clin Pharmacologist, St Vincent's Hosp, Sydney, 1981-90; Dir, Clin Pharm and Toxicology, St Vincent's Hosp, Prof, Clin Pharm, Univ NSW, 1990-. Memberships: Pharm Hlth and Rational Use of Meds Cttee, Dept Hlth Housing and Community Servs, 1992-94; Chmn, NSW Therapeutic Assessment Grp, Res Ethics Cttee, 1991-97, St Vincent's Hosp, Sydney, Drug Cttee, Mbr, Roy Austl Coll Phys, Pres, Austl Soc Clin Experimental Pharmacologists and Toxicologists, 1994-95; Austl Rheumatology Assn. Hobbies: Sailing; Swimming. Address: 33 Woodside Avenue, Lindfield, NSW 2070, Australia.

DAYAL John, b. 2 Oct 1948. Journalist; Film Maker. m. Mercy Mariamma, 7 July 1974, 1 s, 1 d. Education: BSc, hons, Phys; Dip, Jrnlsm. Appointments: Ed-in-Chf, Chf Exec Offr, Delhi Mid Day, 1992-; Natl Sec, All India Catholic Union; Treas, Eds Guild of India. Publications: For Reasons of State; Commission of Enquiry; Indian Cinema; Profile of the Indian Correspondent; Indian Christians; The Culture of Indian Christians. Honours: Keynotes Speaker, UCIP Congress, Aust, 1995; The New Ldr Awd; Best Christian Jrnlst of India, 1995; Natl Excellence Awd, 1999. Memberships: WACC; UCIP; Treas, Eds Guild of India; INTACH; IDPA; India Intl Ctr; India Habitat Ctr. Hobbies: Reading; Travel; Golf; Chess. Listed in: Who's Who In Indian Media; Who's Who In India. Address: 505 Media Appartments, 18 IP Extension, New Delhi 110092, India.

DE ARAUGO Sarah Therese (Tess), b. 26 May 1930, Lismore, Vic, Aust. Writer. m. Maurice De Araugo, 11 Apr 1950, 2 s, 2 d. Education: Notre Dame de Sion Coll, Warragal, Vic. Publications: You Are What You Make Yourself To Be, 1980, revised ed, 1989; The Kurnai of Gippsland, 1985; Boonoorong on the Mornington Peninsula, 1993; Contbr to: Biogs to Encyclopaedia of Aboriginal Australia; Echo of Aboriginal Past, to Weekly Times, 1983; Memories of the Murray River People, to This Australia, 1984-85; Aboriginal Australians and Their Descendants, to Annals Journal, 1990; Articles to newspprs and biogs to Australian Dictionary of Evangelical Biography. Honours: NSW Premier's Awd for Austl Lit, 1985; Banjo Awd, Austl Lit, Natl Book Cncl, 1985; Fellshp, 1987, Writer's Grant, 1989, Austl Lit Bd; Short Story Awd, PEN Intl, Aust, 1991. Memberships: Austl Soc of Auths; Fellshp of Austl Writers; Roy Histl Soc of Vic; Women Writers of Aust; Nepean Histl Soc. Address: 19 Grenville Grove, Rosebud West, Vic 3940, Australia.

DE CANO Maria Cecilia Gallardo, b. 9 Mar 1952. Minister of Education. m. Education: MA, Psychol, Cntrl Amn Univ, El Salvador, 1975. Appointments: Pvte Prac, San Salvador, 1974; Advd Socl Educ Prog, Salvadoran Demographic Assn 1976-84; Psychol, Francisco Mandez Natl Inst, 1977; Dir, Kindergarten, 1979-86; Psychotherapist, 1980-86; Prov Advsr, API Pub Rels Firm, 1986; Mngr, Dept Gen Educ, 1987-89; Vice Min, Educ, Govt El Salvador, 1989-90; Min, Educ, 1990-.

DE CASTELLA (François) Robert, b. 27 Feb 1957. Consultant in Health Promotion and Intervention; Executive Director; Athlete. 2 s, 1 d. Education: Xavier Coll, Univ Melbourne; Swinburne Inst Technol, Univ Melbourne; BSc. Appointments: Winner, Fukuoka Intl Marathon, 1981, setting World Rec 2:08:18, held, 1981-84; Won C'wlth Games Marathon, Queensland, 1982, Edinburgh, 1986, World Championships Marathon, 1983, 4 x OG Marathon, 1984, 1988, 1992, 1996; Boston Marathon, 2:07:51, 1986; Dir, Austl Inst Sport, 1990-95; Dir, Decorp Pty Ltd, 1995-; Dir, RWM Publications, 1996-; Chmn, Hlthpact, ACT Govt Hlth Promotion Fund; Mngng Dir, Smart Start (Aust) Pty, Ltd, 1998-; Dir, Sport Aust's Hall of Fame; Dir, Leisure Australia, 1999-. Publications: De Castella on Running, 1984; Deek, Australia's World Champion, 1984. Honours: MBE, 1983; Top Athlete of Asian Continent, 1983; Austl of Yr, 1983. Memberships: VP, ACT Olympians Club; Patron, NHF ACT Div; Glenhuntly Amateur Athletics Club. Hobbies: Sports science; Reading; Music; Scuba; Golf; Fly-fishing. Address: Smart Start (Australia) Pty, Ltd, PO Box 3808 Weston, ACT 2611, Australia.

DE CRESPIGNY Richard Rafe Champion, b. 16 Mar 1936, Adelaide, S Aust. Academic Scholar; Administrator. m. Christa Charlotte Boltz, 17 May 1959, 1 s, 1 d. Education: MA (Cantab); MA (Oriental Studies), PhD (Austl Natl Univ). Appointments: Lectr; Snr Lectr, Fac of Asian Studies, Rdr, Chinese, ANU, 1973; Dean of Asian Stdies, 1979-82; Master of Univ House, 1991-, ANU; Adjumet Prof of Asian Stdies, 1999-. Publications: Last of the Han, 1969; China This Century, 1975, 1992; Northern Frontier, 1984; Emperor Huan and Emperor Ling, 1989; Generals of the South, 1990; To Establish Peace, 1996. Hobbies: Gardening; Walking; Heraldry. Address: University House, Australian National University, Canberra, ACT 0020, Australia.

DE FREITAS Christopher Rhodes, b. 16 Feb 1948, Trinidad, West Indies. University Professor. m. Nancy, 10 May 1969, 2 s. Education: BA (hons), Univ of Toronto, Can; MA, Univ of Toronto, Can; PhD, Univ of Queensland, Aust. Appointments: Dpty Dean of Sci, Hd of Scis and Technol, Pro-Vice Chan, Univ of Auckland. Publications: Over 100 publs in books and sci jrnl lit. Honours: Lit and Athletic Soc Schlshp, Univ of Toronto, Univ Coll; Brit Commonwealth Postgrad Schl; NZ Assoc of Scientists; Sci Communicator AWd; Fndn for Sci, Rsch and Technol, Sci Cttee Merit Awd. Memberships: VP, Meteorological Soc of NZ. Address: 12 Northgrove Avenue, Auckland, New Zealand.

DE GROEN Alma Margaret, b. 5 Sept 1941, Foxton, New Zealand. Playwright. div, 1 d. Education: Dip, NZ Lib Assn. Publications: Going Home, 1976; Chidley, 1977; Vocations, 1983; The Rivers of China, 1987; The Girl Who Saw Everything, 1992; The Woman in the Window, 1998. Honours: NSW Premiers Awd for Drama, 1988; Vic Premiers Awd for Drama, 1988; Austl Writers Guild Awd, Best Stage Play, 1993. Memberships: Varuna Writers Cntr; Austl Writers Guild; Austl Natl Playwrights Cntr. Hobbies: Reading; Gardening. Address: c/o Hilary Linstead & Associates, Level 18, Plaza II, 500 Oxford Street, Bondi Junction, NSW 2022, Australia.

DE KRETSER David Morritz, b. 27 Apr 1939. Professor. m. Janice, 7 Dec 1962, 4 s. Education: Univ of Melbourne. Appointments: Res Medl Offr, 1963-64, Asst Endocrinologist, 1971-, Physn, 1973-74, Snr Rsch Fell, 1974-78, Assoc Dir Medl Rsch Cntr, 1977-78, Prince Henrys Hosp;, Demonstrator, 1965, Lectr, 1966-68, Snr Lectr Dept Med, Dept Anatomy, 1971-75, Rdr in Anatomy, 1976-78, Monash Univ; Snr Fell, Endocrinology

Dept, Med Univ Wash, 1969-71; Dir Inst of Reproduction and Dev, Chmn, Dept Anatomy, Monash Univ, 1978-91. Publications: The Pituitary and Testis: Clinical and Experimental Studies, 1983; Many chapters and pprs on reproductive bio and male infertility. Hobbies: Squash; Fishing. Address: 1 Leura Street, Surrey Hills, Victoria, Australia 3127.

DE LA MADRID HURTADO Miguel, b. 1935. Politician; Lawyer. m. Paloma C de la Madrid, 5 children. Education: Harvard Univ USA. Appointments: Successively with Bank of Mexico, Petroleos Mexicanos, Asst Dir of Fins, 1970-72; Dir Pub Sector Credit later Under-Sec Min of Fin; Sec for Plng and Fed Budget Govt of Mexico, 1979-80; Instnl Revolutionary Party cand to succeed Lopez Portillo as Pres of Mexico, Sep 1981; Pres of Mexico, 1982-88; Pres Natl Assn of Lawyers, 1989-; Mexican Inst of Culture, 1989-; Dir-Gen Fondo de Cultura Economica, 1990-. Address: Parras 46, Barrio Sta Catarina, Deleg Coyoacan, 04010, Mexico, DF, Mexico.

DE LACY Keith Ernest (The Hon), b. 7 Aug 1940, Cairns, Qld, Aust. Director. m. Yvonne Jarrett, 22 Dec 1962, 3 d. Education: BA Deg, Qld Univ; QDA, Qld Dip of Agric, Gatton Coll. Appointments: Tobacco Farmer, 1960-67; Agric Coll Prin, Papua New Guinea Pub Serv, 1967-76; Agric Educ Cnslt, 1977-82; Mbr for Cairns, Qld Parl, 1983-98; Treas, Qld, 1989-96; Chmn Trinity Funds Mngmnt; Dir, Qld Investment Corp, Securities Exchanges Guarantee Corp Ltd, Cairns Intl Univ; Strategic Advsr, Theiss Contractors Pty Ltd; Chmn, Fndn for Gambling Stdies; Mbr, Salvation Army Advsry Cttee, Cairns; Chmn Red Shield Appeal; Chmn, Ergon Engrng. Honour: Hon DLitt, James Gold Univ. Membership: Fell Aust Inst of Mngmnt. Address: PO Box 256, Cairns, Qld 4870, Australia.

DE LAETER John Robert, b. 3 May 1933. Professor. m. Robin McGrath, 28 Dec 1957, 2 s, 1 d. Education: BSc hons; BEd hons; PhD; DSc; Hon DTech; FTSE; FAIP; Univ of WA; McMaster Univ, Can. Appointments: Inaugural Hd, Dept of Phys, 1968; Dean, Applied Sci, WAIT, 1974; Mbr, WA Post Second Educ Commn, 1978-84; Assoc Dir, Engrng and Sci, WAIT, 1981-87; Pres, Conservation and Environ Cl of WA, 1981-84; Chmn, CSIRO Advsry Cttee, WA, 1983-86; Dir, WA Product Innovation Cntr, 1983-84; Chmn, WA Sc Ind and Technol Cntr, 1984-87; Austl Studies Schl, PA State Univ, USA, 1986-91; Prof of Phys, 1986-, Acting Vice Chan, 1987-88, Dpty Vice Chan, Engrng and Sci, 1987-90, Rsch and Dev, 1991-95, Curtin Univ of Technol; Sec, 1983-87, Chmn, 1987-91, Commn on Atomic Weights and Isotopic Abundances, Intl Union of Pure and Applied Chem; Chmn, Wesley Coll Cl, 1988-94; Patron, Scitech Discovery Cntr, 1998-. Honours: Citizen of the Yr for WA; ANZAAS Medal; Roy Soc Medal; AO; W R Browne Medal, Geol Soc of Aust, 1996. Memberships: Bd of Mngmt, CSIRO, 1992-95; Dir, WA Sands Pty Ltd, 1994-; Dpty Chair, Scitch Discovery Cntr, 1985-97; ASTEC, 1996-98; PMSEC, 1996-97. Hobbies: Hockey; Tennis. Address: 4 The Parapet, Burrendah, WA 6155, Australia.

de LEON CARPIO Ramiro, b. Guatemala Cty. Politican; Lawyer; Professor. m. Appointments: Prof Legal and Soc Scis Fac Polit and Soc Scis Fac Rafael Landivar Univ; Asst consultant Min of Econ, consultant Common Mkt div, 1967-69; Sec Perm Commn of Tarffs, 1968-70; Sec Natl Commn of Econ Integratoin, 1970; Sec-Gen State Cncl, 1974-78; Legal consultant, 1978-81; Gen Mgr Sugar Assn of Guatemala;, 1981-83; Co-fndr Union del Centro Nacional, Union of Natl Cnt Party, 1983; Sec-Gen, 1983-86; Alt Pres, 1984-86; Pres of Guatemala, 1993-96; Fndr Pres Inst de Invest y Capacitacion Atanasio Tzul; Pres Cncl for Cntr Am Civ Soc for Peace.Memberships: Mbr Constituent Natl Assn, 1984-86. Address: c/o Office of the President, Palacio Nacional, Guatemala City, Guatemala.

DE LUCA Anthony, b. 7 July 1963, Melbourne, Aust. Medical Scientist; Consultant. Education: BS (Hons); PhD; Grad Dip; Pharm Sci Drug Ev. Appointments: Rsch Fell, Vic Coll Pharm, 1991-93; Fell RMIT, 1993-97; Dir,

Techlink Australasia, 1995-. Publications: Review for International Encyclopedia of Pharmacology & Therapeutics (Opiate Drugs), 1996. Memberships: ABA; ISHR; ASCEPT; IUPHAR; ARCS. Hobbies: Science fiction; Cycling; Squash; Handball; Coins; DIY. Address: 8 Hosie Street, Richmond 3121, Melbourne, Victoria, Australia.

DE MICHELI Giovanni, b. 26 Nov 1955, Milan, Italy. Professor. m. Marie-Madeline, 1 s, 1 d. Education: PhD, Univ CA, Berkeley, 1983. Appointments: Cnslt in Res, Harris Semiconductor, Melbourne, FL, 1981; Asst Prof, Dept of Electrons of the Politecnico di Milano, Italy, 1983-84; Rsch Staff Mbr, IBM T.J. Watson Rsch Cntr, Yorktown Heights, NY, 1984-85; Project Ldr, D A Workstations, IBM T.J. Watson Rsch Cntr, 1985-86; Asst Prof, Dept of Elec Engrng, Stanford Univ, CA, 1987-89; Guest Schl, Dept of Elec Engrng, Kyoto Univ, Japan, 1992; Guest Prof, Dept of Elec Engrng, Delft Univ, Netherlands, 1994; Assoc Prof, Dept of Elec Engrng, Stanford Univ, 1989-96; Prof, Dept of Elec Engrng, Computer Sci, Stanford. Publications: Over 100 tech pprs incl 5 books. Honours: Best Ppr Awd, 20th ACM/IEEE Design Automation Conf, Miami Beach, 1983; NSF Initiation Awd, 1987; Best Ppr Awd, IEEE Transactions on CAD/ICAS, 1987; NSF Presl Yng Investigator Awd, 1988; IEEE-CS Disting Serv Awd, 1990; Best Ppr Awd, 30th ACM/IEEE Design Automation Conf, Dallas, 1993; IEEE Fell, 1994. Memberships: IEEE; ACM. Address: Stanford University, Gates Computer Science, Stanford, CA 94305, USA.

DE NIJS Eugenie Maria (Jenny), Lecturer in Design. m. Max Pierre de Nijs, 23 Jan 1951, 2 s. Education: DA, Vienna; RMIT, Melbourne; MDIA, Ed. Appointments: Display, Advtng Exec, Myer Emporium, Melbourne, 1942-57; Lectr, Illustration and Des, Roy Melbourne Inst of Technol, RMIT Univ. Publications: Women as Designers in Australia, 1986; Papers publd: Insea NY, 1969; Num Aust, 1971-88; Baden, Austria, 1980; Forum Resumee, Rotterdam, Netherlands and Melbourne, 1981; R and D Memorandum, 1978-79. Honours: Num testimonials. Memberships: Design Inst of Aust, Sec/Treas, Cncl Mbr, Vic Chapt 1983-88; DIA, 1980-; INSEA, 1968-. Hobbies: Drawing; Fashion history research; Community work; Girl Guides; Brotherhood of St Lawrence. Address: 21 King Street, Balwyn, Victoria 3103, Australia.

DE NIRO Robert, b. 1943 NY. Actor. m. Diahnne Abbott, 1976, 1 s, 1 d, 2 children by Toukie Smith. Appointments: Fndr and Pres Tri Beca Prodns, 1989-. Films incl: The Wedding Party, 1969; Jennifer On My Mind, 1971; Bloody Mama; Born to Win, 1971; The Gang That Couldn't Shoot Straight, 1971; Bang the Drum Slowly, 1973; Mean Streets, 1973; The Godfather Part II, 1974; The Last Tycoon; Taxi Driver, 1976; New York, New York, 1900, 1977; The Deer Hunter, 1978; Raging Bull, 1980; True Confessions, 1981; The King of Comedy, 1982; Once Upon a Time in America, 1986; The Untouchables, 1987; Letters Home from Vietnam; Midnight Run, 1988; We're No Angels, 1989; Stanley and Iris, 1989; Good Fellas, 1989; Jacknife, 1989; Awakenings, 1990; Fear No Evil, 1990; Backdraft, 1990; Cape Fear, 1990; Guilty of Suspicion, 1991; Mistress, 1992; Night and the City, 1992; Mad Dog and Glory, 1992; This Boy's Life, 1993; Mary Shelley's Frankenstein, 1993; A Bronx Tale - also dir, co-prodr - 1993; Sleepers, 1997; Jackie Brown, 1998; Prodr Thunderheart, 1992. Honours: Cmdr Ordre des Arts et des Lettres; Acady Awd for Best Supporting Actor for The Godfather Part II, 1974; Acady Awd Best Actor for Raging Bull, 1980. Address: CAA, 9830 Wilshire Boulevard, Beverly Hills, CA 90212, USA.

DE PALMA Brian, b. 11 Sep 1940 Newark NJ. Film Director. m. Gale Ann Hurd, 1991, 1 d. Education: Sarah Lawrence Coll Bronxville; Columbia Univ. Appointments: Directed - short films - Icarus, 1960, 660124: The Story of an IBM Card, 1961; Wotan's Wake, 1962; Feature length: The Wedding Party, 1964; The Responsive Eye - documentary - 1966; Murder a la Mod, 1967; Greetings, 1968; Dionysus in '69 - co-dir - 1969; Hi Mom!, 1970; Get to Know Your Rabbit, 1970; Sisters, 1972; Phantom of the Paradise, 1974; Obsession, 1975; Carrie, 1976; The Fury, 1978; Home Movies, 1979; Dressed to Kill, 1980; Blow Out, 1981; Scarface, 1983; Body Double, 1984; Wise Guys, 1985; The Untouchables, 1987; Casualties of War, 1989; Bonfire of the Vanities, 1990; Raising Cain, 1992; Carlito's Way, 1993; Mission Impossible, 1996. Address: Paramount Pictures, Lubitsch Annex #119, 5555 Melrose Avenue #119, W Hollywood, CA 90038, USA.

DE SILVA Manawaduge Wilmot Arthur, b. 21 Oct 1931, Galle, Sri Lanka. Teacher; Journalist; Astrologer. m. T H W De Silva, 21 Apr 1961, 3 d. Education: Engl Spec Trained Tchr; Admin & Mngmt; Dr Astrology. Appointments: Prin, Mihiripenna Coll; Pres, Sri Kapila Hum Soc; Pres, Young Men's Buddhist Assn (Relig Sect); Dir, Sarasavi Astrological Serv. Publications: (auth) Sammajeewa; How to Live a Healthy Life; The Path to Nirvana; Ed, Sathuta Annual Publication. Honours: Recog of Meritorious Serv to Animals, Amn Hum Assn, 1967; JP, 1991; Dr Astrology, 1997. Memberships: Pres, Sri Kadila Hum Soc, 1961-; Pres, Relig Sect, Young Men's Buddhist Assn, 1997-. Hobbies: Writing to papers; Astrology. Address: Sarasavi Astrological Service, Sri Kapila Humanitarian Society, 257 Circular Road, Magalle, Galle, Sri Lanka.

DE SOTO Alvaro, b. 16 Mar 1943, Buenos Aires, Argentina. United Nations Official. div, 2 s, 1 d. Education: Intl Sch, Geneva; Cath Univ, Lima; San Marcos Univ, Lima; Dipl, Acady Lima & Inst of Intl Studies, Geneva. Appointments: Acting Dir, Maritime Sovereignty Divsn, Min of Fgn Specl Asst to UN Sec-Gen, 1982-86; Asst Sec-Gen, Exec Asst to UN Sec-Gen, 1987-91; Personal Rep of UN Sec-Gen, UN Off for Rsch & Collection of Info, 1991; Rep of UN Sec-Gen in El Salvadore Peace Negotiations, 1990-91; Snr Polit Advsr to UN Sec-Gen, 1992-94; Asst Sec-Gen for Polit Affairs, 1995-. Honour: Hon Deg, St Joseph's Univ, PA, USA, 1992. Memberships: Assoc Mbr, Intl Ist of Strategic Studies, London. Address: United Nations, Room 3527-A, New York, NY 10017, USA.

DEAN John Theodore, b. 25 June 1934, Perth, WA, Aust. Violist. m. Margot Hamilton Robertson, 26 Sept 1959, 1 s, 2 d. Education: Dip Mus, Melbourne Univ Conserv, 1956; MusB 1970, MusM 1981, Univ of WA. Career: Prin Violist, WA Symph Orch, 1970-89; Pub concerts and brdcst recitals for ABC; Quartet recitals for Musica Viva Soc, 1971, 1974; Examiner, AMEB, 1976-96. Memberships: Austl Strings Assn; WA Music Tchrs' Assn. Hobbies: Skin diving; Boating; Fishing. Address: Lot 134 Egan Place, Barragup, WA 6210, Australia.

DEANE William Patrick, b. 4 Jan 1931, St Kilda, Vic. Governor General of the Commmonwealth of Australia. m. Helen, 6 Jan 1965, 1 s, 1 d. Education: BA, LLB; Dip Int Law, The Hague; Trinity Coll, Dublin. Appointments: Acting Lectr, Pub Intl Law, 1956-57; Tchng Fell, Equity Univ, Sydney, 1956-61; Admitted as Barrister, 1957; QC, 1966; Pres, Austl Trade Pracs Tribunal, 1977-82; Judge, Suprme Crt, NSW, 1977; Fedl Crt Aust, 1977-82; Justice High Crt Aust, 1982-95; Gov-Gen, Commonwealth of Aust, 1996-. Honours: KBE, 1982; AC, 1988; KTStJ, 1996; Hon LLD, Sydney, Griffith, Notre Dame; Hon Dr Univ, Southern Cross, Austl Cath Univ, Qld Univ of Technol, 1999; Hon Sac Theol, Melbourne Coll of Div. Address: Government House, Canberra, ACT 2600, Australia.

DEARNLEY Christopher Hugh, b. 11 Feb 1930, Wolverhampton, Eng. Organist. m. Bridget Wateridge, 3 s, 1 d. Education: MA, Worcester Coll, Oxford, Eng; DMus, Lambeth, 1987; DFA, Westminster Coll, USA, 1989; FRCO, FRSCM. Appointments: Asst Organist, Salisbury Cath, 1954-57; Organist and Master of Choristers, ibid, 1957-68; Organist and Dir of Music, St Paul's Cath, 1968-89; Dir of Music, Christ Ch St Laurence, Sydney, Aust, 1990-91; Organist locum tenens, St David's Cath, Hobart, 1991; Dir of Music, Trinity Coll, Univ of Melbourne, Aust, 1992-93; Acting

Organist, St George's Cathedral, Perth, 1994, St Andrew's Cathedral, Sydney, 1995, Christ Church Cathedral, Newcastle, 1996. Compositions: Var ch music; Arrangements and editions of early ch music. Recordings: EMI Great Cathedral Organ Series, nos 112 and 17; Organ Music From Salisbury and St Paul's Cathedrals; Num choir discs. Publications: The Treasury of English Church Music, vol 3; English Church Music, 1650-1750; Contributions to: Var ch music jrnls. Honour: Lt, Roy Vic Order, 1990. Memberships: Pres, Incorp Assn of Organists, 1968-70; Chmn, Friends of Cath Music, 1971-90, VP 1990-; Chmn, Percy Whitlock Trust, 1982-89, Pres 1989-; Dir, Engl Hymnal Co, 1970-94; Chmn, Harwich Fest, 1981-89, Pres 1989-; Patron Natl Accordion Org, 1989-; Hon Gov, Corp of Sons of the Clergy, 1989-; Patron, Organ Histl Trust of Aust, 1990-. Hobbies: Sketching; Gardening. Address: PO Box 102, Wilberforce, NSW 2756, Australia.

DEAS Walter Chalmers, b. 28 July 1933, Monifieth, Angus, Scot. Cinematographer. m. Jane Hannan, 12 Feb 1955. Career: Fndr, w wife Jean, Seawest Prodns Pty Ltd, 1969; One of first underwater photogs in Scot and Aust. Creative works include: (as camera operator, Dir of Photog, Prodr, Dir), in Aust: Australia Take a Bow; HMS Pandora; The Greatest Reef; The Basking Shark (awd winner, Russia & France); Heron Island (Silver Medal); The Quest for Freedom (Gold Medal - Sea Tasmsania '97 Film Fest); Bungee Jump (Gold Medal); BBC: Life on Earth; The Living Planet; Animal Magic Goes Cruising; Where the Fish are Friendly; The Living Isles; Supersense; The Discovery of Animal Behaviour: The Private Life of Plants; USA: Mission Impossible; Mercy Mission; Time Trax (episode won TV Drama of Yr); Earth Force; 20,000 Leagues Beneath The Sea; Japan: Fighting Fish; Sweden: The Man and His Universe; Saga of Life (Intl Emmy NY, 1996); BBC and Israel TV: Reefwatch - The Red Sea; Saudi Arabia: Dugongs and Turtles; CBS Canada: Two Islands. Publications include: Underwater Photography; Australia's Great Barrier Reef; Corals of the Great Barrier Reef and Pacific. Honours: Num awds for prodns; Dive Aust for Cinematography; Padi Hallmark Awd for Photo Jrnlsm, 1994. Memberships: BECTU; Intl Assn of Wildlife Filmakers; PADI; Hon VP, Scottish Sub-Aqua Club. Hobbies: Photography; Writing; Natural history; Reading; Travel; Genealogy; Art. Address: 11 Platypus Avenue, Isle of Sorrento, Gold Coast, Queensland 4217, Australia.

DEASEY Michael Keith, b. 25 Jan 1947, Sydney, Aust. Cathedral Organist. m. Antonia Harman, 30 Aug 1980, 1 s, 2 d. Education: Dip MusEd, NSW Conservatorium of Music, 1964-67; Roy Sch of Ch Music, UK, 1969-71; FTCL, 1969; ARCM, 1969; LRAM, 1970; ARCO, 1971; BEduc (Music), Sydney, 1984. Appointments: Asst Organist, St Andrew's Cath, Sydney, 1967-69; Organist, Choirmaster, Selsdon Parish Ch, Surrey, Eng, 1969-72; Organist and Choirmaster, St Peter's Brockville, Ont, Can, 1973-80; Organist and Master of Choristers, St Andrew's Cath, Sydney, 1981-; Recitals in Aust, NZ, Eng, Iceland, Can, USA. Honours: First Prize, Ernest Truman Meml Organ Playing, RSCM, Eng, 1971. Memberships: Sydney Organ Soc; Roy Coll of Organists. Hobbies: Tennis; Crosscountry skiing. Address: St Andrew's Cathedral, PO Box Q190, Queen Victoria Buildings, Sydney, NSW 2000, Australia.

DEB Kalyanmoy, b. 29 Apr 1962, India. Associate Professor. m. Debjani, 23 Jan 1991, 1 s, 1 d. Education: BTech, 1985; MSc, 1989; PhD, 1991. Appointments: Engrs India Ltd, New Delhi, 1987-85; Univ of AL, 1987-91; Univ IL, 1991-92; Indian Inst of Technol, Kanpur, 1993-. Publications: Optimization in Engineering Design, 1995; Sev pprs in profl jrnls. Honours: Yng Engr Awd, Indian Natl Acady of Engrs, 1996; AICTE Career Awd, 1997; Alexander von Humboldt Fellshp, 1998. Hobbies: Badminton; Soccer; Reading; Research. Address: Department of Mechanical Engineering, Indian Institute of Technology, Kanpur 208016, India.

DEBNATH Lokenath, b. 30 Sept 1935, India. Professor. m. Sadhana, 1 Aug 1969, 1 s. PhD, Pune Math; Phd, Applied, Math. Appointments: Prof, E Carolina

Univ, 1969-83; Prof, Chr, Dept of Maths, 1983-95; Actng Chr, Dept of Stats, Univ of Cntrl FL, 1989-90; Mechl and Aerospace Engrng Prof, 1991-; Maths Prof, 1995-. Creative Works: co-auth, Nonlinear Partial Differential Equationa for Scientist and Engrs; Integral Transform and Their Applications; Nonlinear Water Waves; Introduction to Hilbert Spaces with Applications; Jrnls of Math Analysis and Applications; Integral Transforms and Special Functions; Intl jrnl of Maths and Stats. Honours: Visng Lectr, Math Assn of Am; Snr Fullbright Fellshp for Lectrs and Rsch, India, Korea, Russia; Disting Rsch Awd; Ex in Profl Serv Awd; Disting Tchng Awd; Ex in Profl Awd. Memberships: Amn Maths Soc; Amn Physical Soc; Math Assn of Am; Soc of Indl and Applied Math; Calcutta Maths Soc. Address: Dept of Maths, Central Florida Univ, Central Florida, FL, USA.

DEBONIS Steven Larry, b. 10 Jan 1949, New York, USA. Teacher; Writer. m. Laurie Kuntz, 6 Oct 1987, 1 s. Education: BA, Psychol, Univ CT, 1971. Publications: Children of the Enemy: Oral Histories of Vietnamese Amerasians and Their Mothers, 1995. Address: R115A, 1-28, 2 Chome, Hirahata, Misawa-shi, Aomori-ken 033, Japan.

DEDHIA Navin Shamji, b. 25 Dec 1940, Mumbai, India. Engineer. m. 2 d. Education: BE, Electr Engrng, Univ of Bombay, 1963; MS, Electr Engring, TN Techl Univ, 1968; MBA, Golden Gate Univ, 1983. Appointments: Engr, Polychem Ltd, Mumbai, India, 1963-66; Consolidated Comstock, Pitts, USA, 1967; Jnr Engr, Assoc Engr, Snr Assoc Engr, IBM, NY, 1968-76; Staff Engr, Advsry Engr, San José, CA, 1976-. Publications: Quality World Newsletter, 1982-; Survive Business Challenges with the Total Quality Management Approach, jrnl, 1995; Quality from Many Perspectives, Parts I and II, 1998; Winning in the Market Place, conf proceeding, 1998; articles, proceedings and newsletters since 1980. Honours: CVO Seva Samaj Silver Medal, Mumbai, India, 1958; Sarla Devi Gold Medal, Mumbai, 1960; GPD Achmnt Awd, 1983, San José Plant Mgr MDQ Awd, 1993, IBM; ASQ Testimonial Awds, 1984, 1990, 1995; ASQ Volun of the Month, 1988; ASQ E Jack Lancaster Awd, 1993; Jaina Recognition Awd, 1999. Memberships: Mid-Hudson India Assn, Pres 1974-; Gujarati Cultural Assn, 1983-; Amn Soc for Qlty, Intl Chapt Chair/Tstee, 1984-; Santa Clara Valley Sect, Chair, 1987-88; E J Lancaster Awd Chair, 1993-; Adlibmasters Toastmasters Club, Pres, 1997-98. Hobbies: Playing cards; Bridge; Chess; Swimming; Sightseeing. Listed in: Who's Who in California; Who's Who Among Asian Americans. Address: 5080 Bougainvillea Deive, San José, CA 95111, USA.

DEGALLAIX Serge, b. 5 Sept 1947, Denaim, France. Diplomat. m. F Richard, 6 Apr 1999, 1 s. Education: Grad, Inst of Pol Stdies, Paris, France; Master in Econs, Paris Univ; Natl Admin Sch (ENA). Appointments: 1st Sec in Cameroon, 1974-76; Mbr, French Deleg to UN, 1975; 1st Sec in Tehran, 1976-79; Econ Affairs Dept, French Min of For Affairs, 1979-80; Hd, Dev Mission in Rome, 1982-85; Dpty Dir, then Chf, Econ Serv, French Cooperation Min, 1985-89; French Amb in Bangladesh, 1989-92; Dpty Gen Dir, French Min of For Affairs, 1992-96; French Amb in Vietnam, 1996-. Honours: Kt, Natl Order of Merit; Kt, Legion of Honour; Offr, var for orders. Hobbies: Art history; Modern painting; African art. Listed in: Who's Who in France. Address: French Embassy, 57 Tran Hung Dao, Hanoi, Vietnam.

DEL ROSARIO Jose P Jnr, b. 4 June 1942, Poblacion, Plaridel, Bulacan, Philippines. Diplomat. 3 s, 1 d. Education: BSc, For Serv; MA, Asian Studies. Appointments include: Prin Asst, Off of Consular Affairs, 1973-74; Prin Asst, Off of Protocol, 1982-86; Exec Offr RP-US, Bus Dev Cncl, Manila Off, 1982-86; Dir, Protocol for Ceremonials, 1986; Exec Dir & Dpty Dir Gen, Off of Asean Affairs, 1993-94; Acting Asst Sec, Acting Dir Gen, Off of Asean Affairs, 1993-94; Acting Asst Sec and Acting Dir Gen, Off of Asean Affairs, 1993-94; Asst Sec, Chief of Protocol, Off of Protocol and State Visits, 1995-97. Honour: Great Cross, Orden Libertador Bernardo O'Higgins, Repub of Chile. Memberships: UP Alumni

Assn; Bulacan Histl Assn; Alpha Sigma Fraternity; Lyceum of the Philippines. Hobbies: Antique collection; Singing; Reading; Dancing; Sports. Address: Embassy of the Philippines, 50-N, Nyaya Marg, Chanakyapuri, New Delhi 110221, India.

DEL VALLE ALLIENDE Jaime, b. 2 Jul 1931 Santiago. Politician; Lawyer. m. Paulina Swinburn Pereira, 4 c. Education: Escuela de Derecho de la Universidad Catolica de Chile. Appointments: Taught at Catholic Univ Law Sch from 1955; Appt'd dir, 1969; Dean, 1970; Var posts in Supreme Crt, 1958-64; Pub Prosecutor, 1964-74; Pro-Rector Pontificia Univ Catolica de Chile, 1974; Dir-Gen natl TV channel, 1975-78; Pres Bd Colegio de Abogados, 1982-83; Min of Jus, Feb-Dec 1983; Min of For Affairs, 1983-87. Memberships: Mbr Bd Colegio de Abogados, 1981-. Address: c/o Ministerio de Asuntos Exteriores, Palacio de la Moneda, Santiago, Chile.

DELAHUNT Brett, b. 20 Feb 1950, Wellington, NZ. Pathologist. Education: BSc 1971, BSc Hons 1972, Vic Univ of Wellington; BMedSc 1976, MBChB 1978, MD 1995, Univ of Otago; Fell Roy Coll of Pathologists of Aust. Appointments: Demonstrator in Anatomy, Univ of Otago, 1975; Asst Lectr 1980-81, Lectr 1981-86, Snr Lectr 1986-94, Assoc Prof 1994-96, Prof, 1996-, in Pathol, Dpty Dean, 1999-, Wellington Sch of Med, Univ of Otago; Cnslt Pathologist, Wellington Hosp, Capital Coast Hlth Ltd, 1986-; Mbr, Bd of Mngmt, Wellington Ambulance Serv, 1986-96; Commnr Wellington Dist, St John Ambulance Brigade, 1986-90; Mbr, Med Steering Cttee, Wellington Regl Cncl; Cnslt Pathologist, Pacific Paramed Trng Cntr; Curator, Pathol Mus, Wellington Hosp and Wellington Sch of Med; Visng Sci, Armed Forces Inst of Pathol, WA DC, USA, 1989; Mbr, WHO Renal Tumour Classification Panel, 1989-; Prin Medl Advsr, Order of St John in NZ, 1994-96; Chmn, Dept of Pathol, Wellington Sch of Med, Univ of Otago. Publications: Num publd articles in sci jrnls in the field of Pathol; Ed NZ First Aid Manual, 1994, reprinted 1995. Honours: Med Rsch Schlsp, 1975; Rsch Prize, NZ Soc of Pathologists, 1984; Offr, Order of St John, 1986; Cmndr Order of St John, 1993; Kt Order of St John, 1995; Rsch Awd, NZ Soc of Pathologists, 1994. Memberships: VP, 1991-95, Pres, 1996-, NZ Soc of Pathologists; Biomed Rsch Soc; Intl Acady of Pathol; VP, Intl Soc of Urological Pathology, 1995-; Mbr Sci Advsry Cttee, Cancer Soc of NZ, 1997-; Chmn Sci Advsry Cttee, Wellington Med Rsch Fndn, 1998-. Address: Department of Pathology, Wellington School of Medicine, PO Box 7343, Wellington South, New Zealand.

DELAMERE Tuariki John. Government Minister. m. Jo-ell, 3 children. Education: WA State Univ; Master Bus Admin, Long Island Univ, NY, USA. Appointments: Proj Mngr, Whakatohea Trust Bd; Whakatane Regl Dir Te Puni Kokiri; Mngr, Plcy and Treaty Negotiations, fmr Dept of Jus; Chf Finl Offr, Polynesian Airlines; Snr Finl Acct, Caxton Paper Mill; Staff Mbr, US Mil Acady, Westpoint, 1st in Battalion; Elected to Parl, 1996, Min of Immigraion, Min of Pacific Is Affairs, Assoc Min of Fin, Min in Charge of Pub Trust Off, Assoc Min of Hlth. Address: 4 Toroa Street, PO Box 699, Whakatane, New Zealand.

DELBOURGO Robert, b. 11 Nov 1940, Bombay, India. Professor of Physics. m. Elizabeth Mary Wilkinson, 16 Dec 1967, 2 s. Education: BSc, 1st class hons, ARCS, 1960; PhD, Imperial Coll, London, England, 1963; DSc, London Univ, 1976. Appointments: Rsch Assoc, Univ of WI, USA, 1963-64; Rsch Sci, Intl Cntr for Theoretical Phys, Trieste, 1964-65; Guest Scientist, Weizmann Inst, 1965; Lectr, Rdr, Imperial Coll, London, Eng, 1965-76; Prof, Univ of Tas, Aust, 1976-, Chmn, Natl Cttee for Phys, 1993-96, Dean of Grad Stdies, 1994-96. Publications: Contbr of num articles to profl jrnls and mags. Honours: Walter Boas Medal, Austl Inst of Phys, 1988; Thomas Ranken Lyle Medal, Austl Acady, 1989. Memberships: Fell, Austl Acady of Sci; Fell, Austl Inst of Phys, 1977-; Assn of Math Phys, 1979-; Chmn, Tas Br of AIP; FAA. Hobbies: Table Tennis; Go; Computing. Address: Department of Physics, University of Tasmania, Box 252 C, Hobart, Tas 7001, Australia.

DELINS Emils, b. 15 May 1921, Riga, Latvia. Journalist; Diplomat. m. Nina Sics, 18 Dec 1948, 2 s, 1 d. Education: Univ of Latvia; Technische Hochschule Stuttgart. Appointments: Ed, Austl Latvian News, 1949; Hon Vice-Consul of Latvia, Melbourne, 1979; Hon, Consul-Gen, 1991. Publications: 69 Hours (essays), 1969; President to President (travel notes), 1980; Consul Without a Government, 1997. Honours: Queen's Silver Jubilee Medal, 1977; AO, 1996; Order of Three Stars, Latvia, 1997. Memberships: Latvian Press Soc (Boston); Natl Press Club (Canberra); RACV (Melbourne); Austl Inst of Intl Affairs. Hobbies: Travel; History. Address: PO Box 23, Kew, NC 3101, Australia.

DELL Miriam Patricia, b. 14 June 1924, Hamilton, NZ. Teacher; Community Worker. m. Richard, 3 Aug 1946, 4 d. Education: BA. Appointments: Tchng full/pt-time, 1945-47, 1957-58, 1961-71; Pub appts incl: Socl Security Appeal Authority, 1974-; Chair, Cttee on Women, 1974-81; JP, 1975-; Review, Preparation and Initial Employment of Nurses, 1986-92; Mbr, Mus of NZ Proj Dev Bd, 1988-92; Mbr, Natl Mus Cncl, 1989-92; Wellington Conserv Bd, 1990-99; Chair 1993 Suffrage Centennial Yr Trust, 1991-94; Prime Min's Cttee to Review Hons System, 1995. Honours: CBE, 1975; Adele Ristori Prize, 1976; Queen's Jubilee Medal, 1977; DBE, 1980; 1990 Commemorative Medal, 1990; Suffrage Centennial Medal, 1993; Order of NZ, 1993. Memberships include: Mbr, 1975-, Chair, 1981-86, Sec, 1986-87, Inter-Ch Cncl on Pub Affairs, Co-opted Mbr, Parly Watch Cttee; VP, 1976-79, Pres, 1979-86, Hon Pres, 1986-88, Coord, Dev Prog, 1988-, Cttee of Hon, 1988-, Intl Cncl of Women; Exec, 1971-78, Co-Chair, 1988-, Environ & Conservation Orgn; Fndn Mbr, Hutt Valley Branch, 1958, Pres, Hutt Valley Branch, 1966-68, VP, Bd of Offrs, NCWNZ, 1967-70, Pres, 1970-74, Natl Life Mbr, 1974-78, Natl Cncl of Women. Hobbies: Gardening; Conservation; Family history. Address: 2 Bowline Place, Whitby, Porirua, New Zealand.

DELLA SENTA Tarcisio, b. 2 May 1932, Brazil. Director. m. Iara Maria Correia Della Senta. Education: BSc, Cath Univ, Rio Grande do Sul, Brazil, 1957; MA, Educn, Inst Cath, Paris, France, 1960; PhD, Educl Planning & Admin, Harvard Univ, 1974. Appointments: Asst Prof, Fed Univ of Rio Grande do Sul, 1971-74; Prof, Cath Univ, Sao Paulo, Brazil, 1963-66; Hd, Planning & Budgeting Divsn, 1985-87, Prog Coord, Sci & Technol Devel, 1975-79, Specl Advsr to Min of Educn, 1983-84, Sec of Higher Educn, 1979-83, VP, Postgrad Educn Devel Agcy, 1974-75, Min of Educn; Specl Asst to Rector, 1988-89, Dir of Planning & Devel Divsn, 1989-93, Vice Rector, Acad Divsn, 1994-95, Acting Dir, UN Univ Inst of Adv Studies, 1996-, Dir, 1996-, UN Univ. Publications include: Communications Technology and the Crisis in Education, 1971; Recursos Humanos para a Ciencia e a Tecnologia no Brasil, 1987; Educational Reforms - Strategic Points in Restructuring Educational Systems, 1987; Institutional Strategy of the United Nations University, 1994. Address: UN University, Institute of Advanced Studies, 5-53-67 Jingumae, Shibuya-ku, Tokyo 150-8304, Japan.

DELLOW Ronald Graeme, b. 29 Sept 1924, Auckland, NZ. Retired University Lecturer; Choral Conductor; Organist; Harpischordist. m. Jane Brown Currie Cowan, 1 s, 3 d. Education: MusB, Auckland Univ Coll; Assoc, RSCM; FRCO (Chm); FNZAO; LTCL. Appointments: Lectr, Dept of Music, Auckland Univ Coll, 1949; Adult Educ Tutor, 1950-64; Extension Lectr, Music, Univ of Auckland, 1964-89; Organist and Choirmaster, Pitt St Meth Ch, Auckland, 1964-78; Dir of Music, All Saints Ch, Ponsonby, Auckland, 1986-. Compositions include: 6 recorder trios, 1971; Anthem, Let the Children Come to Me, 1972; Missa Brevis, boys' choir and organ, 1974; Jubilate, chorus and organ, 1977; Magnificat, 1978; Suite, 4 recorders, 1978. Honours: Auckland Centennial Music Schl, 1943; Prize for Fantasia for Viols, Viola de Gamba Soc, Eng, 1958; MBE, 1980; Fell, NZ Assn of Organists, 1996. Memberships: Spec Commnr, 1962-, RSCM; Var offs, Auckland Fest Soc; Past Pres, Auckland Dorian Singers, Auckland Organists Assn; Musical Dir, 1954-89, NZ Soc of Recorder Players; Gov, 1963-,

Dolmetsch Fndn; Auckland Bach Cantata Soc, Music Dir, 1978-91. Hobbies: Tape recording; Singing. Listed in: Who's Who in Music. Address: 8 Lynch Street, Point Chevalier, Auckland 2, New Zealand.

DELOFSKI Edwin Franklin (Ted), b. 19 Nov 1947. High Commissioner. m. Irene, 4 Jan 1980, 1 s, 1 d. Education: BA, 1st Class hons, Econs, Univ NSW; MPhil, Econs, Oxford Univ. Appointments: Asst Sec, Austl Treas, 1985; Min, Econ, Austl High Cmmn, London, 1987; 1st Asst Sec, Dept of For Affairs and Trade, 1990; Aust High Cmmnr to Singapore, 1993-; Amb to World Trade Org, Geneva, 1997-. Address: c/o Department of Foreign Affairs & Trade, Canberra, Australia.

DEMIREL Suleyman, b. 1924. Politician; Engineer. Education: Istanbul Tech Univ. Appointments: Rschr in irrigation and electrification Bur of Reclamation, 1949-50; Engr Elecl Survey Admin; Hd of Dams Dep, 1954-55; Exchange Fell'ship schl; Sev pvt cos and pub deps USA, 1954-55; Dir-Gen Hydraulic Works Turkey, 1955-60; Pvt contractor engr; Lectr Middle East Technol Univ, 1962-64; Chmn Jus Party - AP - 1965-80; Isparta Dep, 1965-80; Dep PM, Feb-Oct 1965; PM - led AP govt - 1965-71; Four coalition govts, 1977-78; Opposition Ldr, 1978-80; PM, 1979-80; Banned from pols, 1980-87; Chmn True Path Party - DYP - 1987-93; Dep for Isparta, 1987-93; PM, 1991-93; Pres of Turkey, May 1993-. Address: Office of the President, Cumhurbas-Kanligi Kosku, Cankaya, Ankara, Turkey.

DENG Anping, b. 14 Feb 1962, Jiangxi Prov, China. Academic; Educator. m. Yang Hong, 6 Oct 1986, 1 s. Education: BS, Nanjing Univ, 1984; MSc, W China Univ Medl Scis (WCUMS), 1990; PhD, Masaryk Univ, Czech Repub, 1999. Appointments: Lectr, WCUMS, 1992; Visng Schl, Gyeongsang Natl Univ, S Korea, May-June, 1997; Visng Schl, Inst of Chemo and Biosensor, Germany, July-Aug, 1998; PhD, postgrad, Masaryk Univ, Czech, 1996-99. Publications: Determination of gentmycin by enhanced chemiluminescent immoassay, 1993; Sensitive ELISA for the determination of atarzine in water samples, 1998. Hobbies: Table tennis; Reading. Address: Department of Inorganic Chemistry, West China University of Medical Sciences, #17 3rd Block, Renmin Nanlu, Chengdu, 610041, China.

DENG Guanghua, b. 24 Nov 1940, Sinan, Guizhou, China. Music Educator; Ethnomusicologist. m. Ke Taixiang, 2 s, 1 d. Education: Grad, Arts Dept, Guizhou Natl Coll, 1959. Appointments: Music Tchr, Sinan County Normal Sch, 1959-70, Sinan HS, 1971-83; Hd, Sinan County Cultural Bur, 1984-85; Music Tchr, Assoc Prof, Prof, Dir, Music Dept, Guizhou Normal Univ, 1985-. Publications: Initiation of Music Education, 1986; Nuo and Arts, Religion, 1993; A Research for Nuo-ritural Music, 1997. Honours: Awd, Guizhou Prov Ex Rsch Achievement, Prizes of Philos and Socl Sci, 3 times, 1990-98; Title, Ex w Spel Contbrn, Guizhou Prov People's Govt, 1993. Memberships: Chinese Musicians Assn; Vice Chmn, Guizhou Musicians Assn, 1995; Chmn, Soc for Music Educn, Guizhou Prov, 1990; Dir, Soc for Minority Natl Music of China, 1993. Address: Guizhou Normal University, Guiyang, Guizhou, China.

DENG Yaoliang, b. 17 Mar 1955, Qingzhou, China. Urologist. m. Gu Ming, Qingzhou, China, 1 May 1984, 1 s. Education: MD, Youjiang Medl Coll, Bose China, 1982; MSc, Hunan Medl Univ, Changsha, China, 1987. Appointments: Res, Guangxi Medl Coll, Nanning, China, 1987-90; Asst Prof, 1990-93; Assoc Prof, 1993-. Publications: Articles to profl jrnls, 1988-. Honours: Awd for Advmnt of Sci & Tech, Guangxi Prov Govt, 1991; Nat Scis Grantee, 1994, 1997; Young Scientist Grant, 1994. Memberships: Chinese Pharm Assn, 1988; Urology Assn, 1989; AAAS, 1995. Hobbies: Music; Fishing; Reading; TV News; Laboratory work; PC Game. Address: Department of Urology, First Hospital, Guangxi Medical University, 6 Binhu Road, Nanning 530027, China.

DENHOLM William Thomas, b. 17 May 1925. Metallurgist. m. Pamela Avalon Mcleod, 21 Aug 1954, dec 18 Apr 1998, 2 d. Education: BMetE, 1947, MEng Sc,

1952, Univ of Melbourne; PhD, Univ of Adelaide, 1960. Appointments: Metallurgist, King Island Scheelite, 1946; Rsch Metallurgist, Austl Paper Mfrs, 1947; Lectr, 1950, Snr Lectr, 1953, Rdr/Hd of Dept of Metall, 1961, S Austl Sch of Mines (later S A Inst of Technol); Prin Rsch Scientist, 1964, Chf Rsch Scientist, 1987, The C'wlth Sci and Indl Rsch Org (CSIRO) Div of Mineral and Process Engrng; Retd, 1990; Cnsltng Metallurgist, 1990-; Hon Snr Rsch Fell, Chem Engrng Dept Monash Univ, 1994-. Publications: Auth of 40 tech papers on Corrosion, Electrochemistry and Extractive Metallurgy, 8 patents on metal extraction and refining, 1956-96. Honours: Forence Taylor Medal (AIM), 1964; Austl Corrosion Medal, 1963; Sir Ian McLennan Awd for Achievement for Ind (CSIRO), 1990; Mbr, Order of Aust (AM), 1996. Memberships: Fedl Cnclr, Austl Inst of Metals (AIM), 1955-63; Hon Life Mbr, Australasian Corrosion Assn (ACA), Australasian Pres, 1964; Fell, Australasian Inst of Mining and Metall (AusIMM), Melbourne Br Cnclr, 1967-74; The Minerals, Metals and Materials Soc (TMS) of AIME. Hobbies: Music; Reading; Sailing; Camping; Corrosion and Metallurgical research. Address: 9 Tallis Close, Camberwell, Vic 3124, Australia.

DENNERSTEIN Lorraine, b. 5 Aug 1947, Melbourne, Australia. Professor. 2 s. Education: MBBS; PhD; DPM; FRANZCP. Appointments: Dir, Off for Gender & Health, Dept of Psych; Univ of Melbourne. Publications: Auth, Co-Auth, 8 books, edited 12; Auth, Co-Auth, over 200 articles in jrnls abd chapts in books. Honours: AO, 1994. Memberships: Rapporteur, Women's Hlth, Bioethics and Human Rights; Intl Bioethics Commn; UNESCO; Women's Hlth Cnslt; C'Wealth Secretariat. Hobbies: Skiing; Bicycling; Opera. Address: Office for Gender and Health, Department of Psychiatry, The University of Melbourne, 6th Floor, Charles Connibere Building, Royal Melbourne Hospital, Vic 3050, Australia.

DENNISON Lucie Elizabeth, b. 30 Apr 1927. m. Arthur Geoffrey Dennison, dec, 1 d. Education: BA; AILA; Dip, Leisure Stdies; CD. Appointments; BBC Ref and Rsch Libn; Ref Libn, Newcastle Lib, Cessnock, NSW; Cty Libn, then self employed as Co-Dir Bldg, Fitness and Hospitality inds. Memberships: Fitness Ind Assn; Bldng Servs Corp; Women in Pols; Bldg Ind Assn; Constructive Women; Lib Assn of Aust; Co Dirs Assn; Mus Soc and Mus of Contemp Art. Hobby: Fitness. Address: Imperial Lodge, 54-58 City Road, Broadway, Sydney, NSW 2010, Australia.

DENTON Derek Ashworth, b. 27 May 1924, Launceston, Tas. Medical Research Scientist. m. Catherine M Scott, 2 s. Education: MM, BS, Univ of Melbourne, Aust. Appointments: Dir and Originating Bd Mbr, Howard Florey Inst, Expl Physiology and Med, 1971-89; Emer Dir, 1990-; VP, HFI, 1993-94; Pres, Howard Florey Biomed Rsch Fndn, 1997-. Publications: The Hunger for Salt, 1982; The Pinnacle of Life, 1993. Honours: Fell, Austl Acady of Scis, 1979; Hon For, Amn Acady of Arts and Scis, 1986; Hon Mbr, Amn Physiological Soc, 1987. Memberships: For Assoc, Natl Acady of Sci, US, 1995; For Med Mbr, Roy Swedish Acady of Sci, 1974; FRS; FRCP; FRACP. Hobbies: Fly fishing; Music; Theatre; Wine. Address: 816 Orrong Road, Toorak, Vic 3144, Australia.

DENTON Noel James, b. 2 Mar 1935, Bendigo, Vic, Aust. Executive Director, Waste Management Council. m. Marilyn Catterall, 17 Aug 1961, 1 s, 2 d. Education: Dip of Pub Admin, RMIT, 1961; BEc, Monash Univ, 1968; BA, Univ of Melbourne, 1984. Appointments: State Rivers and Water Supply Cmmn, 1953-65; Asst Sec, Soil Conservation Authy, 1965-69; Admin Offr, Vic Inst of Colls, 1969-73; Fndng Admnstr, Vic Coll of the Arts, 1973-86; Exec Dir, Pvte Hosps, 1986-89, Waste Mngmt Cncl (Vic), 1994-96. Publication: Lenton Parr, Sculptor (co-ed), 1984. Honours: ED, Efficiency Decoration, 1967; RFD, Reserve Forces Decoration, 1976; City of Waverley Art Acquisition Cttee, 1979-92; Arts Waverley, 1980-92; Elected Cnclr, City of Waverley, 1987-93; Mbr, SE Reg Waste Mngmt Cncl, 1987-93, Chmn 1991-93. Memberships: Rotary Club of Ashburton, 1985-96, Pres, 1995-96; Bone Marrow Donor Inst, Pres, Waverley Br, 1993-96, Sec 1997-; Maj, Roy Austl Infantry Corps (Army Reserve); Naval and Mil Club, Melbourne. Listed in: Who's Who in Australia. Hobbies: Acting; Music; Dance; Fine Arts; Photography; Carpentry; Interesting and Creative People; Local Government Affairs. Address: 3 Leonie Avenue, Mount Waverley, Vic 3149, Australia.

DENTON Richard Norman Hamilton, b. 10 Oct 1928, Sydney, Aust. Chartered Accountant. m. Patricia Eldridge, 22 Jan 1954, 2 s, 2 d. Education: Exams, Inst of Chartered Accts in Aust. Appointments: Ptnr, Irish Young & Outhwaite, 1954-80; Deloitte Haskins and Sells, 1980-85; Deloitte Haskins and Sells Intl, 1985-87; Co Dir. Publications: Var profl jrnls. Honour: AO, 1980. Membership: Life Mbr, Pres 1977-78, Inst of Chartered Accts in Aust. Hobbies: Tennis; Boating; Music. Address: 98 Prince Alfred Parade, Newport, NSW 2106, Australia.

DEOREPATIL Ashok, b. 1 June 1957, Astane, Sakri. Public Servant. m. Shella, 29 May 1985, 2 s. Education: BA (Hons) Econs; MSW. Creative works: Rotary voc progs. Honours: Rotary Voc Awds, 1 June 1992; Best Socl Worker, 22 May 1991. Hobby: Voluntary social work in tribal and slum areas and for the handicapped.

DEPP Johnny, b. 9 June 1963 Owensboro KY. Actor. Appointments: Fmr rock musician. Tv appearances incl: 21 Jump Street. Films incl: A Nightmare on Elm Street; Platoon; Slow Burn; Cry Baby; Edward Scissorhands, 1990; Benny and Joon, 1993; What's Eating Gilbert Grape, 1993; Arizona Dream; Ed Wood; Don Juan de Marco, 1994; Dead Man; Nick of Time; Divine Rapture; The Brave, 1997 - also writer and dir; Donnie Brasco, 1997. Address: c/o Tracy Jacobs, ICM, 8942 Wilshire Boulevard, Beverly Hills, CA 90211, USA.

DERHAM David Mark Brudenell, b. 10 Jan 1950. Barrister. m. Amanda Margaret Crothers, 12 May 1979, 1 s, 2 d. Education: LLB (Hons), Univ of Melbourne, 1973; Legis Drafting Inst, Canberra, 1975. Appointments: Bar and Sol of Supreme Crt of Vic, 1974, High Crt of Aust, 1974, ACT Supreme Crt, 1976, Tas Supreme Crt, 1981; NSW Supreme Crt, 1992, Western Austl Supreme Crt, 1994; Appt QC, Vic, 1994, NSW 1995. Memberships: Cncl of The Advsry Cncl for Children with Impaired Hearing, 1981-; Vice-Chmn, Victorian Bar Cncl, 1996-. Hobbies: Reading; Tennis; Golf; Skiing; Sailing. Address: 205 William St, Melbourne, Vic 3000, Australia.

DERRICOURT Robin Michael, b. 31 Mar 1948, Birmingham, Eng. Publisher. m. Marguerite, 8 Dec 1972, 1 s, 1 d. Education: BA, 1969, MA, 1973, PhD, 1978, Univ of Cambridge. Appointments: Lectr in Archaeology, 1971-73; Dir, Zambia Natl Monuments Commn, 1973-76; Publr, Longman Grp, 1977-79; Publr then Publr Dir, Cambridge Univ Press, 1979-94; Mngng Dir, Fine Arts Press, 1994-97; Mngng Dir, Univ NSW Press, 1997-. Publications: Ideas into Books, 1996; Authors Guide to Scholarly Publishing, 1996; 4 books on archaeology and African history. Memberships: Fell, Soc of Antiquities; Assoc Fell, Aust Inst of Mngmt. Address: University of New South Wales Press, Sydney, NSw 2052, Australia.

DESAI Hasmukhroy Maganlal, b. 10 May 1924, Khamblav. Electrical, Mechanical Engineer. m. (1) Savita, 27 Jan 1947, decd 18 June 1990, (2) Pvamodini, 12 Nov 1992, 1 s, 2 d. Education: LME, Vic Jubilee Tech Inst, 1944; LEE, 1945; HNC, IEE and Min of Educ, 1953; Grad IEE, DIM, IEE, VJT Aluminum Assn, 1973-74. Appointments: Asst Engr, Harbour Power Stn,Belfast, 1951-53; Asst Engr, Supt, BEST, Bombay, 1954-70; Chf Engr, 1970-72; EDPM, 1972-80; Gen Mngr, Acting Gen Mngr, 1980-82; Gen Mngr, Star Textile Inds, Ltd, 1982-86; Hon Sec, Inst of Mechl Engrs, 1957-; Mbr, Tech Bur of Cttee Indian Stands, Delhi, 1967-73; Review Cttee, Chmn, 1972. Creative Works: Hon Ed, Monthly Offic Jrnl of Instn of Mechl Engrs. Honours: Rai Bahadur G M Modi Gold Medal, 1947. Meberships: Instn of Mechl Engrs; Inst of Elecl Engrs; Soc of Power Engrs. Hobbies: Philatalist; Trav; Cricket; Table Tennis; Volley Ball; Ball Room Dancing. Address: 220-222 V Savarkar Marg, 400 016 Mumbai, India.

DESAI Jitendra Thakorebhai, b. 26 Nov 1938. Management Executive. m. Amin Tara I, 7 June 1963, 1 s, 1 d. Education: Samaj Vidya Visharad (BA), LLB, Dip in Books and Periodical Prodn and Mngmt, London. Appointments: Mngmt Trnee, 1959-63, Off Mngr, 1964-69, MMgr-Sales and Copyright, 1970-74, Gen Mngr and Mngng Tstee of Navajivan Trust (publng House and Printing Press) founded by Mahatma Gandhi, the father of the nation; Hon Hd of Dept, Dept of Jrnlsm and Mass Comm, Gujarat Vidyapith (Deemed Univ, Govt of India), Ahmedabad. Publications: Writer, transl, 18 books in Gujurati; Column writer. Honours: Best Children Book in Gujurati, 1965; Best Transl of Stories in Gujurati, 1972; Disting Publrs (Gujurati), 1993. Memberships: Pres Gujurat Printers Fedn, 1981-83; Pres, Fedn of Gujurat Publrs and Book Sellers Assns, 1979-81; Book Dev Cncl, 1991-; Pres, Gujurati Sahitya Prakashak Vikreta Mandal, 1991-; Jrnlsm and Mass Comms Panel, Univ Grants Commn, India. Hobbies: Reading; Writing; Meeting people; Sports; Swimming. Address: Managing trustee's Bungalow, Naajivan Blocks, Stadium Road, Ahmedabad 380 014, Gujurat State, India.

DESCHAMPS Noel St Clair, b. 25 Dec 1908, Brisbane, Aust. Diplomat. Education: Rome and Brussels, 1919-22; Melbourne Grammar, 1923-26; Pembroke Coll, Cambridge Univ, Eng, 1927-31; BA, Hons, 1930, MA 1934, Cambridge Univ. Appointments: Snr Mod Lang Master, Ruthin Sch, N Wales, 1935-36; Joined Dept of External Affairs, Canberra, Aust, 1937; Official Sec, Austl High Commn, Can, 1940-43; Austl Official Rep, New Caledonia, 1944-45; Charge d'Affaires, Moscow, USSR, 1946-47; Hd, Eurn Amn & Mid East Div, Canberra, Aust, 1948-49; Hd, Austl Mil Mission, Berlin, 1949-52; Hd, Austl Mission to Allied High Commn, Germany, Bonn, 1950-52; Hd, West Div, Canberra, 1953; Cnslr, Austl Emb, Paris, France, 1953-58; Ldr, Austl Deleg to First Antarctic Conf, Paris, 1955; Press Liaison Offr, Suez Cttee, London and Cairo, 1956; Austl Alternate UN Cttee for Hungary, 1957; Charge d'Affaires, Dublin, Ireland, 1958-61; Acting High Commnr, S Afr, 1960; Amb to Cambodia, 1962-69; Amb to Chile, 1969-73; Pres, Austl Soc for Latin-Amn Studies, 1974-78. Memberships: Melbourne Club; C'wlth Club, Canberra; Univ Club, Sydney. Honours: Grand Cross, Roy Order of Cambodia, 1969; Grand Cross, Order of Merit, Chile, 1974; Chevalier, Natl Order of Merit, France, 1992. Listed in: Many including: Who's Who in the World; Dictionary of International Biography; Who's Who in Australia; Notable Australians. Hobbies: History; Music; Reading; Travel; Tennis; Squash. Address: 28 Kensington Road, South Yarra, Vic 3141, Australia.

DESHMUKH Ravindrakumar, b. 15 July 1960, Satara. Assistant Teacher. m. Vandana, 17 May 1986, 2 d. Education: MSc; BEd. Appointments: Asst Tchr; Snr Master. Honours: Dir Gen Batton of Hon. Hobbies: Watching Good Prog; Playing var games. Address: R S Deshmukh, Sanjeewan Vidyalaya, Panchgani, Tal-Mahabaleshwar Dist, Satara 412805, India.

DESHMUKH Snehlata S, b. 30 Dec 1938, Mumbai, India. Doctor. m. 21 Nov 1963, 1 s, 1 d. Education: MS; FRCS; FAMS. Appointments: Dean, LTMGMC, Sion, Mumbai, Maharashtra, India; Vice-Chmn, Univ of Mumbai, Fort, Mumbai, Maharashtra, India. Publications; 180 publs and rsch comms; (co-auth) Clinical Pediatric Surgery; Chapt in ASI Textbook of Surgery; Conbr, chapts in textbook of Pediatrics. Honour: Hon FRCS, Coll of Surgs of Edinburgh. Memberships: Natl Acady of Medl Scis; Natl Bd of Exams Medl Cncl of India, New Delhi, India. Hobbies: Reading; Writing. Address: Vice-Chancellor's Lodge, University Sports Pavilion, Jian Patan Mandal Marg, Marine Lines (W), Mumbai-400020, Maharashtra, India.

DETELS Roger, b. 14 Oct 1936, Brooklyn, NY, USA. Professor of Epidemiology. m. Mary M Doud, 2 s. Education: BA, Harvard Univ, 1958; MD NY Univ, NY, 1962; MS, Univ of WA, Seattle, 1966. Appointments: Medl Offr (Rsch), Epidemiology Branch, C&FR, Natl Inst of Neurol Disease and Stroke, Natl Inst of Hlth, Bethseda, MD, 1969-70; Assoc Prof, Epidemiology, 1970-73, Acting Hd, Div of Epidemiology, 1970-72, Hd, Div of

Epidemiology, 1972-80, Prof of Epidemiology, 1973-, Dean, 1980-85, UCLA Sch of Pub Hlth. Honours: Fell, Soc for Epidemiologic Rsch, 1969; Sigma Xi, 1971; Delta Omega, 1971; Selected for: 1983 Distinguished Alumnus Awd, Sch of Pub Hlth, Univ of WA, Seattle, 1983; Fell, Amn Coll of Epidemiology, 1984; Hon Fellshp, Fac of Pub Hlth Med of Roy Colls of Physns of UK, 1992; Selected for: Fac Awd, UCLA Sch of Pub Hlth, Alumni Assn, 1992; Fell, AAAS, 1994. Memberships: AAAS; Amn Assn for Cancer Educ; Amn Coll of Epidemiology; Amn Coll of Preventive Med; Amn Epidemiological Soc; Amn Pub Hlth Assn; Physns for Socl Responsibility; Soc for Epidemiological Rsch, Pres, 1977-78; Intl Epidemiological Assn, Pres, 1990-93. Address: University of California, Los Angeles, Department of Epidemiology, Box 951772, Los Angeles, CA 90095-1772, USA.

DEUBA Sher Bahadur, b. 12 June 1946 Angra Dadeldhura Dist. Politician. Education: Tribhuvan Univ. Appointments: Chmn Far West Students Cttee Kathmandu, 1965; Served a total of nine yrs imprisonment for polit activities, 1966-85; Rsch Fell LSE, 1988-90; Active in Popular Movement for Restoration of Democracy in Nepal, 1991; Mbr Parl, 1991-; Min of Home Affairs; Ldr Parly Party Nepali Congress, 1994; PM, 1995-97. Memberships: Fndr mbr Nepal Students Union, 1970. Address: c/o Office of the Prime Minister, Central Secretariat, Singha Durbar, Kathmandu, Nepal.

DEUTCH Richard, b. 25 Sep 1944. Poet; Author; Teacher; Journalist. m. Maria Trefely, 27 Mar 1982, 1 s. Education: BA (Hons equiv), Langs and Lit, Bard Coll, NY, 1967. Appointments: Lectr, Engl and Comp Lit, Univ of KS, 1968-72; Master of Latin, St Anthony's Prep Sch, Hampstead, Eng, 1973-76; Tutor of Engl as a Secnd Lang, Rome, London and Sydney; Film Critic, Sunday Telegraph, 7 yrs; Editl exp in London and US. Publications: Books: New York: New Rivers, poetry, 1970; Prayers, pamphlet of poetry, 1971; Bedside Blue, anthology, 1989; From Barbecue to Bouillabaisse, 1989; Your Book of Magic Secrets, children's non-fic, 1991; The Australian Magician's Handbook, adult non-fict, 1994; Contbr to num mags in US, UK, France, Can and Aust inclng: Quarterly Review of Literature; Nation; Sud; London Magazine; Stand; Pol; Poetry Australia; Southerly; Overland; Imago; Western Humanities Review; Cleo; Billy Blue; Penthouse; Phoenix Review; Sydney Morning Herald; Reader's Digest. Honours: W J Lockwood Awds in Creative Writing (undergrad); 2 Clenenger Awds for Non-Fic. Membership: Auth's Guild, USA. Listed in: Men of Achievement. Hobbies: Metaphysics; Cookery. Address: 3 Joanne Place, Bilgola Plateau, NSW 2107, Australia.

DEVARAJ Theranya Lakkannagowda, b. 22 Sept 1938, Theranya. Physician. m. Subhadramma, 1 d. Education: GCIM, DAYMCMD, MACHindi; Sahityacharya (Sanskrit). Appointments: Lectr, Asst Prof, Prof, Prin, Goof Apurveda Medl Coll, Bellary of Bangalore; Dpty Dir, Ayurvea. Publications: 20 books and Purveda. Honour: Intl Awd, Ayurveda Bhaskara Awd. Memberships: VP, AYSP Assn, New Delhi; VP, Ayurugda Acady, Bangalore. Hobbies: Publishing books; Articles on Ayurveda; Treatment of patients. Address: Professor, Chidanda Murthy BT, Principal, Jindal Institute of Naturopathy, Bangalore, South India.

DEVARAJAN G, b. 8 Mar 1947. Tchng Prof. m. Sugathakumany S, 8 Feb 1977, 1 s, 1 d. Education: BSc, Botany; MA, Russian Lang and Lit; MLIS, Lib and Info Sci; PhD, Lib and Info Sci. Appointments: Lib Asst, 1973-74; Asst Libn, 1975-83; Lectr in Lib Sci, 1983-96; Rdr in Lib Sci, 1996-; Dean, Fac of Arts, Univ of Kesala, 1998-. Publications: 19 books; 2 rsch rprts; 17 conf papers; 62 jrnl articles. Honour: First Rank Holder in MLIS. Memberships: KLA pres, 1989-90; Life mbr of ILA, IATLIS, IASLIC; Sec of Cntr for Info and Technol Studies (CITS), 1993-. Listed in: Reference India, New Delhi. Hobby: Reading. Address: Reader and Head, Department of Library and Information Science, University of Kerala, Trivandrum 34, India.

DEVE GOWDA Haradanahalli. Politician. m. 6 c. Education: Govt Polytechnic inst; Trained as civ engr. Appointments: Ran contracting bus; Elected to Karnataka State Legis in 1960s; Imprisoned during state of emergency in 1970s; Min of Pub Works and Irrigation Karnataka until 1980; Chf Min of Karnataka, 1995-96; Ldr multiparty United Front, 1996; PM Min of Home and Agric Sci and Tech Personnel and Atomic Energy, 1996-97. Memberships: Fmr mbr Lok Sabha. Address: c/o Office of the Prime Minister, New Delhi, India.

DEVESI Sir Baddeley, b. 16 Oct 1941 East Tathiboko Guadalcanal. Politician; Administrator. m. June Marie Barley, 1969, 4 s, 3 d, 1 d dec. Education: St Mary's Sch Maravovo; King George VI Sch Solomon Is; Ardmore Tchrs Trng Coll Auckland NZ. Appointments: Tchr Melanesian Mission schs Solomon Is, 1965-66; Elected mbr Brit Solomon Is Legis and Exec Cncls, 1967-68; Lectr Solomon Is Tchrs Coll, 1970-72; Asst Sec for Socl Servs, 1972; Internal Affairs, 1972; Dist Offr S Malaita, 1973-75; Perm Sec Min of Works and Pub Utilities, 1976; Min of Transp and Comms, 1977; Gov-Gen of Solomon Is, 1978-88; Chan Univ of S Pacific, 1980-83; Min for For Affairs and Trade Rels, 1989-91; Dep PM and Min for Home Affairs, 1990-92; Min for Hlth and Med Scis, 1992. Honours: Hon D Univ; K St J. Hobbies: Swimming; Lawn tennis; Cricket; Reading; Snooker. Address: c/o Ministry of Health and Medical Sciences, Honiara, Solomon Islands.

DEVESON Ivan Albert, b. 18 Feb 1934. Businessman. m. Mary Ellen Perez, 1 Aug 1959, 3 s, 2 d. Education: MS, Stanford Univ, USA; Masters Deg Mngmt, 1976; Indl Engrng Deg, Gen Motors Inst; Prodn Engrng RMIT. Appointments: Chmn, Importer/Exporter Panel; Premiers Bus Gr; Prodn Mngr, Gen Motors, S Afr; Mngr, Qual Control, Gen Motors Overseas Ops, 1971; Plant Mngr, Gen Motors Intl, Denmark, 1973; Supply Mngr, Gen Motors Continental, Belgium, 1975; Mngr, Mfg Plng Overseas Grp, 1977; Gen Dir, Intl Purchasing, Gen Motors Corp, until 1986; Dir, Materials Mngmt, Gen Motors Holden's Ltd, 1981-86; Mng Dir and Chf Exec, Off Nissan Motor Co (Aust) Pty Ltd, 1987-91; Chmn, Seven Network Ltd, 1991-95; Dir, MIM Holdings. 1991-, Cwlth Bank of Aust, 1991-96; Fndn Chan RMIT, 1992-95; Dir, DG Crane Holdings Ltd, 1993-; Chmn United Construction Grp Ltd, 1994-; Lord Mayor, Cty of Melbourne, 1996-. Publication: Evolution of Australian Management Style, 1997. Honours: AO, 1991; Vic of Yr, 1991. Memberships: Chmn, Bus Skills Assessment panel, Dept Immigration and Ethnic Affairs, 1992-96; Dir, Williamson Community Ldrshp Prog, 1992-; Pres, Asian Assn Mngmnt Orgs, 1995-; Hobbies: Football; Farming; Tennis. Address: 18 Chesterfield Avenue, Malvern, Vic 3144, Australia.

DEVOTTA Sukumar, b. 3 Apr 1948, Madras, India. Scientist. m. Linnet, 18 May 1978, 1 s, 1 d. Education: BTech, 1971; MTech, 1973; PhD, 1978; MSc, Univ Salford, England. Appointments: Lectr, Univ Madras, 1977-79; Snr Rsch Fell, Univ Salford, 1979-84; Asst Dir, 1984-91, Dpty Dir, 1991-, NCL, Pune. Publications: 1 tech book, 1 monograph, over 100 tech rsch pprs. Honour: USEPA Stratospheric Ozone Protection Awd, 1997. Memberships: Maharashtra Acady of Scis, fell; IIChemE, chmn, pune chapt. Hobbies: Music; International Travel. Address: DII 10 NCL Colony, Pune 411008, India.

DEXTER Barrie Graham, b. 15 July 1921, Aust. Retired. m. Judith McWalter Craig, 30 May 1950, 1 s, 2 d. Education: MA, Hons; DipEd, Melbourne, 1947. Appointments: Sch Tchr, Vic, 1940, 1947; 2/6 Commando Squadron, AIF, 1941-43; RAN, 1944-47; Dept of External Affairs, joined 1948; Arabic Studies, London and Lebanon, 1950-51; 3rd Sec, Cairo, 1951-53; 1st Sec, Karachi, 1956-58; WA, 1960-63; High Commnr, Accra, Ghana, 1963-64; Amb, Vientiane, Laos, 1964-68; Exec Mbr, Fed Cncl for Aboriginal Affairs, 1967-76; Estab Fed Off of Aboriginal Affairs, Dir, 1977-73, and Dept of Aboriginal Affairs, Sec, 1973-77; Amb to Yugoslavia, Romania and Bulgaria, 1977-80; High Commnr, Can and Commnr in Bermuda, 1980-83; Visng Fell, Austl Natl

Univ, 1984-87; Aesop Vol, Fedn of Micronesia, 1986; Vice Chmn, CARE Aust, 1987-95; Chmn, Chmn Emer, Fndn for Intl Trng for Third World Cos, Toronto, 1984-96. Creative Works include: Var articles and reports. Honour: CBE, 1981. Memberships include: Assoc Mbr, Austl Inst of Aboriginal and Torres Strait Islander Studies. Hobbies: Music; Gardening; Walking. Address: 11/79 Collings Street, Pearce, ACT 2607, Australia.

DHALL Dharam Pal, b. 8 Dec 1937, Meru, Kenya. Surgeon; Businessman. m. Dr T Z Dhall, 28 Dec 1973, 1 s, 1 d. Education: MBChB, 1961; FRCS, 1965; PhD, 1967; MD, 1968; FRACS, 1994. Appointments: Snr Registrar, Lectr, Univ Aberdeen; Prof of Surg, Univ Nairobi; Snr Cnslt Surg, Canberra Hosp, Aust. Publications: Approx 200 pprs and presentations in profl jrnls; Sai Awareness Programme, 1992; Sai Vision Programme, 1993; Divinity and Love, 1993; Dharma for Integrated Living, 1997; Stepping Stones to Peace, 1998; My Work is My Blessing, 1999. Honours: Hallett Awd, Roy Coll Surg; MD w Commendation. Memberships: Dir, Salkya Sai Inst of Educ; Natl Coordinator for Spiritual Educ, 1990-98; Natl Spiritual Coordinator, Sathiya Sai Orgn, 1994-96. Hobbies: Flute; Harmonium; Vocal singing; Golf; Chess. Address: PO Box 697, Queanbayan, NSW 2620, Australia.

DHANABALAN Suppiah, b. 8 Aug 1937. Politician. m. Tan Khoon Hiap, 1963, 1 s, 1 d. Education: Victoria Sch; Univ of Malaya Singapore. Appointments: Asst Sec Min of Fina, 1960-61; Snr Indl Economist Dep Dir - Ops and Fin - Econ Dev Bd, 1961-68; VP Exec VP Dev Bank of Singapore, 1968-78; MP, 1976-; Snr Min of State Min of Natl Dev, 1978-79; Min of For Affairs, 1979-80; Min of For Affairs, 1980-88; Min for Culture, 1981-84; Min for Community Dev, 1984-86; Also Min for Natl Dev, 1987-92; With Singapore Indian Chamber of Com, 1992-; Min Min of Trade and Ind, 1992-93; Chmn Parameswara Holdings, 1994-; Snr Advsr Nuri Holdings - S - Pte Ltd, 1994-. Hobbies: Reading; Squash; Golf. Address: c/o Singapore Federal Chamber of Commerce and Industry, 47 Hill Street, 03-01 Commerce Building, Singapore 0617.

DHANAGARE Dattatraya, b. 11 June 1936, Washim, Maharashtra, India. Vice Chancellor. m. Nisha, 5 July 1962, 2 s. Education: BA, MA, Nagpur Univ; DPhil, Univ of Sussex. Appointments: Lectr in Sociol, Agra Univ, Inst of Socl Scis, 1961-68; Asst Prof of Sociol, IIT, Kanpur, 1968-77; Prof, Pune Univ, 1977-95; Vice Chan, Shivaji Univ, 1995-. Publications include: Agrarian Movements in Gandhian Politics; Peasant Movements in India 1920-1950; Rural Transformation in India - Challenges and Prospects; Themes and Perspectives in Indian Sociology. Honours include: Shrimati Jayantibai Kolte Silver Medal; N N Wazalwar Gold Medal; Prin V K Joag Awd as Best Tchr in Pune Univ, 1995. Hobbies: Indian classical music; Reading history; Biographics. Address: Shivaji University, Kolhapur 416 004, India.

DHANORKAR Savita, b. 15 Nov 1958, Pune. Scientist. m. Saurabh, 28 Nov 1982, 2 s. Education: BS, 1978; MSc, 1980; DSc, 1994. Appointments: Software Engr, 1980-82; Scientist, 1982-. Publications: Measurement of Mobility and Concentration of all Atmospheric Ions with a single apparatus, 1991; Relations Between Electrical Conductivity and Small Ions in the Presence of Intermediate and Large Ions in the Lower Atmosphere, 1992; Diurnal Variations of the Mobility Spectrum of Ions and Size Distribution of Fine Aerosols in the Atmosphere, 1993; Diurnal and Seasonal Variations of the Small Intermediate and Large Ion Concentrations and their Contributions to Polar Conductivity, 1993; Many other pbls. Honours: IITM Silver Jubilee Awd, Best Sci Contbn in Atmospheric Sci, 1992. Memberships: Indian Aerosol Sci and Technol Assoc; India Meteor Soc. Hobbies: Reading; Traveling. Address: Indian Institute of Tropical Meterology, Dr Homi Bhabha Road, Parhan Pune 411008, India.

DHARMASAKTI Sanya, b. 5 Apr 1907, Bangkok, Thailand. Lawyer; Judge. m. Panga Benjati, 1935, 2 s. Education: Bangkok; London. Appointments include: Fmr

Chf Justice Thailand; Fmr Rector, Thammasat Univ; PM, 1973-75; Pres, Privy Cncl, 1976; World Fell'ship Buddhists, 1984-88. Publications: Law Books. Membership: Thai Bar (Barister at Law). Listed in: International Who's Who. Hobbies: Gardening; Reading. Address: 15 Sukhumvit Road, Soi 41, Bangkok, Thailand.

DHULAYMI Talal, b. 10 June 1951, Dammam, Saudi Arabia. Marketing and Advertising Executive. m. Eman Al Fadll, 14 June 1979, 1 s. Education: MBA Mktng, Univ of Portland, OR, USA, 1978. Memberships: IAA; GCCAA; Jeddah Chmbr of Comm; Jt Media Cttee KSA; Saudi Cncl of Chmbr of Comm. Address: PO Box 3218, Jeddah 21471, Saudi Arabia.

DHUR Dipankar, b. 30 Jan 1972, Calcutta, India. Businessman; Publisher. Education: Grad, Polit Sci, Calcutta Univ. Appointment: 1991. Publications: In medl fields. Memberships: Fedn of Indian Publrs. Hobbies: Music; Travelling. Address: Academic Publishers, 12/1A, Bankim Chatterjee Street, Calcutta 700 073, India.

DHYANI Pushpa, b. 11 Aug 1938. Teacher. m. S N Dhyani, 12 Feb 1959. Education: BA, Agra Univ, UP; MA, Lucknow Univ, UP; MLibSci, Varanasi Univ, UP; PhD, Jaipur Univ, Rajasthan. Appointments: JTC, 1965; STC, 1967; Lectr, 1972; Assoc Prof, 1986-. Publications: Classification Schemes and Indian Libraries, 1985, 1989; Books on DDC, 1985, 1994; Information Science, 2 books, 1984, 1994; Library Classification: Theory and Principles, 1998; Pustkalay Vargikaran (Hindi), 1999; Many articles in profl jrnls in India and abroad. Honour: 1st Indian woman to gain a PhD in Lib Sci. Memberships: Indian Lib Assn; IASLIC; Indian Assn of Lib Sci Tchrs; Intl Soc for Knowledge Org. Listed in: Who's Who in Knowledge Classification; Eminent Personalities of the 20th Century. Hobby: Music. Address: 253 Panditwari, Phase II, Dehradun 248007, Uttar Pradesh, India.

DI BARTOLOMEO Joseph Raymond, b. 31 Aug 1937, NY, USA. Physician. m. Maxine, 3 s. Education: All Hallows Inst, Bronx, NY, 1951-55; BS, St John's Univ, Jamaica, NY, 1959; DMed, Georgetown Medl Sch, Washington, DC, 1963. Appointments: Attng Otolaryngologist, 1968; Chmn, Dept of Otolaryngology Active Staff, 1968; Rsch Assoc, 1969; Sec, 1974-75; Medl Dir, 1975; Asst Clinl Prof, 1976; UCLA Medl Staff, 1976; Instr, 1976-85; Cnslt, 1982; Sec, Treas, 1982-86; Chmn, Dept of Otolaryngology, 1983-85; Chf of Staff, 1986-87; Chmn, Nominating Cttee and Immediate Past Chf of Staff, 1988-95; VP, Triological Soc, 1991; Pres, Amn Neurotology Soc, 1993-94; Clinl Prof, Univ of CA, 1994; SB ENT Reps CMA's Advsry Panel, 1995; Mbr, Exec Cttee, CA Otolaryngology, 1995; Cnslt, Amn Acady of Otolaryngology, 1995; Pres, Amn Nurotology Soc, 1995-96; Past Pres, ANS, 1996-97; Mbr, Bd of Dirs, Proper Meniere Soc, 1996-99. Creative Works: Many Publs. Honours: Outstndng Tchng Awd; Hon Awd Recipient. Memberships: Amn Cncl of Otolaryngology; Amn Auditory Soc; Amn Soc for Laser Med and Surg; Undersea Medl Soc; Amn Neurotology Soc; The Prosper Meniere Soc; The Triological Soc; Many ors. Hobbies: Ear Diseases; Eustachian Tube Disorders. Address: 2420 Castilo Street, Santa Barbara, CA 93105-4346, USA.

DIAS Ivan Cornelius, b. 14 Apr 1936, Mumbai, India. Archbishop of Bombay. Education: Studies at Pontifical Ecclesiastical Acady in Rome, 1961-64; Doct in Canon Law, Lateran Univ, Rome, 1964. Appointments: Ordained a Priest in Mumbai, 1958; Vatican Secretariat of State, preparing vis of His Holiness Pope Paul VI to Mumbai, Intl Eucharistic Congress, 1964; Sec, Apostolic Nunciatures in Denmark, Sweden, Norway, Iceland, Finland, Indonesia, Madagascar, Reunion, Comores, Mauritius, 1965-73; Chf of Desk, Vatican Secretariat of State for USSR, Baltic States, Bielorussia, Ukraine, Poland, Bulgaria, China, Vietnam, Laos, Cambodia, The Philippines, S Africa, Namibia, Lesotho, Swaziland, Zimbabwe, Ethiopia, Rwanda, Burundi, Uganda, Zambia, Kenya, Tanzania, 1973-82; Apptd Titular Archbish, Rusubisir and Apostolic Pro-Nuncio to Ghana, Togo, Benin, 1982-87; Episc Ordination in St Peter's Basilica in Rome, 1982; Apostolic Pro-Nuncio, S Korea, 1987-91;

Apostolic Nuncio, Albania, 1991-97; Apptd Archbish of Bombay, 1997; Installed as Archbish of Bombay, 1997. Address: 21, Nathalal Parekh Marg, Mumbai 400 001, Maharashtra, India.

DiCAPRIO Leonardo, b. 11 Nov 1974, Hollywood. Actor. Films incl: Critters III, 1991; Poison Ivy, 1992; This Boy's Life, 1993; What's Eating Gilbert Grape, 1993; The Quick and the Dead, 1995; The Basketball Diaries, 1995; William Shakespeare's Romeo and Juliet, 1996; Titanic, 1996; Man in the Iron Mask, 1997; The Beach, 1999. TV series incl: Parenthood, 1990; Growing Pains, 1991. Address: c/o AMG, 9465 Wilshire Boulevard, Beverly Hills, CA 90212, USA.

DICKERSON Robert Henry, b. 30 Mar 1924, Sydney, Australia. Artist. m. Jennifer, 8 June 1971, 3 d. Appointments: RAF, Borneo, New Guinea. Publications: Against the Tide (biography), 1995. Honours: Clint Prize; Merit Awd, Chinese Arts Min. Membership: Scottish Hist Assn, Sydney, pres, 1988-91. Hobbies: Horse Racing; Jogging; Farming; Environment. Address: 34 Queen Street, Woollahra, NSW 2025, Australia.

DICKINSON Harley Rivers, b. 20 Oct 1938. m. Nicola Payne, 28 Nov 1964, 3 s, 1 d. Education: GLG Coll; Grad ASOPA, Mosman, NSW; KSJ; AAIM. Appointments: Dept of Admin PNG Pub Serv Dept, 1958-70; Patrol Offr, CI Advsr, Dist Offr, Offr, RPNG Constabulary, Off of Programming and Coord, 1970-71; Exec Offr, Ok Tedi and Bougainville Copper Projects, 1970-71;; Chmn, Highlands Dist Land Disputes Cttee, 1971-76; Res Magistrate, Visng Justice, Coroner Boroko, Popondetta and Mendi Dist Crts, Dist Supvsng magistrate for Sthn Highlands Prov, Exec Offr, Assn Sec, Vic Chamber of Mfrs, 1976-80; Tstee, Ch of England Trusts Corp, 1980-81; Sec to Archbish in CI Annual Synod and Diocesan Mngmt Cttees; Registrar, Ch of England, Diocese of Melbourne; Sec of Local r, VFGA; Intl Police Assn; Mbr, Order of St John of Jerusalem, Austl Inst of Mngmt, United Servs Inst; MLA (Li) for S Barwon, Vic, 1982-92; Deakin Univ Cl, 1984, Joint All-Party Salinity Cttee, 1984, Mbbr Vic Govt Joint House Cttee, 1985; Pres, Geelong Community Orchestra. Creative Works: Private Art Exhibition of 40 acrylic paintings, 1999. Hobbies: Tennis; Antiques; Painting: GLG Fine Art School; Cellist: Geelong Community Orchestra; Eco Tourism; Farming. Address Mount Pleasant, Bannockburn, Vic 3331, Australia.

DICKINSON James Arthur, b. 4 Oct 1950. Professor of Family Medicine. m. 2 s, 2 d. Education: MBBS, Univ of Qld, 1973; Coll of Family Physns, CCFP, 1978; PhD, Newcastle, 1979; FRACGP, 1990. Appointments: Res Princess Alexander Hosp, Brisbane, 1974-75; McMaster Univ Med Cntr, 1976-78; Fell, McGill Univ, 1978-80; Fell, Cmnty Med, Newcastle Univ, NSW, 1980-84; Lectr in Gen Prac, 1984-90; Med Advsr, Gen Prac Br, Dept of Health, Canberra, 1990-94; Prof of Gen Practice, Fremantle Hosp, Univ of WA, 1995-97; Prof of Family Med, Chinese Univ of hong Kong, 1997-. Publications: Ed, Guidelines for Preventive Activities in General Practice, 2nd ed, 1993, 3rd ed, 1994, 4th ed, 1996. Address: Department of Community and Family Medicine, 4/F Lek Yuen Health Centre, Shatin, NT, Hong Kong.

DICKMAN Jorge Camet, b. 23 Sept 1927, Lima, Peru. Minister of Economy and Finance. Education: Natl Engl Univ of Lima. Appointments: Civ Engr, Fndn Mngr, J and J Camet Engrs SA; Pres, Assn of Constrn Engrs of Peru; Pres, Peruvian Constrn Cncl; Pres, Natl Confed of Pvte Entrepreneurial Instns; Dir, num banking, fin and insurance firms; Pres, Pub Wrks Cncl of Lima; Pres, Pub Co for Commercialization of Flour, Oil and Fish; Consultative Cncl, Min of Housing and Constrn; Min of Ind, Com, Tourism and Integration, 1992. Address: Ministry of Economy and Finance, Jirón Junín 339 4, Lima, Peru.

DIJMARESCU Eugen, b. 11 Feb 1948. Economist; Diplomat. m. Gabriela, 5 Oct 1973, 1 d. Education: Dr, Econs, Acady Econs, Bucharest, Romania.

Appointments: Snr Rschr, Inst for World Econ, Bucharest, 1971-89; Min of State, Econ and Fin, Govt of Romania, 1990-91; Senator, Vice Speaker, Romanian Senate, 1992-94; Amb of Romania to Japan, 1994-. Publications: GSP and World Trade, 1978; Limits and Alternatives of Transition, 1990; The Road From State to Market, 1993. Memberships: Romanian Econ Soc; Romanian Assn for Intl Law and For Policy. Hobbies: Economics; Politics; Classical Music; Driving. Address: c/o Embassy of Romania, 3-16-19 Nishi Azabu, Minato-ku, Tokyo 106-0031, Japan.

DIMITRIC Radoslav, b. 4 May 1955, Loznica, Serbia. Mathematician; Translator. Education: BSCI, Univ Belgrade, Serbia, 1978; MSCI, 1980; PhD, Tulane Univ, USA, 1983. Appointments: Tchng Asst, Tulane Univ, USA, 1980-83; Lectr, Dublin Inst Tech, Ireland, 1985-87; Lectr, Univ of Exeter, Eng, 1987-89; Visng Prof, Univ of CA, 1989-90; Visng Schl, Stanford Univ, USA, 1990-92; Visng Prof, PA State Univ, 1992-93; Visng Prof, Rsch Assoc, Univ CA, 1993-. Creative Works: Over 30 publs in profl jrnls; Monograph, Slender Modules, Slender Rings. Honours: Grand Prix Young Math Rschrs; Magna Cum Laude; Prizes in maths Competitions. Memberships: Amn Math Soc; London Math Soc. Hobbies: Swimming; Fishing; Painting; Music; Singing. Address: University of California, Department of Mathematics, Berkeley, CA 94720, USA.

DIMSEY Ross Bernard, b. 10 Oct 1943, Melbourne, Aust. Film and Television Producer. m. Eve Seymour, 29 Sept 1967, 1 s, 1 d. Education: Hampton (Vic) HS, PC, MPS, Vic Pharm Coll. Appointments: Film Prodn Mngr and Dir, 1968-79; Chf Exec, Film, Vic, 1979-82; Film Prodr and Writer, 1982-86; Snr Exec Prodr, ABC TV Drama, 1986-88; Film Prodr and Writer, 1989-; Dir, Film Qld, 1994-97. Publications: The Naked Country, feature film, 1984; A Thousand Skies, tv series, 1985; Kangaroo, feature film, 1986; Warm Nights on a Slow Moving Train, feature film, 1990; Half a World Away (aka The Great Air Race), tv series. Honours: AFI, 1971; Penguin, 1972, Austl TV Soc, Best Documentary, 1973. Memberships: Screen Prodn Assn of Aust; Austl Writers' Guild; Cinema Papers Bd. Address: Apt 4, 19 Oxlade Drive, New Farm, Qld 4005, Australia.

DINAMPO Eladio, b. 18 Feb 1944, Amlan, Negros Oriental, Philippines. Professor. m. Esther Espino, 13 Apr 1973, 1 s, 1 d. Education: MS; BD; BSE; AB; AA. Appointments: Assoc Prof V, Asst Prof I, Asst Prof III, Asst Prof VI; Mngr, DXMU; Print Media Spec, CMU-AEOP. Publications: Writer, Ed, CMU Press Release Bulletin, 1974-78; Auth, Communicating Effectively, 1994. Honours: Valedictorian Elem, 1958; Hon Mention, HS, 1963; Class Hons, BD, 1972; Univ Schlr Coll Schlr, PLB, 1979-80; DXMU Awd of Dist, CMU, 1989. Memberships: Comms for Rural Dev; Philippine Assn of Comm Educrs; UP Alumni Assn. Hobbies: Reading; Writing; Sightseeing. Address: Central Mindamao University, College of Agriculture, University Town, Bukidnon, Philippines.

DINCERLER M Vehbi, b. 2 Aug 1940 Gziantep. Poltician. m. 3 s, 1 d. Education: Dept of Engr Istanbul Tech Univ; Bus Inst Istanbul Univ; Graduate Sch Univ of Syracuse NY. Appointments: Worked for State Plng Org; Joined Proj Studies for Turkey at World Bank; Studied economy of Ireland; Acad at Middle East Tech Univ Gaziantep Campus; Min of Educ Yth and Sports, 1983-85; Min of State, 1985-87; Chmn Natl Assembly For Rels Cttee, 1988-90; Min of State, 1989-91. Memberships: Mbr Natl Assembly, 1983-; Mbr Constl Cttee, 1991-; Mbr N Atlantic Assembly; Mbr Motherland Party. Hobbies: Music; Socl activities. Address: Ahmet Hasim Cad 67/U Dikmen, Ankara, Turkey 06460.

DING Dajun, b. 28 Apr 1923, Anhui Prov. Educator. m. Fan Qi, 16 Apr 1944, 2 s, 4 d. Education: BEng. Appointments: Univ Asst, 1948; Lectr, 1953; Prof, 1978; Doctoral Supvsr, China State Cncl, 1981; Retd. Creative Works: 37 Chinese Text, Ref Books, 1952-97; 265 Chinese Tech Pprs, 1953-98; 140 Pprs, 10 For Langs; 60 in Procs of Inter Conf; 80 in Intl Jrnls, 1982-98. Honours:

Natl Sci Cong Prize, 1978; Natl Prize of Natural Sci, 1982; 1-3 Degs of 8 Prizes, Prov and Ministries, 1981-96. Memberships: China CV Engr Soc; IABSE; INCERC; NY Acady of Sci; CTBUH; HM of FASH. Hobbies: Old Chinese Poems; Trad Chinese Painting; Calligraphy. Address: Civil Engineering College, Nanjing Inst of Technology, Nanjing, Jiangsu, 210096, China.

DING Guangen, b. Sep 1929 Wuxi Co Jiangsu Prov. State Offic. Education: Jiaotong Univ of Shanghai. Appointments: Joined CCP, 1956; Dep Sec-Gen Standing Commn NPC, 1983-85; Min of Railways, 1985-88; Vice-Min State Plng Commn, 1988; Dir Taiwan Affairs Off, 1988; Hd United Front Work Dept of CCP, 1990-; Sec Secr 14th CCP Cntr Cttee, 1992; Hd CCP Propaganda Dept, 1992-; Hd Cntr Ldng Grp for Propaganda and Thought, 1994-. Memberships: Mbr 12th CCP Cntr Cttee, 1985-87; Mbr 13th CCP Cntr Cttee, 1987-92; Alt mbr Polit Bur, 1987; Mbr, 1992-; Mbr 15th CCP Cntr Cttee, 1997-. Address: Central Committee of the Chinese Communist Party, Zhongnanhai, Beijing, People's Republic of China.

DING Henggao, b. 1931 Nanjing Co Jiangsu Prov. Politician; Scientist. m. Nie Lili. Education: Nanjing Uni; USSR. Appointments: Min of State Commn of Sci Tech and Ind for Natl Def, 1985; Party Cttee Sec, 1989-; Rank of Lt-Gen PLA, 1988; Gen, 1994; Min in charge of Commn of Sci Tech and Ind for Natl Def, 1993-96. Memberships: Mbr 13th CCP Cntr Cttee, 1989-92; Mbr 14th CCP Cntr Cttee, 1992-; Mbr Natl Ldng Grp for Sci and Tech Chinese Acady of Eng. Address: c/o Commission of Science, Technology and Industry for National Defence, Beijing, People's Republic of China.

DING Jiaan, b. 19 Nov 1939, Shanghai, China. Thoracic Surgeon. m. Lin Qiaoyun, 1 Sept 1965, 1 s, 1 d. Education: Medl Dr, Shanghai Second Medl Coll, 1961. Appointments: Chf, Thoracic Surg, Dept of Shanghai First Pulmonology Hosp; Chf, Thoracic Surg Rsch Inst of Shanghai Medl Univ. 72 medl articles in jrnls, 1976-98. Honours: 2nd Prize, Hollow Fiber Oxygenator, 1984; 3rd Prize, Niti Self Expanding Stent for Severe Trachea Stenosis, 1994; Lung Volume Reduction Surg for COPD, by Shanghai Sci and Technol Cttee, 1997. Memberships: Dir, Chinese Assn of Biomedl Engrng and Artificial Organ, 1992; Cttee Mbr, Chinese Assn of Organ Transplantation, 1997. Hobbies: Music; Sport. Address: 507, Zheng Min Road, Shanghai 200433, China.

DING Wen-Long, b. 31 Dec 1952, Shanghai, China. m. Luo Na, 1 Feb 1980, 2 d. Education: BM, Undergrad Stdy, Jiangxi Medl Coll; MSc, Grad Stdy, China Acady of Trad Chinese Med, Beijing. Appointments: Asst Lectr, Assoc Prof, Prof, Jiangxi Medl Coll, 1980-99; Dir, Dept of Anatomy, Jiangxi Nedl Coll, 1992-99; Dpty Dir, Fac of Basis Medl Sci, Jiangxi Medl Coll, 1994-98; Dean, Jiangxi Medl Coll, 1998-. Publications: The Nervous Pathways of Angina Pectoris and Refered Pain, 1983; The Segmental Distribution of the Afferent Neurons Traversing the Stellate Ganglion of the Cat, 1985; Regeneration of Peripheral Nerve in Heterogenic Nerve Graft, 1992; Effect of Coirradiation of Nerve Regeneration in Heterograft Nerve, 1994; The Regeneration of Motor end-plate in Denervated Skeletal Muscle after Heterogenic Nerve Graft, 1994; Influence on Nerve Regeneration in the Use of Heterograft Treaged; Retrograde Transportation of HRP in Regenerating Nerve after Transplant with the Heterograft Nerve, 1996; Effect of Tripterygium Wilfordii Hook on Nerve Regeneration After Heterografting, 1999. Memberships: Cncl Mbr, China Soc for Anatomical Scis; Vice Dir, Educl Commn of Chinese Soc for Anatomical Scis; Cncl Mbr, Neuroanatomy Commn of Chinese Soc for Anatomical Scis; Acta Anatomical Sinica; Chinese Jrnl of Anatomy. Hobbies: Music; Football; Swim; Trav. Address: Department of Anatomy, Jiangxi Medical College, Nanchang 330006, China.

DING Xiaxi, b. 25 May 1928, Hunan, China. Research. m. Luo Peizhu, 5 Jan 1957, 3 d. Education: Grad, Dept of Maths, Wuhan Univ. Appointments: Rsch Prof, 1978-; Acad, Chinese Acady of Scis, 1991-. Publications: Over 90 pprs, 4 books, 3 popular sci publns. Honours: 2nd

Class Prize, Natl Sci Prizes, China, 1989; 1st Class Prize, Chinese Acady of Scis, 1988; 2nd Class Prize, Chinese Acady of Scis, 1980; Awd, Natl Sci Conf, 1978. Memberships: Standing Mbr, Cttee of Chinese Soc of Systems Engrng. Hobby: Mathematics. Address: Institute of Applied Mathematics, Academia Sincia, Beijing 100080, China.

DING Yuhua, b. 30 Oct 1948, Wendeng, Weihai, China. Enterprise Management. m. Fufeng Wang, 30 Dec 1975, 1 s, 1 d. Education: Grad, Econ Dept, Shandong Univ, 1987; Grad, Indl Econ Dept, Grad Sch of Chinese Acady of Socl Scis, 1996. Appointments: Techn, Rongcheng Cty Chem Plant, Shandong, 1969-75; Staff, Roncheng Cty Plng Cttee, 1975-76; Chf of Prodn Sect, Rongcheng Cty Chem Ind Bur, 1976-80; Econ, Rongchen Rubber Factory, 1981-85; Dir, Rongcheng City Chem Ind Bur, 1987-89; Dir, Rongcheng Cty Econ Commn, 1989-90; Gen Mngr, Shandong Weihai Rubber Indl Grp Corp, 1991-92; Pres, Shandong Tyre Fac, 1991-92; Snr Econ, Pres, Shandong Tyre Factory, 1992-97, Mngr, Weihai Chem Ind Bur, 1992-97, Gen Mngr, Shandong Weihai Rubber Ind Grp Commn, 1992-97; Snr Intl Commercialist, Mngr.Weihai Chem Ind Bur, Gen Mngr, Shandong Weihai Rubber Indl Grp Corp, Chmn, Dirs Bd and Gen Mngr, Shandong Triangle Grp Co Ltd, 1997-. Publications: Building Up the Profit into the Center of Management Mechanism to Improve Economic Operation Quality, 1995; How to Make Use of Personnel for Enterprises, 1996; The Thinking and Practice to Revive the State Owned Enterprises, 1997; Carring Out the Right Development Strategy to Enhance One's Ability in Commercial Wars and Market Competition; Marching On Towards to the World by Quality. Honours include: Model Worker, Shandong Prov, 1992; Govt Allowance, 1993; Natl Model Wrkr, 1995. Memberships: China Natl Tyre Br Assn; Bd Dir, Beijing Chem Ind Univ; Vice Chmn, Shandong Chem Ind Mag; Prof, Shendong Univ Qingdao Cheml Indl Insts. Hobbies: Reading; Music; Table Tennis. Address: No 56, Qingdao (M) Road, Weihai City, Shandong Province, China.

DINH Gia Khanh, b. 25 Dec 1925, Thai Binh, Viet Nam. Social Sciences Researcher. m. Dac Quy, 8 June 1956, 3 s, 1 d. Education: Univ of Hanoi, 1941-46. Appointments: Prof, Univ of Hanoi, 1956-83; Dir, Inst of Folk Culture, 1983-86; Ed-in-Chf, Review of Folk Culture, 1983-91; Prof, High Rank Rschr, Natl Cntr for Socl Scis & Hums. Publications: 12; Pres, Editl Bd for the compilation and publ of the Gen Anthology of Vietnamese literature (Chu tich Hôi dong biên tâp Bô Tông tâp hoc Viêt Nam), 51 vols publd - 1997; Over 100 articles and pprs in var natl and intl sci and cultural reviews. Honours: Ho Chi Minh Prize for Scis and techniques, highest awd granted to outstndng scientists and schls in Vietnam. Address: National Center for Social and Human Sciences, 36 Hang Chuoi, Hanoi, Vietnam.

DINTE David Ian, b. 29 May 1962, Sydney, Aust. Company Director. m. Judy, 30 June 1985, 2 s, 1 d. Education: BEC (Bachelor of Econs); LLB; Regd Solicitor, Supreme Crt of NSW. Appointments: Dir, Hopetown Spec Sch for Mildly Intellectually Handicapped Children; Dir, Sydney Jewish Mus; Austl Jewish Hist and the Holocaust. Hobbies: Jogging; Family. Address: PO Box 109, Double Bay, 1360, Australia.

DIPLOCK Jane, b. 26 June 1949, Australia. Lawyer. m. Phillip Meyer. Education: BA, hons; LLB; Dip, Educn; Dip, Intl Law. Appointments: Chf Mngr, Westpac Banking Corp; Dir Gen, DTEC; Mngng Dir, Tate NSW; ASIC Region Cmmnr. Memberships: Fell, Natl Inst of Pub Admin; Pres, YWCA Sydney; Chair, Womens Coll Cncl, Univ Sydney. Address: 26 Avenue Road, Hunters Hill 2110, Australia.

DISHION Catherine Diane, b. 10 Aug 1947, Los Angeles, USA. President. m. Don, 10 Dec 1998, 1 s. Education: BA, Bus Admin. Publications: National Career Connections Outplacement Guide. Honour: Bus Person of the Yr, 1998. Memberships: Human Resources Assn; Univ Clup-Yp. Hobbies: Scuba Diving; Boating. Address:

1300 Santa Barbara Street, Santa Barbara, CA 93101, USA.

DIVALL Richard S, b. 9 Sept 1945, Sydney, NSW, Aust. Opera Conductor. Appointments: Debut, Sydney; Prodr, Austl Brdcsting Commn, 1962-70; Musical Dir, Qld Opera Co, 1971-; Vic State Opera, 1972-96; Assoc, Fac of Music, Artist-in-Res, Queen's Coll, Artist-in-Res, Queen's Coll, Univ of Melbourne; Num recdngs for ABC; Assoc Prof, Music, Univ of Melbourne, 1991-; Guest Conductor, Aust Ballet, 1994-; Prin Res Conductor, Opera Aust, 1996-. Publications: Complete works of Linger, 1971; Symphonies, Cipriani Pottrer, Samuel Wesley, 1980; Edited works by Gluck, Rameau, Handel, Wesley; Contbr, var profl jrnls. Honours: Churchill Fell, 1975; French Govt Schlsp, 1972; Aust Cncl Schlsp, 1979; OBE, 1981; Amn Inst of Verdi Studies, 1982; Chevalier, Order of St Lazarus, France, 1986; Fell, Queen's Coll, Univ of Melbourne, 1987; DMus (Hon Causa), Sao Paolo, Brazil, 1987; Fell, Roy Numismatic Soc, 1985; Fell, Roy Asiatic Soc, 1985; Dame Joan Hammond Awd, 1968; Hon Doc Litt, Monash, 1992; Commendatore al Merito, 1989; Kt of Magistral Grace, Order of Malta, 1990; Tracy Maund Fell, Roy Woman's Hosp, 1996. Memberships: Austl Club; Roy Dart Yacht Club; Chmn Marshall-Hall Trust; Chmn, Sylvia Fisher Schlshp. Listed in: Who's Who in Australia; Debretts; Who's Who of Musicians. Hobbies: History; Charity work. Address: 301 Arcadia, 228 The Avenue, Parkville, Vic, Australia 3052.

DIX Belinda Louise, b. 6 Nov 1964, S Aust, Aust. Conference Director, Hills Christian Life Centre. Education: BEd, Dip of Tchng. Appointments: Estab and Mngr, One Vision Dance Co (and dancer), 1987-93; Acct, Westpac Banking Corp, WPC, 1993; Mngr, Grad Recruitment, WBC, 1994; Proj Mngr, Workforce Diversity, WBC, 1995; Conf Dir, Hills CLC, 1995-. Honours: Rotary Yth Ldrshp Awd, 1984; Rotary Yth Merit Awd, 1985. Memberships: Austl Inst of Bankers, 1989-95; Meetings Ind Assn of Aust, 1997-98. Hobbies: Theatre; Dance; Singing; Fitness training; Reading autobiographical or biographical works. Address: 2A Brokenwood Place, Cherrybrook, NSW 2126, Australia.

DIXIT Jyotindranath, b. 8 Jan 1936 Madras. Diplomatist. m. Vijaya Sundaram, 1958, 3 s, 2 d. Education: Univ of Delhi. Appointments: Served in different capacities in Indian Embs in Mexico, Chile, Bhutan, Japan, Aust, 1958-69; Served at Min of External Affairs dealing with China, Pakistan and UN Affairs, 1961-63, 1969-72; First Amb - acting - to Bangladesh, 1972-75; Min Indian Emb WA USA, 1975-78; Spokesman on For Pol Govt of India, 1978-82; Amb to Afghanistan, 1982-85; Amb to Pakistan, 1989; High Commnr to Sri Lanka, 1985-89; Amb to Afghanistan, 1989-91; For Sec to the Govt of India, 1991-94. Publication: Self in Autumn - poems - 1982. Hobbies: Reading; Swimming; Rowing; Hiking. Address: AJH-102-A, Aryun rang, DLF Dunkirk Enclave phase 1, Gurgaon-122002, Haryana, India.

DIXON Donald Douglas, b. 19 Aug 1929, Chester, Eng. Professional Engineer. m. Dr Kathleen Nelson, 14 Dec 1973, 2 s. Education: BSc; Dipl Metall; MBA; MSc; Registered Profl Engr, PE. Appointments: Engr, Caltech; Tech Offr, Austl Atomic Energy Commn; Monitor, UK Atomic Energy. Publications: Technical pprs. Honours: War Medal, Rhine Army and Service Medals, 1945. Memberships: Brit United Servs Club, Exec Cttee, LA. Hobbies: Target shooting; Movies; Borzoi dogs. Address: 1795 Oakdale Street, Pasadena, CA 91106-3569, USA.

DIXON Joan Maureen, b. 4 May 1937, Hobart, Australia. Biologist. Education: BSc, Tas, 1958; BSc, hons, Tas, 1960. Appointments: Demonstrator, Zoology, Univ Qld, 1960; Snr Tchng Fell, Monash Univ, 1961-64; Curator, Natl Mus of Vic, 1966; Curator of Mammals, 1978, Snr Curator, Mammals, 1985, Mus of Vic. Publications: Reproductions of Gould's Mammals of Australia, 1973; Donald Thomsons Mammals and Fishes of Northern Australia, 1985. Honours: Whitley Book Awd, 1985; Rsch Assoc, Hist and Philos of Sci, Univ Melbourne, 1982-. Memberships: Soc for Marine Mammal; Amn Soc of Mammal; Aust Mammal Soc; RSA;

Roy Soc of Vic; Austl Soc of Auths. Hobbies: Swimming; Gardening; Cycling; Reading. Address: 2A Ozone Avenue, Beaumaris, Victoria 3193, Australia.

DO Muoi, b. 1917 Hanoi. Politician. Appointments: Joined movement against French colonial rule, 1936; Imprisoned by French; Escaped in 1945 and took part in anti-Japanese uprising in Ha Dong Prov; Polit and mil ldr in provs of Red River delta during struggle against French, 1951-54; Dep to Natl Ass 2nd 4th 5th 6th 7th and 8th Legislatures; Min of Com, 1969; Dep PM and Min of Bldg, 1976-87; Vice-Chmn Cncl of Mins in charge of Econ, 1987-; Sec-Gen Cntr Cttee CPV, 1987-; PM, 1988-91; Vice-Chmn Natl Def Cncl, Dec 1989; Sec Gen CPV, 1991-98. Honours: Order of the Oct Revolution, USSR, 1987; Sev Vietnamese decorations. Memberships: Alt mbr Cntr Cttee Communist Party of Vietnam, 1955-60; Mbr, 1960-; Alt mbr Polit Bur CPV, 1976-82; Mbr Polit Bur CPV, 1987-. Address: Communist Party of Vietnam, 1 Hoang Van Thu, Hanoi, Vietnam.

DOCHERTY Derrick John, b. 5 Oct 1934, Scotland. Accountant; Company Director. m. Barbara Jean Johnson, 10 Mar 1962, 1 s, 3 d. Education: Qualified Acct, 1959; Cost Acct, 1960. Appointments: Joined IBM Aust, 1961; Dir, IBM Aust Ltd, 1968-90; Chmn, IBM Aust Credit, 1983-90, Chmn, Legal & Gen Aust Ltd, 1996-98; Dir, 1987 Chmn, Hannover Life of Australasia Ltd, 1994; Dir, Burns, Philp & Co Ltd, 1991-97; Coal & Allied Inds Ltd, 1991; GRW Property Ltd, 1993-96; Perm Tstee Co Ltd, 1991-97; Ricegrowers Co-op Ltd, 1987; Rice Mktng Bd for the State of NSW, 1987; Ernst & Young Ins Advsry Bd, 1990; Homecare Servs Advsry Bd, 1995. Memberships: Fell, Austl Soc of Cert Practising Accts; Fin Execs Inst of Aust; Hon Tstee, Cttee for Econ Devel of Aust. Hobbies: Rowing (NSW 1958); Golf (Mbr, Pennant Hills Golf Club); Gardening; Mbr, Australia Club (Sydney). Address: PO Box 672, Pennant Hills, NSW 2120, Australia.

DOCHERTY James Cairns, b. 1 Aug 1949, Gosford, NSW, Aust. Australian Federal Government. m. Kerry Anne Watson, 23 Mar 1991, 1 d. Education: BA, Univ of Newcastle, NSW, 1972; MA, 1974; PhD, 1978, Austl Natl Univ. Publications: Newcastle: The Making of an Australian City, 1983; Historical Dictionary of Australia, 1992, 1998; Historical Dictionary of Organized Labour, 1996; Historical Dictionary of Socialism, 1997. Hobbies: Classical numismatics; Manual labour. Address: 59 Devonport Street, Lyons, ACT, Australia 2606.

DODDS Gregory Ronald, b. 17 Sept 1947, Perth, W Aust. Government Official. Education: BA, Austl Natl Univ; BA (Mil), Roy Mil Coll, Duntroon. Appointments: Offr, Austl Army, 1969-79; Dir, Aust-Japan Fndn, 1979-83; Spec Min of State, 1983-85; Snr Task Commnr, Tokyo, 1986-90; Dpty Hd of Mission, 1990-91; Exec Gen Mngr, Austrade NE Asia, Austl Emb, Tokyo, 1992-. Hobbies: Tennis; Swimming; Reading. Address: Australian Embassy, 2-1-14 Mita, Minato-Ku, Tokyo, Japan 108-8361.

DODDS Raymond Stewart, b. 19 Jan 1922. Managing Director. m. Joan Mallows, 2 Feb 1946, 2 s, 1 d. Education: BEc, Sydney Univ; MA, Univ of IL, USA. Appointments: Cartographer, NSw Dept of Lands, 1938-41, 1946-50; 2nd AIF, 1941-46; Insp, 1950-58, Snr Insp, Dir, Indl Rels Div, Chf Insp, 1960-76, Pub Servs Bd; Rsch Assoc, Univ of IL, USA, 1958-59; Dir, NSW Dept of Decentralisation and Devel, 1973-74; Sec, NSW Cttee of Inquiry into State Taxation, 1975-76 Dpty Under-Sec, Dept of Lab and Ind, 1976-77; Under-Sec and Perm Hd, Dept of Indl Rels, NSW, 1977-82; Advsr, Austl Deleg to Intl Lab Conf, 1979; Mngng Dir, Burnmar Holdings Pty Ltd, 1982-. Hobbies: Golf; Swimming. Address: 12 Westminster Avenue, Dee Why, NSW 2099, Australia.

DOE Hidekazu, b. 26 Aug 1952, Japan. Researcher. m. Kazuyo, 27 Nov 1983, 3 s. Education: DSc, Kyoto Univ. Appointments: Rsch Assoc, 1980; Lectr, 1993; Assoc Prof, 1998. Publication: Ppr in profl jrnl. Membership: Cheml Soc, Japan, 1976. Hobbies: Tennis;

Audio. Address: 356-1 Matoba, Koryo-cho, Kitakatsuragi-gun, Nara 635-0802, Japan.

DOGAN Husnu, b. 1944 Malatya. Politician. m. 1 child. Education: Dept of Constrn Middle East Tech Univ; Proj Eng with State Electricity Bd; Rschr later Dir For Capital Dept State Plng Org; Spec Advsr to Min of Agric Rsch Plng Co-ord and Dir-Gen; Worked for State Procurement Off; Co-ord in Turkish automobile ind; Min of Agric Forestry and Rural Affairs, 1983-89; Min of Def, 1990-91. Address: Tarim, Orman ve Koyisleri Bakanligi, Bakanliklar, Ankara, Turkey.

DOJE Cering, b. 1939 Xiahe Co Gansu Prov. Government Official. Appointments: Worked in Tibet, 1959; Joined CCP, 1960; Co magistrate in Tibet, 1962; First Sec Xigaze Municipality CCP, 1979-82; Vice-Chmn Tibet Autonomous Reg, 1983-85; Acting Admin Hd, 1986-88; Chmn, 1988-90; Dep for Tibet Autonomous Reg 7th NPC, 1988-; Vice-Min of Civ Affairs, 1990-93; Min, March 1993-; Vice-Chmn China Cttee Intl Decade for Natl Disaster Reduction; Dir Ldng Grp for Placement of Demobilized Army Offrs, 1993-; Dep Hd Ldng Grp for the Work of Supporting the Army Giving Preferential Treatment to the Families of Armymen and Martyrs supporting the Govt and Cherishing the People; Dep Hd State Cncl Ldng Grp on Boundary Delimitation. Memberships: Mbr Tibet Autonomous Reg CCP, 1974-90; Mbr Standing Cttee Tibet CCP, 1977-90; Mbr 8th NPC, 1993; Mbr 14th CCP Cntr Cttee, 1992-97; Mbr 15th CCP Cntr Cttee, 1997-. Address: Government of Xizang Autonomous Region, Lhasa City, People's Republic of China.

DOLLING (Charles Hoani) Scott, b. 11 Oct 1925, Adelaide, S Aust. Sheep Geneticist. m. Alwyn Mona King Gow, 12 May 1951, 2 s, 2 d. Education: Roseworthy Dip in Agric(RDA); MAgric Sci (MAgSc), Univ Adelaide. Offr-in-Charge, CSIRO Natl Field Stn, "Gilruth Plains", Cunnamulla, Qld; Prin Livestock Rsch Offr, S Austl Dept Agric; FAO appts in India and China. Publications: Poll Dorset Breeding, 1964; Breeding Merinos, (transl into Russian) 1970. Honours: OAM, 1990; Fell, ASAP, 1986; Fell, AAABG, 1995; Roseworthy Awd of Merit, 1991. Memberships: Austl Soc Animal Prodn, 1956- (Fedl Pres, 1974-76); Assn Advmnt Animal Breeding and Genetics, 1979-. Hobbies: The sheep gene scene; Languages; Family history; Breeding coloured sheep; History of Rome. Address: Box 74, McLaren Vale, SA 5171, Australia.

DOMINGUEZ James Thomas, b. 2 Dec 1938, Junee, NSW, Aust. Company Director. m. Suzanne, 16 Dec 1964, 3 s, 2 d. Education: Assumption Coll, Kilmore; Newman Coll; B Com, University of Melbourne; BA, University of Sydney. Appointments: A C Goode & Co, Melbourne & Sydney, 1962-76; Mbr, Melourne Stock Exchange/ASX, 1971-; Joint Fndng Ptnr, Dominguez & Barry, 1976; Dir, Samuel Montagu London, 1983-91; Chmn, Dominguez Barry Samuel Montagu Ltd, 1983-91; SBC Dominguez Barry Ltd, 1991-94; Ceedata Holdings Pty Ltd, 1996-; Next Fin Ltd, 1998- QuickSmart Online Pty Ltd, 1998-; Dir, Aero Space Tech Aust Pty Ltd, 1986-89; Paladin Aust, 1994-, Capral Aluminium, 1994- Nestle Aust, 1995-, Asea Brown Boveri Asia, 1996-, Scudder Stevens & Clark Aust, 1996, ETrade Aust, 1997, O'Connell Street Associates Pty Ltd, 1997-, PA Consuting, 1997-, Tat Hong Holdings (Singapore), 1997-, Wesfi, 1998; Mbr, C'wlth of Aust Trade Policy Advsry Cncl. 1996, Fuji Xerox Co (Japan) Asia Pacific Advsry Cncl, 1997. Honours: AM, 1987; Kt Sovereign Mil Order Malta, 1989; CBE, 1993; Fell, Senate Univ of Sydney, 1992-95; Pres and Knight, Austl Assn, Sovereign Mil Order of Malta, 1997; Grand Chambellan, Austl Commanderie of Confrerie des Chevaliers du Tastevin, 1998. Memberships: Chifley Adv Cl; Vigneron, Yering Station Vineyard; Dir, Chmn, St Vincents Hosp, Sydney; Adv Cl St Ignatius Coll Riverview; Bd Trustee, Powerhouse Mus, Sydney; Cl Kincoppal Rose Bay Convent. Hobbies: Reading; Fine Wine; Opera; Tennis; Sailing; Philately; Viticulture; Beach. Address: Hunters Hill, NSW, Australia.

DONALD J Robert, b. 24 Apr 1950, Bangalore, Karnataka State. Chairman, Local Boards of Education, SDA Schools and Colleges. Education: BLA, Spicer Mem Coll, Poona; MA, Philos and Psychol, Univ of Poona; Fell, Acady gen Educ, Acady of Higher Educ, manipal, Karnataka; PhD, Hum Psychol, Univ of Poona; DLitt, Hum Psychol (in progress). Appointments: Tchr, Spicer Mem Higher Sec Sch, Poona; Lectr (Philos and Psychol) Registrar, Asst Prof (Philos and Psychol), Spicer Mem Coll, Poona; Assoc Dir, Educ, S India Union of SDA's, Banglaore; Prin, SDA Jnr Coll, Thiruvalla, Kerala (Residential); Dir of Pub Affairs and Relig Liberty, S India Union of SDA's, Bangalore; Prin, Lowry Mem Jnr Coll and Tchr's Trng Inst, Bangalore (Residential); Dir of Educ, S India Union of SDA's, Bangalore. Publications: Pprs presented in seminars and confs; Articles; Books inclng: Understanding the SDA Church Organization in India: Trends and Conflicts; Critical Perspectives of Humanistic Psychology; A Study in Husserl, Heidegger and Binswanger. Honours include: Commendations, Indian Cncl of Socl Scientists, Amn Psychologists; Cited as Prominent Citizen of Karnataka, 1995; Citation of Merit Cert and Serv Pin, for 25 yrs of disting servs to cause of Educ; Man of Yr, ABI, 1999. Memberships include: Exec Cttee, S India Union of SDA; Ed-in-Chf, The Educator; VP, Karnataka Labor Welfare Fedn; Copr Mbr, Pub Rels Soc of India; Gen Sec, Karnataka Christian Political Forum; Bd Dirs, Lions Club of Bangalore; Life Mbr, Indian Red Cross Soc. Listed in: The International Directory of Distinguished Leadership, 1998. Address: 8/4 Spencer Road, Fraser Town, Bangalore 560 005, India.

DONALDSON Anita, b. 2 Jan 1948, Prien am Chiemsee, Germany. Academic. Education: Dip, Tchng, Adelaide Tchrs Coll, 1969; BA, Univ Adelaide, 1970; Assoc, Univ Adelaide, 1970; Dip of Educ, Univ London, Goldsmith's Coll, 1980; PhD, Laban Cntr for Movement and Dance, City Univ, London, 1993. Appointments: Physl Educ, Dance Spec Tchr, Henley HS, 1970; Lectr III, Physl Educ, Salisbury Tchrs Coll, 1971; Lectr I, Physl Educ, Salisbury Coll of Adv Educ, 1976; Lectr I, Dance Studies, S Austl Coll of Adv Educ (SACAE), 1982; Course Co-ord, Allied Arts, SACAE, 1984-85; Lectr I, Dance Perf, SACAE, 1987; Hd, Dept of Dance, SACAE, 1987-89; Acting Hd, Sch of Perf Arts, SACAE, 1990; Snr Lectr, Dance, Fac of Perf Arts, Univ Adelaide, 1991; Assoc Dean, Fac of Perf Arts, 1991; Assoc Dean, Fac of Perf Arts, 1993; Dean, Fac of Perf Arts, Univ Adelaide, 1993-; Tstee, Adelaide Fest Cntr Trust, 1996-99. Publications: Dance Criticism Down Under, 1993; The Choreutic Parameter: A Key Determinant of Choreographic Structural Style, 1993; The Choreological Image: Structure and Meaning in Dance, 1994; Symbolic Meaning in Dance, 1995; Performing Arts- The Australian Perspective, 1996; New Dance from Old Cultures: One Critic's Perspective, 1997; There's More to Dance Than Dancing, 1997. Contributions to: Dance Worlds, 1995; The International Dictionary of Madern Dance, 1998; The Companion to Music and Dance in Australia, 1998. Honours: SACAE Travel Schlshp, Intl Dance Schls Cong, W Germany, 1988; Inaugural PhD Schlshp, Univ Adelaide, 1991; Austl Rsch Cncl Small Grants, 1995, 1998. Memberships: Austl Assn for Dance Educ; Natl Cncl of Tertiary Dance Dirs; Austl Cncl for Hlth, Physl Educ and Recreation; Soc for Dance Rsch; Intl Soc for the Arts; Dance Critics Assn; S Austl Assn for Studies in the Perf Arts; Higher Educ Rsch and Dev Soc of Aust; Soc for Textual Schlshp; Intl Th Inst. Hobbies: Theatre; Music; Dance; Visual arts. Address: School of Performing Arts, University of Adelaide, SA 5005, Australia.

DONALDSON Christine Collett, b. 29 July 1946. Company Director. m. Ivan Donaldson, 17 Feb 1968, 4 s. Education: Regd Gen and Obstets Nurse; Music Theor and Singing. Appointments: Ward Sister (Charge Nurse), 1969; Tutor Sister, 1969-70; Canterbury Opera Chorus, Jubilate Singers. Memberships: Bd Mbr, Canterbury opera Trust, 1988-; Owner and Bus Mngr, Pegasus Bay Winery, Restaurant and Vineyard. Hobbies: Opera; Wine; Classical music. Address: 112 Heaton Street, Christchurch 8005, New Zealand.

DONALDSON Edgar John, b. 13 Nov 1920, Toowoomba, Qld, Aust. Ophthalmic Surgeon. m. Marjorie Bryant, 23 Oct 1948, 1 s, 3 d. Education: MBBS, Hons, 1937; DO, 1947, Sydney Univ; Fell, Roy Austl Coll of Surgs, 1978; Fell, Roy Austl Coll of Ophthalmologists, 1978. Appointments: Ophthalmic Surg, Sydney Eye Hosp, 1949-85; Pres, NSW Ophthalmological Soc, 1961-63; Sec, Ophthalmic Rsch Inst of Aust, 1966-68; Dir, Ophthalmic Studies and Eye Health, Univ of Sydney, 1970-78; Chmn, Crt of Examiners, Roy Austl Coll of Ophthalmologists, 1971-78; Chmn, Visng Staff Sydney Eye Hosp, 1976-85; Pres, Roy Austl Coll of Ophthalmologists, 1978-79. Publications: Pprs in Medl Jrnls. Honours: Education MBBS (Hons), 1943; Sydney Hosp Telfer Prize, 1972; AO, 1985; Medal of Hon, Roy Aust Coll of Opthals, 1997. Membership: Austl Med Assn, 1944. Hobby: Photography. Address: 8 Braeside Street, Wahroonga, Sydney, NSW 2076, Australia.

DONALDSON Francis Gordon, b. 28 Sept 1944. Principal. m. Joyce Fieldhouse, 8 July 1969, 1 s, 1 d. Education: BSc Hons; PhD; MACE; Queen's Univ, Belfast; Univ of Windsor, Can. Appointments: Tchr, Coleraine Acad Inst, N Ireland, 1972-78; Vice Prin, Wallace HS, N Ireland, 1978-82; Prin, Scotch Coll, Melbourne, 1983-. Hobbies: Photography; Music; Gardening; Golf; Swimming. Address: c/o Scotch College, Morrison Street, Hawthorn, Vic 3122, Australia.

DONALDSON Ivan MacGregor, b. 28 Aug 1941. Neurologist. m. Christine Taylor, 17 Feb 1968, 4 s. Education: MD; FRCP; FRACP; MBChB. Appointments: Prof of Med, Otago Univ; Snr Cnslt, Canterbury Hlth. Publications: Health and Wine in New Zealand; Movement Disorders, forthcoming. Memberships: Snr Censor, Roy Austl Coll Physns; Owner Viticulturalist/Oenologist, Pegasus Bay Winery; Intl Wine Judge. Listed in: Who's Who in Aoteroa. Hobbies: Wine; Opera; Classical music generally. Address: 112 Heaton Street, Christchurch 8005, New Zealand.

DONATH Egon Josef, b. 18 May 1906, Vienna, Austria. Retired University Lecturer. m. Martha, 1 child. Education: DipEd; MA. Appointments: Hs Tchr, 1930; Mbr, Staff of Com, Univ of Melbourne, 1947. Publications: William Farrer, 1955; Wheat Industry in Australia, 1960. Membership: Hon Life Mbr, Austl Inst of Export; Life Mbr, Melbourne Bushwalkers Club. Address: 9/155 Power Street, Hawthorn, Vic 3122, Australia.

DONE Kenneth Stephen, b. 29 June 1940, Sydney, Australia. Artist. m. Judith Ann, 1 s, 1 d. Education: Natl Art Sch. Appointments: Chmn, Ken Done Grp Cos, 1979-; Creative Dir, Advtng Samuelson Talbot Syd, QMMS J Walter Thompson, NY, 1960-78; Goodwill Amb Unicef Aust; Paul Harris Fell, Rotary Intl; Hon Mbr, Rotary Syd Cove. Publications: Ken Done: Paintings and Drawings, 1975-87, 1992; Ken Done Paintings, 1990-94, 1994; Ken Done: The Art of Design; Ken Done's Sydney, 1999; num solo and group exhibs throughout galls in Aust, Japan and France. Honours: Rotary Awd for Ex, 1993; Spirit of Aust Awd, 1993; Mosman Citizen of Yr, 1992-93; Father of Yr, 1989; NSW Tourism Awd, 1986; FACTS Awd, Gold and Silver AWARDS; Cannes Gold Lion Awd; Westpac Export Hero's Awd, 1999. Hobbies: Golf; Swimming; Diving; Travelling; Windsurfing. Address: 17 Thurlow Street, Redfern, NSW 2016, Australia.

DONG Fureng, b. 26 July 1927, Ningbo, Zhejiang, China. Economist. m. Liu Ainian, 1 Aug 1957, 1 s, 1 d. Education: Dept of Econs, Wuhan Univ, China, 1946-50; Cand for Doct, Moscow Natl Econ Inst, USSR, 1953-57. Appointments: Asst 1950-52, Lectr 1957-58, Dept of Econs, Prof 1986-, Wuhan Univ; Asst Rschr, Dpty Hd of Grp, Balance of Natl Econ, 1959-77, Dpty Dir 1978-85, VP, Grad Sch 1982-85, Dir 1985-88, Hon Dir 1988-, Inst of Econs, Chinese Acady of Socl Scis; Rsch Fell, Inst of Econs, 1979-; Prof, Beijing Univ, 1979-; Ed-in-Chief, Econ Rsch Jrnl, 1985-88; Dpty to Natl People's Congress, 1988-98, Mbr of Stndng Cttee, NPC, 1988-98, Vice Chmn, Finl and Econ Cttee, NPC, 1988-98; Mbr, 1998-, Vice-Chmn, Econ Cttee, 1998-, Natl Cttee Chinese People's Political Consultative Conf (CPPCC); Short-term Cnslt, The World Bank, 1985; Visng Prof, St Antony's and Wolfson Colls, Univ of Oxford, 1985; Visng Prof, Duisburg Univ, 1988. Publications: Books: Dynamic Analysis of National Income in USSR, 1959; Problems of Socialist Reproduction and National Income, 1980; Theoretical Problems of the Chinese Economy in the Great Transformation, 1982; On Sun Yefan's Socialist Economic Theory, 1983; Selected Works of Dong Fureng, 1985; On Economic Development Strategies, 1988; Industrialisan and China's Rural Modernization, 1992; Studies on Economic Reform, 1995; Reform and Development - on Chinese Economy in the Great Transition, 1995; On Chinese Economy, 1996; Studies on Economic Development, 1997; On Socialist Market Economy, 1998; Talking on Market Economy, 1999; Over 100 essays on Chinese Econ. Honours: Sun Yefan's Prize, 1985; Prize of Econ Rsch, 1985, expert w outstndng achivements, Chinese Sci and Technol Commn, 1984; Palmes Academiques, France, 1987; Awd, Golden Triangle, 1988; Ex Ppr Prize, Beijing Munic Govt, 1989. Membership: Gen Sec, Union of Chinese Socs for Econ Rsch, 1985. Hobbies: Music; Reading. Address: Institute of Economics, CASS, 2 Yuetan Beixiaojie, Beijing 100836, China.

DONG Jian, b. 3 Jan 1936, Daotian, Shouguang, Shandong, China. Professor. m. Huayu, 28 Jan 1967, 1 s. Education: Grad, Nanjing Univ, Dept of Chinese Lang & Lit, 1965. Appointments: Dean, Dept of Chinese Lang & Lit, 1986, VP, 1988, Pres, Sch of Arts, 1993, Nanjing Univ. Publications: A History of Modern Chinese Literature, 1980; A History of Modern Chinese Drama, 1989; Literature and History, 1992; Biography of Tianhan, 1996. Memberships: Chinese Writers Assn; Chinese Dramatists Assn; Chinese Assn of Studies of Tianhan. Address: 9-2 Beijingxilu, Nanjing 210008, China.

DONG Lisheng, b. 18 Mar 1955, Nanjing, China. Researcher. m. Tong Li, 4 July 1985, 1 s. Education: PhD, Pol Sc, Univ Instelling Aniwerpen, Belgium, 1992. Appointments: Rprtr, Ed, China Daily, 1985-88; Rsch Fell, Intl Inst for Asian Rsch, 1993-95; Assoc Prof, Chinese Acady of Soc Scis, 1995-. Administrative Reform in the Peoples Republic of China; Sino-German Administrative Law; Administrative Act Supervision and Judicature. Honours: Fellshp, Univ Instelling Antwerpen, 1988-92; Fellshp, Leiden Univ, 1993. Memberships: China Natl Assn of Pub Admin; Assn of Asian Studies. Hobbies: Swimming; Tab Tennis; Reading. Address: Inst of Political Science, Cass, 15 Shatan Beijie, Beijing 100720, China.

DONG Qizhong, b. 25 May 1935, Taihe Co, Jiangxi Province, China. Artist. m. Yingmei Lei, Feb 1964, 2 s. Education: Grad, Art Dept of Beijing Art Tchrs Coll, 1958. Appointments: Tchr, Shanxi Art Coll and Art Dept, Shanxi Univ, 1958-65; Artist, Shanxi Artists' Assn, 1965-95. Creative Works: Woodcusts exhibited, Natl Art Exhib, more than 30 occasions, over 30 works selected for UN and exhibited in more than 30 countries & regions, more than 120 articles publs; The Selected Woodcuts of Doing Qizhong. Memberships: Mbr, Dir, Natl Artists' Assn of China; Dir, Graphic Soc of China; V Chmn, Shanxi Fedn of Lit & Art Circles; Hon Chmn, Shanxi Artists' Assn; Dir, Ex-libris Rsch Assn of China. Honours: The Autumnal Evening (woodcut), Ex Creative Prize, Natl 9th Art Exhib; The Morning Song of a Mountain Village (woodcut), Silver Medal of Shanxi Provincial Lit & Arts Awds; Luxun Prize, 50-Yr Ex Woodcutter of China, 1996. Hobbies: Music; Writing. Address: Shanxi Artists' Association, No 378 Yingze Street, Taiyuan, Shanxi, China.

DONG Shi-Hai, b. 20 Sept 1939. Computer Scientist. m. Wen-Juan Tu, 1 July 1974, 1 d. Education: BSc, Peking Univ, 1962. Publications: Computer Software Engineering Environment and Software Tools, 1988; Computer User Interface and It's Tools, 1994. Honours: Awd of Natl Sci Technol, Min of Educ, 1991; Specl Finl Asst by the Govt, 1992. Memberships: China Computer Fedn; China Image and Graphics Assn; Editl Bd of Jrnl of Chinese CAD and CG. Hobbies: Chinese Calligraphy; Playing Table Tennis. Address: Department of Computer Science, Peking University, Beijing 100871, China.

DONG Xilin, b. 10 Oct 1960, Xi-an, Shannxi Prov, China. Teacher in Fire Engineering. m. Song Xiaoyan, 25 Dec 1983. Education: BEng, 1982; MEng, 1986; Visng Schl, Edinburgh, 1994. Appointments: Lectr, 1988; Dir of Fire Dynamics, 1994; Assoc Prof, 1995; Ldr, Fire Safety Sci, 1999. Publications: Fire Combustion, 1997; Fire Protection in Nuclear Power Stations; 20 rsch pprs. Honour: Excellent Returned Visng Schl, 1997. Membership: Fire Assn of China, 1987; Intl Assn for Fire Safety Sci, 1999. Hobbies: Fishing; Football. Address: Department of Fire Protection, Intitute of Fire Protection of China 06500, Langfang, PO Box 424, China.

DONG You Qi, b. 21 Feb 1953, Ningbo Cty, China. Paediatrician. m. Shi Hong Yue, 15 May 1980, 1 s. Education: Bach, Medl Sci, Shanghai Tradl Chinese Medl Seminar. Appointment: Chf, Paediat Dept, Ningbo Tradl Chinese Medl Hosp. Publications: The Therapeutic Experience in Treating Children's Skin Mucous Membrane Lumph Node, 1988; The effects of the Colon mixture in curing mycosis enteritis diseases of children, 1993; To cure high fever convulsions sympton of children; Dong ting Yao's experience in treating acute nephritis of children, 1994; Stomach recuperation decocts applied in curing damp-hot type gastritis of children, 1998. Honour: Bathurn-like Medl Wrkr, 1995. Memberships: Tradl Chinese Medl Assn; Vice-Chmn, Tradl Chinese Medl Assn of Ningbo; Vice-Chmn, Yth Union of Ningbo, 4th, 5th and 6th sessions; Cty People's Pol Consultative Conf, 7th, 8th, 9th and 10th sessions. Address: 64 Xiaowen Lane, Ningbo, Zhejiang Province, China.

DONIGJAV Damba, b. 1959, Zuun-Gobisoum, Uvsaimak Prov, Mongolia. Minister of Defence. m. Education: Mil Pol Sch, USSR; Mongolian State Univ. Appointments: Rschr, Rsch and Stdies Cntr, Mongolian Revolutionary Yth League's Cntrl Cttee, 1989; Elected, Small Huval, 1990; Dpty Chair; Prime Min, 1992. Membership: Natl Democratic Party. Address: Ministry of Defence, Dander St, Ulan Bator 61, Mongolia.

DONLEY Joan Elsa, b. 19 Mar 1916. Registered Nurse; Registered Midwife. m. Robert Donley, 22 Nov 1941, 4 s, 1 d. Appointments: Cnslt to Intl Childbirth Educ Assn; Cnslt, NZ Coll of Midwives. Publications: Save the Midwife, 1986; History of NZ Homebirth, 1982; Summary NZ HBA in Women Together History of Women's Organisations in NZ Dept Internal Affairs, 1993; Independent Midwifery in NZ Chapter in Issues on Midwives, 1995. Honours: OBE for Servs to Midwifery, 1989; NZ Commemoration Medal for Servs to NZ, 1990; NZ Suffrage Medal, 1993; Hon Masters Deg, Hlth Sci, Aukland Inst of Technol, 1997. Listed in: New Zealand Who's Who. Hobbies: Research; Politics; Writing; Gardening. Address: 3 Hendon Avenue, Owairaka, Auckland 1003, New Zealand.

DONNE Gaven John (Hon Sir), b. 8 May 1914, Christchurch, NZ. Chief Justice. m. Isabel Fenwick Hall, 1946, 2 s 2 d. Education: Vic Univ; LLB, Auckland Univ, 1937; Admitted Bar, Sol, 1938. Appointments: Served 2nd NZ Expeditionary Force, 36th NZ Survey Battery, Mid E, Italy, 1941-45; Mbr, Takapuna Borough Cncl, Auckland Town Plng Authy and Westlake HS Bd Govs, 1957-58; Stipendiary Magistrate, 1958-75; Puisne Judge, Supreme Crt, W Samoa, 1970-71; Chf Jus, W Samoa, 1972-74, Niue, 1974-82, Cook Is, 1975-82, Nauru, 1985-, Tuvalu, 1985-; Mbr, Crt of Appeal, W Samoa, 1975-82, Kiribati, 1986-; Actng Rep of HM the Queen, 1975-82, Queen's Rep, 1982-84. Honour: KBE, 1979. Hobbies: Golf; Walking. Address: Meneng Nauru, Otaramarae, RD 4, Rotorua, New Zealand.

DONOVAN Anne, b. 5 Sept 1956, Innisfail. Lecturer. Education: MPhil; BN; Dip App Sci; Regd Nurse; Regd Midwife; Child Hlth Nurse. Appointments: Lectr, Griffith Univ; Cnslt, Primary Hlth Care, Myanmar, Nepal, Sri Lanka. Hobbies: Reading; Water sports; Asian cooking. Address: 4 Nitawill St, Everton PK, Brisbane 4053, Australia.

DONOVAN Francis Patrick, b. 1 Feb 1922, Ingham, Aust. Retired. m. M Kozslik, 1 s, 1 d. Education: MA, BCL

(Oxon); LLB (Qld); LLM (Hon, Melbourne). Apointments: Prof, Coml Law, Univ Melbourne, 1952-61; Amb, OECD, 1977-80; VP, Intl Crt of Arbitration, 1985-. Publications: Signed, Sealed and Delivered, 1960; Cases of Materials on Contract, 1961. Honours: AM, 1974; Kt, Sov Mil Order of Malta; Chevalier Legion d'Honneur, France, 1988. Address: 25 Avenue Bosquet, 75007 Paris, France.

DONOVAN Michael John, b. 13 Oct 1954, Melbourne, Australia. Trade Union Secretary. Education: BSc, Monash Univ. Appointments: Rsch Offr, 1977, Asst Sec, Indl, 1992, Br Sec-Treas, 1996. Address: 9th Floor, 53 Queen Street, Melbourne, Australia.

DOOGAN Christopher Matthew, b. 23 Nov 1945, Sydney, Aust. Chief Executive and Principal Registrar, High Court of Australia. m. Maria, 22 May 1974, 2 s, 1 d. Education: St Bernard's Coll; Canberra CAE; Macquarie Univ. Appointments: Dpty Comptroller Gen Customs, 1992-94; Sol Snr Comm Ptnr and Mngng Ptnr, Macphillamy Cummins & Gibson Bars Sols, 1985-92, Bar High Crt, Aust, 1985, Bar and Solr Supr Crt ACT, 1985, Bar Sup Crt, NSW, 1984; Snr Exec Export Inspection Serv, 1984-85; Dir, Investigations, Off C'wlth Ombudsman, 1983-84; Def Fell, 1983. Address: High Court of Australia, Canberra, ACT 2600, Australia.

DOOHAN John James (Hon). Grazier. m. Mena, 1944, dec, 1 s, 1 d. Education: St Joseph's Coll, Hunters Hill. Appointments: Cntrl Cncl Bush Nursing Assn, 1962-74; Mbr, Fauna Protection Panel, 1964-67; Chmn, NSW State Shearing Ind Cttee, 1965-78; Natl Parks and Wildlife Serv Advsry Cncl, 1967-77; Bd of Trees, McGarvie Smith Inst, 1967-; Graziers Assn of NSW: Mbr, Gen Cncl, 1957-78, Vice Chmn, 1965-68, 1971-73, Treas, 1969-71, Chmn, Wool Cttee, 1970-73, Mbr, Exec Cttee, Austl Wool Ind Conf, 1970-78, Pres, 1973-76; Mbr, Exec Cttee, Austl Wool Growers 7 Graziers Cncl, 1973-76; Dir, Grazcos Co-Op Ltd, 1973-80; Tstee, Bush Childrens Educ (NSW), 1973-; Mbr, Natl Trade Dev Cncl, 1976-78; Chmn, Natl Wool Producing Ind Trng Cttee, 1976-78; Chmn, Jnt Wool-Selling Org (Natl), 1977-80; Dir, Farmers Grazcos, 1980-86; MLC (Natl Party) for NSW, 1978-91; W Lands Advsry Bd, 1993-. Honour: OBE, 1977. Memberships: Bourke Oxley; Double Bay Bowling; E Sub Leagues; AJC, STC. Hobbies: Golf; Tennis; Racing; Bowls. Address: PO Box 799, Bondi Junction, NSW 2022, Australia.

DOOLEY Cheryl Dawn, b. 8 Apr 1958, Walsall, Eng. Marketing Consultant. m. Stephen Kevin Dooley, 14 July 1990. Education: Dip, Direct Mktng (Dist), 1989; Co Dirs Dip, 1999; Cert IV in Assessment and Workplace Trng, 1999. Appointments: Mngng Dir, Dooley Dynamics Pty Ltd. Publications: Telemarketing, 1992; Telephone Technique, 1993, 1994, 1996, 1999 (revised ed). Honour: Pan Pacific 1994 Mktng Excellence Achiever, 1994. Memberships: Assoc Fell, Austl Inst Mngmt; Austl Soc of Auths; Fell Austl Inst of Co Dirs; Fell Austl Inst of Trng and Dev.. Hobbies: Reading; Travel; Gardening. Address: 99 Elanora Road, Elanora Heights, NSW 2101, Australia.

DOOLEY James Creswell, b. 30 Jan 1919, Ivanhoe, Victoria, Australia. Retired Geophysicist. m. Nanette E Dooley, 19 Feb 1949, 4 s, 1 d. Education: BSc, 1940, MSc, 1941, Melbourne; BA, Hons, Austl Natl Univ, 1971. Appointments: Rsch Asst, Mt Stromlo Observatory, 1940-44; Mil Serv, 1942-43; Geophysicist, BMR, Geol T Geophys, 1944-84; Snr Lectr, Univ Qld, 1986, Univ PNG, 1987. Publications: Pprs and reports on gravity and magnetic fields. Honours: Pacific Star, 1939-45; Queens Silver Jubilee Medal, 1977; AM, 1987. Memberships: Fell, Austl Inst of Phys; Austl Inst of Geoscis; Inst of Phys, England; Soc of Exploration Geophys; Am Geophysl Union; Roy Astronomical Soc; Geol Soc of Aust; Alumni Assn, Univ of Melbourne; Canberra Legacy Club; ANZAAS. Hobby: Music. Address: 66 Hawker Street, Torrens, ACT 2607, Australia.

DORAI CHETTY Sister John, b. 19 July 1921, Bangalore, India. Pianist; Music Teacher; Social Worker. Education: Fellshp, Trinity Coll of Music, London. Appointments: Prin, Sch of Music, Good Shepherd Convent, Madras, 1950-68; Prin, Sch of Music, Mysore, 1971-; Fndr, Pres, Mysore Music Assn, 1971; Num concerts and lectr demonstrations (Carnatic Ragas on the Piano) in India, London, Singapore and Malaysia. Creative works: Experimented, South Indian Carnatic Ragas on piano in pure Carnatic system; Many perfces of Carnatic Ragas on the piano. Honours: Tchr's Awds, Rotary Mysore S East, 1994; Govt of Karnataka Awd, 1995; Trinity Coll Tchr's Awds, Madras Cntr. Memberships: Mysore Music Assn, 1971-; EPTA, London, 1978; J S Music Acady, Mysore, 1982; Bangalore Sch of Music, -1995. Hobbies: Stamp collecting; Charity work. Listed in: Madras Quiz Programme; Music Directory, Delhi. Address: Good Shepherd Convent School of Music, Mysore 570 001, India.

DORFMAN Ariel, b. Argentina. Writer. Appointments: Rsch Prof of Lit and Latin Am Studies Duke Univ NC, 1992-; Won Time Out and Olivier Prize for Death and the Maiden. Publications incl: Death and the Maiden - play also screenplay; My House is on Fire - short stories; Konfidenz; Reader - play.

DORNEY Kiernan John Joseph, b. 9 Jan 1912, Vic, Aust. Surgeon. m. Joan Calliwan, 8 Mar 1943, 4 s, 1 dec, 2 d. Education: Newman Coll, Univ of Melbourne, Aust, 1930-32; BSc 1934, MBBS 1937, FRACS 1947, MS, Melbourne, 1948. Appointments: Res Med Offr, St Vincents Hosp, 1938; War Serv, 1st Libyan Campaign, Greece, Crete El Alamein, New Guinea, Borneo, 1939-45; Surg, Austn Forces BCOF, Korea, 1953; Chf Surg, Bein Hioa Hosp, S Vietnam, 1971; Commanding Offr, FDAMB, 1952-54; 31 BN, 1954-57; Snr Med Offr, 11 BDE, 1958-60; QC Command Staff Grp, 11 BDE, 1961-63; Supt, La Trobe Hosp, Tas, 1948-50; Townsville Gen Hosp, Qld, 1950-53, 1971. Publications include: Treatment of Severely Wounded Casuality. Honours: CBE, 1977; DSO, 1943; MID (4), 1939-45; Full Blue Football, Half Blue Swimming, Univ of Melbourne; AM, 1992. Memberships include: Pres, Subnormal Childrens Assn, 1958-82; Chmn, N Qld Med Conf, 1966-82; Pres, St Raphael's Coll Cncl, James Cook Univ, 1978-82; Pres, Cntrl Sunshine Coast Cttee on Ageing, 1984-89; Chmn, Day Respite Care and Crisis Respite Care, 1989-; VP, Red Cross Legacy. Listed in: Who's Who in Australia. Hobbies: Golf; Gardening; Community service; Grandchildren. Address: 2 Illawong Street, Buderim, Queensland 4556, Australia.

DORUM Eileen Esther, b. 17 Mar 1917, Melbourne, Aust. Musician. m. Ivar Chepmell Dorum, 10 Jan 1942, 1 s, 1 d. Appointments: Music Critic, Daily Mirror, Sydney; Music Tchr, Melbourne Schs (var); Percy Grainger: the Man Behind the Music (book), 1986; Composers of Australia (book), 1997. Memberships: Austl Cnsl for the Arts, Vic Branch Sec, 1951-54. Hobbies: Horticulture; Watercolour painting. Address: 54 Fordholm Road, Hawthorn, Vic 3122, Australia.

DOST Shah Mohammad, b. 1929 Kabul. Politician. Education: Kabul Univ; Fmr Dep For Min and For Min of the Dem Rep of Afghanistan; Min of State for For Affairs, 1986-88; Perm Rep to UN, 1988-90. Honours: Order of People's Friendship. Memberships: Mbr Cntr Cttee, 1979; Mbr Revolutionary Cnc. Address: c/o Ministry of Foreign Affairs, Shah Mahmoud Ghazi Street, Shar-i-Nau, Kabul, Afghanistan.

DOU Hua-Shu, b. 24 Aug 1958. Research Scientist in Mechanical Engineering. m. Chen Ying-Ying, 11 Oct 1985, 1 son. Education: BSc, 1982, MSc, 1984, Northeast Univ; PhD, BUAA, Beijing, China, 1991. Appointments: Asst 1984, Lectr 1987, NEU, China; Postdoct, 1991, Assoc Prof, 1993, Tsinghu Univ; Visng Rschr, Tohuko Univ, Japan, 1994; Assoc Prof, Hosei Univ, Japan, 1995; Rsch Scientist, Sydney Univ, Aust, 1996. Publications: Contrb articles in profl mags and jrnls. Honour: Outstndng Achmnt Awds, Tsinghua Univ, 1993; 2nd Class prize of Sci and Technol Progress, Min of Mech Ind of China, 1994; 2nd Prize of Sci and Technol, Min of Aeronautical Ind of China, 1994. Memberships: AIAA, 1993; ASME, 1993; CSET, 1988. Hobbies: Music;

Basketball; Literature. Listed in: Who's Who in the World; Dictionary of International Biography. Address: Department Mechanical Engineering, University of Sydney, NSW 2006, Australia.

DOUGLAS Kenneth George, b. 15 Nov 1935. President Trade Union Council. Div. 2 s, 2 d. Appointments: Mbr, PM Enterprise Cncl; Mbr, Trade Devel Bd; Pres, NZ Cncl of Trade Unions. Honours: Order of NZ; JP. Memberships include: Cncl Mbr, Inst of Policy Studies; Bd Mr, Employee Asst Progs Cncl; Indl Rels Fndn; Prince Philip Tree; Cntr for Strategic Studies; Exec Bd, ICFTU and Pres, ICFTU Asia Pacific Reg Org; Var Sports, Cultural and Community Orgs. Address: The New Zealand Council of Trade Unions, PO Box 6645, Education House, 178 Willis Street, Wellington 1, New Zealand.

DOUGLAS Kirk, b. 9 Dec 1916, Amsterdam, NY. Actor. m. (1) Diana Dill, div 1950, 2 s, (2) Anne Buydens, 1954, 2 s. Education: St Lawrence Univ; Am Acady Dramatic Arts. Appointments: Pres Bryna Prodns, 1955-; Dir Los Angeles Chapter UN Assn. Broadway Stage appearances: Spring Again; Three Sisters; Kiss and Tell; The Wind is Ninety; Alice in Arms; Man Bites Dog; The Boys of Autumn - not on Broadway. Films incl: The Strange Love of Martha Ivers; Letter to Three Wives; Ace in the Hole; The Bad and the Beautiful; 20000 Leagues under the Sea; Ulysses; Lust for Life; Gunfight at OK Corral; Paths of Glory; The Vikings; Last Train from Gun Hill; The Devil's Disciple; Spartacus; Strangers When We Meet; Seven Days in May; Town without Pity; The List of Adrian Messenger; In Harms Way; Cast a Giant Shadow; The Way West; War Waggon; The Brotherhood; The Arrangement; There Was a Crooked Man; Gunfight, 1971; Light at the Edge of the World; Catch Me a Spy; A Man to Respect, 1972; Cat and Mouse; Scalawag -dir-1973; Once Is Not Enough, 1975; Posse -prodr actor-1975; The Moneychangers -tv-1978; Holocaust 2000, 1977; The Fury, 1977; Villain, 1978; Saturn, 1979; The Final Countdown, 1980; The Man from Snowy River; Tough Guys, 1986; Queenie -tv mini series- 1987; Oscar; Welcome to Veraz; Greedy, 1994. Publications: The Ragman's Son: An Autobiography, 1988; Dance with the Devil -novel- 1990; The Secret -novel- 1992; The Gift -novel- 1992; Last Tango in Brooklyn -novel- 1994; Climbing the Mountain: My Search for Meaning, 1997. Honours: Acady Awds 1948, 1952, 1956; NY Film Critics Awd; Hollywood For Press Awd; Cmdr Ordre des Arts et Lettres, 1979; Legion d'honneur, 1985; Presl Medal of Freedom, 1981; Am Film Insts Lifetime Achievement Awd, 1991; Kennedy Cntr Honors, 1994; Hon Acady Awd, 1996. Address: The Bryna Co, 141 S El Camino Dr, Beverly Hills, CA 90212, USA.

DOUGLAS Michael Kirk, b. 25 Sep 1944, New Brunswick, NJ. Actor; Film Producer. m. Diandra Mornell Luker, 1977, separated, 1 s. Film appearances: It's My Turn; Hail Heroll, 1969; Summertime, 1971; Napoleon and Samantha, 1972; Coma, 1978; Running, 1979; Star Chamber, 1983; Romancing the Stone, 1984; A Chorus Line, 1985; Jewel of the Nile, 1985; Fatal Attraction, 1987; Wall Street; 1987; Heidi, 1989; Black Rain, 1989; The War of the Roses, 1990; Shining Through, 1990; Basic Instinct, 1992; Falling Down, 1993; The American President, 1995; The Ghost and the Darkness, 1996; The Game, 1997. Films produced incl: One Flew Over the Cuckoo's Nest; The China Syndrome; Sarman, exec prodr; Romancing the Stone; Jewel of the Nile; Flatliners, 1990; Made in America, co exec prodr; Disclosure, 1994. Appeared in tv series Streets of San Francisco. Honours: Acady Awd for Best Film for One Flew Over the Cuckoo's Nest, 1975; Acady Awd for Best Actor, for Wall Street, 1988. Address: c/o Creative Artist Agency Inc, 9830 Wilshire Boulevard, Beverly Hills, CA 90212, USA.

DOUGLAS Sir Roger Owen, b. 5 Dec 1937 Auckland. Politician; Accountant. m. Glennis June Anderson, 1961, 1 s, 1 d. Education: Auckland Grammar Sch; Auckland Univ. Appointments: Entered HoR as Labour mbr for Manukau, 1969 - now Manurewa; Min of Brdcstng, 1973-75; Min of the Post Off, 1973-74; Min of Housing - with State Advances Housing Corp - 1974-75; Min of Fin and Min in Charge of the Inland Revenue Dept and of Friendly Socs, 1984-87; Min of Fin, 1988; Min of Police and Immigration, 1989-90; Dir Brierley Invmnts, 1990-; Dir John Fairfax Ltd, 1997-; Dir Aetna Hlth - NZ - Ltd, 1997-; Dir Tasman Inst, 1997-; Fmr Pres Auckland Labour Regl Cncl Manukau Labour Cttee. Publications: There's Got to be a Better Way, 1980; Toward Prosperity, 1987; Unfinished Business, 1993; Completing the Cirlce, 1996; Sev papers on intl and econ affairs. Honours: Max Schmidheiny Freedom Prize Switzerland, 1995; Ludwig Erhard Fndn Prize Germany, 1997. Hobbies: Cricket; Rugby; Rugby league; Reading. Address: 411 Redoubt Road, R D Papatoetoe, Auckland, New Zealand.

DOW Frederick W, b. 8 Feb 1917, Boston, USA. University Professor; Management Consultant. m. Patricia Rathbone, 9, Feb 1945, 2 s, 2 d. Education: BS, Magna Cum Laude, Boston Coll; AM; PhD, Yale. Appointments: Exec, Dow, Chem Co, 1945-67; Prof, Univ of Notre Dame, 1967-77; Prof, US Intl Univ, 1977-. Honours: FRSA, 1970; Croix de Guerre, 1942. Address: 5080 Carlsbad Blvd, Carlstad, CA 92008-4353, USA.

DOWD John Robert Arthur, b. 12 Nov 1940, Sydney, Aust. Judge of the Supreme Court of New South Wales. m. Jill, 31 Aug 1963, 4 d. Education: LLB (Syd). Appointments: Dpty Chmn, SCIMED Fndn Ltd; Goodwill Ambassador, Former VP, Spastic Cntr of NSW; Chmn, Law Fac Advsry Bd, Univ of West Sydney; Dpty Chmn, Austl Legal Resources Intl; Pres, Austl Sect of Intl Commn of Jurists; MP (Lib) Lane Cove, 1975-91; Ldr of State Opposition, 1981-83; State Atty-Gen and Ldr of Legis Assembly, 1988-91; QC, NSW, 1990; QC, ACT, 1992; Judge of the Suprme Crt of NSW, 1994; Dpty Chmn, NSW Law Reform Commn, 1996. Publications: The Conduct of an Undefended Divorce, 1969; (co-auth) The Status of Border Crossings to PNG, Intl Commn of Jurists, 1985; (co-auth) Count down to 1997, Intl Commn of Jurists, 1992. Honours: Queen's Silver Jubilee Medal, 1977; AO, 1991. Membership: Austl Club. Hobbies: Opera; Theatre. Address: Supreme Court, GPO Box 3, Sydney, NSW 2001, Australia.

DOWIYOGO Bernard, b. 14 Feb 1946. Politician. Education: Austl Natl Univ. Appointments: Lawyer; Mbr of Parl, 1973-; Sec, Nauru Gen Hosp and Gen Mngr Nauru Co-op Soc; Pres, Nauru, 1976-78, 1989-95, 1996-; Min of Jus, 1983, External Affairs, Dev and Ind, Pub Serv and Civil Aviation; Chair, Bank of Nauru, 1985; Fmr Ldr, Nauru Party. Address: c/o Bank of Nauru, Civic Centre, PO Box 289, Nauru.

DOWLING Carolyn Henderson, b. 29 Jan 1943, Melbourne, Aust. University Lecturer. m. John Timothy Dowling, 17 Dec 1966, 2 d. Education: BA, 1962, Grad BEd, 1965, Univ Melbourne; PhD, Monash Univ, 1993. Appointments: Tchr, Vic Educ Dept, 1964-69; Pvte Music Tchr, 1974-78; Freelance Writer, 1978-82; Computing Cnslt, 1983-84; Lectr, Computing Coord, Austl Cath Univ, Vic, 1985-93; Hd, Dept of Maths, Sci and Computing, Austl Cath Univ, 1993-95; Assoc Prof, Hd, Sch of Arts & Scis, Austl Cath Univ, 1996-. Publications: Fun Plus, co-auth, 1978; Weekend Historic Walks, 1979; The Book of the Year, 1980; The Turtle Series, 1983, 1984, 1988; Collecting Things, 1984. Honour: Peter Fensham Prize, 1995. Memberships: Austl Computer Soc; Austl Cncl for Computers in Educ. Hobbies: Horse riding; Cross country skiing; Choral singing. Address: 32 Chrystobel Crescent, Hawthorn, Victoria 3122, Australia.

DOWNER Alexander John Gosse (The Hon), b. 9 Sep 1951. Politician; Former Diplomatist. m. Nicola Robinson, 1978, 1 s, 3 d. Education: Radley Col; Univ of Newcastle-upon-Tyne UK. Appointments: Mbr Austl Dip Serv, 1976-81; Austl Miss to Eurn Communities Emb to Belgium and Luxembourg, 1977-80; Snr For Affairs Rep S Aust, 1981; Polit Advsr to PM, 1982-83; Dir Austl Chamber of Com, 1983-84; Liberal Mbr HoR for Mayo S Aust, 1984-; Shadow Min for Arts Heritage and Environment, 1987; Shadow Min for Housing Small Bus and Customs, 1988-89; Shadow Min for Trade Negotiations, 1990-92; Shadow Min for Def, 1992-93; Fed Shadow Treas, 1993-94; Ldr Liberal Party, 1994-95; Shadow Min for For Affairs, 1995-96; Min of For Affairs, 1996-. Hobbies: Reading; Music; Tennis. Address: Department of Foreign Affairs and Trade, Locked Bag 40, QVT, Canberra, ACT 2600, Australia.

DOWNES Garry Keith, b. 7 Jan 1944, Sydney, Aust. Barrister; Arbitrator. m. Brenda Ann Davis, 23 Aug 1968, 3 d. Education: Newington Coll, Sydney; BA, 1964, LLB, 1967, Sydney Univ. Appointments: Assoc Chf Jus of Aust, Rt Hon Sir Garfield Barwick, GCMG, 1967-70; Bar, 1970-; Mbr of the Bar of Eng and Wales (Inner Temple); Cncl Mbr, NSW Bar Assn, 1981-84; Fac of Law, Sydney Univ, 1982-91; Bars Admission Bd, NSW, 1982-91; Procurator, Presbyterian Ch of Aust, 1982-; Mbr, Hist Bldngs Cttee, Natl Trust of Aust, 1984-91; Cncl of Law Reporting for NSW, 1984-, (chmn, 1993-94); Policy Advsry Grp, Law Cncl of Aust, 1987-91; Chmn, Admin Law Cttee, Law Cncl of Aust, 1987-92; Mbr, Exec, Fed Litigation Section, Law Cncl of Aust, 1989-94 (Chmn, 1992-94); Cncl Mbr, NSW State Cancer Cncl, 1989-94; Regl Sec, Australasia and Pacific Rim Union Internationale des Avocats, 1989-94, Mbr, Exec Cttee, 1990-96, Pres, 1994-95, Hon Life Pres, 1997; Mbr, Intl Crt of Arbitration of the Intl Chamber of Com, 1997-. Creative Works: Austl Cnsltng Ed, Encyclopedia Of International Commercial Litigation. Honours: Queen's Counsel, NSW, 1983, Vic, ACT, Northern Territory, WA, Qld, SA; Fell, Chart Inst of Arbitrators; Mbr of the Order of Aust, 1997. Memberships: VP, 1996-99, Chmn, 1999-, Austl Branch, Chartered Inst of Arbitrators; Austl Panel of Arbitrators; Pres, Anglo Austl Lawyers Society, 1998-. Listed in: Who's Who in Australia. Hobbies: Travel; Conservation of Historic Buildings; Horse Riding; Motoring. Address: 7 Wentworth Chambers, 180 Phillip Street, Sydney, NSW 2000, Australia.

DOWNEY Robert Jnr, b. 4 Apr 1965 NY. Actor. m. Deborah Falconer, 1 child. Films incl: Pound, 1970; Firstborn; Weird Science; To Live and Die in LA; Back to School; The Pick-Up Artist; Johnny B Good; True Believer; Chances Are; Air America; Soapdish; Chaplin; Heart and Souls; Short Cuts; The Last Party; Natural Born Killers; Only You; Restoration; Mussolini: The Untold Story, TV mini series; Restoration; Danger Zone; Home for the Holidays; Richard III; Bliss Vision, 1997; The Gingerbread Man, 1997. Honours: BAFTA Awd for Chaplin. Address: c/o CAA, 9830 Wilshire Boulevard, Beverly Hills, CA 90212, USA.

DOWNTON Peter James, b. 6 Sept 1946. Architectural Educator. m. 14 Aug 1976, Marion Elizabeth Pitt, 1 s. Education: BArch, 1970, MArch, 1976, PhD, 1985, Univ of Melbourne. Appointments: Director, UNESCO Children's Perception of Space Project, Melbourne Stdy, 1972-73; Rsch Fell, Univ of Melbourne, 1973-76; Lectr, RMIT, 1977-80; Snr Lectr, 1980-83; Hd, Dept of Arch, RMIT, 1983-86; Snr Lectr, 1987-91; Assoc Dir, Key Cntr for Des, RMIT, 1990-91; Assoc Prof, Archtl Theory, RMIT, 1991-97; Hd, Sch of Arch and Design, RMIT, 1997-. Publications: Ed (w K Dovey and G Missingham) Place and Placemaking, 1985; Over 40 Jrnl pprs, rprts, book chapts, reviews. Memberships: Fell, Roy Austl Inst of Archts, 1986-, Mbr, 1972-85; Vice Chmn, People and Physl Environment Rsch Assn, 1983-87. Hobbies: Opera; Ballet; Photography; Cars. Address: School of Architecture, RMIT, Box 2476V GPO, Melbourne, Vic 3001, Australia.

DOYAMA Masao, b. 8 Feb 1927, Tokyo, Japan. Professor. m. Eiko, 28 Dec 1953, 1 s, 1 d. Education: PhD, Univ Il, 1962; DEng, Univ Tokyo, 1975; DHon Causa, Denmark Techl Univ, 1982. Appointments: Tchng Fell, Rsch Asst, Univ Notre Dame, IN, 1954-55; Rsch Asst, Assoc, Univ IL, Urban, 1955-63; Res Rsch Assoc, Argonne, IL, Natl Lab, 1963-64; Assoc Physicist, 1964-67; Assoc Prof, Univ Tokyo, 1967-75; Prof, Dept materials Sci, 1975-87; Sci Advsr, Min of Educ, Tokyo, 1984-88; Prof, Dept Materials Sci, Nagoya Univ, 1986-90; Prof, Dept Materials, Nishi, Tokyo Univ, 1990-96; Prof, Dept Teikyo Univ Sci & Technol, 1996-. Publications: Ed/auth: Lattice Defects in Quenched Metals, 1965; Progress in the Study of Point Defects, 1977; Point Defects and Defect Interactions in Metals, 1982; Materials Tech (Japanese), 28 vols. Honours: Decorated, Japanese Govt, Medal w Purple Ribbon, 1985; Recip Royalty Awd, Univ IL Allumni Assn, 1985; Honda Memm Awd, 1993; Japan Inst Metals Awd, Gold Medal, 1995. Memberships: Japan Illini Club, Emeritus Pres, 1972-; Advd Materials Sci & Engrng Soc, Pres, 1989; Materials Rsch Soc, Japan, Pres, 1992; Intl Union on Materials Rsch Soc, Pres, 1995-96. Address: 3-37-2 Wakamiya, Nakano, Tokyo 165-0033, Japan.

DOYLE Douglas Thomas, b. 9 Apr 1919. m. Fay Rennie, 2 Oct 1943, 1 s, 1 d. Education: LFAIV. Appointments: AIF Maj, 1939-45; Pvte Prac in Real Estate and Valuation, 1945-47; C'wlth Treas, 1947-50; Valuer, Tas Valuation Br, 1950-77; Mbr, Gen Cl, 1958-75; Fed Pres, Austl Inst of Valuers, 1967; Valuer-Gen for Tas, 1970-77; Dir-Gen of Lands, Tas, 1977-83; Sullivans Cove Dev Authy, 1977-92; Chmn, Tas World Heritage Area Consultative Cttee, 1984-90. Honour: ISO, 1984; Mbr, 2nd AIF, 1939-46; Retired Maj, Wounded, Tobruk. Hobbies: Golf; Fishing. Address: 11 Circassian Street. St Helen's, Tas 7216, Australia.

DOYLE John Jeremy, b. 4 Jan 1945. Chief Justice of South Australia. m. Marie McLoughlin, 27 June 1969, 2 s, 3 d. Education: LLB; BCL; QC, Univ of Adelaide; Oxford Univ. Appointments: Ptnr, Kelly & Co, 1970-77; Bar, 1977-95; Sol-Gen for SA, 1986-95; Chf Jus, Supreme Crt of SA, 1995-; Pro-Chan, Flinders Univ of SA, 1988-. Address: Supreme Court, 1 Gouger Street, Adelaide, SA 5000, Australia.

DOYLE Louise Madeleine,b. 6 Mar 1970. Producer; Project Manager. Education: BA, Cinema Studies Major, La Trobe Univ, Melbourne. Appointments: Co-dir, The Entire Future Prodn Co. Memberships: Pres, St Kilda Access TV, Melbourne, 1990-91; Austl Film Inst, 1995-. Hobbies: Reading; Body Surfing; Surfing; Writing. Address: c/o B J Doyle, Clayton Utz, 333 Collins Street, Melbourne, Victoria 3000, Australia.

DOYLE Robert Urban, b. Sydney, Can. Professor. Education: BA (summa cum laude), Engl, St Francis Xavier Univ, Can; SW, Maritime Sch of Socl Wrk, Dalhousie Univ, Can; PhD (Socl Wrk), Univ of Toronto. Appointments: Asst Prof, Com and Socl Wrk, Dalhousie, Unv, 1970-72; Exec Dir of Prog Dev, Dept of Socl Scis, Prov of New Brunswick, 1972-76; Snr Lectr, Socl Wrk, Univ NSW, 1976-78; Assoc Prof, Univ of Manitoba, 1978-79; Coord, Neighbourhood Servs, Toronto, 1979-81; Cnslt, DEL Support Cntr, 1981-82; Cnslt, Orgn Systems and Dev Inc, 1985-88; Snr Prog Dir and Acting Exec Dir, Socl Plng Cncl of Metrop Toronto (SPC), 1983-90; Snr Lectr, Grad Sch of Socl Wrk, La Trobe Univ, Melbourne, 1991-94; Currently, Prof of Socl Wrk & Socl Welfare, Dir of Cntr for Rural Socl Rsch, Charles Sturt Univ. Publications include: (book) Behind the Multicultural Mask; Rsch into intl community dev. Honours: Allister McIntyre Trophy, St Francis Xavier Univ; Manuel I Zive Awd, Maritime Sch of Socl Wrk, Dalhousie Univ, NSW; Fellshps, Fac of Socl Wrk Alumni Awd, 1987, Univ of Toronto, Can. Address: Po Box 5393 B/C, Wogga Wogga, NSW 2650, Australia.

DRACHNIK Catherine Meldyn, b. 6 July 1924, Kansas City, USA. Artist; Art Therapist; Teacher. m. Joseph, 1 s, 1 d. Education: BS, Univ MD, 1945; MA, CA Univ, Sacremento, 1975. Appointments: Art Therapist, Vincent Hall Retirement Home, McLean, VA, Fairfax Mental Hlth Day Treatment Cntr, McLean, Arlington (VA) Mental Hlth Day Treatment Cntr, 1971-72, Hope for Retarded, San Jose, CA, Sequoia Hosp, Redwood City, CA, 1972-73; Supvsng Tchr, Adult Educ, Sacramento Soc for the Blind, 1975-77; Instr, CA Univ, Sacramento, 1975-82, 1992-93, Coll of Notre Dame, Belmont, CA, 1975-96; Art Therapist, Mental Hlth Cnslr, Psych W Cnslng Cntr, Carmichael, CA, 1975-93; Ptnr, Sacramento Div of Mediation Servs, 1981-82; Instr, Sacramento City Coll, 1997-. Publications include: Interpreting Metaphors in Childrens Drawings, 1995. Creative Works: Num exhbns. Memberships: Am Art Therapy Assn; CA Art Therapy Assn; CA Arts Inc; Natl Art Educ Assn; Am Assn of Marriage and Family Therapists; Kappa Kappa

Gamma Alumnae Assn; Alpha Psi Omega; Omicron Nu. Hobbies: Swimming; Golf; Theatre. Address: 4124 American River Drive, Sacramento, CA 95864-6025, USA.

DRAKE Bernard John, b. 24 Sept 1918, Christchurch, NZ. Retired Barrister and Solicitor. m. Margery Esther Gowenlock, 24 Feb 1948, 4 d. Education: BA 1940, LLB 1944, LLM 1946, Univ of Canterbury. Appointments: Asst Master Christ's Coll, 1941-43; Pt Lectr Law and Com Facs, Univ of Canterbury, 1946-66; Practising as Bar and Sol either on own account or in ptnrship, 1947-91. Honours: OBE, 1990; Christ's Coll Entrance Schlshp, 1931; Univ Jnr Schlshp, 1936; Travelling Schlshp in Law, 1947. Memberships: Canterbury Rugby Referees Assn, active referee, 1946-60; Pres 1958, 1959; Life Mbr, Canterbury Rugby Football Union Cttee 1958-59, 1965-86, Pres 1980-82, Life Mbr 1986, Pres NZ Rugby Referees Assn 1967, Victory Pk Bd, Lancaster Pk, 1977-85, Chmn 1981, Life Mbr 1986; Canterbury Cricket Assn Cttee, 1950-53, Treas 1953; C'wlth Games Promotion, 1963-72; St Margaret's Trust Bd 1968-81, Chmn 1978-81; Canterbury Dist Law Soc; var cttees inclng Legal Aid Cttee, 1970-91; Pres, Univ of Canterbury Studs Assn, 1942, 1943; Pres, Canterbury Jnr Chmbr of Comm, 1955; Pres, Canterbury Chmbr of Comm, 1966; Pres, Canterbury Prog League, 1962-64. Address: 11 Roa Road, Fendalton, Christchurch, New Zealand.

DRAKE George Warren James, b. 4 Aug 1939, Auckland, NZ. Lecturer in Music and Musicologist. m. Carla Maria Driessen, 1 s, 1 d. Education: BA, 1961, MA, 1963, Univ of Auckland, NZ; PhD, Univ of Il, USA, 1972. Appointment: Snr Lectr, Univ of Auckland, NZ. Publications: The First Books of Motets Petrucci's Motetti a Numero Trentatre (Venice 1502) and Motetti de Passione de Cruce, de Sacramento, de Beata Virgine, de Huiusmodi (Venice 1503; A Critical Study and Complete Edition, 1972). Memberships; Pres, NZ Musicological Soc, 1982-85; Amn Musicological Soc; Musicological Soc of Aust; Aust and NZ Assn for Medieval and Renaissance Studies; Intl Music Libs Assn, NZ br. Address: c/o School of Music, University of Auckland, Auckland, New Zealand.

DRAKE Harold Allen, b. 24 July 1942, Cincinnati, OH, USA. Historian. m. Kathleen Senica, 31 May 1969, 2 d. Education: AB Jrnlsm, 1963, Univ S CA; MA Eng Hist, 1966, MA Classics, 1969, PhD Ancient Hist, 1970, Univ WI, Madison. Appointments: Staff Reporter, UPI, LA,1962-65; Tchng Asst, Univ WI, Madison, 1965-68; Asst Prof, Assoc Prof, Prof Hist, Univ CA, Santa Barbara, 1970-; Chair, Dept Hist, 1987-90, 1997-98. Publications: In Praise of Constantine, 1976; Co-author, Eudoxia and the Holy Sepulchre, 1980; Constantine and the Bishops, 2000. Honours: NEH Fell, Inst Advd Stdy, Princeton, NJ, 1976-77; Snr Fell, Annenberg Rsch Inst, Phil, PA, 1991-92; Plous Awd, Acad Senate, 1976; Prof of Yr, Mortar Bd, 1986-87; Alumni Disting Tchng Awd, 1996. Memberships: Phi Beta Kappa; Phi Alpha Theta; Amn Philol Assn; Soc Promotion Roman Stdies; N Amn Patristics Soc; Amn Soc Ch History. Address: Dept of History, University California, Santa Barbara, CA 93106, USA.

DREW Leslie Raymond Hill, b. 23 Apr 1933, Moonta, SA, Aust. Psychiatrist. m. Josephine Lee Green, 21 Aug 1954, 2 s, 3 d. Education: MBBS 1955, BSc 1959, Dip in Psychological Med 1961, Univ of Melbourne; Fell, Roy Austl & NZ Coll of Psychs, 1986. Appointments: Chf Res, Psych, Boston City Hosp, MA & Tchng Fell, Harvard Univ, MA, 1962-63; Psych Supt, Sunbury Mental Hosp, 1965-70; Snr Med Advsr, C'wlth Dept of Hlth, Canberra, 1975-88; Comm Psych, Queanbeyan, NSW, 1988-90; Dir of Mental Hlth Servs, SE Region, NSW, 1991-94; Cnslt Psych, Canberra Hosp, ACT, 1994-. Publication: Drew L Moon J and Buchanan F, Alcoholism: A Handbook, 1974. Honour: Mbr, Order of Aust, 1986. Memberships: Fell, Roy Austl & NZ Coll of Psychs; Austl Profl Assn on Drugs, Life Mbr. Address: 19 Delprat Cct, Monash, ACT 2904, Australia.

DREW Philip, b. 28 Jan 1943, Coff's Harbour. Architectural Historian. m. Julie, 28 June 1969, 1 d. Education: BArch, UNSW; MArch Univ of Sydney; Chartered Archt, NSW. Publications: Books include: Tensile Architecture, 1979; Two Towers: Harry Seidler: Australia Square, MLC Tower, 1980; The Architecture of Arata Isozaki, 1982-83; Leaves of Iron: Glenn Murcutt, Pioneer of an Australian Architectural Form, 1985, 1986, 1988; Veranda: Embracing Place, 992; Real Space, The Architecture of Martorell Bohigas Makay Puigdomenech, 1993. The Coast Dwellers: Australians Living on the Edge, 1994; Sydney Opera House, 1995; Edward Suzuki: Buildings and Projects, 1996; Church of the Light, Church on the Water, 1996; Gunma Prefecture Museum of Modern Art, 1996; Contbns to encyclopedias and dictionaries. Honours: Dux of Sch, 1959; Best First Yr Result (UNSW), RAIA Awd, 1960; Category A Fellshp, Lit Bd, Aust Cncl, 1989-91; "Veranda", Natl Non-Fiction Short List, 1994; Fest Awds for Lit, Adelaide, SA, 1994. Memberships: Soc Archtl Histns (USA); Austl Soc of Auths; Intl Cttee of Archtl Critics, 1990-; ARAIA, 1986-. Hobbies: Swimming; Tennis; Bushwalking; Travel; Photography. Address: 12 View Street, Annandale, NSW 2038, Australia.

DREWE Robert Duncan, b. 9 Jan 1943, Melbourne, Australia. Novelist. m. Candida Baker, 4 s, 2 d. Education: Hon DLit, Univ Qld. Appointments: Sydney Bur Chf, The Age, 1965-70; Columnist, Lit Ed, The Australian, 1971-75; Writer-in-Res, Univ WA, 1979, LaTrobe Univ, 1986; Film Critic, Sydney Morning Herald, 1996-97. Publications: The Savage Crows, 1976; A Cry in the Jungle Bar, 1979; The Bodysurfers, 1983; Fortune, 1986; The Bay of Contented Men, 1989; Our Sunshine, 1991; South American Barbecue (play), 1991; The Drowner, 1996; Walking Ella, 1998. Honours: Natl Book Cncl Awd, 1987; C'wlth Writers Prize, 1990; NSW, Vic, WA & SA Premiers Lit Prizes, 1997; Book of the Yr, 1997; Adelaide Fest Prize for Lit, 1998. Membership: Austl Soc of Auths. Hobbies: Swimming; Walking; Films; Theatre; Watching Australian Rules Football. Address: c/o Hickson Associates, 128 Queen Street, Woollahra, NSW 2025, Australia.

DREYFUS George, b. 22 July 1928, Wuppertal, Germany. Composer. 2 s, 1 d. Education: Vienna Acady of Music, 1955-56. Appointments: Composer-in-Res, Tianjin, China, 1983; Shanghai, 1987-. Creative Works include: The Last Frivolous Book, 1984; Being George and Liking It!, book, 1998; Rathenau, opera, 1992; Die Marx Sisters, opera, 1995; Compositions include: Garni Sands; The Gilt-Edged Kid, operas; Symphonies Nos 1 & 1; Songs Comic and Curious; Music in the Air; Recdngs incl: Jingles; Homage to Igor Stravinsky; Trio From Within Looking Out; The Seasons Sextet for Didjeridu and Wind Instruments; Rush; Power Without Glory; The Adventure of Sebastian the Fox; Serenade for Small Orchestra; Many other pieces. Honours: Henry Lawson Awd, 1972; Prix de Rome, 1976; Mishkenot Sah'ananim, Jerusalem, 1980; Apra Serious Music Awd, 1986; Order of Aust, 1993. Hobbies: Swimming; Gardening. Address: 3 Grace Street, Camberwell, Vic 3124, Australia.

DREYFUSS Richard Stephan, b. 29 Oct 1947, NY. Actor. m. Jeramie Dreyfuss, 1983, 2 s, 1 d. Education: San Fernando Valley State Coll. Appointments: Alternative mil serv Los Angeles Co Gen Hosp, 1969-71. Stage appearances incl: Julius Caesar, 1978; The Big Fix, also prodr, 1978; Othello, 1979; Death and the Maiden, 1992. Films incl: American Graffitti, 1972; Dillinger, 1973; The Apprenticeship of Duddy Kravitz, 1974; Jaws, 1975; Inserts, 1975; Close Encounters of the Third Kind, 1976; The Goodbye Girl, 1977; The Competition, 1980; Whose Life Is It Anyway?, 1981; Down and Out in Beverly Hills, 1986; Stakeout, 1988; Moon over Parador, 1989; Let it Ride Always, 1989; Rosencrantz and Guildernstern are Dead; Postcards from the Edge, 1990; Once Around, 1990; Randall and Juliet, 1990; Prisoners of Honor, 1991; What About Bob?, 1991; Lost in Yonkers, 1993; Another Stakeout, 1993; The American President; Mr Holland's Opus, 1995; Mad Dog Time, 1996; James and the Giant Peach, 1996; Night Falls on Manhattan, 1997; The Call of the Wild, 1997. Tv movie: Oliver Twist, 1997. Dir produr Nuts, 1987; Hamlet, Birmingham, 1994. Publications: The Two Georges, with Harry Turtledove, 1996. Honours: Golden Globe Awd, 1978; Acady Awd for Best Actor in The Goodbye Girl, 1978. Memberships: Mbr Am Civ Liberties Union Acreen Actors Guild; Equity Assn; Amn Fedn of TV and Radio Artist; Mbr Motion Picture Acady Arts and Scis. Address: c/o ICM, 8942 Wilshire Blvd, Beverly Hills, CA 90211, USA.

DRUMMOND John Dodds, b. 11 Sept 1944, Lancaster, Eng. Music Educator; Composer; Musicologist; Opera Director; Broadcaster. m. Louise Isabel Benny, 28 Jan 1984, 2 s, 2 d. Education: Univs of Leeds and Birmingham; BA Hons, Music; MusB, Univ of Leeds; PhD, Univ of Birmingham. Appointments: Haywood Rsch Fell, Lectr in Music, Univ of Birmingham, 1969-76; Blair Prof of Music, Univ of Otgo, 1976-. Creative works: Plague Upon Eyam, opera in 3 acts, 1984. Publication: Opera in Perspective, London and Mineapolis, 1980. Memberships: NZ Soc for Music Educ; Composer's Assn of NZ; International Soc of Music Educ, Bd Mbr, 1994-96. Hobbies: Walking; Science Fiction; Good Company. Address: Department of Music, University of Otago, PO Box 56, Dunedin, New Zealand.

DRYSDALE Peter David, b. 24 Oct 1938, Grafton, NSW, Aust. Professor; Executive Director. m. Elizabeth Legge, 22 Feb 1979, 1 s. Education: BA, hons, Econs, Univ New England, 1959; PhD, Econs, Austl Natl Univ, 1967. Appointments: Tutor, Econs, 1960-61, Lectr, Econs, 1962, Univ New England; Rsch Schl, Econs Dept, Rsch Sch of Pacific Studies, 1963-65; Lectr, Econs, 1966-69, Snr Lectr, Econs, 1969-74, Rsch Dir, Aust, Japan and Western Pacific Econ Rels Rsch Project, 1972-81, Rdr, Econs, 1974-81, Profl Fell, Exec Dir, 1981-89, Prof, Exec Dir, 1989-98, Aust-Japan Rsch Cntr, Rsch Sch of Pacific and Asian Stdies, Austl Natl Univ; Prof, Exec Dir, Aust-Japan Rsch Cntr, Asia Pacific Sch of Econs and Mngmt, Austl Natl Univ, 1999-; Rsch Schl, Econs Fac, Hitotsubashi Univ, Tokyo, 1965; Adj Prof, Grad Sch of Bus, Columbia Univ. Publications include: Japanese Studies in Australia and the Training of Australians to do Business with Japan, 1987; Japan as a Pacific and World Economic Power, 1988; Japan's Trade Diplomacy: Yesterday, Today and Tomorrow, A Pacific Free Trade Area? (jointly); The Australia-Japan Relationship: Towards the Year 2000 (jointly); International Economic Pluralism: Economic Policy in Asia and the Pacific, 1989; Asia Pacific Regionalism: Readings in International Economic Relations (jointly), 1994; Corporate Links and Foreign Direct Investment in Asia and the Pacific (jointly), 1995; Europe, East Asia and APEC: A Shared Global Agenda (jointly), 1998; The Japanese Economy, Part I, vols I-IV, Part II, vols V-VIII (jointly), 1998. Honours: AM, 1985; Fell, Acady of Socl Scis in Aust, 1989; Winner, Asia-Pacific Prize, Asian Affairs Rsch Cncl and Mainichi Newsppr, Tokyo, 1989; Dunlop Asia Medal, 1995. Memberships: Econ Soc of Aust and NZ; Roy Econ Soc; US Acady of Polit Sci Japan Studies Assn of Aust; Asian Studies Assn of Aust; Korean Studies Assn of Aust. Hobbies: Jogging; Swimming. Address: Australia-Japan Research Centre, Asia Pacific School of Economics and Management, Australian National University, Canberra, ACT 0200, Australia.

DU Anna, b. 17 Jan 1945, Beijing, China. Researcher. m. Wu Shi Jin, 1968, 2 s. Education: Grad, Geophysl Dept, Geol Univ, China, 1967. Appointments: Geol Rsch Dept, Chinese Sci Inst, 1967-70; Cntr for Analysis and Prediction State Seismol Bur, 1970-. Publications: Over 30 articles in profl jrnls. Memberships: Geophysl and Seismol Assn. Hobbies: Oil painting; Piano; Table tennis; Violin; Skiing; Dancing; Singing. Address: No 63 Hai Dian Qyu, Beijing, China.

DU Hanzhong, b. 10 Feb 1937, Wuhan, China. Professional and Technical Engineer. m. Fan Kewen, 10 July 1969, 1 s, 1 d. Education: BEng, S China, Univ of Tech (SCUT), Guangzhou. Appointments: Engr, Snr Engr, Prof, Vice Chf Engr, Vice Dir, 709 Inst of CSSC (China State Shipbuilding Co), 1958-98. Creative works: X-I Computer Series, 1961-66; 908 Shipborne Computer, 1967-77; Position Measuring System, 1978-84; Anti Severe Computers, 1985-98. Honours: Over 10 projs received var awds over 40 yrs; Guang-Hua Prize, 1993. Memberships: Commnr, Wuhan Sci and Tech Assn, 1986-96; Vice Dir, Severe Environ Computer Assn of China, 1991-96. Hobbies: Reading; Music. Address: 74223 Mailbox, Wuhan 430074, China.

DU Shimin, b. 26 Mar 1940, Tonchen, Anxaie Province, China. Radio and Radar Engineer; Designer. Education: Grad, Herbin Polytech Univ, 1963. Appointment: Chf Des, Beijing Inst of Radio Measmts, 1986-. Puiblications: 11 Books incl: Radio and Microwave interference measure (co-auth), 1986;Handbook of Pragmatic TV Receiving Antenna, 1993; Home Satellite TV Receiver, 1994; Handbook of Measurement Technology, Vol 8 (co-auth), 1997; More than 100 pprs incl: A High Performance Antenna for the Monoplus Tracking, 1981; A New Method for Measuring Dielectric Constant Using the Resonant Frequency of a Patch Antenna, 1986; Dual-band Monopulse Feed and Antenna, 1996; Analysis of Multi-band Electromagnetic Compatability, 1996; Chinese Pat: Broadband Planar Microstrip Antenna, 1997. Honours: Ex Ppr, Chinese Inst of Electronics, 1986, Chinese Inst of GCS, 1986; Gold Prize, 97'Fourth News Technol and Prodn Fair, China, 1997; Ex Pat, Hong Kong Intl Spec Technol Investment Dev Grp Ltd, 1998; World Cultural Celebrity Achievement Prize, 1999; The Gold Star Awd, Symbol of Outstndng Achievement, IBC, Cambridge, 1999. Memberships: Snr Mbr, Chinese Inst of Electronics, 1986; Mbr, EMC Cttee of China, 1986; Cttee Mbr, Chinese Sci Writers'Assn; Fell, IBC; Dpty Gov, ABI. Listed in: Zhongguo Zhuanjia Dacidian, 1998; World Cultural Celebrity Dictionary (Chinese), 1998; Worldwide Consultative Expert (China), 1998; Zhonguo Zhuanjia Rencaiku, 1998; Five Hundred Leaders of Influence. Hobby: Huangmei drama. Address: PO Box 142, Branch Box 203-2, Beijing 100854, China.

DU Zhongren, b. 11 Dec 1941, Beijing, China. Researcher; Educator. m. Jizhuang Fang, 18 Mar 1974, 2 d. Education; BS, Nankai Univ, Tianjin, China, 1964; Dip, Electron Engrng, Tianjin Laser Inst, China, 1981. Appointments: Visng Staff MBr, Strathclyde Univ, UK, 1986-87; Lectr, Tianjin Inst Tech, 1987-94; Assoc Prof, Tianjin Inst, Tech, 1994-98. Publications: Robot's Nerves: Optic Fibre Sensors, Fibre Optic Sensors IIAM Scheggi; Ed, Proc SPIE 798, 1987. Honours: Schlshp, Tianjin Higher Educ Bur, 1986; Supvsr Awd of Student Rsch Contest, Tianjin, 1997. Memberships: China Interpreter Assn; China Electrons Soc. Hobbies: Light classical music; Chinese cooking; Walking. Address: 98 Ying Shui Road, 2-1-501, Tianjin 300191, China.

DUAN Baolin, b. 6 Jan 1934. Professor. m. Chin, 6 Aug 1961, 2 d. Education: Grad, Peking Univ, 1958. Appointments: Prof, Peking Univ, Dept of Chinese. Publications: Essentials of the Chinese Folk Literature, 1981; Complete Collected Works of Chinese Folklore (series of books), 1998. Honours: Outstndng Wrk Prize, 1980; Pitrè premio, Centro Internazionale di Etnosteria Palermo Italia, 1996. Memberships: VP, Chinese Folklore Rsch Soc; VP, Chinese Folklore Rsch Soc. Hobbies: Singing; Sports. Address: Department of Chinese, Peking University, 100871, Beijing, China.

DUC Ha Minh, b. 3 May 1935, Thanh Hoa, Vietnam. Professor; Writer. m. Pham Bich Ngoc, 8 Feb 1963, 1 d. Education: Grad, Lit Dept, Ha Noi Tchng Coll, 1957; LLD, 1990. Appointments: Dpty Prof, 1984, Prof, 1990, Dean, Preas Fac, 1990, Dir, Lit Inst, Ed-in-Chf, Lit Review, 1995, Chmn, 1995-2000. Publications include: Professor and His Working Place, 1996; Time and Witness, 1998; Nam Cao Writer - Career and Works, 1998; Treatise in Literature, 1998. Honours: 1st Prize of Lit, 1985; Awd, Vietnamese Writers Assn, 1985; 2nd Grade Medal, 1987; Ex Tchr, 1990; Labour Decoration 3rd Grade, 1995. Memberships: Vietnamese Writers Assn; Vietnamese Jrnlsts Assn; Chmn, Criticism and Theory Cncl, 1985-89; Mbr, Vietnamese Natl Educ Cttee, 1995-200. Hobbies: Writing; Travel. Address: 20Ly Thai To Street, Hanoi, Vietnam.

DUCAT Raymond John, b. 8 Mar 1943, Shepparton, Aust. Owner, Managing Director, Ducats Food Products. m. Carmel, 8 Mar 1969, 1 s, 4 d. Education: Cert of Competancy, Gilbert Chandler Sch of Dairy Technol, 1963. Career: Owner, Mngr, Ducats Food Prods Pty Ltd, Vic, Aust, (founded in 1917), 1957-. Memberships: Treas, Milk Processors Assn of Vic; Treas, Vic Milk Distbrs Assn; Life Govr, Guthrie St Primary Sch. Hobby: Travel to overseas food shows. Address: Ducats Food Products Pty Ltd, 116 Corio Street, Shepparton, VIC 3630, Australia.

DUCK-CHONG Robert Neil, b. 27 Sept 1932, Sydney, Aust. Life Insurance Broker; Financial Planner. m. Barbara, 27 Oct 1986, 1 s, 4 d. Appointments: Pres, Life Underwriters' Assn of Aust (NSW), 1977; Natl VP, Life Underwriters' Assn of Aust, 1978-79; Natl Pres, 1980-81; Regl Monitor, Rosicrucian Order, AMORC, 1979-81, Grand Cnclr, 1981-84; Mbr, Life Ins Consultative Cttee, 1981-89; Chmn, NIBA Life & Employee Benefits Cttee, 1987-90; Accredited Lifewriter, 1991; Grand Cmdr, OSTI Aust, 1992-99; Pres, Delegate Circes Aust, 1992-99. Honour: Life Mbr, Austl Lifewriters Assn. Memberships: Finl Plng Assn; Hon Roll Life Mbr, Million Dollar Round Table; Fell, Natl Ins Brokers Assn; Fell, Austl Inst of Co Dirs; Dipl, Austl Ins Inst; Fell, Assn Fin Advsrs. Hobbies: Teaching Acting; Communication; EMF Balancing; Music; Reading. Address: 3 Blue Ridge Crescent, Berowra Heights, NSW 2082, Australia.

DUCKER William Thomas, b. 18 Mar 1933, NSW, Australia. Judge, District Court. m. (1) Margaret Christine Waugh, 30 May 1964, 2 d, (2) Jennifer Patricia Michel, 3 Sept 1988. Appointments: Admitted to Bar NSW, 1961; Crown Prosecutor, New Eng and Far N Coast, 1967; Dist Crt Judge, 1980. Hobbies: Wine; Music; Reading. Address: Judges Chambers, District Court, Sydney, NSW 2000, Australia.

DUCKWORTH Colin Ryder, b. 20 July 1926, Birmingham, Eng. Writer; Academic. m. Mary Adams, 2 Jan 1954, 1 s, 1 d. Education: BA Hons, MA, Birmingham; PhD, Trinity Hall, Cambridge; DLitt, Melbourne. Appointments: Lecteur Anglais, Montpellier Univ, 1950-51; Lectr, French, Bedford Coll, London Univ, 1954-71; Visng Prof, Univ CA (Davis), 1966-67; Prof of French, Auckland Univ, 1972-77; Prof of French, 1978-88, Emer Prof and Professorial Fell, 1988-, Univ of Melbourne; Hon Visng Prof, Drama, La Trobe Univ, 1992-96. Publications: A Study of Leon Bopp: the Novelist and the Philosopher, 1955; Angels of Darkness: Dramatic Impact in Beckett and Ionesco, 1972; The d'Antraigues Phenomenon: The Making and Breaking of a Revolutionary Royalist Espionage Agent, 1986; Steps to the High Garden (novel), 1992; Digging in Dark Places (novel), 1997; Opera Libretti; Translator: Tardieu, The Underground Lovers and Other Experimental Plays; Critical Eds of Voltaire, Beckett, Flaubert and Renan. Honour: Cmdr, Ordre des Palmes Académiques, 1984. Memberships: Fell, Roy Soc of Arts; Intl Soc for 18th C St, Sec-Gen, 1970-75; Alliance Française Auckland, Pres, 1973-77, Melbourne Cttee, VP, 1978-97; Austl Soc of Auths, 1999. Hobbies: Music; Theatre; Tennis. Address: PO Box 93, Parkville, Victoria, 3052, Australia.

DUCKWORTH Marilyn, b. 10 Nov 1935, Auckland, NZ. Writer. m. (1) Harry Duckworth, 28 May 1955, dissolved 1964, (2) Ian Macfarlane, 2 Oct 1964, dissolved 1972, Daniel Donovan, 9 Dec 1974, dec 1978, John Batstone, 8 June 1985, 4 d. Publications: Novels incl: Disorderly Conduct, 1984; Married Alive, 1985; Rest For The Wicked, 1986; Pulling Faces, 1987; A Message From Harpo, 1989; Unlawful Entry, 1992; Seeing Red, 1993; Fooling (novella), 1994; Leather Wings, 1995; Studmuffin, 1997; (short stories) Explosions on the Sun, 1989; (poems) Other Lovers Children, 1975; (non-fiction) Cherries on a Plate, 1994. Honours include: Katherine Mansfield Fellshp, Menton, 1980; Fulbright Visng Writers's Fellshp, USA, 1987; OBE for servs to Lit, 1987; Aust NZ Writers' Exchange Fellshp, 1989; Vic Univ of Wellington Writer's Fellshp, 1990; Arts Cncl NZ Schlshp in Letters, 1993; Hawthornden Writing Fellshp, Scot, 1994; Sargeson Writing Fellshp, Auckland, 1995; Auckland Univ Lit Fellshp, 1996; Shortlisted Commonwealth Writer's Prize, for Leather Wings, 1996. Membership: NZ Soc of Auths; PEN. Hobby: Violin. Address: 41 Queen Street, Mt Victoria, Wellington, New Zealand.

DUFFY Michael John (The Hon,) b. 2 Mar 1938, Mildura, Vic, Aust. Politician. m. Carolyn Adams, 29 Apr 1965, 1 s, 2 d. Education: Christian Brother's Coll, Albury, NSW; Newman Coll, Univ of Melbourne. Appointments: Solicitor, Michael Duffy & Co, 1968-71; Ptnr, Duffy and Forrest, 1971-80; MHR (ALP), Holt, Vic, 1980-96; Min Comms, 1983-87; Min, Trade Negotiations, 1987-90; Fed Atty-Gen, 1990-93. Honour: Awd'd Order of NZ, NZ Govt, 1990. Memberships: Mbr, Labor Party Victorian Branch Admin Cttee, 1973-76; Mbr HoR Jnt Cttee of Pub Accts, 1980-83. Hobbies: Cricket; Football; Horse racing; Reading; Music. Address: 8 Birdwood, St Mentone, Vic 3194, Australia.

DUGAR Chand Ratan, b. 11 Apr 1953, Sardarshar, Churu Rajasthan, India. Chief Executive Officer. m. Kamala, 2 June 1975. Education: BCom (Hons), Calcutta Univ, India, FCA. Appointments: Audit Articled Clkship as Chartered Acct, M/s Singhi & Co, Calcutta, India, 1971-75; Snr Asst M/S Singhi & Co, 1975-76; Chf Acct; Coml Mngr, VP, Fin and Mktng, Jt Pres, M/S East Spinning Mills, 1976-91; Advsr, Indophils Mills Philppines and Indo-Thai Synthetic Thailand, 1992; Gen Mngr, Pt Elegant Textile Ind, 1992-97; Pres, Dir, Pt Elegant Textile Ind, 1997-; Shawali Awd as Environ Friendly Businessman, Indonesian Environ Mngmt and Info Cntr. Honours: Grid Awd, Grid Org Dev Grp, Malaysia; Best Exec Awd conferred by Asean Prog Cnslt Indonesian Consortium, Indonesian Dev Citra Awds, 1998-99. Memberships: Fell, Inst of Chartered Acct of India. Hobbies: Cricket; Outings; Reading. Address: P T Elegant Textile Industry, Menara Batavia Level 16, Jl K H Mas Manysur, Kav 126 Jakarta 10220, Indonesia.

DUGGINS Robert Kirby, b. 16 Mar 1935, Birmingham, Eng. University Professor. m. Clare Margaret Duggins, 3 Aug 1964, 1 s, 1 d. Education: Coll of Advd Technol, Birmingham; Univ of London, 1953-57; BSc, Hons, Univ of Nottingham, 1963; PhD. Appointments: Lectr, Snr Lectr, Mech Engrng, Univ of Nottingham, 1963-76; NASA Postdoc Rsch Assoc, Univ of Pitts, USA, 1964-65; Prof, Hd Dept, Univ of NSW; Austl Def Force Acady, 1976-; Consultancies incl: Imperial Oil Ltd, Can; Rolls Royce and Assocs, Eng. Publications: 80 pprs in tech lit. Honours: Birmingham Chmbr of Comm Awd, 1957; Fulbright Schlshp, 1964; Hon Mbr, Amn Fraternity of Engrs, 1965; Roy Soc Visng Awd, 1969. Memberships include: Fell, Inst of Engrs; Chartered Engr; Inst of Mech Engrs, UK. Hobbies: Sport; Current Affairs. Address: 23 Holmes Crescent, Campbell, Canberra, ACT 2601, Australia.

DUGGLEBY John Colin, b. 27 Apr 1936, Thorpe Bassett, Eng. Physicist (retd). m. Barbara Ann Hopwood, 22 Dec 1962. Education: BSc (Hons), Phys, London Univ, 1958; PhD, Medl Phys, Leeds Univ, 1962. Appointments: Rsch Asst, Leeds Univ, 1958-62; Rsch Scientist, Austl Atomic Energy Commn, 1962-65; Snr Profl Offr, Austl Radiation Lab, Austl Govt, 1965-96. Publications: Over 50 sci pprs and reports; Hockey in Waverley: The First 25 Years, 1984. Honours: Cty Exhibn Schlshp (York), 1955; Goldsmiths Co Schlshp, 1957; Awd of Merit, Vic Hockey Assn, 1989. Memberships: Inst of Phys (UK), MInstP; Fell, Austl Inst of Phys (FAIP); Australasian Radiation Protection Soc (MARPS); Australasian Coll of Phys Scientists and Engrs in Med (MACPSEM). Hobbies: Hockey; Bridge; Walking. Address: 20 Battery Road, Panton Hill, Vic 3759, Australia.

DUMARESQ John Alan, b. 5 Feb 1914, Tas. Veterinarian. m. Elizabeth, 2 s, 2 d. Education: BVSc. Appointments: Vet Pathol, Tas, 1937-42, 1947-50; Flight Lt, RAAF, 1943-46; Austl Meat Rsch Cttee, 1967-79. Memberships: Tas Farmers Fedn; Austl Ver Assn; Austl Wool and Meat Fedn. Hobbies: Fishing; Gardening. Address: Greenside, Longford, Tas 7301, Australia.

DUMITRU Pavel, 1 Sept 1963, Vaslui, Romania. Research Scientist. Education: Bachelor of Polymer Engrng (Hons), Jasi, Romania; PhD, Polymer Area, 1999.

Appointments: Rsch Engr, Tech Univ of Iasi, 1989; Rsch Scientist, RMIT Univ, Aust, 1998. Publications: 1 sci book (auth) Liquid Crystalline Polymers, 1999; 1 patent in Polymer Sci; Over 30 sci pprs in Polymer Sci. Honours: RMIT Univ Postgrad Awd, 1996-98; Awd for Outsndng Merit, Polytechnical Inst of Iasi, 1988. Memberships: Instn of Engrs, Aust. Hobbies: Art; Reading; Travelling; Soccer. Address: RMIT University, Department of Chemical Engineering, GPO Box 2476V, Melbourne, Vic 3001, Australia.

DUNAWAY Dorothy Faye, b. 14 Jan 1941 Bascom FL. m. (1) Peter Wolf, 1974; (2) Terry O'Neill - qv - 1981. Education: Univs of FL and Boston. Appointments: Spent three yrs with Lincoln Cntr Repertory Co in NY appearing in A Man for All Seasons, After the Fall and Tartuffe; Off-Bradway in Hogan's Goat, 1965; Appeared at the Mark Taper Forum LA in Old Times as Blanche du Bois in A Streetcar Named Desire, 1973; The Curse of an Aching Heart, 1982. Films incl: Hurry Sundown, 1967; The Happening, 1967; Bonnie and Cylde, 1967; The Thomas Crown Affair, 1968; A Place For Lovers, 1969; The Arrangement, 1969; Little Big Man, 1970; Doc, 1971; The Getaway, 1972; Oklahoma Crude, 1973; The Three Musketeers, 1973; Chinatown, 1974; Three Days of the Condor, 1975; The Towering Inferno, 1976; Voyage of the Damned, 1976; Network, 1976; The Eyes of Laura Mars, 1978; The Champ, 1979; The First Deadly Sin, 1981; Mommie Dearest, 1981; The Wicked Lady, 1982; Supergirl, 1984; Barfly, 1987; Burning Secret, 1988; The Handmaid's Tale, 1989; On A Moonlit Night, 1989; Up to Date, 1989; Scorchers, 1991; Faithful, 1991; Three Weeks in Jerusalem; The Arrowtooth Waltz, 1991; Double Edge; Arizona Dream; The Temp; Don Juan DeMarco; Drunks; Dunston Checks In; Albino Alligator; The Chamber. Tv incl: After the Fall, 1974; The Disappearance of Aimee, 1976; Hogan's Goat; Mommie Dearest, 1981; Evita!-First Lady, 1981; 13 at Dinner, 1985; Beverly Hills Madame, 1986; The Country Girl; Casanova; The Raspberry Ripple; Cold Sassy Tree; Silhouette; Rebecca. Publications: Looking For Gatsby - autobiog with Betsy Sharkey - 1995. Honours: Acady Awd Best Actress for Network. Address: c/o ICM, 8942 Wilshire Blvd, Beverly Hills, CA 90211, USA.

DUNCAN Doris G. Professor of Computer Information Systems. Education: PhD; CCP; CDP; CSP; CDE. Appointments: Mngr, Amn Telephone and Telegraph; Comms Cnslt, Pacific Northwest Bell Telephone Co; Snr Staff Cnslt, Prof Mngr, Quantum Sci Corp; Dir of Info Sci, Golden Gate Univ, San Fran; Visng Prof, Univ of WA, Seattle; Prog Coordinator, currently Prof, Computer Info Systs, CA State Univ at Hayward. Publications: Computers and Remote Computing Services, 1983; Over 40 articles in jrnls and pprs in conf proceedings. Honours: Educator of Yr, Intl Assn of Computer Info Systems; Bronze, Silver, Gold, Emerald and Diamond Perf Awds, Assn of Info Technol Profls; Beta Gamma Sigma Natl Scholastic Honorary. Memberships: Assn of Info Technol Profls; AITP Spec Interest Grp in Educ; Editl Review Bd Mbr, Jrnl of Info Systems Educ; Assn of Computing Machinery. Address: California State University, Hayward, CA 94542, USA.

DUNDAS-SMITH Peter, b. 18 Apr 1945. Executive Director. m. Cherry Burdon, 7 Aug 1971, 2 s. Educaton: RAAF Acady, Point Cook, UNE.Appointments: Joined RAAF, 1964; Air Traffic Controller, Butterworth, Malaysia, Williamstown, NSW, Richmond, NSW, 1968-78; Snr Military Control Offr, Sydney Airport, 1976-79; Personnel Plans and Plcy Sect, AF Off, Canberra, 1979-81; Wing Cmndr, 1982; Proj Offr, 1982-84; Dir of Admin Austl Def Force Acady, 1984-85; Controller of Telecom Tower, Black Mountain, Canberra, 1985-87; Chmn, Canberra Visitor Attractions Assn, 1986-; Pres, Canberra Visitor Convention Bur, 1987; Mngr, Telecom Aust, Canberra, 1988-92; Exec Dir, Fisheries Rsch and Dev Corp, 1992-. Honour: Jnt Servs Commendation, 1988. Membership: Canberra Southern Cross Club. Hobbies: Home entertainment; Snow-skiing; Gardening; Golf. Address: 4 Pelham Place, Chapman, ACT 2611, Australia.

DUNFORD John Robert (The Hon Mr Justice), b. 17 Apr 1936. Judge. m. Kathleen Lohan, 20 Apr 1965, 1 s, 4 d. Education: LLB, Univ of Sydney. Appointments: Barrister-at-Law, 1960-86; QC, NSW, 1980, Tas and ACT, 1981, Judge, Dist Crt of NSW, 1986-92; Judge, Supreme Crt of NSW, 1993-. Publication: Landlord and Tenant (NSW) Practice and Procedure, 7th edition (jointly). Hobbies: Surfing; Golf; Music. Address: Judges' Chambers, Supreme Court, Sydney, NSW, Australia.

DUNG Huynh Phi, b. 26 Jan 1961, Buon Me Thuot Prov, Vietnam. Manufacturing, Trading and Import-Export Executive; National Assembly Deputy. m. Tran Thi Tuyet, 3 children. Education: Army Ordnance Sch, 5th Mil Zone, 1979-80. Appointments: Vietnam Mil Offr, Army Corps 7707, 1980-83; Dir, Lime Prod Enterprise, Thu Dau Mot Police Dept, 1983-90; Dir Gen, Thanh Le Trading Import-Export Co, Song Be Prov, 1991-96; Chmn, Bd of Dirs, Binh Duong Assn of Enterprises for Invmnt and Dev, Vietnam, 1996-; Elected, Natl Assembly, Socl Repub of Vietnam, 1997-2002. Honours: Decoration, Vietnam Red Cross; Decoration, Vietnam Labour, War Invalid and Socl Affairs; Awd, Natl Def; Awd, Educ Min. Memberships: Vietnam Red Cross; Barons Fellshp, 1997-98; Binh Duong Assn of Enterprises for Invmnt and Dev; Natl Assembly Dep, Socl Repub of Vietnam, 1997-2002. Address: Binh Duong Association of Enterprises for Investment and Development, 63 Yersin Street, Thu Dau Mot Town, Binh Duong Province, Vietnam.

DUNKIN Ruth, b. 18 May 1953. University Administrator. Education: BA, Hons, Melbourne; GradDipMngmt, UCQ; MPA, Harv. Appointment: Dpty Vice-Chan, Dpty Pres, RMIT, Melbourne, 1998.

DUNMORE John, b. 6 Aug 1923, Trouville, France. Professor (retired). m. Joyce Megan Langley, 22 Apr 1946, 1 s, 1 d. Education: BA (Hons), Univ of London, 1948-50; Assoc, Inst of Banks, UK, 1950-; Vic Univ Coll, Wellington, NZ, 1957-59, PhD, 1962. Appointments: Second Sch Tchr, 1951-56; Lectr, Snr Lectr, Massey Univ, 1961-66; Prof of French, 1966-83; Dean of Hum, 1968-81; Chmn, Higher Salaries Commn, 1986-91. Publications: Over 30 incl: New Zealand: The North Island, 1987; New Zealand: The South Island, 1987; The Book of Friends, 1989; New Zealand and the French, 1990, 1997; Around the Shining Waters, 1991; The French and the Maori, 1992; A Playwright's Workbook, 1993; The Journal of La Pérouse, 1994-95; Visions and Realities: France in the Pacific 1695-1995, 1997. Honours: NZ Book of the Yr, 1970; Legion of Hon, 1976; Acad Palms, 1986; NZ Commemoration Medal, 1990; Massey Medal, 1993. Memberships: Australasia Univs Lang and Lit Assn, Pres, 1980-82; Fedn des Alliances Françaises de NZ, Pres, 1979-98. Hobbies: Drama; Politics. Address: 9b Pounamu Avenue, Greenhithe, Auckland, New Zealand.

DUNN Michael Ronald, b. 2 Mar 1942, Ashburton, New Zealand. University Professor. m. Patricia, 30 Jan 1970. Education: Dip FA, Hons; PhD, Auckland; BA Hons; MA, Melbourne; DipFA Cant. Appointments: Lectr, Art Hist, Univ Auckland, 1970-75; Snr Lectr, 1976-92; Hd, Dept, 1992-93; Prof, Hd, Fine Arts, 1994-. Publications: A Concise History of New Zealand Painting, 1991-93; Contemporary Painting in New Zealand, 1996. Honours: Smithsonian Grantee, 1986; Queen Elizabeth Arts Cncl Grantee, 1966-69. Membership: Bd Mbr, Auckland Art Gall, 1979-96. Hobbies: Swimming; Art Collecting. Address: 18 Bracken Avenue, Epsom, Auckland, New Zealand.

DUNSFORD Cathie Joy, b. 12 Dec 1953. Publishing Consultant. Education: BA, MA (1st class hons), PhD, Auckland Univ, NZ, 1972-83; Fulbright Post-Doct Rsch Schl, Univ CA, Berkeley, USA, 1983-86. Appointments: Lectr, Engl Dept, Auckland Univ, 1976-83; Fulbright Post-Doct Rsch Fell, Lectr, Univ CA, Berkeley, USA, 1983-86; Freelance Ed, Mngng Ed, Black Widow Publns, USA, 1987-89; Dir, Forum N Conf and Cultural Ctr, Whangarei City Cncl, 1989-90; Hd, Community Activities, Arts/Cutural Div, Whangarei City Cncl; Sec, Northland Community Arts Trust; Co-ord, Matakana Community

Scheme, Northland, 1990-92; Dir, Dunsford & Assocs Publng Cnslts, 1990-. Publications include: New Women's Fiction, 1986; Subversive Acts, 1991; Me & Marilyn Monroe, 1993; Cowrie; The Journey Home; Manawa Toa; CMXL; Aust In 2 , anthology. Honours: Univ Schlsps, 1971, 1988; Fulbright Post-Doct Rsch Schlsp, 1983-86; Leading Writers Grant, 1995, Schlshp in Letters, 1997, NZ Arts Cncl; Intl Woman of the Yr in Publng, 1997. Memberships: Mercury Th, 1968-78; Northland Community Trust; NZIM; Life Mbr, NZIBS; NZ Book Eds Assn; Life Mbr, Bloomsbury Writers. Listed in: New Zealand Who's Who; International Who's Who. Hobbies: White Water Rafting; Kayaking; Gardening; Conservation; Internet. Address: Dunsford Publishing Consultants, RD 6, Warkworth, Aotearoa, New Zealand.

DUNSTAN Allan Albert, b. 8 Apr 1924, Donald, Vic, Aust. Newspaper Executive; Farmer. m. Lesley Mavis Hands, 1 Mar 1947, 3 s. Appointments: Cnclr, Shire of Donald, 36 yrs, Shire Pres, 5 times; Pres, Vic Country Football League, 1979-80; Fndr, Donald and Dist Sports Complex; Cricket career 40 yrs; Capt/Mngr, Co Week, 30 yrs; Chmn, Donald Nursing Home Appeal and new ambulance stat; Fndr Donald Ind Estate. Honours: OBE, for servs to comm, 1980; OAM, 1992; Justice of the Peace, 1974-; Natl Merit Awd for serv to country football. Memberships: SPASMS Club, Donald; Vic Co Football League. Hobbies: Cricket; Football. Address: 4 Corack Street, Donald, Vic 3480, Australia.

DUNSTON Arthur John, b. 17 Jan 1922, Reading, Eng. Emeritus Professor. m. Lynette Meryl McAuley, 1 s, 1 d. Education: BA, Univ of Reading, Eng, 1940-41; 1945-47; BA 1949, MA 1951, St John's Coll, Cambridge; MA Hons, Sydney. Appointments: Asst Lectr, Classics, Univ Coll, London, 1949-51; Lectr, Classics, Univ of Reading, 1951-53; Prof, Latin, 1953-86, Dean, Fac of Arts, 1956-62, Dpty Vice Chan, 1981-86, Univ of Sydney, Aust. Publications: Studies in Domizio Calderini, 1968; Four Centres of Classical Learning in Renaissance Italy, 1972; Sir Hermann Black, Selected Addresses, ed, 1996. Honours: Cavaliere nell'Ordine'al Merito della Repubblica Italiana', 1968; Hon DLitt, Sydney, 1987. Hobby: Lawn Bowls. Address: 7/11 Cates Place, St Ives, NSW 2075, Australia.

DUPONT Alan Anthony, b. 7 Oct 1950, London, Eng. Academic. m. Rosemary, 7 Dec 1974, 2 d. Education: BA Hons, Austl Natl Univ; MA; Grad, Roy Mil Coll, 1968-71. Appointments: Army Offr, 1971-79; Jrnlst, Pacific Defence Reporter, 1980-81; Dipl, 1982-94; Dir, Asia Pacific Security Prog, Austl Natl Univ, 1997-. Memberships: Intl Inst for Strategic Stdies; Austl Natl Cttee Cncl for Security Co-op Asia and Pacific. Hobbies: Skiing; Tennis; Running; Reading; Gardening. Address: Research School of Pacific and Asian Studies, The Australian National University, Canberra, ACT 0200, Australia.

DURAI Pushparanee Thambiah, b. 4 Feb 1938. Senior Research Entomologist. m. Dr Suppiah Sinnadurai, 18 Aug 1967. Education: Rsch and Publs, Snr Rsch Fell, ASEAN PLANTI, Malaysia, 1985-86; Cert, Hun Resource Mngmt, INTAN, PLANTI, 1987-88; Study Tour, Dept of Entomology. Univ FL, Gainesville, Dept Primary Inds, FL, 1992, Study Tour, US Dept Agric, USDA-APHIS-PPQ, Hyattsville, MD, USA, 1992. Appointments include: Tchr, Zool Meth Boys Second Sch, Malaysia, 1964-67; Tchr, Chem and Bio, Achimota and St John's Second Sch, Ghana, 1968-78; Tutor, Zool and Medl Dept, Univ of Ghana, Legon, W Africa, 1975-79; Rsch Assoc, Zool Dept, Univ Ghana, Legon, W Africa, 1980-81; Snr Rsch Entomologist, ASEAN Plant Quarantine Cntr and Trng Inst, Min Agric, Post Bag 209, UPM 43400, Serdang, Selangor, Malaysia, 1987-94; Resource Person: Jrnl of Socl Sci and Hum, UPM, Serdang, 1995-96; Malaysian Nat Soc, KL, 1996-97; CAB Intl, Wallingford, Oxon, UK, June-July 1996. Publications: 18 papers incl: (w A Ganapathi) Plant Quarantine and Pest Risk Analysis, Paper presented at MAPPS 4th International Conference on Plant Protection in the Tropics, Kuala Lumpur, Malaysia, 1994. Honours: Presidential Seal of Hon, 1996, Man of the Yr, 1996,

ABI.Memberships: African Assn of Insect Sci (Kenya-Nairobi), 1977-81; Legon Women's Soc (A Socl Welfare Club) Ghana; Malaysian Plant Protection Soc (MAPPS); SAM (Sahabat Alam Sekitar). Listed in: Many Including: Malaysian Who is Who; ASEAN Who is Who; Asia Pacific Who's Who. Address: No 28 Jalan 5/1 Jalan Gasing, 46000 Petaling Jaya, Selangor, Malaysia.

DURAISWAMY Sivanandini, b. 24 Dec 1936, Colombo, Sri Lanka. Coordinating Secretary, Ministry of Duraiswamy Cultural Religious Affairs. m. Yogendra, 26 Aug 1962, 1 s. Education: BA, London; Assoc, Trinity Coll of Music, London; Dip, Carnatic Music, Sri Lanka; Dip, Chinese Brush Work Painting. Appointments: Coordinating Sec, Min of Cultural & Religious Affairs. Publications: Remembering Hindu Traditions, 1997. Honours: Zonta (Intl) Awd for Socl Work; Hon by Hindu Women's Soc. Memberships: Pres, Hindu Women's Soc, 1995; Hindu Voice, Ed, 1997; Sri Lanka Women's Conf. Hobbies: Painting; Writing. Address: 9 Castle Lane, Colombo 4, Sri Lanka.

DURAN Roberto, b. 16 Jun 1951 Chorrillo. Boxer. m. Felicidad Duran, 4 c. Appointments: Profl boxer March 1967-; Won world lightweight title from Ken Buchanan, June 1972; Made record number of championship defs - 12 - before relinquishing title to box as welterweight from Feb 1979; Won World Boxing Cncl version of world welterweight title from Ray Leonard - qv - Montreal, June 1980; Lost it to Leonard New Orleans, Nov 1980; Retained it 1989; 79 fights, 75 wins; Exempt from all taxes received monthly pension for life from Govt. Hobbies: Cars. Address: Nuevo Reperto El Carmen, Panama.

DURAN BALLEN Sixto, b. Boston MA USA. Politician. Education: Columbia Univ. Appointments: Prac'd as archtect; Fmr Mayor of Quito; Fmr offic of Inter-Am Dev Bank NY; Pres of Ecuador, 1992-96. Memberships: Mbr Partido Unidad Republicana - PRU. Address: c/o Office of the President, Palacio Nacional, Garcia Moreno 1043, Quito, Ecuador.

DUREY Peter Burrell, b. 29 Aug 1932, Sunderland, England. University Librarian Emeritus. m. Patricia Mary Antill, 1965, div 1984, 2 d. Education: BA, Durham; FLA; FNZLA, ALAA. Appointments: Grad Asst, Newcastle Upon Tyne, 1956; Snr Asst Libn, Univ Reading, Eng, 1957-63; Sub Libn, Univ of Sussex, Eng, 1963-66; Dpty Libn, Univ of Keele, 1966-70, Univ Libn, Univ Auckland, 1970-98; Em, Univ Auckland, 1998-. Publications: Staff Mngmt, Univ and Coll Libs, 1976; Num articles. Memberships: NZLIA, Pres, 1981; LA; ALIA; Rotary. Hobbies: Theatre; Cinema; Toy Theatres; Painting. Address: 711D Remuera Road, Remuera, Auckland 5, New Zealand.

DUTT Ganesh C, b. 8 July 1931, Dhaka, Bangladesh. Medical Practitioner. m. Susanna, 17 May 1969, 2 d. Education: BSc (Hons); MBBS; DTM&H, Edin; MRCP (UK); MF Hom (UK); Dip in Medl Acupuncture (UK). Appointments: Hosps: House Offr, Med; SHO, Registrar; Med. Psych; Snr Registrar Geriatrics; GP Trng; GP. Publications: Articles; Book: Health Care for Bangladeshis (Engl/Bengali). Memberships: Brit Medl Assn; Overseas Drs Assn; Local Medl Cttee; G P Forum; Small Prac Assn. Hobbies: Writing; Music; Swimming; Travel; Photography. Address: Asian Observe Publications, 47 Beattyville Gardens, Ilford, Essex 1G61JW, England.

DUVALL James Ernest, b. Provo, UT, USA. Test Engineer. m. Doreen Renée Peterson, 29 May 1993, 1 s, 2 d. Education: BS, Computer Sci, Brigham Young Univ, 1984. Address: ATL Ultrasound, 22100 Bothell-Everett Highway, Bothell, WA 98021, USA.

DUYKER Edward Adrian Joseph, b. 21 Mar 1955, Melbourne, Aust. Historian; Author. m. Susan Wade, 30 Oct 1982, 2 s. Education: BA (hons), La Trobe; PhD, Melbourne. Appintments: Hon Consul, Repub of Mauritius, 1996; JP, 1997. Publications: Mauritian Heritage, 1986; Tribal Guerillas, 1987; The Dutch in

Australia, 1987; Of the Star and the Key, 1988; Molly and the Rajah, 1991; The Discovery of Tasmania, 1992; An Officer of the Blue, 1994; A Woman of the Goldfields, 1995; Daniel Solander, 1995; Nature's Argonaut, 1998. Memberships: Austl Soc of Auths; Inst for the Study of the French Austl Rels; Ntl Trust; Austl Mauritian Rsch Grp, Chmn, 1983-. Hobbies: Gardening; Bush regeneration; Reading; Classical music. Address: PO Box 20, Sylvania-Southgate, NSW 2224, Australia.

DWIVEDI Manisha, b. 29 Dec 1952, Allahabad. Medical Doctor. m. Shailesh, 5 Mar 1978, 2 s, 1 d. Education; MB, BS; MD; DM (Gastroeneterology), All India Inst of Medl Sci, New Delhi, 1988. Appointments: Lectr in Med, 1982; Assoc Prof of Gastroenterology, 1990; Prof in Gastroenterology, 1998-, MLN Medl Coll, Allahabad. Publications: 67 full rsch pprs in intl and natl profl jrnls. Honours: Stood 1st and 2nd in profl MBBS exams; Overall 1st in MBBS; Gold Medals in Anatomy, Pathol, Pharmacology, Forensic Med, Socl and Preventive Med, Med, Surg, Gynae, Obstets; P N Berry Schlshp to visit Uk, 1991. Memberships: Pres, UP Chapt of Indian Soc of Gastroenterology, 1998-99; INSAL; ISG; SGEI; API. Hobbies: Reading; Music. Address: 4/403, MLN Medical College, Allahabad 211001, India.

DWYER Judith Margaret, b. 20 Mar 1951, Brisbane, Aust. Health Service Executive. 1 d. Education: BA, Univ of Qld, Aust, 1972; Ass Dip, Vic Coll, 1982; MBusAd, Univ of Adelaide, 1988. Appointments: Rsch Cnslt, Cty of Kensington, 1981; Rsch Admin, Adelaide Womens Hlth Cntr, 1982-85; Dir of Admin, Julia Farr Cntr, 1986; Chief Exec Offr, Family Plng Assn, 1987; Dir, Resources, Plng, Metro Hlth Servs Div, SA, 1989; Dir, Bd Adelaide Med Cntr for Women and Children, 1986-89; Gen Mngr, Queen Vic Hosp, 1991-93; Mbr, Hlth Care Cttee, Natl Hlth and Med Rsch Cncl; Chmn, Women's Hlth Sub Cttee, 1991-94; Dpty Chief Exec Offr, Women's and Childrens Hosp, 1993-95; Chief Exec Offr, Flinders Med Cntr, 1995; Dir, Austl Inst of Hlth and Welfare, 1995-98; Assoc Prof, Pub Hlth, Flinders Univ, 1997; Chf Exec Offr, Southern Hlth Care Network, Victoria, 1999. Publications include: Num papers in profl jrnls. Honours: MBA Soc Prize, 1988; Austl Medl Assn Women's Hlth Awd, 1998. Membership. Assoc Fell, Ausl Coll of Hlth Serv Execs; Austl Pub Hlth Assn. Listed in: Who's Who in Business. Address: 1/49 Marine Parade, St Kilda, Victoria 3182, Australia.

DYETT Francis Gilbert, b. 6 Apr 1933. Judge. m. Rita Ulbrick, 3 Jan 1959, 2 s, 1 d. Education: LLB Hons; Univ of Melbourne. Appointments: Barrister & Sol, Sup Crt of Vic, 1956; Signed Roll of Cnsl, Vic Bar, 1958; Admitted Barrister, Sup Crt of NSW, 1965; Judge, Co Crt of Vic, 1978-; Chmn, Workers Compensation Bd, 1981-84. Memberships: Former Mbr, Legal Aid Cttee; Newman Coll Cl; Mannix Coll Cncl. Hobbies: Squash Golf. Address: 7 Bramley Court, Kew, Vic 3101, Australia.

DZUMAGULOV Apas Dzumagulovich, b. 19 Sep 1934 Arashan Kyrgyz SSR. Politician. m. 2 s. Education: Moscow Gubkin Inst of Oil. Appointments: Worked at Comlex S Geol Expedition USSR Acady of Scs, 1958-59; Snr Geol oil field Changar-Tash; Hd Cntr Rsch Lab; Chf Geol Drilling Div; Chf Engr Oil Co Kyrghizneft Osh Dist, 1959-73; Hd Indl Transp Div Cntr Cttee CP of Kyrgyz SSR, 1973-79; Sec Cntr Cttee CP of Kirgyzia, 1979-85; Dep to USSR Supreme Soviet, 1984-89; First Sec Issyk-Kul Dist Cttee, 1985-86; Chmn Cncl of Mins Kyrgyz SSR, 1986-91; USSR People's Dep, 1989-91; Chmn Org Cttee then Chmn Regl Soviet of Deps; Hd of Admin Chuysk Reg, 1991-93; PM of Kyrgyz Repub, 1993-. Memberships: Mbr CPSU, 1962-91. Address: Office of the Prime Minister, 720003 Bishkek, Kyrgyzstan.

E

EARLE James Heward, b. 31 Aug 1927. Architect. m. Joan Wright, 27 Sept 1952, 5 s, 2 d. Education: Scotch Coll, Vic; RMIT; Univ of Melbourne; Stockholm Tech Coll; BArch; DipArch; Dip T&RP. Appointments: Hon Sec, Vic Grp, Austl Inst of Landscape Archs, 1974-79; Mbr, Advsry Cttee to Town and Country Plng Bd, SA, 1974-80; Lectr, Tropical Arch, Univ of Melbourne, 1974-76; Mbr, Tech Advsry Cttee, Natl Trust of Aust, Vic, 1975-99; Senator, Chmn, Capital Grants (Bldngs) Cttee, State Coll, Vic, 1976-82; Mbr, Archts Panel, Uniting Ch of Aust, 1977-87; Parish Cnclr, Elder, Toorak Uniting Ch, 1981-99; Mbr, Advsry Cttee, Western Port Regl Plng Authy, 1978; Dpty Chmn, Tasma Terrace Restoration Cttee (Natl Trust), 1979-80; Lectr, Cntr of Environ Studies, Melbourne Univ, 1979-81; Fed Cnclr, 1975-79, Pres, Vic Divsn, 1976-78, Fed VP, 1979, Roy Austl Planning Inst; Mbr, Housing Advsry Cttee to Min of Housing, Vic, 1979-80; Chmn of Cncl, Hawthorn Inst of Educ, 1982-88; Mbr, Natl Prac Cttee, 1978-83; Pres, Vic Chapt, 1980-82, Natl Cnclr, 1983-85; Mbr, Vic Chapt Prac Cttee, 1976-99; RAIA. Publication: Buildings for Tonga the Friendly Isles, 1963. Honour: AM, 1981. Hobbies: Photography; Swimming; Travel. Address: 18 Marian Street, Hawthorn, Vic 3122, Australia.

EAST Paul, b. 1946 Opotiki. Politician; Lawyer. m. 3 children. Education: Univ of Virginia Sch of Law. Appointments: Law Clerk Morpeth Gould & Co Auckland, 1968-70; Partner East Brewster Solicitors Rotorua, 1974-; Fmr Rotorua Cty Cnclr and Dep Mayor; Natl Party MP for Rotorua, 1978-; Att-Gen Min responsible for Serious Fraud Off and Audit Dep, 1990-; Ldr of the House, 1990-93; Min of Crown Hlth Enterprises, 1991-96; Min for Def and War Pensions, 1996-. Address: Parliament Buildings, Wellington, New Zealand.

EASTEAL Patricia Lynn, b. 12 Jan 1951. Academic Criminologist. m. Simon Easteal, 10 Aug 1985, 3 s, 1 d. Education: BA, Socl Scis, SUNY, Binghamton; MA, Anthropology, Univ Pitts; PhD, Anthropology, Univ Pitts. Appointments: Lectr, Bowling Green State Univ, 1978-85; Exec Dir, Women's Resource Ctr, Norman, OK, 1985-86; Freelance Rsch Cnslt, 1987-89; Snr Criminologist, Austl Inst of Criminology, 1990-95; Visng Fell, Fac of Law, Austl Natl Univ, 1995-. Publications: Books: Women in Policing, 1981; The Forgotten Few: Overseas-born Women in Australian Prisons, 1992; Killing the Beloved: Homicide Among Adult Sexual Intimates in Australia, 1993; Voices of The Survivors, 1994; Shattered Dreams; Balancing the Scales: Rape, Law Reform and Australian Culture, 1998; 6 others; 48 acad jrnl articles and book chapters; 28 other publns. Honours: Phi Beta Kappa; BA, magna cum laude; Num rsch grants. Memberships: Austl Inst for Women's Rsch and Policy; Austl and NZ Soc of Criminology; Austl Soc of Auths; Natl Women's Justice Coalition. Hobbies: Aerobics; Reading; Volunteer Work with Refuges and Sexual Assault Services. Address: Faculty of Law, Australian National University, ACT 0200, Australia.

EASTICK Bruce Charles, b. 25 Oct 1927, Reade Park, S Aust, Aust. Veterinary Surgeon; Member of Parliament. m. Mary Dawn Marsh, 8 Dec 1951, 3 s, 1 d. Education: Roseworthy Dip, 1st Class Hons, RDA, 1947; BVSc, 2nd Class Hons, Sydney Univ, 1951; Fndn Fell, Austl Coll of Vet Scis, FACVSc, 1970. Appointments: Pvte prac, Vet Surg, 1952-70; Mbr, SA State Parl, 1970-93; Ldr of Opposition, 1972-75; Speaker 1979-82, Opposition Spokesperson on Local Govt, Treas, Emerg Servs, Housing, Environment and Plng. Publications: Vet articles. Honour: Medal for Queen's Silver Jubilee Anniversary; AM, 1996. Memberships: Fell, Austl Vet Assn; Austl Coll Vet Scis; C'wlth Parly Assn; Mayor of Gawler, 1968-72, 1993-. Hobby: Lawn bowls. Address: 6 Goodger Street, Gawler, SA 5118, Australia.

EASTON Alan Keith, b. 15 Aug 1942. Applied Mathematician. m. Grace Raelene Mewett, 12 Apr 1969, 2 s, 1 d. Education: MSc; PhD, Flinders; DipT, ATC; CMath; FIMA; Comp IE Aust. Appointments: Secondary Tchr, SA; Lectr/Snr Lectr, Caulfield Inst of Technol; Prin Lectr/Assoc Prof, Swinburne Univ of Technol. Publications: Co-ed w J M Steiner: The Role of Mathematics in Modern Engineering; Student Litteratur, 1996; Co-ed w R May, Computational Techniques and Applications: CTAC 95, World Scientific, 1996. Honours: Invited Companion Mbr, Inst of Engrs, Aust, 1995; EMG Awd, Austl Engrng Maths Grp, 1996. Memberships: ANZIAM, co-fndr EMG; IMA; AMSA. Hobbies: Scouts; Uniting Church in Australia. Address: School of Mathematical Sciences, Swinburne University of Technology, Hawthorn, Vic 3122, Australia.

EASTON Brian Henry, b. 28 Mar 1943. Research Economist; Social Statistician. m. Jenny du Fresne, 1966, 1 s, 1 d. Education: BSc hons, Univ Canterbury; BA, VUW, C Stat. Appointments include: NZIER, 1963-66, 1981-86; Univ Sussex, 1966-70; Univ Canterbury, 1970-81; Econ and Socl Trust, NZ, 1986-; Hon Rsch Fell, Rsch Proj on Plng, Wellington, 1986-; Assoc, Inst Exec Dev, Massey Univ, 1993-; Hon Lectr, Dept Community Hlth, Wellington Medl Sch, 1994-; Snr Rsch Fell, pt-time, Socl Policy and Applied Econs, Socl Policy Cntr, Massey Univ, 1994-; Visng Snr Lectr, Dept Polit Studies, Univ Auckland, 1995-; Professorial Rsch Fell, Cntrl Inst Technol, 1996-. Publications: Over 29 books and monographs. Honours include: Fndn Mbr, Roy Soc NZ, 1993-; Hocken Lectr, Univ Otago, 1994. Memberships include: Fell, Roy Stats Soc. Address: 18 Talavera Terrace, Wellington, New Zealand.

EASTON Christoper John, b. 3 Sept 1955, Adelaide, Australia. Research Chemist. m. Robyn G, 13 Jan 1979, 1 s, 2 d. Education: BSc, Hons, Flinders, 1977; PhD, Adelaide, 1981; DSc, Adelaide, 1998. Appointments: Harvard Univ, 1980-81; Univ of Canterbury, 1983-86; Univ of Adelaide, 1986-94; Austl Natl Univ, 1995-. Publications: Over 130 pprs and 50 patent applications. Memberships: Fell, Roy Austl Chem Inst, 1993, Roy Soc of Chem, 1994; Sec, Fedn of Austl Sci & Technol Socs, 1996-. Hobbies: Whisky; Wine. Address: Research School of Chemistry, Australian National University, Canberra, ACT 0200, Australia.

EASTON Stephen Andrew, b. 28 Aug 1959, Adelaide, Aust. Finance. m. Diane, 7 Dec 1985, 1 s, 2 d. Education: BEcon (Adelaide); MEcon (Monash); PhD (Monash). Appointments: Lectr, Univ of Adelaide, 1986-88; Assoc Prof, Monash Univ, 1989-96; Hd of Dept of Acctng and Fin, Dpty Dean, 1997-98, Dean, 1998- Fac of Econs and Com, Univ of Newcastle. Memberships: Fell, Austl Soc of CPAs; Snr Assoc, Austl Inst of Banking and Fin. Hobby: Cycling. Address: c/o Department of Accounting and Finance, University of Newcastle, Callaghan, NSW 2308, Australia.

EASTWOOD Clint, b. 31 May 1930 San Francisco. Actor; Film Dir. m. (1) Maggie Johnson, 1953, div, 1 s, 1 d; 1 d by Frances Fisher, 1993; (2) Dina Ruiz, 1996, 1 d. Education: Los Angeles Cty Coll. Appointments: Worked as lumberjack Ore; Army serv; Appeared tv series Rawhide, 1959-65; Owner Malpaso Prodns, 1969-; Co-Chmn UNESCO Campaign to protect world's film heritage; Mayor of Carmel, 1986-88. Films appeared incl: Revenge of the Creature, 1955; Francis in the Navy, 1955; Lady Godiva, 1955;Tarantula, 1955; Never Say Goodbye, 1956; The First Travelling Saleslady, 1956; Star in the Dust, 1956; Escapade in Japan, 1957; Ambush at Cimarron Pass, 1958; Lafayette Escadrille, 1958; A Fistful of Dollars, 1964; For A Few Dollars More, 1965; The Good The Bad and The Ugly, 1966; The Witches, 1967; Hang 'Em High, 1968; Coogan's Bluff, 1968; Where Eagles Dare, 1969; Paint Your Wagon, 1969; Kelly's Heroes, 1970; Two Mules for Sister Sara, 1970; The Beguiled, 1971; Play Misty for Me, also dir, 1971; Dirty Harry, 1971, 1971; Joe Kidd, 1972; High Plains Drifter, also dir, 1973; Dir Film, Breezy, 1973; Magnum Force, 1973; Thunderbolt and Lightfoot, 1974; The Eiger Sanction, also dir, 1975; The Outlaw Josey Wales, also dir, 1976; The Enforcer, 1976; The Gauntlet, also dir, 1978; Every Which Way But Loose, 1978; Escape from Alcatraz, 1979; Bronco Billy, also dir, 1976;

Any Which Way You Can, 1980; Firefox, also dir, 1982; Honky Tonk Man, also dir, 1982; Sudden Impact, also dir, 1983; Tightrope, 1984; City Heat, 1984; Pale Rider, also dir, 1985; Heartbreak Ridge, also dir, 1986; Bird, 1988; The Dead Pool, 1988; Pink Cadillac, 1989; White Hunter Black Heart, also dir, 1989; The Rookie, also dir, 1990; Unforgiven, also dir, 1992; In the Line of Fire, 1993; A Perfect World, also dir, 1993; The Bridges of Madison County, also dir prodr, 1995; The Stars Fell on Henrietta, co-prodr only; Absolute Power, also dir; Dir Midnight in the Garden of Good and Evil, 1997. Honours: Golden Globe Awd Best Dir Breezy, 1989; Acady Awd Best Film and Best Dir The Unforgiven, 1993; Fell BFI, 1993; Irving G Thalberg Awd, 1995; Legion d'honneur; Cmdr Ordre des Arts et des Lettres; Am Film Insts Life Achievement Awd, 1996. Address: c/o William Morris, 151 S El Camino Dr, Beverly Hills, CA 90212, USA.

EATHER Owen Michael, b. 4 Jan 1945, Sydney, Aust. Management Consultant. m. Julian, 13 Dec 1968, 1 s. Education: MBA, Macquarie Univ; Grad, Offr Cadet Sch; Portsea (Austl Regular Army); Army Reserve Cmd and Staff Coll. Appointments: Var line and staff positions (inclng S Vietnam), 1965-75; Mktng Mngr, Shell, Aust; Divisional G M, Fleetexpress; Chf Exec, Exec Task Force; Mngng Ptnr, Search Assocs Asia Pty Ltd. Publications: Aristotelean Logic Based Problem Solving, 1978; Antipodes Deterrent, 1989. Honour: Cross of Gallantry, Repub of Vietnam. Memberships: Fndn Fell, Austl Inst of Co Dirs; Fell, Austl Inst of Mngmt. Hobbies: Reading; Writing; Sailing; Surfing; Skiing. Address: 41 Raglan Street, Mosman, New South Wales, 2088, Australia.

EATON Derek Lionel, b. 10 Sept 1941, Christchurch, NZ. Anglican Bishop. m. Alice Janice Maslin, 24 Aug 1964, 2 s, 1 d. Education: Trained Tchrs' Cert w dist, Christch, 1964; Dip in Theol, Aust, 1966; Cert Français, Switzerland, 1969; Cert, Arabic and Islamics, Tunis, 1970; MA, cum laude, MO, 1978. Appointments: Tchr, Sumner Primary Sch, 1964-; Miss, Tunisia, 1968-70; Ordained, Bristol, Eng, 1971; Curacy, Bristol, 1971-72; Vicar, St Georges, Tunis and Hon Brit Emb Chap, 1972-78; Provost, Cairo Cath, Egypt, 1978-83; Transl Cnslt for N Africa Tyndale House Publrs, 1973-79; Assoc Priest, Parish of Papanui, Christchurch, NZ, 1984-85; Australasian Commissary for Bish of Egypt, 1984; Vicar of Sumner, Redcliffs, 1985-90; Bish of Diocese of Nelson, 1990-. Honours: Provost Em Cairo Cath, 1984; Canon Em Cairo Cath, 1985; Queens Serv Medal, 1985. Hobbies: Swimming; Golf; Reading. Address: Bishopdale, PO Box 100, Nelson, New Zealand.

EBESU Joanne S M, b. 13 Dec 1967, Honolulu, HI, USA. Research Director. m. Eric H, 23 May 1993. Education: BA, Univ of CA, Berkeley, 1989; MS, Univ of HI, 1992; PhD, Univ of HI, 1998. Appointments: Rsch Assoc, Univ of HI, 1993-98; Rsch Dir, Oceanit Test Systems Inc, 1998-. Publications: PhD dissertation: Isolation & Characterization of Novel Ciguateric Compounds From Acanthurus Triostegus (Manini), 1998. Honours: Uchida Fndn Grant, Univ of Tokyo, 1991; Grad Schlshp Awd, Dahu Educl Employees Fedl Credit Union, 1995; Sigma Xi. Memberships: AAAS; NY Acady of Sci; Amn Fisheries Soc (HI chapt). Hobbies: Fishing; Golf; Reading. Address: C/o Oceanit Test Systems, 1100 Alakea Street, 31st Floor, Honolulu, HI 96813, USA.

ECHEVERRI-MEJIA Gilberto. Minister of National Defence. Address: Ministry of National Defence, Centro Administrativo Nacional, 2 Avda El Dorado, Santafé de Bogotá, Colombia.

EDA Satsuki, b. 22 May 1941, Okayama-shi, Japan. Member of the House of Councillors. m. Kyoko Fukagai, 26 Mar 1967, 2 s, 1 d. Education: B of Law, Univ of Tokyo; Dip in Law, Univ of Oxford. Appointments; Mbr, House of Cnclrs, 1977; Mbr, House of Reprs, 1983; Min of State for Sci & Technol, 1993. Publications: 2 books in Japanese. Membership: Pres, Utd Socl Dem Party of Japan. Hobbies: Japanese Calligraphy; Japanese style swimming. Address: 243-7 Yamasaki, Okayama-shi. Japan 703-8267.

EDBERG Stephen J, b. 3 Nov 1952, Pasadena, California, USA. Astronomer. m. Janet Lynn, 23 Dec 1979, 2 s, 1 d. Education: AB, Phys, Univ CA, Santa Cruz, 1974; MA, Astronomy, Univ CA, Los Angeles, 1976. Appointments: Observer, San Fernando Observatory, 1977-79, Jet Propulsion Lab, Galileo Project Sci Coord, 1979-81, 1989-95; Intl Halley Watch Discipline Sci, 1981-88; Comet Rendezvous/Asteroid Flyby Sci Coord, 1986-1992; Cassini Prog Investigation Sci, 1992-; Cassini Prog Outreach Team Lder, 1996-. Publications include: International Halley Watch Amateur Obervers' Manual, 1983; Observing Comets, Asteroids, Meteors and the Zodiacal Light (co-auth w David H Levy), 1994. Honours include: NASA Exceptional Serv Medal, 1995; JPL Awd for Ex, 1998. Memberships: Am Astronomical Soc. Hobby: Bicycling. Address: Jet Propulsion Laboratory, 4800 Oak Grove Drive, Pasadena, CA 91109, USA.

EDELSTEIN Yuli, b. 1958 Ukraine. Politician. m. 2 c. Education: Moscow Inst for Tchr Trng. Appointments: Fmr tchr Melitz Cntr for Jewish-Zionist Educ Sch for Educl Inst Jerusalem; Advsr to Opposition Ldr Benjamin Netanyahu, 1993-94; A fndr of Yisrael Ba-Aliya party, 1995; Hd'd party's election campaign; Min of Immigration and Absorption, 1996-. Memberships: Mbr Knesset, 1996-. Address: Ministry of Immigration and Absorption, P O Box 883, 2 Rehov Kaplan, Kiryat Ben-Gurion, Jerusalem 91006, Israel.

EDGAR Patricia May, b. 11 Mar 1937. Director, Australian Children's Television Foundation, 1982-. m. Donald Edgar, 7 May 1960, 2 d. Education: Univ of Melbourne, Aust; Stanford Univ; La Trobe Univ, BA, Dip Ed BEd Hons, MA, PhD. Appointments: Secnd Sch Tchr, 1959-62; Lectr, Cncl of Adult Educ, Vic, 1965-66; Sec, Vic Assn for Tchng of Engl, 1966; Profl Intern, KQED TV San Fran, 1968; Actng Dir of Rsch, Ford Fndn Proj, Univ of Chgo, USA, 1969; Chairperson, Cntr for The Stdy of Educl Comm and Media, 1970-71; Lectr 1970-71, Snr Lectr 1972-81, Sch of Educ, La Trobe Univ; Visng Prof, Dept of Comm and Dramatic Arts, Univ of IA, USA, 1980; Task Force, Dir, Austl Children's TV Fndn, 1981; Mbr, Austl Natl Commn, UNESCO, Comm Subcttee, 1978-82; Chmn, Children's Prog Cttee, Austl Brdcstng Tribunal, 1978-84; Mbr, Austl Educ Cncl's Children's TV Wrkng Grp, 1980; Mbr, Interim Bd for Educ Film and TV (Vic), 1980-82; Cncl Mbr 1976-82; Chmn, Acad Bd, 1978-79; Chmn, Grad Dip Bd, 1981-82, Austl Film and TV Sch; Bd Mbr, Film Vic 1982; Mbr, UNICEF Natl Educ Cttee 1983-85; Commnr, Vic Post-Secnd Educ Comm, 1985-89; Cnslt, Vic Govt's Socl Dev Cttee, 1988; Dpty Chmn, Austl Film Fin Corp, 1988-95; Assoc Mbr, Austl Brdcstng Tribunal Inquiry into Violence on TV, 1988-89; Mbr, Vic Govt's Bd of Circit Ltd, 1990-93. Publications: Under 5 in Australia, 1973; Media She, 1975; Children and Screen Violence, 1977; The Politics of the Press, 1979; Janet Holmes a Court, 1999. Honours: AM, 1986; Hon DLitt, Univ of WA, 1994; Austl Coll of Educ Medal, 1998. Address: 8 Mount Street, Eaglemont, Vic 3084, Australia.

EDGELL Geoffrey Bayard Gibson, b. 28 Aug 1908. Primary Producer of Wool and Cattle. m. Gwendolyn Courthope, 30 Apr 1935, 1 s, 2 d. Appointments: Cncl Mbr, 1944-77, Exec Mr, 1951-72, Pres, 1962-65, Tas Farmers, Stockowners and Orchardists Assn; Mr, 1952-75, Dpty Warden, 1957, Warden, 1965-75, Bothwell Municipality Cncl; Cnclr and Pres, 1955-56, 1971-73, Hon Life Mbr, 1977, RAS Tas; Dir, Tas AMP Soc, 1962-81; Mbr, Tas Govt Trade Mission to SE Asia, 1963; Chmn, Tas Farmers Cncl, 1963; Exec Mbr, 1964-68, VP, 1965-68, Austl Woolgrowers and Graziers Cncl; Exec, Austl Wool Ind Conf, 1965-69; Chmn, Clyde Water Trust, 1966-72; State Relief (Bush Fires) Cttee, 1967; Bd of Inquiry into Land Valuation in Tas, 1970; Mbr, Rural Reconstruction, 1971-83. Honour CBE, 1971. Address: Dennistoun, Bothwell, Tas 7030, Australia.

EDIRIWEERA Padma Kumar, b. 15 Apr 1930, Sri Lanka. Barrister; Solicitor. m. Sirimavo, 25 Oct 1971, 1 s. Education: Advocate, Supreme Crt of Sri Lanka; Solicitor, Supreme Crt of England and Wales; Barrister and Solicitor, Supreme Crt of Tas, Aust. Appointments: Atty-at-Law, Sri Lanka, 1970-71; Crown Cnsl, Atty Gen Dept, Sri Lanka, 1971-76; Legal Offr, Dept of Justice, Tas, Aust, 1976-93; Cnslt, Wallace Wilkinson & Webster, Barristers and Solicitors, Tas, 1994-95. Honours: Sir Lalitha Rajapakse Gold Medal; Hector Jayawardena Gold Medal. Memberships: Law Asia; Bar Assn of Tas; Law Soc of Tas; UN Assn of Aust, Tas Divsn; Austl Red Cross; Intl Wall of Friendship Devel Cttee, Tas; Ethnic Cttees Cncl of Tas; Fedn of Ethnic Cttees, Cncl of Aust; Bur of Immigration, Multicultural and Population Rsch, Aust; Aust-Asia Soc of Tas; Aust-Japan Soc; Friends of Sri Lanka, Tas; Aust-Tibet Cncl. Hobbies: Public Speaking; Painting; Caricaturing; Cartooning; Music; Photography; Theatre. Address: 61 Liverpool Crescent, Hobart, Tasmania 7000, Australia.

EDMOND Lauris Dorothy, b. 2 Apr 1924, Dannevirke, NZ. Writer. m. Trevor Edmond, 16 May 1945, 1 s, 5 d. Education: Trained Tchr's Cert, 1943; Speech Therapy Dip, 1944; BA, Waikato Univ, 1968; MA (1st Class Hons) Vic Univ, 1972. Appointments: Tchr, Engl and French, Huntly Coll, Heretaunga Coll, 1968-72; Regl Tutor, Massey Univ Engl Dept, 1980-94; Creative Writing Courses and Workshops, Educ Classes, Polytechnics, Summer Schs, Lit Grps, 1982-. Publications: Poetry incl: Salt From the North, 1980; Catching It, 1983; Selected Poems, 1984; Seasons and Creatures, 1986; Summer Near the Arctic Circle, 1988; New and Selected Poems, 1991; Five Villanelles, 1992; Scenes From a Small City, 1994; Selected Poems 1975-94, 1994; A Matter of Timing, 1996; In Position, 1996. Drama incl: The Mountain, radio play; Between Night and Morning, stage play, 1981; Novel: High Country Weather, 1984; Stories, prose writings, reviews; Autobiography: Hot October, 1989; Bonfires in the Rain, Vol II, 1991; The Quick World Vol III, 1992; single vol, 1994; Editls. Honours include: PEN NZ Best 1st Book, 1975; Katherine Mansfield Mem Fellshp, 1981; Writer in Res, Deakin Univ, Melbourne, 1985, Vic Univ, Wellington, 1987; Commonwealth Poetry Prize, 1985; OBE, 1986; Lilian Ida Smith Awd for poetry (PEN) NZ), 1987; Mobil Radio Awd for The Mountain, 1987; Hon Dlitt, Massey Univ, 1988; Schlshp in Letters, NZ Arts Cncl, 1990. Hobbies: Music; Gardens; Grandchildren. Address: 22 Grass Street, Oriental Bay, Wellington, New Zealand.

EDMONDS Philip Hanbury, b. 25 Apr 1940, Sydney, Aust. Real Estate and Business Valuer. m. Janet Gibson, 4 Aug 1973, 1 d. Education: BEcon (Hons), Sydney Univ. Appointments: Mng Dir 1972-, Tasman Securities Pty Ltd, 1981-; Mng Dir, Edmonds & Assocs P/L, 1985; Cnclr, Comm Consultative Cncl of the Hawkesbury Mepean Catchment Mngmt Trust; Mbr, Coml Tribunal of NSW. Memberships: Austl Inst of Valuers and Land Economist; Fell, Chartered Inst of Secs; Cert Practising Acct. Hobbies: Yachting; Breeding, grazing and management of Beef Cattle. Address: 44 Harbour Street, Mosman, NSW 2088, Australia.

EDWARDS Alan Edmund William, b. 17 Jan 1925, Chatham, Eng. Theatre Worker. Appointments: Old Vic Th Sch, 1945-47; The Young Vic Players, 1947; The Young Vic Co, 1948; Actor, Dir in var Brit Repertory Ths, 1948-64; Formed Mngmt Teamwork and presented wrk in W End and The Edinburgh Fest; Made 4 Films; Appeared in over 250 TV Shows for BBC and ITV Network; Taught at var Drama Schs; Tutor in Acting, Natl Inst of Dramatic Art, Sydney, 1964; Appeared w The Old Tote Th, Th Roy Hobart; Apptd Fndng Dir, Qld Th Co, 1969; Co granted the prefix Roy and became Roy Qld Th Co, 1984; Dir of more than 50 prodns for the co and appeared as an actor in over 18 prodns; Freelance Career, 1988. Honours: Adv Aust Awd, 1982; Finalist, Qldr of the Yr Awd; MBE, 1983; AM, 1990 Matilda Awd, Servs to Qld Th, 1994; The Glugs of Gosh Awd for Excellence in Th, 1998; Hon DLitt (USQ), 1998. Memberships include: Prodrs and Dirs Guild of Aust; Th BBd, Aust Cncl, 1978-83; Qld Performing Arts Trust (10yrs); Pres, Actors and Entertainers Benevolent Fund (Qld), 1975-94; Patron, Qld Th of the Deaf; Brisbane Musical Advsry Cncl; Immigration Review Panel (Brisbane), 1988-90; JP; Arts Advsry Panel to State Govt, 1989; Arts Advsry Cttee, State Govt, 1990. Listed in: Who's Who in Australia. Hobbies: Collecting pottery; Cooking; Growing pot plants; Music; Dance. Address: 4 Langham Street, Tarragindi, Queensland 4121, Australia.

EDWARDS John Keith, b. 29 Oct 1924, Melbourne, Vic, Aust. Civil Engineer. m. 14 June 1948, 2 s. Education: Fellshp Dip in Civil Engrng, Melbourne Tech Coll, 1944. Appointments: Engr, Country Roads Bd, Vic, 1944-48; RAAF, 1945 Engr, Marine Bd of Burnie, Tas, 1948-51; Engr, Gen Mngr, Chf Engr, Port of Launceston Authy, Tas, 1951-50; Cnsltng Engr, Pvte Prac, 1980-; Chmn, LBS Statewide Bank, 1982-86; Chmn, Gas Corp of Tas, 1987-96; Chmn, 1987-88, Dir, 1984-93, Tas Dev Authy; Cmmnr, Hydro-Elec Commn, 1980-90; Dpty Chmn, Aust Maritime Coll Cncl, 1978-95. Honour: AO, 1981. Membership: Fell, Inst of Engrs, Aust. Hobby: Manual work. Address: Main Road, Dilston, Tasmania, Australia.

EDWARDS John Reginald, b. 6 Nov 1949. Veterinarian. m. Peta Suzanne Edwards, 15 Dec 1974, 2 d. Education: BS (Agric), West Aust; BVSc, Qld; MVS, Melbourne; PhD, Murdoch. Appointments: Agric WA; Dist Vet Offr, Albany, 1975; Regl Vet Epidemiologist, 1981; Lectr in Vet Epidemiology, Murdoch Univ, 1986; Prin Offr (Vet Services), Agric WA, 1989; Chf Vet Offr, 1992; Mbr Vet Surg's Bd, 1994; Mngr, Surveillance and Preparedness, 1996; Mngr, Animal Ind Protection, 1998 Mbr, of Sen of Murdoch Univ, 1996-99. Publications: In sci jrnls, natl and intl conf proceedings. Honours: Full Blue (Hockey), Univ of Qld, 1974; Univ of Melbourne, 1980; Rep WA (under-21, Veterans), Qld (State); Aust (Masters) in Hockey. Memberships: Austl Vet Assn; Austl Coll of Vet Scientists; Chmn, Epidemiology Chapt, 1988. Hobbies: Hockey; Golf; Fitness. Address: c/o Agriculture Western Australia, Baron-Hay Crt, South Perth, WA 6151,Australia.

EDWARDS Marshall John, b. 17 Jan 1928, Mosman, NSW, Aust. Veterinary Surgeon. m. Marcia, 22 Sept 1951, 1 s, 1 d. Education: BVSc; PhD; DVSc (Sydney); MVSc (Liverpool); MRCVS. Appointments include: Vet farm prac, NSW, WA, Eng, 1950-61; Warden, Nepean Hall, 1972-75, Prof, Vet Clin Scis, 1975-94, Dean, Fac of Vet Sci, 1978-79, 1986-94, Dir, JD Stewart Fndn, 1986-94, Fac Vet Sci, Univ Sydney. Consultancies incl: Sci Cnsl, Natl Cncl for Radiation Protection and Measurement (USA), 1989-92, World Fedn for Ultrasound in Med & Bio, Austl deleg on sci cttee, 1989-92; Chmn of Dirs, Novogen Ltd, 1993-97; Dir, Novogen Ltd, 1997-99. Publications: 1 revised book; 14 book chapts; Over 100 sci rsch pprs on birth defects, animal diseases. Honours: Gilruth Prize, Austl Vet Assn, 1992; AO, 1994. Memberships: Austl Vet Assn, 1950-; Austl Teratology Soc, Chmn, 1980-86; Cncl, Intl Fed of Teratology Socs, 1991-93. Hobbies: Classical music; Gardening; Sport. Address: 21 Almora Street, Mosman, NSW 2088, Australia.

EDWARDS Meredith Ann, b. 10 May 1941, Canberra, Aust. Economist; Deputy Vice-Chancellor. m. 19 Feb 1963, div, 1 s, 1 d. Education: Bachelor of Com (hons), Univ of Melbourne; PhD (Pub Fin), ANU. Appointments include: Snr Tutor, 1964-68, Lectr, 1972-79, ANU; Snr Lectr Canb, CAE, 1979-83: Spec Advsr, Off Yth Affairs, 1983-85; Cnslt to Min Socl Security on Child Support, 1985-87; First Asst Sec, Socl Policy Div, Dept Socl Security, 1987-90; Dir, Natl Housing Strategy Dept Community Servs and Hlth, 1990-92; First Asst Sec Econ and Policy Analysis Div Sept Employment Educ and Trng (DEET), 1992-93. Publications: Financial Arrangements Within Families, 1981; The Income Unit for Australian Tax and Social Security Policy, 1984. Honour: AM, 1992. Memberships: Cl Univ Canberra, 1990; Austl Statistical Adv Cl, 1995-. Hobbies: Walking; Tennis; Music; Photography. Address: University of Canberra, ACT, 2601, Australia.

EFIMOV Vitaly, b. 10 Dec 1938, St Petersburg, Russia. Physicist. m. Albina Shabelsky, 18 Nov 1983, 1 s, 1 d. Education: BS, Radio Engrng, Hons, Leningrad Electrical Engrng Inst, 1962; PhD, Theoretical Phys, Ioffe

Phys-Tech Inst, 1966; Doctorate in Theoretical Phys, Leningrad Nucl Phys Inst, 1976. Appointments: Jnr Sci, Ioffe Phys-Tech Inst, 1962-71; Snr Sci, Leningrad Nucl Phys Inst, 1971-89; Visng Prof, Univ of Minnesota, Minneapolis, 1989-90; Snr Rsch Fell, CA Inst of Technol, Pasadena, 1990; Lectr, Affiliate Prof, Univ of WA, Seattle, 1990-; Lectr, Seattle Univ, 1994-. Publications: Articles in profl jrnls, 1964-. Memberships: Soc for Dissemination of Sci Knowledge, St Petersburg, 1977-84; Sci Cncl on Nuclr Phys, Acady of Scis, Moscow, 1981-89; Amn Phys Soc, 1989-. Hobbies: Music; Reading. Address: 1210 NE 41st St Apt D, Seattle, WA 98105, USA.

EGAN Michael Rueben (Hon), b. 21 Feb 1948, Sydney, Australia. Minister; Treasurer of NSW. Education: St Patricks Coll, Sutherland; BA, Univ of Sydney. Appointments: Mbr for Cronulla in Legislative Assembly of NSW, 1978-84; Chmn, Pub Accounts Cttee, 1981-84; Mbr, Legislative Cncl of NSW, 1986-; Ldr, Opposition in Legislative Cncl, 1991-95; Ldr of the Govt in the Legislative Cncl, 1995-; Treas, 1995-; Min for Energy, 1995-98; Min for State Dev, 1995- VP of the Exec Cncl of NSW, 1995-. Address: Parliament House, Macquarie Street, Sydney, NSW 2000, Australia.

EHRLICH Frederick, b. 23 Mar 1932. Medical Academic. m. Shirley Rose Eastbourne, 4 s, 2 d. Education: MA, MBBS (Hons); PhD, Dip Phys and Rehab Med; FRCS (Eng); FRCS (Edin); MRCPsych; FAFRM (RACP). Appointments: Rotating Res, Roy Newcastle Hosp, Surg Registrar, Charing Cross and Fulham Hosp, Registrar, Surgical Div, RNH; Dir, Surg and Rehab Serv, State Psych Hosp, NSW; Dir, Rehab and Geriatrics, NSW; Visng Orth Surg, Concord Hosp, NSW; Prof, Rehab, Age and Extended Care, UNSW. Publications: Ed, sev books, auth and co-auth, 100 articles and pprs in profl jrnls. Honour: Sydney Univ Exhibitioner, 1949-54. Hobbies: Opera; Theatre. Address: A2011 Sydney South, 1235, Australia.

EICHELBAUM (Johann) Thomas (Rt Hon Sir), b. 17 May 1931, Königsberg, Germany. Retired Judge. m. Vida Franz, 1956, 3 s. Education: Vic Univ Coll. Appointments: Solicitor, 1953; Bar, 1954; Ptnr, Chapman Tripp and Co, 1958-78; QC, 1978; Bar, 1978-82; Pres, NZ Law Soc, 1980-92; Judge, High Crt NZ, 1982; Chf Justice NZ, 1989-99. Publication: Ed in Ch, Mauet's Fundamentals of Trial Techniques. Honours: GBE; PC. Hobbies: Reading; Bushwalking. Address: Lowry Bay, Eastbourne, New Zealand.

EINFELD John Isadore, b. 21 Dec 1915. Solicitor. m. Maadi Sussman, 18 Oct 1945, 1 s, 2 d. Appointments: Sol, Supreme Crt, NSW, 1939; AIF, 1940-46; Cap MID; Life Patron, Austl Fedn of Jewish Ex-Serv Assns, 1959-, Pres, 1951-59, 1994-; Pres, King David Sch, 1966-86; Life Gov, Sydney Hosp, 1971, Freemasons Benevolent Inst, 1977; Mbr, Ethics Cttee, Law Soc, NSW, 1972-82; Chmn, Welfare Co-op Housing Soc Grp, 1975-87 (Dir 1960-87); Pres, NSW Jewish War Mem, 1981-86; Mbr, Solicitors Statutory Cttee, 1982-90; Tstee, Moriah War Mem Coll, 1987-, Life Patron, 1984-, (Immediate Past Pres, 1976-84, Pres, 1971-76); Legal Profl Review Panel, 1990-95; Pres, Double Bay Bowling Club, 1990-93, Life Mbr, 1997-. Honour: AM, 1979. Memberships: RACA; Double Bay Bowls, Hakoah. Hobby: Bowls. Address: 1/5 Coolong Road, Vaucluse, NSW 2030, Australia.

EINFELD Marcus Richard (Hon Justice), b. 22 Sept 1937. Judge Federal Court of Australia. m. 2 s, 2 d. Education: LLB, Sydney Univ; PhD, LLD, USA. Appointments: Barrister, 1962-; Dir, African, Asian and C'wlth Affairs, Dpty Dir, Intl Affairs, London, 1972-75; Dir, Marks and Spencer Ltd, London, 1975-76; QC, Austl States and Territories, UK, 1977-; Chmn, Natl '88 Paralympics Appeal; Fndn Pres, Austl Hum Rights and Equal Opportunity Commn, 1986-90; Mbr, Medl Bd of NSW, 1985-86; Chmn, Legal and Socl Cttee, Austl Natl Advsry Cttee on AIDS, 1986; Justice Fedl Crt of Aust, 1986; Spec Advsr, Austl Delegation, UN Hum Rights Commn, 1987-90; Inaugural Pres, Austl Paralympic Fedn, 1990-94; AUSTCARE's Amb for Refugees, 1990-, investigated situation of Burmese refugees in Bangladesh and Thailand, 1992; Further wrk w refugees in S Afr, 1993, Rwanda and Bosnia, 1994, Bosnia and Croatia, 1995; Judge, Fed Crt of Aust; Judge of the Supreme Crt of the Aust Capital Territory. Memberships: Intl Commn of Jurists; Amnesty Intl; Intl Law Assn; Intl Bar Assn; Cncl for Civil Liberties; Aust Day Amb; Amb of Hope (Jewish Community Servs); Patron of: Children of Chernobyl; Austl Campaign of Tibet; Aboriginal Medl Servs Coop; Victorian Assn for Victims of Torture; Hum Rights Defender (publ of Univ of NSW Human Rights Cntr); Aust-Bangladesh Assn; Sydney hs Cntr for Music, Art and Drama; Ted Noffs Fndn; Mbr Advsry Cncl, Sporting Wheelies (Disabled Sport and Recreation Assn) Queensland; Dir, Sydney 2000 Olympics bid; UNICEF's Amb for Children. Hobbies: Music; Sport; Reading. Address: c/o Judges Chambers, Federal Court of Australia, Sydney, NSW 2000, Australia.

EITAN Raphael, b. 1929 Tel Adashim. Army Officer. m. 4 c. Education: Tel-Aviv and Haifa Univs. Appointments: Joined Palmach when 17; Dep Co Cmdr, 1948; Var posts with paratroops, 1950-53; Cmdr Paratroop Unit Sinai campaign, 1956; Dep Cmdr Paratroop Brigade, 1958; Cmdr, 1964-67; Cmdr Jordan Valley Brigade, 1967-68; Chf Paratroop and Infantry Offr rank of Brig-Gen, 1968-73; Cmdr Div on Golan Heights rank of Maj-Gen Yom Kippur War, 1973-74; CO North Command, 1974-77; Chf of Gen Staff Branch, 1977-78; Chf of Gen Staff, 1996-; Dep PM Min of Environment, 1996-. Address: Ministry of Agriculture, P O Box 7011, 8 Arania Street, Tel-Aviv 61070, Israel.

EIZENBERG David Henry, b. 29 Sept 1943, Sydney, Aust. Obstetrician; Gynaecologist. m. Helen, 21 Mar 1973, 2 s, 1 d. Education: MB BS (UNSW); FRCOG (UK); FRACOG (Aust). Appointments: VMP, St Margarets Hosp, Mater Hosp VMO, Roy Hosp for Women. Publications: Management of Premature Labour, 1978; Goserelin Reduction of Uterine Fibroids Prior to Vaginal Hysterectomy, 1995; Antenatal Umbilical True Knot Leading to Fetal Demise, 1998. Memberships: AAGL; AGES; Bd, St Margarets Hosp, 1984-93. Address: 183 Macquerie Street, Sydney, NSW 2060, Australia.

EL-SAYEH Ramzy Shehata, b. 1 Nov 1921. Professor of Anatomy. m. Fawkia Dawoud Rizk, 25 Jul 1957, 3 s, 1 d. Education: MD, Medl Scis, Anatomy, 1959; Dip of Medl Scis, Anatomy and Embryology, 1954; MB, BCh, 1946. Appointments: Medl Offr, Govt Hosps, 1946-51; Combated Cholera Epidemic, Egypt, 1947; Demonstrator, 1951-60, Lectr, 1960-68, Assit Prof, 1968-73, Prof, 1973-81, Emer Prof, 1981-, Anatomy Dept, Fac Med, Cairo Univ. Publications: 42 rschs in intl jrnls. Honours: Brit Cncl Bursary, 1965; LFABI and Intl Advsr, 1983; LFIBA and Intl Advsr, 1980; Cultural Doct in Philos of Therapeutics, USA, 1984; Medal of the Egyptian Repub, 1983. Memberships: Past Ed, ACTA Anatomica, Switzerland; Past Abstractor, Biol Abstracts, USA; Past Mbr of Perm Cttee of Promotion to Posts of Prof of Anatomy or Histology; Mbr of Cncl of Egyptian Anatomical and Zool Socs. Listed in: Many including: Register of Profiles; Directory of Arab Doctors; International Register of Biographies. Hobbies: Travel; Listening to Music; Visiting Foreign Countries. Address: 35 Mousaddak (Bahlawi) Street, Dokki, Gizza, Cairo, Egypt.

ELDER Jack A, b. 1949. Government Minister. m. 1 child. Appointments: Sch Tchr; Cnclr, New Lynn Borough Cncl; Dpty Mayor; Labour MP, West Auckland, 1984-93, 1993-96; Joined NZ 1st Party, Elected, 1996; Min of Internal Affairs, Min of Civil Dec, Assoc Min of Local Govt. Address: Suite 4, 254 Lincoln Road, PO Box 104-034, Lincoln North, Waitakere City, New Zealand.

ELGAR Mark Adrian, b. 25 July 1957. Academic; Biologist. Education: BSc First Class Hons, Griffith Univ; PhD, Univ of Cambridge, Eng. Appointments: SERC Rsch Fell, Univ Oxford, Eng, 1985; Univ Rsch Fell, Univ NSW, 1987; Queen Elizabeth II Rsch Fell, Univ NSW, 1989; Lectr, Univ Melbourne, 1991; Snr Lectr, Univ Melbourne, 1995; Professeur Visité, Univ Pierre-et-Marie Curie, 1998; Rdr and Assoc Prof, Univ of Melbourne, 1999. Publications: Cannibalism: Ecology and Evolution Among Diverse Taxa, 1992; Over 80 articles in refereed and other jrnls. Honours: Grad Rsch Schlsp, Christs Coll, Cambridge, 1982. Memberships: Corresp Sec, Intl Ethological Congress, 1996; Cnclr, Intl Soc for Behavioural Ecology, 1994; Edl Bd, Behavioral Ecology, 1990; Assoc Ed, Behavioral Ecology and Sociobiology, 1994; Assoc Ed, Austl Jrnl of Ecology, 1996. Hobbies: Bushwalking; Australian Literature; Furniture Renovation. Address: Department of Zoology, University of Melbourne, Parkville, Vic 3052, Australia.

ELKIN Peter Kingsley, b. 5 Mar 1924, Cessnock, NSW, Aust. Professor of English. m. Patricia Judith Bell, 20 Apr 1950, 2 s, 1 d. Education: BA 1st Class Hons, Engl, 1st Class Hons, Anthropology, Univ of Sydney, 1944; BLitt 1949, DPhil 1967, Oxford Univ, Eng. Appointments: AIF, 1944-46; Lectr in Engl, Univ of Ceylon, 1949-50; Lectr in Engl, Univ of WA, 1951; Snr Lectr in Engl, Univ of NSW, Aust, 1952-68; Prof of Engl, 1972-87, Emer Prof of Engl, 1987-, Univ of New Eng. Publication: The Augustan Defence of Satire, 1973. Hobbies: Gardening; Farming; Short story writing; Sport: all games except cricket. Address: Gingunyah, Kelly's Plains, Armidale, NSW 2350, Australia.

ELLIOT (Winston) Rodger, b. 31 May 1941. Writer; Horticulturist. m. Gwen(doline) Parry, 31 Aug 1963, 1 s, 1 d. Appointments: Co-Proprietor, Austraflora Nursery, 1963-72; Co-Proprietor, Austl Tube Plants, 1973-92; Bd, Roy Bot Gdns, Melbourne and Cranbourne. Publications include: Encyclopaedia of Australian Plants Suitable for Cultivation, Vol 3, 1984, Vol 4, 1986, Vol 5, 1990, Vol 6, 1993, Vol 7, 1997; Plant Identikit Series, 1988; Gardening with Australian Plants, 1990; Coastal Gardening in Australia, 1992; Pruning: A Practical Guide, 1993; Attracting Wildlife to Your Garden, 1994; Encyclopaedia of Australian Plants - Supplement I, 1994, Supplement 2, 1995, Supplement 3, 1996, Supplement 4, 1999. Honours: Austl Inst of Hort, Awd of Excellence, 1992; Austl Plants Awd, 1995; Aust Nat Hist Medallion, 1995; Veitch Gold Meml Medal, RHS, 1999. Memberships: Austl Flora Fndn; Austl Garden Hist Soc; Austl Systematic Botany Soc; Burrendong Arboretum Assn; David G Stead Rsch Fndn of Aust; Indigenous Flora and Fauna Assn; Karwarra Austl Plant Garden Advsry Cttee; Maud Gibson (Gardens) Trust Advsry Cttee; Ornamental Plant Collects Assn; Fell, Roy Hort Soc, London; Soc for Growing Austl Plants; The Points Arboretum, Coleraine, Vic. Hobbies: Photography; Botanising; Gardening; Travel; Natural history. Listed in: Who's Who of Australian Writers. Address: c/o Lothian Books, 11 Munro St, Port Melbourne, Vic 3207, Australia.

ELLIOTT John Gregory, b. 9 Nov 1948, Surabaya, Indonesia. Aerospace Engineer. m. Jennifer Lee Austin, 7 May 1988, 2 s. Education: BS, CA Univ, Long Beach; AA, Cerritos Coll, Norwalk, CA. Membership: S CA Profl Engrng Assn. Hobbies: Tennis; Sailing; Skiing; Surfing; Windsurfing; Photography; Guitar; Roller Blading; Ice Skating; Reading. Address: 40717 Mountain Pride Drive, Murrieta, CA 92562, USA.

ELLIOTT Lorraine Clare, b. 9 July 1943, Melbourne, Australia. Member of Parliament. m. John Kiely, 8 Nov 1996, 2 s, 1 d. Education: BA, Univ of Melbourne; BEd, Monash Univ. Appointments: Mbr for Mooroolbank, 1992-; Parly Sec to the Premier for the Arts, 1996-. Membership: C'wlth Parly Assn. Hobbies: Reading; Theatre; Walking; Travel. Address: PO Box 700, 60 Main Street, Croydon, Victoria 3136, Australia.

ELLIOTT Randal Forbes, b. 12 Oct 1922, Wellington, NZ. Ophthalmic Surgeon. m. Pauline June Young, 30 July 1949, 1 s, 6 d. Education MchB (NZ), 1947; DO (London), 1949; FRCS (Eng), 1953; FRACS, 1955; FRACO. Appointments: Snr Res Offr, Moorfields Hosp, 1951; Eye Surgn, Univ Coll Hosp, London, 1952; Eye Surgn, Wellington Hosp, 1953-88; Grp Cap, RNZAF, retd, 1982. Publications Num sci med pprs in profl jrnls. Honours: OBE, 1975; KBE, 1977 KstJ, 1978; GCstJ, 1987. Memberships: Chmn, Pres, NZ Med Assn; Pres, Ophthalmological Soc of NZ; Pres, Wellington Club; Pres,

Wellington Medico-Legal Sec; Chmn, NZ Rd Safety Trust; Chan, Order of St John (NZ). Hobbies: Skiing; Mountaineering; Tramping; Sailing. Address 13B Herbert Gardens, 186 The Terrace, Wellington 1, New Zealand.

ELLIS Niki Maree, b. 22 May 1955. Occupational Physician. m. 24 Dec 1986. Education: MBBS; DOH; FAFOM; FAFPHM. Appointments: Med Off, Tasmanian Dept Hlth, 1980-85; Coord Tasmania's First Aids Strategy; Dir, RSI Natl Strategy, 1985-87, Dir, Preventive Strategies, 1987-90, Worksafe Australia; Cnslt to a number of pvte and pub sect org. Publications: Columnist Occupational Health Magazine, 1992-; Contbr to Aust Dr Weekly; Var Scientific articles and papers. Memberships: World Hlth Org Expert Advsry Panel on Occupational Hlth, 1986-90; Inaugural Pres, Aust FAc of Occupational Med, 1992-94; Chair, Med Advsry Cttee, NSW Workcover Auth, 1995-98. Address: NE & A, 2/11 Kellett Street, Kings Cross, NSW 2011, Australia.

ELLIS William Frank, b. 4 Apr 1928. m. 1 s, 1 d. Education: Univ of Tas. Appointments: Cadet, Phys Dept, Univ of Tas, 1946-50; Sci Offr, Anthropology and Archaeology, 1950-53; Asst Dir 1953-55, Dir 1955-78, Queen Vic Mus and Art Gall, Launceston; Dir, Art Gall of WA, 1978-86; Exec Offr of Dev, Burnie City Cncl, 1986-93; Dir, Burnie Regl Art Gall, 1986-93. Publications: Penal Settlements of Van Diemen's Land, 1954; Diaries of John Helder Wedge (jointly), 1968; Van Diemen's Land Correspondents, Venturing Westward, 1987. Honour: OBE, 1970. Hobbies: Bonsai; Hobby farming; Reading. Address: Westvale, 203 West Ridgley Road, via Burnie, Tasmania 7320, Australia.

ELLISON Christopher Martin, b. 15 June 1954, Bulawayo, Zimbabwe. Senator for Western Australia. m. Caroline, 21 Nov 1992. Education: BJuris, LLB, Univ West Aust. Appointments: Formerly Parly Sec to Atty Gen and Min for Hlth; Min for Customs & Consumer Affairs; Min Assisting the Atty Gen; Presently, Min for Schs, Vocational Educ & Trng. Membership: Law Soc of West Aust.

ELLYETT Clifton Darfield, b. 10 Jan 1915. Emeritus Professor; Physicist. m. Ngaire Frances Warren, 26 June 1947, 2 s, 2 d. Education: MSc, NZ; PhD, Manchester. Appointments: Var levels in Phys, Univ of Canterbury, NZ, 1936-64; Prof of Phys, Univ of Newcastle, NSW, 1964-80; Fndr, Dir, Energy Cnslts of Aust Pty Ltd and Ellyett's Farm. Publications: Energy Policy and Research in Australia and New Zealand, 1982; 68 pprs in sci jrnls. Honours include: Sir George Grey Schlsp, 1935; Natl Rsch Schlsp, 1946; Imperial Chem Inds Snr Rsch Fellshp, 1947; NZ Fulbright Travel Grant to USA, 1957; E R Cooper Mem Awd, 1958; Fell, Roy Soc of NZ, 1962; Michaelis Mem Prize, 1963; Fell Roy Astronomical Soc, 1964; Fell, Austl Inst of Energy, 1979; Hon D, Univ of Newcastle, 1993. Memberships include: NZ Radio Rsch Cttee, 1942-64; Chmn, Christchurch Planetarium Appeal Cttee, 1958-64; Sec, NZ Natl Space Rsch Cttee, 1961-64; Chmn, Central Coast Tertiary Educ Devl Cttee, 1983-96; Pres, Central Coast Community Coll, 1994-95, 1998-; Fndr, Pres, Friends of the Univ (Central Coast), 1990-95; Patron, Natl Herbalists Assn of Aust. Listed in: Who's Who in Australia; Men of Achievement; New Zealand Who's Who; International Who's Who. Address: PO Box 84, Ourimbah, NSW 2258, Australia.

ELMS David George, b. 3 June 1934. Professor of Civil Engineering. m. Margaret Mary Norris, 2 July 1977, 3 s, 1 d. Education: BA, Cambridge; MSE, PhD, Princeton. Appointments: Structural Engr, De Havilland Aircraft Co, Eng, 1957-60; Lectr, 1964-77, Snr Lectr, 1978-, Univ Canterbury; Prof, Civil Engrng, Univ Canterbury. Publications: Linear Elastic Analysis, 1970; The Safety of Nuclear-Powered Ships, 1992; The Environmentally Educated Engineer, 1995; Over 100 pprs. Honour: Medal for Disting Contbrns to Engrng Educ, AAEE, 1993. Memberships: FRSNZ; FIPENZ; MASCE; Pres, AEESEAP, 1991-94. Hobbies: Music; Walking. Address: 61A Kidson Terrace, Christchurch 2, New Zealand.

ELPHICK Harold Robert, b. 9 Apr 1917. Physician. m. Dorothy Charleston, 22 Jan 1943, 3 s, 3 d. Education: MBBS, Melbourne Univ; FRCP (Lon), FRACP. Appointments: Capt, AAMC, 1945-47; RMO, 1941; Surg Registrar, Roy Perth Hosp, 1941-42; Asst Med Supt, Fremantle Hosp, 1943-45; Med Supt State Sanatorium, 1947-58; Physn Supt, Sir Charles Gairdner Hosp, WA, 1958-68; Ret'd. Publications: Rehabilitation of the Tuberculous in Western Australia, 1954; Problems in the Diagnosis and Treatment of Skeletal Tuberculosis. Honour: JP. 1947; CBE, 1978; AM, 1998. Hobbies: Fishing. Gardening. Address: 105 Winthrop Avenue, Nedlands, WA 6009, Australia.

ELVISH Rodney David, b. 17 Mar 1949. Metallurgist. m. Monika, 4 Jan 1986, 1 s, 1 d. Education: AssDipMetall (RMIT), 1970; FellDipPrimMetall (RMIT), 1980; GradDipGeosc (MinEcon) (Macq), 1984; Fell, Royal Melbourne Inst Technol. Appointments: Var Metallurgical posns within the Peko Wallsend Grp, 1971-75; Mngr, Metallurgy, Texasgulf Aust Ltd, 1975-82; Snr Metallurgist, Aquitaine Aust Minerlas Ltd, 1982-84; Mngr, Mineral Processing, Dorr Oliver P/L, 1984-87; Snr Metallurgist, Elders Resources Ltd, 1987; Cnslt Metallurgist, B E Enterprises P/L, 1987-; VP and Cnclr, Australasian Inst of Mining & Metallurgy; Dir, Allstate Explorations NL. Memberships: Fell, Australasian Inst of Mining & Metallurgy (CPMet); Fell, Austl Inst of Co Dirs. Hobbies: Tennis; Music. Address: 12 Hudson Close, Turramurra, NSW 2074, Australia.

EMERY Garry, b. 17 Nov 1939, Perth, West Aust, Aust. Graphic Designer. 1 s, 1 d. Career: Self-employed. Publications: CI Book, 1996; Designing the Corporate Future (jnt auth), 1997; Idiom, 1998. Hobbies: Design, art and architecture. Address: C/o Emery Vincent Design, 80 Market Street, Southbank, Victoria 3006, Australia.

EMILSEN William Wayne, b. 7 Dec 1948. Historian. m. Susan, 1 s, 1 d. Education: BS; Dip Ed (UNSW); MA, BD, PhD, Sydney. Publications: Remodelling God, 1983; Winter Harvest, 1987; Violence and Atonement, 1994; The India of My Dreams, 1995; O'Connor, 1997; Marketing Twenty Years: The Uniting Church in Australia. Memberships: Jrnl of the Relig Hist Assn; Soc for the Study of Early Christianity; Oral Hist Assn of Aust; Austl Assn for the Study of Religion. Hobby: Swimming. Address: 16 Masons Drive, North Parramatta 2151, Australia.

EMMENS Clifford Walter. Physiologist. m. Muriel E Bristow, May 1937, 2 s, 2 d. Education: PhD; DSc. Appointments: Demonstrator, Zoo, Univ Coll, London, Eng, 1936-37; Rsch Biol, MRC, 1937-48; Seconded to Min of Home Sec and RAF, 1941-46; Hd, Dept of Vet Physiol, Univ of Sydney, 1948-78; Pt time OIC of CSIRO Sheep Bio Lab, later Div of Animal Physiol, 1952-54. Publications: Auth, Co-auth, var books and over 200 sci papers. Honours: Oliver Bird Medal and Prize, Eng; Hon W/C RAF, 1946; Hon FACVSc, 1976; Hon DVSc, 1983. Memberships: Pres, Austl Soc for Reprod Bio; Endocrine Soc of Aust; 2nd Asia and Oceania Congress of Endocrinology; Pres, Sydney Assn of Univ Tchrs; Pres, Aust Reg of Intl Biometric Soc. Hobbies: Marine science and aquarium keeping; History of science. Address: 603/22 Sutherland St, Cremorne, NSW 2090, Australia.

EMMERSON Bryan Thomas, b. 5 Sept 1929, Townsville, Qld, Aust. Physician; Scientist; Educator. m. Elva Brett, 28 Apr 1955, 2 s. Education: MBBS, Univ Qld, 1952; MD, 1962; PhD, 1973. Appointments: Snr Lectr, Materia Medica, Therapeutics, 1960-63, Rdr, Med, 1963-73, Prof, Med, 1974-, Chmn, Division Med, 1981-84, 1996-97, Princess Alexandra Hosp; Hd, 1974-94, Hon Rsch Cnslt, 1994-, Dept Med, Univ Qld. Publications: Hyperuricaemia and Gout in Clinical Practice, 1983; Getting Rid of Gout, 1996; Contbns to postgrad textbooks in med, nephrology, rheumatology, and to sci medl lit. Honours: Weinholt Prize, Univ Qld; Masonic Bursary, Univ Qld; Parr Prize, Rsch in Rheumatic Diseases, Austl Rheumatism Assn, 1996; Postdoct Intl Fellshp, US Pub Hlth Servs, 1967; Susman Prize, Contbn to Knowledge, Roy Austl Coll Physns,

1978; Wellcome Visng Prof, Rheumatology, Roy N Shore Hosp, Sydney, NSW, 1985; Snr Medl Fellshp, UK, to Stdy Medl Educ, C'wlth Schlshp Commn; AO 1997. Memberships: Qld Inst Medl Rsch, Cnclr, 1978-94; Austl Medl Assn; Life Mbr, Australasian Soc Nephrology, 1988-; Arthritis Fndn Aust, Qld, Dir, 1985-94, VP, 1994-; Spina Bifida Assn Aust, 1984; Austl Rheumatology Assn; Qld Conservatorium Music, Cnclr, 1981-96.Hobbies: Music; Swimming; Antique collecting. Address: University of Queensland, Department of Medicine, Princess Alexandra Hospital, Ipswich Road, Woolloongabba, Qld 4102, Australia.

EMY Hugh Vincent, b. 5 Nov 1944, Eng. Professor of Politics. m. Elizabeth A Gloster, 14 May 1971, div, 2 s. Education: BSc Econs, 1st Class, 1966, PhD, 1969, London Sch Econs. Appointments: Lectr, 1969-73, Snr Lectr, 1973-75, Prof, 1976-, Dept Pols, Monash Univ, Vic, Aust. Publications: Remaking Australia, 1993. Membership: Polit Studies Assn, Aust. Address: Department of Politics, Monash University, Wellington Road, Clayton, Melbourne, Vic 3168, Australia.

ENCEL Solomon, b. 3 Mar 1925, Poland. Research Worker. m. Diana Helen Hovev, 23 June 1949, 1 s, 3 d. Education: MA; PhD. Appointments: Lectr, Polit Sci, Melbourne, 1952-55; Snr Lectr/Rdr, Austl Natl Univ, 1956-61; Prof, Sociol, Univ NSW, 1966-90. Publications: 20 books on socl or polit issues, (auth or ed), 1961-97. Memberships: Fell, Austl Acady of Socl Scis, 1968-; Austl Sociol Assn, Pres, 1969-70. Hobbies: Walking; Music; Wine. Address: Social Policy Research Centre, UNSW, Sydney 2052, Australia.

ENDERBY Keppel Earl, b. 25 June 1926, Dubbo, NSW, Aust. Retired Supreme Court Judge. m. Dorothy, 17 July 1964, 1 s, 1 d. Education: LLB, Univ of Sydney; LLM, Univ of London. Appointments: Fedl Govt Min, var mins incl Atty-Gen, 1975; Judge of Supreme Ct of NSW, 1982-92; Chmn, Serious Offenders Review Cncl, NSW. Memberships: NSW Br of Austl Inst Int Affairs, Cnclr, 1980-94, Pres, 1983-85; Aust-USSR Soc, Natl Pres, 1986-90; Austl Acady of Forensic Scis, Cnclr, 1990-94; Austl Esperanto Assn, Natl Pres, 1992-98; Pres, Universal Esperanto Assn (Rotterdam); NSW Cncl for Civil Liberties, Pres, 1993-94; NSW Soc of Labor Lawyers, Pres, 1993-94. Hobbies: Esperanto; Flying; Sailing; Farming. Address: 2 Phoebe Street, Balmain, NSW 2041, Australia.

ENDO Masao, b. 1 Feb 1947, Tokyo, Japan. Composer. 1 s, 1 d. Education: Grad, Grad Sch, Music Rsch Course, Tokyo Natl Univ of Fine Arts and Music, 1973. Creative Works: Compositions: Green Sky Dominated by Golden and Red Sun (for piano and orch); Zephyr With Outstretched Wings (for violin and orch); Wind's Corridor (for alto recorder and guitar); Sunspot (for 5 percussion players); Foaming Eternity (for violoncello and marimba); Wind's Corpuscle (electronic music); Aqua Planet (for piano). Honours: 37th Japan Music Composition Awd, Composition Section, sponsored by NHK and Mainichi Shimbun, 1968; Ongaku-no-tome-sha Composition Awd, 1972; 1st Prize, 1st Th Arts Coomp, sponsored by Natl Agency of Cultural Affairs, 1979. Membership: Dir, Vice Sec-Gen, Japan Fedn of Composers Inc. Address: 3-1-14-401 Uehara, Shibuya, Tokyo 151-0064, Japan.

ENEVER Keith James, b. 10 Oct 1941. Research Manager. m. Gillian Enticknap, 29 Aug 1964, 2 s. Education: Queen Mary Coll, London Univ, BSc Engrng 1963, PhD 1966. Appointments: Rsch Engr/Snr Engr, Brit Hydromechs Rsch Assn, 1966-70; Lectr/Snr Lectr, The City Univ, London, 1970-79; Reader in Hydraulic Engrng, Cranfield Univ, 1980-86; Rsch Mngr, BHP Rsch, Port Kembla, Aust, 1986-. Publications: Many papers on Fluid Mechanics, in particular, on Pressure Surges in Pipelines. Honour: Hon Professorial Fell, Univ of Wollongong. Memberships: Inst of Engrs; Chartered Engr, Fell of Inst of Engrs of Aust; Chartered Profl Engr. Hobbies: Choral Singing; Watching cricket; Opera and theatre. Address: 133 Cabbage Tree Lane, Mount Ousley, NSW 2519, Australia.

ENGLISH Bill (S W), b. 1061. Government Minister. m. Mary, 5 children. Education: Bach of Com, Otago Univ; BA, Hons, Engl Lit, Victoria Univ, Wellington. Appointments: Plcy Analyst; Farmer; Elected to Parl, Wallace, 1990; Chair, Parl Socl Serv Select Cttee; Re-elected, Parly Under-Sec, Hlth, Crown Hlth Enterprises, 1993; Min of Crown Hlth Enterprises and Assoc Min of Educ, 1996; Min of Hlth, Co-alition Govt; Assoc Treasurer, 1998; Min of Fin, Min of Revenue, 1999-. Address: PO Box 30, Dipton, New Zealand.

ENGLY Piphal, b. 28 Jan 1944, Kam Pong-Cham, Cambodia (Aust citizen). Minister-Counsellor. m. Syaratt Thanndrak, 22 Jan 1963, 1 s, 1 d. Education: 6 Dips; BA, Aust, 1992; Grad Dip, Asian Studies, 1997; Currently reading for MA at Univ of New Eng (external study). Appointments include: Tchr, PR Offr for Min Pub Hlth, Coord, Pharm/Medl Prods Supvsr, WHO, Cambodia, 1965-75; Hlth Inspector and Interpreter, Transl, Interviewer, Lib Offr at State Lib of Vic, (pt-time), Aust, 1981-83; Univ of Melbourne Offr, 1983-86; Monash Univ Offr, 1986-94; Cnst, Interpreter, Translator, Interviewer, State Govt of Vic, Cnslt and Interpreter, Translator, Ed, for Immigration and Multicultural Affairs, State Govt of Vic and Commonwealth Govt of Aust, 1980-94; Min-Cnslr (or Doty Amb), Roy Emb of Cambodia to Aust and NZ, 1994-98; Admin Serv Offr, Fedl Dept of Workplace Rels and Small Bus, 1998. Publication: Rschr for The Royal Family of Cambodia, by Dr J J Cornfield, 1991, 1993. Honours: Excellent Awd of Primary Sch Cert, Cambodia. Memberships: Acting Pres, Roy Polit Party, Funcin-Aust, 1994-. Hobbies: Scrabble; Reading; Badminton; Flower arrangement; Squash. Address: Unit 13/1 Edwell Place, North Lyneham, ACT 2602, Australia.

ENHSAYHAN   Mendsayhany.   Politician. Appointments: Economist; Chf of Staff to Pres Ochirbat; Prime Min of Mongolia, 1997-. Membership: Democratic Alliance. Address: c/o Great Hural, Ulan Bator, Mongolia.

EPPELBAUM Lev V, b. 18 May 1959, Tbilisi, Georgia. Geophysicist; Investigator; Educator. m. Elina, 16 Mar 1986, 1 s. 1 d. Education: PhD, 1989, Inst of Geophys, Georgian Acady of Sci; Post-doctorate, Dept Geophys, Tel Aviv Univ, 1991-92. Appointments: Geophys, 1982-83, Rschr, 1984-88, Snr Rschr, Inst Geophys, Baku, Azerbaijan; Rschr, 1991-94, Snr Rschr, 1995-, Dept Geophys, Tel Aviv Univ. Publications: Book, Interpretation of Geophysical Fields in Complicated Environments, 1996; 27 pprs and 55 proceedings and abstracts. Honours: Awd, Min of Scis of Israel, 1991-93; Min of Energy of Israel, 1995-99; Waitzman Inst, Rehovot, Israel, 1996-97; UNESCO, 1998-2001. Memberships: Soc of Exploration Geophys; Amn Geophys Union; NY Acady Scis; Soc of Mediterranean Geophys; Soc of Geoinform; Israel Geol Soc. Hobbies: Chess; Basketball; Fantastic literature. Address: Dept of Geophysics and Planetary Sciences, Tel Aviv University, Ramat Aviv 69578, Tel Aviv, Israel.

EPSTEIN June Sadie, b. 29 June 1918, Perth, WA, Aust. Musician; Writer. m. Julius Guest, 2 children, 1 dec. Appointments: Scriptwriter, Brdcstr, Austl Brdcstng Cmmn (Corp); Dir of Music, Melbourne Ch of England Girls Grammar Sch; Snr Lectr in Music, Univ of Melbourne Inst of Educn Sch of Early Childhood Studies. Creative Works: Musical compositions and over 60 books, mainly biographies of disabled people, histories; Childrens books; Adult books incl: The Story of the Bionic Ear; June Epstein, Woman With Two Hats (autobiog); Mermaid on Wheels; Concert Pitch, The Story of the National Music Camp and the Australian Youth Orchestra. Honours: Overseas Schl, Trinity Coll of Music, London, 1936-39; Silver Medal, Worshipful Co of Musicians, 1938; OAM, 1986; Var awds for best childrens books; Hon Life Mbr, St Catherines Old Girl's Assn. Memberships: Fndn Pres, Kew Cottages Parent's Assn; Spina Bifida Assn; Soc of Women Writers (Aust); Austl Soc of Auths; Fellshp, Austl Writers; Hon Life Mbr, Grads Assn Inst of Early Childhood Devel; Noah's Ark Toy Lib; Austl Performing Right Assn. Hobbies: Teaching grandchildren music and accompanying; Working for

people with disabilities. Address: 2 Alexander Street, Bentleigh East, Vic 3165, Australia.

ERATH Hermann, b. 11 Jan 1945, Singen, Germany. Ambassador. Education: 2nd State Law Exam. Appointments: Embassies in S Africa, Kingston, New York, Off in Bonn. Hobbies: Sport, Literature, Art, Classical music and jazz. Address: Embassy of the Federal Republic of Germany, 9 South Sathorn Road, Bangkok, Thailand.

ERBAKAN Necmettin, b. 1926 Sinop. Politician. Education: Inst of Mechs Tech Univ of Istanbul; Technische Univ Aachen Germany. Appointments: Asst lectr Inst of Mechs Tech Univ of Istanbul, 1948-51; Engr Firma Deutz, 1951-54; Prof Tech Univ of Istanbul, 1954-66; Chmn Indl Dept Turkish Assn of Chambers of Com, 1966-68; Chmn of Assn, 1968; Fndr Natl Order Party, 1970 - disbanded 1971; Chmn Natl Salvation Party, Oct 1973 - disbanded 1981; Dep PM and Min of State, Jan-Sept 1974; Dep PM, 1975-77, July-Dec 1977; Detained, 1980-81; Now ldr Refah Partisi - Welfare Party fnd 1983; PM of Turkey, July 1996-. Address: Office of the Prime Minister, Basbakanlik, Ankara, Turkey.

ERDEM Kaya, b. 1928 Zonguldak. Government Official. m. Sevil Sibay, 1956, 2 d. Education: High Sch of Com; Univ of Marmara. Appointments: Fin Dir Sugar Corp, 1960-62; Asst Dir-Gen State Treas, 1963-72; Dir-Gen State Treas, 1972-73; Chf Finl Cnslr Turkish Emb London, 1973-76; Sec-Gen Min of Fin, 1978-80; Min of Fin, 1980-82; Dep PM Min of State, 1983-89; Prominent in drafting and implementation of econ stabilization prog, 1980. Publications: State Economic Enterprise, 1966; Num articles on cost and managerial acctcy. Memberships: Mbr Fac Anatolian Univ, 1959-65; Mbr Cttee for Reorganization of State Econ Enterprises, 1971-72. Hobbies: Bridge; Tennis. Address: c/o Office of the Deputy Prime Minister, Basbakan yard. ve Devlet Bakani, Bakanliklar, Ankara, Turkey.

ERDONMEZ GROCKE Denise Elizabeth, b. 24 July 1946, Melbourne, Aust. Senior Lecturer. 1 s, 1 d. Education: BMus, 1967; BMus Therapy, 1970; MMus, 1987. Appointments: First Austl to Qualify in Music Therapy Practised Larundel Hosp, 1970-80, Inaugural Lectr, Music Therapy, Univ of Melbourne, 1980-; TV appearances, radio broadcasts. Publications: Many articles in refereed jrnls; 7 chapts in books; 1 edited volume. Honour: Hon Life Mbr, Austl Music Therapy Assn. Memberships: Fndng Mbr, Austl Music Therapy Assn; Natl Pres, Austl Music Therapy Assn, 1978-81, 1988-91; Chair, Educ Commn, World Fedn of Music Therapy, 1993-. Address: Faculty of Music, University of Melbourne, Parkville, Vic 3052, Australia.

ERICKSON Dorothy, b. 2 June 1939. Artist; Historian; Writer. m. David Carr, 23 Apr 1973, div 1986. Education: PhD, Univ of Western Aust; BA, Design; AA, Curtin Univ; Tchrs Ctf, Edith Cowan Univ. Creative Works: Jewellery in Collections of: Schmuckmuseum, Pforzeim, Germany; The Victoria and Albert Mus, London; The Australian National Gall; The Art Gall of WA; Art Gall of Qld; Art Gall of SA; Queen Vic Mus, Tas; 16 Solo Exhibns in Aust and Eur, 1977-; Over 150 Grp Exhibns in num countries; Ed of Craftwest, 1994-98; Writing publd in many periodicals, inclg, The Bulletin, Artlink, Oz Arts, Craft Arts International. Honours: Hon Fell, Craft Cncl of WA, 1994. Memberships: Craft Cncl of WA, 1970-, Pres, 1979-81; Intl Soc of Jewellery Histns, 1988-; Craft Cncl of Aust, 1980-81; Art Assn of Aust, 1987-; Intl Assn of Art Critics, 1983-; Austl Histl Assn, 1994-; Jewellers and Metalsmiths Grp, Aust, 1980-. Listed in: The WAY 79 Who's Who; Who's Who of Australian Visual Artists; Who's Who of Australian Writers. Address: 2 William Street, Cottesloe, WA 6011, Australia.

ERNST Eldon Gilbert, b. 27 Jan 1939, Seattle, Washington, USA. Educator. m. Joy, 4 s, 1 d. Education: BA, Linfield Coll; MDiv, Colgate Rochester Divinity Sch; MA, PhD, Yale Univ. Appointments: Grad, Theol Union, 1967-; Am Bapt Seminary of the W, 1967-82, 1990-. Publications: Moment of Truth for Protestant America,

1974; Without Help Or Hindrance, 1977; Pilgrim Progression, 1993. Honours: Howd Sociol Prize, Linfield Coll, 1961; Luthen Wesley Smith Citation for Christian Higher Educn, 1995; Grad, Theol Union Disting Fac Lectr, 1997. Memberships: Am Acady of Relig; Am Histl Assn; CA Histl Soc; Am Soc of Ch Hist. Hobbies: Music; Boating; Antique Cars. Address: 1855 San Antonio Avenue, Berkeley, CA 94707, USA.

ESCURO Pedro Bolivar, b. 2 Aug 1923. Emeritus Professor. m. Manuela Sales-Escuro, 2 s. Education: BSA, magna cum laude, Coll of Agric, Univ of the Philippines, Los Baños, Laguna, 1948-52; MS, Cornell Univ, Ithaca, NY, USA, 1953-54; PhD, Univ MN, St Paul, USA, 1956-59; Studied Corn Breeding at LA State Univ, Baton Rouge, USA, 1954; Studied Rice Breeding at LA Rice Expmt Stn, Crowley, USA, 1954. Appointments include: Rice Improvement Specialist, UNDP/FAO Burma, 1975-78; Plant Breeder, Intl Rice Rsch Inst, 1978-86; Cnslt, 1986, Snr Scientist, 1987-88, Cnsltng Snr Scientist, 1988-91, Philippine Rice Rsch Inst; Rsch Asst Prof, Agronomy, 1959-60, Hd of Agronomy Dept, 1960-64, Rsch Assoc Prof of Agronomy, 1960-67, Prof in Plant Breeding, 1968-75, Professorial Chair in Plant Breeding, 1973-75, Emer Prof, 1980-, Univ of the Philippines; Participant at many confs. Publications: 36 publs as auth or co-auth in var profl jrnls inclng: Co-Auth, Breeding program for medium deepwater logged rainfed lowland rice in Burma, in Progress in Rainfed Lowland Rice. Honours include: Presdtl Plaque of Merit for Outstndng Accomplishments in Rice Improvement, Pres of the Philippines, 1967; Rizal Pro-Patria Medal and Presdtl Citation for Outstndng Contbn in Rice Breeding, Pres of the Philippines, 1968; Hon Fell, Crop Sci Soc of the Philippines, 1972; DSc, hc, Univ of the Philippines, 1979; Academician, Natl Acady of Sci and Technol, 1980-; Dip in Recog of Sci Achmnts, World Cultural Cncl, Mexico, 1988; Disting Serv Awd in Agric, Gamma Sigma Delta, 1993; Natl Scientist, Pres of the Philippines, 1994. Memberships include: Natl Rsch Cncl of the Philippines, 1967-; VP, 1974, Crop Sci Soc of the Philippines, 1970-; Soc for Advmnt of Breeding Rsch in Asia and Oceania, 1969-. Address: Makiling St, Los Baños Subdivision, College, Laguna 4031, The Philippines.

ESLAKE Saul Richard, b. 24 Jan 1958, London, UK. Economist. m. Linda Arenella, 21 Apr 1990. Education: BEcon (Hons), Univ of Tas. Appointments: Chf Economist, McIntosh Securities, 1986-91; Chf Economist (Intl), Natl Mutual, 1991-95; Chf Economist, ANZ Banking Grp, 1995-. Address: Level 10, 100 Queen Street, Melbourne, Victoria 3000, Australia.

ESPLIN Ian George, b. 26 Feb 1914. Air Vice-Marshal RAF (retired). m. 13 May 1944, Patricia Barlow, 1 s, 1 d. Education: MA, Oxon; BEc, Sydney; NSW Rhodes Schl, 1937. Appointments: Volun, RAF, 1939; Aircraftsman 2nd Class, Commn'd Pilot Offr, 1940; Pilot, Night-Fighters No 29 Sqdn, 1942-43; Strategic Air Plans Lord Mountbatten's Staff HQ, SE Asia Command, 1943-45; Policy Staff Air Min, 1945; Sec, Qantas Empire Airways, 1946; CO, RAF Desford, 1947; Dpty, SPSO HQ Reserve Cmnd, 1948; Staff Coll, 1949; Directing Staff, RAF Staff Coll, 1950-51; CO, 148 Wing, Germany, 1952-54; Air War Coll, 1954; CO, RAF Wartling, 1958-60; Dpty Dir, Operational Requirements, Air Min, London, 1955-58; Dir, Operational Requirements, Air Min, London, 1960-62; Brit Air Attache, Wash DC, 1962-65; Dean, Air Attache Corps, 1964-65; Retd at own request, 1965; Mktng Dir, Japan, Aust, SE Asia, India, Ryan Aero Co, USA, 1965-69; Mngng Dir, Computer Scis Austl Pty Ltd, 1970-73. Honours: CB, 1962; OBE, 1945; DFC, 1943. Hobbies: Family; Golf; Tennis; Writing. Address: 12 Ralston Rd, Palm Beach, NSW 2108, Australia.

ESSEX Elizabeth Annette, b. 21 Apr 1940, Grafton, NSW, Aust. Physicist. m. H A Cohen, 3 s, 1 d. Education: BSc, Hons, PhD, Univ New Eng. Appointments: Lectr, Univ W Indies, 1966-68; Rsch Sci, James Cook Univ, 1968; Lectr, La Trobe Univ, 1969-72; Snr Lectr, La Trobe Univ, 1973-. Publications: Over 50 articles in intl jrnls. Memberships: Fell, Austl Inst of Phys; Inst of Phys; Amn

Geophysl Union. Hobbies: Bush walking; Fun runs. Address: Shorts Road, Research, Victoria, Australia.

ESTEVEZ Emilio, b. 1962. Actor. m. Paula Abdul, 1992, div, 1994, 1 s, 1 d. Films incl: Tex, 1982; Nightmares, 1983; The Outsiders, 1983; The Breakfast Club, 1984; Repo Man, 1984; St Elmo's Fire, 1984; That was then ... This is Now, 1985; Maximum Overdrive, 1986; Wisdom, also wrote and dir, 1986; Stakeout, 1987; Men at Work, 1989; Freejack, 1992; Loaded Weapon, 1993; Another Stakeout, 1993; Champions II, 1993; Judgement Night, 1993; D2: The Mighty Ducks, 1994; The Jerky Boys, co-exec prodr only; Mighty Ducks 3, Mission Impossible, 1996; The War at Home, 1996. Address: c/o UTA, 5th Floor, 9560 Wilshire Boulevard, Beverly Hills, CA 90212, USA.

ETCHEGARAY AUBRY Alberto, b. 5 May 1945. Politician; Civil Engineer. m. 4 s, 2 d. Appointments: Univ Prof of Bus Admin; Dir Dept of Stdies Union Social de Empresarios Cristianos; Co-ord of visit of Pope John Paul II to Chile; Dir Hogar de Cristo; Min of Housing and Urban Dev, 1990-94; Pres Natl Cncl against Poverty, 1994-98. Memberships: Mbr Cncl Semanas Sociales de Chile - initiative of Episcopal Conf of Chile. Address: Canada 185-A, Providencia, Santiago, Chile.

ETHERINGTON Norman Alan, b. 27 June 1941, USA. Historian. m. Peggy Brock, 18 July 1980, 2 s. Education: BA, 1963; MA, 1966; MPhil, 1968; PhD, 1971, Yale Univ. Appointments: Lectr, Hist, Yale Univ, 1968-73; Snr Lectr, 1974-78, Rdr, 1979-; Dean, Fac of Arts, 1978, Univ of Adelaide; Prof, Univ of WA, 1989-. Publications include: Preachers, Peasants and Politics in Southeast Africa, 1978; Rider Haggard, 1984. Honours: Phi Betta Kappa, 1961; Carnegie Fell, 1964; Andrew White Prize, 1962; Fell, Acady of Socl Scis in Aust. Memberships: Pres, Austl Histl Assn, 1994-96; Amn Austl Histl Assns Roy African Soc; African Stdies Assn of Australasia and the Pacific; Fell, Roy Histl Soc, Eng; ICOMOS, Aust. Hobbies: Chamber Music; Carpentry. Address: 14 Campbell Street, Subiaco, Perth, WA 6008, Australia.

EVANS Cyril Percival Victorious, b. 27 Apr 1921, Sydney, Aust. Medical Practitioner. m. Beryl Dean Podmore, 20 Dec 1949, 1 s, 3 d. Education: MBBS, Sydney, 1943; DTM, Sydney, 1946; FRCP, London, Eng; FRACP; FRACMA. Appointments include: Med appts: Austl Army Med Corps, Solomon Is, London, Eng; NC, USA, 1943-55; Dpty Dir, Tuberculosis, Qld Dept of Hlth, 1956-63, 1966-69; Med Offr, WHO, Madras, India, 1964-65; Dir, Tuberculosis Servs, SA Dept of Pub Hlth, 1969-73; 1st Asst Dir-Gen, Austl C'wlth Dir of Tuberculosis, Med Servs Div, 1974; Dpty Dir Gen, Austl C'wlth Dept of Hlth, 1974-82; WHO short-term Cnslt, Chronic Diseases/Actng Regl Advsr, Chronic Diseases, WHO Regl Offr, Manila, Philippines, 1983; Cnslt, Roy Adelaide Hosp, 1984; Part-time C'wlth Med Offr, Canberra; Med Dir, Austl Kidney Fndn, 1986-97. Publications include: Var articles to profl jrnls. Honour: OBE, 1978. Memberships include: Med Assn for the Prevention of War; Thoracic Soc of Aust; Austl Soc for Infectious Diseases. Address: 57 Ambalindum Street, Hawker, ACT 2614, Australia.

EVANS David Mylor, b. 20 June 1934, Richmond, Vic, Aust. Member of Victorian Parliament (MLC); Farmer. m. (1) Alison Mary Pullar, 4 Aug 1961, 1 s, 2 d, (2) Marion Mavis Miller, 23 Nov 1984. Appointments: Farmer, Family Property, 1952; Oxley Shire Cncl, 1967-76; Mbr, Legis Cncl, 1976-96; Pres, Vic Natl Party, 1975-76; Chmn, Wangaratta HS Cncl, 1976-98; Mr, Statute Law Revision Cttee, 1976-82; Pub Bodies Review Cttee, 1982-88; Chmn, Legal and Constitutional Cttee, 1988-92; Environ and Natural Resources Cttee, 1992-96; Dpty Pres, Chmn of Cttee, Legislative Cncl, 1992-96; Alpine Natl Park Advsry Cttee, 1999-. Membership: Vic Farmers Fedn. Hobbies: Farming; Skiing. Address: Redcamp, RMB 1230, Moyhu, Vic 3732, Australia.

EVANS Frank Geoffrey, b. 7 Feb 1922. Education: Scotch Coll, Melbourne. Appointments: RAN, 1941-46; RANR, 1947-82 (Cmdr); Snr Offr, Austl Sea Cadet Corps, Naval Reserve Cadets, 1953-75; ADC, 1956, Pvte Sec to Gov of Vic, 1962-63, State Pres, Vic Divsn, Navy League of Aust, 1967-73 (Mbr, Fed Cncl, 1950-); Alternate Pub Mbr, Austl Press Cncl, 1987-96; Fed Pres, Navy League of Aust, 1971-94; Chmn, Fed Advsry Cncl, Navy League of Aust, 1995-. Honours: MBE, 1967; VRD; OBE, 1982. Memberships: Fed Pres, Navy League of Aust, 1971-94; Austl Press Cncl, 1987-96. Listed in: Who's Who in Australia. Hobbies: Tennis; Swimming. Address: 15 Prospect Road, Rosanna, Vic 3084, Australia.

EVANS Gareth John (Hon), b. 5 Sept 1944. Politician. m. Merran Anderson, 15 Jan 1969, 1 s, 1 d. Education: Melbourne HS; BA, LLB hons, Melbourne Univ; MA, Oxford Univ. Appointments: Admitted to Bar, 1968; VP, Vic Cncl of Civil Liberties, 1970-84; Lectr, 1971-74, Snr Lectr in Law, 1974-76, Univ of Melbourne; Cmmnr, Austl law Reform Cmmn, 1975; Senator (ALP) for Vic, 1978-; MHR (ALP) for Melbourne, 1996-; Fndn Pres, Austl Soc of Labor Lawyers, 1980-81; Shadow Atty Gen, 1980-83; QC, 1983; Atty Gen, 1983-84; Min Assisting Min of For Affairs, Min Assisting PM, Min for Resources and Energy, 1984-87; Min for Transp and Comns, 1987-88; Dpty Ldr of the Govt and Mngr of Govt Bus in the Senate, 1987-88; For Min, 1988-96; Ldr of the Govt in the Senate, 1993-96; Deputy Ldr of the Opposition, 1996-98. Publications: Ed, Labor and the Constitution 1972-75, 1977; Law, Politics and the Labor Movement, 1980; Labor Essays, 1980-82; Joint Auth, Australia's Constitution: Time for Change?, 1983; Australia's Foreign Relations, 1991, 2nd ed, 1995; Auth, Cooperating for Peace, 1993. Honours: Supreme Crt Prize, 1966; Austl Humanist of the Yr, 1990; Freedom of City of Sydney, 1993; ANZAC Peace Prize, 1994; Grawemeyer Awd for Ideas Improving World Order, 1995. Hobbies: Reading; Writing; Opera; Golf; Football. Address: c/o Parliament House, Canberra, ACT 2600, Australia.

EVANS Lloyd Thomas, b. 6 Aug 1927. Plant Physiologist. m. Margaret Newell, 2 s, 1 d. Education: Wanganui Coll, Univ Canterbury, NZ; Oxford Univ, Eng; MAgrSc, DPhil, DSc; Hon LLD; FAA; FRS. Appointments: Rhodes Schl, Oxford Univ, Eng, 1951-54; C'wlth Fund Fell, CA Inst Technol, 1954-56; Rsch Staff, CSIRO, 1956-; Natl Acady Scis Fell, Wash DC, USA, 1963-64; Overseas Fell, Churchill Coll, Cambridge, Eng, 1969-70; Pres, ANZAAS, 1976-77; Visng Fell, Wolfson Coll, Cambridge, 1978; Pres, Austl Acady Scis, 1978-82; Currently Hon Rsch Fell, Div Plant Ind, CSIRO, Canberra. Publications: Environmental Control of Plant Growth, 1963; The Induction of Flowering, 1969; Crop Physiology, 1975; Daylength and the Flowering of Plants, 1975; Wheat Science Today and Tomorrow, 1981; Policy and Practice: Essays in Honour of Sir John Crawford, 1987; Crop Evolution, Adaptation and Yield, 1993; Feeding the Ten Billion, 1998. Honour: AO. Address: 3 Elliott Street, Campbell, ACT 2601, Australia.

EVANS Louise, b. San Antonio, TX, USA. Investor; Clinical Psychologist (retired); Philanthropist. m. Thomas Tross Gambrell, 23 Feb 1960. Education: BS, Psychol, Northwestern Univ, 1949; MS, Psychol, Purdue Univ, 1952; Internship in Clin Psychol, Menninger Fndn (1st woman in prog) 1953; PhD, Clin Psychol, Purdue Univ, 1955; Post-doct Fell in Clin Child Psychol, Dept of Child Psychol (1st woman trained), Menninger Clin, 1956; Amn Bd of Examiners in Profl Psychol, Dipl, Clin Psychol (by exam), 1966. Appointments include: Staff Psychol, Child Guidance Clin, Kings Co Hosp, Brooklyn, NY, 1957-58; Hd Staff Psychol, Child Guidance Clin, Kings Co Hosp, Brooklyn, NY, 1957-58; Clin Rsch Conslt, Episc Cty Diocese, St Louis, MO, 1959; Dir, Psychol Clin Barnes-Renard Hosps and Instr in Medl Psychol, Dept of Psych and Neur, Wash Univ Sch of Med, St Louis, MO, 1959; Priv prac, Clin and Cnsltng Psychol, Fullerton, CA, 1960-92. Publications: Articles on clin psychol to profl jrnls. Honours: Elected Sec, Intl Cncl of Phycols, 1962-64, 1973-74, 1974-76; World's Leading Biographee of 1987, IBC, 1987; Citizenship Awd (one of first five), 1975, Disting Alumni Awd, 1993, Old Master Awd, 1993, Purdue Univ; Merit Awd (one of two), Northwestern Univ, Coll of Arts and Scis, 1997; Cntr for Study of Presidency Soc Jewelry Histns USA (charter); Alumni Assn Menninger Sch Psych; Soc Sigma Xi Natl Rsch Hon (emeritus). Memberships include: Fell, Acady of Clin Psychol; Charter Fell, Amn Psychol Soc; Amn Assn of Applied and Preventive Psychol; Life Fell: Amn Orthopsychiatric Assn; World Wide Acady of Schls, NZ; Fell: Amn Psychol Assn; Div of Cnsltng Psychol; Div of Clin Psychol; Div of Psychol of Women. Address: PO Box 6067, Beverley Hills, CA 90212-1067, USA.

EVATT Elizabeth Andreas (Hon), b. Aust. Barrister-at-Law. m. Robert S T Southan, 8 Aug 1960, 1 d. Education: LLB, Univ of Sydney, 1955; LLM, Harvard Univ, USA; Admitted to NSW Bar, 1955; Inner Temple, London, Eng, 1958. Appointments include: Dpty Pres, Austl Conciliation & Arbitration Cmmn, 1973; Chmn, Roy Cmmn on Human Relationships, 1974-77; Chmn, Family Law Cncl, 1976-79; First Chf Judge, Family Crt of Aust, 1976-88; Pres, Austl Law Reform Cmmn, 1988-93; Chan, Univ of Newcastle, 1988-93; Tree, Sydney Opera House Trust, 1977-83; Mbr of Cncl, Macquarie Univ, 1979-85; Mbr, UN Cttee on Elimination of Discrimination Against Women, 1984-92; Fndr, 1984, Bd Mbr, 1985-, Pearl Watson Fndn, to devel projects for community info and educn about marriage, marriage breakdown and family law servs; Bd Mbr, Austl Inst of Family Studies, 1989-91; Mbr, Human Rights Cttee (ICCPR), 1993-; Pt-time Commnr, Human Rights and Equal Opportunity Commn, 1995-. Honours: Univ Medal in Law, Sydney, 1955; AO, 1982; Hon LLD (Sydney), 1985; Hon DUniv (Newcastle), 1988 Hon LLD (Macquarie), 1989; AC, 1995. Address: 13 Glenview Street, Paddington, NSW 2021, Australia.

EVERITT Arthur Vincent, b. 25 Sept 1924. Physiologist. m. Joyce Nutt, 23 Feb 1957, 1 s, 1 d. Education: ASTC, Sydney Tech Coll, 1949; BSc, 1953; PhD, 1959; Univ of Sydney. Appointments: Temp Lectr, 1955-58, Lectr, 1960-64, Snr Lectr, 1965-71, Assoc Prof, 1972-85, Univ of Sydney, Dept of Physiol; Hon Assoc, Anatomy and Histology, Univ of Sydney, 1987-99; Visng Physiol, Concord Hosp, 1986-99. Publications: Hypothalamus, Pituitary and Aging, 1976; Regulation of Neuroendocrine Aging, 1988; 125 Sci pprs and book chapts. Honour: Nuffield Travelling Fellshp, 1959. Memberships: Austl Assn of Gerontology; Fndn Mbr 1964, Life Mbr 1988; Gerontology Fndn of Aust, Pres 1982-86, Life Mbr 1984. Hobbies: Travel; Photography; Popular music, 1930-70; Dogs. Address: 30 Boronia Grove, Heathcote, NSW 2233, Australia.

EVREN Kenan, b. 1918. Army Officer. m. 3 c. Education: Mil Acady; War Coll. Appointments: Artillery Offr, 1938; Served in Korea; Chf of Staff of the Land Forces then Dep Chf of Staff of the Armed Forces; Cmdr Fourth Army - Aegean Army - Izmir, 1976; Rank of Gen, 1974; Hd Turkish mil deleg to USSR, 1975; Chf of the Land Forces, 1977; Chf of Staff of the Armed Forces, 1978; Led coup deposing civn govt, Sept 1980; Hd of State and Chmn Natl Security Cncl, 1980-82; Pres of Turkey, 1982-89. Honours: Num decorations. Address: Beyaz Ev Sokak 21, Armutalan, Marmaris, Turkey.

EWELL A Ben Jr, b. 9 Oct 1941, Ohio, USA. Attorney; Buisnessman. m. Suzanne, 3 s. Education: BA, Miami Univ; LLB, JD, Univ CA, Hastings Coll of Law, San Fran. Appointments: Pres, A B Ewell Jr, The Clarksfield Co Inc, Water Acquisition, Transfer & Exchange Resources; Mbr, State Bar of CA, Fresno County Bar Assn; Admitted, CA State Crts, Fed Dist Crts, US Ninth Circuit Crt, US Supreme Crt; Developer, Millerton New Town & Brighton Crest. Memberships include: Bd Dir, Fresno Volleyball Club, Police Activities League, Fresno; Bldng Ind Assn, San Joaquin Valley; Assn of CA Water Agencies; Clovis Cham of Com; Copper River Country Club. Address: 410 West Fallbrook Avenue, Suite 102, Fresno, CA 93711, USA.

EWING Maurice Rossie. Emeritus Professor. m. Phyllis Parnall, 18 May 1946, 2 s, 1 d. Education: Daniel Stewart's Coll, University of Edinburgh, MB ChB, MSc, MD hons, FRCS, FRACS, FACS(Hon). Appointments: RNVR Surgn Lt-Cmdr, 1940-45; Snr Lectr, Postgrad Med Sch, London, 1947-55, Hunterian Prof RCS, 1950; James Stewart Prof of Surg, Univ of Melbourne, 1955-78; Emer

Prof, Univ of Melbourne, 1978-. Honour: CBE, 1977.
Hobby: Farming. Address: 40 Kneen Street, North
Fitzroy, Victoria 3068, Australia.

F

FABINYI Gavin Christopher Andrew, b. 12 May 1946, Melbourne, Vic, Aust. Neurosurgeon. m Jan Piper, 17 Nov 1973, 2 s, 1 d. Education: Wesley Coll, Melbourne; MBBS, Melbourne Univ, 1970; Fell, Roy Austl Coll Surgs, Neurosurg, 1978; Higher Surg Trng Cert, Roy Coll Surg, UK. Appointments: Res Medl Offr, Alfred Hosp, 1971-72; Snr Prosector, Anatomy, Melbourne Univ, 1973; Neurosurg Registrar, Roy Melbourne Hosp, 1974-76; Snr Registrar, Radcliffe Infirmary, Oxford, and Manchester Roy Infirmary, Manchester, Eng, 1977-80; Neurosurg, Repatriation Gen, Austin and Roy Melbourne Hosps, 1980-87; Dir, Neurosurg, Austin and Repatriation Gen Hosps, 1987-; Dir, Neurosurg, Austin Repatriation Medl Cntr. Publications: Pprs, monographs and presentations on neurosurg subjs, 1976-. Honour: Roy Austl Coll Surgs Fndn Rsch Awd, 1988. Memberships: Neurosurg Soc Australasia, VP, 1987-88, Pres, 1992-94; Austl Brain Fndn, Exec Cncl Mbr, 1984-; Dir; Editl Bd, Jrnl Clinl Neurosci, 1993-. Hobbies: Reading; Neurosurgical history. Address: Epworth Medical Centre, 62 Erin Street, Richmond, Vic 3121, Australia.

FAHD IBN ABDUL AZIZ, b. 1923 Riyadh. King of Saudi Arabia. Appointments: Min of Educ, 1953; Min of the Interior, 1962-75; Second Dep PM, 1967-75; First Dep PM, 1975-82; PM, June, 1982-; Became Crown Prince, 1975; Succeeded to the throne on the death of his brother, 13 June 1982; Assumed title "Servant of the Two Shrines", 1986. Address: Royal Diwan, Riyadh, Saudi Arabia.

FAHEY John Joseph, b. 10 Jan 1945 New Zealand. Politician; Lawyer. m. Colleen McGurran, 1968, 1 s, 2 d. Education: St Anthony's Convent Picton; Chevalier Coll Bowral. Appointments: Min for Indl Rels and Employment and Min Asstng Premier of NSW, 1988-90; Min for Indl Rels Further Educ Trng and Employment NSW, 1990-92; Premier and Treas of NSW, 1992; Chmn Sydney 2000 Olympic Bid Co, 1992-93; Premier and Min for Econ Dev of NSW, 1993-95; Min for Fin, 1996-. Memberships: Mbr Parl of NSW, 1984-95; Fed Mbr for Macarthur. Hobbies: Keen sports follower. Address: Parliament House, Canberra, ACT, Australia.

FAHIM Thimsy, b. 21 Aug 1958. Editor. m. Al Haj Fahim, 14 Sept 1985, 2 s, 1 d. Education: Dip, Jrnlsm, Colombo Univ. Appointments: Sub Ed, 1978-85; Mngng Ed, 1985-95; Ed and Proprietor, 1996-, The Economic Times. Memberships: Asst Treas, Sri Lanka Press Assn, 1980-; Cttee Mbr, Sri Lanka Muslim Media Forum. 1995-96. Hobbies: Reading; Travelling. Address: Albion Publications, 51/1 Sri Dharmarama Rd, Colombo 9, Sri Lanka.

FAICHNEY Graham John, b. 30 Sept 1938. Research Scientist. Div, 3 s. Education: BAgrSc, Melbourne; MScAgr, Sydney; PhD, Melbourne; DAgrSc, Melbourne. Appointments: Tchng Fell, Animal Nutr, Univ Sydney, 1962; Lectr, Animal Husbandry, Univ Melbourne, 1965-66; Postdoct Fell, Rowett Inst, Aberdeen, Scotland, 1967; Rsch Scientist, CSIRO Div of Animal Physiol, 1968; Snr Rsch Scientist, 1971; Prin Rsch Scientist, CSIRO Div of Animal Prodn, 1976; Visng Scientist, ARC Babraham, UK, 1977; Snr Prin Rsch Scientist, 1982; Chercheur Contractuel, INRA de Theix, France, 1986; Chf Rsch Scientist, 1987; Hon Assoc, Dept of Animal Husbandry, Univ Sydney, 1982-87; Cnllr, NSW Animal Welfare Advsry Cncl, 1988-94; Prog Mgr, CSIRO Div of Animal Prodn, 1989-92; Visng Scientist, INRA de Theix, France, 1991; Natl Greenhouse Gas Inventory Livestock Working Grp, 1994-95; Hon Rsch Assoc, Sch of Biol Sci, Univ Sydney, 1995-. Creative works: 125 scientific publications; 62 full pprs in refereed jrnls; 22 invited reviews and chapts; 41 original communications. Honours: Fell, Chartered Biolst, Inst of Biol, 1987-94; Hon Mbr, Nutrition Soc of Aust, 1995. Memberships: Hon Treas, Austl Soc of Animal Prodn, 1964, Editl Cttee, 1965-66, 1986-88; Hon Treas, NSW, 1971-72; Fed Cnslr, 1973-74, 1986-88; Regr, 1986-88; Nutrition Soc of Aust:

Sec, Sydney, 1975-76, Sydney Cttee, 1979-80, 1998, Hon Treas, Sydney, 1999-; Natl Sec, 1981-84, Newsletter Ed, 1981-84, Natl Pres, 1986-89, Editl Bd, 1991-; Austl Fedn for the Welfare of Animals, Cnclr, 1988-94; Intl Symposia on Ruminant Physiol: Treas, 1972-76, Scientific Advsr, 1992-94. Hobbies: Bush walking; Photography; Reading. Address: 18 Gregory Avenue, Baulkham Hills, NSW 2153, Australia.

FAINE Solomon, b. 17 Aug 1926, NZ. Emeritus Professor of Microbiology. m. Eva Rothschild, 17 May 1950, 1 s, 2 d. Education: BMedSc, 1946, MB ChB, 1949, MD, 1958, Univ NZ; DPhil Oxon, 1955; Fell, Roy Coll Pathologists Aust, 1962. Appointments: Asst Lectr, Lectr, Bacteriology, 1950-52, Lectr, Microbio, 1956-58, Otago Univ, 1950-52; Nuffield Dominions Demonstrator, Oxford Univ, Eng, 1953-55; Snr Lectr, Bacteriology, 1959-63, Assoc Prof, Bacteriology, 1963-67, Sydney Univ, NSW, Aust; Prof, Microbio, 1968-1991, Chmn, Dept Microbio, 1968-87, 1989, Emer Prof, 1991-, Monash Univ; Prin, MediSci Cnsltng, 1992. Publications: Num contbns to sci jrnls and textbooks; Books: Guidelines for the Control of Leptospirosis, WHO, in Engl, French, Japanese, Arabic, Chinese, 1982; Leptospira and Leptospirosis, 1994. Honours include: Peter Bancroft Prize, Rsch, Sydney Univ, 1965; Exch Schl, Institut Pasteur, Paris, 1971-72; Fulbright Awd, Amn-Austl Fndn, 1978; Exch Snr Fellshp, W German Govt, 1979; Medallion, Disting Serv, Intl Union Microbiol Socs, 1982. Memberships: Intl Union Microbiol Socs, Exec Bd, 1978-82, Chmn, Div Bacteriology, 1978-82; Austl Soc Microbiol, Fell, 1989-, Hon Life Mbr, 1990-, Chmn, Stndng Cttee Clinl Microbiol, 1984-85; Fell, Amn Acady Microbiol, 1979-. Hobbies: Photography; Music. Address: Department of Microbiology, Monash University, Wellington Road, Clayton, Vic 3168, Australia.

FAIRBAIRN Linda Caroline, b. 4 Aug 1952, Enfield, Middlesex, UK. Longcase Clock Dial Conservator. m. Phil Smyrk, 13 July 1978, 2 s. Education: Dip, Cartography, Oxon, UK. Career: Priv prac, 1984-. Hobbies: Performing and visual arts; The Australian bush. Address: PO Box 707, Parap, NT 0804, Australia.

FAIRFAX James Oswald, b. 27 Mar 1933, Sydney, NSW, Aust. Company Director. Education: MA, Balliol Coll, Oxford, Eng. Appointments: Dir, 1957-87, Chmn, 1977-87, John Fairfax Ltd; Dir, 1958-87, Chmn, 1975-87, Amalgamated Tv Servs Pty Ltd; Dir, Assocd Newspapers Ltd, 1958-87; Dir, 1977-87, Chmn, 1984-87, David Syme and Co Ltd. Honour: AO, Gen Div, 1993. Memberships: Bd Mngmt, Roy Alexandra Hosp Children, 1967-85; Bd, Children's Medl Rsch Fndn, 1986-89; Cncl, Intl House, Sydney Univ, 1967-79; Intl Cncl, Mus Mod Art, NYC, USA, 1971-; Austl Natl Gall, Cncl, 1976-84. Listed in: Who's Who in Australia; The International Year Book and Statesmen's Who's Who. Address: Retford Park, Old South Road, Bowral, NSW 2576, Australia.

FAIRHALL Allen (The Hon Sir), b. 24 Nov 1909, Morpeth, NSW, Aust. Retired Parliamentarian. m. Monica Ballantine, 23 Apr 1936, 1 s. Education: Newcastle Tech Inst, 1924-27. Appointments: Alderman, Newcastle Cty Cncl, 1941-44; Supvsng Engr, Radio and Signals Sect, Min Munitions, 1942-45; Pres, Austl Coml Brdcstng Fedn, 1943; Fmrly Fndr/Mngng Dir, Newcastle Brdcstng Co Pty Ltd; Mbr House Reps (Liberal), for Paterson, NSW, 1949-69; Min Interior and Wrks, 1956-58, Chmn, Pub Wrks Cttee, 1959-61, Min Supply, 1961-66, Min Def, 1966-69. Honours: Hon DSc, Newcastle, 1966; Kirby Medallist, Austl Soc Prodn Engrs, 1967. Memberships: FRSA; Life Mbr, WIA. Hobbies: Amateur radio; Tax reform. Address: 7 Parkway Avenue, Newcastle, NSW 2300, Australia.

FAIRNIE Ian James, b. 9 Mar 1944, Melbourne, Australia. University. m. Helen, 11 Jan 1968, 2 s. Education: BVSc; BEd; PhD. Appointments: Dir, Muresk Inst of Agr, 1985-89; Exec VP, Curtin Univ, N Am, 1989-95; Dir, External and Cmnty Rels, 1995-. Memberships: Austl Vet Assn, natl pres, 1989-90; Fell, Austl Vet Assn. Hobby: Pipe Organ. Address: 2 Pearson Crescent, Bull Creek, WA 6149, Australia.

FAKAFANUA Tutoatasi, b. 20 Jan 1962. Government Official. m. 3 children. Education: BCom, Univ Otago, Dunedin, NZ, 1983; LLB, 1987; LLM (Hon), Univ Auckland, NZ, 1991. Appointments: Lay Preacher, Free Wesleyan Ch; Law Clk, Bar and Solicitor, Clive Edwards & Co, Auckland, 1987-89; Mbr, Bd Dirs, Tonga Dev Bank; Crown Cnsl, Crown Law Dept, Tonga, 1991; Min, Labour, Com and Inds, Govt Tonga, Nuku'alofa, 1991-; Mbr, Legis Assembly, Privy Cncl and Cabinet, Dept Min Fin, Registrar of Co's; Registrar of Inc Socs, 1991-; Min Fin, Treas Commnr, Inland Revenue, Contoller, Post Office, Min i/c Stats Dept. Address: Ministry of Finance, PO Box 87, Vuna Road, Nuku'alofa, Tonga.

FAKES Neville Lewis, b. 30 Nov 1919, Glen Innes, NSW, Aust. Retired Company Director. m. Audrey May Harrison, 23 Mar 1946, 2 d. Education: BSc, 1940, BE Aeronautical, 1942, Sydney Univ. Appointments: Chf Aerodynamicist, Propellor Div, De Havilland Aircraft Co, 1942-44; Engr, Shell Co Aust, 1945-46; Shell Refining Co, UK, 1947; Engr, Burmah Shell, Bombay, India, 1948; Gen Mngr Mktng, Compania Shell de Venezuela, Caracas, 1949-60; Mngng Dir, Shell East Ltd, Singapore, 1961-63; Chmn, Shell Malaysia, Kuala Lumpur, 1964-67; Chmn, Pres, Shell Grp Cos, Japan, 1968-72. Honours: CBE, 1971; Order of the Sacred Treas, Japan, 1973. Memberships: Chartered Engr, Instn Engrs, Aust; Roy Aeronautical Soc, London; Planetary Soc, USA; Dickens Fellshp, London. Listed in: Dictionary of International Biography; Who's Who in the World; Who's Who in Australia; Notable Australians. Hobbies: Astronomy; Collecting antiquarian books; Reading; Golf. Address: 3 Magarra Place, Seaforth, NSW 2092, Australia.

FAKHRO Abdul Rahman Ebrahim, b. 14 Sept 1948, Bahrain. General Surgeon. m. Sahar, 2 s, 1 d. Education: MBBCH; FRCS. Appointments: Snr Cnslt Surg; Asst Prof, Medl Coll; VP, Bahrain Cancer Soc. Memberships: Franco-Arab Du Cancer; Pan-arab Soc for Doctors; Editl Bd, Jrnl of Bahrain Medl Soc; Gulf Assn Form for Cancer Prevention. Hobbies: Sport; Fishing; Reading; Voluntary Works with non-profitable Societies. Address: P O Box 22213, Muharraq, Bahrain.

FAKHRO Ali Ben Yousuf, b. 1924, Bahrain. Businessman. 1 s, 4 d. Appointments: Chmn, Bahrain Chamber of Com and Ind, Bahrain Flour Mills Co, Bahrain Cinema Co; Dir, Mohammaed Fakhroo & Bros, Gulf Union Ins and Reins Co, Gulf Union Ins and Risk Mngmt Co, Gulf Union Ins and Projects Mngmt Holdings; Vice Chmn, Gulf Union Ins Co. Address: PO Box 439, Manama, Bahrain.

FALCAM Leo A. Government Official. Appointment: VP, Federated States of Micronesia, 1997-. Address: POB PS-53, Plankir, Pohnpei, Eastern Carolina Islands, Federated States of Micronesia.

FALCONE Alfonso Benjamin, b. Bryn Mawr, PA, USA. Physician; Biochemist. Education: AB, Chem, 1944; MD (Hons), 1947; PhD, Biochemistry, Univ MN, 1954; Dipl, Amn Bd of Internal Med. Appointments: Intern, Res, PA Gen Hosp, 1947-49; Tchng Fell, Univ of MN Hosps, 1950-52; Lt-Cmdr, US Naval Reserve Medl Corps, 1954-56; Asst Clin Prof, Med, 1956-59, Assoc Clin Prof, 1959-63, Asst Prof, Inst of Enzyme Rsch, 1963-66, Visng Prof, 1967, Univ WI, Madison; Priv prac, cnslt, Fresno, CA, 1968-; Mbr, Medl Staff, Fresno Community Hosp (Chmn, Dept of Med, 1973-) & St Agnes Hosp; Hon mbr staff, Univ Medl Cntr. Publications: Articles to profl jrnls on rsch in mechanisms of energy transduction in biol systmems. Honours: Sigma Xi; Phi Lambda Epsilon; Doct grants, Natl Inst Hlth, 1951-53; Rsch grants, 1958-68. Memberships: Fell, Amn Coll of Physns; AAAS; Amn Soc Biochemistry & Molecular Bio; Cntrl Soc of Clin Rsch; Amn Fedn for Clin Rsch; Amn Chem Soc; Amn Assn for Study of Liver Disease; Endocrine Soc; Amn Diabetes; Assn for Acad Excellence; Univ of CA at Fresno Cttee; Fresno County Assn for Univ of CA Campus; Archaeol Inst of Am; CA Acady of Med. Address: Metabolic and Endocrine Disorders, 2240 E IL Avenue, Fresno, CA 93701-2118, USA.

FALERO Frank, b. 22 Dec 1937, NYC, NY, USA. Economist; Educator. m. Verna Whittier. Education: AA, St Petersburg Junior Coll, FL, USA, 1962; BA Hons, Univ of S Florida, Tampa, 1964; MS, Econs, 1965, PhD, Econs, 1967, Florida State Univ, Tallahassee, 1967. Appointments include: Visng Prof, Econs Inst, Univ of Colorado, USA, Summer 1974; Visng Prof, Econs and Fin, Natl Sch of Fin and Mngt, Fairfield, CT, USA, Summer 1986; Bd of Dirs, Cntr for Econ Educ and Rsch, California State Univ, Bakersfield, 1979-97; Prof, Econs and Fin, California State Univ, Bakersfield, 1974-. Publications include: The Evaluation of Teaching Performance: A Factor Analytic Approach, co-auth, 1977; Book Review of Peruvian Democracy Under Economic Stress: An Account of the Belaunde Administration, 1963-1968, 1978; Marketing Rural Subdivisions: The Influence of Recreational Amenities, co-auth, 1980; Financing Wind Parks, 1985; Selecting a Discount Rate: Relevant Criteria, 1988; Wage Loss in Wrongful Death - A Historical Analysis, 1996. Honours: Dipl, Amn Bd of Forensic Examiners, 1994; Arbitrator, Natl Futures Assn, 1996; Fell, Amn Coll of For Examiners, 1997. Memberships: Fell, Roy Econ Soc, 1964; Amn Arbitration Assn, 1964; NDEA Title IV Fell, 1964-67; AAAS, 1965; Reg Sci Assn, 1965; Southern Econ Assn, 1965; Amn Econ Assn, 1965. Address: PO Box 950, Springville, CA 93265-0950, USA.

FALLOON, John H. Politician; Farmer. Appointments: Natl Party MP for Pahiatua, 1977-; Fmr Assoc Min of Fin and Min of Inland Revenue and Stats; Postmaster-Gen, 1981-2; Min of Agric, 1984-96; Min of Forestry, 1990-96; Min of Racing. Address: Parliament Buildings, Wellington, New Zealand.

FALVEY Lindsay, b. 23 May 1950. Professor; Dean. Education: BAgriSci (hons), 1971; MAgriSc, 1976, La Trobe Univ; PhD, Qld Univ, 1980. Appointments: Intl Mission Mbr, 70 missions in over 20 countries, 1976-95; Ldr, 35 intl missions to Asia and elsewhere, 1981-85; Mngng Dir, MPW Aust, 1983-89; Dir, Fndr, Engl Lang Cntr of Aust, 1985-93; Dir, Fndr, Vic Intl coll Pty Ltd & Vic Coll Ltd, 1986-95; Dir, Calgene Pacific (now FloriGene), 1987-89; Dir, Winsearch Ltd, 1989-91; Mngng Dir, Coffey-MPW Pty Ltd, 1989-93; Intl Mbr, 6th AAAP Congress, Bangkok, 1992; Dir, Ptnr, Hoffmann Andersen & Ptnrs, Copenhagen, 1993-95; Dir, GDMC Pty Ltd; Exec Cnclr, Consult Aust; Bd Mbr, Cntr for Farm Planning & Land Mngmt; Dir, VCAH Ltd; Dir, Sch of Forestry, Creswick Ltd; Dir, CRC for Hardwood Fibre; Dean, Inst of Land and Food Resources, Univ of Melbourne. Publications: Cattle and Sheep in Northern Thailand, 1979; Introduction to Working Animals, 1988; International Consulting Providing Your Services to International Development Agencies, 1994; Food Environmental Education: Agricultural Education in Natural Resource Management, 1996; Land and Food; 70 short tech and other publns. Honours: A H Howard Awd, 1972; Fell, Acady of Tech Sci and Engrng; Fell, Austl Inst of Agricl Sci, 1991; Inaugural Pres Awd for Agricl, Pres of Austl Inst of Agricl Sci, 1992; PM (Thailand) Awd for Company proj; Awd of Ex, Austl Assn of Agricl Cnslts, 1993. Address: Inst of Land and Food Resources, University of Melbourne, Parkville, Vic 3052, Australia.

FAN Chenchen, b. 31 Jan 1944, Shanxi, China. Research Professor; System Manager; Chief. m. Yisheng Chen, 1 Oct 1974, 1 s, 1 d. Education: Maths Fac, Peking Univ, 1967. Appointments: Div Chf, Comprehensive Div, Survey and Stdy Div, Network Div. Publications: Education Management Information System in Japan, USA, Canada and Germany, 1989; Basic Information Set for Management in Chinese University, 1995. Honours: 3rd Grade Awds of Natl Prize, Sci and Technol Progress, 1992. Memberships: Cttee, Natl Info Technol Standardization Tech Cttee, 1992. Hobbies: Swimming; Music; Dance music. Address: c/o Education Management Information Centre, Ministry of Education, Beijing 100816, China.

FAN Jiashen, b. 20 Aug 1929, Kunming, Yunnan Province, China. Professor. m. Ruzhan Zhao, 23 Mar 1936, 2 s, 2 d. Education: Undergrad, Dept For Langs and Lit, Yunnan Univ, Kunming, 1948-50; Mid-S Civil Engrng and Arch Inst, Changsha, 1951-55; Bachelor's deg, 1955. Appointments: Techn, 3rd Railway Des Inst, 1955-57; Tchr, Tianjing Railway Engrng Sch, 1957-59; Lectr, Baotao Railway Engrng Inst, 1959-75; Rsch Engr, Yunnan Provincial Seismological Bur, 1975-84; Assoc Prof, Prof, Yunnan Inst Technol, now Yunnan Polytechnic Univ, 1984-; Visng Schl, US Natl Cntr Earthquake Engrng Rsch, Buffalo, NY, 1988-89. Publications: 78 papers on solid mechs and earthquake engrng inclng 14 w abstracts in SCI Search. Honours: Awd, Prominent Contributive Scientist, Yunnan Prov, 1987; Awd, Prominently Contributive Scientist, People's Repub China, 1989. Memberships: Chinese Assn Earthquake Engrng; Chinese Soc Mechs; Chinese Soc Hwy Engrng; Intl Assn Computational Mechs, 1990-; Gesellschaft für Angewandte Mathematik und Mechanik, Germany, 1955-. Listed in: Five Hundred Leaders of Influence, 1993; International Who's Who of Intellectuals, 1992; Contemporary Who's Who of China, 1994. Hobbies: Swimming; Long distance running; Classical music. Address: Architecture Engineering Department, Yunnan Polytechnic University, Kunming, Yunnan 650051, China.

FAN Tian-You, b. 1 July 1939, China. Professor. m. Z T Li, 22 Mar 1973, 2 d. Education: Dips, Peking Univ, Dept Maths and Mechs, 1963. Appointment: Rsch Cntr of Materials Sci, Beijing Inst of Technol. Publications: Foundation of Fracture Mechanics, 1978; Introduction to Fracture Dynamics, 1990; Mathematical Theory of Elasticity of Quasicrystals, 1999. Honours: Rsch Fell, Alexander Von Humboldt Fndn, 1981-83, 1986, 1993; 2nd Prize of China Book Prize, 1991. Memberships; NY Acady of Sci; Amn Maths Soc; 9th Natl Cttee, Chinese People's Polit Consultative Conf. Hobbies: Classical literature; Classical music. Address: Research Centre of Materials Science, Beijing Institute of Technology, PO Box 327, Beijing.

FAN Tining, b. 3 Apr 1947, China. Professor. m. Li Suying, 23 July 1979, 1 s. Education: BA, Peking Univ; MA, Grad Sch, Chinese Acady of Socl Scis; Snr Visng Schl, Univ Oxford and Cambridge. Appointments: Dean, Prof, Dept of Intl Politics, Inst of Intl Rels. Publications: This is America, 1993; American Government and Politics, 1993; Western Comparative Politics, 1996. Memberships: Chinese Assn of Intl Rels; Stndng Bd, Dir, Assn of Intl Politics of Beijing Univs and Colls. Hobby: Tourism. Address: Department of International Politics, Institute of International Relations, Beijing 100091, China.

FAN Wen Tao, b. 23 Apr 1938, Mianyang, Hubei, China. Professor of Applied Mathematics and System Science. m. Ding Guangying, Jan 1965, 2 s. Education: BS, Dept of Maths, Wuhan Univ, 1957-62. Appointments: Asst Rschr, 1963-79, Vice Rschr, 1979-88, Prof, 1988-, PhD Dir, 1997-. Publications include: Mathematics Model and Industry Control Theory, 1978; System Theory, 1990. Memberships: VP, Hubei Assn of Systems Engrng, Chmn of Acad Cttee; Chmn, Systems Sci Dept, Wuhan Inst of Maths Phys, Academia Sincia. Hobbies: Poetry; Cooking; Table Tennis. Address: Wuhan Institute of Physics & Mathematics, PO Box 71010, Wuhan 430071, China.

FAN Yewei, b. 27 Dec 1945, Daliang, China. Professor and Editor for ancient Chinese music and medicine. m. R Zhang, 5 Sept 1987, 1 d. Education: BS. Appointments: Music Tchr, 1970; Ed, Musical Jrnl, 1980; Rschr, Mngr of Publing, 1990. Publications: Chinese Ancient Healing Therapy by Using Special Rock-Bian Therapy; (book) Healing by Bian Therapy. Memberships: Chinese Musicians, 1986; Snr Mbr, Soc of Chinese Natl Music, 1993; Soc Chinese Med Dev, 1996. Hobbies: Music; Sports; Archeology. Address: No 24, Wenhuiyan Road Hadian District, Beijing 100088, China.

FAN Yiu-Kwan, b. 29 Aug 1944, China. Economist. m. Mary Jing Ying Pan, 20 Sept 1974, 2 s, 1 d. Education: BA, Hons, Univ of Hong Kong, 1967; MA, Univ of Toronto, 1969; PhD, Univ of WI, Madison, 1974. Appointments: Lectr in Econ, Univ of Hong Kong, 1974-80; Visng Asst Prof of Econ, Univ of Southern CA, 1977-78; Adj Assoc Prof of Econ; Vice Pres, Asst Dir of Rsch, Econ Dynamic Inc, Malibu, CA, 1980-81; Assoc Prof of Econ, Univ of WI, Stevens Pnt, 1981-84; Prof of Econ, 1984-89; Dir, Bus Rsch Centre, Sch of Bus, Hong Kong Baptist Univ; Dean, Sch of Bus, Hong Kong Baptist Univ, 1986-. Publications: The Economic Positioning of Hong Kong in the Pacific Community; The Other Hong Kong Report 1998; Higher Education and National Development; Many Jrnl Articles, Contbns to books. Honours: Phi Kappa Phi, 1974; Hon Cnslt, Econ and Law, 1992-; Cnsltng Prof, S China Univ of Technol, 1992-; Fac Rsch Awd, 1983; Schl Access Grnt, 1982-83; Rsch Ppr Prize, 1973-74; Fell, The Pop Cncl, 1972-73; Marie Christine Kohler Res Fell, 1972-74; World Univ Serv Schlshp, 1964-67. Memberships: Hong Kong Cttee for Pacific Econ Co-op; Cttee on Mngmt and Supvsr Trng; Voc Trng Cncl; Bus and Profl Studies; Many other mbrshps. Hobbies: Reading; Golf; Swimming; Hiking; Music. Address: School of Business, Hong Kong Baptist University, Hong Kong Baptist University, Kowloon Tong, Hong Kong.

FAN Zhen-Zeng, b. 19 Sept 1960, Hebei, China. Doctor. m. Zhang Li-Ping, 12 June 1987, 1 s. Education: Dr, Hebei Medl Univ, 1996. Creative Works: Medical Answer; Medical Introcuction; Psychosis and Behaviorism of Neurosurgery. Memberships: China Coll of Med. Hobbies: Music. Address: 223 He-Ping West Road, Xin Hua Dist, Affiliated Hospital, Number 2 He Bei Medical University, Shijiazhuang, Hebei, China.

FANG Cuichang, b. 23 Sept 1928, Cixi, Zhejiang, China. Mechanics Educator. m. 9 Feb 1957, 2 s, 1 d. Education: BEng, Tsinghua Univ, China, 1950. Appointments: Asst, Mechs, 1950-54, Lectr, Mechs, 1954-61, Assoc Prof, Mechs, 1961-86, Prof, Mechs, 1986, Tsinghua Univ; Prof, Mechs, China Univ of Mining, Beijing, 1987-; Tchr of Doctoral Students, China Univ of Mining, Beijing, 1990-. Publications: Moire Method of Strain Analysis, auth, 1983; Moire Method, auth, 1985; Grid Method, auth, 1985; Experimental Stress Analysis, co-auth, 1984; Contemporary Photomechanics, co-auth, 1990; Strength of Materials, chief ed, 1964; Advanced Engineering Mechanics, ed, 1990. Honours: Beijing Sci & Technol Achievements Awd, 1980; Govt Spec Subsidy, 1992-. Membership: Chinese Soc of Mechs, 1979-. Hobbies: Taijiquan; Qigong; Music. Address: Apt 502-1, W Bldng 43, Tsinghua University, Beijing 100084, China.

FANG Da Jun, b. 16 Aug 1951, Suzhou, Jiangsu, China. Teacher. m. Wei Shao, Jan 1980, 1 s. Education: BA. Appointment: Hd of Lib, Lectr. Creative Works: Auspiciousness in the Four Seasons; Auspicious Flowers and Beautiful Line; Relaxation; Charms of Spring in the Southern State; Moonlights; Hatred of Blood; Sui Yang Bathed in Blood; The Story of a Cat and a Crew. Honours: Fine Works Prize, Suzhou Gardeners Art Works Exhbn, 1983; 4th Prize, Fine Works, Suzhou Gardeners Art & Calligraphy Exhbn, 1990; Fine Works Prize, Suzhou Tchrs Art & Calligraphy Exhbn, 1994; 2nd Prize, Suzhou Tchrs Art Works Exhbn, 1996. Memberships: Suzhou Tchrs Art Assn; Suzhou Art & Crafts Assn; Zhongyuan Art & Calligraphy Inst; Jiangdu Art & Calligraphy Inst of China. Hobbies: Literature; Painting; Collecting Stamps. Address: School of Industrial Art, Suzhou, China.

FANG Dingyou, b. 24 July 1935, Zhejiang, China. Teacher. m. Geng Shufan, 25 Dec 1962, 1 s, 1 d. Education: Grad, Coll. Appointments: Lectr, 1978; Assoc Prof, 1985; Prof, 1992. Publications: Two-Phase Flow Dynamics, 1988; Internal Ballistics of Solid Rocket Motor, 1997. Honour: Specl Subsidy, Govt of China. Memberships: Chinese Soc of Astronautics, 1981; Chinese Soc of Aeronautics, 1984. Address: Department of Astronautical Technology, National University of Defense Technology, Changsha, Hunan 410073, China.

FANG Ji-Qian, b. 6 July 1939, Shanghai, China. University Professor. m. Mei-Ying Gong, 27 Oct 1966, 2 d. Education: BS Dept of Maths, Fu Dan Univ, Shanghai, China, 1956-61; Prog of Biostatistics, Univ of CA, Berkeley, USA, PhD, 1982-85. Appointments: Instr of Maths, 1961-79, Lectr of Biomathematics and

Biostatistics, 1979-85, Prof, Chmn, Dept of Biomathematics, Beijing Medl Univ, China, 1985-90; Visng Prof, Univ of Kent, UK, 1987-88; Prof, Chmn, Dept of Medl Stats, Sun Yat-Sen Univ of Medl Scis, Guangzhou, China, 1991-; Visng Prof, Chinese Univ of Hong Kong, 1993-. Publications: Books: The Computer and its Application in the Medical Field, 1981; Advanced Mathematics (chf ed), 1987; Methods of Mathematical Statistics, 1987; Medical Statistics and Computer Experiment, 1997. Honours: Cert of Merit, Beijing Municipal Govt, for Disting Rsch in Sci & Technol, 1985, 1988; Cert of Merit, Min of Pub Hlth, China, 1986, 1992. Memberships: Intl Biometric Soc, Sec of Chinese Grp, 1986-; Intl Inst of Math Stats; Royal Stats Soc. Hobbies: Drama; Literature. Address: Medical Statistics, Sun Yat Sen University of Medical Sciences, Guangzhou 510089, China.

FANG Lei, b. 18 June 1934, Anhui, China. Official. m. Wenying Yan, 8 Dec 1958, 2 d. Education: University Diploma. Vice Dir-Gen, Land Resource Bur of State Plng Commn (SPC), 1984; Dir-Gen, Land Dev and Plng Dept, SPC, 1988; Dir-Gen, Land Plng & Regl Econ Coop Dept, SPC, 1990; Prof, Beijing Snr Profs Consortium, 1986; Pt-time Prof, Peking Univ, Nanjing Univ, 1988. Publication: Land Planning and City Development, 1995. Honours: Spec Awd, SPC, for Contbn to Environ Protection and Regl Ecn Coop of China. Memberships: VP, China Regl Sci Inst, 1980; Vice-Chmn, China Bioecology Econ Assn, 1990; VP, China Investment Environment Inst, 1995. Hobby: Bridge. Address: No 503, Gate 1, A4 Building, Sanlihe, Xicheng District, Beijing 100045, China.

FANG Nenghang, b. 15 July 1935, Shanghai, China. Antenna Engineer. m. Zhu Zhi, 10 Feb 1966, 1 d. Education: DEng, Leningrad Electrotech Inst, Russia, 1959. Appointments: Hd, Antenna Lab, 1964-80; Hd, Lab of Basic Rsch, 1981-95. Publications: Phased Array Antenna, 1966; Electromagnetic Theory, 1985; Vector and Dyadic Analysis, 1995. Honour: Best Ppr Awd, IEEE, 1992. Membership: Snr Mbr, IEEE, USA. Hobby: Radio Amateur. Address: PO Box 1313 Nanjing, 210013, China.

FANG Weiguo, b. 20 Apr 1969, Xiaogan, Hubei, China. Associate Professor. Education: PhD. Appointment: Assoc Prof, Beijing Univ of Aerons & Astrons. Publication: Aircraft Scheme Optimization Design Based on Global Sensitivity Equation Method, 1998. Hobby: Classical Music. Address: Institute of Aircraft Design, Beijing University of Aeronautics & Astronautics, Beijing 100083, China.

FANIBUNDA Kersi, b. 4 Nov 1936, India. Consultant Oral and Maxillofacial Surgeon. m. Mingi, 27 Nov 1969, 1 s. Education: BDS; LDS; RCS; MDS; FDSRCS. Appointments: Snr Lectr and Hon Cnslt, Univ of Newcastle upon Tyne Sch and Hosp, 1978-. Memberships: Elected Mbr, Gen Dental Cncl, 1989-; Brit Assn of Oral and Maxillofacial Surgs; Brit Dental Assn. Hobby: Photography. Address: Department of Oral and Maxillofacial Surgery, The Dental School, University of Newcastle upon Tyne, Framlington Place, Newcastle upon Tyne, NE2 4BW, UK.

FANNING Pauline, b. 18 Jan 1915. Bibliographer. m. 8 May 1941, 2 d. Education: Collegiate Sch, Hobart; Univ of Tas. Appointments: Libn, 1936-41, 1944-80, Prin Libn, 1972-75, C'wlth Natl Lib, Natl Lib of Aust; Dir, Austl Natl Hums Lib, 1975-80; Cnslt to C'wlth Parlty Lib, 1980-81; Bibliographer, Austl Natl Dictionary Austl Natl Univ, 1980-91. Honour: MBE, 1969; ISO, 1978. Hobbies: Gardening. Address: 8 Durville Crescent, Manuka, ACT 2603, Australia.

FAQIH Osama Ibn Jafar Ibn Ibrahim, b. 1943. Politician. Education: BA, Acctng and Bus Admin, Riyadh Univ, 1969; MBA, Univ of AZ, USA, 1973. Appointments: Lectr, Fac of Bus Admin, Riyadh 1969-75; Dir, Dept of Credits and Fin, Saudi Arabian Monetary Agy, 1975; Asst Dpty for Intl Dev Co-op, Min of Fin, 1981; Dpty, Intl Econ Co-op, Min of Fin, 1983; Chmn, Bd of Dirs, Gen Dir, Saudi Arabian Monetary Agy, 1989; Chmn, Bd Dirs,

CEO, Arab Trade Fund, 1989; Chmn, Islamic Dev Bank, 1994; Min of Com, 1995-. Address: Ministry of Commerce, PO Box 1774, Airport Road, Riyadh 11162, Saudi Arabia.

FARDON Ross Stuart Harpur, b. 28 Jan 1938. m. 15 Dec 1962, 2 s. Education: BSc, Univ of Qld; AM, PhD, Harvard Univ. Appointments: Asst Chf Geol, Western Mining Corp; GEN Supt Exploration BHP Co Ltd; Dir Gen, S Aust Dept of Mines and Energy; Exec Gen Mngr, Exploration MIM Holdings Ltd; Cnslt. Honour: Fulbright Schlsp, 1962. Memberships: Fell, Aust Inst Mining and Metall; Geol Soc Aust; Fell, Aust Acady of Technological Sci and Engrng; Chair, Co-operative Rsch Cncl for Landscape Evolution and Mineral Exploration. Hobbies: Astronomy; Evolution; Biography. Address: 9 Mariner Street, Manly West, Queensland 4179, Australia.

FAREED Abdul Sabur. Politician. Appointments: PM in Interim Govt, 1992-93. Memberships: Mbr Hizb-i Islami. Address: Office of the Prime Minister, Kabul, Afghanistan.

FARELL CUBILLAS Arsenio, b. Jun 1921 Mexico City. Politician. Education: Natl Univ of Mexico; Civ Law Iberoamerican Univ Mexico City. Appointments: Pres Natl Chamber of Sugar and Alcohol Inds, 1973; Dir-Gen Fed Electricity Commn, 1973-76; Dir-Gen Socl Security Inst, 1976-82; Sec of State for Employment, 1982-85; Sec of State for Labour and Socl Welfare, 1985-95. Publications: Essays and articles on legal matters. Address: c/o Secretaria del Trabajo y Prevision Social, Edificio A, 4o, Periferico Sur 4271, Coronel Fuentes del Pedregal, 14140 Mexico, DF Mexico.

FARHADI Mohammad, b. 1949, Shahroud, Iran. Minister of Health. Education: Studied med, Mashhad Univ, 1968, Doct Deg, 1975, Specialised, ENT Surg, 1980; Postgrad Stdies, Laser Op, Endoscopic Surg and Coclea Transplantation. Appointments: Acting Hd, Red Crescent; Sec, Medl Educ Cncl; Culture and Higher Educ Min; Chan, Tehran Univ; Hd, Inst for Promotion of Sci and Rsch; Contrb to estab of cntrs for genetic, polymer and medl engrng rsch and higher educ cntrs; Prof, Mashhad Univ; Dir and Mbr, Medl Disciplinary Panel; Sec, Bd of Tstees, Shahed Univ; Mbr, Cntrl Bd of Dirs of Hlth Ministry; Mbr, Medl Trng Cncl; Elected, Min of Hlth.

FARLEY Helen Sara, b. 28 June 1968, Birmingham, England. Journalist; Author. Education: Bach Veterinary Sci. Appointments: Columnist, Rave Magazine; Freelance Music Jrnlst specialising in Blues Music. Publications: The Titillation of Tasseography, 1999. Membership: Pres, Blues Assn of SE Qld Inc, 1997-99. Address: 50 MacDonald Street, Norman Park, Qld 4170, Australia.

FARMER William John, b. 10 June 1947. Secretary, Australian Department of Immigration and Cultural Affairs. m. Elaine Farmer, 21 June 1969, 1 s, 1 d. Education: Univ Sydney; London Sch Econs; Univ London. Appointments: Joined Dept External Affairs, 1969; 3rd Sec, 2nd Sec, Cairo, 1972-75; Dept For Affairs, 1975-78; Dpty High Commnr, Suva, 1979-81; Hd, Plcy Plng Dept, For Affairs, Canberra, 1983; Cnslr, Min, Austl Miss to UN, 1985-86; Dpty Rep Aust, UN Security Cncl, 1985-86; Amb Aust to Mexico, Nicaragua, El Salvador, Costa Rica, Guatemala, Honduras, Cuba, 1987-89; Asst Sec, later 1st Asst Sec, Dept For Affairs and Trade, 1989-93; Austl High Commnr, Papua New Guinea, 1993-95; Austl High Commnr, Malaysia, 1996-97; Dpty Sec, Dept For Affairs and Trade, 1997-98; Sec, Dept of Immigration and Multicultural Affairs, 1998. Membership: C'wlth Club; Natl Press Club, Canberra. Hobbies: Antiques; Books; Music. Listed in: Who's Who in Australia. Address: c/o Department of Immigration and Multicultural Affairs, Belconnen 2616, Australia.

FARNHAM John Peter, b. 1 July 1949, Essex, England. Singer; Entertainer. m. Jillian, Apr 1973, 2 s. Appointments: Apprenticed Plumber; Lead Singer, Strings Unlimited, 1965; Fndr, John Farnham Band, 1978; Lead Singer, Little River Band. Creative Works: Recordings include: Sadie the Cleaning Lady; Friday Kind of Monday; Rose Coloured Glasses; One; Raindrops

Keep Falling on My Head; Comic Conversation; Rock Me Baby; Don't You Know It's Magic; Everything is Out of Season; Pippin; Charlie Girl. Honours: Sev Gold Records; Aust of the Yr, Bicentennial 1998. Address: c/o TalentWorks, Suite 1, 663 Victoria Street, Abbottsford, Victoria 3067, Australia.

FARNWORTH Arthur James, b. 30 Sept 1923, Geelong, Vic, Aust. Former Research Officer and General Manager. m. Enid Hinda Brown, 16 Oct 1946, 2 s, 1 d. Education: Dip Indl Chem, Gordon Inst Technol, 1943; BSc, 1945, MSc, 1946, Melbourne; PhD, Leeds, 1948. Appointments: Lectr, Rsch Chem, Textile Coll, Gordon Inst, Geelong, 1948-54; Rsch Offr to Prin Rsch Offr, C'wlth Sci and Indl Rsch Org, 1954-61; Tech Dir, Dpty Mngng Dir, Gen Mngr, Aust Wool Bd, 1961-72; Gen Mngr, Chf Gen Mngr, Austl Wool Corp, 1982-84; Chmn, Austl Wool Rsch and Dev Cncl, 1986-88. Publications: Var pprs in sci jrnls; Co-auth, monograph, Permanent Setting of Wool, 1971; Contbr to New International Illustrated Encyclopedia; Contbns to GEO Australasia, 1992, 1993, 1995. Honours: MBE, 1959; Silver Medal, Worshipful Co Woolmen, UK, 1985. Memberships: Roy Aust Chem Inst; Fell, Austl Inst Mngmt. Listed in: Who's Who in Australia; Notable Australians - The Pictorial Who's Who; Australian Men and Women of Science, Technology and Engineering. Address: 47 The Boulevarde, Doncaster, Vic 3108, Australia.

FARQUHAR David Andross, b. 5 Apr 1928, Cambridge, NZ. Composer. m. Raydia d'Elsa, 2 June 1954, 1 s, 1 d. Education: BMus, BA U,niv NZ; MA, Cambridge Univ; Guildhall Sch Music. Appointments: Lectr, 1953-, Prof Music, Vic Univ Wellington, NZ, 1976-93. Creative Works: Recd compositions: Concerto for wind quintet; Symphony No 1; Three Improvisations; Three Pieces for violin and piano; Concertino for piano and strings; Evocation; Partita; Ring Round the Moon, dance suite; Three Scots Ballads; String Quartet; In Despite of Death; Suite for guitar; Magpies and Other Birds; Echoes and Reflections; Scherzo for orchestra; Short Suite, Ring Around the Moon; Auras, for piano and orch; Serenade for Strings; Homage to Stravinsky; Anniversary Suite No 2. Other publd compositions: And One Makes Ten; Anniversary Duets, 2 sets; Five Scenes for guitar; On Your Own; Three Pieces for double bass; Three Cilla McQueen Songs; A Folksong Trio (recorders); Eight Blake Songs; Five Canons for two clarinets; Ode for piano; Six Songs of Women; Symphony No 2; Three Echoes for piano; Waiata Maori, choir; Concerto for wind quintet; In Despite of Death; Partita, piano; Dance Suite, Ring Around the Moon; String Quartet No 1; Suite for guitar; Symphony No 1; Three Improvisations; Three Pieces for violin and piano. Memberships: Composers Assn NZ, Fndng Pres; Cntr of NZ Music, bd mbr. Address: 15 Nottingham Street, Wellington 5, New Zealand.

FARRER Keith Thomas Henry, b. 28 Mar 1916, Footscray, Vic, Aust. Scientist. Education: BSc, Chem and Metall, 1936, MSc, Chem, 1938, DSc, Biochemistry, 1954, Univ of Melbourne; MA Hist, La Trobe, 1977. Appointments: Kraft Foods Ltd, Melbourne, 1938-81; Rsch Chem, 1938-44; Snr Rsch Chem, 1945-49; Snr Tech Exec; Mngr, Rsch and Dev, 1949-76; Chf Scientist, 1976-81; Prin, Farrer Cnslts, 1981-87; Freelance Cnslt, Engl and Austl clients, 1987-; Austl Govt Rep, CAB Intl, 1988-. Publications: 4 books; 3 chapts in tech books, 130 sci, tech and histl pprs in Austl, NZ, UK, US and SE Asian jrnls and conf proceedings. Honour: OBE, for servs to sci and ind, 1979. Memberships: Fell, Roy Soc Chem, 1947; Fell, Roy Austl Chem Inst; Fell, Inst Food Sci and Technol, 1966; Fell, Austl Inst Food Sci and Technol, Pres, 1969-71, Life Fell, 1982; Fell, Austl Acady of Technological Scis and Engrng, Hon Fell, 1988; Hon Fell, NZ Inst of Food Sci and Technol, 1985; Fell Roy Soc of Arts; Fell, Whitley Coll (Univ of Melbourne), 1978-87; Profl Mbr, Inst of Food Technologists, Emeritus Mbr, 1981-; Hobbies: Reading; Writing; Listening to classical music. Address: Glen Ebor, 24 Rosemoor Grove, Chandler's Ford, Hampshire, SO53 1TB, England.

FARROW Colin Pyewell, b. 16 June 1919, Wagin, WA, Aust. Company Director. m. (1) Kathleen Murphy, 1944, dec, 3 s, 1 d, (2) Patricia Mary Brearley, 1979, dec, 1998. Education: BEng, Univ WA, 1941. Appointments: Engr, C'wlth Pub Wrks Dept, Perth, WA, 1940-41; Engr, De Havilland Aircraft Corp, Sydney, NSW, 1941-44; Engr, Shell Co Aust, Sydney, Brisbane, Melbourne and Sydney, 1944-57; Ops Mngr, Shell Co Philippines, Manila, 1957-60; Asst Bch Mngr, 1960-64, Asphalt Mngr, 1964-79, Shell Co Aust, Melbourne, Vic; Dir, Pioneer Asphalt PL, 1967-79; Pres, Austl Rd Fedn, 1979-88; Dir, Chemcrete Asia Corp, 1989-93. Honour: WA State Exhib, 1936; Memberships: Inst Engrs Aust; Univ WA Engrng Grads Assn. Hobbies: Golf; Gardening; Travel. Address: 8 Millicent Avenue, North Balwyn, Vic 3104, Australia.

FARUQI Nisar Ahmed, b. 29 June 1936, Amroh, India. Professor of Arabic Studies. m. Razia, 20 Oct 1967, 2 s, 2 d. Education: MA, Arabic; PhD, Historiography. Appointments: Delhi Univ, 1964-66, 1977-; Delhi Coll, 1966-77. Publications: 36 books in Urdu, Arabic, Persian, English & Hindi; Over 500 rsch pprs. Honours include: Ctf of Hon, Pres of India w Life Pension, 1985; Abul Kalam Azad Awd for Rsch. Memberships: Gen Sec, Oriental Soc; Iqbal Acady, Pakistan; Iqbal Adabi Markaz. Hobbies: Reading; Writing; Travel; Music. Address: A-42 (FF) 6th Street, Batla House, Jamia Nagar, PO No 9723, New Delhi 110025, India.

FASOL Gerhard, b. 13 Sept 1954, Vienna, Austria. Company Director. m. Nanako, 27 Nov 1989, 2 s. Education: Dip, Physiker, Univ Bochum; PhD, Univ of Cambridge, UK. Appointments: Lectr, Univ of Cambridge; Lab Mngr, Hitachi Cambridge Lab; Assoc Prof, Univ of Tokyo, 1991-96; Pres, Eurotechnol Japan KK, 1996-. Publications: The Blue Laser Diode (co-auth), 1997. Honours: Fell, Trinity Coll, Cambridge, 1981-86, 1986-90; 2nd Prize, Computer Visualization Contest, Japan, 1996. Memberships: German Chmbr of Com in Japan; IEEE; Amn Chmbr of Com in Japan (ACCJ). Hobbies: Skiing; Mountains; Travel. Address: Eurotechnology Japan KK, Parkwest Bldg 11F, 6-12-1 Nishi-Shinjuku, Shinjuku-ku, Tokyo 160-0023, Japan.

FATIN Wendy, b. 10 Apr 1941 Harvey WA. Politician. 1 s, 1 d. Education: WA Inst of Technol. Appointments: Trnd as regd nurse; Advsr to Min for Repatriation and Compensation and Min for Socl Security, 1974-75; Polit Rsrch, 1975-77, 1981-83; Min for Local Govt, Min Asstng PM for Status of Women, 1990-93; Min for Arts and Territories, 1991-93. Honours: Fell Coll of Nursing Aust. Memberships: Mbr HoR for Canning WA, 1983; Mbr HoR for Brand WA, 1984-96; Mbr Govt Econ Cttee, 1983-87; Mbr HoR Standing Cttee on Community Affairs, 1987-96; Mbr HoR Standing Cttee on Employment, Educ and Trng, 1987-96; Fndr Mbr Women's Electoral Lobby; Labor Party. Address: Lot 46, Soldiers Road, Roleystone, WA 6111, Australia.

FAULKNER Leonard Anthony (Most Reverend), b. 5 Dec 1926, Aust. Roman Catholic Archbishop. Education: Sacred Heart Coll, Glenelg; Corpus Christi Coll, Werribee; Urban Univ, Rome; Consecrated Bish, Townsville, 1967. Appointments: Asst Priest, Woodville, SA, 1950-57; Diocesan Chap, Young Christian Workers, 1955-67; Admor, St Francis Xavier Cath, SA, 1957-67; Bish Townsville, 1967-83; Coadjutor to Archbish Adelaide, 1983-85; Archbish Adelaide, 1985-. Memberships: Cntrl Commn, Austl Cath Bishs' Conf; Chmn, Bishs' Cttee for Family and Life; Natl Fitness Cncl SA, 1958-67. Address: Catholic Church Office, GPO Box 1364, Adelaide, SA 5001, Australia.

FAUNCE Marcus de Laune, b. 5 Dec 1922, Sydney, NSW, Aust. Consultant Physician. m. Marjorie Morison, 1951, dec, 1995, 2 s, 1 d. Education: St Peters Coll; MBBS, Univ Adelaide, 1946; FRACP, 1965; FRCP London, 1968. Appointments: Cap, Austl Army Medl Corps, 1947-49; Snr Registrar, Sydney Hosp, 1950-53; Brompton Hosp, London, Eng, 1954-56; Cnslt Physn, 1957-87, Bd Mngmt, 1967-73, Roy Canberra Hosp, ACT; Medl, Bd ACT, 1963-74; Snr Cnslt Physn, RAAF; Grp Cap, RAAF Medl Serv (Reserve), 1976-84; Emer Cnslt

Physn, Roy Canberra Hosp, 1993-. Honours: OBE, 1969; AM, 1981; CVO, 1996. Memberships: Thoracic Soc Aust; Aust Brit Soc; Univ House, ANU. Listed in: Who's Who in Australia. Hobbies: People; Books; Music. Address: 4 Mayo Street, Weetangera, ACT 2614, Australia.

FAYEZ Mohamad al-Ali al-, b. 1937 Hail. Politician. Appointments: Legal Advsr Cncl of Mins, 1960-70; Gov Chmn Bd Dirs Gen Org for Socl Ins; Dep Min of Labour and Socl Affairs Min, 1983-95. Address: Ministry of Labour and Social Affairs, Omar bin al-Khatab Street, Riyadh 11157, Saudi Arabia.

FEBRES CORDERO RIVADENEIRA Leon. Businessman; Engineer; Politician. Appointments: PSC cand in elections, 1978, 1979; Pres of Ecuador, 1984-88. Memberships: Mbr Partido Social Cristiano - PSC. Address: c/o Oficina del Presidente, Quito, Ecuador.

FEI Kaiyang, b. 5 Mar 1925, Shanghai, China. Editor-in-Chief. m. Hui-zhen Tan, 17 Sept 1960, 2 d. Education: Shanghai Tradl Chinese Medl Sch, 1946. Appointments: Medl Dr, Shanghai Chaozhou Heji Hosp, 1947-52; Beijing Medl Coll, 1952-57; Visng Dr, Xiyuan Affiliated Hosp, Acady Tradl Chinese Med, 1957-59; Ed-in-Chf, Jrnl Tradl Chinese Med, 1960-82; Pres, Guang Anmen Hosp, affiliated Chinese Acady Tradl Chinese Med, 1983-85. Honours: Dpty, People's Congress, E Cty Dist, Beijing; Advsr, Beijing Tong Ren Tang Medl Wine Extract Factory. Memberships: Acad Activities Cttee, China Acady Tradl Chinese Med; Postgrad Fellshp Assessment Cttee, Stndng Cncl, All-China Assn Tradl Chinese Med; Dir, Chinese Medl Assn; Stndng Mbr, Pharmacopaedia Cttee, People's Repub China; Ed-in-Chf, All-China Editl Cttee, Tradl Chinese Med; Ed-in-Chf, All-China Gt Ency, Tradl Chinese Med Theort Bch Vol. Hobby: Appreciating art of Chinese calligraphy. Address: China Academy of Traditional Chinese Medicine, Beijing 100700, China.

FEI Xiang, b. 20 May 1962, Nanning, Guangxi, China. Teacher. m. Tang Jianping, 2 Feb 1986, 1 s. Education: BA, Engl, Guangxi Tchr's Univ. Appointments: Dpty Dir, Tchng Dept, Nanning TVU, 1995. Publications: 6 acad theses, 1997, 1998. Honour: Advd Tchr, 1992, 1996, 1997. Membership: Inst of Radio & TV Higher Educ of Nanning, Guangxi, 1990. Hobbies: Dance; Collecting. Address: Nanning Minzu Road, Nanning TV University, Guangxi, China.

FEIT Michael D, b. 15 Nov 1942, Easton, PA, USA. Physicist. m. Lorraine R Mauriel, 30 Dec 1967, 1 s, 1 d. Education: BA, Phys, Lehigh Univ, 1964; PhD, Phys, Rensslaer Polytechnic Inst, 1970. Appointments: Rsch Assoc, Univ of IL, 1969-72; Physicist, Lawrence Livermore Natl Lab, 1972-; Grp Leader, Theort Optics, 1992-; Grp leader, Laser Damage Modelling, 1997-. Publications: Over 150 profl publs; 1 Pat. Honours: Phi Beta Kappa, 1964; Sigma Xi, 1964; Fell, Amn Phys Soc, 1988; Phys Disting Achmnt Awd, 1990, 1995; Fell, Optical Soc of Am, 1992; Rsch and Dev 100 Awd, 1997. Memberships: Amn Phys Soc; AAAS; Optical Soc of Am. Address: Lawrence Livermore National Laboratory, Mailstop L-477, Livermore, CA 94550, USA.

FELT Bert, b. 7 Mar 1944, St Olai, Sweden. Engineer; Senior Consultant. m. Keiko, 7 July 1975. Education: BE; BS; Msc; DLLb; DEcon; DBA; MPM; Dip Negotiations. Appointments: Techn Mngr, Kanda Gaigo Gakkuin, Tokyo; Dir, Sweco, Stockholm; Snr Cnslt, Proj Dir, Snr Systs Integrator, Telecom; Sect Mngr, CDC, Stockholm; Dir, Nihon TPKK, Tokyo; Govt Advisor, US Dept of the Interior. Publications: Noise and Its Influence on Work, 1970; Technology in Japan, 1971; Object Oriented Analyses, 1995; Performance inprovement of telecommunications systems, 1997; ERP systems, 1997; Venture Taming, 1998. Memberships: IEEE: Life Mbr, Tokyo Amn Club; Past Mbr, FEANI; Life Mbr, Auckland Aero Club. Hobbies: Equine Science; History; Sailing; Languages. Address: PO Box 90-173, Auckland, NZ.

FENG Beiye, b. 27 May 1946, Huaian, Jiangsu, China. Professor. m. Zhang Qingzhen, 24 Dec 1971, 1 s, 1 d.

Education: MS, Peking Univ, 1983. Appointments: Rsch Asst, 1983-86, Asst Prof, 1986-90, Assoc Prof, 1990-95, Rsch Prof, 1995-. Publications: The Stability of a Heteroclinic Cycle for the Critical Case. 1991. Membership: Inst of Appl Maths, Chinese Acady of Scis. Address: Institute of Applied Mathematics, Academia Sinica, Beijing 100080, China.

FENG Boyang, b. 4 Sept 1952, Changchun, Jilin Province, China. Musicologist. m. Wei Wang, 22 Dec 1983, 1 s. Education: Bachelor Degree of Lib Arts, Jilin Coll of Arts, 1978. Appointments: Monitor in Univ, 1978-82; Dean of Stdies, Dean's Off, Jilin Coll of Arts, 1993-98. Publications: The Analysis of the Social Values of Manchu Shaman Music, 1987; Manchu Shaman Music as Viewed from Cultural Anthropology, 1997; Instructions to Musical Works Appreciation. Honours: Chang Bai Shan Lit and Art Awd; Musicians Assn Excellent Tchng Achievements Awd. Memberships: Vice-Board Chmn, Manchu Music Rsch Inst in Chinese Musicians Union; Chinese Relig Inst; Music Hist in Chinese Musicians Assn. Hobbies: Literature; Sports. Address: Jilin Colege of Arts, No 11 Ziyou Road, Changchun 130021, China.

FENG David Dagan, b. 21 July 1948, Nanking, China. Computer Science and Information Engineer. m. Ruki Guo, 15 Sept 1974, 1 s. Education: PhD. Appointments: Asst Prof, Univ of California, Riverside, CA, USA; Lectr, Snr Lectr, Reader, Univ of Sydney, 1988; Prof, Dept of Electric Engrng, Hong Kong Poly Univ, 1997-. Publications: Publs over 100 rsch pprs. Honours: Sev awds inclng: Crump Prize for Ex, Med Engrng, USA. Memberships: Fndr, Dir, Biomed and Multimeda Info Technol Grp, Univ of Syndey; Assoc Ed, IEEE Transactions on Info; Vice Chair, Intl Fedn of Automatic Control Tech Cttee; Pro-Vice Pres, Soc of Chinese-Austl Acads in NSW; Chair, Australasian Chinese Assn of EE and Computer Sci. Address: Department of Electrical & Information Engineering, Hung mom, Kowloon, Hong Kong.

FENG Ji-Kang, b. 21 Aug 1938, Haining, Zhejiang, China. Educator. m. Guilan Fu, 28 Dec 1968, 2 d. Education: BS, Jilin Univ, 1961. Appointments: Asst Tchr, 1961-77, Lectr, Assoc Prof, Prof, 1978-92, PhD Supvsr, 1993-, Jilin Univ. Publications: Elementary Quantum Chemistry, 1987; Sev articles in profl jrnls. Honours: Ex Educ Awd, 1993; Sci and Technol Devel Awd, State Educn Cmmn, 1995; Sci and Technol Dev Awd, Educ Cmmn, 1997. Memberships: Rsch Cntr of Higher Chem Educ, 1986-96. Address: National Key Laboratory of Theoretical and Computational Chemistry, Jilin University, Changchun, China.

FENG Lanrui, b. 16 Sept 1920, Guiyang, Guizhou, China. Economist; Senior Research Fellow, Chinese Academy of Social Sciences. m. Li Chang, 1946, 2 s, 2 d. Education: Snr Party Sch of CPC Cntrl Cttee. Appointments: Ed-in-Chief, Harbin Daily, 1949-54; Dir, Tchng & Rsch Sect of Pol Econ, Harbin Poly Inst, 1956-59; Dpty Dir, Heilongjiang Inst of Econs & Heilongjiang Provl Bur of Stats, 1959-64; Dpty Dir, Rsch Sect, State Cttee for Cultural Religs w For Cos, 1965-75; Mbr, State Cncl Pol Rsch Dept, 1975-80; Dpty Dir, Inst of Marxism-Leninism Mao Zedong Thought, The Chinese Acady of Socl Scis, 1980-82; Advsr, 1983-86; Mbr, Acad Cncl, 1986-89. Publications include: Labor Payments and Employment, 1982; To Each According to His Work, Wage and Employment, 1988; Labor Employment at the Initial Stage of Socialism, 1988; Labor Market in China, 1991. Honours: Sun Yefang Prize, Best Econ Article of Yr, 1984; Most Impressive Article of Yr, 1997. Memberships: Sec Gen, China Cncl of Econ Assns, 1981-91; Stndng Cttee, Chinese People's Friendship Assn, 1986-94; Bd of Dirs, China Soc for Study of Market Econ, 1992-. Hobby: Literature. Address: 34 Dong Zongbu Hutong, Beijing 100005, China.

FENG Sheng Xi, b. 26 Jan 1968, China. Engineer. m. Li Dong Lin, 1 Feb 1992, 1 d. Education: MS, Shanghai Inst of Materia Med, Academia Sinica. Appointment: Engr, Dir, Inst of Synthetic Med, Guangzhou Baiyunshan Pharm Co Ltd. Publications: Synthesis and Anti-Candida

Albicans Properties of L-4-Oxalysine-N3-4-Methoxyfumaroyl-L-2.3-Diaminopropanoic Peptide Analogues, 1998; Improved Synthesis of 7-Aminodesacetoxycephalosporamic Acid, 1998. Hobbies: Sports (playing tennis, table tennis). Address: Institute of Synthetic Medicine, Guangzhou Baiyunshan Pharmaceutical Co Ltd, Guangzhou 510515, China.

FENG Sze-Shiang, b. 6 July 1967, Heqiu, Anhui, China. Teacher. m. Li-Yun Xing, Oct 1994, 1 s. Education: PhD. Appointment: Assoc Prof, Shanghai Univ, 1996-. Publication: General Covariant Conservation Law of Angular-Momentum and Observable 3-Poincare Algebra in General Relativity, 1994. Memberships: Chinese Assn of Gravitation; CCAST. Hobbies: Classical Music; Reading English Essays. Address: Physics Department, Shanghai University, 201800 Shanghai, China.

FENG Xiangdong (Shawn), b. 27 July 1956, Hunan, China. Materials Scientist. m. M Gong, 26 Dec 1984, 2 d. Education: PhD Chem. Appointments: Lectr, Hunan Univ, Rsch Scientist, Catholic Univ of Am; Chem, Argonne Natl Lab; Staff Scientist, Pacific Northwest Nat Lab; Core Technol Co-Chmn, Ferro Corp. Publications: 2 books; Over 100 sci pubs; 4 USA patents. Honours: Materials Rsch Awd, 1998, USA Dept Energy; Discover Awd, 1998; R&D 100 Awd of 1998; Outstndng Perf Awd, 1998, PNNL. Memberships: Amn Chem Soc; Amn Ceramic Soc; Materials Rsch Soc of USA. Hobbies: Table tennis; Swimming; Bicycling. Address: 7500 E Pleasant Valley, Independence, OH 44131, USA.

FENG Zhenxing, b. 11 Sept 1937, Wuxi City, Jiangsu Prov, China. Professor. m. Z X Li, 1963, 1 d. Education: Postgrad student, Mechs, Tsinghua Univ, 1962. Appointments: Standing Cttee, Mechs Soc in Wuhan & Hubei Prov, 1992-. Publication: Continuum Mechanics and its Numerical Simulation. Honours: Rewards of Prog in Nat Sci, 1982-98; 2nd or 3rd Class, Min of Educ/Aviation, 7 x. Membership: Sci Cttee, Occupational Mechs, Hubei Prov. Hobbies: Music; Table tennis. Address: Departmemt of Maths, Wuhan University, China, 430072.

FENG Zong Pu, b. 26 July 1928, Beijing, China. Writer. m. Zhong De Cai, 1 s. Education: BA, Tsing Hua Univ. Publications: Collected Works of Zong Pu, 4 vols (novels, novelettes, essays), 1996. Honours: Natl Prize for Short Stories, 1979. Memberships: Chmn Cttee of Chinese Writers' Assn. Hobbies: Travel; Music. Address: 57 Yan Nan Yuan, Peking University, Beijing 10087, China.

FENNER Frank John, b. 21 Dec 1914, Ballarat, Vic, Aust. Medical Research Worker and Writer. m. Ellen Margaret Bobbie Roberts, 5 Nov 1943, dec 1995, 1 d. Education: MB BS, 1938, MD, 1942, Univ Adelaide; DTM, Univ Sydney, 1940. Appointments: Roy Army Medl Corps, 1940-46; Walter and Eliza Hall Inst, Melbourne, Vic, 1946-48; Prof, Microbio, 1949-67, Dir, 1967-73, Visng Fell, 1980-, John Curtin Sch Medl Rsch, Austl Natl Univ, Canberra; Dir, Cntr Rsch and Environtl Stdies, Austl Natl Univ, 1973-79. Publications: Co-auth, The Production of Antibodies, 1949; Co-auth, Myxomatosis, 1965; The Biology of Animal Viruses, 1968, 2nd ed, 1974; Co-auth, Medical Virology, 1970, 4th ed, 1994; Co-auth, Veterinary Virology, 1987, 2nd ed, 1993; Co-auth, Smallpox and its Eradication, 1988; Co-auth, Human Monkeypox, 1988; Co-auth, The Orthopoxviruses, 1989; History of Microbiology in Australia, 1990; The Australian Academy of Sciences: The First Forty Years, 1995; Co-auth, Biological Control of Vertebrate Pests, 1999. Honours: MBE, 1945; David Syme Prize, 1949; Leeuwenhoek Lect, Roy Soc, 1962; Mueller Medal, 1964; Hon MD, 1964; Britannica Austl Award Medl, 1967; Flinders Lect, Austl Acady Sci, 1967; CMG, 1976; ANZAC Peace Prize, 1980; Florey Lect, Roy Soc, 1983; Burnet Lect, Austl Acady Sci, 1985; ANZAS Medal, Stuart Mudd Awd, 1986; Japan Prize, 1988; AC, 1989; Hon DVSc, 1992; Copley Medal, Roy Soc, 1995; Hon DSc, 1996. Memberships: Fell, Austl Acady Sci; FRS; For Assoc, US Natl Acady Scis. Hobbies: Gardening; Tennis.

Address: John Curtin School of Medical Research, GPO Box 334, Canberra, ACT 2601, Australia.

FENSHAM Peter James, b. 26 Oct 1927, Melbourne, Vic, Aust. Emeritus Professor. m. Dorothy Christine Fairweather, 3 Apr 1954, 3 s, 1 d. Education: BSc, 1948, MSc, 1950, Melbourne; PhD, Bristol, 1953; PhD Cantab, 1958; Dip Ed, Monash, 1982. Appointments: Nuffield Sociolgcl Schl, Cambridge Univ, Eng, 1953-56; Lectr, Snr Lectr, Rdr, Physl Chem, Melbourne Univ, Vic, 1956-67; Prof, Sci Educ, 1967-81, 1989-92, Dean, Fac Educ, 1982-88, Emer Prof, 1992-, Monash Univ. Publications: Auth, 8 books and over 70 pprs. Honours: Nyholm Medal, Roy Soc Chem, 1983; AM, 1985; Chem Educ Medal, Roy Austl Chem Inst, NSW, 1985; Intl Fell, ICASE, 1988; Disting Rschr, NARST, 1999. Memberships: FRACI; FACE; MA Psych Soc; FAARE; FAAEE. Hobbies: Walking; Wood carving; Religious education. Listed in: Several biographical volumes. Address: 20 Stanley Grove, Blackburn, Vic 3130, Australia.

FERGUSON David Alexander, b. 14 Apr 1920, Sydney, NSW, Aust. Occupational Physician; Emeritus Professor. m. Betty Rogalsky, 27 June 1942, 1 s, 2 d. Education: MB BS, 1942, MD, 1971, Univ Sydney; Mbr, 1955, FRACP, 1971; FRCP, London, 1988; FRCP, Edinburgh, 1988. Appointments: Cap, Austl Imperial Force, 1943-46; Gen Medl Prac, Narromine and Sydney, 1946-60; Joined, 1960, Prof, Occupational Hlth, 1976-87, Dir, 1982-85, Emer Prof, 1987-, Sch Pub Hlth and Tropical Med; Cnslt, 1985-89, Cnslt Occupational Physn, 1989-, Worksafe Aust. Publications: About 182 sci publs, maj rprts, abstracts, conf proceedings; book chapts, others. Honour: AM, 1986. Memberships: Fell, fmr Pres, Australasian Coll Occupational Med, Fell, fmr Pres, Ergonomics Soc Aust; Fell, Fac Occupational Med, Roy Coll Physns, London; Brit Occupational Hyg Soc; Amn Coll Occupational Med. Hobbies: Family; Australian flora; Golf; Classical music and literature. Address: 61 Tryon Road, Lindfield, NSW 2070, Australia.

FERGUSON Graeme Robert, b. 18 Aug 1935, Richmond, NZ. Minister. m. Mairi Ferguson, 16 May 1960, 2 s, 2 d. Education: MA, Univ Auckland, 1956; BD, Univ Otago, 1960; PhD, Cambridge Univ, Eng, 1965. Appointments: Min, Kent Tce Presby Ch, 1965-75; Prin, Utd Theol Coll, Sydney, NSW, Aust, 1975-89; Min, St David's Presby Ch, Auckland, NZ, 1989-. Publications: 15 articles in monographs and learned jrnls. Honours: Gordon Watson Schlshp, Univ NZ, 1960; Adam and Catherine Begg Travelling Schlshp, 1960; Lewis and Gibson Schl, 1964. Hobbies: Music; Theatre; Modern dance; Bush walking. Address: 1/18 Dryden Avenue, Papatoetoe, Auckland, New Zealand.

FERGUSON Martin John, b. 12 Dec 1953. Member of Parliament. m. Patricia Jane Waller. Appointments: Fed Rsch Offr, 1975, Asst Gen Sec, 1981, Gen Sec, 1984-90, Fed Miscellaneous Workers Union of Aust; Exec, 1984-90, VP, 1985-90; Pres, 1990-96, Austl Cncl of Trade Unions; ILO Gov Body, 1990-96; Fed Mbr for Batman House of Reps, 1996; Shadow Min for Employment and Trng, 1996-97; Shadow Min for Employment, Trng, Population and Immigration, 1997, 1998-; Asst to Ldr on Multicultural Affairs, 1997; Re-Elected, 1998. Honour: AO, 1996. Membership: Liquor, Hospitality and Miscellaneous Workers Union, 1995. Address: 48 High Street, (Cnr Westgarth and High Streets), Northcote, Victoria 3070, Australia.

FERGUSON Robert Alexander, b. 2 Dec 1945, Sydney, Australia. Managing Director. m. Jennifer Ferguson, 6 Jan 1968, 1 d. Education: Univ Sydney. Appointments: Portfolio Mngmt Invmnt Div, 1972, Dir, Corp Fin, 1977, Dpty Mngng Dir, 1982, Mngng Dir, 1986-, Bankers Trust Aust Ltd. Memberships: AJC Club, Sydney; Sydney Turf Club. Hobbies: Horse racing; Horse breeding; Movies; Books; Wine and food. Address: 8 Eva Lane, Northwood, NSW 2066, Australia.

FERNANDES George, b. 3 June 1930, Mangalore, Karnataka, India. Member of Parliament. m. Leila Kabir, 21 July 1971, 1 s. Appointments: Elected, 4th Lok Sabha,

1967; Mbr, Cttee on Petitions, 1967-70; Gen Sec, Samyukta Socialist Pty, 1969-71; Chmn, Socialist Pty, 1971-77; Pres, All India Railwaymen's Fed, 1973-77; Re-elected 6th Lok Sabha, 1977; Union Cabinet Min, Comms, 1977, Ind, 1977-79; Re-elected, 7th Lok Sabha, 1980, 9th Lok Sabha, 1989; Union Cabinet Min, Railways, 1989-9-; Min of Kashmir Affairs, 1990; Mbr, Railway Convention Cttee, 1990-91; Re-elected, 10th Lok Sabha, 1991; Mbr, Cttee on Fin, 1995-96; Re-elected, 11th Lok Sabha, 1996; Mbr, Cttee on External Affairs, 1997-98; Re-elected 12th Lok Sabha, 1998; Pres, Samata Party, 1998; Union Cabinet Min, Def, 1998-; Mbr Gen Purpose Cttee. Publications: What Ails the Socialists; Railway Strike of 1974; George Fernandes Speaks; Ed, The Otherside; Chmn, Editl Bd, Pratipaksha. Memberships: Fndr Chmn, New India Co-op bank; Co-Chmn, Indo-Libyan, Indo-GDR and Indo-Hungarian Dev Grp, London, 1979; Schumacher Fndn, 1979; Pres, Hind Mazdoor Ki Panchayat; Amnesty Intl; Press Cncl of India; People's Union for Civ Liberties. Hobbies: Human rights; Anti-nuclear and environmental campaigns. Address: 3 Krishna Menon Marg, New Delhi 110011, India.

FERNANDEZ MALDONADO SOLARI Jorge, b. 29 May 1922 Ilo Moquegua. Politician; Army Officer. m. Estela Castro Faucheux, 2 s, 2 d. Education: Chorillos Mil Schl. Appointments: Hd of Army Intell Serv; Dir of Army Intell Schl; Dir Mariscal Ramon Castilla Mil Schl Trujillo; Mil Attache Argentina; Min of Energy and Mines, 1968-75; Army Chf of Staff, 1975-76; PM Min of War Cmdr-Gen of Army, Feb-July 1976; Senator, 1985-; Sec-Gen Intergovernmental Cncl of Copper Exporting Cos, 1990-. Memberships: Mbr Pres Advsry Cttee - COAP. Address: CIPEC, 39 rue de Bienfaisance, 75008 Paris, France.

FERNANDEZ-MURO Jose Antonio, b. 1 Mar 1920. Appointments: Dir Natl Schl of Fine Arts Buenos Aires, 1957-58; Travelled and studied in Eur and Am on UNESCO Fell'ship of Museology, 1957-58; Lives in NY, 1962-; One-man exhibns in Buenos Aires, Madrid, WA, NY, Rome and Detroit; Rep'd in num Grp Shows inclng 50 ans de Peinture Abstraite Paris and The Emergent Decade Guggenheim Mus, 1965. Major works: Superimposed circles, 1958; In Reds Di Tella Fndn Buenos Aires, 1959; Horizonte terroso Mus of Modern Art Caracas, 1961; Circulo azogado Mus of Modern Art NY, 1962; Lacerated Tablet Rockefeller NY, 1963; Elemental Forms MIT, 1964; Silver Field Guggenheim Mus, 1965; Summit Bonino Gall NY. Honours: Gold Medal Brussels World Fair, 1958; Guggenheim Intl and Di Tella Intl awds.

FERNANDO John N L C, b. 27 Dec 1944. Computer Company Director. m. 27 Dec 1968-1990, 2 s. Education: MEng (AIT); BSc Engrng (SL) BSc Eng. Appointments: ICL Chf Computer Engr, Sri Lanka; ICL Customer Engrng Mngr, Indonesia; WANG Dealer Gen Mngr, Sri Lanka; IBM Mktng Mngr, Sri Lanka; AIT Postgrad Schl, Thailand; IBM Plans and Controls Mngr, SEAR/ASPA HQ, Hong Kong; IBM Customer Ops Mngr, Sri Lanka; IBM Acct Mngr, India Offshore Ops; IBM AS/400 Product Mngr, Singapore; IBM AS/400 Brand Mngr, ASEAN/SA HQ, Singapore; IBM Country Dir, Sri Lanka. Publications: Analysis of Computer Resources of Sri Lanka, People's Bank Economic Review, 1981; Computer Education in Elementary Schools (co-auth) proceedings of Annual Conf SEARCC '95, 1995; The Digital Office - Are We Ready for IT?, proceedings 17th Natl Conf, Inst of Chartered Accts of Sri Lanka, 1996. Memberships: Computer Soc of Sri Lanka, Cncl Mbr, 1980-90; Austl Computer Soc; Instn of Engrs, Sri Lanka. Hobbies: Bridge; Horse riding; Meditative relaxation. Address: Marine Drive, Block 65 #06/172, Marine Parade, Singapore 440065.

FERNANDO Sarath Anthony Lyn, b. 20 Aug 1940. Company Director. m. 26 Aug 1970, 1 s, 1 d. Education: BS Econs. Appointments: Exec Mitsubishi Ceylon Ltd, 1960-64; Mngng Dir, Assoc Enterprises Ltd, 1964; Com & Econ Affairs Offr, Royal Netherland Embassy, Colombo, 1964-70; Com & Econ Affairs Offr, Brit High Commn, 1970-77; Served on Panel of Experts of ITC,

Geneva, and the Export Mkt Dev Div, C'wlth Secretariat, London, 1975-79; Chmn, Creations (Pvt) Ltd, L& M Leisurewear Inc USA, L& J Trading Co, (Pvt) Ltd, 1977-; Dir, Adelphi Electronics. Memberships: Chmn, Sri Lanka Apparel Exporters Assn, 1985-87; Chmn, Fedn of Exporters Assn of Sri Lanka, 1991-93; Industrialization Commn. 1992-96; Chmn, Export Sect, Ceylon Chmbr of Comm, 1993-96; Mbr, Sri Lanka Export Dev Bd, 1993-95. Hobbies: Keen tennis player, veterans champion, 1995. Address: No 17/1 Kassapa Rd, Colombo 5, Sri Lanka.

FERNANDO W A Nobert, b. 8 Apr 1934, Moratuwa, Sri Lanka. Surveyor and Leveller. m. Nayani, 7 Mar 1963, 1 s. Education: Surveyors Trng Inst. Membership: Surveyors Inst of Sri Lanka. Hobby: Social Service. Address: 18/A Dheewara Niwahan Pedesa, Koralawella, Moratuwa, Sri Lanka.

FEROS James Nicholas, b. 1 Mar 1932. International Management Consultant; Business Author; Lecturer. m. Agatha Antoniades, 5 Oct 1957, 3 d. Education: Univ Deg, Law, Commerce, Arts, Bus Admin. Appointments: Fmr World Vice Chmn of Matchbox Toys, NY Exch, 1979-92; Profl Ex as a Lawyer, Acct, Merchant Banker, Mngmt Cnslt. Publications: Appraisals of Companies, 1971; Mergers are People, 1979; Business Appraisals, 1984; Strategic Business Decisions, 1995. Memberships: Bar-at-Law; Acct; Mbr of var profl inst in law, acctcy and mngmt. Hobby: Commissioned Officer in Royal Australian Air Force. Address: 24 Ramsay Avenue, West Pymble, Sydney, NSW, Australia.

FEROZE Sleem, b. 13 Aug 1937. Obstetrician and Gynaecologist. m. 26 Apr 1970, 2 s. Education: BSc; MBBS, London: LRCP; MRCS, Eng; FRCOG; FACOG; FRCS(C); FSOGC; DABOG. Appointments: Cnslt, Oakville Trafalgar Mem Hosp, Oakville, Ontario; Visng Cnslt, McMaster's Univ and Milton Dist Hosp. Memberships: Soc of Obstet and Gynae, Can, USA and Eng; Ontario Medl Assn. Hobbies: Tennis; Classical Music. Address: Suite 4, 358 Reynolds Street, Oakville, Ontario L6J 3L9, Canada.

FERRIER Ian Douglas, b. 5 Sept 1940, Sydney, Aust. Chartered Accountant. m. Pam, 3 Feb 1981, 2 s, 1 d. Education: Fell, Inst of Chartered Accts; Offic Regd Liquidator. Memberships: Chmn, Fedl Airports Corp; Port Douglas Reef Resorts; NSW Rugby Union; Hill Young Assocs; Austl Refrigeration PIL; Knotts Pine Warehouse; Dir: Austl Rugby Union; Brian McEugan Wine Ltd; Tourism Asst Holdings; Reef Casino Trust. Address: 7 Victoria Street, Watsons Bay, NSW 2030, Australia.

FERRO Pablo, b. 15 Dec 1935, Cuba. Director; Editor; Producer; Graphic Designer; Animator; Graphic Consultant; Commercial Artist. Appointments include: Animator, Animation Dir, 1955-80; Fndr, Pres, Writer, Prodr, Ferro Mogubgub & Schwarz, 1961; Created Main Title Designs for Dr Strangelove, Midnight Cowboy, Thomas Crown Affair, Bullitt, Being There, Philadelphia, To Die For, Men in Black, LA Confidential, As Good As It Gets, Good Will Hunting, 1997; Fndr, Depablo Prodns, 1998. Honours: Num awds, prizes and hons. Address: Depablo Productions, 738 N Cahuenga Boulevard, Suite H, Hollywood, CA 90038, USA.

FERRY David Sage, b. 21 May 1939, Adelaide, SA, Aust. Retired. m. Gail Eccleston, 30 Sept 1972, 1 s, 1 d. Education: Roy Austl Naval Coll, 1953-56; Roy Naval Coll, Dartmouth, 1958; Roy Naval Engrng Coll, 1961-63; MSc, Cranfield Inst Technol, 1967-68. Appointments: Roy Austl Navy, 1953-90; Retd as Commodore. Honour: AM, 1987. Memberships: Fell, Roy Aeronautical Soc; Fell, Inst of Mechl Engrs. Address: 8/19 Barbara Cr, Batehaven, NSW 2536, Australia.

FERRY Victor Jasper (Hon), b. 11 Jan 1922. Retired Politician. m. Doris Ferry, 8 Feb 1947, 2 d. Appointments: Flt Lt, RAAF, World War II; Liberal Mbr for SW Prov, WA, 1965-87; Chmn, Select Cttee, Examining Potato Ind, WA, 1971-72; Govt Whip, 1974-77; Chmn, Cttee Legis Cncl, 1977-83; Patron, World Aerospace Educ Org, WA Br, 1998-; State Warden, State War Mem. 1998-99. Honours:

DFC, RAF, 1944; JP, 1985. Memberships: Hon Roy Commn into Dept Conservation and Land Mngmt, 1985; State Pres, RAAF Assn, 1994-95; Natl VP, RAAF Assn, 1996-97. Hobby: Lawn bowls. Address: c/o RAAFA Estate, Merriwa, WA 6030, Australia.

FIDGE Noel Hadden, b. 3 Sept 1936, Peterborough, S Aust. Medical Scientist; Composer. m. Heather, 2 s, 1 d. Education: BS, Univ Adelaide (Aust), 1961; PhD, 1965. Appointments: Rsch Fell, Dept Physiol, Medl Sci, Univ Melbourne, Aust, 1968-69; Snr Rsch Fell, Dept Clin Sci, John Curtin Sch Med Rsch Austl Natl Univ, Canberra, 1970-77; Snr Biochemist Cardiovascular Metabolism and Nutrition Rsch Unit, Baker Medl Rsch Inst, Melbourne, Aust, 1977-80; Prin Rsch Fell, Cardiovascular Metabolism and Nutrition Rsch Unit, 1981-87; Snr Prin Rsch Fell, Hd Lipoprotein Structure and Function Lab, 1987-. Creative works; Opera: Boffler & Son; Musical plays: Little Miss April; Chamber works, wind quartets, piano sonatas. Publications: Contbr chapts to books, articles to profl jrnls. Memberships: Overseas Life Fell, Life Ins Medl Rsch Fund Aust and NZ, NY, 1966-68; AHA; Austl Atherosclerosis Soc (Past Pres, 1975, Ed, Atherosclerosis jrnl, 1985); Eurn Atherosclerosis Soc. Hobbies: Piano; Oil painting; Composing. Address: 25 Elizabeth Street, 3185 Elsternwick, Victoria, Australia.

FIELD Michael Walter (Hon), b. 28 May 1946, Latrobe, Tasmania, Aust. Politician. m. Janette Elizabeth Mary Fone, 6 Dec 1975, 1 s, 2 d. Education: BA, Univ Tas. Appointments: Tchr, 1971-75; Cmnty Dev Offr, 1975-76; Mbr, Austl Labor Party; Mbr, House of Assembly, for Braddon, Tas, 1976-; Min Transp, Main Rds, Constrn and Local Govt, 1979-82; Shadow Min Educ and Indl Rels, 1982-86; Dpty Ldr Opposition, Shadow Min Forestry, Indl Rels and Energy, 1986-88; Ldr Opposition, 1988-89; Premier, Treas, Min State Dev and Fin, 1989-92; Shadow Min Econ Dev, 1992-93; Shadow Treas, 1992-96; Tasmanian Ldr Opposition, 1992-97; Shadow Min State Dev, 1993-94; Shadow Min Educ and Trng, 1994-96; Shadow Min Yth Affairs, 1992-97; Bd Mbr, John Curtis House, Ltd; Bd Mbr, John Curtis House, Ltd, Aust; Bd Mbr, Tasmanian Electricity Code Change Panel; Cnslt, Trainer in change mngmt; Chair, Innovations Bd, Tasmania, 1999-. Memberships: Advsry Grp Mbr for Ortus Star Inc (Ldrshp Dev), Univ of Tasmania. Listed in: Who's Who 2000; Who's Who in Australia. Hobbies: Reading; Music. Address: 16 Osprey Rd, Eaglehawk Neck, Tasmania 7179, Australia.

FIFE Wal (Hon), b. 2 Oct 1929, Wagga Wagga, NSW, Aust. Member of Parliament. m. Marcia Fife, 2 s, 2 d. Appointments include: Mbr, NSW Parl, 1957-75; Asst Min for Educ, 1965-67; Min for Mines, 1967-75; Min for Conserv, 1971-72; Min for Power, 1972-75; Asst Treas, 1972-75; Min for Transport and Highways, 1975; Mbr, Farrer, 1975-85, Hume, 1984-93; C'wlth Parl, Min for Bus and Consular Affairs, 1977-79; Min Asstng the PM, 1978-83; Min for Educ, 1979-82; Min for Aviation, 1982-83; Shadow Min, Hsng and Constrn, 1983-84; Vice Chmn, C'wlth Parly Pub Wrks Cttee, 1983-84; Shadow Min, Def, Shadow Min, Primary Ind, 1987; Shadow Min, Adminstv Servs, 1987; Mngr, Opposition Bus, HoR, 1987-92; Shadow Min, ACT, 1990; Shadow Min with Portfolio; Resigned from Shadow Cabinet and as Mngr of Opposition Bus in House of Reprs, 1992; Ceased to be Mbr, House of Reprs, 1993. Honours: Freedom of Cty of Wagga Wagga, 1982; DLit (honouris causa), Charles Sturt Univ, Wagga Wagga, 1993; Knighthood of the Order of Saint Sylvester, 1994. Memberships: Austl Liberal Party; Bd, NZI Ins, 1993-99. Address: Gundary, RMB 416A, Wagga Wagga, New South Wales 2650, Australia.

FIGGIS Brian Norman, b. 27 Mar 1930, Sydney, Australia. Educator. m. Jane Susan, 1 s, 1 d. Education: MSc, Sydney, 1952; PhD, NSW, 1956; DSc, WA, 1966. Appointments: Lectr, Chem, Univ Coll, London, 1958-62; Rdr, Prof, Chem, Univ WA, Aust, 1963-. Publications: Introduction to Ligand Fields, 1966; Over 200 articles in profl jrnls. Honours: Fell, Austl Acady of Scis, 1985; Inorg Awd, 1986; H G Smith Medal, 1989; Walter Burfitt Prize, Roy Soc of NSW, 1987. Address: 9 Hamersley Street, Cottesloe, WA 6011, Australia.

FIGUEROA SERRANO Carlos, b. 28 Nov 1930 Angol. Politician; Lawyer. m. Sara Guzman, 1953, 7 c. Education: Colegio de los Sagrados Corazones; Schl of Law; Univ de Chile. Appointments: Practising lawyer, 1957-; Joined Partido Democrata Cristiano - PDC - 1957; Prof of Procedural Law Catholic Univ of Chile, 1960-76; Under-Sec for Agric, 1967-69; Acting Min of For Rels and of Fin var occasions, 1967-70; Min of Econ, 1969-70; Dir CIC SA, 1971-; Served at Appeals Crt Santiago, 1971-72; Pres Asociacion Radiodifusoras de Chile, 1972-78; Cnslr Asociacion Iberamericana de Radiodifusion, 1973-79; Sec Bd of Dirs, 1975-77; Pres PDC Polit Cttee, 1980; Gen Mngr VEEP SA - bldg contractors - 1980-86; Deleg for Providencia to Prov Bd of East Santiago, 1984-87; Dir Financiera Condell, 1986-90; Dir Pesquera Guafo SA, 1987-89; Hd Comms and Publicity Patricio Aylwin's Presdl Campaign, 1989; Amb to Argentina, 1990-93; Dir Comms and Publicity Eduardo Frei's Presdl Campaign, 1993; Min for For Affairs, Mar-Sep 1994; Min for Interior Sep, 1994-. Address: Ministro del Interior, Palacio de la Moneda, Santiago, Chile.

FINCH Lancelot, b. 14 Sept 1917, Oamaru, NZ. Retired Research Scientist. m. (1) Beryl Mardon Rickman, 11 Feb 1942 (dec 1949); (2)Elizabeth Christina Finlayson, 20 Apr 1957. Education: BArch (Dist in Thesis); BSc, NZ; PhD, Melbourne, Aust. Appointments: WWII, R&D Proj Engr, 1941; Bldng Rsch, 1945-46; Univ NZ/DSIR; Engr Geologist, SMHEA, 1952-56; Rsch Offr/Scientist, CSIRO, 1956-77; Visng Lectr, Univ of Melbourne, 1957-59. Publications: Invitation Papers on Research Findings for Guidance of Architectural Profession 1961-73. Memberships: ANZIA, 1940; ARIBA, 1942; FRSA, c.1955; Geol Soc of Aust c 1955, Roy Soc of Vic, c 1996; Aust Inst Conservation Cultural Material, 1973. Hobbies: Photography; Encouraging cancer research; Compiling memoirs (for archives NZ and Aust); Submission of evidence to Royal Commission and Select Committees, Austl Fedl & State Parls, re law Reforms. Address: 27 Hawdon Street, Heidelberg, Vic 3084, Australia.

FINCKH Ernest Sydney, b. 13 June 1924. Pathologist. m. (1) Nancye, 26 Mar 1955, dec, (2) Heather, 17 Apr 1993. Education: SCEGS; Sydney Univ. Appointments: Med Offr, Red Cross Blood Transfusion Serv, NSW, 1947-48; RMO, 1946-47, Fell in Pathol, 1949-50, Roy Prince Alfred Hosp, Sydney; Pathologist, Walter and Eliza Hall Inst, Melbourne, 1951-54; Nuffield Dominion Travelling Fell, Univ Coll Hosp, London, 1955-56; Snr Fulbright Schl and Guest Investigator, Rockefeller Inst, NY, USA, 1964-65; Dpty Dir, Inst of Clin Pathol and Med Rsch, Lidcombe, NSW, 1969-78; Dir, Inst of Clin Pathol and Med Rsch, Westmead Hosp, NSW, 1978-89; Ed, The Effects of Environ on Cells and Tissues, 1976; VP, 1975-79, Pres, 1979-81, Roy Coll of Pathologists, Australasia; Snr Lectr, 1958-62, Assoc Prof, 1962-78, Clin Prof of Pathol, 1978-89, Sub-Dean, 1961-77, 1984-89, Fac of Med, Univ of Sydney; Mbr, NSW Med Bd, 1987-96; Emer Prof, Univ of Sydney, 1989-. Membership: Sydney Amateur Sailing Club. Hobby: Yachting. Address: 5/1 Krait Close, Nelson Bay, NSW 2315, Australia.

FINERAN Brian Arnold, b. 1 Oct 1937, Christchurch, New Zealand. University Professor. m. (1) Judith Marion Greenall, 22 Feb 1969, dec 12 Dec 1991, (2) Barbara Lindsay Fisher, 12 Apr 1993, 1 s, 2 d. Education: BSc, NZ; MSc, Hons, NZ; PhD, Canterbury. Appointments: Asst Lectr, Univ Canterbury, Christchurch, NZ, 1961-64; Lectr, 1965-71; Snr Lectr, 1972-76; Reader, 1977-91; Prof, 1992-. Publications: Contbr, over 90 pprs to sci jrnls & book chapts. Memberships: Intl Soc Plant Morphologists, Editl Bd, 1985-89, Regl Cnclr, 1975-78; Roy Soc NZ; Roy Microscopical Soc; NZ Soc for Microscopy. Hobbies: Mountaineering & Tramping; Farming; Music. Address: 31 Marama Crescent, Christchurch 8008, New Zealand.

FINGARETTE Herbert, b. 20 Jan 1921, NYC, USA. Philosopher. m. Leslie, 23 Jan 1945, 1 d. Education: BA, UCLA, 1947; PhD, UCLA, Philos, 1949. Appointments: Lectr to Prof, Univ of CA, Santa Barbara, 1948-91.

Publications: The Self in Transformation, 1963; On Responsibility, 1967; Self-Deception, 1969, 1999; Confucius, 1972; The Meaning of Criminal Insanity, 1972; Mental Disabilities and Criminal Responsibility, 1979; Heavy Drinking, 1989; Death Philosophical Soundings, 1996. Honours: Phi Beta Kappa Prof; Fac Rsch Lectr; Disting Tchr; Dr of Humane Letters. Memberships: Pres, Pacific Div Amn Phys Assn, 1976-77. Address: Philosophy Department, University of California, Santa Barbara, CA 93106, USA.

FINLAYSON Robert Frederick, b. 28 Aug 1958, Melbourne, Aust. Writer. m. 18 Aug 1990, div, 1 d. Appointments: Admnstr, Fellshp of Austl Writers, WA; Coord, Katherine Susannah Prichard Fndn. Publications: Songs ov th city ov desire + fear, 1986; In the azure room ov the peacock palace, 1987. Memberships: Fellshp of Austl Writers, WA; Austl Jrnlsts Assn; Fremantle Surf Lifesaving Club. Hobbies: Swimming. Address: PO Box 198, Fremantle WA 6160, Australia.

FINN T Brian, b. 3 Aug 1937, Newcastle-upon-Tyne, Eng. Company Director. m. Ivy E. Finn, 4s, 1d. Appointments: Mktng and Software Dev, 35 yrs, IBM, 1975-93; IBM in Afghanistan, Bangladesh, India, Nepal, Sri Lanka, 1975-78; IBM throughout Asia, 1978-80; Chf Exec, 1980-93, Chmn, Advsry Bd, 1996-98, IBM Aust; Chmn, Austl Natl Trng Authy, 1992-95; Mbr, Bd of Gov, Univ Western Sydney, 1989-95; Chmn, CitiPower Ltd, 1994-95. Honours: FUTS; FIE(Aust); FTS; FACS; Offr, Order of Aust, 1990. Memberships: Bd Dir, Natl Mutual Holdings; Dpty Chmn, Southcorp; Chmn, Impart Corp; Dpty Chmn, Powertel Ltd; Dir, Heytesbury Grp; John Holland Grp. Address: 7 Excalibur Court, The Sovereign Islands, Qld 4216, Australia.

FIROUZ-ABADI Abbas Alex, b. 8 Nov 1927, Iran. Medical Practitioner; Pathologist. Education: MD, Tehran Univ, 1955; Residency in Pathol, Jersey City, 1959-64; Postgrad Course, Seton Hall, Univ NJ, 1961; Cytopathy Course, Johns Hopkins Univ, 1965. Appointments: Asst Prof Pathol, PA Coll Med, 1971-73; Prof Pathol, Tehran Univ, 1972-81; Snr Pathologist, 1981-89; Assoc Prof, Queensland Univ, 1981-; Dir, Cytopathology Dept, Electronmicroscopic Unit, 1981-; Dir, Anatomical Pathol, 1990-93. Publications: Contbr many articles to medl and sci jrnls. Honour: Mycologist of Yr, 1971. Memberships: Fell, Coll Amn Pathologists; Fell, Royal Coll Pathologists, Australasia; Fell, Intl Acady Cytology; Life Mbr, Amn Soc of Cytoloy; Australian Soc Cytology; Aust Soc Electron Microscopy; Thoracic Soc Queensland; Profl Offrs Assn. Listed in American Who's Who. Hobbies: Outdoor activities. Address: 107 Boswell Terrace, Manly, Brisbane, Qld 4179, Australia.

FIROUZDOR Mohammad, b. 10 July 1940, Tehran, Iran. Secretary General. m. Forouzandeh Arbabi, July 1980, 3 s. Education: BA; MA, Econ, USA. Address: Asian Clearing Union, c/o Central Bank of IR, Iran, BO Box 113651/8551, Tehran, Iran.

FISCHER Margaret Charlotte, b. 8 Jan 1952, Sydney, Aust. Writer; Performer; Producer. Education: BA; DipEd. Appointments: Co Artistic Dir, Adelaide Lesbian Gay Cultural Fest (FEAST), 1997. Publications: Many plays inclng: The Gay Divorcee, 1990; Getting Your Man, 1997. Honours: Ros Bower Awd Winner; Natl Awd, Aust Cncl, 1996. Memberships: Bd Mbr, Vitalstaistix Th Co. Hobbies: Working for justice; Reconciliation for indigenous people; Drinking coffee and eating cake. Address: 18 Cave Street, Semaphore 5019, South Australia, Australia.

FISCHER Timothy Andrew, b. 3 May 1946 Lockhart NSW. Politician. m. 1992, 1 s. Education: Boree Creek Schl; Xavier Coll Melbourne. Appointments: Joined Army, 1966; Offr with First Bn Roy Austl Regt Aust and Vietnam, 1966-69; Farmer Boree Creek NSW. MP for Farrer NSW, 1984-; Shadow Min for Veterans' Affairs, 1985-89; Dep Mngr of Opposition Bus, 1989-90; Ldr Natl Party of Aust, 1990-; Shadow Min for Energy and Rescs, 1990-93; Shadow Min for Trade, 1993-96; Dep PM and Min for Trade, Mar 1996-. Memberships: Mbr NSW Legis Assn, 1970-84. Hobbies: Chess; Tennis; Skiing; Water Skiing; Bush-Walking; Mountaineering. Address: Parliament House, Canberra, ACT 2600, Australia.

FISHER Anthony Colin Joseph, b. 10 Mar 1960, Sydney, Australia. Priest; Ethicist. Education: BA, LLB, Univ Sydney; BTheol, Melbourne Coll of Divinity; DPhil. Appointments: Lawyer, Clayton Utz Sydney, 1984; Dominican Friar, 1985-; Cath Priest, 1991-; Lectr in Ethics, Austl Cath Univ, 1995-; Rsch Assoc, John Plunkett Cntr, 1996-; Chaplain to Parly of Vic, 1996-; Episcopal Vicar for Hlth Care, 1997-; Chap to Cath Drs Assn of Melbourne, 1998-; Infertility Treatment Authy of Vic, 1999-; Bd of Eastn Palliative Care, Melbourne, 1999. Publications: Abortion in Australia, 1985; IVF: Critical Issues, 1989; I Am A Stranger: Will You Welcome Me?, 1991; Relevant Ethical Issues in Health Care, 1996. Honours: Jurisprudence Prize, Univ Sydney, 1983; Pres Prize, Yarra Theol Union, 1990; Brewster Schl, Univ Coll Oxford, 1993; Phillipa Brazil Awd, 1997; 21st Century Trust Schlr, 1998. Memberships: Moral Theol Assn of Aust; Austl Bioethics Assn; Soc for Protection of Unborn Child; Order of Preachers. Hobbies: Prayer; Study; Religious Community Life. Address: c/o Australian Catholic University, 412 Mount Alexander Road, Ascot Vale, Victoria 3032, Australia.

FISHER Beatrice Awura Oboshie Allua, b. Nigeria. Attorney-at-Law. m. Babatunde Olanrewaju Fisher, 3 children. Education: Salvation Army Sch, Lagos, Nigeria, 1939-45; Annie Walsh Mem Sch, Sierra Leone, 1946-50; Ophthalmic Nursing Dip, Moorfields Eye Hosp, London, England, 1951-53; SRN, Guys Hosp, London, England, 1953-57; Pt I Midwifery, Rottenrow Maternity Hosp, Glasgow, Scotland, 1957-58; LLB, hons, Univ of Lagos, 1968-71; Nigerian Bar, Bar and Sol, Supreme Crt of Nigeria, 1972; Notary Pub, 1979; ACI Arb, 1997. Appointments: Obafemi Awolowo & Co, Attys-at-Law, Lagos, 1972-75; Beatrice Fisher & Co, Attys-at-Law, Nigeria, 1975-. Honours: FIDA Gold Medal, 1990; Silver Medal of Hon, ABI, 1991. Memberships: C'wlth Lawyers Assn; African Bar Assn; Nigerian Bar Assn; Intl Fedn of Women Lawyers; Intl Bar Assn; Dpty Gov, ABI; Natl Geographic Soc; Nigerian Soc of Univ Women. Listed in: Who's Who of Women; Who's Who in Australia and the Far East. Hobbies: Reading; Gardening; Floral Arrangements; Travel; Theatre; Opera; Classical Music. Address: Beatrice Fisher & Co, PO Box 8032, Marina, Lagos, Nigeria.

FISHER Bruce, b. 24 Dec 1949, Long Beach, CA. Educator. m. Mindi, 1 d. Education: BA, Cum Laude; CA Std elem tchng Credential; Lrng Handicapped Credential. Appointments: CA Technol Asst, Proj Schs of CA, On Line Resources for Educ; CA Curriculum, Frameworks and Instructional. Creative Works: Internaltional Geoscience and Remote Sensing; Health Related Fitness Grades, 1-2, 3-4, 5-6. Honours: Lifetime Educ Achmnt Awd; Natl Educr; Profl Best; CA Tchr of the Yr, 1991; ABC Favorite Tchr; NEWEST. Memberships: Computer Using Educrs; CA Sci Proj; Natl Sci Proj; CA Natl Educr Steering Cttee; CA Maths Cncl. Hobbies: Space and Astronomy; Photography; Curriculum Development. Address: 4810 14th St, Fieldbrook, CA 95519, USA.

FISHER Norman Henry, b. 30 Sept 1909, Hay, NSW, Aust. Geologist. m. (1) Ellice Marguerite Summers, 23 Aug 1937, 1 s, (2) Mary Eldershaw Bowman, 10 Dec 1994. Education: BSc, 1931, MSc, 1933, DSc, 1941, Qld Univ. Appointments: Geol, Mt Isa Mines, 1931-34; Govt Geol and Vulcanologist, Territory New Guinea, 1934-42; Chf Geol, Mineral Rescs Survey, Canberra, ACT, 1942-46; Chf Geol, 1946-69, Dir, 1969-74, Bur Mineral Rescs, Geol, Geophys; Advsr, mineral dev, UN, Bolivia, 1954-55, Israel, 3 months 1963-64. Publications: Num pprs in sci and semi-sci jrnls. Honours: AO, 1976; Spendiarov Prize, Intl Geol Congress, 1976; Pres, Intl Geol Congress, 1976; Pres's Awd, Austl Inst Mining and Metall, 1979; W R Browne Medal, Geol Soc Aust, 1981; Hon Fell, St Johns Coll, Univ Qld, 1985. Memberships: Geol Soc Aust, Past Pres; Australasian Inst Mining and Metall; Soc Econ Geols. Hobbies: Tennis; Geology of ore

bodies; Geological mapping. Address: 19/9 Anderson Street, Neutral Bay, Sydney, NSW 2089, Australia.

FITZGERALD Gerald Edward (Tony), b. 26 Nov 1941, Brisbane, Australia. Judge of Appeal. m. Catherine, 21 Dec 1968, 1 s, 2 d. Education: LLB. Appointments include: Pres, Crt of Appeal, Supreme Crt of Qld, 1991-; Chmn, Qld Litigation Reform Commn, 1991-92; Chmn, Natl Inst for Law, Ethics & Pub Affairs, 1992-95; Mbr, Visng Cttee of Fac of Law, Griffith Univ, 1992-95; Chan, Sunshine Coast Univ Coll, 1994-; Dpty Chmn, Mater Health Servs Govng Bd, 1993-; Visng Schlr, New York Univ Sch of Law, 1997. Honours: Companion, Order of Aust, 1991; DUniv, Qld Univ of Technol, 1995. Hobbies: Reading; Tennis; Music. Address: 43 McCaul Street, Taringa East 4068, Australia.

FITZGERALD Paul Desmond, b. 1 Aug 1922. Portrait Painter. m. Mary Fitzgerald, 2 s, 4 d. Education: National Art Gall Sch, Melbourne. Creative Works: Noted Portrait Commns inclng Roy Jubilee Portrait Queen Elizabeth II, Queen Elizabeth II, 1963; HRH Prince Philip, 1974, 1975; Prince Charles, Pope John XXIII, Sir William and Lady Slim, King Hisamuddin of Malaya, and Prince and Princess Von Baden, Germany; Amn Portraits inclng Cardinal Cooke, Conrad Hilton, Glenn Ford, 5 Chairmen of Governors of New York Hospital; Austl Portraits inclng Sir Robert and Dame Pattie Menzies, Mr Malcolm Fraser, Sir Brian Murray, Sir Henry Bolte, Sir Henry Winneke, Cardinal Knox, Sir Rohan Delacombe, Allan Border, 14 Supreme Crt Judges, 6 Chfs of Air Staff; Sir James Gobbo, 2 Pres Roy Coll Obstet and Gynaecologists and Aust Colls of Surgs, Physns, Obstet, Gynaecologists and a Pres Austl Coll Anaesthetists; Neale Fraser. Honour: Kt Malta, 1973; AM, 1997. Membership: 1st Pres, Austl Guild Realist Artists. Listed in: Who's Who in Australia; Who's Who in the Commonwealth; Debrett's Handbook of Australia and New Zealand. Hobbies: Tennis; Golf. Address: 21 Victoria Avenue, Canterbury, Vic 3126, Australia.

FITZPATRICK James Michael Bede, b. 9 June 1927, Childers, Qld, Aust. Retired. m. 6 Sept 1958, 3 s. Education: BEcon, Univ Queensland. Appointments: Dpty Chmn, Dpty Mngng Dir, 1965-71, Chmn, Mngng Dir, 1971-87, Hsg Loans Ins Corp; Chmn, Credit Lyonnais Fund Mngrs Ltd; Now retd. Honours: Queen Elizabeth II Silver Jubilee Medal, 1977; AM, 1985; Sir Philip Lynch Awd, 1986. Hobbies: History; Walking; Farming. Address: 2 Margaret Street, Woolwich, NSW 2110, Australia.

FLAMM Melvin Daniel, b. 29 Jan 1934, Los Angeles, CA, USA. Cardiologist. m. Carla. Education: BA, Univ of California at Los Angeles, 1956; MD, Stanford Univ Sch of Med, 1960. Appointments include: Clinl Asst Prof, 1969-73, Clinl Assoc Prof of Med, 1974-81, 1986-90, Clinl Prof of Med, 1990-, Cardiology, Univ of California Sch of Med, Davis, CA, USA. Publications include: Noninvasive Myocardial Imaging with Potassium-43 and Rubidium-81 in Patients with Left Bundle Branch Block, 1976; Diagnostic Accuracy of Noninvasive Myocardial Imaging for Coronary Artery Disease: An Electrocardiographic and Angiographic Correlation, 1977; Pulmonary Hypertension and Sudden Death in Aortic Stenosis, 1979. Honours: Phi Beta Kappa, 1956; Alpha Omega Alpha, 1959; Hon Grad, Primary Course in Aerospace Med, 1961; Casimir Funk Awd, 1973. Memberships: Fell, Amn Coll of Cardiology; Fell, Amn Coll of Physns; Fell, Cncl of Clinl Cardiology, Amn Heart Assn; Amn Fedn for Clinl Rsch; Sacramento-El Dorado, California and Amn Med Assn. Address: Northern California Cardiology Associates, 5301 F Street, Suite 117, Sacramento, CA 95819, USA.

FLATTERY Thomas Long, b. 14 Nov 1922, Detroit, Michigan, USA. Lawyer. m. Barbara Jones Flattery, 4 Oct 1986, 4 s, 5 d. Education: BS, US Mil Acady, 1947; JD, Univ CA, Los Angeles, 1955; LLM, Univ S CA, 1965. Appointments: Motor Prods Corp, Detroit, 1950; Equitable Life Assurance Soc, Detroit, 1951; Bohn Aluminum & Brass Co, MI, 1952; Legal Staff, Asst, Contract Admnstr, Radioplane Co, Van Nuys, CA, 1955-57; Corp Cnsl, Gen Cnsl, Asst, Sec, McCulloch Corp, Los Angeles, 1957-64; Sec, Corp Cnsl, Technicolor Inc, Hollywood, CA,

1964-70; Corp Cnsl, Asst, Sec, VP, Sec, Gen Cnsl, Amcord Inc, Newport Beach, CA, 1970-72; VP, Sec, Gen Cnsl, Schick Inc, Los Angeles, 1972-75; Cnsl, Asst Sec, C F Braun & Co, Alhambra, CA, 1975-76; Snr VP, Sec Gen, Cnsl, Automation Ind Inc, Greenwich, CT, 1976-86; VP, Gen Cnsl, G&H Tech Inc, Santa Monica, CA, 1986-93; Temporary Judge, Mcpl Crt CA, Los Angeles, Jud Dist and Santa Monica Unified Crts, 1987-; Settlement Offr, Los Angeles Superior and Mcpl Crts, 1991-; Pvte Prac, 1993-. Publications: Sev articles in profl jrnls. Memberships include: Am Educl League; W Point Alumni Assn; Army Athletic Assn. Hobbies: Golf; Skiing. Address:439 Via De La Paz, Pacific Palisades, CA 90272-4633, USA.

FLEMING Elaine Dawn, b. Sale, Vic, Aust. Director, promotions and advertising. m. Don, 11 Jan 1958, 2 s, 1 d. Education: Dip, Needlecraft. Publications: (Ed) Deciduous Tree Fruit Cultivars, 1991; Deciduous Fruit, Ornamental Trees, 1992. Honours: Life Mbr, Monbulk Rural Fire Brigade; Monbulk Rural Fire Brigade Ladies Auxilary (Pres, 17-18 yrs). Hobbies: Photography (student, professional photography course); Walking. Address: Old Macclesfield Road, Monbulk, Victoria, Australia.

FLEMING (Eric) Donald, b. 8 May 1935, Belgrave, Vic, Aust. Nurseryman. m. Elaine Dawn Fleming, 11 Jan 1958, 2 s, 1 d. Appointments: Ptnr, Eric S Fleming & Sons, 1957-84; Mngng Dir, Owner, Eric S Fleming & Sons, 1984-; Mngng Dir, Owner, Flemings Nurseries, 1984-. Honours: Queens Fire Serv Medal, QFSM; Life Mbr, Monbulk Rural Brigade; Life Mbr, Monbulk Cricket Club. Memberships: Capt, 1961-84, Pres, 1984-89, 1997-, Monbulk Rural Fire Brigade. Hobbies: Fire brigade; Family business; Motorbikes; Tennis. Address: Old Macclesfield Road, Monbulk, Victoria, Australia.

FLEMING Jean Sutherland, b. 11 Apr 1952, Wellington, NZ. Feminist Scientist, 1 s. Education: BSc Hons, Biochem, 1973; MSc, Clinl Biochem, 1981; PhD, 1986. Appointments: Rsch Asst, New Addenbrookes Hosp, Cambridge, Eng, 1975-77; Sci Offr, Wellington Medl Sch, NZ, 1978-81; Temporary Lectr, Vic Univ, Wellington, 1986; ANZAC Fell, Howard Florey Inst, Melbourne, Vic, Aust, 1987; Postdoct Fell, Min Agric and Fisheries, NZ, 1988-90; Scientist, Min Agric and Fisheries Technol, Wallaceville Animal Rsch Cntr, Upper Hutt, 1990-92; Scientist, AgRsch, 1992-93; Lectr, 1994-96, Snr Lectr, 1997-98, Dept Physiology, Snr Lectr, 1999-, Dept Anatomy and Structural Biol, Otago Medl Sch, Dunedin. Publications: 36 sci pprs in intl jrnls. Honours: Kirk Prize, Vic Univ, 1970; Sarah Anne Rhodes Rsch Schlshp, 1973; Medl Rsch Cncl Postgrad Schlshp, 1980; Zonta Natl Sci Medal, 1990; NZ Suffrage Medal, 1993; Roy Soc of NZ Silver Sci and Technol Medal, 1998; Sev Fell'ships. Memberships include: NZ Roy Soc; NZ Assn Women in Scis; Austl Soc Reproductive Bio; NZ Endocrine Soc; Pres, Otago Inst Inc, Roy Soc NZ, 1996-98. Hobbies: Women's studies; Networking; Gardening; Kayaking. Listed in: The World Who's Who of Women. Address: Department of Anatomy and Structural Biology, Otago University School of Medical Sciences, PO Box 913, Dunedin, New Zealand.

FLETCHER Marion Douglas, b. 6 Dec 1910. Former Art Lecturer; Former Curator. Education: Dip, Design and Crafts, Edinburgh Coll of Art, Scotland. Appointments: Tchr Pt-time, Edinburgh Coll of Art, Scotland; Lectr in Art Sch, Roy Melbourne Inst of Technol, Melbourne; Asst Curator, Decorative Arts (Costume and Textiles) Natl Gallery of Vic, Aust. Publications: Creative Embroidery; Books: Costume in Australia 1788-1901; Needlework in Australia. Honours: Life Mbr, Natl Gallery of Vic. Memberships: Arts and Crafts Soc of Vic; Fndn Cttee Mbr, Embroiderers Guild of Vic; Vic Tapestry Wrkshp. Listed in: Who's Who of Australian Writers. Hobbies: Art; Reading. Address: 42 Hope Street, South Yarra, Melbourne, Vic 3141, Australia.

FLETCHER Neville Horner, b. 14 Juy 1930, Armidale, Aust. Physicist. m. Eunice Sciffer, 1 s, 2 d. Education: BSc (Sydney), 1951; PhD (Harvard), 1955; DSc (Sydney), 1973. Appointments include: Rsch Engr, Clevite Transistor Prods, Waltham Massachusetts, 1953-55; Rsch Offr, CSIRO Radiophysics Lab, 1956-60; Snr Lectr, Phys, Univ of New Eng, 1960-63; Prof of Phys (Personal Chair), Univ of New England, 1963-83; Dir, Inst of Phys Scis, CSIRO, 1983-87; Chf Rsch Scientist, CSIRO, 1988-95; Visng Fell, Austl Natl Univ, 1996-; Visng Prof, Univ Coll, ADFA, Univ of NSW, 1996-. Publications: 6 books: The Physics of Rainclouds, 1962; The Chemical Physics of Ice, 1970; The Physics of Musical Instruments, 1991; Acoustic Systems in Biology, 1992; Principles of Vibration and Sound, 1995; (Co-ed) Vocal Fold Physiology: Controlling Complexity and Chaos, 1996; 150 sci pprs in intl jrnls. Honours include: Edgeworth David Medal Roy Soc NSW, 1963; Fell, Austl Acady of Sci (FAA), 1976; Fell, Austl Acady of Technol Scis and Engrng (FTSE), 1987; Mbr of the Order of Aust (AM), 1990; Thomas Ranken Lyle Medal, Austl Acady of Sci, 1993; Disting Alumni Awd, Univ New Eng, 1994; Silver Medal, Accoustical Soc of Am, 1998. Memberships: Fell, Inst Of Phys (London) (FIP); Fell, Austl Inst of Phys (FAIP), Pres, 1981-83; Fell, Acoustical Soc of Am; Fell, Austl Acoustical Soc (FAAS). Hobbies: Music (flute, bassoon, organ). Address: 30 Rosebery Street, Fisher, ACT 2611, Australia.

FLINT David Edward, b. 3 July 1938, Sydney, Aust. Professor of Law. Education: LLB, LLM, Sydney; BS Econs, Londn; DSU, Paris 2. Appointments: Solicitor, Supreme Crt (NSW), 1962-, Eng & Wales, 1966-; Voce-Chmn, Alliance Française de Sydney, 1983-84; Chmn, Austl Press Cncl, 1987-97; Dean, UTS Law Sch, 1987-96; Mbr, Int Legal Servs Cncl, 1990-96; Convenor/Chmn, Cttee of Austl Law Deans, 1989-93; Dir of Studies, Intl Law Assn (Aust & NZ branch), 1991-97; Chmn, Exec Cncl of World Assn of Press Cncl, 1992-; Cnsltng Ed, Austl Intl Law Jrnl, 1994-; Natl Pres (Aust) World Jurists Assn, 1995-; Chmn, Austl Brdcstng Authority, 1997-; Visng Prof, Fac of Laws, UWS Macarthur, July 1998-June 2000. Publications: (co-auth) Business Law of the European Community, 1993; Num chapts in books incl: Freedom of Speech and Media Regulation in India, chapt in V Taylor's Asian Laws Through Australian Eyes, 1997. Honours: World Outsndng Legal Schl, World Jurists Assn, Barcelona, 1991; AM, 1995. Membership: Union Club. Address: ABA, Level 15, 201 Sussex Street, Sydney 2000, Australia.

FLINT Janet Susan, b. 18 July 1935, Sydney, NSW, Aust. Teacher; Librarian. m. John Marsden Flint, 6 Sept 1958, 1 s, 2 d. Education: BA, Univ Sydney, 1956; Dip Educ, Univ New Eng, 1981; Dip Children's Lit, Kuringai Coll Advd Educ, 1984; Registration Cert, Lib Assn Aust, 1975. Appointments: Libn, Dept Primary Ind, Canberra, ACT, 1957-58; Libn, Kuringai Munic Lib, Sydney, 1958; Libn, State Lib NSW, Sydney, 1959; Libn i/c, NSW Dept Labour and Ind, Sydney, 1960-62; Libn i/c, Coopers and Lybrands Chartered Accts, 1968-80; Tchr-Libn, Trinity Grammar Sch, Summer Hill, NSW, 1980-96; Cnslt to Jessie St Natl Women's Lib, 1998. Publications: Report to Fulbright Assn; Article on Tour of American Schools, in Access, Jan 1990; Book review, Austl Soc Archivists; Book reviews, AHISA indep jrnl; Report on Operational Plan for Jessie St Natl Women's Lib, 1999-2001. Honour: Fulbright Schlshp, 1988, taken up 1989. Memberships: Assoc Mbr, Austl Lib and Info Assn; Indep Tchrs Assn; Chmn, Centenary Summer Sch, Women's Coll, Univ Sydney; Visng Evaluation Cttee to Scot's Coll, Warwick, Qld; Visng Evaluation Cttee to St Paul's Sch, Brisbane, Qld; Visng Evaluation Cttee to The Brooks Sch, N Andover, USA; Austl Deleg of Libns to China, 1995; Cttee Mbr, IBBY, Plan Intl Aust; Sec NSW Fulbright Assn; Cmnty Care Br, St Johns Ambulance NSW, PAL and LinkAGE Progs. Hobbies: Reading; Art; Gardening. Address: 3 Nola Road, Roseville, NSW 2069, Australia.

FLOOD Philip James, b. 2 Jul 1935. Australian High Commissioner to the United Kingdom. m. Carole, 24 Mar 1990, 2 s, 1 d. Education: BEc (Hons), Univ of Sydney, 1958. Appointments: Austl Mission to Eurn Communities, Austl Emb, Brussels, 1959-62; Austl Rep, OECD Dev Assistance Cttee, Austl Emb, Paris, 1966-69; Asst Sec, Dept For Affairs, 1971-73; High Commnr of Aust to Bangladesh, 1974-76; Min, Austl Emb, USA, 1976-77; Chf Exec Offr, Dept Special Trade Reps, 1977-80; First Asst Sec, Dept Trade, 1980-84; Dpty Sec, Dept For Affairs, Canberra, 1985-89; Austl Amb, Indonesia, 1989-93; Dir Gen, Austl Agcy for Intl De (AUSAID), 1993-95; Dir Gen, Off of Natl Assessments (ONAO), 1995-96; Sec, Dept of For Affairs and Trade, 1996-98. Honours: Offr of the Order of Aust, 1992; Bintang Jasa Utama, Indonesia, 1993; Fell, Royal Austl Inst of Pub Admin; Fell, Austl Inst of Mngmt. Hobbies: Reading; Music; Golf; Swimming. Address: 96 Jervois Street, Deakin, ACT 2600, Australia.

FLORES TORRES Jorge, b. 11 Apr 1929 Tacna. Government Minister; Army Officer. Appointments: Began mil career as soldier in Cavalry Schl, 1947; Cadet at Chorrillos Mil Schl, 1948-52; Fmr Instructor at Schl of Equitation; Dir of Cavalry Schl; Chf of Natl Def Sec; Maj-Gen First Mil Reg Piura; Rank of Gen, 1984; Min of Def, Army, 1985. Address: c/o Ministry of Defence, Army, Lima, Peru.

FLOYD John M, b. 30 Jan 1941. Scientist. m. 10 Dec 1966, 3 s, 1 d. Education: BSc, MSc, Univ of Melbourne; PhD, Univ of London. Appointments: Rsch Scientist, Prin Rsch Scientist, CIIRO; Prin; CEO, Dpty Chmn, Ausmelt Ltd; Profl Rsch Fell, Profl Assoc, Univ of Melbourne. Publications: Over 70 sci and tech publns. Honours: Clunies-Ross Natl Sci and Technol Awd, 1995; Aust IMM Pres Awd, 1997; AM, 1998. Memberships: Fell, ATS&E; Fell, Aust IMM; CIM; TSM. Listed in: Debrett's Handbook of Australia; Who's Who in Engineering. Hobbies: Farming; Surfing. Address: 70-72 Emerald Road, Upper Beaconsfield, Vic 3808, Australia.

FLYNN Kevin A, b. 3 July 1963, Hartford, USA. Consulting Wood Technologist. Education: BS, Wood Sci and Technol, MS, Forestry, Univ Maine. Appointments: Rsch Assoc, Univ CA, Forest Products Lab; Cnsltng Wood Technol. Publications: Articles in profl jrnls. Memberships: Forest Products Soc; Soc of Wood Sci and Technol; Amn Alpine Club. Hobbies: Mountaineering; Backpacking; Music. Address: PO Box 805, El Cerrito, CA 94530-0805, USA.

FOGARTY John Francis (Hon Mr Justice), b. 9 June 1933. Judge. m. Alicia Fogarty, 3 s. Education: Univ Melbourne. Appointments: Barrister at Law, 1956-76; Ed, Vic Rprts, 1969-76; Vic Bar Cncl, Matrimonial Causes Cttee, 1975-76; Chmn, Family Law Cncl, 1983-86; Presiding Mbr, Bd of Austl Inst of Family Stdies, 1986-89; Judge, Family Crt Aust, Vic, 1976-; Judge, Appeal Div, Family Crt, 1983-; Chmn, Child Support Consultative Grp, 1987-91. Publications: Maintenance, Custody and Adoption, Police Summary Offences. Honour: AM, 1992. Listed in: Who's Who in Australia. Hobbies: Literature; History; Football. Address: c/o Judges Chambers, Family Court of Australia, Melbourne, Vic 3000, Australia.

FONDA Jane, b. 21 Dec 1937. Actress. m. (1) Roger Vadim, 1967, div 1973, 1 d; (2) Tom Hayden, 1973, div 1989, 1 s; (3) Ted Turner, 1991. Education: Vassar Coll. Films incl: Tall Story, 1960; A Walk on the Wild Side, 1962; Period of Adjustment, 1962; Sunday in New York, 1963; The Love Cage, 1963; La Ronde, 1964; Histoires extraordinaires, 1967; Barbarella, 1968; They Shoot Horses Don't They?, 1969; Klute, 1970; Steelyard Blues, 1972; Tout va bien, 1972; A Doll's House, 1973; The Blue Bird, 1975; Fun with Dick and Jane, 1976; Julia, 1977; Coming Home, 1978; California Suite, 1978; The Electric Horseman, 1979; The China Syndrome, 1979; Nine to Five, 1980; On Golden Pond, 1981; Roll-Over, 1981; Agnes of God, 1985; The Morning After, 1986; The Old Gringo, Stanley and Iris, 1990; Prodr Lakota Woman, 1994. Plays incl: There Was a Little Girl; Invitation to a March; The Fun Couple; Strange Interlude. Tv: The Dollmaker, ABC-TV, 1984. Publications: Jane Fonda's Workout Book, 1982; Women Coming of Age, 1984; Jane Fonda's new Workout and Weight Loss Program, 1986; Jane Fonda's New Pregnancy Workout and Total Birth Program, 1989; Jane Fonda Workout Video; Jane Fonda Cooking for Healthy Living, 1996. Honours: Emmy Awd for The Dollmaker; Acady Awd for Best Actress, 1972, 1979; Golden Globe Awd, 1978. Address: Fonda Films Inc, 1438 N Gower Street, Suite 22, Los Angeles, CA 90028, USA.

FOONG Boon Bee, b. 14 Nov 1960, Ipoh, Malaysia. Dermatologist. m. E M Taylor, 12 May 1992, 2 s. Education: MBBS, Univ Malaya, 1985; MRCP, England, 1991. Appointments: Med Offr, 1987; Clin Specialist, Dermatol, 1991; Cnslt Dermatologist, 1993. Honours: Dip in Genitourinary Med, Distinction, England, 1993. Memberships: Malaysian Med Assn; Dermatol Soc of Malaysia; Amn Acady of Dermatol; Acady of Med, Malaysia. Hobbies: Swimming; Gymnasium; Badminton; Travel; Reading; Computers. Address: 30 Jalan Ghazali Jawi, 31400 Ipoh, Malaysia.

FOOTS Kenneth John, b. 11 Aug 1941, Aust. Mining Engineer. m. 1964, 2 s, 2 d. Education: BE, 1964; CPA, 1984. Appointments: Chf Exec Offr, Ensham Resources Pty Ltd, 1991-; Present Dirshps: Austl Coal Rsch, Qld Mining Cncl; 202 Ltd; Lake Resources, NL. Memberships: Chmn, Qld Coal, 1988-90; Chmn, Austl Coal Assn, 1989; Chmn, Qld Coal Operators, 1990-; Dpty Chmn Austl Coal Assn; Fell, Austl Inst Mining and Metall; FAICD; CIMM; ASCPA. Listed in: Who's Who in Australia. Address: 1 Nankin Street, Fig Tree Pocket, Queensland 4069, Australia.

FORBES Dean Keith, b. 26 Nov 1949, Adelaide, Aust. 4 d. Education: BA (Hons); MA; PhD. Appointments: Prof, Schof Geog, Population & Environ Mngmt; Chmn, Intl Bd, Flinders Univ. Publications: China's Spatial Economy, 1991; Multiculturalism, Difference, Postmodernism, 1993; Asian Metropolis, 1996. Honour: Fell, Acady of Socl Scis in Aust, 1994. Hobbies: Walking; Reading. Address: 634 Anzac Highway, Glenelg East, Adelaide, Australia.

FORD David James, b. 1 Dec 1944, Brisbane, Qld. Aust. Medical Scientist. m. Mary-Anne Cook, 7 Dec 1974, 1 s, 1 d. Education: Fell, Austl Inst Medl Lab Sci, 1978; MSc, NSW Inst Technol, 1987. Appointments: Snr Medl Technologist, 1976-91, Prin Scientist, 1991-, Prince of Wales Hosp, Randwick, NSW. Memberships: Intl Soc Hematotherapy and Graft Engrng, 1993; The Bone Marrow Transplant Scientists Assn Australasia, 1993. Hobbies: Aviation - private pilot; Music. Address: Bone Marrow Transplant Laboratory, Prince of Wales Hospital, Randwick, NSW 2031, Australia.

FORD Gerald Rudolph Jr, b. 14 July 1913 Omaha Neb. Politician; Lawyer. m. Elizabeth Bloomer, 1948, 3 s, 1 d. Education: Univ of MI; Yale Univ Law Schl. Appointments: Partner Law firm Ford and Buchen, 1941-42; USN Serv, 1942-46; House Minority Ldr, 1965-73; VP of USA, 1973-74; Pres of USA, 1974-77; Visng Prof in Govt Univ of MI; Chmn Bd of Acady for Educl Devl, 1977; Advsr Am Express Co, 1981; Advsr Texas Com Bancshares Inc. Publications: Portrait of the Assassin - with John R Stiels; A Time to Heal - memoirs - 1979; The Humor and the Presidency, 1987. Honours: Num hon degrees and awds. Memberships: Mbr law firm Butterfield Keeney and Amberg, 1947-49; Mbr US HoR, 1949-73; Mbr Interparl Union Warsaw, 1959; Mbr Interparl Union Brussels, 1961; Mbr Interparl Union Belgrade, 1963; Mbr Warren Comm; Mbr Am Enterprise Ist; Bd Mbr The Traveler's Inc; Bd mbr Alexander & Alexander. Address: P O Box 927, Rancho Mirage, CA 92270, USA.

FORD Harrison, b. 1942 Chicago. Actor. m. (1) Mary Ford, 2 s; (2) Melissa Ford, 1 s, 1 d. Education: Ripon Coll. Appointments: Num tv appearances. Films incl: Dead Heat on a Merry-Go-Round, 1966; Luv, 1967; The Long Ride Home, 1967; Getting Straight, 1970; Zabriskie Point, 1970; The Conversation, 1974; American Graffiti, 1974; Star Wars, 1977; Heroes, 1977; Force 10 from Navarone, 1978; Hanover Street, 1979; Frisco Kid, 1979; The Empire Strikes Back, 1980; Raiders of the Lost Ark, 1981; Blade Runner, 1982; Return of the Jedi, 1983; Indiana Jones and the Temple of Doom, Witness, The Mosquito Coast, 1986; Working Girl, 1988; Frantic, 1988; Indiana Jones and the Last Crusade, 1989; Presumed Innocent,

1990; Regarding Henry, 1991; The Fugitive, 1992; Patriot Games, 1992; Clear and Present Danger, 1994; Sabrina, 1995; Air Force One, 1996. Address: 10279 Century Woods Drive, Los Angeles, CA 90067, USA.

FORD Jonathan Marcus, b. 4 May 1957, Brisbane, Aust. Historian. m. Brenda, 17 Dec 1988, 1 d. Education: Dip, Tchng, BA, Univ Ctrl Qld; MA (Qual), PhD, Hist, Univ Qld. Appointments: Tutor, Univ Qld, 1990-91, Sunshine Coast Univ, 1996; Histn, Geebung RSL, 1997; Histl Cnslt, The Carson Grp, 1998-. Publications: Allies in a Bind - Australia and the Netherlands East Indies Relations in the Second World War, 1996. Memberships: Profl Histns Assn, Qld, pres, 1997-99; Austl Inst of Intl Affairs, Qld, sec, 1988-90. Hobbies: Music; Bushwalking; Reading; Science fiction. Address: 7 Station Avenue, Northgate, Queensland 4013, Australia.

FORD Margaret Ellen, b. 12 Apr 1927. Retired Senior Chemistry Teacher. m. 3 Nov 1951, 3 s. Education: BSc w Hons; Dip in Educ. Appointments: Tchng Fell, Biochem Dept, Univ of Sydney, 1948-50; Austrl Stud Christian Travelling Sec, 1950-51; Snr Chem Tchr, Normanhurst Boys HS, 1974-94. Publications: End of a Beginning, 1963, 3rd edn, 1995; Beyond the Furthest Fences, 1966, 2nd edn, 1978. Hobbies: Opera; Theatre. Address: 34 Morven Rd, Niagara Park, NSW 2250, Australia.

FORDE Mary Marguerite (Leneen), b. 12 May 1955, Ottawa, Can. Former Governor of Queensland. m. (1) Francis Gerard Forde, 1955, 3 s, 2 d, (2) Angus McDonald, 1983. Education: Dip Med Tech, Ottawa; LLB, Qld, Aust, 1970. Appointments: Medl Lab Techn, Ottawa Gen Hosp, 1953-54; Med Lab Techn, Roy Brisbane Hosp, Aust, 1954-56; Sol, 1971-74, Ptnr, 1974-92, Deacons Graham and James (fmrly Cannan and Peterson); Appt Gov of Qld, 1992-97; Pres, Scouts Aust, 1997-; Chmn Commn of Enquiry into Abuse of Children in Govt Licensed Insts, 1998-. Honours: Paul Harris Fell, Rotary Club of Brisbane, 1990; Queenslander of Yr, 1991; AC, 1992; D St J; DUniv, Griffith, 1992; DUniv, QUT, 1993; DLitt, Qld, 1996. Membership: Past Intl Pres, 1990-92, Zonta Intl. Hobbies: Music; Theatre; Ballet; Art. Address: Government House, Brisbane, Qld 4001, Australia.

FORDYCE Horace Spencer Wills, b. 30 Mar 1914. Retired Executive Director. m. June Alison Vinton, 1946, 1 s, 1 d. Education: Melbourne HS; Univ HS. Appointments include: WWII Flt-Lt, RAAF, UK, Malta, ME, shot down at sea, 1942; POW, Italy, until 1943 and Stalag Luft 111 until end of war, was in Great Escape but returned to camp after shooting started; Flew w ANA after war; Cttee, Assn of Austl Philanthropic Trusts, 1977-87; Advsr to Sir William Angliss Charitable Fund, Vic, 1977-89; Exec Dir, Lord Mayors Fund, Melbourne, 1977-89; VP, Heraldry Soc of Aust, 1979-89; Trustee, Vic Blinded Soldier's Welfare Trust, 1978-97; First Sec, Ryder Cheshire Vic Homes Fndn, 1980-89. Homour: AE. Memberships include: Helping Hand for Mentally Retarded; Pres, ML Powell Fndn; Tstee, Vic Assn of Benevolent Socs; Tipping Fndn for the Mentally Retarded. Listed in: Who's Who in Australia; Australian Debretts. Hobbies: Heraldry; Art; Painting. Address: 24 Alexandra Avenue, Canterbury, Vic 3126, Australia.

FORERO DE SAADE Maria Teresa, b. 28 Feb 1939, Vergara, Cundinamarca. Politician; Medical Practitioner. m. Rafael Saade Abdala, 3 s. Education: Instituto Pedagogico Nacional; Colegio Departamental de la Merced; Pontificia Univ, Javeriana. Appointments: Prof, Paediats, Univ of Rosario, 1968-69; Fac of Nursing, Natl Red Cross, 1971-72; Dir Gen, Solsubsidio Clin for Children, 1974-82; Dpty Senator, 1978-82; Vice Min of Hlth, 1982; Min, Ministry of Hlth, 1982; Min of Labour and Socl Security, 1989-90. Address: Ministry of Labour and Social Security, Calle 20, No 8-18, Santafé de Bogotá, Colombia.

FORGAS Joseph Paul, b. 15 May 1947, Budapest, Hungary. Professor of Psychology. m. Letitia Jane Carr, 16 Mar 1974, 2 s. Education: BA (Hons) 1st Class, Macquarie Univ, Sydney, 1974; DPhil, 1977, DSc, 1990,

Univ of Oxford. Appointments: Lectr, Univ of NSW, Sydney, 1977-81; Prof, Univ of Gressen, Germany, 1982-85; Prof, Univ of NSW, Sydney, 1985-. Publications: 7 books inclng: Interpersonal Behaviour, 1985; Emotion and Social Judgement, 1991; Social Cognition, 1981; About 100 sci pprs. Honours: Austl Psychol Soc: Prize, 1974, Early Career Awd, 1980; St Catherine's Coll, Oxford Grad Schlshp, 1974-77; Alexander Von Humboldt Prize, Germany, 1993; Assoc Ed, Cnsltng Ed, 4 jrnls. Memberships: Acady Socl Scis in Aust; Div VIII, Amn Psych Soc; Soc of Experimental Socl Psychol; Eurn Assn for Exp Socl Psychol; Fell, Soc for Personality - Socl Psychol; Intl Soc for Rsch on Emotion; Intl Soc for Rsch on Personal Rels; Fell, Amn Psychol; Fell, Amn Psychol Soc. Hobbies: Gliding; Collecting antique cameras; Travel. Address: University of New South Wales, Sydney 2052, Australia.

FORGHANI-ABKENARI Bagher, b. 10 Mar 1936, Bandar-Anzali, Iran. Research Scientist. m. Nikoo Alavi, 12 June 1969, 2 children. Education: PhD, Virology, Justus Liebig Univ, Giessen, Germany, 1965. Appointments: Chf, Viral Immuno-serology sect of State of CA, Dept of Hlth Servs, Berkeley, CA. Publications: 9 chapts in virological book, auth or co-auth of more than 50 orig publs in natl & intl sci jrnls. Honours: Sci advsry bd of varicella-zoster virus (VZV) Rsch Fndn Inc, NY, NY, 1991. Memberships: Amn Soc for Microbiology, 1969; Regd Spec Microbiologist; Natl Registry of Microbiologist, 1974. Hobbies: Reading; Gardening. Address: 134 Lombardy Lane, Orinda, CA 94563, USA.

FORSYTH Elliott Christopher, b. 1 Feb 1924, SA, Aust. Emeritus Professor of French. m. Rona Lynette Williams, 29 May 1967, 2 d. Education: BA Hons, 1947, DipEd, 1950, Univ Adelaide; Docteur, Université de Paris, France, 1954. Appointments: Tchr, The Friends Sch, Hobart, Tas, 1947-49; Lectr, Snr Lectr, French, Univ Adelaide, SA, 1954-66; Visng Lectr, French, Univ WI, USA, 1963-65; Fndn Prof French, 1966-87, Emer Prof, 1988-, La Trobe Univ, Melbourne, Vic; Visng Prof, Univ of Melbourne, 1992. Publications: La Tragédie française de Jodelle à Corneille (1553-1640): le thème de la vengeance, 1962, 2nd ed, 1994; J de la Taille, Saul le furieux..., critical ed, 1968; Concordance des Tragiques d'A d'Aubigné, 1984; Ed, Baudin in Australian Waters, 1988. Honours: Boursier, Gouvernement Français, 1951-53; Officier, 1971, Commandeur, 1983, Ordre des Palmes Académiques. Memberships: Fell, Austl Acady Hums; Fell, Austl Coll Educ; Uniting Ch Aust; Assn des Amis d'A d'Aubigné. Hobbies: Music; Photography; Church activities. Address: 25 Jacka Street, North Balwyn, Vic 3104, Australia.

FORSYTH Kevin Douglas, b. 20 June 1953, Aust. Professor of Academic Medicine. m. Johanna, 3 s, 1 d. Education: MB ChB; MD; PhD; FRACP; FRCPA. Appointments: Lectr, Pediatric Immunol Univ of London; Hd, Pediatric Immunol, Childrens Hosp, Perth; Prof, Hd of Pediat, Flinders IUniv. Publications: Multiple pprs and books on pediats and pediat immunol/infection. Memberships: Chmn, Pediat Profl Hds Cttee; Chmn, Pediat Interactive Educ; Chmn, Austl Immunisation Forum. Hobbies: Music; Travel.

FORTUNE John A, b. 9 Apr 1929, England. Manager; Consultant. m. Lucy Yan, June 1958, 2 s. Education: RMA Sandhurst, Fell Intl Civil Def Org; FEMA Grad; ACDC Grad. Appointments: Commissioned RMA Sandhurst, 1949; Overseas Civil Serv, Hong Kong Govt, 1953; Gen Mngr, Golf/Mariner, 1989; Dir, Hong Kong Exhib/Convention Orgs Suppliers' Assn, 1994; Mng Dir, J A Fortune Cnslts, 1992. Publications: Sev publs inclng: On Counter; Disaster Planning. Honours: Hong Kong Mountaineering Cncl, Tech Cnslts Hong Kong Comm Chest; ISO, 1978; ED, 1966; Queens Silver Jubilee Medal; CDLSM, 1987. Memberships: Inst Civil Defence, 1988; Pres, Hong Kong Underwater Assn, 1976-, VP. Hobbies: Scuba Diving; Golf; Underwater Photography; Remote Area Exploration. Address: 17F Blk 34 Baguio Villa, 550 Victoria Road, Pok Fu Lam, Hong Kong.

FORTUNE Paul John Alfred, b. 26 Apr 1959, Hong Kong. Lawyer; Solicitor. Education: LLB, Hons, Wales. Appointments: Sol, Supreme Court, Eng, 1985; Supreme Crt, Hong Kong, 1987; Supreme Crt, Singapore, 1995; Ptnr, Richards Butler, Hong Kong, 1992-95; Ptnr, NG and Ptnrs, 1995-98; Ptnr, Sinclair Roche and Temperley, Hong Kong, 1998-. Publications: Contbr for Hong Kong-Lloyds Worldwide Arrest Handbook, 1997. Memberships: Chmn, Hong Kong MLA Arrest Cttee; Hong Kong, MLA Exec Cttee; IMO, UNCTAD Conv, Hong Kong deleg, Geneva, 1999. Hobbies: Politics; Travel; Geography; Music; Film; The sea. Address: Block 36, 10F Lower Baguio Villa, 555 Victoria Rd, Hong Kong.

FORWOOD William, b. 21 Oct 1946, Adelaide, Australia. Member of Parliament. m. Anne, 1 July 1989, 1 s, 2 d. Education: BCom; FCPA. Appointments: MP for Templestowe, 1992; Chmn, Pub Accts and Estimates Cttee, 1996; Parly Sec to the Premier, 1998. Membership: Cncl, Univ of Melbourne, 1993-. Hobbies: Sports; Reading. Address: c/o Parliament House, Melbourne, Victoria, Australia.

FOSTER David John, b. 20 Mar 1957, Hobart, Tasmania, Australia. Professional Axeman. m. Jan, 15 May 1976, 1 s, 3 d. Honours: Order of Aust Medal; Austl Axeman of Yr, 9 times in row; Champion Axeman Awd; World 400mm Underhand Championship; World 600mm Double Handed Sawing Championship; Axeman of the Decade, 1990; Selected as 1 of 15 Austl Achievers of the Yr, 1989; 1989 Lindy Awd; Tasmanian Axeman of Yr, 1990; Announced as first Advance Aust Amb for Tasmania, 1992; Melvin Jones Fellowship Awd, 1994; Commendation from Gov of Tasmania, 1995; Paul Harris Fellowship Awd, 1995; Tasmanian of Yr for 1995; Tasmanian Fndng Mbr and Amb for Olympic Club, 1998; Natl Family Day Ambs, 1998; Dir of Natl Aust Day Cncl, 1998; Tasmanian Sporting Personality of Yr, 1999. Address: David Foster Industries, 389 Manuka Road, Kettering, Tasmania, 7155, Australia.

FOSTER David Manning, b. 15 May 1944, Katoomba, NSW, Aust. Writer. m. Gerda Busch, 1 Sept 1975, 2 s, 4 d. Education: BS (Sydney), 1967; PhD, Austl Natl Univ, 1970. Publications: The Pure Land, 1974; The Empathy Experiment, 1977; Moonlite, 1981; Plumbum, 1983; Dog Rock: A Postal Pastoral, 1985; The Adventures of Christian Rosy Cross, 1986; Testostero, 1987; The Pale Blue Crochet Coathanger Cover, 1988; Mates of Mars, 1991; Self Portraits (Ed), 1991; A Slab of Fosters, 1994; The Glade Within the Grove, 1996; The Ballad of Erinungarah, 1997; Crossing the Blue Mountain (contbr), 1997; In the New Country, 1999; Studs and Nogs (essays), 1999; Short stories: North South West: Three Novellas, 1973; Escape to Reality, 1977; Hitting the Wall: Two Novellas, 1989. Honours: The Age Awd, 1974; Austl Natl Book Cncl Awd, 1981; NSW Premier's Fellshp, 1986; Keating Fellshp, 1991-94; James Joyce Fndn Awd, 1996; Miles Franklin Awd, 1997; Shortlisted, Intl Dublin IMPAC AWd, 1998. Address: PO Box 57, Bundanoon, New South Wales, 2578, Australia.

FOSTER Jodie, b. 19 Nov 1962, Los Angeles. Actress; Film Dir. Education: Yale Univ. Appointments: Acting debut in tv prog Mayberry, 1969. Films incl: Napoleon and Samantha, 1972; Kansas City Bomber, 1972; Menace of the Mountain, One Little Indian, 1973; Tom Sawyer, 1973; Alice Doesn't Live Here Any More, 1975; Taxi Driver, 1976; Echoes of a Summer, 1976; Bugsy Malone, 1976; Freaky Friday Foxes, 1980; Carny, 1980; Hotel New Hampshire, 1984; The Blood of Others, 1984; Siesta, 1986; Five Corners, 1986; The Accused, 1988; Stealing Home, 1988; Catchfire, 1990; The Silence of the Lambs, 1990; Little Man Tate, also dir, 1991; Shadows and Fog, 1992; Sommersby, 1993; Maverick, 1994; Nell, 1994; Home for the Holidays, dir, co-prodr only, 1996; Contact, 1997; The Baby Dance, exec prodr only, 1997; Waking the Dead, exec prodr only, 1998. Honours: Acady Awd for Best Actress for The Accused, 1989; Acady Awd for Best Actress for Silence of the Lambs, 1992; Hon DFA, Yale, 1997. Address: EGG Pictures Production Co, 7920 Sunset Boulevard, Suite 200, Los Angeles, CA 90046, USA.

FOSTER Leo Leslie, b. 25 June 1933, Melbourne, Vic, Aust. Emeritus Professor. m. (1) Mary Lenore Fenselau, dec, 2 s, 1 d, (2) Elaine Betty Roysland, 16 Dec 1987, 1 d. Education: BSc, 1955, BEd, 1960, MEd, 1968, Univ Melbourne; PhD, Univ WI, Madison, USA, 1976. Appointments: Secnd Tchr, 1957-61; Lectr, Snr Lectr, Melbourne Secnd Tchrs Coll, 1962-70; Educ Dev Offr, 1970-71, Hd, Dept External Stdys, 1972-73, Hd, Stud Progs, Fac Educ, 1974-76, Dean, Fac Educ, 1977-81, WA Inst Technol (now Curtin Univ Technol); Dir, Phillip Inst Technol, Bundoora, Vic, 1982-92; Dpty Vice Chan, Acad Servs, RMIT Univ, 1992-94. Honours: Emer Prof, RMIT Univ, 1995; Rotary Fndn Dist Serv Awd, 1997. Memberships: Fell, Austl Coll Educ; Victorian Inst Educl Rsch, VP, 1988-94; Austl Natl Commn UNESCO, 1981-86; Austl Cncl Educl Rsch, 1987-91; Pres, Assn for Intellectually Disabled Adults, 1998-. Hobbies: Walking; Sporting activities; Theatre. Listed in: Who's Who in Australia. Address: Unit 6, 57 Locksley Road, Ivanhoe, Vic 3079, Australia.

FOSTER Michael Leader (The Hon Justice), b. 27 Nov 1928, Sydney, NSW, Aust. Retired Federal Court Judge. m. Ruth Laws, 6 Jan 1960, 1 s, 2 d. Education: Univ Sydney, 1946-52; BA, LLM, Sydney. Appointments: Admitted Bar, NSW, 1955; QC, 1974; Chmn, Cttee Enquiry into Psychosurg, 1977; Mbr, NSW Medl Bd, 1979-81; VP, NSW Bar Assn, 1980-81; Judge, Supreme Crt NSW, 1981-87; Judge, Fed Crt Aust, 1987-99; Pres, Austl Fed Police Disciplinary Tribunal, 1990-99. Hobbies: Sailing; Golf. Address: 19 Ruby Street, Mosman, Australia 2088.

FOTHERINGHAM Brian James, b. 29 Sept 1941. Medical Superintendent. m. Janet Fotheringham, 3 June 1967, 3 s. Education: Univ Adelaide. Appointments: Medl Offr, St John Ambulance Brig, 1961-; Asst Medl Supt, 1971-74, Medl Supt, 1979-96, Dir of Medl Projs, 1996-, Adelaide Children's Hosp, (now known as Women's and Children's Hosp) Adelaide, SA, 1971-74; Medl Supt, Modbury Hosp, 1975-78; Commnr, St John Ambulance Brig, SA Dist, 1987-90. Publication: Co-auth, Casualty Care and Transport, 1975. Honours: AM, 1989; KStJ, 1990. Hobbies: Tennis; Philately. Address: 3 Caithness Avenue, Beaumont, SA 5066, Australia.

FOWLER Murray Elwood, b. 17 July 1928, Glendale, WA, USA. Veterinarian, University of California. m. Audrey Cooley, 5 June 1950, 2 s, 3 d. Education: BS; DVM. Appointments: Student Instr, IA State Univ, Ames IA, 1953-55; Priv Vet Prac, San Fernando Valley, CA, 1955-58; Instr to Assoc Prof, Sch of Vet Med, Univ of CA, Davis, 1958-72; Rsch Assoc, Toxicological Medl Rsch Cncl Labs, Carshalton, Eng, 1964-65; Prof of Vet Med, Univ of CA, Davis, 1972; Rsch Fell, San Diego Zool Gdn, San Diego, 1972-73; Prof, Vet Med, Fac of Vet Med, Makerere Univ, Kampala, Uganda, 1973; Prof Emer, Univ of CA, 1991. Publications: 215 profl pprs; 1 CDROM Interactive prog: Poisonous Plants - A Veterinary Guide to Toxic Syndromes; Auth, co-auth, prin ed of 15 books inclng: Medicine and Surgery of South American Camelids, 1998; Zoo and Wild Animal Medicine, 1998; Color Atlas of Camelid Hematology, 1998. Honours include: Stange Mem Alumni Awd, Vet Sch, IA State Univ, Ames, IA, 1989; Maagizo Awd, Sacramento Zool Soc, 1992; Park Davis Vet Awd, Brit Vet Zool Soc, London, 1994; Murray E Fowler Achievement Awd, Intl Llama Assn, Denver, CO, 1995; Emil P Dolensk Mem Awd, Amn Assn of Zoo Vets, 1995. Alpha Zeta; Gamma Sigma Delta; Phi Zeta; Phi Kappa Phi; Sigma Xi. Memberships: Dipl, Amn Bd of Vet Toxicology; Dipl, Amn Coll of Vet Internal Med; Amn Assn of Zoo Vets, Pres, 1975-76; Charter Dipl, Amn Coll of Zool Med, Pres, 1983-90; Amn Assn of Avian Vets; Intl Assn Aquatic Animal Med; Amn Vet Medl Assn; CA Vet Medl Assn. Hobbies: Photography; Natural History; Cabinet making; Scouting. Address: 427 Cabrillo Avenue, Davis, CA 95616, USA.

FOWLER Thurley, b. 21 Mar 1925, Aust. m. G E Fowler, 18 Aug 1956, 1 s, 2 d. Publications: Books include: The Green Wind, 1985; The Wind is Silver, 1991; Not Again, Dad, 1994; Sev short stories. Honours: Book

of the Yr, 1986; Short List, Book of the Yr, 195. Hobbies: Tenpin bowling; Scrabble; Reading; Home and family. Address: 16 Lee Street, Frankston, Victoria 3199, Australia.

FOWLER-SMITH Louise, b. 2 Dec 1955, Sydney, Australia. Artist; Lecturer. 1 d. Education: MFA, Univ CA, Santa Barbara; BFA, City Art Inst, Sydney; Grad Dip, Profl Art Stdies, Alexander Mackie CAE; Dip, Art Educ, Alexander Mackie CAE. Appointment: Lectr, Coll of Fine Arts, Univ NSW. Creative Works: 7 solo exhbns, 34 grp exhbns. Honour: WC & FW Matthews Fellshp, Univ CA, Santa Barbara, 1983. Membership: Art Gallery of NSW. Hobbies: Fine Arts; Philosophy. Address: The School of Art, College of Fine Arts, University of New South Wales, PO Box 259, Paddington, NSW 2021, Australia.

FOX James Walter, b. 15 Dec 1913, Grimsby, Eng. (NZ citizen). Retired Associate Professor of Geography. m. Emily Louisa Croft, 17 Nov 1945. Education: BA Hons, Univ Coll, Nottingham, 1936; Dip Ed, London Univ Inst Educ, 1937; PhD, Univ Auckland, NZ, 1963. Appointments: Schmaster, Grimsby, Eng, 1937-40; RAF, 1940-45; Lectr, Snr Lectr, Univ Auckland, NZ, 1947-62; Assoc Prof, Univ New Eng, Aust, 1963-77; Univ Ombudsman, 1983-98. Publications include: New Zealand: A Regional View; Western Samoa; 40 papers in learned jrnls. Honours: Hon Life Mbr, NZ Geogl Soc; Hon Life Mbr, NSW Geogl Soc. Memberships include: Inst Brit Geogs; Inst Austl Geogs; Past Hon Ed, NZ Geographer; Past Mbr, NSW Bd Snr Sch Stdys, Geog Syll and Exam Cttees; FRGS. Hobbies: Travel; Photography; Music; Wine; Steam railways. Address: 109 Kentucky Street, Armidale, NSW 2350, Australia.

FOX Russell Walter, b. 30 Sept 1920, Sydney, NSW, Aust. Retired Judge; Writer. m. Shirley Bradfield, 6 Feb 1943, 3 s, 1 d. Education: Grad, Roy Mil Coll, Duntroon, 1940; LLB, Univ Sydney, 1949. Appointments: Lt, Austl Staff Corps, 1940-42; Cap, Austl Imperial Force, 1942-45; NSW Bar, 1949-67; QC, 1963; Lectr, Postgrad Stdys, Univ Sydney, 1963-67; Snr Judge, 1967-77, Chf Judge, 1977, ACT; Judge, Fed Crt, 1977-89; Austl Amb at Large, Nuclear Non-Proliferation, 1977-80; Chf Judge, Norfolk Is, 1982-89; Visng Prof, Univ Technol, Sydney, 1994-. Publications: Gen Ed, Australian Law Journal, 1958-67; Legal Essays; Jntly w I Mathews, Drugs Policy, Fact, Fiction and the Future, 1992; Justice in the 21st Century, forthcoming. Honour: AC, 1989. Memberships: Hon Assoc, Hon Rsch Fell, 1989-92, Univ Sydney; Fac Law, Austl Natl Univ, 1968-77; Pres, Sydney Univ Law Graduates Assn, 1966-68; Fellshp Cttee, Churchill Fndn, 1965-79; Pres, Comnr, Ranger Uranium Environl Inquiry, 1975-79. Hobbies: Swimming; Reading; Writing. Address: PO Box 641, Norfolk Island, Australia 2899.

FOXLEY RIOSECO Alejandro, b. 26 May 1939, Vina del Mar. Politician; Economist. m. Gisela Tapia, 1963, 2 c. Education: Univ of WI; Harvard Univ; Catholic Univ Valparaiso. Appointments: Ford Intl Fell, 1963-64; Daugherty Fndn Fell, 1965-66; Dir Global Plng Div Natl Plng Off Govt of Chile, 1967-70; Ford Fndn Fell, 1970; Dir Cntr for Natl Plng Studies Catholic Univ of Chile, 1970-76; Visng Fell Univ of Sussex, 1973, Oxford 1975, MIT 1978; Pres Corp for Latin-Am Econ Rsch - CIEPLAN - Santiago, 1976-90; Assoc Ed Journal of Development Economics, 1977-; Helen Kellogg Prof of Econs - part-time - and Intl Dev Univ of Notre Dame, 1982-; Min of Fin, 1990-94; Pres Christian Dem - PDC - 1994. Publications: Redistributive Effects of Government Programmes; Income Distribution in Latin-America; Estrategia de Desarrollo y Modelos de Planificacion; Legados del Monetarismo: Artentina y Chile; Para una Democracia Estable, 1985; Chile y su futuro: un pais posible, 1989; Chile puede mas, 1989; Num articles and working papers. Memberships: Mbr Joint Cttee Latin-Am Studies Socl Sci Rsch Cncl NY, 1975-78; Mbr Exec Cncl Latin-Am Socl Sci Cncl - CLACSO - 1975-81; Mbr Exec Cttee Interamerican Dialogue WA; Mbr Intl Advsry Bd Journal Latin Am Studies. Address: Partido Democrata Cristiano - PDC, Carmen 8, 6o, Santiago, Chile.

FRAENKEL Aviezri, b. 7 June 1929, Munich, Germany. Mathematician; Computer Scientist. m. Shaula, 7 June 1956, 5 s, 1 d. Education: BSEE, Dip, Elctr Engr, 1953, MSEE, 1957, Israel Inst Technol; PhD, Maths, UCLA, 1961. Appointments: Weizmann Inst of Sci, Univ of CA, Los Angeles, Univ of OR, Bar Ilan Univ. Publications: 150 publs in sci lit; Mbr editl bd, Discrete Math; Intl Jrnl Appl Math, Electronic Jrnl Combinatorics, Theoretical Computer Science; Fndr, 1963, Dir, 1963-75, Cnslt, 1975-, Response Storage and Retrieval Project. Honours: Feder Fndn Prize, 1972; Israel Jubilee Quality Initiative Prize, 1998. Memberships: Israel Math Union, Chmn, 1970-72; Info Process Assn Israel, Bulletin Fndr, Ed, 1972-75, Cncl Mbr, 1971-82; Amn Maths Soc; Maths Assn Am; Assn Computing Machinery. Address: Department of Computer Science & Applied Maths, Weizmann Institute of Science, Rehovot 76100, Israel.

FRAENKEL Gustav Julius, b. 28 May 1919, Berlin, Germany. Consultant in Medical Education and Services. m. Ruth Marie Gwendolyn Anderson, 4 May 1957, dec 1990, 2 s, 1 d. Education: Univ Oxford, Eng, 1938-43; BA, 1941; BM, 1943; BCh, 1943; FRCS, 1946; MCh, 1949; MA, 1954; FRACS, 1959; FACS, 1962; FRACMA, 1972. Appointments: House Surg, Surg Registrar, Harefield EMS Hosp, 1943-45; Res Surg Offr, Worcester Roy Infirmary, 1945-46; Snr Surg Registrar, Nottingham Gen Hosp, 1946-50; Surg Tutor, Univ Oxford, 1951-55; Nuffield Inst Medl Rsch, 1956; Ralph Barnett Prof Surg, Univ Otago, NZ, 1958-70; Fndn Dean, Sch Med, Flinders Univ, SA, 1970-84; Co-ord Rsch, Roy Children's Hosp, Melbourne, Vic, 1985-90; Rsch Review and Recommendation, Roy Adelaide Hosp, 1986; Queen Elizabeth Hosp, Adelaide, 1987; Univ Hosp, Canberra Hosps, 1989. Publications include: Hugh Cairns, First Nuffield Professor of Surgery, University of Oxford, 1991, reprinted, 1994; The Medical Board of South Australia 1844-1994, 1994; Articles; Chapts in var books. Honours: Disting Serv Awd, Flinders Univ, 1979; Hon MD, Flinders, 1985; AM, 1985; Hon FFARACS, 1986. Memberships: Corresp Mbr, Surg Rsch Soc, UK; Fndng Mbr, Surg Rsch Soc Australasia; Austl Medl Assn. Address: 12 Lochwinnoch Road, Torrens Park, SA 5062, Australia.

FRAME Janet, b. 1924 Dunedin. Writer. Education: Dunedin Trng Coll; Otago Univ. Publications: Lagoon, 1951; Owls do Cry, 1957; Faces in the Water, 1961; The Edge of the Alphabet, 1962; Scented Gardens for the Blind, 1963; The Reservoir, stories; Snowman, Snowman, fables; The Adaptable Man, 1965; A State of Siege, 1967; The Pocket Mirror, poetry; Yellow Flowers in the Antipodean Room, 1968; Mona Minim and the Smell of the Sun, children's book, 1969; Intensive Care, novel, 1971; Daughter Buffalo, novel, 1972; Living in the Maniototo, novel, 1979; The Carpathians, 1988; An Autobiography, 1990. Honours: Hubert Ch Awd for NZ Prose; NZ Schlshp in Letters, 1964; Burns Fell Otago Univ Dunedin.

FRAME Thomas Robert, b. 7 Oct 1962, Stanmore, NSW, Aust. Anglican Clergyman. m. Helen Mary Bardsley, 10 Dec 1983, 2 d. Education: DipEd, Melbourne Univ; MA (Hons), Applied Theol, Kent, UK; MTh, Sydney Coll of Divinity; PhD, Hist, Univ of NSW. Appointments: Roy Austl Navy, 1979-92; Asst Priest, St Johns Wagga Wagga, 1993-95; Rector, St James, Binda, 1995-; Lucas Took Schl, Univ of Kent, Canterbury. Publications: First In, Last Out: The Navy at Gallipoli, 1990; The Garden Island, 1990; Where Fate Calls: The HMAS Voyager Disaster, 1992; Pacific Ptnrs, 1992; HMAS Sydney: Loss & Controversy, 1993; Labouring in Vain: A History of Bishopthorpe, 1996; Binding Ties, 1997. Membership: MACE, 1994. Hobbies: Cycling; Golf. Address: St James' Anglican Rectory, Jarvis Street, Binda, NSW 2583, Australia.

FRANCE Evelyn Christine, b. 23 Dec 1939, Sydney, Australia. Art Historian. m. Stephen France, 22 Dec 1962, 1 d. Education: BA, Sydney Univ. Publications: Justin O'Brien: Image and Icon, 1987; The Art of Margaret Olley, 1990; Marea Gazzard: Form and Clay, 1994; The Art of Jean Appleton, 1998. Address: Old Baerami, Baerami, New South Wales 2333, Australia.

FRANCE George Roger Wayne, b. 27 Dec 1944, Dunedin, NZ. Chartered Accountant. m. Julie Norman, 2 s, 1 d. Education: BCom, Univ of Canterbury. Appointments: Fmr Mbr, Mkt Surveillance Panel of NZ Exchange; Fmr Mngng Ptnr, Auckland Off, Coopers & Lybrand; Currently Dir, Tappenden Holdings Ltd and Team NZ Ltd; Mbr Governance Bd, Pricewaterhouse Coopers, NZ; Ptnr in Charge of Corp Value Cnsltng, Asia Pacific th, Pricewaterhouse Coopers. Membership: Inst Chartered Accts of NZ. Hobbies: Sailing; Skiing; Reading. Address: Pricewaterhouse Coopers, Private Bag 92 162, Auckland, New Zealand.

FRANCIS John, b. 22 May 1915. Emeritus Professor. m. (1) Sarah Anne Comber Hunt, 1940, dec 1984, 2 s, 1 dec, 1 d, (2) Hazel Mellick, 1985. Appointments: Demonstrator, Bacteriology, Roy Vet Coll, 1939-40; Rsch Offr, Foot and Mouth Disease Rsch Stn, Eng, 1940-43; ICI Pharm Division, 1943-52; Prof, Vet Preventive Med and Pub Hlth (now Vet Path), 1952-83, Prof Emer, 1983-, Univ Queensland. Honours include: Medal Hon, US Armed Forces Inst Path, 1949; Assoc Mbr, All Sci Cttees, Intl Union Against Tuberculosis, Paris, 1950-86; Hon Dip, Amn Vet Epidemiology Soc, 1974; CBE, 1976; Gilruth Prize, Meritorious Serv Vet Sci, Aust, 1984; FRS Queensland, Aust, 1989; John Francis Virology Lab and John Francis Dr named by Senate, Univ Queensland, 1990; Fell, Roy Coll Vet Surgs, London; Fell, Austl Coll Vet Scientists; Mbr, WHO Expert Advsry Panel on Zooses, 1967-80. Memberships include: Roy Soc Queensland, Pres, 1969-70; Life Mbr, Drought Master Stud Breeders Soc; Life Mbr, Rural Press Club, Queensland. Hobbies: Breeding cattle; Riding; History. Address: Holkham, 11 Fenchurch Street, Fig Tree Pocket, Queensland 4069, Australia.

FRANJIEH Sleiman, b. 18 Oct 1965. Appointments: Elected to Parl, 1990, 1992, 1996; Min of State for Housing and Coops, Munic and Rural Affairs, Pub Hlth.

FRANKHAM Richard, b. 4 Apr 1942, Singleton, NSW, Aust. University Professor. m. Annette Lindsay, 7 Oct 1994, 2 s. Education: BSc, Agric (Hons), Univ Sydney, 1964; PhD, Univ Sydney, 1968. Appointments: Rsch Scientist, Agric, Can, Lacombe, Alberta, Can, 1967-69; Postdoct Fell, Univ Chgo, 1969-71; Lectr, Macquarie Univ, Sydney, 1973-81; Snr Lectr, MU, 1973-81; Assoc Prof, MU, 1981-97; Prof, MU, 1997-. Publications: Over 90 sci publs in intl jrnls. Honours: Fell Zool Soc of London; Mbr, Editl Bds of Genetical Rsch, Animal Conservation; Mbr, Conservation Breeding Spec Grp; Species Survival Commn; IUCN (World Conservation Union). Memberships: Genetics Soc of Aust, Treas, 1973-75, Auditor, 1987-90; Soc for Conservation Biology (organising cttee), 1998; Intl Prog Cttee, 2nd Intl Conf, Quantitative Genetics, Raleigh, NC, USA. Hobbies: Bushwalking; Travel; Golf; Reading. Address: Key Centre for Biodiversity & Bioresources, Department of Biological Sciences, Macquarie University, NSW 2109, Australia.

FRANKLIN James Ashley (Jim), b. 14 Feb 1959. Composer; Performing Musician. m. Margit Spaeth, 18 Dec 1991. Education: BMus w Hons, 1981, MMus w Hons, 1987, PhD, 1998, Univ of Sydney; Shihan (Master Perf), Intl Shakuhachi Trng Cntr, Japan, 1996. Appointments: Freelance Composer and Perf, 1978-; Tutor and Lectr in Contemp West, Electronic and Computer Music, Sydney Univ, 1987-89, 1991-98; Lectr, 1994-95, Snr Lrctr, 1996-, Music Technol, Univ of West Sydney, Nepean. Creative works include: Across the Swan's Riding, 1981; Fragments of a Broken Land, 1984; Giving Shape, 1986; The Hours of the Sea-Bird, 1988; Der japanische Garten, 1990; Middle Dance, 1992; Fountain of Light, collaboration w Riley Lee, 1993; Naratic Visions, suite vern, 1994; Heart, 1995; Empty Hands No 1 and 2, 1996; Three Treasures: Columns and Webs, 1996; Water Spirits (w Satsuki Odamura), 1997; Hibiki II: Tokyo Inter Arts, Sydney, 1997; Butsuga, 1999; Moon Road to Dawn (co-auth), 1999. Honours: Donald Peart Mem Prize, 1981; Young Composers' Orchl Awd for, Across the Swan's Riding, Austl Brdcstng Commn, 1981; Mention: for Tryptich III: Le Stagioni, Valentine Bucchi Prize, 1985; Selection of Boundaries, for The Child of Flame, For Perf at the Gaudeamus Intl Music Week, Amsterdam, 1986; Innovative Projs Grants, Austl Cncl, 1989, 1992, 1993; Prizes for Best Wrk in Arts and Entertainment Category and Best Orig Soundtrack for Der Japanische Garten, Munich Multi-Media Fest, 1990; Asialink Residency at Kunitachi Coll, Tokyo, 1996. Memberships: Austl Music Cntr, 1987-; Musicians' Union of Aust, 1988-; Fellshp of Austl Composers, 1991-; Austl Performing Rights Assn, 1994-; Intl Computer Music Assn, 1996-. Hobbies: Literature; Languages; Mathematics; Computer programming. Address: 2 Garden Square, Faulconbridge, NSW 2777, Australia.

FRANKLIN James William, b. 19 June 1953, Sydney, Aust. Academic. m. Alexandra, 5 Jan 1985. Education: MA (Sydney); PhD (Warwick). Appointments: Lectr, Snr Lectr, Maths, Univ NSW. Publications: Introduction to Proof in Mathematics, 1988, 1996. Membership: Austl Math Soc. Address: School of Mathematics, University of New South Wales, Sydney 2052, Australia.

FRANKLIN Richard (Bruce), b. 15 July 1948. Film Producer; Director. m. 15 Jan 1972, 2 s,1 d. Education: MA (equiv), Univ South CA. Appointments include: Lectr, Comm, Hawthorn State Coll, 1975-77; Guest Lectr, USC, UCLA, NYU, UN Carolina, VCA Sch Film & TV, 1982-92; Lectr (pt-time), RMIT, 1995-. Creative Works: Films (Dir/Prodr/Co-Prodr): The True Story Of Eskimo Nell, 1975; Patrick, 1978; The Blue Lagoon, 1980; Roadgames, 1981; Psycho II, 1983; Cloak & Dagger, 1984; Link, 1986; F/X2, 1991; Hotel Sorrento (also co-writer) 1994; Brilliant Lies (also co-writer), 1995; TV (Dir): Pilot Episode, Beauty And The Beast (CBS Network, USA), 1987; Pilot Episode, A Fine Romance (ABC Network USA), 1988; Running Delilah (ABC Network), 1992; 9 Shorts; Var TV Commercials incl awd-winning Railway Crossing, 1987. Screenplays: The House On The Strand, 1993; Hotel Sorrento, 1994; Brilliant Lies, 1995; Book: Words Alone, 1995; Sch textbook: Fred Ott Sneezes For Edison, 1974; Report on Film Study in Victorian Secondary Schools, ATFAV, 1973; Articles & Reviews in American Film, Cinema Papers, The Age, National Times, 1969-95. Honours: For Patrick: Grand Prix, Avoriez, France, Best For Film, Acady SF USA, Best Dir, Sitges, Spain, 1978; Prix Spec du Jury, Link, 1986; FACTS Awd, for Coml, Railway Crossing, 1987; Emmy, for Beauty And The Beast, 1988; 10 AFI Awds inclng: Best Screenplay Adaption, Best Supporting Actor, Ldng Nominee for Hotel Sorrento, 1995. Memberships: Dirs Guild Am; Melbourne Cricket Club. Hobbies: Theatre; Musical Theatre. Address: c/o Anthony Williams, 1st Floor, 50 Oxford Street, Paddington, NSW 2021, Australia.

FRANKLIN Richard Langdon, b. 13 July 1925, Melbourne, Vic, Aust. Emeritus Professor of Philosophy (retired). m. Margaret Ann Burgoyne, 20 Dec 1951, dec 1996, 4 s. Education: LLB, 1948, LLM, 1949, BA, 1952, MA, 1955, Univ Melbourne; PhD, Univ WA, 1963. Appointments: War Serv, RAAF, 1944-45; Assoc to Chf Justice of Vic, 1950; Bar, Supreme Crt Vic, 1951-52; Temporary Lectr, Lectr, Snr Lectr, Philos, Univ WA, 1956-67; Prof, Hd, Dept Philos, Univ New Eng, 1968-85. Publications include: Freewill and Determinism: A Study of Rival Conceptions of Man, 1968; The Search for Understanding, 1995; Contbr, articles to legal, philosl and theol jrnls. Memberships: Australasian Assn Philos, Pres, 1969-70; Austl Assn Stdy of Relig; Armidale Decorative and Fine Arts Soc, Chmn, 1992-96; Armidale Univ of the Third Age, Pres, 1993-97. Hobbies: Swimming; Gardening; Reading; Lay Reader, Anglican Church. Address: 8 Lambs Avenue, Armidale, NSW 2350, Australia.

FRANKLYN Edward Morrissey (The Hon), b. 1 Aug 1928, WA, Aust. Retired Supreme Court Judge. m. Margaret Louise Franklyn, 20 Sept 1952, 3 s, 3 d. Education: LLB Aquinas Coll, Univ WA, 1948; Admitted to Prac, 1951. Appointments: Barrister, Solicitor, Geraldton and Perth, WA, to 1967; Joined Indep Bar,

1968; Appointed QC, 1974; Mbr, Barristers Bd WA, 1974-84; Pres, Bar Assn WA, 1975-78; Pres, Austl Bar Cncl, 1976-77; Appointed Bench, Supreme Crt WA, 1984-98; Fmr Chmn, Land Valuers Licensing Bd; Dpty Pres, Natl Native Title Tribunal, 1998-. Memberships: Fmr Mbr, Law Soc WA; Soc Reform Criminal Law; Austl Inst Judicial Admin; Weld Club; Roy Perth Golf Club; Chmn, Advsry Bd, Coll of Law, Univ Notre Dame Aust; Advsry Bd, Law sch, Univ Western Aust; Cncl Mbr, Western Aust Yth Orch Assn; Fmr Tree, Italian Austl Friendshp Awd (WA). Hobbies: Golf; Sailing; Swimming. Address: 8 The Coombe, Mosman Park, Western Australia 6012, Australia.

FRAPPELL Ruth Meredith, (Ruth Teale), b. 8 Mar 1942, Bathurst, NSW, Aust. Academic; Freelance Writer. m. Leighton Frappell, 15 Aug 1970, 1 s, 2 d. Education: BA, 1963; LMusA, Austl Music Exam Bd, 1964; MA, 1968; PhD, Univ of Sydney, 1992. Appointments: Writer, Australian Dictionary of Biography, 1968-; Ed, Journal of Royal Australian Historical Society, 1994-. Publications: Thomas Brisbane, 1971; Colonial Eve, 1979; Contbr to: Australian Dictionary of Biography; Journal of Religious History; Journal of Ecclesiastical History; Journal of Royal Australian Historical Society. Honour: Aust Cncl Lit Bd, 1980. Memberships: Life Mbr, Snr VP, Royal Austl Histl Soc; Assn for Jrnl of Relig Hist; Pres, Macquarie Univ Lib Friends; Austl Histl Assn. Listed in: International Authors and Writers Who's Who; Who's Who of Australian Writers. Address: 22 Ingalara Avenue, Wahroonga, NSW 2076, Australia.

FRASER (John) Malcolm (Rt Hon), b. 21 May 1930, Melbourne, Aust. Australian Politician. m. Tamara Beggs, 1956, 2 s, 2 d. Education: Oxford Univ. Appointments: MP for Wannon, 1955-83; Mbr Jt Parl Cttee of For Affairs, 1962-66; Chair Govt Mbrs, Def Cttee; Sec, Wool Cttee; Mbr, Cncl of Austl Natl Univ, Canberra, 1964-66; Min for the Army, 1966-68, for Educ and Sci, 1968-69, for Def, 1969-71, for Educ and Sci, 1971-72; Parl, Ldr of Liberal Party, 1975-83; PM, 1975-83; Co-chair, C'wlth Eminent Persons Grp, 1985-86; Hon Fell, Magdalen Coll, Oxford, 1982; Hon VP, Oxford Soc, 1983; Snr Adj Fell, Cntr for Strategic and Intl Studies, 1983; Fell, Intl Cncl for Assoc at Claremont Univ, 1985; ANZ Intl Bd of Advice, 1987-93; Chair, CARE Aust, 1987-; Chair, UN Cttee on African Commodity Problems, 1989-90; Pres, CARE Intl, 1990-95-; Mbr, 1993- Chmn, 1997- InterAction Cncl of Fmr Hds of Govt. Honours: PC, 1976; CH, 1977; Hon LLD, SC, USA, 1981; AC, 1988; Hon Dr.Letters, Deakin Univ, 1989; B'nai B'rith Gold Medal, 1980. Membership: Melbourne Club. Hobbies: Fishing; Photography; Vintage Cars and Motorcycles. Address: 44th Floor, ANZ Tower, 55 Collins Street, Melbourne, Vic 3000, Australia.

FRASER Barry John, b. 8 Apr 1945, Melbourne, Australia. University Professor. m. Marilyn, 3 Dec 1974, 2 d. Education: BSc, Melbourne Univ, 1967; BEd, 1972, PhD, 1976, Monash Univ. Appointments: Sci Tchr, Vic Educn Dept, 1969-71; Snr Tutor, Educn, Monash Univ, 1972-75; Snr Lectr, Educn, Macquarie Univ, 1976-81; Prof, Curtin Univ of Technol, 1982-. Publications: Gender, Science and Mathematics, 1996; Improving Teaching and Learning in Science and Mathematics, 1996; International Handbook of Science Education, 1998. Honours: Fell, Austl Coll of Educn, 1994, Am Assn for the Adv of Sci, 1997, Acady of Socl Scis of Aust, 1997, Intl Acady of Educ, 1998. Memberships: Pres, Natl Assn for Rsch in Sci Tchng; Exec Dir, Intl Acady of Educn. Address: c/o Science & Mathematics Education Centre, Curtin University of Technology, GPO Box U1987, Perth 6845, Australia.

FRASER Bernard William, b. 26 Feb 1941, Junee NSW. Bank Governor. m. (1) Edna Gallogly, 1965, div, 1 s, 1 d. Education: Univ of New England Armidale NSW; Austl Natl Univ ACT. Appointments: Joined Dept of Natl Dev, 1961; Joined Dept of Treas, 1963; Treas Rep London UK, 1969-72; First Asst Sec, 1979; Sec Dept, 1984-89; With Dept of Fin, 1976; Dir Natl Energy Off, 1981-83; Gov Reserve Bank of Aust, 1989-96. Hobbies: Farming. Address: c/o Reserve Bank of Australia, 65 Martin Place, Sydney, NSW 2000, Australia.

FRASER Conon, b. 8 Mar 1930, Cambridge, England. Retired Documentary Film Producer and Director; Writer. m. Jacqueline Stearns, 17 Mar 1955, 5 s. Education: Marlborough Coll, 1943-47; Roy Mil Acady, Sandhurst, 1948-50. Publications include: The Underground Explorers, 1957; Oystercatcher Bay, 1962; Looking at New Zealand, 1969; Beyond the Roaring Forties, 1986. Honours: Silver Medal, Documentary Film, Coal Valley, Fest of the Ams, 1979; Silver Screen Awd, US Indl Film Fest, 1980; Mitra Awd of Hon, 26th Asian Film Fest, 1980. Address: Matapuna Road, RD6 Raetihi, New Zealand.

FRASER Dorothy Rita (Dame), b. 3 May 1926, Wairoa, NZ. Consultant. m. The Honourable William Alex Fraser, 29 Nov 1947, 1 s, 1 d. Appointments: NZ Dir, 1975-93, Chairperson, 1991-93, Community Systs Fndn, Australasia, 1975-93; Chmn, Tertiary Liaison Cttee, Univ Otago, Dunedin Coll of Educ and Otago Polytech, 1988-; Cnslt-Advsr, Command Pacific Grp, Utd Hlth Serv, 1989-90; Chairperson, Colls Educ Accreditation Panels, 1996. Honours: JP, 1959; Queen's Silver Jubilee Medal, 1977; Companion, Queen's Serv Order Pub Serv, 1978; DBE, 1987; Hon LLD, Univ Otago Jubilee Ceremony, 1994; Honoured by the Queen 1953-1993. Memberships include: Otago Hosp Bd, 1953-56, 1962-86; Pres, Dunedin Marriage Guidance Cncl, 1966-70; NZ Exec Marriage Guidance, 1967-74; Cncl, Univ Otago, 1974-86; Otago Plunket Karitane Hosp Bd, 1979-87; VP, Hosp Bds Assn NZ, 1981-86; Hosps Advsry Cncl, 1984-86; Hosp and Specialist Servs Cttee, NZ Bd Hlth, 1985-88; NZ Hosp and Related Servs Task Force, 1987-88; Patron, Schizophrenia Fellshp, Otago Bch, 1993-; Chairperson, Roy C'wlth Soc, Otago Bch, 1993. Listed in: New Zealand Who's Who Aotearoa. Hobbies: Gardening; Golf; Reading. Address: 21 Ings Avenue, St Clair, Dunedin, New Zealand.

FRASER Neale Andrew, b. 3 Oct 1933, Melbourne, Vic, Aust. Professional Tennis Player. m. (1) 2 s, 3 d, (2) Thea Fraser, 16 Sept 1989. Appointments include: Mbr, Austl Davis Cup Team, 1955-63; Austl Davis Cup Cap, 1970-93; Won Austl Open Doubles, 1957, 1958, 1962; Won Aust Mixed Doubles, 1956; Won US Open Doubles, 1957, 1959, 1960, Open Mixed Doubles, 1958, 1959, 1960, Open Singles, 1959, 1960; Won French Open Doubles, 1958, 1960, 1962; Won Wimbledon Doubles, 1959, 1961, Singles, 1960, Mixed Doubles, 1962; Dir, Victorian Inst of Sport, 1994-; Mbr Intl Tennis Fedn Davis Cup Cttee, 1994; Chmn Sport Aust Hall of Fame, 1997; Pres, Austl Davis Cup Tennis Fndn, 1998-. Publications: Power Tennis, 1961; Successful Tennis, 1983, 1984. Honours: MBE, 1974; AO, 1988. Hobbies: Golf; Tennis; Racing; Cricket. Address: Tennis Australia, Private Bag 6060, Richmond South, Vic 3121, Australia.

FRASER Robert Donald Bruce, b. 14 Aug 1924. Biophysicist. m. 9 June 1952, 1 s, 2 d. Education: BSc, Math and Phys, 1 Class Hons, London, 1948; PhD, Biophys, London, 1951; DSc, London, 1960. Appointments: MRC Studentship, 1948-51; Nuffield Fndn Fellshp, 1951-52; Rsch Scientist, Chf of Div, CSIRO Div of Protein Chem, 1952-1987. Publications: Keratins, 1972; Conformation in Fibrous Proteins, 1973; Num contbns to learned jrnls and review articles in books, 1948-1996. Honours: Roy Soc of Vic Medal, 1982; S G Smith Mem Medal of the Textile Inst, 1984; Fogarty Schlshp of Natl Insts of Hlth, USA, 1985. Membership: Fell, Austl Acady Sci, 1978. Hobbies: Flying; Fly fishing; Computer programming. Address: 28 Satinay Drive, Tewantin, Qld 4565, Australia.

FRAZER Murray Cornu, b. 2 July 1943, Aust. Academic. m. Dr Anne Brooks, 11 Apr 1983, 2 d. Education: BSc (Hons), Monash Univ, 1966; PhD, Cambridge Univ, 1971; DipEd (Tert) South Queensland Univ, 1981; MAdmin, Monash Univ, 1983; BA, Deakin Univ, 1993. Appointments: Prof of Mngmt, Swinburne Univ, 1992-; Pro-Vice-Chancellor (Acad), 1994-97. Publications: Num acad pprs; Jt ed, 2 books. Membership: Fell, Austl Inst of Mngmt. Address: Swinburne University of Technology, Hawthorn, Vic 3122, Australia.

FRAZIER James Albert, b. 26 Nov 1940, Armidale, NSW, Aust. Wildlife Cameraman and Photographer. Appointments: Co-Dir, Mantis Wildlife Films Pty Ltd, 20-yr ptnrship w naturalist, writer, photogr Densey Clyne. Creative Works: The Australian Ark, 1971; Garden Jungle; Aliens Among Us; Now You See Me Now You Don't; Come Into My Parlour, 1975; Every Care But No Responsibility; Blueprint for Survival, 1977; Butterfly Farming in Papua New Guinea, 1978; Crystal Dancer, 1989; Web of Intrigue, 1992; Involved, folng TV prodns: Life on Earth, 1979; Encounter Underground, 1979; Lady of the Spiders; Funnelweb; Drought, 1982; The Living Planet, 1983; Desire of the Moth, 1984; Frazer Island - The Sands of Time, 1985; The Nature of Australia, 1985-86; To Be a Butterfly; Sounds Like Australia, 1986; Cane Toads - An Unnatural History; Burke's Backyard, 1987; Trials of Life, 1988-89; Specialises, macro and micro filming of small animals; Inv and dev, spec effects lenses and devices inclng Panavision-Frazier Lens Syst, launched USA, 1995. Honours: 3 Golden Tripod Awds, Aust; Golden Camera Awd, USA; Golden Penguin Awd, Garden Jungle; Awd Winning TV Documentary, Cane Toads - An Unnatural History; Golden Tripod Awd, Crystal Dancer; Emmy Awd, Golden Panda Awd and others, Webs of Intrigue; Order Aust Medal, 1995; Tech Achievement Awd, Acady Arts and Scis, USA, 1998. Memberships: Fell, Roy Photo Soc; Austl Cinematographic Soc; Assoc, Austl Mus. Address: c/o Mantis Wildlife Films Pty Ltd, 14 Taylors Rd, Dural, NSW 2158, Australia.

FRECKELTON Ian Richard, b. 1 May 1958, Durban, S Africa. Barrister. m. Helen Malony, 6 Oct 1990, 1 s, 1 d. Education: BA (Hons); LLB, Sydney; PhD, Griffith; Dip ThM, ANH. Appointments: Mbr, Socl Security Appeals Tribunal, 1989-93; Mbr, Mental Hlth Review Bd of Vic, 1996-; Mbr, Psychosurgery Review Bd of Vic, 1997-; Adj Prof, Law and Legal Studies, La Trobe Univ, 1998-; Hon Assoc Prof, Forensic Med, Monash Univ, 1998-; Mbr Psychols Registration Bd of Vic, 1999-. Publications: The Trial of the Expert, 1987; Police in Our Society, 1988; Expert Evidence, 1993; Indictable Offences in Victoria, 1999; Controversies in Health Law, 1999; The Law of Expert Evidence, 1999; Expert Evidence in Criminal Law, 1999; Expert Evidence in Family Law, 1999. Honour: Life Mbr, ANZAPPL, 1997. Memberships: Pres, Austl and NZ Assn of Psych, Psychol and Law (ANZPPL), 1991-97. Hobbies: Swimming; Medieval music; Drama. Address: C/o Barristers Clerk Howells, Owen Dixon Chambers, 205 William Street, Melbourne, Vic 3000, Australia.

FREDERIKSEN Jorgen Segerlund, b. 5 May 1946. Atmospheric Scientist. m. Lorraine Margaret, 20 May 1972, 1 s, 1 d. Education: BScH, Adelaide, 1969; PhD, ANU, 1972; DSc, Adelaide, 1988. Appointments: Postdoct,, Univ of Groningen, Netherlands, 1972; Postdoct, ANU, 1974; Rsch Scientist, CSIRO-DAR, 1974. Publications: 100 scientific articles. Honours: Peter William Straud Prize, 1972; Rothmans Fellshp, 1974; Crafoord Fellshp, 1983; David Rivett Medal, 1984. Memberships: Fell, Austl Inst of Phys; Fell, Roy Met Soc; Austl Math Soc; Austl Met and Ocean Soc. Listed in: Australian Men and Women of Science Engineering and Technology; Dictionary of International Biography; Who's Who in the World. Hobbies: Swimming; Sport; Politics; Reading. Address: CSIRO Division of Atmopheric Research, PMB No 1, Aspendale, Vic 3195, Australia.

FREDMAN Myer, b. 29 Jan 1932, Plymouth, Devon, Eng. Conductor. m. Jeanne Winfield, 26 Aug 1954, 2 s. Education: Opera Sch, London. Appointments: Debut, Cork; Glyndebourne Fest, Operas by Mozart, Verdi, Maw, Von Einem, and Glyndebourne Touring Opera, 1968-74; State Opera SA; Seymour Grp; Guest Conductor throughout Eur, Am, Aust, elsewhere; Appeared, BBC TV, Wexford Fest, Perth Fest, Adelaide Fest, Hong Kong Fest, Poland, Belgium, Romania, Germany, elsewhere; Conducted Cavalli's L'Ormindo, Brussels, 1972, Bizet's Carmen, Hamburg, 1973, Il Barbiere di Siviglia, Sydney, 1974; Recorded Bax Symphs Nos 1 and 2 w London Phil Orch, No 2 w Sydney Symph, H Brian's Symphs Nos 16 and 22 w London Phil Orch, Delius Paradise Gdn w London Phil Orch, Benjamin Overture to An Italian

Comedy, Respighi's Sinfonia Drammatica and Piano Concerto w Sydney Symph, Puccini's Le Villi w Adelaide Symph. Creative Works: CDs: CD for Naxos, Britten, 1996; CD for Naxos, Delius, 1996; Publications: Contrbs to Opera Mag, Twenty-Four Hours and others; The Conductors Domain, 1998. Honour: Bronze Medal, Italian Govt. Hobbies: Walking; Theatre; Scrabble. Address: 38 Plaister Court, Sandy Bay, Tasmania 7005, Australia.

FREEDMAN Saul Benedict, b. 18 June 1949. Cardiologist. m. Alexandra Sharland, 7 July 1994, 1 s, 1 d. Education: BSc, Med; MBBS; Phd: FRACP; FACC; FESC; AMusA. Appointments: Prof of Cardiology, Univ of Sydney; Assoc Dean, Ctrl Clinl Sch, Univ of Sydney. Creative works: Over 50 pprs. Memberships: Cardiac Soc of Aust and NZ; Mbr Bd, NHF of Aust, NSW Div, 1995. Listed in: Who's Who in the World. Hobbies: Tennis; Violin. Address: 461 Darling Street, Balmain, NSW 2041, Australia.

FREEMAN Hans Charles, b. 26 May 1929. Scientist; Teacher. m. Edith Siou Cam San, 31 Mar 1966, 1 s, 1 d. Education: BSc Hons, Univ of Sydney, 1949; MSc, Univ of Sydney, 1952; PhD, Univ of Sydney, 1957. Appointments: Lectr in Chem, 1954, Snr Lectr, 1959, Rdr, 1964, Prof of Inorganic Chem, 1971, Prof of Chem, 1995, Emer Prof, 1998, Univ of Sydney; CA Inst of Technol, Rotary Fndn Fell, 1952-53; George Ellery Hale Rsch Fell, 1958-59; Editl Bd, Jrnl Of Coord Chem, 1971-80; Jrnl of Inorganic Biochem, 1979-; Inorganica Chimica Acta, 1982-88; Editl Bd, Jrnl of Biol Inorganic Chem, 1996-. Publications: Num rsch pprs and reviews on crystal structure analysis, protein structure, biological inorganic chemistry. Honours: Fell, Austl Acady of Sci, 1984; Burrows Medal and Awd for Inorganic Chem, Royal Austl Chem Inst, 1980. Memberships: Fell, Royal Soc for Chem; Fell, Royal Austl Chem Inst; Amn Crystallographic Assn; Intl House, Univ of Sydney , cncl mbr, 1967-98, chmn, 1988-91; Fndn for Inorganic Chem Within the Univ of Sydney, acad dir, 1973-96, dpty pres, 1996-; Soc for Crystallography in Aust, pres, 1976-77; Austl Natl Cttee for Crystallography, 1970-78, 1984-94, chmn, 1984-92; Austl Dept of Ind Sci and Technol Advsry Cttee, 1989-92; Mbr, Mngmt & Prog Cttees, Austl Natl Beamline Facility, 1991-96; Mbr, Prog & Review Bd, Austl Synchrotron Rsch Prog, 1996-. Listed in: Who's Who in Australia. Hobbies: Reading; Travel. Address: School of Chemistry, University of Sydney, NSW 2006, Australia.

FREETH Sir Gordon, b. 6 Aug 1914 SA. Politician. m. Joan C C Baker, 1939, 1 s, 2 d. Education: Univ of WA. Appointment: Bar and Solicitor WA, 1938-; Solicitor Katanning WA, 1939-49; RAAF, 1942-45; Min for Interior and Works, 1958-63; Min asstng the Att-Gen, 1962-64; Min for Shipping and Transp, 1963-68; Min for Air and Min asstng the Treas, 1968; Min for External Affairs, Feb-Oct 1969; Amb to Japan, 1970-73; Practised law Perth, 1973-77; High Commnr in UK, 1977-80; Chmn Austl Consolidated Minerals, 1981-90; Dir Beaconsfield Gold Mines, 1987-90; Liberal.Memberships: Mbr Parl, 1949-69. Hobbies: Golf; Reading. Address: Tingrith, 25 Owston Street, Mosman Park, WA 6012, Australia.

FREI RUIZ-TAGLE Eduardo. Politician. Appointments: Joined Christian Dem, Party, 1958; Fmr Pres; Elected to senate, 1990; CD Presdl cand, Dec 1993; Pres of Chile, Mar 1994-. Address: Office of the President, Palacio de la Moneda, Santiago, Chile.

FREIHA Bassam, b. 26 Nov 1939, Beirut, Lebanon. Publisher. m. Judith Anne Supple, 1983, 1 s, 2 d. Education: BA, Polit Sci, Amn Univ of Beirut, 1961. Appointments: Jrnlst, Pres Mngrng Dir of Dar Assayad SAL (Publng House), Polit Advsr to Hds of 2 Arab States-Spec Envoy of the Lebanese Pres, 1977-; Amb of Belize to the UNESCO, Paris. Publications: Sev articles in profl jrnls and mags. Honours: Lebanese Natl Medal of Cedars, Offr's Order; Tunisian Cultural Medal of 1st Order; Medal commemorating 40th Anniversary of UNESCO; Key to Cty of Sao Paulo; Comoroan Crescent Medal, Cavalier's Order of the Comoro Island. Hobbies: Reading; Music; Sports. Address: Dar Assayad SAL, POB 1038, Hzmieh, Beirut, Lebanon.

FREIMAN Marcelle, b. 20 Oct 1951, S Afr. Academic; Lecturer; Poet. 2 s. Education: BA, Univ Witwatersrand, 1973; MA, Engl Lit, Phd, Engl Lit, Macquarie Univ. Appointment: Lectr, Univ NSW. Publication: Monkey's Wedding (poetry book), 1995. Address: 186 Old South Head Road, Bellevue Hill, NSW 2023, Australia.

FRENCH Claire A M Wieser, b. 14 May 1924, Selb, Germany. Lecturer; Writer. m. Jack French, 2 Apr 1956, 2 s, 1 d. Education: BA (Melb), 1956; MA (Melb), 1971; PhD (Deakin), 1990. Appointments: Tutor, Monash Univ, Melbourne Univ, 1960-62; Lectr, Melbourne Cncl of Adult Educ, 1965-95. Publications: (novels) Der Prinz von Annun; De Grijze Jager; The Queen of the Silver Castle; Die Keltische Goettin; Num articles and pprs in German and Engl. Honours: Hons List Juvenile Lit, Vienna, 1980; Austl Women's Rsch Cntr since Fndn, 1990; CAE Dedicated Serv Awd, 1993. Memberships: FAW (Fellshp of Austl Writers); Adult Educ Tchrs Assn, Sec, 1983-85; AUMLA, 1960-62. Hobbies: Celtic studies; Matriarchal studies; Religious studies; Ecology; Family. Address: 138 Springvale Road, Glen Waverley, 3150, Victoria, Australia.

FRETWELL Elizabeth Drina (Betty), b. 13 Aug 1920, Melbourne, Aust. Opera Singer (Soprano); Adjudicator; Vocal Cnslt. m. Robert Simmns, 7 Feb 1958, 1 s, 1 d. Appointments: Joined Natl Th, Melbourne, 1950; Came to Brit in 1955; Joined Sadler's Wells, 1956 and Elizabethan Opera Co, Aust, 1963; Tours: W Germany, 1963; USA, Can and Covent Garden, 1964; Eur, 1965; Guest Soprano w Cape Town and Durban Opera Cos, S Africa, 1970; Joined Austl Opera, 1970; Roles incl: Violetta in La Traviata; Leonore in Fidelio; Ariadne in Ariadne auf Naxos; Senta in the Flying Dutchman; Minnie in Girl of the Golden West; Leonora in Il Trovatore; Aida; Ellen Orford in Peter Grimes; Leonora in Forza del Destino; Alice Ford in Falstaff; Amelia in Masked Ball; Giorgetta in Il Tabarro, opening season, Sydney Opera House, 1973; Has sung in BBC Promenade Concerts and on TV; Retired, 1998. Publications: Recordings include: Verdi's Il Trovatore; Lehar's Land of Smiles. Honour: OBE, 1977. Membership: Music Bd, Austl Opera Fndn, 1982-. Address: 47 Kananook Avenue, Bayview, NSW 2104, Australia.

FRIEDMAN Milton, b. 31 July 1912, Brooklyn, NY, USA. Economist; Educator Emeritus; Author. m. Rose Director, 25 June 1938, 1 s, 1 d. Education: AB, Rutgers Univ, 1932; AM, Univ Chgo, 1933; PhD, Columbia Univ, 1946. Appointments: Assoc Economist, Natl Resources Cttee, WA, 1935-37; Mbr, Rsch Staff, Natl Bur Econ Rsch, NYC, 1937-45, 1948-81; Visng Prof Econs, Univ WI, Madison, 1940-41; Prin Economist, Tax Rsch Div US Treasury Dept, WA, 1941-43; Assoc Dir, Rsch Stats, Rsch Grp, War Rsch Div, Columbia Univ, NYC, 1943-45; Assoc Prof, Econs and Stats, Univ MN, Mpls, 1945-46; Assoc Prof, Econs, 1946-48, Prof Econs, 1948-62, Univ Chgo; Paul Snowden Russell Distinguished Serv Prof Econs, 1962-82, Prof Emeritus, 1983-. Publications: Num books incl: Price Theory (co-auth), 1976; Milton Friedman's Monetary Framework, 1974; Tax Limitation, Inflation and the Role of Government, 1978; Free to Choose (co-auth), 1980; Bright Promises, Dismal Performance, 1983; Tyranny of the Status Quo, 1984; Money Mischief, 1992; Friedman & Szasz on Drugs: Essays on the Free Market and Prohibition (co-auth), 1992; Two Lucky People: Memoirs, 1998. Honours: Very num incl: Decorated Grand Cordon, 1st Class Order of the Sacred Treasure (Japan); Nobel Prize in Econs, 1976; Priv Enterprise Exemplar Medal Freedoms Fndn, 1978; Preditl Medal of Freedom, 1988; Natl Medal of Sci, 1988; Prize in Moral Cultural Affairs, Instn of World Capitalism, 1993; Templeton Hon Rolls Lifetime Achievement Awd, 1997; Goldwater Awd, 1997; Chmn, BD Dirs, Milton & Rose D Friedman Fndn. Memberships include: Fell Inst Math Stats; Amn Stats Assn; Econometric Soc; NAS, Amn Econ Assn, Pres, 1967; Amn Enterprise Assn, Pres, 1984-85. Address: Stanford University, Hoover Institution, Stanford, CA 94305-6010, USA.

FROGGATT Leslie Trevor (Sir), b. 8 Apr 1920. Business Executive. m. Jessie Elizabeth Grant, 14 Dec 1945. Appointments: Shell Grp, London, 1937; Chf Acct, Shell Singapore, Thailand, Malaya, 1947-54; Chf Acct, Shell Grp Egypt, 1955; Fin Dir, 1958; Gen Mngr, Kalimantan, Borneo, Indonesia, 1961; Dir, Dpty Chf PT Shell Indonesia, 1961-62; Area Co-ord, S Asia and Austl, 1962-63; Dir, Burmah Shell and Grp Coys, 1963-64; Mktng Efficiency Sales, Eur, 1964-65; Mktng Efficiency Div, London, 1966; Hd, Shell Oil Co, Atlanta, GA, 1967-68; Chmn, Chf Exec Offr, Shell Grp of Coys, Aust, 1969-80; Non-Exec Dir, until 1987; Chmn, Ashton Mining Ltd, 1981-94; Dir, 1978-90, Chmn, 1986-90 Pacific Dunlop Ltd; Dir, 1978-90, Austl Ind Devl Corp; Bd Mbr, Intl Bd of Advice of ANZ Banking Grp, 1986-91 and Austl Natl Airlines Cmmn, 1981-87; Vice-Chmn, 1984-87, Gov, 1982-93, Ian Clunies Ross Mem Fndn; Intl Advsry Cncl, Tandem Computers Inc, USA, 1988-98, Chmn of Asia Advsry Cncl; Chmn, Co-op Rsch Cntr for Cochlear Implant, Speech and Hearing Rsch; Vice-Chmn, Care Aust; Chmn, BRL Hardy Ltd, 1992-95; Chmn, Tandem Computers Pty Ltd, 1992-98. Honours: Hon Fell, 1981, AIP Medal, 1985, Austl Inst of Petroleum. Memberships: Fell, Austl Inst of Petroleum, 1981; Melbourne Club; Austl Club; C'wlth Golf Club. Hobbies: Reading; Music; Sports. Address: 20 Albany Road, Toorak, Vic 3142, Australia.

FROST Alan Charles Hamlyn, b. 8 July 1914. Consulting Engineer. m. Edith, 16 Apr 1938, 3 s. Education: University of London. Appointments: Electr Engr, 1936-42; RE India, 1943-46; Snr Engr, Merz and MCLellan, UK, 1947-51; Snr Engr/Engr in Charge, Elecl Engrng Snowy Mountains Authority, 1951-67; Chf Engr, Elecl and Mechl, Snowy Mtns Authy and Snowy Mtns Engrng Corp, 1967-75; Asst Dir, Snowy Mtns Engrng Corp, 1975-78; Prin, A and E Frost Cnsltng Servs. Publication: Hydro-Electric in Australia, 1983. Honours: MBE, 1978; Hon Fell, Inst of Engrng, Aust, 1989. Memberships: FIEE, 1951; Rotarian, 1960. Listed in: Debrett's Handbook of Australia; Who's Who in Engineering, Australia and New Zealand; Five Thousand Personalities of the World. Hobby: Photography. Address: 72 Orana Avenue, Cooma, NSW 2630, Australia.

FU Hao, b. 13 Apr 1916, Shanxi, China. Diplomat. m. Jiao Ling, 12 Feb 1945, 2 s, 1 d. Appointments: Vice Min, For Affairs, 1972-74; Amb to Democratic Repub of Vietnam, 1974-77, Japan, 1977-82; Dpty 6th NPC, Mbr Standing Cttee, Vice Chair, For Affairs Cttee, 1983-93. Publication: Tian Nan Di Bei (poems), 1992. Honour: Grand Cordon of the Sacred Treas, Japan, 1992. Memberships: Assn for Fmr Dipl of China, chair; Inst for Dipl Hist of China; Chinese Chmn, 21st Century Cttee for Sino-Japan Friendship. Hobbies: Poems; Literature. Address: 69 Bao Fang Lane, East District, Beijing 100010, China.

FU Shi Ying, b. 10 Nov 1919, Dehui Cty, Jilin Prov, China. Cardiologist. m. Shun Hua Zhan, 30 Sept 1973, 4 d. Education: MB; CHB. Appointments: Res Dr, Mukden Medl Coll, 1943-44; Physn in Charge, Harbin Pu Du Hosp, 1945-50; Fellshp Peking Union Medl Coll, 1950-52; Assoc Prof, Prof, Pres, Hon Pres, Cardiology Inst of Harbin Medl Univ, 1952-. Publications: Chf Ed, Adv of Cardiology, 1980; Profl jrnls. Honours: Prizes of Hlth Min, China and Heilong Jiang Prov, MONICA Proj. Heilong Jiang prov, 1984-93; Sodium Nitroprusside and Dopamine in the treatment of AMI, Prizes of Heilong Jiang Prov. Memberships: Cncl of Chinese Medl Assn, 1984-89; Hon Pres, Heilong Jiang Branch, Chinese Medl Assn. Hobbies: Swimming; Calligraphy. Address: Department of Cardiology, the 1st Affiliated Hospital of Harbin Medical University, Harbin 150001, Heilong Jiang Province, China.

FU Weiling, b. 17 May 1955, Shenyang, China. Professor of Medicine. m. Yue Xuli, 23 Aug 1984, 1 s. Education: MD; PhD. Appointments: MD, 1984; Intern, 1986; Msc, 1989; PhD, 1992; Assoc Prof, 1994; Prof, 1997. Publications: 3 books; 35 compositions, 1980-. Honours: Sci and Techol Adv Rewards of PLA of China, 1993, 1994, 1995, 1996, 1997; Wu Gieping Medl Reward, 1996. Memberships: Vice Dir, Assn for NosoComial

Infection of China, 1994; Vice Dir, Assn for Medl Lab, Chongqing, China, 1998. Hobbies: Sport; Music. Address: Medical Laboratory, South-Western Hospital, Gao Tan Yan Road, Chongqing 400038, China.

FU Xishou, b. 1931 Beijing. Government Official; Engineer. Education: Dept of Civ Engrng Qinghua Univ. Appointments: Joined CCP, 1959; Dep Sec Anhui Prov CP Cttee, 1987-; Dep Gov of Anhui Prov, 1988-90; Gov, 1991-95; NPC Dep to Anhui Prov; Dep Sec CPC 5th Anhui Provincial Cttee, 1988-; Gov Anhui Provincial People's Govt, 1989-94; Chmn People's Armament Cttee, 1991-. Memberships: Mbr 14th CCP Cntrl Cttee, 1992-. Address: c/o Office of Provincial Governor, Heifei City, Anhui Province, People's Republic of China.

FU Zhihuan, b. Mar 1938 Haicheng Co Liaoning Prov. Vice-Minister of Railways. Education: Moscow Railways Inst USSR. Appointments: Joined CCP, 1966; Chf Engr Sci and Tech Bur Min of Railways, 1984; Dir Sci and Tech Bur Min of Railways, 1985; Dir Harbin Railway Bur, 1989; Vice-Min of Railways, 1991-. Memberships: Mbr CCP Cntrl Commn for Inspecting Discipline, 1992-; Mbr 15th CCP Cntrl Cttee, 1997-. Address: Ministry of Railways, 10 Fuxing Lu, Haidan Qu, Beijing 100844, People's Republic of China.

FUCHS Ephraim, b. 28 Jan 1933, Israel. Advocate; Notary. m. Esther, 28 Mar 1961, 1 s, 1 d. Education: Fac of Law, MJur, Hebrew Univ, Jerusalem; Pre-doct degree in Law, Tel Aviv Univ. Appointments: Presently, Grand Repr of Utd Grand Lodge of Eng in Israel (previously OH, NC, Prince Edward Island). Publications: Num articles & lects on Fremmasonry. Honours: Mbr & Off Bearer of Hon: Grand Lodge Natl France; Grand Lodge, Turkey; Grand Lodge, TX; Grand Lodge, Chile; Hons: G L Orient Brazil; Hon Trustee of Univ La Repub Chile; Medal of Merit Israel Grand Lodge; Dr Leo Müffelman Mem Awd; Jerusalem Lodge, Paris; Jerusalem Lodge Rome; Jerusalem Lodge, Abidjan. Memberships: Grand Master, Grand Lodge of Israel of AF & A Masons, 1994-98; Israel Bar; Intl Orgn of Jewish Jurists; Univ Grads Orgn; Soc for Med & Law in Israel; Fndr & Mbr Veteran Orgn of Engrng Corp (Major). Hobby: Gardening. Address: 129 Haeshel Street, Herzlia, Israel 46644.

FUENTE Juan Ramón de la, b. 5 Sept 1951, Mexico Cty, Mexico. Secretary of Health. Education: Studied Med, UNAM; Spec in Psych, Masters Deg, Sci, Mayo Clin, Rochester, MN, USA. Appointments: Rschr, Instituto Nacional de Nutrición, Instituto Mexicano de Psiquiatria; Dir, Univ Prog of Hlth Rsch, UNAM, Dir, Dept of Med. Publications: Over 100 wrks on med incl books on hlth rsch and educ in Mexico. Honours: WA Awd to Merit in Psych, 1979; Miguel Alemán Valdés Awd in Hlth, 1987; Natl Sci Awd of Acady of Scientific Rsch, 1989; Eduardo Liceaga Awd, Natl Acady of Med, 1992. Memberships: Sistema Nacional de Investigadores, Cnslt, World Hlth Org, 1982; Bd of Govs, Salvador Zubirán Natl Nutr Inst; Techl Cncl of the Fundación Mexicana para la Salud. Address: Office of the President, Mexico.

FUENTES Carlos, b. 11 Nov 1928, Mexico City. Author; Diplomatist. m. (1) Rita Macedo, 1957, 1 d; (2) Sylvia Lemus, 1973, 1 s, 1 d. Education: Mexico Univ; Inst des Hautes Etudes Intls Geneva. Appointments: Asst Hd Press Section Min of For Affairs Mexico, 1954; Asst Dir Cultural Dissemination Mexico Univ, 1955-56; Hd Dept of Cultural Rels Min of For Affairs, 1957-79; Ed Revista Mexicana de Lit, 1954-58; Co-Ed El Espectador, 1959-61; Ed Siempre and Politica, 1960-; Amb to France, 1974-77; Fell Woodrow Wilson Intl Cntr for Schs WA DC, 1974; Fmr Prof of Spanish and Comparative Lit Columbia Univ NY; Prof of Comparative Lit Harvard Univ, 1984-86; Robert F Kennedy Prof of Latin Am Studies, 1987-; Prof-at-Large Brown Univ, 1995-; Pres Modern Hum Rsch Assn, 1989-; Fmr Adj Prof of Engl and Romance langs Univ of Pennsylvania PA; Fell of the Hum Princeton Univ; Virginia Goldersleeve Visng Prof Barnard Coll NY; Edward Leroc Visng Prof Sch of Intl Affairs Columbia Univ NY; Norman Maccoll Lectr Univ of Cambridge Eng. Publications: Los dias enmascarados, 1954; La region mas transparente, 1958; Las buenas conciencias, 1959;

Aura, 1962; La muerte de Artemio Cruz, 1962; Cantar de ciegos, 1965; Zona sagrada,1967; Cambio de piel; Paris La Revolucion de Mayo, 1968; La Nueva Novela Hispanoamericana, 1969; Cumpleanos, 1969; Le Borgne est Roi, 1970; Casa con Dos Puertas, 1970; Todos los gatos son pardos, 1970; Tiempo Mexicano, 1971; Don Quixote or the Critique of Reading, 1974; Terra Nostra, 1975; La Cabeza de la Hidra, 1978; Orchids in the Moonlight - play - 1982; The Old Gringo, 1985; The Good Conscience, 1987; Cristobal Nonato - novel - 1987; Myself With Others - Essays - 1988; Christopher Unborn, 1989; Constancia and Stories for Virgins, 1991; The Campaign - novel - 1991; The Buried Mirror - Essays also tv series - 1992; Geography of the Novel - essays - 1993; El Naranjo - novellas - 1993; Diana: The Goddess Who Hunts Alon, 1995; The Crystal Frontier, 1995; A New Time for Mexico, 1997; Por un Progreso Incluyente, 1997. Honours: The Biblioteca Breve Prize - for A Change of Skin - 1967; The Javier Villaurrutia Prize - for Terra Nostra - 1975; Romulo Gallegos Prize - for Terra Nostra - 1977; Mexican Natl Awd for Lit, 1984; Miguel de Cervantes Prize - for Cristobal Nonato - 1987; Ruben Dario Prize, 1988; IUA Prize - the The Old Gringo - 1989; Hon Dr - Harvard Wesleyan Essex Cambridge. Memberships: Mbr Mexican Deleg to ILO Geneva, 1950-51; Mbr Mexican Natl Commn on Human Rights, 1989-. Address: c/o Brandt & Brandt, 1501 Broadway, New York, NY 10036, USA.

FUH Chiou-Shann, b. 2 Aug 1961, Changhua, Taiwan. Associate Professor. m. Ling-Jen Twu, 17 June 1985, 3 d. Education: MS, Computer Sci, PA Univ, USA, 1987; PhD, Computer Sci, Harvard Univ, USA, 1992. Appointment: Assoc Prof, Natl Taiwan Univ, Taipei, 1993-. Publication: Image Segmentation to Inspect 3-D Object Sizes, 1996. Honour: Fellshp, Harvard Univ, 1987-88. Membership: Inst of Elec and Electron Engrs, 1989-. Hobbies: Private Pilot; Skiing. Address: Department of Computer Science & Information Engineering, National Taiwan University, Taipei, Taiwan.

FUJII Hirohisa. Politician. Appointments: Chmn Fin Cttee HoR; Chmn Fin Ctte House of Cnclrs; Parly Vice-Min of Fin; Min of Fin, 1993-94. Memberships: Mbr HoR; Fmr mbr House of Cnclrs; Mbr Japan Renewal Party - Shinseito JRP. Address: House of Representative, Tokyo, Japan.

FUJIMORI Alberto Kenyo, b. 1939 Lima. Politician; Academic. m. Susana Higushi, div 1996, 2 s, 1 d. Education: Natl Sch of Agric. Appointments: Fmr Rector Natl Agrarian Univ; Pres Natl Assn of Rectors, 1984-89; Pres of Peru, 1990-. Memberships: Fndr mbr Cambio '90 - polit party. Address: Office of the President, Lima, Peru.

FUJIMOTO Takao, b. 1931 Kagawa Pref. Politician. m. 1 s. Education: Fac of Law Tokyo Univ. Appointments: Joined Nomura Securities Co Ltd, 1944; Joined Nippon Telegraph and Telephone Pub Corp, 1957; Elected HoR for 1st constituency Kagawa Pref, 1963; Parl Vice-Min of Sci and Tech Agcy, 1970; Chmn Liberal Dem Party, Sci and Tech Sub-Cttee of the Policy Rsch Cttee, 1972; Parl Vice-Min of the Environment Agcy, 1973; Chmn Standing Cttee on For Affairs, 1976; LDP Standing Cttee on Pub Info, 1983; Min of State Dir-Gen Okinawa Dev Agcy, 1985; Dep Sec-Gen LDP, 1985-86; Min of Hlth and Welfare, 1987-88; Min of Agric Forestry and Fisheries, Nov 1996-. Hobbies: Sports, baseball; Reading; Golf; Karaoke singing. Address: Ministry of Agriculture, Forestry and Fisheries, 1-2-1, Kasumigaseki, Chiyoda-ku, Tokyo 100, Japan.

FUJIOKA Masayuki, b. 9 Nov 1963, Osaka, Japan. Medical Doctor; Neurosurgeon. m. Kazuko, 10 June 1992. Education: DMSc, Nara Medl Univ. Appointments: Chf Dr, Dept of Neurosurgery, Nara Medl Univ, 1993; Assoc Dir, Nara Prefectural Nara Hosp, 1995. Publications: Medl jrnls, 1994-. Honours; Hon Awds, 1995, 1996; Daiger Awds, 1994, 1997; Pioneering Brain Rsch Awds, 1998. Memberships: Amn Heart Assn; AAAS; Intl Stroke Soc. Hobbies: Guitar; Piano; Movies; Travel; Reading; Tennis. Address: Department of Neurosurgery, Nara Medical University 840, Shijo,

Kashihara 634, Nara, Japan.

FUJITA Kazumasa, b. 3 Jan 1932, Udonomura, Japan. Professor. m. 18 Oct 1960, 2 d. Education: Grad, Doshisha Univ. Creative Works: Impressive Social Work; The Philosophy of Social Work in Shingon Mikkyo. Memberships: Buddhist Socl Welfare Soc; Assn of Esoteric Buddhist Stdies. Address: 20-117 Koyasan, Koyacho, Itogun, Wakayama ken, Japan.

FUKADA Naohiko, b. 4 June 1923, Osaka, Japan. Professor Emeritus. m. 10 Oct 1952, 1 s, 1 d. Education: Osaka Normal Coll, 1943; Osaka Coll, Maths, 1947; BA, 1950; PhD, Dooshisha Univ, 1980. Appointments: Clinl Psychol, Kyoto Prefecture Child Guidance Clin, 1960; Lectr, 1961; Assoc Prof, 1964; Prof, Psychol, 1970, Prof Emer, 1989-, Doshisha Women's Coll; Prof, Postgrad Course, 1989-, Pres, 1995-, Osaka Univ Arts; Pres, Naniwa Coll, 1995-. Publications include: Many articles in learned jrnls; The Dictionaries of Psychology; 7 transls; Many essays; Experimental Studies of Drawing Behaviour, 1989. Memberships: Japanese Psychol Assn; Brit Soc Aesthetics; Intl Cncl Psychol, USA. Hobbies: Listening to classical music; Reading. Address: 37-12 Shimootani, Kuze, Jyoyo-shi 610-01, Japan.

FUKAYA Takashi. Politician. Appointments: Min of Posts and Telecomms; Fmr Parl Vice-Min of Labour; Fmr Chmn Cttee on Comms; Min of Home Affairs, 1995-96. Memberships: Mbr HoR. Address: Ministry of Home Affairs, 2-1-2, Kasumigaseki, Chiyoda-ku, Tokyo 100, Japan.

FUKUDA Chiseko, b. 10 Jan 1946, Japan. Lawyer. Education: LLB, Keio Univ, 1969; Legal Trng and Rsch Inst of Supreme Crt of Japan, 1970-72; LLM, NY Univ, Law Sch, 1977. Memberships: 1st Tokyo Bar Assn, 1972-; Cttee to Customs and Tariff Bur, Min of Fin of Japan, 1994-. Address: 505 Tokyo Sakurada Building, 1-3, Nishi-shinbashi I-chome, Minato-ku, Tokyo 105-0003, Japan.

FUKUDA Hitoshi, b. 30 Sept 1951, Hikawa, Shimane, Japan. Neurologist. m. Takako Yoshida, 30 Apr 1983, 2 d. Education: Bach of Electons, Matsue Tech Coll, Japan, 1972; Bach of Med, 1985, Dr of Med, 1990, Shimane Medl Univ. Appointments: Staff, 3rd Dept of Internal Med, Shimane Medl Univ, 1987-90; Staff, Dept of Neurology, Masuda Red Cross Hosp, 1990-. Publications: Articles publd in profl jrnls. Memberships: Societas Neurologica Japonica, Tokyo, 1985-; Japanese Soc of Internal Med, Tokyo, 1985-; Japan Geriatrics Soc, Tokyo, 1985-. Hobbies: Mountain climbing; Reading. Address: Department of Neurology, Masuda Red Cross Hospital, 1-103-1, Otoyoshi, Masuda, Shimane 698-8501, Japan.

FUKUDA Kazuhiko, b. 4 Jan 1958, Tokyo, Japan. Associate Professor. m. 16 Oct 1983, 1 s, 1 d. Education: PhD. Publications: Sleep Paralysis and Sleep-Onset REM Period in Normal Individuals, 1994. Membership: World Fedn of Sleep Rsch Socs. Hobby: Skiing. Address: c/o Fukushima University, Asakawa, Matsukawa-machi 960-1296, Japan.

FUKUHARA Kazuo Henry, b. 25 Apr 1913. Artist. m. Fujiko, 18 Aug 1938, 1 s, 3 d. Education: Attended watercolour workshops by Whitney, Brandt, Post, Wood, Molno. Appointments: Wholesale Florist, 1945-1980; Watercolour Instructor, 1987- Publications: Learn Watercolour the Edgar Whitney; Splash 3-4; Best of Watercolour 2; Watercolour Colour and Light; The Artistic Touch 3, 1999; Exhibition: Rosoh Kai Water Media Exhib, Tokyo, Japan, 1989-99. Honour: Santa Monica HS Disting Alumni, only Asian Hons in Class of 1931, 1994. Memberships: Pittsburgh Watercolour Soc; Watercolour Soc of Alabama; Natl Watercolour Soc; Hon Mbr, Valley Watercolour Soc, Sherman Oaks, CA, USA. Hobbies: Plants; Museums of art; Painting watercolours; Sketching. Address: 1214 Marine Street, Santa Monica, CA 90405, USA.

FUKUI Naoki, b. 9 Oct 1955, Tokyo, Japan. Professor of Linguistics. Education: BA, Linguistics, 1979, MA,

Linguistics, 1982, Intl Christian Univ; PhD, Linguistics, MIT, 1986. Appointments: Postdoct Fell, Cntr for Cognitive Sci, MIT, 1986-87; Asst Prof, Keio Univ, 1988-89; Asst Prof, Univ Of PA, 1989-90; Asst Prof, 1990-94, Assoc Prof, 1994-98, Prof, 1998-, Univ of CA, Irvine. Publications: Theory of Projection in Syntax, 1995; Generative Grammar, 1998; Transformational Generative Theory. Honour: Fulbright, 1982-87, 1998. Memberships: Linguistic Soc of Am; Linguistic Soc of Japan; AAAS; Japanese Cognitive Sci Soc. Address: 3151 Social Science Plaza, Department of Linguistics, University of California, Irvine, CA 92612-5100, USA.

FUKUYAMA Yukio, b. 28 May 1928, Miyazaki, Japan. Paediatrician. m. Ayako Arai, 10 Oct 1954. Education: Fac of Med, Univ of Tokyo, 1948-52; Postgrad Studies, Univ of Tokyo, 1954-57. Appointments: Assoc Prof, Dept of Paediats, Univ of Tokyo, 1964; Dir of Neurology Div, Natl Children's Hosp, Tokyo, 1965; Prof and Chmn, Dept of Paediats, Tokyo Women's Med Coll, Tokyo, 1967-94; Chmn, Bd of Trees, Jap Soc of Child Neurology, 1968-94; Emer Prof, Tokyo Women's Med Coll, 1994-99; Prof, Dept of Paediats, Saitama Med Sch, Saitama, 1994-99. Publications: Epilepsy Bibliography - Books and Monographs, 1945-97, 7th ed, Tokyo, 1998; An Atlas of Child Neurology, 1986; Child Neurology, Amsterdam: Excerpta Med, 1982; Modern Perspectives of Child Neurology, 1991; Fetal and Neonatal Neurology, 1992; EEG and Evoked Potentials in Children, 1992; Crossroads of Child Neurology, 1995; Congenital Muscular Distrophies, 1997. Honours: Em Pres, Asian and Oceanian Child Neurol Assn, 1993-; Em Chmn, Bd of Trees, Jap Soc of Child Neur, 1993-; Duchenne-Erb Prize, Germany, 1999. Memberships: Japan Paediat Soc; Japan Soc of Neur; Japan Soc of Child Neur; NY Acady of Scis; Amn Acady of Cerebral Palsy and Dev Med; Pres, Intl Child Neurol Assn, 1982-86; Pres, Asian and Oceanian Assn of Child Neur, 1983-90; Amn Neurol Assn; Hon Mbr, Amn Acady of Neur; Canad Assn of Child Neurol; Child Neur Soc (USA); Czech Neur Soc. Listed in: Who's Who in the World; Who's Who in Science and Engineering. Hobbies: Philately; Baseball. Address: 6-12-16, Minami-Shinagawa, Shinagawa-ku, Tokyo 140, Japan.

FULCHER Gillian Tempest. Editor; Sociologist. m. 9 Feb 1962, Clive Norman Fulcher, div, 29 Sept 1979, 1 s. Education: BA, 1st Class Hons; PhD. Appointments include: Snr Tutor in Sociol, Monash Univ, 1976-80; Lectr, Sociol, Lincoln Inst of Hlth Scis, 1982-84; Secondment as main Writer/Rschr/Policy Analyst, Victorian Ministerial Review of Educl Servs, 1983-84; Lectr, Sociol, Monash Univ, 1984-88; Dir of Rsch, Assn for the Blind, 1990-91; Hon Rsch Assoc, Monash Univ. Publications include: Book, Disabling Policies? A Comparative Approach to Education Policy and Disability, 1989; Silence and Other Poems, 1996. Honours: Univ Prize for Anthropol and Sociol, Monash Univ, 1965. Memberships: Indep Schlrs Assn of Aust; Soc of Eds, Vic; Victorian Writers Cntr. Hobbies: Reading; Writing; Gardening; Swimming; Cooking; Theatre. Address: Lares Green, 9 The Ridge, Mount Eliza, Vic 3930, Australia.

FUNADA Hajime, b. 22 Nov 1953 Utsunomiya Cty Tochigi Pref. Politician. m. Rumi Funada, 1978, 1 s, 2 d. Education: Keio Univ. Appointments: Hd Yth Sect of Natl Organizing Cttee LDP - 1985-86; State Sec for Mngmt and Co-ord Agcy, 1986-87; State Sec for Min of Educ, 1987-88; Dir Educ Div of Policy Rsch Cncl LDP, 1988-89; Dir For Affairs Div, 1990-92; Chmn Sub-Cttee of Cnslng Japan Overseas Co-op Voluns, 1989-90; Min of State for Econ Plng, 1992-93; Co-fndr of Japan Renewal Party - Shinseito - 1993; Dep Sec Gen for Organizational Affairs, 1993-94; Dep Sec Gen for Polit Affairs, 1994; Vice-Chmn Diet Mngmnt Cttee; 'Reform' In-House Grpng - Kaikaku - 1994; Co-fndr New Frontier Party - Shinshinto - 1994; Vice-Chmn Org Cttee, 1994-95; Dep Sec Gen, 1995; Assoc Chmn Gen Cncl, 1995-96; Resigned from Party, 1996; Hd of '21st Century' In-House Grpng - 21seiki - 1996; Rejoined Liberal Dem Party, Jan 1997; Chmn Sub-Cttee on Asia and the Pacific; Dir Cttee on Hlth and Welfare; HoR, 1998-. Memberships: Mbr HoR from Tochigi, 1979-; Mbr Policy Deliberation Commn; Mbr Gen Cncl, 1997-; Mbr Ruling Parties Consultative Cttee on Guidelines for Japan; US Def Co-op, 1997-. Hobbies: Astronomy; Driving. Address: Shugiin Daini Giinkaikan, Room 412, 2-1-2 Nagata-cho, Chiyoda-ku, Tokyo 100, Japan.

FUNDER John Watson, b. 26 Dec 1940, Adelaide, S Aust. Physician. m. Kathleen Rose Brennan, 11 Dec 1964, 2 s, 1 d. Education: BA, 1964, MBBS, 1965, PhD, 1970, MD, 1971, Melbourne Univ; FRACP, 1978; MRACP, 1995. Appointments: NHMRC Snr Prin Rsch Fell, 1984; Prof of Med, Monash Univ, 1987; Dir, Baker Medl Rsch Inst, 1990. Publications: Over 400 sci pprs. Honours: AO, 1998. Memberships: Pres, Austl Soc for Medl Rsch, 1979; Pres, Endocrine Soc of Aust, 1982-84; Chmn, Exec Cttee, Intl Soc for Endocrinology, 1996-; Chairman, Vic Hlth Promotion Fndn, 1997-. Hobbies: Current affairs; History; Classical music; Cooking. Address: 1022 Drummond Street, North Carlton 3054, Victoria, Australia.

FUNNELL Raymond George (Air Marshal), b. 1 Mar 1935, Brisbane, Qld, Aust. Retired Military Officer; Consultant (Military Affairs; Airpower). m. 27 Nov 1958, 2 s. Education: RAAF Coll, 1953-56; MPSc, Auburn Univ, 1971-72; Grad Dip Admin, Canberra Coll Advd Educ, 1977-78; RAAF Staff Coll, 1967; USAF Air War Coll, 1971-72; Roy Coll Def Stdys, 1981. Appointments: RAAF, 1953-92, Chf, Air Staff, 1987-92; Prin, ACDSS, 1993-99. Honours: AO, 1985; AC, 1989; Cmdr, US Legion Merit, 1991. Memberships: Utd Servs Inst; C'wlth Club; Life Mbr, Schofields Flying Club. Hobbies: Photography; Motor-cycling; Fishing; Camping. Address: 18 Duterrau Crescent, Lyneham, ACT 2602, Australia.

FUSIMALOHI S Tavake, b. 22 Mar 1936. Broadcast Journalist. m. Keiti Tu'i'ile'ila, 2 Feb 1962, 2 s, 3 d. Education: MA, Commn; BA, Jrlsm; Dip in Law. Appointments: Asst Announcer, 1961-66; Snr Announcer, 1967-75; Gen Mngr, Tonga Brdcstng Commn, 1976-. Memberships: Exec Dir, Pacific Islands News Assn, 1985-97; Chmn, Pacific Is Brdcstng Assn, 1987-94. Hobby: Rugby. Address: Tonga Broadcasting Commission, PO Box 36, Nuku'alofa, Tonga, The Pacific Islands.

G

GABEROV Stefan Christov, b. 17 Mar 1949. Diplomat; Economist. m. Elmira Emilova Tomova, 30 Sept 1972, 1 s, 1 d. Education: Univ of Natl & World Econ, Sofia, 1972. Appointments: Rsch Assoc, Inst for For Affairs, Sofia, specializing in Asian Problems, 1973; Attache to the Emb of Bulgaria in Beijing, China, 1976-79; 3rd & 2nd Sec to min of For Affairs of Bulgaria, Sofia, Asian Dept, 1979-82; 2nd Sec, Emb of Bulgaria, Beijing, China, 1982-86; 1st Sec & Cnslr, Min of For Affairs of Bulgaria, Sofia, Chf of the China Desk, Asian Dept, 1986-90; Min Plenipotentiary to the Emb of Bulgaria, Beijing, China, 1990-92; Amb, Repub of Bulgaria, China, 1993-. Hobbies: Reading; Music; History. Address: Embassy of the Republic of Bulgaria, No 4, Xiu Shui Bei Jie, Jian Guo Man Wai, Beijing100600, China.

GADAGIN Basavaraj, b. 1 June 1958, Abbigeri, India. Librarian. m. Girija, 13 May 1989, 1 s, 1 d. Education: MA; MLISc. Appointments: Libn, Dayananda Sagar Engrng Coll, Bangalore, 1984-86; Libn, Veerasiava Coll, Bellary, 1986-. Honours: Man of Yr, ABI, 1998. Memberships: Life Mbr, ILA; IASLIC; DRTC; ALSD; SIS; KSCLA; Kannada Sahitya Parishath, Elected cncl mbr, 1998-99. Hobbies: Reading; Social work. Address: Librarian, Veerasaiva College, Bellary 583104, India.

GADDAM Encik Kasitah bin, b. 18 Oct 1947 Ranau Sabah. Politician. m. Puan Rosnie bte Ambuting, 4 c. Education: Sabah Coll Kota Kinabalu; Univ of Malay. Appointments: Admin Offr Chf Mins Dept Kota Kinabalu Sabah, 1971; Asst Dir of Immigration Sabah, 1971-76; Regl Mngr KPD for Kundasang Ranau and Tambunan; Admin Offr Purng Mngr KPD Hq Kota Kinabalu, 1977-80; Dir of Personnel for East Malaysia and Brunei; Inchcape Malaysia Holding Bhd, 1980-83; VP Parti Bersatu Sabah, 1984; Chmn Sabah Dev Bank Sabah Fin Bd Soilogen - Sabah - Sdn Bhd, 1985; Min PMs Dep, 1986-89; Min of Land and Regl Dev, 1989-90. Memberships: Mbr Parl, 1986-. Address: c/o Prime Minister's Department, Jalan Dato Omn, 50502 Kuala Lumpur, Malaysia.

GADGIL Gangadhar Gopal, b. 25 Aug 1923, Mumbai, India. Economic Adviser. m. Vasanti, 12 Dec 1948, 1 s, 2 d. Education: MA, w Econs as spec subj, Univ of Mumbai, India. Appointments: Prin and Prof of Econs, Narsee Monjee Coll, Mumbai; Hon Prof of Marthi, Univ of Mumbai, 1976-79; Dir, Raval Gaon Sugar Farm Ltd, Walchand Capital Ltd; VP, Sahitya Akad, 1988-93; Mumbai Marathi Grantha Sangrahalaya. Publications: Plays, novels, travelogues, books in Marathi and Eng; Credited w having created the new short story in Marathi. Honours: Rockefeller Fndn Fellshp, 1957; N C Kelkae Awd; Abhiruchi Awd; Sahitya Akademi Awd; Janasthan Awd, 1997. Memberships: Econ Affairs Cttee, CEI; Pres, Mumbai Marathi Sahitya Sangh, Mumbai Grahak Panchayat; All India Lit Conf, Raipur, 1981, 1982; Conf of Maharasgtrians in N Am, Houston, 1995. Hobbies: Reading and writing. Address: c/o Beacons Pvt Ltd, United India Bank Building, 3rd Floor, PM Road, Mumbai 400001, India.

GADRE Rati Kumar, b. 12 May 1984, Akola, India. Student. Education: IXth Std Radio and TV Artist and Intl Awde, Classical Music and Poetry, Cambridge and USA. Appointments: Stud, IXth Std Kendriya Vidyalaya, Bidar. Creative Works: TV and Radio Artist Classical Music Singer Presented 18 times; Radio Prog 3 Times; TV Prog, Yng Poetees; Publd 2 Poetry Books. Honours: CCRT New Delhi Schlshp; Selected for 2 Intl Awds, USA and Cambridge; Succeeded 5th Vocal Exam. Hobbies: Reading; Playing Badminton; Tour; Music and Harmonuim. Address: c/o Dr K M Gadre, Manik Prabhu Niwas, Beside KEB, Infront og Sharanodyana, Bidar 585401, Karnataka State, India.

GAIR George Frederick, b. 13 Oct 1926, Dunedin. m. Esther Mary Fay Levy, 1951, 1 s, 2 d. Education: Wellington Coll; Wairarapa Coll, Vic Univ Coll, Wellington, 1944; BA, Auckland Univ Coll, 1949. Appointments: Mil

Serv, Brit C'Wlth Occupational Force, Japan, 1947-48; Pub Rels Offr, 1953-57; Natl Pres, NZ Pub Rels Inst, 1962-64; Mbr of parl, North Shore, 1966-90; Parly Under-Sec, Mins of Educ and Sci, 1969-72; Min of Customs, Assoc Min of Fin, 1972; Min of Housing, Dpty Min of Fin, 1975-77; Min of Regl Dev, 1975-78; Min of Energy, Min of of Natl Dev, 1977-78; Min of Hlth, Min of Socl Welfare, 1978-81; Min of Transp, Civ Aviation, Railways, 1981-84; Dpty Ldr, Natl Party, 1986-87; NZ High Commnr to UK, Amb to Ireland, NZ High Commnr to Nigeria, 1991-94. Honours: QSO, 1988; CMG, 1994. Memberships: NZ Natl Party; Alumni Assn, Univ Auckland, pres, 1994-96; Mayor, North Shore City, 1995-98. Hobbies: Walking; Travel; Family. Address: 41 Hauraki Road, Takapuna, North Shore City, New Zealand.

GAITONDE Bhikaji Balwant, b. 29 Dec 1926, Banda, Maharashtra, India. Medical. m. Nirmala, 25 June 1953, 2 s, 1 d. Education: MD; MSc. Appointments: Prof, Dir, Clinl Pharm; Advsr, World Health Org; Dean, Fac Med. Publication: Pharmacology for Medical and Dental Students, 1965. Honours: Fell, Acady of Scis, India; Fell, Acady Med Scis, India; Fell, NYAS. Hobbies: Reading; Writing; Social Work. Address: Banda, Sindhudurg, Maharashtra, 416511, India.

GAJWAY Purushottamrao Maniram, b. 20 Jan 1943, India. Lecturer. m. Deekanya, May 1968, 2 s, 1 d. Education: MCom; MA; MLib & Info Sci; PhD. Appointments: Lib Dept, Educ Dept, Govt VMV Amt, Amravati Univ, 32 yrs; Var Cttees. Publications: 10 rsch pprs at var confs. Memberships: Indian Lib Assn; IASLIC, India; Vidarbha Acad Lib Assn. Hobbies: Social work; Reading; Speeches; Religious matters. Address: Shramsaphyalaya, Kishore Nagar, Amravati 444 606, India.

GALE David Peter, b. 13 Dec 1929, Aust. Opthalmic Surgeon. m. Gillian Whitaker, 27 Dec 1958 (diss), 1 s, 4 d. Education: Trinity Coll, Univ Melbourne; MB BS, Melbourne, 1954; DO RCP and S, UK, 1960; FRCS, Edinburgh, 1962; FRACS, 1964; FACS, Opthalmic Surg, 1969; MACO, 1969; FRACO, 1976; FCOpth, 1989; MACO, 1990; FRCopth, UK, 1992. Appointments: Jnr & Snr Res Med Off, Royal Melbourne Hosp, 1955-57; Snr House Off, Royal Eye Hosp, London, Eng, 1958-59; Registrar & Snr Registrar, St Paul's Eye Hops, Liverpool, 1959-62; Hon Asst Opthalmic Surg, Royal Melbourne Hosp, 1962-66; Opthal and Opthalmic Surg i/c Dept, 1963-87; Pres, Med Staff, Queen Victoria Med Cntr, 1970-71; Cnslt Opthal, Monash Medl Cntr, 1988-; Contbr, Eye Injuries, Medicine & Surgery For Lawyers, 1st Ed, 1985; 2nd Ed, 1996. Publications: Co-ed, Proceedings of Medical-Legal Society of Victoria, Vol XI and Vol XII, Estropia in Infancy. Memberships: Melbourne Cricket Club, 1948-; RACV, 1952; Medl-Legal Soc of Victoria, Medl Sec, 1966-84; Cttee, 1984-90; VP, 1987-89; Pres, 1989-90; Aust Medl Assn; Aust Coll Opthals, 1969-; IMMAAO, 1990; FRC Opthal, UK, 1992; Richard Wagner Soc, Vic, Pres 1981-88, Sec 1989-92, 1995-96. Listed in: Who's Who In Australia. Hobbies: Melbourne Symph Orch Subscribers Cttee, Hon Sec, 1952-57, Mbr, 1963-86; Victorian Cncl of Friends of Aust Opera, 1970-84; Hon Sec, 1989-. Address: Alcaston House, 2 Collins Street, Melbourne, Vic 3000, Australia.

GALE Gwendoline Fay, b. 13 June 1932, Balaklava, S Aust, Aust. Academic. 1 s, 1 d. Education: BA Hons, 1954; PhD, 1962; D Univ, Adelaide, 1994; Hon D Litt, UWA, 1998. Appointments: Snr Geog Mistress, Walford C of E Girls Sch, 1954-56; Postgrad Schl, 1957-60; Post Doctoral Fell, 1964-65; Lectr, 1966-70; Snr Lectr, 1971-74; Rdr, 1975-77; Prof, 1978-89; Pro Vice Chan, Univ of Adelaide, 1988-89; Vice Chan, Univ of W Aust, 1990-97; Pres, Austl Vice Chan Cttee, 1996-97; Pres, Acady of the Socl Sci, Aust, 1998-. Creative Works: Woman's Role in Aboriginal Society; The Aboriginal Situation; Urban Aborigines; Race Relations in Australia; Many or publs. Honours: Elin Wagner Fell, 1971; Catherine Helen Spencer Schl, 1972; Emer Prof, Univ of Adelaide; AO; Many or hons. Memberships: Assn of C'wlth Univ Cncl; WA Symph Orch Advsry Bd; PM's Sci

and Engrng Cncl; Many or mbrshps. Hobbies: Walking; Music. Address: Academy of Social Sciences, Canberra, ACT 2601, Australia.

GALLAGHER Monica Josephine (Dame), m. John Gallagher, 24 Jan 1946, 2 s, 2 d. Appointments: Tour Guide, St Mary's Cath, Sydney, 1970-, Fndr and Pres, Flower Fest Cttee, 1986-95, Fest Dir, 1996-, Assoc, 1997-; Fndr and pres, Friends of St Mary's Cath, 1983-87, VP 1988-90, Cttee Mbr, 1991-97, Pres 1998; Most Ex Order of the Brit Empire, Mbr 1978-84, VP, 1985-89; Pres 1989-92, Cttee 1994-; Life Mbr Cath Women's League, Sydney, Natl Pres, 1972-74; Gen and State Pres, 1972-80; Past Pres, Cath Women's Club; Past Pres Assocd Cath Cttee; Cath Inst Nursing Stdies; Fmr Mbr Nursing External Advsry Cttee, Cath Coll Educ, Sydney; Fmr Chmn YWCA Appeals Cttee; Exec Bd Mater Misericordia Hosp, N Sydney, Gertrude Abbott Nursing Home; Bd, Cath Family Life Cntr; Select Cttee, Queen Elizabeth Silver Jubilee Trust; Cath Central Cttee, Care of Aged, Sydney; Austcare; Rd Safety Cncl, NSW; 1st Natl Conf Laity, Daybreak, 1980; Austl Ch Women, Mbr, 1973-91, Assoc 1991-; Fmr Mbr UN NSW Div; Cttee Mbr Dr Horace Nowland Travelling Schlshp; VP, Save the Children Fund, NSW, 1992-94. Honours: DBE, 1976; Good Citizen Awd, 1979; Papal Hon, Augustae Crucis Insigne pro Ecclesia et Pontifice, 1981. Hobbies: Reading; Opera; Ballet; Symphony concerts. Address: 1, Pobert Street, Willoughby, NSW 2068, Australia.

GALLOP John Foster (Hon Justice), b. 31 July 1930. Judge. m. Joy Gallop, 1955, 2 s, 1 d. Education: Sydney Univ. Appointments: Retd Cap, Roy Austl Naval Reserve; Pres, Austl Cncl Soc Servs, ACT, 1975-76; QC, 1976; Pres, Law Soc, ACT, 1976-78; Judge, Supreme Crt, ACT, NT and Christmas Is, and Fed Crt Aust: Def Force Discipline Appeal Tribunal, 1985-; Presdtl Mbr, Admnstv Appeals Tribunal. Honours: RFD, 1985; AM, 1998. Memberships: C'wlth Club, Canberra; Roy Canberra Golf Club; Roy Sydney Golf Club. Hobbies: Cricket; Golf; Tennis. Address: c/o Judges' Chambers, Supreme Court, Canberra, ACT 2600, Australia.

GALSWORTHY Anthony Charles, b. 20 Dec 1944. Diplomat. m. Dawson-Grove, Jan 1970, 1 s, 1 d. Education: Corpus Christi Coll, Cambridge, MA, FCO, 1966-67; Lang Training, Hong Kong, 1968-70; Peking, 1970-72; FCO, 1972-77; Rome, 1977-81; Cnslr, Peking, 1981-84; Hd of Hong Hong Dept, FCO, 1984-86; Prin Pvt Sec to Sec of State for For and C'Wealth Affairs, 1986-88; Seconded to RIIA, 1988-89; Snr Brit Rep, Sino-Brit Jt Liaison Gp, Hong Kong, 1989-93; Chief of Assessments Staff, Cabinet Off, 1993-95; Dpty Under Sec of State, FCO, 1995-97; Amb to People's Repub of China, 1997-. Hobbies: Bird-watching; Wildlife. Address: c/o Foreign and Commonwealth Office, King Charles Street, SW1A 2AH, England.

GAMBLE Robert Thom. m. Betty, 22 June 1944, 1 s, 1 d. Education: Cath Sch, Shanghai; Drummoyne HS, NSW. Appointments: RANR, 1941-46, Commnd, 1943; Pub Acct, 1953-; Capt, RANR, 1966-; ADC to HM Queen Elizabeth II, 1966-67; Dir, Holpitt Pty Ltd. Honours: OBE, 1964; VRD, 1955, and Bar, 1972. Memberships: Fell, Aust Soc of CPAs; Fell, Inst of Chartered Acct, 1974. Hobby: Tennis. Address: 2 Flagstaff Street, Gladesville, NSW 2111, Australia.

GAMBLING William Alexander, b. 11 Oct 1926, Port Talbot, UK. Electrical Engineer. m. (1) Margaret Pooley, 1952, diss 1994, 1 s, 2 d, (2) Barbara Colleen O'Neil, 1994. Education: BS (1st Class Hons), Electr Engrng, Univ of Bristol, 1947; PhD, Electr Engrng, Univ of Liverpool, 1955; DSc, Univ of Bristol, 1968. Appointments: Lectr, Elec Power Engrng, Univ o Lverpool, 1950-55; Natl Rsch Cncl Fell, Univ of BC, 1955-57; Lectr, Snr Lectr, Rdr, 1957-64; Dean of Engrng and Applied Sci, 1972-75; Prof, Electrons, 1964-80; Hd of Dept, 1974-79, Prof, Optical Comms, 1980-95, Dir, Optoelectrons Rsch Cntr, 1989-95, Univ of Southampton; Dir, York Ltd, 1990-97; Roy Soc Kan Tang Po Prof and Dir, Optoelectrons Rsch Cntr, City Univ, Hong Kong, 1996-; Indl cnslt; Visng Prof, Univs inclng: CO, USA,

1966-67; Bhabha Atomic Rsch Cntr, India, 1970; Osaka Univ, Japan, 1977; City Univ, Hong Kong, 1995. Publications: Pprs on electrons and optical fibre comms. Honours include: Acad Enterprise Awd, 1982; J J Thomson Medal, IEE, 1982; Faraday Medal, IEE, 1983; Churchill Medal, Soc of Engrs, 1984 and Simms Medal, Soc of Engrs, 1989, for rsch innovation and ldrshp; Hon Prof, Huazhung Univ Sci and Technol, 1986-, Beijing Univ Posts & Telecomms, 1987-, Shanghai Univ, 1991-. Micro-optics Awd, Japan, 1989; Dennis Gabor Awd, Intl Soc for Optical Engrng, USA, 1990; Rank Prize for Optoelectronics, 1991; Medal and Prize, Fndn for Computer and Commns Promotion, Japan, 1993; Mountbatten Medal, Natl Electrons Cncl, 1993; Dr hc Univ Politèchnic of Madrid, 1994, Aston Univ, 1995, Bristol Univ, 1999. Memberships include: FIERE, 1964; CEng, FIEE, 1967; Pres, IERE, 1977-78, Hon Fell, 1983; FEng, 1979; FRS, 1983; For Mbr, Polish Acady of Scis, 1985; Freeman, Cty of London, 1988. Hobbies: Music; Reading; Walking. Address: Optoelectronics Research Centre, City University of Hong Kong, 83 Tat Chee Avenue, Kowloon, Hong Kong, China.

GAME David Aylward, b. 31 Mar 1926, Adelaide, SA, Aust. Medical Practitioner. m. Patricia Jean Hamilton, 8 Dec 1949, 2 s, 2 d. Education: MB BS, Adelaide, 1949; FRACGP, 1968; FRCGP, 1986; Fell, Hong Kong Coll Gen Practitioners, 1987. Appointments: Res Medl Offr, 1950, Registrar, 1951, Snr Visng Medl Practitioner, 1977-91, Emer Specialist, 1991-, Roy Adelaide Hosp; Gen Medl Prac, 1952-96; Pres, Roy Austl Coll Gen Practitioners, 1974-76; Co-ord, Gen Prac Trng, 1983-89, Snr Visng Practitioner, 1989-, Adelaide Children's Hosp; Pres, World Org Colls Acads and Acad Assns Gen Practitioners, Family Physns, 1983-96; Lorna Laffer Medl Dir, SA Post Grad Medl Educ Assn, 1989-97. Publications: Articles in medl jrnls. Honours: AO, 1983; Rose Hunt Awd, Roy Austl Coll Gen Practitioners; Life Gov, Austl Postgrad Fedn Med, 1994; Kt, Order St John, Kts Hospitaller, 1995; Patron and Fell, Austl Postgrad Fed in Med, 1997. Memberships include: Austl Medl Assn; Austl Geriatric Assn; Roy Austl Coll Gen Practitioners. Listed in: Who's Who in Australia; Who's Who in Australia and the Far East; Who's Who in the World; Debretts Handbook of Australia and New Zealand; International Who's Who in Community Service. Hobbies: Gardening; Painting; Stamp collecting; Tapestry. Address: 50 Lambert Road, Royston Park, SA 5070, Australia.

GAN Vivien Hwee-Yong, b. 13 June 1962, Singapore. Entrepeneur. Education: BA, Econs. Hobbies: Reading; Corresponding. Address: #21-08, Katong Park Towers, 114A Arthur Road (South Tower), Singapore 439826, Republic of Singapore.

GAN Woon Spong, b. 6 Mar 1943, Singapore. Acoustician; Company Director. m. Siu Hui Chiong, 4 Mar 1973, 2 s, 1 d. Education: BS, Phys, 1965, DIC, Acoustics & Vibration, 1967, PhD Acoustics, 1969, Imperial Coll, London. Appointments: Postdoct Rsch Asst in Chelsea Coll, London, 1968-1969; Postdoct Rsch Student, Imperial Coll, 1969-70; Assoc Prof, Nanyang Univ, Singapore, 1970-79; Founding Dir, Acoustical Servs, Pte Ltd, 1976-. Publications: About 100 pprs in acoustical imaging and active noise cancellation. Honour: Postdoct Rsch Fellshp twice, to do rsch in intl cntr for theort phys, Trieste, Italy, 1970, 1973. Memberships: Fell, Instn of Elec Engrs, UK; Fell, Inst of Acoustics, UK; Snr Mbr, Inst of Elec & Electron Engrs, USA. Hobbies: Reading; Listening to classical music. Address: C/o Acoustical Services, Singapore Pte Ltd, 209-212 Innovation Centre, NTU, Nanyang Avenue, Singapore, 639798, Singapore.

GAN Yi, b. 28 Oct 1913, Zhejiang, China. Professor of Mechanical Engineering. m. Yuemei Xiang, 26 Jan 1935, 4 s, 4 d. Education: Grad, Roy Mil Coll, Sandhurst, 1936; BA, 1939, MA, 1941, Cambridge Univ; Grad, Engrng Sch, Ft Belvoir, 1940; Grad, Cmnd & Gen Staff Sch, Ft Leavenworth, 1943. Appointments: Maj Gen, Chinese Army, 1943; Tchr, Anti-Tank Tactics, War Coll, 1944; Hd, Mil Sect, Chinese Deleg to Japan, 1946; Chf of Staff, Trng Command, Chinese Army, 1947; Prof, Mech Engrng Dept, NE Univ of Technol, 1950; Prof, Hd of Mech Engrng Dept, Hunan Univ, 1951; Prof, Huazhong Univ of Sci & Technol, 1953; Retd, 1984. Publications: Machine Design; Ratchet; Heat Engines; Advanced Heat Transfer; Trans, Heat Engine; Steam Turbines and Gas Turbine; Sev sci pprs publ. Listed in: Who's Who in Educational Front of Zhejiang Province. Address: Apt 402, Building 9, W-2, Huazhong University of Science and Technology, Wuhan, Hubei Province, China.

GAN Zhijian, b. 1927 Shanghai. Government Official; Senior Engineer. Education: Zhijang Univ; USSR. Appointments: Joined CCP, 1950; Vice-Min for State Plng, 1985-88; Min for Constrn, 1988; NPC Dep for Shanghai Prov. Memberships: Mbr State Plng Commn, 1982-85; Mbr Finl and Econ Cttee. Address: State Planning Commission, 38 Yuetan Nanjie Street, Sanlihe, Beijing 100824, People's Republic of China.

GAN Ziyu, b. 15 Oct 1929 Canton. Government Official; Senior Engineer. 2 s. Education: Zhongshan Univ. Appointments: Joined CCP, 1953; Vice-Chmn of State Plng Commn, 1978-; Vice-Chmn of Admin Commn on Import and Export Affairs, 1981-82; Vice-Chmn of State For Invmnt Commn, 1981-82; Vice-Chmn Drafting Cttee for Natl Def Law of PRC, 1993-; Dep Chmn Natl Ldng Grp for Work Concerning For Capital, 1994-. Memberships: Mbr Preliminary Working Cttee of the Preparatory Cttee of the Hong Kong Spec Admin Reg, 1993-. Address: State Planning Commission, 38 S Yuetan Street, Sanlihe, Beijing 100824, People's Republic of China.

GANACHARI Neelkantji, b. 10 June 1916, Hosur, India. Social Work. m. Irawa, 1 May 1939, 4 s, 2 d. Honours: Karnatak State Rajyostav Awds; Sirinadu Awds; Freedom Fighters Awds. Memberships: Fndr, 4 Khadi & Vill Inds; Fndr, 6 Second Sch, 3 Gandhian Ashram; Campaigned against Cow Slaughter; Promoted all-round dev of vills in and around Belgaum dist; Introduced prohibition of alcohol in many vills. Address: Gandhi Bhawan, Surebam 591127, India.

GANDEVIA Bryan Harle, b. 5 Apr 1925, Vic, Aust. Consultant Physician. m. Dorothy Virginia Murphy, 2 s. Education: MB BS, 1938, MD, 1953, Melbourne Univ; M, 1953, F, 1963, Roy Australasian Coll of Physns; Austl Coll Allergy, 1975; Fell, Fac Hist of Med, London soc of Apothecaries, 1979; Hon Fell, Fac of Occupational Med, Roy Coll Physns, London, 1991; Hon Fell, Austl Coll of Occupational Med, 1984. Appointments: Cap, RAAMC, BCOF, Japan and Korea, 1949-51; Var Postgrad Appts, Melbourne, 1958-63; Chmn, Dept of Respiratory Med, Prince Henry and Prince of Wales Hosps, Sydney, 1963-85; Mbr, Austl War Mem Cncl, Chmn, Hist and Publns Cttee, 1967-83; Cnslt, Pvte Prac. Publications include: Annotated Bibliography of the History of Medicine in Australia, 1957; Sev other books; Contbr of articles in profl and histl jrnls. Honour: AM, 1985. Memberships include: Roy Soc of Med; Roy Austl Histl Soc; Brit Soc for the Socl Hist of Med; Austl Thoracic Soc; Intl Soc Hist of Med. Hobbies: Wine; Books. Address: Cregganduff, Mount York Road, Mount Victoria, NSW 2786, Australia.

GANDHI Maneka, b. 26 Aug 1956, New Delhi, India. Activist; Author; TV Host; Member of Government. m. Sanjay Gandhi, Sept 1974, 1 s. Appointments: Min for Environ and Forests, 1989-91; Min for Empowerment and Socl Justice, 1998-. Publications: Penguin Book of Hindu Names; Book of Muslim Names; Brahma's Hair; Animal Laws of India; First Aid for Animals; Quiz Books on Animals. Honours: Lord Erskine Awd, RSPCA, 1992; Vegetarian of the Yr, Vegetarian Soc, 1995; Maharana Udai Singh Awd, 1996; Prani Mitra Awd, 1997; Marchig Prize, France and Switz, 1997; Venu Menon LIfetime Achmnt Awd, 1999; Bhadwan Mahaveer Awd, 1999. Memberships: People for Animals, chairperson; Rugmark Fndn, chairperson; Cttee for the Supvsn of Experiments on Animals, chairperson; Eurosolar Bd. Hobbies: Environmental and Animal Protection; Art. Address: A-4 Maharani Bagh, New Delhi 110065, India.

GANDHI Ramniklal K, b. 18 Jan 1929, Wankaner, Gujarat State, India. Pediatric Surgeon. m. Madhu, 23 Nov 1957, 1 s, 2 d. Education: MS, 1957; FCPS, 1957; FRCS, (ED) 1958; FICS (Hon); FACS; FAMS; FIAP. Appointments: Prof, Hd, Dept Pediat Surg, Seth G S Medl Coll, Univ of Mumbai. Creative works: Organised first postgrad dept of pediat surg w ICU for neonatal surg and modern operating th block in India. Honours include: Spec Awd for Promoting Pediat Syrg in Asia, from Prime Min of Thailand, 1978; Dr B C Roy Natl Awd, 1980; Medal of Polish Medl Acady (Academia Medica Polonia), 1980; Copernicus Medal of Craconicusis (Warsaw Univ), 1980; Sir John Bruce Gold Medal, RCS of Edinburgh, for promotion of the Sci of Surg at Global Level, 1990; Sir Denis Browne Gold Medal, Brit Assn of Pediat Surgs for Outstndng Contbn to Pediat Surg, 1993. Memberships: Indian Assn of Pediat Surgs, Pres, 1975-76; Indian Acady of Pediats, 1979; Assn of Surgs of India, Pres, 1980-; World Fedn of Assns of Pediat Surgs, 1980-83; Pres, Asian Assn of Pediat Surgs, 1980-82; Ed, Indian Jrnl of Surg, 1980-; Dean, Fac of Med, Univ of Bombay, 1981-86; Pres, Assn for Trauma Care of India; Pres, Coll Physns & Surgs of Bombay, 1983-84; Pres, Natl Acady of Medl Scis, 1988-90. Hobbies: Playing bridge. Address: 18, India House No 2, Kemps Corner, Mumbai 400 036, India.

GANDHI Sonia. Politician. m. Rajiv Gandhi, dec. Pres Rajiv Gandhi Fndn; Ldr Congress -I- Party, 1998-. Memberships: Mbr Congress -I- Party. Address: Rajiv Gandhi Foundation, Jawahar Bhawa, Dr Rajendra Prasad Road, New Delhi 110001, India.

GANESH P, b. 2 Mar 1965, Bangalore, India. Lecturer; Social Scientist. m. Radha, 25 Feb 1993, 2 d. Education: MA (Sociol); PhD (Socl Scis); PhD (Lit); Dip in Drug and Alcoholic Counselling and Therapy. Appointments: Lectr, Hd, Dept of Sociol, Noorie Coll of Nursing and Physiotherapy, KGF (affiliated to Rajiv Gandhi Univ of Hlth Scis) Suvarna Nursing Inst, KGF. Publications: Book of poems; Rsch articles in jrnls; Souvenirs, mags, newspprs. Honour: Participated in over 100 natl and intl seminars and confs. Membership: Utd Writer's Assn. Hobby: Booklover (collected over 10,000 books). Address: Panpagam, 11th Cross, 1095, Swarna Nagar, Robertsonpet, K G F-563 122, Karnataka, India.

GANGHARA RAO Kotha, b. 10 Feb 1926, Roddam Vill, Ananatapur District, Andhra Pradesh, India. Retired Administrative Officer, Andhra Pradesh, India. m. Manorama, 26 Jan 1945, 1 d. Education: Completed LME Dip Course, CNT Inst, Vepery, Madras, 1943. Appointments: LD Clerk, U D Clerk, Jnr Dpty Off Supt, Snr Dpty Off Supt, Off Supt, Admnstv Offr, Cntrl Excise Dept, Govt of India. Publications: Essays in Telugu on Social Reformers Vemana, Guruzada Appa Rao, Veeresalingam and Poems on Indira Gandhi, Uplift of Women during the period 1957-1975. Honours: 1st prize, Dr Bezewada Gopala Reddy, Fmr Chf Min of Andhra Pradesh for Telugu Essay (Vemana - the poet and socl reformer; Newsppr support in Karnataka and Andhra Pradesh for Eye Donation Campaign. Memberships: Cntrl Govt Pensioners Assn, Mysore; Life Mbr, Telgu Samakruthika Samithi, Mysore; Interested in Body Donation Campaign to Promote Organ Transplantation and Organ Banks, Mysore, India. Hobbies: Reading; Visiting places of interest; Interested in melodious music, social work and the environment. Address: Shree, #40, 5th Mian, 7th Cross, Sraswathipuram, Mysore 570 009, India.

GANGULI Som Nath, b. 16 Dec 1940, Meerut, India. Experimental Physicist. m. Kaberi, 9 June 1971, 1 s. Education: PhD, Phys, 1967. Appointments: Assoc Prof, 1984-90, Prof, 1990-93, Snr Prof, 1993-, TIFR, Mumbai, India; Sci Assoc, 1967-69, 1975-76, 1982-83, 1992-93, CERN, Geneva. Publications: Over 250 rsch pprs in refereed jrnls. Honour: Elect Fell, Indian Acady of Scis, Bangalore, 1992. Membership: Asian Cttee for Future Accelerators, 1996. Hobby: To understand evolutionary nature of mankind. Address: Tata Institute of Fundamental Research, Homi Bhabba Road, Mumbai 400 005, India.

GANGULY Bani Bandana, b. 19 Aug 1959, W Bengal, India. Scientist. m. P Ganguly, 28 June 1989, 2 s. Education: BS, 1982, MSc, 1984, PhD, 1989, Univ of Calcutta. Appointments: JRF, 1984-86; SRF, 1986-87; ARO, 1987-90, RA, 1991-96, Scientist (NGO), 1996-97, Pool Scientist, 1997-. Publications: 8 natl; 18 intl. Honours: Natl Young Scientist Awds, 1987, 1992; Invited as Guest Scientist, Fedl Off for Radiation Protection, Germany. Memberships: Life Mbr, Environ Mutagen Soc of India; Indian Women Scientists Assn. Address: Cell Biology Division, Bhabha Atomic Research Centre, Bombay 400085, India.

GANGULY Sobhakar, b. 31 Jan 1942, Barasat, India. Professor of Mathematics. m. Swati Ganguly, 10 Mar 1974, 2 s. Education: MA; PhD. Appointments: Lectr, W Bengal Jnr Educn Serv, 1965-73; Lectr, CA Univ, 1973-80; Rdr, CA Univ, 1980-86; Prof, Calcutta Univ, 1987-. Publications: Over 30 rsch pprs in profl jrnls. Honours: Gold Medal, CA Univ, 1961. Membership: Calcutta Mths Soc. Hobby: Music. Address: Kailaspuri, Barasat, North 24 Parganas, West Bengal, India.

GANGWAR Santosh Kumar, b. Nov 1948, Bareilly, Uttar Pradesh, India. Member of Parliament. m. Saubhagya Gangwar, 1 s, 1 d. Education: BSc, Agra Univ; LLB, Rohilkhand Univ, Bareilly. Appointments: Mbr, State Wrkng Cttee, Bharatiya Janata Pty, Uttar Pradesh, 1989-; Gen Sec, 1989; Elected, 9th Lok Sabha, 1989; Mbr Cttee of Priveleges, Consultative Cttee, Min of Com, Consultative Cttee, Min of Transp and Tourism, 1990; Re-elected, 10th Lok Sabha, 1991; Whip, BJP Parly Pty, Mbr, Cttee on Welfare of Scheduled Castes and Tribes, Cttee on Estimates, Cttee on Govt Assurances, Consultative Cttee, Min of Civ Aviation and Tourism, 1991-96; Re-elected, 11th Lok Sabha, 1996; Gen Sec, BJP, Uttar Pradesh, 1996-; Chmn, Cttee on Agric, 1996-97; Re-elected, 12th Lok Sabha, 1998; Union Min of State, Pet and Natural Gas, 1998-. Memberships: Chmn, Urban Co-op Bank Ltd, Bareilly; Crt of the Aligarh Muslim Univ; Gov Body, Indian Cncl of Agricl Rsch. Address: 22 Chaudhary Mohalla, Bareilly 243001, Uttar Pradesh, India.

GANI Joseph Mark, b. 15 Dec 1924, Cairo, Egypt. Statistician; Educator. m. Ruth Stephens, 3 Sept 1955, dec, 28 Jan 1997, 2 s, 2 d. Education: BSc, 1947, DIC, 1948, Imperial Coll, London; PhD, Austl Natl Univ, Canberra, 1955; DSc, London Univ, 1970. Appointments: Lectr, Dept of Maths, Univ of Melbourne, Vic, 1948-50; Lectr, Snr Lectr, Rdr, Dept of Maths, Univ of West Aust, 1953-60; Snr Fell, Dept of Stats, Austl Natl Univ, 1960-64; Prof, Dept of Stats and Probability, Michigan State Univ, USA, 1964-65; Prof, Dept of Probability and Stats, Univ of Sheffield, Eng, 1965-74; Dir, Manchester-Sheffield Sch of Probability and Stats, 1967-74; Chf Div of Maths and Stats, CSIRO, Aust, 1974-81; Chmn, Dept of Stats, Univ of KY, USA, 1981-85; Chmn, Dept of Stats and Applied Probability, Univ of CA, Santa Barbara, 1985-91; Prof, 1992-94; Visng Fell, Austl Natl Univ, 1995-97; Univ Fell, 1998-. Publications: The Condition of Science in Australian Universities, 1963; (ed) Perspectives in Probability and Statistics, 1975; The Making of Statisticians, 1982; (co-auth) Essays in Statistical Science, 1982; The Craft of Probabilistic Modelling, 1986; (co-auth) Essays in Time Series and Allied Processes, 1986; (co-auth) Epidemic Modelling: An Introduction, 1999. Honours: Nuffield Fndn Fell, 1956; Fell, Ausl Acady of Sci, 1976; Hon DSc, Univ of Sheffield, 1989; Univ of Wollongong, 1991; Statistical Soc of Aust's Pitman Medallist, 1994. Memberships include: Fell, Roy Statistical Soc; Amn Statistical Assn; Inst of Math Stats. Address: School of Mathematical Sciences, Australian National University, Canberra, ACT 0200, Australia.

GANN Deborah Ellen, b. 25 July 1968, Malaysia. Band Manager; Publicist. Education: Art and Entertainment Mktng Dip. Memberships: Intl Mngrs Forum, Aust; Mngmnt Cttee Mbr. Hobbies: Music. Address: Reservoir Promotions, P O BOx 502, Ashgrove, Qld 4060, Australia.

GAO Dachao, b. 30 Jan 1950, Jilin, China. Physicist. m. Guiqin, 14 Feb 1977, 1 d. Education: PhD, Appl Phys. Appointments: Rsch Assoc, Academia Sinica, China, 1976-86; Visng Scientist, Univ Manchester, Eng, 1987-88; Guest Scientist, 1988-92, Rsch Scientist, 1993-98, Snr Scientist, 1998-, CSIRO, Aust. Publications: 43 articles in profl jrnls. Honours: Sci Rsch Prize, 1979, 1982; Ex Yth Top Prize, 1985; Merit Citation, RSNA, 1997; '98 CSIRO Medal, 1998. Memberships: Austl Crystalography Soc; Austl Inst of Phys. Hobbies: Ice skating; Swimming; Travel. Address: CSIRO Manufacturing Science & Technology, Normandy Road, Claton, Victoria 3168, Australia.

GAO Dezhan, b. 6 Aug 1932. State Official; Senior Engineer. Appointments: Joined CCP, 1950; Worked in chem petrochem and light inds; Dir Jilin Prov Econ Commn Vice-Gov Jilin, 1983-85; Gov, 1985-87; Dep Sec CCP Prov Cttee Jilin, 1985; Min of Forestry, 1987-93; Vice-Chmn All-China Greening Cttee, 1988-93; Dep Hd Cntrl Forest Fire Prevention, 1988-93; Dep Hd State Ldng Grp for Comprehensive Agricl Dev, 1990-; Sec Tianjin Cty CCP Cttee, 1993-. Memberships: Alt mbr 12th CCP Cntrl Cttee; Alt mbr 13th CCP Cntrl Cttee, 1987-92; Mbr 14th CCP Cntrl Cttee, 1992-. Address: Office of the Tianjin Committee of Communist Party, Tianjin, Republic of China.

GAO Fu-An, b. 11 Oct 1944. Professor; Senior Engineer. m. 27 Nov 1969, 3 s. Education: Aircraft Dept, Northwestern Polytech Univ, 1961-66; Math Dept, Xian Jiaotong Univ, 1971-72; Math Dept, Zhejiang Univ, 1984-85; Engl Dept, Xian For Lang Inst, 1986. Appointments: Engr, 1977; Ldr, Sec-Gen, 1st and 2nd Natl Conf on Inverse Problems in China, 1986, 1989; Snr Engr, 1987; Reviewer, Chinese Jrnl of Vibration Engrng, 1987; Prof, 1989; Dir, Chinese Math Prog Soc, 1994. Publications include: Design and Calculation for Helicopter, book, 1976; 80 pprs, inclng: Sensitivity Analysis of Parameters in Solving Inverse Problem of Structural Dynamics, 1987; Research on the Inverse Eigenstate of Lumbocrural Pain Mechanism, 1993; The Theory and the Practice of Inverse Problem of High Dimensional Structural Dynamics, 1994; The Research for Vibration Control and Design of Helicopter Rotor Blade, 1995; Research for Inverse Problems and its Application in Aeronautical Engineering, 1994. Honours: Natl Sci Prize, 1978; 2nd Prize, Achmnt in Sci Rsch, 3rd Min of Machine-Bldng, China, 1981; Spec Theoretical Achmnt Prize, Min of Aeronautical Ind, China, 1983; Natl Invention Prize, China, 1983; 5 Prizes of Achievement in Sci Rsch, Prov, Cty and Inst Level. Memberships: Chinese Math Soc; Chinese Vibration Engrng Soc; AIAA; Intl Soc of Computing Mech; Dir, Chinese Math Prog Soc. Listed in: Famous Engineers in China; Dictionary of Chinese Famous Inventors. Hobbies: Music; Sports; Reading Philosophy, Chinese history and mysterious cultures. Address: Chinese Aeronautical Computation Technique Research Institute, PO Box 90, Xian 710068, Shaanxi Province, China.

GAO Rufeng, b. 23 June 1945, Zhejiang, China. Researcher. m. Zhang Baoqing, 22 Jan 1971, 1 d. Education: Grad, French Dept, Beijing Inst of Fgn Langs, 1968. Appointments: Tchr, Mid Sch, 1971-79; 3rd Sec, Chinese Emb in France, 1980-83; Assoc Rsch Fell, 1987-95, Rsch Fell, Prof, 1995-, Natl Inst of Educl Rsch. Publications: French Education Today, 1986; Comparative Education, 1992; French Cultural Tradition and Modern Education, 1993; On the French Educational Acts System, 1997. Membership: Rsch Cncl of Comparative Educn, Chinese Educl Inst. Hobbies: Sports; Reading. Address: Comparative Education Center, Chinese National Institute of Education Research, Be-San-Huan-Zhong-Lu 46, Beijing 100088, China.

GAO Shangquan, b. 1929 Jia Ding Co Shagnhai. Govt Official; Professor of Econsomics. m. Cha Peijun, 1958, 1 s. Education: St John's Univ Shanghai. Appointments: Rschr Dep Div Chf Div Chf Bur for Mach Bldg Ind of Min of Ind of local N East People's Govt; Policy Rsch Dep First Min of Mach Bldg Ind; Rsch Dept Min of Agricl Mach

Bldg Ind; Off of Agricl Mechanization State Cncl; Policy Rsch Dep State Commn of Mach Bldg Ind; Rsch Fell Rsch Cntr for Agricul Dev; Snr Economist State Commn of Mach Bldg Ind; State Commn for Restructuring Econ System, 1982; Dep Dir and Hd Rsch Inst of Restructuring Econ System; Vice-Min in charge of State Commn for Restructuring Econ System, 1985-93; Hd of Econ Panel, 1993-97; Vice-Grp-Ldr Ldng Grp for Restructuring Housing System under State Cncl; Chmn China Rsch Soc for Restructuring Econ Systems; Pres China Soc of Enterprise Reform and Dev; Pres China Reform and Dev Inst China Soc of Urban Housing System Reform; Pres Assn of Future Market of China; VP Assn of China's Urban Econ; VP Assn of China's Indl Econ; VP Assn for Study of China's Spec Condition; VP Assn of Soc and Econs Publs; Chmn Rsch Grp for Rural and Urban Housing Reform, 1995-; Doct Supvsr Prof Beijing Univ and Shanghai Jiaotong Univ; Prof Nankai Univ; MBA prog advsr of Natl Univ of Aust. Publications: Enterprises Should Enjoy Certain Autonomy, 1956; Follow A Road of Our Own In Agricultural Modernization, 1982; Nine Years of Reform in China' Economic System, 1987; A Road To Success, 1987; Selected Works of Gao Shangquan, 1989; China: A Decade of Economic Reform, 1989; China's Economic Reform, 1991, Engl edition, 1996; Lead to a Powerful Country, 1991; On Planning and Market in China, 1992; From Planned Economy to the Socialist Market Economy, 1993; An Introduction to Socialist Market Economy, 1994; China: The Second Revolution, 1995; Extensive Talk About China's Market Economy, 1998; Two Decades Reform in China, 1999; Market Economy and China's Reform, 1999; Also ed of num publs. Honours: Outstanding Schl Awd Hong Kong Polytech. Memberships: Mbr Natl Cttee of CPPCC prelim wrkng cttee of preparatory cttee of Hong Kong SAR; Mbr Sino-Japanese Econ Exch Commn; Mbr UN Cttee for Dev Policy. Address: State Commn for Restructuring the Econ System, 22 Xianmen St, Beijing 100017, People's Republic of China.

GAO Shou Lun, b. 13 July 1948, Tianquan County, Sichuan, China. Business Manager. m. Yakui-Tan, 16 Apr 1996, 2 s, 1 d. Education: Grad, Corresp Sch, Shangzhen Univ, specialising in Indl Mngmt. Appointments: Vice Mngr, Tianquan Saw-mill Factory, 1965-88; Mngr of multifarious timber factories, 1988-93; Gen Mngr of Erlang Indl Grp, 1993-. Publications: How to Make Artificial Timber with One-Layer Force, 1981; New Technology on Retreatment of Iron Belt, 1993; Improve the Quality of Iron Belt to Treat More Profits, 1993. Honours: Outstndng Scientific Personnel of Yaan Prefecture, 1994; Natl Model Worker, 1995. Hobby: Classical music. Address: Erlang Industrial Group, 27# Zhengxi Street, 625500 Tianquan County, Sichuan, China.

GAO Tianzheng, b. 1931 Tongxian Co Heibei Prov. Army Officer; Party Official. Appointments: Joined PLA, 1948; CCP, 1949-; Dep Polit Commissar PLA Guangzhou Mil Area Command, 1988-96. Memberships: Mbr 14th CCP Cntrl Cttee, 1992-. Address: Political Department of Guangzhou Military Area Command, Guangzhou City, Guangdong Province, People's Republic of China.

GAO Xin, b. 24 Dec 1955, China. Doctor. m. Feng Xiao Yuan, 9 Sept 1983, 1 d. Education: Master Deg, Med. Appointments: Vice Dir, Dept of Endocrinol, Zhongshan Hosp, Shanghai Med Univ, 1994; Dir, Dept of Endocrinol, Zhongshan Hosp, 1998. Memberships: Cttee, Chinese Med Assn of Endocrinol, Shanghai Diabetes Assn. Hobbies: Music; Photography. Address: 136 Yi-Xue-Yuan Road, Shanghai 200032, China.

GAO Yan, b. 1942 Yushu Co Jilin Prov. Government Official; Engineer. Appointments: Joined CCP, 1965; Vice-Gov of Jilin Prov, 1988-92; Gov, 1992-95; Sec CCP Cttee Yunnan Prov, 1995-97; Dir Polit Dept Chinese People's Armed Police Force; Sec CPC 6th Yunnan Prov Cttee. Memberships: Mbr 14th CCP Cntrl Cttee, 1992-97; Mbr 15th CCP Cntrl Cttee, 1997-. Address: c/o Communist Party of China, Yunnan Provincial Committee, Kunming, Yunnan Province, People's Republic of China.

GAO Yi-Tian, b. 6 May 1959. Physicist; Computer Scientist. Education: BS, Nankai Univ, China, 1982; MA, City Univ of New York, USA, 1986; MS, 1988, PhD, 1991 Univ of CA, Los Angeles, USA. Appointments: Postdoct Rsch Fell, Univ of MI and Fermi Natl Accelerator Lab, USA, 1991-93; Guest Sci, Fermi Natl Accelerator Lab, USA, 1993; Full Prof of Phys and Dpty Dir, Inst for Sci and Engrng Computations, Lanzhou Univ, China, 1993-96; Full Prof of Phys and Dpty Dir, Diff Engrng Cntr, Beijing Univ of Aeronautics and Astronautics, China, 1996-; Visng Rsch Prof, Lab of Computational Phys, Inst of Applied Phys and Computational Maths, China, 1996-; Visng Prof, Cath Univ of Taegu, S Korea. Honours: Ou Jou Yi Schlsp, USA, 1990; Julius Goodman Mem Prize in Theort Phys, USA, 1991; Outstndng Young Fac Fellshp, State Educ Commn of China, 1995-97. Address: Department of Applied Physics, Beijing University of Aeronautics & Astronautics, Beijing 100083, China.

GAO Ying, b. 25 Dec 1929 Jiaozuo Henan. Author. m. Duan Chuanchen, 1954, 1 s, 2 d. Appointments: Vice-Chmn Sichuan Br Chinese Writers' Assn; Dep Dir Ed Bd Sichuan Prov Brdcstng Stn, 1983-. Publications: The Song of Ding Youjun; Lamplights around the Three Gorges; High Mountains and Distant Rivers; Cloudy Cliff - long novel; Da Ji and her Fathers - novel and film script; The Orchid - novel; Loving-Kindness of the Bamboo Storey - collect of prose; Mother in my Heart - autobiogl novel; Songs of Da Liang Mountains - collect of poems; Frozen Snowflakes - collect of poems; Reminiscences; Xue Ma - novel; Gao Ying short novel collect. Memberships: Mbr Cncl Chinese Writers' Assn; Mbr Sichuan Polit Consultative Conf. Hobbies: Painting; Music. Address: Sichuan Branch of Chinese Association of Literary and Art Workers, Bu-hou-jie Street, Chengdu, Sichuan, People's Republic of China.

GAO Zhanxiang, b. 1935 Tongxian Co Hebei Prov. Party Official. Appointments: Joined CCP, 1953; Sec Communist Yth League Cntrl Cttee, 1978-82; Sec CCP Cttee Heibei Prov, 1983-86; Vice-Min of Culture, 1986-96; Pres Soc of Mass Culture, 1990-93; VP, 1993-; Chinese Assn for Promotion of Population Culture; Pres Soc of Photo Arts, 1994; Sec Party Grp China Fedn of Lit and Art Cirlces; Vice-Chmn, 1996; Dir Ed-in-Chf Chinese Arts. Memberships: Mbr Communist Yth League Cntrl Cttee, 1964; Alt mbr 12th CCP Cntrl Cttee, 1982-87; Mbr 8th CCP Natl Cttee, 1993-. Address: Ministry of Culture, A83 Beiheyan, Dongamen, Beijing 100722, People's Republic of China.

GAO Zhiqiang, b. 25 Mar 1964, Kaifeng, Henan, China. Educator. m. Pin Li, 23 Jan 1987, 1 s, 2 d. Education: BSc, 1985, PhD, 1990, Wuhan Univ. Appointments: Feingberg Postdoct Fell, 1993-94; Tchng Fell, Lee Kuan Yew Rsch Fell, 1994-97. Publications: Over 70 rsch articles in profl jrnls. Memberships: AAAS; Intl Soc of Electrochem; Union of Pure & Appl Chem. Hobbies: Swimming; Table Tennis; Bridge; Chess. Address: 111 Clementi Road #07-03, Singapore 129792, Singapore.

GARB Khona, b. 9 July 1945, USSR. Physicist. m. Steinbook, 15 May 1971, 2 d. Education: MS, State Univ, Vilnius, 1967; PhD, 1974; DSc, State Univ, Kharkov, 1990. Appointments: Rsch Inst, Radio Measuring Devices, Vilnius, 1967-90; Snr Rschr, Dept Electr Engrng and Physical Electronics, Tel Aviv Univ, Israel, 1991-. Creative Works: Sci Pprs, IEEE Transactions on MTT; IEEE Transactions on Antennas and Propagation; Sov Jrnl of Comms Technol and Electrons, Radiophysics, Quantum Electrons, Electron Letters. Address: Ugav 12-7, 48600 Rosh-Haayn, Tel Aviv, Israel.

GARCES Francisco, b. 30 Aug 1934, Santiago, Chile. Economist, Banker. m. Ysabel, 8 July 1977, 2 s. Education: MSc, Econs, William Coll; Ingeniero Comercial, Univ Catolica. Appointments: Mngr, Capital Mkts, Bank of Central Chile, 1975; Exec Dir, IMF, 1977-81; Intl Dir, Cntrl Bank, Chile, 1981-92; Dir, Intl Econ Inst. Publications: Sev Articles in Econs, Fin and Intl Economy. Memberships: Colegio Ingenieros, 1970-; Instituto Libertad of Desarrollo, 1992-. Hobbies: Arts; Reading; Horse back riding; Television. Address: Chinguihue 6638, Vitacura, Stgo, Chile.

GARCIA PEREZ Alan, b. 23 May 1949 Lima. Politician. m. Pilar Norse, 4 d. Education: Jose Maria Eguren Natl Coll; Univ Catolica Lima; Univ Natl Mayor de San Marcos - graduated as lawyer; Univ Complutense Madrid Spain and Sorbonne; Inst of Higher Latin Am Studies Paris France. Appointments: Returned to Peru and elected mbr of Constituent Ass, 1978; Subsequently apptd Org Sec and Chmn Ideology of Aprista Party; Parly Dep, 1980-85; Became Sec-Gen of Party, 1982; Now Pres; Sen for Life, 1990-; Nominated Presdl Candidate, 1984; Obtained largest number of votes Natl Presdl Elections, Apr 1985; On withdrawal of Izquierda Unida candidate Alfonso Barrantes Lingan proclaimed Pres elect, June 1985; Assuming powers, 1985-89; Granted Polit asylum in Colombia, June 1992. Memberships: Mbr of Partido Aprista Peruano.

GARCIA RAMIREZ Sergio, b. 1938 Guadalajara. Politician; Lawyer. Education: Natl Univ of Mexico. Appointments: Rsch Fell and tchr of penal law Inst of Juridical Rsch Natl Univ of Mexico, 1966-76; Dir Correction Cntr State of Mexico; Judge Juvenile Crts; Asst Dir of Govt Min of Interior; Att-Gen of Fed Dist; Under-Sec Mins of Natl Rescs Interior Educ Indl Dev; Dir Prevention Cntr of Mexico Cty; Fmr Min of Labour; Att-Gen, 1982-88. Publications incl: Teseo Alucinado, 1966; Asistencia a Reos Liberados, 1966; El Articulo 18 Constitucional, 1967; La Imputabilidad en el Derecho Penal Mexicano; El Codigo Tutelar para Menores del Estado Michoacan, 1969; La Ciudadania de la Juventud, 1970; La Prision, 1975; Los Derechos Humanos y el Derecho Penal, 1976; Legislacion Penitenciaria y Correccional Comentada, 1978; Otros Minotauros, 1979; Cuestines Criminologicas y Penales Contemporaneas, 1981; Justicia Penal, 1982. Memberships: Mbr Mexican Acady of Penal Scis; Mbr Mexican Inst of Penal Law; Mbr Natl Inst of Pub Admin; Mbr Ibero-Am Inst of Penal Law etc. Address: c/o Oficina del Procurador General, Mexico, DF, Mexico.

GARE Arran Emrys, b. 15 Jan 1948, Perth, Aust. Academic. m. Jennifer Willett, 11 May 1993, 1 s, 1 d. Education: BA (Hons), Univ West Aust; PhD, Murdoch Univ. Appointments: Lectr, Philos, Univ of Queensland, Murdoch Univ, Curtin Univ, Swinburne Univ; Snr Lectr. Publications: Nihilism Incorporated, 1993; Beyond European Civilisation, 1993; Postmodernism and th Environmental Crisis, 1995; Nihilim Inc, 1996. Honours: Fulbright Postdoct, Boston Univ, 1985. Address: Philosophy and Cultural Inquiry, Swinburne University, Victoria, Australia.

GARFORTH Vivienne Meryl, b. 22 Mar 1947. Auth; Tutor. m. (1) Phillip Chinnery, 30 Jan 1970, (2) Edward Garforth, 9 Dec 1989, 1 s, 2 d. Appointments: Class Tutor in Embroidery and Dècoupage, Perth, WA. Publications: Australian Cross-Stitch Designs, 1989; Colonial Embroidery, 1991; Australian Themes in Cross-Stitch, 1992; Our Heritage in Cross-Stitch and Embroidery, 1993; Dècoupage with Scrapbook Pictures, 1993; Australian Dècoupage; A Source Book for Australian Cross-Stitch, 1996; Num articles on Embroidery to mags inclg: Australian Womens Weekly; The New Idea; Australian Country Craft; Handmade; Embroidery and Cross-Stitch; Needlecraft, UK. Honours: Guest Embroiderer at, The Knitting and Stitching Show, London, 1995. Memberships: Embroiderers Guild of WA, 1980-87. Hobbies: Embroidery; Gardening. Address: 22 Waterhall Road, South Guildford, WA 6055.

GARNAUT Michelle Anne, b. 31 Jan 1957, Melbourne, Australia. Restauranteur. Education: Cert of Catering. Appointments: Trainee Cook, Wentworth Hotel, Melbourne, 1981-82; Hd Cook, Orient Express, London, 1983; Freelance Cook, Melbourne, 1983-84; Restaurant Mngr, Hong Kong, 1984-86; Mngng Dir, M.G. CCC, Hong Kong, 1986-89; Owner, Operator, M at the Fringe, Hong Kong, 1989-, M on the Bund, Shanghai, 1999-. Publications: Ed, Hong Kong Cooks (book), 1996. Memberships: Chairperson, Ft Chefs of Hong Kong Heep Hong Soc, 1996; Cttee, Bela Vista Ball Worldwide Party Prog. Address: M at the Fringe, 2 Lower Albert Road, Hong Kong, China.

GARNER Bruce Le Grange, b. 27 May 1962, Hastings, New Zealand. Genealogist. m. Vicki, 28 May 1983. Memberships: Australasian Assn of Genealogists and Record Agents, Cncl Mbr, 1997-. Hobbies: History of funeral directors; Pro wrestling. Address: 11/99 Neplean Highway, Seaford 3198, Victoria, Australia.

GARNETT Michael Pearson, b. 24 Nov 1938. Chief Executive, Australian Royal Tennis Association. m. 1975, 2 s. Education: Framlingham Coll, Suffolk; Dip Bus and Co Law, Brit Inst of Careers, NSW. Appointments: Mil Serv, Flt Lt, RAF and RAAF; Tea Plantation Mngr, N E India, 1960-67; Govt and Pub Affairs, BP Aust Ltd, 1967-94. Publications: A History of Royal Tennis in Australia, 1983; Tennis, Rackets and Other Ball Games, 1986; Royal Tennis for the Record, 1991; A Chase Down-Under, 1999. Memberships: Roy Melbourne Tennis; Naval and Mil, Melbourne. Hobbies: Tennis; Gardening; Writing. Address: The Chase, Romsey Vic 3434, Australia.

GARNIER RIMOLO Leonardo, b. 4 Feb 1955. Minister of National Planning. m. Education: BSc, Econ Scis, Univ Costa Rica, 1977; MSc, Econs, NY Sch Socl Rsch, 1982; PhD, Econs, 1989. Appointments: Prof, Gen Stdies, Univ Costa Rica, 1975-77; Prof, Econs, 1977-; Advsr, Ministry Natl Plng, 1987-88; Dir, Global Plng, 1988-89; Min, Nalt Plng Econ Plcy, Govt Costa Rica, 1994-; Prof, Rschr, Econs, Natl Univ Caribbean, 1986-87, Tilburg Univ, 1986-87; Dir, Rschr, Alternative Inst Dev, 1985-; Masters' Prof, 1986-; Dir, Econ Plcy, Cntrl Am, 1985-; Rschr, Socl Environ and Technol Rsch Cntr, 1986-; Advsr, Indl Dev Org, UN, 1986; Advsr Dev Prog, 1991; Mbr, Rsch Team, Latin Am Fac Socl Scis, 1990-91; Guest Prof, Cntrl Am Inst Bus Admin, 1991-; Exec Dir, Bipartisan Commn, Costa Rican Reform, 1991-92; Ed, La Republica, 1993-. Address: Ministry of National Planning, Avenida 3 y 5 Calle 4, 1000 San José, Costa Rica.

GARRAN-BROWN Edna Graham, b. Brisbane, Aust. Artist. m. Raymond Farley Thew, 29 Apr 1944, 1 s, 1 d. Education: Studied Painting. Honours include: Over 100 Awds, Latest Frist Prize Awds in Art Competitions incl: Portland, 1985, 1986, 1989; Quirindi, 1986; Scone (Open Bicentennial Prize), 1988; Kogarah, 1988, 1992; Roy Easter Show, Sydney, 1991, other Roy Easter Show Awds, 1983, 1985, 1986, 1988, 1994; Finalist in Archiald Portrait Prize, Sydney, 13 times, incl most recent, 1972, 1973, 1974, 1975, 1977; Finalist in Sulman Art Prize, Sydney, 7 times; Finalist in Wynne Art Prize, Sydney, 4 times. Membership: Fell, Roy Art Soc of NSW, 1984. Listed in: The World Who's Who of Women and others. Address: 77 The Chase Road, Turramurra, NSW 2074, Australia.

GARRETT Peter, b. 16 Apr 1953, Wahroonga, NSW, Aust. Singer. m. Doris Garrett, 1986, 3 d. Education: Law deg, Univ of NSW, 1977. Appointments: Mbr, Rock Is Line; Ld Singer, Midnight Oil, 1976-; Reg tours worldwide inclng: Earthquake Benefit Concert (w Crowded House), NSW, 1990; Solo perfs, Earth Day Sound Action Benefit (w Joan Baez, Steve Miller, The Kinks), Foxboro, MA, USA, 1992; Earth Day Sound Action Benefit, Columbia, 1993; Strong links w ecological grps; Benefit concerts for: Aboriginal Rights Assn; Tibet Cncl; Song proceeds for Deadicated to Rainforest Action Network & Cultural Survival; Protest Concert, Exxon Bldg (Exxon Valdez oil spill), 1990; Ran for Austl Senate, Nuc Disarmament Party, 1984. Publications: Political Blues, 1987; Outlanders (radio drama w T Daly), 1995. Creative works: Albums recorded w Midnight Oil: Head Injuries, 1979; Bird Noises, 1980; Place Without a Postcard, 1981; Red Sails in the Sunset, 1982; 10, 9, 8, 7, 6, 5, 4, 3, 2, 1, 1983; Diesel and Dust, 1987; Blue Sky Mining, 1990; Scream in Blue - Live Earth, Sun and Moon, 1992, 1993; Breathe, 1996; 20,000 Watt RSL, 1997; Hit single: Beds Are Burning, 1989; Contbr: Artists Utd Against Apartheid album, 1985; Deadicated (Grateful Dead tribute album), 1991. Honours: 5 Austl Rec Ind Assn Awds, 1991; Crystal

Globe Awd, Sony Music, 1991; Gold and Platinum Discs. Membership: Pres, Austl Conservation Fndn, 1987; Natl Trust Living Treasure. Listed in: International Who's Who; Who's Who in Australia. Hobbies: Bodysurfing; Australian literature. Address: c/o Gary Morris Management, PO Box 186, Glebe, NSW 2037, Australia.

GASCOIGNE John, b. 20 Jan 1951, Liverpool, England. Academic. m. Kathleen May Bock, 6 Apr 1998, 1 s, 1 d. Education: BA, 1st class hons, Sydney Univ; MA, distinction, Princeton Univ; PhD, Cambridge Univ. Appointments: Lectr, Univ of Papua New Guinea, 1977-78; Tutor, 1980, Lectr, 1984-89, Snr Lectr, 1989-97, Asst Prof, 1997-, Univ NSW. Publications: Cambridge in the Age of the Enlightenment, 1989; Joseph Banks and the English Enlightenment, 1994; Science in the Service of the Empire, 1998. Honour: Austl Histl Assn Hancock Prize. Membership: Review Ed, Jrnl of Relig Hist, 1996-. Address: c/o School of History, University of New South Wales, Sydney, NSW 2052, Australia.

GASCOIGNE Thomas Humphrey, b. 15 June 1945, Canberra, Australia. Scientist. m. Lynette, 15 Nov 1981, 2 s. Education: BA, Aust Natl Univ; Dip.Ed, Univ of Tas. Appointments: Rsch Offr, C'wlth Dept of Housing, 1967-69; Tchr, England and Tas, 1970-90; Freelance Jrnlst, 1982-90; Cmmn Mngr, Cntr Environ Mechs, CSIRO, 1991-94; Exec Dir, FASTS, 1994-. Publications include: Antarctica: Discovery and Exploration, 1985; Dreamtime, 1988; Into the Future, 1990; Bittersweet, 1992. Honours: Media Awd, Landcare, 1991; CSIRO Chf Exec Study Awd, 1994. Memberships: Natl Press Club; Fndng Mbr, VP, Austl Sci Cmmnrs; Sci Cttee, Intl Network for the Pub Cmmn of Sci and Technol; Sci Forum. Address: PO Box 218, Deakin West, ACT 2600, Australia.

GATES Ronald Cecil, b. 8 Jan 1923, Melbourne, Aust. Retired. m. Barbara Mann, 19 Dec 1953, 2 s (1 dec), 2 d. Education: BCom, Univ of Tas, (Interrupted by War Serv), 1941-45; MA, Oxford Univ, 1946-48. Appointments: Clk, Austl Taxation Off, Hobart, 1941-42; Pvt, AIF, 1942-45; Histn, Austl Taxation Off, Canberra, 1949-52; Snr Lectr, Econs, Univ of Sydney, 1952-64; Assoc Prof, 1964-65, Prof, Econs, 1966-77, Univ of Qld; Pres, Professorial Bd, 1975-77; Vice Chan, Univ of New England, 1977-85. Publications: Survey of Consumer Finances (w H R Edwards and N T Drane), 1963-65, Vol 2, 1965, Vols 1, 3, 4, 1966, Vols, 5, 6, 7, 1967; Jointly: The Price of Land, 1971; New Cities for Australia, 1972; Land for the Cities, 1973; Simulation, Uncertainty and Public Investment Analysis (w P A Cassidy), 1977; La Septaga Murdenigmo, 1991, Kolera Afero, 1993, Morto de Sciencisto, 1994, (Detective Novels in Esperanto); Sep Krimnoveloj, 1993, Refoje Krimnoveloj Sep, 1994, Tria Kolekto da Krimnoveloj (Vols of Crime Short Stories in Esperanto), 1996; La Vidvino kaj la Profesoro (novel). Honours: Rhodes Schl, Tas, 1946; Rockefeller Fell in Socl Scis, 1955; Carnegie Travel Grant, 1960; Fell, Acady of Socl Scis in Aust, 1968; Hon Fell, Roy Austl Plng Inst, 1976; AO, 1978; Hon DEcon Qld, 1978; Hon Fell, Austl Inst of Urban Studies, 1979; Hon DLitt, New England, 1987. Memberships include: Chmn, Statutory Consumer Affairs Cncl of Qld, 1971-73; Cmnr, C'wlth Cmmn of Inquiry into Poverty, 1973-77; Chmn, Austl Inst of Urban Studies, 1975-77; Chmn, Advsry Cncl for Inter-Govt Rels, 1979-85; Chmn, Austl Natl Cmmn for UNESCO, 1981-83; Chmn, Local Govt Trng Cncl, 1983-92; Chmn, Armidale City and Dumaresq Shire Joint Plng Cttee, 1992-97; Vice Pres, 1995-98, Pres, 1998- Austl Esperanto Assn; Rektoro, Internacia Kongresa Universitato, 1997. Hobbies: Music; Beef cattle breeding; Esperanto; Bridge. Listed in: Who's Who; Who's Who in Australia; Who's Who in the World; Dictionary of International Biography. Address: Wangarang, MSF 2001, Armidale, NSW 2350, Australia.

GATT Israel, b. 31 Aug 1953, Jerusalem, Israel. Engineer; Data System Analyst. m. Aviva, 13 Feb 1974, 3 s, 1 d. Education: MSc, Data System Analysis, Engrng Mngmt. Publications: ILS Data Resource Management, 1986; DFD & SADT Methods, 1986; Configuration Management, 1988; Engineering Data, 1988; HW & SW Integration, 1988. Memberships: SME; SOLE; ISCM; Israeli Soc of Data Analysts. Address: 17 Bet-El Road, PO Box 78, Kocav Yair 44864, Israel.

GATT Stephen, b. 24 Jan 1952, Malta (arr in Aust, 1975). Anesthesiologist; Intensivist. m. Alice Dingli, 16 Sept 1975, 1 s, 3 d. Education: MD, Roy Univ Malta, 1975; LRCP (London) Lic Roy Coll Physns of London, 1975; MRCS (Eng) Mem Roy Coll Surg of Eng, 1975; FFARACS (Aust) Fell Fac Anaesthesiology Roy Australasian Coll Surgs, 1982; FANZCA (Aust, NZ) Fell Aust and NZ Coll Anaesthesiologists, 1992; FFICANZCA (AUST, NZ) Fell Fac Intensive Care Aust and NZ Coll Anaesthesiologists, 1993; MRACMA (Aust), Mbr Roy Australasian Coll of Medl Admnstrs, 1999. Appointments include: Res, Snr Res, 1977078, Medl Registrar, 1978-79, St Vincent's Hosp, Darlinghurst, Sydney; Anesthetic and intensive care registrar, Prince Henry/Prince of Wales Hosps, Randwick, Sydney, 1979-83; Jnr Cnclt Fell, Intensive Care, Prince of Wales Hosp, 1983; Instr, Anesthesia (attending) Harvard Univ Sch, Brigham and Womens' Hosp, Boston, 1983-85; Clin Lectr, Univ NSW, Kensington, Aust, 1985-89, Snr Lectr, 1989-; Dir Anesthesia, Roy Hosp for Women, Sydney, 1985-89, 1991-97; Estab 1st free-standing obstet intensive care unit, 1991; Anesthesia and Acute Care, 1988-91; Dir, Anesthesia and Acute Care, 1988-91, Snr Staff Spec, 1997-, Roy Hosp for Women; Hd, Div Anesthesia and Intensive Care, prog Dir Acute Servs, Prince of Wales, Prince Henry and Sydney Children's Hosps, Mbr editl bd, Obstet Anesthesia, 1995-. Publications: Contbr over 100 articles and chapts to profl jrnls and sci books. Honours: Recip Griffiths Gold Medal, 1975; Warrent Pres of Repub of Malta, 1975; Matthew Spence Medal in Intensive Care, 1982; Medal of the Order of Aust, 1997; Invested Kt of Order of St John of Jerusalem, Rhodes and Malta (SMOM), 1998; Pres, Obstet Anaethesia Soc of Asia and Oceania. Hobbies: Fishing; Snorkelling. Address: Kensington, A'Orangi, 47 Balfour Rd, Kensington, Sydney, NSW 2033, Australia.

GAUDRON Alfred Wasserman, b. 11 Oct 1947, Sydney, Aust. Retired Librarian. Education: BA (Hons), MA (Hons), Sydney Univ; Dip in Librarianship, Univ of NSW. Appointments: Lib Trainee, 1968-73; Tutor, Univ of Sydney, 1973-74; Libn, Hosp Libs, 1984-90. Publications: No Blunt Invention, 1989; Narrabeen and Other Places, 1990; Qumran Verse, 1992; Translations of Dead Sea Scrolls, 1992. Honours: Hon DLit, World Congress of Poets, 1992. Memberships: Austl Soc of Auths; Life Mbr, Tranby Aboriginal Coll. Hobbies: Chess; Reading; Classical music; Translating Dead Sea Scrolls. Address: 14 Oak Street, Narrabeen North, New South Wales 2101, Australia.

GAUNDER Yashwant, b. 9 Aug 1963. Publisher; Managing Director. Education: Univ of S Pacific, Fiji; Univ of Adelaide, S Aust. Appointments: Publr, The Review, Pacific Bus, Pacific Telecom, Fiji Prod Directory, Fiji Calling, Fiji Magic; Mngng Dir, The Network Ltd, a corp comms co; Mngng Dir, Assoc Media Ltd, publng co; Mngng Dir, Fijilive.com website; Mngng Dir, Freedom Fones Co. Memberships: Pub Rels Inst of Aust; Pub Rels Inst of NZ. Address: GPO Box 12095, Suva, Fiji.

GAUR S N S, b. 29 Jan 1936. University Professor. m. Somlata, 20 Apr 1962, 1 s, 2 d. Education: BVSc, AH; MVSc; PhD. Appointments: Asst Prof, Assoc Prof, Prof; Prof, Hd Dept, Para Sitology, G B Dant Univ; Prof, Parasitology Expert, Shiraz Univ, Iran. Creative Works: 110 Orig Rsch Articles; Prolozoan and Arthropod Diseases of Animals. Honours: B V Rao Awd. Memberships: Indian Assn for Advmnt of Vet Parasitology; Jrnl of Vet Parasitology. Hobbies: Editing; Research articles; Helping collegues. Address: K G-1, 147, Vikaspuri, New Delhi 110018, Inida.

GAUTHMAN M, b. 15 June 1958, Ogalur. Librarian. m. 11 June 1986, 1 s. Education: MA Philos; MPhil Pol Philos; MLIS, Lib Sci. Adult Educ, TNBCE, Chennai, 1984; Supvsr, 2 Libns, Tamil Univ, Thanjavur-5. Memberships: Life Mbr, IASLIC, Calcutta, India; Indian Red Cross Soc, Thanjavur-5, India. Hobby: Volleyball. Address: HIG 255, Marutham, New Housing Unit, Thanjavuur-5, Tamil Nadu, India.

GAVASKAR Sunil Manohar, b. 10 Jul 1949 Bombay. Cricketer; Business Executive. m. Marshniel Mehrotra, 1974, 1 s. Education: St Xavier's High Sch Bombay; St Xavier's Coll Bombay Univ. Appointments: Right-hand opening batsman; Played for Bombay, 1967-87; Somerset, 1980; 125 Tests for India, 1970-97 - 47 as Cap - scoring 10122 runs - average 51.1 - with 34 hundreds - world record - and holding 108 catches; Toured Eng 1971, 1974, 1975 - World Cup - 1979, 1982, 1983 - World Cup; Scored 25834 first-class runs with 81 hundreds; highest score - 236 v Aust, Dec 1983 - by Indian in Test match; First player to score more than 10000 Test runs, 1987; First player to score over 2000 runs against three cos, 1987; Only man to play in a hundred successive Tests. Publications: Sunny Days - An Autobiography, 1976; Idols - autobiog - 1982; Runs 'n Ruins, 1984. Honours: Arjuna Awd, 1975; Padma Bhushan, 1980. Address: Nirlon Synthetic Fibres and Chemicals Ltd, Nirlon House, 254-B, Dr Annie Besant Road, Worli, Bombay-18, India.

GAVIRIA TRUJILLO Cesar. Politician. m. Milena Gaviria. Appointments: Dir Commn for Econ Affairs, 1972; Vice-Min for Dev; Min of Fin and Pub Credit, 1986; Min of the Interior, 1988; Pres of Colombia, 1990-94; Sec-Gen OAS, Mar 1994-. Memberships: Mbr Town Cncl of Pereira; Mbr Chamber of Deps. Address: Organization of American States, 1889 F Street, NW, Washington, DC 20006, USA.

GAYOOM Maumoon Abdul, b. 29 Dec 1937. Maldivian Politician. m. Nasreena Ibrahim, 2 s, 2 d. Education: Al-Azhar University, Cairo; Rsch Asst in Islamic History, Amn Univ of Cairo, 1967-69. Appointments: Lectr in Islamic Studies and Philos, Abdullahi Bayero Coll of Ahmadu Bello Univ, Nigeria, 1969-71; Tchr, Aminiya Sch, 1971-72; Imam at Friday Prayers, 1972-73; Man Govt Shipping Dept, 1972-73; Writer and Translator, Pres Off, 1972-73; Imam at Friday Prayers, 1973-74; Under-Sec, Telecomms Dept, 1974; Writer and Translator, Pres Off, 1974; Dir, Telephone Dept, 1974; Spec Under-Sec Off of the Prime Min, 1974-75; Dpty Amb to Sri Lanka, 1975-76; Under-Sec Dept of External Affairs, 1976; Dpty Min of Transport, 1976; Perm Repr to UN, 1976-77; Min of Transport, 1977-78; Pres of the Repub of Maldives; Gov of Maldives Monetary Authy, 1981-; Min of Def and Natl Security, 1982-; Min of Fin, 1989-93; Min of Fin & Treas, 1993-; Mbr, Constituent Cncl of Rabitat Al-Alam Al-Islami. Honours: Hon DLitt, Aligarh Muslim Univ of India, 1983; Hon PhD in Pol Sci, Marquis Giuseppe Scicluna (1855-1907), Intl Univ Fndn, USA, 1988; Global 500 Hon Roll (UN Environ Prog), 1988; Hon DLItt, Jamia Millia Islamia of India, 1990; Man of Sea Awd, Lega Navale Italiana, 1990; Hon DLitt, Pondicherry Univ of India, 1994; GCMG, 1997; WHO Hlth-for-All Gold Medal, 1988; DRV Intl Environ Awd, 1998. Hobbies: Astronomy; Calligraphy; Photography; Badminton; Cricket. Address: The President's Office, Boduthakurufaanu Magu, Malé 20-05, Republic of Maldives.

GAZIT Shlomo, b. 1926 Turkey. Army Officer; Administrator. m. Avigayil-Gala Gazit, 1 s, 2 d. Education: Tel Aviv Univ. Appointments: Joined Palmach, 1944; Co Cmdr Harel Brig, 1948; Dir Off of Chf of Staff, 1953; Liaison Offr with French Army Deleg Sinai Campaign, 1956; Instr Israel Def Forces Staff and Command Coll, 1958-59; Gen Staff, 1960-61; Dep Cmdr Golani Brig, 1961-62; Instr Natl Def Coll, 1962-64; Hd IDFIntelligence assessment div, 1964-67; Co-ordr of Govt Activities in Admin'd Territories Min of Def, 1967-74; Rank of Maj-Gen, 1973; Hd of Mil Intelligence, 1974-79; Fell at Cntr for Intl Affairs Harvard Univ, 1979-80; Pres Ben Gurion Univ of the Negev, 1981-85; Dir-Gen Jewish Agcy Jerusalem, 1985-88; Snr Rsch Fell Jaffee Cntr for Strategic Studies Tel-Aviv Univ, 1988-94; Fell Woodrow Wilson Cntr WA DC, 1989-90; Disting Fell US Inst of Peace WA DC, 1994-95; Advsr to Israeli PM on Palestinian Peace Process, 1995-96. Publications: Estimates and Fortune-Telling in Intelligence Work, 1980;

Early Attempts at Establishing West Bank Autonomy, 1980; Insurgency Terrorism and Intelligence, 1980; On Hostages' Rescue Operations, 1981; The Stick and the Carrot - Israel's Military Govt in Judea and Samaria - in Hebrew - 1985; The Third Way - The Way of No Solution, 1987; Policies in the Administered Territories, 1988; Intelligence Estimates and the Decision Maker, 1988 - ed; The Middle East Military Balance, 1988-89, 1990-92, 1993-94; Trapped: 30 Years of Israeli Policy in W B and Gaza (Hebrew), 1999. Address: 20 Tarpad Street, Ramat Hasharon 47250, Israel.

GAZZO Yves, b. 17 Dec 1946, Oran. Ambassador. m. Nikola, 4 s. Education: Dip, Inst of Polit Studies, Paris, 1969; PhD, Econs, Paris, 1971, PhD, Applied Econs, 1975. Appointments: Volun, Chad, 1969-70; Cnslt, Bus Org, Arthur Andersen, 1971-72; Hd of Proj, Niger, UNDP, 1973-74; Hd of Proj, FAO, World Bank Invmnt Cntr, 1974-79; Loans Offr, World Bank, 1980-84; Intl Rels Advsr, World Bank, Paris, 1985-88; Econ Cnslr, EC Delegation in Mali, 1988-90; Dpty Hd, EC Structural Adjustment Unit, Brussels, 1990-94; EC Amb, Hd of Delegation, Delegation in Jordan, 1994-98; EC Amb, Hd of Delegation, Manila, Philippines, 1998- . Creative Works: Many Publications. Honours: Great Cross of Independence, Jordan; Chevalier de la Legion d'Honneur, France. Address: 7/F Salustiana D Ty Tower, 104 Paseo de Roxas Cor Perea Street, Legaspi Village, Makati City 1200, Philipines.

GE Hongsheng, b. 1931 Ju'nan Co Shandong Prov. Government Official. Appointments: Joined CCP, 1948; Sect Chf CCP Taizhou Prefectural Cttee, 1949-56; Dir of Propaganda Dept Xin'anjiang Electric Power Engng Bur, 1960; Dep Dir and Dep Sec No 9 Engng Bur Min of Electric Power, 1963-74; Gen Dir and Sec CCP Zhejiang Banshan Power Plant GHQ, 1974-77; Dir Electric Power Bur Zhejiang Prov, 1983; Vice-Chmn Zhejiang Prov Econ Commn, 1983; Sec CCP Ningbo Municipal Cttee, 1983-88; Dep Sec CCP Zhejiang Prov Cttee, 1988-93, removed from off; Gov Zhejiang Prov, 1991-93; Dep Dir Spec Econ Zones Off, 1994-96; Dir, 1996-. Memberships: Mbr Standing Cttee CCP Zhejiang Prov Cttee, 1986-88; Mbr CCP 14th Cntrl Cttee, 1992-. Address: Special Economic Zones Offices, Beijing, People's Republic of China.

GE Qin-Sheng, b. 24 Feb 1917, Shanghai, China. Professor. m. H C Iseng, 2 Sept 1949, 1 s. Education: Grad, Shanghai Med Univ. Appointments: Peoples Hosp, Beijing, 1944; Peking Union Med Coll Hosp, 1948-. Publications: Sev articles in profl med jrnls. Honours: 3rd Place Natl Sci Prize, 1997. Address: c/o Department of Obstetrics & Gynaecology, Peking Union Medical Hospital, Beijing 100730, China.

GE Xian-Kang, b. 25 Nov 1932, Shanghai, China. Professor. m. Cai-Li Yie, 25 May 1953, 1 s, 1 d. Education: Grad, E China Jiaotong Coll, Shanghai, 1952. Appointments: Chmn, Automobile Dept, Nanking Mech Coll, 1952-65; Vice Prof, Chmn, Internal Combustion Engine Dept, Hunan Univ, 1965-85; Prof, Dpty Chmn, Automobile Engrng Dept, Shanghai Univ of Engrng Sci, 1985-; Pt-time Prof, Mech Engrng Dept, Hunan Univ. Publications include: Development of Spark Plug Rating Equipment and Investigation of Method for Spark Plug Rating, 1984; Numerical Simulation of Combustion Process in SI Engines, 1986; Calculation, Analysis and Application of Heat Release Rate in the Swirl Chamber Diesel Engine, 1985; A Study on the Accurate Calculation Method of Heat-Release Rate in Swirl Chamber Indirect Injection Diesel Engine, 1989. Honours: Sci Awd, 1978, 1984, Model Tchr, 1978, Model Worker, 1986, Hunan Prov; Sci Awd, Mech Ind Min of China, 1984; Sci Gold Awd, China, 1993; Invention and Innovation Sci-Tech Star, 1994, UN TIPS Natl Bur in China. Memberships: Tchng Guiding Cttee, Chinese Tech Univ Internal Combustion Engine Speciality; Standing Dir, Shanghai Soc for Internal Combustion Engines. Hobbies: Literature; Art; Music; Sports. Address: Automobile Engineering College, Shanghai University of Engineering Science, No 350 Xian-Xia Road, Shanghai 200335, China.

GEBBIE Gordon Joseph, b. 16 July 1949, Melbourne, Australia. Catholic Priest. Education: Master of Relig, Cath Univ of Am, WA, USA. Appointments: Asst Priest, Bundoora, Brunswick, Ashburton; Asst Dir, Melbourne Liturgy Cntr; Parish Priest, N Noblepark, Bentleigh E. Memberships: Sec, Austl Acady of Liturgy, 1983-84; Chairperson, Melbourne Senate of Priests, 1994-95. Hobbies: Woodturning; Golf; Tennis. Address: St Peter's Church, 844 Centre Road, East Bentleigh 3165, Australia.

GEE Helen Margaret, b. 9 Nov 1950, Launceston, Tas, Aust. Writer; Farmer; Environmentalist. m. Robert Earle Graham, 8 Oct 1979, 1 s, 1 d. Education: BA, 1971, DipEd, 1973, Univ Tas; Bush and Mountain Walking Ldrshp Ctf, Tas, 1990. Appointments: Tchng from Kindergarten to Matriculation; Archaeological Site Recorder, AIAS; Environmental Activism; Campaign Co-ordinator; Writer and Poet; Farmer. Publications: The Franklin: Tasmania's Last Wild River, 1978; The South-West Book, 1978, 1979, 1983; The West Wind and Other Verses for the Tasmanian Bush, 1980; South West Tasmania (ed), 1981; Wild Tasmania and Wilderness (ed), 1982; Forest Echoes (ed), 1988; Magpie Boy (editor), 1989; Prosser River Landcare Survey Riparian Weeds and Erosion (ed), 1995; A History of Tasmanian Forest Campaigns, forthcoming. Other: Num articles in profl jrnls and mags. Honours: Fndr and Hon Life Mbr, The Wilderness Soc, Aust, 1990. Memberships: Aust Greens Party; Aust Conservation Fndn; Convenor, Pedder 2000 and The Lake Pedder Restoration Campaign; Convenor, SE Forest Protection Grp; Tasmania 2010 Forum. Hobbies: Restoration ecology; Bushwalking; Mountaineering; Music; Reading; Travel. Address: Stonehurst, Buckland, Tas 7190, Australia.

GEE Maurice Gough, b. 22 Aug 1931, Whakatane, New Zealand. Writer. m. Margareta, 1970, 1 s (previous m), 2 d. Education: MA, Auckland Univ, 1954. Publications: 14 adult novels; 9 childrens novels. Honour: Hon DLitt, Vic Univ of Wellington, 1987. Address: 41 Chelmsford Street, Ngaio, Wellington, New Zealand.

GEGHMAN Yahya Hamoud, b. 24 Sept 1934 Jahana. Diplomatist. m. Cathya Geghman, 1971, 1 s, 1 d. Education: Law Schs of Cairo Paris Damascus and Boston; Columbia Univs. Appointments: Tchr of Arabic Lang and Lit Kuwait, 1957-59; Dir-Gen Yemen Brdcstng System, 1962-63; Gov Yemen Bank For Reconstruction and Dev, 1962-63; Sec-Gen Supreme Cncl for Tribal Affairs, 1962-63; Spec Advsr Min of For Affairs, 1962-63; Dep Perm Rep to UN, 1963-66, 1967-68; Min Plenipotentiary Yemen Arab Repub - YAR - Emb to USA, 1963-67; Min of For Affairs, 1968-69; Min of State Personal Rep of the Pres, 1969; Dep PM Pres Supreme Cncl for Yth Welfare and Sport, 1969-71; Perm Rep to UN, 1971-73; Amb to USA, 1972-74; Min for For Affairs, 1974-75; Personal Rep of Pres of the Repub, 1977-85; Chf Bur of S Yemen Affairs and Chmn Yemen Reunification Commns, 1980-83; Amb to Switzerland and perm Rep to UN in Vienna and UNIDO, 1985-90; Perm Rep to UN Eurn HQ and Intl Orgs Geneva, 1985-; Gov and Exec Dir UN Common Fund for Commdties Amsterdam, 1989-; Pres Dip Cttee on Host Co Rels, 1991. Publications: Articles on pols econs and lit poems. Memberships: Mbr Governing Cncl UN Compensation Commn, 1991. Hobbies: Reading; Horseback Riding; Swimming; Writing; Chess; Music. Address: Permanent Mission of the Republic of Yemen, 19 chemin du Jonc, 1216 Cointrin, Geneva, Switzerland.

GELIN Ben Ami, b. 15 Jan 1936, Buenos Aires, Argentina. Solicitor; Member, NSW Administrative Decisions Tribunal. m. Martha Montgomery Morrison, 16 Sept 1961, 1 s, 1 d. Education: Bachiller en Humanidades, Buenos Aires, 1952; Lic Phil, Univ of Buenos Aires, 1959; MSW, 1963, PhD, 1970, Univ of PA; B Leg S, Macquarie Univ, 1989; Grad Dip in Legal Prac, Univ of Technol, Sydney. Appointments include: Socl Affairs Offr, Socl Devel Div, UN Secretariat, NY, 1969-70; Offl Vis, Bathurst Gaol, 1986-88; Assoc Prof, 1984-; Dean, 1984-88, Sch of Socl Scis, Charles Sturt Univ-Mitchell; Solicitor, King Cain Richardson &

Gilbertson, Solicitors and Attys, Bathurst. Publications include: La Familia, Anthropologia y Crisis, 1959; A Report on the Richmond Chamber of Commerce Summer Jobs Programme, 1968 (w Linda C Parker and Lois E Wright), 1969; Promoting Social Change Within the Administrative Cadres, 1976; Social Workers and Bureaucrats - The Changing Context of Social Work (w Geophrey Read), 1982; Other pprs, consultation and rsch rprts, wrkng documents for profl meetings, lectrs, stdy guides for external stdy. Honours include: Bard Coll Intl Schlshp, 1959-60; Rsch Schlshp, US Natl Inst of Mental Hlth, 1964-65; Fulbright-Hays Lectrshp, Colombia, 1969; Butterworths Prize for Studies in Litigation, Macquarie Univ Sch of Law, 1989. Memberships include: Bd Dir, Intl Soc for Cmmnty Dev; Fell, Taxation Inst of Aust; Law Soc of NSW. Hobbies: Camping; Water sports; Photography; Breeding Angora goats. Address: PO Box 1319, Bathurst, NSW 2795, Australia.

GELLI Ramesh, b. 16 Nov 1945. Chairman and Managing Director. m. Premkala, 22 Oct 1972, 2 s. Education: BEng, Osmania Univ, Hyderabad, 1967; MBM, Asian Inst Mngmt, Manila, Philippines, 1972; Snr Exec Prog, London Bus Sch, London, 1989. Appointments: Engr, Vazir Sultan Tobacco Co, 1967-68; Engr, Bharat Heavy Elecs Ltd, Hyderabad, India, 1968-69; Mngmt Trainee, Andhra Pradesh State Transpt Corp, Hyderabad, India, 1969-70; Cnslt, Ford Inc, Philippines, 1971; Mbr of Fac Fin, Admnstve Staff, Coll of India, Hyderabad, 1972-74; Gen Mngr, Andhra Pradesh State Finl Corp, Hyderabad, 1974-80; Gen Mngr, Vysya Bank Ltd, Bangalore, 1980-83; Chmn & CEO, Vysya Bank Ltd, Bangalore, 1983-93; Chmn and Mngng Dir, Global Trust Bank Ltd, Secunderabad, India, 1993-. Publications: Financial and Legal Issues Relating to Investments in the Infrastructure Industries in India, 1995; Entry of Private Banks into the Indian Banking Scene, 1995; Rising to the Challenge, 1995; The Role of Private Sector Banks in the Changing Scenario, 1995; New Private Sector Banks - Tomorrow and Beyond, 1995; Indian Banking Industry: Tomorrow & Beyond; Banking Services after 90s - Some Sweeping Changes. Honours include: Hall of Fame, Asian Inst Mngmt; Padma Shri, Govt India, New Delhi, 1991; Indira Gandhi Natl Unity Awd, All India Natl Unity Conf; Udyog Rattan - Golden Awd, Inst Econ Studies, New Delhi, 1988. Memberships include: Bharatidasan Inst Mngmt, Pres, 1995-; Chmn, Intl Rels Cttee, 1995-; Chmn, Bd Govs, Essae Chandran Inst, Bangalore, 1995-; Pres, All India Mngmt Assn, 1992-93; Fndr, Asian Inst Mngmt Alumni Assn of India, 1987-88; Pres, Bangalore Mngmt Assn, 1984-87; Mbr, Stndng Cttee, Indian Banks' Assn, 1988-93; Natl Inst Bank Mngmt, 1990-92; Mbr Andhra Pradesh State Plng Bd; Cncl Mbr, Assian Assn of Mngmt Org; Mbr, Admin Staff Coll of India. Address: 8-2-268/2/B/3A, Road No 2, Banjara Hills, Hyderabad 500034, India.

GEMAYEL Amin, b. 1942 Bikfayya. Politician. Education: St Joseph Univ Beirut. Appointments: MP, 1970-; Pres of Lebanon, 1982-88; Fndr The House of the Future The Amin Gemayel Educl Fndn Le Reveil newspaper. Memberships: Kataeb Party - Phalanges Libanaises. Address: Presidence de la Republique, Palais de Baabda, Beirut, Lebanon.

GEORGE Andrea Z, b. 2 Mar 1946, Los Angeles, CA, USA. Psychologist. m. (1) 3 sons, (2) Irwin Silberman, 13 Nov 1993. Education: BA, UCLA, 1970; MA, CSPP, LA, 1983; PhD, CSPP, LA, 1985. Appointment: Asst Prof, UCLA NPI, 1995-98. Creative work: Mural, Sulphur Springs Elem Sch, 1979. Honours: Pres, SFV CAMFT, 1990, Toastmasters ATM Silver, 1996; APRT, 1993. Memberships: APA, 1981-; SFV CAMFT, 1986-; CAMFT, 1986-; SFVPA Bd, 1988-91; LACPA, 1991-; Bd, 1994-97. Hobbies: Psychoneuroimmunolgy; Gardening; Skiing; LA Marathon. Address: 3716 Beverley Ridge Drive, Sherman Oaks, CA 91423-4509, USA.

GEORGE Janet E G, b. 10 Apr 1937, Sydney, Australia. Assocate Professor. m. Robert, 4 Jan 1958, 2 s, 1 d. Education: BA, New England; MPhil, Hong Kong; PhD, Sydney. Appointments: Lectr, 1985, Snr Lectr, 1988, Assoc Prof, 1998. Publications: States of Health:

Health and Illness in Australia, co-auth, 1988; Num of articles in profl jrnls. Memberships: Asian Pacific Assn for Socl Work Educn; Intl Assn of Schs of Socl Work. Hobbies: Reading; Music; Travel; Walking. Address: Department of Social Work, Social Policy & Sociology, University of Sydney, NSW 2006, Australia.

GER Yeong-Kuang, b. 27 Nov 1954, Taiwan, Repub of China. Professor. m. I-Chin Che, 12 Dec 1994, 2 s. Education: PhD, Dept of Polit Sci, Univ of Wisconsin-Madison, USA. Appointments: Dir, Sch Yth Serv Dept, China Yth Corp, 1986; Sec Gen, Dept of Yth Affairs, KMT, 1988; Sec Gen, World League for Freedom and Dem, Repub of China chapt, 1991; Vice Chmn, IYDU, 1991; Mbr, Cntrl Cttee, KMT, 1993; Mbr, Rsch, Dev an dEvaluation Commn, ROC Govt, 1996; Dir, Grad Inst of San-Min-Chu-I, Natl Taiwan Univ, 1996. Publications: Cultural Pluralism and National Intergration, 1991; Party Politics and Democratic Development, 1996; The Story of Taiwan: Politics, 1998. Honours: Dr Sun Yat-Sen Schlshp Awd, 1980-82; Ten Outstndng Young Persons Awd, 1993; Rsc Awd, Natl Sci Commn, 1992, 1995, 1996, 1997. Memberships: Prof, Dept of Polit Sci, NTU, 1985; Mngng Dir, Bd of Dirs, ROC's Prof Assn, 1991; Mngng Dir, Bd of Dirs, Prof World Peace Acady of ROC, 1995; Pres, UW Alumni Assn of ROC, 1997. Hobbies: Reading; Basketball; Music. Address: No 1, Roosevelt Road, Sec 4, Taipei, Taiwan, China.

GERBRACHT Robert Thomas (Bob), b. 23 June 1924. Artist; Art Instructor. m. Delia M, 27 Nov 1952, 1 s, 2 d. Education: BFA, Yale Sch of Fine Art; MFA, Univ of Southern California, USA. Appointments: Advsr, Pastel Soc of West Coast; Tstee, Soc of West Artists. Publication: Portraits and Figure Paintings. Honour: Master Pastellist, Pastel Soc of Am. Memberships: Pastel Soc of W Coast; Pastel Soc of Am; Soc of West Artists; Oil Painters of Am. Address: 1301 Blue Oak Court, Pinole, CA 94564, USA.

GERE Richard, b. 31 Aug 1949. Actor. m. Cindy Crawford, 1991, div. Education: Univ MA. Appointments: Fmrly played trumpet, piano, guitar and bass and composed music with var grps; Stage perfcs with Provincetown Playhouse and off-Broadway; Appeared in London and Broadway prodns of The Taming of the Shrew A Midsummer Night's Dream and Broadway prodns of Habeas Corpus and Bent; Film debut, 1975; Fndng chmn and Pres Tibet House NY. Films incl: Report to the Commissioner, 1975; Baby Blue Marine, 1976; Looking for Mr Goodbar, 1977; Days of Heaven, 1978; Blood Brothers, 1978; Yanks, 1979; American Gigolo, 1980; An Officer and a Gentleman, 1982; Breathless, 1983; Beyond the Limit, 1983; The Cotton Club, 1984; King David, 1985; Power, 1986; No Mercy, 1986; Miles From Home, 1989; 3000, 1989; Internal Affairs, 1990; Pretty Woman, 1990; Rhapsody in August, 1991; Final Analysis, 1991; Sommersby, co-exec prodr, 1993; Mr Jones, co-exec prodr, 1994; Intersection, 1994; First Knight, 1995; Primal Fear, 1996; Red Corner, 1997. Honours: HonDLit, Leicester, 1992. Address: c/o Andrea Jaffe Inc, 9229 Sunset Boulevard, Los Angeles, CA 90069, USA.

GERRINGER Elizabeth J (Marchioness de Roe Devon), b. 7 Jan 1934, Wisconsin, USA. Songwriter; Poet. m. Roe (Don Davis) Devon Gerringer-Busenbark, 30 Sept 1968 (dec Dec 1972). Education: LA Cty Coll, 1960-62; Santa Monica (CA) Jr Coll, 1963; Bar of CA, 1965; JD Univ of CA, San Fran, 1973; Postgrad, Wharton Sch, Univ PA, 1977; M PhD, Univ of Cambridge, UK, 1979; London Art Coll, 1979; Attended Goethe Inst, 1985. Career: Actress: Actors Workshop San Fran, 1959, 1965; Th of Arts Beverley Hills, 1963; Radio Cnslt and Systems Analyst for banks and acctng agys; Artist; Poet; Singer; Songwriter; Playwright; Dress Designer; Pres, Tchr, Environ Improvement, Originals by Elizabeth; Attny, Dometrik's; Steering Cttee, Explorations in Worship; Ordained Min, 1978. Publications include: Skid Row Minister, 1978; Points in Time, 1979; Special Arrangement - A Clown in Town, 1979; Happenings, 1980; Candles, 1980; The Stranger on the Train, 1983; Votes From the Closet, 1984; Wait for Me, 1984; The Stairway, 1984; The River is a Rock, 1985; Happenings Revisited, 1986; Comparative Religion in the United States, 1986; Lumber in the Skies, 1986; The Fifth Season, 1987; Summer Thoughts, 1987; Crimes of the Heart, 1987; A Thousand Points of Light, 1989; The Face in the Mirror, 1989; Sea Gulls, 1990; Voices on the Hill, 1991; It's Tough to Get a Matched Set, 1991; Equality, 1991; Miss Geranium,1991; Forest Voices, 1991; Golden Threads, 1991; Castles in the Air, 1991; The Cave, 1991; Angels, 1991; Real, 1991; An Appeal to Reason, 1992; We Knew, 1992; Like It is, 1992; Politicians Anonymous, 1993; Wheels Within Wheels, 1994; A Tree for All Seasons, 1995; The Visitor, 1995; Time Frames, 1996; Save the Dance, 1999. Address: 1008 10th Street, Sacramento, CA 95814, USA.

GESCHKE Charles Norman, b. 7 Mar 1924. Ombudsman. m. Audrey, 12 Feb 1949, 3 s, 1 d. Appointments: War Serv, Aust SW Pacific, 1943-45; Bomber Wing, 1953-54; Ops Directorate, Dept Air, 1955-56; RAAF Staff Lon, 1956-57, Hon ADC to Gov Gen, 1959; Cmdng Offr, 6 Squadron, 1959; Cmdng Offr, HQ Support Cmnd Unit, 1960-62; Staff Offr (Dir), Recruiting, 1963-67; Cmdng Offr, 38 Sqdn, 1967-68 (Grp Cap Retd); Staff Offr to AOC Support Cmnd, 1969-71; Bus Mngr, Howard Florey Inst, Melbourne, 1971-74; Chmn, Regular Def Forces Welfare Assn, 1974-79; Dir, Consumer Affairs, 1974-80; Ombudsman for Vic, 1980-. Honours: Queens Commendation, 1954; OBE, 1966. Memberships: Chmn, Vic Interserv Sports Cttee, 1971; Huntingdale Golf Club; Hon Life Mbr, Intl Ombudsman's Inst, Dir, Exec Sec, 1988-92. Hobbies: Golf; Fishing; Home mechanics. Address: 42 Andrew Street, Oakleigh, Victoria 3166, Australia.

GHAFURZAI Abdorrahim. Appointment: Min of For Affairs, Interim Cncl of Mins, Afghanistan, 1997-. Address: Ministry of Foreign Affairs, Shah Mahmud Ghazi Street, Shar-i-Nau, Kabul, Afghanistan.

GHAI Surinder Kumar, b. 18 Apr 1945. Publisher. m. Geeta Ghai, 16 Aug 1968, 2 s. Education: BA, Punjab Univ, 1965. Appointment: Mngng Dir, Sterling Publrs Ltd, 1965-, Chmn, Mngng Dir, 1992-. Publications: Afro-Asian Publishing: Contempary Trends and Future Prospects (co-ed), 1992; Directory of Indian Publishers, 1995, 1997. Honours: Outstndng Dist Pres Awd and 12 other awds, Rotary Club of Delhi Southend, 1994-95. Memberships: Hon Sec Gen, 1994-96, VP, 1998-2000, Chmn, World Book Day 1999, Fedn of Indian Publrs; Regl Rep, Intl Assn of Schl Publrs; VP, Acad of Fine Arts, New Delhi; Life Mbr Chinmay Mission; Life Mbr Intl Soc for Krishna Consciousness. Listed in: Who's Who of Indian Publishing. Hobbies: Walking; Reading; Photography. Address: A1/256 Safalarjang Enclave, New Delhi 110029, India.

GHANDAR Ann, b. 1 Nov 1943, Adelaide, SA, Aust. Composer; Performer; Educator. m. M E Ghandar, 15 Oct 1977, 2 s. Education: BA, hons, Univ of Adelaide, 1964; MA, Austl Natl Univ, 1969; BMus, Southampton Univ, 1974; LMusA, Austl Music Examinations Bd, 1969. Appointments: Num piano perfces and perfces of compositions in Aust and overseas; Lectr in Composition, 1974-, Snr Lectr, 1985-, Univ New England, Armidale. Publications: Compositions: Sonata for flute and piano, 1975; Eshelgharam, in Contemporary Austl Piano, 1985; Sea Suite, for orch, perf'd by State Orch of Vic, conducted by Julia de Plater, 1994; Sinai Music for piano, 1995-97. Honour: John Howard Clarke Prize, Engl, 1964. Memberships: Austl Music Cntr; Australasian Perf Rights Assoc Ltd; Fellshp, Austl Composers; Musicol Soc of Aust; Austl Fedn of Univ Women. Hobbies: Reading; Travel. Address: Music Department, University of New England, Armidale, NSW 2351, Australia.

GHANEM Iskandar Assad, b. 5 June 1913, Saghbin Begaa, West Lebanon. Appointments: Fmr Commndr in Chf of the Army; Fmr Def Min. m. Caunice, 23 Feb 1941, 3 s. Appointment: Fmr Pres, Mil Lebanese Forces Assn. Honours: Higher Lebanese Medal and 14 other medals from different countries. Address: Building Houssaïni, Mar Tacla, Hazmiyé, Lebanon.

GHANIM Faraj Said bin. Politician. Appointment: PM of Yemen, May 1997-; Independent. Address: Office of the Prime Minister, San'a, Yemen.

GHATAK Nitai Chandra, b. 17 Sept 1956. Librarian. m. Bahnisikha, 5 May 1992. Education: MLib and Info Sci; MA, Hlth Sci Libnshp Trained; Ctf, Hindi Lang; Ctf, MEDLAR; Deg, Homoeopath Med and Surg. Appointments: Botanical Survey HQ Lib, Shibpur, Bengal, 1978-80; Libn, Med Coll Lib, Calcutta, 1980-. Publications: Pprs in profl seminars and confs. Honour: Medal and Ctf, Donating Blood to Save Life, 1986. Memberships: Med Lib Assn of India; ILA; BLA; IASLIC. Listed in: Who's Who in USA. Hobbies: Social service; Medicine and allied subjects. Address: Pirtala, Agarpara, North 24 Parganes, West Bengal 743177, India.

GHAZVINIAN Mahmoud, b. 22 May 1955, Shahrud, Iran. Employee, Central Bank. m. Efat Shahsavaran, 30 Oct 1988, 1 s, 1 d. Education: HS Dip. Appointment: Hd, Off Section, Intl Dept. Hobbies: Swimming; Hiking. Address: International Department, Central Bank of Iran, Ferdowsi Avenue, PO Box 11369-8551, Tehran, Iran.

GHISALBERTI Emilio Luciano, b. 6 Jan 1943. Organic Chemist. m. Ann Vivienne Armstrong, 17 May 1973, 1 s, 1 d. Education: BS Hons, 1964; PhD. Appointments: CNR, Postdoct Fell, Italy, 1968; Wellcome Rsch Fell, Liverpool, 1969; Lectr, Univ of WA, 1970; Snr Lectr, 1979; Assoc Prof, 1987. Creative works: Over 180 pprs in Organic Chem, Phytochem, Botany, Biosynthesis, Natural Prods, 1964-1996. Memberships: Roy Soc of Chem; NY Acady of Scis; Amn Soc of Pharmacognosy. Hobbies: Etymology; European language. Address: Department of Chemistry, University of Western Australia, Nedlands, WA 6907, Australia.

GHOLAMI-SCHABANI Raziye, b. 19 May 1925, Tabriz, Iran. Teacher; Nurse. m. Reza Ebrahimzadeh, 12 Dec 1942, 3 s. Education: BA, Hist and Lit, Pedagogical Univ of Tajikestan, 1960; BSc, Nursing, 1969. Appointment: 1st Iranian Women Polit Prisoner. Publications: Khaterat-e yek Zan-e Tude-ee (Memoirs of a Women Member of Tudeh Party), 1994. Honour: Cited, Women's Calender, 1999-2000. Memberships: Ctrl Cttee, Workers and Peasants Cncl, Tehran, 1942; Propaganda Cmmn, Democratic Assn of Women of Iran, 1943; Tudeh People's Party of Iran, 1944; Participant, Autonomous Movement of Azerbaijan, 1945-46. Address: Vogelpothsweg 30, 44149 Dortmund, Germany.

GHOSE Sre Arbindghos, b. 1 Nov 1935, Bangladesh. Teacher. m. Chandrima Ghose, 22 June 1967, 1 s, 2 d. Education: BA; MA. Appointments: Lectr, Asst prof in Banglai, Ishuridi Govt Coll, Patna, 1968-94. Publications: 2 dramas in Bangali; 3 dramas in local lang of Chapai Newalganj; 3 dramas broadcast on Radio Bangladesh. Honours: Certs from Govt of Bangladesh. Address: Kaliganj (Babupara) Po-Rajaram Pur Dist, Chapainawabg Dist (Chapainawabganj) Bangladesh.

GHOSH Ananda Mohan, b. 27 Jan 1941, West Bengal, India. Professor of Computer Software. m. Mira, 7 June 1979. Education: MTech; PhD. Appointments: Des Engr, Hengers (I) Pvt Ltd, 1965; Lectr, Electr Engin, Engrng Dept, B E Coll, 1968; Asst Prof, Electr Engin Dept, B E Coll, 1974. Publications: Sev popular rsch articles in Bengali; About 45 rsch pprs. Honours: Univ Medals, BTech and Mtech results; Glory of India Awd proposed by NGO, 1999. Hobby: Mapping science with Indian Philosophy. Address: Budge Budge Trunk Road, PO Shyampur, Dist 24 PGs, West Bengal 743319, India.

GHOSH Gautam, b. 24 July 1950 Calcutta. Film Director. m. Neelanjana Ghosh, 1978, 1 s, 1 d. Education: Cathedral Miss Sch Calcutta; City Coll Calcutta; Calcutta Univ. Appointments: Offic deleg Cannes and London Film Fests, 1982; Offic deleg Venice and Tokyo Film Fests, 1984; Exec Dir Natl Film Inst, 1987; Dir Natl Film Dev Corp; Dir West Bengal Film Dev Corp. Films incl: Hungry Autumn, 1974; Ma Bhoomi, 1980; Dakhal, 1982; Paar, 1984; Antarjali Yatra, 1988; Padma Nadir Majhi, 1992; Patang, 1994. Publications:

Num articles on the cinema. Honours: Pres Awd, five times; Human Rights Awd - France; Silver Med and UNESCO Awd; Grand Prix Awd, USSR. Memberships: Mbr Intl Jury, Oberhausen, 1979; Mbr Natl Jury, 1985. Hobbies: Music; Reading; Travel. Address: Bock 5, Flat 50, 28/1A Gariahat Road, Calcutta 700029, India.

GHOSH Jayanta Kumar, b. 22 May 1937, Calcutta, India. Researcher; Teacher. m. Ira, 7 Dec 1967, 1 s, 1 d. Education: MA, 1958, DPhil, 1964, Calcutta Univ. Appointments: Lectr, Calcutta Univ, 1962-64; Visng Asst Prof, Univ IL, USA, 1964-66; Assoc Prof, 1966-69, Prof, 1970-84, Indian Stats Inst; Prof, Purdue Univ, 1989-96; Dist Scientist, 1984-96, Dir, 1987-92, Jawaharlal Nehru Prof, 1996-, Indian Stats Inst. Publications: Over 100 pprs in profl jrnls. Honour: Shanti Swarup Bhatnagar Awd, 1981. Memberships: FASc; FNA; FNSc; IMS. Hobbies: Writing poems and stories for children. Address: Indian Statistical Institute, 203 BT Road, Calcutta 700 035, India.

GHOSH Narayan Chandra, b. 14 Sept 1949, Satirpara, India. Scientist. m. Sarmistha Biswas, 6 Dec 1987, 1 s, 1 d. Education: MSc; PhD; ICA. Appointments: Rdr, SN Bose Sch for Maths and Maths Sci; Recorder, Maths Sect, Indian Sci Congress; Prin Investigator, NCERT Project on Maths Educn; Prog Coord, NR Sen Cntr for Pedagogic and Profl Maths; Mbr Editl Bd, Sanbad Krishi O Bijnan; Exec Ed, Jrnl Pure and Applied Phys; Intl Jrnl Env Pol Minimisation; Ponebesh Dushne; Former Admnstr, Govt Sponsered Lib; Former Mbr N Bull Cal Math Soc; Mbr Govt Sponsored Tech Instn. Publications: 23 rsch pprs, 12 articles. Memberships: Indian Stats Inst; Bangladesh Maths Soc; Indian Sci Congress Assn; Inst of Sci Culture and Educ; Indian Assn for Cultivation of Sci; Benaras Hindu Univ Maths Soc; All India Sci Tchrs Assn; Ramanujan Maths Soc; Assn for Improvement of Maths Tchng; Natl Environ Sci Acady; Inst of Indian Environ Engrng; SN Bose Cntr for Rsch and Stdy for Minimising Environ Pollution; Indian Math Soc. Hobbies: Photography; Fluid dynamics; Mathematics education. Address: Aghorsmriti, Raibahadur, SC Mukherjee Road, Hooghly, West Bengal 712103, India.

GHOSH Subrata, b. 8 Apr 1950, Calcutta, India. Research. m. Manju, 10 Feb 1982, 2 s. Education: PhD. Appointments: Rsch Fell, Indian Assn for the Cultivation of Sci (ICS), 1974; Postdoct Fell, Case West Reserve Univ, USA, 1979; Lectr, IACS, 1982; Rdr, IACS, 1987; Prof, IACS, 1994. Honour: Fell, Indian Acady of Scis. Membership: Indian Chem Soc. Hobby: Stamp collection. Address: Department of Organic Chemistry, Indian Association for the Cultivation of Science, Jadavpur, Calcutta 700032, India.

GIBBONS Geoffrey Clifford, b. 10 July 1947, Sydney, Aust. Veterinary Specialist. m. Anne, 30 Dec 1976, 1 s, 2 d. Education: BVSc, Univ Sydney, 1970; Aust Coll of Vet Sci, 1981; Fell, Roy Coll of Vet Surgns, London, 1995. Appointments: Prin, Melba Vet Hosp, 1978-85; Night Supvsr, Tufts Univ Vet Sch, 1987-90; Hd Examiner, Aust Coll of Vet Sci, 1998-. Publications: Sev articles in profl jrnls. Memberships: Austl Vet Assn, 1965-; Apex Clubs. Hobbies: Cycle touring; Running; Camping. Address: 59 Gould Avenue, St Ives, NSW 2075, Australia.

GIBBS Brian Geoffrey, b. 19 July 1933, Katandra West, Vic, Aust. Commodore (retired). m. Jean Mary Boden, 30 Dec 1959, 1 s, 2 d. Education: Scotch Coll, Launceston, Tas; RAN Coll; RN Coll, Greenwich, Eng; Bar, (High Crt of Aust), 1968; Bar and Solicitor, Supreme Crt, NSW and ACT, 1967. Appointments: HM Ships: Devonshire, Indomitable, Swiftsure, Pembroke; HMA Ships: Sydney, Melbourne, Parramatta, Perth (Vietnam, 1968-69); Term Offr, RAN Coll, 1957-59; Exch Serv, Roy Navy, 1963-65, 1972-74, Cmdr, 1968, Cap, 1975, Commodore, 1982; Dir, Naval Legal Servs, 1975-79; Cmdng Offr, HMAS Cerberus, 1980-82; Dir-Gen, Naval Manpower, 1982-84; Snr Mbr, Fed Admin Appeals Tribunal, 1985-. Honours: AM, 1979; Meritorious Unit Citation, HMAS Perth, Vietnam, 1979. Memberships: Fndn Cnclr, Austl Naval Inst; Pres, Melbourne Naval Cntr. Hobby: Horticulture. Address: Chatham House, 259 Myers Road, Bittern, Vic 3918, Australia.

GIBBS Harry Talbot, b. 7 Feb 1917. Justice. m. Muriel Ruth Dunn, 1 s, 3 d. Education: BA, 1937; LLB, 1939; LLM, 1946; Hon LLD, Qld Univ; HonD Univ, Griffith Univ. Appointments: Barrister, Queensland, 1939; Mil Serv: AMF 1939-42, AIF, 1942-45; MID; QC, 1957, Judge, Supreme Crt of Queensland, 1961-67; Judge, Fedl Crt of Bankruptcy and Supreme Crt of ACT, 1967-70; Justice of the High Crt of Aust, 1970-81; Chf Justice, 1981-87; Crt of Appeal, Kiribati, 1988-. Memberships: Australian Club, Sydney, Queensland Club, Brisbane, Australia.

GIBBS Ivan James (Hon), b. 22 Nov 1927. Politician. m. Doris, 20 May 1950, 4 s, 1 d. Appointments: Cncl Mbr, 1967-70; Dpty Mayor, Gold Coast City, 1973-76; NPA for Albert Qld, 1974-; Chmn, NPA Parly Small Bus Cttee; Min, Culture, Natl Pks and Recreation, 1979-80; Min, Mines and Energy, 1980-86; Min, Wrks and Housing, 1986-87; Min for Transp, 1987-89; Min of Hlth, 1989-; Min for Hlth and Atty Gen, 1989. Memberships: Hon Life Mbr, Natl Pty Aust, Qld, 1992; Chmn, Coomera Anglican Coll, Cl, 1996-; Chmn, Mngmt Labrador Snr Citizens Cntr. Hobby: Horse riding. Address: 177 Reserve Road, Coomera, Qld 4209, Australia.

GIBSON Keiko Matsui, b. 9 Apr 1953, Kyoto, Japan. Professor. m. Morgan Gibson, 14 Sept 1978, 1 s. Education: Engl, Kwansei Gakuin Univ, 1976; Comparative Lit, Univ of IL, 1983; Comparative Lit, IN Univ, 1992. Appointments: Assc Prof, Kanda Univ of Intl Studies, Japan. Publications: Stir Up the Precipitable World (poems), 1983; Noma Hiroshi's Struggle for the Total Novel, 1992; River of Stars: Poems of Yosano Akito (translated by KUG and Sam Hamill, 1997. Honours: Phi Kappa Phi, 1982; Rexroth Awd for Poetry, 1982; Fellshp, IN Univ, 1983-84. Membership: Intl Comparative Lit Assn. Address: 202 Excel Negoshi, 3-chome, 148-2 Negishi-cho, Naka-ku, Yokohama-shi, 231-0836, Japan.

GIBSON Mel, b. 3 Jan 1956, Peekskill, New York, USA. Actor; Director; Producer. m. Robyn Moore, 6 s, 1 d. Education: Natl Inst Dramatic Arts, Sydney, NSW. Appointments: Settled Aust, 1968; Actor, films inclng: Mad Max, 1979; Tim, 1979; Attack Force Z; Gallipoli, 1981; The Road Warrior (Mad Max II), 1982; The Year of Living Dangerously, 1983; The Bounty, 1984; The River, 1984; Mrs Soffel, 1984; Mad Max Beyond Thunderdome, 1985; Lethal Weapon; Tequila Sunrise; Lethal Weapon II; Bird on a Wire, 1989; Hamlet, 1990; Air America, 1990; Lethal Weapon III, 1991; Maverick, 1994; Lethal Weapon 4, 1998; Actor, Dir, Man Without a Face, 1992; Actor, Dir, Co-Prodr, Braveheart, 1995; Actor, Ransom, 1996; Actor, Conspiracy Theory, 1997; Actor, Producer, Payback, 1999; Plays inclng Romeo and Juliet, Waiting for Godot, No Names No Pack Drill, Death of a Salesman; Ptnr, Icon Prodns. Honours: Best Dir, Best Picture, Braveheart, Acady Awds, 1996; Best Dir, Braveheart, Golden Globe Awds, 1996; Cmdr, Ordre des Arts et des Lettres. Address: c/o Shanahan Management Pty Ltd, PO Box 478, Kings Cross, NSW 2011, Australia.

GIBSON Robert Dennis, b. 13 Apr 1942, Northumberland, UK. Vice-Chancellor. m. Catherin, 1 s, 2 d. Education: BS (Hons 1), Hull Univ, 1963; MSc, 1965, PhD, 1967, Univ Newcastle-upon-Tyne; DSc, Cncl Natl Acad Awds, UK, 1987. Appointments: Asst Lectr, 1966-67, Lectr, 1968-69, Maths, Univ Newcastle-upon-Tyne; Sci Offr, Culham Plasma Phys Lab, UKAEA, 1967-68; Snr Lectr, Maths and Stats, Teeside Polytechnic, 1969-77; Hd of Dept, 1977-80, Hd of Sch, 1980-82, Maths, Stats and Computing, Newcastle-upon-Tyne Polytechnic; Dpty Dir and Acting Dir, Queensland Inst of Technol, 1982-83; Dir, Queensland Inst of Technol, 1983-88; Dir, Queensland Inst of Technol, 1989-. Publications: Num on applied maths. Honours: Fell, Austl Acady of Technol Scis and Engrng, 1993; Fell, Austl Inst of Mngmt, 1982. Memberships: Austl Inst of Co Dirs, 1990; Soc of Snr Execs, 1996. Hobbies: Cricket; Jogging; Reading. Address: 2 George Street, Brisbane, Australia.

GIBSON William Peter, b. 11 June 1944, England. Professor. m. Alexandra, 15 June 1968, 1 s, 1 d. Education: MBBS; MD, London; FRACS; FRCS. Appointments: Prof, Otocaryngology, Univ of Sydney, 1983-; Dir, Childrens Implant Cntr, NSW. Publications: Var pprs in profl med jrnls. Honours: AM, 1996; Golden Heart Awd, Variety Club of Aust. Memberships: Roy Soc of Med; Collegium Orlas. Hobbies: Boating; Golf. Address: 34/8 Water Street, Birchgrove, NSW 2041, Australia.

GIFFORD Kenneth Harril, b. 8 Mar 1923, Melbourne, Aust. Queen's Counsel; Author; Editor; Lecturer. m. Elizabeth Eleanor Lorraine Caldwell, 26 Mar 1949, 1 s, 1 d. Education: Scotch Coll, Melbourne; Price Alfred Coll, Adelaide; LLB, Univ of Melbourne, 1946. Appointments: Probation Offr, Children's Crts, 1941-45; Austl Mil Forces, 1941-44; Admitted as a Bar in Vic, 1947; Independent Lectr in Law of Planning, Univ of Melbourne, 1955-66; Gen Ed, Town Planning and Local Govt Guide, 1956-97; Ed, Local Govt Reports of Aust, 1956-88; Independent Lectr in Ctrl and Local Govt, Univ of Melbourne, 1957-66; Appointed QC for States of Vic, Qld, Tas, 1964; Cnslt to SA Local Govt Act Revision Cttee, 1965-70; Ed, Vic Planning Appeal Decisions, 1969-82; Admitted to prac in Fiji, 1969; Pres, Old Scotch Collegians Assn, 1972-73, Sec London Br 1991-98; Procurator, Presbysterian Ch of aust, 1967-77; Ed, Aust Planning Appeal Decisions, 1981-91; Visng Prof, Law Sch, Univ HI, USA, 1987; Chmn, Environ Law Cttee, Cncl Mbr, Section on Bus Law, Intl Bar Assn, 1984-85 Chmn, Comparative Govt Law Cttee, Amn Bar Assn, 1987; Grand Registrar, Supreme Grand Chap of Vic, 1982-84, 1985-91; 2nd Grand Prin, Supreme Grand Cap of Vic, 1984-85; Grand Registrar, Grand Lodge Mark Master Masons, Vic, 1993-96. Publications: How to Understand an Act of Parliament (co-auth); How to Understand Statutes and By-Laws. Honours: Hon Fell, Roy Austl Planning Inst; Hon Fell, Inst of Municipal Mngmt; total Community Devel Awd; Freedom of the City of London. Memberships include: Natl Trust, Scotland; Vic Environ Law Assn; UK Environ Law Assn; Austls for Constitutional Monarchy; Melbourne Cricket Club. Hobbies: Freemasonary; Lawn bowls; Music; Reading. Address: 1A Adria Street, Glen Iris, Vic 3146, Australia.

GIFKINS Robert Cecil, b. 30 May 1918. Materials Engineer. m. Elizabeth E Glaisher, 14 Feb 1942, 2 s, 1 d. Education: BSc, London; DSc, Melbourne. Appointments: Lab Asst, Brit Indl Solvents; Expmtl Off, NPL, DSIR, UK; Harwell AAEC; CSIRO Aust; Retd Chief Rsch Scientist, 1978. Publications: Optical Microscopy of Metals, 1969; Jubilee History of IMMA, 1996; 103 research papers in international journals. Honours: Hon Mbr: Instn of Engrs, Aust; Aust Inst of Metal and Materials; Iron and Steel Inst of Japan; Silver Medal, Aust Inst Metals, 1966; Disting Lectr in Metallography, 1991-; Am Soc of Metals; Intl Metallographic Soc; ACTA Metallurgica Intl Lect, 1990-91; Vic Branch IMMA, R C Gifkins Annual Lect, 1996. Memberships: IMMA, 1948; Fell, UK Inst of Materials, 1954; Chmn Editl Cttee, 1954-78; Fed and Branch Pres, 1964, 1956; Chmn, Assessment Cttee, 1982-88; Instn of Engrs Aust, 1989. Hobbies: Bush walking; Gardening; Photography; Music; Lecturing. Address: PO Box 257, Somers, Vic 3927, Australia.

GILCHRIST Hugh, b. 8 Aug 1916, Sydney, Aust. Retired Public Servant. m. Elizabeth, 10 Apr 1950, 1 s, 2 d. Education: BA (Hons); LLB. Appointments: Austl Dept of For Affairs, 1945-79; High Commnr in Tanzania, 1962-66; Amb to Greece, 1968-72; To Spain, 1976-79. Publications: Australians and Greeks, Vols 1, 1992, 2 1997; Vol 3 in preparation. Honours: Grand Cross of King George of the Hellenes, 1997; Gold Cross of St Andrew (conferred by Greek Orthodox Ch of Aust), 1998. Memberships: Lit Bd of Aust Cncl, 1980-83; Cnslt on archives to Dept of For Affairs, 1984-87. Hobby: Historical research. Address: 5 Park Terrace, Telopea Park, Kingston, ACT 2604, Australia.

GILL Graeme Joseph, b. 10 Dec 1947, Melbourne, Aust. University Teacher. m. Heather, 8 Jan 1972, 1 s, 1 d. Education: PhD, London Univ, 1976; MA, Monash

Univ, 1973. Appointments: Lectr, Univ of Tasmania, 1978; Lectr, 1981, Snr Lectr, 1984, Assoc Prof, 1988, Prof of Govt, 1990, Sydney Univ; Pro-Vice Chan (Rsch), Sydney Univ, 1997. Publications: Power in the Party (co-auth); The Collapse of a Single Party System, 1994; The Politics of Transition, 1993: 5 other books. Honour: ARC large grants, 1989-99. Memberships: Fell, Acady of Socl Studies in Aust; Australasian Polit Students Assn; Amn Assn for Advancement of Slavic Studies. Hobbies: Reading; Music; Gardening. Address: Department of Government, University of Sydney, Sydney, NSW 2006, Australia.

GILL Peter Thomas, b. 16 June 1940, Melbourne, Australia. Researcher. m. Janice, 14 Apr 1967, 2 s, 2 d. Education: BA, 1976, BEd, 1979, Monash Univ. Appointments: Tchr, Libn, Admnstr, Victorian Educl Insts, 1962, 1996. Publications: 100 Seasons (History of Yarra Yarra Rowing Club), auth, 1972; Camberwell Resource Manual, ed, 1977. Honour: Life Mbr, Yarra Yarra Rowing Club, 1989. Memberships: Ashburton/Glen Iris Assn Sec, 1984-88; Australasian Assn of Genealogists and Record Agents, 1997. Hobbies: Rowing; Genealogy. Address: 2 Mernda Avenue, Ashburton 3147, Victoria, Australia.

GILLESPIE Lyall Leslie, b. 23 July 1919, Queanbeyan, NSW, Aust. Former Public Servant; Now, Local Historian and Author. m. Norma Joan Bogg, 6 Sept 1941, 2 s, 2 d. Education: Leaving Cert, Qualified Acct Assoc (Tech); Inst of Radio and Elecl Engrs, Aust. Appointments include: Asst Dir of Wrks, Canberra, 1958-60; Asst Admnstr, North Territory, 1960-63; Asst Sec, Dept of Interior, Canberra, 1964-72; Commr for Housing, Dept of the Capital Territory, Canberra, 1973-78; Cty Mngr, Canberra, 1978-82. Publications: A Pictorial History of the Read/Reid Family in Australia, 1849-1979; Aborigines of the Canberra Region; A Pictorial History of Telopea Park School 1923-1983 (co-auth); The Southwell Family, Pioneers of the Canberra District 1838-1988; Canberra 1820-1931; Ginninderra, Forerunner to Canberra; Early Verse of the Canberra Region; Early Education and Schools in the Canberra Region. Honour: Companion of the Imperial Serv Order (ISO), 1983; OAM, 1999. Memberships: Fell, Austl Inst Mngmt; Assoc (Tech), Instn of Radio and Electronics Engrs, Aust; Assoc, Austl Soc of Accts; Life Mbr and Past Pres, Canberra and Dist Histl Soc, Hort Soc of Canberra; Mbr Queanbeyan and Dist Histl Mus Soc; Goulburn and Dist Histl Soc; Austl Rock Art Rsch Assn. Hobbies: Historical research; Archaeology; Gardening; Photography. Address: Lynora, 18 Ferdinand St, Cambell, ACT 2612, Australia.

GILLIES Malcolm George William, b. 23 Dec 1954, Brisbane, Aust. Musician. Education: BA, Aust Natl Univ; MA, Cambridge; MMus, PhD, London; DipEduc; LMusA; LTCL; FLCM; FAHA. Appointments: Prof of Music, Univ of Queensland, 1992-; Dean, Fac of Music, Univ of Qld, 1992-97; Music Critic, The Australian, 1995-; Gen Ed, Oxford Studies in Musical Genesis, 1997-. Publications: Bartok in Britain, 1989; Bartok Remembered, 1990; Ed, The Bartok Companion, 1993; The All-Round Man, 1994; Ed, Grainger on Music, 1999. Memberships: Pres, Austl Acady of the Hum, 1998-; Pres, Natl Acadys Forum (Aust), 1998-. Hobbies: The Arts; Swimming; Languages. Address: School of Music, University of Queensland, St Lucia, Qld 4072, Australia.

GILLILAND Hector Beaumont, b. 30 Dec 1911, Launceston, Tas. Artist. Education: Sydney Tech HS, 1924-28; Natl Art Sch, Sydney, 1935-40; Philos, (Univ of Melbourne Examinations), Canberra Univ Coll, 1946-48; Inst of Contemporary Arts, London, lectrs by Lawrence Alloway, Tate Gall, London, 1953-54; Pvte Stdy, Psychol of Visual Perception, Comm Theory, Phys, Physiol, Cybernetics. Appointments: Survey Draftsman, NSW Pub Serv, Registrar-Gens Off, Sydney, 1929-42; Survey Draftsman, C'wlth Pub Serv, Dept of the Interior, Canberra, 1942-53; Tchr, Adv Art, Canberra Tech Coll, 1949-52; Taught Adv Watercolour, Vic Cncl of Adult Educ Summer Sch, Natl Gall of Vic, Melbourne, 1958; Lectr, Tutor, pt-time, Graphic Comm, 1959-77, Mbr, Comm Stdy Grp, 1975-77, Sch of Arch, Univ NSW, Sydney; Mbr, 1966-75, Hon Mbr, 1975-85, Fine Art Advsry Cttee, Dept of Tech and Further Educ, NSW, 1966-85; Tchr, pt-time, Des, Painting, 1970-74, Drawing, Rsch, 1970, Natl Art Sch, Sydney. Creative Works include: Mural designed and painted w Lorna Nimmo in Basser Coll, Univ NSW, 1959; Wrks in Austl Natl Gall, most State and Regl Galls, Aust, corporate and pvte collects, Aust, USA, Eur. Publications: Alan Davie - Flag Dream No 4: Wheel, 1982; The Canberra Landscape in the Work of Douglas Dundas, 1982, etc. Assisted in updating Graphic Comm Course, Univ NSW. Honours: Over 50 Awds for Art Throughout Aust; Direct Assistance Grants, Visual Arts Bd, Aust Cncl, 1975, 1976. Memberships include: Hon Life Mbr, Aust Watercolour Inst; Soc of Artists, NSW. Hobbies: Reading; Writing; Listening to classical music; Contemplating nature. Address: 26 Lyall Street, Leichhardt, NSW 2040, Australia.

GILLMAN Derek Anthony, b. 7 Dec 1952. Museum Professional. m. Yael Joanna Hirsch, 30 Aug 1987, 1s, 2 d. Education: MA, Oxon; LLM. Appointments: Chinese Specialist, Christie's Auctioneers, London, 1977-81; Curator, Dept Oriental Antiquities, Brit Mus, 1981-85; Keeper, Sainsbury Cntr for Visual Arts, Univ E Anglia, Norwich, 1985-95; Dpty Dir, Intl Art and Collect Mngmt, Natl Gall of Vic, Melbourne, Aust, 1995-96; Dpty Dir, Collect and Curatorial Servs, Natl Gall of Vic, Melbourne, 1996-99; Exec Dir and Provost, Penn Acady of the Fine Arts, Philadelphia, 1999-. Publications: Contrb to exhbn catalogues and articles in jrnls. Memberships: Gov, Norfolk Inst Art and Des, 1990-95; Oriental Ceramic Soc Cncl, 1990-93. Hobbies: Reading; Painting. Address: Pennsylvania Academy of the Fine Arts, 1301 Cherry Street, Philadelphia, PA 19107, USA.

GILMORE Gordon Ray, b. 7 Sept 1935, Mesa, AZ, USA. Naval Officer; Petroleum Engineer; Business Executive. m. Donna, 28 July 1979, 4 ss. Education: BS, Pet Engrng; MSc, Mngmt. Appointments: Ensign to Capt, USN, 1958-80; VP, Lawrence Allison, 1984; Pres, John Brown, US SVCS, 1993. Publication: Article on the dev of the Naval Petroleum Reserves, Navy Civil Engineer, Spring, 1979. Honours: Bronze Star w Combat V; Vietnam Serv Medal; Meritorious Serv Medals, 1974; Legion of Merit, 1983. Hobbies: Hunting; Fishing; Stamp collecting; Volunteer work. Address: 1405 Corte Canalette, Bakersfield, CA 93309, USA.

GILMORE Ian George Charles, b. 30 June 1925, NSW, Aust. Brigadier (retired). m. Alison Shirley Cayley, 17 Apr 1954, 2 s, 1 d. Education: Grad, Roy Mil Coll, Duntroon, 1946; Sydney Univ, 1948-50; Roy Mil Coll Sci, UK, 1954-56; Austl Staff Coll, Ft Queenscliff, 1960; US Command and Gen Staff Coll, 1964-65. Appointments: Served, Austl Regular Army, 35 yrs to 1978; Active serv, Korea and Vietnam; Chf of Staff, ANZUK Force, Singapore and Malaysia, 1973-75; Cmdt, Austl Staff Coll, Ft Queenscliff, 1975-78; Retd Army, 1978; Dir, Austl Counter Disaster Coll, 1978-87; Rep Col Cmdt, Corps of Roy Austl Engrs, 1988-92; Chmn, Bd, Braemar Coll, 1988-94; Chmn, The Field Marshall Sir Thomas Blaney Mem Fund, 1995-. Honours: Mentioned in dispatches, Korea; OBE, Vietnam. Memberships: Fell, Instn Engrs Aust; Fell, Austl Inst Mngmt; Pres, Vic Assn of the Most Excellent Order of the Brit Empire, 1996-99; Chmn, Legacy Co-ord Cncl Aust, 1997-99. Hobbies: Gardening; Legacy. Address: The Laurels, Mount Macedon, Vic 3441, Australia.

GIONG Tran Thi, b. 5 Mar 1947, Hue, Vietnam. Counselling Psychologist. Education: Doct in Cnslng Psychol. Publications: The Happiness is Within Your Reach, 1997; Wild Flower (poems). Memberships: Exec Mbr, Psycho-Educl Assn of Ho Chi Minh Cty; Exec Mbr, Socl Dev Rsch & Cnsltncy, Ho Chi Minh Cty. Hobby: Collections. Address: 228 Nam Ky Khoi Nghia, Q 3 Ho Chi Minh City, Vietnam.

GIORGI Piero Paolo, b. 29 Aug 1941, Bologua, Italy. University Lecturer. m. Parosash, 3 July 1998, 1 s, 1 d. Education: BSc, Hons, Bologua; PhD, Newcastle, England. Appointments: Lectr, Univ de Lousanne; Snr Lectr, Univ Qld. Publications: 2 books on med hist. Membership: Fell, Austl Inst Biol. Hobby: Peace studies. Address: c/o University of Queensland, Qld 4072, Australia.

GIRARD Dominique, b. 28 Jan 1946. Ambassador of France. m. Maud Geslan, 25 Feb 1967, 2 s. Education: Grad Inst d'Etudes Politiques, Paris; Ecole des Langues Orientales (Chinese, Vietnamese). Appointments: Diplomatic Assignments in Hanoi, 1971; Vietnam, 1972; Paris, 1975-78; Singapore, 1978-80; Wash DC, 1980-84; Paris, 1984-86; Beijing, 1986-88; Dpty Dir in Personnel min on For Affairs, Paris, 1988-89; Dpty Dir of Cabinet For Min's Off, Paris, 1988-92; Amb to Indonesia, 1992-95, Aust, 1995. Honours: Chevalier of the Ordre du Mérite, 1986; Offr, Ordre al Merito, Italy, 1990; Areas Offr, Order of Orange Nassau, 1991; MBE, 1992; Chevalier de l'Ordre du Mérite, Senegal, 1992; Chevalier, Legion of Honour, 1996. Listed in: Who's Who in Science; Who's Who in Australia. Hobbies: Collections; Paintings; Ceramics. Address: 6 Perth Avenue, Yarralumla, ACT 2600, Australia.

GIRAY I Safa, b. 5 Mar 1931 Izmir. Politician. m. (1) Sema Giray, 1955; (2) Misler Giray, 1972, 2 s, 1 d. Education: Istanbul Tech Univ. Appointments: Plng engr at Gen Directorate of Electricity Wrks Study Dept, 1968; Wrk'd on proj studies of Keban and Oymapinar Dams; Advsr at Gen Directorate of Electrical Wrks; Mngr Black Sea Copper Enterprises, 1969-74; Gen Mngr Akkardan Co, 1974-80; Gen Mngr Anadolu Mach Co, 1980-83; Dep for Istanbul, 1983-; Min of Pub Wrks and Housing, 1983-89; Min of Def, 1989-90; Min of For Affairs, 1991; MP, 1991-. Hobbies: Music; Games. Address: TBMM, Ankara, Turkey.

GIRGIN Ismail, b. 3 Apr 1950, Bolu, Turkey. Educator; Chemist. m. Aysel, 5 Oct 1978, 3 s. Education: BS, Chem, Mid E Tech Univ, Ankara, Turkey, 1973; MS, Chem, Ankara Univ, Turkey, 1975; PhD, Chem, 1979; Assoc Prof, Mineral Processing, Hacettepe Univ, Ankara, Turkey, 1985; Prof, 1993. Appointments: Asst, Chem Dept, Ankara Univ, 1973-77; Hon Rsch Assoc, Minerals Engrng Dept, Birmingham Univ, 1977-79; Rsch Assoc, Chem Dept, Ankara Univ, 1979-81; Lectr, Mining Engrng Dept, Hacettepe Univ, 1981-85; Visng Rsch Assoc, Dept of Inorganic and Structural Chem, Univ of Leeds, 1985-86; Snr Lectr, Mining Engrng Dept, Hacettepe Univ, 1986-95; Dir, Earth Sci Application and Rsch Cntr, Hacettepe Univ, 1995-. Publications: Ed, Earth Sciences. 11 Technol Rprts; 29 Publshd Articles. Honours: Min of O'seas Dev Fell, 1977; Roy Soc Dev Country Fell, 1985. Memberships: Environl Rsch and Application Cntr, Hacettepe Univ, 1990; Earth Scientists Assn, 1991; NY Acady of Scis, 1995. Hobbies: Playing football; Scientific research. Address: Mining Engineering Dept, Hacettepe University, 06532 Beytepe Ankara, Turkey.

GITTOES George Noel, b. 7 Dec 1949, Sydney, Aust. Artist; Photographer. m. Gabrielle Dalton, 1 s, 1 d. Creative Works: Works rep in pub collects and many pvte collects. Honours: AM; Wynne Prize, Landscape Painting; Blake Prize, Relig Painting (twice). Address: PO Box 2, Bundeena, NSW 2230, Australia.

GLADSTONES John Sylvester, b. 14 Feb 1932, Perth, Aust. Agricultural Scientist. m. Helen Patricia Burns, 19 Dec 1962, 1 s, 1 d. Education: BSc Agric Hons, 1955; PhD 1959, Univ of WA. Appointments: Postdoct Fell, Can Rsch Cncl, 1958-59; Lectr 1960-65, Snr Lectr 1966-71, Univ of WA; Snr Plant Breeder 1971-81, Prin Plant Breeder 1981-91, WA Dept of Agric; Agric and Viticulture Cnslt, 1991-. Creative Works include: Over 100 publs inclng Viticulture and Environment, 1992, breeder, co-breeder, of 20 coml varieties of crop lupins, 11 subterranean clover and 7 of serradella. Honours: Medal of Austl Inst of Agricl Sci, 1974; William Farrer Mem Medal, 1975; Fell, Austl Acady of Technol Scis and Engrng, 1976; Urrbrae Awd, 1985; Mbr, Order of Aust, 1986; Adv Aust Awd, 1987; Hon Doct of Sci in Agric, Univ of WA, 1988; Sheraton Jack Mann Mem Medal, 1989; Fell, Austl Inst of Agric Sci, 1990; Clunies Ross Natl Sci and Technol Awd, 1991; WA Citizen of the Yr (The Professions), 1992; Hon Life Mbr, Intl Lupin Assn, 1996.

Memberships: Austl Inst of Agricl Sci; Roy Soc of WA; Austl and Amn Socs for Viticulture and Oenology. Hobbies: Music; Wine; Gardening. Address: 27 Pandora Drive, City Beach, WA 6015, Australia.

GLARE Kelvin, b. 6 Jan 1938. Director; Executive Chairman. m. Trish, 10 Oct 1959, 2 d. Education: Univ of Melbourne. Appointments: Joined Police Dept, 1957; Divsnl Investigator, CIB, Russell Street, 1966, Sunshine, 1966, Heidelberg, 1967; FBR Superior, Fingerprint Bur, 1969; Stn Supvsr, Russell Street, 1969, 1972, Eltham, 1973; Spec Duties List, CCP Off Personnel Dept, 1976; Admitted Practice Bar and Solicitor, Supreme Crt, Vic, 1977; Divsnl Offr, D Dist No 1 Divsn, 1979; O Dist 1 Divsnl Offr in Charge, Prosecutions Divsn, 1981; Supt R and D Offr i/c Inspectorate, 1984; Asst Cmmnr, IID Internal Investigations Dept, 1984; Asst Cmmnr, Ops Dept, 1985; Dpty Cmmnr, Ops, Chf Cmmnr Off, 1986; Chf Cmmnr of Police, Vic, 1987-92; Dir, Exec Advsr, Corp Security and Dev, FBIS Intl Pty Ltd, 1995-. Honours: Good Conduct and Long Serving Medal, 1980; Austl Police Medal, 1987; AO, 1993. Hobbies: Fishing; Tennis; Bushwalking. Address: FBIS International Issues Management Pty Ltd, Albert Gate Level 5, 150 Albert Road, South Melbourne, Vic 3205, Australia.

GLASKIN Gerald Marcus, b. 16 Dec 1923, Perth, WA, Aust. Author. Appointments: Roy Austl Navy, 1941-43; Roy Austl Air Force, 1944-46; Fremantle Sports Depot, 1946-47; Ford Motor Co of Aust, 1947-48; Wearne Brothers Ltd, 1949; McMullan & Co, 1950; Ptnr, Lyall & Evatt, Stockbrokers, Singapore, 1951-59. Publications: Novels: A World of Our Own; A Minor Portrait (The Mistress); A Change of Mind; A Lion in the Sun; The Beach of Passionate Love; A Waltz Through the Hills; Flight to Landfall; O Love, O Loneliness; No End to the Way (as Nevile Jackson); The Man Who Didn't Count; Short stories: A Small Collection; The Road to Nowhere; Sometimes it Wasn't So Nice; Memoirs; A Many Splendoured Woman: A Memoir of Han Suyin; A Bird in My Hands; The Eaves of Night (in Two Women); One Way to Wonderland; Plays: Turn on the Heat (in Two Women); Kabbarli; Woman of the Dreaming; A Waltz Through the Hills (musical); Sexus; Travel: The Land that Sleeps; Parapsychology: Windows of the Mind; Worlds Within; A Door to Eternity (A Door to Infinity). Honours: C'wlth Lit Awd for A World of Our Own; Var Austl Lit, Film and TV Bd Grants; Writer-in-Res; Pater Intl (TV Series) Awd, 1988 . Memberships: Soc of Auths, UK; PEN Intl; Austl Soc of Auths; Fellshp, Austl Writers, Pres, 1967-68; Austl Writers Guild. Hobbies: Music; Theatre; Literature; Photography; Parapsychology. Address: PO Box 79, Mosman Park, WA 6912, Australia.

GLAZEBROOK Susan Gwynfa Mary, b. 8 Feb 1956, Bowden, Cheshire, Eng. Lawyer. m. Greg Kane, 2 s. Education: Dip Bus, Fin, Auckland Univ, NZ; D Phil, French Legal Hist, Oxford Univ, UK; LLB Hons, Auckland Univ, NZ; MA, 1st Class Hons, Hist, Auckland Univ, NZ; BA, Hist, Auckland Univ, NZ. Appointments: Jr Lectr, Hist, Univ of Auckland, 1976, 1978, 1979; Wrkd in Rouen, France with the Govt Funded Org resp for the resettlement of Polit Refugees, France, 1981-83; Rsch Asst, Late Sir Keith Sinclair; Tutor, Hist, Auckland Univ, 1984; Pt-time Tutor, Acctcy, Engl, 1985; Pt-time Lectr, Dept of Coml Law, Univ of Auckland, 1991-94; Lawyer, Simpson Grierson Butler White, 1986-. Publications: The New Zealand Accrual Regime - A Practical Guide, 1989; Cahiers de droit fiscal international; New Zealand Journal of Taxation Law and Policy; Taxation; New Zealand Society of Accountants 1993 Tax Conferences; Women and Taxation; Many or publs. Memberships: NZ Cttee of the Pacific Econ Co-op Cncl; Intl Bar Assn; Inter-Pacific Bar Assn; Auckland Dist Law Soc; Legal Rsch Fndn; NZ Law Soc; NZ Law Soc and Taxation Cttee; Intl Fiscal Assn; Natl Provident Fund. Hobbies: Music; Theatre; Detective novels; Aerobics. Address: Simpson Grierson Building, 92-96 Albert Street, Private Bag 92-518, Wellesley Street, Auckland, New Zealand.

GLEESON Anthony Murray, b. 30 Aug 1938. Queen's Counsel. m. Robyn, 13 Jan 1965, 1 s, 3 d. Education: St Joseph's Coll, Hunters Hill; Admitted Bar at Law, 1963. Appointments: Cncl Mbr, 1979-; Queen's Counsel, NSW, 1974-; Chf Justice, NSW, 1988-98; Lt Gov, NSW, 1989-98; Chf Justice, Aust, 1998-. Honours: AO, 1981; AC, 1992. Memberships: Pres, NSW Bar Assn, 1984-86; Aust Club, Sydney. Hobbies: Tennis; Skiing. Address: Chief Justices Chambers, Supreme Court, Queens Square, Sydney, NSW, Australia.

GLEGHORN Thomas, b. 2 June 1925, Thorney, Eng. Artist. m. Elsie Mavis Beynon, 27 Dec 1946, 1 s, 1 d. Education: Broadmeadow Jnr Tech Sch; Engrng Apprentice, Broken Hill Co Ltd, Iron and Steel Wrks, Port Waratah, Newcastle, NSW, Aust. Appointments: Dir, Blaxland Art Gall, Sydney, NSW, 1958; Tchr, Art, Des, Natl Art Sch, 1960; Travel and stdys, Eur, 1962-63; Hd, Canberra Art Sch, ACT, 1968; Lectr, Art, 1969, Chmn, Art Dept, 1971-72, Bedford Pk Tchrs Coll, Adelaide, SA, 1969; Snr Lectr, Art, Sturt Coll Advd Educ, Adelaide, 1973-82; Full-time Painter, 1983-; Solo exhibns include Greenhill Gall, Perth, Fest Art, paintings, 1986; Tynte Gall, Adelaide, paintings, 1986; Greythorn Gall, Vic, paintings, 1986; Adrian Slinger Gall, Brisbane, stdys, drawings, 1987; Freeman Gall, Hobart, paintings, 1988; Tynte Gall, Adelaide, Fest Art, paintings, 1988; Num grp exhibns; Wrks incld in many perm collects. Honours: 30 Art Awds throughout Aust; Helena Rubinstein Travelling Schlshp, 1961; Brit Cncl Grant, 1962; Churchill Fell, 1973; Hon Rsch Fell, Life Mbr, Cntr for Rsch in New Lit in Engl, Flinders Univ. Hobby: Wine collecting. Address: 27 Northgate Street, Unley Park, SA 5061, Australia.

GLENN (Joseph Robert) Archibald (Sir), b. 24 May 1911. Company Director. m. (1) Elizabeth, 14 Nov 1939, dec 1988, 1 s, 3 d. (2) Sue, 6 Feb 1992. Education: Scotch Coll, Melbourne Univ. Appointments: Chmn, Scotch Coll Cncl, 1953-82; AMP, Harv, 1957; Cnslr, Indl Des Cncl of Aust, 1958-78; Prov Cncl, Monash Univ, 1958-61; Univ of Melbourne Appts Bd, 1960-72; Mfng Indl Advice Cncl, 1960-75; Hon Dr of the Univ, Chan, La Trobe Univ, 1964-72; Gov, Atlantic Inst of Intl Affairs, Paris, 1970-88; Chmn, Ormond Coll Cncl, 1976-83; Bank of NSW Savings Bank Ltd, 1960-73; Westpac Banking Corp, 1967-84; Dir, ICI Ltd, London, 1970-75; Gen Mngr, 1950-52, Mngng Dir, 1953-73, Dir, 1952-73, Chmn, 1963-73, ICI Aust Ltd; Chmn, 1973-83, IMI Aust, 1970-78; Tioxide Aust Ltd; Hill Samuel Aust Ltd, 1973-83; Dir, Alcoa Aust Ltd, 1973-86; Rocky Dam Pty Ltd, 1974-88; Chmn, Collins Wales Pty Ltd, 1974-83; Newmont Aust Ltd, 1976-; Dir, Westralian Sands Ltd, 1977-85. Honours: OBE; Jas N Kirby Awd, 1970. Memberships: Natl Fin Cttee, Austl Red Cross, 1982-99; Cook Soc; Soc of Collectors; Austl-Japan Bus Co-op Cttee, 1963-75; Austl Club, Melbourne; Melbourne Club; Frankston Golf Club; Snr Golfers Soc; Melbourne Univ Boat Club. Hobbies: Farming; Antiquarian books. Address: 8 Freemans Road, Mount Eliza, Vic 3930, Australia.

GLENNON Alfred James, b. 2 Dec 1920, Sydney, Aust. Anglican Clergyman. Education: Licentiate in Theol, Austl Coll of Theol, 1951; Dip in Socl Studies, Univ of Sydney, 1957. Appointments: Precentor, 1956-62, Chap, St George Hosp, Kogarah, 1962-68; Snr Asst, 1962-88, Fndr of Healing Min, 1960, Minor Canon, 1968-89, Hon Canon, 1989-, St Andrew's Cath, Sydney. Publications: Your Healing is Within You, 1978; How Can I Find Healing?, 1984. Honour: AM, 1987. Membership: Union Club, Sydney. Hobbies: Writing; Heraldry. Address: 59 Boundary Street, Clovelly, Sydney, NSW 2031, Australia.

GLOBUS Yoram, b. 7 Sept 1943. Film Producer. Appointments: Fndr Noah Films with Menahem Golan - qv - 1963; Bought Cannon Films - USA - with Menahem Golan, 1979; Prod'd over 100 motion pictures inclng Over the Top, Barfly, Dancers, Missing in Action I, II & II, Death Wish IV, The Assault, Surrender, Runaway Train, Hanna's War, Masters of the Universe, King Lear, Tough Guys Don't Dance, Shy People, A Cry In The Dark; Chmn CEO Cannon Entertainments, 1989; Offr Cannon Grp Inc, 1989; Co-Pres Pathe Comms Corp; Chmn CEO Pathe Intl until 1991. Honours: Acady Awd for Best For Lang Film for The Assault, 1986.

GLONEK Garique Francis Vladimir, b. 5 Aug 1960, Adelaide, Australia. Statistician. m. Meredith Hoare, 5 Aug 1987, 3 s. Education: BSc, hons; PhD. Appointments: Visng Asst Prof, Univ Chgo, USA, 1987; Lectr, Snr Lectr, Flinders Univ, 1989-. Memberships: Amn Stats Assn; Inst of Math Stats; Stats Soc of Aust. Address: Department of Mathematics and Statistics, Flinders University, GPO Box 2100, Adelaide, SA 5001, Australia.

GLOVER Danny, b. 22 July 1947 Georgia. Actor. m. Asake Bomani, 1 d. Education: San Francisco State Univ. Appointments: Rschr Off of Mayor San Francisco, 1971-75; Broadway debut Master Harold ... and the Boys, 1982; other stage appearances incl: The Blood Knot, 1982; The Island, Sizwe Banzi is Dead; Macbeth; Suicide in B Flat; Nevis Mountain Dew; Jukebox; Appearances in tv movies and series; With his wife fndr Bomani Gall San Francisco. Films: Escape from Alcatraz, 1979; Chu Chu and the Philly Flash, 1981; Out, 1982; Iceman, 1984; Places in the Heart, 1984; Birdy, 1984; The Color Purple, 1984; Silverado, 1985; Witness, 1985; Lethal Weapon, 1897; Bat 21, 1988; Lethal Weapon II, 1989; To Sleep with Anger, 1990; Predator 2, 1990; Flight of the Intruder, 1991; A Rage in Harlem, 1991; Pure Luck, 1991; Grand Canyon, 1992; Lethal Weapon III, 1992; The Saint of Fort Washington, 1993; Bopha, 1993; Angels in the Outfield, 1994; Operation Dumbo Drop. Address: William Morris Agency, 151 El Camino Blvd, Beverly Hills, CA 90212, USA.

GOBBO James (Augustine) (Sir), b. 22 Mar 1931. Governor of Victoria. m. Shirley Lewis, 1957, 2 s, 3 d. Education: Xavier Coll, Kew, Vic; BA Hons, Melbourne Univ; MA, Magdalen Coll, Oxford. Appointments: Called to Bar, Gray's Inn, London, 1956; Bar and Solicitor, Vic, Aust, 1956; Roll of Cnsl, Vict Bar, 1957; Indep Lectr, Evidence, Univ of Melbourne, 1963-68; QC, 1971; Supreme Crt Judge, Vic, 1978-94; Commnr, Vict Law Reform Commn, 1985-88; Gov, Vic, 1997-. Publications: Ed, Cross on Evidence (Austl edn), 1970-78; Num pprs. Honours: Commendatore all'Ordine di Merito, Italy, 1973; Kt Grand Cross, Malto, 1982; AC, 1993; Hon LLD, Monash, 1995; Hon Doct Aust Catholic Univ, 1996. Memberships include: Chmn, Austl Refugee Cncl, 1977; Cncl, Order of Aust, 1982-92; Natl Population Cncl, 1983; Tstee: Victorian Opera Fndn, 1983-97, WWF Aust, 1991-97; Pres, Scout Assn of Aust, 1987-97; Austl Multicultural Affairs Cncl, 1987-91; Austl Bicentennial Multicultural Fnd, 1988-97; Palladio Fndn, 1989-97; Victorian Cmnty Fndn, 1992-97; Austl Banking Ind Ombudsman Cncl, 1994-97; Electricity Ind Ombudsman Cncl, 1995-97. Address: Government House, Melbourne, Vic 3004, Australia.

GODDARD Leonard, b. 13 Feb 1925, Nottingham, Eng. Professor Emeritus. Div, 2 d. Education: MA, 1951, BPhil, 1955, St Andrews. Appointments: Asst Lectr, 1951-56, Prof, Logic, Metaphys, 1966-77, Univ St Andrews; Lectr, Snr Lectr, 1956-61, Prof, Philos, 1961-66, Univ New Eng; Boyce Gibson Prof Philos, 1977-90, Prof Emer, 1990-, Univ Melbourne. Publications: Co-auth: The Logic of Significance and Context, Vol 1, 1973; Philosophical Problems, 1977; The Metaphysics of Wittgenstein's Tratatus, 1982; Articles in Mind, Analysis, Australasian Journal of Philosophy, Notre Dame Journal of Formal Logic, other jrnls. Honour: Fell, Austl Acady Hum, 1980. Memberships: Mind Assn; Australasian Assn Philos. Hobby: Gardening. Address: Department of Philosophy, University of Melbourne, Parkville, Vic 3052, Australia.

GODFREY John Robert, b. 5 Aug 1938, Nadrogin, WA, Aust. Educator; Academic. m. Robyn Jilian Bailey, 17 Dec 1989, 2 s, 2 d. Education: BA; BEd; MA; MEd; PhD. Appointments: Snr Lectr, Avondale Coll, 1977-1988; Lectr, Edith Cowan Univ, Churchlands, 1989-. Publications: Influences on the Development of the New South Wales Examination: 1930-1957, 1989. Honours: NSW Inst of Educ Prize for Best Rsch Thesis, Univ of Newcastle, 1987. Memberships: Pres, Edith Cowan Univ Acad Staff Assn; Cncl Mbr, Edith Cowan Univ Cncl. Hobbies; Horse racing; Tennis; Biography. Address: Edith

Cowan University, Churchlands, Western Australia 6018, Australia.

GODFREY Peter David Hensman, b. 3 Apr 1922, Bluntisham, Huntingdon, Eng. Musician. m. (1) Sheila Margarette McNeile, 1945, dec 1993, 4 d, (2) Elizabeth Jane Barnett, 1994. Education: Kings Coll, Cambridge, 1941-42, 1945-46; Roy Coll of Music, 1946-47. Appointments: Asst Dir, Uppingham Sch, 1947-49; Asst Dir, 1949-54, Dir of Music, 1954-58, Marlborough Coll; Lectr, Auckland Univ, NZ, 1958-71; Assoc Prof, 1971-73, Dean and Hd of Dept, 1974-82, Dir of Music, Auckland Cath, 1958-74; Conductor, Symphonia of Auckland, 1959-68, Auckland Dorian Choir, 1961-83, NZ Natl Yth Choir, 1979-88, Kapiti Chamber Choir, 1992-, Kapiti Chorale, 1995-; Prof Emer, Auckland Univ, 1983-; Dir of Music, Wellington Cath, 1983-89, tours w choir of Eng and Eur, 1972, 1975, 1977, 1982, 1988; Conductor, Wellington Orpheus Choir, 1984-90; Dir of Music, Trinity Coll, Melbourne, 1989-91; Pres, Fndr, NZ Choral Fedn, 1985-. Creative Works: Recdngs: Music of the Church's Year; The Way of the Cross, The Dorian Singers, 1969; Five Centuries of Sacred Music, 1975; Visions 1, 1977; The Blue Bird, Motets of Peter Philips, 1981; The Dorians Sing, 1982. CDs: A Royal Occasion - Kiri Te Kanawa and the National Youth Choir of NZ; Carols, Psalms and Anthems, Trinity Coll Chapel Choir, Melbourne, 1992. Honours: MBE, 1978; CBE, 1988. Hobby: Gardening. Address: 11 Karaka Grove, Waikanae, New Zealand.

GOENKA Vinodini, b. 14 Aug 1935, India. Writer. m. 17 June 1951, 1 s. Publications: 6 story collections, 4 novels, 1 poetry collection, all in Hindi; 2 books trans in Engl. Honours: Yuohvir Awd, 1988; Nirla Awd, 1997. Memberships include: Auth Guild of India. Hobbies: Story writing; Indian classical music. Address: Sriram Sadan, Road No 47, Jubilee Hills, Hyderabad, India.

GOERKE Annette Maureen, b. 8 Sept 1938, Perth, WA, Aust. Musician; Organist; Director of Cathedral Music. m. Vincent Leonard Goerke, 20 Aug 1960, 3 d. Education: A Mus A (Piano), 1958, L Mus A (Organ), 1964, Mus B (Composition), 1971, Univ of WA. Appointments: Organist, St Marys Cath, Perth, 1956-; Frequent Recitals Brdcst by the Austl Brdcstng Corp, 1965-; Soloist, Orch Organist, WA Symph Orch, 1969-; Acting Organist, Univ of WA, 1973; Dir of Music, St Marys Cath, Perth, 1974-; Recitalist, Fest of Perth, 1977; Organist, Univ of WA, 1982-88; Examiner (Organ/Piano) for Austl Music Examiners Bd, 1982-; Specialist Tchr, (Organ Perf) Univ of WA, 1982-; Western Austl Conservatorium of Music, 1989-; Recitalist, Melbourne Intl Fest of Organ and Harpsichord, 1993; Recitalist Sydney Town Hall, 1998. Honours: Churchill Fellshp for Advd Organ Studies in Eur (chfly w Marie-Claire Alain in Paris), attended Master Classes given by Anton Heiller and Werner Jacob at Intl Summer Acady for Organists, Haarlem, Netherlands, 1972; Crucis Insigne pro Ecclesia et Pontifice (Papal Awd), 1996. Membership: Patron, Soc of Organists (Vic) Inc, 1999. Address: 53 Pandora Drive, City Beach, WA 6015, Australia.

GOFF Philip Bruce, b. 22 June 1953, Auckland, NZ. Member of Parliament. m. Mary, 1979, 2 s, 1 d. Education: MA, 1st Class Hons, Univ of Auckland. Appointments: MP for Roskill, 1984-90, 1993-96; MP for New Lynn, 1996-. Memberships: C'wlth Parly Assn; Inter Parly Union. Hobbies: Sports; Gardening; Travel. Address: c/o Parliament House, Wellington, New Zealand.

GOH Chok Tong, b. 20 May 1941, Singapore. Prime Minister. m. Choo Leng Tan, 1 s, 1 d. Education: Raffles Instn, Singapore, 1955-60; BA, 1st Class Hons, Univ Singapore, 1961-64; MA, Williams Coll, USA, 1966-67. Appointments: Admin Offr, Singapore Admin Serv, 1964; Planning & Projects Mngr, Neptune Orient Lines, 1969; MP, 1976; Snr Min of State for Fin, 1977; Min for Trade & Ind, 1979; Min for Trade & Ind, Min for Hlth, 1981; Min for Hlth, 2nd Min for Def, 1981; Min for Def, 2nd Min for Hlth, 1982; 1st Dpty PM, Min for Def, 1985; PM, Min for Def, 1990; PM, 1991. Hobbies: Golf; Tennis. Address: c/o Prime Minister's Office, Singapore.

GOH Keng Swee, b. 6 Oct 1918 Malacca. Politician. m. Alice Woon, 1942, 1 s. Education: Anglo-Chinese Sch Singapore; Raffles Coll London Univ. Appointments: Fmrly Vice-Chmn People's Action Party; Min for Fin, 1959-65; Initiated Singapore's industrialization plan the establishment of Econ Dev Bd; Min of Def, 1965-67; Min of Fin, 1967-70; Min of Def, 1970-79; Concurrently Dep PM, 1973-80; Min of Educ, 1979-81, 1981-84; First Dep PM, 1980-84 and with responsibility for the Monetary Auth of Singapore, 1980-81 - Dep Chmn 1992; Econ Advsr to Chinese Govt, July 1985-. Publications: Urban Incomes and Housing; A Report on the Social Survey of Singapore, 1953-54 1958; Economics of Modernization and Other Essays, 1972; The Practice of Economic Growth, 1977. Honours: Ramon Magsaysay Awd for Govt Serv, 1972. Memberships: Fmr mbr Legis Assembly from Kreta Ayer Div; Mbr Govng Cncl Asian Inst for Econ Dev and Plng Bangkok, 1963-66. Address: c/o Ministry of Foreign Affairs, 2nd Foor, City Hall, St Andrews Road, Singapore 0617.

GOH Kun, b. 2 Jan 1938, Seoul, Korea. Mayor of Seoul; Former Prime Minister. m. 3 s. Education: Seoul Natl Univ. Appointments: Asst Jnr Official, 1962-65; Asst Dir, Plng Off, Min of Home Affairs, 1965-68; Dir, Interior Dept, Jeonbuk Prov, 1968-71; Commnr, New Village Movt, 1971-73; Vice Gov, Kangwon Prov, 1973; Dir, Local Admin Bur, Min of Home Affairs, 1973-75; Gov, Jeonnam Prov, 1975-79; Chf Sec, Pol Affairs, Chong Wa Dae (The Blue House); Chf Advsr, Korea Rsch Inst for Human Settlement, 1980; Min of Transportation, 1980-81, Min of Agric and Marine Affairs, 1981-82, Min of Home Affairs, 1987; Visng Rschr, Harv Univ, USA, 1983; Visng Rschr, MIT, USA, 1984; Mbr, 12th Natl Assembly, 1985-88; Min of Home Affairs, 1987; Mayor of Seoul Metrop Govt, 1988-90; Pres, Myong Ji Univ, 1994-97; Co-Pres, Korea Fedn for Environ Movt, 1996-97; Prime Minister, 1997-98; Mayor of Seoul Metrop Govt, 1998-. Honour: Hon LLD, Won Kwang Univ, 1992. Address: Mayor's Office, Seoul Metropolitan Government, 31 Taepyung-no 1 ga, Chung-gu, Seoul, Korea 100-744.

GOH Lai Yoong, b. 1938, Malaysia. Academic. m. Swee Hock Goh, 1968, 1 s, 2 d. Education: BSc, Hons, Hong Kong; MSc, Malaya; PhD, DSc, London. Appointments: Tutor, 1963-64, Lectr, 1968-76, Assoc Prof, 1976-91, Prof, 1992-95, Univ of Malaya; Snr Rsch Fell, Monash Univ, Aust, 1995-97; Snr Fell, Natl Univ of Singapore, 1997-. Publications: Articles in Chem jrnls. Honours: Loke Yew Schl, 1959-63; C'wlth Schl, 1965-67; William Ramsay Meml Gold Medalist, Univ Coll, London, 1967; Roy Soc C'wlth Devel Countries Fellshp, 1991. Memberships: Fell, Malaysian Inst of Chem, Roy Soc of Chem, London; Mbr, Roy Austl Chem Inst. Hobbies: Music; Sewing. Address: 14 Jalan 17/35, 46400 Petaling Jaya, Selangor, Malaysia.

GOH Mark K H, b. 26 Mar 1960. Educator; Researcher; Consultant. m. 28 Feb 1987, 4 s. Education: PhD; MBA; BSc (Hons). Appointments: VP, OR Soc of Singapore, 1994-96; ASEAN Wrkng Grp on Transport, 1995; Editl Bd, Jrn of Supply Chain Mngmt, 1998-; Editl Bd, Asia Pacific Jrnl of OR, 1995-; VP, Austl Alumni, 1997-99; Bd Mbr, CIT, Singapore, 1999-. Publications: Opportunities in the Growth Triangle, 1993; OR Applications in Singapore, 1995. Honours: Colombo Plan Schl, 1980-84; C'wlth Fell, 1998; Citibank Fell, 1998; Visng Prof, Chulalongkorn Univ, 1999. Hobbies: Reading; Writing; Badminton. Address: Department of Decision Sciences, Faculty of Business Adminstration, National University of Singapore, 10 Kent Ridge Crescent, S 119260 Singapore.

GOH Swee Hock, b. 14 Oct 1940, Malaysia. Academician. m. L Y Goh, 1968, 1 s, 2 d. Education: BSc Hons; MSc; PhD (Chgo). Appointments: Lectr; Prof. Publications: Phytochemial Guide to Malaysian Flora, 1993; Malaysian Medicinal Plants for the Treatment of Cardiovascular Diseases, 1995. Honour: Gold Medal (MIC), 1995. Memberships: Amn Chem Soc; Roy Soc of Chem; Roy Austl Chem Inst; Malaysian Inst of Chem. Hobby: Nature appreciation. Address: Chemistry Department, National University of Singapore, Singapore.

GOHEL Mayur Danny I, b. 14 Apr 1962, Hong Kong. Senior Lecturer. m. Doris Auwai Ting, 6 Dec 1993. Education: BS, Bio; BS Clinl Chem; MPhil; PhD. Appointments: Lectr, 1993; Section Hd, Biomedl Scis, 1997; Snr Lectr, 1998. Honours: Sir Edward Youde Meml Fell, 1992-93; Fell, Inst of Biomedl Sci; Wong Ching Yee Medl Schlshps, 1991-92 1992-93; Hui Pun Hing Chem Schlshp. Memberships: Roy Soc of Chem; Inst of Bio; Chartered Chemist; Chartered Biolst; Fell, Roy Soc of Hlth. Hobbies: Rowing; Swimming; Cricket; Advanced IT teaching. Address: Department of Nursing and Health Sciences; Hong Kong Polytechnic University, Hung Hom, Kowloon, Hong Kong.

GOKBEL Hakki, b. 27 Apr 1964, Nazilli, Turkey. Associate Professor of Physiology. m. Hatice, 29 May 1988, 1 s, 2 d. Education: MD. Publications: 2 books, 60 articles, 39 congress reps. Memberships: Intl Union of Physiol Soc; NY Acady of Scis. Hobbies: Internet; Philosophy; History of Science. Address: Seleuk Univ Tip Fakultesi, Fizyoloji Anabilim Dali, 42080 Konya, Turkey.

GOKHALE Pratibha Ashok, b. 11 Dec 1952. Teacher. m. Ashok Sadashiv Gokhale, 14 May 1975, 1 son, 1 daughter. Education: BSc Chemistry; Master of Library Science. Appointments: Library Assistant, Tata Institute of Fundamental Research, 1974-77; Librarian, ICI, India Ltd Research Centre, 1978-92; Reader, University of Bombay, 1994-. Publications: Articles in professional journals and newspapers. Memberships: Indian Association of Special Libraries and Information Centre; IATLIS; Indian Library Association. Hobbies: Reading; Indian classical music; Medical science. Address: Reader, Department of Library Science, University of Bombay, Vidyanagari, Kalina, Santacauz (E), Bombay 400098, India.

GOKHARU Surendra Sinha, b. 24 Sept 1935, Banera, India. Engineer; Computer Consultant. m. Ratan Gokharu, 10 May 1959, 3 d. Education: BE, Mech Engrng, Birla Coll of Engrng, Pilani, India, 1959; Dip, Computer Programming Syst, Bur of Data Processing, Bombay, 1971. Appointments: Sci Offr, Atomic Energy Estab, India, 1959-66; Planning Mngr, Ass Bearing Co (Unit of SKF, Sweden), India, 1966-73; Proj Mngr, Parrys Bearing Ltd, India, 1974-77; Gen Mngr, P T Sri Riken Wiguna (Unit of RIKEN-Japan), 1977-81; Mngmt Cnslt, P T Pembangunan Jaya, Indonesia, 1982-84; Computer Cnslt PT Harlan Bekti Corp, 1984-91; Mngng Dir, PT Gokharu Microsystems, 1991-97; Exhib sects of fuel elements for atomic power reactors, 3rd Intl Conf on Peaceful Uses of Atomic Energy, Geneva, 1964. Publication: Centreless Grinding, book, 1967. Honours: 1st Prize for highest perf in Mechl Engrng Lab, Engrng Coll, 1958, 1959; Awd for designing extended bore grinding tools, 1968; Socially won for introducing Computer Course at GM Intl Sch, Jakarta, 1987. Hobbies: Scientific study and experimentation to find causes of general helplessness of human thoughts, emotions and actions and related use of hidden human energy to reduce this through awareness development techniques. Listed in: Who's Who in the World; International Directory of Distinguished Leadership; Dictionary of International Biography; 5000 Personalities of the World. Address: 1 A 11 Old Housing Board, Shastri Nagar; Bhilwara 311001, India.

GOLCHHA Hulaschand, b. 15 Mar 1935, Biratnagar, Nepal. m. Pukhraj Devi Golchha, Dec 1956, 4 s. Appointments include: Chmn, Golchha Org; Chmn, Nepal United Co Ltd, Kathmandu; Dir, Sagarmatha Ins Co Ltd. Honours: Gold Medal, 1952; Yuwak Ratna, 1972; His Majesty King Birendra Coronation Medal, 1975; Dharma Diwakar, 1990; Jubilee Medal, 1993; Vijaya Ratna Medal, 1994; Marwari Gaurav, 1994; Spec Hon Awd, 1996; HM King Birendra Accession to throne Silver Jubilee Medal, 1996; Poddar Ratna, 1997; Man of Yr, 1998. Memberships include: Chmn, Ramlal Golchha Eye Hosp, Biratnagar; VP, Nepal Heritage Soc; Fell, Rotary Intl Fndn, USA; Nepal Red Cross Soc; Nepal Cancer Relief Soc; Nepal Heritage Soc; World Hindu Fedn. Address: Golchha House, Post Box No 363, Kathmandu, Nepal.

GÖLCÜKLÜ Ahmet Feyyaz, b. 4 Oct 1926, Lila. University Professor. 2 s. Education: MA; PhD; Doct. Appointments: Prof, 1958; Dir, Sch of Jrnlsm and Brcstng, 1969, 1972; Dean, Fac of Polit Scis, Univ of Ankhara, 1973-76; Now Prof Emeritus, Fmr Judge, Eurn Crt of Hum Rights, 1977-98; Mbr Turkish Consultative Assembly (Constituent Assembly). 1981-83. Publications: Num books and articles on Penal Law, Intl Law of Hum Rights. Address: 1377 Sok NO 7/4 Alsancah, 35210 Izmir, Turkey.

GOLD Henry, b. 3 Dec 1934, Czechoslovakia. Wilderness Photographer. m. 15 Aug 1959, 3 d. Education: Graphic Arts Inst, Vienna, 1964. Appointments: Created photog images for conservation orgns to lobby Govts and for press releases during conservation campaigns against logging and mining in scenic and environmemtally sensitive areas: Colong campaign, 1968-71; Boyd Plateau campaign, 1972-75; Gtr BLue Mts Natl Park campaign, 1975; Kakadu uranium mining, 1976; Colo River Dam, 1978; Rainforest campaign, 1973-82; Nattai Wilderness, 1974; Old Growth Forest campaign, 1992-98. Publications: The McDonnell Ranges, 1973; Colo Wilderness, 1978; Wild Places, 1983; New South Wales Wilderness Calandar, 1980-97. Honours: Hon Photogr, the Colong Fndn for Wilderness, 1984. Memberships: Natl Parks Assn of NSW, 1966; The Colong Fndn for Wilderness, 1978; Natl Assn for the Visual Arts, 1977, Hobbies: Mountaineering; Travel. Address: PO Box 247, Frenchs Forest, NSW 2086, Australia.

GOLDBLUM Jeff, b. 22 Oct 1952 Pittsburgh. Actor. m. (2) Geena Davis, div. Education: NY Neighborhood Playhouse. Films incl: California Split, 1974; Death Wish, 1974; Nashville, 1975; Next Stop Greenwich Village, 1976; Annie Hall, 1977; Between the Lines, 1977; The Sentinel, 1977; Invasion of the Bodysnatchers, 1978; Remember My Name, 1978; Thank God it's Friday, 1978; Escape from Athena, 1979; The Big Chill, 1983; The Right Stuff, 1983; Threshold, 1983; The Adventures of Buckaroo Banzai, 1984; Silverado, 1985; Into the Night, 1985; Transylvania 6-5000, 1985; The Fly, 1986; Beyond Therapy, 1987; The Tall Guy, 1989; Earth Girls are Easy, 1989; First Born - tv - 1989; The Mad Monkey, 1990; Mister Frost, 1991; Deep Cover, 1992; The Favour, the Watch and the Very Big Fish, 1992; Father and Sons, 1993; Jurassic Park, 1993; Lushlife, TV, 1994; Future Quest, TV, 1994; Hideaway, 1995; Nine Months, 1995; Independence Day, 1996; The Lost World, 1997; Prodr, Little Surprises, 1995. Address: c/o International Creative Managements, 8899 Beverly Boulevard, Los Angeles, CA 90048, USA.

GOLDENBERG SCHREIBER Efrain, b. 28 Dec 1929 Lima. Politician; Businessman. m. Irene Pravatiner, 1952, 1 s, 4 d. Education: San Andres - fmrly Anglo-Peruvian - Sch; Univ Natl Mayor de San Marcos. Appointments: Priv Entrepreneur, 1951-; Fmr Dir FOPEX Sociedad Nacional de Pesqueria and other cos; Min of For Affairs, 1993-94; Pres Cncl of Mins - PM - and Min of For Affairs, 1994-95; Working in priv sector, 1995-. Address: Av Javier Prado Oeste 1661, Lima 23, Peru.

GOLDING Raymund Marshall, b. 17 June 1935, Westport, New Zealand. Researcher; Academic. m. Ingeborg, 16 June 1962, 2 d. Education: BS, Univ of Auckland, 1957; MSc, 1958; PhD, Univ of Cambridge, 1963. Appointments: Snr Rsch Scientist, Sect Hd, Theort Chem, 1963-68; Prof, Univ of NSW, 1968-86; Pro-Vice Chan, 1978-86; Vice Chan, James Cook Univ, 1986-96; Dir, PACON Intl; Chmn, Australasian Marine Sci Consortium; Hon Chmn, Austl Chapt PACON Intl; Chmn, Mngmt Cttee, Natl Unit for Multidisciplinary Stdies of Spinal Pain. Publications: Wave Machines, 1969; Chemistry, Multistrand Senior Science for High School Students, 1975; The Goldings of Oakington, 1992; Over 100 Rsch Pprs. Honours: Easterfield Award, 1967; Hon Fell, Korean Chem Soc, 1985; DSc, Univ of NSW, 1986; Awd Offr, AO, 1994; Pacon Intl Awd, 1996. Memberships: NZ Inst of Chem; Roy Austl Chem Inst; Inst of Phys; Roy Soc of Arts; Austl Acady of Technol Scis and Engrng.

Hobbies: Music; Photography; Astronomy. Address: Lot 2 Tolson Rd, Mooloolah, QLD 4553, Australia.

GOLDSMID John Marsden, b. 2 Feb 1937, E London, S Africa. University Lecturer. m. Hilary, 5 May 1962, 1 s, 2 d. Education: BSc, 1957, BSc, (Hons), 1958, MSc, 1963, Rhodes Univ, S Africa; PhD, Univ of London, Eng, 1970; MIBiol, 1972; MRCPath, 1976; MASM, 1978; FRCPath, 1983; FIBiol, 1984; FAIBiol (Fndr Fell), 1987; FASM, 1989; FACTM (Fndr Fell), 1991. Appointments include: Lectr, Medl Parasitology, Dept of Path, 1968, Lectr in Medl Parasitology, Dept of Medl Microbiology, 1971-74, Rdr, 1975, Prof & Hd, 1976-77, Univ of Rhodesia; Snr Lectr, Medl Microbiology, Dept of Path, Univ of Tas, Aust, 1977-78; Hon Microbiologist, Roy Hobart Hosp, Hobart, Aust, 1977-; Rdr, Medl Microbiology, Dept of Path, Univ of Tas, Aust, 1979-94; Prof, Medl Microbiology, Div of Path, Univ of Tas, Aust, 1995-. Publication: The Deadly Legacy, 1988. Honours include: Hon Life Mbr, Assn of Medl Lab Technologists, Zimbabwe, 1968; Hon Life Mbr, Aust Soc for Microbiology, 1988; Ashdown Orator, Australasian Coll of Tropical Med, 1997. Memberships: Roy Soc of Tropical Med and Hygiene; Amn Soc of Hygiene and Tropical Med; Pres, Australasian Coll of Tropical Med, 1998-; Paleopathology Assn; Intl Soc of Travel Med. Hobby: Trout fishing. Address: Div Pathology Clinical School, University of Tasmania, Royal Heart Hospital, 43 Collins Street, Hobart, Tasmania 7000, Australia.

GOLHAN Mehmet, b. 1929 Adapazari. Politician; Engineer. m. 2 children. Education: Istanbul Tech Univ. Appointments: Chf Indl Dept Min of Ind, 1974; Dir-Gen Road Water and Electricity Auth - YSE - Turkish Pet Corp - TPA; Under-Sec Min of Ind and Tech, 1980; Fmr Acting Chmn Grand Turkey Party and Dogru Yol Partisi - DYP; Parly Dep - DYP - 1987; Min of Natl Def, 1993-96. Memberships: Fndng mbr Grand Turkey Party and Dogru Yol Partisi - DYP. Address: c/o Ministry of National Defence, Milli Savunma Bakanligi, 06100 Ankara, Turkey.

GOLIYA Chandmal, b. 10 Aug 1945, Bikaner. Businessman. m. Kusum, 1 June 1967, 2 s. 1 d. Education: BEng. Appointments: Dir, Meco Instruments P Ltd, Mumbai, 1962-85; Mng Dir, Mahavir Instrumentation P Ltd, 1986-. Memberships: Life Mbr, Inst of Engrs, India; Ahmedabad Mngmt Assn; Assn Overseas Trng Scholarship; Hon Sec, All India Instruments Manufacturers and Dealers Assn. Hobbies: Reading; Music. Address: A-72 Chinar, Rafiahmed Kidwai Rd, Mumbai 400 031, India.

GOLLAN Myfanwy Jane Anna, b. 23 July 1933. Writer; Editor. m. Donald Richmond Horne, 22 Mar 1960, 1 s, 1 d. Education: BA, Sydney Univ. Appointments: Cttee, Lib Soc, State Lib NSW; Convenor Lib Soc Symposia, 1985-89; Mbr, Univ of NSW U Comm, 1985-; Ed Cnslt, Aust Encyc, 1972-76; Columnist Aust Book Review, 1969-71; The Observer, 1960-61; Sydney Morning, Herald Jrnlst, 1955-60. Publications: Books: Contbr: The Coming Republic, 1992; Good Reading Guide, 1989; Different Lives, 1987; Ed: Children of Tibet, 1994; Kerr and the Consequences: An Account of a Public Meeting, 1976; Travelling Exhibition, Auth and Ed: The Struggle for Australian Democracy, 1788-1977; Contbr to var jnrls and newspprs. Hobbies: Books; Visual arts; Music; People; Food. Address: 53 Grosvenor Street, Woollahra 2025, Australia.

GONG Fangzhen, b. 2 Dec 1923, Shanghai, China. Social Science; History; Religion. m. Yang, 1 Oct 1954, 1 s. Education: LLB. Appointments: Ed, Tchr of Masters, Fudan Univ; Tchr of Docts, Fudan Univ; Tchr of Masters, Shanghai Acady of Socl Scis. Publications: Wisdom of Byzantine, 1994; Man, Society and Religion, 1995; The History of the Zoroastrians, 1998. Honour: Acad Cnslt, Shanghai Soc of Relg, 1996. Memberships: Hist of Sino Fgn Rels Assn; Shanghai Soc of Relig. Hobby: Classical music. Address: Institute of Religions, Shanghai Academy of Social Sciences, 622-7 Huaihai Road M, Shanghai 200041, China.

GONZALEZ Stella Marise, b. 11 Jan, Philippines. Realtor; Writer. Education: BSc, Com, Univ Santo Tomas; MBA, Ateneo Grad Sch of Bus. Appointments: Liason Offr, Off of the Manila Mayor, Manila Bd of Realtors, 1997; Liason Offr, Manila Bd of Realtors, 1998. Publications: Sev articles in profl jrnls. Honours: Most Popular Lady Realtor, 1997-98; Real Estate Broker of the Yr, 1998. Memberships: Confreire de la Chaine de Rotisseurs; Chinese & Wine Club of the Philippines; Ordre Mondial des Gourmets Degustateurs; Philippine Aust Soc; Roy Soc of St George; Fgn Corresp Assn of Singapore; Philippine Union of Jrnlsts; Philippine Assn of Real Estate Bds; Manila Bd of Realtors; Natl Assn of Realtors, USA; Intl Congress of Overseas Filipinos. Hobbies: Writing; Music appreciation. Address: Suite 511, Prince Tower Condominium, Tordesillas Street, Salcedo Village, Makati 1200, Philippines.

GONZALEZ GINER Ramón Ernesto, b. 16 May 1958. Minister of Foreign Affairs. m. 3 children. Education: Miami Univ, FL, USA. Appointment: Min for Socl and Econ Plng and Co-ord, 1994-95. Memberships: Pres, Credibank, SA; CV Indl Imports; VP, Coml Agricl Bank of El Salvador; Rep for El Salvador, IBRD (World Bank) and IDB. Address: Ministry of Foreign Affairs, Alameda Dr Manuel Enrique Araújo, Km 6, Carretera a Santa Tecla, San Salvador, El Salvador.

GOODFELLOW Geoffrey James, b. 21 Sept 1949, Adelaide, Aust. Poet. 3 s, 1 d. Appointments: Fmr Mbr, S Austl Yth Arts Bd; Fmr Mbr, S Austl Community Cultural Dev Advsry Cttee. Publications: (books) No Collars No Cuffs, 1986; Bow Tie & Tails, 1989; No Ticket No Start, 1990; Triggers, 1992; Semi Madness, 1997. Honours: Austl Cncl Community Writers, 1990; Inaugural Recip of Carclew Fellshp Fest Awds for Lit, 1998. Membership: Inaugural Mbr, S Austl Writers Cntr, Austl Labour Party. Hobbies: Running; Swimming; Jazz. Address: PO Box 1740 Adelaide, South Australia 5001.

GOODHEAD Bernard, b. 20 Oct 1934, Derby, Eng. Physician. m. Arlene, 19 Mar 1978, 1 s, 2 d. Education: BSc; MBSLB; LRCP; MRCS; MSc; ChB; FACS; FRCS; FICS. Appointments: Multiple Hosp, CA and TX. Creative Works: 29 Publd Sci Pprs. Hons: Hunterian Profl, 1968; Fulbright Schlshp. Memberships: FRCS; FACS; FICS. Hobby: Travel. Address: 1395 Park Row, La Jolle, CA 92037, USA.

GOODHEW Richard Henry (Harry), b. 19 Mar 1931, Sydney, NSW, Aust. Anglican Archbishop of Sydney. m. Pamela, 1 Mar 1958, 2 s, 2 d. Education: MA (Hons) Wollongong; ThL; DLitt, hon causa, Wollongong. Appointments: Bishop Wollongong, 1982-93; Archd Wollongong and Camden, 1979-82; Snr Canon, St Michael's Provisional Cath, 1976-79, Rector St Stephen's Corparoo Brisb, 1971-76; St Paul's Carlingford, NSW, 1966-71; w Bush Ch Aid Ceduna, SA, 1963-66; Curate ic St Bede's Beverly Hills, NSW, 1959-63; Curate, St Matthew's Bondi, NSW, 1958. Hobbies: Jogging; Reading; Tennis; Swimming. Address: Anglican Church Office, St Andrews House, Sydney Square, NSW 2000, Australia.

GOODMAN John, b. 20 June 1952 St Louis. Film Actor. m. Annabeth Hartzog, 1989, 1 d. Education: Meramac Community Coll; SW MO State Univ. Appointments: Broadway appearances in Loose Ends, 1979; Big River, 1985; Appearances on tv incl: The Mystery of Moro Castle; The Face of Rage; Heart of Steel; Moonlighting; Chiefs, mini series; The Paper Chase; Murder Ordained; The Equalizer; Roseanne, series. Films incl: The Survivors, 1983; Eddie Macon's Run, 1983; Revenge of the Nerds, 1984; CHUD, 1984; Maria's Lovers, 1985; Sweet Dreams, 1985; True Stories, 1986; The Big Easy, 1987; Burglar, 1987; Raising Arizona, 1987; The Wrong Guys, 1988; Everybody's All-American, 1988; Punchline, 1988; Sea of Love, 1989; Always, 1989; Stella, 1990; Arachnophobia, 1990; King Ralph, 1990; Barton Fink, 1991; The Babe, 1992; Born Yesterday, 1993; The Flintstones, 1994; Kingfish: A Story of Huey P Long, 1995; Pie in the Sky; Mother Night.

Address: CAA, 9830 Wilshire Boulevard, Beverly Hills, CA 90212, USA.

GOODMAN Max A, b. 24 May 1924, Chgo, IL, USA. Professor of Law. m. Marylene, 2 June 1946, 1 s, 2 d. Education: AA; JD. Honour: Spencer Brandeis Family Law Serv Awd, 1988. Memberships: Los Angeles Co Bar Assn, Chair of Family Law Sect, 1975-76; CA State Bar, Amn BA, Beverly Hills Bar Assn. Hobby: Contract bridge. Address: 675 South Westmoreland Avenue, Los Angeles, CA 90005, USA.

GOONERATNE Malini Yasmine, b. 22 Dec 1935, Colombo, Sri Lanka. University Emeritus Professor; Writer. m. Brendon Gooneratne, 31 Dec 1962, 1 s, 1 d. Education: BA, Hons, Ceylon, 1959; PhD, Cambridge, 1962; DLitt, Macquarie, 1981. Appointments: Univ Prof of Engl Lit; Lit Critic; Ed; Bibliographer; Novelist; Essayist; Biographer; Poet. Publications include: Fiction: A Change of Skies, 1991; The Pleasures of Conquest, 1995. Poetry: Word, Bird, Motif, 1971; The Lizard's Cry and Other Poems, 1972; 6,000 Ft Death Dive, 1981; Celebrations and Departures: Selected Poems 1951-1991, 1991; Relative Merits (biog), 1986. Honours: AO, 1990; Marjorie Barnard Lt Awd for Fiction, 1992. Address: Department of English, Division of Humanities, Macquarie University, North Ryde, NSW 2109, Australia.

GOPALAN Coluthur, b. 29 Nov 1918, Salem, Tamil Nadu. Medical Researcher; Nutrition Researcher. m. Mrs Seetha, 1 s, 1 d. Education: FRS; MD (Madras); DSc (London); FRCP (Engl); FRCP (Edin). Appointments: Dir, Natl Inst of Nutrition, Hyderabad, 1974-; Dir-Gen, Indian Cncl of Medl Rsch, New Delhi, -1997; Currently Pres, Nutrition Fndn of India, New Delhi. Publications: Auth of over 200 rsch publs and sev monographs on nutrition. Honours: Basant Devi Amir Chand Prize, 1954, Basant Devi Amir Chand Prize (Snr), 1960, Indian Cncl of Medl Rsch; Amrut Mody Rsch Awd, 1972; Dr B C Roy Natl Awd, 1974; Ambuj Nath Bose Prize, Roy Coll Physns, London, 1976; Dhanvantri Awd for Outstndng Contbn in Medl Rsch and Ldrshp in field of nutrition and medl rsch, 1978; Fedn of Indian Chmbrs of Com and Ind Awd, 1978; WHO-Hlth for All Medal, 1988; Sir C V Raman Gold Medal, Indian Natl Sci Acady, 1988; Intl Union of Nutrition Scis Awd, 1989;R D Birla Awd, 1990. Memberships: Pres, Intl Union of Nutritional Scis, 1975-79; Fndr Pres, Nutrition Soc of India. Address: C-13, Qutab Institutional Area, New Delhi 110016, India.

GOPINATHAN Melethil Sankaran, b. 8 Oct 1942. Professor of Chemistry. m. Dr Kamala, 19 Feb 1974, 1 s. Education: MSc; PhD. Appointment: Prof, IIT Madras, 1977-. Publication: Group Theory in Chemistry, 1986. Honour: Alexander von Humboldt Fell. Memberships: Fell, Indian Natl Sci Acady; Fell, Natl Acady of Sci. Listed in: Who's Who of Asia. Hobbies: Poetry; Dramatics. Address: Department of Chemistry, Indian Institute of Technology, Madras 600 036, India.

GORAON Marilyn, b. 11 Dec 1940, Chgo, IL, USA. Hypnotherapist; Teacher; Author. 1 d. Education: BA, Engl, Univ of MI; Grad Studies in Engl, Univ of CA. Appointment: Fndr and Dir, Cntr for Hypnotherapy Certification. Creative Works: Healing is Remembering Who You Are; Manual for Transformational Healing; Manual for Mind Body Healing; Extraordinary Healing. Honours: Phi Beta Kappa; Phi Kappa Phi; Pi Lambda Theta; Hypnosis Achvmnt Awd. Memberships: Natl Guild of Hypnotists; Amn Cnslng Assn. Hobbies: Yoga; Meditation; Graphic design; Writing; Speaking. Address: P O Box 10795, Oakland, CA 94610, USA.

GORAY Narayan Ganesh, b. 15 Jun 1907 Hindala Maharashtra. Politician. m. Sumati Kirtane, 1935, 1 d. Education: Fergusson Coll Poona. Appointments: Congress Socl Party, 1930; Mayor of Poona; Imprisoned for polit activities before independence; Joint Sec Socl Party, 1948; Gen Sec Praja Socl Party, 1949-54, 1954-65; Chmn, 1965-71; Mayor Pune Municipal Corp, 1967-68; Ed Janata Weekly, 1971-; Led first wave of Satyagrahis against Portuguese Govt in Goa; High Commnr to UK, 1977-79. Publications: History of the

United States of America, 1959, etc. Memberships: Mbr Natl Exec, 1934; Mbr Lok Sabha, 1957-62; Mbr Rajya Sabha, 1970-76. Hobbies: Music; Painting; Writing. Address: 1813 Sadashiv Peth, Pune 30, Maharashtra State, India.

GORDON Henry Alfred, b. 9 Nov 1925, Melbourne, Aust. Editor; Author. m. (1) Dorothy Mae Scott, 11 July 1951, dec 1984, 2 s, 1 d, (2) Joy Ida Milner, 1993. Education: Melbourne HS. Appointments: RAAF, 1943-45; Jrnlst, Sydney Telegraph, Straits Times, Courier-Mail, Melbourne Sun, 1946-; War Corresp, Korea, 1950-51; Algeria, 1960; Ed, Melbourne Sun, 1968, Ed-in-Chf, Qld Newspprs, 1978-84; Ed-in-Chf, Herald - Weekly Times, 1984-86, Chmn AAP, 1983-84; Official Histn, Austl Olympic Cttee, 1994-. Publications: Young Men in a Hurry, 1960; The Embarrassing Australian, 1961; Gold Medal Girl, 1965; Famous Australian News Pictures, 1975; An Eyewitness History of Australia, 1976; Die Like the Carp!, 1978; Bicentennial - An Australian Mosaic, 1981; The Hard Way, 1990; Australia and the Olympic Games, 1994; Voyage From Shame, 1994. Honours: CMG, Servs to Jrnlsm, 1981; Natl Book Cncl 1st Prize for Austl Lit, 1978; Barbara Ramsden Lit Awd, 1976; Roy Austl Coll of Surgs, Graeme Grove Medal for Serv to Road Safety, 1977; UN Media Peace Prize Gold Citations, 1979, 1981, 1988; AM for servs to sport, hist and community, 1993; Foster's Best Olympic Writing Awd, 1998; Olympic Writers' and Photogrs Assn Writer of the Yr Awd, 1998. Memberships: Austl Soc of Auths; Cncl of Austl War Mem; Melbourne Cricket Club. Hobbies: Swimming; Gardening; Reading; Writing; Travel. Address: Sandgate Terrace, 35A Peak Avenue, Main Beach, Qld 4217, Australia.

GORDON Ruth Vida, b. 19 Sept 1926, Seattle, WA, USA. Structural Engineer. m. Michael H Schnapp, 28 Sept 1949, 1 s, 2 d. Education: BS, Civ Engrng, MS, Structures, Stanford Univ, CA; Regd Civil Engr, 1953; First Woman Licensed Structural Engr, 1959. Appointments: Structural Designer, Isadore Thompson San Fran, 1950-51, K P Norrie, Spokane, WA, 1951, Bechtel Corp, San Fran, 1951-51; Civ Engr, CALTRANS, San Fran, 1953-54; Structural Designer, Russell Fuller, San Fran, 1954, Western Knapp Engrng Corp, San Fran, 1954-55; Structural Safety Sect, San Fran, Off of the State Archt, State of CA; Structural Engrng Assoc, 1956-57, Snr Structural Designer, 1957-59, Snr Structural Engr, 1959-76, Dist Structural Engr, 1976-86 (1st woman in these posns); Structural Safety Sect, San Fran, Off of the State Archt, State of CA, 1984-; Pres, Pegasus Engrng Inc, 1984-. Publication: Seismic Safety Regulations for California Hospital and Public School Buildings, 1979. Honours: Margaret Byrne Schlshp, Stanford Univ, 1943-45; Wing and Garland Schlshps for Civ Engrng, Stanford Univ Grad Sch, 1948-49; Woman of Achmnt, Union Square Bus and Profl Women's Club, 1975, 1982; Outstndng Serv Awd, Golden Gate Sect, Soc of Women Engrs, 1979, 1984; CA Fedn of Bus and Profl Women Hall of Fame in field of Scis, 1992; Eminent Engr Awd in Recog of Outstndng Contbns to Field of Engrng and to Soc (1st woman), Tau Beta Pi, 1995. Memberships include: Structural Engrs Assn, Northern CA (1st woman), 1953; Profl Engrs, Chair, Profl Plcies Commn, 1982-83; Dir, Deleg San Fran Bay area Engrng Cncl, 1985-87, Dir, 1977-79, Treas, 1979-80, Sec, 1980-81, VP, 1981-82, Pres (1st woman), 1982-82, Co-Chair, Professionalism, 1977-87; Golden Gate Sect, Soc of Women Engrs, VP, 1976-77; Natl Soc of Women Engrs; Amn Soc of Civ Engrs; Assn for Women in Sci. Hobbies: Sailing; Knitting; Reading; Puzzles. Listed in: Who's Who in California; International Who's Who in Engineering; Two Thousand Notable Americans; International Who's Who of Professional and Business Women. Address: 726-23rd Avenue, San Francisco, CA 94121, USA.

GORMAN Gary Eugene, b. 8 Oct 1944, Carmel-by-Sea, CA, USA. Academic. m. Lynette Chaffey, 7 June 1980, 1 d. Education: BA cum laude, Boston Univ, 1967; MDiv, Gettysburg Theol Sem, 1970; STB Hons, Trinity Coll, Toronto, 1971; Dip Lib, UCL, 1975; MA, London Univ, 1977; ThD, Austl Coll Theo, 1991; Fell, Lib

Assn; FRSA. Appointments: Lectr, Ballarat Coll, Aust, 1984-85; Snr Lectr, Grad Stdys Coord, Charles Sturt Univ, 1986-98; Assoc Dir, Cntr Info Stdys, 1994-96; Snr Lectr, Victoria Univ, Wellington, 1999-. Publications include: The South African Novel in English since 1950: An Information and Resource Guide, 1978; Development Studies: Register of Research in the United Kingdom, 1978-83; Theological and Religious Reference Materials, 3 vols, 1984-86; Index to Development Studies Literature, 1985; Guide to Current National Bibliographies in the Third World, 2nd Revised Ed, 1987; Collection Development for Libraries, 1989; The Education and Training of Information Professionals: Comparative and International Perspectives, 1990; Guide to Current Indexing and Abstracting Services in the Third World, 1992; Collection Development for Australian Libraries, 2nd Revised Ed, 1992; Australian Studies: Acquisition and Collection Development for Librarians, 1992; I Never Asked for This Job: A Study of Serials Librarians and Serials Education in Australia, 1992; No Time for Despair: A Manpower Survey of the Hong Kong Library Workforce, 1992-1996, 1993; Fiji, 1994; Library/Clientele Congruence: CAUL Performance Indicator A, 1995; How Much Did You Say? A Descriptive Survey of Library Buying Patterns and Library Supply in Australia, 1995; Collection Management for the 21st century, 1997; Qualitative Research for the Information Professional, 1997; Ed, 3 jrnls, (Asian Libs, African Book Pub Record, Libr Coll Acq Tech Serv); 2 book ser. Honours include: Outstdng Acad Book, Book on Theol Ref Lit, Choice, 1995; Highly Commended, Book on Austl Stdys, Besterman Medal Lib, 1992. Memberships include: Austl Lib and Info Assn, 1978-; Lib Assn, 1975-; Amn Theol Lib Assn, 1975-; Intl Fedn Documentation, 1993-. Address: Communications and Information Management, Victoria University of Wellington, PO Box 600, Wellington 6001, New Zealand.

GORMAN Michael Stuart Frederic, b. 16 Nov 1944, Christchurch, NZ. Oriental Art Dealer. m. Mizue, 10 Oct 1970. Education: Christ's Coll, Christchurch, NZ. Publication: The Quest for Kibi and the True Origins of Japan, 1999. Membership: Canterbury Club Christchurch, NZ. Hobbies: Chinese and Japanese history; Classical music; Reading. Address: C/o Canterbury Club, Christchurch, New Zealand.

GOSS David Colin, b. 6 Mar 1933. Diplomat. m. Ann Briant, 1 s, dec, 2 d. Education: BA Hons, Univ of Melbourne. Appointments: Cnslt Gen, Chgo, 1977-80; Amb, Israel, 1980-83; Snr Advsr, DFAT, 1984-89; High Commnr, Kenya, Uganda, Tanzania; Amb, Ethiopia, 1989-1992; Dpty High Commnr, London, 1992-96. Membership: AIIA. Hobbies: Tennis; Philately. Address: 37 Candlagan Drive, Broulee, New South Wales, Australia, 2537.

GOSS Zoë Jean, b. 6 Dec 1968, Perth, Aust. Cricket Promoter. Education: BSc; Postgrad Dr of Sci, Environtl Mngmt, ongoing. Career: Included, Bradman XI v World XI, captured Brian Lara'a wicket. Honours: Austl Team Debut, 1987. Hobbies: Surfing; Environmental philosophy; Science; Permaculture; Music. Address: 46 Blencowe Street, West Leederville, WA 6007, Australia.

GOSSET Robyn Margaret Couper, b. Christchurch, NZ. Writer; Freelance Journalist. m. H J Gosset, 26 Jan 1966, 1 s, 2 d. Education: MSc, Dip, Hosp Laborday Prac. Publications: New Zealand Mysteries; The New Zealand Ghost Book; Ex Cathedra; From Boater to Backpacks; Local history. Honour: Sir George Grey Schl, 1954. Hobbies: Writing; Photography; Gardening; Collectables. Address: PO Box 17 567 Christchurch, New Zealand.

GOSWAMI Anjana, b. 17 Apr 1952. Librarian. m. Arun Goswami, 14 May 1983, 1 d. Education: BSc w Hons, Zoo; BLibSc; Currently pursuing MLIS. Appointments: JTA, STA, Tech Offr. Publications: Articles on pop sci, lib and info sci. Memberships: Indian Assn of Spec Lib and Info Cntrs; Assam Sci Soc, Jorhat, Assam; Jorhat Lib Assn, Jorhat, Assam. Hobbies: Reading; Singing; Playing indoor games. Address: Regional Research Laboratory, Jorhat, Assam 785006, India.

GOTODA Masaharu, b. 9 Aug 1914. Politician. Education: Tokyo Univ. Appointments: With Min of Home Affairs, 1939; Chf Sec Home Affairs Min, 1959; Dir Local Tax Bur, 1959-62; Sec-Gen Natl Police Agcy, 1962-63; Dir of Security Bur, 1963-65; Dir-Gen, 1969-72; Dep Chf Cabinet Sec, 1972-73; Min of Home Affairs, 1979-80; Dir-Gen Natl Pub Safety Commn, 1979-80; Hokkaido Dev Agncy, 1979-80; Chf Cabinet Sec, 1982-83, 1985-87; Admin Mngmnt Agcy, 1983-84; Mngr Co-ord Agcy, 1984-85; Min of Jus, 1992-93; Dep PM, Aug-Apr 1993. Memberships: Mbr HoR, 1976-.

GOTTSHALL Alexander Phillip, b. 26 Oct 1949, Sydney, Aust. Public Relations Consultant. Education: BA, 1974, LLB, hons, 1982, Grad Dip in Commn, 1977, Dip of Co Admin, 1976. Appointments: Mngr, Pub Rels & Commns, Price Waterhouse, 1975-84; Mngr, Pub Affairs, Chase AMP Bank, 1985-87; Mngng Dir, Alex Gottshall Communicators, 1987-. Honours: Golden Target Awds for Pub Rels Ex, 1976, 1977, 1978. Memberships: Fell, Pub Rels Inst of Aust; Austl Ins of Profl Communicators. Hobbies: Current Affairs; Reading; Swimming. Address: PO Box 4223, Sydney, NSW 2001, Australia.

GOUGHNOUR Roy Robert, b. 10 May 1928, OH, USA. Civil Engineer; Consultant. m. (1) Marilynn Ruth Knoll, 20 Sept 1948, div Mar 1968, 2 s, 1 d, (2) Mary Rosetta Strahan, 28 June 1968. Education: BS, MI State Univ, 1961; MS, 1965; PhD, 1967. Appointments: Regd Profl Engr, MI; VP, Aukerman Co, Jackson, MI, 1958-64; Assoc Prof, No AZ Univ, Flagstaff, 1967-68; MI State Univ, E Lansing, 1968-72; VP, Aukerman-Goughnour Co, Jackson, 1972-76; Pres, Strahan Mfg Co, Tampa, FL, 1976-77; VP, R&D, Vibroflotation Fndn Cl, Pitts, 1976-86; Exec VP, Geosyst Inc, Sterling, VA, 1986-89; VP, Geotechs Am Inc, Peachtree Cty, GA, 1989-; Cnslt, Hubbell, Roth & Clark, Bloomfield Hills, MI, 1989-91; Publications: Contbr to articles in profl jrnls. Memberships: ASCE; Intl Soc Soil Mechs and Fndn Engrng; SE Asian Geotech Soc Repub. Hobbies: Hunting; Target shooting. Address: 705 Duff Road, NE Leesburg, VA 20176-4907, USA.

GOULD Alan David, b. 22 Mar 1949, London, Eng. Writer. m. Anne Langridge, 17 Jan 1984, 2 children. Education: BA, Hons; Dip.Ed. Appointments: Creative Arts Fell, Geelong Coll, 1978, 1980, 1982, 1985, Austl Natl Univ, 1978, Austl Def Force Acady, 1986. Publications include: The Man Who Stayed Below, 1984; The Enduring Disguises, 1988; To the Burning City, 1991; Closeups, 1994. Honours: NSW Premier's Prize for Poetry, 1981; Fndn for Austl Lit Book of the Year, 1985; Natl Book Cncl Banjo, 1992. Hobbies: Ship modeling; Illustration. Address: 6 Mulga Street, O'Connor 2602, Australia.

GOVINDA Nayak, b. 15 Sept 1956, India. Teacher; Researcher. m. Uma, 12 Nov 1989, 1 d. Education: MSc; PhD. Appointments: Lectr in Phys, 1987-95, Rdr in Phys, 1995-, Univ Mangalore. Memberships: Indian Soc for Radiation Phys; Indian Soc for Atomic and Molecular Phys. Hobbies: Singing; Public speaking; Science popularization programs. Address: Mangalore University, Mangalagangotri 574 199, India.

GOVINDARAJAN Nirmala, b. 22 Mar 1975, Kadur, Karnataka. Trainer in Documentary Film Making. Education: BA, Indl Rels, Econs, Sociol; Dip in Advtng; Dip Jrnlsm; German Lang, Levels, G1, G2, M4, M2; Hons Prog in Personality Dev. Appointments: Via Media, Bangalore. Publications: (poem) Death A Big Blow to Sanity - Mosaic, 1994; Star of Bethlehem - The Quest, 1995; Dream - the Quest, 1996; The Dead End - the Quest, 1997; River - Wanderlust, 1998. Honours: 2nd Place in Odessey, poetry contest, 1990; 1st Place in Crisis poetry contest, 1990; Nehu Bal Songh, creative writing, 3rd Place, 1990. Memberships: Bangalore Little Th; Writers Forum, Ranchi; Old Students Assn of Sacred Heart Girls hs & St Josephs Coll.

GOYAL Rajesh, b. 2 Feb 1950, Dhuri. Doctor. m. Rita, 22 Aug 1977, 1 s, 1 d. Education: MBBS; DOMS; MD. Honours: Hlth Servs, Dr Bachittai Sinps Awd. Memberships: IMA. Hobbies: Magazine Reading; Music. Address: Hira Mahal, Nabha, Punjab, India.

GRACE Patricia (Frances), b. 1937, Wellington, NZ. Novelist. m. 7 children. Education: St Marys Coll; Wellington Tchrs Coll. Appointments: Tchr, primary and secnd schs, King Country, Northland and Porirua; Writing Fell, Victoria Univ, Wellington, 1985. Publications: Mutuwhenua: The Moon Sleeps, 1978; Potiki, 1986; Cousins, 1992; Short Stories: Waiariki, 1975; The Dream Sleepers and Other Stories, 1980; Electric City and Other Stories, 1980; Selected Stories, 1991; The Sky People, 1994; Collected Stories, 1994; Baby No-eyes, 1998 Several publs for children inclng: Areta and the Kahawai (picture book in Engl), 1994; Ko Areta me Nga Kahawai (picture book in Maori), 1994. Honours: NZ Fic Awd, 1987; HLD, Victoria Univ, 1989. Listed in: International Authors and Writers Who's Who. Address: Box 54111, Plimmerton, New Zealand.

GRACIAS Maurice, b. 16 July 1923, Nairobi, Kenya. Economist. m. Angela, 22 Aug 1954, 3 d. Education: BA, Univ of Intl Studies, Geneva, 1962; Grad exams, Inst of Transport, London, Eng, 1956; Cert exams, Assn of C&C Accts, London, Eng, 1958. Appointments: Asst to Controller, E African Railways, Nairobi, 1948-63; Controller, E African Road Servs, 1963-65; Chief Auditor, US State Dept (AID) 16 cos in Africa, 1965-69; Snr Acct, Coopers Lybrand, CPAs, Oakland, CA, USA, 1969; Chief Auditor, Econ Dev Org, San Fran, CA, USA, 1970-71; Corp Audit Mngr, Blue Cross, Oakland, 1971-80; Pres, Intl Investment Assocs; Mngmt Cnslt/Pres, Gracias & Assocs, Oakland, 1976-; Cnslt, Asian Dev Bank (UN), Manila, 1978-; Dir, Land Title Co, Oakland, 1986-. Publications: Life - Search for It's Glory, auth, 1989; Newsppr articles on demography, monetary and fin topics, 1958-60. Honours: Fell, Roy Econ Soc, London, 1964-68. Address: Gracias & Associates, 84 Crestmont Drive, Oakland, CA 94619, USA.

GRAHAM Douglas Arthur Montrose, b. 12 Jan 1942, Auckland, NZ. Attorney General. m. Beverley, 28 May 1966, 2 s, 1 d. Education: LLB, 1965; Hon Doct, Waikato Univ, 1999. Appointments: Min Justice, 1990-99; Min Cultural Affairs, 1990-96; Min for Crts, 1996-98; Min of Treaty of Waitangi, Negotiations, 1991-; Atty Gen, 1998-. Publication: Trick or Treaty, 1997. Honours: Privy Cncl, 1998; Kt Companion, NZ Order of Merit, 1999. Hobbies: Gardening; Golf. Address: Elderslie, Manuwai Lane, Rd 2 Drury, Auckland, NZ.

GRAHAM Ian Vivian, b. 3 Nov 1937. Retired. m. 29 Mar 1969, Edna McGhie Carruthers. Honours: George Medal, 1964; Royal Humane Soc Gold Medal, NZ; Silver Medal, Surf Life Saving Assn, NZ; RLSS Kingsland Mem Medal, NZ. Memberships: RLSS, NZ; CSLSA; NZIM. Hobbies: Yachting; Swimming. Address: 38 Whitewash Head Road, Christchurch 8, New Zealand.

GRAHAM Rod Keith, b. 17 Oct 1952, Adelaide, S Aust. Veterinary Surgeon. m. Di, 15 Oct 1988, 1 s, 2 d. Education: BVSc, Melbourne; LLB, Monash. Appointments: Master of Fox Hound, Mansfield Hunt, 1980; Master of Foxhound Barwon Hunt, 1991; MD, Village Vet Pty Ltd, 1994. Honours: Life Mbrshp, Mansfield Hunt, 1990. Memberships: Austl Vet Assn; Rotary. Hobbies: Horse riding; Swimming. Address: 11 St Georges St, Toorak, Vic 3142, Australia.

GRAHAM-HIGGS Elizabeth Patricia, b. 16 Nov 1929, Jamaica, WI. Social Worker. m. Dr Graham, 3 Oct 1957, 3 s, 1 d. Education: Dip Socl Sci, Liverpool Univ; Cert of Medl Sch Wrk, London. Appointments: Socl Worker, Glasgow Roy Infirmary, Alfred Hosp, Melbourne Fndn, SW Princess Alexander Hosp, Brisbane, Queensland. Publications: Ppr at 1st Natl Aust Conf on Child Abuse, Perth; 1st World Congress, Hong Kong, 1996. Memberships: Sec, Inaugural Cttees of Queensland Paraplegic Assn; Geelong Family Plng; Save the Children, Geelong; WoolSabba Snr Cit; Austl Assn of

Socl Workers. Hobbies: Travel; Letter writing; Reading; Swimming. Address: 4 Warina Place, Mullumbimby, New South Wales, Australia.

GRAMMATER Rudolf Dimitri, b. 29 Nov 1910, Detroit. Retired Construction Executive. m. Fredricka W Cook, 18 Aug 1943, 1 s. Education: Stud, Pace Inst, 1928-32; LLB, Lincoln Univ, 1937. Appointments: Bar CA, 1938; Bechtel Corp, San Fran, 1941-73; Treas, VP, 1955-62; VP, 1962-71; Dir, 1960-73; Cons, 1973; VP Dir, Subsidiaries, 1955-71. Memberships: CPA, CA; ABA, CA Bar Assn; AICPA; Menlo Country Club. Address: The Peninsula Regent #819, One Baldwin Avneue, San Mateo, CA 94401 3852, USA.

GRANROSE Cherlyn Skromme, b. 23 Nov 1942, Michigan, USA. Professor. m. John Granrose, 14 Apr 1963, div. 1 s. 2 d. Education: BS, MS Zool, Univ MI; MS Counselling Psychol, KS State Univ; PhD Psychol, Rutgers Univ, NJ. Appointments: Temple Univ, 1981-93; Claremont Grad Univ, 1993-. Publications: Books, Cross Cultural Work Groups, 1997; Careers of Business Managers in E Asia, 1997; Work - Family Choices for Women, 1996; Job Saving Strategies, 1989; Science, Sex & Society, 1979. Honours: Fulbright Lectr, China, 1997-98; Fulbright Rsch Awd, Singapore, 1993; Radcliffe Fellshp, 1990; Danforth Assoc, 1968-72; Rackham Fell, 1965-66. Memberships: Acady of Mngmt, Careers Div and Gender and Diversity Div Steering Cttees; AIB; APS. Hobbies: Scuba; Poetry; Mystery fiction. Address: School of Behavioural & Organisational Science, 123E 8th Street, Claremont Graduate University, Claremont, CA 19122, USA.

GRANT Bruce Alexander, b. 4 Apr 1925, Perth, Australia. Author. m. (3) Ratih Hardjono, 1 Sept 1997, from previous marriages, 3 s, 2 d. Education: BA, Melbourne Univ, 1951; Fell, Harvard Univ, 1960. Appointments: Fgn Corresp, 1950-65; Film Th Critic, 1951-54; Fell, Univ Melbourne, 1965-69; Columnist, 1969-72; High Cmmnr to India, 1973-76; Auth, 1976-83; Arts Advsr, State Govt Vic, 1983-88; Advsr to Min of Fgn Affairs & Trade, 1988-91; Chmn, Aust-Indonesia Inst, 1989-92; Prof, Monash Univ, 1994-. Publications: Indonesia, 1964; The Crisis of Loyalty, 1972; Arthur and Eric, 1977; The Boat People, 1979; Cherry Bloom, 1980; Gods and Politicians, 1982; The Australian Dilemma, 1983; What Kind of Country, 1988; Australia's Foreign Relations (w Gareth Evans), 1991; The Budd Family, 1995; A Furious Hunger, 1998. Hobbies: Austl Soc of Auths; Austl Inst of Intl Affairs; Pacific Inst; Harvard Club. Hobbies: Swimming; Walking; Observing failed states. Address: c/o Curtis Brown, PO Box 19, Paddington, NSW 2021, Australia.

GRANT James Alexander, b. 30 Aug 1931, Red Cliffs, Aust. Anglican Bishop. m. Rowena Margaret Armstrong, 9 Apr 1983. Education: BA, hons, Univ of Melbourne, 1953; ThL, 1st class, Austl Coll of Theol, 1958; BD, Melbourne Coll of Divinity, 1968. Appointments: Ordained Deacon, 1959, Curate, St Peter's Murrumbeena, Priest, 1960, Curate, W Heidelberg, Broadmeadows, 1961, Ldr, Diocesan Task Force, 1962-66; Domestic and Examining Chap to Archbish of Melbourne, 1966-70; Chap, Trinity Coll, 1970; Consecrated Bish, 1970, Regl Bish, Diocese of Melbourne, 1970-85; Dean of St Paul's Cath, Melbourne, 1985-99; Retd, 1999. Publications: (w Geoffrey Serle), The Melbourne Scene, 1957; Perspective of a Century - Trinity College 1872-1972. Honours: Hey Sharp Prize, 1958; AM, 1994. Membership: Fell, Trinity Club. Hobby: Historical research. Address: St Paul's Cathedral, 209 Flinders Lane, Melbourne, Vic 3000, Australia.

GRANT John McBain, b. 15 Nov 1923, Adelaide, S Aust. Retired. m. Rosamund Hallett, 10 Dec 1952, 3 s. Education: MEcons (Adelaide); Dip Econs (Cambridge). Appointments: Lectr, Univ Adelaide; Prof, Univ of Tasmania; Commnr, Trade Prac Commn. Publications: Inflation and Company Finance, 1958; Topics in Business Finance and Accounting, 1964; Economics - An Australian Introduction, 1964; Economic Institution and Policy, 1969. Honours: Fell, Acady of Socl Scis of Aust,

1975. Memberships: Econ Soc of Aust; Austl Soc of Cert Prac Accts. Hobby: Golf. Address: 33 Parkhill Street, Pearce, Australian Capital Territory 2607, Australia.

GRANT Keith Henry, b. 11 Oct 1927, Melbourne, Aust. Chartered Accountant. m. Denise Kidd, 8 Feb 1963, 1 s. Education: Wesley Coll, Melbourne; BCom, Melbourne Univ. Appointments: Pub Acct, 1951-87; Dir, Austl Devel Ltd, 1957-87; Dir, 1964-82, Chmn, 1967-82, Barrier Exploration N L. Memberships: Fell, Inst of Chart Accts in Aust; Fmr State Cnclr, Inst of Chartered Secs and Admnstrs; VP Vic Chamber of Mines; Snr Steward, Malvern Circuit Methodist Ch; Point Lonsdale Bowling Club; Lonsdale Golf Club. Hobby: Golf; Bowls. Address: 2 Jennifer Crescent, Point Lonsdale, Vic 3225, Australia.

GRASSBY Albert Jaime, b. 12 July 1926, Brisbane, Queensland, Aust. Author. m. Ellnor Louez, 5 Feb 1962. Education: Arts, SW Eng; Agricl Extension, Univ of CA. Appointments include: Brit Army, 1945; Jrnlst, UK; Spec Offr in Info, CSIRO; MIA, Agricl Extension Serv, Dept of Agric, NSW, Aust; Exec Offr, Irrigation Rsch and Extension Orgn; Idep Trade Missions to Asia, Eur and S Am, 1959-60; Attached, US Dept of Agric, Wash DC, sec studies extension, 1962; Spec study mission, Food and Agric Orgn of UN, Italy, 1956; Labour MP; MP, Murrumbidgee, NSW Parl, 1965; Shadow Min for Agric and Conservation, 1968-69; Labour MP, Riverina, 1969; Re-elected, 1972; Min for Immigration, 1972-74; Spec Cnslt to Autl Govt on Community Rels, 1974-75; Apptd Aust's Firs Commnr for Community Rels, 1975; Spec Advsr in Community Rels, NSW Govt, 1986-87. Publications: Griffith of the Four Faces; The Morning After; Tyranny of Prejudice; Six Australian Battle Fields; The Australian Republic; Contbns to many jrnls and ref publs. Honours: Kt of Mil Order of St Agatha of Paterno, 1969; Kt Cmdr of Order of Solidarity of Italian Repub, 1970; Grand Cross of Mil Order, 1974; Citation of Univ of Santo Tomas, Repub of Philippines; Freedom of Sinopoli and Plati, Italy; Platynos & Akrata, Greece; PhD, hc, Munich, 1979; AM, 1985; Kt Cmdr of Order of Isabella of Spain; UN Intl Yr of Peace Medal, 1987; Order of Merit, Ecuador, 1997; Medal of Sarajevo, Bosnia, 1998. Memberships: Canberra Labour Club; Canberra Irish Club; Spanish Club, Sydney; Yoogali Club, Griffith, NSW. Address: 1 Warzi Place, Aranda, ACT, Australia.

GRATION Peter Courtney, b. 6 Jan 1932, Richmond, Vic, Aust. Army Officer. m. Delys Lorraine May, 2 Dec 1961, 2 s. Education: Scotch Coll, Melbourne; Bach, Civil Engrng, Melbourne Univ, 1955; BA, 1961, BEcon, 1966, Univ Qld; Hon DSc, Univ NSW, 1993. Appointments: Lt, Roy Austl Engrs, 1952; CO, Austl Civil Affairs Unit, S Vietnam, 1969-70; Dir of Engrs, 1973-76; Chf of Gen Staff, 1984-87; Chf of Def Force, 1987-93; Chmn, Civil Aviation Authy, 1993-95; Chmn, Mngmt Cttee, Transfield Def Systems, 1993-97; Chmn, Austl War Meml, 1994-99; Dir, Tenix Pty Ltd, 1998-; Chmn, Tenixtoll def Logistics, 1999-. Honours: OBE, 1970; AC, 1987; Yudha Dharma Utama, Indonesia, 1993. Memberships: Hon Fell, Inst of Engrs, Aust, 1986; Fell, Austl Acady of Technol Sci & Engrng, 1988. Hobbies: Skiing; Bush walking; Jogging; Cycling. Address: 21 The Ridgeway, Queanbeyan, NSW 2620, Australia.

GRAY George Lionel, b. 27 Mar 1930, Sydney, Aust. m. Barbara Griffith, 9 May 1959, 1 s, 1 d. Education: MB BS, hons, Univ Qld, 1953; DLO, Univ of Melbourne, 1958; FRCS, 1958; FRACS, Eng, 1959. Appointments: Res Med Offr, 1954; Registrar, 1955-56, Brisbane Cntrl Hosp; Snr Demonstrator, Anatomy Dept, Univ of Melbourne, 1957-58; Snr Registrar, Roy Natl Ear, Nose and Throat Hosp, London, Eng, 1959-60; Snr Surgn, Austin Hosp, Melbourne, 1961-85. Publications include: Otosclerostic Deafness; Ear Nose and Throat. Honours: AO, 1977; Pres, Otolaryngological Soc, 1985-87. Memberships include: Otolaryngological Soc of Aust; Austl Med Assn; Roy Australasian Coll of Surgs; Roy Coll of Surgs, Eng. Hobbies: Golf; Scuba-diving; Snow skiing. Address: 1 Reserve Road, Hawthorn, Melbourne, Vic 3122, Australia.

GRAY Malcolm Alexander, b. 30 May 1940, Melbourne, Aust. Estate Agent. m. Nerida Ellen Steele, 23 Apr 1970, 2 s, 1 d. Education: Dip of Agricl, Dookie Agricl Coll; BComm, Melbourne Univ; Dip of Valuations, Roy Melbourne Inst of Technol. Appointments: Ptnr, Gray & Johnston, 1964-; Dir, Wildsmith Gray Ins, 1966-85; Dir, Robert Barrow Vic, 1985-92; Dir, Resi Statewide Bldg Soc, 1977-89; Dir, Mutual Friendly Soc, 1987-; Dpty Chmn, Bank of Melbourne, 1989-; Dir, Lowndes Lambert, 1992-; Dir, Diabetes Australia, 1995-. Honour: AM, 1993. Memberships: Fell, Real Estate Inst; Fell, Austl Inst of Valuers; Fell, Soc of Land Econs; Pres, Real Estate Inst of Vic, 1973-74; Pres, Real Estate Inst of Aust, 1982-84; Mbr, Exec Cttee, Intl Real Estate Fedn, 1984-86; Mbr, Exec Cttee, 1973-, Vic Cricket Assn, Chmn, 1991-; Dir, 1983-, Chmn,1986-89, Austl Cricket Bd; VP, Intl Cricket Cncl, 1999-. Hobbies: Tennis; Cricket; Reading. Address: 11 Myambert Avenue, Balwyn, Vic 3103, Australia.

GRAY Nigel, b. 9 Apr 1941, Ireland. Author. m. Yasmin, 29 Apr 1978, 2 s, 2 d. Education: BA, Engl, Lancaster Univ, UK; MA, Creative Writing, Univ of E Anglia, UK. Appointments: Writing Fellshps: E Midland Arts, UK, 1977-79; Northampton Dev Corp, UK, 1979-80; C Day Lewis Fellshp, UK, 1980-81; East Arts, UK, 1981-82; WA Coll of Advd Educ, Aust, 1988; Shire of Kalamunda, UK, 1989-90; Edith Cowan Univ, Aust, 1990; Katherine Susannah Prichard Fndn, Aust, 1992; Edith Cowan Univ, Aust, 1994. Publications include: (for adults) The Silent Majority, 1973; Life Sentence, 1984; Happy Families, 1985; The Worst of Times, 1986; Writers Talking, 1989; (for children) The Deserter, 1977; Shots, 1986; Carrot Top, 1987; Private Eye of New York, 1991; Night Music, 1992; Sharon and Darren, 1993; (picture books) I'll Take You to Mrs Cole. 1985; A Country Far Away, 1988; A Balloon for Grandad, 1988; Little Pig's Tale, 1988; Running Away From Home, 1995; The Dog Show, 1996; Full House, 1998; A Walk With Granny, 1998. Honours: Dickens Fellshp Awd; Irish Post Awd for Lit (also var book prizes and hons for individual books). Memberships: Intl PEN, Ex-Pres of the Perth Cntr, 1991-92; Austl Soc of Auths. Address: 171 Orange Valley Road, Kalamunda, Western Australia 6076, Australia.

GRAY Robin Trevor, b. 1 Mar 1940, Melbourne, Australia. Company Director; Consultant. m. Judith, 31 Aug 1965, 2 s, 1 d. Education: BAgriSc, Melbourne; Dip of Agricl; Ctf Practising Agricls. Appointments: Agricl Cnslt, J P Makeham & Assocs Pty Ltd, Colac, Vic, 1965-66; Chmn, R T Gray & Assocs Pty Ltd, Agricl & Farm Mngmt Cnslts, Launceston, Tas, 1966-; Pt-time Lectr, Agricl Econs, Univ Tas, 1966-77; Liberal Pty Mbr, Seat of Lyons, Tas House of Assembly, 1976; Dpty Ldr, Tas Liberal Pty, 1979-81; Ldr, Tas Liberal Pty, 1981-91; Ldr of Opposition, Tas, 1981-82; Premier, Treas, Tas, Min for State Devel, Min for Energy, Min for Racing & Gaming, Min for Forests, 1982-89; Ldr of Opposition, Tas, 1989-91; Min for Energy, Min for Primary Ind & Fisheries, Min for the TT-Line, 1992-95; Ret'd, Tas Parly, 1995; Ptnr, Evers Gray, Cnslts in Govt Rels, 1996-; Dir, Gunns Ltd, 1996-; Dir, Fujii Tas Pty Ltd, 1996-; Chmn, Botanical Resources Aust Pty Ltd, 1996-; Dir, AMC Search Ltd, 1996-; Trustee, Tas Wool Mus, 1996-; Advsry Bd, Austl Agricl Rsch Inst, 1997-; Dir, Tas Global Investments Pty Ltd, 1997-; Dir, Agribus Projects Aust Pty Ltd, 1998-. Hobbies: Gardening; Golf. Address: 11 Beech Road, Launceston, Tasmania, Australia.

GRAYCAR Adam, b. 29 Oct 1946, Brisbane, Aust. Chief Executive Officer. m. Elizabeth Percival, 1987, 2 d. Education: BA; PhD; DLitt, Univ of NSW. Publications: Lectr in Polit Sci, Univ of NSW, 1971-73; Snr Lectr, Socl Admin, Flinders Univ, 1973-80; Visng Prof, Sch of Socl Welfare, Univ of CA, Berkeley, USA, 1978; (Fndn) Dir and Prof, Socl Policy Rsch Cntr, Univ of NSW, 1980-85; Visng Prof, Inst of Socl and Policy Studies, Yale Univ, New Haven, CT, 1982; (Fndn) Commnr for the Ageing, 1985-90, Chf Exec Offr, Min of Higher Educ, 1990-94, Govt of S Aust; Rsch Assoc, Natl Inst of Labour Studies (Flinders Univ), 1990-; Visng Prof, Natl Univ of Singapore, 1992, 1993; Dir, Austl Inst of Criminology, Fedl Govt, 1994-; Adj Prof, Socl Wrk and Socl Plcy, Univ of Qld, 1997-. Publications: Books include: (co-auth) How Australians Live: Social Policy in Theory and Practice, 1989; Look After Yourself: The Health Handbook for Older People, 1990; (ed) Money Laundering: Risks and Countermeasures, 1996; (ed) Protecting Superannuation from Criminal Exploitation, 1996; (co-auth) Crime and Justice in Australia, 1997. Hobbies: Cooking; Walking. Address: GPo Box 2944, Canberra, ACT 2601, Australia.

GREASER Constance Udean, b. 18 Jan 1938, San Diego, CA, USA. Publisher. Education: Bach Deg, San Diego State Univ, 1959; Masters Deg, USC, 1968; Exec MBA Dip, UCLA Grad Sch of Mngmt, 1981. Honours: Naomi Berber Awd, Outstndng Woman in Graphic Arts, Graphic Arts Tech Fndn, 1989. Memberships: Women in Bus, 1974-76; Women in Comm; Graphic Comm Assn; Soc for Scholarly Publng. Hobbies: Travel; Theatre. Address: American Honda Motor Co, Inc, 1919 Torrance Blvd, Torrance, CA 90501, USA.

GREEN Andrew Ashley, b. 25 Dec 1946, Perth, West Aust. Research Scientist. m. Carolyn Gaton-Smith, 17 Nov 1978, 3 d. Education: BS (Hons), PhD, Univ of WA. Appointments: Dpty Chf, CSIRO Div of Exploration Geoscience; Dir, CRC for Aust Mineral Exploration Technols. Publications: Num sci publs on Mineral Exploration, Remote Sensing and Geophysics. Honour: Aust Prize (in Remote Servicing), 1995. Membership: Fell, Austl Acady of Technol Scis & Engrng. Hobbies: Tennis (weak 2nd serv); Postmodern Critical Theory. Address: 8 Lawley Crescent, Pymble, NSW, Australia.

GREEN David Geoffrey, b. 21 Sept 1949, Melbourne, Aust. Scientist. m. Yvonne, 26 July 1980, 2 d. Education: BSc, Hons; MSc; PhD. Appointments: Assoc Dir, Austl Environ Resources Info Network, 1990; Austl Rsch Cncl Snr Fell, 1992; Prof, Info Technol, Charles Sturt Univ, 1994. Publications: Complex Systems - From Biology to, 1993; Patterns in the Sand, 1998; Complex Systems, 1999. Hobbies: Music; Fencing; Reading; Skiing. Address: SEIS/CSU, PO Box 789, Albury, NSW 2640, Australia.

GREEN Guy Stephen Montague, b. 26 July 1937, Lauceston, Tas, Aust. Governor of Tasmania. m. Rosslyn, 21 Dec 1963, 2 s, 2 d. Education: LLB, Univ of Tas, 1960. Appointments: Admitted to Bar, Supreme Crt of Tas, 1960; Ptnr, Ritchie & Parker Alfred Green & Co, 1963-71; Pres, Tas Bar Assn, 1968-70; Magistrate, 1971-73; Chf Jus of Tas, 1973-95; Lieut Gov of Tas, 1982-95; Chan, Univ of Tas, 1985-95; Gov of Tas, 1995-. Publications: Num articles and monographs. Honours: Kt Cmndr of Most Ex Order of Brit Empire, 1982; Kt of Grace in Most Venerable Order of Hosp of StJofJ, 1985; Companion, Gen Div Order of Aust, 1994; Hon LLD, Univ of Tas, 1996. Memberships include: Fac of Law, Univ of Tas, 1974-85; Chmn, Tasmanian Cttee of Duke of Edinburgh's Awd in Aust, 1975-80; Chmn, Tasmanian Regl Cttee, 1975-80, Dpty Natl Chmn, 1980-85, Dir, 1975-85, Winston Churchill Meml Trust; Cncl of Law Reporting, 1978-85; Dpty Chmn, Austl Inst of Judicial Admin, 1986-88, Cncl, 1984-88. Listed in: Who's Who in Australia; Who's Who. Address: Government House, Domain Road, Hobart, Tas 7000, Australia.

GREEN Harry Edward, b. 11 Feb 1935. Electrical Engineer. m. Helen Claire Rees, 25 Nov 1961. Education: MEng, Univ of Adelaide, 1964; Phd, Elec Engrng, OH State Univ, 1968. Appointments include: Snr Rsch Scientist, Weapons Rsch Estab, Austl Dept of Supply, 1965-69; Prin Rsch Scientist Ctrl Studies Estab, Austl Dept of Supply, 1970-72; Prof of Elecl Engrng, Fac of Mil Studies, Univ of NSW, Aust, 1972-86; Chief of High Frequency Radar Div, Surveillance Rsch Lab, Defence Sci and Technol Org, Austl Dept of Defence, 1986-91; Dean, Fac of Engrng, Univ of Adelaide, 1991-95; present pos: Adjunct Rsch Prof, Inst for Telcommunications Rsch, Univ of Sth Aust. Publications: About 50 scientific and engrng pprs in profl jrnls. Honours: Austl Pub Serv Bd Overseas Postgrad Schlshp, 1965; John Madsen Medal, Instn of Engrs, Aust, 1978, 1999; Norman W V Hayes Mem, Instn of Radio and Electric Engrs, Aust, 1981; Centennial Medal, Inst of Elecl and Electron Engrs, 1984. Memberships: Fell, Instn of Engrs, Aust; Fell, Instn of

Radio and Electrons Engrs, Aust; Snr Mbr, Inst of Electrl and Electrons Engrs; Sigma Xi; Assoc Mbr, Assoc of Old Crows; NY Acad of Scis; Austl Joint Servs Staff Coll Assn. Listed in: Who's Who in Australia; Who's Who in the World. Address: 11a Bradfield Street, Burnside, SA 5066, Australia.

GREEN John Douglas, b. 21 Sept 1951. Consultant Engineer. m. Karen Muriel Fredricka Barnes, 6 Jan 1973, 1 s, 1 d. Education: BTech (Elec); MSc (Build); UNSW, 1981. Appointments: JP, (Qld), 1982; Dir, AHW Pty Ltd, 1989-94; Bish, New Apostolic Ch, 1991-; Chmn, ME Br ACEA NSW, 1992-95; Chmn, Natl Cttee on Building Servs, 1995-; Mngng Dir, Green Futures Pty Ltd, 1997-; Dir, NIFI Pty Ltd, 1999. Publications: Maintaining Your Home, 1997. Honours: MBA Schlsp, 1981; Qld Govt Schlsp, 1980-81; Alex Rigby Prize, 1981. Memberships: Fell, Inst of Engrs, Aust; MAIB; MAIPM; AIES Chmn, Coll of Elecl Engrs, IE, Aust. Listed in Who's Who in Australia. Hobbies: Reading; Painting; Water sports. Address: Castle Hill, Australia, 2154.

GREEN Louis Ferdinand, b. 4 Sept 1929, Saint-Cloud, France. Historian. m. (1) Juanita Florence Crook, 31 Mar 1951, (2) Louise McOwan Powell, 2 Feb 1979, 2 s, 3 d. Education: BA, Qld, 1951; MA, Adelaide, 1961; PhD, Monash, 1989. Appointments: Rsch Offr, Dept of Def, Melbourne, 1951-57; Tutor in Hist, Univ of Adelaide, 1958-60; Lectr in Hist, Univ of Tas, 1961-66; Snr Lectr/Rdr, Hist, Monash Univ, 1967-94; Currently, Rsch Assoc, Hist, Monash Univ. Publications: Chronicle into History, 1972; Castruccio Castracani, 1986; Lucca Under Many Masters, 1995. Hobbies: Reading; Writing; Films; Music. Address: 3/82 Millswyn Street, South Yarra, Victoria 3141, Australia.

GREEN Martin Andrew, b. 20 July 1948, Brisbane. Research Engineer. m. Judith, 4 July 1970, 1 s, 1 d. Education: BE, Univ Qld; MEng Sc; PhD. Appointments: Prof, Elecl Engrng, 1986-; Dir, UNSW Photovoltaics Specl Rsch Cntr, 1990-. Creative Works: 4 Books, Solar Cells; Over 200 Sci Pprs. Honours: Austl Prize, 1997; J J Ebers Awd; Wm R Cherry Awd; Pawrsey Medal; Lilley Medal. Memberships: Austl Acady of Sci; Austl Acady of Tech Scis. Hobbies: Swimming; Running; Reading; Writing; Travel. Address: c/o Electircal Engineering, UNSW, Sydney 2052, Australia.

GREEN Philip Richard, b. 1 July 1935, Hobart, Tas, Aust. Roman Catholic Priest. Education: BA, Univ Tas, 1967. Appointments: Asst, St Mary's Cath, Hobart, 1962-63; Archbish's Sec, Dir Cath Educ, 1963-72; Admnstr, Cath, 1972-79; Dean, Southern Tas, 1978-82; Archbish's Sec, 1979-82; Vicar-Gen, 1982-88; Diocesan Admnstr, 1988; Vicar-Gen, Archdiocese Hobart, 1988-84; Parish Priest, Sandy Bay, Tas, 1994-. Publications: Occasional articles, newspapers, mags. Honours: Created Prelate of Hon by Pope John Paul II w title Monseigneur, 1982; MBE, 1988; AM, 1995. Memberships: Austl Coll Educ; Chap, Order St Lazarus of Jerusalem. Hobbies: Reading; Music. Address: PO Box 37, Sandy Bay, Tas 7006, Australia.

GREEN Roger Curtis, b. 15 Mar 1932. Anthropology University Teacher. m. Valerie J Sallen, 20 Jan 1984, 1 s, 1 d. Education: BA, Univ of NM, 1954; BS, Univ of MN, 1955; PhD, Harvard Univ, 1964. Appointments: Snr Lectr in Prehist, Univ of Auckland, 1961-66; Assoc Prof, 1966-67; Prof, Prehist, 1973-92; Prof Emer, 1992-; Anthropologist, B P Bishop Mus, 1967-73; Rsch Assoc, 1973-; RSNZ Capt James Cook Fellshp, 1970-73. Publications: Num articles and monographs on culture historical, anthropology and archaeological subjects. Honours: Fulbright Schl, 1958-59; Elsdon Best Medal, Polynesian Soc, 1973; Hector Mem Medal, Royal Soc of NZ, 1992. Memberships: Natl Acady of Sci (USA), 1984; FRSNZ, 1975; Mbr, Bd Fndn Rsch Sci of Technol, 1993-95. Hobbies: Music; Travel; Walking. Address: Research Associates Pacifica, PO Box 60-054 Titirangi, Auckland 1230, New Zealand.

GREEN MACIAS Rosario. Education: Bach Deg, Intl Rels, Pol and Socl Scis Dept, Universidad Nacional Autónoma, Mexico; Master's Deg, Econs, Centro de Estudios Económicos, Colegio de México; Grad Stdies, Intl Econs and Latin Amn Problems, Columbia Univ, NY, USA. Appointments: 1st Sec, Mexican For Serv, UN Agies in Geneva, 1972-74; Cnslt, Dept of For Rels, 1976-77; Advsrm Center for Third World Econ and Socl Stdies, 1979-89; Assoc Dir, Foro Internacional, 1968-72, 1979-80; Hd, Matías Romero Inst of Diplomatic Stdies; Dir, Mexican Mag of For Plcy; Dir, Intl Affairs Commn, Natl Exec Cttee, Partido Revolucionario Institucional; Exec Dir, Commn of the Future of Mexico-US Rels, 1986-; Mexican Amb to Germany, 1989-; Exec Sec for Latin Am, Cultural affairs and Intl Co-op for Dept of For Rels of Mexico, 1990-; Prof, Rschr, Colegio de México, in charge of courses in Intl Econs and Contemp Problems in Latin Am, 1968-. Publications: 9 books incl: Mexican Foreign Policy Indebtedness: 1940-1973, 1976; State and Transnational Banking in Mexico, 1981, 1984; Foreign Debt in Mexico: From Abundance to a Scarcity of Credit, 1988. Memberships: Fndng Mbr, Mexican Acady of Human Rights; Cnslt, num intl agies incl UN Intl Dev Org, 1981, Latin Amn Econ System, 1982.

GREENBERG Jacob, b. 29 Jan 1938, Odessa, Ukraine, USSR. Chemist. m. Tatyana Ilina, 24 Sept 1961, 2 s. Education: Grad, Cntrl Musical Sch, Tchaikovsky State Conservatoire, Moscow, Russia, 1956; MSc, Moscow Inst Fine Chem Technal, 1962; PhD, 1966, DSc, 1989, Inst Gen and Inorg Chem, Russian Acady Sci, Moscow. Appointments: Jnr Sci, 1962-66, Rsch Sci, 1966-75, Snr Sci, 1975-89, Prin Sci, 1989-92, Inst Gen and Inorg Chem, Moscow; Snr Sci, 1993-99, Prof, 1999-, Hebrew Univ Jerusalem, Israel; Visng Lectr, Inst Crystal Growth Berlin, 1997; Cnslt, 1985-91, Platan Electronics, Moscow, 1985-91; Trucks & Tractor Co, Moscow, 1985-90; II-VI Inc PA, USA, 1996; URIGAL Techn, Rehovot, Israel, 1996-; IMARAD Imaging Systs Ltd, Rehovot, Israel, 1998-. Publications: Co-auth, 4 books; About 150 pprs; 5 Russian patents. Honours: Rsch work of yr, 1967, 1976, 1988, 1991; Inst Gen & Inorg Chem, Russian Acady Sci, Moscow; Expo-USSR Medal, 1977, 1989. Memberships: ACS, 1994-; NYAS, 1995-; AAAS, 1995-97; Israel Assn of Crystal Growth, 1999-. Hobbies: Classical music; Literature; Athletics. Address: 14/6 Hatziltzal St, 98370 Maale Adumim, Israel.

GREENWOOD Arthur Alexander, b. 8 Mar 1920, Corby Glen, Eng. Genealogist. m. (1) Betty Doreen Westrop, 20 July 1946, 1 s, 1 d, (2) Shirley Knowles Fitton, 16 Sept 1976. Education: Sidney Sussex Coll, Cambridge, 1938-39; FCIS, UK, 1970; PhD, USA, 1987. Appointments: Reg Army, Roy Lincolnshire Regt, 1939-59, retd as Maj, served in Norway, Iceland, India, Burma, Mid E, ADC to Field-Marshal Sir Claude Auchinleck, 1943-44, Chf Instr, Sch of Mil Intell, 1954-56. Publications: A Brief History of the 4th Battalion, The Royal Lincolnshire Regiment (TA), 1948; The Greenwood Tree in Three Continents, 1988; Field-Marshal Auchinleck, 1990; Articles in sev profl jrnls; Brdcsts on genealogy for TV. Honours: Mentioned in Despatches, 1944; Freeman of the Cty of London, 1960; Pres, The Old Oakhamian Club, 1960-61; Liveryman of the Pattenmakers Co; Liveryman of the Chart Secs Co; Mbr, Hon Co of Freeman of the Cty of London in N Am, 1983; VP, Reform Party of Can, 1994-96. Memberships: Soc of Auths; Life Fell, Roy Econ Soc; Life Fell, Roy Soc of Arts; Fell, Roy Geogl Soc; Fell, Inst of Dirs; Soc of Genealogists (UK); Assn of Profl Genealogists (USA); Heraldry Soc UK; Carlton Club, London, Eng; Pilgrim Soc. Hobbies: Genealogy; Golf; Cricket. Address: 1419 Madrona Drive, Nanoose Bay, British Columbia V9P 9C9, Canada.

GREENWOOD Barrie Leck, b. 5 Oct 1934, Invercargill, NZ. Choral Singer. m. Susan Nichol, 1978. Education: Priv Piano Tuition. Appointments: 38 yrs Choral Singing; Active Mbr, Choir of Roy Christchurch Musical Soc, 1954-90; Adelaide Harmony Choir and Phil Choir, Aust, 1962; Travelling Chorus, NZ Opera Co, 1964, 1965; Choir, Oxford Terrace Bapt Ch, Christchurch, 1963-70, Choir, Cath of Blessed Sacrament, Christchurch, 1975-77; Christchurch Cty Choir, 1991-92. Publications: Contbr to Studies in Music, Nedlands (WA), Vol 7, 1973; Crescendo No 3, 1982. Honours: 2 Grants-in-Aid, Amn Phil Soc, Phila, 1972, 1973. Memberships: Crt Star of Canterbury No 2309, Ancient Order of Foresters, 1959-; NZ Branch, IAML, 1974-; Treas, 1993-96; Dist Chf Ranger, Canterbury Foresters Friendly Soc, 1995-96. Hobbies: Choral singing; Musicology; History; History of Music; Thinking; Reading. Address: PO Box 7382, Sydenham, Christchurch 2, New Zealand.

GREENWOOD John Ward (The Hon), b. 29 Apr 1934. Barrister; QC. m. Barbara Mary Ellen Conrad, 14 Jan 1961, 1 s, 2 d. Education: CEGS, East Brisbane; BA; LLB, Univ Queensland. Appointments: Pvte Prac, Barrister, 1959-; Pt-time Lectr in Coml Law, 1963-65; Exec, 1970-74, Mbr, 1960-66, 1968-74, Law Fac Bd, Univ Queensland; Counsel in Roy Commns into Petrol Drilling on Grt Barrier Reef, 1970-72; Commn to Prosecute for the Crown, 1972-74; Entered Parl, 1974-83; Cabinet Min, 1976-80; Queensland Deleg to Aust Constl Conventions, 1976, 1983; Resumed Prac at Bar, 1983; Barrister, High crt of Aust and Supreme Crt of Queensland, 1958-; Admitted, Fiji for single causes, 1996, 1997, 1998; Served, Austl Army Res, 1952-94; Reviewing Judge Advocate, Austl Def Force, 1990-94; Promoted to Col 1992; Pt-time Snr Mbr Veterans Review Bd, 1998-. Publication: Land Data Banks, co-auth, 1978. Honours: QC, 1980; RFD, 1989. Memberships: Natl Union of Austl Univ Studs Exec, 1955; Ldr, Austl Deleg to Malaya, Singapore and Indonesia, 1956; Univ Queensland Union, Pres, 1956-57; Queensland Bar Assn, Hon Sec, 1959-60; Queensland Univ Senate, 1960-66; Austl Bicentennial Authy, Queensland Cnclr and Chmn, Histl and Lit Cttee, 1979-90; Roy Geog Soc of Australasia Queensland Inc, Pres, 1986, 1987; Roy Utd Serv Inst of Queensland, Pres, 1995-98. Hobbies: Coral reef and rainforest ecosystems. Address: 17th Level Inns of Court, 107 North Quay, Brisbane, Qld 4000, Australia.

GREER Germaine, b. 29 Jan 1939 Melbourne. Feminist; Author. Education: Melbourne and Sydney Univs; Cambridge Univ Eng. Appointments: Jnr Govt Schlshp, 1952; Diocesan Schlshp, 1956; Snr Govt Schlshp, 1956; Tchr Coll Studentship, 1956; C'wlth Schlshp, 1964; Hon D, Univ of Griffith, 1996; Snr Tutor in Eng Sydney Univ, 1963-64; Asst Lectr then Lectr in Eng Warwick Univ, 1967-72; Brdcstr/jrnlst, 1972-79; Lectr throughout N Am with Am Prog Bur, 1973-78; Visng Prof Grad Fac of Modern Letters Univ of Tulsa, 1979; Lectr to raise funds for Tulsa Bursary and Fell'shp Scheme, 1980-83; Prof of Modern Letters, 1980-83; Fndr-Dir of Tulsa Cntr for the Study of Women's Lit; Fndr-Ed Tulsa Studies in Women's Lit, 1981; Dir Stump Cross Books, 1988-; Spec Lectr and Unoffic Fell Newnham Coll Cambridge, 1989-98; Prof of Engl and Comparative Lit Stdies, Univ of Warwick, 1998-; Num tv appearances and pub talks inclng discussion with Norman Mailer - qv - in The Theatre of Ideas NY. Publications: The Female Eunuch, 1969; The Obstacle Race: The Fortunes of Women Painters and Their Work, 1979; Sex and Destiny: The Politics of Human Fertility, 1984; Shakespeare - Co-Ed - 1986; The Madwoman's Underclothes - selected jrnlsm - 1986; Kissing the Rod: An Anthology of 17th Century Women's Verse, 1988; Daddy, We Hardly Knew You, 1989; The Uncollected Verse of Aphra Behn - Ed - 1989; The Change: Women, Ageing and the Menopause, 1991; Shakespeare and Cultural Traditions: The Selected Proceedings of The Intl Shakespre Assn World Congress, 1991; Slip-Shod Sibyls, 1995; The Whole Woman, 1999; Articles for Listener, Spectator, Esquire, Harper's Magazine, Playboy, Private Eye and other jrnls. Honours: J R Ackerly Prize and Premio Internazionale Mondello for Daddy, We Hardly Knew You. Hobbies: Gardening. Address: c/o Gillon Aitken and Associates Ltd, 29 Fernshaw Road, London, SW10 0TG, England.

GREGORY Reginald Edward, b. 28 Apr 1911, Melbourne, Aust. Accountant; Company Director. m. Laura Read, 27 Dec 1937. Education: Qual'd Acct, 1933; Qual'd Sec, 1934; Lic Co Auditor, 1934. Appointments: Joined Myer Emporium, 1927, Assoc Dir, 1948, Sec, 1949, Dir, 1950, Fin Dir, 1961, Retd as Exec, 1976, Retd as Dir, 1978; Dir, Austl Fndn Invmnt Co, 1976-83; Hon

Sec, 1931-41, Mbr, State Bd, 1939-50, Chmn, 1946-47, Fed Pres, 1948-50, Fed Inst of Accts Stud Soc. Honours: 1st Place, Aust Mercantile Law, Fed Inst of Accts, 1933; JP, 1946; MBE, 1973; Lucy Bryce Awd, Red Cross Blood Bank. Memberships include: Life Mbr, Austl Soc of Accts, 1955-; Utd Givers Fund Investigation Cttee; VP, Freemasons Hosp, 1969-71; Cncl Mbr, Assn of Philanthropic Trusts; Fin Cttee, Girl Guides Austl Assn; Baden Powell Mem Homes Cttee; Grand Master, Utd Grand Lodge of Vic, 1978-80; Former Hon Treas, Girl Guides Assn of Vic; Dir, Baden Powell Soc. Address: 21 Albany Road, Toorak, Vic 3142, Australia.

GREGORY Robert George, b. 25 Sept 1939, Melbourne, Aust. Economist. m. Annette, dec, 3 s, 1 d. Education: BComm, hons, Univ of Melbourne, 1961; PhD, London Sch of Econs and Polit Sci, Eng, 1967. Appointments: Tutor, Asst Lectr, London Sch of Econs, 1964-67; Visng Assoc, Asst Prof, Northwestern Univ, Aust, 1967-69, 1976; First Asst Commnr, Inds Assistance Commn, 1973-75; Visng Schl, Bd of Govs, Fed Reserve System, 1977; Snr Rsch Fell, Snr Fell, Profl Fell, Prof of Econs, 1987-, Austl Natl Univ. Publications: Auth of over 60 pprs in profl jrnls and chapts in books. Honours: Fell, Austl Acady of Socl Scis; Chair, Austl Stdies, Harv Univ, 1983-84; AO, 1996. Memberships: Bd of Reserve Bank of Aust, 1985-95; ASTEC, 1986-92; Bd of Mngmt, Austl Inst of Family Stdies, 1989-98; Cnslt to Chinese Govt on lessons from Austl Welfare System, 1994; Pres, Econ Soc of Aust, 1997-; Cnslt, OECD, Paris, 1998. Address: Economics Program, Research School of Social Sciences, Australian National University, Canberra, ACT 0200, Australia.

GREGORY Robert John, b. 28 Aug 1938, Elmira, NY, USA. Psychologist. m. Janet, 4 July 1975, 3 d. Education: BA, Cornell Univ, IThaca, NY, 1960; MA, 1964, PhD, 1968, Syracuse Univ, Syracuse, NY. Appointments: Fell, Inst of Hum Ecology, Raleigh, NC, USA, 1969-71; Exec Dir, Drug Action of Wake Co Inc, Raleigh, NC, 1971-73; Postdoct Fell, Dept of Psych, Duke Univ Medl Cntr, Durham, NC, 1973-75; Rsch Assoc, Dept of Anthropology, Duke Univ, 1975-78; Snr Extension Assoc, NY State Sch of Indl and Labour Rels, Cornell Univ, Ithaca, 1978-80; Asst Prof, Dept of Cnslng and Rehabilitation, Marshall Univ, Huntington, WV 25701, 1980-83; Snr Lectr, Sch of Psychol, Massey Univ, Palmerston N, NZ, 1983-. Publications: Num pprs, articles, writing and reports. Memberships: Disabled Persons Assembly (Palmerston North) Inc, 1983-; NZ REgd Psychol, 1985-; NZ Rehab Assn, 1984-; Liason Person for NZ Guillain-Barre Syndrome Fndn Intl, 1992-; Intl Affiliate, Amn Psychol Assn, 1994-; Bd Mbr, Audrey Green Soc, 1997-; Info Technol Cttee, Sch of Psychol, 1998- Hobbies: Writing; Tree planting; Fishing. Address: School of Psychology, Massey University, Palmerston North, New Zealnd.

GRIECO-TISO Pina, b. 27 Mar 1954. Secondary School Teacher; Author. m. Alfredo Tiso, 17 Jan 1981, 3 s. Education: BA, Dip.Ed, Monash Univ; For Lang Courses, Melbourne Univ. Appointments: Tchr, Springvale High, Paisley High, Werribee High, Karingal Secondary, Carwatha Secondary, Brighton Secondary, Dandenong High, Dandenong Sch of Fgn Langs, Princes Hill Sch of Fgn Langs, Bon Beach Secondary, Mordialloc-Chelsea Secondary Coll, Parkdale Secondary Coll. Publications include: Blitz: A Bomber's Nightmare, 1991; Time Out, 1993; The Name Givers, 1998; The Honoured Society (Black Pepper 199-). Honours: Faw Regl Prizes, 1st and 2nd, 1987, 1988, 1990; Coolum Short Story and Poetry Prizes, 1989, 1990; Rockhampton Poetry Awd, 1989. Memberships: ASA; NBC; FAW; ALITRA. Hobbies: Graffiti; Reading; Writing; Movies; Music; Taekwondo; Rollerblading; Leadlight art; Travel; Egyptology; Working with youth groups; Astrology; The occult. Address: 18 Daley Street, Bentleigh 3204, Victoria, Australia.

GRIEVE Janet Elizabeth, b. 18 Aug 1950. Public Relations and Company Director, 2 s. Appointments: Mngng Dir, Michels Warren; Dir TAB (SA); Dir, S Smith & Son Pty Ltd, Yalumba Wines; Hon Consul for France.

Memberships: FAICD; FAIM. Hobbies: Theatre; Politics; Keeping Fit. Address: Michels Warren Pty Ltd, 195 Fullarton Road, Dulwich 5065, South Australia

GRIFFIN Robert (Robin) Henry, b. 4 Nov 1935, Trinidad, West Indies. Archivist. m. Gail Irene Hamblin, 14 May 1992, 3 ss. Education: BA; BEduc; Dip Teaching. Appointments: Secondary Tchr; Voc Guidance Offr; Archivist, Bank of NZ, Auckland Coll of Educ . Publications: Bank of New Zealand Banknotes, 1987; Introduction to the History of Banking, 1987; Letters to Granny, 1995. Memberships: Archives and Records Assn of NZ, Pres, VP, Treas; NZ Soc of Archivists. Hobbies: Irish history; Heraldry; Model trains. Address: 10 Charlton Avenue, Mount Eden, Auckland 1003, New Zealand.

GRIFFITH J Gordon, b. 16 Dec 1931, USA. Real Estate. 1 s, 1 d. Education: BS. Memberships: Natl Assn of Home Bldrs; Bldng Ind Assn of S CA. Hobbies: Skiing; Golf; Fishing. Address: Centurion R E & Investment Corp, 2043 Westcliff Drive, Suite 201, Newport Beach, CA 92660, USA.

GRIFFITH John Chadwick, b. 25 Feb 1960, Switzerland. Lawyer. Education: BA, Boston Univ, 1980; JD, Univ VA, 1983; MA, Univ VA, 1999. Membership: MENSA. Address: PO Box 628, Quogue, NY 11959, USA.

GRIFFITHS Alan Gordon, b. 4 Sept 1952. Politician. m. Shirley Griffiths, 2 d. Education: Traralgon High Sch Vic; Monash Univ. Appointments: Wrked as a scaffolder, rigger, labourer, foundry wrker and fruit picker, then as trainee exec before entering univ, 1974; With firm of solicitors speclng in trade union affairs, 1979-82; Indl offr Federated Rubber and Allied Workers' Union of Aust, 1982; Min for Rescs, 1990-93; Min for Tourism, 1991-93; Min for Ind Tech and Regl Dev, 1993-94; Chmn Mining Funds Mngmnt Ltd, 1996-; Chmn Far East Capital Pty Ltd, 1996-; Chmn Griffiths Grp Intl Pty Ltd, 1996-; Labor Party. Memberships: HoR for Maribyrnong Vic, 1983-96. Hobbies: Football; Cricket; Canoeing; Swimming; Golf; Reading; Music; Travel. Address: Level 9, 4 O'Connell Street, Sydney, NSW 2000, Australia.

GRIGG Geoffrey Walter, b. 9 Mar 1926. Director. m. Ailsa-Claire Grigg, 21 Aug 1950, 2 s, 2 d. Education: BSc, MSc, Univ Melbourne; PhD, ScD, Cantab. Appointments: Joined as Rsch Offr, Div Animal Hlth and Prodn, 1952, Chf Rsch Scientist, 1972, Acting Chf, Div Animal Genetics, 1974, Offr i/c, Molecular and Cellular Bio Unit, 1975-83, Chf, Div Molecular Bio, Sydney, 1983-87, Chf, Div Biotechnol, 1987-88, C'wlth Sci and Indl Rsch Org; Seconded, Dept Genetics, Univ Adelaide, 1953-58; Fulbright Fell, Columbia Univ, NYC, USA, 1960-61; Assoc Wine Judge, Roy Easter Show, Sydney, NSW, 1963-76; Dir, Peptide Technol Ltd, Sydney, 1985-96; Dir, Carlbiotech A/S Copenhagen, Denmark, 1986-90; Professorial Fell, Macquarie Univ, 1986-89; Dir, Chmn, Cambridge Antibody Technol Ltd, Cambridge, Eng, 1990-96; Chmn, Beta Peptide Fndn Pty Ltd, Sydney; Fell, Austl Acady Technological Scis and Engrng, 1995. Honour: Medal, Clunies Ross Fndn, 1993. Memberships: Pres, Austl and NZ Environmental Mutagen Soc; Genetics Soc Aust; Aust Soc Biochem Molecular Bio. Hobbies: Music; Sailing; Good wine and food; Science; Reading. Address: c/o CSIRO, Box 184, North Ryde, NSW 2113, Australia.

GRIGG Peter Maxwell, b. 5 Mar 1933, Sydney, NSW, Aust. Management and Government Consultant. m. Ann Beaumont, 2 May 1987, 1 s, 2 steps, 2 d, 2 stepd. Education: Basic Navigation Course, 1953-55; Advd Navigation Course, 1962; RAAF Staff Coll, 1967; RAF Coll Air Warfare, 1969; BA, Maths, 1977; Austl Jnt Servs Staff Coll, 1978. Appointments: Served to Air Commodore, RAAF; RAAF Sqdns, 1953-61; RAAF Aircraft Rsch and Dev Unit, 1962-66; Chf Instr, RAAF Offrs Trng Sch, 1968; Ops and Op Requirements Staff, Depts Air and Def, 1972-78; Dir, Personnel Servs, Dir and Air-Gen, Plcy and Plans, Dept Def, 1980-87; Ptnr, Beaumont & Grigg, 1987-. Honours: Queen's Commendation, Valuable Serv in the Air, 1967; AM,

1987. Membership: Roy Aeronautical Soc. Hobbies: Sailing; Military history. Address: Wongaburra, Lemon Tree Passage, NSW 2319, Australia.

GRIMES Don, b. 4 Oct 1937 Albury NSW. Politician; Doctor. m. (1) Margaret Schofield, 1962; (2) Helen Knight, 1984; (3) Esther Timmersmans, 1991, 2 s, 1 d. Education: NSW High Schs Univ of Sydney. Appointments: Medl Practitioner, 1962-74; Sen for Tasmania, 1974-87; Opposition Spokesman for Socl Security, 1976-83; Opposition Spokesman for Repatriation and Compensation, 1976-77; Opposition Spokesman for Veterans' Affairs and Compensaion, 1977, 1980-83; Dep Ldr of the Opposition, 1980-83; Dep Chmn Asia-Pacific Socl Org, 1981; Min for Socl Security, 1983-84; Dep Ldr of Govt in Sen, 1983-87; Min for Community Servs, 1984-87; Amb to the Netherlands, 1987-91; Chmn Austl Natl Cncl on AIDS, 1992-96; Chmn Bd S East Sydney Area Hlth Serv, 1995-; Chmn AusHealth, 1997-. Memberships: Snr mbr Admin Appeals Tribunal, 1991-96; Bd mbr Austl Inst of Family Studies, 1991-96. Hobbies: Jazz; Reading. Address: P O Box 73, Surry Hills, NSW 2010, Australia.

GRIMWADE Frederick Sheppard, b. 23 June 1958, Melbourne, Australia. m. Alexandra Jane Grimwade, 7 Oct 1989, 1 s, 2 d. Education: LLB, hons; BCom; Dip, Securities Inst of Aust; MBA. Appointments: Solicitor, Mallesons Stephen Jaques, 1981-83; Assoc, McKinsey & Co, 1984; Assoc, Goldman Sachs & Co, NY, 1985-87; VP, Goldman Sachs (Aust), Sydney, 1988-89; Co Sec, Gen Mngr, Shareholder, Relations Western Mining Corp Ltd, 1989-95; Grp Co Sec, Gen Mngr, Legal Affairs, Colonial Ltd, 1996-98; Gen Mngr, Corp Devel, Colonial First State Investments, 1998-. Memberships: Fell, Inst of Corp Mngrs; Sec and Admnstrs Ltd; Securities Inst of Aust; Austl Club; Melbourne Club. Hobbies: Farming; Skiing. Address: Colonial Ltd, Level 12, 330 Collins Street, Melbourne, Australia.

GRINDROD John Basil Rowland (Most Rev), b. 14 Dec 1919, Aughton, Eng. Ecclesiastic. m. (1) Ailsa W Newman, 1949, dec, 1981, 2 d, (2) Dell Judith Cornish, 17 Dec 1983. Education: MA, Univ Oxford; Lincoln Theol Coll. Appointments: Ordained Priest, Manchester; Rector, All Souls, Ancoats, 1956-60; Rector, St Barnabas Parish, Archdeacon, Diocese Rockhampton, Queensland, 1961-65; Vicar, Christ Ch, S Yarra, Melbourne, Vic, 1965-66; Bish Riverina, NSW, 1966-71; Bish Rockhampton, 1971-80; Archbish Brisbane, 1980-89; Primate, Anglican Ch Aust, 1982-89. Honour: KBE, 1983. Address: 14B Thomas Street, Murwillumbah, NSW 2484, Australia.

GROCOTT Stephen Charles, b. 8 Nov 1957. Research Scientist. 1 s, 1 d. Education: BS Hons; PhD. Appointments: Dev Chem; Rsch Chem; Snr Rsch Chem; Snr Cnslt, Chem; Snr Prin Rsch Scientist, Alcoa of Aust Ltd; Mngr, Process Dev, Comalco Aluminium Ltd; Gen Mngr, R and D, Southern Pacific Petroleum. Publications: 27 pprs. Memberships: Roy Aust Chem Inst; Amn Chem Soc; Intl Humic Substances Soc; Amn Assn for the Advmt of Sci; Metall Soc; Amn Inst of Cheml Engrs. Listed in: Marquis Who's Who; Who's Who in Science and Engineering in Australia. Address: 10 Cardigan Place, Sunnybank Hills, Qld 4109, Australia.

GROENEWEGEN Peter Diderik, b. 13 Feb 1939, Kerkrade, Holland. University Teacher. m. Eileen Jennifer Allan, 15 Aug 1962, 1 s, 1 d. Education: BEcon, MEcon, Univ of Sydney; Phd, Econs, London Sch of Econs. Appointments: Lectr, Snr, Assoc Prof, Prof, Univ of Sydney. Publications: History of Aust Econs, 1990' A Soaring Eagle, 1995. Honours: Acady of Socl Scis in Aust, 1982; Roy Dutch Acady of Sci, 1993. Memberships: RES; AEA; Econ Soc, Aust; HETSA; Hist Econ Thought Soc. Hobbies: Art; Reading; Music; Cooking. Address: Department of Economics, University of Sydney, Sydney, NSW 2006, Australia.

GROFMAN Bernard, b. 2 Dec 1944, Houston, Tx, USA. Professor of Political Science and Social Psychology. Education: PhD Polit Sci, 1972, Univ

Chicago. Appointments: Instr Polit Sci, 1970-71, Asst Prof Polit Sci, 1971-76; Adj Asst Prof, Appl Math, 1975, SUNY at Stony Brook; Visng Lectr, Lehrstuhl fuer Polit Wissenschaft, Univ Mannheim, 1973; Visng Asst Prof, Sch Soc Sci, 1975-76, Assoc Prof Polit Sci and Soc Psychol, 1976-80, Univ CA at Irvine; Coll Visng Prof, Dept Polit Sci, Univ Washington, Seattle, 1985; Fell, Cntr for Advd Stdy in Behavioral Scis, Stanford, 1985-86; Visng Prof, Dept Polit Sci, Univ Mich, 1989. Publications: Ed or co-ed, 9 books in field of legislative stdies and intolerance. Honours: Pi Sigma Alpha Awd, Best Ppr, 1979; Co-recip, 1985, Carl B Allendoerfer Awd, Math Assn Am; Awd for outstndng book on intolerance pub in N Am, 1992; Co-recip, Richard Fenno Prize, Legislative Stdies Sect of Amn Polit Sci Assoc, 1995; Lauds and Laurels Awd, 1995; Sch of Soc Scis Awds for Tchng Innovation and Excellence, 1996, 1997. Memberships: Amn Polit Sci Assn; Pub Choice Soc; Law and Society Assn; Amn Inst Parliamentarians. Hobby: International folk art collecting. Address: Dept of Political Science, University of CA, Irvine, 3151 Social Science Plaza, Irvine, CA 92697-5100, USA.

GROOTAERS Willem Anciaux, b. 26 May 1911, St Servais, Belgium. Catholic Priest; Professor of Japanese Dialectology. Education: Philos and Theol, Belgium, 1933-39; Classic Chinese, Brussels-Louvain, 1933-39; DLitt, hon, Louvain Univ, 1981. Appointments: Missionary, Shansi Prov, China, 1941-43; Prof, Fujen Univ, Peking, 1945-48; Missionary, Toyooka, Japan, 1950-55; Rsch Fell, Japanese Lang Inst, Tokyo, 1955-; Prof, Seisen Womens Coll, 1965-76; Sophia Univ, 1973-82; Tenri Univ, 1971-81. Publications include: Linguistic Atlas of Japan (w others), 6 vols, 1966-76; Mistranslations, 1967; Grammar Atlas of the Japanese Dialects (w others) 3 vols, 1988-93; Many articles in profl jrnls. Honour: 3rd Class of Order of Sacred Treas, 1984. Memberships: Assn Teihard de Chardin of Japan; Societe Ling de Paris; Societe Linguistique Romane; Dialectal Soc of Japan; Ling Soc of Japan. Hobby: Cycling. Address: 28-5 2-chome, Matsubara, Setagaya-ku, Tokyo 156, Japan.

GROSS Eric, b. 16 Sept 1926. Composer; Lecturer. m. Pamela Margaret Mary Davies, 22 Feb 1955. Education: MA; MLitt; DMus; FTCL; LMUSTCL. Appointments: Sydney Conservatorium of Music, 1956-60; Assoc Prof of Music, Univ of Sydney, 1960-91. Publications: Num compositions and recordings: Symphony No 1, 1974; Symphony No 2, 1981; Violin Concerto No 1, 1983. Honours: DAAD Schl, Germany, 1974, 1981; Albert H Maggs Composition Awd, Univ Melbourne, 1976. Memberships: Fell, Austl Composers; Asian Composers League; Austl Music Cntr. Hobbies: Stamp collecting; Football. Address: Unit 54, 84 St Georges Street, Drummoyne, NSW 2047, Australia.

GROSS Michael Roderick, b. 21 Nov 1940, Auckland, NZ. Company Manager. Widowed, 2 s. 2 d. Appointments: Chmn, Bay of Is Co Cncl, 1983-89; Chmn, Northland Regl Cncl, 1989-95; VP, NZ Local Gov Assn, 1995; Chmn, Transfund NZ, 1996-; Bd, Northland Port Corp, 1997-. Honours: NZ Medal, 1990; Queen's Serv Order for Pub Serv, 1996. Membership: Fell, Chartered Inst of Transp, 1999. Hobbies: Theatre; Art; Family; History. Listed in: Who's Who in New Zealand. Address: Fairway Drive, Kerikeri, Northland, New Zealand.

GROSSBERG Kenneth Alan, b. 17 Feb 1946, NY, USA. Professor of International Marketing; Consultant. m. Keiko Matsuzaki, 11 July 1975, 1 s, 1 d. Education: BA, summa cum laude, Hobart Coll, 1966; MA, 1969, PhD, 1977, Princeton Univ. Appointments: Prof of Mktng, Tel Aviv Univ; Dir, Asia Progs, Fac of Mngmt, Tel Aviv Univ; Visng Fulbright Rsch Prof, Tel Aviv Univ; Prof of Mktng, Yeshiva Univ; VP, Citibank. Publications: Japan's Renaissance, 1981; Japan Today, 1981. Honours: Jnr Fell, Harv Univ Soc of Fells, 1974-77; Fulbright Awd, 1992-93. Memberships: Acady of Intl Bus; Assn for Asian Stdies; NY Am Global Mktng Ldrshp Cncl. Hobbies: Reading; Music; Theatre; Swimming; Travel. Address: 11-A Hazayit Street, Zichron, Yaakov 30900, Israel.

GROSSER Morton, b. 25 Dec 1931, Philadelphia, PA, USA. Author; Consultant; Venture Capitalist. m. Janet Zachs, 28 June 1953, 1 s. Education: BS, 1953, MS, 1954, MIT; PhD, 1961, Stanford Univ. Appointments: Dir Des, Clevite Transister, 1956; Dir Publs, Boeing Sci Rsch Labs, 1964; Pres, MG Consulting, 1967-. Publications: 8 books; 100 pprs; 7 pats granted or pending. Honours: Coates & Clark Fellow, MIT, 1955; Ford Fndn Fellow, Stanford, 1960; Natl Insts of Hlth Fell, UCLA Medl Ctr, 1961-62; C'Wealth Club Medal for Lit, 1991. Memberships: Assoc Fellow, Amn Inst Aeronautics and Astronautics; Auths' Guild; Fell, Amn Soc Mech; Soc Automotive Engrs. Hobbies: Woodcarving; Model building; Weight training. Address: MG Consulting, 1016 Lemon Street, Menlo Park, CA 94025, USA.

GROVER Gautam, b. New Delhi, India. Businessman. Education: SSC, St Columba's Sch, New Delhi, India. Appointments: Coord, KARE (Kindness to Animals and Respect for Environ), 1995, Tstee, KARE, 1997; Pres, People For Animals, 1998. Publications: First Aid for Animals, 1996. Memberships: KARE; People for Animals. Hobbies: Music; Animal rights activism. Address: BA/1A Ashok, Vihar-I, Delhi 110052, India.

GROVER H R, b. 3 Jan 1946. Publisher. m. Sudesh, 6 May 1968, 2 s, 1 d. Education: MA LLB, PGDs in Book Publng; Mktng and Sales Mngmt. Appointments: Mngr, Publication Bur, Panjab Univ, Chandigarh 160 014, India, 1982. Publications: stdy rsch ppr on Advertisement and Sales Promotion of University Publications in partial fulfilment of the PGD in Marketing and Sales Management, 1989, 1990. Honours: Awarded Cert of Hon by Dept of Laws, PU, Chandigarh, for highest marks in Labour Laws; Best Display Awd at Chandigarh Book Fair, 1993; Intl Man of Yr Awd, 1996-97, 20th Century Awd, 1997-98, IBC, Eng. Memberships: Life mbr, PU Law Alumni Assn, 1981-82; Printing, Prodn, Sales, Promotion, Purchase Cttees of different depts of PU and other instns. Hobbies: Sociall welfare activities; Reading books and newspapers. Address: Manager, Publication Bureau, Panjab Univ, Chandigarh 160 014, India.

GROVER John Charles, b. 25 Nov 1920, Randwick, NSW, Aust. Military Engineer; Earth Scientist; Mining Engineer; Author. m. Caroline Sandon, 20 June 1959, 1 s, 2 d. Education: BEng, Mining and Metall, Sydney, 1950; MSc, Geol and Geophys, Sydney, 1968. Appointments: Roy Austl Engrs, 1 Fd Sqn, 1939; Commissioned in AIF, Serv in Mid E, 1941; Papua, 1942-43, New Guinea, 1944-45; Snr Geol, Brit Solomon Islands, 1950; Chf Geolst, 1951; Dir, 1965, Dir Geol Surveys, Colony of Fiji, 1967; Gen Mngr, Kathleen Investments (Aust) Ltd, 1969; UN Proj Mngr, Ethiopia Geol Survey, 1975; Coord Spec Projs, Peko-Wallsend Ltd, Sydney, 1977. Publications: 5 hard-covered vols on Geol of Solomon Islands, 1953-73; The Struggle for Power, 1980; Struggle for Cargo, 1984; The Hellmakers, 1988, 1993, 1998; Volcanic Eruptions and Great Earthquakes, Advance Warning Techniques to Master the Deadly Science, 1998. Honours: Danish Silver Galathea Medal, 1959; OBE, 1963. Memberships: Fell, Aust Inst of Mining and Metall; Fell Roy Geog Soc; Fell, Geol Soc; Fell, Inst of Mining and Metall; Fell, Inst of Engrs (Aust). Hobbies: Research; Writing; Public speaking. Address: 21 Cotentin Road, Belrose, NSW 2085, Australia.

GRUBB Warren Bruce, b. 11 Dec 1936, Cooranbong, Aust. University Professor of Microbiology. m. Kaye Elston, 12 Dec 1963, 2 s, 1 d. Education: BS (Hons); PhD. Appointments: Snr Tutor, Snr Lectr, Assoc Prof, Prof. Publications: Sci pprs, chapts in books & sci reviews. Memberships: Amn Soc for Microbiology; Austl Biotechnology Assn; Fell, Austl Soc for Microbiology. Hobbies: Photography; Badminton. Address: School of Biomedical Sciences, Curtin University of Technology, Perth, WA, Australia.

GRUZMAN Neville Bruce, b. 14 Nov 1928. Architect. m. Margot, 20 May 1963, 1 s, 1 d. Education: B H Sch, Univ Sydney, UNSW. Appointments: Fndn Chmn, Friends of Natl Art Sch, 1964; Fndn Chmn, Craft Assn of Aust,

1966; Mbr, Cl Assn of Classical Archaeol, Univ Sydney, 1967-87; Lectr, "The Failure of Modern Arch", Art Gall, NSW; Visng Prof, Arch, UNSW, 1987; Fndn 1988, Cl Natl Trust of of NSW, 1992; Mbr, PM's Urban Des Task Force, 1994-; Mayor of Wollahra, NSW; Adj Prof, Sch of Arch, Univ NSW, 1999-. Publications: Selected Writings; Architecture into Millenium 3; Delight or Disaster in the City; An Industrial City Crawls Out of the Ashes; The Threat to Hobart; The Rape of Sydney; Cities in Despair; Why Can't We Be Like Hong Kong; The Last Nail in Sydney's Concrete Coffin; Deconstructing the New and Better. Honours: Hon by Retrospective RAIA (NSW Chapt); 4 of 20 Best Bldgs in Austl Arch and Arts Awd. Memberships: Carlton Club (London); Rose Bay Surf (Sydney). Address: 8 Oswald Street, Darling Point, NSW 2027, Australia.

GU Dao Xiu, b. 2 Nov 1938, Chang de County, China. Teacher. m. Kai Zhi Yao, 12 Dec 1970, 1 s. Education: Dip, Beijing Normal Univ. Publications: The New Classification of Natural Number System and the Construction of Human Body, 1993; Human Social Activities and the Establishment of New Mathematics, 1996. Memberships: Bio & Maths Assn. Hobbies: Music; Sports. Address: Department of Mathematics, Hunan College of Education, Changsha, Hunan 410012, China.

GU Jiadong, b. 15 Sept 1948, Shanghai, China. Economist and Manager. m. 28 Feb 1978, 1 s. Education: MBA, China-Euro Intl Bus Sch. Appointments: Gen Mngr, Shanghai For Serv Co Ltd; VP, Shanghai E Best Intl (Grp) Co Ltd. Publications: The Trend of Human Resource Development in Shanghai With Global Integrated Economy; Substantial Development of Human Resource Service Toward Foreign Investor in Shanghai. Honours: Outstndng Mngr, Min of For Trade and Con Coop, China, 1998; Outstndng Entrepreneur of Shanghai, 1997. Memberships: VP, China Assn of Fgn Serv Trades; Exec Dir, Shanghai World Trade Cntr and Assn of Shanghai Entrepreneur. Hobbies: Research in marketing, investment and human resources; Football. Address: 12th Floor, Jinling Building, 28 Jinling Road (W), Shanghai 200021, China.

GU Jinchi, b. 1932 Xiong Co Hebei Prov. Party and Government Official. Appointments: Joined CCP, 1949; Vice-Gov Sichuan Prov, 1982-86; Dep Sec Sichuan Provincial Cttee, 1988-90; Sec Gansu Provincial Cttee, 1990; Sec Liaoning Provincial Cttee, 1993-97. Memberships: Mbr 13th CCP Cntrl Cttee, 1987-92; Mbr 14th CCP Cntrl Cttee, 1992-. Address: Gansu Provincial Committee, Gansu Province, People's Republic of China.

GU Ming Xin, b. 17 Apr 1937, Shanghai, China. Researcher; Consultant. m. Zhang Jing Fang, 9 Sept 1960, 2 d. Education: Engr Deg, Tsinghua Univ, 1954; Dir Deg, Nanjing Univ of Aeron and Astrons, 1986. Appointments: Metallurgist, Harbin Aircraft Mfg Corp, 1960-67; Metallurgist, 1967-81, Vice Chf Engr, 1981-83, Chf Engr, 1983-85, Pres, 1985-87, AnDa Forging Plant; Dir, Sci and Technol Dept, 1987-92, GAIC; Vice Chair, Sci and Technol Com, 1986-93, Chf Engr, Hong Yuan Aviation Forging & Casting Ind Co, 1993-96; Chair, Sci and Technol Com, 1996-97; Retd, 1997; Cnclr, Technol Devel Cntr of Materials, AVIC, 1995-. Publications: Sev articles in profl jrnls. Honours: 1st Prize, Natl Sci and Technol Progress Awd, 1987; 1st Prize, Ministerial Sci and Technol Progress Awd 1980, 1986, 2nd Prize, 1994; 2nd Def Sci and Technol Ind Improvement Awd, 1981; Natl Outstndng Sci and Technol Contbr Awd, 1993. Memberships: Fell, Cttee on Aeron Forging Technol, 1994-97; CSBTS TG33 on Mould and Die, 1996-; Amn Soc for Testing and Materials. Hobbies: Investigation; Study. Address: Hong Yuan Aviation Forging & Casting Industry Co, Yang Du Village, PO Box 2, Sanyuan, Shaanxi 713801, China.

GU Xiulian, b. 1935 Jiangsu Prov. Party and Government Official. Appointments: Cadre State Cncl, 1970; Vice-Min State Plng Commn State Cncl, 1973-83; Vice-Chmn Cntrl Patriotic Sanitation Campaign Cttee Cntrl Cttee, 1981-89; Dep Sec CCP Prov Cttee Jiangsu, 1982-89; Gov of Jiangsu, 1983-89; Min of Chem Ind,

1989-93, 1993-98 - also Party Cttee Sec at the Min. Memberships: Alt mbr Cntrl Cttee, CCP, 1977; Mbr 12th Cntrl Cttee CCP, 1982-87; Mbr 13th Cntrl Cttee, 1981-89; Mbr 14th Cntrl Cttee CCP, 1992-97; Mbr 15th Cntr Cttee CCP, 1997-; Fmr Standing mbr Natl Fedn of Women. Address: c/o Ministry of Chemical Industry, Hepingli Street, Anding Menwai, Beijing 100723, People's Republic of China.

GU Yingqi, b. 1930 Xinmin Liaoning. Politician. m. 2 s, 1 d. Appointments: Joined PLA, 1948; Joined CCP, 1950; Vice-Min of Pub Hlth, 1984-95; Chf Physician; Pres Chinese Assn of Rehabilitation Med, 1985-; Pres China Rural Hyg Assn, 1986-; Co-ord State Co-ord of Control of Narcotics and Against Drugs, 1987-90; Hd of deleg to UN Intl Conf on Drug Abuse and Illicit Trafficking, 1987; Hd of deleg to Signing of Sino-US Memorandum of Understanding on Co-opn and Control of Narcotic Drugs WA, 1987; Hd Deleg to UN Conf for Adoption of a Convention Against Ilicit Traffic in Narcotic Drugs and Psychotropic Substances, 1988; Hd deleg to 17th Specl Sess of UN Gen Ass on Intl Co-opn against Drugs, 1990; Exec VP Red Cross Soc of China, 1990-; Hd deleg to 44th Gen Ass of WHO, 1991; Hd Deleg to Intl Conf for Protection of War Victims Geneva, 1993; Hd deleg to 9th Sess of Gen Ass of Intl Fedn of Red Cross and Red Crescent Socs Birmingham UK, 1993; Conf Chmn 15th Meeting of Natl Drug Law Enforcement Agcs for Asia and Pacific, 1990; Exec VP Intl Fedn of Red Cross and Red Crescent Socs, 1991-93; Chmn 4th Asia and Pacific Red Cross and Red Crescent Conf Beijing, 1993; Hd of Chinese Red Cross deleg to 26th Intl Conf of Red Cross and Red Crescent Geneva, 1995; Pres Chinese Assn of Hosp Mngr. Address: c/o Red Cross Society of China, 53 Ganmian Hutong, Beijing 100010, People's Republic of China.

GU Yunfei, b. 1930 Wujiang. Government Official. Appointments: Sec Working Cttee of depts directly under CCP Cntrl Cttee. Memberships: Mbr 13th and 14th CCP Cntrl Disciplinary Cttee. Address: Chinese Communist Party Central Committee, Beijing, People's Republic of China.

GUAN Guangfu, b. 1931 Muling Co Heilongjiang Prov. Politician; Banker. Appointments: Joined CCP, 1948; VP Hubei Br People's Bank of China, 1971-78; Pres Hubei Br, 1978-82; Sec Hubei Prov CCP Cttee, 1983-94; First Polit Commissar First Party Sec Hubei Prov Mil Dist, 1983-; Chmn Hubei Prov 8th People's Congress, 1993-. Memberships: Mbr 12th Cntrl Cttee, 1985; 13th Cntrl Cttee, 1987; 14th Cntrl Cttee, 1992; Mbr Presidium 13th and 14th Natl Congresses CCP. Address: Shui Guo Hu, Wuhan, Hubei Province, People's Republic of China.

GUAN Zhaoye, b. 24 Oct 1929, Beijing, China. Architecture. m. Lingzhang Kong, 27 Apr 1957, 2 s. Education: BEng. Appointment: Tchr, Dept of Arch, Tsinghua Univ, 1953-; Tsinghua Univ Lib, 1983-92; Tsinghua Sci Coll, 1994-98; Peking Univ Lib, 1994-97. Honour: Gold Medal, State Cncl, 1993. Memberships: Arch Soc of China, 1982-; Chinese Acady of Engrng, 1996-. Hobbies: Tennis; Music. Address: Department of Architecture, Tsinghua Univ, Beijing, China.

GUE See Sew, b. 3 May 1953. Director. m. Choi Ling Ho, 23 July 1977, 2 s. Education: BSc w 1st Class Hons, Civ Engrng, Univ of Strathclyde, Glasgow, Scotland, 1979; 1st Class Dip in Civ Engrng, Univ of Technol, Malaysia, 1976; Dr Philos, Geotech Engrng, Univ of Oxford, Eng, 1984. Appointments: Surveying Asst, Loh & Loh Constrn SDN BHD, 1974, 1975; Tech Asst, Drainage and Irrigation Dept, Malaysia, 1976-77; Bridge Design Engr, Pub Wrks Dept, Malaysia, 1979-81; Snr Geotech Engr, Pub Wrks Dept, Malaysia, 1984-90; Hd of Rsch and Dev Dept, Pernas Constrn SDN BHD, 1990-92; Mngng Dir, SSP Geotechnics SDN BHD, 1992-. Memberships: Intl Soc of Soil Mechs and Fndn Engrng, 1985-; PEng, Bd of Engrs Malaysia, 1986-; Fell, Instn of Engrs Malaysia, 1990-; Regd Prin, Assn of Cnsltng Engrs, Malaysia and UK, 1993-; Cncl, Bd of Engrs Malaysia, 1993-; VP, Inst of Engrs Malaysia, 1993-. Address: SSP Geotechnics SDN BHD, Level 6, Wisma SSP, 1 Jalan SR 8/3, Serdang Raya Seksyen 8, 43300 Seri Kembangan, Selangor, Malaysia.

GUESGEN Hans Werner, b. 24 April 1959, Bonn, Germany. Senior Lecturer. m. Gaby, 11 Aug 1984, 3 d. Education: Dipl-Inform, 1983; Dr rer nat, 1988; Dr habil, 1993. Appointments: Post Doctoral Fell, ICSI, Berkeley, CA, 1989-90; Sci Rschr, GMD St Augustin, Germany, 1983-92; Snr Lectr, Comp Sci Dept, Univ of Auckland, 1992-. Creative Works: 3 Books; Over 50 Articles; Over 30 Tech Rprts. Memberships: Amn Assn for Artificial Intelligence. Hobbies: Scuba diving; Hiking; Working with wood. Address: Computer Science Department, University of Auckland, New Zealand.

GUESS Jeff, b. 1948, Adelaide, Australia. Poet. Appointments: Org of num writing workshops. Publications include: Leaving Maps, 1984; Four in the Afternoon, 1987; Painting the Town, 1988; Replacing Fuses in the House of Cards, 1988; Rites of Arrival, 1990; Selected Sonnets, 1991; Living in the Shade of Nothing Solid, 1997. Honours: Num 1st Prizes and 5 writing grants. Address: PO Box 1039, Gawler, South Australia 5118, Australia.

GUEVARA Amelia, b. 10 July 1947, Philippines. Professor of Chemistry. m. Gil Guevara, 7 Mar 1976, 3 s. Education: BS, 1967; MS, 1973; PhD, 1988. Appointments: Instr, Dept of Chem, 1968-75, Divsn Sec, Divsn of Natural Scis & Maths, 1983, Coll of Arts & Sci, UP Diliman; Assoc Cnslt, Chem Section Hd, Engrng & Indl Rsch Servs, Econ Devel Fndn, 1975-82; Coll Sec, Coll of Sci, UP Diliman, 1983-84; Asst to VP for Devel, 1989-90; Asst to VP for Acad Affairs, 1990, Univ Philippines; Exec Dir, UP Sci Rsch Fndn, Coll of Sci, UP Diliman, 1989-93; Assoc Prof, Inst of Chem, Coll of Sci, 1988-93; Univ Reg, 1990-93, Dir, Off of Admissions, 1994, Prof of Chem, Coll of Sci, 1993-, Univ of Philippines; Natl Point of Contact Rep, 1993-, Exec Sec, UNESCO Regl Network for the Chem of Natural Products in SE Asia, 1998-. Publications include: Antimutagens From Plumeria acuminata; Antimutagens From Momordica charantia; Structure Elucidation of Acylglucosylsterols from Momordica charantia. Honour: Outstndng Fac Prof, Univ Philippines, 1997. Memberships: Kilusan ng mga Kimiko sa Pilipinas; Integrated Chems of the Philippines; Natl Rsch Cncl of the Philippines; Phi Kappa Phi; Bd Dir, UP Chem Alumni Fndn, 1989-, Natural Products Soc of the Philippines, 1996-; Pres, Philippine Environ Mutagen Soc, 1991-. Hobby: Sewing. Address: Institute of Chemistry, College of Science, University of the Philippines, Diliman, Quezon City, Philippines.

GUGNANI Harish Chander, b. 10 Apr 1939, Lyallpur. Teacher; Researcher. m. Dinesh, 8 May 1966, 2 s, 1 d. Education: BSc Hons, Delhi Univ, 1958; MSc, Pl Pallology and Microbio, BHU, 1960; PhD, Microbio, Delhi, 1970; FRC Path, London, 1990. Appointments: Rsch Asst, JARG, New Delhi, 1960-62; Asst Rsch Offr, AIIMS, New Delhi, 1962-64; Rsch Offr, NICD, Delhi, 1964-72; Lectr, 1973-4; Snr Lectr, 1974-76; Rdr, 1976-78; Prof, 1978-97; Prof, V P Chest Inst, 1997-. Honours: Welcome Nigeria Fndn Awd, Outstndng Rsch in Med; Merit Awd; Univ Rsch Ldrshp Prize, Univ of Nigeria. Memberships: Amn Soc for Microbio; Nigerian Soc for Microbio; Intl Soc for Hum and Animal Mycology. Hobbies: Reading magazines; Helping children with their studies; Community Work. Address: J3/45, Rajouri Garden, New Delhi 110027, India.

GUHA R P, b. 23 June 1929, Calcutta, India. Teacher. m. A Guha, 17 Feb 1960, 1 s, 1 d. Education: PhD, Law, USA; DLitt; MHM. Publications: Sev articles in profl jrnls. Honours: MM Acady Awd, Lit, 1997. Membership: FUWA. Hobbies: Poetry; Music. Address: Patratu School of Economics, PO Patratu Thermal Power Station, PB 13, Hazaribagh 829119, India.

GUI Shiyong, b. Feb 1935 Huzhou Cty Zhejiang Prov. Politician. Education: Chinese People's Univ. Appointments: Joined CCP, 1956; Dir Econs Inst of Chinese Acady of Scis; Dep Ed-in-Chf Renmin Ribao - People's Daily; Vice-Dir Rsch Off of the State Cncl, 1987; Vice-Chmn State Plng Commn; Dir Econs Rsch Cntr, 1989; VP State Admin Inst, 1994-. Memberships: Alt mbr 13th CCP Cntrl Cttee, 1987; Mbr State Plng Commn; Alt mbr 14th CCP Cntrl Cttee, 1992; Mbr 15th CCP Cntrl Cttee, 1997-. Address: Office of the President, State Administrative Institute, Beijing, People's Republic of China.

GUILFORD Colin Michael, b. 3 Apr 1929, Wanstead, Essex, Eng. Chartered Civil Engineer. m. (1) 2 s, 2 d, (2) Patricia Ann Shih, 1994. Education: BA, 1952, MA, 1964, Queens' Coll, Cambridge Univ, Eng; Dip, Harvard Univ, USA, 1963. Appointments: Jnr Asst Engr, Snr Asst Engr, 1952-63, Snr Engr, 1963-65, Assoc, 1965-69, Ptnr, 1970-91, Cnslt, 1991-95, Scott Wilson Kirkpatrick & Ptnrs, Hong Kong, Cnsltng Engrs, UK, 1952, 1956-58, 1961-63; Dir, Scott Wilson Kirkpatrick Co Ltd, 1970-91; Dir, Scott Wilson Kirkpatrick Intl, 1978-91; Cnslt, Scott Wilson Kirkpatrick Asia-Pacific Ltd, 1994-96; Cnslt, Scott Wilson Kirkpatrick Hong Kong Ltd, 1994-96. Honour: JP, Hong Kong, 1982-. Memberships include: Fell, Inst of Civil Engrs, London; Fell, Amn Soc of Civil Engrs; Fell, Hong Kong Inst of Engrs; Hong Kong Club; Marylebone Cricket Club, London. Hobbies: Antiques; Local history. Address: Flat 8C, 44 Fa Po Street, Yau Yat Chuen, Kowloon, Hong Kong.

GUILFOYLE Margaret Georgina Constance, b. 15 May 1926, Belfast, North Ireland. Accountant. m. Stanley Martin Leslie Guilfoyle, 20 Nov 1952, 1 s, 2 d. Education: LLB, Austl Natl Univ; Fell, Chartered Inst of Secs and Admnstrs (FCIS); Fell, Certified Practising Accts (FCPA). Appointments include: Sen for Vic, 1971-87; Min for Educ, 1975; Min for Socl Security, 1975-80; Min for Fin, 1980-83; Bd Mbr, 1989-, Dpty Chmn, 1994-, Austl Children's TV Fndn; Trustee, Mark Fitzpatrick Trust, 1990-; Dir, Jack Brockhoff Fndn Ltd, 1990-; Mbr, Austl Inst Family Studies Bd, 1992-; Chmn, Dept of Justice (Vic) Judicial Remuneration Tribunal, 1995-; Chmn, Austl Polit Exchange Cncl, 1996-; Chmn, Ministerial Advsry Cttee on Women's Hlth (Vic), 1996-; Chmn, Austl Polit Exchange Cncl, 1996-; Mbr, Clin Rsch and Ethics Cttee, Roy Melbourne Hosp Rsch Fndn Inc, 1996-; Mbr, Walter and Eliza Hall Inst of Medl Rsch Ethics Cttee, 1996-. Honours: dame Cmdr of Brit Empire (DBE). Membership: Dpty Chmn, Infertility Treatment Authority, 1995-. Hobbies: Reading; Opera. Address: 21 Howard Street, Kew, Victoria, Australia 3101.

GUILLILAND Karen Mary, b. 16 Oct 1949. Midwife. m. Anthony Ritchie Guilliland, 4 Dec 1970, 2 s, 1 d. Education: Regd Nurse and Obstets Nurse; Regd Midwife; Advd Dip, Maternal Child Hlth; MA, 1998 . Appointments: Midwife, Christchurch Womens Hosp, 1977-83; Tutor, Women's Hlth, Christchurch Polytech, 1983-89; ICM Rep, UN Econ Commn, 1990-; Ministerial Appointee Nursing Cncl of NZ, 1990-93; Natl Dir, NZ Coll of Midwives, 1990-; Co-ord Hlth Care Pactises Task Force, World Alliance, Breastfeeding Action, Malaysia, 1997-; Midwife Cnslt to NZ Fedn of Parent Cntrs, 1998-. Publications: Co-Auth, The Midwifery Partnership - A Model for Practice, 1995; Prodr, Video, Active Birthing, 1988. Honours: Queens Commemorative Medal, 1990; Hon Life Mbr, NZ Coll Midwives. Memberships: Inaugural Pres, NZ Coll Midwives, 1989-91; Chairperson, Bd of Trees, Family Help Trust, 1992-. Listed in: Who's Who. Hobbies: Travel. Address: PO Box 21106, Christchurch, New Zealand.

GUITON Patrick de Carteret, b. 16 Mar 1935, Jersey, Channel Is. Director of External Studies. m. Kate Haslam, 9 Sept 1967, div 1990, 2 d. Education: Christ's Hosp, 1944-52; BA, hons, Univ of York, Eng, 1966; MA, Econs, Univ of Manchester, 1968. Appointments: HM Overseas Civ Serv, Northern Rhodesia, 1957-63; Lectr, Univ of Stirling, Scotland, 1967-72; Dpty Regl Dir, Open Univ, UK, 1972-74; Dir of External Studies, Murdoch Univ 1974-97; Educ Specialist, Higher Educ, The C'wlth of Learning, 1998-. Honour: Austl Acady of Brdcst Arts and Scis Pater Awd, Most Outstndng Radio Innovation, 1985. Listed in: Who's Who in Australia; Who's Who in Distance

Education. Hobbies: Running; Sailing. Address: 12 Smith Street, Hilton, Western Australia 6163, Australia.

GUJRAL Inder Kumar, b. 4 Dec 1919 Jhelum - now in Pakistan. Politican. m. Shrimati Sheila Gujral, 1944, 2 s. Education: Forman Christian Coll; Hailey Coll of Com Lahore; Punjab Univ. Appointments: Jailed for participation in freedom movement, 1930-31 - and again during Quit India movement, 1942; Pres Lahore Students' Union; Gen-Sec Punjab Students' Fedn; Migrated to India, 1947; Helped natl effort for rehabilitation of displaced persons; Co-Chmn Asian Regl Conf of Rotary Intl, 1958; VP New Delhi Municipal Cttee, 1959-64; Helped org Citizens Cttee for Civ Def; Alt Ldr Indian Deleg Inter-Parly Union Conf Canberra, 1966; Alt Ldr Indian Delegs to UNESCO, 1970, 1972, 1974; Alt Ldr Indian Deleg to UN session on Environment Stockholm, 1972; Min of State for Wrks Housing and Urban Dev, 1971-72; Min for Info and Brdcstng, 1972-75; Chmn UNESCO seminar on Mngmnt and Current Comms Systems Paris, 1973; Min for Plng, 1975-76; Amb to USSR - with ministerial rank - 1976-80; Ldr Indian Deleg UNESCO session on Environment and Educ Tbilisi, 1977; Min of External Affairs, 1989-91, 1996-97; PM of India, 1997-98; Fndr-Pres Delhi Arts Th; Treas Fedn of Film Socs of India; VP Lok Kalyan Samiti. Memberships: Mbr Rajya Sabha, 1964-76; Mbr Lok Sabha, 1989-Janata Dal; Mbr Cncl of Mins Govt of India, 1967-76; Mbr Cncl of Mins Govt of India holding portfolios for Comms and Parly Affairs, 1967-69; Mbr Cncl of Mins Govt of India for Info Comms and Brdcstng, 1969-71; Mbr Rajya Sabha, 1970-76; Mbr All India Cntrl Citizens Cncl; Mbr All India Congress Cttee. Hobbies: Theatre; Poetry; Painting; Ecological problems. Address: c/o G 13, Maharani Bagh, New Delhi 110065, India.

GUJRAL Sheila, b. 24 Jan 1924, Lahore, Pakistan. Poetess; Writer; Social Worker. m. Mr I K Gujral, 26 May 1945, 2 s. Education: MA (Econs); Dip in Jrnlsm; Dip in Montessori Trng; DLitt. Career: Fmrly in educ; Socl Welfare; Pt-time Writer. Publications: 26 incl: Niara Hindustan (Punjabi Poetry), 1988; Nishwas (Hindi Poetry), 1989; Signature of Silence (Engl Poetry), 1991, New Ed, 1998; Tapovan Mai Bavanddar (Hindi) Short Stories, 1992; Mehak (Punjabi Short Stories), 1995; Jab Mai Na Rahun (Hindi Poetry), 1995; Throttled Dove (English Poetry), 1995; Barf Ke Chehre (Hindi Poetry), 1997; Canvas of Life (Engl Poetry), 1997; 3 Punjabi books publd in Pakistan (in Urdu & Gurmukhi script); 2 transls; Freelance writer in Hindi & Engl on socl & educl problems; Engl anthology, Two Black Cinders, translated into Arabic; Ed, Sema Raksha, for Citizens Cncl, 1963-64. Honours include: Golden Poet Awd, World of Poetry, 1989, 1990; Nirala Awd, Best Hindi Poetry of Yr, 1989; Mahila Shiromani Awd, 1990; Ed's Choice Awd for outstndng in poetry, Natl Lib of Poetry, MD, USA, 1995; Huh Nansolhoen Poetry Highest Awd (Korea), 1997; Soka Univ (Japan) Awd of Highest Hon, 1997; Shiomani Sahitkar Awd, 1997; Govt of Punjab Delhi Ratan the XVII State Intellectuals Hon, 1998. Hobbies: Poetry writing; Music; Gardening; Social work. Address: 5, Jan Path, New Delhi 110011, India.

GULATI Sunita, b. 4 Feb 1955. Assistant Librarian. m. Dr P K Gulati, 24 Nov 1979, 1 s. Education: MA, Pol Sci; MPhil, Lib and Info Sci. Appointments: Profl Asst, Indian Inst of Mass Comn Lib, 1978-79; Libn, Dayanand Ay Coll, Jalandhar, 1980-; Internee, Amn Cntr Lib, 1982-; Profl Asst Indian Inst of Pub Admin, 1983-; Jnr Asst Libn Indian Inst of Pub Admin, 1983-85; Asst Libn Indian Inst of Pub Admin, 1985-92; Snr Asst Libn, Indian Inst of Pub Admin, 1992-95; Snr Asst Libn, Ref, Info and Circulation Div, 1996-; Conducted 5 trng progs on User Education for Librarians, sponsored by Brit Cncl Div and Govt of India. Publications: 3 articles: AACR -2: A Critical Review, International Library Movement; National Public Administration Information Services Network (PAISNET): A Proposal In All India Library Conference (co-auth), 1990; New Trends in The Management of Public Documents: A Case Study of Indian Institute of Public Administration, In Seminar on New Trends in Management of Indian Official Documents, 1996; 41 bibliographies in var jrnls and books. Memberships:

Indian Lib Assn; Life mbr; Indian Assn of Spec Libs & Info Cntrs, life mbr; Assn of Govt Libns of India, life mbr; Indian Inst of Pub Admin, life mbr. Address: Indian Institute of Public Administration, I P Estate, New Delhi 110002, India.

GUMASHTA Anurag, b. 1 June 1972, Bombay. Intern. Education: MBBS; ND; Dip in Naturopathy. Appointments: Pursuing Internship. Publications: From Minerva to Delilah; Life of Shri Vallabhacharya, Vaishnavite Saint. Honours: Jnr Fellshp, Ecstatic Enjoyment in the Shreemad Bhaagvad Mahapurana. Memberships: Utd Writers Assn. Hobbies: Drugless healing; Research; Reading fiction, Philosophy, Poetry. Address: 47 Ishavasyan Pratapganj, Baroda 390 002, India.

GUNER Osman Fatih, b. 25 Feb 1956, Turkey. Physical Organic Chemist. m. Nazli, 23 Apr 1982, 1 s, 1 d. Education: BS, Chem, Mid E Tech Univ, Turkey, 1979; MS, Organic Chem, 1981; PhD, Physl Organic Chem, VA C'wlth Univ, 1986. Appointments: Postdoctoral Fell, Univ AL, Birmingham, 1986-89; Snr Application Scientist, Molecular Design Ltd, 1989-93; Snr Sci, Mol Information Systems Inc, 1993-96; Snr Prof Mngr, Molecular Simulations Inc, 1996-. Creative Works: Over 24 pprs in sci jrnls. Memberships: Amn Chem Soc; Intl QSAR and Modeling Soc. Hobbies: Golf; Chess; Backgammon. Address: Molecular Simulations Inc, 9685 Scranton Road, San Diego, CA 92121, USA.

GUO Jikang, b. 11 Jan 1936, Fuzhou, China. Senior Engineer. m. Xie Jinhua, 1 s, 1 d. Education: Dept of Elec Engrng, Zhejiang Univ. Appointments: Vice Chf Engr, Vice Dir, Hubei Elec Power Bur, 1980; VP, Hubei Qingjiang Hydroelec Devel Co Ltd, 1989. Publications: Management on Medium-Size Hydropower Station in Hubei, 1994; GeHe Yan Hydropower Station, 1995; Dream Realized in Qingjiang River, 1997. Honours: Hubei Prov Adv Worker, 1994; Natl Model Worker, 1995. Memberships: Hubei Soc of Hydroelec Engrng, vice bd chmn, 1986-91, 1996-; China Soc of Hydroelec Engrng, dir, 1996-. Address: c/o Hubei Qingjiang Hydroelectric Development Co Ltd, 9 Qiaohu 2nd Road, Yichang, Hubei 443002, China.

GUO Qi-Zhen, b. 3 May 1930, Yong-Chun Fujian, China. Teaching. m. Y W Xue, 18 Mar 1956, 2 s, 1 d. Education: MSc. Appointment: Dir, Div of Organic Chem, Dept of Chem, Xiamen Univ. Publications: Chemistry of Plant Growth Regulators, 1962; Organosuphur Fungicide, 1963; Biomimetic Chemistry, 1990; Acids and Bases Principle in Organic Chemistry. Honours: 3rd Awd, Fujian Prov, 1980, 1988; 2nd Awds, Prog Awds of Sci and Tech, Min of Educ, 1985, 1994; Fujian Prov, 1980, 1988. Memberships: Fujian Soc of Chem, 1985-93; Hd Mbr, Rsch Cntr of High Chem Educ, 1986-95. Address: Department of Chemistry, Xiamen University, Xiamen, Fujian, China.

GUO Rixiu, b. 18 July 1924, Nanchang, Jiangxi, China. Teacher; Scientific Researcher. m. Lo Rong Ying, 20 Aug 1948, 1 s, 2 d. Education: Civil Engrng Dept, Tangshan Engrng Coll; BS, Engrng, Jiaotong Univ, 1946. Appointments: Tchng Asst, Tangshan Engrng Coll, 1946; Tsinghua Univ, 1947-50; Lectr, Naval Inst, Dalian, 1950-62; Dean, Dept of Naval Arch, 1953-64, 1979-83, Assoc Prof, 1962-86, Prof, Supvsr of Doct Cands, 1986-; Naval Acady of Engrng; Mbr, Shipping Grp of State Sci and Technol Commn, 1962-66; Dpty, 3rd Natl Peoples Congress, 1964-74; Mbr, Disciplinary Appraisal Grp of Acad Degs Cttee, State Cncl, 1985-97. Publications include: Tensor Analysis and Theory of Elasticity, 1988; A Semi-Analytical Plate-Beam Super-Element, 1995; Hydroelasticity of Rotating Bodies-Theory and Application, 1996; Vibration of Elastic Spherical Shell in Bubbly Layer, 1996; Sub-Region Isoparametric Spline Element Analysis of Strength and Stability of Ring-Stiffened Combined Shell of Revolution, 1998. Honours include: 1st Class Prizes, Ex Sci Pprs, Govt of Hubei, 1988, 1994; 1st Class Prize, Outstndng Tchng Contbrn, Navy of Chinese PLA. Memberships: Naval Archs and Marine Engrs; Marine Mechs Inst, CSNAME.

Hobbies: Music; Peking opera; Novels. Address: 339-100 Jiefang Avenue, Wuhan, Hubei 430033, China.

GUO Si-jia, b. 2 July 1934, Weifang, Shandong, China. Professor; Tutor. m. Cui Wei-xian, 1968, 2 d. Education: Grad, Beijing Agricl Univ, 1956. Appointments: Dpty Dir, Animal Husbandry & Vet Sept, Ningxia Agricl Coll, 1985-88; Vice Dir, Ningxia Animal Husbandry Bur, 1991-95; Hon Dir, Grassland Scis Inst, Ningxia Agricl Coll, 1995-. Publications include: Grassland Resources and Pastures Culture, 1989; Flora of Forage Plants in China, vol 1-6, 1973-95; Rangeland Resources of China, 1996; Resources of Forage Plants in Grassland China, 1996. Honours: Yng-Mid Age Specialist, Human Affairs Min of China, 1989; Adv Sci Rschr, Educn & Sci Technol Cmmn of China, 1990; Model Tchr Awd, Ningxia Govt, 1995. Memberships: Grassland Soc; Grassland Resource & Mngmt Acady Cmmn of China Grassland, vice chmn, 1994-; Grassland Assn of 5th Prov in NW China, advsr, 1992-. Hobbies: Music; Swimming. Address: Ningxia Animal Husbandry Bureau, 48 Yuhongge South Street, Yinchuan, Ningxia, China.

GUO Yanchang, b. 17 Dec 1938, Xinghua, Jiangsu, China. Research Fellow. m. Xiuhua Wang, 8 Feb 1967, 1 s. 2 d. Education: Stud, Nanjing Univ, 1960; PhD, 1982, Univ Coll London. Appointments: Engr, Nanjing Rsch Inst Elect Tech, 1980-87, Snr Engr, 1987-94, Rsch Fell, 1994-. Publications: Co-author, Fundamental Principles of Phased Array Antennas, 1972; Principles of Phased Array and Frequency Scanning Antennas, 1978; Handbook of Antenna Engineering, 1999. Honour: Sci and Tech Prog Awd, Min Electronics, 1983. Memberships: Fell, Chinese Inst Electronics; Snr Mbr, IEEE. Address: Nanjing Research Institute Electron Tech, PO Box 1313, 210013, Nanjing, Jiangsu, China.

GUO Zhenqian, b. Feb 1933, Henan Prov, China. Senator. Education: Bachelor's degree in For Trade, People's Univ, Beijing, China, 1950-54. Appointments: Pres, Hubei Provcl Branch, China Comm Bank, 1980-83; Dir Gen, Hubei Provcl Econ Cttee, Dpty Gov, Hubei Prov, Acting Gov, Hubei Prov, Gov, Hubei Prov, 1983-90; Dpty Gov, Cntrl Bank, China, 1990-94; Auditor Gen, Natl Audit Off, China, 1994-98; Mbr of Standing Cttee, Natl People's Congress, China, Vice Chmn, Finl & Econ Cttee, Natl People's Congress, China; Chmn, Budget Cttee, Natl People's Congress, China, 1998-; Snr Economist, Mbr 13th & 14th Cntrl Cttee, Chinese Communist Party.

GUO Zongru, b. 15 Jan 1938, Hebei, China. Academic Research. m. R Ouyang, 1 Oct 1967, 1 s, 1 d. Education: Grad Sch, Peking Union Med Coll. Appointments: Assoc Prof, 1985, Prof, 1988-. Publication: Medicinal Chemistry. Honour: Awd of Sci & Technol Progress, Min of Pub Hlth, China. Membership: Chinese Pharm Assn. Hobbies: Music; Sports. Address: c/o Institute of Materia Medica, 1 Xiannong Tan Street, Beijing, China.

GUOXUN Peng, b. 23 Aug 1937, Sichuan, China. Professor. m. 30 Dec 1965, 1 d. Education: Dip, Tsinghua Univ, 1960; Visng Schl, Politecnico di Milano, Italy, 1979-81. Appointments: Techn, Design and Rsch Inst of Nuclear Engrng, 1960-70; Prof, Northwest Inst of Light Ind, 1970-, Pres, 1985-96. Publications include: Design of Packaging Machines, 1989; Packaging Dynamics, 1989; Design of Cam Mechanisms in Automotive Machines, 1990. Honours: 1st Prize, Splendid Works, Shaanxi Prov, 1986; Splendid Packaging Worker, 1987; 2nd Sci and Technol Progress Awd, Shanxi Prov, 1995. Memberships include: Dpty Dir, Design Subcttee of Mech Engrng Acady; Dpty Dir, China Packaging and Food Machinery Acady; Dpty Dir, China Light Ind Machinery Assn; Pres, China Leather Acady, 1994-. Address: Northwest Institute of Light Industry, West Renmin Road, No 49, Xianying, Shaanxi 712081, China.

GUPTA Chiranjib Kumar, b. 12 Jan 1939, Commilla, Bangladesh. Metallurgical Engineer. m. Chandrima, 1 s. Education: BSc, Met Engrng, 1962, PhD, Met Engrng, 1969, Banaras Hindu Univ. Appointments: Hd, Metallurgy Div, Bhabha Atomic Rsch Cntr; Assoc Dir, Materials Grp, BARC, 1990-92; Dir, Materials Grp, BARC, 1993-.

Publications: Honours: Binani Gold Medal, 1972; Bralco Gold Medal, 1974; Binani Gold Medal, 1978; Best Metallurgist Awd, 1978; Disting Alumnus Awd, 1981; Vasvik Rsch Awd, 1983; Materials Rsch Soc of India Medal, 1990; Indep Day Awd, 1993; Binani Medal, 1993; Hindustan Zinc Gold Medal, 1995. Memberships: Fell, Indian Natl Acady of Engr; Cncl Mbr, Indian Inst of Metals; Pres, Mumbai Chapt of Materials Rsch Soc of India. Hobbies: Reading; Writing. Address: Materials Group, Bhabha Atomic Research Centre, Trombay, Mumbai 400085, India.

GUPTA Chittar Mal, b. 1 Sept 1944, Bharatpur, Rajasthan. Scientist. m. Savita Gupta, 26 June 1970, 1 s, 1 d. Education: MSc; PhD. Appointments: Sci, CDRI, Lucknow, 1978-92; Dir, IMTech, Chandigarh, 1992-97; Dir, Cntrl Drug Rsch Inst, Lucknow, 1997-. Honours: INSA Young Sci Medal in Chem, 1974; Shanti Swarup Bhatnagar Prize in Biol Sci, 1985; FICCI Awd in Life Sci, 1994-95. Memberships: Fell, Indian Acady of Scis, 1986; Fell, Indian Natl Sci Acady, 1988; Soc of Biol Chems of India, 1992; Indian Biophys Soc, 1992; Indian Pharmacological Soc, 1997. Hobbies: Reading; Writing. Address: Central Drug Research Institute, Chattar Manzil, PO Box 173, Lucknow 226 001, Uttar Pradesh, India.

GUPTA Dipak, b. 2 Oct 1967, Calcutta. Executive Manager. m. Archana, 21 Oct 1995. Education: BSc, Econs, Hons; MBA, Special in mktng. Appointments: Flex Inds Ltd; Jnt Exec Mngr, Designation. Memberships: Confedn of India Inds Fedn of Indian Chmbr of Comm and Ind. Hobbies: Dramatics; Music; Cricket. Address: R-32 Sector XI, Noida (UP) India.

GUPTA Rajen K, b. 8 Apr 1950. Academic. m. Indu, 30 Nov 1983, 1 s, 1 d. Education: BTech; Fell, IIM Ahmedabad. Appointments: Covenanted Off, State Bank of India; Corporate HRD Mngr; Asst Prof; Assoc Prof; Prof. Publication: Implementing Human Resources Development: Action Research into the Process. Honours: Natl Schlsp; IIT Kanpur Schlsp; Dissertation Proposal Awd. Memberships: Academy of Mngmt; Indian Soc, Applied Behavioral Sci; Natl HRD Network. Listed in: International Directory of Business and Management Scholars and Research. Address: Management Development Institute, PB No 60, Gurgaon-122001, India

GUPTA Rakesh, b. 15 May 1954, Ajmer, India. Industralist. m. Usha, 4 Dec 1977, 2 d. Education: BE, hons, Electron Engrng, Birla Inst of Technol & Sci, India. Appointments: Mktng Offr, Electrons Corp of India Ltd, 1976-83; Prodn Mngr, Rajasthan Electron & Instruments Ltd, 1983-89. Memberships: Instn of Engrs, India. Hobbies: Bridge; Reading. Address: 25 Industrial Area, Makhupura, Ajmer 305001, India.

GUPTA Sunil Kumar, b. 13 Oct 1928 Sihipasha. Politician. m. Kamal Gupta, 1958, 4 s, 2 d. Education: Brajo Mohan Coll Barisal. Appointments: VP Barisal Dist Cttee, 1957-72; VP Cntrl Cttee, 1973; Min of State for Pet and Mineral Rescs, 1979, 1985; Min for Min of Comms, 1985-86; Min of Textiles, 1986-88; Min of Yth and Sports, Mar-Dec 1988; Min of Fisheries and Livestock, 1980-90. Memberships: Mbr East Pakistan Dem Party, 1950; Mbr Natl Awami Party; Fmr mbr Cntrl Cttee Bangladesh Nationalist Party. Hobbies: Reading; Gardening; Music. Address: National Audit Office of the People's Republic of China, 1 Beiluyuan, Zhanlan Road, Xicheng District, People's Republic of China.

GUPTA Yogesh Chandra, b. 15 May 1946, Hathras, India. Teacher. m. Sushma, 19 Feb 1972, 1 s, 1 d. Education: PhD; DSc. Appointments: Rdr, Hd, Zool Dept, BSA Coll, Madras. Honours: Best Sec of Rotary Dist. Memberships: Rotary Club. Address: 2096 Dampier Nagar, Mathura, UP 281001, India.

GURGULINO DE SOUZA Heitor, b. 1 Aug 1928. United Nations Official. m. Lilian Maria Quilici, 6 Jan 1960, 2 s. Education: BSc Maths 1949, Licenciado, Sch of Philos and Scis, Univ of MacKenzie, Sao Paulo, Brazil, 1950; Grad and Spec Courses, Solid State Phys and Nucl Phys, Aeronautics Inst of Technols, Jose dos Campos, Sao Paulo, Brazil; Univ of KS, USA and Van de Graaf Lab, Phys Dept, Univ of Sao Paulo, 1956-57. Appointments: Prog Spec, Interamn Sci Prog, Pan Amn Union, WA, DC, 1962-64; Hd, Unit of Educ and Rsch, Dept of Sci Affairs, Org of Amn States, WA DC, 1964-69; Rector, Fed Univ of Sao Carlos, State of Sao Paulo 1979-84; Dir, Dept of Univ Affairs, Min of Educ and Culture, Brasilia, 1972-74; Chmn, Interamn Cttee on Sci and Technol, Cncl for Educ, Sci and Culture, OAS, WA DC, 1974-77; Dir, CNPq, Natl Cncl for Sci and Technological Dev, Brasilia, 1975-78; Spec Advsr to Pres of CNPq, Brasilia, 1979-80; VP, Intl Assn of Univ Pres, 1985-87; Pres, Grupo Univ Latinoamns, Caracas, 1985-87; VP, Fed Cncl of Educ of Brazil, 1980-82; Mbr, CFE, 1982-88; Rector, UN Univ, Tokyo, 1987-97; Spec Advsr to Dir Gen, UNESCO, Paris. Publications: Gamma-rays from the Proton Bombardment of Natural Silicon, 1957; Computers and Higher Education in Brazil, 1984; Present Status of Research in Latin America, 1986; Co-ed, book, Science Policy; Auth, chapt on Brazil, International Encyclopedia of Higher Education, 1978. Honours: Dr Hon Causa, Autonomous Univ, Guadalajara, Mexico, 1986; Dr Hon Causa, Fed Univ Esp Vitoria, Brazil, 1987; Hon Deg of Dr of Laws, CA State Univ, 1996. Hobbies: Swimming; Sailing; Music. Address: 24 Avenue Charles Floquet, 75007 Paris, France.

GURR Geoffrey Michael, b. 21 Dec 1959, Croydon, Surrey, Eng. Academic; Scientist. m. Donna Read, 1 s, 1 d. Education: BSc, Hons, Plymouth Polytech, 1981; PhD, Univ London, 1989; Dip, Imperial Coll, 1989; Grad Ctf, Educl Studies, Univ Sydney, 1998. Appointments: Rsch Sci, Natl Inst of Agricl Bot, Cambridge, Eng, 1982-89; Acad, Univ Melbourne, 1991-92, Univ New Eng, 1992-95, Univ Sydney, 1994-. Publications include: Habitat Manipulation and Natural Enemy Efficiency: Implications for the Control of Pests; Evolution of Arthropod Pest Management in Apples. Honour: Fell, Roy Entomol Soc, 1997. Memberships: Austl Entomol Soc; Entomol Soc of Am; Austl Plant Pathol Soc. Hobbies: Tae Kwon Do; Windsurfing; Fishing. Address: 22 Northstoke Way, Orange, NSW 2800, Australia.

GURRIA TREVINO Jose Angel, b. 8 May 1950 Tampico Tamaulipas State. Politician. m. Lulu Ululani Quintana Pali, 1973, 1 s, 2 d. Appointments: Dir Gen for Pub Credit Min of Fin, 1983-88; Under Sec for Intl Finl Affairs, 1989-92; Pres and CEO Natl Bank for For Trade - Bancomext - 1993; Pres and CEO Nac Financiera, 1993-94; Sec for For Affairs Natl Exec Cttee Instnl Revolutionary Party - PRI - Apr-Nov 1994; Min of For Affairs, 1994-. Publications: The Politics of External Debt, 1994; Articles on Mexican economy. Honours: Decorations from sev cos. Hobbies: Tennis; Reading; Swimming. Address: Foreign Affairs Secretariat, R Flores Magon 1, Ala "A", Nivel 4, 06995 Mexico City, Mexico.

GURVICH (Gurvich-Lishchiner) Sophia D, b. 19 Sept 1929, Moscow, USSR. History; Criticism of Literature. m. Joseph Gurvich, 19 July 1955, decd 1994, 1 s. Education: Grad, Moscow Univ; PhD in Lit, Inst of World Lit, Moscow, Acady of Sci, USSR. Appointments: Tchr, 1951-55; Sci Wrkr, after that grp ldr, Inst of World Lit, Moscow, 1955-90; Sci Advsr, Univ of Tel-Aviv, Israel. Publications: Over 130 rsch books and pprs on Russian lit of XIX century and its intl significance. Membership: Israel Assn of Slavic Lit. Address: PO Box 15245, Rishon Le Zion, 75051, Israel.

GUSSAKOVSKY Eugene, b. 29 Nov 1946, Tashkent, USSR. Biophysicist. m. Shifer L, 6 July 1967, 1 s. Education: MSc, Novosibirsk State Univ, USSR, 1970; PhD, 1976, DSc, 1987, Inst Biochem, Tashkent, USSR. Appointments: Inst Biochem, Tashkent, USSR, 1970-86; Inst Virology, Tashkent, USSR, 1986-91; Bar Ilan Univ Ramat Gan, Israel, 1991-; Inst Hort, The Volcanic Cntr, Bet Dagan, Israel, 1992-. Publications: 64 articles in sci jrnls; 2 books; 1 patent. Honours: Fellshps: Wolfson Fndn, 1991-95; Eurn Molecular Bio Orgn, 1995, 1998; Giladi Fndn, 1995-98; Kamea Prog, 1998-. Memberships: NY Acady Scis, NYC, 1996; Amn Soc Photobiology and Eurn Soc Photobiology; Intl Soc Photosynthesis; Natl Geographic Soc, USA. Hobbies: Music; Paintings;

Literature; Arts. Address: Department of Life Sciences, Bar Ilan University, Ramat Gan 52900, Israel.

GUST Ian David, b. 15 Jan 1941, Melbourne, Aust. Doctor. m. Dianne, 21 Feb 1969, 4 s, 1 d. Education: MDBS; Dip Bact; BS; FRACP; FRCPA; FTS. Appointments: Dir, MacFarlane Burnet Cntr of Medl Rsch, 1985-90; R&D Dir, CSL Ltd, 1990-. Publications: 3 books, over 300 rsch pprs. Honour: AO, 1991. Membership: Pres, Austl Soc for Microbiology, 1998-2000. Hobbies: Golf; Walking; Travel; Reading. Address: 8 The Boulevard, Ivanhoe, Vic 3079, Australia.

GUTHRIE James Ernest, b. 25 June 1952, Melbourne, Victoria, Australia. Accountant. Ptnr, Dianne Hill, 3 d. Education: BBus, Acctng, Roy Melbourne Inst of Technol, 1976; Grad Dip in Acctng, Deakin Univ, 1980; MBus, Curtin Univ, 1983; PhD, Univ of NSW, Aust, 1995. Appointments include: Cnslt, Pub Accts Cttee, Canberra; Indl Rels Commn, NSW; NSW Environmental Plng Auth; Org for Econ Coop and Dev; Dir, Sector Rsch Pty Ltd; Assoc Dir, Cntr for Socl and Environmental Acctng Rsch, Dundee Univ, Scotland. Publications include: Books: The Public Sector: Contemporary Readings in Accounting and Auditing, 1990; Making the Australian Public Sector It Count in the 1990s, 1993; Australian Public Service: Pathways to Change in the 1990s, 1993; Articles: Public Financial Management Changes in OECD Nations, 1998; Public Sector Financial Management Developments in Australia and Britain: Trends and Contradictions, 1996. Honours: Roy Melbourne Inst of Technol Centenary Medallion, 1987; Best Eds Prize, 1993, 1995. Memberships: Fell, Austl Soc of CPAs; Fell, Inst of Chartered Accts, Aust; Austl Evaluation Soc; Roy Inst Pub Inst Aust; Acctng Assn of Aust and NZ; Joint Ed, Acctng, Auditing & Accountability Jrnl; Joint Fndng Ed, Socl Acctng Monitor Newsletter. Hobbies: Music; Reading; Cooking; Push bike racing. Address: Macquarie University Graduate School of Management, North Ryde, NSW 2109, Australia.

GUTHRIE Roy David, b. 29 Mar 1934, Leatherhead, England. Consultant. m. Lyn, 21 May 1982. Education: BSc; PhD; DSc. Appointments: Rsch Offr, Shirley Inst, Manchester, 1958-60; Asst Lectr, Lectr, Dept of Chem, Univ Leicester, 1960-63; Lectr, Rdr, Sch of Molecular Scis, Univ Sussex, 1963-73; Fndn Prof, Sch of Sci, Chmn, Sch of Sci, 1973-78, Pro Vice Chan, 1980-81, Emer Prof, 1982, Griffith Univ, Brisbane; Sec Gen, Roy Soc of Chem, London, 1982-86; Pres, NSWIT, 1986-87; Vice Chan, 1988, Emer Prof, 1996, Univ of Technol, Sydney. Publications: Sev articles in profl sci jrnls. Honours: Fell, Austl Acady of Technol Scis & Engrng, Roy Soc of Chem, Roy Austl Chem Inst, Austl Inst of Mngmt, Roy Soc of Arts, Austl Inst of Co Dirs; AM, 1996. Memberships: Sev. Hobbies: Theatre; Music; Tai-chi, Croquet. Address: PO Box 403, Pymble, NSW 2073, Australia.

GUTNICHENKO Larisa, b. 12 May 1947. Education: Deg, Jurisp, Judge Issyk-Kulskogo oblast crt, 1974-76. Appointments: Pres, Prevalskogo Cty Crt, 1976-83; Dpty to Pres of Supreme Crt, Govt of Kyrgyzstan, Bishkek, 1984-95; Min of Jus, 1995-. Address: Ministry of Justice, ul Orozbekov 37, Bishkek 720400, Kyrgyzstan.

GUZMAN MORALES Jaime, b. 20 Nov 1949. Minister of National Defence. Education: Capt Gen Gerardo Barrios's Mil Sch. Appointments: Num mil posts, 1971-94; Rank of Gen, 1995. Address: Ministry of National Defence, Alameda Dr Manuel Enrique Araújo, Km 5, Carretera a Santa Tecla, San Salvador, El Salvador.

GYIBUG Puncog Cedain, b. 1930 Tibet. Politician. Appointments: Vice-Chmn of People's Govt of Tibet Autonomous Reg, 1983-; Dep for Tibet to 7th NPC, 1988. Address: People's Government of Tibet Autonomous Region, Lhasa, People's Republic of China.

GYNGELL Bruce, b. 8 July 1929 Melbourne. Broadcasting Executive. m. (1) Ann Barr, 1 s, 2 d; (2) Kathy Rowan, 2 s. Education: Sydney Univ; Columbia Univ NY. Appointments: Trainee Austl Brdcstng Corpn,

1950; Joined Channel Nine tv, 1956; First person to appear on Austl tv, 16 Sep 1956; Prog Dir, 1956-66; Mngng Dir, 1966-69; Dep Mngng Dir ATV Eng, 1972-76; Dep Mngng Dir ITC Entertainment, 1972-75; Chmn Network Plng Cttee, 1974-76; Chmn Austl Brdcstng Tribunal, 1977-80; Chf Exec Spec Brdcstng Service - tv service for ethnic minorities - 1980; Mngng Dir tv-am, 1984-92; Chmn, 1990-92; Exec Chmn Nine Network Aust Ltd, 1993-94; Mngng Dir Yorkshire-Tyne Tees tv, 1995-97. Hobbies: Surfing; Skiing; Jogging; Yoga. Address: c/o Yorkshire Television, The Television Centre, Leeds LS3 1JS, England.

H

HA Chang-Sik, b. 30 Jan 1956, Pusan, Korea. Professor. m. Sheonja Han, 13 Jan 1983, 1 s, 2 d. Education: BS, Pusan Natl Univ, 1978; MS, 1980, PhD, 1987, Korea Adv Inst of Sci and Technol. Appointments: Prof, Pusan Natl Univ, Korea, 1982-99; Dept Chmn, Polymer Sci and Engrng, Pusan Natl Univ, 1992-94; Visng Schl, Univ of Cincinnati, 1988-89, Stanford Univ, 1997-98. Publications: Over 200 sci pprs in profl jrnls. Honours: Best Ppr of the Yr, Korean Inst of Rubber Ind, 1990; Polymer Sci Awd, Polymer Soc of Korea, 1994. Memberships: Editl Advsry Bd, Materials Sci Forum; Amn Chem Soc; Soc of Polymer Sci, Japan; Polymer Soc, Korea. Hobbies: Climbing; Classical music. Address: Department of Polymer Science and Engineering, Pusan National University, Pusan 609-735, Korea.

HA Van Lau, b. 9 Dec 1918 Thua Thien. Diplomatist. m. 3 c. Appointments: Served with Viet Nam People's Army, 1945-54; A Deleg of Dem Repub of Viet Nam to Geneva Conf on Indochina, 1954; Deleg Paris Conf on Viet Nam, 1968; Asst Min of For Affairs, 1973; Amb to Cuba, 1974-78; Perm Rep to UN, 1978-82; Dep Min for For Affairs, 1982-84; Amb to France - also accred to Belgium, The Netherlands, Luxembourg - 1984-89. Address: c/o Ministry of Foreign Affairs, Dien Bien Phu, Hanoi, Viet Nam.

HABIB Randa, b. 16 Jan 1952 Beirut Lebanon. Journalist. m. Adnan Gharaybeh, 1973, 1 s, 1 d. Education: French Lycee; Rio de Janeiro; Univ of Beirut. Appointments: Corresp Agence France Press, AFP, 1980; Dir and Hd AFP Off Amman, 1987-; Corresp Radio Monte Carlo, 1988-; Also for sev intl publrs and TV. Publications: Articles in Politique Internationale. Hobbies: Reading; Swimming; Painting. Address: Agence France Press, Jebel Amman, 2nd Circle, P O Box 3340, Amman, Jordan.

HABUKA Hitoshi, b. 25 Mar 1957, Akita, Japan. Researcher. m. 19 Apr 1986, 1 s, 1 d. Education: BA, Niigata Univ, 1979; Master Deg, Kyoto Univ, 1981; Dr Deg, Hiroshima Univ, 1996. Publications: over 10 pprs in sci jrnls. Hobbies: Science; Music. Address: 1-35-4 Asakura, Maebashi Gunma 371-0811, Japan.

HACKMAN Gene, b. 30 Jan 1930 San Bernardino CA. Actor. m. Fay Maltese, 1956, div 1985, 1 s, 2 d. Education: Studied acting at the Pasadena Playhouse. Films incl: Lillith, 1964; Hawaii, 1966; Banning, 1967; Bonnie and Clyde, 1967; The Split, 1968; Downhill Racer, 1969; I Never Sang For My Father, 1969; The Gypsy Moths, 1969; Marooned, 1970; The Hunting Party, 1971; The French Connection, 1971; The Poseidon Adventure, 1972; The Conversation, 1973; Scarecrow, 1973; Zandy's Bridge, 1974; Young Frankenstein, 1974; The French Connection II, 1975; Lucky Lady, 1975; Night Moves, 1976; Domino Principle, 1977; Superman, 1978; Superman II, 1980; All Night Long, 1980; Target, 1985; Twice in a Lifetime, 1985; Power, 1985; Bat 21 Supmeran IV, 1987; No Way Out, 1987; Another Woman, 1988; Mississippi Burning, 1988; The Package, 1989; The Von Metz Incident, 1989; Loose Connections, 1989; Full Moon in Blue Water, 1989; Postcards from the Edge, 1989; Class Action, 1989; Loose Canons, 1990; Narrow Margin, 1990; Necessary Roughness, 1991; Company Business, 1991; The William Munny Killings, 1991; The Unforgiven, 1992; The Firm, 1992; Geronimo Wyatt Earp, 1994; Crimson Tide, The Quick and the Dead, 1995; Get Shorty, Birds of a Feather, Extreme Measures, 1996; The Chamber, 1996; Absolute Power, 1996; Twilight, 1998; TV incls many guest appearances on US series; Also My Father, My Mother CBS Playhouse, 1968 and Shadow on the Land, 1971. Stage Plays incl: Children From Their Games, 1963; Cass Henderson in Any Wednesday, 1964; Poor Richard, 1964; Death and the Maiden, 1992. Honours: Acady Awd for Best Actor; New York Film Critics' Awd; Scarecrow; Natl Review Bd Awd for Mississippi Burning, 1988; Berlin Film Awd, 1989; Acady Awd for The Unforgiven, 1993. Address: c/o Barry

Haldeman, 1900 Avenue of the Stars, Suite 2000, Los Angeles, CA 90067, USA.

HACOBIAN Steven, b. 29 Oct 1916, Soerabaia, Dutch East Indies. Retired Reader in Physical Chemistry. m. Wendy Isabel Wyatt Warren, 19 Sept 1950, 2 s. Education: BSc hons 1950, MSc 1951, PhD 1954, DSc 1978, Univ of Sydney. Appointments: Indl Chem, Shell Co, Singapore, 1937-41; Prisoner of War, 1942-45; Rsch Stud then Tchng Fell, 1950-54, Lectr 1954-63, Snr Lectr in Phys Chem 1963-79, Rdr in Phys Chem 1979-81 retired, Hon Assoc in Phys Chem 1982-89, Univ of Sydney; Rsch into New Riemann Quantum Electrodynamical Theory of Nuclear Quadrupole Spectra. Publications: Contbr to profl jrnls; Abstracts; Presentations. Honour: Long Serv Medal, 30 yrs, awd'd to staff by Canc Sir Hermann Black, Univ of Sydney. Memberships: Fell, Roy Aust Chem Inst; Fell, The Roy Soc of Chem, London; Aust and NZ Assn for Advancement of Scis; Amn Physl Soc. Hobbies: Art (oil painting); Classical music (piano). Address: 14 Stephen Street, Katoomba, Blue Mountains, NSW 2780, Australia.

HADAGAU Prakesh Basappa, b. 12 Feb 1958, Nalaudi (Karnataka), India. Library and Information Scientist. m. Sujata, 3 May 1984, 2 s. Education: BS; BLISc; Drp Mngmt; MLISc. Appointments: Lib & Info servs in var orgns incl: IRMA, 1980; ERDA, 1982; CIS, 1983; GAU, 1988; C-DOT, Mngr Lib & Info Systems, 1992. Honour: Best individual perf C-DOT. Memberships: IASLIC; BMA; KALA; ITILIC Forum; AGLIS. Hobbies: Reading; Social service; Agriculture. Address: Manager (Library and Information Systems), C-DOT 71/1, Millers Road, Sneha Complex, Bangalore, India.

HADINOTO Kusudiarso, b. 13 Aug 1930, Semarang, Java. Senior Business Consultant. m. Nini, 30 Oct 1954, 1 s, 1 d. Education: MSc.E.E, Delft Technol Univ, Netherlands, 1955; War Coll, Jakarta, 1968; Pub and Bus Mngmt Sch, 1974; Eur.Ing. FEANI Chart Profl Engrs, Eur, 1987. Appointments: Univ Prof, Elec Engrng; Sci Advsr, Air Force; Fndr, Dir, Power Rsch Lab, Elec Utility; Dir-Gen, Mfng. Publications: Sci pprs to sci and technol congresses. Honour: Dev Medal, Repub of Indonesia. Memberships: Netherlands Roy Inst of Engrs; FEANI Eurn Chart Profl Engrs; Indonesian Soc of Engrs. Hobbies: Reading; Writing. Address: Jalan Danau Tondano 5, Pejompongan 10210, Jakarta, Indonesia.

HADLEE Sir Richard John, b. 3 July 1951 Christchurch. Cricketer. m. Karen Hadlee. Education: Christchurch Boys High Sch; Middle-order left-hand batsman; Right-arm fast-medium bowler; Played for Canterbury, 1971-72 to 1988-89; Nottinghamshire, 1978-1987; Tasmania, 1979-80; Played in 86 Tests, 1972-73 to 1990; Scoring 3124 runs - average 27.1 - and taking then world record 431 wickets - average 22.9; First to take 400 Test wickets - at Christchurch in Feb 1990 in his 79th Test; Took 5 or more wickets in an innings a record 36 times in Tests; Highest test score 151 v Sri Lanka Colombo, 1987; Best test bowling performance 9-52 v Aust Brisbane, 1985-86; Toured Eng, 1973, 1978, 1983, 1986, 1990; Scored 12052 first-class runs - 14 hundreds - and took 1490 wickets inclng 5 or more in an innings 102 tims; Achieved Double - 1179 runs and 117 wickets - 1984. Publications: Rhythm and Swing - autobiog - 1989. Address: Box 29186, Christchurch, New Zealand.

HADLEY Margaret, b. 4 May 1950. Principal. m. Patrick, 20 Oct 1978, 2 s. Education: BSc Hons (Wales); MSc (Reading). Appointments: Dir, Curric and Hd Sci Melbourne CEGGS, 1991-94; Lectr, LaTrobe Univ, 1989-91; Dauntseys Sch, Wiltshire, Eng, 1985-89, Hd Sci New Engl Sch, Kuwait, 1977-79; Hd Biol, Llandysul Gram Sch, Wales, 1974-77; Prin, Wenona Girls Sch, N Sydney, 1995-. Memberships: MACE; AHIGS; AHISA; ASERA; Roy Soc (Vic). Hobbies: Reading; Sport; Music; Clubs. Address: Wenona School Ltd, 176 Walker Street, North Sydney, NSW 2060, Australia.

HAFIZ Sulayman. Appointment: Min of Fin, Jordan, 1997-. Address: Ministry of Finance, POB 85, Amman 11118, Jordan.

HAGGER Alfred James, b. 16 Nov 1922, Melbourne, Aust. Economist. m. Elsie Rona Clark, 13 Aug 1950, 1 s, 1 d. Education: BCom (Melb), 1942; PhD (London), 1952. Appointments: C'wlth Pub Serv, 1942-48; Personal Asst to Sir Douglas Copland, Vice-Chan, Austl Natl Univ, 1948-49; Lectr, 1952-54, Snr Lectr, 1954-64, Rdr, 1964-82, Dept of Econs, Univ of Tasmania; Dir, Cntr fr Regl Econ Analysis; Tutor in Quantitative Methods I, under contract to AIDAB, Riawunna and Dept of Employment Educ and Trng, 1991-92. Publications include: (books) Unemployment and Inflation in the UK (co-auth), 1983; Macroeconometric Systems (co-auth), 1983; A Guide to Australian Economic and Social Statistics, 1983; Principles of Economics (co-auth), 1985; Contbns to books; Articles in profl jrnls. Memberships: Acady of the Socl Scis Aust, elected, 1980. Address: Centre for Regional Economic Analysis, GPO Box 252-90, Hobart, Tas 7005, Australia.

HAHN Yong Ki, b. 21 Jan 1938, Seoul, Korea. Businessman; Chairman. m. 30 Oct 1967, 1 d. Education: Degree of Engl Lit, Hankuk Univ For Studies. Appointments: Sales Agt, Enso, 1978; Chmn, Enso-Eurocan-Bumjin Co Ltd. Memberships: Kt. 1st Class, Order of Lion of Finland, 1995; Awd of Merit by Assn of For Trade Agcy, 14 Feb 1985, 22 Feb 1988, 10 Apr 1991. Hobby: Golf. Address: 306-903, SamHwan Apt 877, Changdong-Dong, Ilsan-KU, Koyang-Si, Korea.

HAHNEL Roland, b. 5 Oct 1931. Biochemist. m. Erika Thoss, 31 Mar 1955, 2 d. Education: Dip Chem, 1955, Dr rer nat, 1958, Univ of Halle-Wittenberg, Halle, Germany; Fell, Austl Assn of Clinl Biochems, 1975. Appointments: Biochem, Dept of Dermatology, Univ of Halle, 1955-59; Biochem, Dept of Ophth, Univ of Frankfurt, 1959-60; Rsch Fell, Queen Elizabeth Coronation Gift Fund Trust, Perth, Aust, 1961-66; Snr Lectr 1968-72, Assoc Prof 1972-89, Dept of Obstet and Gynae, Univ of WA; Assoc Prof, Dept of Path, Univ of WA, 1990-97; Visng Endocrinologist, King Edward Mem Hosp for Women, Subiaco, WA, 1968-90; Hon Rshc Fell, Cntr for Molecular Immunology and Instrumentation. Publications: Num publs on sci and med jrnls and books. Honours: Intl Fell, US Pub Hlth Serv, 1968; Yamagiwa-Yoshida Fell, Int Union Against Cancer, 1978; Bundesverdienstkreuz, Fed Repub of Germany, 1982, 1st Class, 1997; NY Acady of Scis. Membership: Pres, WA Goethe Soc Inc, 1975-. Listed in: Who's Who in the World; Who's Who in Australia; Who's Who in Science and Engineering. Hobbies: Music; Literature; Art. Address: 27 Templetonia Crescent, City Beach, WA 6015, Australia.

HAIDARI Iqbal, b. 25 July 1929. Research Writer; Publisher. m. Noor Begum, 12 Nov 1955, 1 s, 1 d. Education: MA, Econs; BA, hons. Appointments: Dir, 1956-59, Trade and Ind Ed, 1960-65, Econ Review Ed, 1970-, Franco Feri & Co Ltd; Corresp, Bus Asia, 1970-90; Bus Intl Corresp, Weekly NY, Weekly Hong Kong. Publications include: Coal and Coal-Based Power Projects, 1995; Cotton Textile Industry in Pakistan - II, 1995; Sugar Industry in Pakistan, 1996; Fertilizer Industry in Pakistan, 1996; Power Generation in Private Power Sector, 1996; Food Processing Industry, 1998; Automobile Industry, 1998; Cotton Textile Industry, 1998; Top 100 Companies in Pakistan, 1999; Cement Industry in Pakistan, 1999; Petroleum Industry in Pakistan, 1999. Memberships: Soc for Intl Devel; Thinkers Forum. Hobbies: Poetry; Social service; Literature. Address: Al-Masiha Building, 3rd Floor, 47 Abdullah Haroon Road, PO Box 7843, Karachi 74400, Pakistan.

HAIG Albert Roland, b. 11 Oct 1968, Newcastle, Aust. Neuroscientist. Education: BMedSci (Hons); PhD Student, Univ of Sydney. Appointments: Sci Offr, Commonwealth Sci and Indl Rsch Orgn (CSIRO) Div of Radiophysics; Sci Offr, Cognitive Neuroscience Unit, Westmead Hosp. Publications include: 8 articles to profl jrnls. Honour: 20th Century Awd for Achievement, IBA. Memberships: Intl Orgn of Psychophysiology (IOP); FIBA;

Intl Soc of Neuroimaging in Psych (ISNIP); Australasian Soc for Psychophysiology; Societa Italian di Psicofisiologia; Trinitarian Bible Soc. Hobbies: Theology; Mathematics; Music. Address: 41 Bridge Street, Waratah, NSW 2298, Australia.

HAIRE Ian James Mitchell, b. 2 July 1946. Professor of Theology and College Principle. m. Mary Christine Davies, 28 June 1968, 2 d. Education: BA, 1969, MA, 1973, Worcester Coll, Univ of Oxford; Dipl, Hendrik Kraemer Inst, Leiden, 1972; PhD, Univ Birmingham, 1981. Appointments: Missionary (Theologian), Halmahera, Indonesia, 1972-85; Min, Darwin, 1985-86; Prof of New Testament Studies, Trinity Coll, Brisbane, 1987-; Dean, 1991-97, Pres, 1998- Brisbane Coll of Theol; Prin Trinity Coll, Brisbane, 1992-; Hd, Sch of Theol, Griffith Univ, Brisbane, 1993-; Adj Prof, Griffith Univ, 1994-; Natl Pres Elect, 1997-2000, Pres, 2000- The Uniting Ch in Aust. Publications: Book: The Character and Theological Struggle of the Church in Halmahera, Indonesia, 1941-79, 1981, trans'd into Indonesian, 1998 ; Academic articles. Honours: Open Exhibnr, Worcester Coll, Univ of Oxford, 1965-69; Hon DD, Presby Theol Fac of Ireland, Belfast, 1999. Memberships: Austl and NZ Soc for Theol Studies, Pres, 1992-96; Griffith Asia Pacific Cncl; The Intl Reformed Theol Inst. Listed in: Men of Achievement; Who's Who in Australia; Who's Who in the World. Hobbies: Swimming; Hill-walking. Address: Griffith University, Trinity College, GPO Box 674, Brisbane, Queensland 4001, Australia.

HAKIMELAHI Gholam Hosein, b. 1 Jan 1954, Shiraz, Iran. Professor of Chemistry. m. Zahra Ramezani, 1 Jan 1975, 2 s. Education: BSc, Chem, Natl Univ; MSc, Chem, Shiraz Univ; PhD, Med Chem, McGill Univ. Appointments: Rsch Assoc, McGill Univ, 1980-82; Asst Prof, 1982-83, Assoc Prof, 1983-86, Prof, 1986-91, Shiraz Univ; Vis Prof, Acad Sinica, Taipei, 1992-; Tchr, Dominican Intl Sch, Taipei, 1994-. Publications: Num articles in profl jrnls. Honours: Best Rschr Awd, Min of Sci and Educ, Iran, 1983-85; Best Inventor Awd, Iranian Acady of Sci, 1986; Best Inventor Awd, Iranian Acady of Sci, 1986; Iranian Chem Soc Awd, 1990; French Med Fndn Awd, 1991; Best Tchr Awd, 1997-98. Memberships: Swiss Chem Soc; NY Acady of Scis. Address: Dominican International School, 76 Tah Chih Street, Taipei, Taiwan.

HAKSAR Parmeshwar Narain, b. 4 Sep 1913 Gujranwala Punjab. Government Official; Former Diplomat. m. Urmila Sapru - dec - 1952, 2 d. Education: Univ of Allahabad; Univ Coll London; London Sch of Econs Lincoln's Inn. Appointments: Elected to Dip Conf for Revision of Red Cross Conventions, 1949; Joint Sec in charge of Admin Min of External Affairs, 1959-60; Served as Amb and High Commnr in var cos, 1960-67; Prin Sec to PM, 1967-73; Chf Negotiator India-Pakistan-Bangladesh, 1972-73; Dep Chmn Plng Commn with Cabinet rank Bangladesh, 1972-73; Dep Chmn Plng Commn with Cabinet rank, 1975-77; Chmn Giri Inst, 1976-; VP Cncl of Sci and Tech, 1975-77; Co-Chmn Indo-Soviet Jnt Commn, 1975-77; Fmr Chmn Natl Labour Inst; Co-signatory Global Initiative for Restoration of Morality Tolerance and Humanism in 21st Century Seoul, 1995; Ed Mngmnt Dev; Dir Press Trust of India; VP Krishna Menon Memorial Soc; Chmn Soc Tech and Natl Dev New Delhi; Chmn New Delhi High Powered Cttee to review Sahitya Sangeet Natak and Lakit Akademis; Chmn Natl Sch of Drama; Chmn Cntr for Area Dev and Action Rsch Studies New Delhi; Convenor Sub-Grp Natl Integration Cncl Hony; Fmr Chan Jawaharlal Nehru Univ New Delhi. Publications: Premonitions, 1979; Reflections of our Times, 1982; Problems of Foreign Policy; One More Life - autobiog. Honours: Hon LLD - Patiala Utkal and Kashmir Univs; Hon DLit Andhra Pradesh Open Univ; Katuri Ranga Natl Awd, 1981; Soviet Land Nehru Awd, 1987; Indian Sci Cong Awd, 1989; Indira Gandhi Nalt Awd for Natl Integertion, 1989; Natl Kakasaheb Gadgil Awd, 1995. Hobbies: Cooking; Photography; Reading. Address: 4/9 Shanti Niketan, New Delhi 110021, India.

HALBERG Murray Gordon (Sir), b. 7 July 1933, Eketahuna, New Zealand. Former Champion Athlete. m. Phyllis Korff, 1959, 2 s, 1 d. Appointments: NZ 1 Mile Champion, 1954-57, 1960; NZ 3 Miles Champion, 1958-62; 1st NZer to break 4-minute mile: 3 minutes 57.5 seconds, Dublin, 6 Aug 1958; Empire Games: 5th, 1 mile, Vancouver, 1954; Gold Medal, 3 miles, 5th, 1 mile, Cardiff, 1958; Gold Medal, 3 miles, Perth, 1962; Olympic Games: 11th, 1500 m, Melbourne, 1956; Gold Medal, 5000 m, 5th, 10,000 m, Rome, 1960; 7th, 10,000 m, Tokyo, 1964; Set World Records: 2 miles, 8 minutes 30.0 seconds, Jyväskylä, Finland, 7 July 1961; 3 miles, 13 minutes 10.0 seconds, Stockholm, 25 July 1961; 4 x 1 mile (Gary Philpott, Halberg, Barry Magee, Peter Snell), 16 minutes 23.8 seconds, Dublin, 17 July 1961; Established The Halberg Trust, 1963, to hon sporting excellence, supporting children with disabilities. Honours: NZ Sportsman of Yr, 1958; MBE, 1961; Kt, 1987; Inducted NZ Sports Hall of Fame, 1990. Address: The Halberg Trust, PO Box 11-487, Ellerslie, Aukland, New Zealand.

HALDANE-STEVENSON James Patrick, b. 17 Mar 1910, Cardiff, Wales. Anglican Clergyman. m. (1) Leila Mary Flack, 5 Nov 1938, diss 1967, 2 s, 1 d, (2) Joan Talbot Smith, 6 Aug 1983. Education: BA 1933, MA 1941, St Catharine's Coll, Oxford, Eng; Queen's, Birmingham, 1935. Appointments: Westminster Bank, 1927-30; Roy Tank Corps, Supplementary Reserve, 1931-37; Ordained, 1935; Brit Army Chap, 1937-55 (served Dunkirk, Italy); Austl Ch, 1955; Vicar, N Balwyn, 1959-80; Austl Govt Immigration Dept, 1980-82. Publications: In Our Tongues, 1944; Religion and Leadership, 1948; Crisanzio, poems, 1948; Beyond the Bridge, autobiog, 1973; The Backward Look, family hist, 1976; Contbr to mags, jrnls and var vols of theol and poetry. Honours: Freeman of London, 1937; TD w Clasp, 1948; Order of St Stanislaus of Poland, Class II, 1995, Grand Cross, 1997. Memberships: Athenauem, UK; Inst of Roy Engrs (Assoc), UK; Melbourne Club; Pres, Canberra Welsh Soc, 1985-86. Hobbies: Wales, past and present; The SW Pacific. Address: 4/33 Bruce Street, Toorak 3142, Australia.

HALEFOGLU Vahit M, b. 19 Nov 1919 Antakya. Diplomatist. m. Zehra Bereket, 1951, 1 s, 1 d. Education: Antakya Coll; Univ of Ankara. Appointments: Turkish For Service, 1943-; Served Vienna Moscow Min of For Affairs London, 1946-59; Dir-Gen First Polit Dept Min of For Affairs, 1959-62; Amb to Lebanon, 1962-65; Accred to Kuwait, 1964-65; Amb to USSR, 1965-66; Amb to Netherlands, 1966-70; Dep Sec-Gen Polit Affairs Min of For Affairs, 1970-72; Amb to Fed Repub of Germany, 1972-83; Amb to USSR, 1982-83; Min of For Affairs, 1983-87; MP, 1986. Honours: Dr hc; Legion d'honneur; Other French Finnish British Lebanese Saudi and Italian decorations. Hobbies: Classical lit; Hist; Intl Rels; Music; Walking; Swimming. Address: Cumhuriyet Caddesi 47/2 Taksin, Istanbul, Turkey.

HALL Bernadette Mary, b. 6 Dec 1945, Alexandra, New Zealand. Teacher; Writer. m. John Raymond Hall, 13 Jan 1968, 2 s, 1 d. Education: MA, Hons. Appointment: Poetry Ed, Takahe Mag. Publications: Poetry: Heartwood, 1989; The Persistent Levitator, 1994; Still Talking, 1997. Plays: The Clotheshine, 1990; The Girl Who Sings Water Falls, 1992; Glad and the Angels, 1993; Questing (a musical), 1995. Honours: Writing Fellshp, Canterbury Univ, 1991; Robert Burns Fellshp, Otago Univ, 1996, IWP, IA, USA, 1997. Membership: NZSA. Address: 19 Bryndwr Road, Fendalton, Christchurch, New Zealand.

HALL Hubert Desmond, b. 3 June 1925, Portsmouth, Eng. Director. m. Mavis Dorothea, 24 Dec 1951. Appointments: Enlisted, RAF, 1942; Offr Cmdng 57 Sqdn, 1968-71, Gp Cap Nuc Ops SHAPE HQ 19, 1968-71, Offr Cmdng RAF Waddington, 1971-73, Natl Def Coll, India, 1974, MOD Dir of Establishments, Air Cmdr, Malta, 1977-79; Def Advsr, Aust, 1980-82; Air Vice Marshall (ret'd). Honours: Queens Commendation, 1962; AFC, 1963; CBE, 1972; CB, 1979; K St J, 1983. Memberships: FRAeS; Pres, Aust-Brit Soc, ACT; Dpty Chmn, St John Ambulance, ACT; Fell, Brit Inst of Mngmt; Fell, Austl Inst of Mngmt. Hobbies: Shooting; Gardening; Current affairs. Address: 7 Richardson Street, Garran, ACT 2605, Australia.

HALL Penelope (Penny) Jane, b. 30 Jan 1941. Writer. m. (1) Edward William Patterson, 15 June1962, (2) Robert James Hall, 25 Sept 1976, 1 s, 1 d. Education; BA; Dip Ed; Grad, Dip Tch Libn. Appointments: Sec; Tchr; Educ Offr; Tchr-Libn. Publications: Paper Chaser, 1987; Catalyst, 1989; Sylvia Mystery, 1990; Nim's Time, 1991; Better for Everyone, 1992; Contact, 1993; Cat-Face, 1994; Big Scream, 1995; Fraidy Cats, 1998. Memberships: Austl Soc of Auths; Children's Book Cncl of Aust. Listed In: Who's Who of Australian Children's Writers. Hobby: Children's Literature. Address: 116 Grosvenor Road, Lindfield, NSW 2070, Australia.

HALL Peter Ronald, b. 27 May 1952, Castlemaine, Vic, Aust. Member of Parliament. m. Kay, 26 Feb 1972, 1 s. Education: BA, Maths, Monash Univ; Dip Educ, Monash Univ. Appointment: Dpty Pres, Legis Cncl, 1986. Hobbies: Golf; Running; Furniture restoration. Address: 190 Franklin Street, Taralgon, Victoria 3844, Australia.

HALL Peter Gavin, b. 20 Nov 1951. Statistical Scientist. m. Jeannie Jean Chien Lo, 15 Apr 1977. Education: BS, Univ of Sydney, 1974; MSC, Austl Natl Univ, 1976; DPhil, Oxford, 1976. Appointments: Univ of Melbourne, 1976-78; Austl Natl Univ, 1978-. Creative works: Martingale Limit Theory and its Applications, 1980; Rates of Convergence on the Central Limit Theorem, 1982; Introduction to the Theory of Coverage Processes, 1988; The Bootstrap and Edgeworth Expansion, 1992. Honours: Austl Maths Soc Medal, 1986; Rollo Davidson Prize, 1986; Lyle Medal, 1989; Pitman Medal, 1990; Cttee of Pres of Statistical Socs Awd, 1989; Hannan Medal, 1995; Doct, honoris causa, Université Catholique de Louvain, 1997. Memberships: Fell, Roy Statistical Soc; Fell, Inst of Maths Stats, 1984; Fell, Austl Acady of Sci, 1987; Fell, Amn Statistical Assn, 1996. Listed in: Who's Who in Australia. Hobbies: Railways; Photography. Address: Centre for Mathematics and its Applications, Australian National University, Canberra, ACT 0200, Australia.

HALL Rodney, b. 18 Nov 1935. Writer; Musician; Actor. m. Maureen McPhail, 1962, 3 d. Education: Cty of Bath Sch for Boys UK; Brisbane Boy's Coll; Univ of Queensland. Appointments: Ldr Baroque Music Grp; Published over 500 poems in Aust, UK, USA, USSR, Philippines, France, India; Sev published books of poetry and novels; Creative Arts Fell ANU, 1968; Lit Bd Fell, 1974-80; Tutor New Eng Univ Summer Sch of Music, 1967-71, 1977-80; Lectr Dept of For Affairs; Recorder Canberra Sch of Music, 1979-83; Chmn Aust Cncl, 1991-94. Publications incl: Selected Poems, 1975; Just Relations, 1982; Kisses of the Enemy, 1987; Captivity Captive, 1988; The Second Bridegroom, 1991; The Grisly Wife, 1994; The Island in the Mind, 1996. Honours: Miles Frankln Awd, 1994. Address: Australia Council, 181 Lawson Street, Redfern, NSW 2016, Australia.

HALL-MATTHEWS Anthony Francis Berners, b. 14 Nov 1940, India. Bishop. m. Valerie Joan Cecil, 29 Jan 1966, 2 s, 3 d. Education: ThL, Austl Coll of Theol; G DipA, James Cook Univ, Cairns. Appointments: Ordained Deacon, 1963, Priest, 1964; Curate, Darwin NT, 1963-65; Chaplain, Carpentaria Aerial Mission, 1966-84; Bish's Chaplain, Thursday Island, 1966-67; Priest-in-Charge, St Peter's Normanton, 1968-76; Canon, All Souls and St Bartholomew's Cath, Thursday Island, 1970-76; Priest-in-Charge, Cooktown, 1976-82; Archdeacon, Cape York Peninsula, 1976-84; Bish of Carpentaria, 1984-96; Dir, Carpentaria Consulting Services, 1997-; Bish in Residence, Mareeba, Qld. Publications: Conflict in Agreement, An Analysis of the Cape York Peninsula Heads of Agreement, 1997. Memberships: Soc of St Francis, Third Order; Guild of Air Pilots and Air Navigators; VP, Cape York Peninsula Dev Assn, 1996-97. Hobbies: Flying; Reading; Making compost for organic gardening. Address: 5 Wattle Close, Yungaburra, Queensland 4872, Australia.

HALLIDAY Michael Alexander Kirkwood, b. 13 Apr 1925, Leeds, Eng. Emeritus Professor. Education: BA Hons, Mod Chinse, Univ of London, Eng, 1945-48; PhD, Univ of Cambridge, Eng, 1950-54. Appointments include: Asst Lectr Chinese Univ of Cambridge, 1954-58; Lectr, then Rdr, Gen Lings, Univ of Edinburgh, 1958-63; Rdr then Prof, Gen Lings, Univ Coll, London, 1963-70; Ling Soc of Am Prof, IN Univ, USA, 1964; Visng Prof of Lings, Yale Univ, USA, 1967; Visng Prof of Lings, Brown Univ, USA, 1971; Visng Prof of Lings, Univ of Nairobi, 1972; Prof, Lings, Univ of Sydney, 1976-87; Lee Kuan Yew Disting Vis, Natl Univ of Singapore, 1986; Visng Prof, Natl Univ of Singapore, 1990-91; Visng Prof, Intl Christian Univ, Tokyo, 1992. Publications include: The Language of Chinese Secret History of the Mongols, 1959; The Linguistic Sciences and Language Teaching, w Angus McIntosh & Peter Strevens, 1964; Learning How to Mean: Explorations in the Development of Language, London, 1975; Cohesion in English (w R Hasan), 1976; Language as Social Semiotic: The Social Interpretation of Language and Meaning, 1978; An Introduction to Functional Grammar, 1985, revised ed 1994; Spoken and Written Language, 1985; Writing Science: Literacy and Discursive Power, w J R Martin, 1993. Honours include: DLit, Univ of Birmingham, 1987; DLit, York Univ, Can, 1988; Pres, Eighth World Congress of Applied Lings, Univ of Sydney, Aust, 1987; Guest Prof, Peking Univ, 1995; Hon Dr of Engl Philology, Univ of Athens, Greece, 1995; DLit, Macquarie Univ, 1996; Fell, Aust Acady of the Humanities, 1979-; Corresp Fell of Brit Acady, 1989-; Hon Visng Prof, Macquarie Univ, 1989-; For Mbr of Acad Europaea, 1993-; Hon Fell, Cardiff Univ, 1998. Memberships: Philological Soc, GB; Yorkshire Dialect Soc; Ling Soc of Am, Hon Life Mbr 1978; Applied Lings Assn of Aust, VP 1976-87; Ling Assn of Can and USA, Pres 1982-83; Aust Lings Soc, Pres 1984-86. Address: PO Box 42, Urunga, NSW 2455, Australia.

HALLIDAY Peter Ernest, b. 19 Oct 1947, London, Eng. Police Officer. m. Chau Sin-Ping, 12 Jan 1993, 1 s, 1 d. Education: MA. Appointments: Insp, 1967; Chf Insp, 1975; Suptnt, 1977; Snr Suptnt, 1983; Chf Suptnt, 1988; Asst Commnr, 1996. Honours: Colonial Police Medal, 1980; Queens Police Medal, 1997. Memberships: Hong Kong Mental Hlth Assn; Scout Assn; Hong Kong Coll of Psych; Hong Kong Roy Asiatic Soc. Hobbies: Rock climbing; Scouting; Mental health; Singing; Reading; Research. Address: c/o Information Systems Wing, Police Headquarters, Wanchai, Hong Kong, China.

HALLORAN Richard, b. 2 Mar 1930, Washington, DC, USA. Journalist. 1 s, 2 d. Education: AB, dist, Govt Intl Rels, Dartmouth Coll, 1951; MA, East Asian Studies, Univ of Michigan, 1957; Columbia Univ, E Asia Inst, Ford Fndn Fellowship in Advd Intl Reporting, 1964-65. Appointments: Night Ed, Reporter, Editl Dir, The Michigan Daily, 1955-57; Reporter, Phila Bur, 1958-59, Asst For Ed, New York, 1960-61, Asia Bur Chief, Tokyo, 1962-64; Bus Week; Asia Spec, Washington, 1965-66, Tokyo Bur Chf, 1966-68, Econ Corresp, Washington, 1968-69, The Washington Post; Dip Corresp, 1969-70, Gen Assignment, Washington, 1970-72, Bur Chief for Japan, Korea, Taiwan, Cntrl Pacific, 1972-76, Washington: Investigative Reporter, 1976-77, Energy Corresp, 1978-79, Defense Corresp, 1979-84, Mil Corresp, 1985-89, The New York Times. Publications include: Japan: Images and Realities, 1969; Conflict and Compromise: The Dynamics of American Foreign Policy, 1973; To Arm a Nation: Rebuilding America's Endangered Defenses, 1986; Serving America: Prospects for the Volunteer Force, 1988. Honours: George Polk Awd, 1982; Gerald R Ford Prize, 1988; US Army Medal, for Outstndng Civilian Serv, 1989; Japan's Order of the Sacred Treasure, 1998; Hon Mbr, 100th Infantry Battalion Veterans Assn, 1998. Memberships: Woodrow Wilson Natl Fell, Princeton, NJ, USA; Fell, Furman Univ, SC, USA; Luther Coll, IA, USA; Union Coll, NY, USA; Univ of Redlands, CA, USA; Linfield Coll, OR, USA; Goucher Coll, MD, USA; Ohio Wesleyan Univ, OH, USA; McMurry Univ, TX, USA; Trinity Coll, VT, USA; St Mary's Coll, CA, USA; Wabash Coll, IN, USA; Adj Fell, Pacific Forum, Cntr for Strategic & Intl Studies; Adj Fell, Cntr for War, Peace and News Media; Visng Lectr, Univ

of Hawaii, Manoa. Address: 1065 Kao'opulu Place, Honolulu, HI 96825, USA.

HALLSWORTH Ernest Gordon, b. 1 Oct 1913, Ashton-under-Lyne, Eng. Science Consultant; Writer; Chairman, Hallsworth and Associates m. (1) Elaine Gertrude Seddon, 3 Dec 1943, dec 22 Apr 1970, 2 s, 1 d, 1 ss, (2) Merrily Jeanne Ramly, 18 Dec 1976, 1 sd. Education: BSc, 1st Class Hons, Agricl Chem, 1936; PhD, 1939, DSc, 1964, Univ of Leeds. Appointments: Asst Lectr, Univ of Leeds, 1936-40; Lectr, then Snr Lectr in Agricl Chem, Univ of Sydney, 1940-51; Prof of Agricl Chem, Univ of Nottingham, 1951-64; Chf, Div of Soils, CSIRO, Aust, 1964-73; Chmn, Land Resources Labs, CSIRO, 1973-78; Dir, Save Our Soils Proj, Intl Fedn of Insts of Adv Stdy and Hon Prof Fell, Sci Policy Rsch Unit, Univ of Sussex, Eng. Publications: (ed) Nutrition of the Legumes, 1957; (ed) Experimental Pedology, 1965; (co-auth) Handbook of Australian Soils, 1968; Land and Water Resources of Australia, Australian Academy of Technological Sciences, 1979; Socio-economic Effects and Constraints in Tropical Forest Management, 1982; Anatomy, Physiology and Psychology of Erosion, 1987. Honours: Sir Swire Smith Fell, Univ of Leeds, 1936; Membre d'Academie d'Agriculture de France, 1984; Hon Mbr, Intl Soc of Soil Sci, 1990; Prescott Medal, Austl Soc Of Soil Sci, 1986; Dokuchaev Medal, All-Union Soc of Soil Sci, 1990; Hon Mbr Austl Soc of Soil Sci, 1988. Memberships: Fell, Roy Soc of Chem, London; Mbr, Biochemical Soc, London; Mbr, Soc of Experimental Bio; Mbr, Royal Agricl Soc of Eng; Pres, Intl Soc of Soil Sci, 1964-68; Mbr of Cncl, Flinders Univ, 1963-79; Mbr of Cncl, Aust Acady of Technol Sci, 1977-79; Fell, World Acady of Art and Sci, 1993. Hobbies: Pedology; Tennis; Talking. Address: 8 Old Belair Road, Mitcham, SA, 5062, Australia.

HALPERN Georges Maurice, b. 7 Sept 1935, Warsaw, Poland. Healthcare Consultant. m. Emiko Oguiss, 24 May 1971, 2 d. Education: MD, Silver Medal, Fac of Med, Paris, France, 1964; PhD, Pharm Sci, Highest and Jury Hons, Fac of Pharm, Univ of Paris XI, France, 1992; DSc, Pharm Sci, 1992. Appointments: Asst, Neuroradiology, Gamma-Encephalography, Hôpital Pitie, Paris, 1964-65; Assoc Prof, Fndn Rothschild, Paris, Stanford Univ CA,1965-69; Hd, Allergy and Clinl Immun Clin, Paris, 1969-81; Visng Rsch Schl, 1981-83; Chf Sci Advsr, Allergenetics, Mountain View, CA, 1983-88; Prof of Med, Sch of Med, Univ of CA, 1983-97; Hon Prof of Med, Queen Mary Hosp, Univ of Hong Kong, 1990-; Visng Prof, Sci Rsch Cncl, Taipei, Taiwan, 1991-; Prof of Nutr, Coll of Agricl and Environl Sci, Univ of CA, 1992-97. Creative Works: Ginkgo, A Practical Guide; Cordyceps; 11 Books; 53 Book Chapters; 195 Orig Papers; Hundreds of Reviews and Abstracts. Honours: Spec Guest Awd, 1978; Medal of Vermeil, Cty of Paris, France, 1985; Five Pembicara Awd Peralmuni, 1987; Cmdr, Natl Order of the Merite Agricole, 1999. Memberships: Fell or Mbr of over 36 Acad of Sci Socs. Hobbies: Gourmet cooking; Wine tasting; Oenology. Address: 9 Hillbrook Drive, Portola Valley, CA 94028-7933, USA.

HALTON Brian, b. 9 Mar 1941, Accrington, Eng. Professor of Chemistry. m. Margaret P, 9 May 1970, 2 s. Education: BS (Hons) Southampton, UK; PhD (Organic Chem), Southampton, UK; DSc, Vic Univ of Wellington. Appointments: Postdoct Fell, 1966-67, Asst Prof, 1967-68, Univ FL, Gainesville; Lectr, 1968-71, Snr Lectr, 1972-76, Rdr, 1977-91, Prof, 1991-, Vic Univ; UNESCO Lectr, Univ NSW, Sydney, 1972; Visng Prof, Chem Dept, Univ UT, Salt Lake Cty, 1981-82, Chem Dept, Monash Univ, Melbourne, Aust, 1988-89, Max-Planck Inst, Mainz, Germany, 1993; Cntr for Molecular Arch, CQU, Qld Aust, 1999. Publications: Jt auth: Organic Photochemistry, 1974, 1987; Contbr, Chemistry of the Cyclopropyl Group, 1987, 1995; Series Ed, Advances in Strain and Organic Chemistry; Contbr, rsch articles to sci publs. Honours: Trustee, Newman Trust, 1980-; Fulbright Fellshp, NZ/US Educl Fndn, Univ UT, 1981-82; McCarthy Trust Fellshp, 1989. Memberships: Fell, Roy Soc of NZ, Pres, 1986-87, Cncl Mbr, 1978-81, 1981-87, 1989-91, Trustee, Chem Educ Trust, 1995-; Intl Union Pure and Applied Chem.

Address: 3 Scorian Close, Campbell Street, Karori, 6005 Wellington, New Zealand.

HALTON Charles Christopher, b. 4 Mar 1932. Commissioner. m. Shirley Harden, 9 June 1956, 2 s, 1 d. Education: BSc, Hons Maths, 1953, MSc, Maths, 1955, CEng, Univ of London. Appointments: Hd, Advd Systems and Rsch, Brit Aircraft Corp, Bristol, 1967; Dir, Sci and Technol Rsch Br, Canad Transp Commn, 1969-70; Snr Min, Exec Plcy Plng and Maj Projs, Canad Transp Min, 1970-73; Sec, Austl Dept of Transp, 1973-82; Sec, Dept of Def Support, 1982-84; Mbr, Austl Cl of Def, 1982-84; Chmn, C'wlth Review of Yth Allowance Admin, 1985-86; Aust Tstee, Intl Inst of Comms, 1986-; Sec, Dept of Comms, Aust, 1986-87; Dir, AUSSAT and Commnr, Austl Telecomms Commn, 1986-87; Chmn, C'wlth Task Force on Trng and Educ, 1987-88; Commnr, Overseas Telecomms Commn, 1987-89; Commnr, Snowy Mtns Hydro-elec Authy, 1987-93; Chmn, Employment and Skills Cncl of Aust, 1988-91; Chmn, Dev Allowance Authy, 1992-95; Mbr, Natl Invmnt Cncl of Aust, 1993-96; Chmn, C'wlth Review of Fire Plcy, 1997; Dir, Hydromet Pty Ltd, 1997- Chmn First Regional IIF Mngmnt Pty Ltd, 1997-; Dir, Sky Stn Aust Pty Ltd, 1998-. Honour: CBE, 1983. Memberships: FRAeS; FCIT; FIE (Aust); FAIE. Address: PO Box 234, Curtin, ACT 2605, Australia.

HALVORSEN Carl, b. 9 July 1912. Yachtsman and Boat Builder. m. Glenagh Brown, 25 Feb 1939, 1 d. Appointments: Dir, Halvorsen Gr Cos, 1938-; Austl Champion 5.5 metre yachts, 1967, 1981. Honour: Kt First Class Roy Norwegian Order of Merit, 1992. Hobbies: Yachting; Skiing. Address: 139 Eastern Road, Wahroonga, NSW 2076, Australia.

HAMAD Abdul-Latif Yousef al-, b. 1936. International Official; Banker; Politician. m. 4 children. Education: Claremont Coll CA; Harvard Univ. Appointments: Dir-Gen Kuwait Fund for Arab Econ Dev, 1963-81; Dir then Mngng Dir Kuwait Invmnt Co, 1963-71; Mngng Dir Kuwait Invmnt, 1965-74; Chmn Kuwait Prefabricated Bldg Co, 1965-78; Chmn United Ban of Kuwait Ltd London, 1966-84; Exec Dir Arab Fund for Econ and Socl Dev, 1972-81; Chmn Compagnie Arabe et Internationale d'Investissements Luxembourg, 1973-81; Min of Fin and Plng, 1981-83; Gov for Kuwait World Bank and IMF, 1981-83;Dir-Gen and Chmn Bd of Dirs Arab Fund for Econ and Socl Dev, 1985-; Chmn UN Cttee for Dev Plng, 1987. Memberships: Mbr Bd of Trustees Corporate Property Investors NY, 1975-; Mbr Governing Body Inst of Dev Studies Sussex UK, 1975-87; Mbr Ind Commn on Intl Dev Issues - Brandt Commn - 1976-79; Mbr Bd Intl Inst for Environment and Dev London, 1976-80; Mbr IFC Banking Advsry Bd Grp, 1987-; Mbr Advsry Grp on Finl Flows for Africa - UN - 1987-88; Mbr S Commn, 1987-89; Mbr Grp of Ten - African Dev Bank - 1987-; Mbr World Bank's Priv Sector Dev Review Grp, 1988-; Mbr UN Panel for Pub Hearings on Activities of Transnatl Corps in S Africa and Namibia, 1989-92; Mbr Bd Trustees of Stockholm Environment Inst, 1989-92; Mbr Commn on Global Governance, 1992-. Address: Arab Fund for Economic and Social Development, P O Box 21923, Safat 13080, Kuwait.

HAMAD Esam Zaki, b. 8 Feb 1961, Taif, Saudi Arabia. Professor of Chemical Engineering. m. Maha Abu-Sharkh, 1983, 2 s, 4 d. Education: BS, Chem engrng, King Fahd Univ, 1982; MS, Chem Engrng, King Fahd Univ, 1984; PhD, Chem Engrng, Univ of Illinois, Chgo, USA, 1988. Appointments: Rsch Assoc, Case West Reserve Univ, 1988; Asst Prof, Kuwait Univ, 1989; Asst to Assoc Prof, King Fahd Univ, 1990, 1999. Publications: More than 50 rsch pprs in referred jrnls, 1980-99. Honour: Ex in Rsch Awd, King Fahd Univ. Address: Chemical Engineering Department, King Fahd University, 31261 Dhahran, Saudi Arabia.

HAMADA Taizo, b. 3 June 1944, Yamagachi, Japan. Profesor. M. Hiroko, 6 June 1971, 1 s, 2 d. Education: DDS, Oska Univ, 1969; PhD, Osaka Univ, 1973. Appointment: Prof, Horoshima Univ, 1981-. Publications: Denture Plaque Control, 1983; Duplicate Denture, 1986; Denture Lining, 1991. Honour: Widyakarya Aislangga

Kencana, 1996; IADR Disting Scientist Awd, 1999; Rsch in Prosthodontics and Implants Awd, Vancouver, Can, 1999. Memberships: IADR; Japan Prosthetic Assn. Address: Department of Prosthodontics, Hiroshima University School of Dentistry, 1 2 3 Kasumi Minami Ku, Hiroshima 734 8553, Japan.

HAMAMOTO Manso. Politician. Appointments: Chmn Socl Dem Party of Japan - SDPJ - Diet Affairs Cttee for House of Conclrs; Chmn of SDPJ mbrs in House of Cnclrs; Min of Labour, 1994-96. Address: c/o Ministry of Labour, 1-2-2 Kusmigasekim, Chiyoda-ku, Tokyo, Japan.

HAMBERGER Sydney Maxwell, b. 20 Aug 1929, London, Eng. Retired University Professor. m. Rita, 30 Aug 1953, 2 s, 1 d. Education: BSc (Hons); PhD; DSc, London; FInstP; FAIP. Appointments: Snr Scientist, GEC Rsch Labs, UK, 1952-58; UKAEA Harwell & Culham, 1958-77; Prof, ANU, 1977-94. Publications: Many sci pprs. Honour: Emeritus Professor, ANU, 1999. Hobbies: Music; Gardening; Travel. Address: 9 Castlereagh Crescent, Macquarie, ACT 2614, Australia.

HAMDAN Mohammad Ahmad, b. 3 Nov 1934, Jaffa. Secretary General, HCST. m. Huda, 15 July 1966, 1 s, 1 d. Education: BS (Hons), Maths, Cairo Univ, 1957; PhD, Math Stats, Sydney Univ, Aust, 1963. Appointments: Asst Prof, Maths, Riyadh Univ, Saudi Arabia, 1964-65; Asst Prof, Maths, Amn Univ of Beirut, Lebanon, 1965-69; Assoc Visng Prof, Math Stats, VA Polytechnic Inst and State Univ, USA, 1969-71; Assoc Prof of Maths, 1970-76; Prof, Amn Univ of Beirut, Lebanon, 1976-77; Visng Prof of Maths, Amn Univ of Cairo, Egypt, 1977-78; Dean of Stud Affairs and Prof of Maths, Univ of Jordan, Amman, 1978-82; Dean of Sci Rsch and Prof of Maths, Univ of Jordan, Amman, 1982-84; Dean, Fac of Sci and Prof of Maths, Univ of Jordan, Amman, 1984-86; Pres, Yarmouk Univ, Jordan, 1986-89; Min of Educ and Higher Educ, 1989-90; Prof of Maths, Univ of Jordan, Amman, 1990-92. Publications: 69 in jrnls and confs. Memberships: Intl Statistical Inst; Amn Statistical Assn; Islamic Acady of Scis; Jordan Acady of Arabic Lang; Third World Acady of Scis; Jordan Higher Cncl of Educ; Many sci and educl cncls and cttees in Jordan. Hobby: Tennis. Address: Higher Council for Science and Technology, PO Box 36, Amman 11941, Jordan.

HAMDOON Nizar, b. 18 May 1944 Baghdad. Diplomatist. m. Sahar Hamdoon, 2 d. Education: Baghdad Coll; Univ of Baghdad. Appointments: Iraqi Air Force, 1968-70; Worked at Arab Ba'ath Party Natl Command, 1970-81; Under-Sec Min of Culture and Info, 1981-83; Joined Min of For Affairs, 1983; Hd Iraqi Interests Sect WA DC, 1983; Amb to USA, 1984-87; Under-Sec Min of For Affairs, 1987-92; Fndr and Chmn Soc of Iraqi Architects, 1990; Amb and perm Rep of Iraq to UN, 1992-. Address: Permanent Mission to Iraq at the United Nations, 14 East 79th Street, New York, NY 10021, USA.

HAMEED A C S, b. 10 Apr 1929. Politician. Appointments: MP for Harispattuwa, 1960-; Min of For Affairs, 1977-89; Min of Educ Sci and Tech, 1989-90; Min of Jus, 1990-93; Min of For Affairs, 1993-94; First to hold separate portfolio of For Affairs; Chmn Utd Natl Party - UNP - 1995-. Publications: In Pursuit of Peace, 1983; Foreign Policy Perspectives of Sri Lanka, 1988. Address: United National Party, 400 Kotte Road, Pitakotte, Sri Lanka.

HAMER Clive Arthur, b. 4 Oct 1923, NSW, Aust. Teacher. m. Joan Muriel Ashcroft, 13 Aug 1949, 1 s, 3 d. Education: BA, hons, 1949; MA, hons, 1954; DipEd, 1950. Appointments: Tchr, Nowra hs, NSW, 1950-56; Snr Master, Wolaroi Coll, NSW, 1957-62; Lectr, Adult Educ, Univ of Sydney, 1963-64; Hdmaster, Wesley Coll, Perth, 1965-83. Publication: Hope of the Vale, 1985. Honour: Mbr, Gen Div of Order of Aust, 1985. Memberships: Hdmasters' Conf, Mbr, Stndng Cttee, 1975-81; Fell, Austl Coll of Educ, WA Chapt Chmn, 1980-81; Accredited Local Preacher, Uniting Ch. Hobbies: Reading; History. Address: 106 Monash Avenue, Como, WA 6152, Australia.

HAMER Margaret Elizabeth, b. 11 May 1926, Adelaide, Aust. Community Worker. m. Alan William Hamer, 13 Nov 1948, 3 s, 1 d. Education: SA, Woodlands, 1941; BMechE, Adelaide Univ, 1945; BE, Sydney Univ, 1947; BA, Melbourne Univ, 1966. Appointments: Tutor, Fine Arts Dept, Melbourne Univ, 1967; Bd Mngmt, Queen Vic Med Cntr, 1972-86; Chmn, Planning Team, QVMC, 1974-86; Pres, QVMC, 1977-86; Vic Hosp Assc Dw 1, 1977-86; VHA, Bd 1979-86; Cncl Mbr, Univ of Monash, 1979-83. Honour: Hon LLD, Monash Univ, 1987; AM, 1997. Listed in: Who's Who in Australia. Hobbies: Reading; Music; Skiing; Collecting; Community services; Opera; Ballet. Address: 10A/29 Queens Road, Melbourne, Vic 3004, Australia.

HAMER Rupert James (Sir), b. 29 July 1916, Melbourne, Aust. Lawyer; Politician. m. April, 4 Mar 1944, 3 s. 2 d. Education: LLM, Melbourne; Hon LLD, Melbourne; Hon DUniv, Swinburne. Appointments: Sol; Mbr Victorian Parl, 1958-81; Min for Immigration and Asst Att-Gen, 1962-64; Min for Local Govt, 1964-71; Dep Premier and Chf Sec, 1971-72; Premier, Treas and Min for Arts, 1972-79; Premier and Min for Econ Dev, 1979-81; Retired from parl, 1981; Since then: Natl Pres, Save the Children Fund; Pres: 6 charitable orgs; Chmn: Victoria State Opera, Cancer/Heart Consultative Cncl, Melbourne Intl Chamber Music Competition, Natl Inst of Circus Arts; Tstee: Melbourne Cricket Ground, Yarra Bend Natl Park. Honours: KCMG, 1982; AC, 1995. Hobbies: Reading; Music; Gardening. Address: 35 Heather Grove, Kew, VIC 3101, Australia.

HAMES William George, b. 13 Oct 1942, Adelaide, SA, Aust. City Planner; Architect. m. Helen Kaye Lang, 24 Sept 1969, 1 s, 1 d. Education: BArch Hons, Adelaide; Master of City Planning, Harvard Univ, USA. Appointments: Commenced own prac as Archt and City Planner, 1969; Expanded offices to Adelaide, Perth, Melbourne, also Auckland, NZ; Currently Chmn of Dirs; Chmn of Dirs Cedarwoods Properties Ltd. Creative Works: Des of large scale devs and mngmt of strategic plng proj throughout Aust, NZ, Asia and USA; Extensive publ of rsch and strategic plans in cty plng, urban des and arch. Honours: Kenneth and Hazel Milne Schlsp, Clive E Boyce Fellshp, Adelaide Univ; Milton Fund Schlsp, Harvard Univ. Memberships: Fell, Roy Austl Inst of Archts; Roy Austl Planning Inst; Fell, Austl Property Inst; Austl Inst of Urban Studies. Hobbies: Boating; Sailing. Address: 29 Ridge Street, South Perth, WA 6151, Australia.

HAMILTON Linda, b. 26 Sept 1956 Salisbury Md. Actress. m. Bruce Abbott - div. Stage appearances: Looice, 1975; Richard II, 1977. Films incl: TAG; The Assassination Game, 1982; Children of the Corn, 1984; The Stone Boy, 1984; The Terminator, 1984; Black Moon Rising, 1986; King Kong Lives!, 1986; Mr Destiny, 1990; Terminator 2: Judgment Day, 1991; Silent Fall, 1994. TV series inc: The Secrets of Midland Heights, 1980-81; King's Crossing, 1982; Beauty and the Beast, 1987-90. TV films incl: Reunion, 1980; Rape and Marriage-The Rideout Case, 1980; Country Gold, 1982; Secrets of a Mother and Daughter, 1983; Secret Weapons, 1985; Club Med, 1986; Go Toward the Light, 1988. Address: c/o International Creative Management, 8942 Wilshire Blvd, Beverly Hills, CA 90211, USA.

HAMILTON Mark Eric, b. 4 Apr 1952. Barrister; Solicitor; Vigneron. m. Deborah Ann Roche, 3 Nov 1979, 2 d. Education: BLL, Adelaide Univ, 1975; ML (Coml), Adelaide Univ), 1988. Appointments: Dir, Hamilton's Ewell Vineyards Pty Ltd, 1972-79; Articled Law Clk, 1976; Working Exec Dir, Hamilton's Ewell Vineyards Pty Ltd, 1977; Employed Solicitor, Ouwens Wagnitz & Co Solicitors, 1978-79; Ptnr, Ouwens Wagnitz & Co Solicitors, 1979-82; Mngng Ptnr, Johnsons Solicitors, 1988-90; Ptnr, Finlaysons Solicitors, 1991; Mngng Ptnr and Coml Litigation Ptnr, Grope Hamilton Lawyers, 1991-; Chmn, Hamilton's Ewell Vineyards, 1991-; Cnclr and Alderman of Adelaide City Cncl, 1982-93; Dpty Lord Mayor, Adelaide, 1992; Actng Lord Mayor, Adelaide, periods, 1992; Chmn, var permanent Cttees of Adelaide Cty Cncl, inclng long period as Chmn of Cncl's Policy and

City Dev Cttee and Cty Plng Cttee, 1984-93; Commnr, Dpty Commnr, Cty of Adelaide Plng Commn, SA Govt gazetted appt, 1985-91; Chmn, Cty of Adelaide's Plng Commn's Plan Review Subcttee, 1985-91; Dpty Mbr, Aust Grand Prix Bd, 1992; Dir, Women's and Children's Hosp, Adelaide, SA Govt ministerial appt, 1996-. Memberships: Roy Adelaide Golf Club Inc, S Aust, 1975-; Adelaide Club, SA, 1991-; Dept Mbr, State Heritage Authy, 1996-98, Mbr, 1999-. Address: c/o Ground Floor, 15 Bentham Street, Adelaide, SA 5000, Australia.

HAMMADI Sadoon, b. 22 June 1930 Karbala. Politician; Economist. m. Lamia Hammadi, 1961, 5 s. Education: In Beirut Lebanon and USA. Appointments: Prof of Econs Univ of Baghdad, 1957; Dep Hd of Econ Rsch Natl Bank of Libya Tripoli, 1961-62; Min of Agrarian Reform, 1963; Econ Advsr to Presdl Cncl Govt of Syria, 1964; Econ Expert UN Plng Inst Syria, 1965-68; Pres Iraq Natl Oil Co - INOC - 1968; Min of Oil and Minerals, 1969-74; Min of For Affairs, 1974-83; Speaker of Natl Ass, 1984-88, 1996-; Dep PM, 1991; PM of Iraq, Mar-Sep 1991; Advsr to Pres. Publications: Towards a Socialistic Agrarian Reform in Iraq, 1964; Views about Arab Revolution, 1969; Memoirs and Views on Oil Issues, 1980; About Nationalism and Arab Unity, 1993. Memberships: Revolutionary Command Cncl; Mbr Iraqi Acady. Hobbies: Swimming; Walking; Coin Collect; Reading Novels. Address: National Assembly, Hamorabi Building, Baghdad, Iraq.

HAMMARSTROM Ulf Goran, b. 9 Apr 1922, Landskrona, Sweden. Professor of Linguistics. m. 21 Apr 1951, 1 s, 1 d. Education: Fil Mag, 1943, Fil lic, 1949, Fil dr, 1953, Uppsala Univ, Sweden. Appointments: Asst, 1949, Docent, 1953, Prof, Chmn, 1965-87, Emer Prof, 1988, Dept of Linguistics, Monash Univ, Clayton, Vic, Aust; Lectr, Footscray Inst of Technol, 1988-94; Prof, Romance Langs, Univ of Mainz, Germany, 1994-98. Publications: Auth of over 150 pprs and books. Address: Department of Linguistics, Monash University, Clayton, Victoria 3168, Australia.

HAMPEL Felicity Pia, b. 1 June 1955, Melbourne, Aust. Barrister. m. George Hampel, 22 July 1986. Education: BA, 1976; LLB, 1978. Appointments: Admitted to prac, 1980; Barrister, 1981; QC, 1996. Appointments: VP, Vic Cncl for Civil Liberties, 1996-98; PUC Cncl for Civil Liberties, 1998- Convenor, Women Barristers Assn, 1997-98; Bd Mbr, Austl Women Lawyers, 1997-98; Mbr, Chair Mngmt Cttee, Austl Advocacy Inst; Dpty Convener State Cncl, Austl Repub Movement. Hobbies: Travelling; Skiing; Eating; Drinking; Reading; Music. Address: 205 William Street, Melbourne, Australia 3000.

HAMPEL George (Hon Justice), b. 4 Oct 1933. Judge. Education: LLB, Melbourne Univ. Appointments: Admitted Barrister and Sol, Sup Crt of Vic, 1958; Barrister, Vic, NSW, Tas, WA, ACT, High Crt of Aust; Called to bar (Mid ACT, High Crt of Aust, Called to Engl bar (Mid Temple), 1975; QC, 1976; Vice Chmn, Vic Bar Cl; VP, Law Cl of Aust; Judge, Sup Crt of Vic, 1983-; Chmn, Leo Cussen Inst, 1987; Chmn, Austl Advocacy Inst, 1991; Adj Prof of Law, Univ of Melbourne and Austl Natl Univ; Visng Prof, Coll of Law, London. Address: c/o Judges' Chambers, Supreme Court of Victoria, Vic 3000, Australia.

HAN Huaizhi, b. 1922 Pingshan Co Hebei Prov. Army Officer. Appointments: Asst to the Chf of the PLA Gen Staff, 1980-85; Dep 6th NPC, 1983-87; Dep 7th NPC, 1988-; Dir of the Mil Trng Dept under the PLA Gen Staff, 1984-85; Dep Chf of the PLA Gen Staff, 1985; Lt Gen PLA, 1985-; Chmn Sports Commn, 1990-. Memberships: Mbr Natl Degrees Cttee, Oct 1988-. Address: Chinese People's Liberation Army Gen Staff, Beijing, People's Republic of China.

HAN Kang Hong, b. 24 Jan 1934, Singapore. Academic. 1 s, 1 d. Education: Postgrad. Appointment: Retd, Singapore Nanyang Technol Univ. Publications: Sev books and articles in profl jrnls. Honour: BBM, 1975; Memberships: ACIB; ACIS; FCMA; CPA Aust; CPA Singapore. Hobbies: Golf; Tennis; Swimming; Writing.

Address: 15 Brighton Crescent, Singapore 559159, Singapore.

HAN Pao-Teh, b. 19 Aug 1934. Professor. m. Hsiao Chung-hsing, 1965, 1 s, 1 d. Education: MArch, Har Univ, USA, 1965; MFA, Princeton Univ, USA, 1967. Appointments: Prof, Chmn, Dept of Arch, Tunghai Univ, 1967; Dean, Coll of Sci and Engrng, Natl Chung-Hsing Univ, 1977; Dir, Natl Mus of Natural Sci, China, 1981; Pres, Tainan Natl Coll of The Arts, 1995-. Publications: Spiritual Dimension of Architecture, 1971; Two essays about Ming and Qing Architecture, 1972; The Origin and Development of Bracket System, 1973; Architecture, Society and Culture, 1975; External Forms and Internal Visions - The Story of Chinese Landscape Design, 1992; Recent Reflections on Architecture and Culture, 1995. Creative Works: Youth Activity Cntrs and Hostels, Chitou, Kenting, Penhu, South Garden, 1985; Inst of Ethnology, Academia Sinica; Taiwan Natl Coll of the Arts, Campus Plan, 1996. Memberships: Chinese Inst of Arch; Chinese Inst of Urban Planning; Chmn, Chinese Assn of Mus, CAM, 1995-. Hobby: Chinese Calligraphic Art. Address: 387-3 Fu-chin Street, Taipei, Taiwan, China.

HAN Shao Gong, b. 1 Jan 1953 Chang Sha. Writer. m. Liang Yu Li, 1980, 1 d. Education: Hunan Tchrs Univ. Appointments: Vice-Chmn Hunan Yth Union, 1985; Chf Ed of Hainan Review, 1988; Pres Hainan Lit Corresp Coll, 1988. Publications: Biography of Ren Bi Shi, 1979; - collects of short stories - Yue Nan, 1981; Flying Across the Blue Sky, 1983; Film script Deaf Mute and His Suona, 1984; To Face the Mystical and Wide World - selection of articles - 1985; New Stories, 1986; Trans: The Unbearable Lightness of Being - Kundra - 1987; Other Shore - selection of prose pieces - 1988; The Murder, 1990; Pa Pa Pa and Seduction and Femme Femme Femme, 1990-91; Homecoming, 1992; The Play and Holy War, 1993; Raving of a Pedestrian in the Night, 1994; Fondness for Shoes, 1994; The Thought of the Sea, 1994; Dictionary of Ma-Bridge - novel - 1995. Memberships: Cncl mbr Chinses Writer's Assn, 1984; Mbr Standing Cttee CPCC Hainan Prov, 1988. Honours: Prize for Best Chinese Stories, 1980, 1981; Hobbies: Chinese Calligraphy. Address: Room 2-602, Hainan Teacher's University, Hai Kou 571158, Hainan, People's Republic of China.

HAN Sung-Joo, b. 1940. Politician. Education: Seoul Natl Univ; Univ of CA Berkeley. Appointments: Prof of Polit Sci Korea Univ; Vice-Chmn Intl Polit Sci Assn; Columnits Newsweek; Min of For Affairs, 1993-95; Pres Intl Rels Inst Korea Univ Seoul. Address: Korea University, 1-5 gu, Anam-dong, Sungbuk, Seoul, Republic of Korea.

HAN Taizhan, b. 24 May 1944, Shandong Prov, China. Physiology Professor. m. Haijang Wang, 1 Sept 1969, 2 s. Education; Master Physiology, 1982; PhD, Physiology, 1988. Appointments: Physn, 1969, Tchr of Physiology, 1978, Chmn, Physiology Dept, 1996, Shantou Univ Medl Coll. Publications: Neurobiology of Learning and Memory (Chf Ed), 1998; The Morphological Characteristics of Synapses in the Process from Induction of LTP to Maintenance, 1998. Honour: Provost's Awd, Kent State Univ (USA), 1988. Membership: Cttee Mbr, Physi-psychol Cttee of China Psychol Assn. Hobby: Chinese folk music. Address: Department of Physiology, Xian Medical University, Xian City, China.

HAN Zhicheng, b. 27 Sept 1936, Hardan, Hebei, China. Professor of Hydrogeology and Engineering Geology. m. Shunling Li, 26 Jan 1961, 1 s, 2 d. Education: BS. Appointments: Techn, 1963; Engr, 1977; Snr Engr, 1987; Prof, 1993. Publications: Over 30 pprs and some rsh results inclng: The law analysis on shera between layers and low angle faults and fissures, 1985; The engineering geological investigation and study on clayey intercalcated bed, 1986; The several principal engineering geological problems and its treatment in Mingtombs pumped storage power station, 1992; The Unload rock body and its engineering geological property analysis, 1994; The analysis and study on geological engineering problems of round rock in underground construction. Honours: Natl Sci and Technol Prog Awd (2nd Class), 1987; 1st Class Oustndng People in Natl 9511 Proj, 1995. Memberships: Intl Engrng Geol Assn; Intl Rock Mechs Assn; Intl Pumped Storage Power Stn Assn. Hobby: Sport. Address: Building No 10-2-4, Dingfuzhang West Street, Chaoyang District, Beijing 100024, China.

HAN Zhubin, b. 1935. Government Official. Appointments: Min of Railways, 1993-98; Dpty Hd, Ldng Grp for Beijing-Kowloon Railway Constrn, 1993-; Dpty Sec, Cntrl Commn for Discipline Inspection; Mbr, 15th Cnrtl Cttee, CCP, 1997-. Address: Central Committee of the Chinese Communist Party, Zhongnanhai, Beijing, China.

HANCOCK Herbert Jeffrey, b. 12 Apr 1940 Chicago IL. Jazz Pianist; Composer. m. Gudrun Meixner, 1968. Education: Roosevelt Univ Chgo; Manhattan Sch of Music; New Sch for Socl Rsch. Appointments: Owner and Publr Hancock Music Co, 1962-; Fndr Hancock and Joe Prodns, 1989-; Pres Harlem Jazz Music Cntr Inc; Performed with Chgo Symph Orch, 1952; Coleman Hawkins Chgo, 1960; Donald Byrd, 1960-63; Miles Davis Quintet, 1963-68; Recorded with Chick Corea; Composed film music for: Blow Up, 1966; The Spook Who Sat by the Door, 1973; Death Wish, 1974; A Soldier's Story, 1984; Jo Jo Dancer, Your Life is Calling, 1986; Wrote score and appeared in film Round Midnight, 1986; Action Jackson, 1988; Colors, 1988; Harlem Nights, 1989; Livin' Large, 1991. Albums incl: Takin' Off, 1963; Succotash, 1964; Speak Like a Child, 1968; Fat Albert Rotunda, 1969; Mwandishi, 1971; Crossings, 1972; Sextant, 1972; Headhunters, 1973; Thrust, 1974; The Best of Herbie Hancock, 1974; Man-Child, 1975; The Quintet, 1977; VSOP, 1977; Sunlight, 1978; An Evening with Herbie Hancock and Chick Corea In Concert, 1979; Lite Me Up, 1982; Future Shock, 1983; Perfect Machine, 1988; Jamming, 1992; Cantaloupe Island, 1994; Tribute to Miles, 1994; Dis Is Da Drum, 1995. Honours: Num awds inclng Citation of Achievement Brdcst Music Inc, 1963; Jay Awd Jazz Mag, 1964; Grammy Awd for Best Rhythm and Blues Instrumental Performance, 1983, 1984; Acady Awd Best Original Score for Round Midnight, 1986; Grammy Awd for Best Jazz Instrumental Composition - co-composer - 1987; Grammy Awd Best Jazz Instrumental Performance, 1995. Memberships: Natl Acady of Recording Arts and Scis; Mbr Jazz Musicians Assn; Mbr Natl Acady of TV Arts and Scis; Mbr Brdcst Music. Address: Hancock Music, 1250 N Doheny Dr, Los Angeles, CA 90069, USA.

HANCOCK James Arnold, b. 8 June 1923. Company Director. m. Patricia, 17 Feb 1949, 2 s, 1 d. Education: Univ Melbourne. Appointments: Dir, ABB ASEA Brown Boveri Pty Ltd, 1971-92; Chmn, 1986-92, Chmn Natl Comm Union Ltd, 1984-93, Dir 1968-93, Chmn, State Bank Vic, 1983-89; Ptnr Hancock & Woodward and Successor Firms 1951-84; Inquiry into C'wlth Labs 1983, Melb Underground Railway Loop Auth 1978-82; Mbr Cl Monash Univ, 1985-92; Dpty Chan, 1989-92, Mbr Natl Hlth Res Cl, 1969-78; Chmn Vic Tapestry Wrkshp, 1989-94; Dir, Howard Florry Inst Exptl Physiol and Med, Natl Hlth & Med Res Cl Review Cttee 1984; Chmn Mus Vic Dev Study 1986; State Lib Vic Dev Study 1987; V Chmn C'Wlth Serum Lab Commn 1961-69; RAAF 1942-45. Honour: OBE, 1969. Listed in: Who's Who in Australia. Hobbies: Tennis; Golf; Fishing. Address: Level 45, 55 Collins Street, Melbourne, Vic 3000, Australia.

HANDELSMAN David Joshua, b. 16 Apr 1950, Melbourne, Aust. Academic Physician. m. Penny, 8 Aug 1986, 2 s, 1 d. Education: MB BS, Melbourne, 1974; FRACP, 1980; PhD, Sydney, 1984. Appointments: Rsch Fell, 1980-83; NHMRC Fairley Fell, 1984-85; Dir, Androl Unit, 1985; Wellcome Snr Rsch Fell, 1987-91; Assoc Prof, 1987-96; Prof, Reproductive Endocrinol and Androl, 1996-; Inaugural Prof/Dir, ANZAC Rsch Inst, 1998-. Publications: Over 300 sci publns in profl jrnls and meetings. Honour: Susman Medal, 1994. Memberships: Endocrine Soc of Aust; Endocrine Soc, USA; Intl Soc of Androl. Hobbies: Reading; Cinema. Address: 18 North Arm Road, Middle Cove, NSW 2068, Australia.

HANEGBI Tzachi, b. 1957 Jerusalem. Politician. m. 3 children. Education: Hebrew Univ of Jerusalem. Appointments: Served in an Israeli Def Forces paratroopers unit, 1974-77; Pres Hebrew Univ Student Union, 1979-80; Pres Natl Union of Israeli Students, 1980-82; Advsr to Min of For Affairs, 1984-86; Bur Dir PMs Off, 1986-88; Hd - in rotation - Econ Affairs Cttee; Min of Hlth, 1996-97; Min of Jus, 1997-. Memberships: Mbr Knesset For Affairs and Def Cttee; Mbr Cttee on Constitution Law and Jus Knesset House Cttee; Mbr Cttee on Labour and Socl Welfare; Mbr Cttee on Educ and Culture, 1988-92; Mbr Cttee on Constitution Law and Jus, 1992-96; Mbr Likud-Tzomet-Gesher polit grp. Address: Ministry of Health, 29 Rehov Salahadin, Jerusalem 91010, Israel.

HANIFFA Mohamed Abdulkather, b. 20 Oct 1949. Reader in Zoology. m. 2 children. Education: MSc (Zool) Madras Univ, 1972; PhD (Zool) Madurai Kamaraj Univ, 1975. Appointment: Dir, Cntr for Aquaculture Rsch and Extension, St Xavier's Coll (Autonomous), Tamil Nadu, India; Rsch schemes incl: Tamil Nadu State Cncl for Sci and Technol, Chennai, 1994-97; Dept of Environ and Forests, New Delhi, 1995-98; Dept of Sci and Technol, New Delhi, 1997-2000. Publications: 72 rsch publs. Honours: Gold Medal, Sadakathulla Appa Coll, Palayankottai, 1986; All India Young Sci Awd, MAAS, New Delhi, 1989; Visng Professorship, Sophia Univ, Tokyo, 1991; Fr Theo Mathias Awd, AIACHE, New Delhi, 1992. Memberships: Expert Mbr, Man & Biosphere, Min of Environ and Forests, New Delhi; Utilizing Sci Expertise of Retd Scientists, Min of Sci and Technol, New Delhi; Environ Cttee, Tamil Nadu Pollution Control Bd, Tirunelveli; Asian Fisheries Soc, Philippines; Assn for Advancement of Entomology, India; Assn of Environl Bio, India; Bd of Studies and Bd of Examiners, diff univs. Address: 12 18th Cross St, Maharaja Nagar, Tirunelveli 627 011, Tamil Nadu, India.

HANKEY Graeme John, b. 11 Oct 1957, Collie, WA, Aust. Medical Practitioner. m. Sandra, 29 Nov 1981, 2 d. Education: MBBS, MD, Univ West Aust; FRCP (London); FRCP (Edinburgh);FRACP. Appointment: Cnslt Neurologist. Publications: Transient Ischaemic Attacks of the Brain and Eye, 1994; Stroke - A Practical Guide to Management, 1996. Honou: Winner - Roy Soc of Med Medl Book of the Yr, 1997. Memberships: Assn of Brit Neurologists, 1992-98; Austl Assn of Neurologists, 1987-98; Roy Austrasian Coll of Physns, 1988-98. Hobbies: Music; Painting (Fine Arts) Sport (football, cricket, swimming); Birds. Address: Stroke Unit, Department of Neurology, Royal Perth Hospital, Wellington Street, Perth, Australia 6001.

HANKIN Cherry Anne, b. 30 Sept 1937, Nelson, NZ. Retired University Professor. m. Professor J C Garrett, 18 May 1981, dec. Education: BA, Engl and Latin, Otago Univ, 1958; MA, Engl, Vic Univ, 1959; Tchr's Cert, Auckland, TC, 1960; PhD, Engl, Univ of CA, Berkeley, 1971. Appointments: Lectr in Engl, Univ of Canterbury, Christchurch, 1971-83; Assoc Prof, 1983-94. Publications: Ed, books: Critical Essays on the New Zealand Novel, 1976; It Was So Late and Other Stories (by John Reece Cole), 1978; Life in Young Colony: Selections from Early New Zealand Writing, 1981; Critical Essays on the New Zealand Short Story, 1982; The Letters of John Middleton Murry to Katherine Mansfield, 1983; Auth, Katherine Mansfield and Her Confessional Stories, 1983, 1988; Letters Between Katherine Mansfield and John Middleton Murry, 1988, Introductions to 5 other wrks. Honours: Advd Grad Travelling Fellshp in Engl, Berkeley, 1971; Memberships: NZ Soc of Auths; Dante Aligheri Soc, Univ of 3rd Age. Hobbies: Reading; Art appreciation; Gardening; Bowls; Walking. Address: 22 West Tamaki Road, St Heliers, Auckland, New Zealand.

HANKS Tom, b. Oakland CA. Actor. m. (1) Samantha Lewes, 1978, div 1985, 2 c; (2) Rita Wilson, 1988, 2 s. Appointments: Began acting career with Great Lakes Shakespeare Fest; Appeared in Bosom Buddies ABC tv, 1980. Films incl: Splash; Bachelor Party; The Man with One Red Shoe; Volunteers; The Money Pit; Dragnet; Big; Punch Line; The Burbs; Nothing in Common; Every Time

We Say Goodbye; Joe Versus the Volcano, 1900; The Bonfire of the Vanities, 1990; A League of Their Own, 1991; Sleepless in Seattle; Philadelphia, 1993; Forrest Gump, 1994; Apollo 13, 1995; That Thing You Do - also dir; Turner & Hooch, 1997. Honours: Acady Awd for Best Actor for Philadelphia, 1994; Acady Awd for Forrest Gump, 1995. Address: c/o CAA, 9830 Wilshire Boulevard, Beverly Hills, CA 90212, USA.

HANNAH Daryl, b. 1960 Chgo IL. Actress: Education: Univ of CA at Los Angeles; Studied with Stella Adler; Studied ballet with Marjorie Tallchief. Appointments: Appeared on TV in Paper Dolls. Films: The Fury, 1978; The Final Terror; Hard Country; Blade Runner; Summer Lovers; Splash; The Pope of Greenwich Village; Reckless; Clan of the Cave Bear; Legal Eagles; Roxanne; Wall Street; High Spirits; Steel Magnolias; Grazy People; At Play in the Fields of the Lord; Memoirs of an Invisible Man; Grumpy Old Men; Attack of the 50 ft Woman; The Tie That Binds; Dir The Last Supper, 1994; Dir A Hundred and One Nights, 1995; Grumpier Old Men, 1995; Two Much, 1996; The Last Days of Frankie the Fly, 1996. Address: c/o ICM, 8942 Wilshire Blvd, Beverly Hills, CA 90211, USA.

HANSEN Rodney Harold, b. 13 Mar 1944, Auckland, NZ. Barrister. m. Penelope Jane Berghan, 4 Feb 1971, 3 s. Education: LLB Hons, Univ of Auckland, 1969; ACA, 1969. Appointments: Acct in pvte practice, 1969-73; Assoc, Simpson Coates & Clapshaw, barristers and sols, 1973-75; Ptnr, Simpson, Grierson, Butler, White, barristers and sols, 1975-91; Barrister Sole, 1991-. Publications: Auth, Interpretation of Deeds and Other Documents for Laws of New Zealand. Honours: Alexander Johnstone Schlsp, 1967; Annual Prize in Juris, 1967; Law Soc Prize (best undergrad record), 1968; Appointed Queens Cnsl, 1995. Memberships: NZ Law Soc; NZ Soc of Accts; Pres, C'Wlth Lawyers Assn. Hobbies: Music; Reading; Gardening; Sport. Address: 5 Bellevue Road, Mount Eden, Auckland, New Zealand.

HANSON John Francis Jr, b. 1 Dec 1914, Alameda, CA, USA. Attorney. m. Marilyn. Education: AB, JD, Law, Stanford Univ. Appointments: Ret'd Col, US Army Reserve; Attorney. Honours: Pres, 1957, Lt Gov, 1965, Kiwanis Club, Alameda; Combat Awds, 5 Pacific Landings. Memberships: Amn Bar, 1939-; CA and Alameda Co Bar, 1939-; World Peace Through Law, 1950-92. Hobby: Travel. Listed in: Who's Who in California. Address: 10654 Park View Circle, El Paso, TX 79935, USA.

HANUMANTHA RAO Balanthrapu, b. 15 May 1951, Guntur. Teacher; Researcher. m. Mrs Srigowri, 9 June 1995. Education: MSc, 1973; PhD, 1981. Appointments: Lectr, Botany, Andhra Univ, 1976; Rdr, 1985; Prof, 1993. Publications: Over 50 rsch pprs. Honours: Gold Medalist, Andhra Univ, 1973. Memberships: Fell, Botanic Soc, India; Swamy Botanical Club; Int Soc of Plant Morphologists; Indian Assn of Angiosperm Taxonomy. Hobbies: Sports; Music; Travel; Photography. Address: Department of Botany, Andhra University, Visakhapatnam 530003, AP, India.

HAO Jianxiu, b. 1935 Qingdao. Politician. Appointments: Wrkr State Operated Cotton Factory No 6 Qingdao; Originated Hao Jianxiu Wrk Method; Joined CCP, 1954; Dep Dir Cotton Factory No 6 Qingdao, 1964; Vice-Chmn Qingdao Municipality Revolutionary Cttee 1971; Vice-Chmn Trade Union Sandong, 1975; Chmn Women's Fedn Shandong, 1975; Vice-Min of Textile Ind, 1978-81; Vice-Chmn Women's Fedn, 1978; Min Textile Ind, 1981-83; Alt Sec Sec, 1982; Sec, 1985; Vice-Min Plng Cttee, 1987-; Vice-Chmn Cttee for Women and Children's Wrk, 1987-; Vice-Chmn State Tourism Cttee, 1988; Dep Dir Ldng Grp for the Placement of Demobilized Army Offrs, 1993-. Honours: Natl Model Wrkr in Ind, 1951; Hon Pres Factory Dirs' Study Soc Acady of Socl Scis, 1985. Memberships: Mbr Exec Cncl Women's Fedn, 1953; Mbr Cntrl Cttee Communist Yth League, 1964- Cultural Revolution; Mbr Qingdao Municipality Revolutionary Cttee, 1967; Mbr Standing Cttee Cotton Factory No 6 Revolutionary Cttee, 1968;

Mbr Standing Cttee Shandong Prov CCP Cttee, 1977; Mbr 11th CCP Cntrl Cttee, 1977-82; Mbr 12th Cntrl Cttee CCP, 1982-87; Mbr Politburo 13th Cntrl Cttee CCP, 1985; Mbr Finl and Econ Ldng Grp CCP Cntrl Cttee, 1986; Mbr 13th Cntrl Cttee CCP, 1987-92; Mbr 14th Cntrl Cttee CCP, 1992-97; Mbr 15th Cntrl Cttee CCP, 1997-. Address: Zhong-gong Zhongyang, A8, Taipingjie Street, Beijing 100050, People's Republic of China.

HAQUE Mohammed Hamidul, b. 16 Feb 1956, Bangladesh. Teacher. m. Shahin, 29 Oct 1982, 1 s. 1 d. Education: PhD. Appointments: Lectr; Snr Lectr; Asst Prof; Assoc Prof. Publications: Over 40 rsch articles to profl jrnls and conf proceedings. Memberships: Snr Mbr, IEEE; Snr Mbr, IEAust; Fellow, IE(Bangladesh). Address: Block L #03-05, 100 Nanyang Crescent, Singapore 637819.

HAQUE Rizwanul, b. 20 Aug 1950, Karachi, Pakistan. General Manager. m. Nurun Nahar, 23 Feb 1984, 1 s, 1 d. Education: MBA; Advd Finl Mngmnt Techniques. Appointments: Gen Mngr; Snr Mngr Pur; Co-ord Coml Div; Snr Mngr. Hobbies: Travel; Reading; Sports. Address: C-25 Block 13D, Gulshan B Iqbal, Karachi, Pakistan.

HARA Kenzaburo, b. 6 Feb 1907 Hyogo Pref. Politician. Education: Waseda Univ; OR Univ USA. Appointments: Parly Vice-Min of Transp, 1949; Vice-Speaker, 1961-63; Min of Labour, 1968-70, 1971-72; Vice-Chmn Liberal Dem Party - LDP - Gen Cncl, 1977-78; Min of State Dir-Gen Natl Land Agcy and Hokkaido Dev Agcy, 1980-81; Speaker HoR, 1986-89. Memberships: Mbr HoR, 1946-. Hobbies: Collecting For Whiskies Brandies etc; Keeping dogs and carp. Address: c/o House of Representatives, Tokyo, Japan.

HARA Masanori, b. 13 Apr 1942, Japan. Scientist. m. Takako, 1 s, 1 d. Education: DEng, Kyushu Univ. Appointments: Lectr, 1972-73, Assoc Prof, 1973-75, Kyushu Inst of Technol; Assoc Prof, 1975-86, Prof, 1986-, Kyushu Univ. Publications: High Voltage Pulsed Power Engineering, 1981; Electric Energy Engineering, 1988; High Voltage Phenomena. Honours: Ppr Awd, IEE, Japan, 1980, 1995; Ppr Awd, Inst of Electrostats, Japan, 1982; Outstndng Contbrn Awd, Inst of Electrostats, Japan, 1988. Memberships: IEEE; IEE of Japan; Inst of Electrostats, Japan; Cyogenic Engrng of Japan. Address: c/o Department of Electrical & Electronic Systems Engineering, Kyushu University, Fukuoka 812-8581, Japan.

HARADA Kaoru, b. 19 Sept 1927, Japan. University Professor; Research Chemist. m. Hatsuko, 28 Aug 1958, 2 s. Education: PhD, Osaka Univ. Appointments: Rsch Assoc, FL Univ, 1956; Asst Prof, 1964, Assoc Prof, 1986, Prof, 1971, Rsch Prof, 1973, Univ MI; Prof, Tsukuba Univ, 1978; Prof, Kobeshoin Womens Univ, 1991-. Publications: 335 rsch pprs in intl sci jrnls. Honours: Fell, Intl Soc for the Study of Origin of Life; Prof Emer, Tsukuba Univ. Memberships: Chem Soc of Japan; Intl Soc for the Study of Origin of Life; Japanese Soc for the Hist of Chem. Hobbies: Reading; Writing; Travel; Photography; Drawing; Tennis. Address: Sumiregaoka 2-2-1-912, Takaraguka, 665-0847 Japan.

HARAHAP Rustam Effendi, b. 9 Aug 1937, Gungsitoli, Nias, Indian Ocean. Gynaecologist. m. Soelistijo Rini, 2 s, 1 d. Education: MD; PhD. Career: Priv gynaecologist. Publications: Gynaecological Cancers, 1983; Contbr of articles to var medl jrnls. Honours: Cert of Merit - to Med and Gynae; Decree of Merit - to Med and Gynae; Meritorious Achievement - to Med and Gynae; Pictorial testimonial of Achievement and Distinction; Life Fell, IBA; MOIF; IBC Golden Scroll of Excellence; 2000 Outstndng Achievement Dip and Medal; Life Fell, ABI Rsch Assn; 20th Century Achievement Awd; Ldr in Sci Awd; Medl Excellence Awd; Intl Cultural Dip of Hon. Memberships: Intl Soc for Preventive Oncology, NY, 1979-; AAAS, 1993-; NY Acady Sci, 1994-; World Org of Family Drs; Intl Medl Assn for Ozone Therapy; Planetary Soc, 1995-; Natl Geographic Soc, 1996-. Hobbies: Music;

Videography; Astronomy. Address: 2 Suryopranoto, harmoni Plaza B30-31, Jakarta 10130, Indonesia.

HARAWIRA Makere Winifred, b. 15 Sept 1945, Christchurch, NZ. Lecturer; Researcher; Speaker. m. (1) Christopher Wright, 6 Feb 1971, (2) Clarence Harawira, 25 Jan 1991, 4 s, 2 d. Education: BEduc & Maori Studies, 1993, MA, Edic (1st Class Hons), 1995, PhD, Educ, 1999, Univ of Auckland. Appointments: Tutr, Sociol of Educ, Univ of Auckland, Lectr/Tutor Sociol of Educ, Lectr, Maori Rsch, Auckland Coll of Educ, 1993-95; Acting HOD Maori Bi-Lingual Unit, 1996; Tutor, Sociol of Educ, Univ of Auckland, Lectr/Tutor Sociol of Educ, Auckland Coll of Educ, 1997; Tutor/Guest Lectr, Sociol of Educ, Univ of Auckland, Guest Lectr in Maori Rsch, Guest Lectr, Auckland Coll of Educ, 1998; Lectr in Indigenous Studies, Te Whare Wanaga o Awanuiarangi, 1998-; Visng Lectr, Hum Resource Dev, Univ of Waikato, 1998; Visng Lectr, Intl Issues in Dev, Univ of Waikato, 1999. Publications: Auth, contbns to books inclng: Maori: Who Owns the Identity? in Te Oua, Vol 2, 1993; The Impact of State-Welfare Relations on Whanau in Education Policy in New Zealand: The 1990s and Beyond, 1997; Globalisation and Indigenous Development: The Problematics of APEC, in Linkages in Development, issues of Governance, 1998. Honours: Snr Prize in Educ, 1992; Te Pae O Te Rangi: Snr Maori Student in Educ, 1993; Univ of Auckland Grad Schlshp, 1993; Univ of Auckland Doct Schlshp, 1995. Memberships include: Aotearoa NZ Intl Dev Studies Netwrok; Intl Rsch Inst in Indigenous & Maori Educ; Aust & NZ Hist of Educ Soc; NZ Educl Admin Soc; NZ Assn for Rsch in Educ; Quality Pub Educ Coalition, Auckland Branch. Hobbies: Planetary healing; World Peace; Environmental and biodiversity issues; Developing alternative frameworks for world order; dance; Music; Singing.

HARCOURT John Kenneth, b. 27 June 1931. Dentist. Education: DDSc; MDSc; BDSc, Melbourne; LDS, Vic; FRACDS; FDS RCS Ed (Hon). Appointments include: Rdr, Dept of Dental Prosthetics, 1974-82; Asst Dean, Fac of Dental Sci, 1976; Fac Co-Ord for Audio-Visual Aids, 1976-79; Dpty Dean, Fac of Dental Sci, 1977-79; Reader, Dept of Restorative Dentistry, Univ of Melbourne, 1983-90; Chmn, Dept of Restorative Dentistry, 1985-88; Ed, Austl Dental Jrnl, 1985-98; Dental Bd of Vic, 1987-; Pres 1995-96; Hd, Restorative Dentistry Section, 1989-91; Assoc Prof, Reader, Restorative Dentistry, 1990-96; Continuing Educ Co-Ord, 1991-95; Dir of Continuing Educ, 1996; Ret'd 1996; Snr Assoc, 1997-98; Hon Prin Fell, 1999-, Sch of Dental Sci, Univ of Melbourne. Publications include: Over 40 scientific pprs; 20 abstracts of rsch presentations; Editls, Austl Dental Jrnl, 1985-98; Guest Editl, Jrnl of Dental Rsch, 1995; Num textbooks. Honours include: John Iliffe Schlshp, 1949, 1950, 1952, 1953; T C Adamson Prize, Dental Prosthetics, 1951; W J Tuckfield Prize, 1953; Ernest Joske Mem Prize, 1953; OAM, 1995; Hon Fell, Fac of Dental Surg, Roy Coll of Surgs (Edinburgh), 1998. Memberships: Austl Dental Assn; Austl Dental Assn, Victorian Br; Intl Assn for Dental Rsch; FDI World Dental Fedn; Acady of Dental Materials; Intl Coll of Dentists; Roy Australasian Coll of Dental Surgeons, Pres, 1994-96; Roy Dental Hosp of Melbourne. Address: 24 Faircroft Avenue, Glen Iris, Vic 3146, Australia.

HARDIE BOYS Michael, b. 6 Oct 1931, Wellington, New Zealand. Governor General. m. Edith Mary, 2 Feb 1957, 2 s, 2 d. Education: BA, LLB, Vic Univ. Appointments: Judge, High Crt, 1980; Judge, Crt of Appeal, 1989; Privy Cnslr, 1989; Gov Gen, 1996-. Publication: Courts. Honours: GCMG, 1996; GNZM, 1997; Hon LLD, Vic Univ, 1997; Hon Bencher, Gray's Inn, 1994; Hon Fell, Wolfson Coll, Cambridge, 1995. Hobbies: Art; Outdoors. Address: Government House, Wellington, New Zealand.

HARDIN Ann, b. 2 Aug 1947, Findlay, OH, USA. Social Worker; Therapist. m. John W, 6 Dec 1969, 2 s, 1 d. Education: Bachelors Deg, Socl Wrk, Natl Assn of Socl Wrkrs; Masters Deg, Socl Wrk, Univ of MO. Appointments: Dir, Option Prog, 1975-78; Stud Internship, Univ of MO, 1983; Grad Stud Asst, MO Assn for Socl Welfare, 1984-85; Adj Fac, Univ of Guam, 1990-91; Individual, Marriage and Family Therapist, Navy Family Serv Cntr, 1985-92; Snr Individual Marriage and Family Therapist, Superior Ct of Guam, Client Servs and Family Cnslng Div, 1992-. Creative Works: 2 Chapts, Family Violence on Guam, 1997. Honours: Outstndng Grad Stud; Socl Wrkr of the Yr, 1991. Memberships: Natl Assn of Socl Wrkrs; Guam Assn of Socl Wrkrs; Guam Assn of Individual, Marriage and Family Therapists; Amn Cnslng Assn; Amn Assn of Univ Women; Amn Assn of Christian Cnslrs. Hobbies: Long stitch needlepoint; Playing with son. Address: P O Box 4324, Hagatna, Guam 96932, USA.

HARDING Ann, b. 18 May 1958. Academic. m. John Sekoranja, 1 July 1995, 1 s. Education: BEc Hons, Sydney Univ; PhD, London Sch of Econs. Appointments: Prof, Applied Econ and Socl Policy, Inaugural Dir, Natl Ctr for Socl and Econ Modelling, Univ of Canberra, 1992; Dept of Socl Security, Treasury, Hlth Housing and Cmnty Servs. Publications: Lifetime Income Distribution and Redistribution, 1993; Microsimulation and Public Policy, 1996; Num monographs, book chapters. Honours: 5 undergrad prizes, Schlshps, 1977-78; Shell Prize, 1983; Brit Cncl PhD Schlshp, 1987; DSS Awd, 1987; Fell, Acad of Socl Scis, Aust, 1996. Memberships: Intl Assn for Rsch on Income and Wealth; Austl Econ Soc. Listed in: Who's Who in Australia. Hobbies: Income distribution; Microsimulation; Government policy. Address: National Centre for Social and Economic Modelling, University of Canberra, ACT 2601, Australia.

HARDY Sara Kathryn, b. 30 Jul 1952. Playwright; Performer. Education: Dip in Drama, Dartington Coll of Arts, UK; Tchng Cert, Rolle Coll, UK. Appointments: Writing/Acting Career with var Th Co's in UK and Aust, inclg: Harrogate YPT, Gay Sweatshop, Hormone Imbalance, Half Moon YPT; Australia: Acting Tutor for SUDS; Actor for The Co of Women (Sydney), Troupe Theatre (Adelaide), Radclyffe Theatre Prodns, What's The Deal?, (Melbourne). Creative Works: Plays: Who Know's?, 1979; Radclyffe, Co-Author: Adele Salem, 1987; Vita! - A Fantasy, 1989; She of the Electrolux, 1995; Virtually Ethel, 1998; Radio Plays: She of the Electrolux, 1996; Books: Vita! - A Fantasy, 1991; Rosie Fingered Dawn, 1994. Honours: Writers Fellshp, 1991 and B R Whiting Fellshp, Rome, 1995, Aust Cncl, Fed Govt Funding for the Arts. Memberships: Entertainment and Arts Alliance; Austl Writers Guild; Vic Writers Cntr. Address: c/o Radclyffe Theatre Productions, 16-18 Barnett Street, Kensington, Vic 3031, Australia.

HARDY William David, b. 23 Nov 1950, Adelaide, SA, Aust. Winemaker. m. Merilyn Ann Macrow, 27 May 1972, 2 d. Education: Bachelor of Agric Sci, Univ of Adelaide, 1971; Diplome Nat d'Oenologue, Univ de Bordeaux, France, 1973. Appointments: Trainee Winemaker 1972-74, Winemaker 1974-76, Snr Winemaker, Houghton Wines Pty Ltd, 1977-82; Winemaker 1983-90, Thomas Hardy and Sons Pty Ltd; Gen Mngr, Domaine de La Baume EURL, 1991-94; Prod Coord, BRL Hardy Ltd, 1995-98; Oenologist, 1999. Memberships: Pres 1989, 1990, Austl Soc of Viticulture and Oenology; Vice Chmn, Wetland Care, Aust, 1998-; Hobbies: Wine tasting; Hunting; Bushwalking; Golf. Address: c/o BRL Hardy Ltd, Reynell Road, Reynella, SA 5161, Australia.

HARGRAVE Nathaniel Charles, b. 13 Nov 1915, Adelaide, SA, Aust. Barrister; Solicitor. m. (1) Mary Minto Wyles, 10 May 1941, 1 s, 2 d, (2) Pauline Manning McClaren, 25 Feb 1989. Education: LLB, 1938, BA, 1939, Adelaide Univ. Appointments: Admitted to Supreme Crt of Sa, 1938; RAAF, 1940-45; Sec, Law Soc of SA and SA Hockey Assn, 1945-47; Legal Prac, Alice Springs, North Territory, 1949-63; Mbr, North Territory Legis Cncl and Chmn of var cttees, 1954-63; Mbr, North Territory Delegations on Constitutional Reform, 1958, 1961, 1964; Fndn Chmn, North Territories Reserves Bd (Natl Pks), 1956-63; Ptnr, Knox and Hargrave, Adelaide, 1963-88; Mbr of Cncl, Flinders Univ, 1972-78, 1979-89; Chmn, Flinders Univ Fin and Bldngs Cttee, 1983-88. Honours: Mbr of SA State Hockey Team, 1938; OBE for community serv in North Territory, 1964; Flinders Univ Disting Serv

Medal, 1988; GM's Order of Serv to Masonry, 1988; Past Dpty Grand Master, 1988. Membership: Mbr, Law Soc of SA; Fndn Chmn, North Territory's Reserves Bd. Hobbies: Tennis; Golf; Carpentry; Hockey; Coaching and umpiring; Freemasonry; Bowls. Address: Unit 2, 6 Wynyard Grove, Wattle Park, SA, Australia.

HARIBHAKTI Vishnubhai Bhagwandas, b. 8 Oct 1929. Chartered Accountant. Widowed, 2 s, 1 d. Education: B.COM; A.C.A. Appointment: Fndr, Snr Ptnr, Haribhakti & Co, 1954-; Dir Bajaj Electricals Ltd and other leading pub cos; Cttee Mbr, Assocham, Apex Chamber of Com. Publication: Taxation of Non-Residents in India (book). Honours: G.P. Kapadia Gold Medal; Rotary Plaque, Best Rotarian. Memberships: Inst of Chart Accts of India (Past Pres); Indian Merchants Chamber (Past Pres); Rotary Club, Bombay Mid-Town (Past Pres); Co-Chmn, Dir, Taxes Cttee, Assocd Chambers of Com of India. Hobbies: Writing; Reading; Music; Public Speaking. Address: Haribhakti & Co, 42 Free Press House, 215 Nariman Point, Bombay 400 021, India.

HARIMAN Jusuf, b. 6 Sept 1954, Indonesia. Management Consultant. m. Polly Hariman, 4 Aug 1979, diss 1990, 1 s, 1 d, ptnr, Linda Williams. Education: BA (Psychology), 1977, BA Hons (Philos), 1979; Macquarie Univ; MA (Psychol), 1978; BEC (Acctng) 1986, Univ of Sydney; PhD (Psychol), Columbia Pacific Univ, 1980. Appointments: Assoc Ed, Austl Jrnl of Clinl Hypnotherapy and Hypnosis, 1980-94; Fndr of the fifth force in psychotherapy, Intergrative and Eclectic Psychotherapy; Fndg Ed, Jrnl of Integrative and Eclectic Psychotherapy, 1982-; Editl Cnslt CPU Abstract, 1988-91; Assoc Ed, Aust Jrnl of Transpersonal Psychol, 1981-85; Columnist, AAA Media Network. Publications: How to Use The Power of Self Hypnosis, 1981, 1982, 1983, 1984, 1986, 1988, 1994 (Engl, Spanish and Polish); The Therapeutic Efficacy of the Major Psychotherapeutic Techniques, 1983; Banish That Smoking Habit, 1983; Does Psychotherapy Really Help People?, 1984; Stay Calm and Reach the Top, 1993, 1995; Over 120 scholarly articles in var jrnls. Memberships: Fndng Pres and Fell, Intl Acady of Elect Psychotherapists, 1983; Austl Coll of Pvte Cnsltng Psychols; Writing Fell and Manuscript Assessor, Fellshp of Austl Writers. Hobby: Making friends. Address: Macquarie Centre, PO Box 1677, North Ryde, NSW 2113, Australia.

HARIRI Rafik Bahaa El Din, b. 1944 Sidon Lebanon. Politician; Business Executive. Appointments: Emigrated to Saudi Arabia, 1965; Tchr then auditor with engrng co; Prin Civ Constrn Estab, CICONEST, 1970-78; Fndr Saudi Oger, with Oger Enterprises, 1978; Fndr Hariri Fndn for Culture and Higher Educ, 1979; Prin, Oger Co, 1979; Prin, Oger Liban; Prin Saudi Oger Services UK; Organised Lausanne Conf, 1984 and Taif Conf, 1989 to end civil war in Lebanon. PM of Lebanon and Min of Fin, 1992-. Honours incl: Chevalier Legion d'honneur, 1981; Kt of the Italian Repub, 1982; Natl Cedars Medal - Lebanon - 1983; Saint Butros and Saint Boulos Medal, 1983; Save the Children 50th Anniversary Awd, 1983; King Faisal Medal, 1983; Medaille de Paris, 1983; Beirut Golden Key, 1983; Grande Croix de la Légion d'Honneur, 1996; Many Hon Doctorates. Address: Office of President of Council of Minister, Grand Serail, rue des Arts et Metiers, Sanayeh, Beirut, Lebanon.

HARISH Michael, b. 28 Nov 1936 Romania. Politician; Economist. m. Edith Normand, 1963, 3 s, 1 d. Education: Studies in econs and polit sci. Appointments: Sec-Gen Labour Party's Student Org, 1961-63; Dir and Chmn Intl Dept Israel Labour Party, 1967-82; Dep Chmn Def and For Affairs Cttee, 1984-88; Chmn Fin Cttee, 1988-89; Sec-Gen Israel Labour Party, 1989-92; Min of Ind and Trade, 1992-96; Co-Chmn Jnt Sci and Tech Cttee - US Israel. Memberships: Mbr Knesset, 1974-; Mbr sev ministerial cttees inclng Econ Affairs Immigrants' Absorption Devt Areas Jerusalem Affairs; Mbr Cttee for co-ordng activities between Govt and the Jewish Agcy and the Zionist Org. Hobbies: Sport; Music. Address: 1 Mishmar Hayarden Street, Givatayim, 53582 Israel.

HARJANTO Robby, b. 16 Feb 1963, Surabaya. Deputy Chief Engineer. Education: Satya Wacana Christian University (Electronic Engrng), Salatiga, Indonesia. Memberships: Amn Mngmt Assn, 1996-. Hobby: Reading scientific and technical books. Address: PT Ekamas Fortuna, Ds Gampingan, Kec Pagak, Kab Malang, PO Box 259, Malang - East Java 65101, Indonesia.

HARKIANAKIS Stylianos, b. 29 Dec 1935, Crete, Greece. Greek Orthodox Primate. Education: Theol Sch of Halki, 1958; Postgrad Stdies, Bonn, Germany, 1958-66; Doctorate, Div, Univ of Athens, Greece, 1965. Appointments: Ordained Deacon, 1957 and Priest, 1958; Lectr, Univ of Thessaloniki, 1969; Exarch of Mt Athos, 1970; Titular Metrop of Miletoupolis, 1971; Archbish of Aust, 1975; Dean, St Andrews Theol Coll, Sydney, Aust, 1986. Publications include: Orthodoxy and Catholicism; The Infallibility of the Church in Orthodox Theology, 1965; 20 vols of poetic collects; 55 theol essays in intl periodicals. Honours: Golden Cross of St Andrew, Constantinople, of Thyateira, London, of Holy Sepulchre, Jerusalem; Gottfried von Herder Preis, Vienna, 1973; Prize for Poetry, Acady of Athens, 1980. Memberships include: Perm Mbr, Joint Dialogue between Orthodox and Anglicans. Hobbies: Reading; Walking; Swimming. Address: Greek Orthodox Archdiocese of Australia, 242 Cleveland Street, Redfern, NSW 2016, Australia.

HARLAND David John, b. 6 Jan 1940, Newcastle, NSW, Aust. Professor. m. Barbara Anne de Simone, 16 Aug 1969, 1 s, 2 d. Education: BA, LLB, Univ of Sydney; Bach of Civil Law, Oxford Univ, Eng. Appointments: Instr, Law Sch, Univ of PA, USA, 1965-66; Lectr in Law 1966-68, Snr Lectr in Law 1968-73, Assoc Prof of Law 1974-81, Prof of Law 1981, Challis Prof of Law 1989, Univ of Sydney; Cnslt, Clayton Utz, 1985-. Publications: Law of Minors, 1974; Co-Auth, Trade Practices and Consumer Protection, 3rd ed, 1983; Co-Auth, Contract Law in Australia, 1986, 3rd ed, 1996; Co-Auth, Cases and Materials on Contract Law in Australia, 1988, 3rd ed, 1998. Memberships: Chmn, Natl Consumer Affairs Advsry Cncl, 1977-87; Assoc Commnr, Trade Practices Commn, 1983-86; Chairperson, Australasian Univs Law Tchrs Assn, 1986-89; Commercial Tribunal of NSW, 1989-95; Intl Acady of Commercial and Consumer Law; Tstee, Travel Compensation Fund, 1986-. Listed in: Who's Who in Australia. Address: University of Sydney Law School, 173-75 Phillip Street, Sydney, NSW 2000, Australia.

HARLAND William Bryce, b. 11 Dec 1931, Wellington, NZ. Retired Diplomat. m. Anne Blackborn, 29 June 1979, 3 s. Education: MA (Hons), NZ; AM (Tufts), USA. Appointments: NZ Amb to China, 1973-75; NZ Perm Rep to the UN, 1982-85; NZ High Commnr to UK, 1985-91. Publications: (books) On Our Own, 1992; Collision Course, 1996. Honours: K St J (US), 1985; QSO (NZ), 1992. Hobbies: Reading; History; Walking. Address: 9 Tinakori Road, Wellington, New Zealand.

HARMAN Grant Stewart, b. 4 Oct 1934, Lismore, NSW, Aust. Professor of Educational Administration. m. Kay Maree Hogan, 9 Jan 1965, 3 s. Education: BA, hons, Hist, 1960, MA, hons, Hist, 1965, Univ of New Eng; PhD, Austl Natl Univ, 1969. Appointments: Tchr, NSW Dept of Educ, 1953-60; Lectr, Armidale Tchrs Coll, 1961-69; Rsch Fell, Fell, Austl Natl Univ, 1969-79; Prof of Educl Admin, 1985, Pro Vice-Chan, 1994-98, Univ of New Eng. Publications: Research in the Politics of Education, 1973-78; The Politics of Education, 1974; Regional Colleges, 1975; Academia Becalmed, 1980; Education, Recession and the World Village, 1986; Quality Assurance for Higher Education, 1996. Memberships: Austl Assn for Rsch in Educ; Fell, Austl Coll of Educ. Address: School of Administration and Training, University of New England, Armidale, NSW 2351, Australia.

HARPER Jenny Gwynnydd, b. 27 Apr 1950, Geraldine, NZ. Art Gallery Director; Educator. Div, 1 d. Education: BA, 1973, MA 1st Class Hons, 1978, Univ Canterbury, NZ; Dip Tchng, Christch Tchrs Coll, NZ,

1976; MPhil, Univ London, Eng, 1982; Dip Mus Stdys, Univ Sydney, Aust, 1983. Appointments: Tutor, Univ Canterbury, 1974-77; Tchr, Naenae Coll, 1978-80; Curator, Eurn Art, Queensland Art Gall, Aust, 1983-86; Snr Curator, 1986-88, Dir, 1990-93, Natl Art Gall, NZ; Institutional Plng, Mus NZ, 1988-89; Currently Assoc Prof, Hd, Art Hist Dept, Vic Univ, Wellington. Publications: Imants Tillers: 1930-1, National Art Gallery, New Zealand; Barbara Kruger, National Art Gallery, New Zealand; Bridget Riley: An Australian Context, Queensland Art Gallery; Boyd Webb, Auckland Art Gallery and Museums Aotearoa. Honours: Sir William Hartley Schlshp, 1981-82; NZ 1990 Commemoration Medal, 1990. Listed in: Who's Who in New Zealand; International Women's Who's Who. Hobbies: Reading; Visiting art galleries; Opera. Address: PO Box 9075, Marton Square, Wellington, New Zealand.

HARRELSON Woody, b. 23 Jul 1961 Midland TX. Actor. m. Laura Louie, 1997, 2 children. Education: Hanover Coll. Theatre Incls: The Boys Next Door; 2 on 2 - auth prodr actor; The Zoo Story - auth actor; Brooklyn Laundry; The Rainmaker. TV incls: Cheers. Films incl: Wildcats; Cool Blue; LA Story; Doc Hollywood; Ted and Venus; White Men Can't Jump; Indecent Proposal; The Cowboy Way; Natural Born Killers; Money Train; The Sunchaser; Kingpin; The People vs Larry Flynt; Wag the Dog; Palmetto; Hi Lo Country; Play it to the Bone. Hobbies: Sports; Juggling; Writing; Chess. Address: c/o Creative Artists Agency, 9830 Wilshire Boulevard, Beverly Hills, CA 90212, USA.

HARRIS Anna, b. 21 June 1959, Sydney, Aust. Career Management; Specialist - Psychology. Education: BA, Sydney Univ; MA (Cnslng) Macquarie Univ; DipEd, Sydney Univ. Tchr, NSW Dept of Educ, 1981-84; Sch Cnslr, NSW Dept of Educ, 1984-87; Mngng Dir and Psychologist, Aptitude Grp, 1988-94; Mngr, KPMG, Outplacement Div, 1994-97; Snr Cnslt, Price Waterhouse (Outplacement), 1997; Cnsltng Psychologist, Audrey Page and Assocs, Aust, 1998-. Memberships: Psychologists Registration Bd of NSW and West Aust. Hobbies: Boating; Opera; Violin playing; Bushwalking; Art galleries. Address: Level 23, St Martins Tower, 44 St George's Terrace, Perth, Western Australia, Australia 6000.

HARRIS Donald Dunstan, b. 2 Dec 1906, Adelaide, Australia. Teacher. Education: BA, Hons, Engl; MA; Dip. Ed; Dip. D'Etudes Francaises. Appointments: Tchr, Dpty Hd, Kings College, Adelaide, 1971; Releiving Geog Tutor, SA Coll of Adv Educn. Publications include: Man in Australia, 1974; Southern South Australia, 1975; Patterns of Trade, 1979; Dilemmas of Development, 1987; Your Money or Your Life, 1990; Which Future, 1991. Honours: Silver Kangaroo, Scout Assn; OAM. Memberships: SA Engl Tchrs Assn; SA Geog Tchrs Assn; Aust Soc of Auths. Hobbies: Gardening; Reading. Address: 341 Parade, Kensington Park, SA 5068, Australia.

HARRIS Jocelyn Margaret, b. 10 Sept 1939. University Lecturer. 1 s, 1 d. Education: MA, Otago; PhD, London. Appointments: Lectr, Univ Otago, 1971; Chair, Univ Otago, 1994, Hd of Engl, 1997-. Publications: Samuel Richardson, Sir Charles Grandson, 1981; Samuel Richardson, 1989; Jane Austen's Art of Memory. Memberships: Austl and Pacific Eighteenth Century Soc. Address: English Department, University of Otago, Box 56, Dunedin, New Zealand.

HARRIS Lagumot. Politician. Appointments: MP, 1968-; Pres of Nauru, Apr-May 1978, 1995-96; Fmr Min for Hlth and Educ; Fmr Min Asstng the Pres. Memberships: Mbr Nauru Party now indep. Address: c/o Office of the President, Yaren, Nauru.

HARRISON Ivan George, b. 27 Sept 1927. Retired. m. Barbara Drake, 9 Sept 1950, 1 s, 1 d. Appointments: Pub Servant, 1944-68; Pvte Sec to Min for Works and Housing, 1968-72; Programming Offr, 1972-78; Offr in Charge of Buildings and Sites Br, 1976; Snr Admin Offr, Investigations, 1977-78; Dir, Div of Admin and Finl Dept Works, 1978-80; Dir Gen, Works Dept of Works, Qld, 1980-87; Chmn, Natl Pub Works Conf, 1983-84.

Membership: Past Mbr, Qld Cultural Trust. Honour: ISO, 1988. Hobbies: Fishing; Sport; Lawn bowls. Address: 15 Shepherdson Street, Capalaba, Qld 4157, Australia.

HARRISON Leonard Charles, b. 24 Dec 1944, Sydney, Australia. Physician. m. (1) Dianne Pilgrim, 3 Dec 1966, 2 s, 3 d, (2) Margo Honeyman, 26 June 1994. Education: MB BS, Univ NSW, 1968; MD, 1977, DSc, 1987, Univ of Melbourne; FRACP; FRCPA. Appointments: Snr Prin Rsch Fell, Natl Hlth and Med Rsch Cncl of Aust; Hd, Autoimmunity and Transplantation Divsn, Walter and Eliza Hall Inst of Med Rsch, Roy Melbourne Hosp; Prof, Dir, Burnet Clin Rsch Unit and Dept of Clin Immunol and Allergy, Roy Melbourne Hosp. Publications: 350 sci articles in profl med jrnls. Honours include: C J Martin Fellshp, Natl Hlth and Med Rsch Cncl of Aust, 1976; Welcome Aust Medal and Awd, 1985; Eric Susman Prize for Rsch, Roy Austl Coll of Physns, 1987; Juvenile Diabetes Fndn Awd, 1988; Keillon Medal, Austl Diabetes Soc. Memberships: Austl Diabetes Soc. Hobbies: Family; Sailing; Tennis; Writing; Italian language and culture. Address: c/o Walter and Eliza Hall Institute of Medical Research, Royal Melbourne Hospital, Parkville, Victoria 3050, Australia.

HARRISON Steve, b. 22 Mar 1952, England. Artist. 1 s. Education: MA, Hons, Wollongong Univ. Publications: Laid Back Wood Firing, 1976; Handbook for Australian Potters, 1984. Membership: Potters Soc of Aust, 1975-. Hobby: My work. Address: c/o Hot & Sticky, Balmoral Village, NSW 2571, Australia.

HARRY Ralph Lindsay, b. Mar 1917, Vic, Aust. Retired Diplomat. m. Elsie Dorothy Sheppard, 8 Jan 1944, 1 s, 2 d. Education: LLB, Tas; BA, Oxford Univ, Eng. Appointments: Austl Dept of External Affairs and posts, 1940-53; Cnsul-Gen, Geneva, Switz, 1953; Repr, Singapore, 1956; Dir, Austl Secret Intelligence Serv, 1957-60; Amb, Brussels, 1965; Saigon, 1968; Bonn, 1971; Perm Repr, NY, USA, 1975-78; Visng Fell, Univ of Tas, 1979; Dir, Austl Inst of Intl Affairs, 1979-81; Natl Aust Day Cttee, 1980. Publications include: The Diplomat Who Laughed, 1983; The North Was Always Near, 1994; Aventuroj en Esperantujo, 1995; No Man is a Hero; Profiles of Pioneer Diplomats, 1997. Honours: Rhodes Schl for Tas, 1938; CBE, 1963; AC, 1980; Hon LLD (Tas), 1990; Memberships include: Fell, Austl Esperanto Assn, Past Pres; Cttee of Patrons, World Esperanto Assn, Hon Life Mbr, Austl Inst of Intl Affairs. Listed in: Who's Who in Australia; International Who's Who. Hobbies: Esperanto International Affairs. Address: 319 Bayview Gardens, 36-42 Cabbage Tree Road, Bayview, NSW 2104, Australia.

HART John Arthur Lewis, b. 4 Sept 1957, Melbourne, Australia. Orthopaedic Surgeon. m. Jan, 9 Oct 1965, 1 s, 1 d. Education: Univ of Melbourne. Appointments: Assessor, Natl Hlth abd Med Rsch Cncl, 1982-; Natl Bd Mbr, Austl Orthopaedic Assn, 1992-; Examiner, Orthopaedic Surg, 1992-98, Bd of Orthopaedic Surg, 1994-; Roy Austl Coll of Surgns; Clin Assoc Prof, Dept of Surg, Monash Univ, 1996-. Publications: Sev articles in profl med jrnls. Honours: ALSA Maj Bursary Vic Sci Talent Quest, 1955; The Alped Hosp Travelling Fell, 1988; Intl Cultural Dip of Hon, 1990; Fell, Austl Coll of Sports Physns, 1993; L O Betts Meml Gold Medal, Austl Orthopaedic Assn, 1997; The Evelyn Hamilton Trust Prize, Austl Orthopaedic Assn, 1997; Hon Mbr, The Knee Soc, 1998. Memberships: Kooyong Lawn Tennis Club; Yarra Yarra Golf Club; Vic Ski Club; Lord Baden Powell Soc; Davis Cup Tennis Assn; Healesville Sanctuary Sponsor; Austl Geog Soc; Gold Maroon and Black Patrons Club. Hobbies: Tennis; Golf; Skiing; Philately; Cartography; Indigenous art. Address: 16 Riversdale Court, East Hawthorn, Victoria 3122, Australia.

HART Lynette Arnason, b. 12 Nov 1938, Salt Lake City, UT, USA. Professor. m. Ben, 6 Jan 1983, 1 s, 3 d. Education: BS, Brigham Yng; MA, UC Berkeley; PhD, Rutgers. Appointments: Rsch Assoc, Monell Chem Senses Cntr, 1976-81; Asst Prof, 1990, Assoc Prof, 1995, Dept of Hlth; Dir, Cntr Animals in Soc; Dir, Univ of CA, Cntr for Animal Alternatives. Publications: Co-Auth,

Canine and Feline Behavioural Therapy; The Perfect Puppy; Ed, Responsible Conduct of Research with Animals. Memberships: Intl Soc for Anthro Zool; Acoustical Soc of Am; Animal Behavior Soc. Address: Center for Animals in Society, School of Veterinary Medicine, University of California, Daves, CA 95616, USA.

HARTARTO, b. 30 May 1932 Delanggu Cntrl Java. Politician. Education: Inst of Technol Bandung; Univ of NSW. Appointments: Technol Dir Leces paper factory, 1961; Mngng Dir of Bd dealing with paper inds Dept of Ind, 1965; Dir Silicate Ind Div Directorate-Gen of Basic Chem Inds Dept of Ind, 1974; Dir-Gen for Basic Chem Inds, 1979; Min of Ind, 1983-93; Co-ordng Min for Indl and Trade Affairs, 1993-96; Co-ordng Min for Prodn and Distribution, 1996-. Memberships: Mbr Mngmnt Bd state-owned paper factories of Padalarang and Leces, 1959. Address: Office of Co-ordinating Minister for Production and Distribution, Jalan Jenderal Gatot Subroto Kav 52-53, Jakarta 12950, Indonesia.

HARTSTONGE Mary Ellen (Sister Mary Lucia), b. 16 Oct 1934, Mosgiel, Otago. CEO, Hospital Administration. Education: NZRG and ON, 1960; NZ Reg Midwife, 1965; NZ Postgrad Dip in Nursing, 1967. Appointments: Prin Nurse, Mecy Hosp, Dunedin, 1974-90; Min of Hlth Bed Indiactors Cttee, 1986; CEO, Mercy Hosp Dunedin Ltd, 1990-. Honours: Paul Harris Rotary Fellshp, 1995; Offr NZ Order of Merit (ONZM), 1996. Memberships include: NZ Nurses Assn, 1961-, Cncl Mbr, Otago Branch, 3 yrs, Dpty Chairperson, 1973; Exec Mbr, NZ Priv Hosps Assn, 1983-93; Sisters of Mercy (Diocese of Dunedin) Trust Bd, 1987-; Asst to Superior Gen of Sisters of Mercy (Diocese of Dunedin), 1987-94; Fedn of Sisters of Mercy of NZ, 1987-94; Leadership Team, Sisters of Mercy (Dunedin), 1987-; Dir, Bd of Mercy Hosp Dunedin Ltd, 1994-; Exec Cttee, Bd of Mercy Hosp Dunedin Ltd, 1994-. Hobbies: Leathercraft; Fishing; Gardening. Address: 10 Bellevue Street, Belleknowes, Dunedin, New Zealand.

HARVEY Bryan Laurance, b. 1 Nov 1937, Newport, Gwent, Wales. Professor. m. Eileen, 24 Sept 1960, 2 s. Education: BSA, Horticulture, 1960, MSc, 1961, Univ of Saskatchewan; PhD, Genetics, Univ CA, 1964. Appointments: Asst Prof, Univ of Guelph, 1964-66; Asst Prof, Prof, Univ of Saskatchewan, 1966-, Asst Dean of Agric, 1980-83; Visng Prof, Nairobi, 1975; Hd, Crop Sci and Plant Ecology, 36 varieties of barley regd, Univ of Saskatchewan, 1993-94, Dir, Crop Dev Cntr, 1983-94; Hd Hort Sci, 1994-97, Coord, Agric Res, 1997-. Publications: Sev articles in profl jrnls. Honours include: Fellshps: AIC, 1990, ASA, 1990, CSSA, 1990; MBBA Recog Awd, 1996; Outstndng Sci, CSTA, 1997. Memberships: Chair, CSGA Plant Breeders Cttee; Chair, IOC Intl Barley Genetic Conf; Chair, Cand Cttee on Crops; Pres, Agricl Inst of Can; Life Mbr, SSGA, 1992; Life Mbr, CSGA, 1994; Dir, Accreditation AIC, Chir, Min Advsry Cttee on Plant Breeding Rights, 1997. Address: c/o University of Saskatchewan, 204 Kirk Hall, 117 Science Park, Saskatoon, Saskatchewan S7N 5C8, Canada.

HARVEY John Vernon, b. 3 Jan 1923, Adelaide, Aust. Brewing Consultant. m. Margaret Goudie, 28 June 1947, 3 s, 1 d. Education: St Peters' Coll, Adelaide; S Austl Sch of Mines and Inds (ASASM). Appointments: Analyst, Adelaide Chem Wrks Ltd, 1944-46; Asst Brewer and Analyst, 1946-48; Lab Supt, 1949-67; Techl Supt, 1968-78, Hd Brewer, 1979-85, Retd, 1985, The S Austl Brewing Co Ltd, Adelaide. Publications: Chapt, Analysis of Beers, Vol 2, Brewing Science, 1981; Papers presented at 1953, 1955, 1958, 1960, 1962, 1986 Conventions: Asia Pacific Sect, Inst of Brewing and 1971 Convention Amn Soc of Brewing Chems. Memberships: Fell, Inst of Brewing, sec, Asia Pacific Sect, Inst of Brewing, 1953-57, 1985-95, cttee mbr, 1957-65, mbr, editl sub-cttee, 1958-67, 1969-98, Ed, 1995-98; Fell, Roy Austl Chem Inst; Fell, Austl Inst of Food Sci and Technol; Master Brewers Assn of Ams; Amn Soc of Brewing Chems; Histl Soc of S Aust. Hobbies: Photography; Travel; Colonial history; History of Brewing; Rotarian. Address: 26 Davis Street, West Beach, SA 5024, Australia.

HARVEY Mark Stephen, b. 17 Sept 1958. Scientist. 1 d. Education: BS, PhD, Monash Univ. Appointments: Rsch Fell, Div of Entomology, CSIRO, Canberra, 1983-85; Rsch Fell, Mus of Victoria, Melbourne, 1985-89; Curator, 1989-95; Snr Curator, 1995-, Arachnids, WA Mus, Perth. Creative works: co-author, Worms to Wasps, 1989; Catalogue of the Pseudoscorpionida, 1991; Num scientific papers; Sev edited vols. Honour: Edgeworth David Medal, 1991. Memberships: Editl Advsry Cttee, 1989-95; Arachnology Nomenclature Cttee, 1992-; Austl Heritage Commns Western Austl Environment Panel, 1993-; Fauna Editl Cttee, 1994-; Natl Cttee, Animal and Vet Scis, Austl Acad of Sci, 1996-. Listed in: Who's Who of Australian Writers, 1991; International Authors and Writers Who's Who, 1995; Australian Men and Women of Science, Engineering and Technology, 1995; Who's Who of Australian Writers, 1995; Who's Who and What's What of Western Australia, 1996. Hobbies: Basketball; Old books. Address: Western Australian Museum, Francis Street, Perth, WA 6000, Australia.

HARVEY Suzanne MacLeod, b. 2 Nov 1946, Palmerston, NZ. Nursing. Education: Bachelor Hlth Sci (Mngmt), Mitchell CAE, NSW; Spinal Injuries Cert, Stoke Mandeville Hosp, UK; Regd Nurse, NZ; Intensive Care Cert, Roy Infirmary Edinburgh, Scotland. Appointments include: Staff Nurse, Christchurch Pub Hosp, NZ, 1968; Regd Nurse, Bourke Dist Hosp, NSW, Aust, 1969; Post-Grad courses, UK, 1970-73; Regd Nurse, Shenton Pk Rehab Cntr, Perth, WA, 1973; Nursing Unit Mngr, Intensive Care Unit, Roy Prince Alfred Hosp, Sydney, Aust, 1974-76; Charge Nurse, Intensive Care Unit, Christchurch Hosp, NZ, 1977-78; Supvsr, Intensive Care Unit, Westmead Hosp, Sydney, Aust, 1978-81; Asst Dir of Nursing, Accident & Emergency, Westmead Hosp, Sydney, 1981-85; Asst Dir, Nursing Pediats, Westmead Hosp, Sydney, NSW, 1985-88; Dpty Dir of Nursing, Auburn Dist Hosp, Sydney, 1990; Asst Dir, Nursing Radiology, Nuclear Med, Staff Hlth, Outpatients, Accident & Emergency, Endoscopy, Geriatric Day Care, Radiation Oncology, Westmead Hosp, Sydney, 1989-90; Dpty Dir of Nursing, Roy N Shore Hosp, Sydney, 1990-95; Dpty Dir of Nursing and Patient Servs, Roy N Shore Hosp, Sydney, 1995; Exec Dir of Nursing, Hum Resources & Patient Servs, Austin & Repatriation Medl Cntr, Melbourne, Vic, 1995-; Exec Dir Nursing and Patient Support Servs, 1997-. Honour: Finalist, Victoria Bus Woman of the Yr, Corp and Govt Sect, 1998. Memberships: NSW Coll of Nursing, 1987; Charles Stuart Univ, Mitchell Coll Grads Assn, 1989; Aust Coll of Hlth Serv Execs (Vic), Assoc Fell, 1990; Aust Coll of Hlth Sev Execs, Cert Hlth Exec (CHE), 1991; Roy Coll of Nursing, Aust, 1995; Victorian Nurse Exec Assn, Fell, 1996. Listed in: Contemporary Australian Women, 1996-97. Hobbies: Reading; Walking; Ballet; Opera; Swimming. Address: Austin & Repatriation Centre, Austin Campus, Studley Road, Heidelberg, Vic 3084, Australia.

HASANY Syed Moosa, b. 21 Dec 1942, Tonk, India. Scientist. m. Farhat Aziz Sulemani, 2 Sept 1973, 1 s, 1 d. Education: BSc, hons; MSc; PhD. Appointments: Lectr in Chem, Univ of Karachi, 1964-65; Asst Sci Offr, 1965-66, Sci Offr, 1967-71, Snr Sci Offr, 1971-78, Prin Sci Offr, 1978-92, Chf Sci Offr, 1992-. Publications: Over 88 rsch pprs in profl jrnls. Honours: Colombo Plan Fell, 1968-71; Alexander von Humboldt Fell, 1973-74; 2nd Prize of Rsch in Chem, Govt of Pakistan, 1986; Pinstech Perform Gold Medal, 1994; INFAQ Fndn, Pakistan Acady Joint Gold Medal in Chem Scis, 1995. Memberships: Austl Alumni Assn of Pakistan; Nuclear Soc of Pakistan; Fell, Chart Chem, Roy Soc of Chem, England; Fell, Chem Soc of Pakistan. Hobbies: Reading; Writing. Address: #738 St 10, 9-9/3, Islamabad, Pakistan.

HASEBE Norio, b. 2 Feb 1942, Japan. Professor. m. Misako, 29 Mar 1975, 1 s, 2 d. Education: Dr Engrng. Appointments: Asst, 1964; Lectr, 1971; Assoc Prof, 1975, Prof, 1984, Nagoya Inst of Technol. Publications: Handbook of Stress Intensity Factors I and II, 1987, III, 1992. Memberships: Amn Soc of Civ Engrs; Japanese Soc of Civ Engrs; Japanese Soc of Mechl Engrs. Hobbies: Tennis; Skiing. Address: Umesato 2-14-15, Midoriku, Nagoya 458-0001, Japan.

HASÉGAWA Yasuji, b. 7 Oct 1929, Ôsaka Cty, Japan. Emeritus Professor at Tôka'i University; Retired French Language Educator. m. Yaé Ta'ichi, Mar 1959, (decd) May 1959. Education: Dip, French, Ôsaka For Langs Sch, 1950; Lic of Letters, French Lit, Kyôto Univ, 1953. Appointments: 1st Sec and Tchr, Inst Franco-Japonais du Kansa'i, Kyôto, 1953-60; Instr of French at Tôka'i Univ, Tôkyô, 1960-66; Asst Prof, Tôka'i Univ, 1966-75; Prof, For Langs Tchng Cntr, Tôka'i Univ, 1975-95. Publications: (textbook) Onze leçons de la grammaire du français parlé, 1982. Honours: Dpty Dir Gen, IBC, 1997; Lifetime Dpty Gov, ABI, 1997; Most Admired Man of Decade, 1997. Memberships: Japan Soc of French Lang and lit; Japan Soc of French Lang Tchng. Hobbies: Walking; Studying history of Japan; Translating Japanese writings into French. Address: 2241-14 Minami-Yana Hadano-shi 257-0003, Japan.

HASHIGUCHI Yasuo, b. 31 July 1924, Japan. m. Eiko Uchida, 8 Jan 1957, 1 s, 1 d. Education: BA, Univ of Tokyo, 1948; MEd, Ohio Univ, USA, 1951. Appointments: Assoc Prof, Engl, Kagoshima Univ, 1951-64, 1964-68; Prof, 1968-82, Kyushu Univ; Fukuoka Univ, 1982-88; Pres, Fukuoka Jo Gakuin Jnr Coll, 1988-93; Prof, Yasuda Women's Univ, 1993-96. Publications: Ed, Complete Works of John Steinbeck, 20 vols, 1985. Honours: Dick A Renner Prize, 1976; Spec Recog for Outstndng Publ, 1988; Recog for Many Yrs of Outstndng Ldrshp in Amn Lit and Steinbeck Studies, 1991; Richard W and Dorothy Barkhardt Awd, 1994; John J and Angeline Pruis Awd, 1996. Memberships: Kyushu Amn Lit Soc, Pres 1977-89, Advsr 1989-; Steinbeck Soc of Jap, Pres 1977-91, Hon Pres 1991-; Intl Steinbeck Soc, Snr Cnslt, 1983-; Intl Assoc of Univ Profs of Eng, 1999. Hobbies: Music; Reading; Christian Literature. Address: 7-29-31-105 Iikura, Sawara-ku, Fukuoka 814-0161, Japan.

HASHIM Jawad M, b. 10 Feb 1938. Economist; Politician. m. Salwa Al-Rufaiee, 1961, 2 s. Education: London Sch of Econs and Polit Sci Univ of London. Appointments: Prof of Stats Univ of Baghdad, 1967; Dir-Gen Cntrl Statistical Org, 1968; Min of Plng, 1968-71; Min of Plng, 1972-74; Chmn UN Econ Commn for West Asia - ECWA, 1975; Pres Arab Monetary Fund - AMF - Apr 1977-82; Fell Intl Bankers' Assn. Publications: Capital Formation in Iraq, 1957-70; National Income - Its Methods of Estimation; The Evaluation of Economic Growth in Iraq, 1950-70; Development of Iraq's Foreign Trade Sector, 1950-70; Eighteen articles and sev papers. Memberships: Mbr Econ Off Revolutionary Command Cncl, 1971-72, 1974-77; Mbr Consultative Grp on Intl Econ and Monetary Affairs - Rockefeller Fndn; Mbr Economists Assn Iraq; Mbr Study Grp on Energy and World Econs. Hobbies: Sport; Driving; Reading. Address: c/o Arab Monetary Fund, P O Box 2818, Abu Dhabi, United Arab Emirates.

HASHIMOTO Ryutaro, b. 29 July 1937. Politician. m. Kumiko Hashimoto, 2 s, 3 d. Education: Keio Univ. Appointments: Previous posts incl: Chmn Cttee on Socl and Labour Problems HoR; Dep Chmn Liberal Dem Party - LDP Pol Rsch Cncl; Chmn LDP Rsch Commn on Pub Admin and Fins; Min of Transp, 1986-87; Sec-Gen LDP, Jul-Aug 1989; Min of Fin, 1989-91; Min of Intl Trade and Ind, 1994-96; Pres LDP, 1995-; PM of Japan, Jan 1996-; Liberal Dem Party. Hobbies: Kendo -5th dang; Mountaineering; Photog. Address: Office of the Prime Minister, 1-6 Nagata-cho, Chiyoda-ku, Tokyo 100, Japan.

HASHMI Ziauddin Syed, b. 24 Feb 1960, Pakistan. Manager; Research and Development Worker. m. Shameem, 24 Jan 1987, 1 s, 1 d. Education: BSc, Hons; MSc; PhD. Appointment: Rsch Asst, Pub Hlth Rsch Lab, Univ Karachi, 1983; Microbio, Haj Rsch Proj, Haj Rsch Cntr, KAIA Clin, Jeddah, Saudi Arabia, 1983; Lectr, Dept of Med Scis, Univ of Umm Al-Qura, Makkah Al-Mukarramah, Saudi Arabia, 1984-88; Demonstrator, Dept of Microbiol, Univ Otago, 1989-92; Postdoct Fell, Univ Sydney, 1993-94; Mngr, Pharm Section, Rsch and Devel Dept, BOMAC Labs Ltd. Publications: Sev articles in profl jrnls. Honours: Rsch Studentshp, Pub Hlth Rsch Lab, Univ Karachi, 1983; Summer Studentshp, Otago Med Rsch Fndn, 1989-91; Merit Schlshp, NZ Univ Grants

Cttee, 1990-92; Glaxo Prize, 1992. Memberships: MBIRA; NZ Microbiol Soc; Roy Soc of NZ; ZN Org for Quality; Cnslt, Agric Compounds and Vet Med Act, Min of Agric and Forestry, NZ, 1997; MASM. Hobbies: Reading; Writing; Community work. Address: 31 Watson Place, Papatoetoe, Manukau City, Auckland, New Zealand.

HASKARD Malcolm Rosswyn, b. 22 Apr 1936. Professor; Microelectronics Engineer. m. Georgina Isabella McLaughlan, 25 Jan 1964, 1 s, 1 d. Education: BE, 1st Hons, 1959; ME, 1964; Grad Dip, Maths, 1978. Appointments: Rsch Fell, Univ of Adelaide, 1961; Lectr, SA Technol, 1963; Snr Lect, 1968; Prin Lect, SA Inst Tech, 1983; Assoc Prof, Univ of South Aust, 1990; Prof, 1993; Hd Sch Electron Engrng, 1995; Retired, 1996; Adj Prof Sch Phys and Electronic Systems Engrng, Univ S Aust, 1997. Creative works: 9 books; 2 chapts in other books. Honour: JP, SA, 1978-. Memberships: Fell, Inst Engrs Austl, by invitation ; Fell, Inst Radio and Electrons Engrs, Austl; Fell, Inst Elec Engrs, London. Hobbies: Music; Amateur radio; Lay preacher. Address: Windrush House, Bassnet Road, One Tree Hill, SA 5114, Australia.

HASKELL John Christopher, b. 18 Sept 1931. University Professor and Architect. m. Janetta, 1 ss, 2 d. Education: MA, Dipl TP, (London); Rome Schl in Arch. Appointments: First Asst Commnr (Arch), Natl Capital Dept Commn, Canberra, 1972-75; Prof of Arch, Univ of NSW, 1975-93. Publications: Haskell's Sydney, 1983; Sydney Architecture, 1997. Honour: Rome Schlshp in Arch, 1955. Memberships: Assn Roy Inst of Brit Archts, 1955; Assn Roy Austl Inst Archts, 1975. Hobbies: Travel; Sketching; Music. Address: 5/13 McLeod Street, Mosman, Sydney, NSW 2088, Australia.

HASLETT Stephen John, b. 24 Jan 1951, Wellington. Statistician, Associate Professor, Director. m. Hilary Anne Smith, 1 s. Education: BSc, Otago Univ, 1971; BA, 1977; BA, First Class Hons, Vic Univ of Wellington, 1980; PhD, 1986. Appointments: Chartered Statn; Fell of Royal Stats Soc; Assoc Prof, Surv Sect, Stats Lab, Dept of Stats, IA State Univ, 1988-90; Rsch Statn, Dir of Internal Cnsltng, Inst of Stats and Ops Rsch, Vic Univ of Wellington, NZ. Publications: Theort Stats, Applied Stats. Memberships: Convenor of Surv Appraisals and Pub Questions Cttee, NZ Stats Assoc. Address: 116 Buick Cres, Palmerston North, New Zealand.

HASNAIN Nadeem, b. 20 Mar 1952, Ghazipur, UP, India. Teacher; Researcher. m. Nishat Fatima, 17 Dec 1975, 1 s, 1 d. Education: MA, Socl Anthropology; PhD, Socl Anthropology. Appointments: Rdr, Anthropology, Shia Post-Grad Coll, Lucknow Univ. Publications: Bonded For Ever, 1982; Shias and Shia Islam in India, 1988; Tribal India, 1991; Indian Anthropology, 1991; General Anthropology, 1991; Unifying Anthropology, 1996; 12 rsch pprs; Over 50 articles in newspprs and popular mags. Honours: Cert for Rsch Metgodology, Indian Cncl of Socl Sci Rsch. Membership: Life Mbr, currently Gen Sec, Ethnographical and Folkculture Soc. Hobbies: Sports (cricket); Writing in popular magazines. Address: 5/505 Uikas Nagar, Lucknow, India.

HASSAN IBN TALAL, b. 20 Mar 1947 Amman. Former Crown Prince of Jordan. m. Sarrath Khujista Akhter Banu, 1968, 1 s, 3 d. Education: Christ Ch Oxford Univ. Appointments: Brother of H M Hussein ibn Talal King of Jordan - qv; Heir to the throne; Acts as Regent during absence of King Hussein; Ombudsman for Natl Devt, 1971-; Fndr of Roy Scientific Soc of Jordan, 1970; Fndr Roy Acady for Islamic Civilization Rsch - Al AlBait - 1980; Fndr Arab Thought Forum, 1981; Fndr Forum Humanum - now Araby Yth Forum - 1982; Co-Chmn Indep Commn on Intl Humanitarian Issues; Co-Patron Islamic Acady of Scis; Pres Higher Cncl for Sci and Tech. Publications: A Study on Jerusalem, 1979; Palestinian Self-Determination, 1981; Search for Peace, 1984. Honours: Hon Gen of Jordan Armed Forces; Medal of Pres of Italian Repub, 1982; Kt of Grand Cross of Order of Merit - Italy - 1983; Hon Dr Arts and Scis - Jordan - 1987; Hon DCL - Durham - 1990; Dr hc - Ulster - 1996. Hobbies: Polo; Squash; Scuba Diving; Mountaineering; Archaeology; Karate; Taekwondo; Helicopter Piloting;

Skiing. Address: Office of the Crown Prince, The Royal Palace, Amman, Jordan.

HASSAN SHARQ Mohammad, b. 1925, Farah, Afghanistan. Politician. Appointments: Dep PM, 1974-77; PM of Afghanistan, 1988-89. Address: c/o Office of the Prime Minister, Kabul, Afghanistan.

HASSETT Francis George, b. 11 Apr 1918, Sydney, Aust. Soldier (retired). m. Margaret Hallie Spencer, 18 May 1946, 2 s, 1 dec, 2 d. Education: psc, Staff Coll, Aust; IDC, London. Appointments: Lt Darwin Mobile Force, 1939; AIF Mid E a SWPA (wounded) (mid twice) 2/3 Aust Inf Bn, Bde Maj 18 Aust Inf Bde GSO I HQ 3 Aust Div (Lt Col) Comd I RAR and 3 RAR Korea, 1951-52; Mil Sec, AHQ, 1958; DMA Duntroon, 1953; Cmndr, C'Wlth Bde, 1960-62; Dep CGS, Aust, 1964-66; Hd, Austl Jt Servs Staff, London, 1966-67; Extra Gentlemen Uher to HM the Queen, 1966-68; GOC Northern Comd, 1968-70; Vice CGS Aust, 1971-73; CGS 1973-75; Lt Gen 1977; Ch of Def Force Staff, Chmn Chfs of Staff, 1975-77; Gen 1975. Publications: Var mil papers. Honours: OBE, 1945; DSO, 1953; LVO, 1954; CBE, 1966; CB, 1968; AC, 1975; KBE, 1976. Hobbies: Gardening; Writing. Address: 42 Mugga Way, Red Hill, Canberra, ACT 2603, Australia.

HASUNUMA Kohji, b. 12 Dec 1943, Tokyo, Japan. Molecular Biologist. m. Miyako Abe, 14 Mar 1971, 1 s, 1 d. Education: BS, 1966, MSc, 1968, DSc, 1971, Bio Sci, Fac of Sci, Tokyo Univ. Appointments: Rsch Assoc, Fac of Culture & Sci, Tokyo Univ, 1971; Assoc Prof, Natl Inst for Basic Bio, 1979; Visng Rschr, Lab of Dr Winslow R Briggs, Carnegie Instn of Wash, Dept of Plant Bio, Stanford, USA, 1990; Prof, Kihara Inst for Biol Rsch and Grad Sch of Integrated Sci, Yokohama Cty Univ, 1990-. Publications: Co-Ed, books: Signal Transduction in Plants (in Japanese), 1996; Light Signal Transduction (in Japanese), 1999; Reviews; 8 original pprs on light signal transduction. Honours: 20th Century Achievement Awd, ABI, 1998; Disting Leadership Awd, ABI, 1998; Magnificent and Disting Deeds, ABI, USA, 1998; Dpty Dir Gen, IBC, Mem Silver Medal, 1998; Hall of Fame Hon, ABI, 1998; Amn Biog Inst, 2000 Millenium Medal of Hon, 1998; IBC, Intl Man of Yr 1997/98 Awd, 1998; IBC, Citation of Meritorious Achievement Awd, 1998; Decree of Merit Awd, 1998; 20th Century Awd for Achievement, IBC, 1999. Memberships: NY Acady Scis, NY, 1997-; Life Fell, IBC, 1998-; Bd of Advsrs, Life Fell, ABI, 1998-. Hobby: Enjoys jogging. Address: 438-7 Tsuruma Machidashi, Tokyo 194-0004, Japan.

HATA Eijiro. Politician. Appointments: Chmn Socl and Labour Affairs Ctte; Parly Vice-Min of Posts and Telecomms; Vice-Min of Hlth and Welfare; Min of Agric Forestry and Fisheries, 1993-94; Min Inl Trade and Ind, May-Jun 1994. Memberships: Mbr HoR; Mbr Japanese Renewal Party - Shinseito JRP. Address: House of Representatives, Tokyo, Japan.

HATA Tsutomu, b. 24 Aug 1935 Tokyo. Politician. Education: Seijo Univ. Appointments: Fmr bus tour operator; Elected to HoR, 1969; Fmr Parly Vice-Min of Psts and Telecomms; Vice-Min of Agric Forestry and Fisheries; Fmr Min of Agric Forestry and Fishers;;Chmn Liberal Dem Party - LDP - Rsch Commn on the Election System; Min of Fin, 1991-92; Left LDP to fnd Shinseito - New Life Party; Pres, 1993-94; Shinseito dissolved, 1994 - merged with eight others to form New Frontier Party; Ldr Good Governance Party, 1998-; Dep PM and Min of For Affairs, 1993-94; PM of Japan, May-Jun 1994. Address: House of Representatives, Tokyo, Japan.

HATANAKA Kaoru, b. 4 Nov 1943, Japan. Pharmaceutical Physician. m. Masako, 1970. Education: MD. Appointments: Hd, Toxicology Path Unit, 1996-1998; Medl Advsr, 1998-. Creative Works: Hatanaka K, et al Pathol; Hananaka K, et al, Thromb Res. Memberships: Japanese Soc of Path; Japan Shock Soc; Japanese Assn of Medl Drs in Drus Inds. Hobbies: Tennis; Fishing. Address: Shionogi and Co, Ltd, 5-12-4 Sagisu, Fukushima-ku, Osaka, 553-0002, Japan.

HATANO Yoshio, b. 3 Jan 1932, Tokyo, Japan. President. m. Sumiko Hatano, 16 Apr 1961, 1 s, 1 d. Education: BA, Woodrow Wilson Sch, Princeton Univ; Rsch Assoc, Intl Inst of Strategic Stdies, London. Appointments: Amb, Intl Org, Geneva, 1987-90, UN, 1990-94; Prof, Gakushuin Womens Univ. Memberships: Natl Cncls on Pub Safety and Environ; Pres, Security Cncl of the UN, 1994. Hobbies: Golf; Opera; Classical Music; Sports. Address: 2-14-13 Hiroo, Shibuya-ku, Tokyo, Japan.

HATCH Marshall Davidson, b. 24 Dec 1932, Perth, Aust. Scientist. m. (1) 2s, (2) Lyndall Langman, 23 July 1983. Education: Hon BSc; PhD, Sydney Univ. Appointments: Rsch Sci, CSIRO, 1955-59; Rsch Fell, Univ of CA, USA, 1959-61; Rsch Offr, CSR Co Ltd, Brisbane, 1961-66, 1968-69; Reader, Univ of Qld, 1967; Chief Rsch Sci, CSIRO, Canberra. Publications: 156 publs inclng 24 reviews, chapts or edited books. Honours: Fell, Austl Acady of Sci, 1975; Roy Soc, Eng, 1980; Clarke Medal, 1973; Lemberg Medal, 1975; Charles Kettering Awd, 1980; Rank Awd, 1981; AM, 1981; For Assoc, Natl Acady of Sci, USA, 1990; Intl Prize for Bio, Jap Soc for Promotion of Sci, 1991; Hon Doctorate, Univ of Göttingen, Germany, 1992; Hon Doct, Univ of Qld, 1998. Memberships: Austl Biochem Soc; Austl Soc of Plant Physiologists; Biochem Soc, Eng; Amn Soc of Plant Physiologists. Address: PO Box 480, Jamison Centre, ACT 2614, Australia.

HATOYAMA Kunio. Politician. Appointments: Fmr Parly Vice-Min for Educ; Dir Liberal Dem Party - LDP - Educ Div; Chmn Cttee on Educ HoR; Min of Educ, 1991-92; Min of Labour, May-Jun 1994. Memberships: Mbr HoR; Mbr Renaissance Party, 1993. Address: c/o Ministry of Education, 3-2 Kasumigaseki, Chiyoda-ku, Tokyo, Japan.

HATTAB Faiez Najib, b. 12 Aug 1944, Mosul, Iraq. Dentist; Professor. m. Ayoub Rasha, 21 July 1989, 3 s. Education: BDS, Baghdad Univ; PhD, Odont Dr, Karolinska Inst, Stockholm, Sweden. Appointments: Snr Rschr, Hong Kong Univ, 1985-87; Cnslt, Assoc Prof, Chmn, Dept of Restorative and Pediat Dentistry. Publications: Chapts in books, over 60 articles in profl jrnls. Memberships: Eurn Org for Caries Rsch; Intl Assn for Dental Rsch; NY Acady of Scis. Hobbies: Swimming; Jogging; Travelling. Address: PO Box 6 Husn, Irbid, Jordan.

HATTON Stephen Paul, b. 28 Jan 1948 Sydney. Politician. m. (1) Deborah J Humphreys, 1969, div 1993, 3 s, 1 d. (2) Cathy Huyer, 1995, 1 d. Education: Univ of NSW. Appointments: Personnel Offr James Hardie & Co Pty Ltd, 1965-70; Indl Offr Nabalco Pty Ltd, 1970-75; Exec Dir NT Confedn of Inds and Com Inc, 1975-83; Elected NT Legislaative Ass - Nightcliff - 1983-; Min for Lands Conservation Ports and Fisheries Primary Prodn, 1983-84; Min for Mines and Energy Primary Prodn, 1986; Chf Min for NT, 1986-88; Min for Hlth and Community Servs, 1989; Min for Conservation, 1989; Min for Inds and Dev and for Trade Dev Zone and Liquor Commn, 1990-91; Min for Lands Housing and Local Govt and Min for Aboriginal Devt, 1992; Min for Constitutional Devt, 1994; Att-Gen Min for Educ Min for Sport and Recreation Min for Constitutional Dev, 1995; Min for Correctional Servs Min for Sport and Recreation Min for Parks and Wildlife Min for Ethnic Affairs, 1996-. Hobbies: Sport. Address: Parliament House, State Square, Darwin, NT 0800, Australia.

HAUCK James Pierre, b. 23 Jan 1946, St Cloud, MN, USA. Scientist. m. Ann Stevenson, 29 July 1997, 2 s, 3 d. Education: BS, Phys; BS, Math; MA, Phys; PhD, Phys. Appointments: Prin Engr Spec, 1976-; Pres, Chf Scientist, JPN Profl Scis Inc, 1984-. Creative Works: 10 rfrd jrnl publs, 1973-; PhD Dissertation, 1976. Honours: about 18 Who's Who and Acad awds; NEEA; NOAA; Memberships: Inst of Elecl and Electron Engrs; SPIE; Intl Optios Soc. Hobbies: Biking; Surfing; Diving; Piano. Address: 2658 Del Mar Heights, Rd #192, Del Mar, CA 92010, USA.

HAVEA Sione Amanaki, b. 6 Jan 1922, Tonga. Minister of Religion; President. m. Etina Feaomoetoa Havea, 27 Jan 1947, 3 s, 4 d. Education: Tupou Coll Hon Bd, 1933; Bach of Divinity, St Paul's Univ, 1958. Appointments: Deputation for Overseas Mission, Meth Ch of Australasia, 1941; Delegate to World Cncl of Chs, 1953, 1961, 1975, 1983; Chmn, Pacific Conf of Chs, 1961; Roy Chaplain to the King of Tonga, 1971; Offl Delegate/Assemblies, World Meth Conf, 1971, 1976, 1981, 1986; Elected Pres, 1971, Re-elected Pres, 1982, Meth Ch in Tonga; Mbr of Presidum, World Meth Conf, 1971; Prin, Pacific Theol Coll, Suva, Fiji, 1977. Publications: Ed, Tohi Fanongonongo Church Paper, 1958; Translator, Tongan Bible, 1995; Regular articles to Ch Pprs. Memberships: Regl Mbr, Fndn for Peoples of the S Pacific, 1975; Chmn, Tongan Cncl of Devel Trust, 1983. Hobbies: Reading; Gardening. Address: PO Box 207, Nukualofa, Tonga, South Pacific.

HAWCROFT Timothy James, b. 7 July 1946, Sydney, Aust. Veterinary Surgeon. m. Janette, 10 Apr 1971, 1 s, 3 d. Education: BVSc (Hons); MACVSc. Publications: Complete Book of Horse Care; Complete Book of Dog Care; Complete Book of Cat Care; A to Z Horse Diseases and Health Problems; First Aid Dogs; First Aid Cats; First Aid Horses; First Aid Birds. Honour: Best Gen Reference Book, Dog Writers' Assn of Am, 1992. Membership: Austl Coll of Vet Scientists. Address: 19 Ryde Road, Pymble, NSW 2073, Australia.

HAY David Russell (Sir), b. 8 Dec 1927, NZ. Retired Cardiologist. m. Jocelyn Valerie Bell, 22 Feb 1958, 2 d. Education: MB, ChB, 1951; MD, 1960, Univ of NZ; FRCP, London, 1971; FRACP, 1965. Appointments: Res, Christchurch, Hammersmith, Brompton, Natl Heart Hosps, 1951-55; Snr Registrar, Dunedin and Christchurch Hosps, 1956-59; Physn 1959-64; Cardiologist, 1964-89; Hd, Dept of Cardiology, 1969-78; Chmn of Med Servs, 1978-84, N Canterbury Hosp Bd; Clinl Lectr, Christchurch Clinl Sch, 1973-80; Clinl Reader, Christchurch Sch of Med, 1980-88; Med Dir, Natl Heart Fndn, 1977-92; Past Chmn, Christchurch Hosps Med Staff Assn, 1983-85; Mbr, Advsry Cttee to Min of Hlth on Smoking and Hlth, 1974-87; To Min of Hlth on Prevention of Cardiovascular Diseases, 1985-87; Ed, NHF Tech Rprt Series, 1975-90. Publications include: Over 90 pprs in sci jrnls. Honours: CBE, 1981; NZ, Commemoration Medal, 1990; Kt, 1991; Coll Medal RACP, 1993; WHO Tobacco or Hlth Medal, 1995. Memberships include: Past Pres, Canterbury Div of Brit Med Assn; Past Chmn, Cntrl Specialists Cttee, BMA, 1967-68; Past Chmn, Cardiac Soc of Aust and NZ (NZ Reg); Mbr, WHO Expert Advsry Panel on Tobacco or Hlth, 1977-; Life Mbr, Natl Heart Fndn of NZ, 1992-, Pres, 1996-99. Hobbies: Golf; Writing. Address: 20 Greers Road, Christchurch 4, New Zealand.

HAY Hamish Grenfell (Sir), b. 8 Dec 1927, Christchurch, NZ. Former Mayor of Christchurch. m. Lady Judith Leicester Gill, CNZM, QSO,14 May 1955, 1 s, 4 d. Education: BCom, Univ of Canterbury, NZ; FCA, NZ. Appointments: Mayor of Christchurch, 1974-89; Canterbury Regl Cncl, Dpty Chmn, 1998-, Bd Mus of NZ, 1992-98, Chmn, 1992-94. Publications: (Autobiography) Hay Days, 1988. Honours: Kt Bach, 1982; Order of Rising Sun w Gold Rays, 1990. Membership: NZ Soc of Accts, FCA, Chmn, Canterbury Branch, 1955. Hobbies: Music; Politics. Address: 70 Heaton Street, Merivale, Christchurch, New Zealand.

HAY John Anthony, b. 21 Sept 1942, Perth, Aust. Vice-Chancellor. m. Barbara, 5 June 1965, 3 s, 1 d. Education: Perth Mod Sch; Univ WA; Pembroke Coll, Cambridge. Appointments: Lectr, Engl, 1966; Snr Lectr, 1971; Prof, 1981; Dpty Chmn, Acad Bd, 1985, Univ of WA; Ed, AUMLA, 1985; Dean of Arts, Monash Univ 1987; Dpty Vice Chan, Monash Univ, 1988; Vice Chan, Univ of Qld, 1996-. Publications: Directions in Australian Secondary English, 1975; Western Australian Literature: A Bibliography, 1979; Testing English Comprehension, 1979; K S Prichard, 1984; European Relations, 1985; The Early Imprints at New Norcia, 1986; Australian Studies in Tertiary Education Institutions in Australia, 1987; Western

Australian Writing, 1989; Narrative Issues, 1990; Bibliography of Australian Literature, I and II, 1995. Hobbies: Bushwalking; Cinema; Reading. Address: Brian Wilson Chancellery, University of Queensland, Brisbane, Queensland 4072, Australia.

HAY Judith Leicester (Lady), b. 20 Mar 1927, Timaru, NZ. m. Sir Hamish Grenfell Hay, 14 May 1955, 1 s, 4 d. Education: St Margaret's Coll; Canty Coll, Occupational Therapy Sch. Appointments: Chmn, NZ Regd Occupational Therapists Assn, 1954-1955; Provincial Commnr Girl Guides Assn of NZ, 1974-82; Chair, Intl Women's Yr Cttee, 1974-75; Chair, Reg Women's Decade Cttee, 1975-85; Fndr Tstee, Children's Holiday Camp Trust, 1975-; Mbr, NZ Children's Hlth Camp Bd, 1980-94; Chmn, Glenelg Children's Hlth Camp, 1983-94; Chmn and Bd Mbr Canty Volun Cntr Trust; 1988-94; Mbr, 1993 Suffrage Centennial Trust of NZ, Whakatu Wahine; NZ Natl Rep, Intl Assn of Volun Effort, 1994-. Honour: Companion, NZ Order of Merit; Queen's Serv Order (QSO), 1987; NZ Commemorative Medal, 1990; Suffrage Centennial Medal, 1993. Hobbies: Gardening; Embroidery. Address: 70 Heaton Street, Christchurch 5, New Zealand.

HAYASHI Yoshiro, b. 16 June 1927 Yamaguchi Pref. Politician. m. Mariko Hayashi, 1960, 2 s, 2 d. Appointments: Fmr civ servant Min of Intl Trade and Ind and other depts; Dir Acctng Div Liberal-Dem Party - LDP - for two yrs then Dir Intl Bur of LDP, 1950-69; Sec-Gen Hirakawa Kai - policy study grp; Min of Hlth and Welfare, 1982-83; Min of Fin, 1992-93. Memberships: Mbr HoR, 1969-. Hobbies: Golf. Address: c/o Liberal-Democratic Party, 7, 2-chome, Hirakawacho, Chiyoda-ku, Tokyo, Japan.

HAYASHI Ichiroku, b. 30 Sept 1939, Nagano, Japan. Professor. m. Nobuko, 15 Mar 1965, 2 s. Education: BA, Biol Sci, Chiba Univ, 1962; MS, Biol Sci, 1965, DSc, 1972, Tokyo Kyoiku Univ. Appointments: Instr, Tokyo Kyoik Univ, 1965-72; Assoc Prof, 1972-89, Prof, 1989-, Tsukuba Univ. Publications: Vegetation Geography, 1992; The Fragile Tropics of Latin America, 1995. Memberships: Ecol Soc of Japan; Japanese Assn for Arid Land Studies. Hobby: Haiku. Address: 173-5 Kosato, Ueda, Nagano, Japan.

HAYASHI Takemi, b. 8 Oct 1938, Nagoya, Aichi, Japan. Professor of Physics. m. Mariko, 24 Sept 1978, 1 s, 1 d. Education: BS, 1961, MS, 1963, DSc, 1966, Nagoya Univ. Appointments: Rsch Fell, Hiroshima Univ, 1966-83; Lectr, 1983, Assoc Prof, 1983-85, Prof, 1985-91, Kure Natl Coll of Tech, Hiroshima; Prof, Kogakkan Univ, Ise, 1991-. Publications: Sev articles in profl jrnls. Memberships: Physl Soc, Japan; Am Physl Soc; Am Assn for the Adv of Sci; Am Assn of Phys Tchrs; NY Acady of Sci. Hobby: Tennis. Address: Kogakkan University, 1704 Kodakujimoto-cho, Ise, Mie 516-8555, Japan.

HAYDAR Mohammad Haydar, b. 1931. Politician. Education: Univ of Damascus. Appointments: Tchr Lattakia Hama, 1951-60; With Min of Agrarian Reform, 1960-63; Dir Alghab Estab Hama, 1963; Dir Agrarian Reform Damascus Daraa Suweidaa, 1964; Dir Legal and Admin Affairs Min of Agric and Agrarian Reform, 1965; Gov Alhasakeh, 1966; Tchr Damascus, 1968; Temporary Regl Command of BASP, 1970; Min of Agric and Agrarian Reform until 1973; Dep Premier for Econ Affairs, 1973-76. Memberships: Mbr Command Damascus Branch of Baath Arab Socialist Party - BASP - 1968; Mbr of both Regl and Natl Commands of BASP; Mbr of Cntrl Command Progressive Natl Front of Syria; Mbr of Natl Command of BASP, 1980-; Mbr of the Natl Progressive Front, 1980-. Address: Foreign Relations Bureau, Baath Arab Socialist Party, Damascus, Syria.

HAYDEN William George, b. 23 Jan 1933, Brisbane, Australia. Cattle Farmer. m. Dallas, 7 May 1960, 2 s, 2 d. Education: BEcon, Univ Qld. Appointments: Qld State Pub Serv, 1950-52; Qld Police Force, 1953-61; House of Reps for Oxley, Qld, Aust Natl Parly, 1961-88; Min for Socl Security, 1972-75; Fed Treas, 1975; Ldr, Fed

Opposition, 1977-83; Min for For Affairs, 1983-87; Min for For Affairs and Trade, 1987-88; Gov Gen of Aust, 1989; Retd, 1996; Cattle Farmer, Brisbane Valley, Qld, 1996-. Publication: Hayden: An Autobiography, 1996. Honours: AO; Knight of the Order of St John; Gwanghwa Medal, Korean Order of Dipl Merit; Aust Humanist of the Yr, 1996; Sev hon degs. Membership: Chmn, Edl Cttee, Quadrant Jrnl, 1998. Honours: Reading; Music; Golf; Horse Riding; Cross Country Skiing; Bush Walking. Address: GPO Box 7829, Waterfront Place, Brisbane, Qld 4001, Australia.

HAYES Michael Gordon, b. 18 July 1951, USA. Publisher. Education: Bachelor Intl Stdies, Sch for Intl Trng, USA; MSc, For Serv, Georgetown Univ, USA. Publication: Fndr, Phnom Penh Post, Cambodia's oldest indep newsppr. Hobbies: Bowling; Ping pong; Skydiving. Address: Publisher and Editor-in-Chief, Phnom Penh Post, #10A, St 264, Phnom Penh, Cambodia.

HAYES Ross Abbott, b. 6 May 1921, Sydney, Aust. Medical Practitioner. m. June Broun, 12 Aug 1949, 3 s. Education: MBBS, FRCPA, FRCPath, Melbourne Univ. Appointments: Clinl Pathol, Alfred Hosp, Melbourne, 1950-60; Spec in Path, Sydney, 1960-90; Pathol, Roy S Sydney Hosp, 1961-86; Hon Clinl Asst (Haematol), Sydney Hosp, 1961-88; Sec, Roy Coll of Pathols of Aust, 1962-66; RAAMC (CMF)OC, 1 Mobile Malaria Field Lab, Maj, 1962-66; Specialist Pathologist, Sydney, 1960-88; Retd, 1988. Publications: Articles to med jrnls. Honours include: JP, 1967; Civ Marriage Celebrant, 1995. Memberships: Austl Med Assn; BMA; Affiliate Em Mbr, Coll of Amn Pathols; Hon Fell, Assn Clinl Scientists, USA; Assn Clinl Pathologists, UK; Amn Coll of Heraldry; Advsry Cttees, C'wlth Dept Hlth and Austl Medl Assn; Miscellaneous spec med socs. Listed in: Many including: Who's Who in Australia; Who's Who in the World; Who's Who in Australia and the Far East; Dictionary of International Biography. Hobbies: Gardening; Swimming. Address: 98 Balfour Road, Rose Bay, NSW 2029, Australia.

HAYMET Anthony Douglas John, b. 5 Feb 1956. Professor of Chemistry. Education: BS Hons, Univ of Sydney, 1978; PhD Chem, Univ of Chicago, 1981; DSc, Sydney, 1997. Appointments: Rsch Fell, Harvard Univ, 1981; Asst Prof, Berkeley, 1983; Assoc, Full Prof, Univ of Utah, 1988; Chair, Theoretical Chem, Univ of Sydney, 1991. Creative works: More than 110 articles in refered jrnls on Freezing, Interfaces & Aqueous Solutions. Honours: Masson Medal, 1978; Rennie Medal, 1983; RACI; US Presidential Young Investigation, 1985-90; US Antarctic Serv Medal, 1994. Memberships: Fell, Roy Austl Chem Inst; Chair, Physical Chem Div, 1995-97. Address: School of Chemistry, University of Sydney, NSW 2006, Australia.

HAYWARD Bruce William, b. 18 Jan 1950, Auckland, New Zealand. Geologist; Marine Scientist. m. Glenys Puch, 2 Dec 1972, 3 d. Education: BSc (hons), PhD, Auckland. Appointments: Postdoct Fell, Smithsonian Instn; Micropaleontologist, NZ Geol Survey; Curator, Auckland War Meml Mus; Self-Employed Rschr. Publications: Kauri Timber Dams, 1975; The Maori History and Legends of the Waitakere Ranges, 1979; Cinemas of Auckland 1896-1979, 1979; Kauri Gum and the Gumdiggers, 1982; Granite and Marble: A Guide to Building Stones in New Zealand, 1987; Trilobites, Dinosaurs and Moa Bones. The Story of New Zealand Fossils, 1990; Kauri Timber Days: A Pictorial Account of the Kauri Timber Industry in New Zealand, 1991; Precious Land: Protecting New Zealand's Landforms and Geological Features, 1996; A Field Guide to Auckland, 1997; The Restless Country: Volcanoes and Earthquakes of New Zealand, 1999. Honours: McKay hammer Awd, Geol Soc of NZ, 1979; NZ Assn of Scis Rsch Medal, 1988; James Cook Rsch Fellshp, 1998-2000. Memberships: Geol Soc of NZ, pres, 1989-91; NZ Conservation Authy, 1990-93. Hobbies: Lichens; Tramping; Natural History; Research. Address: 19 Debron Avenue, Remuera, Auckland, New Zealand.

HAZELRIGG Meredith Kent, b. 28 Mar 1942, MI, USA. International Consultant. m. Nimi Junko, 1980, 1 s. Education: BA, 1965; MA, 1967, MI State Univ; PhD 1994, Newport Univ. Appointments: Educr, Lansing Pub Schs Adult Educ Prog; MI Dept of Socl Servs Boys Trng Sch, 1964-68; Lansing Comm Coll, 1966-69; Malcolm X Comms Skills Acady, 1970-71; Staff Writer, Advtng Dir, Westside News, Lansing, MI, 1970-71; Fndng Mbr, Bd Dirs, Allegan Comm Dev Corp; In succession: Commnr, Sec, Chmn, Allegan City Planning Commn; Staff Writer, Allegan Co Photo Jrnl; Adj Prof, Univ of MD, 1980-83, Kanagawa Univ, Jap, 1985-, Natl Univ of Jap, 1987-96; Assoc Prof, Rissho Univ, 1992-. Publications include: Insight through Fiction (with Antico), 1970; NihONSENSE (w Snowden and Atkin), 1987; Understanding NihONSENSE, 1990; English Guide to Pronunciation for Japanese, 1990; Overcoming Miscommunication in English, 1994; Some 250 Japanese Senryu and Then Some (w Hayakawa), 1997; Var articles and columns, Armchair Gardner for newspapers, jrnls. Honours: Natl Hon Soc, 1960; Natl Merit Finalist, 1961; Kikkoman Grand Prix, 1985; Itoen 1st Prize, 1996; Var recog awds. Memberships include: Advsry Bd, Lansing Com Art Gall; Capital Art Gall; Boars Hd Players; Jap Civil Libs Union; Phonetic Soc of Jap; Jap Assn of Practical Engl; Soc of Writers, Eds and Transls; Japanese Assn of Tranlss; Tokyo Engl Lit Soc; Boy Scouts of Am, Japanese Asst Dist Commnr. Listed in: Who's Who in the World; Contemporary Authors; Dictionary of International Biography; International Who's Who of Intellectuals. Hobbies: Graphic and Ceramic Arts; Gourmet Cooking; Oenology; Gardening. Address: 468-1 Mizuno Sayama-shi, Saitama-ken, Japan 350-1317.

HAZELTON Martin Luke, b. 18 Nov 1967, Bath, UK. University Lecturer. m. Ann Kent, 19 Apr 1997, 1 s. Education: BA, 1989, MA, 1993, DPhil, 1993, University of Oxford. Appointments: Lectr, Univ Coll, 1994-97; Lectr, Univ of West Aust, 1997. Membership: Statistical Soc of West Aust, Sec, West Aust Branch. Hobbies: Chess; Opera; Walking; Wine. Address: Department of Mathematics and Statistics, University of Western Australia, Nedlands, WA 6907, Australia.

HAZELTON Michael John, b. 7 Feb 1955. Nurse. m. Carroll Doyle, 15 Dec 1984, 2 s. Education: BA, MA, Macquarie Univ; Regd Nurse, Gen & Psych Nursing Certs. Appointments: Lectr, Nursing, Macarthur Inst of Advd Educ, 1986-87; Snr Lectr, Nursing, Macarthur Inst of Advd Educ, 1988-89; Prin Lectr, Nursing, Tasmanian State Inst of Technol, 1989-90; Acad Dean, Fac of Nursing, Univ of Tas, 1994-96; Assoc Prof, Nursing, Univ of Tas, 1991-97; Hd of Dept, Tasmanian Sch of Nursing, Univ of Tasmania, 1997-. Creative works include: Medical Discourse on Contemporary Nurse Education, 1990; Mental Health Deinstitutionalisation and Citizenship, 1995; Reporting Mental Health: A Discourse Analysis of Mental Health-Related News in Two Australian Newspapers, 1997. Honours: Editl Board, Jrnls Contemp Nurse, 1995-97; Austl and NZ, Jrnl of Mental Hlth Nursing, 1997. Memberships: Austl and NZ Coll of Mental Hlth Nurses, 1992-97; Austl Sociological Assn, 1993-96; Tasmanian Branch Sec, 1994-95; Coll Cnclr, 1996-97; Tasmanian Branch Pres, 1996-97. Address: School of Nursing, University of Tasmania, PO Box 1214, Launceston, Tas 7250, Australia.

HAZLEHURST Cameron, b. 12 Oct 1941, Harrogate, Eng. Historian. m. (1) 1964, 2 s, 1 d, (2) Kayleen McNeil, 7 May 1983. Education: BA, hons, Univ of Melbourne, 1960-63; DPhil, Univ of Oxford, 1966-69. Appointments: Tchng Fell, Monash Univ, 1964-65; Rsch Fell, Nuffield Coll, 1968-70; Rsch Fell, Queens Coll, Oxford, 1970-72; Fell, 1972-88, Snr Fell, 1988-92, Inst of Adv Studies, Austl Natl Univ; Asst Sec, Austl Dept of Urban and Regl Devel, 1974-75; 1st Asst Sec, C'wlth Dept of Commns, 1984-86; Natl Campaign Dir, AIDS Educn and Info, 1988-89; Fndn Prof, Hd, Sch of Hums, Qld Univ of Technol, 1992-97; Histl Advsr, Seven Network, 1998-; CEO, Flaxton Mill House, 1998-. Publications: Politicians at War, 1971; A Guide to the Papers of British Cabinet Ministers 1900-1951 (co-auth Christine Woodland), 1974; Menzies Observed, 1979; The Mastermind Book, 1979;

The Mastermind General Knowledge Book, 1982; Gordon Chalk, 1987; A Liberal Chronicle (co-ed Christine Woodland), 1995; A Guide to the Papers of British Cabinet Ministers 1900-1964 (co-auth), 1996; Gangs and Youth Subcultures (co-ed Kayleen Hazlehurst), 1998. Honours: Wyselaskie Schlsp in Engl Constitutional Hist, 1963-65; Monash Univ Travelling Schlsp, 1966-68; Nuffield Coll Studentship, 1966-68; Visng Fell, Griffith Univ, 1977-80, Univ of Durham, 1990, 1993; Inst of Adv Stdies, ANU, 1992-. Memberships: Fell, Roy Soc of Lit; Fell, Roy Histl Soc; Fell, Roy Soc of Arts. Listed in: Who's Who in Australia. Hobbies: Television; Cricket. Address: PO Box 60, Mapleton, Queensland 4560, Australia.

HAZZARD Shirley, b. 30 Jan 1931, Sydney, Aust. m. Francis Steegmuller, 22 Dec 1963. Appointments: Combined Servs Intelligence, Hong Kong, 1947-48; UK High Commnr's Off, Wellington, NZ, 1949-50; UN Secretariat, NY, 1952-61. Publications: Cliffs of Fall, 1963; The Evening of the Holiday, 1966; People in Glass Houses, 1964; The Bay of Noon, 1970; The Transit of Venus, 1980; (history) Defeat of an Ideal, 1973; Countenance of Truth, 1990; Greene on Capri (biog), forthcoming. Honours: Awd in Lit, Amn Acady Arts and Letters, 1966; Guggenheim Fellshp, 1970; Natl Book Critics Circle Awd for Fiction, 1981. Memberships: Amn Acady of Arts and Letters; Natl Acady of Arts and Scis (USA); Roy Soc of Lit (UK). Hobby: Parthenophile (special interest in the city of Naples). Address: Apt C1705, 200 East 66th Street, New York, NY 10021, USA.

HE Chunlin, b. Aug 1933 Wuxi Cty Jiangsu Prov. Politician. Education: Northeast Agric Coll. Appointments: Joined CCP, 1951; Dir Spec Econ Zone Off of State Cncl; Vice-Sec Gen State Cncl, 1988-. Memberships: Mbr 14th CCP Cntrl Cttee, 1992; Mbr 15th CCP Cntrl Cttee, 1997-. Address: State Council, Beijing, People's Republic of China.

HE Fang, b. 18 Oct 1922, Xian, Shaanxi, China. Senior Research Fellow. m. Song Yimin, 1 May 1953, 2 s. Education: Grad, Inst of Fgn Langs, Yenan, Shaanxi. Appointments: Dept Hd, PRC Emb, USSR, 1950-55; Divsn Hd, Vice Dir of Gen Off, Min of Fgn Affairs, 1955-65; Dir, Inst of Japanese Studies, 1980-88; Vice Dir of China Cntr for Intl Stdies, 1988-95; Snr Fell, CIJ. Publications: On the Epoch We Are In, 1988; Certain Issues of the International Situation in a Transitional Period, 1992; On Issues in Economic Globalization, 1998; The US Factor in Sino-Japan Relations, 1998. Honours: Hon Doct, Inst of Far E Studies, Russian Acady of Scis. Memberships: Natl Cttee, Chinese Peoples Polit Consultative Conf, 1988-97; VP, China-Russia Friendship Assn; Snr Cnslt, China Inst for Intl Strategic Studies. Hobbies: Reading; Meditation. Address: 6-1-501 Tuanjiehu, Beili, Beijing, China.

HE Guangyuan, b. 1930, Anxin Co, Hebei Prov, China. State Official. Appointments: Vice Min of Machinery and Electrons Ind, 1982-88, Min, 1988-93; Min, Machine Bldg Ind, 1993-96; Alt Mbr, 12th CCP Cntrl Cttee, 1982-87, 13th Cttee, 1987-92, 8th NPC, 1993-, 14th CCP Cntrl Cttee, 1992-; Chair, State Exam Cttee for Proj. Address: Ministry of Machine Building Industry, 84 Sanlihe Lu, Xichent Qu, Beijing, China.

HE Guoqiang, b. Oct 1943 Xiangxiang Co Hunan Prov. Politician. Education: Beijing Chem Engrng Inst. Appointments: Joined CCP, 1966; Dir and CCP Sec Shandong Petro-Chem Dept, 1984; Vice-Min of Chem Ind, 1991; Vice-Sec CCP Fujian Provincial Cttee; Acting Gov Fujian Prov, 1996; Gov, 1997-. Memberships: Alt Mbr 12th CCP Cntrl Cttee, 1985; Alt Mbr 13th CCP Cntrl Cttee, 1987; Alt Mbr 14th Cntrl Cttee, 1992; Mbr of the Standing Cttee of CCP Shandong Provincial Cttee; Mbr 15th CCP Cntrl Cttee, 1997-. Address: Office of the Governor, Fuzhou City, Fujian Province, People's Republic of China.

HE Ji-Fan, b. 30 June 1937, Shanghai, China. Solid Mechanics Educator. m. Bang-An Ma, 14 Feb 1972. Education: Master Tsinghua Univ, 1959. Appointments: Asst, 1959-79, Lectr, 1979-86, Assoc Prof,

1986-96, Prof, 1996-, Tsinghua Univ, Beijing. Publications: A refined shear deformation theory of laminated plates and shells, 1989; A twelfth-order theory of bending of isotropic plates, 1996. Honour: Achievements in basic research, Tsinghua Univ, 1996. Memberships: Chinese Soc Theort and Applied Mechs; Chinese Soc Composite Materials; Chinese Soc Vibration Engrng. Hobby: Music. Address: Department of Engineering Mechanics, Tsinghua University, Beijing 100084, China.

HE Jiaming, b. 6 Jan 1978, Hangzhou, China. m. Mingru Zhao, 1 s. Education: ME, 1993, PhD, 1996, Postdoct, 1998, ZheJiang Univ. Appointment: Professor, Info & Electron Engrng Dept, Yuquan, Zhejiang, China. Publications: 14 incl: Technical of Photoelectric Detection (co-auth), 1996. Honours include: Excellent Tchng Achievement of Coll Prizes, two equal prov access priority prizes, 1993; ZheJiang Prov Excellent Disseration of Nat Sci, three equal prov access Priority Prizes for sci ppr, 1995. Memberships: China Inst of Comms (CIC); China Inst of Optics (CIO). Hobbies: Novels; Writing; Music. Address: ZheJiang University, Information & Electronic Engineering Department, Yuquan,, 310027, Zhejiang, China.

HE Jian-Bo, b. 16 July 1965, Taihu, China. Educator; Researcher. m. Xin Ju Huang, 19 Dec 1991, 1 s. Education: BS, Chem, Norm Univ, Wuhu, China, 1985; MS, Applied Chem, Hefei Univ of Technol, China, 1990. Appointments: Asst, Hefei Univ of Tech, 1985-91; Lectr, 1991-97; Assoc Prof, 1997-. Creative Works: Rsch Articles to Profl Jrnls; Chem J of China; Trans NFSoc; Acta Chim Sinica; Electrochemistry. Honours: Ex Grad Awd; 2nd Awd, Writing Contest; 1st Awd, Progress in Sci and Technol. Memberships: Chinese Chem Soc. Hobbies: Lit; Music; Sport. Address: Inst of Chem Engineering, Hefei Univ of Tech, 193 Tunxi Rd, Hefei 230009, China.

HE Jingye, b. 23 Feb 1942, Zhejiang, China. Professor of French. m. Jingdi Zhang, 1971, 1 d. Education: Grad, China E Normal Univ; Second Fgn Lang Coll of Beijing; Third Univ of Paris. Appointments: Vice Dean, Fgn Lang Dept, E China Normal Univ, 1981-84, 1990-92; Guest Prof, ISCID France, 1995-97; Dean, French Dept, Coll Bargde, 1999-. Publications: Vietnamese-Chinese Business Conversation, 1995; France, 1999; The Dictionary of Foreign Modern Literature, 1999; Trans of sev essays. Memberships: Trans Assn of Shanghai; Lit Comparison Soc of Shanghai; Exec Mbr, Chinese-French Culture Comparison Rsch Assn of China. Hobby: Literature. Address: East China Normal University, Foreign Language College, 3663 Zhongshan Road North, Shanghai, China.

HE Kang, b. 26 Feb 1923 Hebei Prov. Government and Party Official. m. Miao Shixia, 1945, 2 s. Education: Agric Coll of Guanxi Univ. Appointments: Chf Dir of Agric and Forestry under Shanghai Mil Control Cttee; Dep Hd Dept of Agric and Forestry under E China Mil and Polit Cttee, 150-52; Dir Dept of Spec Forestry of Cntrl Min of Forestry, 1952-54; Dir Dept of Tropical Plants Min of Agric, 1954-57; Dir S China Tropical Crop Sci Rsch Inst and Tropical Crop Coll, 1957-72; Dep to 3rd Natl People's Congress, 1964; Dep Dir Gen Bur of Land Reclamation Guangdong Prov, 1972-77; Vice-Min of Agric and Forestry, 1978; Dep Dir Natl Commn on Agric and Vice-Min of Agric, 1979; Acting Vice-Chmn Natl Agric Regl Plng Cttee, 1979; Min of Agric Animal Husbandry and Fishery, 1983-90; Dep Dir Natl Plng Commn, 1983-85; NPC Dep for Guangxi Zhuang Autonomous Reg; Vice-Chmn Natl Cttee China Assn for Sci and Tech, 1986-; Vice-Chmn All China Agric Zoning Cttee, 1989; Pres Chinese Village & Township Enterprise Assn, 1990-; Pres Agric Econs Soc, 1990-; Pres China-Bangladesh Friendship Assn; Sci Advsr to Natl Environment Protection Cttee, 1992. Honours: Hon Vice-Chmn Zhongkai Inst of Agricl Tech; World Food Prize, 1993. Memberships: Mbr 12th Cntrl Cttee, 1982-87; Mbr 13th Cntrl Cttee, 1987-93; Mbr 8th NPC, 1993-. Address: Ministry of Agriculture, Nun Zen Nan Li, Beijing, People's Republic of China.

HE Ronghua, b. 2 Jan 1939, Hebei, China. Doctor. m. Huo Xing, 9 Sept 1967, 1 s, 1 d. Education: Bach Deg, Nanjing Med Univ, 1962. Appointments: Hd, Endocrine Dept, 1st Affiliated Hosp, Nanjing Med Univ. Publications: 80 med theses in clin med jrnls, 12 med books. Honour: Ex Dr, Jiangsu Prov Med Assn. Memberships: Chinese Med Assn; Chinese Diabetes Assn. Hobbies: Painting; Music. Address: 300 Guangzhou Road, Jiangsu Province Hospital, Nanjing 210029, China.

HE Shan-An, b. 16 Feb 1932, Changsha, Hunan, China. Botanist; Researcher. m. Gu Yin, 12 May 1956, 1 s. Education: Grad, Zhejiang Agricl Univ, 1954. Appointments: Rsch Asst, 1954-60, Asst Prof, Vice Dir, 1960-82, Vice Dir, 1982-83, Dir, 1983-, Inst of Botany, Jiangsu Prof & Chinese Acady of Scis, Nanjing; Dir, Jiangsu Prov Key Lab for Plant Ex-situ Conservation, Nanjing, 1992-; Vice Hd, Botanical Expedition Team, Chinese Acady of Scis to USA, 1981-82; Supvsr, PhD Deg Students, State Cncl Acad Deg Cttee, Beijing, 1990. Publications include: Olive introduction and breeding, 1984. Honours: Sci Grade III on Olive Introdn & Breeding, Jiangsu Prov Govt, 1980; Sci Grade II, Plant Introdn & Extension of Econ Forests in Huai Bei Zone, Nanjing, 1984; Disting Contbn Sci Awd, State Cncl Spec Allowance, Jiangsu Prov Govt, 1988; Natl Outstndng Mbrs on Environ & Technol, China Environ Sci Soc, Beijing, 1995. Memberships: Chinese Soc of Botany; Botanical Garden Conservation Intl; Species Survival Cmmn Plant Conservation Sub-cttee; Intl Assn of Botanical Gardens. Hobbies: Chinese Calligraphy; Photography; Travel; Chinese Chess. Address: PO Box 1435, Nanjing 210014, Jiangsu, China.

HE Shao-Xun, b. 21 July 1920, Beijing, China. Professor. m. Xiao Qing-Cheng, 15 Sept 1948, 2 s, 1 d. Education: BS, Natl S West Assocd Univ, Kumming, China, 1942. Appointments: Jnr Geol, Geol Surv of Sechuan Prov, China, 1942-46; Lectr, Guangdong Art and Sci Coll, Guangdong, China, 1949-50; Assoc Prof, Guangxi Univ, 1950-52; Prof, Cntrl S Univ of Technol, Changsha, China, 1952-. Creative Works: The Use of Stereographic Projection in Structural Geology, 1979; Duccile Shear Zone Structure and Mecallogeny, 1996; The Origin of the Echelon Structures of Tungsten Veins in Xihuashang Jiangxi; Acta Geologica Sinica; On the Gold Deposits of Shearzone Type and its Classification; Transactions of NF Soc. Honours: Progressive Awd of Sci and Technol; Natl Educ Cttee; Progressive Awd of Sci and Technol; China Natl Nonferrous Metals Ind Corp. Memberships: Geol Soc of China. Hobbies: Classical Music; Football; Tennis; Badminton; Baseball. Address: Department of Geology, Central South University of Technology, Changsha, Hunan 410083, China.

HE Xuntian, b. 15 May 1953, Suining, China. Professor. Education: BA. Appointments: Prof, Chmn, Musical Composition and Direction Dept, Shanghai Conservatory of Music; World premieres of his wrks in Germany, Brit, the Netherlands, New York (USA), Hong Kong, Can, Japan; He Xuntian Symph Concert, Beijing Concert Hall by China Musician Assn and the Cntrl Orch, 1988. Creative works include: (symphs) Tonal Patterns, 1985; Four Dreams, 1986; Telepathy, 1987; (chamber music) Two of the Earthly Branches, 1983; Sounds of Nature, 1986; Phonism, 1989; Imagine the Sound, 1990; The Pattern of Sound Suite, 1997; (folk orch music) Caprice of Dabo River, 1982; (new song albums) Yellow Children, 1992; Sister Drum, 1994; Voice From the Sky, 1996. Honours: Num incl 1st Prize, 3rd Natl Musical Piece Competition, 1984; 1st Prize, First China Phonograph Awds, 1984; Gold Tripod Awd, Taiwan, 1995; 3rd Prize, Intl Carl-Marla-Von-Wettbewerbes fur Kammermusik, Germany, 1987; Outstndng Musical Achievement Awd, Intl New Music Composer Competition, USA, 1990. Address: 20 Fen Yang Road, Shanghai Conservatory of Music, Shanghai 200031, China.

HE Zhi Qian (Zhi-chien Ho), b. 2 Mar 1924, Zhongshan Cty, Guangdong, China. Professor of Nutrition. m. W H Guo, 1 July 1950, 2 d. Education: BA; MD; PhD. Appointments: Lectr, Prof, Dean, Hd of Lib,

Sun Yat-Sen Univ of Medl Scis, 44 yrs. Publications: 97 orig articles (pprs); 4 text books; 8 other books. Honours: 13 hon awds, Chinese authorities and orgns; Highest Hon Awd, Ryerson Univ of Can. Memberships: VP, Chinese Nutrition Soc; Pres, Chinese Maternal and Infant Nutrition Assn. Hobby: Classical music. Address: Department of Clinical Nutrition, Sun Yat-Sen University of Medical Science, Guangzhou, China, 510080.

HE Zuo-Yong, b. 24 Feb 1927, Nanjing, Jiangsue, China. Professor. m. 7 Aug 1958, 1 s, 1 d. Education: Grad, Dept of Maths & Phys, Fudan Univ, 1951. Appointments: Tchr, Rschr, Mil Engrng Inst, 1953-69; Rschr, Tchr, currently Prof, Inst of Acoustic Engrng, Harbin Engrng Univ, 1970-; Mbr, Natl Tech Cttee of Metrology and Test, 1994; Leader, Tech Grp of Advsrs of Metrology of Underwater Acoustics Whole Nation, 1990-. Publications: Theoretical Foundation of Acoustics, 1981; Vibration of Immersed Rectangular Composite Plate Exerted by Underwater Sound, Vol 3 No 1, 1985; Scattering of Near Field of a Rectangular Composite Plate Immersed in Water, Vol 4 No 1, 1985; Underwater Acoustic Calibration and Measurements in HSEI, Proceedings of the Institute of Acoustics, Vol 6, Pt 5, 1984; Study on Vibration and Sound Radiation of Composite Plate with Non-Rigid Baffle Exerted by Random Force, 1987; Predicting the Far-field Sound Radiating and Study on Predicating Underwater Noise of Modelling Ship Structure and Its Review, Underwater Sound Communication of China No 2, 1987, and No 2, 1988; Resonance Oscillation and Sound of Rectangular Cavities Without Flange Induced by Flow, 1989, ICA, 1992; Field Reconstruction by Acoustic Holography Technique and Performance Identification of Sources, Progress in Physics of China, No 3-4, Vol 16, 1996. Honours: Prize for Ex Textbook for Theoretical Fndn of Acoustics, Natl Educ Cncl of China, 1987; Prize for Reward of Sci and Technique, 2nd Class for rsch work Study on Underwater Acoustic Array-Receiving Phased Aray, Natl Educ Cncl of China, 1987; Prize for Reward of Sci and Technique Prog, 2nd Class for rsch work Vibration and Sound Radiation of Elastic Shell in Water, 1st class for Synthetic Analysis of Underwater Noise, Vibration and their control; 2nd class for Investigation of Underwater Sound Sources by Intensity Measurement Technique, by China State of Shipbuilding Co, 1987; Prize for Ex Achievement in Tchng, 1st Class, Heilongjiang Prov, 1989, 1991, 1996; Prize, Natl Model Worker of Educ Syst, Natl Educ Cncl and Min of Natl Personnel, China, 1989; Model Worker, People's Govt of Heilongjiang Prov, 1991. Memberships: Cttee Mbr, Natl Cttee of Acoustic Standards of China; Cttee Mbr, Acoustical Soc of China and Phys Acoustics Commn; Chmn of Acoustical Soc of Heilongjiang Prov; Tech Advsr, China Ship Sci Rsch Cntr and Inst of Applied Acoustics of China; Commn of Mechs, Chinese Soc of Naval Arch and Marine Engrng; Ed, Jrnl of Applied Acoustics of China, 1988-. Address: Institute of Acoustic Engineering of Harbin Engineering University, Harbin, Heilongjiang, China.

HEAD Peter, b. 26 Jan 1946, Adelaide, Aust. Musician. m. Mouse, 14 July 1965, 1 s, 1 d. Publication: CD Recording: King of the Cross, 1996. Hobbies: Art; Ufology; Films; Books. Address: 22 Chisholm Street, Darlinghurst, Australia.

HEALEY Anthony J, b. 10 Sept 1940, London, England. Mechanical Engineering. m. Anne, 1 s, 2 d. Education: BSc, Engrng, PhD, Univ Sheffield, England. Appointments: Asst Prof, PA Univ, 1967-71; Assoc Prof, Prof, Univ TX, Austin, 1971-81; Mngr, Brown & Rooting, 1981-86; Prof, Chmn, Naval Postgrad Sch, 1986-; Dir, Cntr for Autonomous Vehicles, 1994-. Publications: Over 150 in profl jrnls. Honours: Disting Serv Awd, ASME, 1994; Fell, ASME. Memberships: ASME; IEEE; Oceanic Engrng Soc. Hobbies: Golf; Underwater Robotics. Address: Department of Mechanical Engineering, Naval Postgraduate School, Monterey, CA 93943, USA.

HEARDER Jeremy Victor Roblin, b. 6 Dec 1936, Peshawar, Pakistan. Former Diplomat; Writer. m. Kay 4 Dec 1961, 2 s, 3 d. Education: BA (Hons), Melbourne Univ; MA, Stanford Univ, USA. Appointments: In Aust Dip Serv: Vientiane, 1962-64; Canberra, 1964-66; Dar-es-salaam, 1966-68; Bangkok, 1968-70; Nairobi, 1970-71; Canberra, 1972-75; Brussels, 1975-78; Sydney, Snr For Affairs RSP, 1979-80; High Commnr, Harare, 1980-84; H C Suva, 1984-86; Canberra, 1986-88; Consul-Gen, Chicago, 1988-91; Dpty, H C Wellington, 1991-94; Chf of Protocol, Canberra, 1994-96. Honours: Minor Res Schlshp, Trinity Coll, Univ of Melbourne, 1957-58; Rotary Fndn Fellshp and Fulbright Travel Grant, 1959-60. Hobbies: Reading; Sport; Photography. Address: 83 Hilder Street, Weston, ACT 2611, Australia.

HEARN Milton Thomas William, b. 17 Feb 1943. Professor. m. 20 Dec 1968, 1 s, 1 d. Education: PhD, Adelaide Univ, 1970; DSc, 1983. Appointments: NRC Fell, U BC, Vancouver, 1969-71; ICI Fell, Oxford Univ, 1971-75; Snr Rsch Fell, Univ Otago, NZ, 1975-81; Prin Rsch Fell, St Voncent's Inst Med Rsch, Aust, 1981-86; Prof, Biochem, Monash Univ, Aust, 1986-; Prof, Dir, Ctr for Bioprocess Tech, 1987-. Publications: Peptide and Protein Reviews, 1982-88; Protein Purification, 1990; Contrib Chapter, Physical Biochemistry, 1989; HPLC of Proteins and Peptides, 1991; Protein Purification, 1998; Advances in Separation Science, 1999; over 400 articles to profl jrnls; Ed 14 books; 30 patents. Memberships: Fell, Roy Austl Chem Ist; Austl Acady Tech Scis; Amn Chem Soc; Endocrine Soc; Acady Tech Scis. Address: 263 Union Road, Balwyn, Vic 3103, Australia.

HEBBARD Dale Furneaux, b. 29 Jan 1929. Research Physicist. m. Jocelyn Penelope Fancourt Thomas, 11 Dec 1956, 3 s. Education: BA Hons, MSc, PhD, Univ of Melbourne. Appointments: Snr Demonstrator, Melbourne Univ, 1956-57; Rsch Fell, CA Inst of Technol, 1957-60; Rsch Fell, 1960-62, Snr Rsch Fell, 1962-64, Snr Fell, 1964-92, ANU; Visng Fell, CA Inst of Technol, 1967; Visng Prof, Univ of Heidelberg, 1972; Hon Visng Fell, ANU, 1992-97. Creative works: 27 papers publd, referred scientific jrnls, 1955-90. Honour: Fulbright Travel Grant, Post-Doct, 1957-60. Memberships: Austl Fulbright Assn, 1991-; Fell, Austl Inst of Phys, 1960-. Hobbies: Bush Walking; Bird Watching; Travelling; Computing; Sciences. Address: 21 Brand Street, Hughes, ACT 2605, Australia.

HEBESTREIT Lydia Karola Ludewine, b. 31 Dec 1925. Education: DNurs (hon causa, RMIT); BA; MSc; Dip Hosp Admin; Dip N Ed; Univ of S Afr; Pretoria Univ, S Afr; Univ of PA, USA. Appointments: Lectr 1958-59, Prin 1960-66, Gr 1 Baragwanath Coll of Nursing; Asst Dir of Nursing 1967-68; Dir of Nursing 1970-75, Baragwanath Hosp, Johannesburg; Hd, Dept of Nursing, Univ of Witwatersrand, Johannesburg, 1969-70; Hd, Dept of Nursing, Preston Inst of Technol, Melbourne, 1975-79; Hd, Sch of Nursing, Phillip Inst of Technol, Melbourne, 1980-87. Honour: AO, 1987. Hobbies: Gardening; Painting; Music. Address: 245 Fiddlers Green Village, 57 Gloucester Avenue, Berwick, Vic 3806, Australia.

HEENAN Ashley David Joseph, b. 11 Sept 1925, Wellington, NZ. Musician. m. (1) Jean Margaret Ross, 31 Mar 1951, 2 s, 2 d, (2) Maureen Elizabeth Roberts, 8 Nov 1985. Education: DipMus 1954, MusBach 1956, Univ NZ; Roy Coll of Music, London, Eng. Appointments: Musical Dir, Schola Music of NZ Symph Orch, 1961-84; NZ Youth Orch, 1965-75; Musical Advsr and Orchl Coord, QE II Arts Cncl, 1964-65; Musical Dir, NZ Ballet Trust, 1966-68; NZ Writer Dir, APRA, 1966-80; Chmn, NZ Composers Fndn, 1981-95; Diverse musical positions w NZ Radio, orgs, 1942-84; Chmn, NZ Composers Fndn, 1981-96; Dpty Chair, NZ Music Cntr, 1992-97; Pres, World Croquet Feds, 1989-94. Publications: Auth, The New Zealand Symphony Orchestra, 1971; Schola Musica, 1974; Articles in var music mags; Composer: var vocal, instrumental and orchestral works inclng: Jack Winters Dream (radio drama); War and Peace (incidental music); Scottish Dances; A College Overture; Maori Suite; Cindy; Conductor appearing in the Kiwi Pacific catalogue as a conductor and composer. Honours: NZ Music Bursar, 1948-50; UNESCO Bursar, 1961-62; NZ Phonographic Industry Awd, 1976; Composers Assn NZ Citation, 1981; OBE, 1983; NZ Commemorative Medal, 1990. Memberships: NZ Musicans Union (Wgtn Br) Hon Mbr;

Australasian Performing Right Assn; Composers Assn of NZ. Hobbies: Private aviation; New Zealand history; Cricket; Croquet. Address: 11 Kiwi Street, Alicetown, Lower Hutt, New Zealand.

HEENAN Desmond Charles, b. 4 Nov 1930, Perth, WA, Aust. Justice, Supreme Court of WA. m. (1) diss, (2) Dale Evans Bradbury, 29 Feb 1992, 3 s, 3 d. Education: LLB, 1953, BA 1956, Univ of WA. Appointments: Ptnr, EM Heenan & Co, Sols of Perth, 1956-67; Mbr of Indep Bar, Perth, 1967-70; Judge, 1970-82, Chf Judge, 1982-95, Dist Crt of WA; Justice, Supreme Crt of WA, 1995-. Listed in: Who's Who in Australia. Hobbies: Fishing; Swimming; Tennis. Address: Judges' Chambers, Supreme Court, Perth, WA 6000, Australia.

HEFFERNAN Thomas Carroll, b. 19 Aug 1939, Hyannis, MA, USA. Professor, American and English Studies. m. N E Iler, 14 July 1972, div 1977. Education: Dip, Classics, Boston Coll HS, 1957; AB, Engl Lit, Boston Coll, 1961; MA, Engl Lit, Univ of Manchester, 1963; PhD, Engl Lit, Sophia Univ, Tokyo, Japan, 1990. Appointments: Prof, Kagoshima Kenritsu Daigaku, 1994-; Visng Prof, Kagoshima Univ, 1992-94; Lectr, Univ of MD, Asian Div, Tokyo, 1984-92. Publications: Gathering in Ireland, poems, 1996; The Liam Poems, 1981, 2nd ed, 1996; Art and Emblem, 1991. Honours: Mainichi Intl Haiku Awds, 1985, 1987, 1988, 1989, 1990, 1991, 1992, 1993, 1997; Itoen Intl Haiku Awd, 1991, 1995; Roanoke-Chowan Awd, 1982. Memberships: Engl Lit Soc of Japan; Renaissance Inst, Tokyo, Japan; Amn Lit Soc Japan; Japan Shakespeare Soc; MLA. Hobbies: Singing; Travel; Hiking. Address: Kagoshima Kenritsu Daigaku, 1-52-1 Shimo-ishiki-cho, Kagoshima City, 890-0005, Japan.

HEGDE Rama Krishna, b. 29 Aug 1927 Doddamane Siddapur Taluk Uttara Kannada Dist. Politician. m. Saraswati Hegde, 3 c. Education: Kashi Vidyapeeta Benares and Lucknow Univs. Appointments: Active in Quit India movement; Imprisoned twice; Organized Ryots' - Tenants' - movement Uttara Kannada Dist; Pres Dist Congress Cttee Uttara Kannada Dist, 1954-57; Entered State Legis as Dep Min for Plng and Dev, 1957; Gen Sec Mysore Pradesh Congress, 1958-62; Min in charge of Rural Dev Panchayatraj and Co-op Nijalingappa's Cabinet, 1962-65; Min for Fin Excise Prohibition Info and Publicity, 1965-67; Min for Fin Excise and Plng, 1967-68; Min for Fin Plng and Yth Servs, 1968, 1971; Ldr of Opposition, 1971-77; Imprisoned during Emergency; Elected Gen Sec All India Janata Party, 1977; Elected to Rajya Sabha from Karnataka Assn, 1978; Ldr Karnataka Janata Legislature Party, 1983; First ever non-Congress Chf Min in the State; Continued as hd of caretaker min, 1984; Following State Legislature by-electin Chf Min of Karnataka, 1985-88; Dep Chmn Plng Commn, 1989-90; Min of Com, 1998-; Pres World Fedn UN Assns. Address: 229 Kritika Rajmahal Vilas Extension, Bangalore 560080, India.

HEGGEN Alan Edwin, b. 3 July 1932, Kerang, Aust. Consultant; Retired Public Service Officer; Retired, RAAF Officer. m. 18 May 1953, 2 s. Education: Grad, RAAF Coll, 1952; RAAF Staff Coll, 1965; Jnt Servs Staff Coll, 1971; Austl Admin Staff Coll, 1979. Appointments: Roy Aust AF, 1949-89; Snr Appts: Chief of AF Materiel, 1982-87; Chf of AF Dev, 1987; Chf of Logs Dev, 1988-89; Grp Gen Mngr, Safety Regulation Civ Aviation Authy, 1989-91; Dir Off of Austl War Graves, 1991-97. Honour: Offr in Order of Aust (Mil Div), 1987. Memberships: Fell, Roy Aeronautical Soc; Utd Servs Inst of Vic; Rotary Intl; Melbourne Probus; Naval and Mil Club, Melbourne. Hobbies: Gardening; Walking. Address: 5/36 Daniell Place, Kew, Victoria 3101, Australia.

HEGGIE Andrew Alistair Cromie, b. 16 July 1955. Maxillofacial Surgeon. m. Denise, 4 Oct 1979, 1 s, 2 d. Education: MBBS; BDSc: MDSc; FRACDS; FFDRCSI; FACOMS; FRACDS(OMS). Appointments: Asst Surg, Roy Melbourne Hosp; Hd, Maxillofacial Surg, Roy Children's Hosp of Melbourne. Memberships: Austl Medl Assn; Austl Dental Assn; Aust and NZ Assn of Oral and Maxillofacial Surgs. Hobbies: Surfing; Reading; Music. Address: Department of Plastic and Maxillofacial Surgery,

Royal Children's Hospital of Melbourne, Parkville, 3052, Melbourne.

HEIMANN Ariel, b. 6 Sept 1953, Jerusalem. Geologist. m. Revital, 24 Aug 1978, 3 s. Education: BS, Geol & Bio, 1978, MSc, Geol, 1985, PhD, Geol, 1990, Hebrew Univ; Postdoc, Ohio State Univ, USA, 1990-92. Appointments: Geol Rsch Inst, 1985-90; Hebrew Univ, 1985-90; Geol Survey of Israel, 1992-. Publications: Physics of Chemistry of Dykes, book, 1995; Sci articles in sci jrnls. Address: 758 Nahal Arugot St, Maccabbim, 71908, Israel.

HEINZE Ruth-Inge, b. 4 Nov 1919, Berlin, Germany. Researcher. Education: BA, 1969; MA, 1971; PhD, 1974. Appointments: Ed, Follett Publng Co, 1955-56; Lectr, Course Designer, Adult Educ, San Fran, 1956-62; Lectr, Extension Courses, Berlin, W Germany, 1963-68; Prod, Writer, Monthly Educl Radio Prog, Berlin, 1963-73; Rsch Fell, Natl Mus, Bangkok, 1971-72; Lectr, Dept of Hum, Univ of Chiangmai, Thailand, 1971-72; Lectr, Socl Sci Sect, Mills Coll, Oakland, 1974; Staff Rsch Asst, Hum Devel Prog, Univ of CA, San Fran, 1975; Fulbright Hays Rsch Fell, Inst of SE Asian Studies, Singapore, 1978-79; Visng Prof, CA Inst of Integral Studies, San Fran, 1984-93; Rsch Assoc, Cntr for SE Asian Studies, 1974-; Adj Fac, Saybrook Inst, San Fran, 1985-. Creative Works: The Search for Visions; Shamans of the 20th Century; Trance and Healing in Southeast Asia Today; Tham Khwan - How to Contain the Essence of Life. Honours: Fulbright-Hays Rsch Grant; Amn Inst for Indian Studies, Trav Grants; Outstndng Immigrant to the US. Memberships: Assn for Asian Studies Inc; CA Soc for Physl Stdy; Indep Schls of Asia Inc; Inst for Noetic Scis; Intl Assn for the Stdy of Subtle Energies and Energy Med; Natl Coalition of Independent Schls; Natl Pictographic Soc; Spiritual Emer Network. Hobbies: Research; Writing. Address: 2121 Russell #3C, Berkeley, CA 94705-1959, USA.

HEKMATYAR Gulbuddin. Politician; Fomer Guerrilla Leader. Appointments: Ldr Hezb-i-Islam Mujahideen Movement against Soviet-backed regime; PM of Afghanistan, 1993-94, 1996-97; Returned from exile in Iran, 1998.

HELLYER Jill, b. 17 Apr 1925, North Sydney, Aust. Writer. Div, 2 s, 1 d. Appointments: Fndn Exec Sec, Austl Soc of Auths, 1963-71. Publications: Verse: The Exile, 1969; Song of the Humpback Whales, 1981; Novel: Not Enough Savages, 1975. Honours: Grenfell Henry Lawson Awd, 1963; Poetry Mag Awd, 1965. Membership: Austl Soc of Auths. Hobby: Gardening. Address: 25 Berowra Road, Mount Colah, NSW 2079, Australia.

HELM Kenneth Francis, b. 27 May 1945. Winemaker; Viticultural Consultant. m. Judith Mary Williams, 3 May 1969, 1 s, 2 d. Education: Biol Rsch Cert, 1972. Appointments: Local Cnclr, Yass Shire (4 yr terms), 1988-; ACT Liquor Licensing Authority Bd Mbr, 1991; Reappointed 1996; NSW Liquor Consultative Cttee, 1995; Aust Winemakers Forum, 1993-; Mayor, Yass Shire, 1997-. Publications: 10 incl: Cool Climate Wine Growing on the Canberra District, The Australian Horticulture Vol 85, No 8 pp 29-31, 1987; The influence of climatic variability on the production of quality wines in the Canberra district of South Eastern Australia, Proceedings of Second International Cool Climate Viticulture and Oenology Symposium, Auckland, NZ, 1988; The Effect of Drought on Populations of Phylloxera in Australian Vineyards, The Australian & NZ Wine Industry Journal, Vol 6, 1991; Phylloxera: Political or Pest?, The Australian Grapegrower & Winemaker, Oct 1993. Memberships: Fndng mbr, Canberra District Vignerons Assn; The Wine Press Club of Canberra; The Canberra Wine Show (Austl Wine Show); Estab The Indep Wineries Assn, 1993; Fndn Mbr, NSW Winemakers Forum, 1994; Fndn Mbr, NSW Winemakers Assn, 1995; Chmn, NSW Wine Ind promotion cttee, 1995. Listed in: Who's Who in Canberra. Address: Helm's Wines, Butts Road, Murrumbateman, NSW 2582, Australia.

HENARE Tau. Politician. m. 5 children. Appointments: Advsry Offr, Maori Dev, Waitakere Cty Cncl; Yth Educ Co-ordinator, Race Rels Conciliator; Advsry Offr, Dept of Internal Affairs; Elected to Parl, 1993; Ldr, Mauri Pacific; Min of Maori Affairs, Assoc Min of Educ, Assoc Min of Corrections. Address: PO Box 228, Whangarei, New Zealand.

HENDERSON Alexander Scott, b. 7 Dec 1935, Aberdeen, Scotland. Psychiatrist. m. 24 Feb 1963, 2 s, 3 d. Education: MB ChB, 1959, MD, 1967, Univ of Aberdeen, Scotland. Appointments: House Physn, Aberdeen Roy Infirmary, 1959-69; House Physn, Ross Clinic, Aberdeen, 1961-62; Reg, Prince Henry Hosp, Sydney, Aust, 1963-65; Mbr, Sci Staff, MRC Unit for Epidemiol Studies in Psych, Univ of Edinburgh, 1965-68; Fndn Prof of Psych, Univ of Tas, Aust, 1969-74; Dir, Prof, Psych Epidemiology Rsch Cntr, NH MRC, Austl Natl Univ, Canberra, 1975-; Clinl Advsr in Mental Hlth, C'wlth Dept of Hlth. Honour: DSc, 1992. Memberships: Roy Coll of Physns, London; Roy Australasian Coll of Physns; Roy Austl & NZ Coll of Psych; Roy Coll of Psych; Acady of the Socl Scis in Aust. Hobbies: Fly Fishing; Hill Walking. Address: NH MRC Psychiatric Epidemiology Research Centre, Australian National University, Canberra, ACT 0200, Australia.

HENDERSON James Herbert (Jim), b. 26 Aug 1918. Writer; Radio Broadcaster. m. 22 Sep 1948, 2 s, 1 d. Education: Nelson Coll. Appointments: Reporter, Nelson Evening Mail, 1936; Staff, NZ Free Lance, 1937-39; Lost a leg and POW, Sidi Rezegh, 1941; Wrote comedy skit, Wrack and Ruin Castle, produced POW Camp, Italy, 1943; Post war Jrnlsm, Freelance Wrk in Eng and Can; Fndr, Writer, Unofficial History, in NZRSA Review, 1953-95; Originator, Ed, Presenter, natl radio prog, Open Country, 1961-75; Also originated, This is New Zealand (65 radio talks); Writer of over 100 radio documentaries and features; Writer of feature, Home Country, in NZ Farmer, 1971-78; Talk-back Host, Radio Pacific, 1980-85; Writer of weekly feature, Getting in Behind, in NZ Times, 1983-86; 2 series of "Henderson's Country" for TVNZ. Publications include: Gunner Inglorious, 1945, 11th ed 1991; RMR, Official NZ War Hist, 1954; Te Kao, dist hist, 1957; 22 Battalion, Official NZ War Hist, 1958; One Foot at the Pole, 1962; Soldier Country, 1990; Open Country, 1965; Co-Auth, NZ's South Island in Colour, 1966; Return to Open Country, 1967; Open Country Calling, 1969; Our Open Country, 1971; Open Country Muster, 1974; Co-Auth, The New Zealanders, 1975; Swagger Country, 1976; Soldier Country, 1978; The Exiles of Asbestos Cottage, 1981; Jim Henderson's Open Country, 1982; Down From Marble Mountain, 1983; Co-Auth, No Honour, No Glory, 1983; Tales of the Coast, 1984; Jim Henderson's People, 1986; Jim Henderson's New Zealand, 1989; Jim Henderson's Home Country, 1990; Top to Bottom Reinga to Bluff, 1998. Honours: Mobil Radio Awd for Outstndng Contbn to Radio in NZ, 1984; MBE; First leg amputee to reach S Pole, 1960. Listed in: Who's Who in New Zealand. Hobbies: Writing; Reading. Address: 33A Kawau Rd, One Tree Hill, Auckland 5, New Zealand.

HENDERSON Le Roy Freame, b. 6 Nov 1927, Melbourne, Aust. Scientist. m. Una Millicent Henderson, 30 May 1958, 2 s, 1 d. Education: DEng, MEng, BCE, Univ Melbourne; PhD, Univ Sdyney. Appointments: Sci, Aero Rsch Lab, 1952-62; Rdr, Univ Sydney, 1962; Visng Prof, Cornell Univ, 1967, Princeton Univ, 1972, 1985, Tokyo Univ, 1973, Univ CA, Berkeley, 1987, Univ NY, 1991-93, Univ Provence, 1995, Tohoku Univ, 1996, Ben-Gurion, Israel, 1997. Publications: Over 100 pprs in sci jrnls and proceedings of confs. Honours: Fulbright Fell, 1967-68; Leverhulme Fell, 1973; German Acad Exchange Fell. Memberships: Austl Acady of Technol Scis and Engrng. Hobbies: Baroque and Russian Orthodox Church music; Modern art. Address: 8 Damour Avenue, East Lindfield, NSW 2070, Australia.

HENDERSON Margaret Mary, b. 13 Nov 1915. Consultant Physician. Education: MD; FRCP; FRACP. Appointments: RMO, 1939-40; Hon Physn 1947-75, Spec Physn 1976-81, Cnslt 1981-, Roy Melbourne Hosp; AMF Capt, 1941-42; Jnr Rsch Offr, WTE Hall Inst, 1941-42; Hon Phys, Queen Vic Mem Hosp, 1943-59; Fell, Janet Clarke Hall, Univ of Melbourne, 1966-. Honour: OBE, 1976. Address: 12/54 The Avenue, Parkville, Vic 3052, Australia.

HENDERSON Norman Harold, b. 19 May 1920, Sydney, NSW, Aust. Retired. m. Florrie King, 17 Dec 1941, 2 d. Appointments: War Serv, Roy Austl Navy, 1939-46; Bus Equip & Engrng Pty Ltd, 1946-49, Natl Sales Mngr, Salmond & Spraggon (Aust) Pty Ltd, 1949-66; Lt Cmndr, RANR, 1952-80; Hon ADC to Gov of NSW, 1964-70; Mng Dir, Chanel (Aust) Pty Ltd, 1966-85. Publication: Hints for Honorary ADC's. Honours: Vol Reserve Decoration and Bar, 1954; MBE, 1968; Reserve Forces Decoration, 1985. Memberships: JP, NSW; Patron, Sunnyfield Assn for Intellectualy Disabled; Chmn, St Ives Masonic Temple Ltd; Mbr, Roy Sydney Yacht Sqdn; Masonic Club of NSW. Hobbies: Freemasonry; Walking. Address: 227 Alfred Street, Cromer, NSW 2099, Australia.

HENDERSON Paul, b. 2 May 1961, Sydney, Aust. Electrical Engineer. m. Lindy, 7 Oct 1990, 1 s. Education: BEE, Univ of NSW, Aust; Postgrad Dip in Mngmt, Deakin. Appointments: Snr Tech Cons, WANG, 1992; Proj Mngr, DIGITAL, 1996; Prog Mngr, COMPAQ, 1998. Publications: Contbr, sev Austl comm standars, 1996. Honours: MCP, 1998; PMI PMP, 1999. Memberships: MIEEE, 1983-; ATUG, 1990-; Standards Australia, 1996-; APESMA, 1998-; PMI, 1999. Hobbies: Mountain bike; 4WD; Sailing. Address: 39 Marlow Avenue, Denistone 2114, Australia.

HENDERSON Peter Graham Faithfull, b. 1 Oct 1928, Sydney, Aust. Retired Foreign Service Officer; Chancellor St John Ambulance, Australia. Education: MA Oxon, Oxford Univ, 1947-50. Appointments: Joined Austl Dept of For Affirs, 1951; Served at diplomatic posts in Washington, Jakarta, Geneva and London, 1952-70; Austl Amb to the Philippines, 1973-74; Dpty Sec of the Dept, 1976-79; Sec of the Dept, 1979-84. Publication: Privilege and Pleasure (autobiog). Honour: AC, 1985. Listed in: Who's Who in Australia. Hobbies: Walking; Music; Reading. Address: 19 Black Street, Yarralumla, ACT 2600, Australia.

HENDLER Gordon Lee, b. 11 Dec 1946, New York, USA. Biologist. 4 s. Education: BS, Rutgers Univ; PhD, Univ CT. Appointments: Dir, Galeta Marine Lab, Panama, 1974-78; Marine Biol, Smithsonian Inst, 1978-85; Hd, Invertebrate Zoology, Curator, Natural Hist Mus, LA, 1985-. Publication: Sea Stars, Sea Urchins and Allies, 1995. Memberships: Soc for Integrative and Comparative Biol; AAAS; SCAMIT; WSN; SSZ. Address: Natural History Museum of Los Angeles County, 900 Exposition Boulevard, Los Angeles, CA 90007, USA.

HENDRICKSON Lyndall, b. 16 May 1917. Educator. m. 6 June 1946, Graeme Robson, 1 s. Appointments: Lectr and Violin Tutor, S Austl Coll of Advd Educ, 1981-90; Supvsr Music Rsch, 1991-94, Tutor Music Studies, 1993-; Tutor String Methodology, 1994-99, Univ of Adelaide. Fell (Hon), Flinders Univ of S Aust, 1995; Visng Fell, Rsch, Flinders Univ of S Aust, 1996; Schl-in-Residence Univ of WA, 1997. Publications: Children's Stories, 1971-80; Paintings, 1965-95. Honours: Hon Fell, Flinders Univ of S Aust, 1995; Hon Visng Fell, Flinders Univ, 1996. Memberships: Univ of Adelaide Alumni Assn; Austl String Tchrs Assn; S Austl Autism Assn; Post-Polio Assn; The Natl Cncl of Women. Listed in: Who's Who of Australian Women, 1982. Hobbies: Gardening; Reading; Travelling in the Australian desert areas. Address: 12 Parkgate Place, Upper Sturt, SA 5156, Australia.

HENDRY Peter Ian Alexander, b. 29 June 1915. Emeritus Consultant. m Senta Taft, 25 Feb 1972, 1 s, 1 d. Education: MB BS; Hon MD, DU, 1998, (Newcastle); DCP (Lon); FRCPA; FCAP; FAACB. Appointments: RMO 1939-40; Res Pathologist, 1940, Clin Pathologist, 1945-46, Prince Henry Hosp, Sydney; War serv: 2nd AIF Capt 2/10 FD AMB Malayan Campaign, 1940-45; Clin Pathologist, 1945-57, Emeritus Cnslt Pathologist, 1957-85, Royal Newcastle Hosp; Sec, 1960-72, Comn on

World Stands, VP, 1960-72, Intl Soc of Clin Path; Chmn, 1967-71, VP, 1971-73, Bd of Educ, 1973-75, Pres, 1973-75, Royal Coll of Pathologists, Aust; Dpty Chan, Newcastle Univ, 1990-97. Honour: AO, 1985. Memberships: World Assn of Socs of Path, Pres, 1972-75; Pres, World Path Fndn, 1977-79; Mbr Cncl, Newcastle Univ, 1970-72, 1979-97. Hobbies: Golf; Sailing; Swimming. Address: 82 Scenic Highway, Merewether, NSW 2291, Australia.

HENG Samrin, b. 25 May 1934. Politician. Appointments: Polit Commissar and Cmdr of Khmer-Rouge 4th Infantry Div, 1976-78; Led abortive coup against Pol Pot and fled to Viet Nam, 1978; Pres Natl Front for Natl Salvation of Kampuchea, 1978; Pres People's Revolutinoary Cncl, 1979 - took power after Vietnamese invasion of Kampuchea; Chmn Cncl of State of Cambodia, 1991; Sec Gen People's Revolutionary Party of Kampuchea - KPRP - 1981-91. Memberships: Mbr Poliburo of Cambodia, 1991-. Address: Council of State, Phnom-Penh, Cambodia.

HENRY Geoffrey Arama (Sir), b. 16 Nov 1940, Aitutaki, Cook Is. Politician. m. Louisa Olga Hoff, 1965, 4 s, 2 d. Education: Vic Univ, Wellington, NZ. Appointments: Sch Tchr, 1965-67; Active in Pols, 1965-68; Pub Serv, 1970-72; Cabinet Min, 1972-78; Ldr, Opposition, 1978-89; PM, 1983, 1989-; Dpty PM, Coalition Govt, 1984; Organiser, Jnt Coml Commn, USA and Pacific Is, 1990; Chmn, Econ Summit Small Is States, 1992; Chan, Univ S Pacific, 1992. Honours: KBE; Silver Jubilee Medal, 1977; NZ Commemorative Medal, 1990. Listed in: International Who's Who. Hobbies: Golf, rugby and other sports; Reading; Music. Address: PO Box 281, Rarotonga, Cook Islands.

HENSEN Steven Adrian, b. 10 Mar 1960. Environmental Chemist. m. Sharmini Kanniah, 25 Dec 1995, 3 s, 2 d. Education: BS, Chem, CA State Univ, Chico; Grad Courses in Environmental Engrng, Univ of TX, Arlington and Kensington Univ. Appointments: Lab Techn, Harter Packing Co, Yuba Cty, CA, 1978-81; Chem, Roy F Weston Inc, Stockton, CA, 1986-88; Rsch Assoc, Univ of TX Arlington, Arlington, TX, 1988-89; Qual Ass Chem, Hitachi, Semiconductor - US, Dallas, TX, 1988-89; Dir of Tech Servs, CURA Inc, CEL Inc, Dallas, TX, 1989-92; Lab Mngr, Core Labs Inc, Corpus Christi, TX & Anaheim, CA, 1992-93; VP of Lab Ops, Inchcape Testing/NDRC Labs, Dallas, 1993-94; Mngr, Integrated Environmental Chem Servs, 1994-, Mngr Chem Servs, Asia Pacific, 1998-, Core Labs Malaysia Sdn BhD, Shah Alam, Malaysia, 1994-. Memberships: Amn Chem Soc; Amn Inst of Chem; Amn Soc of Qual Control. Listed in: Who's Who in the Environmental Industry. Hobbies: Swimming; Camping; Basketball. Address: 19-17-5 Royale, Mont Kiara Palma, Jalun Mont Kiara, 50480 Kuala Lumpur, Malaysia.

HERBERT Yvonne May. m. Hon John Herbert, dec. Appointments: Assoc w the Welfare Cttee of former premiers' wives, 1957-; Pres, Cttee named for wife of Qld Premier, Senator Flo Bjelke-Petersen, cttees have raised in excess of $175,000 for charity, 1968-. Honours: Awd'd for her contbn to comm & charitable orgs; OBE, 1980; CBE, 1989. Memberships: Girl Guides; Scouts; The Natl Cncl of Women; Children & Yth Welfare Activities. Address: 22 Randolph Street, Graceville, Qld 4075, Australia.

HERCUS John Duncan Andrew, b. 30 Nov 1935, Wellington, New Zealand. International Advisor. m. Ann, 17 Dec 1960, 2 s. Education: MSc. Appointments: Dir, Christchurch Polytech, 1975-94; Advsr, Cnslt, UNDP, UNESCO and ILO, 1990-. Publications: Over 30 reports and policy documents on tech educ in Asia and Pacific countries. Honours: Num schlsps. Memberships: Assn of Polytechs in NZ, life mbr. Hobbies: Sailing; Ship model building; Research. Address: 82A Park Terrace, Christchurch, New Zealand.

HERCUS Luise Anna, b. 16 Jan 1926, Munich, Germany. Linguist. m. Graham Hercus, 1 s. Education: MA, Oxon; PhD, Austl Natl Univ. Appointments: Fell, St Anne's Coll, Oxford, 1954; Rsch Fell, Univ Adelaide, 1969; Snr Lectr, Austl Natl Univ, 1991. Publications: The Languages of Victoria, 1969; The Bagandji Language, 1982; Arabana-Wangkangurru Grammar, 1994; The Wirangu Language from the West Coast of South Australia. Honour: Order of Aust, 1996. Membership: Fell, Austl Acady of the Humanities. Hobby: Native Animals. Address: Kintala, via Gundaroo, NSW 2620, Australia.

HERCUS Dame Margaret Ann, b. 24 Feb 1942 Hamilton. Politician. m. John Hercus, 2 s. Education: Vic Auckland and Canterbury Univs. Appointments: Lawyer and Staff Trng Offr Beath & Co Christchurch, 1969-70; Dep Chmn Com Commn, 1975-78; Chmn Consumer Rights Campaign, 1975; MP for Lyttelton, 1978-87; Opposition Spokesperson on Socl Welfare Consumer Affairs and Women's Affairs, 1978-84; Min of Socl Welfare Police and Women's Affairs, 1984-87; Perm Rep of NZ to the UN, 1989-90; Intl consultant, 1991-. Memberships: Price Tribunal and Trade Pracs Commn, 1973-75; Labour. Hobbies: Collecting original NZ prints; Th; Reading. Address: 82 Park Terrace, Christchurch 1, New Zealand.

HERMANN John Arthur, b. 29 Mar 1943, Melbourne, Australia. Research Scientist. m. Leona M Hermann, 28 Sept 1976, 1 s, 1 d. Education: BSc, Melbourne Univ; MSc, Monash Univ; PhD, Queens Univ, UK. Appointment: Prin Rsch Sci, DSTO Aust. Publications: Over 100 sci pprs, articles and reviews. Memberships: NY Acady of Scis; Optical Soc of Am; Austl Optical Soc; IEEE/LEDS Nonlin Optics Cttee; Edl Bd, Jrnl of Nonlinear Optical Phys and Materials; Cttee on Monetary and Econ Reform; Natl Coord, SA State Sec, Econ Reform Aust. Hobbies: Economic and Monetary Reform; Musical Appreciation. Address: 1106 Lower North East Road, Highbury, SA 5089, Australia.

HERNANDEZ Leopoldo Hernando, b. 4 June 1947, Havana, Cuba. Lawyer. m. Alita, 4 Oct 1982, 2 d. Education: JD; BSc; Bus Admin. Appointment: Judge, Pro tem, CA Dept of Indl Rels, Workers Compensation Appeals Bd, 1985. Honours: Richard Radcliff Meml Ldrshp Awd, 1968; Pres, Cuban Amn Bar Assn, 1984. Memberships: Amn Bar Assn; CA Applicants Attys Assn. Hobbies: Import-export; Investments. Address: 3330 Pico Boulevard, #2308, Santa Monica, CA 90405, USA.

HERNANDEZ Rujher, b. 21 June 1956, Cerete, Cordoba, Colombia. Poet; Teacher. 1s, 1d. Education: Technic Profesional en Idomas, CESCO, Montería, Cordoba, 1983. Appointment: Lang Tchr. Publications: Si En Algun Lugar Del Mundo Me Respondieras (poems), 1988; Detrás De Ese Cielo Profundo...Mas Alla De Tu Nombre (poems), 1993; Mas Alla Del Oscuro Puente (poems), 1997. Honours: Many intl lit awds incl: Accademico di Merito, Intl Acady Trinacria, Messina, Italy, 1997; Diploma, Accademico Benemerito, Accademia Ferdinandea, Catania, Italy, 1998. Hobbies: Reading; Singing; Listening to music. Address: Apartado Postal 273, Cerete, Cordoba, Columbia.

HERNANDEZ CERVANTES Hector, b. Dec 1923 Mexico Cty. Politician. Education: Natl Univ of Mexico; Col de Mexico; Univ of Melbourne. Appointments: Fmrly taught econ theor Univ of Mexico and Cntr of Latin Am Monetary Studies; Economist Banco de Mexico; Asst Dir of Finl Studies min of Fin; Dir-Gen of Ind and Com min of Com; Dir-Gen of Finl and Intl Studies min of Fin; Under-Sec of For Trade min of Com and Indl Dev, 1982-83; Sec of Com and Indl Dev, 1983-88. Address: c/o Secretaria de Industria y Comercio, Avenida Cuauhtemoc 80, Mexico DF, Mexico.

HERON Thomas Anthony Edmond, b. 10 July 1945, Brisbane, Aust. Mechanical Engineer. m. Jean Helen, 14 Sept 1968, div 1990, 1 s. 1 d. Education: BEng Hons; MEngSc; MPubAd; Grad Dip Exec L'ship; First Class Marine Engrs Cert. Appointments: Chf Engr, Slipway Engr, Engr Surv, Marine Bd of QLD; Des Engr, QLD Dept of Works; Prin Advr Engrg, Div Workplace Health and Safety; Snr Prin Advr (Tech), Div WH&S. Publications: Contbr Auth, Small Ship Manual. Honours: NACO Aust

Prize for design analysis, 1979; Aust Inst of Refrigeration, Air Conditioning and Htg Awd, 1979; W W Marriner Awd for Best Tech Paper Aust and NZ, 1985. Memberships: Regd Profl Engr, Bd of Profl Engrs, QLD. Hobbies: Breeding stud cattle; Endurance horse riding. Address: Karrahbil, 807 Upper Brookfield Road, Upper Brookfield, QLD 4069, Australia.

HERRERA Luis Felipe, b. 17 Jun 1922 Valparaiso. Banker; Lawyer; Economist. m. Ines Olmo, 1961, 2 s. Education: Col Aleman de Santiago; Escuela Militar; Univs of Chile and London. Appointments: Legal Dept Cntrl Bank of Chile, 1943-47; Att for Cntrl Bank of Chile and priv law prac, 1947-52; Prof of Econs Schs of Law and Sociol Univ of Chile, 1947-58; Under-Sec for Econ and Com, 1952; Min of Fin, Apr-Oct 1953; Gen Mngr Cntrl Bank of Chile, 1953-58; Gov Intl Bank for Reconstrn and Dev IMF, 1953-58; Exec Dir, 1958-60; Pres Inter-Am Dev Bank, 1960-71; Pres Soc for Intl Dev, 1970-71; Co-ordr Gen ECIEL Prog - Jnt Studies for Latin Am Econ Integration - 1974-; Perm Consultant, 1981-; Pres Admin Cncl Intl Fund for Promotion of Culture - UNESCO - 1976-; Chmn Bd of Trustees UN Inst for Trng and Rsch, 1976-; Pres World Soc of Ekistics Inst for Intl Co-op, 1977-80; Pres Corp Investigaciones para el Desarrollo - CINDE - 1986; Pres Chilean Chapter of SID, 1986; Perm Consultant Emer Intl Am Dev Bank. Publcations: El Banco Cntral de Chile, 1945; Politica economica, 1950; Elementos de Economia Monetaria, 1955; Desarrollo Economico o Estabilidad Monetaria? 1958; America Latina Integrada, 1964; El Desarrollo Latinoamericano y su Financiamiento, 1967; Nacionalismo Latinoamericano, 1968; Chile en America Latina, 1969; Internacionalismo Regionalismo Nacionalismo, 1970; America Latina: Experiencias y Desafios, 1974; America Latina: Viejas y Nuevas Fronteras, 1978; El Ecenario Latinoamericano y el Desafio Cultural, 1981; Despertar de un Continenete: America Latina 1960-1980, 1983; Communidad Latinoamericana de Naciones: presencia de Chile, 1983; Vision de America Latina: 1974-1984, 1985; America Latina: Desarollo e Integracion, 1986. Honours: Num hon degrees; Great Cross Distinguished Service Fed Repub Germany, 1958; Kt Grand Cross Order of Merit Italy, 1966; Medalla Civica 'Camilo Torres' Colombia, 1968; Grand Cross for Educl Merit Brazil, 1969; Bronfman Awd Am Pub Hlth Assn, 1969; Premio 'Diego Portales' Chile, 1971; Gran Cruz de la Orden del Sol Peru, 1971; Gran Cruz Placa de Plata Dominican Repub, 1971; Gran Cruz Orden Ruben Dario Nicaragua, 1971; Al Merito Nacional Paraguay, 1971; Orden del Aguila Azteca Mexico, 1972; Antonio Jose de Irisarri Guatemala, 1975; Orden al Merito Cultural 'Andres Bello' Venezuela, 1978; Offr de l'Ordre du Merite France, 1979; Gran Cruz de Isabel La Catolica Spain, 1980; Premio Serfin de Integracion Mexico, 1987; Premio ONU: Medalla Plata a la Paz Cepal Santiago, 1988; UN Personnel Peace Prize, 1989; Univ Austral de Chile: Condecoracion al Merito Univ, 1990; Dr hc - Santiago de Chile - 1993; Num awds and prizes. Memberships: Mbr Bd of Govs Intl Dev Rsch Cntr - IDRC - 1980; Mbr Bd of Trustees Third World Fndn; Mbr Hon Bd Raul Prebish Fndn, 1986. Address: CONSULT, Calle Europa 2048, P O Box 16.969, Santiago 9, Chile.

HESELTINE William Frederick Payne (Sir), b. 17 July 1930, Western Aust, Aust. Private Secretary to HM Queen Elizabeth II; Keeper of the Queen's Archives. m. Audrey Margaret Nolan, 21 Nov 1959, 1 s, 1 d. Education: BA Hons, Hist, Univ of WA, 1950. Appointments: Prime Mins Dept, Canberra, Aust, 1951-62; Pvte Sec to Prime Min RG Menzies, 1955-59; Asst Info Offr to the Queen 1960-61; Asst Fed Dir, Liberal Party, 1963-64; Asst Press Sec, Press Sec to Queen, 1965-72; Asst, Dpty Pvte Sec to the Queen, 1972-86; Pvte Sec and Keeper of Queens Archives, 1986-90; Dir, 1990-92, Chmn, 1992-98, NZI Aust Ltd; Dir, 1990-97, Dpty Chmn, 1998- P&O, Aust Ltd, Dir, W Coast Telecasters, 1991-95. Honours: MVO, 1961; CVO, 1969; CB, 1978; KCVO, 1981; KCB, 1986; AC, 1988; GCVO, 1989; QSO, 1990; GCB, 1990; Privy Cnclr, 1986. Listed in: Who's Who; Who's Who in Australia. Address: PO Box 35, York, WA 6302, Australia.

HESKIN Kenneth, b. 28 Sept 1945, Belfast, Northern Ireland. Academic. m. Susan, 11 Mar 1967, 2 s, 1 d. Education: BA, hons, Queens Univ, Belfast, 1968; PhD, Univ Durham, 1975; MA, Trinity Coll, Dublin, 1979. Appointments: Rsch Asst, Durham Univ, 1968-72; Lectr, Univ of Ulster, 1972-76; Lectr, 1982-85, Snr Lectr, 1985-87, Hd of Dept, 1987-88, Trinity Coll, Dublin; Hd of Dept, 1988-94, Hd, Sch of Socl and Behavioral Scis, 1992-, Swinburne Univ, Melbourne. Publications: Northern Ireland: A Psychological Analysis, 1980; Sev articles in profl jrnls. Honour: Fulbright Fellshp, 1977-78. Memberships: Assoc Fell, Brit Psychol Soc; APA; Austl Psychol Soc; Reversal Theory Soc. Hobby: Golf. Address: Swinburne University of Technology, PO Box 218, John Street, Melbourne 3122, Australia.

HESTON Charlton, b. 4 Oct 1924 Evanston IL. Actor. m. Lydia Clark, 1944, 1 s, 1 d. Education: Nwest Univ Evanston. Appointments: First Broadway appearance Antony and Cleopatra, 1948; Starred in more than 50 films Hollywood, 1950-; Pres Screen Actors Guild, 1965-71; Trustee Am Film Inst, 1971-; Chmn, 1973; Chmn on Arts Predl Task Force on Arts and Hums, 1981; VP Natl Rifle Assn, 1997-. Stage appearances incl: Macbeth, 1954, 1959, 1976 - London; Mister Roberts, 1954; Detective Story, 1956; A Man for All Seasons, 1965, 1987; Caine Mutiny Court Martial - also Dir - London, 1985. Tv incls: Chiefs - CBS - 1983; Nairobi Affairs - CBS - 1984; The Colbys - ABC-TV; A Thousand Heroes, 1991. Films incl: Julius Caesar, 1950; Dark City, 1950; The Greatest Show on Earth, 1952; The Savage, 1952; Ruby Gentry, 1952; The President's Lady, 1953; Pony Express, 1953; Arrowhead, 1953; Bad for Each Other, 1953; The Naked Jungle, 1953; Secret of the Incas, 1954; The Far Horizons, 1955; Lucy Gallant, 1955; The Private War of Major Benson, 1955; Three Violent People, 1956; The Ten Commandments, 1956; Touch of Evil, 1958; The Big Country, 1958; The Buccaneer, 1958; Ben Hur, 1959; The Wreck of the Mary Deare, 1959; El Cid, 1961; The Pigeon that Took Rome, 1962; Diamond Head, 1962; 55 Days at Peking, 1962; Major Dundee, 1964; The Greatest Story Ever Told, 1965; The Agony and the Ecstasy, 1965; The War Lord, 1965; Khartoum, 1966; Counterpoint, 1967; Will Penny, 1967; Planet of the Apes, 1967; Beneath the Planet of the Apes, 1969; The Hawaiians, 1970; Julius Caesar, 1970; The Omega Man, 1971; Antony and Cleopatra, 1972; Skyjacked, 1972; The Call of the Wild, 1972; Soylent Green, 1973; The Three Musketeers, 1973; The Four Musketeers, 1974; Earthquake, 1974; Airport, 1975; Midway, 1975; Two Minute Warning, 1976; The Last Hard Men, 1976; The Prince and the Pauper, 1976; Gray Lady Down, 1978; The Awakening, 1980; Mother Lode, 1981; Caine Mutiny Court Martial - also dir - 1988; Treasure Island, 1989; Almost an Angel - cameo; Solar Crisis; Wayne's World 2 - cameo; True Lies, 1994; In The Mouth of Madness; Alaska - also dir; Hercules - voice - 1997. Publications: The Actor's Life, 1979; In the Arena, 1995; Charlton Heston Presents the Bible, 1997. Honours: Acady Awd for Best Actor Ben Hur, 1959; Veterans of For Wars Citizenship Medal, 1982; Golden Medal of the Cty of Vienna, 1995; Cmdr Ordre des Arts et des Lettres. Memberships: Mbr Natl Cncl of Arts, 1967. Hobbies: Sketching; Tennis. Address: c/o Jack Gilardi, ICM, 8942 Wilshire Boulevard, Beverly HIllcs, CA 90211, USA.

HETTIARCHCHI Ranjith, b. 24 oct 1949, Colombo, Sri Lanka. Chief Executive Officer. m. Letticia, 22 Oct 1978, 2 s. Education: MEcon. Appointments: Finl Advsr, 1993; Gen Mngr, ACCU, 1994; Gen Mngr, SANSA, Sri Lanka; Asst Proj Dir, TTD Dir of Trng Inst. Creative Works: Professional Management Manual Microfinancing, CUs Development Manual. Address: 1/95 Dewals Road, Makola North, Makola, Sri Lanka.

HETZEL Basil Stuart, b. 13 June 1922, London, Eng. Medical Scientist. m. (1) Helen Eyles, 3 Dec 1946, (2) Anne Gilmour Fisher, 1 Oct 1983, 3 s, 2 d. Education: MD, 1949; Fulbright Rsch Schl, Cornell, NY, 1951-54; Rsch Fell, Chem Pathol, St Thomas' Hosp, London, 1954-55; FRACP, 1958; FRCP, 1972; FFCM, 1980; FTS, 1981. Appointments: Michell Prof of Med, Adelaide Univ, 1964-68; Prof, Socl & Preventive Med, Monash Univ, 1968-75; Chf, CSIRO Div of Hum Nutrition, 1975-85; Exec Dir, Intl Cncl for Control of Iodine Deficiency Disorders, 1985-95; Chmn, 1995-. Publications: Health and Australian Society, 1974; The LS Factor, 1987; The Story of Iodine Deficiency, 1989; SOS for a Billion, 1996. Honours: Companion, Order of Aust, 1990; Lt Gov, S Aust, 1992; Chan, Univ of S Aust, 1992-98; Alwyn Smith Medal, Fac of Pub Hlth, Roy Coll of Physns, 1993; Anzac Peace Prize, RSL, 1997; Hon Doct, Univ of S Aust, 1999. Memberships: Pres, Endocrine Soc of Aust, 1964-66; Pres, Aust Soc for Epidemiology and Rsch in Cmnty Hlth, 1973-75; Dpty Chmn, Intl Epidemiological Assn, 1977-8; Life Mbr, Pub Hlth Assn, 1992; Life Mbr, Austl Nutrition Fndn, 1997; Life Mbr, Austl Epidemiological Assn, 1997. Hobbies: Biographies; History; Music. Address: 139 Kermode Street, North Adelaide 5006, Australia.

HEWETSON Richard William, b. 19 Apr 1921, Tenterfield, NSW, Aust. Veterinary Science. m. Mary, 28 Sept 1957, 2 s, 2 d. Education: BVSc; HDA. Appointments: Cattle Husbandry Offr, Dept Agric Stock, Queensland; Vet Offr in Charge, A I Cntr, Berry, NSW, EOV CSIRO. Publications; Dairy Cattle Breeding Proj Wollongbar, BSW. Honours: Paul Harris Fellow (Rotary), 1991. Memberships: Life Mbr, Aust Vet Assn; Past Pres, Rotary; Probus. Hobbies: Golf; Travelling; Reading; Cattle breeding. Address: 38 Hewetsons Lane, Rous Mill, Alstonville, NSW 2477, Australian.

HEWGILL Frank Richmond, b. 21 Sept 1929. Academic. m. Elizabeth C Barrett, 29 Nov 1958, 1 s, 2 d. Education: MA, Cantab, 1954; PhD, Adelaide, 1955. Appointments: Snr Rsch Offr, C'Wlth Antioxidant Rsch Proj, 1956-59, Univ of WA; Lectr in Organic Chem 1959-65, Snr Lectr 1966-69, Rdr 1970-94, Hon Snr Rsch Fell, 1995-98. Publications: Num publs in chem jrnls. Honours: Roy Soc Travelling Fellshp, 1970; Austl Acady Travelling Fellshp, 1988. Memberships: Roy Soc of Chem; NY Acady of Scis. Listed in: Who's Who in the World. Hobbies: Music; Literature; Woodwork. Address: 2610 Thomas Road, Mahogany Creek, WA 6072, Australia.

HEWITT (Cyrus) Lenox (Simson) (Sir), b. 7 May 1917. Company Chairman and Director. m. Alison Tillyard, 1 s, 3 d, 1 dec. Education: BCom, Melbourne Univ; FASA; FCIS; CPA. Appointments: Broken Hill Proprietary Co Ltd, 1933-46; Asst Sec, C'wlth Prices Br, Canberra, 1939-46; Lectr, Econs and Gost Acctcy, Canberra UC, 1940-49, 1954; Economist, Dept of Post War Reconstrn, 1946-49; Offl Sec, Acting Dpty High Cmmnr, London, 1950-53; C'wlth Treas: Asst Sec, 1953-55, 1st Asst Sec, 1955-62, Dpty Sec, 1962-66; Chmn, Austl Unius Cmmn, 1967; Sec to: PM's Dept, 1968-71, Dept of the Environ, Aborigines and the Arts, 1971-72, Dept of Minerals and Energy, 1972-75; Dpty Chmn, Austl Atomic Energy Cmmn, 1972-77; Acting Chmn, Pipeline Authy, 1973-75, Petroleum and Minerals Athy, 1974-75; Dir, 1973-80, Chmn, 1975-80, Qantas Airways Ltd; Dir, E-Austl Pipeline Corp Ltd, 1974-75, Mary Kathleen Uranium Ltd, 1975-80, Pontello Constructions Ltd, 1980-82, Santos Ltd, 1981-82, Aberfoyle Ltd, 1981-89, Short Bros (Aust) Ltd, 1981-91, Endeavour Resources Ltd, 1982-86, Airship Inds PLC, 1984-88, Qintex Aust Ltd, 1985-90, Brit Midlands Airways (Aust) Pty Ltd, 1985-, Universal Telecasters Securities Ltd, 1985-90, Qintex Am Ltd, 1987-90, Fortis Pacific Aviation Ltd, 1987-, Qantas Wentworth Holdings Ltd, 1975-80; QH Tours Ltd, 1975-80 (Dir 1974-80); Petroleum & Minerals Co of Austl Pty Ltd, 1975; Chmn, Exec Cttee, IATA, 1976-77 (Mbr 1975-80); Orient Airlines Assn, 1977; Austmark Intl Ltd, 1983-88; Northern Mining Corp NL, 1984-85; State Rail Authy of NSW, 1986-90. Honour: OBE, 1963. Hobby: Farming. Address: 9 Torres Street, Red Hill, Canberra, ACT 2603, Australia.

HEWITT Heather Agnes, b. 14 July 1934, Vic, Aust. Academic. m. John R Hewitt, 30 Dec 1959, 2 s, 1 d. Education: BA, DipEd, Univ of Melbourne, 1955. Appointments: Offr in Charge of Cnslng Guidance, Clin Servs, Vic Educ Dept, 1957-79; Psychologist, Roy Children's Hosp, 1960-63; Lectr, Lincoln Inst of Hlth Scis, 1966-70; Lectr, Inst of Early Childhood Devel, 1978-80; Lectr, Vic Coll of Adv Educ, Burwood Campus, 1979-80; Prin, Univ Coll, Univ of Melbourne, 1980-99. Publications: Persons Handicapped by Rubella, 1991; Auth of articles in profl jrnls; Edl Bd, Intl Jrnl of Rehab Rsch, Intl Jrnl of Visual Impairment and Blindness. Memberships include: Exec Mbr, Intl Assn of Deaf/Blind; Exec Mbr, Intl Cncl for Educ of Visually Impaired, 1987-; Austl Psychol Soc; Austl Coll of Educ. Hobbies: Music; Gardening. Address: University College, University of Melbourne, College Crescent, Parkville, Vic 3052, Australia.

HEWITT Joanna Miriam, b. 1 May 1949. Public Servant. m. Mark Pierce, 1 May 1987, 1 s, 2 d. Education: BEcons, Hons I, Univ of West Aust; MSc Econ, London Sch of Econs. Appointments: Joined Dept of For Affairs, 1972; Sub appts, 1983-, Depts of PM Cabinet Ind, Trade and Primary Inds/Energy; Appointed Hd of Div, OECDS Agric Dir, 1993-96; Dpty Sec, Dept For Affairs and Trade, 1996 and concurrently Amb for APEC, 1998-. Memberships: Austl Inst of Intl Affairs, 1996; Export Fin and Ins Corp, Bd of Dirs, 1996-98, Alternate Dir, 1998-; Bd Mbr, Austl Wool Corp, 1990-91. Hobbies: Cinema; Literature. Address: Department of Foreign Affairs and Trade, Barton, ACT 0221, Australia.

HEWITT Leslie Edward, b. 5 Sept 1916, Tas, Aust. m. Marie J Burns, 8 May 1943, 4 s, 2 d. Education: Dip, Tech, 1939; Dip, Motor Engrng, 1936. Appointments: Apprentice Carpenter, Joiner, 1933-38; Fitter, RAAF, 1940-45; Works Supvsr, Arch, 1947-81. Honours: Life Mbrshp, Stello Maris Sch; RAAF Assn, Natl VP; Lions Citizens Awd, 1980; Rotary Awd, 1983; Good Neighbour Cncl Assoc; Rostrum, 1975; Freeman, 1989; Life Mbr, Boy Scouts Assn, 1989; Awd'd Citizenship of Burnie; OAM, 1995. Membership: Burnie Show Soc Cttee. Hobbies: Boating; Antique cars; Golf. Listed in: Australian Roll of Honour; Who's Who in Australia and the Far East. Address: 188 Mount Road, Burnie, Tasmania 7320, Australia.

HEYWARD Oliver Spencer (The Right Reverend), b. 16 Mar 1926, Tas, Aust. Anglican Bishop. m. Peggy Butcher, 27 Sept 1952, 4 s. Education: BA, hons, Univ of Tas, 1946-48; MA, Oxon; Oriel Coll, 1950-52; Cuddesdon Coll, Oxford, 1952-53. Appointments: Deacon, 1953; Priest, Brighton, Eng, 1954; Rector, Sorell, Tas, 1956; Rector, Richmond, 1960; Precentor, St David's Cath, Tas, 1962; Warden, Christ Coll, Univ of Tas, 1963-74; Bish of Bendigo, Vic, 1975-91; Asst to Anglican Primate, Pt-time, 1991-95. Honour: Rhodes Schl, 1949. Memberships: Pres, Bendigo Coll of Adv Educ, 1975-85; Chmn of Socl Response Cmmn, Anglican Ch of Aust, 1977-92; Pres, Austl Cncl of Chs, 1989-92; Cmmnr, Vic Post-Secnd Educ Cmmn, 1981-92; Chmn, Brotherhood of St Lawrence, 1993-97. Hobby: Gardening. Address: 7 Waltham Street, Richmond, Vic 3121, Australia.

HICKEY Barry James. Archbishop. Education: Christian Bros Coll (WA); St Charles Seminary (WA); Licentiate of Sacred Theol, Urbaniana Univ, Rome, 1955-59; BA, Univ WA, 1968-71; MSoc Wk 1971-73. Appointments: Ordained Priest, 1958; Asst Priest, St Brigid's, West Perth, 1959-65; Cptn, Aust Army Reserve, 1962-67; Admnstr, Sacred Heart, Highgate, 1965-68; Dir, Centrecare, 1973-83; Dir, Cath Immigration, 1976-83; Chmn WA Soc Welfare Commn, 1978-82; Bd Mbr Inst of Family Stdies, 1980-83; State Chap to St Vincent de Paul, 1982-83; Episcopal Vicar for Soc Welfare, 1982-83; Chmn Aust Cath Soc Welfare Commn, 1983-85; Parish Priest, Sacred Heart, Highgate, 1983-84; Bish of Geraldton, WA, 1984-91; Archbish of Perth, 1991-; Mbr Austl Citizenshp Cncl, 1998. Bishop's Committees: Soc Welfare, 1985-91; Seminaries, 1985-91; Sec, Migrants and Refugees, 1992-; Liturgy, 1992-; Central Commn, 1992-; Chmn, Aust Cath Liturgy Cttee, 1993-; Great Jubilee 2000, 1995-. Publication: Preparing Couples for Marriage, 1982. Honour: OAM, 1977. Listed in: Who's Who in Australia; Who's Who in the World. Hobbies: Reading; Music; Tennis. Address: St Mary's Cathedral, Victoria Square, Perth, WA 6000, Australia.

HICKS Peter Alastair, b. 20 Aug 1945, Kampala, Uganda. Food Technologist. m. Constance, 16 Sept

1967, 1 s, 1 d. Education: BSc Hons, Reading Univ; MEngSc, Sydney Univ. Appointments: Mngmnt Trnee, H J Heinz Co Ltd, London, 1964-68; Food Engr, IFRPD Kasetsart Univ, Bangkok, 1977-78; Visng Fell, Univ S Pacific, Apia, W Samoa, 1981; Lectr, Univ W Sydney, Aust, 1970-83; Hon Assoc Food Tech, Assn NSW, 1974-84; Dir, Hawkaid R and D Co, Aust, 1982-90; Food Inds Offr, FAO/UN, Rome, 1984-86; Snr Regl Agroinds Offr, FAO/UN, Bangkok, 1987-; Tech Advsr, Asia-Pacific Food Inds Jrnl, 1991-; Advsr, Acady Consortium of Thai Univ, Agro Ind Curric, 1995-. Creative Works: Num Chapts in textbooks; Articles to Profl Jrnls. Memberships: Chmn, Gdn Condominium, Food Engrng Grp, Austl Inst of Food Sci and Technol, Cncl for Educ in World Citizenship; Mbr, Asian Assn Agric Engrs, Thai Assn Food Sci and Technol. Hobby: Numismatics. Address: Maliwan Mansion, Phra Atit Road, Bangkok 10200, Thailand.

HICKS Peter Richard. Telecommunications Engineer. Education: BE 1971, BSc 1975, MEngSc 1982, Monash Univ. Appointments: Snr Engr, Telecom Austl Rsch Labs, 1984; Prin Engr, Data Switching Sect, Telecom Rsch, 1987; Tech Spec, Switching Sect, TRL, 1988; Tech Spec, Broadband Networks, 1996, Proj Mngr, Network Perf and Dimensioning, 1997, Broadband Networks, Telstra Rsch Labs. Honour: Telstra Rsch Labs Outstndng Achievement Awd, 1994. Memberships: Leader, Austl Deleg to ITU-TSG7, 1992-; Rapporteur, Data Network Numbering ITU-TSG7, 1994-96; Rapporteur, Data Network Numbering, ITU-TSG7, 1997-. Hobbies: Skiing; Gardening; Railways. Address: c/o Telstra Research Laboratories, 770 Blackburn Road, Clayton, Vic 3168, Australia.

HICKS Roger George, b. 28 Nov 1945, Gloucester, England. Information Systems Consultant. m. Glenis, 13 Dec 1969, 1 s, 2 d. Education: BSc, hons, Bath Univ, 1968. Appointments: Systems Engr, Plessey Telecomms Rsch, 1968-69; Snr Systems Engr, Rolls Royce, Bristol Engines, 1969-72; Mngr, N Eurn Info Servs, Digital Equipment, 1972-77; Supvsng Software Progr, Dept of Hlth, 1977-78; Systems Mngr, AHI Computer Servs, 1978-81; Tech Mngr, PAXUS, 1981-86; Mngr, Independent Software Divsn, RAKON Computers, 1986-88; Mngr, Open Systems Unit, Digital Equipment, 1988-90; Prin, R N G Cnsltng, 1990-95; Lectr, Auckland Univ, 1991-96; System Arch, CLEAR Cmmns, 1995-. Memberships: Brit Computer Soc; NZ Computer Soc; NZ Hewlett Packard Computer Users Grp; UniForum NZ; NZ Software Standards Cttee; UNESCO, NZ Rep to Regl Informatics Network for SE Asia & Pacific; UNESCO, NZ Natl Com, Cmmns Cttee; Internt Soc of NZ; Asia Pacific Internet Assn. Hobbies: Poetry; Movies; Family Life. Address: PO Box 51480, Pakuranga, Auckland, New Zealand.

HIELSCHER Leo Arthur (Sir), b. 1 Oct 1926. Company Director. m. Mary Pelgrave, 22 May 1948, 1 s, 1 d. Education: D. Univ Griffith (Hon), BComm, AAUQ, FCPA, FAIM. Appointments: Joined Qld Pub Serv, 1942; RAAF, 1945-47; Under Treas of Qld, 1974-88, Retd, 1988; Chmn, Qld Treas Corp, 1988-; Chmn, Austsafe Ltd, Gladstone Spec Steel Corp, Sugar N Ltd, Opera Qld; Dir, Austl Prov Newspprs Ltd, Asea Brown Boveri Pty Ltd Advsry Bd, Davids Ltd, Epic Ltd, Corps of Commissionaires (Qld) Ltd, Retail Servs Ltd; Cnclr, Griffith Univ. Honours: Eisenhower Fellshp, 1973; Knighted, 1987; Hon Doct, Griffith Univ, 1993. Memberships: Brisbane Club; Tattersalls Club; Gailes Golf Club. Hobbies: Fishing; Boating; Theatre; Horse racing; Golf. Address: 8 Silversash Court, Capalaba, Brisbane, Qld 4157, Australia.

HIGGINS Thomas Joseph, b. 12 Sept 1944, Ireland. Scientist. m. Peggy, 3 Feb 1973. Education: B.Agr.Sc; M.Agr.Sc; PhD. Appointments: Rsch Sci, Prog Ldr. Publication: Phytohormones - A Treatise, 1978. Honours: Goldacre Medal, 1978; Rivett Medal, 1982; Amrad-Pharmacia-LKB Medal, 1993; Fell, Acady of Technol Scis and Engrng, 1997. Memberships: Austl Soc of Plant Physiol; Amn Soc of Plant Physiols; Intl Soc of Plant Molecular Bio. Hobbies: Reading; Folk dancing.

Address: 71 Banambila Street, Aranda, Canberra, ACT 2614, Australia.

HIGHTOWER Carol A, b. 22 Sept 1950, USA. Business Owner. m. 26 June 1972, 2 s, 1 d. Education: AA, 1972; BA, 1972; MA, 1977. Appointment: Owner, Fndr, Tower Advtng. Publications: Sev articles in profl jrnls and mags. Honours: Schlsp Awds, 1968, 1972, 1977; Outstndng Achievement Awd, 1987. Memberships: Bd Dir, Life Sci Ind Cncl. Hobbies: Family; Exercise; Boating. Address: Tower Advertising, 21161 Foxtail Mission, Viejo, CA 92692, USA.

HIHARA Katsuji, b. 16 Feb 1949, Taka-gun, Hyogo, Japan. University Professor. m. Masami Yoshida, 13 Nov 1988, 1 s. Education: BCS, Kwansei-gakuin Univ, 1971; MBA, 1973, DBA, 1996, Kobe Univ, Japan. Appointments: Asst, 1975-76, Asst Prof, 1976-79, Assoc Prof, 1979-88, Prof, 1988-89, Toyama Univ, Toyama; Prof, 1989-, Hd Grad Sch of Bus Admin, 1992-93, Hd Dept of Bus Admin, 1992-93, Kobe Univ. Publications: Inflation Accounting (in Japanese), 1984; Income Concepts of Inflation Accounting (in Japanese), 1995. Memberships: Amn Acctng Assn; Japan Acctng Assn. Listed in: Who's Who in Finance and Industry; Who's Who in Japan; Dictionary of International Biography. Hobby: Skiing. Address: Kobe University of Commerce, 8-2-1 Gakuennishi-Machi, Nishi-Ku, Kobe Htogo, 651-2197, Japan.

HILALY Agha, b. 20 May 1911 Bangalore. Diplomatist. m. Malek Taj Kazim, 1938, 3 s. Education: Madras and Cambridge Univ. Appointments: Entered Civ Service, 1936; Appt'd Under-Sec to Fin Min Govt of Begal; Transferred to pre-partition Govt of India and served a Under-Sec in Mins of Agriculture Food and Com, 1941-47; Dep Sec Pakistan For Min, 1947-51; Jnt Sec, 1951-54; Attended sev Intl Confs as Sec-Gen of Pakistan delegs; Amb to Sweden Norway Denmark and Finland, 1956-59; Amb to USSR, concurrently Min to Czechoslovakia, 1959-61; High Commnr in India and Amb to Nepal, 1961-63; High Commnr in UK and Amb to Repub of Ireland, 1963-66; Amb to USA - concurrently to Mexico Venezuela and Jamaica 1966-71; Chmn Bd of Govs Pakistan Inst of Strategic Studies, 1973; Ldr Pakistan deleg to Human Rights Commn, 1981-85; Ldr UN Working Grp on Missing Persons, 1983-. Honours: Hilal-i-Quaid-i-Azam; Grand Cross of Order of Northern Star, Sweden; Grand Cross of Order of Gurkha, Nepal. Memberships: Mbr Bd of Dirs State Bank of Pakistan, 1973-; Bd of Dirs Fed Bank of Co-ops, Islamabad, 1973-. Hobbies: Photography; Hunting. Address: 22B Circular Street, Phase 2, Defence Housing Society, Karachi 6, Pakistan.

HILDEBRAND Clive Perry, b. 27 Oct 1937, Gladstone, Aust. Company Director. m. Nita Lyle Young, 3 s, 1 d. Education: BE, Univ of Qld, 1960; MA, Oxford Univ, Eng, 1967. Appointments: Underground Supt, Mt Isa Mines Ltd, 1967-69; Analyst Mngr, Mng Dir, Austl Anglo Amn, 1969-78; Strategic Planning Mngr, Smelting Project Mngr, Alcoa of Aust Ltd, 1978-81; Chief Exec Offr, Mng Dir, Umal Consolidated Ltd, Qld Coal Trust, QCT Resources Ltd, 1981-94; Chmn, AUSTA Elect, 1995-; Hon Prof of Intl Bus, Griffith Univ, 1995-; Chmn, Sugar Rsch and Dev Corp, 1995; Chmn, Highlands Gold, 1996-97. Memberships: Fell, Aus IMM; Fell, AICD. Hobbies: Music; Sculling. Address: c/o SRDC, 16/141 Queen Street, Brisbane, Qld 4000, Australia.

HILL Barry, b. 19 June 1943, Melbourne, Aust. Writer. m. (1) 1 s, 1 d, (2) Ramona Koval, 23 May 1992. Education: BA; BEd; MA (London). Appointments: Tchr, Educl Psychol, Melbourne, London; Jrlst, Times Educl Supplement; Educ Ed, The Age; Radio Critic. Publications: Poetry, 1988; 1990, 1994; Fiction, 1976, 1980, 1988; Non-Fiction, 1976, 1990, 1995. Honours: Natl Book Cncl, 1978; NSW Premier's Awd for Non-Fiction, 1992, and for Poetry, 1994. Memberships: Austl Soc of Auths. Hobbies: Swimming; Gardening; Karate. Address: Queenscliff, Victoria, Australia.

HILL Brian Victor, b. 20 Aug 1934, Perth, WA. Professor of Education. m. Margaret, 21 Dec 1963, 2 s. 2 d. Education: BA, BEd, WA; MA, Sydney; PhD, IL. Appointments: HS Tchr, WA, 1956-60; Travelling Sec, Inter-Sch Christian Fellshp, NSW, 1961-63; Lectr Educ, Univ WR, 1964-67; Snr Lectr Educ, Univ NSW, 1968-73; Prof of Educ, Murdoch Univ, 1974-99. Publications: 9 books incl Values Education in Australian Schools, 1991; Teaching Secondary Social Studies in a Multicultural Society, 1994. Honours: Bertha Houghton Prize, 1961; Univ Medal for rsch, Univ Sydney, 1968; Fulbright Grant to visit USA in 1980, Stanford Univ in CA; Outstndng Serv Awd, Aust Assn for Religious Educ, 1994. Memberships include: Austl Coll Educ; Fndng Mbr, Philos of Educ Soc of Australasia; Austl Assn for Rsch in Educ, and Stdy of Rels; Fulbright Assn. Hobbies: Music; Tennis. Address: The Australian Institute of Education, Murdoch, Murdoch University, South St, Murdoch, WA 6150, Australia.

HILL Charles Murray (Hon), b. 2 July 1923, Adelaide, Aust. Investor. m. Eunice Pearl, 21 June 1944, 3 s, 1 d. Education: FAIM; FAIV; F Inst D. Appointments: Roy Austl Navy, 1941-45; Real Estate Bus Proprietor, 1946-66; Min, SA Legislative Cncl, 1965-68; Min for Road, Transp & Local Govt, 1968-70; Min for Arts, Housing & Local Govt, 1979-82. Honour: AM, 1990. Memberships: Fell, Inst of Mngmt; Fell, Austl Inst of Valuers. Hobbies: Agriculture; Gardening. Address: 79 Cross Road, Hawthorn, SA 5062, Australia.

HILL David, b. 20 June 1946 Sussex Eng. Sports Administrator. m. Emily Booker, 1985. Education: East Sydney Tech Coll; Univ of Sydney; Dir NSW Govt Ministerial Advsry Unit, 1976-80; Chf Exec State Rail Authy, 1980-86; Commnr Austl Natl Airline, 1984; Chmn Austl Brdcstng Corp, 1986; Mngng Dir, 1986-95; Chmn Austl Soccer Fedn Rockdale NSW, 1995-. Memberships: Mbr Pub Transp Commn, 1979; Mbr Senate Univ of Sydney, 1983. Hobbies: Soccer; Reading; Chess; Opera. Address: Australian Soccer Federation, P O Box 175, Paddington, NSW 2021, Australia.

HILL Douglas John, b. 27 Jan 1927, Queanbeyan, NSW, Aust. Retired Deputy Auditor General; Representative in Thailand of the Australian Expert Service Overseas Program. m. (1) dissolved 1990, 5 s, (2) Kunnika Sarapanich, 28 Sept 1990. Education: BComm (Melbourne), 1956. Appointments: Austl Pub Serv, 1944-89; Asst Sec 1965, First Ass Sec 1969, Treas Dept, First Asst Sec,Fin Dept 1976, Dpty Auditor Gen of Aust, 1980; Currently World Bank Cnslt. Publications: Num addresses publd by the Austl Natl Audit Off; Accountability of Public Enterprises, 1989. Honour: AM, 1986. Membership: Fell, Austl Soc of Certified Practising Accts. Hobby: Gardening. Address: 111/160 Soi Thait, Ratanatibeth Road, Nonthaburi Province, Thailand.

HILL George Everard, b. 20 May 1942. Hospitality Consultant m. Catherine, 1 s, 2 d. Education: Dip Applied Sci; Dip Tech Tchng. Appointments: Chef dr Partie, Sous Chef, Exec chef positions in London and Melbourne, 1957-70; Tchr, Hospitality Studies (Cooking, 1971-80; Hd of Food Dept, William Angliss Coll, 198084; Trng and Dev Servs Prog Mngr William Angliss Coll, 1984-86; Hd of Dept, Hospitality Studies Dandenong (Casey) Inst of Tafe, 1986-94; Sucessfully operating a cnsltng enterprise, 1994-. Publication: Margarine Modelling, 1988. Honours: Gold Medallist Culinary Olympics, 1980; Food Serv Mfrs Assn Awd, 1983; Churchill Fellshp to examine hospitality educ in USA and Can, 1988; Natl Assn of Foodservice Equipment Suppliers Awd (NAFES), 1994. Memberships: Past Pres, Austl Guild of Profl Cooks; VP, Past Pres, Austl Inst of Hospitality Mngmt (AIHM); VP, Dandenong Accommodation Assn (DAA). Hobbies: Chess; Running a 4.5 Star Accommodation (5 Star Food) Bed and Breakfast Guest House. Address: Rosehill Lodge, Kalorama Terrace, Kalorama, Victoria, Australia.

HILL Helen Mary, b. 22 Feb 1945, Melbourne, Aust. Senior Lecturer in Sociology. Education: BA (Hons), MA, Monash Univ; PhD, Austl Natl Univ; Dip of Educ, Univ of Melbourne. Appointments: Course Dir, C'wlth Yth Prog, Suva, Fiji, 1987-90; Sociol Lectr, Vic Univ of Technol,

Melbourne, 1991-. Memberships: Cncl Mbr, Austl Cncl for Overseas Aid, 1986-87; Austl Labour Party, Natl For Affairs & Def Cttee, 1983-85; Commonwealth Assn for Educ & Trng of Adults, Newsletter ed, 1993-; Vic Pres, Women's Intl; League for Peace. Hobbies: Yoga; Swimming; Photography; Singing. Address: 14 Westgarth Street, Fitzroy 3065, Victoria, Australia.

HILL Peter Manners, b. 16 Oct 1945, Perth, Aust. University Professor. m. Alexandra, 14 Dec 1981. Education: MA, Rsch Fell, Univ of Melbourne, 1970; PhD, Hamburg, 1972. Appointments: Rsch Fell, Univ of Melbourne, 1978-79; Fndn Lectr in South-Slavonic Studies, Macquarie Univ, 1983-86; Prof, Univ of Hamburg, 1981-. Publications: Dir Fawörter der russichen und bulgarischen Schriftsprache der Gegewart. Versuch einer Klassifikation und einer strukturell-semantischen Analyse (Words for Colour in Contemporary Standard Russian and Bulgarian. Attempt at Classification and a Structural-Semantic Analysis, 1972; The Macedonians in Australia, 1989; The Dialect of Gorno Kalenik, 1991. Hobby: Swimming. Address: c/o F Stambanis, 44 Leonard Street, Rye, Vic 3941, Australia.

HILL Robert Murray, b. 25 Sept 1946. Politician. m. 1969, 2 s, 2 d. Education: Scotch Coll SA Univ of Adelaide; Univ of London UK. Appointments: Barrister and solicitor, 1970-; Liberal Party Campaign Chmn, 1975-77; Chmn Constitutional Cttee, 1977-81; VP Liberal Party SA Div, 1977-79; Sen for SA, 1981-; Shadow Min for For Affairs, -1993; Shadow Min for Def, 1993-94; Shadow Min for Pub Admin, 1993-94; Ldr of Opposition in Senate, 1993-96; Shadow Min for Educ Sci and Tech, 1994-96; Min for the Environment Ldr of Govt in Senate, Mar 1996-. Memberships: Law Soc SA. Hobbies: Austl and Asian hist. Address: Commonwealth Parl Offices, 100 King William Street, Adelaide, SA 5000, Australia.

HILL Roderick Jeffrey, b. 29 Mar 1949, Adelaide, S Aust. Research Manager; Scientist. m. Monica, 28 Oct 1989. Education: BS (Hons 1st Class); PhD; DSc. Appointments: NSF Postdoct Fell, VA Polytechnic Inst & State Univ; Rsch Scientist, CSIRO Div of Mineral Chem; R&D Mngr, CSIRO Minerals; Chf, CSIRO Minerals. Publications: 95 sci publs. Honours: Klaus-Glass Crystallographic Awd, 1980; David Rivett Medal, 1987; RACI Solid State Medal, 1988. Memberships: Amn Crystallographic Assn; Fell,Mineralogical Soc of Am; Fell, Roy Austl Chem Inst; Chmn, Commn on Powder Diffraction Intl Union of Crystallography, 1993-96. Hobbies: Squash; Bushwalking and camping; Ballroom dancing; Tennis. Address: 18 Malakoff Street, Caulfield North, Victoria 3161, Australia.

HILL Stephen Craig, b. 20 Aug 1943. Regional Director; Representative. m. Jill Hockey, 14 Feb 1982, 2 d. Education: BS, Hons 1, Phys Chem, Univ Sydney; PhD, Bus Admin, Univ Melbourne. Appointments: Asst Prof Sociol, Indl Engrng, Northwestern Univ, Chgo, 1968-69; Rsch Fell, Sci Policy Rsch Unit, Univ Sussex, 1969-70; Snr Lectr, Dept Sociol, UNSW, 1971-74; Dir, Cntr for Technol and Social Change, 1983-89; Prof, Hd Dept Sociol, 1974-89; Dir, Cntr Rsch Policy, 1990-95, Univ of Wollongong; Regl Dir, S E Asian, UNESCO, 1995-. Publications: The Making of Professional Scientists, 1974; Development with a Human Face, 1981; Future Tense?, 1983, 84; Science & Technology in Australia, 1989; The Tragedy of Technology, 1988, 89; Crossing Innovation Boundaries, 1993; Using Basic Research, 1995. Honours: Fulbright Fell, 1968-69; Nuffield Fell, 1975-76; Fell, Austl Acad of Technological Scis and Engrng, 1995; Mbr, Order of Aust (AM), 1997. Memberships: Chmn, Socl Scis and Hums, Pacific Sci Assn, 1987-94; Fndn Chmn, Sci, Technol Policy, Asian Netwrk, 1988-95; Chmn, APEC, Hrd and Ind Technol, 1991-95; Regl Advsry Cncl, UNESCO, 1993-95. Hobbies: Tennis; Music Composition; Reading; Travel. Address: Regional Director, UNESCO, United Nations Building, JL M.H Thamrin 14, Tromolpos 1273/JKT, Jakarta 10002, Indonesia.

HILL Terence Rodney, b. 10 Sept 1946. Vigneron. m. Leah Cashmore, 4 Jan 1969, 2 s. Education; BEd, DEakin; MEd, Monash. Appointments: Headmaster, Wooragee P S, Timor PS, Yanakie P S, Prin, Yarra Glen P S, Yarra Junction P S (Mngng Dir, Yarra Valley Hills P/L). Honours: Paul Harris, Fell, 1986; Grp Study Exchange, Team Ldr to Germany, 1996. Memberships: Charter Mbr, Beechworth Apex, Mbr, Maryborough Apex, 1969-71; Capt/Coach, Carisbrook Football Club, 1969; Charter Mbr, Healesville Rotary, 1976-, Pres, 1971; Foster Football Club, Capt, Coach, 1972. Hobbies: Trout fishing; Food and wine; Sport. Address: Kiah Yallambee, Old Don Road, Healesville, Vic, Australia.

HILLEL Shlomo, b. 1923 Baghdad, Iraq. Politician. m. Tmima Rosner, 1952, 1 s, 1 d. Education: Herzliah High Sch Tel-Aviv; Hebrew Univ Jerusalem. Appointments: Jewish Agcy for Palestine - miss to cos in Middle East, 1946-48, 1949-51; Israel Def Forces, 1948-49; PMs Off, 1952-53; Amb to Guinea, 1959-61; Amb to Ivory Coast Dahomey Upper Volta and Niger, 1961-63; Perm Miss to UN with rank of Min, 1964-67; Asst Dir-Gen Min of For Affairs, 1967-69; Min of Police, 1969-77; Co-ord of polit contacts with Arab ldrship in administered territories, 1970-77; Min of the Interior, Jun-Oct 1974, 1996-97; Chmn Ministerial Cttee for Socl Welfare, 1974-77; Chmn Sephardi Fedn, 1976-; Perm Observer to Cncl of Eu, 1977-84; Chmn Cttee of the Interior and Environment, 1977-81; Chmn of For Affairs and Def, 1981-84; Speaker of the Knesset, Sep 1984-88; Cmdr Natl Order of Repubs of Ivory Coast Upper Volta and Dahomey; World Chmn Keren Hayesod United Israel Appeal, 1989-. Publications: Operation Babylon, 1988. Memberships: Mbr Ma'agan Michael Kibbutz, 1942-58; Mbr of Knesset, 1953-59, 1974-. Hobbies: Tennis; Gardening. Address: Keren Hayesod, P OB 7583, Jerusalem, Israel.

HILLIS William Edwin, b. 9 Feb 1921. Wood Scientist. m. Marjorie Maureen Moore, 15 Nov 1952, 1 s, 2 d. Education: Dip App Chem, Gordon Inst, Geelong, 1942; BSc, Melbourne, 1947; MSc, Melbourne, 1951; DSc, Melbourne, 1966. Appointments: Chem, Colonial Gas Assn, 1939-42; CSIR, 1942- Chf Rsch Scientist, CSIRO Div of Forest Products, 1986; Visng Lectr, Melbourne Univ, 1972-85; Visng Fell, Austl Natl Univ, 1974-85; Visng Lectr, Univ of Lae, Papua New Guinea, 1975-76; Co-ord, Forest Products Div and Exec Bd Mbr, Intl Union of Forestry Rsch Org (IUFRO), 1976-83; Visng Prof, Univ BC, Can, 1983; Edtl Bd Wood Sci and Technol, Germany, 1978-, Hon Rsch Fell, CSIRO, 1986-; Visng Lectr, Monash Univ, 1990-. Publications: Books: Wood Extractives (ed), 1962; Eucalypts for Wood Production (co-editor), 1978, 1984, 1988; Wood: Future Growth and Conversion (co-ed), 1981; Heartwood and Tree Exudates, 1987; Author and Co-auth of over 195 sci pprs in major jrnls and books; Keynote addresses in 8 countries. Memberships: Elected Fell, Austl Acady of Technol Scis and Engrng, 1980; Elected Fell, Intl Acady of Wood Sci, 1970, Pres, 1978-82; Fndn Chmn, Austl Branch, Inst of Wood Sci, 1973-77, cttee, 1977-; Fell, Roy Austl Chem Inst, 1960; Mbr, Austl Inst of Foresters, 1976. Honours: Hon Mbr, Intl Union of Forestry Rsch Orgs (IUFRO), 1986; Hon Mbr, Intl Assn of Wood Anatomists, 1981; Stanley A Clarke Mem Medal, 1986; Hon Mbr, Chinese Soc of Chem and Chem Engrng of Forest Products, 1984. Listed in: Men of Achievement, 1982; Australian Men amd Women of Science Engineering and Technology, 1995. Hobbies: Music; International affairs. Address: 12 Lindsay Street, Bewleigh, Vic 3204, Australia.

HILLY Francis Billy, b. 1947. Politician. Education: Univ of S Pacific. Appointments: Joined pre-indep govt working under Solomon Mamaloni - qv; Later wrked for a priv co in Gizo; Fmr Premier of West Prov; PM of the Solomon Islands, 1993-94. Memberships: Mbr Parl, 1976-84, 1993-. Address: c/o Office of the Prime Minister, Legakiki Ridge, Honiara, Solomon Islands.

HILSON Malcolm Geoffrey, b. 28 Sept 1942, Olney, Eng. Diplomat. m. Marion Freeman, 2 Jan 1965, 2 s. Appointments: Jakarta; Singapore; Bombay; Kuala Lumpur; Kaduna; London; New Delhi; London; Port Vila. Hobbies: Travel; Gardening; Cricket; Golf. Address: British High Commission, PB 567, Port Vila, Vanuatu.

HINDE George William, b. 20 Aug 1929. Educationalist; Emeritus Professor; Barrister. m. Marian Sybil Cranwell. Education: LLM, Univ of NZ, 1953; LLD, Auckland Univ, 1981. Appointments: Bar and Sol, High Crt of NZ, 1952-58; Tutor in Law, 1959; Snr Tutor, Melbourne Univ, 1960; Snr Lectr in Law, Auckland Univ, 1961-67; Visng Fell, Austl Natl Univ, 1963; Nuffield Fndn Dominion Trav Fell, 1967; Hon Mbr, Fac of Laws, Queen Mary Coll, Univ of London, 1967; Prof of Law, Canty Univ, 1968; Prof of Law, Auckland Univ, 1969-87; Mbr, NZ Property Law and Equity Reform Cttee, 1968-78; Ptnr, Nicholson Gribbin Sols, 1987-88; Disting Visng Prof of Law, Bond Univ, 1989-92; Visng Prof of Law, Bond Univ, 1993; Bar, High Court of NZ, 1997. Publications: The New Zealand Torrens System Centennial Essays (Ed and Contrb); Studies in the Law of Landlord and Tenant (Ed and Contrb); Land Law (w D W McMorland and P B A Sim); Introduction to Land Law (w D W McMorland and P B A Sim); New Zealand Law Dictionary (w M S Hinde); Australian Law Dictionary (w H A J Ford and M S Hinde); Butterworths Land Law in New Zealand (w D W McMorland and others). Listed in Who's Who in New Zealand. Hobbies: Concerts; Theatre; Horticulture. Address: PO Box 25-377, St Heliers, Auckland 1130, New Zealand.

HINDE Leonard Thomas, b. 5 Apr 1925, Sydney, Aust. Company Director. m. Norma Doris Dyason, 4 June 1949, 2 s. Education: Fell, Inst of Actuaries, London, Eng, 1956; Fell, Inst of Actuaries of Aust. Appointments: C'wlth Bank of Aust, 1942-60; Mngr, Banking Dept, 1966-70, Chf Mngr, Banking and Fin Dept, 1970-72, Chf Rep, London 1972-73, Advsr and Chf Rep, London, 1973-74; Advsr and Chf Mngr, Personnel Dept, 1974-82; Advsr and Chf Rep in Eur, 1983-84; Advsr, 1984-85, Ret'd 1985, Reserve Bank of Aust. Honour: Harkness Fellshp, C'wlth Fund of NY, 1962-63. Memberships: Inst of Actuaries of Aust, Mbr of Cncl, 1978-80; Inst of Actuaries, London; Mbr of Cncl, Austl Natl Univ, 1975-84, 1990-92; Austl Rep, C'wlth Fund of NY, 1971-85; Mbr of Strategic Advsry Cncl, Austl Photonics Co-op Rsch Cntr, 1993-. Hobbies: Music; Personal Computers; Golf. Address: 13/8 Earl Street, Mosman, New South Wales 2088, Australia.

HINDIN-MILLER Grant, b. 2 July 1950, Auckland, NZ. Writer; Tutor. m. Jennifer, 1 s, 1 d. Education: Dip of Tchng. Publications: Books: Estralita; The Dream Monger. Films: Starlight Hotel, 1987; A Soldier's Tale, 1989; Chunuk Bair, 1992. Music Albums: Sing O Carmel, 1984; Fire and Steel, 1986; Journey, 1988; Rivers of Light, 1998. Hobby: Baha'i Faith. Address: PO Box 31-066, Ilam, Christchurch, New Zealand.

HINDS Geoffrey William John, b. 2 Apr 1950, Auckland, NZ. Composer; Piano Teacher. Education: BA, 1974, MPhil (Mus), 1976, Auckland Univ; BDiv, Melbourne Coll of Divinity, 1980; LRSM (Piano Tchrs), 1983. Creative works: Compositions: held in NZ Music Archive, Canterbury Univ: Sonata for Viola and Pianoforte, 1975; Suite for String Quartet, 1975; String Quartet, 1976; Cantata Upon This Rock, 1982; Held in Mus Lib, Radio NZ, Wellington: Motet for the Lord Has Purposed, 1980-81; Overture into a Broad Place, 1981; String Quartet, 1981; Symphonic Movements of Our Time, 1982; And His Name Shall Be Called, 1981; Through the Grapevine, 1982; Anthems Written for St Barnabas Choir; Song Cycle, Water, Water Everywhere, 1985; Song Cycle, Pieces of Peace, 1986; Colyton Overture, 1985-87; Written for Manawatu Yth Orch: String Quartet, 1983-84; Song cycle: Innocence and Experience, 1987; Blowing in the Wind for wind quartet, 1987; Song Cycle, Nine Mystical Songs, 1988-89; Godzone Re-evaluated for Yth Orch, 1989; Great Outdoors Suite for Pf, 1989; String Quartet, 1989; Creation Cantata, 1990; St Barnabas Ballads, tenor and pf, 1991; Piano Sonata, 1992; Two-Edged Sword, soprano and Pf, 1992; Our Free Land, 1992; Flights of Fancy; Gardens; Holy Ground (organ); Suite for Viola, Our Good Keen Men; Excursions, recorder trio; God is A Sea, 1993; Blessed Spirits, brass band; A Tree for All Seasons; City of...; 5th String Quartet, 1994; The Mind; Reflections; I Lift Mine Eyes; For the Birds, 1995; Kings

Came Riding (SATB), 1995; From the Rising of the Sun, pf, 1996; Creation in Reverse, 1997; Rhapsody in White, 1998. Honour: Recorder Soc Prize, Original Composition, 1996. Memberships: Inst of Regd Music Tchrs, NZ. Composer's Assn of NZ. Hobbies: Political science; Crossword puzzles; Bushwalks; Youth hostelling. Address: 72 Valley Road, Mount Eden, Auckland 3, New Zealand.

HINDS Manuel Enrique, b. 21 Sept 1945. Government Official. m. Education: Deg, Indl Engrng, Univ El Salvador, 1968; MA, Econs, Northwestern Univ, 1973. Appointments: Min of Econ, Govt El Salvador, San Salvador, 1979-80; Min, Treas, 1995-; Alt Govt Intl Monetary Fund. Address: Ministry of the Treasury, Avda Alvarado y Diag Centroamerica, San Salvador, El Salvador.

HINO Ichiro. Politician; Lawyer. Appointments: Min of Posts and Telecomms, Jan-Oct 1996. Memberships: Mbr HoR; Mbr Socl Dem Party of Japan - SDPJ. Address: Ministry of Posts and Telecommunications, 1-3-2, Kasumigaseki, Chiyoda-ku, Tokyo 100, Japan.

HIRAI Kyoko, b. 9 Aug 1946, Nagasaki, Japan. Teacher; Writer. m. Keizo H, 1 d. Education: MA, Showa Womens Univ. Publications: A Dove Hotel, 1992; Iris Murdoch, 1995. Honour: Takayama Lit Prize, 1992. Memberships: Engl Lit Soc of Japan; Am Lit Soc of Japan; IASIL, Japan. Hobbies: Cinema; Painting; Porcelain; Plants. Address: 2-11-27 Sagamiono, Sagamihara, Kanagawa 228-0803, Japan.

HIRAI Takushi, b. 1931. Politician. Appointments: Previous posts incl Parly Vice-Min of Intl Trade and Ind and of Jus; Chmn Cttee on For Affairs House of Cnclrs; Dir Judicial Affairs Div Liberal Dem Party - LDP - Policy Rsch Cncl; Min of Labour, 1986-87; Dir House of Cnclrs Cttee on the Budget, 1990-. Address: 2-2 Kasumigaseki 1-chome, Chiyoda-ku, Tokyo, Japan.

HIRAWAKA Kimiyoshi, b. 18 Aug 1934, Fukuyama Cty, Hiroshima Prefecture, Japan. Neurosurgeon. m. Atsuko Nakatsuka, 30 May 1968, 2 d. Education: MD, DMSc, Univ of Tokyo. Appointments: Asst Prof, Neurosurgery, Univ of Tokyo, 1969; Assoc Prof, 1972, Prof of Neurosurgery, Kyoto Univ of Med, 1978; Prof of Neurosurgery, Tokyo Medl Dental Univ, 1988. Publications: Medl lit. Honour: Igakushoin Publ Co, 1971. Memberships: Japanese Congress of Neurol Surgs, Pres, 1986; Japan Neurosurgical Soc; Amn Assn of Neurol Surgs. Address: Department of Neurosurgery, Tokyo Medical and Dental University, Yushima 1-5-45, Bunkyo-ku, Tokyo 113-8519, Japan.

HIRANUMA Takeo. Politician. Appointments: Fmr Parly Vice-Min of Fin; Dep Chmn LDP Policy Rsch Cncl; Chmn LDP Natl Org Cttee; Min of Transp, 1995-96. Memberships: Mbr HoR. Address: Ministry of Transport, 2-1-3 Kasumigaseki, Chiyoda-ku, Tokyo 100, Japan.

HIRAOKA Atsushi, b. 3 Nov 1948, Tokyo, Japan. University Instructor. m. 23 Mar 1980. Education: BSc, Saitama Univ, Urawa, Japan, 1972; MSc, 1974, PhD, 1979, Tokyo Metro Univ. Appointments: Postdoct Fellshp, Inst of Physl and Chem Rsch, Wako, Japan, 1979-80; Asst, 1980-83, Instr, 1983-, Kyorin Univ Sch of Hlth Scis. Publications: Over 60 articles in profl jrnls. Memberships: Japanese Biochem Soc; Pharm Soc of Japan; Japanese Soc of Electrophoresis; Japanese Soc of Biofeedback Rsch. Address: c/o Kyorin University School of Health Sciences, 476 Miyashita-cho, Hachioji, Tokyo 192-8508, Japan.

HIRASAWA Eiji, b. 22 Aug 1950, Tonami, Toyama, Japan. Researcher. m. Mariko, 28 Sept 1974, 1 s, 2 d. Education: BS, Toyama Univ; MAgr, Kyoto Univ; DAgr, hons, 1977; DSc, hon, 1981. Appointments: Rsch Assoc, Osaka Cty Univ, 1979-88; Instr, 1988-94, Assoc Prof, 1994-96, Prof, 1996-. Publication: Basic Biochemistry, 1998. Honour: Alexander von Humboldt Fell, Germany, 1984-86. Memberships: Botl Soc of Japan; Japanese Soc of Plant Physiol; Amn Assn of Plant Physiol. Hobbies:

Wine; Chronological biology. Address: Yamasaka 3-3-14, Higashisumiyoshi-ku, Osaka 546-0036, Japan.

HIRATA Tatsuya, b. 26 June 1943, Tokyo, Japan. Painter; Ceramic Artist. m. Saeko, 25 Feb, 2 s. Education: Bachelor, French Lang, French Lang Dept, Sophia Univ; Prof, Art Dept, Accademia del Verbano, Italy. Creative works: Paintings; Ceramic art. Honours: Chevalier de l'Ordre Templier, France, 1997; Accademicien del Verbano Italia, 1995; Hon Mbr, Fndn Marabello, Spain. Memberships: Soc Natl des Beaux Arts; Arts-Scis; Lettres; Soc des Artistes, Accademia del Verbeno. Hobbies: Music; Nature. Address: 20 avenue de la Gare, Cae Postale 205-1001 Lausanne, Switzerland.

HISCUTT Hugh James, b. 10 July 1926, Burnie, Tas, Aust. Retired Member, Tasmanian Legislative Council. m. Joan Owen, 12 May 1951, 3 s, 3 d. Education: St Virgil's Coll, Hobart. Appointments: 21 yrs involvement w Local Govt, Elected to Tas Legislative Cncl, 1983, retd, 1995. Hobbies: Gardening; Lawn bowls; Light music. Address: 42 Nine Mile Road, Howth, North West Coast, Tas 7316, Australia.

HJORTH Noela Jane, b. 5 Dec 1940, Melbourne, Aust. Artist. Education: Prahran and Roy Melbourne Insts of Technol, 1958-62; Chelsea Sch of Art, London, Eng, 1969-71. Appointments: 28 Individual Exhbns held in Eng, Aust, Thailand, 1970-94; Sev Grp Exhbns; Collections: Austl Natl Gall, ACT, Natl Gall of Vic, Art Gall of NSW; Art Gall of SA, Qld State Gall, Tas Mus and Art Gall, Mus and Art Gall of NT, Spencer and Gillen Mus, Alice Springs, NT, Burnic Art Gall, Tas, Latrobe Valley Arts Cntr, Morwell, Vic, Newcastle Region Gall, NSW, Swan Hill Regl Art Gall, Vic, Stanthorpe Art Gall, Qld, Wagga Wagga City Art Gall, Qld; Araluen Arts Cntr, Alice-Springs, NT, Vic & Albert Mus, London, Eng. Publications: Artists and Galleries of Australia and New Zealand, 1979; Encyclopedia of Australian Art, 1984; Lasting Impressions, 1988; A Dictionary of Women Artists of Australia, 1991; Contemporary Australian Printmaking, 1994, 1996; Monographs: Noela Hjorth, 1984; Noela Hjorth-Journey of a Fire Goddess, 1989; Sophia and the Seven Serpents, 1998. Honours: Austl Print Prize (2nd), Westmead, NSW, 1978; Commission, Hilton Intl Hotel, Adelaide, 1982; Sculpture for the Peace Circle, Riverbend Park, SA, 1993; Austl Day Awd, 1994. Address: PO Box 6, Clarendon, SA 5157, Australia.

HO Andrew Chung Yin, b, 21 June 1947, Hong Kong. Obstetrician; Gynaecologist. m. Jung Liau, 1 s, 4 d. Education: MBBS (HK); FRCOG (UK); FHKCPG; FHKAM (Obs & Gyn). Appointments: Snr Medl Offr, Queen Elizabeth Hosp, Hong Kong; Now Hon Cnslt Gynnaecologist; Hong Kong Buddhist Hosp; Fell, Hong Kong Acady of Med (Obs & Gynae); Ex-Pres, Hong Kong Yth for Christ. Memberships: Hong Kong Medl Assn; Singapore Medl Assn. Address: Room 705, Argyle Centre, Phase 1, 688 Nathan Road, Kowloon, Hong Kong.

HO David Yau-Fai, b. 23 Mar 1939, Hong Kong. Psychologist. Education: BSc, Phys, Acadia, 1960; MA, Psychol, Roosevelt, 1964; PhD, Psychol, IIT, 1967. Appointment: Prof, Univ of Hong Kong, 1985-. Publications: Sev articles in profl jrnls. Honour: Fulbright Profshp, Philippines, 1980-81. Membership: Pres, Intl Cncl of Psychols, 1988-89. Hobby: Martial Arts. Address: Department of Psychology, University of Hong Kong, Hong Kong.

HO Monto, b. 28 Mar 1927, Hunan, China. Professor. m. Carol Tsu, 28 June 1952, 1 s, 1 d. Education: AB, 1949; MD, 1954. Appointments: Prof, Chmn, Dept of Infectious Diseases and Microbiol, Grad Sch of Pub Hlth, Univ of PA, 1972-95; Dir, Clinl Rsch m Natl Hlth Rsch Inst, Taiwan, 1996-. Creative Works: Cytomegrlo Virus, Biology and Infection. Memberships: Amn Soc for Clinl Investigation; Amn Assn of Physns; Amn Soc of Infectious Diseases; Academia Sinica; Amn Assn for Advmnt of Sci. Address: National Health Research Institutes, 128 Yen-Chin Road Section 2, Taipei 115, Taiwan.

HO Quang Long, b. 30 Dec 1935, Nghe An, Vietnam. Ship Designer; Ship Builder. m. Do Bao Loc, 10 Mar 1962, 2 d. Education: Engr; BMath; Bphys. Appointments: Hd, Bur of Technic Rsch, Inst of Ship Design, 1970; Vice Gen Dir, Mechl Contruction Dept, 1979-94; Vice Gen Dir, Dept of Ind and Materials Equip, Min of Transp and Comms, 1984-85; Chf Cabinet, Min of Transp and Comms, 1986-87; First Vice Gen Dir, Gen Dir, Vietnam Shipbuilding Union, 1988-94; Gen Dir, Ship Technol Dev Cntr, 1994-. Creative Works: Handbook of Shipbuilding Technic, 1978; Handbook of Shipbuilding Technic, 1982; Ship Repair, 1983; Ferro - Cement Boats, 1985; Sea River Navigation Ships, 1986; Aluminium Alloy Boat, 1999; 100 Compositions publd, reviews and mags of Vietnam. Memberships: Vietnam Maritime Sci and Technol Assn. Hobbies: Reading; Music. Address: Shiptech, 14 Lynam De Hanoi Tel 84-4-7330451, Vietnam.

HO Samuel K M, b. 28 Jan 1954, Hong Kong. Professor. m. Catherine, 21 Aug 1980, 1 d. Education: BSC, Engrng; MSc; PhD, Mngmt. Appointments: Engr; Mktng Mngr; Snr Lectr; Prin Lectr, Lectr; Prof of Strategy and Qlty, Visng Prof of Paisley Univ and RMIT. Publications: Over 80 pprs and 8 books; TQM: An Integrated Approach, 3rd ed, 1999; Operations and Quality Management, 1999. Honours: Oshikawa Fellshp Awd, Asian Productivity Org, 1987; Quality Expert to Malaysian Govt, Asian Devel Bank, 1993. Memberships: MBCS; MCIM; FIQA; FAKAAST. Hobbies: Electronic organ; Scuba diving. Address: School of Business, Hong Kong Baptist University; Kowloon Tong, Hong Kong.

HO Teck Heng, b. 8 Dec 1965, Malaysia. Civil and Structural Engineer. m. Mao Meijiao, 5 Dec 1998. Education: MSc; BEng, hons; Dip, CE. Appointments: Project Mngr, Lian Beng Constrn Pte Ltd, 1998, Strahs Constrn Co Pte Ltd, 1999. Publication: Effect of Hydrostistic Pressure on R C Concrete Structure, 1994. Honour: MICE Awd, Tech Ppr, Dundee, England. Membership: Am Soc of Civil Engrs, 1994. Hobbies: Hiking; Skiing; Fishing; Badminton. Address: Blk 341 #03-72, Bukit Batok Street 34, Singapore 650341, Singapore.

HO Zhi Chien, b. 3 Mar 1924, Guangdong, China. Professor of Medicine. m. Guo Wen Hua, 2 d. Education: BA, 1947; MD, 1952; Hon PhD, 1992. Appointments: Lectr to Prof, 1954-97, Dean of Fac of Clinl Nutrition, 1984-97, Sun Yat-sen Univ of Medl Scis, Guangzhou, China. Publications: 97 orig articles; 13 books as ed and writer. Honours: 13 provincial and natl awds; Highest Awd, Ryerson Univ, Can. Membership: Chair, Chinese Infant and Maternal Assn. Address: Department of Clinical Nutrition, Sun Yat-sen University of Medical Science, Guangzhou, China 510089.

HOANG Mai, b. 6 Aug 1920, Hanoi, China. Professor; Writer. m. Pham Kim Trang, 15 Apr 1945, 3 s, 2 d. Education: BLL, Hanoi Univ. Publications: Tieng Trong Ha Hoi (Beat of the Ha Hoi Drum), drama; Tho Mot Thoi (Poet of the Age). Hobbies: Studying about literature and travelling.

HOARE Merval Hannah, b. 17 June 1914. m. Percy Raymond Hoare, 1949, 1 d. Publications: Norfolk Island: An Outline of its History 1774-1987, 1988; Rambler's Guide to Norfolk Island, 1994; The Discovery of Norfolk Island, 1974; Norfolk Island - A History Through Illustration 1774-1974, 1979; The Winds of Change - Norfolk Island 1950-1982, 1983; Elizabeth Robertson's Diary, Norfolk Island 1845, ed, 1989; Thomas Samuel Stewart's Journal - Norfolk Island 1855, ed, 1992; Norfolk Island Hospitals and Public Health from the First Convict Settlement, ed, 1994; Norfolk Island in the 1930's, 1996. Memberships: Norfolk Is Conservation Soc; Norfolk Is Histl Soc; Austl Soc Auths; Austl Republican Movement. Hobbies: Conservation; History; Politics and other social issues. Address: New Cascade Road, Norfolk Island 2899, via Australia.

HOARE Tyler James, b. 5 June 1940, Joplin, MO, USA. Sculptor. m. Kathy, 9 Mar 1963, 1 d. Education:

Univ of CO, 1959; Sculptor Cntr, NYC, 1960; BFA Drawing and Painting, Univ of KS, 1963; Sculpture, CA Coll of Arts and Crafts, 1966. Appointments: Guest Lectr, Many Venues, 1972-84; Guest Curator, CA, 1973-88. Creative Works: Many one man shows, 1964-; Many Exhibitions; Many Publs and Reviews. Honours: 12th Annual Spiva Art Cntr; 15th Annual MO Valley Exhibit; 22nd Annual San Fran Art Festial; West Art Graphics 70; Age of Enlightenment Awd; Dip of Merit. Memberships: Richmond Art Cntr; LA Print Soc; Natl Soc of Lit and the Arts; Metal Arts Guild; Oakland Mus Assn; San Fran Art Inst; San Fran Mus of Art; IBA; Cntr for Visual Arts; Pro Arts. Address: 30 Menlo Place, Berkeley, CA 94707, USA.

HOBBS Marcia Wilson, b. 23 June 1947, Los Angeles, CA, USA. Chairman, Christie's Auction House. Div. 3 s. Education: Univ of California, Berkeley. Appointments: Pres, CEO Gtr Los Angeles Zoo Assn, 1978-87; Mktng Cnslt for Christie's, The Smithsonian Inst, Ferrari N Am, Salvatore Ferragamo, Buccellati Jewelers, KCET Public TV, LA County Mus of Art; Pres, San Vicente Investments, 1988-97; Chmn, Christie's Los Angeles, 1997-. Memberships: Commnr, State of California Dept of Police and Educ; Fedl Advsr, US Sec of Energy, 1985-88; Cmmnr, Former Chmn, CA Tourism Corp; Chmn, LA County HS for the Arts; Bd Mbr, LA Music Cntr Blue Ribbon 400, Mod and Contemp Art Cncl of LA Mus of Art; Bd of Regents for Children's Hosp; Chmn, Amn Women for Intl Understanding; Mbr, Natl Cttee, US-China Rels; Exec Cttee, LA-Guangzhou Sister Cty Assn. Address: Christie's, 360 North Camden Drive, Beverly Hills, CA 90210, USA.

HOBCROFT Rex Kelvin, b. 12 May 1925, Renmark, SA, Aust. Musician. m. Perpetua, 1 s, 3 d. Education: DipMusic, Univ of Melbourne. Appointments: Fndn Hd, Keyboard Dept, Qld Conservatorium of Music, 1957-61; Fndn Hd, Music, Univ of Tas, 1961-70; Fndn Dir, Tasmania Conservatorium of Music, 1963-71; Dir, NSW State Conservatorium of Music, 1972-82; Fndn Dir, Sydney Intl Piano Comp, 1976-. Creative Works: Num piano recitals and concerto perfs. Honours: Churchill Fellshp, 1967; Jap Fndn Fellshp, 1975; Hon Fellshp, NSW State Conservatorium of Music, 1984; AM (Mbr of Order of Aust), 1990. Hobbies: Reading; Table Tennis. Address: 26A Luffingham Street, Melville, WA 6156, Australia.

HOBERG Michael Dean, b. 27 Feb 1955, Pipestone, MN, USA. Management Analyst. m. Janet Hoberg, 5 Mar 1995, 1 s, 1 d. Education: PhD; MPA; BS; CGFM. Appointment: Mngmt Analyst, San Joaquin Co Sheriff's Off. Publication: British Mutants: Evolution of Criminal Justice Systems in Australia, Canada and the US. Honours: Resolution of Commendation, CA State Senate and Assembly; Sacramento Chamber of Com's Athletic Hall of Fame. Membership: MENSA. Hobby: Fencing. Listed in: Who's Who in the West. Address: San Joaquin County Sheriff's Office, 7000 South Canlis Boulevard, French Camp, CA 95231, USA.

HOBSON Peter Ross, b. 11 Feb 1942, Sydney, NSW, Aust. University Lecturer. m. Roswitha, 6 Dec 1969, 1 s, 1 d. Education: BA (1st Class Hons) Educ, 1966, DipEd, 1967, Sydney; MA, 1968, MPhil, 1971, London. Appointments: Lectr, 1971, Snr Lectr, 1977-, Assoc Prof, 1999- Univ of New Eng. Publications: Theories of Education (co-auth), 2nd ed, 1987; Religious Education in a Pluralist Society (co-auth), 1999. Honour: Gowrie Schlshp, Univ of London, 1967-69. Memberships: Philos of Educ Assn of Aust; Austl Assn for the Stdy of Religions; Austl Assn for Profl and Applied Ethics. Hobbies: Philately; Squash rackets; Gardening. Address: School of Education Studies, University of New England, Armidale, NSW 2351, Australia.

HOCKEY Joseph Benedict, b. 2 Aug 1965. Federal Member for North Sydney. m. Melissa Babbage, 18 Dec 1993. Education: St Aloysius Coll, 1974-83; Sydney Univ, 1990. Appointments: Banking and Fin Lawyer, Corrs Chambers Westgarth; Snr Advsr on Govt Trading Enterprise Reform, NSW Premier's Dept; Snr Policy

Advsr, NSW Treas, 1992-94; Dir of Policy to NSW Premier and Min for Econ Devl, 1994-95; Cnslt w Corrs Chambers Westgarth on Privatisation, Infrastructure and Pub Affairs, 1995-96; Chmn Sydney Airport Community Forum, 1996-; Govt Mbrs Taskforce on Taxation, 1997-. Memberships: Austl Conservation Fndn; Amnesty Intl; N Sydney Rotary; N Sydney Leagues Club; Kirribilli Ex-Servicemen's Club; Sydney Inst; Law Soc; Natl Press Club; Friends of the Independent Th; Roy Sydney Yacht Squadron. Listed in: Who's Who in Australia. Hobbies: Scuba Diving; Squash; Cricket; Football; Reading. Address: Level 2, 200 Pacific Highway, Crows Nest, NSW 2065, Australia.

HODGES John Charles, b. 3 Oct 1937. Pharmacist. m. Margaret, 1961, 1 s, 2 d. Appointments: Pharm, 1957-; MHR (Lib) for Petrie, Qld, 1974, 1983, 1984, 1987; Immigration and Ethnic Affairs Min, 1982-83; Regd Migration Agt No 53794. Hobbies: Fishing; Singing. Memberships: Brisbane Club; Tattersalls Club. Address: 2 Handsworth Street, Clontarf, Qld 4019, Australia.

HODGES Raymond John, b. 9 May 1943, Raymond Terrace, Aust. Chartered Chemist (Analytical). m. Delma Mackey, 12 May 1973, 1 s, 1 d. Education: BSc (Hons), Newcastle, NSW, 1964; PhD, Kensington, NSW, 1969; Coml Pilot's Lic (CPL), Civil Aviation Auth, Melbourne, 1980. Appointments: Rsch Trainee (BHP Shortland), 1959; Post-doct Fell, Hull Univ, 1969; Rsch Offr (BHP Shortland), 1972; Lectr, Monash Univ, Gippsland, 1975; Snr Lectr, 1981; Assoc Prof, 1992, w sabbaticals at Univ NSW Aeronautics Eng, 1983, BHP, 1989, Hull, 1996. Publications: Spectrometer Manual, 1992, 2nd edition, 1999; Instrumental Analysis, an introduction, 1997; About 100 publs, 1963-. Creative works: Successful inventions: Labelled hydrocarbons, 1967; Wire analysis, 1975; Hodges volatility tester, 1984; Teaching spectrometer, 1992. Honours: Commonwealth Schl (undregrad, 1960-64, postgrad, 1965-69;; Postdoct fell, organometallic grant, 1969-72; Air Safety awd, 1980; Roy Aeronautical Soc Medal, 1984. Memberships: RACI, 1961-, Fell, 1985; Sec, Gippsland sect, 1978-82, Chairperson, 1982-83, 1994-95; Fndng Mbr, AIE, 1980; AIPet Fell, 1980. Hobbies: Photography; Flying; Christian teaching. Address: RMB 4333 Rickard Drive, Morwell, Vic 3840, Australia.

HODGSON James Day, b. 3 Dec 1915, USA. Diplomat. m. Maria, 24 Aug 1943, 1 s, 1 d. Education: AB, Univ MN; Grad, Univ MN & UCLA. Appointments: US Sec of Labour, 1969-73; US Amb to Japan, 1974-77. Publications: Future of US-Japan Relations. Honours: Order of the Rising Sun, Japan; Sev hon degs. Memberships: Cncl of Fgn Rels; NY Pacific Cncl on Intl Policy. Hobbies: Writing; Foreign Affairs; Golf; Lexicography. Address: 10132 Hillgrove Drive, Beverly Hills, CA 90210, USA.

HOFMEKLER Ori, b. 12 Mar 1952 Israel. Painter. m. Ilana Wellisch, 1977, 1 s, 1 d. Education: Bezalel Acady Jerusalem; Jersualem Univ. Publications: Hofmekler's People, 1983; Contbns to Penthouse Mag since 1983; Contbns to mags in France Germany and USA. Honours: Shtrouk Prize, 1976. Hobbies: Reading; Sports; Travel.

HOGAN Geoffrey, b. 24 Dec 1929, Mosman, Aust. Retired Chairman. m. Joan Maree, 16 Jan 1959, 1 s, 1 d. Education: FAIM, Austl Inst of Mngmt. Appointments: Clerk, Perm Tree Co, 1945-46; Ins Clerk, Wynn Roberts Pty Ltd, 1946-52; Acct, Norman Reynolds Pty Ltd, 1952-55; Acct, Future Films & TV Ltd, 1955-57; Owner, Movie Hire and Sales Co, Apex Telesales, 1957-58; Dir, London Estates, London Chems, Picture Tube Replacement Co, 1958-62; Mngng Dir, E A Ireland Co P/L; Scotts & Irelands P/L, 1962-78; Chmn, Statewide Pool Servs Pty Ltd, 1979-98; Pres, Aboriginal Educ Cncl (NSW), 1991-99; Natl Chair, Rotary Trees for 2000 Inc, 1995-99. Honours: AM, Queen Elizabeth Silver Jubilee Medal; JP; Assn of Apex Clubs, life mbr; Austl Freedom from Hunger Campaign, life mbr. Memberships: Assn of Apex Clubs, Dist Gov, 1967-68; Natl Treasurer, 1970-71; UN Assn of Aust, NSW Pres, 1975-81, Natl Sec, 1976-78; Austl Freedom from Hunger Campaign, Natl

Pres, 1978-82, Sec/Treas, 1987-91; Aboriginal Educ Cncl, Snr VP, 1984-91; Pres, 1991-99; Cmnty Aid Abroad, Mbr State and Natl Exec Cttees, 1991-97. Hobbies: Rotary; Tennis; Golf; Swimming; Snooker. Address: 87 Eastern Valley Way, Castlecrag, NSW 2068, Australia.

HOGAN Paul. Actor. m. Linda Kozlowski, 1990. Appointments: Fmr rigger on Sydney Harbour Bridge; Host of TV shows A Current Affair; The Paul Hogan Show; Filmed TV specs on location in Eng, 1983; Comls for Austl Tourist Commn Fosters Lager. Films: Crocodile Dundee, 1986; Crocodile Dundee II, 1989; Almost An Angel, 1993; Lightning Jack, 1994; Flipper. TV: Anzacs: The War Down Under. Address: Level 29, 133 Castlereagh Street, Syndey, NSW 2000, Australia.

HOGAN Peter, b. 18 Mar 1958, Adelaide, Australia. General Manager. m. Vicki, Nov 1997. Education: BA; BComms. Appointments: Mngr, Adelaide Casino, 1986-88; HR Mngr, Adelaide Casino, 1988-95; Exec Asst Mngr, Reef Hotel Casino, 1995-96; Regl HR Mngr, Accor Asian Pacific, 1996-97; Gen Mngr, Grand Mercure Hotel. Memberships: Bd Mbr, Adelaide Hills Tourism, 1998; Aust Human Resources Inst; JP, SA. Hobbies: Music; Sports; Assistance to the Elderly; Current Affairs. Address: 74 Summit Road, Crafers, SA 5152, Australia.

HOGUE Cavan Oliver, b. 21 Jan 1937. International Consultant. m. Mira Reyes, 28 Sept 1957, 1 s, 2 d. Education: BA, Sydney; MA, Macquarie Univ; Austl Jnt Servs Coll; Harv Univ, USA; CFIA. Appointments: Pub Li, NSW, 1957-59; Dept of For Affairs, 1960, served in Seoul, 1960-62, Rome, 1963-65, Mexico, 1966-68, Santiago, 1968-70, Manila, 1973-75; Min for Jakarta, 1976-78; Asst Sec, Sea, 1979-80; 1st Asst Sec, Immigration, 1981-82; Amb to Mexico and Ctrl Am, 1983-84, to DPR Austl Miss to UN, NY, 1985-86; High Cmmnr, Kuala Lumpur, 1987-90; Amb, Moscow, 1991-94; Amb, Bangkok, 1994-97; Dir, Natl Thai Stdies Cntr, Aust, Natl Univ Canberra; Adjunct Prof, UTS, Sydney. Hobby: Music. Address: ASEAN Focus Group, 140 Sussex Street, Sydney, NSW 2000, Australia.

HOHNEN Ross Ainsworth, b. 21 Oct 1917, Aust. m. Phyllis Whitten, 16 Nov 1940, 3 s, 1 d. Education: BEc; Hon FDIA; Univ of Sydney. Appointments: AIF MID, 1940-46; Registrar, 1949-68, Sec, 1968-75, the ANU; Dir and Hon Sec, 1966-77, Pres, ACT Div, Dpty Natl Pres, 1979-81, Heart Fndn of Aust; Dpty Chmn, 1968-70, Chmn, 1971-77, Canberra Th Trust; Intl Commnr for Aust, 1972-76; Chmn, Asia-Pacific Reg World Scout Org, 1976-78; Pres, ACT Branch, 1981-; Chmn, Planning and Restoration Cttee, Crafts Cncls Gall, The Rocks, Sydney, 1979-81; Chmn, Techl Aid for the Disabled, ACT, 1979-82; Tstee, The Arthur Shakespeare Fndn for Scouting, 1985-; Chmn, Smoking and Heart Disease Cttee, Natl Heart Fndn; Fndr Mbr, Bd of Govs, Dev Cncl, 1986, Heart Rsch Inst. Honours: OBE, 1967; Hon Fell, Des Inst of Aust, 1971; Essington Lewis Awd, 1971; Canberran of the Yr, 1977; Awd'd Silver Kangaroo, Pres's Citation, 1994, Scout Assn of Aust, 1975; AM, 1987; Sir John Loewenthal Awd, 1988; Hon Commnr, ACT Branch, Boy Scouts Assn. Memberships: Natl Cttee, Editl Bd, Austl Dictionary of Biography, Vols 1-9; Mbr, Exec Cttee, Duke of Edinburgh's Third Study Conf, 1968; Fmr Mbr, Canberra-Monaro Diocesan Cncl and Canberra Grammar Sch; Austl Cncl Crafts Bd; Chmn, Community Arts Cttee, 1975-77; Cncl Wollongong Univ, 1975-77; Adv Cncl, Canberra Sch of Music, 1977-78; Hon Fell, Heart Rsch Inst, Sydney, 1991. Address: 71 Empire Circuit, Forrest, ACT 2603, Australia.

HOJJATI Muhammad, b. 1955, Najafabad, Isfahan, Iran. Minister of Transport. m. 4 children. Education: Majored, Civ Engrng, Isfahan Indl Univ, 1975. Appointments: Administrator, Construction Jihad, Chahar Mahal-Bakhtiyari Prov, Mbr, Cntrl Cttee, 1985, helped prepare the 5-yr plan; Gov Gen, Sistan and Baluchestan Prov, 1989-94; Administrator, Karkheh dam; Elected, Min of Roads and Transport.

HOLDING Clyde, b. 27 Apr 1931 Melbourne. Politician. m. (1) Margaret Sheer, div, 2 s, 1 d; (2) Judith Crump, 1 d. Education: Melbourne Univ. Appointments: Solicitor; Ldr State Parl Labor Party and Ldr of Opposition, 1967-77; Pres Victorian Labor Party, 1977-79; Min for Aboriginal Affairs, 1983-86; Min for Arts and Territories, 1988-89; Min of Employment Services and Yth Affairs; Min Asstng the Treas, 1987-88; Min asstng the Min for Immigration Local Govt and Ethnic Affairs, 1988-89; Asstng the PM, 1988-89; Min for Arts, Tourism and Territories, 1989-90. Memberships: Mbr Victorian Parl for Richmond, 1962-77; Mbr Fed Parl for Melbourne Ports, 1977-. Address: 117 Fitzroy Street, St Kilda, Vic 3183, Australia.

HOLDWAY Douglas Alan, b. 23 Jan 1954, Montreal, Can. Professor of Ecotoxicology. m. Tracey Ann, 11 June 1983, 2 s, 1 d. Education: BS (Hons), 1976; MSc, 1978; PhD, 1983. Appointments: Rsch scientist, OSS, 1986; Snr Rsch Scientist, OSS, 988; Snr Rsch Fell, RMIT, 1989-92; Assoc Prof Environ Toxicol, RMIT, 1992-97; Prof of Ecotoxicol, RMIT, 1997-. Publications: 206 publs incl 3 theses and books; 54 refereed pprs; 29 refereed book chapts, monographs and reports; 97 conf abstracts; 5 book reviews; 18 other publs. Honours: Ont Schl, 1972; Ont Grad Schl, 1977-79; Canad Govt Lab Visng Fellshp, 1985-87; Assoc Ed, J Ecosystem Stress and Recovery, 1997-; Regl Ed, Spill Sci and Technol Bull, 1997-99. Memberships: SETAC, 1983-; ASL, 1986-; AIB, 1987-; ASTM, 1987-. Hobbies: Electric and blues guitar; Bush walking; Reading; Scuba diving; Family. Address: Department of Applied Biology & Biotechnology, Royal Melbourne Institute of Technology - City Campus, GPO Box 2476 V, Melbourne, Vic 3001, Australia.

HOLGATE Alan, b. 13 Oct 1935. Chartered Chemical Engineer. Div, 1 s, 3 d. Education: BS(Eng) Chem Eng, ACGI & Imperial Coll, London; CEng. Appointments: Process Engr/Metallurgist, Rhokana Corp; Process Engr, Humphreys & Glasgow; Sales Mngr, Simon-Carves Ltd; Asia Pacific Regl Dir, Simon-Carves. Memberships: Fell, Instn of Chem Engrs; Petrochemical Cttee MICCI. Hobbies: Golf; Music. Address: Simon-Carves, 54A (1st Floor), Jalan SS2/67, 47300 Petlaing Jaya, Selangor Darul Fuhsan, Malaysia.

HOLLAND Alfred Charles, b. 23 Feb 1927, London, Eng. Former Anglican Bishop of Newcastle, NSW. m. 22 Sept 1954, 3 s, 1 d. Education: BA 1950, DipTh 1952. Appointments: Roy Navy, 1945-47; Univ of Durham, 1948-52; Ordained Deacon, 1952; Ordained Priest, 1953; Asst Priest, West Hackney, 1952-54; Rector, Scarborough, WA, 1955-70; Asst Bishop, Perth, WA, 1970-77; Bishop of Newcastle, NSW, 1978-92; Episcopal Chap, St George's Coll, Jerusalem, 1993. Publications: Luke Through Lent, 1980; The Diocese Together (ed), 1987. Membership: Austl Club. Listed in: International Who's Who; Who's Who in Australia. Hobbies: Painting; Reading. Address: 21 Sullivan Crescent, Wanniasea, ACT 2903, Australia.

HOLLAND Dulcie Sybil, b. 5 Jan 1913, Sydney, Aust. Composer. m. A Bellhouse, 26 Oct 1940, 1 s, 1 d. Education: Tchr Dip, Sydney Conservatory of Music, 1933. Appointments: Freelance Broadcaster, Lectr, Adj, Tchr, Accompanist, 1934-; Organist, Choir Dir, 1975-87. Publications: Symphony for Pleasure, 1971; String Quartet, 1996; Master Your Theory: 8 Books, 1981. Honours: LRSM, 1934; AM, 1977; FTCL, 1982; Fell, AMEB, 1994; Hon DLitt, Macquarie Univ, 1993. Membership: Fell, Austl Composers. Address: 67 Kameruka Road, Northbridge, NSW 2063, Australia.

HOLLAND Kevin James (Hon), b. 15 July 1923. m. Joan McKenna, 21 Mar 1952, 2 s. Education: LLB, Univ of Sydney. Appointments: RAAF, 1941-46; Admitted NSW Bar, 1951; Judge, Sup Crt of NSW, 1972-85; Probate Judge, 1977-85; Dpty Chmn, Advtng Stands Cncl, 1986-89; Acting Judge, Land and Environment, 1988; Acting Judge, Sup Crt of NSW, 1989, 1990; Roy Commnr, Inquiry into the Building Ind in NSW, 1991-92; Asst Commnr, Indep Commn Against Corruption, 1993; Acting Commnr, Indep Commn Against Corruption, 1994;

Local Govt Pecuniary Interest Tribunal, 1994. Honour: QC. Hobbies: Skiing; Surfing; Tennis. Address: 50 Melbourne Road, East Lindfield, NSW 2070, Australia.

HOLLICK Ian Bruce, b. 22 Oct 1950, Mildura, Aust. Manager. m. Wendy, 2 d. Education: DipAgScio (DAC). Memberships: Austl Soc Viticulture and Oenology; Viticultural Cncl of the Limestone Coast; Winemakers Fedn of Austl Execs. Address: PO Box 9B, Coonawarra, South Australia 5263.

HOLLIER Donald Russell, b. 7 May 1934, Sydney, Aust. Composer; Performer; Lecturer. m. Sharman Ellen Pretty, 12 July 1978. Education: NSW State Conservatorium, Roy Acady of London, Eng; BMus 1961, DMus 1974, Univ of London. Appointments: Dir, Music, Newington Coll, 1962-63; Hd, Acad Studies, Canberra Sch of Music, 1967; Coord of Studies, 1976; Hd, Musicology, 1978; Canberra Sch of Music; Musical Dir, Canberra Choral Sch, 1978; Musical Dir, Canberra Opera, 1979; Composer in Res, Tas Symph Orch. Compositions: Musicks Empire; Variations for Violin and Piano; Seven Psalms for Choir and Orchestra; Mass in D. Creative Works: 6 Operas inclng The Heiress and For the Term of His Natural Life. Honours: Henry W Richards Prize for Organ; Frank Shirley Prize; Maggs Awd, Churchill Fellshp. Membership: Composers Guild. Hobby: Walking. Address: 59 Ross Street, Glebe, NSW 2037, Australia.

HOLLINGWORTH Peter John, b. 10 Apr 1935, Adelaide, Aust. Clergyman. m. Kathleen-Ann Turner, 6 Feb 1960, 3 d. Education: Scotch Coll, Melbourne, 1947-51; BA, Trinity Coll, Melbourne Univ, 1958; ThL, Austl Coll of Theol, 1960; Dip of Socl Studies, 1969, MA, 1981, Melbourne Univ. Appointments: Priest i/c, St Mary's, North Melbourne, 1960-64; Chaplain and Dir of Yth Wrk, 1964-70, Assoc Dir, Soc Issues, 1970-79, Exec Dir, 1980-90, Brotherhood of St Laurence; Canon, St Paul's Cath, Melbourne, 1980; Bishop in the Inner Cty, Diocese of Melbourne, 1985-90; 8th Archbish of Brisbane, 1990-; Chaplain, Order of St John of Jerusalem, 1997. Publications: Australians in Poverty, 1978, 1979, 1981, 1986; The Poor - Victims of Affluence, 1974; The Powerless Poor, 1972, 1974. Honours: Victorian Father of the Yr, Adv Aust Awd, 1987; OBE, 1976; AO, 1988; Hon LLD, Monash Univ, 1986; Melbourne Univ, 1990; Snr Austl of the Yr, 1990; Hon Dr Univ, Griffith, 1992, QUT, 1993, Cntrl Queensland, 1994. Memberships: Austl Assn of Socl Workers, 1970-78. Hobbies: Writing; Reading; Swimming. Address: Bishopsbourne, PO Box 421 GPO, Brisbane, Queensland 4001, Australia.

HOLLIS Colin Patrick, b. 30 May 1938. Member of Parliament. Education: BSc (Hons); BA; Dip Intl Affairs; Dip in Adult Educ. Appointments: MP, House of Reprs, 1983-. Honours: Adv Aust Awd, 1979; Cmdr, Order Lion of Finland, 1996. Address: PO Box 3000, Albion Park Rail, NSW 2527, Australia.

HOLLYMAN Kenneth James, b. 28 Jan 1922. Retired. m. (1) Miriam Miller, 1946, diss 1969, 1 child, (2) Jeanette Leita Glasgow, 1970, 2 s, 1 d. Education: BA 1942, Snr Schl in French, 1946, MA 1947, Victoria Univ Coll, Univ of NZ; Ex-Serviceman's Postgrad Sch in Arts; Doct in French Ling, Univ of Paris, 1947-51; Courses at Ecole des Hautes Études and Inst de Sociologie. Appointments: Lectr in Mod Langs, 1953-56; Lectr in French, 1957, Snr Lectr, 1958-62, Assoc Prof, 1963-65, Prof of French, 1966-86, Hd of Dept of Romance Langs, 1972-86, Emer Prof, 1987-, Hon Rsch Fell, 1988-; AU Prof Bd/Senate, 1959-62, 1966-86, AU Cncl, 1960-61, 1974, 1976-77, 1979-83, Dean of Fac of Arts, 1969-71, Chmn AU Press, 1975-76, 1982-86, Asst Vice Chan, 1977-78, 1980, Dpty Vice Chair, 1976, 1979, Mbr NZUGC, 1977-81. Publications: Books: Le Développement du Vocabulaire Féodal en France, 1957; A Checklist of Oceanic Languages, 1960; Le Français Régional de l'Indo-Pacifique, 1968; A Short Descriptive Grammar of Old French, 1968; Ed, Observatoire du Français dans le Pacifique, 1983; Les Noms Français des Plantes Calédoniennes, 1993; Co-Auth, Le Lexique du

Bagne à La Nouvelle, 1994; Les Noms Français des Animaux en Nouvelle-Calédonie, 1995; Études sur les Langues du Nord de la Novelle-Calédonie, 1999; Auth of over 100 articles in ling & Pacific jrnls. Honours: Chevalier for Tchng Servs French, Ordre des Palmes Acads, 1981; Dunmore Medal, Fedn of Alliances Françaises of NZ, 1992. Memberships: Fndr, 1958, Sec, Ed, Ling Soc of NZ; Fndr, Dir, 1979, Co-Dir, 1987-; Pacific French Rsch Unit, AU; Auckland Inst & Mus. Hobby: Cooking. Address: 255 Pakaraka Rd, Okoroire, RD2, Tirau 2372, New Zealand.

HOLMES John Dean, b. 29 Aug 1942. m. 7 Aug 1971, 1 s, 2 d. Education: BSc (Eng), Univ Southampton, 1963; PhD, Monash Univ, Melbourne, Aust, 1973. Appointments: Sci Offr, Aeronautical Rsch Labs, Melbourne, 1964-66; Engr, Govt Aircraft Factories, 1966-69; Rsch Fell, Univ of West Ont, Canada, 1973-74; Snr Lectr, James Cook Univ, Townsville, Aust, 1974-81; Prin, Snr Prin and Chf Rsch Sci, CSIRO, 1982-96; Snr Rsch Fell, Monash Univ, 1996-; Dir, JDH Cnsltng. Publications: Book: A Commentary on the Australian Standard for Wind Loads (with W H Melbourne, G R Walker), 1990. Honours: State Schshp (UK) 1960-63; Brit Cncl Travel Grant, 1973; Fulbright Snr Fellowship, 1989; W H Warren Medal (I E Aust), 1990; J S P S Fellowship, Japan, 1996. Memberships: Fell, Instn of Engrs, Aust mbr; Life Mbr, Austl Wind Engrng Soc, chmn, 1984-89. Listed in: Australian Men and Women of Science, Engineering and Technology. Hobbies: Music (Jazz, Blues). Address: 6 Charman Road, Mentone, Vic 3194, Australia.

HOLMES John Leonard, b. 18 Jan 1925, Sydney, Aust. Retired. m. Elise Mayer, 21 Aug 1965, 1 s, 1 d. Education: BSc, Univ Sydney, 1949. Appointments: Trade Commnr, Austl Dept of Trade, 1961-84; Pres, Exec Dir, Austl Countertrade Assn Ltd, 1986-. Publications: Conductors on Record, 1982; Conductors, 1988, (Chinese transl, 1992); Composers on Composers, 1990; Conductors on Composers, 1993. Address: 31 Mawson Drive, Mawson, ACT 2607, Australia.

HOLMES Ralph John, b. 12 Mar 1946. Physicist. m. Yvonne Siok Tin Tan, 27 Nov 1976, 2 d. Education: BSc, PhD, Univ of Melbourne. Appointment: Mngr, Iron Ore Processing, CSIRO Minerals, Aust. Publications: Over 100 sci pprs and rprts; 3 patents. Honours: Inaugural Aust IMM Mineral Ind Operating Technique Awd, 1987; Inaugural Stands Awd, Stands Aust, 1993; Clunies Ross Natl Sci and Technol Awd, 1998. Memberships: Fell, Austl Inst of Phys; Fell, Australasian Inst of Mining and Metall; Soc of Mining Engrng, USA. Hobbies: Music; Travel. Address: 30 Candlebark Crescent, Chapel Hill, Qld 4069, Australia.

HOLT John Foster, b. 9 June 1939, Melbourne, Australia. Genealogist; Family Historian. m. Erzsi Mather, 19 Nov 1960, 1 s, 1 d. Education: Cert of Fin Analysis, Dun and Bradstreet, NYC; Inst of Personnel Cnslts (Aust), 1985. Appointments: Cncl of Austl Assn of Genealogists and Record Agts (AAGRA), 1985; Web-Ed, AAGRA, 1995; Web Ed, Assn of Profl Genealogists, 1998. Honour: Achievement Awd, Camperdown Community House, 1998. Memberships: Cnclr, AAGRA, 1985-; AAGRA Quarterly Newsletter Ed, 1997-98; International Trustee, APG, 1999-2000. Hobbies: Tracing heirs, genealogy; Lecturer; Teacher; Newspaper columnist. Address: 254 White Road, Worthaggi, Vic 3995, Australia.

HOLTON Richard Henry, b. 17 Mar 1926, Columbus, OH, USA. Professor. m. Constance Minzey, 7 June 1947, 1 s, 2 d. Education: BS, Miami Univ, OH, 1947; MA, OH State Univ, 1948; PhD, Harv Univ, 1952. Appointments: Asst Dir, Mktng Proj, Socl Sci Rsch Cntr, Univ of Puerto Rico, 1951-52; Asst Prof of Econs, OH State Univ, 1953; Asst Prof of Econs, Harv Univ, 1953-57; Asst Prof, Sch of Bus Admin, 1957-61, Dir, Inst of Bus and Econ Rsch, 1959-61, Prof, Sch of Bus Admin, 1961-91, Prof Emer, Haas Sch of Bus Admin, 1991-, Univ of CA at Berkeley. Publications: Co-auth: Marketing Efficiency in Puerto Rico, 1955; The Canadian Economy: Prospect and

Retrospect, 1959; The Supply and Demand Structure of Food Retailing Services, 1954; The Characteristic of the New Industrial Firms in the Campania and Their Marketing Problems, 1961; Management Education in Italy, 1973; Num articles, book chapts and book reviews. Memberships include: Chmn, President's Consumer Advsry Cncl, Wash DC, 1965-66; Natl Mktng Advsry Cttee, US Dept of Com, Wash DC, 1968-71; Acad Advsry Cttee, Amn Assn of Advertising Agencies Educ Fndn, 1968-81; Advsry Bd, Econ Inst, Univ of CO, 1974-78; Consumer Advsry Cncl, Bd of Govs, Fed Reserve System, 1978-79; US Dept of Com Advsry Cttee, Natl Cntr for Mngmt Dev at Dalian, China, 1986-89; Acad Advsry Bd, Amn Grad Sch of Intl Mngmt, Phoenix, AZ. 1983-88; Num Cnltng Assignments in ind. Address: 87 Southampton Ave, Berkeley, CA 94707, USA.

HOLUIGUE B Diane, b. 22 Oct 1942, Melbourne, Australia. Teacher; Journalist; Author. m. 30 Aug 1963, 1 s, 1 d. Education: BA, Melbourne Univ. Publications: 9 books and 26 yrs of articles. Membership: Certified Mbr, IACP (Ind Assn for Culinary Profls). Hobbies: Travel; Writing. Address: 3 Avondale Road, Armadale, Victoria 3143, Australia.

HOME Roderick Weir, b. 6 Jan 1939, Melbourne, Vic, Aust. University Professor. m. Marjorie Elaine Mahoney, 1 Sept 1962, 2 s, 1 d. Education: BSc hons, Ormond Coll, Univ of Melbourne, 1959; PhD, IN Univ, USA, 1967. Appointments: Sci Master, Haileybury Coll Melbourne, 1960-64; Lectr, Hist and Philos of Sci, 1967-71; Snr Lectr, 1971-75; Fndn Prof, Hist and Philos of Sci, 1975-, Univ of Melbourne, Parkville. Publications: Aepinus's Essay on the Theory of Electricity and Magnetism, 1979; The Effluvial Theory of Electricity, 1981; Ed, Science Under Scrutiny, 1983; The History of Classical Physics: A Selected, annotated Bibliography, 1984; Ed, Australian Science in the Making, 1988; Physics in Australia to 1945: Bibliography and Biographical Register, 1990; Ed, International Science and National Scientific Identity, 1991; Electricity and Experimental Physics in Eighteenth-Century Europe, 1992; Ed, The Scientific Savant in Nineteenth Century Australia, 1997; Ed, Respectfully Yours: Selected Correspondence of Ferdinand von Mueller, 1998. Num articles in schl jrnls. Honour: DLitt, Univ of Melbourne, 1985. Memberships: Corresp Mbr, Intl Acady of the Hist of Sci; Fell, Austl Acady of Hums; Australasian Assn for the Hist, Philos and Socl Studies of Sci, Pres, 1977-80. Address: Department of History and Philosophy of Science, University of Melbourne, Parkville, Vic 3052, Australia.

HOMOD Al-Turaiki, b. 23 Feb 1955, Al-Zulfi, Saudi Arabia. Professor; Orthopedic Bioengineer. m. Norah and Ratibe, 3 s, 6 d. Education: BS (Hons) Mechl Engrng, Univ of Lancaster, UK, 1980; PhD, Salford Univ, UK, 1984; Postgrad Cert in Orthotics, Postgrad Cert in Prosthetics, Northwestern Univ, Chgo, USA, 1989. Diplomate of Amn Bd of Profl Disability Cnslts, ABPDV, USA, 1995; Professorial Rank, King Saud Univ, 1996. Appointments: Rsch Asst Prof & Supvsr of Biomedl Rsch Projs, Directorate of Sci Rsch, King Abdulaziz Cty for Sci & Technol (KACST), 1984-86; Asst Prof, Chmn, Dept of Biomedl Technol, Coll of Applied Medl Scis, King Saud Univ, Riyadh, Saudi Arabia, 1987-88; Visng Prof, Rehab Egrng Engrng Prog and Prosthetic Rsch Lab, Northwestern Univ Medl Sch, Chgo, IL, USA, 1989; Asst Prof, Orth Bioengineering & Rehab, Dept of Biomedl Technol, Coll of Applied Medl Scis, 1986-90, Cnslt Prosthetist-Orthotist, Coll of Med & King Khalid Univ Hosp, 1992-, Chmn, Dept of Biomedl Technol, Coll of Applied Medl Scis, 1993-98, Assoc Prof, Orthopedic Bioengineering & Rehabilitation, Dept of Biomedical Technol, Coll of Applied Medl Scis, 1990-96, Prof, Orthopedic Bioengineering and Rehabilitation, Dept of Biomedical Technol, Coll of Applied Medl Scis, 1996-, King Saud Univ, Riyadh. Publications: 23 books; 70 pprs; 2 patented inventions. Honours: Best Ppr Gold Medal, India, 1996; Leadership Awd, Temple Univ, USA, 1998. Address: PO Box 65. Al-Zulfi 11932, Saudi Arabia.

HONDA Yuzo, b. 1947, Tokyo, Japan. Professor of Economics. m. 1973. Education: PhD, Econs, Princeton

Univ. Appointments: Assoc Prof, Kobe Univ of Com, 1980-87; Assoc Prof, Prof, Kobe Univ, 1987-96; Prof, Osaka Univ, 1996-. Publications: Large Sample Tests in Econometrics, 1990; Ed, Business Cycles in Japan, 1995. Honour: Nikkei Econs Awd, 1990. Memberships: Japanese Econ Assn, cncl mbr, 1986-89, 1996-, Assoc Ed, Jrnl of the Assn, 1988-94. Hobby: Tennis. Address: c/o School of Economics, Osaka University, Toyonaka, Osaka 560-0043, Japan.

HONE Geoffrey William, b. 20 Nov 1943, Sydney, Aust. Lawyer. m. Anthea, 24 Feb 1973, 1 s, 2 d. Education: LLB, hons, Univ Melbourne. Appointments: Ptnr, Blake Dawson Waldron, 1975-; Dir, SEGC Ltd, 1991-; Dir, The Queens Trust for Yng Austlns, 1994-. Publications: Sev articles in profl jrnls. Memberships: Intl Bar Assn; Law Cncl of Aust. Hobbies: Tennis; Opera; Bridge. Address: Level 39, 101 Collins Street, Melbourne, Victoria 3000, Australia.

HONEY Peter Geoffrey, b. 24 July 1949, Kiama, NSW, Aust. Veterinarian. m. Jeanette, 2 d. Education: BVSc, (Sydney); MS (Texas A&M); Diplomate Amn Coll of Theriogenologists. Appointments: Dist Vet, Lismore, NSW, 1973-74; Dist Vet, Glen Innes, NSW, 1975-77; Vet Clin Assoc, Texas A & M Univ, 1978-79; Asst Prof, LA State Univ, 1980-82; Priv prac, 1983-. Memberships: Austl Vet Assn; Austl Assn of Cattle Vets; Beef Improvement Assn; Amn Coll of Theriohenologists; Amn Soc of Theriogenology; Austl Angus Assn; Vic Farmers Fedn. Hobbies: Triathlon; Snow skiing; Landscape painting; Cattle breeding. Address: Snowy River Veterinary Clinic, Box 278, Orbost, Vic 3888, Australia.

HONEYWOOD Phillip Neville, b. 26 Apr 1960, Gosford, NSW, Aust. Member of Parliament. Div, 1 s, 1 d. Education: BA, Hons, Aust Natl Univ. Appointments: Fin Dir, Yng Liberal Movement, 1987; Estimates Cttee, 1988; Chmn, Conservation and Environ Cttee, 1990-96; Parly Sec to Premier on Ethnic Affairs, 1992-96; Chair, Melbourne Parks and Waterways Advsry Cncl, 1993-96; Min for Tertiary Educn and Trng, Min Assisting the Premier on Multicultural Afffairs, 1996. Membership: Swinburne Univ Gov Cncl, 1991-96. Hobbies: Swimming; Tennis; Bushwalking. Address: 44 New Street, Ringwood, Victoria 3134, Australia.

HONG Hu, b. Jun 1940 Jinzhai Co Anhui Prov. Politician. Education: Beijing Indl Inst. Appointments: Joined CCP, 1965; Vice-Sec-Gen Sec-Gen State Commn for Econ Restructuring, 1982; Vice-Dir State Commn for Econ Restructuring, 1991-. Memberships: Mbr Commn of Securities of the State Cncl, 1992-; Mbr CCP Cntrl Commn for Discipline Inspection, 1992; Mbr 15th CCP Cntrl Cttee, 1997-. Address: State Commission for Economic Restructuring, State Council, People's Republic of China.

HONG Jae-Hyong, b. Chongju Cty N Chungchong Prov. Politician. Education: Seoul Natl Univ. Appointments: Joined For Exchange Bur Min of Fin, 1963; Later wrkd at IBRD WA DC; Admin Korean Customs Admin; Pres Export-Import Bank of Korea; Pres Korea Exchange Bank; Min of Fin, 1993; Dep PM Min of Fin and Econs, 1994-96. Address: c/o Ministry of Finance, 1 Jungang-dong, Gwachon City, Kyonggi Province, Republic of Korea.

HONG Moon-Shin, b. 13 Dec 1942. Company Chairman; President. m. Mrs Myung-Suh Kim, 1 s, 1 d. Education: DEcon, Univ of Bonn, W Germany, 1973. Appointments: Snr Rsch Fell, Korea Dev Inst, 1974; Pres & Chmn, Korea Shipping Corp, 1975; Snr Rsch Fell, Kiet, 1982; Snr Rsch Dir, Kiet, 1984; Pres, Kiet, 1986-88; Pres, Korea Appraisal Bd, 1989-95; Hankuk Real Estate Trust Co, 1991-95; Pres and Chmn, Korean Reins Co, 1995-. Publications: Die Bedeutung des Verkehrssystems fuer die Wirtschaftlice Entwicklung des Ostasiatischen Raums, 1973; An Analysis of Korea Investment Pattern in ASEAN, 1981; The Current Status and the Directions of Development of the Korean Fine-Chemical Industry, 1981. Memberships: Cncl of Technol Promotion, min of Sc & T; Advsry Cttee for Econ Restructuring, Off of the

Pres; Cttee for the Econ and Socl Dev Plan, Econ Planning Bd. Hobbies: Photography; Opera. Address: 22-602 Hanyang Apt, Apkujung-dong, Kangnam-gu, Seoul, Korea.

HONG Pei-Sun, b. 9 June 1932, Nanjing, Jiangsu, China. Engineering Educator. m. Bao-Lin Shu, 28 May 1958, 1 s, 1 d. Education: BS, Nanjing Inst of Technol, 1955; Dr's degree, Tsing-Hua Univ, Beijing, 1964. Appointments: Tchr, Nanjing Coll of Elec Engrng, 1955-60; Hd Dept, Elec Engrng, 1955-60; Vice Rector, 1981-85; Dept Hd, Hohai Univ, Nanjing, 1986-96; Rector, Rural Electrification Coll of Hohoi Univ, 1987-96; Prof, Nanjing Univ tech, 1994-; Wu-Xi Univ of Light Industry, 1994-. Publications: Distance Protection of Transmission Line, 1987; Protective Relaying of Power System, 1986. Honours: Named Advd Educr, Nanjing Municipal Govt, 1960; Advd Scientist, Jiangsu Prov Govt, 1979; Advd Techn, Bur Elec Power Jiangsu, 1978; Winner Govt Spec Allownace, State Cncl of People's Repub of China, 1992. Memberships: Dpty, Nanjing People's Congress, 1983-87; China Soc Elec Engrng (Snr); Soc of Rural Electrification China, Dir, 1989-96; Dir, Jiangsu Soc EE, 1986-. Hobbies: Classical music; Amateur radio. Address: 76 Western Beijing Road, 210013, Nanjing, China.

HONG Seong Chan, b. 25 Apr 1938. Professor of Law. m. Ha Jung Ae, 1 s, 1 d. Education: Coll of Law, Kon-Kuk Univ, 1963; PhD, Yonsei Univ, 1978. Appointments: Lectr, Korea Univ and Yonsei Univ 1972-82; Prof, Dept of Law, Coll of Socl Sci, Kon-Kuk Univ 1984-, Dean, 1988; Visng Prof, Northwestern Univ, USA, 1991; Dir of Lib, Kon-Kuk Univ, 1994; Dean, Grad Sch of Socl Sci, 1996. Publications: General Theory of Law, 1983; The Administrative Law, 1987; Law of the Housing and Land, 1992. Memberships: Korean Pub Law Assn; Korean Assn for Philos of Law and Soc Philos; Korean Assn of Real Estate; Univ of Southern CA Korean Stdies Inst. Hobby: Travel. Address: 451-34 Seokyo-dong, Mapo-ku, Seoul, Korea.

HONG Yi, b. 24 Aug 1943, Fujian, China. Professor. m. Yingxiao, 1972, 2 s. Education: PhD, Wayne State Univ, MI, USA. Appointment: Prof, Dept of Appl Maths, S China Univ of Technol, 1989-. Publications: Tensor Analysis and its Application, 1992; Economic Mathematical Model, 1998. Memberships: Am Math Soc; Chinese Math Soc. Hobbies: Bridge; Chess. Address: Department of Applied Mathematics, South China University of Technology, Guangzhou, China.

HONIMAE Johnson Fataolisa, b. 28 Feb 1959, Auki, Solomon Islands. Journalist. m. Annette, 1 s, 4 d. Education: BA; Dip Jrnlsm; Cert in Brdcst Trng. Appointments: Snr Info, Offr, Ed News and Current Affairs; Dir of Progs; Dir of Info; Gen Mngr SIBC. Honours: Solomon Islands, 20th Indep Anniversary Medal, 7 July 1998. Memberships: Media Assn of Solomon Islands; Solomon Islands, NZ Soc, Hobbies: Reading (non-fiction); Watching TV documentaries; Shortwave radio listening. Address: General Manager, Solomon Islands Broadcasting Corporation, PO Box 654, Honiara, Solomon Islands.

HOOD David John, b. 27 Apr 1945, New Malden, Eng (Austl Res, 1984-). Writer; Pianist; Broadcaster; Public Speaker. Education: Assoc Dip of Liberal Studies, Hartly, SA; AMusA, PNO; Higher qualification for music tchrs, Melbourne; Fndns of profl writing (Homesglen). Appointments: Brdcstr, 3MBS FM, 1984-; artistic Dir, Franz Liszt Exhibn (3 MBS FM), 1986; Co-ord, Friends of Liszt, Melbourne, 1987-; Pre-concert Speaker for Melbourne Symph Orch, 1988-91; Tutor in Music Hist, CAE, Melbourne; Var. Publications: Poetry in: Mouth of the Dragon, June 1975; Poet's Choice (Aust), 1976-78; Meanjin (Melbourne), Jan 1986. Essay on Franz Liszt in Jrnl of the Amn Liszt Soc, 1994. Honours: Franz Liszt Mem Plaque for Liszt Centenary (Hungarian Govt), 1986. Hobbies: Languages; Gardening; European History. Address: 5/245 Barkly Street, North Fitzroy, Victoria 3068, Australia.

HOOGENRAAD Nicholas Dohannes, b. 17 Feb 1942, The Hague, Netherlands. Biochemist; Molecular Biologist. m. Joan, 20 Feb 1965, 1 s, 1 d. Education: BAgric Sci, Melbourne, 1965; PhD Biochem, Melbourne Univ, 1969. Appointments: Asst Prof, Pediats, Stanford Univ, 1971-74; Lectr in Biochem, La Trobe Univ, 974-75; Snr Lectr, 1976-83; Rdr, 1984-91; Prof, 1992-. Honours: AMRA/DPharmacia Biotechnol Medal of ASBMB, 1994. Memberships: Austl Soc Biochem and Molecular Bio, Pres, 1997-98. Hobbies: Grapegrowing and winemaking; Carpentry; Hiking. Address: 460 Hildebrand Rd, St Andrews, Victoria, Australia.

HOOKE John Anthony Lionel, b. 6 June 1933, Sydney, Aust. Company Chairman. m. Maria Teresa Savio, 17 Jan 1976, 2 s. Education: BS, Hons, Sydney Univ. Appointments: Chmn, Chf Exec, Almagamated Wireless Ltd, 1974-88; Dir, GE Crane Holdings Ltd, 1972-97, The Broken Hill Proprietory Co Ltd, 1981-92; Chmn, Tubemakers of Aust, 1986-96; Chmn, Def Ind Cttee, 1986-92; Dpty Chmn, Crane Holdings Ltd, 1989-97. Honours: Queens Silver Jubilee Medal, 1977; Cmdr, OBE, 1979. Memberships include: Fell, Instn of Engrs, Aust; Fell, Austl Acady of Technol Scis; Salvation Army Advsry Cttee, Red Shield Appeal. Hobbies: Reading; Skiing; Photography. Address: 26 Buckingham Road, Killara, NSW 2071, Australia.

HOOKER John Lee, b. 22 Aug 1917 Clarksdale, MS, USA. Education: Studied guitar under Will Moore. Appointments: Extensive tours across N Am, 1951-; Eur and UK, 1961-; Appeared at Newport Folk Fest, 1959, 1960, 1963; Newport Jazz Fest, 1964; Amn Blues Fest, 1964-1965, 1968; Ann Arbor Blues Fest, 1969, 1970, 1973, 1974; At Carnegie Hall, 1971, 1983, 1986. TV appearances incl: Midnight Spec, 1971; Don Kirsher's Rock Concert, 1978; Writer of num blues songs inclng She's Long She's Tall; Boom Boom; Boogie Chillen; Has recorded over 100 albums inclng Folklore of John Lee Hooker, 1962; Big Soul of John Lee Hooker, 1964; Best of John Lee Hooker, 1974; This is Hip, 1980; Tantalising With The Blues, 1982; Solid Sender, 1984; Black Rhythm and Blues, 1984; The Healer, 1988; Never Get Out of These Blues Alive, 1990; John Lee Hooker, 1990; I'm in the Mood, 1991; More Real Folks Blues/The Missing Album, 1991; That's My Story, 1991; Mr Lucky, 1991; That's Where It's At Boom Boom, 1992; Get Back Home, 1992; Graveyard Blues, 1992; Hobo Blues, 1992; The Early Years, 1994; Simply the Truth, 1994; One Way, 1994; Chill Out, 1995; Has also recorded under names Delta John, John Lee Booker, Birmington Sam, Texas Slim, John Williams. Films: The Blues Brothers, 1980. Honours: W C Handy Awd, 1986, 1989, 1990, 1993, 1996; Folk Heritage Awd Smithsonian Inst, 1983; Other awds. Address: c/o Rosebud Agency, P O Box 170429, San Francisco, CA 94117, USA.

HOOKINGS Gordon Alick, b. 28 Oct 1920, Napier, NZ. Retired. m. Margaret Eileen Louise Dodd, 8 Oct 1960, 1 s, 2 d. Education: BSc, Sir Geo Grey Sch, 1940; MSc, First Class Hons in Maths, 1941; MSc, Cambridge Univ, Eng, 1947. Appointments: Snr Lectr in Maths, Auckland Univ, 1948; Assoc Prof of Applied Maths, 1967; Hd of Dept of Maths, 1967-68, 1972, 1975. Publications: J Applied Meterology, vol 4, number, 1965; Aero Revue, vol 41, number 1, 1966. Honours: Cook Meml Prize in Maths, 1941; Sir Henry Wigram Medal, Roy Aeronautical Soc, NZ Div, 1965; MBE, 1989. Memberships: London Math Soc; The Auckland Math Assn; Assn of Univ Lectrs. Hobbies: Gliding; Sailing; Skiing; Secretary, New Zealand Mathematical Olympiad Committee. Address: 8 Helen Place, Auckland 5, New Zealand.

HOPE Bob, b. 29 May 1903, Eltham, Eng. Comedian. m. Dolores Reade, 1934, 2 adopted s, 2 adopted d. Appointments: First film, 1938; Since then has appeared in num films radio tv prodns. Films incl: College Swing; Big Broadcast; Give Me A Sailor; Thanks for the Memory, 1938; Never Say Die; Some Like it Hot; Cat and the Canary, 1939; Road to Singapore, 1940; Nothing But the Truth; Road To Zanzibar; Louisiana Purchase; Caught in the Draft, 1941; My Favourtie Blonde; Star Spangled Rhythm; Road to Morocco, 1942; They've Got Me Covered; Let's Face It, 1943; Princess and the Pirate, 1944; Road to Utopia, 1945; Monsieur Beaucaire, 1946; My Favourite Brunette, 1947; Road To Rio; The Paleface, 1948; Sorrowful Jones; The Great Lover, 1949; Fancy Pants, 1950; My Favourite Spy; Lemon Drop Kid, 1951; Son of Paleface, 1952; Off Limits; Here Come the Girls, 1951; Road to Bali, 1953; Casanova's Big Night, 1954; Seven Little Foys, 1955; Iron Petticoat; That Certain Feeling, 1956; Beau James, 1957; Paris Holiday, 1958; Alias Jesse James, 1959; The Facts of Life, 1960; Bachelor in Paradise, 1961; Road to Hong Kong, 1962; Call Me Bwana, 1963; A Global Affair, 1964; I'll Take Sweden, 1965; Boy, Did I get a Wrong Number!, 1966; Eight on the Lam, 1967; Private Life of Sgt O'Farrell, 1968; How to Commit Marriage, 1969; The Road to Ruin, 1972; Cancel My Reservation, 1972; The Bob Hope Christmas Special, 1987; The Bob Hope Birthday Special, 1988; Bob Hope's Yellow Ribbon Party, 1991; Bob Hope: A 90th Birthday Celebration, 1993. Publications: They've Got Me Covered, 1941; I Never Left Home, 1944; So This Is Peace, 1946; Have Tux Will Travel, 1954; I Owe Russia $1200, 1963; Five Women I Love, 1966; The Last Christmas Show, 1974; Road to Hollywood, 1977; Confessions of a Hooker, 1985; Don't Shoot It's Only Me, 1990. Honours: Num hon degress and awds inclng Am Congressional Medal of Honor, 1963; Awd of Entertainment Hall of Fame, 1975; Four spec Acady Awds; Am Hope Awd, 1988; Medal of Liberty; Hon KBE and 44 hon Docts, 1982; Natl Medal of Arts, 1995. Address: Hope Enterprises Inc, 3808 Riverside Drive, Burbank, CA 91505, USA.

HOPPER Dennis, b. 17 May 1936, Dodge Cty, KS, USA. Actor; Author. m. (3) Katherine La Nasa, 1989, 1 s, 2 d - from prev marriages. Education: Pub schs in San Diego. Appointments: Num TV appearances incl Loretta Young Show. Films incl: Rebel without a Cause, 1955; I Died a Thousand Times, 1955; Giant, 1956; Story of Mankind; Gunfight at the OK Corral, 1957; Night Tide; Key Witness; From Hell to Texas, 1958; Glory Stompers, 1959; The Trip, 1961; The Sons of Katie Elder, 1962; Hang 'Em High, 1966; Cool Hand Luke, 1967; True Grit, 1968; Actor writer dir Easy Rider, 1969; Actor writers dir The Last Movie, 1971; The American Dreamer, 1971; Kid Blue, 1973; The Sky is Falling, 1975; James Dean - The First American Teenager, 1976; Mad Dog Morgan, 1976; Tracks, 1979; American Friend, 1978; Apocalypse Now, 1979; Actor dir Out of the Blue, 1980; Wild Times, 1980; King of the Mountain, 1981; Human Highway, 1981; Rumble Fish, 1983; The Osterman Weekend, 1984; Black Widow, 1986; Blue Velvet, 1986; River's Edge, 1987; Dir Colors, 1988; Blood Red, 1989; Flashback, 1989; The American Wars, 1989; Dir, The Hot Spot, 1990; Actor, Writer, Dir, Paris Trout, 1990; Chattahoochie, 1990; Motion and Emotion, 1990; Superstar: The Life and Times of Andy Warhol, 1990; Hot Spot, 1990; Dir, Catchfire, 1991; Dir, Nails, 1991; Actor, Writer, Dir, The Indian Runner, 1991; True Romance; Boiling Point; Super Mario Bros, 1993; Chasers, 1994; Speed, 1994; Waterworld, 1995; Search and Destroy, 1995; Basquiat, 1996; Carrie Away, 1996. Has held sev pub exhibns of photos. Honours: Named Best New Dir Cannes, 1969; Best Film awds at Venice, 1971; Best Film awds at Cannes, 1980. Address: c/o Creative Artists Agcy, 9830 Wilshire Blvd, Beverly Hills, CA 90212, USA.

HOPPER Ian David, b. 6 Aug 1936, Ballarat, Aust. m. Pam, 28 May 1960, 2 s, 2 d. Education: Techl Tchr Cert, 1965; Dip, 1983. Appointments: Elecl Techn, Eng, 1960; Techl Tchr, 1963; Curriculum Cnslt, Min of Educ, 1976. Honour: Victorian Overseas Fndn Awd, 1959. Memberships include: Victorian Overseas Fndn; Austl Coll of Educ; JP, 1985-; Cnclr, Cty of S Barwon, 1978-93; Mayor, Cty of S Barwon, 1984-86; Royal Assn of Hon Justices; Rotary Intl, 1987. Hobbies: Flying Pilot RAAF Reserve; Tourism; Sen Austl Jaycees; Adult and further education management, 1975-; Current Affairs. Address: 58 Reigate Road, Highton, Vic 3216, Australia.

HOPPER Victor David, b. 13 May 1913. Emeritus Professor. m. Muriel Lloyd, 1 Feb 1939, 3 s. Education: DSc; MSc; F Inst P; FAIP, Univ of Melbourne. Appointments: Dixson Sch, 1938; Lectr, Univ of WA, 1939; Snr Lectr, 1947; Rdr 1957, Dean, Fac of Sci, 1964-68, Univ of Melbourne; Nuffield Rsch Fell, Univ of Birmingham, 1950; Res S Afr and S Am on cosmic rays and upper atmosphere, 1959; Observer, Mediterranean Balloon Exped, Bristol Univ, 1961; Dean of Univ Studs, RAAF Acady, Vic, 1961-78; Prof of Phys, Emer Prof 1978-. Publications: Determination of the Electronic Charge (jointly); Cosmic Radiation and High Energy Interactions. Honours: David Syme Prize and Medal (jointly), 1943; OBE, 1980. Memberships: Nuffield Adv Cttee (Aust); Austl Natl Cttee on Space Rsch. Hobbies: Hockey; Fishing. Address: 16 Hawkins Avenue, Box HIll, Vic 3129, Australia.

HORGAN Daniel C, b. 9 Nov 1963, Leominster, MA, USA. Senior Vice President. Education: BSc, Fin. Appointments: Cert Fund Spec; Soc of Cert Snr Advsrs, USC Alva Assn. Publications: Contbr, writer, var jrnls. Honours: Keystone Funds, 1996; John Hancock Funds, Pres Club, 1997; Evergreen Guards, 1997. Memberships: Investment Mngmnt Cnslts; Intl Assn of Finl Planners. Hobbies: Reading; Wine tasting; Computers. Address: 610 Newport Center Drive, #900, Newport Beach, CA 92660, USA.

HORINOUCHI Hisao. Politician. Appointments: Fmr Min of Agric Forestry and Fisheries: Min of Posts and Telecomms, Nov 1996-. Memberships: Mbr HoR. Address: Ministry of Posts and Telecommunications, 1-3-2 Kasumigaseki, Chiyoda-ku, Tokyo 100, Japan.

HORIOKA Charles Yuji, b. 7 Sept 1956, Boston, MA, USA. Economist; Educator. Education: BA, magna cum laude, Econs, Harv Coll; PhD, Bus Econs, Harv Univ. Appointments: Asst Prof, 1983-85, Assoc Prof, 1985-87, Fac of Econs, Kyoto Univ; Vis Asst Prof, Dept of Econs, Stanford Univ, 1988; Assoc Prof, 1987-97, Prof, 1997-, Inst of Socl and Econ Rsch, Osaka Univ; Vis Assoc Prof, Dept of Econs and E Asian Inst, Columbia Univ, 1993. Publications: Saving and Bequests/Inheritances in an Aging Society, 1996; The Saving Behavior of Japanese and US Households, 1998; Num articles in profl jrnls. Honours: Japan Fndn Lang Fellshp, 1981-82; Fulbright Hays Fellshp, Dept of Educn, 1982-83. Memberships: Amn Econ Assn; Roy Econ Soc; Japanese Econ Assn; natl Bur of Econ Rsch, Tokyo Cntr for Econ Rsch; Intl Econ Review. Hobbies: Stamp and Coin Collecting; Sports. Address: Institute of Social and Economic Research, Osaka University, 6-1 Mihogaoka, Ibaraki, Osaka 567-0047, Japan.

HORIUCHI Toshio, b. Feb 1918 Nara Pref. Politician. 4 s. Education: Nara Normal Sch. Appointments: Mayor of Tenri Cty, 1966; Parly Vice-Min of Econ Plng, 1979; Dep Sec-Gen Liberal Dem Party - LDP; Min of State; Dir-Gen Environment Agcy, 1987-88. Memberships: Mbr Nara Prefectural Ass; Mbr House of Cnclrs, 1976-.

HORN Barbara Constance, b. 19 June 1936, Maitland, NSW, Aust. Retired Company Director; Author. m. Ross G, 11 Oct 1958, 1 s, 1 d. Education: DipAgric. Appointments: Mngng Dir, Prydes Sweets Pty Ltd. Publications: Rambling Around Roses, 1981; Diary of Flowering Bulbs, 1984. Memberships: Hunter Valley Rose Soc, Treas, 1965-67; Maitland Embroiderers Inc, Pres, 1991-94. Hobbies: Gardening; Embroidery; Art; Reading.

HORNABROOK Richard William, b. 1 Dec 1925, Wellington. Physician. m. Fay Marshall, 2 s, 1 d. Education: MD, NZ, 1955; MB, CHB, 1949; FRACP, 1963. Appointments: Res Medl Offr, Natl Hosp Queen Sq, 1958-59; Assoc Prof, Neur, Cornell Univ, NY, 1960-61; Cnslt, Neurologist, Wellington, 1976-90; Dir, Papua New Guinea Inst Medl Rsch, 1969-75. Publications: Ed: Topicals in Tropical Neurology; Essays in Kuru. Memberships: Fell Roy Ent Soc, London; Australasian Assn Neurologists. Hobbies: Natural history; Gardening. Address: 27 Orchard Street, Wadestown, Wellington, New Zealand.

HORNBLOW Andrew Reed, b. 25 June 1942. Psychologist. m. Daphne Tui Skeels, 7 May 1966, 2 s, 1

d. Education: BA (Well); MA; Dip Clin Psych (Cant); PhD (Monash); FNZPsS. Appointments: Stud Cnsllr, Univ of Canterbury, 1971-74; Snr Tchng Fell, Lectr, Monash Univ, 1974-78; Snr Lectr, Assoc Prof, Prof of Pub Hlth, Dean, Christchurch Sch of Med, Univ of Otago, 1978-; Dean of CSM, 1994-. Publications: Over 60 sci publs in refereed jrnls and books in sev langs incl: The role of the community in assessment, prevention and intervention of suicide and attempted suicide, 1995; New Zealand's Health Reforms: A Clash of Cultures, 1997; Tomorrow's Doctors and Beyond: Medical Education in the UK, 1998. Honours: NZ 1990 Commemorative Medal; Elected Fell, NZ Psychol Soc, 1982; Elected Life Mbr, NZ Pub Hlth Assn, 1994; Hon Fell, Lincoln Univ, 1996-. Memberships: NZ Psychol Soc, pres, 1986-91; Mental Hlth Fndn, chmn, 1981-86; Pub Hlth Assn, pres, 1980-81; Pub Hlth Comn, 1993-95; Hlth Rsch Cncl, 1995-; Alcohol Advsry Cncl NZ, 1999-. Listed in: New Zealand/Aotearoa Who's Who. Hobbies: Walking; Tramping. Address: 32 Puriri Street, Christchurch, New Zealand.

HORNE Colin James, b. 31 Oct 1912, Vic, Aust. Professor Emeritus of English. m. (1) Margaret Parsons, 1939, 4 s, (2) Cynthia Werfel, 1968. Education: MA Hons, Dip Ed, Melbourne Univ, 1931-34; MA, MLitt, Oxford Univ, Eng, 1935-39; MA, Adelaide Univ, 1958. Appointments: Tutor, Engl, Melbourne Univ, 1935; Aitchison Travelling Schl, 1935-37; War Mem Schl, Balliol Coll, 1937-39; Lectr, Queens Univ, Belfast, Northern Ireland, 1939-48; Univ of Leicester, Eng, 1948-53; Snr Lectr 1953-57; Prof, 1957-77 Dean, Fac of Arts, 1969-70, Adelaide Univ. Publications include: Swift on His Age, 1953; The Pelican Guide to English Literature, 1957-91; The Progress of Poetry, 1965; The Dunstan Decade, 1981; The Classical Temper in Western Europe, 1983. Honours: Patron, S Aust Eng Tchrs Assn, 1960- Order of Aust, 1979; Hon Life Mbr, Adelaide Fest; Fell, Austl Acady of Humanities, 1972-; Hon Life Mbr, Mt Lofty Dists Histl Soc. Memberships include: Intl Assn of Univ Profs of Engl; Pres, Friends of the State Lib of SA, 1982-94. Hobbies: Book collecting; Local History. Listed in: Many Including: Who's Who in Australia; Who's Who in the World; Australian Roll of Honour; The Dictionary of International Biography. Address: Woodstock, 12 Bracken Road, Stirling, SA 5152, Australia.

HORNE Dennis Edward, b. 3 Nov 1931. Private Consultant. m. Brenda Joy Hembury, 14 Oct 1978, 2 d. Education: Dip Educ (Dist), London Univ; Tchrs Cert of Educ, (Dist), Nottingham Univ; Theory and Practice of Educ, (Hons), Loughborough. Appointments: Secondary Educ Tchr, Eng, 1953-65; Hd of Phys Educ Dept of a number of schs, Eng, 1957-65; Sales Rep, Light Engrng Co, Eng, 1964-65; Tech Rep, Cntrl Cncl of Phys Recreation, 1965-68; Asst Sec, Gtr London and SE Sports Cncl, Eng, 1968-70; Asst Dir, Natl Fitnes Cncl, S Aust, 1970-75; Acting Dir Natl Fitness Cncl, 1975-76; Mngr, Tech Advsry Servs, Dept of Recreation and Sport, S Aust Govt, 1976-90; Snr Recreation Offr, 1976-77, Snr Facilities Offr, 1977-78, Dept Recreation and Sport; Mngr, Facilities and Spec Projects, Off for Recreation, Sport and Racing, SA Govt, 1990-94. Publications: Trampolining - A Complete Handbook, 1968, reprint 1970, new ed 1978; Your Book of Trampolining, 1970; The Other Man's Sport, 1968; The Basic Mechanics Involved in Trampolining; Jump for Joy; Trampolining; Trampolining for Divers; Diving: Pre-Season Training; The Techniques of Springboard & Highboard Diving; The How and Why of Take-off for Springboard Diving; Sports Injuries and their Relation to the Selection of a Suitable Sports Surface; An Introduction to the Use of Psychology in Coaching, 1999. Honours: Patron and Life Mbr, S Aust Trampoline Assn, 1971-; Patron and Life Mbr, S Aust Swimming Tchrs Assn, 1978-; Patron and Life Mbr, Intl Swimming Tchrs Assn, Aust Br, 1980-; S Aust Achievers Awd, 1992; Intl Trampoline Fed, Pub Awd, 1973. Hobbies: Reading; Music; All Sports; Odd Jobbing around the home. Address: 21 Minerva Crescent, Modbury Heights, SA 5092, Australia.

HORNE Donald Richmond, b. 26 Dec 1921. Author; Lecturer. m. Myfanwy Gollan, 22 Mar 1960, 1 s, 1 d. Education: Sydney Univ; Canberra Univ Coll. Appointments: Ed, 1958-61, The Observer, 1960-62, The Bulletin; Contbng Ed, Newsweek Intl; Co-ed, Quadrant, 1963-66; Creative Dir, Jackson Wain Advtng, 1963-66; Rsch Fell, Assoc Prof, Prof, Univ of NSW, 1973-86; Emer Prof, 1987-; Chmn, Aust Cncl, 1985-90; Chmn, Ideas for Aust Prog, 1991-93; Chanc, Univ of Canberra, 1992-95. Publications: The Lucky Country, 1964; The Permit, 1965; The Education of Young Donald, 1967; God is an Englishman, 1969; The Next Australia, 1970; But What If There Are No Problems? 1971; Money Made Us, 1976; Death of the Lucky Country, 1976; His Excellency's Pleasure, 1977; Right Way, Don't Go Back, 1978; In Search of Billy Hughes, 1979; Time of Hope, 1980; Winner Takes All, 1981; The Great Museum, 1984; Confessions of a New Boy, 1985; The Story of the Australian People, 1985; The Public Culture, 1986; The Lucky Country Revisited, 1987; Portrait of an Optimist, 1988; Ideas for a Nation, 1989; The Coming Republic, 1992; The Intelligent Tourist, 1993; The Avenue of the Fair Go, 1997; An Interrupted Life, 1998. Honours: AO, 1982; DLitt Hons, Univ of NSW, 1981; Emer Prof, Univ of NSW, 1987; DUniv, Griffith Univ, 1988; Fell, Aust Acady of Hums, 1995; Hon DLitt Univ of Canberra, 1996. Memberships: Advsry Bd, Aust Ency, 1973-89; Chmn 1987-89; NSW Cultural Grants Advsry Cttee, 1976-79; Pres, Austl Soc of Auths, 1984-85; Chmn, Copyright Agcy, 1983-84; Exec Govt Cttee, Austl Constl Commn, 1985-87; Austl Citizenshp Cncl, 1998-. Address: 53 Grosvenor Street, Woollahra, Sydney, NSW 2025, Australia.

HORNE Paul Anthony, b. 21 Mar 1956, Eng. Entomologist. m. Janet, 4 Mar 1989, 1 s, 1 d. Education: BS (Hons); PhD (La Trobe). Appointments: La Trobe Univ, Antarctic Div; Rural Water Commn; Dept of Agric; IPM Technols P/L. Publication: (book) Backyard Insects, 1996. Membership: Hon Rsch Assoc, Ballarat Univ, 1997-2000. Hobby: Mountaineering. Address: IPM Technologies P/C, PO Box 560, Hurstbridge, Australia 3099.

HORNER David Murray, b. 12 Mar 1948, Adelaide, Aust. Military Historian. m. Sigrid, 12 Apr 1973, 1 s, 2 d. Education: Dip, Mil Stdies; MA; PhD. Appointments: Austl Army, 1966-90; Rsch Offr, 1990-94, Fell, 1994-96, Snr Fell, 1996-, Austl Natl Univ; Hd, Land Warfare Stdies Cntr, Austl Army, 1998-. Publications include: The Gunners: A History of Australian Artillery, 1995; Inside the War Cabinet, 1996; Blamey: The Commander-in-Chief, 1998; Breaking the Codes (co-auth), 1998. Hobbies: Choir; Australian Football; Cricket; Squash. Address: Strategic and Defence Studies Centre, Australian National University, Canberra, ACT 0200, Australia.

HOROWITZ David Charles, b. 30 June 1937, Bronx, NY, USA. Consumer Advocate; Journalist. m. Suzanne, 26 Aug 1973, 2 d. Education: AB, Jrnlsm, Bradley Univ, Peoria, IL, 1959; Medill Sch of Jrnlsm, NW Univ, Evanston, IL, 1961; Postgrad, Columbia Univ, NYC. Publications: Fight Back! and Don't Get Ripped Off, 1979; The Business of Business, 1989; Fight Back! For Your Medical Health, 1993; Fight Back! At Work, 1994. Honours: Angel Awd, Ex in Media, 1998; Golden Halo Awd, Career Achievement, Motion Picture Cncl of S CA, 1998; Quality of Life Awd, Proctor Hlth Care Fndn, 1998; Lifetime Achievement Awd, Kern Cnty Law Enforcement Fndn, 1999. Memberships: Overseas Press Club; Soc of Profl Jrnlsts; Soc of Consumer Affairs Profls; AFTRA; Screen Actors Guild; Writers Guild; Natl News Features Assn. Hobbies: Writing; Photography; Gardening; Theatre; Music; Collecting Contemporary Art; Travel. Address: PO Box 49915, Los Angeles, CA 90049-0915, USA.

HOSER Raymond Terrence, b. 8 Feb 1962, UK. Zoologist. Education: 2/3 BS, Sydney Univ; Var dips. Appointments: Pres, Austls Against Corruption; Cttee positions on about 50 other socs. Publications: Australian Reptiles and Frogs, 1989; Endangered Animals of Australia, 1991; Smuggled - The Underground Trade in Australia's Wildlife, 1993; The Hoser Files - The Fight Against Entrenched Official Corruption, 1995; Co-auth, about 15 other books; Over 130 sci pprs, mainly to do w reptiles. Memberships: Over 100. Hobbies: Reptiles (herpetology); Corruption in Government; Wildlife Conservation. Address: 41 Village Avenue, Doncaster, Vic 3108, Australia.

HOSHINO Eiichi, b. 29 May 1953, Tokyo. Education. m. Michiyo Avakowa, m. 18 Apr 1993. Education: BA, Eng, Sofia Univ, 1976; MA, Law and Pol Sc, Seikei Univ, 1980; MA, Intl Studies, Univ of Denver, 1990. Appointments: Asst Prof, Univ of the Ryaleyus, 1990-91; Assoc Prof, 1991-98; Prof, 1998-. Publications: Debating Human Rights in the US and Asia; China in the 20th Century Tokyo, 1994. Memberships: Intl Studies Assoc; Amn Pol Sc Assn; Japanese Assn of Intl Rels. Address: Department of Political Science and International Relations, Faculty of Law and Letters, University of the Ryukyus, Nishihara, Nakagami, Okinawa 903-0213, Japan.

HOSKING John William, b. 15 Feb 1940. Chem. m. (1) Helen Rowsell, 10 Aug 1963, dec 1987, (2) Janis Ward, 4 Mar 1989, 1 s, 2 d. Education: BSc (Hons), 1962, MSc, 1963, PhD, 1967, Univ Sydney. Appointments: Post Doct Rsch, 1966, 1967; Vanderbilt Univ, Univ NC, Stanford Univ; Univ of West Aust, 1968-70; Lectr, Snr Lectr, West Aust Inst of Technol, 1971-84; Chf, Govt Chem Lab, 1984-88; Dir, Chem Cntr, West Aust, 1988-. Publications: Over 20 sci pprs, 1965-96. Memberships: Fell, Royal Austl Chem Inst, WA Branch Pres, 1983-84; Natl Pres, 1991; Fell, Austl Inst of Mining and Metall; Cncl Mbr, Natl Assn Testing Authorities. Listed in: Australian Men and Women of Science, Engineering and Technology; Who is Who The Way, 1979. Hobbies: Rotary; Tennis; Squash. Address: 11/240 Burke Drive, Attadale, WA 6156, Australia.

HOSKING Michael Desmond, b. 6 July 1959, Singapore. Businessman. m. Rona, 6 July 1997, 1 s. Education: St John's Coll Southsea, Hants UK. Appointments: Estab Midas Promotions in Bahrain, 1978; Opened Asia Offs, 1992. Creative works: Promoted the following: Manchester Utd Asian Tour, 1986; Harlem Globetrotters Mid E Tour, 1989; Paula Abdul in Asia, 1992; Bryan Adams in Asia (1st ever rock concert in Vietnam), 1994; Roxette (inclng China), 1995; Michael Jackson, 1996; Sting, 1996; Boyzone, 1997; Ricky Martin, 1998. Honours: Invited to talk at Midem (Cannes), 1996; MTV Times of India Music Forum, 1998; Sony Music Conf (Singapore), 1997. Hobbies: Manchester United (travels to UK to watch them); Golf; Tennis; Scuba; Family. Address: 112 Sherwood Heights, Jerusalem Street, Multinational Village, Parañaque, Philippines.

HOSKINS Cedric Howard, b. 25 May 1929, Cheviot, NZ. Anaesthetist; Businessman. m. Doreen, 29 Oct 1955, 4 d. Education: MB ChB, Univ of NZ, 1954; FFA, RCS (Dip of Fell, Fac of Anaesthetists, Roy Coll of Surgs), June 1970. Appointments: Trng posts in med and anaesthesia in NZ, London and Sweden, 1955-65; Specialist Anaesthetist, Auckland Area Hlth Bd, 1965-93; Priv Specialist Anaesthetic prac, 1969-98; Mbr, Bd of Trees, Lavington Trust Hosp, 1975-81; Dir, Auckland Surg Cntr Ltd (Day Stay Surg), 1986-89. Publications: Requirements for a Free Standing Day Stay Centre in Anaesthesia for a Day Case Surgery, 1990, History of the Asian and Australasian Regional Section of the World Federation of Societies of Anaesthesilogists, 1962-90. Memberships: Sec, 1968-69, Pres, 1977-79, NZ Soc of Anaesthetists; Chmn, 1978-82, Sec, 1979-86, Bd of Asian and Australasian Regl Sect of the World Fedn of Socs of Anaesthesiologists; Mbr, NZ Regl Cttee, Fac of Anaesthetists, Roy Australasian Coll of Surgs, 1980-92, chmn, 1990-92; Mbr, (repr, NZ, Aust, S Pacific Is), Exec Cttee of 1984-92, VP, WFSA, 1992-96; Vice-Chmn,, Organising Cttee, 6th Asian and Australasian Congress of Anaesthesiolgists, Auckland, 1982; Hobbies: Yachting; Rear Commodore, Royal Akarana Yacht Club, 1986-88, 1990-91. Address: 6 Appleyard Crescent, Meadowbank, Auckland 1005, New Zealand.

HOSOKAWA Morihiro, b. 14 Jan 1938 Tokyo. Politician. m. Kayoko Hosokawa, 1 s, 2 d. Education:

Sophia Univ Tokyo. Appointments: Reporter The Daily Asahi Shimbun; Gov of Kumamoto, 1983-91; Fndr Chmn Japan New Party, 1992; PM, 1993-94. Memberships: Fmr mbr Liberal Dem Party - LDP; Mbr House of Cnclrs, 1971-83. Hobbies: Skiing; Golf. Address: House of Representatives, Ciyoda-ku, Tokyo 100, Japan.

HOSPITAL Janette Turner, b. 12 Nov 1942, Melbourne, Aust. Author. m. Clifford, 5 Feb 1965, 1 s, 1 d. Education: BA (Engl), Univ of Qld, Aust, 1965; MA (Medieval Lit), Queen's Univ, Can, 1973. Appointments: Hs Tchr, Queensland, 1963-66; Libn, Harvard Univ, 1967-71; Lectr in Engl, Kingston, Ont, 1971-82; Full-time Writer, 1982-; Writer in Res: MIT, 1985-86, winter/spring 1987, spring 1989; Univ of Ottawa, 1987; Univ of Sydney, 1989; Adj Prof, Engl, La Trobe Univ, Melbourne, 1990-93; Visng Prof in Writing, Boston Univ, 1991; Writer-in-Res, Queens Univ, Herstmonceaux Castle, UK, fall 1994; Visng Fell and Writer-in-Res, Sch of Engl & Amn Studies, Univ E Anglia, Eng, 1996. Publications: 6 novels: The Ivory Swing, 1982; The Tiger in the Tiger Pit, 1983; Borderline, 1985; Charades, 1988; The Last Magician, 1992; Oyster, 1996; 3 collections short stories: Dislocations, 1986; Isobars, 1990; Collected Stories, 1995; Num articles in intl publs. Honours include: First Prize, Mag Fiction, Fndn for Advmnt of Canad Letters, 1982; The Ivory Swing, $50,000 Seal First Novel Awd, 1982; Named in Can's Best 10 Younger Writers, 1986; Fiction Awd, Fellshp of Austl Writers for Dislocations, 1988; Best Short Stories, 1990, 1992, Heinemann, London, UK; Gold Medal for Travel, Natl Mag Awds, Can, 1991; The Last Magician, listed in Best 16 Novels of 1992, Most Notable Books of the Yr, NY Times, 1992. Address: C/o Jill Hickson, Literary Agent, POB 271, Woollahra, Sydney, NSW 2025, Australia.

HOTTA Kenji, b. 1 Aug 1945, Nagano, Japan. Professor. m. Hiromi, 10 Apr 1980, 2 s. Education: PhD, Engrng. Appointments: Vice Chmn, Engrng Cttee on Oceanic Resources (UNESCO, IOC); Bd Mbr, Pacific Congress on Marine Sci & Technol Intl (USA). Publications: Coastal Management in the Asia-Pacific Region: Issues and Approaches, 1995; Ocean Environment, 1999; 6 other books. Honours: Henry Adams Awd, AIA, USA, 1975; Louis P Price Awd, AIA, USA, 1975; DACON Intl Serv Awd, USA, 1990; Kozai Club Serv Awd on Educ, 1995. Memberships: Archtl Inst of Japan, 1968-; Soc of Naval Archts in Japan, 1980-. Hobbies: Fishing; Diving; Sports. Address: 4-1096-86 Minomi-cho Narashino-shi Chiba 2950002, Japan.

HOU Chaozhen, b. 21 Sept 1938, Sichuan, China. Teacher. m. Ningxi Hu, 15 Jan 1969, 2 s. Education: Grad, Beijing Inst of Technol, China, 1962. Appointments: Dir of Control Lab, 1984-90; Vice Chmn, Dept, 1990-97; Chf Prof, 1998-. Publications: Application Fundamentals of Microcomputer and Single-chip Computer, 1992; Distributed Computer Control Systems, 1997. Honours: Sci and Technol Progress Awds, Min of China, 1994; Tchng Awds of Beijing Inst of Technol of China, 1997. Hobbies: Swimming; Climbing mountains. Address: Department of Automatic Control, Beijing Institute of Technology, PO Box 327, Beijing 100081, China.

HOU Hsiao-hsien, b. 8 Apr 1947 Meihsien Canton Prov. Film Director. Education: Taipei Natl Acady of Arts (film and drama dept). Appointments: Wrked as an electronic calculator salesman; Entered film ind in 1973; Asst to sev dirs from 1974. Films incl: Chiu shih liu-liu-te t'a - Cute Girl - 1981; Feng-erh t'i t''a-ts'ai - Cheerful Wind - 1982; Tsai na ho-pan ch'ing ts'ao'ch'ing - Green Grass of Home - 1982; Erh-tzu-te ta wan-ou - The Sandwich Man - 1983; Feng-kuei-lai-te jen - The Boys from Fengkuei/All the Youthful Days - 1983; Tung-tung-te chia-ch'i - Summer at Grandpa's - 1984; Tung-nien wang-shih - The Time to Live and the Time to Die - 1985; Lien-lien feng-ch'en - Dust in the Wind/Rite of Passage - 1986; Ni-lo-ho nu-erh - Daughter of the Nile - 1987; Pei-ch'ing ch'eng-shih - A City of Sadness - 1989. Honours: Winner of Golden Lion at the Venice Film Fest.

HOU Jie, b. 1931 Luan Co Hebei Prov. Politician. Appointments: Joined CCP, 1948; Vice-Chmn

Revolutionary Cttee Heilongjiang Prov, 1977-78; Vice-Gov Heilongjiang, 1979-85; Sec CCP Cttee Heilongjiang, 1982-83; Dep Sec, 1985-88; Gov Heilongjiang, 1985-89; Dep 7th NPC, 1988-92; Vice-Min of Water Rescs, 1988-93; Dep 8th NPC, 1993-; Min of Constrn, 1993-; Fmr Vice-Dir Natl Greening Cttee and Capital Plng Cttee; Vice-Chmn Natl Afforestation Cttee. Memberships: Mbr 12th CCP Cntrl Cttee, 1985; Mbr 13th Cntrl Cttee, 1987-92; Mbr 14th CCP Cntrl Cttee, 1992-. Address: Ministry of Construction, Baiwanzhuang, Western Suburb, Beijing 100835, People's Republic of China.

HOU Tian Zhen, b. 5 Feb 1940, Hejin Shaxi, China. Biologist. m. Mao Guo Jing, 16 Nov 1969, 2 s. Education: Forestry and Soil Coll, Shenyang, 1960-64; Bach Deg, Inst of Fgn Lang, Xian, 1984-85; Univ MN, USA, 1986-87, 1991-93. Appointment: Dir, Dept of Forest Physiol and Biochem, Xinjiang Acady of Forestry Sci. Publications: Experimental Evidence of a Plant Meridian System, 1994. Honour: Great Achievement of Sci Technol, Xinjiang Govt, 1981. Memberships: Fell, Xinjiang Cttee of Biol Sci and Technol, 1985-88; Fell, China Cttee of Forest Physiol and Biochem, 1988-89. Hobby: Chinese chess. Address: Xinjiang Academy of Forestry Science, Xinjiang 830002, China.

HOUSE Lynda Mary, b. 30 Apr 1949. Film Producer. m. Tony Mahood, 23 Nov 1991. Appointments: Bd, Film Victoria, 1993-96; Bd, Austl Film Fin Corp, 1997- . Creative works: Producer: Proof, 1991; Muriels Wedding, 1994; River Street, 1996; The Missing, 1998. Honour: Best Film, Austl Film Inst, Proof, 1991, Muriels Wedding, 1994. Membership: SPAA, 1990-. Hobbies: Reading; Gardening. Address: House & Moorhouse Films, 117 Rouse Street, Port Melbourne, Vic 3207, Australia.

HOWARD David Andrew, b. 20 Aug 1959, Christchurch, NZ. 1 s. Education: Dip, Cabaret, Christchurch Acady, 1988; Ctf, Hazardous Substances, 1996. Appointments: Ed, Takahe, 1989-93, Des, C'wlth Hds of Govt Meeting, 1995; Proj Dir, Gisborne 2000, 1996-; Special Effects Supvsr, Metallica, 1998, Janet Jackson, 1998. Publications: In The First Place: 1980-1990; Holding Company, 1995; Gisborne 2000: A Design Prospectus, 1997. Honours: 1st Prize, NZ Poetry Soc Intl Comp, 1987; 1st Prize, Gordon and Gotech Poetry Awd, 1984. Memberships: NZ Guild of Des; NZ Soc of Auths. Hobbies: Films; Opera; Travel. Address: PO Box 90672, Auckland Mail Centre, Auckland, New Zealand.

HOWARD John Winston, b. 26 Jul 1939 Sydney. Politician. m. Alison Janette Parker, 1971, 2 s, 1 d. Education: Univ of Sydney. Appointments: Solicitor to Supreme Crt NSW, 1962; Partner Sydney solicitors' firm, 1968-74; VP NSW Div Liberal Party, 1972-74; Liberal MP for Bennelong NSW Fed Parl, 1974-; Min for Bus and Consumer Affairs, 1975-77; Min Asstng PM, 1977; Fed Treas, 1977-83; Dep Ldr of Opposition, 1983-85; Ldr of Opposition, 1985-89; Ldr Liberal Party, Sep 1985-89; Shadow Min for Indl Rels Employment and Trng; Shadow Min asstng the Ldr on the Pub Service; Chmn Manpower and Labour Market Reform Grp, 1990-95; Liberal Party, 1995-; PM of Aust, Mar 1996-. Memberships: Mbr State Exec NSW Liberal Party, 1963-74. Hobbies: Reading; Cricket; Tennis. Address: Department of the Prime Minister and Cabinet, 3-5 National Circuit, Barton, ACT 2600, Australia.

HOWARD Robert Wayne, b. 4 Sept 1953, Auckland, NZ. University Lecturer. Education: BA, MA, Auckland; PhD, Queensland. Membership: Cognitive Sci Soc. Hobbies: Chess; Travel; Music. Address: Education Faculty, University of Newcastle, Callaghan, NSW 2308, Australia.

HOWARD Ron, b. 1 Mar 1954, Duncan, OK, USA. Film Actor; Director. m. Cheryl Alley, 1975, 2 s, 2 d. Education: Univ of S CA; Los Angeles Valley Coll. Appointments: Regular TV series The Andy Griffith Show, 1960-68; The Smith Family, 1971-72; Happy Days, 1974; Dir co-auth star Grand Theft Auto, 1977; Many other TV

appearances. Films dir'd incl: Night Shift, 1974; Splash, 1984; Cocoon, 1985; Gung Ho, 1986; Return to Mayberry, 1986; Willow, 1988; Parenthood, 1989; Backdraft, 1991; Far and Away - also co-prodr - 1992; The Paper, 1994; Apollo 13, 1995. Film appearances incl: The Journey, 1959; Five Minutes to Live, 1959; Music Man, 1962; The Courtship of Eddie's Father, 1963; Village of the Giants, 1965; Wild County, 1971; Mother's Day; American Graffiti, 1974; The Spikes Gang; Eat My Dust, 1976; The Shootist, 1976; More American Graffiti, 1979; Leo and Loree - TV; Act of Love, 1980; Skyward, 1981; Through the Magic Pyramid - dir, exec prodr - 1981; When Your Lover Leaves - co-exec prodr - 1983; Return to Mayberry, 1986; Ransom, 1996. Honours: Outstndng Directorial Achmnt in Motion Picture Awd from Dirs Guild of Am for Apollo 13, 1996. Address: c/o Peter Dekom Bloom, Dekom & Hergott, 150 S Rodeo Drive, Beverly Hills, CA 90212, USA.

HOWAT Peter Aran, b. 23 Feb 1949, Hokitika, NZ. Professor. m. Jeanette Clark, 27 Dec 1975, 1 s, 1 d. Education: Dip Ed, Otago, 1970; BSc, Canterbury, 1971; Dip Tchng, Christchurch, 1971; MSc, Illinois, 1978; PhD, Illinois, 1979. Appointments: Tchr, Greymouth HS, NZ, 1972-75; Hd, Dept Health Promotion, Curtin Univ, Aust, 1980-; Co-Dir, Curtin Univ Cntr for Health Promotion Rsch; Austl Ed, Amn Jrnl of Health Behavior, 1991-. Publications: 150 refereed jrnl articles, book chapts, rprts and conf proceedings. Honours: Avery Brundage Schlsp, Univ of IL, 1978, 1979; Grad, Univ of IL MSc and PhD Progs; Natl Hon Soc, Phi Kappa Phi. Memberships: Austl Hlth Promotion Assn, Natl Sec, 1992-95; Pub Hlth Assn Aust, WA State Pres, 1993-95; Injury Control Cncl of W Aust, Pres, 1992-94. Hobbies: Trumpet; Golf; Rugby Union. Address: School of Public Health, Curtin University, GPO Box U1987, Perth, WA 6845, Australia.

HOWE Brian Leslie, b. 28 Jan 1936, Melbourne, Australia. Professor. m. Renate, 8 May 1962, 1 s, 2 d. Education: BA; MA. Appointments: Snr Lectr, Min, Dpty PM. Membership: VP, Evatt Fndn, 1998. Hobbies: Golf; Cricket; Films. Address: 6 Brennard Street, North Fitzry 3068, Australia.

HOWE Yoon Chong, b. 1923 China. Politician; Banker. m. 3 c. Education: St Francis Inst Malacca; Raffles Coll; Univ of Malaya in Singapore. Appointments: Fmr civ servant; Sec to Pub Service Commn; CEO Housing and Dev Bd, 1960; Perm Sec Mins of Fin and Natl Dev; Dep Chmn Econ Dev Bd; Chmn and Pres Dev Bank of Singapore concurrently Chmn and Gen Mngr Port of Singapore Authy; Perm Sec PM Off and Hd of Civ Service; Min of Def, 1979-82; Min of Hlth, 1982-84; Chmn and Chf Exec Dev Bank of Singapore, 1985-90; Chmn and Chf Exec Straits Trading Co Ltd, 1992-; Chmn Gt East Life Assurance Co Ltd, 1992-. Honours: Malaysia Medal; Meritorious Service Medal; Hon DLitt - Singapore. Memberships: Mbr Parl, 1979-84; Mbr Bd of Trustees Eisenhower Exchange Fellships Inc, 1980-90. Address: c/o Straits Trading Company Ltd, 9 Battery Road, 21-00 Straits Trading Building, Singapore, 049910.

HOWELL David, b. 26 Feb 1928, Sydney. Aust. Medical Specialist. m. Patricia Peet, 9 Dec 1953. Education: MBBS (Hons II), Univ of Sydney, Aust; FRCS Eng; FRCS Edin; FRACS; FRCOG London. Appointments: Visng Specialist, Univ of NSW Tchng Hosps, 1958-93. Publications: Childrens' Sports Injuries, 1989. Memberships: Austl Soc of Auths. Hobbies: Golf; Photography. Address: 12 Longworth Avenue, Point Piper, NSW 2027, Australia.

HOYOS (Bernard) Dexter, b. 17 Jan 1944, Barbados. University Academic. m. Jann Lesley Peterson, 24 Apr 1976, 1 d. Education: BA Hons, Univ of West Indies, Jamaica, 1966; MA, McMaster Univ, Can, 1967; DPhil, Oxford Univ, Eng, 1971. Appointments: Lectr 1972-78, Snr Lectr 1978-83, Assoc Prof 1984-, Acting Hd, Latin Dept 1981-82, Hd Dept 1983-90, Univ of Sydney; Ed, Classicum, 1977-90. Publications include: Unplanned Wars: The Origins of the First and Second Punic Wars, 1998; Latin: How to Read It Fluently, 1998; Articles in learned jrnls, tchrs' jrnls. Honours: Hawkins Prize,

Harrison Coll, Barbados, 1962; Barbados Schlsp, 1963; Postgrad Awd, McMaster Univ, 1966; UWI Stud of Yr, 1965; Juan de Osma Sclshp, Casa Del Velásquez, Madrid, 1970; Univ of Sydney Bronze Serv Medal, 1997. Memberships: Classical Assn of NSW; Classical Langs Tchrs Assn, NSW; Austl Soc for Classical Studies; Soc for Roman Studies, Eng; Amn Classical League. Listed in Who's Who in Australia. Hobbies: History; Current affairs; Geography; Travel; Family; Landscape. Address: 7 Dalleys Road, Naremburn, NSW 2065, Australia.

HRAWI Elias, b. 1930, Zahle, Lebanon. Politician; Businessman; President of Lebanon. Appointments: Fmr Maronite Christian Dpty; Pres of Lebanon, 1989-. Address: Office of the President, Baabda, Beirut, Lebanon.

HRUBY Joy, b. 1 July 1927, Taree, NSW, Aust. Actress; Writer; Producer. m. 1 Sept 1954, 1 s, 2 d. Education: Dip in Dramatic Art, Whitehall Acady, 1948; Licentiate Dip, Trinity Coll of London, 1968; Dip, Hector Crawford Sch of Radio, 1950. Appointments: J C Williamsons Touring Co, 1949-52; Num appearances on stage, film, radio and tv; Creator and Dir, Studio J Theatrical Agcy, 1968-88; Exec Dir and Patron, Cable TV CTV-1, 1990; Music Th Lectre, Univ Sydney; Dir, Joy's Creative Mngmt, multi-cultural medial theat agcy, 1995-; Presenter, Around the World on Saturday Night, for Community TV Sydney. Creative Works: Writer, Prodr, Dir, Sydney Children's Theatre Fairy Stories; Zipman Meets the Dubbo Dazzlers; A School is Born (History of La Perouse School); Producer over 400 Live-to-Air progs on CTV-1. Honours: Gold Medal, Best Tchr's Dip in Trinity of London, 1968; Critics Awd for Best Supporting Actress, 1973; Openfield Documentary featuring Joy Hruby's work in Agcy and Have a Go Show. Memberships: Actors Equity; Randwick Historical Soc; Prompters; Austl Film Inst; Speech and Drama Assn; Aboriginal Evangelical Fellshp Mbr; Drama Dept, Wesley Inst for Min and the Arts; Drama Dept, Actors Coll of Theatre and TV. Hobbies: Writing; Producing; Gardening; Church; Theatre. Address: 48 Elaroo Avenue, Philip Bay, NSW 2036, Australia.

HSIANG Chin-min, (Xiang Jin-min), b. 28 Jan 1914, Hanchwan, Hebei, China. Professor of Virology and Immunology. m. 24 July 1957, 3 s. Education: Dip, Natl Army Med Coll, 1942; Brock Army Med Cntr, San Antonio, TX, USA, 1946-47; Univ TX Med Br, Galveston, USA, 1949-54. Appointments: Asst NAMC, 1942-46; Lectr, Natl Ctrl Univ Med Coll, 1947-48; Assoc Prof, Hubei Med Coll, 1949-54 (on leave from Univ TX Med Br, Galveston); Prof, Wuhn Univ, 1954-78; Dir, Virus Rsch Inst, 1978-88, Hubei Medl Univ; Rsch Prof, Inst of Virol, Academia Sinica, 1960-65. Publications: Books: Cell and Tissue Culture, 1965; Fundamental Immunology, 1978; Medical Virology, 1986; Recent Advances in Medical Virology, 1987; Medical Virology, 3rd ed, 1986, 1990; Molecular Ecology, 1995; Molecular Ecology, Vol II, 1999; Auth of about 200 articles published in Chinese and English. Honours: Delegation to Natl Conf of Med and Pharm Scis, Min of Hlth, 1978; John E Fogarty Intl Cntr Awd as Visng Sci to NIH, 1983-84; Hon Ctf, Min of Hlth, 1987; Hon Ctf, Chinese Med Assn, 1987; Friendshp Medal, US Army Med Rsch Inst of Infectious Diseases, 1988; Hon Ctf for Acady Serv over 40 yrs, 1990; Med for Ex Achmnts in Advs of Scis and Technol, Natl Sci Cttee and Natl Educl Cttee, 1990; Prize, Achmnt in Rsch, Natl Educl Cttee, 1990; Hon Dir, Molecular Ecol Lab, Medl Sch, Hubei Medl Univ; 2nd Class Awd and Certificate, Hubei Prov Sci Cttee, 1998. Memberships: Pres, China Soc of Molecular Ecol; Life Mbr, Chinese Med Assn; Advsr, Hubei Med Br of Chinese Medl Assn; Chmn, Wuhan Soc of Virol; Standing Cttee, Wuhan Med Soc; Sci Cttee, Viral Diseases and Virol, Min of Hlth China; Vice Chmn, Hubei Prov Soc of Genetics; Chinese Soc of Microbio. Hobbies: Music; Sports. Address: Cell Biology and Molecular Ecology Laboratories, Virus Research Institute, Hubei Medical University, Wuchang, Hubei, China 430071.

HSIU-YING Shen Yu, b. 12 July 1936, Taipei, Taiwan, China. Professor. m. Yu-Zen Shen, 1 Oct 1961, 2 s, 1 d. Education: PhD, Pharm Scis, Univ of Tokyo, Japan.

Appointments: Editl Cttee, Chinese Pharmacopoeia, 3rd ed; Trustee: The Chen's Pharmaceutical Rsch Fndn. Honour: Annual Excellent Rsch Achievement Awd, Natl Sci Cncl, China, 1984-. Memberships: Intl Pharm Assn; Pharm Soc, China; Japan Soc of DDS. Address: School of Pharmacy, College of Medicine, National Taiwan University, 1 Jen-Ai Road, Section 1, Taipei, 100 Taiwan, China.

HSU Ching-Chung, b. 19 Jul 1907 Taipei. Politician. m. Huang Tsen, 2 s, 1 d. Education: Taipei Acady Taipei Imperial Univ. Appointments: Prof Natl Taiwan Univ, 1945-47; Dir Agricl and Forestry Admin Taiwan Provincial Govt, 1947-49; Commnr Dept of Agric and Forestry Taiwan Provincial Govt, 1949-54; Commnr, 1954-57; Dep Sec-Gen Cntrl Cttee, 1961-66; Min of the Interior, 1966-72; Vice-Premier of Exec Yuan, 1972-81. Publications: Sev studies on agricl problems in Taiwan. Honours: Medal of Clouds and Banner. Memberships: Mbr Standing Cttee Taiwan Land Bank, 1946-67; Mbr Cntrl Plng and Evaluation Cttee China Nationalist Party, 1955-61; Mbr China Farmers' Bank, 1967-72. Hobbies: Horticulture; Reading; Painting; Golf. Address: 180 Yenping S Road, Taipei, Taiwan.

HSU Li-Teh, b. 6 Aug 1931 Loshan Co Honan. Politician. m. 2 s. Education: Taiwan Provincial Coll of Law and Com; Natl Chengchi Univ; Harv Univ. Appointments: Dir Fifth Dept Taiwan Govt, 1972-76; Admin Vice-Min of Fin, 1976-78; Commnr Dept of Fin Taiwan Provincial Govt, 1978-81; Min of Fin, 1981-84; Min of Econ Affairs, 1984-85; Chmn Lien-ho Jnr Coll of Tech; Chmn Global Invmnt Holding Co Ltd, 1986-88; Chmn Fin Commn Cntrl Cttee Kuomintang, 1988-93; Dep Sec-Gen and Exec Policy Co-ord Commn Cntrl Cttee Kuomintang, 1990-93; Vice-Premier of Taiwan, 1993-97. Address: c/o National Assembly, Taipei, Taiwan.

HSU Paul S P, b. 25 March 1939, Hong Kong. Attorney. m. Pat Tsao, 1 s. Education: MA, Fletcher Sch of Law and Diplomacy, Tufts Univ; LLB, Natl Taiwan Univ; LLM, NY Univ Sch of Law. Appointments: Snr Ptnr, Lee & Li, Taiwan; Prof of Law, Natl Taiwan Univ, 1969-; Exec Dir, Epoch Fndn; Chmn, Asia Fndn, Taiwan; Dir Bd, ROC-USA Econ Cncl; Chmn, ROC-NZ Bus Cncl; Dir of Bd, Europe Asia Trade Org; Mbr, Asia Soc's Corp Cncl and Intl Cncl. Publications: 13 pprs and tech reports. Memberships: Cnslt, Exec Yuan; Mbr, Natl Competitiveness Enforcement Task Force, Exec Yuan; Cnslt, Privatisation Cttee, Exec Yuan; Ind Tech Plng and Assessment Cttee, Min Econ Affairs; Finl Reform Cttee, Min Fin; Advsry Cttee, APEC Cntr, Min For Affairs; and others. Hobbies: Research on war history; Jazz music; Hunting. Address: c/o Lee & Li, 7th Floor, 201 Tun Hua N Rd, Taipei 105, Taiwan, ROC.

HSU Shui-Teh, b. 1 Aug 1931 Kaohsiung Cty. Politician. m. Yang Shu-hua, 2 s. Education: Natl Taiwan Normal Univ; Natl Chengchi Univ; Japan Univ of Educ. Appointments: Offic Pingtung Co Govt, 1968-70; Offic Kaohsiung Cty Govt, 1970-75; Commnr Dept of Socl Affairs Taiwan Provincial Govt, 1975-79; Dir Dept of Socl Affairs Cntrl Cttee Kuomintang, 1979; Sec-Gen Kaohsiung Cty Govt, 1979-82; Mayor of kaohsiung, 1982-85; Mayor of Taipei, 1985-88; Min of the Interior, 1988-91; Rep Taipei Econ and Culture Rep Off in Japan, 1991-93. Publications: The Childhood Education of Emile; My Compliments - Recollections of Those Days Serving as Kaohsiung Mayor; A Thousand Sunrises and Midnights; My Scoopwheel Philosophy; A Study of Welfare Administration for the Aged; Sev wrks on psychol and educ. Honours: Hon LLD - Lincoln Univ - 1985. Address: c/o Kuomintang, 53 Jen Ai Road, Section 3, Taipei, Taiwan.

HSU Tzu-Chi, b. 2 Apr 1948, Taipei. Physician; Surgeon. m. Chien-Hui, 1 s, 2 d. Education: MD, Taipei Medl College. Address: 3F #8 Ln 10 Sect II, Chin-San South Rd, Taipei, Taiwan.

HU Bo, b. 5 Dec 1968, Chengdu, Sichuan, China. Lecturer. m. Bu Xiao, 26 May 1997. Education: BA, Biomed Electrons, 1986-90; Dr, Radio Electrons,

1993-96, Fudan Univ. Appointments: Visng Schl, Hong Kong Univ of Sci and Technol, 1994-96; Lectr, Fudan Univ, 1997-. Membership: Chinese Inst of Electrons. Hobbies: Music; Badminton; Computer Games. Address: c/o CAT Laboratory, Department of Electronic Engineering, Fudan University, #220 Handan Road, Shanghai 200433, China.

HU Jason C, b. 15 May 1948, Yungchi Co, Kirin, China. Minister of Foreign Affairs. m. 1 s, 1 d. Education: LLB, Diplomacy, Natl Chengchi Univ, 1970; Master of Socl Scis in Pol, Univ of Southampton, Eng, 1978; DPhil, Intl Stdies, Oxford Univ, 1984. Appointments: Exec Sec, Natl Union of Studs, China, 1966-68; China Deleg Ldr, UN World Yth Assembly, 1970; Chmn, Chinese Acad and Profl Assn, UK, 1984-85; Rsch Fell, St Anthony's Coll, Rschr, Cntr for Mod Chinese Stdies, Oxford Univ, 1985; Assoc Prof, Sun Yat-sen Inst for Interdisciplinary Stdies, Dpty Dir, Sun Yat-sen Cntr for Plcy Stdies, Natl Sun Yat-sen Inst, 1985-90; Dpty Sec-Gen, Soc for Strategic Stdies, China, 1989; Dpty Dir, 1st Bur, Off of the Pres, Preditl Press Sec, 1991; Dir-Gen, Govt Info Off, Exec Yuan, China Govt Spokesman, 1991-96; Rep, Taipei Econ and Cultural Rep Off in USA, 1996-97; Min For Affairs, 1997-.

HU Jia Xun, b. Feb 1939, Bijie, Guizhou, China. Composer. m. Zhangchen Fen, Jan 1968, 2 s. Education: Coll Deg. Creative Works: The Crooked Horns of an Old Buffalo (song); Probing the Sources of the Structural features (ppr); Investigation on Sitting on the Moon Activity of Miao People (ppr). Honours: 2nd Prize, Natl Songs Selection, Min of Culture, Min of Educ, Min of Broadcasting, Film and TV. Membership: China Musician Assn, 1988. Hobby: Photography. Address: No 2 Primary School, Bijie, 441700 Guizhou, China.

HU Jintao, b. Dec 1942, Jixi Co, Anhui Prov, China. Party and State Official. Education: Qinghua Univ. Appointments: Joined CCP, 1964; Dir Constrn Commn Gansu Prov Govt, 1982; Sec Gansu Prov Branch Communist Yth League, 1982; Sec Communist Yth League, 1982; Pres Soc of Young Pioneers Wrk, 1984-; A VP China Intl Cultural Exchange Cntr, 1984-; Sec CCP Cttee Guizhou, 1985-88; Sec CCP Cttee Tibet, Dec 1988- 98; Sec Secr 14th CCP Cntrl Cttee, 1992-; Pres Cntrl Party Sch, 1993; Vice-Chmn CCP Organizational Cttee, 1993-; Hd Cntrl Ldng Grp for Party Bldg Wrk; VP of People's Repub of China, 1998-. Memberships: Alt Mbr 12th CCP Cntrl Cttee, 1982 and Mbr, 1985; Mbr Standing Cttee 6th NPC; Mbr Presidium; Mbr Standing Cttee CPPCC 6th Natl Cttee, 1983-98; Mbr 13th CCP Cntrl Cttee, 1987-92; Perm Mbr CCP Politburo, 1992-; Mbr 14th CCP Cntrl Cttee, 1992-97; Mbr 15th CCP Cntrl Cttee, 1997-; Mbr 7th Natl Cttee, 1998-. Address: Central Committee of the Chinese Communist Party, 1 Zhong Nan Hai, Beijing, People's Republic of China.

HU Lijiao, b. 1914 Jiangxi. Party Official. m. Gu Min, 1 s. Appointments: Joined CCP, 1930; Took part in Long March as mbr Little Devils, 1934; Dpty Dir Org Dept E China Bur, 1950; Vice-Chmn People's Control Cttee E China Mil and Admin Cncl - ECMAC - 1951; Dir Personnel Dept ECMAC, 1951; Vice-Chmn Labour Employment Cttee ECMAC, 1952; Vice-Min of Fin, 1954-58; Sec CCP Cttee Min of Fin, 1954-58; Prin Cadres Sch Min of Fin, 1957-58; 1st Sec Secr Songjiang Dist Heilongjiang CP, 1958; Dep Dir People's Bank of China, 1961-66; Acting Pres, 1966; Disappeared during Cultural Revolution; Dep Sec CCP Cttee Henan, 1975-77; 2nd Sec, 1977-; Vice-Chmn Prov Revolutionary Cttee Henan, 1977-79; Chmn Standing Cttee People's Congress Henan, 1979; 2nd Sec CCP Cttee Shanghai, 1981-85; Chmn Municipal People's Congress Shanghai, 1981-; Dep to 3rd 5th and 6th NPC. Memberships: Mbr 11th CCP Cntrl Cttee, 1977; Mbr 12th CCP Cntrl Cttee, 1982-85; Mbr Presidium 6th NPC, 1986; Mbr Cntrl Advsry Commn CCP, 1987-. Hobbies: Tennis; Swimming; Chess. Address: 200 The People's Square, Shanghai, People's Republic of China.

HU Ping, b. 1930 Jiaxing Co, Zhejiang Prov, China. Government Official. Education: Jiangsu Ind Inst.

Appointments: Joined CCP, 1950; Vice-Gov of Fujian, 1981-83; Sec CCP Prov Cttee Fujian, 1982; Dpty Sec, CCP Prov Cttee Fujian, 1982; Dir, Fujian Cttee for Econ Reconstrn, 1983; Sec CCP Prov Cttee, 1982-83; Acting Gov of Fujian, 1983; Gov, 1983-87 - removed from post; Chmn Bd of Regents Overseas Chinese Univ, 1986; Vice-Min State Plng Commn, 1987-88; Min of Com, 1988-93; Dir Spec Econ Zones Off, 1993-96. Memberships: Alt mbr 12th CCP Cntrl Cttee, 1982; Mbr, 1985; Mbr 13th CCP Cntrl Cttee, 1987-92; Mbr 14th CCP Cntrl Cttee, 1992-. Address: c/o Ministry of Commerce, 45 Fuxingmen Nei Dajie, Beijing 100801, People's Republic of China.

HU Qili, b. 1929 Yulin Co Shaaxi Prov. Politician. 1 s, 1 d. Appointments: Sec Communist Yth League - CYL - Cttee Beijing Univ, 1954; Vice-Chmn Students' Fedn, 1954; Sec CYL, 1964, 1978; Vice-Chmn Yth Fedn, 1965; Purged, 1967; VP Qinghua Univ Beijing, 1978; Sec CYL, 1978; Chmn Yth Fedn, 1979-82; Mayor Tianjin, 1979-82; Sec CCP Cttee Tianjin, 1981-82; Dir Gen Off Cntrl Cttee CCP, 1982; Elected to Politburo, 1985; Sec Secr CCP, 1982; Vice-Chmn Cntrl Party Consolidation Commn, 1983-89; Dep 7th NPC, 1988-; Vice-Min of Electronics Ind and Mach-Bldg Ind, 1991-93; Min of Electrons Ind, 1993-98. Memberships: Mbr Standing Cttee Yth Fedn, 1958; Mbr Standing Cttee 5th CPPCC, 1979-83; Mbr 12th CCP Cntrl Cttee, 1982; Mbr Politubro Standing Cttee, 1987-89; Mbr Presidium 1st sess 7th NPC, 1988-; Mbr 14th CCP Cntrl Cttee, 1992-97. Hobbies: Tennis; Cycling. Address: c/o Ministry of Electronics Industry, 48 Sanlihe Road, Beijing 100823, People's Republic of China.

HU Qiquan, b. 30 Mar 1942, Jiangsu, Suzhou, China. Scientific Research. m. Wu Huaiying, 4 Feb 1970, 1 s, 1 d. Education: Grad, Univ of Sci and Technol, China, 1964; Visng Schl, Univ of Paris, 1978. Appointments: Asst Prof, 1978, Assoc Prof, 1986, Prof, 1992, Dpty Dir, 1997, Shanghai Inst of Optics and Fine Mechs. Publications include: Solid State Laser, 1975. Honours: Natl Sci Awd of China, 1978; Natl Sci and Technol Progress Specl Grade Awd of China, 1985. Memberships: Optics Assn of China; Vice Dir, Shanghai Infrared and Remote Sensing and Laser Assn, 1996. Hobbies: Music; Literature; Art. Address: PO Box 800-211, Shanghai 201800, China.

HU Richard W X, b. 17 Oct 1957, Nanjing, China. Professor. Education: PhD, Polit Sci. Appointment: Assoc Prof, Dept of Polit and Pub Admin, Univ Hong Kong. Memberships: ISA; APSA. Address: University of Hong Kong, Pokfulam Road, Hong Kong.

HU Shi Zhen, b. 3 Aug 1932, Shanghai, China. Teacher. m. 1959. Education: Grad, Peking Univ, 1956. Appointments: Assoc Prof, 1983, Prof, 1991-. Publications: On Resources Contribution Value Theory, 1994; How to Realize Price Rising in Our Country, 1997; Query the Validity of the Principle of Distribution According to Work, 1997; Socialist Primary Period and Stock System, 1998. Memberships: Cncl, Capital Rsch Assn of High Fin-Econ Coll-Univ of China, 1988-. Hobbies: Music; Arts. Address: c/o Economics Department, College of Economics, Jinan University, Guangzhou 510632, China.

HU Weilue, b. 9 July 1937, Wuhan Cty, Hubei Prov, China. Research Fellow; Professor. m. Liu Xiuwen, 11 May 1965, 4 d. Education: BA, Beijing Univ. Appointments: Univ Tchr, 1960-80; Chf, Population Rsch Off, Beijing Educ Coll, 1980-88; Chf, Population and Econs Dept, Population Rsch Inst, CASS, 1988-98. Publications: The Oasis of Demography, 1982; China's Population, 1993; China's Old Population and Economy, 1993; A Study on China's Family Economy and Fertility, 1997; Human Resources Study, 1998. Memberships: Prof, Grad Sch, CASS; Dir, China Population Assn; Dir, China Soc Econ Culture Exchange Assn; INSSP. Hobbies: Literature; Arts; Music; Volleyball. Address: Population Research Institute, Chinese Academy of Social Sciences, 5 Jian Guv Men Nei Street, Beijing 100732, China.

HU Yisan, b. 12 Feb 1941, Henan, China. Flood Control Engineer. m. Li Fengxian, 12 Jan 1968, 1 s, 1 d. Education: Grad, Hydraulic Engrng, Tianjin Univ. Appointments: Yellow River Conservancy Commn for Flood Control and River Regulation, 1964-; Vice Chf Engr, Yellow River Conservancy Cmmn, 1987-. Publications: The Yellow River Volume of Flood Control in China Series, 1996; Flood Control in the Yellow River, 1996; River Regulation in Meandering Reaches of the Yellow River, 1998. Honours: 1st Class Prize, Adv in Sci and Technol, Min of Water Resources, China. Memberships: Yellow River Rsch Assn; Chinese Assn of Water Conservancy. Hobby: Table tennis. Address: Yellow River Conservancy Commission, 11 Jinshui Road, Zhengzhou 450003, Henan, China.

HU Yizhou, b. 1928 Shanghai. Aviation Adminstr - retd. Appointments: Engr Civ Aviation Admin of China - CAAC - 1949-80; Joined CCP, 1960; Dep Dir Beijing Regl Admin of CAAC, 1980-82; Dep Dir-Gen Civ Aviation Admin, 1982-85; Dir-Gen, 1985-91; Advsr, 1991-94. Address: c/o General Administration of Civil Aviation of China, 155 Dongsi Street West, Beijing 100710, People's Republic of China.

HUA Yunzhang, b. 1911, Wuxi, Jiangsu, China. Railway Chief Engineer. 2 s, 2 d. Education: Grad, Shanghai Jiaotong Univ. Appointments: Hd, Designing Section of Qiangui, Zhegan Railways; Dir, Engrng Dept, Shanghai Railway Bur; Dpty Chf Engr, Railway Const Corps of PLA. Publications: Up-grading of Existing Railway Lines and Construction of New Lines; A Feasible Plan to Build the Beijing-Shanghai High Speed Railway. Memberships: China Railway Soc; China C.E. Soc; Shanghai Assn of Snr Experts. Hobbies: Reading Magazines; Music. Address: 370 Lane #15-101, Middle Yanchang Road, Shanghai 200072, China.

HUA Guofeng, b. 1920 Shanxi. Politician. m. Han Chih-chun. Appointments: Vice-Gov Hunan, 1958-67; Sec CCP Hunan, 1959; Vice-Chmn Hunan Revolutionary Cttee, 1968; Chmn, 1970; First Sec CCP Hunan, 1970-77; Polit Commissar Guangzhou Mil Reg People's Liberation Army, 1972; First Polit Commissar Hunan Mil Dist PLA, 1973; Dep Premier and Min of Pub Security, 1975-76; Acting Premier, Feb-Apr 1976; Premier, 1976-81; Dep Premier, 1981; First Vice-Chmn Cntrl Cttee of CCP Apr-Oct 1976; Chmn, 1976-81; Chmn CCP Mil Affairs Commn, 1976-81; Chmn Politburo 11th Cntrl Cttee CCP, 1977-81; Vice-Chmn, 1981-82. Memberships: Mbr 9th Cntrl Cttee of CCP, 1969; Mbr Politburo 10th Cntrl Cttee of CCP, 1973; Mbr Politburo 11th Cntrl Cttee CCP, 1977-81; Mbr 12th CCP Cntrl Cttee, 1982-87; Mbr 13th CCP Cntrl Cttee, 1987-92; Mbr 14th CCP Cntrl Cttee, 1992-97; Mbr 15th CCP Cntrl Cttee, 1997-. Address: Central Committee, Zhongguo Gongchan Dang, Beijing, People's Republic of China.

HUANG Ai-Lian, b. 13 Oct 1916, Tianjin, China. Nurse. Education: Dip, Sch of Nursing, Peking Union Medl Coll; BS, Tchr's Coll, Columbia Univ, USA. Appointments: Dean, Turner Sch of Nursing, Guangzhou, 1949; Prin, 1st Nursing Sch, Guangzhou, 1956; Vice Supt, Guangzhou Overseas Chinese Hosp, 1978. Publications: Basis of Nursing Psychology, 1981; Psychology for Nurses, 1987; Nursing of Geriatric Patients in Chapt 6, Chinese Traditional Medicine and Western Medicine, 1993. Honours: Forerunner, Guangzhou Hlth Dept, 1962; Forerunner, Jinan Univ, 1979, 1980, 1981; Spec Subsidy, Outstndng Contb of Hlth Affairs by Dept of State, 1992. Memberships: Hon Mbr, Chinese Nursing Assn; Hon Prin, Guangdong Branch of Chinese Nursing Assn. Hobby: Reading. Address: c/o Nursing Department of Guangzhou Overseas Chinese Hospital, Jinan University, Shipai, Guangzhou, China.

HUANG An-Lun, b. 15 Mar 1949 Guangzhou Cty Guangdong Prov. Composer. m. Ouyang Rui-Li, 1974, 1 s. Education: Cntrl Conservatory of Music Beijing; Univ of Toronto Canada; Trinity Coll of Music London; Yale Univ USA. Appointments: Started piano aged 5; Studied with Shaw Yuan-Xin and Chen Zi; Wrks have been widely performed in China Hong Kong Philippines North Africa Aust Eu USA and Can; Res Composer Cntrl Opera House of China, 1976-; Fellship in Composition Trinity Coll London, 1983; Dep Dir State Bur of Materials and Equipment, 1987-88; Vice-Min of Materials, 1990. Compositions: Operas: Flower Guardian op 26, 1979; Yeu Fei op 37, 1986 and 6 others; Symphonic chamber vocal choral and film music inclng: Symphonic Concert op 35; Symphonic Overture; The Consecration of the Spring in 1976 op 25a, 1977; Piano Concerto in G op 25b, 1982; Symphony in C op 25c, 1984; The Sword - symphonic poem - op 33, 1982; Easter Cantata - text by Semuel Tang - op 38, 1986; Psalm 22-A Cantata in Baroque Style op 43c, 1988; Piano Concerto in G; Ballets: The Little Match Girl op 24, 1978; A Dream of Dun Huang op 29, 1980; 7 other records. Honours: Yale Alumni Assn Prize Yale Univ, 1986. Hobbies: Reading; Sport. Address: The Central Opera House of China, Zuojia Zhuang, Out of Dongzhimen Gate, Beijing, People's Republic of China.

HUANG Austin Xiaofeng, b. 10 June 1957, Jilin, China. Engineer. m. Nina Qi Tian, 2 s. Education: BS, Mining Engrng, China Inst of Mining, 1982; MS, Geol Engrng, Univ WI-Madison, USA, 1989; PhD, Geol Engrng, Univ of WI-Madison, USA, 1990. Appointments: Adj Fac Mbr, West WA Univ, USA, 1992-; Pres, Merit Engrng Inc, 1993-. Publication: Rsch ppr: Complete Solution of Pore Pressure in Saturated Medium and a General Poroelastic Medal for Hydrofracturing. Honour: Full Schlshp for Grad Study in USA, Li Fndn, USA, 1984-86. Memberships: Amn Soc of Civ Engrs; Amn Soc of Mining Engrs; Amn Geophysical Union; Amn Cnsltng Engrng Cncl. Hobbies: Violin and classical music. Address: 5315 Bellaire Way, Bellingham, WA 98226, USA.

HUANG Bao-Zong, b. 22 Jan 1939, Jinxi, Liaoning, China. Teacher. m. Zhen-Juan Bing, 8 Jan 1968, 2 d. Education: Grad, Tsinghua Univ, 1963, 1966. Appointments: Techn, Shenyang Aircraft Rsch Inst, 1973-76; Engr, Shenyang Glider Factory, 1977-81; Lectr, 1981-87, Assoc Prof, 1987-91, Prof, 1991-, Northeastern Univ; Visng Prof, GA Tech, USA, 1992-94. Publications: Koiter's Stability Theory and its Application, 1987; Finite Element Analysis of Initial Post-Buckling of Stiffened Plate and Shell Structures, 1990; Localized Analysis of the Buckling and Post-Buckling of Thin-Walled Structures and its Accuracy, 1991; A Quasi-Conforming Triangular Laminated Composite Shell Element Based on a Refined First-Order Theory, 1994; A Computation Method to Identify Limit and Bifurcation Points, 1998. Honours: Awd of Natl Sci Conf, 1978; Awd, Min of Metallurgical Ind for Sci and Technol Adv, 1991; Premium, State Cncl of China, 1996. Memberships: Dpty Bd Chmn, Cncl of Liaoning Prov Soc of Mech, 1994-; Cncl, Chinese Soc of Theort and Applied Mech, 1994-98. Address: College of Science, Northeastern University, Shenyang, Liaoning 110006, China.

HUANG Benli (Ben), b. 21 Sept 1925, Hong Kong. Scientist. m. Peihuan Zhang, 5 Nov 1960, 1 d. Education: BS, Dept of Phys, Lingnan Univ, Canton (now Guangzhou), China, 1949. Appointments: Rrsch Spectroscopist, Assoc Rsch Prof and Grad Rsch Prof, Changchun Inst of Applied Chem, Academia Sinica, Changchun, China, 1950-86; Grad Rsch Prof, Dept of Chem, Xiamen Univ, Xiamen, China, 1986-; Touring USA, UK, FRG, Can, Japan, China, Norway, Russia, Singapore, Malaysia, Korea, Hungary, 1982-; Chairperson, The Fifth Asian Conf on Analytical Scis, Xiamen, China, 1999. Publications: Atlas of Spectral Lines of Rare-Earth Elements, 1964; Spectroscopic Instruments in Analytical Emission Spectroscopy, 1977, 1979; An Atlas of High Resolution Spectra of Rare Earth Elements, 1999; Over 180 pprs on analytical spectroscopy in Chinese and intl jrnls; Patent: A new nebulizer-hydride generator for atomic spectroscopy; Mbr sev editl advsry bds. Honours: Major Achievements in Sci and Technol Awds, Academica Sinica, 1984, 1985, 1986; State Commn for Sci and Technol, China; Awd for Prog in Sci and Technol, Acdemica Sinica; Awds for Prog in Sci and Technol; State Commn for Educ, 1995; Hon Prof, Wuyi Univ, Jiangmen, Guangdong, China. Memberships:

Chinese Acady Scis, 1993-; Chmn, Analytical Chem Div, Chinese Chem Soc, 1994, Pres, 1999-2002; Spectroscopic Soc of China. Hobbies: Photography; Philately; Classical music. Address: Department of Chemistry, Xiamen University, Xiamen 361005, China.

HUANG Chao-Shang, b. 29 Jan 1939, Jiangxi, China. Professor of Physics. m. Xiuping Xu, 5 Sept 1973, 1 d. Education: PhD, Acad Sinica, 1982. Appointments: Asst Prof, 1982-86, Assoc Prof, 1986-91, Prof, 1992-, Inst of Theoretical Phys, Acad Sinica. Publications: Procs of the International Symposium on Heavy Flavor and Electroweak Theory, ed, 1996; Contbr, articles to profl jrnls. Honour: Nature Sci Awd, sec class, Acad Sinica, 1997. Membership: Chinese High Energy Phys Soc. Hobbies: Reading; Swimming. Address: Institute of Theoretical Physics, Academia Sinica, PO Box 2735, 100080, Beijing, China.

HUANG Da, b. 22 Feb 1925, Tianjin, China. Professor of Economics. m. Shuzhen Luo, 20 June 1952, 2 s. Education: MA, North China Utd Univ, 1947. Appointments: Mbr, Acad Degrees Cttee of State Cncl, China; Mbr, Monetary Policy Cttee, People's Bank of China; Dir, Expert Advsry Cttee for the Hum and Socl Sci Stdies, State Educ commn, 1997. Publications: Socialist Fiscal and Financial Problems, 1981; Introduction to the Overall Balancing of Public Finance and Bank Credit, 1984; Economics of Money and Banking, 1992; Macroeconomic Control and Money Supply, 1997. Honours: Awd of Econ Scis, Sun Yefang Fndn, 1986; Awd of Excellent Textbook, State Educ Commn, 1987. Hobbies: Calligraphy; Running. Address: Office of the President, Renmin University of China, Beijing 100872, China.

HUANG Hua, b. 1913 Cixian Co Hebei Prov. Diplomatist. m. He Liliang, 2 s, 1 d. Education: Yanqing Univ Beijing. Appointments: Joined CCP, 1936; Fmr Dir For Affairs Bur of Tianjin Nanking and Shanghai; Later Dir West Eurn Dept Min of For Affairs; Chf Chinese deleg at Panmunjom - Korean War polit negotiations - 1953; Polit advsr to Premier Zhou En-lai; Spokesman of Chinese deleg to Geneva Conf on Indo-China and Korea, 1954; First Afro-Asian Conf Bandung, 1955; Advsr Sino-Am negotiations Warsaw, 1958; Amb to Ghana, 1960-66; Amb to Egypt, 1966-69; Amb to Canada, Jul-Nov 1971; Perm Rep to UN, 1971-76; Min of For Affairs, 1976-83; A Vice-Premier State Cncl, 1980-82; State Cnclr, 1982-83; Vice-Chmn Standing Cttee 6th NPC, 1983-88; Pres Exec Cttee China Welfare Inst, 1988; Pres Chinese Assn for Intl Friendly Contacts, 1992-; Chmn Soong Ching Ling Fndn, 1992-; Advsr Chinese Assn for Promotion of the Population Culture; Hd sev intl delegs; Pres Smedley Strong Snow Soc of China. Honours: Hon Pres China Intl Pub Rels Assn, 1991-; Hon Pres Chinese Environmental Protection Fndn, 1993-; Hon Pres Yenching Alumnae Assn; Hon DHumLitt - MO. Memberships: Mbr 10th Cntrl Cttee CCP, 1974; Mbr 11th, 1978; Mbr 12th, 1983-87; Mbr Standing Cttee of Cntrl Advsry Commn, 1987; Mbr Presidium 14th CCP Natl Congress, Oct 1992. Hobbies: Fishing; Jogging. Address: Standing Committee, National People's Congress, Beijing, People's Republic of China.

HUANG Huang, b. 1933 Linshui Co Jiangsu Prov. Party Offic. Appointments: Joined PLA, 1946; Joined CCP, 1949; Ldng Sec CCP Cttee Anhui Prov, 1983-86; Dep Gov Jianxi Prov, 1987-90; Sec CPC 7th Ningxia Hui Autonomous Regl Cttee, 1990-; Polit Commissar, 1990-96. Memberships: Mbr 12th CCP Cntrl Cttee, 1985-87; Mbr Presidium 6th NPC, 1986; Mbr 14th CCP Cntrl Cttee, 1992-. Address: Ningxia Hui Autonomous Region, Yinchuan, People's Republic of China.

HUANG Jian, b. 12 Apr 1951, Fujian, China. Teacher; Professor. m. Zizhen Lin, 13 Oct 1978, 1 d. Education: BS, 1982, MS, 1987, PhD, 1991, Fujian Agricl Univ. Appointments: Lectr, 1990-92, Assoc Prof, 1993-95, Prof, Vice Dir, Dept of Plant Protection, 1996-, Fujian Agricl Univ. Publications include: Systematic Studies on Aphelinidae of China, 1994; 50 pprs on agricultural pests and biocontrol. Honours: 3rd Awd of Sci and Technol Progress, State Educ Cmmn, 1996; 3rd Awd, Sci and

Technol Progress, Fujian Prov, 1996; Ex Expert of Fujian Prov, 1997. Memberships: Intl Soc of Hymenopterists; Intl Org for Biol Control. Hobbies: Sport; Travel. Address: Department of Plant Protection, Fujian Agricultural University, Fuzhou, Fujian 350002, China.

HUANG Jie, b. 10 May 1955, Fuzhou, China. Professor. m. Qing Weili, July 1985, 2 d. Education: Dr of Philos, Johns Hopkins Univ. Appointment: Assoc Prof, Chinese Univ of Hong Kong, 1995-. Publications: Over 50 rsch pprs in automatic control. Memberships: Mbr, 1990-, Snr Mbr, 1994-, IEEE. Hobbies: Reading; Music; Movies; Swimming; Table tennis. Address: Department of Mechanical and Automation Engineering, Chinese University of Hong Kong, Hong Kong.

HUANG Leting, b. 15 Dec 1959, LongKou, Shandong Prov, China. Scientific Researcher. m. Huo Shumei, 16 Dec 1984, 1 s. Education: Bachelor of Mining, Mining Inst of Shandong, 1982. Appointments: Engr & Hd, 1985, Snr Engr and Hd, 1991, Mining-induced Subsidence and Protection of Surface Bldngs; Asst Dir, 1994, Dpty Dir, 1995, Dpty Dir & Rsch Fell (Prof), 1996, Dir, 1998, Mine Surveying Rsch Inst (MSRI). Publications: Pprs to profl jrnls. Honours: 3rd Grade Prizes for Sci and Technol Prog, for Rsch Achievements incl: Study on Technol for Indirect Prodn of Fndn Bldgs Erected on Base-Rock Fndns in Mining-Affected Areas, 1995, A Study of the Technol Applied for Mining Beneath the Densely-built Vill w High Ground Water Table and its Reconstruction at Pangzhuang Mine, Xuzhou Mining Admin, 1996, Min of the Coal Ind; Outstndng Yth in Sci and Technol Awd, Sun Yueqi Fndn of Sci, Technol & Educ of China Sci and Technol Dev Fndn, 1994; 2nd China Pioneering Work Awd for Outstndng Yth in Sci and Technol, 1996; Winner, Hon title, 1 of 1st Batch of Profl Talents in fmr Coal Ind Sect, 1996; Specialist designated by State Cncl for Spec Govtl Subsidy, 1997. Memberships: China Sci Assn of Yth; China Coal Soc. Hobbies: Sports. Address: No 21 Xinhuaxi Road, Tangshan City, Hebei Prov, China 063012.

HUANG Lu, b. 29 Oct 1936, Shanghai, China. Associate Professor of English. m. 1 Sept 1965, Guo Fuxiang, 1 s. Education: Grad, Russian Lang and Lit Dept, Beijing Univ, 1965. Appointments: Tchr, Engl, Sanhao Middle Sch, Shanghai, 1965-71; Middle Sch of Yunnan Bur of Geol, 1971-86; Lectr, Assoc Prof of Engl, Guilin Inst of Technol (Guilin Coll of Geol), 1987-. Publications: 11 pprs on Engl and Engl tchng. Honours: Ex Tchr of Yunnan Bur of Geol, 1978; Advd Worker of Kunming Cty, 1978, 1980; Top Model Tchr of Guilin Coll of Geol, 1991, 1992; Excellent Tchr of Guangxi, 1993; Excellent Tchr of All China, 1995; Natl Special Allowance for Outstndng Contbn of Engl Tchng, per month, State Cncl of China, 1993-. Memberships: Higher Educ Assn of Engl of Guangxi. Hobbies: Literature; Horticulture. Addrress: c/o Teaching and Research Section of English, Foreign Language Department, Guilin Institute of Technology, Guilin 541004, China.

HUANG Mao, b. 11 Feb 1939, Changsha, China. Scientific Researcher. m. Keling Liu, 1 Oct 1966, 1 s. Education: MS, Dept of Phys, Peking Univ, 1964. Appointments: Vis Sci, IN Univ; Prof of Phys & Info Sci, Lib of Chinese Acady of Scis. Publications include: Microwave Plasmas in Analytical Atomic Spectrometry, 1993. Honours: Natl Achievement in Sci and Technol of China, 1985; Nominated, Spectroscopy Best Ppr Awd, 1992. Memberships: Chinese Soc of Phys; Chinese Soc of Spectroscopy; Chinese Assn of Plasma Phys Study; Chinese Soc of Lib and Info Scis. Hobbies: Peking Opera; Sport; Travel. Address: Documentation and Information Centre, Academia Sinica, Zhong Guan Cun, Beijing 100080, China.

HUANG Minquan, b. 5 Oct 1944, Fujian, Japan. Scientific Researcher. m. Huang Li-Feng, 5 Feb 1971, 2 s. Education: Univ Grad; Visng Schl, Auburn Univ, AL, USA, 1985-88. Appointments: Asst Rschr, 1967-80; Asst Prof, 1981-89; Assoc Prof, 1990-96; Full Prof, 1997-. Publications: (book) Chinese Seed-il Plants, 1987; (Article) A C18 Conjugated Tetraenoic Acid from Ixora

Chinensis Seed Oil, 1990. Honours: Chinese Acady Important Sci Technol Fruit Awd, 1984; Chinese Acady Sci Awd, 1990; Natl Sci Awd, 1991; Guangdong Prov Sci Awd, 1996. Membership: Guangdong Bot Soc. Hobbies: Planting flowers and flowering herbs; Exercise. Address: South China Botanical Garden, Academia Sinica, Longdong, Sha-He, Guangzhou 510520, China.

HUANG Ning-Yi, b. 24 Sept 1937, Wuxi, Jiangsu, China. Microwave Electronics and Television Engineer. m. Ming-Hua Lu, 10 June 1968, 1 s. 1 d. Education: Grad, 1962, Electronics Dept, Tsinghua Univ, Beijing. Appointments: Asst, Tsinghua Univ, Beijing, 1962-76; From Engr to Chf Engr, Hong-Mei Electronics Enterprise, Wuxi, 1977-93; Chmn, Wuxi Branch, Jiu San Soc, 1985-; V Chmn, Standing Cttee, Wuxi City People's Congress, 1986-; Mbr Central Cttee, Jiu San Soc, 1988-. Publications: Microwave Elements and Measurement, textbook, 1972; Principles of the Microwave Tubes, textbook, 1974; Some Problems of Chromaticity in CTV, article, 1990. Membership: Snr Mbr, IEEE. Hobbies: Travel; Swimming; Peking Opera. Address: Wuxi City People's Congress, Jinxing Rd, Qingyang Rd, Wuxi, 214023, China.

HUANG Qitao. Govt Offic. Appointments: Fmr Vice-Min of Nuclear Ind; Fmr Vice-Dir State Sci and Tech Commn; Dir State Bur of Nuclear Safety, Feb 1994-. Address: State Science and Technology Commission, 15B Fuxing Road, Haidian District, Beijing, People's Republic of China.

HUANG Qizao, b. Nov 1933 Baxian Co Sichuan Prov. Politician. Education: Southwest Tchrs Coll. Appointments: Joined CCP, 1952; Sec Communist Yth League Chongqing Cty Cttee; Vice-Dir Dept of Culture of Chongqing Cty, 1980; Vice-Dir Dept of Educ of Chingqing Cty; Vice-Dir Dept of Culture of Sichuan Prov; Dir CCP United Front Wrk Dept of Sichuan Prov; VP Polit Consultative Conf Sichuan Prov; Sec-Gen CCP Sichuan Provncial C ttee, 1988; VP of 6th Exec Cttee; Sec Secr of All-China Women's Fedn, 1988; First Sec Secr of All-China Women's Fedn, 1990-; Vice-Dir Co-ord Cttee for Women's and Children's Wrk of State Cncl, 1990-. Memberships: Mbr 14th CCP Cntrl Cttee, 1992; Mbr 15th CCP Cntrl Cttee, 1997-. Address: All-China Women's Fedn, Beijing, People's Republic of China.

HUANG Shilin, b. 10 May 1933, Henan, China. Doctor. m. Mingiyi Sun, 1 May 1961, 2 s. Education: Univ. Appointments: Chf Physn, 1969, Vice Dir of Hosp, 1983, Prof, 1991, Hd, Dalian Heamotol Chinese Med Inst, 1987. Publication: Study on Pulse Condition of Chinese Medicine, 1986. Honour: Intl Recognised Expert, Oriental Med, USA Chinese Med Assn, 1994. Memberships: Vice Chmn, Assn of Combination of TCM and Western Med, China. Hobby: Sport. Address: Dalian Heamotology Chinese Medicine Institute, 80 Shengli Road, Xigang, Dalian 116021, China.

HUANG Shiping, b. 18 Sept 1946, Min Qing, Fuzhou, China. m. Xi Yan Yang, 1 Jan 1974, 1 s, 1 d. Education: Univ. Appointments: Chief Ed, newsppr; Writer, Fuzhou Writers' Assn; Chf Ed, A Fine Collection of Chinese Poems; Pres, China's Poetry Assn; Spec Hd Ed, Yinhe Publng House, Hong Kong; Leading Writer, Chinese Culture Publng House, Hong Kong; Poet Laureate; Versifier; Muse; Rhymer. Publications: Collection of poems; poetry anthology; Huaxia. Hobbies: Writing; Singing; Dancing; Getting to know people; Playing tennis. Address: No 167 Ming Qing Xi Men Road, 350800 Fuzhou, China.

HUANG Shoumeng, b. 1934, Hunan, China. Professor of Electrical Engineering. Education: Grad, Dept of Elec Machine, Harbin Univ of Technol, 1958; Appointments: Des, Northeastern Hydroelectric Power Des Inst, Min of Hydraulic & Electr Engin, 1958-60; Tech-Cnslt, Des Hydroelectric Power Plant, 1960-63; Prof, Wuhan Univ of Hydraulic & Electr Engin, 1963-; Other positions incl: Ed, Jrnl of Wuhan Univ of Hydraulic & Electr Engin; Snr Cnslt, Jrnl of Elec Power and Its Automation of China; Cncl Mbr, Hydroelectric Power Inst; Cncl Mbr, Hubei Inst of Energy

Resources; Adj Prof, Hubei Univ of Nationality; Supervised over 50 grad students. Publications: 10 books inclng; Digital Signal Processing for Protective Relaying Power Systems (textbook); 2 books appraised as outstndng by Min of Power Ind: Modern Technologies for Construction of Transmission and Distribution; High-Voltage Direct Current Power Transmission; Chinese-English Standard Terms for Hydraulic and Hydroelectric Technologies; Num pprs, many of which have won prizes. Honours include: National Disting Expert w Outstndng Contbns, 1992. Address: Department of Electrical Engineering, Wuhan University of Hydraulic and Electric Engineering, Wuhan, Hubei, 430072, China.

HUANG Tianshou, b. 26 Mar 1932. Teacher. m. Hua Zhifei, 5 Aug 1961, 1 s, 1 d. Education: Grad Stud, People's Univ of China, 1956. Appointments: Dir, Dept of Philos, Scis and Technol, People's Univ of China, 1985-95; Dir of Master, 1979-95; Dir of Dr, 1989-96. Publications: Dialectics of Nature, 1985; Philosophy of Science and Technology, 1991; Introduction to Modern Science and Technology, 1995. Honour: Ex Dir, Grad Sch of People's Univ of China, 1994. Memberships: Philos of Bio Cncl, Chinese Soc for Dialectics of Nature, 1990-. Hobbies: Music; Literature. Address: Department of Philosophy, People's University of China, Beijing 100872, China.

HUANG Xianglu, b. 14 May 1933, Nanjing, Jiangsu Prov, China. Professor. m. Shanging Wang, 1 s. Education: BSDept of Naval Arch, Shanghai Jiao Tong University. Appointments: Lectr, Dept of Naval Arch, Shanghai Jiao Tong University, 1960; Assoc Prof, 1980; Rsch Fell, NHL, Trondheim, Norway, 1981-83; Prof, 1985; Visng Prof, Univ Coll of Santa Barbara, USA, 1987. Publications: Stochastic theory of ship and ocean structure motion, 1994; Over 50 techl pprs. Honour: CSSC Techl Achmnt Awd, 2nd Grade, 1990. Memberships: Chinese Soc of Naval Archts, 1980; Chinese Soc of Ocean Engrng, 1980. Hobby: Classical music. Address: College of Naval Architecture and Ocean Engineering, Shanghai Jiao Tong University, 1954 Hua Shan Road, Shanghai 200030, China.

HUANG Xueyin, b. 7 Feb 1962, Inner Mongolia, China. Museum Museology. m. 10 Oct 1983, 1 s. Education: Schls Deg. Publications: Beyond the Great Wall, The Heritage of Genghis Khan. Memberships: Rsch Soc of Chinese Ancient Ceramics; Mem, Chinese Soc of Mus. Address: Inner Mongolia Museum, Huhhot, China.

HUANG Yaofeng, b. 3 Dec 1949, Puning Cty, Guangdong, China. Surgical Doctor. m. Shunfei Li, 2 Oct 1980, 2 s. Education: Sun Yat-Sen Univ of Med Scis. Appointment: Chf Surgeon. Publications: Hydronephrosis Assoicated With Traumatic Renal Rupture, 1997. Honours: Awds of Sci and Technol Achmnt, Jieyang City, 1996, 1997. Membership: Edl Bd, Jrnl of Med Theory and Practice, 1996-. Hobby: Music. Address: c/o Peoples Hospital of Puning City, Puning 515300, Guangdong Province, China.

HUANG Yuefa, b. 15 Oct 1938, Xiamen, China. Professor. Teacher. m. Sifei Fu, 2 Feb 1969, 1 d. Education: BA, Engl, Hangzhou Univ, 1961; MA, Applied Linguistics, IN Univ, 1984. Appointments: Hd, Tchng and Rsch Sect; Dpty Hd, For Langs Rsch Inst; Exec Dir, K529 TOEFL Test Cntr; Vice-Chmn of For Lang Dept, 1990. Publications: English Vocabulary 10000, 1990; Intensive Training for TOEFL, 1996; Intensive Training for College English Examinations, Bands IV and VI, 1998; A Comprehensive English Course (1-4) (Co-auth), 1994; English Teaching Methodology - Methods and Techniques, 1995; An Essential Vocabulary for Beginners, 1998. Honours: 1st Prize, Tchng Materials of Excllence, HU, 1995; 2nd Prize of Excellent Tchng Materials of Colls and Univs, Zhejiang Provcl Educ Commn, 1995. Memberships: IPA; Zhejiang FLA; IN Univ Alumni Assn. Hobbies: Music; Stamp-collecting; Bowling. Address: Foreign Language Institute, Zhejiang University, West Stream Campus, Hangzhou 310028, China.

HUANG Zhan Yue, b. 1 Dec 1926, Hanan, Fujian, China. Professor. m. Zhang Jia Ling, 2 s. Education: Peking Univ, 1954; Grad, Inst of Archaeol, CASS, 1957-60. Publications: Han Tomb No 1 at Mawangdui, Changsha, 1973; On Ancient Chinese Human Immolation: Mortuary and Non-Mortuary Sacrifices, 1991; Nanyue King's Tomb of the Western Han, 1991; The Earliest Chinese Artifacts Unearthed Archaeolog, 1998; Archaeology and Culture of the Pre-Qin to Han Period, 1998. Honours: Chinese Acady of Socl Scis Awd for Ex Rsch, 1993; Archaeol Excavation & Rsch in New Xia Nai Archaeol Rsch First Awd, 1995. Memberships: Cncl, Chinese Soc of Archaeol, 1979-, Chinese Soc of Overseas Cmmns Hist, 1979-, Chinese Assn for the Study of Ancient Bronze Drums, 1980-. Address: Institute of Archaeology, No 27 Wanfujing Main Street, Beijing, China.

HUANG Zhendong, b. 1935. Politician. Appointments: Joined CCP, 1960; Vice-Min of Comms, 1985-94; Min, 1994-98; Chmn China Merchants Holdings - Hong Kong - Ltd. Memberships: Mbr 14th CCP Cntrl Cttee, 1992-97; Mbr 15th CCP Cntrl Cttee, 1997-. Address: c/o Ministry of Communications, 10 Fuxing Road, Haidian District, Beijing 100845, People's Republic of China.

HUANG Zhi-Zhi, b. 25 Oct 1933, Shantou, China. Doctor. m. Ma Qiong Feng, 15 Aug 1961, 1 s, 1 d. Education: BS, Clin Med, Sun Yat-Sen Univ of Medl Scis, 1958. Appointments: Dpty Chf of Soc of Path Shantou, CMA, 1986-97; Prof of Path, Shantou Univ Medl Coll, 1993-98; Acady Cttee of Intl Rsch and Exchange Cntr of Liver Disease, 1994-98. Publications: 40 articles in profl jrnls; Book: Immunology of Liver Diseases, 1997. Memberships: Acad Cttee, Intl Rsch and Exchange Cntr of Liver Disease; Dpty Chf, Soc of Path, Shnatou, CMA. Hobby: Literature. Address: Department of Pathology, Shantou University Medical College, 10 Xinling Road, Shantou, Guangdong, China 515031.

HUANG Zhishang, b. 12 Dec 1916, Shanghai, China. Professor of Virology and Dermatology. m. Zhang Cuiying, 8 Aug 1959, 2 children. Education: Grad, Natl Med Coll, Shanghai, 1942; MD, Inst of Virol, Acady of Med Scis, Moscow, Russia, 1957. Appointments: Prof, Dermatol, Huadong Med Coll, 1946; Prof of Dermatol, Vice Dean, Shanghai Med Univ, 1949; Snr Rschr, Virol, Acady of Mil Med Sci, Beijing, 1958-88. Publications: Practical Microbiology, 1948; Biological Properties of Hexpes Virus, 1957; Concentration and Purification of Sindbis Virus Cultivated in Chick Embryo Cells, 1980; Review of Human Cytomegalovirus Infections, 1993. Honour: Medal of Hon, Natl Independence, 1988. Memberships: Chinese Scis and Technols Assn; Overseas Returned Schls Assn. Hobbies: Music; Poetry; Literature. Address: No 402, Entrance 2, 50 Handan Road, Shanghai 200437, China.

HUANG Zong-Zhong, b. 13 Oct 1931, Hunan, China. Professor. m. Mar 1964, 1 s, 1 d. Education: BA, Libnshp Sci, Wuhan Univ, 1958. Appointments: Tchr, Rschr, Asst, Lectr, Prof, 1958-; Dir, Lib Dept, 1972-; Deg Judging Cttee, 1980-, Vice Dir, 1984, Mbr of Cttee, 1984, Wuhan Univ; Ed-in-Chf, Libnshp and Info Knowledge, 1987-. Publications: Introduction to Library Science, textbook, 1988; Selected Works of Zong Zhong Huang, 1988; Library Management, textbook, 1992; Documentary Information, book, 1992. Honours: Hubei Socl Sci Prize, 1984; Wuhan Socl Sci Prize, 1985; Hubei Archived Achmnts Prize, 1987; Spec Allowance of Govt, State Cncl, 1992-. Memberships: Standing Bd Dir of Bd Dirs, China Libnshp Soc; Ed, Libnshp Edng Cttee, Great Chinese Encyclopedia; Standing Dir, Archive Soc of Hubei; Pres, Libnshp Soc of Hubei; Assoc, Soc of Socl Sci of Hubei. Hobbies: News; Talking. Address: School of Library and Information Science, Wuhan University, Wuhan, China.

HUCKSTEP Ronald Lawrie, b. 22 July 1926, Chefoo, China. Professor of Traumatic and Orthopaedic Surgery. m. 2 Jan 1960, 2 s, 1 d. Education: Lester Inst of Engrng, Shanghai, 1942; Aurora Univ, Shanghai, 1943; Queens' Coll, Cambridge Univ, 1946-48, BA(Hons) 1948;

Middlesex Hosp, London, 1948-52, MA MB BChir, 1952; MD, Cambridge Univ, 1957; FRCS, Edinburgh, 1957; FRCS, Eng, 1958; FRACS, 1973; Hon MD (NSW), 1988. Appointments include: Middlesex, St Bartholemews and Roy Natl Orth Hosps, London, Eng, 1952-60; Prof of Orth Surg, var other posts, Makerere Univ, Kampala, Uganda, 1960-72; Prof and Chmn, Dept of Traumatic and Orth Surg, 1972-92, Emeritus Prof, 1992-, The University of NSW, Chmn, Sch of Surg; Visng Prof, 1994, Hon Prof of Surg, 1995-, Univ of Sydney. Publications include: 5 books, inclng: Typhoid Fever and Other Salmonella Infections, 1962; Poliomyelitis, 1975; A Simple Guide to Orthopaedics, 1993; Picture Tests - Orthopaedics and Trauma, 1994; Simple Guide Trauma, 5th ed, 1995; Num chapts in books and papers of orth surg and other medl subjects; Corresp Ed, Journal of Bone and Joint Surgery and Injury; Sev films; Inventor of var appliances and implants for crippled patients. Honours include: Irving Geist Awd, 1969; Commonwealth Fndn Travelling Lectr, 1970; CMG, 1971; Betts Medal, Austl Orth Assn, 1983; James Cook Medal, Royal Soc of NSW, 1984; Fell, Sutherland Medal, Austl Acady of Technol Scis, 1986; Paul Harris Fell, Rotary Intl, 1987; Hon MD, Univ of NSW, 1988; Hum Awd Orth Overseas, 1991. Memberships include: Fndng and Hon Mbr, World Orth Concern, 1973; VP, Austl Orth Assn, 1982; Pres, Coast Medl Assn, 1986; num other assns. Listed in: Who's Who; Who's Who in: Australia, the World, the Commonwealth, Australia and the Far East, East Africa, International Who's Who; International Who's Who: of Intellectuals, of Community Service, in Education, International Directory of Distinguished Leadership; International Book Of Honour; Debrett's Peerage; Men of Achievement; num others. Hobbies: Photography; Designing orthopaedic appliances and implants; Swimming; Travel. Address: 108 Sugarloaf Crescent, Castlecrag, Sydney, NSW 2068, Australia.

HUDSON Paul Richard William, b. 4 May 1947. Technology Manager. m. Jill Ruddock, 8 July 1967, div 9 Oct 1989, 1 s. Education: BSc, 1st Class Hons, Southampton Univ, 1969; DPhil, Univ Coll, Oxford, Eng, 1972. Appointments include: Phys Prof, Univ Coimbra, Portugal, 1973-74; Rsch/Tech Controller, Austl Wool Corp, 1978-86; Fndr Mbr, Austl Grape and Wine Rsch Cncl, 1986-89; Gen Mngr and Mng Dir, Montech Pty Ltd, 1987-91; Chmn and Mng Dir, The Wills Record Off Pty Ltd, 1988-90; Exec Dir, Vic Br, Greening Aust, 1991; Gen Mngr, Greening Aust Vic Inc, Melbourne, 1991-96; Mng Dir, Paul Hudson & Assocs, Melbourne, Aust, 1986-. Publications: 58 publs in sci, technological and bus jrnls, 1972-87; Books: Ed, Proceedings of the 2nd National Wool Harvesting R and D Conference, 1982; Ed, Wool Harvesting Research and Development, 1980; Mathematics Required for Advanced Level Physics, 1971. Honours: Laureat du Champagne, Aust, 1981; Rothbury Purple Ribbon 1979. Memberships: Fell, Austl Inst of Mngmt, 1995; Fell, Aust Inst of Co Dirs, 1990; Fell, Aust Inst of Phys, 1976; Companion Fell, Inst of Engrs, Aust, 1983; Clubs: MCC; MCC Golf Club; Riversdale Golf Club; Oxford Soc; Kelvin Club. Hobbies: Science technology management; Theatre; Opera; Music; Archaeology; History; Golf; Skiing; Tennis; Wine and food appreciation. Address: Savernake, 2 Staughton Road, Glen Iris, Melbourne, Vic 3146, Australia.

HUGHES Aneurin Rhys, b. 11 Feb 1937. Ambassador. m. 15 Feb 1964, Jill Christine Hughes, 2 s. Education: Philos, Univ Coll of Wales; Postgrad Rsch for PhD, Univ of London. Appointments: For Off, London; First Sec, Brit High Commn, Singapore; First Sec, Brit Emb, Rome; Hd of Cabinet of EU Commnr Lord Richard; Hd of EU Delegation in Oslo, Norway; Hd of EU Delegation in Canberra, Aust. Publications: Num articles, pamphlets, essays, speeches, editorials on EC related issues. Memberships: C'wlth Club, Canberra. Hobbies: Golf; Cricket; Rugby. Address: 121 Empire Circuit, Yarralumla, ACT 2600, Australia.

HUGHES Anthony Vernon, b. 29 Dec 1936, Eng. Banking Exec; Civ Servant. m. (1) Carole Frances Robson, 1961, div 1970, 1 s; (2) Kuria Vaze Paia, 1971, 1 s, 1 d, 2 adopted d. Education: Queen Mary's Grammar Sch Walsall Eng; Pembroke Coll Oxford; Bradford Univ.

Appointments: Commnr of Lands Registrar of Titles Solomon Islands, 1969-70; Devt Sec Gilbert and Ellice Islands, 1971-73; Hd of Plng, 1974-76; Perm Sec Min of Fin, 1976-81; Regl Econ Advsr UN Econ and Socl Commn for Asia and the Pacific, Jan 1994-. Publications: Num articles on land tenure econ plng devt admin for invmnt especially jnt ventures with spec emphasis on small cos. Honours: Cross of Solomon Islands, 1981. Hobbies: Working outside; Sculling; Sailing. Address: ESCAP, Pacific Operations Centre, PMB 004, Port Vila, Vanuatu, Solomon Islands.

HUGHES Charles Wilson, b. 3 May 1946, Greenville, KY, USA. Procurement Director. m. Daniele, 6 Oct 1973, 1 s, 1 d. Education: BS; JD. Appointments: Procurement and Support Servs Dir, CA State Univ, Long Beach, 1991. Publications: Var articles on Procurement and Logistics. Honour: Cert Purchasing Mngr (CPM), 1998. Memberships: Natl Assn of Purchasing Mngrs; Natl Inst of Govt Procurement; CA Assn of Pub Procurement Offrs; CSU Procurement and Support Servs Offrs Assn, Pres, 1998-99. Hobbies: Stamps; Colas; Computer. Address: CA State University, Long Beach, Purchasing 34-345, 1250 Bellflower Blvd, Long Beach, CA 90846-0123, USA.

HUGHES Colin Anfield, b. 4 May 1930, Bahamas. Political Scientist. m. Gwen Glover, 6 Aug 1955, 1 s. Education: BA, 1949, MA, 1950, Columbia Univ, USA; PhD, London Sch of Econs, Eng, 1952; Bar-at-Law, Gray's Inn, Eng, 1954. Appointments: Lectr, 1956-59, Prof, 1965-74, 1989-95, Emer Prof, 1995-, Univ of Qld; Fell, 1961-65, Professorial Fell, 1975-84, Austl Natl Univ; Electoral Commnr (C'wlth), 1984-89; Mbr, Bd of Dirs Intl Inst for Democracy and Electoral Assistance, Stockholm, 1996-99; Chmn, Qld Constitutional Review Commn, 1999. Publications: Images and Issues, 1969; Mr Prime Minister, 1976; A Handbook of Australian Government and Politics, 1965-74, 1977; The Government of Queensland, 1980; Race and Politics in the Bahamas, 1981; A Handbook of Australian Government and Politics, 1975-84, 1986; The Prime Minister's Policy Speech (co-auth), 1966; A Handbook of Australian Government and Politics, 1890-1964 (co-auth), 1968; The Mass Media in Australia (co-auth), 1972, 2nd ed, 1982. Membership: Australasian Polit Stdies Assn. Address: Department of Government, University of Queensland, St Lucia, Qld 4072, Australia.

HUGHES Edward Stuart Reginald (Sir), b. 4 July 1919, Bruthen, Vic, Aust. Retired Surgeon. m. 30 Dec 1944, 2 s, 2 d. Education: MB BS, 1943, MD, 1945, MS, 1946, Melbourne Univ; FRACS; FRCS; FRCS(c), 1947, FRCS(Eng), 1975; FHES USA; LLD (Hons), Monash Univ. Appointments: Wingfield Morris Hosp, Oxford, 1946; Connaught Hosp, London, 1947; St Marks, London, 1948; Roy Melbourne Hosp, 1950-72; Prof of Surg, Monash Univ, Aust, 1972-84. Publications: Auth of 306 articles and 12 books. Honours: Med; Exhibn Path; Sir Henry Simpson Newland Prize, 1952; Aris and Gale Lectr, Huntarian Lectr; Moynihan Lectr, RCS Eng; CBE, 1970; Kt, 1977. Memberships: Roy Soc of Med; Hon Mbr, Assn of Surgs, GB and Ireland, Hon Fell; Roy Australasian Coll of Surgs, Pres, 1975-77. Hobby: Horse-racing. Address: 308A Glenferrie Road, Malvern, Vic 3144, Australia.

HUGHES Helen Ethelberta, b. 20 Jan 1909, Sunderland, Eng. Teacher. Appointments: Tchr, Sunderland, 1930-36, Hastings, 1936-40; Tech Offr, Ctrl Cncl of Physl Recreation, 1940-45; Uniformed Offr, Soldiers, Sailors and Airmen Help Soc, Welfare Offr, India, 1945-47; Asst Org, Natl Fitness Cncl, Tas, 1949-53; Prin Advsry Tchr, Girls Physl Educ, Perth, WA, 1953-69. Creative Works: Folk Dances, Primary Schools, 1960; Junior Dances, 1962. Honours: Roy Life Saving Medal, Servs Rendered. Memberships: Soldiers, Sailors, Airmens Forces Help Soc; Sec, Tas, WA, HQ, London 1947-98; Roy C'wlth Soc, London; Hon Mbr, 2nd Indian Pathfinders and 44th Indian Airborn Div. Hobbies: Choirs; Volunteer Work. Address: 51 Purser House, Air Force Memorial Estate, Bullcreek, WA 6149, Australia.

HUGHES James Curnow, b. 18 Aug 1929, Adelaide, SA, Aust. Company Director. m. Janice Mary Wardropper, 3 Aug 1955, 2 s, 1 d. Education: Grad, Roy Mil Coll, Duntroon, 1950; Grad, Austl Staff Coll, 1964; Grad, Roy Coll of Def Studies, London, Eng, 1977. Appointments: 3RAR Korea 1951-52, Staff Capt, BCFK, Jap, 1952-53, Adjutant, Adelaide Univ Regiment, 1954-57, 3RAR Malaya, 1957-59; Instr, RMA Sandhurst, 1960-62; Offr Commanding, 2 Spec Air Servs inclng Borneo, 1964-66, Dir, Army Recruiting, 1966-69, Commanding Offr, 4RAR, 1969-72 (including Vietnam 1971 as CO 4RAR/NZ ANZAC), Commandant, Land Warfare Cntr, Canungra, 1972-75; Dir Gen, Trng and Educ Plcy, 1975-76; Dpty Chf, Army Reserves, 1978; Controller of Org and Manpower, Dept of Def, 1978-81; Gen Offr Commanding, Logistics Command, 1981-83; Pres, Melbourne and Metro Fire Brigade Bd, 1983-86; Dir, Roy Agric Soc of Vic, 1987-89; Servs Mbr, Veterans Review Bd, 1990-. Publications: Articles in profl mags. Honours: MC, 1951, Cross of Gallantry (with palm), 1971; DSO, 1972; Army Commendation Awd, 1973; AO, 1982; . Memberships include: Fell, Austl Inst of Mngmnt; United Servs Inst; RSL Def Cttee Vic, 1984-; Hon Col, Roy Vic Regt, 1985-88; Govt, Corps of Commissioncurls, 1986-; Patron, Roy Austl Regiment Assn, Vic, 1987-; Gov, St Michaels Grammar Sch, 1989-97; Patron, Korean Veterans Assn, Aust, 1991-; Patron, Natl Malaya and Borneo Veterans Assn, 1995-; Mbr Korean Veterans Mortality Stdy Consultative Cttee, 1998-; Hon Col, Monash Univ Regt, 1999-. Hobbies: Football, Rowing; Reading; Walking. Address: PO Box 2100, Melbourne, Vic 3002, Australia.

HUGHES Kate, b. 27 May 1949, Adelaide, Aust. Writer; Advocate. m. Peter, 18 Sept 1993, 2 s. Education: BA (Hons); PhD. Appointments: Visng Lectr, Biol Scis, Univ of Newcastle, 1997. Publications: Quick Poison Slow Poison, 1994; Fndr, Ed, Austl Toxic Network News, Sentinel. Memberships: Soc for Environmental Toxicology and Chem; Natl Toxics Network (NGO); Environ Inst. Hobbies: Gardening; Walking. Address: Wollombi Road, St Albans 2775, Australia.

HUGHES Richard Joseph, b. 8 July 1931. Journalist; Jazz Pianist. m. Fay Parsons, 5 June 1962, 3 d. Education: BA (Hons), Univ of Melbourne. Appointments: Reporter, Austl Consolidated Press, Fleet Street, 1952-54; Reporter, Daily Telegraph, Sydney, 1955-66; Sub Ed, Daily Mirror, Sydney, 1966-91; Sub-Ed, Fairfax Cmnty Newspprs, 1993-; Pianist with Cy Laurie and Ian Bell, London, 1952-54; Pianist, Port Jackson Jazz Band, 1955-; Pianist with Ray Price, 1957-62; Own Grp, 1962-87. Publications: Daddy's Practising Again, 1977; Don't You Sing! (Memories of a Catholic Boyhood from Napkins to Long Trousers), 1994. Memberships: Austl Jrnlsts Assn, 1955-; Musicians Union, 1956-; Baritsu Chapt, Baker St Irregulars, 1959-; Sydney Passengers, 1986-. Hobbies: Jazz; Reading; Trains; Sherlock Holmes. Address: Conga Brava, 11 Girilang Avenue, Vaucluse, Sydney, NSW 2030, Australia.

HUGHES Robert Watson, b. 27 Mar 1912, Scotland. Composer. m. 10 Apr 1937, 3 d. Education: Conservatorium of Music, Univ of Melbourne, 1938-40. Appointments: Composer, pt-time, 1934-41; Ed; Composer; Austl Brdcstng Cmmn, Melbourne, 1946-76; Retd as self employed composer, music cnslt. Creative Works: Compositions: Sinfonietta, Fantasia, Forbidden Rite, Xanadu, Sea Spell, and many others. Honours: Austl C'wlth Jubilee Prize, 1951; MBE, 1978; Fac of Music Centennial Awd, Univ of Melbourne, 1995; Life-time Achmnt Awd, Sounds Aust (Austl Music Cntr), 1997. Memberships include: Former Dir, Mbr, Chmn, Austl Performing Rights Assn. Listed in: Who's Who in Australia. Hobby: Music. Address: 4 Arthur Street, Dover Heights, New South Wales 2030, Australia.

HUGO Graeme John, b. 5 Dec 1946, Adelaide, Aust. Professor of Geography. m. Meredith, 27 Dec 1969, 1 d. Education: BA, Hons, Univ of Adelaide; MA, Flinders Univ; PhD, Univ of Adelaide. Appointments: Tutor in Geog, 1968-71, Lectr in Geog, 1975-91, Prof of Geog, 1992-, Univ Adelaide. Publications include: Immigrants and Public Housing, 1996; International Migration Statistics: Guidelines for Improving Data Collection System, 1997; Atlas of the Australian People - 1991 Census: Northern Territory, 1997; Worlds in Motion: Understanding International Migration at Century's End, 1998. Honours: John Lewis Medal and Roy Geog Soc Prize, 1963; Fell, Acady of Socl Scis in Aust, 1987; AISIST Awd, 1994; Stephen Cole the Elder Prize, Univ of Adelaide, 1995. Memberships include: Intl Geog Union's Cttee on Famine and Food Crisis Mngmt; Sci Cttee, Intl Migration of the Intl Union for the Sci Study of Population; Inst of Austl Geogs; Austl Population Assn; Intl Union for the Sci Study of Population; NSW Geog Soc; Population Assn of Am; Roy Geog Soc of Asia; Asian Stdies Assn of Aust; Regl Sci Assn; Austl Assn of Gerontol. Hobbies: Tennis; Running. Address: Department of Geographical & Environmental Studies, University of Adelaide, Adelaide, SA 5005, Australia.

HUH Chan-Hee, b. 6 Jan 1953. Physician. m. Min-Jung Kim, 11 Jan 1979, 1 s, 1 d. Education: MD; PhD. Appointments: Instr of Kyungpook Univ, Sch of Med; Clin Prof, Kyungpook Univ, Sch of Med. Memberships: Intl Fed for Psychotherapy; Korean Acady of Psychotherapists; Treas of Asia-Pacific Assn of Psychotherapists; Psych Assoc of Amn Acady of Psychoanalysis. Hobby: Golf. Address: 1039-10 Manchon-dong, Susung-gu, Taegu 706-023, Korea.

HUI Liangyu, b. 1944 Yushu Co Jilin Prov. Provincial Gov; Economist. Education: Jilin Agricl Sch. Appointments: Joined CCP, 1966; Dep Sec CCP Yushu Co Cttee, 1974-77; Dep Dir Jilin Prov Agricl Bu Prov Agricl and Animal Husbandry Dept, 1977-84; Dep Sec CCP Baichengzi Prefectural Cttee Commnr Baichengzi Admin Off, 1984-85; Elected mbr Standing Cttee CCP Jilin Prov Cttee, 1985; Dir Rural Policy Rsch Off Dir Rural Work Dept CCP Jilin Prov Cttee, 1985-87; Apptd Vice-Gov Jilin Prov, 1987; Dep Dir CCPCC Policy Rsch Off, 1991-93; Dep Sec CCP Hubei Prov Cttee, 1992-94; Chmn 7th Hubei Prov CPPCC Cttee; Elected Dep for Jilin Prov to 7th NPC; Dep Sec CCP Anui Prov Cttee, 1994-; Vice-Gov and Acting Gov Anhui Prov, 1994-95; Gov, 1995-. Memberships: Mbr Alt mbr 14th CCPPCC Cttee; Mbr 15th CCP Cntrl Cttee, 1997-. Address: Office of the Governor of Anhui Province, Hefei, Anhui Province, People's Republic of China.

HULL Andrea Douglas, b. 13 Mar 1949, Sydney, Aust. Director; Professor. Education: BA, Dip, Educ, Sydney. Appointments: Natl Travel Dir, Natl Union of Austl Univ Students, 1970-71; Second Tchr, Borough Haringey, England, 1972-73; Snr Project Offr, 1973-79, Dir, Cmty Arts Bd, Aust, 1979-82; Dir, Plcy and Plng, Aust, 1982-87; Dir Strategic Dev Div Aust, 1987-88; Exec Dir, Dept for the Arts, WA, 1988-94; Dir, Prof, Vic Coll of the Arts, 1995-. Publications: Student Travel Guide to Australia, 1971; A Directory of Festivals Held Throughout Australia, 1975; Review of the Tertiary Arts Education and Training, 1987; Sev articles in profl jrnls. Memberships include: Austl-Korea Fndn; Premier's Cl for the Arts; Bd Mbr, Melbourne Th Co; Tstee, Vic Arts Cntr Trust. Hobbies: Yoga; Tennis; Swimming; Theatre. Address: Victorian College of the Arts, 234 St Kilda Road, Southbank, Victoria 3006, Australia.

HUMPHREYS Leonard Ross, b. 12 Sept 1927, Sydney, Aust. Agricultural Scientist. m. Irene Lyle Allen, 23 Feb 1951, 2 s, 2 d. Education: MSAgr, Sydney, 1958; PhD, Qld, 1966. Appointments: Snr Agrostologist 1956-59, Chf Agrostologist 1959-66, Asst Dir of Agric 1964-66, Qld Dept of Primary Inds; Snr Lectr in Pasture Agronomy 1966-72, Rdr 1973-, Personal Chair 1988-93, Hd, Dept of Agric, 1978-91, Pro-Vice Chan, 1991-93, Univ of Qld. Publications: Environmental Adaptation of Tropical Pasture Plants; Tropical Pastures and Fodder Crops; Tropical Pasture Seed Production; Tropical Pasture Utilisation; Tropical Forages: Their Role in Sustainable Agriculture; Seeds of Progress; The Evolving Science of Grassland Improvement; Contbr of over 100 rsch pprs. Honour: Hon DSc, KKU, 1983. Memberships: Fed Pres 1985-86, Austl Inst of Agricl Sci; Chmn 1981-85, Intl Grassland Congress Continuing Cttee, Pres

1966, Tropical Grassland Soc of Aust. Hobbies: Books; Music. Address: 1/63 Warren Street, St Lucia, Qld 4067, Australia.

HUMPHRIES (John) Barry, b. 17 Feb 1934, Melbourne, Vic, Aust. Actor; Writer; Music Hall Artiste. m. (1) div, (2) div, 2 d, (3) Diane Millstead, div, 2 s, (4) Lizzie Spender, June 1990, 2 s. Education: Univ Melbourne. Appointment: Films: Adventures of Barry McKenzie, 1972; Barry McKenzie Holds His Own, 1974; Sir Les Saves the World, 1986; 1-man shows incl: At Least You Can Say You've Seen It, 1974; Housewife, Super-star, London, NYC, 1976-77; Isn't It Pathetic At His Age, 1978; A Night With Dame Edna, 1978-79; An Evening's Intercourse, 1981-82; Tears Before Bedtime, 1985; Back With A Vengeance, 1987, 1988; Look At Me When I'm Talking To You!, 1993; Edna the Spectacle, 1998; Edna the Royal Tour, San Fransico, 1998-99; Remember You're Out, New York, 1999; TV shows: Dame Edna's Hollywood; The Barry Humphries Scandals; Audience with Dame Edna; Another Audience with Dame Edna; Single Voices; Dame Edna Special; Records: Song of Australia; 12 Inches of Les; The Sound of Edna; The Dame Edna Party Experience; Housewife!; Superstar!. Publications: Bizarre 1, 1965; Innocent Austral Verse, 1968; Wonderful World of Barry McKenzie, 1968; Bazza Pulls It Off, 1972; Adventures of Barry McKenzie, 1973; Bazza Holds His Own, 1974; Dame Edna's Coffee Table Book, 1976; Bazza Comes Into His Own, 1978; Les Patterson's Australia, 1979; Barry Humphries' Treasury of Australian Kitsch, 1980; Dame Edna's Bedside Companion, 1982; Les Patterson: The Traveller's Tool, 1985; Dame Edna: My Gorgeous Life, 1989; Neglected Poems, 1991; More Please, autobiography, 1992; Women in the Background, novel, 1997. Honours: Awd, Comedy Perf Yr, Soc W End Mngmts London, 1979; AO, 1982; TV Personality of Yr, 1990; Most Popular TV Personality in Denmark, 1994; Sir Peter Ustinov Endowment, Banff TV Fest, 1997; Bay Area Th Critics Circle Outstndng Achievement Awd, 1998. Memberships include: Garrick Club, London; Beefsteak Club, London; Savage Club, Melbourne. Listed in: Who's Who in Australia. Hobbies: Reading secondhand booksellers' catalogues in bed; Baiting humourless republicans; Inventing Australia; Trailing his coat. Address: c/o Duet Productions, 20 Young St, Neutral Bay, NSW 2089, Australia.

HUN Sen, b. 1952 Kompang-Cham Prov. Politician. m. Binn Sam Hieng, 1976, 3 s, 3 d. Education: Phnom Penh. Appointments: Joined Khmer Rouges, 1970; Rising to Cmdt; In Viet Nam with prov-Vietnamese Kampucheans, 1977; Returned to Kampuchea - now Cambodia - after Vietnamese-backed take-over; Min for For Affairs, 1979-85; Dep PM, 1981; Chmn Cncl of Mins of Cambodia-PM-1985-93; Second PM Roy Govt of Cambodia, Sept 1993-; Vice-Chmn Cambodian People's Party - CPP. Address: Council of Ministers, Phnom Penh, Cambodia.

HUNG Hon Cheung George, b. 24 July 1934, Guangdong, China. Education: Chung Chi Coll; Dip, Chinese Univ of Hong Kong, 1956. Appointments: Mngr, Intl Engrng Ltd, 1957-79; Dir, System Engrng Ltd, 1979-. Honours: 1st Prize, Intl Inventors Expo, 1991; Awd for Recog, Popular Sci, 1995. Memberships: Heating, Refrigerating and Air Conditioning Engrs; Amn Mngmt Assn; Assn of Energy Engrs. Address: 16 1/F New Henry House, 10 Ice House Street, Central Hong Kong, Hong Kong.

HUNT David Anthony (His Excellency the Hon), b. 15 Feb 1935, Sydney, Aust. Judge of UN International Criminal Tribunal for the Former Yugoslavia. m. Margaret Jennifer Frazer East, 23 Jan 1959, 3 s. Education: BA 1956, LLB, 1958, Univ of Qld. Appointments: Called to Qld Bar, 1958, the NSW Bar, 1958; Signed the Roll of Cnsl in Vic, 1962; Appointed QC for NSW, 1975 and for Vic, Qld and the ACT, 1976; Practised mainly in the common law jurisdiction, specialising in defamation litigation; Snr Cnsl assisting the Roy Commn into NSW Prisons, 1976; Appointed a Judge of the Supreme Crt of NSW, 1979; Assigned to the Common Law, Admnstrv

Law and Criminal Divs; Appointed Chf Judge at Common Law of Supreme Crt of NSW, 1991; Elected Judge of the UN Intl Criminal Tribunal for the Former Yugoslavia, 1998. Publications: Contbr to profl law jrnls. Membership: Aust Club, Sydney. Hobbies: Skiing; Swimming; Reading. Address: PO Box 13888, 2501 EW The Hague, The Netherlands.

HUNT Harold Gordon, b. 29 Dec 1917. Administrator. m. May Catherine Vautier, 16 June 1944, 2 s, 1 d. Education: BCom, Univ of NZ, 1948; FCIS, 1956-; FCA(NZ), 1969-; F Inst D, 1977-; FCCM, 1995. Appointments: Dept of Socl Welfare, 1936-39; Flying Offr, NZ & o'seas war serv, RNZAF, 1940-45; Educ Dept, Auckland, 1946-48; Chf Admnstv Offr, Lincoln Coll (Univ) 1949-76; JP, 1963-; Fndn Dir, A A Canterbury Trav Ltd, serving southern auto assns, 1972-88; Retd from full-time employment, 1977; Mbr of Motor Vehicle Disputes Tribunal, Jus Dept, 1977-96. Publications: Ed, Lincoln Calendar, annual, 1950-65. Honours: Hon Auditor, Lincoln Univ Coll Old Studs Assn, 1950-76; Fell, Roy C'wlth Assn, Inst of Dirs, London; Fell, Inst of Chartered Secs and Administrators, 1956; Fell NZ Soc of Accts; Fell, Chartered Inst of Corporate Mngmt, NZ. Memberships include: Var offs, Assoc, 1949-55, Inst Chartered Secs and Admnstrs; Assoc, NZ Soc Accts, 1946-68; Bd of Mngmt, Traffic Accident Rsch Fndn, 1975-; Vet Life Mbr, AA (Canterbury); Life Mbr, NZ AA, 1991; Hon Life Mbr, Friends of Orton Bradley Pk, 1992-. Hobbies: Golf; Woodworking; Travel. Listed in: Notable New Zealanders; Who's Who in New Zealand; Dictionary of International Biography; New Zealand Who's Who of Justices of the Peace. Address: 25 Tuawera Terrace, Clifton Hill, Christchurch 8008, New Zealand.

HUNT Jonathan Lucas, b. 2 Dec 1938 Lower Hutt. Politician. Education: Auckland Univ. Appointments: Tchr, Kelston Boys High Sch, 1961-66; Tutor, Univ of Auckland, 1964-66; Jnr Govt Whip, 1972; Chmn of Cttees and Dpty Speaker of House of Reps, 1974-75; Acting Speaker, 1975; Labour Opposition Spokesman on Hlth, 1976-79; Labour Opposition Spokesman on Constitution and Parly Affairs, 1978-81; Snr Opposition Whip, 1980-84; Shadow Min of Brdcstng, 1982; Min of Brdcstng and Postmaster-Gen, 1984-87; Min of State, 1987-89; Ldr of the House, 1987-90; Min of Brdcstng, 1988-90; Min for Tourism, 1988-89; Min of Housing, 1989; Min of Comms, 1990; Snr Opposition Whip, 1990-96; Shadow Ldr of the House, 1996-; Chmn, Regulations Review Cttee, 1997. Hobbies: Music; International Affairs; Cricket; Literature. Address: Parliament Buildings, Wellington, New Zealand.

HUNTER Barry Russell, b. 15 Aug 1927, Brisbane, Aust. Anglican Bishop. m. Dorothy Nancy Sanders, 17 June 1961, 3 d. Education: ThL, St Francis Theol Coll, Brisbane, 1952; BA, Univ of Qld, 1966. Appointments: Asst Curate, St Matthews Sherwood, 1953-56; Mbr, Bush Brotherhood of St Paul, Cunnamulla, 1956-61; Rector, Parish of Chinchilla, 1961-66; Rector, Parish of Callide Valley, 1966-71; Archdeacon of E Diocese of Rockhampton, 1969-71; Bish of Riverina, 1971-92; Locum Tenens Parish of Cudal, 1992-96; Retd, 1996; PTO Diocese of Newcastle. Honours: AM, 1992; Hon DLitt, honoris causa, Charles Sturt Univ, 1995. Hobbies: Music; Reading. Address: 27 Telopea Drive, Taree, NSW 2430, Australia.

HUNTER Gregory Preston, b. Deniliquin, NSW, Aust. Magazine Editor. 1 s, 1 d. Education: BA; DipEd, Univ of New Eng, NSW. Appointments: Second Sch Tchr (Engl, Hist Modern), 1979; Snr Writer, Austl Penthouse Mag, 1982; Ed (Founding Ed), Inside Sport Mag, 1991-. Publications: Wrks in jrnls. Memberships: Austl Soc of Mag Eds (ASME); Awds Judge, Mag Publr Assn (MPA). Hobbies: Rugby union; Vocals accompanying piano; Surfing. Address: 15 Therry Street, Avalon, NSW 2107, Australia.

HUNTER Ian Alexander, b. 23 Oct 1939, Dunedin, NZ. Naval Officer. m. Hilary R Sturrock, 13 Mar 1965, 2 s. Education: Royal Naval Coll, Dartmouth, 1958-60; Roy Coll Def Studies, 1985. Appointments: Royal NZ Navy: Cadet, 1957; Midshipman, 1959; Sub Lt, 1960; Lt Cmdr,

1970; Cmdr, 1976; Commanding Offr, HMNZ Waikato, 1979; Capt, 1982; Commanding Offr, HMNZS Southland, 1982-84; Commodore, 1987; Rear Admiral Chf of Naval Staff, 1991-94; Wellington Mus Trust, 1995. Honours: NZ Armed Forces Awd, 1985; Clasp, 1987; NZ 1990 Commemoration Medal, 1990; Companion of the Order of the Bath (CB), Queen's Birthday Hons, 1993. Memberships; Aust Naval Inst; Royal NZ Forest and Bird Soc; Inst Dirs NZ; Friends of Wellington Maritime Mus, Chmn, 1995; Wellington Civic Trust, 1996; Sea Cadet Assn of NZ, Pres, 1998. Listed in Who's Who in New Zealand. Hobby: Youth Sail Training. Address: 108B Messines Road, Karori, Wellington, New Zealand.

HUNTER Robert John, b. 26 June 1933. Research Chemist. m. Barbara Robson, 15 May 1954, div 1995, 1 s, 1 d. Education: BSc, 1954, PhD, Sydney. Appointments: CSIRO Chem, 1954; Lectr 1964, Assoc Prof 1972, Hd, Sch of Chem, 1987-90, Univ of Sydney; Cnsltng Chem, Colloidal Dynamics, 1990-. Publications: Zeta Potential in Colloid Science, 1981; Foundations of Colloid Science, Vol I, 1987, Vol II, 1989; Introduction to Modern Colloid Science, 1993. Honours include: CSIRO Grad Schlshp from Div of Soils, 1957-60; Fndn for Fundamental Stdy of Materials, Rsch Fellshp, Utrecht, Netherlands, 1967; Archibald D Ollé Prize, NSW Br, RACI, 1982; A E Alexander Mem Lectr, RACI, 1987; Liversidge Lectr, Roy Soc of NSW, 1988; Archibald D Ollé Prize, 1994. Memberships: Fell, Roy Austl Chem Inst; Fell, Austl Acady of Sci; Pres, Intl Assn Coll and Interface Sci, 1990-94. Listed in Who's Who in Australia; Who's Who in the World. Hobbies: Music; Reading; Drama and the theatre. Address: School of Chemistry, University of Sydney, NSW 2006, Australia.

HUQ Shamsul, b. 1 Sept 1931 Shugandhi Comilla Dist. Politician; Army Officer. m. 2 s, 2 d. Education: Dhaka Coll. Appointmnets: Commissioned Army Medical Corps, 1955; Served Army and Air Force Medical Services then joined War of Liberaton; Organised Medical Services; Achieved rank of Lt Col, 1971; Rank of Maj-Gen, 1979; Then Dir-Gen Medical Services rank of Col then Brig, 1983; Min of Hlth and Population Control, 1982-86; Min of Relief and Rehabilitation, 1986-87; Min of Com, 1990-91. Hobby: Gardening. Address: c/o Ministry of Commerce and Industry, Shilpa Babour, Motijheel, Dhaka, Bangladesh.

HURFORD Christopher John, b. 30 July 1931. Company Director; Public Affairs Consultant; University Distinguished Visiting Fellow. m. Lorna Seedsman, 17 Dec 1960, 2 s, 3 d. Education: BSc, (Econ), London Sch of Econs; FCA. Appointments: Acct, pub prac, ind, com, 1949-1969, incl Zinc Corp Ltd, Aust, Marks and Spencer's Ltd, UK; Bd Mbr, SA Socl Welfare Advsry Cttee, 1966-69, SA Munic Tramways Trust, 1966-69, Savings Bank of SA, 1966-69; Labor Mbr, Adelaide, SA, Austl Parl, 1969-87; Var appts incl: Vice-Chmn, 1969-72, Chmn, 1973, Jnt Parly Cttee on Pub Accounts; Chmn, Jnt Cttee on Prices, 1973-75; Var Shadow Portfolios, 1976-83: Min for Housing and Construction, 1984-85, Min for Immigration and Ethnic Affairs, 1985-87; Min for Cmnty Servs, 1987, Asst Treas, 1983-87; Aust Consul Gen of NY, 1988-91; Dir of External Rels, Univ of SA, 1991-93; Co Dir and Pub Affairs Cnslt, 1993-. Honour: AO, 1993. Memberships: Taxation Inst of SA, SA Cncl Mbr, 1965-70; Elderly Citizens Homes, SA Inc, Bd Mbr, 1965-69; Workers Educ Assn SA, Chmn, 1967-68; SA Aboriginal Educ Fndn, Inaugural Treas, 1969-72; SA Cncl of Civil Liberties, Fndn Treas, 1969-72; Austl Assn of Adult Educ, Natl Exec, 1966-70; Austcare, App Chmn, 1970-72. Listed in: Who's Who in Australia; Who's Who in the World; Who's Who in Business in Australia. Hobbies: Golf; Cinema; Reading. Address: 65 Hackney Road, Hackney, SA 5069, Australia.

HURLEY Thomas Henry, b. 12 July 1925, Melbourne, Aust. Consultant Physician. m. Yvonne Capon, 1 Dec 1948, 3 s, 1 d. Education: MBBS, 1947; MD, 1951, Univ of Melbourne; MRACP, 1951; FRACP, 1962. Appointments: Physn 1952-, Snr Physn 1966, Pres 1985-92, Roy Melbourne Hosp; Chmn 1986-88, Dpty Chmn 1980-86, Commnr 1969, C'wealth Serum Labs;

Chmn, Med Rsch Cttee, Natl Health and Medl Rsch Cncl, 1975-81; Chmn, COSELCO, Mimotopes, 1988-90. Memberships include: Haematology Soc of Aust; Intl Soc of Haematology; Roy Austl Coll of Physns; Austl Med Assn; Clinl Oncological Soc of Aust; Bd Mbr, AMRAD, 1987-97; Walter and Eliza Hall Inst, 1966-94; Ian Potter Fndn, 1978. Honours: Queens Silver Jubilee Medal, 1977; Fell, Aust Med Assn; OBE, 1980; AO, 1989. Listed in: Who's Who in Australia. Hobbies: Sailing; Skiing; Tennis. Address: 44 Campbell Road, Balwun 3103, Australia.

HURTADO Osvaldo, b. 26 June 1939, Chambo, Chimborazo. Doctor in Law. m. Margarita Perez, 29 Sept 1969, 3 s, 2 d. Education: Bach Deg, Polit Sci, 1964; Dr in Law, 1966; Honoris Causa, Georgetown Univ, 1983. Appointments: VP, 1979-81, Pres, Repub of Ecuador, 1981-84; Pres, Cordes, 1984-; Pres, Consitutent Assembly, 1997-98. Publications: Dos Mundos Super-Puestos, 1969; El Poder Politico en Ecuador, 1977; Politica Democratica, 1990; Gobernabilidad y Defensa Constitucional, 1993. Memberships: Interam Dialogue, bd mbr; S Am Cmmn for Peace, Santiago, Chile, bd of ex pres of state. Hobbies: Tennis; Gardening. Address: Suecia E 813 Y Shyris, Quito, Ecuador.

HURTADO LARREA Oswaldo, b. 26 Jun 1939 Riobamba. Politician. m. Margarita Perez de Hurtado, 3 s, 2 d. Education: Cath Univ Quito.Appointments: Fnd'd Ecuadorian Christian Dem Party, 1964; Pres of Congress, 1966; Prof of Polit Sociol Cath Univ Quito; Dir Instituto Ecuatoriano de Desarrollo Soc - INEDES - 1966; Under-Sec of Labour, 1969; Sub-Dean Fac of Econs and Dir Inst of Econ Rsch Cath Univ Quito, 1973; Invited to form part of World Polit Cncl of Christian Dem, 1975; Joined with other polit grps to form Popular Dem, 1978; Pres Org of Christian Dems of Am; VP Intl Christian Dems; Pres Commn to prepare Law of Referendum of Elections and Polit Parties, 1977; VP of Ecuador and Pres Consejo Nacional de Desarrollo - Natl Devt Cncl - 1979-812; Pres of Ecuador, 1981-84; Pres Cordes - org for study of Latin Am devt problems - Quito; Fmr VP Inst for Eurn Latinam Rels Madrid. Publications incl: El poder politico en Ecuador, 1977. Honours: Dr hc - Georgetown - and var for decorations. Memberships: Mbr cncl of Ex-Pres Atlanta; Mbr Cncl Interam Dialogue WA; Mbr Cncl South Am Peace Commn Santiago; Mbr Cncl Raul Prebisch Fndn Buenos Aires; Mbr Cncl Latin Am Popular Fndn Caracas; Mbr Cncl Cntr for Rsch and Promotion of Latin Am-Eurn Rels Madrid; Mbr var environmental commns. Address: Suecia 277 y Los Shyris, Quito, Ecuador.

HUSAIN Imtiyaz, b. 30 July 1941, Calcutta, India. Stockbroker; Investment Advisor. m. Sharmin, 23 Nov 1968, 2 s. Education: MA, Univ of Dhaka; MBA, Dip in Invmnt Appraisal, Bradford. Appointments: Cnclr, Dhaka Stock Exchange, 1986-90; Vice Chmn, Dhaka Stock Exchange, 1991, 1993-95; Chmn, DSE, 1995-97. Memberships: Trustee, Bangladesh Protibondhi Fndn, 1985-98; Metrop Chmbr of Com and Ind. Hobbies: Reading; Music. Address: 316 AB, Tejgaon IA, Dhaka 1208, Bangladesh.

HUSAIN Sajjad, b. 15 Aug 1950, Sargodha, Pakistan. Doctor; Urologist; Kidney Transplant Surgeon. m. Effat Hussan, 1976, 5 s, 1 d. Education: Pre-medl, Govt Coll, Lahore; MBBS, Ke, Lahore, 1973; MCPs, CPsP Pakistan; FRCS, Glasgow, 1982. Appointments: Asst Prof, Postgrad Medl Inst, Lahore; Assoc Prof, Urology, KE, Medl Coll, LHR; Prof of Urology, Allama Iqbal Medl Coll. Publications include: Infestious Renal Calculi, 1994; Role of Transrectal Utrasonography in Prostatic Diseases, 1994; Estimation of Prostatic Size by Utrasonography, 1995; Role of Double Pigtail Stents in Extracorporeal Shockwave Lithotripsy, 1995; Urodynamics, Role in BPH, 1996; Incidence of Recurrence of Superficial Bladder Tumour Following TUR BT, 1997; Role of DRE, PSA and TRUS, in Ca Prostrate, 1998; Improvement of Symptom Status following TURP in BPH Patients, 1999. Memberships: Life Mbr, Pakistan Medl Assn; Life Mbr, Pakistan Soc of Surgs, VP, 1996; VP, Pakistan Assn of

Urological Surgs. Hobbies: Literature; History. Address: 89-B GOR III, Shadman Lahore, Pakistan.

HUSEIN Mahmood, b. 21 Oct 1948, Mumbai, India. Surgeon (Opthalmic). m. Jumana, 5 Dec 1974, 1 s, 1 d. Education: MB BS; DOMS; FCPS; MSc Opth. Honours: Gold Medal, Fells, Coll of Physns & Surgs, Bombay, 1976. Memberships: Natl Assn for Blind; Logical Soc; Bombay Opth Assn; Assn of Medl Cnslts. Hobbies: Reading; Research, Music; Innovations in his field. Address: 3 Court Royal, Christ Church Road, Byculla, Bombay 400 008, India.

HUSSAIN Manzoor, b. 3 Jan 1953, Dhaka, Bangladesh. Consultant Paediatrician. m. Shermin, 25 Apr 1982, 2 s. Education: MBBS, Dac; DTM&H, Bangkok; DCH, Glasgow; MRCP, UK. Appointment: Dir and Prof, Paediat Med, Dhaka Shishu (Children's) Hosp. Publications: Shishu Paricharja (Bengali), 1989; Shishur Jibon O Swastho (Bengali), 1993; Pediatric Diagnostic Approach, 1993. Honours: FRSTM, 1991; FRCP, Edin, Glasgow, 1998; FRCP, London, 1998. Memberships: Sec Gen, Bangladesh Pediat Assn, 1998; Bangladesh Medl Rsch Cncl; Life Mbr, Bangladesh Medl Assn, Bangladesh Cancer Soc, Bangladesh Asthma Soc, Bangladesh Pvte Medl Practitioners Assn. Hobbies: Reading; Writing. Address: Dir, Dhaka Shishu (Children's) Hospital, Sher-e-Bangla Nagar, Dhaka 1207, Bangladesh.

HUSSAIN Mohamed Zahir. Government Official. Appointment: Min, Presdtl Off, Govt of Maldives. Address: Office of the President, Boduthak ufufaanu Magu, Malé 20-05, Henveyru, Maldives.

HUSSAIN Munir, b. 29 Nov 1929. Cricket Commentator; Publisher. m. 1958, 2 s, 2 d. Education: MBA. Publications: 3 books on cricket; 1 book on boxing. Honour: Pioneer of Natl Lang, Urdu Cricket Commentary. Membership: Karachi Gymkhana and Press Club. Hobbies: Commentary; Writing on Sports. Address: 68-C 13th Commerical Street, Phase-II, Extension Defence, Karachi, Pakistan.

HUSSEIN Abdirizak Haji, b. 1924 Galkayo Dist. Politician; Diplomatist. Appointments: Joined Somali Yth Club which became Somali Yth League, 1944; Pres, 1956-58; Pres of Univ Inst Mogadishu, 1956-59; Frmd Popular Movement for Dem Action; Min of Interior later of Works and Comms, 1960-64; PM, 1964-67; Detained following coup, 1969; Released, Apr 1973; Perm Rep to UN, 1974-80. Memberships: Mbr Natl Assembly, 1959-69. Address: c/o Ministry of Foreign Affairs, Mogadishu, Somalia.

HUSSEIN Abdul-Aziz, b. 1921 Kuwait. Politician; Diplomatist. m. 2 s, 1 d. Education: Tchr Higher Inst Cairo; Univ of London. Appointments: Fmr Dir 'House of Kuwait' Cairo; Dir-Gen Dept of Educ Kuwait; Amb to the UAR, 1961-62; Perm Rep to Arab League Cncl; State Min in Charge of Cabinet Affairs, 1963-64; Min of State for Cabinet Affairs, Feb 1971-85; Cnslr of HM the Amir of Kuwait, 1985-. Publication: Lects on Arab Soc in Kuwait, 1960. Address: Amari Diwan, Seif Palace, Kuwait Cty, Kuwait.

HUSSEIN Queen Noor (HM), b. 23 Aug 1951. m. King Hussein I of Jordan, dec 2 Feb 1999, 4 children. Education: BA, Arch, Urban Plng, Princeton Univ, 1974. Appointments: Arch and Urban Plng Projs in Aust, Iran and Jordan; Founded in Jordan, Roy Endowment for Culture and Educ, 1979; Annual Arab Children's Congress, 1980; Annual Intl Jerash fest for Culture and Arts, 1981; Jubilee Sch, 1984; Noor Al Hussein Fndn, 1985; Natl Music Conservatory, 1986; Chr, Natl Task Force for Children; Chr Advsry, Cttee for the UN Univ Intl Ldrshp Acady, Amman; Patron of the Gen Fedn, Jordanian Women and the Natl Fedn of Bus and Profl Women's Clubs; Patron, Roy Soc for the Conserv of Nature; Hon Pres, Jordan Red Cres; The Jordan Soc, WA, DC, 1980; Patron, Intl Union for the conserv of nat and nat resc, 1988; Fndng Mbr, Intl Commn on Peace and Food, 1992; Pres, Utd World Colls, 1995; Hon Pres, Birdlife Intl, 1996; Dir, Hunger Proj. Honours: num hon

Doctorates, Intl Rels, Law, Humane Letters; Intl Awds and Decorations. Memberships: Intl Eye Fndn Hon Bd; Tstee, Mentor Fndn; Gen Assembly of the SOSKinderdorf Intl; Intl Cncl of the Near E Fndn. Hobbies: Skiing; Horseback Riding; Tennis; Sailing; Reading; Photography. Address: Royal Palace, Amman, Jordan.

HUTCHERSON Raymond Adrian, b. 3 Mar 1924, Sydney, NSW, Aust. Chartered Builder. Consultant. m. Kathleen Milne Smith, 4 Jan 1947, 2 s. Education: Sch Leaving Cert, Barker Coll, Hornsby, Sydney, 1940; Building Sci Dip, 1950; Assoc, Sydney Tech Coll. Appointments: Served RAAF, 1942-46; Commenced Building Career, 1946; Responsible for cnstrn of some of Aust's largest contracts inclng Lucas Heights Nuclr Reactor and NW Cape Comms base for US Navy. Membership: Fell, Roy Austl Inst of Building. Hobbies: Yachting; Cattle Raising; Farming; Bonsai Collecting. Address: c/o Raymond Hutcherson Pty Ltd, 96 Crown St, East Sydney, NSW 2011, Australia.

HUTCHINSON William Arthur, b. 24 Sept 1939. Industrial Marketer. m. 5 Nov 1966, Irene Leslie Gammie, 1 s, 2 d. Education: BSc, 1960; MSc, 1966, Univ of Sydney, 1966; Dip, Petro-Geol, Brit Inst of Engrng Technol, N Sydney, 1970; Dip, Concrete Technol, People's Cmnty Coll, MI, USA, 1978; PhD, Mktng, MI State Univ, 1984; Cert of Mktng Rsch, Univ of Technol, NSW, 1988; Cert, Hotel Licensee, Coll of TAFE, Sydney, NSW, 1988; Cert, Tourism in Regl Areas, Coll of TAFE, Gosford, NSW, 1989; Cert, Intl Mktng, Coll of Profl Studies, Univ of Sydney, 1990. Appointments: Personal Asst, Boral Ltd, 1963-78; Gen Mngr of Concrete Masonry Div, Farley & Lewers Ltd, 1978-79; NSW State Mngr, Silica Lime Brick and Paving Div, Calsil Ltd, 1979-81; Snr Cnslt, Indl Mktng and Mngmnt Cnsltng, Didcroft Grp, Queensland, 1981-83; Gen Mngr, BTR Trading (Qld) Pty Ltd, 1983-84; Natl Product Dev Mngr, ACI Ltd, 1984-87; Asst to Mngng Dir and Hd of Mktng and Promotions, Old Sydney Town, 1988-89; Cnslt, Aaron Duhon Hyodo and Shinagawa, 1989-91; Gen Mngr, Dir of Product Planning, Uniting Ch of Aust, 1991-93; Inds Mngr, Corrections Corp of Aust Pty Ltd, 1993-97; Indl Marketer, 1998-; Wesley Hosp, Dev Offr, 1998-. Publications: Synopsis To Goodbye Mr Chips; The Awakening Giant, 3 Volumes. Honours include: Encouragement Awd for Govt Mktng, Austl Mktng Inst Awds, 1991; Premier of Queensland Awds for Export Achievement, 1991; Order of the Knight Templar of Jerusalem, 1986; Men's Inner Circle of Achievement, 1996; Meritorious Mktng Awd, 1999; 2,000 Outstndng Schls of the 20th Century Medal, 1999. Memberships include: Mktng Rsch Soc; Austl Mktng Inst; Inst of Dirs in Aust; The Masonry Soc, CO, USA; Austl Incentive Assn; Rsch Bd Advsrs, Amn Biographical Inst. Listed in: Many, including: Who's Who in Australia; Who's Who in Marketing (Australia); Intl Bk of Hons, USA; Who's Who in Asia; Who's Who in Australia and the Pacific Nations, 1998; Who's Who in Asia and the Pacific Nations, 1999;. Hobbies: Reading; Swimming; Rugby Union. Address: 61 Dandenong Road, Jamboree Heights, Queensland 4074, Australia.

HUTCHISON Keith Robert, b. 20 Sept 1944, Sydney, Australia. Academic. m. 20 Sept 1969, 2 s. Education: BSc, hons, Austl Natl Univ, 1967; MSc, Monash, 1968; Dipl, HPS, Oxon, 1969; DPhil, Oxon, 1977. Appointments: Tutor, Maths, Monash Univ, 1967-68, The Open Univ, 1970-71; Tutor, Guest Lectr, Maths, Open Univ, 1971, 1972; Lectr, Maths, Stats, Sch of Appl Sci, Riverina Coll of Adv Educ, Wagga Wagga, NSW, 1973-75; Rsch Asst, Univ Melbourne, 1975; Rsch Assoc, Dept of Hist of Sci and Technol, Univ Manchester Inst of Sci and Technol, 1976; Lectr, Hist of Sci, Swinburne Inst of Technol, 1977, 1981, 1982, 1983; Tutor, 1975-84, Lectr, 1978-79, 1983-84, Snr Lectr, 1985-, Univ Melbourne; Gast Prof, Univ of Hamburg, Germany, 1998; Prof Contratto, Univ Pavia, Italy, 1998. Publications include: Temporal asymmetry in classical mechanics, 1995; Differing criteria for temporal reversibility, 1995; Why does Plato urge rulers to study astronomy?, 1996. Honour: Zeitlein-Verbrugge Prize, 1985. Memberships include: Hist of Sci Soc; Brit Soc for the Hist of Sci;

Australasian Assn for the Hist, Philos and Socl Stdies of Sci. Address: HPS Department, University of Melbourne, Parkville 3052, Australia.

HUTTON Pierre Norman, b. 16 July 1928, Hobart, Tas, Aust. Consultant. m. Judith Mary Carnegie, 11 Apr 1964, 1 s, 4 d. Education. BCom, Tas; Dip, Dipl Studies, Canberra Univ Coll. Appointments: Diplomatic Staff Cadet, 1949; Dept of External Affairs, 1950-52; Served in Bangkok, 1952-58; Dept External Affairs, UN Div, 1958-59; Snr Pvte Sec to Min, 1959-60; Indonesia, 1960-62; Hd, Malaysia, Indonesia Sect, 1962-64; Dpty Perm Repr to the UN, Geneva, 1964-67; Pub Info Offr, 1967-70; High Commnr, Nigeria, 1970-73; Amb, Lebanon, Iraq, Syria, Jordan, 1973-75; Asst Sec, Acting First Asst Sec, Dept of For Affairs, 1975-78; Amb, Egypt, The Sudan, 1978-81; Amb, Switzerland, 1981-85; Hd, Eur Branch, Dept of For Affairs, 1985-87; Retd, 1987; Visits Cnslt, Dept of PM, 1990-96; Rsch Assoc, Cntr for SE Asian Studies, Monash Univ, 1990-92; Mbr, Advisory Cttee, Cntr for Asian Pacific Studies, Vic Univ, 1995-. Creative Works: The Legacy of Suez, 1996; After the Heroic Age, 1997; The Forgotten First Australian Official Overseas Representative Outside the British Empire, 1999. Memberships: Austl Inst of Intl Affairs; Genealogical Soc of Vic. Hobbies: Genealogical and Historical Research; Walking; Reading. Address: 5 Kiata Court, Mount Eliza, Vic 3930, Australia.

HWANG Deng Fwu, b. 14 Mar 1953, Taiwan. Professor. m. Lin Shu Hua, 22 Mar 1979, 2 s. Education: BS, 1975, MS, 1981, Natl Taiwan Coll of Marine Sci and Technol; PhD, Tokyo Univ, 1988. Appointments: Lectr, 1981-88, Assoc Prof, 1988-89, Natl Taiwan Coll of Marine Sci and Technol; Assoc Prof, 1989-91, Prof, 1991-, Natl Taiwan Ocean Univ. Publications: Illustration of the Toxic Fish in Taiwan; Illustration of One Hundred Toxic Fish in Taiwan; Environmental Protection of Costal Ecosystem. Honours: Gen Rsch Awd, Natl Sci Cncl, 1988-90; Ex Rsch Awd, Natl Sci Cncl, 1991-92; Outstndng Rsch Awd, Natl Sci Cncl, 1993-98; Rsch Awd, Chinese Inst of Sci and Technol, 1993. Memberships: Fisheries Soc of Taiwan; Toxicol Soc of Taiwan; Intl Soc of Toxicol. Hobbies: Bridge; Philately; Poker. Address: Department of Food Science, National Taiwan Ocean University, 2 Pei-Ning Road, Keelung, Taiwan.

HWANG In-Sung, b. 9 Jan 1926. Politician. Education: Korea Mil Acady; Seoul Natl Univ. Appointments: Army Offr, 1960-68; Asst Min without Portfolio, 1970; Chf Sec to PM, 1973; Gov N Cholla Prov, 1973-78; Min of Transp, 1978; Pres KNTC, 1980; Min of Agric Forestry and Fisheries, 1985-87; Chmn, Asiana Air Lines, 1988-93; Pres, Kumho Air Lines, 1989-93; Chmn, Polit Cttee Dem Liberal Party, 1992; PM of Repub of Korea, Mar-Dec 1993. Memberships: Mbr Natl Ass, 1981, 1985, 1992. Address: c/o Office of the Prime Minister, Seoul, Republic of Korea.

HYAM Frank, b. 22 Aug 1926, Brisbane, Aust. Actor; Cartoonist; Writer; Freelance Lecturer. m. Joyce, 14 Apr 1951, 1 d. Education: Ctf Educ, BA, MA, Univ Qld. Appointments: Clerical Duties, State Pub Serv, RAAF, Law Firm, Newsppr, Car Sales Firm, City Cncl; Tchr, Primary Sch, Secondary Sch, Adult Educ, 1953-67; Tchr, Bavarian Educ Dept Acad HS, Peoples Univ, Munich Cty Cncl Lang Sch, 1968; Lectr, BCAE, 1969-88; Tutor, Univ Qld; Performer, Th, Film, Radio and TV; Advsr, Brisbane Warana Fest. Publications: Readers For Students of English in Germany and French in Australia; Inspiration in Colour and Stitch - A Series of Pieces Based on Lewis Carroll's Alice, 1997. Honour: Life Mbr, Austl Writers Guild. Hobby: Self-education. Address: 21 Elkhorn Street, Enoggera, Queensland 4051, Australia.

HYAM Joyce Rae, b. 18 Jan 1923, Brisbane, Aust. Artist. m. Frank, 14 Apr 1951, 1 d. Education: Fine Art Ctf. Appointments: Art Instr, Coll of Art, Brisbane, 1962-83; Lectr, Bd of Adult Educ, Brisbane, 1963-72; Art Lectr, Kindergarten Tchrs Coll, Kelvin Grove, 1965, 1973; Art and Craft Lectr, Sch Dental Therapy, 1974-87; Judge, Toowoomba Quilters, 1985; Tutor, Quilt Experience, Toowoomba, 1994. Publications include: Interior

Decoration for Australian Homes, 1972; Australian Waters, 1996; The Alice Series: Joyce Hyam, 1997; Inspiration in Colour and Stitch, 1997; Here Be Magic, 1997. Honours: 1st Prizes, 1972, 1978, 1980, 1981, 1998; 2nd Prizes, 1987, 1997; Highly Commended, 1980, 1982, 1993; Commended, 1980, 1987. Hobbies: Gardening; Art. Address: 21 Elkhorn Street, Enoggera, Brisbane, Queensland 4051, Australia.

HYDE Geoffrey Gerard, b. 5 June 1953, Dandenong, Aust. Tourism Adviser; Consultant. m. Jane, 2 s, 2 d. Education: BA, Mngmt; MSc, Tourism. Appointments: Lectr, Tourism Studies, Vic Univ of Technol, 1985-88; Ptnr, Hyde King & Assocs, Melbourne, 1986-90; Tourism Cnslt, World Tourism Org Secretariat, Madrid, Spain, 1988; Snr Cnslt, Touche Ross, Melbourne, 1988-89; Snr Cnslt, Mingatjuta Cnsltng Servs, Gen Mngr, Destination Aust Mktng & Consultancy Pty Ltd, Melbourne, 1989-91; Tourism Devel Advsr, Govt of W Samoa, 1991-94; Tourism Mktng Advsr, W Samoa Vis Bur, 1995; Specl Tourism Cnslt, S Pacific Project Fac, 1995; Tourism Mktng Advsr, Govt of St Vincent & the Grenadines, W Indies, 1996-. Publications: Leisure and Recreation Directory, 1982; Tourism Policy in Australia and the USA - A Comparative Analysis, 1986; Tourism Marketing in a Competitive Environment - The Interdata Leisure and Tourism Handbook, 1989-90; Developing Tourism Projects with Aboriginal Communities, 1990-91; Tourism Marketing in Australia, 1989. Memberships: Austl Inst of Travel an Tdourism; Eco-Tourism Soc; Austl Inst of Mngmt. Hobbies: Scuba Diving; Reading; Blues Music. Address: 4 Rugby Road, Oakleigh, Victoria, Australia.

HYDE Miriam Beatrice, b. 15 Jan 1913, Adelaide, SA. Aust. Composer; Pianist. m. Marcus Bruce Edwards, 26 Dec 1939, 1s, 1 d. Education: LAB, AMUA, 1928, Mus Bac, 1931, Univ of Adelaide; Roy Coll of Music, London, Eng, 1932-35; ARCM, Piano and Composition, LRAM, 1935. Appointments: Brdcstng for ABC, 1929-; Examiner, Austl Music Exams Bd, 1945-82; Advsry Bd 1958-83; Patron, Music Tchrs Assn of NSW and SA, The Austl Musicians Acady; The Eisteddfods of the Blue Mnts and Inner West; Lectr and Recitalist, sems in Aust; Recitals in Jakarta, 1973. Creative works include: 2 piano concertos performed w LPO, LSO and BBC and Aust Orch; 25 piano solos recorded 1986; Recital of own Wrks, RCM, 1997; Composer of num pieces, inclng 4 overtures, chmbr music and songs; 2 CDs of Chamber music, 1997; 2 CDs of own piano works and 2 concertos w the W Aust Symph Orch; Complete Accord (autobiog), 1991. Honours: OBE, 1981; Sullivan, Farrar, Cobbett Prizes, RCM, 1932-35; Anzac Song Prizes, 1951, 1952, 1955; Brewster Jones Prize, 1952; ABC APRA Prizes, 1942-1954, 1955; Shared Prize, Jubilee of Music Tchrs Assn of NSW; Melbourne Sun Song Quest, 1st Prize, 1955; AO, 1991; Hon D Litt, Macquarie Univ, 1993; Hon F Mus A, 1995. Memberships include: Music Tchrs Assn of NSW and Vic; Fellshp of Austl Composers; Australasian Performing Right Assn; Fndng and Hon Mbr Strathfield Symph Orch. Hobbies: Gardening; Italian. Address: 12 Kelso Street, Burwood Heights, NSW 2136, Australia.

HYLAND Matthew Thomas, b. 20 Feb 1920. m. Marjorie Picton, 24 Nov 1951, 1 s, 3 d. Appointments: Joined Dept of Navy, 1938; Var Budget and Acctng posns at Navy Off, Melbourne and Sydney; Course at Admnstv Staff Coll, Mt Eliza, 1963; Royal Coll of Def Studs, London, 1966; Acting Sec, 1960; First Asst Sec (Fin and Material), 1964-73; Acting First Asst Sec (Progs and Budgets), Dept of Def, 1974-82; Acting Dpty Sec, 1982 (retd). Honour: OBE, 1969. Hobbies: Golf; Bowls; Fishing. Address: 83 Jacka Crescent, Campbell, ACT 2612, Australia.

HYLANDS Peter Howard Ronald, b. 20 May 1952. Managing Director. m. Andrea, 28 Sept 1974. Appointments: Partner, Hillgrove Pottery, 1984-; Dir, Longman Cheshire, Longman Aust, 1990-96; Mngng Dir, Pearson Profl, Aust Pty Ltd, incorporating FT Law and Tax, Pitman Publng, Churchill Livingstone, Bus Law Educ Ctr, 1995-; Mngng Dir, Hillgrove Media International, 1997- Hobbies: Natural History; Conservation; Arts;

Design; Architecture. Address: Hillgrove, Henry Street, Chewton, Vic 3451, Australia.

HYNDMAN Robin John, b. 2 May 1967, Melbourne, Vic, Aust. Statistician. m. Leanne, 9 Dec 1989, 2 s, 2 d. Education: BS, Hons, Univ of Melbourne, 1988; PhD, 1992. Appointments: Statistical Cnslt, Statistical Cnsltng Cntr Univ of Melbourne, 1985-92; Lectr, Dept of Stats, 1993-94; Lectr, Dept of Maths, Monash Univ, 1995-96; Snr Lectr, Dept of Maths and Stats, 1997-98; Snr Lectr, Dept of Econometrics and Bus Stats, 1998-; Visng Prof, Dept of Stats, CO State Univ, 1998. Publications: Many publs, Refereed articles, chapts, rsch pprs; Forecasting, Methods and Applications, 1998; Forecasting, Methods and Applications, Instructors Manual, 1998. Honours: Second Maurice H Belz Prize in Stats, Univ of Melbourne, 1986; Norma McArthur Prize in Stats, 1987; First Class Sci Fac Hons, 1987; Dwights Prize in Stats, 1988; First Class Sci Fac Hons, 1988; Finalist, Channel Ten Young Achiever Awds, 1990; Awd for Excellence in Tchng, 1998; Dictionary of Intl Biog, IBC, 1999. Memberships: Statistical Soc of Aust; Amn Stats Assoc. Hobbies: Christadelphian Church; Speaking. Address: Monash Univ Dept of Econometrics and Business Statistics, Wellington Road, Clayton Vic 3168, Australia.

HYSLOP Robert, b. 24 Dec 1918, Pelaw Main, NSW, Aust. Civil Servant. m. Dorothy Fleming, 14 Sept 1946, 2 d. Education: Dip, Acctng, ACT. Appointments: Asst Sec, Dept Navy, 1959; Dpty Sec Gen, SEATO, 1971; Hd, Hons Secretariat, 1977. Publications include: Australian Naval Administration 1900-1939, 1973; Aye Aye, Minister: Australian Naval Administration 1939-1959, 1991; Dear You: A Guide to Forms of Address, 1991; Australian Mandarins: Perceptions of the Role of Departmental Secretaries, 1993; First Encounter: A Guide to Communicating with Institutions and Organizations, 1994; A Very Civil Servant, 1998. Honour: ISO, 1980. Memberships: Assoc, Fed Inst of Accts, 1940; Inst of Pub Admin, 1946-; Aust Soc of Indexes. Hobbies: Sculpture; Lawn bowls; Writing. Address: 33 Hampton Circuit, Yarralumla, ACT 2600, Australia.

I

IANCONESCU Marius, b. 4 Aug 1929, Bucharest, Romania. Physician. m. Elena, 25 Nov 1994, 1 s, 1 d. Education: MD, 1954; PhD, Virology and Immunology, 1960. Appointments: Physn, 1954-55; Rsch in Virology at Inst of Virology, Romania, 1956-62; Rsch at Kimron Vet Inst, Israel, 1963-94; Hd, R&D Lab, Shafit, Israel. Publications: 6 books on virology and cell cultures; Over 90 wrks in sci publs. Honours; Intl Union Cancer, E Roosevelt Intl Awd, 1968-69; Nimron Rsch Prize, 1972, 1974, 1994; Memberships: Hon Mbr, Romanian Acady of Medl Scis, 1994; Var profl assns. Hobbies: Fishing; Photography. Address: Shafit Biological Laboratories, 60990 Kibbutz Shefaim, Israel.

IBRAHIM Encik Anwar bin, b. 10 Aug 1947. Politician. Education: Univ of Malaya. Appointments: Pres UMNO Yth Movement, 1982-; VP UMNO, 1982-; Hd UMNO Permatang Pauh Div, 1982-; Dep Min PMs Dept, 1982; Min of Sport Yth and Culture, 1983; Min of Agric, 1984-86; Min of Educ, 1986-91; Min of Fin, 1991-; Dep PM, Dec 1993-. Address: Ministry of Finance, Block 9, Kompleks Pejabat Kerajaan, Jalan Duta, 50592 Kuala Lumpur, Malaysia.

IBRAHIM Izzat, b. 1942, al-Dour Shire. Politician. Appointments: Ed Voice of the Peasant, 1968; Hd Supreme Cttee for People's Wrk, 1968-70; Min of Agrarian Reform, 1970-74; VP Supreme Agric Cncl, 1970-71; Hd, 1971-79; Min of Agric, 1973-74; Min of Interior, 1974-79; Vice-Chmn Revolutionary Command Cncl, 1979-; Dpty Sec-Gen Regl Command of Arab Baath Socl Party, Jul 1979-. Memberships: Mbr Revolutionary Command Cncl; Mbr Natl Command Arab Baath Socl Party. Address: Arab Baath Socl Party, Office of the Deputy Sec-Gen, P O Box 6012, Al-Mansour, Baghdad, Iraq.

IBRAIMOV Abyt, b. 1 Jan 1948, Kyrghyzstan. Geneticist. m. Baltaeva, 1970, 3 s. Education: Kyrghyz State Medl Inst, 1970; Postgrad Course, Acady Medl Scis, USSR, 1974. Appointments: Snr Rschr, Lab of Med Inst, 1970-74; Hd of Lab, Kyrghyz Cardiology Inst, 1974-. Publications: Human Genetics, 1979, 4th edn, 1986; Cytobios, 1990, 1991; Human Evolution, 1993. Honour: Intl Scientific Fndn, 1991, 1994. Memberships: Natl Acady of Scis of Kyrghyz Repub, 1994; NY Acady of Scis, 1996. Hobby; Hunting. Address: Laborat Human Genetics, National Center of Cardiology and Therapy, Togolok Moldo str 3, Bishkek 720040, Kyrghyzstan CIS.

ICHIKAWA Kon, b. 1915. Film Director. Education: Ichioka Com Sch Osaka. Films incl: Foo-San, 1953; A Billionaire, 1954; The Heart, 1954; Punishment Room, 1955; The Burmese Harp, 1956; The Men of Tohoku, 1956; Conflagration, 1958; Fires on the Plain, 1959; The Key, 1959; Bonchi, 1960; Her Brother, 1960; The Sin, 1961; Being Two Isn't Easy, 1962; The Revenge of Yuki-No-Jo, 1963; Alone on the Pacific, 1963; Tokyo Olympiad, 1964; Seishun, 1970; To Love Again, 1971; The Wanderers, 1973; Visions of Eight - co-dir - 1973; Wagahai wa Neko de Aru, 1975; The Ingunami's, 1976; Gokumon-to, 1977; Joobachi, 1978; Byoin-zaka no Kubikukuri no le, 1979; Ancient City, 1980; The Makioka Sisters, 1983; Actress, 1987; Fusa, 1993; The Forty-Seven Ronin, 1994.

IDE Shoichi. Politician. Appointments: Fmr Parly Vice-Min Econ Plng Agency; Min of Hlth and Welfare, 1994-95; Chmn Sakigake Party in House of Reps; Dir, Budget Cttee. Memberships: Mbr House of Reps for Nagano. Address: c/o Ministry of Health and Welfare, 1-2-2, Kasumigaseki, Chiyoda-ku, Tokyo 100, Japan.

IGARASHI Koza. Politician. Appointments: Fmr Mayor Asahika-wa Cty; Dir Pub Info; Min of Constrn, 1993-94; Chf Sec to CAST, 1994-95. Memberships: Mbr House of Reps; Mbr, Socl Dem Party of Japan. Address: House of Representatives, Tokyo, Japan.

IGGULDEN John Manners, b. 12 Feb 1917, Brighton, Vic, Aust. Author; Industrialist; Environmentalist. m. Helen Carroll Schapper, 1 s dec, 2 d. Appointments: Mngmt, sev cos, 1940-59; Writer, 1959-70, 1980-; Chf Exec, Planet Lighting and Lucinda Glassworks, Bellingen, NSW. Publications include: Breakthrough, 1960; The Clouded Sky, 1965; Summers Tales 3, 1966; Gliding Instructors Handbook, 1968; Revolution of the Good, 1986; The Modification of Freedom, 1993; The Sound of the Rainbow; Good World. Honours: Austl Natl Gliding Champion, 1959-60; Rep, 9th World Gliding Championships, Argentina, 1963. Memberships: Life Gov, Gliding Fedn of Aust; Port Phillip Conservation Cncl. Address: Gleniffer Road, Promised Land, Bellingen, NSW 2454, Australia.

IHARA Yasuo, b. 16 Feb 1945, Matsué, Japan. Neuropathologist. m. Keiko Kato, 29 Mar 1975, 1 s, 1 d. Education: MD, 1971, PhD, 1979, Tokyo Univ Med Sch. Appointments: Asst Prof, Neurol, Univ of Tokyo, 1982-84; Hd, Clin Physiol, Tokyo Metro Inst of Gerontol, 1984-90; Prof, Chmn, Neuropathol, Univ Tokyo, 1991-. Honours: Bälz Prize, 1994; Potamkin Prize, 1995; Metro Life Fndn Awd for Med Rsch, 1997. Memberships: Japan Soc for Neurochem; Japan Soc for Neuropathol. Address: 4-30-5 Utsukushigaoka, Aoba-ku, Yokohama 225-0002, Japan.

IIDA Nobutoshi, b. 14 Nov 1928, Hokkaido, Japan. Medical Doctor. m. Yuri, 15 June 1952, 2 d. Education: MD; PhD. Appointments: Chf, Medl Dept, Yodogawa Christian Hosp; Chf, Nephrology, Osaka Prefecture Gen Hosp; Prof, Ainogakuin Coll. Publications: Num medl textbooks. Honour: Dip of Hon, Japanese Welfare Min, 1997. Memberships: Intl Soc of Nephrology; Amn Soc of Nephrology. Hobbies: Reading history books; Travel. Address: 3-4-33 Bandaihigashi, Sumiyoshi, Osaka 558-0056, Japan.

IKEDA Daisaku, b. 2 Jan 1928 Tokyo. Philos; Auth. m. Kaneko Shiraki, 1952, 2 s. Education: Fuji Coll. Appointments: Pres Soka Gakkai, 1960-79; Pres Soka Gakkai Intl, 1975-; Fndr Soka Univ Soka Univ Am Soka Women's Jnr Coll Tokyo Kansai Soka Schs Soka Kindergartens - Sapporo Hong Kong Singapore and Malaysia - Inst of Oriental Philos Boston Rsch Cntr for the 21st Century Toda Inst for Global Peace and Policy Rsch Tokyo Shinauoka Fuji Art Mus Min-On Concert Assn and Victor Hugo House of Lit. Publications: The Human Revolution Vols I-V, 1972-84; The Living Buddha, 1976; Choose Life, 1976; Buddhism: The First Millenium, 1977; Glass Children and Other Essays, 1979; La Nuit Appelle L'Aurore, 1980; A Lasting Peace vols I-II, 1981, 1987; Life: An Enigma, a Precious Jewel, 1982; Before It Is Too Late, 1984; Buddhism and Cosmos, 1985; The Flower of Chinese Buddhism, 1986; Human Values in a Changing World, 1987; Unlocking the Mysteries of Birth and Death, 1988; The Snow Country Prince, 1990; The Princess and the Moon, 1992; A Lifelong Quest for Peace, 1992; Choose Peace, 1995; A New Humanism: The University Addresses of Daisaku Ikeda, 1996; Ikeda-Gorbachev Dialogue - in Japanese, 1996; New Human Revolution Vol I - in Japanese, 1998; Other writings on Buddhism civilization life and Peace. Honours: Dr hc - Moscow State Univ - 1975; Hon Pres Soka Gakkai, 1979-; Poet Laureate World Acady of Arts and Culture India, 1981-; Dr hc - Sofia - 1981; Hon Prof Natl Univ of San Marcos, 1981; UN Peace Awd, 1983; Order of the Sun of Peru with Grand Cross, 1984; Hon Prof Beijing Univ, 1984; Hon Prof Fudan Univ, 1984; Jebta Irak Kut Awd, 1986; UNHCR Humanitarian Awd, 1989; Dr hc - Buenos Aires - 1990; Grand Cross Order of Merit in May - Argentina - 1990; Natl Order of S Dr hc - Southern Cross - Brazil - 1990; Kt Grand Cross of the Most Noble Order of the Crown - Thailand - 1991; Univ of the Philippines - 1991; Dr hc - Nairobi - 1992; Dr hc - Ankara - 1992; Hon Cross of Sci and the Arts - Austria - 1992; Hon Prof Natl Univ of Lomas de Zamora, 1993; Rosa Parks Humanitarian Awd - USA - 1993; Simon Wiesenthal Cntr Intl Tolerance Awd - USA - 1993; Dr hc - Glasgow - 1994; Dr hc - Tribhuvan - 1995; Dr hc - Hong Kong - 1996; Dr hc - Denver - 1996; Dr hc - Havana - 1996; Dr hc - Univ of Ghana - 1996; Dr hc - Natl Univ of Mongolia - 1996; Other Dr hcs; Hon mbr Club of Rome, 1996-; Kt Grand Cross of Rizal -

Philippines - 1996; Hon mbr Inst of Oriental Studies of Russian Acady of Scis, 1996-; Hon Prof Jilin Univ, 1997; Hon Sen Eurn Acady of Scis and Arts, 1997-; Tagore Peace Awd The Asiatic Soc - India - 1997; Other Awds. Memberships: For mbr Brazilian Acady of Letters, 1993-. Hobbies: Photog. Address: 32 Shinano-machi, Shinjuku-ku, Tokyo 160, Japan.

IKEDA Kazuyosi, b. 15 July 1928, Fukuoka, Japan. Professor of Theoretical Physics; Poet. m. Mieko Ikeda, 20 Oct 1956, 1 s, 1 d. Education: Grad, degree "Rigakusi", Dept of Phys, Fac of Sci, Kyushu Univ, 1951; Postgrad course, Dept of Phys, Fac of Sci, Kyushu Univ, 1951-56; DSc, 1957; Hon Dr Environ Sci, 1993; Hon DLitt, 1995. Appointments: Asst, 1956-60, Assoc Prof, 1960-65, Dept of Phys, Fac of Sci, Kyushu Univ; Assoc Prof, 1965-68, Prof, 1968-89, Dept of Applied Phys, Fac of Engrng, Osaka Univ; Prof, Dept Math Scis, 1989-92, Prof Emeritus, 1992-, Fac of Engrng, Osaka Univ; Prof, 1992-, Pres, 1995-, Intl Earth Environ Univ, Japan. Publications: Over 100 pprs on theort phys; Books: Statistical Thermodynamics, 1975; Mechanics without Use of Mathematical Formulae, From a Moving Stone to Halley's Comet, 1980; Invitation to Mechanics, with Appendix on a Comet in Ancient Times, 1985; Basic Mechanics, 1987; Basic Thermodynamics, From Entropy to Osmotic Pressure, 1991; Bansyoo Hyakusi (collection of poems), 1986; The World of God, Creation and Poetry, 1991; Graphical Theory of Relativity, 1998; Poems on the Hearts of Creation, 1993; Mountains, 1995; North, South, East and West, 1996; Book of Poems, Hearts of Myriad Things in the Universe, 1998; Kazuyosi's Poetry on the Animate and the Inanimate, 1998; Poems on Love and Peace, 1998; Num Poems and essays in Intl Jrnls and Athologies. Honours include: Yukawa Commemorative Schlshp Awd, 1954; Grand Amb of Achievement, 1989; Hall of Fame ABI, 1989; Intl Order of Merit, 1990; Chevalier Grand Cross, 1991; Golden Acady Awd for Lifetime Achievement, 1991; Intl Hons Cup, 1992; 20th Century Awd for Achievement, 1993; Prize Catania e il suo Vulcano, 1994; Prize, Catania Duomo, 1995; Gold Star Awd, 1995; World w/w Hall of Fame, 1996; IBC Dir Gen's Hons List, 1996; Intl Sash of Academia, 1997; Millennium Hall of Fame, 1997; Kt of Templar Order, 1995; Kt of Lofsensic Ursinus Order, 1995; Kt of Holy Grail Order, 1995; Kt of San Ciriaco Order, 1995; Man of Yr, 1990, 1993-95, 1997, 1998; Personality of Yr, 1991, 1998; Intl Man of Yr, 1991, 1992, 1996, 1997, 1998, 1999; Intl Man of Millennium, 1999. Hobbies: Seeing Kabuki and Noh plays; Seeing and performing Noh farces. Address: Nisi-7-7-11 Aomadani, Minoo-si, Osaka 562-0023, Japan.

IKEDA Yukihiko, b. 13 May 1937 Kobe Cty Hyogo Pref. Politician. Education: Univ of Tokyo. Appointments: Overall Co-ord Div Min's Sec min of Fin, 1961; Seconded to Min of For Affairs, served four yrs as Vice-Consul NY, 1964; Priv Sec to Min of Fin, 1974; Dep Chf Cabinet Sec, 1981; Chmn PMs Off Div Policy Rsch Cncl of LDP, 1983; Chmn Cttee on Fin HoR, 1986; Dir-Gen Mngr and Co-ord Agcy, 1989; Dep Sec-Gen LDP, 1990; Dir-Gen Def Agcy, 1990-91; Min for For Affairs, 1996-97; Chmn, Rsch Commn on the Annuities Syst Plcy Rsch Cncl LDP, 1977; Chmn Plcy Rsch Cncl, LDP, 1998-. Memberships: Mbr HoR, 1976-. Address: 1-11-23 Nagata-cho, Chiyoda-ku, Tokyo 100-8910, Japan.

IKEUCHI Tatsuro, b. 20 Jan 1942, Antong, China. Associate Professor. m. Hiroko Aoki, Nov 1976, 1 s, 1 d. Education: MSc, 1966, DSc, 1972, Grad Sch, Hokkaido Univ. Appointments: Rsch Assoc, Roswell Pk Mem Inst, NY, USA, 1968-71; Asst Prof, Fac of Sci, Hokkaido Univ, 1975-79; Assoc Prof, Tokyo Medl and Dental Univ, 1979-. Publications: Over 150 sci pprs in profl jrnls, 1964-. Memberships: Japan Soc Human Genetics; Genetic Soc of Japan; Japan Cancer Assn; Soc of Chromosome Rsch. Hobby: Philately. Address: Division of Genetics, Medical Research Institute, Tokyo Medical and Dental University, Yushima 1-5-45, Bunkyo-ku, Tokyo, 113-0034, Japan.

ILBERY Peter Red, b. 20 Mar 1923, Perth, WA. Medical Practitioner. m. Marianne Boyer, 8 Mar 1951, 2 s, 2,d. Education: MB; BS; DCRA; MD, Sydney; DMRT. Appointments: Assoc Prof, Radiobiology, 1970; Medl Dir Victorian Cancer Inst, 1978; Spec Advsr, NH and MRC, 1988; Cnslt Radiologist. Creative Works: Radiobiology, 1964; Empire Airmen Strike Back, 1999; Over 100 Sci Pprs, Radiation Med. Honours: RFD, 1984. Memberships: AMA; BIR; FRACR; FRACP; FFAFPHM. Address: 93 Hawkesbury Crescent, Farrer, ACT 2607, Australia.

ILES Robert Lindsay, b. 8 Nov 1945. Educator. m. Lesley Ann Thomas, 21 Dec 1968, 2 s, 1 d. Education: BA; BEd; MEd; DipRE; PHD. Appointments: Tchr, St Arnaud hs, 1967-68; Castlemaine hs, 1969-70; Box Hill hs, 1971-85; Exchange Tchr, H A Kostash Sch, Smoky Lake, Alberta, Can; Snr Policy Offr, Min Educ, Vic, 1986-89; Curric Co-ord, Presby Ladies Coll, Burwood, Vic, 1989-93; Prin, The Scots Coll, Sydney, 1994-. Honours: Intl Tchng Fell, 1981; Study Fellowship, Min Educ, Vic, 1982-83. Memberships: Aust Coll Educ; Assn Hds Indep Schs, Aust; Headmasters Conf, UK; Assoc Fell, Austl Inst Mngmt. Hobbies: Cricket; Reading; AFL Football. Address: The Scots College, Victoria Road, Bellevue Hill, NSW, Australia.

ILLUECA Jorge E, b. 17 Dec 1918, Panama City. Politician; Diplomat. m. 4 children. Education: Univ de Panama; Harvard Law Sch; Univ Chgo. Appointments: Dpty Perm Rep to UN, 1957, Perm Rep, 1960, 1976-81, 1994-97; Mbr Del to UN Gen Assembly, 1957, 1961, 1975, Specl Emergency Session; Prof, Univ de Panama, 1962-63, 1966-68; Pres, Natl Bar Assn, 1963-64, 1966-68; Dir, El Panama Am (newsppr), 1963-64 1967-68; Specl Amb to USA for new Panama Canal Treaty, 1964; Specl Envoy, 1972; Hd of Del, 1st Session of 3rd UN Conf on Law of the Sea, 1974; Mbe, Perm Ctr of Arbitration, The Hague, Netherlands, 1974-76; Mbr Del, 4th Session, 1976; Fgn Min, VP of Panama, 1982-83; Pres, 38th Session of UN Gen Assn, 1983; Pres, Panama, 1984. Honour: Univ Thant Awd, 1983. Address: c/o Ministry of Foreign Affairs, Panama 4, Panama.

ILME Anil Bhikuji, b. 26 Sept 1967, Sonegaon Kharda. Chairman; Director. Education: Grad Dip, Export Mngmnt; Dip, Hum Resc Dev; BSc. Appointments: Chem, J B Oil and Vegetabel Prods Ltd; Proj Offr, Gramgita Rural Dev Soc; Chmn, Dir, Bhavishyavedha Rural Dev Soc. Creative Works: Trng Progs, Mushroom Cultivation, 1998. Honours: MSPI Outstndng Personalitites Awd, 1998; Memberships: Mushroom Growers Assoc; Lokmanya Vachanalya Sanstha. Hobby: Rural Development. Address: Development Society, Prithviraj Nagar, Dhamangaon Rly, 444709 MS, India.

IMAI Nobuko, b. 18 Mar 1943, Tokyo, Japan. Violist. m. Aart von Bochove, 1981, 1 s, 1 d. Education: Toho Sch of Music, Tokyo; Yale Univ; Juilliard Sch of Music, NY. Appointments: Mbr of Vermeer Quartet, 1974-79; Soloist w London Symph Orch, Royal Phil, Chgo Symph, Berlin Phil, Concertgebouw Orch, Montreal Symph, Boston Symph, Vienna Symph, Stockholm Phil; Fests incl: Marlboro, Casals, S Bank Summer Music, Bath, Cheltenham, Aldeburgh, London Promenade Concerts, Intl Viola Cong, Houston, Salzburg. Creative works: Recordings: Tippett's Triple Concerto and Berlioz's Harold in Italy, w London Symph Orch under Colin Davis; Mozart and Haydn Duos w Mark Lubotsky; Brahms' Sonatas, Schumann's Märchenbilder; Schubert's Arpeggione, Beethoven's Notturno Op 42 w Roger Vignoles; Shostakovich' Sonata, Glinka's Sonata, Schnittke's Viola Concerto and Mozart Quintets, w Orlando Quartet; Mozart's Sinfonia Concertante, w Iona Brown; Hindemith's Sonatas for Solo Viola, Denisov's Concertos, J S Bach: viola da gamba Sonatas w Roland Pöntinen, Schumann chambermusic w Martha Argerich; Walton's Concerto, Franck's and Vieuxtemps' Sonatas; Viola Bouquet: Works for Viola and Piano, w Roland Pöntinen. Honours: 1st Prize, Munich Intl Viola Competition; 2nd Prize, Geneva Intl Viola Competition; Avon Awd, 1993; Mobil Prize of Japan, 1995; Suntory Hall Prize, 1996; Initiator and Artistic Dir, Hindemith Fests, Tokyo, London, NY, 1995. Hobbies: Golf; Cooking.

Address: c/o Irene Witmer Personal Management in Classical Music, Kerkstraat 97, NL-1017 GD Amsterdam, Netherlands.

IMAM Zafar, b. 1940, Bangladesh. Politician. Education: Punjab Univ. Appointments: Pakistan Army, 1966, CO, 10th Bengal Regt, 1971, Lt-Col, 1975; Mbr, Bangladesh Natl Party Exec Cttee, 1978; MP, 1979; Dpty Min of Relief & Rehab, 1980; Min, 1985-86; Min of Jute, 1986-88, Textiles, 1988-89, Forests & Environ, 1990-91. Honour: Bir Birkram Awd. Address: c/o Ministry of Forests & Environment, Dhaka, Bangladesh.

IMANAKA Makoto, b. 21 June 1951, Amagasaki Cty, Hyogo Pref, Japan. Engineer. m. Yukiyo Uemara, 2 d. Education: BEng, Himeji Inst Tech, 1973; MEng, 1975, DEng, 1986, Nagoya Univ. Appointments: Rschr, Koei Chem Co Ltd, 1975-79; Rschr, Indl Rsch Inst Hyogo Pref, 1979-90; Assoc Prof, Osaka Univ of Educ, 1990-97; Prof, Osaka Univ of Educ, 1997-. Publications: 9 pprs in intl profl jrnls. Memberships: Soc Material Sci, Japan; Soc of Mech Engrs, Japan; Soc of Adhesion of Japan; Chem Engrng Soc of Japan; Amn Soc of Testing Metals. Address: Osaka University of Education, Asahgaoka Kashiwara City, Osaka 582, Japan.

IMANALIYEV Muratbeck Sansyzbayevich, b. 1956, Bishkek. Politician. m. 2 children. Education: Inst of Asian & African Countries; Moscow State Univ, Leningrad; Inst of Oriental Studies, USSR Acady of Scis. Appointments: 2nd Sec, Press & Info, Min of Fgn Affairs, Kyrgys Repub, 1982-88; Hd, Protocol Consulate Divsn, 1988-89; Hd, Consular Divsn, 1989-90; Min of Fgn Affairs, Kyrgyz Repub, 1991-93; Amb to China, 1993-96; Hd, Intl Divsn, Presl Admin, 1996-97; Min of Fgn Affairs, 1997-. Address: Ministry of Foreign Affairs, Erkindik Boulevard 54, 720021 Bishkek, Kyrgyz Republic.

IMBERGER Jörg, b. 10 Sept 1942, Aust. Professor. m. Barbara Edith Sandermann, 28 May 1964, 1 s, 1 d. Education: BCE, Univ of Melbourne, 1963; MEngSc, Univ of WA, 1966; PhD, Univ of CA, Berkeley, USA, 1970. Appointments: Rsch Engr, Dept of Civil Engrng, Univ of Adelaide, 1963-64; Snr Tutor, Dept of Maths, Univ of WA, 1964-67; Lectr, Dept of Maths and Civil Engrng, Univ of CA, Berkeley, USA, 1970-71; Lectr, 1972-76, Snr Lectr, 1975-76, Depts of Maths and Mech Engrng, Univ of WA; Asst Prof, 1976-77, Assoc Prof (w tenure), Univ of CA, Berkeley, USA, 1977-78; Prof, Civil and Environ Engrng, 1978-89, Dir, Cntr for Water Rsch, 1982-, Prof, Environ Engrng, 1989-, Hd, Dept of Environ Engrng, 1992-94, Univ of WA. Publications: Co-auth of 1 textbook; 12 contbns to books, 87 publns in refereed jrnls, 68 conf proceedings, 91 rprts. Honours include: Gledden Fell, 1967-69; Sci Fell, Univ CA, Berkeley, USA, 1969-70; Fairchild Fell, CA Inst of Technol, 1985-86; Elected Fell, Austl Acady of Technol Scis, 1985 Karl Emil Hilgard Hydraulics Prizes, Amn Soc of Civil Engrs, 1988, 1994; Jolly Awd, Austl Soc for Limnology, 1992; AO, 1992; Peter Hughes Water Awd, Austl Water and Wastewater Assn, 1995; Peter Nicol Russell Mem Medal, Inst of Engineers, Aust, 1995; Stockholm Water Prize, Stockholm Water Fndn, 1996; Western Austl Citizen of the Yr Awd, 1996; Clunies Ross Natl Sci and Technol Awd, 1997. Memberships: Fell, Inst of Engrs, Aust; Past-Pres, Austl Marine Scis Assn; Estuarine and Brackish Water Scis; Amn Soc of Limnology and Oceanography; Amn Soc of Civil Engrs; Amn Meterol Soc; Austl Limnology Soc; Amn Geophysl Union; Intl Assn of Hydraulic Rsch; Austl Water and Wastewater Assn. Hobbies: Photography; Travel. Address: Centre for Water Research, University of Western Australia, Nedlands, WA 6009, Australia.

IMRAN KHAN Niazi, b. 25 Nov 1952, Lahore, Pakistan. Cricketer. m. Jemima Goldsmith, 1995, 1 s. Education: Aitchison Coll & Cathedral Sch, Lahore; Worcester Roy Grammar Sch, England; Keble Coll, Oxford. Appointments: Right-Arm Fast Bowler, Mid-Order Right-Hand Batsman, Played for Lahore, 1969-71, Worcs, 1971-76, Oxford Univ, 1973-75 (Capt 1974), Dawood, 1975-76, PIA, 1975-81, Sussex, 1977-88, NSW, 1984-85; 88 Test matches for Pakistan, 1971-92, 48 as

Capt, scoring 3,807 runs (average 37.6) and taking 362 wickets (average 22.8); Toured England, 1971, 1974, 1975 (World Cups, 1979, 1982, 1983, 1987); Scoured 17,771 first-class runs and took 1,287 first-class wickets; 175 ltd-overs ints, 139 as Capt (incl 1992 World Cup victory); 2nd player to score a century and take 10 wickets in a Test 1983; Only 3rd player to score over 3,000 Test runs and take 300 wickets; Specl Rep for Sports, UNICEF, 1989; Ed-in-Chf, Cricket Life, 1989-90; Fndr, Imran Khan Cancer Hosp Appeal, 1991-. Publications: Imran, 1983; All-Round View (autobiog), 1988; Indus Journey, 1990; Warrior Race, 1993. Honours: Fell, Keble Coll, Oxford, 1988; Hilal-e-Imtiaz, 1993. Address: c/o Shankat Khanum Memorial Trust, 29 Shah Jamal, Lahore 546000, Pakistan.

IMWINKELRIED Edward John, b. 19 Sept 1946, San Fran, CA, USA. Law Teacher. m. Cynthia Clark, 30 Dec 1978, 1 s, 1 d. Education: BA, Univ San Fran, 1967; JD, 1969. Appointments: Univ of San Diego; Washington Univ, St Louis; Univ of CA Davis. Creative Works: Uncharged Misconduct Evidence; Evidentiary Foundations; Scientific Evidence. Honours: Outstndng Tchr; Disting Tchr Awd. Memberships: Amn Assn of Law Schs; Natl Coll of Dist Attourneys. Hobby: Jogging. Address: School of Law, University of California Davis, Davis, CA 95616, USA.

INAGAKI Jitsuo, Politician. Appointments: Mbr, House of Reps; Fmr Parl Vice-Min of Hlth & Welfare; Dir Gen, Hokkaido Devl Agcy & Okinawa Devel Agcy, (State Min), 1996-. Address: Hokkaido Development Agency, 3-1-1 Kasumigaseki, Chiyoda-ku, Tokyo 100, Japan.

INAN Kamran, b. 18 Feb 1929, Bitlis, Turkey. Diplomat; Member of Parliament. m. Yasemin. Education: Fac of Law, Ankara; PhD, Pol Sco, Geneva Univ. Appointments: Senator, Min (sev times); Chmn, For Rels Cttee; Amb. Publications: 6 books; Articles and lectures. Honours: Officier, Légion d'Honneur; Gold Medal Eurn Parl. Memberships: Num, natl and intl; Cncl of Eur; NAA. Hobbies: Reading; Writing. Listed in: Turkish Who's Who. Address: Gevre Sokak 56/42, Ankara, Turkey.

ING Huot, Politician. Appointments: Min of Educn, 1993, Fgn Affairs & Intl Co-op, 1995-. Address: Ministry of Foreign Affairs, Phnom-Penh, Cambodia.

INGER Göran Jan Axel, b. 1917, Kungsör, Sweden. Professor. m. Margret, 1976. Education: BA, 1941; DD, 1961; MA, 1962; LLB, 1970; LLD, 1972. Appointments: Clergyman, 1945; Snr Master, 1962-66; Assoc Prof, Uppsala Univ, 1965-70; Prof, Lunds Univ, 1970-76; Prof, Uppsala Univ, 1976-84. Publications: The Ecclesiastical Visitations in the Medieval Sweden, 1961; The Confession in the Swedish Legal Procedure I-II, 1976-94; Swedish Legal History, 1997. Honours: Knight of the Order of the N Star, 1974; Medal, Merit of the Swedish State, 1982; Knight Cmdr of the Finnish Lion Order, 1986. Address: Skolgatan 21, SE-75312 Uppsala, Sweden.

INGERBEKLII Salvador. Government Official. Appointment: Min of Jus, Govt of Palau, Koror. Address: Ministry of Justice, PO Box 790, PW 96940, Palau.

INGRAM David Eric, b. 9 Jan 1939, Miles, Qld, Aust. Applied Linguist. m. Nelly, 1 Aug 1981, 2 s, 3 d. Education: BA; AEd; MA; PhD. Appointments: Tchr, var schs; French Subject Master, Bremer and Brisbane, 1967-71; Colombo Plan Expert, Cambodia, 1968; Lectr, Snr Lectr, Mt Gravatt, CAE, 1972-83; Prin Lectr, Hd, Dept of Educn Studies, Darwin Inst of Technol, 1983-86; Dir, Inst of Appl Lings, Brisbane CAE, 1986-90; Prof of Appl Lings, Dir, Cntr for Appl Lings and Langs, Griffith Univ, 1990-; IELTS Chf Examiner (Aust), 1989-98. Publications: Num articles in profl jrnls and books. Honours: Andrew Mellon Fndn Fell, Natl Fgn Lang Cntr, Wash DC, 1993-94; AFMLTA Medal, Outstndng Serv to Lang Tchng in Aust, 1994; Adj Fell, Natl Fgn Lang Cntr, Wash DC, 1995, 1996, 1997, 1998. Memberships include: Qld Assn for the Tchng of Engl to Speakers of Other Langs, life mbr 1981-; Mod Lang Tchrs Assn of Qld, life mbr, 1983-; Pres, Redlands Cmty Kindergarten

Mngmt Cttee, 1997; Austl Lang and Lit Cncl, 1992-96; Mbr Cleveland State Sch Cncl; Applied Ling Assn of Aust; Brit Assn for Lang Learning. Hobbies: Family; Cricket; Tennis; Surfing; Classical music. Address: c/o Centre for Applied Linguistics and Languages, Griffith University, Nathan, Queensland 4111, Australia.

INOGUCHI Takashi, b. 17 Jan 1944, Japan. Professor of Political Science. m. Kuniko Inoguchi, 8 Aug 1976. Education: BA, 1966, MA, 1968, Univ of Tokyo; PhD, MA Inst of Technol, USA, 1974. Appointments: Assoc Prof, Inst of Intl Rels, Sophia Univ, Tokyo, 1974-77; Assoc Prof, 1977-88, Prof, 1988-, Inst of Oriental Culture, Univ of Tokyo; Affiliate Schl, UN Univ, Tokyo, 1993-95; Snr Vice Rector, 1995-97; Uner-Sec Gen, Univ Mobility in Asia and the Pacific, 1998-2000; VP, Japan's Assn of Intl Rels, 1998-2000. Publications: Auth of 16 books incl: The Metier of a Political Scientist, 1996; Japanese Politics Today, 1997; The Vitality of Japan, co-ed, 1997; United States-Japan Relations in International Institutions after the Cold War, 1997; Co-auth 4 books; Ed 1 vol and co-ed 9 books; Num profl articles in jrnls. Memberships: Japanese Polit Sci Assn; Assn of Intl Rels; Japanese Electoral Studies Assn; Intl Studies Assn; Amn Polit Sci Assn. Listed in: Who' Who in the World. Address: Institute of Oriental Culture, University of Tokyo, 7-3-1 Hongo, Bunkyo-ku, Tokyo 113, Japan.

INOMATA Nobumichi, b. 14 Nov 1936, Ashio Tochigi, Japan. Biology Educator. m. Nobuko, 13 June 1971, 1 s, 1 d. Education: BAgri, 1961; MAgri, 1963; DAgri, 1973. Publications: Experimental Manipulation of Ovale Tissues, 1985; Biotechnology in Agriculture and Forestry, 1990; Breeding Oilseed Brasica, 1993; Recent Advances in Oilseed Brassicas, 1997. Hobby: Appreciation of art and music. Address: 180-3 Shinogoze, Okayoma 703-8201, Japan.

INONU Erdal, b. 1926, Ankara, Turkey. Politician. Education: Ankara Univ; CA Inst of Technol, USA. Appointments: Prof of Phys, Dean, Sci & Lit Fac, Rector, Mid E Tech Univ, 1960-74; Chair, Scol Democratic Party (Socl Democratic Populist Party), 1963-; Dpty for Izmir, 1986, 1987; Dpty PM, State Min, 1991-94; Min of Fgn Affairs, 1995. Address: Ministry of Foreign Affairs, Yeni Hizmet Binasi, 06520 Balgat, Ankara, Turkey.

INOUE Issei, Politician; Civil Servant. Appointments: Fmr Mayor of Settsu City; Mbr, House of Reps; Fmr Dir, Cttee of Fgn Affairs; Fmr Vice Chair, Socl Democratic Party of Japan; Min of Posts & Telecoms, 1995-96. Address: Ministry of Posts & Telecommunications, 1-3-2 Kasumigaseki, Chiyoda-ku, Tokyo 100, Japan.

INOUYE Minoru, b. 10 Jan 1924, Tokyo, Japan. Banker. m. Kazuko Nakase, 15 Nov 1953, 1 s. Education: Grad, Fac of Law, Tokyo Imperial Univ (now Univ of Tokyo), 1947. Appointments: Hd Off, The Bank of Tokyo Ltd, 1947; Dpty Agent, NY Agcy, Gen Mngr, Plng and Coord Divsn, Dir, Gen Mngr, London Off, Res Mngng Dir for Eur and Gen Mngr, London Off, Snr Mngng Dir, Dpty Pres, Pres, 1985-; Advsr, 1990-; Advsr, Bank of Tokyo-Mitsubishi Ltd, 1996. Honours: Orden Mexicana del Aguila Azteca, Mexico, 1986; Ordem Nacional de Cruzeiro do Sul, Brazil, 1989; Medal of Hon w Blue Ribbon, Japan, 1989; Legion d'Honneur, France, 1990; Order of the Rising Sun, Gold and Silver Star, Japan, 1994. Hobbies: Golf; Travel. Address: 11-7 Kohinata 1-chome, Bunkyo-ku, Tokyo 112-0006, Japan.

INSULZA SALINAS Jose Miguel, b. 1943. Politician; Lawyer. m. Georgina Nunez V, 4 children. Education: St Georges Coll, Santiago; Law Sch, Universidad de Chile; Facultad Latinoamericana de Ciencias Sociales; Univ MI, USA. Appointments: Prof of Polit Theory, Universidad de Chile, of Polit Scis, Pontificia Universidad Catolica de Chile, 1973; Polit Advsr to Min of Fgn Rels, Dir, Dipl Acady, 1974; Rschr, Dir, Instituto de Estudios de Estados Unidos, Cntro de Investigacion y Docencia Econs, Mexico, 1981-88; Prof, Universidad Autonoma de Mexico; Hd, Multilateral Econ Affairs Dept, Min of Fgn Rels, Dpty Chair, Intl Co-op Agcy, 1990-94; Under Sec for Fgn Affairs, 1994, Min, 1994-; Bd Dir, Instituto de Fomento de

Desarrollo Cientifico y Technol; Mbr, Consejo Chileno de Relaciones Internacionales, Consejo de Redaccion, Nexos Mag, Mexico, Corporacion de Desarrollo Tecnologico Empresarial. Address: Ministro de Relaciones Exteriores, Morandé 441, Casilla 91, Correo 21, Santiago, Chile.

INTERIANO MARTINEZ Eduardo Rafael, b. 22 Apr 1943. Minister of Public Health. m. 4 children. Education: MD, Natl Univ El Salvador; Spec in Pediats, Autonomous Natl Univ Mexico. Appointments: Pediatn, Munic Govt, San Salvador, 1988-91; Sect Profl Dir, Natl Rep Alliance, 1982-85; Dir, 1993, Gen Dir, Natl Utd Deptmntl Assembly, 1990; 2nd Cnclman, Munic Govt, 1991-94, 1st Cnclman, 1994; Min Pub Hlth, Socl Assistance, Govt El Salvador, 1994-. Membership: Assn Pediat, VP, 1992-93. Address: Ministry of Public Health, Calle Arce 827, San Salvador, El Salvador.

INVERARITY Robert John, b. 31 Jan 1944, Perth, Wa, Aust. Headmaster, Secondary Independent School. m. Jane, 3 Feb 1969, 2 d. Education: BA; DipEd. Appointments: Sheffield Shield Cricketer, 1962-85; Test Cricketer, 1968-72; Capt West Aust, 1971-78; Dpty Hdmaster, Pembroke Sch, S Aust, 1979-88; Headmaster, Hale Sch, West Aust, 1989-. Honour: MBE, 1978. Memberships: Life Mbr, West Aust Cricket Assn; Standing Cttee, Assn of Hds of Indep Schs of Aust (ake HMC), Bd Mbr, West Aust Inst of Sport. Hobbies: Education; Sport, especially cricket. Address: Hale School, Hale Road, Wembley Downs, WA 6019, Australia.

IOANOVICIU Damaschin, b. 28 Jan 1935, Oradea, Romania. Physicist. m. Marina, 19 Mar 1964, 1 d. Education: Grad, Phys, Fac of Maths and Phys, PhD, Phys, Babes-Bolyai, Univ of Cluj-Napoca, Romania. Appointments: Prin Physicist, Snr Rschr III, 1961-88, Snr Rschr III, 1992-, Snr Rschr I, Inst of Molecular Technol, Cluj-Napoca; Prof, Nuclear Phys, Tizi Ouzou Univ Cntr, Algeria, 1978-82; Volunteer, Natl Superc Cyclotron, 1987-90; Rsch Assoc, Chem Dept, MI State Univ. Publications: 70 pprs and book chapts. Memberships: Romanian Soc of Phys; Romanian Soc for Mass Spectrometry, pres, 1995-98; NY Acady of Scis. Hobbies: Airplane modelling; Football; Reading. Address: c/o Institute of Isotopic and Molecular Technology, PO Box 700, R-3400 Cluj-Napoca, Romania.

IORDAN Andrei A, b. 1934, Klarus. Government Official. Education: Grad, Frunze Poly Inst, Bishkek, Kyrgyzstan, 1972. Appointments: Var State Econ Orgs, 1979-88; Dpty Chmn, Cncl of Mins, Govt of Kyrgyzstan, Bishkek; Sec of State, Cncl of Mins; Dpty Prime Min; Min, Trade and Material Rescs, 1992-94; Dpty Prime Min, Trade and Indl Plcy, 1994; Min, Ind and Trade, 1994-. Address: Ministry of Industry Trade, pr Chuy 106, Bishkek 720002, Kyrgyzstan.

IP David, b. 4 Nov 1947, Hong Kong. Professor. Education: Chinese Univ of Hong Kong; MA, Univ of HI, 1970-72; PhD, Univ of BC, Can, 1974-79. Appointments: Asst Lectr, Univ of Hong Kong, 1972-74; Lectr, 1980-91; Snr Lectr, 1992-97, Assoc Prof, Rdr, 1998-, Univ of Qld. Publication: Diaspora Chinese and Mainland China: An Emerging Synergy (co-auth), 1996. Memberships: Intl Assn of Impact Assessment; Austl Asian Stdies Assn, Aust. Hobbies: Arts; Cinema; Literature; Photography. Address: Department of Anthropology and Sociology, University of Queensland, Brisbane 4072, Australia.

IQBAL Abdul Rashid, b. 19 Sept 1942, Bangalore, India. Marketing Manager. m. Rehana, 12 Mar 1973, 2 s, 2 d. Education: BSc (Hons), Chem. Appointments: Medl Repr, Abbott OP John, 1969-77; District Mngr, Servier, 1977-81; Bayer Diag (Diagnostic SPLT, PDT, MGV), Mktg Mngr, 1982-94; Proj Mngr, Lab System. Membership: Pakistan Inst of Mngmt. Hobbies: Stamp collection; Swimming; Reading. Address: 1421 St No 13, 1-107, Islamabad, Pakistan.

IQBAL Mohammad, b. 13 Apr 1950, Okara, Pakistan. University Teacher; Researcher. m. Saeeda, 3 Sept

1982, 2 s, 1 d. Education: PhD; MPhil; MSc; BS. Appointments: Prof, Chmn, Chem Dept, BZ Univ Multan, Pakistan; Rsch Scientist, Tchr, Univ of Saskatchewan, Can, 1997-. Publications: 25 rsch pprs. Memberships: Chem Inst of Can; Assoc Sec, Chem Soc of Pakistan, 1991-94. Address: Chemistry Department, BZ University, Multan, Pakistan.

IQBAL Muhammad, b. 30 Sept 1952, India. Professor of Botany. m. 12 Nov 1975, 3 d. Education: Dip, Langs; BSc, Hons; MSc; MPhil; PhD. Appointments: Lectr in Botany, Govt PG Coll, Uttarkashi, 1981-82, Aligarh Muslim Univ, 1982-87; Rdr in Botany, Aligarh Muslim Univ, 1987-90; Prof of Botany, 1990-, Hd, Dept of Botany, 1990-, Dean, Fac of Scis, 1990-92, 1994-96, Hamdard Univ. Publications: 5 books, 180 articles in profl jrnls. Honours: 4 awds, 4 fellshps. Memberships: Over 20 assns and socs. Hobbies: Urdu literature; Photo collecting; Helping the poor. Address: c/o Department of Botany, Hamdard University, Hamdard Nagar, New Delhi 110062, India.

IRELAND Kevin Mark, b. 18 July 1933, Auckland, NZ. Writer. m. Phoebe Caroline Dalwood, 2 s. Publications: Face to Face, 1963; Educating the Body, 1967; A Letter From Amsterdam, 1972; Orchids, Hummingbirds and Other Poems, 1974; A Grammer of Dreams, 1975; Literary Cartoons, 1978; The Dangers of Art, 1980; Practice Night in the Drill Hall, 1984; The Year of the Comet, 1986; Selected Poems, 1987; Tiberius at the Beehive, 1990; Skinned a Fish, 1994; Anzac Day: Selected Poems, 1997; (fiction) Sleeping With The Angels, 1995; Blowing My Top, 1996; The Man Who Never Lived, 1997; The New Zealand Collection (non-fiction), 1989; Under the Bridge and Over the Moon, 1998. Honours: Commemoration Medal, 1990; OBE, 1993. Membership: Natl Pres, PEN, 1991-93. Address: 8 Domain Street, Devonport, Auckland 1309, New Zealand.

IRIANI Abdul Karim, b. 12 Oct 1934, Eryan. Politician; Economist. m. 3 s, 3 d. Education: Univ GA; Yale Univ. Appointments: Worker, Agricl Project, Yemen, 1968-72; Chair, Cntr of Planning Org, 1972-76; Min of Devel, 1974-76, of Educn & Rector, San'a Univ, 1976-78; Advsr, Kuwait Fund for Arab Econ Devel, 1978-80; PM, 1980-83; Chair, Cncl for Reconstrn of Earthquake Areas, 1983-84; Dpty PM & Min of Fgn Affairs, 1984-90, 1994-; Min of Fgn Affairs, 1990-93, Planning & Devel, 1993-94. Address: Ministry of Foreign Affairs, San'a, Republic of Yemen.

IRLEN Helen Lewis, b. 4 May 1945, Brooklyn, NY, USA. Educational Psychologist; Researcher. m. Robert Irlen, 16 July 1967, 1 s, 1 d. Education: BS, Cornell Univ, 1967; MA, CSU Long Beach, 1969; MFCC. Appointments: Rsch Assoc, Cornell Univ, Ithaca, NY, 1965-67; Instr, Pepperdine Univ, 1970-71; Sch Psychologist, Newport-Mesa Unified Sch Dist, Newport Beach, 1970-81; Asst Prof, Dir, Adult Learning Disabilities, CSU, Long Beach, 1981-85; Exec Dir, Irlen Inst, Long Beach, 1985-; Intl Lectr and Dir, Irlen Clins in Aust, NZ, Ireland, Hong Kong, Austria, Belgium, Can, Iceland, Jordan, Repub of S Africa, Spain, Germany, UK, USA, 1985-. Creative works: Medl/educl syndrome Scotopic Sensitivity, 1981; Irlen Filters, 1983; Irlen Technology for SSS (pat), 1990. Publication: Reading By the Colours (book). Honour: CARS, CA, 1987. Membership: Jnr League Long Beach. Address: Irlen Institute, 5380 Village Road, Long Beach 90808, USA.

IRWIN John Alan Gibson, b. 16 July 1950, Brisbane, Aust. Agricultural Scientist. m. Hilary, 18 May 1973, 2 d. Education: BAgrSc, Hons, MAgrSci, Univ of Queensland; PhD, Univ of WI at Madison, USA; DAgrSc, Univ of Queensland. Appointments: Plant Pathologist/ Snr Plant Pathologist, Qld Dept Primary Inds; Lectr, Snr Lectr, Rdr, Prof, Univ of Qld. Publications: Over 150 articles in refereed jrnls. Honours: Austl Medal, Agricl Sci, 1992; Urrbrae Medal, 1993; Fell, Austl Acady Technol Scis and Engnrg, 1998. Memberships: Fell, AUstl Inst Agricl Sci and Technol, 1995; Fell, Amn Phytopathological Soc, 1995; Fell, Austl Plant Pathol Soc, 1999. Hobby: Gardening. Listed in: Who's Who in Australia. Address: University of Queensland, Queensland 4072, Australia.

ISA Pehin Dato Haji, Politician; Barrister. Appointments: Fmr Gen Advsr to Sultan of Brunei; Specl Advsr w Ministerial Rank in PM Off; Min of Home Affairs, 1988-95; Specl Advsr to PM, 1995. Address: Ministry of Home Affairs, Bandar Seri Begawan, Brunei.

ISAAC Joseph Ezra, b. 11 Mar 1922, Penang, Malaysia. Economist. m. 29 May 1947, 2 s, 1 d. Education: BCom, 1944, BA, hons, 1945, Univ of Melbourne; PhD, Univ of London, 1949. Appointments: Lectr, Snr Lectr, Rdr, Prof of Econs, 1950-64, Professorial Assoc, 1987-, Univ of Melbourne; Prof of Econs, 1965-73, Dpty Chan, 1980-88, Monash Univ; Dpty Pres, Austl Conciliation and Arbitration Commn, 1974-87; Mbr, Austl Commn on Austl Gov Admin, 1975-76; Mbr, Commn on Review of Higher Educ in NZ, 1978; Chair, Gen Ins Claims Review Panel, 1993-99. Publications: Auth of books and pprs. Honours: Fell, Queens Coll, Univ of Melbourne, 1963-; Fell, Acady of Socl Scis in Aust, 1971; Hon Fell, London Sch of Econs, 1977-; Emer Prof of Econs, Monash Univ, 1987-; AO, 1989; Hon DEcon, Monash Univ, 1991; Professorial Fell, Dept of Mngmt, Univ of Melbourne. Memberships: Fndn Pres, Indl Rels Soc of Vic, 1964-65; Pres, Econ Soc of Aust and NZ, 1967; Pres, Acady of Socl Scis in Aust, 1985-87; Patron, Indl Rels Soc of Vic, 1988. Listed in: Who's Who in Australia. Address: 5 Vista Avenue, Kew, Vic 3101, Australia.

ISENBERG Harold, b. 28 Oct 1938, Chgo, IL, USA. Physician. 2 s. Education: BS, Zool; BS, Pharm; BS, Dentistry; DDS; MD. Appointments: Asst Instr, Univ IL, Chgo, 1968-69, Univ IL, Peoria, 1997-80; Clin intr, Harbor UCLA, Torrance, 1983-. Publication: Contbng auth, Amn Acad Family Practice (monograph), 1982. Honours: Rho Chi, Univ IL, 1961; Acad Gen Dentistry Awd, 1968; Schlshp, Univ of E Partial Acady, 1973; Fell, Amn Acady Family Prac, 1982. Memberships: AMA; CMA; Amn Dental Assn, 1968; LA Co Medl Assn, 1980; Amn Acady Family Prac, 1982; Bd Mbr, Asian Amn Physn Assn, 1998. Hobbies: Chess; Audio. Address: 3655 Lomita Blvd, Ste 314, Torrance, CA 90505, USA.

ISHIDA Koshiro, Politician. Appointments: Fmr Vice Chair, Komeito, now Chair; Min of State, Dir-Gen, Man Co-ord Agcy, 1993-94; Fmr Chair, Komei Party; VP, New Frontier Party. Address: House of Representatives, Tokyo, Japan.

ISHIGOHKA Takeshi, b. 10 Mar 1944, Tokyo, Japan. Professor. m. Terue, 28 Nov 1971, 1 s, 1 d. Education: DEng, Dept of Elec Engrng, Seikei Univ, 1971. Appointments: Asst, 1971, Lectr, 1977, Assoc Prof, 1978, Prof, 1989-, Seikei Univ. Honour: Matsunaga Yasuzaemon Meml Prize, 1978. Memberships: IEEE; IEE of Japan; Cryogenic Engrng Assn of Japan. Hobbies: Tennis; Playing musical instruments. Address: 2-4-13 Akatsuki-cho, Hachioji-shi, Tokyo 192-0043, Japan.

ISHII Hajime, b. 17 Aug 1934, Kobe, Japan. Politician. m. Tomoko Sugiguchi, 1961, 1 s. Education: Konan Univ; Stanford Univ Grad Sch. Appointments: Mbr, House of Reps, 1969-; Fmr Parl Vice-Min of Transp; Min of State, Dir-Gen, Natl Land Agcy, 1989-90; Min of Home Affairs, 1994; Fmr Chair, Liberal-Democratic Party Natl Org Cttee; Fmr, Chair, LDP Rsch Comn on Fgn Affairs; Exec Mbr, Japan Renewal Party; Chair, Specl Cttee on Polit Reform (House of Reps). Address: No 1 Diet Building, Room 220, 2-2-1 Nagata-cho, Chiyoda-ku, Tokyo 100, Japan.

ISHII Maki, b. 28 May 1936, Tokyo, Japan. Composer; Conductor. m. Christa Frauke Meinecke, 1963, 1 s, 1 d. Education: Hochschule für Musik, Berlin; DAAD (German Acad Exchange Serv); Berliner Künstlerprogramm, 1969. Appointments: Travelled as Composer, Eur, USA, Asia; Composer, Conductor of Comtemporary Music; Fndr, Japanese Tokk Ensemble, 1973; Composer for Grp, Ondeko-Za, Sado Island, 1975-76; Appearances at Berlin Metamusik Fest, 1978, Maki Ishii Concert, Paris Fest, 1978, Eté Japonais, Geneva, 1983; Presenter, Dir, Here Comes the Orch, TBS-TV, Japan, 1978-84; Conductor w New Japan Philharmonic Orch, 1979; Artistic Dir, Tokyo

Summer Fest, 1985-89; Lectr, Hochschule für Kunste Berlin, 1988, San Fran, 1989; Organizer, Asian Music Fest, Tokyo, 1990; Dir, Prodn of Ballets, Rotterdam, The Hague, Paris, 1991. Creative Works: Compositions incl: Kyo-So, for percussion and orch, 1969; So-Gu II, for Gagaku and orch, 1971; Monochrome, for Japanese drums and gongs, 1975; Mono-Prism, for Japanese drums and orch, 1976; Afro-Concerto, for percussion and orch, 1982; Thirteen Drums, for percussion solo, 1985; Kaguyahime, ballet score, 1985; Floating Wind, symphonic linked work, 1992; String Quartet, 1992. Honours: Sev music and recording awds and other distinctions. Hobby: Walking. Address: 1-24-3 Jiyugaoka, Meguro-ku, Tokyo 152, Japan.

ISHII Michiko, Politician; Member, House of Councillors. Appointments: Fmr Parly Vice-Min of Labour; Dir-Gen, Environ Agcy (State Min), 1996-. Address: Environmental Agency, 1-2-2 Kasumigaseki, Chiyoda-ku, Tokyo, Japan.

ISHIKAWA Tetsuya, b. 27 May 1943, Tokyo, Japan. Professor. m. Sachiko, 5 June 1971, 2 d. Education: MA, Keio Univ; PhD, Waseda Univ. Address: 1-2 Kasuga, Tsukuba, 305-8550, Japan.

ISHIZAKI Teruhiko, b. 9 Jan 1928, Tokyo, Japan. Professor Emeritus. m. Tazuko Suzuki, 4 Nov 1963, 2 s, 1 d. Education: Dr Course, Grad Sch of Econs, 1958, DEcon, 1963, Tokyo Univ. Appointments: Prof, Dept of Econs, 1968-98, Dir, Inst of Econs and Trade, 1992-98, Kanagawa Univ. Publications: The Evolution of Finance Capitalism in the US, 1962; The Japanese Economic Challenge to US Economy, 1990. Membership: Chmn, Soc for Indl Studies, Japan. Address: 5-1-47 Shoudo Sakaeku, Yokohama 247-0022, Japan.

ISLAM AKM Nurul, b. 1925, Khajilpur, Dhaka, Bangladesh. Politician; Judge. m. Jahanara Arjoo, 2 s, 1 d. Education: Calcutta. Appointments: Advocate, Dhaka High Crt, 1951, Supreme Crt, 1956; Additional Judge, Dhaka High Crt, 1968, Judge, 1970; Chf Election Commr of Bangladesh, 1977, 1982; Fndr, Snr Prof, City Law Coll, Dhaka; Active in Independence Movement, 1971; VP of Bangladesh, 1986-88, 1989; Min of Law & Justice, 1986-89. Address: c/o Office of the Vice President, Dhaka, Bangladesh.

ISMAIL Amat, b. 1935, Xinjiang. Politician. Appointments: Active in People's Commune Movt, 1960; Dpty Sec, CCP Cttee, Xinjiang, 1960; Dpty Dir, Dept of Polit Work in Culture & Educn, Xinjiang, 1960; Mbr, 10th CCP Cen Cttee, 1973-77; Sec, CCP Cttee, Xinjiang, 1974-79; Vice Chair, Aubnavan Regl Revolutionary Cttee, Xinjiang, 1974-79; Polit Cmmnr, Xinjiang Mil Region, 1976-85; 1st Dpty Dir, Party Sch, Xinjiang, 1977-85; Chair, People's Govt, Xinjiang, 1979-85; Mbr, 12th CCP Cen Cttee, 1982-87, 13th CCP Cen Cttee, 1987-92, 14th CCP Cen Cttee, 1992-97, 15th CCP Cen Cttee, 1997-; Min of State Nationalities Affairs Comm, 1986-98; State Cnclr, 1993-; Min in Charge of State Natl Affairs Comm, 1993-. Memberships: Pres, China-Turkey Friendship Assn; Hon Pres, Chinese Assn of Ethnic Minorities for External Exchanges. Address: State Nationalities Affairs Commission, 25 Taipingqiao Street, West District, Beijing 100800, China.

ISMOILOV Shavkat, b. 12 May 1951, Dushanbe, Tajikistan. Minister of Justice; Lawyer. m. Jabarova, 20 Sept 1980, 2s, 1d. Education: Grad, doctoral dissertation (Doctor of Law Scis), 1990. Appointments: Asst, Civil Law Chair, 1978-1980; Dean of Fac, Tajik State Univ, 1980-1993; Min of Justice, Repub Tajisikstan, 1993-. Publications: 120 creative works, inclng 7 monographs. Honours: Honoured Scientist. Membership: Pres, Basketball Fedn. Hobbies: Sport; Music. Address: Rudaki 25, Dushanbe, Tajikistan.

ISOKANGAS Tauno Antero, b. 2 Dec 1932. Mining Engineer. m. Raija Anneli Flint, 8 Jan 1965, 3 s. Education: BEng, Mining, 1958; First Class Mine Mngrs Cert, Metalliferous, Qld, 1964. Appointments: Mbr Bd of Examiners, Dept of Mines and Energy, Qld, 1986-; Mbr,

Tech Stndng Cttee No 2, Coal Mine Site Technol of Natl Energy Rsch Dev and Demonstration Cncl, 1978-83. Publications: Mount Isa Cut and Fill, 1968; A Case Study of Reserves Estimation for a Strip Coal Mine, 1979. Honour: C'wlth Schlsp, 1951. Memberships: FAusIMM; CPMin; MAIME; MMICA; MACEA; FAICD; RPEQ. Hobbies: Amateur radio VK4ASI; Gardening; Sailing; Fishing. Address: 16 Shannan Place, Kenmore Hills, Qld 4069, Australia.

ITAKURA Hiroshi, b. 15 Jan 1934, Osaka, Japan. Educationalist; Writer; Professor of Law. m. Akiko Hanawa, 30 July 1961, 2 s. Education: LLD, Tokyo, Univ, Japan. Publications: Bribes, 1986; The Modern Crime, 1990; Corporate Crime, 1995; Criminal Law, 1996; Criminal Law, General part, 1998. Honour: Intl Dip of Hon, 1994. Membership: Dir, Judicial Rsch Inst, Nihon Univ, 1996. Address: 12-24, IChome Kugenuma-Sakuragaoka Fujisawa, 251-0027, Japan.

ITO Kenichi, b. 7 Mar 1938, Tokyo, Japan. Professor of International Practice. m. Yasuko, 7 Mar 1981, 1 s, 1 d. Education: BA, Law Sch, Hitotsubashi Univ, Tokyo, 1980; Dept of Govt & Russian Rsch Cntr, Grad Sch of Arts & Scis, Harvard Univ, 1961-63. Appointments: Japanese For Servs, assigned to Japanese Embs in Moscow, Manila, Wash, 1977-; Dir, 1st SE Asian Div, Min For Affairs, Tokyo (flew to Hanoi to normalize Japans' rels w N Vietnam after collapse of S Vietnam, 1975); Diplomatic commentator, 1977-; Univ Prof, 1980-; Hd, For Policy Think Tank, 1987-; Intl and natl lectr and debater. Publications: 13 books incl: Kokka To Senryaku (State and Strategy), 1985; Taikoku To Senryaku (Great Powers and Strategy), 1988; Futatsu No Shogeki To Nihon (Japan's Response to the Two Shocks), 1991; Chiheisen Wo Koete (Beyond the Horizon), 1993; Cho-Kindai No Shogeki (The Impact of Post-Modern Civilization), 1995. Membership: Pres, Japan Forum on Intl Rels. Address: 17-12-1301, Akasaka 2-chome, Minato-ku, Tokyo 107, Japan.

ITO Manabu, b. 22 Dec 1930, Tokyo, Japan. Professor. m. Atsuko, 10 Feb 1983, 3 d. Education: BEng, 1953, DEng, 1959, Univ of Tokyo. Appointments: Asst Prof, 1959, Prof, 1972, Univ of Tokyo; Prof, Saitama Univ, 1991; Prof, Takushoku Univ, 1997. Publications: Structural Design (In Japanese), 1980; Steel Structures (In Japanese), 1985; Cable-Stayed Bridges, 1991. Honours: Tanaka Prize (JSCE), 1968; Emeritus Prof, Univ of Tokyo, 1991; Awd of Merits (Japan Assn Wind Engrng), 1994. Memberships: Intl Assn for Bridge and Structural Engrng; Engrng Acady of Japan; ASCE; JSCE. Hobby: Classical music. Address: 5-45-2 Sendagi, Bunkyo-ku, Tokyo, 113-0022, Japan.

ITOH Isao, b. 19 Sept 1949, Japan. Professor. m. Nobuko, 26 Mar 1974, 1 s, 1 d. Education: MA, Meijigakuin Univ. Appointments: Asst Prof, Nagoya Jiyu Gakuin Jnr Coll, 1990; Pt-time Lectr, Waseda Univ, 1995-; Prof, Tokyo Seitoku Coll, 1998. Publications: Collected Poems: The Moonlight Reflected in the Stream, 1981; Pater - His Quest for Beauty, 1986; The Collected Poems: The Sound of Oneness, 1991; Nishiwaki Junzaburo the Paterian, 1999. Memberships: Pater Soc of Japan, dir, 1990-; Wilde Soc of Japan, dir, 1995-; Mod Poetry Soc of Japan; Engl Lit Soc of Japan; Japan Writers Assn. Hobby: Judo. Address: 336-0031 Saitama-ken, Urawa-shi, Shikatebukuro 4-11-15, Japan.

ITOH Kazuyoshi, b. 21 Nov 1948, Himeji, Hyogo, Japan. Professor of Applied Physics. m. Kae Itoh, 17 Dec 1972, 1 s, 1 d. Education: DEng, Hokkaido Univ; MEng, Osaka Univ; Engrng and Math Dipl. Appointments: Standing Sec, 1988-89, 1992-94, Ed-in-Chf, Edl Bd of Optical Soc, Japan, 1997-99. Honour: Fell, Optical Soc of Am, 1998-. Memberships: Optical Soc of Japan; Optical Soc of Am; SPIE, Bellingham, USA. Hobbies: Walking; Cycling; Audiophile. Address: 1-27-16 Hanayashiki, Kawanishi, Hyogo 666-0035, Japan.

ITOH Shinji, b. 16 Feb 1912, Ise Cty, Japan. Physiologist; Researcher. m. Eiko Itoh, 9 June 1937, 2 s, 2 d. Education: MD, Nagoya Medl Coll, 1935; PhD, 1941.

Appointments: Nagoya Univ Asst, 1937-41, Assoc, 1941-47, Assoc Prof, 1947-57, Hokkaido Univ; Prof, 1957-75, Prof Emer, 1975-. Publications: Ed, Advances in Climatic Physiology, 1972; Physiology of Cold-Adapted Man, 1974; Circumpolar Health, 1976; Patentee on memory enhancer, 1985; New peptide improves mental functions, 1985. Honours: Sci and Tech Prize, Hokkaido Govt, 1968; Hokkaido Medl Assn, 1971; Sunrising Medal, Japan Govt, 1985. Memberships: AAAS; Japan Physiol Soc; Japan Endocrinology Soc; Japan Neuroendocrinol Soc; Japan Biometeorol Soc; Intl Soc Biometeorol; Neuroscience Soc. Address: 2-6-31 Nishikoori, Otsu 520-0027, Japan.

ITTYERAH Miriam, b. 13 Oct 1953, Thalavady, Kerala, India. Research and Teaching Faculty. m. A Ittyerah, 5 Jan 1976, 1 s. Education: BA, Psychol, Bangalore Univ, 1973; MA, Appl Psychol, Bombay Univ, 1975; PhD, Psychol, Univ of Delhi, 1979. Appointments: 17 yrs of postgrad tchng, Dept of Psychol, Univ of Delhi, on subjs: topics in perception, memory, experimental neuropsychology, developmental psychol, 1979-96. Publications: (book) Laterality in Blind Children, 1994; 24 pprs in intl profl jrnls. Honours: Govt of India Natl Merit Schlshp, Dept of Applied Psychol, Univ of Bombay, 1973-75; UGC Jnr Rsch Fellshp, Dept of Psychol, Univ of Delhi, 1976-79; C'wlth Acad Staff Fellshp, Dept of Experimental Psychol, Univ of Oxford, 1985-86; Invited Mbr, NY Acady of Scis, 1993; Fulbright Snr Rsch Fellshp, John B Pierce Lab, New Haven, CT, 1996-97. Memberships: Intl Study for Study of Behavioural Dev; Indian Acady of Applied Psychol; Oxford and Cambridge Soc of India; Natl Acady of Psychol. Hobbies: Music; Gardening; Theatre; Walking. Address: Department of Psychology, University of Delhi, Delhi 110007, India.

IVANOV Stefan, b. Bejanovo, Lovetch (reg). Physicist. m. Mariana, 15 Dec 1975, 1 s, 1 d. Education; Master, Radiophysics & Electrons, Kharkov Univ, 1968; DMath, Dr Physics, N Lebedev, Moscow, 1976. Appointments: Snr Rsch Assoc, JINR, Dubna, USSR, 1975-77; Chf Asst Prof Fac of Phys, Sofia Univ, 1977-85; Guest Scientist FOM-Inst for Atomic and Molecular Phys, Amst, 1985-86; Assoc Prof, Sofia Univ, 1986-; 60 articles, 30 reports: 2 books, 1991, 1998. Honours include: Man of the Yr, ABI, 1997. Memberships: Union of Scientists of Bulgaria, Bulgarian Union of Phys; C6/Bul/8504 IAEA Vienna, 1984; F-267, 1992; F-408, 1994; Natl Fund for Sci Rsch, Sofia, IMG-94-BG-1048, TEMPUS, Brussels; 324-BG-95-UB, DAAD, Bonn. Hobbies: Skiing; History; Mountains; Bridge. Address: Faculty of Physics, Sofia University, 5 J Bourchier Boulevard, BG-1164 Sofia, Bulgaria.

IVLEV Boris, b. 1 Apr 1947, Elets, Russia. Physicist. m. Irina Pavlova, 18 Sept 1997, 1 d. Education: Dip, Phys Tech Inst, Moscow, 1970; PhD, Phys, Landau Inst, Moscow, 1973; Doct degree, Phys, Landau Inst, Moscow, 1980; Dip, Snr Rschr, Moscow, 1982. Appointments: Rschr, Landau Inst,, 1970-90, Hd, Superconductivity Dept, 1990, Moscow; Rschr, Univ of South CA, Los Angeles, USA, 1991; Cnslt, Los Alamos Natl Lab, USA, 1991-97; Rschr, Swiss Fedl Inst of Technol, Zurich, Switz, 1992-94; Prof, Univ of San Luis Potosi, Mexico, 1994-; Cnslt, Oak Ridge Natl Lab, Oak Ridge, USA, 1995-. Memberships: Amn Phys Soc, 1993-; AAAS, 1995-98; Mexican Acady of Scis, 1997-. Address: Physics Institute, University of San Luis Potosi, A Obregon 64, 78000 San Luis Potosi, SLP, Mexico.

IYER Ramaswamy Rajagopal, b. 18 Oct 1929, Aleppey, India. Civil Servant. m. Suhasini Ramaswamy, 7 Apr 1954, 2 s. Education: MA, Bombay, 1950; Postgrad Dip, Econ & Socl Admin, London Sch of Econs and Pol Sci, 1964. Appointments: Sec, Govt of India, Min of Water Resources, 1985-87; Sec, Econ Admin Reforms Commn, 1981-84; Rsch Prof, Cntr for Plcy Rsch, 1990-. Publications: A Grammar of Public Enterprises, 1991; Mid-Year of Economy, 1993-94; Konark, Delhi, 1994; Harnessing The Eastern Himalayan Rivers, 1993; Num articles in newpprs and learned jrnls, pprs, chapts in books. Memberships: Indian Inst of Pub Admin; Indian Water Resources Soc; Inst of Pub Auditors; Indian Soc of Ecol Econs. Hobbies: Music (Indian classical); Literature (English, Sanskrit, Tamil); The Arts generally; Philosophy (particularly Wittgenstein). Address: A-10 Sarita Wihar, New Delhi, 110044, India.

IYER Sarang Nath, b. 21 June 1926, Pune, India. Consultant. m. Lalitha, 18 May 1951, 2 s. Education: BSc, Chem, 1944, MSc, Chem, 1947, Lucknow Univ; PhD, Microbiol, Univ IA, USA, 1957. Appointments: Analyst, Lab of Pub Analyst, UP Govt, Lucknow, 1945-46; Snr Rsch Asst, Lucknow Univ, 1947-51; Snr Sci Asst, Biochem Div, Ctrl Drug Rsch Inst, Lucknow, 1951-54; Qlty Assurance Mngr, Parke Davis India Ltd, Mumbai, 1957-69; Lab Mngr, Johnson & Johnson Ltd, 1969-80; Gen Mngr, Tech, Johnson & Johnson Ltd, 1980-83; Gen Mngr, Corp Servs, Johnson & Johnson Ltd, 1983-88; Cnslt, 1986-. Publications: 15 rsch pprs. Memberships: Indian Pharm Assn; Assn of Microbiols of India; Soc of Biol Chems of India; Sigma Xi, USA; NY Acady of Scis, USA; Indo-Amn Soc. Hobbies: Reading; Indian music. Address: 63 Bharat Tirtha, 409 V N Purav Marg, Chembur, Mumbai 400071, India.

J

JABER Assem, b. 21 June 1946, Al Bennay, Lebanon. Amb of Lebanon. 1 s, 1 d. Education: lic in Law, 1968; MA, Pub Law, 1969; MA, Pvt Law, 1980; PhD, Pub Intl Law, 1984. Appointments: Legal Dept, min of Plng, 1971; Min, For Affairs, 1972; Sec, Jeddah, 1972-77; C A Havana, 1977-79; Amb, Accra, 1983-87; Dir, Protocol Beirut, 1988-90; Amb Ottawa, 1990; Dean, Arab Diplomatic Corps, Canada, 1994. Creative Works: Consular and Diplomatic Rels. Honours: Dip, Natl Inst of Admin and Dev, Lebanon. Hobbies: Reading; Walking. Address: 640 Lyon Street, Ottawa, K1S 3Z5.

JABER Yassin, b. 1 May 1951. Businessman. Education: BS, Bus Admin. Appointments: Elected to Parl, 1996; Min of Econ and Trade.

JACK Kenneth William David, b. 5 Oct 1924, Melbourne, Aust. Artist. m. Betty Joan Dyer, 14 Jan 1950, 1 s, 2 d. Education: Drawing Tchrs Primary and Second Certs, Art Tchrs cert and Dip, Royal Melbourne Inst of Technol, 1940-51; Trained Tchrs Cert (Manual Arts) Melbourne Tchts Coll, 1947. Appointments: RAAF Survey and Cartographical Draughtsman, War Serv New Guinea and Borneo, 1942-45; Art Tchr, Victorian Educ Dept, 1948-68; 16 years at Caulfield Inst of Technol, Fndr and Hd of Painting and Printmaking Depts, Dpty Hd of Art Dept, 1968, retd from tchng for full-time painting, 1968; Mbr of Cncl, Caulfield (renamed Monash Univ) Inst of Technol, 1969-76. Creative Works: Over 35 large reprodns of paintings of subjects in each Austl State, 1986; Folio of Prints of Fremantle, 1986; 2 Folios of 6 each orig lithographs, Old Mining Towns of Australia; Cover and 4 page article and 4 illustrations, Australian Artist, 1987; Retrospective Exhibitions, Adelaide, 1970, 1978, Melbourne, 1988; Book published on Kenneth Jack with text by Lou Klepac, 1988; 500 paintings and drawings made in World War II in collection of Austl War Memorial, Canberra; Artwork in: Kenneth Jack: World War II Paintings and Drawings, 1990; Queensland Paintings and Drawings: Kenneth Jack, 1994; The Melbourne Book, 1948; The Charm of Hobart, 1949; Kenneth Jack, 1972; The Flinders Ranges, 1984; Kenneth Jack-Printmaker, 1998. Honours include: MBE, 1982; AM, 1987; Over 40 art awds; Cert of Hon, Intl Graphic Art Exhibn, Leipzig, 1965; Sev medals and certs of merit. Memberships: Austl Watercolour Inst; Roy Watercolour Soc, London, 1977-; Past Fndn VP, Austl Guild of Realist Artists, 1974-80; Patron, Victoria Watercolour Soc; Pres, 1978, 1979, 1980; Fndn Mbr, Fed Govt's Art Bank Bd, 1980-83; Hon Life Mbr, Melbourne hs Old Boys Assn, 1988-; Hon Life Mbr, AGRA (Austl Guild Realist Artist), 1989-; Elected Hon Fell, Victorian Artists Soc, 1994-. Address: 50 Linton Court, Doreen, Vic 3754, Australia.

JACKSON David Clements, b. 7 Sept 1912, Brisbane, Aust. Paediatrician (Retired). Education: MB BS, Trinity Coll, Univ of Melbourne, 1937; Dip, Child Hlth, London, 1942. Appointments: Surg-Lt, RNVR, 1941-46; Hon Physn, Mater Childrens Hosp, Brisbane, 1946-75; Snr Lectr, Paediats, Univ Qld, 1953-74; Hon Paediatn, Mater Mothers Hosp, Brisbane, 1960-75; Hon Cnslt Physn Emer, Mater Childrens Hosp, 1975-. Publications: The Six Horseshoes (Memoirs of Personal and Professional Life), 1987; The Discovery of Childhood: A Paediatric Triad, 1990; One Ship, One Company: The Story of HMS Worcester 1650-1950, 1996. Honours: DSC, 1942; AM, 1984. Memberships: FRACP FRACGP; Austl Coll of Paediats, Pres, 1967-68; Fell, Roy Soc of Med; BMA; AMA. Hobbies: Music; Writing; Naval History. Listed in: Who's Who in Australia. Address: 217 Wickham Terrace, Brisbane, Qld 4000, Australia.

JACKSON John, b. 22 July 1946, London, Eng. Professor; Deputy Vice Chancellor. Education: Univ Southampton; Univ London; Univ PA, USA. Appointments: Assoc Prof and Dean, Fac Econs and Comm, Univ WA, 1984-90; Snr Lectr, Aust Dept Econs, 1980-84; Dean of Bus, RMIT, 1991-98; Visng Lectr/Prof

at var, UK/USA Univs inclng NE 1982, London, 1977, PA, 1976; Cnslt, 20 Govt agencies and pvte sector orgs inclng Reports on Educ Plng in Aust; Contbr, Exec Dev Progs for Snr Pub Servants and Adv Mngmt Progs for Pvte Sector Execs. Publications: Economics Problems Principles and Policies, w C R McConnell, 1980, 5 eds; Var tech pprs on econ growth. Hobbies: Classical music; Public radio; Theatre. Address: Royal Melbourne Institute Technology, Melbourne, Vic 3000, Australia.

JACKSON MacDonald Pairman, b. 13 Oct 1938, Auckland, NZ. University Professor. m. Nicole Philippa, 2 Sept 1964, 1 s, 2 d. Education: MA, NZ, 1960; BLitt, Oxford, 1964. Appointments: Lectr, Snr Lectr, Assoc Prof, 1964-89, Prof, 1989-, Hd of Dept, 1990-92, Univ Auckland. Publications include: Shakespeare's A Lover's Complaint, 1965; Studies in Attribution: Middleton and Shakespeare, 1979; The Oxford Book of New Zealand Writing Since 1949, 1983; Companion to Shakespeare Studies, 1986; The Selected Plays of John Marston, 1986; A R D Fairburn: Selected Poems, 1995. Honours: Fell, Shakespeare Lib, 1989, Huntington Lib, 1993, St Catherine' Coll, Oxford, 2000. Membership: Intl Shakespeare Assn. Hobbies: Theatre; Films; Music; Running. Address: 21 Te Kownai Place, Remuera, Auckland 5, New Zealand.

JACKSON Peter Anthony, b. 14 Feb 1956, Sydney, Aust. Academic. Education: BA, UNE, 1977; MA, Macquarie, 1982; PhD, Austl Natl Univ, 1987. Appointments: Exec Offr, Natl Thai Stdies Cntr, Austl Natl Univ, 1992-94; Rsch Fell, Thai Hist Austl Natl Univ, 1995-. Publications: Buddhism, Legitimation and Conflict, 1989; Dear Uncle Go, Male Homosexuality in Thailand, 1995. Address: Research School of Pacific and Asian Studies, The Australian National University, Canberra, ACT 0200, Australia.

JACKSON William Keith, b. 5 Sept 1928, Colchester, Eng. Political Scientist. m. (2) Jennifer Mary Louch, 21 Dec 1990, 3 s. Education: London Univ Tchrs Cert, 1947; BA (Hons) Univ of Nottingham, 1953; PhD, Orago Univ, 1967. Appointments: Orago Univ Asst Lectr, 1956-58; Lectr, 1959-62; Snr Lectr, 1963-67; Prof, Polit Sci, Univ of Canterbury, 1967-94; Emeritus Prof, 1994-. Publications: New Zealand Politics in Action (co-auth), 1962; New Zealand (co-auth), 1969; Fight for Life: New Zealand, Britain and the EEC (ed), 1971; Politics of Change, 1972; The New Zealand Legislative Council, 1972; Beyond New Zealand: The Foreign Policy of a Small State (ed), 1980; The Dilemma of Parliament, 1987; Historical Dictionary of New Zealand (co-auth), 1996; New Zealand Adopts Proportional Representation: Accident, Design of Evolution? (co-auth), 1998. Honours: Mobil Awd, Radio NZ, 1979; Henry Chapman Fellshp, Inst Commonwealth Affairs, 1963; Canterbury Fellshp, 1987; US Govt Intl Vis Grantee, 1980, 1988; NZ Asia 2000 Fellshp, Ritsumeikan Univ, Kyoto, Japan, 1996. Memberships: NZ Inst of Intl Affairs; NZ Polit Studies Assn; NZ Histl Assn; Austl Polit Sci Assn; Australasian Study of Parl Grp; Polit Studies Assn (UK). Address: 92A Hinau Street, Christchurch 4, New Zealand.

JACKSON William Roy, b. 27 Feb 1935, Lancashire, Eng. Professor of Chemistry. m. Heather, 23 July 1960, 2 s, 1 d. Education: BSc, hons; PhD; DSc. Appointments: Postdoct Fell, Oxford Univ, 1958-59; Asst Lectr, 1959-62, Lectr, 1962-70, Rdr, 1970-72, Queen's Univ, Belfast; Prof, Organic Chem, Monash Univ, Melbourne, 1973-95; Sir John Monash Disting Prof, 1995-. Publications: 300 pprs in profl jrnls, sev chapts in books. Honours: Sir Ian Wark Medal, ICI Aust, 1987; H G Smith Medal, RACI Aust, 1991; Baragawanath Awd, Austl Inst of Energy, 1992. Memberships: Fell, Austl Inst of Technol Scis and Engrng, Roy Austl Chem Inst, Austl Inst of Energy. Hobbies: Sport; Music; Bushwalking. Address: 30 Through Road, Burwood, Victoria 3125, Australia.

JACOB Freda Elizabeth, b. 3 Aug 1919. Occupational Therapist. Education: AM, 1981, OTD; MLC (WA), Sch of Occupational Therapy (NSW); Liverpool Sch of Occupational Therapy, UK; WAIT; Tchrs Dip in Occupational Therapy; Occupational Therapy Regd,

USA, 1955. Appointments: Occupational Therapist-i/c, Princess Margaret Hosp, WA, 1950-52; Occupational Therapist-i/c Locums UK and USA, 1952-55; Hd Occupational Therapist, Spastic Cntr, WA, 1955-57; Supt Occupational Therapist, Roy Perth Hosp, WA, 1957-80. Membership: Zonta Intl, WA. Hobbies: Tennis; Fishing; Birdwatching; Bowls. Address: 6/4 Perina Way, City Beach, WA 6015, Australia.

JACOB Kallarackel Thomas, b. 13 May 1944, Karanchira, Kerala, India. Materials Engineer. m. Moire Susan, 2 s, 1 d. Education: BSc; BE; DIC; PhD, London; DSc, London. Appointments: Snr Rsch Assoc, 1972-76, Specl Lectr, 1976-77, Asst Prof, 1977-81, Assoc Prof, 1981-83, Univ Toronto, Can; Prof, 1983-, Chm, Dept of Metallurgy, 1992-98, Chm, Materials Rsch Cntr, 1993-97, KTIDC Chair, 1994-97, Indian Inst of Sci, Bangalore. Publications: 297 in profl sci jrnls, 6 books. Honours include: Extraction and Processing Sci Awd, Minerals, Metals and Materials Soc, 1993; Prof Rustom Choksi Awd, Ex in Rsch, Indian Inst of Sci, 1997; Best Ppr Awd, Mining and Materials Processing Inst, Japan, 1998; Prof Brahm Prakash Mem Medal, Indian Natl Sci Acady, 1998. Memberships: Minerals, Metals and Materials Soc; Amn Ceramic Soc; Natl Inst of Ceramic Engrs, USA; Asia-Pacific Acady of Materials; ASM Intl; Materials Rsch Soc of India; Indian Inst of Metals. Hobbies: Music; Hiking. Address: Department of Metallurgy, Indian Institute of Science, Bangalore 560 012, India.

JACOB Mathew Mundakaal, Politician. Education: Univs of Madras & Lucknow. Appointments: Advocate, High Crt of Cochin; Sec Gen, Bharat Sevak Samaj, Kerala, 1956-66; Indian Rep, World Youth Fest, Moscow, 1957; World Assn of Youth Conf, Delhi, 1958; Convenor Student, Youth Affairs Cttee, Natl Def, Kerala State Govt, 1962; State Sec, Sadachar Samiti, Kerala; Mbr, Kerala State, Sec-Gen, Youth Hostel Assn of India; Bd of Govs, Inst of Socl Work; Chair, Plantation Corpn of Kerala, 1974-78; 1st Chair, Oil Palm India Ltd; Pres, Kerala State Co-op Rubber Mktng Bd, Cochin, 6yrs; Dir, Indian Overseas Bank, 1976-82; Fndr, Dir, Chair, Chitralekha Film Coop, Trivandrum; Publr, Bharat Sevak Socl Work Jrnl,; Mngr, Dir, Publr, Congress Review Newsppr, 1978-86; Fmr Sec-Gen, Congress Party, Kerala State; Fmr Mbr, All India Congress Cttee; Mbr, Indian Parl (Senate), 1982-94; Chair, Parl Cttee on Subordinate Legislation, 1983-85; Del to UN Gen Assn, 1985, 1993, to UN/IPU World Disarmament Symposium, 1985, UN World Human Rights Conf, 1993, C'wlth IPU & Rubber Prodrs Confs; Dpty Chair, Senate, 1986-87; Min of State for Parl Affairs, 1987-93; Min of State for Water Resources, 1988-89; Min of State for Home Affairs, Cncl of Mins, 1991-93; Chair, Parl Standing Cttee on Home Affairs, 1993-94; Gov of Meghalaya, Shillong, 1995-, of Arunachal Pradesh, 1996. Address: Office of the Governor of Meghalaya, Raj Bhavan, Shillong 793001, India.

JACOB Teuku, b. 6 Dec 1929, Peurfulak, Aceh, Indonesia. Anthropologist. m. Nuraini, 17 Dec 1972. Education: MD, 1956; MS, 1960; PhD, 1967. Apointments: Lectr, Gadjah Mada Univ, 1962; Prof, 1971; Dean, Medl Fac, 1975-79; Rector, 1981-86. Publications: Man, Science and Technology, 1992; The Future, 1994; Humane Technology, 1996. Honours: Sci Prize, 1982; Sci Prize, Rsch Indonesian Medl Assn, 1984; Sultan Hamengkubuwono II Awd, 1997. Memberships: AAAS; Indonesian Acady of Scis. Hobbies: Reading; Photography; Travel. Address: Laboratory of Biology and Paleoanthropology, Faculty of Medicine, Gadjah Mada Un, Yogyakarta 55281, Indonesia.

JACOBS Samuel Joshua, b. 6 Dec 1920. Justice. m. Mary Scott, 14 Feb 1946, 3 s, 1 d. Education: Scotch Coll, Adelaide; LLB, Adelaide Univ. Appointments: Mbr of Cncl, Univ of Adelaide, 1961-93; Dpty Chan, 1984-93; QC, 1965; Mbr, Cl of Govs, Scotch Coll, 1966-88; Pres, Law Soc, SA, 1972-73; Judge, Supreme Crt of SA, 1973-90; Hon Col, Univ Regt, 1978-82; Regl Chmn, Winston Churchill Mem Trust, 1979-94. Honour: AO, 1982. Membership: Adelaide Club. Hobbies: Contract

Bridge; Gardening. Address 7 Glebe Road, Glen Osmond, SA 5064, Australia.

JACOBSON Nathan, b. 12 Feb 1916, USSR. Solicitor; Company Director. m. (1) Martha Lederman, 12 May 1945, dec 1991, 1 s, 1 d, (2) Pamela Myer, 2 Nov 1992, 2 d. Education: LLB, Univ of Melbourne. Appointments: Solicitor, 1947-; Fndr, legal firm of Jacobson, Chamberlin & Casem in 1947; Amalgamated w Barker Gosling, Sol, Melbourne in 1982 Dir, number of pub and pvte co's. Honour: OBE, Servs to the Cmnty, 1972. Memberships: Pres, State Zionist Cncl of Vic, 1951, 1956; Pres, Jewish Community Cncl of vic, 1956-60; Pres, Zionist Fedn of Aust, 1964-68; Pres, Exec Cncl of Austl Jewry, 1970-72, 1974, 1976; Treas, Cncl of Christians and Jews of Vic, 1958-68; Law Inst of Vic. Hobbies: Skiing; Fishing; Golf; Bridge. Address: 85/546 Toorak Road, Toorak, Vic 3142, Australia.

JACOBSON Raymond Earl, b. 25 May 1922, St Paul, MN, USA. Entrepreneur; Electronics Executive. m. Maxine Meadows, 1959, Div 1986, 3 s. Education: BE, Yale Univ, 1944; MBA, Harv Univ, 1948, BA, 1950; MA, 1954. Appointments: Asst, Gen Mngr, PRD Electros Inc, 1951-55; Sales Mngr, Curtiss-Wright Electrons Div, 1955-57; Dir Mktng, TRW Computers Co,1957-60; Lectr, Engrng, UCLA, 1958-60; VP, Ops Electro-Sci Investors, 1960-63; Bd Dirs, Tamar Electrons Inc, Rawco Instruments Inc, 1960-63; Pres, Whitehall Electrons Inc, 1961-63; Dir, 1961-63; Chmn, Electrons Control Inc, 1961-63; Staco Inc, 1961-63; Pres, Maxson Electron Corp, 1963-64; Micro Radionics Inc, 1964-67; Jacobson Assoc, CA, 1964-67; Lectr, Bus Admin, UC Berkeley, 1965-66 Co-Fndr, Pres, Chmn, Chf Exec Offr, Anderson Jacobson Inc, 1967-88; Chmn, Anderson Jacobson, SA, Paris, 1974-88; Chmn, London, 1975-85; Chmn, Can, 1975-85; Anderson Jacobson, GmbH Cologne, 1978-83; CXR Corp, 1988-94; Computerman, USA Inc, Reno, 1997-.Honours: Rhodes Schl; Prize for Ex in Mechl Engrng; Tau Beta Pi.Memberships: Underwriting Lloyd's London; Eagle Scout Boy Scouts Am; Assn Amn Rhodes Schls; Harv Bus Sch Assn; Oxford Soc; Yale Club; Sigma Xi; Tau Beta Pi. Hobbies: Courtside Tennis; Seascape Swim; Racquet. Address: 1247 Montcourse Ln, San Jose, CA, 95131-2420, USA.

JAFFERY Muhammad Sayedain, b. 17 May 1926, Sonepat, India. Consultant. Education: BVSc, Univ Panjab, 1947; MSc, Vet Sci, WA Univ, 1959; PhD, Intl Open Univ, Columbo, 1997. Appointments: Vet Offr, Dist Muzaffargarh, Govt of Punjab, 1948-52; Rsch Asst, Biol Products, Coll of Vet Scis, Lahore, 1952-57; Postgrad, USA, 1957-59; Asst Prof, Pathol, 1959-65, Assoc Prof, Microbiol, 1965-68, Coll of Vet Scis, Lahore; Rsch Offr, Vet Rsch Inst, Punjab, 1968-73; Dir, Vet Rsch Inst, Punjab, 1975-79; Hd, Prodn and Tech Divsn, PIA-Shaver Poultry Breeding Farms, Pakistan, 1979-83; Chf Exec, PIA-Shaver Poultry Breeding Farms, 1983-87; Gen Mngr, K&N's Poultry Breeding Complex, Pakistan, 1987-89; Specl Cnslt, Natl and Intl Agencies, 1989-. Publications: Num articles in profl jrnls. Books: First-Ever Report on the Newly Emerged Angara Disease in Broilers, 1989; A Ready Reckoner and Trouble Shooting Guide for Hatchery Men, 1993. Hobbies: Travel; Writing; Editing; Painting; Speaking. Address: D-6 Hasan Square, Karachi 75300, Pakistan.

JAFRI Syed Amjed Ali, b. 1 Jan 1938, Kapurthala, Pakistan. Social Therapist. m. Raisa, 27 Aug 1966, 2 s. Education: BSc; MBHS; MS(SW); Pb; MA, Jrnslm; MComm.Hlth, Liverpool; PhD; Hon PhD, India. Appointments: Socl Therapist, Hlth Educr, Ojha Inst of Chest Disease, 1964-70, Nishtar Hosp, 1970-71, Pakistan Anti Bacterior Assn, 1971-74, Dow Med Coll, 1971-. Publications: 21 books, 39 rsch stdies. Honours: 19 awds for acad work. Memberships: Pres, Karachi Homeo Lions Club; Patron, Sindh Anti TB Assn. Hobbies: Reading; Writing; Travel; Nature watching. Address: GRE/668/2-3 Motomal Garden, Benori Town, Karachi 74800, Pakistan.

JAGADEESH Anumakonda, b. 13 Aug 1947, Nallore, India. Renewable Energy Expert. m. Vaiderbhi, 1 Oct 1979, 1 s, 2 d. Education: BS, 1965; MSc, Phys, 1976; Phd, Wind Energy, 1985. Appointments: Tch, V R Coll, Nellore, India, 1968-89; Rsch, Danish Folkecntr for Renewable Energy, 1989-90; Rsch in Wind Energy, 1990-92; Dir, Murugappa Chettiar Rsch Cntr, 1993-95; VP, Advd Radio Masts Ltd, 1995-96; Dir, Infrastructure Consulting and Engineers Pvt, 1996-97; Freelance Wind Energy Cnslt, 1997-. Publications: Over 100 Rsch Pprs, Intl, Natl Jrnls; Over 150 Pop Articles and Letters. Honours: Awd in Energy Technol; Intl Man of the Yr, IBC, 1997; Golden Jubilee of Indep of India Awd, 1997; Utd Writers Assn; CBR Awd in Sci and Technol. Memberships: Sigma Xi Sci Soc; Roy Meteor Soc; CEU; Solar Energy Soc of India; IPV Prima Viri; Energy Environ Grp. Hobbies: Creative writing; Inventing low cost gadgets; Creative thinking. Address: 2-210 First Floor, Nawabpet, Nellore 524 002 AP, India.

JAGADISH Chennupati, b. 10 Aug 1957. Scientist. m. Vidya, 28 Feb 1989, 1 d. Education: PhD, Delhi; MPhil, Delhi; MSc Tech, Andhra; BSc, Nagarjuna. Appointments: Lectr in Electrics and Phys, S V Coll, Delhi; Rsch Assoc, Queen's Univ, Can; Rsch Sci, Rsch Fell, Fell, Snr Fell, Austl Natl Univ. Publications: Semiconducting Transparent Thin Films, book; Publs 140 rsch pprs in sci jrnls. Honours: Elect Sci Mbr, Bohmische Phys Soc; IEEE Disting Lectr Awd, Electron Devices Soc, 1997. Memberships: Fell, Austl Inst of Phys; Snr Mbr, IEEE; Amn Phys Soc; Fell, Inst of Physics, UK. Hobbies: Gardening; Reading. Listed in: Who's Who in the World; Who's Who in Science and Engineering. Address: Electronic Materials Engineering Dept, Research School of Physical Sciences and Engineering, Australian National University, Canberra, ACT 0200, Australia.

JAGANNATH Mitta Srinivas, b. 12 July 1943, Bangalore. Teacher. m. Mrs Bharathi, 12 Aug 1970, 1 s. Education: BVSc, Univ Agricl Scis, Bangalore, 1966; MVSc, Univ of Madras, 1971; Trained at London Sch of Hygiene and Tropical Med, London and Cntr of Tropical Vet Med, Edinburgh, UK, 1979. Appointments: Vet Asst Surg, Directorate of Animal Husbandry and Vet Servs, Karnataka, India, 1966-68; Instr, Parasitology, Vet Coll, Univ of Agricl Scis, Bangalore, India, 1968-74; Asst Prof, 1974-81, Assoc Prof, 1981-93, Prof-cum-Dir, 1993-, Dept of Parasitology, Vet Coll, Univ of Agricl Scis, Bangalore, India. Publications: 110 rsch articles, 40 pprs presented in natl and intl seminars, confs, symposia; Prin Investigator 2 rsch projs funded by India Cncl of Agricl Rsch and the World Bank; Creative works: Dev and standardised serological tests for var parasitic diseases. Honours: Awd, Karnataka State Govt Merit Schlshp, 1961-66; Recip, Indian Cncl of Agricl Rsch Jnr Fellshp, 1969; A V Mudaliar Gold Medal, Univ of Madras, 1971; Commonwealth Vet Assn Travel Grant to visit UK, 1979; BV Rao Gold Medal for Best Rsch Article in Indian Vet Jrnl, 1994; Apptd Dir, Cntr of Advd Studies in Vet Parasitology, Indian Cncl of Agricl Rsch, 5,000 000 rupees for sci contbn in Vet Parasitology, 1994; Letter of Appreciation, Indian Cncl of Agricl Rsch, 1998. Memberships: Karnataka Vet Assn; Karnataka Vet Cncl; Indian Vet Assn; Acrological Soc of India; Indian Soc of Parasitology. Hobbies: Music; Sports. Address: Director, Centre of Advanced Studies, Department of Parsitology, Veterinary College, University of Agricultural Sciences, Hebbal, Bangalore, 560 024.

JAGANNATHAN Neela, b. 23 Oct 1941. Librarian. m. V R Jagannathan, 27 June 1971, 2 sons. Education: BA, MS Univ, Baroda, 1963; MA 1968, PhD 1978, MLIS 1993, Univ of Bombay; PGDDA, Indira Gandhi Natnl Open Univ, New Delhi, 1994. Appointments include: Asst Libn i/c, Indian Instit of Econs, Hyderabad, 1978-80; Libn i/c, Centre for Econ and Soc Stdies, Hyderabad, 1980-82; Asst Libn i/c, B R Ambedkar Open Univ, Hyderabad, 1984-87; Dpty Libn i/c, 1987-89, Libn i/c, 1989-92, Dpty Libn, 1992-96, Libn 1996-, Central Lib. Publications: Linguistics, 1971; Library and Information Science and Distance Education, 1991, 1993; Women's Stdies, 1991; Women's Stdies and Distance Education, 1995. Honours: Rsch Fellshp, Dept of Linguistics Univ of Bombay; Awd for 1st class first in Dip in Applied Linguistics, Central Instit of Hindi, Agra; Chmn, Sectional Cttee on Consultancy Projects, Indian Lib Assn, New Delhi; Best Univ Libn, Fed of Indian Booksellers and Publrs. Memberships: Linguistic Soc of India, Poona, 1971; Indian Lib Assn, 1980; Indian Assn of Spec Libs and Info Centres, Calcutta, 1981; Andhra Pradesh Acady of Lib Sci and Documentation, Hyderabad, 1984; Women Intl Network, ICDE, 1987; Indian Assn of Distance Educ, Warangal, 1993; Life Mbr, Soc for Info Sci, New Delhi, 1997; Pres, Assn of Indian Univ Libns, New Delhi, 1998. Hobbies: Social work; Reading; Music. Listed in: International Who's Who of Professional and Business Women; 5000 Personalities of the World. Address: G-173 Madanlal Block, Asian Games Village, New Delhi 110 049, India.

JAGETIA Ganesh Chandra, b. 17 Aug 1952, Sawar, India. Medical Researcher. m. Mangla, 27 June 1982, 1 s, 1 d. Education: MSc; PhD; Dip German Lang. Appointments: Rsch Assoc, 1980, Asst Prof, 1982, Rdr, 1987, Assoc Prof, 1989, Prof, 1991-, Kasturba Medical College, Department of Radiobiology. Publications: 60 rsch publs in var intl and natl jrnls. Honours include: Visng Fellshp: Stanford Univ, CA, 1988; Univ of Klinikum Essen, Germany, 1988; Marie Curie Post-Doct Fellshp, Commn of Eurn Commmunities Belgium, 1994; Young Scientist Awd, Eurn Socs of Radiation Bio and Hyperthermic Oncology, 1994; Visng Scientist, Gesellschaft für Forschung, Germany, 1995; 20th Century Outstndng Achievement Awd, IBC; Intl Man of Yr, Global Laureates, India, 1998. Memberships: Life Mbr: Indian Assn Radiation Protection; Indian Soc Radiation Bio; Soc Nuclear Med, India; Indian Soc Cell Bio; Environ Mutag Soc, India. Hobbies: Swimming; Table tennis; Cooking; Tailoring. Address: Department of Radiobiology, Kasturba Medical College, Manipal 576 119, India.

JAGGER (Maglona Patricia) Bryony Phillips, b. 10 Mar 1948, Salford, Lancs, Eng. Composer; Writer. 2 children. Education: BA, 1971, MA, 1974, Univ of Cambridge; Studied composition and Asian Music, Boston, USA, 1971-72. Appointments: Concert perfs of choral vocal and instrument works, Eng and NZ; World premiere, Birds of Enlightenment and Release from Hell, Auckland, NZ, 1979; Var interviews for newspprs, radio and TV; ist oboe, Manukar City Symphony Orch, Leys Inst Orch. Creative Works: Compositions incl: Autumn Floods, oratorio; Chitra, lyric opera; Birds of Enlightenment, th cantata; Release from Hell, operetta; Shosho, chamber opera; A New Zealand Symphony, Requiem Brevis, chamber choir; The Divine Meditations of John Donne, song cycle; Virgin Birth, Christmas cantata; Concertinos for flute, trumpet and orchestra, 1996, for horn and orchestra, 1996, for piccolo and orchestra, 1997, for clarinet and orchestra, 1997-98. Recordings: Num works recorded by Radio NZ; Songs of Parting recorded and broadcast by NZ TV. Publications include: Poetry books: A Nursery of Pain; Purple Bananas; Garden of Love; Mushroom Cellar; Turtle Banquet; Colours; Black Tulip/After Images; A Solo Mother's Guide to the Zoo. Honours: Winner, Dorian Choir's Competition for Choral Work, 1977; Grant, NZ/Japan Exchange Prog, 1983, to assist w visit to Japan to see Trad Japanese Drama; Friends of the NZ Symphony Orch Awd for Servs to Music. Memberships: Past Sec, Composers Assn of NZ; NZ Soc of Auths (PEN); Assoc Mbr, Australasian Performing Rights Assn; Sec, Auckland Lieder Grp. Hobbies: Singing; Playing the oboe and treble recorder; Reading. Listed in: Who's Who in New Zealand; Who's Who of Business and Professional Women; Who's Who in Music. Address: 14 Carmen Avenue, Balmoral, Auckland 4, New Zealand.

JAIN Alok, b. 9 Dec 1966, Vidisha, MP, India. Engineer. m. Ritu Jain, 1 May 1992, 2 s. Education: BE, Electronics and Instrumentation; MTech Computer Sci and Tech. Appointments: Reader, Electronics and Instrumentation Dept, S.A. T.I.Vidisha, 1996-. Publications: Pprs in jrnls, intl conf and natl seminars. Memberships: Assoc Mbr, IEE, UK and IEI, India; ISTE, India; IETE, India. Hobbies: Cricket; Reading. Address: Samrat Ashok Technological Institute, Vidisha (MP) 464001, India.

JAIN Ashok Kumar, b. 12 Aug 1948. Architect; Town Planner. m. Shashi, 1 s, 1 d. Education: BArch (Gold Medallist); PG Town Plng (Hons); FITP; FIIA; Dip, Housing Plng and Bldg, Holland; Dip, Urban Mngmt, Univ of Birmingham. Appointments: Delhi Sch of Plng and Arch; Rajasthan Govt; GOI Design Grp, min of Urban Dev; DDA, 1976-; Visng Fac, Delhi Sch of Plng and Arch; VP, Assn of Brit Schls; Fndr Mbr, Indian Bldgs Cong. Publications: The Making of a Metropolis, 1990; Building Systems for Low Income Housing, 1992; The Cities of Delhi, 1994; The Indian Megacity and Economic Reforms, 1996; School Buildings, 1998. Honours: Stdy Fellshps, Netherlands, 1975, 1980, Belgium, 1980, UK, 1991, Sri Lanka, 1995. Memberships: Fell, Inst of Town Planners, Cncl of Arch; Pres, Asn for Settlement and Housing Activities; Designer and Planner, Dwarka (Papankala) Proj, Delhi; Attended UN Conf on Hum Settlement at Vancouver, Can, 1976 and Istanbul, 1996; Pres, Assn for Settlements and Housing Activities; Pres, IHS Alumni Assn; Governing body: People's Initiative on Dev and Trng. Listed in: Who's Who in India. Address: 180 Asian Games Village, New Delhi 110049, India.

JAIN Atul, b. 26 Mar 1950, Dehradun, India. Scientist. m. Mamta Jain, 11 April 1987, 1 s. 1 d. Education: BS, 1969, MS, 1970, PhD, 1973, Elec Engrg, CA Inst of Technol, Pasadena. Appointments: JPL, 1973-81; Snr Scientist, Hughes Electronics, 1981-. Publications: Numerous. Address: PO Box 45863, Los Angeles, CA 90045, USA.

JAIN Purnendra C, b. 5 Jan 1951, India. Professor. m. Indu, 11 Dec 1975, 2 s. Education: MA, Polit Sci; MPhil; PhD. Appointments: Prof, Japanese Studies Prog, Univ of Adelaide. Publications: 6 books, sev rsch articles in profl jrnls. Honour: Japan Fndn Fell, 1990-91. Memberships: Intl Polit Sci Assn; Asian Studies Assn of Aust. Hobbies: Golf; Tennis; Travel. Address: Centre for Asian Studies, University of Adelaide, SA 5005, Australia.

JAIN Virendra Kumar, b. 5 June 1941, Kanpur. Teacher. m. Alka Jain, 13 July 1972, 2 s. Education: BE, Elect, 1962, ME, Hons, 1966, Roorkee Univ, India; PhD, Elect Engrng, Kanpur Univ, India, 1972. Appointments: Prof, Hd, Computer Sci, HBTI, Kanpur, 1988-; Dir, H B Technol Inst, Kanpur, India, 1996-. Publications: 30 rsch pprs; Basic Programming with Applications, book, 1995. Honour: Pres, India Prize, 1981-82. Memberships: Fell, IE, India; Fell, Inst of Elect and Telecomm Engrs; Computer Soc of India. Hobby: Reading. Address: H B Technological Institute, Kanpur, 208 002, India.

JAIVIN Linda Betty, b. 27 Mar 1955, New London, CT, USA. Writer. Education: BA, Asian Hist, Brown Univ, Providence, RI. Publications: Fiction: Eat Me, 1995; Rock n Roll Babes From Outer Space, 1996; Nonfiction: Confessions of an S & M Virgin, 1997; Co-ed w Geremie Barmé: New Ghosts, Old Dreams: Chinese Rebel Voices, 1992. Address: C/o Cameron Creswll, Suite 5, Edgecliff Court, 2 New McLean Street, Edgecliff, NSW 2027, Australia.

JAKHAR Bal Ram, b. 23 Aug 1923, Panjkosi, Ferozepur, Punjab, India. Politician. m. Rameshwari Jakhar, 3 s, 2 d. Appointments: Elected, Punjab Assn, 1972; Dpty Min of Co-ops & Irrigation, 1972-77; Ldr of Opposition, 1977-79; Speaker, Lok Sabha (House of People), 1980-89; Pres, Indian Parl Grp, Indian Grp of IPU, Indian Br, CPA, 1979-; Chair, Bharat Krishak Samaj, 1979; Ldr, num Indian parl dels overseas, 1980; Min of Agricl, 1991-96. Publication: People, Parliament and Administration. Address: 11 Race Course Road, New Delhi 110011, India.

JAKINS Judith Helen, b. 8 Feb 1940. Former Member of Parliament. 2 s. Appointments: Fndng Offr, ICPA, 1971; Trnd Mothercraft Nurse; JP; Grazier until 1982; Mbr, NSW Legis Cncl, 1984-91; Alderman, Dubbo Cty Cncl, 1991-95; Zool Pks Bd, 1992-95; Cnclr, Roy Flying Dr Serv, 1993-. Honour: First Woman Ever to Rep the Natl Party in NSW. Memberships: C'wlth Parly Assn; Rotary Intl. Address: PO Box 1486, Dubbo, NSW 2830, Australia.

JALAJ Jaykumar, b. 2 Oct 1934, Lalitpur, UP, India. College Principal. m. Preeti Jalaj, 15 May 1959, 2 d. Education: MA; PhD. Appointments: Asst Prof, Alld Univ, 1961-62, Asst Prof, Govt of MP (Different cities), 1959-72, Prof of Hindi, 1972-83, Degree Prin, 1983-84, Postgrad Prin, 1984-94, Govt Coll Ratlam. Publications: Suraj Si Aasthha (Poems); Dhvani Aur Dhvani Gram Shastra (Linguistics); Aitihasik Bhasha Vijnan (Philology); Sanskrit Aur Hindi Natak (Criticism). Honours: MP Govt Kamta Prasad Guru Awd, 1967; MP Govt All India Vishvanath Awd, 1967; MP, Govt Bhoj Awd, 1987. Memberships: Wrking Chmn, Cntrl Sch Ratlam, 1984-94; Hon Mbr, Rotary Club, Ratlam, 1994-; Mbr, Prog Advsry Cttee All India Radio, Indore, India, 1995-97. Hobbies: Reading; Creative writing. Address: 30 Indira Nagar, Ratlam, MP, India.

JAMEEL Fathulla, b. 5 Sept 1942, Maldives. m (1) Aishath Ibrahim, 1969, (2) Fathimath Moosa, 1989, 2 s, 1 d. Education: Al-Azhar Univ; Ein Shams Univ, Cairo. Appointments: Under-Sec, External Affairs, 1973-76, Dpty Hd, 1976-77, Govt, Asian Dev Bank, 1979-83; IMF, 1979-89; IBRD (World Bank), 1979-; Islamic Dev Bank, 1980-; Perm Rep to UN, 1977-78; Acting Min of Plng and Dev, 1982-84; Min of State for Plng and Dev, 1990-91; Mbr of Parl, 1989-. Memberships: Fisheries Bd, 1979-; Natl Plng Cncl, 1981-; Bd Dirs, Maldives Monetary Authy, 1981-; Chair, Natl Telecomm Co, 1981-; Tourism Advsry Bd, 1981-; Natl Educ Cncl, 1989-. Address: Ministry of Foreign Affairs, Boduthakurufaanu Magu, Malé 20-05, Maldives.

JAMES Clive Vivian Leopold, b. 7 Oct 1939. Author; Broadcaster; Journalist. Education: Sydney Univ; Pembroke Coll, Cambridge. Appointments: Pres, Footlights, Cambridge; TV Critic, The Observer, 1972-82; Feature Writer, 1972-. Creative Works: Lyricist for Pete Atkin, Record Albums incl: Beware of the Beautiful Stranger; Driving Through Mythical America; A King at Nightfall; The Road of Silk; Secret Drinker; Live Libel; The Master of the Revels; A First Folio, (songbook w Pete Atkin). TV Series incl: Cinema; Up Sundayp So It Goes; A Question of Sex; Saturday Night People; Clive James on Television; The Late Clive James; The Late Show with Clive James; Saturday Night Clive; Fame in the 20th Century; Sunday Night Clive; The Clive James Show; Num TV Documentaries. Publications: Non-fiction: The Metropolitan Critic, 1974; The Fate of Felicity Park in the Land of the Media, 1975; Peregrine Prykke's Pilgrimage Through the London Literary World, 1976; Britannia Bright's Bewilderment in the Wilderness of Westminster, 1976; Visions Before Midnight, 1977; At the Pillars of Hercules, 1979; First Reactions, 1980; The Crystal Bucket, 1981; Charles Charming's Challenges on the Pathway to the Throne, 1981; From the Land of Shadows, 1982; Glued to the Box, 1982; Flying Visits, 1984; Snakecharmers in Texas, 1988; The Dreaming Swimmer, 1992; Fame, 1993. Novels: Brilliant Creatures, 1983; The Remake, 1987; Unreliable Memoirs (autobiog), 1980; Falling Towards England: Unreliable Memoirs, vol II, 1985; May Week was in June, 1990; Brrm! Brrm! or The Man From Japan or Perfume at Anchorage, 1991; Fame in the 20th Century, 1993; The Metropolitan Critic, 1993; 3 vols of poetry. Criticism: Clive James on Television, 1993; The Silver Castle (novel), 1996.

JAMIALAHMADI Mohammad, b. 6 June 1954, Iran. University Professor. m. Parivash Shoghi, 1991, 1 d. Education: Bachelor, Indl Chem (1st Class Hons), Ferdowsi Univ, Iran, 1977; Post grad Dip of Chem Engrng, Aston Univ, Birmingham, Eng, 1978; MSc, Chem Engrng, Aston Univ, Birmingham, 1979; PhD, Chem Process Engrng, Aston Univ, 1982. Appointments: Lectr, Chem & Pet Engrng, Abadan Inst of Technol, Natl Iranian Oil Co, 1982-87; Visng Prof, Snr Rsch Fell, Dept of Chem and Materials Engrng, Univ of Auckland, NZ, 1987-92; Prof, Chem and Pet Engrng, Univ of Pet Ind, Ahwaz, Iran, 1992-. Publications: 180 pprs in jrnls and intl confs; 6 major confidential reports prepared for var cos. Honours: TMS Awd, Minerals, Metals and Materials Soc, USA, 1992, 1994, 1995; Best Indl Chem Engr In Iran, Iranian Soc of Chem Engrng and Chem, 1993; Visng Professorship, Dept of Chem and Process Engrng, Univ of Surrey, Eng, 1994; Awd, Heat Transfer Soc of Can, 1996; Mick Akrill Awd, Heat Transfer Soc, UK, 1997; Elected, schl employee, Natl Iranian Oil Co, 1998. Memberships: Roy Soc of NZ; Iranian Soc of Pet Engrng; Iranian Soc of Chem Engrng. Hobbies: Reading; Sports. Address: Univeristy of Petroleum Industry, National Iranian Oil Co, Ahwaz , Iran.

JAMIESON Hamish Thomas Umphelby, b. 15 Feb 1932, Glenbrook, NSW, Aust. Anglican Bishop. m. Ellice Anne McPherson, 3 Feb 1962, 1 s, 2 d. Education: Licentiate in Theol, ACT, St Michaels House, Crafers, SA, 1952-56; BA, Univ of New Eng, 1974. Appointments Ordained Deacon, 1955; Priest, 1956; Brotherhood of the Good Shepherd, 1955-62; Gilgandra, 1956-57; Katherine, 1957-62; Rector, Darwin, 1962-67 Canon, All Souls Cath, Thursday Is, 1963-67; Chap, Roy Austl Navy, 1967-74, (HMAS Sydney, 1967-68, HMAS Albatross, 1969-71, Small Ships, 1972, HMAS Cerberus, 1972-74); Bish of Carpentaria, Qld, 1974-84; Bish of Bunbury, WA, 1984-; Chmn, Natl Exec, Anglican Renewal Ministries of Aust, 1984; Liaison Bish to West and Chmn, Austl Cncl to Missions to Seamen, 1992; Exec Mbr, Intl Charismatic Consultation on World Evangelisation, 1994. Hobbies: History; Reading. Address: PO Box 15, Bunbury, WA 6231, Australia.

JAMIR S C, b. 17 Oct 1931. Politician. m. Alemia Jamir, 1959, 3 s, 2 d. Education: Univ Allahabad. Appointments: Mbr, Interim Body of Nagaland, Jt Sec, Naga People's Convention; Vice Chair, Mokokchung Town Cttee, 1959-60; MP, 1961-70, 1987-89; Parl Sec, Min of External Affairs, Govt of India, 1961-67; Union Dpty Min of Railways, of Labour & Rehab, of Cmty Devel and Co-op, Food & Agricl, 1968-70; Re-elected Mbr, Aonglenden Consituency, 1974; Min of Fin, Revenue & Border Affairs; Re-elected, 1977; Dpty Chf Min, UDF Min; Chf Min, ULP Min, 1980; Ldr of Opposition Congress (I), State Legis Assembly, 1980-82; Elected, 1982; Ldr, Congress (I) Legislature Party, Chf Min Nagaland, 1982-86, 1989-92, 1993-. Address: Chief Minister's Secretariat, Kohima, Nagaland, India.

JAMISON Dean Tecumseh, b. 10 Oct 1943, MO, USA. Economist. m. (1), 1 d, (2) Kin Bing Wu, 19 Jan 1997, 2 s. Education: PhD, Econs, Harv Univ, 1970; AB, Philos, 1966, MSc Engrng Sci, 1987, Stanford Univ. Appointments: Acting Asst Prof, Dept of Econs, 1969-70, Asst Prof, Mngmt Sci, Grad Sch of Bus and Asst Prof, Dept of Econs and Sch of Educ, 1970-73, Stanford Univ; Educl Testing Serv, Princeton, NJ, 1973-76; Var posts inclng Chf, Educ Policy Div, Chf, Population, Hlth and Nutrition Div and Dir, World Dev Report Off, The World Bank, Wash DC, 1976-88, 1992-93; Prof, 1988-, Prof, Sch of Pub Hlth; Dir, Cntr for Pacific Rim Stdies, 1993-; Econ Advsr (cnslt), Hum Dev Dept, The World Bank, Wash DC, 1993-98; Dir, Econs Advsry Serv, WHO, 1998-. Publications: Books, monographs, books edited incl: (co-auth) Radio for Education and Development, 1978; Farmer Education and Farm Efficiency, 1982; Disease Control Priorities in Developing Countries, 1993; Investing in Health: World Development Report, 1993. Honours include: Heath Clark Lect, London Sch of Hygiene and Tropical Med, 1990; Edward Kass Mem Lectr, Intl Soc for Infectious Diseases, 1994; Hon Mbr, Inst of Med of Natl Acady of Scis, 1994. Memberships include: Bd on Intl Hlth, Inst of Med, Natl Acady Scis, Co-Chmn, 1992-94; Cttee on Microbial Threats to Hlth, Inst of Med, Natl Acady of Scis, 1991-92; Chmn, Ad hoc Cttee on Hlth Rsch and Dev Priorities for Dev Countries, WHO, 1994-95; Advsry Cttee on Hlth Rsch and Dev for the Poor, WHO, 1996-. Hobby: Tennis. Address: Center for Pacific Rim Studies, 11-292 Bunche Hall, University of California, Los Angeles, Los Angeles, CA 90095-1487, USA.

JAMMALAMADAKA Sreenivasa Rao, b. 7 Dec 1943, Munipalle, India. Professor. m. Vijaya, 1 July 1972, 1 s, 1 d. Education: B STAT, Indian Statistical Inst, Calcutta, India, 1964; M Stat, 1965; PhD, 1969. Appointments: Asst Prof, Indiana Univ, USA, 1969-75; Univ of WI, 1975-76; Asst Prof, Assoc Prof, Univ of CA, Santa Barbara, USA, 1976-82; Prof, 1982-. Publications: Over

100 Rsch Publs, Natl and Intl Jrnls. Memberships: Amn Stats Assn; Inst of Math Stats; Intl Stat Inst. Hobbies: Travelling; Photography. Address: Dept of Statistics, Univ of California, Santa Barbara, CA 93106, USA.

JAMSHED Syed Muhammed, b. 21 May 1962, Pakistan. Business Executive. m. Saadia, 3 s. Education: BE, Aerospace; MBA, Fin, Mktng; Aircraft Maintenance Certs; Courses on Quality Assurance and Total Quality Mngmnt. Appointments: Engrng Offr, Pakistan Air Force, 1984-94; Plnng Info and Control Mngr, Novartis, Ltd, Pakistan, 1995-. Creative Works: Regular Flight Safety Articles in Flight Mags. Honours: Chf of Air Staff Commendation Cert. Memberships: Pakistan Engrng Cncl; Amn Assn of Aeronautics and Astronautics. Hobbies: Reading; Playing squash. Address: H No 44 A, Block II, Pechs, Karachi 75400, Pakistan.

JANABIL Kades, b. 26 Dec 1936, Altay, Xinjiang, China. Vice President, Standing Committee, Peoples Congress. m. Berikbol, 18 Dec 1956, 2 s, 3 d. Education: Grad, Higher Tech Sch, Fin Sch. Appointments: VP, Peoples Bank of China, Altai, 1963-73; Vice Dir of the Off, Vice Sec, Altai, 1973-83; Vice Cmmnr, Cmmnr, Altai, 1983-93; Rep, 13th Congress, Communist Party of China, 1987-91; Rep, 8th Natl Peoples Congress, China, 1993-97; Pres, Peoples Congress, Altai, 1993-96; VP, Standing Cttee, Peoples Congress, Xinjiang Uygur Autonomons Region, Urimqi, 1996-. Publications: The Big Dipper, 1987; The Road of Exploration; History of Abak Kerey, 1994. Memberships: Hon Vice Dir, Assn Soc of China Ctrl Asia Civilization Studies, 1992; Standing VP, Inst of Xinjiang Intl Altai Studies, 1993-97; Xinjiang Writers Soc, 1996. Hobbies: Literature; History. Address: Standing Committee of Peoples Congress, Urmqi 830000, China.

JANAKIRAMAN Ramaswamy, b. 18 Dec 1944, Mayiladuthurai, India. Bank Executive. m. N Premakumari, 16 Apr 1990, 1 s, 1 d. Education: BS, Stats; MA, Linguistics. Appointments: Exec, All India Radio; Chf Mngr (Plng), State Bank of India, Zonal Off, Tiruchirapalli; Chf Mngr, State Bank of India, Thanjavur. Publications: Selection of Tirukkuval (great Tamil poetry); Poems in Engl in Poet, Poet International, Metverse Muse. Honours: Poet of Yr, ISP, USA, 1995; Nom, Intl Man of Yr, ABI, 1998, IBC, 1999. Memberships: Fell of Utd Writers Assn, Chennai, Intl Soc of Poets, USA; Writers Forum, Ranchi; World Poetry Soc; Inter-Continental, Chennai. Hobbies: Social and spiritual philosophy. Address: c/o State Bank of India, Thanjavur, India.

JANARDHANA SWAMY Gajaraj, b. 16 Feb 1936, Mandya. Government Servant; Retired as Assistant Administrative Officer. m. Marayanamma, 1 s, 2 d. Education: SSLC. Appointments: Jnr Asst, Snr Asst, Gen Supt (Class II Post), Asst Admin Offr (Class I Post), Govt of Karnataka. Honours: Var socl orgns. Memberships: Var socl serv orns, last 30 yrs. Hobby: Social service. Address: No, 68, B Cross, UAS Layout, Krishinagar, Sanjayanagar PO, Bangalore 560094, Karnataka, India.

JANJIC Jevrem, b. 9 Oct 1939, Valjevo. Professor of University. m. Nada Perisic, 23 July 1967, 2 d. Education: BS, fac of Sci, beograd, 1964; MS, Univ Novi Sad, Yugoslavia, 1970; PhD, Univ Novi Sad, Yugoslavia, 1972. Asst, 1965-73, Docent, 1973-76, Asst Prof, 1976-81, Dean, 1979-81, Prof, 1981-, Fac of Scis, Novi Sad; Vice Rector, 1987-89, Rector, 1989-91, Univ of Novi Sad. Publications: 15 books of courses of General Physics. Memberships: Academician, Intl Acady of Hums and Nat Scis, Moscow, Russia, 1997; Academician, Intl Acady of Energy and Info Scis, Moscow, Russia, 1997. Address: Balzakova 25/V, 21000 Novi Sad, Yugoslavia.

JANSZ Errol Radcliffe, b. 9 Nov 1941, Colombo, Sri Lanka. Biochemist. m. Oranee, 31 Aug 1967, 1 s, 2 d. Education: BS (Hons), Chem, Univ of Ceylon; PhD, Biochemistry, Dalhousie, Can. Appointments: Dpty Dir, CISIR, 1983-85; Dir (CEO), Ceylon Inst of Sci Ind Rsch (CISIR), 1985-90; Hd, Dept of Biochemistry, Univ of Sri Jayewar dene Pura, 1993-. Publications: Monographs on

essential oils, medicinal plants, cocoa, palmyrah, vitamins, toxins in food. Honours: Lions Gold Medal, 1986; Naresa Grant Proj Report Awd, 1987; Inst of Chem, Gold Medal, 1992; Disting Serv Awds, CISIR, 1994; IChemC, 1997. Memberships: Fell, Inst of Chem, 1977-; Fell, Natl Acady of Scis (Sri Lanka), 1984-. Hobby: Stamp collecting. Address: 29/1, Pietersz Place, Nugegoda, Sri Lanka.

JASENTULIYANA Nandasiri, b. 23 Nov 1938, Ambalangoda, Sri Lanka. Lawyer. m. Shanthi, 3 s. Education: LLB, Univ of Ceylon, Sri Lanka; LLB, Univ of London, UK; LLM, McGill Univ, Can; Atty-at-Law, Ceylon Law Coll, Sri Lanka; Dip Acady of Amn and Comparative Law, Dallas, TX, USA; Attendence Cert, Hague Acady of Intl Law, Netherlands. Appointments: Intern, FJ & G De Sarans, 1960-61; Atty, Julius & Creasy, 1962; Prog Offr, Asia Fndn, 1962-63; UN Offic, 1965-; Exec Sec, UN Conf on Peaceful Uses of Outer Space (UNISPACE), 1981-82; Exec Sec, UN Conf on Nuclear Energy (UNIPICPUNE), 1986-87; Mbr, Bd of Trustees, Intl Space Univ, 1989-; Pres, Intl Inst of Space Law, 1993-; Dir, UN Off for Outer Space Affairs, 1988-; Dpty, Dir-Gen, UN Off at Vienna, 1994-. Publications: 7 books incl: Manual of Space, 4 vols, 1979; Space Law: Development and Scope, 1991; Perspectives on International Law, 1995; Foreign Policy of Sri Lanka and the United Nations, 1998; 12 book chapts; 27 jrnl articles. Honours: Testm Awd, Intl Astronautical Fedn, 1982; Book Awd, Intl Acady Astonautics, 1989; Selected Intl Acady of by UN Natl Space Soc for list of 100 space people who have had the greatest impact on our lives, 1992; Academician, Intl Acady of Astronautics; Academician Russian Acady of Cosmonautics, 1996; Var awds in athletic and scouting fields. Hobbies: Reading (history/biographies); Theatre and opera; Swimming and jogging. Address: United Nations at Vienna, PO Box 600, A-1400 Vienna, Austria.

JASPERT Werner Pincus, b. 21 Mar 1926, Frankfurt, Main, Germany. Writer. m. Barri Clark, 3 Apr 1998, 2 s, 3 d. Education: Coll: Germany, Switz, Eng. Appointments: Asst Ed, Ed, Switz, Germany, Eng, USA, Japan, in books, mag and newspaper publng and printing; Lived in Angola, Germany, Austria, Hungary, Switz, Holland, USA, Japan, Czech Repub. Publications: Encyclopedia of Typefaces (1956-1992); State of the Art (1968-1998); Num assoc editorships worldwide in 28 countries. Honour: Fell, IOP (UK). Memberships: Rsch and Engrng Cnsl for the Graphic Arts; Soc for Imaging Sci and Technol; Fell, Inst of Printing; Tech Assn of the Graphic Arts. Hobbies: Prints; Wordblock. Address: 98C Clifton Hill, London, NW8 OJT, England.

JAVED Miandad Khan, b. 12 June 1957, Karachi, Pakistan. Cricketer. Appointments: Asst VP, Habib Bank of Pakistan; Right-Hand Mid-Order Batsman, Leg-Break & Googly Bowler; Played for Karachi, 1973-76, Sind, 1973-76, Sussex, 1976-79, Habib Bank, 1976-94, Glamorgan, 1980-85; 124 Test Matches for Pakistan, 1976-94, 34 as Capt, Scoring 8,832 Runs (average 52.5) incl 23 Hundreds; Scored 28,647 1st Class Runs (80 hundreds); Toured England, 1975, 1979 (World Cup), 1982, 1983 (World Cup), 1987, 1992 (Capt); 233 Ltd-Overs ints. Hobbies: Hockey; Soccer; Swimming; Reading Sports Books; Television; Spending Time with Family. Address: c/o Pakistani Board of Control for Cricket, Gaddafi Stadium, Lahore, Pakistan.

JAYAKUMAR Shunmugam, b. 12 Aug 1939, Singapore. Diplomat. m. Lalitha Rajahram, 1969, 2 s, 1 d. Education: Univ Singapore; Yale Univ. Appointments: Perm Rep of Singapore to UN, 1971-74; High Cmmr to Can, 1971-74; Dean, Law Fac, Prof of Law, Univ Singapore, 1974-80; MP, 1980-; Min of State for Law & Home Affairs, 1981-83; Min of Labour, 1983-85, of Home Affairs, 1985-94, of Fgn Affairs, & Law, 1994-. Publications: Constitutional Law Cases From Malaysia and Singapore, 1971; Public International Law Cases From Malaysia and Singapore, 1974; Constitutional Law (w documentary material), 1976; Sev articles in profl jrnls. Address: Ministry of Foreign Affairs, 250 North Bridge Road, #07-00 Raffles City Tower, Singapore 179101, Singapore.

JAYALALITHA C Jayaram, b. 24 Feb 1948, Mysore, India. Politician; Actress. Appointments: Appearances in over 100 films; Joined All-India Anna Dravida Munnetra Kazhagam, 1982; Propaganda Sec, 1983; Dpty Ldr, Ldr, Mbr, Rajya Sabha (parl), 1984; Chf Min, Tamil Nadu, 1991-96. Publications: Sev. Honour: Kalaimamani Awd, 1971-72. Address: c/o Chief Minister's Secretariat, Madras, India.

JAYARAMAN Jagadisa, b. 27 Mar 1933, Tamil Nadu, India. Consultant. m. Sushila, 26 Jan 1962, 1 s, 1 d. Education: MSc, Chem. Appointments: Chf Gen Mngr, Gen Mngr, 1964-84, Chf Gen Mngr, Corp Planning, 1984-86, Indian Oil Corp; Chf Exec Offr, Chmn, Mngng Dir, Cochin Refineries Ltd, 1986-91; Cnslt, The World Bank Assignments, 1994-96; Adhoc Task Force on MOU, 1994-98; Bd Dir, var cos, Advsry Bd, Mngmt Cnslts, Ms A T Kearney, Hd, Ms Hydrocarbon Cnslts, Madras, Cttee, Min of Petroleum, Govt of India, Expert Cttee, Govt of Tamil Nadu, Chmn of Cttee, Madras Refineries Ltd, 1997-98. Publications: Organisational Improvements in Productivity; Diversification and Joint Venture Opportunity. Memberships: Sev. Hobby: Social work in the field of Education. Address: 39/4 C P Ramasevamy Road, Madras 600018, India.

JAYASINGHA Indasena, b. 26 Nov 1932, Devinuwara, Sri Lanka. Journalist; Doctor. m. Kanthi, 27 June 1968, 2 s, 1 d. Education: Dip, Jrnlsm, 1965; Dip, Ldrshp, 1984; Youth Trng Courses, 1990. Appointments: JP; Area Cmmnr, St John Ambulance Assn. Publications: Sev articles in profl jrnls. Honours: Bronze Medal, Oratorical Contest of UN, 1970; Rotary Club Intl, Philippines, 1984. Memberships: IOJ, Czech Rep; UN Assn S.L; Searsolin Alumni Soc; Lions Club. Hobbies: Poetry; Stamp and coin collecting. Address: Friends of Nations, Hevana Holiday Home, Debarawewa, Tissamaharama 82600, Sri Lanka.

JAYASINGHE Samson Nicholas, b. 8 Dec 1951, Negombo, Sri Lanka. National Secretary. m. Matilda Adikaram, 10 Jan 1979, 1 s, 2 d. Education: Dip, Engl; Dip, Mngmt; Dip, Mass Media. Appointment: Natl Sec. Publication: Book, 1997. Honours: JP, Min of Justice, 1990. Memberships: Inter-Relig Peace Fndn; Sec, Dist Peace Cncl; Sec, Profl Socl Workers Assn. Hobby: Assisting the poor community to develop. Address: Samasevaya, National Secretariat, Anuradhapura Road, Talawa NCP, Sri Lanka.

JAYASURIYA Dharmasoka Laksiri, b. 27 Oct 1931. Emeritus Professor, University of Western Australia. m. Rohini, 2 s. Education: Roy Coll (Colombo), Univ Sri Lanka, Univ Sydney, Univ London. Appointments include: Asst Lectr, Lectr, Snr Lectr, 1955-66; Prof, Sociol Welfare, 1969; Dean, Fac Soc Scis, Univ Ceylon, 1971; Prof, Socl Wrk & Socl Admin, 1971; Prof, Dept Socl Wrk & Socl Admin, 1974-93; Chmn, Natl Advsry & Coord Cttee Multicultural Educ, 1984-; Dir, Cntr Asian Studies Univ West Aust, 1990-93; Hon Snr Rsch Fell, Univ West Aust, 1993-; Chmn, Inter Univ Consortium Dev Studies, 1994-; Emeritus Prof, Univ West Aust. Publications: Multiculturalism and Ethnic Affairs Policy; Ethnicity, Mental Illness and Migration (jointly); Social Dimensions of Development (w M Lee); Changing Face of Sri Lankan Politics. Honours: Visng Schl, Fulbright Awd, UCL Berkely, 1967-68. Membership: WACA. Hobbies: Music; Social service; Cricket. Address: 30 Sutcliffe Street, Dalkeith, WA 6009, Australia.

JEAN Jau-Ho, b. 20 July 1957, Taipei, Taiwan. Educator. m. Chwenling Kuo, 15 Feb 1985, 1 s, 1 d. Education: PhD, MA Inst of Technol, USA. Appointments: Engelhard Corp, 1986-89; Alcoa, 1989-94; Natl Tsing Hua Univ, 1994-. Publications: 70 in jrnls; 14 US pats; ed, book on electronic ceramics. Honours: Disting Young Ceramist Awd; Chinese Ceramic Soc; Alcoa Pat Awds, 1991-93; Best Ppr Awd, Electronic Devices and Materials Soc, 1996. Memberships: Amn Ceramic Soc; Gen Sec, Chinese Materials Rsch Soc, 1998-. Address: Department of Materials Science and Engineering, National Tsing Hua University, Hsinchu, Taiwan 30043.

JEDIA Shyam Lal, b. 20 Dec 1944, Jodhpur, India. Professor of Sociology. m. Lalita, 1970, 2 s, 3 d. Education: PhD; MA, Sociol. Appointments: Prof in Sociol, Hd, Dept of Sociol, Univ of Rajasthan; Vice-Chan, JNV Univ, Jodhpur, 1996; Chmn, ISRAA, W Bengal, 1996. Publications: Caste and Political Mobilization: The Bhangis, 1981; The Bhangis in Transition, 1984; Education Among Tribal, 1984; The Bhangis, 1992; Tribal and Christian Missionaries, 1993; Maharshi Nawal - A Great Bhangi Saint, 1996; From Higher Castes to Lower Castes, 1997; Over 50 rsch pprs. Honours: Akhil Bharatiya Dalit Sahitya Acady, 1995; Delhi, Mahatma Jyoti Rao Phule Sodh Sansthan, Jodhpur, 1997. Memberships: RAS; ISRAAA; AMWSR. Hobbies: Reading; Writing; Social activities. Address: Jai Narain Vyas Univ, Jodhpur, Rajasthan, India.

JEFFERY Philip Michael (Maj Gen), 12 Dec 1937. Governor of Western Australia. m. Marlena Joy Kerr, 1966, 3 s, 1 d. Education: Roy Mil Coll, Duntroon. Appointments: Served, Infantry, 1958-; Jnr Regtl Appts, 17 Natl Serv Trng Co and SAS Regt, 1959-62; Operational Serv, Malaya, Borneo, Vietnam, 1962-72; PSC, 1972; Cmndng Offr, 2nd Battalion Pacific Is Regt, Papua New Guinea, 1974-75; SAS Regt, Perth, 1976-77; Dir, Spec Forces, 1979-81; Cmnd, 1 Brigade, Sydney, 1983-84; Cmnd, 1 Div, Brisbane, 1986-88; Gov, W Aust, 1993-. Honours: MC, 1971; AO (mil), 1989; AC, 1996. Membership: United Servs Inst, Canberra, 1978-. Hobbies: Golf; Fishing; Music. Address: Government House, Perth, WA 6000, Australia.

JELLY Michael Thomas James, b. 13 May 1939, Semaphore, SA, Aust. Medicine. m. Elizabeth Burns, 15 Dec 1962, 2 s, 2 d. Education: BMed; BSurg; Fell, Roy Austl Coll of Med Admnstrs; Fell, Roy Austl Coll of Gen Practitioners; Fell, Austl Coll of Hlth Execs. Appointments: Jnr RMO, Roy Adelaide Hosp; Jnr Surg Reg, Queen Elizabeth Hosp; Rsch Fell, Univ of Adelaide; Gen Practitioner, Asst Med Adminstr, RAH; Assist Med Admnstr, Adelaide Childrens Hosp; Dir, Chf Med Offr, Hlth Progs, SA Hlth Cmmn Cntr; Mbr, Med Bd of SA. Honours: Natl Medal, 1982; Reserve Forces Decoration, 1985. Memberships: Fell, RACMA, 1978-; AMA; SASMOA; Aust Inst of Emergency Mngmt. Hobbies: Army Reserve Colonel; Golf; Private pilot. Address: 11 Hindmarsh Square, Adelaide, SA 5000, Australia.

JENA Prafulla Kumar, b. 27 Dec 1931. Scientist; Educationist. m. Manju, 9 Mar 1953, 3 s, 1 d. Education: BSc, Honours, MSc, PhD, Utkal Univ, India; MS, Univ of BC, Can. Appointments: Snr Sci, Bhabha Atomic Rsch Cntr, India; Prof (Metallurgy), Banaras Hindu Univ, India; Dir, Regl Rsch Lab, Bhubaneswar, India; Disting Prof (Tata Chair), IIT, India; Snr Vsng Prof; Fndr Pres, Nat Rescs Dev Fndn and Fndr Chmn, Inst of Advd Technol and Environmental Studies, Bhubaneswar, India. Honours: Natl Metallurgist Awd, 1969; PADMASHRI, Govt of India, 1977; Indian Chmbr of Comm and Inds Awd, 1982. Memberships: Pres, Orissa Bigyan Acady, India; Pres, Engrng Sect, Indian Sci Congress, 1988; Life Fell, Indian Acady of Scis, Inst of Engrs, Indian Inst of Metals. Hobbies: Writing popular scientific articles; Social service; Gardening; Cooking; Travelling. Address: Institute of Advance Technology and Environmental Studies Plot No 80A-83A, Lewis Road, Bhubaneswar 751002, India.

JENG Kee Ching George, b. 15 June 1947, Fuchow, Fukien. Researcher. m. Sue Chuan, 17 Dec 1975, 2 s, 1 d. Education: BS, Pharm; MS, Pharm; PhD, Microbiology/Immunology. Appointments: Snr Technician, Assoc Prof, Tunghai Univ; Assoc Investigator, Taichung Veterans Gen Hosp, Taiwan. Publications: Publs in num jrnls. Honour: Rsch awd in Immunology, Taipei, Taiwan, 1991. Memberships: Amn Assn of Immunologist, 1983; Soc of Chinese Bioscis, Am, 1985. Address: 1-30, 10F-C Hsi-Ping S Lane, Hsitung Road Sec 3, Taichung, Taiwan.

JENG Mu-Der, b. 25 June 1961, Taipei, Taiwan. Professor. m. Na-Na Kao, 13 May 1988, 1 s, 1 d. Education: BS, 1983; MS, 1985; PhD, 1992. Appointments: Assoc Engr, Inst of Info Ind, 1987-88;

Rsch Asst, Rensselaer Poly Inst, 1988-92; Assoc Prof, 1992-98, Prof, 1998-, Natl Taiwan Ocean Univ. Publications: Over 70 in profl jrnls. Honours: Rsch Awd, Natl Sci Cncl, 1994-97; Franklin V Taylor Awd, 1993. Membership: IEEE. Hobby: Tennis. Address: Department of Electrical Engineering, National Taiwan Ocean University, Keelong 202, Taiwan.

JENKINS Margaret Anne, b. 20 Apr 1944. Biochemist. m. Ian McPherson Jenkins, 28 Jan 1966, 1 s, 1 d. BS, Monash Univ, 1964; MAACB (Mbr Austl Assn of Clin Biochemists), 1982; Dip, Fin Plng, Deakin Univ, 1992. Appointments: Biochemist, Queen Vic Hosp, Melbourne, Aust, 1965; Sole Technol, 1965-68, Relieving Technol, 1968-72, Sole Biochemist, W Gippsland Hosp, Warragul, Aust, 1972-76; Biochemist, Preston and Northcote Community Hosp, Preston, 1976-83; Biochemist, Repatriation Campus, 1983-95, Biochemist, Austin Campus, Austin and Repatriation Medl Cntr, Heidelberg, Aust, 1995-. Publications: 11 pprs and 3 chapts in profl jrnls incl: Laboratory Investigation of Paraproteins by Capillary Electrophoresis, 1996; Automated Capillary Electrophoresis, 1998; Introduction Chapter: Clinical Applications of Capillary Electrophoresis, 1998. Honours: Travelling Schlshp, Austl Assn of Clin Biochemists Annual Sci Meeting, 1991; Nancy Dale Schlshp, Austl Assn of Clin Biochems, 1993. Memberships: Australasian Assn of Clin Biochems, 1981-, Cttee Mbr, Victorian Br; Br Educ Repr, Victorian Br, 1987-91; Austl Electrophoresis Soc, 1994-, Cttee Mbr, 1996-98. Listed in: Who's Who in the World, 1999. Hobby: Music. Address: Austin Campus, Austin and Repatriation Medical Centre, Studley Road, Heidelberg, Vic 3084, Australia.

JENKINS Paul Ellerby, b. 6 May 1935. Chartered Civil Engineer. m. Janet Etherington, 2 d. Appointments: Engr, KCC Rds Dept, 1958-66; Rd Engr, Pub Wrks Dept, Tas, 1966-69; Dir/Snr Engr, Munro, Johnson, and Assocs, Cnsltng Engrs, 1969-76; Dir/Proj Engr, Elrail Cnslts, Cnsltng Engrs, 1976-90; Mngr, Plng and Admin, Natl Rail Corp, One Nation Proj, E Corridor, 1992-93; Rds Maintenance Engr, GHD, 1994; Preparation of SW Metrop Railway Master Plan, W Austl Govt, 1998-99. Memberships: Instn of Civil Engrs; Student, 1956, Grad, 1962, Mbr 1964, Instn of Engrs, Aust M, 1967, F 1985; Mbr, Natl Cttee on Railway Engrng; Mbr Qld Cttee, Railway Tech Soc of Aust. Address: PO Box 235 Mount Ommaney, Qld 4074, Australia.

JENSEN Rodney Charles, b. 16 Dec 1934. Academic. m. Enid Hamilton, 29 May 1953, 1 s, 3 d. Education: AEd; BEcon; PhD (Univ of Qld); MAgEc (UNE); QDAH; QDA; QDH (QAC). Appointments: Tchr, Qld Educ Dept, 1955-62; Rsch Asst, Temp Lectr, Univ New Eng, 1963-64; Lectr, Snr Lectr, Lincoln Coll, NZ, 1965-69; Lectr, Snr Lectr, Rdr, Prof, Univ Qld, 1969-; Dean, Fac of Com and Econs, 1995-96; Prof Emer, 1997. Publications: Approx 260 pprs, rprts, and other publs in regl/urban econs, econ policy w emphasis on reg econ modelling and rural regs. Honours: Adj Prof in Geog and Reg Sci, Univ of IL, 1989; AZ Reg Sci Assn, Hon Life; Adj Prof, Southern Cross Univ, Univ of Sunshine Coast, Qld Univ Technol. Hobbies: Tennis; DIY; Genealogy. Address: c/o Department of Economics, University of Queensland, Brisbane, Qld 4072, Australia.

JEPHCOTT Barbara Aileen Harpham, b. 17 Sept 1929, Toowoomba, Aust. Veterinary Surgeon; Grazier. m. Hon Sir Bruce Jephcott, 23 Nov 1956, dec 1987, 1 s, 2 d. Education: BVetSc, 1955, BEcon, 1966, Qld Univ. Appointments: Vet offr, Animal Ind Branch, North Territory Admin, Mngng Dir, DUMPV Pty Ltd, Madang Prov, Papua New Guinea, 1956-99. Publications: Sci pprs on beef cattle ind in Papua New Guinea, presented to AVA Conf, Commonwealth Vet Assn Conf, 1998. Honours: Rural Woman of Yr for South Queensland, 1996. Memberships: Austl Vet Assn; Livestock Prodrs Assn, Papua New Guinea Sec and Pres; Utd Graziers Assn, Branch Pres, Qld. Hobbies: Equestrian sports; Tennis; Reading and writing. Address: "Yundah", Warwick, Australia.

JESSUP Bryan Lloyd, b. 19 Nov 1951, Unley, Adelaide, SA, Aust. Physicist. m. Jennifer, 14 May 1983, 3 d. Education: BS, Phys Scis, 1972; HBS, Phys, 1973; PhD, Experimental Plasma Phys, 1978. Appointments: Rsch Physicist, Cntr for Nuclear Studies, Grenoble, France, 1978; Rsch Physicist, Sch of Phys Scis, Flinders Univ, 1980; Austl Inst of Nuclear Sci and Engrng Fellshp, Atomic Energy Commn Lucas Heights, Sydney Univ, 1982; Harry Messel Fellshp, Sch of Phys, Univ of Sydney, 1984; Grp Hd, Mine Warfare Signatures, Maritime Ops Div, AMRL, Def Sci and Technol Org, Pyrmont, NSW. Honour: MRL Awd for Excellence, 1991. Memberships: MAIP, 1985; MAAS, 1997. Hobby: Bushwalking. Address: 34 Neirbo Avenue, Hurstville, NSW 2220, Australia.

JESUS Carlito Gonzales de, b. 21 Sept 1948, Manila, Philippines. Finance Consultant. m. Carmencita C Camañag, 22 Aug 1971, 1 d. Education: AB, Engl, Univ of the Philippnes. Appointments: Pres, Dir, China Southwest Energy Projs Ltd; Mngng Dir, Bus Plaza Inc. Publications: Loans and Capital; The Secrets of Loan Arbitrage; The Complete Guide to Making Money. Honours: Nom for 1997-98 Intl Man of Yr, IBC; Fell, Intl Biographical Assn, US Biographical Inst. Memberships: Lifetime Mbr, APWDBC; Vista Club; Wexas Intl London. Hobbies: Writing; Miniature modelling; Collecting mini-artworks. Address: 2169 Suter, St Ana, Manila, Philippines 1009.

JETHANI Shalini Shalu, b. 20 Dec 1973, Ajmer, India. Lecturer. Education: Cert course in French with Hons; Cert course in Computers; SLET (lectureship exam). Appointments: Pt-time Lectr, Kanoria Girls' Coll, Jaipur, 1997; Lectr in LPS Girls' Col, Rani, 1998-. Publications: Poems in coll magazine, 3 years; Poems in 3 anthologies of Writers' Forum. Honours: Hon by Sindhi Acad Assoc for securing position in JNV Univ at PG level in Eng Lit. Membership: Writer's Forum, Ranchi, Bihar, India, 1993-. Hobbies: Dancing; Watching movies; Cooking; Dreaming; Reading and writing poetry. Address: House No 4/3 Civil Lines, Opp Savitri Girls' School, Ajmer 305006, Rajasthan, India.

JEUNG Eui-Bae, b. 26 Oct 1961, In-Jae , Republic of Korea. Professor. m. Hyunthi Jeung, 27 July 1986, 1 s, 1 d. Education: DVM, Seoul Natl Unv, 1984; MS, Seoul Natl Univ, 1986; PhD, Univ of Brit Columbia, 1993. Appointments: Rsch Assoc, Washington Univ, St Louis, USA, 1993-95; Full Lectr, Chungbuk Natl Univ, Korea, 1995-99; Asst Prof, Chungbuk Natl Univ, Korea, 1995-. Memberships: The Endocrine Soc, 1993; The Korean Soc for Vet Sci, 1995; Korean Assn for Lab Animal Sci, 1995. Hobbies: Hunting; Soccer; Reading; Swimming. Address: c/o College of Veterinary Medicine, Chungbuk National University, Cheougou, 361-763 Korea.

JHA Vashishtha Narayan, b. 20 July 1946, Raiganj, W Bengal. m. Dr Ujjiwala, 15 July 1989, 1 d. Education: MA, Sanskrit; MA, Comparative Philology; PhD, Sanskrit. Appointments: Deccan Coll, Pune, 1970-77; Cntr of Advd Stdy in Sanskrit, Univ of Pune, 1977-. Publications: 24 books inclng monograph, Engl tansl from Sanskrit, eds; 80 rsch pprs in var jrnls. Honour: Natl Lectr, 1991-92. Memberships: Life Mbr, Bhandarkar Oriental Rsch Inst; Ling Soc of India; Lexicographical Soc of India. Hobbies: Reading; Writing; Music. Address: Centre of Advanced Study in Sanskrit, University of Pune, Pune 411007, India.

JI Chen Yang, b. 23 Jan 1954, Guangzhou, China. Professor of Medicine; Oncology Consultant. m. Dan Ji, 1 Sept 1979, 1 child. Education: MD, 1st Medl Coll of PLA; MSc, Sun Yat-sen Univ of Med. Appointments: Physn, Asst Prof, 1977; Lectr and Physn-in-Charge, 1987; Rsch Fell, SGH Singapore, 1992; Snr Sci Offr, Singapore SGH Dept of Surg, 1994; Prof, Oncology and Med, Chf Physn, 1997. Publications: 31 pprs in profl jrnls. Honour: Sci Awd of PLA, China. Memberships: Anti Cancer Soc of China; Chinese Medl Assn Soc. Hobbies: Reading; Music; Travel; Collecting. Address: Department of Oncology and Department of Pathology, Nanfang Hospital, Guangzhou 510515, China.

JI Chuanmao, b. 28 Feb 1934, Hebei, China. Senior Engineer; Geologist. m. Zhaoxin Wang, 16 Jan 1960, 2 s, 1 d. Education: HS Dip, Peking No 2 Mid Sch, 1952; Ctf, Peking For Lang Coll, 1953; BSc, Geol Dept, Leningrad Mining Coll, Russia, 1958. Appointments: Engr, Prin Engr, Bur of Hydrogeol and Engrng Geol, Min of Geol, China, 1958-83; VP, Chf Engr, China Geo-Engrng Corp, 1984-88; Dpty Dir, Dept of Intl Co-op, Min of Geol and Mineral Resources, China, 1989-; Snr Cnslt, Snr Cnsltng Cntr, Min of Geol and Mineral Resources, 1994-. Publications: Groundwater Exploration and Development in Northern Hemisphere, 1989; Successful Organization and Technical Supervision of Overseas Projects in Developing Nations; Principle and Practice for International Technic-Economic Cooperation in the Field of Geology and Mineral Resources, book, 1992; Groundwater Development in the World and Guidelines for International Co-operation, 1996. Honours: 1st Prize, Min of Agric, China; Ctf of Awd for Ex Work, Geol Soc of China, 1988, 1995; Spec Subsidy, State Cncl of China, 1993-. Memberships: Dpty Sec-Gen, Geol Soc of China; Vice Chmn, Chinese Natl Cttee for Intl Assn of Hydrogeologists; IAH Burdon Commn for Dev Nations; China Natl Cttee for Pacific Econ Co-op. Hobbies: Performing in Peking Opera; Collecting stamps; Photography. Address: 64 Funei Street, Xicheng District, Beijing 100812, China.

JI Guoxing, b. 16 Oct 1935, Shanghai, China. International Relations. m. Xiaohan Lu, 25 Jan 1967, 1 s. Education: BA, Shanghai Intl Studies Univ. Appointments: Dir, Asian-Pacific Dept, Shanghai Inst for Intl Studies, 1972; Dir, Inst of Intl Strategic Studies, Mngmt Cntr, Shanghai, 1996. Publications: Survey of Southeast Asia, 1994; Maritime Jurisdiction in the Three China Seas, 1995; Energy Security Cooperation in Asia Pacific, 1996; China Versus South China Sea Security, 1998. Honours: Govt Spec Bonus, China's State Cncl, 1992-; World Cultural Celebrity Acheivement Prize, China Intl Famous Acad Cntr, 1998. Memberships: Cncl Mbr, Shanghai Assn of Intl Rels, 1985-; Cncl Mbr, China's Natl Afro-Asian Assn, 1993-. Hobby: Shadow boxing Taijiquan. Address: 692 Yongjia Road, Shanghai, China 200031, China.

JI Pengfei, b. 1910, Yongji, Shanxi, China. Politician. m. Xu Hanbing, 3 s, 3 d. Education: Mil Med Coll. Appointments: Joined CCP, 1933; Long March in Med Dept, Red Army, 1935; Dpty Polit Cmmr, Army Corps, 3rd Field Army, 1950; Amb to German Dem Repub, 1950-55; Vice-Min of Fgn Affairs, 1955-72; Acting Min of Fgn Affairs, 1968-72; Min 1972-74; Mbr, 10th Cen Cttee, CCP, 1973, 11th Cen Cttee, 1977; Sec-Gen, Standing Cttee, Natl People's Congress, 1975-79; Mbr, Polit & Legal Affairs Grp, Cen Cttee, CCP, 1978-; Vice-Premier, State Cncl, 1979-82; Sec-Gen, 1980-81; State Cnclr, 1982-; Hd of CP Liaison Off, 1981-82; Dir, State Cncl Hong Kong & Macao Affairs, 1983-90; Chair, Cttee for Drafting Basic Law of Hong Kong Specl Admin Region, 1985-90; Mbr, Presidium 14th CCP Natl Congress, 1992. Memberships: Standing Cttee, Cen Advsry Comm, 1987-92; Hon Chair, China Fndn for Intl & Strategic Studies, 1989-; Hon Pres, China-Germany Friendship Assn, 1992-; Pres, Assn for Well Known Chinese Figures, 1993-. Address: State Council, Zhong Nan Hai, Beijing, China.

JIA Chengwen, b. 28 Mar 1954, Yiaoxian, Shaanxi, China. Teacher; Doctor. m. Ma Xian, 1 s. Education: Univ Grad. Appointments: Lectr, 1987-96; Vice-Prof, 1996-. Publications: 6 books inclng: Translation of A-B Classic of Acupuncture and Moxibustion, 1998; Over 10 compositions. Honours: Outstndng Tchr of Shaanxi Coll of Trad Chinese Med, 1985, 1995. Memberships: China Acupuncture Inst; Dir, Shaanxi Provcl Acupuncture Inst. Address: Acupuncture Department, Shaanxi College of Traditional Chinese Medicine, XianYang City, Shaanxi, China.

JIA Chunwang, b. 1938, Beijing, China. State Official. Education: Qinghua Univ. Appointments: Vice Chair, Tibet Autonomous Regl People's Govt, 1984-85; Min of State Security, 1985-; Party Cttee Sec, 1993-; Mbr, 12th

CCP Cen Cttee, 1985, 13th Cen Cttee, 1987-92; Mbr, Cen Comm of Polit Sci & Law, 1991-, 14th CCP Cen Cttee, 1992-97, 15th CCP Cen Cttee, 1997-. Address: Ministry of State Security, 14 Dongchangan jie, Beijing, China.

JIA Huixuan, b. 2 Mar 1941, Hebei Prov, China. Professor. m. Professor J Zhou, 3 Mar 1997, 2 s, 1 d. Education: Grad, Peking Univ, 1966. Appointments: Departmental Hd, Sino-Japanese Friendshp Assn, 1988; Prof, Dpty Dir of Japanese Rsch Cntr, Peking Univ. Publications: Japanese Local Conditions and Customs, 1987; A Comparison of Chinese and Japanese Folklores, 1996. Honour: Japanese Seikyo Culture Awd, 1992. Memberships: Vice-Sec, Gen Chinese Assn for Japanese Stdies; Cttee Mbr, Intl Assn of Asian Folklores. Address: Japanese Research Centre of Peking University, Beijing 100871, China.

JIA Tingchu, b. 10 Aug 1930, Huangyan County, Zhejiang Prov, China. University Teacher; Buddhist Philosophy Scholar. m. Lady Zhou Lixin, 3 d. Education: Grad, Philos Dept of Beijing Univ, 1956; Postgrad stud for Assoc Doct, Hist of Chinese Philos. Appointments: Wrk'd as peasant 1966-79; Tchr, Philos Dept, Hangzhou Univ, 1979-; Mbr, Ldrs in Ed Cttee of Chinese Do Zang Bible, Beijing, 1985-93; Retd from Hangzhou Univ, 1992; Left Beijing and retd, 1993; Personal writing, 1993-. Publications: Articles in jrnls; Chinese draft, Religion, Philosophy of, transl from Great Britain Encyclopedia, used by World Religions Rsch Inst, Chinese Acady Socl Servs, 1981; Compiler, in collaboration w collective, Chinese Do Zang Bible (Chinese Character Part) all 106 vols, 1993; On the Great Wisdom Guide Forward All Living Creatures from the Shore to Faramita, 1997. Honour: 1st Awd for Compilation of Do Zang Bible, 1992. Membership; Soc of Hist of Chinese Philos, 1981-. Hobbies: Reading literary works and historical biographies; Chinese chess. Address: Philosophy Department of Zhejiang University (Xixi Area of School), No 47 Tian Mu Shan Road, Hangzhou, Zhejiang, 310028 China.

JIAN Xin-Chun, b. 26 Feb 1951, Anxiang, Hunan, China. Oral and Maxillofacial Surgeon. m. 1 Jan 1979, 1 s. Education: DDS, 1976, MD, 1986, Hunan Med Univ. Appointments: Res, Peoples Hosp, Hunan, 1976-83; Visng Surgn, Xiang Ya Hosp, Changsha, 1986-91; Assoc Prof, 1991-93, Visng Prof, 1993-94, Med Coll VA, Richmond, USA; Vice Dir, Dept of Stomatology, 1989-92, Chmn, Dept of Stomatology, 1994-, Chmn, Dept of Oral and Maxillofacial Surg, 1994-, Assoc Prof, 1995-96, Prof, 1997-, Xiang Ya Hosp, Hunan Med Univ; Dean, Fac of Stomatology, Hunan Med Univ, 1994-. Publications: Histomorphology of Oral Submucous Fibrosis: Report of 24 Cases, 1988; Neurocristopathy That Manifests Right Facial Cleft and Right Maxillary Duplication, 1995; Management of Deformities and Defects in the Oral and Maxillofacial Regions, 1997. Honours: 2nd Prize, Ex Article, Hunan Med Univ, 1989; 2nd Prize, Ex Article, Hunan Prov, 1996; Prov Grade Prize, Sci and Tech Achievement, Hunan Prov, 1996. Memberships: Fell, Intl Assn of Oral and Maxillofacial Surgns; Amn Assn for the Adv of Sci; NY Acady of Scis; Chinese Med Assn; Chinese Anticarcinogial Assn. Address: Department of Oral & Maxillofacial Surgery, Xiang Ya Hospital, Hunan Medical University, Changsha, Hunan 410008, China.

JIANG Anmin, b. 3 Feb 1937, Xiangtan, Hunan, China. Scientific Research Personnel. m. Wang Xiaoqin, 20 July 1966, 1 s, 1 d. Education: BS, Jilin Univ. Publications: Over 20 articles in profl jrnls. Honour: 3rd Class Prize, Adv Sci and Technol; Sev other prizes and awds. Membership: Shanghai Laser Assn, 1976-. Hobbies: Go; Fishing; Making things. Address: Shanghai Institute of Optics and Fine Mechanics, Academia Sinica, PO Box 800-216, Shanghai 201800, China.

JIANG Chengan, b. 16 Dec 1943. Editor. m. Qu Zhongyan, 1 Mar 1968, 1 d. Education: BA, Dept Chinese Painting, Lu Xun Acady Fine Arts. Appointments: Pres, Ed-in-Chf, Dolphin Press, 1986-95; Pres, Ed-in-Chf, Morning Glory Publrs, 1996-. Publications: Edited and

illustrated king-sized pictorial album: Urban Development in China, 1996; Ed and illustrated, The Wiles of War - 36 Military Strategies from Ancient China, 1994; Ed and illustrated, Ancient Chinese Heroines, 1992; 100 other books. Honours: Japanese Noma World Painting Awd, 1992; First Prize, First Chinese Bookbinding and Design Competition, 1990; First Prize, Southwest China Painting Competition, 1986; 18 other domestic and intl awds; Natl Level Specialist w Outstndng Contrbns, 1986. Memberships: Chinese Artists Assn; Beijing Artists Assn; Chinese Assn for Creative Pop Sci Wrks; Beijing Assn for Creative Pop Sci Wrks; Chinese Film Artists Assn; Chinese Bookbinders and Designers Assn. Hobby: Music. Address: Morning Glory Publishers, 35 Chegongzhuang Xilu, Beijing 100044, China.

JIANG Chenyong, b. 1 July 1956, Yiwu, Zhejiang, China. Teacher. m. Wang Shaoling, 11 July 1986, 1 s. Education: BA, Chinse Dept, Hangzhou Univ; MA, Inst of Lit Rsch, Shanghai Normal Univ. Appointments: Dean of Chinese Dept, 1989-93; VP, Pres, Taizhou Tchrs Coll, 1997-. Appointments: A Modern Interpretation of the 19th Century Realist Literature, 1996; Foreign Literature (Chf Ed), 1997; Western Literature Under the Vision of Modern Culture, 1998. Honours: State Cncl Spec Allowance, 1993; Natl Excellent Tchr, 1994. Memberships: VP, Zhejiang Provcl Tchng and Rsch Inst of For Lit, 1996-; Perm Mbr, Cncl of the For Lit Tchng and Rsch Insns, 1996-. Hobbies: Music; Sports. Address: Taizhou Teachers College, Post Box 84, Linhai 317000, Zhejiang, China.

JIANG Chunyun, b. Apr 1930, Laixi, Shandong, China. Party Official. Appointments: Joined CCP, 1947; Dir, Gen Off Laixi Co, CCP Cttee, 1957-60; Dpty Section Chf, Qingdao Br, China Export Corpn for Local Products, 1957-60; Fgn Trade Bur, Qingdao City, 1957-60; Instr, Inspector, Dpty Dir, Gen Off, Propaganda Dept, Shandong CCP Cttee, 1960-66; Manual Work, Huimin Co, 1969; Revolutionary Cttee, Shandong, 1970-75; Dpty Dir, Gen Off, Shandong CCP Cttee, 1975-77; Dpty Sec-Gen, Sec-Gen, 1977-83; Dpty Sec, 1983-84; Sec, Jinan Municipal CCP Cttee, 1984-87; Acting Gov, Shandong, 1987-88; Gov, 1988-89; Pres, Shandong Party Sch, 1989-; 1st Sec, Shandong Mil Dist, CCP Cttee, 1989-; Vice-Premier, State Cncl, Agricl, 1995-; Standing Cttee, CCP Cen Cttee, Politburo, CCP Cen Cttee Secr; Hd, State Flood-Control & Drought Relief HQ; Mbr, 13th CCP Cen Cttee, 14th CCP Cen Cttee, 15th CCP Cen Cttee, 1997-; Cen, Fin & Econ Ldng Grp; Del, Shandong to 8th NPC. Address: State Council, Beijing, China.

JIANG Da-Yong, b. 9 Feb 1931, Nanchang, China. Weather and Climate Dynamics. m. Xiang-ru Wu, 19 Jan 1963, 2 s, 1 d. Education: BSc, Nnjing Univ, 1955. Appointments: Dynamics Meteorol, Beijing Meteorol Coll, 1956-72; Lectr, Assoc Prof, Prof, Weather and Climate Dynamics, CAMS, 1972-. Publications include: Advance a New Conception - Thermal Current in Terms of Tropical Upper Ocean Thermocline. Honours: State Sci and Technol Adv Encourage and Reward, 1985; Outstndng Person Awd, 1988; Stdies of Air-Sea Interaction Awd, 1995. Memberships: Vice Chmn, Chinese Air-Sea Interaction Rsch Cttee; Vice Dir, Sci Steering Grp, WOCE Chinese Committee. Memberships: Football; Basketball; Volleyball. Address: c/o Chinese Academy of Meteorological Sciences, 46 Baishigao Road, Beijing 100081, China.

JIANG Dingming, b. 1927, Tianjin, China. Professor. Education: Studied, Northeastern and Nankai Univs; Grad, Beijing Univ. Appointments: Prof, Tianjin Inst of Technol and Pt-time Prof, Nankai and Tianjin Univs and Coll of City Cnstrn; Dir, Cncl of Tianjin Transls Assn; Examiner of Collected Oceanic Works; Middle Sch Tchr. Publications: Complete Works of Lenin, transl; Books: English Grammar; English Phonetics; An Analysis to Sentence Patterns in the TOEFL; Oxford Advanced Learner's Dictionary of Current English with Chinese Translation, transl; The Practical Value of Chinese Philosophy, transl; Wrote 20 articles on transl and Engl stdy. Address: Old Cadres' Office, Tianjin Institute of Technology, Tianjin 300191, China.

JIANG Dingxian, b. 10 Nov 1912, Wuhan, China. Teacher of Composition. m. Xiao Shufang, 8 Feb 1943, 1 s, 2 d. Education: Dips for Composition, Shanghai Conservatory of Music, 1934. Appointments: Prof, 1942, Dir of the Compositional Department, 1950, VP. 1961, Cntrl Conservatory of Music, Beijing, China. Publications: Artistic Song, Sui-yue, You-you, 1936; Symphonie for the Poetry, Yan-bo-jiang-shang, 1959; Music for the Film, Zao-chun er-yue, 1965; Symphonie, Cang-Sang, 1981. Honours: Enjoys subsidy for outstndng expert from the govt, 1991-; Lifelong Prof, 1993-. Memberships: Mbr, Dir, assn for Chinese Musicians, 1949-; Mbr, CPPCC, 1978-93. Hobby: Photography. Address: Central Conservatory of Music, 1-1-301, Beijing, 10031, China.

JIANG Enci, b. 25 June 1934, Shanghai, China. Law Professor; Researcher. m. Peiqiu Zhang, 14 Jan 1967, 1 d. Education: LLB, Peoples Univ of China, Beijing, 1956; Dip, Engl Lang and Lit, 1966. Appointments: Lectr, Beijing Inst of Polit Sci and Law, 1956-64; Assoc Prof, Dir of Comparative Law Dept, Shanghai Acady of Socl Scis, 1979-92; Snr Legal Cnslt, New China News Agency, Macau Br, 1988-92; Prof of Intl Law, Dir, Rsch Cntr of Laws of Hong Kong, Macau and Taiwan, 1992-; Snr Legal Cnslt, Law Trans Dept, Macau Govt, 1996-. Publications: Legal Aspects of Foreign Investments in the PRC; On the Legal Protection and Encouragement of Foreign Investments in China; Introduction to Macau Commercial Laws; Introduction to the Biography and Doctrines of Western Jurists. Honours: Awd of Ex Rsch Achievement, SASS, 1984; Awd, Inst of Law, SASS, 1987. Memberships: Law Soc of China; Intl Law Soc of China; Dpty Sec Gen, Econ Law Assn, Shanghai, 1985-88. Hobbies: Music; Golf. Address: Shanghai Academy of Social Sciences, 622 7 Huaihai Road M, Shanghai 200020, China.

JIANG Enzhu, b. 1938, Jiangsu, China. Diplomat. Appointments: Trans, Min of Fgn Affairs, 1965; 3rd & 2nd Sec, London, 1970's; Fmr Dir, W Eurn Affairs, Min of Fgn Affairs, Vice-Min, 1994-95; Amb to UK, 1995-97; Chf Negotiator, People's Repub of China in Sino-Brit Talks Over Hong Kong; Dpty Hd, Preliminary Working Cttee of Preparatory Cttee of Hong Kong Specl Admin Region; Dir, Hong Kong Br, Xinhua News Agcy; Mbr, 15th CCP Cen Cttee, 1997-. Address: Ministry of Foreign Affairs, 225 Chaoyangmennei Dajie, Dongsi, Beijing, China.

JIANG Guorui, b. 8 July 1954, China. Mathematics; Computer. m. 1 Oct 1984, 1 d. Education: Vis, Dept of Computers, Tsinghua Univ, 1997-98; Doct student, Inst of Systems Sci, Academia Sinica, 1992-94. Appointments: Lectr, 1987, Asst Prof, 1992, Dpty Dir of Maths, 1994, Prof, 1996, Dpty Dir of Dept of Computers, 1998. Publication: Classifying involutions fixing some manifolds. Honours: 2nd Class Awd of Sci and Tech Progress, 1991; Outstndng Contb Expert, 1992; Person With Ability Striding Over Century, 1997. Memberships: Maths Inst, Dir, Maths Inst, Hebei Prov, 1992. Hobbies: Shadowboxing; Taiji sword; Volleyball; Swimming. Address: Department, Hebei Teacher's University, Shijia Zhuang, China 050016.

JIANG Jian Min, b. 10 May 1939, Ningguo, Anhui, China. Meteorologist; Educator. m. You Xingtian, 13 May 1966, 1 s, 1 d. Education: MSc, Peking Univ, 1981. Appointments: Weather Forecaster, Meteorological Bur, Xingjiang Reg, Wulumugi, 1962-78; Lectr - Prof, Beijing Meteorological Coll, 1981-99; Dir, Cnslt, Dept Atmospheric Sci, 1987-99. Publications: Essentials of Atmospheric Circulation (in Chinese), 1994; 3 articles in profl jrnls, 1996, 1997. Honour: Invited Mbr, AAAS. Memberships: Dpty Dir, Sec Gen, Meteorology-hydrology Cttee, Chinese Assn for Applied Statistics; Active Mbr, NY Acady Scis. Hobbies: Travelling; Stamp collecting. Address: Beijing Meteorological College, 46 Baishigiaolu, Beijing 100081, China.

JIANG Sen, b. 25 May 1923, Nantong, China. Obstetrician and Gynecologist. m. 10 Mar 1960, 1 s, 1 d.

Appointment: Bach Deg, Shanghai Med Univ. Appointments: Prof, Tutor of MD. Publications include: Practice of Gynecology, 1976; Practice of Obstetrics, 1978. Honours: Top-Notch Person of Qualified Scis and Techns, Shandong Prov, 1978-99; Natl Adv Worker of China, 1983-99. Memberships: Obstectrics Grp, Gynecol Grp, Family Planning Grp for Inpatients. Hobbies: Music; Wine. Address: Wen Hua Xi Lu 107, Jinan, Shandong, China.

JIANG Shiliang, b. 12 Dec 1938, Guilin, China. Teacher. m. Ruzhuang Xue, 15 Apr 1975, 1 s, 1 d. Education: Grad, Normal Univ. Appointments: Prof, 1994; Vice Dean of Phys and Electrics Dept, Guangxi Univ for Nationalities, 1994. Publications: Books: The Research on Some Issues of Theoretical Mechanics, 1994; The Guide for the Study of Theoretical Mechanics, 1997. Honour: Class Provincial Outstndng Instruction Achmnt Awd, 1997; Hon of Provincial Outstndng Tchr, 1998. Membership: Phys Assn. Hobbies: Reading and researching on instruction. Address: Guangxi University for Nationalities, 74 Xixiangtang Road, Nanning, Guangxi, China.

JIANG Xi-Kui, b. 5 Sept 1926, Shanghai, China. Academician; Professor of Chemistry. m. (1) Hua Di Liu, 14 Apr 1957, dec Feb 1997, (2) Yue-Li Kang, 20 May 1999, 2 s. Education: BS (Hons), St John's Univ, Shanghai, China, 1947; PhD, Univ Wash, Seattle, USA, 1952. Appointments: Rsch Worker, Rsch Lab of M W Kellogg Co, 1952-55; Assoc Prof, Beijing Inst of Chem, 1956-63; Prof, Chmn, Acad Cttee, Shanghai Inst of Organic Chem, 1963-. Publications: 171 pprs in profl jrnls. Honours: Natl Nat Sci Awd, State Sci and Technol Cttee of China, 1982, 1987; State Cncl Awd for outstndng overseas Returned Schls, State Cncl of China, 1989. Memberships: Academician, Standing Cttee Mbr, Chinese Acady of Scis, 1991-98; Natl Repr, IUPAC Commn III2, 1980-93; Standing Ctte Mbr, Bd of Dirs, Chinese Chem Soc, 1990-94. Hobbies: Chinese shadow-boxing; Listening to good music; Watching American football. Address: Shanghai Institute of Organic Chemistry, 354 Feng-Lin Lu, Shanghai 200032, China.

JIANG Xin, b. 16 Mar 1917, Ho-Peh Prov, China. Professor. m. S Z Wang, 2 Apr 1939, 2 s. Education: BA, NW Utd Univs, 1943; MA, Educl Rschng Inst, NW Normal Univ, 1947; Sorbonne, France, 1949-53. Appointments: Asst in Pedagogy, Lectr, Educl-Rsch Inst, NW Normal Univ, 1944-48; Prof of French, 1955-90. Publications: Chf Ed, French-Chinese Practical Dictionary of International Life, 1962; The IChing (Book of Changes) has been written only through usurpation and distortion of Fu Hsi's Original eight trigrams system, 1987; It is Right Time Now to Call IChing a "Counterfeit Writing", 1989; New Exploration on Confusius' Relations with IChing, 1990; Leibniz' Binary System is Quite Different from Fu Hsi's, 1994; E Einstein and N Bohr: Two Followers of Fu Hsi, 1999. Memberships: Vice Chmn, Beijing Rsch Soc of Chou (IChing), 1988-; Dpty Dir, Rsch Cntr of I-Ching Rsch Inst of Oriental Tradl Culture, 1989-93; Chinese Learned Soc of Confucius, 1990-. Hobbies: Fishing; Mountain climbing. Address: 242 Grey Building, Foreign Affairs College, Zhan Lan Road, Beijing 100037, China.

JIANG Xinxiong, b. 6 July 1931. Government Official. Education: Nankai Univ. Appointments: Joined CCP, 1956; Dir, Nuclear Fuel Plant, 1979-82; Alt Mbr, 12th Cen Cttee, CCP, 1982, 13th Cen Cttee, 1985-92, 14th Cen Cttee, CCP, 1992-; Vice-Min, Nuclear Ind, 1982-83, Min, 1983; Chair, Bd of Dirs, China Isotopes Co, 1983-; Pres, Natl Nuclear Corp, 1988-; Chair, China Atomic Energy Authy, 1994-; Dpty Hd, Ldng Grp for Nuclear Power Plants. Address: China Isotopes Company, Sanlihe Road, Beijing, China.

JIANG Xuefeng, b. 22 Nov 1946, Zhejiang, China. Teacher; Scientist. m. Guangxia Zhang, 25 Feb 1974, 1 s. Education: Grad, Shanghai Jiao Tong Univ, 1970. Appointments: Software tchng grp ldr in Computer Sci Dept, Guizhou Univ; Dpty Ldr, Lin's Entailment Logic Soc of Guizhou, China. Publications: Software Engineering, 1997; Information Retrieval (English), 1997; English for

Computer Technology and Application, 1997. Honour: Prizewinner of Sci Dev, Guizhou Govt of China, 1994, 1996. Memberships: Chinese Computer Assn, 1987; Phys Sci Assn of China, 1994. Hobbies: Programming with IBM PC; Playing table tennis. Address: Computer Science Department, Guizhou University, Huaxi, Guiyang, Guizhou 550025, China.

JIANG Zemin, b. 17 Aug 1926, Yangzhou, Jiangsu, China. Government Official; Head of State. Education: Jiaotong Univ. Appointments: Joined CCP, 1946; Shanghai Yimin No 1 Foodstuffs Factory, Shanghai Soap Factory, 1st Min of Machine-Bldg Ind; Trainee, Stalin Automobile Plant, Moscow, 1955-56; Dpty Chf, Power Divsn, Dpty Chf, Power Engrng, Dir, Power Plant, Changchun No 1 Auto Works, 1957-62; Dpty Dir, Shanghai Elec Equip Rsch Inst; Dir, Acting Party Sec, Wuhan Thermo-Tech Machinery Rsch Inst, Dpty Dir, Dir, Fgn Affairs Bur, 1st Min of Machine-Bldg Ind, 1962-80; Vice Chair, Sec-Gen, State Comm on Admin of Imports & Exports & State Comm on Admin of Fgn Investment, 1980-82; Mbr, 12th Natl Congress CCP Cttee, 1982, Politburo 1st Plenary Session of 13th Cen Cttee, 1987, Gen-Sec, 4th Plenary Session, 1989, Chair, Mil Cttee, 5th Plenary Session, 1989; 1st Vice-Min, Electron Ind, 1982-83, Min, 1983-85; Mayor of Shanghai, 1985-88; Dpty Sec, Sec, Shanghai Municipal Party Cttee, 1985-89; Dpty to 7th NPC, Chair, Cen Mil Comm, 3rd Session, 7th NPC, 1990; Mbr, Standing Cttee, Politburo, Gen-Sec & Chair, Mil Cttee, 14th & 15th CCP Cen Cttees, 1992-; Pres, People's Repub of China, Chair, Cen Mil Comm, 1st Session of 8th NPC, 1993-; Hd, Cen Fin & Econ, Ldng Grp. Memberships: Hon Chair, Red Cross Soc of China; Hon Pres, Software Ind Assn. Address: Office of the President, Beijing, China.

JIANG Zhenghua, b. 1937, Hangzhou, China. Politician. Education: Jiaotong Univ; Intl Population Sci Coll, Bombay, India, 1982. Appointments: Vice-Dir, State Family Planning Comm, 1991-; Joined Chinese Peasants' & Workers Democratic Party, 1992; Vice-Chair, Chinese Standing Cttee, 8th CPPCC, 1993-. Address: Chinese People's Political Consultative Conference, Beijing, China.

JIANG Zhi Chao, b. 19 Dec 1939, Shanghai, China. Musician (Chinese Bamboo Flute). m. Jin Yu Chuan, 3 Aug 1970, 1 s. Education: Bachelor degree. Membership: Chinese Musician's Association. Address: Rm 1307, New 4 Bldg, No 43, Bao Jia Street, Xi Cheng District, Beijing, China 100031.

JIANG Zhusong, b. 7 June 1962, Nantong, Jiangsu, China. Associate Professor. m. XiaoBing Wu, 8 June 1987, 1 d. Education: MA. Appointments: Asst Tchr, 1986-90; Lectr, 1991-96; Assoc Prof, 1996-. Creative Works: Put Creative Thinking into Basic Teaching of Painting; Seek a Clue for Color Revolution. Honours: Outstndng Work of the 2nd natl Watercolour 2 Gouache Exhibition; Silver medal of the 5th Jiangsu Watercolour Exhibition. Memebrships: Jiangsu Young Artists Assn; Suzhou Artists Assn; China Animation Film Assn. Hobbies: Cinema; Music; Swimming. Address: College of Art, Suzhou University, 178 Ganjiang East Road, Suzhou 215021, China.

JIN Guang Xi, b. 15 Feb 1936, Soochow, Jiangsu Prov, China. Educator, Consultant. m. Gui Xiang Lu, July 1966, 2 d. Education: BS, Northeast Univ, Shenyang, China, 1957; MBA, 1959. Appointments: Asst, 1959-63, Instr, 1963-83, Assoc Prof, 1983-85, Prof 1985-93, Northeast Univ; Prof, Baosteel Grp, 1993-; Rschr, Inst of Productivity Dev, Shanghai, 1994-. Publication: Econometrics, 1990; Practical Handbook of Industrial Engineering, 1993. Honours: Awd for Prog of Sci and Technol, Municipal Cttee of Sci and Technol, Shenyang, 1988; Metallurgical Min of China, Beijing, 1990. Membership: Dir, Chinese Rsch Soc for Modernization of Mngmt, 1988-. Hobbies: Reading; Stamp collecting. Address: 196 Yueyang Road, Education Committee, Bao Steel Group, 200941, Shanghai, China.

JIN Han, b. Mar 1940, Jinan, China. Adviser. m. Xiaohong Ding, 1969, 2 s. Education: Dip, Chinese Lang and Lit, Br of Ctrl Univ for Minorities. Appointments: Prof, Chinese Lit, 1991; Standing Cttee, Chinese Peoples Polit Consultative Conf, Zhejiang Br, 1998. Publications include: A History of Contemporary Chinese Fiction, 1990; Symposium of Contemporary Chinese Literary Works, 1990; Library of Latest Chinese Fiction - A Selection of New Provincial Fiction, 1993; A Collection of Belletristic Reviews on Works of Wang Wenshi. Honours: 1st Prize, Textbooks of Ex in Univs and Colls, Zhejiang; 2nd Prize, Socl Scis Rsch and Stdy, Zhejiang Educl Cttee; 3rd Prize, Socl Scis Rsch and Stdy, Zhejiang Admin; Specl Emoluments, Outstndng Experts, State Dept, 1993. Memberships: Acady of Chinese Fiction; Acady of Contemporary Chinese Lit; Acady of Contemporary Lit in Zhejiang; Assn of Writers in Zhejiang Prov. Address: Chinese Department, Zhejiang Normal University, Jinhua, Zhejiang 321004, China.

JIN Wei Xin, b. 2 June 1938, Jilin, China. Science Researcher. m. Chen Shenqing, 26 Feb 1966, 1 s, 1 d. Education: BS, Phys, Dept of Phys, Univ of Sci and Technol of China, 1963. Appointments: Rsch Assoc, Inst of Semiconductors, Chinese Acady of Sci, 1987; Prof, Inst of Semiconductors, Chinese Acady of Sci, 1990-. Publications: Inventive Title: Development-free Vapor Photoetching (Integrated Circuits Fabrication), 1983. Honours: 3rd Class Prize and Gold Medal for Invention, Fany Yi, Pres, State Sci and Technol Cttee of China, 1983. Memberships: Assn of Engrs; Chinese Acady of Scis, 1985. Hobby: Swimming. Address: Institute of Semi-Conductors of Chinese Academy of Sciences, 7-415 Living Quarters, PO Box 912, Beijing 100083, China.

JIN Wenjing, b. 8 Oct 1937, Jiangsu Prov, China. Professor. m. 1 Oct 1960, 1 s. Education: BS, Dept of Astron, Nanking Univ. Appointments: Asst Prof, 1966-78, Assoc Prof, 1978-86, Prof, 1986-, Shanghai Observatory. Publications: Determination of ERP with the date of LLR, 1986; Combined Solution of ERP During 1983-1985, 1988; Lunar Free Liberations Determined from LLR Data, 1989. Honours: 2nd Prize, Natl Natural Scis, 1982; 1st Prize, Adv Scis and Technique, Chinese Acady of Scis; Memberships: Organising Cttee, IAU Cmmn 19, 1988-94; Bd Dir, Chinese Astronomical Soc, 1989-95; Pres, Cmmn of Astrogeodynamics, 1989-92; VP, Organising Cttee, IAU Commns 8, 24, 1997-2000. Hobby: Listening to classical music. Address: Shanghai Observatory, 80 Nandan Road, Shanghai 200030, China.

JIN Yi, b. 24 Apr 1954, Shanghai, China. Professor. m. Lihua Zhou, 1 Feb 1984, 1 s. Education: Master Deg, Dept of Agronomy, Shenyang Agricl Univ, 1984. Appointments: Lectr, Plant Genetics and Breeding, 1985-91, Assoc Prof, 1992-97, Prof, 1998-, NE Agricl Univ, China. Publications: On the Analysis Method of the Triple Test Design, 1995; Effect of Plant Type on Grain Yield of Maize Hybrid Grown in Different Densities, 1997. Honour: 3rd Grade, China Natl Awd of Sci and Technol Progress, Beijing, 1990. Hobbies: Football; Bridge; Swimming. Address: c/o Agronomy College, Northeast Agricultural University, Harbin 150030, China.

JIN-NO Kenji, b. 29 Aug 1946, Kagawa Pref, Japan. Doctor; Researcher. m. Michiko Kurokawa, 1 s, 2 d. Education: Postgrad course, Medl Sch, Okayama Univ; Medl Dr (MD, PhD). Appointments: Dr, Dept of Internal Med, Natl Iwakuni Hosp, 1976-79; Hd, Internal Med, Natl Shikoku Cancer Hosp, 1979-93; Dir, Internal Med & Clin Rsch, Natl Shikoku Cancer Cntr Hosp, 1993-. Publications: Hepatocellular Carcinoma (in Japanese), 1991. Memberships: Japan Soc of Gastroenterology; Japan Gastroenterological Endoscopy Soc; Japan Soc of Hepatology; Japan Soc of Internal Med; Japan Cancer Assn; World Soc of Gastroenterology; AAAS. Hobbies: Oil painting; Reading. Address: 2-7-27, Iwasaki-cho, Matsuyama, Ehime 790-0854, Japan.

JINDAL Dharam Paul, b. 5 Mar 1942, Bassi Pathana. Teacher. m. Kiran, 9 Oct 1972, 3 d. Education: DPharm, 1962, BPharm, 1967, MPharm, 1970, PhD, 1975, Panjab Univ, Chandigarh, India. Appointments: Demonstrator, Medl Coll, Rohtak, 1967; Lectr, 1972, Rdr, 1984, Prof, 1989, Panjab Univ, Chandigarh, India. Publications: 3 books; 76 rsch pprs; 21 profl articles; 18 pats and applications; 37 conf abstracts; Co-discoverer of new neuromuscular blocking drug, chandonium iodide (WHO name: Candocuronium Iodide). Honours: Jnr Rsch Fellshp, 1968-70; Snr Rsch Fellshp, 1970-72; C'wlth Schlshp, 1981-82. Memberships: Assn of Pharm TChr of India; Pb Univ Pharm Soc; Ind Pharm Assn; All India Tech Educ; Pharm Cncl of India; Dean Fac Pharm Sci. Hobbies: Reading; Gardening. Address: University of Pharmaceutical Sciences, Panjab University, Chandigarh 160014, India.

JO Won-Hee, b. 27 Feb 1956, Korea. University Professor. m. Hyunsook, 15 Apr 1984, 2 d. Education: PhD, Econ, Univ of London. Appointments: Assoc Prof, Kookmin Univ, 1992-; Chmn, Dept of Econ, 1994-96. Creative Works: co-auth, Noo-Liberalism: A Critique, 1996. Honours: Most Prominent 100 Persons in their 30's who will lead Korea in the 21st Century. Memberships: Econ Cttee, Inst for Participating Soc. Address: Dept of Economics, Kookmin University, 861-1 Jeongnung-dong, Sungbok-Ku, Seoul, Korea.

JOEL Asher Alexander (Hon Sir), b. 4 May 1912, NSW, Aust. m. (1) 1937, 2 s, (2) Sybil Jacobs, 1949, 1 s, 1 d. Appointments include: War Serv, 1939-45; AIF, 1942, Roy Austl Navy, Lt RANVR, 1943, RANPRO Staff Gen MacArthur, 1944-45; Chmn, Asher Joel Media Grp Pty Ltd; Carpentaria Newsppprs; Natl Pres, Anzac Mem Forest in Israel; Dir, Roy N Shore Hosp, 1959-81; Mbr, Advsry Cncl, 31st IAA World Advtng Congress, 1984-88, Pub Rels World Congress, 1985-88; Mbr, Appeals Cttee, N Shore Heart Rsch Fndn, 1987; Fndn Gov, Sir David Martin Fndn, 1990-94. Publications: Without Chains, Free, 1977; Australian Protocol and Procedures, 1982, 1988. Honours: King George VI Coronation Medal, 1938; US Bronze Star, 1944; Queen Elizabeth Coronation Medal, 1953; OBE, 1956; Pub Rels Inst of Aust Man of Achievement, 1970; KB, 1971; KBE, 1974; Ancient Order of Sikatuna, Philippines, 1975; Queen Elizabeth Silver Jubilee Medal, 1977; Hon Kt Cmdr, Order of Kts of Rizal, Philippines, 1978; AO, 1986; Hon DLitt, Macquarie Univ, 1988; Kt of the Order of St Sylvester, 1994. Memberships include: Fell, Austl Advtng Inst; Austl Inst of Mngmt; Life Fell, Pub Rels Inst of Aust, 1994; Hon Mbr, Intl Coll of Dentists. Hobbies: Fishing; Gardening; Reading; Writing. Address: 120 Clarence Street, Sydney, NSW 2000, Australia.

JOHN Madhu Joseph, b. 7 Dec 1946, India. Physician; Oncologist. Education: Bd Cert, Radiation Oncology, Amn Bd of Radiology. Appointments: Clin Assoc Prof, Dept of Radiation Oncology, Univ of San Fran. Publications: Chf Ed, Auth, Chemoradiation - An Integrated Approach to Cancer Treatment, 1994. Honours: Best Drs in Am, 1996-97, 1998-99; Best Drs in CA 1996-97. Membership: Prin Investigator, Cntrl CA, Cancer Rsch Grp, GI Cttee, Amn Coll of Radiology. Hobbies: Music; Tennis; Reading; Photography. Address: 7130 N Mill Brook Avenue, Suite 112, Fresno, CA USA 93720.

JOHN Subbiah, b. 31 May 1950, India. Scientist. m. Roselin, 6 Feb 1974, 1 s. 1 d. Education: B Eng. Appointments: JSA, 1972; JSO, 1980; SSO, 1985; Sci E1, 1990; Sci E2, 1995. Honours: Sampath Awd for Meritorious Wrk in Metal Finishing. Memberships: Comp Soc of India; Swadeshi Sci Mov; SAEST; Indian Inst of Metals; AI Assn India. Hobbies: Social work among underprivileged; Prayer. Address: Scientist and Head, IMF Division, CECRI, Karaikudi, Tamil Nadu, India.

JOHN Walter, b. 16 Feb 1924, Newkirk, OK, USA. Retired Physicist. m. Carol S, 23 Jan 1954, 1 s, 3 d. Education: BS, 1950; PhD, 1955. Appointments: Instr, Univ IL, 1955-58; Snr Physicist, Lawrence Livermore Natl Lab, 1958-71; Prof, CA State Coll, 1971-74; Rsch Sci, CA Dept Hlth Servs, 1974-92. Publications: Over 100 articles in profl jrnls and books. Honour: Fell, Amn Physl Soc, 1965-. Memberships: Dir, Amn Assn for Aerosol Rsch, 1987-92; Amn Conf Gov Ind Hygiene; Amn Assn of Phys Tchrs. Hobbies: Music; Art. Address: 195 Grover Lane, Walnut Creek, CA 94596, USA.

JOHNS Robert Keith, b. 24 Apr 1927, Port Pirie, Aust. Geologist; Director-General. m. Barbara Jean Nicolle, 15 Oct 1950, 1 s, 4 d.Education: BSc, hons, 1947, MSC, 1958, Univ of Adelaide. Appointments: Asst Geol, 1948, Res Geol, Leigh Creek Coalfield, 1953; Supvsrng Geol, 1960, Chf Geol, 1972, Dpty Dir of Mines and Dpty Govt Geol, 1973, Dept of Mines; Dir-Gen, Dept of Mines and Energy, 1983-. Publications: Geology and Mineral Resources of Southern Eyre Peninsula, 1961; Limestone Dolomite and Magnesite Resources of South Australia, 1963; Geology and Mineral Resources of the Andamooka-Torrens Area, 1968; History and Role of Government Geological Surveys in Australia (ed), 1976; Cornish Mining Heritage, 1985. Memberships: Roy Soc of SA; Geol Soc of Aust; Australasian Inst of Mining and Metall; Austl Inst of Energy; Austl Inst of Petrol; Petrol Exploration Soc of Aust. Hobbies: Cricket; Tennis. Address: 9 Beckman Street, Glandore, SA 5037, Australia.

JOHNSON Charles Jerome, b. 26 May 1942, Santa Rosa, CA, USA. Energy Economist. m. 1 s, 1 d. Education: BS, San Jose State; MS, Univ CA at Riverside; PhD, Penn State Univ, USA. Appointments: Hd, Energy and Environment Prog; Coord, Environtl Stdies, E-W Cntr, Hawaii, USA, at pres. Publications: About 80 publs. Honour: Centennial Fell Awd, 1996. Hobbies: Travel; Fiction writing; Photography. Address: 1601 East-West Road, Honolulu, HI 96848, USA.

JOHNSON Christine Patricia, b. 23 June 1958, Wagga Wagga, NSW, Aust. Veterinarian. Education: Assoc Dip of Agric; BS; BVMS. Appointments: Equine Practitioner, Epsom Equine Cntr, 1989-94; Equine Practitioner, Goulbourn Valley Equine Hosp, 1994; Race Day Vet, WATC, 1995-99. Memberships: AVA; AEVA, WA Repr, AEVA, 1993-99; Convenor, Bain Fallon Conf, 1999; Austl Palomino Breeders Assn. Hobbies: Horse riding; Music. Address: Epsom Equine Centre, 47 Epsom Avenue, Belmont, WA 6104.

JOHNSON Dorothy Myers, b. 27 Sept 1917, Magna, UT, USA. Jeweller; Accountant. m. H Kenneth Johnson, 7 Apr 1944. Appointments: Acct, Brisacher Advtng, San Fran, CA, 1935-42, Jones & King, Hayward, CA, 1942-43; Jeweller: Co-owner, Johnson Jewellers, Oakland, CA, 1944-56, Ptnr, Parker & Johnson Jewellers, Hollister, CA, 1947-56; Acct: Margaret Kitchen Axell, PA, San Rafael, CA, 1956-79. Honours include: Intl Directory of Disting Leadership (3rd ed), Hall of Fame, 3rd Ed, 4-5th Ed; Two Thousand Notable American Women, 1990; Five Thousand Personalities of the World, 1992. Memberships: East Star, 1962-; Intl Platform Assn, 1992-; Var snr orgns. Hobbies: Studies: finance, science, politics. Address: PO Box 1536, Paradise, CA 95967, USA.

JOHNSON Keith Alan, b. 7 Apr 1942, DC. Home Builder. m. Jame, 1967, 2 s. Education: BSME, Purdue Univ, 1963; Commn, U S Navy Offr Candidate Sch, 1964; MBA, Stanford Univ, 1969. Honours: Constrn Ind, Ldr of the Yr; Spirit of Life Awd; Builder Headliner of the Yr; Disting Serv Awd; Fndn Hall of Fame; Outstndng Cttee Ldrshp Awd; Many or hons. Memberships: Gtr San Diego Chmbr of Comm; Bus Roundtable for Educ; CEO's Roundtable. Hobbies: Fishing; Scuba diving; Hunting. Address: Fieldstone Communities, 14 Corporate Place, Newport Beach, CA 92660, USA.

JOHNSTON Allen Howard, b. 2 Sept 1912, Auckland, NZ. Archbishop. m. Joyce Rhoda Grantley, 1937, 4 d. Education: Seddon Mem Tech Coll, Auckland; Auckland Univ; LTh, St John's Coll, Auckland. Appointments: Asst Curate, St Mark's, Remuera, 1935-37; Vicar, Dargaville, 1937-44, Otahuhu, 1944-49, Whangarei, 1949-53; Archdeacon, Waimate, 1949-53; Bish, Dunedin, 1953-69, Waikato, 1969-80; Primate, Archbish, NZ, 1972-80; Now retd; Chap, Sub-Prelate Order of St John of Jerusalem, 1974-; Mbr, Roy Commn to Inquire into Circumstances of

Convictions of Arthur Allan Thomas for Murders of Harvey and Jeanette Crewe, 1980; Mbr, Cttee of Inquiry to Rprt on Practs and Procedures Following in Insts of DSW, Auckland, 1982. Honours: Hon LLD, Otago Univ, 1969; Fell, St John's Coll, Auckland, 1970; Companion, Order of St Michael and St George, 1977. Address: 3 Wymer Terrace, Hamilton, New Zealand.

JOHNSTON Colin Ivor, b. 28 May 1934, Hong Kong. m. Susan, 12 June 1959, 1 s, 2 d. Education: MBBS, 1957; MRACP, 1962; FRACP, 1970. Appointments; Prof of Med, Monash Univ, 1973-86; Prof of Med, Hd of Dept, Univ of Melbourne, Austin and Repatriation Medl Cntr. Publications: Over 450 articles in sci and medl jrnls in areas of cardiovascular and renal med, hypertension, drug therapy and hormones. Honours: Franz Volhard Prize, Intl Soc of Hypertension, 1992; Richard Bright Awd, Amn Soc of Hypertension, 1995; Coll Medal, Roy Australasian Coll of Physns, 1995; Offr, Gen Div of Order of Aust (AO), 1996. Memberships: Natl Heart Fndn Aust; Intl Soc Hypertension, VP, 1985-90; Amn Soc Hypertension, Exec Cncl, 1988-; High Blood Pressure Rsch Cncl, Aust, Chmn, 1990-93, Treas, 1993-95; Intl Soc Nephrology. Hobbies: Fly fishing; Walnut farming; Collecting. Address: Baker Medical Research Institute, Commercial Road, Prahran, Victoria 3181, Australia.

JOHORE, Sultan Mahmood Iskandar ibni Al-Marhum Sultan Ismail, b. 8 Apr 1932, Johore Bahru, Johore. Malaysian Ruler. m. (1) Josephine Trevorrow, 1956, (2) Tengku Zanariah Ahmad Zanariah Ahmad, 1961. Education: Sultan Abu Bakar Engl Coll, Johore Bahru; Trinity Grammar Sch, Sydney, Aust; Devon Tech Coll, Torquay, England. Appointments: Tengku Makota (Crown Prince), 1959-61, 1981; Raja Muda (2nd-in-line to throne), 1966-81; 5th Sultan of Johore, 1981-; Col-in-Chf, Johore Mil Forces, 1981-; Yang di-Pertuan Agung (Supreme Hd of State), 1984-89; Fndr, Mado's Enterprises & Mados-Citoh-Daiken (timber cos). Hobbies: Hunting; Tennis; Golf; Flying; Water Sports.

JOISHER Vasantlal Haridas, b. 5 Nov 1933, Bombay, India. Trading and Exports Executive. m. Jyotika, 2 June 1959, 1 s, 2 d. Education: BCom; LLB. Appointments: Ptnr, Premji Haridas & Co; Dir, Deccan Plantation P Ltd; Mng Dir, Shri Laxmi Chems & India P Ltd. Honour: Spec Exec Magistrate, Govt of Maharastra, 1980-82. Memberships: Sec, Jolly Gymkhana Bombay; Treas, Sec, Pres, Rotary Club of Kharagpur, 1989-90. Hobbies: Badminton; Table tennis. Address: Shri Laxmi Chemicals & Industries P Ltd, Malancha Road, Nimpura, Kharagpur, 721304, West Bengal, India.

JOLLY Gunita, b. 11 Nov 1964, India. Doctor of Medicine. m. Surinder Paul, 7 Sept 1996. Education: MBBS; DRCOG; MRCGP; FPC. Appointments: House jobs: Roy Utd Hosp Bath, Pembury Hosp Kent; Gen Practitioner Trng, Greenwich, London; Gen Med, Hertford Hosp, Paris, France. Memberships: BMA (Brit Medl Assn); GMC (Gen Medl Cncl); Ordre de Médécines. Hobbies: Sport; Tennis; Scuba diving; Rock climbing; Travel (North and South America, SE Asia, Africa, Europe, Australia). Address: 10 Rue de l'Industrie, Vincennes, Paris, France.

JOLSON Henry, b. 16 Apr 1947, Melbourne, Aust. Barrister; Mediator. m. Carolyn, 2 Feb 1969, 3 s, 1 d. Education: LLB, Monash Univ, 1972; BEcon, Monash, 1972. Appointment: QC, 1991; Tchng Asst, Bond Univ Coml Disputes Resolution Cntr; Tchng Asst to Prof Roger Fisher of Harv Univ in Melbourne, 1994; Tchng Asst, Lawyers Engaged in Alternative Dispute Resolution. Publication: Judicial Determination: Is It Becoming the Alternative Method of Dispute Resolution, 1997. Memberships: Intl Bar Assn, 1993-; Victorian Bar, 1973-; NSW Bar Assn; Chair Victorian Bar Commercial Law ADR Sect; Victorian Exec of LEADR; Victorian Bar ADR Cttee; London Crt of Intl Arbitration; Indep Chairperson, Victorial Elec Supply Ind Dispute Resolution Panel, 1996-97; Natl Elec Mkt Dispute Resolution Panel, 1998-; Vic Legal Prac Act Conciliator; Chairperson, Family Bus Cncl Mediation Cttee. Hobbies: Boating; Commodore of Eildon Boat Club, Vic, 1995-; Golf, Cranbourne Golf Club,

Vic; Natl Golf Club; Skiing; Tennis; Scuba Diving. Address: Owen Dixon Chambers West, 205 William St, Melbourne, Vic 3000, Australia.

JONA Walter (Hon), b. 17 July 1926, Melbourne, Aust. Company Director; Former Cabinet Minister. m. Alwynne Burley, 10 Jan 1972. Education: Scotch Coll; Univ of Melbourne. Appointments: Mbr for Hawthorn, Vic Parl, 1964-85;; Sec for Cabinet, 1973-76; Min of Immigration and Ethnic Affairs, 1976-79; Dpty Min of Hlth, 1976-79; Min for Community Welfare Servs, 1979-82; Shadow Min of Educ, 1982-85; Chmn, Parly Enquiry into Compulsory Wearing of Seat-Belts, 1965-67; Chmn, Dir, sev companies. Publications: Num articles in jrnls. Honours: Queen Elizabeth Jubilee Medal, 1977; AM, 1986; JP; PhD, Hon causa, 1996. Memberships: Life Gov, Assn for the Blind; C'wlth Parly Assn; Chmn, Bd of Advsrs, RSPCA; Dir, 1966-, Pres, 1985-89, Asthma Fndn of Vic; Mbr, Bd of Govs, Tel-Aviv Univ; Chmn, Queen Elizabeth Cntr Fndn. Hobbies: Watching Football; Cricket. Listed in: Who's Who in Australia; Notable Australians; Debrett's Handbook of Australia. Address: 11 Kildare Street, Hawthorn East, Vic 3123, Australia.

JONES Alan Stanley, b. 2 Nov 1946, Melbourne, Australia. Racing Driver. m. Beverly Jones, 1971, 1 s adopted. Education: Xavier Coll, Melbourne. Appointments: Began Racing, Aust, 1964, Brit, 1970; Grand Prix Wins, Aust (Shadow-Ford), 1977, German (Williams-Ford), 1979, Aust (Williams-Ford), 1979, Dutch (Williams-Ford), 1979, Cand (Williams-Ford), 1979, Argentine (Williams-Ford), 1980, French (Williams-Ford), 1980, Brit (Williams-Ford), 1980, Cand (Williams-Ford), 1980, US (Williams-Ford), 1980, US (Williams-Ford), 1981; Can-Am Champion, 1978; Runner-up, 1979, World Champion, 1980; Retd, 1981. Hobbies: Collecting Interesting Cars; Farming.

JONES Albert Walter, b. 2 Sept 1912, Adelaide, SA, Aust. Educator. m. Shirley Walkley, 20 Dec 1941, 1 s, dec, 2 d. Education: BSc, 1932, DipSecEd, 1939, MA, 1944, Univ of Adelaide; PhD, Univ of New Eng, 1986. Appointments: Maths and Sci Tchr, SA Secnd Schs, 1934-48; Insp of Schs, 1948-54; Insp, Secnd Schs, 1954-59; 1st Supt, Recruitment and Trng, 1954-67; Dpty Dir of Educ, 1967-70; Dir Gen of Educ, 1970-77; Univ Fell, Univ of New Eng, 1978; Mbr, Mngmt Cttee to Write Hist of Austl Educ Cncl, 1982-; Chmn, Educn Cttee, Austl Advsry Cncl of Elders, 1984-; Cnslt, Cntr for Brit Tchrs, 1979-; Chmn, Cttee of Inquiry into Yr 12 Exams in SA, 1978; Co-Commn for Human Rights in S Aust, 1999. Publications: Mathematics Text Book for Secondary Schools (w Searle); Influence of the Freedom and Authority Memorandum, 1978; Ebb and Flow: Papers and Addresses by A W Jones, 1977; Decentralization in the Central State, 1980; General Ed: Adelaide High School: The Students of 1938; Development of the Role of Inspectors of Schools, PhD thes, 1985; Articles and book chapts. Honours: UNESCO Fell, Malaysia, 1964; Delegate, UNESCO Gen Assembly, 1973; Study Awds, Goeth Inst to Germany, Japanese Govt to Japan, 1977; AO, 1979; ANZAAS Mackie Medallist for Educn, 1979; ACEA Travel Awd, 1980; Austl Coll of Educn Medallist, 1984; 1st Smith-Mundt and Fulbright Schl from SA; Inaugural A W Jones Lectr, SA Chapt, ACE, 1989; Disting Alumni Awd, Univ of Adelaide, 1992; ACEA Gold Medal, 1995. Memberships: Pres, Hon Fell, Fndn Mbr, Austl Coll of Educn; Fell, Roy Austl Inst of Pub Admin and Austl Inst of Mngmt; Order of Aust Assn; C'wlth Cncl for Educ Admin; Fndn Mbr, Univ of Adelaide Alumni Assn; First Disting Alumni, Life Patron, Friends of the Art Gall of SA; Invited Mbr, Eurn Acady of Arts Scis and Hum. Address: 491 Magill Road, Tranmere, SA 5073, Australia.

JONES Athol James Holtham, b. 18 Mar 1913, Horsham. Educator. m. Margaret, 18 Jan 1941. Education: BA; Dip.Ed; LTH. Appointments: Tchr, Ballarat High, Euroa High, Melbourne High, Camberwell High, Univ High; Prin, Synal High, Macleod High. Publications: ABC of Politics, 1970; Sources For Seventies, 1975. Honours: Blue in Athletics, Melbourne Univ, 1934, Austl Univ, 1935; Rep, Aust Empire Games, 1938. Hobbies:

Sport; Gardening; Poetry. Address: 28 Webster Street, Burwood, Victoria 3125, Australia.

JONES Barry Owen (Hon), b. 11 Oct 1932, Geelong, Vic, Aust. Politician. m. Rosemary Hanbury, 30 June 1961. Education: MA, LLB, Univ Melbourne. Appointments include: HS Tchr, Vic Dept Educ, 1957-67; Bar and Sol, 1968; Lectr, Hist, La Trobe Univ, 1968-70; Mbr, Legis Assembly, Melbourne, 1972-77; Sec, Parly Labor Party, Vic, 1977-98; Mbr (Austl Labor Party) for Lalor, Vic, House of Reps, 1977-98; Chmn, Amnesty Intl Austl Parly Grp, 1980; Shadow Min Sc and Technol, 1980-83; Shadow Min Environment and Conserv, 1983; Min Technol, 1983-84; Min Sci, 1983-90; Min Assisting Treas, Prices, 1987; Min Small Bus, 1987-90; Min Customs, 1988-90; Min Assisting PM, Sci and Technol, 1989-90; Chmn, House of Reps Cttee for Long Term Strategies, 1990-96; Mbr, Natl Commn UNESCO, 1990-98; Mbr, Exec Bd, UNESCO, 1991-95; Natl Pres, Austl Labor Party, 1992-; Pres, Austl and NZ Assn Advmnt of Sci, 1993; VP, World Heritage Cttee, 1995-96; Adj Prof, Monash Univ, 1999-; Visng Fell, Trinity Coll, Cambridge, 1999-. Publications: Decades of Decision, 1965; Joseph II, 1966; The Penalty is Death, 1968; Age of Apocalypse, 1975; Macmillan Dictionary of Biography, 1981; Sleepers, Wake!: Technology and the Future of Work, 1982; Managing Our Opportunities, 1984; Living By Our Wits, 1986; Barry Jones' Dictionary of World Biography, 1994. Honours: DLitt, UTS; DSc, Macquarie Univ; DLitt, Wollongong; 1st and only Austl Min invited address G7 Summit Conf, Ottawa, 1985; Masson Lectr, Univ Melbourne, 1985; AO, 1993. Memberships include: Fell, Austl Acady Sci; Fell, Austl Acad Humanities; FTSE; FRSA; VP, Aust ICOMOS, 1998-. Hobbies: Reading; Music; Travel; Collecting autographed documents and letters, paintings, ancient metal work. Address: GPO Box 496H, Melbourne, Vic 3001, Australia.

JONES David Anthony Talbot, b. 19 Jan 1941, Melbourne, Aust. County Court Judge. m. Jacqueline Patricia Schaefer, 23 May 1964, 1 s, 3 d. Education: LLB, Melbourne Univ. Appointments: Ptnr, Ellison, Hewison & Whitehead, Sols, 1967-80; Chmn, Legal Aid Cmmn of Vic, 1979-80; Chmn, Austl Brdcstng Tribunal, 1980-85; Judge of the Co Crt, 1986-. Honours: Solicitors Prize, 1967; AM, 1987. Hobbies: Golf; Gardening. Address: County Court, William Street, Melbourne, Vic 3000, Australia.

JONES Dean Mervyn, b. 24 Mar 1961, Coburg, Victoria, Australia. Cricketer. m. Jane Jones, 1986, 1 d. Education: Mt Waverley HS. Appointments: Right-Hand Batsman; Played for Vic, 1981-82 to date (Capt 1993-94 to 1995-96), Durham, 1992, Derbyshire (Capt), 1996-97, resigned in season; Played in 52 Tests for Aust, 1983-84 to 1992-93, scoring 3,631 runs (average 46.5) incl 11 hundreds; Toured England, 1989; Scored 18, 292 1st-class runs (52 hundreds), 1997; 164 Ltd-Overs Intls. Publication: Deano: My Call, 1995. Hobbies: Golf; Baseball; Looking After His Two Rottweilers.

JONES Gavin Willis, b. 21 Nov 1940, Armidale, Aust. University Professor. m. Margaret, 24 Aug 1963, 2 s, 1 d. Education: PhD, Austl Natl Univ, 1966. Appointments: Hd, Div of Demography and Sociol Rsch Sch of Socl Scis, Austl Natl Univ, Canberra. Publications: Marriage and Divorce in Islamic Southeast Asia, 1996; Urbanization in Large Developing Countries, 1997. Memberships: Fell, Acady of Socl Scis in Aust; Pres, Austl Population Assn. Hobbies: Running; Tennis; Gardening. Address: 7 Gidja Place, Giralang, ACT 2617, Australia.

JONES Ian Keith, b. 14 May 1943. Biochemist. m. Alison Howell, 2 s. Education: BAgrSc; PhD; Dip Ed. Appointmants: Univ of CA at Los Angeles; Univ Melbourne; Univ Nuremburg; Swinburne Univ of Technol. Membership: Fell, Roy Austl Chem Inst. Hobby: Middle distance running. Address: 125 Rowell Avenue, Camberwell, Vic 3124, Australia.

JONES Ian Stanley Ferguson, b. 3 June 1942. Professional Engineer. m. Cynthia Mary, 3 Sept 1964, 1

s, 1 d. Education: BE, Univ NSW; PhD, Univ Waterloo, Can. Appointments: Rsch Scientist, Boeing Sci Rsch La; Dir, Ocean Technol Grp, Univ Sydney. Publications: Oceanography in the Days of Sail; Satellite Remote Sensing of the Oceanic Environment. Honour: Aust Day Medallion, 1993. Membership: Pres, Austl Meteorological and Oceanographic Soc, 1992-93. Address: Ocean Technology Group, J05, University of Sydney, NSW 2006, Australia.

JONES James Earl, b. 17 Jan 1931, USA. Actor. m. Cecilia Hurt, 1982. Education: Univ MI. Appointments: Num stage appearances on Broadway and elsewhere incl Master Harold...And the Boys, Othello, King Lear, Hamlet, Paul Robeson, A Lesson From Aloes, Of Mice and Men, The Iceman Cometh, A Hand is on the Gate, The Cherry Orchard, Danton's Death, Fences; Sev TV Appearances; Voice of Darth Vader, Star Wars, The Empire Strikes Back, The Return of the Jedi; Films incl: Matewan, Garden of Stone, Soul Man, My Little Girl, The Man, The End of the Road, Dr Strangelove, Conan the Barbarian, The Red Tide, A Piece of Action, The Last Remake of Beau Geste, The Greatest, The Heretic, The River Niger, Deadly Hero, Claudine, The Great White Hope, The Comedians, Coming to America, Three Fugitives, Field of Dreams, Patriot Games, Sommersby, The Lion King (voice), Clear and Present Danger, Cry the Beloved Country, Lone Star, A Family Thing, Gang Related, Rebound. Honours include: Tony Awd. Address: c/o Dale C Olson & Associates, 6310 San Vicente Boulevard, Suite 340, Los Angeles, CA 90048, USA.

JONES Keith Stephen, b. 7 July 1911. Consulting Surgeon. m. Kathleen Abott, 30 Jan 1936, 3 s. Education: Newington College; MB, BS, Univ of Sydney. Appointments: AAMC, 1940-44; Mbr, Cl Newington Coll, 1951-70; Chf Medl Offr, NSW State Emer Servs, 1966-74; Mbr, NSW Medl Bd, 1971-81; Pres, Austl Medl Assn, 1973-76 (Pres, NSW Bd 1962-63); Pres, Australasian Medl Publng Corp, 1976-82; Natl Specialist, Quals Advsry Cttee, 1979-82; Chmn, Austl Natl Specialist Recog Appeals Cttee, 1979-82; Emer Cnslt Surgn, Manly Dist Hosp, 1982-; Chmn, Blue Cross Assn of Aust, 1983-85; Pres, Medl Benefits Fund of Aust Ltd, 1983-85. Honours: Hon Gold Medal, AMA, 1976; Kt, 1980; FRACGP (Hon). Memberships: FRCS, Edin; FRACS; FACEM. Listed in: Who's Who in Australia. Address: 123 Bayview Garden Village, Cabbage Tree Road, Bayview, NSW 2104, Australia.

JONES Lawrence Oliver, b. 20 June 1934, Los Angeles, CA, USA. University Lecturer. m. Marion, 12 Aug 1956, 2 s, 1 d. Education: BA, Pomona Coll, 1956; MA, UCLA, 1958; PhD, UCLA, 1962. Appointments: Asst Prof, Engl, Linfield Coll, 1961-64; Lectr, 1964-67, Snr Lectr, 1967-74, Assoc Prof, 1975-96, Prof, 1996-, Univ of Otago. Publications: Barbed Wire and Mirrors, 1987; From the Mainland, 1995; The Novel, in the Oxford History of New Zealand Literature, 1991, 1998. Honours: Danforth Grad Fell, 1956-61; Phi Beta Kappa, 1956; Rsch Fell, Alexander Turnbull Lib, 1983; Fell, Stout Rsch Cntr, 1994. Memberships: Lit Cttee, Queen Elizabeth II Arts Cncl, 1990-94; Ed, Jrnl of NZ Lit, 1990-. Hobbies: Gardening; Fishing; Music; Sports. Address: 30 Bedford Parade, Brighton, Dunedin, New Zealand.

JONES Quincy, b. 14 Mar 1933, Chicago, USA. Composer; Arranger; Conductor; Trumpeter. m. (1) 3 children, (2) Peggy Lipton, 2 d, 1 d by Nastassia Kinski. Education: Seattle Univ; Berkley Sch of Music; Boston Conservatory. Appointments: Trumpeter, Arranger, Lionel Hampton Orch, 1950-53; Arranger for Orchs & Singers, incl Frank Sinatra, Dinah Washington, Count Basie, Sarah Vaughan, Peggy Lee; Organizer, Trumpeter, Dizzy Gillespie Orch, Dept of State Tour of Near & Mid E & S Am, 1956; Music Dir, Barchlay Disques, Paris; Eurn Tour, 1960; Music Dir, Mercury Records, 1961, VP, 1964; Conductor of num film scores; Composer, Actor in Film, Blues for Trumpet & Koto; Albums incl Body Heat, 1974, The Dude, 1981, Back on the Block, 1989; Prodr Recordings of Off the Wall, 1980, by Michael Jackson, Thriller, 1982, Bad; Videotape, Portrait of An Album: Frank Sinatra w Quincy Jones & Orch, 1986. Honours

include: German Jazz Fest Awd; Edison Intl Awd, Sweden; Downbeat Critics Poll Awd; Downbeat Rdrs Poll Awd; Billboard Trendsetters Awd, 1983; Martell Fndn Humanitarian Awd, 1986; Lifetime Achievement Awd, Natl Acady of Songwriters, 1989; Jean Hersholt Humanitarian Awd, 1995. Address: Rogers & Cowan, 3800 Barham Boulevard, Suite 503, Los Angeles, CA 90068, USA.

JONES Tom, b. 7 June 1940, Treforest, Glamorgan, England. Singer. m. Melinda Trenchard, 1956, 1 s. Appointments: 1st Hit Record, It's Not Unusual, 1965; Other Records incl One Upon A Time; Green Green Grass of Home; I'll Never Fall in Love Again; I'm Coming Home; Delilah; Help Yourself; I Who Have Nothing; Close Up; Body and Soul; A Boy From Nowhere, 1987; Kiss, 1988; Carrying A Torch, 1991; Appeared on TV Shows, Beat Room, Top Gear, Thank Your Lucky Stars, Sunday Night at the London Palladium; Toured USA, 1965; Appeard in Ed Sullivan Show, Copacabana, NY; Variety Show, This Is Tom Jones, in England & USA, 1969; Actor, Singer, Live Performances of Dylan Thomas' Under Milkwood, 1992; Made 26 Singles, 16 Albums; Appeared in Film, Mars Attacks!, 1996. Honours include: Hon Fell, Welsh Coll of Music & Drama, 1994; Brit Most Popular Male Singer, Melody Maker Poll. Address: c/o Tom Jones Enterprises, 10100 Santa Monica Boulevard, Floor 348, Los Angeles, CA 90067, USA.

JONSON Peter David, b. 11 Aug 1946, Melbourne, Aust. Business Executive. m. Elizabeth, 23 Dec, 2 s, 1 d. Education: BComm; MA; PhD. Appointments: MD, ANZ Funds Mngmt; MD, Norwich Union Fin Servs Ltd; Dpty MD, James Capel Aust Ltd; Econ, Reserve Bank of Aust. Honour: Fell, Acady of Socl Scis of Aust. Hobbies: Family; Sport; Writing. Address: L18, 530 Collins Street, Melbourne 3000, Australia.

JORM Anthony Francis, b. 25 Jan 1951, Brisbane, Aust. Research Scientist. m. Betty Kitchener, 1978, 1 s, 1 d. Education: PhD; DSc. Appointments: Dpty Dir, NHMRC Soc Psych Rsch Unit, 1988-96; Prof, NAMRC Psych Epidemiology Rsch Cntr, 1997-. Publications: The Psychology of Reading and Spelling Disabilities, 1983; Understanding Senile Dementia, 1987; The Epidemiology of Alzheimer's Disease and Related Disorders, 1990; Men and Mental Health, 1995. Honours: Ewald W Busse Rsch Awd, Intl Assn of Gerontology, 1997. Memberships: fell, Acady of Socl Scis in Austl, 1994-; Pres-Elect, Australasian Soc for Psych Rsch, 1998. Hobbies: Family history; Peace. Address: NHMRC Psychiatric Epidemiology Research Centre, Australian National University, Canberra, ACT 0200, Australia.

JORY Edward John, b. 20 June 1936, St Ives, Cornwall, Eng. University Professor. m. Marie Therese McGee, 24 May 1964, 3 s. Education: BA 1958, PhD 1967, Univ Coll, London, Eng. Appointments: Lectr, 1959-65, Snr Lectr, Latin and Greek, 1966-73, Assoc Prof, 1974-78, Prof of Classics and Ancient Hist, 1979-91, Dept of Classics and Ancient Hist, Univ of WA; Hon Lectr, Latin and Greek, Univ Coll London, Eng, 1962-63, Hd, Div of Arts and Arch, 1991-93, Visng Prof, Inst of Classical Studies, London, 1989-90; Exec Dean, Fac of Arts, 1994-. Publications: Corpus Inscriptionum Latinarum; Indices Verborum, w D W Moore, 1974; Notae Numerorum, 1989. Honours: C'wlth Fell, Inst of Classical Studies, London, 1962, 1966; Alexander von Humbolt Fell, Kommission fur Epigraphic und alte Geschichte, Munich, Germany, 1974, 1980. Membership: Fell, Austl Acady of Hum, 1983. Hobbies: Cricket; Golf; Sailing; Spear-fishing; Fishing. Address: Faculty of Arts, The University of Western Australia, Nedlands, WA 6907, Australia.

JOSEPH James, b. 28 Oct 1930, Los Angeles, CA, USA. Scientist. m. Patricia Duffy, 2 s. Education: PhD. Publications: Num books, chapts in books, pprs and articles in sci and trade jrnls. Honours: Docteur Honoris Causa, Univ de Bretagne, France; Disting Alumnus Awd, Humboldt State Univ; Nautilus Awd, Marine Technol Soc; Roger Revelle Awd, San Diego Oceans Fndn. Memberships: Am Inst of Fishery Rsch Biols; Sigma Xi.

Address: Inter-American Tropical Tuna Commission, Suite A-302, 8604 La Jolla Shores Drive, La Jolla, CA 92037-1508, USA.

JOSHI Avinash Wasudeo, b. 10 Aug 1942. Professor; Researcher. m. Madhubala, 3 d. Education: Nagpur and Pune Univs, PhD, Phys. Appointments: Visng Fell, Tata Inst of Fundamental Rsch, Mumbai, 1966-67; Rsch Ast, Univ of Bristol (UK), 1967-69; Rdr in Phys, CCS Univ, Meerut, 1969-81; Dean, Students Welfare, 1977-81; Prof Phys, Himachal Pradesh Univ, Shimla, 1981-84; Dean, Sci Fac, 1983-84; Prof, Phys, Pune Univ, Pune, 1984-; Hd, Phys Dept, Pune Univ, 1997-; Supvsr, 3 PhD and over 30 MPhil and MSc theses; Chf Ed, Phys Educ (India); Completed UGC proj on dev of CAL lessons, 1989-92; UNESCO proj on dev of multicomponent comprehensive 1st yr undergrad gen phys course: A World View of Phys; Bd Mbr, Sch of Scis, Indira Gandhi Natl Open Univ, Delhi, 1995-98. Publications: Over 120 articles; Books incl: Our Solar System (co-auth), 1992; Matrices and Tensors in Physics, 1995; Apala Sauraparivar (Marathi), 1996; Elements of Group Theory for Physicists, 4th ed 1997; Ed: Horizons of Physics, Vol 1, 1989, Vol II, 1996. Honour: Mahrashtra State Awd, Best Marathi Book on Phys and Astrophysics, 1996. Memberships: Life Mbr, Indian Phys Assn; Indian Assn of Phys Tchrs; Amn Inst of Phys; Fell, Maharashtra Acady of Scis, 1985. Address: Physics Department, Pune University, Pune 411 007, India.

JOSHI Damayanti, b. 5 Dec 1932, Bombay, India. Classical Dancer. Education: Sev Schs of Classical Dance. Appointments: Ldng Exponent of Kathak Dance; Choreographed Num Prodns, Holding Dance Seminars in India; Tours of Asia, Africa, Eur; Examiner in Music & Dance, Indian Univs; Vis Prof, Indirakala Sangeet Vishwavidyalaya, Khairagarh; Conductor of Tchrs Workshops; Lectr, Demonstrator, England, Germany, China, India. Publications:Madame Menaka (monography); Articles in sev mags, weeklies & dailies. Memberships: Chair, Dancers' Guild of Bombay; Life Mbr, num socs and assns. Hobbies: Reading; Writing; Sitar. Address: D-1 Jeshtharam Baug, Tram Terminus, Dadar, Bombay 400013, India.

JOSHI Mahesh Chandra, b. 6 Apr 1944, Tanakpur. Associate Professor. m. Sudha, 5 June 1972, 1 s, 1 d. Education: BA, MA, Gorakhpur Univ; PhD, JNV Univ, Jodhpur. Appointments: Lectr, Rajasthan Univ, Jaipur; Asst Prof, Jodhpur; Assoc Prof, JNV Univ, Jodhpur. Publications: Princes and Polity in Ancient India, 1986; Yug Yugin Bhartiya Kala, 1995; Sev articles and book reviews. Memberships: Indian Hist Congress; Rajasthan Hist Congress. Hobby: Reading spiritual literature. Address: Department of History, JNV University, Jodhpur, India.

JOSHI Munish Chander, b. 30 Mar 1935, Haldwani, UP, India. Public Servant. m. Mrs Gaura Joshi, 22 Nov 1961, 1 s, 1 d. Education: MA, Ancient Hist and Culture; BA, Indian Hist and Culture. Appointments: Joined Tech Care in Archaeological Survey of India, 1956; Served in var capacities, worked in different areas of the Indian Archaeology, Hist, Culture and Retd as Dir Gen, Archaeological Survey of India; Currently, Mbr, Sec, Indira Gandhi Natl Cntr for the Arts, Janpath, New Delhi. Publications: Tech 1976; Taj Mahal; Indian Archaeology - A Review, 1986-87, 1987-88, 1988-89; King Chandra and Mehrauli Inscription, 1989; over 200 rsch pprs. Honours: Delivered Dr Hiranand Sasiri Mem Lect, 1988; Prof V S Agrawala Mem Lect, 1989; Served as expert mbr, var cttees set up by Govt of India, univs. Memberships: Bd of Hist of Sci, Natl Sci Acady, New Delhi; Chmn, Natl Screening and Evaluation Cttee on Art Objs sent abroad for exhibn, Govt of India; Fndr, Tstee, Mbr, Rasaja Fndn and Art Gall. Address: C-11/64, Shahjahan Road, New Delhi, India.

JOSHI Ram Prasad, b. 14 July 1940, Nepal. Business Executive. m. Indu Joshi, 1 s, 2 d. Education: MCom; LLB. Appointments: Gen Mngr, Nepal Food Corp, 1985-91; Snr Advsr, 1991-95, Chf Exec Offr, 1995-, Salt Trading Corp Ltd. Publications: A Case Study of Nepal

Food Corporation on Improving Marketing and Cost Efficiency; Increasing Access to Foodgrain by the Vulnerable Sections of Population in Nepal; Cost of Government Subsidy on Foodgrain Distribution in Nepal; Three Decades of Agriculture Marketing Development in Nepal; Consultancy Report on Foodgrain Marketing Liberalization and Privatization. Memberships: Charter Mbr, Rotary Club of Patan W; Exec Mbr, VP, Nepal Heart Fndn; Mngnt Assn of Nepal; Number of Socl Orgs. Hobby: Studying. Address: 30 Kwako, Lalitpur 11, Nepal.

JOSHI Shri Krishna, b. 6 June 1935, Anarpa, Pithoragarh, India. Researcher and Administrator. m. 7 Feb 1965, 2 s. Education: MSc; DPhil. Appointments: Lectr, Allahabad Univ, 1957-65; Visng Lectr, Univ of CA (Riverside), 1965-67; Prof, Univ of Roorkee, 1967-86; Dir, NPL, 1986-91; Dir Gen, CSIR, 1991-95; Chmn, RAC, 1997-. Publications: Over 180 pprs in jrnls. Honours: Watumull Mem Prize, 1965; Shanti Swarup Bhatnagar Prize, 1972; Meghnad Saha Awd, 1974; FICCI Awd, 1990; Goyal Prize, 1993; Padma Shri, 1991. Memberships: Fell, Indian Natl Sci Acady, 1974-, Pres, 1993-95; For Mbr Russian Acady of Scis; Fell, Indian Acady of Sci, 1974-; Fell, Third World Acady, 1994-; Pres, Indian Sci Congress, 1996-97. Hobby: Trekking. Address: Chairman, RAC, Lucknow Road, Timarpur, Delhi 110054, India.

JOSHI Shrikant, b. 24 June 1960, Hyderabad, India. Scientist. m. Rashmi, 2 d. Education: BTech, Chem Engrng, Osmania Univ; MS, Chem Engrng, Rensselaer Polytech Inst, NY, USA, 1984; PhD, Chem Engrng, Univ of ID, USA, 1987. Appointments: Rsch Assoc, Univ of ID, USA, 1987-89; Sci, Def Metallurgical Rsch Lab, Hyderabad, 1989-98; Sci, Intl Adv Rsch Cntr for Powder Metallurgy and New Materials, Hyderabad, 1999-. Publications: Over 40 articles in profl jrnls. Honour: Gold Medal, Osmania Univ, 1982. Memberships: Materials Rsch Soc of India; Laser Inst of Am; Indian Inst of Metals. Hobbies: Travel; Cricket; Reading. Address: International Advanced Research Centre for Powder Metallurgy and New Materials, Opp Balapur Village, RR District, Hyderabad 500005, India.

JOSHI Sudha Prabhakar, b. 9 Aug 1939, Mumbai, India. Teacher. m. Prabhakar, 5 May 1963, 1 s. Education: BA (Hons), 1958, MA, 1960, PhD, 1986, Univ of Mumbai, Mumbai, India. Appointments: Lectr, Hd of Dept, 1963-94, Rdr, Hd of Dept, 1994-, Vice Prin, 1994-95, R Jhunjhunwala Coll, Mumbai; Guiding Tchr for Doct Rsch, 1987-; Chairperson, Bd of Stdies, Mbr, Acad Cncl, 1992-93, 1995-; Mbr, Coll and Univ Dev, 1994-; Mbr, Bd of Exams, 1996-, Univ of Mumbai. Publications: Ed, Anthologies: Nivadak Gangadhar Gadgil, 1986; Gangadhar Gadgil: Wangmay Soochi, 1987; Bus Ka Tikat, 1991; Saat Majale Hasyache, 1993; Co-ed: Niradak Marathi Ekankika, 1983; Over 30 critical essays. Honour: Tchr Fell, Univ Grants Commn, New Delhi, 1980-84. Memberships: Exec Cttee, Marathi Rsch Bd, Mumbai, 1992-; Editl Bd, Dictionary of Literary Terms, State Bd of Lit and Culture, Mumbai, 1994-; Lang Advsry Cttee Natl Awd for Lit, Bharatiya Jnanpith, New Delhi, 1997-; Advsry Cttee, Marathi Rsch Cntr, SNDT Univ, Mumbai, 1997-. Hobbies: Reading; Theatre; Visual arts; Travel; Library movement; Teaching languages. Address: 24 Parameshwar Kripa, Tilak Road, Ghatkopar (East), Mumbai 400077, India.

JOSHI Venkatesh Govind-Bhat, b. 27 Feb 1928, Kukanoor, Koppal District, Karnataka, India. Khadi Work (Rural Development through Gandhian constructive activities). m. Padma Joshi, 1 May 1956, 4 s. Education: BCom, w Pub Fin and Admin as spec subj, Bombay Univ, 1954. Appointments: Joined Rastra Seva Dal as active vol, 1940-52, Joined Bombay Vill Inds Cttee, 1954; Trng at Ambar Spinning at Prayaga Samiti, 1954, then at Nasik Vidyalaya and at Dhirendre Mujundar's Ashram in Bihar; Mngr, Cntrl Vastragar, Mngr, Model Inds Cntr at Jamakhandi and Prin of Khadi Vidyalya, 1954-58; Joined Mysore State Khadi and Vill Inds Bd, Mngr, Khadi Prodn Cntr, Khadi Orgnr, Intensive Area Orgnr and Dev Offr, -1983; Proj Dir, Rural Inds, Asian Inst for Rural Dev, Bangalore, 1983-84. Publications: Num articles in local

lang (Kannada). Membership: Chmn, Karnataka Khadi Workers Assn, Gadag-Betgeri, 1985-. Hobbies: Studying rural life; Indian music; Reading. Address: 142 A IInd Block, Rajanagar, Bangalore-10, India.

JOSHUA Edward Mathew Kilmartin, b. 13 May 1960, Aust. Livestock Officer. m. Fiona, 24 Apr 1993. Education: BApp.Sci, 1986; Ctf, Woolchassing; Ctf, Agricl. Appointments: Dist Livestock Offr, Albury, 1987, Warren, 1988, Moree, 1989; NSW Sheep Ectoparasite Control Coord, 1996. Publications: Lice Advance, 1990; Sheep Health Guide, 1992; Flywise, 1998; Licekill, 1998. Membership: Austl Soc of Animal Prodn. Hobbies: Gardening; Sheep and cattle breeding. Address: 179 Heber Street, Moree, NSW 2400, Australia.

JOSKE John Alexander, b. 21 Jan 1969, Casterton, Vic, Aust. Entertainment Promoter. Membership: Treas, Australasian Assn of Campus Activities, 1996, 1997. Hobbies: Travelling; Music; Paragliding. Address: PO Box 12705, A'Beckett St, Melbourne, 8006, Australia.

JOSKE Thomas Roderick (Hon Justice), b. 22 Aug 1932, Melbourne, Aust. Judge. m. (1) 1960, 2 s, 2 d, (2) Gail Frances Robinson, 1978. Education: Wesley Coll, Melbourne, 1940-50; LLB, Univ of Melbourne, 1950-54. Appointments: Admitted to Practice, 1955; Bar at Law, 1957-76; Judge, Family Crt of Aust, 1976-. Memberships: Medico Legal Soc; Fmr Mbr, Legal Aid Cmmn; Bar Civil Juries Sub-Cttee; Chmn, Bar Matrimonial Causes Sub-Cttee. Hobbies: Reading; Golf; Swimming. Address: Family Court, 305 William Street, Melbourne, Vic 3000, Australia.

JOZWIK Maciej, b. 9 Aug 1962, Bialystok, Poland. Medical Doctor; Obstetrician; Gynecologist; Educator. Education: MD, 1986; PhD, 1992; Dipl, Obstet and Gynae, 1994. Appointments: Asst, Regl Womens Hosp, Bialystok, 1986-88; Snr Offr, Dept of Gynae and Septic Obstet, Sch of Med, Bialystok, 1988-94; Lectr, Dept of Gynae and Septic Obstet, Bialystok Med Univ, 1994-98; Lectr, Dept of Gynae, Bialystok Med Univ, Bialystok, 1998-. Publications: More than 40 articles in profl med jrnls. Memberships: Polish Gynae Soc; Intl Continence Soc; Eurn Assn of Perinatal Med; Intr Urogyne Assn. Hobbies: Water Sports; Skiing. Address: Department of Gynaecology, Bialystok Medical University, Sklodowskiej 24A, 15-276 Bialystok, Poland.

JU Ming, b. 20 Jan 1938, Taiwan. Sculptor. m. 8 Dec 1961, 2 s, 2 d. Education: Woodcarver, Potter; Sculptor in Bronze. Creative Works: Num one-man shows, USA and Far E; Maj Exhbn, Hong Kong, 1988; Produced 3 series, The Living World. Honours: Sculpture Awd, Chinese Sculptors & Artists Assn, 1976; Awd, Ten Outstndng Youths, 1987; Natl Culture Awd, China Natl Culture Fndn. Address: 28 Lane 460, Chih Shan Road, Section 2, Taipei, Taiwan.

JU Ti, b. 11 Feb 1942, Shanghai, China. Educator. m. Miaozheng Huang, 1 Sept 1968, 1 s. Education: Double MS. Appointments: Hd, Dept Computer Engnrg, 1985-93; Chmn, Computer Educ Dir Cttee Min of Posts and Telecomms, 1987. Creative works: Computer-Aided Design of Active Network; Computer method for network des, dev and application of PLD. Honour: Govt spec bonus, state cncl, 1992. Address: Department of Computer Engineering, Nanjing University of Posts and Telecommunications, 66 Xing Mufen Road, Nanjing, China 210003.

JUDD Gary James, b. 24 Aug 1946. Queen's Counsel. m. Judge Jan Marie Doogue, 12 Jan 1989, 2 s, 2 d. Education: LLB w Hons, Auckland Univ. Appointments: Chmn, ASB Bank Ltd. Membership: F Inst D. Address: William Martin Chambers, 152 Anzac Avenue, Auckland 1, New Zealand.

JUENGER Friedrich K, b. 18 Feb 1930, Frankfurt/Main, Germany. Professor of Law. m. Baerbel J, 9 Sept 1967, 2 s. Education: Referendarexamen, 1955; MCL, MI, 1957; JD, Columbia, 1960. Appointments: Assoc Prof, Wayne State Univ, 1966-68; Prof, Wayne

State Univ, 1966-75; Prof, Univ of CA, Davis, 1972-92; Edward L Barnett Prof, UC Davis, 1992-. Publications: German Stock Corporation Act, 1969; Zum Wandel des Internationalem Privatrechts, 1974; Choice of Law amd Multistate Justice, 1993. Honours: Volkswagen Fndn Grant, 1972-73; Fulbright Snr Rsch Fellshp, 1981-82; UC Davis Distinguished Tchng Awd, 1985; Humboldt Fndn Fellshp, 1990. Memberships: Amn Soc Comparative Law, Pres, 1992-94, Hon Pres, 1992-94; Titular Mbr and VP, Common Law Grp of Intl Acady Comp L, 1994-. Hobbies: Reading; Travel. Address: 1203 Bucknell Drive, Davis, CA 95616, USA.

JUNANKAR Pramod Nagorao, b. 21 May 1943, Wardha, India. Academic Economist. m. Pauline, 7 Aug 1973, 1 s, 1 d. Education: BS, Econ, Univ of London, 1961-64; MS, Econ, Univ of London, 1964-66; PhD, Econ, Univ of Essex, 1984. Appointments: Lect in Econ, 1964-65; Rsch Asst, 1965; Tutor in Econ, 1965-66; Lect in Econ, 1966-69; Occasional Tchng, 1969-72; Visng Fell, Indian Statistical Inst, 1972, 1976; Visng Asst Prof, Northwestern Univ, IL, USA, 1972-73; Visng Assoc Prof, Queen's Univ, Kingston, Canada, 1978-79; Visng Fell, Dept of Econ, Univ of Warwick, 1981; Visng Fell, Austl Natl Univ, 1984-87; Guest Lect, Univ of Warwick, 1984-85; Prin Rsch Fell, Univ of Warwick, 1984-85; Visng Fell, Univ of Warwick, 1986; Lect in Econ, Univ of Essex, 1969-88; Visng Fell, Univ of London, 1989; Visng Fell, Austl Natl Univ, 1988-92; Rdr in Econ, Austl Natl Univ, 1993-97; Prof of Econ and Fin, Univ of West Sydney, 1998-. Publications: Investment, Theories and Evidence, 1972; Marx's Economics, 1982; From School to Unemployment? The Labour Market for Young People, 1987; Economics of Unemployment, Causes, Consequences and Policies, 1998; Sev Monographs; Many Contbns. Honours: Grad Bursary, London Sch of Econ and Polit Sci, 1964-65; Leverhulme Rsch Studentshp, London Sch of Econ and Polit Sci, 1965-66. Memberships: Amn Econ Assoc; Econ Soc of Aust; Roy Econ Soc. Address: Department of Economics and Finance, University of Western Sydney, Macarthur, P O Box 555, Campbelltown, NSW 2560, Australia.

JUNG Iftikhar Hamidullah, b. 29 Mar 1933, Kurwai, India. Electrical Engineer. m. Elena, 3 Jan 1959, 2 s, 2 d. Education: Dip, Loughborough Coll, 1958; Postgrad, MIEEE, 1959. Appointments: S of Scotland Elec Bd, 1959-65; Foster Wheeler, 1965-69; Cnslt, 1970-72; John Brown, 1972-76; Occidental Oil, Libya, 1976-79; Worly Engrng, 1980-81; Sci Design, 1982-84; Arabian Gulf Oil Co, Libya, 1984-98. Publications: Many articles in profl jrnls. Memberships: MIEEE, USA; Chm, Muslim Educ Bur, London. Address: 60 Pembroke Road, Ruislip HA4 8NE, England.

JUNID Datuk Seri Sanusi bin, b. 10 July 1943, Jerlun Langkawi, Kedah. Politician. m. Mila Inangda Manjam Keumala, 3 children. Education: City of London Coll; Univ of London; Berlitz Sch of Langs, Hamburg. Appointments: Fmr Bank Mngr, 7yrs; Dpty Min of Home Affairs, 1978-81; Min of Rural & Natl Devel, 1981-86; Mbr, UMNO Supreme Cncl, 1981-83; Min of Agricl, 1986-95. Address: Ministry of Agriculture, Wisma Tani, Jalan Mahameru, 50624 Kuala Lumpur, Malaysia.

JURGA Ludovit, b. 17 July 1943, Bratislava. Professor; Oncologist; Radiotherapist. m. Jane, 29 Dec 1995, 1 s, 1 d. Education: MD; PhD; Prof of Radiol; Specialist, Radiotherapy and Clin Oncol. Appointments: Asst Prof, 1967-79, Assoc Prof, 1979-97, Safarik Univ Sch of Med, Kosice; Prof, Fac of Nursing and Pub Hlth, Univ of Trnava, 1996-. Publications: Textbook of Radiology, 1990; Over 120 pprs in profl jrnls. Honours: Hon Acknowledgement, Safarik Univ Sch of Med, 1986; Bronze Medal, Slovak Med Soc, 1993. Memberships: Eurn Soc for Med Oncol; Multinatl Assn of Supportive Care in Cancer; NY Acady of Scis. Hobbies: Body-Building; Swimming; Tennis; Biking; Skiing. Address: c/o Department of Oncology and Radiotherapy, University Teaching Hospital, A Zarnova 11, 917 75 Trnava, Slovakia.

JUUL Kurt, b. 23 April 1944, Denmark. Ambassador. m. Mariela, 2 s. Education: MSc, Engrng; BSc, Econs. Appointments: Hd of Div, Eurn Commn; Amb, Hd of Delegation, Chile, 1993; Amb, Pakistan, 1998. Honours: Order Al Merito. Hobbies: Golf. Address: Delagation of the European Commission, Sector 66/3, Street 88, Honte 9, Islamabad, Pakistan.

K

KAADAN Abdul Nasser, b. 18 Aug 1957, Syria. Doctor of Medicine. m. Rawa Hajjjar, 31 Jan 1985, 1 s, 1 d. Education: MD; CES: Orth Surg; Dip, Hist of Med; MSc, Hist of Med; PhD, Hist of Med. Appointments: Lectr, Aleppo Univ; Natl Deleg of Intl Soc for Hist of Med. Publications: Bone Fractures as Viewed by Old Arab Physician, 1992. Honours: Japanese Schlshp, 1994; Brit Lister Law Schlshp, 1996; ISSLA Schlshp, 1997. Memberships: ISHM; SICOT. Address: PO Box 7581, Aleppo, Syria.

KABARITI Abdul Karim A, b. 15 Dec 1949, Amman, Jordan. Politician. m. 2 children. Education: St Edward's Univ, Austin, TX, USA; Am Univ of Beirut, Lebanon; Lic Fin Advsr, NY, 1986. Appointments: Owner, Money Exchange Co; Bd Dir, sev cos; Mbr, House of Reps, Governorate of Ma'an, 1989-93, 1993-95; Min of Tourism, 1989-92; Min of Labour, 1992-93; Chair, Bd of Socl Security Corp, 1992-93; Chair, Bd of Vocational Trng Corp, 1992-93; Chair, Fgn Rels Cttee, House of Reps, 1994-; Min of Fgn Affairs, 1995-96; PM, Min of Def & Fgn Affairs, 1996-97. Hobbies: Water Skiing; Music. Address: House of Representatives, Amman, Jordan.

KABBANI Sami S, b. 3 Jan 1937, Damascus, Syria. Professor of Cardiac Surgery. m. Sally, 3 Mar 1969, 2 s, 1 d. Education: BS, 1958, MD, 1962, Intern, 1962-63, Amn Univ of Beirut; Residencies: Cleveland Metro, Gen Hosp, Cleveland, OH, 1963-64; St Louis Univ Grp Hosps, MO, 1963-65; St John's Mercy Hosp, MO, 1965-66; Henry Ford Hosp, MI, 1966-68; TX Heart Inst, Houston, 1972-73. Appointments: Asst Prof, 1969-74, Assoc Prof, 1974-79, Dir, Damacus Univ Cardiovascular Surg Cntr, 1975-, Prof, Surg, 1979-, Chmn, Dept of Cardiovascular Surg, 1997-, Damascus Univ Medl Sch; Cardiovascular Surg, West Heart Inst, San Fran, CA, USA, 1982-83. Publications: Num, in profl jrnls in Engl and in Arabic. Honour: 1st Degree Presdtl Appreciation Awd (for starting open-heart surg in Syria), 1972. Memberships: Arab (Syrian) Medl Soc; Amn Assn for Thoracic Surg; Amn Coll Surgs; Denton A Cooley Cardiovascular Soc; Assn of Thoracic and Cardiovascular Surgs of Asia; Eurn Soc for Cardiovascular Surg (Eurn Chapt, Int Soc for Cardiovascular Surg); Soc Thoracic Surgs; CA Medl Assn; San Fran Medl Soc; Arab-Amn Medl Assn; Amn Coll Cardiology; Mid E and N African Chapt (MENA) of Intl Soc for Cardiovascular Surg, Pres, 1989-92, 1996-; Intl Soc Cardio-Thoracic Surgs; Syrian Cardiovascular Assn, Pres, 1994-; Mediterranean Assn of Cardiology & Cardiac Surg, Pres, 1998-99; Sev editl bds of profl medl jrnls.

KABUA Amata, b. 17 Nov 1928, Jabor Is, Jaluit Atoll, Marshall Is. President, Marshall Islands. Education: Mauna Olu Coll, HI. Appointments: Chf Clk, Marshall Is Cncl of Iroji, 1951-58; Mbr, 1st Marshall Is Cong, 1958-63; Senator, Marshall Is, Cong of Micronesia, 1963-78; Pres, Senate of Marshall Is, 1963-70; Mbr of Parl, 1979-; Fndr and Ldr, Pol Movt for Marshall Is, sep from Micronesia, 1972-78; Pres, Marshall Is. Address: Office of the President, Government of the Republic of the Marshall Islands, POB 2, Majuro, MH 96960, Marshall Islands.

KACHORNPRASART Sanan, b. 7 Sept 1944, Phichit, Thailand. Politician. Education: Chulachomklao Roy Mil Acady. Appointments: Aid-de-Camp to Gen Chalard Hiranyasiri; Involved in Attempted Coup, 1981; Democrat Party MP for Phichit, 1983, 1986, 1988; Dpty Commns Min, 1986; Min of Agricl & Co-ops, 1989; Dpty PM, 1990-91. Address: Government House, Nakhom Pathom Road, Bangkok 10300, Thailand.

KADALBAJOO Mohan Krishen, b. 21 Jan 1949, Srinagar, Kashmir. Teaching and Research. m. Usha, 26 July 1978, 2 d. Education: BSc, 1968; MSc, 1970; Post MSc, 1972; PhD, 1976. Appointments: Rsch Assoc, 1976-77; Lectr, Prof, 1978-91; Prof, 1991-. Publications: Over 75 in profl jrnls. Memberships: Amn Mathl Soc; NY

Acady of Scis. Hobbies: Reading; Gardening; Music. Address: Department of Mathematics, Indian Institute of Technology, Kanpur 208016, India.

KAHAN Louis, b. 25 May 1905, Vienna, Austria. m. 24 May 1953, 2 d. Education: La Grande Chaumiere, Paris; Hornsey Coll of Arts, London. Appointments: Tailor and Des, 1920-39; French For Legion, 1939-41; War Artist, 1942-45; Staff Artist, Le Figaro, Paris, 1946; Painter, Printmaker, Stage Des in Aust and Eng, 1947-99. Creative Works: Solo Exhbns in France, London, Aust. Publications: Australian Writers; The Artist; Louis Kahan by Lou Klepac. Honours: Archibald Prize for Portraiture, 1962; AO, 1993; Rep in all maj pub galls in Aust, 14 Austl and Overseas Univs and pub galls in France, Eng, Austria and USA. Address 11 Second Avenue, East Kew, Vic 3102, Australia.

KAHAN Sheldon Jeremiah, b. 5 Mar 1948, Honolulu, Hawaii, USA. Entertainer; Songwriter. Education: Tel Aviv Univ, 1968-70; Merritt Coll, 1971-73. Creative Works: City Lights (album), 1993. Memberships: Musicians Union; AFTRA. Hobbies: Philosophy; Sports. Address: 3915 Fredonia Drive, Los Angeles, CA 90068, USA.

KAILIS Patricia Verne, b. 19 Aug 1933, Castlemaine, Vic, Aust. Neurogeneticist; Company Director. m. Michael George Kailis, 31 Mar 1960, 2 s, 2 d. Education: MB, BS, Univ Melbourne. Appointments: Res Medl Offr, Roy Perth Hosp, Princess Margaret Hosp, King Edward Hosp, 1958-59; Gen Prac, WA, 1960-79; Dir, M G Kailis Grp Cos, 1960-; Chmn, Rsch and Dev Cttee; Hon Geneticist, Dept Neuropath, 1970-80, Roy Perth Hosp; Hon Neurogeneticist, Dept Neur, Roy Perth Hosp and Roy Perth Rehab Hosp, 1980-85; Emer Cnslt Neur, Roy Perth Hosp, 1997; Cncl, WA Soc Crippled Children, 1980-97; Pres, Rocky Bay Inc, 1991-97; Cncl, 1991-, Chair, 1998, PLC, Perth, 1991-; Gov, Univ of Notre Dame Austl, Mbr State Advsry Cttee CSIRO, 1984-87; Hlth Advsry Cttee, Hlth Dept, WA, 1985-92; Ind Living Cntr, WA Inc, 1982-91; Chmn, 1986-91, VP, Liberal Pty WA, 1986-89; Bd Mbr Disability Servs Commn, Chair Ministerial Advsry Cttee for Disability Servs, WA, 1998-. Publications: Pprs on muscular dystrophy, genetic counselling, malignant hypothermia, motor neurone disease. Honours: OBE, 1979; AM, 1996; FTSE, 1996. Memberships: Fndn Mbr, Austl Soc Human Genetics, 1973; Mbr Amn Soc Human Genetics; Life Mbr, Muscular Dystrophy Rsch Assn WA, 1975; Liberal Party WA, 1980, VP 1986-89; Cncl WA Soc Crippled Children, 1980-, Chmn 1991-; Mbr, State Advsry Cttee, CSIRO, 1984-87; Hlth Advsry Network, Hlth Dept WA, 1985-90; WA Providers Cncl, 1985-92; Hellenic Assn WA; Austl Medl Assn, WA; Castellorizian Ladies Assn, WA; Castellorizian Assn, WA; Karrakatta Club, WA; Roy C'wlth Soc. Address: 5 Minim Close, Mosman Park, WA 6012, Australia.

KAJIYAMA Seiroku, b. 27 Mar 1926, Ibaragi Pref, Japan. Politician. m. Harue Kajiyama, 1 s, 1 d. Education: Nihon Univ. Appointments: Mbr, Ibaraki Prefectural Assn, 1955-69; Speaker, 1967-69; Mbr, House of Representatives, 1969-; Dpty Chf Cabinet Sec, 1974; Parl, Vice Min for Constrn, 1976, Intl Trade and Ind, 1979; Chair, House of Representatives Stndng Cttee on Com and Ind, 1983; Chair, Exec Cncl of Liberal Democratic Party, 1986; Min of Home Affairs, 1987-88, Trade and Ind, 1989; Chf Cabinet Sec, 1996-97. Hobbies: Golf; Shogi (4th dan); Reading. Address: Kudun Shukusha, 2-14-3 Fujimi, Chiyoda-ku, Tokyo 102, Japan.

KAJORNPRASART Sanan, b. 7 Sept 1935, Phichit, Thailand. Deputy Prime Minister; Minster of Interior. m. Education: Roy Thai, Mil Acady; Jt Staff Coll, Maj Gen. Appointments: Hd of House Stndng Cttee on Soldiers, 1983; Dpty Min of Transp and Comms, 1986; Min of Agric and Co-ops, 1988; Dpty Prime Min, 1990; Min of Ind, 1992; Min of Interior, 1994, 1997. Honour: Kt Grand Cordon, Spec Class, Exalted Order of the White Elephant, 1989. Memberships: Exec Cttee of Democratic Party, Dpty Ldr, 1985, Sec Gen, 1988. Address: 59/13 Soi Chawal-preecha, Sanambinnam Road, Thacai Sub-District, Muang District, Nonthaburi, Thailand.

KAKIZAWA Koji, b. 26 Nov 1933, Tokyo, Japan. Professor; Former Member, House of Representatives. m. Eiko Kono, 5 Sept 1962, 2 s, 1 d. Education: Grad, Dept of Econ(s), Tokyo Univ. Appointments: Min of Fin, Asst to Chf Cabinet Sec, and others, 1958-77; Elected to House of Cnclrs from Tokyo Dist, 1977; Elected to House of Reps from 6th Dist of Tokyo 1980, re-elected 1983, 1986, 1990, 1994; Chmn, Cttee on For Affairs, 1990; Parl Vice Min for For Affairs, 1991; Min of For Affairs, 1994; Resigned to run for Tokyo Gubernational elections, 1999; Prof, Tokai Univ, Tokyo. Publications include: Tax Office Chief, Just Fresh from France; Bureaucracy and Japan Ship; Nagatacho Funny Stories; Exhortation Toward Police State Japan, all in Japanese. Honours: Chevalier de l'Ordre de la Légion d'Honneur de la République Française; Grand Officier de l'Ordre de Leopold II du Royaume du Belgique; Chevalier de l'Ordre de la Grande Etoile de la République de Djibouti; Grand Officier de l'Ordre Royal du Cambodge de Sahametre I. Memberships: Sec-Gen, Japan-Algeria Assn, Japan-Libya Friendship Assn. Hobbies: Scuba Diving; Swimming; Wine Appreciation. Address: 401 Wakatake Blg, 5-31-17 Toyo cho, Koto-ku, Tokyo 135-0016, Japan.

KAKKAR Poonam, b. 28 Sept 1959, Lucknow, India. Scientist. m. Avinash Kakkar, 16 Apr 1982, 2 s. Education: MSc, Biochem, Lucknow Univ, 1980; PhD, Kanpur Univ, 1985. Appointments: Jnr Rsch Fell, 1981-83, Snr Rsch Fell, 1983-85, Rsch Assoc, 1986-87, Sci B, 1987-90, Sci C, 1990-95, Sci E-2, 1995-. Publications: Toxicity Data Handbooks, vol I and II, 1986; Toxicity Data Handbooks, vol III and IV, 1989; Toxicology Atlas of India, 1990; Num pprs in profl jrnls. Honours: Natl Schlsp, Govt of India, 1974-76; CSIR Fellshp, 1981-87. Memberships: NY Acady of Scis; Intl Soc of Free Radical Rsch, Aust; Soc of Biol Chems, India. Hobbies: Music; Reading. Address: c/o Industrial Toxicology Research Centre, PO Box 80, MG Marg, Lucknow 226001, India.

KAKULAS Byron Arthur, b. 29 Mar 1932, Perth, Aust. Professor of Neuropathology; Medical Director. m. Valerie Anne Patsoyannis, 5 Feb 1961, 1 s, 2 d. Education: MBBS, 1956, Univ of Adelaide; MD, Univ of WA, 1964; MRACP, 1960; FRACP, 1971; MRCPath, UK, 1973; FRCPath, 1975, Appointments: Fell, Harvard Medl Sch, USA, 1963-65; Visng Pathologist, Roy Perth Hosp, 1965-67; Snr Lectr, 1964-66, Rdr, 1967-71, Dean, 1976-78, Univ of WA; Prof and Hd of Neuropath, Roy Perth Hosp, Medl Dir, Austl Neuromuscular Rsch Inst. Publications: Basic Research in Myology; Man, Marsupials and Muscle, 1982; Co-Ed, Pathogensisi and Therapy of Duchenne and Becker Muscular Dystrophy, 1990; Duchenne Muscular Dystrophy - Animal Models and Genetic Manipulation, 1992; Neuromuscular Disorders, Muscle Section: Current Opinion on Neurology, ed, 1996. Honours: Hon Mbr, Rotary Club, W Perth, 1967-; AO, 1975; Didaktora (honoris causa), Hon Prof, Univ of Athens, 1979; Citation of Hon, Rotary Intl; Anzaas Fell, 1987; Adv Aust Awd, 1989; Hellenism Awd, Greek Austl Profl and Bussmen's Assn of WA, 1989; Paul Harris Fell, Rotary Intl Fndn, 1990; Hon Mbr, Hellenic Neurol Assn, 1991; Castellorizian of the Yr, Castellorizian Assn of Vic, 1995; Medicus Hippocraticus Prize, 1st Intl Medl Olympiad, Kos, 1996. Memberships include: VP, 2nd, 3rd, 4th, 5th Intl Congresses on Muscle Diseases, 1971, 1974, 1978, 1982; World Fedn of Neurol, 1967-; Austl Assn of Neurologists, Cnclr, 1972-75; Austl Brain Fndn, Pres, 1980-85; Intl Spinal Rsch Trust, 1983-; Austl and NZ Soc for Neuropath, Pres, 1985-; Pres, XIIIth Intl Cong of Neuropathology, Perth, 1997. Hobbies: Water sports. Listed in: Who's Who in the World; Who's Who in Australia. Address: Department of Neuropathology, Royal Perth Hospital, Box X 2213, GPO, Perth, WA 6001, Australia.

KALAM Akhtar, b. 12 Jan 1950, Calcutta, India. Engineering Educator. m. Shamsha, 27 Dec 1975, 3 d. Education: BSc; BEng; MS; PhD. Appointments: Snr Lectr, 1984-90, Assoc Prof, 1991-96, Prof, 1997-, Dpty Dean, 1999-, Vic Univ, Melbourne, Aust. Publications: Cogeneration and Gas Turbine Operation, 1998; Power System Protection, 1999. Honours: Cleo Cross Fellshp, 1974; Univ of Bath Schlsp, 1978. Memberships: FIEAust;

CPEng; FIEE; CEng; IEEE. Hobbies: Cricket; Reading; Politics. Address: 45 Stuart Street, Moonee Ponds, Victoria 3039, Australia.

KALYONCU Ali Fuat, b. 20 Mar 1959, Eskisehir, Turkey. Chest Physician and Allergolog. m. Alev, 16 Mar 1985, 1 d. Education: Istanbul Univ Med Fac, 1982; Chest Diseases of Hacettepe Univ, Ankara, 1988; Allergic Diseases, Uppsala Univ Hosp, Uppsala, Sweden, 1990. Appointments: Malaria Fighting Service, 1982-84; Hacettepe Univ Hosp Dept of Chest Diseases, 1984-88; Uppsala (Sweden) Univ Hosp, 1989-90. Honour: UCB Inst of Allergy Schlsp, 1994. Memberships: Eurn Acady Allergol and Clinl Immunology, 1991; Eurn Respiratory Soc, 1997; Turkish Thoracic Soc, 1994; Turkish Allergic Soc, 1992. Hobbies: Medical History; Coin Collecting. Address: Hacettepe University Hospital Department of Chest Diseases, Adult Allergy Unit, Sihhiye, 06100 Ankara, Turkey.

KAM Chak Wah, b. 19 Apr 1959, Hong Kong. Doctor. Education: MBBS, Hong Kong; MRCP, UK; FRCSEd; FRCSG; MHKCP; FCSHK; FHKCEM; FHKAM Surg; FHKAM, emer Med. Appointments: Cnslt, A and E Dept, Tuen Mun Hosp, Hong Kong, 1993-. Creative Works: Ed in Chf, Hong Kong Jrnl of emer Med, 1994-. Memberships: Hong Kong Soc for emer med and surg; Hong Kong Coll of emer med; Exam Cttee of Hong Kong Coll of emer med. Hobbies: Gym; Swimming; Squash; Music. Address: Flat C, 1/F BL One, Grand Del Sol, Fung Cheung Road, Yuen Lons, NT, Hong Kong.

KAM John Kaihong, b. 11 June 1955, Hong Kong. Environmental Professional. m. Luo Xun, 1994. Education: PhD. Appointment: Cncl Mbr, Soc of Homes for the Handicapped, 1996-. Publications: Logical Fallacies in Everyday Life; Cults: Their Recognition, Evaluation & Control; ....Warped Space-Time. Address: Morrison Hill, PO Box 47138, Hong Kong.

KAMAL Mustafa, b. 27 Apr 1944, Malang, E Java. Civil Engineer. m. Siti Fadhilah, 25 Sept 1977, 2 s, 3 d. Education: Cert, Jefferson hs, Cedar Rapid, IA, USA, 1963; Grad in Civ Engrng Cert, West Austl Inst of Technol, Perth, WA, 1972. Appointments: Civ Engr, W Autl Govt Railways, Perth, Aust, 1972; Civil Engr, Tugu Co, Hong Kong, 1975-77; Dir, PT Timur Jauh Co, 1977-85; Pres Dir, KAI Co, 1985; Dir, PT Berdikari Co, 1986; Dir, PT Felima Orient Pacific Co, 1987-; Pres Dir, P T Wanamekar Handayani o, 1997. Honours: Amn Field Serv Schlshp, 1963; Colombo Plan Schlshp, 1966. Hobbies: Travelling; Swimming. Address: Jl Pengadegan No 6 Rt08/Rw04 depan Komplex, DPR Kalibata, Pancoran, Jakarta Selatan 12770, Indonesia.

KAMALI Mohammad Hashim, b. 7 Feb 1944. University Professor. m. 24 July 1974, 1 s, 1 d. Education: BA; LLM; PhD. Appointments: Asst Prof, Kabul Univ, 1965; Pub Atty, Min of Justice, Kabul, 1966-68; Lang Monitor, BBC, Eng, 1975-79; Asst Prof, McGill Univ, Montreal, 1979-83; Rsch Assoc, Can Cncl for Socl Scis and Hums, 1984-85; Assoc Prof, Intl Islamic Univ, Malaysia, 1985-86; Prof, 1991-. Publications: Law in Afghanistan, 1985; Principles of Islamic Jurisprudence, 1991; Freedom of Expression in Islam, 1994; Punishment in Islamic Law, 1995; Juristic Preference (Istihsan) and Its Application to Contemporary Issues, 1997; Freedom, Equality and Justice in Islam, 1999; The Dignity of Man: The Islamic Perspective, 1999. Honours: Strategic Rsch Grant, Socl Sci and Hums Rsch Cncl of Can, 1984; Isma'il Al Faruqi Awds for Acad Ex, 1995, 1997. Memberships: Mid East Studies Assn of N Am; Fell, Intl Inst of Islamic Thought, Herndon, VA; Fell, Sch of Oriental and Afr Studies, Lond Univ; Majlis Ilmuan Malaysia. Hobbies: Islamic Calligraphy; Swimming; Tennis. Listed in: Who's Who in Asia and the Pacific Nations; Who's Who in the USA. Address: Apartment 165-1, Sri Wangsaria Condominium, Jalan Ara, Bangsar, 59100 Kuala Lumpur, Malaysia.

KAMATA Satoshi, b. 12 June 1938, Aanori, Japan. Journalism (Freelance). m. Kimiyo Kamata, 1 May 1967, 2 s, 1 d. Education: BA, Russian Lit, Waseda Univ.

Publications: Japan in the Passing Lane, 1983; Toyota y Nissari, 1993; Japan aan de lopende band, 1986. Honours: Nitta Jiro Awd, 1990; Mainichi Cultural and Publng Awd, 1991. Memberships: Japan Pen Club; Japan Labor Pen Club. Hobbies: Photography; Gardening; Watching movies. Address: 1-235-55 Nakazato Kiyose-shi, Tokyo, Japan.

KAMEI Shizuka, Politician. Appointments: Parl Vice-Min of Transp, Min, 1994-94, of Constrn, 1996; Mbr, House of Reps for Hiroshima; Chair, LDP Natl Org Cttee, & Acting Chair, LDP Policy Rsch Cncl. Address: Ministry of Transport, 2-1-3 Kasumigaseki, Chiyoda-ku, Tokyo, Japan.

KAMEI Yoshiyuki. Politician. Appointments: Fmr Parl Vice-Min of Transp, Min, 1996; Mbr, House of Reps; Mbr, LDP. Address: Ministry of Transport, 2-1-3 Kasumigaseki, Chiyoda-ku, Tokyo 100, Japan.

KAMEYAMA Michitaka, b. 12 May 1950, Japan. Professor. m. 29 Apr 1983, 1 s, 2 d. Education: BE, Tohoku Univ; ME, 1975; DEng, 1978. Appointments: Rsch Assoc, 1978-81, Assoc Prof, 1981-91, Prof, 1991-, Tohoku Univ. Publications: Sev articles in profl jrnls. Honour: Fell Awd, IEEE, 1997. Membership: Chair, IEEE Tech Cttee on Multiple-Valued Logic, 1996-97. Hobbies: Piano; Skiing; Hiking. Address: 6-10-8 Minami-Yoshinari, Aoba-ku, Sendai 989-3204, Japan.

KAMLANG-EK Arthit, b. Bangkok, Thailand. Politician. Education: Chulachomklao Roy Mil Acady. Appointments: Senator, 1977, 1986; Supreme Commdr of the Armed Forces & Col-in-Chf of the Army, 1983-86; Thai People's Party MP for Loei, 1988; Dpty PM, 1990-91. Address: Government House, Nakhom Pathan Road, Bangkok 10300, Thailand.

KAMILOV Abdulaziz Khafizovich, b. 16 Nov 1947, Yangiyul. Diplomat. m. 1 s. Education: Moscow Inst of Oriental Langs; Dipl Acady, USSR Min of Fgn Affairs. Appointments: Dipl Serv, 1972; Attache, USR Emb, Lebanon, 1973-76; 2nd Sec, USSR Emb Syria, 1980-84; Mbr, Divsn of Near E, USSR Min of Fgn Affairs, 1984-88; Snr Rschr, Inst of World Econs & Intl Rels, USSR Acady of Scis, 1988-91; Cnslr, Uzbekistan Emb, Russian Fedn, 1991-92; Dpty Chair, Security Serv of Uzbekistan Repub, 1992-94; 1st Dpty Min of Fgn Affairs, 1994, Min, 1994-. Address: Ministry of Foreign Affairs, Uzbekistansky prosp 9, 700029 Tashkent, Uzbekistan.

KAMRA Adarsh Kumar, b. 20 Sept 1944, Kamalia, Punjab, India. Atmospheric Scientist. m. Uma, 31 May 1972, 2 s, 1 d. Education: BS, Coll of Sci, Gurukala, Kangri, 1961; MSc, DAV Coll, Dehradoon, India, 1963; PhD, Univ of Roorkee, India, 1968. Appointments: Rsch Assoc, SUNY, Albany, NY, 1968-71; Pool Offr, Univ of Roorkee, 1971-74; Snr Sci Offr II, 1974-75, Snr Sci Offr I, 1975-80, Asst Dir, 1980-88, Dpty Dir, 1988-99, Dpty Dir, 1999, Indian Inst of Tropical Meteorology, Pune, India. Publications: About 70 rsch pprs. Honours: Proj Grant, Natl Sci Fndn, Wash, 1970-71; WMO Awd for Encouragement to Young Scientists, 1975; Indian Inst of Tropical Meteorology Silver Jubilee Awds, 1989, 1991; Mbr, Commn for Atmospheric Scis, World Meteor Orgn, Geneva, 1997-; Fell, Indian Acady Scis, Bangalore, 1998-. Memberships: Indian Meteor Soc. Hobbies: Reading; Listening to music; Visiting places. Address: Indian Institute of Tropical Meteorology, Dr Homi Bhabha Road, Pune 411 008, India.

KAN Min, b. 5 May 1934, Hefei, China. Research Fellow; Professor. m. D H Wang, 4 Apr 1954, 3 d. Education: BS, Solid State Phys, Fudan Univ, 1956. Appointments: VP, Southwest China Inst of Applied Magnetics, 1980-84; VP, Shanghai Univ of Sci & Technol. Publications: Knowledge of Magnetic, 1984; Notebook of Production Technology of Electronics Industry, 1990. Honours: 1st Awd, Electrons Ind, China (EIMC), 1980; 2nd Awd, EIMC, 1981. Memberships: Standing Cttee, Mianyang Municipal People's Congress, 1983-86; Shanghai Cttee, CPPCC, 1987-2003. Hobby: Application

of Ancient Chinese Ceramic. Address: No 27-102, 440 Tacheng Road, Jiading, Shanghai 201800, China.

KAN Naoto, Politician. Appointments: Fmr Patent Atty; Min of Hlth & Welfare, 1996; Mbr, House of Reps; Mbr, New Party Sakigake. Address: Ministry of Health & Welfare, 1-2-2 Kasumigaseki, Chiyoda-ku, Tokyo 100, Japan.

KANAPATHY Raj Intan, b. 4 Apr 1967, Kuala Lumpur, Malaysia. Banker. Education: LLB, hons, Anglia Polytech Univ, England. Appointment: Credit Recovery Exec and Sec to Credit Cttee. Memberships: Treas, Rotary Club of Brickfields, Malaysia; Brit Grads Assn of Malaysia; Brit Malaysian Ind and Trade Assn; Malaysia Aust Bus Cncl; Malaysia Cand Bus Cncl; Malaysia NZ Bus Cncl; Malaysian Econ Assn; Kuala Lumpur Symph Orch Soc. Hobbies: Collecting Stamps; Plays; Classical Music; Indian Classical Music; Opera; Hockey; Cricket; Swimming. Address: BBMB Leasing Berhad, 28th Floor, Menara Tun Razak, Jalan Raja Laut, Kuala Lumpur 50350, Malaysia.

KANASRI K N Srinivas, b. 3 Jan 1944, Kadalaveni, India. Bank Emloyee. m. Sharada, 16 June 1975, 2 d. Education: BA; LLB. Appointment: Spec Asst, State Bank of Mysore. Publications: Poems; Articles. Honours: Karnataka State Nataka Acady Awd, 1993; Hon, Kannada Sahithya Parishat, 1997. Hobbies: Reading; Organising cultural activities. Address: 402, Srinagagr, Gouribidanur, Kolar District, Karnataka State, India.

KANDA Seiichi, b. 22 May 1927, Kobe, Japan. Professor in Chemistry. m. A Takagi, 29 May 1960, 1 s. Education: BS, Osaka Univ, 1953; DSc, 1963. Appointments: Instr, Osaka Cty Univ, 1953-62; Osaka Univ, 1962-65; Prof, Chem, Tokushima Univ, 1965-93; Kobe Women's Jnr Coll, 1993-. Publications: Synth and prop of coord polym (jrnls), 1957-97. Membership: Chem Soc of Japan. Hobbies: Skiing; Skating. Address: Kamihachiman, Nishiyama 498, Tokushima, Japan 770-8041.

KANDO Noriko, b. 2 Sept 1960, Tokyo, Japan. Information Science Researcher. m. Takashi Kando, 10 Oct 1987. Education: Master, Keio Univ, Tokyo, 1991; PhD, 1995. Appointments: Rsch Fell, Japanese Soc for Promotion of Sci, 1993-94; Rsch Assn, NACSIS, Tokyo, 1994-97; Assoc Prof, 1998-. Creative Works: Phrase Processing Methods for Japanese Text Retrieval; Text-Level Structure of Research Articles and its Implication for Text-based Information Processing Systems. Honours: Rsch Awd, Japan Soc of Librarianship; Outstnding Rsch Awd, Info Processing Soc of Japan. Memberships: ACM-SIGIR; Amn Soc for Info Sci. Hobbies: Swimming. Address: NACSIS 3-29-1 Otsuka, Bunkyo-ku, Tokyo 112-0864, Japan.

KANE-RUZICKA Penelope Susan, b. 23 Jan 1945, Nairobi, Kenya. Consultant. m. Lado Ruzicka, 21 Mar, 1985. Education: MSc, Econs, Univ Wales. Appointments: Min Advsry Cncl on Aid Plcy, 1993-95; Snr Assoc, Offr for Gender and Hlth, 1994-, Assoc Prof, 1998- Univ of Melbourne. Publications include: Ehkaisy, 1988; The Choice Guide to Birth Control, 1988; Famine in China 1959-61: Demographic and Social Implications, 1988; Differential Mortality: Methodological Issues and Biosocial Factors, 1989; Women's Health: From Womb to Tomb, 1993; Victorian Families in Fact and Fiction, 1994. Memberships: Family Planning ACT; Brit Soc for Population Studies; Austl Population Assn; Intl Union for the Sci Study of Population. Hobby: Painting. Address: The Old School, Major's Creek via Braidwood, NSW 2622, Australia.

KANEHARA Yu, b. 3 Jan 1949, Tokyo, Japan. Publisher. Education: BE, Seikei Univ, Japan, 1971. Address: Igaku-Shoin Ltd, 5-24-3 Hongo Bunkyo-Ku, Tokyo, 113-8719, Japan.

KANEKO Kazushige, b. 7 Dec 1925, Yokohama, Japan. Asian Ethno-Forms. m. Chieko, 27 Jan 1952, 1 s, 1 d. Education: BA, Kokugakuin Univ, 1950.

Appointments: Hd, Govt Survey Mission of Intangible SW Asia, 1993; Japanese Deleg at UNESCO, Intl Consultation of Intangible Cultural Heritage in Vietnam, 1994; Chmn, Intl Conf on Preservation; Field Stdy throughout Asia over 300 times in 35 yrs; Tchr, Otsuma Women's Univ, Okinawa Pref Univ of Fine Arts; Visng Prof, Central Univ of Nationalities, China. Publications: Asian Ethno-Forms, 3 vols; Mainichi Shinbonsha, 3 vols. Honours: 3rd Crown Decoration, Roy Thailand. Memberships: Pres, Inst of Asian Ethno-Forms and Culture; Asian Ethno- Forms Soc; Chmn, Asian Ethno-Forms Mus. Address: 100, Makigahara, Asahi-ku, Yokohama, Japan.

KANEKO Koichi, b. 13 Oct 1963, Tokyo, Japan. Assistant Professor. m. Keiko, 11 Oct 1992, 1 s, 1 d. Education: BA, Econs, Seikei Univ, 1986; MA, Sociol, Shukutoku Univ, 1991; Rsch Course, LSE, England, 1991-92; PhD, Socl Welfare, Japan Womens Univ, 1996. Publication: Beatrice Webb's Ideas on Welfare, 1997. Memberships: Japanese Soc for the Stdy of Socl Welfare, 1990; Asian Acad Assn of Socl Servs, 1996. Hobbies: Walking; Music. Address: 200 Daiganji-cho, Chuo-ku, Chiba 260-8701, Japan.

KANEKO Shiro, b. 31 Mar 1943, Tokyo, Japan. Office Worker. Education: Bach, Waseda Univ, Fac of Sci Engrng, 1967; DEng, Waseda Univ, 1994. Appointments: Rschr, Car Brake Lining Materials, Miyasi Asbestos Co, Chiba, 1967-70; Dev of Air Cleaner, Hitachi Co, Kameido Factory, 1970-75; Environmental Measmt and Valuation, Hitachi Plant Eng and Cnstrn Co, Matudo, 1975-98; Chief, Sect, 1990-. Publications: Rsch pprs: Phosphorus Removal by New Crystallization Process, 1985; Phosphorus Removal by Crystallization Using a Granular Activated Mag, 1988; Phosphorus Removal from Secondary Effluent by Crystallization, 1992. Memberships: Amn Chem Soc, 1982; Soc of Chem Engrng of Japan, 1989. Hobbies: Appreciation of classical music; Playing golf. Address: 2-41-3 Tomigaya Shibuya-ku, Tokyo 151-0063, Japan.

KANG Byung Kifa, b. 19 July 1961, Korea. President of the Associations. m. Jenil Yan, 3 s, 1 d. Education: LLD; PhD, IA, USA. Appointments: Prof, Cheungung Univ, 1956-70; Sec-Gen, Aspac Culture Cntr, Seoul, 1968-71; Korea-Japan Cncl, Seoul, Congressman, Natl Assembly, 1971-81; Chmn, Educ & Culture Cmty, 1979-81; Pres, Hansung Univ, Seoul, 1981-85, Korean World Peace Assn, Seoul, 1990-; Prof, Damul Natl Sch, Seoul, 1995-; Visng Prof, Grad Sch Socl SciCY. Publications: Contemporary Foreign Policy, 1965; Political Environment of the Korean War, 1970; Selection of Dr Kang's Writings, 1991. Honour: Kt of the Cmdr, Malta. Memberships: Interactive Studies Assn, USA; Natl Cncl of Korean Utilogists; Korean World Peace Assn. Hobbies: Golf; Fishing. Address: 476-2, Seokyodong, Mepoka, Seoul, Korea.

KANG Hui Jun, b. 30 July 1957, Shanghai, China. Senior Economist. m. Wang Xiaoqin, 1 s. Education: ML, E China Univ of Sci and Technol; Bachelor of Intl Trade, Shanghai For Trad Inst. Appointments: Sec, Yth League, Dir, Publicity Dept, Dir, For Trade Dept, Shanghai Huangpu Dist; Dir, Pudong New Area Econ and Trade Bur. Publications; On the Target Mode and Operation Mechanism of the Economic and Trade System in Pudong, Shanghai, 1995; On National Treatments of Foreign Enterprises, 1997; The Securities of Real Estate, 1999. Honours: 2nd Prize, Excellent Theses, Shanghai Govt, On the Dev of Pudong Tourism, 1994; The Functional Positioning and Mktng of Pudong's Trade, 1996. Memberships: China Dev Zone Assn, Standing Cncl Mbr, 1995-; China Harbour Cty Real Estate Assn, Dpty Chmn, 1998-. Hobbies: Reading; Football; Music. Address: 981 Pudong Da Dao Shanghai, China.

KANG Man-Soo, b. 30 June 1945, Kyong nam, Repub of Korea. Government Official. m. In-Kyung Ha, 8 Apr 1972, 2 s, 1 d. Education: BLL, Seoul Natl Univ, 1965-69; MEcon, NY Univ, 1985-87. Appointments: Passed Snr Govt Offr Exam, started Pub Serv as Dpty Dir, Off Natl Tax Admin, 1970; Fin Attaché, Korean Emb, USA,

1985-88; Dir-Gen, Intl Fin Bur, Fin Bur, Insurance Bur, 1988-90; Spec Cnslr, Natl Assembly, 1993-94; Asst Min for Tax & Customs, Min of Fin, 1994-95; Commnr, Korea Customs Serv, 1995-96; Vice Min, Min of Trade & Ind & Energy, 1996-97; Vice Min, Min of Fin & Econ, 1997-. Publications: VAT: Theory and Practice, 1977. Honours: Order of serv merit red stripes. Hobbies: Tennis; Mountain climbing. Address: Sunkyong Apt, #2-1203, Taechi-dong, Kangnam-gu, Seoul, Korea.

KANG Songshi, b. 26 June 1938. Electrical Engineer. m. Heling Li, 2 d. Education: Radio Engr, Moscow Electrotechnical Inst of Comm; MSEE, OH Univ. Appointments: Rsch Wrkr, Rsch Ldr, Brdcstng Sci Rsch Inst, Min of Radio, Film & TV, Beijing, 1961-84; Dpty Dir, TV Rsch Div, 1984-86; Dpty Dir, TV Rsch Labs, 1986-89; Dir, Tech Policy Rsch Div, 1989-95; Vice-Chmn, Study Grp 12, CCIR, 1990-93; Vice Chmn, Study Grp II ITU-R, Geneva; Chf Engr, Pan Brilliance Co Ltd, 1995-. Publications: 100 pprs. Honour: Many Natl Awds. Memberships: Fell, Chinese Inst of Electrons; Standing Cttee Mbr, Brdcst Technol Soc, China. Hobbies: Sports; Music. Address: No 2, Bei Bin He Lu (3-3-201), West District, Beijing 100045, China.

KANG Young Hoon, b. 30 May 1922. Politician; Diplomat. m. Hyo-Soo Kim, 1947, 2 s, 1 d. Education: Univ of Manchuria; Univ S CA, USA. Appointments: Mil Attaché to Emb, Washing DC, 1952-53; Divsn Commdr, 1953, Corps Commdr, 1959-60, Retd, Rank of Lt-Gen, 1961; Asst Min of Def, 1955-56; Staff Mbr, Rsch Inst of Communist Strategy & Propaganda, Univ S CA, 1968-69; Dir, Rsch Inst on Korean Affairs, Silver Spring, MD, USA, 1970-76; Dean, Grad Sch, Hankuk Univ of Fgn Studies, 1977-78; Chan, Inst of Fgn Affairs & Natl Security, Min of Fgn Affairs, 1978-80; Amb to England, 1981-84, to the Holy See, 1985-88; PM of the Repub of Korea, 1988-91. Honours: Num mil medals.

KANNAN K, b. 15 Apr 1956, Virudhunagar, India. Reader in Pharm. m. Mythili, 2 Dec 1983, 2 d. Education: MPharm; PhD. Appointments: Apprentice, CIBA-GEIGY Ltd, 1978-79; Chem, Astra-IDL Ltd, 1979; Chem, FDC Ltd, 1981-82; Tchng Fac, Annamalai Univ, 1982-. Publications: Sev articles in profl jrnls. Membership: Assn of Pharm Tchrs of India. Address: Pedagogy; Research. Address: c/o Institute of Pharmaceutical Technology, Annamalai University, Annamalai Nagar 608002, India.

KANNO Akisa, b. 1 Dec 1932, Tokyo, Japan. Banking. m. Yasuko, 15 Nov 1957, 1 s, 1 d. Education: BA (Law), Tokyo Univ, 1955; MA (Econs), Yale Univ, 1963. Appointments: Exec Dir, Bank of Japan, 1986; Dpty Gov, Export-Import Bank of Japan, 1992; Vice-Chmn, Snr Exec Dir, Japanese Banking Assn, 1994-. Hobby: Travelling. Address: 4-12-14 Kouyama, Nerimaku, Tokyo 176-0022, Japan.

KANT Shri Krishnan, b. 28 Feb, Kot Mohammed Khan, Tehsil Taran Taran, Amristar, India. Political Activist. m. Suman Kant. Education: Stud, Lahore. Career: Mbr Parl; Attended all India Cong Cttee, Ahmedabad, 1971; Active in fields of For Plcy, Def Plcy, Land Reforms, Freedom of Press, Electoral Reform; Chmn, Jt Parly Cttee, helped into Prevention of Water Pollution Bill; Sec, Indian Parly and Scientific Cttee; Ed, quarterly jrnl, Sci in Parl; Expelled from Cong, 1975; Held off, Cong Pty and Janata Pty; Mbr, Natl Exec, Janata Pty, 1977-88; Mbr Exec Cttee, Janata Parly Pty; Fndg Gen Sec, People's Union of Civ Liberties and Dem Rights; Held Natl Seminar against 49th Amendment of Const; Org, Guru Govind singh Samagam. Publications: Num articles in newspprs and periodicals on natl and intl pol, culture and sci plcy. Memberships: Quit India Movt, 1942; Rajya Sabha, 1966-77; Lok Sabha, -1980; Life Mbr, Pres, Servants of the People Soc; Chmn, Cttee of Railway Reservations and Booking, 1972-76; Exec Cncl, Inst of Def Stdies and Analysis; AICC; Bd of Mngmt, Gandhian Inst of Stdies, Varanasi. Hobby: Urdu Poetry.

KANZAKI Takenori, Politician. Appointments: Mbr, House of Reps; Mbr, Komeito, Chair, Fgn Affairs Cttee; Chair, Diet Policy Cttee; Min of Posts & Telecoms,

1993-94. Address: House of Representatives, Tokyo, Japan.

KAPADIA Ashwinbhat Sakerlal, b. 9 Sept 1941, Surat, Gujarat. Retired Vice Chancellor. 1 s, 1 d. Education: BEd (1st), Univ of Baroda, 1965; MA, Gujarat Univ, Ahmedabad, 1967; PhD (Hon), 1989, DSc (Hon), 1995, Sri Lanka (honoris causa). Appointments: Coll Prof, Hd of Dept of Engl, MK Coll of Com, Bharuch; PG Tchr in Engl; Syndicate Mbr, S Gujarat Univ, Surat as Govt nominee, 1986-88; Vice-Chan, S Gujarat Univ, Surat, 1997-98 (retired). Publications: Booklets & pprs on Savitri Sri Aurobi Do's Sepic. Honours: PhD, Open Intl Univ for Complimentary Meds, Sri Lanka. Memberships: Life Mbr, ISCON. Hobbies: International speaker; Papers, publications and discourses on Sri Aurobindo's philosophy of Savitri. Address: 1 Ananddham Mahadevnagar Housing Society, Opp J P College, at Bharuch (Gujarat), India.

KAPADIA Marie Nirmala Braganza, b. 15 July 1949. Librarian. m. Samir Kapadia, 26 Apr 1980, div. Education: BA (Gen); BEd; BLib Sci; MLib and Info Scis. Appointments: Tchr, Loreto Convent, Darjeeling, 1970-72; Tchr, St Vincent's, Pune, 1973-78; Doc, Philips India Ltd, 1978-80; Libn, Tata Mgmnt Trng Cntr, Pune, 1983-96. Honour: Ist in BLib & MLib, Parkhi Prize. Past Sec, Univ Women's Assn; Indian Fedn of Women; IASLIC; Fndr Mbr, PRERNA. Hobbies: Reading; Theatre; Women's Issues. Address: 37 St Patrick's Town, Sholapur Rd, Pune 411013, India.

KAPI Mari (Sir), b. 12 Dec 1950. Deputy Chief Justice. m. Lady Tegana Kapi, 12 July 1973, 2 s, 3 d. Education: LLM, Univ of London; LLB, Univ of Papua New Guinea. Appointments: Snr Legal Offr, 1974; Acting Dpty Pub Sol, 1975; Assoc Dpty Pub Sol, 1976; Assoc Pub Sol, 1976; Pub Sol, 1978; Judge, Natl and Supreme Crts of Papua New Guinea, 1979; Dpty Chf Jus, 1982; Jus of Appeal of Solomon Is, 1982; Jus of Appeal of Fiji Crt of Appeal, 1992. Honours: CBE; KB; Order of the Solomon Is, 1994. Memberships: Chmn, Bd Dirs, Natl Inst for Continual Legal Educ; Chmn, Continual Judicial Educ Cttee. Address: Supreme Court Chambers, PO Box 7018, Boroko, National Capital District, Papua New Guinea.

KAPIL Dev, b. 6 Jan 1959, Chandigarh, India. Cricketer. m. Education: Punjab Univ. Appointments: Right-Hand Mid-Order Batsman, Right-Arm Fast-Medium Bowler; Played for Haryana, 1975-76 to 1991-92, Northamptonshire, 1981-83, Worcestershire, 1984-85; Played in 131 Tests for India, 1978-79 to 1993-94, 34 as Capt, Scoring 5,248 Runs (average 31.0) incl 8 Hundreds and Taking Record 434 Wickets (average 29.6); Youngest to Take 100 Test Wickets (21 yrs 25 days); Hit 4 Successive Balls for 6 v England, Lords, 1990; Scored 11,356 Runs (18 hundreds) and Took 835 Wickets in 1st class Cricket; Toured England, 1979, 1982, 1983 (World Cup), 1986, 1990; 224 Ltd-Overs Intls. Publication: Kapil Dev -Triumph of the Spirit, 1995. Hobbies: Hunting; Riding; Dancing. Address: Board of Control for Cricket in India, E-4 Radio Colony, Indore (MP), India.

KAPLAN Gisela, b. 25 Aug 1944, Germany. Academic; Writer. m. 14 Dec 1965, 1 d. Education: BA, 1st Class Hons, 1974, DipEd, 1975, MA, 1978, PhD, 1984, Monash Univ, Aust. Appointments: Univ Tchr, 1976-; Monash Univ, Melbourne, ANU, Canberra, Univ NSW, Sydney, 1976-; Ldng role in Educ, 1975-85; Chairperson, Cttees, Vic inst Secnd Educ, 1980-84; Convenor, Women's Affairs Cttee, Ethnic Communities Cncl, Sydney, 1984-85; Mbr, Snr Bd of Educ, NSW, 1984-85; Ed, Sociological Newsletter, 1986-88; Co-Ed, Austl and NZ Jrnl of Sociol, 1989-; Exec Mbr, Sociological Assn of Aust and NZ; VP, Sociological Assn of Aust, 1991; Snr Rsch (Cnslt), 1986-; Mbr, State Govt Advsry Cttees, 1987-89; Mbr, NSW Women's Advsry Cncl, 1989-90; Visng Prof, Sociol, Memphis State Univ, 1990; Fndn Prof of Socl Sci, Queensland Univ of Technol, 1992; Adj Prof, Univ New Eng, Armidale, 1996. Publications: Num sociological articles and contrb of chapts; Books: Hannah Arendt: Thinking, Judging, Freedom, (co-ed), 1989; Contemporary Western

European Feminism, 1992; Women of the World: Australia, 1992; Cultures of the World: Iran, (co-auth), 1993; Spectrum: Bibliography of Women in Australia 1945-1994, 1995; The Meagre Harvest. The Australian Women's Movement 1950s-1990s, 1996; Poetry in anthologies in Germany and Aust; Also Ethologist (primatology and ornithology) with mun publs, incl books, co-written w L J Rogers: Orang-Utans in Borneo, 1994; Not Only Roars and Rituals: Communication in Animals, 1998; The Orang-Utans, 1999. Honours include: C'wlth Undergrad and Postgrad Awds; Natl Austl Lit Awds, 1987; Contrb, Amn Gustavus Myers Hum Rights Awd for Outstndng Publ, 1996. Memberships include: Austl Sociological Assn; Intl Sociological Assn; Amn Sociological Assn; Austl Polit Studies Assn; Intl Ethological Soc. Address: University of New England, Armidale, NSW 2351, Australia.

KAPOOR Shyam Sunder, b. 14 June 1938, Jalesar, UP. Scientist. m. Veena, 22 Apr 1967, 1 s, 1 d. Education: MSc; PhD. Appointments: Hd, Fission Phys Sect, 1974; Proj Dir, MEHIA, 1982; Hd, Nuc Phys Div, 1984-87; Assoc Dir, Phys Grp, 1987-90; Dir, Phys Grp, 1990; Dir, Phys and Electrons and Instrumentation Grp, 1991. Creative Works: Nuclear Radiation Detector; Many publs and repts, Intl Jrnls. Honours: Fell, Indian Acady of Scis; Fell, Indian Natl Sci Acady; Fell, Natl Acady of Scis; Awd, Shantiswarup Bhatnagar Prize; Awd Goyal Prize. Memberships: Indian Phys Assn; Amn Phys Soc; Indian Soc; Indian Soc for Radiation Phys; Indian Sci Congress; Phys Sect, Indian Sci Congress. Hobbies: Reading. Address: 6th Floor, Central Complex, BARC, Trombay, Mumbai 400 085, India.

KAPUDIA Kundanika, b. 11 Jan 1927, Limbadi, Gujarat, India. Writer; Social Worker. m. Makarand, 30 Apr 1968. Education: BA. Appointments: Ed, Yatrik; Ed, Navaneet; Columnist, Janmabhuomi. Publications: Short Story Collections, 1954, 1968, 1978, 1983, 1987, 1990; Novels, 1968, 1972, 1984. Honours: 6 awds for novel, Women's Cause. Membership: Mng Tstee, Nandigram Trust. Hobbies: Nature; Spiritual Journey. Address: Nandigram Trust, P Vankal 396007, Valsad, India.

KAPUR Basant Kumar, b. 24 Jan 1950, Singapore. Professor of Economics. m. Renu, 26 Oct 1977, 1 s, 1 d. Education: Bachelor of Socl Scis, Econs, Univ of Singapore, 1970; PhD, Econ, Stanford Univ, 1974. Appointments: Lectr, Natl Univ of Singapore, 1974-79; Snr Lectr, 1979-86; Assoc Prof, 1987-97; Prof, 1997-. Creative Works: Studies in Inflationary Dynamics, 1986; Communitarian Ethics and Economics, 1995; Over 20 Articles in Intl Econ Jrnls. Memberships: Econ Soc of Singapore, 1997. Hobbies: Chess; Jogging. Address: Department of Economics, National University of Singapore, Kent Ridge Crescent, Singapore 119260, Singapore.

KAR Debabrata, b. 3 Dec 1936, Calcutta, India. Civil Engineer. m. Nandini Ghosh, 9 May 1964, 1 s, 1 d. Education: BEng, Calcutta, India, 1958; Dip in Computer Programming, 1974; Auditor, Quality Systems, Calcutta; Arbitrator, Instn of Engrs, India; Regd Surveyor and Valuer, Hifg Crt, Calcutta. Appointments: Res Mngr, Venezuala, 1975-80; Res Dir, Libya, 1982-88; Techl Dir in Dasteur Engnrg Intl, 1988-96; World Bank Expert on Monitoring and Evaluation, 1999-2000. Publications: Pprs on computerized proj mngmt in India, 1972-75; Pprs on mngmt of intl projs in USA/Venezuala, 1975-80. Honours: Schl, Dir of Pub Instrn, W Bengal, India, 1952 Schl, Calcutta Univ, 1954; Disting Serv Awd, Proj Mngmt Inst, USA, 1980. Memberships: Chartered Engr, UK and India; Fell, Instn of Civil Engrs, UK; Fell, Amn Soc of Civil Engrs. Hobbies: Music; Drama; Outdoor sports; Technical reading. Address: CB78 Sector I, Salt Lake City, Calcutta 700064, India.

KAR Subal, b. 27 Dec 1953, Shillong, India. Engineering Educator; Scientist. m. Rina Pal, 20 Apr 1989, 1 s. Education: BSc (Hons), Gauhati Univ, 1973; BTech, Radio Phys and Elec, 1976, MTech, Radio Phys and Elec, 1978, PhD (Tech) Microwaves, 1989, Univ of Calcutta. Appointments: Snr Rsch Fell, 1980-83, Lectr,

1983-90, Univ of Calcutta; Asst Prof, Delhi Inst of Technol, 1990; Snr Lectr, 1990-94, Rdr, 1994, Univ of Calcutta. Publications: Publd pprs in profl jrnls; Patentee in Microwaves; Presented pprs in Intl Confs in France, USA, Japan; Inv of modified (slotted disc) resonant-cap IMPATT oscillator and amplifier, high efficiency twin-cap IMPATT power combiner; Dev microprocessor controlled AFC for IMPATT oscillator and coax-waveguide type millimeter-wave IMPATT source. Honours: Young Sci Awd, ISSSE'95, Intl Union of Radio Sci (URSI), IEEE, MTT, Army and Naval Rsch of USA; Visng Scientist, Kyoto Univ, Japan, 1997; 1 yr's invitation for rsch, from Hd of Beam Electrodynamics Grp, Cntr for Beam Phys, Lawrence Berkeley Natl Lab, Berkeley, USA, as Fulbright Schlr, 1999-2000. Memberships: Fell, Instn of Electrons and Telecomms Engrs; Indian Sci Congress Assn. Hobbies: Writing poems; Listening to classical music, Reading books. Address: Institute of Radio Physics & Electronics, University of Calcutta, 92 APC Road, Calcutta 700009, India.

KARAMI Omar, Politician. Appointments: Fmr Min of Educn & The Arts; PM of Lebanon, 1990-92. Address: Office of the Prime Minister, Beirut, Lebanon.

KARANTH Gopalakrishna, b. 23 Apr 1943, Udupi, India. Research Scientist. m. Prapulla G Karanth, 5 Feb 1976, 1 s, 2 d. Education: MSc; PhD. Appointments: Lectr in Botany, Sri Bhuvanendra Coll, Karkala, 1966-68; Rsch Fell, Microbiol & Cell Biol Lab, 1969-74, Postdoct Assoc, Dept of Org Chem, 1974, Indian Inst of Sci, Bangalore; Sci, Natl Inst of Oceanography, Goa, 1974-76; Postdoct Fell, Institute fur Bodenbiologie, Braunschweig, Germany, 1976-78; Rsch Sci, Deutsche Fors-chungsgemeinschaft, Braunschweig, Germany, 1978; Sci C, 1979-84, Sci EI, 1985-89, Sci EII, 1990-94, Hd, FPIC Dept, 1993-, Sci F, 1995-, CFTRI, Mysore, India. Publications: Sev articles in profl jrnls. Honours include: Silver Jubilee Prize, Mysore Univ, 1966. Memberships: Intl Soc of Soil Scis, Netherlands; Alexandar von Humboldt Fndn, Germany; Acady of Gen Educn, India; Assn of Food Scis & Technols, India; Assn of Microbiols of India; Soc of Pub Analysts & Analytical Chems, India; Soc of Biol Chems, India; Indian Inst of Sci Alumni Assn; Indian Soc of Soil Biol & Ecol; Soc of Pesticide Sci, India. Hobbies: Yoga; Religious Discourses. Address: c/o Food Protectants & Infestation Control Department, Central Food Technological Research Institute, Mysore 570 013, India.

KARATSU Osamu, b. 25 Apr 1947, Tokyo, Japan. Large Scale Integration Researcher. Education: BS, 1970, MA, 1972, PhD, 1975, Tokyo Univ. Appointments: Rschr, 1975-78; Staff Rschr, NTT Musashino Labs, 1979-82; Snr Rsch Engr, NTT Atsugi Labs, 1983-86; Rsch Grp Ldr, NTT LSI Labs, 1987-88; Snr Mngr, NTT Strategy Plng HQ, 1988-89; Snr Rsch Mngr, NTT LSI Labs, 1989-90, Exec Mngr, 1991-96; VP, Dir, Advd Telecom Rsch Inst Intl, Kyoto, 1997-98; Prin, Stanford Rsch Inst Cnsltng, 1999-. Publications: Introduction to Very Large Scale Integration Design, 1983; Custom Large Scale Integration design, 1986; Encyclopedia of Information Science, 1990 Honour: Best Ppr Awd, 7th Intl Symp, Tokyo, 1985. Memberships: IEEE; Amn Physl Soc; Japan Soc of Applied Phys; Inst of Electrics and Commns Engrs, Japan; Inst of Elec Engrs, Japan. Hobby: Playing and listening to classical music. Address: 3-5-16 Nishi Azabu, Minato-ku, Tokyo, Japan.

KARIEVA Bernara, b. 28 Jan 1936, Tashkent, Uzbekistan. Ballerina. 2 d. Education: Tashkent Choreography Sch, 1947-51; Moscow Sch of Choreography. Appointments: Prin Ballerina, Navoi Th, Tashkent, 1955-86, Coach, 1986-, Dir, Bolshoi Navoi Th of Opera & Ballet, 1994-; Mbr, CPSU, 1967-91; Dancer, Bolshoi & Abroad; Prof, Tashkent Sch of Choreography; Pres Bd, Uzbek Union of Th Workers; USSR People's Dpty, 1989-91; Mbr, UNESCO Natl Comm on Culture, Uzbekistan. Creative Works: Roles incl: Odette/Odile (Giselle); Francesca da Rimini; Young Lady (Young Lady & Hooligan by Shostakovich); Anna Karenina (by Shchedrin); Donna Anna (Don Juan); Zarrina (Love and the Sword by Ashrafi); Cinderella. Honours include: Uzbek State Prize, 1970; People's Artist of USSR, 1973;

USSR State Prize, 1982. Hobbies: Piano Music; Visually Discovering the World. Address: Navoi Opera Theatre, Tashkent, 28 Mustafo Kamol Otaturk Street, Tashkent 700029, Uzbekistan.

KARIM Md Abdul, b. 4 July 1948, Pabna, Bangladesh. Teacher. m. Latifa, 24 Sept 1974, 1 s, 2 d. Education: BA (hons), Polit Sci, 1970, MA, Polit Sci, 1971, Rajashi Univ, Bangladesh. Appointments: Lectr, Polit Sci, Govt Carmichael Coll, Post and Dist, Rangpur, 1974-84; Asst Prof, Polit Sci, Govt BL Coll, Post and Dist Khulna, 1984-89; Asst Prof, Polit Sci, Govt Ed Coll, Post and Dist, Pabna, 1989-92; Assoc Prof, Polit Sci, Govt Nawab Nazimuddin Coll, Post and Dist, Madaripur, 1992; Assoc Prof, Polit Sci, Govt Edward Coll, Pabna, 1992-94; Vice-Prin, Ishurdi Govt Coll, Ishurdi, Pabna, 1994-. Publications: Many songs inclng modern, classical, folk-songs, Mass songs, Baul (Spiritual), Hamd and Nath (Religious), in monthly mags; Some songs brdcst on Radio Bangladesh; Book of Songs: Suryamukhi Futlo (The Sunflower Blooms). Memberships: Regd Lyricist, Radio Bangladesh; VP, Uttar Bangla Shahitya Parishad, Pabna; VP, Bandhan Sangit (Music) Acady, Pabna; Lalan Acady, Pabna. Hobbies: Reading; Singing; Composing songs. Address: Vice Principal, Ishurdi Government College, Post-Ishurdi, Dist Pabna, Bangladesh.

KARIMI Mehdi, b. 6 Nov 1948, Tehran, Iran. Project Management. m. Azra, 27 Sept 1972, 3 s, 1 d. Education: BS, Mechl Engrng. Appointments: Site Supvsr; Proj Mngr; Engrng Gen Mngr; Mngng Dir. Publication: Article: New Methods of Project Scheduling. Hobbies: Mountain climbing; Poetry. Address: #16, 13th Banafshe Alley, Golha Highway, Rah Ahan Complex, Tehran, Iran.

KARIMI Mehrnaz, b. 23 Mar 1967, Tehran, Iran. Audiologist; Translator of English Language. Education: BA, Translation Engl Lang; Assoc of Scis, Audiology, Iran Univ of Medl Scis, Coll of Rehab Scis; BSc, Audiology, Iran Univ of Med Scis Coll of Rehab Scis; MSc, Audiology, Tehran Univ of Med Scis, Coll of Rehab. Appointments: Fac Mbr, Tehran Univ of Medl Scis, Coll of Rehab, Audiology Dept, 1992-99; Engl Sect Dir, Iranian Jrnl of Audiology, 1992-93; Intl Comm Mngr, Audiology Dept, Tehran Univ of Medls Scis, Coll of Rehab Scis, 1992-94; Scientific and Exec Mbr, 1st Iranian Cong of Audiology, 1992; Rschr related to Audiology. Publication: Paintings: Flowers with Oil Color. Honours: Hon Student during Assoc; Bach and Master Deg of Audiology. Memberships: Amn Auditory Soc, 1990; Intl Affairs Assn Related to ASHA, 1991-92; Iranian Audiologists' Soc. Hobbies: Art; Movies; Aerobics; Travelling; Spanish language; Music. Address: Audiology Department, Rehabilitation College, Piche Shemiran, Enghelab Avenue, 11998, Tehran, Iran.

KARIMIAN Seyed M H, b. 16 Mar 1964, Tehran, Iran. Assistant Professor. m. Farnoush, 10 July 1986, 1 s, 1 d. Education: BSc, MSc, PhD, Mech Engrng. Appointments: Asst Prof, 1995-, Hd of Aerodynamic Grp, 1996-97, Assoc Chair, Dept of Educl Affairs, 1997-. Amirkabir Univ of Technol. Publications: Sev articles in profl jrnls and cof proceedings. Memberships: AIAA; Bd of Trustees, Rsch Inst for Geoscis. Hobbies: Swimming; Political and Social Subjects. Address: Department of Aerospace Engineering, Amirkabir University of Technology, Hafez Avenue, Tehran 15914, Iran.

KARIMOV Dzhamshed Khilolovich, b. 4 Aug 1940, Dushanbe. Politician. Education: Moscow Technol Inst of Light Ind. Appointments: Rschr, Ctrl Rsch Inst of Econs & Maths, USSR Acady of Scis; Asst Chair of Econ of Ind, Tajik State Univ; Jnr Rschr, Hd of Divsn of Optimal Planning Inst of Econs, Tajik Acady of Scis, 1962-72; Dpty Dir, Dir, Rsch Inst of Econ & Econ-Mathl Methods of Planning, State Planning Cttee, Tajik, 1972-81; Corresp Mbr, Tajik Acady of Scis; Dpty Chair, State Planning Cttee, 1981-88; Dpty Chair, Cncl of Mins, Chair, State Planning Cttee, 1988-89; 1st Sec, Dushanbe City Cttee of CP Tajikistan, 1989-91; USSR People's Dpty, 1989-92; Dpty, 1st Dpty Chair, Cncl of Mins, Tajik Repub, 1991-92; Rep of Tajikistan in Russia, 1992-93; Chf Advsr on Econs to Pres, 1994; PM of Tajikistan, 1994-96; Advsr to Pres

Rakhmonov, 1996-97; Amb to China, 1997-. Address: Office of the Prime Minister, Dushanbe, Tajikistan.

KARIMOV Islam, b. 30 Jan 1938, Samarkand. Politician. m. Tatyana Karimova, 2 d. Education: Ctrl Asian Polytech; Tashkent Econs Inst. Appointments: Worker, Tashkent Aviation Constrn Factory, 1960-66; Mbr, CPSU, 1964-91; Snr Specialist, Hd of Section, Vice Chair, Uzbekistan Gosplan, 1966-83; Min of Fin, Dpty Chair, Cncl of Mins, Uzbek, 1983-86; 1st Sec, Kashkadarinsk Dist Cttee (obkom), 1986-89; 1st Sec, Ctrl Cttee, Uzbek CP, 1989-91; USSR People's Dpty, 1989-91; Mbr, Ctrl Cttee, CPSU & Politburo, 1990-91; Pres of Uzbek, 1990; Chair, People's Democratic Party of Uzbekistan, 1991-96; Pres of Uzbekistan, Chair, Cabinet of Mins, Hon Chair, Fund of Friendship of Ctrl Asia & Kazakhstan, 1991-. Publications: Uzbekistan's Way of Restoration and Progress; To Complete the Noble Cause; Uzbekistan's Way of Strengthening Economic Reforms, 1995; Stability and Reforms, 1996; Uzbekistan on the Threshold of the Twenty-First Century, 1997. Honours: Var decorations. Address: Office of the President, Uzbekistansky prosp 45, 700163 Tashkent, Uzbekistan.

KARMEL Peter Henry, b. 9 May 1922, Melbourne, Aust. University Vice Chancellor. m. Lena Garrett, 30 Oct 1946, 1 s, 5 d. Education: BA, Melbourne; PhD, Cambridge. Appointments: Prof of Econs, Univ of Adelaide; Vice Chan, Flinders Univ; Chmn, Austl Univ Commn; Chmn Tertiary Educ Commn; Vice Chan, Chmn, Inst of the Arts, Austl Natl Univ. Publications: Texts on stats and econs. Honours: CBE, 1967; AC, 1976. Membership: Fel, Acady of Socl Scis, 1952-, Pres, 1987-90. Address: 4/127 Hopetoun Circuit, Yarralumla, ACT, Australia.

KARNAD Girish, b. 19 May 1938, Matheran, India. Playwright; Film Maker; Actor. m. Saraswarthy Ganapathy, 1980, 1 s, 1 d. Education: Karnatak College, Dharwad; Univ Oxford. Appointments: Asst Mngr, 1963-69, Mngr, 1969-70, Oxford Univ Press; Homi Bhabha Fell, 1970-72; Dir, Film & TV Inst of India, Pune, 1974, 1975; Indian Co-Chair, Media Cttee, Indo-US Subcomm, 1984-93; Vis Prof, Fulbright Schl-in-Res, Univ Chgo, 1987-88; Chair, Sangeet Natak Akademi, 1988-93. Creative Works: Plays: Yayati, 1961; Tughlaq, 1964; Hayavadana, 1971; Anjumallige, 1976; Hittina Hunja, 1980; Nagamandala, 1988; Taledanda, 1990; Agni Mattu Male, 1995. Films: Vamsha Vriksha, 1971; Kaadu, 1973; Tabbaliyu Neenade Magane, 1977; Ondanondu Kaaladalli, 1978; Utsav, 1984; Cheluvi, 1992. Honours: Hon DLitt, Univ Karnataka, 1994; Sev awds for film work. Membership: Pres, Oxford Union Soc, 1963. Address: 301 Silver Cascade, Mount Mary Road, Bombay 400 050, India.

KARNES Barry Gordon, b. 3 Oct 1958, San Jose, CA, USA. Engineer. m. Dawna, 13 June 1981, 2 s. Education: BS, Mechl Engrng, San Jose St Univ, 1980. Appointments: Snr Proj Engr, Underwriters Labs Inc, 1980-; Tstee, Burbank Sanitary Dist, 1988-. Honours: Underwriters Labs Profl Engrng Awds, 1986, 1997. Membership: Amn Soc of Mechl Engrng. Hobbies: Private pilot; Travel overseas; Golf. Listed in: Who's Who in California; Personalities of America. Address: 380 Clifton Ave, San Jose, CA 95128, USA.

KARNIK Charudatta, b. 1940, Pune, India. Chief Executive. m. Vilasini, 27 Mar 1970, 1 s, 2 d. Education: Com Grad; Grad, Law Studies; Chart Acct. Appointment: Chf Exec, Audit Bur of Circulations, 1967-. Publications: Sev pprs in intl confs. Honours: Awd of Merit & Hon Life Mbrshp, IFABC. Memberships: Sec-Gen, Intl Fedn of Audit Bur of Circulations, 1992-97. Hobbies: Indian Classical Music; Travel. Address: 3 Prasnant, 37 Swastik Park, Purav Marg, Chembur, Mumbai 71, India.

KARUNANIDHI Muthuvel, b. 3 June 1924, Thirukkuvalai, Thanjavur, India. Politician; Playwright. m. Dayalu Karunanidhi, 4 s, 1 d. Appointments: Ed-in-Charge, Kudiarasu; Jrnlst; Stage & Screen Playwright in Tamil; Actor in His Own Plays; Writer of

Over 35 Film-Plays; Fndr, Tamilnadu Tamil Manavar Mandram; Fndr Mbr, Dravida Munnetra Kazhagam Legislative Party, 1949, Treas, 1961, Dpty Ldr, 1968, Pres, 1969-; Fndr-Ed, Tamil Daily Organ; Rep, Kulittalai in State Assembly, 1957-62, Thanjavur, 1962-67, Saidapet, 1968; Ldr, kallakkudi Agitation; Fmr Min of Pub Works; Chf Min of Tamil Nadu, 1969-76, 1989-90; Thamizha Vell (Patron of Tamil). Honour: DLitt, Annamalai Univ, 1971. Membership: Assn of Rsch Schls in Tamil, 1971. Address: 7A S Gopalapuram, IV Street, Madras 600086, India.

KARVE Anand Dinakar, b. 7 Aug 1936, Pune, India. Scientist. m. Meena, 26 Jan 1969, 1 d. Education: BS, Univ Pune, India. Appointments: Hd, Botany Dept, Shivaji Univ, Kolhapur, India, 1964; Dir, Nimbkar Agric Rsch Inst, Phaltan, India, 1966-80; Groundnut Agronomist, Agricl Rsch Inst, Yezin, Burma, 1980-82; Fell, A V Humboldt Fndn, Inst of Bio, Univ Freiburg, Germany; Hd, Agric Rsch Sect, Hindustan Lever Ltd, Mumbai, India, 1984-88; Dpty Dir, Cntr for Application of Sci and Technol for Rural Dev, Pune, 1988-90; Cnslt to FAO proj, Sugar from Sweet Sorghum in Iran, 1990; Dir, Cntr for Application of Sci and Technol for Rural Dev, Pune, 1991-96; Pres, Appropriate Rural Technol Inst, Pune, 1996-. Publications: 4 books; 250 popular articles, 150 rsch pprs and reports. Hobby: Writing. Address: 6, Koyna Apartments, Survey No 133, Kothrud, Pune 411029, India.

KASARAVALLI Girish, b. 3 Dec 1950, Karasavalli, Karnataka, India. Film Script Writer; Director. m. Vaishali Kasaravalli, 1978, 1 s, 1 d. Education: Studies, Pharm & Film Direction. Appointments: Began Film Career, 1977; Prin, Adarsh Film Inst, 1978-86; Hon Ed, Chitravihari, 1986-87; Mbr, Advsry Panel, Deep Focus, Rujuvathu (lit & cultural quarterly); Mbr, Film Advsry Cttee, Govt of Karnataka, 1979; Mbr, Gov Cncl, Film & TV Inst of India, Poona, 1981-84. Creative Works: Films: Avashesh (The Ruins), 1975; Ghatashraddha (The Ritual Excommunication), 1977; Akramana, 1978; Mooru Darigalu (Three Pathways), 1981; Tabarana Kathe (Story of Tabara), 1986; Bannada Vesha (The Mask), 1988; Mane, 1990; Ek Ghar, 1991. Honours: Golden Lotus Awd, 1975, 1977, 1986; Intl Cath Jury Awd, 1977; Ducats Awd, Mannheim, 1977; Moitra Awd, 1978; Natl Awd, Silver Lotus, 1990, 1991. Address: 1015 Drishya, 8th Cross, 16th Main BTM Layout, I Stage, I Phase, Bangalore 560 029, India.

KASHYAP Rohit Kumar, b. 28 Sept 1953, Jammu Tawi. Engineering. m. Simran, 22 Feb 1985, 2 d. Education: B Tech, Elec, IIT Kanpur, 1974; Finl Mngmnt, Univ of Bombay, 1977. Appointments: Rsch Assoc, IIT, Kanpur, 1974-; Sales Engr, Advani Oerlikon, 1974-75; Snr Sci Offr, Dept of Atomic Energy, India, 1975-82; Snr Proj Engr, Hd, Snr Mngr, Instruments, Gen Mngr, Proj Engrng, Chf Engr, Natl Organic Chem Inds Ltd, 1982-. Creative Works: Pprs Publd in Ind Application Soc of IEEE; SHELL Confs Automation and Controls; Dept of Atomic Energy Seminar on Process Control. Honours: Chf Guest and Key Role Speaker of Measmt and Control; Confedn of Brit Ind Schl; Cert of Merit, Min of Educ. Memberships: IEEE; ISA. Hobbies: Trekking; Music. Address: PB 73, NOCIL, Thane Belapur Road, Thane 400601, India.

KASPER Wolfgang Ernst, b. 18 Mar 1939, Gablonz. Professor of Economics. m. Regine, 2 Apr 1966, 2 d. Education: Dip, Volkswirt, Univ Saarbrucken, Germany; PhD, Econs, Univ Kiel; Mod Langs, Univ Saarbrucken. Appointments: Staff, German Cncl, 1965-69; Snr Fell, Kiel Inst for World Econs, 1969-71; Advsr, Malaysian Treas, 1971-73; Snr Res Fell, Austl Natl Univ, 1973-77; Prof of Econs, Univ NSW, 1977-. Publications include: Global Competition, Institutions and the East Asian Ascendancy, 1994; Competitive Federalism Promoting Freedom and Prosperity, 1995; Free to Work: The Liberalization of New Zealand's Labour Markets; Institutional Economics: Social Order and Public Policy. Memberships: Sev. Hobbies: Travel; History. Address: Economics & Management, University College, University of New South Wales, Campbell 2600, Australia.

KASSEM Abdul-Rauf al, b. 1932, Damascus, Syria. Politician. Education: Damascus Univ Sch of Arts; Istanbul Univ; Geneva Univ. Appointments: Tchr of Arch, Sch of Fine Arts, Damascus, Dean, 1964-70; Hd, Arch Dept, 1970-77, Rector, 1977-79, Sch of Civil Engrng, Damascus Univ; Mbr, Higher Cncl for Town Planning, 1968-; Mbr, Natl Union of Archs, Perm Comm on Town Planning, 1975-; Hon Prof, Geneva Univ, 1975-; Gov of Damascus, 1979-80; Mbr, Baath Party Regl Cmd, 1979; Ctrl Cmd of Progressive Natl Front, 1980; PM, 1980-87. Address: Office of the Prime Minister, Damascus, Syria.

KASSLER Jamie Croy, b. Neenah, WI, USA. Musicologist. m. Michael Kassler. Education: PhD, Columbia Univ, 1971. Appointments: Postdoct Rsch Fell, Dept of Music, Univ of Sydney, NSW, Aust, 1975-77; Rsch Fell, Sch of Hist and Philos of Sci, 1979-82; Rsch Fell, Sch of Engl, 1982-87, Rsch Fell, Sch of Sci and Technol Stdies, 1988-89, 1991-92, Univ of NSW. Publications: The Science of Music in Britain, 1914-1930, 2 volumes, 1979; Inner Music: Hobbes, Hooke and North on Internal Character, 1995; Metaphor - A Musical Dimension, ed and contrb; Contbr of articles in profl jrnls; Contbr to Roger North's The Musicall Grammarian 1728; Articles in The Wider Domain of Evolutionary Thought, 1983; Ed, The Uses of Antiquity, 1991; Festschrifts for Alice A Moyle, 1984, Paul H Lang, 1984 and Claude Palisca, 1991; North Papers, vol 1, 1986, vol 2, 1987, vol 3, 1988, vol 4, 1989; Ed, The Soft Underbelly of Reason, 1998. Honour: Fac Schl, Columbia Univ, 1966-67. Memberships: Musicological Soc of Aust; Australasian Assn of Hist, Philos and Socl Studies of Sci; Hist of Sci Soc; Fell, Austl Acad of the Hums, 1991. Address: 10 Wollombi Road, Northbridge, NSW 2063, Australia.

KASWAN Hanuman Singh, b. 3 July 1947, Churu, Taranagar. Doctor; Surgeon. m. Vimla, 15 June 1970, 1 s, 2 d. Education: MB BS; MS, Gen Surg; Registrar, Anasthesiology. Appointments: Tutor in Forensic Med; Tutor in Surg; Lectr in Forensic Med; Lectr in Surg; Assoc Prof in Surg. Memberships: FICS (Fell, Intl Coll of Surgs); Fell, Intl Coll of Gerontologists. Hobbies: Jogging; Tennis; Swimming. Address: Kaswan Niwas, Hospital Road, Bikaner 334003 (Raj), India.

KATO Koichi, b. 17 June 1939, Tsuruoka, Yamagata, Japan. Politician. m. Aiko Sugiura, 1967, 1 s, 3 d. Education: Univ Tokyo; Harvard Univ, USA. Appointments: Entered Min of Fgn Affairs, 1964; Vice-Consul, Japanese Consulate Gen, Hong Kong, 1967-69; Dpty Dir, Chinese Divsn, Asian Affairs Bur, 1969-71; MP for 2nd Dist, Yamagata Pref, House of Reps, 1972-; Dpty Chf Cabinet Sec, 1978-80; Dir, House Cttee on Rules & Admin, 1980-81, on Agricl, Forestry & Fisheries, 1981-83; Vice-Chair, Diet Policy Cttee, LDP, 1980-81; Dir, Agricl & Forestry Divsn, LDP Policy Affairs Rsch Cncl, 1981-83; Dir-Gen, LDP Gen Affairs Bur, 1983-84; Min of State for Def, 1984-86; Chf Dpty Chair Polit Rsch Cncl, LDP, 1986-87, Chair, 1994-95; Acting Chair, Rsch Comm on Comprehensive Agricl, 1987-88; Min of State, Chf Cabinet Sec, 1991-92; Acting Sec-Gen, LDP, 1992-94, Sec-Gen, 1995-. Address: Liberal Democratic Party, 1-11-23 Nagata-cho, Chiyoda-ku, Tokyo 100, Japan.

KATO Rykichi, b. 1 Apr 1926, Tokyo, Japan. Clinical Psychotherapist. m. Shach'ko, 1952, 2 s, 1 d. Education: Shinging Medl Sch. Honour: Chf Dir, Inst Hypnosis, Japan, 1978. Publications: Intl Soc of Hypnosis; World Assn of Serology. Hobbies: Yacht; Fishing. Address: 106-12 Sengendai Nishier, Yokohama, perf Kanagawa, Japan 220071.

KATO Shuichi, b. 19 Sept 1919, Tokyo, Japan. Writer. Education: Grad, Tokyo Univ Medl Sch, 1943; MD, Tokyo Univ, 1950. Publications: Chosaku-shu (Selected Works), 27 vols, 1998; A History of Japanese Literature, 3 vols, 1979-83 (available also in Japanese, French, Italian, Chinese, Korean); Jaoan, Spirit & Form, 1994; Schatsgesänge, Begegnung mit Europa, 1997. Honours: Officier des Arts et des lettres, French Govt, 1993; Asahi Prize, ASAHI Newspapers, 1994; Dr hon causa, Univ

Stendhal, Grenoble, 1995. Address: Kamonoge 1-8-16, Sgtagaya-KV, Tokyo, 158 Japan.

KATSURA Ryotaro, b. 1 Nov 1950, Osaka, Japan. Sociologist; Social Worker. m. Itsuko, 31 Mar 1980, 2 s. Education: MA, Kyoto Univ of For Studies; Master Sociol, Kansai Univ. Appointments: Lectr, Nara Univ, 1989; Assoc Prof, Nara Univ, 1992; Visng Fell, Natl Univ of Singapore. Publications: Family and Welfare, 1987; Family Sociology, 1989; Welfare for the Aged, 1992; Welfare Study, 1992; General Introduction of Family, 1996. Honour: Mbr Hyogo Prefecture. Memberships: Japanese Soc for the Study of Socl Welfare, 1980; Japan Sociol Soc, 1985; Asian Acad Welfare Soc, 1996. Hobbies: World trip; Collecting pottery. Address: 2-9-6 Asahicho, Nara, Japan 631-0014.

KATSURA Shigeru, b. 13 Feb 1928, Komatsushima, Japan. Dental Anatomist. m. Sumiko Kawahara, 18 Jan 1957, 1 s, 1 d. Education: Tokushima Medl Sch, 1951; MD, 1957. Appointments: Lectr, Anatomy Dept, Tokushima Univ Sch of Med, 1956-58, Asst Prof, 1958-66, Prof Anatomy Dept, Tokushima Univ Sch of Dentistry, 1978-93, Prof Emeritus, 1993-. Memberships: Intl Soc Developmental Biolsts; Tokushima Bio Soc, Japanese Assn Anatomists, Emer Mbr, 1993-. Hobbies: Walking; Reading; Gardening. Address: Matsushima-cho 14-13, Komatsushima 7730003, Japan.

KATZ Kent Douglas, b. 10 Dec 1954, Twin Falls, ID, USA. m. Carolyn, 23 Nov 1991, 1 s, 1 d. Education: BS, Molecular Bio, Univ of UT; MD, Univ of WA, Med Residency, Mayo Clin; Gastrenterology Fellshp, Univ of CA, Irvine. Appointment: Asst Clin Prof of Med, Univ of CA, Irvine, 1988-. Address: Long Beach, VA Medical Center, 5901, E7th Street Long Beach, Los Angeles, CA 90822, USA.

KATZ-OZ Avraham, b. 1934, Tel Aviv, Israel. Politician. m. 3 children. Education: Hebrew Univ. Appointments: Mbr, Kibbutz Nahal Oz; Kibbutz Sec & Var Offs in Kibbutz Movt; Mbr, Labour Alignment Party; Mbr, Knesset, 1981-; Min of Agricl, 1988-90. Address: Ministry of Agriculture, PO Box 7011, Hakirya, Tel Aviv 61070, Israel.

KATZAV Moshe, b. 1945, Iran. Politician; Economist. m. 5 children. Education: Hebrew Univ, Jerusalem. Appointments: Mayor, Kiryat Malachi, 1969, 1974-81; Mbr, Knesset, 1977-; Cttee, Interior Affairs & The Environ, 1977-81; Cttee, Educn & Culture, 1977-81; Cttee on Def; Cttee on Fgn Affairs; Dpty Min of Housing, 1981-83; Min of Labour & Socl Affairs, 1984-88, of Transp, 1988-92; Mbr, Inner Cabinet, 1990-; Chair, Likud Faction, Knesset, 1992-; Dpty PM, Min of Tourism, 1996-. Membership: Likud Party. Address: Ministry of Tourism, PO Box 1018, 24 King George Street, Jerusalem 91009, Israel.

KATZIR Ephraim, b. 16 May 1916, Kiev, Ukraine. Scientist; Administrator. m. Nina Gotlieb, 1938, dec. Education: Hebrew Univ, Jerusalem. Appointments: Prof, Hd, Dept Biophys, Weizmann Inst of Sci, 1951-73; Chf Sci, Min of Def, 1966-68; Pres of State of Israel, 1973-78; Prof, Weizmann Inst of Sci, 1978-; Prof, Tel Aviv Univ, 1978-; Herman F Mark Chair, Polymer Sci, Polytech Inst, NY, 1979-; Pres, World ORT Union, 1987-90, COBIOTECH Intl Cttee for Biotechnol, 1989-95. Publications: Num pprs and articles in profl jrnls. Honours: Tchernikhovski Prize, 1948; Weizmann Prize, 1950; Israel Prize of Natural Scis, 1959; Rothschild Prize of Natural Scis, 1961; Linderstrom-Lang Gold Medal, 1969; Hans Krebs Medal, 1972; Underwood Prescott Awd, MIT, 1982; Japan Prize, Sci & Technol Fndn of Japan, 1985; Enzyme Engrng Awd, 1987; Commdr Legion d'honneur, France, 1990. Memberships include: Israel Acady of Scis & Humanities; Leopoldina Acady of Scis; Am Soc of Biol Chems; Roy Soc of London; Am Acady of Arts & Scis; Intl Union of Biochem; Acad des Scis, France; Roy Inst of GB. Hobby: Swimming. Address: Department of Biological Chemistry, Weizmann Institute of Science, PO Box 26, Rehovot 76100, Israel.

KAUCIMOCE Jonetani, b. 29 Sept 1946. Government Minister. Education: Fiji Inst of Technol; Univ of Wales, Cardiff. Appointments: Fiji Mil Serv, Mbr, Territorial Force, Active Serv Overseas, Peacekeeping Duties, 1965; Asst Sec, Ministry of Comms, Wrks and Tourism, 1964-74; Admnstv Offr, Fiji Visitors Bur, 1974-76; Dir Ops, Exec Mngmt, Ports Authy of Fiji, 1976-92; Lt Col, Snr Plans Offr, UNIFIL Ops, 1988-90; Min for Transp and Civil Aviation; Mbr of Parl for Suva Cty, 1992-93; Min for Yth, Employment Opportunities and Sports. Address: PO Box 2448, Government Buildings, Suva, Fiji.

KAUL Jawahar, b. 15 Feb 1937, Srinagar, India. Director; Consulting Engineer. m. Raj, 11 June 1962, 1 s, 1 d. Education: BA, BE, Hons; CE, PG Dip, Bus Mngmnt; FIE, FICA, MIRC. Appointments: Dir, Large Cnsltng Co; Span Cnslts Pvt Ltd; Span Travers Morgan Lts; Army Engr. Honour: Vijay Ratuna Awd. Memberships: VP, Cnsltng Engrs Assn of Inida; Inst of Engrs. Hobbies: Th; Lit. Address: K1/29 Chittaranjan Park, New Delhi 110 019, India.

KAUMI Simon, b. 26 Jan 1938, Buna Oro Prov, Papua New Guinea. Minister for Justice. m. 5 children. Education: Admin Coll. Appointments: Chf Electoral Commnr, 1966-72; Sec of Dept of Interior, 1972-74; Self-employed; Elected to Parl, 1992; Min of For Affairs, 1992; Min of Comms, 1994; Min for Transp, Wrks and Civ Aviation, 1995; Min for Jus. Membership: People's Natl Cong.

KAUSHAL Kuldip Chand, b. 8 July 1945. Information Scientist. Education: MA, Sociol; BS, Bio; BLibSc, Gold Medalist; Associateship in Documentation and Reprography; CLibSc, Gold Medalist; Dip, Jrnlsm. Appointments: Jnr Tech Asst, 1964; Snr Tech Asst, 1967; Scientist A, 1972; Scientist B, 1977; Documentalist, Commonwealth Yth Prog, Asia Pacific Cntr, Chandigarh, 1980-82; Scientist C, 1982; Scientist EI, 1988. Publications: Guide to Indian Medicinal Plants, 1976; Sev biennial Status on Science and Technology in India, Medicinal Plants Sourcebook, India; Perspectives of Multi-media Information Services in India; Information Marketing: Status and Prospects. Honours: Gold Medals in CLibSc, 1971 and BLibSc, 1972; Manav Seva Medal, 1993; Fellshp, Soc for Info Sci, 1994. Memberships: Jnt Sec, 1989-90, Ed, SISCOM, 1983-95, Treas, 1988, VP, 1991-94, Soc for Info Sci; Life, Indian Lib Assn; Life, Indian Assn of Spec Libs and Info Cntrs. Hobbies: Reading; Writing. Address: National Institute of Science Communication, Dr K S Krishnan Marg, New Delhi 110 012, India.

KAUSHIK J N, b. 4 Nov 1935, Jahangirpur, Jhakkar, Haryana. Retired. m. Vimla, 21 June 1961, 1 s, 2 d. Education: MA (Hindi & Engl); MEd; JD; PhD Educ. Appointments: Tchr, Dir, Haryana Sahitya Acady. Publications: Haryanvi Hindi Kosh, 1985; Fasts of the Hindus, 1990; Dilli Ki Apni Kahani, 1998; Meri Kailash Mansarovar Yatra, 1999. Honours: Delhi State Tchrs Awd, 1981; Natl Tchrs Awd, 1995; Delhi Hindi Sahitya Acady Lit Awd, 1998. Hobbies: Collection of folk literature; Writing poems and stories. Address: C-605 Saraswati Vihar, Delhi 110034, India.

KAVIYA Somkuan, b. 14 Jan 1935, Suratthani, Thailand. Teaching and Writing. m. Duangjai, 13 Apr 1968, 1 s, 1 d. Education: BA, Jrnlsm, Thammasat Univ, Thailand, 1963; Dip in Pub Info, Cntr Intl d'Enseignement Supérieur du Journalisme, Strasbourg, France, 1966; Dr Jrnlsm (Hon), Univ de Stasbourg, France, 1969; MPA Econs, Inst Intl d'Admin Pub, Paris. Appointments: Announcer Radio-Thailand, Bangkok, 1965; Dean, Assoc Prof, Comms, Thammasat Univ, Bangkok, 1970-92; Asst Rector Pub Rels, Thammasat Univ, Bangkok, 1988-89; Dean Comm Arts, Dhurakijpundit Univ, Bangkok, 1993-98. Publications: Communication Status and Problems in Thailand, 1995; Mass Communication, 1996; Eco-Communication, 1999. Honour: Outstndng People of the 20th Century, IBC, 1999. Memberships: AMIC CTTEE, 1975-85; Chmn, Mass Comm Educ Min of Univ Affairs, 1988-95; Natl Brdcstng Bd Cttee, 1998-99.

Hobbies: Travelling; Writing songs. Address: 3/170, Muangthong 1, Laksi, Bangkok 12010, Thailand.

KAWAI Masao, b. 6 Sept 1942, Osaka, Japan. Professor. m. Mitoko, 28 Apr 1968, 1 s, 1 d. Education: Grad, Kyoto Univ, 1965; Masters, 1967; PhD, 1970. Appointments: Instr, Kwansei Gakuin Univ, 1970-72; Rsch Chem, Mitsubishi Kasei Inst of Life Sci, 1972-83; Assoc Prof, Nagoya Inst of Technol, 1983-89; Prof, Nagoya Inst of Tech, Dept of Applied Chem, 1989-. Creative Works: Has Estd Chem Structures of 15 Physalins, 1969-96. Memberships: Chem Soc of Japan; The Japanese Peptide Soc. Hobby: Amateur Magic. Address: Nagoya Inst of Technology, Department of Applied Chemistry, Gokiso-cho, Showa-ku, Nagoya 466-8555, Japan.

KAWAKATSU Masaharu, b. 20 Jan 1929, Kameoka, Japan. Zoology Educator. m. Kazuko Hatano, 5 Jan 1959, 1 s, 1 d. Education: BEduc, Kyoto Gakugei Univ, 1953; DSc, Hokkaido Univ, 1961. Appointments: Asst, Kyoto Gakugei Univ, Kyoto, Japan, 1953-61; Asst Prof, Fuji Women's Coll, Sapporo, Japan, 1961-66; Prof, Bio, 1966-99. Publications: Red Data Book; Mem Protective Com Environ Agy Prime Min, Off of Wild Plants and Animals, 1994-. Honour: Sec Prize, Biogeo Soc of Japan, 1993, 1994. Memberships: Zoo Soc Japan; Soc Syst Zoo Japan; Biogeo Soc Japan; Speleol Soc Japan. Hobby: Reading of suspense and detective stories. Address: 9jo 9chome 1-8, Shinkotoni, Kita-ku, Sapporo, Hokkaido, 001-0909, Japan.

KAWAMURA Hideto, b. 4 July 1949, Sakai City, Osaka, Japan. Medical Scientist; Educator. m. Michiko, 15 Mar 1981, 2 s. Education: BS, 1973, MS, 1975, Osaka City Univ; PhD, Aichi Med Univ, 1987. Appointments: Rsch Assoc, 1975-93, Lectr, 1994-, Aichi Med Univ. Address: 7-36-12 Wakinoshima-cho, Tajimi City, Gifu-Ken 507-0826, Japan.

KAWASHIMA Seiichiro, b. 20 Nov 1934, Tokyo, Japan. Professor. m. Mitsuko Kawashima, 21 Apr 1961, 2 s. Education: BS, 1958, MSc, 1960, PhD, 1965, Univ of Tokyo. Appointments: Rsch Assoc, 1965-70, Asst Prof, 1970-72, Assoc Prof, 1972-80; Chmn, Zoology Dept, Univ Mus, 1972-81; Mbr, Endocrinol Cttee, Sci Cncl of Japan, 1979-85; Prof, Hiroshima Univ, 1981-89; Prof, Univ of Tokyo, 1988-95; Dir, Rsch Lab, Zenyaku Kogyo Co, 1995-. Publications include: Num pprs and review articles in profl jrnls. Honour: Prize of Zoological Soc of Japan, 1989. Memberships: Pres, Japan Soc for Comparative Endocrinol; Intl Soc of Psychoneuroendocrinology; Soc for Study of Reproduction; NY Acady Sci; Intl Soc for Devel Neurosci; Soc for Experimental Biol and Med; Intl Soc of Andrology. Hobbies: Reading; Travel. Address: Research Laboratory, Zenyaku Kogyo Co Ltd, 2-33-7 Oizumi, Nerima-ku, Tokyo 178-0062, Japan.

KAYANAMA Yosuke, b. 15 Aug 1944, Tokyo, Japan. Physicist, Professor of University. m. Mari Ohori, 8 Niov 1975, 2 s. Education: DSc, Univ of Tokyo, 1975. Appointments: Rsch Assoc, Dept Phys; Assoc Prof, Tohoku Univ; Prof, Coll of Engrng, Osaka Prefecture Univ. Publications: Articles on solid state phys. Hobbies: Skiing; Swimming. Address: 2-26-6, Minami, Sakai, Osaka, 590 Japan.

KAYE Keith Woodhill, b. 8 Feb 1942, Cape Town, South Africa. Professor of Urology. m. Valda, 3 d. Education: BS, (Hons); MB BCh; FRCS (Edin); FRACS, FCS (SA); Cert Amn Bd of Urology. Appointments: Clin Assoc Prof, 1983-92, Clin Prof of Urology, 1992-93, Univ of MN; Prof of Urology, Div of Urolgic Surg, Univ of Urological Rsch Cntr, Univ of WA, 1983-98. Publication: Outpatient Urologic Surgery (Ed), 1985. Creative works: 4 videos on urology; 5 surg devices. Honours: Cotrill Mem Prize, for Acad Merit and Contbns to Medl Sch Activities, 1967; Citation for lect: Renal Anatomy "First Perfect rating", Continuing Medl Educ, Univ of MN, only lect given perfect score by peer evaluation, 1982; Voted one of Mpls-St Paul's Top Drs by peer questionaire. Memberships: MN Urological Soc; Soc for Minimally Invasive Surg; Amn Fertility Soc; Amn Urological Assn;

Endourology Soc; Austl Medl Assn; Urological Soc of Australasia; Australasian Prostate Hlth Cncl. Hobbies: Outdoor activities. Address: Urological Research Centre, Level 2, M Block, Queen Elizabeth II Medical Centre, Nedlands, WA 6009, Australia.

KAZAK Ali Ibrahim, b. 29 Mar 1947, Haifa, Palestine. m. Aminah, 6 Mar 1987, 2 s, 2 d. Education: Coll of Com, Damascus Univ, Syria. Appointment: Hd, Gen Palestinian Deleg and Palestine Liberation Orgn Repr to Aust, NZ, S Pacific; Amb of Palestine to Vanatu. Publications: Free Palestine, 1979-90; Background Briefing, 1987-93; The Jerusalem Question, 1997. Hobbies: Table tennis; Walking; Music. Address: PO Box 4646, Kingston, ACT 2604, Australia.

KAZHEGELDIN Akezhan Magzhanovich, b. 27 Mar 1952, Georgiyevka, Kazakstan. Politician; Economist. m. 2 children. Education: Semipalatinsk Pedagogical Inst; Almaty Inst of Natl Econs. Appointments: Chair, Regl Exec Cttee of Semipalatinsk, 1983; Dir, Ore-Enriching Factory, Dpty Hd, Admin of Semipalatinsk Region, 1991-94; Pres, Kazakstan Union of Indls & Entrepreneurs, 1992-; 1st Dpty PM of Kazakstan, 1993-94, PM, 1994-97. Publications include: Kazakstan in the Conditions of Reforms; Problems of State Regulations in the Conditions of Socio-Economic Transformation; Socio-Economic Problems of Development of Kazakstan in the Conditions of Reforms. Address: Respubliki sq 4, Almaty, Kazakstan.

KAZIEV Naken K, b. 22 Sept 1947, Akelfuz, Narya, Kyrgyzstan. Government Official. Education: Grad, Kyrgyz State Medl Inst, 1970. Appointments: Mil Physn, 1971-73; Chf Physn, Tokmak Hosp, 1973-86; Hd, Maryn Oblast Hlth Administration, 1986-88; Dpty Min of Hlth, Govt of Kyrgyzstan, Bishkek, 1988-90; Min of Hlth, 1991-. Address: Ministry of Health, ul Moskovskaya, 144 Bishkek 120005, Kyrgyzstan.

KAZUHISA Takemura, b. 8 Oct 1960, Kyoto, Japan. Associate Professor. m. Mineko, 18 June 1989, 1 s, 1 d. Education: PhD, Syst Sci, Tokyo Inst of Technol. Creative Works: Psychology of Decision Making. Honours: Grants for yng Scientists, Min of Educ, 1993-99. Memberships: Amn Psychol Assn; Eur Assn of Dicision Making. Hobbies: Swimming. Address: 123-104 Namiki 2 chome, Tsukuba, Ibaraki 305-0044, Japan.

KEARNEY John Basil, b. 11 Dec 1921, Sydney, Aust. Judge, Supreme Court of New South Wales. m. (1) 28 June 1947, 1 s, 4 d, (2) 1 June 1985. Education: Univ of Sydney, 1939-41, 1946; LLB, 1946. Appointments: Lt, AIF (Armoured Div), 1941-45; Admitted to NSW Bar, 1947; Acting Master in Equity, Supreme Crt of NSW, 1968; Appt Judge, Supreme Crt of NSW (Equity Div), 1978; Retd from Supreme Crt, 1992. Memberships: Cncl, NSW Bar Assn, 1969-71, 1977-78; VP, 1978, NSW Bar Assn; Cncl, 1976-81, Pres, 1980-81, St Thomas More Soc. Hobbies: Reading; Swimming; Croquet. Address: 6 Amaroo Crescent, Mosman, NSW 2088, Australia.

KEARNEY William John Francis (Hon Sir), b. 8 Jan 1935. Supreme Court Judge. m. Jessie Yung, 10 Oct, 1959, 3 d. Education: BA, LLB, LLM, Sydney Univ, Univ Coll, London. Appointments: Sol, NSW, 1959; Bar and Sol, Papua New Guinea, 1963; Govt Legal Serv, Papua New Guinea, 1963; Sec for Law, 1972-75; Official Mbr, Papua New Guinea House of Assembly and Exec Cncl, 1972-73; Dormant Commn, Adminr, 1973, High Commnr, Papua New Guinea, 1973-75, and as Admiral, 1973; Chmn, Papua New Guinea Parly Salaries Tribunal, 1977-82; Dept Chf Justice, Supreme Crt, Papua New Guinea, 1980-82, Judge, 1976-82; Judge, Supreme Crt, NT of Aust, 1982-; Aboriginal Land Commnr, 1982-86; Chmn, Law Reform Cttee, 1982-90; Chmn, NT Cncl of Law Rprtng, 1995-99. Honours: CBE, 1976; Kt cr, 1982. Hobbies: Travel; Literature. Address: c/o Judge's Chambers, Supreme Court, Darwin, NT 0800, Australia.

KEATING Paul John, b. 18 Jan 1944, Sydney, Australia. Politician. m. Annita van Iersel, 1975, 1 s, 3 d. Education: LaSalle Coll, Bankstown. Appointments: House of Reps, Fed Seat of Blaxland, 1969-96; Min for N Aust, 1975; Opposition Spokesman on Agricl, 1976, on Minerals & Energy, 1976-83, on Treas Matters, 1983; Fed Treas, 1983-91; Ldr, Austl Labor Party, 1991-96; PM of Aust, 1991-96; Vis Prof, Pub Policy, Univ NSW, 1996-. Membership: Pres, NSW Br of Labor Party, 1979-83. Address: Keating Associates, Level 2, 31 Bligh Street, Sydney, NSW 2000, Australia.

KEATON Michael, b. 9 Sept 1951, Pittsburgh, USA. Actor. m. Caroline MacWilliams, div, 1 s. Education: Kent State Univ. Appointments: Comedy Grp, Second City, Los Angeles; TV Appearances incl: All in the Family; Maude; Mary Tyler Moore Show; Working Stiffs; Report to Murphy; Roosevelt & Truman. Creative Works: Films: Night Shift, 1982; Mr Mom, 1983; Johnny Dangerously, 1984; Touch and Go, 1987; Gung Ho, 1987; Beetlejuice, 1988; Clean and Sober, 1988; The Dream Team, 1989; Batman, 1989; Much Ado About Nothing, 1992; My Life, The Paper, 1994; Speechless, 1994; Multiplicity, Jackie Brown, 1997; Desperate Measures, 1998. Address: c/o Creative Artists Agency, 9830 Wilshire Boulevard, Beverly Hills, CA 90212, USA.

KEATS Reynold Gilbert, b. 15 Feb 1918, Port Pirie, SA, Aust. m. V Joy Brealey, 24 Jan 1948, 2 d. Education: BSc, 1948, PhD, 1965, Adelaide Univ; DMath, honoris causa, Waterloo, 1979. Appointments: Savings Bank of SA, 1934-40; 2/48th Battalion AIF, serving at Tobruk, El Alamein, Finschafen, 1940-45; Rsch Sci, RAE Farnborough, Eng, 1948-51; Dept of Supply, Melbourne, Aust, 1951-52 WRE Salisbury, SA, 1952-61; Snr Lectr, Adelaide Univ, 1961-67; Prof of Maths, 1968-83, Dpty Chmn of Senate, 1977-78, Prof Emer, 1983-, Hon Prof, 1984-88, Univ of Newcastle, NSW. Memberships: FIMA; FCPA; FAustMS; FACS. Hobbies: Mathematics; Travel. Listed in: Who's Who in Australia. Address: 39 Woodward Street, Merewether, NSW 2291, Australia.

KEAY Nigel David, b. 13 June 1955, Palmerston N, NZ. Musician; Composer. Education: Cert of Executant Music, Wellington Polytech, 1978; B Mus, Vic Univ of Wellington, 1982. Appointments: Active Perf, Contemporary Music (Viola); Mozart Fell, Univ of Otago, 1986, 1987; Composer-in-Res, Nelson Sch of Music, NZ, 1988, 1989; Composer-in-Res, Auckland Phil Orch, 1995. Creative works: Variations for Violin and Piano, Four Piano Pieces, 1983; String Quartet, 1983; Variations for Orchestra, 1983; Variations for Piano; Quartet for Piano, Violin, Viola and Cello, 1986; Diffractions for piano and orchestra, 1987; Interludes for Piano, 1988; Two Pieces for Trumpet, Horn and Trombone, 1988; Symph Poem: Ritual Dance of the Unappeasable Shadow, 1993; String Quartet No 2, 1995; Fanfare for Orchestra, 1995; Symphony in Five Movements, 1996. Honours: 1st Prize, Vic Univ of Wellington Music Dept Composition Competition, 1982; 2nd Prize, Wellington Yth Orch Orchestral Composition Competition, 1983; Philip Neill Mem Prize, Music, Univ of Otago, 1985. Membership: Writer Full Mbr, Australasian Performing Right Assn Ltd. Hobby: Instructor, Hapkido (Korean Martial Art of Self Def). Address: 43 Sale Street, Howick, Auckland, New Zealand.

KEDAH H.R.H. b. **28 Nov 1927,** Alor Setar. Ruler of Kedah, Malaysia. m. Tuanku Bahiyah binti Al-marhum, Tuanku Abdul Rahman, 1956, 3 d. Education: Sultan Abdul Hamid Coll; Alor Setar & Wadham Coll, Oxford. Appointments: Raja Muda (Heir to Throne of Kedah), 1949; Regent of Kedah, 1957, Sultan, 1958-; Timbalan Yang di Pertuan Agong (Dpty Hd of State of Malaysia), 1965-70; Yang di Pertuan Agong (Hd of State), 1970-75; Col-in-Chf, Roy Malay Reg, 1975. Honours: 1st Class Order of the Rising Sun, Japan, 1970; Bintang Maha Putera, Klas Satu, Indonesia, 1970; Kt Grand Cross of Bath, England, 1972; Kt of the Order of St John, 1974; Most Auspicious Order of the Rajamithrathorn, Thailand, 1973. Hobbies: Golf; Billiards; Photography; Tennis. Address: Istana Anak Bukit, Alor Setar, Kedah, Darul Aman, Malaysia.

KEELY John Augustine (Hon), b. 2 Oct 1925. Retired Judge. m. Maureen Masters, 6 Dec 1952, 3 s, 4 d.

Education: LLB, Melbourne Univ. Appointments: Admitted to Bar, 1954; QC, 1969; Chmn, Vic Legal Aid Cttee, 1971; VP, Indl Rels Soc of Vic, 1971-72; Chmn, Indl Law Prac Cttee, 1973-77; Judge, Fedl Crt of Aust, 1977-96; Judge, Indl Rels Crt of Aust, 1994-95; Dpty Pres, Trade Pracs Tribunal, 1977-80. Membership: Wrkrs Compensation Standing Cttee, 1972-77; Advsry Bd for Grad Dip in Labour Rels Law, 1990-96. Hobbies: Tennis; Reading. Address: 14A Yarbat Avenue, Balwyn, Melbourne, Vic 3103, Australia.

KEEN Ian David, b. 21 Nov 1938. Anthropologist. m. 30 May 1968, Elizabeth Joy Bayly, 1 s, 1 d. Education: BSc, Anthropology, London; PhD, Anthropology, Austl Natl Univ. Appointments: Art Tchr and Freelance Artist, 1960-70; Tutor, Dept of Anthropology and Sociol, Univ of Queensland, 1979; Lectr and Snr Lectr, Dept of Anthropology and Sociol, Univ of Qld, 1980-87; Snr Lectr, Dept of Archaeology and Anthropology, 1988, Reader, 1997-, Austl Natl Univ. Publications: How Australia Was Settled, 1980; Being Black: Aboriginal Cultures of Settled Australia, 1988; Knowledge and Secrecy in an Aboriginal Religion, 1994. Honour: Stanner Awd, 1997. Memberships: Fell, Royal Anthropological Inst; Austl Anthropological Soc; Austl Evolution Soc; Assn of Socl Anthropologists in Oceania; Eurn Soc for Oceanists. Hobbies: Music; House renovation. Address: Department of Archaeology and Anthropology, Australian National University, Canberra, ACT 0200, Australia.

KEEY Roger Brian, b. 11 Mar 1934, Birmingham, Eng. Professor Emeritus of Chemical Engineering. m. Daphne, 18 Mar 1959, 1 s, 3 d. Education: BSc, Hons, Birmingham Univ, 1954; PhD, Chem Engrng, 1957. Appointments: Chem Engr, DCI, Hull, 1957; Lectr, 1962; Prof, 1978; Chem Engrng, Univ of Canterbury, NZ; Dir, Wood Technol Rsch Ctr, 1997. Creative Works: Drying Principles and Practice, 1972; Introduction to Industrial Deperations; Drying of Loose and Particulate Materials; The Wainui Incident. Honours: Cadman Medal, 1954; Angus Awd, NZ, 1976; Skellerup Awds; Rabone Awd; Proctor and Gamble Awd for Ex. Memberships: Roy Soc of NZ; Inst of Chem Engrs; Inst of Profl Engrs, NZ; NZ Inst of Chem. Hobbies: Alping Botany; Photog. Address: 25 Montclare Avenue, Avonhead, Christchurch 8004, New Zealand.

KEH Huan Jang, b. 3 Nov 1955, Taiwan. Chemical Engineer; Educator; Researcher. m. Sue-Jean Chen, 2 Apr 1989, 1 s. 1 d. Education: BS, 1978, Natl Taiwan Univ; MS, 1980, Univ Fla; PhD, 1984, Carnegie Mellon Univ. Appointments: Prof, Dept Chem Engrng; Dir, Rsch Cntr for Petrochem Ind; Assoc Dean, Coll of Engrng, Natl Taiwan Univ. Publications: Over 60 rsch pprs in Sci jrnls. Honours: Outstndng Rsch Awds, Natl Sci Cncl, Taiwan, 1992, 1994, 1997; Excellence in Tchng Awd, Min of Educ, Taiwan, 1993. Memberships: Chinese Inst of Chem Engrs; Intl Assn of Colloid and Interface Sci. Hobbies: Swimming; Travel; Bridge; Music. Address: Dept of Chemical Engineering, National Taiwan University, Taipei 106-17 Taiwan, China.

KEHAL Harbhajan Singh, b. 25 June 1942, Sandaur, India. Senior Lecturer in Economics. m. Harbans Kaur Kehal, 11 June 1959, 2 s, 1 d. Education: BA, Engl and Econs, 1961, MEcon, 1963, Punjab Univ; PhD, Econs, Univ West Aust, 1984. Appointments include: Rsch Schl, Univ of West Aust Fac of E Cons Com, 1977-84; Snr Fin Offr, Dept of Fin Commonwealth Govt, 1986-87; Lectr in Econs, Fac of Bus and Land Econ, Univ of West Sydney Hawkesbury, 1987-91; Snr Lectr, Econs, Univ of West Sydney, Hawkesbury, Richmond, NSW, Aust, 1992-; Visng Prof, Fukuoka Univ, Japan, 1992; Visng Fell, Univ of Durham, Eng, 1992; Visng Prof, Punjabi Univ, India, 1996; Visng Prof, Delhi Univ, Inst of Rcon Growth. 1996; Visng Fell, Inst SE Asian Studies, Singapore, 1996; Visng Prof, Fac of Econs, Chulalongkorn Univ, Bangkok, Thailand, 1996. Publications: 7 chapts in books; Ed, 2 books, 24 jrnl articles. Honours: Univ West Aust Rsch Schlshp for PhD Rsch, 1977-82. Memberships: Econ Soc of Aust, Cncl Mbr, 1994-95, 1995-96; Austl Inst of Intl Affairs, Cncl Mbr, 1997-98, 1998-99; Fndng Mbr, Indian Ocean Rsch Network. Hobbies: Music; Walking; Current affairs. Address: Faculty of Management, University of Western Sydney, Richmond, NSW, Australia 2753.

KEHLER Dorothea Faith, b. 21 Apr 1936, NY City, USA. Professor of English Literature. m. (1)William Dolid, 1956, div 1961, 1 s, 1d. (2)Harold Kehler, 1962, dec, 1 s, 1 d. Education: BA, 1956, CCNY; MA, 1967, Ohio Univ; PhD, 1969. Appointments: Instr, 1964-65, MacMurray College, Jacksonville, IL; Instr, Tchg Fell, OH Univ, Athens, OH, 1965-68; Lectr, Asst, Assoc, Full Prof, 1969-, San Diego State Univ. Publications: Books: Ed, A Midsummer Night's Dream: Critical Essays, 1998; Problems in Literary Research: A Guide to Selected Reference Works, 1975, 1981, 1987, 1997; Ed, In Another Country: Feminist Perspectives on Renaissance Drama; Over 30 jrnl Articles, book chapts and notes on Shakespeare and his contemporaries. Honours: NEH Fellshp, Harvard Univ, 1983; Folger Libr Inst Grant, 1988; San Diego State Univ Meritorious Performance and Profl Promise Awd, 1988, 1996; SDSU Resch Grants, 1986, 1988, 1990, 1995, 1997, 1998; Outstanding Prof, SDSU Dept English, 1991; Hon Mbr, Phi Beta Kappa, 1997; Advry Bd of Hamlet Studies, 1998. Memberships: Shakespeare Assn of Am; Intl Shakespeare Assn; Southern Comparative Lit Assn; Rocky Mountain MLA; South Central Renaissance Conf; Southeastern Renaissance Conf; Northwest Conf on Brit Studies; Nu Chapt Phi Beta Kappa, Historian 1998-. Hobbies: Travel; Piano; Film; Theatre. Address: English Dept, San Diego State University, San Diego, CA 92182-8140, USA.

KEITH Kenneth James, b. 19 Nov 1937, Auckland, NZ. Court of Appeal Judge. m. Jocelyn Margaret Buckett, 13 May 1961, 2 s, 2 d. Education: LLM, Vic Univ of Wellington. Appointments: Magistrates Crt, Auckland, 1957-60; External Affairs Dept, Wellington, 1960-62; Vic Univ of Wellington, 1962-64, 1966-68; NZ Inst of Intl Affairs, 1972-74; NZ Law Commnr, 1986-96, pres, 1991-96; Judge, Crt of Appeal, 1996-. Publications: Advisory Jurisdiction of the International Council of Justice, 1971; Essays on Human Rights (ed), 1968; New Zealand Defence Policy (ed), 1972; Reports of Law Commission and other law reform bodies. Honours: KBE, 1988; NZ Commemoration Medal, 1990; QC, 1994. Memberships: Intl Inst of Strategic Studies; NZ Inst of Intl Affairs. Hobbies: Reading; Walking; Music. Address: Court of Appeal, PO Box 1606, Wellington, New Zealand.

KEKILBAYEV Abish Kekilbayevich, b. 6 Dec 1939, Ondy, Kazakhstan. Politician; Writer. m. Klara Zhumabaeva, 4 children. Education: Kazakh State Univ. Appointments: Sch Tchr, Kazakh Lang; Worker, Newspprs Kazakh Adebieti & Leninshil Zhas; Ed-in-Chf, Studio Kazakhfilm; CP Offl in Alma-Ata; Dpty Min of Culture, Kazakh; Sec Mngr, Cttee of Kazakh Writers Union; Chair, Presidium of Kazakh Soc for Protection of Monuments of Hist & Culture, 1962-89; Chair, Cttee on Natl Policy, Lang & Culture Devel, Kazakhstan Supreme Soviet, 1991-93; Ed-in-Chf, Egemen Kazakhstan Newsppr, 1992-93; State Cnslr, 1993-94; Chair, Supreme Cncl of Repub, 1994-95; State Cnslr to Pres of Repub, 1995-; Dpty to Majlis (Parl), 1995-; State Sec, Rep of Kazakhstan, 1996-. Publications: Novems, short stories, critical reviews and transl. Address: Government Building, Respubliki Square 4, 480091 Almaty, Kazakhstan.

KELEN Stephen, b. 21 Mar 1912, Budapest, Hungary. Author; Sportsman. m. Sylvia Steuart, 19 Jan 1951, 2 s. Appointment: Freelance Writer. Publications: 7 books incl: Remember Hiroshima, 1983. Honours: OAM, 1986; Intl Table Tennis Hall of Fame, 1993; Writing Fell, Fellshp of Aust Writers, 1995; Champion Forever of Hungary. Memberships: Sydney Cntr, Intl PEN, pres, 1975-85; Austl Jrnlsts Assn; Soc of Auths. Hobbies: Reading; Writing; Drama; Theatre; Concerts; Art Galleries. Address: c/o Australian Society of Authors, PO Box 315, Redfern, NSW 2016, Australia.

KELEN Stephen Kenneth, b. 12 Feb 1956, Sydney, Aust. Poet; Creative Writing Teacher. m. Linda Susan Aflecht, 15 Aug 1987, 2 s. Education: BA, Univ of Sydney, Aust, 1976; DipLibSci, Kuring-gai, 1984; MA, Univ of Sydney, 1990. Publications: (books) The Gods

Ash Their Cigarettes, 1978; To The Heart of the World's Electricity, 1980; Atomic Ballet, 1990; Dingo Sky, 1993; Trans-Sumatran Highway and other poems, 1995; Dragon Rising, 1998. Honours: Poetry Aust Prize, 1973; Univ of Sydney Union Poetry Prize, 1976; Aust Cncl Spec Purpose Writers Grant, 1995; Visng Prof of Poetry, Univ of Sd, 1996; Asialink Writers-in-res, Hanoi, Vietnam. Membership: PEN Intl. Address: 25 Longstaff Street, Lyneham, ACT 2602, Australia.

KELLAS John Gordon, b. 13 Mar 1925, Lismore, NSW, Aust. Pharmacist. Education: PhC, Queensland, Aust, 1948. Appointments: Relieving wrk: Queensland, NSW, Vic, S Aust, West Aust, Northern Territory, Aust; Retd; Present Registrations: Queensland, NSW, incl hosp dispensing. Hobbies: Investor; Reading. Address: 260 Ainsworth Road, Leeville, Via Casino, NSW, Australia 2470.

KELLEHER Bryan John, b. 17 Jan 1924, Caulfield, Vic, Aust. Business Executive. m. Mary Teresa Clare, 18 May 1946, 1 s, 1 d. Education: BComm, 1950, BA, 1952, Univ of Melbourne. Appointments: Offr, Dept of Navy, 1941-59; 2nd Austl Imperial Force, 1942-46; Snr Rsch Offr, Fed Dept of Labour, 1960-64; Snr Inspector, Pub Serv Bd and Indl Advocate, 1964-70; Controller, Indl Rels, Postmaster Gens Dept, 1970-74; Dpty Asst Dir Gen, 1974-75; Mngr, Indl Rels, Dept Aust Post, 1975-82; Bd Dir, Austl Natives Assn, 1972-93; Trustee, 1978-87, Fed Pres, 1978-86; Dir, 1972, Perm Bldng Soc, Chmn of Bd, 1981-82; Dir, 1972-93, ANA Ins Co Ltd; Sec-Treas, Henry Lawson Lit Soc, 1983-; Ed, The Lawsonian, 1984-; Dir, Southern Community Broadcasters, 1984-87. Honours: Queen Elizabeth II Silver Jubilee Medal, 1977; Awd for 40 yr Serv to Community of Aust, 1981; Delivered Adam Lindsay Gordon 150th Anniversary Oration at Mem Cottage, Ballarat, 1983. Memberships: Life Gov, Old Colonists Assn of Vic; Life Mbr, Roy Histl Soc of Vic; Econ Soc of Aust and NZ; Indl Rels Soc of Aust. Hobbies: Gardening; Carpentry; Travel; Australian History; Genealogy. Address: 47 Bowen Street, Chadstone, Vic 3148, Australia.

KELLEHER Graeme George, b. 2 May 1933, Sydney, Aust. Public Servant; Businessman. m. Fleur, 21 Nov 1959, 1 s, 2 d. Education: BEng, Civil Engrng, Wesley Coll, Sydney Univ, 1955. Appointments: Proj Mngr, Googong Water Supply Proj, Canberra, 1973; Asst Sec, Acting First Asst Sec, Water and Soils Resources Div, Dept of the Environment and Conservation, 1974-75; Commnr, Ranger Uranium Environmental Inquiry, 1976-77; Dpty Chmn, Nuclear Non-Proliferation Task Force, 1978; Chmn, Gt Barrier Reef Marine Pk Authy, 1979-94; Vice Chmn, Marine of IUCN's World Comn on Protected Areas (WCPA), 1986-98; Snr Advsr, WCPA, 1999-; Kevin Stark Prof of Systs Engrng, James Cook Univ, 1992-95; Chmn, CSIRO Marine Sector Advsry Cttee, 1995-; Co-Chair, CRC Life Scis Panel, 1996-; Mbr, Cttee on Marine Protected Areas, US Natl Rsch Cncl, 1998-. Publications: A Global Representative System of Marine Protected Areas (co-eds C B Bleakley and S Wells), 1995; Guidelines for Establishing Marine Protected Areas (co-auth), 1992; Num reports, sci publs to profl bodies. Honours: Churchill Fell, 1971; Monash Medal, 1987; Mbr, Order of Aust (AM), 1988; Offr, Order of Aust, 1996; Fred Packard Intl Parks Merit Awd, 1998. Memberships: Fell, Instn of Engrs, Aust; Assn of Profl engrs, Aust; Intl Soc for Reef Studies; Austl Conservation Fndn; austl Marine Scis Assn; Fell, Acady of Technol Scis & Engrng. Hobbies: Tennis; Squash; Badminton; Bushwalking; Scuba diving; Swimming. Listed in: Who's Who in Australia; Dictionary of International Biography. Address: 12 Marulda Street, Aranda, Canberra, ACT 2614, Australia.

KELLY Anne-Maree, b. 18 Dec 1959, Melbourne, Aust. Emergency Physician. Education: MBBS, Melbourne; MClinEd, Univ NSW; FACEM. Appointments: Prof, Dir Emer Med, Western Hosp, Footscray, Melbourne, Aust and Univ Melbourne. Publications: Auth, Ed, 4 books; Auth over 50 refereed pprs in jrnls. Memberships: Pres, ASEM, 1991-93; Treas, ASEM, 1989-91; Chair, Primary Exam Cttee, ACEM, 1998-.

Honours: Tom Hamilton Lectr, ASEM, 1995. Address: Dept of Emergency Medicine, Western Hospital, Private Bag, Footscray 3011, Australia.

KELLY Anthony Bernard, b. 31 Aug 1928, Bondi, NSW, Aust. Philosopher; Theologian. m. Madge Yvonne McConville, 4 Aug 1951, 1 s, 4 d. Education: Waverley Coll, -1943; Clyde Cameron Coll, 1975-83; BA, 1984-87, Hons, 1988, PhD, 1998, Flinders Univ. Appointments: NSW Pub Serv, 1944-50; Northern Territory Police Force, 1950-60; Police Constable, Darwin and Alice Springs, 1950-51; Police Camel Patrol, Finke NT (last Police Cameleer in Aust), 1951-54; Police Sgt, Alice Springs NT, 1954-56; Police Prosecutor, Darwin, NT, 1956-57; OIC Police, Tennant Creek, NT, 1957-60; Personnel and Safety Offr, 1960-65; Indl Offr, 1965-75; Asst Union Sec, 1976-80, Union Sec, 1980-84; Cnslt, Pt-time Lectr and Stud, 1984-94; Indl Rels Cnslt, 1985-91; Guest Lectr, Indl Rels, Univ of SA, 1986-91; Austl Labor Cand for Seat of Davenport, SA, 1993. Creative Work: Auth, The Process of the Cosmos: Philosophical Theology and Cosmology, 1999; Originator of Work Level Analysis System of Job Evaluation. Memberships: Asst Rover Scout Ldr, 1948-50; Cttee Mbr and Ed, NT Police Jrnl, 1950-51; Pres, NT Police Assn, 1956-57; Bd Mbr, Inter-Ch Trade and Ind Mission, SA, 1973-77, Chmn ITIM, 1977-78; SA Indl Rels Soc Sec, 1970-71, VP, 1972-79, Pres, 1980-82; Cncl mbr, Flinders Univ, SA, 1981-84; Mbr, Local Govt, Superannuation Working Party, 1982-84; Bd Mbr, Local Govt, Superannuation Scheme, 1984-85. Listed in: Who's Who in Australia. Address: 6 Chowilla Street, Eden Hills, SA 5050, Australia.

KELLY Charles Norman Davidson, b. 2 June 1945. Education: BA, Jurisp, Exeter Coll, Oxford Univ; LLB, Edinburgh. Appointments: Law Apprentice/Asst Solicitor, W & J Burness, 1968-70; Invmnt Analyst & Fund Mngr, Ivory & Sime, 1970-74; Legal Advsr/Co Sec, Oil Exploration (Holdings) Ltd, 1974-80; Mngr, Legal and Corp Affairs, 1980-82, Gen Mngr, Corp Dev, 1982-86, Dir, Corp Dev, 1986-94, LASMP plc; Grp Gen Mngr, Bus Dev, BHP Petrol, 1995-. Memberships: Law Soc of Scotland. Hobbies: Sheepbreeding; Bagpipe playing. Address: c/o BHP Petroleum Pty Ltd, 120 Collins Street, Melbourne, Vic 3000, Australia.

KELLY Gregory Maxwell, b. 5 June 1930, Sydney, NSW, Aust. Emeritus Professor & Professor Fellow. m. Constance Imogen, 5 Nov 1960, 3 s, 1 d. Education: BSc, 1951, Univ of Sydney; BA, 1953, PhD, 1957, Univ of Cambridge, 1957. Appointments: Lectr in Pure Maths, 1957-60, Snr Lectr, 1961-65, Rdr, 1965-66, Univ of Sydney; Prof of Pure Maths, Univ of NSW, 1967-72; Prof of Pure Maths, Univ of Sydney, 1973-94. Publications: An Introduction to Algebra and Vector Geometry, 1972; Basic Concepts of Enriched Category Theory, 1982; Ed, Journal of Pure & Applied Algebra. Memberships: Fell, Austl Acady of Sci, 1972; Austl Math Soc; Amn Math Soc & Cambridge Philos Soc. Hobbies: Bridge; Music. Address: 319 Mona Vale Road, St Ives, NSW 2075, Australia.

KELLY Jack Lawrence (Hon), b. 25 Sept 1920. m. (1) Mavis 1944 dec 1982, (2) Isobel Gallogly, 6 Jan 1984. Education: BA, LL B, Univ of Qld. Appointments: AIF, 1941-45; Admitted Bar Qld, 1949; Priv Sec to Dpty Prime Min & Fedl Treasurer, 1950-52; Cmdng Offr, 9 INF BN (the Moreton Regt) CMF 1957-60; Chmn, Licensing Commn, Queensland, 1960-70; QC, 1964; Judge, Supreme Crt of Papua New Guinea, 1970-72; Judge, Supreme Crt of Queensland, 1973-90, Snr Puisne Judge, 1985-90; Judge Advocate Gen Austl Army, as Major-Gen, 1976-82; Jus of Appeal, Crt for Appeal, Solomon Is, 1982-84; Chmn, Parole Bd, Queensland, 1983-85. Honours: CBE, 1982; RFD, 1984. Membership: Inc Cncl of Law Rprtng Queensland, 1965-70. Address: 33 Eblin Drive, Hamilton, Queensland 4007, Australia.

KELLY Michael, b. 26 Mar 1946, Newcastle-upon-Tyne. Venue Manager. m. Kathryn, 3 June 1972, 3 d. Education: BA (Hons); CFE. Appointments: Gen Mngr, Regina , 1984; Gen Mngr, Upper Clementy Theme Pk, 1989; Dir, 4th Fac, Univ St

Columbia, 1991; Exec Dir, NCC (NZ) Ltd, 1996. Memberships: IAAM (Intl Assn of Assembly Mngrs) Bd, 1993-95; APECC (Asia-Pacific Exhibn and Convention Cncl), Chmn, 1999-200; Viva (Venue Mngmt Assn). Address: C/o NCE (New Zealand) Ltd, Christchurch, New Zealand.

KELLY Ros, b. 25 Jan 1948, Sydney, Aust. Politician. m. David Morgan, 1 s, 1 d. Education: Univ Sydney. Appointments: HS Tchr, NSW & ACT, 1969-74; Cnslt, Mbr, ACT Consumer Affairs Cncl, 1974-79; Mbr, ACT Legal Aid Comm, 1976-79; Fmr Mbr, ACT Legis Assembly; Mbr, Fed Parl, 1980-95; Sec, Fed Labor Party Parl Caucus, 1981-87; Min for Def Sci & Personnel, 1987-89, for Telecomms & Aviation Support, 1989-90, for Sport, the Environ & Territories, 1990-94, for the Arts, 1990-93, Assisting the PM for the Status of Women, 1993-94; Grp Exec, Dames & Moore, Aust & Asia, 1995-; Mbr, Intl Advsry Bd, Normandy Poseidon Ltd, 1995-; Mbr, Normandy Minerals. Hobbies: Reading; Films; Aerobics. Address: c/o Dames & Moore, 1/41 McLaren Street, North Sydney, NSW 2060, Australia.

KELSALL Merran Horne, b. 12 Oct 1954. Company Director; Chartered Accountant. m. 6 May 1989, 2 s, 1 d. Education: BCom, Hons, 1975. Appointments: Dir, Transport Accident Comm of Vic, 1987-96; Roy Melbourne Inst of Technol Cncl, 1988-96; Citywide Serv Solutions Pty Ltd, Commercial Subsidiary City of Melbourne, 1995-; NW Health Care Network, 1995-; IOOF of Victor, 1995-; Housing Loans Insurance Corp Ltd, 1997-. Memberships: Austl Inst of Co Dirs; Austl Inst of Mngmt. Hobbies: Family; Art; Music; Gardening; Bushwalking. Listed in: Who's Who in Business. Address: c/o 563 Bourke Street, Melbourne, Vic 3000, Australia.

KEMP Bruce William, b. 27 Mar 1943, Melbourne, Aust. Company Executive. m. Dorothy, 26 July 1969, 1 s, 1 d. Education: Dip, Mechl Engrng, Aust; Dip, Indl Engrng, USA; Harvard Univ, Prog Mngmt Dev, USA. Appointments: GM ppr Prods, Rheem, 1979-81; GM PPR & Packaging, Rheem, 1982-85; EGM, Appliances, 1985-92; Chf Exec, Southcorp Wines, 1992-. Memberships: Bd Mbr, Wine Fedn Aust, 1993-; Bd Mbr, Wine Export Cncl, 1994-; Exec Mbr Austl Ind Grp. Hobby: Motorbike riding. Address: 1 Munn Street, Millers Point, NSW 2000, Australia.

KEMP David Ronald, b. 5 May 1946. Scientist; Agronomist. m. 9 May 1970, 2 s, 1 d. Education: BS Agr (Hons), Sydney; MScAgr, Sydney; PhD, West Aust. Appointments: Regl Rsch Offr, Taree, 1967-74; Rsch Offr, Univ WA; Prin Rsch Scientist, Orange Agricl Inst; NSW Agric; Prof of Farm Mngmt, Univ of Sydney, Orange Campus, 1999. Publications: Books: Pasture Management: Technology for the 21st Century; Over 200 articles in jrnls, confs and others. Honours: Howard Fell, 1970; Stapledon Intl Fell, 1985; Fell, Aust Inst Agrcl Sci and Technol, 1995. Memberships: Aust Inst of Agricl Sci Technol, NSW pres, 1993-94; NSW Grassland Soc; Austl Agronomy Soc; Ecological Soc of Aust; Aust Soc Plant Physiologists. Hobbies: Agriculture; Trekking; Gardening. Address: University of Sydney, Orange Campus, Leeds Rd, Orange, NSW 2800, Australia.

KEMP Noel Robert, b. 23 Dec 1940. Geologist. m. Joelle Mason, 14 Dec 1967, 2 d. Education: Dookie Dip Agric, 1960; BSc, Univ of Melbourne, Aust, 1964; Dip Educ, Univ of Melbourne, 1965; MSc, Univ of Melbourne, 1970. Appointments: Secondary Sch Tchr, Melbourne, Aust, 1961; Demonstrator in Geol, Univ of Melbourne, 1966-70; Secondary Sch Tchr, Tipperary, Ireland, 1971; Secondary Sch Tchr, London, Eng, 1972; Curator of Geol, 1973-95, Snr Curator, 1996-, Tasmanian Mus, Hobart, Aust. Publications: 29 pprs, book chapts, sci and popular on geol, Antarctica and Fossilized Sharks' Teeth, 1975-95. Honour: Antarctic Medal of USA, 1979. Memberships: Geol Soc, Aust, 1973-; Assn Australasian Palaeontologists, 1973-; Austl Inst Geoscis, 1981-; Bonsai Soc Vic, 1985-; Fndn VP of Bonsai Soc S Tas, 1985, Pres BSST, 1987-. Hobbies: Bonsai; Travelling worldwide (multiple visits to all 7 continents), 1965-. Listed in: International Who's Who of Intellectuals;

Dictionary of International Biography; Australian Men and Women of Science, Engineering and Technology. Address: 19 Davey Street, Hobart, Tasmania, Australia.

KENILOREA Peter, b. 23 May 1943, Takataka, Malaita, Solomon Islands. Politician. m. Margaret Kwanairara, 1971, 2 s, 2 d. Education: Tchrs Coll, NZ. Appointments: Sch Master, King George CI Second Sch, 1968-70; Asst Sec, Fin, 1971; Admin Offr, Dist Admin, 1971-73; Lands Offr, 1973-74; Dpty Sec to Cabinet & to Chf Min, 1974-75; Dist Commr, E Solomons, 1975-76; Mbr, Legis Assembly, 1976-78; MP for E Are-Are, 1976-; Chf Min of the Solomon Islands, 1976-78; PM, Solomon Islands, 1978-81, 1984-86; Dpty PM, 1986-89; Min of Fgn Affairs, 1988-89, of Fgn Affairs & Trade Rels, 1990; Dir, S Pacific Frum Fisheries Agcy, 1991-94. Publications: Num articles in profl jrnls. Honour: Queens Silver Jubilee Medal, 1977. Hobbies: Reading; Sports. Address: Legislative Assembly, Honiara, Guadalcanal, Solomon Islands.

KENIRY John Stanley, b. 23 June 1943. Chemical Engineer. m. Dianne Cooper, 12 Mar 1966, 1 s, 3 d. Education: BSc Hons, Univ of NSW, 1964; PhD, Cambridge, Eng, 1971. Appointments: Chmn, Ridley Corp Ltd; Var other pub/pvte sector dirs. Memberships: Fell, R Aust Chem Inst; Fell, Aust Acady of Technol Sci and Engrng; Fell, Aust Inst of Co Dirs. Hobbies: Golf; Sailing; Tennis. Address: 81 Mona Vale Road, Pymble, NSW, Australia.

KENNETT Jeffrey (Gibb), b. 2 Mar 1948. Premier of Victoria. m. Felicity, 3 s, 1 d. Appointments: Fndr, KNF Advtng Pty Ltd; Mbr of Parl, Burwood, 1976-; Min for Aboriginal Affairs, Immigration, Ethnic Affairs and Housing, 1981-82; Ldr of Opposition, 1982-89, 1991-92; Premier, Vic, 1992-; Min for Multicultural Affairs and the Arts, 1996-. Address: Office of the Premier, 1 Treasury Place, Melbourne, Vic 3002, Australia.

KENNETT Keith Franklin, b. 18 July 1935. Professor. 2 s, 1 d. Education: DipT, Adelaide Tchrs Coll. 1955; DipEd, 1965, BA, 1967, AUA, 1968, MEd, 1976, Univ of Adelaide; MA, 1969, PhD, 1972, Univ of Saskatchewan. Appointments: Tchr, var positions in Primary Schs in S Aust; Clin Psychol, Pvte Prac, 1970-; Assoc Prof, Psychol, St Francis Xavier Univ and Univ Coll of Cape Breton, Nova Scotia, 1973; Dean of Educ, Nepean Coll of Adv Educ, 1977; Dean, Prof of Educ, Univ of Western Sydney, 1990-91; Snr Cnslt, Marble & Granite Intl Ltd, 1992; Exec Dir, Jeffries Inds Ltd, 1993-94; Mngng Dir, Profl and Corp Educ Cnslts Pty Ltd, 1995-; Dpty Chmn, Kampala Heart Cntr, Uganda, 1996; Chmn, Austl Wine and Living Pty Ltd, 1996-; Mngng Dir, Vital Lifecare Learning and Achmt Cntrs Pty Ltd, 1996-; Mngng Dir, Excelsior Coll Pty Ltd, 1996-; Mngng Dir, RRCS Employment Servs Pty Ltd, 1997-; Chmn, First Oceania Security Ltd, 1997-. Publications: The Family Behavior Profile, 1973; The Work Adjustment Assessment Profile, 1974; Painting Contractors Certification Program Assessment, 1994; Cash-in on Your Career, 1997; Num profl articles and chapts in books. Honours: Can Cncl Doct Fellshp, 1970-72; Visng Schl, Nisonger Cntr, OH State Univ, USA, 1977; Visng Schl, Fac of Educ, Univ S AL, 1983; Prof, Natl Fac, US Sports Acady, 1983-. Memberships: Am Psychol Assn; Am Assn on Mental Retardation; Austl Psychol Soc; Inst of Pvte Clin Psychols of Aust; FCIM; FCIS; MAICD; DABFE. Listed in: Who's Who in Australia. Address: 157B Old Northern Road, Castle Hill, NSW 2154, Australia.

KENZHAYEV Safarali, b. 18 Feb 1942, Tajikistan. Jurisprudent. m. Nazokat, 1965, 3 s, 3 d. Education: DL, Tajik State Univ, 1965. Appointments: Pub Prosecution Offr, Detective, 1965; Procurator of Frunze Dist, Dushanbe, 1975; Trans Procurator, Tajikis, 1983; Advsr, Pres of the Rep of Tajikistan; Chr, Supreme Soviet, Tajikistan; Chr, KGB, Tajikistan, 1991; Chr, Peoples Front, Tajikistan; Procurator, Kairakkum; Chr, Cttee of Legis and Hum Rights, Majlisi Oil, Tajikistan, 1992. Creative Works: 71 Works Publd in Tajik, Russia, Uzbek. Honours: Order of Friendship between Nations, 1985; Disting Wrk Medal. Memberships: Socialist Pty of

Tajikistans; Assn of Lawyers of Tajikistan; Cttee on Legis and Hum Rights; Majlisi Oil of the Rep of Tajikistan. Hobbies: Reading; Gdng. Address: Committee on Legislation and Human Rights, Majlisi Oli, Dushanbe, Tajikistan 734051.

KENZO Takada, b. 1940, Kyoto, Japan. Fashion Designer. Education: Art Sch, Japan. Appointments: Designer, Patterns, Tokyo Mag; Freelance Designer to Louis Feraud, Paris, 1964-70; Owner, Shop, Jungle Jap, 1970. Creative Works: Trans trad designs into origl contemporary garments and for ready-to-wear knitwear.

KEOGH Anne, b. 18 June 1957, Broken Hill, NSW, Australia. Cardiologist. Education: MBBS; MD; FRACP. Appointments: Snr Cardiologist, Heart Transpl Unit, St Vincent's Hosp, 1990; Assoc Prof, Univ of NSW, 1998-. Memberships: Cnclr, Intl Soc of Heart and Lung Transplants, 1995-98; Fed Cnclr, Cardiac Soc of Aust and NZ, 1995-2001. Address: St Vincent's Hospital, Heart and Lung Transplant Unit, Sydney Darlinghurst 2010, Australia.

KERIN John Charles, b. 21 Nov 1937, Bowral, NSW, Australia. Politician. m. (1) 1971, 1 s, 3 d, (2) June Raye Verrier, 1983. Education: BA, Univ New Eng; BEc, Austl Natl Univ. Appointments: Axeman, farmer and businessman, 1952-71; Rsch Economist, Bur of Agric Econs, 1971-72; Mbr for Macarthur, House of Representatives, 1972-75; Prin Rsch Economist, Bur of Agric Economics, 1976-78; MHR (ALP), Werriwa, 1978-93, Min, Primary Ind, 1983-87, Min Primary Inds and Energy, 1987-91, Treas, 1991, Min, Transp and Commns, 1991, Min for Trade and O'seas Dev, 1992-93; Chmn, Austl Meat and Livestock Corp, 1994-97; Dpty Chmn, Coal Mines Aust Ltd, 1994; Chmn: Corporate Investment Aust Funds Mngmt Ltd, 1994-; Bio-Logic Intl Inc, 1996-99; Co-op Rsch Cntrs for Sustainable Plantation Forestry, Weed Mngmt, Tropical Savannas, Sensor Signals and Info Processing; NSW Water Advsry Cncl; ReefMAC; Macarthur Cncl UWS and Mbr Bd of Governors UWS. Publications: Economic and Rural Policy Statement, 1986; Primary Industries and Resources: Policies for Growth, 1988; Research Innovation and Competitiveness, 1989. Honours: Hon Dr Rural Sci, Univ New Eng; Hon DLetters, UWS. Memberships: Ind and Econ Plcy Cttees Cabinet and Caucus, 1983; Cabinet Cttees: Expenditure Review Cttee; Structural Adjustment Cttee; Ecologically Sustainable Dev Sub-Cttee; Socl and Family Plcy Cttee. Hobbies: Bushwalking; Classical music; Performing arts; Reading. Address: 28D Hilly St, Mortlake, NSW, Australia.

KERIN Robert Gerard, b. 4 Jan 1954, Jamestown, S Aust. Minister of Primary Industries, Nat Resources & Regl Dev, SA. m. Catherine, 8 July 1978, 4 d. Appointments: Elected to Parl, 1993; Min for Primary Inds, 1995; Min for Primary Inds, Nat Resources and Regl Dev, 1997-; Dpty Premier of S Aust, 1998-. Address: 57 Railway Terrace, Crystal Brook 5523.

KERKVLIET Benedict, b. 28 Oct 1943, Montana, USA. Social Scientist. m. Melinda Castro Tria, 16 June 1972, 1 s, 1 d. Education: MA, PhD, Univ of WI, Madison, USA; BA, Whitman Coll. Appointments: Dept of Pol Sci, Univ of HI, 1972-92; Rsch Sch of Pacific and Asia and Studies, Austl Natl Univ, Canberra, Aust, 1992-. Publications: The Huk Rebellion; Everyday Politics in the Philippines; sev jrnl articles and edited books. Honours: Phi Beta Kappa, 1965; Natl Defense Educ Act Title 4 and Title 6 Fellships, 1966-69; For Area Fellship, 1969-71; Woodrow Wilson Cntr Fell, 1973-74; Natl Endowment for the Hum Fell, 1978; Snr Fell, ANU, 1984-85. Memberships: Assn for Asian Stdies; SE Asia Cncl. Hobbies: Gardening; Hiking; Flyfishing. Address: Research School of Pacific and Asian Studies, Australian National University, Canberra, ACT 0200, Australia.

KERR Alexander McBride, b. 23 Apr 1921, Perth, Aust. Economist. m. Joan Ivy Langridge, 9 Aug 1947, 2 s, 3 d. Education: Ctf of Socl Scis, hons, Oxford Univ, Eng, 1944; BSc, Econ, hons, Univ of London, 1947; BA, hons, 1948, MA, 1949, PhD, 1957, Univ WA. Appointments Citizen Mil Forces Army, 1937-39, 1947-54; Roy Austl Air Force, 1939-45; C'wlth Statsn Economist, 1950-52; Lectr, 1952-53, Snr Rsch Fell, 1954-55, Snr Lectr, 1956-63, Rdr, 1964-71, Assoc Prof, 1971-74, Univ WA; Fndn Prof of Econs, 1975-81, Dpty Vice Chan, 1980-83, Murdoch Univ; Dir, 1975-83, Dpty Chmn, 1984-86, Perth Bldng Soc; Dpty Chmn, Challenge Bank, 1987-89; Dir, Vincent Corp, Nusantaqua (Singapore), Daya Dakti Barnuna Nusantara (Indonesia), Atlas Pacific Ltd (Aust) Dir, 1993-96, Chmn, 1997-, Cendana Indopearls, Indonesia; Chmn, Biomngmt Systs, 1996-; Cnslt to: OECD; UNDP; ILO; ECAFE; ESCAP; Colombo Plan; Fed and State Govts in Aust and abroad; Pvte Ind: Has worked on assignments worldwide. Publications: Personal Income of Western Australia, 1951; Northwestern Australia, 1962; Regional Income Estimation, 1963; The Southwest Region of Western Australia, 1965; Australia's Northwest, 1967, 1975; The Texas Reefshell Industry, 1968; The Indian Ocean: Resources and Development, 1981; We Flew, We Fell, We Survived, Vol II, In The Bag, 1991. Honours: Fulbright Fellshp, 1960; Leverhulme Fellshp, 1969; Life Mbr, Econ Tchrs Assn of WA, 1980; Life Mbr, Austl and NZ Sect, Regl Sci Assn, 1981; Econ Soc Awd, 1984; Austin Holmes Awd, 1995. Hobbies: Golf; Fishing. Address: 146 Alderbury Street, Floreat, WA 6014, Australia.

KERR Duncan James Colquhoun, b. 26 Feb 1952, Hobart, Tas. Member of Parliament; Barrister; Solicitor. m. Celia Grace Taylor, 8 Nov 1987, div 1994, 1 s. Education: LLB, Tas Univ, 1975; BA Socl Work, Tasmanian Coll Adv Educ, 1977. Appointments: Socl Worker, Tasmanian Educ Dept, 1977; Lawyer, 1978-80, Crown Cnsl, 1980-82, Solicitor-Gen's Dept, Tas; Lectr 1982-85, Dean 1985, Fac of Law, Univ of Papua New Guinea; Prin Sol, Aboriginal Legal Serv, NSW, 1986; Lawyer, Hobart Comm Legal Serv, 1987; Elect Mbr, House of Reps, Electorate of Denison, 1987-; Min for Justice, 1993-96; Atty-Gen, 1993; Shadow Min for Immigration, 1996-97; Min Asstng Ldr of Opposition, Multicultural Affairs, 1996-97; Shadow Min, Environment, 1997-98; Shadow Min for Justice and Customs, Shadow Min for the Arts, 1998-. Publications: As Natural as Breathing (w C Grey), 1974; Annotated Constitution of Papua New Guinea (w B Brunton), 1985; Essays on the Constitution (w R Devere, J Kaburise, eds), 1985; Reinventing Socialism, ed, 1992. Memberships: Law Soc of Tas; Tasmanian Bar Assn; Admitted to Practice, Papua New Guinea, NSW, Tas. Hobbies: Cricket; Scuba diving; Tennis; Squash; Poetry; Theatre. Address: GPO Box 32A, Hobart, Tas 7001, Australia.

KESARWANI Sarojkumar, b. 17 July 1936. Information Scientist. m. Kumudini, 1 June 1959, 2 s, 2 d. Education: Associateship in Documentation and Reprography, INSDOC, Delhi, India; PG Dip in Lib Sci. Appointments: Libn, G S Coll of Comm, 1962-63; Libn, Jrnlsm Dept, Hislop Coll, Nagpur, 1963; Tech Asst, Natl Environmental Engrng Rsch Inst, Nagpur, 1963-74; Documentation Offr, Snr Documentation Offr 1974-85, Asst Dr 1979-85, Snr Asst Dir 1985-90, Natl Environmental Engrng Rsch Inst, Nagpur; Visng Lectr, Dept of Lib and Info Sci, Nagpur Univ. Publications: 25 jrnl articles & conf papers; 27 info access tools compiled & ed; 3 chapts in books. Honoura: WHO Fellshp, 1981; Lib of Yr Awd, 1995, Indian Assn of Spec Libs and Info Cntrs. Memberships: Indian Lib Assn; Indian Assn of Spec Libs and Info Cntrs; Soc for Info Sci; Acady of Info Sci, Mysore; Indian Assn of Environ Mngmt, Nagpur; Indian Assn of Tchrs of Lib and Info Sci. Hobbies: Excursion; Reading literature. Address: 72-B Tapovan Complex, Jai Prakash, Nagar, Nagpur 440 025, India.

KESORNTHONG Pancha, b. 5 Aug 1931. Deputy Prime Minister; Minister of Education. Appointments: Mbr of Parl, 1969, 1975, 1976, 1979, 1983, 1986, 1988, 1992, 1995, 1996; Dpty Min of Educ, 1975; Mbr, Natl Legislative Assembly, 1977; Speaker, House of Representatives, 1988-91; Min, Prime Min's Off, 1994-95; Dpty Prime Min, 1997. Honours: Kt Grand Cordon, Spec Class, Most Exalted Order of the White Elephant; Hon Doctorates, Ratchapat Phetchabun, Ramkhamhaeng. Address: 131-133 Lardprod 18, Lardprod Road, Lard Yao Chatuchak, Bangkok, Thailand.

KESRI Sitaram. Politician. Appointments: Min of State for Parl Affairs, 1985; Min for Welfare, 1991; Treas, All-India Congress Cttee; Pres, Congress Party, 1996-98; Parl Ldr, 1997. Address: All-India Congress Committee, 24 Akbar Road, New Delhi 110011, India.

KESSAR Yisrael, b. 1931, Yemen, emigrated to Israel, 1933. Politician; Economist; Sociologist. Appointments: Served in the Histadrut (Gen Fed of Labour), 1966-92; Chair, Manpower Dept & Youth & Sports Dept, 1966-71, Treas, 1973-77; Chair, Trade Union Dept, Dpty Sec-Gen, 1977-84; Sec-Gen, 1984-92; Mbr, Knesset, 1984-; Min of Transp, 1992-96. Address: Ministry of Transport, Klal Building, 97 Rehov Jaffa, Jerusalem 94342, Israel.

KEYS Alexander George William (Sir), b. 2 Feb 1923, Sydney, Aust. Company Director. m. Dulcie Beryl Stinson, 12 Sept 1950, 3 d. Appointments: War Serv: WWII, 1941-46, Korean War, 1950-51; Natl Sec, 1961-78; Natl Pres, 1978-88; The Returned Servs, League of Aust; Dir, 4 Pub Co's, 4 Pvte Co's. Publications: Biog book: Flowers in Winter, 1995. Honours: Mil Cross, Korea, 1951; Order of Natl Security Merit (Korea), 1951; OBE, 1970; KB, 1980; Chevalier de Polonia Restituta (Poland), 1980; Amn Legion Amity Awd, 1982; AC, 1988. Memberships: Nuffield Schl, 1956; Churchill Fell, 1969; Cncl of Austl War Memorial, 1974-93; Cncl of Austl Def Force Acad, 1984-97. Hobbies: Tennis; Painting. Address: Glenlee, Captains Flat Road, via Queanbeyan, NSW 2620, Australia.

KHADDAM Abdel Halim, Politician. Appointments: Min of the Econ & Fgn Trade, 1969-70; Dpty PM, Min of Fgn Affairs, 1970-84; VP, Polit & Fgn Affairs, 1984-. Membership: Regl Cmd, Baath Party, 1971-84. Address: Office of the President, Damascus, Syria.

KHAIL Muhammad Ali Aba al, b. 1935, Buraidah, Saudi Arabia. Politician. Education: Cairo Univ. Appointments: Min of Commns, Inst of Pub Admin, 1961; Dir-Gen, Inst of Pub Admin, 1962-63; Dpty Min of Fin & Natl Econ, 1964; Vice Min, 1970; Min of State, 1971; Mbr, Cncl of Mins, 1971; Min of Fin & Natl Econ, 1975-76; Chair, Saudi Intl Bank (London), Pub Investment Fund, Inst of Pub Admin, Pension & Retd Fund;Saudi Arabia-US Joint Comm on Econ Co-op; Saudi Arabian-German Joint Comm on Econ & Tech Co-op; Saudi Arabian-Sino Perm Jt Cttee on Econ & Tech Co-op. Honours: Num medals and decorations. Memberships: Sev bds. Hobbies: Reading; Indoor Sports. Address: Ministry of Finance & National Economy, Airport Road, Riyadh 11177, Saudi Arabia.

KHAIRAT Taha al, b. 1936, Daka'a, Syria. Diplomat. m. Khadija Salamat, 1957, 3 s, 3 d. Education: Univ Damascus. Appointments: Tchr, Min of Educn, 1957-69; Dir, Socl Affairs & Security, 1969-70; Sec, Baath Party Br, Daraa, 1970-71; Mbr, Regl Ldrshp, Baath Arab Socialist Party, 1971-80; Min of Local Admin, 1976-80; Amb to Bulgaria, 1982-89; Dir, Arab Dept, Min of Fgn Affairs, 1990-96. Hobby: Reading. Address: Ministry of Foreign Affairs, Damascus, Syria.

KHAITAN Suman Jyoti, b. 9 Feb 1959, Calcutta, India. Advocate. m. Seema, 27 Feb 1990. Education: BA Hons, Econs. LL B. Appointments: Asst, Khaitan and Co, 1977; Advocate, 1985. Creative Works: Article, After the Honeymoon; Running the Agent and Distribution network; Case Study, IBA Conf, Vancouver, Can. Memberships: Bar Assn of India; Bar Cncl of India; Bar Cncl of Delhi; CEGAT Bar Assn; Delhi High Crt Bar Assn; ICC India; Incorporated Law Soc; Inter Pacific Bar Assn; Indian Cncl of Arbitration; Indian Law Inst; Indian Soc of Intl Law; Intl Bar Assn; MRTP Commn Bar Assn; Supreme Crt Bar Assn; Union Intl Des Advocates. Hobbies: Reading; Music; Yoga; Walking. Address: W-13 Greater Kailash Part II, New Delhi 110 048, India.

KHALEGHIAN Peyvand, b. 29 Mar 1973, mash-had, Iran. Physician. Education: BHB (Bachelor Hum Biol), Univ of Auckland, 1990-92; BMed, MBchB (Bachelor Med, Bachelor Surg), Univ of Auckland, 1993-95. Appointment: Mbr, Natl Spiritual Assembly, Baha'is of NZ, 1996-. Honours: Univ Entrance Schl, 1989; Snr Prize in Hum Biol, 1993; JDK North Prize in Clin Med, 1995; Masonic Prize in Geriatric Med, 1995. Address: 1 Santa Monica Place, Manukau 1701, New Zealand.

KHALIFA Brig Gen Khalifa bin Ahmed al, b. 20 June 1945, Bahrain. Army Officer. Education: Roy Mil Acady, Sandhurst, England. Appointments: Platoon Cmdr, trng to Cmdr; Infantry Co Cmdr; Bn 2nd in Cmd; Battalion Cmdr; Fmr Chf of Staff, Bahrian Def Force. Address: Ministry of Defence, PO Box 245, West Rifaa, Bahrain.

KHALIFA Khalifa Bin Sulman al (Sheikh), b. 1936. Prime Minister of Bahrain. m. 3 children. Appointments: 1st Pres, Educ Cncl, 1957-60; Hd of Fin, 1960-66; Chmn, Admnstv Cncl, 1966-70; Co-ord, For Aid and Techl Assistance; Chmn, Cttee for Register of Com; Chmn, Jt Cttee for Econ and Finl Stdies; Pres, State Cncl, 1970-73; Prime Min, 1973-; Hd Supreme Def Cncl; Chmn, Bahrain Monetary Agcy. Honour: Khalifite Medallion, highest Order of Merit, the Amir, 1979. Hobbies: Reading; Travel; Motoring. Address: Office of the Prime Minister, PO Box 1000, Manama, Bahrain.

KHALIFA Sheikh Hamad bin Isa al, b. 28 Jan 1950, Bahrain. Crown Prince of Bahrain; Heir Apparent to His Highness the Amir of Bahrain. m. Sheikha Sabeeka bint Ibrahim Al-Khalifa, 1968, 6 s, 4 d. Education: Cambridge Univ. Appointments: Mons Offr, Cadet Sch, Aldershot, England, US Army Cmd, Gen Staff Coll, Ft Leavenworth, KS, USA. Fndr, Bahrain Def Force, 1968; Cmdr-in-Chf, 1968-, Raised Def Air Wing, 1978; Mbr, State Admin Cncl, 1970-71; Min of Def, 1971-88; Dpty Pres, Family Cncl of Al-Khalifa, 1974-; Fndr, Histl Documents Cntr, 1976; Fndr Mbr, Pres, Bahrain High Cncl for Youth & Sports, 1976-; Initiated, Al-Areen Wildlife Parks Reserve, 1976; Fndr, Salman Falcon Cntr, 1977, Amiri Stud, Bahrain, 1977, Bahrain Equestrian & Horse Racing Assn, Pres, 1977-; Fndr, Bahrain Cntr for Studies & Rsch, 1989. Honours: Order of the Star of Jordan (1st class), 1967, Al-Rafidain of Iraq (1st class), 1968, Natl Def of Kuwait (1st class), 1970, Al-Muhammedi of Morocco (1st class), 1970, Al-Nahdha of Jordan (1st class), 1972, Qiladat Gumhooreeya of Egypt (1st class), 1974, The Taj of Iran (1st class), 1973, King Abdul-Aziz of Saudi Arabia (1st class), 1976, Repub of Indonesia (1st class), 1977, Repub of Mauritania (1st class), El-Fateh Al-Adheem of Libya (1st class), 1979, Kuwait Liberation, 1994; Hon KCMG, UK; Ordre nationale du Mérite de la République Francaise (1st class), 1980; Grand Cross of Isabel la Catolica of Spain (1st class), 1981; Freedom of the City of KS, USA; Army Ctf of Hon. Membership: Helicopter Club of GB. Hobbies: Horse Riding; Golf; Study of Ancient History and Prehistory of Bahrain; Water Skiing; Swimming; Fishing; Falconry; Shooting; Football; Tennis. Address: The Crown Princes Court, Al-Zahir Palace, PO Box 28788, Bahrain.

KHALIFA Sheikh Isa bin Salman al, b. 3 June 1933, Bahrain. Ruler of the State of Bahrain. m. 5 s, 4 d. Appointments: Appointed, 1958; Succeeded as Ruler on the death of his father, 1961; Title of Amir Aug, 1971. Honour: KCMG. Memberships: Chair, Manama Mun Cncl, 1955-61; Vice Chair, Bahrain Admin Cncl. Address: PO Box 555, Rifa'a Palace, Manama, Bahrain.

khalifa Sheikh Khalifa bin Sulman al, b. 1935, Bahrain. Politician. Appoitments: Dir of Fin, Pres, Elec Bd, 1961; Pres, Cncl of Admin, 1966-70; Pres, State Cncl, 1970-73; PM, 1973-; chair, Bahrain Monetary Agcy. Address: Office of the Prime Minister, PO Box 1000, Government House, Government Road, Manama, Bahrain.

KHALIKYAR Fazle Haq, b. 1934, Shahr-e Naw, Herat, Afghanistan. Politician. Education: Kabul Univ. Appointments: Govt Employee, Min of Planning, 1958-60; Min of Internal Affairs, 1962-64; Min of Comms, 1966-67; Gen Auditor, Kabul Prov; Admin Pres, Min of Fin, 1969; Gov, Baghlan Prov, 1971; Dpty Min of Fin, 1971-72; 1st

Dpty Min of Fin, 1972-81; Min Cnslr, Cncl of Mins & Gov-Gen, N Western Zone, 1981-90; PM of Afghanistan, 1990. Honour: Hero of the Repub. Address: Office of the Prime Minister, Shar Rahi Sedarat, Kabul, Afghanistan.

KHALIL Muhammad Khalil, b. 14 Dec 1925, Tayibah, Palestine. Ex-Professor of Law, Judge and Legal Advisor. m. Rudaina Tibi, 14 Feb 1956, 2 s, 2 d. Education: Palestine Intermediate, Arab Coll, Jerusalem, 1945; LLB, (Hon), Liverpool Univ, 1948; Barrister-at-Law, Middle Temple, London, 1949; LLD, Leyden, 1952. Appointments: Sec Gen, Libyan Roy Crt, 1952-54; Legal Advsr to H M King Idriss Sanusi, Libya, 1954-55; Asst Prof, Intl Law, Amn Univ of Beirut, Lebanon, 1956-59; Advocate, Amman, Jordan, 1959-61; Legal Advsr: Shell Co of Qatar, 1961-63; Iraq Natl Oil Co, Baghdad, 1964-65; SONATRACH, Algiers, 1965-71; Mngng Dir, Pan Arab Cnslts for Pet, Econ and Indl Dev, Beirut, 1972-77; Cnslt, Orgn of Arab Pet Exporting Countries (OAPEC), Kuwait, 1975-77; Legal Advsr, Qatar Pet Producing Authority and The Qatar Gen Pet Corp, Doha, 1977-86; Judge, OAPEC Judicial Tribunal, Kuwait, 1981-87. Publications: The Arab States and the Arab League: a Documentary Record, 2 vols, 1962, 1987, 1990; Ed, The General Agreement on participation in Respect of Crude Oil Concessions in the Arabian Gulf States: A Legal, Economic and Financial Appraisal (ed), 1973; Towards an Optimal Production and Investment Strategy of the Arab Petroleum Exporting Countries in the Light of Alternative Energy Sources the Year 1985, 1974; Sev articles, rsch pprs, lectures, reviews. Honours: Hon Pres, First Pan Arab Students' Congress in Eur, Leyden, 1950; Fndng Mbr, Shaybani Soc of Intl Law, Germany, 1954; Mbr, Select Cttee, Abdul Hamid Shoman Fndn's Awds of Excellence for Disting Young Arab Schlrs, 1992. Hobbies: Reading; Photography; Music; Sports watching (especially football/soccer); Travel. Address: PO Box 140978, El-Biader, Amman 11814, Jordan.

KHALILOV Erkin Khamdamovich, b. 1955, Bukhara, Uzbekistan. m. 3 s. Education: Tashkent State Univ. Appointments: Engr, Rsch Prodn Unit, Cybernetics, 1977-79; Jnr, Snr Rschr, Hd of Divsn, Inst of Philos & Law, Uzbek Acady of Scis, 1979-90; People's Dpty, Repub of Uzbekistan; Chair, Cttee on Law, Dpty Chair, Oliy Majlis (Supreme Soviet), 1990-93, Acting Chair, 1993-95, Chair, 1995-. Address: Oliy Majlis, 700008 Tashkent, Uzbekistan.

KHAMBATI Nitin, b 12 Oct 1945, Bombay, India. Managing Director. m. Chandrika, 22 Dec 1969, 2 d. Education: BE (Electr). Appointments: Trnee, Des and Mfng of Railway Elect Equip, Beni Ltd, Calcutta, 1967; Trnee, Switchgear Factory, L&T Ltd, 1968; Electr installations, 1969-71, Mktng Mngr, 1971-78, Mktng, 1978-89, Promotion of Optical Fibre Cable Test Equip, 1989-, Trinity Electr Syndicate. Honours: Platinum Jubilee Endowment Trust Awd; Indian Merchants Chamber Jhulelel Awd, Intl Sindhi Panchayat. Memberships: IEE, UK, Cttee, Hon Sec, Treas; Assoc Mbr, IEEE, USA; Fell, Inst of Engrs, India; Fell, Inst of Electron and Telecom Engrs; Soc of Power Engrs, Hon Treas, 1992-94; Hn Sec, Dir, Electr Contractors Assn, Maharashtra; Sec, Electr Merchants Assn; Fed of All India Electr Traders Assn; Tstee, Forum Against Drugs and AIDS; Tstee, Kushtrog Nivaran Samiti; Dist Gov, 1987-88, Active Mbr, Lions, Chmn, Multiple Cncl; Partic and org'd num Eye Camps in rehab for the Blind, num fundraising activities.

KHAMENEI Ayatollah Seyed Ali, b. 1940, Mashad, Khorassan, Iran. Politician; Religious Leader. m. 1964, 4 s, 1 d. Appointments: Fmr Personal Rep, Ayatollah Khomeini, Supreme Def Cncl; Friday Prayer Ldr, Teheran, 1980-; Sec-Gen, Pres, Ctrl Cttee, Islamic Repub Party, 1980-87; Pres of Iran, 1981-89; Wali Faqih (Relig Ldr), 1989-; Mbr, Revolutionary Cncl; Rep of Revolutionary, Min of Def. Hobby: Traditional Persian Athletics. Address: Office of the Religious Leader, Teheran, Iran.

KHAMOUANE Boupra. Government Official. Appointment: **Min,** Ministry of Jus, Laos. Address: Ministry of Justice, Lane Xang Ave, Vientiane, Laos.

KHAN Abdul Waheed, b. 1 Jan 1947. Government Service. m. Asya Khatoon, 3 d. Education: BSc, Agricl, 1963; MSc, Agricl, 1965; MS, 1970; PhD, 1973. Appointments: Lectr, Agricl Extension, Agra Univ, Shamli, India, 1965-66; Rsch Fell, Indian Inst of Mass Commn, New Delhi, 1966-69; Rsch Asst, Dept of Agricl Jrnlsm, Univ WI, USA, 1969-73; Assoc Dir, GB Plant Univ of Agric and Technol, Patnagar, USA, 1973-75; Dir, All India Radio, New Delhi, 1975-79; Commns Cnslt, UNEPA, Dhaka, Bangladesh, 1979-81; Commns Specl, UNESCO, Dhaka, Bangladesh, 1981-84; Expert, FAO of UN, Kathmandu, 1984-86; Visng Prof, Sci, Natl Inst of Multimedia Educ, Chiba, Japan, 1990-91; Prof, Dir, Comms Divsn, IGNOU, New Delhi, 1986-92; Snr Prog Offr, 1992-96, Acting Hd, 1995-96, Prin Comms Specialist, 1996-98, C'wlth of Learning, Vancouver, Can; Vice Chan, Indira Gandhi Natl Open Univ, New Delhi, 1998-. Honours: Vilas Travel Fellshp, USA, 1972; Rsch Grant, Univ WI, 1972; COL Fellshp, 1989; Disting Serv Awd, C'wlth of Learning, 1998; Natl Integration Awd, 1998; Millennium Awd for Educl Plng and Mngmt, 1998. Memberships: Pres, AAOU, CDE, Dev Comm India. Address: Indira Gandhi National Open University, New Delhi 110 068, India.

KHAN Inamullah, b. 17 Sept 1914, Rangoon, Burma. Religious Leader. m. Khadija Khalik, 1939, 1 s, 5 d. Education: Rangoon Univ. Appointments: Ed-in-Chf, Burma Muslim Daily, 1942; In India, 1942-46; Pakistan Citizen, 1948-; Fndr, Modern World Muslim Congress; Pres, World Conf on Religion & Peace. Honours: Niwano Peace Prize, Japan; Templeton Prize, Bahamas. Hobbies: Reading; Writing. Address: D-26, Block 8, Gulshan-e-Iqbal, Karachi 75300, Pakistan.

KHAN M Shamsul Islam, b. 1 Dec 1949. Librarian; Information Specialist. m. Nilufar Akhter, 30 May 1976, 3 d. Education: MA, Lib Sci, 1974; Dip, Personnel Mngmt, 1979. Appointments: Acting Hd Libn, Cholera Rsch Lab, 1977-79; Hd Libn, 1979-84; Hd, Lib and Publ Branch, 1984-89; Mngr, Intl Diarrhoeal Disease Info and Documentation Ctr Project, 1982-89; Hd, Diarrhoeal Diseases Info Servs Ctr, 1989-95; Hd, Dissemination and Info Servs Ctr, ICDDR B, 1995-. Honours: Govt Jnr Schlsp, 1963-65; Lib Assn of Bangladesh Schlsp, 1970; Project Grants: Intl Dev Rsch Ctr, Canada, 1982-91; Swiss Dev Corp, Switzerland, 1988-91. Memberships include: Life Mbr: Nepal Lib Assn; Bangladesh Soc of Microbiologists; Population Assn of Bangladesh; Indian Lib Assn; Bengal Lib Assn; Bangladesh Assn for the Advancement of Sci; Editing and Publn Assn of Bangladesh; Bangladesh Assn of Libns, Info Scientists and Documentalists; Donor and Life Mbr, Lib Assn of Bangladesh; Bangladesh Environl Soc; VP, Editing and Publn Assn of Bangladesh; Gen Sec, 1988-91, Pres, 1991-95, Lib Assn of Bangladesh. Hobbies: Reading; Outdoor games. Address: Dissemination and Information Services Centre, International Centre for Diarrhoeal Disease Research, Bangladesh, Mohakhali, Dhaka 1212, Bangladesh.

KHAN Mahbubur Rahman, b. 2 Mar 1940, Dhaka, Bangladesh. Managing Director. m. Delara Begum, 1 June 1961, 1 s, 2 d. Education: MA, Econs, Dhaka Univ, 1960; MA, Econs, Yale Univ, USA, 1967. Appointments: Lectr, Econs, Govt Colls, Bangladesh, 1961-62; Rsch Offr, State Bank of Pakistan, 1962-63; Snr Exec, 1963-86, Dpty Gov, 1987-92, Bangladesh Bank (Ctrl Bank); Mngng Dir, Rupali Bank Ltd, Dhaka, 1992-93; Prin IMF Advsr to Ctrl Bank of Guyana, SA, 1993-94; Dpty Gov, Bangladesh Bank (Ctrl Bank), 1994-97; Mngng Dir, Sonali Bank, Dhaka, 1997-. Publications: Sev articles in profl jrnls. Memberships: Bangladesh Econ Assn; Asiatic Soc of Bangladesh; Bangla Acady; Fell, Inst of Bankers, Bangladesh; Dir, Eastern Bank Ltd, Dhaka, Investment Corp of Bangladesh, Dhaka; VP, Inst of Bankers, Bangladesh; Gov Bd, Bangladesh Inst of Bank Mngmt, Dhaka; Bd Dir, Grameen Securities Mngmt Ltd, Dhaka. Hobbies: Reading; Gardening; Collecting Books and Rare Plants; Preservation of Classic Paintings. Address: Sonali Bank, Head Office, Motijheel Commercial Area, Dhaka 1000, Bangladesh.

KHAN Mohammad Mohabbat, b. 16 Jan 1949, Dhaka. Teaching (University). m. Rokeya, 28 May 1977, 2 s. Education: BA, 1968, MA, 1970, Univ of Dhaka; MPA, Syracuse Univ, 1974; PhD, MPA, Univ of South CA, 1976. Appointments: Prof, Pub Admin, Univ of Dhaka, 1983; Prof, Pub Admin, Yarmouk Univ, Jordan, 1990-91; Snr Fulbright Fell, Univ of TX, Austin, 1989-90; Assoc Prof, Pub Admin, Univ of Benin, Nigeria, 1981-82. Publications: Bureaucratic Self-Preservation, 1980; Politics of Administrative Reform, 1991; Administrative Reforms in Bangladesh, 1998. Honours: Univ of Dhaka Grad Schlshp, 1968-69; Asia Fndn Grad Schlshp at Syracuse Univ & Univ of South CA, 1972-76; Tchng Asstshp, Univ of South CA, 1976. Memberships: Amn Soc for Pub Admin, 1974; Intl Inst of Admin Scis, 1984; Intl Polit Sci Assn, 1985; Commonwealth Assn for Pub Admin, 1994. Hobbies: Watching movies; Cricket on TV; Jogging; Reading posts. Address: Department of Public Administration, University of Dhaka -1000, Bangladesh.

KHAN Mosaddeque, b. 5 June 1959, Chittagong. Consultant. m. C Khan, 1985, 1 d. Education: MS, State Tech Univ, Astrakhan, Russia, 1981; PhD, Moscow State Univ, 1991. Appointments: Cnslt, Longreach Grp, Sydney, 1995-; Internet Mngr, Longreachgold, Sydney, 1998-. Honours: State Schlshp, Govt of USSR, 1975-81; USSR Govt Schl, 1986. Memberships: Bd of Eds, Cntr for Integrated Rural Dev for Asia and The Pacific, 1984-85; Pres, Bangladesh Assn, Astrakhan, 1987-89. Hobbies: Computing; Travel; Cricket. Address: 5/1 Noela Place, St Marys, NSW 2760, Australia.

KHAN Muhammad, b. 10 Feb 1926, Domel, Attock, Pakistan. Agriculture. m. Aziz Khanum, 15 Aug 1963, 1 s, 1 d. Appointments: Brit Army; Trans, Greek Emb at Islamabad; Var Shipping Cos. Honours: War Serv Medal, 1939-45; Pak Medal, Kashmir Medal, 1948. Hobbies: Agriculture; Gardening. Address: Village & PO Domel Mohallah Tamna, Tehsil Jand, District Attock, Pakistan.

KHAN Muhammad Fahim, b. 15 Aug 1947, Delhi, India. Islamic Economics & Finance. m. Tahira, 18 Nov 1973, 1 s. Education: MA, Stats (Punjab-Pakistan); MA, Pol Econ, Boston, USA; PhD, Econs, Boston, USA. Appointments include: Snr pos in Min of Planning, 1969-81; Prof, Dir Sch of Econs, Intl Islamic Univ, Islamabad, 1981-88; Div Chief, Islamic Rsch & Training Inst, Islamic Dev Bank, Jeddah, 1989-. Publications include: Human Resource Mobilization through Profit-Loss Sharing Based Financial System, 1991; Essays in Islamic Economics, 1994; Islamic Futures and Their Markets, 1995; Islamic Financial Institutions, 1995; Counter Trade - Policies and Practices in OIC Member Countries, 1995. Honour: Punjab Univ Gold Medal, 1968. Membership: Life Mbr, Intl Assn of Islamic Econs. Hobbies: Travel; Literature. Address: PO Box 9201, Jeddah, 21413, Saudi Arabia.

KHAN Muhammad Mansoor, b. 10 Apr 1939, Wadhona, India. Teaching. m. Tahira Aidrous, 12 May 1966, 2 s. Education: MA; PhD, Engl. Appointments: Asst Lectr, Govt Sci Coll, Nagpur; Asst Lectr, 1961, VMV Govt Coll; Asst Lectr, Amravati, 1962; Lectr and Asst Prof, Govt Coll Ambikapur; Asst Prof and Prof, Govt Autonomous Postgrad Coll Chhindwara, 1969-. Publications: Emily Dickinson's Poetry, book, 1983; The Butterfly Throb, collection of English poems, 1996; Sev poems and articles publs in jrnls. Honours: Life Mbr, Amn Stdies Rsch Cntr, India; Erstwhile Mbr, Indian Assn of Amn Studies; Life Mbr, Amn Cntr (USIS) and former Amn Book Club; Hon Dir, Bd of Editl Dirs of Dickinson Studies and Higginson Jrnl of Poetry, until 1995. Hobbies: Reading and Writing; Writing poetry in English and Urdu; Reciting poetry in poetry conferences; Speaking on literary and social topics; Literary and poetry broadcasts and telecasts. Address: 5 Mehta Colony, Parasia Road, Chhindwara MP 480001, India.

KHAN Salil Chandra, b. 2 Mar 1953. Library and Information Science. m. Smriti Khan, 18 June 1984, 1 d. Education: B Lib Sc, Jadavpur Univ, Calcutta, 1975; M Lib and Inf Sci, Jadavpur Univ, 1988. Appointments: Udayan Lib, Calcutta, 1971; Natl Atlas and Thematic

Mapping Org, Calcutta, 1975; Cntrl Mine Planning and Design Inst Ltd, Reg Inst I, Asansol, WB, 1982; Natl Test House, Calcutta, 1993; Rabindra Bharati Univ, Calcutta, 1995; Guest Tchr, Vidyasagar Univ, Mindapore, 1995-96, 1996-97, 1997-98. Publications: 1 book, 19 papers. Honour: Awd, Drama Competition. Memberships: Indian Assn of Spec Libs & Info Cntrs, Life Mbr; Cncl Mbr 1990-91, 1994-95, Sec, Docum Div 1994-95, Asst Sec and Convenor Exec and Fin Cttee 1996-97; Bengal Lib Assn, Life Mbr; Indian Assn of Tchrs in Lib and Info Sci, Life Mbr; Bengal Sci Assn, Life Mbr. Hobbies: Stamp Collection; Acting in drama. Address: Department of Library & Information Science, Rabindra Bharati University, 56A, B T Road, Calcutta 700050, India.

KHAN Tanveer Nasir, b. 15 June 1944, Varansi, India. Manager, Crop Breeding Group. m. 15 July 1985, 1 s, 1 d. Education: BSc, Agric, MSc, Agric, Agra Univ; PhD, Univ of West Aust. Appointments: Farm Mngr, Agric Coll, Kanpur, India, 1964-65; Rsch Fell, Univ of WA, 1968-70; Lectr, Makerere Univ, Uganda, 1970-72; Snr Lectr, Univ of Papua, New Guinea, 1973-76; Plant Path, 1976-87, Snr Plant Breeder, 1988-96; Mngr, Crop Breeding Grp, Agric WA; Rsch Coord, Mbr, Winged Bean Steering Cttee, Intl Cncl for Dev of Underutilised Plants, San Fran, USA, 1976-90; Cnslt, Intl Dambala (Winged Bean) Inst, Sri Lanka on appt w FAO, UN, Rome, 1984-. Publications: Over 166 sci pprs; Auth: Winged Bean Production in the Tropics. Honours: 3 Gold, 1 Silver Medal for var acad distinctions when doing BS, MSc. Memberships: Fell, Indian Soc of Genetics and Plant Breeding; Austl Inst of Agricl Sci; Pisum Genetics Assn. Listed in: Reference Asia; Asian/American Who's Who; International Directory of Distinguished Leadership. Address: Agriculture Western Australia, 3 Baron-Hay Court, South Perth, WA 6151, Australia.

KHANI Abdallah Fikri El, b. 25 Jan 1925, Damascus. Politician; Diplomat; Judge. m. 2 d. Education: Syrian Univ, Damascus; St Joseph, Beirut; Am Univ, Beirut. Appointments: Lawyer, 1947-49; Sec-Gen in Presidency of Repub, 1949-59; Lectr, Sch of Law, Syrian Univ, 1954-58; Min Cnslr, Min, Plenipotentiary, Madrid, Brussels, Ankara, London, Paris, 1959-69; Perm Rep to UNESCO, 1966-69; Hd Del to UN Gen Assembly & Security Cncl, 1970; Chair, Syro-Lebanese Perm Comm, 1969-72; Min for Tourism, 1972-76; Sec-Gen, Min of Fgn Affairs, 1969-72; Min of Fgn Affairs, 1973-74, Dpty Min, 1976-77; Amb to India, 1978-81; Mbr, Vice Chair, UN Sub-Comm on Prevention of Discrimination & Protection of Minorities, 1978-81; Mbr, Intl Crt of Justice, The Hague, 1981-85; Mbr, Intl Crt of Arbitration of ICC, 1991-93. Honours: Order of Merit, Syria, Egypt, Jordan, Indonesia; Order of the Egyptian Repub; Grand Cross of the Argentine Order of May; His Holiness Pope Paul VI Bronze Medal. Membership: Am Law Soc. Hobbies: Music; Sport; Reading; Philately. Address: 46 Argentine Street, Damascus, Syria.

KHANNA Akshaye, b. 28 Mar 1975, Bombay, India. Professional Actor. Education: BCom. Honours: Sev awds inclng Filmfare, Screen, Zee. Hobbies: Reading; Flying; Squash; Art. Address: 12A Sumangal, Ridge Road, Bombay 400006, India.

KHANUKAEV Sergey, b. 26 Aug 1952, Makhachkala, Russia. Conductor; Musicologist. m. Elena Medvedovski, 3 Jan 1999. Education: MA, Musicology, Moscow Tchaikovsky Conservatory, 1969-74; PhD, Musicology, Moscow Gnessin Music Inst, 1976-79; MA, Conducting, Hon Dip, St Petersburg Conserv, 1981-85. Appointments: Music Dir, Nalchik Music Theater, 1986-89; Conductor, Moscow Stanislavski and Nemirovich-Danchenko Music Theater, 1989-91; Music Dir, Israel Camerata Women String Orch, 1992--95; Conductor, New Israeli Opera, 1992-94; Mngr, Israeli Music Publs, 1993; Music Dir, Israel Classica Chamber Orch, Hadera, 1997-. Recording: Recordings on Israel Broadcasting Auth w Jerusalem Symph Orch, 1992-97. Honour: Spec Prize, Austrian Courses for Conductors Mürzzuschlag, 1992. Membership: Amn Conductors Guild, 1997-. Hobbies: Driving; Reading; Diving; Swimming. Address: PO Box 46261, Jerusalem, 91461, Israel.

KHARRAZI Kamal, b. 1944, Tehran, Iran. Minister of Foreign Affairs. m. 2 s. Education: BA, Persian Lang and Lit, 1969, MA, Educ, 1971, Tehran Univ; PhD, Educ, Houston Univ, TX, USA, 1972-79. Appointments: Var Posts incl Dpty for Plng of Islamic Repub of Iran Brdcstng, Dpty For Min for Pol Affairs, Mng Dir, Cntr for Intellectual Dev of Children and Young Adults, 1978-80; Mbr, Supreme Def Cncl, Hd, War Propaganda HQ; Mng Dir, Islamic Repub News Agy, Irna, 1980-89; Perm Rep and Amb to UN, 1989-; Elected, Min of For Affairs. Publications: Sev essays and books on psychol and educ.

KHATAMI Hojjatoleslam Seyyed Mohammad, b. 1943, Ardkan, Yazd, Iran. Politician. m. 1974, 1 s, 2 d. Education: Qom & Isfahan Seminaries; Univ Teheran; Man Islamic Cntr, Hamburg. Appointments: MBr for Ardakan & Meibod; 1st Islamic Consultative Assn (Parl); Rep, Imam Khomeini; Dir, Kayhan Newsppr; Fmr Min of Culture & Islamic Guidance; Cultural Dpty HQ of C-in-C; Hd, Def Publicity Cttee; Fmr Min of Culture & Islamic Guidance; Fmr Advsr to Pres Rafsanjani & Pres, Natl Lib of Iran; Fmr Mbr, High Cncl of Cultural Revolution; Pres, Islamic Repub of Iran, 1997-. Publications: Fear of Wave; From World to City to World City; Faith and Thought Trapped by Selfishness. Address: Office of the President, Pastor Avenue, Teheran, Iran.

KHATAMI Seyyed Mohammad, Politician. Education: Relig Sci Cntr; Qom. Appointments: Involved in Resistance to Shah's Govt, 1970s; Fmr Min of Culture & Islamic Guidance; Pres of Iran, 1997-. Address: Office of the President, Teheran, Iran.

KHATIB Hisham, b. 5 Jan 1936, Palestine. Engineer; Economist. m. Maha, 21 Aug 1968, 2 s, 1 d. Education: BS, Engrng, BS, Econs, PhD, Engrng, Univ of London. Appointments: Min of Energy, Gov of Jordan, 1984-90; Min of Plng, Gov of Jordan, 1993-95. Publications: 2 books on engrng econs; 100 pprs. Honours: Achievement Medal, Instn of Elec Engrs (UK), 1998; Decorated in Italy, Sweden, Indonesia, Austria, Jordan, Victoria. Memberships: Fell, IEE (UK); Fell, IEEE (USA). Hobbies: History and art of the Holy Land. Address: PO Box 925 387, Amman 11110, Jordan.

KHATOON Akram, b. 26 Sept 1937, India. Banking. Education: Master Deg, Econs; Dip, Inst of Banking, Pakistan. Appointments: Lectr in Econs, 1958-59; Muslim Cmty Bank Ltd, Karachi, 1959-89; Exec VP, Pres, First Womens Bank, Karachi, 1989-. Publications: Sev articles in profl jrnls. Honours include: Woman of the Yr Awd, 1990; Awd, Bus & Profl Women, Karachi, 1998. Memberships: Inst of Bankers; Fedn of Bus & Profl Women; Bd Gov, Natl Inst of Pub Admin. Hobbies: Reading; Music. Address: First Women Bank Ltd, A-115 7th Floor Mehdi Towers, Sindhi Muslim Co-operative Housing Society, Sharah e Faisal, PO Box 15549, Karachi, Pakistan.

KHATTAK Saifullah Khan, b. 15 Sept 1942, Karak, Pakistan. Federal Government Servant. m. 1 s. Education: MSc, Am Univ of Beirut; BSc, Hons, Peshawar Univ; Adv Trng, Agricl Planning, Japan, 1975; Ctf of Higher Trng, Agricl Policy Plng and Project Appraisal, 1984. Appointments: Agricl Offr, Asst Dir, Econ and Plng, Snr Mktng Offr, Agricl Econ, Snr Mktng Offr, Dpty Agricl Mktng Advsr, Agricl and Livestock Mktng Advsr. Publications: Sev articles and reports. Memberships: Am Soc for Agricl Econs, 1973-75; AFMA. Hobbies: Reading; Discussions. Address: Block 6-A, 2nd Floor, F/7 Markaz, Islamabad, Pakistan.

KHAVARI-NEJAD Ramazan Ali, b, 21 Jan 1943, Babol, Mazandaran, Iran. Botanist. m. Behnaz Eshragh, 17 Oct 1974, 2 d. Education: BSc, Bio, Tehran Univ, Tehran, 1963; MSc, Bio, Tehran Univ, 1965; MSc, Botany, Imperial Coll, London Univ, 1969; DIC, Botany, Imperial Coll, London, Eng, 1969; PhD, Botany, Imperial Coll, London, 1972. Appointments: Asst Prof, Isfahan Univ, Isfahan, Iran, 1972-76, 1978-79; Adj Prof, MI State Univ, MI, E Lansing, USA, 1976-77; Asst Prof, 1979-84, Assoc Prof, 1984-94, Prof, 1994-, Univ Tchrs Educ,

Tehran. Publications include: Growth Parameters in Sunflower Plants as Affected by Ca^{2+} Na^+ Interactions Under NaCl Salinity, 1990; Effects of NaCl on Photosynthetic Pigments, Saccharides and Chloroplast Ultrastructure in Leaves of Tomato Cultivars, 1998. Honours: Roy Coll Schlshp in Bot, Imperial Coll, London, 1970; Hon of Disting Prof, Univ of Tchrs Educ, Tehran, Iran, 1992. Membership: Active Mbr, Bio Cttee, Min of Higher Educ, Tehran, 1980-87. Hobbies: Computer Programming; Biostatistics; Music. Address: Department of Biology, University for Teachers Education, 49 Mobarezan (Roosevelt) Avenue, Tehran 15, Iran.

KHAYATA Abdulwahab, b. 24 Feb 1924, Aleppo, Syria. Banking. m. Lamya Zakri, 2 s, 2 d. Education: DEcon, Bach Deg, Fin, Belgium; LLB, France. Appointments: Dpty Chmn, Ctrl Bank of Oman, 1978-92; Dpty Dir, UNDP, NY; Dpty Gov, Cntrl Bank of Syria. Publications: Balance Sheet Analysis, 1960; Principles of Economics, 1964; Technology of Planning, 1968. Honour: H H Sultan Qaboos of Oman Awd, 1984. Memberships: Assn of Econs, Syria; Soc of Econs, Syria; Assn of Arbitrage. Hobbies: Swimming; Chess; Reading; Walking. Address: PO Box 16006, Aleppo, Syria.

KHAYOYEV Izatullo, b. 22 June 1936, Khodzhaikhok, Tajikistan. Official. Education: Tajik Univ; Higher Party Sch. Appointments: Fin Instns, 1954-61; Mbr, CPSU, 1961-91; Hd, Min og Agricl, 1961-63; Chair, Collective Farm, 1963-65; Snr Posts in State & CP Insts, 1966-78; Min of Meat & Dairy Ind, Tajik, 1978-83; 1st Sec, Kulyab Dist, 1983-86; Dpty, USSR Supreme Soviet, 1984-89; Cand Mbr, CPSU Ctrl Cttee, 1986-91; Chair, Cncl of Mins, Tajik, 1986-90; VP, Tajik, 1990-91; PM, 1991-92; Min of Fgn Econ Rels, 1992-94; Hd of Staff, of Pres Rakhmonov. Address: Office of the President, Dushanbe, Tajikistan.

KHAYRULLOYEV Sherali. Appointment: Min of Def, Tajikistan, 1995-. Address: Ministry of Defence, Dushanbe, Tajikistan.

KHETRAPAL CL, b. 25 Aug 1937, Sahival, India. Distinguished Professor; Vice-Chancellor. m. Shashi, 29 May 1963, 2 s. Education: PhD; MSc. Appointments: Vice Chan, Allahabad Univ, India; Distin Prof, SGPGI, Lucknow; Prof, Indian Inst of Science. Publications: Almost 250 rsch pprs, 20 books, reviews, monographs. Honours include: S S Bhatnagar Awd Chem scis; R K Asundi Lect Awd, INSA, 1990; Shastrabudhey Awd, Magpur Univ, 1994; Dr Jagdish Shankar Lect Awd, INSA, Local Chapt, Bombay; fell, Indian Natl Sci Acady; Natl Acady of Scis. Memberships: Fell, Indian Natl Sci Acady, New Delhi, 1981; Governing Cncls, Intl Socs of Magnetic Resonance and Magnetic Resonance in Biol Systems; Sec Gen, Intl Conf on Magnetic Resonance in Biol Systems, 1990-92; Fndr Pres, Natl Magnetic Resonance Soc, India; Nom Convenor, Bangalore Chapt (INSA), 1997-1998. Address: Vice Chancellor, University of Allahabad, Allahabad, India.

KHIEU Samphan, b. 1932, Svay Rieng, Cambodia. Politician. m. Khieu Ponnary. Education: Paris Univ. Appointments: Fndr, French-Lang Jrnl, Observer, Cambondia; Dpty, Natl Assembly on Prince Sihanouk's Party, Sangkum Reastr Nyum (Popular Socialist Cmty); Sec of State for Com; Joined Khmer Rouge, 1967; Min ofDef, Roy Govt, Natl Union of Cambodia, 1970-76; Dpty PM, 1970-76; Exile, 1970-75, 1975-76; Mbr, Politburo Natl United Front of Cambodia, 1970-79; C-in-C, Khmer Rough High Cmd, 1973-79; Pres of State Presidium (Hd of State), 1976-79; PM of the Khmer Rouge Opposition Govt, 1979-91; VP, Govt of Democratic Kampuchea, 1982-91; Pres, Khmer Rouge, 1985-91; Mbr, Supreme Natl Cncl, 1991-97; VP, Fgn Affairs, Natl Govt of Cambodia, 1991; Chair, Cambodian Natl Union Party, 1993-97; PM, Illegal Provisional Govt of Natl Unity, 1994-. Pres, Fndr, Natl Solidarity Party, 1997-.

KHIN-NWE-OO, b. 30 Aug 1950, Yangon, Myanmar. Microbiologist; Researcher. Education: MBBS, Inst Med, Yangon, 1974; DBact, 1982; MmEdSci, Microbiology, 1994. Appointments: AS, Ag San Tb, 1978-81; MO, NHL,

1981-83; RO, DMR, 1983-91; SRO, DMR, 1991-94; RS, DMR, 1994-97; DD?hd, DMR, 1997-. Publications: Pprs in intl profl jrnls. Honours: Fellshp, JICA, Japan, 1991-92; Best Poster Awd, Myanmar Hlth Rsch Congress, 1993; Medal for Pub Sev Awd, Govt of Myanmar, 1995. Memberships: Myanmar Medl Assn, 1978-; Myanmar Medl Micro Assn, 1992-. Hobby: Reading. Address: 90 Sabaichan 2nd Lane, Hlaing Township, Yangon, Myanmar.

KHISAMUTDINOV Amir Aleksandrovich, b. 16 Feb 1950, Krasnoiarsk, Russia. Researcher. Education: Grad, Navigator, Vladivostok Marine Coll, 1972; Grad, Econs, Vladivostok Far Eastern Fishing Higher Tech Inst, 1980; Grad, Hist, Far Eastern State Univ, Vladivostok, 1985; Cand in Hist, Far Eastern Tech Univ, 1999. Appointments: Navigator, Captains Mate, Far Eastern Shipping Co, 1973-74; Captain, 1974-75, Fleet Captain, 1975-80, Chf Marine Inspector, 1980-85, Maritime Regl Fishing Co; Acad Sec, 1985-90, Chmn, 1991, Far Eastern Br, USSR Geog Soc; Lectr, Far Eastern State Univ, Jrnlsm Dept, 1991; Pres, Far Eastern Studies Soc, 1991-93; Specl Reporter, Vladivostokskoe vremia, 1994-96; Snr Lectr, Engl, 1994, Japanese, 1995-96, Vladivostok Univ of Econs & Servs; Snr Bibliographer, Gorky Maritime Lib, 1995-; Rschr, Lectr, Oriental Studies, Far Eastern Tech Univ, 1998-. Publications: Sev articles in profl jrnls. Honours include: Lit Awd, 1985; Arthur L Andrews Disting Vis Prof of Asian & Pacific Studies Chair, Univ HI, 1992; MacArthur Fndn Travel Grant, 1997. Address: Far Eastern Technological University, Ul Gogolia 41, 690600 Vladivostok, Russia.

KHOO Khee Ming, b. 19 July 1942. Director. m. Chen Lee Lee, 1 s. Education: BAgrSci, Malaysia. Appointments: Rsch Offr, Harrisons & Crosfield Ltd, 1966; Snr Agronomist, SDP, 1972; Mngr, SDP, 1978; Planting Adviser, SDP, 1980; Estates Dir, SDP, 1987; Bus Dev Dir, Sime Darby Plantations, 1997-98; Chf Operating Offr, PPB Oil Palms Berhad, 1999-. Memberships: Agric Inst of Malaysia; Assoc, Malaysian Sci Assn; Malaysian Soils Sci Soc; Incorp Soc of Planters; Pres 1996-98, United Planting Assn of Malaysia; Cncl, Malayan Agric Prodrs Assn; Malaysian Cocoa Growers Cncl; Bd Mbr 1989-92, Malaysian Cocoa Bd; Bd Mbr 1988-91, Malaysian Rubber Rsch Dev Bd; Bd Mbr 1988-91, Intl Rubber Rsch Dev Bd. Hobby: Golf. Address: PPB Oil Palms Berhad, 15th Floor Wisma Jerneh, 38 Jalan Sultan Ismail, 50250 Kuala Lumpur, Malaysia.

KHUE Doan, Minister of National Defence. Appointment: Mbr, Politburo, Natl Def and Security Cncl. Address: Ministry of National Defence, 1 Hoang Dieu, Hanoi, Vietnam,

KHUNKITTI Suwit, b. 17 Oct 1957, Khonkaen, Thailand. Deputy Prime Minister; Minister of Science, Technology and Environment. Education: BA, Chem, Univ of KY, USA. Appointments: Mbr of Parl, 1983, 1986, 1988, 1991-92, 1995, 1996; Parly Sec, Min of Com, 1985, Min of For Affairs, 1986; Advsr, For Min, 1987; Parly Sec, Min of For Affairs, 1990; Min of Jus, 1992, 1996; Dpty Sec Gen, Prime Min for Pol Affairs, 1992; Dpty Min of Agric and Co-ops, 1995, Min, 1996; Dpty Prime Min, Min of Jus, Dpty Min, then Min, of Agric and Co-ops, Sec gen Socl Action Party, 1997. Memberships: Elected Mbr, Exec Cttee, Socl Scis Assn of Thailand, 1991; Chmn, Parly Rsch Plcy Cttee; Chmn, Stndg Cttee, House of Representative Affairs; Chmn, 1st Parly Dev Plan Drafting Cttee; Chmn, Stndng Cttee, Women and Yths Affairs; Chmn, Sub-Cttee, Econs for Tapioca Plcy; Khon Kaen Provl Assembly; Hon Pres, Thai Bar Assn, 1992, 1996-; Chan, Law Soc of Thailand, 1992, 1996-. Address: 99/99 Ngamwongwan Road, Chatuchak, Bangkok 10900, Thailand.

KHURSHID AHMED. Trade Unionist. m. Saihra Khurshid, 2 s, 4 d. Education: Law Grad, Univ of Punjab. Appointments: Gen Sec, Pakistan Workers Confederation, All Pakistan Fedn of Trade Unions and Pakistan WAPDA Hydro Elec Labour Union. Publications: Var books inclng Dignity of Labour; Labour -

Management Relations in Australia, Germany and Japan; Chf Ed, monthly, Pak Workers; Regular writer of articles in natl newpprs on labour issues. Honours: Elected VP, ILO Conf, 1986; Repr Workers Grp, ILO Governing Body as spokesman of var cttees. Memberships: ILO Governing Body, Workers Grp; Tripartite Standing Labour Commn of Pakistan; Natl Indl Rels Commn. Hobby: Trade Unionism. Address: Bukhtiar Labour Hall, 28 Nisbat Road, Lahore, Pakistan.

KHUSSAIBY Salim Bin Mohammed Bin Salim al, b. 11 Mar 1939. Diplomat. m. 3 children. Education: Tchrs Coll, Zanzibar; Police Offrs Coll, Kenya. Appointments: Tchr, Second Sch, Dubai, 1964-70; Roy Omani Police, 1970, Apptd Dpty Inspector Gen of Police & Customs; Min Plenipotentiary, Min of Fgn Affairs, 1976; Chargé d'affaires, Omani Emb, Nairobi; Consul Gen, Bombay, 1979; Amb to Kuwait, 1980, to Pakistan, 1982-87; Perm Rep to UN, 1987-. Address: Permanent Mission of Oman to the United Nations, 866 United Nations Plaza, Suite 540, NY 10017, USA.

KHUWEITER Abdul Aziz Abdallah al, b. 1927, Onaizah, Saudi Arabia. Politician. m. Fatima al-Khuweiter, 1963, 1 s, 3 d. Appointments: Vice Rector, King Saud Univ; Hd, Directorate Supervision & Follow-up; Fmr Min of Hlth; Min of Educn, 1987-95, of State, 1995-. Publications: Fi Turuk al Bahth; Tarikh Shafi Ibn Ali (ed); Al-Malik al-Zahir Baybars (in Arabic & English); Al-Rawd al Zahir (ed); Min Hatab al-Layl; Ayy-Bunayy; Qiraah Fi Diwan al-Sha'ir Muh; Uthaymin. Honours: King Abdulaziz Order of Merit (2nd class); Repub Order, Sudan (1st class). Hobby: Reading. Address: Council of Ministers, Murabba Riyadh 11121, Saudi Arabia.

KIBBLE Robert Maclean, b. 9 Dec 1935, Sydney, Australia. Veterinary Surgeon. m. Mathilde Kearny-Kibble, 14 Jan 1978, 2 s, 1 d. Education: Hawkesbury Dip in Agric; BVSc; MACVS; Fell, Austl Veterinary Assn, Justice of the Peace. Honour: Fell of AVA, 1991. Memberships: Pres, Austl Vet Assn, 1990-91; Pres, Animal Welfare League, 1990-97. Hobbies: Human Animal Interactions; Veterinary Politics. Address: 107 Fox Valley Road, Wahroonga, 2076, Australia.

KIBRIA Shah A M S, b. 1 May 1931, Sylhet. United Nations Official. m. 1 s, 1 d. Education: Univ of Dacca; Fletcher Sch of Law and Diplomacy, Boston, MA, USA. Appointments: Joined Diplomatic Serv of Pakistan, 1954; Served Var Embs until 1971; Declared Allegiance to Bangladesh, Joined Bangladesh Mission, Wash DC, 1971; Dir-Gen, Polit Affairs Dept, Min of For Affairs, 1972; Sec, Min of For Affairs, 1972-73; High Commnr in Aust, 1973-76; Perm Rep to UN Offs, Geneva, 1976-78; Chair, Preparatory Cttee, Grp of 77 for UNCTAD V, Geneva, 1978; Fgn Sec, Min of For Affairs, 1978-81; Exec Sec, UN Econ and Socl Commn for Asia and The Pacific, 1981-92; Specl Rep of UN Sec-Gen for Coordination of Cambodian Humanitarian Assistance Progs, 1987; Polit Advsr to Pres of Awami League, 1994-; Min for Fin, Govt of People's Repub of Bangladesh, 1996. Address: House No 58, Road No 3/A, Dhanmondi Residential Area, Dhaka 5, Bangladesh.

KIDD Doug, b. 1941, Levin. Politician; Lawyer. m. 3 children. Appointments: Wisheart MacNab & Ptnrs, law firm, 1965-79; Fmr Pt-time Mussel Farmer, Marlborough Sounds; Natl Party MP for Marlborough/Kaikoura, 1978-; Min of State-Owned Enterprises of Fisheries, Assoc Min of Fin, 1990-91; Assoc Min of Fin, Min of Maori Affairs, 1991-94; Min of Energy, of Fisheries & Labour, 1994-96, for Accident Rehab & Compensation Ins; Speaker, House of Reps, 1996; Chair, Parl Serv Comm. Membership: Fmr Fndn Pres, Marlborough Forest Owners Assn. Address: Parliament Buildings, Wellington, New Zealand.

KIDMAN Fiona Judith, b. 26 Mar 1940, New Zealand. Writer. m. Ian Kidman, 20 Aug 1966, 1 s, 1 d. Appointments: Dpty Libn, Rotorua Pub Lib, 1958-62; Sec, Organizer, NZ Book Cncl, 1972-75, Pres of Hon, 1997; Prodr, Radio NZ, 1976-81. Publications include: A Breed of Women, 1979; Mandarin Summer, 1981; Paddy's Puzzle, 1984; The Book of Secrets, 1987; True Stars,

1990; Ricochet Baby, 1996; The House Within (short stories), 1997; The Best of Fiona Kidman's Short Stories, 1998; Sev short stories, poems, plays and non fiction. Honours: Schlsp in Letters, 1981, 1996; Vic Writers Fell, 1988; DCNZ, 1998. Memberships: PEN NZ Cntr; Pres, NZ Book Cncl, 1992-95; Pres of Hon, NZ Book Cncl; Patron, Cambodia Trust. Hobbies: Gardening; Theatre; Promoting New Zealand Writing. Address: PO Box 14-401, Kilbirnie, Wellington, New Zealand.

KIDMAN Nicole, b. 20 June 1967, Hawaii, USA (Austl). Actress. m. Tom Cruise, 1990, 1 s adopted, 1 d adopted. Education: St Martin's Yth Th, Melbourne; Austl Th for Young People, Sydney. Appointments: Goodwill Amb, UNICEF; Actress, TV mini-series, Vietnam, 1987; Bangkok Hilton, 1989; Film appearances incl: Emerald City; The Year My Voice Broke; Flirting; Dead Calm, 1990; Days of Thunder, 1990; Billy Bathgate, 1991; Far and Away, 1992; Malice, 1993; My Life, 1993; Batman Forever, 1995; To Die For, 1995; Portrait of a Lady, 1996; Peacemaker; Eyes Wide Shut, 1997; Practical Magic, 1998. Theatre: The Blue Room, 1999. Honours: Actress of the Yr for Vietnam, Aust; Seattle Intl Film Fest Awd, 1995; London Film Critics Awd, 1996; Brdcst Film Critics Awd, 1996; BAFTA Nom, 1996; Best Actress for To Die For, Golden Globe Awd, 1996; People's Choice Awds, Favourite Austl Movie Star (female), Favourite Intl Movie Star (female), 1998. Address: c/o Ann Churchill-Brown, Shanahan's Management, PO Box 478, Kings Cross, NSW 2011, Australia.

KIDMAN Robert Conway, b. 18 Aug 1934, Port Lincoln, Aust. Former General Manager. m. Helen, 26 Feb 1960, 3 s, 1 d. Appointments: Natl Aust Bank Ltd: Mngr, N Terrace Br, Adelaide, 1966-68, Asst Mngr, Adelaide Off, 1968-70, Asst Mngr, Investment Servs, Melbourne, 1970-72, Mngr, Investment Servs, Sydney, 1972-73, London, Eng, 1973-77, Mngr, Intl Banking, Sydney, Aust, 1977-81, Asst State Mngr, NSW, 1981-83, State Mngr, Retail Banking, 1984, Gen Mngr, Qld, 1984-90; Dir, Life Plan Finl Grp, St Andrews Hosp Inc; Cmmnr of Charitable Funds; Dir, Friendly Soc Medl Assn Ltd. Memberships: Fell, Austl Inst of Bankers; Fell, Austl Inst of Mngmt; Fell, Austl Inst of Co Dirs. Hobbies: Tennis; Swimming; Reading. Address: 48 Molesworth Street, North Adelaide, SA 5006, Australia.

KIERNAN Ian Bruce Carrick, b. 4 Oct 1940, Sydney, NSW, Aust. m. Judy, 2 d. Career: Builder; Competitive yacht racer, repr Aust at the Admiral's Cup, South Cross Cup, Trans Pacific yacht races; Solo yacht racer, 1970s-; Repr Aust in BOC Challenge solo around the world yacht race sailing the Spirit of Sydney, finished 6th, set Austl record for solo circumnavigation (156 days), 1986-87; Chmn, Clean Up Aust (natl non-profit orgn), coord Clean-Up Aust Day, 9x 1990-99; Spokesperson, Clean Up Aust and Clean Up the World; Presenter, Living Earth segments on Discovery Channel, Aust, NZ. Publication: (autobiography) Coming Clean (w Phil Jarratt), 1995. Honours: OAM, 1991; Austl of Yr, 1994; AO, 1995; Natl Living Treas, 1998; Utd Nations Global 500 Laureate; Adv Aust Awd; UN Sasakawa Environmental Awd. Memberships: Cncl Mbr, Ausl Natl Maritime Mus; Mbr, Premier's Olympic Bus Roundtable; Chmn, Coop Rsch Cntr for Waste Mngmt & Pollution Control (CRC); Cttee Mbr, NRMA's Clean Air 2000 initiative; Patron, Stream Watch; Patron, Sailors w disabilities, Together Alone Expedition Icebound and Lord Howe Island Pub Sch. Hobbies: Sailing; Skiing; Swimming; Surf. Address: Clean Up Australia Ltd, 18 Bridge Rd, Glebe, NSW 2037, Australia.

KIERULFF Stephen, b. 17 June 1942, Los Angeles, California, USA. Psychologist; Writer. 1 s. Education: BA, Cultural Anthropol; MA, Tchng; PhD, Psychol. Appointments: Adj Prof, Psychol, CA Univ, Long Beach, Antioch Univ, Los Angeles. Publications: Sev articles in profl jrnls. Memberships: Amn Psychol Assn; Assn for Humanistic Psychol; CA Psychol Assn; Psi Chi. Hobbies: Walking; Reading; Writing. Address: 3201 Wilshire Boulevard, Suite 201, Santa Monica, CA 90403, USA.

KIHARA Yasuki, b. 8 Feb 1955, Hiroshima, Japan. Cardiologist. m. Miho Yukitoshi, 7 Oct 1979, 1 s, 2 d. Education: BSc, Kyoto Univ, 1973-75; MD, Kyoto Univ Sch of Med, 1975-79; PhD, Grad Sch of Med, Kyoto Univ, 1982-86. Appointments: Jnr Res in Med, 1979-81, Snr Res, 1981-82, Tenri Hosp, Nara, Japan; Clin Fell, Kyoto Univ Hosp, 1986; Rsch Fell in Med, 1986-87, Instr in Med, 1987-89, Harvard Med Sch, USA; Asst Prof, Toyama Med and Pharm Univ, Japan, 1993-; Asst Prof, Kyoto Univ Fac of Med, 1993-. Publications: Sev articles in profl med jrnls. Honours: Rsch Awd, Yamanouchi Fndn, Tokyo, 1986; Rsch Fellshp, Amn Heart Assn, 1987-88; Finalist, R I Bing Awd, 1989; Rsch Awd, Japan Heart Fndn, Tokyo, 1991; Rsch Awd, Yokoyama Fndn, Nagoya, 1992; Sagawa Yng Investigator Awd, 10th Intl Conf of Cardiovascular Syst Dynamics Soc, Kobe, 1992. Memberships: Japan Soc of Internal Med; Japanese Circulation Soc; Am Heart Assn; Am Coll of Cardiol, assoc fell; Am Assn for the Adv of Sci; Sigma Xi; Intl Soc for Heart Rsch, Tokyo. Address: 4-9-2 Minamishiga, Otsu Shiga 520, Japan.

KIJIMA Takashi, b. 24 Dec 1920, USA. Photographer. Publications: (photo books) The Orchid, 1975; Yoshitsune Senbon Sakuka, 1981; The Original Orchids, 1987. Honours: Life Advtng Awd, USA, 1960; Annual Awd, The Photog Soc of Japan, 1976; The Order of the Sacred Treasure Gold Rays w Rosette, Japan, 1991. Memberships: Japan Profl Photogrs Soc; Japan Advtng Pgotogrs Assn; The Photog Soc of Japan. Address: 2-7 Tomihisa-Cho, Shinjuku-ku, Tokyo 162-0067, Japan.

KILE Glen Ashley, b. 2 Dec 1946, Hobart, Tasmania. Chief, CSIRO Forestry and Forest Products. m. Jane Elizabeth, 1 s, 1 d. Education: BAgrSc (Hon); PhD (Tas). Appointments: Rsch Sci, Prog Mngr, CSIRO Div of Forest Rsch, 1972-90; Dir, Co-op Rsch Cntr Temperate Hardwood Forestry, 1991; Chf, CSIRO Forestry and Forest Prods, 1996-. Publications: Over 100 publs (rsch spec on forest hlth and related issues). Memberships: Standng Cttee Forestry, 1992-; Chmn, Forest Hlth Cttee of SCF; Natl Cncl of Greening Aust; Natl Plantations Advsry Cttee, 1991. Address: CSIRO Forestry and Forest Prods, PO Box E 4008, Kingston, ACT 2604, Australia.

KILMER Val, b. 31 Dec 1959, Los Angeles, USA. Actor. div, 1 d. Education: Hollywood's Profl Sch, Juilliard. Appointments: Stage Appearances incl: Electra & Orestes, Henry IV Part 1, 1981; As You Like It, 1982; Slab Boys, 1983; Hamlet, 1988; Tis Pity She's A Whore, 1992; Sev appearances on TV. Creative Works: Films: Top Secret, 1984; Real Genius, 1985; Top Gun, 1986; Willow, 1988; Kill Me Again, 1989; The Doors, 1991; Thunderheart, 1991; True Romance, 1993; The Real McCoy, 1993; Tombstone, 1993; Wings of Courage, 1995; Batman Forever, 1995; Heat, 1995; The Saint, 1996; The Island of Dr Moreau, 1996; The Ghost and the Darkness, 1996; Dead Girl, 1996. Address: c/o CAA, 9830 Wilshire Boulevard, Beverly Hills, CA 90212, USA.

KIM Chae-Han, b. 16 Feb 1962, Pusan, Korea. m. Cho, 9 Apr 1996, 1 d. Education: BA, Seoul Natl Univ; PhD, Univ of Rochester. Appointments: Fell, Hoover Instn, USA, 1987-88; Prof of Polit Sci, 1991-, Acting Dir, 1997-, Hallym Univ, Korea. Publications: Game Theory and Inter-Korean Relations, 1995; Rationality and Irrationality in the Korean Society, 1998. Membership: Dir, Korean Assn of Intl Studies, 1999. Address: Department of Political Sciences, Hallym University, Chunchon 200-702, Korea.

KIM Chol Yong, b. 28 Nov 1935, Japan. Tourism Researcher. m. M H Hahn, 20 May 1961, 2 s. Education: Grad, Seoul Natl Univ, 1954-59; MA, George Washington Univ, 1986-88; PhD, VA Polytech Inst and State Univ, 1987-92. Appointments: Snr Staff, Bur of Tourism, Min of Transp, 1957-69; Dir, Plng Dept and Tourism Promotion Dept, Bur to Tourism, Min of Transp, 1969-77; Dir-Gen, Bur of Inspection, Land Transp Bur, Bur of Tourism, Transp Policy Bur, Civil Aviation Bur, Min of Transp, 1977-86; Lectr, Hanyang Univ, Pres, Korean Air Transp Rsch Inst, 1992-93; Admnstr, Korea Maritime and Port Admin, 1993-95; Pres, Korea Tourism Rsch Inst, 1996-98; Dean, Grad Sch of Tourism, Sejong Univ, 1999-. Publication: International Tourism, 1996. Honours: Order of Serv Merit, Green Stripes, 1972; Order of Serv Merit, Yellow Stripes, 1996. Hobby: Golf. Address: 708-404 Sadang 3 Dong, Dongjak-xu, Seoul, Korea.

KIM Dae-Jung, b. 3 Dec 1925, Hugwang-ri, Ha-ui-myon, Shin-an-gun, South Cholla Prov, Korea. President of Korea. Education: Attended grad prog, bus admin, Korea Univ, Seoul, 1964; Non-degree grad prog, Inst of Indl Mngmt, Kyunghee Univ, Seoul, 1967; MA Prog, Econs, Kyunghee Univ, 1970; Visng Fell, Cntr for Intl Affairs, Harvard Univ, MA, USA, 1983-84; PhD, Polit Sci, Dipl Acady of For Min of Russia, Moscow, 1992; Visng Fell, Clare Hall Coll, Cambridge Univ, 1993. Appointments include: Pres, Mokpo Merchant Ship Co, 1948; Arrested by N Korean Communists, broke out of jail to escape execution, 1950; Pres, Mokpo Daily News, 1950; Dpty Cmdr, S Cholla Reg, Maritime Def Force, 1950; Pres, Heungkuk Merchant Shipping Co, 1951; Pres, Dae-yang Shipbuilding Co, 1951; Mbr, Cntrl Cttee Dem Party, 1957; Spokesman, ruling Dem Party, 1960; Elected to 5th Natl Assembly (diss by mil coup), 1961; Re-elected, 6th Natl Assembly, 1963; Chmn, Policy Plng Cncl, Mbr Cntrl Exec Bd Minjungdang, 1966; Elected Mbr, Party Cntrl Exec Bd, elected 7th Natl Assembly, 1967; Survived assassination attempts, 1971, 1973; Exile, 1972-73; Prison sentence, suspended, under house arrest, 1977-79; Further imprisonment, exile to USA, return to house arrest, 1980-87; Fndr, Party for Peace & Dem, 1987; Fndr, New Dem Party, 1991; Merged into Dem Party (DP), 1991; Estab, Kim Dae-jung Peace Fndn for Asia Pacific Reg, 1994; Elected pres, Repub Of Korea, 1997. Publications: Num in Korean, Engl and other langs. Honours: Num intl awds incl: Bruno Kreisky Hum Rights Awd, Austria, 1981; George Meany Hum Rights Awd, AFL-Clo, USA, 1987; 9 noms for Nobel Peace Prize, 1987-95. Address: Chong Wa Dae, 1 Sejongno, Chongno-gu, Seoul, Korea.

KIM Dong-Kun, b. 3 Oct 1930, Seoul, Korea. Government Official; Politician. m. Ko Wha-Young, 2 s, 5 d. Education: BA, Korea Mil Acady; MPA, Yonsei Univ, Grad Sch, 1970-71. Appointments: Asst Dpty Dir, Dir-Gen Agcy, Natl Security & Plng, 1966; Consul-Gen, Repub of Sudan, Min of For Affairs (MOFA), 1976-77; Amb, Repub of Sudan, MOFA, 1977-79; Amb, Repub of Finland, MOFA, 1979-84; Amb at Large, MOFA, 1984-85; Chf Sec to Pres, New Dem Repub Party, 1988-90; Chf Sec to Co-Chmn, Dem Lib Party, 1990-; Mbr, 14th Ntl Assembly, Natl Assembly, For Aff & Unification Cttee, Natl Assembly, Natl Def Cttee, 1992-96; Dir-Gen, Cntrl Polit Trng Inst, New Korea Party, 1995-96; New Korea Party, Grand Natl Party, Ntl Policy Advsry Cttee, Chmn, For Affairs & Unification Cttee, 1996-; Standing Advsr, Korea Airport Constrn Auth, 1996-. Address: Gaepo Woosung Apt 8-1305, Taechi-Dong, Kangnam-ku, Seoul, Korea.

KIM Hak-Hoon, b. 8 June 1956, Seoul, Korea. Professor. 2 s. Education: BA, Seoul Natl Univ, 1981; MA, CA State Univ, Los Angeles, 1986; PhD, Univ of AZ, 1993. Appointments: Geog Tchr, Kumho Mid Sch 1981-82; Tchng Asst, Univ of AZ, 1987-92; Rsch Specialist, Univ of AZ, 1992-93; Prof in Geog, Chongju Univ, 1994-. Publications: Articles in var jrnls; Man and Environment. Honours: Alumni Cert of Hon, CA State Univ, 1986. Memberships: Assoc of Amn Geogs, 1988-; Korean Geogl Soc, 1991-; Korean Regl Sci Assoc, 1994-. Hobbies: Tennis; Tvl; Classical Guitar. Address: Chongju Univ, Dept Geography, Chongju 360-764, Korea.

KIM Hyong-O, b. 30 Nov 1947, Kosung, South Korea. Member, National Assembly. m. Jhee In-Kyong, 31 Jan 1978, 2 d. Education: MA, Polit Sci, Grad Sch, Seoul Natl Univ, 1975; Dr Course, Polit Sci, Kyong-Nan Univ, 1988. Appointments: Reporter, Dong-a Ilbo, Newsppr, 1976-78; Snr Rschr, Inst of Fgn Affairs & Natl Security, Min of Fgn Affairs, 1978-82; Dir, Off of Press Sec to the Pres, Polit Affairs Sec to the Pres, 1982-86; Sec, Off of Polit Affairs to the PM, 1986-90; Specialist, Democracy & Harmony Promotion Cttee, 1988; Chf, Off of the Admin for the '89 Parly Inspection, 1989; Sec, Off of Polit Affairs to the Pres, 1990. Publications: The Parliament, Party and Politics in England, 1983; The Future of Conservative Party in Korea, 1989. Memberships: Korean Assn of Intl Studies; Korean Polit Sci Assn; Chmn, Pusan Yongdo-Ku Dist Chapt, New Korea Party, 1990-. Hobby: Reading. Address: E-605, Mi-Sung Apt, Youido dong, Youngdungpo-ku, Seoul, Korea.

KIM Jae-Ho, b. 26 Dec 1936, Seoul, Korea. Opthalmology. m. K S Suh, 15 Oct 1966, 2 d. Education: PhD, MD, Sci Med Dr/MSc, BS, Grad Sch, Cath Univ Medl Coll. Appointments: Chmn, Cath Fndn, Eye Rsch; Dean, Grad Sch, Cath Univ. Publication: Textbook of Opthalmology Eye-Health. Honours: Distinguished Awd, APAO; Dong-Back-Chang, Natl Awd, Korea. Memberships: Korean Medl Assn; Korean Opthalmology Soc; IIIC; ASCRS; AAO; APAO. Hobby: Golf. Address: Department of Opthalmology, Catholic University Medical College, Kangnam, St Mary's Hospital, 505 Banpo-dong, Seocho-Ku, Seoul, 137-040, Korea.

KIM Jong Il, b. 16 Feb 1942, Korea. Politician. m. 1 child. Education: Kim Il Sung Univ, Pyongyang. Appointments: Dpty Dir, Dir, Dept of Ctrl Cttee, Workers' Party of Korea, 1964-73; Sec, Ctrl Cttee, 1973; Mbr, Polit Comm Ctrl Cttee, 1974; Mbr, Presidium of Politburo of Ctrl Cttee of Korean Workers Party, 1980-, Sec-Gen, 1997-; Sec, Korean Workers Party, 1980-; Mbr, Mil Comm Ctrl Cttee at 6th Party Congress, 1980; Dpty to Supreme Peoples Assembly, 1982; 1st Vice Chair, Natl Def Comm, 1990-93, Chair, 1993-; Supreme Cmdr, Korean Peples Army, 1991-; Marshal, Democratic Peoples Repub of Korea, 1992-. Publications: Selected Works of Kim Jong Il (8 vols); For the Completion of the Revolutionary Cause of Juche (8 vols). Honours include: Kim Il Sung Order (3 times); Title, Marshall, 1992; Orden de Solidaridad, Cuba; Grand Croix de l'Ordre nat des Mille Collines; Rwanda Necklace. Address: Central Committee of the Workers Party of Korea, Pyongyang, Korea.

KIM Ke Bom, b. 4 June 1936, Seoul, Korea. Stockbroker; Financial Planner. m. Myung So Chung, 6 June 1964, 2 s. Education: BS, Univ of Redlands, CA, 1959; MS, Yale Univ, 1961; MIA, 1963. Appointments: CFP, 1984; Snr VP, 1986. Memberships: Stockbroker Assn. Hobbies: Reading; Tennis; Music. Address: Morgan Stanley Dean Witter, 601 S, Figueroa St, Los Angeles, CA 90017-5704, USA.

KIM Kwang Sik, b. 9 June 1947, Seoul, Korea. Medicine. m. Aeran, 30 June 1983, 1 s, 1 d. Education: BS, Seoul Natl Univ, 1967; MD, 1971. Appointments: Asst Prof, Pediats, Harbor UCLA Medl Cntr, 1980-86; Attng Physn, 1980-86; Assoc Prof, Pediats, Childrens Hosp LA, 1986-91; Attng Physn, 1986-; Prof, Pediats, 1991-; Hd, Div of Infectious Diseases, 1992-; Prof, Molecular Microbiol and Immunology, USC Sch of Med, 1997-. Creative Works: 118 Orig Articles; 14 Book Chapts; 2 Book Reviews; 101 Abstracts; Many invited talks and sems. Honours: The Mead Johnson Labs Awd for Outstndng Pediat Res, 1977; Advd Rsch Fellshp, 1981; Basil O'Connor Rsch Grant, 1982; Snr Investigator, Amn Heart Assn, 1983; The 1996-97 Fac Rsch and Innovation Fund, 1986; Fogarty Snr Intl Fellshp, 1996; NIH Grantee, 1984-. Memberships: Amn Soc for Microbiol; The Lancefield Soc; W Soc for Pediat Rsch; Infectious Diseases for Pediat Rsch; Infectious Diseases Soc of Am; NY Acady Sci; Amn Assn for the Advmnt of Sci; Pediat Infectious Disease Soc; Soc for Pediat Rsch; Amn Fndn for Clinl Rsch; Amn Pediat Soc; Amn Soc for Cell Bio; NIH Stdy Sect, FDA Vaccine and Related Biol Products Advsry Cttee. Address: Division of Infectious Diseases, Children's Hospital Los Angeles, 4650 Sunset Blvd, Mailstop #51, Los Angeles, CA 90027, USA.

KIM Kwang Ung, b. 20 July 1944, Korea. Researcher. m. Y J Kim, 19 Dec 1970, 1 s, 1 d. Education: BS; MS; PhD. Appointments: Lab Hd (KIST); Adj Prof (sev univs); Visng Prof, MMI, USA; Dir Gen, MOST; Dir, KIST. Publications: Mysterious Engineering Plastics, Kyumjisa, Jan 1988; Polymer Rheology, Moonwoon-Dang, 1994. Honours: Min of Def, 1966; Min of Sci and Technol, 1990, 1991; Decoration of Hon, 1993. Memberships: Polymer

Proc Soc; Soc of Plastics Eng; Soc of Rheology. Address: Korea Institute of Science and Technology, 39-1 Hawolgok-Dong, Sungbuk-Ku, Seoul, Korea 136-791.

KIM Kwang-Iel, b. 6 Dec 1936. Psychiatrist; Professor. m. 10 May 1965, Haeshin, 2 s, 1 d. Education: MD, Sch of Med, Seoul Natl Univ, 1961; PhD, Postgrad Sch, Seoul Natl Univ, 1967. Appointments: Assoc Prof, Kyung Hee Univ Medl Sch, 1971-74; Prof, Hanyang Univ Medl Sch, 1974-; Pres, Korean Neuropsych Assn, 1985-86; Pres, Mental Hlth Rsch Inst, Hanyang Univ, 1974-97; Cttee Mbr, Transcultural Psych Sect, WPA, 1985-; Ed in Chf, Korean Neuropsych Assn Jrnl, 1989-95. Publications: Books: Psychoanalytic Study of Traditional Korean Culture, 1983; Family Violence, 1989; Mental Health of Salaried Men, 1995; Anthropology of Madness, 1981; Beyond the Fantasy, 1979; The Fact and Structure of Pentacostalism in Korea, 1979; Numerous Articles; 400 Papers. Honours: Awd of Medl Rsch, 1974; Awd of Best Psych Rsch, 1985; Today's Book for Psychoanalytic Stdy of Korean Tradl Culture, 1984; Baeknam Awd, 1988; 1st prize, Wyeth Ayerst Awd, 1989; Byokbong Awd, 1993. Memberships: Korean Neuropsych Assn, 1961-; Transcultural Sect, WPA, 1983-; Korean Anthropological Assn, 1964-; Active Mbr, Korean Acady of Sci & Technol, 1994-. Address: Department of Neuropsychiatry, Hanyang University Medical School, Seoul 133-792, Korea.

KIM Kyong-Dong, b. 11 Nov 1936, Andong Cty, Korea. University Professor of Sociology. m. On-Jook Lee, 28 Mar 1970, 2 d. Education: BA, Sociol, Seoul Natl Univ, 1955-59; MA, Sociol, Univ of Michigan, 1961-62; PhD, Sociol, Cornell Univ, 1969-71. Appointments: Prof, Seoul Women's Univ, 1961-67; Instr, Seoul Natl Univ, 1968-69; Prof, NC State Univ, 1971-77; Prof, Seoul Natl Univ, 1977-; Adj Prof, Duke Univ, 1996-. Publications: Rethinking Development, 1985; Social Change in Korea, 1993; Education in Korea, 1998. Honours: Fell, W Wilson Intl Cntr for Schls, 1986-87; Grand Prize for Schl Achievement, 19th Chung-Ang Grand Prize, 1993. Memberships: Amn Soc Assn, 1962-; Alpha Kappa Delta, 1972-; Korean Sociol Assn, Pres, 1989; Assn for Info Soc, Pres, 1997-. Hobbies: Singing; Drawing; Golf. Address: Department of Sociology, Seoul National University, San 56-1, Shilling-dong, Kwanak-Ku, Seoul 151-742, Korea.

KIM Kyung-Ho, b. 3 Feb 1961, Eui-Jung-Bu. Senior Engineer. m. Chan-Joo Park, 26 Sept 1987, 1 s, 1 d. Education: PhD. Appointments: Samsung Electrons, 1983-. Publications: Many patents and techl pprs in IEEE Jrnl. Honour: Samsung Grp CAd Prize, Seoul, 1995. Memberships: KITE, 1987-; IEEE, 1988-. Hobby: Golf. Address: Kuk-Dong Apt 102-204, mai-tan 2 Dong, Pal-Dal Gu, Suwon, Korea 442-372.

KIM Nam-Hyun, b. 20 June 1935, Korea. Professor; Medical Doctor. m. Keum-Bong Han, 17 May 1962, 1 s, 4 d. Education: Med Dr, 1961; Master of Med Sci, 1966; Spec of Orthopaedic Surg, 1966; Doctorate of Med Sci, 1973. Appointments: Internship, Severance Hosp, 1962; Res, 1966; Instr, 1970; Asst Prof, 1973; Assoc Prof, 1977; Prof, 1980; Prof, Chmn, Dept of Orthopaedic Surg, 1988, Yonsei Univ; Elder, Chung Dong First Meth Ch, 1977; Med Cnslt, Korean Min of Defence, 1989; Med Cnslt of Korean Air, 1990; Pres, Soc of Korean Traffic Med, 1990; Pres, Korean Christian Med Assn; Pres, Korean Soc of Spine Surg, 1993; Pres, Korean Orthopaedic Assn, 1997-98. Publication: Text Book of Orthopaedics, in Korean, 1982; Textbook of Spine Surgery, in Korean, 1998. Honours: ManRae Acad Awd, ManRae Fndn, 1992, 1994; Acad Awd, Korean Orthopaedic Assn, 1993, 1996; Koream Fedn of Sci and Technol Socs, 1992. Memberships: Korean Medl Assn, 1961; Korean Orthopaedic Assn, 1966; Western Pacific Orthopaedic Assn, 1974; Societe Intl de Chirurgie Orthopedique et de Traumatologie, 1978; Korean Acady of Rehab Med, Seoul, Korea, 1984; Intl Soc for Study of Lumbar Spine, 1992; Intl Assn for Accident and Traffic Med, Uppsala, Sweden, 1992; AO Alumni Assn, Switzerland, 1993; Aerospace Medl Assn of Korea, 1994; Intl Affiliate Mbr, Amn Acady of Orthopaedic Surgs, 1997. Listed In: Many including: International Register of Profiles, 1994; Men of Achievement, 1994; Dictionary of International Biography, 1996. Address: 109-15 Yonhee-Dong, Seodaemoon-ku, Seoul 120-111, Korea.

KIM Sang-Joon, b. 12 July 1932, Unyang, Kyongnam, Korea. Professor of Political Science. m. Jung Sun Shen, 27 Dec 1967, 2 s. Education: BSFS, Georgetown, 1957; PhD, Yale, 1964. Appointments: Instr, St Joseph Coll, 1962-64; Asst Prof, St John's Univ, 1964-69; Prof, Sogang Univ, 1969-. Publications: Theories of International Politics I & II, 1977-80; Korean Politics, 1993. Memberships: Pres, Korean Polit Assn, 1989-90; Pres, Korean Fedn of Cath Profs Assn, 1993-94. Address: Hansol 701, 177-4 Bang Yidong, Songpa-Gu, Seoul 138-052, Korea.

KIM Seock Sam, b. 7 Feb 1949, Kimchon, Korea. Professor. m. Moohyun Chang, 24 Feb 1973, 1 s, 2 d. Education: DEng, Tohoku Univ, Japan. Appointments: Rschr, Korean Inst of Machine and Metal, 1974-79; Prof, Kyungpook Natl Univ, 1979-99. Publications: Precision Measurement Theory and Application, 1986. Honour: Excellent Ppr, 1997. Memberships: Korean Soc of Mechl Engrs; Japanese Soc Tribologists; Korean Soc Tribologists and Lubrication Enngrs. Hobby: Mountain climbing. Address: Sangin Chunggu Town 103-702, 1520 Sangin-Dong, Dalseo-Ku, 704-370 Taegu, Korea.

KIM Won-Bae, b. 17 Dec 1949, Pusan, Korea. Research Professor. m. Young S, 2 s. Education: Master Deg, City & Regl Planning; PhD, Urban & Regl Econs. Appointments: Rsch Fell, E-W Cntr, 1985-86; Asst Prof, Univ HI, 1986; Fell, E-W Cntr, 1987-95; Assoc Prof, Snr Fell, Univ HI. Publictions: Asian NIEs and the Global Economy, 1995; Culture and the City in East Asia, 1997. Memberships: Regl Sci Assn; Assn for NE Asian Econ. Address: Korea Research Institute for Human Settlements, 1591-6 Kwanyang-dong, Dongan-ku, Anyang-shi, Kyoggi-do, Korea.

KIM Yong Nam, Politician. Appointments: Mbr, Ctrl Cttee, Workers Party of Korea, 1970; Polit Commnr, 1977; Mbr, Polit Bur, 1980; Vice-Premier, Min of Fgn Affairs, 1983-; Del to Supreme Peoples Assembly. Address: Ministry of Foreign Affairs, Pyongyang, Korea.

KIM Young Koo, b. 26 June 1939, Seoul, Korea. Professor of International Law. m. Sung Suk Lee, 9 Oct 1969, 1 s, 1 d. Education: JD, Hanyang Univ Grad Sch, 1984. Appointments: Staff Judge Advocate, ROK Fleet, 1971-75; Dpty, ROK Navy, 1975-80; Dean, Fac of Naval War Coll, 1981-87; Prof, Intl Law, Korean Maritime Univ, 1989-. Publications: Treaties and Documents on the Law of the Sea, 1998; Korea and the Law of the Sea, 1999. Honours: Medal of Merit, 1982; Best Working Schl Awd, Korean Assn of Intl Law, 1997; Best Purisprudence Dissertation Awd, Korean Legal Cntr. Memberships: VP, Korean Assn of Intl Law, 1996-98. Hobby: Tennis. Address: 202 Building 6, Whashin Villa, 213-35 Tongsamdong Youngdoku, Pusan 606-080, Korea.

KIM Young Sam, b. 20 Dec 1927, Koje-gun, Korea. Politician. m. Myoung Soon Sohn, 2 s, 3 d. Education: Pusan Univ; Seoul Natl Univ. Appointments: Mbr, Natl Assembly, 1954-79; Fndr Mbr, Democratic Party, 1955; Pres, New Democratic Party, 1974, 1979; Co-Chair, Cncl for Promotion of Democracy, 1984; Presl Cand, 1987; Fndr Pres, Reunification Democracy Party, 1987-90; Exec Chair, Democratic Liberal Party, 1990-97, Pres, 1992-97; Pres, Repub of Korea, 1992-97. Publictions: There is No Hill We Can Depend On; Politics is Long and Political Power is Short; Standard-Bearer in His Forties; My Truth and My Country's Truth. Honours include: Martin Luther King Peace Prize, 1995. Hobbies: Calligraphy; Mountain Climbing; Jogging; Swimming.

KIMES (PEARSON) Casey, b. 5 June 1954, W Germany, Bad Kreunach. Educational Training Consultant. Education: BA, Linfield Coll, USA; ME, Linfield Coll, USA; MSc, Oxford Brookes Univ, UK; PhD, MacQuarie Univ, Aust. Appointments: Served on Bds: Pacific Children's Cntr; Oakland Yth Chorus; AITD; AITDO; Oxford Brookes Prog Review Bd Sch of Hotel & Catering Inst. Publication: (co-auth) Winning the 5 Star Way. Memberships: NY Acady of Scis; Amn Mngmt Assn; Austl Inst of Trng & Dev; Asian Rim Trng & Dev Org. Hobbies: Travel; Wine; Cultural diversity. Address: 11 Fingal Avenue, Glenhaven, NSW 2156, Australia.

KING Geoffrey Moore, b. 15 Sept 1920, Brisbane, Aust. Retired Company Director. m. Rae Benjamin, 4 Jan 1947, 2 s, 1 dec, 1 d. Appointments: Dir, H M King & Son P/L 1947-57; Mkt Dev Dir, Brit Motor Corp Ltd, 1959-60; Gen Mngr, Angus & Robertson (Booksellers) Ltd, 1961-63; Exec Chmn Austl and NZ Book Co Pty Ltd, 1964-83; Chmn, Craftsman Press and Craftsman House P/L, 1981-94. Honours: Serv 2/2 Austl Anti-tank Regt, 1940-45; Awd'd Paul Harris Fell, Rotary Intl, 1994; Mbr Order of Aust (AM), 1997. Memberships: Fed Cncl, 1947-49, Exec Lib Pty of Aust, 1946-51; Bd, Flying Doctor Serv (Q'ld), 1951-52; Advsry Cttee, YWCA, 1952-56; Pres, Austl Jaycees, 1954; Intl VP JCI, 1955; JC Senator No 386; Pres, Rotary Club of Lane Cove, 1972-73; Life Mbr, Aust Amn Assn, 1973-; Life Mbr, Natl Trust of Aust, 1979-; Pres, Austl Book Publrs Assn, 1979-80; VP Intl Publrs Assn, 1981-85; Dir, Gordon & Breach Sci Publrs P/L, 1981-94; Patron, Cnclr, Mus Contemporary Art, 1989-; Austl Dir, Fine Arts Press, P/L 1992-94; Bd Mbr and Treas, Asthma Fndn of NSW, 1985-97 Hobbies: Cricket; Book collecting; Music. Address: 19 Ben Nevis Circuit, Bundanoon, NSW 2578, Australia.

KING Jonathan Leslie, b. 28 Dec 1942, Geelong, Aust. Writer; Film producer. m. Jane Lewis, 23 Feb 1975, 4 d. Education: Dip, Jrnlsm, BA (Hons), PhD, Melbourne Univ; MSc, London Univ. Appointments: Ed, "Australasian Express", London, 1974; Lectr, Polit Sci, Melbourne Univ, 1977; Fndr, Creative Dir, 1st Fleet Re-enactment Co, 1985; Ldr, 1st Fleet Tall Ship Re-enactment Expedition London to Sydney, 1987; Austl Dir, Rainforest Fndn, 1990; Prodr, Presenter, The Gt Clumbus Race, Genoa to NY, 1992; Dir, Life Educ Cntrs NSW, 1993; Dir, Marco Polo Fndn, 1993; Dir, Waltzing Matilda Centenary, 1994; Dir, Man From Snowy River Centenary, 1995; Dir, Film Prodn, Webster Publng, 1996. Publications: Books incl: Waltzing Materialism: attitudes that shaped Australia, 1978; Governor Philip Gidley King, 1982; The First Fleet, 1982; Founding of Australia, 1986; Australia's First Fleet and the Re-enactment, 1988; The Battle for the Bicentenary, 1989; The Man from Snowy River, 1995; The Fight for Federation, 1998; TV documentaries/CD-ROMS: Bound for Botany Bay, 1984; First Rite of Passage, 1988; The Great Columbus Race, 1992; Waltzing Matilda: The Song that Shaped a Nation, 1995; History of Australia, 1997. Honours: Austl of Yr, Austl Day Cncl, Vic; Oustndng Austl, Portland Cty Cncl; Austl Achiever, Austl Event of Yr, Natl Austl Day Cnsl, 1989. Memberships: Pioneers Club of Aust; Roy Austl Histl Assn; Fellshp of First Fleeters; Avalon Sailing Club Awds. Hobbies: Horse riding; Square-rig sailing; Bush walking; International travel. Address: Dunhevd, 131 Upper Clontarf Street, Seaforth, Sydney, NSW 2092, Australia.

KING Leonard James, b. 1 May 1925, SA, Aust. Retired Judge. m. Sheila Therese Keane, 1953, 2 s, 3 d. Education: LLB, Admitted to Bar, Univ of Adelaide, 1950. Appointments include: Appointed Queens Counsel, 1967; House of Assembly, 1970; Atty Gen, 1970-75; Min of Socl Welfare & Aboriginal Affairs, 1970-72; Min of Community Affairs, 1973-75; Judge, 1975-78; Chf Jus, 1978, Retd, 1995, Supreme Crt of S Aust. Honour: AC, 1987. Address: 19 Wall Street, Norwood, SA 5067, Australia.

KING Pamela Graham, b. 12 Mar 1929. Author; Artist; Businesswoman. m. 20 July 1951, Donald D King, 1 s, 1 d. Education: Dip of Arts (Creative), Univ of Southern Queensland; BA, Univ of Queensland; Litt B, Univ of New Eng; MPhil, Griffith Univ. Appointments: Art Critic for Daily Newspapers, 1978-87. Publications: Books: Co-Author, Downs Artists: A Changing Landscape, 1985; Co-Author, Nut Harvest Cook Book, 1986; Co-Author, Ginger for A Tropical Taste, 1993; Like Painting, Like Music..., Joseph Conrad and the Modernist Sensibility,

1996; Exhibition of Paintings, Downs Art Centre, 1977. Honours: Num Art Awds, 1960-70. Hobbies: Farming. Listed in: Artists and Galleries of Australia. Address: 29 Mcllwraith Street, Moffat Headland, 4551 Australia.

KING Poppy, b. 24 May 1972, Melbourne, Australia. Cosmetic Company. Honour: Yng Austl of the Yr, 1995. Membership: Austl Repub Movement. Hobbies: Arts; Films; Politics. Address: 6 Kirks Lane, Melbourne, Victoria 3000, Australia.

KINGSLAND Richard (Sir), b. 19 Oct 1916, NSW, Aust. m. 1 s, 2 d. Education: RAAF, Flying Sch, Vic, 1935-36; RAAF, Staff Coll, 1945; Imperial Def Coll, London, England, 1955. Appointments: RAAF Pilot, UK and SW Pacific, 1939-42; Grp Cap, 1943; Dir, Ops Trng, 1943-44; Air Force Intell, 1945-46; Dir Gen of Org, 1946-48; Mngr, Sydney Airport, 1948; Airline Transp Pilot, 1949; Regl Dir, Civil Aviation, SA, 1950-51; Asst Sec, Dept of Air, 1954-58; UK Min of Def, 1954-56; 1st Asst Sec, Dept of Def, 1958-63; Sec, Dept of Interior, 1963-70; Dept of Veterans Affairs, 1970-81; Chmn, Repatriation Cmmn, 1970-81. Honours: DFC, 1940; CBE, 1967; Knight Bach, 1978; AO, 1989. Memberships include: Bd Mngmt, Canberra Th Trust Natl Heart Fndn; Austl Films Bd Review; ACT Arts Dev Bd; C'wlth Uranium Advsry Cncl; Independent Air Fares Cttee; Aust Day Cttee; Natl Cncl, Austl Opera; RAAF Educ Fund; Barnardos Canberra Cttee, Canberra Fest. Address: 36 Vasey Crescent, Campbell, ACT 2612, Australia.

KINGWELL Bronwyn Anne, b. 5 Mar 1966. Medical Research Scientist. m. Andrew Nicholas Plant, 26 July 1996. Education: BSc Hons; PhD. Appointments: Rsch Assoc, Dept Med, Hon Lectr, Dept Physiology, Monash Univ; Rsch Fell, Baker Med Rsch Inst. Publications include: Papers: Exercise and Baroreflex Sensitivity, 1991; The Effect of Hypertensive Episodes and Cardiac Hypertrophy the Blood Pressure-Heart Rate Baroreflex, 1994; Arterial Compliance May Influence Baroreflex Function in Athletes and Hypertensives, 1995; Enhanced Dilatation to Acetylcholine in Athletes is Associated with Lower Plasma Cholesterol, 1996; Four Weeks of Cycle Training Increases Basal Production of Nitric Oxide From the Forearm, 1997. Honours: Vic Young Achiever Sci & Technol Awd, 1992; Vic Young Achiever of the Yr, 1992. Memberships: High Blood Pressure Rsch Cncl of Aust; Intl Soc of Hypertension; Austl Soc for Medl Rsch; Intl Soc of Heart Rsch; Sec, Austl Soc for Medl Rsch, Victoria Div. Hobbies: Running; Aerobics; Weight Training; Singing. Address: Alfred & Baker Medical Unit, Baker Medical Research Institute, Commercial Road, Prahran, Vic 3181, Australia.

KINI Manjunatha R, b. 7 May 1956, Shimoga, India. Scientist. m. Nobue, 21 June 1987. Education: BSc; MSc; PhD. Appointments: Snr Scientist, Biosci Cntr, 1997-; Affiliate Assoc Prof, Medl Coll, VA, USA, 1998-. Publications: Book, Venom Phospholipase A2 Enzymes: Structure, Function and Mechanism, Ed, 1997. Honours: Gold Medal in MSc; Sev Schlshp Awds and Visng Scientist Awds. Memberships: Intl Soc on Toxinology; Intl Soc on Thrombosis and Hemostasis, Co-Chair of a subcttee. Hobbies: Tennis; Volleyball; Other outdoor sports. Address: Bioscience Centre, Facility of Science, National University of Singapore, Singapore 119260.

KIRBY Michael, b. 18 Mar 1939. Honourable Justice. Education: BA, LLM, BEc, Sydney Univ. Appointments include: Govnr, Intl Cncl for Computer Commns, Wash, 1984-; Cmmnr, Intl Cmmn of Jurists, 1984-; Pres, Crt of Appeal, 1984-96; Judge of Appeal, 1984-96; Judge, 1984-96; Acting Chf Justice, Supreme Crt, NSW, 1988, 1990, 1993; Mbr, ILO Fact-Finding and Conciliation Cmmn on Freedom Assn, 1991-, Inquiry into S Africa, 1991-92; Mbr, Perm Tribunal of Peoples, 1992-; Advsry Bd, Austl Cntr for Media and Telecomms Law and Policy, 1993-; Spec Rep of Sec-Gen for Human Rights in Cambodia, 1993-96; Hon Prof, Natl Law Sch, India Univ, Bangalore, 1994-; Mbr, Ethics Cttee, (fmrly Human Genome Org), London, 1995-; Pres, Crt of Appeal, Solomon Islands, 1995-96; Pres, Intl Cmmn of Jurists, 1995-; Mbr, UNESCO Intl Bioethic Cttee, 1996- Justice, High Crt of Aust, 1996-; Hon Fell, Acady of Socl Scis, Aust, 1996-. Publications: Reform the Law, 1983; The Judges, 1984; Industrial Index Australian Labour Law, 2nd ed, 1984; A Touch of Healing (Sir Zelman Cowen's Vice Regal Speeches), co-ed. Honours: CMG, 1983; Hon Fell, NZ Rsch Fndn, 1984; Hon DLitt, Univ Newcastle, NSW, 1987; AC, 1991; Austl Human Rights Medal, 1991; Hon LLD, Macquarie Univ, 1994, Sydney Univ, 1996, Natl Law Sch, India, 1997; Laureate, UESCO Prize for Human Rights Educ, 1998; Hon LLD. NH Law S Univ, India, 1997. Address: c/o High Court of Australia, PO Box E435, Kingston, ACT 2604, Australia.

KIRKGOZ Mehmet Salih, b. 10 July 1947, Kemaliye, Turkey. Civil Engineer. m. Yasemin Kirkgoz, 10 Aug 1974, 1 s, 1 d. Education: MSc, Civil Engrng, Tech Univ of Istanbul, 1970; PhD, Civil Engrng, Liverpool Univ, 1978. Appointments: Design Engr, Pvte Co, Istanbul, 1971-73; Rsch Asst, Tech Univ of Istanbul, 1974; Rsch Asst, 1979-81, Asst Prof, 1982-84, Assoc Prof, 1985-89, Prof, 1990-, Cukurova Univ Adana; Vice Dean, Fac of Engrng and Arch, 1987-89; Hd, Civil Engrng Dept, 1991-. Publications: Turbulent Velocity Profiles for Smooth and Rough Open Channel Flow, 1989; Breaking Wave Impact on Vertical and Sloping Coastal Structures, 1995. Address: Cukurova University, Civil Engineering Department, Adana 01330, Turkey.

KISHI Masumi, b. 9 Jan 1944, Aichi Prefecture, Japan. Professor, Faculty of Commerce, Chuo University. m. Etsuko Goto, 13 Mar 1976, 1 s. Education: BA, Econs, 1967, MA, Econs, 1972, PhD, Econs, 1987, Keio Univ. Appointments: Assoc Prof, Sch of Polit Sci & Econs, Tokai Univ, 1974-77; Visng Fell, Yale Univ, 1979-81; Prof, Sch of Polit Sci & Econs, 1985-93; Cnslt, Asian Dev Bank, 1993; Prof, Fac of Com, 1994-. Publications: Economic Development and Financial Policies, 1990; Contbr, Financial Markets and Policies in the Newly Industrializing Economies in Financial Sector Development in Asia (ed S Zahid), 1995; Contemporary Monetary Economics (w Prof N Hayashi), 1997; Ed, The Economic Development Process of Financial and Capital Markets of Thailand (in Japanese), 1998. Memberships: Eec Ed, Jrnl of Asian Econs, 1994-; Rsch Mbr, Rsch Inst of Contrn and Econ, 1997-98; Rsch Mbr, Inst of Monetary and Fiscal Policies, Min of Fin, 1997-98; Rsch Mbr, Inst of Dev Econs, 1998-99; Mbr, seminar on Asian Fin Plcy and Macroeconomic Mngmt, Japan Intl Coop Agcy, 1998-99. Hobby: Golf. Address: 4-27-12 Azamino, Aoba-ku, Yokohama-shi, Kanagawa Prefecture, 225-0011, Japan.

KISHIKAWA Toshiaki, b. 3 Feb 1939, Fukui, Japan. Professor of Radiochemistry. m. Atsuko, 23 Sept 1970, 2 s, 1 d. Education: BEng, Kumamoto Univ, 1965; MEng, Kumamoto Univ, 1967; DSc, Tohoku Univ, 1973. Appointments: Rsch Assoc, 1967-74, Lectr, Kurokami Radioisotope Lab, 1974-84, Radiation Safety Supvsr, 1975-, Kumamoto Univ; Lectr, Yatsushiro Natl Tech Coll, 1974-76; Assoc Prof, Kumamoto Univ Fac of Engrng, 1984-; Hon Rsch Fell, Radiation Cntr, Univ of Birmingham, UK, 1986-87; Assoc Prof, Kumamoto Univ Grad Sch of Sci and Technol, 1988-; Mbr, Cnsltng Cttee, Kyushu Energy Forum, Econ Fedn Kyushu-Yamaguchi (The Kyu-Kei-Ren), 1989-; Mbr, Tech Cttee, Rsch Cntr for Nuclear Sci and Technol, Univ of Tokyo, 1996-; Assoc Ed, Jrnl of Radioanalytical and Nuclear Chem, 1997-; Chmn, Organizing Cttee, Asia-Pacific Symp on Radiochem '97 (APSORC'97), 1997; Organizer and Chmn, Steering Cttee, The 41st Symp of Radiochem (Japan), 1997; Mbr Intl Tech Advsry Cttee, 2nd Intl Conf on Isotopes (2ICI), Syney, Aust, 1997; Mbr, Steering Cttee, Heisei 10 Annual Conf of Radiation Safety Supvsrs, Japan Radioisotope Assn, 1998. Publications: (auth) Fundamentals of Radiochemistry, 1994; (ed) Proceedings of the Asia-Pacific Symposium on Radiochemistry '97, 1997; Articles to profl jrnls. Honour: Fellshp Awd, Sakkoukai Fndn, 1970. Memberships: Chem Soc of Japan, 1964-; Atomic Soc of Japan, 1966-, Bd Dirs, Kyushu Branch, 1993-95, 1996-99; Japan Radioisotope Assn, 1970-, Bd of Dirs, RSS Sect, Kyushu Branch, 1994-97; Japan Soc of Applied Phys, 1990-; Japan Assn of Activation Analysis, 1995-. Hobbies: Oil and pastel painting; Do-it-yourself fun; Committee member, 3rd Kumamoto Scout Group. Address: Kokai-honmachi, Kumamoto 860-0851, Japan.

KISIM Marwan al, b. 12 May 1938, Amman, Jordan. Education: E Ml Univ; Columbia Univ; Georgetown Univ. Appointments: Min of Fgn Affairs, 1962; Consul-Gen, NY, 1964-65; Dpty Dir of Protocol, 1966; Polit Offr, Jordanian Emb, Beirut, 1967-68, USA, 1968-72; Sec to Crown Prince Hassan, 1972-75; Dir-Gen, Roy Hashemite Crt, 1975-76, Chf, 1988; Min of State, 1976; Min of Supply, 1977-79; Min of State for Fgn Affairs, 1979-80; Min of Fgn Affairs, 1980-83; Dpty PM, Min of Fgn Affairs, 1988-90. Honours: Jordanian, Syrian, Mexican, Lebanese, Chinese, Italian Decorations. Address: Ministry of Foreign Affairs, Amman, Jordan.

KITAGAWA Naofumi, b. 12 Jan 1935, Hiroshima, Japan. University Professor. m. Kazumi, 30 Mar 1965, 2 d. Education: DSc, Kyoto Univ, 1967. Appointment: Prof, Nara Univ of Educ, 1975. Memberships: Japanese Bryological Soc (Fac of Sci, Univ of Hiroshima, Higashi), 1972. Hobbies: Go, Shogi (Japanese chess). Address: 624-1-302, Nara, 6309-8301, Japan.

KITAMURA Teitaro, b. 15 Nov 1933, Tokyo, Japan. Professor, Tokyo Univeristy of Agriculture. 1 d. Appointments: Asst Prof, Kyoto Univ, 1961; Assoc Prof, 1967, Prof, 1981, Kyoto Univ; Ret'd, Prof Emeritus, Kyoto Univ, 1997-. Publication: Systems of Land Use Planning for Rural Development. Honours: NIRA Policy Rsch, TOHATA Mem Awd, 1988; Awd for Assn of Rural Plng, 1991. Memberships: Assn of Rural Plng; Assn of Regl Sci. Hobby: Gardening. Address: 35 Hanazomo-cho, Iwakura, Sakyo-ku, Kyoto 606-0024, Japan.

KITANO Hirohisa, b. 28 Jan 1931, Toyama Cty, Japan. Professor of Tax Law. m. Hachie Aoyama, 28 Jan 1962, 3 s. Education; LLD, Ritsumeikan Univ, Kyoto, Japan, 1974. Appointments: Mbr, Tax Bur of Tax, Min of Fin, Japan, 1955-60; Lectr, Univ of Tokyo, Japan, 1963-64, 1977-79; Full-tine Lectr, Nihon Univ, Japan, 1964-66; Asst Prof, Nihon Univ, 1966-71; Prof, Nihon Univ, 1971-; Pres, Inst of Comparative Law, Nihon Univ, 1996-; Visng Schl Univ of California, Berkeley, Sch of Law, USA, 1975-76. Publications: Rights of Taxpayers, 1981; Fundamental Theory of Science of Task Law, 1984. Memberships: Pres, Taxpayers' Union to Correct Unfair Tax System, Tokyo, 1977-; Dir, Japan Civil Liberties Union, Tokyo, 1978-; Tokyo Bar Assn, 1981-; Intl Fiscal Assn, Rotterdam, 1983-; Tokyo Bar Assn, 1981-; Pres, Japan Assn of Pub Fin Law, 1991-; Repr Dir, Japan Dem Lawyer's Assn, Tokyo, 1993-; Sci Cncl of Japan, 1994-; Pres, Japan Assn of Sci of Taxation, 1995-; Tokyo Assn of Tax Profls, 1996-. Hobbies: Baseball critic. Address: 5-9-25 Kitamachi, Koubunji, Tokyo 1850001, Japan.

KITCHING Roger Laurence, b. 1 Feb 1945, Hornsea, UK. Professor of Ecology. m. Beverley (née Craig), 12 Apr 1969, 1 s, 1 d. Education: BS, Zool, London, 1966; DPhil, Oxford, 1969; ARCS, Imperial Coll, London, 1966; DIPL.COMP, Canberra, 1976. Appointments: Rsch Scientist, CSIRO, 1971-76; Lectr, Snr Lectr, Asst Prof, Griffith Univ, 1976-86; Prof, Ecosystem Mngmt, Univ of New Eng, 1986-92; Prof of Ecology, Griffith Univ, 1992-; Spec Commnr, Kakadu Inquiry, Resource Assessment Commn, 1991-92; Chmn, Natl Biodiversity Cncl, 1993-95; Chmn, Commonwealth Biodiversity Advsry Cncl, 1995-. Publications: Ecology of Pests (co-auth), 198-; Systems Ecology, 1983; Ecology of Exotic Animals and Plants, 986; Insect Ecology (co-auth), 1984; Ecology of Australia's Wet Tropics, 1988; Num sci articles. Memberships: Austl Inst of Bio, Fell, 1991-, Pres, 1991-98; Austl Entomological Soc, Treas, 1973-75, Pres, 1996-99; Austl Ecological Soc, Ed, 1978-81; Roy Entomological Soc of London, Fell, 1984-. Hobbies: Bibliography; Butterflies; Carpentry. Address: 118 Teys Road, Holmview, Queensland, 4207, Australia.

KITTANI Ismat, b. 1929, Emadieh, Mesopotamia, Iraq. Diplomat. m. 1 s. Education: Knox Coll, USA. Appointments: Tchr, HS, Iraq; Min of Fgn Affairs,

Baghdad Emb, Cairo, 1954-57; Perm Mission of Iraq to UN, 1957-61; Perm Rep of Iraq, UN Geneva, 1961-64; Joined UN Secr, 1964; Sec, Socl and Econ Cttee, 1965-66; Dpty Asst Sec Gen, Office of Inter-Agency Affairs and Coord, 1969-70 Asst Sec-Gen, UN, 1971-73; Exec Asst to Sec Gen, 1973-75; Amb, For Min of Iraq, Baghdad, 1975-80; Pres, 36th Gen Assembly of UN, 1981-82; Perm Rep to UN, 1985-90; UN Sec-Gen's Specl Rep to Somalia, 1992-93; Specl Envoy to Tajikistan, 1993; Specl Advsr to UN Sec-Gen, 1996-. Address: United Nations, Palais des Nations, Room 190, Avenue de la Paix 8-14, 1211 Geneva 10, Switzerland.

KIZAWA Makoto, b. 18 Apr 1925, Kiryu, Japan. Former University Professor. m. Yukiko Nishi, 21 Jan 1951, 2 s, 1 d. Education: BA, Dept of EE, Univ of Tokyo, 1948; DEng, Univ of Tokyo, 1969. Appointments: Electrotech Lab, 1948-70; Prof, Osaka Univ, 1970-80; Prof, 1980-83, VP, 1983-87, Univ of Lib and Info Sci. Publications: Digital Magnetic Recording, 1979; A Treatize of Data in Science and Technology, 1983. Honours: Niwa Prize, Japan Info Cntr of Sci and Technol, 1969; Standardization Awd, Min of Intl Trade and Ind, Japan, 1989. Memberships: ICSU/CODATA Test Grp on Computer Use, 1967-69; Sec, ICSU/CODATA Task Grp on Accessibility and Dissemination of Data, 1972-80. Address: 3-13-6 Hachimanyama, Setagaya-ku, Tokyo, 156-0056, Japan.

KLEIN Anthony George, b. 14 Dec 1935, Timisoara, Romania. Physicist. Education: Univ of Melbourne. Appointments: Rsch Assoc, Argonne Natl Lab, 1960-61, Oak Ridge Natl Lab, USA, 1961-62; Snr Lectr, 1965-76, Rdr Phys, 1976-83, Assoc Dean Fac Sci, 1985-86, Hd Sch Phys, 1987-96, Cncl Mbr, Univ Melbourne, 1995-; Hon Fell, Univ Coll London, 1971; Snr Sci Fell, Inst Laue-Langevin Grenoble, 1975, 1979; Visng Prof, MIT, 1983. Honour: Walter Boas Medal AIP Shared, 1990; Fell, Austl Acady of Scis, 1994. Memberships include: Austl Inst of Phys Chmn, Vic Br, 1980-82, VP, 1987-88, Pres, 1989-91; Pres, Austl Optical Soc, 1985-86; Hobbies: Reading; Boating; Bushwalking. Address: 2 Rochester Street, Kew, Vic 3101, Australia.

KLINE Kevin Delaney, b. 24 Oct 1947, St Louis, USA. Actor. m. Phoebe Cates, 1989, 1 s, 1 d. Education: IN Univ; Julliard Sch, Drama Divsn, NY. Appointments: Fndng Mbr, The Acting Co, NY, 1972-76; Sev Broadway appearances. Creative Works: Films: Sophie's Choice; Pirates of Penzance; The Big Chill, 1983; Silverado, 1985; Violets Are Blue, 1985; Cry Freedom, 1987; A Fish Called Wanda, 1988; January Man, 1989; I Love You to Death, 1989; Soapdish, 1991; Grand Canyon, 1991; Consenting Adults, 1992; Chaplin, 1992; Dave, 1993; Princess Caraboo, 1994; Paris Match, 1995; French Kiss, 1995; Fierce Creatures, 1996; The Ice Storm, 1997; In and Out, 1997. Honours include: Obie Awd, Sustained Achievement; Will Awd, Classical Th; Tony Awd, 1978, 1980; Acady Awd, Best Supporting Actor, 1989. Address: c/o Jeff Hunter, William Morris Agency, 151 El Camino, Beverly Hills, CA 90212, USA.

KLUMPP Robert Lloyd, b. 3 Mar 1958, Moree, NSW, Aust. Veterinary Surgeon. m. (1) Kim Taylor, 31 Dec 1919, (2) Belinda Rowe, 2 Aug 1997, 1 s. Education: BVSc; MACVS; Currently studying for Grad Dip Psychol. Memberships: AVA; AEVA; ACVSc; Vic Endurance Riders Assn (Hon Vet). Hobbies: Equine Endurance Drive, Torquay, Vic, Aust.

KNECHT Monica Mary Elizabeth Hopper de, b. 24 Aug 1951, Vic, Aust. Student; Volunteer Worker. m. (1) 2 s, 3 d, (2) Johannes, 18 June 1993. Education: Stott's Secretarial Dip, Stott's Bus Coll, Melbourne, Aust, 1968; Vic Cert of Educ, Coll of Tech and Further Educ, Frankston, Vic, Aust, 1995; Presently in 4rd yr of BA Hons, majoring in Hist, admitted to BA Hum, 1998, La Trobe Univ, Bundoora, Vic, Aust. Career: Sec to var profl firms and corps, 1969-90; Disabled in hit-run accident, 1991; Vol worker, student. Publications: (poem) Bad King John, Intl Lib of Poetry, 1998. Honours: Golden Key Natl Hon, 1997; Soc at La Trobe Univ, Aust. Memberships: Sec, Holland Fest Sub-cttee, Netherlands Soc, Vic, Aust.

Hobbies: Voluntary worker in Dutch community for past 6 years, fundraiser for the Dutch Elderly. Address: 37 Arcadia Avenue, The Basin, Victoria, Australia.

KNIGHT Edwin Walter, b. 1 Nov 1934, Perth, Aust. Occupational Physician. m. Maureen Ann Malone, 7 Feb 1959, 3 s (1 decd), 3 d. Education: MB BS, Univ Adelaide, Aust, 1957. Appointments: Jnr Res Med Offr, 1958, Snr Res Medl Offr, 1960, Footscray and Dist Hosp, Melbourne; Gen Prac, Melbourne, 1961-72; Medl Cnslt, The Herald & Weekly Times, Melbourne, 1972-; Medl Cnslt: David Syme & Co, Melbourne, 1973-96; Nissan Motor Mgf Co, Melbourne, 1977-85; Hon Snr Lectr Dept Epidemiology and Preventive Med, Monash Univ, Melbourne, 1987-; Natl Safety Cncl Vic, 1979-84; Satff Hlth Physn, Alfred Hosp, Melbourne, 1996-. Publications: Dollar Doctor, 1974; Childrens Doctor, 1977, 1992; Emotional Illness, 1979; Emergency Doctor, 1983; Family Doctor, 1986; Living With Stress, 1987; The Family Medical Diary, 1991; (co-auth) Square Pegs Square Holes, 1981; Look Good Feel Great, 1987; Medl Columnist num jrnls. Memberships: Fell, Roy Austl Coll Gen Practitioners; Austl Coll Occupational Med; Austl Fac Occupational Med; Austl Med Assn; Austl and NZ Soc Occupational Med; Melbourn Club; Vic Racing Club; Melbourne Cricket Club; Kooyong Lawn Tennis Club. Hobbies: Running; Reading; Bridge. Address: 9 Ranfurlie Crecent Glen Iris, Melbourne, Vic 3146, Australia.

KNIGHT Keith Edwards, b. 20 June 1954, Brisbane, Aust. Veterinary Surgeon. m. Ann 1 Oct 1983, 2 s. Education: BVSc. Memberships: Vetmark, Pres, 1997-98; Austl Vet Assn; Animal Chiropractor Assn; Austl Greyhound Assn; Austl Vet Acupuncture Assn. Hobbies: Greyhound racing; Surfing. Address: 34 A, Liewa Drive, Loganholme, QLD, Australia.

KNOWLES Brian Henry, b. 6 Jan 1931. Accountant. m. Nancy Weitemeyer, 21 Feb 1955, 1 s, dec, 1 d. Education: Acctcy Qual. Honour: Polio-Free World Intl Serv Awd. Memberships: Joined Rotary, 1960, Gov, Dist 9600, 1969-70, Bd Dirs, Rotary Intl, 1986-88, Treas, 1987-88, Chmn, Convention Cttee, Melbourne, 1993, Chmn, Western Pacific Polio Plus Cttee, 1991-, Volun, polio vaccine factory, Kunming, China, 1990-; Pres, Qld Squash Assn, 1960-69, Austl Squash Selector, 1966-74; Exec Cttee, 1966-80, Pres, 1974-80, Austl Cncl Co-op Housing and Building Socs; Qld Govt Housing and Building Soc Advsry Cttee. 1976-92; Bd Govs, 1971-89, Treas, 1972-85, Dpty Pres, 1985-89, Intl House, Univ Qld; VP, Guide Dogs for Blind Assn, 1972-80; Chmn, WHO Interagcy Co-ord Cttee, Western Pacific Reg, 1991-; Assoc, Austl Soc Accts; Fell, Inst Finl Servs. Hobbies: Cricket; Boating. Address: 43/17 Bayview Street, Runaway Bay, Queensland 4216, Australia.

KNOX David Montgomery, b. 28 Dec 1953, Melbourne, Aust. Actuary. m. Carol, 10 Dec 1977, 2 s, 1 d. Education: BA; PhD; FIA; FIAA. Appointments: Natl Mutual, 1975-78; Macquarie Univ, 1979-92; Univ of Melbourne, 1992-. Honour: Actuary of the Yr, 1996. Membership: VP, Inst of Actuaries of Aust, 1998. Address: Centre for Actuarial Studies, University of Melbourne, VIC 5052, Australia.

KOBAYASHI Atsushi, b. 22 Aug 1958, Tokyo, Japan. Executive Search Consultant. m. Rumiko, 28 Apr 1985, 1 s, 1 d. Education: BA, Sophia Univ, Tokyo, 1984; MPA, Harvard Univ, Kennedy Sch of Govt, 1991. Appointments: Nissho Iwai Corp Tokyo, 1984-93; Dir, Gen Mngr, Datatec Corp, Tokyo, 1993-94; Mngr, The Kansai Elec Power Co Inc, Osaka, Japan, 1994-98; Prin, Korn/Ferry Intl, Toyko, 1999-. Publications: (auth) Business in English, 1987; (transl) The Making of a Japanese Prime Minister, 1994. Address: E-708, 4-1 Honmokuhara, Naka-ku, Yokohama 231-0821, Japan.

KOBAYASHI Toshiro, b. Sapporo, Hokkaido, Japan. University Professor. m. Fumiko Fukuda, 1 May 1969, 1 s, 1 d. Education: BEng, 1962, DEng, Hokkaido Univ. Appointments: Assoc Prof, Nagoya Univ, 1973; Prof, Toyohashi Univ of Technol, 1982; Chmn, Dept Prodn

Systems Engrng, Toyohashi Univ Tech, 1999. Publications: Zairyo-System-Gaku, 1997. Honours: Japan Invention Awd, Japan's Inv Soc, 1981; Iidaka Prize, Japanese Foundryman's Soc, 1993; Mishima Prize, Japan Inst Iron and Steel, 1997; MOIF; DDG. Memberships: Inst Mat (Eng); ASTM (USA); Fell, ASM (USA). Hobby: Classical music. Address: 21-16 Kodare, Ogasaki, Toyohashi, Aichi 441-8580, Japan.

KOCH Grace, b. 14 July 1945, Indpls, IN, USA. Teacher; Musicologist; Media Archivist. m. Harold James Koch, 26 Aug 1972, 1 d, dec. Education; BSc, Hons, Music Educ, East Nazarene Coll, Wollaston Pk, Quincy, MA, 1967; MMus, Boston Univ, Boston, MA, 1973. Appointments: Elem Vocal Music Supvsr, Cohasset Pub Schs, MA, 1967-69; Dir, Music Educ Curric Lab, Boston Univ, 1970-72; Tutor in Music Educ, Canberra Coll of Advd Educ, 1974-75; Archives Mngr (Music and Oral Hist) Austl Inst of Aboriginal and Torres Strait Islander Series, 1975-; Snr Cncl, Cntrl Land Cncl, Alice Springs, 1979-; Lectr, Univ of Vienna, Course on Austl Aboriginal Music, 1993. Publications: On Ethnomusicology and Aboriginal music, oral hist, sound archiving; Reviews, books, compact discs and cassettes. Honours: Elks Ldrshp Awd, 1963; Austl Inst of Aboriginal and Torres Strait Islander Studies, 1983; Stanner Prize, 1999. Memberships: Musicological Soc of Aust, ACT Chapt, VP, 1988-89; Intl Assn of Sound Archives (Intl)Exec Bd Mbr, 1987-93; Chair, 1992; Australasian Sound Recordings Assn/Intl Assn of Sound Archives Conf Orgng Cttee, 1990-92; Intl Assn of Sound Archives (Austl Branch) Treasurer, 1982-84, VP, 1984-87; Australasian Sound Recordings Assn, VP, 1988-90; Profl Mbr, Austl Soc of Archivists. Hobbies: Peoples Warden, Ch of St John the Bapt, Canberra; Choral singing; Solo performance with Baroque and Medieval music ensembles; Travel; Cooking; Reading. Address: 67 Argyle Square, Reid, ACT 2612, Australia.

KODAMANOGLU Nuri, b. 16 Aug 1923, Ulukisla. Politician. m. Ayten, 1 Nov 1951. Education: Fac of Scis, Univ of Istanbul; Higher Tchrs Trng Coll, Istanbul. Appointments: Perm Under Sec, min of Educ; Dpty Grand Natl Assembly; Min of Energy and Nat Rescs; Chf Advsr of Pres, Turkish Rep. Creative Works: Educ in Turkey; Financial Problems of National Education; Var Reports. Memberships: Soc of Grads of Tchr Trng Coll of Turkey; Ataturk Rsch Cntr; Soc of Paliamentors Turcs. Hobbies: Handicrafts; Gdng. Address: Burkes Sokak No 6 Daire 8, Cankaya, 06680 Ankara, Turkey.

KODELA Phillip Gerhard, b. 24 Aug 1962, Merewether, Aust. Geographer. Education: BSc hons, 1985, PhD, 1997, Univ NSW. Appointments: Tutor, Univ NSW, 1985-90; Botanist, Natl Herbarium of NSW, Roy Botanic Gdns, Sydney, 1990-; Cnslt Scientific Ed, Flora of Australia, Volumes on Acacia, Sydney, 1998. Publications: Auth of sci pprs and rprts in the fields of geog, bot and conservation, 1985-. Honours: Warrane Coll Schl, 1983-84; Univ Medal, 1985. Memberships: Coast and Wetlands Soc; Natl Pks Assn of NSW; Robertson Environl Protection Soc. Hobbies: Swimming; Bushwalking; Camping; Gardening; Philately. Address: National Herbarium of New South Wales, Royal Botanic Gardens, Mrs Macquaries Road, Sydney, NSW 2000, Australia.

KOSUGI Takashi. Politician. Appointments: Mbr, House of Reps; Fmr Parl Vice-Min of Environ; Min of Educn, 1996-97. Address: Ministry of Education, Science & Culture, 3-2-2 Kasumigaseki, Chiyoda-ku, Tokyo 100, Japan.

KOGA Makato, Politician. Appointments: Mbr, House of Reps; Fmr Chair, House of Reps Cttee on Constrn; Min of Transp, 1996. Address: Ministry of Transport, 2-1-3 Kasumigaseki, Chiyoda-ku, Tokyo 100, Japan.

KOGA Shinji, b. 24 Sept 1953, Fukuoka, Japan. Assistant Professor. Education: BS, Kyushu University, Japan, 1977; MS, Kyoto Univ, Japan, 1979; PhD, Kyoto University, Japan, 1983. Appointments: Rsch Assoc, Osaka Kyoiku Univ, Japan, 1987-94; Asst Prof, Osaka

Kyoiku Univ, 1994-. Publications: Pprs in profl jrnls. Memberships: Phys Soc of Japan, Tokyo, 1981-; NY Acady of Scis, 1995-; AAAS, 1996-; IBA, 1999-. Hobby: Table tennis. Address: Osaka Kyoiku University, Department of Physics, 4-698-1, Asahi ga oka, Kashiwara, Osaka 582-8582, Japan.

KOGIKU Kiichiro, b. 30 July 1927, Okayama, Japan. Economist. Education: PhD, Univ of WI, Madison, USA. Appointments: Asst Prof, Univ of CA; Assoc Prof; Prof, Aoyama Gakuin Univ, Tokyo. Creative Works: Introduction to Macroeconomic Models; Microeconomic Models, Resource Allocation Models. Honours: Bookings Rsch Prof. Memberships: Amn Econ Assn; Japan Econ Assn; Western Econ Assn Intl; Econometric Soc. Address: Aoyama Gakuin University, Tokyo 150-8366, Japan.

KOH Kun, b. 2 Jan 1938, Okgu-gun, Korea. Politician. m. 3 s. Education: Seoul Natl Univ. Appointments: Pres, Gen Students Assn, Seoul Natl Univ, 1959; Asst Jnr Offl, Min of Home Affairs, 1962-65; Asst Dir, Planning Off, 1965-68; Dir, Interior Dept, Jeonbuk Prov, 1968-71; Commr, New Village Movt, 1971-73; Vice-Gov, Kangwon Prov, 1973; Dir, Local Admin Bur, 1973-75; Gov, Jeonnam Prov, 1975-79; Chf Sec of Polit Affairs, Chong Wa Dae (The Blue House); Chf Advsr, Korea Rsch Inst for Human Settlement, 1980; Min of Transp, 1980-81, of Agricl & Marine Affairs, 1981-82; Vis Fell, Harvard Univ, 1983; Vis Prof, MIT, 1984; Mbr, 12th Natl Assembly, 1985-88; Min of Home Affairs, 1987; Mayor, Seoul Metro Govt, 1988-90; Pres, Myong Ji Univ, 1994-97; Co-Pres, Korea Fedn for Environ Movt, 1996-97; PM of S Korea, 1997-98. Honour: LLD, Won Kwang Univ, 1992. Address: Samchong-dong, Chongno-gu, Seoul, Korea.

KOH Sung-Kun, b. 2 Mar 1937, Seoul, Korea. Medicine (Urologist). m. O-Young Kwon, 14 Dec 1966, 1 s, 3 d. Education: MD, Korea Univ, 1961; PhD, Korea Univ, 1969; Rsch Fell: Saarbrucken Univ, 1974; Mainz Univ, Germany, 1978. Appointments: Instr Asst Prof, Assoc Prof, Prof, Korea Univ, Coll of Med, 1969-; Chmn, Dept Urology, Korea Univ Hosp, 1983-93; Supt, Korea Univ Hosp, 1986-89; Pres, Korean Urol Assn, Dean Korean Univ Med. Publication: Urology, 1991, 1996. Memberships: Korean Urol Assn, 1969; Intl Soc of Urol, 1982; Korean-Japan Urol Soc, 1984; German Soc Urol, 1995. Hobby: Music. Address: Department of Urology, Korea University Hospital, 126-1, 5-Ka, Anam-Dong, Sungbuk-Ku 136-705, Korea.

KOIDE Hitoshi, b. 2 Feb 1940, Tokyo, Japan. Government Official. m. Sumiko, 19 Dept 1970, 2 d. Education: BA, Engrng, Univ of Tokyo, 962; Dr degree, Engrng, Univ of Tokyo, 1968. Appointments: Geol Survey of Japan, 1969-; Dir, Environ Geol Dept, Gel Survey of Japan; Lectr, Univ of Tokyo, 1971-74; Visng Prof, Cty Univ of NY, 1973-76. Publication: Earthquakes and Active Faults (in Japanese and Chinese). Membership: Inst of Geosphere Assessment, Toyko, 1997. Hobby: Paintings. Address: 2-6-1-602, Higashi-Ikebukuro, Toshima, Tokyo 170-0013, Japan.

KOIRALA Girija Prasad. Politician. Appointments: Fmr Gen Sec, Nepal Congress Party; PM of Nepal; Responsible for Def, Fgn Affairs & Roy Palace Affairs, 1991-94. Address: Office of the Prime Minister, Central Secretariat, Singh Durbar, Kathmandu, Nepal.

KOIRALA Matrika Prasad, b. 1 Jan 1912. Politician; Diplomat. Education: Banares & Patna, India. Appointments: Fmr Pres, Nepali Congress Party; PM & Min of Gen Admin & Fgn Affairs, 1951-52, 1953-55; Nominated to Upper House of Parl; Amb to US, 1962-64; Perm Rep to UN, 1962-64; Fmrly Exiled in India; Pres, Natl People's Cncl, 1992-94.

KOIZUMI Jun'ichiro, Politician. Appointments: Mbr, House of Reps from Kanagawa; Fmr Parl Vice-Min of Fin & Hlth & Welfare; Min of Posts & Telecomms, 1992-93; Chair, House of Reps, Fin Cttee; Mbr, Mitsuzuka Faction of LDP; Min of Hlth & Welfare, 1996-. Address: Ministry

of Health & Welfare, 1-2-2 Kasumigaseki, Chiyoda-ku, Tokyo 100, Japan.

KOIZUMI Masatoshi, b. 10 June 1964, Sendai, Japan. Associate Professor. m. Chikako, 5 Apr 1997. Education: PhD, Dept of Lings and Philos, MA Inst of Technol, USA, 1995. Appointments: Asst Prof, 1995, Assoc Prof, 1996-, Tohoku Gakuin Univ. Publications: Formal Approaches to Japanese Linguistics, Vol I, 1994, Vol II, 1996; Phrase Structure in Minimalist Syntax, 1999. Memberships: Ling Soc of Am; Am Assn for the Adv of Sci; Japanese Cognitive Sci. Hobby: Mountain Climbing. Address: Department of English, Tohoku Gakuin University, 1-3-1 Tsuchitoi Aoba-ku, Sendai 980-8511, Japan.

KOJIMA Katsuyaki, b. 8 Apr 1944, Kyotanabe-shi, Kyoto, Japan. University Professor. Education: BEng, 1967, MEng, 1969, PhD, 1983, Ritsumeikan Univ, Kyoto, Japan. Appointments: Tech Offr and Rsch Asst, Kyoto Inst of Technol, 1969-76; Assoc Prof, Intl Coll of Bio-Medl Technol, Seki-shi, 1977-85; Lectr, 1983-86, Assoc Prof, 1986-89, Grad Coll of Bio-Medl Technol, Seki-shi; Assoc Prof, 1989-92, Prof, 1992-, Univ of Hamamatsu, Hamamatsu-shi. Publications: books: Experiments of Radiograph Technology, 1985; Radiograph Technology, 1986; Digital Radiograph Technology, 1998; Articles: Study on Correction of Spectral Images Formed by Spectroscopic Systems by means of Optical Transfer Functions, 1983; Study on Coltman's Correction by Simulation. Honour: Ucida Awd, Pres of Japan Soc of Medl Imaging and Info Sci, 1991. Memberships: Japan Soc of Medl Imaging and Info Scis, 1973-; Soc of Photo-Optical Instrumentation Engrs, 1990-; Inst of Elec and Electronics Engrs Inc, 1994-. Address: Department of Administration and Informatics, University of Hamamatsu, 1230 Miyakodacho, Hamamatsu-shi, Shizuoka, 431-2102, Japan.

KOK Chong Meng, b. 26 Sept 1950. Polymer Scientist. m. Cheng Suan Ooi, 3 May 1975, 1 d. Education: HNC, Hatfield; Grad PRI, N London; MSc, Loughborough; PhD, Waterloo. Appointments: Rsch Asst, Malaysian Rubber Producers' Rsch Assn, Eng, 1970-74; Lectr in Polymer Sci, Univ Sains Malaysia, 1976-87; Chairperson, Polymer Sci, 1985-87; Snr Rsch Sci, Sola Intl Holdings Ltd, 1987-. Publications: Kimia Polimer, 1987; Pengantar Teknology Getah, 1981; 19 publs in Polymer Sci; 5 Pats. Honours: Cabot Carbon Prize, Loughborough Univ, 1975; WB Pearson Medal, Univ of Waterloo, 1983. Membership: MRAIC, Organizing Cttee of 20th Austl Polymer Symp. Hobbies: Tennis; Reading; Classical Guitar. Address: 17 Georgiana Street, Flagstaff Hill, SA 5159, Australia.

KOLLEK Theodore (Teddy), b. 27 May 1911, Vienna. Politician. m. Tamar Schwarz, 1937, 1 s, 1 d. Appointments: Fndr Mbr, Kibbutz Ein Gev, 1937; Polit Dept, Jewish Agcy for Palestine, 1940; Fndr, Jewish Agcy Off, Istanbul, 1942; Mission to USA for haganah, 1947-48; Hd, US Div, Israel Fgn Min, 1950; Min, WA, 1951-52; Dir-Gen of PM Off, Jerusalem, 1952-65; Chair, Israel Govt Tourist Corp, 1955-65; Chair, Israel Govt Water Desalination Jt Project w US Govt, 1964-66; Chair, Bd of Govs, Israel Mus, Jerusalem, 1965-93; Mbr, Advsry Bd, Inst on Global Conflict and Co-op, 1982-92. Publications: Jerusalem: A History of Forty Centuries (co-auth); Pilgrims to the Holy Land (co-auth), 1970; For Jerusalem (autobiog), 1978; My Jerusalem; Twelve Walks in the World's Holiest City (co-auth); 180 polit sci articles. Honours: Sev doctorates, prizes and awds. Hobbies: Archaeology; Reading; Collecting Ancient Maps and Books on Holy Land. Address: 3 Guatemala Street, Kiryat Yovel, Jerusalem 96704, Israel.

KOLOBOV Alexander, b. 10 Apr 1955, Armavir, Russia. Physicist. m. V Makarova, 6 Nov 1989, 1 d. Education: MSc, 1979; PhD, 1983, DSc, 1991. Appointments: Jnr Rschr, Rschr, Ioffe Phys-Tech Inst, St Petersburg, Russia, 1979-94; Snr Visng Fell, Univ of Cambridge, England, 1 yr; Rschr, Ecole Superieure de Physique, Paris, France, 1991-92; Vis Prof, Belgium, 1993; Snr Rschr, Natl Inst for Adv Interdisciplinary Rsch, 1994-. Publications: Over 110 sci publns in profl jrnls.

Honour: Kapitza Fellshp Awd, Roy Soc of London, 1993. Hobbies: Travelling; Linguistics. Address: 1-1-4 Higashi, Ibaraki, Tsukuba, Japan.

KOMURA Masahiko, Politician. Appointments: Fmr Parl Vice-Min, Def Agcy; Min of State; Dir-Gen, Econ Planning Agcy, 1994-95; Mbr, House of Reps for Yamaguchi; Dpty Sec-Gen, LDP, Chair, LDP Specl Cttee on Disasters. Address: Economic Planning Agency, 3-1 Kasumigaseki, Chiyoda-ku, Tokyo, Japan.

KONDO Yoshio, b. 17 Feb 1924, Kyoto, Japan. Professor Emeritus. m. Noriko, 24 Oct 1951, 1 s, 1 d. Education: BEng, DEng, Kyoto Univ. Appointments: Assoc Prof, Prof, Kyoto Univ; Rsch Assoc, MIT. Publications: Human Motivation, 1991; Companywide Quality Control, 1995. Honours: EMDS Sci Awd, 1971; Deming Prize, 1971; E L Grant Awd, ASQC, 1977; ASQC Fell, 1988; Hon Mbr, JSQC, 1994. Memberships: Pres, Japanese Soc for Quality Control, 1992-93; Pres, Intl Acady for Quality, 1994-96. Hobbies: Tennis; Mountain Climbing; Skiing. Address: 29 Hihashi-Takagicho, Shimogamo, Sakyo-ku, Kyoto 606-0865, Japan.

KONG Fan Rang, b. 10 Nov 1951. Educr. m. Zhang Xiao Dong, 1 Oct 1980, 1 d. Education: PhD. Publication: Sleep Colour Map Technology, 1995. Hobbies: Computers; Swimming. Address: Department of Precision Instrumentation, University of Science & Technology of China, Hefei, Anhui 230026, China.

KONG Fanhu, b. 1 Aug 1924, Hebei, China. Plastic Surgeon. m. Kang Qiyu, 30 Dec 1948, 1 s, 2 d. Education: MD, Beijing Med Univ, 1950. Appointments: Vice Dir, Dept of Plastic Surg, 3rd Hosp, Beijing Med Univ, 1968-84; Med Cttee, Chinese Min of Pub Hlth, 1981-87; Med Technique Apprasal and Consultative Specl, Chinese Min of Public Hlth, 1988-; Edl Bd, Chinese Jrnl of Surg, 1985-; Vice Ed, Chinese Jrnl of Plastic Surg and Burns, 1995-; VP, Plastic Surg Inst of Chinese Med Assn, 1992-96; Cnslt, Chinese Jrnl of Reparative and Reconstructive Surg, 1995-; Cnslt, Chinese Jrnl of Practical Aesthetic and Plastic Surg, 1997-. Publications: Practical Plastic Operative Surgery, 1965; Plastic Surgery Volume of Chinese Encyclopedia, 1986; Over 50 pprs in var jrnls. Honour: Adv Worker, Beijing Govt, 1960. Memberships: Chinese Med Assn; Chinese Plastic Surg Inst. Hobbies: Travel; Calligraphy. Address: c/o Dormitory of 3rd Hospital 1-2-401, Beijing Medical University, Hua Yuan North Road 49, Beijing 100083, China.

KONG Ing Chung, b. 4 Mar 1965, Malaysia. Geologist. Education: BSc, hons, Appl Geol, Univ Malaya. Appointment: Geol, Global Minerals (Sarawak) Pty Ltd, 1992-. Memberships: Geol Soc of Malaysia; Malaysia Inst of Geol. Hobbies: Travel; Swimming. Address: No 480 Jalan Brayun, 95000 Sri Aman, Sarawak, Malaysia.

KONG Jackson, b. 19 Jan 1965, Hong Kong. Engineer. m. Sara Chan, 6 May 1995. Education: BS, Engl, (1st Class Hons), Univ of London, UK; MASc, Univ of Waterloo; MEng, Univ of Toronto; PhD, Univ of Hong Kong. Appointments: Univ of Hong Kong, 1994-95; Univ of Toronto, 1995-96; Maunsell Cnslt Aria Ltd, 1996-. Publications: Over 20 articles in var intl jrnls and conf proceedings. Honours: Dennis Gadd Prize, 1984; Anthony Gordon Pooley Mem Prize, 1986; Croucher Fndn Fllshp, 1995-96; Memberships: NY Acady of Sci. Address: Block 48, 26/F, Baguio Villa, Victoria Road, Hong Kong, China.

KONG Lingren, b. Nov 1924, Qufu County, Shandong, China. Politician. Education; Tsinghua Univ. Appointments: Chinese Democratic League, 1952; Lectr, Assoc Prof, Shandong Univ; Vice Chair, Shandong Prov CPPCC; Vice Chair, China Confucius Fndn; Mbr, 7th CPPCC, 1988; Mbr, Standing Cttee, 8th CPPCC, 1993-; Vice Chair, 7th Exec Cttee, All-China Womens Fedn, 1993-; Vice Chair, 8th Chinese Democratic League Ctrl Cttee, 1997-. Address: All-China Womens Federation, Beijing, China.

KONO Toshihiko, b. 8 Nov 1930, Ashiya, Japan, came to USA, 1966. Cellist. m. Edna Libby, 20 June 1968, 2 d. Education: LLB, Kyoto Univ, 1953; Student, Mannes Coll Music, Stanford Univ, Kneisel Hall Sch; DFA (Hon), London Inst Applied Rsch; Studied w Gaspar Cassado, Zara Nelsova. Career: Appearances throughout world in recitals, chmbr music, w symph orchs; Also radio, TV, fest concerts; Prin cellist w num Orchs incl Kyoto Symph Orch, Amn Symph Orch (In-sch concerts), Westchester Phil Orch, S I Symph Orch, 1990-; Drs Orch Soc, NY, 1991-; Cntr Symph Orch, 1992-; Yonkers Phil Orch, 1997-; Asst Prin Cellist, New Orleans Phil Orch, 1967-68; Cellist, Amn Symph Orch (Leopold Stokowski, Carnegie Hall, NYC), 1968-90, Trustee, 1975-90; Res artist mbr, Acadia String Quartet, Bar Harbor (Maine) Fest, 1971-; Prin Cellist, Fest Orch, 1984-. Publications: Num articles to profl jrnls and periodicals. Honours: Decorated Count Lofsensic Ursinius Order; Baron, Roy Order of Bohemian Crown; Count Order of San Ciriaco; Fromm Fell, Fest Contemporary Music, Tanglewood, 1970, 1971; van Beethoven Medal, Dip of Hon and Silver Medal for Disting Serv to Music, 1974; Awd for Contemporary Achievement, 1975; US Pres' Medal of Merit, 1990; Legion of Merit, 1991; IBC Gold Medal, 1991; ABI Gold Medal of Hon, 1991; Serv Awd, BHF, 1991; Named Man of Yr, ABI, 1991. Dpty Dir Gen, IBC, 1997-; Order of Intl Fellshp, 1998. Memberships include: Acady Maison Intl des Intellectuals; Assoc Musicians Gtr NY; Amn Fedn Musicians; Violoncello Soc; Intl Platform Assn; NY Cttee for Young Audiences. Address: 400 W 43rd St, New York, NY 10036, USA.

KONO Yohei, b. 15 Jan 1937, Japan. Politician. Education: Waseda Univ; Stanford Univ. Appointments: Mbr, House of Reps from Kanagawa; Fmr Parl Vice-Min of Educn; Dir-Gen, Sci & Technol Agcy; Chf Cabinet Sec, 1992-93; Chair, LDP Rsch Comm on Fgn Affairs, Pres, 1993-; Dpty PM, Min of Fgn Affairs, 1994-96; Co-Fndr, New Liberal Club; Mbr, Miyazawa Faction of LDP. Address: Liberal Democratic Party, 1-11-23 nagata-cho, Chiyoda-ku, Tokyo 100, Japan.

KONUK Nejat, b. 1928, Nicosia, Turkey. Politician; Lawyer; Writer. Education: Turkish Lycée, Cyprus; Law Fac, Ankara Univ, Turkey. Appointments: Legal Advsr, Turkish Civil Serv; Sec-Gen, Acting Dir-Gen, Turkish Communal Chamber, Cyprus; Under-Sec to Rauf Denktas, 1968-69; Min of Justice & Internal Affairs, Turkish Cypriot Admin, 1969-75; Mbr for Nicosia, Turkish Communal Chamber, Constituent Assembly, Turkish Cypriot Legislative Assembly, 1970-; Fndr Mbr, Natl Unity Party, 1975, Ldr, 1976-78; PM, Turkish Fed State of Cyprus, 1976-78; Ldr, Democratic Peoples Party, 1979-82; Pres, Legis Assembly, Turkish Fed State of Cyprus, 1981, 1982-83; PM, Turkish Repub of N Cyprus, 1983-85. Publications: Essays on lit, var pprs on Cyprus polit articles, 1953-77. Hobbies: Reading; Swimming. Address: Kumsal, Lefkosa, Mersin 10, Turkey.

KOO L C, b. 26 Oct 1947, Hong Kong, China. Consultant. m. Christine, 22 Sept 1973, 1 d. Education: PhD; MBA; DipMS; AHK1B; DipMmt. Appointments: Belgian Bank; Poon Kam Kai Inst of Mngmt; HKU; Hong Kong Bank; Hsin Chong; HKECIC; WT Aircargo; Emery Airfreight; Jebeen & Co Ltd. Publication: Balanced Scorecard. Honours: Master Tchr, IMC, 1998; Doct Supvsr. Memberships: HKQMA, Vice Chmn, 1997-98. Hobbies: Business; Research. Address: Quality Service Department, Belgian Bank, Belgian Bank Tower 27th Floor, 77-79 Gloucester Road, Hong Kong, China.

KOPEIKA N S, b. 12 Nov 1944, Baltimore, USA. Electrical Engineering Professor. m. Miriam, 13 Mar 1966, 2 s, 1 d. Education: BSc, 1966, MSc, 1968, PhD, 1972, Elec Engrng, Univ PA, USA. Appointments: Lectr, 1973, Snr Lectr, 1976, Assoc Prof, 1981, Prof, 1987, Dept of Elec and Computer Engrng, Ben Gurion Univ of the Negev, Israel. Publications: Over 130 pprs in intl jrnls. Honours: Rsch Grants, Israel Min of Sci, US Air Force, Wolfson Fndn, DIP (Germany). Memberships: IEEE; OSA; SPIE. Hobbies: Jewish Studies; Sports. Address: Ben Gurion University of the Negev, Department of

Electrical & Computer Engineering, PO Box 653, Beer-Sheva, Israel.

KOPEKOV Danatar, b. 12 May 1933, Ashgabat. Minister of Defence. Education: Chardzhou Pedagogical Inst and Spec Sch of Turkmen KGB. Appointments: Mbr, CP, 1958-91; Geog Tchr, Kum Dag Raion and Ashgabat, 1954-59; Chr, KGB Res,Meshkhed, Iran, 1959-84; Dpty Chair, Personnel, Operational Questions, Turkmen KGB, 1984-90; 1st Dpty Chair, Chair, Turkmen KGB, 1991. Memberships: Auditing Commn for Turkman CP, 1991; Chair, Turkman Natl Security Cttee, 1991. Address: Ministry of Defence, Ashgabat, pr Magtymguly 83, Turkmenistan.

KORASANI Nematollah, b. 16 Nov 1945, Iran. Academic Staff. m. A Matin, 1 Oct 1982. Education: PhD. Appointments: Hd of Environl Dept, Univ of Tehran. Publications: Many Books; Articles; Text. Honors: SKI; Memberships: IUFRO; MAB; IEES. Hobbies: Football; Singing. Address: Islamic Azad Univ, P O Box 14515 775, Tehran, Iran.

KORN Israel, b. 2 Mar 1934, Zamosc. Electrical Engineering. m. Nurit, 4 May 1961, 2 s, 1 d. Education; BSc, 1962, MSc, 1964, DSc, 1968, Technion-Israel Inst of Technol, Haifa, Israel. Appointments: lectr, 1968; Vis Asst Prof, 1969-71; Rsch Assoc, 1971-72; Snr Lectr, 1972-76; Assoc Prof, 1976-95. Publication: Digital Communications, 1985. Honour: Fell, IEEE. Membership: IEEE. Hobby: Philosophy. Address: 188 Military Road, Dover Heights, NSW 2030, Australia.

KOSAI Akio, b. 19 Apr 1931, Okayama, Japan. Business Executive. Education: Univ of Tokyo. Appointments: Joined Sumitomo Chem Co Ltd, 1954, Dir, Gen Mngr, Indl Chems & Fertilizers Divsn, 1983; Pres, Petrochem Corp of Singapore (Pte) Ltd, 1984-87; Mngng Dir, 1987, Snr Mngng Dir, 1991, Pres, 1993-, Sumitomo Chem Co Ltd. Address: 27-1 Shinkawa 2-chome, Chuo-ku, Tokyo 104, Japan.

KOSHI Masaki, b. 16 Nov 1934, Tokyo, Japan. Engineering Educator. Yoko Sato, 10 Oct 1959. Education: MSc, Univ of Tokyo, 1959. Appointments: Chmn, Road Rsch Grp, Orgn Econ Coop Dev Advocator; Ldr, Rsch and Dev, Automated Underground Freight Transport System. Publications: Auth, sev books on road traffic engrng; Contbr, articles to profl jrnls. Honours: Recip, article awd, Intl Assn Traffic and Scis, Tokyo, 1984. Memberships: Japanese Soc Civil Egrng; Jaan Soc Traffic Engrs; Intl Assn, Traffic and Safety Scis. Hobbies: Skiing; Sailing. Address: Nihon University, 7-24-1, Natashinodai, Funabashi-shi, Chiba, 274-8501, Japan.

KOSHIRO Matsumoto IX (born Teruaki Fujima), b. 1942, Japan. Actor. Appointments: As Child Acted Under Name "Kintaro; Became Koshiro IX, 1980. Creative Works: Plays Acted In incl: Kanjincho (and many other Kabuki plays); Man of La Mancha (incl 10 weeks run on Broadway); The Passion of Dracula; The King and I; Half a Sixpence; Sweeney Todd; Fiddler on the Roof; Amadeus (Salieri). AddressL c/o Kabukiza Theatre, No 12-15 Ginza 4-chome, Chuo-ku, Tokyo 104, Japan.

KOSHIYAMA Hiroyuki, b. 13 Oct 1956, Fukuchyama, Japan. Physician. m. Sonoko, 20 Apr 1986, 2 d. Education: MD, Kyoto Univ, 1982; PhD, Kyoto Univ, 1989. Appointments: Staff, Kurashiki Cntrl Hosp, 1983-85; Visng Scientist, Harvard Sch of Pub Hlth, 1989-91; Chf Physn, Kyoto Cty Hosp, 1991-94; Chf, Div Endo & Metal Dept Intern Med, Hyogo Prof Amagasaki Hosp, 1994-; Clin Instr, Dept Med & Clin Sci, Kyoto Univ Grad Medl Sch, 1994-. Honours: Lilly Intl Fell, 1989; Sandoz Co Geriatric Med Grantee, 1989; Hyogo Pref Medl Sch Rsch Grantee, 1996; Rsch Awd Dept Medl Clin Sci, Kyoto Univ Grad Medl Sch, 1997. Memberships: Japan Diabetes Soc; Japan Intl Medl Soc; Japan Endocrine Soc; Endocrine Soc Intl Endocrinology Soc. Address: 6-27-9 Tsukumo-dai, Suita, Osaka 565, Japan.

KOSSATZ Leslie George, b. 10 Jan 1943, Melbourne, Australia. Artist (Sculptor). Education: Dip Art RMIT,

TSTC. Appointments: Lectr, Sch of Fine Art, Roy Melbourne Inst of Technol, 1967-90; Hd of Sculp, Monash Univ, 1994-. Creative works: Ceremonial doors, High Crt of Aust, 1988; Archtl Glass, Austl Emb, RIYADA; Other pub sculps in all major Austl art mus. Address: 90 Kay Street, Carlton, Vic 3053, Australia.

KOTCHEFF Ted, b. 7 Apr 1931, Toronto, Canada. Film & Stage Director. Appointments: CBC TV, 1952-57; ABC-TV, London, 1957. Creative works: Plays: Play With A Tiger; Maggie May; The Au Pair Man; Have You Any Dirty Washing; Mother Dear?. Films incl: Life At The Top, 1965; Two Gentlemen Sharing, 1968; Wake In Fright, 1971; The Apprenticeship of Duddy Kravitz (in Can), 1973-74; Fun with Dick and Jane, 1977; Who is Killing the Great Chefs of Europe?, 1978; North Dallas Forty (dir & wrote), 1979; First Blood, Split Image, 1982-83; Uncommon Valour, 1984; Joshua Then and Now, 1985; Weekend at Bernie's, 1989; Winter People (dir), 1990; Folks! (actor), The Shooter, 1996. TV Plays Incl: The Human Voice, 1966; Of Mice and Men, 1968; Edna The Inebriate Woman, 1971. Address: ICM, 8942 Wilshire Boulevard, Beverly Hills, CA 90211, USA.

KOTESWARA RAO Tumuluru, b. 23 Aug 1964. Librarian. m. Ms Latha, 26 June 1994. Education: MSc, Dist, Andhra Univ; BLISc, Rank Holder, AndhraUniv; MLISc, Annamalai Univ; MBA, Pursuing, IGNOU. Appointments: Jnr Lectr in Bio, Guntur, AP, India, 1989; Apprentice, The Brit Cncl, Madras, 1989; Lib Assoc, Citibank, Madras, India, 1989; Asst Mngr, Customer Servs, The Brit Cncl Lib, Hyderabad, India, 1991-. Publications: Regular Contbr to Brit Cncl's Inhouse Jrnls, Current Awareness Bulletins. Honours: Winner, Serv Ex & Citistar Awds Citibank, Madras, 1991; Proj Leader, Quality Improvement Projects; Brit Cncl Lib, Hyderabad, 1996. Memberships: IASLIC, Calcutta; ILA, New Delhi; ALSD, Hyderabad; HMA, Hymark, Hyderabad. Hobbies: Reading; Writing; Articles; Listening to Music; Playing Carrom & Cricket; Interested in contributing to British Council's Objectives. Address: The British Library, 5-9-22, Sarovar Centre, Secretariat Road, Hyderabad 500 004, Andhra Pradesh, India.

KOTHARI Hemraj, b. 10 Nov 1933, Sujangarh, Rajasthan. Management and Technical Consultant; Chartered Engineer; Valuer; Arbitrator. Education: BS; DWP (Lon); CE (Lond and India); FIMEChE (Lon); FCI (Lon); FRAS (Lon); FBIS (Lon); FIE; FAE; MASME (USA); PhD (Hon), USA; FISE; FSEI; LMIIM; FGMS; MMMGI. Appointments: Fndr, Owner, Orgn Controller, India Intl News Serv; Ed, Dir, Kothai Publ; Kothsi Cnslt. Publications: 11 books, inclng Fndr, Ed, Who's Who series in India; Ed, over 7 profl jrnls. Honours: Apptd Assessor of Municipalities in W Bengal by the Gov over 7 yrs on panel of Arbitration; Amn Arbitration Assn; Indian Cncl of Arbitrators. Memberships: Life Fell, Fell, Life Mbr, Cttee Mbr of over 100 profl and trade orgns worldwide, inclng: NY Acady of Scis; Natl Acady of Sci (India). Hobbies: Films; Journalism; Travel. Address: Kothari Organisation, 12, India Exchange Place, Calcutta 700001, India.

KOTHS Kirston, b. 24 Dec 1948, LaFayette, IN, USA. m. Catherine, 24 Aug 1985, 1 s. Education: BS, Amherst Coll, 1971; PhD, Biochem, Molecular Bio, Harv Univ, 1971. Appointments: Mngr, Protein Chem Dept, Cetus Corp; Dir, Rsch; Dir of Rsch, Therapeut Div, Chiron Corp. Creative Works: num sci pprs and pats. Hobbies: Photography; American traditional dance; Fly fishing. Address: 2646 Mira Vista Dr, El Cerrito, CA 94530, USA.

KOUMOTO Kunihito, b. 12 Nov 1949, Okayama, Japan. Professor. m. Tomoko, 30 Apr 1976, 1 s, 1 d. Education: BS, MS, DEng, Univ of Tokyo, Japan. Appointments: Asst Prof, 1982, Assoc Prof, 1986, Univ of Tokyo; Prof, Nagoya Univ, 1992. Publications: Ceramic Materials Science, 1996; Solid State Chemistry, 1996. Honour: Richard M Fulrath Pacific Awd, 1993. Memberships: AAAS, 1996-; Chem Soc Japan, 1980-; Amn Ceramic Soc, 1980-; Ceramic Soc Japan, 1975-. Hobbies: Golf; Music; Baseball; Skiing; Art. Address:

Department of Applied Chemistry, Nagoya University, Nagoya, 464-8603, Japan.

KOYAMA Sadao, b. 20 May 1936, Yokohama, Japan. Vice President, Professor of Law. m. Yoshiko Muto, 20 Oct 1960, 2 d. Education: LLB, 1959, LLD, 1969, Tohoku Univ. Appointments: Lectr, 1963, Assoc Prof, 1968, Prof of Law, 1975, Dean, Fac of Law, 1992-94, Dir, Univ Lib, 1994-97, VP, 1997-, Tohoku Univ. Publications: Local Government of Medieval England, 1968; The Formation of English Law and its Modern Transformation, 1983; Studies in the Legal History of Tudor and Early Stuart England, 1992. Memberships: Japan Legal Hist Assn, cnclr, 1976-84, 1988-, auditor, 1987-88; Chmn, Bd of Cnclrs, 1996-; Selden Soc. Address: 11-1002 Kawauchi-jutaku, 35 Kawauchi-Motohasekura, Aoba-ku, Sendai 980-0861, Japan.

KRAIVICHIEN Thanin, b. 5 Apr 1927, Thailand. Politician; Jurist. 5 children. Education: Suan Kularp Sch; Thammasat Univ; Univ of London, Gray's Inn. Appointments: Snr Judge, Civil Crt, 1969; Snr Judge, Crt of Appeal, 1972; Judge, Supreme Crt, 1972-76; Snr Judge, 1976; Mbr, Investment Bd of Thailand, 1976-77. Publications: Democracy; Communist Ideology and Tactics; The Language of the Thai Law; The Use of Anti-Communist Law; Constitutional Monarchy; The Reform of the Legal and Judicial Systems During the Reign of King Chulalongkorn. Address: Office of the Prime Minister, Government House, Bangkok, Thailand.

KRAMER Leonie (Judith), b. 1 Oct 1924. m. Harold Kramer, 1952, 2 d. Education: BA, Melbourne Univ, 1945; DPhil, St Hugh's Coll, Oxford, 1953; FAHA; FACE. Appointments: Tutor, Lectr, Univ of Melbourne, 1945-49; Tutor & postgrad, student, St Hugh's Coll, Oxford, 1949-52; Lectr, Canberra Univ Coll, 1954-56; Lectr, Subseq Snr Lectr & Assoc Prof, Univ of NSW, 1958-68; Prof, Austl Lit, Univ of Sydney, 1968-89; Dpty Chan, 1989-91, Chan, 1991, Univ of Sydney Sen; Dir, Austl & NZ Banking Grp, 1983-94; West Mining Corp Ltd, 1984-96; Chmn, Quadrant Mag, 1988-. Publications: (as L J Gibson) Henry Handel Richardson and Some of Her Sources, 1954; A Companion to Australian Felix, 1962; Myself When Laura: fact and fiction in Henry Richardson's school career, 1966; Henry Handel Richardson, 1967, repr as contbr to Six Australian Writers, 1971; (w Robert D Eagleson) Language and Literature: a synthesis, 1976; A D Hope, 1979; (ed and intro) The Oxford History of Australian Literature, 1981; (co-ed) The Oxford Anthology of Australian Literature, 1985; (Ed and intro) My Country: Australian poetry and short stories - two hundred years, 1985; (ed and intro) James McAuley, 1988; (ed) Collected Poems of David Campbell, 1989; (ed) Collected Poems of James McAuley, 1995. Hnours include: OBE, 1976; Hon DLitt: Tasmania, 1977; Queensland, 1991; NSW, 1992; Hon LLD: Melbourne, 1983; ANU, 1984; DBE, 1983; Britannica Awd, 1986; AC, 1993. Memberships include: World Book Encyclopedia Britannica Advsry Bd, 1989-; Intl Advsry Cttee Encyclopedia Britannica, 1991-; Cncl of Aust Inst of Co Dirs, 1992-; Chmn, Op Rainbow Aust Ltd, 1996-. Hobbies: Gardening; Music. Address: 12 Vaucluse Road, Vaucluse, NSW 2030, Australia.

KRAMER Stanley, b. 29 Sept 1913, New York, USA. Film Producer; Director. m. (1) Ann Pearce, 1950, 2 s, (2) Karen Sharpe, 1966, 2 d. Education: NY Univ. Appointments: Film Cutter, Film Ed, Radio Writer, MGM Rsch Dept; US Signal Corp; Fndr, Film Prodn Co; Fndr, Pres, Dramer Pictures, 1949-. Creative Works: Films incl: So Ends Our Night, 1941; The Moon and Sixpence, 1942; So This is New York, 1948; Home of the Brave, 1949; The Men, 1950; Cyrano de Bergerac, 1950; Death of a Salesman, 1951; High Noon, 1952; The Happy Time, 1952; Eight Iron Men, 1952; The Caine Mutiny, Not As A Stranger, 1955; The Pride and the Passion, 1957; The Defiant Ones, 1958; On The Beach, 1959; Inherit the Wind, 1960; Judgment at Nuremberg, 1961; It's a Mad, Mad, Mad, Mad World, 1963; Ship of Fools, 1965; Guess Who's Coming to Dinner, 1967; The Secret of Santa Vittoria, 1969; R.P.M, 1971; Bless the Beasts and Children, 1971; Oklahoma Crude, 1973; The Domino

Principle, 1977; The Runner Stumbles, 1979. Address: c/o Paul Kohner, 9169 West Sunset Boulevard, Los Angeles, CA 90069, USA.

KREBS Stephen Jeffrey, b. 29 July 1950, Belvedere, Illinois, USA. Professor. m. Julie. Education: BSc, Plant Sci, 1976, MSc, Horticulture, 1977, PhD, Ecology, 1995, Univ CA, Davis. Appointments: Student Asst, Loan Dept, Peter J Shields Main Lib, 1970-72, Lib Asst II, Night & Weekend Supvsr, Loan Dept, Peter J Shields Main Lib, 1972-77, Tchng Asst, Pomology, 1977, Univ CA, Davis; Viticulturist, Mngr, San Pasqual Vineyards, Escondido, CA, 1977-79; Viticulturist, Mngr, Mayacamas Vineyards, Napa, CA, 1980-83; Viticulturist, Rschr, Jancis Robinson, 1984; Viticulturist, Mngr, Matanzas Creek Winery, Santa Rosa, CA, 1984-85; Viticulturist, Mngr, Sunny Slope Ranch, Glen Ellen, CA, 1986-89; Coord, Viticulture & Winery Technol, Napa Valley Coll, 1986-. Honours: Schslps, 1989-90, 1989, 1990; McPherson Disting Tchr Awd, Napa Valley Coll, 1994. Memberships: Am Soc for Enology & Viticulture; Napa Valley Grape Growers Assn; Napa County Farm Bur; Advsry Cttee, Napa County Resource Conservation Dist. Address: c/o Napa Valley College, Napa, CA 94558, USA.

KRIANGSAK Chomanan, b. 1917, Thailand. Politician; Army Officer. Education: Thai Roy Mil Acady; US Army Staff Coll. Appointments: Served, WW II, Korean War; Dpty Chf of Staff, Supreme Cmd HQ, 1974, Chf of Staff, 1974-76; Dpty Supreme Cmdr of Roy Thai Armed Forces, 1976-77, Supreme Cmdr, 1978; Participated, Mil Coups, 1976, 1977-78; Gen Sec, Natl Admin Reform Cncl, 1976; Vice Chair, PM's Advsry Cncl, 1976-77; Sec-Gen, Revolutionary Cncl, Natl Dir of Peacekeeping, 1977; Sec-Gen, Natl Policy Cncl, 1977-79; PM, 1977-80; Min of Fin, 1979-80, of the Interior, 1977-78, of Def, 1978-79, of Agricl, 1979-80; MP for Muang Roi Et, 1981; Ordained as Monk, Japan, 1983; Ldr, Natl Democratic Party. Address: National Assembly, Bangkok, Thailand.

KRIEGER David, b. 27 Mar 1942, Los Angeles, CA, USA. Peace Leader. m. Carolee, 14 Aug 1967, 2 s, 1 d. Education: MA, PhD, Polit Sci, Univ of HI, Manoa; JD, Santa Barbara Coll of Law. Appointments: Fndr, Nuclear Age Peace Fndn, Pres, 1982-; The Fndn has initiated projs for peace inclng: a World Campaign to Abolish Nuclear Weapons (later Abolition 2000 Global Network); Assoc, Cntr for Study of Dem Instns; Coord, Disarmament and Dev Proj, Fnd for Reshaping the Intl Order (RIO Fndn); Fmr Fac Mbr, Univ of HI and San Fran State Univ; Adj Fac Mbr, Univ of CA at Santa Barbara and Santa Barbara Cty Coll; Tchr through Cntr for the Study of the Future; Lectr worldwide. Publications include: Nuclear Weapons and the World Court: Countdown for Survival; The Challenge of Control and Management of Dual-Purpose Technologies; The Oceans: A Common Heritage; Preventing Accidental Nuclear War; Ed, The Tides of Change, Peace, Pollution and Potential of the Oceans; Waging Peace I; Waging Peace II. Honours: Bronze Medal, Hungarian Engrs for Peace, 1995; Peace Awd, War and Peace Fndn, 1996; Soka Gakkai Intl Peace and Culture Awd, 1997; Soka Univ Awd of Highest Hon, 1997. Memberships include: Judge, Arbitrator, Santa Barbara Superior Crt; Amn Soc for Intl Law; Amn Arbitration Assn; CA Bar Assn; Advsry Cnsl, Global Resource Action Cntr for thr Environ, NY; Intl Cncl of Inst on the Holocaust and Genocide (Israel)l Intl Inst for Peace (Vienna); Peace Resources Coop (Japan); Transnatl Fndn for Peace and Future (Sweden); War and Peace Fndn (NY; Whistler Fndn (Can); Dpty Chair, Intl Network of Engrs and Scientist for Global Responsibility (Germany); Bd Mbr, Lawyers Cttee on Nuclear Policy (NY). Address: Nuclear Age Foundation, PMB 121, 1187 Coast Village Rd, Ste 1, Santa Barbara, CA 93108-2794, USA.

KRIPALANI Ramesh Hiranand, b. 18 Aug 1948, Pune, India. Scientist. m. Sarla, 21 July 1980, 1 s, 1 d. Education: BSc, Phys, 1969; Msc, Maths, 1974; PhD, Phys (Atmospheric Scis), Univ of Poona, 1992. Appointments: Jnr Sci Offr, 1981-86, Snr Sci Offr Grade II, 1986-91, Snr Sci Offr Grade I, 1991-, Indian Inst of

Tropical Meteorology. Publications: 30 in natl and intl jrnls; 30 in conf proceedings on climate change and forecasting. Honours: 6th SAARC (S Asia for Regional Coop) Awd for a ppr publd in USA jrnl, 1986; UNDP Fellshp FL State Univ, USA, 1994; Attd conf in USA, Aust, Italy, China, Finland. Memberships: Indian Meteorological Soc, Sec of Pune chapt, 1993-95. Hobbies: Listening and collecting old (1945-1960) Hindi film songs. Address: Indian Institute of Tropical Meteorology, Pashan, Pune 411008, India.

KRISHNA Daya, b. 17 Sept 1924, Delhi, India. Retired Teacher. m. 8 May 1964, 2 d. Education: MA; PhD. Appointments: Lectr, Philos, Sagar Univ; Prof of Philos, Univ Rajasthan. Publications include: India's Intellectual Traditions, 1987; The Art of the Conceptual: Explorations in a Conceptual Maze Over Three Decades, 1989; Samvada: A Dialogue Between Two Philosophical Traditions, 1991; Indian Philosophy: A Counter Perspective, 1991. Honours: Sev fellshps. Memberships include: Rsch Cttee, Indian Cncl of Philos Rsch, New Delhi; Cncl, Sahitya Akademi, New Delhi; Bd of Govs, Tibetan Inst for Higher Studies, Sarnath. Address: B-189A University Marg, Bapunagar, Jaipur 302015, India.

KRISHNA Rozeline Devi, b. 21 Feb 1974, Nausori, Fiji. Management Accountant. Education: BCom, 1992-95, Dip, Bus Studies, 1994, Ctf in Banking, 1995, Dip, Mngmt, 1995, Nelson Polytech, NZ. Appointments: Acct, HLB Crosbie & Underhill, Chart Accts, 1996-97; Mngmt Acct, Consolidated Textiles (Fiji) Ltd, 1997-. Membership: Fiji Womens Rights Movement. Hobbies: Volleyball; Soccer; Badminton; Netball. Address: PO Box 654, Nausori, Fiji.

KRISHNAMURTHY Bangalore Laxminarayan Sastry, b. 1 Feb 1919, Bangalore, India. Senior Citizen (Retired Officer). m. Mrs Radhamma, 3 Sept 1941, 2 s, 3 d. Appointments: Police Constable; Hd Constable; Police Sub Inspector; Circle Inspector of Police; Asst Commnr of Police. Publications: Articles of 27 sensational crimes he investigated, publd in Indian Police Journal and mags, 1973, 1981, 1982, 1983, 1984. Honours: Indian Indep Medal, 1947; Pres, Police Medal, 1960; Best Investigation Awd for 1973, Home Min, Govt of India, 1975; 100 Rewards and Commendation Certificates. Hobbies: Reading; Sightseeing. Address: No 45, Mico Layout, Maha Laxmi Pura, Banglaore 86.

KRISHNAN Ayyathurai, b. 17 Nov 1923, Tiruchirappalli, India. m. 1 s, 1 d. Education: MS, Columbia Univ; Dip, Lib Sci, BSc, Hons, Calcutta Univ. Appointments: Libn; Documentation Offr; Sci in Charge. Honour: Fulbright Schlsp. Memberships: Indian Lib Assn; Indian Assn of Specl Libs and Info Cntrs. Hobby: Carpentry. Address: 4 Nethaj Street, Srirangam, Trichy 620006, India.

KRISHNASWAMY K S, b. 23 Apr 1938, Bangalore, Inida. Astrophysicist. m. Shyamala, 2 s. Education: BSc Hons, Phys, Delhi Univ, 1957; MSc, Phys, 1959; PhD, Astron, Univ CA, 1965. Rsch Assoc, CA Tech Inst, 1965; Univ Chgo, 1965-66; Snr Rsch Assoc, Rice Univ, 1966-69, 1973-75, 1986-88; Snr Visng Fell, SERC, 1974, 1980-81; Snr Prof, Tata Inst Fund Rsch, Bombay, India, 1992-; Visng Scientist, Intl Cntr for the Theort Phys, Italy, 1995. Creative Works: Physics of Comets, 1986; Ed, Astrophysics: A Modern Perspective, 1996. Honours: Dr Vikram Sarabhai Rsch Awd, Phys Rsch Lab, 1979; Fell, Indian Acady Scis. Memberships: Intl Astron Union. Address: 301 Satyendra, TIFR Housing, Colony Homi Bhabha Road, Bombay 400 005, India.

KRITHIVASAN Narayanaswamy, b. 20 Dec 1941, Marathurai, India. Engineer. m. Meenakshi, 10 Nov 1972, 2 s. Education: BEng; Master Deg in Structural Engrng; Postgrad Dip, Bus Mngmt; Dip of Proficiency in German. Appointments: Divl Railway Mngr, Chennai Div, Southern Railway, 1988; Chief Proj Mngr, Gauge Conversion, Southern Railway, 1992; Gen Mngr, IRCON, 1993; Chief Admstv Offr, Cnstrn, 1995; Gen Mngr, West Railway Mumbai, 1996; Gen Mngr, Southern Railway,

Chennai, 1997-. Honours: Spec Awd, Hon Min for Railways, Govt of India, 1994; Best Railway Awd, Southern Railway, 1997-98. Memberships: Fell, IE, India; Indian Railway Permanent Way Engrs. Hobbies: Chess; Cricket; Badminton; Music; Gardening; Reading. Address: Kaveri, 23 Haddows Road, Chennai, 600006, India.

KRON Tomas, b. 24 Sept 1958, Mainz, Germany. Medical Physicist. Education: Dipl Phys, Mainz, 1983; Dr phil nat, Frankfurt, 1989. Appointments: Snr Sci Offr, Illawarra Cancer Care Cntr, 1991-92; Chf Phys, Newcastle Mater Hosp, 1993-; A/Prof Dept of Phys, Univ of Newcastle, 1998-. Publications: Co-auth, book: Physics of X-Rays from Linear-Acceloratars, 1997; 40 sci articles in intl jrnls. Honours: Boyce Worthly Awd (ACPSEM), 1995; Agfa Schl (AIR), 1996. Memberships; ACPSEM (Chmn, Educ Cttee);AAPM; ESTRO; DGMP; AIP; ARPS. Address: Department of Radiation Oncology, Newcastle Mater Hospital, Locked Bag 7, Hunter Region Mail Centre, NSW 2310, Australia.

KRUL Stephen John, b. 5 Oct 1960. Educational Administration. m. Susan Winton, 1 s. Education: BA (1st Class Hons), Massey Univ, 1982; Univ of Melbourne Postgrad Schlshp, 1984. Appointments: Exec Asst to Vice Chancellor, Swinburne Univ of Technol, 1990-94; Rsch and Grad Studies, Univ of Adelaide, 1994-95; Chf Exec Offr and Registrar, Roy Austrasian Coll of Medl Adminstrs, 1995-. Memberships: MAITEA, 1986, 1990, 1995. Hobbies: Literature; Poetry; Music; Reggae; Football. Address: 35 Drummond Street, Carlton, Victoria 3053, Australia.

KUA-PENNY Angelin P L, b. 6 Oct 1964. Sales and Marketing Manager. m. Neil Penny, 26 June 1996. Education: Chartered Inst of Mktng CIM (UK). Appointments: Inventory Controller, Mktng Exec Sales and Mktng Exec, Snr Sales and Mktng Exec, Mktng Mngr, Intl Sales Exec, Snr Sales and Mktng Mngr. Honours: Cert Purchasing Mngr Course w Distinct, 1987; Chartered Inst of Mktng, 1994. Memberships: Chartered Inst of Mktng, 1994; Singapore Inst of Mktng; Singapore Mfrs Assn; Singapore Inst of Materials Mngmt. Hobbies: Reading; Boating; Diving; Tennis; Travelling; Waterskiing. Address: 49 Watten Estate Road, Singapore 287524.

KUAN Ping-Yin, b. 10 Dec 1955, Taichung, Taiwan. University Professor. m. Barbara Cho, 28 July 1988, 1 d. Education: BA, Fu Jen Cath Univ, 1977; MSc, VA C'wlth Univ, 1982; PhD, Univ of VA, 1993. Appointments: Lectr, Dept of Sociol, Fu Jen Cath Univ, 1986-87; Assoc Prof, 1992-; Dir, Socio-Cultural Rsch Cntr, 1996-; Ed, China News Analysis, 1997-98. Publications: Choosing Rules of Distributive Justice, 1993; Whose Fairness? Whose Justice?, 1994; Stratification Beliefs in Taiwan, 1996; Handling Interpersonal Disputes: A Study of Attitudes Towards Formal and Informal Social Controls in Taiwan, 1999; Other articles. Honours: Phi Tau Phi Hon of Soc; Phi Kappa Phi; Alpha Kappa Delta. Memberships: Intl Ricci Assoc for Chinese Studies; Amn Sociolgcl Assoc; Taiwan Sociolgcl Assoc. Address: Department of Sociology, Fu Jen Catholic University, Taipei, Taiwan, China.

KUANG Jao-Hwa, b. 25 Sept 1948, Keelung, Taiwan. Professor. m. Yu-Hwa Pan, 11 Apr 1975, 2 d. Education: BS, MS, natl Chenkung Univ; PhD, Univ of Cincinnati, USA. Appointments: Mech Engr, 1973-74; Assoc Rschr, 1974-76; Instr of Univ, 1976-78; Assoc Prof, 1982-89; Prof, 1989-; Chmn, 1995-. Publications: 27 jrnl pprs, 68 intl conf pprs, 95 tech reports. Memberships: SAE, USA; IFTOM, USA; ASME, USA; CSME, Taiwan. Address: 13F No 302 Her-Ti Road, San-Min District, Kaohsiung 807, Taiwan.

KUANG Yu Zhong, b. 1 Aug 1835, Beijing, China. Musician. m. Chen Yuan, 1963. Education: Grad, Cntrl Conservatory of Music, China. Appointments: Vice Chmn, Folk Music Dept, 1983-89; Hd, Plucking Instrument grp. Creative Works: Performance Method of Pipa, 1995. Honours: Disting Tchr of Beijing, 1993; Won Yang Xuelan Musical Educ Awd. Memberships: Chinese Musicians

Assn; Beijing Photog Assn. Hobbies: Photog. Address: 43 Bao Jia Street, Central Conservatory of Music, Beijing 100031, China.

KUBIK Kurt Karl, b. 13 Dec 1942, Vienna, Austria. Engineer. m. Heleen, 1970, 2 s, 1 d. Education: Dip Engr, Tech Univ Vienna, 1964; Dr Tech Sci, Tech Univ Vienna, 1967. Appointments: Tech Dir, Div of Info Processing, The Hague, Netherlands, 1973; Chairs, Survng Engrng in Denmark, OH State Univ; QLD Univ of Technol. Creative Works: 3 Books; More than 250 Sci Publs; 2 Pats. Honour: Hon Prof, Wuhan Tech Univ. Address: 35 Marlborough St, Sherwood, QLD 4075, Australia.

KUBO Junichi, b. 12 May 1937, Ako-shi, Japan. Senior Counsellor. m. Michiko, 25 Nov 1964, 1 s, 1 d. Education: Doct, Kyoto Univ. Appointments: Snr Rsch Assoc, Cntrl Tech Rsch Lab, 1980; Snr Rsch Cnslr, Cntrl Tech Rsch Lab, Nippon Oil Co Ltd, 1992; Snr Cnslr, Ako Kasei Co Ltd, 1997-. Publications: About 50 tech pprs in tech and sci jrnls. Honours: Awds from Japan Pet Inst; Awds from Ind Tech Agcy, Japan. Memberships: NY Acady Sci; Amn Chem Soc; Japan Pet Inst. Hobbies: Tennis; Golf; Walking; Painting. Address: Kariya Nakasu 5-59, Ako-shi, Hyogo-ken, 678-0233, Japan.

KUBO Ken-ichi, b. 18 May 1936, Kumamoto, Japan. Professor of University. m. Kimie Amano, 23 May 1964, 2 s. Education: DSc, Tokyo Inst of Technol, 1969. Appointments: Rsch Asst, Univ Tokyo, Japan, 1967-78; Rsch Fell, Max-Planck Inst, Heidelberg, 1972-74; Rsch Sci, TX A&M Univ, 1975-78; Snr Visng Fell, Nuc Phys Lab, Oxford, Eng, 1980; Visng Fell, Oxford Univ, Eng, 1990; Assoc Prof, 1978-85; Prof of Phys, 1985-. Tokyo Met Univ. Publications: Rsch pprs in jrnls; Books on Spin Phys, World of the Modern Physics, in Japanese. Memberships: Japan Phys Soc; Amn Phys Soc; AAAS. Hobbies: Opera; Jogging. Address: 2-7-7-803 Yakumo, Meguro-ku, Tokyo, 192-0023, Japan.

KUBODERA Ken'ichi, b. 10 Aug 1947, Kanagawa, Japan. Executive Researcher. m. Mariko Sakaue, 23 Apr 1974, 1 s, 1 d. Education: BS, 1970, MS, 1972, PhD, 1983, Univ Tokyo. Appointments: Rsch Engr, Nippon T & T Corp, Tokyo, 1972-99; Exec Mngr, New Tech Rsch Lab, Sumitomo Osaka Cement Co Ltd, 1999-. Publications: Diode-Pumped Solid-State Laser, 1979; Measurement of Nonlinear Optical Efficiencies, 1991. Memberships: IEEE, snr mbr, 1997-; IEICE. Hobbies: Golf; Skiing. Address: 3-14-102 Tsutsujino, 259 Kamihirose, Sayama-shi, Saitama 350-1321, Japan.

KUBOTA Manae, Politician. Appointments: Mbr, House of Cnclrs; Fgn Affairs Cttee; Budget Cttee; Vice Chair, Socl Democratic Party of Japan; Min of State, Dir-Gen, Econ Planning Agcy, 1993-94. Address: House of Representatives, Tokyo, Japan.

KUBU Vonivate, b. 8 Aug 1935, Nadroga, Fiji Islands. Labourer. m. Naqoqo, 27 July 1978, 2 s, 1 d. Appointment: Asst Treas, Cagimaira Devel Assn, Fiji. Hobbies: Reading; Playing Soccer; Television. Address: c/o Cagimaira Development Association, PO Box 1038 BA, Fiji.

KUBUABOLA Ratu Inoke, b. 16 June 1948. Government Minister. Education: Auckland Univ, NZ; Univ of S Pacific. Appointments: Mngmt Trnee, NZ Insurance Co Ltd, Auckland Br, 1972-75; Asst Mngr, Suva Br, 1975; Distbn Sec, Bible Soc, 1975-80; Exec Sec, Bible Soc in S Pacific, 1981-87; Min for Info, TV and Brdcstng, 1987; Telecomm, Interim Govt, 1988-92; Min for Yth, Employment Opportunities and Sports, Mbr of Parl, Cakaudrove Prov, 1992; Elected Mbr of Parl, 1994; Min for Regl Dev and Multiethnic Affairs, 1995. Address: Private Mail Bag, Samabula, Fiji.

KUFTARO Ahmad, b. Damascus, Syria. Grand Mufti of Syria. m. Sabah Jabri, 8 s, 3 d. Education: Self taught. Appointments: Mufti of Damascus, 1951; Elect as Grand Mufti of Syria, 1964. Publication: Spiritual and Intellectual Guidance of Muslims and People at Large. Memberships: Founder, Hd of Abu Nour Islamic Fndn; Co-Chair, Global

Forum for Environment. Hobbies: Reading; Walking; Swimming. Address: Sheikh Amin Kufturo Street, Rukn Eddeen, Damascus, Syria.

KUIPER Koenraad, b. 22 Feb 1944, Hannover. Academic. m. Alison Clare Wylde, 11 May 1968, 3 d. Education: MA (Hons), Engl, Vic Univ of Wellington, 1967; PhD, Linguistics, Simon Fraser Univ, 1972. Appointments: Master, Riccarton hs, Christchurch, 1969-70; Tchng Asst, Depts of Engl and Modern Langs, Simon Fraser Univ, 1973-74; Tchr, Burnside hs, Christchurch, 1975-79; Snr Lectr, Engl Dept, Univ of Canterbury, 1981; Visng Instr, Linguistics Dept, Univ of MA, Amherst, 1989; Visng Prof and Bard Coll Cntr Fell, Bard Coll, NY, 1993; Visng Prof, Bethany Coll, WV, 1993-95; Snr Lectr, Dept of Linguistics, Univ of Canterbury, 1996-; Assoc Prof, Linguistics Dept, Univ of Canterbury, 1997; Visng Prof, Dalian Univ of For Langs. Publications: Signs of Life, 1981; Mikrokosmos, 1990; Smooth talkers, 1996; An Introduction to English Language: Sound, Word and Sentence, 1996. Honours: Can Cncl Doct Fellshp, 1971-72; Fulbright Fellshps, 1988, 1993; Rsch Fellshp, NWO, 1995-96; China-NZ Travel Awd, 1997. Memberships: West Conf on Linguistics, 1970-72; Linguistic Soc of NZ, 1978-; Pres, 1981-82, 1989-91; Linguistic Soc of Am, 1979-; NZ Soc of Auths, 1995-. Hobbies: Swimming; Tennis; Gardening; Classical music. Address: 16 Tui Street, Christchurch, New Zealnd.

KUKKONEN Carl A, b. 25 Jan 1945, Duluth, MN, USA. Physicist; Research Director; Businessman. m. Noreen, 22 June 1968, 2 s. Education: BS, Phys, Univ of CA, Davis, 1968; MS, Phys, 1971, PhD, Phys, 1975, Cornell Univ, Ithaca, NY. Appointments: Dir, Cntr for Space Microelectrons, Jet Propulsion Lab, Pasadena, CA, 1984-98; Pres, Chf Exec Offr, ViaSpace Technols, Altadena, CA, 1998-. Honour: NASA Exceptional Achmnt Medal, 1992. Membership: Amn Phys Soc. Address: 33841 Mercator Isle, Monarch Beach, CA 92629, USA.

KULASEKHAR John Meshach, b. 30 Sept 1948. Commissioner. Education: BA, Econs, 1965-68, MA, Engl, 1968-70, St Josephs Coll, Tiruchirapalli; Dip, Ecumenical Studies, Univ of Geneva, 1978-79; MSc, Fiscal Studies, Univ of Bath, Eng, 1992-93. Appointments: Probationer, Indian Revenue Serv, 1972-75; Asst Cmmnr, Cntrl Excise, 1975-83; Dpty Cmmnr, Central Excise, 1983-94; Additional Cmmnr, Customs & Excise, 1994-96; Cmmnr, Customs & Excise, 1996-. Publication: Export Processing Zone, 1994. Honour: Pres of India's Awd, Meritorious Serv, 1996. Memberships: Mngmt Cttee, Cntr for Rural Hlth & Socl Educ, Tirupathur; VP, Soc for Upliftment of Econ Backward, Chennai; Cntr for Human Devl & Socl Change, Chennai; Pres, Anawim Trust, Kulasekarapattinam; Life Mr, YMCA; Mngng Cttee, Community Environ Monitoring Cntr. Hobbies: Reading; Rural Development; People's Organizations. Listed in: Directory of British Scholars. Address: 390/1 Green Gardens, Anna Nagar, Madras 6000102, India.

KULKARNI Ashwini, b. 16 July 1961, Pune, India. Scientist. m. Aniruddha, 1 Mar 1985, 1 d. Education: BSc (Stats), 1981; MSc (Stats), 1983; MPhil (Stats), 1986; PhD (Stats), 1992. Appointments: Snr Scientific Asst, 1988-94, Sci Offr, 1994-, Indian Inst of Tropical Meteorology, Pune, India. Publications: 10 in jrnls; 10 in proceedings, newsletters, rsch reports. Honour: Hon Prof, Univ of Poona. Membership: Indian Meterological Soc. Hobbies: Hindi film music; Classical Indian music. Address: Indian Institute of Tropical Meteorology, NCL PO, Pashan, Pune 411008, India.

KULKARNI Muralidhar Laymanrao, b. 8 Sept 1947, Munavalli, India. Doctor of Medicine. m. Bhagyavathi, 13 Aug 1976, 1 s, 1 d. Education: MBBS; MD; FIAP; FRCPCH; FICPCC; FAMS. Appointments: Prof, Hd, Dept of Paediats, JJM Med Coll. Publications: Pediatric Cardiology, 1997; Manual of Neonatology, 1998; Clinical Methods, 1999. Honours: B C Roy Natl Awd as Eminent Medl Tchr, Medl Cncl of India, 1994. Memberships: Roy Coll of Paediats, Eng; NY Acady of Scis; Skeletal

Dysplasia Grp, Eng; Intl Coll of Paediats. Hobbies: Reading; Travel; Music. Address: 2373 MCC A Block, Davangere 577004, Karnataka, India.

KULKARNI Ravindra, b. 12 Mar 1948, Mandusar, M P, India. Business. m. Alka, 20 May 1978, 1 s, 1 d. Education: PhD, Engl, Columbia Univ, USA. Appointments: Rsch Fell, Columbia Univ, NY, 1970-74; Proj Scientist/Snr Engr, Union Carbide, NY, 1974-80; Dir of Technol, EPID Inc (Exxon Corp), CA, 1980-86; Adv Dev Mngr, IBM, San Jose, CA, 1986-90; Mnging Dir, Elkay Chems, Pvt Ltd, Pune, India, 1990-. Publications: 31; 13 pats in silicone field. Honours: Best Scientist Awd, USA, 1985; Outstndng Entrepeneurs Awd, India, 1995. Hobbies: Reading; Walking. Address: Elkay Chemicals Pvt Ltd, j-152 MIDC, Bhosari, Pune 26, India.

KULKARNI Shrikrishna Ramchandra, b. 25 Mar 1927, Maharashtra, India. Career: Reorganised Bombay Dock Workers' Union, 1946; Organised All India Port & Dock Workers' Federation; Employed at all 11 major ports of India, President, 1962-; Trustee representing labour on Board of Trustees, Port of Mumbai, 1958-. Address: PD'Mello Bhawan, PD'Mello Road, Carnac Bunder, Mumbai 400 038, India.

KUMAGAI Hiroshi. Politician. Appointments: Mbr, House of Reps; Fmr Dpty Sec-Gen, Japanese Renewal Party (Shinseito) (JRP); Fmr Mbr, House of Cnclrs; Min of Intl Trade & Ind, 1993-94; Chf Cabinet Sec, 1994. Address: House of Representatives, Tokyo, Japan.

KUMAR Ananth, b. 22 July 1959, Bangalore, India. Member of Parliament. m. Tejaswini A, 15 Feb 1989, 2 d. Education: BA, K S Art Coll; LLB, JSS Law Coll, Karnataka Univ, Hubli. Appointments: Sec, 1982-85, Natl Sec, 1985-87, Akhil Bharatiya Vidhyarathi Parisha; Sec, 1987-88, Gen Sec, 1988-95, Natl Sec, 1995-, Bharatiya Janata Pty; Elected, 11th Lok Sabha, 1996; Mbr, Cttee on Ind, Consultative Cttee, Min of Railways, 1996-97; Re-elected, 12th Lok Sabha, 1998; Union Cabinet Min, Civ Aviation, 1998-. Publications: Num articles in newsppprs; Auth, num pamphlets and booklets on socio-pol and educl issues. Memberships: Cntrl Silk Bd, 1996-98; Gov Cncl, Indian Inst of Sci, Bangalore, 1996-98. Hobbies: Reading; Writing poetry; Travelling. Address: 16 Sati, 3rd Main Vyalikaval, Bangalore 560003, India.

KUMAR Cecilia, b. 17 July 1953, Lautoka, Fiji Is. School Teacher. m. Sushil, 28 Apr 1984, 2 s. Education: BEd; Dip in Mngmt; Cert in Tchng Engl as 2nd Lang; Tchrs Cert. Appointments: Pres, Soroptimist Intl Lautoka, 994-95; Pres Elect and Trng and Dev Coord, Soroptimist Intl, Fiji, 1998-99; Fedn Cttee Mbr, Soroptimist Intl of SW Pacific Trng and Dev Bd, representing Fiji, 1999-2000. Honours: Kathleen/Elliot Schlshp, 1994, 1996; Soroptimist Int Schlshp. Memberships: Soroptimist Intl of Fiji, Pres Elect, 1988-99. Hobbies: Social work; Cultural dancing; Reading. Address: PO Box 11372, Suva, Fiji Is.

KUMAR Girja, b. 27 Apr 1925, Dera Ghazi, Khan, India. University Librarian. m. Kuntirani, 15 Feb 1948, 1 s, 1 d. Education: MA, Econs; Dip.Lib.Sci. Appointments: Libn, Indian Cncl of World Affairs, 1947-71; Jawaharlal Nehru Univ, 1972-85. Publications: Ranganathan: An Intellectual Biography, 1992; The Book On Trial, 1997; Gandhi and His Women (forthcoming). Honour: Disting Serv Awd, Punjab Lib Assn. Hobbies: Theatre; Music; Cinema. Listed in: Who's Who in India; Who's Who of Indian Writers; Dictionary of International Biography. Address: K-14 Rajouri Garden, New Delhi 110027, India.

KUMAR Krishan, b. 5 Dec 1933, Dera Ghazi Khan, Pakistan. Retired Information Scientist. m. Brij Bala dec, 27 June 1963, 1 sm 2 d. Education: MA; MLibSc. Appointments: Lectr, Inst of Lib Sci, 1961-64, Dept of Lib Sci, Univ of Delhi, 1964-73; Dpty Libn, Panjab Univ, 1973-74; Rdr, Dept of Lib Sci, Univ of Delhi, 1974-84; Prof, Univ of Delhi, 1984-98. Publictions: Research Libraries in Developing Countries, 1973; Theory of Classification, 1988; Research Methods in Library & Information Science, 1992. Honours: ILA Diamond

Jubilee Awd, 1994; IATLIS Motivale Best Tchr Awd, 1994. Memberships: Indian Assn of Tchrs of Lib & Info Sci, 1985-89; Pres, Indian Lib Assn, 1988-90. Hobby: Reading Spiritualism. Address: K-14, Rajouri Garden, New Delhi 110027, India.

KUMAR Krishnan, b. 5 Dec 1933. Teacher (Retired). m. Brij Bala, 27 June 1963, 1 s, 2 d. Education: MA; MLibSc. Appointments: Lectr, Inst of Lib Sci, Univ of Deli, 1961-64; Lectr, Dept of Lib Sci, Univ of Delhi, 1964-73; Dpty Libn, Panjab Univ Lib, 1973-74; Rdr, Dept of Lib and Info Sci, Univ of Delhi, 1974-84; Prof, Dept of Lib and Info Sci, Univ of Delhi, 1984-98. Publications: Research Libraries in Developing Countries, 1973; Theory of Classification, 1988; Research Methods in Library and Information Science, 1992. Honours: ILA Diamond Jubilee Awd, 1994; IATLIS Motivale Best Tchr Awd, 1994. Memberships: Pres, Indian Lib Assn, 1988-90; Pres, Indian Assn of Tchrs of Lib and Info Sci, 1985-89; Sci Advsry Bd, ISKO, Frankfurt. Address: K-14, Rajouti Garden, New Delhi 110007, India.

KUMAR Mahesh, b. 29 Nov 1974, Jalandhar City, Punjab. Teacher. Education: Dip, Elem Educ. Creative Works: Writing a Book of Poems. Honours: Pahal, For Blood Donation. Memberships: Roy Club NGO; Pahal, NGO. Hobbies: Writing Verse; Blood Donation; Motivation. Address: 355 56 Preet Nagar, Sodal Road, Jalandhar, Punjab India.

KUMAR R P, b. 15 Mar 1948, Amritsar, India. Librarian. m. Neena, 23 Nov 1979, 2 d. Education: MSc, Zoology, Banaras Hindu Univ, 1970; MLib.Sc, 1977, PhD, 1983, Panjab Univ. Appointments: Lectr, DAV Coll,Amritsar, 1972-74; Libn, DAV Coll, Batala, 1975-76; Lectr, Libn, DAV Coll, Kangra, 1977-78; Ref Libn, ICRISAT, 1980-82; Chf Libn, AIIMS, 1983-. Publications: 5 books, 40 rsch pprs. Honours: ILA-Kaula Best Libn Awd, 1994; Gold Medal, Educl Awd; Prize, Educl Awd; 1st Annual SALIS Intl Achmnt Awd, 1998. Memberships: Sec, Med Lib Assn of India, 1993-98; Pres, ITLISA, 1985-87; Gen Sec, ILA, 1996-98. Hobbies: Badminton; Swimming; Cooking. Listed in: Who's Who in the World. Address: All India Institute of Medical Sciences, Ansari Nagar, New Delhi 110 029, India.

KUMAR Rajiv, b. 7 July 1965, Gaya, India. Researcher. m. Jyoti, 13 Mar 1994, 1 s, 2 d. Education: MA, Ancient Indian & Asian Studies, 1988; MA, Buddhist Studies, 1990; PhD, 1992; Dip, Jrnlsm, 1994. Appointments: Univ Rsch Schl, 1990-92; VGC Rsch Fell, 1993-97; Rsch Assoc, 1998-. Publications: 35 pprs in rsch jrnls. Memberships: Indian Hist Congress; Bhandarkar Oriental Rsch Inst; Panchal Sodha Sansthan; Exec Bd, Acady of Art & Arch, Mysore, 1992-93. Hobbies: Reading; Collecting Coins and Stamps. Address: No A-17, Magadh Univeraity Campus, Gaya (Bihar), India.

KUMAR Santosh, b. 8 Aug 1936. Professor. m. Veer Bale Kumar, 12 Dec 1966, 1 s. Education: BSc (Raj); MSc (Vikram); PhD (Delhi). Appointments: Lectr, K R Coll, 1959-60; Snr Sci Asst, 1960-67; Jnr Sci Offr, 1967-70; Lectr, RMIT, 1970-73; Snr Lectr, 1973-89, Prin Lectr, 1989-90, Assoc Prof, 1990-95, RMIT; Prof, 1995-, NUST, Zimbabwe; Fndn Prof and Chair, Applied Maths, 1995, Chmn of Dept, 1995-. Publications: 110 pprs; 2 books. Honours: RMIT 25 yrs serv awd, 1996; Snr Mbrshp. ORSI. Memberships: INFORM; ORSI; ASOR; ZAAM; Pres, APORS, 1995-97; Fell, Inst of Maths. Hobbies: World religion; Travel. Address: Department of Applied Mathematics, National University of Science & Technology, Ascor, PO Box AC 939, Bulawayo, Zimbabwe.

KUMAR Suresh, b. 17 Nov 1950. Senior Cadre Assistant Librarian. Education: MA ECon; MLISC. Appointments: Doc Asst, Indian Cncl of Socl Sci Rsch, 1978-80; Asst Libn, Indian Inst of Pub Admin, 1980-85, 1985-93; Snr Cadre Asst Libn, Indian Inst of Pub Admin, 1993-. Publications: BSI and BIS: a sample evaluation of standardisation of Library and Information Services (ppr, ILA seminar), 1989; Evaluation of Indexing and Abstracting Services in Public Administration, 1989;

National Public Administration Information Services Networks (PAISNET), ILA seminar, 1990; Rsch projs available in SSDC, 1980; Compiler, Indian Educ Index (1947-78); Bibliographies. Memberships: Life Mbr, Indian Lib Assn (ILA); Assn of Govt Libns and Info Servs (AGLIS). Address: B-24, Shivam Apts, D-Block, Vikaspuri, New Delhi 110018, India.

KUMAR Sushil, b. 14 Dec 1940. Director. m. Pushpa, 8 Feb 1972, 1 s. Education: PhD. Appointments: Sci S-2, S-3, S-4, Indian Agricl Rsch Inst, 1971-89; Sci-G, Cncl of Sci and Indl Rsch; Dir, Cntrl Inst of Medicinal and Aromatic Plants, Lucknow, 1993-. Publications: 28 books, 143 sci rsch and review articles, 25 pats; Auth: Nature 209: 1966; Journal of Bacteriology 125: 1976; Tropical Diseases: Molecular Biology and Control Strategies (book) Ed: Journal of Medicinal and Aromatic Plant Sciences. Honours: Medal awarded by IARI, 1962; Medal awarded by Indian Soc of Genetics and Plant Breeding IARI, New Delhi, 1965; Shanti Swarup Bhatnagar Prize, CSIR, New Delhi, 1981; Disting Scientist Awd, Natl Acady of Scis, Allahabad, 1986. Memberships: Fell, Indian Acady of Scis, Bangalore, India, 1981; Natl Acady of Agricl Scis, New Delhi, India, 1992; Natl Acady of Scis Allahabad, India, 1993; Indian Natl Sci Acady, New Delhi, India, 1994; Pres, Indian Soc Genetics and Plant Breed, 1994; Soc for Medicinal and Aromatic Plant Rsch; Soc for Conservation of Biodiversity; Soc for Nat Product Rsch. Hobbies: Reading; Music; Badminton. Address: Central Institute of Medicinal and Aromatic Plants, PO CIMAP, Lucknow, UP, India, 226015.

KUMAR Vijayananda Perikala, b. 1 June 1949, Neppalli, India. Doctor. m. Sandhya, 3 Dec 1976, 2 d. Education: MBBS; MD. Appointment: Prof. Publications: 3 books; 79 pprs. Honour: Best Tchr Awd. Membership: Intl Acady of Cytology. Address: Department of Pathology, Shiraz Medical School, Shiraz University of Medical Sciences, Shiraz, Iran.

KUMARASINGHE Gamini, b. 23 June 1944, Sri Lanka. Medical Doctor. m. Sepalika, 2 Sept 1971, 2 s. Education: MBBS; DPath; FRC Path; FRCPA. Appointments: Registrar, Snr Registrar, The Hosp for Sick Children, Great Ormond St, London; Cnslt, Min of Hlth, Saudi Arabia; Hd, Div of Microbiol, Natl Univ Hosp, Singapore. Memberships: Hosp Infection Soc, UK; Amn Soc of Microbiol; Intl Soc for Hum Animal Mycology. Hobbies: Tennis; Jogging; Music; Travelling. Address: Division of Microbiology, National University Hospital, Lower Kent Ridge Road, Singapore 119074, Singapore.

KUMARATUNGA Chandrika Bandaranaike, b. 29 June 1945, Colombo, Sri Lanka. President of Sri Lanka. m. Vijaya Kumaratunga, 1978, dec 1988, 1 s, 1 d. Education: St Bridget's Convent, Colombo; Univ of Paris. Appointments: Exec Cttee, Women's League of SLFP, 1974, Exec Cttee, Working Cttee, 1980, Ctrl Cttee, 1992; Chair, Mngng Dir, Dinakara Sinhala (daily newsppr), 1977-85; VP, Sri Lanka Mahajana (Peoples) Party (SLMP), 1984, Pres, 1986; Ldr, SLMP & Peoples Alliance; Chf Min, Min of Law & Order, Fin & Planning, Educn, Employment & Cultural Affairs of the W Prov Cncl, 1993-94; PM, 1994; Min of Fin & Planning, Ethnic Affairs, Natl Integration, 1994-, of Def, of Buddha Sasana, 1994-; Pres of Sri Lanka, 1994-. Publications: Sev rsch pprs on land reform and food policies. Hobbies: Piano; Guitar; Tennis; Swimming; Kandyan Dance; Music; Reading; Art; Sculpture; Drama; Cinema. Address: Presidential Secretariat, Republic Square, Colombo 1, Sri Lanka.

KUNARATNAM Kanthia, b. 30 Apr 1934, Erlalai, Sri Lanka. Senior Professor of Physics. m. Pushpawathy, 9 Sept 1964, 1 s, 2 d. Education: BSc (Cey) Spec Phys, 1st Class Hons, 1958; PhD (Lond) Imperial Coll, 1963; DIC (Lond), 1963; FRAS (Lond), 1998. Appointments: Asst Lectr, 1958-63, Lectr, Gr I, 1969-75, Univ of Colombo; Lectr Gr II, 1963-68, Univ of Peradeniya; Prof of Phys, 1975-85, Snr Prof, Phys, 1985-, Univ of Jaffna; Fndr Hd Dept Phys, 1975-85, Dean, Fac of Sci, 1977-78, 1984-88, Fndr, Hd, Dept Computer Sci, 1991-93, Vice-Chancellor, 1994-96, Univ of Jaffna, Sri Lanka. Publications:

Acclaimed PhD thesis on application of digital electronic computers to geophysical data interpretation, 1963; Rsch articles in intl jrnls on interpretation of magnetic anomalies and spatial and time variations of geomagnetic fields. Honours: Dr Hewavitharne Mem Prize for Phys, Univ of Colombo, 1958; Commonwealth Univs Acad Staff Fellshp, UK, 1971; Associateship of the ICTP, Italy, 1986-93; Roy Soc of London Dev Country Fellshp, 1988-89; Sev travel awds by prestigious intl orgns or for govts. Memberships: Sri Lanka Assn for Advancement of Sci, 1958-93; Assoc Mbr, ICTP, Italy, 1986-93; Fell, Roy Astronomical Soc, London, 1998-. Address: Department of Physics, University of Jaffna, Thirunelvely, Jaffna, Sri Lanka.

KUNDU S C, b. 2 Nov 1947, Pardaha, India. Teaching; Researcher. m. Shikha, 19 Jan 1976, 2 s. Education: MSc, PhD, Genetics, BHU. Appointments: Asst Prof, Prof, Manipur Univ, 1976-93; Prof, Indian Inst of Technol, Kharagpur, 1994-. Honours: USSR Govt Postdoct, 1976-77; NRC-Can Postdoct, 1980-81; AVH Fellshp, Germany, 1982-83; Intl Cancer Rsch Fellshp, 1993-94. Membership: Chmn, E Zone, All India Biotech Assn. Hobby: Travel. Address: Biotechnology Centre, Indian Institute of Technology, Kharagpur 721302, India.

KUNE Gabriel Andrew, b. 21 Dec 1933. Cancer Prevention Educator; Company Director; Author. m. Susan Bannerman, 8 Apr 1967, 1 s, diss May 1992. Education: Univ of Melbourne, 1952-57; Queens Coll, 1955-57; MB BS, Melbourne, 1957; FRACS, Melbourne, 1962; FRCS (London), 1963; FACS, San Fran, 1966; MD, Melbourne, 1988. Appointments include: Surg in trng, Roy Melbourne Hosp, Aust, St Mary's and Guy's Hosps, London, Eng, Lahey Clin, Boston, USA, 1958-66; Surg, Roy Melbourne Hosp, 1966-77; Prof of Surg, Univ of Melbourne and Cnslt Surg, Roy Melbourne Hosp and Repatriation Gen Hosp, Melbourne, 1977; Emer Prof of Surg, Univ of Melbourne, 1989-; Dpty Chmn and Dir, Saunders Fndn and Terracc Tower Grp of Co's, 1998. Publications include: Current Practice of Biliary Surgery, 1972; Practice of Biliary Surgery, 1980, transl Italian and Japanese; The Melbourne Colorectal Cancer Study, 1986; Causes and Control of Colorectal Cancer: A Model for Cancer Prevention, 1996; Reducing the Odds: A Manual for the Prevention of Cancer, 1999; chapts in multi-auth books, 200 papers in sci jrnls, mainly on gastrointestinal surg, cancer prevention, cancer treatment. Honours: Arris and Gale Lectr, Royal Coll of Surgs, 1970; Guy Miller Lectr in Surg, Univ of Melbourne, 1970; Hunterian Prof, Royal Coll of Surgs, 1976; Visng Prof, Eurn and N Amn univs, 1981-97. Memberships: Roy Soc of Med; Collegium Intl Chirugie Digestivae; Oncological Soc of Aust; Fndn Fell, Australasian Epidemiological Assn. Listed in: Who's Who in Australia; Marquis Who's Who in the World, 1996. Hobbies: Listening to music; Bushwalking; Swimming; Skiing; Cycling; Travel; Writing; Talking to interesting people; Reading; Cancer prevention and discovering causes of cancer. Address: 41 Power Street, Toorak, Vic 3142, Australia.

KUNHIKRISHNAN V V, b. 1 July 1948, Cherutazham, Kannur Dist, India. Professor. m. Leela, 25 May 1975, 3 d. Education: MA; BEd; PhD. Appointments: Tutor in Hist, 1969; Lectr in Hist, 1972; Rdr, 1990; Mbr, MA Bd of Exams in Hist, M G Univ, Kottayam and Annamalai Univ, Tamil Nadu. Publications: Men Who Fought for Freedom, 1987; Tenancy Legislation in Malabar, 1992; 10 rsch pprs on theme, Tenancy Legislation in Malabar in Indian jrnls; 2 books in Malayalam on Peasant Movements in Kerala; 2 articles in Dravidian Encyclopedia, 1981; Presented pprs in 20 natl seminars. Honour: Awd for Best Coll Tchr in Kannur Univ, 1996. Memberships: Indian Hist Congress; S Indian Hist Congress, 1980-; Treas, Assn for Peasant Stdies; Life Mbr, Inter Disciplinary Studies Soc, Trivandrum; Treas, Assn for Peasant Stdies, Univ of Calicut; Exec Mbr, S Indian Hist Congress, 1990. Hobbies: Reading; Research in history; Peasant studies. Address: Reader and Head, Department of History, K M M Govt, Womens College, P Kannur-4, Kerala, India.

KUO Gloria Liang-Hui, b. 10 July 1926, Kaifeng, Henan, China. Author. m. 1949, 2 s. Education: BA, Natl Szechuan Univ, Chengtu, 1948. Appointment: Jrnlst, Hsin Ming Evening News, Shanghai, 1948-49. Publications: 34 Novels, 20 novelettes, 2 non-fic books, some in Engl inclng: Debt of Emotion, 1959; The Lock of a Heart, 1962; Far Far Way to Go, 1962; Stranger in Calcutta, 1973; Taipei Women, 1980; Appreciating Chinese Art (non-fic), 1985; Untold Tales of Chinese Art, 1987; Blue Flowers are Blue, 1988; Beauties are Everywhere, 1997; Contbr to major newspprs: China Times United Daily News (Taiwan); World Journal (NY); Sing Tao Daily News; Sing Tao Evening News; Sing Tao Express (Hong Kong); Morning Post; Sabah Times (Malaysia); Major mags incl: Artist (Taiwan); Art of China Monthly (Hong Kong & Taiwan). Memberships: Chinese Lit Assn, Taiwan; Exec Dir, Chinese Antique Collectors Assn, 1978-. Address: 11F, 126-23 Chung Hsiao East Road, Sec 4, Taipei, China.

KUO Wan-Rong, Politician. Education: MA Inst of Technol, USA. Appointments: Fmr Min of Fin; Mbr, Kuomintang Ctrl Standing Cttee, 1994-. Address: Ministry of Finance, 2 Ai Kuo West Road, Taipei, Taiwan.

KUO Wei-Fan, b. 3 Sept 1937, Tainan City, China. Politician; Educator. m. Mei-Ho L Kuo, 1969, 1 s, 1 d. Education: Taiwan Normal Univ; Univ of Paris. Appointments: Assoc Prof, 1967-70, Prof, 1970-72, 1977-78, Dir, 1978, Pres, 1978-84, Grad Inst of Educn, Natl Taiwan Normal Univ, Univ of Paris; Admin Vice Min of Educn, 1972-77; Pres, Chinese Assn of Spcl Educn, 1973-75, 1979-81, Chinese Assn of Comparative Educn, 1981-82, 1993-; Min of State, 1984-88, 1993; Chair, Cncl of Cultural Planning & Devel, 1988-93. Membership: Pres, Chinese Educn Soc, 1985-87. Hobbies: Table Tennis; Tennis; Music.

KUPERS Terry Allen, b. 14 Oct 1943, Phila, PA, USA. Psychiatrist. m. Arlene Shmaeff, 3 s. Education: BA, Stanford Univ, 1964; MD, UCLA, Med Sch, 1968; MSP, Masters in Socl Psych, UCLA, 1974. Appointments: Asst Prof, Charles Drew Postgrad Medl Sch, 1974-77; Prof, Grad Sch of Psychol, The Wright Inst, 1981-. Creative Works: Public Therapy; Ending Therapy; Revisioning Mens Lives; Prison Madness. Honours: Alpha Omega Alpha. Memberships: Amn Psych Assn; CA Psych Soc; E Bay Psych Soc; Amn Orthopsychiatric Assn; Natl Org for Men Against Sexism. Hobbies: Jewich rec; Playing flute; Wilderness. Address: 8 Wildwood Ave, Oakland, CA 94610, USA.

KURATA Hiroyuki, Politician. Appointments: Fmr Parl Vice-Min of Intl Trade & Ind; Min of Home Affairs, 1996; Mbr, House of Cnclrs; Mbr, LDP. Address: Ministry of Home Affairs, 2-1-2 Kasumigaseki, Chiyoda-ku, Tokyo 100, Japan.

KURATSUNE Masanori, b. 4 Aug 1920, Kitakyushu, Fukuoka, Japan. Medical Doctor; Public Health Researcher. m. Akiko Miwa, 11 Oct 1946, 1 s, 2 d. Education: MD; DMedSc. Appointments: Dept of Pub Hlth, Fac of Med, Kyushu Univ; Nakamura Gakuen Coll. Publication: YUSHO, book. Honours: Prize for Merits, Min of Labour, 1980; Prize for Achmnts, Min of Labour, 1975; NCI Grantee, USA, 1961-64; Prize for Hlth Sci Promotion, Nakatomi Fund, 1999. Memberships: Japan Assn Pub Hlth, Hon Mbr, Chmn, 1981-82; Japan Soc Indl Health, Hon Mbr, Chmn, 1968-69; Japan Soc Hyg, Hon Mbr. Hobbies: Music; Fine arts. Address: 24-6, 7 Chome, Nagazumi, Minami-ku, Fukuoka, 811-1362, Japan.

KURE Reuben Navoge, b. 9 June 1945, Siassi, Papua New Guinea. Administrator. m. Jacobeth, 27 Nov 1967, 1 s, 3 d. Education: Tchng Ctf, Govoka Tchrs Coll, 1969; Mngmnt Ctf, Westhill Coll, Selly Oak. Appointments: Tchng, 1970-74; Educ Sec, 1975-76; clk, Ch Cncl, 1977-79; Ch Sec, 1980-91; Chf Sec, 1996-. Creative Works: Management Dissertation; Parish Administration Articles. Memberships: Papua New Guinea Cncl of Chs; Pacific Conf of Chs. Hobbies: Gardening; Food and Flowers; Reading books; Sports; Cricket. Address: P O Box 80, LAE, Papua New Guinea.

KURODA Tatsuaki, b. 11 Mar 1955, Shirakawa, Japan. Professor of Economics, Nagoya University. m. Junko Otani, 18 Oct 1980, 2 s. Education: BS, 1978, MSc, 1980, Kyoto Univ; PhD, Univ of PA, 1989. Appointments: Urban Planner, Japan Regl Dev Corp, 1980-85; Rsch Assoc, Kyoto Univ, 1985-89; Asst Prof, Toyohashi Univ of Tech, 1989-91; Assoc Prof, Nagoya Univ, 1991-98. Publications: Urban Planning Promoting Amenity, 1984. Honour: Grad Prize, Dept of Regl Sci, Univ of PA, 1987. Memberships: Amn Econ Assn; Japan Econ Assn; Regl Sci Assn Intl. Hobbies: Music; Books. Address: 4-4-18 Takamoridai, Kasugai, 487-0032, Japan.

KURODA Yukiaki, b. 22 May 1926, Nara, Japan. Emeritus Professor. m. Sachi, 15 Apr 1954, 2 s. Education: BSc, Kyoto Univ, 1950; DSc, Osaka Univ, 1959; Postdoct Rsch Fell, Univ Chgo, 1961. Appointments: Assoc Prof, Osaka Univ, 1963; Hd of Lab, Natl Inst of Genetics, 1966; Prof, Natl Inst of Genetics, 1984; Emer Prof, 1990, Prof, 1990, Azabu Univ. Publications: Invertebrate and Fish Tissue Culture, 1988; Antimutagenesis and Anticarcinogenesis, 1990. Honour: Appreciation for Efforts, World Congress of Cell and Tissue Culture, 1991; Awd, Japan Environmental Mutagen Soc, 1998. Memberships: Japanese Tissue Culture Assn; Genetics Soc, Japan; Environ Mutagen Soc, Japan; Japan Soc of Cell Biol. Hobbies: Travel; Photography. Address: 24-8 Hatsunedai, Mishima, Shizuoka 411-0018, Japan.

KUROSAWA Akira, b. 23 Mar 1910, Japan. Film Director. Education: Keika Mid Sch. Appointments: Asst Dir, Toho Film Co, 1936. Creative Works: Films: Sugata Sanshiro; Ichiban Utsukushiku; Torano Owofumu Otokotachi; Waga Seishun ni Kuinashi; Subarashiki Nichiyobi; Yoidore Tenshi; Shizukanaru Ketto; Norainu; Rashomon, 1950; Hakuchi; Ikiru; The Seven Samurai, 1954; Ikimono no Kiroku; Kumonosu Jio; Donzoko; Kakushi Toride no San Akunin; The Throne of Blood, 1957; The Hidden Fortress, 1958; The Bad Sleep Well, 1959; Yojimbo, 1961; Sanjuro, 1962; High and Low, 1962; Akahige, Redbeard, 1964; Dodes'ka-den, Derzu Uzala, 1976; Barkerousse, 1977; Kagemusha, 1979; Ran, 1984; Dreams, 1989; Rhapsody in August, 1991; Madadayo, 1993. Publication: Something Like an Autobiography, 1982. Honours include: Am Motion Picture Acady Awd; Golden Palm Awd; Order of the Yugoslav Flag; David di Donatello Awd; Order of Culture, Japan; Brit Film Inst Fellshp, 1986; Imperial Prize, Japan, 1992. Address: 21-6 Seijo 2-chome, Matsubara-cho, Setagaya-ku, 150 Tokyo, Japan.

KUROYANAGI Tetsuko, b. 9 Aug 1933, Tokyo, Japan. Actress. Education: Tokyo Coll of Music; Th Trng, Bungakuza Th, Tokyo, Mary Tarcai Studio, NY, USA. Appointments: Depbut w Japan Broadcasting Corp, 1954; Host, Tetsuko's Rm (TV chat show), Asahi Natl Broadcasting Co, 1976-94; Regular Guest, Discover Wonders of the World (quiz show), Tokyo Broadcasting System, 1987-; Fndr, Pres, Totto Fndn, 1981-; Trustee, World Wide Fund for Nature, Japan; UNICEF Goodwill Amb, 1984-; Dir, Chihiro Iwasaki Art, Music & Picture Books, 1995-. Publications: From New York With Love, 1972; totto-Chan: The Little Girl at the Window, 1981; Animal Theatre (photographic essay), 1983; Totto-channel, 1984; My Friends, 1986. Honour: Min of Fgn Affairs Awd. Hobbies: Travel; Calligraphy; Study of Giant Pandas. Address: Yoshida Naomi Office, No 2 Tanizawa Building, 4th Floor, 3-2-11 Nishi-Azabu, Minato-ku, Tokyo 106, Japan.

KURRLE Stanley Wynton, b. 30 Sept 1922, Aust. Headmaster in Holy Orders (retired). m. Lorna Mary Wallis, 6 Oct 1951, 1 s, 3 d. Education: BA, DipEd, Melbourne Univ, 1947; MA, Oxford Univ, Eng, 1950. Appointments: Served Austl Mil Forces, 1941-43; Asst Master, Liverpool Coll, Liverpool, Eng, 1948; Curate, Parish of Sutton, Diocese of Liverpool, 1952-54; Hdmaster, Caulfield Grammar Sch, Melbourne, Vic, Aust, 1955-64; Headmaster, The King's School, Parramatta, Sydney, NSW, 1965-82. Honour: OBE, 1982. Memberships: Canon Emer, St Andrews Cath, Sydney; Fell, St Pauls's Coll, Univ of Sydney. Listed in: Who's

Who in Australia. Address: 24 Marieba Road (PO Box 53), Kenthurst, NSW 2156, Australia.

KUSHNER Kames A, b. 14 Apr 1945, Phila, PA, USA. Professor of Law. m. Jacqueline Fregeau, 15 May 1970, 2 s, 1 d. Education: BBA, Univ of Miami, 1967; LLB, JD, Univ of MD, 1968. Appointment: Professor of Law, Southwestern Univ Sch of Law. Publications: Apartheid in America, 1980; Government Discrimination, 1983; Subdivision Law and Growth Management, 1991; Fair Housing, 2nd ed, 1995; Housing and Communty Development, 3rd ed, 1999; Land Use Regulation, 1999. Honour: Apptd Irwin R Bechalter Prof of Law, 1989. Hobbies: Travel; Study of comparative urban planning. Address: 675 Westmoreland Avenue, Los Angeles 9005, USA.

KUSUMAATMADJA Mochtar, b. Feb 1929, Jakarta, Indonesia. Politician. Education: Univ of Indonesia; Yale Univ; Harvard Univ; Univ Chgo Law Sch. Appointments: Min of Justice, 1974-77; Acting Fgn Min, 1977-78; Min of Fgn Affairs, 1978-88; Fmr Hd of UN Comm, 1992; Indonesian Rep, Law of the Sea Conf, Geneva, Seabed Cttee Sessions, NY. Address: Ministry of Foreign Affairs, Jalan Taman Pejambon 6, Jakarta, Indonesia.

KUVALEKAR Vijay, b. 22 Jan 1952. Journalist. m. Sanjeevani, 18 Aug 1978, 1 s, 1 d. Education: BA. Appointments: Trainee Sub Ed, Pudhari, Kolhapur, 1971; Sub Ed, Kesri, Pune; Snr Sub Ed, Sub Ed, Sakal; Ed, Kolhapur, 1981-87; Ed-in-Chf, 1994-. Publications: 3 books, 1979-96; 2 plays, 1975-76; Writer of regular columns for grp publns; Epic poem presentation and show; Stories, screenplays and lyrics. Honours: Sushiladevi Deshmukh Awd, Outstndng Contbrn in the field of Jrnlsm, 1996; Shahu Modak Purskar, 1996; State Govt Awds for Best Story, Screenplay and Lyrics, 1997. Memberships: Press Club, Pune, Chmn, 1992-95; Maharashtra State Wrkers Welfare Bd. Hobbies: Literature; Drama; Cinema; Development and Rural Journalism. Listed in: Who's Who in the World. Address: Sakal Papers Ltd, 595, Budhwar Peth, Pune 411 002, Maharashtra, India.

KUWAIZ Abdullah Ibrahim el, b. 1939, Saudi Arabia. Politician; International Official. 2 s, 2 d. Education: Pacific Lutheran Univ, USA; St Louis Univ, USA. Appointments: Acct, Pensions Dept, 1959-67. Econ, Min of Fin & Natl Econ, 1967-81; Exec Dir, Arab Monetary Fund, Abu Dhabi, 1977-83; Co-Chair, Fin Coop Cttee, Euro-Arab Dialogue, 1978-83; Asst Under-Sec for Econ Affairs, 1981-87; Dpty Min of Fin & Natl Econ, Saudi Arabia, 1987-; Dir Gen, 1987, Chair of Bd, Arab Monetary Fund, Abu Dhabi, 1987; Mbr of Bd, Exec Cttee, Gulf Intl Banks, Bahrain, 1977-; Asst Sec-Gen for Econ Affairs, Coop Cncl for the Arab States of the Gulf, 1981-; Bd Mbr, Gulf Coop Cncls Org for Measures & Standards, 1984-; Oxford Energy Inst, UK, 1985-; Intl Maritime Bur, London, 1985-88. Publications: Num pprs in intl jrnls. Address: Arab Monetary Fund, PO Box 2818, Abu Dhabi, United Arab Emirates.

KUWAYAMA George, b. 25 Feb 1925, New York, USA. Art Museum Curator. m. Lillian, 5 Dec 1961, 2 s, 1 d. Education: BA, MA, PhD. Appointments: Parachute Infantry, Army of the US; Curator of Oriental Art, Los Angeles County Mus; Snr Curator, Far Eastern Art, Los Angeles Mus of Art; Emer. Publications: Far Eastern Language, 1982; Japanese Ink Paintings, 1985; The Quest for Eternity, 1987; Imperial Taste, 1989; Chinese Ceramics in Colonial Mexico, 1997. Honours: NEA & NEH Rsch Travel Grants; Asian Cultural Cncl Grant; Charles Freer Fell; Louise Hackney Fell; Inter-Univ Fell. Memberships: Coll Art Assn; Assn for Asian Studies; Am Oriental Soc; Far Eastern Art Cncl. Hobbies: Music; Reading. Address: 1417 Comstock Avenue, Los Angeles, CA 90024, USA.

KWAN Anne, Siu-King, b. Hong Kong. Anaesthesiologist. m. N K Mak, 1 d. Education: MBBS; FANZCA; FHKCA; FHKAM (Anaesthesiol); DPM; Dip Acup; Dip E&AS; DPaM. Appointments: Chf of Serv, Dept Anaesthesiol, UCH; Hon Assoc Prof in Anaesthesiol,

CUHK. Publications: In jrnls. Honours: Conf grant, SAHK; Schlshp, HAHO; Examiner, HKCA. Memberships: Chmn, UCHDA; Chmn, Guidelines Cttee, HKCA; Ed, Newsletter HKCA. Hobby: Hiking. Address: 180 Hip Wo Street, Kwun Tong, Hong Kong SAR.

KWAN Vincent Po Chuen, b. 24 July 1959, Hong Kong. Solicitor. m. Nikki Tan, 22 Nov 1993, 1 d. Education: LLM; MSc. Appointments: Civil Serv, Hong Kong Govt, 1983-87; Solicitor, Deacons Graham & James, 1988-93; Exec Dir, Chuang's Grp, 1993-97; Gen Mngr, Sino Grp, 1997-. Honours: Ho Fook Prize, 1991; Cty Bank Schlshp, 1991-93. Memberships: Solicitor, Hong Kong, 1990-; England and Wales, 1991-; FCCA, 1992-; ACIArb, 1995-. Hobbies: Reading; Travel. Address: Flat E, 1st Floor, Blessings Garden Phase I, 95 Robinson Road, Mid-Levels, Hong Kong.

KWEI Randolph Chen Chi, b. 25 Nov 1935, China. Investment Management. m. Teresa, 1972, 1 s, 1 d. Education: BE, Yale Univ, 1958; MBA, Columbia Grad Sch of Bus, 1960. Appointments: VP, Citibank, 1976; Snr VP, Am Express Bank, 1980; Mngng Dir, Summa Intl Fin Ltd, 1984; Mngng Dir, Asian Oceanic Grp, 1985; Mngng Dir, Pacific Capital Mngmt Ltd, 1992-. Honour: McKinsey Schl, 1960. Memberships: Rotary Club of Hong Kong; Yale Club of Hong Kong, pres, 1986-90; Fin Execs Inst, Hong Kong Ltd, dir, 1994-96. Hobbies: Tennis; Music; Reading; Hiking. Address: 119A Repulse Bay Road, Apt C11, Hong Kong.

KWOK Alvin, b. 12 Jan 1957. Music Composer. m. Hilda, 5 May 1988, 1 d. Education: Music, Capiloo Coll, Vancouver, Can. Appointments: Composer, Arranger, Over 50 Musical Compositions for Top Recording Artists, Hong Kong & Taiwan, 1986-92; Prodr, 20 Top Recording Artists, Hong Kong & Taiwan, 1986-90; Singer, Songwriter, 6 Solo Albums, Sony Music, 1986-90; Composer, Arranger, Over 300 Musical Compositions for TV Commercials, Hong Kong, China, Japan, Taiwan, Singapore & Korea, 1988-99. Honours: Disting Performance Awd, Yamaha Electone Intl Concours, Japan, 1974; Clio Awd, 1990; Best of the Best, Asian Advt Awds, 1994; 4As Creative Awds, 1995, 1996; 2 Platinum & 2 Gold Albums, Hong Kong, 1988-90; Asia-Pacific Advt Awds, China, 1995; London Intl Advt Awd, 1995. Membership: Composers, Auths Assn of Hong Kong, 1988-. Address: 1B Tower 1, 18 Old Peak Road, Hong Kong.

KWOK Douglas L F, b. 29 Oct 1950, Hong Kong. I T. m. Man Cheng, 28 Oct 1993, 1 s, 1 d. Education: MBA, Univ of Ottowa, Can. Appointment: Mngng Dir, Intergraph, HK Ltd. Memberships: Hong Kong Inst of Engrs; Hong Kong Info Technol Fedn; Amn mngmt Assn. Hobbies: Sports; Swimming. Address: C/o Intergraph HK Ltd, 401-4, HKITC, 72 Tat Chee Ave, Kowloon, Hong Kong.

KWON Yong-tae, b. 12 Feb 1937. Senior Staff Director, National Assembly. m. Cheong-Woi Kim, 17 Oct 1964, 1 s, 1 d. Education: Chung-ang Univ, 1959; Chung-ang Grad Sch, 1961. Appointments: Natl Assembly Seretariat, 1967; Legislative Cnslr, Educ & Pub Affairs Cttee, Natl Assembly, 1983; Staff Dir, Educ & Pub Affairs Cttee, 1992; Dir, Intl Pen Club, Korea, 1993; Snr Staff Dir, Culture, Sports & Info Cttee, Natl Assembly, 1993; Dir, Korean Contemporary Poets Assn, 1993. Publications: Response Song in the Morning, 1968; To The South Wind, 1980; The Moral of Criticism; Meditation on Contemporary Poetry. Honours: Chung-Ang Lit Awd, 1959; Order of Serv Merit Awd w Green Stripes, 1980; Nosan Lit Awd, 1989. Memberships: Broadcasting Cttee, Dir, Intl Pen Club, Korea;Dir, Korean Contemporary Poets Assn. Hobbies: Promenade; Versification. Address: 932-16 Daechi-4-dong, Kangnam-gu, Seoul, Korea.

KWON Young-Hae, b. 1937, Korea. Politician; Army Officer. Education: Korea Mil Acady. Appointments: Commissioned, 1959; Cmdr, 6th Army Divsn, 1984-86; Chf of Staff, 3rd Army, 1986-88; Cmdr, Olympic Support Cmd, 1988; Rank of Gen, retd, 1988; Hd, Planning & Mngrs Off, Min of Def, 1988; Vice-Min of Def, 1990, Min,

1993. Address: Ministry of Defence, 3-1 Yong San-dong, Yongsan-ku, Seoul, Korea.

KWONG Daniel W, b. 1 Aug 1958, Hong Kong. Business Entrepreneur; Professor of Law. div. 1 d. Education: BA, 1982; JD, 1993. Appointments: Snr Advsr, Xnet Corp (USA); Co-Chmn, 1st Convention of Overseas Chinese in Guangzhou, China; Chmn, Golden Harvest Holdings Ltd; Chmn, Global Investment and Mngmt Inst Inc; Hon Chmn, US House Speaker's Victory Circle; Hon Co-Chmn, Amn Bus Tax Force; Natl Chmn Advsr Repub Presdtl; Prof of Law, La Salle Univ Task Force. Publications: A Hidden Tool, 1990; The Tales of Marshlands (co-translator from Chinese into Eng of very famous Chinese folklore), 1990; Songs: Cassandra; Cass' Story, 1991. Honours: US Repub Presdtl Awd, 1994; Honoree, Ronald Reagan Eternal Flame of Freedom, 1992. Memberships: Life Mbr: Repub Natl Cttee; Repub Presdtl Task Force; Fell, Acady of Polit Sci; Hong Kong Assn; Chinese Chmbr of Com; Invited Mbr, Natl Cttee on US China Rels. Complimentary Mbr, Orgn of Chinese-Amn Entrepeneurs Network (OCEAN); Amn Soc of Composers Auths and Publrs; Advsr: IBC; ABI. Hobbies: Gamesmanship; Travel; Reading. Address: 601 South Cecil Street, Monterey Park, CA 91755, USA.

KWONG Peter K K (Rt Rev). Ecclesiastic. Education: Chung Chi Coll; Kenyon Coll; Bexley Hall, Colgate, Rochester; MTh; DD. Appointments: Ordained Priest, Anglican Ch, Hong Kong, 1965; Clergy i/c, Crown of Thorns Ch, Hong Kong, 1956-66; Vicar, St James's Ch, Hong Kong, 1967-70; Curate, St Paul's Ch, Hong Kong, 1971-72; Mbr, Tchng Staff, 1972-79, Chinese Univ Hong Kong; Mbr, Crt, Hong Kong Univ, 1981-; Diocesan Sec, Anglican Diocese Hong Kong and Macao, 1979-81; Bish, Hong Kong and Macao, 1981-; Mbr, Exec Cttee, 1985-89, Chmn, Fin Cttee, 1987-89, Mbr, Basic Law Drafting Cttee of Hong Kong Spec Administrative Reg; Consultative Cttee Basic Law of Hong Kong; Advsr on Hong Kong Affairs, State Dept People's Repub China, 1992-; Mbr, Preparatory Cttee for Spec Admnstv Reg, 1996-; Mbr, Chinese People's Pol Consultative Conf, 1998-; Archbishop and Primate, Hong Kong Sheng Kung Hui (Anglican Ch), 1998-; Num appts in hlth, soc welfare, yth orgs, others. Membership: Ch Miss Soc, VP, 1995-; Mbr, Selection Cttee for Spec Admin Reg. Address: Bishop's House, 1 Lower Albert Road, Hong Kong.

KYI Tun, b. 1 May 1938, Monywa, Sagaing Div, Myanmar. Minister of Trade. Education: Def Servs Acady. Appointments: Cmndr, Cntrl Regl Mil Cmnd; Mbr, State Law and Order Restoration Cncl, 1988; Min of Trade. Address: Ministry of Trade, 228-240 Strand Road, Yangon, Myanmar.

KYUMA Fumio. Politician. Appointments: Mbr, House of Reps; Fmr Parly Min of Transp; Dir-Gen, Def Agcy, 1996-. Address: Defence Agency, 9-7-45 Akasaka, Minato-ku, Tokyo, Japan.

L

L'ESTRANGE Timothy Ignatius, b. 24 Nov 1955. Partner; Lawyer. m. Elizabeth Jill Campbell, 18 Aug 1985, 1 s, 2 d. Appointments: Allen Allen & Hemsley Ptnr, 1987-; Mng Ptnr, 1993-96, joined 1981; Assoc Hon Mr Justice J S Lockhart, Fed Crt Aust, 1979; Perm Sec Crt of Arbitration for Sports Oceania Reg; Tstee Cttee for Econ Dev Aust (CEBA), 1993. Memberships: Insolvency Cttee Bus Law Sect; Law Cl Aust, 1990-93; Sec, NSW Bar Maritime Law Assn Aust and NZ, 1988-90. Hobbies: Golf; Cricket; Rugby; Reading; Clubs: Australian, Royal Sydney Golf. Address: c/o Allen Allen & Hemsley, PO Box 7082, Riverside Centre, Brisbane, Qld 4001, Australia.

LABELLE Jean-Paul, b. 21 June 1920, Montreal, Can. Professor; Priest. Education: BA, Montreal Univ, 1943; LCL, Canon Law, St Thomas Pontifical Univ, Rome, Italy, 1950; Dip, Japanese Lang, 1955. Appointments: Stagiaire, Ecclesiastical Prov Tribunal, Montreal, 1950-51; Prof, Canon Law, Moral Theol, St Sulpice Regl Seminary, Fukuoka, Japan, 1951-94; Defender of Bond, Diocesan Tribunal, Fukuoka, 1957-94; Sec, Episcopal Cmmn on Ch Admin and Legislation, 1978-86; Mbr, Episcopal Cmmn for the Transl of the Code of Canon Law into Japanese, 1983-92; Promoter of the Faith, Fukuoka, 1985-94; Asst to the Admin Sec, Fndn of the Major Seminary of Montreal, Can, 1995-. Publications include: Marriage Registration and Naien in Japan, 1958; Christian Family, 1985; Var articles in USA, Japanese and French Publns. Honours: Hons List, Dictionary of Intl Biography; Biographee of Yr, 1986-87; Ctf of Merit, 1986; World Fellshp Awd, FAI, 1987. Memberships include: Cand Canon Law Soc; Societe Internationale De Droit Canonique et de Legislation Religieuse Comparees; Cath Theol Soc of Am. Address: 2065 Sherbrooke Street West, Montreal, Quebec H3H 1G6, Canada.

LAHIRI Amitava, b. 2 Mar 1957, Howrah. Geologist. m. Sarmistha, 15 July 1985, 1 s. Education: BS (Geol); Msc (Geol); PhD(Sc). Appointments: Rsch Fell, Calcutta Univ; Geologist in Geol Survey of India. Publications: The Occurence of Discocyclina in the Middle Eocene Fulra List of Cutch, Gujarat, India; A Review of Foram Genus Borelis with a Note on its Occurrence in India; The Occurrence of Nummulites in Mid Eocene Har Form and Fulrallst of Cutch, Gujarat, India: Biostratinomic Significance of Bioeroded Gastropod Shells from Coastal Region of Pondi, India; Climatic Zonation of Sediments of Arabian Sea with the Help of Pteropod. Membership: FGMS, 1980; MGNI, 1985. Hobbies: Writing poems and music. Address: Flat #3A, Aashiyana, Garia Station Road, Balia, Calcutta 700084, WB, India.

LAI Chun-Loong, b. 20 May 1943. Engineer. m. Yung Pek-Lum, 1 s, 1 d. Education: BEng, Univ Auckland, 1967; MBA, Univ CA, 1980; Adv Mngmt Prog, Harvard Univ, 1987. Appointments: Mech Engr, 1968-69, Chf Inspection Engr, 1969-70, Quality Control Mngr, 1970-74, Snr Mngr, 1974-75, Works Mngr, 1975-78, Gen Mngr, 1980-82, Pres, 1989-93, Chart Ind of Singapore Ptu Ltd; Mngng Dir, Singapore Technol Corp Pty Ltd & Chart Ind of Singapore Pty Ltd, 1983-89; Dpty Chmn, Pres, 1993-97, Pres, 1997-, Sembawang Indl Pty Ltd. Honours: Colombo Plan Schlsp Awd, 1965-67; Fellshp Awd, Chart Ind of Singapore, 1978-80; Pub Serv Medal, 1992. Memberships: Chmn, Clementi Cmty Cntr Welfare Fund Mngmt Cttee, 1991-; Vice Chmn, Citizens Consultative Cttee, Clementi Constituency, 1993-; China Projects Coord Meeting, Singapore Econ Devel Bd, 1994-; India Bus Grp Steering Cttee Meeting, Singapore Trade Devel Bd, 1994-; Malaysia Singapore Yng Snr Execs, 1994-; Singapore Aust Bus Alliance Forum, 1995-; Indonesia Singapore Tourism Coop, Singapore Tourism Promotion Bd, 1995-; Chmn, Tanjong Pagar Cmty Devel Cncl Liaison Subcttee, 1997-. Hobbies: Reading; Music; Tennis. Address: 48 Faber Avenue, Singapore 129551, Singapore.

LAI Dae, b. 7 Dec 1944, Da Jiang Village, Xiang Dong Dist, Ping Xiang Cty, Jing Xi Prov, China. Mining. Education: Grad, Jiang Xi Coal Mine Coll, 1962. Appointments: Ping Xiang Mineral Bureau, Deep Actual Measurement Technique in Coal Mining, 1962-1999; Techn Engr, 1962-83; Expert Snr Engr, Zong Engr, 1984-95. Honours: Awds incl entry in Dictionary of Prominent Chinese Scientists and Techns, 1996; Worldwide Consultative Expert, 1998; World VIP, 1998; Sci and Technol for Progress in China, 1999; Present of Talent Musical Notation of China, 1999; Outstndng Achmnt mine pressure for Rsch Accomplishment (Intl Prize, Jiang Xi Prov 1st Prize); Thesis: A Test of Composite Support and An Approach to Working Resistance (intl prize, Prov 1st Prize); Proj: QZJ-1 Type Composite Support to Working Resistance (intl prize); Approach for affirming the support to the working resistance of face in Da Chao seam in An Yuan Mine (Pingmine 1st Prize, prov 1st Prize, Ptoi): Mine Support Pressure and On the Spot Actual Measurement Summary of Technique at Ping Mine. Membership: Coal Mine Inst of China.

LAI In-Jaw, b. 24 Aug 1946, Taiwan. Education: SJD, Harvard Univ, 1981; Chmn, Grad Sch of Laws, NCHU, 1982-84; Dir Gen, Customs Dept, MOF, 1984-89; Admin V Min of Fin, 1989; Pol V Min of Fin, 1989-93; The Grand Justice, 1999-. Publications: Annotations of the ROC Sec Exchange Law, 4 vols; Essays on the Corp Law: Taiwan's Financial Map: Prospect & Retrospect; Judicial Yuan Taipei.

LAI Shih-Kung, b. 15 Nov 1957, Taiwan. Professor. m. Chiung-Ku Lee, 15 Oct 1993. Education: PhD, Regl Plng. Appointment: Dir, Cntr for Land Mngmt and Technol, Natl Chung Hsing Univ. Publication: Meanings and Measurements of Multiattribute Preferences, 1996. Honour: Rsch awds of Natl Sci Cnsls, Repub of China, 1993-99. Memberships: Amn Plng Assn; Informs. Hobby: Sports. Address: 67, Section 3, Min Sheng East Road, Taipei, Taiwan, China.

LAI Yukman, b. 25 Feb 1949, Canton, China. Artist. m. Ming-Yan Ng, 18 Jan 1997, 3 d. Education: Dip, Hong Kong Sir Robert Black Coll of Educ, 1974; BA, Univ of E Asia, Macau, 1986. Appointments: Bd Dir, Richmond Art Gall Assn, 1997-98; Curator, CC Arts Gall; Pres, Chinas Canad Artists Fedn, Vancouver, Can; Lectr of Art, Simon Fraser Univ, Vancouver, Can. Publications: Paintings, Calligraphy and Seals of Yukman Lai; My Rockies, Landscape Paintings by Yukman Lai; Yangtze River, A Sentimental Journey, The Landscape Paintings of Yukman Lai. Honours: 1st Class Prize, The Whole China Tabai Cup Competition of Chinese Painting, 1989. Memberships: Life Mbr, Chinese Canad Artists Fedn in Vancouver; Fell, Huang Pu Art Acady, Shanghai, China. Hobbies: Travelling; Reading; Painting. Address: 1280, Eastlawn Drive, Burnaby, BC, Canada.

LAIDLAW Diana Vivienne (Hon), b. 2 Sept 1951. Government Minister. Education: BA, Flinders Univ of S Aust. Appointments: W Potter Ptnrs, Sharebrokers, 1971-72; Rsch Asst to 3 SA Fed MPs, 1976-79; Ministerial Asst to State Min, 1979-82; Lib Party Mbr Legislative Cncl, 1982-; Var Shadow Portfolios, Transport, Marine and Harbours, Arts and Cultural Heritage, Local Govt Rels, Status of Women, 1986-93; Min for Transport, The Arts and the Status of Women for S Aust, 1993-97; Min for Transport and Urban Planning, Min for the Arts, Min for the Status of Women, 1997-; Patron: Handknitters Guild of SA; The Austl Inst of Traffic Plng and Mngmt; SA Soc of Model and Experimental Engrs; Victor Harbour Horse tram Soc; Indep Th Inc; Food and Writers Fest. Memberships: Chatered Inst of Transport in Aust Inc; Queen Elizabeth II Silver Jubilee Trust for Young Australians, SA Bd; Austl Pol Exchange Prog to China, Delegation Ldr; VP, Sturt Football Club; Num community assns, arts and Cultural heritage insts and women's orgs. Hobbies: Performing/visual arts and craft; Bushwalking; Tapestry; Travel. Address: 12th Floor, Roma Mitchell House, 136 North Terrace, Adelaide, SA 5000, Australia.

LAING William Peter, b. 8 Oct 1948. Geologist. m. Susan Kay Turner, 1 s, 1 d. Education: BSc (Hons 1st Class), Sydney Univ; PhD, Univ Adelaide. Appointments: Exploration Geol, Hastings Exploration, NL, 1970-72; Snr Geol, CRA Exploration Pty Ltd, 1979-82; Snr Lectr, Geol, James Cook Univ, 1983-89; Mngng Dir, Prin Cnslt, Laing Exploration Pty Ltd, 1989-99; Hon Rsch Fell, James Cook Univ, 1993-99; 87 Geol Consultancies, Aust, Pacific, Asia, S Am, N Am, Africa. Publications: Num scientific pprs in intl jrnls; Transactions of the Institute of Mining and Metallurgy, Benchmark Papers in Geology, 1975-97; Monographs: Structural Geology in Drillcore; Ore Systems Analysis, 1989-97; Co-des, Drillcore Orientometer (intl export), 1989; Musical recdngs (LP, audio cassette, CD), folk bands: Hammer'n'Tap, 1981; Threepenny Bit, 1988; Mango Jam, 1996; Producer and Artistic Dir, SOCOG Sea Change Concert, Queensland, 1998. Honours: Hon Rsch Fell, James Cook Univ, 1993; Aust Day Awd, Thuringowa City, 1997; Event of the Yr, Townsville City Cncl, 1998. Memberships: Fell, Soc of Econ Geols; Fell, Australasian Inst of Mining and Metall; Fell, Austl Inst of Geoscientists; Geol Soc of Aust; Austl Soc of Exploration Geophysicists; Scientists for Global Responsibility, Convenor, N Qld Br, 1986-90; North Queenslanders for Reconciliation, 1997-99. Hobbies: Community musician (choral singer, soloist, bush band musician, music director); Community activist in peace, indigenous and local community issues; Surfing; Birdwatching; The bush. Address: 11 McLauchlan Crescent, Kelso, Qld 4815, Australia.

LAJCAK Miroslav, b. 20 Mar 1963. Diplomat; Slovak Ambassador. m. Jela Lajcakova, 13 Sept 1986, 1 d. Education: Fac Law, Comenius Univ, Bratislava State Inst Intl Rels, Fac Intl Rels, Moscow; Master of Law, Comenius Univ. Appointments: Attaché, Czech Emb, Sofia, 1986; Desk Offr, Asst to Dir of E Eurn Dept, Fed Min For Affairs, Prague, 1987; 3rd Sec, Asst to Amb, Czech Emb, Moscow, 1991; Emb of Slovak Repub, Moscow, 1993; Dir Gen, Dir of Min Secratariat, Min of For Affairs of the Slovak Repub, Bratislava, 1993; Cslr, Emb of Slovak Repub, Athens, 1994; Dir of the Secretariat of the PM of the Slovak Repub, 1994; Amb of Slovak Repub to Japan, 1994-98; Returned to Slovakia, 1998. Membership: Slovak For Policy Assn. Hobbies: Reading; Music; Tennis.

LAKAS BAHAS Demetrio Basilio, b. 29 Aug 1925, Colon. Politician; Administrator. m. Elizabeth Fannia Roger de Lakas, 1959, 2 s, 1 d. Education: TX Wesleyan Coll; TX Tech Coll. Appointments: Fmr Dir of Socl Security; Pres, Prov Govt Cncl, 1969-72; Pres of Panama, 1972-78. Hobbies: Sailing; Fishing. Address: Palacio de las Garzas, Panama City, Panama.

LAKDAWALA Aftab, b. 11 Feb 1948, Bombay, India. Vice President, New Drug Discovery. m. Rehmat, 20 Apr 1974, 1 s, 1 d. Education: PhD. Appointments: Prin Rsch Sci, Hoechst Rsch Cntr, 1971-93; Hd, Pharm & Toxicology, Wockhardt R&D Cntr, 1994-97; VP, Cadila R&D Cntr, 1997-. Honours: Best Rsch Ppr, Indian Pharm Soc, 1982; Best Rsch Ppr, Maharashtra Pharm Soc, 1983, 1986. Memberships: Rsch Cncl, ITRC; Intl Soc of Immunopharmacology; Indian Pharm Soc. Hobbies: Stamp Collection; Music. Address: Tara Manzil, 4th Floor, 22/26 1st Dhobi Talao Lane, Bombay 400002, India.

LAKE Philip (Sam), b. 11 Sept 1941, Canberra, ACT, Aust. m. Marilyn Calvert, 10 Oct 1968, 2 d. Education: BS, (ANU); PhD, (So'ton). Appointments: Lectr/Snr Lectr, Zool, Univ of Tasmania, 1967-76; Lectr, Snr Lectr, Rdr, Monash Univ, 1976-97; Prof in Ecology, 1997-. Publications: Co-auth, 2 books on wetlands; 134 refereed pprs in ecology and conserv. Honours: Thomas Henry Huxley Awd, Zool Soc of London, 1967-; Jolly Awd, Austl Soc for Limnology, 1980. Memberships: Austl Soc for Limnology, VP, Pres, 1979-81; Ecological Soc Aust, VP, 1988-93. Hobbies: Reading; Fishing; Bushwalking; Music. Address: Department of Biological Sciences, Monash University, Clayton, Vic 3168, Australia.

LAKING George Robert (Sir), b. 15 Oct 1912, NZ. Chief Ombudsman (retired). m. Alice Evelyn Patricia

Hogg, 13 Apr 1940, 1 s, 1 d. Education: Auckland Univ; LLB, Vic Univ of Wellington, 1935. Appointments: PM's and External Affairs Depts, 1940-49; Cnslr, 1949-54, Min, 1954-56, NZ Emb, Wash DC Dpty Sec of External Affairs, Wellington, NZ, 1956-58; Actng High Cmmnr for NZ, London, 1958-61; NZ Am to EEC, 1960-61; NZ Amb to Wash DC, 1961-67; Sec of For Affairs and Perm Hd, PM's Dept, NZ, 1967-72; Ombudsman, 1975-77; Privacy Cmmnr, 1977-78; Chf Ombudsman, 1977-84; Chmn, Legislation Advsry Cttee, 1986-91. Publications: Num articles on for policy and admin law. Honours: CMG, 1969; KCMG, 1985. Memberships: Hum Rights Cmmn, 1978-84; Pub and Admin Law Reform Cttee, 1980-85; Chmn, NZ-US Educl Fndn, 1976-78; NZ Oral Hist Archive Trust, 1985-90; Wellington Civic Trust, 1985-88; Pres, NZ Inst of Intl Affairs, 1980-84. Hobbies: Music; Reading; Golf. Address: 3 Wesley Road, Wellington, New Zealand.

LAKKIS Carol, b. 22 Mar 1970, Melbourne, Aust. Optometrist. Education: BS, Optometry, Univ of Melbourne, 1991; PhD, Univ of Melbourne, 1999. Appointments: Clin Assoc, Vic Coll of Optometry, 1992-; Rsch Fell, Dept of Optometry and Vision Scis, 1993-96; Lectr, 1992-, Clin Instr, 1993-, Dept of Optometry and Vision Scis, Univ of Melbourne. Honours: Melbourne Rsch Schlshp, 1997-99; Contact Soc of Aust Rsch Awd, 1997-98. Memberships: Assoc Cnclr, Optometrists Assn Aust, 1991-; Conact Lens Soc of Aust, VP, 1993-94; Intl Assn Contact Lens Educrs, 1993-. Hobbies: Music; Art; Theatre; Football. Address: C/o Department of Optometry and Vision Sciences, University of Melbourne, Parkville, Victoria 3052, Australia.

LAKSANAWISIT Jurin, b. 15 Mar 1956. Minister to Prime Minister's Office. Education: BA, Pol Sci, Thammasat Univ, Thailand; Master Deg, Pub Admin Plcy and Plng, NIDA. Appointments: Mbr of Parl, 1986, 1988, 1992, 1995, 1996; Sec to Min of Pub Hlth, 1988; Dpty Sec-Gen to Prime Min for Pol Affairs, 1989; Sec to Min of Agric and Co-ops, 1990; Dpty Min of Com, 1992; Dpty Min of Agric and Co-ops, 1994. Honour: Kt Grand Cordon, Spec Class, Most Exalted Order of the White Elephant. Address: 43/20 Mubanpramualsuk Road, Tumbol Watchalor Amphur, Bangkruay, Nonthaburi, Thailand.

LAKSHMINARAYANA Grasthu, b. 2 May 1937, Kurnool. Teacher. m. Ramanamma, 1 Mar 1964, 2 s, 2 d. Education: MA, Engl Lit; Cert in ELT. Appointments: Lectr, 1963, Rdr, 1983, Prof, 1991, Osmania Univ, Hyderabad. Publications: Poems publd in The Quest, 1997, December, 1997, Wanderlust, 1998. Honours: Participated in Poets Meets, Hyderabad, 1997; Recited own poems on All India Radio, 1997, 1998. Memberships: Engl Forum, Osmania Univ, 1965-97. Hobbies: Drawing; Reading and writing poetry in English and Telugu. Address: Kusum Kunj 21-106-1, Sharadanagar, Gaddiannaram, Hyderabad, AP, India.

LAL Bansi, b. 26 Aug 1927, Golagarh, Bhiwani, India. Politician. m. Smt Vidya Devi, 1945, 2 s, 4 d. Education: Punjab Univ & Law Coll, Jullundur. Appointments: Sec, Loharu Praja Mandal, 1943-44; Gen Sec, Tosham Mandal Congress Cttee, 1955-58; Started Practice, Bhiwani, 1956; Pres, Mandal Congress Cttee, Jural, 1958-62; Mbr, Punjab PCC, 1958-62, Rajya Sabha, 1960-66, 1976-80, Haryana Assembly, 1967; Chf Min Haryana, 1968-75, 1986-87; Min without portfolio, Govt of India, 1975; Min of Def, 1975-77; Chair, Cttee on Pub Undertakings, 1980-82, Cttee on Estimates, 1982-84; Min of Railways, 1984-85; Min of Transp, 1985-86; Mbr, 9th Lok Sabha, 1989-. Honours: LLD, Kurukshetra Univ, Haryana, 1972; DSc, Haryana Agricl Univ, 1972. Hobby: Reading. Address: c/o B N Chakravarty Road, Hissr, Haryana State, India.

LAL Devendra, b. 14 Feb 1929, Varanasi, India. Research Teaching. Education: BS, 1947, MSc, 1949, Banaras Hindu Univ; Rsch Student, 1949-50. Appointments: Fell, Assoc Prof, Prof, Snr Prof, 1950-72, Tata Inst Fundamental Rsch; Visng Prof, Univ CA, Los Angeles, 1966-67; Prof, Scripps Instn of Oceanography, 1967-; Dir, Phys Rsch Lab, 1972-83; Visng Prof, Univ of CA, Los Angeles (Inst of Geophys and Planetary Phys), 1983-84; Snr Prof, Phys Rsch Lab, 1987-89; Mbr Editl Bd, num profl jrnls inclng: The Moon and Planets; Jrnl Nuclear Track Detection; Space Sci Reviews; Il Nuovo Cimento. Honours: Krishnan Medal for Geochemistry, 1965; Bhatnagar Mem Awd for Phys, Cncl of Sci and Indl Rsch, Govt of India, 1967; Padma Shri Govt of India, 1971; Outstndng Scientist, 1974; Fedn of Indian Chmbr of Comm and Ind Awd in Sci and Technol; NASA Spec Recog Awd for Prin Investigators, Lunar prog, 1979; DSc (hon causa) Banaras Hindu Univ, 1981; KS Krishnan Mem Lectureship, 1981; NASA Grp Achievement Awd (Skylab III), 1986; Pandit Jawaharlal Nehru Awd for Scis, 1986; H Burr Steinbach Visng Schl, Woods Hole Oceanographic Instn, 1988; Sir C V Raman Birth Centenary Awd, 1996-97; K R Ramanthan Mem Lect, 1997; V M Goldschmidt Medal, 1997. Memberships include: FRS (London); For Assoc, Natl Acady of Scis, USA; Fell, Indian Acady of Scis; Fell, Indian Natl Sci Acady; Assoc, Roy Astron Soc of London; Fndr Mbr, Third World Acady of Scis; Fell, Meteoritical Soc; Fell, Indian Geophysical Union; Fell, Natl Acady Scis (India); Fell, AAAS; Fell, Geochemical Soc (USA); For Hon Mbr, Amn Acady Arts and Scis; Fell, Phys Rsch Lab, Ahmedabad, India. Address: Graduate Department and Geosciences Research Division, Scripps Institution of Oceanography, University of California, San Diego, USA.

LAL Devi, b. 1914, India. Politician. Appointments: Mbr, Punjab Legis Assembly, 1952-65; Chf Parl Sec of Punjab, 1956; Chair, haryana Khadi & Village Ind Bd, 1968-71; Chf Min of haryana, 1977-79; Mbr, Parl, 1980-82; haryana Assembly, 1982, re-elected, 1985; Dpty PM of India, 1989-90, 1990-92; Min of Agricl & Tourism, 1990-92. Address: Office of the Prime Minister, South Block, New Delhi 110 011, India.

LAL Vinay, b. 19 Apr 1961, New Delhi, India. Professor. m. Anju Relan, 19 Feb 1996. Education: BA, MA, 1982, Johns Hopkins Univ; PhD, Univ Chgo, 1992. Appointments: William R Kenan Fell, Columbia Univ, 1992-93; Asst Prof of Hist, Univ CA, Los Angeles, 1993-. Publications include: South Asian Cultural Studies, 1996. Honours: Amn Inst for Indian Stdies Snr Fellshp, 1995; Natl Endowment for the Hums Fellshp, 1996; Postdoct Fellshp, Japan Soc for the Promotion of Sci, 1999. Memberships: Amn Histl Assn; Intl Forum on Globalization; Intl Network for Cultural Alternatives to Dev. Hobbies: Reading; Photography; Cinema; Travel. Address: Department of History, University of California, 405 Hilgard Avenue, Los Angeles, CA 90095-1473, USA.

LAM Chun Man, b. 11 Dec 1948, Hong Kong. Fire Service. m. Chan May Ching, 17 Mar 1973, 1 s, 1 d. Education: FIFireE. Appointments: Asst Station Offr, 1968, Station Offr, 1971, Asst Divisional Offr, 1980, Divisional Offr, 1986, Snr Divisional Offr, 1989, Dpty Chf Fire Offr, 1992, Chf Fire Offr, 1995, Hong Kong Fire Serv. Memberships: Instn of Fire Engrs, 1968; Soc of Homes for the Disabled; Cncl Mbr, Chmn, Dev and Maintenance Cttee, 1998. Hobbies: Travel; Bridge. Address: Hong Kong Fire Services Department, 1 Hong Chong Road, Tsimshatsui East, Hong Kong.

LAM Chung Yau, b. 4 Aug 1955, Hong Kong. Associate Professor. m. Yuen-Yee Tse, 18 Dec 1984, 2 s, 1 d. Education: BSc, 1st class hons, Engrng; PhD. Appointments: Tutor, Univ of London, 1979-83; Lectr, 1984-88, Snr Lectr, 1989-98, Assoc Prof, 1999-, Nanyang Technol Univ. Publication: Applied Numerical Methods for Partial Differential Equations, 1994. Honours: Draper's Rsch Grant, Univ London, 1979-82; Appl Rsch Grant, Nanyang Technol Univ, 1989, 1993. Memberships: MIMechE; Snr, MAIAA. Hobbies: Stamp collecting; Music; Jogging. Address: Nanyang Technological University, School of Mechanical & Production Engineering, Nanyang Avenue, Singapore 639798, Singapore.

LAM Samuel Mong-Dig, b. 13 Apr 1958, Hong Kong. Management Consultant. m. Shirley Yan, 26 Apr 1985, 2 d. Education: BA, Univ S CA; MA, Natl Univ of Singapore. Appointments: Mngng Dir, Am Hosp Supply, 1983-85; Mngng Ptnr, Hlth Search Intl, 1986-95; Dir, Hay Grp, 1995-. Memberships: Am Mngmt Assn; Am Hosp Assn; Singapore Inst of Mngmt. Hobbies: Tennis; Reading; Social and Church Work. Address: 69 One Tree Hill #11-69, Singapore 248706, Singapore.

LAMBLE Reginald (John), b. 18 Sept 1930, Sydney, Aust. Company Director. m. Philippa Patricia, 10 Apr 1953, 1 s, 1 d. Education: Sydney Univ. Appointments: Cadet Trainee, Atlantic Union Oil Co, 1952-54; Clk, Insp, Edward Lumleys, 1954-56; Mngr, Robert Paxton Ins, 1956-59; Gen Mngr, NRMA Ins Ltd, 1968-87; Dir, Macquarie Bank Ltd, 1985-93; CEO, NRMA, 1987-92; Illawarra Mutual Bldg Soc, 1992-93; RGC Ins Brokers (UK), 1992-; Chmn, State Bank NSW, 1993-94; Dir, Email, 1993-; Chmn, SGIC Holdings Ltd, SA, 1992-1995; Chmn, Perpetual Tstees Aust Ltd, 1995-; Chmn, Suncorp-Metway Ltd, 1996-. Publications: Pprs on ins, mngmt and the solvency of ins co's. Memberships: Pres, Non-Tariff Ins Assn, 1972-73; Cr, UNSW, 1977-93; Pres, Sydney Chmbr of Com, 1984; Cl Aust Ins Inst, 1980-85; Chmn, Bldg Cttee, 1981-85; Chmn, Fin Cttee, 1985-93. Hobbies: Opera; Tennis. Address: 6 Oak Hill Close, St Ives, NSW 2075, Australia.

LAMONT Byron Barnard, b. 2 Jan 1945, Perth, Aust. Plant Ecologist. m. Heather Herrmann, 12 May 1973, 2 s. Education: BAgrSc; PhD; DSc. Appointments: Snr Tutor in Botany, Univ of West Aust, 1973; Lectr, Bio, WA Inst of Technol, 1974; Promotion to Personal Chair in Plant Ecology, 1996. Publications: Over 100 jrnl pprs; 25 book chapts; 250 reports and articles, 1972-98. Honours: Snr Fulbright Awd, 1987; Fell, Inst of Bio, 1985; Visng Lectr Awd, Brit Ecological Soc, 1995; Intl Man of the Yr, 1997. Membership: Hon Mbr, S African Assn of Botanists. Hobbies: Scientific writing; Teaching; Fieldwork; Music; Sport. Address: School of Environemntal Biology, Curtin University, PO Box U1987, Perth 6845, Australia.

LAMUG Corazon, b. 25 Nov 1944, Tarlac, Phillippines. Sociology Professor. 1 s, 1 d. Education: MA, 1975; DPhil, 1980. Appointments: Chr, Dept of Socl Scis, 1980-82; Dir, Learning Resources Cntr, 1985-87; Dir of Rsch, Univ og Phil, 1987-91; Assoc Dir, CAS, 1995-. Creative Works: A Path Analysis to Test a Model of Helping Behaviour. Honours: Outstndng Tchr Awd; Post-doctoral Fellshp. Memberships: Phil Sociolgcl Soc. Hobbies: Reading; Rsch. Address: Dept of Social Sciences, CAS U P Los Banos College, Laguna, Philippines.

LANCASTER Henry Oliver, b. 1 Feb 1913, Sydney, NSW, Aust. Retired Professor of Mathematical Statistics. m. Joyce Mellon, 20 Dec 1940, 5 s. Education: MB, 1936, BS, 1947, BA, 1947, PhD, 1954, MD, 1966, DSc, 1972, Univ Sydney. Appointments: Res Medl Offr, Sydney Hosp, 1937-39; Pathologist, Roy Austl Army Medl Corps, 1940-46; Lectr, Snr Lectr, Assoc Prof, Sch Pub Hlth and Tropical Med, Sydney, 1946-59; Rockefeller Fell, Med, London Sch Hyg, Eng, 1948-49; Prof, Math Stats, Univ Sydney, 1959-78. Publications: Bibliography of Statistical Bibliographies, 1968; The Chi-squared Distribution, 1969; An Introduction to Medical Statistics, 1974; Expectations of Life, 1990; Quantitative Methods in Biological and Medical Sciences, 1994; Series of 60 articles on medl stats in Med Jrnl of Aust; Some 80 articles on maths and related subjs. Honours: Fell, Austl Acady Sci, 1961; T R Lyle Medal, Maths and Phys, 1961; Hon Life Mbr, Statl Soc Aust, 1972; E J G Pitman Medal, Stats, 1980; Hon Fell, Roy Statl Soc, 1975; Hon Life Mbr, Austl Math Soc, 1981; Fell, AAAS, 1988; AO, 1992. Memberships: Statl Soc NSW, Pres, 1952-53; Statl Soc Aust, Pres, 1965-66; Austl Math Soc, Gen Sec, 1959-63, Pres, Amn Statl Assn, 1966-67, VP 1968; Inst Math Stats. Hobbies: Reading; History; Biography. Address: The Garrison, 13 Spit Road, Spit Junction, NSW 2088, Australia.

LANCASTER-BROWN Peter, b. 13 Apr 1927, Cue, West Aust. Author. m. Johanne Nyrerod, 15 Aug, 1953. Publications: Twelve Came Back, 1957; Call of the Outback, 1970; What Star is That?, 1971; Australia's Coast of Coral and Pearl, 1972, 1974, reprinted 1995; Astronomy in Colour, 1972; The Seas and Oceans in Colour, 1973; Comets, Meteorites and Men, 1973, 1974;

Star and Planet Spotting, 1974, reprinted 1990; Planet Earth in Colour, 1976; Megaliths, Myths and Men, 1976, 1978; Megaliths and Masterminds, 1979; Fjord of Silent Men, 1983; Astronomy, 1984; Halley's Comet and the Principia, 1986; Skywatch, 1992, 1994. Address: 10 St Peters Road, Aldeburgh, Suffolk 1P15 5BG, England.

LANCE Godfrey Newby, b. 17 Sept 1928. Computer Scientist. m. Margaret Brenda Wells, 6 Oct 1957, 1 s, 3 d. Education: BSc; MSc; PhD; DSc. Appointments: Hawker Aircraft Ltd, 1952; UCLA, Los Angeles, 1954; Univ Southampton, 1955; UKAEA, Winfrith, Dorset, 1960; CSIRO, Canberra, 1963; Min, Sci, Aust House, London, 1972; Resumed as Chf of Div of Computing Rsch, CSIRO, 1973; Univ of Bristol, 1979; Retired 1992. Publication: Numerical Methods for High Speed Digital Computers, 1960. Memberships: FACS (Hon); FBCS; CEng. Hobbies: Carpentry; Gardening; Genealogy. Address: PO Box 54A, Bermagui, NSW 2546, Australia.

LANCE James Waldo, b. 29 Oct 1926, Wollongong, Aust. Neurologist. m. 6 July 1957, 1 s, 4 d. Education: The Kings Sch, Parramatta; MB BS, 1950, MD, 1955, Univ of Sydney; FRCP (London); FRACP; FAA. Appointments: Chmn, Dept of Neurol, Prince Henry and Prince of Wales Hosps, 1961-91; Prof of Neurol, Univ NSW, 1975-91; Emer Prof, Univ of NSW, 1992-. Publications: Introductory Neurology (w J G Mcleod), 3rd ed, 1995; A Physiological Approach to Clinical Neurology; Migraine and Other Headaches, revised ed, 1998; The Mechanism and Management of Headaches (w P G Goadsby), 6th ed, 1998. Honour: CBE, 1978; AO, 1991; Hon DSc, 1992. Memberships: Past Pres, Intl Headache Soc; Past VP, Austl Acady of Sci; VP, World Fedn of Neurology; VP, World Fedn of Neurol, 1991-94. Address: 15 Coolong Road, Vaucluse, NSW 2030, Australia.

LANCELEY Colin John, b. 6 Jan 1938, Dunedin, NZ. Artist. m. Kay Morphett, May 1970, 2 s. Education: Dip of Painting; Natl Art Sch, ASTC, Sydney. Appointments: Lectr, Bath Acady of Art, UK, 1966; Lectr, Chelsea Sch of Art, London, UK, 1975; Chmn, Natl Art School, Sydney, NSW, 1996-. Creative works: Exhibns, Aust, Eur, UK, USA; Wrks in most major contemporary collects from MOMA, NY, Tate Gall, London, Austl Natl Gall. Honours: Young Contemporaries Art Prize, CAS, Sydney, 1963; Helena Rubenstein Schlshp, AGNSW, 1964; Edinburgh Open 100 Art Prize, Edinburgh Fest, 1967; 1st Prize and Prize for Best Suite of Prints, 2nd Annual Graphics, Krakow, Poland, 1968; Eur Prize for Painting, Belgium, 1980; Faber-Castell Prize for Drawing, 1983; AO, 1989. Memberships: Served on Visual Arts Bd, Aust Cncl; Cncl of Natl Gall of Aust; Chelsea Arts Club, Painting and Sculptors Assn of Aust. Hobbies: Gardening; Growing orchids; Long lunches with friends; Chinese ceramics. Address: 2 Esther Lane, Surry Hills, NSW 2010, Australia.

LANDER Hartwell George, b. 24 Sept 1913, Melbourne, Aust. Solicitor. m. Marjorie Smith, 24 Sept 1946, 1 s, 2 d. Education: LLB, Melbourne Univ, 1936. Appointments: As Legal Practitioner, Fndr, Snr Partner, Lander and Rogers Sol, Melbourne; Law Inst Cncl, 1962-69, Pres, 1967-68, Life Mbr, 1983; Motor Car Traders Cttee, Chmn, 1972-85; Co Dir, Chmn, Glaxo Austl Ltd, 1976-83; Brook Bond Ltd, 1973-79. Publications: Co-auth w Dr Gordon Trinca, Road Trauma: The National Epidemic, 1982, 1985. Honours: CAMS Order of Merit, 1985; AM, 1987; RACS Medal, 1987. Membership: Law Inst of Vic, 1938-; Chmn Austl Motor Sport Appeal Crt, 1971-85; Mbr, Roy Aust Coll of Surgs Road Trauma Cttee, 1973-1997. Listed in Who's Who in Australia. Hobbies: Golf; Lawn Bowls; AFL Football; International Cricket. Address: 2A Boston Road, Balwyn, Vic 3103, Australia.

LANDY Peter James Bunworth, b. 30 Apr 1923. Neurologist. m. Cecily O'Connor, 23 Oct 1954, 4 s. Education: MB BS, St Joseph's Coll, Univ Qld. Appointments: Mater Misericordiae Hosp, Brisbane, 1953-73; Repatriation Dept, Qld, 1958-; Visng Neurologist, Princess Alexander Hosp, 1960-82, Chmn, Visng Staff, 1973; Qld Cl of Professions, 1976-77; Mbr, Cl

Qld Br, Austl Medl Assn, Pres, 1980-81; Pres, Medico-Legal Soc, Qld, 1981. Honour: OBE, 1983. Memberships: MRCP (Lon); MRACP; FRACP; FRCP, London; Utd Serv (Qld) Club. Address: Alexandra, 201 Wickham Terrace, Brisbane, Qld 4000, Australia.

LANE Patrick Harding, b. 25 June 1923, Vic, Aust. Author. m. Patricia, 11 Feb 1956, 3 s. Education: BA, 1953, LLB, 1957, LLM, 1960, LLD, 1973, Univ Sydney; SJD, Harv Law Sch, 1965. Appointments: Tchr, Advice Clk, Lectr, Snr Lectr, Assoc Prof, Prof, Constl Law, Univ Sydney. Publications: Introduction to the Australian Constitutions, 1995; Manual of Constitutional Law, 1995; Digest of Constitutional Cases, 1996; Commentary on the Australian Constitution from 1901. Honour: Univ Medal, Sydney, 1957. Hobbies: Writing; Music; Swimming. Address: 337 Rainbow Street, Coogee, NSW 2034, Australia.

LANE William Ronald, b. 15 Feb 1923. Dean. m. Joan Eales, 21 May 1956, 4 d. Education: MCom (Qld); MA (Cantab); Univ of Qld; Univ of Cambridge. Appointments: Dean, Fac of Com & Econs, Univ of Qld; Qld Pub Serv, 1939-45; Brit Cl Sch, Univ of Cambridge, 1951-53; Chf Fin Offr, C'wlth Treas, 1964-65; Mbr, pt-time C'wlth Grants Cmmn, 1966-94; Lectr in Econs, Univ of Qld, 1947-66, Rdr, 1968-. Honour: CBE, 1979. Membership: Univ of Qld Club. Hobbies: Gardening; Music. Address: 228 Harts Road, Indooroopilly, Qld 4068, Australia.

LANG Dazhong, b. Mar 1933, China. State Official. Appointments: Alt Mbr, 12th CCP Ctrl Cttee, 1982, Mbr, 1983-87, Mbr, 13th Ctrl Cttee, 1987-; Dir, Dehong Dai & Jingpo Autonomous Pref Cttee, 1978-83, Party Sec, 1983-; Sec, Comm for Discipline Inspection, 1992-; Standing Cttee, Ctrl Comm for Discipline Inspection, 1992-; Vice Chair, CPPCC 7th Yunnan Prov Cttee. Address: Dehong Dai & Jingpo Autonomous Prefectural Peoples Government, Yunnan, China.

LANG Donald Wilson, b. 3 Mar 1933. Theoretical Physicist. m. Jean Charlotte Spencer, 9 June 1966, 2 s, 1 d. Education: PhD, Austl Natl Univ, Canberra, Aust, 1961; Univ of NZ, Auckland Univ Coll, BSc 1954, MSc 1956. Appointments: Univ of NZ, 1961; Bartol Rsch Fndn, Phila, 1962-64; Argonne Natl Lab, Chgo, 1964-66; Univ of KS, USA, 1966; Harwell, 1966-67; KS State Univ, 1967-69; PA State Univ, 1969-71; Austl Atomic Energy Comm, 1971-92. Publications: Num papers in statistical nuc phys & applied maths. Honours: Life Mbr, NSW Fedn of Parents Citizens Assn, 1994. Memberships: Fell, Austl Inst of Phys; Sec, Sci Plcy Cttee, 1981-83. Hobbies: Education: Science; Broadcasting; Historical Reading. Address: 22 Tulong Place, Kirrawee, NSW 2232, Australia.

LANGE David Russell, b. Sept 1942, Otahuhu, New Zealand. Politician; Lawyer. m. (1) Naomi Lange, 1968, 3 children, (2) Margaret Forsyth Pope, 1992, 1 d. Education: Otahuhu Coll, Auckland Univ. Appointments: Barrister, Solicitor, Kaikohe, 1968, Auckland, 1970-77; Labour Party MP for Mangere, Auckland, 1977-; Opposition Spokesman on Justice, 1978, on Fgn Affairs, 1993-; Dpty Ldr, Parl Labour Party, 1979-83, Ldr, 1983-89; Fmr Opposition Spokesman on Fgn Affairs, Overseas Trade, Justice, Pacific Islands Affairs, Regl Devel; PM, 1984-89; Min in Charge of the Security Intelligence Serv, 1984-89; Min of Fgn Affairs, 1984-87; Min of Educn, 1987-89; Atty-Gen, 1989-90; Min of State, 1989-90; Min in Charge of Serious Fraud Off, 1989-90. Publication: Nuclear Free the New Zealand Way, 1990. Address: 14 Ambury Road, Mangere Bridge, Auckland, New Zealand.

LANGE Jessica, b. 20 Apr 1949, Cloquet, USA. Actress. 1 s, 2 d. Education: Univ MN; Student, Mime w Etienne DeCroux, Paris. Appointments: Dancer, Opera Comique, Paris; Model, Wilhelmina Agcy, NY. Creative Works: Films incl: King Kong, 1976; All That Jazz, 1979; How to Beat the High Cost of Living, 1980; The Postman Always Rings Twice, 1981; Frances, 1982; Tootsie, 1982; Country, 1984; Sweet Dreams, 1985; Crimes of the Heart, 1986; Everybody's All American, 1989; Far North,

1989; Music Box, 1989; Men Don't Leave, 1989; Blue Sky, 1990; Cape Fear, 1991; Far North, 1991; Night and the City, 1993; Losing Isaiah, Rob Roy, 1995; A Thousand Acres; Star Showtime TV Prodn Cat On A Hot Tin Roof; In Summer Stock Prodn Angel On My Shoulder; A Streetcar Named Desire (play). Honours include: Acady Awd, Best Supporting Actress, 1982; Th World Awd, Golden Globe, 1996. Address: c/o CAA, Ron Meyer, 9830 Wilshire Boulevard, Beverly Hills, CA 90212, USA.

LANGLEY Steven Kenneth, b. 17 July 1926, Melbourne, Aust. Consultant. m. Deirdre Dellit, 14 Mar 1958, 2 s, 1 d. Education: RMIT, Dip of Mechl Engrng, 1956. Appointments: Dir, Shedden Pacific Pty Ltd, 1986-94; Chmn, 1983-85. Mngng Dir, 1978-83, Global Eng (Aust) Pty Ltd; Chmn, Miadna Pty Ltd, 1984-87; Bus Dev Mngr, Austin Anderson Pty Ltd, 1973-78. Honours: AO, 1982; Pres, Instn of Engrs Aust, 1981-82; VP, W Inds Assn, 1971-84; Pres, Soc of Chem Ind, 1970. Memberships: Fell; Austl Acady of Technol Scis and Engrng; Austl Inst of Mngmt; Aust Inst of Energy; Hon Fell, Instn of Chem Engrs (London); Hon Fell, Inst of Engrs (Aust). Hobbies: Reading; Walking. Address: 927 Punt Road, South Yarra, Vic 3141, Australia.

LANHAM David, b. 8 Nov 1938, Oxford, Eng. Professor of Law. m. Gillian, 22 Sept 1962, 2 s. Education: LLB, Leeds, 1962; BCL, Oxford, 1964; Barrister, Lincoln's Inn, 1970. Appointments: Asst Lectr, Nottingham Univ, 1964-65; Lectr, Nottingham Univ, 1965-73; Snr Lectr, Nottingham Univ, 1973-75; Prof, Melbourne Univ, 1975-. Publications: Study Guide to Criminal Law, 1967; Practical Forensic Medicine (co-auth), 1971; General Principles of Administrative Law (co-auth), 1979, 1984, 1989, 1997; Criminal Fraud (Co-auth), 1986; Taming Death by Law, 1993; Cross Border, Criminal Law, 1997. Hobbies: Violin and saxophone playing. Address: Faculty of Law, University of Melbourne, Parkville, Victoria, Australia 3052.

LANSDOWN Robert Broughton, b. 10 May 1921, E Maitland, NSW, Aust. Director. m. Gloria Alice Jones, 6 Mar 1943, 1 s, 1 d. Education: BEcon, Univ of Sydney, 1946. Appointments: Assoc Commnr Natl Capital Dev Commn, 1965-72; Sec, C'wlth Dept of Urban Dev, 1972-75; Sec, C'wlth Dept of Environment and Housing, 1975-78; Sec, C'wlth Dept of Commns, 1979-85; Chmn, Austl Postal Planning Auth, 1985-90; Chmn, Natl Capital Planning Authority, 1989-91; Chmn, Telecomms Ind Dev Auth, 1992-97; Chmn, Asia Pacific Smart Card Forum, 1996-. Honours: CBE, 1978; AO, 1991. Membership: Fell, Acady of Technol Scis. Hobbies: 3/36 Shackleton Circuit, Mawson, ACT 2607, Australia.

LAO Francisco, Jr, b. 10 Oct 1963. Rsch Engr. Education: BSc, Chem Engrng, magna cum laude. Appointments: Rsch and Devel Engr, Paramount Vinyl Prods Corp, 1985-87; Mngmt Cnslt, SGV & Co/Andersen Cnsltng, 1987-91; Snr Rsch Engr, Procter and Gamble Phils Inc, 1991-; Cnslt, Lectr, Phil Fndn for Sci and Technol, 1991-; Snr Rsch Engr, Proctor and Gamble Far East Inc, Japan, 1997-. Publications: Ed-in-Chf, The Appulse, 1988-, The Thomasian Engineer, 1984-86. Honours: Deans Awd, 1980-84; Rectors Awd, Acad Ex, 1985; Quezon Awd, Ldrshp, 1985; Padre Faura Awd, Astronomy, 1996. Memberships: Pres, Philippines Astronomical Soc, 1991-94, 1996-97, Bd Dir, 1990-; Planetary Soc; Astro Soc of the Pacific; Intl Amateur Astronomers Network; Solar Observers Network. Listed in: Who's Who; Who's Who in Science and Engineering. Hobbies: Astronomy; Photography; Orchid Growing. Address: 680 Manga Avenue, Saint Mesa, Manila 1016, The Philippines.

LARCO COX Guillermo, b. 19 Feb 1932, Peru. Engineer; Politician. Appointments: MBr, Alianza Popular Revolucionaria Americana; Mayor, Trujillo, 1964-66, 1967-68; Civil Engr; Parl Dpty for Dept of La Libertad, 1980-85; Senator, 1985; PM of Peru, 1987-88, 1990; Min for Presidency, 1987-88; Min of Fgn Affairs, 1989-90. Address: Ministry of Foreign Affairs, Ucayali 363, Lima, Peru.

LARGE Jane Marie Dewey, b. 25 Nov 1941. Public Servant. m. Bryan Robert Large, 28 June 1969, 1 s. Appointments: Govt Coms HQ, 1959, 1964; Brit Embassy, Wash DC, USA, 1961-63; Emigrated to Aust, 1967; W ub Serv, 1968; Atty Gen's Dept, 1970; Austl Legal Aid Commn, 1974; Dept of Mines and Energy, 1979; NT Treasury, 1982; Snr Dir, NT Treas, 1996. Memberships: Justice of the Peace; Legal Aid Commnr. Hobbies: Reading; Spectator sports. Address: 73 Tiwi Gardens Road, Tiwi, NT, Australia.

LARI Abdolvahed Mussavi, b. 1954, Larestan, Fars Prov, Iran. Interior Minister. m. 5 children. Education: Advd Theo. Appointments: Preacher; Dir, Theol Seminary, Qom; Staff Mbr, Ayatollah Khomeini's Off; Construction Crusade; Dpty Culture and Islamic Guidance Min; Mbr, Bd of Tstees, Islamic Culture Fndn, Islamic Thought Fndn; VP, Legal and Parly Affairs; Elected, Min of Interior. Memberships: Islamic Culture Fndn; Islamic Thought Fndn.

LARKIN John Terence, b. 21 Sept 1935, Manly, NSW, Aust. Economist. m. Elaine, 27 Feb 1965, 3 s, 5 d. Education: BEc, Sydney Univ; MA, MPA, Harv. Appointments: First Asst Sec, Dept of Trade, 1975-87; Dir, Austl Bur of Agric and Resource Econs, 1987; Chf Economist, KPMG Peat Marwick, 1988-90; Econ Cnslt, 1991-; Agribusiness Food Dev in SE Asia, 1993. Publications: Investing in Australia's Future (Bus Cncl of Aust), 1994; Refocussing Microeconomic Reform, 1995; Corp Strategies and Structures: Penetrating Asian Markets, 1996. Honour: Harkness Fell, Harv Univ, 1965-67. Memberships: Fell, Harv Club of Aust; Fell, Austl Soc of Accts; Econ Soc of Aust. Hobbies: Surfing; Golf. Address: 46 Creswell Street, Campbell, ACT 2612, Australia.

LARMOUR Ian, b. 24 Dec 1945, Wycheproof, Vic, Aust. Pharmacist; Pharmacologist. m. Laurise Zelle Humphreys, 9 May 1972, 2 s. Education: BPharm, Monash Univ, Melbourne, 1969; MSc, Pharm, 1986; Regd Pharmacist, Vic, Aust. Appointments include: Dpty Dir, Pharm Prince Henry's Hosp, Melbourne, 1973-81; Dir, Pharm, 1981-88; Mngr, Pharm Servs, Monash Med Cntr, Melbourne, 1988-; Dir, Pharm Servs, Jessie McPherson Priv Hosp, Melbourne, 1988-; Snr Mngr, S Hlth Care Network Pharm Servs, 1997-; Cnslt, Monash Healthcare Consultancy, Melbourne, 1994-; Mngng Dir, Enzal Prods & Servs/Larmour Enterprises, Melbourne, 1994-; Lectr in field. Publications: Contbr, num articles to profl jrnls. Honours: Sigma Awd, 1974; Fell, Soc Hosp Pharmacists, Aust, 1995, 1975, Chmn Vic Branch, 1976-79; Samuel Wynn Awd, Prince Henry's Hosp, 1976; SMPA Glaxo Medal of Merit, 1991; Natl Hosp Quality Mngmt Prog Rsch Grantee, 1994. Memberships include: Vic Hosps Assn; Pharm Soc Aust; Pharm Def Pty Ltd; Hosp Pharmacists Assn; Austl Soc Parenteral and Enteral Nutrition; Austl Soc Clin and Exerimental Pharmocologists; Naval and Mil Club; Amnesty Intl; Melbourne Cricket Club; Melbourne Football Club. Hobbies: Reading; Writing; Gardening; Photography; Cricket. Address: Surrey Hills, Melbourne 3127, VIC Australia.

LAROYA Chander Vinod, b. 26 March 1948, Phillaur, Punjab, India. Company Director. m. Madhu, 12 Sept 1975, 1 s. 1 d. Education: BSc; MBA. Appointments: Pres and Dir, P T Indorama Synthetics, Jakarta; Dir, P T Indorama Teknologies, Jakarta, Indo-Poly (Thailand) Ltd, Bangkok, Indorama Iplik San ve Tic A S, Istanbul. Memberships: Rsch Advry Cttee, Ahmedabad Textile Ind Rsch Assn, India; Bd Mgmt, Assn of Synthetic Fiber Prodrs of Indonesia, Jakarta. Hobbies: Music; Reading; Playing Tennis;Cricket. Address: P T Indorama Synthetics, Graha Irama 17th Floor, Jl H R Rasuna Said Blok X-1, Kav 1&2, Jakarta 12950, Indonesia.

LARSEN Walter Harold (Wal), b. 20 Jan 1915, Melbourne, Aust. Scribe. m. Thelma, 24 Dec 1936, 1 s, 1 d. Publications: May Day Hills Railway, 1976; The Ovens Valley Railway, 1983; Change Here For -, 1985; Watching Trains, 1987. Memberships: Puffing Billy Preservation Soc; Pres, Bright & District Histl Soc; Pres, Bright Branch Red Cross. Hobbies: Railways; History (and writing history for magazines and newspapers). Address: 29 Delaney Avenue, Bright, Australia 3741.

LASHER John Steven Robert, b. 18 Oct 1943, El Paso, Texas, USA. Composer; Film Director; Music Producer. Education: Roosevelt Univ, Chgo, IL, USA; Am Conservatory of Music, Chgo, IL, USA. Appointments: Pres, Entr'acte Recording Soc, 1974; Fifth Continent Music Corp, 1982; Mngng Dir, Fifth Continent Aust, 1992-. Creative Works: Compositions: Celluloid Fanfare, 1991; Kinopanorama Logo, 1997; Starcharts, 1999. Film Director: I Am Australian, 1999; Our Scenic Wonders, 2000. Honours: Preis der Deutsche Schallplatten Kritik, 1991, 1992; APRA Best Soundtrack Album of the Yr, 1993. Memberships: Austl Guild of Screen Composers, assoc mbr, 1999; APRA, composer mbr, 1999; Austl Film Inst. Hobbies: Cricket; Soccer; Photography; Train Travel; Film Preservation; Music. Address: c/o Fifth Continent Australia, 28 Gardiner Crescent, Blackheath, NSW 2785, Australia.

LASLETT Lawrence, b. 17 Apr 1942, Boston, MA, USA. Physician; Professor. 1 s, 1 d. Education: MD. Appointments: Prof, Clin Med (Cardiology), Univ of CA, Davis. Publications: Multiple medl jrnl articles and book chapts. Memberships: Amn Coll of Cardiology; Amn Heart Assn; Amn Coll of Physns. Address: Division of Cardiology, University of California, Davis, 4860 Y St, Suite 2800, Sacramento, CA 95817, USA.

LAST Jerold Alan, b. 6 May 1940, NY Cty, NY, USA. Professor of Medicine. m. Elaine, 6 Jan 1975, 3 s. Education: BS, Chem, 1959; MSc, Biochemistry, 1961; PhD, Biochemistry, 1965. Appointments: Prof, Univ of CA at Davis, 1976-; Dir, UC Toxic Substances Prog, 1985-. Publications: About 160 var sci pprs; Ed, Methods in Molecular Biology, 1971-73. Honours: FASEB Visng Prof, Cath Univ of Puerto Rico (Ponce), 1985; Univ of CA, Davis Sch of Med Fac Rsch Awd, 1990; Tuskegee Univ, AL, 1991; Sc f Toxiclogy, ICI Traveling Lectureship Awd, 1992; Fulbright Prof, Univ of Repub, Montevideo, Uraguay & Argentina, 1999; Sigma Xi; Phi Sigma. Memberships: Amn Soc for Biochem & Molecular Bio; Soc of Toxicology; Amn Thoracic Soc; Amn Fedn for Clin Rsch; West Soc for Clin Rsch; West Connective Tissue Soc. Hobbies: Tennis; Baking sourdough; Bread. Address: 510 Hubble Street, Davis, CA 95616, USA.

LATIEF Abdul, b. 27 Apr 1940. Education: Deg in Indl Mngmt, Indonesian Ministry Ind, Jakarta, 1963; BA, Econs, Univ Krisnadwipayana, Jakarta, 1965. Appointments: Hd, Div, Sales Promotion and Expert Dev, PT DSI Sarinah Corp, 1963-71; Dir, Acady Indl Mngmt, Indonesial Ministry Ind, 1969-71; Pres, Alatief Co, 1972-93; Min, Manpower, Govt of Indonesia, Jakarta, 1993-. Memberships: Chmn, Var bureaucratic assns; Fndr, Indonesian Young Businessmen's Assn. Address: Embassy of Indonesia, 2020 Massachusetts Avenue NW, Washington, DC 20036, USA.

LATUKEFU Ruth Annette (Fink), b. 25 Nov 1931. Anthropologist. m. Rev Dr Sione Latukefu, 4 June 1966, dec 1995, 1 s, 1 d. Education: BA w Hons, MA w Hons, Sydney Univ; PhD, Columbia Univ, NY, USA. Appointments: Rsch Fell, Univ of WA, 1955-57; Lectr, Austl Sch of Pacific Admin, 1960-64; Lectr in Anthropology, Univ of Sydney, 1965-66; Snr Lectr, Univ of Papua New Guinea, 1967-85. Publications: Pprs on Aboriginal and New Guinea rsch, 1956-66. Membership: Austl Inst of Aboriginal and Torres St Islander Studies, 1964-. Hobbies: Music; Painting; Writing. Address: 153 Queens Parade, PO Box 644, Newport Beach, NSW 2106, Australia.

LAU Hing Wah, b. 23 Mar 1952, China. Education, Chinese Literary Criticism. m.27 Dec 1979. Education: BA; DipEd; MPhil; PhD. Appointments: Ying Wa Coll, 1981-84; S K H Bishop Baker Second Sch, 1994-95; Hong Kong Inst of Educ, 1995-. Publications: The Practical Writing, 1996; The Listening Training, 1997; Conf pprs, 1996-; Essays. Memberships: Hong Kong Educl Rsch Assn; Sec, Hong Kong Ethnomusicology Soc.

Hobbies: Playing Chinese musical instruments such as Zheng and Chin; Writing. Address: Flat B, 37/F, Blk 3, East Point City, Tseung Kwan O, Kowloon, Hong Kong.

LAU Jerman, b. 25 Dec 1953, Hong Kong. Engineer. m. Velusamy Maha Devi, 21 Mar 1987. Education: Tech Col. Appointments: Tech Cttee of Inst of Intl Container Lessors. Membership: Inst of Intl Container Lessors. Hobbies: Music; Sports. Address: 35/F, 118 Connaught Road West, Hong Kong.

LAU Ki-chit Sebastian, b. 27 June 1930. Chairman of Executive Board. m. Shirley S L Lau Sa, 8 Aug 1978, 2 s, 1 d. Education: Aeronautical Engr, A&C; Far E Aeronautical Engrng. Appointments: Underwriter, Malayan Insurance Co Ltd, 1954-59; Mngr, Asia Ins Co Ltd, 1959-61; Mngr/Dir, Asia Ins Co Ltd, 1961-68; Mng Dir, Asia Ins Co Ltd, 1968-95; Chmn of Exec Bd, Asia Ins Co Ltd, 1996-. Memberships: Ins Claims Complaints Bur; Motor Insurer's Bur of HK; Tung Wah Grp of Hosp; Ruttonjee Hosp HK Tuberculosis Chest and Heart Diseases Assn; Wan Chai Kaifong Welfare Assn; HK Chiu Chow Chmbr of Comm; Chinese Gen Chmbr of Comm; Chiu Chow Merchants Mutual Asst Soc; Chiu On Assns; Am Fau Clansmen Assn; Chiu Sheung Sch; Rotary Club of HK Island West; Assn of Chmn of Tung Wah Grp of Hosps; HK Fedn of Insurers Gen Ins Cncl; HK Expoert Credit Ins Corp; Panel of Assessors. Hobbies: Travel; Music; Golfing. Address: 16th World Wide House, 19 Des Voeux Road Central, Hong Kong.

LAU San-Ching. Politician; Artist. m. Christine Tang. Education: Univ of Hong Kong. Appointments: Fmr Tchr; Admin Asst, Mental Hosp, Hong Kong; Full Time Activist, Revolutionary Marxist league; Vis, S China, 1980-81; Goal in China for Polit Activities, 1981-91; Returned to Hong Kong, 1991; Barred by Govt of Hong Kong for Contesting Dist Be of Elections, 1994; Lodged Election Petition at High Crt, 1994.

LAU Siu Kai, b. 7 June 1947, Hong Kong, China. Education: m. Sophie Kwok, 15 July 1972, 1 s. Education: PhD, Univ of MN, USA. Appointments: Prof of Sociol, Chinese Univ of Hong Kong, 1990-; Assoc Dir, Hong Kong Inst of Asia-Pacific Studies, 1990-; Chmn, Dept of Sociol, CUHK. Publications: 107 pprs to profl jrnls. Memberships: Prel Working Cttee, Hong Kong Spec Admin Reg, 1993-95; Preparatory Cttee, Hong Kong Spec Admnstv Reg, China, 1996-97. Hobbies: Reading; Walking. Address: Room 712 7/F Tin Ka Ping Building, Hong Kong Institute of Asia-Pacific Studies, Chinese University of Hong Kong, Shatin, Hong Kong, China.

LAUDICO Adriano Victor, b. 17 Nov 1941. Physician; Surgeon. 1 s, 2 d. Education: MD; Dipl in Gen Surg; Certs in Cancer Epidemiology, Esophageal and Hepatic Surg. Appointments: Prof of Surg, Univ of the Philippines; Hd, Rizal Cancer Registry and Manila Cancer Registry; Chmn, Off of Rsch Servs, Univ of the Philippines, Manila; Tech Dir for Rsch Mngmt and Dev, Philippine Cncl for Hlth Rsch and Dev; Ed in Chief, Philippine Jrnl of Surg Specialties. Publications: 98 publs in natl and intl biomed publs mainly in cancer and surg infections, 1975-; Editl Bd, Philippine Textbook of Surg, 1990. Honours: Outstndng Publsd Ppr, Natl Acady of Sci and Technol, 1993; Outstndng Cancer Rschr, Philippine Soc of Oncologists, 1994; Outstndng Rschr, Univ of the Philippines Med Alumni Assn, 1994. Memberships: Philippine Coll of Surgs, Pres 1993; Surg Oncology Soc of the Philippines, Pres 1994-95; Amn Coll of Surgs; Intl Soc of Surg. Hobbies: Tennis; Music; Ornamental plants; Food; Reading. Address: Department of Surgery, Philippine General Hospital, Taft Avenue, Manila 1001, Philippines.

LAUDICO Minerva Guysako, b. 4 July 1912, Manila, Philippines. Educator; Social Worker. m. Adriano P, 4 Apr 1940, 1 s, 1 d. Education: BS Educ, Cert in Socl Wrk; MA; EdD honoris causa. Appointments: Exec Sec, Natl Fedn Woman's Clubs, 1935-45; Dir, Home & Mil Welfare Servs, Philippines Natl Red Cross, 1945-65; Dean, College of Socl Wrk, Centro Escolar Univ, 1948-68, Exec VP, 1963-73, Acad VP, 1973-93; Repr Woman Sect,

Congress of the Philippines, 1994-95, 1995-98. Honours: Dr Educ hc, 1973; Hon Pres Fedn Asian Women's Assns, 1976-; Cncl of Welfare Agcys Outstndng Profl Worker of the Yr, 1958; Presdtl Merit Awd, 1966; Philippines Assn Univ Women Outstndng Civic Worker, 1984; Girl Scouts of the Philippines Hall of Fame, 1990. Memberships: Charter Mbr, Girl Scouts of Philippines, 1940; Pres, Fndn for the Elderly, 1995-; Stop Trafficking of Filipinos, 1983-96; Cath Tchrs Guild, 1980-84; Phil Assn of Socl Workers, 1952-53; Chmn, Nutrition Fndn of Philippines, 1985-86. Hobbies: Keeping scrapbooks; Gardening; Travel; Collecting friends. Address: 209A Carriedo Street, San Juan, Metro Manila 1500, Philippines.

LAUER Anthony Raymond, b. 19 Dec 1935, Newcastle, New South Wales, Australia. Retired Commissioner of Police. m. Joy, 4 Apr 1955, 2 s, 2 d. Education: FBI's Natl Exec Inst, VA, USA, 1994; Univ of Sydney Austl Police Coll, 1996; Austl Police Staff Coll, 1997. Appointments: Chf Supt in Charge, Criminal Investigation Br, 1986-88; Asst Cmmnr, 1988-90; Dpty Cmmnr, 1990-91; Cmmnr of Police, 1991-96. Honour: Austl Police Medal, 1990. Memberships: Pres, Police Assn of NSW, 1979-82; Dir, NSW Police Credit Union, 1998-. Hobbies: Motor Cycle Touring; Gardening. Address: PO Box 653, Penrith, NSW 2751, Australia.

LAUGERUD GARCIA Kjell Eugenio, b. 24 Jan 1930, Guatemala. Politician; Army Officer. m. Helen Losi, 1951, 3 s, 2 d. Appointments: Min of Def, Chf of Gen Staff, Army, 1970-74; Pres Cand of Movimiento de Liberacion Nacional/Partido Institucional Democratico, 1974; Pres of Guatemala, 1974-78. Honours include: Legion of Merit, USA, 1971; Gran Collar Orden del Quetzal, Guatemala, 1974; Gran Cruz Brillantes Orden de El Sol, Peru; Orden del Mérito, Chile, 1978. Hobbies: Horseback Riding; Collecting Small Arms; Military History. Address: Oficina del Presidente, Guatemala City, Guatemala.

LAUREL Salvador Hidalgo, b. 18 Nov 1928, Manila, Philippines. Politician. 8 children. Education: Univ of the Philippines; Yale Univ. Appointments: Senator, 1967-73; Prof of Law & Jurisprudence; Fndr, Legal Aid Soc of the Philippines; Mbr, Interim Natl Assn, 1978; Active in Opposition Politics, 1982-; Ldr, United Nationalist Democratic Org, 1981-91, Union for Natl Action, 1988-91; VP of Philippines, 1986; PM, 1986; Min of Fgn Affairs, 1986-87; Pres, Nacionalista Party, 1989.

LAURENT Simon Lyall, b. 5 June 1964, Auckland, New Zealand. Barrister. Education: BSc Phys, 1985; LLB Hons, 1996. Appointments: Cncl of Auckland Dist Law Soc, 1998. Honours: Gold Medal, World Blind Sailing Championships, Fremantle, 1994; Winner, Radio NZ Short Story Competition, 1980. Hobbies: Philosophy; Choral singing; Theatre; Computing. Address: 16 Windsor Street, Parnell, Auckland, New Zealand.

LAURIE Robert Stephen, b. 5 Nov 1936, Sydney, Aust. Diplomat. m. Diana Doyne, 6 June 1969, 1 s, 1 d. Education: BA (Hons). Appointments: Amb to Burma, 1975-77, to Poland, 1977-80; High Commnr to Can, 1985-89;, to NZ, 1989-92; to India, 1997-. Hobbies: Golf; Gardening. Address: Australian High Commissioner, New Delhi, India.

LAUSCH Hans, b. 24 Nov 1941, Vienna, Austria. Mathematician; Educator; Historian of Mathematics. m. Elisabeth, 20 Nov 1971, 1 s, 1 d. Education; PhD, Vienna, 1964; Doz habil phil, Vienna, 1971; Doz habil rer nat, 1982. Appointments: Asst Prof, Univ Vienna, 1965-72; Rsch Fell, ANU, Canberra, 1967-70; Snr Lectr, Monash Univ, 1972-73; Rdr, Monash Univ, 1973-93; Assoc Prof, Monash Univ, 1993-. Publications: Algebra of Polynomials (co-auth), 1973; The Asian Pacific Mathematics Olympiads 1989-1993, 1994; Austl Mathematical Olympiads, 1979-95, 1997. Honours: Prize of Austrian Maths Soc, 1970; Bernhard H Neumann Awd (servs to maths enrichment in Aust & reg), 1998. Memberships: Austl Maths Soc: Ed, J Aust MS, SerA, 1980-82; Vic Algebra Grp, Sec, 1996-. Hobbies: Strategy games; Bushwalking; Byzantine studies. Address: 20 Nonna Street, Clayton, 3168, Australia.

LAVER William Graeme, b. 3 June 1929, Aust. Medical Researcher. m. Judith Garrard Cahn, 1954, 1 s, 2 d. Education: BS, MSc, Univ of Melbourne; PhD, Univ of London, Eng. Appointments: Techl Asst, Walter and Eliza Hall Inst of Medl Rsch, Melbourne, Vic, 1947-52; Rsch Asst, Dept of Biochem, Melbourne Univ, 1954-55; Rsch Fell, 1958-62, Fell, 1962-64, Snr Fell, 1964-, Hd, Influenza Rsch Unit, 1983-, John Curtin Sch of Medl Rsch, Austl Natl Univ, Canberra, ACT; Organizer, intl meetings: Rougement, Switz, 1976; Baden, Vienna, 1977; Thredbo, Aust, 1979; Beijing, China, 1982; Banbury Cntr, Cold Springs Harbor, NY, 1985; Kona, Hawaii, 1989. Publications: Pprs on the structure of influenza virus antigen and molecular mechanisms of antigenic shift and drift in A type influenza articles; Num rsch articles. Honour: Aust Prize, 1996. Hobbies: Raising beef cattle; Viticulture and wine-making; Skiing; Climbing; Volcanoes. Address: Barton Highway, Murrumbateman, NSW 2582, Australia.

LAVIS John Frederic, b. 15 Jan 1923. m. Nanette Reid, 3 June 1959, 3 d. Education: MDS; Prince Alfred Coll, Adelaide Univ. Appointments: Em Specialist, Roy Adelaide Hosp; Hon Cnslt in Dentistry, SA Dental Servs; Mbr, Fac Dentistry, 1957-81; Pres, SA Br, 1962, Mbr, Fedn Cl ADA, 1962-72; Curriculum Cttee, Adelaide Univ, Roy Adelaide Hosp, 1962-76; Hon Treas, Roy Austl Coll of Dental Surgs, 1968-70, VP 1970-72, Pres 1972-76; Chmn, Hon Dental Staff Soc, 1967-78; Dentists Act Stat Cttee, 1975-85; Mbr, Advise Cttee to Adelaide Univ & Roy Adelaide Hosp, 1977-82; Bd of Mngmt, Roy Adelaide Hosp, Chmn, Dental Cttee, 1979-82; Examiner in Final Exams, 1981-86; SA Dental Servs Bd of Mngmt, 1982-84; Dental Profl Conduct Tribunal, 1985-88; Visng Rsch Fell, Univ of Adelaide, 1993-. Honours: AM, 1981; Disting Serv Awd, 1984; ADA, 1993. Memberships: FRACDS; FICD; FADI; Adelaide Club. Address: 157 Strangways Terrace, North Adelaide, SA 5006, Australia.

LAW Chi Kwong, b. 1 Nov 1953. Social Worker; University Teacher. m. Grace Lai-Yun Ling, 20 May 1978, 1 s, 1 d. Education: BSoc Sc; MSW; MBA; DSW. Appointments: Legis Cncl Mbr, 1995-97, 1998-; Hd of Dept of Socl Wrk & Socl Admin, Univ of Hong Kong, 1993-97. Memberships: Hong Kong Socl Workers Assn, 1981-; Pres, 1991-93; Bd Mbr, 1982-86; 1988-; Registrar, 1991-95; Bd Mbr, Socl Workers Registration Bd, 1997-. Hobbies: Swimming; Singing. Address: c/o Department of Social Work and Social Administration, University of Hong Kong, Pokfulam Road, Hong Kong.

LAW Phillip Garth, b. 21 Apr 1912, Tallangatta, Aust. Physicist Educator; Antarctic Explorer. m. Nellie Isabel Allan, 20 Dec 1941. Education: Ballarat Tchrs Coll, 1931; BSc, 1939, MSc, 1941, Melbourne Univ. Appointments: Sci Master, State Secnd Schs, Vic, 1933-38; Tutor, Phys, Newman Coll, Melbourne Univ, 1940-47; Lectr, Phys, 1943-48; Rsch Physicist, Asst Sec, Sci Instrument and Optical Panel, Austl Min of Munitions, 1940-45; Snr Sci Offr, ANARE, 1947-48; Cosmic Ray Measurements in Antarctica & Japan, 1948; Dir, Antarctic Divsn, Dept of Exernal Affairs, Aust, Ldr, ANARE, 1949-66; Expedition Relief Voyages to Heard and Macquarie Is, 1949, 1951, 1952, 1954; Austl Observer w Norwegian-Brit-Swedish Antarctic Expedition, 1950; Ldr, Expedition to Establish First Perm Austl Stn in Antarctica at Mawson, MacRobertson Land, 1954, 2nd Continental Stn at Davis, Princess Elizabeth Land, 1957 taking over Wilkes Station from USA, 1959, to relieve ANARE Stns and to Explore Coast of Austl Antarctic Territory, annually, 1955-66); Chmn, Austl Natl Cttee for Antarctic Rsch, 1966-80; Exec VP, Vic Inst of Colls, 1966-77. Publications include: ANARE (w John Bechervaise), 1957; Antarctic Odyssey, 1983; The Antarctic Voyage of HMAS Wyatt Earp, 1995; You Have To Be Lucky, 1995; Chapts in books, sci rprts and num pprs on Antarctica and Educ. Honours include: AO, 1975; CBE, 1961; Hon DAppSc, Melbourne Univ; Hon DEd, Vic Inst Coll; Hon DSc, Latrobe Univ, 1995; AC, 1995; Num Gold Medals incl: Fndr's Gold Medal of RGS; Queen's Polar Medal. Memberships include: Cncl of Melbourne Univ, 1959-78; Cncl of Latrobe Univ, 1964-74; Pres, Roy Soc of Vic, 1967-68; Pres, Vic Inst of Marine Sci, 1978-80 Austl and NZ Schs Exploring Soc, 1977-82; Dpty Pres, Sci Mus of Vic, 1979-82 (Tstee 1968-83) Pres, Grad Union, Melbourne Univ, 1972-77; Patron, Brit Schs Exploring Soc; FAA; FTSE; FAIP; FRSV; FANZAAS. Hobbies: Tennis; Skiing; Music; Photography. Address: 16 Stanley Grove, Canterbury, Vic 3126, Australia.

LAW Yu Wing, b. 8 Oct 1954, Hong Kong. Electrical Engineer. m. Edith, 18 Nov 1980, 2 d. Education: Higher Dip, Elecl Engrng, Hong Kong Polytechnic. Appointments: Mngng Dir, Alberta Eng Ltd, 1987-. Memberships: Inst of Elecl Engrs, UK. Hobbies: Swimming. Address: Flat A, 6F, Block 20, Wonderland Villas, Kwai Chung, NT, Hong Kong.

LAWRENCE Bruce Cassels, b. 2 Aug 1932, Sydney, Aust. Composer; Artist. m. Denise Lawrence, 14 Jan 1963, 2 s. Education: Royal Coll of Music, 1953-57; LTCL, 1966; FTCL, 1974; AMus A, 1958. Appointments: Viola, Tasmanian Orch and Sydney Symph Orch, 1958-59; Tchng, Sydney, 1960-65; Tchng, Composing, Painting, Freelance playing, Aust, 1975-; String Examiner for Aust Music Exam Bd. Creative works: Orchestra: 3 Aylesbury Sketches; Ballets inclng: Primavera; The Genius, 1959; Choral Music, Salvator Mundi, 1969; Communion Serv, 1990; Psalms; Chmbr Music; String Quartet; Quartet for Cor Anglais and Strings; Two String Trios; Sonatas for Flute (2); Viola; Cello (2); A Large Body of Teaching Music; Exhibitions of Paintings, one man shows in Sydney and 6 in Newcastle. Memberships: Austl String Tchrs's Assn; Amn Viola Soc; Austl Music Cntr. Hobbies: Swimming; Reading. Address: 38 Bangalla Street, Warrawee, NSW 2074, Australia.

LAWRENCE Carmen Mary, b. 2 Mar 1948, Western Australia. Politician; Psychologist. m. 1979, 1 s. Education: Santa Maria Coll, Perth. Appointments: Snr Tutor, Dept of Psych & Behavioural Sci, Univ WA, 1979; Lectr, Course Controller, Behavioural Sci Appl to Med, 1980-83; Rsch Psych, Rsch & Evaluation Unit, Psych Servs, Hlth Dept, WA, 1983-86; Mbr, House of Reps, 1986-; Min of Educn, 1988; Fmr Min of Educn & Aboriginal Affairs, Premier of WA, 1990-93; Treas, Min for the Family & Womens Interests; Ldr of the Opposition, Shadow Treas, Shadow Min for Employment, for Fed Affairs, 1993-94; Fed Min of Hlth, 1994-96, on Status of Women & Environ & The Arts, 1996-97; Mbr, Fed Parl for Fremantle, 1994. Publications: Sev acad pprs on psychol. Honours: Benjamin Rosenstamm Prize in Econs; Brit Psychol Soc Prize for Psychol; Austl Psychol Prize for Psychol; H I Fowler Prize, Rsch in Psychol; J A Wood Meml Prize. Hobbies: Reading; Theatre; Music. Address: Parliament House, Perth, WA 6000, Australia.

LAWRENCE Denise, b. 10 May 1942, Sydney, Aust. Musician. m. Bruce Lawrence, 14 Jan 1963, 2 s. Education: NSW Conservatorium of Music, Sydney; DSCM; AMusA. Appointments: Cellist, Austl Yth Orch; Cello Tchr, Buckinghamshire, Eng, 1965-75; Cello Tchr, NSW Conservatorium, Chf Examiner in Strings, Austl Music Exam Bd, until 1997; Mbr, Advsry Bd, Min of Educ, until 1997; String advsr, Cty of Sydney, Cultural cncl; Adjudicator for many Music Competitions, Eistedfoddau etc; Cellist in both solo and orch capacity in Eng, Czechoslovakia and Aust. Honours: Layman Martin Harrison Schlshp, 1954-58; Queen Vic Club Schlshp, 1959. Memberships: Austl String Tchrs Assn (AUSTA); Amn String Tchrs' Assn (ASTA); Amn Viola Soc; Music Tchrs' Assn of Aust. Address: 38 Bangalla St, Warrawee, NSW 2074, Australia.

LAWRENCE Joan Miro, b. 19 May 1949, Dunedin, New Zealand. Archaeologist; Illustrator; Editor. m. Tony, 9 May 1970, 1 s, 1 d. Education: Dip of Tchng; BA, Otago; MA, Auckland. Appointment: Ed, Archaeol in NZ. Memberships: Auckland Inst & Mus; Historic Places Trust; Roy Forest & Bird Soc. Hobbies: Gardening; Travel; Music. Address: 34 Park Road, Titrangi, Auckland, New Zealand.

LAWRENCE John, b. 10 Apr 1929, Essex. UK. Ceramist. m. Ann, 3 Oct 1959, 1 s, 1 d. Education: Dip of Arts and Crafts, London, Eng, 1957; Dip of Ceramics,

1958. Creative Works: Continual Prodn of Ceramics, Bronzes, Drawings, Paintings. Memberships: New Assn of Potters, 1968; Hobbies: Black Sheep Breeding; Farming; Photog; Video. Address: Rosevillia, Rawhiti Street, Dannevarke, NZ.

LAWRENCE Stephen John, b. 17 Feb 1958, Adelaide, South Australia. Speechwriter; Editor. m. Celine Elizabeth Lawrence, 8 June 1985, 1 s, 1 d. Education: BA Hons, Eng; Dip App Psychol; MA; Dip Educ. Appointments: Tutor, Funders Univ & Univ of Adelaide, 1981-96; Speechwriter, Editor, S Austl Govt, 1997-. Publications: Her Mother's Arms, a verse narrative, 1997; Beasts Labial, poems, 1998. Honours: Runner-up, 12 var Austl lit comps, 1993-98. Hobby: Music. Address: 22 Bushy Park Drive, Auldana, SA 5072, Australia.

LAWS Richard John Sinclair, b. 8 Aug 1935. Radio Broadcaster; Television Host; Author; Poet. m. (2) 2 s, 1 d, (3) Caroline, 27 Nov 1976. Appointments: 3BO Bendigo, Vic, 1953; 2UE, 1957; 2SM, host of syndicated prog from 2KO, 1959; 2GB, host of first coaxial cable broadcast from Nashville to Sydney, 1962; 2UE, 1964; 2UW, 1969; 2UE, 1979; 2GB, 1985; 2UE, 1988; Host of 3 Natl TV Progs, 1962-1985; Columnist, Sunday Telegraph, Sydney, 1991-; Host of Laws Cable TV Prog, Foxtel, 1998- Publications: Book of Irreverent Logic, 1994; Book of Uncommon Sense, 1995; John Laws Limited Edition, 1996. Honours: OBE, 1974; CBE, 1978. Listed in: Australian Who's Who. Hobbies: Travel; Reading; Farming; Motorcycling; Photography. Address: PO Box 1313, St Leonards, New South Wales 2065, Australia.

LAWSON Alan John, b. 29 Sept 1948, Newcastle, NSW, Aust. Academic; Writer. m. (1) Carolyn Dixon, 1970, div 1993, (2) Joanne E Tompkins, 25 Jan 1995, 1 s, 1 d. Education: BA, Hons, Univ of Newcastle, 1970; MA, Austl Natl Univ, 1972; PhD, Univ Qld, 1987. Appointments: Tutor, Austl Natl Univ, 1973-74; Lectr, 1975-86, Lectr, 1987-94, Rdr, Assoc Prof, 1995-, Dean, Postgrad Studs and Dpty Dir, Univ Qld. Publications include: Patrick White, 1994; De-Scribing Empire: Post-Colonialism and Textuality, 1994; Australian & New Zealand Studies in Canada, 1994; Annotated Bibliography of Comparative, General and Theoretical Writing on the Post-Colonial Literatures in English, 1997. Honours: Assn for Study of Austl Lit; Aust and S Pacific Assn for Comparative Lit Stdies; Cand Lit Grp; Mod Lang Assn. Hobbies: Reading; Bird watching. Address: The Graduate School, University of Queensland, Queensland 4072, Australia.

LAY Maxwell Gordon, b. 14 Oct 1936, Aust. Civil Engineer. m. Margaret Ann Ryan, 17 May 1961, 3 s, 1 d. Education: BCE; MEngSci; PhD. Appointments: Engr i/c, Maj Steel Structures, SECV; Engrng Rsch Mngr, BHP; Exec Dir, Austl Rd Rsch Bd; Dir, Techl Resources Roads Corp of Vic, 1989-92; Dir, Maj Projs, 1992-96; Prin, Sinclair Kt Merz, 1996-; Dpty Chmn and Dir, RACV; Chmn and Dir, Intelmatics. Publications: Handbook of Road Technology, Vols 1 and 2, 3rd ed; Source Book for Australian Roads, 3rd ed; Structural Steel Fundamentals; Structural Steel Design (co-auth); Source Book for the Australian Steel Structures Code; Ways of the World, 1992. Honours: Monash Prize; Moisseiff Medal; Warren Medal; Sigma Xi; Transp Medal of the Instn of Engrs, Aust, 1995. Memberships: Fell, Instn of Engrs, Aust; Fell, Chartered Inst of Transp; Fell, Austl Acady of Technol Scis; Amn Soc of Civ Engrs. Hobbies: Reading; Writing; Dir, RAC of Vic, 1985-; Pres, Roy Soc of Vic, 1995-97. Address: 18 Bruce Street, Bulleen, Victoria 3105, Australia.

LAYT James Edward, b. 29 Dec 1935, Sydney, Aust. Company Director. m. Barbara Shanley, 28 Feb 1959, 2 s, 3 d. Education: BS, 1959, MBA, 1969, Univ of NSW; Adv Mngmt Prog, Harvard Univ, USA. Appointments: GKN Ltd, -1965; Joined Co, 1965, Dir, 1970, Dpty Mngng Dir, 1980, Mngng Dir, 1981, Blue Circle S Cement Ltd; Dir, Boral Resource and Energy Grps until 1994. Honours: AM, 1986. Memberships: Chmn and Fell, Austl Inst of Mngmt; Past Pres, Employers Fedn of NSW; Pres,

Cement and Concrete Assn of Aust; Tstee, Cttee of Econ Dev of Aust; Cnclr, Univ of NSW. Hobbies: Golf; Swimming; Tennis. Address: 3 Risorta Avenue, St Ives, NSW 2075, Australia.

LAYTON Roger Alexander, b. 1 Nov 1934, Sydney. Professor. m. Merrilyn Fay, 23 May 1959, 3 d. Education: BEc, Hons, Sydney, 1957; MEc, 1960. Appointments: Lectr, Snr Lectr, Stats, Univ NSW, 1967; Prof, Mktng; Dean, Fac of Com and Econ, 1992-. Many Publs. Honours: Ram Cty Friendship Awd; Order of Aust, 1998. Memberships: Austl Inst of Mngmnt; Mkt Rsch Soc of Aust; Austl Mktng Inst. Hobbies: Reading; Philately. Address: 29 Loquat Valley Road, Bayview, NSW 2104, Australia.

LAZENBY Alec, b. 4 Mar 1927, Yorks, Eng. Principal Consultant, International Development Programme (IDP); Consultant on Higher Education and Agricultural Research and Development. m. Ann Jennifer Hayward, 1957, 1 s, 2 d. Education: BSc, 1949, MSc, 1952, Univ of Wales; MA, 1954, PhD, 1959, ScD, 1984, Univ of Cambridge, Eng. Appointments: Sci Offr, Welsh Plant Breeding Station, 1949-53; Demonstrator, Lectr, Agricl, Botany, Cambridge Univ, Eng, 1953-65; Prof, Agronomy, 1965-70, Vice Chan, 1970-77, Univ of New England, NSW, Aust; Dir, Grassland Rsch Inst, Eng, 1977-82; Vice Chan, Univ of Tas, Aust, 1982-91. Publications: Intensive Pasture Production (joint ed), 1972; Australian Field Crops (joint ed), Vol I, 1975, Vol II, 1979; Australia's Plant Breeding Needs, 1986; The Grass Crop (joint ed), 1988; Pprs on pasture plant breeding, agronomy and weed ecology in var sci jrnls. Honours: HonD, Rural Sci, Univ of New England; AO; Hon LLD, Univ of Tas, 1992. Memberships: Fell, Austl Acady of Technol Sci and Engrng, 1976 (Cnclr 1986-89); Fell, Inst of Biol, 1983; Fell, Aust Inst of Agricl Sci and Technol, 1992. Hobby: Golf. Address: IDP Education Australia, GPO Box 2006, Canberra, ACT 2601, Australia.

LE Kha Phieu. Army Officer; Politician. Appointments: Fmr Chf of Army Polit Dept; Sec-Gen, CP of Vietnam, 1997-. Membership: Politburo Standing Bd. Address: Communist Party of Vietnam, 1 Hoang Van Thu, Hanoi, Vietnam.

LE VAN To, b. 18 Dec 1940, Hue Cty, Vietnam. Food Processing. m. Nga, 26 Jan 1980, 1 s. Education: PhD, 1976; DSc, 1984. Appointments: Dir, Food & Commodities Control Cntr (FCC), Vietnam; Dir, Post Harvest Technol Inst, Ho Chi Minh Cty (PHTI HCMC) Vietnam. Publications: 4 books; 35 sci intl pprs; Intl reports. Honours: Natl sci Awd, 1991; Awd of Ho Chi Minh Cty, 1993; Excellent Study for Prodn, Gold Medal, 1994; Complimetray Cert from Prime Min, 1995; Agric Dev of Vietnam, 1996; For Sci Wrk, 997. Memberships: Vice-Chmn, Vietnam Natl Assn for Food Storage & Processing (VAFSP); Intl Mycological Inst Link Scientist; Proj Coord, 5-yr Natl Prog on Food Processing 1996-2000; Sci Cttee, Min of Agric & Rural Dev. Hobby: Research on food processing. Address: 45, Dinh Tien Hoang Street, Dist 1, Ho Chi Minh Cty, Vietnam.

LEACH David Willoughby (Vice Admiral), b. 17 July 1928. Naval Officer (retired). m. Pamela Prentice, 5 June 1954, 1 s, 1 d. Education: RAN Coll. Appointments: Cmdr, HMAS Vendetta, 1964-66; Commanding Offr, HMAS Perth, 1968-69; Austl Nav Repr UK, 1971-74; Cmdr Nav Operational Requirements, 1975, Dir Gen, 1975-76; Chf Nav Material, 1978; Flag Offr Commanding Nav Fleet, 1979-80; Nav Personnel, 1980-82; Chf Nav Staff, 1982-85; Cl Mbr of Austl War Mem, 1986; Mbr, Crimes Commn, NSW, 1986-89; Cnclr, Woollahra, 1991-; Chmn, Vietnam Veterans Trust, 1997. Honours: CBE, 1969; AO, 1981; AC, 1984; LVO; Vietnam Awd US Meritorious Unit Comm. Membership: Austl Club. Hobbies: Tennis; Fishing. Address: 140 Windsor Street, Paddington, NSW 2021, Australia.

LEAL Robert Barry, b. 9 Feb 1935, Sydney, Aust. University Academic. m. Roslyn, 1 Jan 1965, 1 s, 1 d. Education: Hon DLitt; PhD; MA; BD; Dip Ed. Appointments: Lectr, Snr Lectr in French, Univ of Qld,

1964-74; Prof of French, Univ of Wollongong, 1974-85; Dpty Vice-Chan, Macquarie Univ, 1986-92; Vice-Chan, Univ of S Qld, 1992-96; Visng Prof, Macquarie Univ, 1997-. Publications: 2 books on French Literature, 1973, 1983; 2 vols, Australian Government Report, 1991; Num articles on French and comparative lit, educ, lang plcy. Honours: AM, 1996; Officier dans L'Ordre des Palmes Académiques, 1985; Hon DLitt, Univ S Qld, 1996; Emer Prof; Univ of Wollongong, 1992. Memberships: Patron, Italo-Austl Writers Assn of Aust, 1985-92; Pres, Australasian Univs Lang & Lit Assn, 1986-91. Hobbies: Tennis; Theology; Family history; Bushwalking; Gardening. Address: 28 Greenhaven Drive, Pennant Hills, NSW 2120, Australia.

LEAVER Ian Hamilton, b. 30 July 1941. Scientist. m. Barbara Rosemary Allen, 22 Oct 1964, 3 s, 1 d. Education: BSc, Melbourne; MSc, Keele, Eng. Appointments: Prin Rsch Sci, CSIRO Div of Wool Technol, 1961-91; Grp Leader, Analytical Servs, Dulux, Aust, 1992-98; PPG Ind Aust, 1998-. Publications: Photochemistry of Dyed and Pigmented Polymers, 1980; 75 sci and tech papers. Memberships: Fell, Roy Austl Chem Inst; Amn Soc Photobio, 1975-91; Editl Bd, Dyes and Pigments, 1992-. Address: 11 Ikara Court, Cheltenham, Vic 3192, Australia.

LEAVER Kenneth Batten, b. 17 Sept 1914. Minister of Religion. m. 3 Feb 1940, 2 s, 2 d. Education: Kings Coll, Parkin Theol Coll; BA, 1942, Univ of Adelaide, BD; MCD, 1965; STM, Andover-Newton, 1966. Appointments: Min, Medindie, S Aust, 1939-43; N Balwyn, Vic, 1943-45; Geeveston, Tas, 1945-50; Launceston, 1950-55; N Adelaide, SA, 1955-58; Prin, Parkin Coll, 1958-69; Co-Prin, 1969-72, Prin, 1973-76, Parkin-Wesley Coll; Chaplain, Flinders Medl Cntr, 1977-82; Lectr in Psychol, Kindergarten Tchrs Coll, 1968-70; Lectr in Psychol, Adelaide Childrens Hosp, 1970-71; Pres, Congregational Union of Tas, 1950-51, SA, 1965-66, Aust, 1976-77; Chmn, Rehabilitation Commn, S Austl Soc for Mental Hlth, 1978-88; Patron, Marjorie Black Rehabilitation Club, 1988-. Honour: AM, 1983. Hobbies: Gardening; Interior decoration; Antiques. Address: 49/254 Greenhill Road, Glenside, SA 5065, Australia.

LECKEY Robert Charles George, b. 25 Mar 1938, Bangor, N Ireland. Physicist. m. May, 17 Mar 1964, 2 d. Education: BS; PhD. Appointments: lectr in Phys, La Trobe Univ, 1967; Snr Lectr, 1969; Rdr, 1975; Personal Chair, 1993. Membership: Fell, Austl Inst of Phys, Hon Registrar, 1990-95. Address: Physics Department, la Trobe University, Bundoora, 3083.

LEE Arthur Geoffrey, b. 22 Sept 1928, Sydney, Aust. Company Director. m. (1) Christine, 1953, dec, 1 d, (2) Judith, 14 Apr 1984. Appointments: Fndr, Hodgson & Lee, 1950; Chmn, Halmac Servs Ltd, 1970-81; Scout Area Cmmnsr, E Metro Area, NSW Br, 1963-76; Intl Cmmns,r Aust, 1976-82; Chmn, Elec Equipment Ltd, 1982-84; Natl Cmmnr Resources, 1982-88; Chmn Baden Powell Soc, 1984-; Mbr, World Scout Fndn, Switz, 1986-; Natl Ctr Scout Assn, Aust, 1988-; Dir, Devel Capital of Aust Ltd, 1984-, Ramtron Aust Ltd, 1985-92, Ramtron Intl Corp (USA), 1988-92; Manettas Ltd, 1991-94; Chmn, Maritime Soc, 1990-93; Gov, Maritime Mus, 1990-; Gov, Heart Rsch Inst, 1993-; Chmn Global Imports Ltd, 1999-. Honour: Silver Kangaroo, 1980; OAM, 1984; AM, 1989; Life Mbr Scouts, Aust, 1999. Memberships: FAIM; FAICD; Roy Sydney Yacht Sqdn; Roy Prince Alfred Yacht Club; Cruising Yacht of Aust; Roy Ocean Racing (UK); Lakes Golf Club. Hobbies: Scouting; Yachting. Address: 73 Yarranabbe Road, Darling Point, NSW 2027, Australia.

LEE Bu-Young, b. 26 Sept 1942, Seoul, Korea. Member of National Assembly. m. Su-Hyang Son, 9 Apr 1973, 1 s, 1 d. Education: BA, Polit Sci, Seoul Natl Univ, 1961. Appointments: Vice-Chmn, Dem Party, 1991; Mbr, Supreme Cncl, Dem Party, 1991; Elected Mbr, Natl Assembly, 1992; Vice-Chmn, Dem Party, 1995; Re-elected Mbr, Natl Assembly. Publications: A Critical Biography of Composer Yong-Ha Yoon, 1978; The Roel of the Mass Media, 1983; Towards Better Politics, 1992.

Memberships: Spokesman, Dong-Ah Struggle Cttee for the Freedom of Press, 1974; Co-Chmn, Natl Cncl of People's Movement for Democracy, 1984; Chmn, Fedn of Popular Movements for Dem and Reunification, 1985; Exec Chmn, Cttee for Fedn of Dem Orgns, 1990. Address: #234 Members Building of National Assembly, 1 Yoido-Dong, Youngdungpo-ku, Seoul, Korea.

LEE Byung Kee, b. 12 Jun 1947. Vice-Director, National Security Agency. m. 20 May 1974, Shim Jae Ryung, 1 s, 1 d. Education: BA, Intl Rels, Seoul Natl Univ; Inst of For Affairs & Natl Security. Appointments: Sec, Korean Mission in Geneva, Switz, 1978; Sec, Korean Emb, Nairobi, Kenya, 1980; Served at the min of Pol Affairs, 1981; Served at the min of Home Affairs, 1982; Snr Sec to the Pres of Seoul Olympic Organizing Cttee, 1983; Sec to the Pres of the Democratic Jus Party, 1985; Snr Protocol Sec to the Pres (Blue House), 1988; Rsch Commnr, Inst of For Affairs & Natl Security, min of For Affairs, 1993; Special Asst to the Dir of NSP (Agcy of Natl Security Planning), 1994-96; Vice Director, NSP, 1996-. Honour: The Yellow Stripes Order of Serv Merit, 1992; Gug-Seon Medal, Order of Natl Security Merit, 1997. Membership: Rsch Commn of IFANS. Hobbies: Listening to Music; Reading. Address: 8-1204 Asia Sonsuchon Apt, Chamshil-7 dong, Songpa-gu, Seoul, Korea.

LEE Chang Woo, b. 29 June 1947, S Korea. m. Professor. m. Park Y S, 6 Apr 1974, 1 s, 1 d. Education: MD, 1972; PhD, 1981. Appointments: Prof, Chmn, Dept of Dermatology, Hanyang Univ, 1994; Pres, Seoul Regional Soc of Dermatology, 1998. Creative Works: Autoimmune Disease of the Skin, 1993; 40 Medl Articles, Intl Jrnls. Honours: Medl Publ Awd. Memberships: Korean medl Assn; Korean Dermatological Assn; Amn Acady of Dermatology; Eur Acady of Dermatology and Venerology. Hobbies: Listening to Music; Swimming. Address: Department of Dermatology, Hanyang University College of Medicine and Hospital, Sungdong-Ku, Seoul 133-792, S Korea.

LEE Chin-Teh, b. 2 Dec 1962, Sabah, Malaysia. Engineer. m. Siah S C, 8 Aug 1987, 1 d. Education: BS (Civil Hons); MSc (Civil). Appointments: CEO/Dir, Jurutera Konsult Maju Sdn bhd, 1993-. Memberships: Inst of Engrs, Malaysia; Amn Soc of Civil Engrs, Prfl Engr. Hobbies: Reading; Fishing. Address: 19B SS21/1A, Damansara Utana, 47400 Petaling Jaya, Selangor, Malaysia.

LEE Ching Kwan, b. 1 Aug 1963, Hong Kong. Professor of Sociology. Education: BA, Chinese Univ of Hong Kong, 1987; MA, 1988, PhD, 1994, Univ CA, Berkeley. Appointment: Asst Prof, Sociol, Chinese Univ of Hong Kong, 1993-. Publication: Gender and the South China Miracle, 1998. Memberships: Am Sociol Assn; Assn for Asian Studies. Hobbies: Distance Running; Travel. Address: 147 Hong Ning Road, B5, 21/F, Kowloon, Hong Kong.

LEE Chong-Won, b. 26 Feb 1948, Kunsan, Korea. Professor. m. Namdeuk Woo, 25 June 1981, 1 s. 1 d. Education: BS Mech Engrng, 1970, MS Mech Engrng, 1972, Seoul Natl Univ; MS Applied Mech, 1975, Yale Univ; PhD Mech Engrng, 1980, Univ of CA at Berkeley. Appointments: Instr, Korea Mil Acady, 1972-74; Visng Prof, Univ MI at Ann Arbor, 1985-86; Prof, Korea Adv Inst of Sci and Tech, 1980-. Publications: Book, Vibration Analysis of Rotors, 1993; Auth or co-auth 120 jrnl pprs and 72 intl conf pprs. Honours: KSME Medal in recog outstndng tech pprs, 1984; KSNVE Kangwol Awd, 1992; KAIST Awd for Excellence in Rsch and Dev, 1996; KAIST Awd for excel in tchg, 1997; Mayor's Awd, Cty of Taejon, 1998. Memberships: Korean Acady of Sci and Tech; Candidate Mbr, Korean Acady Engrng; Korea Soc for Noise and Vibration Engrng; Korean Soc Mech Engrs; and many others. Hobbies: Golf; Korean traditional music. Address: Dept of Mechanical Engineering, Korea Advanced Institute of Science & Technology, Science Town, Taejon 305-701, Korea.

LEE David Tawei, b. 15 Oct 1949, Taipei, Taiwan. Government Official. m. 1 s, 1 d. Education: Natl Taiwan Univ; Univ VA, USA. Appointments: Mngng Ed, Asia & The World Forum, 1976-77; Staff Cnslt, Co-ord Cncl for N Am Affairs, Wash DC, 1982-88; Prin Asst to Min of Fgn Affairs, 1988-89; Adj Assoc Prof, Intl Politics, Grad Sch of Socl Scis, Natl Taiwan Normal Univ, 1988-93; Dpty Dir, Dept of Intl Info Servs, Govt Info Off, 1989-90; Dpty Dir, Dept of N Am Affairs, Min of Fgn Affairs, 1990-93; Assoc in Rsch, Fairbank Cntr for E Asian Rsch, Harvard Univ, 1993-96; Dir-Gen, Taipei Econ & Cultural Off, Boston, 1993-96; Dir, Dept of N Am Affairs, Min of Fgn Affairs, 1996; Dpty Dir-Gen, Govt Info Off, Exec, Yuan, 1996-97; Dir-Gen, Govt Info Off, Exec Yuan & Govt Spokesman, 1997-. Address: Government Information Office, 2 Tientsin Street, Taipei, Taiwan.

LEE Dong Wook, b. 11 Jan 1950, Kyung-Ju, Korea. Research Scientist. m. Y J Yu, 5 May 1979, 1 s, 1 d. Education: BS, Han-Yang Univ, Seoul, 1979; MS, Chung-Ang Univ, 1982; PhD, Chung-Ang Univ, 1984. Appointments: Chf, Lab of Biochem, 1980, Prin Sci, 1984, Dir, Chem Rsch Divsn, 1998, Korea Ginseng & Tobacco Rsch Inst. Publication: Smoking and Health, 1993. Memberships: Sev. Hobby: Painting. Address: c/o Korea Ginseng & Tobacco Research Institute, Taejeon 305-345, Korea.

LEE Edward, b. 20 Mar 1947, Singapore. Diplomat. m. Sonya Maria Mallal, 1978, 4 children. Education: Raffles Instm; Univ of Singapore; Cornell Univ. Appointments: For Serv offr, 1970-; Posted to Canberra, 1971-74, Jakarta 1974-77, 1980-82; High Commnr to Brunei, 1984-90; Amb to Philippines, 1990-93; Amb to Indonesia, 1994-. Hobbies: Books; Golf. Address: Block X/4 Kav No 2, Jalan H R Rasuna Said, Kuningan, Jakarta 12950, Indonesia.

LEE Fook-Hou, b. 16 Mar 1955, Singapore. University Lecturer. m. Linda Lim, 5 Nov 1989, 2 s, 1 d. Education: BEng, Monash Univ, Aust, 1978' MEng, Natl Univ of Singapore, 983; MPhil, Cambridge, 1984; PhD, Cambridge, 1986. Appointments: Lectr, 1986-89, Snr Lectr, 1989-97, Assoc Prof, 1998-; Dir, Cntr for Soft Ground Egrng, 1994-97. Publications: Over 40 articles in jrnls, confs, seminars; Inclng 8 invited/keynote addresses. Honours: Snr Engrng Cnslt, Yangtze Water Resources Commn Archtl Des Inst. Memberships: SE Asian Geotech Soc; Profl Engr, Singapore. Hobbies: Reading; Music. Address: 12, Lengkong Lima, Singapore 417548.

LEE Hae-Koo, b. 1937, Ansong, Kyonggi, Korea. Politician. Education: Korea Univ Law Coll. Appointments: Var Posts, Police Dept; Natl Chf of Police, 1983; Gov, Kyonggi Prov, 1st Vice-Dir, Agcy for Natl Security Planning, 1986-87; Min for Home Affairs, 1993. Address: Ministry of Home Affairs, 77 Sejong-no, Chongno-ku, Seoul, Korea.

LEE Helen Dorothy, b. 4 Nov 1967. American Diplomat. Education: BA Econs, 1989, MA For Affairs, 1991, Univ of VA. Appointments: Rsch Asst, World Bank (IBRD), 1990; Intl Trade Specialist, 1991-92, Intl Economist, Desk Offr of El Salvador, Guatemala, Honduras, 1992-95, Coml Attaché, US Emb in Seoul, S Korea, 1995-, US Dept of Com. Publications: For US Dept of Com; Ed, Export Programs: A Business Directory of US Government Resources, 1992; Ed, Country Commercial Guide (for) Korea, 1995-98; (co-auth) How to Set Up an Office in Korea (w W K Cho), 1997; How to Solve Your Trademark Problems in Korea; Articles and reprts also publd in jrnls. Honours: Presdtl Mngmt Intern (PMI), 1991-93; Cert of Recog for Super Perfce, 1995, for Meritorious Serv, 1996-97, US Dept of Com. Memberships: Omicron Delta Epsilon, 1989; Women in Intl Trade (WIT), 1991-; N-S Cttee Co-chair, 1994-95; Co-fndr, Univ of VA Club of Korea, Pres, 1996-97; Co-fndr, Korean Assn of Women in Intl Trade (KAWIT), Pres, 1997. Hobbies: Gardening; Music; Charities; Fitness. Address: American Embassy in Seoul, Foreign Commercial Service, 82 Sejong-ro, Chongro-ku, Seoul 110-050, Republic of Korea.

LEE Hian Kee, b. 11 Apr 1954, Penang, Malaysia. Chemist; Educator. m. Hui Leong Sia, 2 June 1990, 1 d. Education: BS (Hons), PhD, Univ of Canterbury, NZ. Appointments: Tchng Fell, Univ of Canterbury, 1979; Visng Fell, 1983; Lectr, 1984, Snr Lectr, 1990. Assoc Prof, 1996, Dpty Hd, 1998, Natl Univ of Singapore. Publications: Over 130 in sci jrnls; Editorships of conf proceedings. Honours: Ralph P Earle Seminar Prize, Univ of Canterbury, 1978; Referee for sci jrns; Rsch-grant orgns. Memberships: AAAS; Amn Soc for Mass Spectrometry; NZ Inst of Chem; Singapore Natl Inst of Chem. Hobbies: Reading; Chemistry and society; Environmental science. Address: Department of Chemistry, National University of Singapore, Kent Ridge, Republic of Singapore 119260.

LEE Hock Lye, b. 5 Apr 1960, Penang, Malaysia. Airline Executive. m. Lai-Eng Ng, 14 Dec 1985, 3 s. Education: Bachelor, Acctcy, Natl Univ of Singapore, 1982; Dip in Educ, Inst of Educ, Singapore, 1983. Appointments: Tchr, Hwa Chang Jnr Coll, 1983-88; Singapore Airlines: Asst Stn Mngr, Hong Kong, 1989-91, Stn Mngr, Seoul, 1991-93, Snr Mngr, Tokyo, 1993-95, Snr Mngr, London, 1995-99; Mngr Loyalty Servs Unit, 1999-. Honours: Singapore Govt Pub Serv Commn Schlshp, 1979-82; Amn Biog Inst Distinguished Leadership Awd, 1986. Hobbies: Reading; Jogging. Address: 831B Bagnall Court, Upper East Coast Road, Singapore, 466618.

LEE Hong-Koo, b. 9 May 1934, Seoul, Korea. Politician; Political Scientist. m. 1 s, 2 d. Education: Seoul Natl Univ; Emory Univ, USA; Yale Univ, USA. Appointments: Asst Prof, Emory Univ, 1963-64, Case Western Reserve Univ, 1964-67; Asst Prof, Assoc Prof, Prof of Polit Sci, Seoul Natl Univ, 1968-88; Dir, Inst of Socl Scis, 1979-82; Fell, Woodrow Wilson Intl Cntr for Schls, Smithsonian Inst, 1973-74; Harvard Law Sch, 1974-75; Min of Natl Unification, 1988-90; Specl Asst to Pres, 1990-91; Amb to UK, 1991-93; Snr Vice Chair, Advsry Cncl for Unification, Chair, Seoul 21st Century Cttee, The World Cup 2002 Bidding Cttee, 1993-94; Dpty PM, Min of Natl Unification, 1994, PM, 1994-95. Publications: An Introduction to Political Science; One Hundred Years of Marxism; Modernization. Memberships: Comm on Global Goverance, 1991-; Chair, New Korea Party, 1996. Address: New Korea Party, 14-8 Yoido-dong, Yongdeungpo-ku, Seoul, Korea.

LEE Hong-Yi, b. 25 Nov 1952, Shanghai, China. Chemistry Educator. m. Qiu Wen-Ying, 28 Nov 1983, 1 d. Education: BS, Shanghai Tchrs Univ. Publications: Sev articles in profl jrnls. Membership: NY Acady of Scis. Hobby: Music. Address: Shanghai Second Polytechnic University, 80 Shanxi Road, Shanghai 200041, China.

LEE Hsien Loong, b. 1952, Singapore. Politician. m. (1st) dec 1982, 1 s, 1 d, (2) Ho Ching, 1985, 1 s. Education: Cambridge Univ; Harvard Univ. Appointments: Asst Chf of Gen Staff, Ops, 1981-82; Chf of Staff, Singapore Army, 1982-84; Resgnd as Brig-Gen, 1984; Polit Sec to Min of Def; MP for Teck Ghee, 1984-; Min of State for Def & for Trade & Ind, 1985-86, for Trade & Ind, 1986-93; Dpty PM, 1990-; Min of Def, 1993-95; 2nd Min of Def. Hobbies: Swimming; Reading; Jogging; Computers. Address: Office of the Prime Minister, Istana Annexe, Istana, Singapore 238823, Singapore.

LEE Huan, b. 8 Feb 1917, Hankow City, Taiwan. Politician. m. 2 s, 2 d. Education: Natl Chengchi Univ; Columbia Univ. Appointments: Dir, Shenyang Daily News, 1946-48; Chf Sec, Dpty Dir-Gen, Dir-Gen, China Youth Corps, 1952-77; Prof, Natl Chengchi Univ, 1962-79; Chair, Comm for Youth Assistance & Guidance, Exec, Yuan, 1967-72; Exec Offr, Alumni Assn of Natl Chengchi Univ, 1977-80; Pres, Natl Sun Yat-sen Univ, 1979-84; Min of Educn, 1984-87; PM of Taiwan, 1989-90; Sec-Gen, Ctrl Cttee, Kuo-Min-Ta-Hui, 1987-. Honours: Hon PhD, Tan Kok, 1978; Hon LLD, Sun Kyun Kwan, 1981.

LEE Hwan-Kyun, b. 22 Jan 1942, Haman-kun, Korea. Government Official. m. Sung Jung-Sook, 9 Jan 1970, 2 s. Education: BA, Law, Seoul Natl Univ; MA, Pub Admin, Grad Sch, Seoul Natl Univ. Appointments: Sec to Pres for

Econ Affairs, Off of the Pres, 1988; Asst Min, Min of Affairs, 1991-94; Cmmnr, KCS, 1994; Vice Min, MOFE, 1995; Chf Asst to the PM for GPC, 1996; Min, MOCT, 1997-. Hobby: Sports. Address: 111-402 Mido Apt, Taechi 2 dong, Kangnam-ku, Seoul, Korea.

LEE Jack Austell (Hon Justice), b. 15 June 1921, Wellington, NSW, Aust. Retired NSW Supreme Court Judge. m. Nancy Rosemary Wolrige, 8 July 1978. Education: BA, 1940; LLB, 1st Class Hons, Univ of Sydney, 1944; Admitted as Solicitor, 1945; Admitted as Bar, 1946. Appointments include: Appt QC: NSW, 1962, Vic, 1965; Appt Judge, Supreme Crt of NSW, 1966; Appt Chf Judge of Common Law at Supreme Crt, 1988; Appt Roy Commnr to preside over Blackburn Roy Commn, 1989-90; Rep NSW Supreme Crt on Fac Law, ANU. Publications: Lee's Law and Practice of Stamp, Death and Estate Duties; 4th ed of Hammond and Davidson's Law and Practice: Landlord and Tenant (co-auth). Honour: AO, 1992. Memberships: Dir, Sutherland Hosp, 1966-76; Pres, Judge Rainbow Mem Appeal Fund, 1974-82; Pres, Austl Crime Prevention Cncl, 1975-86; Dpty Chmn, Sydney Univ Inst of Criminology, 1976-; Chmn of the Fndn for Austl Constitutional Rsch and Stdies, 1995-98; Union Club, Sydney; Australasian Pioneers Club; Mbr, Natl Cncl and Pres, Sydney Metrop Area, Scout Assn of Aust. Hobbies: Boating; Bush walking; Skiing; Reading novels in German. Address: Supreme Court of New South Wales, Queen's Square, Sydney, NSW 2000, Australia.

LEE Jark Pui, b. 8 July 1939, Macau. m. Rita Lee, 1 s, 1 d. Education: BA (1st Class Hons), Econs, Polit Sci & Sociol. Appointments: Sales Exec, Jardine, Matheson & Co Ltd, 1962-63; Asst Trade Offr, Com & Ind Dept, 1962-63; Sec-Gen, Chinese Mfrs Assn of Hong Kong, 1969-85; Dpty Gen Mngr, 1986, Gen Mngr (Mktng, Pub Rels, Intl Banking), 1986-87; Exec Dir of Bd, 1987-93, Hongkong Chinese Bank Ltd; Exec Dir of Bd, Tobacco Inst of Hong Kong, 1988-94; Dir of Bd: Lippo Inds Ltd, 1989-97, Alexander Lippo (HK) Ltd, 1991-97, HKCB Bank Holding Co Ltd, 1993-97, Lippo Capital Ltd, 1991-, Lippo Ltd, 1992-. JP, 1984; MBE, 1986; OBE, 1997. Memberships include: Cncl, Queen Elizabeth Fndn for Mentally Handicapped, 1988- 2000; Appeal Bd (Nosie Control) Environmental Protection Dept, 1989-2001; Dir of Bd, Hong Kong Indl Technol Cntr Corp, 1993-98; Mbr of Cncl, Hong Kong Quality Assuarnce Agcy, 1994-99; Trade Advsry Bd, Trade Dept, 1994-98; Chmn, Legal Aid Servs Cncl, 1996-98; Dir, Po Leung Kuk Chmn Ltd, 1997-98; Hospital Authority, 1997-99; Advsry Cttee on Corruption, Indep Commn Against Corruption, 1997-98; Hong Kong Cttee for Pacific Econ Coop, 1998-20. Address: Tower I, 24/F, Lippo Centre, 89 Queensway, Hong Kong, China.

LEE Jon-Ha, b. 23 Mar 1922, Kong-Ju, Chung-Nam Prov, Korea. Business. m. Mrs Taesuk, 18 July 1948, 2 s, 2 d. Education: Grad, Sch Bus Admin, Korea Univ, Seoul; Grad, Law Sch of Konkuk Univ, Seoul, Korea. Appointments: Mbr, Advsry Cttee of Kyonggi Prov, 1981; Chmn, Policy Cttee of Suwon Cty, 1984; Mbr, Natl Unification Cncl, 1995. Publications: Customs and Manners in Global Villages, 1995; Auxiliary textbook on Filial Education, 1997. Honours: Kyonggi Prov Gov's Spec Awd, 1985; Awd by PTP Intl HQs for goodwill activities, 1995. Memberships: People-To-People (PTP), Korea Natl Chapt Pres, 1994; PTP Intl Bd Mbr, Kansas, MO, USA, 1995-. Hobbies: Baddok (oriental chequer game); Reading. Address: 390-1 Songjuk-dong, Jangan-ku, Suwon, Kyonggi Province, Korea.

LEE Keun, b. 12 Oct 1960. Associate Professor of Economics. Education: BA, Econs, Seoul Natl Univ, 1983; PhD, Econs, Univ of California, Berkeley, 1989. Appointments: Rsch Fell, E-W Cntr, Honolulu, USA, 1989-92; Lectr, Econs, Univ of Aberdeen, Eng, 1992; Asst Prof, 1992-97, Assoc Prof, 1997-, Seoul Natl Univ. Publications: Enterprise Reform and the Social Security System in China, 1996; An Assessment of the State Sector Reform, 1996; Contrasting Northeast and Southeast Asian Capitalism, 1996; Economic Reforms, Structural Adjustment and Regional Economic Growth in

China: Cross-Province Regressions, 1996; Between Collapse and Survival in North Korea: An Economic Assessment of the Dilemma, 1997. Address: Department of Economics, Seoul National University, Shrinrim-dong, Kwanak-ku, Seoul 151-742, Korea.

LEE Ki-Taek, b. 25 July 1937, Pohang, Korea. Politician. m. Lee Kyung-Ui, 1968, 1 s, 3 d. Educationm: Korea Univ; Univ PA, USA. Appointments: Mbr, Korean Natl Assn, 1967-; Chair, Specl Cttee, Investigation of Polit Corruption of the 5th Repub, 1988, Specl Investigation Democratic Party, Sec-Gen, 1976, VP, 1979; Chair, Inst of Democratic Thoughts, 1979; VP, New Korea Democratic Party, 1984, 1986; VP, Reunification Democratic Party, 1988-89, Floor Ldr, 1989; Chair, Democratic Party of Korea, 1990, 1993, Co-Chair, 1991, Advsr, 1995-96, Pres, 1995, 1996-. Publications: The Bridge of No Return, 1978; History of Minority Parties in Korea, 1987. Honours: Natl Fndn Medal, 1963; Hon Prof, Yonbyun Univ, China, 1995. Hobby: Calligraphy. Address: 51-5 Yong Kang-dong, Mapo-ku, Seoul, Korea.

LEE Kian Seng, b. 10 Aug 1948, China. Malaysian Artist. m. Shoko Lee, 1972, 2 d. Education: Self-taught in Painting, Batik/Dyes and Sculpturing; Artist of Malaysian Pavilion Expo'70, Japan; Independent Study and rsch on Comparative Study on Dyeing Art inclng lithography, prints and dyeing art, 1969, 1972, 1974, 1976, 1977. Creative Works: Many intl and natl exhbns worldwide, inclng: NZ, India, Aust, Eng, Korea, Singapore, ASEAN, Hong Kong, Japan, Germany, Canada, USA; Sev one-man exhbns. Honours include: 3rd Prize, Category B Arts Cncl of Malaysia, 1964; Best Exhibit Prize and 1st in Oil, Young Artists Awd, Malaysia, 1966; Hon Mention, Mixed Media, 3rd Prize, Batik, 3rd Prize, Sculpture, Saloon Malaysia, 1968; Maj Awd, Natl Art Competition, 1972, 1977; Japan Fndn Profl Fellshp, 1976-77; Malaysian Natl Repr, Asean Sculpture Symp, Indonesia, 1984; 2nd Prize, Intl Sand Sculpture Competition, Hong Kong, 1988; Tokyo Creation Awd Overseas Prize, 1993; Commission for Sculpture, Vision 2020, 1993. Membership: Intl Sculpture Cntr, USA. Address: 57 Jalan Rajawali, Taman Bukit Raja, 41150 Klang, Selangor, Malaysia.

LEE Kim Sai Datuk, b. 1 Mar 1937, Selangor, Malaysia. Politician. m. Appointments: Fmr Tchr; Mbr, State Assembly for Rawang, Selangor, 1974-82; MP for Ulu Selangor, 1982-; Dpty Min, PM's Dept, 1983; Min of Labour, 1986-89, of Housing & Local Govt, 1989-90, of Hlth, 1990-95. Membership: Sec-Gen, Malaysian Chinese Assn. Address: Ministry of Health, Jalan Cenderasari, 50590 Kuala Lumpur, Malaysia.

LEE Ko Shan, b. 26 July 1962, China. Musician. m. Leung Yin Yuk Terry, 4 Mar 1995. 1 d. Education: BA, Senzoku Gakuen Coll. Memberships: Hong Kong Ethnomusicology Soc. Hobbies: Music; Reading; Violin. Address: Rm 715, Kam Chun House, Tung Chun Court, Yiu Tung Estate, Shaukiwan, Hong Kong.

LEE Kuan Yew, b. 16 Sept 1923, Singapore. Politician; Barrister. m. Kwa Geok Choo, 1950, 2 s, 1 d. Education: Fitzwilliam Coll, Cambridge, Eng. Appointments: Called to Bar, Middle Temple, London, 1950; Hon Bencher, 1969; Advocate and Solicitor, Singapore, 1951; Fndr, People's Action Party, 1954, Sec Gen, 1954-92; Mbr, Legis Assembly, 1955-; 1st Prime Min, Repub of Singapore, 1959, Re-elected, 1963, 1968, 1972, 1976, 1980, 1984, 1988; Resigned as Prime Min, 1990; Snr Min in Prime Min's Off, 1990-. Honours: Fell, Inst of Pol, Harv Univ, 1968; Hoyt Fell, Berkeley Coll, Yale Univ, 1970; Hon Fell, Fitzwilliam Coll, Cambridge, 1969; Bintang Republik Indonesia Adi Pradana, 1973; Order of Sikatune, Philippines, 1974; Hon Freeman, Cty of London, 1982; Most Hon Order of Crown of Johore, 1st Class, 1984; Num Hon Docts. Memberships: Singapore Internal Security Cncl, 1959-; Fell, Roy Austl Coll Surgeons, 1973; Chair, Singapore Invmt Corp, 1981-. Hobbies: Jogging; Swimming; Golf. Address: Prime Minister's Office, Istana Annexe, Singapore 238823, Republic of Singapore.

LEE Kuen-Jong, b. 21 July 1959, Taiwan. Professor. m. Ling-Huei Huang, 1985, 1 s. Education: PhD. Appointments: Assoc Prof, 1991-97, Prof, 1997-. Publications: Over 70 tech pprs. Honours: NSC A-Class Awd, 1991-99; Best Ppr Awd, HD Media Workshop, 1994. Membership: IEEE. Hobbies: Chess; Bridge. Address: 247-428 Tsu-Zu Jao, Hsinhwa, Tainan, Taiwan.

LEE Martin, b. 8 June 1938, Hong Kong. Politician; Lawyer. m. Amelia Lee, 1969, 1 s. Appointments: Mbr, Hong Kong Legis Cncl, 1985-95, Hong Kong Law Reform Comm, 1985-91, Basic Law Drafting Cttee, 1985-90; Fndr, United Democrats of Hong Kong, Ldr, 1990-. Publication: The Basic Law: Some Basic Flaws (co-auth). Honours: Intl Human Rights Awd, Am Bar Assn. Address: Democratic Party of Hong Kong, Rooms 401/413 Central Government Offices, West Wing, 11 Ice House Street, Hong Kong.

LEE Min Sup, b. 28 Feb 1939, Korea. Advisor; Director. m. Soon Young Hong, 24 Aug 1967, 1 d. Education: Polit Sci, Seoul Natl Univ, Chung-Ang Univ, Kyung-Hee Univ. Publications: The First Principal of the Culture, 1992-94. Honour: Awd of Nation. Address: 33 Da-dong, Jung-ku, Seoul, Korea.

LEE Oi Hian, b. 7 Feb 1951, Ipoh, Perak, Malaysia. Executive Chairman. m. Sandra Ling, 2 s, 2 d. Education: Degree in Agricl Sci; MBA. Membership: Amn Oil Chemists Soc. Hobbies: Golf; Fishing; Tennis. Address: Kuala Lumpur Kepong Berhad, Wisma Taiko, No 1 Jalan S P Seenivasagam, 30000 Ipoh, Perak, Malaysia.

LEE Ryang, b. 2 Jan 1941, Seoul, Korea. Diplomat. m. Lena Kim, 20 Aug 1967, 1 s, 1 d. Education: MA, Grad Sch, Regl Studies, Harvard Univ. Appointments: 1st Sec, Korean Mission to UN in NY, 1977; Cnslr, Korean Mission to UN in Geneva, 1988; Amb to Kuwait, 1996. Hobbies: Tennis; Golf; Music. Address: A-302, Changmi Apt, Yoido-dong, Yongdung po-gu, Seoul, Korea.

LEE Sanghack, b. 11 Feb 1958, Seoul, Korea. Professor of Economics. m. Kyounghee, 26 Aug 1984, 1 s, 1 d. Education: BA, Econs, Seoul Natl Univ, 1980; PhD, Econs, State Univ of New York at Buffalo, 1989. Publications: Pprs publs in sci jrnls. Membership: Bd of Eds, Intl Econ Jrnl, 1993-. Address: School of Economics, Kookmin University, Seoul 136-702, South Korea.

LEE Seung-Kyu, b. 19 Nov 1944, Anyang, Korea. Professor. m. Hye-Kyong, 11 May 1974, 1 s, 1 d. Education: BS, 1971, MS, 1975, Seoul Natl Univ; PhD, Kyoto Univ, Japan, 1986. Appointments: Rschr, Inst of Agric Mechnization, 1971-74; Prof, Gyeongsang Natl Univ, 1974-; VP, Korean Soc of Agricl Machinery, 1998-. Publication: Analysis and Design of Field Machinery, 1992. Honour: Acad Prize, Korean Soc of Agricl Machinery, 1987. Memberships: Korean Soc of Agricl Machinery; Japanese Soc of Agricl Machinery; Amn Soc of Agricl Engrs. Hobby: Mountain Climbing. Address: Department of Agricultural Machinery Engineering, College of Agriculture, Gyeongsang National University, Chinju 660-701, Korea.

LEE Soo Sung, b. Korea. Politician; Academic. Appointments: Fmr Pres, Seoul Natl Univ; PM, Repub of Korea, 1995-97. Address: Office of the Prime Minister, 77 Sejong-no, Chongno-ku, Seoul, Korea.

LEE Soon-Bok, b. 17 Dec 1951, Korea. Professor. m. Jin-Sun Lee, 12 Apr 1980, 1 s, 1 d. Education: BS, Seoul Natl Univ, 1974; MS, KAIST, 1976; PhD, Stanford Univ, 1980. Appointments: Hd, KIMM, 1981-88; Prof, KAIST, 1988-. Publications: 25 jrnl pprs. Honour: Natl Hon Awd, Pres of Korea, 1985. Memberships: Korea Soc of Mech Engrs; ASME; SEM; IEEE. Hobbies: Swimming; Golf. Address: Mechanical Engineering Department, Korea Advanced Institute of Science & Technology, Science Town, Taejon 305-701, South Korea.

LEE Teng-hui, b. 15 Jan 1923, Sanchih, Taiwan. President. m. Tseng Wen-fui, 1949, 1 s, dec, 2 d. Education: Kyoto Imperial Univ, 1945; BS, Natl Taiwan

Univ, 1948; MA, IA State Univ, 1953; PhD, Cornell Univ, 1968. Appointments: Rsch Fell, Taiwan Coop Bank, 1955-57; Assoc Prof, 1956-58; Specialist, Joint Cmmn on Rural Reconstrn, 1957-61, Snr Specialist, Cnslt, 1961-70; Prof, Natl Chengchi Univ, 1958-78; Chf, Rural Econs Div, JCRR, 1970-72; Min Without Portfolio, 1972-78; Mayor, Taipei City, 1978-81; Gov, Taiwan Provincial Govt, 1981-84; VP, ROC, 1984-88; Pres, ROC, 1988-; Chmn, Kuomintang, 1988-. Publications: Agricultural Development and its Contributions to Economic Growth in Taiwan; An Analytical Review of Agricultural Development in Taiwan; Intersectoral Capital Flows in the Economic Development of Taiwan; Initial Conditions of Agriculture and Development Policy; Process and Pattern of Growth in Agricultural Production of Taiwan; Agricultural Diversification and Development; On the Problems of Agricultural Price Policy and Price Level. Honours include: Intl Disting Achmnt Citation, IA State Univ, 1993; Disting Alumni Awd, Cornell Univ, 1995. Hobby: Golf. Address: 122 Chungking South Road, Section 1, Taipei 100, Taiwan, China.

LEE Yau Lung George, b. 3 June 1931. Professional Engineer. m. Valerie Ann Webb, 1 Sept 1979, 3 s. Education: 1st Class Hons Associateship, Sch of Metalliferous Mining, Camborne, Eng. Appointments: Chmn, Mngng Ptnr, George Y L Lee & Co, 1954-; Supvsr, Tun H S Lee Tin Mines, 1954-; Chmn, Sungai Tiram Sand & Quarry Sdn Bhd, 1972-; Chmn, Konsortium Perunding (M) Sdn Bhd, 1974-; Exec Chmn, George Lee, Ariffin & Assoc Sdn Bhd, 1975-; Dir, Tun H S Lee & Sons Sdn Bhd, 1975-; Dir, Syarikat Melaka Timah Sdn Bhd, 1976-85; Dir, On Tai Dev Sdn Bhd, 1978-82; Cnslt, Assoc Pan Malaysia Cement Sdn Bhd, 1978-; Cnslt, Golden Plus Granite Sdn Bhd, 1994-. Publications include: Economic Policy of Malaysia: The Second Malaysia Five-Year Plan, 1971; Contribution of the Tin Mining Industry to the Economic Development of Malaysia; Consultants engaged by Borrowers; Issues and Problems in the Provision of Continuing Education for Management Needs. Honour: Kesatria Mangku Negara, His Majesty The King of Malaysia, 1972. Memberships include: Assn of Cnsltng Engrs; Malaysian Inst of Mngmt; Malayan Mining Employers Assn; All Malaya Chinese Mining Assn; Asian Assn of Mgmnt Orgs. Hobbies: Golf; Swimming. Address: No 1 Lorong Cinta Alam A, Country Heights, 43000 Kajang, Selangor Darul Ehsan, Malaysia.

LEE Yee Loun, b. 22 Dec 1954, Kuala Lumpur. Lecturer; Head of Concrete Lab. m. Guan Whee Teoh, 20 Nov 1982, 1 s, 2 d. Education: Dip Civ Engrng, UTM, 1976; BSc, Hons, Strathclyde, 1980; Dip Ed, Malaya, 1982; MSc, Construction Proj Mngmnt, UMIST, 1991. Appointments: Lectr, Poly Ungku Omar Ioph, 1976-83; Poly Batu Pahat, 1983-84; Hd of Dept, Poly A Setar, 1984-90; Poly Batu Pamat, 1992-93; Hd of Devel, Maintenance, 1993-95; Hd of Concrete Lab, 1993-. Creative Works: Tech Pprs. Honours: Ex Serv Awds; Rsch Grants. Memberships: Inst of Engrs; Concrete Soc Malaysia. Hobbies: 15 Jalan Bintang 10, Taman Koperasi, Bahagia 83000, Batu Pahat, Johor, Malaysia.

LEE Yock Suan, b. 1946, Singapore. Politician. m. 1 s, 1 d. Education: Queenstown Second Tech Sch; Raffles Instn; Imperial Coll, Univ London, England; Univ of Singapore. Appointments: Divsn Dir, Econ Devel Bd, 1969-80; MP for Cheng San, 1980; Dpty Mngng Dir, Petrochem Corp of Singapore (Pte) Ltd, 1981; Min of State, Natl Devel, 1981-83, Fin, 1983-84, Snr Min of State & Acting Min of Labour, 1985-86, Min for Labour, 1987-92, 2nd Min of Educn, 1991-92, Min of Educn, 1992. Membership: Dpty Chair, Peoples Assn, 1984-. Hobby: Badminton. Address: Ministry of Education, Kay Siang Road, Singapore 1024, Singapore.

LEE DOW Kwong Chiu, b. 7 May 1938. m. Joanna McLean, 18 Aug 1962, 2 d. Education: BSc, hons, BEd, Melbourne Univ. Appointments: Lectr, Chem, Secnd Tchrs Coll, Parkville, 1961-66; Snr Lectr, Ctr for Stdy of Higher Educ, Univ of Melbourne, 1967-71; Nuffield Travelling Fell, London Univ Inst of Educ, 1972; Intl House Cl, 1973-, (Chmn, 1987-92); Mbr, Senate State Coll of Vic, 1973-78; Prof of Educ, 1973-, Dean, Fac of Educ, 1978-98, Univ of Melbourne; World Hlth Org Cnslt on Med Educ, Japan, 1974; Chmn, Vic Inst of Secnd Educ, 1977-83; Mbr, Cl Univ Melbourne, 1979-86, Pro-Vice Chan, 1983-86; Educ Rsch and Dev Cttee, 1980-81; Austl Org for Econ Co-op and Dev Educ Cttee, 1980-86; Chair, Victorian Bd of Stdies, 1997-; Mbr, Natl Review of Higher Educ, Financing and Policy, 1997-98; Dpty Vice-Chan, Univ of Melbourne, 1998-. Publications: Chemistry, A Structural View (jointly); Teaching Science in Australian Schools; The Assessment of University Teaching. Honour: AM, 1984. Memberships: ARACI; FACE; Mbr, HK Cncl for Acad Accreditation, 1992-; Mbr, Cncl of HK Inst of Educ, 1994-98. Hobby: Music. Address: 7 Victor Road, Glen Iris, Vic 3146, Australia.

LEECE David Ronald, b. 10 June 1942. Agricultural Scientist; Public Administrator. m. Priscilla Ann Overman, 21 June 1969, 1 s, 1 d. Education: MScAgr, Sydney; PhD, MI State Univ. Appointments: Univ Trainee, 1960-63, Fruit Offr, 1964-65, Chem, 1965-72, Rsch Sci, Snr Rsch Sci, 1972-79, Asst Dir of Chem, 1979-80, Dept of Agric, NSW; Hd, Rsch and Stdies Branch, 1980-81, Dpty Chf, Sci and Tech Div, 1981-82, Mngr, Projs Unit, 1983-85, Environmental Co-ord, Murray-Darling Basin, 1986-87, Chf, Co-ord Div, 1987-88, Chf, Indland, Servs and Nat Rescs Div, 1988-90, Chf, Coast and Inland Div, 1990-92, State Pollution Control Commn, NSW; Dir, Waters and Catchments Branch, 1992-95, Dir, Environ Sci and Chf Sci, 1996-99, Environ Protection Authy, NSW; Dpty Commnr, Murray-Darling Basin Commn, 1990-99; Dir, Co-op Rsch Cntr for Waste Mngmt and Pollution Control Ltd, 1998-99. Publications: 30 sci rsch pprs in refereed jrnls. Honours: ED, 1973; RFD, 1984; 3rd Clasp, 1992. Memberships: Amn Soc for Hort Sci; Aust Soc of Ecotoxicol; Austl Soc of Soil Sci; Austl Inst of Biol; Inst of Biol, Eng; Inst of Pub Admin, Aust; Fell, Austl Inst of Agricl Sci and Tech. Hobbies: Defence and Foreign Affairs; Rugby; Gardening; Sailing. Address: Environment Protection Authority (NSW), Locked Bag 1502, Bankstown, NSW 2200, Australia.

LEECH Stewart Andrew, b. 21 Apr 1946, Melbourne, Aust. Professor of Accounting. m. Susan Mary Klein, 27 Aug 1977. Education: BCom, Melbourne; MEc, Tas; FCA; FCPA; MACS. Appointments: Snr Tutor, Univ Melbourne, 1970-72; Lectr, Univ of Tas, 1970-79; Snr Lectr, Univ of Sydney, 1979-80; Snr Lectr, Univ of Tas, 1980-84; Rdr in Acctng, Univ Tas, 1985-92; Prof of Acctng, Univ Tas, 1992-; Hd, Dept of Acctng and Fin, 1989-. Publications include: Introduction to Accounting Method, 1984; The Tac System, 1985. Memberships: Amn Acctng Assn; Acctng Assn of Aust and NZ; Fell, Inst of Chart Accts, Aust; Fell, ASCPAs; ACS; AIS. Hobbies: Tennis; Golf; Travel; Antiques; History; Music. Address: Thirsk House, 3 Heathorn Avenue, Sandy Bay, Tasmania 7005, Australia.

LEGGAT Peter Adrian, b. 2 Dec 1961. Public Health Physician; Medical Educator. m. Ureporn Kedjarune, 25 Nov 1993. Education: BMedSc, Dept of Socl and Preventive Med, Medl Sch, Univ Qld, Aust, 1985; MB BS, Medl Sch, Univ Qld, 1987; DipEd (Tert), Grad Dip in Educ (Tertiary), Sch of Educ, Darling Downs Inst of Adv Educ, 1988; DipClNutr, Intl Acady of Nutrition, Sydney, 1988; DTM&H, Bangkok Sch Tropical Med, Thailand, 1990; MMedEd, Univ Dundee, Scotland, UK, 1992; CertAddSt, Sch of Psychol, Curtin Univ of Technol, 1992; DIH, Occupational Hlth Unit, Dept of Preventive and Socl Med, Univ of Otago, NZ, 1993; FAICD(Dip), Univ of New Eng, Armidale, Aust Inst Co Dirs; Grad DipCDA, New Eng, 1996; MPH, Univ of Otago, NZ, 1998. Appointments include: Pt-time Clinl Tutor and Lectr, Dept Socl and Preventive Med, Univ Qld, 1985-89; Medl Offr, N Qld, RAMC, Austl Regular Army, 1987-91; Lt Col RAAMC Austl Army Reserve, 1999-; Medl Offr, Repatriation Gen Hosp, Greenslopes, Dept Veterans Affairs, 1988-89; Snr Lectr, Pub Hlth and Tropical Md, Sch of Pub Hlth and Tropical Med, James Cook Univ, 1992-98; Assoc Prof, 1999-; Assoc Dean, Fac of Biomedl and Hlth Scis, James Cook Univ, (Pt-time), 1995-97; Dpty Hd, Sch of Pub Hlth and Tropical Med, James Cook Univ, 1997-; Acad Advsr, Fac of Hlth, Life and Modular Scis, James Cook Univ, 1997-; Visng Medl Offr (pt-time), Dept of Def (Army), 4 Field Regiment, Brig Admin Support Cntr, N Qld, 8 Army Reserve Recruiting Unit, Lavarack Barracks Medical Centre, 1992-; WSO Dpty Dir-Gen, 1993-97; Dir Gen, 1997-; WSO Liason Offr to UN (Pt-time), Thailand, 1994-; Visng Prof (pt-time) Facs of Dentistry and Med, Prince of Songkla Univ, Hat Yai, Thailand, 1995-. Publications: Ed, 17 books; Over 100 pprs nationally and internationally. Honours include: World Safety Org Awds, 1988, 1992; ACTM Prudential Medallion, 1999. Memberships include: MSIA, 1986; World Safety Org, Warrensburg, MO, USA, 1993-; R Austl Coll of Medicine Administrations, 1997-; Fellowships: Austl Coll of Tropical Medicine, 1991-, Austl Faculty of Publioc Health Medicine, 1995-, Austl Coll of Rural and Remote Medicine, 1998-, Safety Inst of Aust, 1998-, Austl Inst of Company Directors, 1991-; Life Fellow, IBA, 1995; Honary Mbr, NZ Soc of Travel Medicine, 1998. Address: School of Public Health and Tropical Medicine, James Cook University, Townsville, Qld 4811, Australia.

LEGGE John David, b. 24 May 1921, Murchison, Vic, Aust. Retired Professor of History. m. (1) Alison Hale, 10 May 1953, (2) Jane Drakand, 20 Feb 1982, 3 children. Education: BA (Melbourne), 1942; MA (Melbourne), 1945; DPhil (Oxford), 1953; Hon DLitt (Monash), 1991. Appointments: Lectr, Snr Lectr, Rdr, Hist, Univ of West Aust, 1946-80; Fndn Prof of Hist, Monash Univ, 1960-77; Dean, Fac of Arts, Monash Univ, 1978-86; Dir, Singapore Inst of SE Asian Studies, 1969-70. Publications: Australian Colonial Policy, 1956; Britain in Fijim 1858-1880, 1958; Central Authority and Regional Autonomy in Indonesia, 1961; Indonesia, 1964, 1977, 1980; Sukarno: A Political Biography, 1972, 1985; Intellectuals and Nationalism in Indonesia, 1988. Memberships: Austl Inst of Intl Affairs, Chmn, Vic Branch, 1963-66, Rsch Chmn, 1973-78; Fell, Acady of Socl Scis in Aust; Asian Studies Assn of Aust, Pres, 1976-78. Address: 7 Eileen St, Armadale, Victoria, Australia 3143.

LEGHARI Farooq Ahmed, b. 2 May 1940, Pakistan. Politician. m. 1965, 2 s, 2 d. Education: Punjab Univ; Oxford Univ. Appointments: Mbr, pakistan Peoples Party; Chf, Baluchi Leghari Tribe; Pakistan Civil Serv, 1963-73; Elected to Senate, 1975, to Natl Assembly, 1977; Min for Prodn, 1977; Sec-Gen, Pakistan Peoples Party, Mbr, Exec Cttee, 1978; Elected Mbr, Natl Assn & Prov Assn, 1988-, Ldr of Opposition, Prov Assn, 1988, Min for Water & Power, 1988-90, Dpty Ldr of Opposition, 1990-93, Min of Fin, 1993, Min of Fgn Affairs, 1993; Pres of Pakistan, 1993-97. Hobbies: Hunting; Horseriding. Address: Office of the President, Constitution Avenue, Islamabad, Pakistan.

LEHMAN Ellen J, b. 21 Feb 1944, Pittsburgh, USA. Psychologist; Psychoanalyst. m. Charles Kennel, 14 Aug 1991. Education: AB, Vassar Coll, 1966; PhD, Cornell Univ, 1975. Appointments: Intern, James Jackson Putnam Childrens Cntr, Boston, 1968-69; Postdoct Fell, Clin Child Psychol, Reiss-Davis Child Study Cntr, Los Angeles, 1972-74; Staff Psychologist, Marianne Frostig Cntr for Educl Therapy, Los Angeles, 1974-75; Pvte Prac, Psychotherapy, Psychoanalysis and Diagnostic Testing, Santa Monica, 1974-; Clin Supvsr, Wright Inst, Los Angeles, 1983-; Asst Clin Prof, Dept of Psych, Univ CA, Los Angeles, 1990-; Supvsr, Trng Analyst, Inst of Contemporary Psychoanalysis, Los Angeles, 1993-; Trng, Supvsng Analyst, 1996-, Mbr Bd of Tstees, 1997-, Grad Inst for Child Dev and Psychotherapy. Publications: Separation Anxiety in Nursery School Children, 1971; The Effects of Rooming-In and Anxiety on the Behavior of Children Hospitalized for Tonsillectomy, 1975. Memberships: Phi Kappa Phi; Am Psychol Assn; Soc for Rsch in Child Devel. Hobbies: Hiking; Photography; Scuba Diving. Address: 1132 26th Street, Santa Monica, CA 90403, USA.

LEHMAN Ronald Frank II, b. 25 Mar 1946, Napa, California, USA. Government Official. m. Susan Yong, 1979. Education: Claremont Men's Coll; Claremont Grad Sch. Appointments: Army Serv, Vietnam, 1969-71; Legis Asst, US Senate, 1976-78; Mbr, Profl Staff, US Senate Armed Servs Cttee, 1978-82; Dpty Asst Sec of Def, Off of Intl Security Policy, 1982-83; Snr Dir, Def Progs & Arms

Control, Natl Security Cncl, 1983-86; Dpty US Negotiator for Strategic Nuclear Arms, Dept of State, Wash DC, 1985-86, Chf US Negotiator, Geneva, 1986-88; Dpty Asst to Pres for Natl Security Affairs, 1986; Asst Sec, Dept of Def, 1988-89; Dir, Arms Control & Disarmament Agcy, Wash DC, 1989-93; Asst to Dir, Lawrence Livermore Natl Lab, 1993-, Dir, Cntr for Global Security, 1996-; Mbr, Presl Advsry Bd, Arms Proliferation Policy, 1995-96. Memberships include: Intl Inst for Strategic Studies; Intl Advsry Bd, Inst of Global Conflict & Coop, Univ CA, San Deigo. Address: Lawrence Livermore National Laboratory, PO Box 808, L-1, Livermoore, CA 94551, USA.

LEI Jie Ming, b. 26 Feb 1950. Professor of History. m. Xu Zhong Yu, 1 s, 2 d. Education: Univ Virgin Is; CWS Univ; BA, Univ New Brunswick, Fedn Can & WSU; MA, Intellectual Hist, PhD Cand, 1975; Univ HI, EW Cntr; PhD Univ WA. Appointments: Lectr, Univ HI, CBA, Honolulu, 1989; Educ, Dist Liason Offr, Pub Sch Statn, 1990; Assoc Prof, N Marianas Coll, CNMI, Trade, Tourism, Mktng, 1991; Assoc Prof, TIFT, Engl Writing Compositors, ORAC Speaking, 1993; Nankai Univ, Tianjin, For Trade and Bus Engl, Writing Oral Lit, TESOL, ESL, 1994; Prof and For Expert-in-Resn, Peking Univ, Grad Sch, Dept Engl/For Lit, 1995-96; Dir, Mngr, Intl Bus Affairs & Dev, CITIC (China Intl Trade & Invmnt Corp, Beijing; PCEC-TMC, Staffordshire Univ; Prof, ASEAN Econ Environ, Bus Enterprise Mngmt Skills Cntr, Shanghai, China, 1998. Publications: Poetry, Nexus, lit publ, 1972; Writing a Business Plan; Fine Arts Soc; 3 poems, 1975; For the 5 Minute Reader, 1991; Language Bending Vs Bilingualism; The Debate, 1991; Writing a Business Plan for the Five Minute Reader, w bus plan checklist; Thoughts on the Business of Life, 1991; China Treaty Port - Tientsin: Mystery Unravelled, 1997; The Collectors Club, Journal of Philately; Chinese Philately is RED Hot, An Insiders Roadmap to Collectors Markets in the PR of China, 1997. Honours: Ed's Awd, Grad newsppr, Univ New Brunswick, Miyazana, 1973; CNMI Fac Tchng Exch Excellence, 1991; Gold Medal, INDIPEX, New Delhi Lit Exhibn, 1997. Memberships include: Amn & China Philos Assn, Beijing; Amn & China Assn of Univ Fac Profs, NY; RPSL (Roy Philatelic Soc), London. Hobbies: Aviation; Writing; International economics and relations. Address: No 101, 2 Men, 7 Hao Lou, 9 Qiu Wan Xin Cun, He Dong Qu, Tianjin 300162, China.

LEI Jieqiong, b. 1905, Guangzhou, China. Politician; Jurist. Education: USA. Appointments: Prof, Yenching Univ, 1931-52; Vice Dean, Inst of Politics & Law, 1953-72; Mbr, Cttee for Implementation Campaign of Marriage Laws, 1953; Dpty Dir, Bur of Fgn Experts Admin, Under State Cncl, 1956-66; Prof, Beijing Univ, 1973-; Vice Mayor, Beijing, 1979-83; Chair, China Assn for Promoting Democracy, 1987-97. Memberships include: Hon Pres, China Assn of Women Judges, Assn for Intl Understanding of China, Western Returned Students Assn, China Socl Workers Assn. Address: 19 Xi Jiaomen Xiang Street, Xicheng District, Beijing, China.

LEI Kechang, b. 3 July 1936, Nanjing, China. Teacher. m. Chen Baojuan, 30 Jan 1968, 1 s, 1 d. Education: Master deg. Appointments: Pres, Nanchang Water Conservancy and Hydroelectric Power, Higher Training Sch, 1979; VP, N China Inst of Water Conservancy and Hydroelectric Power, 1992-97. Publication: Structural Mechanics; Basis of Management. Honour: Allowance from Govt, 1992. Hobby: like playing weigi. Address: No 20 Zhenghua Road, Zhengzhou, China.

LEI Weizong, b. 5 Nov 1927, Sangjiang, Jiangsu, China. Mechanical Engineering. m. Chang Yunqing, 1952, 1 s. Education: Bach, Chaotung Univ. Appointments: Techn, 1951; Engr, 1953; Chf Engr, Dpty Dir, Snr Engr, Prof, 1991-. Publications: Fatigue as a Design Criterian: Mechanical Engineering Industries in China; Mechanical Structure Strength Design; Mechanical Engineering Handbook; Bases for Machine Design. Honours: Govt Specl Subsidy, 1991; Specl Class Tech Progress Min Awd, 1994. Membership: Reliability Engrng Inst. Hobbies: Fine Arts; Music. Address: Academy of Machinery Science & Technology, 2 Shou Ti

Nan Lu, Beijing 100044, China.

LEIBLER Mark Matthew, b. 26 Dec 1943. Lawyer. m. Rosanna Weiss, 5 June 1966, 2 s, 2 d. Education: LLB (Hons); LLM (Hons); Mt Scopus Coll (Vic); Melbourne Univ; Yale Univ (USA). Appointments: VP, Natl Union of Austl Jewish Studs, 1963; Pres, Univ Jewish Studs Soc, 1963; Ed, Melbourne Univ Law Review, 1965; Mbr, Exec Vic Jewish Bd of Dptys, 1969-; Ptnr, 1969- 81, Snr Ptnr, 1981-, Arnold Bloch Leibler; Cr Exec Cncl of Austl Jewry, 1970-; Visng Lectr, Fac of Law, Monash Univ, 1979-80; Pres, State Zionist Cncl of Vic, 1980-84; Deleg, World Zionist Congress, 1982 (1978, 1972); Co-Chmn, Makor Lib and Resource Cntr of Vic, 1983-93; Mbr, Editl Bd of Jrnl Austl Tax Forum, 1984-93; Aust-Israel Chmbr of Comm, 1984-; Gov, Utd Israel Appeal, 1984-; Mbr, World Zionist Gen Cncl, 1984-; Pres, Zionist Fedn of Aust, 1984-94; Pres, Utd Israel Appeal of Aust; Natl Chmn, Aust/Israel and Jewish Affairs Cncl (AIJAC); Mbr of Exec, World Zionist Org, 1988-; Bd Govs, Jewish Agcy for Israel, 1992-; Governing Cncl, Cntr for Coml Law and Applied Legal Rsch, 1985-; Mbr, Natl Tax Liason Grp, 1986-92; Chmn, Taxation Cttee Law Cncl of Aust, 1986-91. Publication: Australian Capital Gains Tax; Traps and Planning Techniques. Honour: AO, 1987. Membership: RACV. Hobby: Reading. Address: 11 Oulton Street, Caulfield, Vic 3161, Australia.

LEIGH Jennifer Jason, b. 5 Feb 1962, Los Angeles, CA, USA. Actress. Creative Works: TV Films incl: The Young Runaways; The Killing of Randy Webster, 1981; The Best Little Girl in the World, 1981. Films incl: Eyes of a Stranger, 1981; Fast Times at Ridgemont High, 1982; Grandview, USA, 1984; Flesh and Blood, 1985; The Hitcher, 1986; The Men's Club, 1986; Heart of Midnight, 1989; The Big Picture, 1989; Miami Blues, 1990; Last Exit to Brooklyn, 1990; Crooked Hearts, 1991; Backdraft, 1991; Rush, 1992; Single White Female, 1992; Short Cuts, 1993; The Hudsucker Proxy, 1994; Mrs Parker and the Vicious Circle, 1994; Georgia, 1995; Kansas City, 1996; Washington Square, 1997. Address: c/o Tracey Jacobs, 8942 Wilshire Boulevard, Beverly Hills, CA 90211, USA.

LELLA Venkateswara Rao, b. 15 Sept 1957, Konayapalem, India. Lecturer. m. Monakumari, 1 Aug 1982, 1 s. Education: MCom, Nagarjuna Univ, 1978-80; PGDCRS, 1980-81; BLISc, 1981-82; Andhra Univ; MLISc, Univ of Madras, 1990. Appointments: Lectr, Lib Sci, 1984-92, Snr Lectr, Lib Sci, 1992-, Sir C.R.R.P.G. Coll, Eluru. Publications: Nearly 20 articles published in seminars, jrnls and souvenirs. Honours: Gold Medal, Janma Bhoomi Activities; Felicitation, Alapati Kalavati Raveendra Petam; Felicitation, Sir C.R.R.P.G. Coll. Memberships: ILA; IASLIC; IATLIS; APLA; ALSD; APPLA. Hobbies: Reading; Making Friends; Social Activities. Address: Sir C.R.R.P.G. College, Eluru 534007 AP, India.

LEMARI Kunio David, b. 29 Nov 1942, Jabor, Jaluit, Marshall Is. Federal Official. m. (1) Helisa A Kaious, 21 June 1967, div Feb 1985, 4 2, 3 d, (2) Christina Maryrose Myazoe, 24 Apr 1987, 1 d. Education: Deg in Theol, Bethel Bible Inst, Manila, 1967. Appointments: Gen Supt, Micronesian Assemblies, Marshall Is, 1976-80; Co-ord, Food Servs, Min of Socl Serv, Marshall Is, 1980-82; Asst Hosp Admnstr, Min of Hlth Serv, Marshall Is, 1982-83; Offr, Pub Wrks Admin, Min of Pub Wrks, Marshall Is, 1983-84; Senator, Parl of Marshall Is, 1984-86; Min Jus, Govt of Marshall Is, 1986-87; Min Transp and Comm, 1987-. Address: PO Box 648, Majuro MH 96980-0648, Marshall Islands.

LEMMON Jack, b. 8 Feb 1925, Boston, USA. Actor. m. (1) Cynthia Boyd Stone, 1950, 1 s, (2) Felicia Farr, 1962, 1 d. Education: Phillips Andover Acady; Harvard Univ. Appointments: Actor, Stage, Radio & TV, 1948-. Creative Works: Films incl: It Should Happen to You, 1953; Three for the Show, 1953; Phffft, 1954; My Sister Eileen, 1955; Mister Roberts, 1955; You Can't Run Away From It, 1956; Fire Down Below, 1957; Bell, Book and Candle, 1958; It Happened to Jane, 1958; Some Like it Hot, 1959; The Apratment, 1960; The Notorious Landlady, 1962; Days of

Wine and Roses, 1962; Irma La Douce, 1963; Under the Yum Yum Tree, 1964; Good Neighbour Sam, 1964; How to Murder Your Wife, 1965; The Great Race, 1965; The Fortune Cookie, 1966; Luv, 1967; The Odd Couple, 1968; The April Fools, 1969; The Out-of-Towners, 1969; Kotch, 1971; The War Between Men and Women, 1972; Avanti, 1972; Save the Tiger, 1973; The Prisoner of Second Avenue, 1974; The Front Page, 1975; The Entertainer, 1975; Alex and the Gypsy, 1976; Airport 77, 1977; The China Syndrome, 1979; Tribute, 1980; Buddy Buddy, 1981; Missing, 1982; Mass Appeal, 1984; Macaroni, 1986; Film Crisis, 1986; That's Life, 1986; Long Day's Journey Into Night, 1986; Dad, 1989; Glengarry Glen Ross, 1989; JFK, 1991; The Player, 1993; Grumpy Old Men, 1993; Short Cuts, 1994; Getting Away with Murder, 1995; The Grass Harp, 1995; Grumpier Old Men; A Weekend in the Country; Hamlet; My Fellow Americans; Out to Sea. Plays incl: Veterans Day, 1989. Honours include: Acady Awd, 1956, 1974; Best Actor, Cannes Film Fest, 1979; Am Film Inst Life Achievement Awd, 1988. Address: CAA, 9830 Wilshire Boulevard, Beverly Hills, CA 90212, USA.

LEMOS SIMMONDS Carlos, b. Popayan, Cauca, Colombia. Politician. m. Martha Blanco Guake, 4 children. Education: Lycée, Cauca Univ. Appointments: Prof, Colombian Polit Hist, Universidad javeriana; Prof, Colombian Econ Hist, Free Univ of Colombia; Mbr, Bogota Cncl, 1972-74, 1986-88; Mbr, House of Reps, 1974-78; Gov of Cauca Prov, 1976-77; Sec-Gen, Presidency, 1978-79; Senator, 1978-81; Min of Fgn Affairs, 1981-82; Dir, Consigna Mag, 1982-87; Amb to the OAS, 1987-89; Min of Commns, 1989; Min of Govt (Interior), 1989-90; Del to Natl Constitutional Assembly, 1990-91; Chair, Bogota Cncl, 1992; Cand for Pres of Colombia, 1992; Amb to Austria, 1995, England, 1995; VP of Colombia, 1996-. Publications include: Francisco de Paula Santander; An Iconography; The Pre-Columbian Economy. Honours: Orders of Boyaca, San Carlos, Civil Merit (Spain), Independence (Equatorial Guinea), Merit (Italy, Chile, Ecuador), Sol (Peru), Balboa (Panama); Cmdr, Order of Isabel la Catolica. Address: Palacio de Narino, Carrera 8A, 7-26, Santafé de Bogota, DC, Colombia.

LENDVAY Paul Gabriel, b. 26 Aug 1938, Budapest, Hungary. Plastic and Reconstructive Surgeon. m. Anna Raza, 19 May 1964, 3 d. Education: MB, BS, Univ Sydney, 1962; Trng, Queen Vic Hosp, E Grinstead, Eng, 1965-68; FRCS, London, 1966; FRACS, 1970; Appointments: Jnr and Snr Residency, Sydney Hosp, NSW, Aust, 1960-61; Lectr, Univ NSW, 1964; Prac in Plastic and Reconstructive Surg, Sydney, 1968-; Established Replantation Serv, 1968, Hon Plastic Surg, 1968-77, Auburn Dist Hosp, Sydney; Hon Plastic and Reconstructive Surg, Prince Henry Hosp, Prince of Wales Hosp, East Suburbs Hosp, 1968-; Dir, Microsurg, Prince of Wales and Prince Henry Hosps; Hd, Dept Plastic and Reconstructive Surg, Prince Henry, Prince of Wales and Sydney Children's Hosps, 1992-. Publications include: Sev papers in medl jrnls. Memberships include: Australasian Soc Aesthetic Plastic Surg; Austl Hand Surg Soc; Austl Soc Plastic Surgs; Intl Microsurg Soc; Roy Coll Surgs, Eng. Hobbies: Skiing; Water-skiing; Tennis. Address: 117 O'Sullivan Road, Bellevue Hill, NSW 2023, Australia.

LENG Yihou, b. 18 July 1936, Gaizhou, Liaoning, China. Technician. m. Jiang Yumei, 17 Sept 1964, 1 s, 1 d. Education: BSc, Xian Comm Univ, 1963. Appointments: Dir, Rsch Dept, 1984; Dir, Info Cntr, 1992. Publications: Over 50 pprs. Honours: A total of 30 rsch topics completed, inclng 8 winners of Provcl Technol Prog 3rd Class Prizes and 1 winner of 1st and 2nd Class Prizes from the China Natl Tax Admin and 1st Class Prize of the 2nd Natl Electrons Info Technol Exhibn, and 1 winner of the Provcl Invention and Creation Prize in 1994; Rsch Dept and Info Cntr led by Mr Leng was selected as model unit 5 x; Govt Spec Allowance from State Cncl, 1992; Title of Advd Sci and Technol Rschr of Natl Tax Trade, 1996. Memberships: Advsry Mbr, Liaoning Provcl Info Theory Soc, 1989 Snr Mbr, China Electrons Soc, 1991; Vice-Chmn, Liaoning Provcl

Electrons Soc, 1991; Vice-Chmn, Liaoning Provcl Software Soc, 1994; VP, Liaoning Provcl Econ Info Expert Advsry Cttee, 1996; Guest Prof, Liaoning Provcl Tax Affairs Higher-learning Profl Sch, 1996. Address: No 8, Ningshan Zhong Lu, Huanggu District, Shenyang Liaoning Province, China 110031.

LEONARD Elmore, b. 11 Oct 1925, New Orleans, USA. Novelist; Screenwriter. m. (1) Beverly Claire Cline, 1949, div 1977, 3 s, 2 d, (2) Joan Leanne Lancaster, 1979, dec 1993, (3) Christine Kent, 1993. Education: Univ Detroit. Publications: 31 novels incl: Hombre, 1961; City Primeval, 1980; Split Images, 1982; Cat Chaser, 1982; La Brava, 1983; Stick, 1983; Glitz, 1985; Bandits, 1987; Touch, 1987; Freaky Deaky, 1988; Killshot, 1989; Get Shorty, 1990; Maximum Bob, 1991; Rum Punch, 1992; Pronto, 1993; Riding the Rap, 1995; Out of Sight, 1996. Memberships: Writers Guild of Am; Auths Guild; Mystery Writers of Am; W Writers of Am. Address: c/o CAA, 9830 Wilshire Boulevard, Beverly Hills, CA 90212, USA.

LEONTIEFF Alexandre, b. 20 Oct 1948, Teahupoo, Tahiti. Politician. m. Demecia Jurd, 1972, 2 s. Appointments: Mbr, Territorial Assn, French Polynesia, 1977-; VP, Govt of Polynesia, 1984-86; Min of Econ, of the Sea & Tourism, 1986-87; Pres, Govt of Polynesia, 1987-91; Dpty to French Natl Assembly, 1986. Address: Residence Taina, BP No 2737, Papeete, French Polynesia.

LEPPING George, b. 22 Nov 1947, Solomon Islands. Politician; Government Official. m. Margaret Kwalea Teioli, 1972, 2 s, 5 d. Education: Agricl Coll, Vudal; Reading Univ. Appointments: Field Offr, Dept of Agricl & Rural Econs, 1968; Pres, Solomon Islands Amateur Athletics Union, 1970-73, 1981-82; Snr Field Offr, Under-Sec, Agricl, Min of Agricl, 1979-80; Perm Sec, Min of Home Affairs & Natl Devel, 1981-84; Project Dir, Rural Serv Project, 1984-87; Min of Fin, 1988; Ldr, Peoples Alliance Party, 1996-. Honours: Kt St John; Sports Medals. Hobbies: Peoples Alliance Party, PO Box 722, Honiara, Solomon Islands.

LESBIREL Sidney Hayden, b. 25 Oct 1957, Townsville, Aust. Associate Professor. m. Edith Rainer, 29 Nov 1986, 1 s, 1 d. Education: BA, Sch of Mod Asian Stdies, Giffith Univ, 1981; PhD, Austl Japan Rsch Cntr, Austl Natl Univ, 1986. Appointments: Lectr, Sch of Mod Asian Stdies, Griffith Univ, 1984-86; Lectr, Rsch Fell, Dept of Polit Sci and Austl Japan Rsch Cntr, Austl Natl Univ, 1986-88; Lectr, Snr Lectr, Dept of Japanese Stdies, Natl Univ of Singapore, 1988-94; Assoc Dir, Austl Japan Rsch Cntr, Austl Nat Univ, 1994-95; Assoc Prof, Polit Sci, Sch of Hum, Fac of Soc Sci, James Cook Univ, 1996-. Publication: NIMBY Politics in Japan, 1998. Honours: Austl, Japan Bus Co-op Cttee Schlshp, 1978-79; Adj Mbr, Rsch Advsry Bd, Inst of Energy Econs, Tokyo, 1989-; Cntr Assoc, Austl, Japan Rsch Cntr, Austl Natl Univ, 1998-. Memberships: Austl Inst of Intl Affairs, 1996; Austl Polit Sci Assn, 1997. Hobbies: Swimming; Bicycle riding. Address: School of Humanities, Faculty of Social Sciences, James Cook University, Townsville, QLD 4811, Australia.

LESSELS John Douglas Gordon, b. 14 Dec 1930, Melbourne, Aust. Consultant Engineer. m. Beris Frances Biddlecombe, 16 Mar 1963, 4 d. Education: BCE, Melbourne Univ, 1953; Psc, RAAF Staff Coll, 1966. Appointments: RAAF, Citizen Air Force, Melbourne Univ Sqdn, 1951-52; RAAF Perm Air Force Works Offr, Leverton, 1953-54; Admiralty Is, 1954-56, Malaya, 1956-58, Snr Works Offr, No 2 Airfield Constrn Sqdn, 1958-61, No 5 Airfield Constrn Sqdn, 1961-62, CO, No 5 Airfield Constrn Sqdn, 1971-73, Dir Gen, Air Force Facilities, 1973-84; Dir Gen, Nat Disasters Org, 1984-87. Honour: OBE, 1963. Membership: Fell, Inst of Engrs, Aust. Hobbies: Golf; Fishing. Address: 45 Argyle Square, 1 Allambee Street, Reid, ACT 2601, Australia.

LETTS Richard Albert, b. 3 Aug 1935, Sydney, NSW, Aust. Executive Director, Arts Organizations. Education: ASTC, Univ of NSW, Sydney, 1957; Univ of Sydney, 1961-63; BA, 1965, PhD, 1971, Univ of CA, Berkeley, USA; Cntr for World Music, Berkeley, 1977-78. Appointments: Dir, E Bay Cntr for Performing Arts, Richmond and Berkeley, CA, USA, 1972-80; Dir, MacPhail Cntr for the Arts, Univ of MN, Minneapolis, 1980-82; Dir, Music Bd, Aust Cncl, Sydney, 1982-87; Dir, Austl Music Cntr/Sounds Austl, Sydney, 1987-93; Proprietor, Zabfray PL, Sydney, 1990-. Publications: A Study into the Future Development of Symphony Orchestras in Australia, 1985; Medium Range Plan for Music, 1985-89; Mngng Ed, Sounds Austl Jrnl, qtrly, 1987-93; Your Career as a Composer, 1993; The Arts on the Edge of Chaos, 1995; The Art of Self Promotion: Successful Promotion by Musicians, 1996; Ed, Music Forum Mag, 1994-; Ed, Resonance Mag, Intl Music Cncl, 1997-. Honours: Albert Prize for Music, Sydney Univ, 1961; Hons List, Music, Univ of CA, Berkeley, 1965; Richmond Letts Th, Richmond, CA, 1980; AM, 1996. Memberships: Bd Mbr, Bay Area Review, San Fran, 1978-80; Natl Guild of Cmnty Schs of Arts, NY, Natl VP, 1980-82, Fndr and Chmn, W Coast Chapt, 1978; Bd Mbr, Pres, Austl Inst of East Music; Bd Mbr, The Song Co, Sydney; Pres, The Song Co, 1991-; UNESCO Intl Music Cncl, exec cttee, 1991-; Chmn, Regl Cncl for Asia and Oceania, 1993-98; Music Cncl of Aust, fndr and chmn, 1994-. Hobbies: Swimming; Running; Music; Theatre; Dance; Literature; Cultural development. Address: 12/23 McLeod Street, Mosman, NSW 2088, Australia.

LEUNG Beatrice Benedict Kit-fun, b. 15 Aug 1938, Hong Kong. Educator (University). Education: Dip Ed, 1967, MA, 1985, BA, 1996, Univ of Hong Kong; PhD, Univ of London, London Sch of Econs & Polit Sci, 1988. Appointments: Asst Prof, Univ of Macau, 1992-93; Lectr, Lingnan Coll, 1993-95; Snr Lectr, 1995-97, Prog Dir, 1996-, Fac of Socl Scis, Lingnan Coll; Assoc Prof, Lingnan Coll, 1997-. Publication: Sino-Vatican Relations 1976-86, 1992. Membership: Perm mbr, Sisters of Precious Blood (Hong Kong), relig orgn of Roman Cath Church. Address: Sister of Precious Blood, 86 Un Chau St, Kowloon, Hong Kong.

LEUNG Chun Fai, b. 23 Nov 1954. University Lecturer. m. Tan Anna, 24 Mar 1984, 2 s, 1 d. Education: BEng Civil Engrng 1977, PhD Geotech Engrng 1981, Univ of Liverpool, Eng. Appointments: Dept of Civil Engrng, Natl Univ of Singapore, Lectr 1981-86, Snr Lectr 1987-96, Assoc Prof 1997-. Memberships: Inst Civil Engrs, 1988-; Inst of Engrs Singapore, 1989. Hobbies: Bridge; Tennis. Address: Department of Civil Engineering, National University of Singapore, 10 Kent Ridge Crescent, Singapore 119260.

LEUNG Clement, b. 10 May 1949. University Professor. m. Q H Choo, 24 Mar 1979, 2 s. Education: BSc, Maths, McGill Univ, Can, 1972; MSc, Maths, Oxford Univ, 1973; PhD, Computer Scis, Univ of London, 1980. Appointments: Computer Systs Techn, Kodak, 1973-76; Analyst, Programmer, Unilever, 1976-78; Cnslt in Mngmt Scis, Brit Oxygen, 1978; Lectr in Computer Sci, Univ of Reading, 1979-82; Lectr in Computer Sci, 1982-86, Prof of Computer Sci, 1986-93, Birbeck Coll, Univ of London; Prof of Computer Sci, Vic Univ of Technol, 1993-. Publications: Quantitative Analysis of Computer Systems, book, 1988; Visual Information Systems, 1997; Over 90 rsch articles publd. Honours: Rsch funded by: UK Sci and Engrng Rsch Cncl; Eurn Cmntys ESPRIT; UK MoD; Brit Lib Rsch and Dev; Eastman Kodak, USA; Served as Prog Chair, on Prog Cttee, Panel Expert, Invited Speaker at major intl confs and workshops; Co-ed, sev intl jrnls. Memberships: Fell, Brit Computer Soc; Chartered Engr; Fell, Roy Soc of Arts, Mfres and Com. Hobbies: Jazz piano; Badminton; Table tennis. Address: Victoria University of Technology, Department of Computer and Mathematical Sciences, Ballarat Road, Footscray, PO Box 14428, MCMC, Melbourne, Vic 8001, Australia.

LEUNG Frankie Fook-Lun, b. 20 Oct 1949, Guangzhou, China. Lawyer. m. Dora, 1 s. Education: BA, Psychol, Hong Kong Univ, 1972; MSc, Clin Psychol, Birmingham Univ, 1974; BA, 1976, MA, 1981, Oxford Univ. Appointments: Visng Schl, E Asian Legal Studies, Harvard Law Sch, 1983; Pt-time Lectr, Chinese Law, Fac of Law, Hong Kong Univ, 1984-85; Cnslting Prof, Chinese Law Dip Prog, Univ of E Asia, Macao, 1985-86; Adj Prof of Law, Loyola Law Sch, CA, 1987-; Assoc, 1987-89, Ptnr, Dir, 1991-99, Cnsl, 1999-, Lewis, D'Amato, Brisbois & Bisgaard, Los Angeles; Adj Prof of Law, Pepperdine Univ CA, 1988; Assoc, Cnsl, Carlsmith Wichman Case Mukai & Ichiki, Los Angeles, 1989-91; Lectr, Chinese Law, Stanford Univ Sch of Law, 1995; Adj Prof in Chinese Law, Univ of Southern CA Law Sch, 1998. Publications: 6 books and sev articles in profl jrnls. Honour: Wiley W Manuel Awd, 1993. Memberships: Fndng Chmn, Hong Kong Univ Alumni Assn of Southern CA, 1991-93; Jonathan Club of Los Angeles, 1993; Bd of Advrs, Southern CA Chinese Lawyers Assn, 1995-96; Bd Dir, YMCA, Pasadena, 1996-99; Dir Amn Arbitration Assn, 1999-. Hobbies: Reading; Writing. Address: 545 South Figueroa Street, Los Angeles, CA 90071, USA.

LEUNG Oi Sie (Elsie), b. 24 Apr 1939, Hong Kong. Legal Official. Education: Univ of Hong Kong. Appointments: Admitted as Solicitor, Supreme Crt of Hong Kong, 1968, Overseas Solicitor, UK Supreme Crt, 1976; Notary Pub, 1978; Admitted as Bar and Solicitor of Vic, Aust, 1982; Fndng Mbr, Hon Sec, Hong Kong Fed of Women Lawyers, 1978; 1st VP, 1992, Pres, 1994-; Deleg, 7th Natl People's Cong, Guangdong, China, 1989, 8th Cong, 1993; Fndng Mbr, Mbr Exec Cttee, Hong Kong Fed of Women, 1993; Sec for Justice of Hong Kong Spec Admin Region, 1997-. Membership: Fell, Intl Acad of Matrimonial Lawyers, 1994. Address: Department of Justice, Secretary of Justice's Offices, 4th Floor, High Block, Queensway Government Offices, 66 Queensway, Hong Kong Special Administrative Region, China.

LEUNG Paul, b. 18 Sept 1923, Hong Kong. Businessman; Composer; Lyricist; Author; Columnist; Lecturer; Record Producer. Appointments: Proprietor, Amo Record Corp; Columnist, Hong Kong Econ Jrnl; Tchr of Engl. Creative Works: Composed over 400 original songs collectively known as Paul Leung's Sing Song Learn English. Publications: Sev books in Chinese. Memberships: Performing Right Soc, London; Brit Acady of Songwriters, Composers and Auths; IFPI; CASH. Hobbies: Musical Composition; Studies of Theories and Practices of Melody Writing; Philosophy; Stamp Collecting. Address: Amo Record Corporation, PO Box 95170, Tsim Sha Tsui Post Office, Kowloon, Hong Kong.

LEUNG Suiwah Edna, b. 10 Dec 1947, Hong Kong, China. Economist. m. Ron Dean, 31 July 1982, 1 s, 1 d. Education: BComm (Hons), MCom (Hons), Univ of NSW; PhD, MA, Johns Hopkins Univ. Appointments: Rsch Offr, Reserve Bank of Aust; Asst Natl Assessment Offr, Austl Govt; Post-doct Fell, Austl Natl Univ; Rsch fell, Austl Natl Univ; Fell, Dir, Grad Studies, Econs of Dev, Austl Natl Univ; Non-exec Dir (pt-time), ACT Elec and Water Corp. Publications: Books: Vietnam Assessment - Creating a Sound Investment Climate, 1996; Vietnam and the East Asian Crisis, 1999; Articles and chapts in books on econ topics in Vietnam, Aust and NZ. Memberships: Austl Inst of Co Dirs. Hobby: Music. Address: National Centre for Development Studies, Australian National University, ACT 0200, Australia.

LEUNG Ying Keung, b. 18 July 1954, Hong Kong, China. Principal Lecturer. m. Guay, 4 Mar 1980, 2 s. Education: BS (Hons) Elec Engrng, Aston, 1978; MSc, Heriot-Watt, 1982; BA, Open, 1986; MBA, Monash, 1990; PhD, Massey, 1995. Appointments: Engr, Burroughs Machines Ltd, Glenroth, 1978-81; Lectr, Vic Univ of Technol, 1982-90; Prin Lectr, Swinburne Univ of Technol, 1989-. Memberships: Instn of Electr Engn, 1985; Chartered Elecl Engr, 1985. Address: 2 Reddington Terrace, East Doncaster, 3109 Victoria, Australia.

LEUNG KAM CHUNG Antony, b. 29 Jan 1952, Hong Kong. Banker; Official. m. Sophie Leung. Education: Univ Hong Kong; Harvard Bus Sch. Appointments: Mngng Dir, Regl Mngr, Greater China & The Philippines, Chase Manhattan Bank; Dir, Hong Kong Futures Exchange, 1987-90, Hong Kong Policy Rsch Inst, 1996-; Chair, Univ Grants Cttee, 1993-; Trustee, Queen Mary Hosp Charitable Trust, 1993-, Hong Kong Cntr for Econ Rsch, 1995-; Hong Kong Affairs Advsr, 1994-; Arbitrator, China

Intl Econ & Trade Arbitration Comm, 1994-. Memberships: Indl Devel Bd, 1985; Univ & Polytech Grants Cttee, 1990-93; Bd, Prov Airport Authy, 1990-95, Airport Authy, 1995-; Ctrl Policy Unit, 1992-93; Bd, Hong Kong Cmty Chest, 1992-94; Educn Comm, 1993-; Standing Cncl, Chinese Soc of Macroecons; State Planning Comm, 1994-; Exchange Fund Advsry Cttee, 1995-; Prep Cttee of Hong Kong Specl Admin Region, 1996-97; Exec Cncl, Hong Kong Specl Admin Region, 1997-. Address: Executive Council Secretariat, 1st Floor, Main Wing, Central Government Offices, Hong Kong.

LEVERSHA Anne, b. 19 Nov 1949, Toorak, Melbourne, Aust. Pharmacist. m. Ian Francis Leversha, 29 Apr 1972, 2 s, 1 d. Education: BPharm, 1971. Appointments: Trainee, 1971, Pharmacist, 1972-75, Snr Pharmacist, 1976, Casual Pharmacist, 1977-81, Roy Children's Hosp, Melbourne; Est'd Drug Info Cntr, Roy Children's Hosp; Pt-time in retail pharm, 1981-85; Clin Pharmacist Grade 2 (pt-time), La Trobe Valley Hosp, Moe, Vic, 1985-87, Ctrl Gippsland Hosp, Traralgon, Vic, 1987-91, La Trobe Regl Hosp, 1985-98; Asst Lectr, Pt-time, 1993, 1994-; Rural Advsr to Soc of Hosp Pharmacists of Aust, 1997-; Snr Lectr Pt-time, 1998-, Monash Univ, Fac of Med Cntr for Rural Hlth; Pt-time Assoc, Pharm Prac, Monash Univ, Victorian Coll of Pharm, 1997; Dpty Mngr Pahrm Servs La Trobe Regl Host, 1998-. Publications: An Analysis of Clinical Pharmacist Interventions and the Role of Clinical Pharmacy at a Regional Hospital in Australia; Articles: Comparison of Activated Charcoals (co-auth), 1974; Comparison of Cardiovascular Toxicity of Three Tricyclic Antidepressant Drugs: Impramine, Amitrityline and Doxepin (co-auth), 1979; The Challenge of Clinical Pharmacy at Regional Hospital, poster exhibt, 1989, 1990; Rural Pharmacist Training and Support Program, 1996. Honour: Winner, CSL Poster Awd, Biennial Fed Conf, Austl Soc of Hosp Pharmacists, 1989. Memberships: Soc of Hosp Pharmacists of Aust; Austl Coll of Pharm Practice; C'wlth Pharm Assn, Chapt of Pharm Prac Tutors; Pharm Soc of Aust. Hobbies: Bushwalking; Member, Uniting Church and Community Aid Abroad; Reading Music. Address: 35 Phillip Crescent, Traralgon, Vic 3844, Australia.

LEVY Anne, b. 29 Sept 1934, Perth, Aust. Former Member of S Aust Parliament. m. Keith Percival Barley, 3 May 1957, dec 1975, 1 s, 1 d. Education: MSc, Univ of Adelaide. Appointments: Tutor in Genetics, 1959-64, Snr Tutor in Genetics, 1965-75, Univ of Adelaide; Elected Mbr of Legis Cncl of S Aust, 1975, re-elected, 1982, 1989; Retired, 1997; Pres Legis Cncl of S Aust, 1986-89; Min of Local Govt, 1989-92, Min for the Arts, 1989-93, Min of State Servs, 1989-92, Min for Consumer Affairs, 1992-93, Min for the Status of Women, 1992-93. Honour: Austl Humanist of Yr Awd, 1986. Memberships: Austl Labor Party; Abortion Law Repeal Assn (SA); S Austl Vol Euthanasia Soc; Humanist Soc; Women's Electoral Lobby; World Women Parliamentarians for Peace. Hobbies: Women's Issues; Theatre; Tennis; Reading. Address: 356 Carrington Street, Adelaide 5000, S Australia; Australia.

LEVY David, b. 1938, Morocco. Politician. Emigrated to Israel, 1957. Appointments: Constrn Worker; Joined Histadrut; Elected to Knesset; Rep Herut (Freedom) Grp of Gahal, 1969-; Likud Cand for Sec-Gen of Histadrut, 1977, 1981; Min of Immigrant Absorption, 1977-78, of Constrn & Housing, 1978-90, of Fgn Affairs, 1990-92, 1996-97; Dpty PM, 1981-84, 1988-92; Fndr, Gesher Party, 1996. Address: c/o Gesher, Jerusalem, Israel.

LEVY Jane, b. 31 Jan 1945, Chgo, IL, USA. Curator; Librarian. m. Neil, 19 Oct 1969, 1 s. 2 d. Education: BA, MLS, Univ CA. Appointments: Curator, Libn, Blumenthal Rare Books and Manuscript Lib, Magnes Museum, Visual Resources Lib, CA Coll of Arts and Crafts. Publications: The Jewish Illustrated Book, 1986; Photo-ed, Gold Rush: a Literary Anthology. Memberships: Visual Resources Assoc; Amn Assoc Mus. Hobbies: Oceanic art; Quilting. Address: California College of Arts & Crafts, 450 Irwin, SF 94107, USA.

LEVY Shlomo, b. 16 Aug 1943, Iraq. Chemist; Forensic Scientist. m. Judith, 7 Mar 1977, 4 s. Education: PhD, Organic Chem (Nat Prods); MPharm, Sch of Pharm, Hebrew Univ of Jerusalem. Appointments: Standardization an Characterization Inst of Drugs, Min of Hlth, 1969-70; Dept of Nat Prods, Sch of Pharm, Hebrew Univ in Jerusalem, 1970-77; Cnslt, Makor Chms LTD, Israel, 1973-78; Fac Rsch Assoc, Chem Dept, Sch of Med, Univ of MA, USA, 1978-79; Fac Rsch Assoc, Chem Dept, Worcester Polytechinique Inst, Worcester, USA, 1979-80; Asst-in-Radiopharmaceuticals, MA Gen Hosp, Boston, USA, 1980-82; Pharmacist, CTS Inds, Israel, 1982-85; Hd, Analytical Lab, Div Identification & Forensic Sci, Israel Police HQ, 1985; Hd, Quality Assurance Unit, Div Identification & Forensic Sci, Israel Police HQ, 1995-. Publications: Articles in profl jnls. Hobbies: Classical music; Martial arts; Scuba diving. Address: 10, Brand Street, Harnof, Jerusalem, Israel.

LEVY Yitzhak, b. 1947, Morocco. Rabbi; Politician. Emmigrated to Israel, 1957. m. 5 children. Education: Kerem B'Yavne; Yeshivat hakotel. Appointments: Ordained Rabbi; Served, Israeli Def Forces to Rank of Maj; Natl Relig Party Mbr, Knesset, 1988-; Mbr, Knesset House Cttee; Cttees on Fin, Constitution, Law & Justice, Labour, Socl Welfare, 1988-92; Knesset House Cttee & Cttee on Constitution Law & Justice, 1992-96; Min of Transp, 1996-. Memberships: Bnei Akiva; Gen Sec, Natl Relig Party; Chair, Israel-Argentina Parl Friendship League. Address: Ministry of Transport, Klal Buinding, 97 Rehov Jaffa, Jerusalem 91000, Israel.

LEWENIQILA Militoni, 29 June 1932. Appointments: Asst Min for Fijian Affairs and Rural Dev, 1972-77; Min of State for Lands and Mineral Rescs, 1978; Min for Urban Dev and Housing, 1979; Min for Urban Dev, Housing and Socl Welfare, 1980-82; Min for Lands, Local Govt and Housing, 1982-83; Min for Home Affairs and Immigration, 1984-85; Mbr of Parl, 1986; Speaker, House of Representatives, 1987; Min for Lands and Mineral Rescs, 1992; Min for Labour and Indl Rels, 1993; Min for Agric, Fisheries and Forests, and ALTA, 1996; Min for Agric, Fisheries and Forests, 1997. Address: PO Box 5442, Raiwaqa, Fiji.

LEWER Walter John, b. 1 Nov 1919. m. Janette Allen, 3 Aug 1956, 3 s, 1 d. Education: LLM, hons, Univ Sydney. Appointments: RAAF and AIF, 1940-46; Stip Magistrate and Coroner, 1960; Dpty Chmn, Bench of Stip Magistrates, NSW, 1971-79 (held inquiry under Pub Servs Act into allegations of corruption, Dept of Motor Transp, 1979); Chmn, Disciplinary Appeals Bds, Overseas Telecoms Commn and Austl Brdcstng Corp, 1980-87; Chmn, NSW Govt Cttee of Inquiry into the use and safety of the pesticide 2,4,5-T, 1981-82. Honour: AM, 1981. Hobbies: Reading; Music; Travel; Fishing; Astronomy. Address: 1 Mayleen Street, Clontarf, Qld 4019, Australia.

LEWIN Klaus Jonathan, b. 10 Aug 1936, Jerusalem,, Israel. Surgical Pathologist. m. Dr Patricia Lewin, 2 s, 1 d. Education: MBBS; MRCS; LRCP; MD; FRCPath. Appointments: Prof, Path & Med, UCLA Sch of Med; Chf Gastroenterologist, liver & pancreas sect. Publications: (co-auth) Gastrointestinal Pathology and its Clinical Implications, 1992; Tumour of the Oesophagus and Stomach, AFIP fascicle, 1996. Memberships: US Acady Path; Assn Clin Pathologists; Path Soc, GB; CA Soc of Path; Amn Gastroenterological Soc; Gastroenterological Path Soc. Hobbies: International pathology; Travel; Swimming. Address: Department of Pathology, Center for Health Sciences, UCLA 10833, Le Conte Ave, Los Angeles, CA 90095, USA.

LEWIS Gordon Charles, b. 5 Aug 1920, Melbourne, Aust. Retired Federal Secretary, National Safety Council of Australia. m. 3 Mar 1942, 3 s, 1 d. Education: Roy Melbourne Inst of Technol. Appointments: Gen Mngr, TV GLV10, 1960-63; Announcer, Copywriter, Programmer, Chf Exec, Radio Brdcstng Ind, 1938-79; C'wlth Brdcstng Corp, Sydney, Netwrk Mngr, 1972-78, Mngng Dir, Sales, 1972-78, Mngr, 2KA, 1978-79; Fed Sec, Natl Safety Cncl of Aust, 1979-89. Honours: Cnclr, Cty of Sale; Pres, Sale

Chmbr of Com; Fed Pres, Fedn of Austl Radio Brdcstrs. Memberships Fedn of Austl Com TV Stns, 1960-63; Fedn of Austl Radio Brdcstrs, State Chmn, WA, 1964-68, Fed Pres, 1970-71; Fell, Advtng Inst of Aust; Fell, Soc of Snr Execs; VP, Claremont, WA Football Club; Treas, Austl Football League, NSW; Probus Club, N Balwyn; Melbourne Cricket Club; Naval Mil Air Force Club of WA; Melbourne RACV, Returned Servs League. Hobby: Australian Football. Address: 19 Nevada Street, North Balwyn, Vic 3104, Australia.

LEWIS Hilda Frances (Present), b. Bridgeport, CT, USA. Professor. 3 s, 1 d. Education: BA, 1948, MA, 1952, PhD, 1959, Univ CA, Berkeley. Appointments: Tchr, Richmond Sch Dist, 1950-52; Lectr, 1957-59, Coll of the Holy Names; Asst Prof, Assoc Prof, Prof, Dept Chair, San Fran State Univ, 1962-. Publications: Child Art: The Beginnings of Self-Affirmation, 1966; Understanding Children's Art for Better Teaching, 1973; Art for the Pre-Primary Child, 1972. Honours: June King McFee Awd, 1982; Meritorious Performance Awd, 1985; Getty Cntr for Educn Grant, 1989; AT&T Grant, 1990. Memberships: Chair, Disting Fells of the Natl Art Educn Assn, 1996; VP, US Soc for Educn Through Art, 1983. Hobbies: Music; Painting; Art History. Address: 17749 Chateau Court, Castro Valley, CA 94552, USA.

LEWIS Hurtle John, b. 2 Jan 1926. University Warden. Education: ThL; BDLon; Prince Alfred Coll. Appointments: RANVR, 1943-46; Ordained 1951; Novice Master, 1957; Prior, St Barnabas Sch, Ravenshoe, 1958-60; Provl Aust Prov Soc of the Sacred Mission and Warden SSM Theologl Coll, SA, 1962-68 (Mbr Col, 1951, joined 1947); Prior of Sacred Mission House, Kobe, Japan, 1969-70; Bish of N Qld, 1971-96; Warden, St Mark's Coll, James Cook Univ, 1996-97. Address: 1/4 Stuart St, North Ward, Townsville, Qld 4810, Australia.

LEWIS Keith William, b. 10 Nov 1927, Adelaide, Aust. Civil Engineer; Retired. m. Alison Bothwell Fleming, 11 Oct 1958, 2 d. Education: BE, Civil, Adelaide Univ, 1952; Fell, SA Sch of Mines, 1952; Dip, Imperial Coll, London Univ, Eng, 1955. Appointments: Engr, Water and Sewage Treatment, Engrng and Water Supply Dept, 1968-74; Dir-Gen, Engr-in-Chf, Engrng and Water Supply Dept, 1974-87. Honours: Hon Fell, Instn of Engrs, Aust; Fell, Austl Acady of Technol Sci. Honours: CB, 1981; AO, 1994. Memberships include: State Plng Authy, 1974-82; Electricity Trust of SA, 1974-84; SA Environment Protection Cncl, 1974-84; Austl Water Rescs Cncl Stndng Cttee, 1974-87; Chmn, SA Water Rescs Cncl, 1976-87; Golden Grove Jnt Venture Cttee, 1984-97; Chmn, Austl Water Rsch Advsry Cncl, 1985-90; Chmn, Energy Plng Exec, 1987-93; Bd, Amdel Ltd, 1987-94; Chmn, Mbr, SA Urban Land Trust, 1984-94; Dpty Chmn, Mbr, Electricity Trust of SA, 1993-95.Listed in Who's Who in Australia; Who's Who. Hobbies: Golf; Tennis; Reading; Ornithology; Fishing. Address: 24 Delamere Avenue, Netherby, SA 5062, Australia.

LEWIS Milton James, b. 15 Oct 1941, Newcastle, NSW, Aust. Academic. m. Elizabeth Anne Beadman, 6 Oct 1969, 1 d. Education: BA, Hons, Univ NSW; MA, PhD, Austl Natl Univ. Appointments: Austl Rsch Cncl Snr Rsch Fell, 1991-95, Snr Rsch Fell, 1996; Natl Hlth and Med Rsch Cncl Snr Rsch Fell, 1997-. Publications include: A Rum State: Alcohol and State Policy in Australia, 1992; Sex, Disease and Society: A Comparative History of Sexually Transmitted Diseases and HIV/AIDS in Asia and the Pacific, 1997; Thorns on the Rose: The History of Sexually Transmitted Diseases in Australia in International Perspective, 1998. Address: Department of Public Health and Community Medicine, University of Sydney, Sydney, NSW 2006, Australia.

LEWIS Sally Elizabeth, b. 12 Oct 1967, Australia. Marketing Director. Education: BA; Dip, Bus Mngmt. Appointments: Mktng Mngr, 1993, Mktng Dir, 1995. Memberships: Austl Mktng Inst; Assoc, State Econ Devel Ind Prog. Hobby: Water Sports. Address: c/o Novotel-Ibis, Olympic Boulevard, Homebush Bay, NSW 2140, Australia

LEYDEN Michael J II (Lei Jie Ming), b. 26 Feb 1950. International Business and Economics Professor. m. Xu Zhong Yu, 1 s, 2 d. Education: Univ Virgin Is; CWS Univ; BA, Univ New Brunswick, Fedn Can and WSU; MA, Philos, Intellectual Hist, ABD, 1974; Univ HI EMBA, E W Cntr; Rsch Fell, Univ WA; Doct, Bus Admin, Newport Univ. Appointments: Visng Schl, Univ Guam, 1988; Lectr, Univ HI, CBA, Honolulu, 1989; Educ, CNMI-PSS Liaison Off, Pub Schl Statistician, 1990; Assoc Prof North Marianas Coll, CNMI, Trade, Tourism, Mktng, 1991; Assoc Prof, TIFT, Intl Bus and Engl Writing Compositors, (ORAL) Speaking, 1993; Nankai Univ, Tianjin, China, For Trade & Bus, Writing Oral Lit, TESOL, ESL, 1994; Prof & For Expert, Peking Univ, Grad Sch, Dept Engl/For Lit, 1995-; Tsinghua Univ Grad Sch For Lang, 1996. Publications: China's Environmental Crisis: International Relations and Business, 1995; APEC-Sino-American Perspectives: Economics and Trade, 1996; Dynamics and Implications for China in the 21st Century with new Telecommunications Technology, 1996; Basic Research Opens Your Eyes I & II, 1996; Sino-American Relations in APEC Forum, 1995; Poetry, Nexus, 1972; Writing A Business Plan; Fine Arts Soc, Duboque, IA; 3 poems, The Poet, 1975; For the 5 Minute Reader, 1991; Language Bending Vs Bilingualism: The Debate, 1991; Writing A Business Plan for the Five Minute Reader; Thoughts On The Business of Life, 1991; Contrb articles in profl jrnls. Honours: Ed's Awd, Sophia Grad Newspaper, Univ New Brunswick, 1973, Miyazawa, Japan; CNMI Fac Tchng Exch Awd for Excellence, 1991. Memberships: Ed, Newsletter, N Cntrl Oriental Rug Soc, 1979-81; Amn & China Philos Assn, Beijing, NY; Amn & China Assn's of Univ Fac Profs, NY; N Cntrl WA Writers Assn, Ellensburg, WA, 1970-72. Hobbies: Aviation; Writing; International Economics; International Relations. Address: No 101, 2 Men, 7 Hao Lou, 9 Qiu Wan Xin Cun, He Dong Qu, Tianjin 300162, China.

LHAGVAJAV Chultem, b. 1947, Bulgan Aimag, Mongolia. Government Executive. m. Education: Grad, Moscow State Univ, 1980; PhD, Physics and Maths. Appointments: Rsch Fell, Cntr Phys and Maths, 1973; Hd, Sect, 1980; Ed, Ug Newsppr, 1990; Rsch Sec, Cntr for Astronomy, 1991; Min of Educ, Govt Mongolia, Ulan Bator, 1996-; Rsch Lectr, Acady Pol Educ, 1993-95. Address: Ministry of Education and Science, Barilgachdyn Talbal 15, Ulan Bator 44, Mongolia.

LHO Shin Yong, b. 28 Feb 1930, Korea. Politician; Diplomat. Education: Law Coll, Seoul Natl Univ; KY State Univ, USA. Appointments: Joined Dipl Serv, 1956; Dir, Planning & Mngrs Off, Min of Fgn Affairs, 1967; Consul-Gen, Los Angeles, USA, 1969-72; Amb to India, 1973, to Geneva, 1976; Vice-Fgn Min, 1974, Fgn Min, 1982-85; PM, 1985-87; Hd, Agcy of Natl Security Planning, 1982-85; Democratic Justice Party (now New Korea Party). Address: New Korea Party, 14-8 Yoido-dong, Yongdeungpo-ku, Seoul 150-010, Korea.

LI An Bo, b. 10 Oct 1923, Heng Non, China. Professor of Preventive Medicine. m. 4 May 1953, 1 s, 2 d. Education: Grad, Xiong Ya Med Coll, 1951. Appointments: Prof, Dir, Fac of Preventive Med, Expert Advsry Cttee Xian Med Univ; Dir, Shaanxi Labour Hygiene and Occupational Disease Cttee; Dir, Br of Air Ions of Environ Biophys Acady, China. Publications: Air Ions, 1995; Air Ions and Air Conditioning Disease, 1995. Honours: Ex Tchng Prize, 1975; 2nd Class Prize, Sci and Technol Progress, Min of Pub Hlth, China, 1982. Memberships: 15. Address: c/o Xian Medical University, Xian 710061, China.

LI Baoqing, b. 17 Dec 1942, Shanghai, China. Professor. m. Zhenying Fang, 25 Apr 1993, 1 d. Education: BS, E China Univ of Sci and Technol, 1964; PhD, Appl Sci, Belgium, 1990. Appointments: Inst of Coal Chem, Chinese Acady of Scis, 1964-86, 1991-, Assoc Prof, 1992, Prof, Chf of Coal Chem Lab, Vice Chmn, Acad Cttee, 1994. Publications: Sev articles in profl jrnls. Honour: Specl Allowance, State Cncl, 1993. Memberships include: Chem Soc, Shanxi; Natl Coal Chem Cttee. Hobby: Music. Address: c/o Institute of Coal

Chemistry, Chinese Academy of Sciences, 27 Taoyuan Nan Road, Taiyuan 030001, China.

LI Bingzheng, b. 18 Aug 1965, Shanxi, China. Professor. m. Jianping Yu, 28 Sept 1993, 1 s. Education: PhD, Maths, Zhejiang Univ, 1994. Publications: 10 pprs in profl maths jrnls. Honours: Ex Ppr Awds, Natural Sci, Zhejiang, 1995, 1997. Hobbies: Music; Sports. Address: Mathematical Institute, Zhejiang University, Hangzhou 310027, China.

LI Boyong, b. 1932, Tianjin, China. State Official; Engineer. Education: Air Force Inst of Mil Engrng. Appointments: Fmr USSR Vice-Min, Labour & Personnel, 1986-93; Mbr, 14th CCP Ctrl Cttee, 1992-; Min of Labour, 1993-98. Address: Ministry of Labour, 12 Hepingli Zhongjie Street, Dongcheng Qu, Beijing 100716, China.

LI Changchun, b. 1944, Jilin, China. Government Official. m. Zhang Shurong. Education: Harbin Polytech Univ. Appointments: Joined CCP, 1965; Mayor, Shenyang Municipality, 1983-86; Sec, Shenyang Municipality CCP Cttee, 1985; Dpty Sec, Liaoning Prov CCP Cttee, 1985-86; Dir, Fgn Affairs Off, 1988-; Gov of Liaoning Prov, 1986-90; Gov of Henan Prov, 1991-93; Sec, CPC 5th Henan Prov Cttee, 1992-; Chair, Standing Cttee, Henan Prov Peoples Congress, 1993-. Address: Office of Provincial Governor, Zhengzhou City, Henan, China.

LI Chengzhi, b. 15 Jan 1951. Research Worker. m. 5 Sept 1984, Suzhen Fan, 1 s, 1 d. Education: Harbin Coll of Elecl Engrng, 1977. Appointments: Serv in 38th Grp Army of CPLA, 1968; Shanxi Provl Bur of Measures and Stands, 1971; Shanxi Provincial Inst of Metrology & Measurement Rsch, 1979; Grp Ldr, Provincial Assignment on Sc & T Rsch, 1982; Dir, Non-Govtl Inst of Clinl Med and Insp, 1984; Grp Ldr, State Assignment Rsch Grp on Natl Stand and Measuring Instruments, 1986; Chf Engr, Non-Govtl Inst of Metrology and Control Technol, 1987; Vice Dir, Cncl of Radio and Computer Speciality, Shanxi Provincial Learned Soc of Metrological Measurement, 1993; Grp Ldr, Rsch on Natl Stand Instrument, 1996. Publications: ZCS: A Intellectual Ultrasonic Power Meter, 1987. Honours: Progress Awds, the First Metrology in Sc and T, Shanxi Prov, 1992; First Advd Yth Workers in Sc and T, Shanxi Prov, 1992; Letter Secret Patent of Invention, 1993; Letter Patent of Invention, 1994. Memberships: Chinese Soc of Biomedl Engrng; Chinese Soc of Cognitive Sci Rsch; Shanxi Learned Soc of Metrological Measurement; Taiyuan Soc Extraordinary Function of Hum Body Rsch. Chinese Contemporary Inventors. Hobbies: Classical Music of Europe; Dance of the Chinese Nation. Address: No 131 Fuxi Street, Taiyuan, Shanxi 030002, China.

LI Chongxiao, b. 7 Nov 1939, Zhunyi, Guizhou, China. Professor of Mathematics. m. 2 Nov 1968, 2 s. Education: Maths Dept, Yunnan Univ, 1956-60. Appointments: Tchr, Jilin Univ, Jilin Corresp Coll, 1962-71; Yunnan Inst of Technol, Kunming, 1978-94; Yunnan Polytech Univ, 1994-. Publications: Higher Mathematics (tchng materials), 1990; Many articles to profl jrnls. Honours: Ex Tchr of Yunnan Univs & colls, 1985; Profl Tech Talent w Outstndng Devotion, Yunnan, 1987. Memberships: VP, Yunnan Polytech Univ; Standing Dir, Yunnan High Educ Assn; Standing dir, Yunnan Maths Soc; Cncl Mbr, Yunnan Educ Assn for Intl Exchange. Hobbies: Playing Weiqi & Bridge. Address: Yunnan Polytechnic University, Kunming, Yunnan 650051, China.

LI Chunting, b. Oct 1936, Luotang, Zhaili, Shandong, China. Governor. Appointments: Joined CCP, 1958; Farmer; Fmr Dpty Sec, CCP Qixia Co Cttee, Dpty Sec, CCP Yantai Pref Cttee, Hd, Prov Metallurgical Dept; Vice-Gov, Shandong Prov, 1988-95, Gov, 1995-; Dpty Sec, CCP Shandong Prov Cttee, 1992-; Alt Mbr, 14th CCPCC; Mbr, 15th CCP Ctrl Cttee, 1997-. Address: Shandong Provincial Committee of the CCP, Jinan, Shandong, China.

LI Cunshan, b. 10 May 1951, Beijing, China. Editor of Social Sciences and Researcher of History of Chinese

Philosophy. m. Gao Rexiang, 21 Jan 1981, 1 s. Education: MPhil, grad student. Dir, Philos Dept, Doty Ed-in-Chf, Socl Scis in China (mag of the Chinese Acady of Socl Scis). Publications: Qi Theory of Chinese Philosophy, 1990; A Critical Biography of Shang Yang, 1997; A Survey of Chinese Philosophy. Honour: Young and Middle-Aged Expert w Disting Accomplishments, granted by Min of Personnel of China. Memberships: Intl Confucian Assn; Intl Assn of Chinese Philosophy; Chinese Confucian Fndn. Hobby: Playing weqi. Address: Social Sciences in China, Jia 118, Gulouxidajie, Beijing, 100720, China.

LI De Tao, b. 16 Jan 1934. Teaching; Research. m. 16 May 1959, 2 d. Education: Grad Sch, Timisoara Politechnics Univ, Romania, 1982. Appointments: Mbrshp of Edl Bd of Chinese Soc of Internal Combustion Engine, 1986-99; Mbrshp Cttee of Natl Nat Scis Fndn of China, 1988-92. Publications: Over six books and ninety papers, 1962-. Honours: Natl Awds of Invention; Advanced Personal Citation of Natl Mech Cong of Sci & Technol. Hobbies: Literature; Music. Address: Jiangsu University of Science & Technology, 2-19-302, Zhenjiang, Jiangsu 212013, China.

LI Delun, b. 6 June 1917, Peking, China. Conductor; Symphony Orchestra Advisor. m. Li Jue, 1 July 1947, 1 s, 2 d. Education: Studied cello at Shanghai Conservatory of Music, 1940; Pursued grad studies in conducting under Prof N Anosow at Moscow Conservatory, Russia, 1953-57. Appointments: Conductor w th orchs in Shanghai, 1943-46, w Yannan Orch, 1946-49, and Cntrl Opera, Peking, 1949-53; Trainee Conductor w Russian State Symph, 1957; Artistic Dir, China Cntrl Phil Symph Orch, 1958; Guest Conductor w over 20 orchs in Russia and in Finland, Cuba, Czech, Germany, USA, Can and Portugal; Led the Symph Orch tour to Japan, Spain and Korea; Advsr, China Natl Symph Orch. Honours: Liszt Mem Medal, Hungarian Govt; Natl Medal of friendship, Russia, 1997. Memberships: Music Advsr, Peking Symph; Hon Advsr, Guanzhou Symph Orch; VP, Chinese Musicians Assn. Listed in: International Who's Who in Music; Who's Who in Asia and the Pacific Nations. Hobby: Photography. Address: 11-1 Heping Street, Central Philharmonic Society, Beijing 100013, China.

LI Dezhu, b. 1943, Wangoing, Jilin, China. Government Official. Education: Yanbian Univ. Appointments: Joined CCP, 1965; Vice-Gov, Jilin Prov, 1988-93; Dpty Hd, United Front Work Dept, 1992-; Pres, Chinese Assn of Ethnic Minorities for External Exchange, 1992-; Mbr, 14th CCP Ctrl Cttee, 1992-97, 15th CCP Ctrl Cttee, 1997-. Address: Jilin Provincial Government, Changchun City, Jilin, China.

LI Dong-Ye, b. 24 Apr 1954, Xuzhou Cty, Jiangsu Prov, China. Chief Physician. m. Tian Yimin, 30 Sept 1973, 1 d. Education: Postgrad grad, Jiangxi Medl Coll, 1986. Appointments: Dpty Dir, Affiliated Hosp, Xuzhou Med Coll, 1993; Assoc Ed, Chinese Jrnl of Prac Electrocardiology. Publications: Rsch wrk in Echocardiography; Pprs in medl jrnls, 1986-. Honour: Spec Subsidy, Chinese Govt. Memberships: Assn of Chinese Med, 1986; Perm Cnclr, Assn of Hosp Admin, Jiangsu Prov. Hobbies: Sport; Chinese chess. Address: Affiliated Hospital of Xuzhou Medical College, Xuzhou City, Jiangsu Province, China 221002.

LI Dongfeng, b. 24 May 1958, Changchun, China. Professor. m. Che Di, 30 Jan 1984, 1 s, 1 d. Education: BA, 1982; MS, 1988. Appointments: Asst Prof, 1986-90, Assoc Prof, 1990-94, Prof, 1994-, Northeast Normal Univ. Creative works: The Neural Connections between Neosturiatum Field L Complex and Vocal Control System in Songbird, 1997. Honours: CAPS, 1988; CSN, 1996; Awd of Sci & Technique Adv of Natl Educl Cttee of China, 1992, 1994. Memberships: AAAS, 1996-98; IBRO, 1997. Hobbies: Music; Sport. Address: School of Life Science, Department of Biology, Northeast Normal University, Changchun 130024, China.

LI Gang, b. 22 Mar 1963, Beijing, China. Businessman. m. Fang Li, 28 Nov 1996. Education: BA,

Mechl Engrng, Univ of Tsinghua, 1986; MBA, Univ of Intl Bus & Econs, 1991; Dipls, Intl Trade, Inst Natl per Il Commercio Estro (ICE), 1993. Appointments: Asst Engr, Beijing Inst of Heavy Duty Automobiles, 1986-88; Fin Analyst, Minmetals, 1991-95; Mngr, Cheemimet Fin Ltd, 1995-98; Asst Mngng Dir, Minmetals LTd, 1995-98. Creative works: Comparison between the Chinese and Amn Acctng System. Memberships: E'Associazione dei Partecipanti Cinesi al Corsi Realizzati Dall'Italian Inst for For Trade (ICE). Hobby: Sports. Address: 16/F The Prudential Assurance Tower, Chatham Road South, Tsimshatsui, KLN, Hong Kong.

LI Gang, b. 24 Sept 1957, Hebei, China. Mechanical Engineer; Ceramics. m. Zhang Qiufang, 28 Dec 1983, 1 s. Education: PhD, Tianjin Univ. Appointments: Rsch Fell, 1989-91; VP, 1991-. Publications: Grinding Dynamics; High Precision Processing of Super-hard Material. Honours: 2nd class Sci & Tech Dev Awd, Natl Educ Cttee and Natl Sci Cttee. Hobby: Singing. Address: C402, Haixing Gardens, Shekou, Shenzhen, China 518067.

LI Gang, b. 1926, Fuzhou, China. State Official. Education: Qinghua Univ. Appointments: Joined CCP, 1949; Alt Mbr, 12th CCP Ctrl Cttee, 1982-87; Gen Mngr, China Automotive Ind Corp, 1982, Chair of Bd, 1985-87; Dpty Gen Mngr, China Investment Corp for Machinery, Elec Equip, Light & Textile Ind, 1988; Vice Chair, Econ Cttee; Mbr, Standing Cttee, CPPCC 8th Natl Cttee, 1993-; Acting Dir, Bur of Cultural Rels w Fgn Countries, 1994-. Address: Chinese Investment Corporation, Beijing, China.

LI Guixian, b. 23 Aug 1937, Yingkou, Liaoning, China. Education: Mendeleyev Chem Technol Inst, Moscow. Appointments: Joined CCP, 1962; Vice-Gov, Liaoning, 1982-83; Sec, CCP Cttee, Liaoning, 1983-85; Sec, CCP Cttee, Anhui Prov, 1985-88; State Cnclr, Gov, PRC Ctrl Bank, 1988-93; Mbr, 14th CCP Ctrl Cttee, 1992-; State Cnclr, 1993-98; Chair, China Cttee of Intl Decade for Natl Disaster Reduction, 1993-; Vice Chair, Ctrl Org Cttee, 1994-; Pres, State Admin Coll, 1994-; Hd, State Cncl Ldng Grp on Boundary Delimitation, 1995-; Mbr, 15th CCP Ctrl Cttee, 1997-. Address: Central Bank of China, Fucheng Mennei Street, Beijing, China.

LI Guoguang, Judge; Vice President. Appointment: Mbr, Judicial Cttee, Supreme Peoples Crt, 1995-. Address: Supreme Peoples Court, Beijing, China.

LI Hong, b. 29 July 1940, Beijing, China. University Professor. m. Song Guiyun, 1 Oct 1968, 1 d. Education: BS, Dept Chem, Fudan Univ, China, 1964; Visng Prof, Dept Chem, McGill Univ, Can, 1991-92; Waseda Univ, Japan, 1997-98. Appointments: Instr, Tianjin High Tech Sch of Organic Chem, 1964-71; Engr, Tianjin Bur of Chem Ind, 1971-78; Lectr, Assoc, Prof, Nankai Univ, 1979-. Publications: Publ 88 acad pprs, translated 2 books of Engl to Chinese. Honours: 2nd Prize, Prog in Sci & Technol, 1988, 3rd Prize, 1997. Membership: Chinese Chem Soc; Chinese Soc of Chem Engrng. Hobbies: Stamp Collecting; Friendship. Address: Institute of Polymer Chemistry, Nankai University, Tianjin, 300071, China.

LI Hua, b. 31 Dec 1959, Sichuan, China. Professor. m. Wang Hua, 26 July 1984, 2 d. Education: Grad, Horticultural Dept, Sichuan Agricl Univ, 1982; Dr of Enology and Viticulture, Inst of Enology, Univ of Bourdeaux II, France, 1985. Appointments: Coll Pres, Enological Prof, Coll of Enology; Dir, Assoc Prof, Viti-vinicultural Major, N-West Agricl Univ, Shaanxi, Yangling, 1986-; Creator of 1st Viti-vinicultural Major in China; Tutor, PhD Grads, 1994; Dean, Coll of Enology, NW Agric Univ, 1994; Set up only Enology Coll in Asia, 1994; Peoples Rep, Ninth Chinese People's Natl Conf. Publications: About 100 in field of viticulture and enology incl: Wine-Making and Controlling, 1990; Wine Tasting, 1992; Modern Enology, 1995; 4 patents for wine-making. Honours: 1st Sci and Technol Awd for Yth, 1988; 1st Natl Star-Fire Awd (Outstndng Yth Awd), 1988; Title of Natl Outstndng Yth in Sci, Technol and Educ, 1989; Some 10 prize medals for wines made w his techniques.

Membership: Life Fell, Amn Biographical Inst. Hobbies: Athletic sports; Bridge. Address: The College of Enology, The North-Western Agricultural University, Shaanxi, Yangling 712100, China.

LI Hui-Zhen, b. 16 Sept 1944, Jilin, China. Electronic Science Educator. m. Xiang-wen Chen, 1 May 1972, 2 d. Education: Physl Schl, Nankai Univ. Appointments: Acad, 1969-79; Asst, Physl & Electron Sci Dept, 1979-86, Lectr, 1986-92, Assoc Prof, 1992-, Nankai Univ. Publications: Lotus 1-2-3 Macro-Order Program Design, 1989; Electromagnetics, 1994; Sev articles in profl jrnls. Honours: 3rd Ppr Awd, 1981; Ex Tchng Material Awd, 1993; 8th Five-Yr Plan, Sci & Technol, Tackle-Key-Problems Tremendous Achievements Awd, 1996. Membership: Physl Inst, 1987-. Address: Nankai University, Electronic Science Department, Weijin Road #94, Tianjin 300071, China.

LI Jian, b. 15 Oct 1957, Beijing, China. Obstetrician; Gynaecologist. m. Li Zhiping, 18 Sept 1984, 1 d. Education: MB, Beijing Med Univ, 1982. Appointments: Res, 1982-88, Snr House Offr, 1988-95, Reg, 1995-, Assoc Prof, 1997-. Publications: Sev articles in profl med jrnls. Honour: 2nd Awd, Sci and Technol, Beijing Hlth Bur, 1995. Membership: Chinese Med Assn, 1983. Address: Beijing Obstetrics and Gynaecology Hospital, 17 Qi He Lou, Beijing 100006, China.

LI Jian-Bin, b. 13 July 1933, China. Polymer Processing Machinery Speciality; Professor. m. Ming-Xiu Zhao, 20 Aug 1961, 2 d. Appointments: Asst, Chem Machinery Dept, 1957-78, Lectr, 1978-83, Asst Prof, 1983-91, Prof, 1992-; Hd of Chem Machinery Dept, 1981-86; Hd of Lib, South China University of Technology, 1989-98. Publications: Design of the Rubber Machinery, 1984. Honours: State Third Class Sci Invention Awd, 1982; Awd of Guangdong Prov for Managing Lib, 1997. Memberships: Chem Ind and Engrng Soc; Vice-Dir Gen of Guandong Prov Second Light ind Assn; Nat Rubber and Plastics Machinery Standardization Technol Cttee; Ed Mbr, China Rubber Technol and Equipment Jrnl. Hobbies: Physical exercise. Address: Library, South China University of Technology, Guangzhou, Gunagdong Province, China.

LI Jing Neng, b. 9 Dec 1927, Canton, China. Professor. m. Shi Fang Chen, 30 Jan 1954, 2 s. Education: BA, Econs, Nankai Univ, 1950; MA, Econs, Nankai Econs Inst, 1952; Postdoct Prog Study, Population Stdies and Trng Cntr, Brown Univ, Providence, RI, USA, 1988-89. Appointments: Assoc Prof, Hist of Econs, 1978-82, Prof, Population Econs, 1983-, Dir, Inst of Population and Dev Rsch, Nankai Univ, 1984-93; Supvsr of PhD Prog of Population Econs, 1986. Publications: Outline of Demography, (co-ed), 1982; Population Economics (co-ed), 1983; Course of Population Theories (co-ed), 1985; Tianjin Volume of China's Population, 1987; History of Tianjin's Population, 1990; Contemporary Western Theories of Population (chf-ed), 1992; On Population Economic Problems in Recent China, 1999. Honour: Schlshp of CEESP, Natl Acady of Scis, USA, Ford Fndn, 1988-89. Memberships: Standing Cncl, Population Assn of China; Population Advsry Cttee, State Family Plng Commn; Cncl, China's Union for Stdy of For Econs; Vice Chmn, Tianjin's Population Assn; IUSSP; VP, Population Assn of China, 1995-. Hobbies: Research; Collecting stamps; Travelling. Address: Institute of Population & Development Research, Nankai University, 94 Weijin Road, Tianjin 300071, China.

LI Jing-Wen, b. 12 May 1926, China. Medical Doctor. m. Ma Yong-hai, 28 Apr 1951, 1 s, 1 d. Education: Guiyang Medl Coll, 1950; MD. Appointments: Res Dr, 1950-54; Visng Dr, 1955-60; Chf Dr, 1961-80, Hd of Guiyang 1st People's Hosp, 1981-84. Publications: Over 30 medl pprs; (book) Tongue Films of Digestive Diseases. Honours: Superman Cup, 2nd Conf World Tradl Med, 1995. Memberships: Earliest Mbr, Digestive Assn and Combined Tradl-Chinese Med and West Med. Address: Guiyang 1st People's Hosp, Guiyang, Guizhou, China.

LI Ke, b. 14 Nov 1931, Mishan Cty, Heilongjiang, China. Teaching and Study of Philosophy and Social Sciences. m. Zhang Guilian, 19 Nov 1951, 2 s, 1 d. Education: Cert for Completing Studies on Philos, Party Sch, CCCP, June 1956. Appointments: Asst Dir, Rsch Dept, Nanching Univ; Dpty Dir, Acad Cttee, Party Sch, Jiangxi; Pres, Acady of Socl Sci, Jiangxi; Pres, Party Sch, Hainan; Chf Ed, Hainan Encyclopedia. Publications; How to Learn Philosophy: Questions and Answers on Philosophy; Essentials of Marxist Philosophy; Knowledge to Make You Wise; Studies on Mao Zedong's Philsophical Thinking; Initial Studies on the Thoughts of Deng Xiaoping; Modern Personnel for Rural Economics Management. Honours: 2nd Class Awds, State, for "Knowledge to Make You Wise"; Top Awds by Jiangsu Prov for "Studies on Mao Zedong's Philosophical Thinking, 1985; Top Awds, Jiangsu Prov, for Excellent Advice to Government's Policy Decision. Memberships: Standing Cttee, Jiangsu Assn for Sci & Technol, 1981; Pres, Hainan Philos Soc, 1989-92. Hobbies: Reading and studying; Sports. Address: Party School of Hainan, Haikou City, Hainan 570001, China.

LI Laizhu, b. 1932, Shen County, China. Army Officer; Party Official. Education: PLA Mil & Polit Acady. Appointments: Joined PLA, 1946, CCP, 1948; Dpty Cmdr, Beijing Mil Area Cmd, 1985; Rank of Lt-Gen, PLA, 1988; Gen Mbr, 14th CCP Ctrl Cttee, 1992-97; Cmdr, Beijing Mil Region, 1994-97; Rank of Gen, 1994. Address: Beijing Military Area Command, Peoples Liberation Army, Beijing, China.

LI Lanqing, b. May 1932, Zhengjiang, Jiangsu, China. Government & Party Official. Education: Shanghai Fudan Univ. Appointments: Joined CCP, 1952; Vice-Mayor, Tianjin, 1983-85; Alt Mbr, 13th CCP Ctrl Cttee, 1987-92; Vice-Min, Fgn Econ Rels & Trade, 1986-90, Min, 1990-93; Mbr, 14th CCP Ctrl Cttee, 1992-97, 15th CCP Ctrl Cttee, 1997-; Mbr, Politburo, 1992-; Vice Premier, 1993-; Mbr, 8th NPC, 1993-; Hd, Natl Ldng Grp for Fgn Investments, 1994-; Dpty Hd, Ctrl Ldng Grp for Party Bldg Work, 1994-; Chair, Acad Degs Cttee, 1995-. Address: Central Committee of the Chinese Communist Party, Zhong Nan Hai, Beijing, China.

LI Lemin, b. 28 May 1932. Professor. m. Peng Shui-Zen, 10 Aug 1957, 1 d. Education: Grad, Jiao-Tong Univ, Shanghai, China, 1952. Appointments: Dir, Info Rsch Cntr, 1985; Dir, Natl Key Lab of Optical Fiber Comms, 1990; Dir of Acad Cttee of Natl Key Lab of Optical Fiber Comms, 1995, Univ of Elect Sci and Technol China, Chengdu, China. Publications: Equalizers in Digital Transmission Equipments, 1980; Digital Transmission Systems, 1986. Honours: Natl Expert w Outstndng Contbn in China, 1986; Natl Advd Worker, China, 1989. Membership: Fell, China Inst of Comms; Mbr, Chinese Acady of Engrng. Hobby: Chinese Chess. Address: University of Electronic Science and Technology of China, National Key Laboratory of Optical Fiber Communications, Chengdu, Sichuan 610054, China.

LI Ming, b. Nov 1927, Tienjin, China. State Official. m. 2 s, 1 d. Appointments: Dpty, Chf of Prodn Off, Anshan Iron & Steel Corp, 1949-68; Chf Engr, Pres, Panzhihua Iron & Steel Complex, 1968-82; Vice Min, Metallurgical Ind, 1982; Alt Mbr, 12th CCP Ctrl Cttee, 1982-85, Mbr 1985-87; Gen Dir, Ldng Off, Shanghai Baoshan Steel Complex Project, Pres, Baoshan Steel Complex, 1983; Alt Mbr, 13th CCP Ctrl Cttee, 1987-92, 14th CCP Ctrl Cttee, 1992-97; Chair, Baoshan Iron & Steel Complex Corp (Grp), 1988-; Dir, Radio & TV Dept, Hubei Prov Peoples Govt, 1994-. Hobby: Swimming. Address: 2 Mundangjiang Lu, Shanghai 201900, China.

LI Ming Yi, b. 26 July 1951, Tai Kang, Henan, China. Teacher. m. Jichilan, 1 Jan 1978, 1 d. Education: Econ Master Deg. Appointments: Tchr, Beijing Inst of Bus, 1982-; Hd, Bus Rsch Inst, 1987-92; Dean, Econs Dept, 1992-95; Chf, Sci Rsch Sect, 1995-. Publications include: The Relations Between Chinese Economic System Reform and Administrative System Reform, 1991; Approach a Few Questions on Enterprises Change

Mechanism of Administration and Management, 1991; About Promoting Cultural Consume, 1994. Honours: Outstndng Expert, Com Min, 1992; Specl Allowance, State Cncl of China, 1993. Memberships include: Chinese Bus Assn; Chinese Vegetable Assn. Address: Scientific Research Section, Beijing Institute of Business, Fu-Cheng Road No 33#, Beijing 100037, China.

LI Mingde, b. 5 Dec 1940, Hebei, China. Scholar. m. Zhenggiu, 13 Mar 1971, 1 d. Education: BA, Nankai Univ, Tianjin, China. Appointments: Div Hd, Chinese Acady of Scis, 1979-85; First Sec, Acting Sci Cnslr, Chinese Emb, USA, 1986-90; Dir, Inst of Latin Amn, 1995-. Creative Works: US Science and Technology Policy and Management; U S Granting and Contracting System in Support of Research; US Science and Technology. Honours: Grants, Ford Fndn, 1992, 1996, 1999. Memberships: Chinese Assn of Latin Amn Studies; Chinese Soc of Amn Econ Studies. Hobbies: Reading Novels; Listening to Music; Peking Opera. Address: Apt 2-3-209, Guanghui Nanli, Chaoyang Dist, beijing 100022, China.

LI Peiquan, b. 31 Feb 1953, Yangcheng, Henan Prov, China. Materia Medica. m. Du Xianghong, 1 May 1980, 1 d. Education: Chem Dept, Henan Univ, China. Appointments: Hd of Med Rsch Off, Vice Dir, Family Plng Rsch Inst of Henan, China. Publications: Yuanhuacine Pellicle and Its Clinical Practice, 1992; Quantitative Analysis on Chinese Patent Medicine, 1997; The Preparation of Yuanhuacine Pellicle and Its Clinical Application. Honours: 100 Advd Sci Workers in Family Plng of State family Plng Commn, 1991; Spec w Prominent Contbns to the Country, 1993. Membership: Dir, Henan Branch, Materia Medica Inst of China, 1996. Hobbies: Jogging; Bowling. Address: 26 Jingwu Road, Zhengzhou, Henan Province, China.

LI Qin-Zu, b. 14 Feb 1936, Linqing, Shandong, China. Geophysicist. m. Jian-Tai Wang, 10 Feb 1966, 1 s, 1 d. Education: Grad, Dept of Geophys, Peking Univ, 1962. Appointments: Asst Seismol, Inst of Geophys, Academia Sinica, Beijing, 1962-77; Asst Prof, 1978-80, Assoc Prof, 1981-82, Dir, 1983-88, Prof of Geophys, 1987-, Seismol Bur, Hebei. Publication: Stress Field in the Crust of North China, 1980. Honours: 5 Awds, Adv Sci and Technol, State Seismol Bur of China, 1985, 1986, 1995. Memberships: Seismol Soc, Hebei; Seismol Soc of China; Am Geophysl Union. Hobbies: Peking Opera; Chinese Calligraphy. Address: Seismological Bureau of Hebei, 31 Huaizhonglu, Shijiazhuang, Hebei 050021, China.

LI Qiyan, b. 15 Oct 1938, Qihe, Shandong, China. Politician. m. Wu Yuhuan, 1 s, 1 d. Education: Beijing Tchrs Coll. Appointments: Joined CCP, 1961; Dpty Sec, CCP Beijing Municipality Cttee, 1987-; Mbr, 14th CCP Ctrl Cttee, 1992-97; Mayor, Beijing Municipality, 1993-96; Vice Min of Labour, 1996-. Hobbies: History Books; Biographies. Address: Ministry of Labour, 12 Hepingli Zhongjie, Beijing 106716, China.

LI Rong, b. 3 May 1937, Kirin Prov, China. Geologist. m. Teng Shuhua, Jan 1959, 1 s, 2 d. Education: Changchun Geol Sch. Appointments: Geol Tech, 1958-80; Geol Engr, Vice-Capt, 6th Geol Brig of Liaoning Geol Survey Bur, Mngr, Dalian Binhai Diamond Co, 1981-87; Snr Geol Engr, Dpty Dir, Liaoning Geol Survey Bur, Gen Mngr, Dalian Wafangdian Diamond Co Ltd, Chmn, Bd of Dirs of the Co, 1988-96; Snr Geol Engr of Professional Rank, Dpty Dir, Liaoning Geol Survey Bur, Gen Mngr, Dalian Wafangdian Diamond Co Ltd, Chmn, Bd of Dirs of the Co, Chmn, Bd of Dirs of Sino-Diamond Gems & Jewellery Co Ltd, 1997-. Publications: China Wafangdian Classifying and Appraising Stand, 1992. Honours: Elected into 500 Enterprise Fndrs of China; Silver Prize, Natl Sci & Tech Industrialists Fndn Prize, 1994. Memberships: VP, China Gemmological Assn. Hobby: Sports. Address: No 1, Sec 1, Wuyi Road, Wafangdian City, Dalian, China.

LI Ruihuan, b. Sept 1934, Baodi, Tianjin, China. Government & Party Official. Appointments: Vice Chair,

Beijing Trade Union, 1973; Dir-Gen, Work Site for Mao Zedong Meml Hall, Beijing, 1977; Dpty, Beijing 5th NPC, 1978; Sec, Communist Youth League, 1978-; Mbr, Standing Cttee, 5th NPC, 1978-; Dpty Mayor, Tianjin, 1981, Acting Mayor, 1982, Mayor, Tianjin, 1982-; Sec, CCP Cttee, Tianjin, 1982-83, Dpty Sec, 1983-87, Sec, 1987-. Honours include: Named, Natl Model Worker, 1979. Memberships include: VP, All-China Youth Fedn; Hon Pres, Chinese Fedn for the Disabled, 1993-; Hon Pres, Chinese Table Tennis Assn. Address: National Committee of Chinese Peoples Consultative Political Committee, 23 Taiping Qiao Street, Beijing, China.

LI Shangying, b. 5 Mar 1942, Jin County, Liaoning Prov, China. Copy Editor; Professor. m. Gu Li, 16 Apr 1972, 1 s, 1 d. Education: Hist Dept, Grad Sch, Chinese Acady of Socl Scis. Appointments: Ed, 1982-88, Assoc Ed, 1989-94, Copy Ed, 31 Aug 1994, Dir, Editl Dept, Acad Jrnl Grad Sch, CASS. Publications: (co-auth) Institutions of the Qing Dynasty, 1993; Folk Religions and Associations, 1997; History of China' Qing Dynasty, 1994. Honour: 2nd Prize, Good Books, Jilin Prov. Memberships: Assn of Hist of Ming Dynasty. Address: Graduate School, Chinese Academy of Social Services, No 1 Wangjing Zhonghuan Nanlu Dongzhimen wai, Beijing, China.

LI Shihong, b. 25 Nov 1943, Wu Zhou, Guangxi, China. Teacher. m. Jiazhang Tang, 10 Feb 1969, 1 s, 1 d. Education: Grad, Normal Univ. Appointments: Dir, Sci Rsch Off, Guangxi Univ for Nationalities; Dir, Mod Educl Technol Cntr, GUN. Publication: The Application of Multimedia Technology in Physics Education, book. Honour: Second Class Provincial Outstndng Instruction Achmnt Awd, 1997. Hobbies: Sports (Tai Ji Shadow Boxing). Address: No 74, Xixiangtang Road, Nanning, Gangxi, China.

LI Shu, b. 15 Dec 1956, Fuzhou, Fujian, China. Psychology Researcher, Educator. m. Shen Lei, 3 July 1983, 1 s. Education: BEng, Fuzhou Univ, 1982; MEd. Hangzhou Univ, 1988; PhD, Univ of NSW, 1994. Appointments: Lectr, Hwa Nan Women's Coll, 1988-91; Vice Chan, Post-Doctoral Rsch Fell, 1995-1996; ARC Austn Post-Doctoral Rsch Fell, 1997-98; Asst Prof, Nangyang Technological Univ, 1999-. Publications: Contbr Articles. Honours: Austn Rsch Cncl Postdoctoral Rsch Fell. Memberships: NY Acady of Sci; Am Assn for the Advmnt of Sci. Hobbies: Laying in Bed. Address: Nanyang Business School, Nanyang Technological University, Singapore 639798.

LI Siao-Jong, b. 10 Mar 1923, Kaifeng, Honan, China. Professor of Botany and Evolution. m. Miss Huang, 12 Apr 1964, 2 s. Education: MSc, Forest Genetics, Univ of ID, Moscow, USA. Appointments: Lectr, Assoc Prof, Dept of Bot, Natl Taiwan Univ, Taipei, Taiwan. Publications: a Brief Introduction to Plant Science; Introduction to Population Genetics. Membership: Life Mbr, Chinese Forestry Assn, Taipei, Taiwan. Hobby: Classical music. Address: 3 Lane 58, Wen-Chou Street, Taipei, Taiwan, China.

LI Tiecheng, b. 27 Sept 1936, Haicheng Cty, Liaoning Prov, China. Teacher. m. Shen Lihua, 1963, 1 s, 1 d. Education: Grad, Dept of Hist, Peking Univ, 1960. Appointments: For Affairs Coll, 1960-73; Beijing Lang & Culture Univ, 1973-. Publications: 26 books inclng: United Nations Chronicles, 1993; Fifty Years of the United Nations, 1995; Chronicle of the Important Events of the UN, 1998. Honours: Outstndng Tchrs of Beijing Cty, 1988; The First Awd of Socl Sci Rsch Achievement, Beijing, 1994; First Awd of China Natl Cttee of Educ in Socl Scis, 1995. Memberships: China Soc of Intl Rels, 1986; CUNS, 1990; UN Assn of China, 1995. Hobbies: Reading; Thinking; Walking. Address: Center for United Nations Studies, Beijing Language and Culture University, HaiDian District, Beijing 100083, China.

LI Tieying, b. Sept 1936, Yanan, Shaanxi, China. State Official. m. Qin Xinhua. Education: Charles Univ, Czech Repub. Appointments: Fmr Dpty Dir, Electron Rsch Inst; Sec, CCP Cttee, Shenyang Municipality, 1981-85; Alt Mbr, 12th CCP Ctrl Cttee, 1982, Mbr, 1985;

Mbr, 13th CCP Ctrl Cttee, 1987-92, 14th CCP Ctrl Cttee, 1992-97, 15th CCP Ctrl Cttee, 1997-; Sec, CCP Cttee, Liaoning Prov, 1983-86; Min of Electrons Ind, 1985-88; Min in Charge of State Educn Comm, 1988-93, of State Comm for Econ Reconstrn, 1987-88; Chair, Ctrl Patriotic Pub Hlth Campaign Cttee; State Cnclr, 1988-98; Min of State Educn Comm, 1988-93, of State Comm for Econ Restructuring, 1993-; Hd, Ldng Grp for the Reform of the Housing System, 1993-; Dpty Hd, Natl Ldng Grp for Anti-Disaster & Relief Work, 1991-; Mbr, Politburo of CCP, 1992-. Memberships: Hon Pres, Athletics Assn; Soc of Natl Conditions. Address: State Commission for Economic Restructuring, Beijing, China.

LI Weilin, b. 24 Aug 1963, Hebei, China. Senior Geologist. m. Li Peng,, 14 Sept 1987, 1 s. Education: BS, Dept of Pet Geol, China Univ of Geoscience, 1985. Appointments: Snr Geol, Inst of Pet Geol, 1995-99; Vice Dir, Database Div, Inst of Pet Geol, MGMR, China, 1998-; Vice Dir, Data & Info Cntr, China Natl Star Pet Corp, China. Publications: Strategy Data File System of Nature Gas Resource Exploration District Report, 1993; Dream of Computer Management of Domestic Jewelry Products and Commercial Market Becomes Reality, China Gems and Jewelry, Vol 6, 1993. Honours: 3rd Grade Prize, Sci & Technol Prog, Min of Geol & Min Resources for proj: Strategy Datafile System of Nature Gas Resource Exploration, 1994. Membership: China Geol. Hobbies: Cooking; Computer programming. Address: Petroleum Institute, China National Star Petroleum Corporation, 31 Xueyuan Road, Haidan District, Beijing 100083, China.

LI Wenchu, b. 7 Sept 1936, Hunan Prov, China. Professor of Chinese Literature Department of Jinan University. m. Wu Meilan, 3 Aug 1970, 2 d. Education: BA, MA, Chinese Lit Dept, Beijing Univ. Apointments: Lectr, Jinan Univ; Assoc Prof, Jinan Univ; Prof, Jinan Univ. Publications include: On Tao Yuanming, 1986; The History of Chinese Landscape Poetry, 1991; The Chinese Landscape Culture, 1996. Honours: Excellent Achievements in Social Science Research of Guangdong Prov, 1989, 1995; Spec Premium Cert, State Cncl of China, 1997. Memberships: Mngng Dir, Inst of Chinese Landscape and Travelling Lit, 1992-98. Hobbies: Cycling; Sightseeing. Address: Chinese Literature Department, Jinan University, Guangzhou, China.

LI Wen Ping, b. 23 Mar 1912, Hui-an, Fu-jian, China. Professor; Engineer. m. Jiang Pei-Yi, 3 Oct 1937, 1 s, 3 d. Education: BSCE Tangshan Univ, 1934; MSE 1936, PhD 1939, Univ Michigan, USA. Appointments: Stud Engr, Longbai Railrd, China, 1934; Engrng Observer, Pa Railrd, USA, 1935-36; Prof, Hunan Univ and Tangshan Coll and Asst Engr, Hunan, Kweichou Railrd, China, 1936-38; Assoc Engr, Engr, Supvsng Engr, 1938-43, India Hwy so called victory to Tokyo Stilwell Rd, 1944-45; CO, 1st Engrng, War Trans Bd and Prof Da-Sia Univ, 1946-53; Shanghai, Beijing and Chungqing Min Bldng Cnstrn Chief Engr Bur Mech, 1953-64; Min Bldng Materials Bur Cnstrn Materials, Chf Engr, 1965-86; Chinese People's Political and Consultative Conf 5th and 6th Sess, 1980-87; Retired. Publications: Co-auth, Co-transl, Principles and Practices of American Building Construction Management and Engineering; Modern Scientific Technology Dictionary; Encyclopedia; Construction Material Section. Honours: Army, Navy and Air Kuang Hwa 1st gr, Natl Mil Cncl; Medal of Freedom, US Pres Truman, 1946; Accomplishment in Reopening the supply arteries to China, 1945; Large Embroidery Banner presented by BRE SOS, US Forces in China; Medal of Victory over Jap; Pres of Chinese Govt, 1946; Outstndng Old Age Contbn, Chinese People's Gt Hall; Cert, 1989 Cert Outstndng Contbn in Engr Field, w life monthly Bonus, 1993. Memberships: China Soc of Civil Engrs, 1948; Amn Soc Explosive Engrs, 1981. Hobby: Playing Tennis. Address: 11 Bei Shun, Chen Jei 100035, China.

LI Wen-Ren, b. 30 May 1914. Cardio-Thoracic Surgeon. m. Pan Pei-Zhen, 2 Aug 1941, 4 d. Education: DMed w Hons, Obstets & Gynae, Peking Union Medl Coll, 1941. Appointments: Res in Surg, Peking Cntrl Hosp; Assoc Prof in Surg, San-Dong Univ Medl Coll; Dir,

Fuzhou Union Hosp; Dir, Fujian Provincial Hosp; Prof of Surg, VP, Fujian Medl Coll, Fuzhou, China; Fndr, Dir, Fujian Provincial Rsch Inst for Cardiovascular Diseases. Publications: Atlas of Cardiac Operation, 1982; Atlas of Coronary Bypass Operative Procedures, 1985; Pre and Post Operative Care of Cardiac Patients, 1986; Cardiac Surgery and Anaethesia, 1988. Honours: 2 Hons, Natl Cong on Sci, 1978; First Surg to dev technique of Transplantation of Transverse Colon to replace excised thoracic oesophagus for carcinoma, 1964; First Surg in Asia to construct hyperbaric chmbr for medl and surg use w clin application of it to save num pateitn's lives due to carbon monoxide poisoning and severe toxic shock; Dpty, 5th, 6th, 7th, 8th Chinese Natl People's Congress. Memberships: Snr Mbr, Chinese Medl Assn; Life, Intl Cong on Hyperbaric Med; Pres, XI Intl Cong on Hyperbaric Med; Chmn, Soc of Chinese Hyperbaric Med; Chmn, Soc of Cardio-Thoracic Surg, Fujian Prov. Address: Dept of Cardio Surgery, Fujian Prov Hosp, 134 East St, Fuzhou, Fujian 350001, China.

LI Xian Dong, b. 14 July 1938. Research Fellow. m. Wang Xin Hua, 1 Jan 1961, 2 s, 2 d. Education: Zhangjiakou Agricl Coll, 1958; Tianjin Corresp Inst, 1963. Appointments: Tchr, Apiculture, Shexian Co Forestry and Animal Husbandry Sch, 1958-62; Dir, and Rsch Fell in Shexian Co Agric and Forestry Bur, Hebei Province, 1962-70; Rsch Fell, Hebei Province Agric Inst, 1961-64; Dir Apiculture, Technol Cntr of Shanxi province, 1981-82; Dir of Agric Project surveying the nectar source in over 100 cos in Shanxi Province, 1982-; Dir, Yanguan Apiculture Inst, N China, 1988. Publications: Books: The Prevention and Treatment of Bee Diseases, 1981; Technology of the Science of Apiculture, 1982; Nectar Source in Shanxi Province, 1989; The Nectar Source in China and its Utilization, 1993; 10 Theses. Hobbies: Music; Calligraphy; Painting; Sports. Address: Yanguan Agricultural Institute, Shanxi, China.

LI Xilin, b. 23 Nov 1948, Dachuan, Sichuan, China. Professor of Conducting; Conductor. m. Luo Caiwen, 16 Jan 1970, 1 s. Education: MA Composition & Conducting, 1981, Shanghai Conservatory of Music. Appointments: Dir Composition and Conducting Dept, Sichuan Conservatory of Music. Creative Work: Rschd and Publd Saito Hideo's A Course of Conducting Pedagogy, 1993. Honours: 2nd Prize, 1986, 2nd Beijing Chorus Festival; 1st Prize, 1993, 1st China Children's Chorus Festival; Gold Prize, 1998, Chorus Compt for Old People. Memberships: Chinese Musicians Assn; Permanent Mbr, Chinese Chorus Assn; Dir, Sichuan Provincial Chorus Assn. Hobbies: Reading; Composing. Address: Sichuan Conservatory of Music, 6 Xinsheng Rd, Chengdu, Sichuan 610021, China.

LI Xinfu, b. 8 Jan 1935. Teacher; Researcher. m. Dai WanYing, 1 Jan 1961, 1 s, 1 d. Education: Dip of Chinese Dept, ShanDong Univ, 1959; Dip of Corresp Postgrad of ShanDong Univ, 1960. Appointments: Vice Rsch on Aesthetic, 1987; Ed of A Series of Works on Chinese Aesthetics, 1993; Prof, Confucius Correspondence of China. Publications: Dynamics of Aesthetics and Artistic Thinking, 1988; History of Human Thinking in Images, 1997; History of Category On Chinese Aesthetics, 1997; On the Maximum, 1997; A Discussion about the Values of Traditional Homonology, 1997; 122 acad thes inclng: Thinking in Images and Information Theory, 1983; A Brief Account of the Categorical of Chn Aesthetics, 1985-86; Aesthetic in Formation Patterns Three Worlds, 1994; On the Philosophical Reformation, 1995. Honours: Ex Reward of Socl Scis, 1983-85; Ex Reward, Educ Dept of Shandong Prov, 1986; Awd, 85 Sci Tecn of China. Membership: Aesthetic Assn of China, 1994. Listed in: Many Incl: Who's Who in the Present Age Culture in China; Who's Who in Social Sciences in China. Hobbies: Chinese Chess; Football; Table Tennis; Music; Calligraphy. Address: Institute of Education and Science Research, Qufu Teacher's University, Shandong, China.

LI Xue Yuan, b. Mar 1932. Professor. Appointments: Grad, Dept Soil Sci and Agrochem, Huazhong Agricl Univ, 1953. Appointments: Prof, Student Advsr, Hd of Soil Resource Utilization and Protection Rsch Div, Mbr, Acad Cttee and Acad Deg Cttee, Huazhong Agricl Univ; Dpty Dir Acad Cttee, Key Lab Subtropical Soil Resources and Environment, Chinese Min of Agric. Publications: Auth, Chf Ed or Coop Ed of 10 tech books and over 140 scientific papers in field of soil sci. Honours: Excellent Textbook Prize, Natl Educ Cttee; 2nd Grade Awd, Acady Sinica Natural Sci; Awds of Sci and Technol Adv, Min of Agric and Natl Educ Cttee; Title of Outstndng Tchr of Key Agricl Univs, Min of Agric, 1985; Natl Outstndng Tchr, 1991. Memberships: Cncl Mbr, CSSS; Pres and Stndng Cncl Mbr, Chinese Soil and Fertilizer Soc, Hubei Prov, China. Address: Huazhong Agricultural University, Wuhan, Hubei 430070, China.

LI Xueling, b. 28 May 1934. Chinese Specialist in Law and Arbitration. m. Tan Yaozi, 23 Jun 1956, 3 d. Education: Grad, Chinese People's Univ. Appointments: Cnslt, Law Cttee, Shenzhen Municipal People's Congress; Decision-Making Cnslt, Guangzhou Municipal Govt; Concurrent Lawyer of Guangdong Lingnan Law Off; Dir, Guangzhou Arbitration Cttee; Arbitrator, China Intl Econ and Trade Arbitration Commn; Prof, S China Sc and T Univ; Leading Person of Econ Law Sci; Instr of Postgrads; Prof; Chmn of Econ Law Tchng Off, Law Dept, Zhongshan Univ; Dir, Econ Law Rsch Cntr, People's Govt of Guangdong Prov. Publications: Books: Great Dictionary of International Trade Law, 1995; Economic Law Concerning Foreign Factors, 1990; Co-Author, Chinese Economic Law Encyclopaedia, 1992; Economic Law, 1993; Chinese Modern Economic Law; Forty-Year History of Guangdong Social Science 1989; Law of Special Economic Zones, 1997; Numerous Creative Compositions. Honours: Conferred title of Specialist w Gt Contrbn, PRC's State Cncl; Awd'd Prize of Excellent Book of Guangdong Prov and Prize of Excellent Textbook of Zhongshan Univ for Economic Law Concerning Foreign Factors, 1990; 1st Class Awd of Guangdong Legal Sci Assn, 1988; 2nd Class Awd of Socl Sci Achievements of Guangdong Prov, 1990; 2nd Class Awd of Guangdong Ind and Com Assn, 1989; 2nd Class Awd, Natl Dictionary Awd, 1997. Memberships: Dir, Chinese Labour Law Assn, 1983-; Dir, Chinese Econ Law Assn, 1984-; Dir, Guangdong Socl Sci Assn, 1984-; Dir and Mbr of Editing Cttee of Academic Rsch, 1984. Listed in: Who's Who of Intellectuals. Hobbies: Collecting Books; Literature. Address: Law Department, Zhongshan University, Guangzhou 510275, China.

LI Yi, b. 26 Mar 1958, Sichuan, China. Education. m. Mai Wong, 3 s. Education: BSc; MSc; PhD; MBA. Appointments: Lectr, Rsch Sci, Snr Rsch Sci, Assoc Prof. Publication: The Science of Clothing Comfort, 1999; More than 100 rsch pprs. Honours: ORS Schlsp; Tetley & Lupton Schlsp. Memberships: ATI; FTI; LFIBA; Fiber Soc. Hobbies: Sport; Entertainment. Address: 15G, Block 9, Site 9, Whampoa Garden, Hung Hom, Hong Kong.

LI Yong, b. 8 Dec 1959. College Teacher (Assistant Professor). m. Dou Hua, 1 d. Education: BS, 1982; Master degree of Palaeontology, 1989; Currently reading for PhD, Dept of Geol, Northwest Univ. Appointment: Tchr, Dept of Geol, Xian Coll of Geol, 1982. Publications: Over 30 rsch pprs, books inclng: Sinian Miaohe Biota, 1996; Discussion about classification and nomenclature of Trace Fossils, 1996; Sponge Spicule Fossils from the Lowest Cambrian, 1993. Honours: 3rd Class Prize, Min, Advmt of Sci and Technol of Geol and Minerals. Memberships: Paleontology Assn of China; Sec Gen, Palaeontology Assn of Shaan Xi Prov. Hobby: Fishing. Address: Department of Geology, Xian Engineering University, No 6, Yanta Road, Xian City, China.

LI Yu, b. 15 Apr 1961, Beijing, China. Oncology. Education: PhD. Publication: (co-auth) The LEc Rat. Honours: Awd, Japanese Cancer Assn, 1992; Awd of Hokkaido Medl Assn, 1992. Memberships: Japan Surg Soc, 1987-; Japanese Cancer Assn, 1988-; Japanese Assn of Hepatology, 1988-. Address: Wakasa 19-1, Saroma, Hokkaido 091, Japan.

LI Yuanchao, b. 1950, Lianshui, Jiangsu, China. Politician. Education: Shanghai Fudan Univ. Appointments: Joined CCP, 1978; Sec, Communist Youth League, 1983; Sec, Shanghai Br of the Communist Youth League, 1983; Dir, Natl Cttee for Yng Pioneers, Communist Youth League, 1984; Vice-Chair, Youth Fedn, 1986-; Dpty Dir, 1st Bur, Info Off, 1993-, Ctrl Off for Overseas Publicity, 1994-; Vice Min, Info Off, State Cncl, 1993-96, of Culture, 1996-; Vice Chair, Women & Youth Cttee. Address: Central Committee, Communist Youth League of China, Beijing, China.

LI Yude, b. 2 May 1962, Shehong County, Sichuan Prov, China. Engineer. m. Min Hong, 18 Aug 1988, 1 d. Education: MS. Appointments: Asst Engr, 1985-88; Engr, 1989-94; Snr Engr, 1995-. Creative Works: Engineering Fracture Mechanics; Intl Jrnl of PVP. Honours: Grade 1 Reasonable Suggestion and Sci Retrofit Awd; Grade 3 Sci Awd. Memberships: NY Acady Sci; Amn Assn for the Advmnt of Sci. Address: 80 Xing Qing Street, Xian 710032, China.

LI Yufen, b. 11 Feb 1928, Shanghai, China. Teacher. m. Zhang Liquan, June 1955, 2 s. Education: Bach, Jiaotong Univ, Shanghai, China, 1950. Appointments: Asst Prof, Dept Chem, Jiaotong Univ, 1950-52; Asst Prof, Lectr, Dept Chem, Fudan Univ, 1952-60; Lectr, Assoc Prof, Nuclr Sci Dept, Fudan Univ, 1960-70; Assoc Prof, Prof, Dept Phys, Fudan Univ, 1970-. Publications: More than 80 pprs publs in sci jrnls in fields of chem & phys. Honours: Natl Invention Awd, 1984; Outstndng Achievement in Sci & Technol, 1984; Progress in Sci & Technol Awds, 1986, 1994. Address: Department Physics, Fudan University, Shanghai 200433, China.

LI Yun Wei, b. 10 Mar 1930. Professor. m. 29 Apr 1930, 1 s, 3 d. Education: Grad, Hua Zhong Coll of Agric. Appointments: Chg, Forest Protection Grp, Comprehensive Survey Team, Min of Forestry, 1954-58; Chf, Disease and Insect Pest Control Rsch Grp, Fujian Rsch Inst of Forestry, 1959-77; Dir, Forest Protection Rsch Sect, Engr, Snr Engr, 1978-91. Publications: Over 30 pprs. Creative Works: Took pt in compiling: The Study, Production and Application of Beauveria bassiana; Forest Insects in Fujian; The Forestry Volume of the Large Chinese Encyclopaedia; Forests in Fugian; Study and Application of Entomogenous Fungi in China; The Comprehensive Management of Dendrolimus Punctatus. Honours: Natl Sci Congress Awd, Prov Sci and Tech Achievement Awd, 1978; Natl Sci Cttee and Agricl Cttee Sci and Tech Popularization Awd, 1982; 2nd Awd,Sci and Tech Progress, Min of Forestry, 1987; 3rd Awd, Comprehensive Sci Observation of Wuyishan Natural Reserve, Prov Sci Cttee, 1989; 1st Awd, 6th Session Natl Fine Sci and Tech Books, 1994. Memberships: Bd Mbr, Forest Entomological Soc, CSF; Stndng Mbr, Fujian Soc of Forestry; Stndng Mbr, Fujian Soc of Ecol; Mbr, Major Cttee Forest Entomol, Chinese Forestry Assn; Stndng Cncl Mbr and Dir Major Cttee, Forest Protection, Fujian Forestry Assn. Hobby: Stamp Collecting. Address: Fujian Research Institute of Forestry Science, Xidian, Fuzhou, Fujian 350012, China.

LI Zaiting, b. 15 Sept 1933, Shanghai, China. Petroleum Refining. m. Weiping Wu, 1956, 1 s, 1 d. Education: Grad, Chem Engrng, Qinghua Univ, 1956. Appointments: Grp Ldr, 1960-83, Tech Dir, 1984-88, Dir, 1989-93, Ed-in-Chf, 1994-, Rsch Inst of Petroleum Processing. Publications include: Novel Catalytic Process for Maximum Light Olefins Production, 1994; Growth of Industrial Units Marks DCC Advance, 1995; Petrochemical Extension of FCC, 1996; Deep Catalytic Cracking for Light Olefins, 1996. Honours: Outstndng Contbrn Ctf, State Cncl of China, 1990; Gold Prize, Natl Patent Off, China, 1991; Special Prize, 1st Prize, Sci & Technol, China Petrochem Corp, 1992; 1st Invention Prize, Natl Sci & Technol Cttee, China, 1995. Memberships: FCC; Petroleum Processing & Petrochems. Hobby: Music. Address: PO Box 914, Beijing 100083, China.

LI Zhao Jie, b. 28 Aug 1955, Changchun, Jilin, China. International Law. m. Shuxuan Xu, 5 Sept 1985. Education: LLB; LLM; MLIS; SJD. Appointments: Prof of Intl Law; Co-Ed-in-Chf, Chinese Yrbook of Intl Law; Dir, Cntr for Intl Legal Materials & Documents. Publications:

Sev articles in profl jrnls. Memberships: Chinese Soc of Intl Law; Am Soc of Intl Law. Hobbies: Photography; Classical Music; Computers. Address: International Law Institute, Peking University, Beijing 100871, China.

LI Zhi Shan, b. 19 Sept 1933, Zhen Jiang, Jiangsu, China. Cardiologist. m. Z Y Lin, 24 Sept 1961, 1 s, 1 d. Eduction: Grad, Fac of Med, Shanghai First Med Coll, 1959. Appointments: PUMC Hosp, CAMS, PUMC, Beijing, 1959-72; Zhong Shan Hosp, Shanghai Med Univ, 1973-. Publications: Arrhythmias, 1986; Antianginal Agents and Inotropic Agents, 1990. Honours: State and Min of Pub Hlth Awd, Progress of Sci & Technol, 1991. Memberships: Soc of Cardiol; Chinese Med Assn; Chinese Pharmacol Assn; Chinese Clin Pharmacol Soc; Shanghai Bd of ADR Monitoring. Hobby: Light Music. Address: Department of Cardiology, Zhong Shan Hospital, Shanghai Medical University, 180 Feng Lin Road, Shanghai 200032, China.

LI Zhishen, b. 21 Nov 1935, Weiyuan, Sichuan Prov, China. Teacher; Professor. m. Jinglin Zhan, 1 May 1966, 2 d. Education: BS, Maths, Lanzhou Univ, China, 1957. Appointments: Tchng Asst, 1957-77; Lectr, 1978-84; Assoc Prof, 1985-89, Prof, 1990-, Maths Dept, Lanzhou Univ. Publications: Equations of Mathematical Physics, Vol I, 1986, Vol II, 1987; Comments in Maths Reviews, num articles. Honours: 1st Awd in Achievements in Sci and Technol, Higher Educ, 1985; 2nd Awd in Achievements in Sci and Technol, Chinese Supvsry Bur on Technol, 1989. Membership: Chinese Techl Cttee for Standardization of Quantities and Units, Chmn, 7th Br Cttee. Hobbies: Travel; Sport. Listed in: Who's Who in the World. Address: Mathematics Department, Lanzhou University, Lanzhou 730000, China.

LI Zhong Lian, b. 11 May 1938, Feng Ren, Hebei, China. Professor. m. Li Zhou, 1 Feb 1965, 1 s, 1 d. Education: Grad, Tchr Trng Univ, Hebei, 1961. Appointments: Asst, 1961-78; Lectr, 1978-87; Assoc Prof, 1987-94; Prof, 1998-. Publication: Probability and Statistics, 1987. Honours: Sci and Technological Progress Awd, Bank of China, 1995; Tianjin; Beijing. Memberships: Soc for Indl and Applied Maths. Hobbies: Classical Music; Bring up Flowers. Address: Dept of Economic Information and Management, Inst of Finance and Banking of China, #10 Xui Xin Dong Jie, Chaoyang Dist, Beijing, China.

LI Zhongying, b. 5 Oct 1943, Wuxi, Jiangsu Prov, China. Nuclear Physicist. m. Jingyang Zhang, 1 Feb 1970, decd 1983, 1 s, 1 d. m. Kegin Shi, 29 Dec 1992. Education: BS, Nanjing Univ, China, 1966. Appointments: Rschr, Inst of Nuclear Phys and Chem (INPC), China Acady of Engrng Phys (CAEP), 1968-88; Prof, INPC, CAEP, 1989-; Dir, Ionizing Radiation Measurement Lab, INPC, CAEP, 1993-; Dpty Dir Gen, IBC, 1999. Publications: Over 20 pprs in sci publs; 2 awarded Major Sci Academic Achievements of for Chinese, Intl Econ Estimate (HK) Cntr, 1999. Honours: Natl Def Gt Achievement Awd, Sci and Technol, 1983; Scis and Technol Advmnt Awd, China Natl Nuclear Corp, 1986; Scis and Technol Advmnt Awd, Sci and Indl Commn of the Natl Def, 1992, 1995; Sci Fnd Awd, China Acady of Engrng Phys, 1994; Outstndng People of the 20th Century, IBC, 1998; Gold Awd of 2000 Outstndng People of 20th Century, IBC, 1999; ABI Rsch Bd of Advsrs, 1999. Memberships: NY Acady of Scis, 1996-; AAAS, 1996-97; Intl Radiation Phys Soc, 1997-. Address: PO Box 919-215, Mianyang, Sichuan 62190, China.

LI Zhou, b. 22 Apr 1936, Hebei, China. Professor. m. Zhong-Lian, 1 Feb 1965, 1 s, 1 d. Education: Grad, Tsinghua Univ. Appointments: Asst, 1960; Lectr, 1978; Assoc Prof, 1986; Prof, 1992-. Creative Works: Liquid Extraction Process and Equipment; Handbook of Chemical Engineering; Extraction and Leaching. Honours: Awd of Ex Book; Sci and Technol of Chem Engrng Awds. Memberships: Nuc Chem Engrng Assn of China; Non-Ferrous Metals Assn of China; Bioengrng Assn of China. Hobbies: Sports; Listening to Classical Music. Address: Department of Chemical Engineering, Tsinghua University, Beijing 100084, China.

LI Zhunyi, b. 3 Oct 1927, Wangqing Co, Jilin Prov, China. Professor of Medicine. Education: Grad, Yanbian Univ; Worked in Yanbian Medl Coll Branch Coll. Career: Tchr, Tradl Chinese Med tchng and clin, over 40 yrs; Treated wide var of illness inclng, 1 case prostatic carcinoma late period patient, 1994; 1 of acute coronary heart disease in Seoul, Korea. Publications: 1 thesis in Japan Tokyo No 6th Intl East Asia Medl Seminar and Korea Seoul No 8 Intl East Asia Medl Seminar. Honours: Good Tchr, Jilin Prov; Sci & Technol Hon Cert, State Labour & Personnel Min. Excellent Result No 1 Prize, China Spec Drugs Pang Ashi Med King Cup; Med King Prize, Hong Kong; World Sci & Technol Cnslt Expert, China Spec Drugs; Golden Book, Ed, Cttee Mbr, China Jiuyang Intl Publng House Supvsr. Membership: Yanbian Medl Coll Branch. Address: 133000 Jilin Province, Yanbian Hygiene School Safety Department, Li Yuanzhi, China.

LIANG Xiao-Tian, b. 28 July 1923, Wu-Yang Co, Henan, China. Professor. m. Xiu-Zhang Yang, 1947, 1 d. Education: BSc, Chem Engrng, Natl Cntrl Univ, Chonqing, 1946; PhD, Organic Chem, Univ of WA at Seattle, USA, 1952. Appointments: Postdoct Fell, Chem Dep, Harvard Univ, 1952-54; Beijing Inst of Materia Medica, 1955-; Guest Prof, Peking Univ & Lanzhou Univ; Ed-in-Chf, Chinese Cheml Letters; Cnltng Ed, 4 Tetrahedron Jrnls; Pres, Chinese Chem Soc, 1991. Honour: Fell, Academia Sinica, Chem Div, 1980. Address: Institute of Materia Medica, Nan-wei Road, Beijing 100050, China.

LIANG Yingming, b. 28 May 1931, Indonesia. Professor. m. Yao Chaozhen, 31 Jan 1960, 2 d. Education: BA, Hist Dept, Peking Univ, 1960. Appointments: Lectr, 1978-84, Assoc Prof, 1985-89, Prof, 1990-, Inst of Afro-Asian Stdies, Peking Univ. Publications: Dictionary of Overseas Chinese, 1993; Modern History of Southeast Asia, 1994; The Chinese in Southeast Asia in Postwar Period, 1999. Honours: Acad Awd, Best Publn, Peking Univ, 1993, 1994. Memberships: Cttee, Cntr for Asia-Pacific Stdies, Peking Univ; Standing Cttee, Soc of Overseas Chinese Hist Stdies. Hobbies: Classical Music; Badminton. Address: c/o Institute of Afro-Asian Studies, Peking University, Beijing, China.

LIANG Yuerong, b. 5 Sept 1957, Guangxi, China. Professor. m. 25 Dec 1986, 1 d. Education: BSc 1982, MSc 1985, Zhejian Agric Univ. Appointments: Sch Tchr, Guangxi, 1974-78; Tchng Asst 1985-87, Lectr 1987-90, Zhejian Agric Univ; Visng Schlr, Unilever Rsch, Eng, 1990-91; Assoc Prof 1991, Chmn, 1994, Dept Chmn 1995, Prof, 1996, Dept of Tea Sci, Zhejiang Agric Univ; Mbr, Polit Consultation Cttee, Zheijiang Prov, 1997-. Publications: Var articles in profl jrnls; Tea Biology, 1995; All About Tea, 1995; Ed-in-Chf, Jrnl of Tea, 1998-. Honours: 3rd Prize, Ex Thes, Zhejian Sci and Technol Assn, 1987; Ex Thesis Awd, Zhejiang Tea Assn, 1987, 1988; 1st Prize and 2nd Prize, Tea Zhejian Tea Assn, 1987, 1989; Awds for Ex Young Sci of Zhejiang Prov, 1992; 1st Prize and 2nd Prize of Ex Thes, Zhejiang Assn of Sci Technol, 1992, 1993, 1994; Awds for Ex Achievements of Sci and Technol, Zhejiang Agric Univ, 1992, 1993. Memberships: Chinese Agronomists Assn; Chinese Tea Assn; Mbr Stndng Cttee, Chinese Teaman Friendship Assn, 1995-; Sec-Gen, Tea Sci Soc, Zhejiang Prov, 1997-. Hobbies: Photography; Cycling. Address: Department of Tea Science, Zhejiang Agricultural University, Hangzhou 310029, China.

LIAO Changyong, b. 25 Oct 1968, Si Chuan Province, China. Teacher of Voice. m. Jia Wang, 10 Nov 1995. Education: Master Deg, Voice. Appointments: Voice Tchr, Shanghai Conservatory of Musc; Guest Baritone, Shanghai Opera House. Creative Works: Performances worldwide. Honours: Ex Prize, Voice of Pacific Natl Comp, 1992; 2nd Prize, Asia Intl Singing Comp, 1992; Golden Prize, Spring Apr Art Fest, Korea, 1993; 1st Place, Spring Magnolia Songs & Singer Comp, 1993; 1st Prize, French Song, 20th Paris Intl Singing Comp, France, 1994; 1st Prize, Natl Audition for the Intl Singing Comp, 1995; 1st Prize, 41 French Intl Toulouse Singing

Comp, 1996; 1st Prize, 97 World Opera Contest Placido Domingo, 1997; 1st Prize, The Queen Soja Intl Music Comp, 1997. Hobby: Sports. Address: 20 Feng Yang Road, Shanghai Conservatory of Music, Shanghai 200031, China.

LIAO Jiqiao, b. 25 Apr 1970, Hunan, China. Powder Metallurgy. m. Zhou Zijun, 1 Jan 1995, 1 s. Education: Master of Powder Metallurgy. Appointments: Vice Dir, 1993, Off Dir, 1995, State Cntr of Quality Supvsn and Testing, P/M Products; Dir, 5th Dept of Powder Metallurgy Rsch Inst, 1997. Publication: Standard Powder Metallurgy Vocabulary, 1997. Membership: Hunan Prov Standard Assn. Hobby: Swimming. Address: c/o Powder Metallurgy Research Institute, Central South University of Technology, Changsha, Hunan 410083, China.

LIAO Shutsung, b. 1 Jan 1931, Tainan, Taiwan. Biochemist. m. Shuching Liao, 19 Mar 1960, 4 c. Education: BS Agricl Chem, Natl Taiwan Univ, 1953; MS Biochem, 1956; PhD in Biochem, Univ Chgo, 1961. Appointments: Rsch Assoc, 1960-63; Asst Prof, 1964-69; Assoc Prof, 1969-71; Prof, 1972-, Dept Biochem and Molecular Biol Ben May Inst for Cancer Rsch, Univ Chgo, 1972-2-; Cnslt to var natl and intl confs, agcys, fndns and workshops. Publications: Mbr, Edtl Bd Jrnl Steroid Biochemistry and Molecular Biology, The Prostate and Receptors; Assoc Ed, Cancer Research, 1982-89; Contbr, over 200 articles to profl jrnls. Honours: NIH Grantee, 1962-; Amn Cancer Soc Grantee, 1971-81; Recip, Sci-Technol Achievement Prize, Taiwanese-Amn Fndn, 1983; Pfizer Lect Fell Awd, Clin Rsch Inst, Montreal, 1972; Gregory Pincus Medal and Awd, Worcester Fndn for Exptl Biol, 1992; Tzongming Tu Awd Formosan Med Assn, 1993; C H Li Mem Lect Awd, 1994. Memberships: Mbr, Amn Soc Biochem and Molecular Biol; Amn Assn Cancer Rsch; Endocrine Soc; N Amn Taiwanese Profs Assn, Pres, 1980-81, Exec Dir, 1981-; Advsry Cttee, Taiwan-US Cultural Ex Cntr, 1984-; Fell, Amn Acady Arts and Scis, 1997-; Acad achievements include Discovery of Androgen Activation Mechanism and Androgen Receptors; Cloning and Structural Determination of Androgen Receptors and other Novel Nuclear Receptors and Their Genes and Receptor Gene Mutation to Hereditary Abnormalities and Cancers; Cancer Prevention and Suppression. Address: University of Chicago, Ben May Institute for Cancer Research, 5841 S Maryland Avenue, Chicago, IL 60637-1463, USA.

LIAO SuSu, b. 8 Aug 1955, Beijing, China. Professor. m. Mr Jing-yang Bai, 30 Dec 1985, 1 d. Education: MD, Beijing Medl Univ, China, 1986; PhD, Peking Union Medl Coll, Beijing, 1991. Appointments: Nurse, Peking Union Medl Coll Hosp, 1977-80; Lectr, Assoc Prof, Full prof, Peking Union Medl Coll, 1991-. Membership: Natl Advsry Cttee on STD & AIDS, 1998. Hobbies: Reading; Collecting stamps. Address: 5 Dong Dan San Tiao, Beijing 10005, China.

LIAQATH D M, b. 6 Jan 1950, Chikballapur. Development Work. m. Frahat Begum, 3 s. Education: Dip in Rural Dev Mngmt. Appointments: Served sev orgns in var capacities. Publications: chf Ed, non-formal educ jrnl. Memberships: Chmn, Farmers Dev Agcy; Life Mbr, Indian Inst of Pub Admin. Hobbies: Social work; Letter writing; Football.

LIBAI David, b. 1934, Tel Aviv, Israel. Politician; Lawyer. Education: Chgo Univ, USA. Appointments: Hd, Israel Bar Assn; Dpty Atty-Gen; Dir, Inst of Criminol & Criminal Law, Tel Aviv Univ, Dean of Students; Chair, Labour Party Constitution Cttee; Chair, Israel-Brit Parl Friendship Assn; Chair, Pub Audit (Control) Cttee, 1984-92; Spokesman, Min of Justice, 1992-96; Fmr Mbr, Natl Comm of Inquiry on Prison Conditions, Press Cncl, Knesset, 1984-. Publications: Num articles in legal jrnls. Address: Knesset, Jerusalem, Israel.

LIDBURY Brett Andrew, b. 23 Nov 1963, Waratah, NSW, Aust. University Lecturer. Education: BSc, 1989; BSc (Hons), 1990; PhD, 1993. Appointments: Rsch Scientist, 1994-95; Postdoct Fell, 1995-96; Univ Lectr, 1996-. Publications: Num jrnl articles in refereed sci jrnls,

1993-; Memberships: Australasian Soc of Immunology, 1989-; NY Acady Sci, 1995-97. Hobbies: Dancing; Music (guitar/mandolin); Golf. Address: School of Human & Biomedical Science, Division of Science and Design, University of Canberra, ACT 2601, Australia.

LIEBIG Phoebe S, b. 28 Dec 1933, Cambridge, Massachusetts, USA. University Professor. m. A E Liebig, 19 June 1954, div, 1 s. Education: BA, MA, UCLA; PhD, Univ Southern California. Appointments: Rsch Asst Prof; Snr Policy Analyst; Asst Prof; Assoc Prof. Publications: Co-auth: California Policy Choices for Long Term Care, 1990; Housing Frail Elders: International Perspectives, Policies and Programs, 1995. Honours: Hansen Family Asst Prof; Fell, Gerontol Soc of Am; Fulbright to India, 1997-98. Memberships: Am Soc on Aging, Sec, 1982; Gerontol Soc of Am, SRPP Cttee; Assn for Gerontol in Higher Educ, Exec Cttee 1990-93. Hobbies: Gardening; Choral singing; Reading; Travel. Address: Andrus Gerontology Centre, University of Southern California, Los Angeles, CA 90089-0191, USA.

LIEBLICH Steve, b. 15 May 1950, Tel Aviv, Israel. Engineer. m. 1980, 2 s, 1 d. Education: BE (Hons); MSc. Appointments: Electrical Engr, Austl Iron and Steel, Port Kembla, NSW, 1971-73; Sales Engr, Snr Sales Engr, Proj Mngr, Sales Mngr, Indl Automation Systems and Control Prods, Honeywell Ltd, Perth, West Aust, 1978-82; Snr Elecl Engr, Elecl and Instrumentation, Fluor Aust Pty Ltd, Perth, West Aust, 1982-83; Acct Exec, Indl Automation Systems, 1983-85, Branch Mngr, Com Div, 1986-89, WA Sales/Mktng Mngr, Indl Automation and Control, 1989-95, Honeywell Ltd, Perth, West Aust; Bus Dev Mngr, Motherwell Systems Pty Ltd, 1995-. Memberships: Instn of Engrs Aust, 1980-, West Austl Div Elecl Engrng Branch Cttee, 1985-98, Natl Cttee for Automation, Control and Instrumentation, 1987-98; Inst of Instrumentation and Control Aust, 1980-; Pet Club of West Aust, 1985-. Address: 49 Woodsome Street, Mt Lawley, Western Australia 6050, Australia.

LIEN Chan, b. 27 Aug 1936, Sian, Shansi, Taiwan. Politician. m. Yui Fang, 2 s, 2 d. Education: Natl Taiwan Univ; Univ Chgo, USA. Appointments: Assoc Prof, 1968-69, Prof, Chair, Dept of Polit Scis, Dir, Grad Inst of Polit Sci, Natl Taiwan Univ; Amb to El Salvador, 1975-76; Dir, Dept of Youth Affairs, Ctrl Cttee, Kuomintang, 1976-78, Mbr, Ctrl Standing Cttee, 1983-; Chair, Natl Youth Comm, Exec, Yuan, 1978-81; Min of Commns, 1981-87; Vice-Premier, 1987-88; Min of Fgn Affairs, 1989-90; Gov, Taiwan Prov Govt, 1990-93; Premier of Taiwan, 1993-97; VP of Taiwan, 1997-. Publications: The Foundation of Democracy; Taiwan in China's External Relations; Western Political Thought. Membership: Pres, Chinese Assn of Polit Sci, 1979-82. Hobbies: Golf; Swimming; Music. Address: Office of the President, Chiehshou Hall, 122 Chungking South Road, Sector 1, Taipei 100, Taiwan.

LIEU Samuel Nan Chiang, b. 4 Mar 1950. Professor. m. Judith Margaret Bending, 24 July 1976, 1 d. Education: BA (Cantab), 1971; MA, 1977; DPhil (Oxford), 1981, Emmanuel Coll, Cambridge, 1969-723; Queen's Coll, Oxford, 1973-74; Wolfson Coll, Oxford, 1974-81. Appointments: Jnr Rsch Fell, Wolfson Coll, Oxford, 1974-76; Lectr, 1976-89, Snr Lectr, 1989-92, Reader, 1992-94, Prof of Ancient Hist, 1994-95, Warwick Univ, Eng, 1996-; Prof of Ancient Hist, Macquarie Univ, NSW, Aust; Co-Dir, UNESCO sponsored Intl Corpus Fontium Manichaeorum Proj, 1991-; Co-Dir, Ancient Hist Documentary Rsch Cntre, Macquarie Univ, 1997-. Publications: The Religion of Light, 1979; Manichaeism in the Later Roman Empire and Medieval China, A Historical Survey, 1985, 1992; The Emperor Julian: Panegyric and Polemi (Mamertinus, Chrysostom and Ephrem Syrus on Julian, 1986; The Roman Eastern Frontier and the Persian Wars, 1991, 1994; Manichaesim in Mesoptamia and the Roman East, Religions in the Graeco-Roman World 118, 1994; From Constantine to Julian: Pagan and Byzantine Views, 1996; Manichaeism in Central Asia and China, 1998; Constantine - Historiography and Legend, 1998; Dictionary of Manichaean Texts, Vol I , 1998. Memberships: Roy Overseas Mbr, Roy Overseas League, London; Fell, Roy Asiatic Soc, 1981-; Fell, Roy Histl Soc, 1983-; Fell, Soc of Antiquaries, 1989-; Fell, Austl Acady of the Hums. Hobbies: Walking; Cycling; Music. Address: Department of Ancient History, Macquarie University, Sydney NSW 2109, Australia.

LIEW Geok Heok, b. 15 Mar 1953, Singapore. Advocate; Solicitor. Education: LLB, Hons, Univ of Singapore. Appointments: Cmmnr for Oaths; Notary Pub. Publications: Men, Women & Violence; Voices & Choices, History of Singapore's Women's Movement; Women's Inspirations . Memberships: Law Soc; Singapore Acady of Law; Medico Legal Soc; Crescent Girls Sch Alumni Assn; Old Rafflesian Assn; Univ Womens Assn, Singapore; Singapore Nature Soc; Soroptimist Intl; Quota Intl; Singapore Assn of Womens Lawyers. Hobbies: Travel; Aquarium fish rearing; Music; Reading; Gardening. Address: 5001 Beach Road, #03-54 Golden Mile Complex, Singapore 199588, Singapore.

LIFVON Guo, b. Taiwan. Singer. m. Appointments: Cowherd; Performs Folk Songs & Folk Chants mixed w mod dance beats; Toured Switz, France, Germany, Netherlands, Italy, 1987. Creative Works: Albums incl: Return to Innocence; Cross of Changes. Address: Taitung, Taiwan.

LILLEE Dennis Keith, b. 18 July 1949, Perth, Australia. Cricketer. m. Helen Lillee, 1970, 2 s. Appointments: Right-Arm Fast Bowler, Lower Order Right-Hand Batsman; Played for WA, 1969-84, Tas, 1987-88, Northants, 1988; 70 Tests for Aust, 1970-84, Taking Then World Record 355 Wickets (Average 23.9), incl Record 167 Wickets in 29 Tests Against England; Toured England, 1972, 1975, 1980, 1981, 1983 (World Cup), Took 882 1st-Class Wickets. Publications: Back to the Mark, 1974; The Art of Fast Bowling, 1977; Dennis Lillee's Book of Family Fitness, 1980; My Life in Cricket, 1982; Over and Out, 1984. Address: c/o WACA, WACA Ground, Nelson Crescent, East Perth, WA 6000, Australia.

LILLIE Mildred L. Education: AB, 1935, JD, Boalt Hall of Law, 1938, Univ of CA, Berkeley; State Bar of CA, 1938; Fedl Crt, 1942; US Supreme Crt, 1961. Appointments: Cty Atty's Off, Alameda, CA, 1938-39; Priv prac, Fresno, CA, 1939-42; Asst US Atty, US Dept of Justice, US Atty, South District of CA, 1942-46; Priv prac, Los Angeles, 1946-47; Judge, Municipal Crt, Cty of Los Angeles, 1947-49; Judge, Superior Crt, County of Los Angeles, 1949-58; Assoc Justice, Crt of Appeal, Div One, 2nd Appellate District, 1958-84; Judicial Cncl, Satte of CA, mbr, 1961-63, 1987-89; Presiding Justice, Crt of Appeal, Div Seven, 2nd Appellate District, 1984-. Honour: LA Alumni Chapt, Phi Alpha Delta Law Fraternity. Memberships: Los Angeles Bar Assn; Amn Bar Assn; Fed Bar Assn; CA Judges Assn; Women Lawyers Assn of Los Angeles; Natl Assn of Women Judges; Pepperdine Univ Sch of Law Bd of Vis; Pepperdine Univ Assocs, Pepperdine Univ; Bd of Trustees for the Boalt Hall Fund; Boalt Hall Alumni Assn; Soroptomist Intl of Los Angeles; Ebell Club; Les Dames of Los Angeles.

LIM Hng Kiang, b. 9 Apr 1954. Minister for National Development; Second Minister for Finance. m. Lee Ai Boon, 2 s. Education: Pres's Schlshp, 1973; Singapore Armed Forces Schlshp, Engrng, Cambridge Univ, Eng, Grad, 1st Class Hons, (Distinction), 1976; Schlshp, Postgrad Stdies, Mason Fell, Kennedy Sch, Harv Univ, Master Pub Admin. Appointments: 9 Yrs, Singapore Armed Forces, Cmnd and Staff Appts; Hd, Air Plans Dept, Singapore Air Force; Min of Def, 1986; Dpty Sec, Min of Natl Dev, 1987; Chf Exec Offr, Housing and Dev Bd, 1991; Returned to Parl, 1991; Min of State for Natl Dev, 1991; Acting Min for Natl Dev, Snr Min of State and For Affairs, 1994; Min for Natl Dev and 2nd Min For Affairs, 1995; Re-elected, 1997; Min of Natl Dev, 2nd Min For Affairs, 1997; 2nd Min Fin, 1998. Memberships: Nanyang Technological Inst Cncl; Mass Rapid Transit Corp Bd; Chmn, Natl Yth Cncl; People's Assn Bd. Hobbies: Swimming; Golf.

LIM Keng Yaik Dato, b. 8 Apr 1939, Tapah, Perak, Malaysia. Politician. m. Wong Yoon Chuan, 3 children. Education: Queens Univ, Belfast. Appointments: Senator, 1972-78; Min w Specl Functions, 1972-73, of Primary Ind, 1986-; Mbr, State Exec Cncl, Perak, 1978-86; Mbr, Parl, 1986-. Membership: Pres, Gerakan, 1980-. Address: Ministry of Primary Industries, 6th-8th Floors, Menara Daya Bumi, Jalan Sultan Hishamuddin, 50654 Kuala Lumpur, Malaysia.

LIM Kim San, b. 30 Nov 1916, Singapore. Politician. m. Pang Gek Kim, 1939, 2 s, 4 d. Education: Anglo-Chinese Sch; Raffles Coll, Singapore. Appointments: Dir, United Chinese Bank Ltd, Chair, Batu Pahat Bank Ltd & Pacific Bank Ltd, 1940-; Mbr, Dpty Chair, Pub Serv Comm, Singapore, 1959-63; Chair, Housing Devel Bd, 1960-63; Dpty Chair, Econ Devel Bd, 1961-63; Min for Natl Devel, 1963-65, for Fin, 1965-67, for the Interior & Def, 1967-70, for Educn, 1970-72, for the Environ, 1972-75, 1979-81, of Natl Devel, 1975-79, for Commns, 1975-78; Acting Pres, 1989; Chair, Cncl of Presl Advsrs, 1992-. Honours: Darjah Utama Temasek, 1962; Ramon Magsaysay Awd, Cmty Ldrshp, 1965. Memberships include: Bd Trustee, Consumers Co-op Ltd; Dewan Ra'ayat. Hobby: Golf. Address: Singapore Press Holdings Ltd, New Centre, 82 Genting Lane, Singapore 349567, Singapore.

LIM Kyung Ho, b. 26 Jan 1940. Ex-Governmental Official. m. 23 Jan 1970, 3 d. Education: PhD Pub Admnin, Dankook Univ, 1987. Appointments: May, Songnam City and Puchon City, 1983-87; Dpty May, Taegu City, 1987; V Gov, N Kyongsang Prov, 1988; Insp Gen, Min of Home Affairs, 1988; Dir Gen, Local Admin Trng Inst, Min of Home Affairs, 1992; Asst Min, Min of Home Affairs, 1993; Gov, Kyonggi Prov, 1994; Pres, Kyonggi Dev Inst, 1995; Pres, Korea Rsch Inst for Local Admin, 1996-; Pres, Rsch Inst of Local Cncls, 1998. Publications: Local Council, 1991. Honour: Order of Serv Merit, Green Stripes, 1977. Membership: Korean Assn for Policy Studies, 1992. Hobby: Mountain climbing. Address: 1-402 Chinhung Apt, Samsong-dong, Kangnam-gu, Seoul, Korea.

LIM Pin, b. 12 Jan 1936, Penang. Vice Chancellor. m. Shirley, 21 Mar 1964, 2 s, 1 d. Education: MBBChir, Cambridge; MA; MD; FRCP, London; FRCPE; FRACP; FACP. Appointments: Registrar, Diabetic Dept, Kings Coll Hosp, London, 1965; Med Offr, Min of Hlth, Singapore, 1965-66; Lectr in Med, Univ of Singapore, 1966-70; C'wlth Med Fell, Dept of Med, Roy Infirmary, Edinburgh, 1970; Snr Lectr in Med, Univ of Singapore, 1971-73; Assoc Prof of Med, 1974-77, Prof, Hd, Dept of Med, 1978-81, Dpty Vice Chan, 1979-81, Vice Chan, 1981-, Natl Univ of Singapore. Honours include: Queens Schl, 1957; Gold Medal, Singapore Pub Admin, 1984; Officier dans l'Ordre des Palmes Academiques, 1988; Meritorious Serv Medal, Singapore, 1990; Friend of Labour Awd, NTUC, 1995; Hon Fell, Roy Coll of Physns and Surgeons, Glasgow, 1997; Hon Fell, Roy Coll of Surgeons of Edinburgh, 1997; Hon Fell, Intl Coll of Dentists, USA, 1999; Hon Dr of Sci, Univ of Hull, 1999. Memberships: Singapore Med Assn; Acady of Med, Singapore; Brit Med Assn; Singapore Profl Ctr. Hobbies: Swimming; Badminton. Address: c/o Vice Chancellor's Office, National University of Singapore, 10 Kent Ridge Crescent, Singapore 119260, Singapore.

LIM Sang Ho, b. 22 Dec 1959, Sangjoo, Korea. Research Scientist. m. Yeon Ok Cho, 20 Feb 1983, 1 s. 1 d. Education: BS, 1981, Korea Univ; MS, 1983, Korea Adv Inst Sci and Technol; PhD, 1989, Univ Newcastle. Appointments: Rsch Scientist, KIST, 1983-86; Natl Rsch Fell,, CSIRO, Aust, 1990; Prin Rsch Scientist, KIST, 1990-. Publications: include: Accurate and Fast Calculations of Phase Diagrams by Monte Carlo Method; Development of Excellent Driving Materials of Micro Devices. Honours: Ppr of Yr Awd, KIST, 1994; Recom Rschr, Korean Min of Sci and Tech, 1995. Memberships: IEEE; Korean Magnetics Soc; Korea Inst of Metal and Materials. Hobbies: Jogging; Environmental protection. Address: Thin Film Tech Research Centre, Korea Institute of Science & Technology, 39-1 Hawolgok-dong,

Sungbuk-gu, Seoul, Korea.

LIM Sang-Seok, b. 15 Mar 1955, Kyungbook, Korea. Professor. m. Yeon-Hee, 10 June 1982, 1 s, 1 d. Education: BS, 1976; MASc, 1984; PhD, 1990. Appointments: Agency for Def Devel, 1976-82; Rsch Assoc, Roy Mil Coll of Can, 1990-92; Sci, DREO, 1992-95; Prof, Hankuk Aviation Univ, 1995-. Publication: Avionics, 1997. Memberships: IEEE; KONI. Hobbies: Hiking; Travel. Address: Hankuk Aviation University, Department of Avionics, 20-1 Whajun-dong, Koyang-si, Kyungki-do 412-791, Korea.

LIM Say Wan Reginald, b. 7 June 1939, Penang, Malaysia. Anaesthesiologist. m. Jeannie Chung, 7 June 1969, 3 s. Education: MBBS, Univ of Singapore, 1963; Univ of Liverpool, Eng, 1966-68; FFARCS, Ireland, 1967; FFARCS, Eng, 1967; FFARACS, 1974; FFAM, 1997. Appointments: Housemanship, Penang Gen Hosp, 1963-64; Med Offr, Min of Health, Malaysia, 1964-66; Lectr, Univ of Malaya, 1966-70; Hon Lectr, Natl Univ of Malaysia, 1986-. Publications: sci papers in profl jrnls, served on var edtl bds. Honours: Hon Fellshp, Roy Australasian Coll of Physns, 1988; Hon Fell, Amn Coll of Physns, 1989; Fell, Roy Coll of Physns and Surgs of Glasgow, 1990 Key to City of Havana, Cuba, 1995; Corresp Mbr, Cuban Soc of Anaesthsiology and Reanimation, 1995; JSM, 1997. Memberships include: Pres, Malaysian Soc of Anaesthesiologists, 1974-75; Pres, Malaysian Med Assn, 1982-83; Pres, Confedn of Med Assns of Asia and Oceania, 1983-85; Chmn, Asian-Australasian Reg Sect of Anaesthesiologists, 1982-86; Chmn, Exec Cttee, World Fedn of Socs of Anaesthesiologists, 1984-88; Sec 1988-92, Pres 1992-96; Master of Acady of Med of Malaysia, 1984-90; Pres, Roy Lake Club, Kuala Lumpur, 1990-92; Pres, Asian and Oceanic Soc of Reg Anaesthesia, 1989-91. Hobbies: Squash; Golf. Address: Pantai Medical Centre, 59100 Kuala Lumpar, Malaysia.

LIM Siew Leng Franklin, b. 17 Sept 1915, Kuching, Malaysia. Computer Scientist; Computer Engineer; Computer Mathematician. m. 8 June 1954, 1 s, 1 d. Education: PhD, MIT, Princeton, Berkeley, Cornell, Caltech, Tokyu, Paris, Heidelberg; Gakushuin, Keio, yale, Qinghua, Stanford, Purdue, Cambridge, Georgetown, Munich, Oxford, Waseba. Appointments: Chf Sci, Lawrence Livermore Natl Labs, Thomas J Watson Labs, IBM Winchester Sci Cntr, Hitachi Computing Labs, NASA, CIA, Fairchild, MIT Media Labs, Fujitsu Labs, Palo Alto Labs, RCA. Publications: The Invention of the 5th-Generation Computer Using Chaos Dynamics/Theory, 1985; Sev articles in profl jrnls. Honours: Nobel Phys Prize, 1953; Norel Chem Prize, 1954; Nobel Peace Prize, 1955; Nobel Lit Prize, 1956; US PResl Medal of Freedom, 1957. Memberships: Fell, Roy Soc, London, Max Planck Inst, Cavendish Lab, Sigma Xi; Dir, Nobel Phys Prize Cttee, 1958. Hobby: Classical Music. Address: IBM East Asia Labs (Research), 15A Jalan Geneng, Singapore 538322, Singapore.

LIMON ROJAS Miguel, b. 17 Dec 1943, Mexico Cty, Mexico. Secretary of Public Education. Education: Law Deg w Hons, UNAM; Grad wrk, Aix Univ, Marseilles, France. Appointments: Tchr, Law Sch, UNAM; Tchr, Dir of Socl Scis and Hums, Universidad Autónoma Metropolitana; Gen Dir, Natl Indiginist Inst, 1983-88; Undersec, Population and Migratory Servs, Dept of Interior, 1988-93; Undersec, Urban Dev and Infrastructure, Dept of Socl Dev, 1993-94. Memberships: PRI, Subdir of Socl Stdies, Inst for Pol, Econ and Socl Stdies; Pres, Natl Forum of Profl and Techl People; Subcommn of UN for Prevention of Discrimination and Protection of Minorities; Pres, Mexican Br, Intl Dev Soc. Address: Office of the President, Mexico.

LIN Bingyi, b. 8 Jan 1937, Fuzhou, China. Professor. m. Zhang Meizhen, 2 s. Education: BA, Fudan Univ, 1962. Appointments: Tchr, 1962; Lectr, 1980; Assoc Prof, 1986; Dir of Hist Dept, 1987; Prof, 1995. Publications: Chinese History; History Textbooks for Schools; Evaluation of the Reform of Historical Curriculums and

Textbooks in Secondary Schools. Honours: Natl Exemplary Tchr Prize, 1991; Educ Fndn Prize, 1993. Memberships: Shanghai Inst of Educ, 1978; E China Normal Univ, 1998. Hobbbies: Music; Classical poetry. Address: Room 102, Building 405, Chifeng Road, Shanghai 200083, China.

LIN Bor-Luh, b. 4 March 1935, Xiamen, Fujian, China. Professor of Mathematics. m. Hsin Lee, 24 Aug 1963, 3 s. Education: BS, Natl Taiwan Univ; MS, Univ Notre Dame; PhD, Northwestern Univ. Appointments: Asst Prof, 1963, Assoc Prof, 1967, Prof, 1972, Chair Dept, 1994-, Univ Iowa. Publications: Ed, Banach Space Theory; Contemporary Mathematics 85, 1989; Ed, Amn Math Soc Proceedings of Intl Workshop on Banach Space Theory; Contemporary Mathematics 144, 1993. Honours: Hon Prof, Harbin Univ of Scis and Tech, 1996. Memberships: AMS. Hobbies: Reading; Swimming; Gardening. Address: 15 Valley View Knoll, NE, Iowa City, Iowa 52240, USA.

LIN Chin-Sheng, b. 4 Aug 1916, Taiwan. Government Official. Education: Law Coll, Tokyo Imperial Univ. Appointments: Magistrate, Chiayi Co Govt, 1951-54; Chair, Yunlin Co HQ, Kuomintang, 1954-57; Magistrate, Yunlin Co Govt, 1957-64; Dir, Cheng-Ching Lake Indl Waterworks, 1964-67; Commr, Taiwan Prov Govt, 1966-70; Sec-Gen, Taiwan Prov HQ, Kuomintang, 1967-78, Chair, Taipei Municipal HQ, 1969-70, Dpty Sec-Gen, Ctrl Cttee, 1970-72, Mbr, Standing Cttee, Ctrl Cttee, 1976-; Min of the Interior, 1972-76, of Commns, 1976-81, without Portfolio, 1981-84; VP, Exam Yuan, 1984-93; Snr Advsr to Pres of Taiwan, 1993-. Honour: Order of the Brilliant Star. Membership: Standing Cttee, Kuomintang Ctrl Cttee, 1976-. Address: 25 Lane 62, Hsinsheng North Road, Sector 3, Taipei, Taiwan.

LIN Ching-Hsia, b. 1955, Taiwan. Film Actress. Creative Works: Films incl: Outside the Window; Dream Lovers; Police Story; Stary, Stary Night. Address: c/o Taiwan Cinema & Drama Association, 10/F 196 Chunghua Road, Sector 1, Taipei, Taiwan.

LIN Ching-Jiang, b. 2 Dec 1940, Yunlin Co, Taiwan. Minister of Education. m. 2 s, 1 d. Education: PhD, Liverpool Univ, Eng, 1968. Appointments: Assoc Prof and Prof, Natl Taiwan Normal Univ, 1968-72; Dir, Dept of Higher Educ, Min of Educ, 1972-75; Vice Min of Educ, 1975-76, 1987-89; Dir-Gen, Dept of Overseas Affairs, Cntrl Cttee, Kuomintang, 1976-78; Prof and Dir, Grad Sch of Educ, Natl Taiwan Normal Univ, 1978-81; Pres, Chinese Comparative Educ Soc, Taipei, 1979-80, 1993-95; Pres, Natl Kaohsiung Normal Coll, 1981-83; Commnr, Dept of Educ, Taiwan Provicial Govt, 1983-87; Pres, Natl Chung Cheng Univ, 1989-96; Pres, China Educ Soc, 1991-92; Pres, Chinese Adult Educ Assn Taipei, 1995; Mbr, (Ministerial rank), Examination Yuan, 1996-98; Min of Educ, 1998-. Honour: Hon Doct in Law, Liverpool Univ, 1997.

LIN Dingyi, b. 31 July 1936. Professor. m. Gong Lizhen, 7 Nov 1967, 1 s, 1 d. Education: BTech, Huazhong Univ of Sci and Technol, China, 1955-60. Appointments: Lectr 1980-85, Assoc Prof 1985-93, Prof, 1993-. Publications: On the Evaluation of Scientific Theories, 1986; Introduction to Methodology of Scientific Research, 1986; Problem Structure and Problem Logic of Science, 1988; On the Aim Model of Scientific Progress, 1990; Scientific Progress and Targets, 1990; The Rising and Decline of View of Nature of Modern Scientific Mechanism, 1995. Honours: Second Prize of Ex Achmnts in Humanities and Socl Sci of Chinese Educ, 1995; Second Prize of Ex Achmnts in Humanities and Socl Sci of the Syst of Higher Educ of Guangdong Prov of China, 1995. Memberships: PT Study Prof of Chinese Mngmt Sci Study Inst; Sci Methodology Cttee, Assn of Dialectics of Nature of China; Assn for Fndns of Sci, Lang and Cognition; Inst of Hist of Sci and Technol, China. Listed in: Contemporary Who's Who of China; Who's Who in Social Sciences in Culture. Hobbies: Playing Volleyball; Swimming. Address: Department of Philosophy, Zhongshan University, Guangzhou 510275, China.

LIN Fuyong, b. 13 Sept 1960, China. Professor. m. Chen Ye, 5 Feb 1991, 1 d. Education: BSc, Fuzhou Univ, 1983; MSc, 1991, PhD, 1993, Shanghai Jiaotong Univ. Appointments: Asst Engr, 1983, Lectr, 1993, Assoc Prof, 1995, Prof, 1999-. Publications: The Structural Model of General Systems and its Proof, 1998; The Structural Theory of General Systems, 1998; The Principles and Laws of General Systems and Their Applications, 1999. Honour: Rsch Awd, Fok Ying Tung Educn Fndn, 1996. Membership: Educn Cttee, Systems Engrng Soc, China, 1998-. Hobby: Carving. Address: Department of Business Administration, Jinan University, Guangzhou 510632, China.

LIN James Peicheng, b. 30 Sept 1949, NYC, NY, USA. Professor of Mathematics. m. Julie Sano Lin, 2 d. Education: BS, Univ of CA, Berkeley, CA, USA; PhD, Princeton Univ, USA. Appointments: Asst Prof, 1974, Assoc Prof, 1978, Full Prof, 1981, Univ of CA, San Diego. Publication: Steenrod Connections and Connectivity in H Spaces, 1987. Honours: Phi Beta Kappa; Sloan Fndn Fell; Chan's Assoc Awd for Ex in Tchng, Univ of Pan Asian Comms Commitment in Educ Awd. Hobbies: Tennis; Camping; Home Remodelling. Address: James Lin, 8239 Paseo del Ocaso, La Jolla, CA 92037, USA.

LIN Jinxian, b. 24 Mar 1925, China. Professor. Education: BS, Engrng, Chiao-Tung Univ, 1946. Memberships: Chinese Ceramic Soc; Chinese Electron Soc. Hobbies: Music; Travel. Address: University of Electronic Science & Technology, Chengdu, Sichuan 610054, China.

LIN Kwang-Lung, b. 23 Feb 1954, Taiwan. Educator. m. Jui-Yu Chiang, 28 Dec 1986, 3 d. Education: BS Chem, 1977, Tunghai Univ; MS Chem, 1979, Catholic Univ of Am; PhD, Metall, 1984, Penn State Univ. Appointments: Post Doc, Ames Lab, DOE, Iowa State Univ, 1984; Assoc Prof, Cheng Kung Univ, 1985; Prof, 1989-. Publications: Over 100 pprs in jrnls and conf proceedings; 11 pats. Honours: Outstndng Rsch Awd, NSC, China, 1998; Outstndg Engrng Prof, Chinese Engr Assn, 1997; Best Ppr Awd, Silver Medal, AESF, 1997. Memberships: IEEE; CPMT; TMS, Warrendale, PA; ASM, Materials Park, OH; AESF, Orlando, FL. Hobbies: Swimming; Music; Hiking. Address: Dept Materials Science and Engineering, National Cheng Kung University, Tainan, Taiwan 701, China.

LIN Liangzhen, b. 4 Aug 1935, Zhejiang, China. Professor. m. Chu Zonglan, 6 Jan 1961, 1 d. Education: Dept of Electr Engin, Harbin Inst of Technol, China. Ldr, rsch grp, Dpty Hd of Div, Hd of Div, Pres of Degree Awarding Cttee, Inst of Electr Engin, Chinese Acady of Scis; Visng Scientist: Inst of Tech Phys, Forschunszentrum Karlsruhe, Germany, 1980-82; Deutsches Elektronen - Synchrotron DESY, Hamburg, 1985-87, 1989-90. Publications: Inductive Energy Storage, High Field Superconducting Magnet, Superconducting Magnet for MHD Generator, HTSC Magnet and Applications; Ed, Proceedings of 15th Intl Conf on Magnet Technol MT-15, 1997; Superconductivity and Applications (book in Chinese), 1998. Honours: Important Achievement Prize, Chinese Acady of Sci, 1978; 2nd Class Prize, Sci & Technol Dev, Chinese Acady of Scis, 1990, 1994; 3rd Class Prize, Natl Sci & Technol Dev, 1991; Intl Cultural Dip of Hon, ABI, 1994; Citation of Meritorious Achievement, IBC, 1994. Hobbies: Classical music; Reading. Address: Institute of Electrical Engineering, Chinese Academy of Sciences, PO Box 2703, Beijing 100080, China.

LIN Liyun, b. 1933, Taizhong, Taiwan. State Official. Education: Kobe, Japan; Beijing Univ. Appointments: Cncl Mbr, Sino-Japanese Friendship Assn, 1973-; Mbr, 10th CCP Ctrl Cttee, 1973; Mbr, Standing Cttee, 4th NPC, 1975; Dpty for Taiwan to 5th NPC, 1978, 6th NPC, 1983; VP, Womens Fedn, 1978-; Pres, Fedn of Taiwan Compatriots, 1981-; Mbr, 12th CCP Ctrl Cttee, 1982-87; Standing Cttee, NPC, 1984-88; Mbr, Credentials Cttee, NPC, 1984-88; Mbr, Overseas Chinese Cttee, NPC, 1986-; Mbr, Presidium 6th NPC, 1986-; Mbr, 13th CCP Ctrl Cttee, 1987-92, 14th CCP Ctrl Cttee, 1992-97, 15th

CCP Ctrl Cttee, 1997-; Mbr, Exec Cncl, 1988-; Vice Chair, 14th NPC Overseas Chinese Affairs Cttee; Advsr, Assn for the Promotion of the Peaceful Reunification of China, 1988-. Memberships include: VP, All-China Sports Fedn; VP, All-China Fedn of Returned Overseas Chinese. Address: Chinese Communist Party Central Committee, Beijing, China.

LIN Paul Kuang-Hsien, b. 12 Nov 1946, Taiwan. Professor, National Assemblyman. m. Dr Catherine Jen, 5 Aug 1978, 1 s, 1 d. Education: BS, Fu-Jen Cath Univ; MS, Brigham Young Univ; PhD, Wayne State Univ. Appointments: Asst Prof, West Michigan Univ; Asst Prof, Univ of Michigan, Dearborn; Assoc Prof, Univ of Michigan, Dearborn. Publications: Many statistical pprs publ in profl jrnls. Honour: Outstndng Tchng Awd, 1996. Memberships: Amn Stat Assn; Amn Math Soc; Natl Assembly, Taipei, Taiwan, 1996-. Hobbies: Playing Piano; Reading. Address: Department Mathematics & Statistics, University of Michigan, Dearborn, MI 48126, USA.

LIN Shi Cheng, b. 3 Mar 1922, Shanghai, China. Professor. 1 s, 1 d. Education: Bachelor Degree, China Med Inst. Appointments: Prof, Cntrl Conservatory of Music; Chmn, Chinese Pipa Inst. Publications: Over 20 on var subjs inclng: Pipa Playing Techniques, 1959; A Selection of Pipa Music, Vols 1 & 2; On the Chinese Gongche Notations; Articles and dissertations. Creative works: Cassettes, CDs, VCD. Honour: One of 1st recipients of State Spec Allowance, granted to outstndng citizens. Memberships: Chmn, Chinese Pipa Inst; Educationist & Performer, Ethnic & Pipa Music; Noted Repr, Pudong Sch of Pipa. Hobbies: Calligraphy; Painting. Address: 43 Bao Jia Jie Beijing, China.

LIN Thomas Wen-shyoung, b. 3 June 1944, Taichung, Taiwan, China. University Educator. m. Angela, 19 May 1969, 1 s, 1 d. Education: BA, Bus Admin, Natl Taiwan Univ, Taiwan, 1966; MBA, Natl Chengchi Univ, Taiwan, 1970; MS, Accts and Inf Systems, UCLA, USA, 1971; PhD, Acctng, Ohio State Univ, USA, 1975. Appointments: Asst Prof, Univ of South CA (USC), 1975-80; Assoc Prof, USC, 1980-86; Dir of Acctng, PhD Prog at USC, 1982-86; Prof, USC, 1986-90; Acctng Circle Prof of Acctng, USC, 1990-. Publications: Planning, Budgeting and Control for Data Processing, 1984; The Use of Mathematical Models, 1986; Using Accounting Information in Business, 1991; Cost Management, 1998; Over 60 articles. Honours: Congressional Awd for Outstndng Community Serv, 1988; Taiwan Natl Econ Dev Sem Capt, 1989; The USC Acctng Circle Professorship, 1990-; Hon Bd of Dir, Chinese (PRC) Acctng Prof's Assn, 1995-96. Memberships: Bd of Dirs, Fndng Pres, N Am Chinese Acctng Profs Assn, 1976-; Advsr, Taiwan Benevolent Assn of Am, 1990-; Advsr, Amn Chinese Cultural and Econ Soc, 1997-; External Examiner, Chinese Univ of Hong Kong, 1998-. Hobby: Gardening. Address: Marshall School of Business, University of Southern California, Los Angeles, CA 90089-1421, USA.

LIN Wei, b. 7 Sept 1934. Professor; Director. m. Wu Jin-yi, 6 Sept 1965, 1 s, 1 d. Education: Grad, Zhongshan Univ, 1956; Grad, Grad Sch of Zhongshan Univ, 1960. Appointments: Lectr, Math Dept, Zhongshan Univ, 1961-78; Assoc Prof 1978-83, Prof 1983-, Zhongshan Univ; Visng Assoc Prof, Univ Delaware, USA, 1982-83; Visng Prof, Kazan Univ, 1988-89; Chmn, Math Dept, 1984-92; Dir of Math Inst, 1992-. Publications: The Distributed Control Systems, 1981; Second Order Systems of Partial Differential Equs, 1985; Systems of Equs of Composite Type, 1989. Honours: Prize, Guangdong Sci Conf, 1979; Prize, Sci and Technol, Guangdong Prov, 1992; Prize, Nat Sci, Guangdong Prov, 1998. Memberships: Cncl Mbr, Chinese Math Soc; Cncl Mbr, Chinese Automatics Soc, 1985-; Chmn, Guangdong Math Soc; Mbr Bd Dirs, ISAAC, USA, 1997. Hobbies: Swimming; Music. Address: Mathematics Department, Zhongshan University, Guangzhou 510275, China.

LIN Xianshu, b. 20 Jan 1937, Fuzhou City, Fujian Province, China. University Teacher. m. Yan Wenhua, 7

Feb 1963, 2 s. Education: Diploma, Xi'an Jiao-tong Univ, China. Appointments: Assoc Prof, 1987, Prof, 1992-, N China Electric Power Univ. Publications: Pprs in profl jrnls. Honour: Awd of Min of Power Ind, China, 1995. Address: North China Electric Power University, Beijing 102206, China.

LIN Yang-Kang, b. 10 June 1927, Nantou, Taiwan. Politician. m. Chen Ho, 1945, 1 s, 3 d. Education: Natl Taiwan Univ. Appointments: Chair, Yunlin Co HQ, Kuomintang, 1964-67; Magistrate, Nantou Co, 1967-72; Cmdr, Dept of Reconstrn, Taiwan Prov Govt, 1972-76; Mayor of Taipei, 1976-78; Gov, Taiwan Prov, 1978-81; Min of Interior, 1981-84; Vice-Premier of Taiwan, 1984-87; Pres, Judicial Yuan, 1987-94; Snr Advsr to Pres, 1994-95; Pres Cand, 1996. Hobbies: Hiking; Reading; Study; Music; Films. Address: 124 Chungking South Road, Sector 1, Taipei, Taiwan.

LIN Zhi Ying, b. 23 July 1935, Zhen Jiang, Jiangsu, China. Oncologist; Gastroenterologist. m. Z S Li, 24 Sept 1961, 1 s, 1 d. Education: Grad, Fac of Med, Shanghai First Med Coll, 1959. Appointments: Dept of Internal Med, Zhong Shan Hosp, 1959-72; Liver Cancer Rsch Inst, Zhong Shan Hosp, 1973-; Sloan-Kettering Cancer Cntr, NYC, USA, 1984-85. Publications: Immunity to Subclinical Hepatocellular Carcinoma, 1988; Clinical Features and Diagnosis of Primary Liver Cancer, 1994. Honour: Pub Hlth Awd, Progress of Sci and Technol, 1985, 1994. Memberships: Soc of Gastroenterol; Chinese Med Assn; Cttee, Shanghai Immunol Assn. Hobby: Light Music. Address: Institute of Liver Cancer, Zhong Shan Hospital, Shanghai Medical University, 180 Feng Lin Road, Shanghai 200032, China.

LIN Zi Yun, b. 20 Aug 1927, Taiwan, China. Doctor. m. Shao Qingxiang, 2 Apr 1996, 2 s. Education: Medl Univ, Beijing. Appointment: Hd, Dept of Clin Lab, 1963-93. Publications: 3 books. Membership: Intl Commn for Prevention of Alcoholism. Hobbies: Playing violin; Interest in music. Address: Institute of Cancer of Medical Academy, Chao Wai Shui Zhui Zi Bldg 13 201, Beijing 100026, China.

LINCOLN John Francis, b. 30 July 1916, Aust. Judge. m. Joan Alison Scott, 24 Jan 1952, 1 s, 1 d. Education: Balliol Coll, Oxford Univ, Eng, 1939-40; Bar-at-Law, Hon Soc of Lincolns Inn, London; Hon LLD, Macquarie Univ, Aust, 1987. Appointments: Dpty Asst Judge, Advocate-Gen, 1946-47; Assoc to Chf Jus of NSW, 1949; Mbr, NSW Bar, 1949-86; Acting Judge, Supreme Crt, NSW, 1967; Judge, Dist Crt, 1968-86; Chmn, Northolm Grammar Sch Cncl, 1981-98; Chmn, Parole Bd of NSW, 1984-85; Chmn, Elect Districts Commnrs, 1990-91; Chmn, Lincoln Cntr for Rsch into Bone and Joint Diseases, 1998-. Honours: Order of Aust, 1985; Fell, Austl Inst of Welfare Offrs; Hon Rotarian, 1986. Memberships include: Mayor of N Sydney, 1956-58; NSW State Treasurer, Liberal Party of Aust; Mbr, Fedl Cncl, Dpty Chan, Macquarie Univ, 1976-; Chan, Diocese Newcastle, NSW, 1978-; Chmn, N Sydney Community Hosp, 1962-; Scout Assn, Regl Pres; Former Pres, Marriage Guidance Cncl; VP, Order of Aust Assn; Pres, Prisoners Aid Assn of NSW, 1981-; Pres, Austl Univ Grad Conf, 1977-80. Listed in: Many including: Who's Who in Australia; Who's Who in the World; Who's Who in the Commonwealth. Hobby: Swimming. Address: Stone Lodge, 30 Stanley Street, St Ives, NSW 2075, Australia.

LINDBECK Keith, b. 7 Oct 1931. Food Consultant. m. Jean Gloria Riepon, 12 Jan 1953, 4 s. Education: BS, Univ WA. Appointments: Sanitarium Hlth Food Co: Lab Techn, 1949-59; Prodn Supvsr, 1959-71; Techl Supt, 1972-78; R&D Asst Dir, 1979-90; R&D Dir, 1990-95; Corp Tech Servs Mngr, 1996-97. Memberships: Roy Aust Chem Inst; Inst Food Technol. Hobbies: Numismatics; Bushwalking; Photography. Address: 17 Babers Road, Cooranbong, NSW 2265, Australia.

LINDSEY Timothy Charles, b. 12 May 1962, Melbourne, Aust. Lawyer. m. Lanita, 2 d. Education: PhD, BA (Hons), BLitt(Hons), LLB, Melbourne Univ. Appointments: Barrister-at-Law, 1990; Assoc Dir, Asian

Law Cntr, 1994; Snr Assoc, Fac of Law, Univ of Melbourne, 1994. Publications: How Companies Work, 1992; The Romance of Ktut Tantri and Indonesia, 1997. Membership: Bd Mbr, Aust Indonesia Inst, 1996-. Hobbies: Painting; Writing. Address: 45 Egan Street, Richmond, VIC 3121, Australia.

LING Francis C C, b. 2 Oct 1966, Hong Kong. Physicist; Teacher. m. Amy N L Lee, 13 Sept 1997. Education: BSc, hons; MPh; PhD. Appointments: Tutor, 1990-93, 1993-96, Instr, 1996-98, Lectr, 1998-, Hong Kong Univ; Sci Offr, Hong Kong Govt, 1993. Publications: Var rsch pprs in profl jrnls. Membership: Inst of Phys. Address: Department of Physics, Hong Kong University, Pokfulam Road, Hong Kong.

LING Liong Sik Dato, b. 18 Sept 1943, Kuala Kangsar, Perak, Malaysia. Politician. m. Datin Ee Nah Ong, 1968, 2 children. Education: King Edueard VII Sch; Roy Mil Coll; Univ Singapore. Appointments: Parl Sec, Min of Local Govt & Fed Territory, 1976-77; Dpty Min of Info, 1978-82, of Fin, 1982-84, of Educn, 1985-86; Dpty Pres, Malaysian Chinese Assn, 1985-87, Pres, 1987-; Min of Transp, 1986-. Hobbies: Reading; Golf. Address: Ministry of Transport, 5th-7th Floors, Wisma Perdana, Jalan Dungun Bukit Damansara, 50616 Kuala Lumpur, Malaysia.

LING Peihong, b. 6 Oct 1918. Professor. m. C C Wang, 12 Mar 1947, 2 s, 3 d. Education: BSc; MSc; Cand for PhD. Appointments: Am No 69 Gen Hosp, 1944-45; Techn, Yunan Tin Mine, 1945; Engr, Jiangxi Coal Mine, 1946; Snr Engr, Kailuan Mining Admin, 1950; Prof, Tangshan Jaiotong Univ, 1952; Hd, Dept of Coal Preparation and Utilization, Tangshan Coal Rsch Inst, 1956-81; Chf Engr, China SW Energy Dev Corp, 1981-86; China Tech Cnsltng Cntr, 1986-91; Snr Engr, Specialist, China Coal Contruction and Dev Corp, 1991-; Dir, W Returned Schls Assn, 1991-; Advsr, Clean Coal Technol Rsch Cntr, 1996-. Publications: 45 pprs published in Chinese and Engl Mags and Proceedings. Honours: Model Worker, K.M.A, 1945; 1st Prize, Min of Coal Ind, 1958; Reward, Min of Coal Ind, 1985. Memberships: AIMME; Dir, China Coal Soc; Dir, China Coal Preparation and Utilization Assn. Hobbies: Athletics; Music. Address: China Technical Consulting Committee of Coal Industry, Hepingli, Beijing 100013, China.

LING Ying Tong, b. WuHe County, Anhwei Prov, China. Financial Management. Education: Bachelor degree, HeFei Normal Inst. Appointments: Pres, BengBu For Trade Bur, 1983-86; Chmn BengBu Suburb, 1986-89; Pres, BengBu Housing Deposit Bank, 1989-. Publication: Reverberation of Practice and Thought. Honours: 1st Chinese Econs Treatise Prize, 1987; 1st Econs Treatise of Socl Sci Assn Prize, 1998. Memberships: Standing Cttee of Chinese Real Estate and Rescience Rsch Inst, 1995; Cncl of Chinese Cty and Town Housing System Reformation Rsch Inst, 1995; Chinese Calligraphy Assn, 1998. Address: BengBu Housing Deposit Bank of China, 155 ZhouRong Street, BengBu, Anhwei Province, China.

LING Yong Yong, b. 3 Feb 1935, Shanghai, China. Professor of Mathematics. m. Neng Di Zhang, 1 Aug 1965, 3 d. Education: Grad, BSc, Dept of Maths and Mechs, Peking Univ, 1957. Appointments: Rsch Asst, Inst of Maths, Chinese Acady of Scis, Peking and Dept of Appl Maths, Chinese Scis and Technol Univ, Peking, 1957-63; Asst Lectr, Dept of Maths, Hebei Univ, Tianjing, 1963-70; Lectr, Assoc Prof, Prof, Dept of Appl Maths, Tongji Univ, Shanghai, 1971-. Publications include: The Theory of Time-Dependent Stochastic Dymanics of Radiation Damage and Repair of Biological System (I), 1992; The Theory of Time-Dependent Stochastic Dymanics of Radiation Damage and Repair of Biological System (II), 1992; Nonlinear Partial Differential Equation and the MWR, 1997; Fundamental Problems of the Method of Weighted Residuals (MWR) in Sobolev Spaces I, II, 1998. Honours: Sci and Technol Progress Prize, 2nd Class, Cttee of Natl Educn, China, 1991; Natl Achievement in Sci and Technol, Dip, Cttee of Natl Sci and Technol, China, 1992. Memberships: ISOPE, USA; Sci and Technol Soc, China; Soc of Relativistic Astrophys and Gravitation, China; Maths Assn, Shanghai; Maths Soc, China. Hobbies: Poetry; Music; Calligraphy. Address: Department of Applied Mathematics, Tongji University, Shanghai 200092, China.

LING Yue Lun, b. 26 Dec 1929. Professor of Economics. m. 7 Feb 1957, 2 d. Education: BA, Econs. Appointments: Vice Prof, Sichuan Univ, 1955-84; Prof, Sichuan Univ, 1984-96; Vice Dean of Econs Dept, Sichuan Univ, 1987-91. Publications: History of Chinese Recent Economics; History of Misheng Company; Chinese State Capitalism Economics and its Management. Honours: Special Bonus of Outstndg Schl; 2nd Awd of Philos and Socl Sci, Sichuan, four times. Memberships: VP, Chinese Recent Econs Hist Inst; Pres, Chinese Econs Hist Inst, Sichuan. Hobbies: Playing Football; Travel. Address: Department of Economics, Sichuan University, Chengdu, Sichuan 610064, China.

LING Zhi-Guang, b. 29 May 1933, Zhejiang, China. Professor; University Vice President; Research Institute Director. m. Gao Hua, 15 Aug 1963, 1 s. Education: Grad, Dept of Mech Engrng, Shanghai Jiaotong Univ, 1953; Postgrad Study, Dept of Power Engrng, Harbin Tech Univ, 1953-57. Appointments: Inst of Power Engrng, 1957-60, Inst of Mechs, 1960-80, Inst of Engrng Thermophys, 1980-85, Chinese Acady of Scis, Beijing; Prof, VP, Dean, Dept of Mech Engrng, Shanghai Univ of Engrng Sci, 1985-; Dir, Shanghai Inst of Energy Rsch, Shanghai Acady of Sci, 1987-. Publications: About 50 pprs in natl and intl jrnls, conf proceedings and symposia on aerothermodynamics of internal flows and multiphase flow of turbomachines, thermodynamic and energy system, gas turbines, cyclone separators, power recovery; Mechanics vol, Chinese Encyclopedia (section auth); Lecture notes; Books. Honours: 1st Rank Awd, 1979, 2nd Rank Awd, 1986, Sci Achievements, Chinese Acady of Scis; 1st Rank Awd, Min for Sci and Technol Achievements, 1980, 1983, 1990; 1st Recipient, Natl Awd for Sci and Technol Achievements, 1985, 1987. Memberships: Energy and Thermodynamics Cttee, Multiphase Flow Cttee, Chinese Soc of Engrng Thermophys Fluid Dynamics Cttee, Chinese Soc of Mechs Bd Chmn, Shanghai Soc of Engrng Thermophys, Shanghai Soc of Mod Design Technol; Shanghai Assn of Energy Rsch; Ed-in-Chf, Energy Rsch and Info. Hobbies: Violin Playing; Listening to Music; Chinese Tai-Ji Chuan Exercise; History and Historical Stories. Address: Shanghai University of Engineering Science, No 350 Xian-Xia Road, Shanghai 200336, China.

LING Zhongzhuan, b. 25 Nov 1938, Fujian Prov, China. Research Professor; Pathologist; Rice Breeder. m. Yan Haijun, 5 Jan 1967, 1 s, 1 d. Education: BS, Biol, Huandong Normal Univ, Shanghai, 1961; MS, Bot, Beijing Normal Univ, Beijing, 1964. Appointments: Asst Rschr, Assoc Rschr, Rsch Prof, Inst Crop Breeding and Cultivation, Chinese Acady of Agric Scies, 1965-92; Rsch into Blast Disease and Rice Breeding for Blast Resistance, Natl Inst for Agric Scis of Japan, 1980-1982; Visng Sci, Intl Rice Rsch Inst, Philippines, 1994; Co-op Rsch in Natl Rsch Cntr of Japan, 1995; Mbr, Cntrl Cttee, Dem Union of China, 1998; Specialist of Specialist Grp in Chinese Assn of Sci and Technol, 1999. Publications: Practical Dictionary of Agricultural Biology, 1986; Rice Breeding for Resistance to Blast Disease, 1990; Advances in Researches on Resistance to Diseases in Major Crops, 1990; Many translations from Engl to Chinese and Japanese to Chinese; 65 pprs in domestic and intl mags, 1978-1998. Honours: Excellent Returned Student Having Outstndng Contbn in Educl and Sci System of China's Agric Min, 1992; 5 Sci and Technol Progress Awds, Agric Min of China, 1 Sci and Technol Progress Awd, Natl Cttee of Sci and Technol. Memberships: Japanese Soc of Breeding, 1982-; Chinese Soc of Plant Path. Hobbies: Basketball; Table tennis. Address: Section of Rice Breeding, Institute of Crop Breeding and Cultivation, Chinese Academy of Agricultural Sciences, 30 Baishiqiao Road, Beijing 1000081, China.

LING-STUCKEY Ian, b. 27 Dec 1959. Minister for Public Services. m. 2 children. Education: BSc, Griffith Univ, Brisbane, Aust, 1981. Appointments: Exec Chmn, Monian Grp, property dev and mngmt and gaming ops; Min for Pub Servs. Membership: Pangu Party.

LINI Walter Hadye, b. 1942, Pentecost, Vanuatu. Politician; Ecclesiastic. m. Mary B Ketu, 1970, 4 s, 2 d. Education: Anglican Priesthood, Solomon Islands, NZ; Ordained Deacon, 1968, Priest, 1970. Appointments: Dpty Chf Min, Min of Socl Servs, New Hebrides (now Vanuatu), 1979; Chf Min, Min of Justice, 1979-80; PM of Vanuatu, 1980-91; Min of Justice & Culture, 1996-. Publication: Beyond Pandemonium, 1980. Memberships: Pres, Vanuaaku Pati; Pres, Natl United Party. Address: c/o National United Party, Port Vila, Vanuatu.

LINIAL Shimon, b. 8 Aug 1922. Advertising and Public Relations Executive. Widower, 1 s, 2 d. Appointments: Chmn, Bd Dirs, Linial DDB Advtng Ltd; Honour: Hon City Tower of Haifa, Univ of Haifa. Memberships: Advtng Assn; Rotary Assn PR; Pres, Israeli Friends Assn, Univ of Haifa. Dir, Friends Assn, Rambam Medl Cntr. Hobbies: Bridge; Tennis. Address: A22 Tel Maneh, Street, 34364 Haifa, Israel.

LINN M David, b. 5 Sept 1943, Adelaide, Aust. Chartered Professional Engineer. m. Elizabeth, 1 s, 1 d. Education: B Eng Civil, 1964; M Eng Rsch, 1981. Appointments: Elec Trust of S Aust, 1965-66; Snowy Mountains Hydro-Elec Authority, 1967-69; Macmahon Construction Pty Ltd, 1972-81; Ops Mngr, Aust and Overseas, Austl Mineral Fndn, 1981-88; Mngng Dir, LETService Pty Ltd, 1988-, Main area of Speciality Continuing Educ and Trng in techl managerial and Hum Resource Dev Related Consulting and Mngmt of Trng Prog, Quality Assurance Trng and Cnsltng. Publications: Lime-Flyash Stabilization of Fine-Granes Soils (Thesis), 1981. Membership: Instn of Engrs. Hobbies: Music; Reading; Woodwork. Address: 15 McGowen Avenue, Unley, SA 5061, Australia.

LINUS Suryadi Agustinus, b. 3 Mar 1951, Yogyakarta, Java, Indonesia. Writer. Education: For Lang Acady; IKIP, Sanata Dharma HS Tchrs Coll. Appointments: Started writing poetry and essays w Persada Studi Klub, Pelopor Yogya weekly, 1970; Cultural Ed, Berita Natl Newspaper, 1979-86; Mbr, Yogya Arts Cncl, 1986-89; Chmn, Ed, Citra Yogya Cultural Mag, 1986-; Poetry readings and sems, Indonesia and USA; Judge, Poetry writing and poetry reading comps. Publications: Langit Kelabu, lyric, 1980; Pengakuan Pariyem, lyrical prose, 1981; Perkutut Manggung, lyric, 1986; Dari Desa Ke Kote, essays, 1986; Tugu, poetry anthology, ed, 1986; Tonggak, poetry anthology, 4 vols, ed, 1987; Kembang Tunjung, lyric, 1989; Rumah Panggung, 1989; Di Balik Sejumlah Nama, poetry criticism, 1989; Nafas Budya Yogya, essay, 1993; Pesta Emas Sastra, Jawa DIY, ed, 1995; Dari Pujangga Ke Penulis Jawa, essay, 1996; Yogya Kotaku, lyric, 1997; Tirta Kamandaru, lyric, 1997. Verses in On Foreign Shores and Walking Westward in the morning, anthologies. Honours: Participant, Intl Writing Prog, Iowa Univ, Iowa City, USA, 1982; Art Prize in Indonesian Lit, Yogyarta Provl Govt, 1984; Rumah Panggung Prize, Pusat Bahasa Jakarta, 1994. Hobbies: Watching Javanese puppet shadow plays; Good films; Listening to Music; Talking to old and young in villages to absorb traditional Javanese and Balinese oral wisdom; Reading books; Birdsong in the wild and on the market; Corresponding with friends; Informal research of Javanese Arts (Ketoprak, wayang kulit, dalang); Travel. Address: Kadisobo Village, Trimulyo, Sleman, Yogyakarta, Indonesia.

LIOSI Napoleon B, b. 7 Feb 1945, Fergusson Island, Papua New Guinea. Labour Leader; Trade Unionist. m. 25 Mar 1972, 3 s, 1 d. Appointments: Natl Disaster Cttee for Papua New Guinea, 1972-74; Govt Law and Order Cttee, 1974; Natl Exec Cttee, Boys Scouts Assn, Papua New Guinea, 1974-76; Pres, Soccer Club, 1980-81; Natl Culture Cncl, Papua New Guinea, 1981-84; Pres, PNG Football (Soccer) Refs Assn, 1982-86; Natl Pres, Public

Employees Assn, Papua New Guinea, 1982-99; Chmn, Pub Employees Assn Superannuation Fund, 1989-99; Natl Minimum Wages Bd, 1991; Cmmnr, Natl Capital Dist Cmmn, 1991-93; Natl Tripartite Consultative Cncl, 1991-95; Papua New Guinea Natl Trng Cncl, 1991-99; Dir, Dpty Chmn, Investment Corp, Papua New Guinea, 1995-98; Chmn of Bd Dirs, Workers Mutual Ins (PNG) Ltd, 1996-99; Dir, Dpty Chmn of Bd Dirs, Solomons Mutual Ins Ltd, 1997-99. Memberships: Austl Inst of Dirs. Address: c/o Public Employees Association of PNG, PO Box 965, Boroko, Papua New Guinea.

LIOTTA Ray, b. 18 Dec 1955, Newark, USA. Film Actor. Education: Univ Miami. Creative Works: TV Appearances incl: Another World, NBC, 1978-80; Hardhat & Legs, CBS Movie, 1980; Crazy Times, ABC Pilot, 1981; Casablanca, NBC, 1983; Our Family Honour, NBC, 1985-86; Women Men = In Love There Are No Rules, 1991. Films: The Lonely Lady, 1983; Something Wild, 1986; Arena Brains, 1987; Dominick and Eugene, 1988; Field of Dreams, 1989; Goodfellas, 1990; Article 99, 1992; Unlawful Entry, 1992; No Escape, 1994; Corrina, Corrina, 1994; Operation Dumbo Drop, 1995; Unforgettable, 1996; Turbulence, 1997; Phoenix, 1997; Copland, 1997. Address: Creative Artists Agency Inc, 9830 Wilshire Boulevard, Beverly Hills, CA 90212, USA.

LIOU To-hai, b. 6 Jan 1957, Yunling, Taiwan. Professor. m. Yu-ling Lee, 24 Dec 1995, 1 s. Education: BA, Dept of Oriental Lang & Cultures, Natl Chengchi Univ; MA, Asian Studies, Univ IL; PhD, E Asian Studies, Univ AZ, Tucson. Appointments: Vis Instr, Dept of Oriental Lang & Lit, Univ CO, Boulder, USA, 1987; Assoc Prof, Dept of Diplomacy, Natl Chengchi Univ, Taiwan, 1991-. Publications: International Politics, 1996; South Korea's Foreign Relations Since the Mid 1980s, 1997. Honour: Dr Mackay Cand Studies Grant, 1994; Korean Fndn Fellshp for Korean Studies, 1995. Memberships: Sec Gen, Standing Mbr of the Bd, Chinese Assn for Korean Studies. Hobbies: Reading; Writing. Address: Department of Diplomacy, National Chengchi University, Taipei, Taiwan.

LIPCHIK Harold, b. 17 Apr 1928, NY, USA. m. Elaine, 23 Mar 1952, 1 s, 1 d. Education: BS, Mechl Engrng, Carnegie Mellon Univ, 1948. Appointments: Pres, Water Treatment Corp, 1968-71; Pres, Halco Assn, 1971-; Chf Admin Offr, Natl Tech Systs, 1984-. Memberships: Assn for Corp Growth; Amn Mngmnt Assn. Address: 4429 Trancas Pl, Tarzana, CA 91356, USA.

LIPSON Menzie, b. 15 Feb 1915. University Fellow. m. Margaret Maxwell, 5 Oct 1950, 3 s. Education: BSc, Sydney; PhD, Leeds. Appointments: CSIRO Div Animal Hlth and Nutrition, 1937-39; CISRO Div of Indl Chem, 1939-41; Chf Chem, Cntrl Wool Cttee, 1941-45; Rsch Fell, Leeds Univ, 1946-48; Offr i/c, CSIRO Wool Rsch Labs, Geelong, 1948-58; Chf, CSIRO Div of Textile Ind, 1958-76; Snr Rsch Fell, CSIRO Div of Animal Hlth, 1976-85. Honours: AO, 1976; Textile Inst Medal, 1977; Hon DSc, Deakin Univ, 1984. Memberships: FTS; FRACI; FTI. Hobbies: Reading; Landscape painting; Bushwalking. Address: 3 Montague Street, Highton, Vic 3216, Australia.

LITCHFIELD Ruby Beatrice (Dame), b. 5 Sept 1912, WA, Aust. Company Director. m. Kenneth Lyle Litchfield, 1940, dec 1976, 1 d. Appointments include: VP, Bd Mbr, Queen Vic Maternity Hosp, 1953-72; Life Mbr, 1972; Mayoress of Prospect SA, 1954-57; Bd Mbr, The Adelaide Repertory Th, 1951-68, Life Mbr, 1957; Mbr, Div Cncl, Red Cross Soc SA, 1955-71; Cnclr, Roy Dist Bush Nursing Soc, 1957-64; Bd Mbr, S Austl Housing Trust, 1962-70; Mbr, Bd of Govs, Adelaide Fest Of Arts, 1966-90, Cttee Mbr, 1960-; Mbr, Kidney Fndn, 1968-; Bd Mbr, Telethon Channel 9, 1969-86; Pres, Sportswoman's Assn, 1969-74; Tstee, the Adelaide Fest Cntr Trust, SA, 1971-82, first woman appointed; Bd of Carclew Yth Performing Arts Cntr, 1972-88; Bd Dirs, Fest Cty Brdcstrs Ltd SA, 1975-86; first woman appointed; Cncl Mbr, Sudden Infant Death Syndrome Rsch Fndn, 1979-; Hon Life Mbr, Spastic Paralysis Welfare Assn Inc; Mbr, Roy C'wlth Soc; Chmn, Families, Relig, Cultural Cttee, SA

Jubilee Cttee, 1981-86; Bd mbr, Mary Potter Fndn, Chmn, Mary Potter Hospice Appeal Cttee, 1988-. Honours: OBE, 1959; Queens Silver Jubilee Medal, 1977; Royal C'wlth Soc; DBE, 1981; Adv Aust Awd, 1985; S Aust Gt Awds, 1987. Hobbies: Art; Community Service; Sports; Tennis (hardcourt tennis champion, 1932-35). Address: 33 Hallett Road, Burnside, SA 5066, Australia.

LITHGOW Bruce Whyte, b. 23 Aug 1929. Chartered Accountant; Company Director. Education: Scotch Coll, Melbourne, Aust. Appointments: Dir, Beswick Grp, 1989-99, GUD Holdings Ltd 1980-98; Chmn, Pacific BBA Ltd, 1989-98; Chmn, Sunbeam Victa Holdings Ltd, 1997-98, Sonoco Aust Grp; Mbr, Austl Bd of Advice Korn/Ferry Intl; Mbr Bd of Advice Vic Br AMP Soc, 1978-92; Commnr, Austl Natl Airlines (TAA), 1980-85; Dir, David Mitchell Grp (Chmn), 1974-86; Hertz Aust Pty Ltd (Chmn) 1982-85; Humes Ltd, 1984-88; Lawrence & Hanson Ltd, 1967-72; Pak Pacific Grp, 1965-88; Fndng Ptnr & Chmn, Parkhill Lithgow & Gibson, 1953-87 (now renamed BDO Nelson Parkhill); Bd Mngmt St Andrew's Hosp, 1962-77, Hon Treas 1964-77; Vic State Cncl Inst of Chartered Accts, 1973-82, State Chmn 1979-80; Natl Cncl Inst of Chartered Accts, 1977-80; Scotch Coll Cncl, 1976-90 (Chmn 1981-90); Chmn, Housing Admissions Canterbury Citizen's Welfare Cttee, 1963-70; Pres, Old Scotch Collegian's Assn, 1979-80; Hon Treas, 1982-84, Chmn, Assn of Indep Boys' Schs, Assoc of Vic, 1988-90, Hon Treas, Metropolitan Golf Club, 1989-94, Pres, 1999-. Hobbies: Golf; Tennis; Walking; Reading; Theatre; Clubs: Australian, Athenaeum, MCC, Metropolitan Golf; Frankston Golf; RACV. Address: BDO House, 563 Bourke Street, Melbourne, Vic 3000, Australia.

LITTLE John Miles, b. 28 Dec 1933, Sydney, Aust. Surgeon; Medical Ethicist. m. Penelope Ann, 29 July 1978, 1 s, 3 d. Education: MB, BS, Univ of Sydney, 1959; FRACS, 1963; MS, 1969; MS, 1977; FACS, 1986; FRSM, 1992; FRSA, 1993. Appointments: Res, Registrar, Clinl Supt, Roy Prince Alfred Hosp, 1959-66; Rsch Fell, Univ of Glasgow, 1966; Snr Lectr in Surg, Univ of Sydney, Roy Prince Alfred Hosp, 1967-71; Assoc Prof, 1971-78; Visng Surg, 1974-80; Fndn Prof Surg, Westmead Hosp, 1978-96; Fndn Chmn, Dept of Surg, 1978-90; Visng Surg, 1979-96; Conslt Surg, Roy Prince Alfred Hosp, Roy Alexandra Hosp for Children, Blacktown Dist Hosp, Mt Druitt Hosp, Bowral Hosp, Dist Hosp; Dir, Cntr for Vals, Ethics and the Law in Med, Univ of Sydney, 1995-. Publications: The Management of Liver Injuries, 1971; Major Amputations for Vascular Diseas, 1975; Humane Medicine, 1995; More than 200 Articles. Honours: Nuffield Dominion Travng Fell in Med, 1966; Glissan Mem Prize, 1967; Coupland Medal, 1985; Hon Prof of Surg, 1987; Silver Medal, Univ of Bologna, 1988; Gold Medal, Chinese Medl Assn, 1994; Silver Medal, Roy Australasian Coll of Surgs, 1994. Memberships: Roy Australasian Coll of Surgs, 1974-84; Asian Surg Assoc; World Assoc Hepatic Pancreatic and Biliary Surgs; Intl Hepatic, Biliary and Pancreatic Assoc; Many other mbrshps. Hobbies: Photography; Philosophy; Medicine. Address: Centre for Values and the Law in Medicine, University of Sydney, Sydney, NSW 2006, Australia.

LITZ Charles Joseph Jr, b. 5 Nov 1928, Philadelphia, USA. Aerospace Engineer. m. Ronalda Clara, 17 Apr 1971, 1 s, 1 d. Education: AE, Martin Coll, 1948; BME, Univ DE, 1951; Postgrad, TX Western, 1954-56; MS, La Salle Coll, 1959; MIT, Cambridge, MA, 1958-62. Appointments: Mech Engr, US Naval Air Devel Cntr, Johnsville, PA, 1951-54; Mil Serv, US Army, Instr, Army Air Def Sch, 1954-56; Elec-Mech Engr, Brown Inst, Minn-Honeywell, Phila, 1956-58; Rsch Assoc, Project Engr, US Army Adv Rsch Agcy, Phila, 1956-60; Cnslt, Ballistic Missile Cmnd for Minute Man Missiles, USAF, Phila, 1959-63; Snr Mech Engr, US Army Frankford Arsenal, Phila, 1959-77; Snr Design Engr, Ford Motor Co, Dearborn, MI, 1977-81; Snr Mfg Engr, Ford Aerospace Co, Newport Beach, CA, 1981-86; Snr Engr, Sci, Space Systems Lab, Boeing Co, Huntington Beach, 1986-. Publications include: Simulation Modeling & Testing of a Satellite Despin System, 1989. Honours: Awd, Sci Rsch, Secty US Army, 1968. Membership: ASME. Hobbies: Music; Reading; Fitness; Writing; Philosophy. Address: Boeing Company, 5301 Bolsa Avenue, Huntington Beach, CA 92647, USA.

LIU Bing, b. 13 Dec 1962, Xian, China. Mechanical Engineer. m. X J Zheng, 5 May 1987, 1 s. Education: PhD. Appointments: The Japan Soc of Mechl Engrs (JSIYE), Tokyo, Japan, 1991-; Mbr, Soc of Material Sci of Japan, Kyoto, Japan, 1994-; Cnslt, Kansai Branch of JSME, Osaka, Japan, 1995-97. Publications: Articles in var profl jrnls. Honours: Lectr, Northwest Inst of Archtl Engrng, Xian, China, 1987-89; Engr, Daiho Indl Co Ltd, Osaka, Japan, 1994-. Hobby: Soccer. Address: 2-25-9 Ikuno, Katano, Osaka 5/6-0054, Japan.

LIU Bo Li, b. 29 Jan 1931, Jiangsu, China. Professor. m. Shu Hua Chen, 19 June 1954, 3 s. Education: BS. Appointments: Prof, 1983, Dir, Inst of Appl Sci and Technol, 1986, Dean, Coll of Appl Sci and Technol, 1993. Publications: Over 130 articles in profl jrnls. Memberships: Vice Chmn, Chinese Nuclear and Radiochem Soc; Standing Tstee, Chinese Isotope Soc; Academician Chinese Acady of Engrng. Address: Beijing Normal University, Department of Chemistry, Beijing 100088, China.

LIU Changling, b. 23 Sept 1926, China. Geologist. m. Wangy Menbin, 30 Dec 1954, 2 s, 1 d. Appointments; Engr, 1960; Snr Engr, 1980; Prof, 1987. Publications: 155 theses incl books on spec topics: Discovery of Al-si spinel; The General Types of Bauxite Deposits; High-Al Clay and Bauxite; Fire Clay Deposits; Burnt Rock and Burnt Deposit. Honours: Sci Dev Prize, 1985. Membership: Dir, Chinese Soc of Sedimentology. Hobbies: Music; TV. Address: Tianjin Geological Academy of Metallurgical Industry, Tianjin, China.

LIU Chun-Wan, b. 16 Nov 1931, Jilin, China. Professor. m. Prof You-Xue, 29 Aug 1958, 2 s. Education: Grad, Beijing Normal Univ, 1956; PhD, Dept of Chem, Moscow State Univ, 1963. Appointments: Asst, Kunming Normal Inst, 1956; Asst, Fuzhou Univ, 1963; Joined Staff, Fujian Inst of Rsch on the Structure of Matter, Chinese Acady of Sci, 1976; Assoc Prof 1979-86; Prof of Chem, 1986-. Creative Works: Proposed a new method for calculating the NMR chem shifts of condensed aromatic hydrocarbons; Contbr, Nitrogen Fixation and It's Research in China, book; Guo-Fan Hong, Ed, 1992; Publs 100 pprs on bonding theory. Honours: Prizes for Achievement in Sci and Technol, Chinese Acady of Sci, 1979, 1983, 1991; Prize for Natl Nat Sci of China, 1993. Memberships: World Assn of Theort Organic Chem and Chinese Chem Soc; Edl Cttees, Chinese Jrnl of Chem; Acta Chimica Sinica; Jrnl of Molecular Scis; Jrnl of Structural Chem. Hobby: Penmanship. Address: Fujian Institute of Research on the Structure of Matter, Chinese Academy of Sciences, Fuzhou, Fujian 350002, China.

LIU Daoyu, b. 7 Oct 1933, Hubei, China. Professor. m. Gaowei Liu, 1 Jan 1961, 2 s. Education: Grad, Dept of Chem, Wuhan Univ, 1958; Russian Lang Trng, Beijing For Lang Inst, 1961-62; Grad Studies, Inst of Elemento-Organic Chem, Acady of Russia, 1962-63. Appointments: Tchng Asst, Lectr of Chem, Vice Provost, VP, 1958-77, VP, Pres, Assoc Prof, Prof of Chem, Wuhan Univ, 1979-; Dir, Higher Educn Dept, Educn Min, China, 1977-79; Fndr, Prin, Wuhan New Century For Langs Boarding Sch. Publications: Theory and Practice of Reform of Higher Educantion in China, 1987; New Technical Revolution and Future; Management of Chinese Universities and Colleges; Knowledge, Intelligence and Creative; A Pioneering and Design of Life, 1995; Loving School, 1996; Over 40 pprs on Organometallic Chemistry and 100 pprs on Higher Education. Honours: Pprs of Ex in Chem, Wuhan City, 1984; Pprs of Ex in Pedagogy, Hubei Prov, 1983; Supreme Glory Medal, Pres Valery Giscard D'Estaing of France, 1985; Acad Prize of Philos, E Philos Rsch Inst, Japan, 1987; Prize for Ex Book in the field of Arts and Socl Sci, Prov of Hubei, 1988; 2 First Prizes for Ex Pprs in Pedagogy, Guangming Daily and Education Times, 1997. Memberships: Dir, China Chem Soc; Hon Ed, Young Chems; Standing Dir, Higher Educn Study Assn of China; Standing Dir, China Study Soc of Dialectics of Nature; Chmn, Bd of Dirs, Sci-Tech Devel Corp Ltd, Zhong Xing; Chmn, Acad Cttee of Experts, Wuhan E Lake High Technol Devel Zone; Chmn, Fndn for Paving-Stone Educ Reform. Listed in: The Grand Dictionary of Chinese Education. Hobbies: Reading and Pondering; Writing; Communicating with Young People. Address: Department of Chemistry, Wuhan University, Hubei 430072, China.

LIU De-quan, b. 17 Dec 1938, Liaoning, China. Biology. m. Xu Gui-rong, 20 Aug 1965, 2 d. Education: Dip, Biol, Liaoning Univ. Appointments: Prof, Dpty Dir, Inst of Parasitic Diseases, Chinese Acady of Preventive Med, 1984-. Publications: Practical Malariology, 1978; Manual of Malaria Control, 1988; Geographical Distribution of Chloroquine-resistant P Falciparum in China and Resistance Degree; Current Situation of Sensitivity of P Falciparum to Antimalrials in China. Membership: VP, Chinese Assn of Rat Hazard & Sanitary Pests, 1998-. Hobbies: Table tennis; Chess. Address: 207 Rui Jin Er Lu, Shanghai 200025, China.

LIU Deming, b. 28 Oct 1935. Researcher. m. 1 Jan 1961, 3 s, 2 d. Education: Shenyang Agricl Univ, 1960. Appointments: Asst Rsch Fell, 1980; Assoc Rsch Fell, 1986; Rsch Fell, 1993. Publications: Cotton Destructive Insect Forecast, the Method and Area Divisional Standard (Co-Author), 1992. Honours: Awd of Agricl Soc of Liaoning, 1986. Memberships: Entomological Soc of China and Liaoning; Plant Protection Soc of China and Liaoning; Argicl Soc of China; Protection Soc of Liaoning. Hobbies: Literature; Tourism. Address: Institute of Soil and Water, Conservation of Liaoning Province, Chaoyang, Liaoning 122000, China.

LIU Fangren, b. 1936, Wugong, Shaanxi, China. Party Official. Appointments: Joined CCP, 1954; Dpty Sec, Jiangxi Prov CCP Cttee, 1985; Alt Mbr, CCP Ctrl Cttee, 1987-; Sec, CPC 7th Guizhou Prov Cttee, 1993-; Mbr, 15th CCP Ctrl Cttee, 1997-. Address: Central Committee of the Chinese Communist Party, Zhong Nan Hai, Beijing, China.

LIU Guoguang, b. 16 Oct 1923, Nanjing, China. Research Fellow. m. Guoxian, 25 Sept 1948, 2 s, 1 d. Education: Dept of Econs, SW Assoc Univ, Kunming, China; Postgrad, Dept of Natl Econ Planning, Moscow Inst of Econs. Appointments: Dir, Inst of Econs, Ed-in-Chf, Econ Rsch, 1982-85; VP, Chinese Acady of Socl Scis, 1982-93; Specl Advsr, Chinese Acady of Socl Scis, 1993-. Publication: Studies on Models of Chinese Economic System Reform, 1987. Hobby: Music. Address: Chinese Academy of Social Sciences, 5 Jianguomenkei Dajie, Beijing, China.

LIU Guoquan, b. 4 May 1952, Shandong Prov, China. Higher Educator. m. Li Hongxiang, 26 July 1978, 1 s. Education: MEng, 1983, PhD, 1984, Univ of FL (USA). Appointments: Lectr, 1984-87, Assoc Prof, 1987-91, Full Prof, 1991-, Dir, Acad Affairs, 1995-98, Dpty Dean of Grad Sch, 1995-, Sec-Gen & Mbr, Acad Degrees Cttee, 1995-, Univ of Sci & Technol, Beijing, China; Mbr, State Steering Cncl for Postgrad Educ w MEng Degree, 1999-. Publications: Over 90 sci publs in intl jrnls and confs. Honours: 1st Class Awd, Fok Ying Tung Educ Fndn, 1989; Offic Citation w Spec Allowance, State Cncl of China, 1992; Natl Excellent Tchr Medal, 1995; Sci-Tech Advmnt Awd, 1994; Natl Outstndng Young Scientist, 1997. Memberships: Chinese Soc for Stereology, 1988-; Cncl Mbrs, Chinese Mechl Engrng Soc, 1990-; Chinese Soc for Acad Degrees & Postgrad, 1995-. Address: Graduate School, University of Science and Technology, Beijing 10083, China.

LIU Hong-Xu, b. 23 Oct 1934. Senior Civil Engineering Researcher. m. 7 May 1963, Liu Shaoping, 1 s, 1 d. Education: BEng, Dept of Civ Engrng, Qinghua Univ, Beijing, 1959. Appointments: Asst Engr, 1959-77, Engr, 1977-84, Heilongjiang Prov Low Temp Cnstrn Sci Rsch Inst, Harbin; Dir, Civ Engrng Rsch Dept, 1977-84; Snr Engr, Heilongjiang Cold Reg Cnstrn Rsch Inst, Harbin and Vice Gen Engr, 1984-94; Prof, Snr Rschr,

Heilongjiang Cold Reg Cnstrn Rsch Inst and Vice Gen Engr, 1994-. Publications: Books: Geocryological Glossary, 1994; The National Code for Design of Soil and Foundation of Building in Frozen Soil Region of China, 1995; Undertaken Research Program: The Theorectical Calculation of Frost Heaving Force in Frozen Soil Foundation and the Research of Design of Reasonable Burying Depth of Foundation in Seasonally Frozen Soil Region, Great Progress and Leading Position in the World being Recognised, 1974-92. Honours include: Awd of Snow, Ice and Frozen Soil of Chinese Soc of Glaciology and Geocryology, 1988; Awd of Sci and Technol Cttee of Heilongjiang Prov, 1993; 1st Awd of Sci and Technol Adv in Civ Engrng of Heilongjiang Prov, 1994; 1st Awd of Sci and Technol Adv of the Min of Cnstrn of China, 1994. Memberships include: Soil and Fndn Acad Cttee of the Archtl Soc of China, 1980-; Standing Cncl Mbr, Sub Cttee of Glaciology and Geocryology, Geogl Soc of China, 1980-95; Acad Cttee of Key Natl Lab of Frozen Soil Engrng, Lanzhou Rsch Inst of Glaciology and Geocryology, Chinese Acady of Scis, 1990-; Nat Soil and Fndn Engrng Cttee of Chinese Soil and Fndn Tech Stand Cttee, 1991-. Hobbies: Vocal Music; Painting; Gymnastics; Body Building. Address: Heilongjiang Cold Regional Construction Research Institute, 60 Qingbin Road, Harbin 150080, China.

LIU Huaqiu, b. Nov 1939, Wuchuan, Guangdong, China. Diplomat. Education: Fgn Affairs Inst. Appointments: Joined CCP, 1965; 2nd Sec, Emb Ghana, 1973; Clk Gen Off, State Cncl, 1981; Cnslr, Min, Emb Aust, 1984; Dir, Dept of Affairs of the Ams & Oceania, Min of Fgn Affairs, 1986; Asst to Min of Fgn Affairs, 1988; Vice-Min of Fgn Affairs, 1989; Alt Mbr, 14th CCP Ctrl Cttee, 1992; Dir, Fgn Affairs Off, State Cncl, 1995-; Mbr, 15th CCP Ctrl Cttee, 1997-. Address: Foreign Affairs Office, State Council, Beijing, China.

LIU Jia-qi, b. 5 June 1909. Doctor. m. Prof Irving Chu, 1 July 1939, 1 s, 2 d. Education: BS, Ginling Coll, Nanking, China, 1932; MD, Peking Union Med Coll, 1937; Univ of State of NY. Appointments: Prof of Ophthalmology, Beijing Med Univ; Chmn of Dept of Ophthalmology, Beijing Med Univ; VP, Chinese Ophthalmology Soc; V Ed in Chief, Chinese Jrnl of Ophthalmology, 1968-84. Publications: Primary Glaucoma, 1964; Text Book of Practical Ophthalmology, 1984, 2nd ed 1996. Honours: Hon, Univ of CA, Berkeley, 1982; Awd, Natl Educ Bur, 1984; Awd, Natl Pub Hlth Min, 1985; Hon, States Cncl, 1990. Hobby: Sports. Address: Department of Pediatric Ophthalmology, First Teaching Hospital, Beijing Medical University, Beijing 100034, China.

LIU Jiang, b. 1940, Beijing, China. Government Official. Appointments: Mbr, CCP, 1978; Vice-Min of Agricl, Animal Husbandry & Fishery, 1986-90; Vice-Min, State Planning Comm, 1986-93; Min of Agricl, 1993-98; Dpty Hd, State Working Grp for Comprehensive Agricl Devel; Mbr, 15th CCP Ctrl Cttee, 1997-. Address: Ministry of Agriculture, Nongzhanguan Nanli, Beijing 100026, China.

LIU Keling, b. 4 May 1941. Chemist; Physicist. m. 1 Oct 1966. Education: Grad, Phys Dept, Peking Univ. Appointments: Hd, Spectroscopic Lab. Publication: Published over 80 acad pprs, 1964-98. Honours: 2 Achievements in Sci and Technol, Chinese Acady of Scis, 1991, 1993; A Natl Achievement Cert of Sci and Technol, 1994. Memberships: Spectroscopy Lab, Inst of Chem Metall, Chinese Acady of Scis, Beijing, 1964-81, 1983-99; Mbr of Dr R M Barnes Grp, Dept of Chem, Univ of MA, USA, 1981-82; Mbr of Dr H D Winforedner Grp, Dept of Chem, Univ of FL, USA, 1982-83. Hobby: Swimming. Address: Institute of Chemical Metallurgy, Chinese Academy of Sciences, 1# Bei Er Tiao, Zhong Guan Cun, Beijing 100080, China.

LIU Keming, b. 28 July 1919, Liaoning, China. Social Scientist. m. 1944. Appointments: Rsch Fell, Econ and Socl Sect WFTU, 1953-58; Dir, Sect in Organ of CPC Cntrl Cttee, 1958-76; Dir, Inst of Soviet Studies, 1976-80; Dir, Inst of Soviet and E Eurn Stdies, Chinese Acady of

Socl Scis, 1981-83; VP, Chinese Soc for E Eurn, Russian and Cntrl Asian Stdies, 1983-; Prof, Peking Univ, 1979-; Prof, Inst of For Affairs, 1985-. Publications: Publd series of pprs in Chinese acad jrnls specializing in the polit econ and theort fields of Soviet Studies. Membership: Cncl Mbr, Chinese Assn for Intl Understanding. Address: No 4 Fuxing Road, Beijing, China.

LIU Laifu, b. 23 July 1938, Beijing, China. Educator; Researcher in Applied Mathematics. m. Xueqin Zhang, 1 Aug 1969, 1 s. Education: Bachelor, Dept Math, Beijing Normal Univ. Appointments: Asst Prof, 1979, Assoc Prof, 1983, Full Prof, 1989, Chair, 1995-98, Dept Math, Beijing Normal Univ. Publications: Books: Quantitative Genetics for Crop Science, 1984; Biostatistics, 1988; Mathematical Models and Mathematical Modeling, 1997; 70 scientific pprs. Honours: Exemplary Tchr in Beijing, 1993; Outstndng Tchng Achmnt in Beijing, 1997; Baogang Educl Prize in China, 1998. Memberships: V Dir, Beijing Math Soc, 1997; Mbr Cncl, Chinese SIAM, 1995. Address: Dept Math, Beijing Normal University, Beijing 100875, China.

LIU Long Fu, b. 30 Nov 1932, Shenyang Cty, Liaoning Prov, China. Teacher. m. Guan Shu Juan, 16 Jan 1963, 1 d. Education: Cand Dr to grad from Maths Dept of Jilin Univ, 1959. Appointments: Instr, 1962; Assoc Prof, 1979; Prof, 1986. Publications: Reductive operators and reductive algebras, 1986; Reflexive operators and reflexive algebras, 1988; Hyporeflexive operators and hyporeflexive algebras, 1990. Honours: Title: Natl Excllent Tchr, 1989; Governmental Spec Allowance, 1992-. Memberships: Ed, Northeastern Math Jrnl and Jrnl Mtah Rsch & Exposition; Cncl Mbr, Chinese Math Soc, 1991-99; Pres, Cncl of Liaoning Prov Math Soc, 1991-99. Hobbies: Enjoys reading Chinese classical novels; Tang poetry and Song Ci. Address: Maths Department of Liaoning University, Shenyang, Liaoning, China.

LIU Mengjun, b. 25 Apr 1965, Wangdu, Hebei, China. Researcher. m. Qi Jinbe, 30 May 1989, 1 d. Education: Bachelor, Master, Hebei Agricl Univ, China; Dr, Beijing Medl Univ, China; Postdoct, Natl Horticultural Rsch Inst, S Korea. Appointments: Asst Prof, Hebei Agricl Univ (HAU), 1987; Lectr (HAU), 1991; Assoc Prof (HAU), 1993; Prof (HAU), 1995. Publications: A Taxonomic Study on the Genus Ziziphus, 1995; Flora of Wild Fruit Tree in China, 1998. Honours: One of 100 Natl Good Example for Young Rschrs, 1994; One of 10 Most Oustndng Young People of Hebei Prov, 1995. Memberships: Vice-Chmn, Fruit Cttee, Chinese Assn for Agricl Technique Popularization, 1996; Hebei Provincial Yth Assn for Sci and Technol, 1997. Hobbies: Touring; Table tennis. Address: Research Centre of Chinese Jujube, Hebei Agricultural University, Baoding, Hebei, 07001, China.

LIU Ming, b. 14 Mar 1958, Shanghai, China. Researcher. m. Sun Li Ping, 12 May 1990, 1 d. Education: ML; Postgrad, Fudan Univ, China. Appointments: Ed in Chf, Asia Pacific Forum, 1991-92; Dpty Sec, Gen of Cntr, Amn Studies, 1996-98. Creative Works: On Models of International and Political Conflict in Post War Era, ppr. Honours: Third Prize, Shanghai Ex Socl Scis Wrks, 1998. Memberships: Shanghai Soc of Intl Studies. Hobbies: Music; Reading Books. Address: 7/622 Huai-hai Road (M), Shanghai 200020, China.

LIU P Dong-Guang, b. 27 Apr 1953, China. Businessman. Education: BA; MBA. Appointments: Mngng Dir, Eisho Trading Co Ltd, 1987; Pres, China Sports Devel Co Ltd, 1988. Honours: Patentee, 1984, 1985, 1989. Membership: World Ten Pin Bowling Assn; FIQ. Hobbies: Skiing; Golf; Reading. Address: 5-29-15 Shiba, Minato-ku, Tokyo, Japan.

LIU Qi, b. 14 Dec 1940, Shanghai, China. Information Retriever. m. Hu Cheng, 5 Jan 1968, 1 d. Education: BA, 1962. Appointments: Chinese Acady of Agricl Scis; Chinese Acady of Med Scis; Chinese Acady of Scis. Publication: Chinese Thesaurus of Computer Science and Technology, 1990. Address: Institute of Computing

Technology, Academia Sinica, PO Box 2704-19, Beijing 100080, China.

LIU Ruixun, b. 23 Feb 1938, Jiamusi Cty, China. Professor of Peking University. m. Shizhang Ding, 2 Feb 1970, 1 d. Education: MSc, Peking Univ, 1963. Appointments: Chmn, Dept of Geol, Peking Univ, 1991-95; Vice-Chmn, Editl Cttee, Acta Scientiarum Naturalium Universitatis Pekinensis, 1995-. Publication: Microstructural Geology (in Chinese), 1988. Hobby: Painting. Address: Department of Geology, Peking University, 100871, Beijing, China.

LIU Shengwu, b. 15 Oct 1925, Beijing, China. Professor; University Library Director. m. Peiguang Ge, 3 Apr 1953, 2 d. Education: BS, Aeronautical Engrng, Cntrl Univ, Nanjing, 1949; Visng Schl, Moscow Aeronautical Inst, USSR, 1956-58; Visng Schl, Braunschweig Techl Univ, W Germany, Sept-Dec 1988. Appointments: Asst, fmr Nanjing Univ, 1949-52; Asst and Lectr, fmr E China Aeronautical Inst, 1952-57; Lectr, Assoc Prof, Prof, NWest Polytechl Univ, 1957-91; Vice-Dean, Depts of Electron Engrng, Automatic Control, Aerospace Engrng and Aircraft Engrng, 1959-66; Hd, Tchng-Rsch Sect of Gyroscopes and Inertial Navigation, 1978-80; Vice-Dean, Dean, Dept Automatic Control, 1981-87; Dir, NWest Polytechl Lib, 1987-90; Hd Rsch Grp of Sensors, UAV Inst, NPU, 1991-; guest prof, Mechl Engrng Dept, Essen Univ, Germany, Aug-Nov, 1992. Publications include: Co-auth: Dictionary of Aeronautical Science and Technology, 1982; Co-auth: Doppler/Strap-down Hybrid Inertial Navigation System Research, 1984; Co-auth: Chinese Encyclopedia, Vol on Aerospace, 1985; Experimental Study of A Precision Magnetic Heading System Aided by Strap-Down Flux-gate Magneto Meters, 1985; Performance Analysis and Simulation Study of GPS/SINS Integrated Inertial Navigation Systems, 1989; A High Accuracy Magnetic Heading System Composed of Fluxgate Magnetometers and microcomputer, 1989; Finite Element Analysis and Computer-aided Optimal Design of Magnetic Field Fluxgate Magnetometers (IECON), 1989; Compass Deviation Analysis and Compensation for a Three Axis Strapdown Magnetic Heading System (IFAC Congress), 1990; Research on High Precision Intelligent Diigital Magnetic Heading System (IEE, ICIT) 1994. Honours: Third Prizes, Min of Aviation of China, 1983, 1994; Adv Fell-Worker, Shaanxi Prov Sci and Technol Assn, 1987; Third Prize, Min of Weapons Ind of China, 1993. Memberships include: Chinese Automation Assn; Mbr Cncl, Chinese Inertial Technol Assn; Xian Vice Chmn, Branch CITA; Snr Mbr, Chinese Elec, Electron and Info Sci Fedl Assn; Mbr, Tech Cttee on Systems and Applications on Automatic Control of Industrial Electronics Soc of IEEE. Hobbies: Chinese Opera (amateur actor); Music; Weiqi; Football. Address: Department of Automatic Control, Director, Library, Northwestern Polytechnical University, Xian, Shaanxi 710072, China.

LIU Shi-Kuo, b. 12 Apr 1938, Jiangsu, China. Professor. m. Xue-Min Zhang, 3 July 1971, 2 s. Education: Grad, Dept of Geophys, Peking Univ, China, 1962. Appointments: Tchng Asst, Sect of Meteor, 1962-77, Instr of Dynamic Meteor and Spec Function, 1978-83; Assoc Prof of Dynamic Meteor and Spec Function, 1983-89; Prof of Dynamics Meteor and Spec Function, 1989-; Chf of Meteor, Peking Univ, Beijing, China, 1991. Publications: Spiral Structure of Planetary Waves, 1979; Spiral Structure of Tropical Cyclone, 1980; Inertial Gravity Waves in Tropical Cyclone, 1981; Nonlinear Waves in Barotropic Model, 1983; Nonlinear Waves in Geophysical Fluid, 1984; Linear and Nonlinear Waves in Geophysical Fluid, 1984; Linear and Nonlinear Stability Problems for Barclinic Rossby Waves, 1985; Wave Action and Stability of Inertia-Internal Gravity Waves, 1986; Nonlinear Waves with Semi-Geostrophic Flow, 1987; Special Function, 1988; A Simple Nonlinear Model of Inertial Oscillation of Atmosphere in Low-Latitudes, 1989; Advances in Studies on Nonlinear Atmospheric Waves, 1990; Dynamic Teaching Material (D-S Yang); Atmospheric Dynamics (book), 1991; Dissipation and Dispersion Effects of Turbulence (ppr),

1992; Two-Dimensional Asymetric Stream Field in Tropical Cyclone (ppr), 1993; Heteroclinic Orbits and Evolution of Atmospheric Motions(ppr), 1994; On the Dispersion Effects of Atmospheric Motion (ppr), 1995. Honours: 1st Class Prize for Sci & Tech (China), 1990; 3rd Class Prize of the State Awds for Nat Sci (China), 1991. Memberships: Roy Meteor Soc, 1994; Active Mbr, NY Acady of Scis, 1996. Address: Department of Geophysics, Peking University, Beijing 100871, China.

LIU Shi-Yue, b. 2 Aug 1935, Tientsin, China. Music Archaeologist; Musicologist; Pianist. Education: Dip, Univ of Logic and Lang, Peking, 1982-83; Self-taught, piano, violin comp, 1956-66; Adv studies w V Ashkenazy by corresp, 1965, w J Squier in Tientsin, 1982; Debut: Tientsin, 1956. Appointments: Tianjin TV, 1986-99, Tianjin Radio, 1986-96; CCTV, 1986-93; Jilin TV, 1993; Cntrl Radio, Peking, 1987, Hong Kong TV, 1986, Hong Kong Radio, 1986, VOA (Chinese Sect), 1986; Radio Aust (Chinese Sect), 1988; Cnslt Ed, 1996-; Rschr, World Cultural and Arts Cntr, 1999-; Publications: Report on Archaeological Finds of Bone Flutes in China, 1985; Bone Flutes of Hemudu in Cheking, China, 1986; Anal bet Mus and other Arts in China, 1988; English Poem, Okay, Vanquish All Things At Once, 1985, 1988; Apollo and Pianist, 1993; Ppr: Human Ecology Past and Present, S Africa, 1998. Honours: Lu Hsun Lit and Art Prize (spec prize), 1988; The World Lifetime Achievement Awd, ABI, USA, 1992; Dip for Outstndng Serv to Culture and Art, State Cncl of China, 1993; 2 Commemorative Rsch Fell Coins, ABI, USA, 1994; Gold Awd, Chinese Hero and Model, PRC, 1998; World Cultural Achievement Prize, PRC, 1999. Memberships: Intl Cncl for Tradl Music (UNESCO); ICTM Study Grp on Music Archaeology (UNESCO); Beethoven Soc for Pianists, USA, 1993; Rsch Bd Advsrs, ABI, USA, 1991-; Edtl Advsry Bd, ABI, USA, 1991-; IBC Advsry Cncl, Cambridge, Eng, 1995. Hobbies: Classical Music; Fine Arts; Art Appreciation; Stamp Collecting; Playing Piano & Violin. Address: 87 Changsha Road, Tientsin 300050, China.

LIU Suzhen, b. 5 Jan 1965, Tongnan, Chongqing, China. Nursing. m. Yang Chengwen, 6 Dec 1988, 1 d. Education: Master Deg, Med & Surg Nursing, Qi Chiang Mai Univ, Chiang Mai, Thailand. Publication: Knowledge and Lifestyle of Chinese Women with Osteoporosis, 1998. Address: Faculty of Nursing, West China University of Medical Sciences, Chengdu, Sichuan, 610041, China.

LIU Timon Cheng-Yi, b. 2 Oct 1963, Grt Bamboo, Sichuan, China. Teacher. m. Mian Tang, 9 July 1993, 1 d. Education: BSc, Chem, Nanjing Univ; MSc, Quantum Chem; PhD, Laser Technol, Huazhong Univ of Scis and Technol. Appointments: Editl Bd Mbr, Chinese Laser Jrnl; Natl Ctteeman of Laser Med and Surg Subsoc of Chinese Optical Soc. Publications: Research on System-Specific Property of Time of Radiation-Matter Interaction (doct disseration), 1993. Memberships: Chinese Optical Soc; Chinese Medl Soc. Hobbies: Cold shower; Music; Playing cards; Research on time nature. Address: Laboratory of Light Transmission Optics, South China Normal University, Guangzhou, GD 510631, China.

LIU Ts'ui-jung, b. 5 Dec 1941, Changhwa, Taiwan. Researcher; Teacher. Education: BA, Natl Taiwan Univ, 1963; MA, 1966; MA, Harv Univ, 1970; PhD, 1974. Appointments: Asst Rsch Fell, Academia Sinica, 1966-68; Assoc Rsch Fell, 1974-78; Post-doctoral Fell, Univ of Pennsylvania, 1976-77; Assoc Prof, Natl Taiwan Univ, 1977-79; Assoc Prof, Soochow Univ, 1978-79; Assoc Rsch Fell, Academia Sinica, 1978-79; Prof, Natl Taiwan Norm Univ, 1979-80; Visng Prof, Ecole des Hautes Etudes en Sciences Sociales, Paris, 1980; Fulbright Fell, Georgetown Univ, 1984; Visng Prof, Univ of CA, 1989; Rsch Fell, Academia Sinica, 1979-; Prof, Dept of Hist, Natl Taiwan Univ, 1980-; Rsch Fell, Academica Sinica, 1998-. Creative Works: 51 Publs. Honours: Mbr, Academia Sinica, 1996-. Address: Inst of Taiwan History, Academia Sinica, No 128 SEc 2 Yen Chiuy Yuan Road, Taipei, Taiwan.

LIU Wan Quan, b. 6 Feb 1965, Shangdong, China. Researcher. m. Wen Wang, 1 Jan 1991, 1 s. Education: PhD, Shanghai Jiaotong Univ, 1993. Appointments: Rsch Assoc, Univ of WA, 1993-98; Rsch Fell, Univ of Sydney, 1998-. Creative Works: Many pprs in Intl Jrnls, 1994-. Honours: Ex yng schl, Shandong Prov, 1993; Univ Fellshp, Sydney Univ, 1998. Memberships: IEEE. Hobbies: Soccer; Reading. Address: School of Electrical and Information Engineering, The University of Sydney, NSW 2006, Australia.

LIU Wei-Yi, b. 13 June 1950. Professor; Computer Software Scientist. m. (2) Ning Song, 25 Jan 1999. Education: BS. Publications: The Reduction of Fuzzy Data Domain and Fuzzy Consistent Join (Fuzzy Sets and Systems Vol 50 No1, 1992). Honours: Yunnan Advd Sci Achievement Awd, 1993; Yunnan Outstndng Scientist and Techn Awd, 1994; Yunnan Natl Sci Achievement Awd, 1995. Hobbies: Research interests include databases and information modelling. Address: Department of Computer Science, Yunnan University, Kunming, Yunnan 650091, China.

LIU Weiqian, b. 28 Mar 1940, Shandong, China. Teacher. m. Hanchong Huang, 31 Aug 1967, 2 d. Education: Bach Deg. Appointment: VP, Dept of Appl Maths, Maths & System Sci Coll, Shandong Univ. Publications: Over 20 pprs in profl jrnls. Honours: Awds, Adv Individual, Soc of Shandong Civil Engrng Computer Appl Br. Memberships: Chinese Soc of Theoretical & Appl Mechs; Chinese Soc of Civil Engrng. Hobby: Qigong. Address: c/o College of Mathematics, Shandong University, Jinan 250100, China.

LIU Weixin, b. 15 Aug 1931. Professor. m. Wenmin Bai, 29 Sept 1960, 2 d. Education: Dalian Tech Inst, 1950-53; Moscow Auto-Mech Inst, 1954-59; Mech Engr Deg; Master Deg. Appointments: Engr, the first Automobile Works in China, Changchun, 1959-62; Lectr, Assoc Prof, Prof, Dept of Automobile Engrng, Tsinghua Univ, Beijing, 1962-; Dean, Dept of Automobile Engrng, Tsinghua Univ, 1985-91. Publications include: Bevel and Hypoid Gears, 1980; Automobile Clutch Design, 1981; Automobile Drive Axle Design, 1987; Optimization of Mechanical Design, 1986; Automobile Dynamics, 1981, 1990; Measurement and Design of Automobile Gears and Spline, 1987; Optimal Design of Mechanism and Automobile Construction, 1994; Mechanical Reliability Design, 1996; Articles: Handbook of Mechanical Engineering, 1980, 1997; Handbook of Automobile Design, 1984; Automobile Encyclopedia, 1992; Japanese Chinese Dictionary of Mechanical Engineering, 1983; Over 40 rsch pprs. Honours include: Many Awd's for Books; Sci and Tech Progress Prize, China Automotive Ind, 1991; Spec Subsidy and Hon Ctf, Spec Contbrn, State Cncl of China, 1992. Memberships: Standing Mbr, Cncl of China SAE; Advsr, Automotive Ind Advsry Cttee, Beijing Municipality; Vice Chmn, Higher Educl Guiding Cttee of Automobile and Tractor Engrng, China; Standing Mbr, Cncl of Reliability Soc of China Rsch Soc of Mod Des Methods. Hobbies: Classical Music; Reading Books; Travel. Address: Department of Automobile Engineering, Tsinghua University, Beijing 100084, China.

LIU Wen, b. 7 Jan 1937. Professor. m. Fu Shaozhen, 26 Apr 1963, 1 s, 1 d. Education: BSc, Nankai Univ, 1959. Appointments: Asst 1959-78, Assoc Prof, 1979-83, Full Prof, 1983-, Hebei Univ of Technol. Publications: Boolean Algebra, 1981; Sequence and Limit, 1980; Algebra, Vol I, 1980, Vol II, 1983; An Introduction to Inequality, 1985; Nowhere Differentiable Continuous Functions, 1987; Basic Measure Theory, 1985; Probability and Statistics, 1990; 190 rsch papers. Honours: Awds for Sci and Technol, Hebei Prov and Tianjin, 1979, 1980, 1985, 1992; Winner of title, Natl Outstndng Expert of Sci and Technol of China. Memberships: Pres, Assn of Engrng Probability and Statistics of China, 1998-; Chmn, Math Assn of Hebei Prov, 1999-. Listed in: Who's Who of Intellectuals; Who's Who in Australasia and the Far East. Address: Department of Maths, Hebei University of Technology, Tianjin 300130, China.

LIU Xiaoqing, b. 30 Oct 1955, Chengdu, Sichuan, China. Actress. Education: Sichuan Music Sch. Publications: My Way; My Eight Years; From a Movie Star to Billionaire. Honours: 10th Hundred Flowers Best Actress Awd, 1986; 7th Golden Cock Best Actress Awd, 1986; 11th Hundred Flowers Best Actress Awd, 1988; 12th Hundred Flowers Best Actress Awd, 1989. Address: PO Box 38, Asia Sport Village, Beijing, China.

LIU Yanpei, b. 1 Feb 1939, Tianjin, China. Mathematician; Educator. m. Li Fengxiu, 1 July 1967, 1 s, 1 d. Education: Grad, Univ of Sci and Technol of China, 1963. Appointments: Prof, Northern Jiaotong Univ, Academia Sinica, 1986; PhD Advsr, Natl State Cncl, 1989; Rsch Scientist, Rutgers Univ, 1987; Univ Rome Sa Sapienza, 1989; Visng Disting Prof, Univ Cincinnati, USA, 1997. Creative Works: Embeddability in Graphs; Enumerative Theory of Maps; Discrete Mathematics in China; Handbook of OR Foundations. Memberships: Amn Math Soc, 1994; NY Acady of Sci. Address: North Jiaotong University, 801 Tower 2, 100044 Beijing, China.

LIU Yansheng, b. 23 Nov 1945, Hebei, China. Professor. m. 1 May 1971, 1 s, 1 d. Education: BA. Publications: The Development From the Confucian Ethics to the Confucian Philosophy; On the Difference Between the Ethical Outlooks of Eastern and Western Philosophy; On Lao Zi's Thinking of Taoism and its Beauty Connotation; The Subjective Development of Roman Philosophy in Ancient Greek and Christian Belief. Honours: Sev awds of ex. Memberships: Ethics Assn of Tianjin; Rsch Assn of Chinese and Western Civilization; Dir, Tianjin Assn of Philos Hist. Hobbies: Chinese Calligraphy; Music; Painting. Address: c/o Department of Social Science, Tianjin University, Tianjin 300072, China.

LIU Yi Ding, b. 31 Mar 1934, Liuyang, China. Researcher of Ethnic Music. m. Luo Bing Lian, 8 Feb 1971, 2 s. Education: Bach Deg Courses. Appointments: Sec in Charge of Culture, Dir of Cultural & Educn Off, Asst Educr, Dir of Off, Gen Sec. Publications: Research of the Buyi People's Folk Music, 1992; Collected Works of Research of Buyi Drama, 1993. Honours: Awd, Collection of Instrumental Music of Chinese Natl Minority, 1993. Memberships: Inst of Chinese Musicians, 1985; Rsch Assn, Chinese Natl Minority Music, 1987. Hobbies: Literature; Music. Address: 69 (6) Guanyin Road, Xingyi City, Guizhou, China.

LIU Yi-Lun, b. 11 May 1913, Fukien, China. Educator. m. Xiao Qian Wang, 10 Oct 1942, 2 d. Education: BSEE, dist, EE Sch, Purdue Univ, USA, 1936; MSE, Grad Sch, Purdue Univ, 1937; MS Comm Engrng, Grad Sch of Engrng, Harv Univ, USA, 1938. Appointments: Tech Staff w a rank corresp to Col, Comms Lab, Min of Mil, 1942-44; Prof and Hd of EE Dept, Chongqing Univ, 1941-55; Prof, Rsch Inst of Telecomms, Chongqing Jiaotong Univ, 1945; Vice Dir and Chief Engr, 4th Dist Admin of Telecomms, Min of Comms, 1946-50; Dpty Dir, Chongqing Telecomms Bur, Min of Posts and Telecomms, 1953; Prof, Asst Pres, Beijing Inst of Posts and Telecomms, 1955-63; Prof, VP, Pres, Advsr, Chongqing Inst of Posts and Telecomms, 1963-85; Prof and Chmn of Acad Cttee, Dpty Dir and Chief Engr, 9th Rsch Inst, MPT, 1973-79; Profl visits to USA, Eng and W Germany. Publications: Theory of Network Sunthesis, 1962; Radio for Navigation, 1945; Mathematics for Electrical Engineering, 1951; More than 40 pprs. Honours: Awd for Advd Rschr, 9th Rsch Inst, MPT, 1977; Attending Awd Prize, Natl Sci Conf, 1978; Prize, Sichuan Sci Conf, 1978; Awd Medal, Sichuan Prov Govt and Chongqing City Govt, disting work in Sci and Technol, 1978; Praised by State Govt and awd'd 1st Class spec payment. 1990-. Memberships include: Vice Chmn, Chongqing Sci and Technol Assn, 1978; Hon Dir, Chongqing Inst of Posts and Telecomms, 1982-; Exec Mbr, China Natl Inst of Posts and Telecomms, 1989-; Vice-Dir, Assn Chongqing Snr Profs, Hon Dir, Assn Chongqing Elder Mbr Higher Educ, Adv Rsch Assn, Chongqing Higher Educ. Hobbies: Football; Bridge. Address: Chongqing Institute of Posts and Telecommunications, Chongqing, Sichuan 400065, China.

LIU Yongchao, b. 30 Sept 1951, Chengdu, Sichuan, China. Engineer (Senior Engineer). m. Li Wei, 1 d. Education: Univ. Appointments: Chmn, New Hope Grp; Pres, Hope Grp. Honours: Golden Prize for Application of Technol, 1993; The Most Excellent Pvte Entrepeneurs, 1993; Outstndng in Chinese Reform, 1994; China Outstndng in Poverty-fighting, 1997. Memberships: Natl Polit Cnslt Standing Cttee Mbr; Vice Chmn of Chinese Ind and Com Fedn; Vice-Chmn, China Minsheng Bank; Vice-Chmn, China Feed Ind Assn. Hobbies: Swimming; Playing badminton. Address: No 45, Sec 4, Renmin Nan Road, Chengdu, Sichuan, China 610041.

LIU Yu, b. 23 May 1964, Jinzhou City, China. Educator; Researcher. m. Yajuan, 21 Nov 1997. Education: BEng, BILI, 1987; MPhil, INSA, Toulouse, 1990; PhD, 1994; Post-doctoral Cert, HKUST, 1996. Appointments: Rsch Assoc, HKUST, 1996-; Prof, BILI, 1997-; Invited Visng Schl, HKUST, 1998-; Lee Kuan Yeu Fell, NTLI, 1998-. Publications: Biofilm Reactor Engineering, 1999. Honours: Yng Acad Leading Expert Awd; Lee Kuan Yew Fellshp. Memberships: NY Acad of Sci, 1999; Hobbies: Tennis; Swimming; Reading. Address: Beijing Inst Light Industry, Dept of Chemical Engineering, II Fucheng Rd, Beijing 100037, China.

LIU Yuan-An, b. 20 Dec 1963, Sichuan, China. Professor. m. Buhua, Feb 1988, 1 s. Education: PhD, Electr Engrng, Univ of Electron Sci and Technol of China, Cheng-Du, Sichuan, China. Appointments: Engr, 1984-86; Assoc Prof, 1992-95; Visng Schl, Ottawa, Can, 1995-97; Full Prof, Beijing, 1997-. Publications: Over 25 techl pprs in jrnsa; Book: Mobile Communication Principle, 1998. Honours: Ho Ying-Dong Awd, Min of Educ of China, 1994; Yth Scientist Awd, ITU Assembly, Toronto. Memberships: Snr Mbr, CIE of China; Cttee, ITU, Beijing Reg. Hobbies: Swimming; Reading. Address: School of Telecommunications Engineering, Beijing University of Posts and Telecommunications, Beijing, China.

LIU Yuecui, b. 26 Jan 1949, Chenxi, Hunan, China. Teacher; Researcher. Education: BAgric, Southmiddle Forest Coll, 1982. Appointments: Tutor of Postgrads, Forestry Mngmt Major, Northwest Forest Coll, 1995-. Publications: Forest Inventory Plan Teach-Yourself Books, 1992; Forest Mensuration and Forest Management, 1996; Forest Calculating and Measuring Management, 1998. Honours: Prov Sci & Technol Awd, 1994; Intl Outstndng Artistic Wrk Awd, 1998; Intl Outstndng Acctng Treatise Awd, 1998; 20th Century Spec Studying Field Contbn Big Awd, 1998; Natl Outstndng Treatise Wrks Awd, 1999. Memberships: China Soc of Forest Mngmt, Cncl Mbr, Branch Soc; China Educationalist Assn, Cncl Mbr; China Systems Engrng Soc Forestry Systems Engrng Spec Field Commn, Cncl Mbr. Hobbies: Computers; Photography. Address: Department of Forestry, 93#, Northwest Forest College, Yangling, Shaanxi, China.

LIU Zhengjie, b. 19 Apr 1958, Dalian, China. Educator; Scientist. m. Yan Jin, 24 Jan 1986, 1 d. Education: BEng; MEng. Appointments: Tchng Asst, Lectr, Assoc Prof, Prof; Guest Prof. Publications: 46 pprs in profl jrnls and confs. Memberships: ISMM; IFIP/TC13; ACM/SIGCHI/IIC. Hobbies: Travel; Photography. Address: Department of Computer Science, Dalian Maritime University, Dalian 116026, China.

LIU Zhixiong, b. 18 Nov 1944, Hunan, China. Vice President. m. Caiyun Wang, 12 Nov 1973, 1 s. Education: BSc, Northwestern Polytech Univ, 1967. Appointments: Engr, Rsch Prof, VP, Chf Engr, Pres, Beijing Spacecrafts, 1967-93; VP, China Great Wall Ind Corp, 1993-. Publications: Mould Design for Superplastic Forming of Titanium Alloy, 1989; Evolution on Superplastic Forming Technology of Large-Size Structure Titanium Alloy, 1993. Honours: 3 Awds, 1988; Spec Awd, Chinese Govt, 1992. Address: c/o China Great Wall Industry Corp, 30 Haidian Nanlu, Beijing 100080, China.

LIU Zhongde, b. 1933, Jian, China. Administrator. Appointments: Dpty Sec-Gen, State Cncl, 1988-92; Dpty Hd, Propaganda Dept, 1990-; Mbr, Ctrl Grp for Propaganda & Thought; Vice-Min of Culture, 1992-93, Min, 1993-98; Mbr, 14th CCP Ctrl Cttee, 1992-97; Pres, Assn for Artists of Min of Culture, 1993-. Membership: VP, Party Bldg Rsch Soc. Address: A83 Beiheyan Street, Beijing 100722, China.

LIU Zhongde, b. 11 May 1914, Henan, China. Professor of English; Writer and Translator. m. Shufeng Chen, 1 May 1942, 3 s, 1 d. Education: BA, For Langs and Lit Dept, Natl Peking Univ, 1938. Appointments: Tchr of Engl, Yunnan Zhaotong Mid Sch, 1938-41; Off Staff Yunnan-Burma Highway Bur, 1941-42; Min of Org, Chongquing, 1942-44; Lectr, Assoc Prof and Full Prof in sev univs and Hunan Tchrs Univ, 1944-; attended four intl confs, 1987-96. Publications: Auth of books: A Study of the Various Uses of the English Word As, 1979; A Free Talk on Translation, 1984; A Collection of Essays in Celebration of the 80th Birthday, 1994; and scores of essays on translation, 1979-90; Translator of: Emma by Jane Austen, revised ed, 1993; Uncle Tom's Cabin, abridged edn, 1981; The Confessions of an English Opium Eater, by Thomas de Quincey, 1988; Chf Ed: Comparative Study of English and Chinese Languages, 1994; A Collection of Papers on Translation by Hunan Scholars, 1995; Comparative Studies of English and Chinese Languages and Translation, 1996; A Dictionary of English-Chinese Translation with Examples, 1999. Honours: A Merit Cert awd'd by Hunan For Lit Soc, 1983; A Second-Class Prize, awd'd by Provl Educ Commn for publ of the book A Tree Talk on Translation; A Merit Cert, awd'd by Univ for a ppr on translation. Memberships: V Chmn, Chinese Translators Assn; Chmn, Hunan Translators Assn; Advsr to Provl For Lit Soc; Advsr to Hunan Lings Assn; Ling Assn of China; Provl Rsch Inst of Culture and Hist. Hobby: Table Tennis. Address: Foreign Languages Department, Hunan Teachers University, Changsha 410006, Hunan, China.

LIVNAT Limor, b. 1950, Haifa, Israel. Politician. m. 2 children. Education: Tel Aviv Univ. Appointments: Advtng & Pub Rels; Mbr, Knesset Educn & Culture Cttee, Labour & Socl Affairs Cttee, 1991-96; Mbr, Knesset, 1992-; Chair, Knesset Cttee for Adv of Women, 1993-94, Sub-Cttee on Women's Rep, Parl Comm of Inquiry into Murder of Women by their Spouses, 1995; Min of Commns, 1996-; Fmr Vice-Chair, World Likud Movt. Membership: Likud-Tzomet-Gesher Grp. Address: Ministry of Communications, 23 Jaffa Street, Jerusalem 91999, Israel.

LLOYD Barbara Lynne, b. 10 Aug 1949, Corryong, Vic, Aust. School Teacher (Primary). m. Greg Flattley, 19 Dec 1970, 1 s, 1 d. Education: Trained Tchr-Libn Cert; Trained Primary Tchr's Cert; BEduc (Primary). Appointments: Bennttswood PS; Collingwood PS; Tecoma PS; Corryong Consolidated Sch; N Melbourne PS; Maidstone PS; Richmond W PS. Publication: Pirate Edna of Old Tallangatta, 1984. Memberships: Austl Educ Union; Austl Literacy Educ Assn; VipperMurray Princess Grp. Hobbies: Reading; Gardening; VCooking; Travelling. Address: Yuppy Views, 81 Market Street, Kensington, Victoria, Australia 3031.

LLOYD Brian Edmund, b. 30 June 1929. Professional Engineer. m. 9 Feb 1952, Elizabeth G Ince, 3 s, 1 d. Education: DipEE; MA; PhD. Appointments: Elecl Engr, Ford Motor Co, Geelong, 1950; Elecl Engr, Austl Cement Ltd, Chmn, Geelong, 1951-54; Elec Engr, Hydro-Elec Commn, Tas, 1955-57; Elecl Engr then Mngr, Sc and T Servs, MMBW, 1957-84; Chmn Dirs, TAFE Natl, Cntr Rsch and Dev, 1982-85; Chmn, Vic Div Inst Engrs Aust, 1981, VP, 1989-91, Dpty Pres, 1992, Natl Pres, 1993; Chmn, TAFE Accrediation Bd, Vic, 1983-87; Dpty Chmn, Vic Post Secnd Accreditation Bd, 1987; Dir, EPM Cnsltng Grp, 1986-94; Adj Prof, Sch Engrng and Technol, Deakin Univ, 1994-. Publications: The Education of Professional Engineers in Australia, 1959, 1962, 1968; Gold at the Ten Mile, 1978; The Organisation of Engineering Work, 1979; Engineering Manpower in Australia, 1979; Manpower and Education for the Water Industry, 1980; Gold at Gaffneys Creek, 1981; Letters of John Maxwell, 1982; Gold at Harrietville, 1982; TAFE and the Technical Workforce, 1984; Rutherglen: A History of Town and District, 1985; Labour Market Roles of Professional Engineers, 1986; Bright Gold, 1987; New Pathways in Engineering Education, 1989; Professional Engineers in Australia: Population Analysis, 1990; Engineers in Australia: A Profession in Transition, 1991; Professional Engineers in Australia: Projections of Supply, 1991; Justice of Jamieson, 1992; A Gallant Life, 1998; Tales of the Ten Mile: Ballybeg to the Bush, 1995. Honours: Mbr of the Order of Aust. Memberships: FIEE; Hon FIEAust. Listed in: Who's Who In Australia; Who's Who in the World. Hobbies: Historical and managerial research. Address: 13 Connor Street, Brighton East, Vic 3187, Australia.

LLOYD Christopher, b. 22 Oct 1938, Stamford, USA. Actor. m. Carol Lloyd. Education: Neighbourhood Playhouse, NY. Creative Works: Films incl: One Flew Over the Cuckoo's Nest, 1975; Butch and Sundance: The Early Days; The Onion Field; The Black Marble; The Legend of the Lone Ranger; Mr Mom; To Be or Not To Be; Star Trek III: The Search for Spock; Adventures of Buckaroo Banzai; Back to the Future; Clue; Who Framed Roger Rabbit?; Track 29; Walk Like a Man; Eight Men Out; The Dream Team; Why Me?; Back to the Future, Part II; Back to the Future, Part III; The Addams Family; Twenty Bucks; Dennis the Menace; Addams Family Values; The Pagemaster; Camp Nowhere; The Radioland Murders; Things To Do in Denver When You're Dead; Cadillac Ranch; Changing Habits. TV incl: Taxi; Best of the West; The Dictator; Tales From Hollywood Hills: Pat Hobby - Teamed with Genius; September Gun; Avonlea. Honours include: Drama Desk & Obie Awds, 1973. Address: Guild Management Corporation, Penthouse A, Los Angeles, CA 90035, USA.

LLOYD Ivor Maurice, b. 9 Jan 1928. Architect. m. Pamela Gordon, 21 July 1971, 1 s, 1 d. Education: ASTC; Sydney Tech Coll. Appointments: Fndr Ptnr, Alexander & Lloyd, 1960, Dir, 1967; Fndn Mbr, Inst of Arbitrators, 1975 Delegate Cr, 1976; Inaugural Chmn, Austl Profl Cnslts Cncl, 1978-80; Chmn, Alexander & Lloyd Aust Pty Ltd, Dir, 1978; Dpty Chmn, Austl Overseas Projects Corp, 1981, Dir, 1978, Chmn, 1984-86. Honour: AM, 1987. Membership: FRAIA. Hobbies Golf; Trout Fishing; Tennis. Address: 1/592 Pacific Highway, Killara, NSW 2071, Australia

LLOYD James Eric (Jim). Federal Politician. m. Kerry Diane, 20 Oct 1975, 2 s. Education: Ship's Master, USL Master Class 4. Appointments: Dairy Product's Distbr, 1980's; 1st Offr, Master of Cruise Ship, MV Lady Hawkesbury, 1987-92; Ops Mngr, Ferry Master, Hawkesbury River Ferries, 1991; Serv STN Proprietor, 1992-95; Mbr, House of Reps, Aboriginal and Torres Strait Islanders Affairs; Sec, Govt Mbrs Transp and Regl Dev Cttee; Mbr House of Reps Stndng Cttee, Ind, Sci and Resources, 1999-; Jnt Stndng Cttee Publ; Chmn, Internation Parly Union for Pacific Island Nations and New Guinea. Memberships: Kariong Prog Assn; Kincumber Action Grp; Rotary (Kariong); Patron, Mooney Mooney Workers; Patron, Gosford Coastal Patrol. Listed in: Who's Who in Australia. Hobbies: Swimming; Jogging; Waterskiing; Hockey. Address: 61 Mann Street, Gosford, NSW 2250, Australia.

LLOYD Russell David Ferrers, b. 31 Jan 1930, Perth, WA, Aust. Retired Brigadier. m. Stephanie Stokes, 27 July 1955, 4 s. Education: Royal Mil Coll (RMC), Duntroon, 1948-51; Austl Staff Coll, Queenscliff, (psc), 1961-62; Jt Servs Staff Coll, 1970 (jssc). Appointments: Grad RMC, 1951; Commissioned Lt, Austl Staff Corps; A/Adjutant, 17 Natl Serv Battalion, 1952; Pl Comd 2RAR, 1952; Pl Comd 3RAR Korea, 1952-53; Capt, 1953; HQ GSO 3 Brit C'wlth Force Korea, Tokyo, 1953-54; Instr, Sch of Infantry, Seymour, Aust, 1954-55; Instr, RMC Duntroon, 1955-57; Adjutant, Corps of Staff Cadets, RMC Duntroon,, 1958; Adjutant, 16 Bn Cameron Highlanders of West Aust, 1959-60; Adjutant, 1 Bn Roy W Aust Regt (RWAR), 1960-61; Attended Austl Staff Coll, Queenscliff, 1961-62; Major, 1961; Army Team of Lectrs, 1962-63; Co Cmdr, Pacific Is Regt (PIR), Papua New Guinea, 1963-64; 21C 1PIR, 1965-66; Lt Col, 1967; GSO 1 Army HQ, Canberra, 1967-69; Cmdr Aust, Army Trng Team,

Vietnam, 1969-70; Attended Jt Servs Staff Coll, Canberra, 1970; CO 2 PIR, 1971-73; Col, 1974; Commandant, 1 Recruit Trng Battalion, 1974-77; Austl Def Attache, Philippines, 1977-79; Brig, 1980; Dir of Security, Dept of Def, 1980-82; Cmdr 5th Mil Dist, 1982-84; Retd from Army, 1985; Servs Mbr of Veterans Review Bd, 1985-89; Mbr, Admin Appeals Tribunal, 1991-; Honours: Mil Cross (Korea), 1953; PSC, 1962; JSSC, 1970; OBE (Vietnam), 1970. Membership: Cnclr, Most Excellent OBE WA Assn, 1985-96; Hon Col, Spec Air Serv Regt, 1985-91; Hon Col, RWAR, 1991-94; Patron, Rats of Tobruk Assn (WA), 1996-; Patron, 2/28 Bn and 24 A TK Coy Assn, 1996-. Hobby: Fishing. Address: 1 C Woodhouse Road, East Fremantle, WA 6158, Australia.

LO James C I, b. 20 Apr 1930, Hualien, Taiwan. Banker. m. Kin-Lan Chen, 4 Mar 1956, 3 d. Education: BA, Natl Taiwan Univ; Pacific Rim Bankers Prog, WA Univ, USA. Appointments: Chmn, Taiwan Coop Bank, 1991; Chmn, Hua Nan Coml Bank, 1994; Chmn, Bank of Taiwan, 1995. Publication: The Credit and Management of Bank, 1995. Honours: Outstndng Banker, Min of Fin, China, 1973. Memberships: Chmn, Bankers Assn of China; Dir, Asia Bankers Assn; Bd Mbr, Cntrl Bank of China. Hobbies: Golf; Reading; Music. Address: 3rd Floor, No 18, Alley 7, Lane 240, Roosevelt Road, Section 3, Taipei, Taiwan.

LO Kenneth C M, b. 10 Apr 1942, Taipei, Taiwan. Vice Chairman; President. m. Christine Lo, 2 Oct 1969, 3 d. Education: MBA, Fin, Univ AL. Appointments: Pres, China Trust Co, 1988-92; Pres, China Trust Cmcl Bank, 1992-. Memberships: Chf Execs Org; World Pres Org; Rotary Club. Hobbies: Golf; Music. Address: 2nd Floor, 3 Sung-Shou Road, Taipei, Taiwan.

LO WONG Yee-Ching Virginia, b. 13 May 1934, Hong Kong. Social Worker. m. John, 9 June 1972, 2 d. Education: DA, Socl Welfare, Univ of CA; Master, Socl Wrk, NY Univ. Appointments: Asst Lectr, Field Instr, Chinese Univ of Hong Kong, 1965-67; Supvsr, Hong Kong Christian Servs, 1967-68; Asst Supt, Socl Servs, Soc for the Aid and Rehab of Drug Abusers, 1969-92; Hd of Dept, Socl Wrk, Hong Kong Shue Yan Coll, 1992-. Publications: Treatment of Drug Dependence in a Therapeutic Community and Aftercare; The Female Addicts in Hong Kong; Rehabilitation of Young Addicts. Memberships: Drug Awareness Cttee of Lions Club Intl; Drug Awareness Cttee; Wrkng Grp on Risk Factors of Adolescent Drug Abusers; Cncl of Socl Serv. Address: Wai Tsui Crescent, Braemar Hill Road, North Point, Hong Kong.

LOADER David Norman, b. 26 Jan 1941, Brisbane, Aust. School Principal. m. Roslyn Helen Kerle, 11 Jan 1964, 2 s. Education: BSc, 1963; DipEd, 1964; Tchrs Ctf, NSW, 1965; Alberta, Can, 1969; MEd, Univ of Sydney, 1971. Appointments: Cranbrook Sch, NSW, 1962-63; Cabamatta HS, NSW, 1964-67; Eastglen Composite Sch, Alberta, Can, 1967-69; The Kings Sch, Parramatta, 1969-70; Prin, Kinross Wolaroi Sch, incorp PLC Kinross and Wolaroi, 1971-78; Prin, Meth Ladies Coll, Melbourne, Vic, 1979; Prin, Wesley Coll, Melbourne. Publications: The Inner Principle; Var articles in profl jrnls. Honours: Fell, Austl Coll of Educ; Fell, Austl Coll Educ Admin, Vic; Fell, Austl Inst of Mngmt. Hobbies: Drama; Walking. Address: 577 St Kildas Road, Prahran, Vic 3181, Australia.

LOBENDAHN Vincent, b. 16 Nov 1937. Government Minister. Education: Victoria Univ of Wellington, NZ. Appointments: State Min for TV and Telecomm, 1992-94; Asst Min, Off of the Prime Min, 1995; Min for Pub Wrks, Infrastructure and Transp, 1995; Min for Labour and Indl Rels, 1996-. Address: PO Box 2216, Government Buildings, Suva, Fiji.

LOCKETT David Robert, b. 13 Jan 1951, Adelaide, Aust. Concert pianist; Senior Lecturer in Piano. m. Alison June Sandow, 13 Jan 1973, 1 s, 1 d. Education: Licentiate in Music Dip, Austl Music Exams Bd, 1970; ARCM, Tchrs Dip, Roy Coll of Music, London, 1972;

Bach of Music, 1st Class Hons, 1972; Master of Music, 1981, Univ of Adelaide. Appointments: Tchng Fell, Univ New England, 1973-74; Lectr, Murray Pk CAE, 1975-83; Snr Lectr, SACAE, 1984-90; Snr Lectr, Univ of Adelaide, 1991-92; Dir, Elder Conservatorium, 1993-96; Assoc Prof, Univ of Adelaide, 1997- Concert appearances throughout Aust and in NZ, UK, US, Canad, Japan, Lorea, China, Malaysia, Singapore, HK, Taiwan, Brunei. Creative Works: Recordings for radio and TV, 1970-; articles for var publs; Margaret Sutherland: The Piano Music, CD recording and notes, 1997. Honours: Hon Life Mbrshp of Piano Tchrs Natl Assn of Jap, 1989; Stephen Cole the Elder Prize for Ex in Tchng, Univ of Adelaide, 1998; Nominated for Recording of the Yr, ABC 24 hrs/Classic FM Recording Awds, 1998. Memberships: Piano Tchrs Natl Assn of Japan; S Austl Music Tchrs Assn; Austl Soc for Keyboard Music; Dpty Chair, SA Cttee and Fed Examiner, Austl Music Exams Bd. Listed in: International Who's Who in Music and Musicians Directory; Who's Who in Australia and the Far East. Hobbies: Picture framing; Reading, esp 19th C Engl fiction. Address: 31 College Drive, Rostrevor, SA 5073, Australia.

LOCSIN Enrique, b. 28 Jan 1946, Manila. Publisher. m. Susan, 22 May 1978, 1 s, 2 d. Education: Asian Inst of Mngmt, 1990. Address: 3G Makati Tuscany Condominium, Ayala Ave, Makati City, Philippines.

LODHA Bhopal Chand, b. 17 Feb 1937, Jodhpur, India. University Management. m. Mrs Meenaxi, 23 Nov 1960, 1 s. 2 d. Education: MSc, PhD, Postdoct work, Univ Toronto; Vstg Prof, Univ Exeter, UK through Brit Counc, 1988. Appointments: Lectr Botany, Rajasthan Univ, 1964-77; Assoc Prof, Plant Pathol, Haryana Agricl Univ; Prof Plant Pathol, Rajasthan Agricl Univ, 1984-97; Vice-Chancellor, Jain Vishna Bharti Inst, 1997-. Publications: 38 rsch pprs in natl and intl jrnls. Memberships: Pres, Mycol Soc of India, 1992-93; Exec Cttee, Intl Mycol Soc, 1990-94; Asia Cttee, 1994-98; Mbr First Intl Cttee on Plant Pathol Tchg and Trng, 1988-93, 1993-98; Participated in sev natl and inlt confs. Hobbies: Gardening; Photography. Address: Jain Vishva Bharati Institute, Ladnun, India.

LOEWENSTEIN Walter Bernand, b. 23 Dec 1926, Gensungen, Germany. Physicist; Engineer. m. Lenore, 21 June 1959, 1 s, 1 d. Education: BS, Univ of Puget Sound; PhD, OH State Univ. Appointments: Argonne Natl Lab, 1954-73; Elec Power Rsch Inst, 1973-89; Prof Cnslt, 1990-. Publications: Over 50 profl publs. Honours: Alumnus Cum Laude, Univ Puget Sound, 1976; Mbr Natl Acady of Engrng, 1991. Memberships: Amn Nuclear Soc, Pres, Pres Elect, 1988-90; Amn Assn of Engrng Socs, Sec-Treas, 1990. Address: 515 Jefferson Drive, Palo Alto, CA, USA.

LOHA-UNCHIT Chesada, b. 27 Nov 1948, Bangkok, Thailand. Economist. m. Thasanee, 22 Dec 1974, 1 s, 1 d. Education: PhD, Econs. Appointments: Assoc Prof, Fac of Econs, Thammasat Univ, 1978-85; VP (Rsch & Plng), Indl Fin Corp of Thailand, 1985-89; Mngng Dir, Tara Siam Bus Info Ltd, 1989-98; Pres, Mutual Fund Pub Co Ltd, 1998-. Honours: Rockefeller Fndn Fellshp, 1972-77. Memberships: Econs Soc of Thailand; Securities Analysts Assn, Thailand. Hobbies: Reading; Swimming; Meditation. Address: 452 Onnuj 6 Sukhumvit 77 Rd, Bangkok 10250, Thailand.

LOHIA Renagi Renagi, b. 15 Oct 1945, Papua New Guinea. Broadcasting Executive; Former Diplomat. m. 1969, 3 s, 2 d. Education: Univ Papua New Guinea; London Univ; MA. Appointments: Rsch Asst, Univ Papua New Guinea, 1970-73; Snr Tutor, 1973, Lectr in Educ, 1974-82, Pro-Vice-Chan, 1976, Dpty Vice-Chan, 1977, Vice-Chan, 1977-82, Chair, Educl Plng Cttee, 1974-75, Educ Fac Rep Jt Cttee on Tchr Educ, 1975-76; Chair, Pub Servs Commn, 1982-83; Amb to USA and Mexico, High Commnr in Can, 1983-89; Perm Rep to UN, 1983-94; Chair, UN Decolonization Cttee; Spec Asst, dept For Affairs, 1986-87; Chf of Staff, Off of PM, 1994-95; Chair, Chf Exec, Natl Brdcstng Commn, 1995-97; VP, Asia Pacific Broadcasting Union, 1997; Mbr

Bd Trstees C'wlth Broadcasting Assn. Honours:, OBE, 1982; CBE, 1994. Memberships: Asia Pacific Broadcasting Union; C'wlth Broadcasting Assn. Address: National Broadcasting Corporation, PO Box 1359, Boroko, Papua New Guinea.

LOKE Kean Hooi, b. 18 Nov 1963, Malaysia. Engineer. m. Jenny Ng Siew Cheng, 13 Mar 1988, 1 s. Education: PhD, Univ of Strathclyde, UK, 1991; BEng (1st Class), Univ of Strathclyde, 1987. Appointments: Rsch Asst Univ of Strathclyde, UK, 1987-91; Tech Mngr, Polyfelt Geosynthetics, 1991-94; Dir, K H Loke Cnslt, 1998-; Regl Tech Mngr, Polyfelt Asia Sdn Bhd, 1995-. Publications: Engineering Design manuals for Geotextile Filters, 1992; Design manuals for Soft Soil Stabilizations, 1993. Honours: Dean's List, Univ of Strathclyde, 1986; Best Thesis Awd, Strathclyde Univ, 1986; Overseas Rsch Awd, 1988-91; David Livingston Awd for Rsch, 1990. Memberships: Intl Geosynthetics Soc, 1992; SE Asia Geotechnical Soc, 1993; Corp Mbr, Instn of Engrs, Malaysia, 1998; Regd Profl Engr, Bd of Engrs, Malaysia, 1998. Hobbies: Reading; Computer; Swimming; Travelling. Address: 99 Jalan USJ 11/1G, Subang Jaya, 47620 Petaling Jaya, Selangor, Malaysia.

LOKESH Belur R, b. 29 Feb 1952, Secunderabad, India. Scientist. m. Pushpa, 15 Nov 1989. Education: PhD, Biochemistry; MSc, Biochemistry. Appointments: Rsch Scientist, Austria, 1980-83; Rsch Assoc II, USA, 1983-89; Scientist, EI, 1989-94; Scientist, EII, India, 1994-. Publications: Rsch articles in sci jrnls. Honours: Dr J C Ghosh Medal, Indian Inst of Sci, 1976-77. Memberships: Soc of Biol Chemists (I); AFSTI (I); Nutrition Soc of India; Indian Assn of Cancer Rsch. Hobbies: Stamp collection; Travelling; Listening to classical music. Address: Department of Biochemistry and Nutrition, Central Food Technological Research Institute, Mysore 570013, India.

LOKUANG Stanislaus, b. 1 Jan 1911, Hunan, China. Philosopher; Educator; President; Professor. Education: PhD, Philos, Urban Univ, Rome, 1936; PhD, Canon Law, 1939, Lateran Univ, Rome; PhD, Sacred Theol, 1942. Appointments: Prof, Urban Univ, 1936-61; Cnslt, Chinese Emb, 1943-61; Bishop of Tainin, Taiwan, 1961-66; Vice Chmn, Commn of Missions during Vatican Cncl II, 1962-66; Prof, Univ of Chinese Culture, 1963-88; Fu Jen Cath Univ, 1963-; Archbishop of Taipei Archdiocese, 1966-78; Mbr, Cttee for Revision of Canon Law, 1966-78; Gen Sec, Pres, Commn of Asian Bishops, 1974-78; Pres, Fu Jen Cath Univ, 1978-; Dean, Coll of Liberal Arts, 1978-81; Prof, Soochow Univ, 1982-88; Pres, Chinese Bishops Conf, 1983-87. Publications: Many books, inclng Confucian Metaphysics, 1959; The History of Chinese Philosophy, 9 vols; The Metaphysic Philosophy of Life Su; Sev biographical writings; Poems, essays and collections; Pprs in jrnls. Honours: Cultural Awd, 1982; Hon Deg, Hyosung Womens Univ, Korea, 1985; Hon Deg, St Vincent Coll, USA, 1985. Memberships include: Commn for Educ and Culture, Pres; Assn for Restoration and Dev of Chinese Culture; Grand Alliance for Reunification of China under the Three Principles of the People; Press Cncl of Repub of China. Hobbies: Chinese painting and writing. Address: Fu Jen Catholic University, Hsin-Chuang, Taiwan 24205, China.

LOMU Jonah, b. 1975, Mangere, New Zealand. Rugby Football Player; Athlete. m. Tanya Rutter, 1996. Appointments: Bank Offr, ASB Bank of NZ; Youngest Ever Capped All Black; Intl Debut, NZ v France, 1994; Semi-Finalist, World Cup, S Africa, 1995; Affil to Rugby Union; Ran 100m in 10.7 Seconds.

LONDONO PAREDES Julio, b. 10 June 1938, Bogota, Colombia. Politician. Education: San Isidro Hermanos Maristas Sch; El Carmen Inst; Mil Cadet Sch, Bogota. Appointments: Prof, Intl Politics, Univ Jorge Tadeo Lozano, Bogota; Prof, Intl Pub Law, Univ El Rosario, Bogota; Served in Army, retd, 1981 w rank of Lt-Col; Hd, Frontier Divsn, Min of Fgn Affairs, 1968-79, Sec-Gen, 1979-82, Vice Min, 1982-83, Min, 1986-90; Amb to Panama, 1983-86; Perm Rep to UN, 1994-. Publications: History of the Colombo-Peruvian Conflict of

1932; Colombian Territorial Law; Colombian Border Issues. Address: Permanent Mission of Columbia to UN, 140 East 57th Street, 5th Floor, NY 10022, USA.

LONEY Peter James, b. 3 Feb 1948, Daylesford, Vic, Aust. Shadow Minister for Energy and Resources and for Tourism. Education: BA, Deakin Univ; Trained Primary Tchrs Cert, Geelong Tchrs Coll. Appointments: Assembly, 1991-93; Primary Sch Tchr, 1966-92; Mbr, Austl Labour Party, 1977-; Commnr, Geelong Regl Commn, 1984-92; State Conf Deleg, 1989-93; Pres, Corio Fedl Electorate Assembly, 1991-93; Elected MLA for Geelong N, 1992, re-elected, 1996; Law Reform Cttee, 1992-; Fedl Campaign Dir (Corio), 1993; Shadow Min for Small Bus and Enterprise Dev and Shadow Min for Energy and Resources and Shadow Min for Tourism, 1996-; Pub Accounts and Estimates Cttee, 1999. Memberships: State Cnclr, Fed Tchrs Union of Vic, 1986-92; Pres, Geelong Trades Hall Cnsl, 1988-89; Asst Snr Timekeeper, Geelong Football Club, 1978; Team Mngr, Mazda Otway Classic, 1986-93. Address: Level 1, Corio Village Centre, Bacchus Marsh Road, Corio 3214, Australia.

LONG Don, b. 5 Jan 1950, Walla Walla. Writer; Editor. m. Michèle, 3 s. Education: MA Hons, Canterbury Univ. Appointments: Co-Ed, Into the World of Light, Te Ao Marama; Ed, Edge; Ed, Pacific Rescs, Learning Media. Publications: Borrow Pit: Poems from the Fifth Season; A Quilt for Kiri; A Gift for Aunty Nga; Cat Talk; Mum's Octopus; Fishing Off the Wharf. Memberships: NZ Soc of Auths; NZ Childrens Books Writers and Illustrators Assn. Hobby: Fly Fishing. Address: 22 Marine Dr, Day's Bay, Eastbourne, New Zealand.

LONG Gui Lu, b. 26 Apr 1962, Muping County, China. Educator; Physicist. m. Shuang Shi, 24 Apr 1986, 1 s, 1 d. Education: BS, Shandong Univ; MSc, Tsinghua Univ, 1985; PhD, 1987. Appointments: Lectr, Tsinghua Univ, 1987-89, 1993-95; Rsch Fell, Univ of Sussex, 1989-93; Assoc Prof, Tsinghua Univ, 1995-98; Div Dir, 1997-; Prof, Tsinghua Univ, 1998-. Publications: Over 50 rsch pprs in nuclear phys and math phys. Honours: Natl Awd and Medal for Prog in Nat Sci, 1997; Educl Min Awd for Prog in Sci and Technol, 1998. Memberships: Chinese Phys Soc, 1987-; Inst of Phys (UK), 1991-; Amn Phys Soc, 1996-. Hobbies: Reading classical Chinese books; Listening to music. Address: Department of Physics, Tsinghua University, Beijing 100084, China.

LONG Ho Quang, b. Nghe An Province, Vietnam. General Director. m. Do Thi Bao Loc, 2 d. Education: Grad, Shanghai Shipbldng Coll; Grad, Maths & Phys, Hanoi Univ, 1964. Appointments: Ship Designer, Ship Design Bur, Min of Transp & Commn, 1959-70; Vice Gen Dir, Mech Dept, Vice Gen Dir, Dept of Ind, Materials & Equipments, Chf, Cabinet of the Ministry of Transp & Commn, 1970-87; 1st Vice Gen Dir, Vietnam Shipbldng Union & Vietnam Shipbldng Sci & Prodn Union, 1987-93; Gen Dir, Ship Technol Devel Cntr, 993-. Publications: Shipbuilding Handbook vl 1, 1978, vol 2, 1982; Ship Repair, 1983; Ferro-Cement Boats, 1985; Sea-River Navigation Ships, 1986; Aluminium Alloy Boats, 1999. Address: Shop Technology Development Centre, Hanoi, Vietnam.

LONG Stephen Ingalls, b. 11 Jan 1946, Alameda, CA, USA. Professor, Electrical Engineering. m. Molly S Long, 17 Dec 1966, 1 s, 1 d. Education: BS, Univ of CA, Berkeley, 1967; MS, PhD, Cornell Univ, 1969, 1974. Appointments: Prof, Univ of CA, Santa Barbara, Elecl/Computer Engrng, 1981-; Mbr, Techl Staff, Rockwell Intl Sci Cntr, 1978-81. Publications: Gallium Arsenide Digital Integrated Circuits, 1990; Over 100 jrnl and conf pprs. Honours: IEEE Microwave Application Awd, 1977; Fulbright Rsch Fellshp, 1994. Memberships: IEEE, Snr Mbr, Amn Sci Affiliation. Address: 895, N Patterson Avenue, Santa Barbara, CA 93111, USA.

LONG Wenpei, b. 10 Nov 1926. Professor of English. m. 29 Jan 1981, Xu Yaozhou, 5 step s. Education: BA, Nanjing Univ, 1952. Appointments: Fac Mbr, Dept of For Langs and Lit, Fudan Univ, 1952-90; Vice Chair, Dept of For Langs and Lit, Fudan Univ, 1964-80; Hd of the Section of Western Lits, 1980-84; Advsr, Eugene O'Neill Rsch Cntr, Cntrl Acady of Drama, 1985-. Publications: Selected Readings in American Literature (Co-Editor), Vol I, 1985, Vol II, 1987, Vol III, 1995; Eugene O'Neill: A Collection of Critical Essays, 1988; Late Plays of Eugene O'Neill, 1988; Theodore Dreiser: A Collection of Critical Essays, 1989; Several articles on Eugene O'Neill and other Engl and Amn Writers for Literary Journals and Collections. Honours: Two Thesis: The Tragic Vision of Eugene O'Neill and On O'Neill's Late Plays were Awd'd prizes for Ex Thes, Shanghai Higher Educl Bur, 1984 and by All China Assn of For Lit Tchng and Rsch in Inst's of Higher Learning, 1995. Memberships: Cncl Mbr, China Assn for the Stdy of Amn Lit, 1979-, VP, 1991-; Advsr to the T S Eliot-E Pound Soc in China, 1995-. Listed in: The International Who's Who of Women. Hobbies: Reading Chinese Classics; Watching Stage Plays. Address: Department of Foreign Language and Literature, Fudan University, Shanghai 200433, China.

LONGLEY John Francis, b. 20 July 1945. m. Jennifer Wilders, 24 Nov 1978, 2 s. Education: Claremont Tchrs Coll, WA; Churchland Tchrs Coll, WA. Appointments: St Paul's Sch, London, 1971; Project Offr, Bond Corp, 1972-74; Inner London Educn Authy, 1975; WA Dept of Educn, 1976-79; Mngr, Am Cup (Challenge) 1983 Ltd, 1980-83; Gen Mngr, Am Cup (Challenge) 1991 Ltd, 1984-; Gen Mngr, The Endeavour Replica Pty Ltd; Chmn, Sport Intl, WA, 1998. Honour: AM, 1984; Freemantle Citizen of the Yr, 1994. Memberships: Roy Freshwater Bay Yacht Club, WA; RSBCA, Fndng Mbr. Hobbies: Sailing; Wind Surfing; Golf; Tennis; Photography. Address: 22 Walker Street, South Fremantle, WA 6162, Australia.

LONGWORTH Graham Peter, b. 18 Oct 1953, Perth, WA, Aust. Data Processing Executive. m. 1994, 1 d. Appointments: Treasury Analyst, 1977-80; Proj Mngr, 1980-86; Info Cntr Mngr, 1986-87; Data Base Admnstr, 1987; Data Processing Exec, 1987-. Publications: Contbns to Austl Rostrum Publs, Sri Lankan Assn newsppr, West Aust. Honours: Awd'd Schlshp to complete hs, 1968; Elected Freeman of Rostrum, 1989. Memberships: Austl Computer Soc; Austl Rostrum. Hobbies: Canoeing; Bushwalking; Teaching Public Speaking; Landscape gardening; Restoring and driving MG cars. Address: 63-65 Lacey Street, Cannington, WA 6107, Australia.

LONGWORTH John William, b. 8 Jan 1940, Marrabri, NSW, Aust. Agricultural Economist. m. Naomi Jill Eames, 8 Dec 1965, 1 s, 4 d. Education: HDA; BS Agric (Hons I); PhD (Sydney). Appointments: Dean, fac of Agric Sci, 1987-88, Pro Vice-Chan, Socl Sci, 1989-96, Exec Dean, Fac of Bus, Econs & Law, 1997-, Univ of Queensland. Publications: China's Rural Development Miracle, 1989; The Wool Industry in China, 1990; China's Pastoral Region, 1993; Agribusiness Reforms in China, 1995. Honours: Univ of W Sydney Gld Medal, 1960; Univ of Sydney Gold Medal, 1964; Austl Inst Agricl Sci Medal, 1984; Farrer Mem Medal, Farrer Trust, 1991. Memberships: Pres, Austl Agric Econ Assn, 1976; Pres, Int Assn of Agric Econ, 1988-91. Hobbies: Geneology; Athletics; Gardening; Tennis. Address: 231 Swann Road, Taringa 4068, Australia.

LOOI Lai-Meng, b. 28 July 1950. Histopathologist. m. Andrew Chang Kwong-Choong, 13 June 1981. Education: MBBS, 1975; MPath, 1979; MRCPath, 1981; MIAC, 1985; FRCPA, 1985; MD, 1987; AM, 1989; FRCPath, 1993; FASc, 1995. Appointments: Lectr, 1979-85, Hd, Path, 1984-, Assoc Prof, 1985-86, Prof, Chair in Path, 1986, Senate, 1998-2000, Univ of Malaya; Snr Cnslt Pathologist, Univ Hosp Kuala Lumpur, 1986-. Publications: Over 120 in sci medl jrnls, technical aid reports and books; Over 200 presentations at Scientific Conferences, sev as guest speaker. Honours: Univ of Singapore: Albert Lim Liat Juay Bronze Medal, for 3rd Profl Exam in Med on subjs of Path and Socl Med and Pub Hlth, 1973-74; King Edward VII Hall, Univ Singapore, Cert of Merit (Serv); Cultural Awd (Literary Wrks); Cultural Awd (Art Forms); Commendation (Poetry); Best Pre-Clinl lectr, by Medl Studs, Univ Malaya, 1983-84, 1989-90, 1994-95, 1995-96; Best Medl Lectr, by Dental Studs, Univ of Malaya, 1987-88, 1989-90, 1990-91; Visng Prof, Harvard Medl Sch, USA, 1991-92; Visng Clin Fell, Univ of Tasmania, 1997. Memberships include: Ed, Malaysian Jrnl Path, 1986-; FRCPath, UK, Mbr Panel of Examiners in Histopath, 1988-; Malaysian Soc of Pathologists: Pres, 1990-91, 1993-95, 1995-97, 1997-99; Acady of Med of Malaysia, Cncl Mbr, 1993-94, 1994-95, 1999-; Malaysian Medl Assn; Fndn Fell, Acady Scis, Malaysia, 1995, Cncl Mbr 1998-2000; Fell, Roy Coll of Pathologists of Australasia, Malaysian rep (corresp mbr) to Bd of Educ and Bd of Censors; Mbr, panel of examiners in Histopathology, 1995-; Intl Acady Pathologists (Aust Branch). Hobbies: Music; Reading; Swimming. Address: Department of Pathology, Faculty of Medicine, University of Malaya, 50603 Kuala Lumpur, Malaysia.

LOOSLI Robert Geoffrey, b. 21 Feb 1926. Naval Executive. m. Jocelyn Paton, 15 May 1951, 2 s, 1 d. Education: RANC, UK JSSC, US Naval War Coll. Appointments: Exec Offr, HMAS Anzac, 1957-58; Cmdng Offr, HMAS Gascoyne, 1960-62; Exec Offr, RANC, 1964-66; Cmdng Offr, HMAS Stuart, 1967-68; Dir, Staff Austl Joint Servs Staff Coll, 1970; Cmdng Offr, HMAS Brisbane, 1971-72; HMAS Supply, 1972-74; Offr-i/c, RAN Trials and Assessing Unit, 1974; Naval Attaché, Austl Emb, Wash DC, 1975-78; Chf, Naval Opl Requirements 1979-81 and Repatriation Review Tribunal and Veteran's Review Bd, 1983-93. Honour: CBE, 1972. Hobbies: Golf; Tennis. Address: 1303 Eastpoint Tower, 180 Ocean Street, Edgecliff, NSW 2027, Australia.

LOPEZ-PORTILLO Y PACHECO Jose, b. 16 June 1920, Mexico City, Mexico. Politician; Lawyer. m. Carmen Romano, 1 s, 2 d. Education: Natl Law Fac, Univ Nacional Autonoma de Mexico; Univ Chile. Appointments: Prof, Gen Theory on the State, Univ Nacional Autonoma de Mexico, 1954, Assoc Prof, Polit Scis, 1956-58; Fndr Prof, Admin Scis Doct, Comm Sch of the Natl Polytech Inst, 1961; Partido Revolucionario Institucional, 1959-64; Tech Assoc, Hd, Off of Min of Patrimony, 1960; Co-ord, Border Urban Devel Cttee, 1962; Mbr, Intersecretarial Comm for Natl Devel, 1966; Under-Sec of the Presidency, 1968; Under-Sec, Min of Patrimony, 1970; Gen Dir, Elec Fed Comm, 1972-73; Sec for Fin & Pub Credit, 1973-75; Pres of Mexico, 1976-82; Fmr Gov for Mexico IMF. Publications: Valoracion de la Estatal; Génesis y Teoria del Estado Moderno; Quetzalcoatl; Don Q. Honour: Ordem Nacional do Cruzeiro do Sul, Brazil, 1978. Address: c/o Palacio de Gobierno, Mexico DF, Mexico.

LORELL Mark Allen, b. 7 Mar 1947, Pasadena, CA, USA. Senior Research Analyst. m. Mary Chenoweth, 12 Aug 1990, 1 s. Education: BA, Hist, Yale Univ, 1969; MA, Hist, Univ of CA, Berkeley, 1971; PhD, Hist, Univ of Washington, 1976. Appointment: Snr Rsch Analyst, Rand Corp, Santa Monica, CA, 1978-. Publication: Troubled Partnership: A History of US-Japan Collaboration on the FSX Fighter, 1996; The Cutting Edge: A Half-Century of US Fighter Aircraft R&D, Rand, Santa Monica, 1998. Membership: CA State Advsry Grp on Japanese - Amn Internment in WWII, 1999. Hobbies: Travel; Reading; Hiking. Address: Rand, 1700 Main Street, Santa Monuica, CA 90407, USA.

LORENZ Andrew Bela, b. 17 Oct 1951, Melbourne, Aust. Violinist. m. Wendy Joy Lorenz, 1 s. Education: DSCM, Performers Dip and Tchrs Dip, Sydney Conservatory of Music, 1970. Appointments: Recitals, concerto, Radio and TV perfs; Dpty Ldr, Melbourne Elizabethan Trust Orch, 1972; Led for D'Oyly Carte Opera Co, Sadler's Wells, Eng, 1973-74; Ldr, New Eng Ensemble (res piano quartet) and Lectr, Music Dept, Univ of New Eng, Armidale, NSW, Aust, 1975-82; Founding Mbr and Ldr, New Eng Sinfonia; World tours w New Eng Ensemble; Assoc Concertmaster, Adelaide Symph Orch, 1983-86; Ldr, Austl Piano Trio, 1983-87; Snr Lectr in Strings, Univ of South Queensland; Currently, Ldr, Darling Downs Ensemble, Dir of McGregor Chmbr Music Sch, Conductor, USQ Sinfonia. Creative works: Recordings: Works by Beethoven, Turina, Margaret

Sutherland, Mozart, Faure, John McCabe, Mendelssohn, Goossens, Rorke. Honours include: Victorian ABC Concerto Competition Winner, 1972. Address: Faculty of Arts, USQ, PO Darling Heights, Toowoomba, Qld 4350, Australia.

LORENZ Wendy Joy, b. 25 Oct 1950, Sydney, Aust. Pianist; Teacher. m. Andrew Bela Lorenz, 1 s. Education: LMusA, 1968; DSCM Hons, Performing and Tchng, Sydney Conservatory, 1970; Studied w Maria Curcio, London, 1973-74. Appointments include: Recital, brdcst, TV and Concerto Soloist; Appearances in Aust, Eur, Asia and Am; Pianist, Young Sydney Piano Trio, 1968-71; Piano Tchr, NSW Conservatory, 1971; Pianist, New England Ensemble and Lectr in Piano, Univ of New England, Armidale, NSW, 1975-82; Pianist, Austl Piano Trio, 1983-87; Pianist, Darling Downs Trio and Snr Lectr in Piano, Univ of Southern Qld, Toowoomba (current). Creative Works: Recdngs: 7 coml releases inclng sundry chmbr wrks and concerto soloist w Adelaide Symph Orch and Slovak Radio Symph Orch and Queensland Symph Orch. Honours include: Beethoven Bicentary Medallion, W German Govt for Outstndng Musical Work, 1970; NSW Winner, ABC Concerto Competition, 1971; 1st Prize, Natl Beethoven Bicentary Chmbr Music Competition, 1970. Membership: Natl Cttee, Austl Natl Piano Pedagogy Conf. Address: 6 Merlin Court, M/S 852 Toowoomba, Qld 4350, Australia.

LOS Cornelis Albertus, b. 14 Dec 1951, Purmerend, Netherlands, Came to USA, 1977. Economist; Portfolio Risk Manager; Educator. m. (1) Diane Nichols, 10 June 1979 (div 1984), 1 d, (2) Elizabeth M Ten Houten, 18 June 1986 (div 1991), 1 d, (3) Rose Lee Haubenstock, 5 May 1994. Education: Cand cum laude (Fell), Univ Groningen, 1974; Doctorandus, 1976; Rsch Student, London Sch Econs, Sch Slavonic and E Eurn Studies, 1975-76; Dip, Inst Socl Studies, The Hague, 1977; MPhil, Columbia Univ, 1980, PhD, 1984. Appointments include: Adj Prof, Baruch Coll, NYC, 1985-86; Ecomomist, Fedl Rsch Bank of NY, NYC, 1981-85; Snr Economist, 1985-87; Snr Economist, Nomura Rsch Inst (Am) Inc, 1987-90; Chf US Economist and Econ Advsr, ING Bank, NYC, 1991-93; Rsch Assoc, Cntr for Math System Theory, Univ FL, Gainesville, 1986-92; Pres, EMEPS Assocs Inc, 1986-; Assoc Prof Banking and Fin, Nanyang Techl Univ, Singapore, 1995-; Lectr, num profl confs, US and for countries; Bd Dirs, Netherland-Am Fndn Inc, 1989-95. Publications: Articles in profl jnls. Honours: Lady Van Renswoude of the Hague Fndn awds, 1974-75; MAOC Countess Van Bylandt Fndn Awd, 1976; Scholten Cordes Fndn awds, 1976-77; Fulbright-Hays Schl, 1977. Memberships: AIMR; IEEE; Math Assn Am; Econometric Soc; Intl Assn for Math & Computer Modelling; Amn Stats Assn; Amn Econ Assn; Amn Fin Assn; NY Acady Scis. Hobbies: Russian and Chinese languages and literature; Yoga; Jogging; Hiking; Golf; Photography. Address: Block B Nanyang Avenue, 10-04 Singapore 639611.

LOTHIAN Thomas Robert Noel, b. Melbourne, Vic, Aust. Director, Adelaide Botanic Gardens (retired); Botanist Horticulturist. Education: Burnley Hort Coll, Vic, 1934; Natl Dip of Hort, NZ, 1945. Appointments: Fitzroy Gdns, Melbourne Cty Cncl, 1934-36; Christchurch Bot Gdns, NZ, 1936-37; Roy Bot Gdns, Kew, England and Munich Bot Gdns, Germany, 1938-40; Adelaide Bot Gdns, SA, 1948-80; Snr Lectr in Hort, Lincoln Agricl Coll, NZ. Publications: Practical Home Gardener, 3rd ed, 1967; Growing Australian Plants (joint auth), 1967; Commonsense Gardening, 1974; Complete Australian Gardener, 1976, 2nd ed, 1980; Num profl pprs in austl and overseas hort and bot jrnls. Honours: OBE, 1961; Veitch Mem Gold Medal, Roy Horticultural Soc of London, 1975. Memberships: Roy Soc, SA; Roy Geogl Soc, SA; Hon Life Mbr, Field Naturalists Soc, SA; Soc for Growing Austl Plants; Intl Camellia Soc; Austl Camellia Rsch Soc; Hon Life Mbr, Rhodendron Soc, Aust; Hon Life Fell, Roy Austl Inst of Parks and Recreation; Pres, 1988-90, Hon Life Mbr, Friends of Bot Gdns, Adelaide. Hobbies: Gardening; Reading. Address: PO Box 27A, Crafers, SA 5152, Australia.

LOTHROP Gloria Ricci, b. 30 Dec 1934, Los Angeles, CA, USA. University Professor. Education: Doctorate in Hist of Am West and CA, 1970, Univ S CA. Appointments: Tchr; Rschr; Cnslt, Time Life Books, NEH, Columbia Pictures, CA Mus of Photography, CA Cncl for Humanities, public and pvt tv; Co-host for spec projects, KFAC's Evening Concert, 1981-91; Exec Cttee, Acad Senate, CA State Univ system; Mbr Bd Govs, CA Maritime Acady; Exec Bd, LA 200 Cttee, LA Cncl for Intl Visitors, Photofriends of LA Pub Lib, CA Hist Soc, Hist Soc of S CA and others. Publications: Recollections of the Flathead Mission, 1979; Pomona: A Centennial History, 1988; Historic Outings in Southern California, 1991; Los Angeles Profiles: A Tribute to the Ethnic Diversity of Los Angeles, 1994; Over 100 articles and chapters; Co-ed, A Guide to the History of California, 1989; Co-author, California Women: A History, 1987. Honours: Outstndng Prof, CA State Poly Univ, 1981; Outstndng Alumna of Immaculate Heart Coll; Fell, S CA Hist Soc, CA Hist Soc; Targhe d'Oro Awd, Govt of Puglia, Italy; Columbian Awd, Federated Italo Americans of LA; Fulbright Fellshp; Haynes and Oakley Fellshps; 2 Haynes/Huntington Rsch Fellshps. Hobbies: Theatre; Travel. Address: Dept of History, CSU Northridge, Northridge, CA 91330-8250, USA.

LOTON Brian Thorley, b. 17 May 1929, Perth, WA, Aust. Company Director. m. Joan Kemelfield, 12 Jan 1956, 2 s, 2 d. Education: BMetEng, Melbourne Univ, 1953. Appointments include: Cadet through to Chf Gen Mngr, 1954-82, Mngng Dir, 1982, Mng Dir and CEO, 1984, Dpty Chmn, Mngng Dir, CEO, 1989-91, Dpty Chmn, 1991, Chmn, 1992-97, Broken Hill Pty Co Ltd; Vice Chmn, Natl Aust Bank Ltd, 1992-99; VP, Aust-Japan Bus Co-op Cttee, 1991-97; Patron, Hale Sch (WA) Des and Technol Cntr Appeal, 1992-; Dir, Austl Fndn Invmnt Co Ltd, 1993-; Mbr, Bd of Govs, Ian Clunies Ross Mem Fndn, 1993-99; Chmn, Cncl of Mining and Metallurgical Instns, 1994-98; Dir, Amcor Ltd, 1992-99; Dir, Chmn, Atlas Copco Aust Pty Ltd, 1996-; Dir Hoechst Aust Ltd, 1996-97. Honours: BRW Businessman of the Yr, 1988; Willis Connolly Medal, 1988; Inst Medal, AusIMM, 1989; Kernot Mem Medal, 1989; AC, 1989; Melbourne Univ Grad Sch of Mngmt Awd, 1991; Hon DSc, Univ of Wollongong, 1992; Gold Tower Order of Indl Serv Merit, Govt of Korea, 1992; Hon LLD, Monash Univ, 1993; Gold Medal, Inst of Mining and Metall (Eng), 1993; Intl Iron and Steel Inst Medal, 1994; Silver Medal, Inst Metals and Materials Australasia Ltd, 1996; Intl Disting Life Mbrshp Awd, Amn Soc for Metals, 1996; Austl Inst Co Dirs Awd, 1997. Memberships include: Hon Fell, IE Aust Fell, Inst of Dirs in Aust; Fell, Austl Acady of Technol Scis; Intl Cnclr Emer, Conf Bd; Fmr Bd Mbr and Chmn, Intl Iron and Steel Inst; Fmr Cnclr, Australasian Inst of Mining and Metallurgy; Exec Cttee, Aust-Japan Bus Co-op Cttee, 1984-97; Pres, Vic Branch, The Scout Assn of Aust, 1997-99. Address: c/o GPO Box 86A, Melbourne, Vic 3001, Australia.

LOVAT Terence John, b. 29 Mar 1949, Sydney, Aust. University Professor. m. Tracey, 4 Jan 1986, 1 s, 2 d. Education: BEd; BLitt; ThM; MA; PhD. Hd, Dept of Relig, MSA Coll, Sydney, 1981; Hd, Dept of Educ, Univ of Newcastle, 1992; Dean, Fac of Educ, Univ of Newcastle, 1996. Publications: Teaching and Learning Religion, 1995; Curriculum (w D Smith), 1995; Bioethics (w K Mitchell & I Kerridge), 1996. Honours: Outstndng Serv, Austl Assn for Relig Educ, 1994; Bd Mbr, Austl Cncl of Deans of Educ, 1997. Memberships: Pres, New Tchr Educ Assn, 1997-98; Bd Mbr, Austl Cncl of Deans of Educ, 1997-. Hobbies: Music; Sport. Address: Faculty of Education, University of Newcastle, NSW 2305, Australia.

LOVE Courtney, b. 1967, USA. Rock Musician. m. Kurt Cobain dec, 1 d. Appointments: Mbr, Rock Band, Hole. Creative Works: Recordings: Retard Girl, 1990; Pretty on the Inside, 1991; Beautiful Son, 1993; Live Through This, 1994. Films: The People vs Larry Flynt, 1996; Basquiat, 1996; Life, 1997. Address: c/o David Geffen Co, 9130 West Sunset Boulevard, Los Angeles, CA 90069, USA.

LOVELL David William, b. 9 Jan 1956, Adelaide, S Aust. Academic. m. Christine K DeBono, 9 Jan 1998, 2 s, 1 d. Education: PhD, Austl Natl Univ, 1985. Appointments: Snr Lectr, Univ Coll, UNSW, 1991-. Publications: Marx's Proletariat, 1988; The Transition from Socialism (co-ed), 1991; The Australian Political System (co-auth), 1995, 1998. Honours: Fell, Austl Polit Stdies, 1992. Memberships: Australasian Polit Stdies Assn, Treas, 1994-95; Intl Soc for Stdy of Eurn Ideas, 1992. Hobbies: Reading; Travel. Address: School of Politics, Australian Defence Force Academy, Canberra, ACT 2600, Australia.

LOVELL Patricia Anne. Film Producer. m. Nigel Lovell, 16 Apr 1956. 1 s, 1 d. Appointments: Actress, TV Presenter and Reporter, 1959-74; Film Prodr, 1971-; Exec Prodr, Picnic at Hanging Rock, 1975; Prodr, Break of Day, 1976, Summerfield, 1977; Co-Prodr, Gallipoli, 1980; Prodr, Monkey Grip, 1981, The Perfectionist, 1985; Hd of Producing, Austl Film, TV and Radio Sch, 1997-98. Publication: No Picnic, autobiography, 1995. Honours: AM, 1986; MBE, 1978. Hobbies: Theatre; Gardening; Walking dogs. Address: PO Box 701, Avalon Beach, NSW 2107, Australia.

LOW Huoi Seong, b. 13 Nov 1956, Kuala Lumpur, Malaysia. Executive Director. m. Monica Ng, 24 Dec 1983, 1 s, 2 d. Education: BSc, hons, Physiol, Newcastle-upon-Tyne, 1978; MSc, Mngmt Sci, Imperial Coll, London, 1979; MSc, Human & Appl Physiol, Kings Coll, London, 1980. Appointments: SGV Kassim Chan Mngmt Servs; Vision Grp of Cos. Memberships: Imperial Coll Alumni Assn Malaysia; Yng Pres Org; Malayan Sub Aqua Club. Hobbies: Diving; Arts; Fine Dining; Travel. Address: 73 Lorong Lai Tet Loke, 54100 Kuala Lumpur, Malaysia.

LOWE Douglas Ackley, b. 15 May 1942, Hobart, Tasmania, Australia. Chief Executive Officer. m. Pamela, 2 Mar 1963, 2 s, 2 d. Education: Trade Ctf, Hobart Tech Coll. Appointments: ALP State Sec, 1965-69; MHA, 1969-86; Min, 1972-81; Dpty Premier, 1975-77; Premier of Tas, 1977-81; MLC, 1986-92. Publication: The Price of Power, 1984. Honour: Queen's Silver Jubilee Medal, 1977. Memberships: Chair, Lady Clark Geriatric Cntr Assn, 1968-77; Appointd Sen, Austl Jaycees, 1980; Sacred Heart Coll, Bd, 1982-90; Pres, Tas Swimming Inc, 1990-98. Hobbies: Swimming; Football; Family Relaxation. Address: 1 Michele Court, Berriedale, Tasmania 7011, Australia.

LOWEN Ian Hartridge, b. 8 Jan 1917. Company Director. m. Meryl Frances Morgan, 2 s, 1 d. Education: PSC; Wellington College, NZ.Appointments: Gilbert Lodge & Co Ltd, 1934; Enlisted Vic Scottish Regiment, 1935; Commnd, 1939; AIF, 1939-45; Served Palestine, N Afr, Greece, Syria, New Guinea, Philippines; Maj Vic Scottish Regiment, 1948-54; Cmndg Offr, 1950-54; Mngr, Melbourne Br, Gilbert Lodge & co Ltd, 1952; Assoc Dir, 1953; Dir, 1955-82; Gen Mngr, 1966; Mngng Dir, 1968-81; GSOI Trng CMF HQ Vic, 1954-56; Cmndr 4 INF BDE, 1956-59; Hon ADC to Gov-Gen, 1958-61; Hon Col, Austl Cadet Corps (S Comd), 1965-72 Hon Col, Monash Univ Regiment, 1973-81; Pres, Citizen Mil Forces Assn (Vic), 1976-84; Natl Pres, 1984-87. Honours: OBE; ED; AM, 1988. Memberships: Melbourne Cricket Club; RACV; RSL; United Servs Club (Melb); Naval and Mil Club. Hobbies: Motoring; Tennis; Golf. Address: 38 The Eyrie, Eaglemount, Vic 3084, Australia.

LOWENTHAL Raymond Michael, b. 11 Nov 1941, Sydney, Aust. Medical Practitioner. m. Dianne, 18 Aug 1943, 1 s, 3 d. Education: MB BS, 1965, MD, 1978, Sydney; FRACP, 1978; FRCP, 1992. Publications: Cancer: What to Do About It, 1990, 2nd ed, 1996; Nearly 100 sci pprs in peer-reviewed jrnls. Memberships: Austl Medl Assn, Tasmanian Pres, 1996-98; Cancer Cncl of Tasmania, Chmn, 1996-; Amn Soc of Hematology, Hematology Soc of Aust; Clin Oncological Soc of Aust; Austl Soc for Medl Rsch; Austl Leukemia Trials Grp. Hobbies: Bushwalking; Gardening; Cooking; Royal tennis. Address: Haematology/Oncology Unit, Royal Hobart Hospital, Hobart, Tasmania, Australia 7000.

LOWKE John James, b. 3 Apr 1934. Physicist. m. Karil Mary Garrett, 12 Jan 1963, 2 s. Education: PhD; BSc Hons; DipEd. Appointments: Snr Physicist, Fell Sci, Westinghouse Rsch Labs, Pitts, PA, USA, 1964-75; Snr Lectr, Rdr, Dept EE, Univ of Sydney, Aust, 1976-80; Chf of Div, CSIRO Div of Applied Phys, Sydney, Aust, 1980-88; Chf Rsch Sci, CSIRO Telecomms and Ind Phys, 1988-. Address: CSIRO Division of Telecommunications and Industrial Physics, Box 218, Lindfield, NSW 2070, Australia.

LOWRIE Kenneth Francis (Hon), b. 4 Sept 1926, Irishtown, Tas, Aust. Legal Practitioner. m. Jean, 2 July 1955, 2 s, 3 d. Education: LLB, Univ of Tas, 1953. Appointments: Mayor, City of Glenorchy, 1965-75; Legis Cncl Parl of Tas, 1968-86, Ldr, Govt, 1982-86; Chmn, Southern Cross Homes, Tas, 1968-98; Chmn State Coastal Advsry Cttee, Tas; Chmn Tassies Home Loans Pty, Ltd.. Honours: Freedom, City of Glenorchy, 1975; OBE, 1989; OAM, 1998. Membership: Athenaeum Club, Hobart. Listed in: Who's Who in Australia. Hobbies: Lawn bowls; Reading. Address: 30 Bay Road, New Town, Tas 7008, Australia.

LOWY Frank P, b. 22 Oct 1930. Co Chmn. m. Shirley Rusanow, 7 Mar 1954, 3 s. 7 Mar 1954, 3 s. Appointments: Exec Chmn, Westfield Holdings Ltd, Westfield Trust, Westfield Am Trust, Westfield Am Inc; Dir, Daily Mail & Gen Trust PLC; Mbr Bd, Reserve Bank of Aust. Honour: AM, 1980; AO 1988. Membership: Fell, Austl Inst of Co Dir, Hakoah Club; Philips Soccer League. Hobbies: Boating; Tennis. Address: c/o Westfiield Ltd, GPO Box 4004, Sydney, NSW 2001, Australia.

LOYN Richard Henry, b. 30 Apr 1951. Biologist. m. Debbie Tully, 14 Apr 1991, 1 d. Education: MA, 1975. Appointments: Cnslt Biolst, Western Port Environ Stdy, 1973-75; Wildlife Biolst, Forest Commn, Vic, 1975-86; Cnslt Biolst, Kinhill Planners/ICI Aust, 1978-80; Biolst, Arthur Rylah Inst for Environ Rsch, 1986-96; Acting Flora, Fauna and Fisheries Co-ord, Melbourne, 1995; Acting Gen Mngr, 1995; Mngr, 1996-; Wildlife Rsch, Arthur Rylah Inst for Environ Rsch. Over 100 reports, pprs, book chaps and articles on wildlife and forestry. Honour: Whitley Awd, 1988. Memberships: Roy Australasian Ornithol Union; Bird Observers Club of Aust; Austl Mammal Soc; Australasian Wildlife Mngmt Soc; Inst of Foresters, Aust. Hobbies: Travel; Wildlife; Birds; Ecology. Address: Arthur Rylah Institute, 123 Brown Street, Heidelberg, Vic 3084, Australia.

LU Bin, b. 27 Oct 1932, Suzhou Cty, Jiangsu Prov. Educator. m. Xiucen Yang, 25 Aug 1957, 1 s, 2 d. Education: Grad, Dept of Pharm, Shandong Medl Coll, 1952. Appointments: Lectr, 1960; Assoc Prof, 1983; Prof, 1987. Creative Works: New Techniques and New Dosage forms of Drugs; Microencapsulation of Drugs; Pharmaceutics; Sci Articles; Over 50 Pprs. Honours: Lead Taking Sci of Sichuan Prov, 1998; Lead Taking Sci of Pharm. Memberships: Natl Pharmacopoeia of China; Pharm Assn of China. Hobbies: Reading; Music. Address: School of Pharmacy, West China Univ Med Scis, 17 Renminnanlu 3 Duan, Chengdu, 610044, China.

LU Daofa, b. 5 Jan 1940, Shandong, China. Senior Vice President, Shanyong Aircraft Corporation. m. Gao Meihua, 14 Sept 1971, 1 d. Education: Beijing Univ, 1960-66. Appointments: Aircraft Assembler, 1966-70; Aircraft Des, 1970-95; Asst to Chf Engnr, 1975-77; Tech Dir, Aircraft Stuctural Shop, 1977-79; Tech Dir, New Aircraft Dev Shop, 1979-82; Mngr, Aircraft Mfng Engrng, 1982-84; Dpty Dir, Tech Updates, 1984; Dir, NC Machining Cntr, 1984-85; Dir, Technol Off, 1985; Snr VP, Gen Mngr of Prodn Support, 1986-96; Snr VP, Gen Mngr, Aeronautic Prodn, 1997-; Publications include: (all 1st prize winners from Min of Aviation or corp) Discussions on Technical Updates for Large-Scale Enterprises; Study on Aircraft Accessories Supply System Engineering; On How to Improve Supplies for Military Aircraft Manufacturing; Test of Aircraft Rocket Sliding Vehicle; Summary of the Development of a Jet Fighter. Honours include: Worker of Yr, Natl Plng Cttee, Natl Econ & Trade Cttee, Natl Sci Cttee; Worker of Yr, Min of Aviation; 1st

Prize, Sci & Technol Adv, Min & Provincial Govt for Aircraft Accessories Supply System Engrng; Many achievement and safety awds. Memberships include: VP, China Aviation Ind Tech Equip Engrng Assn; Exec Gen Dir, China Aviation Ind Northeast Reg Econ & Technol Soc; Snr Cnslt, China Successful People Study Assn Spec Cnslts Regiment; Grad Instr, Beijing Univ of Aeronautics and Astronautics; Visng Prof, SAC Leadership Sch. Hobbies: Sports (gymnastics, volleyball, decathlon). Address: No 1, Lingbei Street, Huanggu District, Shenyang City 110034, Liaoning Province, China.

LU Hong Jiu, b. 26 Nov 1934, Liaoning Prov, China. Theory Study on China National Music. m. Rina Su, 8 Feb 1964, 2 d. Education: Degree, Music Composing, Shenyang Conservatoire of Music. Appointments: Tchr, then Prof, Art Coll of Inner Mongolia; Chf Ed, Grassland Art Circle (acad jrnl of Inner Mongolia). Publications: Books: Monglian National Folk Mode Study, 1981; Art of Liu Yinwei's Vocal Music of Song-and-dance Duet Popular in Inner Mongolia, 1987; Melody Composing (co-auth), 1997; 6 pprs on natl music; Contbr, Chinese Fork Songs and Music Corpus - Inner Mongolia, Chinese Fork Art Forms Corpus - Inner Mongolia, 1985-95. Honours: Inner Mongolia Autonomous Reg Lit & Artistic Sarina Prize, 3 x, 1984, 1987, 1990; 1st prize, for achievements in ed of Chinese Art Corpus, Natl Art Sci Plng Cttee, 1997. Memberships: Mbr, 1982-, Dir, 1985-, Exec Dir, 1985-, Dpty Exec Pres, 1990-, China Soc of Musicians. Hobbies: Reading; Travelling. Address: Art College of Inner Mongolia, No 29 Dongfeng Rd, Xincheng Dis, Hohhot 010010, China.

LU Huisheng, b. 19 Nov 1935, Shanghai, China. Education. m. Wu Xiujing, 20 Dec 1965, 2 d. Education: Dip, Dept of Naval Arch, Shanghai Jiaotong Univ, 1954-59. Appointments: In Charge, Ship Model Towing Tank, 1959-60, Flying Mechs Section, 1960-61; Dpty Chf, Ship Hydrodynamics Section, 1961-85; Vice Ed-in-Chf, Ocean Engrng, 1982-85. Publications include: A Study of Efficiency of MHDS Propulsion, 1991; Ship Manoeuvrability Criteria and Their Application in Primary Design, 1992. Honours: Sev Sci and Technol Progress Prizes. Memberships: Naval Arch Engrng Assn; Chinese Ocean Assn; Chinese Navigation Assn; Chinese Hydraulic Electrogenerating Assn. Hobbies: Reading; Literature; Sports. Address: College of Naval Architecture & Ocean Engineering, Shanghai Jiaotong University, 1954 Hua Shan Road, Shanghai 200030, China.

LU Jining, b. 18 May 945, Shanghai, China. Researcher. m. Ms Li Shuhua, 20 July 1974, 2 s. Education: PhD. Appointments: Mid Sch Tchr; Asst Prof of Chinese Acady of Socl Sci; Assc Prof, Natl Def Univ; Prof of Natl Def Univ. Publications: 9 books inclng: The Structure of Practice-Cognition Activity, 1988; The New Chapter of Reforms and Opening Policy, 1992; The New Development of Marxism Philosophy in China, 1994; Selected Military Poems Research Through Ages, 1997; Selected Military Prose Research Through Ages, 1997; About 200 pprs. Honours: Natl Spec Prize, China State Cncl (monthly) & offic cert, 1993; Over 10 awds in acad rsch, People's Liberation Army & Natl Def Univ. Memberships: Standing Dir, Histl Materialism Rschng Unit of China; Standing Dir, Natl Assn for Hist Rsch of Modern Chinese Philos. Hobbies: Reading; Travelling; Mountain-climbing; Swimming. Address: A8-3-5, No 83 Fu Xing Road, Beijing 100856, China.

LU Lester Yongliang, b. 7 July 1946, Meitan, Guizhou Prov, China. Communication International Trading. m. Kathyleen Kaiguima, 26 Jan 1973, 1 s. Education: BS, Shanghai Jiao Tong Univ, China, 1970. Appointments: Engr, Liaoning Wire 1# Factory, Fuxin, China, 1970-79; Salesman, China Electrons Technol Ip & Exp Corp, Shanghai Branch, 980-82; Tchr, Shanghai Jiao Tong Univ, Ind & For Trade Dept, 1982-84; Dpty Gen Mngr, Forte Trade & Dev Corp (Can), Shanghai Off, 1984-90; Pres, Forte Trade Intl (Can) Inc, 1990-; Pres, Shanghai Forte Commn Equipment Co Ltd, 1995-; Gen Mngr, Beijing High Speed Way (Can) Trade Ltd, 1996-; Gen

Mngr, Watt Trade Harbin (Can) Ltd, 1999-. Hobbies: Volleyball; Majiang.

LU Liansheng, b. 21 Sept 1930, Shandong Province, China. Professor. m. Sui Shunxia, 12 Oct 1960, 1 s, 2 d. Education: Grad, Dept of Biol, Shandong Univ, 1955. Appointments:Prac Rsch Fell, Rsch Inst of Expmtl Bio, Chinese Acady of Sci, 1955-56; Ed, Sci Publng House, The Chinese Acady of Sci, 1956-61; Tchr, E N Agricl Univ, 1961-78; Prof, Shandong Tchrs Univ, 1978-98; Visng Schl, Univ of Tas, 1991-. Publications: Embryo Transfer in the Linging Cat; Cell Differentiation Development; Studies on Supervaluation in Cats. Honours: Cert of Merit, Devel Sci and Technol. Memberships: Soc of Dev Bio, 1983; Soc of Rep Bio. Hobbies: Chinese Chess. Address: Dept of Biology, Shandong Teacher's University, Jinan 250014, China.

LU Longshi, b. 19 Sept 1956, Longjing Cty, Jilin Prov, China. University Teacher. m. Huang Renzi, 25 Mar 1984, 2 d. Education: Master Agronomy, Spec Field of Crop Inheritance and Breeding, Shenyang Agric Univ, 1987; PhD, Spec Field of Insect and Ecology, SW Agricl Univ, 1993; Postdoct Fell, Inst Agric Sci and Technol, Kyungpook Natl Univ, Korea, 1996. Appointments: Lectr, 1988, Assoc Prof, 1993, Prof, 1998, Tchng and rsch: Crop Inheritance and Breeding 1987-90, Agricl Insects and Ecology 1990-, Dean, Agronomy Dept, 1996-98, Vice-Pres, 1998-, Yanbian Univ Agricl Coll. Publications: Pprs to profl jrnls; Co-auth, wrks inclng Biodiversity Catalogue in Korea, 1996; Chf Ed, Biological Statistics and Field Experiment, 1998. Honour: 3rd Prize, Sci Prog, Min of Agric. Memberships: China Agronomy Soc, 1987; Vice-Chmn, Bd Dirs, Yanbian Bio Soc, 1997; Cncl, Yanbian Agronomy Soc, 1998. Honours: Football; Volleyball. Address: Bashu Book Press Publishing House.

LU Ruihua, b. Nov 1938, Chaozhou, Guangdong, China. Politician. Education: Zhongshan Univ. Appointments: Joined CCP, 1972; Fmr Engr, Dpty Dir, Dir, Foshan Analytical Instrument Factory; Fmr May of Foshan, Vice-Chair, Foshan City Econ Cttee; Standing Cttee, CCP Foshan City Cttee; Dpty, 7th NPC, 1988, 8th NPC, 1996; Alt Mbr, 14th CCP Ctrl Cttee, 1992-97, Mbr, 15th CCP Ctrl Cttee, 1997-; Vice Gov, Guangdong Prov, 1991-96, Gov, 1996-. Address: Peoples Government of Guangdong, Guangzhou, Guangdong, China.

LU Youjie, b. 26 Feb 1945, Jilin, China. Professor; Architect; Structural Engineer. m. Wu Ping, 15 Jan 1977, 1 d. Education: Dip, 1970, MS, 1981, Tsinghua Univ; MS, Polytech Inst of NY, 1983. Appointments: Structural Engr, 1986; Assoc Prof, 1991. Publications: Affordable Housing in China, 1996; Systems Engineering for Urban Development, 1997; Project Risk Management, 1998; Project Financing, 1998. Hobby: Sports. Address: Department of Civil Engineering, Tsinghua University, Beijing 100084, China.

LU Yuan, b. 8 Nov 1922, Huanpi, Hubei, China. Editor; Translator; Freelance writer. m. Lou Hui, 12 Dec 1944, 2 s, 2 d. Education: BA, For Lit Dept, Natl Fu Tan Univ, Chungking, 1944. Appointments: Ex-Dpty Ed-in-Chf in charge of for publ, People's Lit Publng House; Co-copy Ed, SHIKAN (poetry mag). Publications: Innocent Talk, 1942; Starting Point, 1947; Songs of Man, 1983; Another Song, 1985; Onion with Honey, 1986; Deutschland-Gedichte, 1988; Espoir, 1988; Sketchbook by a Doppel Ganger, 1992; Finger Logik, 1995; Selected Poems, 1998; Transls: Rilke, 1993; Faust, 1994; Schopenhauer, 1995. Honours: Natl Poetry Prize for Another Song, 1986; Golden Wreath Awd of Struga Poetry Evenings in Macedonia. Memberships: PEN Club China Cntr; Goethe-Gesellschaft in Weimer EV; Intl Assn for Germanic Study. Hobbies: Random reading. Address: c/o People's Literature Publishing House, 166 Chao Nei Street, Beijing 100705, China.

LU Zhen-Hua, b. 21 July 1961, Zhongwei, Ningxia, China. University Professor. m. Wei-Na Cheng, 10 June 1986, 1 d. Education: BS, Engrng, Xian Univ of Highway & Transp, 1982; MS, Engrng, 1985, DS, Engrng, 1990,

Jilin Univ of Technol, Changchun. Appointments: Assoc Lectr, 1985-86, Lectr, 1990-91, Assoc Prof, 1991-92, Prof, 1992-96, Coll of Automotive Engrng, Jilin Univ of Technol; Vis Prof, Ctr for CAD, Coll of Engrng, Univ IA, USA, 1995-96; Prof, Dept of Automotive Engrng, Tsinghua Univ, Beijing, 1996-; Acad Advsr, Jilin Univ of Technol, 1996, Tsinghua Univ, 1997. Publications: 60 rsch pprs in profl jrnls. Honours include: Govt Specl Allowance, 1993-; Outstndng Rschrs in Sci & Technol Awd, Govt of Jilin, 1994; Yng Chinese Sci Expert in Mech Engrng Awd, Min of Machine-Bldng Ind, 1995; Rsch Fund Awd, Trans-Century Trng Prog, 1995-97. Memberships: Exec Cncl, Beijing Soc for Vibration Engrng; Snr Mbr, Chinese Soc for Mech Engrng; Chinese Soc for Automotive Engrng; Chinese Soc for Vibration Engrng; Chinese Soc for Mechs. Hobbies: Reading; Music; Table tennis; Photography. Address: Department of Automotive Engineering, Tsinghua University, Beijing 100084, China.

LU Zhenrong, b. 8 Jan 1946, Changshu, Jiangsu Prov, China. Professor of Chemistry. m. Tan Xingfeng, 1 May 1971, 1 s, 1 d. Education: Postgrad MSc. Appointments: Vice Chmn, Chem Dept, Suzhou Univ, 1985-89; Dir, Testing and Analysis Cntr, Suzhou Univ, 1990-95. Publications: Pprs in profl jrnls. Honours: 2nd Awd of Sci and Technol Prog, Jiangsu Dept of Electrons Ind. Memberships: Chem Thermodynamic and Thermal Analysis (CTTA); Chinese Chem Soc, 1998; Analysis and Testing Assn of Jiangsu Prov. Hobbies: Table tennis; Literature; Music; Chinese calligraphy. Address: Testing & Analysis Centre, Suzhou University, Suzhou, Jiangsu Province, 215006 China.

LU Zhong Yi, b. 1 Oct 1928, Tianjin, China. Vice Director; Coach. m. Li Qin Fang, 16 May 1953, 2 s, 1 d. Education: Bus Mngmt, 1950. Appointment: Chmn, Shanghai Aero Model Assn. Publications: Wooden Craft of Model Plane, 1985; Optimization of 25cc Speed Engine, 1985. Honours: 2nd Class Prize, Sci & Techniqug Progress, Shanghai. Address: #1, 175 Lane, Wan Hong Du Road, Shanghai, China.

LU Zuomei, b. 5 Sept 1941, Taicang, Jiangsu, China. Teacher. m. Taojin, 1 Aug 1967, 1 s. Education: Postgrad. Appointments: Dir, Div of Plant Breeding, 1990; Vice-Dir, Seed Assn of China, 1992; Mngr, Seed Corp of Nau, 1993; Dir, Seed Rsch Cntr of Nau, 1993. Publications: The Application of three-line-seven-nursery-method system in the production of elites of hybrid rice. Honours: Chinese Xinghuo Awds (2nd Class); Progressive Awds (1st Class), Chinese Educ Cttee; Sci & Technol Progressive Awds (3rd Class), Chinese Agricl Min; Outstndng Worker of Nation. Memberships: Seed Assn of China; Seed Assn of Jiangsu; Genetics Assn of Jiangsu. Address: Apt 201, Building 65, Nanjing Agricultural University, Nanjing, Jiangsu, China.

LUBRANI Uri, b. 7 Oct 1926, Haifa, Israel. Diplomat. m. Sarah Levi, 1953, 4 d. Education: Univ of London. Appointments: Fmr Hd of Chancery, Off of Fgn Min, Off of PM, Advsr to PM on Arab Affairs; Amb to Uganda, Rwranda, Burundi, Ethiopia, Iran; Govt Coord for Lebanese Affairs. Address: Office of the Government Coordinator for Lebanese Affairs, Ministry of Defence, Hakira, Tel Aviv, Israel.

LUCAS George, b. 14 May 1944, Modesto, California, USA. Film Director. Education: Univ S CA. Appointments: Warner Bros Studio; Asst to Francis Ford Coppola on The Rain People; Dir, Documentary of The Rain People; Fndr, Lucasfilm Ltd; Dir, Co-Auth, Screenplay Films. Creative Works: THX-1138, 1970; American Graffiti, 1973; Star Wars, 1977; Exec Prodr, American Graffiti, 1979, The Empire Strikes Back, 1980, Raiders of the Lost Art, 1981, Return of the Jedi, 1982, Indiana Jones and the Temple of Doom, 1984, Howard the Duck, 1986, Labyrinth, 1988, Willow, 1988, Tucker: The Man and His Dream, 1988; Co-Exec Prodr, Mishima, 1985, Indiana Jones and the Last Crusade, 1989; Exec Prodr, The Young Indiana Jones Chronicles, 1992-93, Radioland Murders, 1994. Honours include: Irving Thalberg Awd,

1992. Address: Lucasfilm Ltd, PO Box 2009, San Rafael, CA 94912, USA.

LUCKINS Maree Therese, b. 14 Mar 1968. Member of Parliament. m. Jeffrey Luckins, 18 Aug 1990, 1 s, 1 d. Education: Licensed Agt, Real Esate Inst of Vic, Aust. Appointments: Elected Mbr, Legislative Cncl, Vic, for Waverley Prov, Mar 1996-; Mbr, Scrutiny of Acts and Regulations All-Party Cttee; Chmn, Redundant Legislation Cttee, 1996-; Youngest female elected to Vic Parl; First to give birth while serving w the Legislative Cncl. Memberships: Zonta Intl; YWCA; Victorian Womens Trust, Liberal Party of Aust (Vic); Patron Bonnie Babes Fndn; Rotary Club, Monash; RSL, Clayton. Hobbies: Family; Swimming; Reading; Current affairs. Address: 63 Murrumbeena Road, Murrumbeena, Vic 3163, Australia.

LUEGGE Willard Arthur, b. 19 Mar 1931, Oak Park, IL, USA. Consultant, Extractive Metallurgical Chemistry. m. Joanna C Wechter, 9 Jan 1951, 2 d. Education: BA, IN Univ, 1953; Grad Wrk, In Univ, Univ of Louisville, UCLA, 1954-64. Appointments: VP, Bryman Refining Co Inc, 1992; Bd of Dirs, Bryman Refining Co Inc, 1993; Owner, Dir of Precious Metals Labs, 1968-90. Publications: Gravimetric Method of Analysis for the Precious Metals, 1983; Atomic Absorption Method of Analysis for the Precious Metals, 1988; Inventor, Field Assay Kit, 1970. Honours: Chem Tchr of Yr, 1967; Amn Chem Soc; Natl Sci Fndn Grantee, 1963, 1964. Memberships: West Mining Cncl; West States Pub Lands Coalition. Hobbies: Mining History; Jazz; Basketball; Football; Baseball. Address: 560 E Avenue J-1, Lancaster, CA 93535, USA.

LUFT Herbert, b. 17 Aug 1942, Frankfurt, Germany. Professor of European History. m. Yvonne Otratowitz, Aug 1991, 1 s, 1 d. Education: BA; MA; PhD. Appointments: Asst Prof, Assoc Prof, Prof, 1967-. Publications: Var publns and profl presentations. Memberships: Phi Alpha Theta, 1965; Am Hist Assn; Kiwanis Club. Hobbies: Theology and Church History. Address: 24 255 Pacific Coast Highway, Malibu, CA 90263-4225, USA.

LUKITTO Pisi, b. 28 Feb 1933, Indonesia. Surgeon. m. (1) Jetty Oct Witarto, 23 Dec 1962, dec, 1 s, 2 d, (2) Lie Tjoen Hwa, 4 Oct 1995. Education: MD, Univ of Indonesia, 1961; Mil Trng, 1963; Gen Surg, Univ of Padjadjaran, 1969; Surg Oncology, Amsterdam, The Netherlands, 1972; Sev other trng courses in var countries. Appointments: GP, 1961-62; Mil Dr, 1963-64; Lectr, Medl Sch, Univ of Padjadjaran, 1969; Cnslt in Surg Oncology, Hd and Neck Surg and Digestive surg. Publications include: over 90 pprs in profl jrnls. Memberships: Eurn Soc of Surg Oncology; Indonesian Soc of Surg Oncology; Assn of Surgs of SE Asia; Indonesian Cancer Soc; Indonesian Soc of Oncology; Indonesian Soc of Digestive Surgs; Indonesian Surgs Assns and Medl Assns. Hobbies: Reading; Movies. Address: Jalan Dago Asri 21, Kompleks Istana Dago, Bandung 40135, Indonesia.

LUO Ching-Hsing, b. 1 Oct 1958, Taiwan. Instrumentation. m. Shio Shiin Lee, 7 June 1989, 4 s. Education: PhD, Biomedl Engrng. Creative Works: Engineering Mathematics; Introduction to Takuchi Quality Engineering. Honours: Li Fndn Fellshp. Memberships: Chiense Biomedl Engrng. Hobbies: Tai Chi Kun Fu; Buddhism; Ping Pong; Go Game. Address: Dept of Electrical Engineering, National Cheng Kung University, Tainan, Taiwan 701, China.

LUO Gan, b. 14 July 1935, Jinan, Shandong, China. State & Party Official. m. He Zuozhi, 1965, 1 s, 1 d. Education: Leipzig Univ. Appointments: Joined CCP, 1960; Metallurgical & Casting Engr; Vice-Gov, Henan Prov, 1981-83; Alt Mbr, 12th CCP Ctrl Cttee, 1982-87; Mbr, 13th Ctrl Cttee, 1987-92, 14th Ctrl Cttee, 1992-97, 15th CCP Ctrl Cttee, 1997-; Sec, CCP Cttee, Henan, 1983-85; Min of Labour, 1988-89; Mbr, CCP Politburo Sec, Secr CCP Ctrl Cttee, 1997-. Memberships include: VP, All-China Fedn of Trade Unions, 1983-88; Sec Gen, State Cncl, 1988; Spty Hd, Natl Ldng Grp for Anti-Disaster & Relief Work, 1991-. Address: State

Council, Zhong Nan Hai, Beijing, China.

LUO Haocai, b. Mar 1934, Anxi, Fujian, China. Judge; Politician. Education: Beijing Univ. Appointments: Tchng Asst, Lectr, Assoc Prof, Prof, Dept of Law, VP, Beijing Univ; Chair, Beijing Fedn of Returned Overseas Chinese; Vice-Chair, China Law Soc; Mbr, Standing Cttee, China Admin Mngrs Assn; VP, 4th Cncl, All China Fedn of Returned Overseas Chinese, 1989, 5th Cncl, 1994; Vice-Chair, China Zhi Gong Dang, 1992-97, Chair, 1997-; Mbr, Standing Cttee, Dpty Sec-Gen, CPPCC 8th Natl Cttee, 1993-; Vice-Chair, CPPCC Overseas Chinese Cttee, 1993-; VP, Mbr, Judicial Cttee, Supreme Peoples Crt, 1995-. Address: Supreme Peoples Court, Beijing, China.

LUO Huizhao, b. 4 Dec 1929, Tangjiang, Jiangxi, China. Cardiac Surgeon. m. 3 Dec 1950, 3 d. Education: Shandong Medl Univ, 1951-56; Beijing Fuwai Hosp, 1962-63; Yale Univ, Sch of Med, 1988. Appointments: Vice-Dir, No 2 Hosp of Hunan Medl Univ, 1984-86; Dir, Vice Dir, Hunan Provcl Inst of Cardiovac Disease, 1986-92; Prof & Chf Dr, 1987-. Publications: Primary Cardiac Tumors, 1995; Traumatic AI, 1996; Congenital Left Ventricular Diverticulum, 1997; TCPC for Complex Congenital Heart Disease, 1998. Honours: Spec Allowance, Chinese Govt, 1992-; Chinese Natl Sci Techl Achievements Prize, 2nd Class, 1995. Memberships: Cttee, Chinese TCSS, 1996-; Vice-Dir, S-Cntrl TCSS, 1997-; Dir, Hunan TCSS, 1997; Profl Soc, 1997-. Hobbies: Sports; News; Reading. Address: Department of TCS, No 2 Hospital of Hunan Medical University, 156 Renmin Road, Changsha, Hunan 41001, China.

LUO Jiansheng, b. 5 June 1953. Professor of English. m. Li Binjiang, 1 May 1982, 1 d. Education: BA Engl Lang and Lit, Huazhong Normal Univ; MA Engl Lang and Lit, Wuhan Univ; Visng Schl, Strathclyde Univ, Britain; Visng Mbr, Portland Univ, Am. Appointments: Dean, Engl Dept of S-Cntrl Coll for Nationalities, 1993; Mbr, Acad Cttee of the Coll, 1993. Publications: 24 articles on the tchng and rsch of Engl Lang and Lit. Honours: Third Prize for Hubei Prov Transl Competition, 1987; First Prize for Tchng of S-Cntrl Coll for Nationalities, 1995; 2nd Prize Rsch on Tchng Engl, Govt of Hubei Prov. Hobby: Reading. Address: English Department, South-Central College for Nationalities, Wuhan, Hubei 430074, China.

LUO Jiashun, b. 19 Jan 1940, Shanghai, China. Teacher. m. Du Zang, 16 Aug 1967, 1 s, 1 d. Education: BSc, Maths Dept, Nankai Univ. Appointment: Dir, Educl Admin, Nankai Univ, 1993-. Publications: A Geometric Theory of Conjugate Took Surfaces; On Straight Line. Tooth Worm Drive with Arc Surface of Parabolic Modification. Honour: Prize, Chinese Sci Conf, 1978. Membership: Standing Rsch Cttee, Chinese Higher Educn of Scis. Hobby: Computers. Address: 52-1-402 Xi Nan Cun, Nankai University, Tianjin 300071, China.

LUO Shaoji, b. 31 Dec 1933, Guangzhou, China. m. D Z Hu, 1 s, 1 d. Education: BSc, Hydro Engrng, Tsinghua Univ, 1955. Appointments: Engr, Chf Engr, VP, Pres, Mid S Des Inst; Chmn, S China Power Grid; Gen Mngr, GPSJVC. Publications: Design of Hollow Gravity Arch Dam, 1979; Economic Evaluation of Pumped Storage Projects, 1997. Honours: Natl Prize for Tech Prog, 1985; Provincial Prize for Tech Prog, 1996; Natl Prize for Tech Prog, 1997. Memberships: Chmn, Guangdong Hydro Engrng Assn, Snr Tech Advsr Panel to Guangdong Provl Govt, 1985-98. Hobby: Swimming.

LUO Shi Qi, b. 23 Nov 1937. Neurosurgery. m. Long Ling, 1 s, 1 d. Education: Bachelor, Beijing Medl Univ, 1960. Appointments: Vice-Chf, Dept of Neurosurgery, Beijing Tiantan Hosp. Publication: Intracranial Tumors in Children, 1992. Honours: Spec of Inportant Contbn in Sci & Tech (Beijing Govt Awd). Membership: Ed, Chinese Jrnl of Neurosurgery. Address: Beijing Taintan Hospital 100050, China.

LUO Xian Rong, b. 25 Feb 1961, Heng Yany, Hunan, China. Physician. Education: Heng Yang Med Coll, China, 1982. Appointments: Registrar, 1990; Snr

Registrar, 1996; Dir, Respiratory Dept, 1998. Publications: Contemporary Pulmonal Infection, book; Measurement of Intrinic Positive and Expiratory Pressure in Patients with Corpulmonale During Mechanical Ventilation and It's Clinical Significance, 1998. Honours: 4 mil sci progress prizes. Address: Department of Respiratory Medicine, Guangzhou Air Force Hospital of PLA, Guangzhou.

LUO Yao Tiu, b. 3 May 1925, Jian. Professor. m. Huang Song Ying, Fen 1953, 2 d. Education: BA, Jiang Jiesh Univ, 1948. Appointments: Assoc Lectr, Xiamen Univ, 1948-54; Lectr, 1954-78; Prof, 1978. Creative Works: Over 90 acad pprs, articles publd in acad jrnls; 1 Monograph; Ed, 3 books; co-auth 1 book. Honours: Achmnt in Soc Sci, Fujian Prov; 2nd Prize Disting Achmnt, Xiamen Soc Sci Fedn; Hon of Outstndng Tchr, Tert Instns. Memberships: Wuzhenren Rsch Assn; Yanfu Acad Rsch Assn. Hobbies: Classic Chinese Lit; Poetry. Address: Jianxian 8-201, Xiamen University, Xiamen 361005, China.

LUO Yi Feng, b. 11 July 1937, Ning Bo Cty, Zhe Jiang, China. Scientific Research and Information. m. Wang Hui Lan, 18 Jan 1968, 1 s, 1 d. Education: Grad, Beijing Univ, 1964. Appointments: Techn, Engr, Snr Engr, Prof, Vice-Dir, Chf Ed, Dpty to Natl Peoples Congress; Mbr, Overseas Chinese Cttee, NPU. Publications: Handbook of Foreign Specialty Synthetic Fibers, 1973, 1980; Selected articles on Speciality Synthetic Fibers Information Research, both at home and abroad, 1978-85; Hi-Tech Fibers, 1995. Honours: Beijing Spec Class Model Worker, 1985; Model Worker of Whole Nation, Chem Ind Min, 1985; Natl Model Worker, 1989; Natl Grade Expert prominently dedicated to Sci & Technol. Memberships: Satnding Cncl Mbr, Chinese Sci & Technol Info Soc, 1993-98; Cncl Mbr, Chinese Composite Materials Soc, 1994-99; Hon Prof, Sandong Univ of Technol, 1995-. Hobbies: Swimming; Mountain climbing; Enjoying light music. Address: Beijing Synthetic Fiber Experimental Factory, Yan Ting Jing Li Zhong Jie, No25, Beijing 100025.

LUO Yun, b. 15 Oct 1928, Nanchang, China. Professor. m. Xu Ye, 15 Jan 1978, 1 d. Education: BEng, Tsinghua Univ, Beijing, 1950. Hobbies: Music; Walking. Address: c/p Faculty 304, Naval Academy of Engineering, Wuhan 430033, China.

LUO Zhi-Shan, b. 20 Aug 1936, Da-Pu, Guangdong, China. Teacher; Researcher. m. Xiu-Yin Wang, 1 May 1968, 2 s. Education: Grad, Tianjin Univ, 1958. Appointments: Asst, 1958-79, Lectr, 1979-85, Assoc Prof, 1986-93, Dir, Lab of Mechs, 1984-85, Dir, Tchng and Rsch Sect, 1985-86, Prof of Mechs, 1993-, Tianjin Univ. Publications: The Principle and Application of Sticking Film Moire Interferometry, 1990; Ultra-High Sensitivity Moire Interferometry for Subdynamic Tests in Normal Light Environment, 1994. Honours: Gilding Medal, 15th Intl Exhbn of Invention and New Techniques, Geneva, 1987; Gold Medal, 2nd Invention Exhbn of China, 1986; Natl Awd of Invention, China, 1987; Advd Awd of Sci and Technol, China, 1986, 1997. Memberships: Soc of Exptl Mechs; Hong Kong Press Publng Co; Hong Kong sun Wah Publng Co. Hobby: Research. Address: Four Season Village, 29-5-401 Tianjin University, Tianjin 300072, China.

LUO Zongming, b. 9 Dec 1936. Head of Department; Professor. m. Yang Shunan, 8 July 1965, 2 s. Education: Dept of Chem, Yunnan Univ, 1959. Appointments: Asst Tchr, 1959-80; Lectr, 1981; Assoc Prof, 1986; Prof, 1991. Publications: Ternary complexes and their applications in analytical chemistry, book, 1981; Book, Organic Reagents and Their Applications, 1995; Num pprs. Honours: Sci and Technol Prize, Guangdong Prov Govt, 1981; Natural Sci Prize, Guangdong Prov Govt, 1993; Outstndng Expert, Chinese Govt, 1993; Ex Tchr Awd, Guangdong Prov Govt, 1995; Sci and Technol Prize, Gangdong Prov Govt, 1996. Memberships: Chmn, Fine Chem Engrng Assn, 1997; Stndng Cncl Mbr, Guandong Chem Engrng Assn, 1997. Hobbies: Music; Quyi; Gymnastics. Address: 729 Dongfeng East Road,

Department of Chemical Engineering, Guangdong University of Technology, Guangzhou City, 510090, China.

LUXTON John (M J F). Government Minister. m. 3 children. Education: Bach Deg, Postgrad Dip, Agricl Sci, Massey Univ. Appointments: Elected to Parl, 1987; Min for Housing and Energy, 1990; Assoc Min of Educ; Min of Police and Maori Affairs, 1993; Assoc Min of Educ, -1996; Min of Com and Ind, Fisheries and Lands, 1996; Min for Biosecurity, 1997; Min of Food, Fibre, Biosecurity and Border Control incl Agric, Land, Forestry, Fisheries, Customs, Assoc Intl Trade and Assoc Immigration responsibilities, 1998; Bus'man, Farmer, Agricl Cnslt in pub and pvte sectors. Memberships: Directorships incl: Chj=mn, Tatua Dairy Co; Dpty Chmn, Wallford Meats Ltd. Address: 49 Broadway, PO Box 117, Matamata, New Zealand.

LYMAN David, b. 25 Sept 1936. Lawyer. m. 10 Nov 1979, Yubol Pumsathit. Education: BS, Elecl Engrng, Duke Univ, 1958; Cert, US Naval Offrs Submarine Sch, 1960; JD, Univ CA, San Fran, 1965; Postgrad, For & Comp Law, Columbia Univ, 1974. Appointments: US Navy, Minesweepers and Submarine force, 1958-62; Regd Elecl Engr, Thailand Assn Fitzsimmons & Petris, Oakland, CA, 1965-66; Bar, CA, 1966; Lempres & Seyranian, Oakland, 1966-67; Assoc Ptnr, 1967-84, Snr Ptnr, 1984-, Tilleke & Gibbins, ROP Advocates & Sols, Bangkok; Dir, Goodyear (Thailand) Ltd, Truimph Intl (Thailand) Ltd; Fndng Mbr, PM Thailand's For Invmnt Advsry Cncl, 1975; Chmn, For C of C, Thailand Law Change Proj for PM, 1992; Mbr, USAID Advsry Cttee on US-Thai Trade and Invmnt, 1988; Fndr, US Asia Environment Ptnrshp Prog, 1994. Publications: Contributed numerous articles to Professional Journals. Honours include: Recip US Naval Inst Prize, 1958; Amn Jurisp Prize, 1965; US Dept Com Cert, 1987; Paul Harris Fell, 1987; Thai PM's Cert of Achievement, 1990, 1992; Amn C of C Disting Serv Awd, 1990; Beta Gamma Sigma Natl Hon Soc, 1995; Women Secs Assn of Thailand, Boss of the Yr, 1997. Memberships include: Chmn, King Bhumiphol Rama IX Park US Geodesic Dome Pavillion Cttee, 1987; Fndng Mbr, Thailand Bus Cncl, Sustainable Dev, 1993-; Fndr, Davos Grp World Econ Forum on Anti-Corruption Standards for Global Bus, 1995-; ICC Standing Cttee on Extortion and Bribery, 1997-; Fndr, Bd Mbr, ICC Thailand Natl Chapt, 1999; Thailand Rep to ICC Intl Crt of Arbitration, 1999; Co-Fndr, Advsr on Cmnty Servs, Bangkok, 1985; Sec-Gen, Thailand Soc Prevention of Cruelty to Animals; Chaine des Rotisseurs (Charge de Mission); CA Bar Assn; Intl Bar Assn; Thailand Trademark Assn; US Naval Inst; Intl Oceanographic Fndn; Tau Epsilon Phi; Phi Alpha Delta; Thailand Bus Coalition AIDS Assn. Hobbies: Scuba Diving; Swimming; Outdoor Photography. Address: Tilleke and Gibbons ROP, 64/1 Soi Tonson, Ploenchit Road, Bangkok 10330, Thailand.

LYNAM Darryl Frederick, b. 24 June 1926, Melbourne, Aust. Company Director. m. 18 Apr 1962. Education: BE, Sydney Univ. Appointments: Served Roy Austl Navy, retiring as Rear-Admiral, 1983, inclng: Ships Melbourne and Sydney (Aircraft Carriers), and Destroyers Tobruk and Perth; Shore appts at GID, Austl High Comm, London, Navy Off; Dir, Forward Des; Dir, Naval Weapons Des; Dir, Gen Fleet Maintenance; Chf of Naval Tech Servs; Dpty Chmn, Stanilite Pacific; Dir, STN Atlas; Pres, NSW Indl Mobilisation Course Assn. Honour: CBE, 1983. Listed in: Who's Who in Australia. Hobbies: Music; Modern History. Address: 24 Peters Place, Maroubra, NSW 2035, Australia.

LYNCH John Dominic, b. 8 July 1946, Sydney, Australia. Linguist; University Administrator. m. Andonia Piau, 21 Sept 1977, 2 s. Education: BA, hons, Univ Sydney; PhD, Univ HI, USA. Appointments: Prof of Lang, 1978-86, Vice Chan, 1986-91, Univ Papua New Guinea; Dir, Pacific Lang Unit, 1991-, Prof of Pacific Langs, 1994-, Pro Vice Chan, 1996-, Univ of the S Pacific. Publications: Pacific Languages: An Introduction, 1998; Sev articles in profl jrnls. Honour: 10th Anniversary of Independence Medal, Papua New Guinea, 1985. Hobbies: Cricket;

Cryptic Crosswords; Post-Cyclone Garden Reconstruction. Address: University of the South Pacific, PMB 072, Port Vila, Vanuatu.

LYNCH Stanley Peter, b. 28 Fe 1945. Research Associate. m. 6 Mar 1981, 2 d. Education: BSc, hons; MSc, PhD. Appointments: Prin Rsch Sci, Aeron & Maritime Rsch Lab; Rsch Assoc, Dept of Materials Engrng, Monash Univ. Pulications: Over 60 pprs in sci jrnls and conf proceedings; 1 Patent. Honour: Disting Lectr in Metallography Awd, 1988. Memberships: Inst of Metals & Materials, Aust; Am Soc of Materials; Intl Metallographic Soc; Am Soc of Metals; Intl Metallography Soc. Hobbies: Tennis; Skiing; Travel. Address: Aeronautical & Maritime Research Laboratory, PO Box 4331, Melbourne, Vic 3001, Australia.

LYONS John Francis, b. Aust. Barrister-at-Law. m. Elizabeth Ann Baxter, 15 Apr 1964, 2 s, 1 d. Education: BA, Hons, 1958, LLB Hons, 1960, Melbourne Univ. Appointments: Admitted to Prac, Vic, 1962; Vic Bar, Roll of Practitioners, High Crt of Aust, 1963; Admitted as Bar, NSW, 1969, WA, 1984, Qld, 1991; QC, Vic, 1976, NSW, 1977, WA, 1985, Qld, 1992; Admitted to Prac, NZ, 1990, QC, 1994. Memberships: Vic Bar; NSW Bar; Austl Bar Assn; Law Cncl of Aust; Intl Bar Assn. Address: 205 William Street, Melbourne, Vic 3000, Australia.

LYONS Lawrence Ernest, b. 26 May 1922, Sydney, Aust. University Professor. m. Alison Hargreaves, 7 Jan 1956, 2 s. Education: BA, MSc, Univ of Sydney, 1948; PhD, 1952, DSc, 1964, Univ of London, Eng. Appointments: RAAF, 1944-45; Lectr, Snr Lectr, Rdr, Univ of Sydney, 1945-63; Mbr, New Univ Colls Cncl, 1960 also Inst for the Stdy of Christianity in an Age of Sci and Technol, 1960-87; Prof, Physl Chem, 1963-87, Emer Prof, 1987-, Univ of Qld; Mbr of Edl Bds, Molecular Crystals and Liquid Crystals, 1966-83, Chem Phys Letters, 1967-77; Visitor, Dept of Physl Chem, Oxford, 1967; Visng Prof, Univ of BC, Can, 1967, Univ of Waterloo, Can, 1985-86; Leverhulme Snr Fell, Univ of Tokyo, 1970; Visng Fell, Clare Hall and Visng Schl, Physl Chem Dept, Cambridge Univ, England, 1986. Publications: Organic Semiconductors (w F Gutmann), 1967, Russian edition, 1970, reprint, 1980; Organic Semiconductors Part B (w F Gutmann and H Keyzer), 1983; Contbr of 150 pprs in Physl Chem. Honours: Fulbright Travel Awds, 1957 and 1979; Ramsay Fell, UK, 1952-53; H G Smith Medal for Chem, 1968; Burfitt Prize for Sci, 1968; Leverhulme Snr Fell, Tokyo, 1971; Debye Lectr, Cornell Univ, 1979. Memberships: Austl Acady Sci Cttee on Spectroscopy, 1962-81; Fell, RACI, 1962-; Fell, Austl Acady of Sci, 1971-; Natl Energy Rsch Devel and Demonstration Cncl, 1978-81; Pres, ANZAAS Chem Section, 1967; Sci and Ind Forum, 1978-82; Austl Natl Cttee for UNESCO, 1982-84. Listed many inclng: Who's Who In Australia, Who's Who in the World; Men of Achievement. Hobby: Reading. Address: 2172 Moggill Road, Kenmore, Qld 4069, Australia.

M

MA Bao Jiao, b. 26 Oct 1935, China. Research. m. Z X Zhang, 17 Sept 1965, 1 s, 1 d. Education: Dr-Ing, Inst of Technol, Germany. Appointments: Hd, Chem Machinery Dept, Shanghai Rsch of Chem Ind, 1978-95. Publication: Dry Performance and Heat Transfer of Vibrational Fluidized Bed, 1992. Honour: Awd, Sci & Technol Adv, Min of Chem Ind. Memberships: Cncl, Chinese Soc of Chem Ind. Address: Shanghai Research Institute of Chemical Industry, 345 Yun Ling Road East, Shanghai 200062, China.

MA Dayou, b. 1 Mar 1915, Beijing, China. Research Professor. m. Wang Ronghe, 1 Aug 1947, 1 s, 1 d. Education: BS, Phys, Peking, 1936; MA, 1939, PhD, 1940, Harvard, USA. Appointments: Assoc Prof, Prof, Tsinghua and Natl SW Univ, 1940-46; Prof, Dean of Engrng, Beijing, 1946-52; Prof, Dean of Harbin, Polytechnic Inst, Harbin, 1952-55; Rsch Prof, 1955-, Dpty Dir, Inst of Acoustics, Academica Sinica, 1956-84. Publications: 160 papers in sci jrnls; sev handbooks and textbooks. Honours: Mbr, Acadmeica Sinica, 1955; Conf of Sci prize, 1978; Hon Pres, Acoustic Soc of China, 1988; Hon Mbr, Chinese Soc of Metrology, 1988. Memberships: Chinese Phys Soc; Fell, Chinese Electrons Soc; Acoustics Soc of China; Fell, Acoustic Soc, Am; NY Acady Scis, 1980-; Disting Corresp Mbr, Inst of Noise Control Engrng, USA, 1993-. Hobbies: Bridge. Address: Institute of Acoustics, Academica Sinica, PO Box 2712, Beijing 100080, China.

MA Huancheng, b. 28 Dec 1962, Hunan, China. Education. m. Wu Jianrong, 14 Apr 1991, 1 s. Education: PhD, Forestry, Beijing Forestry Univ. Appointment: Assoc Prof, Silviculture, 1997. Publications: The Physiology of Salt Resistance in Pupulus Euphratica, 1998. Honour: Ldng Sci for 21st Century, Yunnan, 1998. Membership: Cncl Dir, Silviculture Divsn, Chinese Forestry Assn. Hobby: Football. Address: c/o Department of Forestry, Southwest Forestry College, Kunming 650224, China.

MA Lin, b. 8 Feb 1925, China. Emeritus Professor of Biochemistry. m. Meng Hua Chen, 24 Jan 1957, 3 d. Education: BSc, W China Union Univ, 1947; PhD, Leeds, Eng. Appointments: Snr Lectr, Rdr, Prof of Biochem, 1964-, Vice Chan, 1978-87, Chinese Univ of Hong Kong; Chmn, Bd of Tstees, Shaw Coll, Chinese Univ of Hong Kong. Publications: Various papers in learned jrnls in chem and biochem. Honours: JP, 1978; CBE (Hons), 1984; Order of the Rising Sun, Jap, 1985; Cmndr's Cross, Fed Repub of Germany, 1987; Hon Degs, DSc, 1984; DLitt, 1985; LLD, 1987, 1995; DHumL, 1988. Memberships: Chem and biochem socs/assns. Hobbies: Swimming; Table Tennis. Address: 95 Sunderland Estate, 1 Hereford Road, Kowloon Tong, Kowloon, Hong Kong.

MA Mao Yang, b. 1964, Hebei, China. College Teacher; Writer; Poet; Theorist. Education: Dbl Bachelor, Philos, Shanghai Jiaotong Uni Litv, 1992; Master, Classical Lit, Beijing Tchr Trng Univ, 1996. Appointments: Coal Miner; Ed, Econ Lit, Lit Review Monthly, Lit Review Ppr; Chf Ed, Hebei Coal Poem, The New Century Poem Monthly. Publications: There is No Way for Love; It Is in Fact A Pity; Contrb, Multiplex Thoughts Anthology. Honours: Gold-Cow Lit Awd, 1993, 1995; 20th Century Awd for Achmnt, 1997. Memberships: Beijing Writers Assn; Shanghai Writers Assn; China Writers Assn; China City Poem Rsch Assn. Hobbies: Tourism; Running. Address: c/o Beijing Youth College, Beijing 100102, China.

MA Ruzhang, b. 20 Oct 1923, Henan, China. Education. m. Yang Zhizang, 1 s, 1 d. Education: Bach, Tangshan Jiaotong Univ, 1945-50; PhD, Moscow Inst of Iron and Steel, 1951-55. Appointments: Vice Dean, Fac of Phys and Chem, 1957-81; Assoc Prof, Prof, 1982-; Publications: Handbook of Mossbauer Spectroscopy, 1993; Mossbauer Spectroscopy, 1996; Modern Research Techniques for Materials Characterization, 1997; Over

100 sci pprs. Memberships: Chinese Assn of Nuclei; Chinese Assn of Metals; Beijing Assn of Metallurgy; Chiense Assn of Nuclear Phys. Hobbies: Taichi'chuan (Chinese boxing); Taichi sword; Weiqi (chess). Address: 30 Xueyuan Road, Building 30-406, Beijing 100083, China.

MA Sun, b. 7 June 1947, Hunan, China. President; Professor of Chemistry. Education: BSc, Chem Engrng, Natl Taiwan Univ, 1966; Dipl Chem, T H Aachen, 1977; Dr rer nat, T H Aachen, Germany, 1980. Appointment: Prof, Natl Cheng Kung Univ, Tainan; Visng Prof, T H Darmstadt, Germany; Chmn, Tainan Regl Instrument Cntr, Natl Sci Cncl; Pres, Huafan Univ, 1995-. Publications: Over 50 reports on chem, educ, Buddhism; Books in Chinese: Dust and Sand in the Shadow, 1997; Stars, Moon and the Clear Sky, 1998; Brief Recollection at Ta-Lun, 1998. Honours: Die Förderung des Wissenschaftlichen Nachwuchs, 1977-80. Memberships: Rsch Fell, Inst of Sino-Indian Studies, Taiwan. Address: Huafan University, No 1, Huafan Road, Shihtin, Taipei Hsien, Taiwan, China.

MA Yunxiang, b. 5 June 1938, Zhengzhou, China. Preventive Medicine. m. Wang Lan, 1 Oct 1961. University Diploma. Appointments: Dir, Sci Rsch and Educ Bur, Provincial PHD, 1983-85; Dir, Provincial EPS, 1985-. Publications include: Applied Hygiene; Applied Cysticercology; Applied Neuromedicine; Smoking or Health; Latrine Revolution Starting in Henan; Prevention and Research of Malaria in Henan; Ed: Illness; A Manual for Management of Country Fair; A Manual for Prevention and Treatment of Parasites; Applied Manual of Health Care; Applied Administration on Epidemic Prevention; More than 80 pprs in natl and intl publs. Honours: Advd Worker, parasite prevention and treatment in China, 1992; First degree prize of MOPH, 1996. Memberships: Fell, Roy Soc of Tropical Med and Hygiene; Chinese Medl Assn. Hobby: Music. Address: Henan Provinicial Epidemic Prevention Station, 47 Weuwu Road, Zhengzhou 450003, China.

MA Yuzhen, b. 26 Sept 1934, Beijing, China. Diplomat. m. Zou Jichun, 1961, 1 s, 1 d. Education: Beijing Inst of Fgn Langs. Appointments: Info Dept, Min of Fgn Affairs, 1954-63, Dpty Divsn Chf, Divsn Chf, 1969-80, Dir, 1984-88; Attaché, 3rd Sec, Emb of Burma, 1963-69, 1st Sec, Cnslr, Emb of Ghana, 1980-84, Consul-Gen, 1988-91, Amb to UK, 1991-95; Dpty Dir, State Cncl Info Off, 1995-97; Fgn Min Commr for China, Hong Kong, 1997-. Hobbies: Reading; Music. Address: Ministry of Foreign Affairs, Beijing, China.

MA'ARAMO Nicholas Mark, b. 9 Aug 1948, Lede, Solomon Islands. General Secretary. m. Maisie, 31 July 1983, 4 s, 4 d. Education: BA. Appointments: Asst Budgets Offr, Advsr, Rsch Cttee, Univ Papua New Guinea, 1973-76; Admin Offr, Min of Home Affairs, 1976; Hong Kong Bank, 1977-87; Supermkt Mngr, Solomon Islands Consumers Coop, 1987; Asst Mngr, Westpac Banking Corp, 199-91; Loans Mngr, Home Fin Corp, 1991. Memberships: Dir, Devel Bank of Solomons Islands, Ctrl Bank of Solomon Islands; Exec Mbr, Solomon Islands Cham of Com; Solomon Islands Govt Schlsp Selection Cttee; Solomon Islands Govt Tender Bd. Address: c/o Church of Melanesia, PO Box 19, Honiara, Solomon Islands.

MAANI Sholeh Arjomand. Associate Professor, Economics. m. K E Maani, 2 children. Education: BS, Univ IL, 1975; MS, 1976; PhD, 1978. Appointments: Asst Prof, Occidental Coll, Los Angeles, CA, 1980-84; Rsch Dir, Fndn for Econ Rsch, Univ of Concepcion, Chile, 1981-82; Visng Schl, Harvard Univ, 1990-91; Snr Lectr, Econs, Univ of Auckland; Assoc Prof. Publications: Rates of Return to Higher Education in New Zealand: A Study of the Census Years 1981-1991, 1994; A Research Agenda, Methodologies, Models and Data Requirements for Estimating Participation in Post-compulsory Education in New Zealand, 1996; Private and Social Rates of Return to Secondary and Higher Education in New Zealand: Evidence from the 1991 Census, 1996; The Effect of Fees on Participation in Higher Education: A

Survey of OECD Countries, 1996; Investing in Minds: The Economics of Higher Education in New Zealand, 1997. Membership: Pres, NZ Assn of Economists, 1995-97. Address: Department of Economics, University of Auckland, Private Bag 92019, Auckland, New Zealand.

MAASTRICHT Susan Margaret, b. 15 Apr 1951, Melbourne, Aust. Veterinarian. m. Jacobus, 16 Nov 1985, 2 s, 1 d. Education: BVSc; MACVSc. Appointments: Newcastle Univ; Monash Univ; Univ NSW. Memberships: Anzslas, pres, 1992-95. Hobbies: Reading; Walking; Painting; Poetry. Address: c/o Biological Resources Centre, University of New South Wales, Sydney 2052, Australia.

MABBETT Ian William, b. 27 Apr 1939, London, England. University Academic. m. Jacqueline Towns, 11 Dec 1971, 2 d. Education: BA, 1960, DPhil, 1963, MA, 1965, Oxon. Appointments: Lectr, 1965-70, Snr Lectr, 1971-80, Rdr in Hist, 1981-, Monash Univ. Publications: Short History of India, 1968, 2nd ed, 1983; Truth, Myth & Politics in Ancient India, 1971; The Khmers, (co-auth), 1995. Honours: Boden Sanskrit Prize, 1958; Boden Sanskrit Schlsp, 1960; Rsch Fellshp, Humanities Rsch Cntr, Austl Natl Univ, 1994; H H Raychaudhuri Gold Medal Awd, for Contbn to Indology, The Asiatic Soc, 1999. Memberships: Fedn of Austl Writers; Austl Soc of Auths. Hobby: Short Story Writing. Address: c/o Department of History, Monash University, Clayton, Victoria 3168, Australia.

MACALISTER Robert Stuart, b. 22 May 1924, Los Angeles, CA, USA. Engineer; Executive. m. (1) Catherine Vera Willby, 15 Nov 1947, decd 24 Nov 1994, 1 s, 1 d, (2) Grace V LeClerc, 4 Dec 1995. Education: Cert of Completion, Brighton Techl Coll, BSME CA Inst of Technol. Appointments: VP, Occidental (Pet) of Libya Inc, 1968; Mnng Dir, Occidental of Brit, Caledonian Occidental, 1971; Pres, Occidental Intl Oil Inc, 1976; Pres, Chmn of Bd, Canad Occidental Pet PLC, 1978; Mnng Dir, Austl Occidental Pet PLC, 1982; Mnng Dir, Hamilton Brothers Oil & Gas Ltd, 1983; Pet Bus Cnslt, 1986. Memberships: Soc of Pet Engrs, 1947-98; Regd Profl Engr, TX, 1965-96; VP, UK Offshore Operators Assn, 1973-78, 1983-86; Bd of Govs, Canad Pet Assn, 1978-81; Dir, Canad Occidental Pet Ltd, Dir, Petrogas Processing Ltd, 1978-81, Scoutmaster, Boy Scouts of Am, 1963-68. Hobbies: Watercolour painting; Crafts; Gardening; Golf; Crossword puzzles; Grandchildren. Address: 78 Lopaco Court, Camarillo, CA 93010, USA.

MACALPIN Rex Nere, b. 25 Apr 1932, Glendale, CA, USA. Physician; University Professor. m. Carol W, 22 June 1957, 1 s, 1 d. Education: BA; MD. Appointments: Prof of Med/Cardiology, UCLA Sch of Med, Los Angeles, 1963-88; Prof (Emeritus) of Med/Cardiology, 1988-. Publications: Over 100 sci articles in medl jrnls, 1958-93. Hobbies: Tennis; Classical music. Address: Division of Cardiology, 10833 Le Conte Avenue, Los Angeles, CA 90095-1679, USA.

MACBRIDE Dexter DuPont, b. 18 Aug 1917, Elizabeth, NJ, USA. Lawyer; Mediator. m. Grace Anderson, 23 Dec 1963, 1 s. 2 d. Education: LLB; MA; JD; Diploma, Colegio de Ingenieros de Venezuela, Soc de Tasadores. Appointments: Chf Appraiser, CA Pub Works, 1968; Ex VP, Amn Soc Appraisers, 1970; VM, Intl Exec Serv Corps, 1987; Pres Bd Tstees, Mt San Antonio College, 1998; Pres, Bd Tstees, Greater LA County Vector Control Dist, 1999. Publications: Power and Process, 1969; Freedom USA, 1976; Opportunities in Appraising, 1982; MacBride's Musings, 1998-; Lecture Series as Adam Smith, 1776 Wealth of Nations; Free Lance Writer. Honours: CA Ldrshp Awd, 1971; Pub Serv Awd of Intl Right of Way Assn, 1982; Chan, ASA Coll of Fells, 1983; L A County Outstndng Volun Serv Awd, 1992. Memberships: ABA; VA Bar Assn; Amn Soc Appraisers; Amn Soc of Assoc Execs. Address: 435 Willapa Lane, Diamond Bar, CA 91765, USA.

MACCORMACK Terrance William, b. 18 Feb 1946, Ottawa, Ontario, Can. Pshchologist. m. Judy, 29 Oct

1997, 1 s, 1 d. Education: BA, Hons, Psychol; BA, Engl Lit; PhD, Clinl Psychol. Appointments: Lectr, Univ of New Eng, NSW, Aust; Clinl Psychol, Univ of Sydney, NSW. Creative Works: Articles, Photos Publd in var mags. Hobbies: Writing; Photog. Address: 19 Marielle Court, Ottawa, Ontario, K2B 8P3, Canada.

MACDONALD Ronald James, b. 31 Mar 1941, Branton, NSW, Aust. Physicist. m. Beverley, 12 Jan 1963, 3 d. Education: BS (Hons 1, Phys); PhD (UNSW). Appointments: Lectr, Snr Lectr, Rdr, ANU, 1966-80; Prof of Phys, Univ Newcastle; Pro Vice Chan, (Rsch); Dpty Vice Chmn (Rsch). Publications: 130 sci pprs, book chapts. Honours: Univ Newcastle Medal, 1990. Memberships: Austl Inst of Koysus, Pres, 1995-96; AINSE. Hobbies: Fishing; Family; Furniture Restoration. Address: 20 The Quarterdeck, Casey Bay, NSW 2283, Australia.

MACDUFF Roderick Alexander, b. 20 Sept 1955, Glasgow, Scotland. Electronic Engineer. m. Valerie, 7 June 1982, 1 d. Education: BS, Electrons, Glasgow Univ, 1977; BA, Hum, Open Univ, 1989. Appointments: Electrons Engr, Racal Ltd, Eng, 1977-86; Snr Scientist, Kodak Ltd, Eng, 1986-89; Cnslt, PSI Fremantle, 1989-92; R&D Mngr, Barrett Comms, Perth, 1992-94; CEO and Tech Dir, Q-MAC Electrons, Perth, 1994. Honours: Instn of Eng Aust Engrng Excellence Awd, 1987; Austl Des Awd, 1997. Hobbies: Cycling; Reading; Amateur radio. Address: 50 Kinshall Road, Attadale, WA 6156, Australia.

MACER Darryl Raymond Johnson, b. 22 July 1962, Christchurch, NZ. University Professor. m. Noburo Yasuhara Macer, 23 Nov 1987. Education: BS (Hons) Lincoln Coll, Univ of Canterbury, NZ; PhD, Trinity Coll, Univ of Cambridge. Appointments: Dir, Eubios Ethics Inst, 1990-; Cnslt, NZ Dept Indl and Sci Rsch, 1990-91; For Prof, Univ of Tsukuba, 1990-. Publications: Shaping Genes, 1990; Bioethics for the People by the People, 1994; Bioethics is Love of Life, 1998. Memberships: UNESCO Intl Bioethics Cttee, 1993-; Human Genome Orgn Ethics Cttee, 1995-; Intl Union Biol Sci (IUBS) Bioethics Prog Chairperson, 1997-. Hobbies: Gardening; Music. University of Tsukuba, Institute of Biological Sciences, Tsukuba Science City, Ibaraki 305, Japan.

MACFARLANE Ian John, b. 22 June 1946, Sydney, Aust. Governor. m. Heather, 16 Jan 1970, 1 s, 1 d. Education: BEc Hons, Monash Univ; MEc. Appointments: Inst for Econs and Stats, Oxford Univ; OECD; Var Positions, Reserve Bank of Aust; Gov, 1996-. Memberships: Chmn, Reserve Bank of Aust Bd; Chmn Payment System Bd; Mbr Austl Prudential Regulation Authority Bd. Address: Reserve Bank of Australia 65 Martin Place, Sydney 2000, Australia.

MACH Martin Henry, b. 10 Feb 1940, NY, USA. Chemist. m. Susan, 17 Dec 1995, 1 d. Education: BS, Chem, Cty Coll of NY, 1961; MA, Physl Organic Chem, Clark Univ, Worcester; MA, 1965; PhD, Physl Organic Chem, Univ of CA, Santa Cruz, 1973. Memberships: Sigma Xi, 1975-; CA Assn of Criminalists, 1975-77. Address: TRW, Bldg 01/2010, 1 Space Park, Redondo Beach, CA.

MACINTYRE Andrew James, b. 19 Aug 1960, Sydney, Australia. Academic. m. Julia, 1984, 3 s. Education: BA Hons, Aust Natl Univ; MA; PhD. Appointments: Assoc Prof, Univ of CA, San Diego. Publications: Business and Politics in Indonesia, 1991; Business and Government in Industrializing Asia, 1994. Memberships: APSA; AIIA. Hobbies: Sailing; Gardening. Address: 1255 Calle Christopher, Encinitas, CA, USA.

MACINTYRE Stuart Forbes, b. 21 Apr 1947, Melbourne, Aust. Academic. m. Martha Adele, 16 Aug 1976, 2 d. Education: BA (Hons), Univ of Melbourne, 1968; MA, Monash, 1971; PhD, Cambridge, 1975. Appointments: Rsch Fell, St John's Coll, Cambridge, 1977-78; Lectr, Sch of Socl Inquiry, Murdoch Univ, 1979; Lectr, Hist Dept, Univ of Melbourne, 1980-81; Rsch Fell, Rsch Sch of Socl Scis, Austl Natl Univ, 1982-83; Snr Lectr, 1984-87; Rdr, 1988-90; Hist Dept, Ernest Scott

Prof of Hist, 1990-, Dean, Fac of Arts, 1999-, Univ of Melbourne. Publications: 10 books incl: Militant: The Life and Times of Paddy Troy, 1984; Winner and Losers: the Pursuit of Social Justice in Australian History, 1985; The Oxford History of Australia, Volume 4, 1901-1942: The Succeeding Age, 1987; The Labour Experiment, 1988; A Colonial Liberalism: The Lost World of Three Victorian Visonaries, 1991; A History for a Nation: Ernest Scott and the Making of Australian History, 1994; The Reds, 1998; A Concise History of Australia, 1999. Memberships: Fell, Acady Socl Scis in Aust, 1987-; Cncl, Constitutional Centenary Fndn, 1991-; Exec Cttee, Evatt Fndn, 1997-; Corresp Fell, Roy Histl Soc. Hobbies: Running; Reading. Address: History Department, University of Melbourne, Parkville, Victoria 3052, Australia.

MACK Eric Charles Thomas, b. 3 Feb 1932, Bega, NSW, Aust. Writer. m. Marie, div, 1 s, 1 d. Publications: The Rock, 1976; National Treasure, 1987; Picaresque Adventures of Mr Cootes, 1988. Memberships: Dir, Mack Art Gall, 1951; Sydney sect, Austl Anarchists Assn, 1952; Fndr, Keep S Aust Beautiful, 1962; Initiated Keep Aust Beautiful, 1963; Convenor, Getting Together, natl green conf, 1982. Hobbies: Painting; Sculpture; Sailing; Green politics. Address: 80 John Street, Eltham, Victoria, Australia 3095.

MACKAY William Morton, b. 26 Mar 1934, Dundee, Scotland. Educator. m. Catherine, 30 July 1959, 2 s, 1 d. Education: MA (hons), St Andrews Univ; Dip Ed, St Andrews Univ, 1957; Dip of Theol Stdies, Free Ch of Scot Coll, Edinburgh, 1959. Appointments: Tchr, Buckhaven HS, 1959-61; Tchr, Supvsr of Sec Stdies and Headmaster (1966-78), St Andrew's Coll, Lima, Peru, 1961-78; Tchr, Lothian Reg, 1978-85; Prin, Presby Ladies Coll, Melbourne, Aust, 1986-97. Publication: Thomas Chalmers: A Short Appreciation. Honours: Hon Mbr, Brit Schls' Assn of Peru, 1971; Dip of Hon for servs to Educ in Peru, Peruvian Govt, 1981; Moderator of Synod, Presby Ch of East Aust, 1993. Memberships: Assn of Hds of Indep Schs of Aust, 1986-97; Austl Prins Cntr, 1996-; Assoc of Roy Scottish Geog Soc, 1998. Hobbies: Music; Photography; Cricket; Rugby; Reading; Walking. Address: 53 Lauderdale Street, Edinburgh EH9 1DE, Scotland.

MACKELLAR Michael John Randal, b. 27 Oct 1938, Sydney, Australia. Politician. m. Robin Morey Smith, 1969, 2 s, 1 d. Education: Sydney Univ; Balliol Coll, Oxford. Appointments: NSW Dept of Agricl, 1961-69; Mbr for Warringah, NSW, House of Reps, 1969-94; Mbr, Cncl of Austl Natl Univ, 1970-76; Mbr, House of Reps Select Cttee on Wildlife Conservation, 1970-72, Standing Cttee on Environ, Recreation & The Arts, 1982-83, 1987-89, on Selection Cttee, 1988-90, House, 1990; Mbr, Jt Parl Cttee on Fgn Affairs & Def, 1971-74, 1983-88, Fgn Affairs, Def & Trade, 1987-94; Jt Standing Cttee on Pub Accts, 1972-74, on Electoral Reform, 1985-87, on the Natl Crime Authy, 1985-89, on New Parl House, 1989-90; Mbr, 1st Austl Parl Del to China, 1973; Parl Sec to Ldr of Opposition, 1973-74; Shadow Min for Immigration, 1974-75; Min for Immigration & Ethnic Affairs, 1975-79; Min Asst the Treas, 1978-79, Min of Hlth, 1979-82, Min Asst the PM, 1979-80; Min for Home Affairs & Environ, 1981; Shadow Min for Fgn Affairs, 1983-84, for Sci & Specl Min of State, 1984-85; Dpty Opposition Ldr of the House, 1985; Opposition Whip, 1989. Memberships include: Cncl, Roy Blind Soc, NSW, 1970. Hobbies: Tennis; Cricket; Golf; Reading; Photography. Address: 2A West Street, Balgowlah Heights, Sydney, NSW 2093, Australia.

MACKENZIE Cortlandt John Gordon, b. 6 Sept 1920. Physician in Public Health. m. Jean Barker, 6 Jan 1945, 3 s. Education: MD, CM, Queens at Kingston, 1951; DPH, Toronto, 1955; FRCPC, 1961, FRSH. Appointments: Dir, Peace River Hlth Unit, 1954-55; Dir, W Kootenay Hlth Unit, 1956-59; Dir, Selkirk Hlth Unit, 1956-58; Dir, Cntrl Vancouver Is Hlth Unit, 1959-63; Rsch Fell, Dept of Hlthcare and Epidemiology, UBC, 1961, Asst Prof, 1963, Assoc Prof, 1967; Acting Chmn, 1969, Dept Hd, 1973-80, Emer Prof, 1986, Visng Prof, Univ Papua New Guinea, 1976; Prof, Univ Papua New Guinea, 1981;

Visng Prof, Natl Univ of Malaysia, 1983; WHO Cnsltn to Cook Islands, Pollution Control Bd of BC (Mbr 1967-82, Chmn 1977-82); Cnslt Cntrl Austl Aboriginal Cttee, 1976. Publications: Numerous Articles in CPHA Journal, Journal of AMA, Annals of Medicine, Singapore, Papua New Guinea Medical Journal. Honours: CPHA Defries Medal, 1986; James Robinson Meml Awd, UBC, 1988. Memberships: BCMA; CMA; CPHA, Exec BC Bd, 1960-62; IEA Exec, 1981-84; Tchr of Social and Preventative Med, Pres, 1976. Listed in: Who's Who in Canada. Address: 3140 West 55th Avenue, Vancouver BC, V6N 3W9, Canada.

MACKENZIE John Weston Seaforth, b. 19 July 1935. Agricultural Consultant. m. Aija Valija Cipants, 16 Dec 1962, 1 s, 1 d. Education: BSc Agric Sci (Hons), Univ of Sydney, 1966. Appointment: 46 yrs in coml agric in Fiji and Aust; Dir, Agricl Cnsltng Firm of Sloane Cook and King Pty Ltd, 1986-. Honour: Natl Farmers Fedn Awd of Hon, 1999. Memberships: Australasian Assn of Agricl Cnslts; Austl Inst of Agricl Sci and Technol, Fed Pres, 1981, Elected Fell, AIAST, 1985, Awd'd CPAg, 1994; Austl Shareholders Assn, chmn, 1974-81; Cncl on Bus Regulation (Fedl Govt), 1995-96; SCK Superannuation Fund, Tstee, 1986-; Exec Cttee, Natl Farmers Fedn, 1983-, Treas, 1984-98; Chmn, Aboriginal Affairs Cttee/Task Force, 1985-; Mbr, NFF Indl Cttee, 1985-; Tstee, Austl Farmers Fighting Fund, 1985-98; North Territory Cattlemens Assn, Exec mbr, 1983-; Rural Rsch Cncls Selection Cttee; CSIRO Agricl Sect Advsry Cttee, 1989-96; Agricl Rsch Strategy for Aust, Steering Cttee; Rural Trng Cncl of Aust. Hobbies: Golf; Music. Address: 93 Bestmann Road East, Sandstone Point, Queensland 4511, Australia.

MACKERRAS Colin Patrick, b. 26 Aug 1939, Sydney, Aust. Academic. m. Alyce Barbara, 29 June 1963, 2 s, 3 d. Education: BA, Univ of Melbourne, 1961; BA, hons, 1962, PhD, 1970, Austl Natl Univ; MLitt, Univ of Cambridge, England, 1964. Appointments: Engl Tchr, Peking For Lang Inst, 1964-66; Rsch Schl, 1966-69, Rsch Fell, Austl Natl Univ, 1969-73; Fndn Prof, Griffith Univ, 1974-; Chmn, Sch of Mod Asian Stdies, 1979-85; Co-Dir, Key Cntr for Asian Langs and Stdies, Griffith Univ, 1988-96; Hd, Sch of Mod Asian Studies, Griffith Univ, 1996-. Publications: Auth of many books, incl: China Observed 1964-67, 1967; Modern China: A Chronology, 1982; The Cambridge Handbook of Contemporary China, 1991; China's Minority Cultures, 1995; Peking Opera, 1997; China in Transformation 1900-1949, 1998; Dictionary of the Politics of the People's Republic of China, 1998; Many pprs in profl jrnls and chapts in books. Honours: Intl Visitor, US, 1977; Gold Citation, Media Peace Prize, UN Assn of Austl, 1981; Einstein Intl Acady Fndn Cross of Merit Awd, 1993. Memberships: Asian Stdies Assn of Aust, VP, 1990-92, Pres, 1992-95; Qld Hist Tchrs Assn; Chinese Stdies Assn of Austl, Pres, 1991-93. Hobbies: Music; Jogging. Address: School of Modern Asian Studies, Griffith University, Nathan, Queensland 4111, Australia.

MACKIE Elizabeth Ruth, b. 3 Dec 1929, Melbourne, Aust. Writer. m. 10 Aug 1957, div, 1 s. Education: BA, Melbourne Univ; Trained Nurse. Publications: Koalas; Illustrated Rhymes for Children; Charles & Louise, the Love Story of Charles II and Louise de Keroualle, My Ancestors. Honour: Red Cross Long Serv Medal. Hobbies: Painting; Poetry; Needlework; Red Cross. Address: 18 Corangamite Street, Colac, Victoria, Australia 3250.

MACKIE Ian John, b. 16 Oct 1932, Belmont, Australia. Cardiologist. m. Ruth, 11 Mar 1961, 2 s, 2 d. Education: FRACP; MBBS. Appointments: Med Advsr, Surflifesaving Aust and Roy Lifesaving Soc, 1976-80; Med Chmn, Intl Lifesaving Fedn, 1976-98. Publications: Many pprs of Drowning, Resuscitation Use of Oxygen, Safety of Aquatic Athletes and Hyperthermia. Honour: AM, 1989. Memberships: Cardiac Soc of Aust, 1976-99; Austl Resuscitation Cncl, 1982-95; Fac of Med Review. Hobbies: Golf; Water Safety. Address: 17 Waratah Street, Cronulla, 2230, Australia.

MACKIE John Bullamore, b. 3 Sept 1910. Mining Engineer; Land Surveyor. m. Susie Gainsford Bacon, 16 June 1947, 1 s, 1 d. Education: MSc, 1st class hons; BEng; Assoc, Otago Sch of Mines. Appointments: Field Engr, Malaya, 1935-36; Brit Colonial Serv, Malaya, 1936-47; Acad Staff 1947-75, Prof, Land Surveying 1969-75, Emer Prof 1976-, Univ of Otago, NZ. Publications: The Elements of Astronomy for Surveyors, 5 eds, 1953, 1964, 1971, 1978, 1985. Honours: ED and Bar, 1954; Queen's Silver Jubilee Medal, 1977; OBE, 1995. Memberships: Pres, FRASNZ, 1969-70; Hon Life Mbr, Scout Assn of NZ, 1974-; Pres, FNZIS, 1977-79; FGS; MIPENZ. Hobbies: Golf; Reading; Writing; Amateur Radio. Address: 8 Tarata Street, Stoke, Nelson 7001, New Zealand.

MACKIE Richard Falconer, b. 23 Nov 1921, Waipukurau, NZ. Barrister; Solicitor; Notary Public. m. Gwen Mary Andrew, 20 May 1949, 4 s. Education: Canterbury Univ, Christchurch, 1940-41 (part) and Vic Univ, 1946-48, LLB, 1949. Appointments: War Serv, 1939-45; Law Clk, 1946; Practised Law as qualified lawyer, 1949-99; Suffered spinal injury in 1971, although a quadraplegic continued w own legal prac. Honours: DSC, 1944; Life Memberships NZ Golf Assn, Pres, 1983-84; Waipukurau Golf, Jockey and Gentleman's Clubs; Appt Capt (non-playing), NZ Golf Team, 1963; Commonwealth and 1966 Eisenhower Tournaments; Won Duffers Cup, 1966. Memberships: Hawkes Bay and NZ Law Socs, Rotary Club; Fndr Mbr, local Chmbr of Com and Outward Bound Cttees; Pres, Local Returned Servs Assn, Area Naval Rels Offr, 1951-99; Pres, Hawkes Bay Provl Golf Assn, mbr, 1952-77; NZ Golf Assn, 1954-77; World Golf Cncl Admnstv Cttee, NZ Repr, World Amateur Golf Cncl, 1966-68; R&A Golf Club, 1967, Estab People to People Sports Inc in NZ w var Golf Clubs, 1968; NZ Golf Assn Deleg on Rules of Golf and Amateur Status Cttees, 1977-84; NZ Deleg, First World Amateur Golf Conf, St Andrews, 1980; NZ Rep, Opening of Fleet Air Arm Mus, Yeovilton, Eng, 1980. Hobbies: Family; Watching sport; Listening to music; Reading. Address: PO Box 66, Waipukurau 4176, New Zealand.

MACKINNON Alison Gay, b. Shepparton, Australia. Historian; University Teacher. m. Malcolm Mackinnon, 21 Dec 1964, 3 s. Education: BA, Dip Ed, Melbourne; MEd, PhD, Adelaide. Appointments: Tutor in Educn, 1976-82, Lectr in Lib & Info Mngmt, 1983-94, Dir, Inst for Socl Rsch, 1994-, Dir, Hawke Inst, 1998-, Prof, Hist & Gender Studies. Publications: One Foot on the Ladder, 1984; The New Women, 1986; Love and Freedom: Professional Women and the Reshaping of Personal Life, 1997; Sev profl jrnl articles. Honours: AARE Outstndng Thesis Awd, 1990; NSW Premiers Lit Awd, 1997. Memberships: Pres, Aust & NZ Hist of Educn Assn, 1997-98; Austl Histl Assn. Hobbies: Vineyard Owner; Bushwalking; Travel. Address: 13 Blyth Street, Glen Osmond, Adelaide, SA 5064, Australia.

MACLELLAN Robert Roy Cameron (The Hon), b. 8 Mar 1934, Melbourne, Aust. Member of Parliament. m. 22 June 1963, 2 s, 1 d. Education: LLB, Melbourne Univ. Appointments: Bar, Sol, MP, 1970-; MLA Gippsland W, 1970-76, MLA Berwick, 1976-92, Min for Labour and Ind and of Consumer Affairs, Vic, 1976-78, Transp, 1978-82; Dpty Ldr of Opposition, 1982-85; MLA, Pakenham, 1992-; Min for Plng, 1992-96; Min for Plng and Local Govt, 1996-; Farmer. Honour: Hon Mbr, Exec Cncl. Address: The Mount, Bonwick Avenue, San Remo, Victoria 3925, Australia.

MACLEOD Ian Donald, b. 16 Oct 1948. Research Chemist. m. Evelyn Ruth MacLeod, 7 Jan 1978, 2 d. Education: BSc (Hons); PhD. Appointments: Rsch Fell, Univ of Glasgow, 1974-75; Rsch Fell, Murdoch Univ, 1976-78; WA Mus, 1978-88; Hd of Conservation, 1988-; Dir, Mus Servs, 1998-. Publications: Over 85 sci pprs. Memberships: Fell, Roy Austl Chem Inst, 1986; Fell, Intl Inst for Conservation of Artistic and Historic Wrks, 1987. Honours: Var rsch grants in conservation of shipwreck materials and Aboriginal rock painting conservation over the past 15 yrs. Hobbies: Scottish Country Dancing; Change ringing on tower bells. Address: Department of

Materials Conservation, Western Australian Museum, Cliff Street, Fremantle, Western Australia 6160.

MACNAB Francis Auchline, b. 21 June 1931, Aust. Psychotherapist; Minister; Author. m. Sheila, 17 July 1958, 1 s, 2 d. Education: PhD; MA; Hon DSc; HonDD. Appointments: Exec Dir, The Cairnmillar Inst, 1961-; Exec Min, St Michaels Ch, Melbourne, 1971-. Pubications: Estrangemnt and Relationship, 1965; Setting People Free, 1975; Change, 1979; Between Two Lives, 1979; Sexual Desire, 1982; Getting There, 1982; Being Together, 1982; I Felt the Eagle's Heart, 1983; Conflict and Stress, 1984; Coping, 1985; Inner Searching and Inner Strength, 1988; Life After Loss, 1989; Psychotherapy: New Directions for Clinical Practice, 1991; Thirty Vital Years, 1992; Streams of Energy, 1993; Footprints, 1994; Hope, 1996; Messages to the Mind and Spirit, 1997; Work - What it does for us, what we do for it, 1998. Honours: AM, 1992; The Sir James Darling Medal for Outstndng Contbns to Educ. Address: 993 Burke Road, Camberwell 3124, Victoria, Australia.

MACONAGHIE Ronald Derek Armstrong, b. 18 Nov 1931. m. Georgina O'Carroll, 25 May 1957, 2 s, 2 d. Education: London Opera Sch. Appointments: NZ Vocal Champion, 1951 NZ Govt Schlsp, 1953-56; Dame Joan Hammond Schlshp, 1954-56; Austl Operatic Baritone, 1956-; Sadlers Wells Opera Co, Engl Opera Grp, 1956-59; NZ Opera Co, 1961-63; Prin Artist, Austl Opera, 1963-86; Juror, Vocal Adjudicator, Auckland, NZ and N Qld Eisteddfods; Austl Singing Competition; Winston Churchill Mem Schlsp; Prodr of Opera and Opera Workshops; Tchr, Vocal Technique, N Qld Conservatorium of Music and Adult Educ in Tas, 1976-78; TV and Radio Recordings for BBC, ABC, NZBC; Lectr, Canberra Sch of Music, 1979-; Artistic Dir, Canberra Opera, 1980-84; Prin Artist, Sutherland Williamson Intl Opera Co, Hong Kong Fest Opera, 1985; Hd of Opera and Vocal Studies, 1991-, Dpty Dean of Music, 1992-, Vic Coll of Arts, Univ of Melbourne. Honour: AM. Membership: Conservatorium of Music, Univ of Sydney, 1997. Hobbies: Golf; Reading. Listed in: Who's Who in Australia. Address: 19A Steward Avenue, Hornsby, NSW 2077, Australia.

MACPHERSON Elle, b. 29 Mar 1963, Killara, Sydney, Australia. Fashion Model; Business Executive. 1 s. Appointment: Chf Exec, Elle Macpherson Inc. Creative Works: Films: Sirens, 1994; Jane Eyre, 1994; If Lucy Fell, 1996; Video: Stretch and Strenghten, The Body Workout, 1995. Address: c/o Women Model Management, 107 Greene Street, Floor 2, NY 10012, USA.

MACROSSAN John Murtagh, b. 12 Mar 1930. Chief Justice. m. Margery Newton, 4 Jan 1961, 1 s. Education: BA; LLB (Qld); BCL Oxon; St Columban's Coll, Brisbane; Qld Univ; Oxford Univ. Appointments: Admitted to the Bar, 1951; Mbr, Bar Bd, 1967-79; QC, 1967; Chmn, Incorp Cncl of Law Reporting, 1972-78; Cttee Mbr, 1965-78, VP, 1974, Pres, 1976-78, Bar Assoc; Pres, Qld Art Gall Soc, 1978-82; Judge, Supreme Court of Qld, 1980-; Chf Justice, 1989-; Chmn, Qld Cttee, Churchill Trust, 1985-92; Dpty Chan, 1985, Chan, 1988-98, Griffith Univ. Memberships: Qld Club; United Oxford & Cambridge Club. Hobbies: Farming; Literature; Films; Wine. Address: 28 Killara Avenue, Hamilton, Brisbane, Qld 4007, Australia.

MADAN Vinod Kumar, b. 4 Dec 1948, Delhi, India. Electronics Engineer. m. Param Jyothi, 8 July 1977, 2 d. Education: BTech, Elec Engrng; PhD. Appointments: Sci Offr, 1971-76; SD, 1976-83; SE, 1983-90; SF, 1990-97; G, 1997-. Publications: Sev articles in profl jrnls. Memberships: IEEE; Fell, IETE, India; Indian Phys Assn; Nuclear Rsch Soc of India; Navi Mumbai Sports Assn. Hobbies: Reading; Swimming. Address: Electronics Division, Bhabha Atomic Research Centre, Mumbai 400085, India.

MADDERN Guy John, b. 20 July 1957. m. Lesley Taylor, dec, 1 s, 2 d. Education: MBBS; PhD; MS. Appointments: Oberartz Univ of Berne, Switzerland, 1989-91; Chef de Clinique, Univ of Rennes, France,

1991-92; RACS Travelling Fell, 1991-92; Cnslt Surg, Hepatobiliary Pancreatic Unit, Royal Adelaide Hosp and Liver Transplantation Unit, Flinders Medl Cntr, 1992-93; RP Jepson Prof of Surg, 1993-. Publications: Questions You Should Ask Your Surgeon, 1994. Honours: Jepson Medal (RACS, SA Branch), 1982; Nimmo Prize (Roy Adelaide Hosp), 1982; RACS John Mitchell Crouch Fellshp, 1998. Memberships: Surgical Rsch Soc of Australasia, 1983-; NHMRC Panel of Assessors, 1986-; Intl Liver Transplantation Soc, 1994-; Intl Soc of Surg, 1994-; Intl Hepato Pancreatic Biliary Soc, 1995-. Hobby: Golf. Address: 35 Seventh Avenue, St Peters, SA 5069, Australia.

MADILL Francis Leslie (Frank) (The Hon), b. 5 Sept 1941, Packenham, Vic, Aust. Member of Parliament. m. Linda Marion, 1965, 2 d. Education: MBBS, Melbourne Medl Sch, 1965. Appointments: Res Medl Offr, Launceston Gen Hosp, 1966-67; GP, 1968-86; Govt Back Bencher, 1986-89; Shadow Min, Police and Emergency Servs, 1989-92; Min for Transport, 1992-93; Min Assisting the Premier, 1993-96; Min for Police and Emergency Servs, Min for Multicultural and Ethnic Affairs, Min for Consumer Affairs, 1992-96; Speaker, House of Assembly, 1996-98. Hobbies: Var cmnty orgs; Motorcycling; Model building; Australian football; Music. Address: 10 Egan Street, Launceston, Tas 7248, Australia.

MADIX Robert, b. 22 June 1938, Beach Grove, IN, USA. Chemical Engineer; Educator. 3 s, 1 d. Education: BS, Univ IL, 1961; PhD, Univ CA, 1964; NSF Postdoct Fell, Max Planck Inst, Göttingen, Germany, 1964-65. Appointments: Asst Prof, Chem Engr, Stanford (CA) Univ, 1965-72; Assoc Prof, Chem Engr, 1972-77; Cnslt, Monsanto Chem, St Louis, 1975-84; Prof Chem Engrng, Stanford Univ, 1977-; Prof, Chem, 1981-; Chmn, Chem Engr, 1983-87; Shell Oil Co, Houston, 1985-86; Peter Debye Lectrshp, Cornell Univ, 1985; Eyring Lectr, Chem, AZ State Univ, 1990; Chmn, Gordon Rsch Conf on Reactions on Surfaces, 1995; Barnett Dodge Lectr, Yale Univ, 1996; Walter Robb Disting Lectr, Penn State Univ, 1996. Publications: Assoc Ed, Catalysis Review, 1986-; Catalysis Letters, 1992-; Research on Chemistry Intermediates, 1994; Num articles, profl jrnls. Honours: Ford Fndn Fell, 1969-72; Humboldt US Snr Scientist Prize, 1978; Irving Langmuir Disting Lectr Awd, Amn Chem Soc, 1981; Paul Emmett Awd Catalysis Soc, N Am, 1984; Alpha Chi Sigma Awd AIChemE, 1990; Arthur Adamson Awd, 1997; Henry J Albert Awd, Precious Metals Inst, 1997. Memberships: Amn Phys Soc; Amn Vacuum Soc; AIChE; CA Catalysis Soc. Address: 3364 Emerson St, Palo Alto, CA 94306-3526, USA.

MADONNA (Madonna Louise Veronica Ciccone), b. 16 Aug 1958, Detroit, USA. Singer; Actress. m. Sean Penn, 1985, div 1989, 1 d by Carlos Leon. Education: Alvin Ailey Dance Sch. Appointments: Sold over 55 million records worldwide; Toured UK, 1983, 1987, France, 1987, Fed Germany, 1987; Appeard in Play Speed-the-Plow, 1988; Coml for Pepsi Cola, 1989; VP, ICA, London. Creative Works: Albums: Madonna - The First Album; Like A Virgin; True Blue; You Can Dance; I'm Breathless, 1990; The Immaculate Collection, 1990; Erotica, 1992; Bedtime Stories, 1994; Something to Remember, 1995; A Ray of Light. Singles incl: Everybody; Burning Up; Holiday; Borderline; Like a Virgin; Material Girl; Into the Groove; Dress You Up; Crazy for You; Papa Don't Preach; La Isla Bonita; Who's That Girl?; True Blue; Like A Prayer; Justify My Lofe, 1990; Erotica, 1992; Bedtime Stories, 1994; Frozen, 1998. Films incl: Desperately Seeking Susan; Shanghai Surprise; Who's That Girl?; Bloodhounds of Broadway; Dick Tracy, 1989; Soap-Dish, 1990; Shadows and Fog, 1991; A League of Their Own; In Bed with Madonna, 1991; Body of Evidence, 1992; Snake Eyes, 1994; Dangerous Game, 1994; Evita, 1996; Four Rooms, 1996; The Girlie Show. Publication: Sex, 1992. Address: ICM, 8942 Wilshire Boulevard, Beverley Hills, CA 90211, USA.

MAEDA Isao, Politician. Appointments: Fmr Vice-Min of Intl Trade & Ind; Min of Justice, 1994-95; Mbr, House of Cnclrs, Dir LDP Press Dept-Newsppr Divsn. Address:

Ministry of Justice, 1-1-1 Kasumigaseki, Chiyoda-ku, Tokyo 100, Japan.

MAGAREY Brian Attiwill, b. 8 Nov 1918. m. Betty McIntosh, 12 July 1945, 1 s, 2 d. Education: LLB; St Peter's Coll; Univ of Adelaide. Appointments: AIF, 1940-45; Cr and Past Pres, Law Soc, SA, Hon Life Mbr, 1974. Honour: MBE, 1982. Memberships: Naval, Mil and Air Force Club; Roy Adelaide Golf Club. Hobby: Golf. Address: 347 Glynburn Road, Kensington Park, SA 5068, Australia.

MAGEN David, b. 1945, Morocco. Politician. m. 4 children. Appointments: Mayor, Kiryat Gat, 1976-86; Mbr, Knesset, 1981-; Mbr, Cttee on Fgn Affairs & Security, 1981-, Cttee on State Control, 1981-84; Min of Econ & Planning, 1990-92. Address: Ministry of Economy & Planning, Knesset Buildings, Jerusalem, Israel.

MAGGS Vicki, b. 1 Aug 1953. Science Teacher. Education: BS (Educ); MED. Appointments: Sci Tchr, Sydney Girls' HS, 1976-89; Sci Tchr, Cromer HS, 1990-. Publications: Studymate: 2 unit Biology, 1995. Honour: UK/Aust Fellowship for Sci Educ, 1991. Memberships: Sci Tchrs Assn of NSW; Austl Sci Tchrs Assn; The Austl Mus Soc; Roy Zool Soc, NSW. Hobbies: Netball; Swimming; Keeping fit. Address: 12/8 The Crescent, Dee Why, 2099, NSW, Australia.

MAHAJAN Pramod, b. 16 Oct 1951, Achalpur Cty, India. Scientist (Satellite Meteorology). m. Aschana, 20 Dec 1981, 1 s, 1 d. Education: BS, Phys, Chem Maths; MSc, Phys; PhD, Phys. Appointments: Tchr, 1973-74; Snr Observer, 1974-80; Snr Sci Asst, 1980-84; Jnr Sci Offr, 1984-88; Snr Sci Offr GS II, 1988-93; Snr Sci Offr GS I, 1993-. Publications: Pprs in profl jrnls. Honours: Indian Inst of Tropical Meteorology (IITM), Silver Jubilee Awd, 1991. Memberships: Indian Meteorological Soc, 1997; Indian Remote Sensing Soc, 1997-98. Hobbies: Playing table tennis; Reading books on modern science. Address: Indian Institute of Tropical Meteorology, Dr Homi Bhabha Road, Pashan, Pune 411008, India.

MAHAJAN Shantaram Gajanan, b. 9 Oct 1932. Librarian. m. Prabha, 10 June 1958, 2 s, 1 d. Education: Dip, Libnshp, 1959; MLiSc, 1970; MA, 1972; PhD, 1979. Appointments: Libn, Prof, Hd, Dept of Lib & Info Sci, Pune Univ, 1982-92; Dir, Pune Lib Network, 1992-93; Hon Co-ord, Lib Sci Prog, YC Maharashtra Open Univ, 1993-96; Cnslt, IGNOU, New Delhi, 1993-96. Publications: History of the Public Library Movement in Mahavashra, 1984; Socio-Economic Study of Pune City: Annotated Bibliography, 1998; History, Growth and Development at Pune City, 768-1988: A Handbook of Sources of Information, 1999. Non profl articles and 15 books. Honours: Best Tchr Awd, 1992; 2 Prizes for Best Books in Marathi; Encyclopardist Ketkar Besr Libn Awd, 1999. Memberships: Indian Lib Assn; IATLIS; IASLIC; Micrographic Congress of India. Hobby: Local History. Listed in: Who's Who in India. Address: Sarasvati Vihar, 27 Swastishri Society, Ganeshnagar, Pune 411 052, India.

MAHATHIR Bin Mohamed, b. 20 Dewc 1925, Alur Setar, Kedah. Prime Minister. m. Siti Hasmah binti Haji Mohd Ali, 1956, 3 s, 2 d. Education: Sultan Abdul Hamid Coll; Univ of Malaya, Singapore. Appointments: Medl Offr, Kedah, Langkawi and Perlis, 1953-57; Pvte Prac, 1957-64; Mbr, UMNO (now Umno Baru) Supreme Cncl, 1965-69, 1972-; Pres, 1981-; Mbr, House of Representatives, Kota Setar Selatan, 1964-69, Kubang Pasu, 1974-; Mbr Senate, 1973; Chair, Food Inds of Malaysia Sbn Bhd, 1973; Min of Educ, 1974-77, Trade and Ind, 1977-81, Def, 1981-86, Home Affairs, 1986-, Jus, 1987, Natural and Rural Dev; Dpty Prime Min, 1976-81; Prime Min, 1981-. Publication: The Malay Dilemma, 1969. Address: Department of the Prime Minister, Jalan Dato Onn, 50502 Kuala Lumpur, Malaysia.

MAHER Robyn Leigh, b. 06 Oct 1959, Ballarat, Vic, Aust. Basketballer. m. 5 Feb 1983, 1 s, 1 d.

MAHESWARAN Kalaranji, b. 5 Dec 1959, Sri Lanka. Consultant; Researcher. Education: MSc, Agronomy, Patrice Lumumba Univ, Moscow. Appointments: Rsch Offr, Agrarian Rsch and Trng Inst, Colombo, 1983-84; Rsch Sci, Natl Agric Rsch Inst, Guyana, 1984-86; Ptnr, Cnslt, Agribus, Colombo, 1990-. Publication: Farmer Organizations and its Viability, 1996. Membership: Natl Agricl Soc of Sri Lanka, 1995-. Hobbies: Writing; Reading; Sewing. Address: Agribusiness, 2B1/1 10th Lane, Colombo 3, Sri Lanka.

MAHESWARAN Rita Nagarani, b. 20 Dec 1931, Kandy, Sri Lanka. Teacher. m. Murugesu Maheswara, Jan 1959, 1 s, 2 d. Education: Dip, Art, Kandy Sch of Art, Sri Lanka. Career: Self-employed Engl Tchr. Membership: Police Families Welfare Assn, Colombo, Sri Lanka. Hobbies: Painting; Knitting; Crocheting. Address: 2B, 1/1, 10th Lane, Colombo-3, Sri Lanka.

MAHONEY Dennis Leslie, .b. 26 Dec 1924, Aust. Queen's Counsel; Retired Judge; President, Court of Appeal. m. Maré Nesta Stacey, 1991. Education: BA, 1945, LLB, Hons I, 1948, Sydney Univ. Appointments: Bar, Supreme Crt of NSW, 1948-60; QC, 1960-72; Chmn, Roy Cmmn on Landlord and Tenant Law, 1960-61; Dir, Taxation Inst of Aust, 1969-72; Judge, Supreme Crt of NSW, 1972-74; Dir, Austl Opera Co, 1973-88; Pres, Intl Cmmn of Jurists (Aust Sect), 1973-75; Judge, Crt of Appeal, 1974-96; Pres, 1996, Actng Chf Jus, 1996, Supreme Crt of NSW; Co-Chmn, Judicial Sect, Law Asia Assn, 1977-90; Chmn, Austl Remmuneration Tribunal, 1982-92; Mbr, Exec Cncl, Intl Law Assn (Austl Sect); Dpty Chmn, 1984-86, Chmn, 1987-8, Austl Inst of Judicial Admin; Visng Prof, Sch of Law, Univ of NSW, 1998. Honours: Knight Grand Cross (ribbon) Sovereign Mil Order of Malta; Univ Medal on Grad, Sydney Univ, 1948; AO, 1993. Membership: Pres, 1974-80, Austl Natl Assn, Sovereign Mil Order of Malta. Hobbies: Golf; Skiing. Address: National Disputes Cntr, 233 Macquarie Street, Sydney, NSW 2023, Australia.

MAHONY John Francis, b. 6 June 1940, Sydney, Aust. Renal Physician. m. Marie Therese Brereton, 18 Aug 1967, 4 s, 5 d. Education: MB BS (Hons), Sydney Univ, 1963; MRACP, 1966; FRACP, 1972. Appointments: Res and Registrar, St Vincent's Hosp, 1963-68; Renal Fell, Univ of CO Medl Cntr, 1968-70; Renal Physn, 1970-79, Dir, Renal Unit, 1979-83, Assoc Dir, Dept of Medl Rsch, 1981-83, Sydney Hosp; Dir of Sydney Dialysis Cntr, 1979-; Renal Physn, Roy N Shore Hosp, 1983-; Clin Assoc Prof of Med, Sydney Univ, 1993. Publications: Hormones and the Kidney (ed w G S Stokes), 1980; Auth of about 100 pprs on Renal Diseases, Dialysis and Transplantation. Memberships: Fell, Roy Australasian Coll of Physns; Exec Offr, 1988-90, Austl and NZ Soc of Nephrology; The Transplantation Soc; Mbr, Cnclr, Transplantation Soc of Aust and NZ, 1993-. Hobbies: Cricket; Tennis; Golf. Address: Duntroon Avenue, Roseville, NSW 2069, Australia.

MAHUTA Nanaia Cybele, b. 21 Aug 1970, Auckland, New Zealand. Labour Member of Parliament. Education: BA, Auckland Univ, 1993; MA, hons, Socl Anthropol, 1995. Appointments: Archivist, Libn, Auckland Univ, 1994; Rschr, Tainui Mauori Trust Bd, 1995-96. Memberships: UN, Friends of Tibet. Address: c/o Parliament Buildings, Wellington, New Zealand.

MAHUTA Robert Te Kotahi, b. 26 Apr 1939, Te Kuiti, New Zealand. Raupatu Research Professor. m. Eliza Irimana Edmonds, Dec 1963, 1 s, 2 d. Education: BA, MA, Auckland Univ; BLitt, Oxford Univ. Appointments include: Te Roopu Manukura; Chmn, Maaori Devel Corp, 1992-; Cmmnr, Treaty of Waitangi Fisheries Cmmn, 1993-. Publications: Sev articles in profl jrnls. Honour: KNZM, 1996. Hobbies: Reading; Rugby League; Fishing. Address: Centre for Maaori Studies & Research, University of Waikato, Private Bag 3105, Hamilton, New Zealand.

MAI Thuc, b. 15 Mar 1950, Quang Ninh, Vietnam. Journalist; Writer. m. Vuthuy, 9 May 1969, 1 s, 1 d.

Education: Vietnam Natl Univ; Vietnam Natl Inst of Politics. Appointment: Ed-in-Chf, Capital Womens newsppr, Hanoi, 1995. Publications: Literature Samples, 1990; Hanoi - Its Beauty and Culture, 1994; The Soul of Hanoi, 1996; Go to Find the Beloved Land, 1998; Hanoi's Essence, 1998. Honours: Labour Order, 1997; Prize, Hanoi's Jrnlsts Assn, 1998. Memberships: Vietnam's Jrnlsts Assn; Hanoi's Writers Assn; Vietnam-US Friendship Soc. Hobbies: Reading; Music; Culture. Address: No 103-36 Hai Ba Trung Street, Hanoi, Vietnam.

MAI Yiu-Wing, b. 5 Jan 1946, Hong Kong. University Professor. m. Louisa Lui, 12 Mar 1980. Education: BSc, (Eng); PhD; DSc; DEng. Appointments: Lectr, 1976-78, Snr Lectr, 1979-82, Assoc Prof, 1983-87, Prof, 1987-, Engrng Fac, Univ of Sydney. Honour: FTSE, elected 1992. Memberships: FIEAust; FMKIE; FASME. Hobbies: Reading; Walking. Address: Department of Mechanical Engineering, University of Sydney, Sydney, NSW 2006, Australia.

MAIBACH Howard, b. 18 Sept 1992, NY, USA. Professor, Dermatology. m. Siesel Wite, 8 July 1953, 2 s, 1 d. Education: AB; MD, Tulane Univ, 1955. Appointments: Intern, William Beaumont Army Hosp, El Paso, TX, 1955-56; Fellshp, USPHS, Hosp of Univ of PA, 1959-61; Asst Instr, Sch of Med, 1958-61, Lectr, Grad Sch of Med, 1960-61, Univ of PA; Clin Prac, Univ of CA Hosps, 1961-; Asst Prof, 1961-66, Assoc Prof, 1967-73, Dermatology Dept, Rsch Assoc, Cancer Rsch Inst, 1967-98, Prof, Dermatology Dept, 1973-, Snr Mbr Bd of Dirs, Univ of CA, Fac Club, 1979-80, Vice Chairperson, Dermatology Dept, 1973-, Acad Vice Chan, Ad Hoc Peer Review Cttee, 1983-, Snr Mbr, Subcttee on Quality of Care, 1983-96, Chf, Occupational Dermatology Clin, 1984-, Univ of CA Schs of Med. Publications: over 1000 in fields of Dermatopharmaocology, Dermatotoxicology, Psoriasis, Exogenous Dermatoses. Memberships: Pacific Dermatologic Assn; Soc for Investigative Dermatology; CA Medl Assn; Amn Coll Physns; Amn Fedn for Clin Rsch; AMA; San Fran Medl Soc; Amn Dermatological Assn; Intl Soc Topical Dermatology; Intl Soc for Digital Imaging of Skin (ISDIS), Bd of Dirs, 1992-, Hon Mbr, 1993; Intl Commn on Occupational Hlth (ICOH), Sci Cttee on Occupational Dermatoses, 1993-. Address: University of California Hospital, Dermatology Department, San Francisco, CA 94143, USA.

MAIR Catherine May, b. 12 Aug 1938, Katikati, BOP, North Island, NZ. Poet. m. 20 Dec 1958, 3 s, 1 d. Education: Dip of Tchng, Ardmore Tchrs Coll. Appointments: Ed winter SPIN, 1995-; Judge of Haiku Sect, NZ Intl Poetry Competition, 1999. Publications: Glimpses (poetry), 1988; Caterpillar (haiku verse), 1990; The Shortcut Home (poetry), 1996; Shadow Patches (haibun), 1998; Every Stone, Drop Pebble (haiku), 1999, Short stories in Another 100 New Zealand Short, Short Stories, 1998, 1999 Takahe, 1998. Honours: Publd in 1st and 2nd NZ Haiku Anthologies, 1993, 1998; Invited speaker at haiku fest, Romania, 1994; Co-winner, Whitireia Poetry Competition, 1996. Memberships: NZ Poetry Soc. Hobbies: Tennis; Swimming; Boating; Music; Art; Reading. Address: PO Box 62, Katikati BOP, North Is, New Zealand.

MAITY Bimalananda, b. 8 Jan 1939. Engineer. m. Renvka, 12 Dec 1963, 1 d. Education: MSc, Advd Structural Analysis, London Univ, 1970. Appointments: Ove Arup & Ptnrs, London; Cnstng Engrng Servs, New Delhi; BHP Pet; Kinhill Dorris; Flour Daniel; Sinclair Knight Merz, Aust. Publications: Bengal for Tourists and Students, 1986; Mimi's World, 1989; Bengali Phrasebook, 1995. Memberships: Inst of Engrs of Aust, 1985; Inst of Engrs of India. Hobbies: Teaching and promoting Bengali; Creating study material for young children; Playing contract bridge. Address: 74 Centre Dandenong Road, Cheltenham, Vic 3192, Australia.

MAJALI Abdel Salam al, b. 1925, Karak, Jordan. University President; Prime Minister. m. Joan M Lachlan, 1956, 2 s, 1 d. Education: Med Coll, Syrian Univ, Damascus. Appointments: Dir-Gen, Ear, Nose & Throat

Cnslt, Roy Med Servs, Jordanian Armed Forces, Amman, 1960-69; Min of Hlth, 1969-71; Pres, Univ of Jordan, Amman, 1971-76, 1980-90; Min of Educn, Min of State for PM Affairs, 1976-79; Chair, Mbr, UN Univ Cncl, Tokyo, 1977-83; PM of Jordan, 1993-95, 1997-; Min of Def & Fgn Affairs, 1993-95; Min of Def, 1997-. Honours: Jordan Independence Medal; Medal of St John of Jerusalem. Memberships: Fell, Am Coll of Surgns. Address: Office of the Prime Minister, PO Box 80, 35216 Amman, Jordan.

MAJOR Malvina Lorraine, b. 28 Jan 1943, Hamilton, NZ. Opera Singer (Soprano). m. Winston William Richard Fleming, 16 Jan 1965, 1 s, 2 d. Education: Hamilton Tech Coll, Waikato; Stdied Music, Ngaruawahia Convent; Stdied singing w Dame Sister Mary Leo, St Mary's Music Sch, Auckland, 1960-65, and Ruth Packer, Roy Coll of Music, London; London Opera Cntr, Eng, 1965-67. Career: Debut, Camden Town Fest, 1968; First non-Mormon soloist w Mormon Tabernacle Choir, 1986; Opera perfs incl: La Bohème, Madame Butterfly, Faust, Il Seraglio, Die Fledermaus, Barber of Seville, Merry Widow, Elizabetta Regina d'Inghiterra, Rigoletto, Don Pasquale, Lucia di Lammermoor, Magic Flute, Tosca, La Traviata, Eugene Onegin, Marriage of Figaro. Creative Works: Num recdngs incl: To the Glory of God, 1964; Signature, 1969; Mahler Symphony No 4, 1976; La Finta Giardiniera, 1989; I Remember, 1991; Casta Diva, 1993; Dame Malvina Major, 1994; Christmastime, 1994; Alleluia, 1996; Recital 1968: Malvina Major and Gerald Moore, 1998. Honours: Winner, NZ Mobil Song Quest, 1963; Melbourne Sun Aria Contest, Aust, 1964; Kathleen Ferrier Awd, London, 1966; OBE, 1985; DBE, 1991; NZ Intl Perf of Yr 1992; NZ entertainer of Yr, 1992; NZ Classical Disc Awd, 1993, 1994; Amb, Amn Express Village, America's Cup, NZ, 2000. Membership: Estab Dame Malvina Major Fndn, 1992. Listed in: Who's Who in New Zealand; New Zealand Who's Who of Aotearoa; Who's Who 2000. Address: PO Box 11-175, Wellington 1, New Zealand.

MAJUMDER Uma, b. 8 Nov 1944, Calcutta, India. Library & Information Scientist, working at the National Library, Calcutta. Education: MA, Polit Sci; MS, Info Studies, Sheffield, UK; Fulbright Schl, Chgo Univ, USA. Appointments: Employed: Bibliography Div, 1966-68; Processing Div, 1968-71; Indian Offic Documents Div, 1971-78; Reading Room Ref Div (Main), 1978-88; Lectr, Ref & Info Sci, Bengal Lib Assn, Calcutta, 1981-85; Pt-time Lectr, Dept of Lib & Info Sci, Jadavpur Univ, 1986-; Working in the Computer Cntr, 1988-; Fulbright Fell, Univ Chgo Lib. The Joseph Regenstien Lib, 1989-90. Publications: Select bibliography on May Day (compiled w others), 1986; India's National Library: Systemization and Modernization, 1987; Articles and pprs. Honour: Fulbright Awd, USA. Memberships: Life Mbr: ILA; IASLIC; BLA: IAWS; Permanent UNIMARC Cttee, IFLA UBC 1M. Hobbies: Music; Reading. Address: SM Nagar Govt Housing Estate, Block N1, Flat No 11, PO Sarkarpool, 24 Paraganas, PIN 743352, West Bengal, India.

MAK Kam (Mak Hoon Ting) (The Hon), b. 28 June 1939, Perak, Malaysia. Senator; Chartered Architect. m. Saw An Nie, 1968, 2 s. Education: Matriculation, Leederville Tech Coll, WA, 1961; Arch, WA Inst of Technol, 1967; PhD, Archl Engrng, Kennedy Western Univ, USA, 1989. Appointments: Practised as Chartered Arch; Lifetime Dpty Gov, ABI Rsch Assn; Elected Mbr of Malaysian Parly for Tanjong Malim Constituency, Perak, 3 consecutive terms, 1974-86; Appt Dpty Min of Culture, Yth & Sports, 1978-79, Dpty Min of Fin, 1979-82, Min of Labour, 1981-85, Min of Hlth, 1985-86; Polit Party Posts: Chmn, 1972-85, VP, 1977-82, Dpty Pres, 1983-85, Treas-Gen, 1985-87, Malaysian Chinese Assn, Perak; Mbr, Natl Front Supreme Cncl, 1980-85; Left MCA and joined Poeple's Progressive Party, 1988; Pres, PPP, 1986; Senator, 1986-; Exec Chmn, FACB Co Ltd. Honours: JMM by the Supreme Hd of Malaysia, 1978; Datoshp (DPMP) by Sultan of Perak, 1980; Gwangha Medal Awd, by Pres of Korea, 1983. Memberships: Fell, Roy Australasian Inst of Archs; Assoc, Roy Inst of Brit Archs; MSIA; APAM; DG, (ABI). Hobby: Swimming.

Address: No 29 Jalan Batai Barat, Damansara Heights, 50490 Kuala Lumpur, Malaysia.

MAKI Misako, b. 3 Mar 1933, Yamanashi Pref, Japan. Lecturer; Translator. m. Sanehiko Maki, 31 Oct 1958, 1 s, 2 d. Education: BA, Tokyo Inst of For Studies (Russian Dept). Appointments: Lectr, Japanese Lang, Tokyo Inst of For Studies, 1955, Fukishima Medl Inst, 1966; Lectr of Russian, Fukushima Univ, 1987; Lectr of Russian Lang, East Japan Intl Univ, 1996. Publications: Transl from Bulgarian lit, 1957; poems by Phist Boteb, 1976; Short Stories, 1977; The Wild Stories, 1983; Roman Bath, 997. Memberships: Assn of Russian Lit in Japan (Tokyo). Hobbies: Mountain climbing; Dyeing and making cravat; Knitting. Address: 3-3 Higyodan, Kitaswamata, Fukushima-city, 960-8251, Japan.

MAKIHARA Minoru, b. 1930, Hampstead, Eng. Business Executive. m. Kikuko Makihara. Education: England; Japan; Harvard Univ, USA. Appointments: Joined Mitsubishi Corpn, Marine Prod Dept, 1956-59, London Br, 1959-70, Rep, Mitsubishi Intl, Seattle & WA, 1970-80, Gen Mngr, Marine Prod Dept, Tokyo, 1980-87, Pres, Mitsubishi Intl, WA, 1987-90, Res Snr Mngng Dir, Am Mitsubishi Corpn, Chair, Mitsubishi Intl, 1990-92, Pres, Mitsubishi Corpn, 1992-. Address: Office of the President, Mitsubishi Corporation, 2-6-3 Marunouchi, 2-chome, Chiyoda-ku, Tokyo 100 86, Japan.

MAKKI Mohammed Hassan, b. 22 Dec 1933. Politician; Diplomat. Education: Univ Bologna; Univ Rome. Appointments: Advsr, Min of Econs, 1960-62, Dpty Min, 1962, Min, 1963-64; Min of Fgn Affairs, 1966, 1967-68; Amb to Italy, 1968-70, 1977079, to Fed Repub of Germany, 1970-72; Dpty PM, 1972-74; PM, 1974; Dpty PM for Econ Affairs, 1974, 1980-84; Perm Rep to UN, 1974-76, Amb to USA, 1975-76; Dpty PM of Yemen Arab Repub, 1985-90; 1st Dpty PM of Repub of Yemen, 1990-93. Address: Office of the Deputy Prime Minister, San'a, Republic of Yemen.

MAKTOUM Maktoum bin Rashid al- (Sheikh), b. 1941. m. 1971. Career: 5th Sheikh of Dubai, 1990; Prime Min, United Arab Emirates, 1971-79, 1991-; Dpty Prime Min, 1979-90, VP, 1990-. Address: Ruler's Palace, Dubai, United Arab Emirates.

MALAEK Seyed Mohammad, b. 29 May 1958, Tehran, Iran. University Faculty. m. Mojdeh, 29 Nov 1984, 2 s. Education: PhD, Aerospace Engrng. Appointments: Hd of Aerospace Engrng Grp, Engrng Dept; Dir, Acad Affairs, Sharif Univ. Creative works: 2 regd inventions, WIPO, Switz, 1995. Honours: Top Ten Student Awd, 1984; Strobel Awd, USA, 1986; PhD w Hons, 1989. Address: Mechanical & Aerospace Engineering Department, Sharif University of Technology, Azadi Avenue, Tehran, Iran.

MALALI Hanumantgouda, b. 20 July 1965, Vasan, Tal-Nargund, Dr St-Gadag, India. Naturopathy Practitioner. m. Kasturi, 18 June 1997. Education: SSLC; ITI; ITI; Apprenticeship; Hal; Bangalore. Appointments: Practising Naturopath. Publications: Articles; Writer on diseases; Auth, philos poems (Vachan Sahitya). Honours: Drama Awd, 1988-89; Tech suggestion Awd from Hal Bangalore, 1988-89. Memberships: Shi Vanand Yoga Samitiya; Gandhi Sevashrama Trust Sureban; Vi Shwachetana Siddharoodh Satsang Balag, Ramdurg. Address: PO Vasan, Taluka-Nargund, Dist Gadag, India.

MALANI Natasha, b. 24 June 1974, Adelaide, Australia. Sales Executive. Education: Dip, Bus Mngmt. Appointments: Fest City Conventions, 1992-96; Hotel Adelaide Intl, 1997-. Memberships: O'Connell Street Traders Assn, cttee. Hobbies: Travel; Sport; Public Speaking; People. Address: 6A French Street, Broadview, SA 5083, Australia.

MALCOLM Clifford Keith, b. 18 Aug 1943. Teacher. m. Marie Lynette Wilson, 28 Jan 1969, dec 1992, 2 s, 1 d. Education: BSc, hons, 1965, BEd, 1969, Melbourne Univ; PhD, Univ of Saskatchewan, Can, 1973. Appointments: Asst Lectr, Primary Sci, 1973, Lectr, Phys,

1974-77, Snr Lectr, Phys, 1978-83, Melbourne State Coll; Visng Prof, Univ MN, USA, 1979-80; Project Mngr, Cntr for Prog Evaluation, Melbourne State Coll, 1980-83; Snr Curriculum Offr, Sci, 1983-86, Dir, Curriculum Frameworks Project, 1987, Curriculum Coord, 1988-90, Min of Educ, Vic; Asst Mngr, John Gardiner Cntr for Sci, Maths and Technol Educ, Hawthorn, Vic, 1991; Coord, Austl Sci Curriculum and Tchng Prog, Curriculum Corp, Carlton, 1992-96; Curriculum Mngr, Min of Educ, Vic, 1996; Visng Prof, Univ of Witswatersrand, S Africa, 1997. Publications: Science Teaching and Technology, 1992; They Don't Tell the Truth About the Wind, 1995; What Happens When You..?, 1995; There's An Emu in the Sky, 1995; Could We? Should We?, 1996; Integrating Technology and Enhancing Learning, 1996; Making Curriculum 2005 Work, 1998; Making Groupwork Work, 1998; Over 50 articles in profl jrnls. Honours: Hon Assoc, Fac of Educ, Monash Univ, 1991-; STAV Awd, 1993. Memberships: Sci Tchrs Assn of Vic; Austl Sci Tchrs Assn. Hobbies: Singing; Guitar; Tennis; Reading; Sketching. Listed in: Who's Who in Science Education Around the World; Australian Men and Women of Science and Technology. Address: 3 Zodiac Street, Burwood, Vic 3125, Australia.

MALCOLM Clive Vincent, b. 26 Dec 1933. Agricultural Research Officer. m. 7 Apr 1962, 4 s, 1 d (adopted). Education: MSc, Agric; MSc, Pollution and Environmental Control. Appointments: Prin Rsch Offr, West Austl Dept of Agric. Publications: Halophytes & Biosaline Agriculture, (Eds; R Choukr-Allah, C V Malcolm, A Hamdy), 1996. Honours: Food and Agric Org, André Mayer Fellshp, 1966; Robert Gleddin Fellshp, 1974. Memberships: Fell, Austl Inst of Agricl Sci; Roy Soc of WA; Austl Soc of Soil Sci; Aust Rangeland Soc. Hobbies: Drama; Environment; Museum curation. Address: RMB 1054, South Coast Highway, Denmark, WA 6333, Australia.

MALCOLM David Kingsley, b. 6 May 1938. Chief Justice of Western Australia. m. Jennifer Birney, 1965, 1 s. Education: LLB, 1st Class Hons, Univ of Western Aust; Rhodes Schl, BCL 1st Class Hons, Oxford Univ. Appointments: Ptnr, Muir Williams Nicholson, 1964-67; Cnsl, Asst Gen Cnsl, Dpty Gen Cnsl, Asian Dev Bank, Manila, 1967-70; Ptnr, Muir Williams Nicholson & Co, 1970-79; Indep Bar, 1980-88; QC, WA, 1980, NSW, 1983. Publications: Articles in learned jrnls incl Austl Law Jrnl, Austl Bar Review, Austl Bus Law Review. Honour: AC, 1992. Memberships include: Law Reform Commn of WA, 1966-67, 1975-82, Chmn, 1976, 1979-82; Cncl of Law Soc of WA, 1966-67, 1985-88, VP, 1986-88; Copyright Tribunal, 1978-86; Chmn, Town Plng Appeal Tribunal, 1979-86; Pres, WA Bar Assn, 1982-84; VP, Austl Bar Assn, 1984; Senate, Univ of WA, 1988-94; Dpty Chmn, 1990-95, Chmn, 1995-, Judicial Sect, LAWASIA; Chmn, Advsry Bd, Neuromuscular Res Inst of Aust, 1989-95, Crime Res Cntr, Univ of WA, 1991-; Cncl Soc for Reform of Criminal Law, 1992-; Patron, var sport and cmnty orgns. Hobbies: Rugby Union; Equestrian sports; Windsurfing. Address: Chief Justice's Chambers, Supreme Court, Perth, WA 6000, Australia.

MALCOLM Laurence Mian, b. 8 Nov 1929, Richmond, NZ. Consultant, health services. m. Lyn Wright, 3 s, 1 d. Education: MBChB; MD; DTM7H; FFPHM; DHA; FRCP (Edin). Appointments: Dist Hlth Offr, Pub Servs, Papua New Guinea, -1966; Regl Hlth Offr, 1967-74; Hd Hlth Plng Unit Pub Servs, Christchurch, NZ, 1975-83; Prof, Community Hlth, Univ Otago, 1984-95; Prof Emer, 1995-; Cnslt to num orgns incl WHO; Chmn, Pacific Reg Advsry Cttee on Hlth Rsch, Manila; Mbr, Global Advsry Cttee in Hlth Rsch, Geneva. Publications: Over 100 articles to medl jrnls; Chapts to books. Honour: Commemoration Medal, Govt of NZ. Memberships: FRCP (Edin); Australasian Fac Pub Hlth Med; UK Fac Pub Hlth Med; NZ Medl Assn, natl cncl, 1980-82. Hobbies: Music; Hiking; Skiing; Travel. Address: Governors Bay, Ernest Adams Dr, Lyttelton RD 1, New Zealand.

MALCOLMSON John Wardell, b. 16 Feb 1931. Electrical Engineer; Manager. m. Jean Margaret Rye, 22 Apr 1957, 2 s, 1 d. Education: BE (Elec), Auckland Univ,

1954; NZ Regd Engr, 1961; Chartered Engr, 1961. Appointments: Prin Des Engr (Thermal), 1978, Asst Chf Engr (Des Constr), 1984, Asst Gen Mngr (Construction), 1986, Elec Div, Min Energy; Engrng and Dev Mngr, Elec Corp NZ Ltd (retd), 1987-91; Dir, Transpower NZ Ltd, 1994-97. Honour; MBE, Servs to Enrng, 1990. Memberships: Inst Elec Engrs, London, 1961; Fell, Cncl Rep, NZ, 1991-97. Honours: Honoured by the Queen, NZ, 1953-93. Hobbies: Gardening; Genealogy; Home handyman. Listed in: Who's Who in New Zealand. Address: 78 Pope St, Plimmerton, Wellington, NZ.

MALIELEGAOI Tuilaepa Sailele, b. 14 Apr 1945, Lepa, Western Samoa. Prime Minister. m. 8 children. Education: Bach of Com, 1968, Master of Com, 1968 Auckland Univ, NZ. Appointments: CPA, Western Samoa; Ptnr, Coopers & Lybrands, Western Samoa; Investigating Offr, Treas Dept, Apia, 1970; Dpty Dir, Econ Dev, Apia, 1971-73; Dpty Finl Sec, Treas Dept, Apia, 1973-78; Expert Intra-ACP Trade, Transp and Comms, ACP Gen Secretariat, Brussels, Belgium, 1978-80; Mbr of Parl, Lepa Dist, 1981; Min of Econ Affairs, Transp and Civil Aviation, Assoc Min of Fin, 1982-83; Min of Fin, 1984-85, 1988-91; Dpty Prime Min, Min of Fin, Tourism, Trade, Com and Ind, 1991-95, 1996; Prime Min, Min of Fin, 1998-. Memberships: Chmn, Pacific Mins of African Caribbean Pacific Grp, 1988-; Co-Pres, Jt Cncl of Mins of ACP-EU, 1990, 1992; Chmn Natl Disaster Cncl, 1991-; Chmn, ADB's Bd of Govs, Manila, Philippines, 1998. Hobbies: Music; Reading; Fishing; Planting; Tennis; Golf; Cricket. Address: Office of the Prime Minister, Apia, Western Samoa.

MALIK Richard, b. 4 Mar 1958. Veterinary Surgeon. m. Dr Geraldine Hunt, 13 Apr 1981. Education: BVSc (Hon 1); DipVetAn; MVetClinStud; PhD; FACVSc; MASM. Appointment: Valentine Charlton Snr Lectr in Vet Med, Univ Sydney. Honour: Clunies Ross Medal from Austl Coll of Vet Scientists. Memberships: Austl Physiological & Pharmaceutical Soc; Austl Microbiology Soc; Austl Neuroscience Soc. Hobbies: Horse riding; Herpetology; Cinema. Address: Department of Veterinary Clinical Sciences, the University of Sydney, Australia 2006.

MALIETOA Tanumafili, b. 4 Jan 1913, Samoa. Head of State. Education: Wesley Coll, Auckland, NZ. Appointments: Advsr, Samoan Govt, 1940; Mbr, NZ Del to UN, 1958; Fmr Mbr, Cncl of State; Jt Hd of State of Western Samoa, 1962-63, Sole Hd, 1963-; Fautua of Maliena. Address: Government House, Vailima, Apia, Samoa, South Pacific.

MALLICK Bibhuti Bhusan, b. 1 Aug 1935, Bengal, India. Vice Chancellor. m. Mira Mallick, 26 Jan 1962, 1 s, 1 d. Education: BSc; GVSc; Assoc IVRI; DSc, Paris. Publications: 237 rsch pprs and sev book chapts. Honours: Webar Prize, Natl Vet Acady, France, 1968; Medal of Hon & Citation, Pres of France; K S Nair Prize, Indian Vet Assn, 1974, 1976; Dr R Eswaran Meml Medal, Indian Vet Assn, 1997; Oration Gold Medal, Indian Coll of Allergy & Appl Immunol, 1998; Dr S K Sengupta Oration Medal; Dr P Richard Massillamony Oration Gold Medal, Indian Soc for Vet Immunol & Biotechnol. Memberships: Fell, Natl Acady of Vet Scis, Indian Coll of Allergy & Appl Immunol; Former Pres, Indian Soc for Vet Immunol & Bacteriol; Former Pres, Life Mbr, Med & Vet Scis, Indian Sci Congress Assn; Former VP, Indian Virol Soc; Life Mbr, Indian Soc of Vet Microbiol, Immunol & Infectious Diseases, Indian Soc of Immunol. Hobbies: Reading; Travel. Address: West Bengal University of Animal & Fishery Sciences, 68 Kshudiram Bose Sarani, Calcutta 700 037, West Bengal, India.

MALOUF David, b. 20 Mar 1934, Brisbane, Aust. Writer; Poet; Lecturer. Education: BA, Univ of Queensland, 1954. Appointments: Jnr Lectr, Engl Dept, Queensland Univ, 1955; Clk, Brit Petroleum; Supply Tchr, London, 1959-61; Tchr, Latin and Engl, Holland Park Comprehensive, 1962; Tchr, St Anselm's Grammar Sch, 1962-68; Snr Tutor & Lectr, Engl, Univ of Sydney, 1968-78. Publications: Novels: Johnno, 1975; An Imaginary Life, 1979, USA ed, 1978; Fly Away Peter, 1982; Child's Play with Eustace and the Prowler, 1982;

Harland's Half Acre, 1984; The Great World, 1990; Remembering Babylon, 1993; The Conversations at Curlow Creek, 1996; Short stories: Antipodes, 1985; Poetry: Interiors, in Four Poets, 1962; Bicycle and Other Poems, 1970; Neighbours in a Thicket, 1974; Poems 1976-1977, 1977; First Things Last, 1981; Selected Poems, 1981; Selected Poems, 1982; Poems 1959-1989, 1992; Play: Blood Relations, 1987; Opera Libretti: Voss, 1986; Mer de Glace; Baa Baa Black Sheep, 1993. Honours: NSW Premier's Awd for Fic; James Cook Awd, 1975; Grace Leven Awd, 1975; Gold Medal of the Austl Lit Soc, 1975, 1982; Victorian Premier's Awd, Vance Palmer Prize for Fic, 1986; C'wlth Writer's Prize, 1991; Miles Franklin Awd, 1991; Prix Femina Etranger, 1991. Address: c/o Rogers, Coleridge and White, 20 Powis Mes, London, W11 1SN.

MALTESH Motebennur, b. 15 Nov 1957, Kajjari, Karnatak, India. Assistant Librarian. m. Mrs Kaveri, 18 Nov 1987, 1 s. Education: MSc (Geol); MLISC. Appointments: Jnr Tchr, 1986, Jnr Tchr cum Libn, 1987, Techl Asst (Lib), 1988, Asst Libn, 1995. Creative work: Paintings: Seascape, 1986, Landscape, 1987, Portrait, 1988, Seascape (on oil), 1987; Portrait Ink and Brush, 1997. Memberships: AISLIC; ILA. Hobbies: Paintings; Dramatics; Television production; Calligraphy. Address: Assistant Librarian, Arunachal University, Rono Hills, Itanagar, Arunachal Pradesh, India.

MAMALONI Solomon Sunaone, b. 1943, Macedonia Village, Arosi, West Makira, Solomon Islands. Politician. Education: King George VI Sch, Malaita; Te Aute Coll, NZ. Appointments: Joined Brit Colonial Admin Serv, Honiara, 1966; Exec Offr, Civil Serv, Clk to Legis Cncl, 1970; Governing Cncl Mbr for Makira, 1970-76; Chf Min, (Brit) Solomon Islands, 1974-76; MP for W Makira, 1976-77, 1980-; Mngng Dir, Patosha Co, 1977; Parl Ldr, Peoples Alliance Pty, 1980; PM of Solomon Islands, 1981-84, 1989-93, 1994-; Acting PM, 1994; Fndr, Ldr, Peoples Progress Pty. Publication: AEDO, Census Day, 1978. Honours: Grand Gwanghwa Medal; Order of Dipl Serv Merit, Korea. Address: Office of the Prime Minister, PO Box G1, Honiara, Guadalcanal, Solomon Islands.

MAN Hou Xiao Chang, b. 5 Oct 1922, Guangzhou, China. Education. m. Cao de Qun, 10 June 1951, 1 s, 1 d. Education: Grad, Dr Su Yet-Sen Univ. Appointment: Prof. Publications: Agricultural Marketing; Agricultural Trade. Honours: First-Class Prize, Ex Tchng, Min of Agricl of China, 1992; Awd, Contbn in agricl educ, State Cncl of China, 1992. Memberships: Spec Artist, China Painting and Calligraphy Rsch Inst; Assn Cncl Mbr, Intl Econ & Trade Soc of GD. Hobbies: China's Calligraphy; Violin. Address: College of Economics and Trade South China Agricultural University, Guangzhou, China.

MANASIKARN Yingpan, b. 23 Nov 1937. Government Executive. m. Mayura Manasikarn. Education: Grad, Chulalongkorn Univ, Bangkok. Appointments: Auditor, Provl Elec Authy, 1975; Sec to Prachakorn Thai-Party Ldr, Samak Sundaravej, 1976; Mbr of Parl, Govt of Thailand, 1979-95; Min of Univ Affairs, 1991-92; Min of Sci, Technol and Environt, 1996-. Honour: Kt Grand Cordon, Spec Class, Most Exalted Order of the White Elephant, 1993.

MANDAL Satyananda, b. 25 Feb 1947. Freelance. Education: BA, CU, 1968; MA, RBU, 1970; Cert French, BLIS, BU, 1976; MLIS, AMU, 1979; Cert Psychological Counselling, Samikshani, 1994; PhD, JU, 1997. Appointments: Bagnan College, WB, 1981-86; BU, WB, Jan, 1983-87; Guest Lecturer; VU, WB, 1986-93, Lecturer in Library and Information Science; Pt-time Lectr, RBU, WB; JU, WB; BU, WB. Publications: Book, Folk Art and Craft of South 24 Parganas of WB, 1984; Sev pprs publd in jrnls. Honours: Stood first in first class in BLIS exam, 1976; Stood second in first class in MLIS exam, 1979; Sonali Rod Award, 1985; Tincori Datta Smarak Award, 1992. Memberships: IASLIC; Affiliate of Indian Psycho-Analytical Society; Vice-President of Metropolitan Institute for Psychiatric Research, 1993-94. Hobbies: Psychiatric social work and Psychological Counselling;

Yoga; Travel; Sports. Address: 189A Kalighat Road, Calcutta, PIN 700 026, West Bengal, India.

MANE Uday Harishchandra, b. 21 Oct 1949, Kolhapur, India. Service. m. Aruna, 26 Jan 1982, 1 s, 1 d. Education: BSc, 1968; MSc, 1970; PhD, 1973; High Spec Student, USSR, 1978; High Level Rsch, France, 1984. Appointments: Rsch Asst, 1973-79; Curator, Marine Rsch Lab, Marathwada Univ, 1979-80; Reader, Zoo, Marathwada Univ, 1980-. Publications: num chapts; over 100 rsch pprs in natl & intl sci jrnls. Memberships: Asian Fish Forum, Manila, 1986; Acady Environ Bio, India, Lucknow, 1984; Intl Acady Sci, India, Allahabad, 1995; Indian Assn Aquatic Bio, Hyderabad, 1995. Address: Department of Zoology, Dr B A M University, Aurangabad 431 004, Maharashtra, India.

MANGAN Louis Joseph, b. 26 May 1922, Aust. Company Director. m. Cecile Joan Wykes, 2 Oct 1964. Education: BCom, Univ of Melbourne, 1951; Assoc, Austl Soc of Cert'd Practising Accts, 1952; MCo, Prelim, Univ of Melbourne, 1955; Fell, Austl Soc of Accts. Appointments: Dir, Associated Cos, C & UB Ltd, 1960-85; Mngng Dir, Carlton and United Breweries Ltd, Aust, 1972-85; Chmn, Austl Associated Brewers, 1973-85; Dir, Elders IXL Ltd, 1981-85; Govt Remuneration Tribunal, Canberra, 1983-92. Honour: Offr, Order of Aust, 1984. Memberships: Fell, Austl Inst of Mngmt; Regd Cos Auditor. Hobbies: Sailing; Golf; Tennis. Address: 24 Hopetoun Road, Toorak 3142, Victoria, Australia.

MANIKFAN Hussein, b. 16 June 1936, Maldives. Politician. m. (1) Aminath Shareefa, 1959, (2) Haseena Ali, 1971, 6 children. Appointments: Civil Serv, Min of Educn, Dept of Info, Min of Fin, Off of the Pres of the Repub, 1953-58; Sec, Min of Trust & Pub Endowment, 1958; Tchr, Min of Educn, 1959; Served, Min of Home Affairs, Dept of Posts & Telecom & Pres's Offl Res, 1959-74; Mbr, Maldives Parl, 1970-; Sec, Dept of Elec, 1974; Under-Sec, Min of Transp, 1978; Dir, Unit, Malé Intl Airport, 1978; Mngng Dir, Govt Fishing Corpn, 1982; Dpty Min of Trade & Ind, 1982-88; Perm Rep to UN, 1988-91; Min of State in Charge of Customs, 1991-. Hobbies: Reading; Tennis. Address: H Thuniya, Boduthakurufaanu Magu, Malé 20-05, Maldives.

MANIVACHAKAN Kutti Muniswami, b. 15 July 1941, Pernamallur, Tamil, Nadu, India. Univ Prof. m. Malathi Devi, 1 s, 1 d. Education: MSc, Math, MSc, Engrng Math, Madras Univ; PhD, Indian Inst of Sci. Appointments: Lectr, 1962-84; Asst Prof, 1985-94; Prof, 1994-. Publications: Publ articles in Science Ency, 1993, Engrng Math, 1998. Membership: Elected Mbr, New York Acady of Scis, USA, 1995. Address: Professor of Mathematics, Anna University, Channai 600 025, Tamil Nadu, India.

MANLEY Kenneth Ross, b. 3 Oct 1935, Sydney, Aust. Minister of Religion; College Principal. m. Margaret Alice Stewart, 6 Jan 1962, 2 d. Education: Balmain Tchrs Coll, 1952-53; Bapt Theol Coll, NSW, 1958-61; BA, Theo, Bristol Univ, 1964; PhD, Univ of Oxford, 1967. Appointments: Bapt Min, NSW, 1959-62, 1967-68; Vice Prin, Bapt Theol Coll, SA, 1969-71; Lectr, Bapt Theol Coll, NSW, 1972-81; Min, Epping Bapt Ch, 1981-86; Prin Whitley Coll, Univ of Melbourne, 1987-; Pres, Melbourne Coll of Divinity, 1993-95; Pres, Bapt Union of Vic, 1996-97. Publications: Baptists: Their Faith and Heritage, 1968; In the Heart of Sydney: Central Baptist Church, 1987. Honour: Dr Williams Exhibn, London, 1964. Membership: Assn for Jrnl of Relig Hist. Address: Whitley College, 271 Royal Parade, Parkville, Victoria 3052, Australia.

MANLY Bryan Frederick John, b. 27 May 1944, London, Eng. Academic. 3 d. Education: BS; DSc; CStat. Appointments: Fisons Ltd, 1966-67; Univ of Salford, 1967-69; Univ of Papua and New Guinea, 1970-72; Univ of Otago, 1973-. Publications: 6 books inclng: Randomization, Bootstrap and Monte Carlo Methods in Biology, 2nd ed, 1997. Honours: Fell Roy Soc of NZ, 1994; Disting Statistical Ecologist, 1993. Hobbies: Wining and dining; Travel to exotic places. Address: Department of Mathematics and Statistics, University of Otago, PO Box 56, Dundedin, New Zealand.

MANN Jeffrey Gordon, b. 31 Dec 1944, Melbourne, Vic, Aust. Law. m. (1) 1 s, 1 d, (2) Antonetta, 16 Nov 1996, 1 d. Education: BA, LLB, LLM, Univ Queensland; PhD, Bond University; Solicitor of Supreme Crts of Queensland and NSW; Barrister and Solicitor, Supreme Crts of Vic, West Aust, ACT. Appointments: In prac in Brisbane w Tully & Wilson, 1969; Ptnr, Tully & Willson, 1970; Firm merged w Chambers Macnab & Co, Ptnr, -1989; Ptnr, Mallesons Stephen Jaques (Corp/Com and Revenue Law prac) 1990-. Publications: Book: Law of Stamp Duties in Queensland, 1981 (37 revisions), 1981; 2 book chapts; 4 articles in profl jrnls; 9 conf proceedings. Hobbies: Acad Fell, Univ Queensland; Adj Prof of Law, Univ Queensland; Jt Awd, Henderson Prize, Univ Queensland; Hon Life Mbr, tax Inst of Aust. Memberships: Fell, Austl Inst for Co Dirs; Cttee, Econ Dev of Aust; Law Cncl of Aust; Queensland Cncl for Civil Liberties; Queensland Law Soc; Hon Life Mbr, Taxation Inst of Aust; Univ of Queensland Law Grads Assn. Hobbies: Music; Architecture; Cycling. Address: Palmer Street, Windsor, Brisbane, Australia.

MANNING Clarence Morcom, b. 18 Apr 1917, Brisbane, Aust. Retired. m. Catherine Sheila Moray Murray, 14 Oct 1943, 2 s, 3 d. Education: BA, Dip, Jrnlsm. Appointments: Jrnlst, 1939-40; War Serv, 1940-45; Jrnlst, 1946-48; Ed, 1949, Mngng Ed, 1969-81, Daily Mercury, Mackay; Dir, 1957-, Chmn, 1973-, Mackay Printing & Publng Co Pty Ltd; Dir, 1968, Chmn, 1970-89, Mngng Dir, 1980-87, Provincial Newspprs (Qld) Ltd; Var other Chmnshps, Dirshps, Newspprs, TV, Radio. Honours: Twice mentioned in dispatches, World War II; OBE. Memberships: MEOBE Assn, Qld. Hobbies: Gardening; Rose Growing. Address: 11 Dart Street, Auchenflower, Qld 4066, Australia.

MANOHARAN Arumugam, b. 14 Jan 1944, Salem, India. Consultant Physician. m. Vasantha, 9 Sept 1971, 1 d. Education: MD; MRACP; FRACP; FRCPA. Appointments include: Postgrad Trnee, Internal Med, Govt Stanley Hosp, Madras, 1968-70; Tutor in Med, Kilpauk Medl Coll and Asst to Physn Govt Royapettah Hosp, Madras, 1970-71; Asst Prof, Med, Madras Medl Coll & Asst Physn, Govt Gen Hosp, Madras, 1971-74; Registrar, 1976-77, Snr Registrar, 1978, 1981-82, Haematology, St George Hosp, Sydney, Aust; Snr Registrar Haematology, Roy Postgrad Medl Sch and Hammersmith Hosp, London, Eng, 1979-80; Staff Clin Haematologist, 1982-85; Dir, Clin Haematology, 1985-; Assoc Prof of Med, Univ of NSW, 1999. Publications: Over 135 in peer-reviewed medl jrnls. Memberships: Austl Intl Soc of Haematology. Hobbies: Classical music; Jazz; Walking; Tennis. Address: Sr George Hospital, Kogarah, Sydney, NSW 2217, Australia.

MANOHARAN Periyakaruppan Thangiah, b. 12 June 1935. Researcher; Teacher. m. Kanagavalli, 25 Oct 1965, 1 s, 1 d. Education: BSc, MA, Univ of Madras; PhD, Columbia Univ, NY. Appointments: Lectr, Thiyagarajar Coll, 1959; Asst Prof, MI Univ, 1966; Asst Prof, IIT, Kanpur, 1969; Prof, IIT, Madras, 1972; Dean of Students, IIT, Madras, 1979; Sec, INSA, 1997-99. Publications: Over 146 original pprs of rsch. Honours: Palit Awd, 1988; FICCI Awd, 1989; Rangadhama INSA Awd, 1990; Sadhan asu Mem INSA Awd, 1996. Memberships: Fndr, 1st Regl Sophisticated Instrumentation Cntr, 1974; Fell, Indian Acady of Scis, 1981; Fell, Indian Natl Sci Acad, 1985; Vice Chan, Univ of Madras, 1997-99. Hobbies: Environment; Music; Reading Books. Address: Regional Sophisticated Instrumentation Centre, Indian Institute of Technology, Madras 600 036, India.

MANSELL Chris, b. 1 Mar 1953, Sydney, Aust. Writer. m. Steven Sturgess, 23 Dec 1986, 1 s, 1 d. Education: BEcon, Univ of Sydney, 1975; DipEd, Sydney Tchrs Coll, 1976; NIDA (Natl Inst of Dramatic Art), Playwright's Studio, 1988. Appointments: Sch talks, visits, workshops throughout Aust, res, readings, 1982-; Writer in res or artist in the community, var Austl locations, 1985-96; Lectr, Creative Writing, Univ of Wollongong (pt-time), 1987-89; Lectr in Creative Writing, Univ of West Sydney, Macarthur, 1989; Lectr, Creative Writing, Univ West Sydney (pt-time) Adult writing courses, Shoalhaven Cty Lib, schs, colls, writers grps, TAFE, 1992-. Publications: Fndr, Compass Poetry & Prose, 1978; Ed, Compass, 1978-87; Freelance writer & ed, 1981-; Ed in Res, Roy Austl Histl Soc, Sydney, 1992; Books of poetry: Head, Heart & Stone, 1982; Redshift/Blueshift, 1988; Day Easy Sunlight Fine in Hot Collation, 1995; Mortifications & Lies; Children's book: Little Wombat, 1996; Selections of poetry & prose incl: On the railway near the sea, 1992; The event horizon, 1992; Words on Words, 1998; Being there at Birth, 1998; Contbns to major anthologies of poetry & prose and to jrnls; Playscripts. Honours include: Amelia Chapbook Awd (USA), 1988; Queensland Premier's Poetry Awd, 1993; Writing Fellshp, Lit Bd, Aust Cncl, 1993; Shoalhaven Intl Women's Day Awd, 1998. Memberships include: NSW Poets Union, Treas, 1983-85, Sec, 1978-79; Austl Soc of Auths; NSW Writers Cntr; Women in Publng. Address: PO Box 94, Berry 2535, NSW, Australia.

MANSFIELD Bruce Edgar, b. 30 Mar 1926, Brisbane, Qld, Aust. Professor. m. Joan Isobel Wood, 19 May 1950, 3 s. Education: BA hons, Univ Medal, 1949; MA hons, 1951, Univ of Sydney. Appointments: Temp Lectr of Hist, 1949, Lectr, 1951, Snr Lectr, 1958, Assoc Prof, 1964, Univ of Sydney; First Prof, Hist, 1965-75, Dpty Vice Chan (Acad), 1976-85, Macquarie Univ; Visng Prof, Hist, Univ of Sydney, 1986-91, Hon Assoc, 1992-. Publications: Australian Democrat - The Career of Edward William O'Sullivan 1846-1910, 1965; Knox - A History of Knox Grammar School, 1974; Phoenix of His Age - Interpretations of Erasmus C 1550-1750, 1979; Interpretations of Erasmus C 1750-1920: Man on His Own, 1992; Liberality of Opportunity: A History of Macquarie University 1964-1989 (w Mark Hutchinson), 1992; Ed, Jrnl of Relig Hist, 1959-87. Honours: Nuffield Dominions Travelling Fellshp, 1953; Fulbright Awd, 1965; Emer Prof, Macquarie Univ, 1976; Hon Fell, Mitchell Coll of Adv Educ, 1986, Dunmore Lang Coll, Macquarie Univ, 1986; Hon DLitt, Univ of Sydney, 1991, Macquarie Univ, 1992; Hon D Univ, Charles Sturt Univ, 1995. Memberships: Austl Histl Assn, Pres, 1977-78; Renaissance Soc of Am; Erasmus of Rotterdam Soc, Exec Cttee, 1986-. Hobbies: Walking; Tennis; Music. Listed in: Who's Who in Australia; Who's Who in the World. Address: 60 Darnley Street, Gordon, New South Wales 2072, Australia.

MANSFIELD Janet Winifred, b. 19 Aug 1934, Sydney, Aust. Artist; Author. m. Dr Colin Mansfield, 23 Sept 1955, 1 s, 3 d. Education; Trng in Ceramics, Nat Art Sch, ESTC, 1964, 1965. Appointments: Ed, Ceramics Art and Perception, 1990-; Ceramics Technical, 1995-; Invited spkr, juror; 33 solo exhibns inclng Aust, Japan, 1985, 1988, 1997, NZ, 1972, 1973, 1986, 1968-; Exhibns incl: Gal le Vieux-Bourg, Switz, 1992; Kunst & Keramiek, Holland, 1993; Mus in Oslo, Lillehammer, Norway, 1993; Mino Kami Cty Fest, Japan, 1994; Contemporary Ceramics, London, UK, 1994; Faenza Mus of Ceramics, Italy, 1995; The Scottish Gall, Edinburgh, Scot, 1995; Galerie b15, Munich, 1996; Green Gall, Tokyo, 1996; Vessel Exhibn, ANU, 1996; Saga Prefectural Mus, 1996; Galerie Hadwerk, Munich, 1997; Tachikichi Gall, Kyoto, 1997; Gres au sel, Touring France, 1997; Other exhibns in countries inclng: USA, Germany, Hungary, Czech Repub, Denmark, Korea. Honours: Aust Ceramic Soc Awd, 1986; OAM, 1987; Aust Cncl Emeritus Awd, 1990. Memberships: VP, Intl Acady of Ceramics. Address: 35 William Street, Paddington, NSW 2021, Australia.

MANSUROV Tair Aimukhametovich, b. 1 Jan 1948, Sarkand, Taldyorgan, Kazakhstan. Diplomat. m. 3 children. Education: Kazakh Polytech Inst; Higher CP Sch, Ctrl CPSU Cttee. Appointments: Constrn Orgs, Alma-Ata; Chf Engr, Almaatacentrostroi, 1965-79; CP Functionary, 1979-88; 2nd Sec, Karaganda Region CP Cttee, Hd of Sector, Ctrl CPSU Cttee, 1989-91; Dpty to Kazakhstan Supreme Soviet, Co-ord, Interparl Comm of Russia & Kazakhstan, 1990-93; Pres, Fndn of Devel, Kazakhstan, 1991-93; Amb to Russian Fedn, 1994-; Amb to Finland, 1996-. Publications: Faces of Sovereignty: Sovereignty in Terms of Social Sciences; Kazakhstan and Russia: Sovereignization, Integration, Experience of Strategic Partnership. Memberships: Acady of Creativity; Intl Acady of HS; Acady of Socl Scis. Hobbies: Literature; Philosophy; History; Memoirs. Address: Embassy of Republic of Kazakhstan, Chistoprudny Boulevard 3A, 101000 Moscow, Russia.

MANUELI Paul, b. 30 Jan 1934. Education: Roy Mil Acady, Sandhurst, Eng, 1953-55; NZ Army Schs, 1958, 1964; Austl Army Staff Coll, 1969. Appointments: Joined BP SW Pacific Ltd, Mngr, Plng and Mktng Mngr, Spec Projs, 1979; Chf Exec and Dir, 1981, Retd, 1989; Elected to parl, appointed var ministries, 1992; Min for Jus and Home Affairs, 1997. Honours: OBE; KStJ; MSD. Address: PO Box 2349, Government Buildings, Suva, Fiji.

MAO Bing Xiang, b. 16 Apr 1935, Shanghai, China. Researcher; Educator. m. Zhou Ciao, 10 Nov 1961. Education: Grad, Lt, Mil Acady of Engrng, PLA, 1960. Appointments: Probation Asst, Asst, Lectr, Naval Acady of Engrng, PLA, 1960-84; Snr Engr, Dir of Div, Naval Rsch Cntr, PLA, 1984-98. Honours: Var prizes of adv of sci and technol; 2nd and 3rd Prize, State Level; 1st Prize, Min Level. Memberships: Dpty, 8th Natl Peoples Congress of China, 1993-98; Technol Commn for Standardization of Human-Machine-Environ System Engrng. Address: PO Box 1303, 15, Beijing 100073, China.

MAO Ping, b. 9 Apr 1957, Changde Cty, China. Professor. m. Professor Xiong Zhixiang, 1 s. Education: BA, Philos, Xiang Tan Univ, 1977-82; Postgrad Dip in Aesthetics, Beijing Univ, 1982-84; MPhil, Xiang Tan Univ, Hunan Prov, 1985-88. Appointments: Lectr, Dept Philos, Xiang Tan Univ, 1988; Prof and Dpty Dean in Sch of Socl Scis, Foshan Univ, 1989-. Publications: Books: The Art History of Shiwan Ceramics, 1996; Friedrich Schiller's Aesthetics and Modern Philosophy, 1999; Articles in jrnls incl On Overstepping One's Authority of the Modern Science and Technology: The Studies on Dialectics of Nature, 1000 The Age of Technology and Life Materialization of Human Beings, The Battleline of Social Sciences, Vol 3, 1996. Honours: Model Tchr, Foshan Cty Govt, 1992; Runner-Up, Competition of Aesthetic Rsch Pprs among Natl Higher Educ Instns, 1997. Membership: Natl Aesthetic Assn. Hobbies: Poetry and poems. Address: School of Social Sciences, Foshan University, Foshan 528000, China.

MAO Xiang Hua, b. 9 Feb 1957, Fujian, China. Research; Management. Education: Master. Appointments: Dpty Gen Mngr; Snr Engr; Magistrate. Creative Works: Tea Processing Machinery; Regulations of a Business Company; A Chinese Pat. Honours: Top Prize Bus Mngmnt, For Investment. Memberships: Chinese Tea Soc; Quanzhou Yth Bus Assn. Hobbies: Trav; Music; Sport. Address: VIP Office Building, Qianban, Wenling Road, Quanzhou, Fujian 362000, China.

MARA Ratu, b. 13 May 1920, Fiji. Politician. m. Adi Lala Mara, 1951, 3 s, 5 d. Education: Queen Vic Sch; Ctrl Med Sch, Suva, Fiji; Sacred Heart Coll; Otago Univ; Oxford Univ; London Sch of Econs. Appointments: Brit Colonial Serv, 1950; Admin Offr, Dist Offr, Commr, Fiji, 1951-61; Mbr, Legis Cncl, Fiji, 1953-59; Mbr, Exec Cncl, Fiji, 1959-61; Fndr, Alliance Pty, 1960; Mbr for Natural Resources, 1964-66; Ldr, Fiji Del Constitutional Conf, London, 1965; Chf Min, 1967-70; PM, 1970-87; PM & Min of Fgn Affairs, 1977-87, 1987-92, and of Fgn Affairs and the Pub Serv, 1987-89, of Fgn Affairs & Home Affairs, 1989; Ldr of Opposition, 1987; Pres of Fiji, 1994-. Honours include: Kt St John Grand Master; Order of the Natl Lion, Senegal, 1975; Order of Dipl Serv Merit, Korea, 1978; Meritorious Serv Decoration, Fiji. Memberships include: Hon Fell, Wadham Coll, 1971. Hobbies: Fishing; Golf. Address: Government House, Suva, Fiji.

MARAK Salseng Chada, b. 16 Jan 1941, Baghmara, India. Politician. m. Truitline K Sangma, 1968, 2 s, 4 d. Appointments: Tchr, Hdmaster, 1965-71; Mbr, Meghalaya Legis Assembly, 1972-76; Indian Natl Congress,

1976-78, re-elected to Assembly, 1978-; Chf Min of Meghalaya, 1993-. Hobbies: Reading; Music; Farming. Address: Meghalaya Secretariat, Main Building, Shillong, Meghalaya, India.

MARCEAU Jane, b. 6 Mar 1943, England. Pro-Vice Chancellor, Research. m. John, 26 Mar 1994, 1 s, 1 d. Education: BA, hons, London, 1964; PhD, Cambridge, 1969. Appointments: Lectr, Univ of Essex, 1967-72; Var posns in France, 1970's; Proj Offr, OECD, 1976-80; Snr Rsch Fell, Austl Natl Univ, 1980-82; Eleanor Rathbone Prof of Sociol, Univ of Liverpool 1982-84; Fndn Prof, Austl Natl Univ, 1984-96. Publications include: Masters of Business: Business Schools and Business Graduates in Britain and France; Education, Urban Development and Local Initiatives; A Family Business?: The Creation of An International Business Elite; Reworking the World: Organizations, Cultures and Technologies in Comparative Perspective. Honours: Fell, Austl Inst of Mngmt, 1993. Memberships: Acady of Socl Scis, Aust. Hobbies: Walking; Opera; Theatre; Reading. Address: 11/3 Wylde Street, Potts, NSW 2011, Australia.

MARGOLIS Donald L, b. 13 Nov 1945, Washington, DC, USA. Professor of Mechanical Engineering. div, 2 s. Education: MS, Mech Engrng; Mech Engrng Deg; PhD. Appointments: System Dynamics: A Unified Approach, 1990; Over 120 articles in profl jrnls. Honour: SAE Ralph Teetor Awd, 1986; Fell, ASME, 1991. Memberships: ASME; SAE. Hobbies: Squash; Sports. Address: University of California, One Shields Avenue, Davis, CA 95616, USA.

MARIMUTHU M Suriyamoorthy, b. 16 Aug 1944, Neidayasal. World Research, Art History. m. 2 Feb 1961, 1 s, 3 d. Career: Fine art and world hist. Publications: Num in intl publs. Honour: 46-Time, Justice Time of the World. Membership: One Man in the World. Address: Kaidaikadu, Neidayasal-Post, Sikau-JK, Nagai-Dist, Tamil Nadu State, S India 609105.

MARKEN Gideon A, b. 24 June 1940, Hampton, IA, USA. Advertising; Public Relations. m. Jeannine Hill, 28 Dec 1966, 1 s. Education: BS; MBA. Appointments: Fairchild Instrumentation, 1967-68; Barnes-Hind Pharms, 1968-69; Bozell Jacobs, 1970-77; Marken Comms, 1979-. Creative Works: Auth of 100 Articles on Advtng, Pub Rels, Mktng, Mngmnt. Honours: PRSA, 1977, 1979, 1986; ABC, 1978, 1980. Memberships: PRSA; AAAA. Hobbies: Sailing; Scuba Diving; Aerobics. Address: 3375 Scott Blvd, #108 Santa Clara, CA 95054, USA.

MARKER Jamsheed K A, b. 1922, Pakistan. Diplomat. m. Education: Doon Sch; Forman Christian Coll, Lahore. Appointments: Navy, Home Dept of Govt of India, 1946-47; Dir, Family Bus, Pakistan, 1947; Del of Pakistan to ILO Confs, Geneva, 1958-62; High Commr in Ghana, 1965-67; Amb to Romania, 1967-69, to USSR, 1969-72, to Can, 1972-73, to GDR, 1973-76, to Japan, 1976-78; Perm Rep to UN, Geneva, 1979-80; Amb to Fed Repub of Germany, 1980-82, to France, 1982-86, to USA, 1986-89; Perm Rep to UN, 1990-95. Address: Ministry of Foreign Affairs, Constitution Avenue, Islamabad, Pakistan.

MARKHAM Philip, b. 18 Dec 1941, Dunedin, NZ. Artist. m. Nahleen Georgina Walton, 18 Jan 1964, 1 s, 1 d. Education: King Edward Tech Coll, 1953; Fay Mackay Sch of Ballet, 1959. Career: Roy NZ Ballet, 1960-61, 1967; Covent Gdn Opera and Ballet, 1964-65; Pact Ballet, 1965-67; Hd of Art Dept, Wellington Coll, 1970-85; Self employed, 1986-. Creative works: 1st solo art exhibn, Wellington Cultural Cntr, 1969; Regular annual and bi-annual solo art exhibns in Molesworth Gall, Wellington, Downtown Hilton Gll, Auckland, Moray Gall, Dunedin, 1985-98; Num grp exhibns annually, NZ Acady of Fine Arts and Wellington Soc of Watercolour Artists, 1985-98; Th des, Roy NZ Ballet, Duo Concertante, 1982, Napoli Divertissement, 1983, Festive Dances, 1985, Tranzformations, 1986, Bacchus and Ariadne, 1987, Le Papillon, 1989, La Sylphide, 1990, Tosca, 1992, Un Ballo in Maschera and Turandot, 1994, Carmen, Eugene Onegin, Don Giovanni, 1997; Madame Butterfly, 1999.

Honours: Williams Art Awd, 1980. Memberships: NZ Acady of Fine Arts, elected to cncl, 1986, VP, 1989, Pres, 1994-97; VP, Wellington Soc of Watercolour Artists, 1983-87. Hobbies: Crosswords; Classical music; Gourmet cooking; Travel. Address: Apart Q, 8 Egmont Street, Wellington, NZ.

MARKWELL John Robert, b. 31 July 1948. Information Technology Management; Applied Research & Development. m. Deborah D Walker, 17 Dec 1977, 1 s, 1 d. Education: BS, Phys, James Cook Univ, NQ, 1970; Dip in Info Processing, Univ Qld, 1972; Intl Exec Prog, INSEAD, France, 1991; Snr Exec Bus Study Course, Tsinghua Univ, Beijing, 1996. Appointments: Shift Supvsr, Univ Qld Computer Cntr, 1972; Trainee Progmr, Systs Progmr, Prin Progmr (Systems & Comms), TAB of Qld, 1972-77; Dir, Hong Kong Jockey Club Systems (Aust) Pty Ltd, 1992-; Systs Analyst/Des, Software Mngr, Software Devel Mngr, Systs Devel Mngr, Info Systs Controller, Hd, Info Technol, Roy Hong Kong Jockey Club, 1978-93; Dir of Info Technol, Hong Kong Jockey Club, 1994-97; Dir of IT & Technol, New World Telephone Ltd, 1997-. Honour; Global 100 Top Users of Info Technol, to RHKJC by Computerworld, 1985. Memberships: HKMA Telecomms Users Grp, Exec Cttee, Hon Treas, 1983-85; Cttee, Info Technol Trng, Vocational Trng Cncl, Hong Kong, 1988-95; Co-opt Mbr, Sub-Cttee on Info Technol of Cttee on Sci & Technol, Trade & Ind/Cntrl Govt Off, Hong Kong, 1988-91; Hon Info Technol Advsr to Urban Cncl, 1990-; Advsry Cttee for Cntr of Computing Servs & Telecomms, Hong Kong Univ of Sci & Technol, 1991-97; Hong Kong Country Club, Fin Cttee, 1994-, Gen Cttee, 1995-97; Deptl Advsry Cttee for Dept Computer Sci, City Univ Hong Kong, 1995-97; Advsry Cttee on Computing, Dept Computing, Hong Kong Polytechnic, 1995-97; Hong Kong Jockey Club; Hong Kong Mngmt Assn; Austl Inst of Co Dirs; Aust Chmbr of Comm in Hong Kong; INSEAD Alumni Assn HK. Hobbies: Technology Education; Asian Furniture & Textiles; Photography & Multimedia; Travel; Golf; Skiing. Address: New World Telephone Ltd, 17/F Chevalier Commercial Centre, 8 Wang Hoi Road, Kowloon Bay, Kowloon, Hong Kong.

MAROUF Taha Muhyiddin, b. 1924, Sulaimaniyah, Iraq. Politician; Diplomat. Education: Coll of Law, Univ of Baghdad. Appointments: Lawyer; Dipl Serv, 1949; Min of State, 1968-70; Min of Works & Housing, 1968; Amb to Italy, Non-Res Amb to Malta & Albania, 1970-74; VP of Iraq, 1974-; Mbr, Higher Cttee of Natl Progressive Front, 1975-; Chair, African Affairs Bur of Revolutionary Cmd Cncl, 1976-. Address: Office of the Vice President, National Assembly Building, Baghdad, Iraq.

MARR David George, b. 22 Sept 1937, GA, USA. University Teacher; Researcher. Education: BA, Dartmouth Coll, Hanover, NH, USA, 1959; MA, 1966, PhD, 1968, Univ of CA, Berkeley. Appointments: US Marine Corps Offr, 1959-64; Lectr, Univ of CA, Berkeley, 1968-69; Visng Prof, Cornell Univ, Ithaca, NY, 1969-71; Co-Dir, Indo-China Resource Cntr, Wash DC and Berkeley, 1971-75; Fell, Snr Fell, Prof, Rsch Sch of Pacific and Asian Stdies, Austl Natl Univ, 1975-. Publications: Vietnamese Anticolonialism 1885-1925 (Berkeley), 1971; Vietnamese Tradition on Trial 1920-1945 (Berkeley), 1981; Vietnam 1945: The Quest for Power (Berkeley), 1995. Honours: Phi Beta Kappa, 1959; BA cum laude, 1959; Fulbright Fellshp, 1967-68, Austl Acady of the Hums, 1991; John K Fairbank Prize for Asian Hist, 1997. Membership: Asian Stdies Assn of Aust. Hobbies: Tennis; Travel. Address: Division of Pacific and Asian History, Research School of Pacific and Asian Stdies, Australian National University, PO Box 2, Canberra, ACT 0200, Australia.

MARSDEN Marina, b. 13 Apr 1966. Violinist. Education: DSCM, 1984; Dip in Performance, Vienna Musikhochschule, 1989. Appointments: Assoc Prin, 2nd Violin, Vienna Chmbr Orch, 1988-90; 2nd Concertmaster, Bruckner Orch, Linz, Austria, 1990-92; Assoc Concertmaster, Melbourne Symph Orch, 1994; Acting Concertmaster, Adelaide Symph Orch 1995; Asst Concertmaster, Sydney Symph Orch, 1995-. Creative

works: Compact discs: Marina Marsden - Violin Recital, 1995; Homage to Brahms, 1995; Margaret Sutherland-The Chamber Music with Strings, 1998. Honours: Austrian Govt Stipends, 1985-86; Austl Cncl Grant, 1987; Ernest Llewellyn Memorial Awd, 1987; Queen Elizabeth II Silver Jubilee Trust Awd for Young Australians, 1987; Churchill Fellshp, 1997; Austl Cncl Grant, 1997. Memberships: Roy Overseas League; Austl Music Cntr; Austl Strings Assn. Hobbies: Golf; Films; Books; Art. Listed in: International Who's Who in Music and Musicians' Directory - Vol I. Address: 8 Crana Avenue, East Lindfield, NSW 2070, Australia.

MARSDEN Robin Bruce, b. 10 June 1936, North Sydney, NSW, Aust. Editor. m. Ian Bruce Marsden, 14 Dec 1957, div 1977, 2 d. Education: BA Hons, Engl Lit, Sydney Univ, 1957. Appointments: Libn in Charge, Wolstenholme Lib, Fac of Econs, Sydney Univ, 1957-61; Asst Ed, 1977-78; Assoc Ed, 1982-90, Hon Assoc Ed, 1991-97, Quadrant Mag; Rsch Cnslt, 1978-82; Cnslt, The Sydney Inst, 1987-90. Publications: Articles in Quadrant, Southerly, Craft Aust. Memberships: NSW Publs Classification Bd, 1987-92; Exec Cttee Mbr, VP, Federated Music Clubs of Aust, NSW Cncl. Hobbies: Reading; Creative writing; Art; Music. Address: 41 Calga Street, East Roseville, NSW 2069, Australia.

MARSH Frank Raymond, b. 5 Aug 1938, Waterville, ME, USA. Technical Writer; Artist. Education: BGS, Polit Sci and Hist, Chaminade Univ, Honolulu, 1968; BFA, MFA, Des and Graphics, Otis Art Inst of Parsons Sch of Des, Los Angeles, 1971, 1973; Profl Certs, Applications Programming, System Programming, Univ of CA, Los Angeles (UCLA), 1981, 1982; BS, MS, Computer Sci, 1984, 1986; MIBA, Intl Bus Admin, 1987; MMIS, MSMIS, Mngmt, Info Systems, 1988-1990; BS Electr Engin, West Coast Univ, Los Angeles, 1993. Appointments: Cartographer: USAF, USA, Japan, 1961-69, Thomas Bros Maps, Los Angeles, CA, 1974-84; Freelance artist, priv & corp commns, 1974-; Engrng Writer, Singer Co, Glendale, CA, 1983-87; Snr Tech Writer, Amperpif Corp, Chatsworth, CA, 1987-89; Prin Engr, Writer, Litton Data Systems, Agoura Hills, CA, 1990-96; USC, Multimedia and Creative Technols Fellshp Prog, 1997-99. Creative works: One-man shows incl: Westwood Art Ass, 1973; Westwood Cntr of the Arts, 1975; Villa Montalvo, Saratoga, 1975; Snr Eye, Long Beach, 1979, 1981; Glendale Community Coll, 1983; Studio 1617 Gall, Los Angeles, 1984; Permanent collections incl: Detroit Mortgage Co, MI; Gulf & Western, Chgo; Utd CA Bank, Los Angeles. Honours: Artist of Yr, Westwood Art Assn, 1971; Downey Art Mus, 1973; Westwod Open, 1973, 1974, 1975; Purchase Awd, Brand Lib, Glendale, 1976; Outstndng Grad Student Achievement Awd, Coll of Bus and Mngmt, Acad Yr 1988-89, W Coast Univ, Los Angeles. Memberships: Soc for Tech Comm, 1988-; IEEE, 1992-; Bowers Mus of Cultural Art, Collector' Cncl, 1997-. Hobbies: Travel; Collecting. Address: 2800 Lambert Drive, Los Angeles, CA 90068, USA.

MARSH Neville Alexander, b. 5 Mar 1943. Physiologist. m. Alison Martin, 8 July 1982, 3 s, 1 d. Education: BSc, Univ of London, 1965; PhD, Univ of London, 1968; Grad Cert Educ, QUT, Brisbane, 1995. Appointments: Lectr in Physiology, Queen Elizabeth Coll, London, 1968-85; Snr Lectr, King's Coll, London, 1986-91; Hd of Anatomy and Physiology Dept, Qld Univ of Technol, Brisbane, Aust, 1992-. Publications: Monograph on Fibrinolysis, 1981; History of Queen Elizabeth College, 1986; 200 referred pprs and abstracts. Honours: Hon Prof, Univ of St Marks, Lima, Peru, 1990. Memberships: Brit Haemostasis Club, UK, Chmn and Sec, 1981-91; Austl Soc of Thrombosis and Haematostasis cnclr, 1995-, Sec, 1997-; Chair, Intl Soc of Thrombosis and Haemostasis Scientific Sub-Cttee Registry on Exogenous Haemostatic Factors, 1996-. Hobby: Genealogy. Address: School of Life Sciences, Queensland University of Technology, 2 George Street, GPO Box 2434, Brisbane Q4001, Australia.

MARSH William Barry (Bill Swampy), b. 1 June 1950, Sydney, Aust. Writer (freelance). Publications: Books: Beckom Pop. 64, 1988; Old Yanconian Daze,

1995; Looking for Dad, 1998; Great Flying Doctor Stories, 1999; Short stories. Honours: North Territory Lit Awds (Open Sect), 1988; Winner, Papyrus Publng Short Story Awd, 1994; Fndrs News Prose Awds, 1994. Memberships: Austl Soc of Auths; S Austl Writers Cntr; S Austl Folk Fedn; SCALA (Songwriters Composers and Lyricists Assn). Hobbies: Cricket; Swimming; Golf; Tai Chi; Yoga; Gym. Address: PO Box 52, Stepney, South Australia 5069, Australia.

MARSHALL Lucy Carlile, b. 28 Sept 1930. Book Importer. m. Lindsay John Marshall, 22 Dec 1951, 2 s, 4 d. Education: MA. Publication: Walter Lawry: Cornwall, Australia, Tonga, New Zealand, 1967. Honours: QSM, 1989; Niel T Hansen Awd for a Significant Contbn to Family Hist, 1990. Membership: Fndr, 1st Pres, Ed of Newsletter, NZ Genealogist, NZ Soc of Genealogists, 1967-86. Hobbies: Church activities; Family history research. Address: 6 Ellangowan Road, Torbay, Auckland 1310, New Zealand.

MARTHOMA Alexander, b. 10 Apr 1913, Kuriannoor, Kerala, India. Bishop. Education: BA; BD; Dip in Tchng (LT); Master of Systematic Theol (STM); PhD. Appointments: Tchr, 1933-45, Vicar, Bangalore Mat Thoma Ch, 1946-48, 1952-53; Diocesan Bishop, Mat Thoma Ch, 1953-75; Suffragan Metrop, 1973-76; Metrop, 1976-. Publications: Mar Thoma Ch Heritage & Mission; 3 eds; Autobiography (Malayalam); Articles in mags and pprs. Memberships: Pres, Bible Soc of India, 1973-82; Deleg to World Cncl of Chs: Evanston, 1954, Nairobi, 1975, Vancouver, 1983. Hobbies: Sacred music; Writing articles in church magazines; Reading. Address: Mar Thoma Metropolitan, Mar Thoma Church, Poolatheen, Tiruvalla, Kerala, 689 101, India.

MARTIN A Lynn, b. 5 Oct 1942, Onawa, IA, USA. Academic. m. Noreen, 22 June 1963, 1 s, 2 d. Appointments: Lectr to Rdr, Hist, Univ of Adelaide, 1973-; Dir, Rsch Cntr for the Hist of Food & Drink, 1997-. Publications: The Jesuit Mind, 1988; Plague?, 1996. Honours: FR Hs+S; FAHA. Memberships: Austl Hist Assn; Amn Hist Assn; Aust & NZ Assn of Medieval & Early Modern Schls. Hobby: Wine. Address: History, University of Adelaide, Adelaide, SA 5005, Australia.

MARTIN Elaine Miriam (Wilson), b. 4 July 1937, Melbourne, Aust. University Lecturer and Administrator. m (1), 1 s, 2 d, (2) Ian Charles Schomburgk, 1998. Education: BA, 1st class hons, Univ of Melbourne, 1958; Dip in Socl Studies, 1959; MA, Socl Admin, London Sch of Econs, Eng, 1962; PhD, Univ of Melbourne, 1991. Appointments: Rsch & Tchng in Socl Work & Socl Welfare, Univ of Melbourne & Var Welfare Agencies, 1962-72; Lectr, Snr Lectr, Socl Admin, 1974-, Mbr, Univ Cncl, 1982-89, Dean, Sch of Socl Scis, 1985-87, Acting Pro-Vice-Chan, 1989, Hd, Sch of Socl Admin and Socl Wrk, 1990-92, Flinders Univ of SA, Bedford Park; Chmn or Mbr, var SA Govt Advsry Cttees and Acad Bodies; Hd. Publications: High Living (co-auth); Changing Relationships, 1998; Cntbr to books and schl jrnls. Honours: Var Prizes, Univ of Melbourne; Postgrad Schlsp, Canteens Trust Fund, 1959; Disting Serv Awd, Flinders Univ, 1995. Hobby: Historical Architecture. Address: School of Social Sciences, Flinders University of South Australia, Bedford Park, South Australia 5042, Australia.

MARTIN Frank, President, American Chamber of Commerce in Hong Kong. m. Noriko. Appointments: Pres, Chf Exec Offr, Bank of Canton for Security Pacific Natl Bank; Snr Offr, Security Pacific's Ops in Asia. Memberships include: Hong Kong Intl Sch Bd of Mngmt; Boy Scouts of Am; Inland Revenue Review Bd; Am Chamber of Com; Am Club; Hong Kong Am Cntr; Bus Assn of Hong Kong Univ; AIESEC. Address: American Chamber of Commerce in Hong Kong, 1904 Bank of America Tower, 12 Harcourt Road, Hong Kong.

MARTIN Joseph Jnr, b. 23 May 1915, San Fran, USA. Attorney. m. Ellen Chandler, 6 July 1946, 1 s, 1 d. Education: BA, Yale, 1936; LLB, 1939. Appointments: Asoc, Cadwalader, Wickersham & Taft, NYC, 1939-41; Lt

Cmdr, USNR, 1941-46; Ptnr, Wallace Garrison, Norton & Ray, San Fran, 1946-55; Pettit & Martin, San Fran, 1955-70, 1973-95; Gen Cnsl FTC, Wash, 1970-71; Amb, US Repr, Disarmament Conf, Geneva, 1971-76; Retd; Mbr, Pres' Advsry Cttee for Arms Control and Disarmament, 1974-78. Honours: Recip Offic Commendation for Outstndng Serv as Gen Cnsl FTC, 1973; Disting Hon Awd, US ACDA, 1973; Lifetime Achievement Awd Legal Assistance to the Elderly, 1981. Memberships include: Fell, Amn Bar Fndn; Repub Natl Comitteman for CA, 1960-64; Bd Dirs, Patrons of Art & Music, CA Palace of Legion of Hon, 1958-70, Pres, 1963-68; Bd Dirs, Arms Control Assn, 1977-84; Pres, Friends of Legal Assistance to Elderly, 1983-87; Burlingame County Club; Pacific Union VClub. Address: 331 Greer Road, Woodside, CA 94062-2441, USA.

MARTIN Philip John Talbot, b. 28 Mar 1931, Melbourne, VIC, Australia. Retired Acad; Poet. Education: BA, Melbourne. Appointments: Tutor in Engl, Univ of Melbourne; Lectr in Engl, Austl Natl Univ; Lectr, Snr Lectr, Monash Univ. Publications: Voice Unaccompanied; Bone Flute; Flag for the Wind; Shakespeare's Sonnets, Self Love and Art; News Selected Poems. Hobbies: Art. Address: 25/9 Nicholson St, Balmain, 2041 NSW, Australia.

MARTIN Raymond Leslie, b. 3 Feb 1926. m. Rena Laman, 20 Feb 1954, 3 s, 1 d. Education: MSc Melb; PhD; ScD Cantab; DSc ANU; Scotch Coll, Melbourne; Univ of Melbourne; Cambridge Univ. Appointments: Res Tutor, Chem, 1947-49; Exhibn of 1851 Overseas Sch, 1949-51; Res Fell, 1951-54; 1851 Snr Sch Sidney Sussex Coll, Cambridge, 1952-54; Snr Lectr, Inorganic Chem, Univ NSW, 1954-59; Ldr, Physl and Inorganic Chem Sects, 1959-60; Assoc Rsch Mngr, ICIANZ, Melbourne, 1960-62; Prof Inorganic Chem, Univ Melbourne, 1962-72; Dean Fac Sci, 1971; Fed Pres RACI, 1969; Visng Prof, Columbia Univ, NY, 1972; Dean, Rsch Sch of Chem, Inst of Advd Studies, 1976-77; Prof, Inorganic Chem, 1972-77; Vice-Chancellor and Prof, Monash Univ, 1977-87; Victorian Vice-Chancellors Cttee, 1983-84; Dir, Circadian Technologies Ltd, 1986-; Chmn, Austl Sci and Technol Cncl, 1988-1992; Prof, Chem, Monash Univ, 1987-1991; Mbr, Cncl Victoria Coll of the Arts, 1984-, Pres, 1992-94; Churchill Mem Trust, 1995-; Chmn, Syngene Ltd, 1996-; Chmn, Optiscan Imaging Ltd, 1997-; Honours: H G Smith Medal 1968;A Olle Prize, 1975; Silver Jubilee Medal, 1977; Inorganic Chem Medal RACI, 1978; AO, 1987; A E Leighton Medal; Hon LLD Monash, 1992; Hon DSc, Melbourne, 1996. Memberships: FAA; FTSE; FRSC; FRACI; Melbourne Club; Hawks Club (Camb). Hobbies: Golf; Tennis. Listed in: Who's Who. Address: PO Box 98, Mt Eliza, Vic 3930, Australia.

MARTIN Steve, b. 1945, Waco, Texas, USA. Actor; Comedian. m. Victoria Tennant, 1986, div 1994. Education: Long Beach State Coll; Univ CA, Los Angeles. Appointments: TV Writer, sev shows; Nightclub Comedian. Creative Works: Recordings: Let's Get Small, 1977; A Wild and Crazy Guy, 1978; Comedy is Not Pretty, 1979; The Steve Martin Bros. Film Appearances incl: The Absent Minded Waiter; Sgt Pepper's Lonely Hearts Club Band, 1978; The Muppet Movie, 1979; The Jerk, 1979; Pennies From Heaven, 1981; Dead Men Don't Wear Plaid, 1982; The Man With Two Brains, 1983; The Lonely Guy, 1984; All of Me, 1984; Three Amigos, 1986; Little Shop of Horrors, 1986; Roxanne, 1987; Planes, Tains and Automobiles, 1987; Parenthood, 1989; My Blue Heaven: LA Story; Grand Canyon; Father of the Bride; Housesitter, 1992; Leap of Faith, 1992; Twist of Fate, 1994; Mixed Nuts, 1994; Father of the Bride 2, 1995; Sgt Bilko, 1995. Honours include: Georgie Awd, Am Guild of Variety Artists, 1977, 1978; Sev Grammy Awds. Address: ICM, 8942 Wilshire Boulevard, Beverly Hills, CA 90211, USA.

MARTIN Victor Eadric, b. 13 Nov 1923. Retired Company Director. m. Lola Turnbull, 3 Jan 1951, 1 s, 2 d. Appointments: Chmn, Aust Bankers Assn, 1976-77, 1981-82; Mngng Dir, Comm Banking Co, Sydney, 1976-83; Jt Mngng Dir, Natl Coml Banking Corp Aust Ltd,

1981-83; Chmn, MLC Life Ltd, 1983-94; Chmn, Rprt Review Grp, Austl Fin Syst, 1983; Dir, Lendlease Corp Ltd, 1984-94; Austl Bank Ltd, 1985-88. Honour: AO, 1985. Memberships: Union Club; Austl Club. Hobby: Golf. Address: 464 Galston Road, Dural NSW 2158, Australia.

MARYTN Laurel, b. 23 July 1916, Toowoomba, Qld. Aust. Dance Teacher; Author. m. Lloyd D Lawton, 14 Nov 1945. Appointments: Mbr Saddler's Wells Ballet, 1935; Prin, Borovensky Ballet, 1940; Artistic Dir, Ballet Victoria, 1946; Tchr, 1976-81; Iniated Young Dancers Th (fndng mbr), 1982; Classical Dance Tchrs Aust became incorp Choreographer for YDT, 1983, Pres and Examiner, CDTA, Choreographer for YDT, 1984; Guest Artist, Austl Ballet, Prodr and Choreographer, Nutcracker, YDT; Pres, Examiner, CDTA, 1985; Guest Artist, Austl Ballet, Prodr, Choreographer, Cinderella, YDT; Pres, Examiner, CDTA; Tchr, Theor and Syll Stdies, VCA, 1986; Pres, Examiner, CDTA; Tchr, Young Dancers Th, Vic, Examiner, Austl Ballet Sch, 1987, Box Hill Assoc Dip Coure, Tchr of Theory and Syllabus Studies, Vic Coll of the Arts, Cncl Mbr, Vic Coll of the Arts, Pres, Examiner, CDTA, 1988, Tchr, Utassy Mem Ballet Sch; Guest Artist, Austl Ballet, Pres, Examiner, CDTA, Tchr of Theor and Syll Stdies, Vic Coll of the Arts, 1989, Dance Co-ord, Tchr, Classical Dance and Dance Analysis for the Assoc Dip in Dance Instrn and Mngmt Course, Box Hill Coll of TAFE, Pres, Classical Dance Tchrs Aust Inc, Examiner for CDTA, 1990; Reproduced Carnaval after Michael Fokine for Austl Ballet, Co-ord, Tchr, Assoc Dip in Dance Instrn and Mngmt, Box Hill Coll of TAFE, Melbourne, 1991; Natl Cttee Mbr, Austl Inst of Classical Dance, 1990-; Chair, Vic Br, AICD, 1990-95; Retd, 1994. Publications: Let Them Dance, 1985, revised edition, 1998; A Theory of Classical Dance, 1991. Honours: Choreographer Schslp, RAD, 1934; Adeline Genee Gold Medalist, RAD, 1936; Adv Tchr, Roy Acady of Dancing, London, 1938 Assoc, Imperial Soc of Tchrs of Dancing, London, 1960; OBE, 1976 Fell, Classical Dance Tchrs Aust Inc, 1983; Lifetime Achievers Awd, Green Room Awds, 1997; Lifetime Achmt, Natl Dance Awds, 1997. Address: 99 Panoramic Road, North Balwyn, Victoria 3104, Australia.

MARTYN Shona Jean, b. 30 June 1957. Book Publisher; Journalist. Ptnr, Christopher Read, 1 d. Education: Dip of Jrnlsm, Auckland Tech Inst. Appointments: Reporter, The Auckland Star, 1975; The NZ Herald, 1978; Features Ed, The Review, St Albans, Eng, 1983; Feature Writer, Arts Ed, Vogue Aust, 1984; Dpty Ed, Ed, Good Weekend, 1988; Publr, Transworld Publrs, 1996-98; Hd of Publng, Transworld Publrs Div, Random House, Aust. Honours: NZ Jrnlst of the Yr, 1979; Commendation, Human Rights Awds, 1989; Outstndng Entry-Spec Category, 1994; Women and the Media Awds, 1995. Membership: Austl Soc of Mag Eds. Hobbies: Books; Journalism; Food; Travel; Exercise; Film; Theatre. Address: 20 Alfred Street, Milsons Point, NSW 2061, Australia.

MARUTA Hiroshi, b. 8 Nov 1942, Tokyo, Japan. Molecular Oncologist. m. Elvera Ralph, 7 June 1987, 2 s, 2 d. Education: PhD, Biochem, Univ Tokyo, 1972. Appointments: NIH, 1973-80; Max-Planck Inst, 1980-84; Yale Univ, 1985-86; UCSD, 1986-87; Ludwig Inst, 1988-. Publications: Regulation of the RAS Signaling Network, 1996; Anti-Cancer Proteins and Drugs, 1997; G Proteins, Cytoskeleton and Cancer, 1998; Anti-Cancer Molecules, 1999. Honours: NIH Intl Fellshp, 1973; NHMRC Rsch Grant, 1992; ACCV Rsch Grant, 1992; US NNFF Rsch Grant, 1995. Memberships: NY Acady of Scis; Amn Men and Women in Scis; Japanese Cancer Assn; Japanese Biochem Soc. Hobbies: Marathons; Mountain climbing; Tennis; Painting; Photography; Writing. Address: c/o Ludwig Institute for Cancer Research, PO Royal Melbourne Hospital, Victoria 3050, Australia.

MARUYAMA Ryo, b. 1 Apr 1945, Nagano, Japan. Composer; Video Artist; Critic. m. Naoko, 20 May 1997. Education: Bachelor, Kyoto Univ; Certificat de Ministère des Affaires Etrangères de la France. Appointments: Tech Offr, Min of Labor, 1968; Examiner, Japanese Pat Offr, 1974; Snr Appeal Examiner, Japanese Pat Off, 1994. Creative Works: Video, Music Theater, Travels of

Orphens, 1995; Woman of the Wind, 1997; Music Score, Sorrowful Elephants. Honours: Eisaku SATO Prize, 1982; Effective Promotion of Technol Trans. Memberships: Soundscape Assoc of Japan. Hobbies: Game of IGO; Travel. Address: 1-506, 2-5-8 Fujimidai Nagarayama, Chiba-Ken 270-0127, Japan.

MARY T Nirmala, b. 22 Oct 1948, Phirangipuram, India. Professor of Botany. m. Mani Kumar, 12 June 1975, 1 s, 1 d. Education: MSc; PhD; Postgrad Ctf in Stats. Appointments: Lectr, 1976-83, Rdr, 1983-92, Prof, 1992-, Nagarjuana Univ. Publications: 60 rsch articles; 73 reviews; BSc Textbook of Genetics (for Open Univ), 1985. Honours: Gold Medal, MSc in Botany, Udaipur Univ; Intl Woman of the Yr, ABI; 2000 Millennium Medal of Hon, ABI. Memberships: Indian Jrnl of Botanical Soc; Indian Jrnl of Cytology and Genetics; Current Sci Soc. Hobbies: Recent developments in biological sciences; Bible reading. Address: Dept of Botany and Microbiology, Nagarjuana University, Nagarjuananagar, 522510 AP, India.

MARYANTO Rusmanto, b. 23 July 1963, Sragen, Central Java. Journalist. m. Idah S Z, 3 s, 1 d. Education: BPhys, Fac of Maths & Sci, Univ of Indonesia, Jakarta, 1988. Appointments: Instr, Nuclear Techns Sch, 1989-94; Rschr, Nuclear Assessment Cntr, 1994-95; Ed & Jrnlst, Electro Indonesia Mag, 1994-. Publications: Graphics Design of Elektro Indonesia Magazine, 1994-; Graphics Designer of Elektro Online, 1996-. Memberships: World Energy Cncl, Indonesian Natl Cttee, 1995-; Indonesian Elecl Power Soc, 1998-; Vice Chmn, Linux User Grp, Jakarta, Indonesia, 1998-. Hobbies: Reading; Writing; Music. Address: Elektro, Grha Citra Lt M, Jl Gatot Subroto 52 Jakarta, Indonesia.

MASDIT Khunying Supatra, b. 9 Jan 1950. Minister to Prime Minister's Office. Education: MA, Comms, USA. Appointments: Mbr of Parl, 1979, 1983, 1986, 1988, 1995, 1996; Sec, Min of Prime Min's Off, 1986-88; Min to Prime Min's Off, 1988-91. Honour: Kt Grand Cordon, Spec Class, Most Exalted Order of the White Elephant. Address: 145/27 Amnuaysongkram Road, Dusit, Bangkok, Thailand.

MASON Anthony Frank (Sir), b. 21 Apr 1925, Sydney, Australia. m. Patricia McQueen, 4 July 1950, 2 s. Education: BA 1946, LLB 1949, Univ of Sydney. Appointments: Flying Offr, RAAF, 1944-45; Admitted, NSW Bar, 1951; Queen's Counsel, 1964; C'wlth Solicitor Gen, 1964-69; Vice-Chmn, UN Commn on Intl Trade Law, 1968; Judge Court of Appeal, Supreme Court of NSW, 1969-72; Justice, High Court of Austl, 1972-87; Austl Lectr, Menzies Lect Studies, Univ of VA, 1985; Chf Justice, High Court of Austl, 1987-95; Leon Ladner Lectr, Univs, British Columbia and Victoria, Can, 1989; Chan, Univ of NSW, 1994-; Singapore Acady of Law Lectr, 1995; Chmn, Natl Lib of Aust, 1995-; Natl Fell, Rsch Sch of Socl Scis, Austl Natl Univ, 1995-; Jus, Supreme Crt of Fiji, 1995-; Arthur Goodhart Prof in Legal Sci, Cambridge Univ, 1996-97; Visnt Fell, Gonville and Caius Coll, Cambridge, 1996-97; Pres, Solomon Is Crt of Appeal, 1997-; Jus, Hong Kong Crt of Final Appeal, 1997-. Honours: CBE, 1969; KBE, 1972; AC, 1988; Hon LLD ANU, 1980; Hon LLD, Sydney, 1988; Hon LLD, Melbourne, 1992; Hon DCI, Oxford, 1993; LLD, Monash, 1995; Hon LLD, Griffith, 1995; Hon LLD Deakin, 1995. Memberships: Cncl, ANU, 1969-72; Pro-Chancellor, ANU, 1972-75; Hon Bencher Lincolns Inn, 1987; Cncl, Mngmnt of British Inst of Intl & Comparative Law, 1987; Fell, Acady of Socl Scis, 1990. Hobbies: Gardening; Tennis; Swimming. Address: 1 Castlereagh Street, Sydney 2000, Australia.

MASON Harold Frederick, b. 15 Feb 1925, Porterville, California, USA. Physical Chemist. m. Marian Caldwell, 30 Jan 1954, dec 4 Dec 1998, 2 s, 1 d. Education: Bach Deg, Chem Engrng, Cornell Univ, 1950; PhD, Physl Chem, Univ WI, 1955. Appointments: Rsch Chem, 1954-67, Section Supvsr, 1967-70, Rsch Mngr, 1970-86, Retd, 1986, Process Rsch Dept, Chevron Rsch Co, Richmond, CA. Publications: Sev articles in profl jrnls. Memberships: Am Chem Soc; Am Inst of Chem Engrs;

Sigma Xi; Tau Beta Pi. Hobbies: Astronomy; Photography; Botany. Address: 535 Silverado Drive, Lafayette, CA 94549, USA.

MASON John Charles Moir (Sir), b. 13 May 1927, Manchester, Eng. Company Director. m. 15 Nov 1954, 1 s, 1 d. Education: MA, Cambridge, 1953. Appointments: HM Diplomatic Serv, 1952-84; HM Amb to Israel, 1976-80; Brit High Commnr to Aust, 1980-84; Chmn, Thorn EMI Aust Ltd, Prudential Assurance Co Aust; Multicon Ltd, Sydney; Bd of Advice, Spencer Stuart & Assocs Ltd; North Shore Heart Rsch Fndn; Lloyds Bank NZA Ltd, Sydney, 1985-90; Dir, Fluor Daniel Ltd; Wellcome Aust Ltd, 1985-90; Pirelli Cables Aust Ltd; Churchill Mem Trust, Aust. Publication: Diplomatic Despatches from a Son to his Mother, 1998. Honours: CMG, 1976; KCMG, 1980. Memberships: Union Club, Sydney; Austl Press Cncl; Profl Conduct Cttees; Law Soc; Bar Cncl, NSW. Address: 147 Dover Road, Dover Heights, Sydney, NSW 2030, Australia.

MASON Kenneth Bruce, b. 4 Sept 1928. Education: BA, DipDiv; ThL; Tchrs Coll, Sydney; St John's Coll, Morpeth; Qld Univ. Appointments: Brotherhood of the Good Shepherd, 1953-64; Priest-i/c, Gilgandra, 1954-58, Darwin, 1959-61, Alice Springs, 1962, St Francis Coll and Brisbane Univ, 1963-64; Asst Chap, Trinity Coll, Melbourne, 1965; Dean, 1966-67, Bish, NT, 1968-83; Chmn, Austl Bd of Miss, 1983-93. Honour: AM, 1984. Hobbies: Music; History. Address: PO Box 544, Glebe, New South Wales 2037, Australia.

MASON Malcolm Geoffrey, b. 3 Mar 1943, Adelaide, Aust. Geology. m. Kay (née Ebsary), 18 June 1968, 3 s, 2 d. Education: BS (Hns), Adelaide Univ, 1965. Appointments: Chf Geol, Seltrust Mining Ltd, -1980; Mngng Dir, Sundowner Minerals NL, -1984; Mngng Dir, Tindals Gold Mines NL, -1993; Dir, Lynas Gold NL, -1996; Mngng Dir, Acclaim Uranium NL, -1997. Memberships: Fell, Geol Soc Aust; Fell, Aust Inst Mining & Met; Fell, Aust Inst Co Dirs; Roy Soc S Aust. Address: 9 Sellenger Court, City Beach, Western Australia 6015.

MASON Raymond, b. 8 Oct 1926, Nebraska, USA. Writer; Investor; Publisher. m. Marilynn, 22 July 1945, 1 d. Education: BA, MA, San Fran State Coll, CA. Publications: 5 novels, num short stories, hundreds of poems, illustrations for lit mags. Honours: 2 mil awds. Hobby: Art. Address: 30 Saroni Court, Oakland, CA 94611-1415, USA.

MASRI Taher Nashat, b. 5 Mar 1942, Nablus, Jordan. Diplomat. m. Samar Bitar, 1968, 1 s, 1 d. Education: N TX Univ. Appointments: Ctrl Bank of Jordan, 1965-73; MP, Nablus Dist, 1973-74, 1984-97; Min of State, Occupied Territories Affairs, 1973-74; Amb to Spain, 1975-78, to France, 1978-83, to Belgium, 1978-80, Rep to EEC, 1978-80; Perm Del to UNESCO, 1978-83; Amb to UK, 1983-84; Min of Fgn Affairs, 1984-88, 1991; Dpty PM, Min of State for Econ Affairs, 1989; Chair, Fgn Rels Cttee, 1989-91, 1992-93; PM, Min of Def, 1991; Speaker, Natl Assembly, 1993-. Honours include: The Jewelled AlNahda, Jordan; Order of Al-Kawkab, Jordan, 1974; Gran Crux de Mérito, Spain, 1977; Order of Isabela la Catolica, Spain, 1978; Cmdr, Légion d'honneur, 1981; Grand Offr, Order Natl du Mérite; GBE. Address: PO Box 5550, Amman 11183, Jordan.

MASSAD Carlos, b. 29 Aug 1932, Santiago, Chile. Economist. m. Lidia, 6 May 1956, 1 s, 4 d. Education: MA, Dept of Econs, Univ Chgo, 1958; PhD Cand, Dept of Econs, Univ Chgo, 1959. Appointments: Exec Pres, Fundacion Eduardo Frei Montalva, 1993-94; Min of Hlth, 1994-96; Gov, Ctrl Bank of Chile, 1996-. Publications: Macroéconomia, 1979; Nociones de Economia, 1980; Adjustment with Growth, 1984; Analisis Economico: Introduccion a la Microeconomia, 1986. Honours: Gestion, como la autoridad de gobierno mas destacada del ano, 1994; Premio al mejor Banquero Central de A. Latina otorgado por Euromoney, 1997. Hobby: Fishing. Address: Agustinas 1180, Santiago, Chile.

MASSEY John Bruce, b. 25 July 1949. Civil Engineer. m. Mang Lai Ping, 15 Apr 1979, 1 d. Education: BEng, Univ WA, Aust, 1970. Appointments: Govt Geotech Engr, Govt of Hong Kong, 1989-. Publications: Contrb 14 tech papers and co-auth of sev Hong Kong Govt publns. Honours: Hong Kong Instn Engrs Pres' Prize, 1988; JP, 1997. Memberships: Fell, Hong Kong Instn Engrs, 1992; Chmn, Geotech Div, 1993. Hobbies: Tropical soils; Landslide prevention; Dredging; Marine environmental studies. Address: 101 Princess Margaret Road, Ho Man Tin, Kowloon, Hong Kong.

MASSIER Paul F, b. 22 July 1923, Pocatello, ID, USA. Engineer. m (1) Miriam Parks, 1 May 1948, decd 5 Aug 1975, 2 d, (2) Dorothy Hedlund Wright, 12 Sept 1978. Education: Mechl Engrng Cert, Univ of ID South Branch (ID State Univ), 1943; BS (Hons), Mechl Engrng, Univ of CO, 1948; MS, Mechl Engrng, MIT, 1949. Appointments: US Army, 1943-46; Engr, Constrn and Maintenance Dept, Pan Am Refining Corp, Texas Cty, TX, 1948; Des Engr, Maytag Co, Newton, IA, 1949-50; Rsch Engr, Boeing Co, Seattle, WA, 1950-55; Snr Rsch Engr, Grp Supvsr, Mbr Tech Staff, Task Mngr, Jet Propulsion Lab (JPL), CA Inst of Technol, Pasadena, CA 1955-89; Retired, 1989; On call mbr, Tech Staff, JPL, 1989-94. Publication: Auth/co-auth, 39 profl tech articles in jrnls and book series; Auth, 4 fam hist/genealogy documents. Honours: Mil Unit Citation Awd, 1946; Apollo Achievement Awd, NASA, 1969; Life Mbr Serv Awd, CA PTA, 1970; Layman of Yr Awd, Arcadia Congrl Ch, 1971; Sustained Serv Awd, AIAA, Los Angeles Sect, 1980-81; Basic Noise Rsch Team Awd, NASA, 1980; Engrng Profl Achievement Awd, ID State Univ, 1991; Sigma Xi; Tau Beta Pi; Sigma Tau; Pi Tau Sigma. Memberships include: NY Acady Scis; Planetary Soc; Assoc Fell, Amn Inst Aeronautics and Astronautics (AIAA); Order of the Engnr; FIBA; Life Fell, ABI Rsch Assn; Intl Bd, Life Mbr, Bukovina Soc of the Ams (genealogy). Hobbies: Travelog and documentary motion picture production and presentations; Genealogy and family history research; Travel; Old sheet music and other antique collectables. Address: 1000 North First Avenue, Arcadia, CA 91006, USA.

MASSOUD Ahmed Shah, b. 1953, Afghanistan. Guerrilla Commander. Education: Engrng Dept, Kabul Polytech. Appointment: Guerrilla Cmdr in Panjshir Valley Against Soviet-Backed Regime of Fmr Pres Najibullah, 1979-92; Min of Def, 1992; Guerrilla Cmdr Against Taliban Islamic Regime, 1996-. Memberships: Muslim Youth League; Jamiat-i-Islami. Address: Ministry of Defence, Darulaman Wat, Kabul, Afghanistan.

MASTERS Margaret, b. 3 Dec 1924, Canton, China. Medical Doctor; Paediatrician. m. Joseph Masters, 1 s, 2 d, 1 dec. Education: AA, William amd Mary Coll, 1945; MD, Medl Coll of VA, VA C'wlth Univ, 1950; Paediat Res, Children's Hosp, San Fran, 1951-54. Appointments: Chf, Paediat Sect, 98th Gen Hosp, US Army, Germany, 1955-57; Medl Cnslt, Sacrament Cty sch Educ Progs, Asst Clinl Prof, Paediats, Univ of CA at Davis, 1971-75. Honour: Cert, Amn Bd of Paediats, 1964. Memberships: Sacrament Co Medl Soc; CA Medl Assn; Amn Medl Assn; Sacramento Paediat Soc; Amn Acady of Paediats. Hobbies: Oil painting; Gardening; Roses. Listed in: Who's Who in the USA. Address: 3937 Orangewood Drive, Fair Oaks, CA 95628, USA.

MASUNAGA Shigeki, b. 16 Aug 1952, Fukui Cty, Japan. Professor. m. Yuko, 18 Nov 1981, 1 s, 2 d. Education: DSc, Univ of Tokyo. Appointments: Rschr, Natl Rsch Inst for Pollution and Rescs, Japan, 1980-85; Snr Rschr, 1985-91; Snr Rsch Assoc, Environ Res, Lab, USEPA, Athens, GA, USA, 1990-91; Snr Rschr, Natl Inst for Resources and Environ, Japan, 1991-96; Assoc Prof, 1996-97, Prof, 1997-, Inst of Environ Sci and Tech, Yokohama Natl Univ, Japan. Publications: Num sci pprs in profl jrnls. Honours: Culture Awd, Inst of Oriental Philos, Japan, 1988; Thesis Awd, Japan Soc on Water Environ, 1992; Evironmental Chem Thesis Prize, Japan Soc for Environ Chem, 1995. Memberships: Amn Chem Soc; Soc of Environ Toxicology and Chem; Japan Soc for Water Environ. Hobby: Philately. Address: Yokohama

National University, Institute of Environmental Science and Technology, 79-7 Tokiwadai, Hodogaya-ku, Yokohama 240-8501, Japan.

MATA'AFA Fiame Naomi, b. 29 Apr 1957, Apia, Western Samoa. Minister of Education. Education: Pol Sci, Victoria Univ, Wellington, NZ. 1976-79. Appointments: Pt-time Employee, Natl Party HQ, Wellington, 1977; Mbr of Parl, Lotofaga Dist, 1985-87, Re-elected, 1988-90, Parly Under-Sec for Fin; Ministerial Portfolios, Yth, Sports and Culture, Mus and Archives, Labour (Accident Compensation), 1991-92; Re-elected to Parl, 1991-96; Min of Educ, 1995-. Memberships: Snr Mbr, Human Rights Protection Party; Natl Pres, Young Women's Christian Assn of W and Amn Samoa, 1984-88; Exec Bd Mbr, Pacific Reg, YWCA, 1987-91; Pacific Regl Pres, C'wlth Women Parliamentarian's Grp, 1995; Regl Pres, PAC "Y", 1995; Natl Pres, Natl Cncl of Women of Western Samoa, 1995-. Hobbies: Reading; Music; Tennis; Watching rugby. Address: Office of the Minister of Education, PO Box 1869, Apia, Western Samoa.

MATAIKA Jona Uluinairai, b. 30 July 1925, Suva, Fiji Is. Retired Medical Officer. m. Kelera Loma, 13 Dec 1953, 2 s, 4 d. Education: Fiji Sch of Med, 1943-46. Appointments: Med Offr, Levuka Hosp and other rural hosps, 1947-51; Med Offr, Fiji Infantry Reg, Malaysia, 1952-53; Med Offr, Fiji Filariasis Rsch, 1954-58; Second to Brit Solomon Is Med Servs, Malaria Prog, 1961-67; Wellcome Virus Lab/Fiji Filariasis Control Prog, 1967-90; Retd, 1995. Publications: Co-auth: An Epidemic of Ross River Virus Infection in Fiji, 1979; Recent Situation of Filariasis in Lau and Rotuma Provinces of Fiji, 1985; Epidemiological Survey of Angiostrongylus Cantonensis in Fiji. Honour: OBE, Civ. Memberships: Asian Grp for Rapid Viral Diagnosis; Gideon Intl Suva Camp. Hobbies: Gardening; Fishing. Address: 9 Vaivai Place, Flagstaff, Suva, Fiji Islands.

MATANE Paulias Nguna (Sir), b. 21 Sept 1931, Viviran, Rabaul, Papua New Guinea. Diplomat. m. Kaludia Peril, 1957, 2 s, 2 d. Appointments: Snr Positions, Depts of Educ, 1957-69; Mbr, Pub Serv Bd, 1969; Hd, Dept of Lands, Surveys and Mines, 1969; Of Bus Dev, 1970-75; Amb to USA and Mexico, 1975-80; Perm Rep to UN, 1975-80; High Commnr in Can, 1977-80; Sec Dept of For Affairs and Trade, 1980-85; Chmn, Cttee of Philos of Educ in Papua New Guinea, 1986; Cocoa Ind and Investigating Cttee of Cocoa Qual in Papua New Guinea, 1987; Chmn of Dirs, Treid Pacific (PNG) Pty Ltd, 1986-91; Mbr, Natl Investment and Dev Authority, Natl Tourism Authority, Natl Citizenship Advsry Cncl; Chmn, Censorship Bd of Papua New Guinea, 1984-97; Mbr, Advsry Review Grp, Papua New Guinea Natl Govt, 1997-99. Publications: Travels Through the Bible Lands, 1997; A Trip of a Lifetime, 1997; The Word Power, 1998; The Other Side of Port Moresby - in Pictures, 1998; Amazing Discoveries of Marriage, 1998; Valiling Community United Church, 1998; Chit Chat, Vol 3, 1999; Coach Adventures Down Under, 1999; Management Problems in Papua New Guinea: Some Solutions, 1999; Further Management Problems: Their Solutions, 1999. Honours: Kt, 1986; CMG; OBE; 10th Indep Anniversary Medal, 1985; UN 40th Anniversary Medal. Memberships: HonDTech (PNG); HonDPhil (PNG). Hobbies: Reading; Squash; Writing; Travel. Listed in: International Who's Who; Who's Who in Australia. Address: PO Box 680, Raband, ENBP, Papua New Guinea.

MATH Mata Amritanandamayi, b. 27 Sept 1953, Idamannel, Kollam, Kerala, India. Spiritual Leader. Career: Fndr, Charitable Trust Mata Amritanandamayi Math, and assoc instns. Publications: Mata Amritananandamayi (biog); Awaken Children (ser); May Your Hearts Blossom; Unity is Peace; Over 10 vols on tchngs in many langs. Honours: Hindu of the Yr, 1993; Speaker, Interfaith Celebrations, NY, 1995; 50th Anniv, UN; Share and Care Humanitarian of the Yr Awd, 1998. Memberships: Pres, Assembly of Global Religions, 1993; Parl of World Religions. Address: Amritapuri PO, Quilon District, 690525 Kerala, India.

MATHER Robert, b. 28 Sept 1914, Hobart, Tas. m. Eileen Walton Bird, 10 Apr 1937, 2 s, 2 d. Education: BCom, Univ of Tas, 1936. Appointments: Economist, Bank of NSW, 1936-46; Dir, 1955-72, Andrew Mather & Co Pty Ltd, 1947-72; Mbr, Tasmanian House of Assembly, 1964-82; Austl Mutual Provident Soc, Mbr Tas Bch Bd, 1964-69, 1972-85; Min, Educ, 1969-72; Dir, Perpetual Tstees Ltd, 1976-89; Chmn, 1984-86, Savings Bank of Tas; Chmn, State Grants Commn, 1982-90; Chmn, Tas Bank, 1987-91. Honour: CBE, 1984. Hobbies: Reading; Bushwalking; Native flora. Address: 5 Hanlon Court, Sandy Bay, Tas 7065, Australia.

MATHESON Audrey Elizabeth (Lady), b. 19 Dec 1913. m. Louis Matheson, 3 Apr 1937, 3 s. Appointments: McCulloch House, 1970-75; VP, Natl Cncl of Women, Vic, 1971-74, 1974-77; Mbr, Deafness Fndn, Vic, Advise Cttee, 1974-86; Chmn, Equal Opportunities Advise Cncl, 1978-81; Chmn, Vic Advise Cncl on Status of Women, 1978-82; Pres, Vic Family Cncl, 1978-82; Mbr, Bd of Dirs, YWCA (Melb), 1982-93; Tstee, World Wildlife Fund, 1982-87; Pres, Family Plng Assn, Vic, 1984-87. Honour: Queens Jubilee Medal, 1977. Membership: Lyceum Club (Melbourne). Hobbies: Music; Theatre. Address: 26-166 West Toorak Road, South Yarra, Vic 3141, Australia.

MATHESON (James Adam) Louis (Sir), b. 11 Feb 1912, Eng. Retired. m. Audrey Elizabeth Wood, 3 Apr 1937, 3 s. Education: MSc; PhD; Hon FICE; Hon FIEAust; FTS; FEng; Hon DSc, Hong Kong; Hon LLD, Manc, Melbourne, Monash. Appointments: Civil Engr, 1933-36; Lectr, Birmingham Univ, 1938-46; Prof, Civil Engrng, Melbourne Univ, Aust, 1946-50; Beyer Prof, Engrng, Manchester Univ, 1950-59; Vice Chan, Monash Univ, 1959-76. Publications: Hyperstatic Structures, 1959; Still Learning, 1980. Honours: Kernot Mem Medal, 1970; CMG, 1972; KBE, 1976; Peter Nicol Russell Mem Medal, 1977. Memberships: Tstee, Sci Mus of Vic, 1964-83; Pres, Cncl, 1969-73; Cncl Instn Engrs, Aust, 1965-81, Pres, 1975-76; Institution of Civil Engrs, 1966-68; Chmn, Austl Sci and Technol Cncl, 1975-76. Hobbies: Music; Woodwork. Address: 26/166 West Toorak Road, South Yarra, Vic 3141, Australia.

MATHEW Thomas, b. 15 Feb 1941, Maramon, Kerala, India. Service. m. Valsa, 25 May 1970, 2 s. Education: BE, Kerala Univ; ME Hons, Roorkee; MBA, Hawaii; Dip, Syst Mngmt; PG Cert, Urban Planning, Hawaii; PhD, IE, NITIE Mumbai; PhD, Proj Mngmt, IIT Mumbai. Appointments: Engr, Pub Works; Fell, E-W Cntr; Fell, Min of HRD; Prof, IIT Mumbai; Prof, XLRI Jamshedpur; Prof, NITIE; Dean, NITIE; Dpty Dir, NITIE; Dir, NITIE, Mumbai, India. Publications: Managerial Skills for Technical Personnel, 1994; 29 rsch projs, 1976-90; 11 pprs in intl jrnls, proceedings, sev articles. Honours: Lilian Gilberth Awd, 1992. Memberships: Pres, IIIE; Chmn, IIIE, 1988, 1989, 1990; Num profl assns & acad cncls. Address: National Institute of Industrial Engineering, Vihar Lake, PO NITIE, Mumbai 400 087, India.

MATHEW Timothy Hamish, b. 10 June 1937. Education: MB BS; Scotch Coll (Melbourne) Univ; Univ Melbourne. Appointments: Res Registrar, 1962-65; Fell in Nephrology Georgetown Univ Hosp, Wash DC, 1967-70; Dept Nephrology, Royal Melbourne Hosp, 1970-77; Physn to Profl Unit, Royal Women's Hosp, 1973-77; Dir, Renal Unit Queen Elizabeth Hosp, S Aust, 1977-; Hd, Div of Med, Queen Elizabeth Hosp, 1992-95. Membership: FRACP; Chmn, Adverse Drug Reaction Advsry Commn, 1994-; Core Mbr, Aust Drug Evaluation Commn, 1994-. Address: 45 Wakefield Street, Kent Town, SA 5067, Australia.

MATHEWS (Charles) Race (Thorson), b. 27 Mar 1935, Melbourne, Aust. Writer. m. (1) Geraldine McKeown, 1956, dec, 1 s, 2 d, (2) Iola Lindsay Hack, 1 Sept 1972, 1 s, 1 d. Education: TPTC, Toorak Tchrs Coll, 1954; Lic, Austl Coll of Speech Therapists, 1961; BEd, Melbourne Univ, 1978, MA, 1990; ThD, Monash Univ, 1999. Appointments: Prin Pvte Sec, Ldr of Opposition, Austl Parl, 1967-72; Mbr, Casey, House of Reps, Austl Fed Parl, 1972-75; Prin Pvte Sec, Ldr of Opposition, Vic State Parl, 1976-79; Mbr, Oakleigh, Vic State Parl, 1979-92; Min, Police and Emergency Servs, Min, Arts, 1982-87; Min, Cmnty Servs, 1987-88; Visng Fell, Pub Sector Mngmt Inst, Monash Univ, 1990-93; Dir, Inst of Pols and Current Affairs, Grad Sch of Govt, Monash Univ, 1994-95; Snr Rsch Fell, Grad Sch of Govt, Monash Univ, 1995-97. Publications: Australia's First Fabians: Middle Class Radicals, 1994; Labour Activists and the Early Labour Movement, 1994; Labor's Troubled Times (co-auth), 1991; Whitham Revisited (co-auth), 1993; Jobs of Our Own: Building and Stakeholder Society, 1999. Memberships: Sec, 1959-68, 1980-86, 1998-, Austl Fabian Soc; Exec Mbr, 1966-68, Vic Assn of Youth Clubs; Austl Cncl for Inter-Govt Rels; Vic Chmn, Austl Inst of Polit Sci, 1977-78; Bd Mbr, H V Evatt Fndn, 1990. Hobbies: Theatre; Music; Reading; Gardening. Listed in: Who's Who in Australia. Address: 123 Alexandra Avenue, South Yarra, Vic 3191, Australia.

MATHEWS Russell Lloyd, b. 5 Jan 1921. m. Joan Tingate, 13 Dec 1947, 1 s, 1 d. Education: BCom, Melbourne Haileybury Coll; Univ Melbourne. Appointments: AIF, Cap MID, 1941-45; Prof, Com, Univ Adelaide, 1958-64; Prof, Acctng and Pub Fin, 1965-78; Mbr, C'wlth Grants Commn, 1972-90; Dir, Cntr for Rsch on Fed Fin Rels, Austl Natl Univ, Canberra, 1972-86; Mbr, Commn of Inquiry into Land Tenures, 1973-76; Chmn, Cttee of Inquiry into Inflation and Taxation, 1975; Chmn, Advsry Cncl for Inter-Govt Rels, 1977-79; Advsr on Taxation/Fiscal Federalism to Govts of Fiji, Tonga, Cook Islands, Papua New Guinea, Cyprus, Newfoundland, Labrador; Chmn, Review of Acctng Discipline in Higher Educ, 1990-91. Publications: Inflation and Company Finance (jointly); Militia Battalion at War; Accounting for Economists; Taxation in Australia (jointly); Public Investment in Australia; The Accounting Framework; Revenue Sharing in Federal Systems; Fiscal Equalisation in Education; Immigration and State Budgets; The Public Sector in Jeopardy (co-auth). Honours: AO, 1987; CBE, 1978. Membership: FASSA, 1959. Address: 22 Cobby Street, Campbell, ACT 2612, Australia.

MATIN A C, b. 8 May 1941, Delhi, India. Professor. m. Mimi Keyhan, 21 June 1968. Education: BS, Microbiol, Zool, Univ of Karachi, Pakistan, 1960; MS, Microbiol, 1962; PhD, Microbiol, Univ CA, LA, 1969. Appointments: Lectr, Microbiol, St Josephs Coll for Women, Pakistan, 1962-64; Postdoctoral Rsch Assoc, Postgrad Bacteriologist, Rsch Asst, Dept of Bacteriol, Univ of CA, LA, 1964-71; Sci Offr, First Class, Dept of Microbiol, State Univ of Groningen Biol Cntr, The Netherlands, 1971-75; Participating Fac Mbr, West Reg Hazardous Substance Rsch Cntr, Stanford Univ, 1989-. Publications: 64 Orig Papers; 32 Invited Articles, Book Chapts, Rsch Rprts; 62 Meeting Abstracts. Honours: MS Deg in First Div; Fulbright Schl; PhD with Distinction. Memberships: Fell Am Acady of Microbiol; Editl Bd, Annual Review of Microbiol; Editl Bd Mbr, Jrnl of Bacteriol; Editl Bd Mbr, Jrnl of Microbiol; ASM Fndn for Microbiol Lectr; Review Cttee of the Accreditation Bd for Engrs and Technol; Intl Visng Bd of ABET; Bd Mbr, Northern Br of the Soc for Indl Microbiol; UN Fell for Tech Transf to Developing Countries; Dept of Energy Stdy Sect; Dept of Energy NABIR Stdy Sect. Hobbies: Reading; Hiking; Music. Address: Stanford University, Dept for Microbiology and Immunology, Fairchild Science Building D317, Stanford, CA 94305-5402, USA.

MATISONS Jani Gunars, b. 13 Aug 1955, Adelaide, South Australia. Polymer Scientist. m. Ina Zandersons, 16 Dec 1978, 1 s, 1 d. Education: BS, Adelaide Univ, 1976; Dip in Educ, 1978; PhD, 1983. Appointments: Phys Tutor, 1977, Rsch Asst, 1978, Adelaide Univ; Postdoct Fell, Univ Alberta, Can, 1983-85; Tchng Fell, Sola Inst, SA, 1985-87; Snr Rsch Fell, Polymer Sci Grp, 1987-92, Rsch Dir, 1993. Honours: SA Educ Schl, 1972-75; William Culross Prize, Adelaide Univ, 1983; George Murray Travel Sch, Adelaide, 1983. Memberships: AAAS; Roy Austl Chem Inst; Chmn, 10th Natl Convention, Polymer Div, 1994; Standing Cttee, Polymer Div, 1994. Hobbies: Bible Study; Basketball; Bushwalking. Address: Polymer Science Group, Ian Wark Research Institute,

University of South Australia, Levels Campus, Mawson Lakes, SA 5095, Australia.

MATSUI Akira, b. 23 May 1948, Fukui, Japan. Paediatrician. m. Tomoko Matsui, 13 Nov 1977, 2 s, 1 d. Education: MD, 1975, DMSc, 1983, Fac of Med, Univ of Tokyo. Appointments: Asst Prof, 1983, Assoc Prof, 1990, Dept of Paediats, Jichi Med Sch, Tochigi, Japan; Prof and Chmn, Dept of Paediats, Inst of Clinl Med, Univ of Tsukuba, 1997. Memberships: Japan Paediat Soc; Japan Soc of Hepatology; Japanese Soc for Paediatric Gastroenterology and Nutr; Treas, Asian and Pan-Pacific Soc for Paediat Gastroenterology and Nutr. Address: Department of Paediatrics, Institute of Clinical Medicine, University of Tsukuba, 1-1-1 Tennodai, Tsukuba, Ibaraki, 305-8575, Japan.

MATSUMURA Kendo, b. 3 Sept 1946, Hofu City, Japan. Marine Biology. m. Kazuko, 13 Oct 1975, 3 s, 1 d. Education: DVM, Yamaguchi Univ, 1970; PhD, Azabu Vet Coll, 1979. Appointments: Rschr, 1976-, Snr Rschr, 1979, Lectr, 1979-, Yamaguchi Univ. Publications: Sev articles in profl jrnls. Honours: Yamaguchi Pref Off, 1991; Chiyoda Fndn, 1993. Memberships: Japan Soc of Vet Sci; Japan Soc of Vet Epideiol. Hobby: Fishing. Address: Yamaguchi Prefectural Research Institute of Health, 2-5-67 Yamaguchi 753-0821, Japan.

MATSUMURA Masanobu, b. 8 June 1939. Engineering Educator. m. 10 May 1970, 2 s. Education: BA, Hiroshima Univ, 1962; MA, Tokyo Inst of Technol, 1964; Dr, Tokyo Inst Technol, 1987. Appointments: Lectr, Hiroshima Univ, 1967-69; Assoc Prof 1969-82, Prof 1982-; Mbr, Dean's Cncl, 1995-96; Dean, 1996-. Publication: Jet-in-Slit Test For Studying Erosion-Corrosion, 1985. Honour: Best Tech Ppr Awd, Japan Soc of Corrosion Engrs, 1989. Memberships: Soc of Chem Engrs, Japan; Japan Soc of Corrosion Engrs; Amn Soc of Testing Materials. Hobby: Yachting. Address: Saijo, Fukumoto 237-101, Higashi-Hiroshima 739, Japan.

MATSUO Toshihiko, b. 21 Mar 1961, Okayama, Japan. Opthalmologist. m. Chie Nakago, 24 Sept 1989. Education: MD, Okayama Univ Medl Sch; PhD, Grad Sch of Okayama Univ. Appointment: Asst Prof, Opthalmology, Okayama Hosp, 1994-. Publications: In intl profl jrnls. Honours: Yuge Awd, Japanese Assn of Strabismus and Amblyopia, 1989; Suda Awd, Japan Soc of Glaucoma, 1996. Memberships: Amn Assn for Advmt of Sci; Assn for Rsch in Vision and Opthalmology. Hobbies: Skiing; Diving; Hiking. Address: Kyoyama 2-3-3-301, Okayama City, 700-0015, Japan.

MATSUOKA Masato, b. 9 May 1958, Kitakyushu, Fukuoka, Japan. Physician; Researcher. m. Education: MD, 1984, PhD, 1988, Univ Occupational and Environtl Hlth, Fukuoka, Japan. Address: Dept of Environmental Toxicology, University of Occupational and Environmental Health, 1-1 Iseigaoka, Yahatanishi-ku, Kitakyushu 807-8555, Japan.

MATSUURA Isao, b. Japan. Politician. Appointments: Mbr, House of Cnclrs; Fmr Chair, House of Cnclrs Cttee on Local Admin; Min of Justice, 1996. Address: Ministry of Justice, 1-1-1 Kasumigaseki, Chiyoda-ku, Tokyo 100, Japan.

MATTHAU Walter, b. 1 Oct 1920, New York, USA. Actor. m. Carol Marcus, 1959, 2 s, 1 d. Education: NY. Creative Works: Stage Appearances in: Anne of a Thousand Days, 1948; The Liar, 1949; Season in the Sun, 1950; Fancy Meeting You Again, 1951; Twilight Walk, 1951; One Bright Day, 1951; In Any Language, 1952; The Grey-Eyed People, 1952; The Ladies of the Corridor, 1953; Will Success Spoil Rock Hunter, 1955; Once More with Feeling, 1958; Once There Was a Russian, 1960; A Shot in the Dark, 1961; My Mother, My Father and Me, 1963; The Odd Couple, 1964. Films incl: The Kentuckian, 1955; Bigger than Life, 1956; A Face in the Crowd, 1957; Slaughter on Tenth Avenue, 1957; Ride a Crooked Trail, 1958; Lonely are the Brave, 1962; Charade, 1963; Fail Safe, 1964; Mirage, 1965; The Fortune Cookie, 1966; A Guide for the Married Man,

1967; The Odd Couple, 1968; The Secret Life of an American Wife, 1968; Candy, 1968; Hello Dolly, 1969; Cactus Flower, 1969; A New Leaf, 1971; Plaza Suite, 1971; Kotch, 1971; Pete 'n Tillie, 1972; Charley Varrick, 1973; The Laughing Policeman, 1973; Earthquake, 1974; The Taking of Pelham One Two Three, 1974; The Front Page, 1975; The Sunshine Boys, 1975; The Bad News Bears, 1976; Casey's Shadow, 1978; House Calls, 1978; California Suite, 1979; Hopscotch, 1980; Little Miss Marker, 1980; First Monday in October, 1980; Buddy Buddy, 1981; I Ought to be in Pictures, 1981; Movers and Shakers, 1984; Pirates, 1986; The Couch Trip, 1987; JFK, 1991; Dennis The Menace, 1993; Grumpy Old Men, 1993; Incident in a Small Town, 1995; IQ, 1995; The Grass Harp, 1995; I'm Not Rappaport, 1996; Grumpier Old Men, Out to Sea, 1997. Honours include: NY Drama Critics Awd, 1951, 1958; Antoinette Perry Awd, 1961, 1964; Acady Awd; Brit Soc of Film & Tv Arts Awd. Address: c/o The Matthau Co, 1999 Avenue of the Stars, Suite 2100, Los Angeles, CA 90067, USA.

MATTHEWS Anthony (Tony), b. 26 Jan 1949, Swansea, S Wales. Author. m. Lensie, 28 Apr 1973. Education: BA(Hons); PhD. Appointments: Lectr, Hervey Bay Campus, Univ of South Queensland, 1989. Publications: 12 books: This Dawning Land, 1986; Crosses, 1987; Beyond the Crossing, 1988; Cry of the Stormbird, 1990; Shadows Dancing, 1993, 1994; River of Dreams, Vol 1, 1995, Vol 2, 1995; A Cleft of Diamonds, 1996; The Coffee Pot Mill, 1997; Landscapes of Change, vols 1 and 2; Letters, Deaths and Dialogue, 1998; TV documentaries incl: This Dawning Land; Black Death; Dark Cargoes; The Mandarins of New Golden Mountain; Centaur; Images and Reflections; Panorama of Progress; The Last of the Bullockies; Over 400 progs for ABC Radio, all brdcst 2x, 1986-90. Memberships: Austl Soc of Auths; Fellshp of Austl Writers. Hobbies: Reading; Writing; Historical research. Address: 32, Marshall Street, Warwick, Queensland 4370, Australia.

MATTHEWS Jill Julius, b. 15 Jan 1949, Adelaide, S Aust. Historian. Education: BA (Hons), 1970, PhD, 1978, Adelaide. Appointments: Dir, Cntr fo Women's Studies, the Facs, ANU; Rdr, Hist Dept, Facs, Austl Natl Univ. Publications: Good and Mad Women, 1984; Sex in Public, (ed), 1997. Address: History Department, The Faculties, Australian National University, Canberra, ACT 0200, Australia.

MATTHEWS Justus, b. 13 Jan 1945, Peoria, IL, USA. University Professor. m. Barbara, 15 Aug 1971, 1 s, 1 d. Education: BA, MA, CSU Northridge; PhD, SUNY, Buffalo, USA. Appointment: Prof, Music Theory & Composition, CSU, Long Beach, USA. Publications: Num musical compositions; Sound designs for theatre. Honours: Num awds for theatrical sound designer. Membership: SESAC (writer affiliate). Address: 245 Harvard Lane, Seal Beach, CA 90740, USA.

MATTINGLEY Christobel Rosemary, b. 26 Oct 1931, Adelaide, South Australia. Writer. m. David, 17 Dec 1953, 2 s, 1 d. Education: BA (Hons), Univ of Tas, 1951; Registration Cert, Assoc, Lib Assoc of Aust, 1971. Appointments: Libn, Dept of Immigration, Canberra, 1951; Regl Libn, Latrobe Valley, 1953; Libn, Prince Alfred Coll, 1966-70; Libn, St Peter's Girls Sch, 1971; Rdr Serv Libn, Murray Park; Libn, Wattle Park Tchrs Coll, 1973-76. Creative Works: 41 Books Publshd; 2 Books Forthcoming. Honours: Christobel Mattingley Awds for Yng Writers; Adv Aust Awd; Hon Doct, Univ of S Aust; AM. Memberships: Pub Lending Right Cttee; Natl Book Cncl; Austl Conserv Fndn; The Wilderness Soc. Hobbies: Nature Observation; Bird Watching; Swimming; Walking; Classical Music; Reading; Gardening. Address: 10 Rosebank Terrace, Stonyfell, South Australia 5066.

MAUNDERS David Edward, b. 31 Mar 1946, Hampton, UK. University Lecturer; Youth Worker. m. Patricia, 21 Feb 1970, 2 d. Education: MA (Cantab); Cert Ed (Nottingham); DipEd Rsch (Surrey); MEd, PhD (La Trobe). Appointments: Yth Worker, 1969-74, Area Yth Offr, Surrey, 1974-77; Lectr in Yth Wrk, Coburg, PIT, 1977-87; Snr Lectr in Yth Affairs (RIT, RMIT), 1987-;

Visng Schl, Univ Brit Columbia Univ, MN, 1993; Moderator, Commonwealth Yth Prog Pacific Region, 1998; Visng Fell, Techn, South Africa, Johannesburg, 1998. Publications: Keeping Them Off the Streets (co-auth), 1989; An Asset to the State (co-auth), 1995; Youth in Australia (co-auth), 1998; Leaving Care. Memberships: ANZMES; AARE. Hobbies: Golf; Cooking; Theatre. Address: 22 Meander Road, Hurstbridge, Victoria, Australia 3099.

MAUNG Kha U, b. Burma. Politician. Appointments: Mbr, Ctrl Exec Cttee, Burma Socl Prog Pty; Min for Ind & Labour, 1973-74, for Ind, 1974-75, for Mines, 1975-77; PM of Burma (now Myanmar), 1977-88; Mbr, State Cncl, 1977-88. Address: Office of the Prime Minister, Yangon, Myanmar.

MAXWELL John Howard, b. 6 July 1920, Wellington, NZ. Retired Company Director. m. Joan Boyes Woods, 6 Jan 1945, 2 s, 2 d. Education: Fell, Austl Inst of Mngmt. Appointments: Mngr, NSW, 1956; Agcy Mngr, Aust, 1957-59; Life Mngr, Aust, 1959-71; Mbr, Austl Bd, Legal & Gen Assurance Soc Ltd, 1969-71; Mngng Dir, 1972-85, Dpty Chmn, 1983-86, Chmn, Aetna Life of Aust & NZ Ltd; Aetna Life & Casualty Ltd, and Subsidiaries, 1986-89. Honour: DFC, 1944. Membership: Fell, Austl Inst of Mngmt. Hobby: Swimming. Address: 2 Ralston Road, Palm Beach, Sydney, NSW 2108, Australia.

MAY Kenneth Spencer (Sir), b. 10 Dec 1914. m. Betty, 26 June 1943, 1 s, 1 d. Appointments: Polit Writer, 1946-59; Asst Mngr, News Ltd, 1959-64; Mngr, 1964-69, Dir, 1969-87, Chmn, 1969-80, Mirror Newsprrs Ltd and Nationwide News Pty Ltd; Dir, Ind Newsprrs Ltd NZ, 1970-84; Mngng Dir, News Ltd (Aust), 1976-80; Dir, The News Corp Ltd, 1979-89; Dir, Santos Ltd, 1980-83; Dir, Advertiser, Newspapers Ltd, 1988-. Honours: CBE, 1976; Knighted, 1980. Address; 26 Waterfall Terrace, Burnside, SA 5066, Australia.

MAYER James Hock, b. 1 Nov 1935, Neptune City, USA. Mediator; Attorney. m. Patrisha, 28 Mar 1981, 2 s. Education: JD, Harvard Univ; AB, Dartmouth Coll. Appointments: Rear Admiral, Supply Corps USNE; Superior Crt Judge; Ptnr, Pillsbury, Madison & Sutro. Publication: Society of Professionals in Dispute Resolution. Honours: Rufus Choate Schl; Deg w Distinction; Def Superior Serv Medal; Legion of Merit. Address: 1328 Sun Valley Road, Solana Beach, CA 92075, USA.

MAZENGARB Peter, b. 20 Jan 1925, Sydney, Aust. Army Officer, Major (retired). m. (1) Margaret, 1947, div, 2 s, (2) Shirley, 1961, 1 s, 1 d. Appointments: Enlisted, Austl Imperial Force, 1942; Served in Aust, Papua New Guinea, 1942-45; Commissioned Regular Army Spec Reserve, 1953; Austl Regular Army, 1960-75; Served in Aust, S Vietnam, Papua New Guinea; Hon State Sec, 1987-90, Pres, 1990-94, Life Mbr, 1994-, Hon Natl VP for Life, 1998-, Returned Servs League of Aust, ACT Br; Mbr, Dept of Veterans Affairs, Med Ethics Cttee, 1993-; Chmn, Commemorative Cttee, Aust Remembers, ACT, 1994-95. Honours: MID, 1968; JP, NSW, ACT; AM, 1995. Memberships: Legacy Club of Canberra; Legacy Club of Sydney; Roy Mil Coll, Duntroon; Golf Club. Listed in: Who's Who in Australia. Address: 16 Beaney Street, Macgregor, ACT 2615, Australia.

MAZID Muhammad Abdul, b. 12 July 1953, Satkhira, Bangladesh. Government Official (Diplomat). m. Selima Mazid, 10 May 1981, 1 s, 2 d. Education: Grad w Hons, English Lit; Postgrad, Univ of Dhaka, 1977; Masters in Pub Fin, 1982; Cert Course, Acctng & Computer, Abingdon Coll of Further Educ, Oxford, Eng, 1986. Appointments: Chief Accts Offr, Min of Fin, 1986-90; Dir, Econ Rels Div, 1990-94; Commercial Cnslr, Emb of Bangladesh, Tokyo, Japan, 1994-. Publications: 5 books on Bengali Lit publ by Bangla Acady, Dhaka, 1989-94; Country Aid Accountability Report. Honours: Best Natl Awd on Essay Writing, 1978; Janabarta Shahitya Awd, 1981; Lit Awd, Kathashilpi Sanistha, 1978. Memberships: Cncl Mbr, Asiatic Soc of Bangladesh, 1991-93; Life Mbr, Bangla Acady; Assoc Mbr, Inst of Training & Dev, Eng,

1986-87; Bangladesh Histl Soc, 1981-. Hobbies: Reading; Sightseeing; Research work. Address: Commercial Counsellor, Bangladesh Embassy, 4-15-15 Meguro, Meguro-ku, Tokyo 153-0063, Japan.

MAZUMDAR Madhusree, b. 7 Sept 1944. Urban Planner. Education: BA, Engl; MA, Geog; PhD, Devel Stdies. Appointments: Lectr, Miranda House, Delhi, Loreto Coll, Lucknow, Bangalore Univ; Snr Rsch Offr, Natl Inst of Urban Affairs, New Delhi. Publications: Rsch and publns on Urban and Regl Plng, and Environment Mgmnt. Honour: Snr Postdoct Fulbright Schlsp. Memberships: Indian Regl Sci Assn; Assn of Brit Schls; Fulbright Alumni; Assn of Indian Geographers. Hobbies: Music; Drama. Address: National Institute of Urban Affairs, India Habitat Centre, Core 4B, First Floor, Lodhi Road, New Delhi 110003, India.

MCBRIDE David Maxwell (Max), b. 15 Dec 1949, Sydney, Aust. Musician; Lecturer in Double Bass. m. Johanna Eltz, 23 Apr 1979, 2 s. Education: NSw Conservatorium of Music, 1965-69; Vienna Musikhochschule, 1975-76, 1978-79; Übertrittsprüfung in Conducting, 1979; Former tchrs incl Prof Frieda Valenzi and Roswitha Heintze (piano); Prof Ludwig Streicher (double bass); Prof Karl Östereriecher and Prof Otmar Suitner (conducting). Career: Double bass w Sydney Symph Orch, 1969; Conductor, ABC, Aust, 1979; Conductor: Sydney Symph Orch, Vic State Orch, Canberra Symph, Queensland Phil; Christchurch Symph Orchs; Conducted Austl premiere of Oratorio, Thamo, King in Egypt, w Sydney Phil Choir; regular guest at Sydney's Mostly Mozart Fest; Twice invited to direct Mozart concerto sect, Sydney Intl Piano Competition; Operatic debut, conducting Don Giovanni, Austl Opera, Brisbane, 1987; Conducted operas inclng: Barber of Seville, Sydney Opera House, 1989; Marriage of Figaro, Vic State Opera, 1991; The Happy Prince, Opera North, Mackay, 1996; Conducts yth orchs in Sydney, Canberra; Currently, Lectr in Double Bass and Conducting, Canberra Sch of Music; Tour, Italy, w Canberra Youth Orch, 1998; Tour USA, 1999. Creative works: Recordings inclng double bass on 1st CD of Brandenburg Orch, 1992; Num w Austl Chmbr Orch and Aust Ensemble. Hobbies: Collecting CDs; Geographyl Languages. Address: 79, Pridham Street, Farrer, ACT 2607, Australia.

MCCALL William David Hair, b. 29 Feb 1940, Yea, Vic, Aust. Anglican Bishop. m. Marion Carmel Le Breton, 15 Aug 1969, 2 s, 3 d. Education: ThL, 1963, SSM, Theol Coll. Appointments: Ordained Deacon, 1963; Ordained Priest, Diocese of Riverina, NSW, 1964; Asst Curate, Griffith, 1963-64; Asst Priest, Broken Hill, 1965-67; Priest-i/c, Barellan-Weethalle, 1967-73; Rector, Corowa, 1973-78; Rector, St George's Goodwood, 1978-87; Pastoral Chaplain, St Barnabas' Theol Coll, 1980-87; Bish of Willochra, 1987-. Hobbies: Reading; Walking; Gardening. Address: Bishop's House, Gladstone, South Australia 5473, Australia.

MCCALLUM John Neil, b. 14 Mar 1918, Brisbane, Aust. Actor; Producer; Manager. m. Georgette Withers, 24 Jan 1948, 1 s, 2 d. Education: Roy Acady of Dramatic Art, London, Eng. Appointments: Actor, Engl Repertory Ths, 1937-39, Stratford on Avon, 1939, Old Vic, 1940; AIF, 1941-45; Ldng Roles, Brit Films, 1946-55; London Ths; Jnt Mngng Dir, JC Williamson Ths, 1958-65; Mngng Dir, 1966; Chmn, 1966-, Fauna Films; Chmn, Mngng Dir, John McCallum Prodns, 1971-; Engl and Austl Th and Films, 1970-. Publication: Life with Googie, 1979. Honours: CBE, 1971; AO, 1993. Memberships: Fndr Pres, Austl Film Cncl, 1971; Pres, Asst Prodrs and Dirs Guild, 1971. Hobbies: Golf; Reading; Writing. Address: 1740 Pittwater Road, Bayview, NSW 2104, Australia.

MCCARDLE Peter M, b. 1955, Te Puke, New Zealand. Government Minister. m. 2 d. Appointments: Cntr Mngr, NZ Employment Serv; Elected to Parl, 1990; Joined NZ 1st Party, 1996; Min of Employment, 1996; Mbr, Select Cttees, Socl Servs, Offrs of Parl and Labour; Min of Bus Dev, Min of Consumer Affairs, Assoc Min of Socl Servs,

Work and Income. Address: Shop 6, City Plaza, Main Street, Upper Hutt, New Zealand.

MCCARTHY Gavan John, b. 17 Sept 1956. Science Archivist. m. Liz James, 23 Apr 1983, 1 s, 1 d. Education: BA (Hons); MA. Appointments: Univ of Melbourne Archives, 1979-85; Austl Sci Archives Proj, Archivist in Charge, 1985-96, Dir, 1996-99; Austl Sci and Technol Heritage Cntr, Univ of Melbourne, Dir, 1999-. Publications: Guide to the Archives of Science in Australia: Records of Individuals, 1992. Memberships: Austl Soc of Archivists Inc, fedl cncl, 1994-; Intl Cncl on Archives Scis, Technol and Med Archives, cttee, 1995-. Hobbies: Music; Gardening; Playing double bass. Address: 5 Camden Road, Hawthron, Victoria 3122, Australia.

MCCARTHY Patrick Francis, b. 1 July 1938, Invercargill, NZ. Journalist. Appointments: Reporter, Southland Daily News, Invercargill, 1958-63; Reporter, Evening Post, Wellington, 1964; Wellington Ed, Zealandia, 1965-68, News Ed, 1969; Reporter, Feature Writer, Ldr Writer, NZ Herald, 1969-75; Freelance Jrnlst, 1975-78; Ed, Humanity, 1978-96, AID, 1980-86, NZ Disabled, 1986-96, NZ Catholic, 1996-. Creative Works: I'd Love Her Back, Though (film, co-auth). Memberships: Hon Life Mbr, Soc for the Protection of the Unborn Child, Auckland; Bd of Mngmt, Zealandia, 1985-90, New Zealandia, 1991-96. Hobby: Wine. Address: PO Box 845, Auckland, New Zealand.

MCCARTHY Thaddeus Pearcey (The Rt Hon Sir), b. 24 Aug 1907, Napier, NZ. Retired President, New Zealand Court of Appeal. m. Joan Margaret Miller, 25 Aug 1938, 1 s, 3 d, 1 dec. Education: LLM, Vic Univ Coll, Wellington, NZ. Appointments: Served, WWII in 22 Infantry BN, later HQ 2 NZ EF; Practised as Bar and Sol until 1956; Jus, Supreme Crt of NZ, 1957; Jus, Crt of Appeal, 1962, Pres, 1973-76, NZ Crt of Appeal; Privy Cncl, 1968-. Publications: Auth of var rprts while Chmn, 7 Roy Cmmns on different functions of Govt in NZ, also Chmn of many NZ Cttees and Orgs. Honours: KB, 1964; KBE, 1974; Hon Bencher, Mid Temple, 1974; Hon LLD, Vic Univ of Wellington, 1978; Fell, NZ Inst of Pub Admin, 1984; ONZ, 1994. Memberships: NZ Law Soc; Judicial Cttee of Privy Cncl; Vice-Patron, NZ Sect, Intl Cmmn of Jus. Hobbies: Golf; Gardening; Sailing. Listed in: Who's Who; Who's Who in New Zealand; Who's Who in the World. Address: 6B Wharenui, Oriental Parade, Wellington, New Zealand.

MCCAUGHAN James Bernard, b. 6 July 1939, Sydney, Australia. Physicist; Educator. m. 10 Dec 1983, 8 s, 2 d. Education: BSc, 1961, MSc, 1962, PhD, 1974, Univ Sydney. Appointments: Tchng Fell, 1961-63, Snr Tutor, Demonstrator, 1965-74, Prin Tutor, 1975-79, Lectr, 1979-86, Snr Lectr, 1987-, Univ of Sydney. Publications: The Messel Era, 1987; Sev articles in profl jrnls and chapts in books. Memberships: Aust Inst of Phys; Am Assn of Phys Tchrs; Asst Dir, Cntr for Human Aspects of Sci and Technol, 1986-91. Hobbies: Architecture; Classical music; Cricket. Address: School of Physics, University of Sydney, Sydney, NSW 2006, Australia.

MCCLEAN Andrew, b. 7 Apr 1961, Melbourne, Aust. Bibliographer; Research Scholar. Education: BA, MA, Univ of Melbourne. Appointments: Rsch Asst, Dept of Hist, Austl Def Force Acady; Peace Rsch Cntr, Austl Natl Univ; Intern, PRIUB, Bonn. Publications: Security, Arms Control and Conflict Reduction in East Asia and the Pacific: A Bibliography, 1993. Memberships: Intl Studies Assn; Asian Studies Assn of Aust; Assn of Asian Studies. Address: School of Australian and International Studies, Deakin University, Geelong, Victoria 3270, Australia.

MCCLINTOCK Eric Paul (Sir), b. 13 Sept 1918, Gulong, Aust. Investment Banker. m. Eva Trayhurn Lawrence, 18 Apr 1942, 2 s, 1 d. Education: Dip, Pub Admin, Sydney Univ. Appointments: Dept of the Navy, 1936-44; Dept of Com, Trade, 1944-62; Exec Dir, Dir, Dpty Chmn, Dev Fin Corp, 1962-87; Dir, Chmn, Var Co's; Chmn, McClintock Assocs; Dir, O'Connell Street Assocs. Honour: KB, 1981. Memberships: Fell, Inst of Dirs; Past

Chmn, Trade Dev Cncl; Pres, Roy Life Saving Soc, NSW; Past Gov, Sydney Inst; Fell, Roy Soc of Arts. Hobbies: Work; Family; Tennis; Music. Address: 2 O'Connell Street, Sydney, NSW 2000, Australia.

MCCOLL Donald H, b. 10 Feb 1939. Mineralogist. m. Lois E McColl, 16 Dec 1961, 2 s, 2 d. Education: BSc, Melbourne; Dip of Gemmology, Aust. Appointments: Mus Curator, Adelaide Univ, 1963-69; Curator of Mineralogy, Bur Mineral Resources, Canberra, 1972-82; Curator of Minerals, Mus of Qld, 1996-98. Publications: Monographs and popular mag articles on Geology, Mineralogy and Meteoritics, 1968-96. Membership: Fell, Austl Inst of Mining, Metallurgy, 1984-94. Hobbies: Gemmology; Meteoritics. Address: PO Box 252, Glenside, South Australia 5065.

McCONKEY Kevin Malcolm, b. 7 Mar 1952. Psychologist. m. Dr J Cranney, 1 s, 1 d. Education: BA (Hons), PhDm Univ of Qld, Aust. Appointments: Lectr, Snr Lectr, Assoc Prof, Psychol, Macquarie Univ, Aust, 1984-92; Prof and Hd, Sch of Psychol, Univ of NSW, Aust, 1993-. Publications: Hypnosis and Experience: The Exploration of Phenomena and Process, 1982; Readings in Australian Psychology, 1991; Australian Psychology: Selected Applications and Initiatives, 1994; Applications and Initiatives, 1994; Hypnosis, Memory and Behaviour in Criminal Investigation, 1995; Truth in Memory, 1998. Honours: Arthur Shapiro Awd, Soc for Clinl and Experimental Hypnosis, 1983; Early Career Awd, Austl Psychol Soc, 1984. Memberships: Fell, Acady of Socl Scis in Aust, 1996- Fell, Austl Psychol Soc, 1988-, Pres, 1993-94; Fell, Amn Psychol Assn, 1987-; Fell, Amn Psychol Soc, 1989-. Hobby: Film. Address: School of Psychology, University of NSW, Sydney, NSW 2052, Australia.

MCCONNELL John Douglas, b. 13 May 1932, Dimboola, Australia. Business Owner. m. 12 Oct 1968, 1 s, 4 d. Education: BA, Univ Melbourne, 1955; PhD, Stanford Univ, 1967. Appointments: Prin Cnslt, SRI Intl, 1967-82, 1986-91; Chmn, Exec Cttee, Sungene Technols Corp, 1986-91; Pres, Owner, Remnant World Inc, 1991-. Honours: Boy Scouts of Am Awd of Merit, 1983; Silver Beaver, 1985; Cmdr, Most Venerable Order of St John of Jerusalem, 1995. Memberships: Life Gov, Roy Vic Inst for the Blind; St Andrew's Soc of San Fran; Roy Scottish Country Dance Soc; Queen's Club, San Fran; Army and Navy Club, WA DC. Hobbies: Scouting; Tennis; Scottish Country Dance; Skiing. Address: 4174 Oak Hill Avenue, Palo Alto, CA 94306, USA.

MCCRORY Paul Robert, b. 11 Apr 1959, Melbourne, Aust. Neurologist; Sports Physician. m. Dr Margaret Bird, 9 Sept 1996, 1 d. Education: MB BS;FRACP; FACSP; FASMF; FRSM. Appointments: Neurologist, Gen Physn, Hyperboric & diving med physn, sports physn. Honours: SMA-Syntax Young Investigator of Yr, 1995; NH+MRC Postgrad Schl, 1995-98. Memberships: Pres, Sports Med Aust, 1993-95; Roy Australasian Coll of Physns, Cnclr, 1995-; Austl Coll of Sports Physns, Crt of Examiners, 1995-. Hobbies: Alpine skiing; Australian football; Mountain climbing. Address: 31 Grosvenor Pole, Blowyn, Victoria, Australia.

MCCULLOUGH Colleen, b. 1 June 1937, Wellington, NSW, Aust. Author. m. Ric Robinson, 1984. Education: Sydney Univ; Inst of Child Hlth; London Univ. Appointments: Neurophysiologist, Sydney, London, Yale Univ Medl Sch, New Haven, CT, USA, 1967-77; Relocated to Norfolk Island, S Pacific, 1980-. Publications: Tim (later filmed), 1974; The Thorn Birds (major best-seller, filmed as TV series loathed by the author), 1977; An Indecent Obsession (later filmed), 1981; Cooking With Colleen McCullough and Jean Easthorpe, 1982; A Creed For The Third Millennium, 1985; The Ladies of Missalonghi, 1987; The First Man in Rome, 1990; The Grass Crown, 1991; Fortune's Favorites, 1993; Caesar's Women, 1996; Caesar, 1997; The Song of Troy, 1998; Roden Cutler, VC (biog), 1998. Honour: DLit hc, Macquarie Univ, Sydney, 1993. Address: PO Box 333, Norfolk Island, Oceania, via Australia.

MCCULLOUGH Colleen, b. 1 June 1937, Wellington, Australia. Author. m. Ric Robinson, 1984. Education: Holy Cross Coll, Woollahra; Sydney Univ; Inst of Child Hlth, London Univ. Appointments: Neurophysiol, Sydney, London, Yale Univ Med Sch. Publications: Novels: Tim, 1974; The Thorn Birds, 1977; An Indecent Obsession, 1981; A Creed for the Third Millennium, 1985; The Ladies of Missalonghi, 1987; The First Man in Rome, 1990; The Grass Crown, 1991; Fortune's Favorites, 1993; Caesar's Women, 1996; Caesar, 1997; The Song of Troy, 1998; Cooking with Colleen McCullough and Jean Easthope. Honour: DLitt, Macquaire Univ. Address: "Out Yenna", Norfolk Island, Oceania, Via Australia.

MCCULLY Murray S, b. 1953, Whangarei, New Zealand. Government Minister. Education: LLB. Appointments: Qualified Bar and Solicitor; Prin, Pub Rels Co; Elected to Parl, 1987; Min of Customs and Assoc Min of Tourism, 1991; Min of Housing, 1993; Caretaker Admnstr, Housing and Customs, Tourism, Local Govt, Civil Def and Sport, Fitness and Leisure, 1996; Min of Tourism and Min of Sport, Fitness and Leisure, Min of Housing, 1996; Min of Housing, Tourism, Sport, Fitness and Leisure, 1997, Min for Accident Rehab and Compensation Insurance. Memberships: Fmr Chmn, Young Nationals; Commns Dir, Natl Party HQ. Address: 85 Beachfront Lane, O Box 35-657, Browns Bay, Auckland, New Zealand.

MCCUSKER Charles Brian Anthony, b. 24 Dec 1919, Stockton-on-Tees, England. Physicist. m. Mary, Apr 1944, 2 s, 1 d. Education: BSc, 1st class hons; MSc; DSc. Appointments: Lectr, Wigan Tech, 1942-46, Univ Liverpool, 1946-48; Asst Prof, Dublin Inst of Adv Studies, 1948-59; Prof, Sydney Univ, 1959-. Publications: Over 110 sci pprs in profl jrls. Honour: Emer Prof, Sydney Univ, 1984. Membership: Roy Irish Acady, 1953. Address: 45/17-25 Spring Street, Bondi Junction, NSW 2022, Australia.

MCDERMOTT David Ian, b. 14 Oct 1954, Darwin, Australia. Engineer. m. Suzanne, 5 Sept 1983, 2 d. Education: Advd Cert of Mngmt; Lic Aircraft Maint Engr. Appointments: Dir; Gen Mngr. Memberships: Austl Inst of Co Dirs. Hobbies: Motor Racing; Scuba Diving. Address: 35 Centenary St, Seaford, Vic 3198, Australia.

MCDERMOTT Francis Thomas, b. 30 Sept 1931, Melbourne, Australia. Medical. m. Mary Sophia, 4 Oct 1961, 2 s, 1 d. Education: MBBS, Melbourne Univ, 1955; FRCS, 1960; FRACS, 1964; FACS, 1970; MD, Monash Univ, 1975. Appointments: Res Med Offr, St Vincents Hosp, Melbourne, 1956-58; Surg Reg, Roy Sussex County Hosp, Brighton, England, 1960-61; Surg Reg, Ipswich and E Suffolk Hosp, England, 1961-63; Snr Lectr, Dept of Surg, Alfred Hosp, Monash Univ, 1967-79; Clin Assoc Prof, 1979-93, Assoc Prof, 1994-96, Hon Assoc Prof, 1997-, Surg, 1980-96, Alfred Hosp, Melbourne. Publications: Clinical Science for Surgeons: Basic Surgical Practice, 1988; Colo-Rectal Surgery, 1983; Num articles in profl jrnls. Honours: Awd, Hunterian Profshp, Roy Coll of Surgs, England, 1978, 1994; AM, 1994. Memberships: Am Assn of Surgs for Trauma; Austl Med Assn; Chair, Vic Road Trauma Cttee, Roy Austl Coll of Surgs, 1982-97; Co-Chair, Consultative Cttee on Road Traffic Fatalities, 1992-; Chmn, Surg Consultative Cncl, Vic, 1997-. Hobbies: Music; Literature; Theatre; Travel. Address: Suite 9, 5th Floor, Medical Centre, 517 St Kilda Road, Melbourne, Victoria 3004, Australia.

MCDONALD Geraldine, b. 31 May 1926. Academic Education and Research Consultant. m. Gordon Russell McDonald, 20 Dec 1948, 1 s, 2 d. Education: BA, Univ of NZ, 1948; BA w Hons, 1967, MA, 1969, PhD, 1976, Vic Univ of Wellington. Appointments: Secnd Sch Tchr, 1946-51; Asst Prin, Wellington Free Kindergarten Tchrs Coll, 1964; Lectr, Wellington Tchrs Coll, 1971-73; NZ Cncl for Educl Rsch, 1974; Asst Dir, 1977-92; Educl and Rsch Cnslt, 1992-; Lectr in Tchr Educ, Vic Univ of Wellington, 1995. Publications: Books and articles on many aspects of educ inclng women in educ and early childhood educ. Honours: J R McKenzie Fellshp, 1970; Queen Elizabeth II Postgrad Fellshp, 1972-73; Fulbright Snr Schl, 1981-82; McKenzie Awd for Rsch in Educ; NZ 1990 Medal; Hon LittD, Vic Univ of Wellington, 1993; Hon Fell, Educl Inst, 1994; Companion, NZ Order of Merit, 1997. Memberships include: Arohata Parole Bd, 1969-71; Advsry Cttee on Maori Educ, 1973-74; Inaugural Pres, 1981, Life Mbr, 1987, NZ Assn for Rsch in Educ; Cncl, Wellington Tchrs Coll, 1982-87; Bd, Stout Rsch Cntr, Vic Univ of Wellington, 1983-93; Educ Review Off Advsry Cncl on Qlty in Educ, 1992-; Tchr Registration Bd, 1993-. Hobbies: Research; Writing; Travel. Address: 50 Highbury Rd, Wellington 6005, New Zealand.

MCDONALD Neil Ewer, b. 12 Nov 1922. Royal Australian Navy Former Deputy Chief of Naval Staff. m. Enid Kellar, 28 Feb 1948, 1 s, 2 d. Education: RAN Coll. Appointments: Served WWII Mediterranean, Pacific & Indian Oceans, Atlantic, North Sea, Navigator, 1945; Fleet Navigating Offr, HMAS, Aust, 1950; Vengeance, 1952-54; Cmdr, 1955; HMAS Sydney, Voyager, Queensborough, 1957-59; Im Command Queensborough, Snr Offr, 1st Frigate Sqdn; Dir, Tactics, Trials and Staff Requirements, Canberra, 1959-61; Captn, 1961; Austl Naval Attache, Jakarta, 1961-63; Dir, Naval Intelligence, Canberra, 1963-65; HMAS Supply, 1966; HMAS Vampire, 10th Destroyer Sqdn, 1967; Dpty Chf, Naval Personnel, 1968; IDC, London, 1969; Chf of Staff to Cmdr Austl Fleet, 1970-72; Cmdng Offr, HMAS, Melbourne, 1972-73; OIC RAN Trials and Assessing Unit, 1973; Dir-Gen, Operations and Plans, Navy Off, 1974-75; Flag Offr, Cmdng East Austl Area, 1975-77; Flag Offr, Cmdng Austl Fleet, 1977-78; Chmn Indl Mobilisation Course, NSW, 1980-83; Mbr, Defence Force, Remuneration Tribunal, 1985-1992. Honour: AO, 1977. Hobbies: Cricket; Golf; Squash; Tennis. Address: 132 Fletcher Street, Woollahra, NSW 2025, Australia.

MCDONALD SMITH Paul, b. 26 Nov 1956, Melbourne, Aust. Artist. Education: Scotch Coll Melbourne Gaining HSC (Hons), 1975; Fine Art (Painting) RMIT, 1976-78; Priv study under guidance of D Cameron, S Ballard, R Rowton and Sir William Dargie CBE, 1973-79; Eurn stdy tours, 1975, 1978-79, 1986, 1991; Camberwell Travel Schlshp, 1986. Career: Curator; Var retrospective exhibns, 1994-96; Num grp exhibns and competitions, 1976-; Self-employed Artist, 1978-; 6 major solo exhibns, Melbourne, 1980, 1982, 1983, 1987, 1990, 1993; Adelaide Fest, 1980; Num Community Arts Appts, 1981-; Many judging appts throughout Vic, 1982-; Tutor, Victorian Artists Soc, 1990-; Cncl Mbr, Vic Artists Soc, 1992-; Var cttees and convenorships; Ed, VAS Publs, 1997-99; Featured guest artist at many exhibns. Publications: Oils - The Medium of the Masters, 1989; Alan Moore (biog catalogue), 1994; Ludmilla Meilerts (biog catalogue), 1994; Eugene Fromentin, 1996, editl contbns, 1997, 1998, 1999, VAS Newsletter. Honours: Over 100 awds for painting incl: Outstndng Achievement Awd, 1998; Sorrento, 1998; Drysdale, 1998; Camberwell Club Awd, 1998; Peninsula Arts Soc, 1998; Mt Eliza Zonta, 1998; Brighton 1998; Ballarat, 1998; Norman Kaye Mem Medallion, 1998; Bright Art Awd, 1999. Memberships: Twenty Melbourne Painters Soc; Bottlebrush Club; Bd Dpty Dirs Gen, IBC; MOIF; Fell, Vic Artists Soc, Pres, 1999; Fell, IBA; Fell, ABIRA (USA); Mbr Roy Art Soc, NSW; Hon Mbr, AAA; CAG; BHAG; Fell, Roy Soc of Arts (London). Hobbies: Music (classical and baroque); Travel. Address: 3 Perry Court, Kew, Vic 3101, Australia.

MCDOUGALL Derek John, b. 1 Nov 1945, Melbourne, Aust. University Lecturer. m. Anne, 31 May 1969, 2 d. Education: BA (Hons), 1967, MA, 1969, DipEd, 1977, Univ of Melbourne; PhD, Duke Univ, 1975. Appointments: Snr Tutor in Pols, Melbourne State Coll, 1974-75; Lectr, Pols, Melbourne St Coll, 1975-82; Lectr, Pols, Melbourne CAE, 1983-88; Lectr, Pols, Inst of Educ, Univ of Melbourne, 1989; Snr Lectr, Inst of Educ, Univ of Melbourne, 1990-91; Snr Lectr, Polit Sci, Univ of Melbourne, 1992-. Publications: Foreign Policies in the Asian-Pacific Region, 1982; Harold D Lasswell and the Study of International Relations, 1984; Soviet-American Relations since the 1940s, 1986, 1989; Australian Foreign Policy, 1987; Studies in International Relations, 1991, 1997; Intl Pols of the New Asia Pacific, 1997; Australian Foreign Relations, 1998. Memberships: Intl Inst for Strategic Studies; Intl Studies Assn; Brit Intl Studies Assn; Austl Inst of Intl Affairs; Australasian Political Studies Assn; Review Ed, Australian Jrnl of Polit Sci. Hobbies: walking; Reading; Theatre. Address: Department of Political Science, University of Melbourne, Parkville, Vic 3052, Australia.

MCDOUGALL Gregory John, b. 14 Jan 1956, Nambour, Queensland, Aust. Inventory Controller and Genealogist. m. Phuong Yen, 26 Jan 1996. Education: Assoc Dip in Local and Applied Hist, Univ of New Eng, Armidale, NSW; Advd Cert of Mngmt, Granville Coll of TAFE, Granville, NSW; Purchasing and Supply Cert, Blacktown Coll of TAFE, Blacktown, NSW. Appointment: JP, State of NSW, 1987. Creative works: Paintings: The Windmill, 1983; Kittens, 1983; The Fruit Platter, 1983. Memberships: Australasian Assn of Genealogists and Record Agts; Soc of Austl Genealogists. Hobbies: Family Trees; Gardening. Address: PO Box 16, Merrylands, NSW 2160, Australia.

MCDOUGALL Trevor John, b. 1 July 1952. Physical Oceanographer. m. Brita Kathryn Hack, 20 May 1978, 1 s, 2 d. Education: BE (Hons), Adelaide Univ, 1974; PhD, Univ of Cambridge, Eng, 1978; Grad Dip Econ, ANU, 1981. Appointments: Queen's Fell, Marine Sci, ANU, 1978; Snr Rsch Sci, CSIRO Div of Oceanography, 1983; Chf Rsch Sci, CSIRO Div of Marine Rsch, 1996. Honours: Frederick White Prize, Austl Acady of Sci, 1988; David Rivett Medal, CSIRO, 1992; Fell, Austl Acady Sci, 1997. Memberships: Sci Steering Grp, World Ocean Circulation Experiment, a part of the World Climate Rsch Prog. Address: 14 Acushla Crt, Sandy Bay, Tas 7005, Australia.

MCDOWELL David Keith, b. 30 Apr 1937, Palmerston North, New Zealand. Diplomat. m. Jan Ingram, 1960, 1 s, 3 d. Education: Vic Univ of Wellington. Appointments: Joined Min of Fgn Affairs, 1959, Hd, UN & African & Md E Divsns, 1973, Dir of External Aid, 1973-76, Hd, Econ Divsn, 1980-81, Specl Asst to Sec-Gen, C'wlth Secr, London; High Commr in Fiji, 1977-80, in India, Nepal & Bangladesh, 1983-85; Asst Sec of Fgn Affairs for Asia, Aust & The Americas, 1981-85; Perm Rep, Mission to UN, 1985-88; Dir-Gen, Dept of Conservation, 1988-89, CEO, Dept of PM & Cabinet, 1989-91; Amb to Japan, 1992-94; Dir-Gen, World Conservation Union, Switz, 1994-. Hobbies: Fishing; Boating; Tennis; Conservation; Gardening; Music. Address: c/o World Conservation Union, Rue Mauverney 28, 1196 Gland, Switzerland.

MCDOWELL Graham H, b. 7 Dec 1944. Deputy Vice Chancellor. m. Mary Elizabeth, 4 Aug 1967, 1 s, 1 d. Education: BAgrSci, Melbourne; PhD, Sydney. Appointments: Rsch Fell, Norway, 1970-71; Rsch Fell, Snr Rsch Fell, 1971-75, Lectr, Snr Lectr, Assoc Prof, 1975-89, Dir, Dairy Rsch Unit, 1979-89, Univ Sydney; Prof, 1989-95, Pro Vice Chan, 1991-95, Dpty Vice Chan, 1995-, La Trobe Univ. Publications: Over 170 sci pprs, reviews and abstracts in the fields of: The Physiology of Milk Production; Factors Affecting Milk Production; Physiology of Growth; Immune Mechanisms in the Mammary Gland and Gut. Honour: Hon Prof, Kunming Medl Coll, Kunming, Yuhnan Prov, China, 1997. Address: La Trobe University, Vic 3083, Australia.

MCELLIGOTT (Daniel) Philip, b. 26 May 1925, Cork, Ireland. Former Honorary National Secretary, National Heart Foundation of Australia; Former National Director, AIIA. m. Beryl Marjorie Porter, 28 Feb 1953, 3 s. Education: Sch of Com, Cork; BA, Austl Natl Univ, Aust. Appointments: RAF, 1943-66; Asst Sec, Dept of the Prime Min and Cabinet, 1970-76; Dpty Offic Sec to the Gov-Gen of Aust, 1976-80; Natl Dir, Austl Inst of Intl Affairs, 1982-88. Honour: MBE, Civil Div, 1980; AM, June 1994. Memberships: Natl Life Mbr, Austl Inst of Intl Affairs; Life Mbr, Natl Heart Fndn (ACT). Hobbies: Astronomy; Reading; International politics. Listed in: Who's Who in Australia; 5000 Personalities of the World; Australian Roll of Honour. Address: PO Box 129, Hawker, Canberra, ACT 2614, Australia.

MCEWAN Andrew Craig, b. 16 May 1942, Christchurch, NZ. Health Physicist. m. Rachel Horne, 8 Sept 1967, 3 s. Education: BS (Hons), Phys; PhD, Medl Phys, Cantab; Dip Hlth Admin. Appointments: Sci, Natl Radiation Lab, 1963; Team Ldr, NRL radiation survey, Christmas Island, Kiribati, 1981; Mbr, S Pacific Sci Mission to Mururoa Atoll, Oct -Nov 1983; Dir, NRL, 1984-; Radiation Protection Advsry Cncl, 1984-; Chmn, Intl Sci Advsry Panel, Repub Marshall Islands, 1989-94; Interagency Advsry Cttee on Extremely Low Frequency Fields, 1989-; Jt Aust-NZ Stands Cttees on radiofrequency radiation exposure limits and radiofrequency radiation measurements (Chmn), 1993-; Natl Coord, IAEA Regl Coop Agreement proj on radiation protection, 1995-; IAEA Advsry Grp, Radiological Conditions of Bikini Atoll, 1995-96; Chmn, Task Grp A, IAEA coord study, Mururoa and Fangataufa atolls, 1996-98; Roy Soc Working Grp on Radiation, 1996-98; Cttee 4, Intl Commn on Radiological Protection, 1997-. Publications: Radiation Protection and Dosimetry in New Zealand: A History of the National Radiation Laboratory, 1983; Ed: Radiation Protection News and Notes, 1988-. Memberships: Australasian Coll of Phys Scientists & Engrs in Med; Fell, Austl Radiation Protection Soc. Hobbies: Farm/Forestry Block; Biblical studies; Church involvement. Address: 24 Ranfurly Street, Christchurch, New Zealand.

MCEWAN Angus, b. 20 July 1937, Alloa, Scot. Marine Scientist. m. Juliana Britten, 1 Aug 1961, div 1983, 2 d. Education: Dip Mech E, (Caulfield), 1957; BE (Melbourne), 1960; MEngSc (Melbourne), 1961; PhD (Cambridge), 1965. Appointments: Chf, CSIRO Div, Oceanography, 1981-95; Snr Sci Advsr, Bur of Melcorology, 1995-; Hd of Austl Deleg to Intergovernmental Oceanographic Commn, 1995-; Chmn, Intergovernmental Cttee, Global Ocean Observing System, 1997-. Honours: Queen Elizabeth Fell, 1969-71; Rossby Fell, 1975. Memberships: Fel Austl Acady Sci, 1984-, Cncl Mbr, 1997-; Fell, Austl Acady Technol Sci & Engrng, 1994-; Chmn, Austl Natl Cttee for Atmospheric and Oceanic Sci, 1997-; Pres, Austl Meteorology and Oceanographic Soc, 1998-. Hobbies: Sailing; Horology; Sketching. Address: c/o Bureau of Meteorology, Box 727 G, Hobart, Tasmania, Australia 7005.

MCEWAN Lena Elizabeth, b. 11 Aug 1927, Adelaide, S Aust, Aust. Plastic Surgeon. Education: MB BS, Univ of Adelaide, 1949; FRCS, Eng, 1954; FRACS, 1958. Appointments: Cnslt Plastic Surg, Queen Vic Mem Hosp, 1959-82; Plastic Surg, Peter MacCullum Cancer Inst, Melbourne, 1964-, Hd of Skin Unit, 1987. Publications: Num articles in medl jrnls. Memberships: AMA; BAPS; AAPS; Lyceum Club. Hobby: Protea Grower. Address: 20 Wimble Street, Parkville, Vic 3052, Australia.

MCFADDEN Phillip Lyle, b. 1 Mar 1950. Research Geophysicist. m. Helen Georgina Cracknell, 26 Aug 1978, 1 s, dec, 1 d. Education: BS, Hons, London, 1st Class, 1970; DPhil, Rhodesia, 1975. Appointments: Dept Phys, Univ of Rhodesia, 1975; Rsch Sch of Earth Scis, Aust Natl Univ, 1981; Aust Geol Survey, 1983; Currently, Chf Rsch Sci, Aust Geol Survey (AGSO). Publications: Book: (Co-auth) Magnetic Field of the Earth: Paleomagnetism, the Core, and the Deep Mantle, 2nd ed, 1996; Over 70 (many invited) in jrnls such as Nature; Science; Journal of Geophysical Research; Geophysics Journal International; Earth and Planetary Science Letters; Physics of the Earth and Planetary Interiors; Encyclopaedia of Solid Earth Geophysics. Honours: Jubilee (Gold) Medal of Geol Soc of S Africa, 1977; Elected Fell of Amn Geophys Union, 1991; Elected a Fell of Aust Acady of Sci, 1996. Memberships: Amn Geophys Union (AGM), 1983-; Austl Soc Exploration Geophysicists, 1986. Hobbies: Swimming; Snorkelling; Scuba diving (Master Instructor); Computing. Listed in: Who's Who in Science and Engineering; Who's Who in the World. Address: 2 Tingha Place, Fisher, Canberra, ACT 2611, Australia.

MCGIBBON Ian Callum, b. 7 Dec 1947, Dannevirke, NZ. Historian. m. (1) Helen Mary Sherriff, 8 July 1972, div 1987, 3 d, (2) Sonia Ochoa, 28 Mar 1998. Education: BA, 1968, BA (Hons) 1969, MA, 1971, LitD, 1994, Vic Univ of Wellington. Appointments: Def Histn, Min of Def, 1971-79; Snr Histn, Histl Branch, Dept Intl Affairs, 1979-; Mngng Ed, NZ Intl Review, 1981-; Assoc Lectr, Hist Dept, Massey Univ, 1990-. Publications: Bluewater Rationale, the Naval Defence of New Zealand 1914-1942, 1981; The Path to Gallipoli, Defending New Zealand 1840-1915, 1991; New Zealand and the Korean War, Volume I: Politics and Diplomacy, Volume II: Combat Operations, 1992, 1996; Undiplomatic Dialogue, Letters Between Carl Berendsen and Alistair McIntosh 1943-52, 1993; Unofficial Channels, Letters between Alister McIntosh and Foss Shanahan, George Laking and Frank Corner 1946-66, 1999; Num articles in intl and NZ jrnls. Honours: ONZM (Offr NZ Order of Merit) servs to histl rsch, 1997. Memberships: NZ Histl Assn; NZ Inst of Intl Affairs, MBr Standing Cttee, 1981-, Hon VP, 1995-. Hobbies: Golf; Cricket; Jogging; Travel. Address: 26 Olivia Crescent, Tawa, Wellington, New Zealand.

MCGILL Albert Ernest Joseph, b. 9 May 1942. Dean; Professor, Food Scientist. m. (2) Margaret Langston. Education: BSc, hons, Chem, Queen's Univ, Belfast, 1965; MSc, Food Sci, Univ of Nottingham, 1968; PhD, Agricl & Food Chem, Queen's Univ, Belfast, 1973; Dip, Adv Studies in Educ, New Univ of Ulster, 1976; MA, Educ, New Univ of Ulster, 1979; DSc, Food Sci, Univ of Pretoria, S Africa, 1991. Appointments: Sci, Shell Rsch Ltd, Kent, England, 1965-69; Rsch Fell, Queen's Univ, Belfast, 1969-72; Lectr, Dept of Food Technol, Loughry Coll, N Ireland, 1972-78; Lectr, Food Studies, Dept of Home Econs, Univ of Surrey, 1978-83 and Dept of Biochem, 1982; Visng Lectr, Dept of Home Econs and Dept of Internal Med, Univ of Stellenbosch, S Africa, 1982; Snr Lectr, Dept of Food Sci, Univ of Pretoria, S Africa, 1983-86; Prof, Dept of Food Sci, 1986, Dir, Cereal Foods Rsch Unit, 1990, Univ of Pretoria; Prof, Hd, Food Dept, Polytech SW, 1991; Hd, Dept of Agricl & Food Studies, Polytech SW, 1993-95; Dir, SW Regl Food Technol Transfer Cntr, 1994; Dean, Prof, Food Sci, Fac of Sci, Vic Univ of Technol, Melbourne, 1995; Dean, Fac of Engrng and Sci, 1997. Publications: Treatment of Egg-Processing Wastewater by Anaerobic Digestion: An Evaluation of a Laboratory-Scale Bioreactor, 1991; Heat-Irradiation Combination Processing as an Effective Method of Producing High Quality, Shelf-Stable, Low-Acid Food Products, 1995; Measurement of the Adulteration of Olive Oils, 1996; Evaluation of Partnerships, Internships and Cooperative Education between Universities and the Food Industry in the UK, South Africa and Australia, 1997. Memberships: Roy Austl Chem Inst; Austl Inst of Food Sci & Technol; Inst of Food Technologists; Inst of Food Sci & Technol (UK); Food & Nutrition Grp, Roy Soc of Hlth; UK Fedn of Food Sci & Technol; S African Cttee, Intl Assn of Cereal Sci & Technol; Am Assn of Cereal Chems; Am Assn for the Adv of Sci. Hobbies: Music; Reading; Calligraphy; Theatre; Cinema. Address: Dean, Faculty of Engineering Science, Victoria University of Technology, PO Box 14428, MCMC, Melbourne, Vic 8001, Australia.

MCGIMPSEY Ronald A, b. 7 June 1944. m. 20 Apr 1974. Education: BS Mngmt Sci; MS Mngmt. Appointments: Grp Controller, Brit Petroleum, 1989-91; Snr VP, BP Aust, 1991-93; Mng Dir, BP Aust, 1994-. Memberships: Aust Inst of Petroleum, Chmn, 1995-; Bus Cncl of Aust. Address: BP Australia, 360 Elizabeth Street, Melbourne, Vic 3191, Australia.

MCGLASHAN Neil Davidson, b. 4 Nov 1929. Academic. m. Helen Stanton, 1 s, 1 d. Education: PhD, 1968, DSc, 1986, Univ of London. Appointments: Cadet-Lt RN, 1947-54; Emer Dist Offr, Kenya, 1956-60; hs Tchr, Luanshya, 1962-65; Lectr in Geog, Univ of Zambia, 1966-69; Lectr, Rdr, Univ of Tas, 1970-96. Publications: Medical Geography (ed), 1972; Geographical Aspects of Health (co-ed), 1983. Honours: Offr, Order of Socl Merit, Belgium, 1976; Fell of the Collegium Ramazzini, Bologna, Italy, 1996. Memberships: IGU Commn for Medl Geog, 1970-88, Sec, 1984-88. Hobbies: Yachting; Scottish Country Dancing. Address: 2 Protea Place, Kingston, Tas 7050, Australia.

MCGOWAN Michael Robert, b. 9 Mar 1957, Tamworth, Australia. Veterinarian; University Lecturer. m. Lynne, 2 May 1987, 4 d. Education: BVSc; MVSc; G Cert Ed; PhD. Appointments: Vet Intern, Res, Univ Saskatchewan, 1981-84; Vet, 1988-90; Lectr, 1990-94; Snr Lectr, Univ Qld, Aust, 1995-. Publications: Auth, Co-auth, 2 books, 28 intl refereed sci pprs, 17 intl conf pprs, 22 natl conf pprs. Honours: Treas, AACV, 1989-91; Corp Team Achievement Awd, Qld Health, 1995; Prize, Austl Coll Vet Scis, 1996; Meritorious Serv Awd, Aust Vet Assn, 1998. Memberships: Canadian Vet Med Assn, 1982; Austl Assn Cattle Vets, 1988-. Hobbies: Bushwalking; Horseriding. Address: University of Queensland, School of Veterinary Science and Animal Protection, Veterinary Science Farm, Puijarra Hills, 4060, Australia.

MCGRATH William Desmond, b. 1936, Minyip, Victoria, Australia. Member of Parliament; Farmer. m. Ivy, 1960, 1 s, 3 d. Appointments: Mbr for Lowan, 1979-92; Mbr for Wimmera, 1992-; Min for Agricl, 1992-96; Min for Police and Emergency Servs, Min for Corrections, 1996-. Address: RMB 5382 A, Horsham, Victoria 3401, Australia.

MCGREGOR John Leonard, b. 22 Mar 1947, Geelong, Australia. Climate Modeller. m. Jill, 13 Aug 1977, 2 d. Education: BSc, Hons, ANU, 1967; PhD, Monash Univ, 1974. Appointments: Tutor, Maths, Monash Univ, 1972; Lectr, Maths, Swinburn, Membourne, 1975; Rsch Sci, ANMRC, 1975; Snr Rsch Sci, CSIRO, 1985. Honour: CSIRO Medal, 1992. Membership: Austl Meteorol Soc. Hobbies: Guitar; Bridge. Address: c/o CSIRO, Atmospheric Research, Station Street, Aspendale, Victoria 3195, Australia.

MCGUIRK Pauline, b. 11 Sept 1965, Dublin, Eire. Geographer. Education: BA(Hons); HDipEd; PhD (Dublin). Appointments: Univ of Wollongong, 1992-93; Univ of Newcastle, 1993-. Publications: Range of articles, Book chapts on urban plng & policy, local govt & urban dev. Memberships: Fell, Inst of Brit Geog; Inst of Austl Geogs; VP, Geog Soc of NSW. Hobby: Music. Address: Department of Geography, University of Newcastle, Callghan, NSW 2308, Australia.

MCHENRY Malcolm Michael, b. 5 Feb 1934, San Fran, CA, USA. Physician. m. Anne. Education: BS, Stanford Univ; MD, Univ of Southern CA. Appointments: Adj Prof, Elec Engrng, CA Coll, Sacramento; Assoc Clin Prof, Med, Univ CA, Davis. Publications: 40 articles in profl med jrnls. Honours: Disting Serv Awd, Amn Heart Assn, 1984; Clin of the Yr, Univ CA, Davis, 1992. Memberships: Amn Coll of Cardiol; Amn Coll of Physns; Roy Soc of Med. Hobbies: Travel; Art collecting. Address: 436 Hopkins Road, Sacramento, CA 95864, USA.

MCINNES Neil Donald, b. 6 Sept 1924, Sydney, NSW, Aust. m. Juliet Turner, Mar 1951, 1 s, 2 d. Education: Sydney Univ, 1942-46. Appointments: Ed, Capital, Calcutta, India, 1951-55; Assoc Ed, Barron's, NY, USA, 1965-78; Dpty Dir, Off of Natl Assessments, 1978-82; First Asst Sec, Policy Co-ord, Dept of Def, 1982-83; Dpty Sec, Dept of PM, Cabinet, 1983-86; Insp-Gen of Intell and Security, 1987-89. Publications: The Western Marxists, 1972; The Communist Parties of Western Europe, 1975; Eurocommunism, 1976; French Politics Today: the Future of the Fifth Republic, 1977. Honour: AM, 1989. Address: 35 Godfrey Street, Campbell. ACT 2612, Australia.

MCINTYRE Arthur Milton, b. 31 Oct 1945. Education: Dip, Art Educ, Sydney, 1996. Appointments: Sydney Art Critic, The Australian, 1977; Lectr, NIDA, Univ of NSW, Sydney, 1979-97; Sydney Art Critic, The Age, Melbourne, 1981-90. Publications: Books: Australian Contemporary Drawing, 1988; Contemporary Australian Collage, 1990; Exhibited numerous Paintings and Drawings at major Pub and Pvte Collections. Honours: ABC C'wlth Art Awd, 1962; 3 Austl Cncl Grants, 1974, 1980, 1987. Memberships: NGA, Canberra; NAVA, Sydney; IBA, Cambridge; WLA, Cambridge. Hobbies: International

Cinema; Afro-American Music. Address: 18 Malvern Avenue, Croydon, NSW 2132, Australia.

MCKAY Kirsten, b. 23 Mar 1973, Castlemaine, Aust. Art Curator. Education: BScAppl, Conservation of Cultural Materials, Univ of Canberra, 1994; Postgrad Dip, Arts Univ of Melbourne, 1995. Appointments: Conservator, State Lib of Vic, 1994; Curator, Castlemaine Art Gall, 1998. Publications: Women Printmakers 1910 to 1940 in the Castlemaine Art Gall Exhibition catalogue , 1995. Honour: Harold Wright Schlshp, Univ of Melbourne. Memberships: Mus Aust (Vic); Austl Inst Conservation Cultural Materials (AICCM). Hobbies: Computer games; Internet; Bushwalking; Reading; Singing. Address: c/o Castlemaine Art Gallery, Castlemaine, Victoria, Australia.

MCKAY Marjory Grieve, b. 23 June 1951, Edinburgh, Scotland. Opera Singer. m. Frederick Charles McKay, 17 July 1981. Education: Roy Manchester Coll of Music, 1969-74; Roy Northern Coll of Music, 1974-75. Appointments: Debut as Esmeralda in Bartered Bride, Scottish Opera, 1980; Concerts and Recitals; Other Scottish Opera Roles: Belleza in L'Egisto and Feklusa in Katya Kabanova; Violetta in La Traviata, Scottish Opera Go Round and Welsh Natl Opera Workshop; Many concerts and recitals, Scotland & N of England; Now living in Sydney, NSW, Aust; Debut in Austl Opera as Gerhilde in Die Walkure, 1985, also Xenia in Boris Godunov, 1986; Debut w WA Opera as Cio Cio San in Madame Butterfly; Created title role in Alan Holly's new opera based on the Austl poetess and auth Dorothea Mackellar's life story. Membership: Music Tchrs Assn of NSW. Hobbies: Dressmaking; Knitting; Picture framing; Bakers clay modelling; Various handicrafts; Gardening; Swimming; Creating rag dolls. Address: 4 Pelican Street, Gladesville, Sydney, NSW 2111, Australia.

MCKECHNIE John Roderick (The Hon Justice), b. 1 Nov 1950, Perth, Western Australia. Judge of the Supreme Court of Western Australia. m. Suzanne Elizabeth McKechnie, 5 children. Education: LLB. Appointments: Bar, Sol, Supreme Court of WA, 1974; Bar, Sol, High Court and Fed Courts, 1977; Queens Cncl, 1989; Dir of Public Prosecutions, 1991-99; Judge of the Supreme Crt of W Aust, 1999-. Publication: Director of Public Prosecutions, Independent and Accountable, 1997. Membership: Austl Inst of Judicial Admin. Hobbies: Music and Yachting. Address: Judge's Chambers, Supreme Court of Western Australia, Barrack Street, Perth 6000, Australia.

MCKERN Reginald (Leo), b. 16 Mar 1920. Actor. m. Jane Holland, 9 Nov 1946, 2 d. Appointments: Num worldwide performances, inclng: Baron Bolligrew, in The Thwarting of B B, Roy Shakespeare Co, Aldwych, 1965; Gov Bligh, in Man Who Shot The Albatross, Melbourne Th Co; Shylock, in The Merchant of Venice, Oxford Playhouse; Unvle Vanya, Inspector in Crime and Punishment, Roy Exchange Th, Manchester; Father, in The Housekeeper, Apollo, 1982; Number One, (play), Anouilh, Queen's, 1983; Hobson's Choice (play), 1996; When We Are Married (play), 1997; 28 films inclng: Ryans Daughter, Help, French Lieutenant's Woman. Publication: Just Resting (memoirs), 1983. Honour: AO, 1983. Memberships: Life Mbr, Order of Aust Assn, 1985; Jersey Preservation Trust; Wildfowl and Wetlands Trust; CPRE; RSPB; Gov, RNLI; WWF. Listed in: Who's Who; Distinguished People of Today; International Who's Who; Handbook of Australia; Dictionary of International Biography. Address: c/o Richard Hatton Ltd, 29 Roehampton Lane, London SW15 5JR, England.

MCKIBBIN Warwick James, b. 21 Apr 1957, Sydney, Aust. Professor of Economics. m. Jennifer, 29 May 1982, 1 s, 2 d. Education: PhD, AM, Harvard; BComm (Hons 1), UNSW. Appointments include: Computer Programmer, 1975-78, Rsch Economist, 1978-87, Hd of Spec Projs, 1987-89, Spec Leave, 1989-91, Reserve Bank of Aust; Rsch Assoc, 1986- V88, Visng Fell, 1989-91, Snr Fell, 1991-93, Brookings Instn; Pres, McKibbin Software Grp Inc (USA), 1990-; Snr Rsch Assoc, Cntr for Intl Econs, Aust, 1990-; Dir, McKibbin Software Grp Pty Ltd (Aust), 1993-; Non-Res Snr Fell, Brookings Instn, USA, 1993-; Prof, Intl Econs, 1993-, Hd, Dept Econs, 1995-, Rsch Sch of Pacific & Asian Studies, Austl Natl Univ; Vsng Schl: Japanese Min of Fin, 1986, US Congressional Budget Off, 1990-91; Adj Prof, Sch of Advd Intl Studies, Johns Hopkins Univ, 1991-93. Publications: (co-auth, books) Global Linkages; Arms Trade and Economic Development. Honours: Univ Medal, UNSW, 1980; Fell, Acady Socl Scis, 1997. Memberships: Amn Econ Assn; Econ Soc of Aust, exec cncl, 1996-. Hobby: Computers. Address: 84 Dominion Circuit, Deakin, ACT 2600, Australia.

MCKIERNAN James Philip, b. 11 Oct 1944, Cavan, Repub of Ireland. Senator. m. (1) 2 s, 1 d, (2) Jackie Watkins, 26 Jan 1985. Education: Tech Sch, England. Appointments: Migrated to Eng, 1961; Apprenticeship as 1st Class Machinist; Migrated to Perth, WA, 1969; Machinist, Fitter, Turner; State Educ Offr, Amalgamated Metal Workers and Shipwrights Union, 1976-85; Austl Labor Party Senator for WA, 1984; Dpty Govt Whip in the Senate, 1987-91; Returning Offr, Fed Parly Labor Party, 1990-96; Temp Chair Cttees Senate, 1993-; JP. Honour: Irish-Aust of the Yr, 1990-91. Memberships: Irish Club of WA, Perth; Canberra Irish Club; Celtic Club. Hobbies: Reading; Listening to classical and folk music; Golf; Gardening. Address: 11/22 Chesterfield Road, Mirabooka, WA 6061, Australia.

MCKIMM-BRESCHKIN Jennifer Lois, b. 21 Mar 1953. Microbiologist; Virologist. m. Alan M Breschkin, 15 July 1978, 2 s. Education: BSc Hons, Monash Univ, 1974; PhD, PA State Univ, USA, 1978. Appointments: Postdoct Fell, Microbio Dept, Melbourne Univ, 1979-81; Postdoct Fell Walter & Eliza Hall Inst of Medl Rsch, 1981-84; Scientist: Therapeutic Goods Admin Labs, Melbourne, 1985-87; Snr Rsch Scientist CSIRO Div of Biomolecular Engrng, 1987-91; Prin Rsch Scientist Biomolecular Rsch Inst, 1991-95; Snr Prin Rsch Sci, 1996-. Publications: Contrb articles in sci jrnls. Honours: Fulbright Fell, 1975-78; Queen Elizabeth II Postdoct Fellshp, 1979-81; Colin Syme Jnr Fell, Walter & Eliza Hall Inst, 1982-84. Membership: Austl Soc for Microbiol (MASM). Hobbies: Classical music; Opera; Gardening; Tennis; Aerobics. Address: Biomolecular Research Institute, 343 Royal Parade, Parkville 3052, Australia.

MCKINLAY Brian John, b. Geelong, Aust. Historian; Lecturer. m. Moira, 3 Jan 1959, 3 s. Education: BA; BEd; DipEd. Appointments: Lectr, Melbourne Tchrs Coll; Dir, Educ Hist Serv, Melbourne. Publications: The First Royal Tour 1967-68, 1970; Documentary History of the Australian Labor Movement, 1989; Sweet and Simple Pleasures, 1994. Memberships: Soc for the Study of Labour Hist; Bd of Cncl of Adult Educ. Hobbies: Music; Gardening; Travel. Address: 2 Deblonay Crescent, Greensborough 3088, Melbourne, Victoria, Australia.

MCKINNON Don, b. New Zealand. Politician. m. (1) 3 s, 1 d, (2) Clare de Love, 1995, 1 s. Appointments: Estate Agent; Farm Mngr; Cnslt; Natl Party MP for Albany, 1978-; Fmr Jnr & Snr Govt Whip, Spokesperson for Hlth, Snr Opposition Whip, 1984-87; Ldr of the House, 1993-96; Min of Fgn Affairs & Trade, of Pacific Island Affairs, of Fgn Affairs, 1991-, for Disarmament & Arms Control, 1996-. Hobbies: Rugby; Cricket; Jogging; Tennis. Address: Ministry of Foreign Affairs & Trade, Private Bag 18901, Wellington, New Zealand.

MCKINNON Don C, b. 1939, London, Eng. Government Minister. (1) 4 children, (2) Clare de Lore, 1995, 1 s. Appointments: Elected to Parl, 1978; Jnr Govt Whip, 1980, Snr Whip, 1982, Dpty Ldr, Natl Party, 1987; Opposition Spokesperson, Hlth and Def, 1987; Dpty Prime Min, 1990-96; Min of Pacific Is Affairs, 1991-98; Ldr of House, 1992-96; Min of For Affairs and Trade, 1990-; Min of Disarmament and Arms Control, 1996-; Min in Charge of War Pensions, 1998-. Honour: Nom, Nobel Peace Prize, 1998. Memberships: Privy Cncl, 1992-; UN Security Cncl, 1993-94.

MCKINNON Malcolm Arthur, b. 10 Sept 1950, Wellington, NZ. Historian. Education: BA, Hons, Vic Univ of Wellington; B Phil, Oxon; PhD, Vic Univ of Wellington. Appoitments: Lectr, Hist, Vic Univ of Wellington, 1979; Visng Fell, Harv Univ, Cntr for Euro Studies, 1982; Snr Lectr, VUW, 1984; Ed, NZ Historial Atlas Proj, 1990; Ed, Millenium Proj, 1999. Creative Works: New Zealand and Japn 150 Yrs; Independence and Foreign Policy; New Zealand Historical Atlas; Immigrants and Citizens. Honours: Harknen Fell, 1982. Address:7 Percival Street, Wellington 6001, New Zealand.

MCLACHLAN Ian Murray, b. 2 Oct 1936, Australia. Politician. m. Janet Lee, 1964, 2 s, 1 d. Education: Collegiate Sch; St Peters, SA; Cambridge Univ, UK. Appointments: Mngng Dir, Nangwarry Pastoral Co Pty Ltd, 1983-90; Dpty Chair, SA Brewing, 1983-90; Dir, Elders IXL Ltd, 1980-90; Mbr, House of Reps (Liberal) for Barker, SA, 1990-; Shadow Min for Infrastructure & Natl Devel, 1993-94, for Environ & Heritage, 1994-95; Min of Def, 1996-. Membership: Pres, Natl Farmers' Fedn, 1984-88. Hobbies: Golf; Photography. Address: Department of Defence, Russell Offices, Canberra, ACT 2600, Australia.

MCLAY James Kenneth, b. 21 Feb 1945, Auckland, New Zealand. Director; Consultant. m. Marcy, 17 Dec 1983, 1 s. Education: LLB, Univ Auckland; EMP, PA Univ. Appointments: Barrister, 1968; MP, 1975-87; Atty Gen, Min of Justice, 1978-84; Dpty PM, 1984; Ldr of Opposition, 1984-88; Cnslt, 1987-; Chair, Macquarie NZ Ltd, 1994-; Facilitator, Bldg Ind Authy review of law relating to earthquakes and bldgs, 1997; Chair, Roading Advsry Grp, 1997-. Honours: Queen's Serv Order, 1987; Suffrage Medal, 1993. Hobby: Fishing. Address: Box 8885, Auckland 1, New Zealand.

MCLEAN Mervyn Evan, b. 17 June 1930, Invercargill, NZ. Retired Ethnomusicologist. m. Patricia Anne Taylor, 15 Feb 1964, 1 s, 1 d. Education: BA, Univ NZ, 1957; MA, 1959, PhD, 1965, Univ of Otago. Appointments: Rsch Fell, Snr Rsch Fell, Snr Lectr, 1968-74, Fndr, Hd, Archive of Maori and Pacific Music, 1970-92, Assoc Prof of Ethnomusicol, 1975-92, Univ of Auckland; Visng Asst Prof, Univ IN, USA, 1967, Univ HI, 1968. Publications: Traditional Songs of the Maori (w Margaret Orbell), 1975; Oceanic Entries in New Grove Dictionary of Musical Instruments, 1984; Tikopia Songs (w Raymond Firth), 1990; Diffusion of Musical Instruments...in New Guinea, 1994; An annotated Bibliography of Oceanic Music and Dance, revised and enlarged, 2nd ed, 1995; Maori Music, 1996; More than 100 other publns on Maori and Pacific Music. Honours: Winner (w Margaret Orbell), non-fiction sect, Inaugural NZ Book Awds, 1975; Elsdon Best Mem Awd, 1978; Harold White Fell, Austl Natl Lib, 1986. Hobbies: Music; Computing. Address: 17 Vienna Place, Birkenhead, Auckland 1310, New Zealand.

MCLELLAND Malcolm Herbert, b. 5 July 1937, Sydney, Aust. Retired Judge, Supreme Court of New South Wales. m. Margaret Roslyn Newell, 8 Jan 1965, 3 d. Education: BA, 1958, LLB, 1961, Univ of Sydney. Appointments: Solicitor, NSW, 1961; Bar, NSW, 1963, WA, QC, NSW, 1974, ACT, 1975, Northern Territory, 1975, Vic, WA, Northern Territory, 1976; Judge, Supreme Crt of NSW, 1979-97; Chf Judge in Equity, Supreme Crt of NSW, 1993-97. Memberships: Mbr Bar Cncl, 1967-72; NSW Bar Assn, Hon Sec, 1970-72. Hobbies: Music; Metaphysics; Windsurfing; Tennis. Address: 37 Mahratta Avenue, Wahroonga, NSW 2076, Australia.

MCLEOD James Graham, b. 18 Jan 1932, Sydney, Aust. Medical. m. Robyn Edith Rule, 13 Jan 1962, 2 s, 2 d. Education: BSc, Univ of Sydney, 1953; DPhil, Oxon, 1956; MB BS, 1959, DSc, 1997, Univ Sydney; Hon DUniv, Aix Marseilles, 1992. Appointments: Visng Physn, Roy Prince Alfred Hosp of Sydney, 1965-98; Snr Lectr, 1967-70, Assoc Prof, 1970-72, Bosch Prof of Med, 1972-97, Bushell Prof of Neurology, 1978-97, Univ of Sydney; Hd, Dept of Neur, Roy Prince Alfred Hosp, 1978-94. Publications: A Physiological Approach to Clinical Neurology, 1981; Introductory Neurology, 1983; Peripheral Neuropathy in Childhood, 1990; Inflammatory Neuropathy, 1991. Honours: Rhodes Schlshp, 1953; AO, 1986; Hon Dr Univ of Aix-Marseille. Memberships: Fell, Roy Austl Coll of Physns, 1971; Fell, Roy Coll of Physns,

1977; Fell, Austl Acady of Sci, 1981; Fell, Austl Acady of Technol Scis, 1986; Pres, Austl Assn of Neurologists. Address: Department of Medicine, University of Sydney, NSW 2006, Australia.

MCMICHAEL Donald Fred, b. 28 Jan 1932, Qld, Aust. Environment and Heritage Consultant. m. Helen Craighead, 16 May 1953, 2 d. Education: BS, Hons, Univ of Sydney, 1948-51; MA, PhD, Harv Univ, USA, 1953-55. Appointments: Curator Molluscs, 1952-67; Dpty Dir, 1966-67, Austl Mus, Sydney; Dir, Austl Conserv Fndn, 1967-68; Natl Pks and Wildlife Serv of NSW, 1969-72; Sec, Dept of Environment, 1975-78; Actng Chmn, Gt Barrier Reef Marine Pk Authy, 1976-78; Sec, Dept of Home Affairs and Environment, 1978-84; Dir, Natl Mus of Aust, 1984-89; Chmn, Taxation Incentives for the Arts Scheme Advsry Cttee, 1990-92; Biol Diversity Advsry Cttee, 1991-92; Univ Mus and Collects Review Cttee, 1995-96. Publications include: Sev books; Num sci articles. Honours: CBE, 1981; Fulbright Schl, 1953; Fell, Harv Univ, USA, 1954-55; Yale Univ Bish Mus Fellshp, 1956-7; Nuffield Fndn Roy Soc C'wlth Bursary, 1961-62; Mbr, Global 500, 1989; Mbr, Administrative Appeals Tribunal, ACT, 1996-. Memberships: Worldwide Fund for Nat, Aust; Environment Inst of Aust; Mus Aust; Exec Cncl, Intl Cncl of Mus, 1992-95; Pres, Yachting Assn of the ACT, 1994-98. Hobbies: Sailing; Bridge; Theatre. Address: 244 La Perouse Street, Red Hill, ACT 2603, Australia.

MCMICHAEL Melvin Eugene, b. 14 Aug 1929, OH, USA. Company Chairman and Managing Director. Norma Louise, 1960, 2 s, 1 d. Education: BA, Hiram Coll, 1955; MBA, Univ Chgo, 1956; PhD, Univ TX, 1961. Appointments: Dir, Intl Bus Cntr, Univ of the Ams, Mexico City, 1961-70; Pres, Latin Am Productivity Assocs, 1963-70; Fndn Dean, Fac of Bus, Univ of Technol, Sydney, Aust, 1971-78; Prof of Mngmt, CA Univ, San Luis Obispo, 1978-84; Dpty Vice Chan, Charles Stuart Univ, Prin, Charles Stuart Univ-Mitchell, 1984-90. Publications include: The Dynamics of International Business Management, 1981; The Entrepreneurship Challenge; Num articles in profl jrnls. Honours: Fell, Univ Chgo; Sigma Iota Epsilon, Hon Mngmt Frat. Memberships include: Acady of Intl Mngmt; Acady of Mngmt; Roy Inst of Pub Admin; Soc for Long-Range Planning; Am Inst of Indl Engrs. Listed in: Who's Who in the West; International Leaders of Achievement; 5,000 Personalities of the World; Debretts Handbook of Australia; Men of Achievement; Who's Who in Australasia and The Far East; Who's Who in Australia. Hobbies: Barbershop Quartet Singing; Water Skiing; Swimming; Hiking; International Business Research. Address: 16 Booral Street, Buderim, Queensland 4556, Australia.

MCMILLAN Stuart William, b. 7 Mar 1933, Dunedin, NZ. Journalist and Academic. m. Nancy Rouse, 26 July 1960, 1 s, 3 d. Education: BA, Engl & Philos. NZ reporter, 1959-61, Cable sub-ed, 1961-76, ldr writer and sec on for affairs, 1976-97, The Press, Christchurch; Visng Schl, Lincoln Univ, Canterbury, NZ, 1997-. Publications: Neither Confirm or Deny: The nuclear ships dispute between New Zealand and the United States, 1987; Other pprs on intl & security affairs. Honours: Anzac Fellshp, 1976; MBE, 1987; PACDAC Fell, 1993. Memberships: Pres, Christchurch branch of NZ Inst of Intl Affairs, 1993-; Intl Inst for Strategic Studies; Natl Cttee of Cncl for Security Co-op in Asia Pacific; Pub Advsry Cttee on Disarmament and Arms Control. Address: 5 Stambridge Place, Cashmere, Christchurch 2, New Zealand.

MCMULLIN Duncan Wallace (Rt Hon Sir), b. 1 May 1927, Auckland, NZ. Retired Court of Appeal Judge. m. Isobel Margaret McMullin, 12 Mar 1955, 2 s, 2 d. Education: LLB, Univ of NZ; Admitted as Bar and Solicitor, Supreme Crt, NZ, 1950. Appointments: Bar, Solicitor, 1950-65; Bar, Sole, 1965-70; Judge, Supreme Crt of NZ, 1970-79; Judge, Crt of Appeal of NZ, 1979-89; Privy Cnslr, 1980; Chmn, Roy Commn on Contraception, Sterilisation and Abortion, 1975-77; Chmn, Wanganui Computer Ctr Policy Cttee, 1989-92; Chmn, Market Suveillance Panel of NZ Electricity Mktng, 1994-; Chmn, NZ Conservation Authy, 1996-; Judge, Crt of Appeal, FIST, Crt of Appeal, Cook Is. Honours: Jubilee Medal; NZ Commemoration Medal; KB, 1987. Memberships: Fell, Arbitrators' Inst of NZ Inc. Hobbies: Conservation; Forestry; Farming. Address: 707 Remuera Road, Auckland, New Zealand.

MCNAUGHTON Neil, b. 16 Apr 1947, Stockport, Eng. Psychologist; Neuroscientist. m. Julia Clare, 30 July 1971, 1 s, 1 d. Education: BA, Oxon; MA, Oxon; PhD, Southampton. Appointments: Demonstrator, 1970-73; Rsch Assoc, 1973-78; Roy Soc C'wlth Bursar, 1978-79; Rsch Assoc, 1979-82; Tutor, 1979-82; Assessor, 1980-81; Lect Course, 1981; Lectr, 1982-84; Snr Lectr, 1985-93; Assoc Prof, Dept of Psychol, Univ of Otago, 1994-. Creative Works: Biology and Emotion, 1989; Anxiety, 1990; Anxiety, 1995-96; The Neuropsychology of Anxiety, forthcoming, 2nd edition; Var book chapts; Jrnl Articles. Honours: Roy Soc C'wlth Bursar, 1978; Sir Thomas Hunter Awd, 1988; Fellshp, NZ Psycol Soc. Memberships include: Brit Neurosci Assn; Eurn Neurosci Assn; Intl Brain Rsch Org; NZ Jrnl of Psychol; Otago Pharm Assn; Roy Soc of NZ; Soc for Neurosci. Address: Dept of Psychology, University of Otago, POB 56, Dunedin, New Zealand.

MCPARLAND Stephen John, b. 15 Nov 1951, Sydney, Australia. Author. m. Margaret, 5 Jan 1974, 2 d. Appointments: California Music, ed; Beach Boys Australia, ed. Publications: Beach Street & Strip, 1983; It's Party Time, 1992; Illustrated Discography of Hot Rod Music, 1990; The Wilson Project, 1991; Brian Wilson Tape 10, 1993. Hobbies: Surfing; Esoterica. Address: 2 Kentwell Avenue, Concord, NSW 2137, Australia.

MCPHEE David Ross, b. 6 Apr 1930, Lansing, MI, USA. Bookseller (retired). m. Ute Bartholemy, 31 Oct 1963, 1 s, 1 d. Education: Barker Coll, 1946. Appointments: Mngr, Antiquarian Dept, Angus & Robertson; Mngr, Swains Book Dept; Mngr, Henry Lawson's Australiana Bookshop. Publications: Some Common Snakes and Lizards of Australia, 1959, 1963; Observer's Book of Snakes and Lizards of Australia, 1979; Contbns to jrnls. Memberships: Sci Mbr, Roy Zool Soc of NSW. Hobbies: Natural history; Bushwalking; Reading; Gardening. Address: 64 Catherine Street, St Ives, New South Wales 2075, Australia.

MCPHEE Ian Bruce, b. 4 August 1942, Brisbane, Aust. Orthopaedic Surgeon. m. Roslyn, 1968, 3 s. Education: MB, Univ of Qld, 1967; BS, 1967; FRACS, 1973. Appointments: Dir, Orth Surg, Roy Brisbane Hosp, 1975-82; Visng Orth Surg, Roy Brisbane Hosp, 1983-; Assoc Prof, Dept of Orth Surg, Univ of Qld, 1990-. Publications: Sev articles and book chapts on Spinal Surg. Honours: Sir George Bedbrook Oration, 1999. Memberships: Roy Austl Coll of Surgs; Austl Orth Assoc; Spine Soc, Austl; Scoliosis Rsch Soc. Address: Ladhope, 131 Wickham Ter, Brisbane, Qld 4000, Australia.

MEARES Russel Ainslie, b. 24 May 1936, Melbourne, Aust. Professor of Psychiatry. m. Susanne Hicks, 29 Apr 1990. Education: MBBS, MD, Melbourne; Acad DPM, London; FRCPsych; FRANZCP. Appointments: RMO, Alfred Hosp, Melbourne, 1961-62; Regr, Maudsley and Bethlem Roy Hosp London, 1963-68; Snr Hon Psych and Hd, Psych Staff and Servs Austin Hosp, 1969; 1st Asst, Depts Psych and Med, Univ of Melbourne, 1969; Rdr in Psych, Austin Hosp, 1975; Chmn, Dept Psych, Univ Melbourne, 1977; Dir, Psych, Westmead Hosp, 1981-; Clin Prof, Univ Sydney, 1981; Prof, Univ of Sydney, 1985; BD, Intl Fedn Medl Psychotherpay, 1985; Fndn Pres, Aust and NZ Assn Psychotherapy, 1989; Visng Prof, Harv Univ, 1989. Publications: The Pursuit of Intimacy: An Approach to Psychotherapy, 1977; Night of No Home, 1990; The Metaphor of Play, 1992; Intimacy of Alienation, forthcoming. Hobbies: Poetry; Boating; Skiing. Address: Department of Psychiatry, Westmead Hospital, Westmead NSW 2145, Australia.

MEASHAM Terence Leonard, b. 30 Dec 1939, Leicestershire, Eng. Museum Director. m. 3 Sept 1966, 3 s. Education: Leicester Coll of Art, 1960-64, Natl Dip of Des, 1964; London Univ, Courtauld Inst of Art, 1964-67, BA, hons, Hist of Art, 1967. Appointments: Asst Keeper, The Tate Gall, 1971-80; Snr Curator, Austl Natl Gall, 1980-88; Dir, Mus of Applied Arts and Scis, Sydney (Powerhouse Mus), 1988-; Chmn, Cncl of Austl Mus Dirs, 1995. Publications: Books: John Latham, 1976; The Moderns 1945-75, 1976; Looking at Paintings (w Frances Kennet), 1978; Van Gogh and His World, 1980; Picasso and His World, 1980; Treasures of the Powerhouse Museum, 1994; Discovering the Powerhouse Museum, 1997. Honours: Dorrance Visng Prof of Fine Art, Trinity Coll, Hartford, CT, USA, 1971; Hon MA, Open Univ, Eng, 1981; FRSA, 1998; AM, 1999. Memberships: Austl Heritage Collections Cncl, 1997; Austl Cultural Heritage Cttee, 1998. Address: Museum of Applied Arts and Sciences, PO Box K346, Haymarket, New South Wales 1238, Australia.

MEDCALF Ian George (Hon), b. 12 July 1918, WA, Aust. Barrister; Solicitor; Notary Public; Queens Counsel. m. Winifred Maxine Love, 13 Apr 1944, 1 s, 2 d. Education: LLB, Univ WA, 1941. Appointments: Ptnr, Robinson Cox Bars and Solicitors, 1950-75; Elected to Legislative Cncl, 1968; Appointed Hon Min, 1975; Atty Gen, Min for Fed Affairs, 1975-83; Min for Police, 1982-83; Ldr Govt in Legislative Cncl, 1980-83; Ldr of Opposition, 1983-84; Former Dir, Pub Cos, incl Perpetual Tstees Ltd, Elder Smith Goldsbrough Mort Ltd; Chmn, Colonial Mutual Life Assurance Soc Ltd; Retd, 1986; Pres, Natl Trust of Aust (WA), 1987-93. Publications: Ed, Cntbr, num mags and jrnls; Delivered address to 5th C'wlth Law Conf, Edinburgh, Scotland, 1977. Honours: ED, 1961; AO, 1992. Memberships include: Law Soc of WA; Bars Bd of WA; Perth Legacy; Fndn Mbr, 1st Dpty Chmn, Chmn, VP, Natl Trust of Aust, WA, Pres, 1987-93; Life Mbrshp, Returned and Servs League of Aust, 1997; Elected Life Mbr, Law Soc of WA, 1998. Hobbies: Heritage History; Gardening; Farming. Listed in: Who's Who in Australia; Dictionary of International Biography; Australian Roll of Honour; Debrett's Handbook of Australia and New Zealand. Address: 42 Gallop Road, Nedlands, WA 6009, Australia.

MEDNIS Karlis, b. 1 Apr 1910. Artist. m. Taissa von Demidoff, 11 June 1969. Education: Univ of Riga, Latvia; Riga Sch of Art. Appointments: Rep in Perm Collections, Natl Collection, Canberra; Univs Melbourne, Monash, La Trobe, Cambridge (UK), TAA, ICI, SEC, Melbourne Club, Repco, Civic Cntr, Camberwell & State Galleries in Aust; Fndr Mbr, Tchr, VAS Sch of Art, 1958-72; VAS Cncl Mbr,, 1960-; Judge, Vic Artists Soc, 1962, 1968, 1972, 1982; Commissioned to Roy Austl Armored Corps to paint presentation of the Standard by the Price of Wales, 1981. Honours: ET Cato Prize, 1950, 1967; Latvian Art Fest Prize, Aust, 1958, 1960, 1961; VAS Artist of the Yr, 1979; Gold Medal, Art Acady of Italy, 1980; Kiwanis Club of Keilor Prize, 1981, 1982; Dip of Merit, Univ of Arts, 1982. Hobbies: Classical Music; Reading; Exploring Australian Outback; Fossicking Opals, Rocks and Minerals. Address: 16 Rockwood Street, North Balwyn, Vic 3104, Australia.

MEDY Loekito, b. 21 July 1962, Surabaya, Indonesia. Poetess. m. Asmian, 22 Dec 1985, 1 s, 1 d. Education: Bachelor degree. Publications: In Soliotude, 1993; Troatoar, 1996; Jakarta, Jangan Lagi, 1996; Antologi Puisi Indonesia, 1997. Memberships: Organisasi Pembina Seni, 1993; Komunitas Sastra Indonesia, 1996. Hobbies: Reading; Travelling; Cultural. Address: Jl Pulo Asem Utara XII No 27, Jati, Jakarta Timur 13220, Indonesia.

MEECHAM William Coryell, b. Detroit, MI, USA. Engineering Educator. m. (1) Barbara Jane Brown, 4 Sept 1948, dec 1965, 1 s, 1 d, (2) Della Fern Carson, 11 Sept 1965. Education: BS, Univ of MI, 1948; MS, 1948; PhD, Phys, 1954. Appointments: Hd, Acoustics Lab, Willow Run Labs, An Arbor MI, 1959-60; Asst Prof, Univ MI, Ann Arbor, 1958-60; Prof, Univ MN, Mnpls, 1960-67; Prof, Fluid Mechs and Acoustics, UCLA, 1967-;. Chmn, Dept of Mechs and Structures, 1972-73; Cnslt, Aerospace Corp, El Segundo, CA, 1975-80, Rand Corp, Santa Monica, CA, 1964-74, Bolt, Beranek and Newman,

Cambridge, MA, 1968-73, Arete Assocs, Encino, CA, 1976-, CRT Cort, Chatsworth, CA, 1985-. Publications: Co-auth, Lasar Systems, 1973; Over 120 pprs on fluid mechs and acoustics. Honours: MI Alumni Schl, 1942-44; Donovan Schl, Univ of MI, 1944-45; UCLA Senate Rsch Grantee, 1968-78; NASA Rsch Grantee, 1971-; Off Naval Rsch Grantee, 1977-; Recip, Disting Serv Awd. Memberships: CA Space and Def Cncl; Fell, Acoustical Soc Am; Assoc Fell, AIAA; Amn Phys Soc, Fluid Dynamics Div; Inst Noise Control Engrng; Sigma Xi; Tau Beta Pi. Address: 927 Glenhaven Drive, Pacific Palisades, CA 90272, USA.

MEHDIZADEH Parviz, b. 15 Sept 1934, Tehran, Iran. Executive. m. Manijeh, 12 Sept 1962, 2 s, 1 d. Education: PhD; MSc; BSc. Appointments: Dist Mngr, Amn Family Life Assurance Co, 1981; Point Intl Corp, 1986; Pres, Active Universal Corp, 1990. Honours: Medal of Merit, 1984; Paul Harris Fellow, 1989. Memberships: Rsch Inst of Natural Rescs, Tehran, 1968; Rancho Park Rotary Club; Resolution Commn; US Senatorial Club. Hobbies: Tennis; Golf. Address: 9301 Wilshire Blvd, #508, Beverley Hills, CA 90210, USA.

MEHER-HOMJI Vispy Minocher, b. 18 Jan 1932, Mumbai, India. Ecologist. m. Kashmira, 9 Dec 1965, 1 s, 2 d. Education: BSc, hons; MSc; PhD; DSc. Appointments: Rsch Assoc, Inst of Sci, Mumbai, 1955-56; Rsch Asst, French Inst, 1956-57; Dir of Rsch, French Inst, Pondicherry, 1991-97; Hon Dean, Sch of Ecol, Pondicherry Univ, 1987-90. Publications: Forest Ecology, vol 1, 1984, vol 2, 1989, vol 3, 1999; Plant Geography of Peninsular India, 1999. Honours: Eduljee Dinshaw "D" Schlsp, Bombay Univ, 1958-61; Pitambar Pant Natl Environ Fellshp, 1991-92; Swami Pranavananda Awd, Univ Grants Cmmn, 1996. Hobbies: Photography; Gardening. Address: 20-D Sagar Sangeet, 58 Colaba Road, Mumbai 400 005, India.

MEHTA Anilkumar, b. 3 Mar 1941. Publisher. m. 3 Mar 1941. m. Anjali Mehata, 26 Feb 1963, 1 s, 1 d. Education: Bach of Commerce. Appointments: Pres, Marathi Prakashak Parishad, Pune; VP, Fedn of Indian Publrs, Delhi. Honour: Disting Publrs Awd; Memberships: Prakashak Parishad; Fedn of Indian Publrs. Hobby: Reading. Address: 1216 Sadashiv Peth, Pune 411 030, India.

MEHTA Surendra Nath, b. 12 Nov 1931. Librarian. m. Suman Mehta, 27 Nov 1960, 1 s, 1 d. Education: BSc 1953; Dip, Lib Sci, 1957; Ctf, French, 1959; Ctf, German, 1960; Ctf, Bulgarian, 1976; Advd Dip, Russian, 1967; Dip, Serbo-Croatian, 1968; Magistar, Yugoslavia, 1972; Pt III, Croatia-Serbian, 1972. Appointments: Jnr Sci Offr, 1963-72; Snr Sci Offr, 1972-80; Dpty Dir, 1980-85; Jnt Dir (Scientiste), 1985-91; Lib Cnslt, 1992-. Publications: 83 pprs in var jrnls and books, 1964-95; Conf pprs for Natl Conf on Sci Info for Def, 1986; Union Catalogue of Patents in DRDOLABS/ESTTS, 1987; Union Catalogue of Aerospace Periodicals, 1988. Honours: Schlshp for specialization in Croatia-Serbian, Govt of Yugoslavia, 1969-72; Alternate Mbr, EC2:9, Indian Standard Instn, 1967-68; Mbr of Documentation Serv Advsry Cttee, INSDOC, 1974-80; Editl Bd Mbr, Informatologia Yugoslavica, 1981-; Chair, IFLA Subcttee on Confs and Seminars, 1992. Publications: Union Catalogue of Periodicals Held in DRDO Libraries in India, 1987; Index of Publications of DESIDOC Scientists, 1987. Memberships: Life, UP Lib Assn; Indian Assn of Spec Libs and Info Cntrs; Indian Lib Assn; Assn of Govt Libs and Info Specialists; Exec Cncl, 1963-67, 1975-77, 1990-92, Asst Sec, 1967-69, Sec 1987-90, Govt of India Lib Assn; Editl Bd, AGLISFOCUS, New Delhi, 1987-90; Editl Bd, DESIDOC Bulletin, 1987-90; Advsry Grp for Documentation and Info Servs Cntrl Road Rsch Inst, New Delhi, 1989-92; Exec Cncl of Soc for Info Sci, New Delhi, 1991-92; Editl Bd, SISCOM, New Delhi, 1991-92. Hobbies: Photography; Indian music; Western music; Travel. Listed in: Directory of the Delhi Library Association; Leaders in Library Science; Reference India; Reference Asia. Address: Sanjay Villa, B149, Sector 36, Noida 201303, UP, India.

MEHTA Vrajendra Raj, b. 19 Aug 1944, Jodhpur. Vice-Chancellor. m. Snehlata, 2 s. Education: Univ of Delhi; Univ of Cambridge (UK). Appointments include: Lectr, Pol Sc, Delhi; Assoc Prof, Himachal Pradesh Univ; Prof, Himachal Pradesh, 1973-; Dean, Fac of Arts & Socl Scis, Mbr, Exec Cncl, Himachal Pradesh Univ; Prof, Dept of Pol Sc, Rajasthan Univ, Jaipur, 1978-; Hd, Dept of Pol Sc, Coord, UGC sponsored Prog in Pol Sc, Rajasthan Univ, Hon Dir, Cntr of Gandhian Studies, Univ of Rajasthan; Dir, Inst of Corresp Studies, Univ of Rajasthan, Jaipur (for 1 yr); Chf Warden in the Univ for 2 yrs; 1st Vice-Chan Kota Open Univ, 1987-90; Vice-Chan, Jodhpur Univ, 1991-93. Publications: 5 books inclng: beyond Marxism: Towards an Alternative Perspective, 1978; Ideology, Modernisation and Politics in India, 1983; Foundations of Indian Political Thought, 1993. Honours include: VKRV Rao Awd, 1983; Swami Pravanandra Awd, Univ Grants Commn of India, 1989; Nahar Samman Puruskar, Rajasthan Welfare Assn, 1990; Rajiv Gandhi Sadbhavana Awd, Indian Solidarity Cncl, 1995; Rajiv Gandhi Excellence Awd, Shromani Inst; Super Achievers of India Front of Natl Prog, 1995; Rajiv Gandhi Natl Unity Awd for Excellence, all India Unity Conf, 1996; Bharat Vikas Excellence Awd, Cncl for Natl Dev, New Delhi, 1996; Shromani Awd, 1996; Dr Ambedkar Distinguished Servs Awd, Bhartiya Dalit Sahitya Acady; Intl Man of Yr, IBC, 1996-97; Man of Yr, ABI, 1997; Awd of Highest Hon and Medal, Soka Univ, Japan. Address: Vice-Chancellor, University of Delhi, Delhi 1100007, India.

MEI Hou-Jun, b. 18 July 1935, Kaifeng, China. Geologist. m. Yi-Win Fang, 3 Apr 1963, 4 d. Education: Beijing Coll Geol, 1952-56. Appointments: Trnee Rschr, 1956-61, Asst Rschr, 1962-65, Inst Geol, Academia Sinica, Beijing; Asst Rschr, 1966-78, Assoc Rschr, Asst Prof, 1979-85, Rschr, Prof, 1986-89, Inst Geochem, Academia Sinica, Guiyang; Rschr, Prof, Inst Geochem, Academia Sinica, Guangzhou, 1990-. Publications: Book, Geological Evolution of Qinghai-Xizang (Tibet) Plateau, 1991; Mica of Granites in S China, 1997; Lamproites in China and Genesis of Diamond, 1998; Articles: Types and Distribution of Ultra-Basic Intrusions in China, 1963; Mantle Peridotite Xenoliths in Alkali Basalt and in Lamprophyry in Maguan County, Yunnan Province, China, 1966; The Relationship between Two Trap Series in SW China, 1973; Telluro-Stibnite of Palladium and Nickel, 1974; Ophiolite of Xizang (Tibet), 1981; Geochemistry of Hongge Layered Ultramafic-Mafic Intrusion in Panzihua Area, 1984; Ultrapotassic Rocks in Qinghai-Xizang (Tibet) Plateau, 1989; On the Transition Relationship from Kimberlite to Ultrapotassic Rocks in China, 1990; Ophiolites and Cenozoic Rift Magmatism in Qing-Zang Plateau, 1991; Distribution of Podiform Chromite Deposits in World and Classification of Chrome Ore Deposit in China, 1995. Honours: Cert of Merit, Significant Achievements, Academia Sinica, 1978; Cert of Hon, Advs Sci and Technol, Academia Sinica, 1986; Cert of Merit, 1st Grade, Geological Evolution of Qinghai-Xizang Plateau, Academia Sinica, 1993. Memberships: Chinese Soc Geol, 1959-; Chinese Soc Mineralogy, Petrology and Geochem, 1966-; Amn Geophysl Union, 1985; Amn Assn of Adv Sci, 1996-. Hobbies: Reading, especially Chinese classical literature. Listed in: Who's Who in China. Address: Guangzhou Institute of Geochemistry, Academia Sinica, PO Box 1131, Wushan, Guangzhou 510640, Guangdong, China.

MEIER Eric John, b. 14 Oct 1946, Hindmarsh, S Aust. MHA (Lib) for Goyder, South Australia. m. Ruth, 3 Sept 1971, 2 s, 1 d. Education: Flinders Univ and Bedford Pk Tchrs Coll, 1966-69, Dip of Tchng (Sec), 1970; Grad Dip Ed Admin, Adelaide Coll of Advd Educ, 1978; BA, Pols and Jrnlsm, Deakin Univ, 1988. Appointments: Tchr, Gawler hs, 1970-73; Snr Master, Yorketown Area Sch, 1974-80; Dpty Prin, Immanuel Coll, 1981-82; Mbr, Parly Lib Cttee, 1982-88; MP, Goyder, 1982-; Mbr, Subordinate Legislation Cttee, 1986-92; Shadow Min for Agric, Fisheries and Marine, 1990-91; Mbr, Legislative Review Cttee, 1992-94, 1997-; SA Govt Whip, 1993-; Mbr, Legis Review Cttee, 1996-; Mbr, Standing Orders Cttee, 1996-. Honour: Robert McDonald Prize, for Excellence in the Area of Journalism, for top student at Deakin Univ, 1988. Memberships: Lions Club of Yorketown and District, 1974-80, Pres, 1979-80; Hon Mbr, Maitland Rotary Club. Hobbies: Gardening; Renovating. Address: 6 Barbican Close, Wallaroo, SA 5556, Australia.

MEJIA María Emma. Minister of Foreign Affairs. Appointments: Min of Educ; Min of For Affairs. Address: Ministry of Foreign Affairs, Placio de San Carlos, Calle 10A, No 5-51, Santafé de Bogotá, Colombia.

MELLICK Selim Abraham, b. 15 Aug 1925. m. Patricia Bulmer, 11 Dec 1954, 2 d. Education: MB, BS, 1st class hons, Univ Qld. Appointments: Mbr AMA, 1949; Tchng Registrar, Surg Registrar, RMO, Brisbane Gen Hosp, 1949-52; Res Surg Offr, Essex Co Hosp, Eng, 1953-54; Mbr, 1960, Chmn, Princess Alexandra Hosp Soc, 1964-68; Mbr, Surg Rsch Soc of Aust, 1964; Cnsltng Vascular Surg, No 1 Mil Hosp, Brisbane, 1965; Mbr, Austl Assn of Surgs, 1972; Mbr, Trng and Accreditation Cttee; Fndn Chmn, Sect of Vascular Surg, 1972-76, Mbr, 1972; Henry John Windsor Lectr, 1976; Cncl Mbr, 1977; Chmn, Bd of Gov, 1980-83; Visng Surg, Snr Vascular Surg, Chmn of Vascular Surg, Princess Alexandra Hosp, 1978-81; Assns of Surgs of SE Asia, 1978; Mr, Societe Intl de Chirurgie, 1979; Chmn, Vascular Soc Qld, 1980; Hunterian Prof, Roy Coll of Surgs of Eng, 1980; Censor-in-Chf, 1983-86; Hon Fell, St John's Coll, Univ Qld, 1985; Mbr, Coll Cncl (Clin Tutor in Surg, 1955-85, Chf Tutor, 1955-65, Snr Lectr, Operative Surg and Surg Anatomy, 1955-65); External Examiner, Roy Coll of Surgs, Ireland, Snr VP, RACS, 1987; Chmn, Cttee on Applicants for Fellshp Am Coll of Surgs, Aust and NZ Chapt, 1987; Fndn Mbr, Austl and NZ Chapt, Intl Soc for Cardiovascular Surg, Pres, 1987; Pres, Qld Div, Austl Archaeol Inst, Athens, 1987; Bancroft Orator AMA, 1987; Mbr, Michael E DeBakey Intl Cardiovascular Soc, 1987; Snr VP, Roy Australasian Coll of Surgs, 1987-. Honours: CBE, 1987; Vietnam Logistic Support Medal, 1995. Memberships: World Pres, Intl Soc for Cardiovascular Surg, 1991-93; FRCSEng; FRACS; FACS; FRCS(I) Hon; Qld Club; Utd Servs Club (Qld); Fndn Pres, State Lib of Qld Soc, 1989-; StatLib of Qld Fndn Cncl, 1989-; Bicentennial Visng Prof, RCS, Ireland, 1991-. Hobbies: Reading; Bird watching; Bushwalking. Listed in: Who's Who in Australia. Address: Lindismead, 34 Towers Street, Ascot, Qld 4007, Australia.

MELLISH Raoul Oakeley John, b. 29 Feb 1928, Brisbane, Aust. Landscape Painter. m. (1) Patrica Mary, 1962, dec, 3 s, (2) Constance Valerie, 1979. Education: St Joseph's Coll, Brisbane; Churchill Fell, 1973; Austl Rep, US Dept of State and Am Assn of Mus, For Mus Profls Proj. 1975. Appointments: Qld Pub Serv, 1947-68; Asst Dir, Qld Art Gall, 1968-74; Dir and Fndng Dir, New Qld Art Gall, 1974-86. Creative works: Regular exhbns of landscape paintings at home and abroad. Honours: Qld Art Gall Awd, 1986. Memberships: Fell, Roy Soc of Arts, London; Mbr, Qld Art Gall Fndn; Life Mbr, Qld Art Gall Soc. Hobbies: Wilderness travel; Photography; Romanesque and Gothic architecture. Address: 12 Sykes Street, Ascot, Brisbane, Queensland 4007, Australia.

MELVILLE Leslie Galfreid (Sir), b. 26 Mar 1902. m. Mary Scales, 20 Aug 1925, 2 s. Education: BEc; Hon LLD, Toronto, ANU; Hon DSc; Univ Sydney. Appointments: Pub, Actuary, SA, 1924-28; Prof Econs, Univ Adelaide, 1929-31; Mbr Advsry Cttee, Finl and Econ Policy, Dept Treas, 1939; Econ Advsr, C'wlth Bank of Aust, 1931-48; Asst Gov Cntrl Banking, 1949-53; Mbr C'wlth Bank Bd, 1950-53; Vice-Chan, ANU, 1953-60; Chmn, Austl Tarriff Bd, Canberra, 1960-63; Dev Adv Serv of Intl Bank, 1963-65; Mbr Reserve Bank Bd, 1965-74; Chmn C'wlth Grants Comm, 1966-74; Mbr, 1979-82. Honours: CBE, 1953; KBE, 1957. Membership: C'wlth Club, Canberra. Address: Unit 61, The Grange, 67 Macgregor Street, Deakin, ACT 2600, Australia.

MENG Jiqing, b. 25 Dec 1926, Qingdao, China. Journalist; Publishing Executive. m. Han Le, 1945, 3 s. Education: BA, St John's Univ, Shanghai. Appointments: Dpty Ed-in-Chf, New World Press, 1979-83; Cultural Cnslr to Chinese Emb, India, 1983-86; Pres, Ed-in-Chf, China Today, 1987-92. Publications: Sev articles in profl jrnls. Honours: Specl Govt Subsidy, 1992-. Memberships:

Cncl, Chinese Assn for Intl Understanding, 1981-; Cncl, Soong Ching Ling Fndn, 1991-. Hobbies: Classical Music; Country Songs. Address: Apt 308, Building 8, Chegongzhuang Zhongli, Beijing 100044, China.

MENSH Ivan N, b. Washington, DC, USA. Medical Education. m. Frances L Mensh. Education: AB; MA; PhD. Appointments: Prof, Hd, Dept of Psych, WA Univ Sch of Med and Med Psychol, 1948-58, Dept of Psych and Biobehavioral Scis, UCLA Sch of Med, 1958-. Publications: 2 texts, over 180 articles in profl jrnls. Honours include: Silver Psi Awd, CA Psychol Assn, 1972; Sev ctfs of appreciation. Memberships: State and Natl Psychol Assns. Address: Department of Psychiatry and Biobehavioral Sciences, University of California at Los Angeles, School of Medicine, 760 Westwood Plaza, Los Angeles, CA 90024-1759, USA.

MENZIES Mona, b. 4 June 1920. Education: BCom, Univ of Melbourne, 1967; Gen Nurse, Roy Prince Alfred Hosp Sydney, 1938-42; Midwife, Queen Vic Mem Hosp, Melbourne, 1944-45. Appointments: Registrar, Nurses Bd, Vic, 1952-58; Registration Offr, Vic Nursing Cncl, 1958-67; Chf Nursing Offr, Vic Nursing Cncl, 1968-85; Fndn Chmn, Austl Nursing Cncl of Cttee on Overseas Profl Quals, Dept of Immigration, Aust, 1982-85; Mbr, Expert Panel on Nursing, COPQ, Canberra, 1972-82. Publication: Facts on Nurses and Nursing in Victoria, 1976, 4th Ed, 1984. Honours: AM for servs to nursing, 1986; Honoured by Nurses Bd of Vic w naming of Mona Menzies Post-doctoral Rsch Grant, 1998. Memberships: Expert Panel on Nursing, Cttee on Overseas Profl Qualifications, 1972-82; Cmmnr, (Pt-time), Hlth Cmmn, Vic, 1978-84; Cncl, Lincoln Inst of Hlth Scis, 1981-85; Life Mbr, Grad Union, Univ of Melbourne; Chmn, Fin Cttee, Airdrie House Soc (Retd Nurses Residence), 1987-; Body Corp Cttee, Forest Hills Retirement Village, 1994-. Listed in: Who's Who in Australia; Who's Who of Women of Australia. Address: Unit 60/264-272 Springvale Road, Nunawading, Victoria 3131, Australia.

MENZIES Rosemary Laura, b. Auckland, New Zealand. Teacher; Poet; Humanitarian Worker. m. Robert, 8 May 1967, 2 d. Education: Dip PE, Otago Univ; Dip Tchng, NZ; Dip ELT, Auckland Univ. Appointments: Takapura Grammer Sch; Lectr, Tchrs Coll in Art; Sloreditch Soc Med, UK; Birkdale Int Sch; AK Inst Tech. Publications: 8 Collects of Poetry; 2 Exhibns, Paintings. Honours: ACCP Cup, Pub Speaking; Hon Mbr Rotary; Hon Mbr Bosnian Cultural Club. Memberships: NZSA. Hobbies: Philos of Rudolf Steiner; Humanitarian Work, Bosnia; Poetry; Music; Dance; Trav. Address: 21 Wernham Place, Birkenhead, Auckland 10, New Zealand.

MEREDITH Eleanor Elizabeth, b. 4 Aug 1931. Hospital Scientist; Biology Educator; Author. m. (1) John Clements, 30 May 1957, (2) William Meredith, 25 Aug 1983, 1 s, 3 d. Education: BSc; Dip of Educ. Appointments: Microbio Rsch, Univ of Melbourne, 1952; Westminster Hosp, London, Eng, 1955; Snr Microbiolst, Wellesley Hosp, Toronto, Can, 1957; Snr Biolst, Kingswood Coll, Melbourne, 1974; Biol Curric Cttee of Vic, 1978. Publications: Books (as E E Clements): Co-Auth, A Guide to HSC Biology, 2 eds, 1982; Author, Year 12 Biology Examination Questions, 4 eds, 1985; Co-Author, VCE Biology Review Questions, 3 eds, 1992. Memberships: Sci Tchrs Assn, Vic, 1978; Austl Coll of Educ, 1984. Hobbies: Gardening; Reading; Tennis. Address: Harding Street, Surrey Hills, Melbourne, Victoria 3127, Australia.

MEREDITH Gwenyth Valmai, b. 18 Nov 1907, Orange, NSW, Aust. Playwright. m. Ainsworth Harrison, 24 Dec 1938. Education: BA, Sydney Univ, 1929. Appointments: Freelance Jrnlst & Writer for coml radio, 1927-42; Owner, Chelsea Book Club, Sydney, 1932-39; Socl Sec, Indep Th, Sydney, 1940-41; Radio Playwright under contract to Austl Brdcstng Cmmn, 1943-76. Creative Works include: Best-known radio serials: The Lawsons, 1943-49; Blue Hills, 1949-76. Publications: The Lawsons; Blue Hills; Beyond Blue Hills; Into the Sun; Inns and Outs; Stage Plays: Wives Have Their Uses; Ask No Questions; Cornerstone. Honours: MBE, 1967; OBE,

1977. Membership: Austl Soc of Auths. Hobbies: Gardening; Reading; Painting; Bridge. Address: Unit 45, Kenilworth Gardens, Kangaloon Road, Bowral, New South Wales 2576, Australia.

MERIAM James Lathrop, b. 25 Mar 1917, Columbia, MO, USA. Retired Professor of Engineering Mechanics. m. Julia E Powers, 25 Dec 1940, 2 d. Education: BE, 1939, MEng, 1941, PhD, 1942, Yale Univ. Appointments: Asst to Instruction, Yale Univ, 1940-42; Instr to Prof, Univ of CA, Berkeley, CA, 1942-63; Lt(jg) US Coast Guard Reserve, 1944-45; Prof & Dean, Sch of Engrng, Duke Univ, 1963-72; Prof, CA State Univ, 1972-80; Visng Prof, Univ CA, Santa Barbara, 1980-90. Publications: Mechanics, Statics, Dynamics, Engineering Mechanics (4th ed), 1952-98. Honours: Pi Tau Sigma, 1939-; Sigma Xi, 1939-; Tau Beta Pi, 1939-; Awd for Advmnt of Basic and Applied Sci, Yale Engrng Assn, 1952; 1st recip, Outstndng Fac Awd, Tau Beta Pi, Univ of CA at Berkeley, 1963; Outstndng Serv Awd, Southeastern Sect, 1975; Fell, 1976, Life Mbr, 1980, Amn Soc of Mechl Engrs; Distinguished Educr Awd for Outstndng Contbn to Tchng of Mechs, 1978, Life Mbrshp Awd, 1980, Hon Mbshp Awd, 1982, Charter Fell Mbr, 1983, Amn Soc Engrng Educ; Benjamin Garver Lamme Awd, ASEE, 1992; Serv Awd, Mechs Div, 1989. Memberships include: Charter Fell Mbr, Amn Soc Engrng Educ; Amn Soc of Mechl Engrs. Hobbies: Wood and metal working; Wooden boat design and building. Address: 4312 Marina Drive, Santa Barbara, CA 93110, USA.

MERIDOR Dan, b. 1947, Jerusalem, Israel. Politician; Lawyer. m. 3 children. Education: Hebrew Univ. Appointments: Mbr, Likud Pty; Sec of Govt, 1982-84; Mbr, Knesset, 1984-; Min of Justice, 1988-92, of Fin, 1996-97. Address: Ministry of Finance, PO Box 883, 1 Rehov Kaplan, Kiryat Ben-Gurion, Jerusalem 91008, Israel.

MERNAGH Terrence Patrick, b. 25 Mar 1959, Waratah, Aust. Geochemist. m. Lynette, 14 Apr 1984, 2 s. Education: BS (Hons), Univ of Newcastle, 1980; PhD, Univ of Newcastle, 1984. Appointments: Sci-2 Bur of Mineral Resources; Snr Rsch Scientist, Austl Geol Survey Org. Honours: NSW Dept of Educ Schlshp; CSR Chem Prize; C'wlth Postgrad Schlshp. Memberships: Fell, Geol Soc of Aust; Roy Austl Chem Inst. Hobbies: Computing; Photography; Bush walking. Address: Australian Geological Survey Organisation, GPO Box 378, Canberra, ACT 2601, Australia.

MERRY Donald Henry, b. 22 Dec 1909. Member, Archives Board of Managment and Investment Committee, University of Melbourne. m. (1) Barbara, dec 1937, 2 s, 1 d. (2) Alison Mitchell, dec 1956. Education: BCom; Scots Coll, Sydney; Scotch Coll, Melbourne; Melbourne Univ; London Sch of Econs. Appointments: Econ Staff, Bank of NSW, Sydney and London, 1933-45; Asst Sec, C'wlth Prices Br, 1940-42; Sec, Army Inventions Directorate, 1942-43; Dpty to Treas Rep, Dept of Def, 1943-45; Fin Ed, Melbourne Argus, 1945-47; Melourne Chmbr of Com, Economist, Union Bank of Aust, 1947-51; Inspector, Snr Economist, 1951-55; Chf Economist, 1955-68; C'wlth Decimal Currency Cttee, 1959; Mbr, Woll Mktng Cttee of Inquiry, 1961; ANZ Bank, 1968-70; Asst Gen Mngr, Econ Advsr, ANZ Banking Grp Ltd, 1970-72; Dir, Barclays Aust Ltd, 1973-80. Publications: Co-auth, A Survey of Business and Economic Trends; Penguin Book Investment in Australia. Honour: OBE, 1977. Memberships: Pres, Cttee for Econ Devel of Aust, 1974-80; Vic Govt, Westernport Bay Environ Stdy Review Cttee, 1974; Vic Govt Dairy Ind Inquiry, 1974; Econs Soc of Aust and NZ; Vic Devel Corp Bd, 1977-81. Hobby: Farming. Address: RMB 930, Lot 7 Tooborrac Road, Lancefield, Vic 3435, Australia.

MESSEL Harry, b. 3 Mar 1922. Education: BA; BSc; PhD; RMC, Can; Queens Univ, Ont; St Andrew's Univ, Scotland; Inst of Adv Studies, Dublin. Appointments: Can Armed Forces Overseas Serv, 1942-45; Snr Lectr, Math Phys, Univ of Adelaide, 1951-52; Prof, Phys, Hd, Sch of Phys, 1952-87; Fndr, Dir, Sci Fndn for Phys, Univ Sydney, 1954-87; Sci Advsr, Austl Govt, 1973-75;

Cmmnr, Austl Atomic Energy Cmmn, 1975-81; Vice Chmn, (Aust) Survival Serv Cmmn Intl Union for the Conservation of Nature, 1978-; Chan, Bond Univ, 1992-97, Exec Chan, 1993-96. Publications including: The Biological Manipulation of Life, 1981; Science Update, 1983; The Study of Population, 1985; Highlights in Science, 1987; Num pprs in profl jrnls. Honours: RMC, 1942; CBE, 1979; Hon DSc, Sydney, 1992; Hon DHI, Schiller, 1994; ANZAAS Medal, 1995. Memberships: Austl Atomic Energy Cmmn, 1974-81; Vice Chmn, Spec Survival Cmmn, World Conserv Union, 1978-90; SSC Steering Cttee, 1978-; Chmn, Crocodile Spec Grp of SSC/IUCN, 1989-; Snr Vice Chmn, SSC, 1991-. Hobbies: Water Skiing; Hunting; Fishing; Photography. Address: PO Box 255, Bond University, Gold Coast, Queensland 4229, Australia.

MESSER Jane Harcourt, b. 26 Nov 1960. Writer. m. Michiel Gerber, 8 Jan 1993. Education: BA, Sociol, Maquerie Univ; MA, Fiction Writing, Johns Hopkins Univ. Publications; Night by Night (novel), 1994; Bedlam, Anthology of Sleepless Nights, 1996; Certifiable Truths: Stories of Love and Madness. Honours: Writers Fellshp, Tchng Fellshp, Johns Hopkins Univ, 1992; Writers Fellshp, Vavona Writers Cntr, 1994. Memberships: ASA; NSW Writers Cntr; Greenpeace. Hobbies: Yoga; Reading; Gardening. Address: PO Box 451, Leichardt, NSW 2040, Australia.

MESSERLE Hugo Karl, b. 25 Oct 1925, Aust. Professor of Electrical Engineering. m. 6 Aug 1955, 2 d. Education: BEE, 1951; MEngSc, 1953; DSc, 1968; PhD, 1958. Appointments: Snr Demonstrator, Tutor, Univ of Melbourne, 1951-52; Lectr, Snr Lectr, 1952-60, Rdr, 1960-66, Prof, 1966-, Hd of Sch, 1970-83, 1987-90, Dir, Elec Engrng Fndn, 1983, Emer Prof, 1992-, Univ of Sydney; Fulbright Schl, 1958; Visng Prof, Cornell Univ, USA, 1964-65; Guest Prof, Inst fur Plasmaforschung, Univ of Suttgart, Germany, 1973. Publications: Dynamic Circuit Theory; Energy Conversion Statics, 1969; Magnetohydrodynamic Electrical Power Generation, 1995. Honours: Dixon Schlshp, Univ of Melbourne, 1950; Elec Engrng Premium, 1953; Prizes, IE Aust, 1961, 1970; Fell, Austl Acady of Technol Scis; Centenary Medal, IEEE USA, 1984; Fellshp, ATSE, IEEE, IEE, E Aust; Medal, Australasian Assn of Engrng Educ, 1994. Memberships include: Austl Acad of Technol Scis and Engrng; Inst of Elec Engrs, Eng; Austl Inst of Phys; Intl Liason Grp on Engrng Educ; ATSE Cttee on Sustainable Dev, 1992-, Chair, 1995-97. Hobbies: Music; Swimming. Listed in: Who's Who in Asia; Who's Who in Australia. Address: 35 Howson Avenue, Turramurra, New South Wales 2074, Australia.

METGE Joan, b. 21 Feb 1930, Auckland, NZ. Anthropologist. Education: BA, MA, Univ NZ, 1952; PhD, London, 1958. Appointments: Jnr Lectr, Geog, Auckland Univ Coll, 1952; Lectr, Univ Extn, Univ of Auckland, 1961-64; Snr Lectr, Anthropol, 1965-67, Assoc Prof, Anthropol, 1968-88, Vic Univ of Wellington; Cap James Cook Rsch Fell, 1981-83; Rsch and Advsry Work, 1988-; Hon Visng Prof, Maori Educ, Univ of Auckland, 1995-. Publications: A New Maori Migration, 1964; The Maoris of New Zealand, 1967, revised ed, 1976; Talking Past Each Other (w Patricia Kinloch), 1978; In and Out of Touch: Whakamaa in Cross-Cultural Context, 1986; Te Kohao o Te Ngira, 1990; New Growth From Old: The Whanau in the Modern World, 1995. Honours: Hutchinson Medal, London Sch of Econs and Polit Scis, 1959; Dame Cmdr of the Brit Empire, 1987; Elsdon Best Mem Medal, Polynesian Soc, 1987; Te Rangi Hiroa Medal, Roy Soc of NZ, 1997. Memberships: Roy Anthropol Inst; Assn of Socl Anthropol of the C'wlth; NZ Assn of Socl Anthropols; NZ Fedn of Univ Women; Polynesian Soc; Intl Union of Anthropol and Ethnol Scis. Listed in: International Authors and Writers Who's Who; International Who's Who of Professional and Business Women; Dictionary of International Biography. Address: 3 Mariri Road, Onehunga, Auckland, New Zealand.

MEWTA Sanjay, b. 14 Mar 1967, Magrota Bagwan, India. Service, (Assistant Manager LIC Housing Finance Ltd). m. Mirupma, 8 Mar 1995, 1 d. Education: BS Medl;

MS, Engl; Post Grad Dip in Personnel Mngmt, AMA Labour Welfare; Lic from Ins Inst. Publications: Poems in jrnls and anthologies inclng: Dayspring, Wonderlust, 1994-. Memberships: Writer's Forum, Ranchi; Jrnl, Poetcrit. Hobbies: Watching cricket; Relaxing in the countryside. Address: c/o LIC Housing Finance Ltd, Royal Hotel Building, Nerr Bus-Stand, Shimla 171001, India.

MEYER George Rex, b. 15 Mar 1928, Sydney, Australia. Retired Educationalist. Education: BSc, 1951, Dip Ed, 1952, BA, 1954, Med, 1955, MA, 1983, Sydney Univ; PhD, London Univ, 1959; MSc Soc, Univ NSW, 1986. Appointments: Tchng Fell, Sydney Univ, Sch of Biol Scis, 1952-55; Lectr in Zoology, Biol, 1956-63, Snr Lectr, 1964-66, Sydney Univ; Fndn Dir, Cntr for Adv of Tchng, Macquarie Univ, 1967-69; Fell in Continuing Educ, Macquarie Univ, 1979-88; Freelance Educl Cnslt, 1988-95; External Cnslt in Biol Edun to Univ of Papua New Guinea, 1972-75; Consultancies for UNESCO in Sci Curriculum in Asian and African Countries, 1968-95; Mbr, NSW State Devel Cttee for In-Serv Educ, 1975-80; Chmn, Natl Sci Curriculum Materials Project, 1969-99; Mbr of Cncl, Mt St Mary's Tchrs Coll, Strathfield, 1977-81; Freelance Educl Cnslt, 1988-95; Freelance Auth, Family History, 1996-. Publications include: Field Work in Animal Biology (co-auth), 1954; Introducing Biology (co-auth), 1961; Science and the Environment of Man, 1966; Objective Tests in Science (co-auth), 1967; Basic Genetics for Schools and Colleges (co-auth), 1975; Quiz Yourself About East African Mammals (co-auth), 1975; Processes of Teaching and Learning (co-auth), 1978; Modules From Design to Implementation, 1984; Teaching Science Out-of-School (co-auth), 1984; Teaching Biology for Social Relevence, 1996; Scientific Orientation Test, 1996; the Cribbon Family of Coleraine, Ireland, 1998; George Wilkins and Emma Johnstone of Oakbourne, 1998; The Watts Family of Ryde and Beecroft, 1999. Memberships: Patron, Educl Suppliers Assn of Aust, 1970-90; Fndn Pres, Educl Rescs Assn of NSW, Pres, 1972-75; Assn of Environ Stdies, NSW, Pres, 1972-74; Cmmn for Biol Educ of the Intl Cncl of Sci Unions, 1979-, Mbr Emer, 1989-. Hobbies: Record collecting; Music appreciation; Gardening; Family history. Listed in: Many including: Who's Who in Australia; Notable Australians. Address: PO Box 154, Beecroft, New South Wales 2119, Australia.

MI Baoyong, b. 25 Nov 1939, Liaoyang, Liaoning, China. Professor; Researcher. m. Zhixiong Jiang, 1 Oct 1970, 1 s. Education: Grad, 1964, Beijing Univ Tech. Appointments: Asst Engr, Changchun Inst Optics and Fine Mech, 1964-67; Engr, 1968-86, Assoc Prof, 1986-95, Prof, 1996-, Dir, Rsch Grp. Publications: Optical endpoint detection of plasma etching, 1994; A computerised photoelectric refractometer, 1991; Photon counter at VUV Bang, 1987; and others. Honours: 2nd advance awd in sci and tech, Academia Sinica, 1989; 3rd awds, 1990, 1995; Reward in excellent product for yr 1991, Min of Electronic Ind of China. Memberships: China Instrument Soc; Chinese Optical Soc; Cnslt ed, Chinese Figures Dictionary. Hobbies: Theatre; Classical music; Literature. Address: Changchun Institute of Optics and Fine Mechanics, Academia Sinica, Renmin St, Gongnong Rd, Changchun, Jilin, 130022 China.

MI Jie, b. 12 June 1961, Beijing, China. Epidemiologist. m. Zhu Renbo, 18 Mar 1989, 1 d. Education: BMedSc, Harbin Medl Univ, 1985; MD, Peking Union Medl Coll, 1998. Appointments: Asst Rschr, 1985-91; Assoc Rschr, 1992-98. Publications: More than 20 pprs, Chinese medl jrnls. Memberships: China Preventive Med Assn. Hobbies: Swimming; Skating; Classic Music; Tennis. Address: No 2 Ya Bao Lu, Dept of Epidemiology, Capital Inst of Pediatrics, Beijing 100020, China.

MI Zhengyu, b. 22 Jan 1942, Shanghai, China. Scientific Research. m. Huang Lijuan, 27 May 1972, 1 d. Education: BS, 1964, MSc, 1967, Fudan Univ. Appointments: Rsch Asst, 1968-78, Shanghai Inst Tech Phys; Rsch Assoc, 1979-85, Dir, Dept Info, 1984-, Assoc Prof, 1986-1994, Prof, 1994-, Ed-in-Chf, 1987-96, Exec

Ed-in-Chf, 1997-, Chinese of Infrared Journal Millimeter Waves. Publications: Fundamentals of Optoelectronic Devices, 1989; Fundamentals of Infrared Radiation Heating and Drying, 1996. Honours: Prize of Nat Sci; Chinese Acad Scis, 1995; Prize of Info Sci and Tech; Municipality Sci Tech Cttee of Shanghai, 1984. Memberships: Sec-Gen, Infrared and Optoelectronic Cttee, Chinese Phys Soc, 1988-; Chinese Medl Assn, 1990; Chinese Optical Soc, 1991-; SPIE, 1992-; OSA, 1997-; IEEE, 1997-. Hobby: Music. Address: 420 Zhong Shan Bei Yi Rd, Shanghai 200083, China.

MIAN Jamat Ali, (Mustakim Zihadi), b. 13 Apr 1941, Pabna, Bangladesh. Service. m. Begum Jahanada Khatun, 6 Oct 1968, 2 s, 1 d. Education: Matriculation, G C Inst, Pabna, 1962; BA, Edward Coll, Pabna, 1968. Appointments: Mbr, Socl Dev Org, 1957; Socl Welfare Assn, 1984; Muslim Sanghati Parishad, 1996. Creative Works: Namaz Porbo Na; Cultural Articles, Column; Answer to Taslimanasrin, unpub. Honours: Shahittya Bhushan; Sponsored by Pabna Dist Cultural Acady. Memberships: Muslim Sanhati Pabishad; Bangladesh Cultural Assn. Hobbies: Reading; Writing; Travelling; Listening to Others Keeping Silent. Address: Pabna Purashvava, PO & Dist Pabna 6600, Bangladesh.

MICHALEWICZ Marek Tadeusz, b. 1 Mar 1957, Wrockaw, Poland. Physicist; Computational Scientist. m. Agnieszka Piotrowska, 29 Mar 1980, 1 s, 1 d. Education: MSc, La Trobe Univ, 1984; PhD Theort Phys, Austl Natl Univ, Canberra, 1987. Appointments: Computer Cnslt, Sci Software, Canberra, 1987-88; Rsch Assoc, Univ MN, Minneapolis, 1988-90; Rsch Scientist, 1990-93, Snr Rsch Scientist, 1993-96; Prin Rsch Scientist, CSIRO Aust, 1996-. Publications: Plants to Ecosystems (ed), 1997; Humans to Proteins, 1998; Over 35 orig sci pprs in intl jrnls. Honours: Visng Fell, Theort Phys, ANU, Canberra, 1987-88. Memberships: Amn Physl Soc; Fell, Austl Inst of Phys. Hobbies: Kayaks; Jazz; Skiing. Address: CSIRO, Molecular Science, 343 Royal Parade, Parkville, Vic 3052, Australia.

MICHOUTOUCHKINE Nicolai, b. 5 Oct 1929, Belfort, France. Artist; Painter. Education: High Coml Sch as painter; Wrk w var masters, E France. Appointments: Co-fndr, Michoutouchkine-Piliecko Fndn for Preservation of Art Values in Pacific; 100 exhibns around the world. Honours: Mérite National, France; Chevalier des Arts et Lettres, France. Hobby: Collector, Oceanic art. Address: Box 224, Port Vila, Vaceatic.

MIDDENWAY Ralph, b. 9 Sept 1932, Sydney, NSW, Aust. Composer. m. (1) Gillian Kennedy, 1957, 3 d, (2) Aina Dambitis, 1983. Education: BA, Sydney Univ, 1958. Appointments: Freelance Composer, 1958-, Full-time, 1983-89, Pt-time, 1990-; Tchr of Music & Drama, Tudor House, Moss Vale, NSW, 1958-64; Sec, later Warden, Adelaide Univ Union, 1965-77; Gen Mngr, The Pks Community Cntr, 1977-82; Freelance Jrnlst, 1968-; Hon Th Cnslt, Th's at Adelaide Univ Union & The Pks, 1968-82. Publications: Many Feature Articles in the Adelaide Advertiser, Austl and Cand Educl, Arts and Conservation Jrnls and Performing Arts Progs; Many Perfs and Brdcsts, some Telecasts; Prin Compositions: 2 Operas: The Letters of Amalie Dietrich and Barossa, both w poet Andrew Taylor; Current Projects (1999): Third Opera: Love's Coming; A Trilogy of Novels: Future Perfect, Future Imperfect, Future Conditional. Memberships: Australasian Performing Rights Assn; Austl Jrnlsts Assn; Austl Music Cntr; Fellshp of Austl Composers; Fndng Chair, Richard Wagner Soc of S Aust Inc. Hobbies: Farmer, interested in conservation and revegetation; Lobbyist in arts and conservation at State and Federal level. Address: Springhill, Inman Valley, PO Box 753, Victor Harbor, SA 5211, Australia.

MIDDLETON Colin Edward, b. 20 July 1920, Warragul, Vic, Aust. Licensed Surveyor. m. (1) Alma Watt, 23 Mar 1946, dec 1989, 1 s, (2) Harriette Hooper, 7 Sept 1996. Education: Roy Melbourne Inst of Technol, 1937-40; Lic Surveyor, 1946. Appointments: Joined Dept of Crown Lands and Survey, 1936; Lt, AIF, 1940-45; Staff Surveyor, 1946-64; Chf Photogrammetrist, 1965-66, Dpty

Surveyor Gen, 1967, Surveyor Gen, 1968-72, Sec for Lands, Vic, 1972-81. Publications: Chmn, Cttee publng the first Atlas of Vic, 1982 and contrb chapt on Topography. Honour: Companion, Imperial Serv Order, 1981. Memberships: Fell, Inst of Surveyors, Aust; Life Mbr, Austl Admin Staff Coll Assn. Hobbies: Oil Painting; Gardening; Golf. Address: 20 Russell Street, Camberwell, Victoria 3124, Australia.

MIKAZUKI Akira, b. Japan. Politician; Lawyer; Academic. Appointments: Fmr Dean, Fac of Law, Tokyo Univ; Prof Emer; Min of Justice, 1993-94. Address: House of Representatives, Tokyo, Japan.

MILCHIKER Marcia, b. 22 Aug 1946, Cleveland, OH, USA. Board of Trustees, South Orange County Community College District. m. Dr Benjamin Milchiker, 3 s. Education: BS, Bio, OH State Univ; MS, Bio, Cleveland State Univ. Appointments: Bd of Trustees, SOCCCD, 1985-, Pres, 1990-91, 1993-94; Fndr, CeWaer O C, Pres, 1987-90; CeWaer Bd, Com Ch, 1989-91; Utd Way SOC Bd, 1990-96; OCSBA Bd, Sec, 1990; ACCT Intl C Bd, 1997. Honours: Woman of the Yr, Saddleback Bus & Profl Women, 1986; Judge, Tchr of Yr OC, 1993. Memberships: OC Bd Assn, 1990-; Community Coll Repr, 1991-; YWCA Bd Mbr, 1996; Perf Art Guild PAJ; Soroptomist; WROC; AAUW; JCC; ORT AJC; SHARE; Angels; Lib Friend. Hobbies: Scientific and biological research; Fine arts. Address: 28000 Marguerite Parkway, Mission Viejo, California 92692-3635, USA.

MILES Jeffrey Allan, b. 20 Mar 1935, NSW, Aust. m. Patricia Freebairn, 15 Apr 1976, 1 s, 1 d. Education: BA, Master of Laws, Univ of Sydney. Appointments: Sol, 1958-59; Lectr, Indonesian Civil Aviation Coll, 1959-60; Sol, 1960-65; Bar, 1965-78; Pub Defender, 1978-80; Judge, Natl Crt of Papua New Guinea, 1980-82; Supreme Crt of NSW, 1982-85; Chf Justice, Surpeme Crt ACT, 1985-; Chf Justice, Austl Cahitoe Territory. Publications: Co-auth, Smail Miles and Shabolt, Summanryu Offences in New South Wales. Honour: AO, 1995. Address: c/o Chief Justices Chambers, Supreme Court of ACT, Canberra, ACT, Australia.

MILES John Arthur, b. 24 Aug 1942, Erith, Kent, UK. Writer. m. Kay, 18 Feb 1972, 1 s, 2 d. Education: Urrbrae Agricl Coll, Adelaide. Appointments: Adelaide Fest Writers Week, 1992; Poetry Ed Austl Writer, 1994; Varuna Fell, 1996; Victorian Fest of Writing, 1997. Creative Works: Anthology, 1987; Going Down Swinging, 1991; Homecoming, 1993; He Dares, 1994; Harvest Five Seasons, 1995; Honour, A Vanuatu Suite and Envoi, 1996; Lost Angry Penguins, 1998. Honours: Bicentenary Poetry Prize, 1988; 10th Anniversary Poetry Prize, 1990; Haiku Awds, 1992; Max Harris Lit Awds, 1993; Shire of Eltham Alan Marshall Short Story Awds, 1994; Natl Lib Illustrated Poetry Exhibn, 1994; Max Harris Lit Awds, 1994; Haiku Awds, 1994; Natl Lib Travng Exhibn Illustrated Poetry 1995; Max Harris Lit Awds 1995; Haiku Awds, 1996; Armidale Fest of Words and Music, Poetry, 1997; Fiction, 1997; Eyre Writers Fest, Fiction, 1998. Memberships: Austl Soc of Auth; S Austl Writers Cntr. Hobbies: Writing; Reading; Vegetable and Fruit Gardening. Address: 17 Nunyah Drive, Banksia Park, South Australia 5091, Australia.

MILIANO Mary Elizabeth Anne, b. 13 Nov 1952, E Melbourne, Aust. Audiovisual Archivist. m. Chris Miliano, 6 May 1989, 2 s, 1 d. Education: BMus, Univ Melbourne, 1976; Grad, Dip Lib, Canb CAE, 1979. Appointments: Lib, Natl Lib of Aust, 1978; Snr Libn, Cataloging, Natl Lib of Aust, 1984; Snr Sound and Radio Cataloguer, Natl Film and Sound Archive, 1985; Asst Mngr, Cataloguing/Collection Info, Natl Film and Sound Archive, 1993. Publications: 11 in profl jrnls, 1981-. Memberships: Dance band Musician, 1976-93; Ldr, St Anthony of Padua Sunday 6pm Music Min, 1988-95; RA (Australasian Sound Recordings Assn) (fmrly IASA Aust, -1988), Sec (IASA), Aust, 1982-84, Vice-Chair (IASA), 1984-88, Treas (ASRA), 1988-90, Vice-Chair (ASRA), 1990-92; IASA (Intl Assn of Sound and Audiovisual Archives), (fmrly Intl Assn of Sound Archives), 1995), Sec, IASA Cataloguing and Documentation Cttee, 1991-94,

Convenor, The IASA Cataloguing Rules: A Manual for Description of Sound Recordings and Related Audiovisual Media, 1993-99, Chair, IASA Cataloguing and Documentation Cttee, 1996-99. Hobbies: Walking; Music; Cross stitch. Address: 12 Clutterbuck Crescent, Oxley, ACT, Australia.

MILLARD Neal Steven, b. 6 June 1947, Dallas, TX, USA. Attorney. m. Janet Keast, 1 d. Education: BA, Univ of CA, LA, 1966; JD, Univ of Chicago Law Sch, 1972. Appointments: Insr, Sch of Admin, CA State Coll, 1975-76; Fac, Real Esate for Legal Assts Practicing Law Inst, 1983-90; Chair, 1989-90; Fac, Negotiation Workshop, Practicing Law Inst, 1987-89; Mbr, PLI Advsry Cttee on Real Estate, 1992-; Adj Prof, Univ of Southern CA Law Cntr, 1994-; Mbr, Advsry Bd Letters of Credit Update, 1995-; Mbr, Editl Advsry Bd, Documentary Credit World, 1997-. Publications: Co-auth: Requesting a Construction Loan, 1983; Validation of Mechanics Liens, 1986; How Letters of Credit are Treated in FRB Risk Based Capital Guidlines, 1989; The New Risk Based Capital Framework and its Application to Letters of Credit, 1989; Letters Perfect, 1996. Honours: Phi Beta Kappa; Pi Gamma Mu; Ephebian Soc of Los Angeles. Memberships: Amn Bar Assoc, Stdy Grp on Legal Assts; State Bar of CA, Resolutions Cttee of the Conf of Deleg; Los Angeles County Bar Assn, Bd of Tstees; Many other mbrshps. Address: White and Case, 633 W Fifth Street, Ste 1900, Los Angeles, CA 90071, USA.

MILLENDER Roy J Jnr, b. 23 July 1938, Riverton, Kansas, USA. College Professor; Attorney. m. Sandra, 30 June 1957, 2 s. Education: AB, Stanford Univ, 1960; JD, Univ CA, Berkeley, 1963. Honours: Air Force Commendation Medal, 1964; Tchr of the Yr, Westmont Coll, 1989. Memberships: Christian Bus Fac; Small Bus Inst. Hobbies: Reading; Travel. Address: 129 Calle Bello, Santa Barbara, CA, USA.

MILLER Alfred Lee, b. 5 Feb 1924, Ontario, California, USA. Rancher; Investment Broker. m. R Jacqueline, 25 July 1958, 2 s. Education: BS, Animal Sci, Univ CA, Davis, 1950; Supvsr Ctf, CSU, Sacramento, 1952-56. Appointments: Owner-Mngr Dairy, 1950-74; Civilian Supvsr, Electron Divsn, Army, 1951-59; Bd Dir, Dairyman Feed & Supply Coop, 1962-74; Steward, CA State Grange, 1978-99. Publications: Economic Cycles and Their Relation to Investments, 1985; Fifty-Year Cycles and Today's Investments, 1987. Honours: Galt Cham of Com, 1988-98; Good Conduct Medal, Am Th, Mid-E Th. Hobbies: Financial Investments; Youth Advising. Address: 9650 Harvey Road, Galt, CA 95632-8861, USA.

MILLER David Niven John, b. 19 Oct 1952, Zimbabwe. Computers; Economist; Businessman. m. Sep, 1 s, 1 d. Education: BS (Hons), Econ; MA, Econ. Appointments: Systems Mngr, Shell Co, Aust, 1987-90; Mngr, Micro Magic Aust, 1990-. Publications: What the Computer Salesman Doesn't Tell You, 1989; How to Buy a Personal Computer, 1990-98. Address: PO Box 139, Cotteloe 6911, Australia.

MILLER George "Kennedy", b. 3 Mar 1945, Brisbane, Australia. Film Director; Producer; Writer; Doctor. m. Sandy Gore, 1985, 1 d. Education: Univ NSW Med Sch. Appointments: Res Med Offr, St Vincent's Hosp, Sydney, 1971-72; Fndr, Kennedy Miller Film Co w late Byron Kennedy, 1977, Chair, 1977-; Writer, Dir, Violence in the Cinema, Pt 1, 1975; Co-Writer, Dir, Mad Max, 1979, Mad Max II, 1981; Exec Prodr, Dir, The Dismissal, 1982; Dir, The Twilight Zone Movie, 1983; Prodr, Bodyline, 1983, The Cowra Breakout, 1984; Co-Writer, Prodr, Co-Dir, Mad Max Beyond Thunderdome, 1985; Prodr, Vietnam, 1986; Dir, Witches of Eastwick, 1986; Prodr, The Riddle of the Stinson, The Clean Machine, Fragments of War, 1987; Co-Prodr, Dead Calm, The Year My Voice Broke, 1988, The Bangkok Hilton, Flirting, 1989, Over the Hill, Dir, Co-Writer, Co-Prodr, Lorenzos Oil, 1990; Co-Prodr, Co-Writer, Babe, 1994; Dir, Contact, 1996. Honours include: Best Dir, TV Drama, Penguin Awds, 1983; Grand Prix Avoriaz, 1983; Best Fgn Film, LA Film Critics, 1983. Memberships: Pres, Jury Avoriaz Film Fest, 1984; Chair, Byron Kennedy Meml Trust, 1984-; Bd Dir, Mus of Contemporary Art, Sydney, 1987-; Jury Cannes Film Fest, 1988. Hobbies: Art; Music; Sport. Address: 30 Orwell Street, King's Cross, NSW 2011, Australia.

MILLER Jacques Francis Albert, b. 2 Apr 1931, Nice, France. Medical Researcher. m. Margaret, 17 Mar 1956. Education: BSc, 1953, MB, BS, 1955, Univ Sydney; PhD, Ex Pathol, 1960, DSc, 1965, Univ London; BA, Univ Melbourne, 1985. Appointments: Jnr Res Med Offr, Roy Prince Alfred Hosp, Sydney, 1956; Pathol Rsch, Univ Sydney, 1957; Lectr, Chester Beatty Rsch Inst, London, 1960; Eleanor Roosevelt Intl Fellshp, Natl Cancer Inst, Natl Inst of Hlth, Bethesda, MD, USA, 1963; Rdr, Ex Pathol, Univ London, 1965; Hd, Dept of Ex Pathol, 1966-, Prof to the Chair of Ex Immunol, 1990, Prof Emer, 1996, Walter and Eliza Hall Inst of Med Rsch, Melbourne. Publications: Over 390 publns in sci jrnls. Honours include: Esther Langer-Bertha Teplitz Mel Prize for Cancer Rsch, Chgo, 1965; Sci Medal, Zoological Soc of London, 1967; Burnet Medal, Austl Acady of Scis, 1971; Rabbi Shai Shacknai Meml Prize, Hebrew Univ, Jerusalem, Israel, 1978; Inaugural Sandoz Prize for Immunol, 1990; J Alwyn Taylor Intl Prize for Med, London, Ont, Can, 1995. Memberships include: Amn Assn of Immunols; Collegium Intl Allergologicum; Transplantation Soc; WHO Expert Advsry Panel on Immunol. Hobbies: Art; Music; Photography; Literature. Address: Walter and Eliza Hall Institute of Medical Research; Post Office Royal Melbourne Hospital, Victoria 3050, Australia.

MILLER John Anthony, b. 12 Apr 1950, London, Eng. Civil Servant. m. Nga-Ching, 2 Apr 1975. Education: Dip, Institu Bourguiba des langs Vivants, Tunisia, 1971; BA, hons, Sch of Oriental & African Studies, London Univ, England, 1972; MPA, Harvard Univ, USA, 1984. Appointments: Admin Offr, Hong Kong Govt, 1972; Dist Offr, 1976-78; Pvte Sec to Gov of Hong Kong, 1979-82; Asst Dir, Housing Dept, 1982-83; Admin Servs & Info Bur, 1984-85; Dpty Dir of Trade, 1985-; Info Coord, Chf Secs Off, 1989-91; Dir of Marine, 1991-93; Dir Gen of Trade, Chf Trade Negotiator, 1993-96; Chf Exec of the Housing Authy, 1996-. Publications: Var articles on trade and econs in intl jrnls and Econ and Pub Affairs textbooks for Second Schls. Honours: JP, 1985; OBE, 1997. Memberships: Asia Soc; Roy Asiatic Soc; Roy C'wlth Soc. Hobbies: Hiking; Travel; Reading; White Jade. Address: c/o Hong Kong Government Secretariat, Lower Albert Road, Central, Hong Kong.

MILLER John Holmes, b. 11 July 1945, Aurora, IL, USA. Researcher; Lecturer in Biology. m. Julie M Quilter, 1 s. Education: BA, N Cntrl Coll, 1967; PhD, Stanford Univ, 1971. Appointments: Postdoct Fell (NIH) UCSD; Postgrad Rsch Nephrologist, UCSD; Lectr, Snr Lectr, Vic Univ. Publications: 31 in sci jrnls. Honours: NSF Predoct Fellshp, 1970; NIH Postdoct Fellshp, 1972; Natl Kidney Fndn Fellship, 1975. Memberships: Cncl Mbr, Physiological Soc of NZ, 1979-84, 1986-94, 1995-97; Cncl Mbr, Wgtn Soc for Biomedl Rsch, 1985-93, 1999-; Cttee Mbr, Natl Cttee, Physiology of the Roy Soc of NZ (IUPS), 1988-93; Chmn, Soc for Biomedl Rsch, Wellington, 1990-92; Cncl Mbr, Wellington Medl Rsch Fndn, 1994-; Cttee Mbr, NZ Physiology Conf Soc (IUPS 2001), 1995-. Hobbies: Tennis; Bridge; Hiking. Address: School of Biological Sciences, Victoria University, PO Box 600, Wellington, New Zealand.

MILLER Walter Geoffrey Thomas, b. 25 Oct 1934, Queenstown, Tas, Aust. Diplomat. m. Rachel Caroline Webb, 13 Aug 1960, 3 s, 1 d. Education: BA, hons, Tas; MA, Oxford Univ, Eng. Appointments: Austl High Cmmn, Kuala Lumpur, 1960-62; Austl Emb, Jakarta, 1965-67; Austl Perm Miss to the UN, NY, USA, 1967-70 Dpty High Cmmnr, New Delhi, India, 1973-75 Austl Amb to Korea, 1978-80; Dpty Sec, Dept of For Affairs, Canberra, Aust, 1983-86; Austl Amb to Japan, 1986-89; Dir-Gen, Off of Natl Assessments, Canberra, Aust, 1989-95; Austl High Cmmn to NZ, 1996-. Honours: Tas Rhodes Schl, 1956; AO, 1993. Membership: Austl Inst of Intl Affairs. Hobbies: International Relations; Literature; Ballet; Tennis; Golf. Address: Australian High Commission, Wellington, New Zealand.

MILLHOUSE Robin Rhodes, b. 9 Dec 1929, Adelaide, Aust. Supreme Court Judge. m. Margaret Ann Radford, 2 Mar 1957, 2 s, 3 d. Education: St Peter's Coll, Adelaide; LLB, St Mark's Coll, Univ of Adelaide, 1951. Appointments: Mbr, Mitcham in South Austl House of Assembly, 1955-82; Atty-Gen, Min for Community Welfare and Min of Aboriginal Affairs, 1968-70; Ldr, Austl Democrats, 1977-82; Judge of Supreme Crt of S Aust. 1982-; Cmdng Offr, Adelaide Univ Regiment, 1972-75. Honour: Reserve Forces Decoration, 1985. Hobbies: Triathlon; Nude bathing; Bike riding; Swimming. Address: 8 Whistler Avenue, Unley park 5061, Australia.

MILLIGAN Robert James, b. 31 Aug 1940, Windermere, Eng. m. Marie-Lou Travers, 2 s, 1 d. Education: London Coll of Printing; Westminster Bus Coll. Appointments: HMSO, printing apprentice, 1957-61; McGraw Hill, Prodn Mngr, 1962-66; J Sainsbury Grp, Printing Mngr, 1967-70; Woolworths Divisional Mngr, 1973-79; Esselte Aust, Mng Dir, 1979-81; NCR Aust, Dir, 1982-88; Gen Mngr and NSW Govt Printer, 1990-. Memberships: Printing Inds Assn; Lithographic Inst of Aust; Assoc Fell, Aust Inst of Mngmt, Justice of the Peace. Hobbies: Coaching Soccer; Bushwalking; Reading. Address: NSW Government Printing Service, PO Box 256, Regents Park, NSW 2143, Australia.

MILLINGTON Alan Fred, b. 22 Feb 1935, Stourport-on-Severn, Eng. Professor of Land Economy. Education: BSc, Estate Mngmnt, Urban, 1965, BSc, Estate Mngmnt, Rural, 1967, Coll of Estate Mngmnt, Univ of London. Appointments: Bus, 1955-59; Lloyds Bank Ltd, 1960-62; Surv, Pvte Prac, 1965-68; Lectr, Coll of Estate Mngmnt, London, 1968-72; Lectr, Univ of Reading, 1972-78; Prof of Land Economy, Paisley Coll, Scotland, 1978-84, 1985-86; Superintending Estates Surv, Dept of Hlth and Socl Security, London 1984; Dean, Faculty of Bus and Land Economy, Univ of Western Sydney, NSW, Aust, 1986-92; Prof of Land Economy, 1989-96. Publications: An Introduction to Property Valuation, 1975, 3rd Edition, 1988, 4th Edition, 1994, 5 other impressions, Malaysian translation, 1987; Chinese translation, 1989; Retail Property in Australia, 1995. Honours: VP, 1982-83, Pres, 1983-84, BSc Estate Mngmnt Club. Memberships: Fell, Roy Instn of Chartered Survs; Fell, Brit Inst of Mngmnt; Fell, Austl Inst of Valuers and Land Economists, 1987-96; Inst of Revenues, Rating & Valuation. Hobbies: Swimming; Motor-Sport; Motorcycling; Reading; Photography; Travel; Listening to music. Address: 43 Keda Circuit, North Richmond, NSW 2754, Australia.

MILLIS Nancy Fannie, b. 10 Apr 1922, Melbourne, Aust. Microbiologist. Education: BAgricSc. 1946, MAgricSc, 1948, Univ of Melbourne; PhD, Bristol, 1952. Appointments: Lectr, 1953, Rdr, 1968, Personal Chair, 1982, Prof Emer, 1987, Univ of Melbourne; Chmn, Genetic Manipulation Advsry Cttee, 1987; Chan, La Trobe Univ, 1992; Dir, Melbourne Pks and Waterways, 1995; Mbr, Food Safety Cncl, 1998. Publications: Auth of 40 rsch pprs; Co-auth of 2 books; Auth of 4 chapts in 4 monographs; Auth of 7 maj reports for Govt Agcies. Honours: AM, White Schl, 1947; Boots Rsch Schl, 1950; Fulbright Travel Grant and Austl Fedn Univ Womens Schl, 1954; MBE, 1977; Fell, Austl Acady Technol Sci and Engrng, 1977; Hon Life Mbr, Austl Soc of Microbiol, 1987; AC, 1990; DSc, honoris causa, Univ of Melbourne, 1993. Memberships: Austl Soc for Microbiol; Austl Biotechnol Assn. Hobbies: Gardening; Sitting in the sun; Listening to music; Science policy; Genetic engineering. Address: Microbiology Department, University of Melbourne, Parkville, Victoria 3052, Australia.

MILNE Douglas James Wood, b. 1 Jan 1944, Dundee, Scotland. Theology College Lecturer. m. 31 July 1969, 1 s, 1 d. Education: MA, hons, 1967, BDiv, 1970, Aberdeen Univ; Dip, Free Ch of Scotland Coll, Edinburgh, 1970; MTh, Westminster Theol Seminary, Phila, USA, 1971; ThD, Potchefstroom Univ, S Afr, 1989. Appointments: Parish Min, Glen Urquhart, Scotland, 1972-79; Visng Prof, 1979-82, Prof, 1982-91, New Testament, Vice Prin, 1985-, Prof, Theol and Ethics, 1991-, Presby Theol Coll, Melbourne; Chmn, Middle East Reformed Fellshp, Aust Inc, 1991. Publication: 1 & 2

Timothy, Titus, 1996. Honours: Robert Donaldson Prize, Biblical Study, Aberdeen Univ, 1964, 1965; Ewan Prize, Biblical Study, Aberdeen Univ, 1967; Duncan Fraser Prize, Old Testament, Free Ch of Scotland, 1978. Hobbies: Ornithology; Reading. Listed in: Who's Who in Australia. Address: 621 Punt Road, South Yarra, Melbourne, Vic 3141, Australia.

MILNE Henry James Ogston, b. 31 Jan 1942, Moshi, Tanganyka. Lecturer. m. Heather L, 7 May 1969, 2 s. Education: Bachelor Educl Studies, Univ Queensland, 1975; Grad Dip Spec Educ (Mildly Mentally Handicapped), Mt Gravatt Coll of Advd Educ, 1976; Master Educl Studies, Univ Queensland, 1983; Grad Dip in Distance Educ, S Austl Coll of Advd Educ, 1987; MA (Educ, Gifted & Talented), Univ of CT, 1996. Appointments include: Primary sch tchr, Queensland Dept of Educ, 1969-72; Tchr, Opportunity Schs (Mildly Intellectually Handicapped), Div of Spec Educ, 1972-74; Acting Prin, Dutton Pk Opportunity Sch, 1973; Tchr, in Charge Opportunity Classes, Div, Spec Educ, Queensland Dept of Educ, 1974-77; Lectr, Spec Educ, Mt Gravatt CAE, 1977-81; Lectr, Psychol & Spec Educ, Brisbane CAW, MT Gravatt CAE, 1981-89; Lectr, Griffith Univ, Fac of Educ, Sch of Cognition, Learning and Spec Educ, Mt Gravatt Campus, 1989-; Visng Rschr, Assoc NRC-GT, Univ CT. Publications: Num books, monographs, book chapts, conf pprs, presentations, referred jrnl articles; contbns to non-refreed jrnls. Honours include: Intl Man of Yr, 1992-1993, IBC, 1993; Inaugural Mbr, Editl Cttee, Australasian Jrnl of Gifted Educ. Memberships include: NZ Territorial Force, 1959-70; Eurn Cncl for High Ability; World Cncl for Gifted and Talented Children; Intl Assn for Spec Educ; Austl Assn for Educ of Gifted and Talented Ltd; Austl Assn for Spec Educ Inc; Queensland Assn for Gifted and Talented Children Inc; Natl Assn for Gifted Children (USA); Assn for Educ of Gifted Underachieving Students; Natl Assn for Gifted Children (UK). Address: Griffith University, Faculty of Education, School of Cognition, Language and Special Education, Mt Gravatt Campus, Australia.

MILTON Peter, b. 22 Sept 1928, London, Eng. Politician. m. Winifred Ellen Spinks, 28 Mar 1953, 2 s, 1 d. Education: BA, Univ of Melbourne, 1978. Appointments: RAF, 1946-49; Clk, Merchant Bank, 1950-60; Acct, 1961; Asst Registrar, Univ of Melbourne, 1962-80; Mbr, Austl Parl, 1980-90; Chmn, House of Reps Standing Cttee on Environ, Recreation & The Arts, 1983-90. Memberships: Assoc, Chart Inst of Secs & Admnstrs; C'wlth Parly Assn. Hobbies: Jogging; Reading; Music. Address: 3 Burston Road, Boronia, Vic 3155, Australia.

MIN Pingqiu, b. 24 Oct 1935, Chongching, China. Chief Engineer. m. Liu Zheng Fang, 8 Feb 1965, 2 d. Education: Grad, Beijing Pet Coll, 1960. Appointments: Techn, Lanzhou Oil Refinery, 1960-65; Engr, Lanzhou Oil Refinery, 1965-74; Engr, Engrng Co of Archtl Installation of Beijing Yanshan Petrochemical Co (AIBYPC), 1974-83; Vice Chf Engr (AIBYPC), 1983-88; Chf Engr (AIBYPC), 1988-95. Publications include: Stress Corrosion and Crevice Corrosion of the Non-penetration Weld of the Tee Fittings, 1981; Iron Contamination on the Titanium Equipment, 1983; Inspection of Equipment and Fittngs, 1984; Quality Control in the Course of Large Spherical Storage Tank, 1985; Corrosion Category of Equipment for Polyester Plant, 1988; Low Stress Brittle Fracture of Pressure Vessel, 1991; Inspection and Evaluation of the Oxidising Reactor Made of Titanium Cladding Steel Plate, 1995; Corrosion Category of Oil Refinery, 1996. Honour: Outstndng Expert Subsidy, Chinese Cntrl Govt, 1993-. Memberships: Exec, Beijing Petrochemical Inst, 1986-95; Mbr of Exec, Sino Petrochemical Mechl Inst, 1986-95. Hobbies: Photography; Music. Address: Beijing PO Box 276, 3 Yandong Road, Yanshan, Fangshan District, Beijing, China Post Code 102502.

MINAGAWA Sitiro, b. 2 Jan 1928, Kashiwazaki, Japan. Applied Mathematics. m. Miyako, 24 Jan 1960, 1 d. Education: DEng, Univ Tokyo. Appointments: Asst Prof, Tohoku Univ; Prof, Univ of Electro-Commn, Prof,

Niigata Univ of Intl and Info Studies. Publications: Num articles in profl jrnls. Honour: Emer Prof, Univ of Electro-Commns. Memberships: Pres, Materials Sci Soc of Japan, 1995-97. Address: Sakuradai 1-33-9, Nerimaku, Tokyo 176-0002, Japan.

MINCHIN Devon George, b. 28 May 1919, Sydney, Aust. Farmer. m. Margo, 3 s, 3 d. Education: BA. Appointments: Gen Patterson Advtng, 1934; Vick Chem, 1937; RAAF, 1940; Dir, Colonial Timbers, Sarawak, 1946; Chmn and MD, MSS Aust, 1954; Retd, 1970. Publications: The Potato Man (novel), 1943; The Money Movers, 1972; Isabel's Mine, 1989. Membership: Austl Club. Hobbies: Swimming; Golf. Address: Wappa Falls Farm, Yandina, Qld 4501, Australia.

MINERS John Oliver, b. 31 Oct 1948, Wellington, New Zealand. Pharmacologist; Toxicologist. m. (1) 2 s, (2) Kathleen Knights, 4 Apr 1987. Education: BSc, 1969, MSc, 1971, PhD, 1974, Vic Univ of Wellington. Appointments: Postdoct Rsch Sci, Oxford Univ, 1974-76; Toxicologist, Dept of Med Biochem, 1977-78, Chf Pharmacologist, Dept of Clin Pharmacol, 1979-, Flinders Medl Cntr, Adelaide; Prof of Pharmacol, Sch of Med, 1992-, Profl Hd, Unit of Environ Hlth, Sch of Med, 1996-98, Flinders Univ of SA, Adelaide. Publications: Over 250 rsch pprs, reviews, book chapts and published abstracts. Honour: DSc, Flinders Univ of SA, 1997. Memberships: Austl Soc of Clin and Experimental Pharmacols and Toxicols, Chair, Scientific Advsry Cttee; Intl Soc for the Study of Xenobiotics; Amn Soc of Clin Pharmacol and Therapeutics; Gastroenterol Soc of Aust; NZ Inst of Chems, fell; Intl Soc for Therapeutic Drug Monitoring and Clin Toxicol; Drug Metabolism Section of IUPHAR, Chmn Elect; Pacific Rim Assn for Clin Pharmacogenetics. Hobbies: Rugby Union; Cricket; Golf. Address: Department of Clinical Pharmacology, Flinders Medical Centre, Bedford Park, SA 5042, Australia.

MINHAJ UDDIN Shiekh Mohammad, b. 5 Oct 1952, Karachi, Pakistan. Business. m. Fauzia, 12 Oct 1979, 1 s, 1 d. Education: MBBS. Appointment: Dir, The Times Press Pvt Ltd. Membership: Exec Cttee, Pakistan Assn of Printing & Graphic Arts. Hobbies: Swimming; Golf; Yoga. Address: C-18 Al Hilal Society, University Road, Karachi, Pakistan.

MINHAS Sukhdev Singh, b. 7 July 1961, Paldi. Teacher. m. Manjit, 29 Nov 1989, 2 d. Education: BA, Hons; MA; Mphil; PhD; Dip in Transl. Creative Works: Articles in Eng, Hindi, Panjabi Dailies and Mags. Hobbies: Writing; Watching cricket; Music. Address: Kothi No 3374/1, Sector 40-D, Chandigarh, India.

MINOGUE Dannii (Danielle Jane), b. 20 Oct 1971, Melbourne, Victoria, Aust. Singer; Actress; Fashion Designer; TV Presenter. Appointments: Actress, Austl TV dramas: Skyways, 1978; The Sullivans, 1978; All the Way, 1988; Home and Away, 1989; TV Presenter: Young Talent Time, Aust, 1979-88; New Generation, Aust & USA, 1988; Co-Host: Big Breakfast, UK, 1993; Fan T C, UK, 1994; Disney's Dannii on Safari, 1995; It's Not Just Saturday, 1995-96; Scoop, 1996; Disney's Cirque du Monde, 1996; BBC's Electric Circus, 1996-98; Disney Villains, 1997; Top of the Pops (host), 1997; Film: Secrets, 1993; Perfs incl: Royal Children's Variety Perf, 1991; Cesme Fest, Turkey, 1992; Gay Pride Fest, London, 1993, 1994; Promotional tours of Aust, SE Asia, USA & UK. Creative works: Album recordings: Love and Kisses, 1991; Get into You, 1993; Girl, 1997; Singles recordings: Love and Kisses, 1990; This Is It, 1993; This is the Way, 1993; All I Wanna Do, 1997; Everything I Wanted, 1997; Disremembrance, 1998; Contbr: The Gift of Christmas, Child Liners, 1995. Honours: Gold Discs, UK & Aust; Young Variety Awd, Austl Variety Club, 1989. Membership: Austl Actor's Equity, APRA. Address: c/o Terry Blamey Management Pty Ltd, 329 Montague Street, Albert Park, Victoria, Australia.

MINOGUE Kylie (Ann), b. 28 May 1968, Melbourne, Victoria, Aust. Singer; Actress. Appointments: Actress, Austl TV dramas: Skyways, 1980; The Sullivans, 1981; The Henderson Kids, 1984-85; Neighbours, 1986-88;

Film appearances: The Deliquents, 1989; Streetfighter, 1994; Bio Dome, 1995; As Singer: biggest selling single of decade in Aust, Locomotion, 1987; Highest UK chart entry for female artist, Locomotion, 1988; Highest debut album chart entry, Aust and UK, Kylie, 1988; First ever artist w 4 top 3 singles from an album; First female artist w first 5 singles to receive Silver Discs; Perfs incl: Austl Royal Bicentennial Concert, 1988; John Lennon Tribute, Liverpool, 1990; Cesne Music Fest, Turkey, 1992; Sydney Gay Mardi Gras, 1994; Prince's Trust Concert, 1994; T in the Park Fest, Glasgow, 1995; Tours of UK, Eur, Asia and Aust; Perf at Sydney Gay and Lesbian Mardi Gras, 1998; Sell-out tour of Aust, 1998; London Shepherd's Bush Empire, 1998; Creative works: Album recordings: Kylie, 1988; Enjoy Yourself, 1989; Rhythm of Love, 1990; Let's Get To It, 1991; Kylie - Greatest Hits, 1992; Kylie Minogue, 1994; Impossible Princess, 1998; Singles recordings incl: Locomotion, 1987; I Should Be So Lucky, 1988; Je Ne Sais Pas Pourquoi, 1988; Especially For You (w Jason Donovan), 1988; Never Too Late, 1989; Confide In Me, 1994; Put Yourself In My Place, 1995; Where is the Feeling, 1995; Where the Wild Roses Grow (duet w Nick Cave), 1995; Some Kind of Bliss, 1997; Did it Again, 1997; Breathe, 1998; Honours: Num Platinum, Gold & Silver Discs; 6 Logies, Aust; 6 Music Week Awds, UK; 3 Smash Hits Awds, UK; 3 Austl Record Ind Assn Awds; 3 Japanese Music Awds; Irish Record Ind Awd; Canad Record Ind Awd; World Music Awd; Austl Variety Club Awd; MO Awd (Austl Showbusiness); Amplex Golden Reel Awd; Diamond Awd, Belgium; Woman of the Decade, UK; MTV Austl Video of the Yr, 1998. Address: c/o Terry Blamey Management Pty Ltd, 329 Montague Street, Albert Park, Victoria, Australia.

MINTON Yvonne Fay, b. 4 Dec 1938, Sydney, Aust. Opera and Concert Singer (Mezzo Soprano). m. William Barclay, 21 Aug 1965, 1 s, 1 d. Education: Sydney Conservatorium. Appointments: Soloist w major Austl orchs; In 1964 appeared in premiere of Nicholas Maw's One Man Show; Soloist w Royal Opera, Covent Garden, notably as Mussorgsky's Marina, Mozart's Dorabella, Strauss' Octavian, Wagner's Waltraute and Thea, in premiere of Tippett's Knot Garden, 1970; Has appeared w most major symph orchs in the world and at all major opera houses; Sang Octavian at the Metrop, 1973; Brangaene at Bayreuth Fest, 1974; Fricka and Waltraute in Centenary Ring, 1976; Octavian at Paris Opéra, 1976; Countess Geschwitz in premiere of the 3-act vern of Lulu; Kundry at Covent Garden, in new prodn of Parsifal; Waltraute at Turin Opera, 1988; Sang Fricka in Die Walküre at Lisbon, 1989; Leokadja Begbick in Mahagonny at 1990 Maggio Musicale, Florence; Season 1993-94 as Marguerite in La Damnation de Faust at Wellington and Mme Larina in Eugene Onegin at Glyndebourne. Creative works: Recordings: Concert recordings w Chgo Symph Orch, BBC Symph Orch and others; Opera recordings incl: Rosenkavalier; La Clemenza di Tito; Wagner's Ring; Tristan and Isolde. Honours: Hon RAM, 1977; CBE, 1981. Hobbies: Gardening; Reading. Address: c/o Ingpen and Williams, 26 Wadham Road, London SW15 2LR, England.

MINTZ Leigh Wayne, b. 12 June 1939, Cleveland, Ohio, USA. University Administrator; Professor. m. Carol, 4 Aug 1962, 1 s, 1 d. Education: BS, Geol, 1961, MS, 1962, Univ MI; PhD, Paleontol, Univ CA, Berkeley. Appointments: Asst Prof, 1966-70, Assoc Dean of Instrn, 1969-70, of Sci, 1970-71, Assoc Prof, 1970-75, Dean, Undergrad Stdies, 1972-79, Prof, 1975-, Assoc VP, 1979-, CA Univ, Hayward. Publications: Historical Geology, 1972, 1977, 1981; Physical Geology, 1982; Sev articles in profl jrnls. Honours: Natl Sci Fndn Grad Fellshp; Woodrow Wilson Fndn Fellshp (declined); Morris Miller Wells Schlsp; Palmer Prize. Memberships: Geol Soc of Am; Paleontol Soc; Sigma Xi. Hobbies: Travel; Photography. Address: California State University, Hayward, CA 94542, USA.

MINTZ Shlomo, b. 30 Oct 1957, Moscow, Russia. Violinist. m. Corina Ciacci, 2 s. Education: Juilliard Sch of Music, NY. Appointments: Premio Accademia Musicale Chigiana, Siena, Italy, 1984; Music Dir, Conductor,

Soloist, Israel Chamber Orch, 1989-. Creative Works: Recordings incl: Violin Concertos by Mendelssohn & Bruch, 1981, J S Bach Complete Sonatas & Partitas for Solo Violin, The Miraculous Mandarin by Bartok, Compositions & Arrangements by Kreisler, The Four Seasons by Vivaldi. Honours include: Grand Prix du Disque, Diapason d'Or, 1981. Address: ICM Artists Ltd, 40 West 57th Street, NY 10019, USA.

MIR Abdul Aziz, b. 13 Jan 1924. Journalist. m. Surayya, Nov 1954, 5 s, 2 d. Education: BA, hons, Punjab Univ. Appointments: Ed, Weekly Millat, FREEOM, Times of Kashmir, INSAF Weekly. Publications: Kashmir Freedom Struggle; Murder of Human Rights in Kashmir; Kashmir Needs Attention; The Kashmiri Language; How to Learn Kashmiri; Sheikh Nooruddin Wali of Kashmir. Honours: Shield and Awd, Kashmir Freedom Movement, 1986; Pres Awd, Pride of Perf in Field of Jrnlsm, Pres of Pakistan, 1996; PM of Pakistan Spec Lit Awd, 1999. Memberships: Gen Sec, Muslim Conf Jamu and Kashmir, 1950, 1956; Gen Sec, Kashmir Muslim Students Union; Sec, Kashmir Cultural Cntr; Pres, Kashmir Cncl of Newsppr Eds. Hobby: Human Rights. Address: Times of Kashmir, P-929 Banni, Rawalpindi, Pakistan.

MIRANI Aftab Shahban, Politician. m. 1 s, 3 d. Education: Farm Mngmt, Agricl, USA. Appointments: Fmr Pres, Shikarpur Municipality; Mbr, Sindh Prov Assembly, 1977-90; Chf Min of Sindh, 1990; Mbr, Natl Assembly, 1990-; Min of Def, 1993-96. Hobbies: Walking; Swimming. Address: Ministry of Defence, Pakistan Secretariat, No 11 Rawalpindi, 46000 Islamabad, Pakistan.

MIRAVALLES Lemuel M, b. 16 July 1946, Philippines. Consultant; Educator; Industrial Development Specialist. Myrna P Miravalles, 20 May 1973. Education: BSChE, Univ of Philippines, Manila, 1962-67; MEng (IE & OR), 1968-71; Princeton Univ, WWS, NJ, 1977-78; World Bank, EDI, Wash DC, 1981; Harvard Univ, HIID Cambridge, MA, 1989. Appointments include: (Acad appts) Fac Mbr, Univ Philippines, Coll of Engrng, 1967-73, Grad Sch of Engrng, 1971-73, 1987-88; Profl Lectr, Ateneo de Manila Univ, MBA prog, 1974-80, 1988-96; (Govt of Philippines appts) Prog Dir, Info Systems, Dev Acady of Philippines, 1973-75; Prog Dir, Plng Support Servs, Hum Settlements Commn, 1975-77; Prog Dir, Technobank, Technol Resource Cntr, 1977-80; Dir Gen/Dpty DG, Natl Manpower and Yth Cncl, 1980-86; (Cnslt appts) World Bank, India, 1988; USAID, Manila, 1989, 1990-92; Govt of Kenya, 1992; Govt of Philippines, BTVE, BNFE, NEDA, 1993-96; Colombo Plan Staff Coll, 1992-95; UNESCO, Bangkok, 1994-95; ADB, Team Leader, Bangladesh NFE TA Proj, 1996-2001. Honours: Coll Schl, RP-US Fac Dev Fell, JICA, Japan, 1974; Phi Kappa Phi, Univ Philippines; Parvin Fell, Princeton, 1977-78; Study vis Fellshps incl Brit Cncl, London, 1979, 1984; IDRC, Ottawa, 1979; Japan's Min of Labour, Tokyo, 1980, 1985; French Min of External Rels, Paris, 1983, 1985; Italian Trade Commn, Rome, 1982; Provl Govt of Ont, Can, 1982; Johnson Fndn, Wisconsin, 1983; APSDEP ILO, West Samoa, 1980, Tokyo, 1981, Jakarta, 1985; US Trade and Dev Prog, Wash DC, 1983; ACCC, Ottawa, 1997. Memberships include: Assn of Princeton Grad Alumni, Cambridge, MA; Soc Intl Dev, Wash DC; Univ of Philippines Alumni Engrs. Hobbies: Swimming; Golf; Reading. Address: Asian Development Bank, NFETA Project, ADB BRM Office, Sheraton Annex, Minto Road, Dhaka, Bangladesh.

MIRSAIDOV Shukurulla Rakhmatovich, b. 14 Feb 1938, Leninabad. Politician. m. 4 children. Education: Tashkent Fin & Econ Inst. Appointments: Mbr, CPSU, 1962-91; Staff, State Planning Org, 1964-84; Hd, Ctrl Stats Dept, Uzbek SSR, 1984-85; Chair, Tashkent City Cncl, 1985-86; Hd of Dept, CP of Uzbekistan, 1988-89; Dpty Premier of Uzbekistan SSR, 1989-90; Chair, Cncl of Mins, 1990-92; VP of Uzbekistan, 1991-92; State Sec for Pres Karimov, 1992; Rep, Intl Fund for Privatization & Investments in Uzbekistan, 1992-95. Address: International Fund for Privatization, Tashkent, Uzbekistan.

MIRZA Mahmud-ul-Hassan, b. 15 Nov 1927, Lahore, Pakistan. Business Consultant. m. Tasawar Sultana, 11 Nov 1962, 3 s, 2 d. Education: Punjab Coll Engrng & Technol, 1944-49; Cty & Guilds, London, 1947; Inst Mech Engrs Sect, London, 1950-51. Appointments: Tech Dir, Pakistan Publr, 1968-81; Mngng Ptnr, 1988; Owner, 1988; Cnslt, Mirza Book Agcy; Lectr, Trng Courses, Natl Book Cncl of Pakistan, Brit Cncl, US Info Agcy. Publications include: He Saw Much to Improve, 1958; Booktrade in Pakistan, 1962; Making of a Bookstore in Pakistan, 1964; Problems of Imported Books and Magazines in Pakistan, 1961. Honours: Num hons, awds & prizes. Memberships: Life Mbr, Pakistan Assn for Adv of Sci, Pakistan Life Assn, Pakistan Assn of Scis & Sci Profession; Bangladesh Lib Assn; Assoc Mbr, Intl Bookseller Fedn, Brussels; Natl Assn of Coll Store, Oberlin; Logas Intl Advsry Bd; Pakistan Am Alumni Assn; Lahore Chmbr of Comm & Ind; Govt Import Grp; Pakistan Publr & Bookseller Assn. Hobbies: Listening to Foreign Radio Stations; Watching Games; Travel. Address: Mirza Book Agency, 65 Shahrah e-Quaid-Azam, PO Box 729, Lahore 54000, Pakistan.

MIRZAKHANIAN Edmond, b. 5 Dec 1972, Tehran, Iran. Economic Development & Planning. Education: MS, Econ Dev & Plng; BA, Econs; BSc, Computer Science. Appointments: VP, SAT Consulting Engrs; Econ Rsch Mngr, AZAD Islamic Univ, Tehran Cntrl Branch. Publications: Num articles on Econs. Honour: Islamic Azad Univ, BS Hon Student Awd, 1994. Memberships: Iranian Econ Soc, 1990; Iranian Econ Dev Assmn, 1993; Armenian Soc of Univ Grads, 1991. Hobbies: Travel; Books; Internet Navigation. Address: #1.92 16th Avenue, Mirzaye Shirazy Street, Tehran 15967, Iran.

MISHIMA Hiroyuki, b. 8 Jan 1952, Koriyama, Fukushima, Japan. Assistant Professor. m. Amiko, 6 Mar 1983, 1 s, 2 d. Education: BS, Tokai Univ, 1974. Appointments: Priv hs Tchr, 1974-75; Prefectural hs Tchr, 1975-77; Asst, 1977-78, Instr, 1978-88, Nihon Univ Sch of Dentistry at Matsudo, 1977-78, Asst Prof. Publications: Tooth Enamel IV, 1984; Profl jrnl. Memberships: Intl Assn for Dental Rsch; Japanese Assn Anatomists; Japanese Assn Oral Bio; Microscopy Soc Am; NY Acady Sci. Hobbies: Jogging; Climbing; Reading; Fishing. Address: Department of Anatomy, Nihon University School of Dentistry at Matsudo, 2-870-1 Sakaecho-Nishi, Matsudo, Chiba 271-8587, Japan.

MISHRA Ahilya, b. 16 Sept 1948, Sagarpur Madhubani, Bihar, India. Hon Director, NVA. m. Shri R D Mishra, 1 July 1964, 1 s. Education: MA; MPhil; PhD; PhD; MEd. Appointments: VP & Dir, Inst. Publications: Patthar patthar patthar, 1988; Cactus par Gulab, 1996; Nari dansh dalan dayitwa. Honours: Hon by Lion Club of Hyd, Good Tchr, 1998 & Achray Upadhi Gemini Acady Arriyana; Intl Woman of Yr, 1998. Memberships: Bihar Assn, former Joint Sec; Mahila Samaj-Pres, Nagar Zilla Samithi. Hobbies: Poetry; Essay; Reading; Stroy. Address: 93/C Vengalrao Nagar, Hyd 500890, India.

MISHRA Purnananda, b. 29 June 1961, Bhubaneswar, India. Doctor. m. S Mishra, 30 May 1991, 1 s. Education: MS, Ophthalmol. Appointments: Rdr in Ophthalmol; Prof in Ophthalmol. Honours: Best Postgrad in Ophthalmol, 1989; Fell, Retina Fndn, Ahemedabad. Memberships: All India Ophthalmol Soc; Intraocular Implant and Refractive Soc. Memberships: Intra-Ocular Implant Surgery; Retinal Surgery. Address: RMMCH, Annamalai nagar 608 002, Tamil Nadu, India.

MISHRA Raghu Nath (Mt Hon Lord Sir), b. 7 Apr 1947, Amwa Digar, India. Engineering Educator. m. Ms Abha, 30 Jan 1973, 2 s, 1 d. Education: BSEE, hons, 1965-69; MTEE, 1969-71; PhD, 1971-75; DCT, 1988. Appointments: Snr Rsch Asst, Indian Inst of Technol, Kanpur, 1973-75; Asst Prof, Dept of Elec Engrng, 1975-87, Assoc Prof, Disting Prof, Dept of Computer Engrng, 1987-97, Prof Computer Engrng, 1997-, Coll of Technol, GBPUAT, Pant Nagar. Publications: Estimation, Detection and Identification Methods in Power System Studies, 1975; Assumptions in Theory of Ballistic Galvanometer, 1980; Num other profl articles in sci jrnls.

Honours: Intl Biographical Roll of Hon, Goldtone Plaque; Ctf, Intl Register of Profiles, 1982; Ctf of Merit, 1984; 1st 500 Silver Medal w Commemorative Personal Plaque, 1985; IBC Paperweight & Letter Opener, 1987; IBC Ctf of Appreciation, 1988; Intl Who's Who of Intellectuals Gilt Medal, Intl Leaders of Achmt Gilt Medal, 1989; Bharat Gaurav Awd. Memberships: Doctl Mbr, World Univ Roundtable; Life Mbr, Indian Soc for Tech Educn; Fell, United Writers Assn, Madras. Hobbies: Photography; Euthenics; Social and community service. Listed in: Reference Asia; Indo-European Who's Who; Who's Who in the Commonwealth. Address: V & P O Amwa Digar, Tehsil, Tamkuhi Raj, District Kushinagar UP 274 302, India.

MISRA Sri Prakash, b. 29 June 1957, Mughalsarai, India. Medical Doctor. m. Vatsala, 17 Apr 1983, 1 s, 1 d. Education: MB BS, 1980; MD, 1984; DM, 1988. Appointments: Asst Prof, Gastroeneterology, 1990-98; Assoc Prof, 1999-. Publications: Over 90 profl medl jrnls. Honours: Hoechst Om-Prakash Mem Awd, 1992, Olympus-Mitra Awd, 1996, Indian Soc of Gastroeneterology; SN Gupta Awd, 1995, N N Gupta Awd, 1996, Assn of Physns of India (UP Chapt); Fell, Natl Acady of Sci (India), 1996; Intl G I Trng Grant Awd, Amn Coll of Gastroenterology; Postdoct Fell, Mayo Clin, Rochester, MN, USA; Sisco-Pentax Oration, Soc of Gastrointestinal Endoscopy of India, 1998; Investigators Awd, Asia Pacific Assn of Gastroenterology, Manila, Philippines, 1998; Searle Oration, Assn of Physns of India, 1999. Memberships: Indian Soc of Gastroenterology; Indian Assn for Study of the Liver; Indian Acady of Gastroenterology; Soc of Gastrointestinal Endoscopy of India; Assn of Physns of India; Indian Medl Assn. Hobbies: Music; Sports. Address: 4/411, MLN Medical College Campus, Allahabad, 211 001, India.

MISRA Ushakant, b. 10 Apr 1952, Azamgarh, UP, India. Medical Doctor. m. Sunita, 2 s. Education: MBBS; MD; FAMS. Appointments: Scientist Neurotoxicology, 1980-87; Lectr Neurol, 1987; Addl Prof, Neur, 1987-93, Prof Neur, 1993-, SGPGI. Publications: Clinical Neurophysiology: Nerve Conduction. Memberships: Corresp Fell, Amn Acady of Neur; Assoc Mbr, Amn Acady of Electrodiagnostic and Med. Address: Department of Neurology, Danjay Gandhi PGI, Lucknow 126014, India.

MITA Katsushige, b, 6 Apr 1924, Tokyo, Japan. Business Executive. m. Toriko Miyata, 1957, 2 d. Education: Univ Tokyo. Appointments: Joined, 1949, Gen Mngr, Omika Wrks, Aug-Nov 1971, Gen Mngr, Kanagawa Wrks, 1971-75, Dir, Kanagawa Wrks, 1975, Mngr, Computer Grp, 1976-78, Exec Mngng Dir, 1977-79, Snr Exec Mngng Dir, 1979-80, Exec VP, 1980-81, Pres, 1981-91, Rep Dir, 1981-99, Chmn, 1991-99, Chmn Emer, 1999- Hitachi Ltd. Honours: Blue Ribbon Medal, Japan, 1985; Dr honoris causa, Tufts Univ, USA, 1991; Officier, Légion d'honneur, 1993; DSPN Dato, Malaysia, 1993; Will Rogers Awd, USA, 1994; Dr, honoris causa, Univ OK, USA, 1996. Membership: Keidanren (Japanese Fedn Econ Orgs). Hobbies: Golf; Gardening. Address: 2423-277 Nara-machi, Aoba-ku, Yokohama-shi, Kanagawa-ken 227, Japan.

MITA Mahamuda Nasrin, b. 6 May 1979, Dilal Pur, Pabna, Bangladesh. Student. Education: SSC, 1994; HBC, 1996. Appointments: Mbr, Bangladesh Cultural Assn, Pabna, Bangladesh; Reporter, Weekly Priobhashi, Dhaka, Bangladesh. Publications: Poems, columns, cultural articles, story. Membership: Bangladesh Cultural Assn, 1998. Hobbies: Collection of Stamps; Coins; Reading; Writing; Gardening. Address: Manamuda Nasrin Mita, Hamida Manzil-1, Dilalpur, Pabna 6600, Bangladesh.

MITCHELL Bruce Tyson, b. 6 Nov 1928, San Francisco, USA. Attorney at Law. m. Adrienne, 14 Oct 1951, 1 s. Education: AB Econs, 1949 JD, 1951, Stanford Univ. Appointments: Snr Cnsl, UT Intl Inc, 1958-87; Corp Sec, 1974-87. Memberships: C'wlth Club of CA; Am Soc of Corp Secs; San Mateo County Repub Ctrl Cttee; San Fran Jnr Cham of Com; State Bar of CA;

Am Bar Assn; Bar Assn of San Fran; Am Judicature Soc; St Francis Fndn; Arthritis Fndn; Alternate Del, Repub Natl Convention, 1968; Pacific-Union Club, San Fran; Olympic Club, San Fran; Capitol Hill Club, WA, DC. Hobby: Travel. Address: 165 Redwood Drive, Hillsborough, CA 94010, USA.

MITCHELL Edwin Arthur, b. 26 May 1948, Abadan, Iran. Paediatrician. m. Hilary, 8 Dec 1979, 1 s, 1 d. Education: BSc, MB, BS, DCH, FRACP, DSc, FRCPCH. Appointment: Assoc Prof, Paediats, Univ Auckland. Publications: Over 150 rsch pprs in profl jrnls. Memberships: Fell, RACP, RCPCH; PSNZ. Hobbies: Sailing; Skiing. Address: Department of Paediatrics, University of Auckland, Private Bag 92019, Auckland, New Zealand.

MITCHELL (Sibyl) Elyne Keith, b. 30 Dec 1913, Melbourne, Aust. Author; Grazier. m. Thomas Walter Mitchell, 4 Nov 1935, 2 s, 2 d. Publications: Australia's Alps; Speak to the Earth; Soil and Civilization; Images in Water; Flow River, Blow Wind; Light Horse; The Story of Australia's Mounted Troops; The Silver Brumby series; Colt from Snowy River series; A Vision of Snowy Mountains, 1988; Towong Hill, Fifty Years on an Upper Murray Cattle Station, 1989. Honours: 2 Books Highly Commended; OAM, 1990; Hon Doct, Sturt Univ, 1993. Membership: Soc of Auths. Hobbies: Skiing; Alpine wild flowers; Bush walking; Travel; Literature; Poetry; Soil conservation. Listed in: Who's Who in Australia; Who's Who in Australian Children's Literature, Writer's Directory. Address: Towong Hill, Corryong, Victoria 3707, Australia.

MITCHELL Graham Frank, b. 22 Aug 1941. Medical Research; Biotechnology. m. Judith Ann Mitchell, 8 Jan 1971, 1 s, 1 d. Education: Roseworthy Dip of Agric, RDA, 1960; BVSc, Sydney, 1965; PhD, Melbourne, 1969. Appointments: Rsch Fell, Snr Rsch Fell, Prin Rsch Fell and Snr Prin Rsch Fell, The Walter and Eliza Hall Inst of Medl Rsch, Melbourne, 1973-90; Dir, The Roy Melbourne Zool Gdns, 1990-93; Dir of Rsch, R&D Div, CSL Ltd, Melbourne, 1993-96; Prin, Foursight Assocs Pty Ltd, Melbourne, 1996-. Publications: 360 in Immunology; Immunoparasitology; Biotechnology; Conservation. Honours: Fell, Austl Acady of Technol Scis and Engrng, FTSE, 1987; Fell, Austl Acady of Sci, FAA, 1988; Fell, Austl Coll of Vet Scis (FAVSc), 1994. Hobbies: Birdwatching; Australian flora; Football; Tennis; Cricket. Address: 21 Sinclair Avenue, Lower Templestowe, Vic 3107, Australia.

MITCHELL J J, b. 1 May 1970, Sydney, Australia. Adult Entertainment Executive. Education: BA, Media Studies, Univ Cambridge, England, 1992. Appointment: Chf Admnstr, Home Video Enthusiasts Cncl. Publications: Num. Honours: Life Fell, IBA; Intl Cultural Dip of Hon, ABI. Membership: Assn of Video Arts. Hobbies: Polo; Star Wars; Walking. Address: 5124 Bur Oak Cr, Raleigh, NC 27612, USA.

MITCHELL Malcolm Gregg, b. 7 Apr 1928, San Fran, CA, USA. Retired Teacher. m. Maybelle, 25 Mar 1956, 1 s, 1 d. Education: AA, City Coll, San Fran; AB, MA, San Fran State Univ; MA, Stanford Univ. Appointments: Socl Studies Tchr, Trinity Co HS, Weaverville, 1952-54; Socl Studies Tchr, Sequoia HS, Redwood Cty, 1954-88; Rsch Asst, 1961-62, Res Supr, 1963-68, Stanford Univ; Citizenship Tchr, Sequoia Adult Sch, 1972-88; Tchr, Assoc, Stanford Univ, 1984-86; Cnslt to CA Dept of Educ, Golden State US Hist Com, 1989-95. Publications: Sev articles in profl jrnls; Propaganda, Polls and Public Opinion. Honour: Unitarian Fellshp, Redwood City. Memberships include: Stanford Alumni Assn, San Mateo County Histl Assn; Natl Cncl of Socl Studies. Address: 164 Corte Madera Road, Portola Valley, CA 94028, USA.

MITCHELL Neil, b. 21 Nov 1951, Melbourne, Aust. Journalist; Broadcaster. m. Selina, 30 Apr 1983, 1 s, 1 d. Appointments: News Ed, Sports Ed, The Age; Ed, The Herald; Radio Commentator and Interviewer, 3AU. Honour: Radio Tack Personality Aust, 1997. Hobbies: Sports; Cars; Family. Address: 43 Bank Street, South Melbourne, Victoria, Australia.

MITCHELL Dame Roma, b. 2 Oct 1913, Adelaide, Aust. Former State Governor; Judge. Education: Adelaide Univ. Appointments: Called to the Bar of S Aust, 1934; Made QC, 1962; Supreme Crt Judge, S Aust, 1965-83; Criminal Law and Penal Methods Reform Cttee Chair, 1971-77; S Aust Parole Bd, 1974-81; Commnr of Hum Rights, 1981-86; Adelaide Univ Chan, 1983-90; S Austl Cncl on Child Protection, 1988-90; Gov of S Aust, 1991-96. Honours: DUniv, Adelaide, 1985; D hc, S Aust, 1994; LL D hc, Queensland, 1992, Flinders, 1993; Inst of Engrs Medal, 1994; Cmndr, Légion d'Honneur, 1997. Hobbies: Theatre; Opera; Walking; Swimming. Address: Box 7030, Hutt Street PO, Adelaide, SA 5000, Australia.

MITRA Asoke Nath, b. 15 Apr 1929, Rajshahi, Bangladesh. Freelance Scientific Research. m. Anjali, 27 Nov 1956, 2 d. Education: BA Hons, Maths, Delhi Univ, 1947; MA, Maths, 1949; PhD, Phys, 1954, Phd, Phys, Cornell Univ, 1955. Appointments: Rdr, Phys, Aligarch Univ, 1955-60; Rdr, Phys, Delhi Univ, 1960-62; Visng Prof, Indiana Univ, 1962-63; Prof, Phys, Delhi Univ, 1963-89; Visng Prof, Phys, UIC Chica, 1986-87; INSA Einstein Prof, Delhi Univ, 1989-94; Visng Prof, Natl Inst Adv Studies, Bangalore, 1995. Creative Works: Over 200 Rsch Pprs, Intl Jrnls; Reviews; 3 Books; Monographs. Honours: Bhatnagar Awd; Meghnad Saha Awd; S N Bose Medal; INSA Einstein Profshp; Sisim Mitra medal. Memberships: Fell, Indian Natl Sci Acady, Indian Acady Sci, Amn Phys Soc, Natl Acady of Sci, Third World Acady of Sci. Hobbies: Stamp and coin collecting; Philosophy of Science. Address: 244 Tagore Park, Delhi 110009, India.

MITRA Banasree, b. 1 Jan 1965. Social Development Services. m. 6 Dec 1985. Education: MSS. Appointments: World Univ Serv Proj, Chittagong Univ; ADAB Comilla, Bangladesh; Trner, dev sector and mngmt. Publications: Sev profl articles to local jrnls. Honours: Awd, Best Volun in Bangladesh, Intl Voluntary Servs. Memberships: SSC; Chittagong Univ. Hobbies: World tours; Social development work. Listed in: World Who's Who of Women. Address: 188 Station Road, Bagichagaw, Comilla, Bangladesh.

MITRA Ramon, b. 4 Feb 1928, Inagawan, Palawn, Philippines. Lawyer (Government official). m. Cecilia Blanco, 14 Apr 1959, 6 s. Education: LLB. Appointments: Congressman from Palwan, 1964-71; Philippine Senator, 1972; Mbr, Batasan Pambansa, 1984; Sec, Dept of Agric Food, 1986; Speaker, House of Reprs, 1987-92; Practising Lawyer, 1992-98; Pres, CEO, Philipine Natl Oil Co, 1998-. Publication: Purpose in Government, An Agenda to Get the Philippines Moving, 1991. Address: 38 Bonifacio Street, Ayala HGeights, Quezon City, Philippines.

MITSUZUKA Hiroshi, b. Japan. Politician. Appointments: Mbr, House of Reps; Fmr Min of Transp, Min of Intl Trade & Ind, Min of Fgn Affairs; Min of Fin, 1996-98. Address: Ministry of Finance, 3-1-1 Kasumigaseki, Chiyoda-ku, Tokyo 100, Japan.

MITTMAN Brian S, b. 16 Feb 1960, Chicago, Illinois, USA. Health Policy Researcher. m. Deborah C Michlin, 8 May 1993, 2 s, 1 d. Education: BSE, Engrng and Ops Rsch, Princeton Univ; MA, Sociol, Stanford Univ; PhD, Mngmt, Stanford Univ Grad Sch of Bus. Appointments: Socl Sci, RAND Corp, 1987-; Assoc Dir, VA Cntr for the Stdy of Hlthcare, 1992-. Publications: Var articles in profl jrnls. Honours: Sigma Xi, 1981; Tau Beta Pi, 1981; Rotary Fndn Intl Fellshp, 1982. Memberships: Assn for Hlth Servs Rsch; Acady of Mngmt. Hobbies: Piano; Hiking; Travel. Address: RAND, 1700 Main Street, Santa Monica, CA 90407-2138, USA.

MIYAKE Issey, b. 22 Apr 1939, Tokyo, Japan. Fashion Designer. Education: Tama Art Univ, Tokyo; La Chambre Syndicale de la Couture, Paris. Appointments: Asst Des to Guy Laroche, Paris, 1966-68, to Hubert Givenchy, Paris, 1968-69; Des, Geoffrey Beene, NY, 1969-70; Est, Miyake Des Studio, Tokyo, 1970; Dir, Issey Miyake Ints, Issey Miyake and Assocs, Issey Miyake Eur, Issey Miyake, USA, Issey Miyake On Limits, Tokyo; Exec Advsr, Plnr, First Japan Culture Conf, Yokohama, 1980;

Wrk exhib in Paris, Tokyo, NY, London. Honour: Japan Fashion Eds' Club Awds, 1974, 1976; Mainichi Des Prize, 1977; Pratt Inst Awd, NY, 1979, Hon Doct, Roy Coll of Art, 1993.

MIYAMOTO Kenji, b. 17 Oct 1908, Yamaguchi, Japan. Politician. m. Sueko Miyamoto, 1956, 2 children. Education: Tokyo Imperial Univ. Appointments: Mbr, Japanese CP, 1931- (imprisoned 1933-45); Mbr, Cntrl Cttee, 1933-; Gen Sec, Cntrl Cttee, 1958-70; Chmn, Presidium Cntl Cttee, 1970-82; Mbr, House of Cnclrs, 1977-89; Chmn, Cntrl Cttee, 1982-97, Chair Emer, 1997-. Publications include: Prospect of Japanese Revolution; Road towards a New Japan (3 vols); Kenji Miyamoto's Literary Critique (4 vols); World of Yuriko Miyamoto; Kenji Miyamoto before the Court under Militarism; Memoirs from Abashiri; Kenji Miyamoto on the 1980s (9 vols); Road to Elimination of Nuclear Weapons; People in Retrospect; Fundamental Questions of Communist Movement; From 12 Years in the Diet; The Twentieth Century and Vitality of Scientific Socialism; Japanese Situation and its Future Course; Basic Course for Party Building (2 vols); Features of Some Party Members; Toward the Progressive Future. Hobby: Walking. Address: 1-31-28 Renkoji, Tama-shi, Tokyo 206, Japan.

MIYAMOTO Tadaomi-Alfonso, b. 6 Oct 1936, Mexico. Physician; Neurobiologist. m. Kazue, 3 Oct 1975, 2 s, 1 d. Education: MD, Sch of Med, Natl Univ of Mexico, 1960. Appointments: Intern, Grasslands Hosp, Valhalla, NY, USA, 1961-62; Res Gen Surg, Montefiore Hosp & Medl Cntr, Bronx, NY, USA, 1962-65; Fell, Cardiac Surg, Tokyo Women Medl Coll, Tokyo, Japan, 1965-67; Res Thoracic & Cardiovascular Surg, Montefiore Hosp & Medl Cntr, Bronx, NY, USA, 1967-69; Fell, Anaesthesiology, Iwate Medl Univ, Morioka, Japan, 1969-71; Assoc Investigator, Natl Inst of Cardiology, Mexico Cty, 1971-72; Snr Staff Surg, Dept of Cardiovascular Surg, Cedars-Sinai Medl Cntr, Los Angeles, CA, 1974-82; Prof, Thoracic & Cardiovascular Surg, Saga Medl Univ, Japan, 1982-84; Hd, Dept of Cardiovascular Surg, Kokura Mem Hosp, Kitakyushu Cty, Japan, 1984-91; Hd, Rsch Dept, Kokura Mem Hosp, Kitakyushu Cty, Japan, 1991-. Hobbies: Wood carving; Making research tools. Address: Research Department, Kokura Memorial Hospital, 1-1 Kifunecho, Kokurakitaku, Kitakyushu, Japan.

MIYATA Takahisa, b. 13 Mar 1962, Yamaguchi, Japan. Mathematics; Computer Science. m. Shigeri, 20 July 1986, 1 d. Education: PhD, Maths. Appointments: Lectr, Univ of Wash, 1993-94; Lectr, Chubu Univ, Nagoya Cty Univ, 1994; Assoc Prof, Numain Coll of Tech, 1994-97; Assoc Prof, Shizuoka Inst of Sci & Tech. Honour: Phi Kappa Phi Hon, 1988. Memberships: Amn Math Soc; Soc of Indl & Applied Maths; Math Inst of Japan. Hobby: Piano.

MIYAZAKI Shigeki, b. 21 Oct 1925, Nigataken, Japan. Cheif of Human Rights Center. m. Setsuko, 27 May 1951, 2 s. Education: Docter Jr. Appointments: Pres, Meiji Univ; Chperson, Consultive Cncl, Regn Improvement Meas. Creative Works: International Law, 1997; Protection of Human Rights, 1998. Memberships: Intl Law Assn. Hobbies: Collect of Stamps. Address: 26-19, Daita 5 Chome, Setagaya-Ku, Tokyo 155-0033, Japan.

MIYAZAKI Shunichi, b. 31 Jan 1955, Kochi, Japan. Cardiologist. m. 4 Nov 1988, 3 d. Education: MD; PhD. Appointments: Assoc Prof, Kochi Medl Sch, 1997. Membership: Amn Physl Soc; Japanese Circulation Soc; Japanese Soc of Internal Med. Hobby: Golf.

MIYAZAWA Kiichi, b. 8 Oct 1919, Tokyo, Japan. Politician. m. Yoko Miyazawa, 1943, 2 children. Education: Tokyo Imperial Univ. Appointments: Fin Min, 1942-52; Pvt Sec to Min of Fin, 1949; Mbr, House of Cnclrs, 1953-65; Parl Vice-Min of Educn, 1959-60; Min of State, Dir-Gen of Econ Planning Agcy, 1962-64, 1966-68, 1977-78; Mbr, House of Reps, 1967-; Min of Intl Trade & Ind, 1970-71, of Fgn Affairs, 1974-76, of Fin, 1986-88; Dpty PM, Min of Fin, 1987-88; Min of State, Chf Cabinet Sec, 1980-82; Chair, Exec Cncl, LDP, 1984-86; Pres, 1991-93; PM of Japan, 1991-93. Publications:

Tokyo-Washington no Mitsudan (Tokyo-Washington Secret Talks), 1956; Shakaito tono taiwa (Dialogue with the Socialist Party); Utsukushii Nippon heno Chosen (Challenge for Beautiful Japan), 1984. Hobbies: Noh Theatre; Reading. Address: Liberal Democratic Party, 1-11-23 Nagata-cho, Chiyoda-ku, Tokyo 100, Japan.

MIYOSHI Toru, b. 31 Oct 1927, Japan. Judge. Education: Univ Tokyo. Appointments: Asst Judge, Tokyo Dist Crt, Tokyo Family Crt, 1955; Judge, Hakodate Dist Crt, Hakodate Family Crt, 1965; Judge, Tokyo Dist Crt, Presiding Judge of Divsn, 1975; Pres, Rsch & Trng Inst for Crt Clks, 1982; Pres, Oita Dist Crt, Oita Family Crt, 1985; Pres, Nagano Dist Crt, Nagano Family Crt, 1986; Chf Judicial Rsch Offl, Supreme Crt, 1987; Pres, Sapporo High Crt, 1990, Tokyo High Crt, 1991; Justice, Supreme Crt, 1992; Chf Justice, Sypreme Crt, 1995-97. Address: Supreme Court of Japan, 4-2 Hayabusa-cho, Chiyoda-ku, Tokyo 102, Japan.

MIZUTANI Yukio, b. 27 Nov 1929, Nagoya, Japan. m. Ritinko Mizutani, 6 Jan 1957, 1 s, 2 d. Education: BS, Tokyo Univ; PhD, Kyushyu Univ. Appointments: Rschr, Toknyarma Soda Co Ltd, Japan, 1953-76; Mngr, Rsch Lab, 1976-80; Dir, Rsch and Dev, 1980-86; Mngng Dir, Rsch and Dev, 1986-93; Cnslt, Toknyarma Corp, 1993-98; Retd, 1998. Publications: Many original pprs. Honours: Awd, Technol Dev, Chem Soc Japan, 1976; Prize, Acad Achmnt, Soc Sea Water Sci, 1979; Recip, Commendation, Min of State for Sci and Technol, 1979. Memberships: Chem Soc Japan; Soc Polymer Sci Japan. Hobbies: Reading; Walking. Address: Oiso Okanoue Terasu 503, Oiso 2115-1, Oiso-Machi, Naka-Gun, Kanagawa-Ken 255-0003, Japan.

MO Pei-Sheng, b. 13 June 1929, Canton, China. Clinical Pathologist. m. Lai Wen Wu, 1 s, 1 d. Education: MD. Appointments: Res Physn, Beijing People's Hosp; Hd, Rsch Lab of Clin Biochemistry, Beijing Friendship Hosp; Dir, Natl Cntr for Clin Labs, China. Publications: Articles in profl jrnls. Honours: Sci Improvement Awds from Min of Pub Hlth, China, 1994; Sci Improvement Awds from Municipal of Beijing, China. Memberships: Chinese Medl Assn; Amn Assn for Clin Chem. Hobby: Music. Address: #202 #1 Apt #1 Building, Dong Jiao Ming Xiang, Beijing, China 100730.

MO Sin Chi, b. 19 Mar 1950, Hong Kong. Shipping; Arbitration; Transport. m. Yung Shin Yue, 11 Jan 1976, 1 d. Education: Fell, Inst of Chart Shipbrokers. Appointments: Chmn, Inst of Seatransp, 1990-91, 1996-98; Panel of Experts, Inst of Chart Shipbrokers, 1999. Memberships: Inst of Chart Shipbrokers, 1983; Fell, Hong Kong Inst of Arbitrators, 1998. Hobbies: Investments; Tennis. Address: 21/F Western Centre, 40-50 Des Voeux Road West, Hong Kong.

MOCHIDA Tohru, b. 27 Aug 1939, Shenyan. Professor of University. m. Lucy Kato Kuniko, 21 Aug 1993. Education: BS, Engrng Sci, 1966, MS, Engrng Sci, 1968, DSc, Engrng Sci, 1973, Hokkaido Univ. Appointments: Instr, 1971-83, Assoc Prof, 1984-92, Prof, 1993, Hokkaido Univ; Guest Rschr, Tech Univ of Denmark, Copenhagen, 1989; Visng Fell, J B Pierce Lab, Yale Univ, New Haven, USA, 1989. Publications: The Human-Environemnet System, 1991; Cyclopedia of Biometeorology, 1992; Heating and Air-Conditioning Engineering, 1996. Honour: Awd of Soc of Heating, Air-Conditioning and Sanitary Engrs of Japan, 1994. Memberships: Soc of Hum-Environ System, Dir, 1989-; Ashrae, USA Tech Cttee Mbr, 1994-; Soc of Heating, Airconditioning and Sanitary Engrs of Japan, Pres, Hokkaido Chapt, 1996-. Address: Graduate School of Hokkaido University, North-13, West-8, Kita-ku, Sapporo, 060-8628, Japan.

MOE Kyaw Thu, b. 26 Nov 1964, Pathein, Myanmar. Petroleum and Marine Scientist. Education: BSc, Hons, Geol, Univ of Yangon, 1985; MS, 1994, DSc, 1999, Geol, Univ of Tokyo. Appointments: Demonstrator, Geol Dept, Univ of Yangon, 1986-89; Mngr, Geocomp Myanmar, 1989-90; Petroleum Geol, Geoservs Eastern Inc, 1990-91. Publications: Sev articles in profl jrnls. Honour:

Japanese Govt Schlsp, 1991-97. Memberships: Amn Assn of Petroleum Geols; SE Asia Petroleum Exploration Soc; Geol Soc of Japan. Hobbies: Reading; Travel; Writing Articles; Swimming. Address: 3-30-10-203 Higuchi So, Yayoi-cho, Nakano-ku, Tokyo 164, Japan.

MOELJOPAWIRO Sugiono, b. 25 Nov 1947, Yogyakarta. Plant Breeder. m. Asseta S 15 June 1976, 1 s, 1 d. Education: BS, Plant Breeding, 1970; Ir in Plant Breeding, 1973; MSc, Plant Breeding, 1979; PhD, Plant Breeding, 1986. Appointments: Rice Breeder, 1977-; Ldr, Biotech Res Prog, 1990-95; Hd, Mol Biol Div, 1995-; Ldr, Natl Biosafety Drafting Team, 1997-. Memberships: ASA, 1984-; ISPMB, 1989-; Indonesian Soc Agricl Biotechnology, Sec, 1992-97, Pres, 1997-. Hobbies: Easy music listening; Cooking. Address: Jalan Cimanggu 7A, Bogor 16114, Indonesia.

MOFFITT Athol Randolph (The Hon), b. 25 June 1914, Lismore, NSW, Aust. Retired Judge; Author. m. Heather Williams, 29 Apr 1946, dec, 2 s. Education: BA, LLB, 1st class hons, Sydney Univ; Calld to NSW Bar, 1938. Appointments: War Serv, AIF-RAA (Cap), 5 yrs; Prosecutor, Sandakan, Japanese War Trials (Borneo-Labuan), 1946; QC, 1958; Acting Jus, 1959, Perm Jus, NSW Supreme Crt, 1962-84; Pres Crt of Appeal, NSW 1974-84; Roy Commnr, Organised Crime, NSW Regd Clubs, 1973-74; Acting Chf Jus, Aug-Sept 1979; Admnstr, NSW, Sept 1979. Publications: A Quarter to Midnight, 1985; Project Kingfisher, 1989; Drug Precipice, 1998; Drug Alert, 1998; Current affairs articles. Honour: CMG, 1979. Memberships: NSW Bar Assn; Australasian Pioneers Club; Elanora County Club; Austl Soc of Auths. Hobbies: Writing, including Current Affairs; Bowls. Address: 26A Powell Street, Killara, Australia.

MOHAMED Isha, b. 30 Oct 1933, Konnagar, West Bengal, India. Artist (Painter). m. Noorjehan, 24 Nov 1972, 1 s, 1 d. Education: Dip, Drawing & Painting, Govt Coll of Art & Craft, Calcutta; Art Appreciation Course, Calcutta Univ; Training in Graphic Art, West Germany. Appointments: Lectr, Drawing & Painting, 1962; Asst Prof, Vice Prin & Offr-in-Charge, 1979; Prin, 1992; Retired, 1994. Publications: Paintings - engaged in creative works, 1956-. Honours: Awd in Graphic Art, Calcutta Univ Inst, 1956; Awd in Painting, Birla Acady of Fine Art & Culture, Calcutta, 1972. Memberships: Mbr of Senate, Calcutta Univ, 1987-88; Acady of Fine Arts, Calcutta. Hobbies: Photography; Reading; Cinema; Theater. Address: AC-38, Flat-4, Sector-1, Salt Lake City, Calcutta, 700 064, India.

MOHAMED Suhaila, b. 12 Sept 1954, Malaysia. Professor. m. Dr Baharuddin Ali, 6 Dec 1975, 4 s, 2 d. Education: BS (Hons), Food Sci and Physiology, Leeds Univ, 1977; PhD Food Sci (Biophys Chem of Food) Leeds Univ, 1981. Appointments: Lectr, 1981; Snr Lectr, 1986; Prof, Food Sci, 1996; Mngr, Technol Commercialisation, 1996-97; VP, R & D Gelatechs Corp, 1998; Dir, Galatechs R & D Co Ltd. Publications: Food and its Healing Power, 1997; 10 books; 50 articles in refereed sci jrnls; Over 100 publs in proceedings, mass media, mags, related to food. Honours: 21st Century JICA Friendship Prog Awd, 1986; UNESCO Awd, 1987; IFS Awd, 1990; FAD Awd, 1992; Asian Dev Bank Awd, 1992; George Weston, Can, ACH, 1993; Excellent Academician of the Yr Awd, 1995. Memberships: Profl Mbr, Malaysian Inst of Food Technol, Technologist; Publ Cttee, Malaysian Acady of Muslim Scis, 1986; Exec Cttee, Inst of Food Tech, USA; NY Acady Scis. Hobbies: Squash; Reading; Science; Swimming; TV; Cooking. Address: Faculty of Food Science and Biotechnology, University Putra, Malaysia, 43400 Serdang, UPM, Selangor, Malaysia.

MOHAMMAD SIDDEEQUE Saqib Zirvi, b. Apr 1919, Zira, India. Journalism. m. Iqbal Begum, 1945, 4 s. Education: Grad, Punjab Univ. Appointment: Fndr Ed, Lahore, 1952-. Publications: Hamare Naghmay; Mahekamil; Dure Khusravi.

MOHAMMADI FAZEL Asghar, b. 16 Aug 1965, Tehran. University Lecturer. m. M Namazi, 23 Sept 1985,

2 d. Education: HND, Lab Sci; BS, MSc, Environ Sci. Appointment: Gen Dir, Nat Hist Museums, Dept of the Environ (DOE). Publications: (books) Sahife Nour, 1994; Environment in Divine Instructions, 1996. Honours: Hon MSc, Univ of Tehran, 1994. Memberships: ICOM (Intl Cncl of Museums) Natl Energy Cttee. Hobbies: Computer; Sport. Address: Environment Department, Natural Resources Faculty, Daneshkadeh St, Karaj, Iran.

MOHAMMED Zahir Shah, b. 15 Oct 1914. Fmr King of Afghanistan. m. Lady Homira, 4 Nov 1931 7 children. Education: Istiqlal Coll, Kabul; Lycée Janson-de-Sailly; Lycée, Montpellier, France; Infantry Offrs Sch, Kabul, 1932. Appointments: Asst Min, Min of Natl Def, 1932-33; Acting Min of Educn, 1933; Deposed 1973, Abdicated 24 Aug 1973, Stripped of Citzenship, 1978, Restored, 1991; King, 1993.

MOHANAN P K, b. 19 Nov 1948, Vadakkekara, India. Stenographer. m. S Devi, 6 Dec 1977, 1 s. Education: PU, Arts. Publication: Love Lyrics. A Book of Romantic Poems, 1993. Honour: Ed Choice Awd, Natl Lib of Poetry, MD, USA. Memberships: Poetry Soc, India; Hon Sec, Poets Guild, Guwahati. Hobbies: Photography; Contract Bridge. Address: 75/B Hathat Colony, Rest Camp, Guwahati 781-012, Assam, India.

MOHANTA Guru Prasad, b. 12 June 1960, Talkunda, India. Teacher. m. Reena, 18 June 1986, 1 s. Education: MPharm. Appointments: Demonstrator, Coll of Pharm Scis, Orissa, 1982-83; Lectr, V L Coll of Pharm, Karnataka, 1984-85; Lectr, Annamalai Univ, 1985-94, Rdr, 1994-. Honours: Natl Rural Talent Schlshp, 1972-76; Merit Schlshp, 1976-78; Orissa Givt Stipend, 1978-82; UGC Fellshp, 1982-84. Memberships: Indian Soc for Tech Educ; Assoc, Instn of Chems, India; Indian Pharm Assn. Hobbies: Writing; Social activities. Address: Institute of Pharmaceutical Technology, Annamalai University, Annamalai nagar, Tamil Nadu 608 002, India.

MOHSIN Muhammad, b. 8 Dec 1942. Journalist; Teacher. m. Gulnahar Begum, 4 Jan 1968, 1 s, 1 d. Education: MSc; BSc Hons in Phys. Appointments: Ed, The Daily Uttara, 1974-; Mbr, Bangladesh Press Commn, 1983 Mbr, Nominating Cttee, Intl Raymon Magsaga Awd, 1985. Publications: Third International Theory, 1978; Bangladesh and Right of Self-determination, 1991; Confession of a Citizen - A Collection of Poems; Voice from the North - Collection of Published News Articles. Honours: Pres Citation, 1993-94; 20th Century Achievement Awd, ABI, 1995. Memberships: Life & Exec, Dinajpur Redereasent Soc; Diabetic Assn Heart Fndn; Family Planning Assn; Pres, Press Club, 1991-93; VP, Bangladesh Cncl of Eds, 1994-96; VP, Bangladesh Cncl of Newspapers, 1993-97. Hobbies: Reading; Writing; Social Works. Address: The Daily Uttara, Dinajpur, Bangladesh.

MOKDAD Abdul-Karim, b. 1 Dec 1937, Haret Hreik. Officer in Interior Security Forces. m. Sadika Daneshyar, 29 Mar 1973, 2 s, 3 d. Education: ML; Cert Criminology, Sorbonne; Langs: French, Engl, Arabic, German. Appointments: Former Pres, Cntrl Admin in FSI (interior security forces). Publications: Articles in nom mags and jrnls. Honours: Lebanese Medal of Merit (1st, 2nd, 3rd degree); Medal of Natl Cedars w grade of Offr and Kt; Commemorative Medal; Hon and Merit Medal from Repub of Haiti (Cmdr degree). Hobbies: Reading; Antiques; Persian carpets. Address: Airport Avenue, Al-Amir Bldg, 3rd Floor, Area 6, No 58, Bldg 6, Beirut, Lebanon.

MOL Johannis (Hans), b. 14 Feb 1922, Netherlands. Professor. m. L Ruth McIntyre, 2 s, 2 d. Education: BD, MA, Union Theol Seminary, 1956; PhD, Sociol, Columbia Univ, 1961. Appointments: Univ of Canterbury, NZ; Fellshp, Sociol, Rsch Sch of Socl Scis, Inst of Adv Studies, Austl Natl Univ, 1963; McMaster Univ, Can, 1970-87; Visng Prof, Univ CA, Santa Barbara, Univ AZ, Tucson, Marquette Univ, WI, Univ Sydney, Univ Ottawa, Can. Publications: 15 books incl: Western Religion, 1971; The Fixed and the Fickle, 1982; How God Hoodwinked Hitler (war experiences), 1987; num articles in profl jrnls.

Memberships: Sociol Assn of Aust and NZ; Sociol of Relign Rsch Cttee, Intl Sociol Assn. Address: 23 Mol Crescent, Queanbeyan, NSW 2620, Australia.

MOLENT Loris, b. 18 Oct 1960, Melbourne, Aust. Aerospace Engineer. m. Catherine, 2 May 1992, 1 s, 1 d. Education: Bachelor, Aerospace Engrng; Grad Dip in Mngmt-Sci Ldrshp. Appointments: Experimental Offr, Aero Rsch Lab, (ARL), 1983-89; Snr Engrng, Naval Air Systems Command, Wash DC, 1989-91; Snr Offr, ARL, 1991-97; Snr Rsch Scientist, ARL, 1997-. Honour: Outstndng Serv to NAVAIR, 1991. Membership: NY Acady of Scis. Hobbies: Travel; Surfing; House renovations. Address: Aeronautical and Maritime Research Laboratory, PO Box 4331, Melbourne, Victoria 3001, Australia.

MOLES Ian Newton, b. 10 Feb 1935. Historian; Writer. m. Phania, 9 Oct 1962, 1 s, dec, 1 d. Education: BA (1st Class Hons), Hist; MA, Univ of Queensland. Appointments: Tutor/Rsch Asst, Univ of Queensland, 1956-57; Tchng Asst, Univ of MN, 1957-58; Lectr, Austl Sch of Pacific Admin, 1959-60; Acting Prin and Prin, Cromwell Coll, Univ of Qld, 1958-59; Stuart House, Olsen House and Univ Hall, James Cook Univ, 1961-68; Lectr, Snr Lectr, Assoc Prof, Univ Coll of Townsville and James Cook Univ of N Qld, 1961-95. Publications: Auth, A Majority of One, (first book-length Australian Study of the Independent's Role in Politics) 1979; Auth and Co-Auth to var other books and articles. Honours: Fulbright Schl, Univ of MN, 1957-58; IKY Schl, Univ of Athens, 1967; Hon Life Mbr, Natl Trust of Queensland, 1989. Memberships: Austl Histl Assn; Roy Histl Soc of Qld; Natl Trust of Qld; Fndr, Townsville Natl Trust Cntr. Hobbies: Swimming; Walking; Gardening; Reading; Music. Address: 358 Stanley Street West, Townsville, Qld 4810, Australia.

MOMMA Takahiro, b. 8 Sept 1960, Fukushima, Japan. Civil Engineer; Architect. m. Naoko Ichihara, 9 May 1987, 2 d. Education: BEng, Waseda Univ, Tokyo, 1983; MEng, Waseda, 1985; PhD, Univ of Nottingham, 1991. Appointments: Civil Engr, Kajima, Tokyo, 1985-87; Rschr, Japan Atomic Energy Rsch Inst, Tokai, 1987-88; Exchange Vis to USDOE, 1988-89; Civil Engr, 1989-95, Snr Engr, 1995-98, Dpty Chf, 1998-, Kajima Corp. Publications: Rsch articles on Cavitation in Wear (profl jrnl). Membership: Archtl Inst fo Japan, Tokyo. Hobbies: Wine; Golf. Address: Kajima Corporation, Nuclear Power Dept, Construction Group 6-5-30 Akasaka, Minato-ku; Tokyo 107-8502, Japan.

MOND Bertram, b. 24 Aug 1931. Professor of Mathematics. m. Haya Lorberbaum, 23 Sept 1970, 2 s, 1 d. Education: BA, 1951, MA, 1959, PhD, 1963. Appointments: Prof Maths, La Trobe Univ, Bundoora, 3083, Melbourne, Aust, 1969-; Chmn, Dept of Maths, La Trobe Univ, 1970-73; Chmn, Dept of Pure Maths, La Trobe Univ, 1973-82; Dean, Sch of Phys Scis, La Trobe Univ, 1976-78; Dean, Sch of Mathl & Info Scis, La Trobe Univ, 1990-94. Publications: Over 200 mathl pprs in jrnls. Honours: Ed, Austl Sch of Maths, 1969-74; Cncl Mbr, Austl Math Soc. Memberships: Amn Math Soc; Maths Programming Soc; Austl Math Soc; Austl Soc Ops Rsch. Address: 22 Crotonhurst Avenue, Caulfield, Vic 3161, Australia.

MONDAL Rabin, b. 1 Jan 1929, Howrah, W Bengal, India. Painter. m. Bani Mitra, 1976. Education: Com Grad, Calcutta Univ; Indian Art Coll, Calcutta; Ashutosh Mus, Calcutta Univ. Appointments: Tchr in Sch; Serv in Indian Railways; Pt-time Lectr, Visual Art, Rabindra Bharati Univ, Calcutta. Creative Works: Ed, Drawings by 14 Contemporary Artists; Drawings by Rabin Mondal, 1970-88. Honours: Eminent Painter, All Indian Fine Arts and Crafts Soc; Mbr, Gen Cncl; Natl Acady of Art, New Delhi. Memberships: Calcutta Painters; Calcutta Art Fair; Calcutta Metropolitan Art Fest. Hobbies: Writing on art; Music; Film; Theatre. Address: IB-6, Flat No 3 Sector III, Salt Lake, Calcutta 700091, W Bengal, India.

MONDO Ludger, b. 18 Aug 1957, Kerangu Mugl Vill, Kamtai Dist, Simtu Prov, Papua New Guinea. Minister for

Health. m.3 children. Education: Major Cath Sem, Bomana, Port Moresby, 1976-80; Urbaniana Univ, Rome, 1982-84, Biblical Stdies, Deg in Theo, 1988. Appointments: Dir, Kefamo Pastoral Cntr, Goroka, 1986-89; Natl Dir, Cath Commn for Jus, Peace and Dev, Cath Bish Conf, 1990-96; In Charge, Jus, Dev and Relief Wrk, Cath Ch; Min for Hlth.

MONEGHETTI Stephen James, b. 26 Sept 1962. Education and Sports Consultant. m. Tanya Moneghetti, 4 Nov 1989, 2 d. Education: BCE; Dip of Educ. Appointment: Chair of Review, Sport & Physl Educ in Vic Schs, 1993-. Honours: 4 times to C'wlth Games, 1986, 1990, 1994, 1998, w medals; 5 times to World Championships, 1987, 1991, 1993, 1995, 1997 (w Marathon Bronze Medal); 3 times Olympian, 1988, 1992, 1996; Winner, Berlin and Tokyo Marathons, 1990, 1994; Age Vic Sportstar of the Yr, 1990; Confedn of Austl Sport, Sportstar of the Yr, 1990. Hobbies: Music; Wine. Address: 2 The Court, Ballarat, Victoria 3350, Australia.

MONGCOLTAM Chingchai, b. 29 Nov 1966. Government Executive. Education: BA, Educ, Srinakharinwirot Univ. Appointments: Asst Sec to Min of Com, Govt of Thailand, 1994; Dpty Min of Def, 1995-96; Min to Prime Min's Off, 1997-.

MONTAGUE Ronald Henry, b. 6 July 1917, Surrey, Eng. Retired. m. (1) Joan Hutart, 4 May 1943; (2) Lilian Ongley, 16 Oct 1971. Education: Dip Pod Med, 1953; Fell, Austl Podiatry Assn, 1968. Appointments: NSw Ed, A Pod A Jrnl, 1967-70. Publications: Dress and Insignia, 1981; How to Trace Your Military Ancestors, 1989. Membership: Mil Histl Soc of Aust. Hobbies: Military and family history. Address: 169 New England Highway, Rutherford, NSW, Australia, 2320.

MONTES Manuel F, b. 9 Dec 1949, Manila, Philippines. Economist. m. Cynthia Alabanza, 18 Dec 1971, 1 s. Education: AB, Econs, Ateneo De Manila Univ; PhD, Econs, Stanford Univ. Appointments: Spec, Budgets and Measurements, Gen Elec Phils, 1974; Assoc Prof, Money and Banking, Univ of Philippines, 1984; Snr Fell, East-West Cntr, 1994. Publications: The Currency Crisis in Southeast Asia, 1998; The Asian Crisis Turns Global, w Vladimir V Popov, 1999. Honour: Outstndng Young Sci, Natl Acady for Sci and Technol, 1988. Hobby: Swimming. Address: East-West Center, 1601 East-West Road, Honolulu, Hawaii, 96848-1601, USA.

MOON Kwang Soon, b. 18 Apr 1942. Scientist. m. Sunok Moon, 28 Dec 1970, 1 s. Education: BSc, Seoul Natl Univ, Korea 1964; MSc, Univ BC, Can, 1976; PhD 1985, Univ CA at Berkeley, USA. Appointments: Rsch Sci, CANMET, Ottawa, Can, 1980; Pres, Korea Interfacial Sci and Engrng Inst, KISEI, Seoul, Korea, 1991. Publications: US Patent No 4, 845,040; Canadian Patents, No 1, 252, 705 and No 1 316, 800. Honours: Pub Servant Invention Awds, CANMET, Can, 1989; Evan Just Awd, AIME, San Fran, USA, 1978. Memberships: Pres 1992, Assn of Korean-Canad Scis and Engrs; Mbr, Korean Acady of Sci and Technol, 1995. Hobby: Hiking. Address: 175-13 Nonhyum-dong, Kangnam-ku, Seoul 135-010, Korea.

MOON Milton, b. 29 Oct 1926, Melbourne, Aust. Ceramic Artist. m. Betty Pestell, 10 Sept 1948, 1 s. Appointments: Snr Pottery Instr, Ctrl Tech Coll, Brisbane, 1962-69; Snr Lectr, Ceramics, South Austl Sch of Art, Adelaide, 1969-75. Creative Works: Rep, Austl Japan Fndn, Tokyo, C'wlth Art Collect; Art Galls of NSW and Vic; ANG Canberra; Art Gall of WA; Art Gall of SA; Qld Art Gall; Tasmanian Art Gall and many others; Works contained in Collect of Govt of Shanghai, Emb Collects, Univ Collects; Intl Ceramic Exhibs in Japan, Germany, USA. Honours: Fndn Winston Churchill Fellshp, 1966; Myer Fndn GEIJUTSu Fellshp, 1975; Mbr, OA, 1984; Austl Govt Creative Arts Fellshp, 1994-. Memberships: Life Mbr, Crafts Cncl of SA. Hobbies: Art; Writing; Physical Fitness; Dogs. Address: 4 Osborn Avenue, Beulah Park, Adelaide, Australia.

MOORE C Bradley, b. 7 Dec 1939, Boston, MA, USA. Professor of Chemistry. m. Penelope Percival, 27 Aug 1960, 1 s, 1 d. Education: BA, Magna cum laude, Harv Univ, 1960; PhD, Univ CA at Berkeley, 1963. Appointments: Asst Prof, 1963-68, Assoc Prof, 1967-72, Prof, 1972-, Chem, Chmn Dept of Chem, 1982-86, Univ of CA, Berkeley; Prof, Associé Fac des Scis, Paris, 1970, 1975; Miller Rsch Prof, Berkeley, 1972-73, 1987-88; Fac Snr Scientist, Dir, Cheml Sci Div, Lawrence Berkeley Natl Lab, 1974-, Div Dir, 1998-; Visng Prof, Inst for Molecular Sci, Okazaki, Japan, 1979, Fudan Univ, Shanghai, 1979; Adv Prof, 1988-; Visng Fell, Jt Inst for Lab Astrophys, Univ CO at Boulder, 1981-82; Dean, Coll Chem, 1988-94. Publications: Ed, Chemical and Biochemical Applications of Lasers; Assoc Ed, Annual Review of Physical Chemistry, 1985-90; Contbr articles to profl jrnls. Honours: Fell, Alfred P Sloan Fndn, 1968, Guggenheim Fndn, 1969; Coblenz Awd, 1973; CA Sec Awd, ACS, 1977; NAs, elected, 1986; E O Lawrence M Awd, 1986; Lipincott Awd, 1987; 1st Awd, Inter-Am Photochem Soc, 1988; Plyler Prize, 1994; Humboldt Rsch Awd for Snr US Scientists, 1994; Spiers Mem Lect, Faraday Div of the Chem Soc, 1995. Memberships include: Fell, AAAS, Amn Phys Soc; NSF Advsry Commn for Educ and Human Rescs, Directorate, Chair, Subcttee, Plcy and Plng; Amn Cheml Soc. Hobby: Cycling. Address: Department of Chemistry, California, Berkeley, CA 94720-1460, USA.

MOORE Christopher George, b. 8 July 1950. Novelist. Education: BCL 1st Class, Oxford Univ. Career: Law Prof, Univs in Can & Eng, -1985; Full-time writer, 1985-. Publications: (novels) His Lordship's Arsenal, 1985; Enemies of Memeory, 1990; A Killing Smile, 1991, 1992, 1996; A Bewitching Smile, 1992; Spirit House, 1992; Asia Hand, 1993; A Haunting Smile, 1993, 1998; Cut Out, 1994, (Thai ed) 1995; Saint Anne, 1994; Comfort Zone, 1995, 1997; The Big Weird, 1996; God of Darkness, 1998; (non-fiction) Heart Talk, 1992, 1998; (radio drama on CBC) Sticks and Pucks, 1979; Taking a Dive for the Queen, 1980; The Semi-Detached Barrister, 1981; The Clairvoyant, 1982; View from Cambie Bridge, NHK, Japan, 1983; On The Bamboo Pillar, 1983. Address: 27 Soi 27 Sukhumvit Road, Bangkok 10110, Thailand.

MOORE Clive Robert, b. 29 Nov 1951. Associate Professor. Education: BA; PhD. Appointments: Lectr, Univ of Papua New Guinea, 1981-85; Snr Lectr, Univ of Papua New Guinea, 1984-87; Lectr, 1987-94, Snr Lectr, 1991-95, Assoc Prof, 1996-, Univ Qld. Publications: Kanaka: A History of Melaresian Mackay, 1985; Labour in the South Pacific, 1990; A Papua New Guinea Political Chronicle, 1998. Memberships: Austl Histl Assn; Pacific Hist Assn. Address: History Department, University of Queensland, Qld 4072, Australia.

MOORE Demi, b. Roswell, New Mexico, USA. Actress. m. Bruce Willis, 3 d. Creative Works: Films: Blame it on Rio; No Small Affair; St Elmo's Fire; One Crazy Summer; About Last Night...; Wisdom; The Seventh Sign; Ghost; Mortal Thoughts; The Butcher's Wife; A Few Good Men; Indecent Proposal; Disclosure; The Scarlet Letter; Striptease, 1995; The Juror, 1996; G I Jane, 1996; The Hunchback of Notre Dame; Now and Then. TV: General Hospital; Bedroom. Theatre: The Early Girl. Honours include: Th World Awd. Address: Creative Artists Agency Inc, 9830 Wilshire Boulevard, Beverly Hills, CA 90212, USA.

MOORE Dudley Stuart John, b. 19 Apr 1935, England. Actor; Composer; Musician. m. (1) Suzy Kendall, 1958, (2) Tuesday Weld, 1975, 1 s, (3) Brogan Lane, 1988, (4) Nicole Rothschild, 1994, 1 s. Education: Magdalen Coll, Oxford. Creative Work: Stage Work: Composed Incidental Music for Roy Crt Th Prodns; W Vic Lewis & John Dankworth Jazz Bands, 1959-60; Beyond the Fringe, London, 1960-62; Broadway, NY, 1962-64; Play It Again Sam, Globe Th, 1970; Behind the Fridge, Cambridge Th, 1972-73; Good Evening Broadway, 1973-74; Tour of USA, 1975; Roy Cmd Performance; Tours w own jazz piano trio. TV Work: Not Only...But Also (series w Peter Cook), 1965, 1966, 1970; Goodbye Again; It's Lulu; Not To Mention Dudley Moore, 1972.

Films: The Wrong Box, 1966; Thirty is a Dangerous Age Cynthia, 1967; Bedazzled, 1968; Monte Carlo or Bust, 1969; The Bed-Sitting Room, 1969; Alice's Adventures in Wonderland, 1972; The Hound of the Baskervilles; Foul Play; 10; Wholly Moses; Arthur; Six Weeks; Lovesick; Romantic Comedy; Unfaithfully Yours; Micki and Maude; Best Defense; Santa Claus; Like Father, Like Son; Arthur 2: On the Rocks; Crazy People; Blame It on the Bellboy; The Pickle; A Weekend in the Country. Albums: Beyond the Fridge and All That Jazz; The Other Side of Dudley Moore; Today; Dudley Moore Trio-Down Under; Dudley Moore and Cleo Laine - Smilin Through; The Music of Dudley Moore; Songs Without Words. Publications: Dud and Pete: The Dagenham Dialogues, 1971; Dudley Moore - Offbeat, 1986; The Complete Beyond the Fridge, 1987; Voices of Survival. Honours include: Golden Globe Awds. Hobbies: Films; Theatre; Music. Address: c/o Loi is Pitt, ICM, 8942 Wilshire Boulevard, Beverly Hills, CA 90212, USA.

MOORE Eva Beate, (Eva May), b. 11 May 1925, Mannheim, Germany. Author. m. John Martin Moore, 21 Oct 1960, 2 d. Education: Dip, Kindergarten Trng Coll, Melbourne, 1945. Publications: Of This and That, 1973; Thank You God, 1973; Don't Tell Me About Goldilocks!, 1974; Old Things, Visitors and Drinks of Water in the Middle of the Night, 1977; 7 Kids, 9 Garbage Bins, 1979; Tell Me My Story, 1986; Cassettes: The Violet Fountain, 1981; The Golden Column, 1981; Short stories; Articles; Poems; Contbn to Anthologies for children. Memberships: Austl Soc of Auths; Fellshp of Austl Writers; Austl Soc of Women Writers, Cttee Mbr, 1977-80. Hobbies: Painting; Sculpture; Reading; Gardening; Walking; Travel; Metaphysics. Address: 1/48 Glen Iris Road, Glen Iris, Vic 3146, Australia.

MOORE Felicity St John, b. 7 Oct 1933, Melbourne, Aust. Art historian; Curator. m. John D, 25 Feb 1955, 2 s, 1 d. Education: BA (Hons), Univ of Melbourne, 1955; MA, Fine Art, Univ of Melbourne, 1980; Dip Hist of Fine and Decorative Arts, London, 1973. Appointments: Curator, Spec Exhibns, Natl Gall of Vic, 1990-96; Hon Fell, Dept of Fine Art, Univ of Melbourne, 1991-; Dir of Educ, Christies, 1994-. Publications: Vassilieff and His Art, 1982; Classical Modernism: The George Bell Circle, 1992; Charles Blackman, 1993; Sam Fullbrook, 1995. Memberships: Canberra Th Tstee, Austl Bicentennial ACT Cncl, 1977-85; Canberra Coll of Advd Educ, Cncl Mbr, 1975-78. Hobbies: Theatre; Chamber music; Tennis. Address: 6/112 Millswyn Street, South Yarra, Victoria 3141, Australia.

MOORE Gloria Jean, b. 8 Jan 1935, Lucknow, India. Educational Consultant; University Tutor. m. Terence, 16 Mar 957, 2 s, 1 d. Education: DipEd; BA (Hons); PhD. Appointments: Educl Cnslt; Univ Tutor; Univ Rschr; Auth (acad and other publs incl hist). Publications: The Anglo Indian Vision, 1986; The Lotus and the Rose, 1986; I Was a Stranger, 1994; Num acad and other articles in leading jrnls. Memberships: Roy C'wlth Soc, Aust. Hobbies: Images of religion in literature; Anglo India history; Literature, history, heritage, issues of human rights. Address: PO Box 155, North Mulgrave, Victoria, Australia.

MOORE John Colinton, b. 16 Nov 1936, Australia. Politician. m. (1) 2 s, 1 d, (2) Jacquelyn Moore. Education: Qld Univ. Appointments: Stockbroker, 1960; Mbr, Brisbane Stock Exchange, 1962-74; VP, Treas, Qld Liberal Pty, 1967-73, Pres, 1973-76, 1984-90; MP for Ryan, Qld, 1975-; Min for Bus & Consumer Affairs, 1980-82; Opposition Spokesman for Fin, 1983-84, for Cmmns, 1984-85, for Northern Devel & Local Govt, 1985-87, for Transp & Aviation, 1987, for Bus & Consumer Affairs, 1987-89, for Bus Privatization & Consumer Affairs, 1989-90; Shadow Min for Privatization & Pub Admin, 1995-96; Min for Ind, Sci & Tourism, 1996-97, of Ind, Sci & Tech, 1997-; VP, Exec Cncl, 1996-; Dir, William Brandt & Sons (Aust), Phillips, First City, Brandt Ltd, Merrill Lynch, Pierce, Fennell & Smith (Aust) Ltd, Citinat, Agricl Investments Aust Ltd. Hobbies: Tennis; Cricket; Reading; Golf. Address: Parliament House, Canberra, ACT 2600, Australia.

MOORE Michael Kenneth (Mike) (Rt Hon), b. 28 Jan 1949, Whakatane, New Zealand. Politician. m. Yvonne Dereany, 1975. Appointments: Social Worker, Freezing Worker; Mbr, Auckland Trades Cncl, age 17; 1st Yth Rep, Labour Party NZ Exec; Later VP, Labour Party, and off holder every level; MP, Labour, Eden, 1972-75, Papanui, 1978-84, Christchurch N, 1984-: Govt Min, Overseas Trade and Mktng, 1984-90, Tourism, Sport and Recreation, 1984-87, i/c Publicity, 1984-88, Ext Rels and Trade, 1988-90, for the Am's Cup, 1989-90; Dpty Min Fin, 1988-90; Mbr, NZ Plng Cncl, 1989-90; Min For Affairs, 1990, PM, Min i/c NZ Security Intell Serv, Sept-Nov 1990; Ldr, Opposition, 1990-. Publications: On Balance, 1980; Beyond Today, 1981; The Pacific Parliament, 1982; The Added Value Economy, 1984, Hard Labour, 1987; Children of the Poor. Honour: PC, 1990. Address: Parliament Buildings, Wellington, New Zealand.

MOORE Willis Henry Allphin, b. 14 Dec 1940, NY, USA. Educator. 2 s, 1 d. Education: M Ed, 1971. Appointments: Instr, HI Prison Syst, 1997; Adj Prof, Hist and Pol Sci, Chaminade Univ, Honolulu, HI, 1986-. Creative Works: Desd, Publd, Maps of the Pacific; Co-Auth, 2 Books; Sev Booklets; Articles for Publs. Memberships: Amn Corrections Assn; HI Hist Soc; Intl Map Trade Assn; Natl Soc of Arts and Letters; HI Geo Soc. Hobbies: Music; Hiking; Snorkel diving. Address: P O Box 37214, Honolulu, HI 96837-0214, USA.

MOORTHY Aragonda Lakshmana, b. 1 July 1952. Information Scientist. m. Mrs K Shailaja Reddy, 15 May 1986, 1 s. Education: BS (MPC): SV Univ, Tirupati, 1974; MSc, Phys, SV Univ, Tirupati, 1976; BLISc-SV Univ, Tirupati, 1978; ADISC (MLISC): DRTC/ISI, Bangalore, 1984. Appointments: Sci Asst A: ISRO/DOS, 1979-82; Sci Asst B: ISRO/DOS, 1982-84; Scientist B: DLRL (DRDO/MOD), 1984-86; Scientist C: DESIDOC (DRDO/MOD): 1987-89; Scientist D: DESIDOC (DRDO/MOD), 1989-95; Scientist E: DESIDOC (DRDO/MOD), 1995. Publications: Books, conf proceedings, spec publs incl: KAV Pandalai, The Other Side of Science (w D S Bedi), DRDO, New Delhi, 1994; Radiological Protection, A Summary Handbook of IRCP Publications and Recommendations (Ed), DRDO, New Delhi, 1995; (Co-Ed) SHAPE 95: Papers presented at National Seminar on Hospital Architecture and Engineering, New Delhi, 1995, Institution of Military Engineers, MES, New Delhi, 1995. International Directory of Defence-Related Institutions and Industries (Ed), DESIDOC, Delhi, 1996; Ed, periodicals: Defence Science Journal, 1987-95; AGLIS Journal, 1990-91; DRDO Newsletter, 1991-95; DRDO Samachar, 1991-95; DESIDOC Bulletin of Information Technology, 1991-95; Technolgy Focus, 1992-95; DESIDOC News, 1995; Popular Science and Technology Series, 1991-95; ILA Newsletter, 1996-2000. Memberships: Mbr, Natl Geog Soc, USA, 1992-94, 1997-, RRC, 1993-; Life Mbr, AGLIS, IASLIC, SIS, ILA, ISWA, SWATI, IPA, Assn of Lib Sci and Documentation, Hyderabad, Indian Sci Cong Assn, Calcutta. Hobbies; Numismatics; Philateley; Reading. Listed in: International Who's Who of 20th Century Achievement; International Directory of Distinguished Leadership. Address: Joint Director, Defence Scientific Information & Documentation Centre (DESIDOC), Ministry of Defence, Metcalfe House, Delhi-110054, India.

MORA RODRIGUEZ Arnoldo, b. 30 Apr 1937, Buenos Aires, Argentina. Minister of Culture, Youth and Sport. Education: Deg in Ecclesiastics, Cntrl Sem Paso Ancho, 1960; BA, 1961, MA, 1963, PhD, Philos, Univ Louvain, Belgium. Appointments: Prof Sys, Hist, Philos, Greater Sem, Paso Ancho, 1965-69; Prof, Philos, Univ Costa Rica, 1968-; Chair, Fundamental Philos, Dpty Dir, 1971-73, Dir, 1973-76; Vice Dean, Fac Letters, 1975, Chair, 1982-; Min Culture, Youth and Sport, Govt Costa Rica, 1994-. Address: Ministry of Culture, Youth and Sport, Apartado 10227, San José, Costa Rica.

MORAN Rachel Fay, b. 27 June 1956, Kansas Cty, MO, USA. Professor of Law. Education: AB, Psychol w Hons and w Distinction, Stanford Univ, 1978; JD, Yale Law Sch, 1981. Appointments: Prof of Law, Boalt Hall, 1982-; Visng Prof, UCLA Sch of Law, 1988, Stanford Law Sch, 1989, NYU Sch of Law, 1996, Univ of Miami Sch of Law, 1997; Robert D and Leslie-Kay Prof of Law, 1998-. Publications: Articles and book chapts; Ed, book: Perspectives on Diversity, 1998. Honours include: Phi Beta Kappa, 1977; Distinguished Tchng Awd, Univ of CA at Berkeley, 1995; JT Canales Awd for Inspiration and Outsndng Serv to Latino Community, Hispanic Law Student Assn, Univ of MI, Ann Arbor, MI. Memberships: Amn Law Inst, 1998-; Exec Cttee, Assn of Amn Law Schs, 1999-2001. Hobbies: Reading mysteries; Listening to music; Walking her dog. Address: University of California School of Law (Boalt Hall), Berkeley, CA 94720-7200, USA.

MORDECHAI Yitzhak, b. 1944, Iraq. Politician; Fmr Army Officer. 2 children. Education: Staff & Cmd Coll, Tel-Aviv & Haifa Univs. Appointments: Israeli Def Forces, 1962-95; Cmdr, Paratroop Unit, Sinai, 1967 Six Day War, Paratroop, Suez Canal Front, 1973 Yom Kippur War; Chf Infantry & Paratroopers Offr, 1983-86; Hd, IDF HQ Trng Dept, Rank of Maj-Gen, 1986; Offr in Cmd of IDF S Cmd, 1986, of Ctrl Cmd, 1989, of Northern Cmd, 1991; Joined Likud Party, 1995; Mbr, Knesset, 1996-; Min of Def, 1996-; Mbr, Likud-Tzomet-Gesher Grp. Address: Ministry of Defence, Kaplan Street, Hakirya, Tel Aviv 67659, Israel.

MORENA Gita Dorothy, b. 1 Aug 1947, Los Angeles, California, USA. Psychotherapist. 2 s. Education: MS, Clin Psych; PhD, Transpersonal Psych. Appointments: Pvte Prac, 1974-; Adj Prof, 1994-. Publications: Open Channel (audiotape), 1990; The Wisdom of Oz, 1998. Memberships: Psi Chi; Intl Soc of Sand Play Therapists; Sand Play Therapists of Am. Hobbies: Yoga; Meditation; Music; Writing. Address: 5100 Marlborough Drive, San Diego, CA 92116, USA.

MORGAN Anthony Tregerthen, b. 15 Oct 1956, England. Chartered Accountant. m. Susan, 1 d. Education: FHKSA; ACA; BA, Hons. Appointments: Chartered Acct, Price Waterhouse, 1977-87; Chartered Acct, Acceptor Grp Ltd, 1987-94; Mngng Dir, Asia Sports Grp, 1994-. Memberships: Fell, H K Soc of Accts; Inst of Chartered Accts of Eng and Wales. Hobbies: Sport; Films; Wine. Address: 15th Floor One Harbourfront, 18 Tak Fung St, Hung Hom Kowloon, Hong Kong.

MORGAN David Raymond, b. 14 Mar 1947, Melbourne, Aust. Banker. m. Roslyn J Kelly, Nov 1982, 1 s, 1 d. Education: BEc, hons, La Trobe; MSc, distinction, PhD, London; AMP, Harvard. Appointments: Snr Econ Fiscal Affairs Dept Intl Monetary Fund, USA, 1976-79; Asst Sec, For Invmnt Br, Fedl Treas Canberra, 1980-81; Sec, Govt Task Force Aust, Fin Syst Inquiry, 1981; Asst Sec, Fiscal and Monetary Policy Br, GFEP Treas, 1982-83; Taxation Policy Div, Treas Dept, Canberra, 1983-85; 1st Asst Sec, Gen Fin & Econ Policy Treas, 1986-87; Dpty Sec (Fin) Treas, 1987; Dpty Sec, (Econ) C'wlth Treas, 1989; Dpty Mngng Dir, 1990, Chf Gen Mngr, Asia-Pacific Div, Westpac Mngng Dir, Westpac Fin Svces Grp, 1990-91; Grp Exec, Retail Banking Grp, Westpac Banking Corp, 1992-94; Grp Exec, Institutional & Intl Banking, Westpac Banking Corp, 1994-; Exec Dir, 1997-, Mngng Dir, Chf Exec, 1999-, Westpac Banking Corp. Publication: Overtaxation by Inflation, 1977. Honour: Ely Devons Prize, London Sch of Econs, 1973. Hobbies: Tennis; Wine; Classical music. Address: Level 27, 60 Martin Place, Sydney, NSW 2000, Australia.

MORGAN Frank Gilmore, b. 11 Oct 1940, Launceston, Tasmania, Aust. Academic; Writer; Film-maker. m. Margot Le Lievre, 25 Jan 1965, 2 s, 1 d. Education: BS (Melbourne); MEd (Canberrra); TSTC (Melbourne). Appointments: TV writer/Prodr, ABC and com channels, Melbourne, 1963-70; Freelance Film and TV Prodr, 1971-; Lectr, Film & TV, Melbourne, 1971; Snr Lectr in Media, Canberra, 1972-80; Visng Lectr, Univ of the S Pacific, 1973-75; Visng Rsch Fell, Open Univ, UK, 1978; Dpty Dir, Austl Film, TV and Radio Sch, Sydney, 1981-86; Cnslt, Pacific Community (fmr S Pacific Commn) Noumea, 1986-; Media Cnslt, Sydney, 1987; Prof, Comm and Media Arts, Univ of Newcastle, 1988-; Cnslt, UNESCO Div for Comm, Info and Informatics,

Paris, 1992-; Hon Fell, Asia-Pacific Inst for Brdcstng Dev, Kuala Lumpur, 1993-. Publications include: Communication in the Pacific, 1997; Matters of Life and Death: Vital factors in the education of journalists and communication professionals, 1997; Globalisation and the Media in the Pacific, 1997; Towards a Pacific Media Association: A strategic plan for the Pacific Islands Broadcasting Association, 1998. Creative works: Films include: Inner Light: Port Stephens Heritage, 1993; Newcastle in the Asia-Pacific Century, 1996; Asia-Pacific Century I, 1996; A Smarter Way to Work, 1997; Asia-Pacific Century II, 1997. Memberships: Pres, Profl Educ Sect, Intl Assn for Media and Comm Rsch, 1986-; Austl Writers Guild; Pacific Islands Brdcstng Assn; Pacific Islands News Assn; Austl & NZ Comm Assn; Commonwealth Assn for Educ in Jrnlsm & Comm; Jrnlsm Educ Assn (Aust & NZ). Hobbies: Boating; Bushwalking; Photography; Reading; Surfing. Address: 24 Alpha Close, Warners Bay, NSW, Aust 2282.

MORGAN Gary Cordell, b. 8 Dec 1941, Melbourne, Aust. Market Research. m. Genevieve, 27 Oct 1977, 2 s, 2 d. Education: BCom, Univ of Melbourne. Appointment: Exec Chmn, Day Morgan Rsch Cntr, 1985-; Chmn, Haoma Mining NL, 1992-. Publications: (presented to clubs, confs) Now There's Democracy in Russia, Australia Must Be Next!, 1990; The Monarchy the Media and the Polls, 1993; Polling and the Political System (in textbook, The Australian Political System), 1994; The Asian Crisis Means We Need Major Change for Australia - If Not, We Need a Republic to Destroy the Parliamentary System as We Know It - And Start Again, 1998. Membership: Amn Mktng Assn; Eurn Soc for Opinion and Mkt Rsch (ESOMAR); Fell, Austl Inst Co Dirs (fndr); Hon Fellin the Behavioural Sci, Univ of Melbourne, 1999; Mktng Assn Aust and NZ. Hobbies: Skiing; Australian pottery and furniture. Address: 193 George Street, East Melbourne 3002, Australia.

MORGAN John Aloysius (Most Rev), b. 9 Oct 1909. Roman Catholic Bishop of the Australian Defence Forces. Education: DD, St Joseph's Coll, Melbourne; St Kevin's Coll, Melbourne; Corpus Christi Theol Coll, Werribee. Appointments: Ordained Priest, 1934; Army Chaplain, 1941; Chaplain 15th Brigade, 58 Battalion, 1941-42; Snr RC Chaplain, 3 Austl Div serving NG, 1942-44; Snr Chaplain 6 Div, 1944-46 NG(MID); Southern Command, 1948-55; Dpty Chaplain Gen, AHQ, 1955-64; Chaplain; Gen (RC) Austl Army, 1964-81; Bishop, 1969; Auxiliary Bishop of Canberra Archdiose, 1969-85; RC Bishop of the Austl Defence Forces, 1969-1985. Honours: AO, 1976; ED; RFD. Address: St Christopher's Cathedral, 55 Franklin Street, Manuka, ACT 2603, Australia.

MORGAN Rex Henry, b. Devon, England. Educator; Author. m. Mary Elizabeth Cottrell, 29 Mar 1958, 2 s, 1 d. Education: C'wlth Schl, Univ of Sydney, Aust; DiptTG, Tchrs Guild of NSW; ATCL; LTCL, Trinity Coll, London, Eng; Assoc, Roy Photographic Soc; Hon MSc, Brooks Inst, CA, USA. Appointments: Fndr, Pittwater House Schs, NSW, 1962; Freelance Broadcaster, Lectr, Author, Ed, Shroud News; Led Hermes expeditions, and to Jordan, Israel. Publications include: Perpetual Miracle, 1983; Jubilee Picture Book, 1987; Frank Mason's Churt, 1988; Shroud Guide, 1983; The Hermes Adventure, 1985; With Man and Beast on the Oregon Trail, 1993; The History of Bathurst 1815-1915 (ed), 1994. Contbr to num booklets, pprs, articles, brdcsts. Honours: Dux of Course, Tchrs Guild of NSW; Justice of the Peace, NSW; Fell, Aust Coll of Educ; MBE, 1969. Memberships include: Fell, Roy Geographical Soc; Fell, Roy Soc of Arts; Pres, SE Asia Rsch Cntr for the Holy Shroud, 1986; Pres, Rex Morgan Fest Cttee, 1992-; S E Asia Writers Awd Cttee, Thailand, 1995; Rex Morgan Fndn, 1999-. Hobbies: Writing; Public Speaking; Travel; Antiques; Vintage Cars; Collecting. Listed in: Who's Who in Australia. Address: Abercrombie House, Bathurst, NSW 2795, Australia.

MORGAN Vincent Thomas, b. 10 May 1923, London, England. Research Scientist; Consultant. m. Jeanette Simmons, 31 Mar 1951, 2 s, 3 d. Education: Dip EE, BSc, PhD, DSc, Univ London. Appointments: Rschr, Telecom London, 1945-51; Grp Ldr, CE GB, Leatherhead, Eng, 1951-64; Snr Rsch Sci, CSIRO, Sydney, 1964-73; Prin Rsch Sci, 1973-84; Snr Prin Rsch Sci, 1984-88; Hon Rsch Fell, 1988-. Publications: Overhead Line Charts, 1952; Thermal Behaviour of Electrical Conductors, 1991. Honours: Hooker Disting Visng Prof, McMaster Univ, 1989-90; Intl Sci Exchange, NSERC, Can, 1994; IEEE Herman Halperin Awd, 1998. Memberships: Fell, Inst of Elec Engrs, 1962, Austl Inst of Phys, 1970; Inst of Elec and Electron Engrs, 1990. Hobbies: History; Travel. Address: 64 Clanville Road, Roseville, NSW 2069, Australia.

MORIMOTO Akihiro, b. 27 Feb 1949, Wakayama Prefecture, Japan. Mechanical Engineering Educator. m. Hiroe Matsushima, 11 Feb 1978, 2 s. Education: Dr Eng; Assoc Prof. Appointments: Sumitomo Metal Industries Ltd, 1977; Kinki Univ, 1991. Publications: Articles and pprs in profl jrnls and transactions. Honours: Awd of Tech Devel, Japan Soc Civ Engrs, 1988. Memberships: Japan Soc Mechl Engrs; Soc Materials Sci Japan. Hobbies: Travel; Radio Control. Address: 4-15-4 Nakano, Higashisumiyoshiku, Osaka 546-0012, Japan.

MORITA Akio, b. Jan 1921, Nagoya Cty, Aichi Prefecture, Japan; Founder and Honorary Chairman, Sony Corporation. m. Yoshiko, 2 s, 1 d. Education: Grad, Phys Dept, Osaka Imperial Univ, 1944. Appointments: Founded Tokyo Tsushin Kogyo (Tokyo Telecomms Engrng Corp) w Mr Masuru Ibuka, 1946; Co name officially changed to Sony Corp, 1958; Exec VP, 1959, Pres, 1971, Chmn & CEO, 1976, Chmn of Bd, 1989, Fndr & Hon Chmn, 1994, Sony Corp. Honours include: Medal of Hon, H M Emperor of Japan, 1976; DL, Williams Coll, 1982; Albert Medal, Roy Soc of Arts, 1982; Legion d'Honneur (Officier) Govt of France, 1984; Cmdr's Cross, Order of Merit, Fedl Repub of Germany, 1987; Kt Cmdrs Cross 1st Class, Order of Merit, Repub of Austria, 1987; Orden Nacional do Cruzeiro do Sul, Govt of Brazil, 1988; DL, Univ of PA, 1990; La Gran Cruz de la Orden del Merito Civil, H M King of Spain, 1990; 1st Class Order, Sacred Treas, H M Emperor of Japan, 1991; Intl Awd, Instn of Mfng Engrs, 1991; Cmdr, Order of Orange Nassau, H M Queen of Netherlands, 1991; Hon Kt Cmdr, Most Excellent Order, Brit Empire, H M Queen of Eng, 1993; DEng, Univ II, 1993; Cmdr of Order of Leopold, H M King of Belgians, 1993; IEEE Fndrs Medal; Creu de Sant Jordi, Govt of Catalonia, Spain, 1996; Distinguished Medal of Honor, Japanese Natl Mus, 1996. Memberships include: Chmn, 1988-95, Hon Chmn, 1995-, Cncl for Better Corp Citizenship; Japan Chmn, Trilateral Commn, 1992-97; Hon Mbr, IEEE. Address: Sony Corporation, Corporate Communications, 6-7-35 Kitashinagawa, Shinagawa-ku, Tokyo, 141 Japan.

MORLEY Brian Derek, b. 16 June 1943. Botanist. m. June Archer, 19 Apr 1965, 3 s. Education: BS (Hons), Univ Wales, 1964; PhD, Univ West Indies, 1968; Appointmemts: Freelance auth, 1968-69; Taxonomist, Natl Bot Grdn, Glasnevin, Ireland, 1969-75; Hort Bot, 1975-78; Asst Dir, 1978-81; Dir, 1981-; Bot Gdn of Adelaide, S Aust; Bd, Austl Arid Lands BG, 1996-. Publications: Wildflowers of the World, 1970; Flowering Plants of the World, contrb, 1978; Flowering Plants in Australia, coed, 1983. Honours: Visng Trevelyan Fell, Durham Univ, 1983; Cosmos Awd Cttee, Osaka, 1993-94; Sec Gen, Intl Assn Bot Gdn, 1984-94. Memberships: Fell, Linnean Soc, London, 1968-; Fell, Soc of Fellows, Univ Durham, 1983-; Life Mbr, Roy Agric & Hort Soc SA, 1981-. Address: Botanic Gardens and State Herbarium, North Terrace, Adelaide, South Australia 5000.

MORRIS Brian James, b. 14 July 1950, Adelaide, Aust. Academic. m. Lilian, 14 Feb 1993, 1 d. Education: BSc (Hons); DSc; PhD. Appointments: C J Martin Fell of Natl Hlth Med Res CL of Aust (to USA), 1975-77; Amn Heart Assn Adv Fell, 1977-78; Lectr, Snr Lectr, 1978-87; Rdr 1987-99; Prof, 1999-. Publications: Over 180 incl 160 in intl jrnls, 1972-99. Honour: Edgeworth David Medal for 1985 (State sci prize). Memberships: Exec Cttee, High Blood Pressure Rsch Cncl of Aust; Austl Soc Medl Rsch; Austl Soc Biochem Molecular Bio. Address: Department of Physiology (F 13), University of Sydney, NSW 2006, Australia.

MORRIS David Charles, b. 23 Aug 1957. Winemaker. m. Alma Jean Morris, 3 Dec 1989, 1 s, 1 d. Education: Assoc Dip in Wine Mrktng and Prodn, Roseworthy Coll. Appointments: Winemaker, Orlando Wines, 1981; Winemaker, Mngr, Wickham Hill Cellars, 1987; Winemaker/Mngr, Morris Wines, 1993. Memberships: Austl Soc of Oenology and Viticulture. Hobbies: Cattle production; Lawn bowls. Address: Mia Mia, Vineyard Rutherglen, Vic, Australia.

MORRIS Grant H, b. 10 Dec 1940, Syracuse, NY, USA. Professor of Law. m. Phyllis, 4 July 1967, 1 s, 1 d. Education: AB, Syracuse Univ, 1962; JD, 1964; LLM, Harv Univ, 1971. Appointments: Asst Prof of Law, 1967-68; Assoc Prof of Law, 1968-70; Prof of Law, Wayne State Univ, 1970-73; Prof of Law, Univ of San Diego, 1973-; Acting Dean, Univ of San Diego, 1977-78, 1988-89, 1997-98. Publications: The Insanity Defense: A Blueprint for Legislative Reform, 1975; Mental Disorder in the Criminal Process, 1993. Honours: Univ Prof for 1996-97, Univ of San Diego. Memberships: Chair, Law and Psych Sect Assn of Amn Law Schs, 1973-74; San Diego County Super Crt Mental Hlth Hearing Offr, 1992-97. Hobbies: Jogging; Cycling. Address: University of San Diego Law School, 5998 Alcala Park, San Diego, CA 92110-2492, USA.

MORRIS Jill, b. 28 Mar 1936, Brisbane, Aust. Teacher; Author. m. (1) John Morris, 26 May 1960, div, (2) Richard Dent, 4 May 1988, 1 s, 2 d. Education: BA, DipEd, Univ of Queensland, 1957. Tchr, Bundabug State hs; Prodr, Brdcstng Commn; Pt-time Tertiary Tchng, Lecturing; Var contracts publng & editing. Publications: Num incl: Mystery of the Patriarch (screenplay), 1984; Freelance articles for newspprs & mags, 1985; Almost a Dinosaur (play), 1987, (book), 1989; Numbat Run!, 1989; Dugong Dive!, 1990; Golden Wombats, 1990; Street Children of Brazil (video script), 1990; Dido Has Diabetes, 1991; Australian Bats, 1992; Australian Owls Frogmouths & Nightjars, 1994; Australian Frogs, Amazing Amphibians, 1995; Green Air, 1996; Velvet the Flying Gecko, 1997; The Wombat Who Talked to the Stars, 1997; Rainbow Warrior - Battle for the Planet, 1998; The Ghost of Drop Choc, 1998. Honours: Churchill Fellshp, 1972; Sunshine Coast Univ Coll UK Cncl, 1994-96, 2nd Cncl, 1997-99. Memberships: Co-fndr, Grtr Glider Prodns, 1983; Fndr, Book Farm, 1988. Hobbies: Bushwalking; Gardening; Sewing; Books and films. Address: Book Farm, 330 Rusville Road, Maleny, Qld 4552, Australia.

MORRIS Julie Dianne, b. 17 Jan 1945, Adelaide, South Aust. Wildlife Artist. m. Gary Whitby, 1 May 1992. Education: Dip, Fashion Art (South Aust Inst of Technol). Publications: Bushland Secrets (children's book, illustrator), 1984; Possums on the Roof (auth, illustrator), 1990; Puddy (illustrator, co-auth), Puddy, 1986; Australian Mammals (auth, illustrator), 1986; The Wollondilly Bunyip and the Koala (illustrator and co-auth), 1990. Hobbies: Photography; Gardening; Travel; Theatre; Animals. Address: Lot 3 Buangi Road, Dooralong, NSW, Australia.

MORRIS Katherine Emily, b. 9 Apr 1913. Retired Teacher. m. Vincent Darcy Morris, 17 Jan 1942, 1 s, 1 d. Education: Sydney Tchrs Coll, 1931-33. Publications: Down by the River (with E Laird), 1967; The Frog, 1968; The Platypus, 1974; Mudeye: The Story of a Dragonfly, 1978; The Wonderful Caterpillar, 1978; Buzzy the Honey Bee, 1978; Pep, Joe and Ana: The Ant's Story, 1980; Tip, the Long Necked Tortoise, 1983; Ringo, the Ringtail Possum, 1983; The Fairy Penguins; How The Sun Was Made, 1984; Why Rabbits Nose Twitches, 1984; Collins Childrens Annual: Little Friend Tortoise, 1984. Hobbies: Reading; Drawing; Painting; Writing. Address: 39 Hawkesbury Road, Springwood, NSW 2777, Australia.

MORRIS Philip Leo Patrick, b. 13 Mar 1949. Psychiatrist. m. Carole Olland Morris, 8 Aug 1987, 2 s, 3 d. Education: BSc (Med); MBBS; PhD; FRANZCP; Dip, Amn Bd Psych & Neurol. Appointments: Prof, Dir, Gold

Coast Mental Hlth Serv, 1997-. Publications: Over 60 publd wrks (articles and others). Honour: Univ NSW, Alumni Awd, 1975. Memberships: Austl Medl Assn; Royal Austl & NZ Coll of Psychs. Hobbies: Surfing; Tennis; Golf. Address; Gold Coast Hospital, PO Box 554, Southport, Qld 4215, Australia.

MORRIS Roger Stewart, b. 29 Nov 1943. Veterinarian. m. Gwenyth Elsie Tanner, 29 Jan 1966, 1 s, 1 d. Education: BVSc (Hons), Sydney; MVSc, Melbourne; PhD, Reading, UK. Appointments: Asst Lectr, 1966-70, Lectr, 1970-73, Snr Lectr, 1973-76, Vet Med, Univ of Melbourne; Asst Dir, Austl Bur of Animal Hlth, 1976-81; Prof and Chmn, Dept of Large Animal Clin Scis, Univ of Minnesota, USA, 1981-85; Gilruth Prof of Animal Hlth, Massey Univ, NZ, 1986-. Publications: 300 sci publs. Honours: Fell, Amn Coll of Epidemiology, 1984; Fell, Austl Coll of Vet Scientists, 1990; Fell, Roy Soc of NZ, 1997. Memberships: Inaugural Chmn, Intl Soc for Vet Epidemiology and Econs, 1979-82. Hobbies: Gardening; Swimming; Wood-carving. Address: EpiCentre, Institute of Veterinary, Animal and Biomedical Sciences, Massey University, Private Bag 11-222, Palmerston, North New Zealand.

MORRIS-SUZUKI Teresa, b. 29 Oct 1951. Historian of Japan. m. Hiroshi Suzuki, 2 June 1975, 1 s. Education: BA, hons, Bristol Univ, 1972; PhD, Univ of Bath, 1980. Appointments: Lectr, Snr Lectr, Assoc Prof, Univ New Eng, 1981-92; Snr Fell, 1992-95, Prof, 1995-, Austl Natl Univ.Publications: Beyond Computopia, 1988; A History of Japanese Economic Thought, 1989; The Technological Transformation of Japan, 1994; re-Inventing Japan, 1998. Honour: Fell, Austl Acady of the Hums. Memberships: Japanese Stdies Assn of Aust; Austl Stdies Assn of Aust. Hobby: Poetry. Address: Pacific and Asian History, Research School of Pacific & Asian Studies, Australian National University, Canberra, ACT 0200, Australia.

MORRISON Charles Edward, b. 4 March 1944, Billings, MT, USA. Researcher; Educator. m. Chieko, 10 March 1984, 2 s. 2 d. Education: PhD, Johns Hopkins Univ. Appointments: Profl Lectr, Johns Hopkins Sch Adv Intl Stdies, 1977-80; Legislative Asst to Sen William V Roth Jr, 1972-80; Snr Rsch Assoc, Japan Cntr for Intl Exchange, Tokyo, 1980-84, 1985-92; Spec Asst to Pres, 1986-92, Dir, Prog on Intl Pols and Econs, 1992-95, Pres, 1998-, East-West Cntr; Dir, Asia Pacific Econ Cncl, Study Cntr and Chair, US Consort of APEC Stdy Cntrs, 1996-98. Publications: Wide range of books, book chapts, reports and other pubs in field of intl rels. Memberships: Var advsry cttees and cncls; Pres, Two Valleys Realty, MT. Address: East West Centre, 1601 East West Rd, Honolulu, HI 96848-1601, USA.

MORSE Richard Jay, b. 2 Aug 1933, Detroit, USA. Human Resources & Organizational Development Consultant. Education: BA, Univ VA, 1955; MA, Clin Psychol, CA Univ, Los Angeles, 1967. Appointments: Area Persons Admnstr, Gen Tele Co of CA, Santa Monica, 1957-67; Snr VP, Human Resources, The Bekins Co, Glendale, CA, 1967-83; Pvte Cnslt, Human Resources & Org Devel, Cambria, 1983-. Publications: Sev articles in profl jrnls. Memberships: Intl Soc of Performance Improvement. Hobbies: Travel; Tennis; Walking; Swimming. Address: 6410 Cambria Pines Road, Cambria, CA 93428-2009, USA.

MORTIMER-DUNN Gloria (nee Smythe), b. 22 July 1928, Sydney, NSW, Aust. Designer; Teacher; Writer. m. Bernard Mortimer-Dunn, 24 Dec 1954. Education: Hons Dipl, Art (Des and Crafts), ASTC, E Sydney Tech Coll (Sydney Inst of Technol, E Sydney Campus), NSW, Aust; Postgrad stdies Barrett Street Coll, now London Sch of Fashion, Eng, 1953. Appointments: Des Tchr, E Sydney Tech Coll, 1947-52, 1956-78; Freelancer Fashion and textile Des, 1948-62; Asst to Hd Designer, Horrockses, London, 1953-56; Hd Designer, Intl Co, Speedo (Aust), 1962-91; Pt-time Tchr, Adult Educ Classes in Fashion, Sydney, 1991-93. Publications: Pattern Design, 1960, 1966, Canad ed, 1970, 1980, 1998/1999; Fashion Making, 1975, 1980, revised 1996; Fashion Design, 1972, 1974, revised as ABC's of Fashion and Design,

UK, 1978; Pattern Design for Children, 1993, revised as Fashion Design for Children's Clothes, UK Ed, 1996. Hobbies: Art; Painting; Sculpture; Literature; Music; Theatre; Travel. Address: 15 Roberts Street, Rose Bay NSW 2029, Australia.

MORTLEY Raoul John, b. 25 Sept 1944, Sydney, Australia. Consultant. m. Miranda, 16 Nov 1983, 1 s, 2 d. Education: BA, hons; MA; DLitt, Strasbourg; Hon Doc, Univ Newcastle, Aust. Appointments: Monash Univ, Univ of Strasbourg, Macquarie Univ; Former Vice Chan, Pres, Univ of Newcastle, Bond Univ. Publications include: From Word to Silence, vols I & II, 1986. Memberships: Fell, Acady of Humanities, Aust; Asutl Inst of Co Dirs. Address: 26 Ben Lexcen Place, Robina, Qld 4226, Australia.

MORTLOCK Harold Bryce, b. 14 Oct 1921. m. Peggy Worley, 22 May 1948, 3 s. Education: BArch, Sydney Univ; DArch, Melbourne Univ. Appointments: Ptnr, Ancher Mortlock and Murray Archts, 1952; Master Planner, Univ of Melbourne, 1968-98; Dir, Ancher Mortlock and Woolley Pty Ltd, 1969-82; NSW Chapt RAIA, Pres, 1970-72; Pres, RAIA, 1975-76; Dir, Austl Bldg Ind Specifications Pty Ltd, 1975-92; Visng Prof, Univ of NSW, 1981; Ed-in-Chf, Austl Bldg Specification, 1982-92. Honours: Sydney Univ Medal, 1951; UCL Alfred Blossom Medal, 1951; RAIA Sulman Awd, 1960; NSW Chapt RAIA, Merit Awd, 1972; Gold Medal, 1979; Victorian Chapt RAIA, Bronze Medal Awd, 1981; AM, 1982. Memberships: LFRAIA; MRAPI. Hobbies: Walking; Reading; Music. Listed in: Who's Who in Australia. Address: 5 Vernon Street, Cammeray, NSW 2062, Australia.

MORTON Alan Ridley, b. 10 Sept 1934, Queanbeyan, MSW, Aust. University Professor. m Jill, 27 Dec 1965, 1s, 2d. Education: Dip PE; MSc; EdD; DSc (HC); FACSM; FASMF; CBIIOL; FIBIOL; FAIBIOL; FACHPER; MAAESS. Appointments include: Lectr, PE, Sydney Tchrs Coll, 1965; Tchng Fell, Functional Anatomy and Physiol of Exercise, Univ Oegon Eugene USA, 1966-67; Asst Prof Educ Univ Vic, Can, 1967-68; Lectr, PE, 1969-1970, Snr Lectr PE, 1971-75, Snr Lectr and Hd, Dept PE and Recreation, 1977-78, Hd Dept, 1978-81, 1985, Assoc Prof, 1978-94, Dept Hum Movement Stdies, Univ WA; Visng Rsch Physiologist, Inst Environ Stress, Univ CA, Santa barbara, USA, 1976; Visng Prof, Univ AZ, Tuscon, AZ, 1979; Snr Fell, Nanyang Technol Univ, Singapore, 1992; Prof Hum Movement, Univ of WA, 1994-. Publications: The Increased Daily Living Plan (co-auth), 1966; Get Fit the Champions Way (co-auth), 1968; Rugby for Teachers, Coaches and Players (co-auth), 1977; Health Assessment for Adults (jtly), 1989; Athletics, Growth and Development in Children (jtly); Num Books, booklets, chapts in books, rsch pprs and jrnl articles. Memberships: Wembly Downs Tennis Club (Perth); Old Golds Rugby Club; Univ Club; WA Rugby Club. Hobbies: Rugby; Fitness; Reading; Jazz music. Address: 208 Weaponess Road, Wembley Downs, WA 6019, Australia.

MORTON Henry Albert, b. 20 July 1925, Gladstone, Manitoba, Can. Farmer; Lecturer. m. Peggy Stuttard, 4 d. Education: BA, BEd, Univ Manitoba; MA, Univ Cambridge, Eng; PhD, Univ Otago, NZ. Appointments: War Serv, Pilot, RCAF, Flying Offr, Bomber Cmnd, 1942-45; Prin, Glastone W Morton Collegiate, Can, 1961; Assoc Prof, Otago Univ, NZ, 1978. Publications: And Now New Zealand, 1969; The Wind Commands, 1975; Which Way New Zealand, 1975; Why Not Together?, 1978; The Whale's Wake, 1982; The Farthest Corner, 1988. Honour: Sir James Wattie Awd, Book of the Yr, 1976. Memberships: Blenheim Club; NZA; Roy NZ Air Force Assn; Bomber Cmnd Assn; ProBus; RSA. Hobbies: Wood Carving; Billiards. Address: 55B Brooklyn Drive, Blenheim, Marlborough, New Zealand.

MOSER Michael Joseph, b. 31 Aug 1950, USA. Lawyer. m. Yvonne Wei, 17 Aug 1973, 3 d. Education: JD, Harvard Law Sch; PhD, Columbia Univ; BSFS, Sch of Fgn Serv, Georgetown Univ. Appointments: Mbr, Panel of Arbitrators, Am Arbitration Assn, Cntr for Intl Coml

Arbitration, Cairo Regl Cntr for Intl Coml Arbitration, China Intl Econ & Trade Arbitration Cmmn, Beijing, China Securities Regulatory Cmmn, Beijing, Hong Kong Intl Arbitration Cntr, The Mauritius Cham of Com & Ind Perm Crt of Coml Arbitration, Singapore Intl Arbitration Cntr, World Intellectual Property Org Arbitration Cntr, Geneva; Fell, Chart Inst of Arbitrators, London, Hong Kong Inst of Arbitrators Ltd, Roy Geographical Soc. Publications include: China Business Law Guide, 1990; Foreigners Within the Gates: The Legations At Peking, 1993; Hong Kong and China Arbitration, 1994; International Arbitration in the People's Republic of China. Honours: Phi Beta Kappa, 1972; Rotary Fell, Rotary Intl, Japan, 1978-79. Memberships: Adj Prof of Law, Peking Univ; Hong Kong Intl Arbitration Cntr, Gov Cncl & Mngmt Cttee; UN Working Grp on Offl Trans of Chinese Fgn Investment Legislation; Hong Kong Arbitration Ordinance Review Cttee. Hobbies: Opera; Poetry; Sports; Anthropology. Address: Baker & McKenzie, 14th Floor, Hutchinson House, 10 Harcourt Road, Central Hong Kong.

MOSTAFIZUR Rahman A S M, b. 8 Jan 1934, Bangladesh. Politician. m. Sufia Ruby, 1 s, 1 d. Education: St Xavier's Coll, Calcutta; Dhaka Govt Coll; Pakistan Mil Acady. Appointments: Army, 1955, Artillery Offr, 1956; Inter-Serv Intelligence; Lt-Col, retd 1973; Bus Man, 1973-77; Dpty Advsr in Charge of Home Affairs, Govt of Pakistan, 1977-78; Min-in-Charge, Min of Home Affairs, 1978-81; Mbr, Parl, 1979-82, 1991-; Mbr, Standing Cttee, Bangladesh Natl Party, Sec-Gen, 1985-86; Min of Fgn Affairs, 1991-96. Hobbies: Shooting; Reading; Photography. Address: Ministry of Foreign Affairs, Topkhana Road, Dhaka, Bangladesh.

MOTT Hamilton Charles, b. 5 Dec 1936, Albury, Aust. Academic; Diplomat; Journalist. m. Elspeth Hall Lewis, 27 Apr 1963, 2 s, 1 d. Appointments: Jrnlst, Herald, Melbourne, Aust, 1957-59; Jrnlst, Reuters, London, England, 1960-61; Jrnlst, Daily Telegraph, London, 1961; Dept of External Affairs, 1962; Third Sec, The Hague, Holland, 1963-65; Second Sec, Karachi-Rawalpindi, Pakistan, 1965-67; UN Section, Dept of For Affairs, 1968-70; First Sec, Cnslr, Mission to UN, NY, USA, 1970-74; Rapporteur, First Cttee, UN Law of the Sea Conf, 1973-75; Asst Sec, Info Br, Dept For Affairs and Snr Dept Spokesperson, 1975-77; Min, Austl High Commn, London, England, 1977-79; Spec Rep and Head, Austl Liaison Offc, Salisbury, Rhodesia (now Zimbabwe), 1979-80; High Commnr to Nigeria, 1979-82; Asst Sec, Intl Orgs and Humanitarian Affairs, 1983-86; Amb, Perm Delegate to UNESCO, 1986-87; Amb to Spain, 1988-92; Asst Sec, Environment and Antartica, 1992-95; Amb to Brazil, 1995-98; Adj Prof and Advsr to Vice Chan on Intl Affairs, La Trobe Univ, Bundoora, Vic, 1998-. Hobbies: Tennis; Gardening. Address: 67 Perth Street, Prahran, Vic 3181, Australia.

MOTT Tony, b. 26 Apr 1956, Sheffield, Eng. Photographer. Education: OND Hotel Mngmt, City & Guilds 147 & 151. Appointments: Sauce Chef, Oriana P&O Ships, 1978-80; Tour Phila Rolling Stones, 1991, 1994, 1995; Publr, Loudmouth and Drum Media Mag, Fleetwood Mac, 1994; Paul McCartney, 1995. Publication: Still Noise. Honours: Ram Photogr of the Yr, 1986, 1988; Photogr Rock of the Yr, AMA Awds, 1988, 1990, 1991, 1992, 1994; Nom Freelance Photogr of Yr, 1997. Hobbies: Trains; Music; Nepal. Address: 775, Bourke Street, Redfern, NSW 2016, Australia.

MOTTERAM Raymond William, b. 14 Mar 1943, Perth, West Australia. Accountant; Business Owner. m. Wilma Kathlyn Steel, 6 Jan 1969, 2 d. Education: Assoc, Aust Soc of Accts, 1970; Reg'd as Tax Agent, 1972; Cert Practising Acct, 1987. Appointments: Asst Acct, Kodak (Aust); Asst Acct, Swan Taxis; Bought into family bus Signal Tyre Service, 1967. Honours: Mbr of the Yr, Field and Game, West Aust, 1985; Greatest Contbr, Field & Game Fed, 1986; Natl Pres, 1982-87, Treas 1988-89, Field and Game Fed of Aust; Life Mbr, Perth Amateur Football Club; AO, 1993. Memberships: Exec Cttee (Intl), FITASC; Roy Aust Ornithologists Union; Pres, Field and Game Fed of Aust, 1989-93, WA Pres, 1989-; Level 1

Shooting Coach, sporting clays. Address: 1 Moran Street, Embleton, WA 6062, Australia.

MOUNT Graham Jaunay, b. 19 Dec 1924, Adelaide, Aust. Dentist. m. Margaret Wilson Jones, 12 Nov 1949, 3 s, 1 d. Education: Bach, Dental Surg, Univ of Sydney, 1945; Fell, Roy Australasian Coll of Dental Surgs, 1986. Appointments: Pvte Prac, Adelaide, SA, 1945-94; Lectr (Pt-time), Univ of Adelaide, 1950-80; Guest Assoc Prof, Northwestern Univ, Chgo, 1970; Visng Rsch Fell, Univ of Adelaide, 1980. Publications: 82 sci pprs published in refereed jrnls; 18 educl video tapes in Restorative Dentistry; 2 books, An Atlas of Glass Ionomer Cements: The Clinician's Guide, 2nd ed, 1994; Preservation and Restoration of Tooth Structure (co-auth), 1998; Chapt, Glass Ionomer Cements, 1999. Honours: Disting Serv Awd, Austl Dental Assn (SA Br), 1984; Graham Mount Oration, Postgrad Cttee in Dentistry, Univ of Adelaide, 1985; Meritorious Serv Awd, Austl Dental Assn, 1987; Mbr of the Order of Aust, 1988; DDS, Univ of Adelaide, 1992; Hon Life Mr, Austl Dental Assn (SA Br). Memberships: Austl Dental Assn; Am Acady of Restorative Dentistry; Fell, Intl Coll of Dentists; Fell, Acady of Dentistry Intl; Gen Prac Study Grp. Hobbies: Gardening; Photography; Writing. Address: 13 MacKinnon Parade, North Adelaide, South Australia 5006, Australia.

MOUSAWI Faisal Radhi al, b. 6 Apr 1944, Bahrain. Government Minister; Orthopaedic Surgeon. 1 s, 3 d. Education: Univ Cairo, Egypt. Appointments: Fmr Rotary Intern, Cairo Univ Hosp; House Offr, Snr House Offr, Dept of Surg, Govt Hosp, Bahrain; Snr House Offr, Accident & Orthopaedic Surg, Ctrl Middlesex Hosp, London, Orthopaedic Surg, St Helier Hosp, Carshalton, Surrey, Gen Surg, Nelson Hosp, London, St Bartholomew's Hosp, London; Reg, Orthopaedic Surg, Whittington Hosp, London; Gen & Traumatic Surg, Wexford Co Hosp, Ireland; Locum Cnslt, Whittington Hosp, 1983-84; Cnslt, Orthopaedic Surgn, Salmaniya Med Cntr, Bahrain, 1976-, Char, Dept of Surg, 1982-84; Chf, Med Staff, 1982, Chair, Dept of Orthopaedic Surg; Asst Prof, Coll of Med & Med Scis, Arabian Gulf; Asst Under-Sec, Min of Hlth, 1982-85, Min of Hlth, 1995-. Publications: Num pprs and articles. Memberships include: Eur Soc for Sport Med, Knee Surg & Arthroscopy; Fell, brit Orthopaedic Assn. Hobby: Tennis. Address: Ministry of Health, PO Box 12, Sheikh Sulman Road, Manama, Bahrain.

MOUSSAVI Mir Hussein, b. 1942, Iran. Politician. Education: Natl Univ, Teheran. Appointments: Joined Islamic Soc; Fndr Mbr, Islamic Repub Pty, 1979; Chf Ed, IRP Newsppr, Islamic Repub, 1979; Fgn Min, 1981; PM, 1981-89; Advsr to the Pres, 1989-. Address: Office of the President, Teheran, Iran.

MOXHAM Gwenyth Constance, b. 3 Sept 1943, Adelaide, Australia. Teacher. m. 14 May 1966, 1 s, 1 d. Education: BA, Adelaide; Dip T TC, MACE. Publications: Sir Claude Gibb (Biog entry in Australian Dictionary of Biography, Vol 14); They Built South Australia: Engineers, Technicians, Manufacturers, Contractors and Their Work. Membership: Austl Coll of Educn. Hobbies: Reading; Writing School Plays; Gardening; History; Travel. Address: 6 Barr Smith Dirve, Urrbrae, South Australia, Australia.

MOZAFAR Hossein, b. 1953, Tehran, Iran. Minister of Education. Education: BA, Islamic Jurisp and fundamentals of Islamic Law; MA, Mngmt. Appointments: HS Tchr, 26 yrs; Hd, Educ Off, Dists 6, 7, 16, Cty of Tehran; Dir Gen, Tehran Prov's Educ Off, 1982; Dir Gen, Inspection and Evaluation Dept of Min of Educ, 1986; Min of Educ; Dpty Hd, Co-operatives of Shahid Fndn.

MU Dong, b. 30 Dec 1962, Shandong, China. Associate Professor. m. Du Zhiping, 4 Apr 1986, 1 s. Education: Bach Deg, 1983; Master Deg, 1985. Appointments: Vice Dir, Dept of Bus Admin & Econ Rsch Cntr, Shandong Inst of Mining Technol, Taian. Publications: The Theory and Exploitation of Coal Enterprise Technology Progress, 1996. Honours: 1st

Prize, Ex Achievement in Mod Mngmt, Chinese Coal Ind, 1995; Ex Tchr of Shandong Inst of Mining Technol. Hobbies: Swimming; Music. Address: c/o Department of Business Administration, Shandong Institute of Mining & Technology, Taian, Shandong, China.

MUBARAK ALI Rahamathulla b. 15 Apr 1961, Dharmapuri, India. Lecturer. m. 1 s. Education: BA, Pub Rels; MA, Socl Wrk; MPhil, Socl Wrk; PhD, Socl Wrk. Appointments: Socl Worker, 1985; Rsch Offr, 1988; Socl Worker, 1992; Lectr, 1993. Publications: Conducted rsch on psych patients and publd in form of books and rsch articls. Membership: Asia Pacific Assn of Socl Wrk Educ. Hobbies: Music; Reading. Address: School of Social Sciences, University Sains Malaysia, 11800 Minden, Pulau Pinang, Malaysia.

MUCKLESTONE Robert Stanley, b. 15 May 1929. Lawyer. m. Megan Kruse, 25 June 1983, 1 s, 3 d. Education: BS, JD, Univ of WA. Publications: Community Property - General Considerations, Tax Management Portfolio, revised ed, 1985; Washington Probate Procedure and Tax Manual, revised ed, 1998. Memberships: Amn Bar Assn; fmrly, House of Delegs; Amn Coll of Trust and Estate Counsel; Intl Acady of Estate and Trust Law, Exec Cncl, 1994-98. Hobby: Flying (holds the record for solo single engine plane around the world, 19-26 May 1978 in 7 days, 13 hours, 13 minutes). Address: 17/F Standard Chartered Bank Building, 4 Dex Voeux Road, Central Hong Kong, Central Hong Kong.

MUDHOLKAR Shivdas Shivling Elias Rajas, b. 17 Oct 1946, Gadhinglaj. CEO; Group Director. m. Snehal, 15 Dec 1970, 1 s, 1 d. Education: BCom, Shivaji Univ, Kolhapur; LLB, Univ of Poona; BSc Econs, London Sch Econs; MBA, Harvard Univ, USA; Advd Mngmt Dip, AIM Manila; Hard Core Top Mngmt Trng, ASTC Hyderabad, India; Doct in Mngmt; Chartered Acct; Chartered Sec. Appointments: A F Ferguson & Co Mngmt Cnslts, 1968-71; Mngmt Exec, Kirloskar Grp, 1971-73; Finl Controller, Co Sec, Consolidated Pneumatics Co Ltd, 1973; Fin Dir, Pfizer (India) Ltd, 1973-81; Treas Dir, Mitsubishi Corp, Osaka, Japan, 1982-83; Proj Dir, Tandon Corp, Singapore, 1983-84; Grp VP, CEO, Nobel Grp of Cos, Bandung, Indonesia, 1984-. Publications: Articles and pprs in profl and periodicals worldwide on var subjs in mngmt; 2 books on mngmt acctng and corp fin; Num articles in Marathi Lit. Honours: 1st Prize, State/Cntrl Govt's UGC Schlshp, Peace Essay Contest, Lions Intl; Schlshp in Yth Exchange Plan, Rotary Intl; Natl schl; Macmillan Prize, London Sch of Econs; GP Kapadia Gold Medal, CA Inst; NC Kelkar Gold Medal in LLB, Univ of Poona. Memberships include: FCA (Eng & Wales); FCA (India); Fell, Inst Co Secs, India; Fell, Inst Co Secs, UK; Fell, Admnstv Acctng, UK; Fell, Brit Inst of Mngmt, London; Fell, Inst Internal Auditors, USA; Assoc, Indian Inst of Pub Admin, New Delhi; Fell, All India Mngmt Assn; Fell, Roy Econ Soc, Eng; Fell, Chartered Assn of Cert Accts, Eng; Assoc Mbr, Finl Club of Indonesia. Address: B-12 Tapasya, Paranjape B Scheme, Road No 4, Vile Parle (East), Bombay 400057, India.

MUHAMMAD Mari'e, b. 3 Apr 1939, Surabaya, E Java, Indonesia. Education: Grad, Univ Indonesia, 1969. Appointments: Hd, Sub-Directorate, Indl Cos, 1973-79; Dir, Shareholder, State Owned Co;, 1979-87; Dir Gen, Taxation, 1988-93; Min of Fin, Indonesia, 1993-. Address: Department of Finance, JL Lapangan Banteng Timur, 2-4 Jakarta, Indonesia.

MUHAMMAD ALI, b. 3 Aug 1957, Rawalpindi, Pakistan. Retired Army Officer. m. Sadia Bibi, 1 Jan 1990, 2 s, 1 d. Education: BA, BS (Hons), War Studies; LLB; MA, in 5 subjs, Hist, Arabic, Islamic Studies, Econs, Polit Sci; MPhil, Islamic Studies; PhD, Hist; 2½ yrs Arabic Lang, NIML, Islamabad, & 8 mths from Amn Univ Cntr, Cairo. Appointments: Cadet, Pakistan Mil Acady, 1975-77; Army Offr, 1977-95; Coord, Intl Islamic Relief Orgn, 1995-. Publications: Islamic Resistance in the Former Soviet Union in the Twentieth Century, 1993; Soviet Military Involvement in Afghanistan and its Impact on the Security of Pakistan, 1997. Memberships: Army medals inclng Tagma Haji, Tama Golden Jubili, Tagma

Sad Salah Gashan-e Birth of Quaid-e-Azam and Tagma Jamuriate, 1975-95. Hobbies: Sufism (Tasawaf); Spirituism. Address: 286-D, Satellite Town, Rawalpindi, Pakistan.

MUHITH Abul Maal Abdul, b. 25 Jan 1934, Bangladesh. Consultant on Finance, Planning, Development and Management. m. Syed Sabia Begum, 19 Nov 1961, 2 s, 1 d. Education: BA, hons 1st class, 1954, MA, 1955, Dhaka Univ; MPA, Harv Univ, 1964. Appointments: Sub Divsnl Offr, Bagerhat, 1959-60; Dpty Sec to Gov of E Pakistan, 1961-62; Dpty Sec, Chf Plng Commn, Karachi, 1964-66; Dpty Sec to Cabinet, Pindi, 1966-69; Econ Cnslr, Pakistan Emb, 1969-71; Charge d'Affaires, Bangladesh Emb in USA, 1972; Alternate Exec Dir, World Bank, 1972-73; Econ Min, Bangladesh Emb, USA, 1972-74; Exec Dir for India and Bangladesh, Asian Dev Bank, Manila, 1974-77; Sec, Econ Rels Div, Dhaka, 1977-81; Min of Fin and Plng, Dhaka, 1982-84; Visng Fell, WW Sch, Princton Univ, 1984-85; Mbr, Experts Grp on Support Cost Stdy, UNDP, NY, USA, 1989; CEO, Delta Brac Housing Corp, Dhaka, 1996-97. Publications: The Deputy Commissioner in East Pakistan, 1968; Bangladesh: Emergence of a Nation, 1978, revised ed, 1992; Thoughts on Development Administration, 1981; Problems of Bangladesh: An Attempt at Survival, 1986; Bangladesh Reconstruction and National Consensus, 1991; American Response to Bangladesh Liberation War, 1996; Unblemished Memories - 1971, 1996; In Search of National Consensus, 1998; Bangladesh in the Twenty First Century, 1999. Honours: Pope Gold Medal, Acad Distinction, 1954; Tamgha-e Pakistan Awd, 1966; Paul Harris Rotary Fellshp, Colombo, 1982. Memberships: Intl Life Mbr, SID; Life Mbr, Bangla Acady, Dhaka; Life Mbr, Econ Assn of Bangladesh; Fndr, Chmn, POROSH envirntl platform for citizens and NGO's in Bangladesh, 1997-. Hobbies: Tennis; Swimming; Reading; Travelling. Address: 61/B Kemal Ataturk Avenue, Banani, Dhaka, Bangladesh.

MUIR Laurence MacDonald (Sir), b. 3 Mar 1925, Morwell, Victoria, Australia. Company Director. m. 1948 (diss 1989), 2 s, 2 d. Education: Scotch Coll, Univ of Melbourne, 1942-46; VRD; LLB; FSIA; FAIM. Appointments: Dir, Hudson Conway Ltd; Chmn, Templeton Global Growth Fund Ltd; Dir, Publng & Brdcstng Ltd, Focus Book Pty Ltd; Former Dir, ANZ Banking Grp Ltd, ANZ Pensions Ltd; ACI Ltd; Herald & Weekly Times Ltd; Wormald Intl Ltd; Natl Comm Union Ltd; Elders Aust Chartering Pty Ltd; Liquid Air Aust Ltd, l'Air Liquide Intl; Admitted Bar & Solicitor, Supreme Court, Victoria, 1950; Sharebroker & Ptnr, Potter Ptnrs, 1960-80; Fndng Chmn, The Canberra Dev Bd and Mbr Parl House Construction Auth, 1978-90; Dept Chmn Natl Sci & Tech Ctr Adv Cttee. Memberships: Fndr & Bd Mbr, Delta Soc Aust; Mbr, Commn for the Future; Bd Mbr, The Fndn for Dev Co-op; Bd Mbr, Sir John Monash Bus Ctr; Patron Microsurgery Fndn; Patron Baker Med Rsch Inst; Mbr, Gen Motors Aust; Adv Cl, Trustee Earthwatch Aust; Bd Mbr, Menzies Fndn; Hon Life Trustee, CEDA; MCC; Melbourne Club. Hobbies: Gardening; Reading. Address: Unit 3, 61 Black Street, Brighton 3186, Australia.

MUIR Robert, b. 27 May 1933, Nedlands, Western Aust. Antiquarian Bookseller. m. Helen Durack, 2 s. 2 d. Appointments: Cncl, Roy Western Aust Hist Soc Inc. Publications: Articles in profl journals and catalogues. Memberships: ILAB; ABA; ANZAAB; AICCM; RWAHS; WA Art Gallery Soc; Ephemera Assn; Custodian WA State Lib. Hobbies: Photography; Underwater diving; History; Blacksmithing. Address: 69 Broadway, Nedlands, Western Australia 6009.

MUKAMBAYEV Usup, b. 28 Jan 1941, Kyrghyzstan. Lawyer. m. Mukambayeva, 2 d. Education: Kyrghyz State Univ, Law Dept, 1964-68. Appointments: KGB Offl, 1968-91; 1st Dpty to KGB VChmn; Min of Just, 1991-93; MP, 1995-96; Speaker, Legis Assembly, Parl of Kyrghyzstan. Publications: Over 10 articles in judicial reform. Honours: Red Star, Orden; Medal for Labor Distinction; 7 other USSR Medals. Membership: Academician of Intl Turkic Acady, 1997. Hobbies: Mountaineering walking. Address: 34, Umetaliyev str,

Ap-t 29, Bishkek, Kyrghyzstan.

MUKERJEE Chitta Mohan, b. 1 Feb 1927, India. Consultant Thoracic Physician. m. Chhaya Banerjee, 15 Jan 1955, 1 s, 2 d. Education: LMF, Bengal, 1946; MB BS, Univ Calcutta, 1956; DTCD, Univ Lucknow, 1966; FCCP (USA), 1980. Appointments: House Surg, CMS Hosp, Calcutta, 1947; Govt Epidemic Order, Bihar; Medl Offr, Anti Malaria Unit, Dist Bd, Ranchi; Medl Offr, Dist Bd, Gaya; Medl Offr on Epidemic Duty, Govt UP; Medl Offr, Dist Bd, Deoria (UP), -1958; Asst Surg Grp J North Railway Divisional Hosp, Jodhpur and Lucknow (Surg Ward, Medl Ward inclng Chest Ward and Children's Ward); Asst-Medl Offr (Chest) North Railway Divisional Hosp, Bikaner, 1958-70; Snr Medl Offr i/c NSWAM Hosp Cnsltnt Chest Physn; Regl Chest Physn, Cntrl Reg, Ghana (W Africa), 1970-73; Resident Medl Offr, Registrar, Roy S Sydney Hosp, Sydney, 1973-74; Medl Offr/Snr Medl Offr, Tuberculosis Div, Dept Hlth, Govt of NSW, Sydney, 1975-87; Visng Medl Offr, Randwick Chest Hosp, Sydney, 1977-80; Visng Medl Offr, Chest Clinic, Liverpool Hosp, Sydney, 1979-95; Visng Medl Off, Chest-Clin, Prince of Wales Hosp, Sydney, 1980-92. Publications: Var orig articles on chest diseases in different medl jrnls inclng Punjab Med Journal; Brit J Dis Chest; Med J Aust; Aust NZ J Med; CHEST; Amn Rev Resp Dis; Pprs var confs and seminars, Aust and abroad 1980-98. Honours: Full Mbr, Thoracic Soc Aust and NZ, for Worthwhile Contbn to Thoracic Med, 1992; Cnslt Emeritus, Liverpool Hosp (Tchng Hosp, NSW) for Meritorious Servs to hosp, 1995; WHO invited to wrkshp of IUATLD, wrkng grp on Clin trials in Tuberculosis, Paris, 1995. Memberships: Thoracic Soc Aust and NZ; Aust Tub and Chest Assn; IUATLD; OAMGA; Amn Coll Chest Physns. Listed in: International Who's Who of Professionals; Who's Who in Australia and the Far East; Australasian Who's Who. Hobby: Gardening. Address: Bhabla-Lucknow House, 1296 Bunnerong Rd, Phillip Bay, NSW 2036, Australia.

MUKHERJEE Devasis, b. 14 Apr 1969, Naihati, India. Artist. Education: BFA; MFA. Creative Works: Num paiting exhbins and one man shows. Honours: Lalit Kala Akademi, New Delhi, 1995; Lalit Kala Akademi Panjab, 1995; S Cntr Zone Cultural Cntr Nagpur, 1995. Membership: Lalit Kala Akademi, New Delhi. Hobbies: Reading; Writing. Address: c/o S K Mukherjee, 308/1 Hori Nagar, Gorifa PO, Gorifa District 24, West Bengal, India.

MUKHERJEE Sanat Kumar, b. 15 Mar 1998, Calcutta, India. Vice Chancellor. m. Sutapa, 2 Mar 1982, 2 s. Education: BME, Hons; MME, Gold Medallist; Fell (PhD) in Mngmt. Appointments: Lectr, Mech Engrs, 1979-84, Reader, Prodn Engrs, 1984-92, Prof, Prodn Engrs, 1992-97, Jadarpur Univ; Vice Chan, Birla Institute of Technology, Bihar, India, 1998-. Honours: Sir R N Mookerjee Gold Medal, 1981. Memberships: Fell, Inst of Engrs, India; Sec, West Bengal State Cntr Inst of Engrs, India, 1996-98. Hobbies: Reading; Social Activities. Address: Vice Chancellor, BIT Mesra Ranchi 835215, Bihar, India.

MUKHERJEE Subhash Chandra, b. 1 Jan 1935. Documentation and Information Scientist. m. 21 July 1968, 1 s. Education: BA Econ and Hist, 1958; BLibSci, Calcutta Univ, 1960; Assocshp of Dip Documentation Rsch and Trng Cntr, 1965; MA Hist, 1969; DMS Hon, Calcutta Univ, 1976. Appointments: Libn, Dept Appl Chem, Calcutta Univ, 1959-69; Lib-in-Charge, Saha Inst of Nucl Phys, 1967; Sci Offr, Lib and Doc, Saha Inst of Nuc Phys, 1979-93. Publications: Number of articles publd in Lib Sci Jrnls, 1968-. Honours: Hon Asst Sec, IASLIC, 1968-71; Hon Lectr Course of Spec Libn and Documentation; Cert Course in LibSc, 1966-68; Tincowri Dutta Mem Gold Medal for best article on LibSci, Bengali, 1971. Memberships: Life Mbr, Indian Assn of Spec Libs and Info Cntrs, 1967-; Life Mbr, Bengal Lib Assn, 1967-; Assoc Ed, Indian Lib Sci Abstract, 1967-68. Hobbies: Photography; Homeopathy; Reading. Address: 12A/15 Pashupati, Bhattacharjee Road, Calcutta 700 034, India.

MUKHOPADHYAY Pinaki Nath, b. 16 Mar 1951, Shibpur, Howrah, India. Teacher. m. Sampa, 24 Feb 1984, 1 d. Education: BSc; MSc; Ctf, Lib Sci; BLib.Sc; MLib.Sc. Appointments: CU Press, 1979; CU Lib, 1980; RE Coll, 1984; JU, 1987; RBU, 1992. Publications: 35 articles in var profl jrnls Honours: 3 Gold Medals. Memberships: ILA; IASL; ATLIS; Bangiya Bijnan Parishad; Bangiya Sahitya Parishad; BLA. Hobbies: Stamp and Coin Collecting. Address: Flat 2B, 22 Type IV, HIT Housing Estate, Echapur Kadamtal, Howrah 711 101, India.

MUKHOPADHYAY Samyasam, b. 19 Mar 1947. Librarian. m. Meena Mukhopadhyay, 16 Jan 1978, 1 s. Education: BSc, Calcutta Univ, 1967; BLibSc, Jadarpur Univ, 1969; MA, Pol Sci, Rajasthan Univ, 1976; MA, Sociol, Rajasthan Univ, Jaipur, 1986; MLIS, IGNOU, New Delhi, 1996. Appointments: Trnee, Amn Lib, USIS, Calcutta, 1969; Cntrl Drugs Lab, Calcutta, Snr Lib Asst 1970-73; Profl Asst, Jawaharlal Nehru Univ Lib, New Delhi, 1973-97; Asst Libn, Jawaharlal Nehru Univ, 1997-. Publications: Ed, Sociological Literature: South Asia, 1993; Articles, bibliographies. Membership: Life Mbr, Indian Assn of Spec Libs and Info Cntrs, Calcutta. Hobbies: Reading; Music. Address: 757 New Campus, Jawaharlal, Nehru University, New Delhi 67, 110067, India.

MUKHOPADHYAY Saroj Kumar, b. 4 Aug 1940, Dhaniakhali, India. Professor. m. Madhabi, 2 June 1967, 1 s, 1 d. Education: BEng, 1966, MEng, 1972, PhD, Engrng, 1982, Jadavpur Univ; Ctf, Mngmt, Intl Cntr for Mngmt Dev, Bucharest, Romania, 1979. Appointment: Prof, Natl Inst of Indl Engrng, Mumbai, 1980-. Publications include: Machine Component Grouping in Cellular Manufacturing by Multidimensional Scaling, 1994; Moments Based Clustering Techniques for Manufacturing Cell Formation, 1995; Design and Implementation of an Integrated Production Planning System for a Pharmaceutical Manufacturing Concern in India, 1998. Honours: Univ Gold Medal; Sir RN Mookerjee Meml Gold Medal, 1975; Ctf of Merit, 1983; Prodn Engrng Div Gold Medal, 1994-95; Ctf of Merit, 1998. Memberships: NY Acady of Scis; Operational Rsch Soc of India; Instn of Engrs, India. Address: National Institute of Industrial Engineering, Vihar Lake, Bombay 400087, India.

MUKUMBAYEV Usup Mukambayevich, b. 28 Jan 1941, Dzholgolot, Kyrgyzia. Politician. Education: Kyrgyz State Univ; Higher Courses, USSR Cttee of State Security. Appointments: Army Serv; Shepherd, Kolkhoz Ak-Suy Region; Sec, CP Cttee of State Security Cttee, Kyrgyz Repub, 1970-78; Dpty Dir, Dept of State Security Cttee, Osh Region, 1978-80; Dir, Dept of State Security Cttee, Talass & Osh Regions, 1980-86; 1st Dpty Dir, State Security Cttee, Kyrgyz Repub, 1986-91; Min of Justice, 1991-92; Dpty Parl (Zhogorku Kenesh) of Kyrgyzstan, 1990-, Chair, 1996-; Chair, Legis Assn, Kyrgyz Parl. Address: Zhogorku Kenesh, 720003 Bishkek, Kyrgyzstan.

MULCAHY Maurice Joseph, b. 4 May 1921, Plymouth, Eng. Environmental Scientist. m. Patricia Leahy, 18 Aug 1952, 1 s, 2 d. Education: Prior Pk Coll, Bath, Eng; BS, Forestry, Univ of Aberdeen, Scotland, 1949; PhD, Univ of West Aust, 1960. Appointments: Royal Navy, 1942-46, Lt (A) RNVR; Soil Rsch, Macaulay Inst, Aberdeen, 1949-53; Soil Rsch, CSIRO Div of Soils, 1953-76; Visng Lectr, Hon Rsch Fell, Agric, Univ of West Aust, 1957-92; Offr in Charge, CSIRO WA Rural Scis Lab, 1964-74; Fac of Agric, Univ of West Aust, 1966-93; Staff, 1976-84, Bd Mbr, WA Environmental Protection Authority, 1984-91. Publications: Num sci papers on soil rsch in sci jrnls; Num reports for WA Government on land resource management and planning; Ed, Atlas of Natural Resources, Darling System, WA, 1980. Honours: AM, 1987; Fell, Austl Inst of Agricl Sci (FAIAS), 1983; Hon DSc, Murdoch Univ, 1996-. Memberships: Austl Inst of Agricl Sci; Royal Soc of West Aust; Royal Perth Yacht Club. Hobbies: Bushwalking; Sailing. Address: 6B Airlie Street, Claremont, WA 6010, Australia.

MULCAHY Richard John, b. 30 June 1952. National Executive Director. m. Rose Marie, 5 Mar 1977, 2 s, 2 d. Education: Univ Tas. Appointments: Snr Hon Marriott, 1975; Res Advsr Ldr, Opposition Tas, 1976; Res & Pub Rels Offr, MHR Denison, 1976-77; Press Off, Emb of the US Canb, 1977-78; Pub Affairs Off, Cand H Commsn Canb, 1979-80; Prin Personal Asst to Premier Vic, 1980-81; Fed Dir, Advtng Ind Employers Assn, 1982-83; Dir, Natl Peanut Cl Aust Ltd, 1983-87; CEO, Fed Dir, Confectionery Mnfrs Aust Ltd, 1983-87; Dir, Dental Progs, W Wrigley Jnr Co, Chgo, IL, USA, 1988-89; CEO, Tobacco Inst Aust Ltd, 1989-90; Natl Exec Dir, Austl Hotels Assn, 1992-. Membership: Ministerial Tourism Adv Cl, 1994-. Hobbies: Swimming; Music; Cinema. Address: Australian Hotels Association, 24 Brisbane Avenue, Barton, ACT 2600, Australia.

MULFORD Therese Odile, b. 11 Feb 1947, Can. Painting Conservator. m. Bill, 21 Feb 1969, 1 s, 1 d. Education: BA, BEd, Master of Applied Sci, Dip of Bus. Appointments: Art Tchr and lectr, Can and Aust; Paintings Conservator at the Queen Vic Mus and Art Gall, Launceston, Tasmania, 1987-. Memberships: AICCM; IIC; AFUW. Hobbies: Tai Chi; Bush walking; Gardening; Thinking; Reading and drinking coffee. Address: 48 Beach Road, Legana, Tasmania, Australia 7277.

MULKEARNS Ronald Austin, b. 11 Nov 1930, Caulfield, Aust. Former Catholic Bishop of Ballarat. Education: De La Salle Coll, Malvern, 1938-48; Corpus Christi Coll, Werriee, 1949-56; Pontifical Lateran Univ, Rome, Italy, 1957-60; DCnL, 1960, DD, 1968. Appointments: Ordained Priest, 1956; Asst Priest, Parish of Mentone, 1957; Asst Priest, Parish of N Melbourne, 1960-62; Sec, Melbourne Archdiocese Tribunal, 1962-68; Sec, Metro Tribunal, Prov of Melbourne, 1962-68; Coadjutor Bish of Ballarat, 1968-71; Bish of Ballarat, 1971-97; Retired, 1997-. Memberships: Canon Law Soc of Aust and NZ. Listed in: Who's Who in Australia. Address: PO Box 411, Aireys Inlet, Vic 3231, Australia.

MULLAN James (Very Reverend), b. 5 Aug 1921, Hamilton, NSW, Aust. Presbyterian Minister. m. Nenufar Clark, 5 July 1948, 2 s. Education: BA, 1942; DipRE, 1970; BLitt Hons, 1991. Appointments: Patrol Min, Western Riverina, 1945-48; Parish Min: Kiama, 1948-52; Liverpool, 1952-58; West Strathfield, 1958-74; Beecroft, 1974-87; Clk of NSW Gen Assembly, 1977-94; Min Emer, 1987. Honour: Moderator Gen, Presby Ch of Austl, 1979-82. Address: Windemere Villa 5, 15 Leo Road, Pennant Hills, NSW 2120, Australia.

MULLANE Graham Robert. Judge. Education: BA; LLM (Syd); MJS (Nev). Appointments: Solicitor, 1971-86; Civil Claims Arbitrator, NSW Dist Crt and local crts, 1984-86; Judge, Fam Crt of Aust, 1986-; Chmn, Fam Cntr. Honour: Scout Assn Medal of Merit, 1996. Memberships: Sec, Newcastle Law Soc, 1977-86; Chmn, Bd, Roy Newcastle Hosp, 1981-86; Judge's Rules Cttee, 1992-96. Memberships: Bd Mbr, Tinonee Gdns Multicultural Hotel, 1989-, Chmn, 1989-1988. Address: Family Court of Australia, 61 Bolton Street, Newcastle, NSW 2300, Australia.

MULLER Hans Konrad, b. 16 July 1937, NSW, Aust. Professor; Head of Pathology. m. Margaret Jill Brady, 23 Apr 1962, 4 s, 3 d. Education: BMedSc, 1961; MB, BS, 1963, Univ of Adelaide; PhD, Univ of NSW, 1970; FRCPA, 1971; MRCPath, 1981; FRCPath, 1991; FFOP (RCPA), 1996; MRACMA, 1997; BA, 1993. Appointments: Res Med Offr, Roy Adelaide Hosp, 1963; Temp Lectr, Univ of Adelaide, Hon Clin Asst, Roy Adelaide Hosp, 1964; Rsch Fell, Univ of NSW, 1965-68; Lectr, Snr Lectr, Monash Univ, 1968-75; C'wlth Med Fell, Univ of Cambridge, Eng, 1972-73; Assoc Prof, Monash Univ, 1975-83; Snr Visng Rsch Fell, Univ of Bristol, 1978-79; Visng Pathol, Roy Hobart Hosp, 1983-; Visng Prof, Dept of Immunol, Univ TX and MD Anderson Cancer Cntr, Houston, USA, 1991-92, 1997-98; Pres, Roy Coll of Pathol of Austl, 1993-95; Acad Dean, Fac of Med & Pharm, 1994-97. Publications: Over 140 pprs on immunopathol and cancer studies. Honours: C'wlth Med Fellshp, 1972-73; Inaugural Dick Buttfield Meml Fell, Tas. Memberships include: Chf Examiner, Bd Censors, 1980-82; Past Chmn, Bd of Censors and Mbr Cncl, Roy

Coll of Pathol of Australasia, 1982-88; VP, Roy coll of Pathol of Australasia, 1989-93, Pres, 1993-95; FRCPath, 1991; Hon FHKCPath, 1993; Austl Med Assn; Fell, Acady of Med, Singapore, 1994; Fndn Fell, Fac of Oral Path, RCPA, 1996; Roy Australasian Coll of Medl Administrators, 1997. Hobbies: Medical history; Biography. Listed in: Who's Who in Australia; Who's Who in the World. Address: Department of Pathology, University of Tasmania, 43 Collins Street, Hobart, Tas 7000, Australia.

MULLER Phillip Henry, b. 2 Jan 1956, Majuro, Marshall Is. Federal Official. m. Yolenda DeBrum, 2 s, 2 d. Education: Deg in Bus Econs, Rockhurst Coll, 1979. Appointments: Dpty Sec, For Affairs, Govt of Marshall Is, 1982-84; Min in Assistance to Pres, 1984-86; Min of Educ, 1986-94; Min For Affairs, 1994-. Embassy of the Marshall Islands, 2433 Massachusetts Avenue NW, Washington, DC 20008, USA.

MULRONEY Graham William, b. 31 Oct 1946, Melbourne, Australia. Professor. m. Mary, 3 Jan 1970, 2 s. Education: BSc; MSc. Appointments: Tchr, Min of Educn, Vic, 1968-69; Asst Lectr, 1969-74, Lectr, 1974-79, Snr Lectr, 1979-82, Dept of Appl Chem, Preston Inst of Technol; Snr Lectr, 1982-86, Prin Lectr, 1986-89, Hd of Dept, 1989-90, Dept of Appl Chem, Philip Inst of Technol; Dean, Sch of Appl Sci & Technol, Phillip Inst of Technol, 1991-92; Assoc Dean, Fac of Appl Sci, 1992-94, Dir, Northern Ptnrshps, 1994-95, Dir, Cmty Servs, 1996-, RMIT Univ. Publications include: Science/Technology-Education: Education and Industry, 1995; Education and Industry Partnership Models in Victoria, 1996; Teacher Internships for Science and Education, 1996; Partnerships in Science and Technology Education, 1996. Memberships: Roy Austl Chem Inst; Soc of Chem Ind of Vic; Intl Org for Sci and Technol Educn, 1984; Austl Assn for Instl Rsch; Vic Chem Coords Cttee; Vic Ind Educn Ptnrshps. Address: RMIT University, PO Box 71, Bundoora, Victoria 3083, Australia.

MULVANEY Derek John, b. 26 Oct 1925, Yarram, Vic, Aust. m. Jean Campbell, 6 Feb 1954, 4 s, 2 d. Education: BA, hons, 1948, MA, 1951, Univ of Melbourne; BA, 1953, MA, 1959, PhD, 1970, Univ of Cambridge, Eng. Appointments: Served as Aircrew, RAAF, 1943-45; Lectr, Snr Lectr in Hist, Univ of Melbourne, 1954-64; Snr Fell in Prehist, 1965-70, Prof of Prehist, 1971-85, Emer Prof, 1986, Fac of Arts, Austl Natl Univ, Canberra; Sec, Austl Acady of the Hums, 1989-96. Publications: The Prehistory of Australia, 1969; So Much That Is New, 1975; Sir Baldwin Spencer 1860-1929 (w J Calaby), 1985; Encounters in Place, 1989; Over 170 archaeological rprts, histl articles. Honours: Rsch Medal, Roy Soc, Vic, 1963; CMG, 1982; Vic Premiers Awd for Austl Hist, 1987; ANZAAS Medal, 1988; AO, 1991. Memberships: Fell, Brit Acady; Fell, Soc of Antiquaries; Fell, Austl Acady of the Hums; Austl Soc of Auths. Hobbies: Gardening; Historical and Environmental Conservation. Address: 128 Schlich Street, Yarralumla, ACT 2600, Australia.

MUNRO Robert Keith, b. 20 Jan 1954, Aust. Veterinary Scientist. m. Philippa, 20 Dec 1991, 2 s, 1 d. Education: BVSc, Sydney Univ; PhD, Sydney Univ. Appointments: Rsch Scientist, CSIRO, 1981-86; Lectr, Univ of New Engl, 1987-90; Scientist w C'wlth Govt, 1990-. Honours: Sir Ian Clunes Ross Awd, 1988; Intervet Awd of Akzo-Nobel, 1986. Memberships: Austl Vet Assn; Aust Soc for Reproductive Bio; Life Mbr, RSPCA. Hobbies: Family; Gardening. Address: 4 Eucumbene Drive, Duffy. ACT 2611, Australia.

MUNZ Peter, b. 12 May 1921. Professor Emeritus of History. m. Anne, 1 s. Education: MA, NZ; PhD (Cantab). Appointment: Prof of Hist; Retd 1986. Publications: The Place of Hooker in the History of Thought, 1952; Problems of Religious Knowledge, 1959; The Origin of the Carolingian Empire, 1960; Relationship and Solitude, A Study of the Relationship between Ethics, Metaphysics and Myth, 1964; Frederick Barbarossa, a Study in Medieval Politics, 1968; Life in the Age of Charlemagne, 1968; (Ed) The Feel of Truth, 1969; When the Golden Bough Breaks, Stucturalism or Typology?, 1973; Boso's Life of Pope Alexander III, 1973; The Shapes of Time, A New Look at the Philosophy of History, 1977; Our Knowledge of the Growth of Knowledge, Popper or Wittgenstein?, 1985; Philosophical Darwinism, On the Origin of Knowledge by Means of Natural Selection, 1993; Critique of Impure Reason: An Essay on Neurons, Somatic Markers and Consciousness, 1999. Hobbies: Tennis; Skiing. Address: 128 Ohiro Rd, Wellington, New Zealand.

MUOI Nguyen Van, b. 15 Sept 1948, Quang-Nam, Danang. University Professor. m. Phan Thi Hoa, 1970, 4 s. Education: BAE; BAT; MA; PhD. Creative Works: 6 Eng Books, 1971-86; 1 Transl Novel, 1988; 1 Book on Vietnamese Culture, 1999; 15 Rsch Pprs. Memberships: Alumni, Univ of Pittsburgh, USA; Rsch Sch of Pacific and Asian Studies; The Austl Natl Univ. Hobbies: Pingpong; Cultural Studies. Address: Dept of English Linguistics and Literature, College of Social Sciences and Humanities, Vietnam National University, Ho Chi Minh City, 12 Dinh Tien Hoang St, Distric 1, Ho Chi Minh City, Vietnam.

MURADOV Sakhat Nepesovich, b. Ivanovo, Russia. Turkmanestan Government Official; Educator. m. Sona Höwme, 2 s, 1 d. Education: Dip in Higher Educ, Turkmen Agricl Inst, Ashbagat, Turkmenistan. Appointments: RschWrkr, 1953-65; Rector, Turkmen State Univ; Rector Turkmen Polytech Inst; Min, Higher Educ, 1970-90; Chmn, Mejlis of Turkmenistan (Parl). Publications: 3 books; 50 articles to profl jrnls. Honours: Decorated 6 times w orders. Memberships: Shmn, Solidarity Commn for African Asian Nations, Ashgabat, 1971-93; Turkmen-Indian Friendshp Soc; Ashgabat Cty Soc of Knowledge; Dpty Chmn, Turkmenistan Rep Soc Knowledge. Hobbies: Sports; Travel; Literature. Listed in: Who's Who in the World; Who's Who in America. Address: Mejlis of Turkmenistan, 17 Bitarap Turkmenistan St, 744000 Ashgabat, Turkmenistan.

MURAKAMI Masakatsu, b. 6 May 1945, Nanjin, China. m. Midori, 29 Apr 1977, 1 s, 1 d. Education: BS Engrng, 1968, MS Engrng, 1970, Hokkaido Univ; MS, Stats, Stanford Univ, 1973; PhD, Engrng, Hokkaido Univ, 1977. Appointments: Rschr, 1974-82, Chf Rschr, 1982-85, Assoc Prof, 1985-94, Prof, 1994-, Inst of Statistical Maths, 1994-; Prof, Grad Univ for Advd Stdies, 1994-. Publications: Engineering Statistics, 1985; Data Analysis Using Personal Computer, 1988; Introduction to Social Survey, 1990; Quantitative Analysis for Authorship Problem, 1994; Quantitative Analysis for Humanities, 1998. Honours: Shara-juin Awd, 1992; Sakamoto Nishin Awd, 1997; Hon Visng Prof, People's Univ of China, 1995; Japan Soc for Archaeological Info Awd, 1997; The Behaviormetric Soc of Japan Awd, 1997. Memberships: Intl Statistical Inst, 1987; Japan Statistical Soc, Regent, 1982-84, Cnclr, 1982-88, 1990-94, Chmn, Cttee of Stats Educ; Behaviormatic Soc of Japan, Ed, 1991-93, Regent, 1991-; Japan Soc for Archaeological Info, Regent, 1996-. Address: 3-11-8 Bessho, Urawa, Saitama Pref, 336-0021, Japan.

MURAKAMI Masatoshi, b. 16 Mar 1935, Kasai, Hyogo, Japan. News Agency. m. Yoko, 5 Mar 1960, 2 d. Education: BA, Waseda Univ. Appointments: NY Corresp, 1964-66; Ed, Econ News Desk, 1978-82; Dir, Pres Secretariat & Planning Off, 1982-86; Mngr, Osaka Regl Br, 1986-88; Exec Dir, Sales & Mktng & Enterprises, 1988-91; Exec Dir, News Reporting, Mngng Ed, 1992-96; Snr Exec Dir, Mngng Ed, 1993-96; Snr Exec Dir, Mass Media, 1996; Pres, CEO, 1996-. Memberships: Intl Press Inst; Japan Newsppr Publrs & Eds Assn, bd mbr; Japan Natl Press Club, bd mbr. Hobbies: Reading; Golf; Watching Rugby Matches. Address: 5-17-19 Asagaya-kita, Suginami-ku, Tokyo 166-0001, Japan.

MURAKAMI Yoichiro Paul, b. 9 Sept 1936, Tokyo, Japan. University Professor. m. Kimiko, 26 Apr 1975, 1 s. Education: Grad, Hist & Philos Dept, Univ of Tokyo, 1962; Doct Prog, Univ of Tokyo, 1968. Appointments: Rsch Asst, 1965, Asst Prof, 1972, Sophia Univ; Asst Prof, Univ of Tokyo, 1986; Prof, Intl Christian Univ, 1995; Professor Emeritus, Tokyo Univ. Publications: 34 books; Over 200 pprs on hist, philos, sociol of sci. Memberships: Pontifical Acady of Socl Scis; Japan Assn, Philos of Sci. Address: Mitaka-shi, Shimorejaku, 3-3-47 Tokyo, 181-0013, Japan.

MURALEEDHARAN N, b. 25 May 1947, Trivandrum, India. Scientist. m. Sobha, 2 s. Education: PhD. Appointments: Asst Zool; Zool, Zool surv of India, Govt of India; Hd of Entomology Div, Utd Planters Assn of India; Asst Dir; Jt Dir; Dir. Creative Works: Post Management in Tea, 1991. Honours: Scroll of Hon, Entomology Rsch Inst, Loyola Coll, Madras. Memberships: Indian Soc for Plantation Crops. Hobbies: Reading Novels; Malayan Poetry; Watching TV. Address: UPASI Tea Research Inst, Nira and Dam, Valparai 642127 Coimbatore District, Tamil Nadu, India.

MURARI P, b. 19 Aug 1934, Chennai. Retired Civil Servant. m. Mrs Sita Murari, 11 Feb 1963, 1 s. Education: MA, Econs, Madras Univ, 1954. Appointments: Indian Admnstv Serv, 1957-; Major positions in Govt both at Cntr and in Tamil Nadu; Sec to Pres of India; Sec, Min of Info and Brdcastng, Govt of India; Sec, Min of Food Processing Inds, Govt of India; Chmn, Tamil Nadu Elec Bd; Hlth Sec, Govt of Tamil Nadu (over 4 yrs); Gen Mngr, State Trading Corp & Handicrafts and Handlooms Export Corp of India (on deputation to Min of Com, Govt India based in NY, for over 4 yrs); State level coord for introduction of Mngmt by Objectives in Govt of Tamil Nadu, 1972-82; Dir, sev pub ltd cos; Advsr to the Pres FICCI; Chmn, Cttee of Deep Sea Fishing Ind, Min of Food Processing Inds; Mbr, Govt of India Cttee of Food Processing. Publications: Shakthi Pipes - A Resurgence, 1974; Monographs: Handicrafts of India and Socio-Economic Surveys of Tribal Villages; Management by Objectives, 1983; Articles. Honours include: Census of India Medal, Pres of India, 1963. Hobbies: Sports; Reading; Music; Travel. Address: Advisor to President, Federation of Indian Chambers of Commerce & Industry, Federation House, Tansen Marg, New Delhi 11000, India.

MURAYAMA Tomoya, b. 25 Feb 1963, Tokyo. Correspondent. Education: BA, Tokyo Univ, 1988. Appointments: Rprtr, NHK Brdcstng Co, Tokushima, Tokyo, 1985-96; Corresp, NHK Brdcstng Co, NYC, 1996-97; Corresp, NHK, Rio de Janiero, 1998-. Creative Works: Corresp, S Amn Technol Aircraft, 1994; NASA, After the Cold War Era, 1996; Hostage Crisis in Peru, 1997; Environl Crisis in Indonesia, 1997. Hobbies: Swimming. Address: c/o NHK Rio de Janeiro, Av Nilo Pecanha 50/1208, Rio de Janeiro, RJ 20044-900, Brazil.

MURCH Graeme Elliott, b. 2 Feb 1948, Adelaide, S Aust. Academic (Personal Chair). m. Christine, 2 s. Education: BS (Hons), 1969, PhD, 1973, DSc, 1982, Flinders Univ; DEng, Newcastle Univ, 1991. Appointments: Rsch Fell, Flinders Univ, 1973-75; Scientist, Argonne Natl Lab, USA, 1975-85; Prin Rsch Scientist, ICI Aust, 1985-86; Acad, 1986-; Personal Chair, Materials Engrng, Newcastle Univ, 1993. Publications: 175 intl jrnl pprs/book chapts; Auth: 1 book, Ed, 7 books. Honours: Ed: Materials Sci Forum, Diffusion and Defect Data; 15 invited lects at intl confs. Memberships: ASM Intl, Chmn, Atomic Transport Activity, 1983-86; Fell, Inst of Engrs, Aust; Materials Rsch Soc. Hobbies: Piano performance; Antiques; Musicology. Address: Department of Mechanical Engineering, The University of Newcastle, Callaghan, NSW, Australia 2308.

MURDOCH (Keith) Rupert, b. 11 Mar 1931, Melbourne, Australia. Publisher. m. Anna Maria Torv, 1967, 2 s, 2 d. Education: Worcester Coll, Oxford. Appointments: Inherited Adelaide News, 1952; Fndr, Cruden Investments, 1979-; Owner, Newspprs, mags in Aut, England, USA, Hong Kong, incl: The Australian; Daily Telegraph; Sunday Telegraph; Daily Mirror; The Chicago Sun-Times; NY Post; Boston Herald; Mirror Newspprs Ltd; TV Week; Sun; News of the World; CEO, Mngng Dir, News Intl PLC (UK), Dir, 1969-, Chair, 1969-87, 1994-95; Chair, Pers, News Am Publng Inc; Dir, United Technols (US), 1984; Dir, Reuters Holdings PLC, 1984-90. Honours include: Cmdr of the White Rose (1st class), 1985. Address: 1 Virginia Street, London E1 9XY, England.

MURDOCH Elisabeth Joy, b. 8 Feb 1909, Melbourne, Aust. m. Keith Arthur Murdoch, 6 June 1928, 1 s, 3 d. Education: St Catherines, Toorak, 1920-22; Clyde Sch, Woodend, Vis, 1922-26. Appointments: Pres, C of M Royal Children's Hosp, 1954-65; Tstee Natl Gall of Victoria, 1968-76; Tstee, McClelland Regl Art Gall, Founding Bd Mbr, Victorian Tapestry Workshop. Honours: CBE, 1961; DBE, 1963; AC, 1989; Hon LLD, Hons Causa, Univ of Melbourne, 1982; AC, 1989. Memberships: Fell, of RSA, Vic, Aust; Freeman, Victorian Coll of Arts; The Patron of the Murdoch Inst for Rsch into Birth Defects. Hobbies: Gardening; Visual Arts; Performing Arts; Medical Research; Education; Landscape Architecture; Health and Welfare of Children and the Handicapped. Address: Cruden Farm, Langwarrin, Vic 3910, Australia.

MURPHY Lizz, b. 7 Aug 1950. Poet. m. 21 Sept 1968, Bill Murphy, 1 s, 1 d. Publications: Do Fish Get Seasick?, 1994; Ed: She's A Train and She's Dangerous: Women Alone in the 1990's, 1994; Wee Girls: Women Writing from an Irish Perspective, 1996; Eat the Ocean, 1997; Pearls and Bullets, 1997; Everyone Needs Cleaners, Eh!, 1997. Honours: Anutech Poetry Prize, 1994; ACT Creative Arts Fellshp in Lit, 1998. Memberships: ASA; NBC; FAW, Canberra; NSW Writers Cntr; ACT Writers Cntr; Poets Union; Shellharbor Multi Arts Soc; YASS Yth Assn. Address: PO Binalong, NSW 2584, Australia.

MURPHY Peter Anthony, b. 5 Aug 1945, Melbourne, Aust. Writer; Teacher. m. Helen Manassa, 11 Mar 1973, 2 s. Education: BA, Monash Univ, 1966; DipEd, Monash Univ, 1967; Assoc Dip in Librarianship, RMIT, 1971. Appointments: Asst Libn, RMIT, 1968-71; Tchr, Dept of Educ, 1971-. Publications: Escape Victim (poetry), 1974; Glass Doors (poetry), 1975; Black Light (stories), 1979; Lies (poetry), 1983; The Moving Shadow Problem (stories), 1986; Snapshots (poetry), 1994. Honours: Commendation, State of Vic Short Story Awd, 1974; Additional Prize, State of Vic Short Story Awd, 1975; Short Story Awd (Shared) West Aust 150th Anniversary Lit Competiton, 1979. Memberships: Austl Assn of Auths; Fellshp of Austl Writers; Austl Educ Union. Hobby: Photography. Address: 3 The Panorama, Eaglemont 3084, Victoria, Australia.

MURR Michel, b. 1932. Engineer; Politician. Education: BA, Pol Sci; PhD, Engrng. Appointments: Prof, Engrng Sch; Elected to Parl, 1968, 1992, 1996; Min of Post and Telecomm, Housing and Coops, Agric, Natl Def, Interior, Vice Prime Min.

MURRAY Bill, b. 21 Sept 1950, Evanston, Illinois, USA. Actor; Writer. m. Margaret Kelly, 1980, 2 s. Education: Loyola Acady; Regis Coll, Denver; Second City Workshop, Chgo. Appointments: Performer, Off-Broadway Natl Lampoon Radio Hour; Regular Appearances TV Series Saturday Night Live; Appeared in Radio Series Marvel Comics' Fantastic Four; Co-Prodr, Dir, Actor, Quick Change, 1990; Writer, NBC-TV Series Saturday Night Live, 1977-80. Creative Works: Films: Meatballs, 1977; Mr Mike's Mondo Video, 1979; Where the Buffalo Roam, 1980; Caddyshack, 1980; Stripes, 1981; Tootsie, 1982; Ghostbusters, 1984; The Razor's Edge, 1984; Nothing Lasts Forever, 1984; Little Shop of Horrors, 1986; Scrooged, 1988; Ghostbusters II, 1989; What About Bob?, 1991; Mad Dog and Glory, 1993; Groundhog Day, 1993; Ed Wood, 1994; Kingpin, 1996. Honours include: Emmy Awd, Best Writing for Comedy Series, 1977. Address: c/o William Carroll Agency, 139 N San Fernando Road, Suite A, Burbank, CA 91502, USA.

MURRAY Frank, b. 16 Nov 1950, Middlesbrough, UK. University Professor. m. Lesley, 2 s. Education: BS, Univ London, 1973; PhD, N'Cle, 1986. Appointments: Cnslt, UN Env Prog, 1984-; Lectr, 1985-94, A/Prof, 1995-, Murdoch Univ; Visng Rsch Fell, Univ of London, 1990; Cnslt, WHO, Geneva, 1994-; Visng Prof, WHO, Geneva, 1995. Publication: Ed, Fluoride Emissions. Honours: Editl Bd, Env Exp Bot; Editl Bd, Fluoride Jrnl. Membership:

Trustee, Allergy Rsch Fndn. Address: Environmental Science, Murdoch Univ, Perth, WA 6150, Australia.

MURRAY James Alexander (Rev), b. 9 Sept 1918. m. (1) Janet, 1941, dec 1985, 1 s, 1 d, (2) Dorothy Lee Mills, 24 Sept 1992. Education: FRGS; ThB. Appointments: Army Serv, 1941-45; Joined Min, 1949; Pastor: Qld, 1951-52; Utd Ch of Scotland Parish, Shetland Is, 1952-54; Qld, 1954-59; S Melbourne Presby Ch, 1960-63; St Aidan's Presby Ch, Claremont, WA, 1964-70; Chap, Scotch Coll, 1964-68; Mbr, Fed Relig Adv, Commn of the ABC, 1965-67; Snr Army Chap, CMF, 1967-69; Moderator Gen Assembly, Presby Ch, WA, 1968-69; St Columba Ch, Woolahra and Double Bay, NSW, 1970-74; Min, St Ninian's Presby Ch, Canberra, 1974; Pres, Canberra Rotary Club, 1976-77; Fmr Moderator WA, Union Min, St Ninian's Uniting Ch; Chap, ANU, Canberra, 1980-81; Chap, Mirinjani Retirement Village; Chmn, TV Assn, ACT, 1977-86. Honour: AM, 1983. Membership: Natl Press, Canberra. Hobbies: Reading; Book reviewing. Listed in: Who's Who in Australia. Address: PO Box 42, Fisher, ACT 2611, Australia.

MURRAY John Stewart, b. 5 Nov 1929. Minister of Religion. m. Shirley Erena Cockroft, 3 s. Education: MA, NZ; MA, Cantab; Cert d'Etudes Oecuméniques, Geneva. Appointments: Moderator of the Gen Assembly, Presby Ch of Aotearoa, NZ, 1990-91. Publications: Break Camp and Move On, 1965; Num articles. Honour: Churchill Fell, 1988. Memberships: Chmn, St Andrews Trust for the Stdy of Relig and Soc; Chmn, St Andrews Music Trust; Chmn, NZ Hymmbook Trust; Natl Co-convenor, World Crt Proj and Abolition 2000 (NZ). Hobbies: Singing; Lying in the sun. Address: 168 Rosetta Road, Raumati, Aotearoa, New Zealand.

MURRAY Meredith Girvan Peter Hugh, b. 19 Aug 1939. Justice of the Peace, Company Director. m. 3 children. Appointments: Prin, Chmn, Murray and Co and Murray and Assocs, pvte bus mngmt cnslts, 1972-81; Chmn NRCC 1977-80; Mbr NSW Local Govt Electricity Assn, Exec Mbr, 1974-80, Treas and VP, 1977-80; Mbr, World Energy Congress, 1977-80; Chmn, NSW Local Govt Water Resources, 1979-82; Mnng Dir, Chf Exec, Fndn Dir, Hortex Pty Ltd, 1981-85; Mnng Dir, Chf Exec, Nursey Ind Assn of NSW, 1981-85; Chmn, Chf Exec, Murray Corp Ltd, 1986-94; Prin Ptnr, Murray Ptnrs, Exec Chmn, Murray Grp of Cos; Ldr and Endorsed Candidate Natl Party of Aust, Tasmania, 1995-96; Pres, Natl Party of Aust, Tasmania, 1996-1997; Federal VP Natl Party of Aust, 1996-97; Currently Pub Speaker in Aust. Memberships: FRMA; FCIPSIA; FAICD; FAIM; Caledonian Soc of Devonport. Hobbies: Rugby; Game fishing; Boating; Motoring; Classical music; Theatre; Scottish history. Address: c/o Murray Partners, 60 Main Street, Sheffield, Tas 7306, Australia.

MURRAY Michael John, b. 16 Jan 1942, Perth, WA, Aust. Judge. m. Dale Randell, 16 Jan 1965, 2 s, 1 d. Education: LLB, Univ of West Aust. Appointments: Admitted to Bar, WA and Aust, 1965; Crown Prosecutor for WA, 1973; Crown Cnsl for WA, 1980, Supreme Crt, 1990. Honours: QC, 1984; LRD (Hon), Murdoch Univ, 1999. Memberships: Dpty Asst, Dir of Legal Servs (Army), 1973-80; Sen, 1990, Pro-Chan, 1993, Murdoch Univ. Hobbies: Reading; Music; Gymnasium. Address: c/o Supreme Crt of WA, Stirling Gardens, Barrack Street, Perth, WA 6000, Australia.

MURRAY Shirley Erena, b. 31 Mar 1931. Hymnwriter. m. Rev John Stewart Murray, 21 July 1954, 3 s. Education: MA (Hons), Otago Univ, NZ; Assoc, Trinity Coll of Music, London. Creative works: Hymn Collections: In Every Corner Sing, 1987, 1992; Every Day in Your Spirit, 1996; Work publd in more than 50 hymnals worldwide. Honour: Routley Lectr in Hymnology, USA, 1996. Membership: Ed Bd, NZ Hymnbook Trust, 1987-. Hobbies: Music; Choral singing; Theatre; Work for Amnesty International. Listed in: Who's Who in Aotearoa. Address: PO Box 2011, Raumati 6450, New Zealand.

MURRELL Janice Marie (Dame), b. 29 Nov 1937. Education: Dip, Vocal Music, Kroeger Inst of Mus, 1972;

Dip, Vocal Music, Julliard Sch of Music, 1979; Bernard Lu Taylor Instr, NYC; Citation, Vocal Music, WA Univ, St Louis, MO, 1972. Appointments: Actress, Singer, Summer Stock Theatre, Municipal Opera Co, St Louis, MO; Perm Instr of the Arts and Acads, St Louis Bd of Educ; Concert Opera Presenter (Internationally); Writer for Natl Lib of Poetry Anthologies - Owings Mills Maryland; St Louis Symphony Orch; Yth Ldr, Concert Participation for Yth aspiring artists. Creative Works: World Distributed Poetic Anthologies, Natl Lib of Poetry - Owings Mills Maryland, 1992-95; Parnassus of World Poets, Madras, India, 1994; Poetic Album - Visions, 1995. Honours: Dame Dr Hon, 1989; Kt of Jerusalem, St Benhamin; Gold Medalion of Hon, 1993; Intl Poetry Awd, 1990; Intl Mus of Musician, 1989; Intl Hall of Fame of Poets, 1997. Memberships: St Louis Symph Orch, 1995; Concert Presenter, Young Audience; Platform Assn, 1989-96; Metrop Opera Guild, 1990-96; Natl Lib of Congress, Wash DC, 1996; Intl Lib of Disting and Famous Poets, 1998. Hobbies: Painting; Sculpture. Address: 5556 Riverview Boulevard, St Louis, MO 63120, USA.

MURTHY C R L, b. 17 Feb 1947, Santharavur. Associate Professor. m. C Padma, 24 Mar 1971, 2 s. Education: PhD, Engrng; MSc, Elecl, Engrng; BE; BSc, maths, Phys, Chem. Appointments: Tech Asst, 1972-73; SO, 1973-83; Lectr, 1983-87; Asst Prof, 1987-92; Assoc Prof, 1992-. Creative Works: Trends in NDE Science and Technology; Non Destructive Evaluation and Quality Assurance; Aerodynamics testing and Structural Dynamics. Honours: Best Ppr Awd; NDE of Composites and NDE of Non Metals; Accoustics Emission Wrkng Grp Gold Medal. Memberships: AEWG. Address: Department of Aerospace Engineering, Indian Institute of Science, Bangalore 560 012, India.

MURTHY Sistla Satynarayana, b. 9 Nov 1939. Director. m. Mrs S N Lakshmi, 2 s, 1 d. Education: MS, Agra Univ, Agra, 1963; Assocshp in Documentation & Reprography, Indian Natl Sci Documentation Cntr, New Delhi, 1971; PhD, Gulbarga Univ, Gulbarga, 1990. Appointments: Documentation Offr, Indian Petrochems Corp, Baroda, 1972-75; Snr Info Offr & Dpty Mngr, Bharat Heavy Electricals Ltd, Hyderabad, 1975-79; Dir, Def Sci Info & Documentation Cntr (DESIDOC), Min of Def, 1979-. Publications: Auth: Report on the Need of a Natl Documentation Cntr for Techl Reports, 1990; Ed, Bibliographic Databases and Networks: Proceedings of the International Conference, 1990; Over 50 pprs in Indian and intl jrnls. Honours: Fellshp, Soc of Info Sci, 1989; Best PhD Thes Awd, Gulbarga Univ, Gulbarga, 1990. Memberships: Amn Soc for Info Sci, 1975-77; Inst of Info Scientists, UK, 1977; Pres, Assn of Govt Libns & Info Specialists, 1987-90. Hobbies: Reading; Listening to Indian music. Address: Director, DESIDOC, Metcalfe House, Delhi - 110054, India.

MURTI K V Suryanarayana, b. 9 May 1925, India. Teacher; Researcher. Education: MA, Engl, 1963; PhD, 1972; Ctf, Lings, Ctrl Inst of Engl, Hyderabad, India. Appointments: Asst Prof, Engl, 1980, Assoc Prof, Engl, 1985, Andhra Univ; Prof, Engl, MMA Law Coll, Madras. Publications include: Sword and Sickle: Critical Study of Mulk Raj Andnd's Novels, 1983; Kohinoor in the Crown: Critical Studies in Indian English Literature, 1987; Alienation and Absolute: Critical Study of William Golding's Novels. Honours include: Awd for Lit, Madras Telugu Acady, 1995; 20th Century Achievement Awd, IBC, 1997; Two-Thousand Mullennium Achievement Awd, ABI, 1998. Memberships include: Fell, Intl Acady of Poets, England, 1976, IBC, 1977; World Poetry Soc Intercontinental, Madras; World Univ Round Table, USA; Indian PEN; Auth Guild of India; Am Rsch Cntr; Bd of Studies in Engl, Andhra Univ. Address: 43-21-9A Venkataraju Nagar, Visakhapatnam 560 016 AP, India.

MURTY Bhyravabhotla Radhakrishna, b. 4 Apr 1928, Gudivada, Andhra Pradesh, India. Agricultural Research and Management. m. Lakshmi, 8 June 1951, 2 d. Education: PhD, Cornell Univ, USA; Assoc IArl (Indian Agricl Rsch Inst, New Delhi); BS, Agric, Madras Univ. Appointments: Hd, Biometrics Unit, 1961-74; Dir, Nuclear

Rsch Lab, New Delhi, 1974-84; Expert Intl Atomic Energy Agcy, Vienna, 1979-88; Prof, Indian Natl Sci Acady, 1988-91. Publications: Monograph, Classifying Genetic Stocks of Sorghumand Pennisetum, 1968; Plant Breeding Perspectives, 1979. Honours: S S Bhatnagar Awd in Sci, 1973; Distng Visng Prof, Cornell Univ; Nuffield Professorial Fell, 1973-74; Chmn, IBP (India); Mbr, UM Sect IBP (Rome); Mbr, Editl Bd, Theort & Applied Genetics, Genetics and Breeding. Memberships: fell, Roy Statistical Soc; Fell, Indian Natl Sci Acady; Indian Acady of Scis; Biometrics Soc; Amn Statistical Assn; Brit Genetic Soc. Hobbies: Nature conservation; Music. Address: Professor INSA and Emeritus Professor (IARI), 5087, B-7 Vasat Kunj, New Delhi 70, India.

MURUGESAN A G, b. 10 Apr 1960, Ariyapuram, India. Researcher; Teaching Consultant. Education: MSc, Zool, Madurai Kamaraj Univ, India; PhD Indl Toxicology; DSc, Alternative Meds, Intl Open Univ; Postdoct Rsch, Manonmaniam Sundaranar Univ; Dip, Gandhian Thought; Dip, Raionalistic Thought; Dip, Hlth and Hygiene. Appointments: Asst Prof, Sri Paramakalyani Coll; Scientist Pool Offr, Manonmaniam Sundaranar Univ; Lectr, Manonmaniam Sundaranar Univ, Alwarkurichi, India. Published: 165 rsch pprs. Honours: Awd for Best Rsch Pprs; Man of Yr, 1998; Distinguished Leadership Awd, 1998. Memberships: Fell, Acady of Environ Bio; Acady of Zool; Soc of Environl Scis; Ethological Soc; Sec, Exnora Intl; Dir, Acady of Sustainable Agric and Environ. Hobbies: Conducting group discussions on environmental safety; Singing. Address: Manonmaniam Sundaranar University, Sri Paramakalyani Centre for Environmental Sciences, Alwarkurichi 627412, Tamilnadu, India.

KHOKAN Muhammad N Chowdhury, b. 20 Oct 1947, Bangladesh. Professor. m. Monwara Zaman, 9 Nov 1975, 1 s, 2 d. Education: BA, 1969; MA, Bengali, 1971. Appointments: Lectr, 1974-76, 1976-78, 1978-81, 1981-98; Asst Prof of Bengali, 1998-. Publications: Sev books and articles in profl jrnls. Honours: Prize and Ctf, Bangladesh Jatio Sahitto Prarishad Tangail, 1991; Trophy and Ctf, Pabna Zila Sahitto Parishad, 1992; Ctf,Kashinathpur Uttaran Pub Lib, 1994; Prize, Islamic Fndn Bangladesh-Pabna; Medal, Bhangura Upozila Parishad. Memberships include: Chmn, Bhangura Kobita Club; Vice-chmn, Bhangura Press Club. Mbr, Pabna Zila Sahitto Parishad; Pabna Zila Kobita Club; Uttar-Bangla Sangscriti (cultural) Parishad; ADG, Bangladesh Sangscriti (cultural) Parishad. Hobbies: Writing; Art; Music; Gardening; BTV and Bangladesh Radio broadcasting; Poetry and Drama. Address: Baitul Musafir, Saratnagar Bazar, Post Bhangura, Pabna 6640, Bangladesh.

MUSSATAYEV Murat Khabdilrhapparovich, b. 21 Mar 1963. Vice Minister. m. Gulmara, 16 Dec, 2 s, 1 d. Appointments: Vice-Min, 1997. Honours: Medal. Hobbies: Sports; Chess; Reading Books. Address: Karl Marx Str 81, Kazakhstan.

MUTALOV Abdulkhashim Mutalovich, b. 1947, Telyau, Tashkent, Uzbekistan. Politician; Business Executive. Education: All-Union Inst of Food Ind. Appointments: Factory Worker, Tashkent Factory of Bread Products; Army Serv, 1965-79; Dir, Akhangaran Enterprise of Bread Products, 1979-86; Dpty Min of Bread Products, Uzbek SSR, 1986-87, Min, 1987-91; Dpty Chair, Cabinet of Mins, 1991-92; PM of Uzbekistan, 1992-96; Chair, State Grain Co Uzdon Makhsulot, 1996-. Address: Government House, 700008 Tashkent, Uzbekistan.

MUTO Kabun, b. 18 Nov 1926, Japan. Politician. m. Hisako Koketsu, 1951, 2 s. Education: Kyoto Univ. Appointments: Brewing Bus; Mbr, House of Reps, 1967-; Parl Vice-Min of Home Affairs, 1972-73; Chair, Liberal Democratic Party, Com & Ind Divsn, 1974-76; Dpty Sec-Gen, LDP, 1978-79; Min of Agricl, Forestry & Fisheries, 1979-80, of Intl Trade & Ind, 1990, of Fgn Affairs, 1993; Dir-Gen, Man & Cord Agcy, 1996-; Mbr, Standing Cttee on Budget, House of Reps, LDP Fin Cttee; VP, LDP Cttee on Small & Medium Enterprises, LDP Tax Policy Cttee. Publications: Kusa-no-Ne

Minshushugi (Grassroots Democracy); Jiminto Saisei no Teigen; Nihon no Sentaku (Japan's Choice). Address: Ministry of Foreign Affairs, 2-2 Kasumigaseki, Chiyoda-ku, Tokyo, Japan.

MYERS John L, b. 8 Aug 1928, Columbus, IN, USA. Retired. m. Donna, 9 Apr 1976, 1 s, 3 d. Education: BSChE, Purdue Univ, 1951. Appointments: Tech Supvsr, Union Carbide Corp, Oak Ridge TN, Padicah, KY, 1951-66; Rsch Engr, Niagara Falls, NY plant, 1966-67; Tech Supt, King Cty, CA plant, 1967-70; Mktng Mngr, Niagara Falls, NY, 1970-81; Bd Chmn, Asbestos Info Assn of N Am, 1981-95; Amn Chem Soc Am Inst of Chem Ops Engrs; Mngr, King Cty, CA, 1981-85; Appt King Cty Plng Commn, 1984-86; Pres, Dir, KCAC Inc (mining, milling & mktng of mineral fibers), King Cty, 1985-93 (retired); Tec Cnslt, 1994-; Elected King Cty Cncl, 1986, 1990, 1994, Mayor, King Cty, 1993-. Publication: 2 US pats. Memberships: Pres, Somoco Community Concerts Assn, 1987; Trustee, 1982-, Chmn, 1987-88, Mee Mem Hosp. Hobbies: Golf; Furniture restoration. Address: 102 River Drive King City, CA 93930-3512, USA.

MYERS Rupert Horace (Sir), b. 21 Feb 1921. m. Io King, 9 Dec 1944, 1 s, 3 d. Education: BSc; MSc; PhD; DSc Hon, DEng Hon, DLitt Hon, LLD (Hon), Univ Melbourne. Appointments: Stawell Engrng Rsch Schlr, 1942; C'wlth Rsch Fell, Univ Melbourne, 1942-47; Prin Rsch Offr, CSIRO, AERE, Harwell, UK, 1947-52; Fndn Prof of Metall, 1952-81; Pro-Vice Chan, Univ NSW, 1961-69; Vice-Chan and Prin, Univ NSW, 1969-81; Fed Pres, Austl Inst of Metals, 1963; Dir, Prince Henry and Prince of Wales Hosps, 1966-83; Mbr, Cncl Scout Assn of Aust, NSW, 1970-80; Dir, Sir William Tyree Fndn, 1971-94; Chmn, NSW State Pollution Control Commn, 1971-89; Dir, Sir James N Kirby Fndn, 1973-; Mbr Sydney Opera House Trust, 1976-83; Chmn, Austl Vice-Chancellors' Cttee, 1977-79; Chmn, Cttee of Inquiry into Technological Change in Aust, 1979-80; Mbr, Natl Energy Advsry Cttee, 1980-83; Chmn NSW Coastal Cncl, 1981-86; Dir, Energy Resources of Aust Ltd, 1981-97; CSR Ltd, 1981-93, IBM (Aust) Ltd, 1987-91, Chmn, Unisearch Ltd, 1989-93; Emer Prof, Univ of NSW, 1981-; Mbr, Cttee Review Natl Capital Dev Commn, 1982-83; Fndn Pres, Friends of Roy Botanic Gdns, Sydney, 1982-85; Chmn, Consultative Cttee for Natl Conservation Strategy for Aust, 1983-86; Dpty Natl Chmn, Winston Churchill Mem Trust, 1983-93 (Mbr Bd, 1975-83); Pres, Austl Acady of Technological Scis and Engrng, 1989-94, VP, 1984-88; Cttee of Review of NZ Univs, 1987; Rothmans Fndn, 1987-94; Austl Natl Botanic Gardens Advisy Cttee, 1987-90; Mbr, PM's Sci and Engrng Cncl, 1992-94. Honours: Grimwade Prizeman, 1947; Florence Taylor Medallist, 1965; CBE, 1976; KBE, 1981; AO, 1995. Memberships: FAA; FTSE; FRACI; FIMMA; FAIM; FAICD; FAusIMM; Hon FIEAust; Austl Club. Hobbies: Music; Lawn bowls; Working with silver. Address: 135 Neerim Road, Castle Cove, NSW 2069, Australia.

MYO-KHIN, b. Rangoon, Burma. Researcher; Physician. m. Khin-May-Oo, 18 Nov 1979, 1 s, 2 d. Education: MBBS, 1976; DCH, 1986; MD, NSW, 1998. Appointments: Rsch Offr, 1981-90; Snr Rsch Offr, 1990-93; Rsch Scientist, 1992-98; Dpty Dir, 1998-. Honours: WHO Fell, 1989, 1993, 1997; Medal for Pub Serv, 1997. Memberships: Myanmar Medl Assn, 1978-; Pediat Sect Exec Cttee, 1991-; Pediat Bulletin Editl Cttee, 1993-. Hobbies: Reading; Sports. Address: Department of Medical Research, No 5, Ziwaka Road, Yangon 11191, Myanmar.

N

NAAMAN Naji Mitri, b. 19 May 1954, Harissa, Lebanon. Poet; Writer; Publisher. m. Fadia Tawfic Al-Hawa, 19 July 1981, 1 d, 2 s. Education: Auditing and Acctng Degree, Cntr Supérieur d'Études Commerciales, Beirut, 1977; LLB, Lebanese Univ, 1979; Master, Pol Scis, La Sorbonne Univ of Paris, France, 1980; Lic en Scis Commerciales, 1979, MBA, BA, Hist, 1979, Holy Spirit Univ, USEK, Kaslik; Dip d'Études Approfondies en Histoire, Univ of Nantes, France, 1980. Appointments: Jrnlst, Al-Jumhur Mag, 1970-74; Exec, Jordan Natl Bank, 1973-74; Tchr, École Profl Pauliste, Junié, Lebanon, 1974-77; Dir, Al-Manshuratul Arabiyya, Beirut, Lyon, 1978-79; Prof, Econs and Mngmt, Al-Markaziyya Coll, Junié, 1978-79; Cntr Intl des Scis Techniques (CIT), Dora, 1980-85; Publr, Fndg Mbr, Dar Na'man Lith Thaqafa (Maison Naaman pour le Culture - Publing House), 1979; Sole owner, 1983-; Fndr, Owner, Galerie d'Art Naaman, 1987-; Fndr, Cntr d'Educations Technique, 1987; Fndr, Owner, NBC - Naaman Biographical Cntr, 1997-. Publications include: Khams wa'Ishun (poetry), 1979; Anti wal Watan (poetry), 1980; Informative and Biographical Directory of the Arab World, 1985, 1990; Ai-Rasa'il (letters), 1995; Al-Mun'atiq (The Emancipated), 1997; Ed, Mawsu'atul Alamil Arabiyyil Mu'asser (Encyclopedia of Contemporary Arab World, 1983-; Arab Press Directory, 1988; Ethnic and Confessional Groups of the Arab World, 1990; One Hundred Arab Figures in a Century, 1993; The Arab World at the Threshold of the 21st Century, 1993; One Hundred Arab Events in a Century, 1996; The Independence of the Arab World, 1996; Courses; Articles; Tranls. Memberships: Fndr, Al Harakatul Insaniyya (Humanitarian Movement), 1971; Wahdatul Insanil Alamiyya, Universal Unity of Man, 1976; Lebanese Publrs Assn, 1979-; Fndng Mbr, Al-Yunbu (Charity Assn), 1991. Hobbies: Painting; Music; Watching sports. Address: Maison Naaman pour la Culture, PO Box 567, Jounieh, Lebanon.

NABENU Simione, b. 18 July 1950, Nadroga, Fiji Islands. Labourer. m. Nakai, 9 July 1968. Appointment: VP, Cagimaira Devel Assn, Fiji. Hobbies: Playing Soccer; Rugby; Reading. Address: c/o Cagimaira Development Association, PO Box 1038 BA, Fiji.

NADEBAUM Peter Robert, b. 25 Sept 1946. Environmental Engineer. m. Lorraine Elizabeth Hodgson, 5 Aug 1972, 1 s, 1 d. Education: BEng, hons, Chem, Monash Univ, 1968; MSc, Chem Engrng, 1971, PhD, Chem Engrng, 1974, Univ of Waterloo, Can. Appointments: Environ Auditor, Process Facilities and Contaminated Land, Vic, 1991-; Mbr IR&D Bd, Engrng, Infrastructure and Environ Grant Cttee, 1992-95; Mbr, Fac of Engrng, Univ of Melbourne, 1993-96; Mbr, DPIE Land Care Grant Cttee for New Technol Demonstration Projs, 1993-94; Mbr, Hazardous Waste Techl Grp, Basel Convention Env Aust, 1997-. Publications: Over 100 publs in the fields of water quality and treatment, wastewater treatment, indl waste, contaminated land, hazardous waste mngmt and environ mngmt. Memberships: MRACI; MIChE; Env Inst Aust; Clean Air Soc; Pres, AWWA, Vic Branch, 1987-88. Hobbies: Family; Music; Travel. Address: Egis Consulting Australia, 390 St Kilda Road, Melbourne, Vic 3004, Australia.

NAG Dilip Kumar, b. 23 Oct 1940, Dacca, Bangladesh. Senior Lecturer in Civil Engineering; Consultant. m. Sati, 13 Aug 1970, 2 d. Education: BTech (Hons) Civil Engrng, IIT Kgp; MSc, Structural Engrng, Wales; MSc in Engrng Rock Mechs, London; DIC London. Appointments: Asst Engr, 1961-66; Asst Bridge Engr, 1967-68; Civil Engr, Rock Mech Engr, 1970-79; Snr Rock Mech Engr, 1979-86; Lectr, 1986-97, Snr Lectr, 1998-. Publications: In jrnls and intl conf proceedings; Over 50 tech pprs. Honours: Indian Copper Schl, 1970-71; Colombo Plan Fell, 1974. Memberships: Instn of Engrs, Aust, Gippsland Grp, Sec, 1995, 1996, Chmn, 1997; Amn Soc of Civil Engrs, Instn Structural Engrs, London; Indian Sci Congress. Hobbies:

Music; Travelling; Gardening. Address: 18 Rae Crescent, Churchill, Vic 3842, Australia.

NAGAHATA Yoshi, b. 30 Jan 1955, Okayama, Japan. Gastrointestinal Surgery, 12 Feb 1983, 2 s. Education: MD, 1979; PhD, 1989. Appointments: Asst Prof of Surg, Kobe Univ Sch of Med, 1989-98; Dir of Surg, Mitsubishi Kobe Hosp, 1998-. Publications: My Treatment for Gastrointestinal Hemorrhage, 1990; Actions of H2 Receptor Antagonists, 1992; Syndrome of Alimentary Tract, 1994; Heliobacter Pylori, 1996; Paradox of H. Pylori, 1998. Memberships: Asian-Pacific Congress Gastroenterology; Fell, Japan Surg Soc; Cnclr, Japanese Soc Gastroenterology; Cnclr, Japan Soc Coloproctology. Address: 6-1-34, Wadamiya-Dori, Hyogo-ku, Kobe 652-0863, Japan.

NAGAI Jun, b. 1 Apr 1931, Hokkaido, Japan. Medical Doctor of Radiology. m. Ti Kashio, 10 Oct 1951, 1 s, 1 d. Education: MD; PhD. Appointments: Prof, Teikyo Univ Sch of Med, 1977; Prof, Jichi Medl Sch, 1989. Publications: Three-Dimensional CT Angiography, 1995; Plain Film Diagnosis of the Abdomen, 1994. Honour: Hon Prof, Jichi Medl Sch, 1 Apr 1998. Membership: Japan Radiological Soc. Hobbies: Enjoyment of music; Golf. Address: 2-9-2, Akitsu-cho, Higashimurayama-shi, Tokyo, 1890001, Japan.

NAGAMI Akira, b. 12 July 1944, Aichi, Japan. Artist; Painter. m. Keiko Iwai, 12 Mar 1971. Education: Art Vocational Coll. Career: Exhibns: Keishouhaten, Nagoya, 1965-79; Genten, Tokyo, Nagoya, 1980-86; Japanese Contemporary painting, Spain, Holland, Mexico, Tahiti, 1984-90; France: Fest of Japanese Art, Paris, 1988; Salon d'Automne, 1990-98; Le salon, 1993-95; Intl Art Selection (one-man show), NY, 1991. Honours: A Prize; 19 incl Exposition Intl d'Art Portugal, 1986; Exposition Hawaii Art Acady, 1997; Le Japon a Monaco, Diplôme d'Honneur, 1998. Membership: Repr, Exposition Konnichi, Nagoya, 1980. Address: 2-274-1 Onogi Nishi-ku Nagoya-shi, Aichi 452-0803, Japan.

NAGAOKA Shinichi, b. 1 Jan 1956, Kyoto, Japan. Associate Professor. m. Yumiko Okada, 19 Oct 1985. Education: BS, 1978, MS, 1980, DS, 1983, Kyoto Univ. Appointments: Rsch Assoc, Hokkaido Univ, Sapporo, Japan, 1983-85; Rsch Assoc, Inst of Molecular Sci, Okazaki, Japan, 1985-89; Assoc Prof, Ehime Univ, Matsuyama, Japan, 1989-99; Visng Prof, Univ of MN, Minneapolis, USA, 1994-95; Assoc Prof, Inst of Molecular Sci, Okazaki, Japan, 1999-. Publications: In profl jrnls. Honours: Chem Frontier VII Awd, Chem Soc of Japan, 1990; Young Schl Lectr Awd, Chem Soc of Japan, 1991. Memberships: Chem Soc of Japan; Vitamin Soc of Japan. Hobby: Calligraphy. Address: Institute for Molecular Science, Okazaki 444-8585, Japan.

NAGASHIMA Shigeo, b. 20 Feb 1936, Chiba, Japan. Baseball Player; Manager. m. Akiko Nishimura, 1965, 2 s, 2 d. Education: St Paul's Univ, Tokyo. Appointments: Profl Baseball Player, Tokyo Yomiuri Giants, 1954-74, Mngr, 1975-81, 1993-. Honours: Rookie of the Yr, 1958; Most Valuable Player of the Yr (5 times); Best Average Hitter of the Yr (6 times); Most Runs Batted in Hitter of the Yr (5 times); Mngr of Champion Team of the Yr (3 times). Hobby: Golf. Address: 3-29-19 Denenchofu, Ohta-ku, Tokyo 145, Japan.

NAGATSUKA Ryuji, b. 20 Apr 1924, Nagoya, Japan. m. Yoko, 28 July 1950. Education: Tokyo Imperial Univ. Appointment: Prof, Nihon Univ. Publications: George Sand, sa Vie et Ses Oeuvres; Napoleon; Tallyrand; Joseph Fouché, Caméléon Politique. Honours: Cmdr des Arts et des Lttres (France); Officier des palmes académiques (France). Membership: Assn Intl des Critiques Littaires. Hobby: Music. Address: 7-6-37, Oizumgakuen-cho, Nerima-ku, Tokyo, Japan.

NAGAYAMA Mokuo, b. 14 Dec 1929, Kurashiki, Japan. School Teacher. m. Kazuko, 3 May 1960, 1 s, 1 d. Education: Doshisha Coll of For Affairs, Kyoto. Publications: Snow Bridge, 1976; Mist on the Ridge, 1985; To The Zodiac Animals, 1988; Lost Ledge, 1999.

Honour: 1st Prize, Am Poetry Assn Contest, 1985. Memberships: Poetry Soc of Japan; Brit Haiku Soc. Hobby: Mountaineering. Address: 1168 Ouchi, Kurashiki, Okayama, Japan.

NAGESWARA RAO Boggarapu, b. 1 June 1952, Cumbum, India. Scientist; Engineer. m. Satyabhama, 17 Aug 1980, 2 s. Education: MSc, IIT Bombay; PhD. Appointments: Scientist, Engr, Vikram Sarabhai Space Cntr, India, 1979-. Creative Works: More than 140 articles to sci jrnls, 1975-. Honours: Jnr Rsch Fellshp, Dept of Atomic Energy, 1975; Snr Rsch Fellshp, Cncl of Sci and Ind Rsch, 1979. Memberships: Rsch Guide, Univ of Kerala; Aeronautical Soc of India. Hobbies: Reading; Trav; Music. Address: E-37, VSSC, Housing Colony, Trivandrum 695586, India.

NAGY Kenneth A, b. 1 July 1943, California, USA. Professor of Biology. m. Patricia, 12 Aug 1967, 2 s. Education: AB, Zoo, 1967; PhD, Bio, 1971. Appointments: Asst Prof, 1971-77; Assoc Prof, 1977-83; Prof, 1983-96; Disting Prof, 1996-. Publications: Auth, Co-auth, over 130 rsch articles, chapts and books on physiol of wild animals. Honours: Fulbright Fell, 1986-87; Visng Disting Prof, Chengdu Inst, China, 1990. Memberships: AAAS; Soc for Integrative and Comparative Biol; Amn Soc Mamm. Hobbies: Photography; Surfing. Address: UCLA Department of Organismic Biology, 621 S Young Drive, Los Angeles, CA 90095-1606, USA.

NAHMIAS Steven, b. 19 June 1945, NYC, USA. Professor. m. Vivian Siloh, 21 Jan 1988, 1 s. Education: BA, Maths, Phys, Queens Coll, 1968; BA, Ind Engrng, Columbia Univ, 1968; MS, Ops Rsch, NWest, 1971; PhD, Ops Rsch, 1972. Appointments: Asst Prof, Univ of Pittsburgh, 1972; Assoc Prof, 1976; Assoc Prof, Santa Clara, 1979; Prof, 1981. Creative Works: Production and Operations Analysis; 50 Tech Publs. Honours: Univ Awd for Schl, 1998; Deans Awd for Rsch; 1st Prize Stud Pprs. Memberships: INFORMS; POMS; MSOM. Hobbies: Golf; Swimming; Biking; Play Jazz Trumpet. Address: OMIS Dept, Santa Clara Univ, Santa Clara, CA 98053, USA.

NAHYAN Zayed bin Sultan an- (Sheikh), b. 1926. Ruler of Abu Dhabi. m. Appointments: Appointed as personal rep to Ruler of Abu Dhabi (his brother), Al Ain, 1946; Ruler, 1966-; Pres, Fed of United Arab Emirates, 1971; Helped estab Gulf Co-op Cncl. Hobbies: Hunting; Falconry. Address: Presidential Palace, Abu Dhabi, United Arab Emirates.

NAIDU Richard Krishnan, b. 28 June 1963. Barrister; Solicitor. m. Judy Teresa Tam, 8 Jan 1994, 1 s, 1 d. Education: BCom, Univ of Auckland, 1987; LLB, Univ Auckland, 1989. Appointments: Jrnlst, 1981-87, Sol, Bell Gully Buddle Weir, Auckland, NZ, 1988-89; Russell McVeagh, McKenzie Bartleet & Co, Auckland, NZ, 1989-95; Ptnr, Munro, Leys & Co, 1995-. Hobbies: Media; Current affairs; Lawn tennis. Address: c/o Box 149, Suva, Fiji.

NAIK Manjanath Krishnappa, b. 1 July 1961, Konalli, Karnataka, India. Scientist (Teaching & Research). m. Uma Naik, 4 Mar 1993, 1 d. Education: BSc, Agric, 1983, MSc, Agric, Plant Path, 1985, Univ of Agric Scis, Bangalore; PhD, Indian Agricl Rsch Inst, New Delhi; Postdoc Fell, Intl Crops Rsch Inst, ICRISAT, Asia Cntr, Hederabad PGDHRM, Indira Gandhi Natl Open Univ, New Delhi, India, 1995. Appointments: Rsch Fell, UAS, Dharwad, 1985-86; Sci, Plant Path, ICAR, New Delhi, 1990-91; Postdoc Fell, ICRISAT Asia Cntr, Hyderabad, 1991-93; Sci, Indian Cncl of Agricl Rsch, ICAR, New Delhi, 1995-96; Prof, Assoc Prof, Univ of Agricl Scis, Dharwad, 1996-. Publications: 43 rsch pprs in natl & intl jrnls; 11 conf pprs; 25 conf presentations; 3 book chapts; 3 review pprs. Honours include: ISCA Young Sci Awd, Indian Sci Cong Assn, Calcutta, 1991; KAAS Young Sci Awd, Karnataka Assn for Advancement of Sci, Bangalore, 1994. Memberships: Indian Phytopathological Soc, IARI, New Delhi; Soc of Mycology and Plant Path, Rajasthan; Plant Protection Assn, Hyderabad; Indian Sci Cong Assn, Calcutta; Soc of Soil Bio and Ecol, Bangalore; Plant Path

Club UAS, Dharwad; Karnataka Jrnl of Agricl Scis, Dharwad. Hobbies: Swimming; Reading; Group Discussion. Address: Department of Plant Pathology, UAS, College of Agriculture, Raichur, Karnataka, 584 101, India.

NAIK Ram, b. 16 Apr 1934, Sangli, Maharashtra, India. Member of Parliament. m. Kunda, 17 May 1960, 2 d. Education: BCom, Brihan Maharashtra Coll of Com; LLB, Kishinchand Chellaram Law Coll, Mumbai. Appointments: Organising Sec, Bharatiya Jana Sangh, Mumbai, 1969-77; Gen Sec, Janata Pty, Mumbai, 1977-78; Mbr, Maharashtra Legislative Assembly, 3 times, 1978-89; Mbr, Pub Accounts Cttee, Estimates Cttee, Priveleges Cttee, Rules Cttee, Maharashtra Legislative Assembly, 1978-89; Pres, Janata Pty, Mumbai, 1979-80; Pres, Bharartiya Janata Pty, Mumbai, 1980-86, VP, 1986-89; Elected, 9th Lok Sahba, 1989; Mbr, Railway Convention Cttee, 1989-95; Mbr, Railway Convention Cttee, 1989-95; Mbr, Consultative Cttee, Min of Railways, 1989-97; Mbr, Ctte on Sci and Technol, 1990-91; Re-elected, 10th Lok Sabha, 1991; Mbr, Jt Parly Cttee on Security Scam, 1992-94; Mbr, Cttee on Railways, 1993-95; Chmn, Jt Cttee on Catering in Parly Complex, 1993-95; Chmn, Pub Accounts Cttee, 1995-96; Re-elected, 11th Lok Sabha w highest votes in reg, 1996; Chf Whip, BJP Parly Pty, 1996-97; Mbr, Bus Advsry Cttee, Cttee on Railways, Jt Parly Cttee on Women's Reservation Bill, Cttee on Empowerment of Women, Rules Cttee, Convenor, Stdy Grp of Cttee on Railways for Suburban Railway Servs in Metrop Cties, 1996-97; Re-elected, 12th Lok Sabha, 1998; Union Min of State, Railways, Parly Affairs, Plng and Prog Implementation, 1998-; Spec Invitee, Gen Purpose Cttee, Mbr, Natl Exec, 1998-99. Hobbies: Reading; Travelling; Sports and games. Address: 9 Shiv Smriti, 51 Jai Prakash Nagar, Goregaon East, Mumbai 400063, India.

NAIK Vihang, b. 2 Sept 1969, India. Lecturer. Education: BA, Univ of Baroda; MA, Univ Baroda. Appointments: Lectr, MC Desai Arts and Com Coll, N Gujarat Univ, 1996-97; Ambaji Arts Coll, N Gujarat Univ, 1998-. Publications: City Times, 1993; Sev articles in profl jrnls. Honour: Michall Madhusudan Awd, Calcutta, 1998. Memberships: Poetry Soc, India; Gujarati Sahitya Parishad, Ahmedabad; Forum on Contemporary Theory, MSU, Baroda; Poetry Circle, Bombay; PEN, India; Writers Forum, Ranchi; World Poetry Soc Intercontinental, Madras; United Writers Assn, Chennai. Address: 3 Kamdurga Society 2, Naranpura, Ahmedabad 380 013, India.

NAIKA Penaia, b. 21 July 1935, Nadroga, Fiji Islands. Market Vendor. m. Nai, 14 July 1958, 1 s. Appointments: Retd Customs Offr; Pres, Cagimaira Devel Assn, Fiji. Hobbies: Reading; Television; Driving. Address: c/o Cagimaira Development Association, PO Box 1038 BA, Fiji.

NAIMI Ali Ibrahim al, b. 1935, Eastern Province. Politician. m. 1962, 4 children. Education: Intl Coll, Beirut; Am Univ, Beirut; Lehigh Univ; PA Univ; Stanford Univ. Appointments: Asst Geol, Exploration Dept, Aramco, 1953; Hydrol & Geol, 1963-67; Econ & Pub Rels Dept, 1967-69, VP, 1975, Snr VP, 1978, Dir, 1980, Exec VP, Ops, 1982, Pres, 1984, CEO, 1988, Aramco; Min of Petroleum & Mineral Resources, 1995-. Hobbies: Hunting; Hiking. Address: PO Box 247, Riyadh 11191, Saudi Arabia.

NAKAGAWA Ichiro, b. 8 Feb 1932, Nara City, Japan. Science Educator; Consultant. m. Keiko Fujimori, 4 Oct 1959. Education: BS, 1954, MS, 1956, DS, 1962, Kyoto Univ. Appointments: Rsch Assoc, 1958-63, Lectr, Fac of Sci, 1963-65, Assoc Prof, 1965-88, Prof, 1988-95, Kyoto Univ; Dir, Beppu Geophys Rsch Lab, 1990-94; Dir, Aso Volcano Lab, 1990-95; Prof Emer, Kyoto Univ, 1995-; Tech Advsr, Daiichi Fukken Engrng Co Ltd, 1995-. Publications: Some Problems on Time Change of Gravity, 1962; Free Oscillations of the Earth, 1964; International Gravimetric Connections, 1983. Memberships: Fell, Intl Assn of Geodesy; Geodetic Soc of Japan, pres, 1991-95; Japanese Assn of Surveyors, vp, 1995-; Japan Fedn of

Surveyors, vp, 1996-. Hobbies: Photography; Classical Music; Travel. Address: Nango 4-11-14, Otsu, Shiga 520-0865, Japan.

NAKAGAWA Yuzo, b. 27 Mar 1932. Professor. m. Atsuko, 2 d. Education: Lic, Pharm, Japan, 1955; PhD, Org Chem, 1960. Appointments: Rsch Assoc, Kyoto Univ; Lectr, Mukogawa Womans Univ; Rsch Assoc, Stanford Univ, CA, USA; Rsch Assoc, Rsch Dir, Shionogi Rsch Labs; Lectr, Kyoto Univ; Rsch Mngr, Matsushita Technoresch; Dir, Innovation Ptnrs Intl; Prof, Osaka Bioengrng Coll; Dir, Nakagawa Rsch. Publications: Sev books and num articles in profl jrnls. Honours: Disting Contbrn Medal, Japan, 1996. Memberships: LC/MS Soc, Japan; Mass Spectrom Soc, Japan; Am Soc of Mass Spectrom; Am Chem Soc; Roy Soc of Chem; Pharm Soc, Japan; Med Mass Spectrom Soc, Japan; Intl Mass Spectrom Soc. Hobbies: Tennis; Photography; Pottery. Address: Takenodai 5-18-20, Nishi-ku, Kobe 651-2274, Japan.

NAKAJIMA Osamu, b. 1 Aug 1962, Shinmori, Asahi-ku, Osaka, Japan. Physician; Cardiologist. m. Chise Sagawa, 29 Sept 1996, 2 d. Education: MD, Osaka Med Coll, Takatsuki, 1989. Appointments: House Staff, Osaka Med Coll, 1989-90; Res, Mishima Critical Care Cntr, Takatsuki, 1990-92; Chf, Nissay Hosp, Osaka, 1993-. Honour: Nissay Med Awd, 1997. Memberships: Japanese Soc of Internal Med; Japanese Circulation Soc; Japanese Assn for Acute Med; Japanese Endocrinol Soc; Japan Med-Dental Assn for Tobacco Control. Address: c/o Nissay Hospital, 3-8 6-chome, Itachibori, Nishi-ku, Osaka 550-0012, Japan.

NAKAJIMA Toshinori, b. 18 Nov 1943, Chiryu-shi, Aichi, Japan. University Professor. m. Hiroko Nakajima, Dec 1974. Education: BEng, 1966; MEng, 1968; DEng, 1976. Appointments: Rsch Sci, Inst of Physl & Chem Rsch, Japan, 1968-96; Rsch Fell, Alexander von Humboldt Fndn, Germany, 1978-79; Prof, Bunkyo Univ, Japan, 1996-. Honour: Optics Prize, Ex Pprs, Japan Soc of Appl Phys, 1975. Hobby: Arts. Address: 2-27-20-306 Hasune, Itabashi-ku, Tokyo 0046, Japan.

NAKAMURA Keiichi, b. 18 Mar 1960, Okazaki City, Japan. General Manager. m. Machiko Nakamura, 29 Apr 1982, 1 s. Education: BA, Econs, Hokkaido Univ, 1982. Appointments: Mngr, 1989, Gen Mngr, Sales Divsn, 1992, Gen Mngr, Labour Dept, 1997-. Publications: Open Eye, 1995; Homage to Toru Takemitsu, 1996; Sev one man exhbns. Hobbies: Mail Art; Painting; Reading. Address: 1-18-7-402 Kamiochiai, Shinjuku-ku, Tokyo 161-0034, Japan.

NAKAMURA Masao, b. 1 Jan 1945, Matsuda, Japan. Professor. m. Alice, 22 Dec 1971, 1 s, 1 d. Education: PhD, Johns Hopkins; MS, Keio; BS. Appointments: Syst Engr, Toshiba Corp, 1969-72; Prof, Univ of Alberta, 1972-93; Prof, Univ of Brit Columbia, 1994-. Creative Works: The Second Paycheck, 1985; Japanese Economic Policies and Growth, 1994. Honours: Konwa-kai Japan Rsch Chr, Inst of Asian Rsch, Univ of Columbia. Memberships: Cntr for Japanese Rsch. Address: Faculty of Commerce and Business Administration, University of British Columbia, 2053 Main Mall, Vancouver, BC, Canada, V6T 1Z2.

NAKARMURA Kuniwo, b. 24 Nov 1943, Peleliu State, Palau. m. Elong Ngiratecheboet Nakarmura, 3 d. Education: BA, Univ of HI at Manoa, USA. Appointments: Mbr, House of Representatives, Cong of Micronesia, 1975-78; 6th and 7th Palau Legislature, 1978-80; Senate, 1st Palau Natl Cong, 1980-84; 2nd Natl Cong, 1985-88; VP, 1988-92. Hobby: Fishing. Address: Office of the President, POB 100, Koror, PW 96940, Palau.

NAKASONE Yasuhiro, b. 27 May 1918, Takasaki, Gumma Prov, Japan. Politician. m. Tsutako Kobayashi, 1945, 1 s, 2 d. Education: Tokyo Imperial Univ. Appointments: Mbr, House of Reps; Fmr Min of State, Dir-Gen of Sci and Technol Agcy; Chair, Natl Org Lib-Dem Party (LDP), Jt Cttee on Atomic Energy, Spec Cttee on Sci Technol, Chair LDP Exec Cncl, 1971-72,

Sec-Gen LDP 1974-76, Chair, 1977-80; Min of Transport, 1967-68; Min of State and Dir-Gen Defence Agcy, 1970-71; Min of Intl Trade and Ind, 1972-74; Min of State and Dir-Gen of Admin Man Agcy, 1980-82; PM of Jap, 1982-87; Chair, and Pres Int Inst for Polit Stdies, 1988-. Publications: Ideal of Youth, Frontier in Japan; The New Conservatism, Human Cities: a proposal for the 21st Century, 1980; Politics and My Life, 1992. Hobbies: Golf; Swimming; Painting. Address: Takada 2-18-6, Toshimaku 171-0033, Tokyo, Japan.

NAKATA Toshihiko, b. 12 Oct 1960, Hatano, Kanagawa. Associate Professor. m. Chika Ando, 1990, 3 d. Education: BEng, 1983, MEng, 1985, DrEng, 1993, Tohoku Univ, Mech Engrng. Appointments: Rschr, Tokyo, 1985-86, Rschr, 1986-92, Snr Rschr, 1992-93, Yokosuka, Central Rsch Inst of Electric Power Ind; Assoc Prof, Grad Sch Engrg, Tohoku Univ, Sendai, Japan, 1993-; Fulbright Schl, Lawrence Livermore Natl Lab, Livermore, CA, 1997-98. Publications: 4 pats; 19 articles in jrnls or contrbr to books; 14 contrbr to acad confs; 48 rsch reports; 5 misc articles. Honours: Pres Awd, Central Rsch Inst of Elec Power Ind, 1991; Acad Awd, Combustion Soc Japan, 1993; Fulbright Awd, 1997-98. Memberships: 8 profl socs incl Intl Assn for Energy Econ; Am Soc Mech Engrs; Japan Soc Energy and Resources; var cttees. Address: Tohoku University Graduate School of Engineering, Sendai 98077, Japan.

NAKATANI Kei, b. 14 Jan 1952, Nara, Japan. Associate Professor. m. Yumiko. Education: BS, MSc, Okayama Univ; PhD, Tokyo Women's Medl Coll. Appointments: Rsch Asst, Tokyo Women's Med Coll, 1978-82; Postdoct Fell, Univ of TX Medl Branch, 1982-86; Rsch Assoc, Johns Hopkins Univ, Sch of Med, 1986-92; Assoc Prof, Univ of Tsukuba, 1992-. Publications: Sci pprs in profl jrnls. Memberships: Soc for Neuroscience (USA); NY Acady of Sci; Physiological Soc of Japan; Biophysical Soc of Japan. Hobbies: Horseback riding; Classical music. Address: Institute of Biological Sciences, University of Tsukuba, Tsukuba, Ibaraki 305-8572, Japan.

NAKATO Yoshihiro, b. 2 Nov 1942, Mie, Japan. Professor. 1 s, 2 d. Education: DEng, Osaka Univ, Japan. Appointments: Rsch, 1969-81, Assoc Prof, 1981-90, Prof, 1990, Osaka Univ, Japan. Publication: New Type Solar Cells. Memberships: Amn Chem Soc; Electro-chem Soc of USA; Intl Soc of Electrochem; Japanese Photochem Assn, 1991; Chem Soc of Japan, 1997. Address: Department of Chemistry, Graduate School of Engineering Science, Osaka University, 1-3 Machikaneyama, Toyonaka, Osaka 560-8531, Japan.

NAKATSU Ryohei, b. 19 Oct 1946, Himeji, Hyogo, Japan. Research Company President. m. Yukiko Katoh, 10 Feb 1971, 1 d. Education: BS, 1969, MS, 1971, PhD, 1982, Kyoto Univ. Appointments: Dir, NTT Basic Rsch Labs, Musashino, Japan, 1990-94; Pres, ATR Media Integration and Commns Rsch Labs, Kyoto, Japan, 1994-. Publication: Toward the Creation of a New Medium for the Multimedia Era, 1998. Honour: Best Ppr Awd, Intl Conf on Multimedia Computing and Systems, 1986. Membership: IEEE, snr mbr, 1992-. Hobbies: Golf; Tennis; Skiing. Address: 2-2 Hikaridai, Seika-cho, Soraku-gun, Kyoto 619-0288, Japan.

NAKAYAMA Hideaki, b. 31 Oct 1946, Kitakyusyu, Japan. Academic Administrator. m. Akiko, 14 Oct 1975, 2 s. Education: DEng, Ritsumeikan Univ. Appointments: Asst Prof, 1975-76, Assoc Prof, 1976-84, Prof, 1984-, Dean, 1990-93, Osaka Sangyo Univ Jnr Coll; Mngng Trustee, Dir of Exec Off HQ, Sch Juridical Person, Osaka Sangyo Univ, 1993-. Publications: Introduction to Fracture Mechanics, 1979; Handbook of Fatigue Crack Propagation in Metallic Structures, 1994; Current Japanese Materials Research vol 14. Cyclic Fatigue in Ceramics, 1995. Memberships: Japan Soc of Mech Engrng; Dir, Japan Friction Welding Assn, 1988-, Soc of Materials Sci, Japan, 1996-. Hobby: Golf. Address: 1-12 Miyanoshita-cho, Hirakata, Osaka 573-0046, Japan.

NAKRA Bahadur Chand, b. 31 Mar 1939, Mianwali. Teaching; Research. m. Sharda, 9 Sept 1967, 2 s. Education: PhD (London); MTech (IIT KGP); BSc Engrng (Punjab); DIC (London). Appointments: Prof, IIT Delhi, 1971-; Hd, Mechl Engrng Dept, 1975-78; Dpty Dir, IIT Delhi, 1991-95. Publications: Books: Instrumentation, Measurement and Analysis, 1985; Automatic Controls, 1998; Over 100 pprs. Honours: Instn of Engrs Prize, 1994-95; C V Raman Awd, 1994. Memberships: Fell, Indian Natl Sci Acady, 1987-; Fell, Indian Natl Acady of Engrng, 1987. Hobbies: Fiction; Movies. Address: Mechanical Engineering Department, Indian Institute of Technology, Hauz Khas, New Delhi 110016, India.

NAMAZI Hossein, b. 1944, Shiraz, Fars Prov, Iran. Minister of Economic Affairs and Finance. Education: BA, MA, PhD, Univ in Austria. Appointments: Fac Mbr, Chan, Al-zahra Univ, Tehran, 1974-81; Min of Econ and Fin; Dpty Hd, Strategic Rsch Cntr in charge of Econ Affairs, 1989-92; Elected, Min of Econ Affairs and Fin; Fac Mbr, Beheshti Univ, Dpty Chan in charge of Rsch.

NAMBOOTHIRI Parameswaran Sankaran, b. 2 Feb 1962, Mavelikara, Kerala, India. Researcher. m. Ushadevi, 25 June 1988, 1 s, 1 d. Education: BSc; MSc; PhD. Appointments: Rsch Asst, 1990-91, Postdoct Fell, 1991-93, Univ of Saskatchewan, Can; JSPS Fell, Kyoto Univ, Japan, 1994-95; Rschr, Natl Inst for Environ Studies, Japan, 1996-99, Comms Rsch Lab, Japan, 1999-. Publications: Rsch articles to sci jrnls. Honour: Awd, Best Rsch Ppr, Natl Space Sci Symposium, Ahmedabad, India, 1987. Memberships: Astron Soc of India; Austl Inst of Phys. Hobbies: Reading; Classical Music; Cricket; Badminton. Address: Space Science Division, Communications Research Laboratory, 4-2-1 Nukui-kita, Koganei-shi, Tokyo 187-8795, Japan.

NAMJIL Hurelsha, b. 28 Feb 1950, Huria Banner, Inner Mongolia, China. Teacher. m. B Sechin, 20 Dec 1970, 2 s, 1 d. Education: Master's degree. Appointments: Dean of Mongolian Lang and Lit, Inner Mongolian Tchr's Coll for Nationalities. Publications: Monographs: The Monasteries of Jirim, 1993; Studies of Mongols Mythology, 1996; Studies of Korchin Shamenism, 1998. Honours: Title: Middle-Aged Outstndg Specialist of Inner Mongolia, 1994; Outstndg Young Intellectual of Inner Mongolia, 1995. Memberships: Hd of Inst of Khorchin Culture, 1998; Standing Cttee, Assn of Mongolian Lit of China. Hobbies: Sport; Travelling. Address: Department of Mongolian Language and Literature, Inner Mongolia Teacher's College for Nationalities, Tongliao City, Inner Mongolia, China.

NAN Cang, b. 1924, Hefei, China. Teacher. m. Yang Rongfang, 1953, 1 s, 1 d. Education: Postgrad Deg, Chinese Peoples Univ. Appointments: Chmn, Philos Section, Philos Dept, Wuhan Univ, 1964; Vice Chmn, Polit Dept, 1978, Chmn, Philos Dept, 1986, Xiangtan Univ. Publications: Philosophic Knowledge of Farmers, 1959; The Philosophic Thought of Mao Zedong, 1993; Sev articles in profl jrnls. Honours: Govt Hon Allowance, 1992; 3rd Grade Awd, Socl Sci, Hunan Prov, 1992; Ex Tchr of China Awd, 1993; Hon Expert of Socl Sci, Hanan, 1998. Memberships: Mao Zedong's Philos Thought Rsch Soc of China; VP, Philos Inst of Hunan Prov. Hobby: Stamp Collecting. Address: Philosophy Department, Xiangtan University, Hunan, China.

NANAYAV Kelembek, b. 7 Nov 1945, Merke, Kazakhstan. m. 3 children. Education: Grad, Kyrgyz State Univ, 1967; Postgrad, Moscow State Univ, 1967-70. Appointments: Prof and Dean of Econs, Kyrgyz State Univ, 1970-80; Dpty Chf, Inst Econ Acady sci, Kyrgyz, 1981-82; Dpty Dir, Inst Economy, 1982-90; Chmn, Bd First Kyrgyz Coml Bank, 1990-91; Chmn, State Property Fund, 1991-92; Chmn, Bd, Natl Bank of Kyrgyz, 1992-94; Min Fin, Govt of Kyrgyzstan, Bishkek, 1994-97; Dpty Prime Min, 1997-. Address: Office of the Prime Minister, Perromayskaya 57, Bishkek 720003, Kyrgyzstan.

NANDA Sudarsan, b. 29 June 1945, Balasore. Teacher; Researcher. m. P Nanda, 20 Feb 1979, 3 d. Education: DSc; PhD; MSc; BSc. Appointments: Lectr,

REG, RKL, 1970-80; Asst Prof, IIT, KGP, 1980-88; Prof, Utkal Univ, 1988-90; Prof, IITKGP, 1990-. Creative Works: 150 Rsch Pprs; Functional Analysis; General Topology; Topics in Algetra; Number Theory; Real Analysis; Mechanics. Honours: FIMA. Memberships: FIMA; AMS; ORSI; IMS; NAtl Acady of Scis; Allahalad Maths Soc; Orissa Math Soc. Address: Department of Mathematics, IIT Kgaragpur, Kharagpur 721302, India.

NANDI Sambhu Nath, b. 21 Oct 1918, Calcutta, India. Cancer Research Worker (Veterinary Surgeon). m. Bina Nandi, 1 Feb 1948, 1 d. Education; BS, Hons (Calcutta); MRCVS (London); BS, Vet Sci, (London); PhD, Vet Path. Appointments: Prof Anatomy, Bengal Vet Coll, 1947; Prof, Comparative Anatomy & Path, 1948-62; Prof, Path & Vice Prin Admin, 1962-74; Supdt Hosp & Dean Agric Univ, 1976; Univ Prof Path, 1977-82. Publications: Cancer rsch; Obstructions to Carcinogenesis Electronic Clouds in Carotene Pigments, cum electron stimulators. Honours: Law Schl, Presdtl Coll, 1934-38; Gowalior Mem Prize, Presdtl Coll, 1936; State Schl of Bengal Govt to Brit, 1939-44; French Govt Schl, Haematuria Cancer, 1962-63. Memberships: Ex-Fell, Brit Chem Soc; Life Mbr, Indian Assn of Vet Pathologists; World Assn Vet Pathologists, Cedex, France. Hobby: Remission of Electro Magnetic Waves by GENES, by application of Quantum Mechanics. Address: 64/1/12, Belgachia Road, Calcutta 700 037, India.

NAORA Hiroto, b. 16 Nov 1927, Tokyo, Japan. Emeritus Professor. m. Hatsuko Terao, 22 Feb 1956, 1 d. Education: BSc, Tokyo Univ of Lit and Sci, 1950; DSc, Univ of Tokyo, 1956. Appointments: Rsch Assoc, The Cancer Inst, 1956-57; Intl Fell, Rockefeller Fndn, Belgium, 1957-58; Assoc, The Rockefeller Univ, NY, USA, 1958-60; Mbr, Cancer Inst, Tokyo, 1960-62; Fndn Chief, Div of Bio, Natl Cancer Cntr Rsch Inst, 1962-68; Profl Fell 1968-91, Prof, Austl Natl Univ, 1991-92. Publications include: Many contbns to sci jrnls: Ed, sev books, inclng Cell Biology, Biochemical Genetics and others. Honours: Asahi Sci Promotion Awd, 1953, 1954; Tamiya Prize, 1966; Toyota Fndn Awd, 1985. Memberships include: VP, Asian and Pacific Orgfor Cell Bio; Jap Soc for Cell Bio; Cncl, Exec Mbr, Jap Biochem Soc; Biophys Bio; Cancer Assn. Hobbies: Mountaineering; Photography. Address: 89 Hilder Street, Weston, ACT 2611, Australia.

NAPATHORN Sophon, b. 18 May 1959, Bangkok, Thailand. m. Dr Sujittra Sombuntham, 1 s, 2 d. Education: MD, Chulalongkorn Univ, 1982; MSc, 1990; Dip Bd, Internal Med, Thailand, 1988; Dip, Bd of Nephrology, 1994. Appointments: Lectr, 1993-96, Asst Prof, 1996-99, Assoc Prof, 1999; Sec to the Fac Bd of Med, 1997-99. Honour: Visng Assoc Awd, Fogarty Intl Cntr, USA, 1993. Memberships: Roy Coll of Physns of Thailand; Nephrology Soc of Thailand; Intl Soc of Nephrology; Natl Kidney Fndn, USA. Hobbies: Jogging; Painting. Address: Division of Nephrology, Department of Medicine, King Chulalongkorn Memorial Hospital, Bangkok 10330, Thailand.

NAPIER Robert John, b. 19 July 1945, Tasmania, Aust. Associate Professor in Farm Management. m. Dimity Jane Teesdale Smith, 20 Dec 1969, 1 s. Education: BAgrSc, Univ of Tas, 1967; Dip, Agricl Stud, Cambridge Univ, Eng, 1968; MEc, Univ New Eng, Aust, 1974. Appointments: Animal Rsch Offr, Tas Dept of Agric, 1967; Agricl Extension Offr, Vic Dept of Agricl, 1969-71; Jnr Rsch Fell, Univ New Eng, 1971-73; Lectr, Farm Mngmt, 1973-76, Prin, 1976-90, Orange Agricl Coll; Pro Vice Chan (Planning), Univ New Eng, 1991 (Seconded from Prin Univ of New Eng-Orange Agricl Coll); Assoc Prof in Farm Mngmt, Orange Agricl Coll, Univ of Sydney, 1992-. Memberships: Austl Inst of Agricl Sci and Technol; Fndn Mbr, Cnclr, Agribus Assn of Aust; Rural Aust Fndn; VP, Intl Farm Mngmt Assn, 1997-. Hobbies: Horse riding; Snow skiing; Small area farming; Travelling; Reading. Address: Orange Agricultural College, University of Sydney, PO Box 883, Orange, NSW 2800, Australia.

NAPTHINE Denis Vincent, b. 6 Mar 1952, Geelong, Victoria, Australia. Member of Parliament. m. Peggy, 12

Nov 1977, 3 s. Education: BVSc, 1974; MVS, 1979; MACVSc, 1983; MBA, 1989. Appointments: MP, 1988-; Parly Sec for Hlth, 1992-96; Min for Youth & Cmty Servs, 1996-. Address: 104 Percy Street, Portland, Victoria, Australia.

NARAIN Yogendra, b. 26 June 1942, Meerut, India. Government Official. m. Neena, 2 Dec 1967, 2 s, 1 d. Education: BSc; MA, Polit Sci; Dip, Econs; PhD, Pub Admin. Appointments: Sec, Govt of India, Min of Surface Transp, 1997-98; Chf Sec, Govt of Uttar Pradesh, India. Publication: ABC of Public Relations for Civil Servants, 1998. Honours: OISCA Awd, 1998; Natl Integration Awd, 1998. Memberships: Inst of Pub Admin; Chmn, Lucknow Club; Pres, Intl Goodwill Soc of India. Hobbies: Writing Poetry; Watching Plays; Reforms in Public Administration. Address: Government of Uttar Pradesh, Secretariat Annex, Lucknow UP, India.

NARASIMHAIAH N, b. 28 May 1938, Magadi, Bangalore, India. Ex ITI employee. m. N Lakshamma, 13 May 1963, 2 s, 2 d. Appointment: Indian Telephone Inds. Creative works: Participation in dramas; Social service and crime prevention; Apprehended a bank robber, 4 Jan 1980; Currently operates a huge network in Krishnarajapuram under the cty police's Neighbourhood Watch Scheme, known as the Vill Def Party (VDP). Honours: Awd of Dalapathy, 1989; Spec Police Offr, 1991, 1999; 2nd Place Spec Police Offr, 1991; Chf Coord, NWS, 1995; Best Coord, NWS, 1996; Best Night Beat Grp Rolling Shield, Police Commnr, 1996-97, 1997-98; Awd Police Nere-Hore Kaualu Sarathi, 1999. Memberships: Traffic Bd Cttee, K R Pura; R M Nagar, Welfare Assn; News of Serv India, Bangalore - 16. Hobbies: Interest in crime prevention for peace and harmony among the public. Address: Chief Coordinator (NWS), No 14, Gayathri Extension, Kalkere Road, R M Nagar, Dooravaninagar Post, Bangalore - 16, India.

NARASINGARAJA NAIDU B, b. 13 Oct 1942, Tambaram (Madras 59), India. Teaching. m. Chandrika, 10 July 1970, 2 d. Education: PhD, Wilson Coll, Bombay, 1988; MA, Madras Christian Coll, 1966. Appointments: Tutor in Hist, 1966-67; Asst Prof of Hist, 1968-72; Prof of Hist, 1993; Hd of Dept; Lectr, 1974, to Prof, 1993, Bangalore Univ. Publications: 3 books: Stand Watie: An Analytical Study, 1984; Essays on Karnataka, 1984; Intellectual History of Colonial India 1831-1920, 1996; 8 rsch articles; 1 book review. Honours: Best Cadet Cup, ACC; Tchr Study Grant, 2 x, Awds Cttee, ASRC, Hyderabad; Thurso & MacPhail Prizes for Hist. Memberships: Life Mbr, Amn Studies Rsch Cntr, Hyderabad; Life Mbr, Mythic Soc, Bangalore; Tamilnadu Hist Congress; S Indian Hist Congress. Hobbies: Lecture tours; Writing; Researching; Watching World News on TV. Address: Professor of History, Department of History, University of Bangalore, Banglaore 560056, India.

NARAYANA Jothi, b. 2 Nov 1955, Bangalore, India. Business. m. Gowramma, 23 Nov 1983, 1 s, 1 d. Education: SSLC. Honours: Specl Police Offr, Karnataka; Police Night Watch Cttee Awd. Memberships: Gen Sec, Kannada Jrnlsts Assn; Pres, Karnataka for Kannada; VP, Gokula Welfare Assn. Address: No 16 Vivekanda Road, Gokula Extn, Devasandra, K R Puram, Bangalore 560036, India.

NARAYANAN Rajendran, b. 25 May 1956, Sri Kalahasti. Teaching. m. J Shanti, 27 Jan 1991, 1 s, 1 d. Education: MA, Hist, Pachaiyappa's Coll, Madras, 1978; MPhil, 1981, PhD, 1988, Hist, Indian Hist Dept, Univ of Madras. Appointments: Asst Prof of Hist, Pachaiyappa's Coll, Madras, 1982-89; Asst Prof of Hist, Vivekananda Coll, Madras, 1985; Lectr, Dept of Futurology, Bharathidasan Univ, Tiruchirappalli, 1989-95; Rdr and Hd Cntr for Hist, Bharathidasan Univ, Tiruchirappalli, 1998. Publication: National Movement in Tamil Nadu: Agitatinal Politics and State Coercion 1905-1914, 1994. Memberships: Indian Hist Congress; Tamil Nadu Hist Congress; S Indian Hist Congress; Assn of Third World Studies; S Indian Numismatics Soc; Exec Mbr, Epigraphical Soc of India, 1994-95; Exec Mbr, Tamil Nadu Hist Congress, 1996; Exec Mbr, S Indian Hist

Congress, 1997; Jt-Sec Tamil Nadu Hist Congress, 1998. Hobbies: Cricket played for college and Tamil Nadu Cricket Association League Cricket; Chess (College Champion); Music; Reading. Address: Centre for History, Bharathidasan University, Tiruchirappalli 620 024, India.

NARAYANAN Melappalayam, b. 17 Aug 1951, Puduppalayam, India. Associate Professor. m. Jayanthi, 31 Jan 1982, 1 s. Education: BEng; MTech. Appointments: Assoc Prof, 1988-, Vice Prin, 1989-94; Cnsltng Engr, 1994-98. Membership: IEEE. Hobby: Indian Astrology. Address: Srivgnesh, Flat B4, Plot No 4, 42nd Street, Nanganallur, Chennai 600 061, India.

NARAYANAN Shri Kocheril Raman, b. 27 Oct 1920, Uzhavoor, Kottayam Dist, Kerala, India. President of India. Education: MA, Engl Lit, Univ of Travancore; BSc, 1st Class Hons, Econ, London Sch of Econs, Eng. Career: Lectr, Univ of Travancore, 1943; Jrnlst, The Hindu, Madras, The Times of India, Bombay; London Corresp, Socl Welfare, 1945-48; Indian For Serv, Indian Embs in Rangoon, Tokyo, London, Canberra and Hanoi, 1949-; Min of External Affairs; Tchr, Econ Admin, Delhi Sch of Econs, 1954-55, Jt Dir, Orientation Cntr for For Techns; Amb to Thailand, 1967-69, Turkey, 1973-75, China, 1976-78; Sec, Min of External Affairs, 1976-78; Vice-Chan, Jawaharlal Nehru Univ, New Delhi, 1979; Pres of India, 1997-.

NARIN Cengiz, b. 9 May 1957, Istanbul, Turkey. Marketing. m. Ayse, 31 July 1986, 2 d. Education: Meister Sticker; Textile Kaufman. Memberships: Textile Inst; Turkish, Am & Swiss Buisnessman Assn. Hobbies: Horse Breeding; Show Jumping. Address: Eski Londra Asfalt 77, TR 34600, Istanbul, Turkey.

NARULA Pornthep, b. 4 Mar 1972, Bangkok, Thailand. Researcher. Education: BEng, King Mongkuts Inst of Technol Ladkrabang, 1994. Appointments: Rschr, NECTEC, Bangkok, 1994-; Cache BOF Chmn, APNG, Asia-Pacific Region, 1997; R&D Chf, Govt IT Servs, 1998-; Advsr, Embeded Systems Lab, 1998-, Adj Lectr, Computer Engrng Dept, 1998-, King Monkut's Inst of Technol Ladkrabang. Membership: IEEE. Address: NECTEC Bangkok Thai Tower, 11th Floor, Rangnam Phyathai, 10400 Bangkok, Thailand.

NASHAR Beryl, b. 9 July 1923. Emeritus Professor of Geology. m. Ali, 13 July 1952, dec, 1 s. Education: Newcastle Girls HS; Univs of Sydney, Tas and Cambridge, BSc, Dip Ed, Sydney; PhD, Tas; Hon DSc, Newcastle. Appointments: Demonstrator in Geol, Univ of Sydney, 1945, 1947; Rotary Fndn Fell, Univ of Chambridge, 1949-50; Demonstrator in Geol, 1949, Rsch Geologist, 1950-52, Univ of Tas; Mbr, Bd of Dirs, Roy Newcastle Hosp, 1965-81; Lectr, 1955-60, Snr Lectr, 1960-63, Newcastle Univ Coll; Hd, Dept of Geol, Newcastle Univ Coll and Newcastle Univ, 1961-80; Assoc Prof, 1964-65, Prof of Geol, 1965-80, Dean, Fac of Sci, 1969-70, Emer Prof of Geol, 1980-, Univ of Newcastle; Mbr, Bd of Dir, Gtr Newcastle Bldng Soc, 1981-86, Chmn, 1983-86; Mbr, Acad Cttee, NSW Higher Educn Bd, 1982-87; Mbr, Bd of Dirs, Dpty Chmn, 1985-94, Newcastle FM Pty Ltd; Chmn, N Reg Country Customer Cncl, NSW Police Serv, 1993-97. Publications: Geology of the Hunter Valley, 1964; Geology of the Sydney Basin, 1967; Man's Island in Space (jointly), 1975; Man and Movement, 1975. Honours: OBE, 1972; UN Assn of NSW Woman of the Yr Awd, 1975. Memberships: Hon Mbr, Geol Soc of Aust; Roy Soc of NSW; Past Pres, Austl Fedn of Bus and Profl Womens Clubs; Intl Fedn of Bus and Profl Women. Hobbies: Gardening; Fishing. Address: 43 Princeton Avenue, Adamstown Heights, NSW 2289, Australia.

NASIR Agha, b. 9 Feb 1937, Meerut, India. Television Executive; Playwright. m. Safia Sultana, 1957, 1 s, 2 d. Appointments: Prog Mngr, Pakistani TV, 1967-68; Additional Gen-Mngr, 1967, Gen Mngr, 1969-72, Dir, Progs Admin, 1972-86, Dpty Mngng Dir, 1986-87, Mngng Dir, 1987-88; Mngng Dir, Natl Film Devel Corp, 1979; Dir-Gen, Pakistan Broadcasting Corp, 1989-92; Chf Exec, Shalimar Recording Co, 1992-. Publications: Saat Dramey (plays); TV Plays. Honours: Num awds for radio and TV plays; Pride of Performance Awd, Pres of Pakistan, 1993. Hobby: Reading. Address: House No 23, Street No 3, F-8/3, Islamabad, Pakistan.

NASIR Mijit, b. 20 Oct 1938, Gulja, Xinjiang, China. m. Parwen, 28 Jan 1968, 3 s. Education: Studies, Tashkent Agricl Inst, 1957-62. Appointments: Sci Cadre, Agricl Sci Inst, 1962-86; Hd, Xinjiang Agricl Dept, 1986-93; Vice Chmn, Xinjiang Uygur Autonomous Region, 1993-98; VP, Xinjiang Peoples Congress, 1998-. Publications: Cotton Cultivation, 1986; Transl and Ed, Cultivating Vegetables in Plastic Awning, 1986; Cotton Breeding and Improved Varieties of Cotton Breeding, 1989; Transl and Ed, Xinjiang Agricultural Items. Honour: Awd, Title: Excellent Scientist of Xinjiang Agricl Sci Academy, 1980. Membership: Pres, Chmn, Chinese Agricl Acadmy, 1992. Hobbies: Translation; Music. Address: 74 Tuanjie Road, Urumqi Xinjiang, Uygur Autonomous Region, China.

NATARAJAN Kalyanasundaram, b. 21 Aug 1948, Tirunelveli, Tamilnadu, India. Engineering Educator; Researcher. m. Aparna A, 5 Apr 1976, 1 s, 1 d. Education: BSc, Kerala Univ, 1969; BE, hons, 1972, ME, 1974, PhD, 1980, Indian Inst of Sci, Bangalore. Appointments: Lectr, Univ Cochin, 1980; Rdr, Regl Engrng Coll, Trichy, 1980-97, Prof, 1997-, Chmn, Dept of Elec & Commn Engrng, 1998-. Publications: Sev articles in profl jrnls. Honours: 20th Century Awd, IBC, 1997; Rsch Bd of Advsrs, ABI, 1998-. Memberships: Electromagnetics Acady, USA, 1993-; NY Acady of Scis, 1994-. Hobby: Bridge. Address: Department of Electronics & Communication Engineering, Regional Engineering College, Tiruchirappalli 620015, India.

NATH Ajit Kumar, b. 22 Jan 1956, Senior Assistant Librarian. Education: MA (Polit Sci); MLib, Info Sci; LLB. Appointments: Jnr Lib Asst, Parly Lib of India, 1980-82; Asst Libn, Supreme Crt of India Lib, 1982-84; Jnr Asst Libn, Indian Inst of Pub Admin, 1984-85; Asst Libn, Indian Inst of Pub Admin, 1985-93; Asst Libn (Snr Cadre) Indian Inst of Pub Admin, 1993-. Publications: Prepared bibliography; Asst Ed of Documentation in Pub Admin Jrnl. Memberships: Life Mbr, AGLIS, participated actively in var seminars, confs, natl and intl workshops. Address: F-1091, C R Park, New Delhi 110019, India.

NATH Ananda Chandra, b. 30 June 1953, Rupaibori, India. Service. m. B Devi, 23 Feb 1981, 2 s. Education: MSc, Anthropol; LLB. Publications include: Handicrafts of the Tiwas of Gobha: With Special Reference to Basketry and their Customary Laws, 1995; A Study on the Variation of Ear Lobe Attachment Among the Karbis of Karbi Anglong in Assam, 1996; A Study of the Ao Foot, 1997; A Study on Occipital Hair Whorl of Kaibartas of Assam, 1998; Radical Constitutional Change Among the Tiwas of Gobha Kingdom, 1998; A Comparative Study of the Muslim Foot of Lower Assam, India, 1999; A Study of Some Behavioural Traits Among Kaibartas of Assam, India, 1999; A Comparative Study of the Genetic traits Among Kaibartas of Assam, 1999. Hobbies: Reading; Playing; Basket Works. Address: Assam Institute of Research for Tribals & Scheduled Castes, Jawaharnagar, Guwahati 781022, Assam, India.

NATHAN Roderic (Rory) John, b. 22 June 1958. Hydrologist. m. Julienne Patricia Kinna, 21 May 1988, 1 s, 1 d. Education: BE(Agr); DIC; MSc; PhD. Appointments: Tutor, Dept of Civ Engrng, Univ of Melbourne; Engr, Cementation Intl Ltd, London, Eng and Muscat, Oman; Engrng Hydrologist, Gutteridge Haskins & Davey, Melbourne and Perth, Aust; Rsch Fell, Cntr for Environ Applied Hydrology, Univ of Melbourne; Engrng Hydrologist, Rural Water Cmmn, Armadale; Snr Hydrologist, Sinclair Knight Merz, Armadale. Publications: Over 50 publns in refereed jrnls, books, book sects and conf proceedings. Honours: W H Warren Medal, Inst of Engrs, 1992; G N Alexander Awd, 1997. Memberships: Snr Mbr, Inst of Engrs, Aust; River Basin Mngmt Soc; Am Geophysl Union. Listed in: Who's Who in the World. Hobbies: Reading; Woodworking; Bushwalking. Address: 8 Pascoe Avenue, McKinnon, Vic 3204, Australia.

NATORI Yasuo, b. 26 Dec 1933, Hokkaido, Japan. Nutrition Biochemistry Professor. m. Mitsuko, 1965. Education: BA, Intl Christian Univ, 1957; PhD, Univ of CA, 1963. Appointments: Instr, Biochem, Univ of CA, 1963; Hd, Biochem, Intl Rice Rsch Inst, 1965; Prof, Nutr, Univ of Tokushima, 1966-. Creative Works: Many books and pprs on Biochem and Nutr. Honour: Prize, Outstndng Achmnt, Japanese Soc of Nutr and Food Sci, 1995. Memberships: Japanese Biochem Soc; Japanese Soc of Nutr and Food Sci; Vitamin Soc of Japan. Hobbies: Playing Go; Classical Music. Address: Department of Nutrition, School of Medicine, The University of Tokushima, Kuramoto, Tokushima 770-8503, Japan.

NAUSS Allen Henry, b. 5 Nov 1923, Fango, ND, USA. Theological Education. m. Victoria (nee Hinck), 24 Aug 1958, 1 s, 3 d. Education: BA, 1947, MDiv, 1948, Concordia Sem, St Louis, MO, USA; MEd, Univ of Oregon, Eugene, OR, USA, 1950; PhD, Univ of Missouri, Columbia, MO, USA. Appointments: St Paul's Coll, Concordia, MO, USA, 1948-59; Concordia Sem, Ft Wayne, IN, USA, 1960-77; Concordia Univ, Irvine, CA, USA, 1978-88. Honour: Behnden Fellowship, 1970-71. Memberships: Amn Psychol Assn; Religious Rsch Assn; Sci Soc of Relig, Inst of Gen Sementic. Hobby: Gardening. Address: 261 N Malena Drive, Orange, CA 92869, USA.

NAVALANI Kishni, b. 20 Mar 1935. Teacher, Library & Information Science. Education: MA Hist, Univ of Rajasthan, Jaipur, 1964; Master of Lib Sci, Delhi Univ, 1968; PhD, Lib Sci, Karnataka Univ, Dharwad, 1983; UNISIST/IFLA Intl Sch of Advd Info, Univ of Sheffield, Engl. Appointments: Tech Asst, Univ of Rajasthan Lib, Jaipur, 1961-68; Libn, Gargi Coll, New Delhi, 1968-70; Dean, Fac of Arts and Socl Sci, Punjabi Univ, Patiala, India, 1991-93; Hd, Dept of Pol Sci and Dept of Socl Work, 1993-94; Lectr 1970-74, Reader 1974-83, Prof 1983-95, Retired Prof 1995-, Dept of Lib and Info Sci. Publications: Auth, compiler, Ed of 10 books; Contbr, 60 papers in jrnls, sems, confs: Guided Research Work for Awarding PhD and Master of Library and Information Science Degrees. Honours: UNESCO Fellshp, 1981; Postdoc Fulbright Fellshp, US Info Agcy, Bd of For Fellshp, USA, 1988; Univ Grants Commn, Panel Expert; Net Panel Expert. Memberships: Indian Lib Assn; Soc for Info Sci; Indian Assn of Spec Libs and Cntrs; Indian Assn of Tchrs of Lib and Info Sci; AGLIS; PLA. Hobbies: Reading; Writing; Travelling; Social Work; Spiritualism. Address: 437 Urban Estate, Phase I, Patiala 147002, Punjab, India.

NAWAZ SHARIF Mohammed, b. 25 Dec 1949, Lahore, Pakistan. Politician; Industrialist. m. 1971, 2 s, 2 d. Education: Govt Coll; Punjab Univ; Law Coll, Lahore. Appointments: Worker, Ittefaq Faction Indl Grp, 1969; Fin Min, Govt of the Punjab, 1981-85; Chf Min of Punjab, 1985-90; Pres, Pakistan Muslim League, Punjab, 1985, Islami Jamhoori Ittehad, 1988; PM of Pakistan, 1990-93, resgnd, 1993, PM, 1997-. Hobbies: Social Work; Photography; Hunting; Cricket. Address: Office of the Prime Minister, Islamabad, Pakistan.

NAZAYBAYEV Nursultan Abishevich, b. 6 July 1940, Chemolgan, Almaty Reg, Kazakhstan. President, Republic of Kazakhstan. m. Sara Alpysovna, 3 d. Education: DSc, Econs; PhD, 1992. Appointments: Wrker, Construction Directorate, 1960; Iron Founder, Karagandy Blast Furnace and Metallurgical Wrks, Dispatcher, Gas Operator, Snr Gas Operator, blast furnace okabtm 1965-69; Party activities, Komsomol, 1969-73; Sec of Party Cttee, Karagandy Iron and Steel Wrks, 1973-77; Sec, 2nd Sec, Karagandy Regl Pary Cttee, 1977-79; Sec, Cntrl Cttee, Communisty Party of Kazakhstan, 1979-84; Chmn, Cncl of Mins, Kazakh SSR, 1984-89; 1st Sec, Cntrl Cttee of Communist Party, 1989-91; Chmn, Supreme Cncl of Kazakh SSR, 1990; Pres of Repub, 1991, Re-elected, 1995-2000. Publications: Steel Profile of Kazakhstan; With Neither the Right nor the Left; Stategy of Resource Saving and Market Transition; Stategy of Formation and Development of Kazakhstan as a Sovereign State; Market and Social and Economic Development; On the

Threshold of the XXIst Century; N Nazarbayev: Eurasian Union - ideas, practice, prospects 1994-97; Num sci articles. Honours include: Gold Medal Guild of Econ Dev and Marketing, Nurnberg, Germany, 1993; Academician, Intl Engrng Acady, 1993, Acady of Socl Scis, Russian Federation, 1994, Natl Acady of Scis, Kazakhstan, 1995; Ctf and Breastplate, Hon Citizen of Almaty, 1995; Hon Mbr, Byelorussian Acady of Scis, 1996; Awd of Crans-Montana Intl Forum, 1996; Order of Yaroslav Mudryi, Ukraine, 1997; Hon Mbr, Natl Acady of Applied Scis of Russia, 1997; Order of a Big Cross Holder w Big Ribbon, Italy, 1998; Num hon doctorates. Memberships include: USSR People's Dpty, 1989-92; Dpty of USSR Suopreme Cncl, 10th and 11th convocations; Chmn, World Assn of Kazakhs, 1992; Hon Chmn, Friendshp Fund, Peoples of Cntrl Asia and Kazakhstan; Pres, Intl FUnd for Rehab of Aral Area, 1993-97; Supreme Cmndr-in-Chf, Armed Forces of Kazakhstan, 1993; Chmn, Assembly of Peoples of Kazakhstan, 1995. Hobby: Big tennis.

NAZAROV Talbak, b. 15 Mar 1938, Kulyab. Politician; Academic. m. Tatyana Grigorievna Teodorovich, 1959, 1 s, 1 d. Education: Leningrad Inst of Fin & Econs. Appointments: Asst Dpty Dean, Econs Fac, Tajik State Univ, 1960-62, Hd of Dept, Dean, 1965-80; Rector, Tajik State Univ, 1982-88; Chair, Supreme Soviet Tajik SSR, 1986-88; Min of Pub Educn, 1988-90; 1st Dpty Chair, Cncl of Mins, Chair, State Planning Cttee, 1990-91; Min of Fgn Affairs, 1994-. Publications: Books and articles on Tajikistan's econ and external policies. Honours include: Merited Worker of Sci. Membership: Tajikistan Acady of Scis. Address: Ministry of Foreign Affairs, Rudaki 42, 734051 Dushanbe, Tajikistan.

NAZER Hisham Mohi ed-Din, b. 1932, Saudi Arabia. Politician. Education: Univ CA, USA. Appointments: Legal Advsr, 1958; Fndr, OPEC, 1960; Dpty Min of Petroleum, 1962-68; Pres, Ctrl Org for Planning, 1968-; Mbr, Supreme Cncl for Petroleum & Minerals, 1968-; Min of Planning, 1975-, Acting Min of Planning, 1986-91; Min of Petroleum & Mineral Resources, 1986-95; Chair, SAMAREC, Saudia Arabian Oil Co. Address: Ministry of Petroleum & Mineral Resources, PO Box 247, Riyadh 11191, Saudi Arabia.

NAZIR Badiuddin, b. 19 May 1950, Bagnan, Howrah, West Bengal. Publishing Consultant. m. Zaharat Ara, 2 Oct 1977, 1 s, 1 d. Education: Master Deg, Dhaka Univ; Assoc in Info Scis, New Delhi. Appointments: Natl Book Cntr of Bangladesh, 1972-94; Chf, Materials Dept, Gonoshahajjo Songstha, 1994-98; Cnsltng Ed, Univ Press Ltd, Dhaka, 1999-. Publications: 1 book on publng, 5 trans books on classics, 1 trans book on printing. Memberships: Bangladesh Lib Assn; All Indian Assn of Specl Libs and Info Cntrs; Afro-Asian Book Cncl. Hobbies: Reading; Cricket. Address: Road No 11, Old 32, House No 13, Dhanmondi R/A, Dhaka 1205, Bangladesh.

NEAL Eric James, b. 3 June 1924, London, England. Governor of South Australia. m. Thelma Joan Bowden, 4 Mar 1950, 2 s. Education: CEng; CPEng; FIE Aust; FIE GasE, London. Appointments: SA Gas Co, Elec Trust, 1940-49; Gas Ind, Broken Hill, Ballarat, 1950-63; Asst Gen Mngr, Boral Gas Ltd, 1963-68; Gen Mngr, 1968-71; Chf Gen Mngr, Boral Ltd Grp, 1972-74; Chf Exec, Mngng Dir, 1974-87; Cttee Mbr, C'wlth Govt Review of Aust's Higher Def, 1981-82; Mbr, C'wlth Prices and Incomes Advsry Cttee, 1983-86; Chf Commnr, Cty of Sydney, 1987-88; Cnclr, Sydney County Cncl, 1987-88; Mbr, Def Ind Cttee, 1988-90; Mbr, Senate, Sydney Univ, 1991-92; Chr, Cncl of Aust Govt's Wrkng Grp on Water Rescs Policy, 1993-95; Chr, Sugar Ind Review Cttee, 1995-96; Gov, SA, 1996-. Honours: Kt Bachelor, 1982; AO, 1988; The Austl Gas Assn Gold Flame Awd, 1988; Hon, DEng, Univ of Sydney, 1989; Dr of the Univ, Univ of SA, 1996; Kt of Grace, 1997. Memberships: Inst of Gas Engrs; Austl Inst of Mngmnt; Inst of Engrs, Aust; Austl Acady of Technol Scis and Engrng; Austl Inst of Co Dirs; Union Club; Melbourne Club; Adelaide Club. Hobbies: Soccer; Sailing; Naval and engineering history; Opera; Travel; Reading; Walking. Address: Government House, GPO Box 2373, Adelaide, SA 5001, Australia.

NEALE Robert George, b. 7 Mar 1919. Emeritus Professor. m. (1) Darthea Shanahan, 1942, Dec 1974, 2 s, (2) Ann Lahey, 19 May 1979. Education: MA, Dip Ed, Melbourne Univ. Appointments: War Serv, 1941-45; Lectr, 1945-65, Prof of Hist, 1965-70, Univ Qld; Ed, Histl Documents, Dept of For Affairs, Canberra, 1970-75; Dir-Gen, Austl Archives, 1975-84; Emer Prof. Publications: Britain and American Imperialism 1898-1900, 1965; Documents on Australian Foreign Policy 1937-49, Vol I, 1937-38, Vol II, 1939. Honour: AO, 1985. Listed in: Who's Who in Australia. Address: PO Box 7, Garran, ACT 2605, Australia.

NEALL Vincent Ernest, b. 17 June 1947, Bristol, England. Earth Scientist. m. Annabel, 12 Feb 1972, 1 s, 1 d. Education: BSc, Hons; PhD. Appointments: Lectr, 1973, Assoc Prof, Massey Univ. Publications: 50 sci pprs in profl jrnls. Honours: McKay Hammer Awd, 1981; Hochstetter Lectr, 1981; Taranaki Regl Cncl Environ Awd, 1997; NZ Sci & Technol Medal, 1998. Memberships: Fell, Geol Soc of Am, NZ Soc of Soil Sci. Hobbies: Camellia's; Croquet; Philately; Golf. Address: Institute of Natural Resources, Massey University, Private Bag 11-222, Palmeston North, New Zealand.

NEEMAN Yaakov, b. 1939, Tel-Aviv, Israel. Politician; Lawyer. m. 6 children. Education: Hebrew Univ of Jerusalem; NY Univ Law Sch. Appointments: Israeli Bar Assn, 1966-; Snr Ptnr, Herzog Fox & Neeman, 1972-; Vis Prof of Law, Univ CA, Los Angeles, 1976, Tel-Aviv Univ, 1977-79, NY Univ, 1989-90, Hebrew Univ of Jerusalem, 1990, 1994; Dir-Gen, Min of Fin, 1979-81; Chair, Cttee of Inquiry into Inter-Rel Btwn Tax Laws & Fgn Currency Restrictions, 1977-78; Pub Cttee on Allocation of Distrbns by Min of Interior, 1991-92; Mbr, Investigation Cttee on Temple Mt Affair, 1991; Min of Justice, 1996, of Fin, 1997-. Publications: 7 books, over 30 articles in profl jrnls. Memberships include: Ctrl Cttee, World Bank. Address: Ministry of Finance, PO Box 13191, 1 Rehov Kaplan, Kiryat Ben-Gurion, Jerusalem 91008, Israel.

NEER SHABNAM Nirmala Shankarrao Chandekar, b. 9 Nov 1939, India. Professor; Principal. Education: MA, Eng Lit. Appointments: Lectr, Eng, 1966-; Prin of Arts, Sci and com Coll, 1999-. Creative Works: Gulmohari Sham; Band Lifafa; Baki Sab Kushal Hai; Guftagu; Ek tha balak Dhrav; Seven Stars of Galaxy; Wonderlust; Kasturigandh. Honours: Jainendra Kumar Prize for Novel, Gulmohar Antak Ke; Gyanbharti Prize; Mata Kusum Kumari Awd; Mahadevi Verma Rashtriya Shikhar; Intl Woman of the Yr, IBC. Memberships: Cmnty Educ, ICEA; People for Animals. Hobbies: Writing Short Stories, Novels, Poems and Plays; Painting; Music; Photography; Visiting Historial Places. Address: Chandrapur 442402, India.

NEGRI SEMBILAN Yang di-Pertuan Besar, Tuanku Jaafar ibni Al-Marhum Tuanku Abdul Rahman, b. 19 July 1922, Malaysia. Ruler. m. Tuanku Najihar binti Tunku Besar Burhanuddin, 1943, 3 s, 3 d. Education: Malay Sch Sri Menanti; Malay Coll; Nottingham Univ. Appointments: Malay Admin Serv, 1944; Asst Dist Offr, Rembau, 1946-47, Parti, 1953-55; Chargé d'Affaires, Wash DC, 1947; 1st Perm Sec, Malayan Perm Mission to the UN, 1957-58; 1st Sec, Trade Cnslr, Dpty High Commr, London, 1962-63; Amb to United Arab Repub, 1962; High Commr, Nigeria & Ghana, 1965-66; Timbalan yang di-Pertuan Agong (Dpty Supreme Hd of State), 1979-84, 1989-94; Yang di-Pertuan Agong (Supreme Hd of State), 1994-. Hobbies: Well-Planned Housing Schemes; Sports. Address: Seremban, Malaysia.

NEILSON William A W, b. 30 Dec 1938, Montreal, Canada. Professor of Law. m. Coline, 9 May 1964, 1 s, 3 d. Education: B Com Hons, Toronto, 1960; LLB, 1st Class, Brit Columbia, 1964; UM, Harv, 1965. Appointments: Prof, Osgoode Hall, Toronto, 1971; Prof, Univ of Vic, Canada, 1977; Dpty Min, Consumer Affairs, Brit Columbia, 1973-76; Dean, Univ Vic Law Fac, 1985-90; Exec Dir, Cntr for Asia-Pacific Initiatives, Univ of Vic, 1992-. Honours: Visng Prof, Chula Long Korn Univ, Bangkok, 1988-; UMEA Univ, 1998; Melbourne Univ, 1998. Memberships: Law Soc of Brit Columbia, 1966-; Intl Acady of Com and Consumer Law, 1982-. Hobbies: Photography; Mountain Hiking. Address: University of Victoria, Begbie Building Room 131, P O Box 1700, Victoria, BC V8W 2Y2, Canada.

NEKHAMKIN Yuri, b. 1 Mar 1947, Leningrad, USSR. Mechanical Engineer. m. Ludmila, 1 s. Education: MSc (Hons) Mechl Engrng, Fac of Phys and Mechanics, Leningrad Polytechnic Inst, Leningrad, USSR, 1971. Appointments: R&D Inst of Chem Engrng, Leningrad, 1971; R&D Inst of Electron Machinery, Leningrad, 1986; Valve Mfng Corp, Leningrad, 1987; Technion-Israel Inst of Technol, Haifa, 1991; Israel Elec Corp Ltd, Haifa, 1994; HTC Ltd, Jerusalem, 1996. Publications: Over 60 articles in profl jrnls and proceedings of sci confs. Membership: Israel Nuclear Soc, 1992-. Address: Str Ofakim 7/32, PO Box 1449, 36770 Nesher, Israel.

NENA Jacob, b. Oct 10 1941, Lelu, Micronesia. Government Official. m. Lerina Jack, 9 children. Education: BA, Polit Sci, Coll of Guam; Grad Deg in Pub Admin and Bus Mngmt. Appointments: Tchr, FICS hs; Polit Affairs Offr, Pohnpei Dist; Acting Dist Rep, Kosrae Dept Dist Rep; Exec Dir, Kosrae Transp Authy; Senator, Cong Federated States of Micronesia, 1987-91; VP, Fed States Micronesia Govt, 1991-97; Pres, 1997-. Memberships: Commn Polit Status and Transition; Chmn, Lelu Munic Govt Constl Conv; Mbr, Kosrae State Constl Cong; Chmn, Gommn Govt Structure and Ops; Chmn, Commn of Hlth and Socl Affairs; Mbr, Commns on Rescs and Dev and External Affairs. Address: National Government, PO Box P9-53, Palikir, Pohnpei 96941, Federated States of Micronesia.

NETANYAHU Benjamin, b. 21 Oct 1949, Israel. Politician; Diplomat. m. 2 children. Education: MIT, USA. Appointments: Mngng Cnslt, Boston Cnsltng Grp, 1976-78; Exec Dir, Jonathan Inst, Jerusalem, 1978-80; Snr Mngr, Rim Inds, Jerusalem, 1980-82; Dpty Chf of Mission, Israeli Emb, Wash DC, 1982-84; Perm Rep to UN, 1984-88; Dpty Min of Fgn Affairs, 1988-91; Dpty Min, PM's Off, 1991-92; Ldr, Likud March, 1993, Fighting Terrorism, 1996; PM of Israel, Min of Housing & Constrn, 1996-. Address: Office of the Prime Minister, PO Box 187, 3 Rehov Kaplan, Kiryat Ben-Gurion, Jerusalem 91919, Israel.

NETTHEIM Robert Garth, b. 4 Feb 1933, Sydney, Australia. Emeritus Professor. 2 s, 1 d. Education: LLB, hons, Univ Sydney, 1954; MA, Fletcher Sch of Law and Diplomacy, Tufts Univ, USA, 1957. Appointments: Radio Prodr, Cand Broadcasting Corp, Vancouver, 1958-60; Lectr, Snr Lectr, Fac of Law, Univ Sydney, 1963-70; Prof, Fac of Law, Univ NSW, 1971-96; Visng Prof, 1996-. Publications: Understanding Law (co-auth), 1973-97; Indigenous Legal Issues (co-auth), 1991. Honour: Emer Prof, 1997. Memberships: Intl Commn of Jurists, Austl Sect, 1965-; Indigenous Law Cntr, Chair, 1981-; Rsch Advsry Cttee, Austl Inst of Aboriginal and Torres Strait Islanders. Hobbies: Music; Walking; Theatre. Address: c/o Faculty of Law, University of New South Wales, NSW 2052, Australia.

NETTLE Charles Alexander, b. 3 Dec 1920. Former Deputy Director General, Australian Department of Health. m. Dorothy Akeroyd, 20 Apr 1946, 2 s, 1 d. Education: Wesley Coll, Perth; Univ of WA, LLB, FCPA. Appointments: RAAF, 1942-45; Off of P S Bd, 1947-54; Tutor, Pub Admin, Univ of WA, 1952-53; HQ Insp, Repatriation Dept, 1954-56; Asst Cmmnr, Instns, 1956-65; 1st Asst Cmmnr, Treatment Servs, 1965-73; 1st Asst Sec, Prog Mngmt and Def Facs, Dept of Def, 1973-74; Dpty Dir Gen, Austl Dept of Hlth, 1974-82; Retd. Honour: MBE. Membership: FCPA, 1966. Listed in: Who's Who in Australia. Address: PO Box 60, Torrens, ACT 2607, Australia.

NEUMANN Bernhard Hermann, b. 15 Oct 1909, Berlin, Germany. Mathematican. m. (1) Hanna von Caemmerer, 22 Dec 1938, dec 1971, 3 s, 2 d, (2) Dorothea Frieda Auguste Zeim, 24 Dec 1973. Education: Univ Freiburg, 1928-29; DrPhil, Univ of Berlin, 1929-32; PhD, Univ of Cambridge, Eng, 1933-35; DSc, Univ of Manchester, 1954. Appointments: Temp Asst Lectr, Univ

Coll, Cardiff, Wales, 1937-40; Army Serv, Pioneer Corps, Roy Artillery, Intelligence Corps, 1940-45; Lectr, Univ Coll, Hull, Eng, 1946-48; Lectr, Snr Lectr, Rdr, Univ of Manchester, 1948-61; Prof, Hd of Dept of Maths, Inst of Adv Studies, Aust Natl Univ, Aust, 1962-74; Hon Fell, Emer Prof, 1975-; Snr Rsch Fell, CSIRO Div of Maths and Stats, 1975-77; Hon Rsch Fell, 1978-, (now Mathematical and Info Scis). Publications: Contbr of over 120 papers in mathematical jrnls; Selected works of B H Neumann and Hanna Neumann, 6 vols, 1988. Honours: Prize, Wiskundig Genootschap to Amsterdam, 1949; Matthew Flinders Lectr, Aust Acady of Sci, 1984; Adams Prize, Univ of Cambridge, 1952-53; Hon DSc, Univ of Newcastle, NSW, 1974, Monash Univ, 1982; Hon Dr Math, Univ of Waterloo, 1986; Hon DSc, Univ of West Aust, 1995; Univ of Hull, Eng, 1995; Dr rer nat hon causa, Humboldt Univ, Berlin, 1992; Hon Mbr, Canberra Math Assn, 1975-; Hon Mbr, NZ Math Soc, 1975-; Hon Mbr, Aust Assn of Maths Tchrs, 1975-; Hon Mbr, Aust Math Soc, 1981-; FAustMS, Fell of Aust Math Soc, 1994; Companion of Order of Aust, 1994. Memberships: FRS; FAA; FACE; FTICA (Hon); London Math Soc; Wiskundig Genootschap; Amn, Canadian, Aust, NZ and SE Asian Math Socs; Math Assn; Math Assn of Am; Aust Assn of Maths Tchrs. Hobbies: Chamber Music; Chess; Cycling; Camping. Address: The Australian National University, School of Mathematical Sciences, ACT 0200, Australia.

NEUTZE Graeme Max, b. 8 Apr 1934, NZ. Professor. m. (1) Margaret Eileen Murray, 23 June 1959, dec 15 Mar 1994, 2 s, 1 d, (2) Mary Marjorie O'Halloran, 9 Nov, 1996. Education: BAgrSc, 1956; MAgrSc, 1957, NZ; DPhil, Oxford, Eng, 1960. Appointments: Lectr, Econs, 1960-63; Snr Lectr, 1963-66; Snr Fell, Hd, Urban Rsch Unit, 1967-72; Professorial Fell, Hd, 1973-79, Prof, 1979-80, 1985-88, 1992-96, Ret'd; Dir, Rsch Sch of Socl Scis, 1980-85; A/Dep Vice Chan, 1988-89; Dpty Vice Chan, 1989-92, Austl Natl Univ. Publications include: The Suburban Apartment Boom, 1968; Australian Urban Policy, 1978; Funding Urban Services, 1997. Honour: AO, 1994. Memberships: Fell, Acady of Socl Scis in Aust; Hon Fell, Roy Austl Planning Inst; Austl Inst of Urban Studies; Chair, Aust Inst, 1994-98. Hobbies: Bushwalking; Tennis; Classical music. Listed in: Who's Who in Australia. Address: Urban and Environmental Program, Australian National University, Canberra, ACT 0200, Australia.

NEVIN Robyn, b. 25 Sept 1942, Melbourne, Australia. Actor; Director. Education: Grad, Natl Inst Dramatic Art, 1960. Career: Assoc Dir, MTC, 1995-96; Currently, Artistic Dir, Queensland Th Co and Sydney Th Co; Acting roles incl: (th) Cleopatra, Caesar and Cleopatra, Miss Julie, Miss Julie, Old Tote Th Co; Martha, Who's Afraid of Virginia Wolf, Lady Macbeth, Macbeth, Sydney Th Co; Hedda, Hedda Gabler, State Th Co of SA; Lady Windamere, Lady Windamere's Fan, 1995, Miss Docker, A Cheery Soul, 1996, Mark Antony in Julius Casear, 1996, Melbourne Th Co; Master Class, Queensland Th Co and Sydney Th Co Co-prodn, 1997; Amy's View and The Marriage of Figaro,Queensland Th Co, 1998; Long Day's Journey into Night, Queensland Th Co, 1999 (TV) Lady Kerr, The Dismissal, Kennedy Miller Entertainment, 1982; Margot, Seven Deadly Sins - Sloth, Generation Films, 1993; The Burning Piano, ABC TV Documentaries, 1993; Irene, Over the Hill, Gary Reilly Prodns, 1994; Angela, Halifax f.p., Simpson Le Mesurier Films, 1994, 1995, 1996; (films) Wiley, Resistance, Macau Light Film Corp Ltd, 1991; Mum, Greenkeeping, Cntrl Prl Films, 1991; Anne-Marie LePine, Lucky Break, Weis Films Pty Ltd, 1994; Dr Norberg, Angel Baby, Astral Films, 1994; Fedl Crt Judge, The Castle, Frontline Films, 1996; Dir, plays, film: The More Things Change, 1986. Honours: 2 Logie Awds; Natl Th Awd, Best Actress NSW, 1976; Sammy, Penguin and Logie Awds for Best Actress for Shasta in Water Under The Bridge (TV mini series); Sammy Awd, Best Actress in A Toast to Melba; AM, 1981; Annual Sydney Critics Circle Awds, 1987, 1991, Nom, 1992; Green Room Awd Noms: Best Dir, Scenes from a Separation, 1995, Best Actress, Julius Caesar, 1996; Variety Club Hearts Awds, Stage Awd, 1998; Sidney Meyer Perf Arts Awd, 1998. Address: Queensland

Theatre Company, PO Box 3310, South Brisbane, Queensland 4101, Australia.

NEWBRUN Ernest, b. 1 Dec 1932, Vienna, Austria. Dentist. m. Eva M, 17 June 1956, 1 s, 2 d. Education: BDS; MS; DMD; Odont Doc (hc); DDsc (hc). Appointments: Assoc Prof, 1965-70; Prof, 1970-94; Prof Emeritus, 1994-. Publications: Ed: Fluorides and Dental Caries, 3rd ed, 1986; Auth: Cariology, 3rd ed, 1989. Honours: Commonwealth Schl, 1951-53; Fell, AAAS, 1983; Odont Dr, 1988; Univ Lund hon causa; Rsch in Dental Caries Awd, IADR, 1992. Memberships: Intl Assn for Dental Rsch (IADR), VP, 1987-88, Pres-Elect, 1988-89, Pres, 1989-90. Hobbies: Opera; Skiing; Tennis; Gardening. Address: 1823, 8th Avenue, San Francisco, CA 94122, USA.

NEWELL William Hare, b. 21 Dec 1922, Varanasi, India. Social Anthropologist. m. Pauline Marsh Prosser, 8 July 1958, 1 s, 3 d. Education: MA, New Zealand, 1943; DipAnt, Oxon, Eng, 1947; Dip, Chinese, W China Union Univ, 1950; PhD, Manchester, 1958. Appointments: Meteorologist, R NZ Air Force, 1942-45; Lectr, W China Union Univ, 1947-53; Lectr, Univ of Manchester, Eng, 1954-55, 1957-59; Socl Rsch Unit, Univ of Singapore, 1955-57; Hd, Dept of Sociol, Intl Christian Univ, Japan, 1959-69; Visng Prof, Tokyo Metropolitan Univ, 1963-69; Assoc Prof, Dept of Anthropol, Univ of Sydney, 1969-88; Yu Shan Theol Coll, Hua Lien, Taiwan, 1988-89. Publications: Scheduled Castes and Tribes of Himachel Pradesh, (Gaddi), 1961; Treacherous River, 1962; Sociology of Japanese Religion, 1968; Ancestors, 1976; Japan in Asia 1942-1945, 1980. Honours: Overseas Fell, Churchill Coll, Oxford, 1968-69; Visng Prof, Delhi Sch of Econs, 1973, Univ of Ryukyus, 1976, Dept of Sociol, Univ of Hong Kong, 1978; Fell, Inst of Ethnol, Academia Sinica, Nankang, Taiwan, 1985-. Memberships: Roy Anthropol Inst; Amn Anthropol Assn; Japan Ethnol Soc; (Nihon Minzoku Gakkal), NSW Soc of Indl rels; Aust-Japan Studies Assn; Chinese Studies Assn of Aust; Assn of Socl Anthropologists of Brit C'wlth. Address: 4 Fort Street, Petersham, NSW 2049, Australia.

NEWMAN Jocelyn Margaret, b. 8 July 1937, Australia. Politician. Education: Melbourne Univ. Appointments: Senator, Liberal Pty, for Tas, 1986-; Shadow Min for Def, Sci & Personnel, 1988-92, Veterans' Affair, 1990-92; Shadow Min Asst Ldr on Status of Women, 1989-93; Shadow Min for the Aged & Vet Affairs, 1992-93; Shadow Min for Family Hlth, Shadow Min Asst Ldr on Family Matters, Chair, Hlth, Welfare & Vet Affairs Grp, 1993-94; Shadow Min for Def, 1994-96; Min for Socl Security & Min Asst PM on Status of Women, 1996-. Address: Parliament House, Canberra, ACT 2600, Australia.

NEWMAN Michael Frederick, b. 28 Oct 1934, Heidelberg, Germany. Research Worker. m. Marion Shakespeare, 13 Mar 1958, 2 s (1 dec), 2 d. Education: MSc, Sydney, 1957; PhD, Manchester, 1960. Appointments include: Asst Lectr, Univ Coll of N Staffordshire, Eng, 1959-61; Lectr, Snr Lectr, Reader, Snr Fell, Prof, Maths, Austl Natl Univ, 1961-. Publications: Over 90 rsch pprs and sev edited monographs. Memberships: Pres, 1971-73, Hon Life Mbr, 1984-, Canberra Math Assn; Pres, 1974-76, Austl Assn of Maths Tchrs; Chair, 1980-8, Austl Subcommn, Intl Commn on Maths Instruction, 1972-94; Exec Cttee Intl Commn on Math Instruction, 1982-86; Amn Math Soc; London Math Soc; Math Assn of Am; Math Assn of GB. Address: School of Mathematical Sciences, Australian National University, ACT 0200, Australia.

NEWMAN Peter James, b. 11 Dec 1938, Melbourne, Aust. Supreme Court Judge. m. Helen, 8 July 1969, 1 s, 1 d. Education: LLM (Hons), Sydney Univ, Aust. Appointments: QC, NSW & NT, 1981, ACT, 1982; Supreme Crt of NSW, 1987; Capt, RANR, 1993; Def Force Discipline Tribunal, 1996. Honour: Res Force Decoration (RFD), 1988. Memberships: NSW Bar Assn, Cncl Mbr, 1969-76, 1981; Hon Sec, 1972-76. Hobbies: Golf; Cricket; Bloodhorse Breeding; Reading. Address: C/o GPO Box 3, Sydney, NSW 2001, Australia.

NEWMAN Stanley Franklin, b. 2 Sept 1916. Engineering Consultant. m. Elizabeth Lyall, 21 July 1943, 1 s, 1 d. Education: MCEGS; Swinburne Tech Coll, FAIM, F Inst DA, FAIP. Appointments: RANR, 1939-46, MID, 1942, Engr Lt, 1944-46; Mngr, 1946, Chmn, Mngng Dir, Engrng Prods Pty Ltd, Burnley, 1963-78; Mbr, 1955, Chmn, 1963-68, Engrng Sect, Vic Chmbr of Mfrs; Cmmnr, Apprenticeship Cmmn, Vic, (now Indl Trng), 1963-79; Pres, Metal Inds Assn, Vic, 1965-67; Rotary Dist Gov, Dist 980, 1975-76; Mbr of Cncl, Vic O'seas Fndn, 1977-; Chmn, State Cncl for Tech Educ and TAFE Bd, 1977-82; Cmmnr, Vic Post-Secnd Educ, 1978-82; Assoc Mbr, Inst Marine Engrs, London. Honour: OBE, 1980. Hobbies: Golf; Tennis; Swimming. Address: 8/740 Orrong Road, Toorak, Vic 3142, Australia.

NEWNHAM Michael Jeffery, b. 31 Mar 1957, Gawler, S Aust. Motion Picture Film Conservator. m. Suzanne, 14 Mar 1981, 1 s, 1 d. Memberships: Mbr, Tech Cttee, SEAPAVAA (SE Asia Pacific Audio Visual Archives Assn); Corresp Mbr, Tech Cttee FIAF (Fedn Intl Archive du Film). Hobbies: Collecting photographica; Painting; Woodworking; Gardening. Address: C/o National Film and Sound Archive, GPO Box 2002, Canberra, ACT 2601, Australia.

NEWSON Marc Andrew, b. 20 Oct 1963, Sydney, Australia. Designer. Education: Sydney Coll of the Arts. Appointments: Designer, Tokyo, 1987-91, Paris, 1991-. Creative Works: Designs worldwide. Address: 5 Passage Piver, Paris, France.

NEWTH Melville Cooper, b. 3 Aug 1914, Manly, NSW, Aust. Clergyman; Headmaster. m. Mona Hope Kirkwood, 3 Oct 1942, 3 d. Education: BA, Sydney Univ, 1938; ThL, Austl Coll of Theol, 1942; MACE, 1965; FACE, 1978. Appointments: Tchr, NSW Educn Dept, 1934-39; Ordained in St Andrew's Cath, Sydney, 1941; Hdmaster, St Andrew's Cath Sch, 1941-79; Precentor, St Andrew's Cath, 1947-54; Minor Canon, 1954-89, Hon Canon, 1989-; Life Gov, Roy NSW Inst for Deaf and Blind Children, 1960-. Publications: Societas: Thomas Moore Centenary, 1940; Serving a Great Cause, 1980; Centenary Supplement, 1985. Honour: OBE, 1978. Memberships: Fell, Austl Coll of Educ; Fndn Pres, Hungerford and Assoc'd Families Soc, 1990-; Fndn Mbr and Fell, Ch of Eng Histl Soc. Hobbies: Music; Astronomy. Address: 10 Laurel Close, Hornsby, NSW 2077, Australia.

NEWTON John Oswald, b. 12 Feb 1924, Birmingham, England. Professor of Nuclear Physics. m. Silva Dusan Sablich, 23 Dec 1964, 2 s, 1 d. Education: MA, 1946, PhD, 1952, Cambridge Univ; DSc, Manchester Univ, 1966. Appointments: Jnr Sci Offr, TRE, Great Malvern, 1943-46; Harwell Fell, 1951-54; Prin Sci Offr, 1954-59, AERE Harwell; Visng Physicist, Lawrence Berkeley Lab, 1956-58, 1965-67, 1972, 1976, 1980-81; Visng Prof, Manchester Univ, 1985-86; Snr Lectr, 1959-67, Rdr, 1967-70, Univ of Manchester; Prof, 1970-89, Hd, Dept of Nuclear Phys, 1970-88, Emer Prof, Visng Fell, 1990-, Inst of Adv Stdies, Austl Natl Univ. Publications: Over 100 profl works inclng book chapts. Memberships: Fell, Austl Acady of Sci; Physl Soc, Eng; Austl Inst of Phys. Hobbies: Painting; Chess; Music; Walking; Tennis. Address: Department of Nuclear Physics, Research School of Physical Sciences & Engineering, Canberra, ACT 0200, Australia.

NG Alan Beh Puan, b. 8 Feb 1934. Pathologist. m. Enid Katherine Charters, 10 May 1958, 2 s, 2 d. Education: MBBS, Univ Melbourne, 1958; FSCAP, 1972; FIAC, 1973; FASD, 1981; FRCPA, 1981. Appointmemts include: Res Mdl Offr, 1959, 1960; Path Registrar, 1961-62, St Vincent's Hosp, Melbourne; Visng Fell, in Path, Inst of Path, Case West Reserve Univ, Cleveland, OH, 1963-64; Lectr in Path, Dept of Path, Fac of Med, Univ of Malaya, Kuala Lumpur, Malaysia, 1965, 1966; Pathologist, 1967-75, Asst Prof, 1967-69, Assoc Prof, 1969-74, Prof, 1975-, Univ Hosps of Cleveland, Case Western Reserve Univ, Cleveland, OH; Hd, Div of Cytopathology, Dept of Path, Univ Hosps of Cleveland, OH, 1970-75; Prof of Path, Dept of Path, Univ of Miami,

FL, 1975-81; Prof of Obstets-Gynae, Dept of Obstets-Gynae, Univ of Miami, FL, 1975-81; Dir, Surg Path and Cytology, Dept of Path. Jackson Mem Hosp, Miami, FL, 1975-81; Dir, Univ of miami, FL, 1975-81; Dir, Anatomic Path, Dept of Path, Jackson Mem Hosp, Miami Sch of Med, 1976-77; Dir, Sch of Histotechnol, Dept of Path, Jackson Mem Hosp, Miami, FL, 1975-81; Professorial Cnslt (Path), The Women's Hosp, Sydney, Aust, 1981-83; Chf Gynecologic Pathologist, Dept of Gynae and Women's Clin, Univ of Zurich, Switz, 1987-88; Hd of Dept, Dept of Anatomic Path, Royal Priince Alfred Hosp, Sydney, Aust, 1981-95; Prof of Path, Univ of Sydney, Aust, 1981-98; Snr Staff Specialist, Dept of Anatomical Path, Royal Prince Alfred Hosp, Sydney, Aust, 1981-98; Cnslt Pathologist, 1998-. Publications: Over 190 sci publs in Path and Cytol incl, 40 chapts in books and co-auth of 3 books. Honours: ICN Can Lectrship Awd, Canad Soc of Lab Technolsts, 1973; Homer A Pearson Mem Lectureship Awd, Miami Obstetrical and Gynecological Soc, 1979; George N Papanicloaou Awd, Amn Soc of Cytology, 1980. Listed in: Many Including: Who's Who in Australia; International Who's Who in Medicine; Who's Who in Australasia and the Pacific Nations. Hobbies: Reading; Travel; Theatres; Tennis. Address: 9/25 Milson Road, Cremorne, NSW 2090, Australia.

NG Man Lun, b. 14 Oct 1946, Hong Kong. Psychiatrist. m. Sui-May, 19 Sept 1972, 1 s, 1 d. Education: MD, Hong Kong; FRCPsych, Eng; FRANZCP; DPM; Dip. Amn Bd Sexol; FAACS; FHKAM, Psych. Appointments: Med Offr, Univ Psych Unit, Queen Mary Hosp, Hong Kong, 1972-73; Lectr, Psych, 1973-81, Snr Lectr, 1981-93, Rdr in Psych, 1993-96, Prof of Psych, 1996-, Univ of Hong Kong. Publications include: Sexuality in Asia, 1993; Sexual Behavior in Modern China - A Report of the Nationwide Sex-Civilization Survey on 20,000 Subjects in China, 1997. Memberships: Hong Kong Coll of Psych; Med Soc, HKUSU; Auxiliary Med Serv, Govt of Hong Kong; Hong Kong Medl Assn Mental Hlth Assn of Hong Kong; Musicol Soc, HKUSU; Hong Kong Family Plng Assn. Hobbies: Music; Computers. Address: Department of Psychiatry, University of Hong Kong, Pokfulam Road, Hong Kong.

NG Yew-Kwang, b. 7 Aug 1942, Kedah, Malaysia. Professor of Economics. m. Seok Hean Low, 30 Mar 1967, 2 d. Education: BCom, Econs, Nanyang Univ, Singapore, 1966; PhD, Econs, Univ of Sydney, Aust, 1971. Appointments: Lectr, Univ of New Eng, NSW, Aust, 1970-71; Snr Lectr, Univ of New Eng, 1972-73; Visng Nuffield Fndn Fell, Nuffield Coll, Oxford, Eng, 1973-74; Rdr, Monash Univ, Vic, Aust, 1974-85; Visng Prof & Fulbright Schl, Tulane Univ, New Orleans, USA, 1987-88; Prof, Personal Chair in Econs, Monash Univ, Vic, Aust, 1985-. Publications: Auth/co-auth 8 inclng: Social Welfare and Economic Policy, 1990; Welfare Economics (Chinese version), 1991; Specialization & Economic Organization, 1993; Economics and Reforms: Collected Papers of Professor Yew-Kwang Ng, 1994; The Unparalleled Mystery, 1994; Mesoeconomics, 1996; Co-Ed, Increasing Returns and Economic Analysis, 1998; Auth of over 100 jrnl articles in econs, philos, psychol, maths, bio; Ed, editl bds of intl jrnls. Honour: Fell, Acady of Socl Scis in Aust, 1981-. Memberships: Life Mbr, Amn Econ Assn; Roy Econ Soc. Hobbies: Bridge; Chess; Badminton; Chinese poetry. Address: Department of Economics, Monash University, Clayton, Victoria, Australia.

NG Ying Chu, b. 19 Dec 1963, Hong Kong. Associate Professor. Education: BS, Computer Sci, 1987; MA, Econs, 1988; PhD, Econs, 1991. Appointments: Asst Prof, 1997-98, Assoc Prof, 1998- Hong Kong Bapt Univ. Cnslt, World Bank, 1991, 1992; Visng Prof, Univ of Alberta, 1997; Visng Prof, Univ of SC, 1997. Publications: In profl jrnls. Memberships: Amn Econ Assn; Soc of Labour Econs; CSWEP; HK Econ Assn. Hobbies: Badminton; Tennis; Reading. Address: Department of Economics, Hong Kong Baptist University, Kowloon Tong, Kowloon, Hong Kong.

NGAN Man Hung Raymond, b. 17 June 1954, Hong Kong. Academic Teaching (Social Work). m. Irene Ip, 14

Apr 1984, 3 d. Education: BSoc Sc (HK), 1977; MSc, Socl Admin (London), 1981; PhD, Socl Wrk, 1990. Appointments: Chf Ed, Hong Kong Jrnl of Socl Wrk, 1994-96; Acting Hd, Dept of Applied Soc Studies, Cty Univ of HK, 1998. Publications: The Vision of Social Policy in Hong Kong, 1986; Applied Gerontology: Casework, 1992; Applied Gerontology: Groupwork, 1994. Honour: Outstndng Rsch Awd in Gerontology, Hong Kong Assn of Gerontology, 1997. Memberships: VP, Hong Kong Assn of Gerontology, 1992-; Chmn, Cttee on Socl Security, Hong Kong Cncl of Socl Serv, 1994-97. Hobby: Vision to improve the well-being of minority groups. Address: Department of Applied Social Studies, City University of Hong Kong, Tat Chee Avaenue, Kowloon, Hong Kong.

NGAPOI Ngawang Jigme, b. 1911, Tibet. Politician. Appointments: Vice Chair, Qamdo Liberation Cttee, 1950; 1st Dpty Cmdr, Tibet Mil Region, 1952, Vice Chair, Sec-Gen, 1959; Dpty for Xizang, 1st NPC, 1954; Mbr, Natl Def Cncl, 1954-; Sec-Gen, Preparatory Cttee for Establishment of Xizang Autonomous Region, 1956, Vice Chair, 1959, Acting Chair, 1965; Vice Chair, Standing Cttee, 3rd NPC, 1965-75, 4th NPC, 1975-78, 5th NPC, 1978-86, 6th NPC, 1983-87, 7th NPC, 1988-93; Chair, Xizang AR, 1965; Vice Chair, Xizang AR Revolutionary Cttee, 1968-79; Chair, Peoples Congress, Xizang AR, 1979; Exec Chair, Presidium 6th NPC, 1986; Chair, Tibet Autonomous REgl 5th Peoples Congress, 1988-93. Publication: Tibet (w others). Memberships: Sev cttees. Address: Office of the Governor, Peoples Government, Lhasa, Xizang Autonomous Region, China.

NGENMUNE Sutasn, b. 18 May 1945. Minister of Justice. m. Education: LLB, Thammasat Univ. Appointments: Mbr of Parl, 1975, 1983, 1988, 1992, 1995, 1996; Asst Sec, Min of Pub Hlth; Dpty Min, Pub Hlth, 1988-90; Dpty min, Agric and Co-ops, 1990-91; Dpty Min of Interior, 1992-95; Chmn, Stndng Cttee on Jus and Human Rights, House of Representatives, 1996-97; Min of Jus, 1996-; Dpty Ldr, Democrat Party. Honours: Kt Grand Cordon, Spec Class, Most Noble Order of the Crown of Thailand, 1990; Kt Grand Cordon, Spec Class, Most Exalted Order of the White Elephant, 1992. Address: 97/54 Sri Bandhit 3, Bang Greut, Sai noi Road, Amphur Muang, Nonthaburi, Thailand.

NGO Manh Lan, b. 9 Nov 1934, Hanoi. Painter; Film Director. m. Ngoc Lan, 15 Dec 1962, 1 s, 3 d. Education: Vietnam Fine Art Sch, 1950-54; Inst of Cinema, Moscow, 1956-62; PhD, 1984; Assoc Prof, 1991. Appointments: Film Dir, Vietnam Animated Film Studio, 1962-86; Prof, Hanoi Cinema Higher Sch, 1963-; Dir, Vietnam Film-Video Tape Import Export Co, 1987-92; Film Dir, 1993-. Honours: Silver Prize, Film, The Little Cat, 1966; Gold Prize, Film, The Legend About Giong, 1971; 3 Gold Prizes; 4 Silver Prizes; Natl Prize, Illust. Memberships: The Vietnam Fine Arts Assn; The Vietnam Cinema Assn of Film Makers; Hanoi Art and Lit Utd Fedn. Hobbies: Painting; Research; Critic Animated Films. Address: 2, To 42 Dai Yen, Ba Dinh, Hanoi, Vietnam.

NGUYEÑ DIÑH Chu, b. 29 Sept 1932, Nghi Hop-Nghiloc NgheAn. Teacher; Researcher in Literature. m. Nguyên Minh Tham, 26 Mar 1952, 2 s, 1 d. Education: BA, Univ of Educ. Appointments: Dean of Moderm-Classical Lit of Univ Pedagogue of Hanoi, 1965-71; Team Ldr, Lit Grp, Min of Higher Vocation of Educ; Mbr, Cttee Sci & Training, Hanoi Natl Univ, 1994-. Memberships: Linguistics Cttee, Min of Educ & Trng, 1980-; Chmn, Copyright Protection Cncl Vietnam Folk Cultural Assn, 1996-. Hobbies: Studying history of literature and ideology. Address: Literature Department, Teacher Training College, Vietnam National University, Hanoi.

NGUYEN Co Thach, b. 15 May 1923, Vietnam. Politician. m. Phan Thi Phuc, 1947, 3 s, 1 d. Appointments: Gen Consul, Delhi, 1956-60; Vice Min of Fgn Affairs, 1960; Peace Talks, Geneva, 1961-62, on Laos, Paris, 1968-72; on Vietnam; Chair, Cttee to Investigate US War Crimes, 1966; Min of Fgn Affairs, 1980; Alt Mbr, Politburo, 1982-86, Mbr, 1986-91; Vice

Premier, State Cncl, 1987-91; Asst to Gen Sec of Pty, 1991-94; Mbr, Advrs Cncl to PM, 1991-; Comm for New Asia, Kuala Lumpur, 1993-; Vice Chair, Cncl of Mins. Hobbies: Reading; Travel. Address: Ministry of Foreign Affairs, Ton That Dan, Hanoi, Vietnam.

NGUYEN Dung Luong, b. 23 Mar 1948, Hanoi, Vietnam. Scientist; Educator. m. Huong Tra Le-Nguyen, 30 Oct 1993, 1 s. Education: Dipl Ing, 1973, Stuttgart; Dr Ing, 1981, Hannover, W Germany. Appointments: Visng Prof, HCM City Univ of Tech, 1992-; Dir, Ctr Computational Mech, 1992-. Publications: Sci books and pprs. Honour: Ring of Honour, German Soc Engrs, 1987. Memberships: NYAS, 1995-; GAMM, 1979-; German Soc Engrs, 1986-. Hobbies: Classical music; Skiing. Address: Ho-Chi-Minh City University of Technology, 268 Ly Thuong Kiet, Q10, Ho-Chi-Minh City, Vietnam.

NGUYEN Nhuy, b. 14 June 1942, Hongson, Ha Tiuls, Vietnam. Scientific Researcher; Editor. m. Nguyen Thi Nhi, 1 s. Education: BA, Hanoi Univ, 1966; PhD, USSR Acad Inst, 1983; Prof, 1996. Appointments: Dpty Dir, Linguistics Inst, 1985; Dpty Dir, Educ Publng House, 1994; Dpty Dir, Ed-in-Chf, Educ Publng House, 1996-. Publications: Researching on Chinese original and French original terms in Vietnamese language, 1983; Language Policy: The Policy for Ethnic Languages in Vietnam; Dictionary of Vietnamese Idioms, 1992; Vietnamese Great Dictionary, 1998. Memberships: Linguistics Assn; Vietnamese Folklore Assn; Chmn, Assn of Tchng Vietnamese Lang; Dpty Dir, Rschng Cntr for Self-educ. Hobbies: Writing books; Poems; Researching; Listening to classical music. Address: Trich Sai Village, Buoi Quarter, Tay Ho District, Hanoi, Vietnam.

NGUYEN Thi Binh, b. 1927, Vietnam. Politician. Education: Saigon. Appointments: Organizer, Anti-Am Demonstration, 1950; Imprisoned, French Authys, 1951-54; VP, S Vietnamese Cttee for Solidarity w the Am People; VP, Union of Women for the Liberation of S Vietnam; Mbr, Ctrl Cttee, Natl Liberation Front (NLF); NLF Spokesman, Paris, 1968; Min of Fgn Affairs, Prov Revolutionary Govt of S Vietnam, 1969-76, in Saigon, 1975-76; Min of Educn, Socialist Repub of Vietnam, 1976-87; VP, Vietnamese Womens Union, Hanoi, 1976-; VP of Vietnam, 1992-93; VP, OSPAA. Address: Ministry of Education, 21 Le Thanh Tong, Hanoi, Vietnam.

NI Chang-I Johnny, b. 17 Dec 1941, Kuang-Si, China. Civil Service. m. Yvonne, 20 Aug 1966, 1 d. Education: MBA, Stanford Univ, USA. Memberships: Pres, Stanford Alumni Assn; Pres, Taiwan MBA Assn. Hobbies: Golf; Singing; Socialising. Address: 3F, 95 Roosevelt Road, Sec 2, Taipei, Taiwan.

NI Xiusheng, b. 11 Nov 1935, Haiyan County, Zhejiang, China. Teacher. m. Qiu Weihua, 6 Aug 1970, 1 d. Education: Undergrad, bachelor degree, grad from Biol Dept, Hanzhou Univ. Appointments: Vice-Dir, Dept of Histology & Embryology, Zhejiang Medl Univ, 1992-94; Dir, 1994-97. Publications: Tchng book of hist and embryology for undergrads, 1991-95; 5 theses on Immunohistochemistry, 1995-96. Memberships: China Anatomical Assn; China Genetic Assn. Hobbies: Listening to news and music. Address: 265 Hai Er Xiang #203, Hangzhou 310006, China.

NI Yongnian, b. 1 Nov 1945, Wuxi, Jiangsu, China. Educator; Teacher. m. Fuji Ma, 5 Jan 1975, 2 d. Education: BS, 1969, MS, 1982, E China Univ of Sci and Technol. Appointments: Lectr, Jiangxi Univ, China, 1984; Nom to Assoc Prof, Jiangxi Univ, China, 1995; Nom to Prof, Nanchang Univ, China. Publications: Principles of Chemometrics, 1995; Electroanalytical Chemistry, 1995; 80 pprs in jrnls. Memberships: Chinese Chemical Society; Chinese Metal Society. Hobbies: Swimming; Painting; Stamp collecting. Address: Department of Chemistry, Nanchang University, Nanchang, Jiangxi 330047, China.

NI Yun Ling, b. 17 Feb 1928, Shanghai, China. Engineer; General Manager. m. Anna Pu, 4 Feb 1954, 2 s. Education: Acad Deg, Shanghai, 1948. Appointments: Techn, Shanghai Textile Mill No 15, Wool Dept, 1948-54;

Chf of Workshop, Shanghai Wool Textile Mill No 3; Hd of Divsn, Engr, Shanghai E China Textile Admin Bur, Tech Dept, Wool, Jute and Silk Div, 1954-55; Hd of Div, Engr, 1956-60, Dpty Mngr, Chf Engr, Gen Mngr, 1960-90, Shanghai Wool and Jute Textile Ind Corp; Vice Chf Engr, Shanghai Textile Ind Bur, 1979-96; Snr Engr, Vice-Chmn of Bd, Xinjiang Jinta Wootex Co Ltd, 1991-. Publications: Handbook of Wool Spinning, Weaving, Dyeing and Finishing, 2 vols; A Techincal Digest of the Foreign Wool Industry; A Series of Forums on Research of Wool Technical Processing. Hobbies: Reading; Music. Address: Hwa Yun Road 89 Apt 3-203, Shanghai 200083, China.

NI Zhengmao, b. 19 June 1940, Pirgyang, Zhejiang, China. Professor. m. Lin Gu, 9 Dec 1962, 1 s, 1 d. Education: BA, Dept of Law, Fudan Univ, 1957-61. Appointments: Vice Chmn, Polit & Legal Cttee, Ctrl Cttee of Jiusan Soc; Lawyer, Shanghai United Law Off. Publications: Research of Law in Sui Dynasty, 1987; Philosophy of Right-Longitude and Latitude, 1996; The Principle of Science and Technology Law, 1998. Honours: Shanghai Municipal Expert w Outstndng Contbrn, 1988; Nominated, Book Awd of China, 1997. Memberships: Dir, Hist of Law Cncl of China, Sci & Technol Law Cncl of China. Hobby: Table Tennis. Address: 77-18-507 Zichang Road, Shanghai 200065, China.

NI Zhifu, b. 1933, Chuansha, Shanghai, China. Party Official. Appointments: Errand Boy, Japanese Oil Co, 1944; Apprentice, Shanghai Printing Machine Factory, 1948; Trades Union Mbr, 1950; Mech, Yongding Machine Tool Factory, 1953; Joined CCP, 1958; Engr, 1962; Mbr, 9th Ctrl Cttee, CCP, 1969; Chair, Municipal Trade Union Cncl, Beijing, 1973; 2nd Sec, CCP Cttee, Beijing, 1973-76; Alt Mbr, Politburo, 10th Ctrl Cttee, CCP, 1973; Vice Chair, Municipal Revolutionary Cttee, Beijing, 1974-78; 2nd Sec, CCP Cttee, Shanghai, 1976-78; 1st Vice Chair, Municipal Revolutionary Cttee, Shanghai, 1976-78; Mbr, Politburo, 11th Ctrl Cttee, CCP, 1977; 2nd Sec, CCP Cttee, Beijing, 1977; Dpty for Beijing, 5th NPC, 1978; Pres, All-China Fedn of Trade Unions, 1978-90; Mbr, Politburo 12th CCP Ctrl Cttee, 1982-87; Sec, Tianjin Municipal Cttee of CCP, 1984-87; Mbr, Presidium, 6th NPC, 1986; Mbr, 13th CCP Ctrl Cttee, 1987-92, 14th CCP Ctrl Cttee, 1992-97, 15th CCP Ctrl Cttee, 1997-; Dpty for Shandong to 7th NPC; Vice Chair, 7th NPC Standing Cttee, 1988-92; Vice Chair, Standing Cttee, 8th NPC, 1993-. Memberships include: Advsr, Chinese Assn for Promotion of Population Culture, 1993-. Address: 10 Fuxingmenwai Street, Beijing, China.

NICHOLLS Dale William Pollard, b. 23 Mar 1950, Hancock, MI, USA. Lawyer. m. Linda Bardo, 16 Nov 1979, 2 s, 1 d. Education: BA, Yale Univ; LLB, Univ Melbourne; MBA, Harv Univ; JD, Univ MI. Appointments: Repub Cnslt, US House of Reps Subcttee on Mines and Mining, 1975-77; Asst to the Pres, AMAX Copper Inc, 1979-81; Arthur Robinson and Hedderwicks Assoc, 1982-87; Ptnr, 1988-. Memberships: Intl Trade and Bus Cttee, Law Cncl of Aust, 1990-; Section on Energy and Natural Resources Law, Intl Bar Assn, 1991-; Vic Cttee Mbr, Austl Mining and Petroleum Law Assn, 1997-. Hobbies: Skiing; Reading. Address: c/o Arthur Robinson & Hedderwicks, 530 Collins Street, Melbourne, Vic 3000, Australia.

NICHOLLS Frank Gordon, b. 1 Jan 1916, Melbourne, Aust. Scientist. m. Yvonne Isabel Miles, 20 Feb 1940. Education: BSc, 1936, MSc, 1938, Melbourne Univ. Appointments: Radio Rsch C'wlth Cncl for Sci and Indl Rsch, 1936-40; Offr-i/c, Austl and NZ Sci Liaison Off, London, 1941-44; Asst Sec, Rsch Sec, C'wlth Sci and Indl Rsch Org, 1945-70; UN Chf Advsr, Applied Sci Rsch, Spec Gov, Applied Sci Rsch Corp, Thailand, 1960-70; Dpty Dir Gen, Intl Union for Conservation of Nature and Natural Resources, Morges, Switz, 1970-76; Mngng Dir, Trans Knowledge Assocs Pty Ltd, Melbourne, 1977-. Publications: Sci pprs. Honour: Cmmndr, Most Noble Order of Crown of Thailand. Memberships include: Fell, Illuminating Engrng Socs of Aust; Roy Austl Chem Inst; Austl Inst of Phys; Intl Pub Rels Assn. Hobbies: Music; Reading; Computer Programming. Address: 61/4 Sydney Street, Prahran, Vic 3181, Australia.

NICHOLLS Stan(ley Linton), b. 16 June 1911, Ballarat, Vic, Aust. Champion Veteran Athlete. m. Arley Jane Rodda, 14 Feb 1942, 1 s, 1 d. Career: 5th, 1938 Brit Empire Games 3 miles Track championship, 1st Austl to finish; Vic 3 miles Track Champion, 1938; 5 miles Vic Cross Country Athletics Champion, 1939; Worlds Veteran Athletics 3000 metres steeplechase Champion (NZ) World Age Rec, 1981; World Veteran 2000 metres steeplechase Champion (Melbourne) world age rec, 1987; Holder, 32 World Veteran Age Athletic recs, 1990; Ran 26 mile marathon aged 66 in 3 hours 7 mins 48 secs world age rec, 1977; Best time in race walking, 7 miles in 59 min 49 secs aged 55, 1966; Ballarat Track and Cross Country Champion, num times; Veterans Austl Athletics Champion num times; Ballarat Athletics Timekeeper, 20 yrs; Melbourne Olympics athletics timekeeper, 1956; Brisbane C'wlth Games Athletics Offl, 1981; Mbr, 1928-, Life Mbr, 1951- Ballarat Harriers; Ballarat Deleg to Vic Athletics for over 30 yrs; Served, AIF, WWII, 1939-45; Ret'd Businessman. Honours: Life Gov, Freemasons Homes, 1971; 50 yrs Serv Awd, Vic Athletics Assn, 1978; Merit Awd, Vic Athletic Assn, 1983; Cty of Melbourne Awd, 1983; Aust Day Sports Medallion, 1984; Adv Aust Logie Awd and Plaque, 1985; Masonic 50 yrs Serv Awd, 1985; Ballarat Athletics Cntr Life Mbr, 1986; Vic Athletics Assn Life Mbr, 1988; Tattersalls Logie Awd, 1990; OAM; Life Mbr, Marathon Club. Membership: Ballarat Masonic Lodge; Mark Lodge, Ballarat. Hobby: Athletics. Address: 510 Windermere Street, Ballarat, Vic 3350, Australia.

NICHOLLS William Anthony (Tony), b. 17 May 1944, Brisbane, Australia. Veterinarian. m. Lorraine, 16 May 1969, 4 s. Education: BVSc, 1972; QDA, 1962. Appointments: Dir, Morningside Vet Clinic, 1977; Dir, Provet Ltd, 1982; Dir, Pacific Meridiam, 1999. Membership: AVA. Hobbies: Golf; Rugby; Theatre. Address: 560 Wynnum Road, Morningside, Brisbane, Australia.

NICHOLSON Jack, b. 22 Apr 1937, Neptune, New Jersey, USA. Actor; Film Maker. m. Sandra Knight, 1961, div 1966, 1 d. Creative Works: Films incl: Cry-Baby Killer, 1958; Studs Lonigan, 1960; The Shooting; Ride the Whirlwind; Hell's Angels on Wheels, 1967; The Trip, 1967; Head, 1968; Psych-Out, 1968; Easy Rider, 1969; On a Clear Day You Can See Forever, 1970; Five Easy Pieces, 1971; Drive, 1971; He Said, 1971; Carnal Knowledge, 1971; The King of Marvin Gardens, 1972; The Last Detail, 1973; Chinatown, 1974; The Passenger, 1974; Tommy, 1974; The Fortune, 1975; The Missouri Breaks, 1975; One Flew Over the Cuckoo's Nest, 1975; The Last Tycoon, 1976; Goin' South, 1978; The Shining, 1980; The Postman Always Rings Twice, 1981; Reds, 1981; The Border, 1982; Terms of Endearment, 1984; Prizzi's Honor, 1984; Heartburn, 1985; The Witches of Eastwick, 1986; Ironweed, 1987; Batman, 1989; The Two Jakes, 1989; Man Trouble, A Few Good Men, 1992; Hoffa, 1993; Wolf, 1994; The Crossing Guard, 1995; Mars Attacks!, 1996; The Evening Star, 1996; Blood and Wine, 1996; As Good As It Gets, 1997. Honours include: Acady Awd, Best Supporting Actor, 1969; Acady Awd, Best Actor, 1976. Address: Bresler Kelly Kipperman, 15760 Ventura Boulevard, Suite 1730, Encino, CA 91436, USA.

NICHOLSON Robert David, b. 7 Aug 1937, Perth, West Aust. Judge of the Federal Court of Australia. m. Lynette Trumble, 27 Dec 1967, 1 s, 2 d. Education: BA, 1959, LLB, 1961, Univ of West Aust; MA, Georgetown Univ, Wash DC, 1963; LLM, Univ of Melbourne, 1981. Appointments: Ptnr, Freehill Hollingdale & Page (Perth), 1964-75, 1981-86; Sec-Gen, Law Cncl of Aust, 1975-80; Dpty Pres, Austl Admnstv Appeals Tribunal, 1986-88; Inaugural Chairperson, Guardianship & Admin Bd, West Aust, 1992-94; Judge, Supreme Crt of West Aust, 1988-94; Judge, Fedl Crt of Aust, 1995-. Publications: Var articles in Austl legal periodicals). Honours: Hon Life Assoc, Guild of Undergrads, UWA, 1960; Pi Sigma Alpha Hon Soc, 1962; Rotary Fndn Grad Fellshp and Fulbright Travel Grant, 1961-62; Fulbright Snr Schls Awd, 1992; 1st Visng For Judicial Fell, US Fedl Judicial Cntr, Wash DC, USA, 1992; Visng Fell, Corpus Christi Coll, Cambridge, 1997; Advsry Bd, Jrnl of Law & Med, 1998-. Memberships include: West Austl Hist Fndn (Chair), 1991-; WA Fulbright Select Cttee (Chair), 1994-97; Malcolm Sargent Cancer Fund for Children, WA (Chair); LAWASIA Judicial Sect (Sec); Austl Fulbright Assn, Natl Pres, 1994-; Trustee, Francis Burt Law Educ Cntr; LAWASIA, Mbr, Govr, Rsch Inst, 1995-; Edith Cowan Univ, Chan, 1996-. Hobbies: Music; History; Tennis; Swimming. Address: Federal Court of Australia, 1 Victoria Avenue, Perth, Western Australia 6000.

NICKS Stevie (Stephanie Nicks), b. 26 May 1948, California, USA. Singer; Songwriter. Appointments: Songwriter w Lindsey Buckingham; Recorded Album, Buckingham Nicks, 1973; Joined Grp, Fleetwood Mac, 1973. Creative Works: Albums w Fleetwood Mac: Fleetwood Mac, 1975; Rumours, 1977; Tusk, 1979; Fleetwood Mac Live, 1980; Mirage, 1982; Tango in the Night, 1987; Behind the Mask, 1990; 25 Years - The Chain, 1992. Solo Albums: Bella Donna, 1981; The Wild Heart, 1983; Rock a Little, 1985; Time Space, 1991; Street Angel, 1994. Composer: Rhiannon; Landslide; Leather and Lace; Dreams; Sara; Edge of Seventeen; If Anyone Falls; Stand Back; I Can't Wait; The Other Side of the Mirror; Time Space; Street Angel; Seven Wonders. Address: Modern Records, c/o WEA, 111 North Hollywood Way, Burbank, CA 91505, USA.

NICKSON Noel John, b. 5 Jan 1919, Melbourne, Vic, Aust. Emeritus Professor of Music. m. Margaret Graham Wortley, 19 June 1948, 1 s, 1 d. Education: BMus, 1st class hons, Univ of Melbourne, 1938; ARCM, Violin Perform, Roy Coll of Music, London, Eng, 1940; BMus, 1948, DMus, 1949, Trinity Coll, Dublin, Ireland. Appointments: Austl Mil Forces, Army Educ Serv, Warrant Offr I, 1942; Organist, Christchurch Cathedral, Newcastle, NSW, 1950; Lectr, Examiner, Conductor, Sydney Conservatorium, 1951; Snr Lectr of Music, Univ Melb, 1959; Fndn Prof, 1966-84, Hd of Dept, 1966-76, Fndn Dean of Fac, 1967-74, currently Emer Prof, Hon Rsch Cnslt, Univ Qld, St Lucia. Creative Works: Prin publns in Music from the Tang Court, vols 2-6, 1981-97; Miscellanea Musicologica, Adelaide; Austl Jrnl of Music Educ; Compositions inclng: Piano Sonatina; Sonata for Violin and Viola. Honours: Hon Life Mbr, Austl Soc for Music Educ, 1974; Hon Fell, Roy Coll of Music, 1977; Visng Grants: The Brit Cncl, 1970, 1975; Japan Fndn, 1970, 1975; Min of For Affairs, France, 1970, 1975; Inst of Culture, Hungary, 1977; Qld China Cncl, 1990. Memberships include: Past Mbr: Austl Music Exams Bd; Advsry Cttee, Qld Conservatorium of Music; ABC Fed Advsry Cttee; UNESCO Natl Advsry Cttee; Austl Inst of Aboriginal Studies. Hobbies: Reading; Writing; Walking; Listening. Address: School of Music, University of Queensland, St Lucia, Qld 4072, Australia.

NIELSEN Ron, b. 1 Nov 1932, Poland. Nuclear Scientist. m. Lorna, 2 Sept 1982, 1 s, 1 d. Education: MSc; DSc. Appointments: Rsch Fell, Inst of Nuclear Rsch, Poland, 1956-63; Rsch Fell, Dept of Nuclear Phys, Austl Natl Univ, Aust, 1964-67; Fell, Dept of Nuclear Phys, Austl Natl Univ, Aust, 1967-89; Visng Fell, Dept of Phys, Birmingham Univ, Eng, 1970-71; Visng Prof, Eidgenessische Technische Hochschule, Zürich, Switz, 1975-76; Visng Prof, Max-Planck-Inst für Kernphysik, Heidelberg, Germany, 1983-84. Publications: Num in profl jrnls. Honour: Peaceful Use of Atomic Energy Awd, 1959. Memberships: Fell, Austl Inst of Phys; Active Mbr, NY Acady of Scis; AAAS. Hobbies: Human Physiology; Medicine; Biology; Cosmology; Particle Physics. Address: 4 Murdoch Place, University Shores, Robina, Qd 4226, Australia.

NIGAM Shyam Behari Lal, b. 7 Apr 1924, India. Manpower and Employment Consultant. m. Prem Kumari, 2 s. Education: MA Econs, MCom, PhD, London Sch of Econs, Eng. Appointments: Lectr, Econs, Univ of Agra, India, 1945-47; Univ of Lucknow, 1950; Hd Econs Dept, Univ of Sagar, 1951; Asst Ins Commnr, Employees State Ins Corp, 1952-54; Asst/Dpty Econ and Stat Advsr, Min of Food and Agric, 1954-57; Joint Dir, Indian Econ Serv,

1958-63; Dir, Indian Econ Serv, 1964-72; ILO Manpower Planning Advsr to Govt of Somalia, 1963-69; ILO Reg Manpower Advsr, Addis Ababa, Ethiopia, 1969-72; First Mbr, Employment Team, ILO, 1973; Dpty Chief, Jobs and Skills Prog for Afr, 1974-77; Chf of Prog, 1978-84; Vising Fell, Inst of Dev Stdies, Univ of Sussex; also held a number of pub appts inclng, Sec, Govt of India, Working Grp on Unemployment Ins; Mbr-Sec, Jute Enquiry Cttee; Ldr and Mbr of sev inter-agency and intdisciplinary ILO/UNDP employment and Basic Needs Miss in Kenya, Tanzania, Somalia, Sudan, Lesotho, Nigeria, Togo, Sierra Leone, Zambia, Swaziland, 1972-84; Guest Lectr at Govt of India's Inst for Applied Manpower Rsch, New Delhi, 1985-; ILO Cnslt in Malaysia and Indonesia; Cnslt, UNDP NY, 1987, Nigeria, 1988-89, Uganda, 1989, Namibia, 1989; Ldr of UNDP/ILO Core Grp on Human Resource Dev in Malaysia, 1990, and of a similiar Asian Dev; Bank Mission in Sabah and Sarawak, 1990-91; Mbr UNDP/ILO Employment Miss to Papua New Guinea, 1991; Snr ILO Manpower Cnslt to Govt of Bhutan and Myanmar, 1992-93. Publications include: Employment and Income Distribution Approach in African Development Plans, 1975; The Manpower Situation in Somalia, 1995; Sev, pprs, articles and contbns to Encyclopaedia Britannica. Honour: A vol of essays, The Challenge of Employment and Basic Needs in Africa, issued by ILO in his hon, 1986. Memberships include: Pres, Indian Assn, Addis Ababa. Address: K-118 Hauz Khas Enclave, New Delhi 110016, India.

NIJS Eugenie (Jenny) Maria de, b. Vienna, Austria. Lecturer in Design. m. Max Pierre de Nijs, 23 Jan 1951, 2 d. Education: Studies w Prof Cizek, Sch of Applied Art and Fashion Acady Kalous, Vienna; Dress Design and Coml Art Media, Melbourne Tech Coll and Emily McPherson Coll, Aust, 1939-42. Appointments: Display and Advtng Exec, Myer Emporium, Melbourne, 1942-57; Lectr in Illustration and Design, Roy Melbourne Inst of Technol, 1962-88; Dir, Childrens Art Classes, Roy Melbourne Inst of Technol and Vic Artists Soc, 1962-72; Lectr, RMIT Univ, 1988-92; Guest Lectr, Natl Gall of Vic, 1989, 1990; Co-ord, Lectr, Decision by Des, RMIT Univ, 1992-99; German brdcst inverviews. Publications: Pprs presented/publ: INSEA, NY, 1969, num, Aust, 1971-79, Baden, Aust, 1980, Forum Resume, Rotterdam, Netherlands and Melbourne, 1981; Research and Development Memorandum: History of Fashion, 1978-79; The History of Design and Art in Education, 1980; Women as Designers in Australia, 1987. Memberships: Des Inst of Aust, Sec/Treas, Cncl Mbr, Vic Chapt, 1983-88; INSEA, Vic State Rep ASEA, 1971-81. Hobbies: Drawing; Fashion History Research; Community Work; Girl Guides; Brotherhood of St Laurence. Address: 21 King Street, Balwyn, Vic 3103, Australia.

NIMMANAHAEMINDA Tarrin, b. 29 Oct 1945, Chiengmai, Thailand. Minister of Finance. m. Education: MBA, Fin, Stanford Univ, USA; BA, Hons, Govt, Harv Univ, USA. Appointments: Pres, CEO, Siam Coml Bank Ltd, 1984-95; Min of Fin, 1992-95; Mbr of Parl, Bangkok Metrop, 1996; Min of Fin, 1997. Honour: Kt Cmndr, 2nd Class, Most Illustrious Order of Chula Chom Klao. Address: Ministry of Finance, Rama VI Road, Bangkok 10400, Thailand.

NIND Leigh Shirley, b. 1970. Education: BVSc (Hons); PhD. Appointments: Vet Cnslt, Univ of Queensland, 1993; In-country Virologist & Supvsr, Vietnam, Austl Cntr for Intl Agric Rsch, 1996; Snr Prod Evaluator, Natl Registration Authority, 1999. Honours: PRDC, Undergrad Encouragement Awd; PRDC, Postgrad Schlshp. Memberships: AVA; AAPV; AAV. Hobbies: Badminton; Squash; Travel; Art. Address: C/o NRA, PO Box E240, Kingston, ACT 2604, Australia.

NING Chunde, b. 14 Apr 1947, Tianjin, China. Dentist. m. Ruxiu Zhao, 8 Jan 1971, 1 d. Education: Trng Coll. Appointments: Res Dentist, 1980; Attending Dentist, 1988. Publications: 2 natl patents; 31 medl theses. Honours: Ex Inv Awd of Jianjin, 1995; Gold Awd, First Intl Einstein New Invs Awd Technols, 1997; United Gold Awd of New Invs and Techs of Am Addison Invention Ctr and Canad Intl Exhibn Ctr. Membership: Chinese Medl Assn.

Hobby: Table tennis. Address: Stomatology Dept, Tianjin Port Hospital, Xingang, Tanggu, Tianjin, China 300456.

NING Sao, b. 8 May 1943. Teacher. m. Zhou Lei, 1 May 1971, 1 s, 1 d. Education: BA, Polit Sci, Peking Univ, 1969. Asst Lectr, 1969-83, Lectr, 1983-85, Assoc Prof, 1985-90, Dept of Intl Polit, Peking Univ; Assoc Prof, 1990-91, Prof, 1991-, Dept of Polit Sci, Peking Univ; Chmn, Dept of Polit Sci, Peking Univ, 1994-97; Dir Inst for Pub Policy Stdies, Beijing Univ, 1998-. Publications: Ethnicities and States: A Comparative Study for Ethnic Relations and Ethnic Policies Among Contemporary Nations, 1995; African Black Culture, 1995. Honours: Prize, Outstndng Achievement Awd, State Cncl of China, 1992; Prize, 1st Natl Educ Cncl of China Wrks Awd, 1995. Memberships: Exec Cncl, Natl Polit Sci Assn of China; Vice-Chmn, Natl Assn for Global Ethnic Stdies of China; Vice-Chmn, Natl Assn for African Hist Stdies. Hobbies: Reading; Travel. Address: Department of Political Science & Public Administration, Peking University, Beijing 100871, China.

NISHIGAKI Akira, b. 30 Oct 1929. President, Chairman of the Board, Overseas Economic Cooperation Fund. Education: Fac of Law, Univ of Tokyo, 1953. Appointments: Joined the Min of Fin, 1953; Dpty Dir Gen Budget Bur, MOF, 1979-82; Dpty Vice Min, Econ Planning Agcy, 1982-83; Dir Gen, Fin Bur, MOF, 1983-84; Dpty Vice Min for Fin, 1984-86; Dir Gen, Budget Bur, MOF, 1986-88; Vice Min for Fin, 1988-89; Pres, Chmn of the Bd, Overseas Econ Coop Fund, 1990-. Publications: Kaihatsu Enjo No Keizaigaku; Yuhikaku, 1993. Hobby: Golf. Address: 4-19-13 Daizawa, Setagaya-ku, Tokyo, Japan.

NISHIHARA Masashi, b. 4 Aug 1937, Osaka, Japan. Scholar. m. Suzuko Osawa, 21 Dec 1968, 2 d. Education: MA, PhD, Polit Sci. Appointments: Assoc Prof, Prof, Kyoto Sangyo Univ, 1973-77; Prof, Natl Def Acady, 1977-; Dir, 1st Rsch Dept, Natl Inst for Def Studies, 1993-97. Publications: The Japanese and Sukarno's Indonesia, 1976; The Japan-US Alliance, 1998. Honour: Fulbright Schlshp, 1959-60. Membership: Cncl, Intl Inst for Strategic Stdies, 1986-95. Hobbies: Reading; Sailing. Address: 3-16-11 Shonan Takatori, Yokosuka-shi 237-0066, Japan.

NISHIYAMA Misuzu, 15 Dec 1951, Sapporo, Japan. Anethesiologist. m. Hiroaki Nishiyama, 2 July 1978, 1 d. Education: Grad, Hokkaido Univ, Sapporo, Japan, 1976. Publication: Anesthesiology Resident Manual, 1994. Address: 1009 2-18-1 Kachidoki Chuo-ku, Tokyo 104-0054, Japan.

NITISH KUMAR, b. 1 Mar 1951, Bakhtiarpur, Patna Dist, Bihar, India. Member of Parliament. m. Manju Kumari Sinha, 22 Feb 1973, 1 s. Education: BSc, Engrng, Bihar Coll of Engrng, Patna. Appointments: Mbr, Bihar Legislative Assembly, 1985-89; Mbr, Cttee on Petitions, Bihar Legislative Assembly, 1986-87; Pres, Yuva Lok Dal, Bihar, 1987-88; Mbr, Cttee on Pub Undertakings, Bihar Legislative Assembly, 1987-89; Sec-Gen, Janata Dal, 1989, Gen Sec, 1991-93; Elected, 9th Lok Sabha, 1989; Mbr, House Cttee, 1989-90; Union Min of Stte, Agric and Cooperation, 1990; Re-elected, 10th Lok Sabha, 1991; Re-elected, 11th Lok Sabha, 1996; Mbr, Cttee of Dec, 1996-97, 1997-98; Re-elected, 12th Lok Sabha, 1998; Union Cabinet Min, Railways, 1998-. Memberships: Fndr-Mbr, Samata Pty; Activist and Mbr, Steering Cttee, J P Movt. Address: Vill Hakikatpur, PO Bakhtiarpur, Dist Patna 800001, India.

NIU Maosheng, b. 1939, Beijing, China. Government Official. Education: Beijing Agricl Inst. Appointments: Joined CCP, 1961; Vice-Min, Water Resources, 1988-93, Min, 1993-98; Dpty Hd, Natl Gen HQ for Flood Prevention & Drought Control; Mbr, 15th CCP Ctrl Cttee, 1997-. Address: Ministry of Water Resources, 1 Baiguang Lu, Ertiao, Xuanwu Qu, Beijing 100761, China.

NIWANE Joseline, b. 3 Apr 1964, Baguio Cty. Social Worker. Education: BSc Socl Wrk. Appointments: Community Dev Worker; Socl Worker; Socl Welfare

Supvsr; Socl Welfare Prog Analyst; Provcl Socl Welfare & Dev Offr. Honours: Cert of Merit, 1996; Dangal ng Byan Awd, Pride of the Country Awd, 1997. Membership: PASWI, Philppne Assn of Socl Workers Inc. Hobbies: Reading; Watching; Films; Hiking. Address: Provinicial Social Welfare & Development Office, Provincial Capital, Lagawe, Ifugao.

NIXON Helena June Rose, b. 20 May 1942. Organist; Composer. m. 14 May 1966. Education: Bmus Org; Dip Mus (Piano); FRCO (CHM); ARCM. Apointments: Dir of Music, St Paul's Cath, Melbourne, 1973; Tchng Staff, Melbourne Univ. Honours: 1st Prize, Austl Natl Organ Comp, 1968; Nickson and Bentwich Schl, Melbourne Univ, 1970; Percy Jones Awd, Cath Archdiocese of Melbourne, 1995; AM, 1998; D Mus (Cantuar), 1999. Address: 115 Canterbury Road, Middle Park, Vic 3206, Australia.

NIYAZOV Saparmurad, b. 19 Feb 1940, Ashkhabad, Turkmenistan. Politician. m. Muza Alexeevna, 1 s, 1 d. Education: Leningrad Polytech Inst. Appointments: Instr, Trade Union Org of Mineral Prospecting Works, Turkmenistan, 1959-67; Mbr, CPSU, 1962-91; Instr, Dpty Hd, Ctrl Cttee, Turkmen CP, 1970-79; Hd of Section, 1st Sec, Ashkhabad City Cttee, Turkmen CP, 1979-84; Pty Work, Ctrl Cttee, CPSU, 1984-85; Mbr, Ctrl Cttee, CPSU, 1986-91; Mbr, CPSU Politburo, 1990-91; Pres, Cncl of Mins, Turkmen SSR, 1985; 1st Sec, Ctrl Cttee, Cp, Turkmen SSR, 1985-91; Chair, Turkmen Supreme Soviet, 1990; Pres of Turkmenistan, 1991-; PM, 1991-; Chair, Democratic Party of Turkmenistan, 1991. Honours: Mukhtumikuli Prize, 1992; Title, Turkmenbashi (Father of Turkmen People), 1993. Membership: Pres, Humanitarian Assn of Turkmen People of the World. Address: Office of the President, Karl Marx Str 24, 744017 Ashgabat, Turkmenistan.

NO Soo Young, b. 27 June 1955, Korea. Professor. m. Yong Sook Suh, 18 Dec 1982, 2 d. Education: PhD, Divsn of Mech Engrng and Energy Studies, Univ of Wales, Cardiff, 1990. Appointments: Asst Prof, 1984-90, Assoc Prof, 1990-95, Prof, 1995-. Publications: 3 books, 35 pprs. Memberships: KSME; KSAE; Combustion Inst; Japan Energy Soc; KSAM; KSEE; ILASS-Korea; ILASS-Japan. Hobby: Cycling. Address: c/o Department of Agricultural Machinery Engineering, Chungbuk National University, Cheongju 361-763, Korea.

NOBLE James Chattan, b. 26 Nov 1937, Sydney, Australia. Rangeland Ecologist. m. Glennis, 22 Aug 1968, 3 s, 1 d. Education: HDA, 1958, BA, 1972, LittB, 1974, Univ NE; PhD, Univ Wales, 1976; Grad Dip, Mngmt, Univ Cntrl Qld, 1984. Appointments: Agronomist, NSW Dept of Agricl, 1958-64; Rsch Sci, CSIRO Deniliquin, 1964-89; CSIRO Wildlife and Ecol, Canberra, 1990-2000. Publications: Plants for Sheep in Australia, 1972; Mediterranean Landscapes in Australia, 1989; The Mallee Lands, 1990; Landscape Ecology, Function and Management, 1997; The Delicate and Noxious Scrub, 1997. Address: 30 Norman Place, Deakin, ACT 2600, Australia.

NOERPER Stephen Eric, b. 8 Dec 1965, USA. Professor of International Relations. m. Debi, 21 Oct 1989. Education: PhD, Fletcher Sch of Law & Diplomacy; MALD, Fletcher Sch; MSc, Econs, London Sch of Econs. Appointments: Assoc Prof, Intl Rels, Asia-Pacific Cntr, 1997; Asst Prof, 1996. Publications: Regime Security and Military, Tension in North Korea; Understanding Regime Dyamics in North Korea, 1998; The Tiger's Leap, 1996. Honours: Asia-Pacific Cntr Serv Awds, 1997, 1998. Memberships: Assn of Asian Studies; Amn Pol Sci Assn; Korea Soc. Hobbies: Jazz; Wine; Art; Philanthropy. Address: Asia-Pacific Center, 2255 Kuhio Avenue, Suite 1800, Honolulu, HI 96815, USA.

NOICHAIBOON Kietphong, b. 20 Jan 1949, Bangkok, Thailand. Chairman; Chief Executive Officer. m. Timaporn Aranyakanond, 10 Aug 1974, 2 d. Education: Natl Def Coll; BEng, Kasetsart Univ. Appointments: Plant Mngr, Siriwiwat Transformer; Mngng Dir, CEO, Ekarat Engrng Pub Co Ltd. Honour: Outstndng Alumni Awd,

Kasetsart Univ, 1993. Memberships: Exec Cttee, Fedn of Thai Inds, 1996-98; Elec Grp, 1996-98; Vice Chmn, Fedn of Thai Inds. Hobbies: Badminton; Reading; Sports; Golf. Address: 1875/239 Charansanidwong 75, Bangplad, Bangkok 10250, Thailand.

NOLCH Guy Rodney, b. 12 Aug 1987, Melbourne, Aust. Publishing. m. Jennifer. Education: BS (Hons), Univ of Melbourne; Assoc Dip of Arts (Profl Writing and Editing), Roy Melbourne Inst of Technol. Appointments: Prodn Ed, Blackwell Sci, 1991-92; Ed, Search: Sci & Technol in Aust & NZ, 1992-98; Ed, Austl Sci, 1998. Honour: Young Achiever Awds, Sci & Technol Category, 1993. Memberships: Austl & NZ Assn for Adv of Sci, 1992-; Cttee Mbr, Victorian Div, 1993-98; Austl Sci Communicator, 1994-. Hobbies: Media; Current affairs; Science; Football; Tennis. Address: PO Box 6122, Doncaster MDC, Vic 3108, Australia.

NOLLER Patricia (Tate), b. 13 Mar 1938. Psychologist; Academic. m. Charles Geoffrey Noller, 14 May 1960, 1 s, 3 d. Education: Tchr's Cert, Sydney Tchr's Coll, 1957; BA (Hons I), 1976; PhD, 1981. Appointments: Crown St Infants' Sch, Aust St Nursery Sch, W Como Infants' Sch; Woolwich Infants Sch; Lectr, Snr Lectr, Rdr, Prof, Dept of Psychol, Dir, Family Cntr, 1996-, Univ of Qld; Ed, Personal Relationships, Jrnl of Intl Soc for the Sty of Personal Rels, 1993-98. Publications: 9 books on Psychology, Family Relationships, family Communication; Over 70 articles and book chapts in acad jrnls. Honours: Austl Postgrad Rsch Awd, 1977-79; Early Career Awd, Austl Psychol Soc, 1985; Fell, Acad of The Socl Scis in Aust, 1994-; Fell, Natl Cncl on Family Rels (USA), 1998. Memberships: Intl Soc for the Study of Personal Relationships, pres-elect, 1996; Intl Commn Assn; Austl Psychol Soc; Soc for Experimental Socl Psychol; Soc of Austl Socl Psychologists. Hobbies: Reading; Walking. Address: 34 Middle Street, West End, Qld 4101, Australia.

NOLTE Nick, b. 1942, Omaha, USA. Actor. m. Rebecca Linger, 1984, div 1995, 1 s. Education: Pasadena City Coll; Phoenix City Coll. Creative Works: Stage Appearances, The Last Pad, 1973; TV Films, 1974-75; Drama Series, Rich Man, Poor Man, 1976. Films: Return to Macon County, 1975; The Deep, 1977; Who'll Stop the Rain, 1978; North Dallas Forty, 1979; Heartbeat, 1980; Cannery Row, 1982; 48 Hours, 1982; Under Fire, 1983; The Ultimate Solution of Grace Quigley, 1984; Teachers, 1984; Down and Outin Beverly Hills, 1986; Weeds, 1987; Extreme Prejudice, 1987; Farewell to the King, 1989; New York Stories, 1989; Three Fugitives, 1990; Everybody Wins, 1990; Q & A, 1990; Prince of Tides, 1990; Cape Fear, 1991; Lorenzo's Oil, 1992; Blue Chips, 1994; I'll Do Anything, 1994; Love Trouble, 1994; Jefferson in Paris, 1994; Mulholland Falls, 1996; Mother Night, 1996; Afterglow Affliction; U-Turn. Address: 6153 Bonsall Drive, Malibu, CA 90265, USA.

NOMURA Junji, b. 10 Apr 1947, Kagawa Prefecture, Japan. Director. m. Mie, 14 Oct 1973, 3 s, 1 d. Education: DEng, Kyoto Univ; BS, Dept of Electrons, Kyoto Univ. Appointments: Dir, Operating Offr of Elecl Cnstrn Materials Co, Matsushita Elec Wrks Ltd. Publications: Virtual Housing, 1996; Virtual Reality, 1997. Honours: Excellent Applications Awds of Operations Rsch Soc, 1986; Fell, Operations Rsch Soc of Japan, 1995. Memberships: Virtual Reality Soc of Japan; Operations Rsch Soc of Japan. Hobby: Golf. Address: 1-16-15 Tamdo-nishi, Nishinari-ku, Osaka, Japan.

NONAKA Hiromu, b. Japan. Politician. Appointments: Fmr Vice-Gov, Kyoto Pref; Min of Home Affairs, 1994-95; Mbr, House of Reps for Kyoto; Dir-Gen, LDP Election Bur. Address: Ministry of Home Affairs, 2-1 Kasumigaseki, Chiyoda-ku, Tokyo, Japan.

NONG Liangqin, b. 5 Aug 1946, Chongzuo, Guangxi, China. Professor. m. Shizhen Chen, 16 Jan 1974, 2 s. Education: Master Deg; Postgrad Dip. Appointments: Vice Dean, Phys Dept, Dean, Tchng Affairs Dept, Dean, Phys Dept, Guangxi Univ for Nationalities. Publications: A Part of Room Temperature Section of Phase Diagram

of Y-Cu-Ni System, 1985; X-Ray Powder Diffraction Data for Com DyNiSn, 1997. Honour: Natl Natural Sci Awd, China, 1987. Memberships: Exec Cncl, Guangxi Phys Assn of China; Metal Assn of China. Hobbies: Sports; Watching Sport Games. Address: Guangxi University for Nationalities, 74# Xixiangtang Road, nanning, Guangxi, China.

NOOR Dato Mohamad Yusof, b. 5 Feb 1941, Raja, Terangganu, Malaysia. Politician; Teacher. m. 2 children. Education: Islamic Coll, Klang, Selangor; Al Azhar Univ; Ein Shams Univ; Univ Cairo. Appointments: Second Sch Tchr, 1969-70; Insp of Second Schs, Terengganu State, 1970; Prin, Sultan Zainal Abidin Second Relig Sch, 1970; Lectr, Hd of Coll, 1974, Dean, Fac of Islamic Studies, 1975-79, Dpty Vice-Chan for Student Affairs, 1980-84, Natl Univ of Malaysia; Mbr, Senate, 1984; Dpty Min for Islamic Affairs, PM's Dept, 1984; Mbr, House of Reps, 1987-; Mbr, Supreme Cncl, United Malays Natl Org, 1987-; Min, PM's Dept, 1987; Chair, Relig Cncl for Fed Territory. Publications: Num articles in profl jrnls. Address: House of Representatives, Parliament Building, Kuala Lumpur, Malaysia.

NORLING Robin Carl, b. 1 May 1939, Windsor, NSW, Aust. Artist. 1 s, 2 d. Education: ASTC (Hons); ARCA London. Appointments: Tchr, NSW Second Schs; Lectr, Alexander Mackie Tchr Trng Coll; Cty Art Inst; Art Gall of NSW; NSW Tafe; Sydney Univ Sch of Educ; Julian Ashton's Art Sch. Publications: Young Persons Guide to Art In Australia, 1986; Australian Artists, 1989. Honours: Robert Le Gay Brereton Drawing Prize and Sulman Prize; NSW Travelling Art Schlshp; Sun Herald Cook Bicentenary; Lady Fairfax Prize. Memberships: Assoc, Roy Art Soc; Austl Watercolour Inst. Hobbies: Music; Surfing. Address: 83 Albert Drive, Killara 2071, NSW Australia.

NORMAN Gregory John, b. 10 Feb 1955, Queensland, Australia. Golfer. m. 2 s. Appointments: Turned Profl, 1976; Won Westlakes Classic, Aust, 1976; Martini Intl NSW Open, S Seas Classic, Fiji, 1978, Martini Intl Hong Kong Open, 1979, Aust Open, French Open, Scandinavian Open, 1980, Austl Masters, Martini Intl, Dunlop Masters, 1981, Dunlop Masters, State Express Classic, Benson & Hedges Intl, 1982, Austl Masters, Natl Panasonic NSW Open, Hong Kong Open, Cannes Invitational, Suntory World Match Play Championship, 1983, Can Open, Vic Open, Austl Masters, Toshiba Austl PGA Championship, 1984, Toshiba Austl PGA Championship, Natl Panasonic Austl Open, 1985, Eur Open, Brit Open, Suntory World Matchplay Championship, Panasonic-Las Vegas Invitational, Kemper Open, 1986, Austl Masters, Natl Panasonic Austl Open, 1987, Palm Meadows Cup, Aust, PGA Natl Tournament Players Championship, Aust, Pansonic NSW Open, Lancia Italian Open, 1988, Austl Masters, PGA Natl Tournament Players Championship, 1989, Austl Masters, The Meml Tournament, 1990, Cand Open, 1992, Brit Open, Taiheyo Masters, Japan, 1993, Johnnie Walker Asian Classic, The Players Championship, 1994, Austl Open, Meml Tournament, Canon Greater Hartford Open, 1995. Hobbies: Fishing; Hunting; Scuba Diving. Address: Hobe Sound, FL, USA.

NORMAN Neville Robert, b. 18 Mar 1946, Melbourne, Aust. Economist. m. Margaret Goodfellow, 8 Jan 1969, 2 s, 2 d. Education: MA (1st Hons), Econs, BCom (1st Hons), Melbourne Univ; PhD, Cantab. Appointments: Univ Classmaster in Econs Stats, 1971; Educr in Econs, 1973; Snr Lectr, 1976, Rdr, 1984, Assoc Prof, 1992, Melbourne Univ. Publications: Economics of Tour Escalation, 1986; Refusing Fiscal Reform, 1995. Honours: Full blues, athletics, University of Cambridge, Eng, 1971, 1972, 1973. Memberships: Econ Soc of Aust, 1966-; Athenaeneum Club, 1977-; Low Cncl of Aust, 1979-. Hobbies: Family history; Classical music. Address: 97 Dendy Street, Brighton, Vic 3186, Australia.

NORMAN Philip Thomas, b. 16 Oct 1953, Christchurch, NZ. Professional Composer and Musician. m. Alison Budge, 18 Dec 1982. Education: BA, MA, 1972-76; DipTch, Christchurch Tchrs Coll, 1977;

LMusTCL, 1978; PhD, Univ Canterbury, 1984. Appointments: Th Conductor, Musical Dir; Fndr, Dir, Nota Bene Music Publng Co-op, 1979-; Prin Music Critic, Christchurch Press, 1982-91; Musical Dir, Christchurch Sch of Music, 1991-95; Composer-in-Res, Christchurch Symph Orch, 1992. Creative Works: Var compositions; 6 Ballets incl Peter Pan; 13 stage musicals inclng Footrot Flats, 1983; Love Off The Shelf, 1987; Dirty Weekends, 1997; Opera: A Christmas Carol, 1993; Orchl, choral and chmbr music; Compiler of Bibliography of New Zealand Compositions, Nota Bene, Christchurch, 1980, 1982, 1991. Honours: Composers Assn Citation for Servs to NZ Music, 1989; NZ Commemoration Medal, 1990. Membership: Pres, Composers Assn of NZ, 1981-82, 1986-87. Address: 14 Bishop Street, Christchurch 1, New Zealand.

NORMAN Robert John, b. 19 June 1949, Woking, Eng. Medical Specialist. m. Susan, 24 June 1972, 2 s, 1 d. Education: BSc, Hons; MBChB, Hons; FRACOG; FRCOG; FRCPA; FRCPath; MD; CREI. Appointments: Intern, Harare Hosp; Reg, Harare Hosp; Assoc Prof, Natal; Prof and Hd, Reproductive Med, Univ of Adelaide. Publications: Over 150 in profl jrnls. Memberships: Endocrine Soc of Aust; Fertility Soc of Aust; Austl Soc of Reproductive Biol, cttee mbr; Austl Menopause Soc, sec. Hobbies: Sport; Art; Politics; Christianity. Address: c/o Department of Obstetrics and Gynaecology, The Queen Elizabeth Hospital, Woodville, SA 5073, Australia.

NORODOM SIHANOUK Samdech Preah, b. 31 Oct 1922, Cambodia. King of Cambodia. m. Princess Monique, 14 children (6 dec). Education: Saigon; Vietnam; Paris; Mil Trng, Saumur, France. Appointments: Elected King, 1941, Abdicated, 1955; PM, Min of Fgn Affairs, 1955, 1956, 1957;Perm Rep to UN, 1956; Hd of State, 1960; Deposed by Forces ofLon Nol, 1970;Resided in Peking; Fndr, Roy Govt of Natl Union of Cambodia, 1970; Restored as Hd of State, 1975, Resigned, 1976; Specl Envoy of Khmer Rouge to UN, 1979; Fndr, Natl United Front, 1981-89; Hd of State in exile of Govt of Democratic Kampuchea, 1982-88, 1989-90; Self-Styled Pres, Natl Govt of Cambodia; Pres, Tripartite Natl Cambodian Resistance; Exile 13 yrs, Returned to Cambodia, 1991; Chair, Supreme Natl Cncl, 1991-93; Pres of Cambodia, 1991-93; Crowned King of Cambodia, 1993-; Col-in-Chf, Armed Forces, 1993-. Publications: L'Indochine vu de Pékin, 1972; My War With the CIA, 1973; War and Hope: The Case for Cambodia, 1980; Souvenirs doux et amers, 1981; Prisonnier des Khmers Rouges, 1986; Charisme et Leadership, 1989. Hobbies: Badminton; Film Making; French Style Cooking. Address: Khemarindra Palace, Phnom Penh, Cambodia.

NORRIS Raymond Paul, b. 11 Jan 1953. Astrophysicist. m. Priscilla Margaret Metford, 2 Sept 1974, 1 s, 1 d. Education: BA, Cambridge, 1975; MA, Cambridge, 1978; PhD, Jodrell Bank, Univ Manchester, 1978. Appointments: Rsch Assoc, Univ of Manchester, 1978-83; Rsch Scientist, CSIRO Div of Radiophysics, 1983-88; Rsch Scientist, CSIRO Aust Telescope Natl Facility, 1988-; Hd of Astrophys, CSIRO Aust Telescope Natl Facility, 1995-; Hon Rsch Assoc, Univ of Tas, 1994-. Publications: Approx 150 in jrnls; About 80 radio and TV appearances. Memberships: Intl Astronomical Union, 1978-; Austl VLBI Cncl, 1991-; aips++ Steering Cttee, 1992-95; Intl Union of Radio Sci (Austl Repr, Commn J, 1993-); Natl Cttee for Radio Sci, 1993-; Intl Acady of Astronautics SETI cttee, 1995-; Intl SETI post-detection cttee, 1995-. Hobbies: Popularising science; Moving walls; Bushwalking. Address: 19 Munro Street, Baulkham Hills, NSW 2153, Australia.

NORRISH Dilys Margaret, b. 6 Nov 1954, Cambridge, Eng. Teacher (Adult Basic Education). m. Simon Emsley, 20 Jan 1978, 3 s. Education: BA, Vic Univ of Wellington, 1976; DipTESL, Vic Univ of Wellington, 1978; Grad Dip Ad Ed (Basic) Sydney Coll of Advd Educ, 1990; MA, Univ of Technol, Sydney, 1998. Appointment: Tchr, TAFE, NSW, 1984-. Publications: Unemployment and Beyond, 1993; Finding Your Library Books on the Shelves, 1994; Learning about Learning, 1994; Positive Thinking - Language, Literacy and Numeracy Resources on

HIV-AIDS for Teachers of Adult Education, 1996; Ed, Literacy Broadsheet, 1997-98; The Never Too Late Show Workbook, 1999. Memberships: NSW Adult Literacy and Numeracy Cncl; ACAL (Austl Cncl for Adult Literacy). Address: 12 Edith Street, Leichhardt, NSW 2040, Australia.

NORTH Thomas (Lindsay) (Sir), b. 11 Dec 1919, Rutherglen, Aust. Retired Company Chairman. m. Kathleen Mabel Jefferis, 10 Jan 1944, 2 d. Appointments: Joined G J Coles & Co Ltd, 1938, Supermarket Dir, 1963, Chmn, 1979-83; AIF, 1941-44; State Mngr, Assoc Dir, 1961, Mngng Dir, 1961, Matthews Thompson & Co Ltd; Dir, Gen Mngr, 1968-73, Mngng Dir, 1975-80, Dir, K'Mart (Aust) Ltd; Viscount Holdings Ltd, 1980-. Honours: FAIM, 1972; FA Inst Dirs, 1979; FRMIA, 1980; Kt, 1982. Hobby: Horse Racing. Address: Chiltern, 5/627 Toorak Road, Toorak, Vic 3142, Australia.

NORTHCOTE Keith Hawke, b. 29 June 1919. Soil Scientist. m. Monica Agnes Hemmings, 20 Dec 1947, 2 s. Education: BAgrSci, 1942; DAgrSci, 1982 Melbourne Univ. Appointments: Rsch Asst, Prof of Agric, Univ of Melbourne, 1942-43; Rsch Scientist to Snr Prin Scientist, Div of Soils, CSIR-CSIRO, 1943-84. Publications: Atlas of Australian Soils, 1960-68; A Factual Key for the Recognition of Australian Soils, 1960, 3rd ed, 1979; Australian Soils with Saline and Sodic Properties, 1972; Description of Australian Soils, 1975; Soils, Soil Morphology and Soil Classification, 1984. Honours: Sir Joseph Verco Medal, Roy Soc of S Aust, 1983; Life Mbr, AIAS, 1989; Life Mbr ASSA, 1989; J A Prescott Medal of Soil Sci, 1997. Memberships: AIAS; ASSSI; Roy Soc of S Aust. Listed in: Dictionary of International Biography. Hobbies: Orchids; Soils. Address: 4 Eucla Avenue, Warradale, SA 5046, Australia.

NORTON Jerry William, b. 16 May 1946, North Bend, OR, USA. Journalist. m. Kim Thoa, 18 Nov 1982, 1 s. Education: MS, Columbia Univ; BA, Univ of OR Hons Coll. Appointments: Reporter, Commodity News Servs, 1974-76; VP and Mng Ed, Phillips Publng, 1976-79; Ed Asia, Unicom News, 1979-82; Exec Ed, Unicom News, 1983-83; Bus Ed, S China Morning Post, 1984-86; Sub Ed, Reuters, Hong Kong, 1986-87; Desk Ed, Reuters Japan, 1987-89; News Ed, Reuters Japan, 1989-93; Bur Chf, Reuters Singapore, 1993-99; Dpty Ed, Reuters Asia Desk, 1999-. Memberships: Pres, For Corresp Assn, Singapore, 1995-97; Sec, 1994-95; For Corresp Club Hong Kong; Phi Beta Kappa; Natl Press Club; Exec Cttee, Hong Kong Jrnlsts Assn, 1980-82. Address: #09-02 Orchard Bel-Air, 245 Orchard Boulevard, Singapore 248648.

NOUJEIM Ziad, b. 2 Nov 1958, Beirut Lebanon. Oral Surgeon, University Professor, Journalist, Television Host and Producer. Education: DDS, St Joseph Univ Dental Sch, Beirut, 1981-82; Oral Bio Advd Cert, Univ of Paris VII, 1982-83; Oral Surg Advd Cert, Univ of Paris VI/Pierre et Marie Curie, Inst of Stomatology & Maxillofacial Surg, Paris, 1991; Clin Fell, Oral & Maxillofacial Surg, Harvard Univ, MA Gen Hosp, Boston, USA, 1993; Fell, Oral & Maxillofacial Pain, Lab of Orofacial Physiology, Univ of Auvernge-Cermont I, Fac of Dental Surg, Clermont-Ferrand, France. Appointments include: Clin Asst Prof & Lectr, Oral Surg, Skull Anatomy & Pain Control, Lebanese Univ, Fac Medl Scis, Beirut, 1985-92; TV Host, Prodr & Ed, Lebanese Brdcstng Corp, 1986-91, Mashreq TV, Lebanon, 1993-, Channel 33, 1995-96; LBCI & LBC SAT, 1996-; Oral Surg Clin Chf, Lectr & Dissection Demonstrator, 1993-94, Snr Lectr, 1994-, St Joseph Univ Dental Sch, Beirut; Editl Bd Mbr, Dental News, Beirut, 1994-; Chmn, Sci Coord, Intl Hd & Neck Pain Symposium of Mid E, 1994-; Cert, Spec in Oral Surg, Lebanese Min of Pub Hlth, Beirut, 1996-; Jrnlst at An Nahar & Nachar Achabab, Beirut, 1997-. Publications: 3 intl pprs. Memberships: Lebanese Dental Assn; Intl Assn of Oral & Maxillofacial Surgs (FIAOMS); Amn Coll of Oral & Maxillofacial Surgs (MACOMS); Amn Assn of Hosp Dentists; Lebanese Assn for Adv of Sci. Address: PO Box 166496 Ashrafieh, Beirut, Lebanon.

NOYE Laurence Richard (Larry), b. 28 July 1928. Journalist. Appointments: Copy Boy at Truth, Melbourne, 1945-46; Jrnlst on Footscray Mail, 1946-52; Bendigo Advertiser, 1952-55; Geelong Advertiser, 1955-56; Austl Utd Press, 1958-59; Launceston Examiner, 1959-60; Hobart Mercury, 1960-64; Western Suburbs Advertiser, 1964-80; Spasmodic Reporter in Canberra with ABC, AAP, Depts of Transp, Primary Ind (Fisheries), Def (Navy), 1981-93. Publications: Biography O'Malley, MHR on US-Australian Statesman Mr King O'Malley, 1985. Memberships: Austl Jrnlsts Assn; Media and Arts Assn; Yulunga Cmttee for Elderly Care Cntr, Sec, 1966-75; Lions Intl, 1969-99. Hobbies: Australian Football; Politics; Windsurfing. Address: 92 Simmons Drive, Altona, Vic 3018, Australia.

NUAIMI Humaid bin Rashid an, Ruler of Ajman. Appointments: Ruler of Ajman, 1981-; Mbr, Supreme Cncl of United Arab Emirates, 1981-; Patron, Sheikh Humaid bin Rashid Prizes for Culture & Sci, 1983-. Address: Ruler's Palace, PO Box 1, Ajman, United Arab Emirates.

NUAMI Rashid Abdullaj an-. Minister of Foreign Affairs. Address: Ministry of Foreign Affairs, POB 1, Abu Dhabi, United Arab Emirates.

NUGAPITIYA Mano, b. 6 Apr 1961, Colombo, Sri Lanka. Civil Engineer; Management Consultant. m. Chandini Kapuwatte, 8 Aug 1991. Education: BSc, Engrng, Univ of Moratuwa, Sri Lanka, 1985; MEng, Civil and Mining; Univ of Sydney, Aust, 1993; PhD Student, Proj Mngmt, UTS Aust, 1996. Appointments: Proj Engr, Aruradhapura Airport Proj, Sri Lanka, 1985-87; Offr Commanding Civil Engrng, Sri Lanka Airforce, 1987-91; Asst Proj Mngr, Sydney Intl Airport Refurbishment, Aust, 1993-95; Mngmt Cnslt, New Southern Railway, Sydney, 1996; Proj Cnslt, Homebush Bay Infrastructure Dev, Sydney 2000 Olympics, Aust, 1996-97; Proj Cnslt, Thredbo Landslide Repairs and Alpine Way Reconstruction, Aust, 1998-99; Proj Cnslt, SA2000 Proj, Sydney Intl Airport, Aust, 1999-; Research in Behavioral Science in Project Teams, 1996-. Honours: Partnering Ex Commendation, 1994; Engrng Ex Awd, 1998. Memberships: CPEngr, Aust; MASCE; M Insts of Engrs Aust. Address: 16/76 Lenthall Street, Kensington, NSW 2033, Australia.

NUGENT Michael Richard, b. 1944. Investor. m. Helen Marion Nugent, 1971, 1 s, 1 d. Education: FCPA. Appointments: Gen Mngr, Margarine and Oils Div, Provl Traders Holdings ltd, 1976-80; Mng Dir, Food Grp Henry Jones (IXL) Ltd, 1981-84; Mng Dir, Intl Grp Elders (IXL) Ltd, 1984-88; Mng Dir, Elders Agribus Grp, Elders, (IXL) Ltd, 1988-89; CEO and Mng Dir, Goodman Fielder Ltd, 1990-93; Chmn, Westmeath Holdings Pty Ltd, Dir, Snow Mountains Engrng Corp and J Boag & Son Ltd, 1994-97; Rail Access Corp, 1996-; formerly Dir of Natl Commercial Union Ltd. Membership: formerly Mbr, Bus Cncl of Aust and Agrifoods Cncl. Hobbies: Reading; Opera; Cinema; Golf; Tennis. Address: 81 Victoria Road, Bellevue Hill, NSW 2023, Australia.

NUNN Kathryn Evelyn, b. 30 Mar 1958, Carmarthan, Wales. Author; Teacher. m. Christopher Nunn, 30 Apr 1983, 1 s, 1 d. Education: MA, Monash Univ; BA (Hons), Univ of Wales; PGCE, Univ of Bristol, UK; RSA; TEFLA (RMIT) Aust. Appointments: Engl Tchr, 1980-81; Educ Offr, Bomana Police Coll PNG, 1981-85; Engl Tchr, 1986-90; Lectr, Trinity Fndn Course, 1990-92. Publications: Radio plays for PNG Radio, 1981-85; Co-auth w Brian Lloyd, Bright Gold, 1987; History of William Angliss Coll, 1990. Hobbies: Writing; Bridge. Address: 62 Victoria Street, Sandringham, Vic 3191, Australia.

NUSSBAUM Luther James, b. 13 Jan 1947, Decatur, IN, USA. Executive. m. Ginger, 24 Aug 1968, 2 d. Education: BA, Rhodes Coll; MBA, Stanford Univ. Appointments: Cummins Eng Co, 1972-83; Businessland, 1983-86; Ashton Tate, 1986-89; Evernet Systs, 1989-93; Nussbaum and Assoc, 1993-95; First Cnsltng Grp, 1994-. Honours: Phi Beta Kappa, 1968; CRN, Top 25 Execs in Computer Ind, 1990, 1991. Memberships: Yng Pres Orgs,

1986-97; WPO, 1997-. Hobbies: Skiing; Golf; Running. Address: 5818 E Bay Shore Walk, Long Beach, CA 90803, USA.

NUSUPOV Erkin, b. 12 Sept 1940, Kyzgyzstan. Mechanics Engineer. m. Maria, 16 July 1962, 2 s, 1 d. Education: Master Deg, 1962, Dr Deg, 1968; Dr Deg. Appointments: Engr, 1962; Prof Asst, 1971; Hd of Dept, 1972; Prof, 1993. Publications: Traktors and Automobiles Theory, textbook, 1998; Automobile Design, 1999. Honours: Kyrguz Tech Univ, 1978; Kyzgyz Agricl Acady, 1999. Memberships: Acad of Intl Higher Educ Acady of Scis, 1994; Kyrgyz Engrng Acady, 1998. Hobbies: Reading; Sport. Address: #26 Apt 60, Microdistrict #6, Bishkek, Kyzgyzstan.

NYAMBAVAA Galsandagva, b. 1958, Hovd Aimag, Mongolia. Government Executive. m. Education: Grad, Moscow Inst Energy, 1983. Appointments: Engr, Transp Mngmt, Bd of the Cty, 1983; Chf Expert, Min of Transp, 1984; Chf Engr, Cty's Trolley Co, 1987; Hd Dept, State Security Bd, 1993; Advsr, Agi Co, 1995; Chmn, Gen Bd, Transp and Road, 1990. Membership: People's Ih Hural-Parl, 1990-92. Address: Ministry of Infrastructure Development, PO Box 1104, Negsden Undestny St 49, Ulan Bator, Mongolia.

NYAMOSOR Tuya (Her Excellency), b. 8 Feb 1958, Ulaanbaatar, Mongolia. International Journalism. m. N Ayush, 1976, 2s, 1d. Education: Dip, Intl Jrnlst, Moscow Inst of Intl Rels; Dip, French Culture and Civilisation, Univ of Sorbonne, Paris; MA, Pol Sci, Leeds Univ, Eng. Appointments: Mngng Ed, Overseas Brdcstng Serv; Rschr, Stategic Stdies, For Min; Mbr Gen Cncl Natl Democratic Party; Dir, Dept of Plcy Plng and Co-ordng, MER; Cabinet Mbr and Min of External Rels. Publication: Democratization Process in Mongolia (rsch work). Membership: Hd, Natl Assn of Info and Comm Technol. Hobbies: Literature; Art. Address: Ministry of External Relations, Enkh Taivny Str 7A, Ulaanbaatar-11, Mongolia 210648.

NYAMSAMBUU Luvsanbaldan, b. 1948, Selsng Aimag, Mongolia. Government Executive. Education: Stud, Mongolian State Univ, Inst of Party, Moscow, 1986. Appointments: Techn, Secnd Sch, 1969; Expert, Min of Constrn, 1974, Hd Dept, 1986; Chmn, Constrn Co, 1988; Min of Constrn, Govt of Mongolia, 1990; Pres, Mongolian Pvte Owners' Assn, 1990-; Min of Agric and Ind, Govt of Mongolia, 1996-. Address: Ministry of Agriculture and Industry, Enkhtalvan St 16, Ulan Bator, Mongolia.

NYLAND Margaret Jean, b. 9 Nov 1942, SA, Aust. Judge. Education LLB, 1964. Appointments: Bar and Solicitor, 1965-87;; Judge, Dist Crt of SA, 1987-93; Justice, Supreme Crt of SA, 1993-. Memberships: Dir, Austl Assn of Women Judges; Chairperson, Law Fndn of SA; Chairperson, Bd of the Austl Dance Th; Cncl Mbr, St Ann's Coll Inc, Univ of Adelaide Res Hall; Pres, John Bray Law Chapt Univ of Adelaide Alumni Assn; Patron, Flinders Univ Law Soc; Patron, Women in Insurance, S Aust. Hobbies: Arts; Travel; Cats. Address: Supreme Court of South Australia, 1 Gouger Street, Adelaide, SA 5000, Australia.

NYMADAWA Pagbajabyn, b. 11 Jan 1947, Barunburen, Mongolia. Physician; Medical Virologist; Presidential Advisor. m. T Oyunbat, 3 s. Education: MD, Natl Med Univ, Ulaanbaatar, Mongolia, 1971; PhD, Med Virology, Med Fac, Humboldt Univ, Berlin, Germany, 1977; DSc (Med) in Med Virology and Epidemiology, D I Ivanosky Inst of Virology, Russian Acady of Med Scis, Moscow, 1989. Appointments: Asst, Chair of Physiol, Natl Med Univ, Ulaanbaatar, 1971-74; Chief, Dept of Virology, 1978-85; Dpty Dir for Rsch and Dev, 1985-87; Natl Inst for Hyg, Epidemiology and Microbiol, Ulaanbaatar; Dpty Min, Min of Health, Mongolia, 1987-90; Min of Health, Govt of Mongolia, Ulaanbaatar, 1990-96; Prof, Natl Medl Univ, Ulaanbaatar, 1997; Chmn, Subassembly of Medl Scis, Mongolian Acady Scis, 1997; Advsr to Pres of Mongolia, 1998. Publications: Over 200 inclng 10 books (mostly in Mongolian). Honour: Hon Doct in Med, Rangsit Univ, Thailand, 1994; Order of the Polar Star, Pres of

Mongolia, 1996. Memberships: Advsry Cttee on Hlth Rsch, WHO SEARO, 1985-88; World Peace Cncl, 1985-89; NY Acady of Scis, 1984; Mongolian Acady Scis, 1991; Exec Bd, 1992-95, WHO; Pres, Alumni Assn, Mongolian Medl Univ, 1998; VP, Mongolian Red Cross Soc, 1998. Listed in: Who's Who in the World. Hobbies: Envelope collection; Collecting children's sayings. Address: Central Post, PO Box 596, Ulaanbaatar, Mongolia.

O

O'BRIEN Philip Michael, b. 5 Jan 1940, Albion, NE, USA. Academic Librarian. m. Ann Topjon, 2 d. Education: BA, Whittier Coll, 1961; MSLS, 1962, Phd; 1974 Univ of S CA; BA, Sociol; MSLS, Lib Sci; PhD, Lib Sci. Appointments: Asst Libn, Whittier Coll, 1962-66; Head Soc and Bus Dept, Chico State Lib, 1966-67, US Army Lib Europe, 1967-70; Spec Collections Libn, Whittier Coll, 1970-74, Coll Libn, Whittier Coll, 1974-. Publications: T E Lawrence and Fine Printing, 1980; T E Lawrence, bibliography, 1988; Jessamyn West, bibliography, 1998. Honours: Besterman Medal, for T E Lawrence bibliography, 1989; HEW Fellowship, 1972-74; Rsch Grant Brit Acady, 1997. Hobbies: Cycling; Book Collecting. Address: Wardman Library, Whittier College, Whittier, CA 90608, USA.

O'COLLINS Gerald Glynn, b. 2 June 1931, Melbourne, Aust. Theologian. Education: MA, Univ of Melbourne, 1959; PhD (Cantab), 1968. Appointments: Rsch Fell, Pembroke Coll (Cantab), 1967-69; Visng Prof, Weston Sch of Theol, 1968-72; Prof, Gregorian Univ, 1974-. Publications: 33 books incl: Patrick McMahon Glynn, 1965; Fundamental Theology, 1981; Christology, 1995. Honours: PhD (Hon) Univ of San Fran, 1991. Membership: Soc of Auths. Hobby: Walking. Address: Universita Gregoriana, Piazza Della Pilotta 4, 00187 Roma, Italy.

O'CONNOR Charmian J, b. 4 Aug 1937, Woodville, NZ. University Administrator; Chemistry Professor. m. P S O'Connor, 1963, div 1970, 1 s, 1 d. Education: Auckland Univ; PhD, DSc, FRSNZ, C Chem, FRSC; FNZIC. Career: Auckland Univ, 1958-66; Snr Lectr, 1967-71; TX A&M Univ Visng Prof, 1972; Assoc Prof, 1972-85; Visng Prof at Nagasaki Univ, 1982, 1986, 1987; Tokushima Univ, 1987; Chem Prof, 1986-; Asst Vice Chan, 1988-96; Dpty Vice-Chan, 1997. Publications: Numerous articles and book chapters. Honours: JP, 1981; CBE, 1989. Memberships: Fedn of Univ Women; NZ Inst Chem; Postdoct Fellshps, Univ Coll, London, 1967, Univ of Santa Barbara, USA, 1967-68. Listed in: International Who's Who of Professional and Business Women; Who's Who in New Zealand. Hobbies: Watching TV; Swimming; Knitting. Address: Department of Chemistry, University of Auckland, Private Bag 92019, Auckland, New Zealand.

O'CONNOR Daryl John, b. 15 Apr 1952, Newcastle, Aust. University Academic. m. Susan, 13 May 1983, 1 s, 1 d. Education: BSc, hons, 1975, PhD, 1979, DSc, 1999, Austl Natl Univ. Appointments: Pt-time Phys Tutor, Austl Natl Univ, 1975-78, Univ of Sussex, England, 1979-80; Lectr in Phys, 1981-85, Snr Lectr, 1986-91, Assoc Prof in Phys, 1992-, Univ of Newcastle, NSW; Lectr to 3rd Yr Solid State Students, Avondale Coll, 1995-. Honours: Ctf of Merit, Univ Divsn, Sch of Maths Comp, Univ NSW, 1969; Prize and Ctf, Univ NSW, 1970; Natl Undergrad Schlshp, Austl Natl Univ, 1971; C'wlth Univ Schlshp, 1971; Austl Natl Univ Postgrad Schlshp, 1975; Alexander von Humboldt Rsch Fellshp, 1988; Bede Morris Fellshp, 1996. Memberships: Fell, Austl Inst of Phys; Am Vacuum Soc; Vacuum Soc of Aust; Austl Assn of von Humboldt Fells; Fndn Mbr, Assn of Sci Communicators. Hobbies: Squash; Bike riding; Boomerangs. Address: 3 Bambara Close, Lambton, NSW 2299, Australia.

O'DONAHOO Ian Peter Scott, b. 26 Feb 1959, Melbourne, Aust. Solicitor. m. Suella, 6 Mar 1987, 1 s, 1 d. Education: BEcon, LLB, Monash Univ. Appointments: Solicitor, 1986, Snr Assoc, 1988, Ptnr, 1991, Arthur Robinson & Hedderwicks. Memberships: Past Pres, Natl Prod Liability Assn Inc; Chmn, Medai & Comms Cttee, Law Cncl of Aust; Prod Liability Cttee, Defamation Law Cttee, Law Inst of Vic; Assoc Mbr, Amn Trial Lawyers Assn; Assoc Mbr, Austl Soc of Accts; LEADR (Lawyers Engaged in Alternative Dispute Resolution); Assoc Mbr, Def Rsch Inst Inc; Inst of Technol Law and Ins (Vienna); Austl Ed, Jrnl of Intl Soc of Technol Law and Ins. Hobbies: Sailing; Golf; Travel. Address: Arthur Robinson

& Hedderwicks, Stock Exchange Centre, Level 27, 530 Collins Street, Melbourne, VIC 3000, Australia.

O'DONNELL Roderick Macduff, b. 14 Jan 1946, Sydney, Aust. University Academic. Education: BE, MEngSc, Qld Univ; BA, BEc, Sydney Univ; PhD (Cantab). Publications: Books: Keynes: Philosophy, Economics and Politics, 1989; Keynes as Philosopher-Economist, 1991. Membership: Econ Soc of Aust. Address: Economics Department, Macquarie University, North Ryde, Sydney, NSW 2109, Australia.

O'FLYNN Mark Oliver, b. 17 Sept 1958, Aust. Writer; Teacher. m. Barbara Fitzgerald, 21 Jan 1990, 1 s, 1 d. Education: BA, Engl, Swinburne Inst, 1979; Dip Arts, Perf Arts, Vic Coll of the Arts, 1984; MA, Engl, Univ of NSW, 1991. Publications: Captain Cook, 1987; Paterson's Curse, 1988; The Too Bright Sun, 1996; Perpetua, 1999. Honour: Writer-in-Res, Deakin Univ, 1985, 1987. Memberships: AWA, 1986-91; Poets Union, 1996-; Varuna Writers Cntr, Bd Mbr, 1997-. Hobbies: Reading; Bushwalking. Address: Elphin, Kanimbla Street, Leura, NSW, Australia 2780.

O'GRADY Irenia B, b. 18 Jan 1931, S Aust, Aust. Writer; Freelance Journalist. m. Michael, 27 Jan 1925, 1 d. Publications: Poems in var magazines and jrnls. Memberships: Engl Speaking Union, Vic; Heritage Club, SA. Address: Elphin Cottage, Black Hill Road, c/o Houghton Post Office, South Australia 5131, Australia.

O'KANE Dene Philip, b. 24 Feb 1963, Christchurch, New Zealand. Snooker Player. Appointments: Youngest Ever Champion, 1980; Turned Profl, 1984; Twice World Championship Quarter-Finalist, 1987, 1992; Finalist, Hong Kong Open, 1989; Quarter-Finalist, Many Other World Ranking Events, incl Brit Open, Eurn Open, Asian Open. Honour: Overseas (non-Brit) Player of the Yr, 1987. Hobbies: Golf; Skin-Diving; Formula One Motor Racing; Wine; Clothes.

O'KANE HALE Frances, b. 4 Aug 1928, Cobram, Vic, Aust. Former Primary and Secondary Teacher (retired); Now Historical Rsearcher. m. Douglas Hale, 10 Mar 1977, 1 ss, 2 sd. Education: BA (Hons) Hist, 1970; MA, Hist, Univ of Melbourne; DipEd, 1972; Regd Primary Tchr, 1949. Appointments: Tchr, Cath Schs, 1949-66; Tutor (Hist), St Mary's Coll, Parkville (Tertiary Coll), 1970-71; Secnd Tchr, St Aloysius Coll, N Melbourne, 1973-79. Publications: A Path is Set: The Catholic Church in the Port Phillip District and Victoria 1839-1862, 1976; Wealth Beneath the Soil, 1981, 1983, 1984, 1985, 1987, 1989; Contbr, Catholic Education in Victoria: Yesterday, Today and Tomorrow, 1986; Contbr to mags and jrnls and Australian Dictionary of Biography, vol 9, 1983. Memberships: Melbourne Diocesan Histl Commn of St Patrick's Cath, 1970-; The Hist Inst of Vic. Hobbies: Reading; Historical research. Address: 19 Denman Avenue, Glen Iris, Victoria, Australia 3146.

O'REILLY William John, b. 15 June 1919, Gladstone, Qld, Aust. Retired. Education: Assoc in Acctncy, Univ of Qld, 1952. Appointments: Taxation Off, Qld State, 1936-46; Served RAAF, 1942-44; Joined Staff, 1946, Asst Commnr, 1961; First Asst Commnr, 1963, Second Commnr (Stat Off), 1967; Commnr, 1976-84. Honours: OBE, 1971; CB, 1981. Membership: Fell, Soc of Accts. Hobbies: Reading; Walking. Address: 7/48 Glen Road, Toowong, Qld 4066, Australia.

O'SULLIVAN Lance Anthony, b. 28 Aug 1963, NZ. Jockey. m. Bridgette O'Sullivan, 5 Feb 1995. Appointments: Jockey, riding over 1890 winners in last 19 yrs inclng 50 Grp 1 winners. Honours: Champion Jockey of NZ, 10 times; Racing Personality of Yr, 1994-95 season; BMW Jockey of Yr, 3 times. Hobbies: Most sports; Planted several thousand trees on farm. Address: 69 Findlater Street, Matamata, New Zealand.

OATES Ronald Kim, b. 16 Sept 1943, Sydney, Aust. Professor of Paediatrics and Child Health. m. Robyn Buttsworth, 16 Dec 1966, 2 s, 1 d. Education: MB, BS, MD, Sydney; MHP, Univ NSW; FRCP, FRACP,

FRACMA, DCH, FAFPHM. Appointments include: Res Med Offr, 1968, Snr Res Med Offr, 1968, St George Hosp, Sydney; Registrar, Snr Paediat Registrar, St Mary Hosp, London, Eng, 1971-73; Snr Res, Childrens Hosp, Boston, 1974-75 Community Paediatn, 1975-78, Hd, Dept of Med, 1977-78, Hd, Child Devel Unit, 1977-81, Dir, Med Servs, 1978-85, Dpty Chf Exec Offr, 1980-85, Chmn, Divsn of Med, 1984, Roy Alexandra Hosp for Children, Sydney; Var visng posts; Clin Fell, Harvard Med Sch, 1974-75; Hd, Child Protection Unit, Childrens Hosp, Camperdown, NSW, 1983-90; Hd, Dept of Paediats and Child Hlth, 1985-, Prof, 1985-97, Hon Prof, 1998-, Univ of Sydney; Chf Exec, Roy Alexandra Hosp for Children, 1997-. Publications include: Care for Your Child (co-auth), 1979; Child Abuse A Community Concern (ed), 1982; Understanding and Managing Child Sexual Abuse, 1990; The Spectrum of Child Abuse, 1996; Ed of sev publns and auth or co-auth. Honours: Nathalie Masse Prize, 1983; C Henry Kempe Visng Prof, Univ CO, USA, 1990; Hon Prof of Paediats, Kunming Med Sch, China, 1992; Brandt Steele Awd, Univ CO, USA, 1994; Mbr Order of Aust, 1996. Memberships include: Roy Austl Coll of Physns; Intl Soc for the Prevention of Child Abuse and Neglect, Pres, 1988-89; Def for Children Intl; NZ Child Hlth Rsch Fndn. Hobbies: Travel; Reading; Amateur Theatre. Address: The New Childrens Hospital, PO Box 3515, Paramatta, NSW 2124, Australia.

OBEIDAT Ahmad Abdul-Majeed, b. 1938, Hartha, Irbid, Jordan. Politician. m. 5 children. Education: Salahiyah Sch; Univ of Baghdad. Appointments: Tchr, Min of Educn, 1957; Customs Offr, 1961; 1st Lt, Gen Security Serv, 1962-64; Asst Dir, Gen Intelligence Serv, 1964-74, Dir, 1974-82; Min of the Interior, 1982-84; PM of Jordan, Min of Def, 1984-85; Ptnr, Law & Arbitration Cntr, 1985-. Address: Law & Arbitration Centre, PO Box 926544, Amman, Jordan.

OBERG Leon Erik, b. 5 Jan 1944, Goulburn, NSW, Aust. Newspaper Editor. m. Tricia, 14 Oct 1967, 2 s, 2 d. Education: TAFE. Publications: Locomotives of Australia, 1975, latest edn, 1998; Diesel Locomotives of Australia, 1980; TRAINS, 1984; Australia Rail at Work, 1995; Motive Power, 1994; Co-auth: Among Their Favourites, 1989; Num compositions. Memberships: Rotary Intl; Goulburn Mulwaree Club; Publicity Dir/Bulletin Ed, 1992-94; Dir, 1997, 1998, 1999, 2000. Hobbies: Photography; Railways; Music. Address: 102 Taralga Road, Bradfordville 2580, NSW, Australia.

OBREGON Alejandro, b. 4 June 1920, Colombia. Painter. 3 s, 1 d. Education: Stonyhurst Coll, England; Middlesex Sch; Concord; Mus Sch of Fine Arts, Boston, USA. Appointments: Dir, Sch of Fine Arts, Bogota, 1949-51, Barranquilla, 1956-57. Creative Works: One Man Exhbns in Bogota, Barranquilla, Cali, Paris, Milan, Washington, NY, Lima, Madrid, Barcelona, Munich, Sao Paulo, Rio de Janeiro; Rep in num galleries worldwide. Honours include: 1st Natl Prize, Guggenheim Intl, 1959; Prize, Sao Paulo Biennial, 1967. Address: Apartado Aéreo 37, Barranquilla, Colombia.

OBST Kevin Eric, b. 7 Nov 1938, Tanunda, Aust. Accountant. m. Rosslyn Ellen Walker, 18 Apr 1964, 3 s. Education: Assocshp Dip in Accty, SA Inst of Technol, 1966. Appointments: Chf Sec Off, 1956; Dept of Pub Hlth, 1960-63; Pub Serv Bd, 1963-65; Chf Sec Off, 1965-74; Premier's Dept, 1974-79; Dept of Transp (formerly Highways Dept), 1979-97. Honour: CVO, 1977. Memberships: Austl Soc of Certified Practising Accts. Hobbies: Travel; Reading; Football; Tennis. Address: 16 Stewart Avenue, Vale Park, SA 5081, Australia.

OCAMPO José Antonio, b. 20 Dec 1952. m. 3 children. Education: Notre Dame Univ; Yale Univ, CT, USA. Appointments: Prof of Econs, Univ de los Andes, 1976-; Dir, Cntr for Devl Stdies, 1980-82; Dpty Dir, FEDESARROLLO, 1983-84; Natl Dir, Employment Mission, 1985-86; Exec Dir, 1988-89; Snr Rschr, 1988-89; Min of Agric, 1993-94; Mbr, Mission to Nicaragua, Swedish Intl Dev Authy, World Inst for Dev and Econ Rsch, 1989, Hd, 1989-93; Advsr, Gov, on Coffee Affairs, 1989-90; Cnslt, Inter-Amn Dev Bank, UN;

Advsr, Min of For Trade, 1993; Visng Rschr, UN Conf on Trade and Dev, 1992. Publications include: Colombia and the World Economy 1830-1910, 1984; Co-ed, Economic Policy at the Crossroads, 1984; Co-ed, Post-Keynesian Economics, 1988; Introduction to Colombian Macroeconomics, 1994. Address: Ministry of Finance and Public Credit, Carera 7A, No 6-45 Of 308, Santafé de Bogotá, Colombia.

OCHI Hiroshi, b. 14 Oct 1957, Toyonaka Cty, Osaka Prefecture, Japan. Researcher. 29 Mar 1987. Kumiko, 29 Mar 1987, 1 s, 1 d. Education: BS, 1979, MS, 1983, PhD, 1997, Osaka Univ. Publication: Immunopharmarology of Allergic Diseases. Address: 3-11 Kanda-Surugadai, Chiyoda-ku, Tokyo 101-8319, Japan.

ODAWARA Ken'ichi, b. 8 Mar 1933, Tokyo, Japan. University Professor. m. Tsuneko Kurosawa, 25 Sept 1965, 2 s. Education: BA, 1955, MA, 1957, Jochi Sophia Univ; MA, Boston Coll, MA, USA, 1958; Postgrad, Columbia Univ, 1958. Appointments: Rsch Asst, Jochi Sophia Univ, Tokyo, 1956-59; Instr, 1959-65, Assoc Prof, 1965-70, Prof, 1970-97; Lectr, Univ Tokyo, Komaba Campus, 1973-84, 1990-93; Prof, Econs and Intl Rels, Nihon Univ, Tokyo, 1997-. Publications: Ppr and prelim draft agmt for Asian Payments Arrangement, UN, 1970; The Great American Disease, 1980; International Comparison of Companies and Labor Unions, 1997; An Overview on International Economics, 2nd edition, 1999; Other profl articles. Memberships: Japan Econ Assn; Amn Econ Assn. Hobbies: Gardening; Travel. Listed in: Who's Who in the World. Address: 1-3-4 Fujigaya, Kugenuma, Fujisawa-shi, Kanagawa-ken 257-0031, Japan.

ODGERS Sally Patricia, (Tegan James), b. 26 Nov 1957, La Trobe, Tas, Aust. Freelance Writer and Lecturer. m. Darrel Allan Odgers, 26 May 1979, 1 s, 1 d. Publications include: Dreadful David, 1984; Five Easy Lessons, 1989; Kayak, 1991; Shadowdancers, 1994; Anna's Own; Tasmania, a Guide; Drummond; Timedetectors (w D Odgers); Trinity Street, 1997; In Search of a Husband , 1997; Hero, 1998; Translations in Celadon, 1998; Mix and Match, 1998; Contbr to var mags and jrnls. Honours: Jrnlsm Awd, Circular Head Fest, 1993; Shortlisted, Talking Book Awds, 1995, 1996; Commended, Christian Book of Yr Awd, 1996. Memberships: Austl Soc of Auths; Soc of Women Writers; RWA. Hobbies: Reading; Writing; Cockatoos; Pet rats; Names. Address: PO Box 41, La Trobe, Tas 7307, Australia.

OGAWARA Hiroshi, b. 11 Sept 1935, Tokyo, Japan. Professor. m. Hiroko, 2 d. Education: DPharmSc. Honour: Soc for Actinomycetes Japan Awd, 1996. Memberships: Soc for Actinomycetes, Japan, pres; Am Soc for Microbiol; Japanese Soc of Biochem. Address: Meiji College of Pharmacy, Nozawa-1, Seragaya-ku, Tokyo 154, Japan.

OGDEN Kenneth Wade, b. 4 July 1945, Ashfield, NSW, Aust. Civil Engineer; Manager. m. Elaine, 3 s. Education: Dip, Civil Engrng, 1965; BE, 1968, MEngSc, 1970, Melbourne; PhD, Monash, 1976. Appointments: Monash Univ, 1969-96; Roy Automobile Club of Vic, 1996-. Publications include: Urban Goods Movement, 1991; Safer Roads, 1996. Honour: Fulbright Snr Awd, 1990-91. Memberships: Fell, Instn of Engrs, Aust; Ist of Transp Engrs. Address: RACV Ltd, 550 Princes Highway, Noble Park, Victoria 3174, Australia.

OGG Wilson Reid, b. 26 Feb 1928, Alhambra, CA, USA. Lawyer; Poet; Lyricist; Mediator; Arbitrator; Retired Judge. Education: AA, 1947, AB, 1949, JD, 1952, Univ of CA, Berkeley; Hon DD, Univ Life Chu, 1969; Doctorate in Relig and Humanities, 1970. Appointments: Psychol Instr, US Armed Forces Inst, Taegu, Korea, 1953-54; Engl Instr, Taegu Engl Lang Inst, 1954; Trustee/Sec, 1st Unitarian Ch of Berkeley, 1957-58; Rsch Atty, Continuing Educ of the Bar, Univ of CA, 1958-63; VP, Intl House Assn, 1961-62; Pres, Bd Chmn, CA Soc for Phys Study, 1963-65; Pvte Law Prac, 1955-78; Dir of Admissions, Intl Soc for Philosophical Enquiry, 1981-84; Creator-in-Res,

Pinebrook, whose Oriental gdns (of Chinese and Japanese des) are of outstndng beauty. Publications: Auth and Ed, num legal articles and publs; Poetry in num jrnls and anthologies; Owner, Pinebrook Press. Honours: Commendation Ribbon w Medal Pendant; Cultural Doct, World Univ. Memberships: Amn Mensa; The Triple Nine Soc; World Future Soc; Parapsychological Assn; World Acady of Arts and Culture; Intl House Assn; NY Acady of Scis; Intl Platform Assn; San Fran Bar Assn; Fell, Intl Acady of Law and Sci; Amn Soc of Composers and Publrs. Address: Pinebrook at Bret Harte Way, 1104 Keith Ave, Berkeley, CA 94708-1607, USA.

OGROD Eugene Stanley, b. Bloomington, IL, USA. Physician. m. Jean, 9 Sept 1969. Education: MD; JD; MA. Appointments: Chf Medl Offr, Sutter Medl Fndn, 1995-. Memberships: Amn Soc of Internal Med; CA Medl Assn; Amn Medl Assn; Cncl on Medl Servs. Address: Box 19275, Sacramento, CA 95819, USA.

OH Choo Hiap, b. 4 Jan 1944, Malaysia. Professor of Physics. Education: PhD. Appointments: Assoc Prof, Univ of Sci, Malaysia; Prof, Natl Univ of Singapore. Publications: Over 50 rsch pprs in profl jrnls. Membership: Amn Physl Soc. Address: Physics Department, National University of Singapore, Kent Ridge, Singapore 268198, Singapore.

OH Myung-Seok, b. 15 Apr 1955, Seoul, Korea. Professor. m. Kim Sun-Ok, 1 s, 1 d. Education: PhD, Anthropol, Monash Univ, 1993. Appointments: Asst Prof, 1994-97, Hd, SE Asian Prog, Grad Inst for Intl and Area Stdies, 1997-, Assoc Prof, 1998-, Seoul Natl Univ. Publications: Asian Studies in the Age of Globalization, 1997; Religion, Ethnicity and Modernity in Southwest Asia, 1998. Memberships: Korean Soc for Cultural Anthropol; Korean Inst of SE Asian Stdies. Address: Department of Anthropology, Seoul National University, Kwanak-gu, Seoul 151-742, Korea.

OHAMA Yoshihiko, b. 29 Mar 1937, Shimonoseki, Japan. Professor; Associate Dean. m. Ikuko Ohama, 24 Mar 1966, 1 s, 2 d. Education: BE, Yamaguchi Univ, 1959; PhD, Tokyo Inst of Technol, 1974. Appointments: Rsch Engr, Cntrl Rsch Lab, Onoda Cement Co Ltd, 1959-66; Rsch Engr, Dept Hd, Bldng Rsch Inst, Japanese Govt, 1966-76; Assoc Prof, Prof, Coll of Engrng, Nihon Univ, 1976-. Publications: Polymeric Waterproofing Work, 1972; Building Materials, 1981; Modern Construction Materials, 1990; Handbook of Polymer-Modifield Concrete and Mortars, 1995; Polymers in Concrete, 1995. Honours: Rsch Prize, Soc of Materials Sci, Japan, 1980; CANMET/ACI Awd, 1992; Hon Dip, Russian Acady of Engrng, 1992; Rsch Prize, Japan Soc for Finishing Technol, 1993; Hon Doct, Cath Univ, Leuven, 1996; Prize, Arch Inst of Japan, 1997. Memberships: ASIM; Am Concrete Inst; Materials Rsch Soc; SAMPE; RILEM; CIB; Japan Concrete Inst; Archtl Inst, Japan; Soc of Materials Sci, Japan. Hobbies: Travel; Mountaineering. Address: 14-10-402 Hiyoshi 2-chome, Kohoku-ku, Yokohama, Kanagawa-ken 223-0061, Japan.

OHARA Ichizo, b. Japan. Politician. Appointments: Fmr Parl Vice-Min, Natl Land Agcy; Min of Agricl, Forestry & Fisheries, 1996; Mbr, House of Reps; Mbr, LDP. Address: Ministry of Agriculture, Forestry & Fisheries, 1-2-1 Kasumigaseki, Chiyoda-ku, Tokyo 100, Japan.

OHASHI Shoichi, b. 7 Mar 1932, Seto, Japan. Professor of Kansai University. m. Kimiko Misaki, 20 Nov 1957, 1 s, 1 d. Education: BEcon, Wakayama Univ, 1955; MBA, Kobe Univ, 1957; DBA, Kobe Univ, 1967. Appointments: Tchr, 1957-70, Prof, 1970-, Dean of Fac of Comm, 1979-80, Dean of Vocational Div, 1982-86, Acad VP, 1986-92, Dean of Bus Sch, 1993-94, Dean of Div of Admission, 1994-, Kansai Univ. Publications: (auth) Theories of Works Community, 1967; Business Administration, 1992; (co-auth) Workers Participation, 1979; (ed) Business Administration in Germany, 1991; Business: the Story of H Nicklisch, 1996; (co-ed) Information, Society, Business, 1988; Fundamentals of Business Administration, 1991; Business and

Management of Today, 1992; Lexicon of Business Administration, 1994; Fundamentals of Modern Business Administration, 1995; Japanese Management and German Management, 1995; Introduction to Japanese Management, 1995; Business Theory in Germany of Today, 1997. Memberships: Japan Soc of Bus Admin, VP, 1995-; Japan Soc of Bus Theory Hist, VP, 1996-; Japan Assn for Comparative Stdy of Mngmt, Pres, 1994-96, Exec Cttee, 1996-. Hobbies: Wood handiwork; Observing machines. Address: 5-4-602 Mukogawacho, Takarazuka, 665-0844, Japan.

OHASHI Tetsuya, b. 21 Aug 1951, Sapporo, Japan. Materials Scientist. m. Yoshie, 26 Mar 1978. Education: BS, 1974, MS, 1976, PhD, 1981, Hokkaido Univ. Appointments: Snr Rschr, Hitachi Rsch Lab, 1991; Rsch Fell, Natl Rsch Inst of Metals, 1997; Prof, Kitani Inst Technol. Memberships: Japan Soc of Mech Engrs, Cttee, Computational Mechs Divsn; Japan Inst of Metals. Hobbies: Stringed Instruments; Wood Working. Address: 1-14-12 Midorigaoka, Kitami 090-0067, Japan.

OHGA Norio, b. 29 Jan 1930, Japan. Business Executive. m. Midori Matsubara, 1957. Education: Tokyo Natl Univ Art; Kunst Univ, Berlin; BMus. Appointments: Cnslt, Advsr, Tokyo Tsushin Kogyo KK (Tokyo Telecoms Engrng Corp), 1953; Co name chaned to Sony Corp, 1958; Gen Mgr, Tape Recorder Div and Prod Plng, 1959; Dir, 1964; Snr Mngng Dir, CBS/Sony Inc, 1968; Pres, 1970; Mngng Dir, Sony Corp, 1972; Snr Mngng Dir, 1974; Dpty Pres, 1976; Pres, 1982-95; Chmn, 1995-; Chmn, CBS/Sony Grp inc, 1980-90; Chmn, Sony USA Inc, 1988-; CEO, Sony Corp, 1989-; Pres, 1989-95; Chmn, Sony Software Corp, 1991-; Chmn and Rep Dir, CEO, Sony Corp, 1995-; Vice Chmn, Tokyo Chmn Com and Ind, 1989-97; Chmn, Cttee on New Bus, Keidanren, 1994-, Electric Indl Assn of Japan, 1995-; Chmn, 1995, Vice Chmn, 1997, Electronic Inds Assn of Japan; Vice Chmn, Bd of Cnclrs, Keidanren, 1997. Honours: Intl CEO of Yr, Geo Wash Univ, 1994; Cmdr's Cross 1st Class Order of Merit, Aust, 1987; Medal of Hon w Blue Ribbon, Japan, 1988; Cmdr's Cross Order of Merit, Germany, 1994; Hon DMusic, Univ of Rochester, 1996; Officier de l'Ordre National de la Legion d'Honneur, France, 1996. Address: Sony Corporation, 6-7-35 Kita Shinagawa 6-chome, Shinagawa-ku, Tokyo 141, Japan.

OHRIA Tatsuya, b. 13 Apr 1964, Kagoshima, Japan. Research Industrial Engineer. m. Emi Itagoki, 15 Mar 1992, 1 d. Education: DEng, Dept of Nuclear Engrng, Univ Tokyo, Japan. Appointments: Snr Rsch Engr, Mitsubishi Heavy Inds Co Ltd, Yokohama. Publications: Sev articles in profl jrnls. Memberships: Materials Rsch Soc, USA; Japanese Soc of Mech Engrng. Hobbies: Soccer; Singing; Books. Address: Mitsubishi Heavy Industries, Advanced Technology Research Centre, 8-1 Sachiura, 1 Chome, Kanazawa-ku, Japan.

OHKOSHI Masaaki, b. 23 Sept 1912, Tokyo, Japan. Director General. m. T Mitsuyo, 2 s, 1 d. Education: MD, Med Fac, Tokyo Univ. Appointment: Dir Gen, Shohwa Med Corp. Honour: Meritorious Awd, Japanese Urol Assn. Memberships: Japanese Urol Assn; Japan Soc of Chemotherapy; Japanese Soc of Nephrol. Hobby: Golf. Address: Minamiyukigaya 4-22-17, Ohta-ku, Tokyo 1450066, Japan.

OHKUBO Nobuyuki, b. 17 Mar 1961, Tokyo, Japan. Medical Doctor. m. Ki Takahashi, 8 June 1991. Education: MD; PhD. Appointments: Instr, keio Univ, 1991-98; Chf Medl Staff, Saitama Chuo Hosp, 1998-; Lectr, Saitama Hygienic Coll, 1994-. Publications: (ppr) In vivo effect of chronic administration of vasoactive intestinal peptide on gut-associated lymphoid tissues in rats, 1994. Honour: Grantee for Sci Rsch, Min of Educ, 1992. Memberships: Japanese Soc Intl Med, 1989-; Japanese Soc Gastroenterology, 1990-; NY Acady Scis, 1994-; AAAS, 1997-. Hobbies: Diving; Endoscopy; Driving. Address: 2-25-5 Nishi-Ikebukuro, Toshima-ku, Tokyo 171, Japan.

OHKURO Shigeru, b. 29 Nov 1940, Sendai, Japan. Associate Professor. m. Noriko, 26 June 1965, 2 d.

Education: MSc, Tohoku Univ, Sendai, Japan, 1965. Appointments: Rsch Asst, Tohoku Univ, Sendai; Assoc Prof, Hachinohe Inst Tech, Hachinohe; Expert Chmbr of Com and Ind, Hachinohe, Sendai. Publications: Fuzzy Process, 1996; Computer Algebra and Experimental Mathematics, 1998; New Equation of Motion, 1999. Honours: World Lifetime Achmnt Awd, ABI, 1998; Individual Awd, IBC, 1998; Pictorial Testimonial of Achmnt and Distinction, 1998. Memberships: Fell, IBA (Eng), 1998; Lifetime Achmnt, Acady of ABI, USA, 1998; Intl Fedn Nonlinear Analysts (USA). Hobbies: Tennis; Skiing; Music. Address: Hachinohe Institute of Technology, Myo, Hachinohe, 031-8501 Japan.

OHNISHI Hiroshi, b. 31 July 1956, Kyoto, Japan. Professor. m. 5 Jan 1987, 1 s. Education: DEcon, Kyoto Univ, 1989. Publications: The Rise and Fall and Interdependence of the Pacific Rim Countries; Socialism as Pre-Capitalism and Socialism as Post-Capitalism. Memberships: E Asian Econ Assn; Western Econ Assn Intl; Assn for Stat Computing. Hobbies: Travel; Chinese history. Address: Graduate School of Economics, Kyoto University, Sakyo-ku, Kyoto, Japan.

OHNISHI Minoru, b. 28 Oct 1925, Hyogo, Japan. Business Executive. m. Yaeko Yui, 1951, 2 s. Education: Sch of Econs, Tokyo Univ. Appointments: Joined Fuji Photo Film Co Ltd, 1948, Mngr, Tokyo Sales Dept of Consumer Products Divsn, 1957-61, Sales Dept of Indl Products Divsn, 1961-62, Fukuoka Br Off, 1962-64, Exec VP, Fuji Photo Film USA Inc, 1964-68, Mngr, Export Sales Divsn, Fuji Photo Flm Co Ltd, 1968-76, Dir, 1972-, Mngng Dir, 1976-79, Snr Mngng Dir, 1979-80, Pres, 1980-96, Chair, 1996-. Membership: Pres, Photo-Sensitized Materials Mfrs Assn of Japan, 1980-. Hobbies: Golf; Reading. Address: Fuji Photo Film Co Ltd, 26-30 Nishiazabu, 2-chome, Minato-ku, Tokyo 106, Japan.

OHSUMI Haruyasu, b. 25 Apr 1930, Osaka, Japan. Education: Fac of Law, Kyoto Univ, 1953; Bus Sch, Columbia Univ, 1957-58. Appointments: Kureha Spinning Co Ltd, Osaka, 1953; Rep of Kureha, Hamburg, 1963-66; Toyobo, 1966-68; Exec Asst, Pres, Bruck Mills Ltd, 1976-79; Gen Mbgr, Overseas Op Div, Toyobo Co Ltd, 1979-80; Pres, Toyobo NY Ltd, Chmn, Rosewood Fabrics Ltd, NY, Pres, Transco Textile Inds Ltd, Augusta, GA, 1980-85; Bd Dir, Toyobo Co Ltd, 1984-87; Snr Mngng Dir, Kansai Econ Fed, Osaka, 1988-94; Snr Advsr, Gov of Hyogo Prefecture, Dir, Hyogo and Kobe Intl Assns, 1994-; Dpty Exec Dir, Great Hanshin-Awaji Earthquake Reconstruction HQ, Hyogo Prefectural Govt, 1995-96; Vice Chmn, Bd Dirs, Hanshin-Awaji Econ Revitalization Org, 1995-. Honours: Hon Citizen of Augusta, GA, 1984; Chevalier de l'Ordre National du Merite, 1989; Verdienstkreuz 1, Klasse des Verdienstordens der Bundesrepublik Deutschland, 1991. Address: 3-19-9 Katsuragi, Kita-ku, Kobe, Hyogo 651-12, Japan.

OHTA Tomoko, b. 7 Sept 1933, Aichi, Japan. Professor Emeritus. Div, 1 d. Education: PhD, NC Univ. Appointments: Rschr, Kihara Inst for Biol Rsch, 1958-62; Natl Inst of Genetics, 1967-97. Publication: Evolution and Variation of Multigene Families, 1980. Honours: Saruhashi Prize, 1981; Japan Acady Prize, 1985; Weldon Meml Prize, 1986. Memberships: For Hon Mbr, Am Acady of Arts and Scis; Assoc Ed, Jrnl of Molecular Evolution. Hobby: Reading. Address: 20-20 Hatsunedai, Mishima 411-0018, Japan.

OHTAHARA Shunsuke, b. 11 Feb 1930, Okayama, Japan. University Professor. m. Sachiko, 28 May 1961, 1 s, 2 d. Education: MD, Okayama Univ Medl Sch, 1956; PhD, 1961. Appointments: Asst Prof, Paediat, 1962, Assoc Prof, Pediat and Child Neurology, 1978, Prof and Chmn, Dept Child Neurology, 1979, Okayama Univ Med Sch; Prof Emer, 1995, Prof, Kibi Intl Univ Health Sci Sch, 1995-. Publications: Over 400 publs on child neurology, clinl neurophysiology, epileptology and child hlth. Memberships: Intl Child Neurological Assn; Intl League against Epilepsy; Japan Soc Child Neurology; Japan Epilepsy Soc; Japan Soc EEG and EMG; Japan Paediatric Soc; Intl Soc Brain Electromagnet Mapping;

Rotary Club of Okayama-Chuo. Hobbies: Classic Camera collection and study; Photography; Travel; Golf. Address: 2-5-17 Tokuyoshicho, Okayama 703-8291, Japan.

OHTSUKA Toshiyuki, b. 28 Sept 1967, Tokyo, Japan. Engineering Educator. Education: BEng, 1990, MEng, 1992, DEng, 1995, Tokyo Metropolitan Inst of Technol, Hino, Tokyo. Appointments: Asst Prof, Univ of Tsukuba, Tsukuba, Ibaraki, Japan, 1995-; Visng Prof, CA Inst of Technol, Pasadena, CA, USA, 1996-97. Publications: 17 articles in profl jrnls. Honour: Young Investigator Awd, Japan Soc for Aeronautical and Space Scis, 1996. Memberships: Japan Soc for Aeronautical and Space Scis; Amn Inst of Aeronautics and Astronautics; Soc for Instrument and Control Engrs; NYAS; Japan Soc of Mech Engrs; IEEE. Hobbies: Reading; Driving. Address: Institute of Engineering Mechanics, University of Tsukuba, 1-1-1 Tennodai, Tsukuba, Ibaraki 305-8573, Japan.

OHWAKI Junichi, b. 15 Mar 1953, Tokyo, Japan. Electrical Engineering. m. Nobuko, 29 Apr 1982, 1 s. Education: Bach Deg, 1976, Master Deg, 1978, Nihon Univ, Tokyo. Appointments: Engr, 1978-85, Snr Rsch Engr, 1985-, Nippon Telegraph and Telephone Corp. Publications: Sev articles in profl jrnls. Honours: Phosphor Prize, 1996. Memberships: Japan Soc of Applied Phys, Tokyo, 1977; Inst of Electrons, Info and Commn Engrs, Tokyo, 1985; Phosphor Rsch Soc; Electrochem Soc of Japan. Hobby: Jogging. Address: 3-10-2 Sekimachi-kita, Nerima-ku, Tokyo 177-0051, Japan.

OHWAKI Kaz, b. 20 Sept 1964, Tokyo, Japan. Finance and Internet Consultant. Education: MA, Waseda Grad Sch. Publications: Mailing List Guide; Management Analysis by Excel. Hobbies: PC; Internet; Guitar. Address: 1-5-10 Komatsugawa, Edogawa-ku, Tokyo 1320034, Japan.

OKA Masahiro, b. 15 Feb 1924, Hiroshima, Japan. Professor. m. Kazuko Oka, 1 s, 2 d. Education: MA, Kyoto Imperial Univ, Fac of Lit, Dept of Philos (Ethics). Appointments: Prof of Philos, Hiroshima Shudo Univ, 1960; Postgrad course, Hiroshima Shudo Univ, 1978. Publications: Advocacy of Business Ethics, 1986; Business Ethics, 1996; Social Philosophy, 1996 and many others. Memberships: Philos Assn of West Japan, Dir, 1965; Japan Soc of Whiteheads Philos, Dir, 1990. Honour: The Third Cosmos Publ Prize. Hobby: Reading. Address: Fujidanchi 3-4 2-chome Ohmachi-nishi, Asaminami-ku, Horoshima 731-0125, Japan.

OKAI Makoto, b. 15 Oct 1959, Kobe, Japan. Researcher. m. Namiko So, 15 Oct 1989, 1 d. Education: Dr of Electron Engrng. Appointments: Staff Mbr, 1984-89, Rschr, 1989-91, Grp Ldr, 1991-94, Snr Rschr, Unit Ldr, 1995-, Ctrl Rsch Lab, Hitachi Ltd; Exchange Rschr, BT Lab, 1994-95. Publications: Semiconductor Lasers, 1994, 1994; Frequency Control of Semiconductor Lasers, 1996. Honours: Ex Ppr Awd, Inst of Electron, Info and Commn Engrng of Japan, 1991; Ex Ppr Awd, Optical Soc of Japan, Japan Soc of Appl Phys, 1995. Memberships: Japan Soc of Appl Phys; Optical Soc of Japan; Inst of Electron, Info and Commn Engrng of Japan; IEEE. Hobbies: Horse riding; Swimming; Ceramics. Address: 319-13 Kume, Tokorozawa, Saitama 359-1131, Japan.

OKAMOTO Koji, b. 25 Feb 1936, Kyoto, Japan. Professor. m. Kazuko, 19 Jan 1981, 2 s, 1 d. Education: LLD, Kyoto Univ. Appointments: Mitsui & Co; Kyoto Sangyo Univ; Osaka Pref Univ; JN Univ, India; Ehime Univ. Publications: Conditions for Discarding the Postwar Stigma, 1995; KITA IKKI, 1996; Changes and Problems in Contemporary China, 1996. Memberships: Japan Pol Sci Assn; Japan Assn for Intl Rels; Japan-Asia Soc for 21st Century; Japanese Assn for S Asian Studies. Hobby: Meeting with unique personalities. Address: 30 Murasakino-Imamiya-cho, Kita-ku, Kyoto 6038243, Japan.

OKAMOTO Tadashi, b. 30 Aug 1941, Hyogo, Japan. Professor. m. Noriko, 16 Apr 1967, 1 s. Education: DSc,

Kyoto Univ. Appointments: Rsch Assoc, Chgo Univ; Instr, Kyoto Univ; Visng Prof, Univ Paris VII; Dept Mngr, Hitachi Chem Co; Prof, Kinki Univ. Publications: About 100 articles in profl jrnls. Memberships: Forest Products Soc; Chem Soc of Japan; Am Chem Soc; Japan Wood Soc; Adhesive Soc, Japan. Hobby: Gardening. Address: Department of Agricultural Chemistry, Faculty of Agriculture, Kinki-Daigaku University, Nakamachi, Nara 631-8505, Japan.

OKANO Yutaka, b. Japan. Politician. Appointments: Mbr, House of Cnclrs; Fmr Chair, House of Cnclrs Cabinet Cttee; Min of Labour, 1996. Address: Ministry of Labour, 1-2-2 Kasumigaseki, Chiyoda-ku, Tokyo, Japan.

OKAWARA Taichiro, b. Japan. Politician. Appointments: Admin Vice-Min of Agricl, Forestry & Fisheries, Min, 1994-95; Mbr, House of Cnclrs; Chair, Fin Cttee, LDP, Policy Deliberation Cttee. Address: Ministry of Agriculture, Forestry & Fisheries, 1-2 Kasumigaseki, Chiyoda-ku, Tokyo, Japan.

OKAZAKI Motoaki, b. 17 July 1937, Tokyo, Japan. Developing Researcher. m. Keiko, 3 d. Education: Bach Deg, Keio Univ, 1961. Appointments: Staff, Yokoyama-Kogyo, 1961-63; Snr Engr, Japan Atomic Energy Rsch Inst, 1963-97. Publication: Analysis of Density Wave Instability in a Boiling Flow Using a Characteristic Method. Memberships: Fell, Japan Soc of Mech Engrs, Atomic Energy Soc of Japan. Hobbies: Classical music; Hiking; Chess. Address: Ichigaya Sanai-cho 29-10, Shinjuku-ku, Tokyo F162-0846, Japan.

OKUDA Mikio, b. Japan. Politician. Appointments: Fmr Parl Vice-Min of Intl Trade & Ind; Min of Educn, 1996; Mbr, House of Reps; Mbr, LDP. Address: Ministry of Education, Science & Culture, 3-2-2 Kasumigaseki, Chiyoda-ku, Tokyo 100, Japan.

OKUDAIRA Masahiko, b. 28 Aug 1927, Hiroshima, Japan. Pathologist; Researcher. m. Hiroko Naitou, 28 Apr 1955, 1 s, 1 d. Education: MD, Med Sch, Tokyo Univ, 1950; PhD, Tokyo Univ, 1958. Appointments: Med Examiner, Tokyo Metropolitan Govt, 1955-72; Prof, Chmn, Dept Pathol, Kitasato Univ Sch of Med, 1972-93; Hd, Div Path, Japan Bioassay Rsch Cntr, 1993-. Publications: Contbr, articles to medl jrnls. Honours: Acad Awd, Japan Soc Medl Mycology, 1987; Japan Soc Hepatology, 1998; Hon, Japan Soc of Medl Mycology. Memberships: Intl Soc Human and Animal Mycology, 1996; Japan Soc of Med Mycology, Hepatology. Address: 3-23-19, Nakano, Nakano-ku, Tokyo, 164-0001, Japan.

OKUTAN Mehmet, b. 21 Jan 1972, Ankara, Turkey. Mechanical Engineer. m. Eda, 1997. Education: BS, Mech Engrng, METU, Turkey; MS, Bldng Technol, MIT, USA. Appointments: Tchng Asst, MIT, 1993-95; Des Coord, MNG, 1995-97; Coord-Cnslt, Okutan Engrng, 1997-; Pt-time Instr, METU, Turkey, 1999-. Publications: 3 tech pprs, 1995, 1996, 1997; Over 20 tech articles, 1993-99. Honours: Tucker Voss Bldng Sci Awd, MIT, USA, 1995; TTMD Recog Awd, TTMD, İstanbul, Turkey. Hobbies: Skiing; Piano; Tennis. Address: Suleyman Nazif, St 11/2, Cankaya, 06550, Ankara, Turkey.

OLDFIELD Keith Arthur, b. 3 May 1938, Yorkshire, Eng. Electrical Engineer. m. Elaine, 29 June 1957, dec 1998, 1 s, 2 d. Education: DipEE; CEng. Appointments: Brook Motors Ltd, Eng; Huddersfield Univ, Eng; Plymouth Univ, Eng; Hong Kong Poly Univ, Hong Kong. Memberships: MHKIE; MIEE; MIEEE. Hobbies: Philately; Railway modelling; Music; Walking. Address: c/o Department Electrical Engineering, Hong Kong Polytechnic University, Hung Hom, Kowloon, Hong Kong.

OLDFIELD Michael Barrie, b. 23 Apr 1933, Rochdale, Eng. Filmmaker. m. Sallie, 20 May 1961, 2 s. Education: Magdalen Coll, Oxford. Appointments: Fndr, Lesmurdie 2000, 1975; Organist, Anglican Ch of St Swithun; Cnclr, Shire of Kalamunda, 1978-81; Filmmaker. Creative Works: Films incl: On the Edge of the Forest, 1977; Wheat Today, What Tomorrow?, 1987. Honours include: Order of Aust Medal for serv to conservation and the environment; Arbor Day Awd, USA. Memberships: Chmn, Salinity Forum; Fndr Mbr, The Men of the Trees, Pres, 1987-. Address: 3 Over Avenue, Lesmurdie, WA 6076, Australia.

OLDMEADOW Maxwell Wilkinson, b. 3 Aug 1924, Dandenong, Aust. Retired. m. Pam, 11 Dec 1948, 3 s. Education: BA; DipEd; TPTC. Appointments: Tchr, 1948-72, Pt-time Lectr/Tchng Fell, Monash Univ, 1964-72; Mbr, Austl Parl, 1972-75; Prin, hs, 1977-82; Dpty pres, Vic Tchng Serv Conciliation and Arbitration Commn, 1982-85. Publications: (jnt-auth) The Human Adventure; Australian Government - Decision Making in Action. Honour: OAM, 1993. Membership: MACE (Austl Coll of Educ). Address: 62 King Street, Dandenong, Victoria, Australia.

OLDROYD David Roger, b. 20 Jan 1936, Luton, Eng. Historian of Science. m. Elizabeth Jane Dawes, 5 Sept 1958, 2 s. Education: MA, Cambridge; MSc, London; PhD, DLitt, Univ of NSW. Appointments: Sci Master, John Lyon Sch, Harrow, 1958-62; Sci Master, Hastings Boy's hs, NZ, 1962-65; Sci Master, Christ's Coll, Christchurch, NZ, 1966-69; Lectr, 1969-76, Snr Lectr, 1976-85, Assoc Prof, 1986-94, Prof, 1995, Hon Visng Prof, 1996-, Univ NSW. Publications: Darwinian Impacts, 1980; The Arch of Knowledge, 1986; The Highlands Controversy, 1990; Thinking About the Earth, 1996; Sciences of the Earth, 1998. Honours: Fell, Geol Soc, 1993-; Fell, Austl Acady of Hums, 1994-; Sue Tyler Friedman Medal, Geol Soc, 1994; Hist of Geol Awd, Geol Soc of Am, 1994. Memberships: Austl Assn for the Hist, Philos and Socl Stdies of Sci, Pres, 1993-95; Hist of Earth Scis Soc, Cnclr, 1993-95. Intl Commn on the Hist of Geol Scis, Sec-Gen, 1996-. Hobby: Music (cello playing). Address: 28 Cassandra Avenue, St Ives, NSW, 2075, Australia.

OLFAT Manoochehr, b. 24 Mar 1939, Esfahan, Iran. Environmentalist. m. Taherpoor, 25 June 1958, 1 s, 1 d. Education: MSc, Pet Engrng, Univ of Tehran, Iran, 1961. Appointments: Hydrogeologist, Min of Energy; Rschr, Snr Rschr, Hd, Environ Pol Rsch Dept, Natl Iranian Oil Co. Honours: Authorship Recog, granted by the Iranian Pet Inst, Tehran, Iran, 1974. Memberships: Energy Commn of Natl Rsch Cncl of Iran; Iranian Soc of Environmentalists. Hobbies: Gardening; Stamp collecting; Instrument maintenance. Address: 13 Niloofar Street, Mina Avenue, Modarres Expy, 19188 Tehran, Iran.

OLIVA Dominador P, b. 7 Aug 1920, Pateros, Metro Manila, Philippines. Communications Engineer; Educator. m. Clemencia M Oliva, 4 s, 2 d. Education: Comms Engrng, OK Cty Univ, OK, USA, 1948; BS, Elec Engin, Mapua Inst of Technol, Manila, Philippines, 1957; BS, Radio & Elec Engin, Feati Univ, Manila, 1965; MPA, Feati Univ, 1968. Appointments include: HD/Dean, Radio TV & Electrons Dept, Feati Univ, Manila; Prof, Electrons and Comms Engrng Dept, Feati Univ; Reviewer, Lcensure Exam for Electrons and Comms Engrs, Reviewmasters, Manila; Spec Lectr, Air Traffic Servs and Comms Servs; Cnslts, Teleconsultants Inc; Cnslt, Electrochem Mngmt and Manpower Servs Inc; Cnslt, Techl Educ Advsry Bd, Technol Univ of the Philippines, Manila. Publications: (co-auth) The Electronics and Communications Engineering Law of the Philippines, 1969; Articles ot profl jrnls. Honours: Num incl: Plaque of Achmnt, 1992 Most Outstndng Techl Tchr of Philippines and cash awd, 1992; Plaque of Recog as Spec Son of Pateros, 1993; Outstndng Electrons and Comms Engr of Philippines for 1993, Profl Regulation Commn; Lifetime Achievement Awd, 1994; Outstndng Engrng & Techl-Vocational Educr, Marquis, Who's Who in World, 1995. Memberships include: Life Mbr, PSAT/PCAT/Technol Univ of Philippines Alumni Assn; Life Mbr, Inst of Electrons and Comms Engr of Philippines Inc (ICEP); Dir, Philippine Assn of Priv Techl Instns Inc (PAPTI); Dir, Techl and Vocational Schs Admnstrs Assn Inc (TEVSAA); Dir, Rizal hs Alumni Assn Inc (RHSAAI). Hobbies: Amateur (ham) radio; Reading; Lawn tennis; Table tennis. Address: 520 M Almeda Street, Pateros, Metro Manila, Philippines.

OLIVER Archibald Robert, b. 31 Oct 1920, SA, Aust. Civil Mechanical Engineer. m. Daphne Marie Althofer, 3

Sept 1947, 1 s, 3 d. Education: BE, 1941, ME, 1952, Adelaide Univ. Appointments: Sev as Engr, E&WS Dept, SA and WC and IC, NSW, 1940-47; Lectr, 1947-52, Snr Lectr, 1952-56, Rdr, Acting Prof, 1956, Prof, 1956-83, Univ of Tas. Publications: Var pprs. Honours: Emer Prof, Univ of Tas, 1983; Mbr Order of Aust, 1999. Memberships: FIE Aust; Fell, Inst of Engrs. Hobbies: Timber Seasoning; Compressor Aerodynamics; Gardening. Address: 197 Tolosa Street, Glenorchy, Tas 7010, Australia.

OLIVER Max Robert, b. 31 Dec 1938, Wanganui, NZ. Real Estate Executive. m. Pamela, 3 Oct 1964, 2 s, 1 d. Education: AREINZ, 1965; MPLEINZ, 1989; FREINZ, 1996. Appointments: Caltex Oil, 1957-63; Real Estate Salesman, 1963-70; Area Mngr/Real Estate (Beton Real Estate), 1970-80; Sales Mngr, Beton Real Estate, 1980-86; Prin Offr, Utd Realty World, 1986-93; Owner, M R Realty Ltd, 1993-. Honour: Fellshp Awd, Real Estate Inst of NZ, 1996. Memberships: Pres, Real Estate Inst of NZ; Prop and Land Econ of NZ. Hobbies: Tennis; Golf; Watching rugby; Art. Address: 547 Remuera Road, Remuera, Auckland 1005, New Zealand.

OLLEY John William, b. 26 July 1938, Sydney, Aust. Minister of Religion. m. 20 Jan 1962, 1 s, 2 d. Education: BSc, hons, 1959, PhD, 1963, Univ of Sydney; BD, hons, Bapt Theol Coll of NSW, 1965; TheolM, Melbourne Coll of Divinity, 1975. Appointments: Pastor, Bapt Chs, NSW, 1963-68; Missionary, Amn Bapt Chs, Lectr, Chinese Univ of Hong Kong, 1968-78; Hd, 1978, Old Testament Dept Vice Prin, 1984, Prin, 1991, Bapt Theol Coll of WA; Snr Lectr, Old Testament, Murdoch Univ, 1994-. Publications include: Articles in sev jrnls, books, inclng: What...On Earth?, 1982; Elders in Baptist Churches, 1984. Memberships include: Cncl Mbr, Evang Alliance of WA; Soc of Biblical Lit; Cncl Mbr, Bapt Chs of WA; Bd Chair, Austl Bapt Missionary Soc. Hobbies: Crossword puzzles; Music. Address: Baptist Theological College, Hayman Road, Bentley, WA 6102, Australia.

OLLIF Lorna Anne, b. 19 Mar 1918. Writer; Publisher. m. Frank Edward Ollif, 19 Oct 1946, 2 d. Education: Hassetts Coll Melbourne, Vic, var tech course and quals. Appointments: Stenographer and Printer to sols, 1936; Sec to Marine Ins Co, 1943; Mil Intell Sec, Aust Women's Army Serv, 1946; Sec to Ins and Publrs, 1975. Publications: 9 books publs, 1968-92; Num short stories, reviews, articles, Talking Books for Blind. Honours: Adv Aust Awd, 1990; BHP Awd and Roy Hist Soc Awd, 1988; Num prizes. Memberships: Ldr Girl Guides Assn; Pres, Horsby Shire Histl Soc; VP, NSW Mil Hist Soc. Address: 41 Galston Road, Hornsby, NSW 2077, Australia.

OLMERT Ehud, b. 1945, Binyamina, Israel. Politician; Lawyer. m. 4 children. Education: Hebrew Univ. Appointments: Columnist, Yediot Achronot (daily evening ppr); Mbr, Likud Pty; Mbr, Knesset, 1973-; Min of Minorities, 1988-90, of Hlth, 1990-92; Mayor of Jerusalem, 1993-. Address: Knesset Jerusalem Office, 29 November Street, Jerusalem, Israel.

OLMI Aiwa Elaiyes, b. 4 Nov 1957, Drima, Gumine District, Simbu Prov, Papua New Guinea. Career Diplomat; Papua New Guinea Ambassador to Japan. m. Bernadette, 1977, 1 s, 2 d. Education: Civil Engrng, Advd Mngmt Dip. Appointments: Joined PNG For Serv, 1980-; Trade Consul, 1984-86; Dir-Op Branch, 1987-88; Dir Gen, Immigration and Citizenship, Dept of For Affairs, 1989-90; Consul-Gen, Jayapura, Indonesia, 1991-93; Amb to Japan, 1994-. Hobbies: Rugby League; Lawn tennis; Golf; Gardening. Address: 2-21-22, Yoga, Setagaya-ku, Tokyo 158-0097, Japan.

OLOYEDE Olayinka Adedeji Adekunle, b. 29 June 1957, Lagos, Nigeria. Academic Engineer. m. Omolade, 25 Apr 1985, 1 d. Education: BSc, Hons; MSc; DIC Lond; PhD. Appointments: Lectr, Bayero Univ, Kano, Nigeria; Rsch Fell, Univ of Auckland, NZ; Snr Lectr, Qld Univ of Technol, Brisbane, Aust. Publications: 40 sci pprs. Honours: Schlshp, Fedl Govt of Nigeria, 1981-86; Rsch Fellshp Awd, Univs Grant Cttee of NZ Vice-Chan. Memberships: Nigeria Soc of Engrs; NY Acady of Scis;

AAAS. Hobbies: Soccer; Running; Chess; Swimming. Address: School of Mechanical, Manufacturing and Medical Engineering, Queensland University of Technology, Brisbane, Q4001, Australia.

OLSEN John Wayne, b. 7 June 1945, Kadina, S Aust. Premier of South Australia. m. Julie, 15 May 1968, 2 s, 1 d. Education: Fell, Natl Inst of Accts. Appointments: Mngng Dir, J R Olsen & Sons Pty Ltd, 1968-79; Pres, S Aust Liberal Party, 1976-79; MP (L) Rocky River, 1979-85; Ldr of the Opposition, 1982-90; MP (L), Custance, 1985-90; Sen for SA, 1990-92; Min for Infrastructure, Min for Ind, Mfng, Small Bus and Regl Dev, 1993-96; Premier of SA, 1996-; MP (L) Kavel, 1992-. Hobby: Barefoot water skiing. Address: GPO Box 2343, Adelaide, South Australia 5001, Australia.

OLSSON Annabelle Roslyn, b. 10 Dec 1962, Canberra, ACT, Aust. Veterinarian (wildlife). m. Richard Allanson, 7 Apr 1990, 1 s, 3 d. Education: BVSc, Sydney Univ; Completing MSc, JCU, 1999. Appointments: Vet-Gen Prac, 1985-92; Boonagrry Vet Surg (sole vet), 1993; Wildlife Consultancy; Trng Co-ord, FNQ Wildlife Rescue, 1993. Honours: Environ Awd, Aust Day, Serv to Wildlife, 1998; Cert of Excellence, Intl Womens Day, 1999. Memberships: Far N Queensland Wildlife Rescue, Assoc Pres, 1993-97; AVA; WDA; AAVCB; QWPA; QWPS. Hobbies: Scuba diving (rescue level); Offshore sailing; Bush hiking; Wilderness camping. Address: C/o Boongarry Vet Surgery, 427 Mayers Street, Edge Hill (Cairns), Queensland 4870, Australia.

OLSSON Bo Michael, b. 15 Feb 1964, Sweden. CEO. m. Endang, 6 May 1994, 2 s, 1 d. Education: MSc, Chem Engrng, Lunds Univ. Appointments: Gen Mngr, 1989-91; Devel Mngr, 1988-90, Sleansha Oak Enterprises; CEO, Atlantis Grp, 1992-. Menberships: IEEE; Jakarta Prog Soc. Hobbies: Family; Computers. Address: 11 Pasar Baru Timar No 9, Jakarta 10710, Indonesia.

OLSSON Leslie Trevor, b. 31 July 1931, Adelaide, S Aust. Judge. m. Marilyn Joan Evans, 24 July 1964, 1 s, 1 d. Education: LLB, Certs in Microcomputing, Mediation. Appointments: Dpty Master, Supreme Crt of S Aust, 1963; Chmn, Tchrs Salaries Bd, 1969; Pub Serv Arbitrator (S Aust), 1969; Dpty Pres, 1969, Chmn, Childhood Servs Cncl, 1974; Pres, Indl Crt and Commn of S Aust, 1975; Asst Cmdr (Ares) Cntrl Cmd, 1982; Puisne Judge Supreme Crt of S Aust, 1984. Honours: MBE, 1960; RFD; ED. Memberships: Pres, Indl Rels Soc of S Aust, 1982-84; Mbr, Cncl of Univ of Adelaide, 1985-97; Pres, Austl Inst of Judicial Admin, 1994-96. Hobbies: Computing; Powerboating; Fishing; Campervanning. Address: 1 Gouger Street, Adelaide, South Australia 5000, Australia.

OLVER Ian Norman, b. 10 May 1953, Melbourne, Aust. Medical Oncologist. m. Jennifer, 14 Jan 1978, 3 s. Education: MBBS, 1976; MD, 1991; PhD, 1997; FRACP, 1984; MRACMA, 1993. Appointments: Clin Dir, Roy Adelaide Hosp Cancer Cntr, 1993-; Clin Assoc Prof, Univ of Adelaide. Publication: Conquering Cancer - Your Guide to Treatment and Research, 1998. Memberships: Anti-Cancer Fndn, SA; Am Soc of Clin Oncol. Hobbies: Photography; Science Fiction; Travel. Address: c/o Royal Adelaide Hospital Cancer Centre, Adelaide, SA 5000, Australia.

OMAR Dato Abu Hassan Bin Haj, b. 15 Sept 1940, Bukit Belimbing, Kuala Selangor, Malaysia. Politician. m. Datin Wan Noor bint Haj Daud, 5 children. Education: Univ of Hull. Appointments: Fmr Dpty State Sec, State of Selangor, Dpty Sec-Gen, Min of Land & Fedl Devel; Mbr, Parl, 1978-; Parl Sec, Min of Com & Ind, 1978-80; Mbr, UMNO Supreme Cncl, 1978-; Dpty Min of Def, 1980-81, of Transp, 1981-84; Min of Welfare Servs, 1984-86, of Fedl Territory, 1986-87, of Fgn Affairs, 1987-91, of Domestic Trade & Consumer Affairs, 1991. Honours: Sev Awds. Hobbies: Gardening; Photography. Address: Ministry of Domestic Trade & Consumer Affairs, Tingat 19, 22-24 & 40 Menara Maybank, 100Jalan Tun Perak, 50050 Kuala Lumpur, Malaysia.

OMAR Dato Napsiah binti, b. 21 Apr 1943, Malaysia. Politician. widow. Education: Austl Natl Univ, Canberra; Cornell Univ, NY. Appointments: Admin Offr, Fed Land Devel Authy, Kuala Lumpur, 1967-69; Fndr, Women's & Family Devel Prog, 1967; Lectr, Agricl Coll, Malaya Serdang, 1972; Coord, Food Tech, Home & Food Tech Divsn, Agricl Univ, 1972-73, Dpty Hd, Dept of Home Tech, 1973-76, Hd, Dept of Human Devel Studies, 1978-80; Warden, 4th Residential Coll, 1974-82; Assoc Prof, Human Devel Studies, 1981; Dpty Min of Housing & Local Govt, 1981-87; Min of Pub Enterprises, 1988-90. Memberships: Exec Cttee, UMNO Women Malaysia; Chair, Econ Bur, UMNO, 1986-88; Chair, Unity Bur, UMNO Malaysia, 1987-90. Address: Ministry of Public Enterprises, WISMA PKNS, 3rd Floor, Jalan Raja Lant, 50652 Kuala Lumpur, Malaysia.

OMIRBEK Baigeldi, b. 15 Apr 1939, Yernazar, Kazakhstan. Politician. m. 3 children. Education: Almaty Inst of Vet Scis; Acady of Socl Scis, Ctrl CPSU Cttee. Appointments: Var posts in Dist Dept of Agricl Mngmt, 1962-74; 1st Dpty Chair, Regl Dept on Agricl Mngmt, 1974-75; 1st Sec, Zhambyl Regl Cttee, CP of Kazakhstan, Zhambyl Soviet of Peoples Deputies, 1975-92; Hd, Zhambyl Regl Admin, 1992-95; Cnslr to Pres of Kazakhstan, 1995-96; Chair, Senate (Parl), 1996-. Address: Respubliki Square 4, Almaty, Kazakhstan.

OMORI Koichi, b. 8 July 1959, Kobe. Medical Doctor. m. Fujiko, 7 Nov 1987, 1 s, 1 d. Education: MD, 1985; PhD, 1992. Appointments: Instr, Kyoto Univ Hosp, 1991-; Dir, Dept of Otolaryngology, Nishi-koke Medl Cntr, 1996-. Publications: Articles to profl jrnls. Honours: Young Fac Awd, Amn Laryngological Assn, 1995. Memberships: Amn Laryngological, Rhinological and Otological Soc. Hobby: Golf. Address: Dept of Otolaryngology, Nishi-Kobe Medical Center, 5-7-1 Kouji-dai, Nishi-ku, Kobe 651-2273, Japan.

OMPRAKASH Bina, b. 7 Sept 1952, Mangalore, India. Professional. 1 s. Education: MLitt; Postgrad Mngmt; Dip in Pub Rels. Appointments: UB Group, India, 1987. Memberships: Pub Rel Soc of India; Assn of Bus Communicators; Indian Soc of Advt. Hobbies: Gardening; Interiors. Address: Public Affairs Dept, The UB Group, 1 Vittal Mallya Road, Bangalore 560001, India.

ONDOH Tadanori, b. 3 Jan 1935, Okayama-Ken, Japan. Director. m. Takako, 7 Jan 1968. Education: BS, Geophysical Inst, Kyoto Univ, Kyoto, Japan; MS; DSc. Appointments: Rsch Assoc, NAS NASA, 1968-70; Dir, Lab for Space Sci, RRL, 1984; Dir, Commns Rsch Lab, 1987-95; Dir, Space Earth Environ Lab, 1995-; Min of Sci and Technol, Japan. Publications: Geospace Environmental Science, 1999. Honours: Tanakadate Gold Medal; Gold Medal, Disting Scientist. Memberships: Amn Geophysical Union; Japanese Soc for Planetary Sci; Assoc, COSPAR, 1994-. Hobbies: Tennis; Travel. Address: 5186 Kitano, Tokorazawa Saitama 359, Japan.

ONG Hean-Choon, b. 10 Nov 1945, Penang, Malaysia. Doctor. m. Lim It-Tean, 2 s. Education: MBBS, Malaysia; FRCOG, Eng; FAMM, Malaysia; FICS, USA; M MEd O&G, Singapore. Appointments: Cnslt, Obstetrician & Gynaecologist, PANTAI Med Cntr, KL, 1986-; Taman Desa Med Cntr, KL, 1996-. Publications: Patient Information Brochures on Menopause, 1, 2, and 3, 1998; Chief Ed, Obstetrics for Asia, textbook, in progress. Honours: Bernhard-Baron Travelling Fellowship, Roy Coll of Obstet and Gynaecol, Eng, 1979. Memberships: Chmn, Malaysian Rep Cttee, RCOG, 1997-2002; Exec Cncl, Malaysian Menopause Soc, 1997-99. Hobbies: Reading; Listening to music. Address: Klinik Wanita H C Ong, 142 Jalan Ipoh, 51200, Kuala Lumpur, Malaysia.

ONG Kah Lam, b. 14 Aug 1936, Malaysia. Consulting Polymer Technologist. 2 s, 1 d. Education: Dip, Natl Coll of Rubber Technol, London, UK; MSc, Chem, Univ of Akron, OH, USA; PhD, Engrng, Case Western Reserve Univ, OH, USA. Appointments: Prodn Chem, Durable Rubber Mfng Co, UK, 1960; Devel Chem, Gen Tire and Rubber Co, OH, USA, 1962; Rsch Fell, Case Inst of

Technol, OH, USA, 1965; Snr Lectr, Rubber and Plastics Div, Singapore Polytechnic, Singapore, 1968; Hd, Chem Process Technol Dept, 1971; MD, Allied Chem Products, Malaysia, 1974; Mngng Ptnr, Goodrich Ent, Malaysia, 1984; Dir of Mfng, Super Latex Co, Malaysia, 1988; Cnslt, Monash Univ, Melbourne, Aust, 1992; Cnslt, RMIT Univ, Melbourne, 1993; Ptnr, Blendrich Cnsltng, Melbourne, 1994-. Memberships: Fell, Plastics and Rubber Inst, UK; Fell, Inst of Materials, UK; Fell, Austl Plastics and Rubber Inst. Hobbies: Reading; Stamp collecting; Classical music; Surfing the Internet. Address: 9 Lovell Close, Rowville, Vic 3178, Australia.

ONG S L, b. 2 Aug 1954, Singapore. Environmental Engineer. m. Jean, 26 Apr 1979, 1 s, 1 d. Education: BEng Hons; MESc; PhD. Creative Works: Books. Honours: ASEAN Engrng Awd, 1997. Memberships: Environmental Engrng Soc of Singapore; Water Environment Fedn; Intl Assn on Water Quality. Hobby: Computers. Address: Dept of Civil Engrng, Natl Univ of Singapore, 10 Kent Ridge Crescent, Singapore 119260, Singapore.

ONG Teng Cheong, b. 22 Jan 1936. President of Singapore. m. Ling Siew May, 1963, 2 s. Education: BArch, Univ Adelaide, 1961; MCD, Univ Liverpool, 1967. Appointments: Archt, Adelaide, SA, Aust, and Singapore, 1962-65; Town Planner, Singapore CS, 1967-71; Archt, Town Planner, pvte sector, 1971-75; MP for Kim Keat, 1972-88, Toa Payoh Gp, 1988-93; Snr Min of State, Comms, 1975-78; Min Comms, 1978-83; Acting Min Culture, 1978-80; Min Labour, 1980-83; Chmn, People's Action Party Cntrl Exec Cttee, 1981-93; Sec-Gen, NTUC, 1983-93; Min Without Portfolio, 1983-85; 2nd Dpty PM, 1985-90; Dpty PM, 1990-93; Pres Singapore, 1993-. Address: Office of the President, Istana, Singapore 238823.

OPITZ Favio Philip, b. 15 Oct 1910, The Rocks, Sydney, Aust. Retd Orthopaedic Surgeon. m. Robin Shaw, 3 Jan 1988, 1 s, 1 d. Education: MB, BS, Sydney Univ, 1936. Appointments: Snr Surg, Wallsend Dist Hosp, 1946; Orth Surg, 1960, Emer Cnslt, Orth Surg, 1980, Hon Med Offr, Newcastle Mater Misericordiae Hosp, 1940; Hon Orth Surg, 1946; Emer Cnslt, Orth Surg, 1980; Asst Orth Surg, Cessnock Dist Hosp, 1967; Mbr, Advsry Med Cncl, Newcastle and Dist Assn for Crippled Children, 1964. Publication: Osteochondritis in the Foot, 1970. Honours: OStJ, 1965; Fell, Austl Orth Assn; Fell, Intl Coll of Surgs; Mbr, Western Pacific Orth Assn. Memberships: Brit Med Assn; Austl Med Assn, since inception. Hobbies: Music; Languages. Address: 43 Tyrrell Street, Newcastle, New South Wales 2300, Australia.

OPPENHEIM Alan Peter, b. 29 Dec 1957, Melbourne, Aust. Manufacturing Chemist (Pharmaceuticals). m. Victoria Marie Jane Robson. Education: BSc, 1st Class Hons, Monash Univ, 1980. Appointments: Sci Dir, Ego Pharms P/L, Braeside, Vic; Mng Dir, Ego Pharms Pty Ltd. Publications: Contbr, Jrnl of Organometallic Chem, 1982. Honours: Dists, Phys, Applied Maths, Higher Sch Cert, 1975; Snr Schlshp, Educ Dept, 1976; Dists, Chem, Phys, Maths, Computer Sci, Monash Univ, 1977-80. Memberships: Cnclr, Aust Soc of Cosmetic Chems; Fell, Roy Aust Chem Inst; Past Pres, Intl Fedn of Socs of Cosmetic Chems. Hobbies: Skiing; Sailing; Bridge; Horticulture. Address: Ego Pharmaceuticals P/L, 21-31 Malcolm Road, Braeside, Vic 3195, Australia.

ORANGE Claudia Josepha, b. 17 Apr 1938, Auckland, NZ. Historian; Educator. m. Rodney David Orange, 17 Jan 1959, 2 s, 1 d. Education: Qualified as State Sch Dental Nurse, 1957; Secnd Tchng Dip, 1973; PhD, Hist, Univ of Auckland, 1984. Appointments: Asst Lectr, Univ of Auckland, 1975-83; Asst Ed, 1984-87, Assoc (Dpty) Ed, 1987-89, Gen Ed, 1990-, Dictionary of NZ Biog; Acting Chf Histn, Histl Branch, Dept of Intenal Affairs, 1997-. Publications: The Treaty of Waitangi, 1987; The Story of a Treaty, 1989; An Illustrated History of the Treaty of Waitangi, 1990; Cntbrns to hist jrnls and other publns on NZ hist. Honours: Goodman, Fielder, Wattie Annual Book Awd, 1988, 1991; Waitangi Awd, 1988; OBE, 1993. Memberships: Fndn Chmn, NOHANZ

(Natl Oral Hist Assn of NZ); NZ Histl Assn; Stout Rsch Cntr for NZ Studies; Zonta. Hobbies: Swimming; Walking; Reading; Travel; History. Address: 2 Kilmister Avenue, Thorndon, Wellington, New Zealand.

ORCHARD John William, b. 22 Jan 1967, Melbourne, Aust. Sports Physician. Education: MBBS, Melbourne Univ, 1989; BA, Melbourne Univ, 1989; FACSP; FACSM. Appointments: Fell, Austl Inst of Sport, 1993; Medl Dir, Sydney Swans Football Club, 1994-97; Medl dir, Sydney Cty Roosters, 1998-. Publications: Articles in sports med jrnls. Honour: Life Mbr, Sports Med, Aust. Memberships: Fell, Austl Coll of Sports Physns; Fell, Amn Coll of Sports Med. Hobbies: Football; Cricket; Injury surveillance databases. Address: South Sydney Sports Medicine, 111 Anzac Parade, Kensington, NSW 2033, Australia.

ORD Alison, b. 21 Mar 1955. Geologist. Education: BSc Hons, 1977; PhD, UCLA, 1981. Appointments: Postdoct Fell, Austl Rsch Cncl, Monash Univ, 1981-84; Rsch Scientist, C'wlth Scientfc and Indl Rsch Org, Aust; Div Geomechs, 1984-93; Div Exploration and Mining, 1993-. Memberships: Sec, Geol Soc Aust; Rep of Tstees, Austl Fndn Sci, 1992-. Address: CSIRO Exploration and Mining, PO Box 437, Nedlands, WA 6009, Australia.

ORDIA Anita, b. 2 Oct 1958, Bhilwara, Rajasthan, India. Classical Dance Exponent (Kathak). m. Ravijhan Kal, 20 June 1985, 1 d. Education: Bhushan Degree in Dance, 1973; Prabhakar Degree, 1975; 3 yr Dip in Kathak; MA (Sociol), 1980; Disciple of Padam Bhushan Birju Maharaj, 1977-80; Spec in Kathak Late Pt DUrgacal, 1980-82. Career: Danced major roles w New Delhi's Shri Ram Bhartiya Kala Kendra in Canden Fest (London), Fest of India (S Korea), Cntrs of performing arts in Japan, Holland, E and W Germany, Belgium, France, Eng, Am, Mid E, Singapore, Hong Kong, Malaysia, Bangkok; Conducts Dance workshops in var towns of Rajasthan and wrk w deaf and dumb children; Only Kathak Dancer givin servs free to UNESCO to create cultural awareness among young, has conducted 150 dance workshops, w 5000 students in Rajasthan and other states. Honours: Awds of Desert Queen; Nritya Bhushan; Nritya Prabhakar; Nritya Shivali; Dagar Gharana Awd of Maharana Mewar Fndn; Fellshp of Hum Resource Dev, Dept of Culture Govt of India, 1997. Memberships: Kinkani Bhilwara (Cultural); Rotary Club, Bhilwara, 1993; UNESCO Fedn, Rajasthan, 1993. Hobbies: Reading literature; Music; Gardening; Travelling. Address: 1, Kranti, Model Town, Seven Bungalow Anddheri(W), Bombay 53, India.

ORDONEZ Juan Mauricio Wurmser, b. 8 Nov 1951, Guatemala. Minister of Economy. m. 4 children. Education: Trenton State Coll, NJ, USA. Appointments: Mktng Dir, Spain, 1984-86, Monterey, Mexico, 1986, Buenos Aires, 1986-89; Pres, Gen Mngr, Tabacalera Nacional SA, Guatemala Cty, 1990-93; Dir, Guatemalan Chmbr of Ind, 1991-93; Pres, Guatemalan Chmbr of Entrepreneurs, 1993; Pres, Cigarette Manufacturers Guild, 1990-93; Gen Mngr, Campero Intl restaurant chain, Guatemala, 1993-96. Address: Ministry of Economy, Palacio Nacional 6a Calle y 7a Avda, Zona 1, Guatemala City, Guatemala.

OREAMUNO Rodrigo. Government Official. Appointment: 1st VP, Govt of Costa Rica, San José, 1994-. Address: Office of the President, Casa Presidencial Apt 5 20-2-1, 1000 San José, Costa Rica.

ORMISTON William Frederick (Hon Mr Justice), b. 6 Oct 1935, Melbourne, Aust. Supreme Court Judge. m. Sarah Jane Doran, 18 Aug 1959, 3 s. Education: MCEGS, Univ of Melbourne; London Univ. Appointments: Bar, 1961; QC, Vic, 1975; WA, 1978; Judge, 1983, Judge of Appeal (Crt of Appeal), 1995, Supreme Crt of Vic. Membership: Hon Fell, Inst of Arbitrators of Aust, 1988-. Hobbies: Music; Reading; History; Cricket; Travel. Address: Judges Chambers, Supreme Court, William Street, Melbourne, Vic 3000, Australia.

ORR Kevin B, b. 17 July 1927, Australia. General Surgeon. m. Shirley, 16 Dec 1950, 2 s, 3 d. Education:

MBBS, Univ Sydney, 1951; FRCS Eng, 1955; FRACS, 1974; FACS, 1979. Appointments: Surg Tutor, Univ NSW; Snr Surg, St George Hosp, NSW; Snr Examiner, Austl Med Cncl. Publications include: Gastrointestinal Lavage Reduces Total Body Water, 1997; Management of Haematemesis and Melaena, 1998; Hazards From Surgical Gloves, 1998; Death is a Journey to be Undertaken, 1998; Prevention of Deep Leg Vein Thrombosis, 1998; Acute Colonic Pseudo-Obstruction, 1998. Memberships: Austl Medl Assn; Gastroenterol Soc of Aust; Clin Oncol Soc of Aust; Roy Soc of Med. Hobbies: Bushwalking; Photography; Sports; Theology and Science. Address: 42 Castle Street, Blakehurst, NSW 2221, Australia.

ORR Wendy Ann, b. 19 Nov 1953, Edmonton, Can. Author. m. Thomas, 11 Jan 1975, 1 s, 1 d. Education: BSc, Dip Occupational Therapy. Appointments: Occupational Therapist, Albury Cmnty Hlth, 1976-80; Lang and Dev Clin, Shepparton, 1982-92. Publications: Amanda's Dinosaur, 1988; The Tin Can Puppy, 1990; Mindblowing!, 1994; Ark in the Park, 1994; Yasou Nikki, 1995; Peeling the Onion, 1997; Arabella, 1998. Honours: Children's Book Cncl of Aust Book of the Yr Awds, Shortlisted, 1993, Winner, 1995; Hon Book, 1997; Amn Lib Assn Best Book for Young Adults, 1998. Memberships: Austl Soc of Auths; Children's Book Cncl of Aust. Hobbies: Reading; Walking; Friends and pets. Address: RMB 1257 Cobram, Vic 3644, Australia.

ORREGO VICUNA Francisco, b. 12 Apr 1942, Santiago, Chile. Lawyer; Diplomat. m. Soledad Bauza, 3 children. Education: Schs in Chile, Argentina, Spain, Egypt; Univ of Chile; LSE. Appointments: Fmr Dir, Inst of Intl Studies, Univ of Chile; Fmr, Vis Prof, Stanford Univ, Univ of Paris II Law Sch, Univ of Miami Law Sch; Projects for Acady of Intl Law, The Hague, UNITAR; Var studies and projects undertaken by univs in Eur, USA, Asia, Latin Am; Fmr Legal Advsr to OAS; Fmr Del Law of Sea Conf; Fmr Intl Ed of El Mercurio (daily newsppr); Amb to UK, 1983-85; Prof of Intl Law, Inst of Intl Studies, Law Sch, Univ of Chile, 1985-; Pres, Chilean Cncl on Fgn Rels; Mbr, Chilean-US Comm for Settlement of Disputes; Conciliator, Arbitrator, ICSID, 1995-; Judge, Admin Tribunal of IBRD. Publications: Antarctic Resources Policy, 1983; Antarctic Mineral Exploitation, 1988; The Exclusive Economic Zone, 1989. Membership: Assoc, Inst of Intl Law. Address: Institute of International Studies, University of Chile, PO Box 14187 Suc 21, Santiago 9, Chile.

ORTEGA Maritza, b. 7 Jan 1956, Talcahuano. Social Worker. Education; Direccion y Supervision del Personal "La Mediacionfamiliar: Una Intervencion Cociliadora en Conflictos conyugales no resueltos"; Curso Internacional de Bioetica. Appointments: Chf, Well-Being French Clin. Publications: Estudio Clinico Psicosocial en Pacientes Discapaciados por Accidentes del Trabajo: El Elaboracion del Duelo. Memberships: Intl Fedn Socl Wrkrs; Socl Wrkrs Fedn; Socl Wrkrs Concepcion; Cttee for Old People; Socl Workers for Conapran (Natl Corp for Old People); Socl Wrkr for ACHS (Safety Chilean Assn); Chf, Well-Being French Clin. Hobbies: Gym; Dancing; Music; Reading poetry; Painting; Travelling. Address: Casilla No 1902 Concepcion, Chile, Sudamerica.

OSBORN Eric Francis, b. 9 Dec 1922, Melbourne, Australia. Theologian. m. Lorna, 20 Dec 1946, 2 s. Education: MA, Univ Melbourne; PhD, DD, Cambridge Univ. Appointment: Prof, New Testament and Early Ch, Queens Coll, Univ Melbourne, 1958-87. Publications include: Ethical Patterns, 1976; Christian Philosophy, 1981; Christian Theology, 1993. Membership: FAHA. Address: 2 Ocean Road, Point Lonsdale 3225, Australia.

OSBORN Francis d'Arenberg, b. 27 Dec 1926, Adelaide, S Aust. Winemaker. m. Pauline, 16 Aug 1958, 1 s, 1 d. Honours: Queens Jubilee Medal, 1978; Patron, Austl Wine Ind, 1994-. Memberships: S Austl Wine and Brandy Ind, Treas, 1967-70, VP, 1971-72, Pres, 1972-75. Hobby: Fishing. Address: PO Box 195, Osborn Road, McLaren Vale, South Australia, Australia.

OSBORNE Charles Thomas, b. 24 Nov 1927. Author. m. Marie Korbelarova 1970, diss 1975. Education: DUniv, Griffith Univ, Brisbane. Appointments: Writer, poetry and criticism, Aust, NZ; Co-owner, Ballad Bookshop, Brisbane, 1947-51; Actor, London, provincial rep, tours, TV and films, 1953-57; Asst Ed, London Mag, 1958-66; Asst Lit Dir, Arts Cncl GB, 1966-71; Lit Dir, 1971-86; Brdcstr, musical and lit progs, BBC, 1957-; Dir Poetry Intl, 1967-74; Mbr, Editl Bd, Opera, 1971-; Sec, Poetry Book Soc, 1971-84; Opera critic, Jewish Chronicle, 1985-. Creative Works: Ed: Australian Stories Of Today, 1961; Opera 66, 1966; Fifty Works Of English Literature We Could Do Without, 1967; Kafka, 1967; Swansong (poems), 1968; The Complete Operas of Verdi, 1969; Ned Kelly, 1970; Ed: Letters Of Giuseppe Verdi, 1971; The Bram Stoker Bedside Companion, 1973; Stories And Essays By Richard Wagner, 1973; The Concert Song Companion, 1974; Masterpieces By Nolan, 1976; Masterpieces Of Drysdale, 1976; Masterpieces of Dobell, 1976; Wagner And His World, 1977; Verdi, 1977; Ed, Masterworks of Opera: Rigoletto, 1979; The Opera House Album, 1979; W H Auden: The Life Of A Poet, 1980; Co-ed, Klemperer Stories, 1980; The Complete Opera Of Puccini, 1981; The Life And Crimes of Agatha Christie, 1982; The World Theatre Of Wagner, 1982; How To Enjoy Opera, 1983; The Dictionary Of Opera, 1983; Letter To W H Auden And Other Poems, 1984; Schubert And His Vienna, 1985; Giving It Away (memoirs), 1986; Ed, The Opera Book Of Best-Loved Verse, 1986; Max Oldaker: Last Of The Matinee Idols, 1988; The Complete Operas Of Wagner, 1989; The Bel Canto Operas, 1994; The Pink Danube (novel), 1998; Poems in var anthols; Jrnls and newspprs. Address: c/o Aitken Stone & Wylie, 29 Fernshaw Road, London SW10 0TG, England.

OSBORNE Michael John, b. 25 Jan 1942, Eastbourne, Sussex, Eng. University Vice-Chancellor. m. Dawn, 23 Feb 1978. Education: BA Literae Humaniores (Class 1), 1965, MA Literae Humaniores, Oxford, 1968; PhD Philos and Letters (summa cum laude) Katholieke Univ te Leuven, Belgium. Appointments: Lectr, Classics, Univ Bristol, 1965-66; Lectr, Classics & Archaeol, Univ of Lancaster, UK, 1978-82; Prof, Hd of Classical Studies, Univ of Melbourne, 1983-89; Prof Emer, Univ of Melbourne, 1989; Vice-Chancellor, Pres, La Trobe Univ, 1990-. Publications: Naturalization in Athens, 4 vols, Belgian Royal Academy; Vol I, A corpus of the Decrees Granting Citizenship, pp257, 1981; Vol II, A Historical Commentary on the Decrees Granting Citizenship, pp 198, 1982; Vol III, The Testimonia for Naturalisation in Athens, pp 135, 1983; Vol IV, A History of the Law and Practice of Naturalization in Athens, pp 110, 1983; (w S G Byrne) Lexicon of Greek Personal Names Vol II, 1994; The Foreign Residents of Athens, Studia Hellenistic Vol 33, 1996. Honours: Laureate, Belgian Roy Acady of Scis, Letters and Fine Arts, 1980; Hon Prof, Yunnan Univ, 1994, 1997, Kunming Medl Univ, 1995-. Memberships: Austl Vice-Chancellors' Cttee (AVCC), 1990-; Chair, AVCC Standing Cttee for Intl Affairs, 1997-; Vic Vice-Chancellors' Cttee (VVCC), 1990-; Mbr, Bd Dirs, Bus Higher Educ Round Table, 1995-. Hobbies: Tennis; Travel; Football (all types). Address: Office of the Vice-Chancellor, La Trobe University, Bundoora, Vic 3083, Australia.

OSPANOV Marat Turdybekovich, b. 17 Sept 1949, Aktyubinsk, Kazakhstan. Politician; Economist. m. Bahyt Akhmetkalievna, 1975, 1 s, 1 d. Education: G Plekhanov Moscow State Inst of Natl Econ; S Kirov Kazakh State Univ. Appointments: Lectr, Aktyubinsk State Inst of Med, 1973-90; Dpty Chair, Cttee Supreme Soviet of Kazakhstan, 1990-91; Dpty Hd, Hd Chf Taxation Inspection, 1st Dpty Min of Fin, Repub of Kazakhstan, 1991-94; Dpty Chair, Supreme Soviet of Kazakhstan, 1994-95; Chair, Cttee on Fgn Investments Cabinet of Mins, 1995-96; Chair, Majilis (Lower Chamber of Parl), Repub of Kazakhstan, 1996-; Mbr, Intl Econ Acady Eurasia, 1997-. Publications: 5 monographs, over 50 publns on econ and agrarian problems, taxation, budget and investment policies. Hobby: Music. Address: House of Parliament, Akmola, Almaty, Kazakhstan.

OTA Masahide, b. 12 June 1925, Okinawa, Japan. Researcher; Former Governor of Okinawa; Professor Emeritus of the University of the Ryukyu. m. Keiko, 7 June 1958, 3 s, 1 d. Education: MA, Jrnlsm, Syracuse Univ, NY, USA. Appointments: Instr, 1958-64, Asst Prof, 1964-68, Prof, 1968-90, Dean of Coll of Law & Letters, 1983-85, Chmn of the Sociology Dept, 1987-90, Univ of Ryukus; Rsch Fell, Univ of Tokyo, 1968-70; Visng Prof, AZ State Univ, 1978-79; Snr Fell, EW Cntr, Univ of HI, 1973-74; Gov of Okinawa Prefecture, Japan, 1990-98; Pres, Ota Peace Rsch Inst & Mbr, Advsry Bd of Japan Policy Rsch Inst, 1998-. Publications: 12 books incl: Consciousness of the Okinawan People, 1967; The Pres of Okinawa, 1966; The Okinawa Mind, 1972; The Political Structure of the Modern Okinawa, 1972; Who are the Okinawans, 1980; A Comprehensive History of the Battle of Okinawa, 1982; Okinawa-War and Peace, 1982; The High Commissioners of the Ryukyus, 1984; (Co-auth) Democratizing Japan: The Allied Occupation, 1987; Articles in jrnls. Honours: Okinawa Times Bunka Sho (Cultural Awd), 1972; SGI Peace Cultural Awd, Soka Gakkai Intl, 1988; Higashionna Kanjun Awd, Ryukyu Shinpo, 1987; Hon Prof, Univ of Ryukyus, 1990-. Memberships: Peace Studies Assn of Japan; Japan Soc for Studies in Jrnlsm and Mass Comms; Japan Soc for Studies in Sociol. Hobbies: Playing golf; Reading books. Address: Ota Peace Research Institute, 2-22-4 Izumizaki, Suite 202, Naha, Okinawa 900-0021, Japan.

OTANI Yoshihiko, b. 10 Jan 1938, Fukui, Japan. Professor. m. Junko Amaike, 22 Oct 1969, 2 s. Education: BA, Kobe Univ, 1960; PhD, Univ MN, USA, 1969. Appointments: Asst Prof, Univ MN, USA, 1969-70; Asst Prof, 1970-74, Assoc Prof, 1974-76, Purdue Univ; Assoc Prof, 1976-81, Prof, 1981-94, Univ KS; Prof, Univ Tsukuba, 1981-. Publications: Sev articles in profl jrnls. Honour: Woodrow Wilson Fell, 1968-69. Memberships: Japanese Econ Assn, cncl, 1993-; Am Econ Assn; Econometric Soc; Am Sci Affiliation. Hobby: Walking. Address: Institute of Policy and Planning Sciences, University of Tsukuba, Tsukuba, Ibaraki 305-8573, Japan.

OTUNBAYEVA Rosa Isakovna, b. 23 Aug 1950, Krygyzstan. Politician; Diplomat. m. 1 s, 1 d. Education: Moscow Univ. Appointments: Snr Tchr, Hd of Chair, Kyrgyzstan Univ, 1975-81; 2nd Sec, Regl CP Cttee in Frunze, Sec, City CP Cttee, 1979-86; Vice Chair, Cncl of Mins, Min of Fgn Affairs of Kyrgyz SSR, 1986-89; Exec Sec, USSR Comm on UNESCO Problems, 1989-90, Chair, 1990-91; Amb of USSR to Malaysia, 1991-92; Vice-PM, Min of Fgn Affairs, Repub of Kyrgyzstan, 1992; Amb of Kyrgyzstan to USA, 1992-94; Min of Fgn Affairs, 1994-97. Address: Ministry of Foreign Affairs, 205 Abdumomunov Street, Bishkek 720003, Kyrgyzstan.

OU Jian-Ping, b. 24 May 1956, Hunan Prov, China. Dance Critic; Historian. m. Ning Ling, 29 Sept 1985, 1 d. Education: BA, Engl Lang and Lit, Cntrl China Tchrs Coll, 1982; MA, Dance Hist and Theory, China Natl Arts Acady, 1985. Appointments: Jade Des and Carver, 1975-78; Dance Rschr, Asst Rsch Fell to Assoc RF to RF, 1985-. Publications: 22 books incl: Modern Dance: Theory and Practice, 1994; How to Appreciate Modern Dance ?, 1996; Dance Aesthetics, 1997. Honours: Fellshps from China-India Govts, 1986; NYC-based Asian Cultural Cncl, 1988, 1993; German, 1988; Israeli, 1995; China-Aust Govts, 1996; Korean, 1997, 1998; British, 1998; French, 1998. Memberships: Standing Mbr, Theory Cttee under China Natl Artists Assn, 1994-; Dir, China Intl Cultural Exchange Cntr, 1994-; All-China Yth Fedn, 1990-. Hobbies: Reading; Writing. Address: 7-2-801 Sizhuyuan, Dewai, Beijing 100101, China.

OVERALL John Wallace (Sir), b. 15 July 1913, Sydney, Aust. Architect; Town Planner; Company Director. m. 17 Sept 1943, 4 s. Education: Dip, Arch, Sydney Tech Coll, 1935; Overseas Travelling Schlshp, 1939; Austl Medallion for Wrk Done, Arch, 1949. Appointments: Archt, Pvte Prac, 1935-40; War Serv, 1940-46; Chf Archt, SA Housing Trust, 1946-49; Ptnr, Overall & Walkley, 1949-51; Chf Archt, C'wlth Govt, Aust, 1951-57; Cmmnr, Natl Capital Devel Cmmn, 1958-72;

Chmn, Natl Capital Plng Cttee, 1973; Co Dir, Ptnr, John Overall & Ptnrs, 1973-85; Mbr, Parly House of Constrn Authy, 1979-85; Chmn, New Parly House, Aust Des Competition, 1979-80. Honours: MC, 1941; Bar to MC, 1942; Austl Medallion, 1949; CBE, 1962; Sydney Luker Mem Medal, NSW Town Plng Awd, 1964; KB, 1968; Sir James Barrett Medal, 1970; Gold Medal, Roy Austl Inst of Arch, 1982; Hon Fell, AIA, 1984. Memberships: Life Fell, Roy Austl Inst of Arch; Roy Austl Plng Inst. Hobbies: Golf; Tennis. Address: 1/9 Jardine Street, Kingston, ACT 2604, Australia.

OWEN Elizabeth Anne, b. 18 Dec 1951. m. 26 Feb 1977, 1 d. Education: BA (Hons), Univ of Melbourne; MAd, Monash Univ. Appointments: Co-ed, Compass Poetry Mag, 1970, 1971, Melbourne Univ Mag, 1973, Melbourne Jrnl of Politics, 1973; Jrnlst, The Age, 1977-81; Publs and Publicity Offr, Lib Cncl of Vic, 1981; Technol Ed, BRW, 1984; Actng Pub Rels Offr, Chisholm Inst of Technol, 1986; Comms Mngr, Austl Lead and Zinc Assocs, 1986-88; Mbr Editl Cttee Luna Lit Mag, 1985-89; Judge, State Short Story Comp, 1978, 1979, Anne Elder Poetry Comp, 1990, 1991, 1992, The John Shaw Nielson Poetry Awd, 1993, The C J Dennis Poetry Awd, 1998, 1999. Publication: A Strawberry in the Shower, 1994. Honours: 1st Prize, Begonia Fest Esso Lit Competition, 1982, Commended, 1984; 2nd in John Shaw Neilson Poetry Awd, 1982; Poem judged outstndng in Daffodil Day Arts Awds, Anti-Cancer Cncl, 1999. Memberships: Fellshp of Austl Writers. Hobbies: Reading; Swimming; Theatre; Listening to music. Address: 11 Smith Street, Hampton, Vic 3188, Australia.

OWEN Jan Jarrold, b. 18 Aug 1940. Writer. 2 s, 1 d. Education: BA, Univ Adelaide; Assoc, Lib Assn of Aust. Appointments: Libn, Univ and Coll Libs, 1961-84; Writer-in-Resn, Venice Studio of the Lit Bd of the Aust Cncl, 1989; Tas Writers Union, 1993; Rome B R Whiting Lib, 1994; Rimbun Dahan, Malaysia, 1997-98. Publications: Poetry books: Boy With A Telescope, 1986; Fingerprints on Light, 1990; Blackberry Season, 1993; Night Rainbows, 1994. Honours: Ian Mudie Prize, 1982; Jessie Litchfield Prize, 1984; Grenfell Henry Lawson Prize, 1985; Harri Jones Mem Prize, 1986; Anne Elder Awd, 1987; Mary Gilmore Prize, 1987; Wesley Michel Wright Poetry Prize, 1992. Memberships: S Austl Writers Ctr; Adelaide Writers' Week Cttee, 1990-93; Lit Arts Advsry Cttee of S Aust, 1988-92. Listed in: International Who's Who in Poetry; International Authors and Writers Who's Who. Hobbies: Languages; Travel; Gardening; Reading. Address: Box 351, Aldinga Beach, SA 5173, Australia.

OWEN Meriel, b. 23 Dec 1932, Toronto, NSW, Aust. Musician; Pianist; Teacher. 3 s. Education: AMusA; LMus; Dip, State Conservatorium of Music (Sydney) (Performer and Tchr); Postgrad study w Lidia Baldecchi, Genoa, Italy, 1978, 1979. Appointments: Examiner for AMEB, 1965; Lectr for Remote Areas Scheme, Sydney Conservatorium of Music, 1983-98; Adjudicator in Metrop and County Eisteddfodau. Publication: Pianoforte Works Suitable for Small Hands, 1995. Memberships: Bus and Profl Women's Assn, 1975; Zonta, 1975-85; Exec and Pres, Warringah Branch, Music Tchrs Assn of NSW, 1980-95; Cncl Mbr, 1997 (re-elected); Pres, for 2 terms of 3 yrs; Received Arts Cncl Grant for study w L Baldecchi, 1978. Hobbies: Travel; Skiing; Family gatherings; Playing 4-hand repertoire. Address: 7 Talgarra Place, Beacon Hill, 2100 NSW, Australia.

OWEN Robert John Richard, b. 11 Feb 1940, London, Eng. Investment Banker. Div, 2 s, 1 d. Education: MA (1st Class Hons), Oxford Univ, 1961. Appointments: Brit For Serv, 1961-68; HM Treas, 1968-77; Dir, Morgan Grenfell & Co Ltd, 1970-79; Dir, Lloyds Bank Intl Ltd, 1980-84; Chmn, Lloyds Merchant Bank and Dir of Investment Banking of Lloyds Bank Grp, 1984-88; Chmn, Securities and Futures Commission of Hong Kong, 1989-92; Dpty Chmn, Nomura (Asia) Holdings NV, 1993-; Dir, Eurn Capital Co Ltd, 1992-; Dir, Intl Securities Consultancy Ltd, 1995-; Dir, Regent Pacific Grp LTd, 1998-; Mbr of Cncl and Regulatory Bd, Lloyds of London, 1993-96. Hobbies: Mountain walking;

Collecting oriental paintings. Address: C/o Nomura International Ltd, 21/F Garden Road, Central, Hong Kong.

OYAKE Tsuneo, b. 29 Oct 1932, Tokyo, Japan. Diplomat. m. Anne-Marie, 8 Aug 1960, 4 d. Education: BA, Univ Tokyo. Appointments: Amb to Zaire, Iran, Argentina; VP, Overseas Econ Coop Fund; Snr Advsr to Chubu Elec Power Co Inc, Kumagai-Gumi Constrn Co Ltd; Specl Rep, World Exposition 2005. Membership: Intl House of Japan. Hobby: International Cooperation. Address: 1-21-3 Kyonancho, Musashino-shi, Tokyo 180-0023, Japan.

OZAKTAS Haldun M, b. 18 June 1966, Ankara, Turkey. Electrical Engineer. Education: BS, Mid E Tech Univ, 1987; MS, 1988, PhD, 1991, Stanford Univ. Appointments: Rsch Asst, Stanford Univ, 1988-91; Prof, Bilkent Univ, 1991-; Postdoct Fell, Univ Erlangen, 1992; Cnslt, AT&T Bell Labs, 1994. Publications: Over 100 in profl jrnls and proceedings. Honours: Parlar Awd, 1994; ICO Prize, 1998. Memberships: Optical Soc of Am; Fndr, Pres, Optical Cttee, Turkey. Hobbies: Cinema; Literature. Address: Bilkent University, Department of Electrical Engineering, Bilkent, Ankara 06533, Turkey.

P

PACHECO Maximo, b. 12 Feb 1953, Santiago, Chile. Economist. m. Soledad Flanagan, 1976, 4 d. Appointments: Mngr, Banco Osorno; Mngr, Planning, Banco Talca; Exec Dir, Cabildo SA, 1982-90, Jucosa, 1987-90; Gen Mngr, Leasing Andino, 1983-90; Pres, Chilean Leasing Assn, 1984-90; Fac Mbr, Univ de Chile; COO, Codelco-Chile; Exec VP for Chile & Latin Am, Carter Holt Harvey, 1994-. Address: Miraflores 222, 13th Floor, Santiago, Chile.

PACINO Al (Alfredo James), b. 25 Apr 1940, New York, USA. Actor. Education: HS for the Performing Arts, NY; Actors Studio. Appointments: Messenger, Cinema Usher; Co-Artistic Dir, The Actors Studio Inc, NY, 1982-83; Mbr, Artistic Directorate Globe Th, 1997-. Creative Works: Appearances incl: Does a Tiger Wear a Necktie?, 1969; Kilroy in Camino Real, 1970; The Connection; Hello Out There; Tiger at the Gates; The Basic Training of Pavlo Hummel, 1977; American Buffalo, 1981; Julius Caesar, 1988; Salome, 1992; Richard III; Arturo Ui; Rats. Films incl: Me, Natalie, 1969; Panic in Needle Park, 1971; The Godfather, 1972; Scarecrow, 1973; Serpico, 1974; The Godfather Part II, 1974; Dog Day Afternoon, 1975; Bobby Deerfield, 1977; And Justice For All, 1979; Cruising, 1980; Author! Author!, 1982; Scarface, 1983; Revolution, 1985; Sea of Love, 1990; Dick Tracy, 1991; The Godfather Part III, 1990; Frankie and Johnny, 1991; Glengarry Glen Ross, 1992; Scent of A Woman, 1992; Carlito's Way, 1994; City Hall, 1995; Heat, 1995; Donny Brasco, 1996; Looking for Richard, 1996; Devil's Advocate, 1997. Honours include: Acady Awd, Best Actor, 1996; Tony Awd, 1996; Natl Soc of Film Critics Awd; Brit Film Awd. Address: c/o Rick Nicita, CAA, 9830 Wilshire Boulevard, Beverly Hills, CA 90212, USA.

PACKER Kerry Francis Bullmore, b. 17 Dec 1937, Sydney, NSW, Aust. Publishing and Broadcasting Director. m. Roslyn Weedon, 30 Aug 1963, 1 s, 1 d. Appointments: Chmn, Consolidated Press Holdings Ltd, 1974-; Dir, Publng and Brdcstng Ltd, 1974. Memberships: Roy Sydney Golf Club; Austl Golf Club; Elanora Country Club; Tattersall's Athaneum (Melbourne) Club. Hobbies: Golf; Tennis; Cricket; Polo. Address: Consolidated Press Holdings Ltd, 54 Park Street, Sydney, NSW 2000, Australia.

PADILLA Roberto Aquino, b. 6 Nov 1947, Manila, Philippines. Lawyer; Labor Leader. m. Cristylinda, 3 s, 2 d. Education: BLL; BA. Appointments: Natl Pres, Natl Mines and Appied Workers Union; Mbr, Exec Cttee, Intl Fedn of Chems, Energy and Mining; VP, Trade Union Congress of Philippines. Honour: Most Outstndng Silver Jubilarian Awd, 1989. Memberships: Integrated Bar of Philippines; San Beda Coll Alumni Assn; Phil Demo Socialist Party. Hobby: Precision shooting. Address: Unit 201-A Dunville Condominium, Castilla St Cor Valencia St, New Manila, Quezon City, 1112, Philippines.

PADMANABHAN Ananadom, b. 30 Dec 1943, Kanyakumary. Teacher. m. Velammal, 19 Oct 1968, 2 d. Education: BPharm, 1968; MPharm, 1973. Appointments: Pharmacist, Medl Coll, Calcut, 1969-70; Pharmacist, 1970-71, 1973, Medl Coll, Trivandrum; Tutor, 1973-74; Asst Prof, 1974-84, Assoc Prof, 1984-89, Prof, 1989-, Coll of Pharm Scis, Medl Coll, Trivandrum. Honour: Best Ppr Awd of III Annual Natl Conf of Assn of Pharm Tchrs of India. Membership: Assn of Pharm Tchrs of India. Hobbies: Music; Reading. Address: Souparnika, V M R Lane, Mangattukadavu Road, Thirumala, Trivandrum 6, India.

PADMANABHAN Thanu, b. 10 Mar 1957, Trivandrum, Kerala, India. Scientist; Researcher; Teacher. m. Vasanthi Padmanabhan 21 Mar 1983, 1 d. Education: BS, 1977, MSc, 1979, Kerala Univ; PhD, TIFR, Bombay Univ, 1983; Postdoct Rsch, Inst of Astron, Cambridge, UK, 1986-87. Appointments: Var positions at TIFR, Bombay, 1980-92; Prof and Dean, Core Acad Progs, IUCAA Pune; Visng positions abroad incl: Rsch Assoc,

Astron Cntr, Univ of Sussex, 1991; Snr Visng Fell, Inst of Astron, Cambridge, UK, 1993; Visng Prof, Princeton Univ, USA, Sept-Nov, 1994, May, 1996; Visng Prof, PA State Univ, USA, 1995; Visng Prof, Caltech, USA, June 1996, Apr-May, 1997, Apr-May, 1998. Publications: Over 120 pprs in refereed intl jrnls, 1982-99 on quantum theory, gravitation, astrophysics; 5 books incl: Structure Formation in the Universe, 1993; Cosmology and Astrophysics through Problems, 1996; After the first three minutes - the story of our universe, 1998; Course on Theoretical Astrophysics, vols I, II, III, 1999; ed, 2 books. Honours include: Gold Medalist Kerala Univ, 1977, 1979; INSA Young Sci Awd, 1984; Gravity essay 5th awd, Gravity Rsch Fndn, USA, 1984; Fell, Indian Acady Scis, 1991-; Birla Sci Prize, 1991; Fell Natl Acady of Scis, 1993-; Fell, Maharashtra Acady of Sci, 1995-; Shanti Swarup Bhatnagar Awd, 1996; A C Banerji Mem Lect Awd, 1997. Memberships include: Intl Astron Union. Hobbies: Chess; Origami. Address: Inter-University Centre for Astronomy and Astrophysics (IUCAA), Post bag 4, Ganeshkhind, Pune 411 007, India.

PADOLINA William Gonzales, b. 15 Nov 1946. Secretary for Department of Science and Technology. Education: BSc, magna cum laude, Agricl Chem, Univ of the Philippines, Los Baños, 1968; PhD, Botany and Phytochem, Univ of TX, Austin, USA, 1973. Appointments: Vice Chan for Acad Affairs, Univ of the Philippines, Los Baños; Prof IX of Chem, on secondment to Dept of Sci and Technol; Undersec for Rsch and Dev, 1992-94, Acting Sec, 1994, Currently Sec, Dept of Sci and Technol; Chem and Biotechnol Cnslt for some pvte cos in the Philippines; Intl Expert Panelist in Biotechnol, Biosafety, Technol Transfer; Served on var intl advsry cttees; Delivered many pprs in intl sci confs. Honours: Outstndng Young Scientist in the Field of Phytochem, 1982; Outstndng Young Men Awd for Sci and Technol, 1985; Outstndng Rsch-Admnstr Awd, Philippine Fedn of Chem Soc, 1989; Pantas Awd for Rsch and Mngmt, 1989; NRCP Achmnt Awd in Chem, 1994; Benigno S Aquino Jr Fellowship Awd for Profl Dev, 1994; Academician, Natl Acady of Sci and Technol; Elected Pres, 40th Annual Conf of IAEA, 1996. Address: Department of Science and Technology, Bicutan, Taguig, Metro Manila, Philippines.

PAENIU Bikenibeu, b. 10 May 1956, Bikenibeu, Tarawa, Tuvalu. Politician; Economist. m. Foketi Paeniu, 2 s, 2 d. Education: King George V Sch, Tarawa; Univ of S Pacific, Suva; Univ HI, USA. Appointments: Agricl Divsns, Tuvalu; Asst Econ, S Pacific Comm, Nouméa; PM of Tuvalu, 1989-93. Address: Office of the Prime Minister, Fongafale, Tuvalu.

PAHANG Sultan Haji Ahmad Shah Al-Mustain Billah ibni Al-Marhum Sultan Abu Bakar Ri'Ayatuddin Al-Muadzam Shah, b. 24 Oct 1930, Istana Mangga Tunggal, Pekan. Malaysian Ruler. m. Tengku Hajjah Afzan binti Tengku Muhammad, 1954. Education: Malay Coll, Kuala Kangsar; Worcester Coll; Oxford Univ. Appointments: Tengku Mahkota (Crown Prince), 1944; Capt, 4th Battalion, Roy Malay Regt, 1954; Mbr, State Cncl, 1955; Regent, 1956, 1959, 1965; Cmdr, 12th Infantry Battalion of Territorial Army, 1963-65, Lt-Col; Succeeded as Sultan, 1974; Timbalan Yang di Pertuan Agong (Dpty Supreme Hd of State of Malaysia), 1975-79, Yang di Pertuan Agong (Supreme Hd of State), 1979-84, 1985; Constitutional Hd of Intl Islamic Univ, 1988. Honours: DLitt, Malaya, 1988; LLD, Northrop, USA, 1993. Address: Istana Abu Bakar, Pekan, Pahang, Malaysia.

PAHLAVI Farah Diba, b. 14 Oct 1938, Iran. Empress of Iran. m. HIM Shah Mohammed Resza Pahlavi, 1959, dec 1980, 2 s, 2 d. Education: Jeanne d'Arc Sch; Razi Sch, Teheran; Ecole Spéciale d'Architecture, Paris. Appointments: Fng Assoc Mbr, Fine Arts Acady, France, 1974; Fmr Patron, Farah Pahlavi Assn, Iran Cultural Fndn, and 34 other educl, hlth and cultural orgs; Left Iran, 1979; Living in Egypt, 1980-.

PAIK Kun Woo, b. 10 Mar 1946, South Korea. Pianist. Education: Juilliard Sch, NY; London; Italy. Appointments: Interpreter of Piano Works of Ravel, Liszt, Scriabin,

Prokofiev; Played w Orchs in N Am & Eur, incl: Indianapolis Symph, BBC Symph, Orchestre Nat de France, Polish Radio Natl Symph; Recitals at all maj Eurn music fests. Honours: 3 Diapason d'Or Awds. Address: c/o Worldwide Artists Ltd, 12 Rosebery Avenue, Thornton Heath, Surrey CR7 8PT, England.

PAINE Gordon Allan, b. 4 Jan 1955, Dunedin, NZ. Barrister; Solicitor. m. (1) 8 Mar 1980, (2) Diane, 24 Oct 1998, 1 s. Education: LLB, Otago. Appointments: Staff Solicitor, Sinclair, Horder & O'Malley, 1980-85, Wheller & Pahl, 1985, Row McBride, 1985-88; Ptnr, Fitzherbert Rowe, 1988. Publications: Sev articles in profl jrnls. Memberships: Manawatu Dist Law Soc, 1993-; Regent Th Trust Bd; Birthright (PN) Inc. Hobbies: Hot Air Ballooning; Music; Rugby. Address: Fitzherbert Rowe, Private Bag 11016, Palmserston North, New Zealand.

PAK Po-Hi, b. 29 Dec 1929. Social Development Planner; Professor, Retired. m. Chae-Kyung Oh, 28 Apr 1988, 1 s. Education: BA, Ewha Womans Univ, Seoul; MSW, Univ of Toronto; DSW, Columbia Univ, NY, USA. Appointments: Instr, Asst Prof, Assoc Prof, Prof, Ewha Womans Univ, 1956-84; Cnslt, UN Hq/UNICEF, 1975, 1977-78; Mbr of Advsry Cttees on Socl Security, Min of Hlth and Socl Affairs, Korea Dev Inst, 1976-79; Chf, Women in Dev, Social Dev Policy and Plng, UN Econ and Socl Commn for Asia and the Pacific, 1979-88; Cnslt, UN Hq (DESPICA)/UN ESCAP/UNICEF, 1988-96; Mbr of Natl Commn on Women's Policies, Govt of Korea, 1989-91, 1994-; Chairperson of the Bd, Dir, Korea Inst for Socl Info and Rsch, 1992-; Mbr of Govt Deleg to the 4th World Conf on Women, Beijing, 1995. Publications include: A Study of Income Maintainance Policy Formation in Selected Under-developed Countries, doct dissertation, 1973; Source Book for Korean Children and Youth for the 1990s, 1992; Planning and Management of Social Development Programmes with Particular Reference to the Agenda for Action on Social Development in the Asia-Pacific Region; Targeting and Target-Setting in Social Development Planning and Management, 1996; Social Development Perspectives and Strategies into the 21st Century, 1998. Honour: Ewha Womans Univ Dev Decade Fell, 1969-72. Memberships: Exec Cttee, Fin Cttee and Plng Cttee, Korean Fedn of YWCA, 1994-; Fndr, Advsr, 1991-, Pres, 1998-, Korea Cncl of Children's Orgs; Women in Future Soc Cttee, Rotary Intl, 1996-97. Hobbies: Literature; Music; Ballet; Spectator sports; Baduk. Address: 22-76 Hewha-Dong, Jongro-ku, Seoul 110-530, Korea.

PAK Song Chol. Politician. Appointments: Amb to Bulgaria, 1954; Min of Fgn Affairs, 1959; Mbr, Ctrl Cttee, Workers Pty of Korea, 1961, Mbr, Polit Bur, 1980-; Vice-Premier, Min of Fgn Affairs, 1966; 2nd Vice-Premier, 1970; Polit Commissar of WPK, 1970; Premier, 1976; Mbr, Ctrl Peoples Cttee, 1977; VP, Democratic Peoples Repub of Korea, 1977-; Mbr, Presidium, Democratic Front for Reunification of Fatherland, 1991. Address: Office of the Vice President, Pyongyang, Korea.

PAL Sankar Kumar, b. 15 Sept 1950. Researcher and Teacher. m. Amita Pal, 19 Feb 1986, 2 s. Education: PhD, Sc; PhD, Engg; DIC. Appointments: Disting Scientist Prof, NASA-NRC; Assoc, Assoc Prof, Fulbright Fell, Computer Engr. Publications: 200 rsch pprs; 3 books; 1 US pat. Honours: SS Bhatnagar Prize, 1990; Jawaharlal Nehru Fell, 1993; Fell, IEEE, USA, 1993; Vikram Sarabhan Rsch Awd, 1994; IEEE TNN, USA; Outstndng Ppr Awd, 1994; FNA, 1994; Ramal Wadhara Gold Medal, 1997; TWAS, 1999; Om Bhasin Awd, 1999. Memberships: FIEEE; FNASC; FNAE; FNA. Address: Machine Intelligence Unit, Indian Statistical Institute, 203 B T Road, Calcutta 700035, India.

PAL SINGH Krishna, b. 2 Aug 1922, India. Politician. Appointments: Pres, Students Union, Rewa; Organized, Congress & Congress Volunteer Corps; Worker w Sindhi Refugees, 1947-48; Joined Quit India Movt; VP, MP, Unit of All India Trades Union Congress; Joined Socialist Pty, 1946, Pres, Fmr Vindya Pradesh & Samyukta Socialist Pty, MP; Joined Congress Pty, 1965; Mbr, AICC & MPCC, later Gen Sec, VP, MPCC, Specl invitee, AIC

Working Cttee; MP, Vidhan Sabha, 1962-90. Memberships: Pres, Friends of Soviet Union, India-Chia Soc; India Africa Friendship Assn; All India Indo-Arab Friendship Soc. Address: Raj Bhavan, Gandhinagar, Gujarat, India.

PALLOTTA-CHIAROLLI Maria, b. 13 Aug 1960, Adelaide, Aust. Lecturer; Writer; Consultant. m. Rob 17 Dec 1983, 1 d. Education: MA; Grad Dip A; Dip Ed; BA; Currently completing a PhD. Appointments: Gender and Equity Exec Offr, 1992-93; Univ of SA, 1992-93; Univ of Adelaide, 1991-93; Macquarie Univ, 1995, 1997-98; Deakin Univ, 1998-. Publications: Someone You Know, 1991; Girl's Talk, 1998; Tapestry: Interweaving Lives, 1999; Num book chapts and jrnl articles. Honours: 1st runner-up, Women's Library Short Story Competition, 1997; Austl Bisexual Network Awd for Serv to Cmnty, 1996. Memberships: Many assns inclng: women's, Italian, queer, educl. Hobbies: Reading; Writing; Dancing; Eating; Film. Address: 15 Mountain Ash Avenue, Ashwood, Victoria 3147, Australia.

PALMER Ernest Lawrence, b. 6 Oct 1923, Perth, WA, Aust. Retired Army Officer. m. Rosa Doris Luck, 10 Aug 1946, 2 s, 1 d. Appointments: Messenger, Post Master Gens Dept, 1937-38, 1939; Clk, Austl Taxation Dept, 1938-39; Storeman, Def Dept, 1939-42; Pvte, Corporal Sergeant, Staff Sergeant WO 11, Lt, Cap, Maj, Lt Col, Col, Brigadier, Austl Army, 1942-78. Honours: Queens Silver Jubilee Medal, 1977; AO, 1978; Mil Barracks, Guilford, WA, named Palmer Barracks, 1988. Membership: FAIM. Hobbies: Fishing; Golf; Gardening; Music. Address: 16A Castlemain Heights, Leemnig, WA 6149, Australia.

PALMER Geoffrey Winston Russell, b. 21 Apr 1942, Nelson, New Zealand. Plitician; Professor. m. Margaret E Hinchcliff, 1963, 1 s, 1 d. Education: Nelson Coll; Vic Univ of Wellington; Univ Chgo, USA. Appointments: Solicitor, Wellington, 1964-66; Lectr, Polit Scis, Vic Univ, 1968-69; Prof of Law, Univ IA, Univ VA, USA, 1969-73; Prin Asst to Austl Natl Comm of Inquiry on Rehab & Compensation, 1973; Prof of Engl & NZ Law, Vic Univ, 1974-79; Vis Fell, Wolfson Coll, Oxford, 1978; Mbr, Parl for Christchurch Ctrl, 1979-90; Dpty Ldr, NZ Labour Pty, 1983-89; Dpty PM, Min of Justice, Atty-Gen, 1984-89, for the Environ, 1987-90; PM of NZ, 1989-90; Min in Charge of NZ Security Intelligence; Prof of Law, Vic Univ, 1991-, Univ IA, 1991-95; Ptnr, Chen & Palmer, Wellington, 1995-. Publications: Unbridled Power? - An Interpretation for Incapacity - A Study of Law and Social Change in Australia and New Zealand, 1979; Environmental Politics - A Greenprint for New Zealand, 1990; New Zealand Constitution in Crisis, 1992; Public Law in New Zealand, 1993; Environment - The International Challenge, 1995; Bridled Power, 1997. Honours: Ida Beam Disting Vis Prof of Law, Univ IA, 1991; UN Environ Prog Global 500 Laureate, 1991. Hobbies: Cricket; Golf; Trumpet; Fishing. Adress: 63 Roxburgh Street, Mount Victoria, Wellington, New Zealand.

PALMER Glen, b. 23 Sept 1945, Temora, NSW, Aust. University Lecturer. m. Robert Anderson. Education: PhD; MEd; BEd; TCert. Appointments: Snr Lectr, Univ of S Aust; Lectr, Griffith Univ (current). Publications: On Home Ground, 1990; Reluctant Refuge: unaccompanied refugee and evacuee children in Australia, 1933-1945, 1997. Address: PO Box 1179, Oxley, Qld, Australia.

PALMER John M, b. 1 Aug 1933, Oakland, CA, USA. Professor, Chair of Urologic Pediatrics. m. Susan Sutton, 6 Feb 1982, 2 s, 1 d. Education: AB, Dartmouth Coll, Hanover, 1955; MD, Stanford Univ, 1960. Appointments: Instr, Asst Prof of Surg, Stanford Univ, 1965-70; Cnslt, Palo Alto Vets Admin Hosp, Santa Clara Med Cntr, 1965-70; Fndr, Dir, Artificial Kidney Unit, Stanford Univ, 1966-69; Dir, Chmn, Dept of Urol, 1970-84, Dir, Renal Transplant Serv, 1970-74, Prof, Dept of Urol, 1973-, Asst Dir, Hosp and Clin Med Advsr for Surg Servs, 1987-, Univ CA, Davis Med Cntr, Sch of Med, Sacramento; Cnslt, Vets Admin Med Cntr, Martinez, CA, 1972-91; Sacramento, 1993-96; Cnslt, Kaiser Permanente Med Cntr, Sacramento, 1972-. Honours: Alpha Omega Alpha,

1960; AOA, Eta Chapt, Treas, 1983-93. Memberships include: Amn Acady of Pediats; Amn Assn of Univ Profs; Amn Coll of Surgns; Amn Med Assn; Amn Soc of Nephrol; Amn Soc of Trauma Surgns. Hobbies: Golf; Fishing; Hunting; Travel. Address: University of California at Davis, Department of Urology, 4860 Y Street, Suite 3500, Sacramento, CA 95817, USA.

PALTA Jairo A, b. 23 Nov 1953, Cali-Colombia. Plant Biologist (Physiologist). Education: PhD, LaTrobe Univ, Melbourne, Aust; MSc, Cinestav, Mexico DF Mex; BS, Univ del Valle, Cali-Colombia. Appointments: Post-doct Rsch Fell, Univ of N Wales, Bangor, Wales; Post-doct Rsch Assoc, UCLA-LBES, Los Angeles, CA, USA; Rsch Scientist, Snr Rsch Scientist and Prin Rsch Scientist, CSIRO Plant Ind, Perth, WA, Aust. Publications: Over 60 publd pprs inclng 2 books, chapts in books and rsch pprs. Honours: PNUD-UNESCO Schlshp; Austl Oil-Seeds Rsch Schlshp; GRDC Snr Fellshp. Memberships: ASPP, USA; ASPP, Canberra, Aust; ASA, USA; Austl Soc of Agronomy. Hobbies: Tennis; Bushwalking; Jogging. Address: CSIRO Plant Industry, Private Bag, PO Wembley, WA 6014, Australia.

PALTRIDGE Brian Richard, b. 28 May 1947, Auckland, NZ. University Lecturer. Education: BA (VUW); RSA Dip TEFLA; Dip TESOL (UTS); Asst Dip Comm Lang (MIHE); MA (Sydney); PhD (Waikato). Appointments: Lectr, Univ of Sydney, 1989; Snr Lectr, Intl Pacific Coll, NZ, 1990-91; Snr Lectr, Univ of Waikato, 1992-94; Snr Lectr, Univ of Melbourne, 1995-. Publications: Genre, Frames and Writing in Research Settings, 1997; Num refereed jrnl articles. Honour: MAK Halliday Schlshp, 1991. Memberships: Applied Ling Assn of Aust, TESOL; TESOL Assn of Aotearos, NZ; Applied Ling Assn of NZ. Address: Department of Linguistics and Applied Linguistics, University of Melbourne, Parkville, VIC 3051, Australia.

PAN Austin De-En, b. 4 Aug 1960, Taiwan, China. University Teacher. m. Penny, 20 Dec 1986, 1 d. Education: BS, Univ of Texas, Austin; MSc, Univ of California, Berkeley; PhD, Univ of California, Berkeley. Appointments: Structural Engr, T Y Lin Intl, 1982; Asst Prof, Purdue Univ, 1989; Assoc Prof, Univ of Hong Kong, 1995. Memberships: Profl Civil Engr (CA), 1984; Amn Soc of Civil Engrs, 1989; Amn Concrete Inst, 1989; Cntr for Asian Tall Buildings and Urban Habitat, 1997. Hobbies: Swimming; World traveller. Address: Department of Civil Engineering, University of Hong Kong, Pokfulam Road, Hong Kong.

PAN Chang Yu, b. 6 Jan 1934. Doctor; Physician; Endocrinologist; Diabetologist. m. Lei Shilian, 3 s. Education: Grad, Harbin Medl Univ, 1956. Appointments: Res Physn, 1956; Chf Physn, 1961; Physn in Charge, 1963; Dpty Chf Dr, 1974; Chf Dr, 1986; Mbr, Consultant Cttee of Diabetologists, Min of Hlth, China, 1997. Publications: Study of the Prevalence of Diabetes Mellitus in Adults in the Corporation in Beijing, 1996; Human Epidermal Keratinorytes in Culture Convert Thyraxine. Honours: Chinese PLA Sci and Technol Advmnt Awd, 1989, 1993, 1997, 1998. Memberships: Cncl Mbr, Chinese Medl Assn; Soc of Endocrinology of CMA; Soc of Diabetes; Soc of Endocrinology of Chinese PLA; Amn Diabetes Assn. Hobbies: Music; Dancing. Address: Chinese PLA General Hospital, Beijing 100853, China.

PAN Du Wu, b. 2 June 1935, Hubei Prov, China. Professor. m. Liu Huayun, July 1968, 2 s. Education: MPhys. Appointments: Asst, Lectr, Prof, Dept of Phys, 1960-. Creative Works: Optics, Co-op and Transl; 6 Textbooks; Dictionaries; 30 Sci Pprs. Honour: Educl Prize, China and Shanghai, 1993. Memberships: Phys Soc of Sci and Technol; Philos of Sci Soc of China; Hist of Sci and Technol. Hobbies: Music; Painting; Swimming; Gate ball. Address: 503/40 The 2nd Teachers Apt, Fudan University, 101 Quonian Road, Shanghai 200433, China.

PAN Hong, b. 4 Nov 1954, Shanghai, China. Actress. m. Mi Jingshan, div 1990. Education: Shanghai Drama Acady, 1973-76. Appointments: Actress, Shanghai Film Studio, 1977-80, Omei Film Studio, Chengdu, 1980-; Mbr,

5th Natl Cttee, Fedn of Lit & Art Circles, 1988-. Creative Works: Films incl: The Last Aristocrat; A Slave's Daughter; Camel Bell in the Desert; A Bitter Smile. Honours: 3rd Golden Rooster Best Actress Awd, 1983; 8th Golden Rooser Best Actress Awd, 1988. Address: Omei Film Studio, Tonghui Menwai, Chengdu City, Sichuan, China.

PAN Jie, b. 2 Apr 1960, Najing, China. Dentist. m. Xiao Hong, 26 Dec 1985, 1 s. Education: Mid Med Sch. Appointments: Dir of Dept, Huangyan Hosp of TCMS. Publications: Planting the Artificial Root of HA-Ti; Be Filled the Imperfection of Jaw Bones Cavity with the Artificial Bone of Hydroxy Phosphatic Rock; Treating Forty Eight Examples of Baby's Goose Mouth Fester. Address: Huangyan Hospital of Traditional Chinese Medical Sciences, Huangyan, Zhejiang 318020, China.

PAN Kuo-Liang, b. 19 Nov 1941. Geotechnical Engineer. m. Mei-Lan Hwang, 1 s, 2 d. Education: BS, Natl Cheng Kung Univ, Tainan, Taiwan; PhD, Univ of IA, IAC, IA, USA. Appointments include: Dir, Energy and Resources Labs (Resources Div), 1986-94; Prof, Inst of Applied Geo, Natl Cntrl Univ, Taiwan, 1991-; Rschr, Sci and Technol Advsry Grp, Exec Yuen, Taiwan, 1987-92; Tstee, Geotech Rsch and Dev Fndn, 1990-; Tree, Civil Engrng Technol Fndn, 1994-; VP, Moh and Assocs Inc, 1994-95; Reviewer, Natl Sci Cncl, 1995- Snr VP, Moh and Assocs Inc, 1995-99; Owner, Dir, Entire Geotekers, 1999. Publications: Geologic Analysis of Slopeland, 1986; Development and Investigation of Slopeland, 1991; Environmental Geology, 1993. Honours: Disting Achievement Awds, 1984; Tech Innovation Awds, 1982; Ed-in-Chief, Sino-Geotechs, 1993-96; Cood, Oceanology Intl, 1994. Memberships: Cnclr, 1997-, Geological Soc of China; Chinese Inst of Civil and Hydraulic Engrng; Chinese Inst of Mining and Metallurgical Engrs; Chinese Taipei Tunnelling Assn; Chinese Soc of Earthquake Engrng; SE Asian Geotech Soc; Fell, Geo Soc of Am; Assn of Engrng Geo; Intl Assn of Hydrologists; Sigma Xi, The Sci Rsch Soc; Exec Dir, Sino Geotech Rsch and Dev Fndn, 1996. Listed in: Who's Who in the World. Hobbies: Hiking; Photography. Address: 2F, 4 Alley 5, Lane 265, Hsin Yi Road, Sec 4, Taipei, Taiwan.

PAN Zhong Ming, b. 25 Feb 1935, Tianjin, China. Educational Researcher. m. Wan Peng Li, 28 Dec 1958, 1 s, 1 d. Education: MA, Fudan Univ, Shanghai, China. Hobby: Literature. Address: Fang Xing Yuan 1-10-1903, Fang Zhuang, Beijing, China.

PAN Zushan, b. 22 Nov 1935, Zhejiang, China. University Professor. m. Zhiqing Li, 10 Feb 1959, 1 s, 1 d. Education: Bachelor's deg, Nanjing Inst Technol, 1958; Visng Schl, Univ New Brunswick, Can, 1980-82; Exch Rsch Prof to Fed Repub Germany. Appointments: Fac Mbr, Electr Engin Dept, 1958-, Dir, Electrotechnics Lab, 1982-84, Vice-Chmn, Electr Engin Dept, 1984-85, Chmn, Electr Engin Dept, 1985-87, Dpty Dean, College Elecl Power Engrng, 1987-, Shanghai Jiao-Tong Univ; Concurrently Dir, Inst Power Electrons Theor and Snr Mbr, Municipal Sci and Technological Advsry Bd, Yantai and Liuzhou. Publications: A Microprocessor Based Myoelectric Signal Processor with Kalman Filter, 1982; Signal Processing for Proportional Myoelectric Control, 1984; A Model for Generation of Myoelectric Signals, 1985; Monograph, Filtering Technique, 1995. Honours: 1st Prize, Ex Tchng, Shanghai Jiao-Tong Univ, 1983, 1986; Recip, Govt Spec Allowance, Outstndng Intellectual. Memberships: Assn Electr Engin China; Educl Assn Grad Studs Shanghai; Review Bd, Natl Sci and Technological Inv Awd, Electrotechnics Bch. Address: Rm 503, No 18, Lane 51, N Xu-Hong Rd, Shanghai 200030, China.

PANCHANATHAM Natarajan, b. 25 Apr 1962, Kumbakonam, India. Teacher; Researcher. m. A Angayarkanni, 18 Mar 1991, 1 s. Education: PhD; MBA; MCom; MSc; MEd; MA; PGDG&C; DLL; DTD; DCPA. Appointments: Bus Mngr, 1988-89; Lectr, 1989-98; Rdr, 1998-. Publications: 70 pprs in profl jrnls. Honours: Subject Proficiency Awd, 1982; Best Rsch Ppr Awd, 1994; Best Rsch Ppr on Mngmt, 1997. Memberships:

AMIMA; MISTE; MIAAP; MISTD; MAPA, USA; FIASS; MISC; MAEPTP; MFASOHD. Hobbies: Social gathering; Watching television. Address: Annamalai University, Annamalainagar 608 002, Tamil Nadu, India.

PANDEY Deo Narayan, b. 25 Dec 1935, Paras Rampur, Pratapgarh, India. Public Servant. m. Mrs S Devi, 1 s, 3 d. Education: Dip in Cooperation, 1958. Appointments: Supvsr, 1953; ADO, 1988. Publications: Num short stories. Honour: Merit Awd, Cooperation. Membership: UP Cooperation Fed. Hobbies: Gardening; Social work. Address: WU and PO Paras Rampur, Dist Pratapgarh, UP, India.

PANDEY Vijay Narayan, b. 16 Feb 1973, Pratapgarh, UP, India. Service Computer Scientist. Education: BSc, 1993; MSc, Botany, 1995; Dip, NIIT, 1998. Appointments: Environment Protection Grp, 1995-97; Rsch Asst, Dept of Botany, DDU Gorakhpur Univ, UP, India. Publications: Rsch pprs on environmental pollution, 1996. Honour: Environment Awareness Awd, 1997. Memberships: Exec Mbr, Environmental Protection Grp, Health Awareness Soc. Hobbies: Music; Gardening. Address: c/o Professor J N Pandey, Uttarayan, Shivalanagar, Mohaddipur, Gorakhpur, UP, India.

PANDHE Madhukar Kashinath, b. 11 July 1925. Trade Unionist. m. Pramila Pandhe, 14 July 1956, 1 s, 1 d. Education: MA; PhD Econs. Appointments: Sec, All India Trade Union Congress, 1966-70; Sec, Cntr of Indian Trade Unions, 1970-91; Gen Sec, CITU, 1991-; ILO Deleg, 1978, 1979, 1996; Vice Chmn, Intl Energy and Miners Org. Publications: Social Life in Rural India; Child Labour in India; Bonded Labour in India; Political Content of Education. Honours: Gen Sec, Cntr of Indian Trade Unions; Cntrl Cttee, Communist Party of India (Marxist). Memberships: Natl Safety Cncl of India; Natl Shipping Bd; Natl Maritime Bd; Bd of Govs, Soc for Environmental Hlth. Hobbies: Reading; Writing; Travelling. Address: 15 Talkatora Road, New Delhi 110001, India.

PANG Xiao-Feng, b. 31 Dec 1945. Researcher. m. 6 May 1975, 2 s. Education: Grad, Stud Sch of Chinese Acady of Scis, Beijing. Appointments: Dean, Biol Molecular Lab of Atomic and Molecular Physl Inst. Publications: Non-Linear Quantum Mechanical Theory, 1994; The New Theory of Bio-Energy Transport in Living System, 1986-93; The Theory of Bio-Photon Emission of Living Bodies, 1995; Soliton Physics, 1998. Honours: Ex Articles Prize, Sichuan Prov and Chengdu Cty, 1991, 1992; 2nd Deg Prize of Advmt of Sci and Technol, 1993; 1st Deg Prize of Advmt of Sci and Technol, China, 1996. Memberships: NY Acady of Scis; Amn Assn for Advmt of Sci; Chinese Cntr of Advd Sci and Technol; Intl Cntr for Material Phys; Academia Sinica. Hobbies: Study of Biophysics and non-linear sciences; Basketball. Address: Department of Physics, Southwest Inst for Nationalities, Chengdu 610041, Sichuan, China.

PANG Zhiyuan, b. 31 Oct 1938. Professor. m. Ruping Wan, 18 May 1967, 2 d. Education: Dip, Math, Peking Univ. Appointments: Dept of Maths and Mechs, Peking Univ, 1960-61; Dept of Maths, Guizhou Univ, 1961-85; Dept of Maths and Computer Sci, Guizhou Normal Univ, 1985-. Publications: Error Estimates for the Finite Estimate Element Method of Lines, 1993; The Direct Integral Expressions of Stress Intensity Factors in Antiplane Shear for Bi-Materials, 1995; The Direct Integral Expressions of Nth-order SIF's in Bi-Materials (II): General Case, 1996. Honours: 2nd Class Prize, Sci and Technol, Guizhou Prov, 1987; 1st Class Prize, Ex Tchng Material, Natl Educl Cttee, 1987; Natl Prize, Ex Achievement in Tchng, 1989; Outstndng Contbrn in Guizhou Prov, 1990; 3rd Class Prize, Sci and Technol, Guizhou Prov, 1990; Spec Allowance, State Cncl, 1991. Memberships: Chinese Soc of Maths; Chinese Soc of Indl and Applied Maths; Chinese Assn of Bridge. Hobbies: Playing bridge and chess. Address: Department of Mathematics and Computer Science, Guizhou Normal University, Guiyang 550001, China.

PANIGRAHI Chintamani, b. 22 Mar 1922, Biswanathpur, India. State Governor. m. Radhamani

Panigrahi, 1946, 4 s, 1 d. Education: Ravenshaw Coll, Cuttack; Vidyasagar Coll, Calcutta; Univ Calcutta. Appointments: Ed, Daily Prajatantra, Cuttack, 1947-51, Daily Matrubhumi, Cuttack, 1951-56; Mbr, Lok Sabha, 1957-62, 1967-70, 1971-77, 1980-84, 1984-89; Pres, Keonjihar Mining & Forest Workers Union, 1958; VP, World Democratic Youth Fedn, 1958; Treas, Indian Natl Rural Labour Fedn, 1958; Vice Chair, Fedn of Indian Youth, 1959; Chair, Orissa Bharat Sewak Samaj & Vice Chair, Ctrl Bharat Sevak Samaj, 1975; Mbr, Orissa Legis Assembly, 1977-80, Ldr of Opposition, 1978; Pres, Orissa Gramina Majdoor Sangh, 1979; Min of Home Affairs, 1986-88, Min of Def, 1988-89; Gov of Manipur, 1989-93; Chair, Orissa Pradesh Bharat Sevak Samaj; Vice Chair, Bharat Sevak Samaj. Publications: Orissa Speaks; The Tragedy of the Orissa Floods; Sev articles in profl jrnls. Hobbies: Reading; Writing; Travel; Gardening; Farming; Volleyball; Chess. Address: Srima Nibas, Samantrapur, Bubaneswar 2, Puri District, Orissa, India.

PANITCHPAKDI Supachai, b. 30 May 1946. Deputy Prime Minister; Minister of Commerce. Education: BA, MA, Econs, PhD, Dev Plng, Netherlands. Appointments: Mbr, House of Representatives, 1986, 1995, 1996; Dpty Min of Fin, 1986; Mbr, Natl Legislative Assembly, 1991; Senator, 1992; Dpty Prime Min, 1992; Min of Com. Honours: Kt Grand Cordon, Spec Class, Most Exalted Order of the White Elephant; Hon Doct, Econs Dev, India. Address: 25 Sukumvit Soi 5, Sukumvit Road, Klongtoey, Bangkok, Thailand.

PANKAJA Shankarappa, b. 29 July 1979, Mysore, Karnataka, India. Secretary. Education: Dip in Modern Off Prac (Coml Prac); II Yr BCom. Appointment: Sec, M M Interior Furnishers Pvt Ltd, Bangalore, Karnataka, India. Honour: Top Rank Holder in Dip in Modern off Prac (Coml Prac), ABI. Memberships: Rotary Club, Mysore; JSS Polytecnic for Women; PKTB Sanitorium Chest and Heart Disease Hosp. Hobbies: Sports; Interested in writing articles and other literary works. Address: c/o Srinivasacharya, D/No 54, 3rd Main, Nanjappa Block, Kempegowdanagar, Bangalore 560 018, Karnataka, India.

PANOV Alexander Nikolaevich, b. 6 July 1944. Diplomat. 1 d. Education: PhD, Hist, Moscow State Univ of Intl Rels. Appointments: Diplomat, 1968-; Dir, Dept of Pacific Ocean and SE Asian Countries of Min of For Rels of the USSR; Amb, Russia to the Repub of Korea, 1992-93; Dpty For Min of Russian Fedn, 1994-96; Amb, Russia to Japan, 1996-. Publications: Auth, num publs on world diplomatic Hist and issues of the Asian-Pacific reg. Honour: Order of Honor, 1998. Memberships: Moscow State Inst, Univ of Intl Rels, 1971-1977. Address: Azabu-dai, 2-1-1, Minato-ku, Tokyo.

PANT Divya Darshan, b. 18 Oct 1919, Ranikhet, India. Teacher; Scientific Researcher. m. Radha, 4 Dec 1946, 1 s, 2 d. Education: BSc, 1939; MSc, Botany, 1941; DPhil, 1950. Appointments: Stud Demonstrator, 1941-44; Lectr, 1945-64; Rdr, 1964-65; Prof, Botany, Hd of Dept, 1965-82. Creative Works: Studies in Gymnospermous Plants Cycas, 1962; Cycas and Cycadales, 1973; About 300 Pprs in Sci Jrnls. Honours: Silver Medallion; Gold Medal, Indian Botany Soc; Gold Medal, Paeleobotanical Soc; Birbal Sahni Medal, Indian Sci Congress; Lectr and Snr Scientist Awd, Indian Natl Sci Acady. Memberships: Fell, Indian Natl Sci Acady; Fell, Indian Acady of Scis; Fell, Natl Acady of Scis; Fell, Linnean Soc, London; Hon For Mbr, Cycad Socs of Am and S Africa. Hobbies: Gardening; Cycad Collecting and cultivation. Address: Botany Department, Allahabad University, Allahabad.

PANYARACHUN Anand, b. 9 Aug 1932, Thailand. Diplomat; Politician. m. M R Sodsee Panyarachun Chakrabandh, 1956, 2 d. Education: Bangkok Christian Coll; Dulwich Coll, London; Univ Cambridge. Appointments: Min of Fgn Affairs, 1955; Sec to Fgn Min, 1959; 1st Sec, Perm Mission to UN, 1964, Cnclr, 1966, Acting Perm Rep, 1967-72, Amb to Can (concurrently); Amb to USA, Perm Rep to UN, 1972-75, Amb to Fed Repub of Germany, 1977; Perm Under-Sec of State for Fgn Affairs, 1975-76; Del to sev sessions of UN Gen

Assembly & SEATO Cncl; Chair, Grp of 77 on Law of Sea, 1973; Rep to UN Econ & Socl Cncl, 1974-75; Chair, Thai Del to 7th Specl Session of UN Gen Assembly, Vice Chair, Ad Hoc Cttee, 7th Specl Session, 1975; Chair, Textport Intl Corp Ltd; Vice Chair, Saha-Union Corp Ltd, 1979; Pres, ASEAN-CCI Cncl, 1980; VP, Assn of Thai Inds; Vice Chair, ASEAN-US Bus Cncl, 1980; Dir, Sime Darby, 1982; Acting PM, 1991-92; PM of Thailand, 1992; UNICEF Amb for Thailand, 1996. Honour: Ramon Magsaysay Awd, 1997. Hobbies: Tennis; Squash; Reading. Address: Government House, Thanon Nakhon Pathom, Bangkok 10300, Thailand.

PARDON Daniel Bruno, b. 16 Feb 1955. Editor. m. 23 Oct 1982, 1 s. Education: Ecole Française des Attachés de Presse. Appointments: La Dépêche de Tahiti, Reuters (Stringer in French Polynesia); Geomundo (Mexico) Reports and Pictures - Apnéa and Océans (two French diving mags); Mineraux et Fossiles (French Monthly Magazine). Publications: 3 books: Tahiti, Portraits et Danses, 1986; Tahiti Entre ciel et mer, 1992; Mururoa, Fangataufa: Etat des Lieux, 1995. Hobbies: Diving; Precious stones. Address: c/o La Dépêche, PO Box 50, Papeete, Tahiti, French Polynesia.

PAREEK Om Prakash, b. 15 July 1939, Jobner. Agricultural Scientist. m. Kamla, 20 May 1959, 2 s, 1 d. Education: MSc, Agric; PhD, Hort. Appointments: Proj Coord; Hd Offr on Spec Duty and Dir. Publications: The Ber, 1983; Advances in Horticulture, Fruits Vol 1-4, 1993; Wasteland Horticulture, 1998; Underutilized Fruits and Nuts, 1998. Honour: G L Chadha Mem Awd, 1993; Isheer Awd, 1995. Memberships: Hort Soc of India; Haryana Hort Soc and Rajasthan Hort Soc. Hobbies: Reading; Gardening. Address: Director, NRC for Arid Horticulture, Beechwal, Bikaner 334006, India.

PAREKH Atul, b. 7 Jan 1952, Bombay, India. Jeweller. m. Hema, 24 Dec 1989, 1 s, 1 d. Education: BCom. Creative works: Spec jewellery collections: Heart of Africa; Romance of India; Queens of Egypt. Memberships: Hon Sec, Indian Cmnty, Tokyo; Dir, Indian Jewellers Assn, Tokyo. Hobbies: Reading; Music. Address: Noa Bldg, Azabudam 2-3-5, Minato ku, Tokyo.

PARER John Gartlan, b. 19 July 1931, Melbourne, Aust. Surgeon. m. Ann, 5 Oct 1985, 5 s, 3 d. Education: MBBS, Melbourne; FRACS; FRCSE; FACS. Appointments: Nepean Hosp; Jamison Hosp; Minchinbury Hosp. Memberships: RACS; AAS; AMA; S Pacific Underwater Soc; Sydney Colorectal Soc; Colorectal Soc of Aust. Hobbies: Skiing; Boating; Photography; 4WD vehicles. Address: 218 Derby Street, Penrith 2750, Australia.

PARER Julian Thomas, b. 2 Sept 1934, Melbourne, Aust. Obstetrician. m. Robin, 23 Apr 1962, 1 s. Education: BAgriSc; MRurSc; MD; PhD. Appointments include: Rsch Asst, Rural Sci, Univ New England, 1958-61; Grad Fell, Dept of Animal Sci, OR Univ, 1961-63; Grad Asst, 1961-63, Summer Fellshp, 1962, Rsch Fell, 1963-66, Heart Rsch Lab, Univ OR Med Sch; Visng Sci, OR Regl Primate Rsch Cntr, 1964-66; Instr, Dept of Obstet and Gynae, 1966-68, Snr Fell, 1969-71; Mbr, Med Rsch Unit, Child Dev and Med Retardation Cntr, 1969-71, Mbr, Anesthesia Rsch Cntr, 1969-71, Univ WA; Rsch Affiliate, WA Regl Primate Cntr, Seattle, 1969-71; Res, Dept of Obstet and Gynae, LA County-Univ of S CA Sch of Med, 1971-74; Asst Prof, 1974-76, Assoc Prof, 1976-82, Prof, 1982-, Dept of Obstet, Gynae and Reproductive Scis, Assoc Staff, Cardiovascular Rsch Inst, 1976-, Dir of Obstet, 1980-87, Dir, Maternal-Fetal Med Fellshp Trng Prog, 1983-, Co-Dir, N Coast Perinatal Access Syst, 1984-89, Univ CA, San Fran; Visng Sci, Nuffield Inst for Med Rsch and John Radcliffe Hosp, Univ Oxford, 1981-82. Publications: Num articles in profl jrnls. Memberships include: Amn Coll of Obstet and Gynae; Amn Physiol Soc; Pacific Coast Obstet and Gynae Soc; Soc of Maternal-Fetal Med. Hobbies: Hiking; Birding; Desert travel; Australian History. Address: Department of Obstetrics, Gynecology and Reproductive Science, Box 0550, University of California, San Francisco, CA 94143-0550, USA.

PARK Cheol Ho, b. 20 Feb 1956, Youngwol, Korea. Professor. m. Hi Jin Kim, 6 Oct 1985, 1 s, 1 d. Education: PhD, Univ Alberta, Can. Appointments: Asst Prof, 1990-95, Assoc Prof, 1996-, Kangwon Natl Univ, Korea; Ed-in-Chf, Plant Resources Soc of Korea, 1996-98. Publications: Five Books on Wild Plants; Plant Genetic Resources, 1997. Memberships: Korean Breeding Soc; Plant Resources Soc of Korea; Korean Soc of Med Crop Sci. Hobbies: Poetry; Essay writing. Address: c/o Division of Applied Plant Science, Kangwon National University, Chunchon 200-701, Korea.

PARK Choong-Hoon, b. 19 Jan 1919, Cheju-do, Korea. Politician. m. Chung Kyungsook, 1943, 2 s, 4 d. Education: Doshisha Coml Coll, Japan. Appointments: Trade Affairs Dir, Min of Com & Ind, Korea, 1948; Retd Air Force Maj Gen, 1961; Vice-Min of Com & Ind, 1961, Min of Com & Ind, 1963; Dpty Premier, Min of Econ Planning, 1967-69; PM, 1980; Acting Pres, 1980. Memberships: Standing Mbr, Econ & Sci Cncl, 1970-71; Chair, AIRC, 1971-73; Pres, Trade Press, 1973-; Chair, Korea-Saudi Arabia Econ Coop Cttee, 1974-, Korea US Econ Cncl, 1974-80; Korean Tchrs Assn; Naeoe Bus Jrnl; Korea Indl Devel Rsch Inst, 1980-; Advsry Cncl of State Affairs, 1981-. Hobby: Golf. Address: 1-36 Seongbuk-dong, Seongbuk-ku, Seoul, Korea.

PARK Dosik, b. 16 Aug 1935, Kyongbuk, Korea. Professor. Education: PhD, Univ of Sorbonne, Paris. Appointment: Pres, Cath Univ, Taegu, Korea. Publication: Atheism of Karl Marx. Hobby: Golf. Address: 618 Dongsei Hayang Up, Kyongsan, N Kyongsang Province, 712-900, Korea.

PARK Jong Kyun, b. 16 Apr 1963, Jinryong, Kyungbuk, Korea. Professor. m. So Young Kim, 15 Dec 1991, 1 s, 1 d. Education: BS, 1986, MS, 1989, DAgri, 1995, Kyungpook Natl Univ. Appointments: Advsry Cttee, Ex Off, Sericulture and Entomol of Kynugbuk Prov, 1997; Chmn, Dept of Sericulture and Entomol Resources, Sangju Natl Univ, 1998. Publications: Books: Environmental Science, 1999; Natural Science 1995-1999, 1999; Over 30 articles in profl jrnls. Memberships: Entomol Soc of Korea; Japanese Soc of Appl Entomol and Zoology; Ed, Apicultural Soc of Korea. Hobbies: Collection of Insects; Tennis. Address: c/o Department of Sericulture and Entomology Resources, Sangju National University, Sangju City, Kyongbuk 742-711, Korea.

PARK Kyu Tae, b. 11 June 1933, Kochang, Korea. Professor of Computer Engineering. m. Moon Ja Shon, 25 Oct 1970, 2 s. Education: BS (Electr Engin), Yonsei Univ, Korea, 1957; MSc (Eng), Univ Coll, London, 1964; PhD, Southampton Univ, UK, 1969. Appointments: Rsch Engr, MO Valave Co, GEC, London, 1964-67; Prof of Computer Engrng, 1969-98; Chmn, Dept of Electron Engrng, 1973-77; Dean of Univ Admin, 1980-84; Dean of Engnrg, 1988-92; Yonsei Univ, Mbr Presdtl Cncl, Sci and Technol, 1992-93; Pres, Korea Natl Assn of Univ Engrng, 1992-93; Vice Chmn, Korea Sci and Enrng Fndn, 1992-98. Publications: Digital Logic, 1975; Digital Logic and Circuits, 1983; Digital Circuits and Systems, 1988; Computer Architecture-I, 1989; Computer Architecture II, 1990; Over 200 pprs. Honours: Acad Excellence Awd, IEEK, 1973, 1974; Order of Merit, Tongbaeck Medal, Repub of Korea, 1988; Haedong Acady Awd, 1997. Memberships: Chartered Engr (UK), 1983; IEEE, Mbr, Snr Mbr, Fell, 1983-; Inst of Electronic Engrng Korea, Pres, 1986; IEE Fell (UK), 1995; Korea Info Sci Soc; Korea Brit Soc. Hobby: Golf. Address: 651-2 Shinsa-dong Kangnam-ku, Seoul, 135-120, Korea.

PARK (Rosina) Ruth (Lucia), b. Aust. Author; Playwright. Publications: The Uninvited Guest (play), 1948; The Harp in the South, 1948; Poor Man's Orange (in USA as 12 and a Half Plymouth Street), 1949; The Witch's Thorn, 1951; A Power of Roses, 1953; Pink Flannel, 1955; The Drums Go Bang (autobiographical with D'Arcy Niland), 1956; One-a-Pecker, Two-a-Pecker (in USA as the Frost and the Fire), 1961; The Good Looking Women, 1961; The Ship's Cat, 1961 (in USA as Serpent's Delight, 1962); Uncle Matt's Mountain, 1962;

The Road to Christmas, 1962; The Road Under the Sea, 1962; The Hole in the Hill (in USA as The Secret of the Maori Cave), 1964; The Muddle-Headed Wombat series, 11 vols, 1962-76; Shaky Island, 1962; Airlift for Grandee, 1964; Ring for the Sorcerer, 1967; The Sixpenny Island (in USA as Ten-Cent Island), 1968; Nuki and the Sea Serpent, 1969; The Companion Guide to Sydney, 1973; Callie's Castle, 1974; The Gigantic Balloon, 1975; Swords and Crowns and Rings, 1977; Come Danger, Come Darkness, 1978; Playing Beatie Bow, 1980; When the Wind Changes, 1980; The Big Brass Key, 1983; The Sydney We Love, 1983; Missus, 1985; My Sister Sif, 1986; The Tasmania We Love, 1987; Callie's Family: James, 1991; A Fence Around the Cuckoo, 1992; Fishing in the Styx, 1993; Home Before Dark, 1996; Ruth Park's Sydney, 1999. Address: c/o Curtis Brown Pty Ltd, PO Box 19, Paddington, NSW 2021, Australia.

PARK Yeung-Ho, b. 30 May 1930, Kyongbuk, Korea. Professor. m. Yeung-Seng Moon, 21 Jan 1958, 1 s, 3 d. Education: BS, Natl Fisheries Univ of Pusan (NFUP), 1952; MSc, 1969, DSc, 1973, Grad Sch, NFUP; Studied Tokyo Univ of Fisheries, Japan, 1971-72. Appointments: Asst Prof, 1969-72, Assoc Prof, 1972-78, Prof, 1978-85, 1989-95, NFUP; Hd, Dept of Food Sci and Technol, NFUP, 1973-75; Dir, Seafood Rsch Inst, NFUP, 1975-77; Dean, Fac of Engrng, NFUP, 1981-84; Dean, Grad Sch, NFUP, 1984-85; Pres, NFUP, 1985-89; Mbr, Presdtl Commn on Sci and Technol, Repub of Korea, 1989-90; Mbr Natl Acady of Scs, Korea, 1989-; Cncl Mbr, Advsry Cncl for Dem and Peaceful Unification, Korea, 1991-95; Mbr, Korea Acady of Sci and Technol, 1994-; Prof Emeritus, Pukyong Natl Univ, 1996-. Publications: 147 pprs; Rsch articles; Critical and info reviews; 51 articles; 14 books incl Processing and Utilization of Marine Products, 1994. Honours: Prize of Repub of Korea for Sci and Technol, 1986; Order of Civil Merit of Moran Medal, 1990; Prize of Wolhae for Fisheries Sci, Wolhae Fndn, 1996. Memberships: Pres, 1982-84, Cnclr, 1975-, Korea Fisheries Soc; Cnclr, Korea Soc of Food Sci and Technol, 1978-; Dir, Korea Soc of Food Sci & Nutrition, 1978-95; Pres, Korea Educl Assn for Fisheries and Marine Scis, 1985-87; Cnclr, Korea Soc of Dietry Culture, 1986-. Hobbies: Pot-planting; Golf. Address: #7-107 Samick Apt, 148 Namcheon-Dong, Suyong-Gu, Pusan, Korea.

PARKER David Henry, b. 25 Feb 1934, Auckland, NZ. University College Principal. m. Kathleen Alison Stevens, 19 Dec 1962, 3 d. Education: MA, Auckland Univ; MLitt, Queens Coll, Oxford Univ, Eng. Appointments: Asst Master, Auckland Grammar Sch, 1958-65; Asst Master, Kings Sch, Chester, Eng, 1961; Lectr, Snr Lectr, Dept of Engl, Univ of Waikato, NZ, 1966-79; Master, Ormond Coll, Univ of Melbourne, Aust, 1980-89; Cnslt, 1993-. Honours: Shirtcliffe Fell, Univ of Auckland, 1968; Hon Rsch Fell, Univ of Exeter, 1977. Hobby: Fly-fishing. Address: 8 Gifford Street, St Heliers, Auckland, New Zealand.

PARKER David Heywood, b. 5 Aug 1943, Adelaide, Aust. Academic. m. Helen, 19 Jan 1970, 2 s, 1 d. Education: BA, Dip, Educn, Adelaide; BA, Flinders; DPhil, Oxford. Appointments: Tutor, Flinders Univ; Lectr, Snr Lectr, Rdr, Aust Natl Univ; Prof, Austl Cath Univ. Publications: Building on Sand, 1988; Mighty World of Eye, 1990; Ethics, Theory and the Novel, 1994; Shame and the Modern Self, 1996. Hobbies: Bushwalking; Football; Tennis. Address: 84 Boldrewood Street, Turner, ACT 2612, Australia.

PARKER Lee David, b. 18 Mar 1949, Berri, Aust. University Professor. m. (1) 2 s, 1 d, (2) Gloria June Parker, 18 Mar 1992. Education: BEc, Adelaide; MPhil, Dundee; PhD, Monash; FCA, Aust; FCPA; FAIM. Appointments: Profl Prac, 1970-73; Lectr, Glasgow Univ, 1973-74, Dundee Univ, 1974-76, Monash Univ, 1976-85; Prof of Acctng, Griffith Univ, 1985-88; Prof of Com, Flinders Univ, 1988-96, Univ Adelaide, 1997-. Publications: Over 120 books and jrnl articles. Memberships include: Aust Soc of CPAs; Austl Inst of Mngmt; Inst of Chart Accts in Aust; Austl and NZ Acady of Mngmt; Acctng Assn of Aust and NZ; Brit Acctng Assn; Amn Acctng Assn; Acady of Acctng Histns, past pres,

1991. Hobbies: Tennis; Singing; Tapestry; Antiquarian book collecting. Address: School of Commerce, University of Adelaide, Adelaide, SA 5005, Australia.

PARKER Vivienne Margaret, b. 7 Nov 1943, Heswall, Cheshire, Eng. Editor; Geneological Researcher. m. (1), Hedley, (2) Keith Robert Vautier, 2 s. Education: Dip in Radiography, 1962; Dip Window Dressing, 1985. Appointments: Radiographer, David Lewis N Hosp, 1962-68; Window Dresser, Own Bus, 1985-90; Ed, The NZ Genealogist, 1991-97; Genealogical Rsch Inst of NZ, 1996-98; Genealogical Rsch Co, Viva Rsch, 1997-. Creative Works: Writing Lectrs; Articles for mags; Pprs for Genealogical Confs, 1985-. Honours: Elizabeth Simpson Awd for Best Genalogical and Family Hist Jrnl, 1993. Memberships: The NZ Soc of Genealogists. Hobbies: Genealogy; Family Historical Research; Cross Stitch; Jigsaw Puzzles. Address: PO Box 87-220 Meadowbank, Auckland 1130, New Zealand.

PARKES Elizabeth Kay, b. 16 Dec 1951, Nelson, NZ. Professional Genealogist. m. Dirk van Straten, 1 s. Education: Grinz Dip in Family Hist (Prof). Publications: Book: Better Prospects: The Parkes Family History, 1986. Honours: Awd of Merit, NZ Soc of Genealogists, 1989; Self-Employed Woman of Yr Awd, 1997. Memberships: Genealogical Rsch Inst of NZ; Australasian Assn of Genealogists and Record Agts; Assn of Profl Genealogists (USA). Hobbies: Genealogy; Seido karate; Gardening; Sketching. Address: Quest House, 211 Vanguard Street, Nelson 7001, New Zealand.

PARKINSON Roger Henry, b. 28 Feb 1959, San Fran, CA, USA. Winegrower. m. Carol, 30 Jan 1994, 1 s. Education: BA (Hist, French), Canberra Univ, 1980; Grad Dip in Wine, Roseworthy Agricl Coll, 1989. Appointments: Mngng Dir, Nga Waka Vineyard Ltd, 1988-. Honour: Penfolds Viticultural Schlshp, 1988. Memberships: Dir, Toast Markinborough Ltd, 1995-97, Chmn, 1997-. Hobbies: Golf; Tennis. Address: Lot 7, Hawkins Drive, Martinborough, New Zealand.

PARKINSON Wilfred Dudley, b. 29 Apr 1919, Perth, WA, Aust. Geophysicist. m. Mary Lucila Lastenia Tamayo-Lagos, 21 Sept 1951, 2 s. Education: PhD; BSc (Hons). Appointments: Observer, DTM Carnegie; Rsch Asst, Fordham Univ; Geophysicist, Bur of Mineral Resources, Canberra; Rdr, Univ of Tas. Publication: Introduction to Geomagnetism. Membership: Aust Inst of Phys. Hobby: Esperanto. Address: 68 Risdon Road, New Town, Tasmania 7008, Australia.

PARRY Mervyn Henry, b. 2 Sept 1913. Consulting Architect. m. 1 s, 2 d. Education: Perth Tech Coll; Regent St Polytech. Appointments Dir, Parry & Rosenthal Pty Ltd, until 1981. Honours: Gold Medallist, Roy Austl Inst of Archts, 1978; AO, 1983; DFC and Bar, AFC. Memberships: Life Fell, Roy Austl Inst of Archs, 1978-; Weld Club, WA; Roy Freshwater Bay Yacht Club, WA. Hobbies: Boating; Fishing. Address: 13 Goldsmith Road, Claremont, WA 6010, Australia.

PARSLOW Thomas, b. 12 Mar 1920, Melbourne, Aust. Lawyer; Soldier. m. Margaret Fraser (Brown), 7 Dec 1946, 2 d. Education: BL, Univ of Qld, 1950. Appointments: Snr Crown Prosecutor, Dpty Parly Draftsman, Crown Sol, Sol-Gen for Qld (QC); Co Queensland Uni Regt, Cmdr, 2 Support grp, Cmdr, 7 Task Force (Brigadier); Hon Col, QUR, Hon ADC Gov Gen Aust. Honours: Reserve Forces Decoration; Efficiency Decoration (2 bars); QC. Memberships: Utd Servs Club, Qld Irish Assn; State Cnsllr; Returned Servs League. Hobbies: Music; Water colour painting. Address: 27 Southerden Street, Sandgate, Australia 4017.

PARSONS Nicholas Stephen Brisbane, b. 9 Jan 1961, Perth, Aust. Writer; Director. m. Joanna Arrowsmith, 2 d. Education: BA, hons, Philos, Sydney Univ, 1982; BA, Film and TV, Austl Film, TV and Radio Sch, 1986; Dip, Directing, NIDA, 1989. Appointments: Dir-in-Res, NIDA, 1994; Chmn, Currency Press Pty Ltd, 1994-. Creative Works include: Written and directed: Little Horrors (short video), 1985; The Visitor (one act stageplay), 1988; Dead Heart (feature film), 1996; Written: The White Room (radio play), 1988; Requiem (short film), 1990; Dead Heart (stageplay), 1992; The Hollow Ground (stageplay), 1998; Directed: The Removalists (stageplay), 1990; Norm and Ahmed (one-act stageplay), 1991; A Handful of Friends (stageplay), 1994. Honours: Ctf of Merit, St Kilda Film Fest, Melbourne, 1987; 1st Prize, Fiction, Toowoomba Fest, 1987; Ian Reed Meml Grand Prize, 1988; Ctf of Merit, Melbourne Film Fest, 1991; Amy McGrath Schlshp for Overseas Travel, 1991; NSW State Lit Awd, 1993; AWGIE Awd, 1994; Human Rights Awd, 1994; Film Critics Circle Awd, 1997. Memberships: Austl Writers Guild; Austl Screen Dirs Assn. Address: Currency Press Pty Ltd, 201 Cleveland Street, Redfern 2016, Australia.

PARTLETT Launa, b. 19 May 1918, Miles, Qld, Aust. Author; Artist; Historian. m. C H Partlett, 19 June 1943, 1 s, 1 d. Publications: (books) Guluguba Pioneers, 1986; John Jones and Family - Rocky River Gold, 1987; Sev poetry anthologies. Honours include: Gold Medal, ABI, 1995; Two Gold Keys, 1996. Memberships: Canterbury and Dist Histl Soc; Stockman's Hall of Fame; Sec, Owner's Corp, 1987-98. Hobbies: Reading; Writing; Gardening; Family history; Painting. Address: 3/11 Parry Avenue, Narwee, NSW 2209, Australia.

PARTON Kevin Anthony, b. 24 Aug 1951, Middlesborough, Eng. University Professor. m. Bev Parton, 18 Aug 1975, 4 s. Education: BCom, Liverpool; MSc, Newcastle upon Tyne; PhD, Univ of New Eng; Dip Econ Stats (Univ of New Eng). Appointments: Rsch Fell, Univ New Eng (UNE), 1980; Rsch Assoc, Univ Newcastle, 1981; Rsch Fell, 1983, Lectr, 1984, Snr Lectr, 1987, Assoc Prof, 1995, UNE. Publications: 4 books: Cost of the Common Agricultural Policy, 1981; Aggregative Programming, 1981; Price Policy in Indonesia, 1993; Particulate Pollution in Australia, 1998. Honours: Drummond Prize, 1981; Sir John Crawford Awd, 1992. Memberships: AAAS; NY Acady of Scis; Modelling and Simulation Soc of Aust; Aust Agricl Econ Soc. Hobbies: Soccer; Orienteering. Address: Dir, Centre for Health Research and Development, University of New England, Armidale, NSW 2351, Australia.

PARVIN Selina, b. 13 Aug 1977, Nator. Student. Education: Degree examinee. Hobbies: Writing poems; Reading books.

PARVIN Shahnaz, b. 22 July 1980, Pabna, India. Student. Education: Dip, Com. Publications: Poems, short stories and articles in profl jrnls, weeklys and magazines. Memberships: Gen Sec, Bangladesh Poets Club, Pabna; Lit Ed, N Bengal Lit Assn, Pabna. Hobbies: Recitation; Writing. Address: c/o Mr Wazuddin Gopalpur, Himsagar Lane, Pabna 6600, Bangladesh.

PASK Raymond Frank, b. 27 May 1944, Melbourne, Aust. Teacher; Writer. Education: BA; DipEd. Appointments: Melbourne hs, 1982-. Publications: 25 books in print inclng: A Handbook of Geography, 1993; A Geography of Victoria, 1995; Heinemann Atlas (exec ed), 1996; Outcomes Geography 1, 1997, 2, 1998. Membership: Geog Tchrs Assn of Vic. Hobbies: Travel; Photography; Gardening; Renovation. Address: 41 Yarra Street, Abbotsford, Australia 3067.

PASWAN Chandra Prakash, b. 3 June 1955, Kharaita, Chautham, Khagaria, Bihar. Police Inspector; Freelance Writer. m. Premwada, 23 May 1977, 3 s, 2 d. Education: BA (Hons) Hist, Tribeniganj, 1985, MA, Hist, 1993, LNMU, Darbhanga; LLB, RMS Coll Saharsa, LNMU, 1999. Appointments: Sub-Inspector of Police, 1976-82; Inspector of Police, 1982-. Publications: Books: Sath Samay Ke (poetry), 1994; Barse Kammal Bhinge Pani (poetry), 1997; Akhari Sawal (poetry), 1999; In collaboration w others; Smarika - Saharasa (poetry), 1999; Sopan - Katihar (poetry), 1999; Others in num publs. Honours: Kameshwar Poddar Sansmritti, Madhepura, For Hindi Lit Wrk Bihar, 1996; Dr Ambedkar Fellshp, Delhi, For Hindi Lit and Socl Wrk, 1996; Awd w Cert and a Cap for Hindi Lit Wrk by Kshetriya Rachnatmak Vikash Manch Dist Branch Araria, at

Forbesganj, Araria, Bihar, 1997; Nirala Samman, Jamalpur, 1997; Awd w a Cert Rajiv Gandhi "Sansmritti Samman" for Lit and Socl Wrk by Kshetriya Rachnatmek Vikas Manch District Ariria, Bihar. Memberships: VP, Akhil Bhartiya Sahitya Sammelan Forbesganj, Araria, Bihar; Fndr Mbr, Renu Sahitya Parishad, Araria, Bihar. Pres, Police Assn, Araria; Fmr Sec of Police Assn, Sharsa; Fmr Pres, Bharat Vikas Parishad. Hobbies: Study of magazines and books; Games; Journeys; Historical places. Address: Kharaita, PO Chautham, District, Khagaria, Bihar, India.

PASZKOWSKI Lech, b. 18 July 1919. Writer; Editor. m. Ursula Janina Trella, 17 Nov 1956, 1 s, 1 d. Education: Caulfield Tech Coll, 1967; Jrnlsm, Roy Melbourne Inst of Technol, 1968-69. Appointment: Hon Ed, Aust Felix Lit Club, Melbourne, 1973-88. Pulications: Polacy w Australii i Oceanii 1790-1940, 1962; Strzelecki's Ascent of Mount Kosciusko 1840 (ed), 1973; Dr John Lhotsky - The Turbulent Australian Writer Naturalist and Expolorer, (co-auth), 1977; Social Background of Sir Paul Strzelecki and Joseph Conrad, 1980; Poles in Australia and Oceania 1790-1940, 1987; Sir Paul Edmund de Strzelecki: Reflections on His Life, 1997; Conbr to sev profl jrnls and books. Honour: Spec Purpose Grant, Lit d of Aust Cncl for the Arts, 1973; Memberships: Quill Club Writers of Aust, 1969-72; Friends of the State Lib of Vic, 1966-99; Roy Histl Soc of Vic, 1972-99. Hobby: Historical Studies. Address: 28 Darling Road, East Malvern, Vic 3145, Australia.

PATEL Manilal Haridas, b. 9 Nov 1949, India. Teacher; Reader. m. Gopi Patel, 21 May 1972, 2 s, 1 d. Education: MA; PhD. Appointments: Lectr in Guajarati, 1973; Rdr in Guajarati, 1990. Publications: 38 books, 5 novels, 3 collecs of short stories, over 50 essays, 15 books of criticisim. Honours: 15 hons and awds for poetry, essays, short stories, novels by Sahitya Parishad and Sahitya Acady. Memberships: Guajarat Sahitya Parishad. Hobbies: Nature; Travel; Music; Reading. Address: Shastri Marg, Bakrol Road, Vidyanagar 38812, India.

PATEL Mrugank Maganlal, b. 1 Nov 1972, Valsad. Engineering Consultant. Education: Dip, Electrons and Telecomm Engrng, MCA. Appointments: Lectr (IET, Valsad) Admission Cnclr (IET valsads), Dir SMT G M Patel I T Engrng, Blimora di, Navsari, 1996-. Honour: Best Achmnt Awd, IET, Valsad, 1995. Memberships: Inst of Engrng and tech, Valsad; Valsad Dist Consumer and Protection Cncl; Patron Mbr IMechE, India; Affiliate, ASME (USA). Hobbies: Reading books; Attending seminars and conferences in other countries. Address: Hanuman Street, Nr Dixit Street, Valsad, Tadi Valsad, 396001, India.

PATERSON Alistair Ian Hughes, b. 28 Feb 1929. Writer. m. Alison Blaiklock. Education: BA; DipEd; Dip Tchng; Fmr Assoc of NZ Inst of Mngmt; Passed RNZAF Armed Servs Cmnd and Staff Course. Career: Tchr of courses in novel writing, Educ Dept, Auckland Univ, 1996-97; Full-time writer and ed. Publications: Fiction, poetry, articles incl: (novel) How to be a Millionaire by Next Wednesday, 1994, issued as talking book by the NZ Fndn for the Blind, 1995; (poetry) Qu'appelle, 1982; Odysseus Rex, 1985; Incantations for Warriors, 1986; (poetics) The New Poetry, 1981; Ed: 8 wrks inclng: Short Stories from New Zealand, 1988; Poetry NZ issues 8-19, 1994-99; included in anthologies inclng: Penguin Book of NZ Verse, 1985; Contemporary NZ poetry, 1989; Blue Mesa Review, 1991; Literary Olympians, 1992; Articles incl: Rob Jackaman, An Introduction to the Poetry and the Poet, 1992; Social Constraints on Literary History, 1995; (play) The Toledo Room, stage and radio, 1978. Honours: Fulbright Awd to USA, 1978; Winner, Auckland Univ's John Cowrie Reid Mem Awd for poetry, 1981; Runner-up, Lilian Ida Smith Awd for fiction, 1991; BNZ Katherine Mansfield Awd for short stories, 1993; 1996 Creative NZ Grant of $20,000 to write fiction, 1996. Memberships include: Deleg repr NZ non govtl orgs to UN Cttee on Rights of Child at Geneva, 1996. Hobbies: Being with his family; Yachting; Community activities;

Politics (Alliance candidate, 1993). Address: 34B Methuen Road, Avondale, Auckland, New Zealand.

PATERSON Mervyn Silas, b. 7 Mar 1925, S Aust. Aust. Geophysicist. m. Katalin Sarosy, 19 Jan 1952, 1 s, 1 d. Education: BE, Adelaide, 1945; PhD, Cambridge, 1949; DSc, Cambridge, 1968. Appointments: Aeronautical Rsch Labs, Melbourne, 1945-53; Austl Natl Univ, 1953-90; Retd, 1990; Visng Fell, Austl Natl Univ, Cnslt, Austl Sci Instruments Pty Ltd, 1990-. Publications include: Experimental Rock Deformation - The Brittle Field, 1978. Honours: Schlshp, Adelaide Univ, 1946; FAA, 1972; Hon Fell, Geol Soc of Am, 1987. Memberships: Amn Geophysl Union; Mineralogical Soc of Am; Geol Soc of Aust. Hobbies: Walking; Reading. Address: Research School of Earth Sciences, Australian National University, Canberra 0200, Australia.

PATHAK Chitta Ranjan, b. 11 June 1935, Sonardanga, Bankura, India. Teacher and Researcher. m. Chhabi, 5 d. Education: MA; PhD. Appointments: Snr Fell, ICSSR, 1996-98; Prof, 1975-95; Assoc Prof, 1971-75; Asst Prof, 1968-71. Honours: Fulbright Schlr, 1961-64; Snr Smith Fund Schl, 1978-79. Memberships: Regl Sci Assn India; Life Mbr, Sec and Mng Ed, Publr, Geo Soc of India; Pres, Natl Assn of Geos; Indian Geo Assn. Hobbies: Reading; Writing; Football. Address: CK-134, Salt Lake City, Sector II, Calcutta, 700 091, India.

PATIL Shankar Vithoba, b. 9 Nov 1926, India. Retired Teacher. m. Laxmi, 14 Feb 1949, 3 s, 4 d. Education: BA, BT, Rastra Bhasha Kovid. Appointments: Tchr, A E S HS, Shelgaon Bazar, Talua-Motala, Buldana, 1956-86. Publications include: Lewa Patidaranch Itihas, 1999. Hobbies: Reading; Writing; Historical Research. Address: PO Dudhalgaon Bk, TQ Malkapur District, Buldana MS, India.

PATIL Suresh, b. 1 Apr 1951, Asoda. Librarian. m. Suhasini, 10 May 1979, 1 s, 1 d. Education: MA; MLiblsc; DCM; PhD. Appointments: Librn, VWS Coll, 1980; Asst Libn, Poona Univ, 1982; Dpty Libn, Pune Univ, 1995. Publications: Precious Thoughts, Convocation Address, 1949-94. Memberships: ILA, 1989; IASLIC, 1990; PULISAA, 1997. Hobbies: Reading; Cricket. Address: Jayakar Library, University of Pune, Pune 411007, India.

PATNAIK Lalit Mohan, b. 22 July 1946, Kasinagar, India. Professor. m. Ganga, 23 Apr 1977, 1 d. Education: BSc, Engrng; ME; PhD; DSc. Appointments: Asst Prof, Assoc Prof, Prof. Publications: 5 books, sev profl articles in jrnls. Honours: Dr Vikram Sarabhai Rsch Awd, 1989; Ram Lal Wadhwa Gold Medal, 1992; Info Technol Man of the Yr, 1998. Membership: Fell, IEEE. Hobby: Music. Address: Department of Computer Science and Automation, Indian Institute of Science, Bangalore 560012, India.

PATRA Pradip Kumar, b. 1 Apr 1966, Balasore, India. Teacher. m. Tanushree Patra, 10 June 1994. Education: MA, MPhil, PhD, Dlitt in Engl, Utkal Univ, Bhubaneswar, India. Appointments: Snr Lectr and Hd, Engl Dept, B B Kishan Coll, Jalah, Dt Barpeta, Pin 781327, Assam, India; Guest Lectr, Engl Dept, Gauhati Univ, India. Publications: Books of poems: Panoramic Shillong, 1996; Summer Implications, 1996; The Winding Path, 1996; Denouement, 1998; Dewy Morning, 1998; Midnight Divinity, 1999. Memberships: Life Mbr, ASRC, Hyderabad; Writers Forum, Ranchi, India; Cncl of Courses of Studies, Gauhati Univ, India. Hobbies: Writing poetry; Watching movies; Sight seeing. Address: At-Jyotinagar, Po-Pathsala, DT-Barpeta, PIN 78132, Assam.

PATSANI Bipin, b. 16 Feb 1951, Badatota, Khurda, Orissa, India. Teacher. m. Manjula, 2 May 1974, 1 s, 2 d. Education: BA (Hons), Engl; MA (Engl). Appointment: Engl Tchr, Arunachal Pradesh, India, 1978-. Publications: Poems in Engl, widely publd in India and abroad; Book of poetry, Voice of the Valley. Honours: Poesie India and Intl WA; Recip, Michael Madhusudan Dutha Awd, MM Acady, Calcutta, 1996. Memberships: Indian PEN; Intl Writers &

Artists Assn; World Poetry Soc; Writers Forum (Ranchi); Paradoxist Movement. Hobbies: Reading, Writing; Listening to music; Sightseeing. Address: Government Hr Sec School, Doimukh 791112, Dist Papum Pare, Arunachal Pradesh, India.

PATTABHI Vasantha, b. 30 Sept 1944, Tamil Nadu, India. Teacher; Researcher. m. R Pattabhi, 22 Jan 1967, 1 s, 1 d. Education: MSc; PhD. Appointments: Lectr; Rdr; Prof. Publications: Aspects of Biomolecules, ed; 1 book and sev articles in profl jrnls. Honours: Univ Grants Commn Career Awd; Natl Merit Schlshp; Roy Soc Nuffield Fndn Fellshp. Memberships: Fulbright Alumni Assn; Intl Union of Crystallography; TWOWS; Indian Biophysl Soc. Hobbies: Music; Reading. Address: Department of Biophysics, University of Madras, Guindy Campus, Chennai 600025, India.

PATTABI Manjunatha, b. 1 Oct 1961, Napoklu Coorg, India. Researcher; Teacher. m. Rani, 18 Nov 1988, 1 s, 1 d. Education: BSc, Mysore Univ, 1981; MSc, Managalore Univ, 1983; PhD, Indian Inst Technol, Madras, 1988. Appointments: Lectr, Mangalore Univ, 1988-95; Rdr, Mangalore Unv, 1995-. Publications: Over 30 pprs in jrnls. Honours: Visng Assoc Inter Univ Consortium for Dept of Atomic Energy Facilities at Indore, India, 1995. Hobby: Photography. Address: Materials Science Faculty, Mangalore University, Mangalagangotri 574 199, India.

PATTEN Bebe Harrison, b. 3 Sept 1913, Waverly, TN, USA. Minister; Chancellor. m. Carl Thomas Patten, 23 Oct 1935, 1 s, 2 d. Education: DD, Mckinley-Roosevelt Coll, 1941; DLitt, Temple Hall Coll and Sem, 1943. Appointments: Ordained to min, Ministerial Assn of Evangelism, 1935; Evangelist, var cities of US, 1933-50; Fndr, Pres, Christian Evang Chs Am Inc, Oakland, CA, 1944-; Patten Acady Christian Educ, Oakland, 1944-; Patten Bible Coll, Oakland, 1944-83; Chancellor, Patten Coll, Oakland, 1983-; Fndr, Pastor, Christian Cath of Oakland, 1950-; Held priv interviews w David Ben-Gurion, 1972; Menachim Begin, 1977; Yitzhak Shamir, 1991; Condr, Stn, KUSW world-wide radio min, 70 countries around world, 1989-90; Stns WHRI and WWCR world coverage short wave, 1990-. Publications: (auth) Give Me Back My Soul, 1973; (ed) Trumpet call, 1953-; Composer: 20 gospel and relig songs, 1945-. Creative works: Radio prog, The Shepherd Hour, 1934-; Daily TV, 1976-; Nationwide telecast, 1979-. Honours include: Ben-Gurion Medallion, Ben-Gurion Rsch Inst, 1977; Dr Bebe Patten Socl Action Chair, estab Bar-Ilan Univ, 1982; Golden State Awd, Who's Who Hist Soc, 1988; Disting Leadership Awd, Ch of God Sch of Theol, 1996. Memberships: Amn Assn for Higher Educ; Relig Educ Assn; Amn Acady Relig and Soc Bible Lit; Zionist Orgn Am; Amn Assn Pres of Indep Colls and Univs; Amn Jewish Hist Soc; Am-Israel Pub Affairs Cttee. Address: 2433 Coolidge Avenue, Oakland, CA 94601-2630, USA.

PATTISON Andrew David, b. 21 July 1952, Melbourne, Aust. Medical Practitioner. m. Carolyn Mary Weir, 22 Dec 1975, 2 s, 1 d. Education: MBBS, Univ Melbourne, 1975; DObst RCOG, 1978; FRACGP, 1978. Appointments: Clin Instr, Dept Community Med, Melbourne Univ; Lectr, Dept Community Med, Monash Univ. Publications: Doctor Toby Books for children (9 titles), 1988, 1989; An Apple a Day, 1995; The M Factor - Men and Their Health, 1998. Memberships: Roy Aust Coll of Grand Practitioners; Austl Medl Assn; Bd Mbr, Transplant Promotion Cncl of Vic; AMa Repr, Austl Children's TV Fndn, 1992-93; GP Working Party, Vic Hlth Promotion Fndn, 1993-95; Educ, Cttee Asthma Fndn of Vic, 1994-95. Hobbies: Medical commentator, Radio 3AW Melbourne, 1989-92; Medical Writer, AGE newspaper, 1993-95; Tennis; Walking. Address: 3 Beauview Parade, East Ivanhoe 3079, Australia.

PATTON Laurence John, b. 14 Oct 1952, Sydney, Aust. Television Executive. m. Robyn Johnson, 15 Dec 1990, 1 s. Education: BA, UNSW, MComm, UNSW, Grad Cert Mngmt, Univ of New Eng. Appointments: Gen Mngr, Sunshine TV; Mktng Dir, Seven Network, Aust; Gen Mngr, Channel Seven, Sydney; Gen Mngr, Pan TV.

Membership: Fell, Austl Inst of Co Dirs. Address: PO Box 466, Drummone, Sydney, Australia 1470.

PAUL Graeme Allan Lindsay, b. 1 Sept 1943, Chemical Engineer; Industrial Chemist. m. 12 Dec 1970, 1 s, 2 d. Education: Dip Sci (Tech); BSc (Applied). Appointments: Ops Mngr/ Asst Wrks Mngr/Plant Supt, 1972-87; Site Mngr, 1988-95; Ops Mngr, 1996-. Publications: Cleaner Production in Chemical Industry, Manila, Philippines, 1995; Cleaner Production, Surface Coatings, Australia 50th Anniversary, 1996; IC 98, Occupational Health, Safety and the Environment. Honours: Fell, RACI, 1991; Fell, I Chem E, 1989; Mbr, Inst of Pet, Australia; Whiffen Medallist for Chem Engrng, 1992; Mbr, Fedn of Asian Chem Soc, 1996; Sci Mbr, Roy Zool Soc; Mbr, Geol Soc of Aust; RK Murphy Medal for Chem Engrng, 1997. Hobbies: Chemistry; Photography; Bushwalking. Address: 46 Cannons Parade, Forestville, NSW 2087, Australia.

PAUL Joanna Margaret, b. 1945. Painter; Poet. 3 d. Education: BA, Auckland Univ; Dip, Fine Arts. Publications: Imogen (poems); Unpacking the Body, 1976; A Chronology: Survey of Paintings, 1990. Honour: 1st Prize, Book of Poetry, 1977. Membership: Wanganui Arch Heritage. Address: 3 Maxwell Avenue, Wanganui, New Zealand.

PAUL Willi, b. 15 July 1966, Trichur, Kerala, India. Research Associate. m. Flower, 18 Aug 1996. Education: BSc, 1986; MSc, 1991. Appointments: Serv Engr, 1986-89; Rsch Assoc, 1989-. Memberships: Soc for Biomaterials and Artificial Organs; Soc for Polymer Sci, 1998-. Hobbies: Paintings; Electronics. Address: Biomedical Technology Wing, Sree Chitra Tirunal Institute for Medical Sciences & Technology, Trivandrum, 695012, India.

PAUPUA Tomasi, b. 10 Sept 1938, Tuvalu. Politician. m. 1971, 2 s, 2 d. Education: Fiji Sch of Med; Univ of Otago, NZ. Appointments: Med Practitioner; PM of Tuvalu, 1981-90; Min for Civil Serv Admin, Local Govt, Min for Fgn Affairs; Speaker of Parl, 1993-. Hobbies: Athletics; Rugby; Tennis; Volleyball; Cricket; Soccer; Fishing; Pig and Poultry Farming; Gardening. Address: Office of the Prime Minister, Vaiaku, Funafuti, Tuvalu.

PAVIOUR Paul, b. 14 Apr 1931, Birmingham, Eng. Composer. m. Janet Margaret Muncaster, 19 June 1954, 3 s. Education: Trinity Coll, London, 1954; BMus, London Univ, 1962; MMus, Roy Coll of Music, 1960; DMus, Univ of GA, USA, 1977. Appointments: Dir of Music, The Newnham Sch, 1961-64; Dir of Music, Normanton Grammar Sch, 1964-69; All Saints Coll, Bathurst, NSW, 1970-74; Lectr, Musical Composition, Goulburn Coll of Adv Educ; Dir of Music, Goulburn Cath, 1993-. Creative Works: Orchl wrks: Symphony Academica, for full orch, 1948; Symphony No 4, for full orch, 1972; Sir Arthur Lives, Ballet Suite from music of Sullivan, arranged for wind band; September Romance, for string orch; Symphony No 6; Vocal wrks: Crazy Jane, for soprano and piano; The Bargain, song for voice and piano; Threnody for Good Friday, Litany of Our Lady of The Cross; Chmbr music: String Quartet No 1; Soliloquy on a theme of Elgar for unaccompanied Oboe; Choral wrks: Four Carols; Swing Praises; So I Walk On; Christ For The World We Sing; Anthem for 2 trebles and organ; The Pyramid Rave, for chorus and var instruments; Requiem for chorus and orch; Keyboard wrks: Piano Sonate No 2; Six Children's Pieces for piano; Lynaldia, for organ; Caroline, opera. Honours: Harding Prize, Roy Coll of Organists, 1961; McKenzie Prize, 1972; Aust Cncl Awd, 1981. Memberships: Pres, Austl Soc for Music Educ; Incorp Soc of Musicians; Roy Soc of Organists; Music Lectrs Assn; Fellshp, Austl Composers. Hobbies: Walking; Reading; Hockey. Address: 4 Beppo Street, Goulburn, NSW 2580, Australia.

PAVLOV Aleksandr, b. 1 Jan 1953, Pavlodar. Government Official. Education: Grad, Byelorussian Inst Natl Econ. Appointment: Min Fin, Govt Kazakhztan, Almaty, 1994-. Address: Ministry of Finance, pr Ablaikhana 97, Almaty 480091, Kazakhstan.

PAYES Shirley, b. 9 June 1937, Wellington, NZ. Volunteer; Housewife. m. Maurice, 3 Mar 1959, 1 s, 1 d. Appointment: Chmn, Safer Community Cncl. Honours: Hutt Cty Civic Awd, 1992; Queen Serv Order (QSO), 1994; Jewish Woman of the Yr, NZ, 1995. Memberships: Cncl of Jewish Women, Natl Pres, 1989-, Intl VP, 1987-93; Asian Pacific Regl Chmn, 1993-99; Pres, Hutt Ethnic Cncl, 1991-97, 1998-. Hobbies: Embroidery; Porcelain art; Gardening. Address: 11 Parnell Street, Lower Hutt 6009, New Zealand.

PAYNE James Richmond, b. 1 June 1921, Aust. Clergyman; Commissary. m. Joan Elliott, 16 Jan 1943, 3 s. Education: Sydney Univ; Metro Bus Coll; ThL, Austl Coll of Theol; Moore Theol Coll, Sydney. Appointments: Chaplain, RAAF, Malta-Aust, 1952-56; Rector, Coorparoo, Brisbane, 1957-62; Dean of Perth, 1962-67; Austl Gen Sec, Bible Soc, 1968-88; Commissary in Aust for Anglican Bish of Ctrl Tanganyika (E Afr), 1988- Chmn, UBS, Global Exec Cttee, 1976-88. Publication: Around the World in Seventy Days, 1965. Honour: MBE, 1982. Hobbies: Reading; Walking; Spectator Sports. Address 10/42 Jinka Street, Hawker, ACT 2614, Australia.

PAYNE John Wilson, b. 9 Sept 1953, Sheparton, Aust. Conservator of Paintings. m. Elsbeth, 7 Mar 1981, 1 s, 2 d. Education: Dip Art, Deakin Univ, 1975; Assoc Dip of Appl Sci, Canberra Univ, 1985. Appointment: Snr Conservator of Painting, Natl Gall of Vic. Publications: Num articles on examination and treatment of paintings. Honour: Fell, Sch of Fine Arts, Classical Studies and Archaeology, Univer of Melbourne, 1999. Membership: Austl Inst for Conservation of Cultural Material (AICCM). Address: c/o Conservation Department, National Gallery of Victoria, 180 St Kilda Road, Melbourne, Victoria, Australia.

PAYTON Phillip W, b. 26 Dec 1929, Santa Barbara, CA, USA. University Administrator. m. (1) Gertrude Crombie, 1 s, (2) Marie A Rowe. Education: BA, Reed Coll, Portland, OR, 1951; MA, Stanford Univ, 1954; DEd, Stanford Univ, 1959-60. Appointments: Full Prof, 1982-, Dept Hd, 1987-, Dean, 1998-, Lincoln Univ, San Fran; Coord Bus Prog, Natl Univ, 1987. Publications: Book on funding of public state universities: Student and Faculty Hope, Faculty and Public Responsibility, 1999; 85 page study on faculty negotiation and bargaining; Articles on hum resc mngmt and higher educ. Memberships: Amn Assn for Higher Educ; Assn for Continuing Higher Educ; Natl Bus Educ Assn. Hobbies: Research on higher education; Collecting historical newspapers and music. Address: Lincoln University, 281 Lincoln Avenue, San Francisco, CA 94118, USA.

PEACOCK Andrew Sharp (Hon), b. 13 Feb 1939. Australian Ambassador to US. m. Susan Peacock, div, 3 d, (2) Margaret Peacock, 1983, div. Education: LLB, Univ Melbourne. Appointments: Fmr Ptnr, Rigby & Fielding; Chmn, Peacock & Smith Pty Ltd, 1962-69; Pres, Vic Liberal Party, 1965-66; Cap, Army Reserve, 1966-94; Mbr, House Reps, for Kooyong, Vic, 1966-94; Ldr, many delegations abroad, 1968-94; Min assisting PM, 1969-71; Min Army, 1969-72; Min assisting Treas, 1971-72; Min External Territories, 1972; Min Environment, Nov-Dec 1975; Min For Affairs, 1975-80; Min Indl Rels, 1980-81; Min Ind and Com, 1982-83; Ldr Opposition, 1983-85, 1989-90; Chmn, Stndng Cttee For Affairs, 1983-86, Intl Dem Union, 1989-92, Pacific Dem Union, 1985-87; Shadow Min For Affairs, 1985-87; Dpty Ldr Opposition, Shadow Treas, 1987-89; Shadow Min Justice, 1990-92; Shadow Atty-Gen, 1990-92; Shadow Min Trade, 1992-93; Fed Shadow Min For Affairs, 1993-94; Chmn, Parly Polit Strategy Cttee, 1994; Chmn, Austl Horse Cncl, 1996-. Memberships include: MCC; VRC; VATC; MVRC. Address: Embassy of Australia, 1601 Massachusetts Avenue NW, Washington, DC 20036, USA.

PEACOCK William James, b. 14 Dec 1937. Research Scientist. m. 1 s, 2 d. Education: BSc, 1st class hons; PhD, Univ Sydney, 1963; DSc, honoris causa, Sturt Univ, Wagga Wagga, 1996. Appointments include: Visng Rsch Sci, Genetics Sect, 1963, Snr Rsch Sci, Div of Plant Ind, 1965-69, Prin Rsch Sci, Div of Plant Ind, 1969-73, Snr

Prin Rsch Sci, Div of Plant Ind, 1973-77, Chf Rsch Sci, Div of Plant Ind, 1977-78, Chf, Div of Plant Ind, 1978-, CSIRO Canberra; Chmn, Sci Advsry Bd, AGEN Biomedical Ltd, 1986-; Adj Pro/Co-Dir, Co-op Rsch Cnte for Plant Sci, Rsch Sch of Biol Dir Scis, The Austl Natl Univ, 1990-; Gene Shears Pty, Ltd, 1991-; Mbr, Rsch Advsry Bd, Goodman Fielder, Ltd, 1992-. Publications: Over 250 sci publns, 1959-. Honours: Edgeworth David Medal, Roy Soc of NSW, 1967; Lemberg Medal, Austl Biochem Soc, 1978; Univ Seal, Louvain, Belgium, 1982; FRS, 1982; 10th Anniversary Medal, Intl Bd of Plant Genetic Resources, 1984; Univ of GA Bicentennial Medal, 1985; NI Vavilov Medal, Vavilov Inst, 1987; BHP Bicentennial Prize, 1988; Burnet Medal, Austl Acad of Sci, 1989; CSIRO Medal, 1989; Companion, Order of Aust, 1994. Memberships: Intl Soc for Plant Molecular Biol; Aust and NZ Soc for Cell Biol; Austl Inst of Agric Sci and Technol; Austl Biotechnol Assn; Austl Biochem Soc; Austl Acady of Technol Scis and Engrng; Austl Acady of Sci; Genetics Soc of Aust; Austl Soc for Biochem and Molecular Biol; Hon Fell, Indian Soc of Genetics and Plant Breeding; Austl Soc of Plant Physiologists; Agronomy Soc of Aust; AAAS; Mbr Sci Advsry Cttee to the Rockefeller Fndn for the Intl Prog on Rice Biotechnol. Listed in: Who's Who in Australia. Hobbies: Bushwalking; Squash. Address: CSIRO Plant Industry, GPO Box 1600, Canberra, ACT 2601, Australia.

PEAKE-JONES Kenneth, b. 7 June 1914, London, Eng. Schoolmaster. m. June McArthur Reid, 9 May 1960, 1 s, 2 d. Education: MA (Cantab). Appointments: Snr Classics Master, St George's Sch, Harpendon, Eng, 1945-49; Snr Classics Master, St Peters Coll, Adelaide, 1957-75. Publications: To the Desert with Sturt, 1975; Recollections of D G B, 1843, 1981; The Branch Without a Tree, 1985. Honour: (RGS of SA) John Lewis Gold Medal for Lit Wrk in Geog, 1985. Membership: RGS of S Aust, Pres, 1965-67; Classical Assn of S Aust, Pres, 1973-75. Hobbies: Athletics; Exploration; Polar research (member of Australian National Antarctic Research Expedition, 1959). Address: Neemana, Mount Torrens, South Australia 5244.

PEARCE Iris Evelyn, b. 14 Aug 1930, Nathalia, Vic, Australia. Genealogist; Record Agent. m. Ron, 22 Mar 1952, 1 s, 2 d. Education: Dip Family Hist Stdies. Publications: 150 Years in Australia, 1982; Oceans Between, 1990; Brushing Up On Brooms, 1994. Honours: Life Mbr, Gen Soc Vic, 1982; Life Mbr, Echuca Gen Grp. Memberships: Pres, Sec, Nathalia Gen Grp. Hobbies: Reading; Bird watching; Native plants; Geology; Genealogy. Address: RMB 1003, Picola, 3639, Victoria, Australia.

PEARCE John Trevor Archdall, b. 7 May 1916, Sydney, Aust. British Colonial Administration Service (retired). m. (1) Isabel Bundey Rankin, 18 Oct 1948, dec 1983, (2) Judith Burland Kingsley-Strack, 16 Mar 1984. Education: MA, Keble Coll, Oxford, 1935-39. Appointments: Dist Offr, Tanganyika, 1939; War Serv, Kenya, Abyssinia, Ceylon, India, Burma, Maj (RE), 1940-46; Dist Cmmnr, Tanganyika, 1950; Prov Cmmnr, 1959; Perm Sec, Off of the VP, 1961; Chmn, Pub Serv Cmmn, Basutoland, 1963; Chmn, Pub Serv Cmmn, Swaziland, 1965; Registrar, Papua New Guinea Univ of Technol, 1969-73. Honour: CMG, 1964. Address: Clippings, 14 Golf Street, Buderim, Qld 4556, Australia.

PEARN John Hemsley, b. 18 Mar 1940, Brisbane, Qld, Aust. Medical Practitioner; Surgeon General, Australian Defence Force. m. Vena Beatrice White, 1 Dec 1966, 2 s, 1 d. Education: BSc, 1962, MBBS 1st Cl Hons, 1964, Univ Qld; MD, 1969; FRACP, 1970; PhD, Univ London, 1974; FRCP (UK), 1974; DCH (London), 1974; FACTM (USA), 1982; FACTM (Aust), 1991. Appointments: Res, Medl Offr, Brisbane Gen Hosp, 1965; Clinl Path, 1966-67, Dept Ch H, 1968-, Univ Qld; Prof, Univ Qld, 1986-. Publications: Arms and Aesculapius, 1966, 1997; Pioneer Medicine in Australia, 1988; First in First Aid, 1988; New Horizons, 1992; Watermen of War, 1993; Milestones of Australian Medicine, 1994; Islands Of Incarceration, 1995; Reflections of Rwanda, 1995; Of Heart and Mind, 1999. Honours: AM, Gen List, 1979; Natl

Medal, 1980; RFB and Bar, 1984; K St J Herbert Moran Medal, RACS; Ashdown Medal, Aust Coll Trop Med, 1995; Hon Fell, Univ of Oxford (Green Coll), 1998; The Sir Edward "Weary" Dunlop Asia-Pacific Medal, 1998. Memberships: Human Genetics Soc Australasia, Seal-Holder, 1980-98, Natl Pres, 1983-85; Austl Coll Paediatricians, Chmn, State Cntr, 1993-95; Qld Father of Yr, 1994; Austl Soc for Hist Med, Natl Pres, 1995-97; Austl Defence Medl Ethics Cttee, Chairperson, 1998. Hobbies: Medical history; Medical philately. Address: Department of Paediatrics and Child Health, Royal Children's Hospital, Brisbane, Queensland 4029, Australia.

PEARSON William Harrison (Bill), b. 18 Jan 1922, Greymouth, NZ. Writer; Retired University Teacher. Education: MA, NZ; PhD (London). Appointments: Snr Rsch Fell, Dept of Pacific Hist, ANU, 1967-69; Tchr, Blackball Sch, 1942, Oxford Dist hs, NZ, 1948-49; Lectr, Snr Lectr, Assoc Prof Engl, Univ of Auckland, 1954-66, 1970-86. Publications: Coal Flat, 1963, 5th ed, 1985; Ed, Frank Sargeson Collected Stories, 1935-63, 1964; Henry Lawson Among Maoris, 1968; Roderick Finlayson, Brown Man's Burden, 1973; Fretful Sleepers and Other Essays, 1974; Rifled Sanctuaries, 1984; Six Stories, 1991; Gen Ed, NZ Fiction Series, AUP, 1973-86. Honours: Landfall Rdrs Awd, 1960; NZ Book Awd, 1975. Hobbies: Reading; Listening to music. Address: 49 Lawrence Street, Herne Bay, Auckland, New Zealand.

PECK Marilyn Cecilia, b. 18 Sept 1932, Windsor, Vic, Aust. Artist. m. Colin Henry Peck, 20 Sept 1958, 1 s, 1 d. Education: Coml Art, Caulfield Tech Coll, Vic, 1947-49; Apprentice, Lithographic Artist, 1949-54. Appointments: Initiator of the Soc and Fndn Pres, 1988-90; Pres, 1991-92; Aust Soc of Miniature Art (Qld). Creative Works: Exhibns: Grp showings nationally and internationally inclng the World Exhibition of Miniature Art, Roy Miniature Soc, London, 1995; Llewellyn Alexander Million Brushstrokes, Waterloo, London, Annual Exhib; Solo Exhibns: Univ of NSW Snr Common Room Club, Sydney, 1983, 1986; Ku-Ring-Gai Motor Yacht Club, Sydney, 1983, 1985; Boronia House, Sydney, 1983, 1984; Deans Gall, Gold Coast, 1991; Ensemble Th, Sydney, 1992; Hibiscus Gall, Hobart, 1996; Duo showings w Colin Peck, BC Fine Art Gall, Southport, Qld, 1997, 1999. Honours: over 50 awds w 14 1st prizes inclng: Sydney Roy Easter Show, 1st Lady Fairfax Prize, Aust Birds and Wildflowers; Macquarie Awd 1000, 1st Contemporary, 1985; Murwillumbah Art Prize, 1st Natl RE Acquisition Awd; GA MAS 7th Intl Miniature Art Show, 1st Abstract, 1992; Best in show overall wrk, 1st in Mixed Media, GA MAS, 1997; 1st Miniature, Bendemeer, NSW. Memberships: Exhibiting mbr of: Assn Fine Artists Inc, Queensland; Aust Socs of Miniature Art (NSW, Qld, Tas, Vic); GA Miniature Art Soc (USA); Miniature Art Soc of FL (USA); Miniature Painters, Sculptors and Gravers Soc, Wash DC. Listed in: World Who's Who of Women. Address: Buckenham, Darwalla Road, Mount Nathan, Qld 4211, Australia.

PECK Michael Laurence, b. 27 June 1938, Melbourne, Aust. Architect. m. (1), 1 s, 1 d, (2) Elizabeth Mary McPherson, 15 Sept 1974, 2 s. Education: BArch, Wesley Coll and Melbourne Univ, 1962. Appointments: Fndng Ptnr, Whitford & Peck, 1963; Cnclr, Roy Austl Inst of Archts, Vic Chapt, 1970-83, VP, 1974-76; Natl Cnclr, RAIA, 1978-83, Pres Elect, 1980, Pres, 1981; Bd Mbr, RAIA Servs Co, 1978-86; Bd Mbr, Assn of Cnsltng Archts, 1985-91; Fndng Chmn, Victorian Bldng Professions Cttee; Bd Mbr, Archts Registration Bd of Vic, 1986-91, Dpty Chmn, 1990-91; Natl Mngr Prac RAIA, 1991-; Chf Exec, RAIA, 1993-. Honours: RAIA Vic Desig Awd, 1980; Life Fellshp, Roy Austl Inst of Archts, 1982; Pres Awd, RAIA Vic Chapt, 1988; Mbr in the Order of Aust, 1990; Charles Joseph La Trobe Des for Living Awd for the Warrandyte Cmnty Cntr, 1992; CIDA Ind Assn Ldrshp Awd, 1995. Memberships: Roy Austl Inst of Archts; Austl Construction Ind Forum; Austl Cncl of Bldng Des Professions; Austl Cncl of Professions; Profl Practice Cmmn Intl Union of Archts. Hobbies: Architecture; Beef cattle farming; Horse riding; Tennis. Address: 27 Fawkner Street, South Yarra, Vic 3141, Australia.

PECKOVER William Sydney, b. 31 May 1922, Sydney, Aust. Ornithology. m. Joan M, 8 Feb 1950, 1 s, 1 d. Appointments: Retd as Chf Gen Mngr, Posts and Telecomms Corp of Papua New Guinea, 1983. Publications: Birds of New Guinea and Tropical Australia, 1976; Birds of Paradise, 1998; Natural History Gazeteer: New Guinea, The Bismarck Archipelago and the Solomon Islands, 1998. Honour: OBE, 1981. Hobbies: Ornithology and geography of New Guinea, Bismarck Archipelago and Solomon Isles. Address: 14 Balanda Street, Jindalee, Queensland, Australia.

PEEL Margaret Mary, b. Kingary, Qld, Aust. Microbiologist. Education: Dip, Medl Lab Sci; BSc (Hons); Postgrad Dip in Bacteriology, London Univ; PhD, London. Appointments: Medl Scientist, Master Pub Hosp; Lectr, Queensland Univ of Technol; Prin Microbiologist, Microbiological Diagnostic Unit, Melbourne. Publications: Book: Sterilization, Disinfection and Infection Control, 1986, 1991, 1998; Co-auth, 50 publs in medl and sci lit. Honour: Hon Life Mbr, Sterilising Rsch Advsry Cnsl of Aust (SRCA). Memberships: Fell, Austl Soc for Microbiology (FASM); Austl Inst of Medl Scientists (MAIMS); Amn Soc for Microbiology. Hobbies: Voice training; Singing; Astronomy; Cake decorating. Address: Unit 2, 9 Silverdale Road, Ivanhoe, Victoria, Australia 3079.

PEH Wilfred, b. 21 Apr 1958, Singapore. Radiologist. m. Angeline, 28 July 1988, 2 s, 1 d. Education: MB BS; DMRD; MRCP (Glasgow); FRCR; FHKCR; FHKAM; FAMS. Appointments: Medl Offr, Singapore Gen Hosp, 1984-87; Tan Tock Seng Hosp, 1987-88; Registrar, West Infirmary & Roy Infirmary Glasgow, 1988-90; Snr Registrar, Birmingham, 1990-91; Lectr, Univ of Hong Kong, 1991-93; Snr Lectr, 1993-96, Assoc Prof, 1996-97, Prof, 1997-. Publications: 101 Years of a New Kind of Rays, 1996; Clinics in Diagnostic Imaging, 1998; Over 200 articles in profl jrnls. Honour: First Editl Fell, Radiological Soc of N Am, 1998. Memberships: Brit Inst of Radiology, 1988; Amn Roentgen Ray Soc, 1993; Intl Skeletal Soc, 1996; Ed-in-Chf, Jrnl of the Hong Kong Coll of Radiologists, 1998; World Assn of Medl Eds, 1998. Hobbies: Horseback riding; Golf. Address: Department of Diagnostic Radiology, The University of Hong Kong, Room K406, Queen Mary Hospital, Pokfulam Road, Hong Kong, China.

PEHL Richard Henry, b. 27 Nov 1936, Raymond, USA. Physicist. m. Paula Bhatia, 1 July 1980. Education: BS, Chem Engrng, WA Univ, Pullman, 1958; MS, Nuclear Engrng, 1959; PhD, Nuclear Chem, 1963, Univ CA, Berkeley. Appointments: Grad Asst, Lawrence Berkeley Lab, 1960-63; Rsch Assoc, 1963-65, Staff Mbr, 1965-78, Snr Sci, 1978-93, Rsch Physicist, Univ CA, Berkeley; Mbr, Instrument Devel Sci Team, NASA, 1984-94; Adj Staff Physicist, IN Univ, Cyclotron Fac, 1987-; Space Sci Lab, 1994-. Publications: Over 215 articles in profl jrnls. Honours: AEC Fellshp, 1958-59; Sigma Xi; Phi Lambda Upsilon; Sigma Tau; Tau Beta Pi; Phi Kappa Phi. Memberships: Am Physl Soc; IEEE. Hobbies: History; Sports. Address: University of California, 2550 Dana Street 6D, Berkeley, CA 94704, USA.

PEI Yanling, b. Aug 1947, Shuning, Hebei, China. Actress. Appointments: Mbr, 7th CPPCC, 1987-92, 8th, 1993-; Vice Chair, Hebei Fedn of Lit & Art Circles, 1993-. Creative Works: Performances: The Man and the Ghost; Lotus Lantern. Address: Hebei Federation of Literary & Art Circles, Shijiazhuang City, China.

PEIRIS Gamini Lakshman, b. 13 Aug 1946, Colombo, Sri Lanka. Academic. m. Savitri N Amarasuriya, 1971, 1 d. Education: St Thomas's Coll, Mount Lavinia; Univ of Ceylon; New Coll, Oxford, Eng. Appointments: Prof of Law, Univ of Colombo, 1979-; Dean, Fac of Law, 1982-88; Vice Chan, Univ of Colombo, -1994; Dir, Natl Film Corp of Sri Lanka, 1973-88; Commnr, Law Commn of Sri Lanka, 1986-; Visng Fell, All Souls Coll, Oxford, 1980-81; Butterworths Visng Fell, Inst of Advd Legal Stdies, Univ of London, 1984; Disting Visng Fell, Christ's Coll, Cambridge, 1985-86; Smuts Visng Fell in C'Wlth Stdies, Univ of Cambridge, 1985-86; Chair, Cttee of

Vice-Chans of the Univs of Sri Lanka; Vice-Chair, Janasaviya Trust Fund. Publications include: General Principles of Criminal Liability in Ceylon, 1972; The Law of Evidence in Sri Lanka, 1974; Criminal Procedure in Sri Lanka, 1975; Landlord and Tenant in Sri Lanka, 1977; Num articles on comparative and admin law, and law of evidence. Honour: Presdtl Awd, 1987. Memberships: Press Commn on Yth Unrest, 1989; Natl Educ Commn; Exec Cttee, Assn of Tchrs and Rschrs in Intellectual Property Law; Bd of Govs, Inst of Fundamental Stdies; Assoc Mbr, Intl Acady of Comparative Law. Hobby: Walking. Address: 37 Kirula Place, Colombo 5, Sri Lanka.

PEIRIS Premanie, b. 27 May 1944, Colombo, Sri Lanka. Welfare Officer. m. Kenneth, 12 Dec 1970, 1 s, 2 d. Education: Dip, Youth Serv and Psychol, Birmingham Univ, Eng. Appointment: Welfare Off, Unilever Ltd. Publications: Pprs at intl IFSW confs, Bangkok, Japan, Stockholm, Philippines. Membership: Intl Fedn of Socl Work, Oslo, Norway. Hobbies: Painting; Nature; Travel. Address: 57/16 Nimala Mariya Mu, Wattala, Sri Lanka.

PEKAR Peter Jnr. Expert in Strategic Alliances. Education: MA, Maths, Univ of IL (Urbana); PhD, Bus and Econs, IL Inst of Technol Stuart Sch of Bus (Chgo). Appointments: Snr mngmt positions in Fortune 500 firms inclng: Esmark, Quaker Oats Co; Hd of Alliances and Venture Capital for Dun & Bradstreet; Pres, BT-USA Inc, Amn Holding Co for a global Dutch conglomerate; Snr Advsr, Booz Allen & Hamilton Inc, 1993-; Visng Prof, London Bus Sch; Guest Spker num orgs and grps inclng: Bus Weeks Pres' Forum; Natl Assn Corp Dirs; Los Angeles and Chgo Bars. Publications: 50 articles; (co-auth) 3 Viewpoints; (co-auth) Smart Alliances: Practical Secrets to Repeatable Success. Address: Booz, Allen & Hamilton, 5220 Pacific Con Drive, 390 Los Angeles, CA 90045, USA.

PELIKA Thomas, b. 14 May 1955, Kawakama Vill, Morobe Prov, Papua New Guinea. Minister for Police. m. 4 children. Education: Grad as Police Offr, Jt Servs Coll, Igam. Appointments: Mbr, Police Force, 18 yrs; Offr in Charge, CID, 1987; Operational Cmndr, Combined Def and Police Ops, 1988; Subsistence Farmer; Min for Energy Dev, 1992-94; Shadow Min for Forests, Environ and Conservation, 1995-97; Min for Internal Affairs; Min for Police. Membership: League for Natl Advmt Party.

PENDAL Phillip George, b. 4 Feb 1947, Bunbury, WA, Aust. Member of Parliament. m. Maxine Mayrhofer, 23 Aug 1969, 1 s, 2 d. Appointments: Jrnlst, 1966-80; MP, 1980-; Shadow Min for Tourism, 1983-84; Shadow Min for Tourism, Arts, Family, 1986-90; Shadow Min for Environ and Heritage, 1990-93. Publications: A R G Hawke - Son of Labor; Sir Eric Smart - Farmer; A Clean Break, (Family History); Uniform Law in Australia - An Alternative Approach, 1996; Leave Granted, 1997. Honours: Winner, Provincial Press Awd, WA, 1967; US State Dept Travel Fellshp, 1990. Memberships: Bd of Tstees, Fund for Faith AIDS Prog; Francis Burt Law Cntr; Constl Centenary Fndn Chapt Exec; Advsry Bd, Law and Pols, Notre Dame Univ, Aust; Chmn, May Gibbs Trust; Austl Jrnlsts Assn; Kts of the Southern Cross; WA Cricket Assn. Hobby: Writing Historical Research. Address: 27 York Street, South Perth, WA 6151, Australia.

PENG Chong, b. 1909, Zhangzhou, Fujian, China. Politician. Appointments: Joined CCP, 1933; Polit Commr, Regt of New 4th Army, 1938; Dpty Sec-Gen, Prov Peoples Govt, Fujian, 1950; Mayor of Nanjing, 1955-59; 1st Sec, Muncipal CCP Cttee, Nanjing, 1955-60; Dpty for Jiangsu, 2nd NPC, 1958; Alt 2nd Sec, CCP Cttee, Jiangsu, 1960; Polit Commr, Nanjing Militia, 1960; 1st Sec, Municipal CCP Cttee, Nanjing, 1962-68; 2nd Sec, CCP Cttee, Jiangsu, 1965-68; Vice Chair, Prov Revolutionary Cttee, Jiangsu, 1968-74; Alt Mbr, 9th Ctrl Cttee CCP, 1969; Sec, CCP Cttee, Jiangsu, 1970-74; Alt Mbr, 10th Ctrl Cttee CCP, 1973; Chair, Prov Revolutionary Cttee, Jiangsu, 1974-76; 2nd Polit Commr, PLA Nanjing Mil Region, 1975-80; 3rd Sec, CCP Cttee, Shanghai, 1976-79; 2nd Vice Chair, Municipal Revolutionary Cttee, Shanghai, 1976-79; Chair, Municipal CPPCC Cttee, Shanghai, 1977-79; Mbr, 11th Ctrl Cttee

CCP, 1977; Hd, Grp in Charge of Snail Fever Prevention, Ctrl Cttee CCP, 1978-; Dpty for Shanghai, 5th NPC, 1978; Dpty for Shanghai, 5th NPC, 1978; Vice Chair, Natl Cttee, 5th CPPCC, 1978-80; 1st Sec, CCP Cttee, Shanghai, 1979-80; Chair, Municipal Revolutionary Cttee, Shanghai, 1979-80; Mayor of Shanghai, 1980; Sec, 11th Ctrl Cttee CCP, 1980-82; Vice Chair, Standing Cttee, 5th NPC, 1980-83; Mbr, 12th Ctrl Cttee CCP, 1982-87; Vice Chair, Standing Cttee, 6th NPC, 1983-88; Mbr, Presidium 6th NPC, 1986-. Honours: China Fndn for Heroism Awds. Memberships include: Soc for Ind & Com Admin; Gymnastics Assn; China Welfare Inst; China Intl Cultural Exchange Cntr. Address: Standing Committee, National Peoples Congress, Tian An Men Square, Beijing, China.

PENG Fred C C, b. 9 July 1934, Fongshan, Taiwan. Neurolinguistics. m. Carol V, 2 Mar 1963, 1 d. Education: PhD, State Univ of NY, Buffalo (SUNY Buffalo), 1964. Appointments: Asst Prof of Ling, Intl Christian Univ, 1966-70; Visng Assoc Prof, Tulane Univ, New Orleans, LA, USA, 1971-72; Assoc Prof of Ling, 1970-74; Prof of Ling, 1974-, Intl Christian Univ (Japan). Publications: (jt auth) Folk Song Style and Culture, 1964; On the Nature of Sign Language, 1976; The Ainu: The Past in the Present (jt auth), 1977; Sign Language and Language Acquisition in Man and Ape: New Dimensions in Comparative Pedolinguistics (Ed for AAAS symposium), 1978. Honour: Spec Awd, Disting Contbns to Medl Rehab, A W F Krakow, Poland, 1994. Memberships: Elected Mbr, NY Acady Scis; Life Mbr, AAAS Societa Neurologica Japonica; Neuropsychological Assn of Japan; Taiwan Stroke Soc; Editl Bd, Asia Pacific Jrnl of Speech, Lang and Hearing; Advsry Bd of Ling and Lang Behaviour. Hobbies: Jogging; Chi Kung; Yoga; Research; Violin; Classical guitar. Address: 10-3, 4-chome Osawa #471, Mitaka-shi, Tokyo 1810015, Japan.

PENG Guoxun, b. 23 Aug 1937, Yibin, Sichuan, China. Professor. m. Xu Shuhui, 30 Dec 1965, 1 d. Education: Dip, Tsinhua Univ, 1954-60. Appointments: Techn, Des and Rsch Inst of Nuclear Engrng; Prof, NW Inst of Light Ind, 1970-. Publications: Design of Packaging Machines, 1986; Des of Cam Mechanisms in Automative Machines, 1990; Dynamics of Cashioning Package, 1989. Honours: 1st Class Prize of Splendid Work, Shaanxi, 1986; 2nd Class Prize, Sci and Technol Progress, Shaanxi, 1995. Memberships: Dpty Dir, Packaging and Food Machinery Commn, CMEA; Dpty Pres, China Light Ind Machinery Assn, 1988-. Address: Northwest Institute of Light Industry, Xiangyang, Shaanxi 712081, China.

PENG Han Chu, b. 8 July 1930, Hu-Nan Prov, China. Clinic Doctor. m. Dr Liu, Nov 1961, 2 s. Education: MD, Hu-Nan (Xiang-Yale) Medl Univ. Appointment: Prof, 1980-. Publications: An Electron Microscopic Study of Thyroxine Against Ototoxicity of Kanamycin, 1988; Forensic Medical Appraisal on Ecoch G and ABR of 113 Ears in 76 Traumatic Cases, 1992. Honour: Two 2nd Awds, Sci and Technol Cttee of Shanxi Prov, China. Membership: Zhong Hua Medl Assn, 1957; China Laser Medl Assn, 1980. Hobbies: Singing songs and listening to music. Address: ENT Department First Teaching Hospital, Shanxi Medical University, Taiyuan Shanxi, 030001, China.

PENG Huihong, b. 20 July 1959, Shanghai, China. Senior Mechanical Engineer. m. Jiping H, 21 Jan 1987, 1 d. Education: Master Deg. Appointments: Dir, Rsch Dept, Shanghai Nonferrous Metals Rsch Inst, 1990-96; Mngr, Project Dept, Granges (Shanghai), 1996-. Publication: Researching the Contact Stress and Heat Deformation of Rolls in Rolling Mill, 1998. Memberships: Shanghai Ferrous Metals Assn; Shanghai Nonferrous Metals Assn; China Nonferrous Metals Assn; Shanghai Mech Engrng Assn. Hobby: Photography. Address: No 6-402, Lane 260, Nan Ma Tou Road, Shanghai 200125, China.

PENG Kunren, b. 12 Sept 1933. Teacher. m. Huang Shu-qiong, 19 Jan 1963, 1 s, 1 d. Education: Grad, Dept of Politics, S China Tchr's Coll, Guangzhou, 1955; Advd Stdy, People's Univ of China, 1961-62. Appointments:

Lectr, Assoc Prof, Prof; Dir of Tchng and Rsch Sect of Polit Econs; V Dir, Propaganda Dept of Zhongshan Univ. Publications: Comprehensive Development of City Real Estate, 1988; Practical Studies of Guangdong Real Estate Investment, 1995; Over 50 other papers. Honours: Ex Tutor for Master Stud, Zhongshan Univ, 1992; Ex works by, Guangdong RA of Agric Econs, 1990; China RA of Labor, 1991; Guangzhou RA of Real Estate, 1995. Memberships: V Chmn, Guangdong Rsch Assn of Real Estate; Rsch Assn of Labor; V Sec in Gen, GRA of Real Estate Evaluation. Hobbies: Reading; Music. Address: Department of Economics, Lingnan College, Zhongshan University, Guangzhou, China.

PENG Ming-Min, b. 1923, Taiwan. Politician. Education: Japan Univ; Natl Taiwan Univ. Appointments: Fmr Chair, Polit Sci Dept, Natl Taiwan Univ; Arrested for activities supporting self-determination for Taiwan, 1964; 8 yrs imprisonment; Sentence commuted to house arrest; Escaped into exile in USA; Returned home, 1992; Joined Democratic Progressive Pty, 1995; DDP Cand, Pres Elections, 1996. Address: Democratic Progressive Party, 14th Floor, 128 Ming Sheng East Road, Sec 3, Taipei, Taiwan.

PENG Ming-Tsung, b. 28 Nov 1917, Taiwan. Professor Emeritus. m. S C Yuan, 3 Oct 1946, 3 s, 1 d. Education: MD; PhD. Appointments: Prof of Physiol, Dir of Stdies, Dean, Coll of Med, Natl Taiwan Univ. Honours: Best Rsch Awd in Med, Min of Educ, China, 1975; Mbr, Academia Sinica, China, 1978. Memberships: Endocrine Soc, USA, 1985-97; Intl Brain Rsch Org, 1985-; Formosan Med Assn, Pres, 1980-83. Hobby: Classic music. Address: 1 Lane 91, Jen-ai Road, Sect 2, Taipei, Taiwan.

PENG Shi Lu, b. 18 Nov 1925, Guangdong, China. Chief Engineer. m. Ma Shu Ying, 14 June 1958, 1 s, 1 d. Education: Chem Mech Engrng Dip, Chem Engrng Inst of Moscow; Inst of Power Engrng, Moscow, 1956-58. Appointments: Techn, Chem Plant, 1947; Dpty Dir, Nuclear Power Lab Inst of Atomic Energy, 1958-64; Assoc Prof, Phys, China Sci and Tech Univ, 1962-65; Chf Engr, Vice Dir, Nuclear Energy Rsch Inst, 1964-73; Vice Dir, Shipbldg Rsch and Devel Admin, 1974-79; Vice Min, Min of Mech Ind No 6, 1979-83; Chf Designer, Nuclear Submarine, 1979-83; Alternative Mbr, 12th Ctrl Cttee of CCP, 1982-87; Vice Min, Min of Water Resource and Electric Power, 1983-86; Dir and Gen Mngr, Daya Bay Nuclear Power Plant, 1983-86; Stndng Cttee Mbr, CCP of Guangdong Prov; Chmn, Sci Technol Cmmn; Chf Engr, Min of Nuclear Ind, 1986-; Snr Advsr, Sci and Technol, CNNC, 1992-; Mbr Environ Protection Cttee, NPC, 1993-; Standing Cttee, 8th NPC, 1993-; Mbr. Chinese Acady of Engrng, 1994-. Publications: Prospects for Nuclear Power Development in China; Calculation and Analysis of Electricity Price in Connection Grid of 2x600 Mwe PWR Nuclear Power Plant; Economic Analysis and Evaluation of Nuclear Energy Industry. Honours: State Sci Awd, 1978 Top Grade Awd of Natl Prize of Sci and Tech Progress, 1985; Natl Def Disting Serv Awd, 1988; Ho Leung Ho Lee Fndn Sci and Tech Progress Awd, 1996. Memberships: Hon Pres, Chinese Nuclear Soc; Pres, Chinese Nuclear Power. Hobbies: Reading; Classical Music. Address: Ministry of Nuclear Industry, PO Box 2102, Beijing, China.

PENG Yuxing, b. 11 Nov 1962, Sichuan, China. Researcher; Chemist. m. Dai Meng, 10 Oct 1985, 1 d. Education: BS, 1978-82, MS, 1982-85, Sichuan Univ, China; PhD, Univ Pierre et Marie Curie (Paris VI), 1990-92. Appointments: Rsch Asst, Assoc Prof, Prof, Chengdu Inst of Organic Chem, Chinese Acady of Scis, 1985-90, 1993-. Publications: Over 30 pprs, 20 indexed by SCI. Membership: Chinese Chem Soc. Address: Chengdu Institute of Organic Chemistry, Chinese Academy of Sciences, PO Box 415, Chengdu 610041, China.

PENGILLEY Warren James, b. 7 Nov 1938, Quirindi, Aust. Lawyer; Professor. m. Jan, 6 Jan 1966, 1 s, 1 d. Education: BA, LLB, Sydney; DJur, Vanderbilt, USA; MCom; DSc, Newcastle, NSW; Fell Austl Soc of Cert

Prac Accts. Appointments: Ptnr, Newman & Pengilley Solicitors, 1964-75; Commn Austl Trade Prac Commn, 1975-82; Parker Deacon Graham & James, Sydney, 1983-93; Prof of Law, Newcastle Univ. Publications: Num books and articles in Aust, NZ, UK, USA, Can. Honours: Austl Reserve Force Decoration, 1986, w clasp for serv to Austl Reserve Forces, 1990. Memberships: Num Univ positions; Commnd Offr, RAAF Reserve, 1970-93; Sec, NSW N and NW Law Soc, 1974-75; Sec, ACT Law Soc, 1981-82. Hobbies: Travel; Writing; Tennis. Address: Faculty of Law, University of Newcastle, NSW, Australia 2308.

PENICKA Miloslav, b. 16 Apr 1935, Ostrava, Czech. Composer. m. S E Parton, 19 Mar 1977, 1 s, 2 d. Education: Dip, Composition, high distinct, Prague Conservatorium of Music, 1958 and Acady of Music, Prague, 1964. Appointments: Emigrated to Aust, 1964; Worked in ABC Music Lib, Sydney Symph Orch, 1965-68; Composition, Abbotsleigh Coll, 1968-77. Creative Works: Compositions: Symphony; 3 Overtures; 2 Piano Concertos; Clarinet Concerto; Divertimento for violin and wind; 3 Orchl Serenades; 2 orchl suites; 3 String Quartets; Clarinet Quintet; Piano Quartet; 2 Piano Sonatas; Four Pieces for flute and piano; Four pieces for oboe and piano; Piano Sonatina; Violin and Piano Sonatina; Sonatina for Cello and Piano; Partita for cello solo; 2 piano cycles: Kookaburras Friends and Musings; Dance Suite for string orch, 1998; Vocal Music; Educl Pieces. Memberships: Assoc Mbr, Austl Performing Rights Assn Full Mbr, Austl Music Cntr. Listed in: Who's Who in Music; Who's Who in Australia. Hobbies: Photography; Fishing; Tropical fish; Chess; Nature. Address: 9 Warraroon Road, Lane Cove, Sydney, NSW 2066, Australia.

PENROSE John, b. 16 June 1942, Tulsa, OK, USA. College Professor. m. Margaret, 15 June 1983. Education: BSJ; MS; PhD. Appointments: OH Univ; S IL Univ, Edwardsville; Univ TX, Austin; San Diego State Univ. Publications: Advanced Business Communications, 3rd ed, 1997; Business Communication Strategies & Skills, 5th ed, 1997. Honours: Disting Mbr, 1983, Francis W Weeks Awd, 1985, Fell, 1989, Assn for Bus Commns. Membership: Assn for Bus Commns, Pres, 1989. Hobbies: Sailing; Classic Cars. Address: c/o IDS Department, San Diego State University, San Diego, CA 92182-8234, USA.

PERAK Sultan Azlan Muhibbuddin Shah ibni Al-Marhum, b. 19 Apr 1928, Batu Gajah, Malaysia. Malaysian Ruler. m. Tuanku Bainun Mohamed Ali, 1954, 2 s, 3 d. Education: Govt Engl Sch; Malay Coll; Univ of Nottingham. Appointments: Called to Bar, Lincoln's Inn; Magistrate, Kuala Lumpur; Asst State Sec, Perak; Dpty Pub Prosecutor; Pres, Sessions Crt, Seremban & Taiping; State Legal Advsr, Pahang & Johore; Raja Kechil Bongsu (6th in line), 1962, Raja Muda (2nd in line to the throne), 1983; Pro-Chan, Univ Saina Malaysia, 1971; Mngr, Malaysian Hockey Team, 1972; Fed Crt Judge, 1973; Chf Justice of Malaysia, 1979; Lord Pres, 1982-83; Sultan of Perak, 1984-; Chan, Univ of Malaya, 1986; Yang di-Pertuan Agong (Supreme Hd of State), 1989-94. Honour: Hon Col-in-Chf, Malaysian Armed Forces Engrs Corps. Memberships: Pres, Malaysian Hockey Fedn, Asian Hockey Fedn; VP, Intl Hockey Fedn; Olympic Cncl of Malaysia.

PEREIRA Benedict Martin Joseph, b. 12 Jan 1957, Mangalore, India. Teacher; Researcher. 2 s. Education: MSc; MPhil; PhD. Appointments: Lectr, 1984, Asst Prof, 1996, Chmn, 1997. Publications: Educl TV Films. Memberships: Acoustical Soc of India; Soc of Bioscis; Soc of Reproductive Biol and Comparative Endocrinol. Hobbies: Music; Cricket. Address: Department of Biosciences & Biotechnology, University of Roorkee, Roorkee 247667, India.

PERERA Liyanagé Henry Horace, b. 9 May 1915, Yatiyantota, Ceylon. International Official. m. Sita Trixie Senarat, 1942, 1 s, 3 d. Education: St Benedict's Coll, Colombo; Univ Coll, London; Univ of Ceylon. Appointments: Snr Master in Govt & Hist, Ceylon,

1936-59; Asst Reg, Aquinas Univ Coll, Colombo, 1960-61; Educn Dir, World Fedn of UN Assns, 1961-63, Dpty Sec-Gen, Educn Dir, 1963-66, Sec-Gen, 1966-76; Cnslt, Pontificial Comm for Peace & Justice, 1969-76; Specl Asst for Asia & The S Pacific, World Confed of Orgs of the Tchng Profession, 1976-84; Cnslt to World Fedn UN Assns, 1985-; Sec, Masaryk Study Cntr for UN Studies, Geneva. Publications: Ceylon Under Western Rule; Guides to the Study of the Status and Working Conditions of the Teacher; ILO Conventions and Trade Unionism; The Convention on the Rights of the Child; The Convention on the Elimination of all Forms of Discrimination Against Women; Human Rights in Hinduism, Buddhism, Christianity and Islam (ed), 1988; Num pprs in profl jrnls. Honours include: William Russel Awd, 1974; Intl Assn of Educrs for World Peace Awd; Gold Medal, Czech Soc for Intl Rels. Memberships include: WFUNA. Hobbies: Swimming; Tennis; Photography; Stamp Collecting; Reading. Address: 22 Avenue Luserna, 1203 Geneva, Switzerland.

PERES Shimon, b. 1923, Poland, immigrated to Palestine, 1934. Politician. m. Sonia Gelman, 2 s, 1 d. Education: NY Univ; Harvard Univ. Appointments: Fmr Sec, Hano'ar Ha'oved Movt; Mbr, Haganah Movt, 1947; hd, Israel Naval Serv, Min of Def, 1948; Hd of Def Mission in USA; Dpty Dir-Gen, Min of Def, 1952-53, Dir-Gen, 1953-59, Dpty Min of Def, 1959-65; Mbr, Knesset, 1959-; Mbr, Mapai Pty, 1959-65; Fndr Mbr, Sec-Gen, Rafi Pty, 1965; Mbr, Labour Party, 1968, Chair, 1977-92, 1995-97; Min for Econ Devel in the Admin Areas & for Immigrant Absorption, 1969-70, of Transp & Comms, 1970-74, of Info, 1974, of Def, 1974-77, of Fgn Affairs, 1992-95; Acting PM, 1977; Ldr of Opposition, 1977-84, 1996-97; PM of Israel, 1984-86; Min of the Interior & Relig Affairs, 1985-85, of Def, 1995-96; Vice Premier, Min of Fgn Affairs, 1986-88; Vice Premier, Fin Min, 1988-90; PM, 1995-96. Publications: The Next Step, 1965; David's Sling, 1970; Tomorrow is Now, 1978; From These Men, 1979; Witness (autobiog), 1993; The New Middle East, 1993; Battling For Peace, 1995. Honours: Nobel Prize for Peace (shared), 1994; Intl Cncl of Christians & Jews Interfaith Gold Medallian, 1997. Address: The Knesset, Jerusalem, Israel.

PERETZ Yitzhak Haim, b. 1939, Morocco. Politician. m. 4 children. Appointments: Ordained Rabbi; Fmr Chf Rabbi of Raanana; Mbr, Shas Pty; Mbr, Knesset, 1984-; Min without Portfolio, 1984, of the Interior, 1984-87, without Portfolio, 1987-88, of Immigrant Absorption, 1988-92. Address: The Knesset, Jerusalem, Israel.

PEREZ BALLADARES Ernesto, b. 29 June 1946, Panama City, Panama. Politician. m. Dora Boyd, 2 s, 3 d. Education: Univ of Notre Dame; Univ PA. Appointments: Dir, Corp Credit Offl for Ctrl Am & Panama Citibank, 1971-75; Min of Fin & the Treas, 1976-81, of Planning & Econ Policy, 1981-82; Fndng Mbr, Partido Revolucionario Democratico (PRD), 1979, Sec-Gen, 1982, 1992; Dir-Gen, Instituto de Recursos Hidraulicos y Electrificacion, 1983; Pres of Panama, 1994-. Honours: Order of Sacred Treas, 1st class, Japan, 1980; Orden Aguila Azteca en Grado de Bando, Mexico, 1981. Memberships include: Pres, Golden Fruit SA Inversionista el Torreon, SA. Address: Office of the President, Palacio Presidencial, Valija 50, Panama 1, Panama.

PERKINS James Oliver Newton, b. 11 July 1924, Bedford, Eng. Economist. m. Ruth Williams, 15 Jan 1955, 1 d. Education: BA, MA, PhD, Cambridge. Appointments: Editl Staff, The Economist, 1952-53; Rsch Fell, Austl Natl Univ, 1953-56; Lectr, Snr Lectr, Rdr, Prof, Univ of Melbourne, 1956-89; Emer Prof, 1990-. Publications: 19 books incl: The Macroeconomic Mix in the Industrialised World, 1985; Contemporary Macroeconomics (co-auth), 1986; Australian Macroeconomic Policy 1974-1985, 1987; The Deregulation of the Australian Financial System, 1989; A General Approach to Macroeconomic Policy, 1990; Budget Deficits and Macroeconomic Policy, 1997; The Wallis Report and the Australian Financial Sustem, 1998. Membership: Fell Socl Scis in Aust, 1973. Hobbies: Music; Watching cricket and rugby football.

Address: Department of Economics, University of Melbourne, Parkville 3052, Victoria, Australia.

PERL Martin Lewis, b. 24 June 1927, Brooklyn, NY, USA. Physicist; Engineer. 3 s, 1 d. Education: BChem Engrng, Polytechnic Inst, 1948; PhD, Phys, Columbia Univ, 1955. Appointments: Instr Asst Prof, Assoc Prof, Univ of MI; Full prof, Stanford Univ. Publications; High Energy Hadron Physics, 1974; Reflections on Experimental Science, 1996. Honours: US Natl Acady of Scis; Amn Acady of Arts and Scis; Wolf Prize, Phys, 1982; Nobel Prize, Phys, 1995. Memberships: Inst of Phys; Amn Phys Soc; US Natl Acady of Scis. Address: Stanford Linear Accelerator Center, Stanford University, Stanford, CA 94309, USA.

PERLIS The Raja of Tuanku Syed Putra ibni al-Marhum Syed Hassan Jamalullail, b. 25 Nov 1920, Arau, Perlis, Malaysia. Malaysian Ruler. m. Tengku Budriah Binti al-Marhum Tengku Ismail, 1941, 8 s, 6 d. Appointments: Appointed Bakal Raja (Heir-Presumptive) of Perlis, 1938; Attached to Crts in Kangar, 1940; Land Off, Kuala Lumpur, 1 yr; Magistrates Crt, Kuala Lumpur, 1 yr; Pvte Bus; Ascended Throne, 1945; Timbalan Yang di-Pertuan Agung (Dpty Paramount Ruler) of Malaya, 1960, Yang di-Pertuan Agung (HM the Paramount Ruler), 1960-65, of Malaysia, 1963-65; Chan, Univ of Sci, Malaysia, 1971-. Honours: Num. Hobbies: Golf; Tennis; Fishing; Shooting. Address: Istana Arau, Perlis, Malaysia.

PERLMAN Edwin Francis, b. 4 Nov 1931, Chgo, USA. Retired Aeronautical Engineer. m. Elka Aharoni, 8 Aug 1974, dec, 18 Feb 1992. Education: BS, Univ IL, 1953; Postgrad, UCLA, 1955-59, Univ IL, 1961-64; MS, Univ IL, 1963. Appointments: Engr, Douglas Aircraft, Santa Monica, CA, 1953-61, MacDonnell Douglas, Long Beach, CA, 1964-71. Publications: Reports pertaining to stress analysis and external, internal loads. Honour: Fell Hon Univ Judaism, Los Angeles, 1968-70. Memberships: VP, Temple Beth Shalom Men's Club, Long Beach, 1967, Bd Dirs, 1968; Mbr, Congl Cabinet, Univ Judaism, Los Angeles, 1968; Bd Dirs, Utd Synagogue of Am, 1968; AIAA (snr); IEEE Computer Soc; Assn for Computing Machinery; Univ IL Alumni Assn; UCLA Alumni Assn; Assn Am and Canad in Israel; Assn of Engrs, Archts, Grads of Technol Scis in Israel. Address: PO Box 22162, Tel Aviv 61221, Israel.

PERLMAN Itzhak, b. 31 Aug 1945, Tel-Aviv, Israel. Violinist. m. Toby Lynn Friedlander, 1967, 2 s, 3 d. Education: Tel-Aviv Acady of Music; Juilliard Sch, USA; Studies w Ivan Galamian & Dorothy De Lay. Appointments: Recitals on Radio, 10 yrs old; 1st Recital, Carnegie Hall, 1963; Played w maj Am orchs, 1964-; Toured Eur, playing w maj Eurn orchs, 1966-; Debut in UK w London Symph Orch, 1968; Toured Poland, Hungary, Far E; Played w Israel Philharmonic Orch in fmr Soviet Union; Appearances at Israel Fest & Eurn Fests; Num Recordings. Honours: Sev hon degs; Sev Grammy Awds; Medal of Liberty, 1986. Address: c/o IMG Artists, 22 East 71st Street, NY 10021, USA.

PERNG Chin-Lin, b. 15 Oct 1957, Hsinchu, Taiwan. Gastroenterologist. m. Hsiao-Feng, 18 Nov 1988, 1 s, 2 d. Education: MB, 1983. Appointments: Attending Phys of Med, Veterans Gen Hosp, Taipei, Taiwan; Instr, Med, Natl Yang-Ming Univ. Publications: Publs in jrnls. Honours: 2nd Prize of publ in natl sci inst, 1995, 1997. Memberships: Gastroenterological Soc, China, 1995; Amn Coll of Gastroenterology, 1997. Hobby: Research of Helicobacter pylori. Address: Division of Gastroenterology, Department of Medicine, Veterans General Hospital-Taipei, Taipei, 11217, Taiwan.

PERRY Valerie Barbara, b. 30 June 1952, Tristan da Cunha. Education Officer. m. Wayne, 11 Jan 1975, 2 s, 1 d. Education: Tchng Ctf, 1970; BA, Educ, 1989; BEd, 1991. Appointments: Tchr, NSW Dept of Educn, 1971-75, ACT Dept of Educ, 1975-97; Educ Offr, 1997-. Publications include: A.C.T. Electricity and Water Kit, 1995; X-Rays The Inside Story, 1995; Colour; Let There Be Light; Water; Hands-On Astronomy. Honours: CRA Fellshp, 1989; BHP Awd, 1992; ACT Highly Commended

Govt Serv Awd. Hobbies: Reading; Astronomy. Address: 76 Perry Drive, Chapman, ACT 2611, Australia.

PERVAN Graham Peter, b. 20 Dec 1950, Perth, Aust. University Academic. m. Elizabeth, 27 Nov 1976, 1 s, 1 d. Education: BS (Hons); BComm; MSc; PhD. Appointments: Snr Tuir, Lectr, Snr Lectr, Assoc Prof, Hd of Sch, Prof. Publications: Over 100 acad publs, 1 book, 3 ed proceedings, jrnl and conf pprs. Honours: Pres, Austl Cncl of Profs and Hds of Info Systems; Rotary Intl Grad Fell; Best Ppr Nominee at Is Natl Conf. Memberships: Austl Soc for Ops Rsch, WA State Pres, 1986-89; Natl VP, 1988-92; Asst Fell, Aust Inst of Mngmt. Hobbies: AFL; Internet; Travel. Address: School of Information Systems, Curtin University of Technology, GPO Box U1987, Perth, WA 6845, Australia.

PESTELL George Stanley, b. 17 Mar 1921, Perth, WA, Aust. Surgeon (retired). m. Miss T Marum, 3 Apr 1954, 2 s, 1 d. Education: MB BS, Melbourne, 1945; FRCS (Eng), 1952; FRACS, 1957; Soc of Hd and Neck Surgs, USA, 13 Apr 1965. Appointments: Roy Perth Hosp, Visng Staff, 1953-77; Retd Emer Cnslt Surg, Hollywood (Veterans) Hosp, 1962-86; Retd Emer Cnslt Surg; Dir, Surg Stdies, Univ Tchng Unit, 1977-89. Honours: Apptd Surg to H M the Queen on her visit to West Aust, 1977. Membership: Austl Medl Assn. Hobbies: Astronomy; Electronics; Classical piano studies. Address: 29 Cygnet Crescent, Dalkeith, Perth, Western Australia, Australia.

PETERS Mark Alan, b. 27 May 1968, Sydney, Aust. Management Consultant. Education: BE (Hons), Univ of Sydney; Grad Dip in Applied Corp Fin and Investment, Securities Inst of Aust; MBA, INSEAD. Appointments: Snr Mngr, Strategy, Anderson Cnsltng, 1997; Prin, Kalehas Grp, 1999. Membership: Assoc, Securities Inst of Aust. Address: c/o Kalehas, Summit House, 70 Wilson Street, London EC2A 2DB, England.

PETERS Winston R, b. New Zealand. Politician; Lawyer. Appointments: Fmr MP for Tauranga; Min of Maori Affairs, Min in Charge of Iwi Transition Agcy, Chair, Cabinet Cttee on Treaty of Waitangi Issues, 1990-91; Independent MP, 1993-, now NZ 1st Pty; Ldr, NZ 1st Pty, 1993-, Dpty PM, Treas, 1996-. Address: Parliament Buildings, Wellington, New Zealand.

PETERSEN George Bouet, b. 5 Sept 1933, Palmerston N, NZ. Professor of Biochemistry. m. Patricia Jane Egerton Caughey, 16 Apr 1960, 4 d. Education: BSc, 1955, MSc, 1956, Univ of Otago; DPhil, 1960, MA (by decree), 1962, Univ of Oxford, Eng. Appointments: Scientist, Dept of Sci and Indl Rsch, Plant Chem Div, Palmerston N, 1959-61, 1963-68; Dept Demonstrator, Biochem, Univ of Oxford, Eng, 1961-63; Prof of Biochem, Univ of Otago, Dunedin, NZ, 1968-; Hd, Dept of Biochem, Univ of Otago, 1968-90; Dpty Dean, Otago Med Sch, 1991-95. Honours: Visng Rsch Fell, Harv Univ, 1963; Travel Grant, Carnegie Corp of NY, 1963; Elected Fell, NZ Inst of Chem, 1967; C'wlth Bursary, Roy Soc, London, 1973, Nuffield Inst, 1981; Elected Fell, 1985, Pres Acady Cncl, 1998, Roy Soc of NZ, 1985; DSc, Univ of Oxford, 1993; NZ Assn of Scis Marsden Medal, 1995; ONZM, 1997. Memberships: Biochem Soc, UK; Roy Soc of Chem, London, NZ Inst of Chem; NZ Biochem Soc. Hobbies: Music; Literature. Address: Otoitu, 47 Maori Road, Dunedin, New Zealand.

PETERSON Richard Byron, b. 10 May 1933, Sioux Cty, IA, USA. University Professor. m. Barbara, 7 Apr 1957, 1 s, 1 d. Education: BA, Augustana Coll, IL; MA, Univ of Il; PhD, Univ of WI. Appointment: Univ of WA, Bus Sch, 1966-. Honour: Phi Kappa Phi. Memberships: Indl Rels Rsch Assn; Intl Rels Assn; Acady of Mngt (IM Div Chair, 1987-88); West Acady of Mngmt. Hobbies: Cross-country skiing; Tennis; Swimming; Reading. Address: 4737 49th NE, Seattle, WA 98105, USA.

PETFIELD Ross Matthew, b. 1 July 1944, Brisbane, Aust. Stockbroker. m. Elaine, 3 Sept 1966, 1 s, 2 d. Education: FSIA; FAIM; FAICD; FSSE. Appointment: Mngng Dir, Credit Suisse First Boston Aust Equities Pvte

Ltd. Address: Gold Creek Road, Brookfield, Qld 4069, Australia.

PETTIT Philip Noel, b. 20 Dec 1945, Ireland. Professor of Social and Political Theory. m. Eileen McNally, 1 July 1978, 2 s. Education: BA, 1966, MA, 1967, Natl Univ of Ireland (Maynooth Coll); MA (ex officio), Cambridge Univ, 1972. Appointments: Asst Lectr, Queens Univ, Belfast, N Ireland, 1967-68; Lectr, 1968-72, 1975-77, Univ Coll, Dublin, Ireland; Rsch Fell, Trinity Hall, Cambridge, Eng, 1972-75; Prof of Philos, Univ of Bradford, 1977-83; Prof, Fell, 1983-89, Prof of Socl and Polit Theory, 1989-, Rsch Sch of Socl Scis, Austl Natl Univ; Vising Prof of Philos, Columbia Univ, NY, 1997-. Publications: The Concept of Structuralism, 1975; Judging Justice, 1980; Semantics and Social Science (w G Macdonald), 1981; Not Just Deserts: A Republican Theory of Criminal Justice (w John Braithwaite), 1990; Rawls: A Theory of Justice and Its Critics (w C Kukathas), 1990; The Common Mind, 1993; Republicanism, 1997. Honours: Elected Fell, Acady of Socl Scis of Aust, 1987; Elected Fell, Austl Acady of the Humanities, 1988. Memberships: Australasian Assn of Philos; Australasian Polit Sci Assn; Mind Assn; Aristotelian Soc. Hobbies: Walking; Music; Child Rearing. Address: Research School of Social Sciences, Australian National University, Canberra, ACT 2601, Australia.

PEZZUTTI Brian Patrick Victor, b. 6 Jan 1947, Casino, NSW, Aust. Member of Parliament; Specialist Aneasthetist. m. Christine, 21 Feb 1976, 2 s, 2 d. Education: MBBS (Sydney), 1970; FFARCS, 1975; FANZCA, 1993. Appointments include: RMO, Registrar Rostings, var Austl hosps, 1970-75; Spec in Anaesthesia and Intensive Care, 1980-87; Elected NSW Legis Cncl (Lib), 1988-; Parly Sec for Hlth, 1993-95; Liberal Spokesman of Hlth and Yth Affairs in Upper House, 1995-; Chmn, 1991-93, Dpty Chmn, 1995-, Legis Cncl Standing Cttee on State Dev; Chmn, Legis Cncl Printing Cttee, 1991-95; Mbr, 1991-, Chmn, 1992, Jt Estimates Cttee; Legis Cncl elected mbr, Univ NSW Cncl, 1991-95; South Cross Univ Interim Cncl, 1993-94; Law Soc, NSW Profl Conduct Cttee, apptd mbr, 1991-93; Mbr, Govt Advsry Cttees inclng: Hlth, 1988- (Chmn, 1991-93, 1995-); Transport, 1988-91 (Chmn, 1990-91); Family and Cmnty Servs, 1988-95 (Chmn, 1991); Ethnic Affairs, 1988-; Status of Women, 1993-95; Indl Rels, 1995-; Mil Serv: Enlisted A/Res, 1965; Lt-Col, SO1 HSSC-A, 1993-; Col Dir Hlth Servs RHSA-NSW, 1997-; Full-time Army called up to serv in Mid E, 1991; Served w Austl Contingent of UN Peacekeeping Force in Rwanda, July-Sept 1995; Served Bouganville, 1998. Publications: 8 as Chmn of Standing Cttee on State Dev, 1991-93; 7 as mbr of Jt Standing Cttee on Rd Safety (STAYSAFE). Honours: Natl Medal, 1978; Res Force Decoration, 1986; Austl Serv Medal (Rwanda), 1995. Memberships include: Austl Medl Assn, 1970-; Fndn Mbr, Aust and NZ Intensive Care Soc, 1974-; Austl Soc of Anaesthetists, 1974-; Fndn Mbr, West Pacific Assn of Critical Care Med, 1978; Fndn Mbr, Sect of Intensive Care RACS, 1980-; Patron, Summerland Early Intervention Prog, 1990-; Patron, HANDITAL, 1994-. Hobbies: Gardening; Reading; Tennis; Fishing. Address: Parliament House, Sydney 2000, NSW, Australia.

PFANNER Louise, b. 6 Mar 1955, St Leonards, NSW, Aust. Illustrator. m. Tim, 4 s. Education: BS, Visual Cmmns; MA, Childrens Lang and Lit. Publications: Louise Builds a House, 1987; Louise Builds a Boat, 1988; Kids First Gardening Book, 1996; The Little Red Hen, 1997; The Green Book, 1998; The Country Mouse. Memberships: SOBI; ASA. Hobby: Reading. Address: c/o Barbara M0665, PO Box 126, Edgecliffe 2027, Australia.

PFEIFFER Michelle, b. 29 Apr 1957, Orange County, California, USA. Actress. m. (1) Peter Horton, div 1987, 1 adopted d, (2) David Kelly, 1993, 1 s. Creative Works: Films incl: Grease 2; Into the Night; The Witches of Eastwick; Sweet Liberty; Married to the Mob; Tequila Sunrise, 1989; Dangerous Liaisons, 1989; The Fabulous Baker Boys, 1989; The Russia House, 1989; Love Field, 1991; Frankie and Johnny, 1991; Batman Returns, 1992; The Age of Innocence, 1993; Wolf, 1994; My Posse Don't

Do Homework, 1994; Dangerous Minds, 1997; Up Close and Personal, 1997; To Gillian On Her 37th Birthday, 1997; One Fine Day, 1997. Address: ICM, 8492 Wilshire Boulevard, Beverly Hills, CA 90211, USA.

PFISTER Lauren Frederick, b. 8 Nov 1951, Denver, CO, USA. Philosopher; Religion Teacher; Researcher. m. Mirasy Miranda, 5 Nov 1977, 1 s, 1 d. Education: BA, Amn Studies cum laude, Denver Univ, 1973; MDiv, cum laude, Denver Cons Bapt Sem, Denver, 1978; MA, Philos, San Diego State Univ, 1982; PhD, Comp Philos, Univ of HI, 1987. Appointments: Prof, Biblical Lang, Ethics, Ch Hist, Intl Coll and Grad Sch of Theology, 1982-86; Lectr, Assoc Prof, Relig and Philos Dept, Hong Kong Bapt Univ, 1987-; Assoc Ed, Jrnl of Chinese Philos, 1997-. Creative Works: Critical Ed of James Legge's Chinese Classics Forthcoming; Feng Youlan's A History of 20th Century Chinese Philosophy. Honours: DFG Grant, Bonn Univ; Visng Fell, Univ NSW; NEH Grant; Short Term Fell to Oxford; Collaborative Rschr, Nanjing Univ. Memberships: Am Philos Assn; Soc for Asian and Comp Philos; Amn Acady of Relig; Soc of Chris Philos; Intl Soc for Chinese Philos Assn of Asian Studies. Hobbies: Singing; Running; Hiking; Numismatics; Philatelics. Address: Religion and Philosophy Dept, Hong Kong Baptist University, 224 Waterloo Road, Kowloon, Hong Kong.

PHAD Bharat, b. 15 Feb 1954, Telghana. Service in MSEB. m. Sukumar, 2 s, 2 d. Career: Profl Artisan, Maharashtra State Elec Bd; Folk artist performing (w younger son, Gopal) Songi Bharud, inherited talk art, originating some 700 yrs ago, Songi Bharud is musically enacted form of Bharud, which is recited as musical theme, 1972-. Honours: State Level awds, 1993, 1998. Address: MSEB Staff Quarter No III/1/2, At Post Girwali PIN 43519, Tehsil Ambajogai, Dist Beed, Maharashtra, India.

PHAN Mai Phuong, b. 4 Dec 1947. Businesswoman. m. 1 s. Education: Dip, Engr. Appointments: Dpty Gen Dir, 1987; Gen Dir, 1997-. Honours: Ctf of Hon, Vietnam PM, 1998. Membership: Chamber of Com and Ind of Vietnam, 1987. Hobbies: Reading; Music; Sport. Address: Vietnam National Complete Equipment & Technics Import-Export Corporation, 16-18 Trang Thi Street, Hanoi SR, Vietnam.

PHAN Tam Dong, b. 1 Mar 1942, Nghe An Prov, Vietnam. 1 d. Education: Chem Engr, Hanoi Univ of Technol, 1963; DSc, Soviet Union, 1973. Appointments: Dpty Gen Dir, Vietnam Natl Salt Corp (VISALCO), 1985-86; Gen Dir, VISALCO, 1987-96; Chmn, Bd of Mngmt, VISALCO, 1997-; Lectr, salt technique, Chem Chair, Hanoi Univ of Technol. Publications: Num pprs related to sci rsch. Creative works: Inventors dips for Sat prodn, gypsums and bittern mfng from sea water; method and equip of grinding and washing salt; Orgr, prodn and distbn of iodized salt, Vietnam; Further salt prodn rsch. Honours: Prof in Sci, Govt of Socialist Repub of Vietnam, 1992; Lab Order, 3rd Class, Pres of SR Vietnam, 1996; Gold Medal, Best Invention and Apparatus for Mixing Iodised Salt, World Intellectual Prop Orgn. Memberships: Trade Leaders Club, Editl Off, Spain, 1995; Barons Fell, Barons Who Who, USA. Address: 27-B2 CatLinh Str, Hanoi, Vietnam.

PHAN Van Khai, b. 25 Dec 1933, Saigon. Politician. Education: Moscow Natl Univ of Econs, 1960-65. Appointments: Revolutionary Activities, N Vietnam, 1954-60; Joined CP, 1959; Fmrly w Gen Dept of State Planning Cttee; Fmr Econ Rschr; Dpty Dir, Aid Planning Dept, Natl Reunification Cttee, 1974-75; Dpty Dir, Planning Dept, Ho Chi Minh City, 1976-78, Dir, 1979-80; Dpty Mayor, Ho Chi Minh City, 1979-80, Perm Mayor, 1981-84, Mayor, 1985-89; Chair, Peoples Cttee of Ho Chi Minh City, 1985-89; Perm Mbr, Ho Chi Minh City CP Cttee, 1979-80, Dpty Sec, 1981-84; Alt Mbr, CP Ctrl Cttee, 1982-84, Mbr, 1984-; Mbr, Polit Bur, 1991-; Dpty Chair, Cncl of Mins, 1991-92; Perm Dpty PM of Vietnam, 1992-97; PM of Vietnam, 1997-. Address: Office of the Prime Minister, Hanoi, Vietnam.

PHANTHUMCHINDA Kammant, b. 28 Feb 1952, Bangkok, Thailand. Professor. Education: BSc; MD; MSc; FRCPCT. Appointments: Prof of Med, 1988-, Hd, Div of Neurol, Chulalongkorn Univ. Publications: Sev articles in profl jrnls. Honour: Best Tchr Awd, Chulalongkorn Univ, 1993. Memberships: Roy Coll of Physns, Thailand; Neurol Assn, Thailand. Hobby: Classical music. Address: Division of Neurology, Department of Medicine, Chulalongkorn University, Bangkok, Thailand.

PHELAN Peter Duhig, b. 12 Nov 1936, Brisbane, Aust. Medical Practitioner. m. Astrid, 18 Apr 1970, 1 s, 1 d. Education: BS; MD; BS; FRACP. Appointments: Vis Fell, Fitzwilliam Coll, Cambridge, 1982; Stevenson Prof, Hd, Dept of Paediats, 1983-97, Asst Dean, Postgrad Studies, Fac of Med, Dentistry and Hlth Scis, 1992-97, Emer Prof of Paediats, 1997-, Univ of Melbourne; Adj Prof, Sch of Hlth Scis, LaTrobe Univ, 1997-; Med Dir, Vic Med Postgrad Fndn, 1998-. Publications: Respiratory Illness in Children, 4 eds. Honours: Rsch Medal, Thoracic Soc of Aust, 1996; Medal, Eurn Respiratory Soc, 1997. Memberships: Austl Coll of Paediats; Thoracic Soc of Aust; Roy Austl Coll of Physns; Cttee of Pres, Med Colls. Hobbies: Theatre; Music; Travel; Gardening. Address: Victorian Medical Postgraduate Foundation, PO Box 27, Parkville, Victoria 3052, Australia.

PHILIP John Robert, b. 18 Jan 1927, Ballarat, Aust. Physicist; Mathematician. m. Frances Julia Long, 30 Apr 1949, 2 s, 1 d. Education: BCE, 1946, DSc, 1960, Univ Melbourne. Appointments: Grad Rsch Asst, Univ Melbourne, 1947; Engr, Qld Irrigation Cmmn, 1948-51; Mbr, Rsch Staff, C'wlth Sci and Indl Rsch Org, Canberra, 1951-; Snr Prin Rsch Sci, 1961-63, Chf Rsch Sci, Asst Chf, Divsn of Plant Ind, 1963-71, Chf, Div of Environ Mechs, 1971-80, 1983-91, Assoc Exec Mbr, 1978, Dir, Inst for Physl Scis, 1980-83, Fell, 1991-92, Emer Fell, 1992-, CSIRO, Canberra. Publications: Over 300 rsch pprs in sci jrnls. Honours: David Rivett Medal, CSIRO Offs Assn, 1966; Eminent Rschr Awd, Austl Water Resources Advsry Cncl, 1990; Univ Medal, Agricl Univ of Athens, 1993; Vis Fell, Trinity Coll, Cambridge Univ, England, 1994; Intl Hydrol Prize, Intl Assn of Hydrol Scis, WMO and UNESCO, 1995; AO, 1998. Memberships: Fell, Austl Acady of Scis; Fgn Mbr, Russian Acady of Agricl Scis, US Natl Acady of Engrng; Fell, Am Geophysl Union, Soil Sci Soc of Am, Roy Meteorol Soc; Hon Mbr, Am Water Resources Assn. Hobbies: Reading; Writing; Architecture; Cooking. Address: CSIRO Land and Water, GPO Box 1666, Canberra, ACT 2601, Australia.

PHILIP William Graeme, b. 20 June 1928, Melbourne, Vic, Aust. Chartered Accountant. m. Mary Louise Doggett, 11 Oct 1957, 2 s, 1 d. Education: BComm, Melbourne Univ, 1951. Appointment: Ptnr, Price Waterhouse, Chart Accts, 1963- Bd, Melbourne Univ Press and Baker Med Rsch Inst. Honour: AM, 1986. Memberships: Inst of Chart Accts, Natl Pres, 1980-81; Legal Aid Commnr, 1979-82; La Trobe Univ Cncl, 1971-78; Pres, Alfred Hosp Bd, 1984-. Hobbies: Golf; Swimming; Tennis; Woodwork. Address: 23 Denham Place, Toorak, Vic 3142, Australia.

PHILLIPS Anthony John, b. 26 Oct 1942, W Bromwich, Eng. Optometrist. m. Susa, 30 July 1967, 4 s. Education: MPhil; FBOA, HD; F C Optom; FCLSA; FAAO; FVCO; DCLP. Appointments: Hd of Contact Lens Unit, Flinders Medl Cntr, Adelaide; Hd of Contact Lens Unit, Adelaide Womens and Childrens Hosp, Adelaide. Publications: (Co-Ed), Contact Lenses (textbook), eds 1, 2, 3, 4; (co-auth) Vision and Aging; (co-auth) Physics for Ophthalmologists, 1994. Honours: Churchill Fell, 1992; Pres, Churchill Fells Assn of S Aust, 1993-96. Memberships: Fell, Brit Optometric Assn; Fell, Amn Acady of Optometry; Fell, Contact Lens Soc, Aust; Optometric Assn of Aust. Hobbies: Gardening; Woodwork; Philately; Numismatics. Address: 24 Centre Way, Belair, South Australia 5052.

PHILLIPS Ian Andrew, b. 29 Oct 1954, Melbourne, Aust. Director of Sales. Membership: Bd, Variety Club of Qld. Hobby: Golf. Address: Surfers Paradise Marriott Resort, 158 Ferny Avenue, Surfers Paradise, Qld 4217, Australia.

PHILLIPS Mervyn John, b. 1 Apr 1930, Sydney, Aust. Company Director. m. Moya Bleazard, 1956, 1 s, 1 d. Education: BEc, Univ of Sydney. Appointments: C'wlth Bank of Aust, 1946-60; Reserve Bank of Aust, 1960-92, Dpty Gov and Dpty Chmn, 1987-92; Chmn. Note Printing Aust, 1990-93; Senate, Austl Cath Univ, 1991-98; Dir, 1992, Chmn, 1996-, Austl Gas Light Co; Chmn, IBJ Aust Bank Ltd, 1992-; Dir, Alcoa of Aust Ltd, 1992-96; O'Connell Street Assocs Pty Ltd, 1992-, Chmn, 1994-; Woolworths Ltd, 1992-, Dpty Chmn, 1995- QBE Ins Grp Ltd, 1992-, Dpty Chmn, 1998-; GRW Property Ltd, 1994-98; WMC Ltd, 1996-; Chmn, For Invmnt Review Bd, 1997-; Hon Treas, Caritas Aust, 1993-; Mbr, Pontifical Cncl COR UNUM, 1994-. Honours: AM, 1987; BEc; FAIBF; FCPA; FAICD. Memberships: PNG Currency Conversion Commn, 1965-66; NSW Credit Union Advsry Cttee, 1968-72; Govt Cttees on PNG Banking, 1971-72; Off-shore Banking in Aust, 1984-; Cncl of Advice, Austl Grad Sch of Mngmt, 1991-; Gov, Natl Gall of Aust Fndn, 1992-94; PM's Task Force on Intl Fin Reform, 1998. Address: O'Connell Street Associates Pty Ltd, 6th Floor, 2 O'Connell Street, Sydney, NSW 2000, Australia.

PHILLIPS Richard Tavener, b. 3 May 1949, Rhiwbina, Cardiff, Wales. University Lecturer; Singer. m. Lesley A M Wilson, 1 Sept 1990, 3 d. Education: MA, PhD, Cambridge. Appointments: Lectr, 1975, Snr Lectr, 1980, Univ Auckland. Publication: China Since 1911, 1996. Memberships: NZ Histl Assn; NZ Asian Stdies Soc. Hobbies: Music; Travel; Family. Address: History Department, University of Auckland, Private Bag 92019, Auckland, New Zealand.

PHILPOT Christopher Ross, b. 21 Oct 1944, Adelaide, Aust. Medical Practitioner. m Suzanne, 3 Oct 1970. Education: B Med Sci, 1965, MB BS, 1968, Prince Alfred Coll; ECFMG, 1969; FRACP, 1973; MASM, 1978; FACSHP (fmrly FAC Ven), 1988, FAFPHM, 1990. Appointments: Intern, Roy Adelaide Hosp, 1969; RMO, Repatriati Hosp, Adelaide, 1970; Registrar, Darwin Gen Hosp, 1971; Registrar, Roy Adelaide Hosp, 1972-73; Cnslt Physn, Darwin, 1974; Cnslt Physn, Adelaide, 1975; Infectious Disease Physn, Flinders Med Cntr, 1976-84; Dir, Sydney STD Cntr, Sydney Hosp, 1984-90; Infectious Diseases Physn, Adelaide, 1990-. Honours: Lucy Osburn Medal, 1989; IUVDT Asia-Pacific Awd, 1997; Asia-Pacific Regl Dir, Intl Union Against Venereol Diseases and the Treponematoses, 1987-95; Fndn Pres, Natl Venereol Cncl of Aust, 1981-84; Fndn Pres, Venerol Soc of SA, 1979-84; World IUVDT Treas, Asst Sec, 1993-95, Sec Gen, 1995-; Pres, A C Venereol, 1991-94. Memberships: Fell, Roy Australasian Coll of Physns; Fndr Fell, Australasian Coll of Venereologists, 1988, (renamed Coll of Sexual Hlth Physns, 1996; Fndr Fell, Austl Fac Pub Hlth Med; Austl Med Assn. Hobbies: Photography; Medical History; International Relations; Travel. Address: SA Infectious Diseases Centre, 135 Hutt Street, Adelaide, SA 5000, Australia.

PHILPS Barry Roy, b. 25 Mar 1942, Coventry, Eng. Veterinary Surgeon. m. Jennifer 19 Aug 1965, 3 d. Education: BVMS; MRCVS; Dip Bus Mngr. Memberships: WPSA; WVPA; AVPA; AVA; Rotary International. Hobbies: Running; Music; Diving. Address: 32 Galahad Crescent, Castle Hill, NSW 2154, Australia.

PHOON Wai On. Medical Consultant. m. Molly Koh Soh Choo. Education: Am, Singapore; MBBS, Malaya; FRCP, London; FRCP, Edinburgh; FRCP, Glasgow; DI H, Eng; DIHSA, London; DCH, Engl; FRACP, Aust; Hon FACOM, Aust; FRFPS, Glasgow; FFOM, London; FFPHM, Eng. Career: Lectr, Bacteriol & Pediatrics; Snr Medl Offr, Shell Intl Pet Ltd; Prof Socl Med & Pub Hlth, Natl Univ Singapore; Acting Dir, Natl Inst Occupational Hlth, Aust; Prof Occupational Hlth, Univ Sydney; Clin Prof, Univ Hl; Cnslt, Westmead, Royal Prince Alfred, St Joseph's and Sydney Hosp; Clin Rsch interests; Clin Toxicology, Solvent Intoxication, Indoor Air Quality; Rehabilitation; Cnslt to sev inds in Asia-Pacific Reg in Occupational and Environmental Hlth. Publications: Auth, Co-auth, Ed, 12 books; 24 sci papers; Fndr, Ed-in-Chf, Asia-Pacific Journal of Public Health. Honours: Hon Fell, Aust Coll Occupational Hlth; Hon Prof, Univ Queensland; Hon Mbr, Asian Assn Occupational Hlth; Hon Prof Tropical Hlth, Univ Queensland; Hon Chmn, Singapore Profl Cntr; Lucas Lectrs RCP Fac Occupational Med, London; Num fellowships. Memberships: Past pres, Singapore Med Assn; Asian Occupational Hlth; Assn of Schs of Pub Hlth, Afro-Asia; Past Chmn, ILO/WHO Commn Occupational Hlth; Cnslt to WHO, ILO, World Bank in Vietnam, China, Saudi Arabia, Thailand; Chmn, Bd Trees, Aust Chinese Medl Assn; Charitable Trust; Past Pres, Singapore Chess Fedn; Fndr Pres, Grad Christian Fellowship, Singapore. Address: PO Box 818, Pymble, NSW 2073, Australia.

PHOTCHAITHAM Samart, b. 30 Oct 1961, Bangkok, Thailand. Executive Director. m. Mingkwan, 8 Oct 1990, 1 s. Education: MBA, Intl Bus, S CA Univ for Profl Servs, USA. Appointments: Asst Prof, Suthon Viriyasomboon, 1984-85; Asst Import Dir, The Coml Co of Siam Ltd, 1985-88; Mngng Dir, Brighton Intl Corp Ltd, 1988-91; Gen Mngr, Teo Hong Silom Co Ltd, 1991-96; Exec Dir, Thai Summit Hirotec Co Ltd, 1996-. Honours: Friendship Prog, 21st Century, Japanese Govt, 1993; Guest Speaker, Roy Thai Airforces, 1995-96. Membership: AMA. Hobbies: Golf; Reading. Address: 2508/345 Dindaeng 1 Road, Dindaeng, Bangkok 10320, Thailand.

PIAN Rulan Chao, b. 20 Apr 1922, Cambridge, MA, USA. Professor Emerita of East Asian Languages, Civilizations and Music. m. Theodore H Pian, 3 Oct 1945, 1 d. Education: BA, 1944, MA, 1946, PhD, 1960, Radcliffe, Harv. Appointments: Lang Asst, 1947-58, Instr in Chinese, 1959-61, Lectr on Chinese, 1961-74, Prof, E Asian Langs, Civilization and Music, 1974-92, Fac Mbr, Cttee on Degrees in Folklore and Mythology, 1976-92, Harvard Univ; Visng Prof, Music, Chinese Univ of Hong Kong, 1975 (Spring), 1978-79, 1982 (Fall), 1994 (Spring); Visng Prof, Inst of Lit, Natl Tsing Hua Univ, Taiwan, 1990 (Spring); Visng Prof, Sch of Hum, Natl Cntrl Univ, Taiwan, 1992 (Fall). Publications: 2 textbooks on Chinese lang tchng; 1 book on Sonq Dynasty Musical Sources; A Compilation of the Complete Musical Works by Yuen Ren Chao; Over 30 schl ethnomusicological studies; 20 field briefs, brief writing gen musicological issues, book reviews. Honours: Caroline I Wilby Pize from Radcliffe for Dissertation, 1960; PBK, 1961; Otto Kinkeldey Awd, 1968; Radcliffe Grad Soc Medal for Disting Achievement, 1980; Academician, Academica Sinica, Taiwan, 1990; Hon Prof, Cntrl China Univ of Technol, Wuhan, 1990; Hon Prof, Cntrl S Univ of Technol, Changsha, 1991; Hon Rsch Fell, Inst of Music Rsch, Shanghai Conservatory of Music, 1991; Hon Prof, SW Jiaotong Univ, Chengdu, 1994, Hon Prof, Shah-shih Univ, Hupei, 1996; Hon Rsch Fell, Inst of Music Rsch, China Acady of Art, 1997; Conf on Chinese Oral and Performing Lit, Assn for Chinese Music Rsch. Memberships include: Soc for Ethnomusicology; Amn Musicological Soc; Soc for Asian Music; Intl Cncl Tradl Music; Assn for Asian Studies. Address: 14 Brattle Circle, Cambridge, MA 02138-4625, USA.

PICKERING David, b. 30 Jan 1937. Government Minister. Appointments: Pub Wrks Dept, Dpty Sec for Wrks, 1952-79; Chf Exec, Fiji Elec Authy, 1979-88; Min for Tourism, Civil Aviation and Energy, 1988-91; Mbr of Parl, 1991-97; Min for Tourism and Civil Aviation, 1996-97; Min for Tourism and Transp, 1997-. Honour: CBE, 1984. Memberships: Past Mbr: Dir, Sedgewick, Dir, Civil Aviation Authy, Fiji, Dir, Air Terminal Servs, Dir, Econ Dev Bd; Dir, Bain and Hogg. Address: PO Box 1260, Suva, Fiji.

PIDCOCK Michael Elliott, b. 25 Mar 1945, Lismore, NSW, Aust. Specialist Haematologist. m. Mary Agnes Micallef, 9 Aug 1980, 3 s, 2 d. Education: MBBS, Univ of Sydney, 1970; MRCP, London, 1973; FRACP, 1974; FRACPA, 1978. Appointments: Res Med Offr, Lewisham Hosp, Aust, 1970, 1971; Snr House Offr, Registrar, Guys Hosp, London, Eng, 1972; Haematology Registrar, Repatriation Hosp, Concord, Sydney, NSW, 1974; Roy N Shore Hosp, 1975, 1976; Roy Prince Alfred Hosp,

1977-78; Currently Clin and Lab Haematologist, Woden Valley Hosp, ACT; Visng Cnslt, Calvary Pvte Hosp, ACT. Publications: Methaemoglobinoemia Resulting from Heterozygosity for Two NADH-Methaemoglobin Reducatase Variants: Characterization as NADH-Ferricyanide Reducatase (w P G Board), 1981; Genetic Hetrogeneity of Human Prothrombin (FII) (w P G Board and M Coggan), 1982; An Evaluation of the Coulter Diff3 50, An Automated Differential Leukocyte Counter (w Stuart J Galloway & G J Rossiter), 1985; Extramedullary Hemopoiesis Arising in the Gut Mimiking Carcinoma of the Cecum (w K Sunderland and J Barratt), 1994. Memberships: Haematol Soc of Aust; Austl Soc of Blood Transfusion; Austl Thalessaemia Assn, Pres, 1983-87; Hum Genetics Soc of Aust. Hobbies: Piano and Organ Playing; Choral Singing; Swimming; Surfing; Theatre; Concerts; Gardening. Address: Haematology Department, The Canberra Hospital, Woden, ACT 2605, Australia.

PIEROTTI Susan Catherine, b. 4 Mar 1958, Melbourne, Vic, Aust. Violinist. Education: Dip in Fine Arts, hons, 1977, Grad Dip in Fine Arts, distinction, 1982, Vic Coll of the Arts; Studies Violin w Emanuel Hurwitz, London, 1978-80. Appointments: Regular live broadcasts, ABC Radio, 1981-85; Fndr Mbr, 1983, Co-Ldr, tour to Spoleto Fest, Italy, 1987, Rantos Collegium Chamber Orch; Fndr Mbr, Trio Nova (1st all-Aust piano trio to enter Intl Chamber Music Competition, Colmar, France), 1986; Fndr Mbr, Elision Contemporary Music Grp, 1986; Mbr, 1990, Dpty Assoc Concertmaster, 1993-, Acting Assoc Concertmaster, 1998-, State Orch of Vic; Commissioning, recdng and performing Aust/World Premieres for piano trio and for solo violin. Honours: State Finalist, ABC Instrumental and Vocal (Concerto) Competition, 1977, 1981; As Mbr of Trio Nova, 5th Place, 22nd Intl Competition for Piano Trios, Colmar, 1989. Membership: Musical Soc of Vic. Hobbies: Reading; Knitting; Cooking. Address: 3A McKean Street, Box Hill North 3129, Australia.

PIESSE Kendrick Bruce, b. 7 Aug 1955, Melbourne, Aust. Journalist; Commentator. m. Susan, 1 s, 4 d. Education: Dip Jrnlsm. Appointment: Ed, Austl cricket mag. Publications: Warne Sultan of Spin, 1995; Wildmen of Cricket, 1997; More Than a Game (ed), 1998; 27 other sporting titles: Cricket and Australian Football. Honour: Vic Cricket Assn Media Awd, 1995. Membership: Peninsula Golf Club. Address: 22 Bareena Drive, Mt Eliza, Victoria 3930, Australia.

PIETROBON Steven Silvio, b. 5 Oct 1963, Naracoorte, Aust. Electronic Engineer. Education: BEng, 1986, MEng, 1989, Elecron Engrng, S Austl Inst of Technol, The Levels, S Aust; PhD, Elecl Engrng, Univ of Notre Dame, IN, USA, 1991. Appointments: Thorn EMI Electrons, 1984-85; Digital Comms Grp, S Austl Inst of Technol, 1985-86; Proj Engr, Rsch Fell, Satellite Comms Rsch Cntr, Univ of S Aust, The levels, S Aust, 1990-97; Adj Rsch Fell, Inst for Telecommunications Rsch, Univ of S Aust, 1997-. Publications: 8 pprs in profl jrnls. Honours: Natl Semiconductor Prize for best 1st yr Electron Engrng student, SAIT, 1982; S Austl Inst of Technol Medal for oustndng acad achievement, 1986; C'wlth Schlshp, 1986-90; NASA Rsch Asstshp, 1988-90; Austl Postdoct Rsch Fellshp, 1993-96. Memberships: Snr Mbr, IEEE; Austl Space Rsch Inst; Brit Interplanetary Soc. Hobbies: Space; Classical guitar; Stamp and coin collecting; Model building; Amateur rocketry. Address: Small World Communications, 6 First Avenue, Payneham South, SA 5070, Australia.

PILIOKO Aloisio, b. 11 June 1935, Wallis Island, S Pacific. Artist; Painter. Career: 40 yrs as S Pacific leading artist (painter); Co-Fndr, Pilioko - Michoutoucakine Fndn for Preservation of Artistic Values in Pacific, 1975; Exhibns, worldwide. Creative works: Decorated Credit Union Sch, Fiji, 1972; 1st Artist in Resn, USP Fiji; Decoration of hotels in Tahiti, Indonesia. Honours: Gold Medal, Min Educ, France, 1975; Gold Medal Univ of S Pacific, 1980; Gold Medal, Salon de Mai Noumea, 1981; Chevalier Arts and Lettres of France, 1995; Selected by Ti Mtca to represent Vancuatu by painting in UN and

UNESCO exhibd Paris, 1998; Contributed to proj, LIBEATE '98 for UN, 1998. Address: Box 224, Port Vila, Vanuatu.

PILLAY Leigh, b. 15 Feb 1959. CEO. Education: Dips, Mktng, Gen Mngmt. Appointments: Mngng Dir, LeMedia Inst; CEO, Legole Ent Aust and S Africa; Gen Mngr, Airport Publns; CEO, Venture Asia Mktng Pty Ltd. Memberships: MIAA; SCNB. Hobbies: Roller Skating; Gym; Cycling; Photography; Videos; Golf. Address: PO Box 2148, Rose Bay, NSW 2030, Australia.

PILOWSKY Issy, b. 4 June 1935. Professor; Psychiatrist. m. Marlene Noar, 1957, dec 1997, 1 s, 3 d. Education: MB; ChB; MD; FRANZCP; FRCPsych; DPM; FRACP. Appointments: Lectr, Univ of Sheffield, 1964-66; Snr Lectr, Univ of Sydney, 1966-70; Assoc Prof, Univ of Sydney, 1970-71; Prof of Psych, Univ of Adelaide, 1971-97; Hd, Psych Serv, Roy Adelaide Hosp, 1971-97; Dir, Clin Serv, Eastern Reg Mental Hlth Serv; Visng Prof, Dept Psychol Med, 1998-. Publications: Psychiatry and the Community (ed), 1969; Cultures in Collision (ed), 1974; Abnormal Illness Behaviour, 1997; Sev articles in sci jrnls. Honour: AM, 1989; Hon Fell, Fac of Pain Med of the Austl and NZ Coll of Anaesthetists, 1999. Membership: Fell, Acady of the Socl Scis in Aust. Hobbies: Cinema; Music; Reading; Swimming. Address: 10 Emmerick St, Leichhardt, NSW 2040, Australia.

PINANSKY Thomas, b. 10 Dec 1958, Portland, ME, USA. Attorney. m. Roxanne Holland. Education: JD, Univ of PA; BA (Sociol), Harvard Univ.

PINCHASI Raphael, b. 1940, Kabul, Afghanistan. Politician; Business Man. m. 7 children. Appointments: Dpty Min of Labour & Socl Affairs, 1981-84, of Interior Affairs, 1990; Dpty Mayor, Bnei Brak, 1983-84; Mbr, Knesset, 1984-; Mbr, Cttee on Interior Affairs & Quality of the Environ, Cttee on Fin, 1984-88; Mbr, Knesset House Cttee, 1984-90; Mbr, Cttee on Fgn Affairs & Security, 1988-90; Dpty Speaker of Knesset, 1988-90; Min of Comms, 1990-92; Mbr, Shas Pty. Address: The Knesset, Jerusalem, Israel.

PINKHAM Clarkson Wilfred, b. 25 Nov 1919, Los Angeles, CA, USA. Structural Engineer. m. EmmaLu (Hull), 8 May 1942, 2 s, 1 d. Education: Civil Engrng, Univ of CA, Berkeley, 1947. Appointments: US Navy, 1941-46; Consulting Structural Engrng Firm in Los Angeles, 1947-, Pres, firm known as S B Barnes Assocs from 1985. Publications: 6 articles in profl jrnls. Honours: Hon Mbr, SEASC, 1984, Stephenson B Barnes Awd for Rsch, 1985, 1990; ACI Fell, 1983, Henry L Kennedy Awd, 1986; ASCE Fell, 1983, Life, 1991; Lifetime Achievement Awd, Amn Inst Steel Constrn, 1999. Memberships: Structural Engrs Assn of South CA, Pres, 1971; Fell, Amn Soc of Civil Engrs (ASCE); Intl Assn of Bridge and Structural Engrng (IABSE); Earthquake Engrng Rsch Inst (EERI); Bldg Seismic Safety Cncl (BSSC); Fell, Amn Concrete Inst (ACI); Amn Soc of Testing and Materials (ASTM); Amn Welding Soc (AWS); The Masonry Soc (TMS); Structural Stability Rsch Cncl (SSRC); Seismological Soc of Am (SSA); Profl Mbr, Intl Conf of Bldg Officials; Profl Mbr, Amn Inst Steel Cnstrn; Inst Advmnt Engrng (IAE); Charter Mbr, Consultative Cncl, Natl Inst of Bldg Scis (NIBS). Hobbies: Philately; Genealogy. Address: 2236 Beverly Boulevard, Los Angeles, CA 90057, USA.

PINOLI Arthur Burton, b. 23 Nov 1954, Santa Raca, CA, USA. Airline Executive. m. Suzanna, Su Yen, 29 May 1987, 1 s. Education: Masters Intl Mngmt, Thunderbird Campus AGSIM, Glendale, AZ, USA; Bachelors Agribusiness, CA State Univ, Fresno, CA, USA; IATA Airline Mktng course cert, 1997. Appointments: Loan Ofrr, Mngmt Trainee, Lloyds Bank CA, Sanger, CA, 1979-81; Mngr, Intl Bus Dev and Sales, Transamerica Ag Dev Corp/Transamerica Airlines, Oakland, CA, 1981-86; Coml Loan Ofrr/Credit Analyst, Farm Credit Bank, Ukiah, CA, 1986-87; District Mngr, Beijing, Northwest Airlines Inc, Beijing, China, 1988-90; District Mngr, Shanghai, Cntrl and South China Northwest Airlines Inc, Shanghai, China, 1991-94; Gen Mngr, People's Repub of China, Northwest Airlines Inc, Beijing, China, 1994-96; Gen

Mngr, China, Hong Kong and Taiwan, Delta Air Lines Inc, Beijing, China, 1997-. Honours: Intl Farm Yth Exchange deleg to India, 1976; Blue Key & Alpha Zeta Hon Socs; Alpha Gamma Rho Profl Fraternity. Address: Lido Center-Holiday Inn, Apartment #352, Jichang Road & Jiangtai Road, Beijing 1000040, China.

PINTAVIROOJ Kitti, b. 5 May 1955, Bangkok, Thailand. Vice President, Legal Department. m. Wikanda, 1 s, 1 d. Education: LLM, Tulane Univ; LLM, Univ MI, USA. Appointments: Dir, Provident Fund Mngr Assn; Dir, Bangkok Investment Pub Co Ltd; Chmn, Marine and Aviation Dept. Memberships: Thai Bar Assn; Lawyer Assn of Thailand; Law Soc; Asia-Pacific Lawyer Assn. Hobby: Reading. Address: American International Assurance Co Ltd, No 181 Ai Tower 20 Fl, Surawong Road, Bangrak District, Bangkok 10500, Thailand.

PIRAMAL Dilip, b. 2 Nov 1949, Bombay, India. Industrialist. m. Gita, 20 May 1972, 2 d. Education: BCom, hons. Memberships: Pres, All India Plastic Mnfrs Assn, 1980; Pres, Rotary Club of Bombay Mid Town, 1981-82; Pres, Org of Plastics of India, 1992. Hobbies: Travel; Music; Photography; Swimming. Address: DGP House, Old Prabhadevi Road, Mumbai 400-025, India.

PIROZZO Ralph Steve, b. 26 Dec 1946. Managing Director. m. Sandra Lynn Ellwood, 24 Feb 1973, 1 s. Education: BSc, 4 Yr Grade A Standing; BEd, Grad Dip, Resource Tchng, Respiratory Technologist; Grad Cert, Mngmnt. Appointments: Sci Tchr, Pimlico State HS, 1975-1977, Wavell State HS, 1977-78; Resource Tchr, Contarf Beach HS, 1978-83; Hd of Sci, Morayfield State HS, 1983-88; Regl Cnslt, Sunshine Coast Reg, 1988-92; Hd of Curriculum, Deception Bay HS, 1992-94; Dir of Dev, Nudgee Coll, 1994-97; Mngng Dir, Pirozzo Consultancy Servs, 1997-. Publications: Sunshine Coast Reg Mentor Prog, 1991; Contrb 63 articles in natl and intl jrnls. Honours: Jaycees Outstndng Young Australian, 1981; CRA Fell, 1988; Paul Harris Fell, 1992; Citizen Amb Deleg, People to People Intl, China, 1992. Memberships: Fndr, Pres, 1979-99, Peninsula Enrichment Prog for Bright Needy Children. Austl Coll of Educ; ADAPE; FIA; Sci Tchrs Assn, Qld. Listed in: Australian Men and Women of Science Engineering and Technology; Who's Who in Australasia and the Pacific Nations. Hobbies: Gardening; Helping needy children. Address: 3 Cathedral Street, Bridgeman Downs 4035, Queensland, Australia.

PISCOS Eusebia Quilab, b. 15 Dec 1954, El Salvador, Misamis Oriental. Social Worker. m. Rustico, 27 Sept 1980, 1 s, 1 d. Education: BSc, Socl Work; Master, Govt Admin, Valencia Coll, Valencia, Bukidnon, at pres. Appointments: Socl Worker, 1976-82; Supervising Socl Worker, 1982-97; Munic Socl Welfare Offr, 1998. Honour: Plaque of Recog. Memberships: VP, Philippine Assn of Socl Workers, Bukidnon Chapt; Philippine Assn of Socl Workers Inc, Manila, Philippines, 1990. Hobbies: Playing lawn tennis, Volleyball; Working with the poor Manobe families. Address: Municipal Social Welfare and Development Office.MSWD San Jernando, Bukidnon, Philippines.

PITAKAKA Moses Puibangara, b. 24 Jan 1945, Zaru Village, Solomon Islands. Politician. m. 1967, 3 s, 4 d. Appointment: Gov-Gen, Solomon Islands. Hobbies: Walking; Reading. Address: Government House, PO Box 252, Honiara, Solomon Islands.

PITCHFORTH Roger John, b. 30 Apr 1942, Purley, Eng. Arbitrators Mediator; Associate Professor. m. Joan, 16 May 1970, 3 s. Education: LLB; MBA Hons. Appointments: Bar, Sol, 1977; Snr Lectr in Bus, 1993; Dir, Dispute Resources Cntr, Massey Univ. Creative Works: Meetings, Practice, Procedures in New Zealand. Memberships: Rotary Club; Arbitrators' and Mediators' Inst of NZ Inc; Hobby: Croquet. Address: 68 Rangitane St, Palmerston North, New Zealand.

PITSUWAN Surin, b. 28 Oct 1949, Nakorn Si Thammarat, Thailand. Minister of Foreign Affairs. m. Alisa Ariya. Education: Grad cum laude, Pol Sci, Claremont

Men's Coll, Claremont, CA, USA, 1972; PhD, Harv Univ, 1982. Appointments: Tchr, Thammasat, Columnist, Nation, Bangkok Post, 1980-92; Congressional Fell, 1983-84; Acad Asst, Dean of Fac of Pol Sci, Acad Asst, Vice Rector for Acad Affairs, 1985-87; Elected Mbr of Parl, 1986; Sec to Speaker of House of Representatives, 1986; Dpty For Min, 1992; Min of For Affairs, 1997. Honours: Kt Grand Cordon, Spec Class, Most Noble Order of Crown of Thailand; Kt Grand Cordon, Spec Class, Most Exalted Order of the White Elephant. Address: 1 Sanamchai Road, Saranrom palace, Bangkok 10200, Thailand.

PITT Brad, b. 18 Dec 1963, Shawnee, Oklahoma, USA. Film Actor. Education: Univ MO, USA. Creative Works: TV Appearances incl: Dallas (series); Glory Days (series); Too Yong to Die? (film); The Image (film). Films incl: Cutting Glass; Happy Together, 1989; Across the Tracks, 1990; Contact, 1991; Thelma and Louise, 1991; The Favor, 1992; Johnny Suede, 1992; Cool World, 1992; A River Runs Through It, 1992; Kalifornia, 1993; Legend of the Fall, 1994; Interview With The Vampire, 1994; 12 Monkeys, 1995; Seven, 1996; Sleepers, 1996; Mad Monkeys, 1996; Tomorrow Never Dies, 1996. Address: Creative Artists Agency, 9830 Wilshire Boulevard, Beverly Hills, CA 90212, USA.

PITT John Ingram, b. 13 Mar 1937, Aust. Research Scientist; Mycologist. m. Patricia Anne Milgate, 20 Apr 1963, 2 s. Education: BSc, 1962, MSc, 1965, Univ NSW; PhD, Univ CA, Davis, USA, 1968. Appointments: Tech Asst, 1954, Experimental Scientist, 1963, Rsch Scientist, 1970, Snr Rsch Scientist, 1972, Prin Rsch Scientist, 1978, Snr Prin Rsch Scientist, 1986-92, Chf Rsch Scientist, 1992-, C'wlth Sci and Indl Rsch Org, Div of Food Sci, Sydney. Publications: The Genus Penicillium, 1979; Fungi and Food Spoilage (co-auth A D Hocking), 1985, 2nd ed 1997; Modern Concepts in Penicillium and Aspergillus Classification (co-ed, R A Samson), 1990; Methods for the Mycological Examination of Food (co-ed), 1986; A Laboratory Guide to Common Penicillum Species, 2nd ed, 1988; Modern Methods in Food Mycology (co-ed, R A Samson), 1992. Honours: Natl Insts of Hlth Fellshp, US Dept of Agricl, Northern Regl Rsch Cntr, Peoria, IL, USA, 1968-69; Disting Serv Awd, Austl Soc for Microbiol, 1991; Awd of Merit, Austl Inst for Food Sci and Technol, 1996, Austl Acady Technol Sci and Engrng, 1998, Intl Acady Food Sci and Technol, 1998. Memberships: Austl Soc for Microbiol; Austl Inst for Food Sci and Technol; Amn Soc for Microbiol; Amn Mycological Soc; Brit Mycological Soc; Soc for Applied Bacteriol; Intl Cmmn on Taxonomy of Fungi; Intl Commn on Penicillium and Aspergillus, Chmn; Intl Commn on Food Mycol, Chmn; Intl Commn on Microbiol Specifications for Foods. Hobbies: Squash; Skiing; Sailing. Address: CSIRO Division of Food Science Australia, PO Box 52, North Ryde, NSW 2113, Australia.

PIYADASA Rohana Luxman, b. 13 Aug 1954, Kandy, Sri Lanka. Head of Department. 1 s. Education: BA (Hons), 1978, MA, Mass Comms, 1983, Univ of Kelaniya; PhD, Moscow State Univ, 1993. Appointment: Snr Lectr, Dept of Mass Comm, Univ of Kelaniya, 1980-. Presenter and Designer, Vivaranaya, weekly radio prog, Sri Lanka Brdcstng Corp, 1987-88; Presenter and Designer, Vahalkada (art and cultural prog), Cntrl Prov Regl Brdcstng Cntr, 1996; Presenter and Interviewer, Ayobowan (Good Moaning) Natl TV Corp; Presenter and Designer, Visam Wada (Dialogue), Sinhala Prog A socio econ and cultural prog, 1996-. Publications: Anti-Imperialist Era and Suriyami Campaign, 1987; Pitteniya Ape Pasweni Pantiya (short stories), 1987; Ath Welak Tanamy Api, 1995; Wiswa Darshani (Hundred Questions from World First Prime Minister, Mrs Sirimavo R D Bandaranayaka), 1996; Ed, var newsletters; 7 articles in jrnls; Contbns to print media. Creative works: Documentary films include: Doren Dora (Door to Door), 1993; Voice of Fisher, 1994; Women in Sri Lanka, 1994; Diyawara, 1997. Hobbies: Filming; Travelling. Address: 37 1st Lane Aruppola Kandey, Sri Lanka.

PIZER Marjorie, b. 3 Apr 1920, Melbourne, Aust. Psychotherapist. Widow, 1 s, 1 d. Education: BA, Univ

Melbourne. Publications: Co-ed, Come Listen, 1966; Thou and I, 1967; To Life, 1969; Tides Flow, 1972; Seasons of Love, 1975; Full Summer, 1977; Gifts and Remembrances, 1979; To You the Living, 1981; The Sixtieth Spring, 1982; Co-ed, Below the Surface, Reflections on Life and Living, 1982; Selected Poems, 1963-83, 1984; Co-ed, Poems of Lesbia Harford, 1985; Equinox, 1987; Fire in the Heart, 1990; Journeys, 1992; Winds of Change; Await the Spring, 1998. Memberships: Fell, Austl Writers; Austl Soc of Auths. Hobbies: Painting; Drawing. Address: 6 Oaks Avenue, Cremorne, NSW 2090, Australia.

PLAISTED Joan M, b. 29 Aug 1945. Diplomat. Education: MA, Asian Studies, BA, Intl Rels, Am Univ. Appointments: Chargé d'Affairs, Dpty Chf of Miss, Rabat, Morocco, 1991-94; Dir, Dept of State, 1994-95; Snr Advsr. US Miss to the UN, 1995. Amb to the Repub of the Marshall Is, Repub of Kiribati, 1996-. Honours: Lode Star Awd, Amn Univ, 1993; Prsdtl Meritorious Serv, Superior and Meritorious Hon Awds, Dept of State. Memberships: Asia Soc; Natl War Coll Alumni Assn; Hong Kong Wine Soc. Listed in: Who's Who in America; Who's Who in Women; Who's Who in the World. Hobbies: Wine Tasting; History; Skiing; Scuba Diving. Address: American Embassy, PO Box 1379, Majuro, MH 96960, The Marshall Islands.

PLANT John Walter, b. 22 Nov 1939. Veterinary Specialist (Sheep Medicine). m. Elizabeth, 15 May 1965, 2 s, 1 d. Education: Univ of Sydney, 1956-62. Appointments: Vet Insp, Gundagai Rural Lands Protection Bd, 1962-68; Vet Rsch Offr, NSW Agricl, 1968-82; Spec Vet Offr (Sheep Hlth), NSW Agricl, 1982-92; Vet Specialist, (Ovine Med), 1988-; Prog Ldr (Flock Hlth), NSW Agricl, 1992-. Publications: Vade Mecum - Diagnosis of Diseases of Sheep, 1992; Over 35 rsch pprs. Honours: AVA Meritorious Serv Awd, 1981; Fell, Austl Vet Assn; Serv Medallion, NSW PSPOA, 1994; Hon Life Mbr, Sheep Vet Soc, UK. Memberships: Exec, NSW Div, Austl Vet Assn, 1969-80; Pres, NSW Div, Austl Vet Assn, 1974-75; Fed Exec, Austl Vet Assn, 1981-83; Fed Pres, Austl Vet Assn, 1991-92; Cncl, Exec, NSW Pub Serv Profl Offrs Assn. Hobbies: Cricket; Golf; Sports; Gardening. Address: 6 Lisle Court, West Pennant Hills, NSW 2125, Australia.

PLATZKER Arnold, b. 26 Aug 1936, NY, USA. Medical Doctor. m. Marjorie A Sanek, 1 s, 1 d. Education: AB Hons, Brown Univ, 1958; MD, Tufts Univ, 1962; Medl Lic, MA, 1963; CA, 1964. Appointments: Asst Prof, Pediats Univ CA, San Fran, 1971-73; Asst Prof, Pediats, USC Sch of Med, Los Angeles, 1973-78; Assoc Prof, 1979-85; Prof, 1986-; Hd, Div of Pediats, Pulmonology, 1995-; Attnd Staff, Childrens Hosp, Los Angeles; Visng Prof, Chief Pediat Pulmonology Div, UCLA Childrens Hosp, 1996-; UCLA Medl Cntr; Bd Dirs, Univ Childrens Medl Grp, 1982-; Exec Commnr, 1982-93; Pres, 1982-86; Steering Commnr, Exec Commnr, NHLBI Stdy of Pediat Pulmonary and Cardiac Complications of Vertically Transmitted HIV Infection. Publications: Over 70 Peer Reviewed Articles and Book Chapters. Honours: Life Mbr, Clare Hall, Cambridge Univ, UK, 1986; Best Drs in Am, 1996-. Memberships: Western Soc for Pediats Rsch, 1973; CA Thoracic Soc; Los Angeles Pediat Soc; CA Perinatial Assn; Amn Lung Assn of Los Angeles Co; Amn Lung Assn of CA; Amn Acady of Pediats; Amn Coll of Chest Physns; Amn Thoracic Soc; AAAS; NY Acady Scis; AAUP; Roy Soc of Med; Eurn Respiratory Soc. Hobbies: Swimming; Photog. Address: Childrens Hospital, 4650 Sunset Boulevard, Box 83, Los Angeles, CA 90027, USA.

PLAYER Theresa Joan, b. 17 Nov 1947, Great Lakes, IL, USA. Law Professor. Education: AB, San Diego State Univ, 1970; JD, UCLA Sch of Law, 1973. Appointments: Staff Atty, Legal Aid Soc, San Diego, 1974-78; Pvte Prac w Meaney & Player, 1979-80; Law Prof, Univ of San Diego, 1980-. Publication: California Trial Techniques, co-auth, 1991. Memberships: ABA; CA State Bar; Lawyers Club; Amn Assn of Law Schs; Clin Sec Exec Cttee. Hobbies: Running; Biking; Swimming; Yoga; Travel. Address: University of San Diego, School of Law, 5998 Alcala Park, San Diego, CA 92110, USA.

POCKLEY Leonard Antill, b. 12 Nov 1915, Sydney, Aust. Rural Management; Veterinary Consultant. m. Mary Brodley Kitchen, 5 July 1947, 1 s. Education: BVSc, Sydney Univ; Fell, Orang Agricl Coll. Appointments: Vet Practitioner, 1937-38; Mngr, Pyara Stud, 1939, 1945, 1980; War Serv, 1939-45; Cnslt, 1980-. Publications: Handbook for Jackeroos; Handbook for Farm Managers; Short History of New South Wales Stud Merino Breeders. Honour: OBE, 1978. Memberships: Roy Agricl Soc of NSW, Hon VP; Life Gov, NSW Stud Merino Breeders Assn. Hobbies: Fishing; Horse racing. Address: 19 Boomerang Drive, Goulburn, NSW 2580, Australia.

PODDAR Mrinal Kanti, b. 3 July 1949, Calcutta, India. Teacher and Researcher. m. Anjana, 21 Nov 1981, 2 d. Education: BS, Hons, 1968; MSc, 1970; PhD(Sc), 1974; DSc, 1978; CChem, FRSC, London, 1992; Chartered Chem, Fell, Roy Soc of Chem (London). Appointments: Rsch Assoc, 1974-75, Asst Rsch Offr, 1975-77, Dept of Biochem, Univ of Calcutta; Visng Scientist, VA Commonwealth Univ, Richmond, USA, 1977-78; Rsch Scientist, Rutgers Medl Sch, Rutgers Univ, 1978-80; Lectr, 1980-86, Rdr, 1987-, Dept of Biochemistry, Univ of Calcutta. Publications: 139 on rsch in Neuroscience, 1971-98; 14 chapts in books; 107 in intl jrnls; 18 in natl jrnls. Honours: Jnr Rsch Fellshp, Indian Cncl of Medl Rsch, New Delhi, 1971-74; Awd, Intl Brain Rsch Orgn, UNESCO, Paris, 1977; Gold Medal (Gananath Sen Mem) for Best Presentation in Intl Seminar on Tradl Med, Calcutta, India, 1992. Memberships: Fell, Roy Soc of Chem, London, 1992; Fell, Inst of Chem India, 1992; 10 intl sci orgns inclng: Intl Brain Rsch Orgn, Intl Soc for Neurochemistry; Exec Mbr, Roy Soc of Chem (London) Eastern India Sect, Calcutta. Hobbies: Reading; Writing; Papers; Books. Address: Department of Biochemistry, University of Calcutta, 35 BC Road, Calcutta 700019, WB, India.

PODMORE Valerie Noelle, b. 13 Nov 1947, Otahuhu, Auckland, NZ. Senior Researcher. m. David, 8 May 1972, 2 d. Education: BA, Massey; BA, hons, Vic; MA, Vic; PhD, Educ, Massey, 1984. Appointments: Rsch Offr, 1985-93, Snr Rschr, 1993-, NZ Cncl for Educl Rsch. Honours: Postgrad Schlsp, Univ Grants Cttee, NZ, 1975; Sarah Anne Rhodes Rsch Fellshp, Vic Univ, 1976. Membership: VP, NZ Assn for Rsch in Educ, 1998-. Hobbies: Tramping; Music; Literature; Snorkelling; Swimming; Fishing. Address: NZCER, PO Box 3237, Wellington, New Zealand.

POK Fabian, b. 22 Feb 1963, Ambang, Western Highlands Prov, Papua New Guinea. Minister for Forests and Public Enterprises. Education: Doct Deg in Acctng and Finl Mngmt. Appointments: Snr Lectr, Com Dept, Univ of Papua New Guinea; Dpty Dir, Constl Review Commn; Min for Forests and Pub Enterprises.

POKHAREL Gyaneswor, b. 27 June 1963, Pokhara, Nepal. Civil Engineer; Researcher. m. Ila, 27 June 1989, 1 s, 1 d. Education: BE, hons, Civil Engrng; MEng; DEng. Appointments: Civil Engr, HMG/Nepal, 1988-89; Rsch Assoc, AIT Bangko, 1991-92; Rsch Assoc, Nagoya Univ, 1995; Rsch Engr, Yahagi Cnstrn Co Ltd, 1995-97; Rsch Fell, PWR, Japan, 1997-. Publications: Rsch pprs in profl jrnls and intl confs. Honour: Mahendr Vidye Bhusan, H.M. King of Nepal, 1999. Memberships: Fndr, Nepal Geotech Soc; Assoc, ASCE; Fell, NGS; JGS; JSCE; ISSMGB; NEA; NGS; IGS. Hobbies: Football; Golf; Driving; Internet Web Page Building; Public Relations. Address: House No 52, Chhinedanda, Pokhara 18, Nepal.

POLANSKY Patricia, b. 6 Apr 1944. Bibliographer. Education: BA, Lib Sci, 1967; MLS, 1969, Univ HI. Appointments: Bibliographer, UH Hamilton Lib, 1970-; Dir, Cntr for Russia in Asia, Sch of HI, Asian and Pacific Stdies, Univ HI, 1988-92. Publications include: Regionalism and Siberian Publishing in Late Imperial Russia, 1880-1917; Published Sources on Russian America; Resources for Current Research on Siberia and the Soviet Far East: A Bibliographic Profile; The Russians and Soviets in Asia. Honours: Fellshp, Cncl on Lib Resources, 1979; Fujio Matsuda Fellshp, 1986; Sev IREX Grants. Memberships: Am Assn for the Adv of Slavic

Stdies; Western Slavic Assn; Intl Assn of Orientalist Libns. Address: University of Hawaii, Hamilton Library, Room 408, The Mall, Honolulu, HI 96822, USA.

POLASEK Oldrich F, b. 26 Nov 1921, Hranice, Czech. Economist. m. Betsy, 19 July 1957. Education: Com and Econs degree, Charles Univ, Prague, 1948. Publication: Skiing. Hobbies: Skiing; Tennis; Golf; Windsurfing; Ice skating; Swimming; Sailing. Address: 121 William Street, Melbourne 3000, Australia.

POLGLASE Adrian Laird, b. 18 Apr 1946, Aust. Colorectal and General Surgeon. m. Cherylin, 24 Dec 1968, 1 s, 1 d. Education: MS; FRACS; FRCS (Eng); FRCS Ed; FACS. Appointments: Prof of Surg, Monash Univ; Vis Surgn, Cabrini Hosp. Memberships: AMA; AAS; Med Def Assn of Vic; Gastroenterol Soc of Aust; Colorectal Surg Soc of Aust. Address: Suite 20, Cabrini Medical Centre, Isabella Street, Malvern, Victoria 3144, Australia.

POLITES Colin George, b. 10 Mar 1946, Geelong, Vic, Aust. Senior Deputy President, Australian Industrial Relations Commission. m. Susan Patrick, 6 Feb 1971, 1 s, 1 d. Education: LLB, Univ of Melbourne. Appointments: Solicitor, Moule, Hamilton & Derham, 1969-72; Ptnr, Freehill Hollingdale & Page, 1972-89; Dpty Pres, Austl Indl Rels Commn, 1989-94; Snr Dpty Pres, Austl Indl Rels Commn, 1994-. Memberships: Chmn, Fedl Costs Advsry Cttee; Past Pres, Indl Rels Soc of Aust; Past Pres, Indl Rels Soc of Vic. Hobbies: Music; Golf; Australian Rules football. Address: Australian Industrial Relations Commission, level 42, Nauru House, 80 Collins Street, Melbourne, Victoria 3001, Australia.

POLLACK Sydney, b. 1 July 1934, Lafayette, USA. Film Director. m. Claire Griswold, 1958, 1 s, 2 d. Education: Neighborhood Playhouse Th Sch, NY. Appointments: Asst to Sanford Meisner, 1954, Acting Instr, 1954-57, 1959-60; Army Serv, 1957-59; Exec Dir, The Actors Studio, W Coast Br. Creative Works: Broadway Appearances: The Dark is Light Enough, 1954; A Stone for Danny Fisher, 1955. TV Appearances: Aloa Presents. Films Directed: The Slender Thread, 1965; This Property is Condemmed, 1966; The Scalphunters, 1967; Castle Keep, 1968; They Shoot Horses Don't They?, 1969-70; Jeremiah Johnson, 1971-72; The Way We Were, 1972-73; The Yakuza, 1974; Three Days of the Condor, 1974-75; Bobby Deerfield, 1976; The Electric Horseman, 1978-79; Absence of Malice, 1981; Tootsie, 1982; Song Writer, 1984; Out of Africa, 1985; Havana, 1989; The Firm, 1993; Sabrina, 1996. Produced: The Fabulous Baker Boys, 1989; The Last Ship, 1990; King Ralph, 1990; Dead Again, 1990. Acted in: The Player; Death Becomes Her; Husbands and Wives. Honours include: Acady Awd for Best Dir; Acady Awd for Best Picture. Address: Mirage Enterprises, De Mille Building 110, 5555 Melrose Avenue, Los Angeles, CA 90212, USA.

POLLAK Michael Peter, b. 23 Oct 1948, Bratislava, Czech. Journalist. m. Margaret McNab, 10 Nov 1996. Education: BA, Univ Sydney. Publications: Sense and Censorship, 1990. Membership: Media Entertainment and Arts Alliance (of Aust). Hobbies: Environment; Music; Golf. Address: 5 Elisha Close, Carina Heights, Qld 4152, Australia.

POLLARD Edna Margaret Jessie, b. 11 Feb 1931, Heathcote, Vic, Aust. Author; Former Landscape Architect. Education: Postgrad Dip, Landscape Archt, RMIT, 1981. Publications: Planning Your New Garden, 1970; Potamus, 1988. Memberships: Austl Soc of Auths; Fell, Austl Writers. Hobbies: Quilling; Photography. Address: 156 Summerhill Res Park, Gremel Road Reservoir, Vic 33073, Australia.

POLLARD Howard Frank, b. 2 Sept 1920. Physicist. m. 8 Jan 1949, 2 d. Education: BS (Hons), Univ West Aust, 1943; MSc, Univ WA, 1946; PhD, Univ NSW, 1963. Appointments: Asst Rsch Offr, CSIRO, Sydney, 1943-45; Rsch Offr, CSIRO, 1945-46; Lectr in Phys, Sydney Techl Coll, 1946-50; Lectr in Phys, NSW Univ of Technol, 1950-59; Snr Lectr in Phys, 1959-72, Assoc Prof, 1972-80, Univ NSW. Publications: Auth; Sound Waves in Solids, 1977; Co-auth (w R W Harris) An Intro to Physical Acoustics, UNSW, 1979; Chf Ed, Acoustics Aust, 1981-93. Honours: Rsch Schlshp Netherlands Govt, Delft, 1958; Rsch Fellshp ISVR Southampton, 1969; Rsch Grants, Aust Rsch Cncl, 1970-82. Memberships: Fell, Austl Inst of Phys; Fell, Austl Acoustical Soc; Inst of Phys (UK); Acoustic Soc of Am. Hobbies: Photography; Organ recitalist. Address: 6 Wren Place, Cronulla, NSW 2230, Australia.

POLLARD Irina, b. 2 Sept 1939. Academic Professor, Assocate Professor. 1 s. Education: BSc, First Class Hons; PhD, Bio, Univ of Sydney. Appointments: Acad, Assoc Prof of Bio, Macquarie Univ, Sydney, Aust. Creative Works: More than 50 Articles in Sci Jrnls, Field of Reproductive Bio; Textbook: A Guide to Reproduction, Sociological Issues abd Human Concerns. Memberships: Austl Inst of Bio; Austl Soc of Reproductive Bio; Intl Bioethics Assn. Hobbies: Reading; Art; Bushwalking; Camping. Address: Marcquarie University, Department of Biological Science, 2109 Sydney, Australia

POLLARD John Hurlstone, b. 14 June 1942, Sydney, NSW, Aust. Professor of Actuarial Studies. m. Carys Mary Griffiths, 2 June 1967, 1 s, 3 d. Education BSc, 1st class hons, Univ of Sydney, 1964 PhD, Univ of Cambridge, 1967; Fell, Inst of Actuaries, London, 1972. Appointments: Rsch Assoc, Univ Chgo, USA, 1967-68; Assoc Prof, Actuarial Studies, 1968-76, Prof, Actuarial Studies, 1977-, Macquarie Univ, Sydney; Dir, Swiss Re Austl Ltd, 1983-; Dir, Swiss Re Life and Hlth Aust Ltd, 1997-. Publications: Mathematical Models for Growth of Human Population, 1973; Handbook of Numerical and Statistical Techniques, 1976; Mortality and Other Actuarial Statistics (w B Benjamin), 1979; The Actuarial Management of a Life Office (w A H Pollard), 1977; Introductory Statistics with Applications in General Insurance (w I Hsossack and B Zehnwirth), 1983; Mortality and Other Actuarial Statistics (w B Benjamin), 1993. Honours: Belgian Actuarial Assn 75th Anniversary Prize, 1971; H M Jackson Awd, Inst of Actuaries of Aust, twice; Kulp Awd, Amn Risk and Insurance Assn. Memberships: Inst of Actuaries of Aust, Cncl, 1979-81, Pres, 1986-87; Stats Soc of Aust, Pres, 1974-75; Roy Stats Soc; Intl Stats Inst; Intl Actuarial Assn; Acady of Socl Scis in Aust. Hobbies: Squash racquets; Handyman; Organ. Address: School of Economic & Financial Studies, Macquarie University, Sydney, NSW 2109, Australia.

POLMEAR Ian James, b. 19 Feb 1928. Materials Engineer. m. (1) Valerie J Roeszler, 28 July 1951, 1 s, 2 d, (2) Margaret C Wark, 27 Aug 1988. Education: BMetE; MSc; DEng, Melbourne. Appointments: Indl Metallurgist, Melbourne, 1949-51; Fulmer Rsch Inst, UK, 1951-53; Exp Offr to Prin Rsch Scientist, Aeronautical Rsch Lab, Melbourne, 1953-67; Prof of Materials Sci, Monash Univ, Melbourne, 1967-86; Fndn Chmn, Dept Materials Engrng, Monash Univ, 1970-86; Dpty Vice-Chan, 1987-90, Emer Prof, 1992-, Monash Univ; Cnsltng Engr, 1992-; Visng Prof, Tohuku Univ, Sendai, Japan, 1993-95. Publications: Books: Light Alloys: Metallurgy of the Light Metals, 1st ed, 1981, 2nd ed, 1989, 3rd ed 1995. Honours: Silver Medal, Inst of Metals and Materials, Australasia, 1988; AO, 1993. Memberships: Fell, Inst Engrng, Aust, 1970; Fell, Austl Acady of Technol Scis and Engrng, 1978; Hon Fell, Austl Inst Nuc Sci and Engrng, 1996. Hobbies; Bushwalking; Tennis; Travel; Gardening; Writing. Address: 3 Aumann Court, Box Hill North, Vic 3129, Australia.

PONG Yuen Sun Louis, b. 5 May 1957, Hong Kong, China. Qualified Lawyer. m. Pong Chan Lai Kuen Grace Brigid, 5 Aug 1985, 1 s, 1 d. Education: BSc, Univ of Hong Kong, 1979. Appointments: Trainee Sol, Asst Sol, Messrs Johnson Stokes Master, 1984-87; Asst Sol, Ptnr, Messrs Liau, Ho & Chan, 1987-. Memberships: Pres, Hong Kong Chinese Family for Christ, 1997-; Synod of Diocese of Hong Kong and Macao, 1994-98; Law Soc of Hong Kong, 1993; Synod of Prov of Hong Kong Shing Kung Hui, 1998-; Synod, Diocese of Hong Kong Island, 1998-. Hobbies: Couples and family ministry; Singing. Address: Flat A, 5th Floor, Avon Court, 2 Fessenden Road, Kowloon Tong, Hong Kong.

PONGPANIT Montri, b. 9 Nov 1943, Thailand. Politician; Engineer. m. Thida Pongpanit, 2 children. Education: Germany. Appointments: Highways Dept; Snr Position B, Grimm & Co; Joined Socl Action Pty, 1979; Off of the PM; Dpty Commn Min; Dpty Interior Min, Dpty Pty Sec-Gen, 1983; Fmr Com Min; Min of Transp & Commns, 1988-90; Ldr, Socl Action Pty. Address: Social Action Party, Bangkok 10300, Thailand.

PONNATTU CHACKO Joseph, b. 19 Sept 1949, Thodupuzha, Kerala, India. Advocate; Social Worker. m. Pouly, 22 June 1975, 2 s. Education: Law Deg. Appointments: Mbr, Kerala Legis Assembly, 1977-80; Mbr, Kerala Univ Senate, 1975-76; Mbr, Gen Cncl, Kerala Agricl Univ, 1980-82, 1997-; Mbr, Kerala Univ Union, 1971-72; Chmn, S H Coll Union, Thevara, 1971-72; State Pres, Kerala Studs Cong, 1975-77; Pres, Kerala Yth Front, 1978-81; Gen Sec, Kerala Cong, 1982-; Chmn, Kerala Agro Inds Corp Ltd, 1996-. Publications: Contbr articles to var publs. Hobbies: Reading; Writing; Delivering public speeches. Listed in: Legislative Assembly (Kerala) Who's Who. Address: Ponnattu House, Vazhithala, Thodupuzha, Idukki District, India.

POOLE Barry Leslie, b. 2 May 1941, Darlinghurst, Sydney, NSW, Aust. Company Director. m. Kulliki Riis, 30 Dec 1966, 1 s, 2 d. Education: Sydney Tech Coll, 1959-68; Dip, Printing Admin, 1968. Appointments: Asst Prod Mngr, Bartlett Murphy & Mackenzie Pty Ltd, Sydney, 1959-60; Prod Mngr, MAC Merchandising Advtng Pty Ltd, Sydney, 1960-61; Asst to Mngng Dir, Westmead Printing Servs Ltd, London, Eng, 1961-62; Sales Mngr, Joint Governing Dir, Hogbin Poole (Printers) Pty Ltd, Sydney, 1963-80; Self-employed in own family Co, Bodlian Holdings Pty Ltd, Aust, 1981-; Dir, Love Typesetting Servs Pty Ltd, Sydney, 1982-87; Chmn, Mngng Dir, Hideaway Island Resorts Ltd, Port Vila, Vanuatu, 1982-90, and Pacific Paradise, Travel Div of Hideaway Is Resorts Ltd, 1982-90; Dir, Sec, Well Connected Travel Pty Ltd, incl: Baltic Connections, Coral Connections and Backpacker Connections, 1995-. Publications: The Work Value Concept, 1968; Mergers, Takeovers and Company Acquisitions Within the Australian Printing Industry, 1975. Memberships: Pres, NSW Divsn, 1972-75, Fell, 1985, Austl Inst of Graphic Arts Mngmt. Hobbies: Motor Boat Cruising; Initiating Aid arrangements and commercial/tourism contacts with the newly independent Baltic States. Address: 89 Ferguson Street, Forestville, NSW 2087, Australia.

POOLE Eric Houguet, b. 10 Aug 1942, Kington, Eng. MLA. m. Elizabeth, 2 s, 1 d. Appointments: Chmn, NT Tourist Comn, 1979-86; Mbr, NT Legis Assembly, 1986-; Curr Min for Tourism, 1988; Min Cntrl Aust, 1994-; Min Correctional Servs, Min Sport and Recreation, Min Responsible for Racing and Gaming, Min Rgs Liquor Commn, 1996; Min Asian Relations Trade and Industry, 1997-98; Min for Resource Dev, Min for Essential Servs (Current). Membership: Fell, Aust Inst of Mngmt. Hobbies: Reading; Swimming; Boating. Address: 10 Armstrong Court, Alice Springs, NT 0870, Australia.

POOLTHUPYA Srisurang, b. 15 Oct 1936, Bangkok, Thailand. Professor Emeritus of History. m. Col Jumpol Poolthupya, 16 Apr 1964, 3 s. Education: BA, Trinity Coll, 1962; Higher Dip in Educ, Dublin Univ, Ireland, 1963; MA, Indian Stdies, Univ of WI, Madison, USA, 1970. Appointments: Mbr, Fac Bd, Fac of Liberal Arts, 1973-78, 1983-87, Hd, Dept of Hist, 1983-87, Dir, Indian Studies Cntr, 1993-97, Thammasat Univ; Publications: Essays on Eastern Civilization (co-auth), 1979, 1983, 1986, 1993, 1994, 1996; 1999; The Origins and Behaviours of the Characters in the Ramakien (w Sumalya Bankloy), 1980; Social and Political Problems in Lebanon, 1985; Love and More Love (collected poems), 1986; Impact of Ataturk's Reforms on Modern Turkey, 1989; Niras New Zealand and Other Poems, 1991; Translation of Collected Poems by Yunus Emre, 1991; Ed, Thammasat Univ Jrnl, 1988-92; Ed, Ed Bd, Encyclopaedia of Asian Hist, Roy Inst, 1988-; The Chao Phraya River (collected poems in

Thai and English). Honours: Kt Grand Cross, 1st Class of the Most Noble Order of the Crown of Thailand, 1985; Kt Grand Cross, 1st Class of the Most Exalted order of the White Elephant, 1988; Kt Grand Cordon of the Most Noble Order of the Crown of Thailand, 1991; Kakasaheb Gadgil Centenary memento Awd, Promoting India-Thailand Rels; Fell, Roy Inst (Rajpandit), 1996; Kirtyacharya Awd, Thammasat Univ, 1997; Kt Grand Cordon (Special Class) of the Most Exalted Order of the White Elephant, 1997. Memberships: Histl Soc of Thailand; PEN Intl, Thai Cntr, Sec-Gen, 1976-78, 2nd VP, 1983-98, Pres, 1998-; Exec Mbr, Thai-Bharat Cultural Lodge; Perm Mbr, World Congress of Poets, 1991-; Mbr, Cttee of Fulbright Thai Assn, 1998-. Hobbies: Writing Poetry, literary essays, children's books; Translating literary works; Swimming. Address: 2/49 Ranong 1 Road, Dusit, Bangkok 10300, Thailand.

POON Chung-Kwong, b. 28 Feb 1940, Hong Kong. Educator; Administrator; Chemist. m. Vivien, 1965, 1 s, 2 d. Education: BSc, 1963; BSc, 1964; PhD, 1967; DSc, 1979; Chart Chem, 1979. Appointments: Lectr, 1968-75, Snr Lectr, 1975-77, Rdr, 1977-82, Prof, 1982-90, Fac Deam, 1983-90, Univ Hong Kong; Dir, Hong Kong Polytech, 1991-94; Pres, Hong Kong Polytech Univ, 1994-. Honours: UK C'wlth Schlsp, 1964-67; US Fulbright Schlsp, 1967-68; Ten Outstndng Yng Persons in Hong Kong Awd, 1979; UK Cncl for Intl Coop in Higher Educn Visitorship, 1984; JP, 1989; OBE, 1991; Fell, Univ Coll, Univ of London, 1996. Hobbies: Reading; Swimming. Address: c/o Hong Kong Polytechnic University, Hung Hom, Kowloon, Hong Kong.

POON Wai Sang, b. 20 Dec 1953, Canton, China. Neurosurgeon. m. Gillian Kew, 15 Sept 1984, 1 s. Education: MB, ChB, Univ of Glasgow Med Sch, Scotland, 1973-78. Appointments: Career trng in Neurosurg, Inst of Neurol Scis, Glasgow, Scotland, 1983-86; Neurosurg, 1986-, Professor and Chf, Neurosurg, Dept of Surg, Prince of Wales Hosp, Chinese Univ of Hong Kong. Publications: Secretion of ADH in Neurosurgical Patients, 1989; Primary Intrasellar Germinoma, 1988; The Human Factor in the Accuracy of ICP Monitoring, 1989; Water and Sodium Disorders in Patients with Pituary Tumour, 1996. Memberships: Fell, Roy Coll of Physns and Surgns, Glasgow, 1983; Cncl Mbr, 1988-, Pres, 1996-2000, Hong Kong Neurosurg Soc. Address: Department of Surgery, Prince of Wales Hospital, CUHK, Shatin, Hong Kong.

POONAWALA Ismail, b. 7 Jan 1937, Godhra, India. Teacher; Professor. m. Oumayma, 6 Jan 1981, 1 s. Education: MA, Bombay Univ; MA, Cairo Univ; PhD, Univ of CA, LA. Appointments: Asst Prof, McGill Univ; Rsch Assoc, Harv Univ; Prof, Univ of CA, LA. Publications: Al-Sultan al-Khattab, 1967; Bibliography of Ismaili Literature, 1977; Last Years of the Prophet, 1990. Honour: Fulbright Rsch Fell, 1995-96. Memberships: Mid E Studies Assn of N Am; Amn Inst of Yemeni Studies. Hobbies: Classical music; Basketball; Ice hockey. Address: Department of Near Eastern Languages and Cultures, University of California, Los Angeles, CA 90095, USA.

PORRA Robert John, b. 7 Aug 1931, Adelaide, Aust. Scientist. m. Margaret Elizabeth Hunter, 11 Apr 1977, 1 s, 2 d. Education: PhC, AUA, 1952; BS, Hons, Univ of Adelaide, 1957; PhD, Austl Natl Univ, 1963. Appointments: Prin Rsch Scientist, CSIRO, 1957-93; CSIRO Hon Rsch Fell, 1994-; CSIRO, Postdoct Fell, Oxford Univ, 1963-64; Leverhulme Snr Fell, Warwick Univ, 1969-70; Sci Rsch Cncl Fell, Bristol Univ, 1970-71; SFB Fell, Marburg Univ, 1979; SFB and DAAD Fell Munich Univ, 1989, 1992, 1993, 1995, 1997. Publications: Over 60 pprs in biochemical jrnls, also 5 in Austl rowing jrnls. Memberships: Austl Soc for Biochem and Molecular Bio. Hobbies: Rowing; Swimming; Bushwalking; Camping. Address: CSIRO Division of Plant Industry, GPO Box 1600, Canberra, ACT 2601, Australia.

PORTE Thierry Georges, b. 28 June 1957, NY, USA. Investment Banker. m. Yasko Tashiro, 1 s, 2 d. Education: AB, Magne Com Laudr, Phi Beta Kappa, Harv Coll; MBA, High Hons, Baker Sch, Harv Bus Sch. Appointments: Mngng Dir, Pres, Morgan Stanley Dean Witter, Japan. Memberships: Amn Chmbr of Comm; Harv Bus Sch Alumni Assn; Amn Sch in Japan. Hobbies: Reading; Opera; Running. Address: Morgan Stanley Japan, Yenbisu Garden Place Twr, 20-3 Ebisu 4-chome, Shibuya-ku Tokyo 150, Japan.

PORTER Colin Francis, b. 11 Oct 1930, London, Eng. Consulting Engineer. m. Christine Stell Whitmore, 25 May 1967, 1 s, 2 d. Education: BSc, London Univ, 1951. Appointments: Signals Offr, RAF, 1951-54; Engr in Charge, Hydraulics Res, Port of London Authy, 1955-62; Pollution Control Offr, 1964-68; Engr in Charge, Hydraulics Res, Maritime Servs Bd, NSW, Aust, 1969-71; Dir of Ops, Environ Protection Authy, Vic, 1972-76; Dir of Conservation and Environ, WA, 1977-86; Town Planning Appeal Tribunal, 1994-. Publications include: Rowing to Win, 1959; Environmental Impact Assessment, 1985; Contbr of num articles. Honours: For Rowing: Gold Medal, C'wlth Games, 1958; Silver Medal, Eurn Championships, 1954 Bronze Medal, Euron Championships, 1953; Bronze Medal, C'wlth Games, 1962; Olympic Record, Coxless IVs Rome, 1960. Memberships: Inst of Engrs, Aust; Austl Water and Wastewater Assn. Hobbies: Woodwork; Film Making; Rowing. Address: 3 Villiers Street, Bassendean, WA 6054, Australia.

PORTER Nyree Dawn, b. 22 Jan, Napier, New Zealand. Actress. m. (1) Bryan O'Leary, 1958, dec 1970, (2) Robin Halstead, 1975, div 1989, 1 d. Creative Works: Appearances in: Look Who's Here!, Fortune Th, London; Ducks and Lovers, Arts Th; Come Blow Your Horn. Leading Role: Sunday in the Park With George, Natl Th, 1990; The Winslow Boy, 1994; Great Expectations, 1994. TV & Film Appearances: Lady Bertram in Mansfield Park, 1996. Honours: Var drama awds and nominations. Hobby: Reading. Address: c/o Jean Diamond, London Management, 2-7 Noel Square, London W1V 3RB, England.

PORTER Rockne, b. 13 Mar 1932, Crossplains, TN, USA. Business Executive. m. Judy, 28 Feb 1974. Education: BS, Middle Tennessee State Univ, 1957; MA, Peabody Coll (now part of Vanderbilt Univ), 1963. Appointments: ITT Corp, 1961-80; Var intl positions, 1981-86; Dir, Indl Prod Mktng Asia, Alactel Trade Intl (Jt Venture w ITT), 1987-89; Dir of Indl Prod Mktng Asia, Tuthill Asia Ltd, 1990-; Mngng Dir. Publications: 5 in jrnls, related to Japanese indl trng, based on MA thesis. Memberships: Amn Chmbr of Com, Japan, 1963-67; Chmn, Jt venture and Licensing Cttee, 1965; Amn Japan Soc, 1968-72; Amn Soc of Trng Dirs, Japan, 1962-68; Res Offrs Assn (Major-AUS retd), 1992-. Hobbies: Hiking; Reading related to Asian history and culture. Address: Grand Plaza Apartments, 2025, Kornhill Road #2, Quarry Bay, Hong Kong.

POSE Kevin S, b. 16 Sept 1946, Melbourne, Aust. Solicitor. m. Evelyn Semsey, 7 Nov 1973, 3 d. Education: BJuris (1st Class), LLB (1st Class), Monash Univ; BCL, Oxon. Appointments: Lectr, Fac of Law, Monash Univ, 1973-77; Snr Lectr, Melbourne Univ, 1977-86; Barrister, 1975-87; Snr Tax Ptnr, Arthur Robinson & Hedderwicks, 1987-. Publications: Cases and Materials on the Legal Process, 1978, 1994; Cases and Materials on Taxation, 1978, 1984; Revenue Law Cases and Materials, 1990; Asst Ed, Australian Tax Review, 1996-. Honours: Supreme Crt Prizes BJuris and LLB, 1967, 1969; Brit C'wlth Schl, 1971-73; Shell Schl, 1969. Memberships: Law Cncl Aust; Law Cncl Tax Cttee, Chmn, 1991-95; Natl Tax Liason Cttee; Commr's Advsry Panel, 1991-95; Intl Tax Cttee (ATO) Fac Bd Mbr, Monash Law Fac, 1997-. Hobbies: Reading; Sport; Travel. Address: 6 Power Avenue, Toorak, Victoria, Australia.

POSINASETTI Nageswara Rao, b. 15 June 1947, Palakol, India. Manufacturing Engineering Educator. m. P V R Lakshmi, 18 Aug 1976, 2 s. Education: BSc, 1967; BE, 1970; ME, 1973; PhD, 1981. Appointments: Asst Lectr, BITS, Pilani, 1973-75; Lectr, 1975-81, Asst Prof, 1981-90, Prof, 1990-97, Indian Inst of Technol, Delhi;

Visng Fac, Asian Inst of Technol, Bangkok, 1993, Mara Inst of Technol, Shah Alam, 1995-. Publications: Numerical Control and Computer Aided Manufacturing, 1985; Manufacturing Technology Foundry Forming and Welding, 1987; Computer Aided Manufacturing, 1995; AutoCAD Made Easy for Engineering Drawing, 1999. Membership: Indian Soc of Mech Engrs. Hobbies: Computers; Literature; Music. Address: c/o Faculty of Mechanical Engineering, Mara Institute of Technology, 40450 Shah Alam, Malaysia.

POSSINGHAM John Victor, b. 28 Oct 1929. Scientist; Vigneron. m. Carol A Summers, 25 Mar 1977, 2 s, 1 d. Education: B Ag Sci, Hons; MSc Adelaide Univ, Aust; DPhil, DSc, Oxford Univ, Eng. Appointments: Sci, Div Plant Ind, Canberra, 1952-62; OIC Com Res St Merbein Vic, 1962-64; Ch, Div Horticulture, Adelaide, 1964-91; Chf Sci, Inst Plant Prod and Proc, Adelaide, 1991-94; Vigneron, McLaren Vale, SA, 1994; VP Intl Soc for Horticulture Sci. Publications: 180 pprs in sci jrnls; Book: Bibliography of Viticultural Res Member of Scientific Journal Boards. Honours: AM, 1990; Siro Medal, 1992; Sir Ian McLennan Awd for Ind, 1994. Memberships: FTSE, Fell Aust Acady Tech Sci and Engrng; Fell, Aust Inst Agricl Sci; Russian Acady of Agricl Sci; Bd Mbr Intl Soc for Horticulture Sci, 1994-98. Hobbies: Boating; Travel; International Horticulture. Address: 31 Thornber Street, Unley Park, SA 5061, Australia.

POTTIER Bernard M, b. 11 July 1942, Vernon, France. Diplomat. 2 s. Education: Dips, Paris Inst of Pol Scis, Natl Sch for Oriental Langs, Alumnus of Natl Sch of Admin. Appointments: Attaché French Embassy in Laos; 1st Sec, French Emb in Indonesia; Personal Advsr, Min of Overseas Territories; French Res, Commnr, New Hebrides; 1st Cnslr, French Emb, Cameroon; Head, Francophone Dept For Min; Dir, Comms, For Min Gen Consul in Frankfurt and Mainz, Germany; Amb, Burma, Myanmar. Honours: Kt, Natl Order of Merit, 1978; Offr, Order of Palmes Académiques, 1991; Kt, Natl Order of Legion d'Honneur, 1998. Membership: Sec Gen, Richelieu Club of Paris, 1986-89. Hobbies: Music; Tennis; Reading. Address: Embassy of France, 102 Pyidaungsu Yeiktha Road, BOB 858, Yangon, Mayanmar, Burma.

POTTS Charles, Poet. Education: BA, Engl, ID Univ, 1965; Real Estate Broker, Real Estate Inst, Spokane, WA, 1978; ATM, 1990; Master Practitioner, Soc of Neuro-Ling Progs, 1991. Appointments: Fndr Dir, Litmus Inc, 1967-77. Publications include: How the South Finally Won the Civil War; Loading Las Vegas; The Dictatorship of the Environment; Rocky Mountain Man; Little Lord Shiva. Honours: Intl Lit Awd, 1991; Disting Profl Achievement Awd, Coll of Arts & Scis, ID Univ, 1994. Address: PO Box 100, Walla Walla, WA 99362-0033, USA.

POTTS Daniel Thomas, b. 10 Feb 1953, New York, NY, USA. Professor of Archaeology. m. Hildreth Burnett, 2 June 1979, 2 s, 1 d. Education: AB, 1975; PhD (Harvard), 1980; DPhil (Copenhagen), 1990. Appointments: Lectr, Free Univ Berlin, 1981-86; Univ of Copenhagen, 1986-91; Prof, Middle East Archaeology, Univ Sydney, 1991-. Publications: The Arabian Gulf in Antiquity, 1990; Mesopotamian Civilization, 1997; Archaeology of Elam, 1999. Honours: FSA, 1993; Fell, Austl Acady Humanities, 1994. Hobbies: Rugby; Fishing; Music. Address: 29 Henry Street, Queen's Park, NSW 2029, Australia.

POTTS Timothy Faulkner, b. 17 June 1958. Art Gallery Director; Archaeologist; Investment Banker. m. Olivia, 15 Sept 1990, 1 s. Education: BA Hons, Sydney; DPhil, Oxon. Appointments: Hist Master, Cranbrook Sch, Sydney, 1981; Co-Dir, Univ Sydney Excavations at Pella Jordan, 1982-87; Res Lectr, 1985-87, Brit Acady Fell in Near Eastern Archaeology and Art, 1987-89 Christchurch Coll, Oxford; Dir, Media and Comms Grp Investment Banking Dept, Lehman Bros, NY and London, 1989-94; Dpty Dir, Intl Art Nat Gall, Vic, 1994-95; Dir, Natl Gall of Vic, 1995-98; Dir, Kimbell Art Mus, Fort Worth, TX, 1998-. Publications: Civilization: Ancient Treasures from the British Museum, 1991; Pella in Jordan 2 (w P C

Edwards), 1993, Mesopotamia and the East, 1994. Address: Kimbell Art Museum, 3333 Camp Bowie Boulevard, Fort Worth, TX 76107, USA.

POULOS Harry George, b. 27 Ar 1940, Katoomba, Aust. Civil Engr. m. Maria, 8 Nov 1964, 3 s, 1 d. Education: BE, PhD, DSc Eng, Univ of Sydney. Appointments: Lectr, Rdr, Prof, Univ of Sydney, 1965-; Snr Prin, Coffey Ptnrs Intl, 1989-. Publications: 3 books; Over 200 tech pprs. Honours: Snr Fulbright Schl, 1969; E H Davis Lectr, 1987; Jaeger Awd, 1988; Rankine Lectr, 1988; AM, 1993; State of Art Awd (ASCE), 1995. Memberships: Fell, Austl Acady of Sci; Austl Acady of Tech, Scis and Eng; Inst of Engrs of Aust; Amn Soc of Civil Engrs. Hobbies: Reading; Music; North American sociology. Address: 11 Alexandra Place, Carlingford, NSW, Australia 2118.

POUND Gregory David, b. 25 Sept 1950, Victoria, Australia. Accountant. m. Lyn, 1 s, 1 d. Education: BEcons, hons, 1973; MEcon, 1978. Appointments: Acct, Melbourne, 1971-75; Lectr, Dept of Acctng and Fin, Monash Univ, 1976-77; Lectr, Dept of Acctng and Fin Mngmt, Univ New Eng, 1978-80; Assoc Prof, Dept of Acctng and Fin, Monash Univ, 1987-90; Dir, Auditing Standard, Austl Acctng Rsch Fndn, 1982-87, 1990-. Publications: Auditing Concepts and Methods, 1983; Sev articles in profl jrnls. Memberships: Fell, Inst of Chart Accts, Aust, Austl Soc of CPAs. Hobbies: Sports. Address: 211 Hawthorn Road, Caulfield, Victoria, Australia.

POWELL Howard William, b. 16 Dec 1945, Sydney, NSW, Aust. Executive. m. Lillian Powell, 20 June 1973, 2 s. Education: BSc, Tchrs Ctf, NSW; Mngmt Dips, Univ VA, USA. Appointments: HS Tchr, NSW, 1965-69; Mktng Analyst, Caterpillar Tractor Co, Vic, 1970-71; Systems Analyst, 1971-74; Br Mngr, 1975-82; IBM; Dir, Computer Power Grp, 1983-96; Gen Mngr, Profl Servs Computer Power Grp, Austl and NZ, 1987-96; Gen Mngr, IBM Global Servs Aust, 1996-. Honour: AM, 1994. Hobbies: Music; Tennis; Cricket; Theatre. Address: 44 National Circuit, Forrest, ACT 2603, Australia.

POWELL J(ohn) Craig, b. 16 Nov 1940, Wollongong, NSW, Aust. Psychoanalyst; Poet. m. Janet, 16 Oct 1965, 1 s, 1 d. Education: BMed, Bachelor of Surg, Sydney Univ, 1965; Mbr, Austl and NZ Coll of Psychs, 1971; Mbr, Intl Psychoanalytical Assn, 1981; Fell, Roy Aust and NZ Coll Psychs, 1982. Appointments: Psych, Parramatta Psych Cntr, Sydney, 1968-72; Brandon Mental Hlth Cntr, Manitoba, Can, 1972-75; London Psych Hosp, Ont, Can, 1976-82; Visng Medl Offr, Dept of Psych, Westmead Hosp, 1984-88; Priv prac, 1982-. Publications: 7 books poetry inclng Minga Street - New and Selected Poems, 1993. Honours: Mattara (Newcastle) Poetry Prize, 1983; Co-Winner, Quarterly Review of Lit, Princeton, NJ, Intl Poetry Comp, 1989. Memberships: Canad Austl and Intl Psychoanalytic Assns; NSW Inst of Psychotherapy, Pres, 1992-94. Address: 24 Minga Street, Ryde, NSW 2112, Australia.

POWELL Joseph Michael, b. 27 Dec 1938, Bootle, Eng. University Teacher. m. Suzanne Margaret Geehman, 28 Dec 1967, 1 s, 1 d. Education: BA Hons, 1960; MA 1962, Liverpool Univ; PhD, 1969; DLitt, 1983, Monash Univ. Appointments: Asst Lectr in Geog, St Mary's Coll, Middlesex, Eng, 1962-63; Snr Tchng Fell, 1964; Lectr, 1965-69; Snr Lectr 1970-79, Rdr 1977-92, Prof 1992-98, Emer Prof, 1999-, Monash Univ. Publications include: Over 250 publs in jrnls and books inclng: The Public Lands of Australia Felix, 1970; An Historical Geography of Modern Australia, 1988; Watering the Garden State, 1989; MDB The Emergence of Bioregionalism in the Murray-Darling Basin, 1993; Watering the Western Third. Honour: Rsch Medal, Roy Soc of Vic, 1988; Thomson Medal, Roy Geogl Soc of Qld, 1998; Macdonald Holmer Medal, Geogl Soc of NSW, 1999. Memberships include: Inst of Austl Geographers; Austl Studies Assn; Roy Austl Histl Soc; Roy Vic Histl Soc; Fell, Acady of Socl Scis in Aust; Inst of Austl Geogs, Pres 1984-85. Hobbies: Football; Gardening; Walking; Reading. Address: Department of Geography and

Environmental Science, Monash University, Clayton, Vic 3168, Australia.

POWLES Stephen Bruce, b. 5 Apr 1950. Scientist. m. Wendy, 11 Jan 1980, 1 s, 2 d. Education: BS; MSc; PhD. Publications: Num. Address: Faculty of Agriculture, University of Western Australia, Nedlands, 6907, Australia.

PRABHU Suresh, b. 11 July 1953, Bombay, India. Member of Parliament. m. Uma, 5 July 1984, 1 s. Education: BCom, Hons; FCA, Inst of Chartered Accts of India, New Delhi. Appointments: Chmn, Maharashtra State Fin Commn, 1995-96; Elected, 11th Lok Sabha, 1996; Union Cabinet Min, Ind, 1996; Re-elected 12th Lok Sabha, 1998; Union Cabinet Min, Environ and Forests, 1998-. Publications: Num pprs in econs, sociol and taxation. Memberships: Chmn Konkan Kala Acady; Vice-Chmn, All India Cntrl; World Chamber of Com and Ind; Treas, Confed of UNESCO; Frmr Chmn, Saraswat Co-op Bank; Bd Dirs, sev cos; Exec Cttee, Intl volun serv in Paris; Boat Club; Khar Gymkhana; New Bombay Sports Assn; MIG Sports Club. Hobbies: Reading; Travelling; Music and drama; Table tennis; Chess; Cricket; Tennis; Football. Address: 15 Ashoka Road, New Delhi 110001, India.

PRADAN Dasho Om, b. 6 Oct 1946, Neoly, Bhutan. Government Official. m. Education: BA, Hist, Delhi Univ, India, 1968. Appointments: Trnee Offr, Min of Trade, Ind and Forests, Bhutan, 1969-70; Acting Sec, 1970-72, Sec, 1972-79; Dpty Min, 1979; Perm Rep of Bhutan to Un, NYC, 1980-84; Amb to India, Nepal and Maldives, Govt of Bhutan, 1984-85; Dpty Min, Trade and Ind, 1985; Min, Ministry of Trade, Ind and Tourism, 1989-; Chf Co-ord, Settlement of landless people in S Bhutan, 1976. Honour: Recip, Gold Medal, Meritorious Serv, Govt of Bhutan, 1974. Address: Ministry of Trade Industry and Tourism, Thimphu, Bhutan.

PRAEGER Cheryl Elisabeth, b. 7 Sept 1948, Toowomba, Qld, Aust. Professor of Mathematics. m. John David Henstridge, 9 Aug 1975, 2 s. Education: AMusA, Piano Perf, 1970; BSc, 1970, MSc, 1972, Univ Qld; MSc, 1972, DPhil, 1974, Oxford Univ; DSc, Univ WA, 1989. Appointments: Rsch Fell, Aust Natl Univ, Canberra, 1973-75; Visng Asst Prof, Univ VA, USA, 1974; Lectr, 1976-81; Snr Lectr, 1982-83; Prof, 1983-, Hd Dept, 1992-94, Dean, Postgrad Rsch Studies, 1996-98, Univ WA, Nedlands; Mbr, Curriculum Dev Cncl (C'wlth Schs Commn), 1984-88; Mbr, Prime Min's Sci Cncl, 1989-91; Publications: 170 pprs, intl maths jrnls; 2 books, Math rsch monographs. Honours: Open Schl, 1966-69, Medal, 1970, Rsch Schl, 1970, Univ Qld; CSFP (C'wlth) Schl to St Anne's Coll, Oxford, 1970-73; Cert Merit, Royal Hum Soc, NSW; DSc Honoris Causa, Maths, Prince Of Songlai Univ, Thailand, 1993; Fell, Austl Acady Sci, 1996; Mbr Order of Aust, 1999. Memberships: Aust Math Soc, Cncl Mbr, 1978-79, 1998-2001; Actng Hon Sec, 1984, 1987, Policy Cttee, 1985-87, VP, 1990-92, 1994-95, Pres, 1992-94, Fell, 1997-; Combinatorial Maths Soc Australasia, Dir, 1984, 1991; London Math Soc; Amn Math Soc; Inst Combinatorics And Its Applications, Fndn Fell, 1992-; Cncl Mbr, 1992-. Listed in: Who's Who in Australia; Who's Who in the World. Hobbies: Hiking; Cycling; Spinning; Choral singing; Keyboard playing (piano, organ). Address: Department of Mathematics and Statistics, University of Western Australia, Nedlands, WA 6907, Australia.

PRAKASA RAO B S L, b. 6 Oct 1942, India. Scientist. m. Vasanta, 13 Mar 1971, 3 s. Education: MA; MStat; PhD. Appointments: Disting Sci, Indian Stats Inst, 1992-; Dir, Indian Stats Inst, 1992-95. Publications: Statistical Inference for Stochastic Processes, 1980; Non-Parametric Functional Estimation, 1983. Honours: Fell, Inst of Math Stats, 1983, Indian Natl Sci Acady, 1984; Bhatnagar Awd, Govt of India, 1982. Memberships: Intl Stats Inst; Inst of Math Stats. Address: Indian Statistical Institute, 7 SJS Sansanwal Marg, New Delhi 110016, India.

PRAKASA RAO Bosukonda Surya, b. 1 July 1949, Dangeru, India. Teacher; Researcher. m. Krishna Veni, 31 Dec 1982, 2 s. Education: MSc, Tech, Geophys; PhD. Appointments: Tech Asst, 1979, 1996-98, Hd of Dept, 1990-93, Assoc Prof, 1990, Chmn of the Bd, 1998-2001. Publication: Application of Mathematical Morphology for Pattern Studies (ed); 12 rsch pprs. Honour: Best Rschr Awd, Andhra Univ, 1995. Memberships: AEG; ISTE; ISRS. Hobbies: Research; Teaching; Homeo practice. Address: c/o Department of Geo-Engineering, College of Engineering, Andhra University, Visakhapatnan 530003, India.

PRAKASH T N, b. 3 Jan 1945, Chamarajanagar, India. Senior Manager. m. Rajeshwari K N, 4 Apr 1983, 1 s, 1 d. Education: PhD. Appointments: Natl Aerospace, 1964-86; Aeronautical Dev Agcy, Bangalore, India, 1986-. Publications: (book) Design and Development of Bibliographic Database for Engineering. Memberships: Coord, Aerospace Info Panel, AR and DVB, New Delhi; Karnataka Lib Assn, Bangalore, India; Indian Assn of Spec Libs and Info Cntr; Soc of Info Scis, New Delhi, India. Hobby: Sports. Address: Senior Manager, Aeronautical Development Agency, PO Box No 1718, Bangalore 560017, India.

PRANAB Ray, b. 27 Mar 1937, Basudevpur (Daspur), Dist Midnapur, W Bengal, India. Professor (retired). m. Sadhāna Ray (formerly Banerjee), 12 June 1966, 1 s, 1 d. Education: MA (CU), BA (Hons) (CU) 1st Class First, Gold Medallist, Jubilee Schl and UGC Schl; Kavyatirtha Vangiya Sanskrit Siksha Parishat, Calcutta, under Govt of W Bengal, stood 1st class second, won prizes. Appointments: Lectr, Ranaghat Coll (Nadia); Asst Prof, ND Coll (Howrah); Lectr, Jhargram Raj Coll, Lectr, Kishnagar Coll; Lectr, Maulana Azad Coll, Calcutta; Asst Prof, Hooghly Mohsin Coll; Asst Prof, Maulana Azad Coll, Calcutta; Sec, Vangiya Sanskrit Siksha Parishat Coll, Calcutta; Rdr, Govt Sanskrit Coll, Calcutta. Publications: Political and Social History of Ghatal (Ghataler Katha); The Archaeological Treasures of Midnapur Dist (Medinipur Jelar Pratnasampad); Banglar Khabar; Medinipur: Itihas O Samskritir Vivartan, Vol I and II (ed and written); About 400 articles in jrnls. Honours: Won Michael Madhusudan Awd from Michael Acady, Calcutta; Felicitated by Vangiya Sahitya Parishat (Midnapur); Int Man of Yr, IBC, Cambridge. Memberships: Life Mbr, Asiatic Soc; Life Mbr, Indian Hist Congress; Life Mbr, Vangiya Sahitya Parishat; Life Mbr, W Bengal Itihas Samsad. Hobbies: Collecting archaeological objects, old manuscripts from many an ancient site; Photographing of temples, mosques, churches, old buildings; Writing articles in journals. Address: A5/16 Dankuni Housing Estate, PO Dankuni, Dist Hooghly, West Bengal, India PIN 711224.

PRASAD Satendra, b. 7 Apr 1962, Fiji. University Lecturer. m. Kushma Ram, 2 d. Education: BA, Sociol and Pols, Univ of S Pacific, Fiji; MA, Sociol, Univ of NB, Can; PhD, Warwick Univ, Eng. Appointments: Lectr, Sociol and Indl Rels, Univ of S Pacific, 1987-98. Membership: Secretariat of Citizens Constitutional Forum of Fiji. Address: SSED, IJSP, PO Box 1168, Suva, Fiji.

PRASAD Suman Prabha, b. 21 May 1941, Gaya. University Professor. m. Kameshwar, 6 Feb 1964, 1 s, 1 d. Education: PhD, Engl, Leicester Univ, Eng; MA; BA Hons, Engl, Patna Univ. Appointments: Lectr, Engl, Bihar Univ, Patna Univ; Rdr, Prof, Engl, Patna Univ; Prof, Sanaa Univ, Yemen; Hd, PG Dept Engl, Patna Univ; Dean of Fac, Hum, Patna Univ, Patna. Creative Works: Hardy and Lawrence; Kathghore Ka Vijeta; Hukum ka Ekka; Mutthi Bhar Shabd. Honours: Prizes in Chess, Table tennis; Engl Essay Competition. Memberships: Amn Studies Intl; Amn Studies Assn; Intl Soc for Humor Studies; Indian Assn of Engl Studies; Amn Studies Rsch Cntr. Hobbies: Games; Music; Creative Writing. Address: 210 MIG House, Lohanagar, Patna 800020, India.

PRASAD Venus, b. 23 Feb 1972, Jamshedpur, India. Teacher in Jamshedpur Womens College. Education: PG in Polit Sci, 1st Class; P G Dip in Software (Computer); BLL. Honours: Bsic Leadership Awd in NCC (Natl Cadet

Corps), Awd in Painting, 1990; Awd in Craft, 1992. Hobbies: Painting; Doing craft; Reading biographies. Address: N/142/1, Telco Colony, Jamshedpur 831004, India.

PRASAD SINGH Devendra, b. 25 Jan 1958, Muzaffarpur, Bihar, India. Journalist. m. Renu, 25 Feb 1982, 2 s, 2 d. Education: Sahityacharya (equiv to master degree), Kameshwar Singh, Darbhanga Sanskrit Univ, Darbhanga, Bihar. Appointments: Jrnlsm, 1987-; Hindustan Hindi Daily, Patna, Awaz; Hindi daily, Dhanbad and Jamshedpur. Publications: Many articles in Indian newspapers and mags. Hobby: Writing about the atrocities against women and the poor. Address: C/o Chamakta Aiha, 36 New Development Area, Golmuri, Jamshedpur, Bihar.

PRATHAP Gangan, b. 6 June 1951, Singapore. Aeronautical Engineer. m. Latha, 19 Aug 1979, 1 s. Education: BTech, Indian Inst of Technol, Madras, 1974; PhD, 1978. Appointments: Rsch Asst, Indian Inst of Technol, Madras, 1977-78; Rsch Assoc, 1978-80, Sci, 1980-, Natl Aerospace Lab, Bangalore. Publication: The Finite Element Method in Structural Mechanics, 1993. Honours: S S Bhatnagar Prize, 1990; Disting Alumnus Awd for Aerospace Engrng, IIT Madras, 1996. Memberships: Fell, Indian Acady of Scis, 1991-, Indian Natl Sci Acady, 1999-. Hobbies: Reading; Writing. Address: National Aerospace Laboratories, Bangalore 560 017, India.

PRATT Craig, b. 10 Apr 1970, Suva, Fiji. Environmental Consultant. Education: BSc, USP, S Pacific; Postgrad Dip, Bio, USP, S Pacific; PostgradDip, Environmental Studies, Macquarie NSW, Aust; MSc, Macquarie, NSW, Aust. Appointments: Demonstrator, Bio, Univ of S Pacific, 1991-93; Toxics Campaigner, Greenpeace Pacific, 1997-98; Environmental Cnslt, S Pacific Geosci Commn, 1998-; sev environmental consultancies. Address: South Pacific Applied Geoscience Commission (SOPAC), Private Mail Bag, Suva, Fiji.

PRAWIRADILAGA Dewi Malia, b. 3 Jan 1955, Bogor, Indonesia. Research Worker. Education: Ir (Engr) in Animal Sci, 1978; Master of Rural Sci, 1985; PhD, Ecology, 1997. Appointments: Working at Cntr for Biol Rsch and Dev, Indonesian Inst of Scis (LIPI), 1978-; Fauna Flora Intl-Indonesia Prog, 1997. Creative works: Diversity of birds in the lowland and highland rice fields of Java, Indonesia, presented at XXth Intl Ornithological Congress, Christchurch, NZ; Diet of Pied Currawongs (Strepera graculina) in newly occupied parts of their range, presented, XXIst Intl Ornithological Congress, Vienna, 1994; Feeding ecology of the Javan Hawk Eagle (Spizaetus bartelsi) presented at the Vth World Conf on Birds of Prey and Owls, S Africa, 1998. Memberships: Roy Australasian Ornithologists Union; Australasian Soc for Stdy of Animal Behaviour; Indonesian Zool Soc. Hobbies: Collecting stamps; Listening to music; Watching birds. Address: PO Box 230, Bogor 16002, Indonesia.

PREBBLE Richard William, b. 7 Feb 1948, Eng. Leader, ACT, New Zealand. m. Doreen Prebble, 2 Dec 1995, 2 s, 1 d. Education: BA, LLB, Auckland Univ, NZ. Appointments: MP, Auckland Cntrl, 1975-93; Sev Ministerial Posts in 4th Labour Govt; MP, Wellington Cntrl, 1996-; Ldr, ACT, NZ. Publications: (books) I've Been Thinking, 1996; Now It's Time to Act, 1996; What Happens Next, 1997. Honour: CBE, 1994. Hobbies: Theatre; Ballet; Writing. Address: 43 Tinakori Road, Thorndon, Wellington, New Zealand.

PREMATILLEKE Leelananda, b. 7 June 1922, Mahara, Sri Lanka. Archaeologist. m. Nanda, 1 s, 1 d. Education: BA (Ceylon); MA (Calcutta); PhD (London). Appointments: Lectr, Snr Lectr, Assoc Prof, Prof, Univ of Peradeniya, 1960-89; Dir/Archaeology, Cntrl Culturl Fund, 1981-98. Publications: Books, 1982-98; Paintings, 1942, 1989. Honours: Visng Prof, Inst of Archaeology, Univ of Waseda, Tokyo, 1934; Snr Visng Fell, Intl Inst of Asian Studies, 1997; Gold Medal, Sri Lanka Cncl of Archaeologists. Memberships: Roy Asiatic Soc; Life Mbr,

(RASC Cey Branch), Advsry Bd, Dept of Archaeology; Fndr Pres, Sri Lanka Cncl of Archaeologists. Hobbies: Writing; Painting. Address: 532/2 Siebel Place, Kandy, Sri Lanka.

PRENTIS Malcolm David, b. 27 June 1948, Auchenflower, Qld, Aust. Educator; Historian. m. Marion Anne Bird, 7 Jan 1978, 2 s, 1 d. Education: BA, hons, Univ of Sydney, 1970; MA, hons, 1973, PhD, 1980, Macquarie Univ; DipTertiaryEd, Univ New Eng, 1982. Appointments: Pt-time Tutor, Macquarie Univ, 1971-74; Lectr in Hist, Cath Coll of Educ, Sydney, 1975-90; Snr Lectr in Hist, Austl Cath Univ, 1991-. Publications: A Study in Black and White: The Aborigines in Australian History, 1975, 2nd ed, 1988; Fellowship, 1977; St David's Kirk, 1977; The Scots in Australia, 1983; The Scottish in Australia, 1987; Warringah History (ed), 1989; Scots to the Fore, 1993; The Forest Kirk, 1993; Science Race and Faith, 1998; Other monographs and articles. Memberships include: Fell, Roy Histl Soc; VP, Uniting Ch Recs and Histl Soc, NSW; Austl Histl Assn; Roy Austl Histl Soc; Hobbies: Reading; Genealogy; Cinema; Cricket; Swimming; Soccer; Elder, Uniting Church. Address: Australian Catholic University, 25A Barker Road, Strathfield, NSW 2135, Australia.

PRESCOTT Dorothy Francis, b. 11 Jan 1931. Map Curator. m. John Robert Victor Prescott, 12 Sept 1953, 1 s, 1 d. Education: BA (Hons), Geog, Dunelm; ALAA; MAIC; MAusS. Appointments: Map Libn, Univ of Ibadan Lib, Nigeria, 1956; Map Curator, Univ of Melbourne Lib, Aust, 1964; Map Curator, Natl Lib of Aust, Canberra, Aust, 1979; Dir, Map Info and Rsch, 1983-; Mbr, Surveyors Bd of Vic, 1987-. Publications: Approximately 30 Articles on Map Librarianship; Author: Spencer Scott Sandilands Important Catalogue of Maps with Particular Reference to Australia, 1982; The Asutralian Early Map Portfolio, 1987; Co-Author, Frontiers of Asia and South East Asia, 1977; Checklist of Australian Map Catalogues and Indexes, 1982; Preliminary Environmental Report on a Proposed Gold Mining Project in the Ovens Valley, Victoria, 1985; Austl Mbr of Editl Grp which prod Cartographic Materials: A Manual of Interpretation for AACR2, Chicago, American Library Association, 1982; A Guide to Maps of Australia in Books Published 1780-1830, 1996. Honours: Hon Life Mbr, Austl Map Circle, 1991. Memberships: Austl Map Circle, 1973-, Pres, 1978-89; Austl Lib and Info Assn, 1964-; Austl Soc of Indexers, 1970-; Austl Inst of Cartographers, 1981-95 (name changed to Mapping Scis Inst of Aust, Mbr, 1995-); Soc of Woman Geographers, 1992-; Austl Mbr, Intl Commn on Hist of Cartography; Intl Cartographic Assn, 1980-. Hobbies: Gardening; Fishing; Travel. Address: 44 Lucas Street, East Brighton, Vic 3187, Australia.

PRESCOTT John Robert Victor, 12 May 1931. Lecturer. m. Dorothy Prescott, 12 Sept 1953, 1 s, 1 d. Education: BS (Hons); Dip Ed; MA, Durham Univ; Ph London Univ; MM, Melbourne Univ. Appointments: Lectr, Univ Coll, Madan, Nigeria, 1956-61; Lectr, Snr Lectr, Rdr, Prof, Prof Emer, Univ of Melbourne, 1961-. Publications: 14 books incl: Political Frontiers and Boundaries, 1986; Aboriginal Frontiers and Boundaries in Australia (w S Davis); Secret Hydrographic Surveys in the Spratly Islands (w D Hancox). Hobbies: Fishing; Reading. Address: Department of Geography, University of Melboune, Parkville, Vic 3052, Australia.

PRESCOTT John Russell, b. 31 May 1924, Cairo, Egypt. Professor Emeritus of Physics. m. Josephine Wylde, 4 oct 1947, 1 s, 2 d. Education: BSc (Hons), Adelaide, 1945; PhD, Melbourne, 1950; DPhil, Oxon, 1953. Appointments: CSIRO, Aust, 1947; Austl Atomic Energy Commn, 1953; Phys Dept Univ BC, 1956; Univ of Calgary, Can, 1961; Univ of Adelaide, 1971. Publications: 200 in learned jrnls on phys educ, nuclear phys, cosmic rays, instrumentation, archaeometry. Honours: Hon Fell, Austl inst Phys; Elder Prof, Univ of Adelaide. Memberships: Brit Inst of Phys; Austl Inst of Phys; Canad Assn Physicists. Hobbies: Gardening; Music; Cabinet making; Sometime international hockey umpire. Address:

Department of Physics and Mathematical Physics, University of Adelaide, Australia 5005.

PRESS Lloyd Douglas (Skip), b. 26 July 1950, Commerce, TX, USA. Writer. m. Debra, 30 July 1989, 1 s, 1 d. Education: UCLA Tchng Ctf. Appointments: Instr, sev univs and colls; Playwright, Dir; Featured Speaker; Panelist; Opening Speaker. Auth. Publications (as Skip Press) include: Cliffhanger; Knucklehead; The Kuwaiti Oil Fires; The Importance of Mark Twain; A Rave of Snakes; Star Families; How To Write What You Want and Sell What You Write; Writer's Guide to Hollywood Producers, Directors and Screenwriters' Agents; Your modeling Career (w Debra Press). Honours: State Championship, Team Golf, W L Roper HS, Anna, TX; Silver Medal, NY Intl Film Fest, 1987; The Hon Order of KY Cols, 1995. Memberships: Dramatists Guild; Mystery Writers of Am; Natl Writers Union; Poets, Essayists and Novelists; Sci Fiction Writers of Am; Eligible for Writers Guild of Am. Hobbies: Golf; Helping Other Writers.

PRESSING Jeffrey Lynn, b. 30 Nov 1946, CA, USA. Scientist; Musician. m. Gillian Wigglesworth, 21 June 1986, 1 s, 1 d. Education: BS, Caltech, 1966; PhD, Univ of CA, San Diego, 1972. Appointments: Postdoct Rsch Fell, Dept of Phys, Univ of Rochester, 1972-74; Postdoct Fell, Dept of Chem, Univ CA, San Diego, 1974-75; Lectr, 1975, Snr Lectr in Music, Chairperson of Dept, 1980-81, 1986, La Trobe Univ, Melbourne, Aust; Rsch Affiliate, MIT Media Lab, Snr Lectr in Psychol, Univ of Melbourne, 1994-; Columnist for Keyboard Mag; AI Researcher with Intelligenesis Corp, 1998-. Publications: Surface Tension and Interfacial Density Profile of Fluids Near the Critical Point, 1973; Cognitive Isomorphisms in World Music, 1983; Cognitive Process in Improvisation, 1984; Improvisation: Methods and Models, 1987; Non-linear Maps As Generators of Musical Design, 1988; Spectral Properties of Human Cognition and Skill, 1997; The Referential Dynamics of Cognition and Action, 1999. Honours: Fulbright Fellshp, 1966-67; Composition Commissions from the Austl Cncl, 1983, 1985, 1987 Artist and New Technol Awd, 1985. Hobbies: Tennis; Creative writing. Address: 42 Darling Street, Fairfield, Vic 3078, Australia.

PRESSLEY Lynne, b. 28 May 1953, Melbourne, Vic, Aust. Cardiologist. m. John Haydon Lennard, 27 Nov 1982. Education: MB BS, 1st Class Hons; BMedSci, 1st Class Hons, 1976; ECFMG, 1976; DPhil, Oxon, 1980; FRACP, 1985. Appointments: Intern, 1977, Registrar, 1981-83, Flinders Medl Cntr, South Austl; Rhodes Schl, Nuffield Dept of Med, Oxford, Eng, 1978-80; Registrar, 1984-85, Visng Medl Off, Cardiology, 1987, Roy Prince Alfred Hosp, Sydney, NSW. Publications: Contbr of num sci articles in jrnls. Honour: Rhodes Schl, Vic, Aust, 1977. Memberships: Fell, Roy Australasian Coll Physns; Mbr, Cardiac Soc of Aust and NZ; Natl Heart Fndn of NSW; Bd, Natl Heart Fndn of Aust (NSW Div); Bd, Natl Heart Fndn of Aust. Hobbies: Tennis; Entertaining. Address: 56 Addison Road, Manly, NSW 2095, Australia.

PRESTON Robert Arthur, b. 29 June 1944, NYC, USA. Astronomer. m. Ann Lee, 18 July 1970, 1 d. Education: BS, 1966, MSc, 1967, Cornell Univ; PhD, MIT, 1972. Appointments: Supvsr, Astron Measurement Grp, 1975-, Space VLBI Proj Scientist, 1991-, Jet Propulsion Lab, CA Inst of Technol. Publications: Over 200 sci pprs. Memberships: Amn Astron Soc; Intl Astron Union. Hobbies: Archaeology; Sports. Address: 238-332, Jet propulsion Laboratory, 1800 Oak Grove Drive, Pasadena, CA 91109, USA.

PRICE John Charles, b. 14 May 1939, Mayfield, NSW, Aust. Member of the Legislative Assembly of NSW. m. Elizabeth, 6 Jan 1989, 1 s, 1 d, 1 step d. Education: Ctf of Marine Engrng Technol. Appointments: Shadow Min for Pub Wrks, 1988-91; Dpty Speaker and Chmn of Cttees, 1995-. Memberships: AMI Marx Eng (Lond); IEng; Assoc I E Aust; FSE. Hobbies: Music; Swimming. Address: Booyong, Flying Fox Lane, Vacy 2421, NSW, Australia.

PRIDER Rex Tregilgas, b. 22 Sept 1910, Narrogin, WA, Aust. Emeritus Professor of Geology. m. Catherine Esther Walton, 19 Aug 1936, 1 s, 1 d. Education: BSc, hons, Univ WA, 1928-31; PhD, Cambridge Univ, Eng, 1936-39. Appointments: Mine Surveyor, Kalgoorlie, 1932-33; Asst Lectr, Geol, 1934-38, Lectr, Geol, 1939-45, Snr Lectr, Geol, 1945-48, Prof, Geol, Hd of Dept, 1949-75, Emer Prof, Geol, 1976-, Univ WA. Publications: Elements of Geology for Australian Students (w E de C Clarke and C Teichert); Practical Geology (w E de C Clarke and C Teichert); Mining in Western Australia (ed); Contbr of num rsch pprs. Honours: Lyell Fnd, Geol Soc of London, 1951; Medal, Roy Soc of WA, 1970; Rex T Prider Medal, Univ of WA, 1975. Memberships: Hon Life Mbr, Geol Soc of Aust, Roy Soc of Aust, Gemmological Soc of Aust; Hon Life Fell, Mineralogical Soc of Am; Fell, Geol Soc of London; Mineralogical Soc of GB. Hobby: Gardening. Address: 89 Broadway, Nedlands, WA 6009, Australia.

PRIEST Graham George, b. 14 Nov 1948, London, Eng. Philosopher. m. Anne Catherine, Sept 1970, sep 1994, 1 s, 1 d. Education: BA, 1970, MA, 1974, St Johns Coll, Cambridge; MSc, Bedford Coll, London, 1971; PhD, London Sch of Econs, 1974. Appointments: Univ of St Andrews, 1974-76; Univ WA, 1976-88; Univ Qld, 1988-. Publications: In Contradiction, 1987; Beyond the Limits of Thought, 1995. Honours: Life Mbr, Clare Hall, Cambridge, 1991; Fell, Austl Acady of Hum, 1995. Hobbies: Music; Karate. Address: Department of Philosophy, University of Queensland, Qld 4072, Australia.

PRIEST Joan Frances, b. 28 Sept 1920, Brisbane, Aust. Author. m. Eric N Priest, 7 Apr 1945, 1 s, 2 d. Education: Engl, Univ Qld. Publications: From Balliol College to Brisbane Grammar, 1993; Without Fear or Favour (biog, Sir Harry Gibbs, Chief Justice High Court Australia, 1981-87), 1995; The Literary Precipice, 1998; Passports Please (musical play). Honour: OAM, 1998. Address: 106 Kadumba Street, Yeronga, Qld 4104, Australia.

PRIMLANI Gulab, b. 14 Dec 1924. Publishing Executive; Education Society Chairman. m. Chandra Primlani, 26 Nov 1977, 1 s, 1 d. Education: BA. Appointments: Mngng Dir, Amerind Publng Co Ltd; Chmn, Tagore Educ Soc. Publications: Num articles in profl jrnls. Memberships: Chmn, Tagore Educ Soc, Cttee Mbr, Fedn of Indian Publrs. Hobbies: Classical Music; Golf; Bridge. Address: Amerind Publishing Co Ltd, Oxford Building, N-56 Connaught Circus, New Delhi 110 001, India.

PRINGLE Eric James, b. 27 July 1941. Company Director. Appointments: Dir, Fndr, Eric Pringle Assocs Sdn Bhd (Pub Rels Cnslts), Malaysia, 1983; Dir, Econ Pub Affairs Pte Ltd, Singapore, 1985; Dir, Sepang Laris Sdn Bhd (Fin Advsry Serv), Malaysia, 1995; Dir, Match Plan Sdn Bhd, (Sport Event Mktng), Malaysia, 1996. Membership: MPRI. Hobbies: Sport; Classical Music; Chess; Reading; Politics. Address: Eric Pringle Associates Sdn Bhd, PO Box 11324-90742 Kuala Lumpur, Suite 7 20 7th Fl-Wisma Central Jalan, Ampang 50450 Kuala Lumpur, Malaysia.

PRIOR Roger Arnold, b. 15 Mar 1938, Temora, NSW, Aust. Executive Search Consultant. m. Jane, 16 Mar 1981, 2 s, 1 d. Education: BCom, Econ, UNSW, Sydney, Aust. Appointments: IBM Corp, Aust, UK, US; MSA Intl, 1979-82; Fndr and Mng Dir, Roger Prior Assocs, 1983. Memberships: Amn Chmbr Singapore; Commanderie de Bordeaux; Singapore Aust Bus Cncl; Tanglin Club; Singapore Cricket Club; Computer Soc, Singapore. Hobby: Scuba. Address: 4 Cable Road, 249888, Singapore.

PROBYN Clive Trevor, b. 27 Mar 1944, Birmingham, Eng. Professor of English. 1 s, 2 d. Education: BA, hons, 1965; MA, Univ of VA, USA, 1966; PhD, Nottingham Univ, 1968; FAHA, 1994. Appointments: Lectr, 1968-78, Snr Lectr, 1978-82, Univ of Lancaster, Eng; Prof, Univ of Sokoto, Nigeria, 1978-80; Univ of Monash, Aust, 1982-;

Fac Profl Assoc, Melbourne Univ, 1988; Visng Prof, Univ of VA, USA, 1988. Publications include: The Art of Jonathan Swift, 1978; Gullivers Travels: A Critical Study, 1987; English Fiction of the Eighteenth Century, 1987; The Sociable Humanist: The Life and Works of James Harris, 1709-80, Provincial and Metropolitan Culture in 18th Century England, 1990; The Correspondence of Henry and Sarah Feidling (w M Battestin), 1993. Honours: Fulbright Travel Schl, 1966; Engl Speaking Union Fell; FAHA, 1992; Academy Edition of The Works of Henry Handel Richardson (w Bruce Steele), 1998, 1999. Memberships: Pres, Johnson Soc of Aust, 1988-; Brit Soc for 18th Century Stdies. Hobby: Theatre. Address: Department of English, Monash University, Clayton, Vic 3168, Australia.

PROMBOON Sumonta, b. 27 Mar 1946, Thailand. Professor of Biology. m. Dr Suebsang, 2 s. 1 d. Education: BA, Zool; MS, Genetics; PhD, Genetics; Ctf in Pop Stdies. Appointments: Dean of Sci, 1983-87, VP Acad Affairs, 1993-97, Pres, 1998-, Srinakharinwirot Univ, Bangkok. Publications: Co-author, Biology, 1987; Ed, Biodiversity, 1991; Population Genetics and Evolution, 1996; Co-auth, Participative Learning, 1997. Honour: Outstndg Sci Tchr Awd, 1996. Memberships: Sci Soc Thailand; Genetics Soc Thailand; Preecha-Prapai A Sci Foun; Sigma Xi; NY Acady Sci. Hobbies: Music; Reading. Address: Srinakharinwirot University, Sukhumvit 23, Bangkok 10110, Thailand.

PROUDFOOT Helen Colleen, b. 3 May 1930. Writer; Urban Historian; Town and Landscape Planner. m. Peter Proudfoot, 3 Feb 1968, 2 d. Education: BA, Hons; Master of Town and Country Plng; PhD. Appointments: Cumberland Co Cncl; NSW State Planning Authy; Advsr, Dept of Urban Affairs on Natl Estate Prog; Urban Hist Cnslt. Publications: Old Government House, 1971; Exploring Sydney's West, 1987; Gardens in Bloom: Jocelyn Brown, 1989; Australia's First Government House, 1991; Contributes chapts to var books and jrnls. Honours: Sydney Luker Medal, 1990; Natl Trust Life Mbr Medal. Memberships: RAHS; RAPI; Natl Parks Cncl, 1982-90. Hobbies: Italian gardens; Colonial culture; Architectural history. Address: 1 Ontario Avenue, Roseville, Sydney, NSW 2069, Australia.

PROUDFOOT Peter Reginald, b. 24 Nov 1936, Sydney, Aust. University Professor. m. Helen, 3 Feb 1968, 2 d. Education: BArch, Sydney; MArch, PA; PhD, NSW. Appointments: Design Arch, NSW Govt Arch Off, 1960-63; Supvsr Arch, Sheppard Robson & Ptnrs, London, 1963-65; Lectr, Snr Lectr, Prof, Univ NSW, 1968-. Publications include: The Secret Plan of Canberra, 1994; Seaport Sydney: The Making of the City Landscape, 1996. Honours: C'wlth Schl, Univ Sydney, 1954-60; Rome Schl in Arch, 1965-66; Visng Fellshp, Univ PA, 1982; Awds, Austl Rsch Cncl, 1988-92. Memberships: Soc of Rome Schls; Soc of Arch Histns; Roy Austl Histl Soc; Austl Assn of Maritime Histns. Hobbies: Squash; Chess. Address: 1 Ontario Avenue, Roseville, NSW 2069, Australia.

PRUSINER Stanley B, b. 28 May 1942, Des Moines, IA, USA. Professor. m. Education: AB, cum laude, Univ PA, The Coll, 1964; MD, Univ PA, Sch of Med, 1968. Appointments: Asst Prof, Neurol in Res, 1974-80, Lectr, Dept of Biochem & Biophys, 1976-88, Assoc Prof, Neurol in Res, 1980-81, Assoc Prof, Neurol, 1981-84, Prof of Neurol, 1984-, Prof of Virol in Res, 1984-, Prof of Biochem, 1988-, Univ CA, Sch of Med, San Fran; Asst Prof, Virol in Res, 1979-83, Assoc Prof, Virol in Res, 1983-84, Prof of Virol in Res, 1984-, Univ CA, Sch of Pub Hlth, Berkeley. Publications: Num articles in profl med jrnls. Honours include: Franklin Inst Gold Medal, 1988; DSc Honoris Causa, Univ PA, Phila, 1998; UCSF Medal, 1998; Medalla Recoral, Universidad de Chile, Santiago, 1998. Memberships include: Am Soc of Biochem and Molecular Biol; Am Soc for Clin Investigation; Amn Chem Soc; Amn Assn for the Adv of Sci; Amn Soc of Neurol; Amn Soc for Microbiol; Intl Soc for Neurochem; Amn Neurol Assn; Amn Soc of Human Genetics; Protein Soc; Assn of Amn Physns; Genetics Soc of Am. Address:

University of California, School of Medicine, Department of Neurology, San Francisco, CA 94143-0518, USA.

PU Chaozhu, b. 1929, Huaning, China. Government Official. Appointments: Joined CCP, 1949; Gov of Yunnan, 1983-85; Sec, Prov CCP Cttee, 1985-95; Mbr, 12th CCP Ctrl Cttee, 1985-87, 13th Ctrl CCP Cttee, 1987-92, 14th Ctrl Cttee, 1992-; 8th NPC Dpty, Yunan Prov, 1993-. Address: Office of the Secretary, CCP, Kunming, Yunnan, China.

PU Haiqing, b. 1940, Sichuan, China. Politician. Education: Chongqing Univ. Appointments: Joined CCP, 1973; Mngr, Chongqing Iron & Steel Co; Vice-Gov, Sichuan Prov; Mayor of Chongqing Municipality, Vice-Sec CCp Chongqing Municipal Cttee, 1997-; Mbr, 15th CCP Ctrl Cttee, 1997-. Address: Chongqing Municipal Government, Chongqing, China.

PU Shan, b. 27 Nov 1923, Economist. m. Chen Xiuying, 10 Feb 1951. Education: PhD, Harv Univ. Appointments: Dir, Inst World Econs and Pols, Chinese Acady Socl Scis, 1982-88; Mbr, Natl Cttee, Chinese People's Pol Consultative Conf, 1988-98; Pres, Grad Sch of Chinese Acady of Socl Scis, 1991-94; Stndng Cttee Mbr, Natl Cttee, Chinese People's Consultative Conf, 1993-98. Honours: Phi Beta Kappa; Phi Kappa Phi, 1943; LLD, Carleton Coll, 1981. Membership: Pres, 1985-97, Hon Pres, 1997- Chinese Soc of World Econ, 1985-9. Address: 24 Zhan Lan Road, Beijing 100037, China.

PU Ta-Hai, b. 3 Apr 1922, Meihsien, Kwangtung, Taiwan. Government Official. m. 1 s, 2 d. Education: Chinese Mil Acady; Chinese Army Cmd & Gen Staff Coll; Chinese Armed Forces Staff Coll. Appointments: Section Chf (Col), Taiwan Peace Preservation HQ, 1956-57; Dept Hd (Col), Gen HQ, Chinese Army, 1957-60; Dept Hd (Maj-Gen), Personnel Divsn, Min of Natl Def, 1963-68; Dept Hd (Maj-Gen), Taiwan Garrison Gen HQ, 1968-72; Dept Hd, Ctrl Personnel Admin Exec, Yuan, 1972-78; Dir, Dept of Personnel, Taipei City Govt, 1978-81, Taiwan Prov Govt, 1981-84; Dpty Dir-Gen, ctrl Personnel Admin Exec, Yuan, 1984, Dir-Gen, 1984-93; Natl Policy Advsr to the Pres, 1993-. Hobbies: Tennis; Badminton. Address: Office of the Director General, Central Personnel Administration Executives Yuan, 109 Huai Ning Street, Taipei, Taiwan.

PUCKETT Richard Edward, b. 9 Sept 1932, Klamath Falls, OR, USA. Artist. m. Velma Hamrick, 14 Apr 1957, dec 1985, 1 s, 3 d. Education: BA, Pub Serv, Arts and Educn. Appointments: Asst Arts and Crafts Dir, Ft Leonord Wood, 1956-97; Arts and Crafts Br Dir, Asst Specl Servs Offr, Mus Dir, US Govt Civil Serv, Ft Sheridan, IL, 1957-59; Arts and Crafts Br Dir, US Govt Civil Serv, Ft Irwin, CA, 1959-60; Arts and Crafts Br Dir, Recreation Exec, US Govt Civil Serv, Ft Ord, CA, 1960-86; Des'd and opened 1st Ft Sheridan Army Mus and 1st Presidio of Monterey Mus. Honours include: Golden Acady Awd for Lifetime Achievement, 1991; 1st Place, Dept of the Army Progmng and Publicity Awd, five times; 19 Awds for Outstndng Performance. Memberships: Am Parks and Recreation Soc; Salinas Valley Fine Arts Assn; Monterey Peninsula Art Assn; Am Craftsman Assn; Glass Arts Soc. Address: 110 Ashland Avenue, Medford, OR 97504, USA.

PUDLOWSKI Zenon Jan. b. 23 May 1943, Pruchnik, Poland. Professor; Director. Education: M Elec Engrng, 1968, Acady of Mining and Metall, Cracow, Poland; PhD, 1979, Jagiellonian Univ, Cracow. Appointments: Lctr, Inst Technol, Univ Pedagogy, Cracow, 1969-76; Rschr, Inst Vocational Educ, Warsaw, 1976-79; Adj Prof, Inst of Pedagogy, Jagiellonian Univ, 1979-81; Snr Lctr, Dept Elec Engrng, Univ of Sydney, 1981-93; Assoc Prof, Assoc Dean Engrng Educ, 1994-98, Dir, UNESCO Intl Cntr for Engrng Educ (UICEE), Fac of Engrng, Monash Univ, Clayton, Australia, current; Estabd an Intl Fac of Engrng, Tech Univ of Lodz, Poland, 1992, Fndn Dean and Prof (in absentia); Hon Dean of Eng Engrng Fac, Donetsk State Tech Univ, Ukraine, 1995. Publications: Books, manuals, over 200 sci pprs in refereed jrnls and conf proceedings. Honours: Fell, Inst of Engrs, Aust;

AAEE Medal for Disting Contbn to Engrng Educ, Australasia, 1991; Order of the Egyptian Syndicate of Engrs for Contbns to the Dev of Engrng Educ on both Natl and Intl levels, 1994; HonD, Donetsk State Tech Univ, 1996; Hon DTech, Glasgow Caledonian Univ, Scotland, 1998. Memberships: Mbr editl advsry bds many intl jrnls; Fndr, Australasian Assn for Engrng Educ; UNESCO Intl Cttee on Engrng Educ; Ukrainian Acady Engrng Scis. Address: UICEE, Faculty of Engineering, Monash University, Clayton, Victoria 3168, Australia.

PUGNO Perry A, b. 28 Apr 1948, San Bernardino, CA, USA. Physician Educator; Executive. m. Terry G, 3 s. Education: BA; MD; MPH. Appointment: VP, Grad Med Educ and Med Affairs, Cath Hlthcare W. Publications: Sev articles in profl med jrnls. Honours: Meade Johnson Awd, 1977; Large Med Publn Awd, 1974; Nominee, CA Family Physn of the Yr, 1995, 1996, 1998. Memberships: Assn of F P Residency Dirs; Fndng Chair, Natl Inst for Dir Dev; Chair, Residency Review, ACGME/AMA. Hobbies: Bioethics; Medical informatics. Address: Mercy Healthcare, 7500 Hospital Drive, Sacramento, CA 95823, USA.

PUNG Adeline Shuk Ken, b. 16 Mar 1949. Librarian. m. Casey Leong, 31 Mar 1975, 1 d. Education: BA Hons, Asian Studies, Austl Natl Univ, Canberra, Aust, 1971; Postgrad Dip in Libnshp, Roy Melbourne Inst of Technol, Melbourne, Aust, 1972. Appointment: Dir, Sabah State Lib, 1973-; Pres, Kota Kinabalu Municipal Cncl, 1998-. Publications: Current Public Library Services in Sabah, 1977; Library Services in Sabah, 1977; Public Library Development in Sabah, 1981; Development of Libraries in Sabah, joint auth w Mr Wong Vui Yin, 1989; Challenges to Public Libraries in Creating a Reading Society: The Context of Sabah, joint auth w Flora Fung, 1996. Honours: Jaycee Awd, 1980; Ahli Darjah Kinabalu, 1982; Outstndng Exec VP Awd, Jaycees Intl, 1987; Ahli Setia Darjah Kinabalu, 1988; Outstndng Young Malaysian Awd, 198; Hennessy Cert of Hon, 1989; Most Active Working Mother Awd, 1989; Ahli Mangku Negara, 1989; Panglima Darjah Gemilang Kinabalu, 1993; Finalist, Woman Mngr of the Yr, 1994; Spirit of Hakka Women's Awd, 1995; Competent Toastmaster, 1995; Outstndng Woman Awd, 1995; Able Toastmaster Awd, Toastmasters Intl, 1997. Memberships: Bd of Dirs, Inst for Dev Studies, 1989; Chmn, Sabah Rhino and Wildlife Pub Relations Conservation Cttee, 1986-88; Chmn, Bd of Vis, Taman Seri Putri, 1987-89; Chmn, Sabah Women's Assn Rsch and Dev Bur, 1987-89; Chmnm Intan Building Cttee, Intan Jaycees, 1987-89; Chmn, Jaycees Malaysia Senate Assn, 1991-93; Chmn, Sabah Women Advsry Cncl, 1988-91; Chmn, Round Table on Mobile Libs of Intl Fedn of Lib Assn, 1988-91; Assoc, Austl Lib and Info Assn; Intl Fedn of Lib Assn; Lib Assn of Malaysia; Gen Legal Cnsl, Sabah Women's Assn, 1985-88; SOS Heart Fund Assn; Exec VP, Jaycees Intl, 1987; Pres, Kota Kinabalu Toastmasters Club, 1994-95; Area Gov, PAN-SEA Toastmasters Dist 51P, 1995-96; Div Gov, PAN-SEA Toastmasters Dist 51P, 1996-; Lt Gov Mktng, PAN-SEA Toastmasters Dist, 1997-98; Dist Gov PAN-SEA Toastmasters Dist 51, 1998-99. Hobbies: Reading; Travelling; Jaycees and Toastmasters. Address: No 1 Jalan Bandaran, Majlis Pernandaran Kota Kinabalu, 88675 Kota Kinabalu, Malaysia.

PUNSALMAAGIIN Ochirbat, b. 23 Jan 1942, Zavhan, Mongolia. Mining Engineer; Politician. m. Tsevelmaa, 15 Dec 1965, 2 d. Education: Mining Inst of USSR. Appointments include: Elect Dpty to Gt People's Hural 9th, 10th and 11th elects; Chmn, Presidium, 1990-; Pres, Repub and Cmndr-in-Chf of the Army Forces, 1990-; Pres, nationwide elect, 1993-97; Charity funds, ecological rsch, bus, 1997-. Publications: Black Gold, 1970; Art of Management; Development of Fuel-Energy Industry of Mongolia; Organisation and Management of Fuel and Energy Complex; Development of Democracy in Mongolia; Heavenly Hour; Historical Volte-Faces of the Development of Mongolian Government and Independent; Without the Rite to Mistakes: Years, Which are Equal to Decades; Ecology-Steady Development; Some Theoretical and Practical Ecology Questions in Mining Industry; Theoretical Basis of Formation and

Exploitation of Thechnogennical Deposits: Ecological and Legal Aspects. Honours: Altan Gadas of Mongolia, 1972; Mu Gung Hwa of Korea, 1991; Honoured Order of Labour, Hungary, 1988; Miner's Hon of Russia, Grs I, II, III, 1972-78; Liberty Awd from Am, 1995. Memberships: Hon Pres, Mongolian Mining Assn; Advsr, Mongolian Amn Assn. Hobbies: Hunting; Reading; Travelling. Address: Olympic Street 14, Tengeriin Tsag Centre, Ulaanbaatar, Mongolia.

PURBRICK Alister John, b. 25 May 1954. Wine Producer. m. Rosa Dalfarra, 30 Oct 1982, 1 s, 1 d. Education: Dip of Oenology, Roseworthy Agricl Coll, 1975. Appointments: Winemaker, Mildara Wines (Cooawarra and Mildara), 1976-77; Winemaker, 1978-, Prodn Mngr, 1978-79, Gen Mngr, 1979-80, Mngng Dir, 1980-, Tahbilk Pty Ltd; Phil McGrath Fine Wines Pty Ltd, 1986-; Mngng Dir, Eastcoast Cellers Pty Ltd, 1987-, AHN Pty Ltd, 1989-; Chmn, Statmer Vineyards Pty Ltd, 1992-, McPherson Wines Pty Ltd, 1993-. Memberships include: Pres, Goulburn Valley Viticultural Assn, 1982-83; Bd, Austl Winemakers Forum, 1984-; Select Cttee, Austl Wine and Brandy Corp, 1989-; Pres, Austl Winemakers Forum, 1989-92, 1994-96; Bd, Winemakers Fedn of Aust, 1990-; Bd, Goulburn Tourism Inc, 1990-97; Bd, Austl Wine Export Cncl, 1993-; VP, Winemakers Fedn of Aust, 1994-; Melbourne Cricket Club; Melbourne Club; Viticultural Wine Soc of Vic. Address: Chateau Tahbilk Wines, Tabilk, Vic 3608, Australia.

PURCELL Malcolm Roy, b. 10 Feb 1945, SA, Aust. Writer. m. 17 Jan 1970, 1 s, 1 d. Education: Undergrad Stud, 1968-71; BA, 2nd class hons, 1973; Postgrad Stud, 1973-75; MA, Drama, 1976; RSA/Cambridge CTEFLA. Appointments: Secnd Tchr, 1972; Freelance Writer, 1977-87; ESL Tchr, SA Coll of Engl, 1995-98. Creative Works: Stage plays: Just Throw Money, 1978; Happy as Larry, 1980; Lolly Day, 1982; The Old Macs, 1985; Diver, 1990. Radio plays: The Tall Stranger, 1979; Roger Marsh, 1981; Happy as Larry, 1983; Gordon, 1991; Short story: About Roger, 1995; Films: 12 documentaries, SA Film Corp, 1978-86. Membership: Austl Writers Guild Ltd. Hobbies: Playing Member, Senior Captain, 1982-86, Flagstaff Cricket Club; Reading; Running. Address: 35 Sunshine Avenue, Warradale, SA 5046, Australia.

PURCELL Stuart, b. 16 Feb 1944, Santa Monica, CA, USA. Financial Planner. Education: AA, Santa Monica City Coll, 1964; BS, CA Univ, Northridge, 1967; Grad, CPA Adv Personal Fin Plng Curriculum, San Fran, 1985. Appointments: Snr Acct, Pannell Kerr Forster, San Fran, 1970-73; Fin Cnslt, Purcell Fin Servs, San Fran, 1973-74, San Rafael, CA, 1980-81; Controller, Decimus Corp, San Fran, 1974-76, Grubb & Ellis Co, Oakland, CA, 1976-78, Marwais Steel Co, Richmond, CA, 1979-80; Owner, Fin Cnslr, Purcell Wlth Mngmt, San Rafael, 1981-; Guest Lectr, Golden Gate Univ, San Fran, 1985-. Publications: Sev articles in profl jrnls and newspprs. Honours: Named Eagle Scout, 1959; Outstndng Achievement Awd, United Way, 1984; Top Prodr, Unimarc, 1986; Best Fin Advsr, Marin County Independent Jrnl Newsppr, 1987. Memberships include: AICPA; Natl Speakers Assn; Intl Assn for Fin Planners; Intl Soc of Pre-Retd Planners. Hobbies: Travel; Auto Racing; Skiing; Gardening. Address: 45 Vineyard Drive, San Rafael, CA 94901-1228, USA.

PURNOMO Hari, b. 20 Nov 1943, Malang (E Java). Senior Lecturer. m. Dina Sri Rahayu, 12 June 1971, 2 s. Education: IR (equivalent BS) Animal Sci, Unibraw, Indonesia; PhD, Food Technol, MAppsci, Food Technol, UNSW, Aust. Appointments: Cnslt, Herbal Med Factory Air Mancur Solo, Meat Processing, Bernardi, Eloda Mitra, Sidoarjo. Publications: Translator: Ilmu Pangan (Food Sci); Auth: Water activity and its role in food preservation. Honours: 3rd Best Lectr Model Univ Brawijaya, 1987; 25 yrs meritorious serv to AAUCS, AUIDP, IDP, IAPUDP (Aust), 1994; 30 yrs meritorious serv as pub serv of Repub of Indonesia, 1997. Memberships: Assn of Austl Inst of Food Sci and Technol (AAIFST), 1980-; Indonesian Food Technol, 1987. Hobby: Music. Address: J/ Puncak Yamin 4, Malang, 65146, Jawa Timur, Indonesia.

PUROHIT D N, b. 29 Mar 1938. Professor. m. Sodra, 6 Feb 1953, 2 s. Education: BSc; MSc; PhD. Appointments: Asst Prof, 1966; Assoc Prof, 1968; Prof, 1983. Publications: 116 Rsch pprs incl: Spectrophotometric Determination Methods of Metals, Ed, 1993; 15 reviews; 20 PhD cands supervised. Honours include: Nom, Nobel Prize for Chem, 1988, 1994. Memberships: Mbr, Advsry/Ed Bd, Asian Jrnl of Chem, Oriental Jrnl of Chem; Acta Chimica Indica; Mbr Natle Acady of Scis, India; Fell, Indian Chem Soc. Hobbies: Chess; Astrology; Geobiomancy. Address: M L Sukhadia University, Udaipur 313001, India.

PUROHIT Umraomal, b. 1 Mar 1928, Jodhpur, Rajasthan, India. Trade Unionist. m. Mohini, 1 May 1945, 2 s, 2 d. Education: Intermediate and Indl Engrng. Hobbies: Industrial Relations; Politics; Social Activities.

PURVES Daphne Helen, b. 8 Nov 1908, Dunedin, NZ. m. Herbert Dudley Purves, 16 Dec 1939, 1 s, 2 d. Education: MA, 1st class hons, Engl and French, Univ NZ, 1931. Appointments: Secnd Sch Tchr, 1931-63; Lectr, 1963-66, Snr Lectr, 1967-73, Dunedin Tchrs Coll. Publications: Auth of var publns in Educl Jrnls, Newspprs; Brdcster on Radio and TV. Honour: DBE, 1979. Memberships Alliance Francaise (Cttee Mbr and VP); Otago Inst of Educl Rsch; UN Assn; Zonta Intl; Post-Prim Tchrs Assn (Pres DTC Br); Pres, Friends of Olveston; Theomin Gallery Mngmt Cttee, NZ Natl Cmmn for UNESCO, 1964-68; Exec, NZ Natl Cmmn for Intl Yr of the Child; Telethon Trust; Intl Fedn of Univ Women (VP and Convenor of IFUW Cttee, Pres, 1977-80); Pres, Fedn of Univ Women natl and locally. Hobbies: Reading; Bridge; Travel; Croquet. Address: 12 Grendon Court, 36 Drivers Road, Dunedin, New Zealand.

PURY Guillaume George de, b. 5 May 1933, Melbourne, Aust. Grazier; Biochemist; Wine grower. m. Katherine Frances Neal, 8 Jan 1958, 1 s, 2 d. Education: BAgric Sci (Melb), 1955; PhD (Melb), 1965. Appointments: Grazier, at Yeringberg, Coldstream, Vic, 1956-; Ed, Jrnl Austl Inst Agric Sci, 1956-57; Rsch Assoc, Enzyme Inst, Univ of Wisconsin, 1967-68; Rsch Fell (pt-time), Dept of Biochem, Univ of Melbourne, 1969-70; Cnclr, Shire of Lillydale, 1970-94; Shire Pres, Shire of Lillydale, 1975, 1979, 1992; Upper Yarra and Dandenong Ranges Planning Authority, 1977-95; Viticulturist and Wine Maker, Yeringberg Wines, 1969-; Dir and Chf Exec, Yeringberg Pty Ltd, 1972-; Chmn, Lilydale Mus Trust, 1989-. Publications: PhD Thesis, Univ of Melbourne, 1965; Var pprs on biochem of essential fatty acids and phospholids in sci jrnls, 1963-72; Biography of Frederic-Guillame de Pury, Australian Dictionary of Biography Vol 4, 1972; The History of the Pury in Australia, 1970; Chronique de la Caisse de Famille Pury, Neuchatel, Switzerland; Regional Planning at the Local Level, Symposium of Regional Planning, Austl Inst of Agric Sci, 1976; Wine Growing in Australia, 1977. Honour: Hon Freeman of Shire of Lillydale, 1994. Memberships: Austl Inst of Agric Sci; Austl Soc of Viticulture and Oenology; Yarra Valley Wine Growers Assn; Grasslands Soc of Vic; Austl Soc of Animal Prodn; Viticultural Soc of Vic; Wine and Food Soc of Vic; Atheneum Club, Melbourne; Life Mbr: Lilydale Agricl and Horticultural Soc; Lilydale Histl Soc. Hobbies: Travelling; Camping; Squash; Wine; Food; Local history. Address: Yeringberg, Coldstream, Vic 3770, Australia.

PUTTANARASAIAH Sri, b. 8 Apr 1952, Maragondana Guni. Teacher. 1 s, 1 d. Education: TCH, Trng, Siddartha Trng Coll Gollahally, Tumkur Dist, 1971; BA, Bangalore Univ, 1978; BEd, 1980; MA. Appointments: Tchr, Prema HPS, 1971-83; Asst Master, Seshadripurama Boys hs, 1983-88; HdMaster, Ambedkar mem High Sch, 1988-1994; Hd Master, Brahmo Samaj Appau Pillai Girls High Sch, 1994-. Creative Works: Many educl articles; Chinthana. Honours: Best Actor Awd; Best Drama Dir Awd; Many Felicitations; Best Tchr Awd; Intl Talented Tchr Awd. Memberships include: Primary Tchrs Assn; Nagarabhavi Site Owners Welfare Assn; Hd Master's and Prin Assn. Hobbies: Singing drama songs; Monoacting. Address: No 26 1st Main Road, Kamakshipalaya 11 Stage, Meenakshinagar Bangalore 560079, India.

PYNE Christopher Maurice, b. 13 Aug 1967. Member of Parliament. m. Carolyn Jane Twelftree, 23 July 1994. Education: BLaw, Adelaide; Grad Dip of Legal Prac, Univ of SA; LLB; GDLP. Appointments: Mbr for Sturt, 1993-; Parly Sec for Socl Security, Opposition, 1994-96; Mbr, Liberal Party Fed Exec, 1990-91; Mbr, Liberal Party SA Exec, 1988-92; Mbr, Fed Cncl, 1988-92; Chmn Govt Cttee on Att-Gen, Justice and Customs, 1998-; Chmn, House of Reps Stndng Cttee on Procedure, 1998-. Publications: Articles publs in newspapers and jrnls. Memberships: Roy Adelaide Golf Club; SA Cricket Assn; Adelaide Cty Soccer Club; UNICEF; Amnesty; C'wlth Parly Assn; Intl Parly Union; Aust-Israel Chmbr of Com; Chmn, Aust/Israel Parly Grp, 1996-; Many local clubs. Listed in: Who's Who in Australia. Hobbies: Theatre; Films; Sport (Golf, Tennis); Gardening; Writing. Address: 38 The Parade, Norwood, SA 5067, Australia.

Q

QABOOS Bin Said, b. 18 Nov 1940, Salalah. Omani Ruler. m. 1976. Education: Pvte, England, RMA Sandhurst. Appointments: Sultan of Oman, 1970-; PM, Min of Fgn Affairs, Def & Fin. Honour: KCMG. Hobbies: Reading; Horse Riding; Music. Address: Diwan of the Royal Court, PO Box 632, Muscat, Sultanate of Oman.

QASIMI Sultan bin Mohammed al- (H H Sheikh), b. 1 July 1939. Education: Exeter Univ. Appointments: Min of Educ, 1972; Ruler of Sharjah, 1972-. Honours: Fell, Doram Univ; Doct honoris causa, Khartoum Univ, Faisalabad Univ, Pakistan; Disting Personality Prize, Exeter Univ, 1993. Address: Ruler's Palace, Sharjah, United Arab Emirates.

QASSIMI Sheikh Saqr bin Muhammad al, b. 1920. Ruler of Ras Al-Khaimah. Appointments: Ruler of Emirate of Ras Al-Khaimah, 1948-; Chair, Rulers Cncl of Trucial States, 1971; Mbr, Supreme Cncl of United Arab Emirates, 1972-. Address: The Rulers Palace, Ras Al-Khaimah, United Arab Emirates.

QI Guan-Rong, b. 3 Oct 1940, Jiangsu, China. Professor. m. Wu Gui Fang, 26 Nov 1958, 2 s, 1 d. Education: BSc, Nanking Univ. Appointments: Vice Dir, Shanxi Obs, 1987-89; Dir, Shaanxi Obs, 1989-96; VP, Chinese Astronomy Soc, 1989-. Publications: Time Measurement; Handbook of Astronomy and Physics; The Time; The Radio Navigation Signals. Honours: Sci Prize, 1987; 1st Prize Natl Sci Rsch, 1988. Hobbies: Literature; Bridge. Address: PO Box 18, Lintong, Xian 710600, China.

QI Haodong, b. 2 Nov 1960, Laizhou, Shandong, China. Agriculture Economics; Accounting. m. Wang Lejin, 18 June 1987, 1 s. Education: Econs Dr, 1997. Appointments: Dean, Dept of Acctng of Econs & Trade, Coll of Shandong Agricl Univ, Dpty Dir, Rural Econs Rsch Inst, 1993-. Publications: Agricultural Policy, 1990; Rural Modernization, 1994; Accounting Principles, 1995; Financial Accounting, 1996. Honours: Shandong Prov Univ and Coll Ex Young Tchr Awd, 1992; Shandong Prov Socl Sci Ex Awd, 1996, 1997, 1998. Memberships: China Agricl Acctng Assn; China Agricl Econs Assn, 1995-. Hobby: Basketball. Address: Economics and Trade College of Shandong Agricultural University, Taian, Shandong, China.

QI Zhouyue, b. Nov 1945, Shaanxi, China. Animal Medicine. m. Zhang Fengxian, Oct 1968, 1 s, 1 d. Education: MSc Northwest Agricultural Univ. Appointments: Dpty-Dir, Shaanxi Animal and Vet Medl Inst; Div Chf of Sci Rsch Mngmt Div, Shaanxi Acady of Agric Scis (SAAS); Gen Sec, VP, SAAS. Publications: Participated in writer and compiling 3 acad books; 50 pprs in acad jrnls and periodicals in China. Honours: 6 rewards above prov and min level from Shaanxi Prov, Chinese Min of Agric, 1983-97; Awd, Chinese Sci Congress, 1998. Memberships: Chmn, Shaanxi Assn of Animal Sci and Vet Med, 1997-; Standing Chmn, Shaanxi Assn of Animal Sci and Vet Med; Chinese Assn of Animal and Vet Med. Hobby: Calligraphy. Address: Shaanxi Academy of Agricultural Sciences, Yangting, Shaanxi, China.

QIAN Cheng-De, b. 5 Dec 1942, Beijing, China. Professor of Physics. m. Lu Zhen-Huan, 8 Feb 1975, 1 s. Education: East China Normal Univ, Shanghai, 1961-67; Masters, Suzhou Univ, 1981. Appointments: Lectr, 1981-90, Assoc Prof, 1990-98, Shanghai Jiao Tong Univ. Publications: Auth, Advanced Quantum Mechanics, 1998; Contbr articles to profl jrnls. Honours: Ex Tchr, Shanghai Jiao Tong Univ, 1991, 1994. Memberships: Chinese Nuc Phys Soc; Chinese High Energy Phys Soc; Chinese Phys Soc; BES Collaboration, 1994-. Hobby: Sport. Address: Dept Applied Physics, Shanghai Jiao Tong University, 1954 Hua Shan Rd, 200030 Shanghai, China.

QIAN Jia Pu, b. 8 Apr 1937, Jiangsu, China. Educator; Scientific Research. m. Sun Kun Zhe, 5 Sept 1962, 1 s, 1 d. Education: BSc, Tsinghua Univ, Beijing, China, 1960; DSc, Harbing Univ of Technol, China, 1964. Appointments: Lectr, Harbing Univ of Technol, China, 1964-67; Prog Hd, 1967-85, Assoc Prof, 1985-90, Div Hd, 1985-, Prof, 1990-, Southwestern Inst of Phys, Leshan, China; Dir, China Natl Prog, Fusion Technol and Materials, China, 1990-. Publication: Physical Experiments and Analysis of Nuclear Reactors, in Chinese, 1965. Honours: Prize, State Cttee of Sci and Technol, 1990; Prize, Sci and Technol Prog, China Natl Nuclr Co, 1988, 1991, 1992, 1993, 1994, 1998; Spec Prize, Outstndng Scis, State Cncl of China, 1995. Hobbies: Taking photographs; Literature; Gardening; Tour; Chinese Drawing; Handwriting Appreciation. Address: Southwestern Institute of Physics, PO Box 432, Chengdu, 610041, Sichuan, China.

QIAN Jian, b. 20 Nov 1939, Wuxi, Qiangsu, China. Physicist; Educator. m. Jun Wei Qiu, Oct 1971, 2 s. Education: BS, Beijing Univ, 1963; MSME, CCNY of USA, 1981; MSEE, CCNY of USA, 1982; PhD, CUNY of USA, 1984. Appointments: Rschr, Inst Mechs, Academia Sinica, China, 1963-79; PhD Prog and Adj Lectr, CUNY, USA, 1979-84; Rschr, Chmn, Theort Dept, Beijing Inst Environ Features, 1985-88; Prof, Rschr, Grad Sch Academia Sinica, Beijing, 1988-. Publications: Num inclng 30 in Engl, inclng: Scaling exponents of second-order structure function of turbulence, 1998; Normal and Anomalous Scaling of Turbulence, 1998. Hobbies: Reading; Chinese chess; Music. Address: Department of Physics, Graduate School of Academia Sinica, PO Box 3908, Beijing 100039, China.

QIAN Qichen, b. Jan 1928, Tiading, Shanghai, China. Diplomat; State Official. m. Zhou Hanqiong, 1 s, 1 d. Education: Shanghai Datung Mid Sch; USSR. Appointments: Joined CCP, 1942; 2nd Sec, Emb USSR, 1955-62, Cnslr, 1972-74; Amb to Guinea & Guinea Bissau, 1974-76; Dir, Info Dept, Min of Fgn Affairs, 1977-82; Vice Min, Fgn Affairs, 1982-88, Min, 1988-98, Vice Premier, 1991-98; Alt Mbr, 12th CCP Ctrl Cttee, 1982, Mbr, 1985, Mbr, 13th Ctrl Cttee, 1987-92, 14th Ctrl Cttee, 1992, Dpty Hd, Ctrl Fgn Affairs Ldng Grp; Mbr, Politburo CCP, 1992-; Mbr, 15th CCP Ctrl Cttee, 1997-; Ldr, Specl Admin Region Preparatory Cttee, 1993-, Chair, 1995-; Mbr, 8th NPC, 1993-; Vice Premier of State Cncl, 1993-; Min of Fgn Affairs, 1993-; Mbr, Cttee to Form Post 1997 Governorship of Hong Kong. Address: Ministry of Foreign Affairs, 225 Chaonei Street, Dongsi, Beijing, China.

QIAN Renyuan, b. 19 Sept 1917, Changshu, Jiangsu, China. Professor. m. (1) Miaozhen Hu, Oct 1951, div 1956, (2) Qicong Ying, 30 Apr 1961, div 1994, 1 d, (3) Yansheng Yu, 18 Nov 1996. Education: BS, Zhejiang Univ, 1939; Postgrad studies, Univ of WI, Madison, USA, 1944-47. Appointments: Assoc Prof, Zhejiang Univ, 1949-51; Prof, Inst of Phys Chem, 1951-53; Prof, Inst of Organic Chem, 1953-56, Prof, 1956-, Dir, 1981-85, Inst of Chem, Academia Sinica. Publications: Contbr of over 260 pprs. Honours: Phi Lambda Upsilon; Sigma Xi; Sci Premium, 3rd Class, Academia Sinica, 1956; Sci Awd, Natl Sci Congress, 1978; State Invention Awd, 3rd Class State Commn of Sci and Technol, 1980; SINOPEC Sci & Technol, Prog Awd, 1st Class, 1987; State Nat Sci Awd, 2nd Class, 1988, 1995; State Sci and Technol, Prog Awd, 1st Class, 1989; Nat Sci Awd, Academia Sinica, 1st Class, 1989, 1993, 1998, 2nd Class, 1992; Qiushi Awd for Disting Scientists, 1994; Intl Awd, Soc of Polymer Sci, Japan, 1995. Memberships: Div of Chem, Academia Sinica, 1981-; Chinese Chem Soc, Pres, 1982-86. Hobby: Classical music appreciation. Address: Institute of Chemistry, Academia Sinica, Zhong Guan Cun, Beijing, China.

QIAN Yao Nian, b. 30 Nov 1930, Jiangsu, China. Textile Researcher. m. Shi Xiu-Zhi, 1 May 1954, 1 s, 2 d. Education: Grad, China Textile Univ, 1952. Appointment: Dir, Textile Technol and Econs Rsch Dept, China Textile Acady, 1991 (retired). Publications: China's Textile Industry in Year 2000, 1987; Statistical Handbook on Textile Technology and Economy, 1st ed, 1987, 2nd ed, 1991. Honours: Sci and Tech Prog Prize, 1989; Allowance from China State Cncl, 1992. Memberships: Dpty Dir, Textile Tech and Econs Commn; China Textile Engrng Assn, 1988-97. Address: BaliZuang 311 Blg 4-303, Chao Yang District, Beijing, China.

QIAN Yu, b. 2 Oct 1957, Jiangsu, China. Educator; Scientist. m. Yang Jilin, 10 Dec 1984, 1 d. Education: PhD, Chem Engrng, Tsinghua Univ, Beijing, 1987. Appointments: Prof, Chem Engrng, S China Univ of Tech; Dir, Sch of Grad Studies, S China Univ of Technol. Publications: Advances in Chemical Engineering and Environmental Engineering, 1997. Honour: Outstndng Young Prof Awd, State Educ Commn, China, 1996. Membership: Fell, Chinese Soc of Computers Application in Chem Engrng (CSCACE). Hobbies: Swimming; Bridge; Biking. Address: Chemical Engineering Research Center, South China University of Technology, Guangzhou 510641, China.

QIAN Zong Yu, b. 23 Oct 1925, Jiangsu, China. Mechanical Engineer. m. He Cheng Ying, 2 May 1954, 1 s, 2 d. Education: Bach Deg, Mech Engrng, Shanghai Inst of Technol. Appointments: Techn, Engr, Tech Dept Ldr, Hd of Designing Rm, Snr Engr in Textile Bur. Publications: Enlarge Milling Machine Stroke by Pinion Mechanism; Cutting Slots 2-Side, Square, Hexagon on Common Lathe by Hypo-Cyloidal Theory; Change Rotary Motion to to-and-fro Motion With Variable Speed (Accelerating in the Middle and Retarding at Both Terminals). Honours: Tech Innovation Awds, 1953, 1954, 1955, 1956. Memberships: Shanghai Textile Engrng Assn; Shanghai Mech Engrng Assn. Hobby: Coin Collecting. Address: Room 201, No 54 Xin Zhuang, Nan Ma, Ping Yang 3 Cun, Shanghai 201102, China.

QIN Qing Hua, b. 22 Mar 1958, Guangxi, China. Physical Scientist. m. Yi Xiao, 3 Feb 1989, 1 d. Education: PhD, Huazhong Univ of Sci and Technol, China, 1990. Appointments: Assoc Lectr, 1984-87, Lectr, 1987-94; DAAD/KC Wong Postdoc Fell, Univ of Stuttgart, Germany, 1994; Postdoc Fell, Tsinghua Univ, China, 1995-96; Queen Elizabeth II Fell, Univ of Sydney, 1997-. Publications include: Book: Qin Qinghua and Yiu-Wing Mai, 1999; Articles: Nonlinear Analysis of Thick Plates by HT FE Approach, 1996; Coupled Torsional-Flexural Vibration of Shafts in Mechanical Engineering--II: FE-TM Impedance Coupling Method, 1996; Application of Hybrid-Trefftz Element Approach to Transient Heat Conduction Analysis, 1996. Honours: DAAD/KC Wong Postdoc Fellowship, 1994; Postdoc Fellowship, 1995; Visng Schlr, Univ of Sydney, Aust, 1996; Queen Elizabeth II Fell, 1997; J G Russell Awd, 1998. Membership: Chinese Mechs Soc, 1992-. Hobbies: Reading novels; Walking; Playing chess; Music. Address: University Sydney, Department Mechanical Engineering, Sydney, NSW 2006, Australia.

QIN Wen-Han, b. 23 Feb 1926, Wuxi, Jiangsu, China. Thoracic Surgeon. m. Yun-Hua Lu, 31 May 1953, 1 s, 1 d. Education: BS, MD, Sch of Med, St John's Univ. Appointments: Chf Surg, Gen Hosp of Air Force, 1980; Cnslt, Thoracic Surg Cntr of Air Force, PLA, 1990. Publications include: The Comparison of Parenteral and Enteral Nutritional Support after Resection of Oesophageal and Gastric Cardiac Cancer, 1992; Computer Assisted Expert System in the Diagnosis of Pulmonary Solitary Nodule, 1992; The Monitoring of Immune Globulin Complement and Prealbumin in the Nutritional Support of Oesophageal and Gastric Cardiac Cancer Perioperatively, 1995; Chf Ed: Contemporary Throracic Surgery, 1997; Handbook of Chest Surgery, 1998; Chf Ed, Handbook of Physician's Prescription, 1998; Vice Chf Ed, The Sketch of Medical Science, 1998. Honours: Awds of Sci and tech, 3rd Awd, 2 x; 4th Awd, 5 x. Memberships: Chinese Soc of Thoracic and Cardiovascular Surg, Chinese Medl Assn. Hobbies: Chinese literature; Chinese chess. Address: Department of Thoracic Surgery, General Hospital of Air Force, 30 Fucheng Road, Beijing 100036, China.

QIN Xiao-Rong, b. 19 Aug 1960, Suzhou, China. m. D T Jiang, 5 June 1986, 1 d. Education: PhD, Condensed Matter Phys, Simon Fraser Univ, 1992; MSc, Electrons and Laser Phys, Tsinghua Univ; BS, Electrons and Laser Phys, Tsinghua Univ, Beijing, China. Appointments: Rsch Asst, Dept of Phys, Simon Fraser Univ, Burnaby, BC, Can, 1986-92; NSERC Postdoct Fell, Univ of West Ont, 1993-95; Rsch Assoc, Univ WI, 1995-. Publications: (co-auth) Adatom Pairing Structures for Ge on Si (100); The Initial Stage of Island Formation, 1997. Honours: Postdoct Fell, Nat Sci and Engrng Rsch Cncl of Can (NSERC), 1993-95. Memberships: Amn Phys Soc, 1989-; Amn Vacuum Soc, 1997-. Hobbies: Drawing; Swimming; Music. Address: Department of Materials and Engineering, 1500 Engineering Drive, University of Wisconsin, Madison WI 53705, USA.

QIN Yi, b. 2 Feb 1922, Shanghai, China. Film Actress. Appointments: Mbr, 6th CPPCC, 1983-87, 7th, 1987-92, 8th, 1993-. Creative Works: Films: Remote Love; Song of Youth; Fog is no Fog, 1993. Honour: Outstndng Film Artist Prize, 1992. Address: Shanghai Film Studio, 595 Caoxi North Road, Shanghai 200030, China.

QIN Yuyuan, b. 4 May 1924, Yangchow, China. Professor of Mathematics. m. 31 Dec 1960, 2 d. Education: Grad, Dept of Maths, Utopia Univ, Shanghai, China, 1950. Appointments: Lectr, 1953-78, Assoc Prof, 1978-82, Prof, 1982-, Vice Dean, 1982-84, Hd of Dept of Mngmt Engrng, 1984-87, Vice Chmn of Acad Cttee, 1984-94, Wuhan Iron and Steel Univ. Publications: 5 books on maths transl from German into Chinese; Book On Algebraic Equations, in Chinese, 1984; Jar-Metric Principle (A Unified Approach to Multistage Decision Problems of Finite Type), book (in Chinese), 1991; Optimum Path Problems in Networks, 1992; Over 60 articles in dynamic programming and graph theory. Honours: 3rd Prize, Sci and Technol Progress, Natl Educ Cttee, 1993; Spec Subsidy, State Cncl, 1993; 2nd Prize, Sci and Technol, Bur of Surveying and Mapping, 1997. Memberships: Maths Assn of China; Hon Mbr, Co-ord, Ctrl S China Prog, Ops Rsch Assn of China; Chmn, Cttee of Math Progng, Maths of Hubei Prov; Hon Mbr, Rsch Assn of China, 1995. Hobbies: Classical music; Stamp collecting. Address: Department of Management Engineering, Wuhan University of Science and Technology (Wuhan Iron and Steel University), Wuhan, Hebei 430081, China.

QIN Zeng-fu, b. 16 Dec 1937, Shanghai, China. Mathematician. m. Zhu Li-ping, 7 May 1984, 1 d. Education: Grad, Fudan Univ, Maths Dept, 1960. Appointments: Maths Prof, 1988-; Dir, Fudan Univ Lib, 1992-; Dpty Dir, Cttee of Dev and rsch, Fudan Univ, 1997-. Publications: (co-auth) Mathematical Analysis, Vols, I, II, III, 1992; (co-auth), Lectures on Higher Mathematics, 1996. Membership: Reviewer, Math Reviews of Amn Math Soc, 1983-. Hobby: Philosophy. Address: Jiao-Tong Xi Road, Lane 48, No 2, Room 2902, Shanghai, 200433, China.

QIU Feng Chang, b. 27 June 1931, Tienjin, China. Teacher. m. Chen Ye, 13 Aug 1956, 1 d. Education: Grad, Yenching Univ, 1952. Appointments: VP, NUST; Dean, Tchng Section, NUST; Chmn, Mech Engrng Dept, NUST. Publications: Machine Design, 1962; Transfer Matrix Method of Multibody System Dynamics, 1992; Launch Dynamics of Multibody System, 1995. Memberships: Standing Cncl, China Ordnance Soc, 1988-92; Edl Bd, Acta Armamentarii, 1988-97. Hobbies: Classical Music; Stamp Collecting. Address: No 6# Building 501, Nanjing University of Science and Technology, Nanjing 210014, China.

QIU Jing Hui, b. 27 May 1947, Nanjing, China. Professor of Mathematics. m. Mei Ling Qi, 10 Jan 1978, 1 s. Education: Grad, Dept of Maths, Suzhou Univ. Appointments: Engaged in Agricl, 1968-72; Tchr, Dept of Maths, Suzhou Univ, 1974-. Publications: Auth of num rsch pprs; Reviewer for Math Reviews (USA), 1988-. Honours: 3 First Prizes, Ex Sci Treatises, 1992; 1st Prize, Suzhou Assn for Sci and Technol, 1994; Top Prize and 2 First Prizes, People's Govt of Suzhou, 1997; Ex Scientific

and Technological Specialist, Jiangsu Assn for Sci and Technol, 1998. Address: Department of Mathematics, Suzhou University, Suzhou, Jiangsu, China.

QIU Yi-Jun, b. 8 Nov 1936, Shanghai, China. Chief Engineer. m. Wang Hui-Fang, 7 Apr 1957, 1 s, 1 d. Education: Grad, Zhejiang Univ, 1955. Appointments: Technol, Magnetic Material and Device, N China Radio Appliances Combine Factory, Beijing, 1955-70; Dir, Chf Engr, Jinshan Radio Elements Factory, Baoji, Shaanxi, 1970-85; Chf Engr, Changzhou Electron Indl Bur, 1985-. Publications: The Thermal Treatment Technology for Alnico Alloy, 1963; The Technology of Permanent Magnet Alloy, 1975. Honour: Sci Achmnt Awd, 1982. Memberships: China Magnetic Material and Device Ind Assn; IEEE; Chinese Electron Inst. Address: 272 Qingtan Road, Changzhou, Jiangsu, China.

QU Hailin, b. 8 Nov 1951, Shanghai, China. Educator. m. Fang Weifen, 22 Nov 1982, 1 s. Education: AA, Shanghai Inst of tour, 1981; 1989; BSc, N AZ Univ, 1987; MSc, 1989; PhD, Purdue Univ, 1992. Appointments: Shanghai Inst of Tour, 1981-86; Hong Kong Polytechnic Univ, 1992-96; San Fran State Univ, 1996-99; Full Prof, OK State Univ, 1999-. Publications: Many Pprs publd in refereed jrnls; Book Chapts. Honours: Hon Lectr, OK State Univ, Hong Kong Univ; Hon Guest Prof, Beijing Inst of tour; Hon Guest Prof, China tour mngmnt Inst; Awd, Hon Citizenship. Memberships: Cncl on Hotel, Restaurant and Instl Educs; Shanghai tour Assn; China Tourism Assns; China Hotel Assns. Hobbies: Reading; Classical music; Teaching. Address: 408 Richmond Drive #1, Millbrae, CA 94030, USA.

QU Liangsheng, . b. 28 Jan 1931, China. Professor; Advisor of Doctorate Students. m. 30 Sept 1956, 1 s. Education: Grad, Mech Engrng Dept, Jiaotong Univ, Shanghai, 1952; Postgrad, Harbin Univ of Technol, 1955. Appointments: Asst, Jiaotong Univ, Shanghai, 1955-56; Lectr, 1956-63, 1965-78, Assoc Prof, Dean, Mech Engrng Dept, Chmn, Mech Engrng Rsch Inst, 1979-87, Prof, 1985-, Xian Jiaotong Univ; Rsch Engr, Shanghai Machine Tool Works, 1964. Publications: Mechanical Faults Diagnostics, 1986; Contbr of 140 profl pprs, 1980-96. Honours: Awd, Sci and Technol Prog, State Cmmn of Educ, 1986; Awd, Sci and Technol Prog, Min of Mech Ind, 1986; Awd, Sci and Technol Prog, Min of Electron Ind, 1997; Ctfs of Merit for Textbooks of Ex and Outstndng Postgrad Advsrs, granted by the Univ, 1984; Awd of Sci and Technol Progress, Min of Chem Ind, 1996; Natl Awd, Sci and Technol, 1998. Memberships: Snr Mbr, Soc of Mech Engrs; Co-Chmn, Soc of Dynamic Signal Processing. Hobby: Music. Address: Research Institute of Diagnostics and Cybernetics, Xian Jiaotong University, Xian 710049, China.

QUAN Shuren, b. 1930, Xinmin, Liaoning, China. Party & Government Official. Appointments: Joined CCP, 1949; Mayor of Fushun, 1980-81; Sec, CCP Cttee, Fushun City, 1981-82; Gov of Liaoning, 1983-86; Sec, 7th CCP Prov Cttee, Liaoning, 1983-85, Dpty Sec, 1985-86, Sec, 1986-93; Alt Mbr, 12th CCP Ctrl Cttee, 1985-87, Mbr, 13th Ctrl Cttee, 1987-92, Mbr, 14th Ctrl Cttee, 1992-; Dpty to 6th NPC to 8th NPC, Liaoning Prov; Chair, Liaoning Prov 8th Peoples Congress Standing Cttee, 1993-. Address: Liaoning Provincial Committee, Shenyang, Liaoning, China.

QUE HEE Shane Stephen, b. 11 Oct 1946, Sydney, Aust. Educator; Researcher. Education: BS, 1968, MSc, 1971, Univ Qld, Aust; PhD, Univ Saskatchewan, Can, 1976; Post-doct, Chem Dept, McMaster Univ, 1976-78. Appointments: Asst Prof, 1978-84, Assoc Prof, 1984-89, Univ Cincinnati; Assoc Prof, 1989-94, Prof, 1994-, Univ CA, LA. Publications: Books: The Phenoxyalkanoic Herbicides, 1981; Biological Monitoring: An Introduction, 1993; Analysis of Hazardous Wastes, 1999. Honours: Fell, Amn Inst of Chemists, 1986; Cert Awd, Recog Noteworthy Contbn US EPA, 1981; Mbr, Toxnet (Hazardous Substances Data Bank) Peer Review Cttee, 1985-89; Fell, Amn Ind Hyg Assn, 1999. Memberships: Amn Chem Soc; Bio Monitoring Cttee, Amn Ind Hygiene Assn; Amn Conf Gov Ind Hygienists. Hobbies: Tennis;

Civil rights. Address: Department of Environmental Health Sciences and Center for Occupational and Environmental Health, UCLA School of Public Health, 10833 Le Conte Avenue, Los Angeles, CA 90095-1772, USA.

QUILLIAM (James) Peter (Hon Sir), b. 23 Mar 1920, New Plymouth, NZ. Retired High Court Judge; Chief Justice; Former Police Complaints Authority. m. Ellison Jean Gill, 2 June 1945, 2 s, 1 d. Education: LLB, 1944. Appointments: Lt, 2nd NZ Expeditionary Force, 1943-44; Bar & Sol, 1945-69; Crown Prosecutor, Taranaki Prov, 1955-69; Judge of High Crt of NZ, 1969-88; Snr Puisne Judge, 1987-88; Police Complaints Authy, 1989-92; Fiji Crt of Appeal, 1992-95; Judge, High Crt of Cook Is, 1988-; Chf Jus of Cook Is, 1995-. Honour: KB, 1987. Membership: Wellington Dist Law Soc. Hobbies: Golf; Gardening; Reading. Address: 9 Puketiro Avenue, Northland, Wellington 5, New Zealand.

QUINN Brian Francis William, b. 19 Jan 1934, Melbourne, Vic, Aust. Clinical Pathologist. m. Anne Adele Lakeland, 14 July 1962, 3 d. Education: MB BS, 1959, DCP, 1964, Univ of Sydney; FRCPA, 1966; MIAC, 1993. Appointments: Res Medl Offr, St Vincent's Hosp, Sydney, 1959-60; Registrar, 1961-64, Dir, 1969-83, Visng Pathologist, 1983-, Mater Hosp, N Sydney; Staff Pathologist, St George Hosp, Sydney, 1964-67; RAAF Cnslt Pathologist, Visng Pathologist, No 3 RAAF Hosp, Richmond, NSW; Retd Grp Capt, RAAF Reserve, 1967-89; Visng Pt-time Lectr, Path, Univ of Sydney, 1969-84; Clin Pathologist in Priv Prac, 1983-. Publications: In Medical Journal of Aust; Listeria Monocytogenes in Neonate, 1964; Argentaffin Carcinoma in Ovary, 1965; Homozygous α-Thalassaemia in Aust, 1974; Immune Red Cell Aplasia in Proceedings of the Haematology of Australia, 1978; RFD Reserve Forces Decoration, 1989. Memberships: Austl Medl Assn; Intl Acady of Path; Haematology Soc of Aust; Intl Soc of Haematology; Fell, Roy Coll of Pathologists, Australasia; Aust Soc of Cytology; Intl Acady Cytology; Intl Soc of Blood Transfusions; Austl Soc of Blood Transfusion. Hobbies: Music; Skiing. Address: 9 Noonbinna Crescent, Northbridge, NSW 2063, Australia.

QURAISHI Abdul Aziz Bin Said al, b. 1930, Hail, Saudi Arabia. Government Official. m. Amal Aziz al-Turki, 1965, 1 s, 2 d. Education: Univ S CA, USA. Appointments: Gen Mngr, State Railways, 1961-68; Pres, Gen Personnel Bur, 1968-74; Min of State, 1971-74; Gov, Saudi Arabian Monetary Agcy, 1974-83; Fmr Gov, Saudi Arabia, IMF, Arab Monetary Fund; Fmr Alt Gov for Saudi Arabia, Islamic Devel Bank; Fmr Mbr, Bd of Dirs, Supreme Cncl for Petroleum & Mineral Affairs, Gen Petroleum & Mineral Org, Pub Investment Fund, Pension Fund; Mngng Dir, Ali Zaid Al-Quraishi & Bros, Riyadh, 1983-; Chair, Natl Saudi Shipping Co, Riyadh, 1983; Vice Chair, Saudi Intl Bank, London, 1983-; Intl Advsry Bd, Security Pacific Natl Bank of Los Angeles, 1983-. Honours: King Abdul Aziz Medal (2nd class); Order of Brilliant Star w Grand Cordon, Taiwan; Order of Dipl Merit; Gwan Ghwa Medal, Korea; King Leopold Medal (Cmdr class), Belgium; Emperor of Japan Awd; Order of Sacred Treas (1st class), 1980. Address: Malaz, Riyadh, Saudi Arabia.

QURESHEY Taha Fazal, b. 4 Feb 1955, Dhahran, Saudi Arabia. Director. m. S Islam, 8 Aug 1985, 1 s, 2 d. Education: BA, 1984; Dip, Univ Leyden, Hague, 1985. Appointments: Material Inspector, Taif, Saudi Arabia, 1974-75; Quality Control Inspector K Intergreen/US Corps of Engrs, Jubail, Saudi Arabia, 1975-77; Supvsr, Ground handling Worldair, Jeddah, Saudi Arabia, 1977-78; Snr Sales and Coord-in-Charge, KLM, Roy Dutch Airlines, Jeddah, 1978-91; Dir, Sales and Mktng, K F Qureshey Trading Corp, Jeddah, 1991-; Cnslt, NG Hosp, Umalsalam Saudi Arabia, 1993-94. Honour: Recip of Gold Medal, Alethad Club. Membership: Hon Mbr, Darel Hanan Sch. Hobbies: Computer graphics; Designing; Animation; Water sports. Address: PO Box 1489, Jeddah 21431, Saudi Arabia.

QURESHI Iqbal Hussain, b. 27 Sept 1936, Ajmer, Pakistan. Scientist. m. Khurshid, 9 June 1987, 2 s.

Education: BSc, Chem and Phys, 1956, MSc, Chem, 1958, Univ of Sind Pakistan; MS, Nuclear Chem, Univ MI, USA, 1962; PhD, Nuclear Chem, Tokyo Univ of Educn, Japan, 1963. Appointments: Lectr, Govt Coll, Hyderabad, 1958-60; Offr on Specl Trng, 1960-63, Snr Sci Offr, 1963-68, Prin Sci Offr, 1968-76, Chf Sci Offr, 1976-88, Chf Sci, 1988-96, Mbr Tech, 1991-95, Snr Mbr, 1995-96, Sci Emer, 1996-, Pakistan Atomic Energy Cmmn; Rsch Sci, NBS Wash DC, USA, 1967-68; Hd, Nuclear Chem Div, 1972-84; Dir, Pakistan Inst of Nuclear Sci and Technol, 1984-91; Vis Sci, AEK, RISO, Denmark, 1970-72. Publications: 150 sci rsch pprs. Honours: 2 Gold Medals, Univ of Sind, 1956, 1958; Open Gold Medal, Pakistan Acady of Scis, 1988; Sitara-e-Imtiaz, Govt of Pakistan, 1992; Fell, Pakistan Acady of Sci, 1994; Platinum Jubilee Specl Awd, Govt Coll, Hyderabad, 1995; Fell, Chem Soc of Pakistan, 1995; Kharazmi Intl Awd, UNDP-IROST, Iran, 1997; Fell, Pakistan Nuclear Soc, 1997; Shield of Hon, Pakistan Nuc Soc, 1999. Memberships include: Intl Union of Elementols; Pakistan Nuclear Soc; Chem Soc of Pakistan. Hobbies: Music; Sports. Address: H. No 211, Street No 18, F-10/2, Islamabad 44000, Pakistan.

QURESHI Moeen Ahmad, b. 26 June 1930, Lahore, Pakistan. Economist; International Official. m. Lilo Elizabeth Rjchter, 1958, 2 s, 2 d. Education: Islamia Coll; Govt Coll; Univ of Punjab; Indian Univ, USA. Appointments: Socl Sci Cnslt, Ford Fndn, Pakistan, 1953; Hon Lectr, Univ of Karachi, 1953-54; Asst Chf, Planning Comm, Govt of Pakistan, 1954-56, Dpty Chf, 1956-58; Econ, IMF, 1958-61, Divsn Chf, 1961-65, Advsr, Africa Dept, 1965-66, Res Rep, Ghana, 1966-68, Snr Advsr, 1977-81; VP, Fin, World Bank, 1979-80, Snr VP, Fin, 1980-87, Snr VP, Ops, 1987-91; Acting PM of Pakistan, 1993. Publications: Var articles in profl jrnls. Hobbies: Tennis; Collecting Antiques. Address: Office of the Prime Minister, Islamabad, Pakistan.

R

RABBANI Burhanuddin. Politician; Academic; Professor. Appointments: Chair, Jamiat-i Islami (Islamic Union of Afghan Mujahidin) IUAM; Pres of Afghanistan, during civil war by Ldrshp Cncl, 1992, elected by Cncl, 1992-; Fled from Kabul w govt during heavy fighting, 1996; Now based in Mazar-i-Sharif.

RABINOWITZ Mario, b. 24 Oct 1936, Mexico Cty, Mexico. Physicist. m. Laverne, 2 s, 1 d. Education: BS, Phys, Univ of WA, 1959; MS, Phys, 1960; PhD, Phys, 1963. Appointments: Snr Physicist, Westinghouse Rsch, PA, 1963-66; Mngr, Gas Discharges and Vcm Varian Assoc, 1966-67; Rsch Physicist, Stanford Linear Accelerator Cntr, 1967-74; Snr Scientist, Mngr, Elec Power Rsch Inst, 1974-95; CEO, Armor Rsch, 1996-; Adj Prof, GA Inst, Tech Univ Houston, VA; C'wlth Univ; Case Western Reserve; Boston Univ. Creative Works: 135 Sci Articles; 34 pats. Honours: Baker Schl, WA Univ 1955-58; Alumni Achievement Awd, 1992. Hobbies: Philosophy; Mathematics. Address: 715 Lakemead Way, Redwood City, CA 94062-3922, USA.

RABUKA Sitiveni Ligamamada, b. 13 Sept 1948. Prime Minister. Appointments: Served, var snr capacities, Peacekeeping Missions in UNIFIL and MFO; Mil Serv, attained rank, Maj-Gen, 1968-88; Prime Min, 1992-. Honours: OBE; MSD; OStJ. Address: PO Box 2513, Government Buildings, Suva, Fiji.

RADFORD Robin, b. 9 Aug 1937. Historian. m. Anthony, 31 Dec 1960, 2 s, 1 d. Appointments: Cnslt Histn; Archivist, Anglican Diocese of Adelaide, S Aust. Publication: Highlanders and Foreigners, 1987. Memberships: Oral Hist Assn of Aust; Profl Histns Assn. Address: PO Box 223, Torrens Park, SA 5062, Australia.

RADHAMANI Shatdharsanam, b. 30 June 1949, Madras, India. Professor of English. m. S Subrahmanya Salmo, 3 Dec 1970, 3 s. Education: MA, Sri Venkateswara Univ, Tiupati, 1973; Rsch Degree PhD, Madras, 1987; PSCTE, 1991, PGDTE, 1993, (CIEFL) Hyderabad. Appointments: Asst Prof of Engl, Chellamal Women's Coll, Pachiayappa's Trust, Chennai, 1975-; Prof of Engl, Pachiayappa's Coll Chennai-30, Postgrad & Rsch Dept. Publications: Books: (Poems) The Times Ahead Are Propitious; Thistle and Transformation; Article: The Theme of Quest in W H Auden's plays; Pprs on Engl Lit presented at confs. Memberships: Life Mbr, Posetry Soc, India; Life Mbr, Writer's Forum, Ranchi.

RADIC Thérèse, b. 7 Sept 1935, Melbourne, Australia. Writer. m. Leonard Radic, 2 Feb 1957, 1 s. Education: BMus, 1958, MMus, 1969, PhD, 1978, Univ Melbourne. Appointments: Archival Asst, Grainger Mus, Univ Melbourne, 1978-79; Course Cnslt, Austl Cultural Studies, Deakin Univ, Vic, 1980-81; Cnclr, Aust Cncl, 1984-87; Sessional Lectr, Musicol, Fac of Music, Univ Melbourne, 1985; Music Advsry Panel, Vic Min for the Arts, 1991-92; Austl Rsch Cncl Fell, Music Dept, Monash Univ, 1991-95; Assoc, Fac of Music, Univ Melbourne, 1996-. Publications include: G.W.L. Marshall-Hall: Portrait of a Lost Crusader; A Treasury of Favourite Australian Songs; Melba: The Voice of Australia; Bernard Heinze; Songs of Australian Working Life. Honours: Num grants, fellshps, schlsps. Address: 2 Gaynor Court, Malvern, Victoria 3144, Australia.

RADZHABOV Safarali, b. 1955, Tajikistan. Education: Dushanbe Pedagogical Inst. Appointments: Dir, Prodn-Technol Trust, Faizabad Region; Dpty, Tajikistan Supreme Soviet, 1990-93, Sec, Chair, Cttee on Law & Human Rights, 1992-93; Dpty Chair, Chair, Majlisi Oli (parl) of Tajikistan, 1995-. Address: Majlisi Oli, Rudaki prosp 42, 734023 Dushanbe, Tajikistan.

RAE Ian David, b. 21 Sept 1937. Academician. m. Joan Caroline Veal, 16 Jan 1960, 1 s, 1 d. Education: Dip of Applied Chem (Footscray); BS, MSc, Melbourne; PhD, Austl Natl Univ. Appointments: Snr Lectr, Assoc Prof,

Prof and Dean of Fac of Sci, Monash; Dpty Vice-Chan, Vic Univ of Technol; Hon Professorial Fell in Hist and Philos of Sci, Univ Melbourne. Publications: Over 170 schl articles and book chapts; 3 patents. Memberships: Fell, Austl Acady of Technol Scis and Engrng; Fell, Roy Austl Chem Inst. Hobbies: Reading; Writing; Walking; Travel. Address: 16 Bates Drive, Williamstown, Vic 3016, Australia.

RAFSANJANI Hojatoleslam Ali Akhbar Hashemi, b. 1934, Rafsanjan, Iran. Politician. Education: Qom. Appointments: Speaker, Islamic Consultative Assembly, 1980-89; Dpty Chair, Cncl of Experts; Mbr, Islamic Repub Pty; Acting C-in-C of the Armed Forces, 1988-89; Vice Chair, Cttee to Revise the Constitution, 1989; Pres of Iran, 1989-97; Chair, Cncl to determine the Expendiency of the Islamic Order; Fmr 1st Dpty Speaker Majlis-E-Khobregan. Address: Islamic Republican Party, Dr Ali Shariati Avenue, Teheran, Iran.

RAHARDJO Harianto, b. 21 Oct 1955, Jakarta, Indonesia. Engineer. m. Chuan Bee Rahardjo, 3 Aug 1985, 1 s, 1 d. Education: PhD, Civil Engrng; MSc, Civil Engrng; IR, Civil Engrng, Univ of Sask, Can. Appointment: Dir, NTU-PWD Geotechnical Rsch Cntr. Publications: Co-auth, Soil Mechanics for Unsaturated Soils (book), 1993. Honours: Undergrad Schlshp, Technol, Bandung Inst, 1975-77; Postgrad Schlshp, Natl Scis and Engrng Rsch Cncl of Can, 1988, 1989. Memberships: Profl Engr of Sask, Can and Singapore; Canad Geotech Soc; SE Asian Geotech Soc. Address: Sch of Civil and Structural Engrng, Nanyang Technological University, Nanyang Avenue, Singapore 639798, Singapore.

RAHBAR Faramarz, b. Tehran, Iran. Electrical Engineer. m. Omekolsum, 5 Aug 1977, 1 s, 2 d. Education: BS, Elec Engin, 1970; MSc, Energy Mngmt & Policy, 1976; PhD Cand, 1977. Appointments: Mngr of Plng, 1977-79, Dir Engrng & Inpestion, 1980, Dir of Transmission Engrng, Tavanir, -1991; Dir of Engnrng. Niroo Cnsltng Engnrs, 1991- . Honours: 1st Degree Rsch Awd, Iran Min of Energy, 1989-. Memberships: IEEE; PSE; ASME; CIGRE; Iranian Soc of Elecl & Electrons Engrs. Hobbies: Swimming; Gardening. Address: NIROO Consulting Engineer, No 84, Ebnesina Avenue, Yusefabad, Tehran 14338, Iran.

RAHMAN Afifa, b. 15 Nov 1941, Bogra. University Teaching. m. Dr A Rahman, 29 June 1962, 2 s, 1 d. Education: Dip, Lib Sci; MA, Lib Sci; MA, Hist; PhD, USC (USA); CU (WAIT) w Aust Coll of Libnshp, Wales, UK. Appointments: Lib Asst; Asst Libn; Libn; Lectr (Univ); Asst Prof; Asst Prof, Prof. Publications: Handbook of Indexing, 1978; D U Library Guide, 1985; Documents on War of Bangladesh, 1993; Library Book Selection, 1997. Honours: Woman of the Yr, ABI, 1997, 1998. Memberships: ALA; ILA; IASLIC; BLA; LAB; Asiatic Soc, Bangladesh; ABCS; BAAA Hist Soc, Bangladesh. Hobbies: Reading; Writing; Travelling; Gardening. Address: Department of Library and Information Science, Dhaka University, Dhaka 1000, Bangladesh.

RAHMANI Mawlawi Mohammed Arsala. Politician. Appointments: Fmr Dpty PM; Min of Relig Guidance, Endowment & The Haj; PM of Afghanistan, 1994-95. Address: Office of the Prime Minister, Shar Rahi Sedarat, Kabul, Afghanistan.

RAHONG Somboon, b. 21 May 1932. Mnister of the Prime Minister's Office. m. Khunying Nongyaw Rahong. Education: Naval Acady, RTAF's Fellshp, Flying Trng Sch, ARTF, Class N 25, 1957; Flying Trng Sch, Randolph Air Force Base, TX, USA, 1963; Jt Combat Sch, Operational Wing, Class 13, 1964; Cmndr of Sqdrn Sch, Class 13, 1966; Air Cmnd and Staff Coll, Class 16, 1971-72; RTN Coll, Class 10, 1978; Natl Def Coll, Class 28, 1985-86. Appointments: Pilot, Tchr, Flying Trng Sch, RTAF, 1958-63; Cmndr, Wing 1, 1965; Tchr and Air Staff for Ops, Wing 1, 1966; Aide de Camp, Cmndr for Ops, 1968; Cmndr, Airlift Unit in Coop w USA, Korean War Grp, 1968; Test Pilot, 1969; Dpty Cmndr, Wing 1, Acting Aide de Camp, Dpty Cmndr in Chf, RTAF, 1974; Aide de

Camp, Def Min, 1975-76; Dir, RTAF Acady, 1978; Def Attaché to Tokyo, Actng Def Attaché to Seoul, 1981; Dir of Transportation of RTAF, 1983; Snr Advsr, 1986; Mbr, 1986, Mngng Dir, 1987, Bd of Airports Authy of Thailand; Mbr, Bd of Thai Airways Intl Ltd, 1987; Mbr, Bd, Express Way and Rapid Transit Authy of Thailand, 1988; Chmn, Sub Cttee, Express Way Proj Phase 4, 1989; Snr Mil Offr to Roy Aide de Camp Dept, ATAF Acady, 1991; Mbr, Natl Legislative Cncl, 1991; Ldr, Chat Thai Party, 1992; Dpty Prime Min and Min of Educ, Pol Advsry of Chat Thai Party, 1992; Dpty Prime Min, 1995. Honours: Kt Grand Cordon, Spec Class, Most Noble Order of the Crown of Thailand, 1990; Kt Grand Cordon, Spec Class, Most Exalted Order of the White Elephant. Memberships: Bd, Laemthong Public Co Ltd; Pres, SAS Trading Co Ltd; Pres, SAS Starmug Co Ltd. Address: 256/19 Moo 6, Saimai, Bangkhen District, Bangkok 10220, Thailand.

RAICHE Rosemary Jane, b. 11 Apr 1935. Poet; Artist. m. Dr Arthur P Raiche, 18 June 1985, 2 s, 2 d. Education: BA, Macquarie Univ; Postgrad Dip (Profl Studies) in Painting & Drawing, Coll of Fine Arts, Univ of NSW. Appointments: Engl Dept, Univ of Sydney, 1980-94. Creative Works: Selected Solo Art Exhibitions: Holdsworth Galleries, Sydney, 1992, 1994, 1995; Montserrat Gallery, NYC, 1994; Work included in various Anthologies of Poetry including: Poets Choice, 1977; Refractory Girl, 1978; Hermes, 1986; Angry Women Anthology, 1989; Southerly, 1989, 1991, 1994. Honours: Finalist in Winsor & Newton Austl Painting Awd, 1994; Finalist in Jacaranda Drawing Prize, 1994. Hobbies: Animal Rights Activist; Bushwalking; Yoga; Reading; Drawing. Address: 18 Blaxland Road, Killara, NSW 2091, Australia.

RAIDI, b. 1938, Biru, Tibet. Politician. Education: Ctrl Nationalities Inst, Beijing. Appointments: Sec, CCP Cttee, Nagu Region, 1972; Sec, CCP Cttee, Tibet Autonomous Region, 1975-77, Dpty Sec (Exec), 1977-; Chair, Peasants' Fedn of Tibet, 1975; Alt Mbr, 11th CCP Ctrl Cttee, 1977-82; Vice Chair, Revolutionary Cttee, Tibet Autonomous Region, 1977-79; Vice Chair, Peoples Congress of Tibet, 1979-83, Chair, 1986; Mbr, 12th CCP Ctrl Cttee, 1982, 14th, 1992-97, 15th, 1997-; Chair, Tibet Autonomous Regl 6th Peoples Congress, 1993-; Dpty Sec, CCP Tibet Autonomous Region. Address: Tibet Autonomous Region Chinese Communist Party, Lhasa, Tibet, China.

RAJ Janak, b. 7 Jan 1939. Librarian. Education: MA, Philos, 1976; MA, Ling, 1970; Ctf, French, 1971; PhD, Ling, 1979; MLib Sci, 1980. Appointments: Libn, GGD Coll, Baijnath, 1962-63; Libn, Vaish Coll, Bhiwani, 1963-67; Asst Libn, 1967-68, Officiating Libn, 1968, Libn, 1968-81, Regl Engrng Coll, Kurukshetra; Dpty Libn, 1981-88, Pt-time Lectr, 1984-88, Univ of Kurukshetra; Univ Libn, Thapar Inst of Engrng & Technol, Deemed Univ, 1988-. Publications include: Promoting Reading Habit and Library Use, 1995; Library Movement in Haryana, 1996; State Central Library, Haryana, 1996; Practical Aspects of Library Automation in the Indian Context, 1997; Internet and Subject Resource Guides, 1997. Honours: Sev. Memberships: Indian Lib Assn; Vice Chmn, Engrng & Technol Libs, State Sectional Cttee, ILA; IASLIC; HLA; INDAAL; PLA. Address: c/o Thapar Institute of Engineering & Technology, Deemed University, Patiala 147 001, Punjab, India.

RAJ Rishi, b. 9 Mar 1950, Sigatoka, Fiji. Hydrologist. m. Unnat, 11 Mar 1983, 3 s, 3 d. Education: BSc, Waikato; Cert Eng Hydrology, NSW, Aust. Appointments: Snr Hydrologist, 1984; Govt Hydrologist. Publications: Many pprs on Hydrology & Tropical Cyclones. Memberships: WMO Working Grp on Hydrology, 1986-, Elect Chmn, and Reg Hydrological Advsr, 1998. Hobbies: Fishing; Gardening; Travelling. Address: PO Box 987, Nausori, Fiji Islands.

RAJAGOPAL Indira, b. 29 Oct 1938, Katuputhur. Research Scientist. m. S R Rajagopalaw, 11 Sept 1970. Education: SSLC, Govt of Madras; BSc, Madras Univ; Charted Chem, Roy soc of Chem, London; MSc, Bombay Univ; PhD. Appointments: Jnr Scientist, CECRI,

Karaikudi, 1958-66; Scientust B, 1966-71; Scientist C, NAL, Bangalore, 1971-81; Scientist EI, 1981-87; Scientist EII, 1987-90; Scientist F, 1990-95; Scientist G, 1995-. Creative Works: 180 Rsch Pprs; 22 Pats. Honours: N M Sampat Natl Awd; V M Gatage Awd; CSIR Technol Prize for Engrng Technol; NAL Outstndng Technol Awd; VASVIK Awd; NDRC Natl Republic Day Awd; MRSI Medal; ASI Awd; Woman of the Yr, ABI; Many others. Memberships: Roy Inst of Chem; Inst of Chem; Advmnt of Sci and Technol; Inst of Metal Finishing; Chartered Chem Roy Soc of Chem; Metal Finishers Assn of India; Electrochem Soc of India; Aluminium Assn of India; Inst of Metal Finishing, London; others. Address: Scientist G, Head of Surface Engineering, National Aerospace Laboratories, Bangalore 560017, Inida.

RAJAN Ayilliath, b. 1 Dec 1937, Kannur, Kerala, India. Veterinary Science Professor. m. Valsala, 24 June 1968, 3 s. Education: BVSc; MVSc; PhD; Fell, Natl Acady of Vet Sci. Appointments: Vet Surgn, 1959-63; Lectr, Pathol Dept, Vet Coll, 1963-68; Rdr, Assoc Prof, 1968-78, Pathol Dept, Dir, 1987-97, Cntr of Ex in Pathol; Dean, Fac of Vet & Animal Scis, Agricl Univ, Kerala, 1993-97. Publications: Sev articles in profl jrnls. Honours: Best Rsch Articles, Indian Vet Assn, 1981, 1983, 1984, 1997; Awd, Outstndng Rsch Contbrn, Dept of Sci Technol, 1981. Memberships: IAVP; FUWAI; IVA; Ed, Jrnl of Vet Sci, 1972-86. Hobby: Reading. Address: Block Road, Ollukkara, Thrissur, Kerala 680655, India.

RAJARAMAN Vaidyeswaran, b. 8 Sept 1933, Erode, T N, India. Information Technologist. Education: BS (Hons) Phys, Delhi Univ, India; SM (MIT, USA), Associateship Indian Inst of Sci, Bangalore; PhD, Univ of WI, USA. Appointments include: Asst Prof, Stats, Univ WI, USA, 1961-62; Asst Prof, Elec Engin and Computer Cntr, Indian Inst of Technol, Kanpur, 1963-65; Visng Asst Prof, Univ of CA, Berkeley, USA, 1965-66; Assoc Prof, Elec Engin and Computer Cntr, Indian Inst of Technol, Kanpur, 1968-72; Visng Fell, IBM Systems Dev Inst, Canberra, Aust, 1972-73; Snr Prof, Computer Scis and Elec Engin and Convenor, Computer Sci Prog, Indian Inst of Technol, Kanpur, 1972-82, Hd of Computer Cntr, 1976-79; Prof and Chmn, Supercomputer Educ and Rsch Cntr, Indian Inst of Sci, Bangalore, 1982-94; Dir, CMC Ltd, 1990-95; Dir, Ncore Technols (Pvt) Ltd, 1991-; Dir, Canbank Computer Servs Ltd, 1996-. Honours include: Shanti Swarup Bhatnagar Prize, 1976; Homi Bhasha Prize, 1984; Lifetime Achievement in Info Technol, Dataquest Ind Panel, 1997; Pradma Bhushan, Presdtl Awd, 1998; Fell, Indian Acady Scis; Fell, Computer Soc India; Fell, Indian Natl Sci Acady; Fell, Natl Acady of Scis; Fell, Indian Natl Acady of Engnrng.. Hobbies: Music (classical); Fiction. Address: Supercomputer Education & Research Centre, Indian Institute of Science, Bangalore 560 012, India.

RAJENDRA Cecil, b. 25 Jan 1941. Barrister. m. Rebecca Lim, 23 June 1972, 1 s, 1 d. Education: Bar-at-law, Lincoln's Inn, London, Eng. Appointments: Chmn, Hum rights, Malaysia Bar Cncl; Chmn, Legal Aid, Malaysian Bar Cncl. Publications: Poetry: Embryo, 1965; Eros and Ashes, 1975; Bones and Feathers, 1978; Refugees and Other Despairs, 1980; Hour of Assasins, 1983; Songs for the Unsung, 1983; Postscripts, 1984; Child of the Sun, 1986; Dove on Fire, 1987; Lovers Lunatics and Lallang, 1989; Papa Moose's Nursery Rhymes for Our Times, 1991; Zerbrochentraume, 1992; Broken Buds, 1995; Shrapnel, Silence and Sand, 1999; Poems also publd and broadcast in over 50 countries and translated intl sev langs inclng: French, German, Swahili, Japanese, Tamil, Chinese, Malay. Hobbies: Music; Football; Tantra; Drinking. Address: c/o Cecil Rajendra & Assocs, Advocates & Solicitors, 2 Che Em Lane, 10200 Penang, Malaysia.

RAJENDRUDU Gedupudi, b. 6 July 1950, Ravillavari Palle. Teaching and Research. m. Dr P Kumari, 29 Nov 1981, 2 s. Education: BSc, 1972; MSc, Botany, 1974; Dip in German, 1976; PhD, Plant Phys, 1980. Appointments: Jnr Rsch Fell, 1974-78; Snr Rsch Fell, 1978-80; Postdoc Fell, ICRISAT, 1980-83; CSIR Pool Sci, 1984; Lectr, 1985-88; UGC Career Awardee, 1988-91; Snr Lectr,

1991-92; Assoc Prof, 1992-. Publications: Biology Textbook for Class IX 1989; Plant Physiology Textbook for BSc Degree Students, 1993; Botany Laboratory Manual for BSc Students. Honours: Selected for Career Awd, Univ Grants Commn, Govt of India, Young Talented Sci. Memberships: Bd of Stdies in Botany; Indian Soc for Plant Phys; Environmental Club of Tirupati. Hobbies: Gardening; Playing Shuttle Badminton; Listening to Classical Music. Address: Department of Botany, Sri Venkateswara University, Tirupati 517 502, Andhra Pradesh, India.

RAJORIA Krishna Behari, b. 26 Aug 1940. Engineer. Education: BE(Civil) (Hons), MBM Engrng Coll, Jodhpur Univ of Rajasthan, 1961; ME (1st in order of merit, Gold Medal), Univ of Roorkee, 1963. Appointments: Lectr, Univ of Roorkee, 1962-63; Asst Exec Engr, 1963-66, Exec Engr, 1966-76, CPWD; Suptng Engr; Cnslt, WAPCOS, 1977-81; Suptng Surveyor of Wrks, Delhi Admin, 1981-82; Chf Engr, Govt of Arunachal, Pradesh, 1987-89; Chf Engr, IT Dept, 1989-93; Chf Engr, 1991-93; Chf Engr, Govt of Delhi, 1993-97; Engr-in-Chf, PWD, 1997-. Publications: 43 pprs publd or presented. Memberships: Indian Bldg Congress, VP, 1996-97, Pres, 1998-2000; Indian Rds Congress, VP, 1993-94, Pres, 1999-2000; Fell, Instn of Engrs, India, Chmn, Delhi State Cntr, 1998-2000; Inst of Valuers; Indian Cncl of Arbitrators; Indian Inst of Bridge Engrs; Indian Geotech Soc (Delhi Chapt); Mbr, Delhi Cntr Unit, Natl Inst for Cnstrn Mngmt & Rsch (NOCMAR); Senate for Univ of Roorkee.

RAJPUT Chandra B S, b. 11 Apr 1939, Sihora, Nurabad, India. Teaching. m. Jeevan, 21 May 1959, 2 s, 4 d. Education: BSc, Vikram Univ, 1959; MSc, Horticul, 1961; PhD, Horticul, 1965. Appointments: Asst Prof, Horticul, 1964-70, Rdr in Horticul, 1970-77, Prof of Horticul, 1977-, Hd, Dean & Dir, Agricl Sci, Inst of Agricul Scis, Banaras Hindu Univ. Publication: Citriculture, 1985; Sev articles in profl jrnls. Honours: C'wlth Nuffield Fndn Rsch Assoc, 1975-76; CIDA Fellshp, 1983-85; Man of the Yr, 1997. Memberships: Horticul Soc of India; Vegetable Soc of India. Hobbies: Reading; Working. Address: c/o Department of Horticulture, Institute of Agricultural Sciences, Banaras Hindu University, Varanasi 221 005, India.

RAJYALAKSHMI Desaraju, b. 17 June 1949. Information Officer. m. D S R Krishna, 2 Dec 1973, 1 s, 1 d. Education: BSc Bot, Zoo, Chem, 1969; MSc Zoo, 1971; BLisc, 1984; MLisc, 1985; PhD Lib & Info Sci, 1992. Appointments: Demonstrator, Milind Coll of Sci, 1971-73; Zoo Lectr, St Francis Coll, Secundrabad, 1975-76; Asst Libn 1986-89, Univ of Qatar, DOHA; Lectr, Dept of Lib Sci, 1989-; Zoo Lectr, Dr Ambedkar Coll, Nagpur, 1990-92; Info Offr, NEERI, Nagpur, 1992-. Publications: Prepared course material for mngmt of libs for Dr Ambedkar Open Univ, Hyderabad, 1995; Publ & presented 25 papers in natl jrnls & natl & intl confs. Honours: Univ First MSc, Zoo, 1971-73; Natl Merit Schlsp Univ First BLisc, 1984; Gold Medal, Univ First MLisc; First PhD in Lib Sc, NU. Memberships: Life Mbr, ILA; Life Mbr, IATLIS; AP Lib Assoc Mbr IASLIC; IWSA. Hobbies: Music; Housekeeping; Knitting; Gardening; Reading; Creative writing. Listed in: Reference Asia; Who's Who in Asia. Address: Distributed Information Sub-Centre, Neeri, Nehru Marg, Nagpur 440 020, Maharashtra, India.

RAKHMONOV Emomali, b. 5 Oct 1952, Dangara, Tajikistan. Politician. Education: Tajik Univ. Appointments: Electrician, Salesman, Sec, Trade Union & CP Cttees; Dir, Sovkhoz in Dangar Region, 1988-92; Chair, Kulyab Regl Exec Soviet, 1992; Chair, Supreme Soviet (Majlisi Oli) Repub of Tajikistan, 1992-94; Pres of Tajikistan, 1994-. Address: Office of the President, Dushanbe, Tajikistan.

RALPH Eric Kodjo, b. 7 Nov 1960, Accra, Ghana. Economist. Education: BEc, 1983, MEc, 1987, Monash Univ; PhD, Duke Univ, 1996. Appointments: Rsch Asst, Tutor, Monash Univ, 1980-84; Economist, Telecom Aust, 1985-87; Rsch Fell, Monash Univ and Pvte Cnsltcy, 1988-90; Assoc Prof, George WA Univ, 1995-98. Honours: Monash Philos and Brit Publrs Book Prize,

1982; C'wlth Postgrad Rsch Awd, Aust, 1984; Most Outstndng Contbrn to the Fin Directorate, Telecom Aust, 1987; Bronfenbrenner Fellshp, Duke Univ, 1990; Summer Fellshp, Duke Univ, 1991; Acad Schlsp, Duke Univ, 1990-94; Glasson Fellshp, Duke Univ, 1993; 2nd Prize, Grad Student Ppr Comp, Telecom Policy Rsch Conf, 1995; Jnr Schlsp Incentive Awd, George WA Univ, 1997. Address: 2323 Audubon Street, New Orleans, LA 70125-4117, USA.

RAM Abha Devi, b. 21 Mar 1956, Suva, Fiji Islands. Medical Doctor; Specialist Family Physician. m. Mr Daya Singh, 2 s. Education: MBBS, Monash Univ, Vic, Aust, 1979. Appointments: Dr, Spec, Family Physn, Cnslr; Runs medl spec cntr; Advsr to women's forum in Fiji. Honours: Rsch Chairperson, Fiji Coll of GPs, Aug 1988. Memberships: Rsch Chairperson, Fiji Coll GPs; Fiji Coll of GPs; Assoc Mbr RACAP. Hobbies: Talking to and meeting people; Family sports; Family outings. Address: PO Box 1391, Labasa, Fiji.

RAM Gurupad Sambhav, b. 15 Mar 1959, Indore, MP, India. Social Service. Memberships: Pres, Avdhoot Bhagvan Ram Kushta Seva Ashram, Shree Sarveshwary Samooh, Baba Bhagwan Ram Trust and Aghor Parishad Trust, Parao, Varanesi, UP, India. Hobby: To serve humanity. Address: President, Avadhoot Bhagvan Ram Kusth Seva Ashram, Parao, Varanesi, UP, India.

RAMA Rama, b. 25 Nov 1968, Horahalli. Yoga Teacher; Special Educator. m. Gowramma, 9 June 1996, 1 d. Education: SSLCPUC Dip in Mental Retardation Spec Tchr; Yoga Cert Course; MA. Appointments: Socl Wrkr, 5 yrs; Yoga Instr, 10 yrs; Spec Tchr Physio Therapist, 5 yrs. Publications: Yoga for Mentally Handicapped; Yoga for Cancer; Yoga for Aids; Yoga for Epilapsy; Yoga for Diabetes. Honour: Best Socl Wrkr. Memberships: Kannada Sahithya Parishad; Bharathiya Karnataka Sangha; Subramanyesh Credit Co-op Bank Ltd. Address: No 86 III Cross, West of Chord Road, Junction of Indiranagar and Rajajinagar, Bangalore 560 010, India.

RAMA SARMA Morra Venkata, b. 6 Sept 1920, Morra, Andhra Pradesh, India. University Teaching and Administration. m. Lakshmi, Nov 1937, 2 s, 2 d. Education: PhD, Wales; Hon DLitt, Andhra Univ, Waltair. Appointments: Lectr, Rdr, Prof of Engl; Prin, S V Univ Coll; Vice Chan, S V Univ, Tirupati. Publications: 6 novels; 11 plays; 16 critical wrks mostly on Milton, Shakespeare, Heywood and Shaw. Honours: Disting Miltonist, 1981; Fell, Univ Coll, Cardiff, 1982; DLitt, Andhra Univ, 1982; Meritorious Tchr, Andhra Pradesh Govt, 1980, 1981; Sev other awds. Memberships: Milton Soc of Am; Fell, Univ of Wales, Cardiff, UK. Hobbies: Tennis; Badminton; Literary interests; Reading and writing in English. Address: Padmanilayam, 18/96 K T Road, Tirupati, India.

RAMACHANDRA Kanakanahali, b. 18 Aug 1933, Mandya Town. Research in Mathematics. m. K Sarailathi, 5 June 1958, 1 d. Education: PhD, Bombay Univ, 1965. Appointments: Retd as Snr Prof, TIFR, Bombay; Hon Vis Prof, Natl Inst of Adv Studies, IISC Campus, Bangalore. Publications: LN85 (for TIFR). Honours: Ramanujan Birth Centenary Awd, ISCA; Ramanujan Medal (INSA); Sir M Vishveshwaraiah Awd of Karnataka State Govt. Membership: Fell, Biographical Acady of Commonwealth. Hobbies: Listening to Karnatic music; Chanting Vedic mantras. Address: 955 Selberg House, Second Cross Third Main (D Block), Rajajinagar, Bangalore 560 010, India.

RAMACHANDRAN Komaralingam Gopalan, b. 26 May 1945, Bangalore, India. m. Balamani, 9 Feb 1972, 2 s. Education: BCom; BLL; Assoc Mbr, Indian Inst of Bankers. Appointments: State Bank of India, 1968-83; Bank of Bahrain & Kuwait, Bahrain, 1983-86; Currently, BHEL; CMD of BHEL. Memberships: Govng Cncl of All India Mngmt of Assn (AIMA); Hon Treas & Chmn, Fin Cttee, AIMA, 1996-98; Govng Cncl of Bharatidasan Inst of Mngmt (BIM). Hobbies: Reading; Music; Scrabble; Management Development. Address: Chairman &

Managing Director, Bharat Heavy Electricals Limited, BHEL House, Siri Fort, New Delhi 110 049, India.

RAMAKRISHNAN Moni, b. 27 Apr 1940, Madurai, Tamil Nadu, India. Geologist. m. Saroja, 20 Aug 1969, 2 s. Education: MSc, Geol, Presidency Coll, Chennai, 1962; PhD, Geol & Geochem, Indian Inst of Sci, Bangalore, 1981. Appointments: Geo Jnr, Geol Survey of India, 1965-69; Geo Snr, 1969-81; Dir, 1981-86; Dir, Sel Gr, 1986-92; Dir, Cntr for Earth Sci Studies, 1987-89; Dpty Dir Gen, 1992-97; Snr Dpty Dir Gen, 1997-98; Retired 1998; Ed, Geol Soc of India, Bangalore, at pres. Publications: 6 books; 66 publs; over 30 reports. Honours: Mysore Geos Gold Medal, 1984; Natl Mineral Awd, 1989. Memberships: Fell, Indian Acady of Sci; Cncl Mbr, Geol Soc of India; Indian Geophys Union; Sci Bd Mbr, Intl Geol Correlation Prog, UNESCO, Paris, 1992-97; Edl Bd, Current Sci. Hobbies: Travel; Movies; Reading. Address: #201, Skyline Surabhi Apts, Vidyapeetha Road, BSK III Stage, Bangalore 560 085, India.

RAMAKRISHWAN Vayanayi K, b. 7 Feb 1944, Kannur, India. Engineer. m. Nina, 12 Dec 1974, 1 s, 1 d. Education: Postgrad Dip, Quality Assurance, Reliable Engrng; Proj Mngmnt; Technol Mngmnt; Pert CPM Techniques. Appointments: Plant Engr; Quality Assurance Engr; Prodn Engr, 1967-86; Design Engr; Naral Armont Stores; Artillery at Air Defence ; Infantry, RKD Capacity. Publications: Productive Technology; Quality Control; Use of Computers in Project Management. Honours: Safety Awd; Recog for Infantry Design Contbn. Membership: Inst of Mechl Engrs. Hobbies: Sports; Swimming; Movies; Reading; Computers; Music; Socl Servs. Address: Design Engineer, DRDO, Flat No 2 Vibha Apts, 128/4-Sanewadi, Aundh, Pune 411007, India.

RAMALINGASWAMI Vulimiri, b. 8 Aug 1921, Srikakulam, India. Medical. m. Prabha, 13 Jan 1947, 1 s, 1 d. Education: MD, Andhra Univ; DPhil, DSc, Oxford Univ; FRCP, FRCPath, London. Appointments: Prof, Chmn, Dept of Pathol, 1957-79, Dir, 1969-79, All India Inst of Medl Scis, New Delhi; Dir-Gen, Indian Cncl of Medl Rsch, New Delhi, 1979-86; Schl-in-Res, Fogarty Intl Cntr, Natl Inst of Hlth, Bethesda, MD, USA, 1986-87; Visng Prof, Intl Hlth Policy, Harvard Sch of Pub Hlth, Boston, USA, 1987-88; Specl Advsr to Exec Dir on Child Survival and Dev, UNICEF, NY, USA, 1988-89; Prof Emer, All India Inst of Med Scis, New Delhi, 1990-; Sec-Gen, Intl Conf on Nutrition, Rome, 1991-92; Pres, Natl Inst of Immunol, New Delhi, 1991-; Natl Rsch Prof, 1995-. Publications: Over 200 articles in profl sci jrnls. Honours: FRS; For Assoc, Natl Acady of Scis, USA; For Mbr, Acady of Medl Scis, USSR; Past Pres, Indian Natl Sci Acady; Hon Fell, Amn Coll of Physns; Chmn, Global Advsry Cttee on Medl Rsch, WHO, Geneva; Hon Doct of Med, Karolinska Inst, Sweden. Memberships: Fell, Roy Soc of London, Roy Coll of Physns, London, Roy Coll of Pathols, London; Hon Fell, Amn Coll of Physns. Hobbies: Walking; Literature; Reading; Music. Address: X-29 Hauz Khas, New Delhi 110 016, India.

RAMAMOORTHY Narayani, b. 5 May 1966, Madras, India. Educator. Education: BSc, Biochem, 1987; MSc, Biochem, 1989; PhD, Biochem & Biomaterials, 1994; PGDBM, 1998. Appointments: Jnr Rsch Fell, 1989-91, Snr Rsch Fell, 1991-93, Rsch Assoc, 1995-96, Asst Prof, 1996-97, VMKV Med Coll, Salem; Rdr, Hd, PNC & KR Coll. Publications: 14 pprs in profl jrnls. Honours: Best Ppr Awd, Soc for Biomaterials & Artificial Organs, 1990; Sev fellshps and assocshps. Memberships: Soc for Biomaterials & Artificial Organs; NY Acady of Scis. Hobbies: Indian Classical Dance; Classical Music; Reading. Address: 16 Thumbia Reddy Street, West Mambalam, Madras 600033, India.

RAMAMURTHY Shanta, b. 4 Apr 1945, Mysore, India. Sports Player. m. S R Rad, 18 June 1964, 1 s, 1 d. Education: BA, Mysore Univ, India. Career: Successfully captained Karnataka Women's Team to victory 13 times in Natl Ball-Badminton Championships, 1980. Honours: Mysore Dasara State Awd, 1970; Karnataka Sports Cncl Awd, 1978. Membership: Karnataka State Ball Badminton Awd, 1978. Hobbies: Table-tennis; Gardening; Cookery. Address: 134, Giri Nivas, II Cross Road, III Block, Jayanagar, Bangalore 560 011, India.

RAMAMURTHY V V, b. 27 June 1952, Coimbatore, New Delhi, India. Scientist. m. M V Kalyani, 1 Feb 1989, 2 s. Education: MS, Agric, Entomology; PhD, Entomology. Appointments: Instr, INAV, Coimbatore, 1975-76; Scientist SI, 1976-82, Snr Scientist, 1982-, Div of Entomology, IARI, New Delhi. Honours: Darwin Fell, Biosystematics, CAB Intl Inst of Entomology, 1995-96. Memberships: Coleopterists Soc, USA; Entomological Soc of Am, USA; Eurn Assn of Coleopterists, Spain. Address: Division of Entomology, Indian Agricultural Research Institute, New Delhi 110012, India.

RAMAN NAIR R, b. 18 Apr 1955, Trivandram. Library and Information Scientist. m. L Sujochana Devi, 13 Sept 1992, 1 s. Education: MLISc; MA; LLB; DPA. Appointments: Cochin Univ of S and T, Cochin, 1979; Cntr for Dev Studies, Trivandrum, 1979-80; Kerala Legislature secretariat, 1981; State Cntrl Lib of Kerala, 1983; Govt PG Coll, Kasaragod, 1987; H H Maharajas Coll for Women, 1991; Kerala Agric Univ, 1995. Publications: 15 books, inclng: Computer Application to Library and Information Services; Academic Library Automation; Sustainable Library Development; Basis of CD/ISIS for DOS; Internet for Library and Information Services; Transl of Khalil Gibran's Nastikanaya Khalil and Alanju Tiriyunnavar; Herman Hesse's Siddartha, Pullamkuzhal Swapnam; Gertrudinu Snehapoorvam; 125 rsch pprs and articles; 21 natl sem presentations Memberships: Natl Geog Soc; Rural Dev Forestry Net; Asian Watershed Mngmt Net; ILA; IASLIC; AALDI; Fndr Mbr, Cntr for S Indian Studies; Cntr for Informatics R and D. Hobbies: Reading; Writing; Translation. Address: Gayathri Hut, Kudappanakynnu, Trivandrum 695005, Kerala, India.

RAMANA Devalla Venkata, b. 19 Nov 1935. Teacher; Researcher. m. Kusuma, 30 Jan 1964, 1 s, 1 d. Education: BSc; MSc; PhD. Appointments: Lectr, 1970, Asst Prof, 1980, Prof, 1988, Emer Prof, 1996-, Indian Inst of Technol, Madras, India. Publications: 2 chapt contrbs, Introduction to Mass Spectrometry; 1970-96: 101 original rsch publs in intl jrnls; 5 review articles in rsch jrnls; 60 rsch pprs presented in natl and intl confs. Honour: Gold Medal and Citation, Indian Soc for Mass Spectometry, 1996. Membership: Life Mbr, Indian Soc for Mass Spectrometry. Hobbies: Reading; Music; Gardening; Sports. Address: 8 Ayodhya Colony, Velacheri, Madras 600042, India.

RAMASUBBAN Radhika, b. 26 June 1948, Pudukkottai, India. Sociological Research. m. 14 Dec 1979, 1 s. Education: MA, PhD, Univ of Bombay, India. Appointments: Tchng & Rsch Fac pos, St Xavier's Coll, Bombay; Sch of Planning, Ahmedabad; Univ of Bombay, Bombay; Univ of Sussex, Eng, 1970-88; Snr Fell, then Dir, Cntr for Socl & Technol Change, Mumbai, 1988-; Cnslt, World Bank, 1990-94. Publications: Public Health and Medicine in Colonial India; War on Disease; Readings on Women's Reproductive Health in India; Over 30 rsch pprs publs in books & jrnls, India & overseas. Honours: Snr Fell, Indian Cncl for Socl Sci Rsch, 1986-88. Memberships: Pres, Intl Rsch Cttee on Sociol of Sci & Technol; Prog Cttee, Intl Sociol Assn, 1994-98, 1990-94; Govt of India Leather Technol Mission; Intl Union for Sci Study of Population. Hobbies: Indian Classical Music; Yoga; Walking. Address: 14 Bandstand Apartments, BJ Rd, Bandra, Mumbai 400050, India.

RAMESH BABU S, b. 12 Feb 1957, Bangalore, India. Metallurgical Scientist. m. Usha Govind Tumkurkar, 9 July 1982, 2 d. Education: BSc, Bangalore Univ, 1977; BE (Metallurgy) Indian Inst of Sci, Bangalore, 1980; PhD, Metallurgy, Indian Inst of Sci, Bangalore, 1985. Appointments: Visng Scientist: NE Univ of Technol, Shenyang, China, 1986; Visng Scientist, Tohoku Univ, Japan, 1986, Monbosho Postdoct Rsch Fell, 1987, Sendai, Japan; Postdoct Rsch Fell, Univ of BC, Vancouver, Can, 1989; Rsch Engr and Assoc Hd, Thapar Corp Rsch and Dev Cntr, Patiala, India, 1989-90; Asst Dir, Natl Metallurgical Lab, Jamshedpur, India, 1990-91; R&D Mngr, Jindal Strips Ltd, Hisar, India, 1991-94; Dpty Gen Mngr (Tech servs), NSL Ltd, Patancheru, Medak Dist, AP, India, 1994; Gen Mngr, R&D, Isapt Profiles India Ltd, Sansawadi, Dist Pune, India, 1994; Prof (Mech), MS Ramaiah Int of Technol, MSR Nagar, Bangalore, 1995-97; Prof (Mech), PES Inst of Technol, Bangalore, 1997-98; Snr Res Scientist Advd Forming Technol Cntr, Bangalore, 1999-. Publications: Profl jrnls; 23 rsch reports; 29 conf pprs; 4 pats; 7jrnl pprs. Honours: Holder of 16 world records in Badminton, Table Tennis, Kite Flying; Carroms; Tennis; Oratory; Cycling; Scooter driving; Vegetable cutting; IISc ME Entraance Test Topper, Metall, 1980; IISc Rsch Entrance Test Topper, Metall, 1980; Rated Outstndng for Rsch at Jindal Strips Ltd, 1992; Best Rsch Ppr Awd, Indian Inst of Metals, Calcutta, 1993; 1st Indian Scientist Invited by Govt of China for longterm rsch in Metall; Outstndng Indian Achiever Awd, 1998. Memberships: Iron and Steel Soc, USA; Inst of Indian Foundrymen; Life Mbr: Inst of Engrs; Indian Inst of Metals; Indian Soc of Theort and Applied Mechs; Indian Inst of Sci Alumni Assn; Uluchukamme Brahmana Maha Sbah; Hon Life Mbr, Hokkaido Intl Friendship Assn Japan. Hobbies: Writing; Acting in Kannada plays; Long distance running and backhand swimming; Interior decoration; South Indian cooking; Photography; Art pieces using stamps and coins; Organising exhibitions about India in China and Japan; Lecturing on India while abroad. Address: # 27 Jaladarshini Layout (near Old Punjab National Bank), New BEL Road, Bangalore, 560094, India.

RAMESH BABU Nagalamadaka, b. 5 May 1960, Y N Hosakota. Biotechnologist. m. S R Shanthala Murthy, 22 Sept 1993, 1 d. Education: BVSc, MVSc, Univ of Agricl Scis, Bangalore; PhD, Tamil Nadu Vet and Animal Scis Univ, Madras, India, 1997. Appointments: Scientist 1, Inst of Animal Hlth and Vet Biologicals, Hebbal, Bangalore, 1986-98; Scientist 2, Institute of Animal Hlth and Vet Biologicals, Bangalore, 1998-. Publications: Num pprs to profl jrnls. Memberships: NY Acady of Sci; Assn for Promotion of DNA Finger Printing and Other DNA Technologies; Indian Soc of Vet Immunology and Biotechnology; Indian Assn of Vet Microbiologists, Immunologists and Specialists in Infectious Diseases. Address: Scientist, Institute of Animal Health and Veterinary Biologicals, Hebbal, Bangalore, 560024, Karnataka, India.

RAMIREZ Dolores, b. 20 Sept 1931, Calamba, Laguna, Philippines. Professor Emeritus. Education: BS, Agricl, Univ of the Philippines Coll of Agricl, 1952-56; MS, Univ MN, 1957-58; PhD, Purdue Univ, 1961-63. Appointments: Rsch Fell, 1956-57, Rsch Instr, 1958-64, Rsch Asst Prof, 1964-68, Assoc Prof, 1969-73, Rschr IV, 1977-79, Prof, 1979-95, Univ Prof, 1995-98, Prof Emer, 1998-, Univ of the Philippines Coll of Agricl; Assoc Prof, 1973-74, Prof, 1974-77, Univ of Philippines, Los Banos Coll of Scis & Humanities. Publications include: Gene Introgression in Maize, 1997; The Macapuno Mutant Coconut, 1998. Honours include: Outstndng Women of Calamba Awd, Calamba Maria Clara Jaycees, 1985; Outstndng Tchr, Univ of the Philippines, 1996; Recog Awd, Philippine Soc for the Adv of Genetics, 1996; Natl Sci, Pres, Repub of the Philippines, 1997. Memberships include: Philippine Biochem Soc; Philippine Biol Tchrs Assn; UP Los Banos Alumni Assn; Third World Org for Women in Sci; Philippine Soc for the Adv of Genetics; Philippine Assn of Univ Women. Hobby: Reading. Address: Institute of Plant Breeding, University of the Philippines, Los Banos College, Laguna, Philippines.

RAMON Haim, b. 1950, Jaffa, Israel. Politician; Lawyer. Appointments: Chair, Pub Cncl for Youth Exchanges; Natl Sec, Labour Pty's Young Guard, 1978-84; Mbr, Knesset, 1983-; Coord, Fin Cttee, Labour Pty, 1984-88, Chair, Labour Pty, 1988-92; Min of Hlth, 1992-94, of the Interior, 1995-96. Address: Knesset, Jerusalem, Israel.

RAMOS Fidel, b. 1928, Philippines. Politician; Army Officer. m. 5 d. Education: Natl Univ, Manila; US Mil

Acady, W Point; Univ IL, USA. Appointments: Active Serv, Korea, Vietnam; Dpty Chf of Staff, 1981; Chf of Staff, Philippines Armed Forces, 1986-98; Ldr, Peoples Power Pty; Sec, Natl Def, 1988-98; Cand for Pres, 1992; Pres of the Philippines, 1992-98. Honour: Légion d'honneur, 1987. Address: Office of the President, Presidential Guest House, Malacanang Palace Compound, J P Laurel Street, San Miguel, Metro Manila, Philippines.

RAMPRASAD Boilahalli S, b. 6 Apr 1938, Bangalore, India. Scientist. Education: BSc; AMIE; MS, Mech Engrng, Worcester Poly Inst, USA; PhD, Optical Engrng. Appointments: Proj Engr, Crompton and Knowles Corp, Worcester, MA, USA, 1964-65; Sci Offr, Indian Inst of Sci, Bangalore, 1965-74; Snr Sci Offr, 1974-81; Prin Rsch Sci, 1981-. Publications: Ed, Advances in Instrumentation, 1996. Memberships: Indian Vacuum Soc; Instrument Soc of India. Hobbies: Writing poetry; Stereo photography. Address: Department of Instrumentation, Indian Institute of Science, Bangalore, 560012, India.

RAMSAY Renato, b. 6 Aug 1947, Sydney, Aust. Company Director. m. 21 Sept 1968, 3 d. Education: MSc (Hons), Socl Ecology; DipEd. Appointments: Sci Tchr, 1974-84; Curric Cnclt, 1985-88; Hd Tchr, Sci, 1989-90; Mngr, Streamwatch, 1991-. Publication: Agriculture and You Books, 1, 2, 3, 1987-89. Hobby: Music. Address: 380 Moreton Park Road, Menangle, NSW, Australia 2568.

RAMSDEN Michael John, b. 17 Apr 1935, Leeds, Eng. Librarianship. m. Sylvia Shirley Brisley, 2 s, 1 d. Education: BA (Hons), Southampton Univ, 1957; MSocSc, RMIT, 1978. Appointments include: Snr Asst, Bexley Pub Lib, 1961-62; Cntrl Lending Libn, Bexley Pub Lib, 1962-65; Regl Libn, Sherwood Reg, Nottinghamshire County Libs, 1965-67; Lectr/Snr Lectr, Coll of Librarianship, Wales, 1967-71; Lectr - Snr Lectr, Dept Librarianship, 1971-77, Hd, Dept of Librarianship, RMIT, 1977-85, Dean, Fac of Applied Socl Scis & Comm, 1985-94, Acting Pro-Vice Chan (Acad Progs), 1994-95; Prof (as mbr Fndn Professoriate), 1991-95, RMIT; Freelance Indexing Cnslt, 1995-. Publications: Monographs include: An Introduction to index language construction, 1974; PRECIS: a handbook for students of Librarianship, 1981, Chinese transl, 1986; Book chapt; 12 pprs in profl jrnls and conf proceedings. Memberships: Assn of Asst Libns, Pres, 1969; Lib Assn, Cnclr, 1965-70; Lib Assn of Aust, Gen Cnclr, 1976-77, Exec Sec, Conf Cttee, 1973-75; LAA Vic Branch, Cnclr, 1972-77, Pres, 1974; Austl Soc of Indexers, Cttee Mbr, 1995-97. Hobbies: Reading; Cricket; Opera. Address: 104 Lakeview Drive, Lilydale, Victoria, Australia 3140.

RAMU Mavally G, b. Bangalore, India. Deputy Director of Staistics. m. V Susheela, 28 Feb 1977, 1 s, 1 d. Education: BA, MA , Econs. Appointments: Asst Dir of Stats; Dpty Dir of Stats. Publications: Mavalli Kshetrea (histl), 1981; Bhagyada Siri (poems), 1984; Baduku (novel), 1987; Trimurthy (poems), 1996. Honours: Awds for essays in Engl in competition review, monthly mags. Memberships: Poets Intl Orgn; PEN; Karnataka Secretariat Club Study Circle. Hobby: Organising literary programmes. Address: G Ramu, D:NO:33, Kempanna Street, Dodda Mavally, Banglaore 560004, India.

RANA Kashri Ram, b. 7 Apr 1938. Member of Parliament. m. Pushpa, dec, 2 s, 4 d. Education: BCom, LLB, South-Gujarat Univ, Surat. Appointments: Mbr, Gujurat Legislative Assembly, 1975-80; Chmn, Cttee on Pub Undertakings, Gujarat Legislative Assemble, 1977-80; Pres, Bharatiya Janata Party, Gujarat, 1985-87, 1993-96; Elected, 9th Lok Sabha, 1989-91; Mbr Rules Cttee, Consultative Cttee, Min of Railways, 1990-91; Re-elected, 10th Lok Sabha, 1991; Mbr, Pub Accounts Cttee, Consultative Cttee, Min of Ind, 1991-92; Re-elected, 11th Lok Sabha, 1996; Mbr, Estimates Cttee, Cttee on Com, Jt Parly Cttee on Brdcstng Bill, 1996-97; Re-elected, 12th Lok Sabha, 1998; Union Cabinet Min, Textiles, 1998-. Memberships: Pres, All India Rana Samaj; Chf Tstee, Deendayal Smarak Trust; Fndr, Ex Ed, Rana Jagat jrnl. Hobbies: Reading; Writing; Sight-seeing; Old film songs; Mushaira; Classical music and ghazals; Wrestling; Weight lifting. Address: 7 Ashoka Road, New Delhi 110001, India.

RANADE Y P, b. 4 May 1935, Kahnuwan, Punjab. Businessman. m. Kamlesh, 22 May 1957, 2 s. Education: IBAM, RMP; Dip on Exports; Dip in Atomic Biol Chem, Protection and Damage Control. Appointments: Indian Navy, 1953-63; Mngr, Publng Co, 1964; MD, Schl Publng Hs, 1968; FICCI, 1984-86; VP, FPBA, 1985-86; Sec Gen, FEPI, 1987-92; Pres, FEPI, 1992-95; Ex Mbr, Afro Asian Book Cncl, 1992-; Chmn, Cntrl Acady Intl Educ Soc, 1998. Publications: Childrens Books; School Text Books, 1966-. Honours: Outstndng Awd, 1983; Bihar Rajaya Pustak Vyavasayi Sangh; Awd for one of the fndr fathers of FEPI; First Exhibn Awd; Publrs of India Awd; Ex Awd in Prodn; Exporter of the Yr; Ex Awd, Indian Cncl for Small and Medium Exporters. Memberships: Afro Asian Cncl; All India Map Charts Publr Assn; Akhil Bhartiya Hindi Prakashan Sangh; Chem and Allied Products Export Promotion Cncl; Educl Publrs Assn; Fedn of Educl Publrs in India; Indian Cncl for Small and Medium Exporters; Indian Econ Studies; Jain Co-op Bank Ltd; Manav Vikas Kendra; Natl Book Devel Cncl. Hobbies: Marketing Research; Travelling; Reading; Teaching. Address: M/S Scholar Publishing House (P) Ltd, 85 Model Basti, New Delhi 110 005, India.

RANCHOD Bhadra G, b. 11 May 1944, Port Elizabeth, S Africa. High Commissioner. m. Vibha Manilal, 2 d. Education: BA, Univ of Cape Town, 1966; LLB, 1967; Doctorandus Iuris, Doctor of Laws, (LLD), Leiden, The Netherlands, 1969. Appointments: Snr Lectr, Univ of Durban-Westville, 1972; Advocate of the Supreme Crt of S Africa; Prof, Hd, Dept of Pvt Law, 1974; Dean of Fac; Visng Schl, Columbia Law Sch, NY, 1980-81; Amb, Eur Union, Brussels, 1987-92; Min, 1993; Mbr, Natl Assembly, Kwazulu, Natal; Dpty Speaker of Parl, 1994; High Commnr, Austl, 1996; High Commnr, NZ, 1996; High Commnr, Fiji, 1997; High Commnr, Cook Is, 1998; Solomon Islands, 1999; High Commnr, Samoa, 1998. Publications: Wide Range of Social Issues. Memberships: Lawyers for Hum Rights; C'wlth Club; Natl Press Club. Address: South African High Commission, cnr State Circle and Rhodes Place, Canberra, ACT 2600, Australia.

RANE Ganish P, b. 5 July 1943, Karwar, India. Business Consultant to UN System Organiser. m. Suchita, 19 May 1974, 1 d. Education: Adv DME, 1964; Grad Adv Engrng, 1965; PGDIM (BOM), 1974; DOM (BOM), 1975; EDP-Prof Mgt (USA), 1976; EDP-Prod Mgt (BOM), 1975; PhD, CA, USA, 1995. Appointments include: Des & Dev Engr, 1965-76' Prodn Mngr, Chubb-Steelage, India, 1976-1980; Mngmt Educr/Entrepeneurship Trainer to Mngmt Insts in Mumbai & Overeas, 1976-82; Chf Chartered Engr & Mngmt Cnslt, Somalia, 1980-82; UNIDO Chf Tech Advsr to PDR Yemen, 1982-88; UNDP/UNIDO Chf Tech Advsr (CTA) to Vietnam, 1990-94; Chf Exec Dir, Pres, Entrepeneur, RRR Inds, 1987-; ULTRA-EDM Tools & Components Co Pvt Ltd, 1994-; RANE Cnsltncy Servs Pvt Ltd, 1988-; MITSUCHI EDM Technols Pvt Ltd, 1996-. Publications: 7 pprs presented publd. Honours include: State Hon, Pres of Somalia, 1982; State Hon, Min of Ind & Trade of Govt of PDR Yemen, 1988; Vijaya Shree Awd (Enriching Hum Life & for Outsndng Intl Achievement), 1994; Paul Harris Fell, Rotary Fndn, Rotary Inl (RI), 1994; RI Presdtl Citation Awd, 1996; RI Dist Disting Serv Awd, 1997; RI Predtl Citation Awd, 1997. Memberships include: Lic Profl Engr, ASME Intl, USA; Lic Indl Engr, Euro IE, Eurn Inst of Indl Engrs; Fndr, Permanent Trustee, Roatry Club of Mumbai W Coast Charitable Trust, 1997-; Inst Mechl Engrs (UK); Inst Mngmt Servs (UK); Intl Golfing Fellshp of Rotary; Intl Travel & Hosting Rotary Fellshp. Hobbies: Third World development efforts; Work on HIV/AIDS awareness and intervention programme; International friendship and goodwill; Travelling. Address: G3/105 Residency-B, Lokhandwala Complex, Andheri West, Mumbai 400053, Maharastra, India.

RANGASHREE, b. 16 May 1967, Bangalore, India. Artistic Director and Performing Artist (Classical Indian Dance). m. Mr M K Srinivas, 4 Mar 1990, 2 s. Education: BCom, 1989; Pre-Masters in Masters Comms & Jrnlsm, 1998. Career: Artistic Dir and Performing Artist, 1983-; Perfs at concerts, fests throughout India; Recitals at Sharjah, Dubai, Abu Dhabi, Untd Arab Emirates (invited by Stage of Sharjah), 1987; 21 perfs, malaysia, Sri Lanka, Singapore, Thailand, July-Aug 1994; On Ref Panel of Artists of the Indian Cncl for Cultural Rels (ICCR) for engagements abroad; Tours of USA, Can, UK incl 12 recitals, conducted 3 workshops, sev lec-dens; Took part in Indo Soviet Fest and World Kannada Meet, Mysore; Teaches Bharathanatyam in her instn Kinkini Nrithyashala. Creative works: Choreographic wrks (Solo & Grp), Shanthala, Malavika-Agnimitra, 1987; Ananada Thirtha Vauhini, 1991; Krishnanjali, 1994; Ramayan Drashana, 1996; Ushas, 1998. Honours: Best Dancer Awd, IFCA, Chennai, 1992; Selected to vis USA, CAn, by Rotary Intl under GSE Prog, 1998. Memberships: Life Mbr, Karnataka NRithya Kala Parishad and Assn of Bharathantyam Dancers of India. Hobbies: Singing; Reading; Cuisine. Address: 308, 10th Main, III Block, Jayanagar, Banglaore 560 011, India.

RANKINE Bryce Crossley, b. 23 Dec 1925, SA, Aust. Consultant. m. Ellaine Bosisto, 22 Feb 1950, 1 s, 2 d. Education: BSc 1945, MSc 1953, DSc 1971. Appointments: F H Faulding & Co Ltd, 1945-49; CSIRO Oeological Investigations, 1950-56; Austl Wine Rsch Inst, 1956-77; Roseworthy Agricl Coll, 1978-86; Dean, Fac of Oenology; Cnslt 1987-. Publications: 6 books on wine; Over 300 sci and tech pprs. Honours: AM, 1986; Awd of Merit, 1973; Fed Pres AIFST, 1982-83; Pres, Burnside Rotary Club, 1988; Dean, Fac of Oenology, Roseworth Agricl Coll, 1982-; McWilliam's Wines Maurice O'Shea Awd, 1998. Memberships: Fell, Roy Austl Chem Inst; Fell, Austl Inst of Food Scis and Technol; Fell, Austl Acady of Technol Scis and Engrng; Exec Dir, Austl Soc of Wine Educrs,1991-96. Hobbies: Wine; Golf; Swimming. Address: 227 Victoria Grove Estate, 254 Greenhill Road, Glenside, SA 5065, Australia.

RANSON David Leo, b. 23 Oct 1956, England. Forensic Pathologist. m. Sally, 25 June 1981, 1 s, 1 d. Education: BMedSci, 1978; BM, BS, 1980; LLB, 1987; MRCPath, 1987; DMJ, 1987; FRCPA, 1989; FRCPath, 1997. Appointments: Dpty Dir, Hd, Forensic Pathol Divsn, Vic Inst of Forensic Med; Hon Clin Assoc Prof, Dept of Forensic Med, Monash Univ; Snr Assoc, Sch of Dental Scis, Assoc, Dept of Pathol, Univ of Melbourne; Hon Assoc, Fac of Law, Monash Univ; Convenor, Forensic Pathol, Bd of Censors, Roy Coll of Pathols of Aust. Memberships: Fell, Roy Coll of Pathos, Aust, Roy Coll of Pathols UK; Assn of Clin Pathols; Intl Acady of Pathol; Brit Acady of Forensic Sci; Brit Assn of Forensic Med; Forensic Sci Soc; Assn of Police Surgns of GB; Austl & NZ Forensic Sci Soc; Am Acady of Forensic Scis; Austl Coll of Legal Med; Austl Acady of Forensic Sci. Hobbies: Amateur Radio; Singing; Early Music; Computing. Address: Victorian Institute of Forensic Medicine, 57-83 Kavanagh Street, Southbank, Victoria 3006, Australia.

RAO Chintamani Nagesa Ramachandra, b. 30 June 1934, Bangalore, India. Teacher. m. Indumati, 15 May 1960, 1 s. 1 d. Education: MSc, Banaras, 1953; PhD, Purdue, 1958; DSc, Mysore, 1960. Appointments: Hd, Dept Chem, Dean of Rsch, Indian Inst of Tech, Kanpur, 1963-77; Chmn, Solid State and Structural Chem Unit and Materials Rsch Cntr, Indian Inst Sci, Bangalore, 1977-84; Dir, Indian Inst of Sci, 1984-94; Pres, Jawaharlal Nehru Cntr for Advd Sci Rsch, 1994-. Publications: Over 950 rsch pubs and 34 books. Honours: Hon doctorates 23 univs in India and abroad; Marlow Medal, Faraday Soc; Bhatnagar Awd, CSIR, India; Jawaharlal Nehru Fellshp; Padma Vibhushan, Pres of India; SN Bose Medal, UGC, India; RSC, London, Medal; GM Modi Awd; Hevrovsky Gold Medal of Czech Acady Scis; Einstein Gold Medal, UNESCO; Hon Fellshp, Cardiff, Univ Wales; Linnett Visng Prof, Cambridge Univ. Memberships: Editl Bd over 15 profl journals; Fell, RS London, Indian Natl Sci Acady, Indian Acady Scis; FORN Assoc, Natl Acady Scis, USA; Amn Philos Soc; Acady Europaea; FORN Mbr, Russian, Polish, Czech, Slovenian, Serbian Academies of Scis; and many more natl and intl acadys and socs. Hobbies: Gourmet cooking; Gardening; Music. Listed in: International Book of

Honour; Men of Achievement; 5000 Personalities of the World; Who's Who in Science and Engineering. Address: J N Centre for Advanced Scientific Research, Bangalore 560012, India.

RAO Digamber, b. 4 Jan 1942, Kotgir, AP, India. Teaching; Research. m. Chandrakala, 2 s. Education: BS; MSc; PhD. Appointments: Lectr, 1967; Rdr, 1976; Prof, 1985-. Publications: 2 books; 180 rsch publs; Articles to books. Honours: Best Tchr Awd, Govt of AP, India, 1983-84; Snr Fulbright Fell, USA, 10 mths; Awd'd Visitorship under Indo-USSR Cultural Exchange Prog, 1982. Memberships: Acad Sen of 2 univs; Subj expert to var univs; Mbr, Chmn of Bd of Studies. Hobbies: Teaching; Reading; Writing; Listening to music. Address: Department of Botany, Kakatiya University, Warangal 506009, AP, India.

RAO Kakaraparti Visweswara, b. 1 July 1938. Reseacher. m. K Sita, 20 May 1958, 1 s, 2 d. Education: FA; BA; MA; MS, Hygiene; PhD; FIS; FISMS. Appointments: Rsch Asst, Asst Rschr, Rsch Offr, Snr Rschr, Asst Dir, Dpty Dir, Snr Dpty Dir, Natl Inst of Nutrition; Cnslt, NIMS, WHO. Publications: Diet Atlas of India, 1969, 1972; Statistics in Health and Nutrition, 1990; Biostatistics Manual, 1996; Nutrition Statistics in India, 1998; 200 rsch pprs. Honours: Prof Prasad's Gold Medal, Indian Soc for Medl Stats, 1986; Fell, Inst of Stats; Fell, Indian Soc Medl Stats; Gold Medals and Fellshps; Padmabhushan Prof P V Sukhatme's Awd, 1996. Memberships: Biometric Soc; Soc for Dev of Stats; Soc of Clin Biostats; Indian Soc for Med Stats; Nutrition Soc of India. Hobby: Writing. Listed in: Who's Who in the World; Who's Who in India; Harvard Alumni; Curriculum Vitae International; World Who's Who of Men and Women of Distinction, 1997. Address: House no 9-79, Fourth Crossroads, HMT Nagar, Nacharam Post, Hyderabad 500076, India.

RAO Kanury Venkata Subba, b. 27 Sept 1958, Lucknow, India. Scientist. m. Indu Rao, 5 June 1983, 1 s, 1 d. Education: PhD. Appointment: Hd, Immunology Grp, Intl Cntr for Genetic Engrng and Biotechnology. Publication: Optimalia, 1997. Honours: NII Snr Oration Awd, 1994; Shanti Swarup Bhatnagar Awd fr Biol Scis, 1997. Memberships: Fell, Indian Acady of Scis; Fell, Natl Acady of Scis. Hobby: Writing. Address: International Centre for Genetic Engineering and Biotechnology, Aruna Asaf Ali Marg, New Delhi 110 067, India.

RAO Prakash Krishna, b. 27 Jan 1951, India. Managing Director. m. Jyothi, 22 May 1981, 2 d. Education: Bach of Sci; Postgrad, Mktng Mngmt. Appointments: Dir, Indian Ops, Tolaram Grp, Singapore, 1981-; Mngng Dir, Tashi Grp of Co's, Bhutan, 1988-. Hobbies: Reading; Music. Address: Tashi Group of Companies, TCC Complex Building, Phuentsholing, Royal Kingdom of Bhutan.

RAO Raman, b. 26 May 1955, Visakhapatnam, India. Research, Teaching. m. Lalita, 9 Dec 1980, 2 s. Education: PhD (Animal Nutrition). Appointment: Jnr Rsch Offr. Memberships: Animal Nutr Assn of India; IVRI; Izatnagar. Hobbies: Sports; Tennis; Music. Address: Department of Animal Science, Agriculture College, Pantnagar 263145, India.

RAO Shakunthala Bai Panduranga, b. 25 Apr 1921, Bangalore, India. Musician. m. B S Panduranga Rao dec, 5 May 1930, 1 s, 3 d. Appointments: Num Concerts Worldwide. Publications: Gamaka Rasayana; Gamaka Kalae mattu Mahilae. Honours: State Sahitya Acady Awd, 1971; Rajyotsava Awd, 1996. Hobbies: Reading; Music. Address: No 825 Kumara Vyasa Krupa II Stage "E" Block, III Main Road, Rajainagar, Bangalore 10, India.

RAO Srinath, b. 15 Dec 1954, Raichur, India. Teaching; Research. m. Kavitha, 1 s, 1 d. Education: MSc; PhD. Appointments: Lectr, 1980; Reader, 1986, Prof, 1994. Membership: Life Mbr, Indian Botanical Soc. Hobbies: Cricket; Music. Address: Department of Botany, Gulbarga, Gulbarga.

RAO Suresh, b. 12 Sept 1945, Mangalore, India. Business Manager. m. Sudha, 28 May 1972, 2 s. Education: BE, EE; MBA, IIMA; Postgrad Dip, Bus Admin. Appointments: Head of Sales, Electric Bus Equips, Godrej; VP (West) Maxworth Orchards; Grp Pres, Easycall Paging, India. Hobbies: Business and Social Writing; Studying different cultures. Address: 402A Savera, Picnic Cottage, Seven Bungalows, Mumbai 400061, India.

RARES Steven David, b. 15 Nov 1953, London, Eng. Barrister-at-Law. m. Madelein Willis Jones, 20 Apr 1985, 1 s. Education: BA, 1975, LLB, 1978, Univ Sydney. Appointments: Sol, Dudley Westgarth and Co, 1979; Admitted NSW Bar, 1980; Snr Cnsl, NSW, 1993; QC, WA, 1995. Membership: Hon Asst, Austl Inst Judicial Admin Inc, 1984-87. Hobbies: Chess; Skiing; Reading; Swimming. Address: 180 Phillip Street, Sydney, NSW 2000, Australia.

RASHEED Natheer al, b. 19 June 1929, Jordan. Business Executive; Civil Servant. m. Rabia al-Rasheed, 1961, 4 s, 1 d. Education: Brit Army & Staff Mil Coll. Appointments: Dir Gen, Intelligence, Jordan, 1969-73; Chf, Bd of Dirs, Jordan Mines Phosphate Co, 1976; Senator, 1989-. Honours: 3 medals. Hobbies: Horse Riding; Shooting. Address: PO Box 6583, Amman, Jordan.

RASMOD NIDI Anant Ram Saran, b. 7 May 1949, Janakpur Dham, India. Service. Appointment: Reliable Sources or Dr Bhanudatt Tripathe Madhwesh. Publications: Sev. Hobby: Religion. Address: Mani Ram Printing Press, Shastrinagar, Myodhiyaji, India.

RASMUSSEN Finn Basse, b. 1 June 1956, Copenhagen, Denmark. m.Antonieta, 1 d. Education: HS, Aalborg (Denmark) Univ, 1976; BSch EE Eng Sch, Aarhus, Denmark, 1979. Appointments: Proj Engr, 1979-81, 1989-90, F L Smidth & Co A/S Copenhagen; Erection Mngr, F L Smidth & Co A/S worldwide, 1981-89; Prodn Mngr, Junckers Inds A/S, Koege, Denmark, 1991-94; Plant and Proj Mngr, P T Sumalindo, Jakarta, Indonesia, 1994-96; Owners Repr, P T Nityasa Mandiri, 1995-96; Owner, FBR-Cnsltng Medellin, Columbia, 1996-. Honours include: IBC, Cambridge, 1997; ABI, 1997; MOIF, IBC, 1998; Outstndng Achievement Awds, People of the 20th Century, IBC, 1998/99; DB, Dpty Gov, ABI Rsch, 1998; Nom: Order of Intl Ambs, 2000 Millennium Medal of Hon, Gold Record of Achievement for 1998, 1998. Hobbies: Family; Computing; Software; Fishing; Tennis; Golf. Address: Cr 43A 12A Sur 190, Bosque del Campestre, El Poblado-Medellin, Colombia.

RASTOGI Raghunath Prasad, b. 4 June 1926, Lucknow, India. Scientist. m. Kamla Rastogi, 19 May 1944, 2 s, 1 d. Education: MSc; PhD. Appointments: Lectr in Chem, Lucknow Univ, 1949-59; Rdr, Punjab Univ, 1959-61; Prof, Hd, Chem Dept, Gorakhipur Univ, 1962-85; Vice Chan, Banaras Hindu Univ, 1985-91. Publications: Introduction to Chemical Thermodynamics, 1978; An Introduction to Quantum Mechanics of Chemical Systems, 1986. Honours: Khosla Natl Awd, 1974; Fedn of Indian Cham of Com & Ind Awd, 1975; Prof S R Palib Awd, 1985; UGC Meglmad Saha Awd, 1985; Indian Natl Sci Acady Awd, 1992; Indian Chemical Soc, P C Ray Mem Medal, 1998. Memberships: Fell, Indian Natl Sci Acady; Indian Acady of Scis; Natl Acady of Scis. Hobbies: Scientific Research; Meditation. Address: Chemistry Department, Lucknow University, Lucknow, India.

RASTOGI Ram Gopal, b. 26 Dec 1929, Allahabad, India. Research Scientist. m. Malati, 14 Dec 1951, 4 s, 1 d. Education: BSc, 1947, MSc, 1949, Allahabad Univ; PhD, Gujarat Univ, 1956. Appointments: Lectr, Phys, Saugar Univ, 1949-51; Rsch Schl, Physl Rsch Lab, Ahmedabad, 1951-58; Postdoct Fell, NRC Can, 1958-60, HAO Boulder, CO, USA, 1960-61; Fell, Assoc Prof, PRL, 1961-77; Snr Rsch Assoc, NRC at AFGL, Bedford, USA, 1977-80; Dir, Indian Inst of Geomagnetism, 1980-90; Emer Sci, CSIRO India, 1990-93; Snr Sci, Indian Natl Sci Acady, 1995-. Publications: 360 rsch pprs in intl jrnls.

Honours: Hari Om Ashram Awd, Gujarat Univ, 1977. USSR Acady of Sci Medal, 1984; Japanese Geophysl Medal, 1985. Memberships: Fell, Indian Natl Sci Acady, New Delhi, Indian Acady of Sci, Bangalore, Indian Geophysl Union, Hyderabad, Assn of Exploration Geophys, Hyderabad; Life Mbr, Indian Phys Assn, Bombay; Co-Chmn, Divsn III of IAGA, 1979-83; Exec Cttee, IAGA, 1983-87; Chmn, Cmmn on Devel Countries, 1983-87. Hobbies: Photography; Gardening. Address: 51 Spring Field, Vastrapur, Ahmedabad 380 054, India.

RASTOGI Shekhar, b. 10 Mar 1964, Kanpur, India. Ophthalmologist; Doctor. m. Vibha, 13 July 1994, 1 s. Education: MBBS; MS, Ophthalmol; Fell, AEH; FCLI. Appointments: Res, Ophthalmol, GSVM Med Coll, 1989-92; Fell, Arauihd Eye Hosp, 1993-95; Fell, Contact Lens Soc, 1995; Cnslt, Eye Hosp, Kanpur, 1995-96; Regency Hosp, 1996-. Publications: 12 rsch pprs. Memberships: Eye Bank Assn of India, 1996-97; All India & UP State Ophthalmol Soc; Delhi Ophathalmol Soc; Intraocular Implant & Refractive Soc; Austl Contact Lens Soc. Hobbies: Reading; Computers; Swimming. Address: 118/374-A Kaushal Puri, Kanpur 208012 UP, India.

RASTOGI Vibha, b. 23 Sept 1969, Kanpur, India. Doctor. m. Shekhar, 13 July 1994, 1 s. Education: MBBS; MS, Ophthalmol. Appointments: Res, Ophthalmol, King George Med Coll, 1992-95; Jnr Cnslt, Dr J L Rohatgi Eye Hosp, 1995-96; Practising Paediat Ophthalmol, 1997-. Membership: Eye Bank Assn of India, 1997-98. Hobbies: Reading; Watching Nature; Painting. Address: 110/374-A Kaushal Puri, Kanpur UP 208012, India.

RATCLIFFE John, b. 12 Apr 1941, Quetta, India. Pediatric Radiologist. m. Dr Helen Kerr, 24 Aug 1972, 1 s, 1 d. Education: MBBS (London); MRCS (Eng); LRCP (London); D(Obstet) RCOG; MRCGP; FRCS (Edin); FRCR; FRACR. Appointments: Medl and Surg Residencies, UK, 1964-69; Surg Registrar in Pediats, Saigon, 1969-70; Trainee Registrar, Radiology, Bristol and Sheffield; Cnslt Radiologist, Booth Hall Hosp, Manchester, 1980-85; Dir of Radiology, Roy Children's Hosp, Brisbane, Aust. Publications: Multiple pprs and chapts in books on pediatric radiology. Honours: Gold Medal, Back Pain Soc, 1982; Boris Rajewshi Medal, Eurn Soc of Radiology, 1983. Memberships: RCR; RACR; Brit Inst of Radiology; RSNA; Roentgen Ray Soc; Australasian Soc of Pediatric Imagery. Hobbies: Paediatric Radiology; Teaching; Bush walking; Wines; Family pursuits. Address: The Radiology Department, The Royal Children's Hospital, Brisbane 4029, Australia.

RATEAVER Bargyla, b. 3 Aug 1916, Madagascar. Writer. 1 s. Education: AB, Botany, Univ CA, Berkeley, 1938-43; MS, 1945-50, PhD, 1950-51, Univ MI, Ann Arbor; MSLS, 1958-59. Appointments: Organized and Introduced num extension and trng progs in univs and colls. Honours: Awd, Plant Introduction, USDA and Joel Spingarn Clematis Collection, 1935; Hon Student, Univ CA, Berkeley, 1938; Grant, Longwood Gardens, 1955; Awd, Chgo Mus of Natural Hist, 1955; Awd, Am Acady of Arts and Scis, 1955; 1st Prize, Della Sizler Graphic Arts Collection, Univ CA, Berkeley, 1959; 1st Prize Awd, Cttee for Sustainable Agricl, 1988; 1st Prize Awd, Acres USA, Lifetime Achievement, 1994. Hobbies: Gardening; Bible Study. Address: 9049 Covina Street, San Diego, CA 92126, USA.

RATHER Mehraj-ud Din, b. 27 Aug 1960, Kashmir, India. Teaching and Research. Education: PhD, Botany. Appointments: Lectr, Dept of Botany, Univ of Kashmir, Seinagar. Publications: 25 rsch publs in field of botany. Honours: Young Scientist Awd, Dept of Sci & Technol, 1995; Young Scientist Fellshp, Dept of Sci & Tech, J & Govt. Memberships: Hon Mbr, Exec Cttee & Editl Bd of rsch jrnls: Nature & Biosphere and Vigyau Paridhi, India. Hobbies: Cricket; Gardening. Address: Lecturer, Department of Botany, University of Kashmir, Srinagar, Kashmir, 190011, India.

RATTAKUL Bhichai, b. 16 Sept 1926. Education: St Stephen Coll, Hong Kong. Appointments: Mbr of Parl, 1969, 1975, 1976, 1983, 1988, 1995, 1996; Mbr, Natl

Legislative Assembly, 1973; Min of For Affairs, 1975, 1976; Dpty Prime Min, 1983, 1986, 1988. Honours: Kt Grand Cordon, Spec Class, Most Exalted Order of the White Elephant; Hon Doct, Law, Ramkhamhaeng Univ, Pol Sci, USA. Address: 231 Panya Village, Pattanakan Suan Leung Road, Bangkok, Thailand.

RATTANAKOSES Mana, b. 16 Sept 1925, Thailand. Politician. m. Pol Col Chalerm, 4 children. Education: Chulachomklao Roy Mil Acady. Appointments: Mil Career, until 1986; MP for Nakhon Prov, 1986-; Fmr Dpty educn min; Min of Educn, 1988-90; Dpty PM, 1990; Co-Fndr, Sec-Gen, Rassadorn Pty. Address: Office of the Deputy Prime Minister, Rassadorn Party, Bangkok, Thailand.

RAU Dar-Chin, b. 31 July 1950, Taipei, Taiwan. Education. m. Long-Mei Lo, 1976, 1 s, 1 d. Education: DEd. Appointments: Hd, Dept of Indl Educ, 1986-92, Grad, Inst of Indl Educ, 1988-92, Dir, Tech and VocEd Rsch Cntr, 1992-99, Natl Taiwan Normal Univ; Cnslt, Bus Automation Technol, Exec Yuan, 1995-99; VP, Intl Vocl Educ and Trng Assn (IVETA), 1997-2000. Publications: Over 10 books; 240 pprs, 1979-99. Honours: Valued Supporter, IVETA, 1998; Century Awds ABI. Memberships: Intl Vocational Educ and Trng Assn, USA, 1990; Chinese Vocational Indl Educ Assn, Taipei. Hobbies: Reading; Badminton. Address: 162, Hoping E Road, Sec 1, Taipei, Taiwan, China.

RAVEENDRAN Kaithoorknam, b. 1 Feb 1945, India. Social worker; General Secretary. m. Sumathy, 10 Dec 1977, 1 s, 2 d. Education: Ctf Courses. Hobbies: Kalaripayathu; Sidha Vaidya. Address: Chief Editor, Gold Star, Sreekamaraj Service Society, Pravachambalam, Thiruvananthapuram, India.

RAVEENDRANATHAN Puthanpurayil Choyan, b. 30 Oct 1944, Tellicherry. Engineer. m. P K Shylasa, 30 Oct 1975, 2 d. Education: Deg, Elecl Engrng, Regional Engrng Coll, Calcut, Kerala, India, 1967. Appointments: First Grade Over Seer, Kerala State Elec Bd; Jnr Engr; Asst Engr; Asst Ex Engr; Ex Engr; Dpty Chf Engr. Memberships: Inst of Elecl and Electrons Engrs Inc, USA; NY Acady of Sci; World Wide Fund for Nature; Water Resource Mngmnt Soc of India; Energy Conserv Soc of India; Admin Staff Coll of India Assn. Hobbies: Thinking; Strategy Making; Developments of All. Address: Poyyeri Buildings, PO REC Calcut 673601, Kerala, India.

RAVENSCROFT Peter John, b. 25 Apr 1942. Director of Palliative Care. m. Dr Elizabeth Ravenscroft (Nicholson), 27 Mar 1989, 1 s, 1 d. Education: MB, BS, 1966, MD, 1989, Qld; FRACP, 1975. Appointments: Dir of Clin Pharmacology, Princess Alexandra Hosp, 1983-92; Assoc Prof of Clinl Pharm, Univ of Qld, 1989-92; Prof of Palliative Care, Univ of Newcastle, Dir of Palliative Care, Newcastle Mater Hosp, 1992-. Publications: Guide to Symptom Control in Advanced Disease, co-auth, 1995. Honours: Merck, Sharpe and Dohme Rsch Fellshp in Clinl Pharm, 1972-72; Natl Hlth and Medl Rsch Cncl Fellshp, 1974-77. Memberships: Past Pres, Austl Soc of Clin Expmntl Pharmacologists, 1958-89; Pres, Austl and NZ Soc for Palliative Med, 1994-. Hobbies: Bushwalking; Tennis. Address: 9 Whiley Close, Merewether, NSW, Australia.

RAVINDRANATHAN Thottappillil, b. 27 Apr 1940, Trichur, Kerala, India. Scientist. m. Geeta, 1 Jan 1974, 1 s, 1 d. Education: BSc, Kerala Univ, 1959; BSc, Tech, 1962, PhD, Tech, 1967, Bombay Univ. Appointments: Jnr Rsch Fell, Snr Rsch Fell, CSIR, 1962-67; Postdoct Fell, Cambridge Univ, 1967-69, Harvard Univ, 1969-70; 1970-73; Sci C, 1973-79, Sci E-I, 1979-84, Sci E-II, 1984, Sci F, 1989-, Hd, Divsn of Org Chem Tech, 1991-, CSIR/NCL. Publications include: Biotransformation derived useful drug and pesticide intermediates, 1992; New Synthetic Strategies Towards (+)-Artemisinin, 1994; Polymer Supported Nitrobenzaldehyde: Efficient, Highly Selective Catalytic Deprotection of Oxathioacetals, 1994. Honours: 2 ICMA Awds; Vis Fellshp, 1990-91; Ranbaxy Rsch Awd, 1991; K G Naik Gold Medal, 1990; Dr R C Shah Meml Lectrshp, 1992; Prof K Venkataraman

Lectrshp, 1995. Memberships: Indian Chem Soc; Am Chem Soc; Britannica Soc. Address: B-1 Bungalow, NCL Colony, Pune 411008, India.

RAWAT Anil, b. 7 May 1962, Dhar (MP), India. Computer Engineer. m. Rashmi, 24 May 1989, 1 s, 1 d. Education: BEng, Electrons & Telecomms, 1984; MEng, Computer, 1990. Appointments: Larsen & Tonbro Ltd, Mumbai, 1984-85; Fac, Univ of Indore, 1985-88; Sci Offr, Cntr for Advd Technol, 1988-. Honour: MP, Young Scientist Awd, 1994; Membership: Computer Soc of India. Hobbies: Reading; Philately; Playing chess & quigging; Tourism. Address: D-26/6, Cat Colony, PO Cat, Indore, MP 452013, India.

RAWAT Pheku Prasad, b. 23 July 1947. Library and Information Scientist. m. Kamalesh Rawat, 1970, 2 s, 2 d. Education: MA Sociol and Hist; Master Deg in Lib and Info Sci; PhD, Lib and Info Sci. Appointments: Chf Libn, Bundelkhand Ayurvedic Coll, Jhansi, 1976-88; Hon Prin, Lib Sci, Jhansi, 1977-88; Chf Libn, Sanjaygandhi Postgrad Inst Medl Scis, Lucknow, 1988-. Publications: International Encyclopaedia of Information Technology and Library Science; 20 pprs; 25 reviews. Honours: Bhamasa Awd for First in Deg in Lib Sci. Memberships: Indian Lib Assn; Medl Lib Assn of India; Indian Assn of Spec Lib and Info Cntrs; Assn of Govt Lib and Info Cntrs. Hobbies: Touring; Reading. Address: Sanjay Gandhi, Postgraduate Institute of Medical Sciences, Post Box No 375, Lucknow 226014, India.

RAWSTRON Richard Ewart, b. 3 Mar 1916, Christchurch, NZ. Physician; Anaesthetist. m. Jessie D Gunn, 18 Apr 1945, 3 s. Education: MB CHB, 1942; FFARACS, 1956; MD, 1973; FANZCA, 1992. Appointments: Visng Anaesthetist, Waikato Hosp, 1948-54, 1956-57; Dir of Anaesthetics, Palmerston N, 1957-80; Visng Anaesthetist, Horowhekua Hosp, 1982-90. Publications: Sev articles in profl med jrnls. Honours: Fellshp, Western Reserve Univ Hosp, 1961; NZ Soc of Anaesthetists, Pres 1964-65; DAAD Fellshp, Johannes Gutenberg Univ, 1977; Rotary, Paul Harris Fell, 1996. Memberships include: NZ Med Assn. Hobby: Gardening. Address: 66 Te Awe Awe Street, Palmerston North 5301, New Zealand.

RAY Pamela May, b. 1 May 1936, Sydney, NSW, Aust. Librarian. m. Alan, 23 Feb 1957, 3 d. Education: BA. Appointments: Dept of Primary Inds, 1973-77; Natl Lib of Aust, 1977-88; Austl War mem; 1988-98. Creative Works: Num Pubs on mil hist recs. Honours: Fell, Heraldry and Genealogy Soc of Canberra. Memberships: Austl Lib and Info Assn; Austl Soc of Archivists, Heraldry and Genealogy Soc of Canberra. Hobbies: Genealogy, Local Hist. Address: 67 Hopetoun Circuit, Yarralumla, ACT 2600, Australia.

RAY Purnima, b. 3 Jan 1959, Bajitpur, India. Teaching. m. Mohit Ray, 25 Sept 1981, 1 s, 1 d. Education: BA, hons, Engl, 1978, MA, Engl, 1981, Burdwan and Visva-Bharati Univs; Adv Dip, French, 1991; Ctf course in German, BU, 1999. Appointments: Tchr, Higher Second Sch, 1981; Pt-time Lectr, French, Burdwan Univ, 1993-. Publications: 4 books and sev essays, poems and transl. Honours: 20th Century Achievement Medal, IBC, 1997; Sev distinctions and awds. Memberships: Writers Forum, Ranchi; Intl Soc of Greek Writers, Athens. Hobbies: Cooking; Reading; Singing. Address: U5A Tarabag, Burdwan 713104, India.

RAY Ranjan, b. 16 Aug 1949, Calcutta, India. Professor of Economics. m. Maitraee, 21 July 1988, 1 d. Education: BA, Univ Calcutta; MA, Delhi Sch of Econs; PhD, London Sch of Econs. Appointments: Lectr, Manchester Univ, England, 1979-89; Prof, Delhi Univ, 1989-95, Univ Tas, 1995-. Honour: Competitive Grant, Austl Rsch Cncl. Memberships: Indian Econometric Soc; Fndng Mbr, Cntr for Devel Econs, Delhi. Address: School of Economics, University of Tasmania, GPO Box 252-85, Hobart 7001, Australia.

RAY Robert Francis, b. 8 Apr 1947, Melbourne, Australia. Politician. m. Jane Ray. Education: Rushden

State Coll. Appointments: Fmr Sch Tchr; Senator, Vic, 1980-; Mbr, Austl Labour Pty Natl Exec, 1983-; Min for Home Affairs, Dpty Mngr of Govt Bus in the Senate, 1987-88, for Transp & Comms, 1988, for Immigration, Local Govt & Ethnic Affairs, Min Asst PM for Multicultural Affairs, 1988-90, for Def, 1990-96; Dpty Ldr of Govt in Senate, 1993-96. Hobbies: Films; Billiards; Tennis; Watching Australian Rules Football; Golf; Cricket. Address: Suite 3, Level 2, Illoura Plaza, 424 St Kilda Road, Melbourne, Victoria 3004, Australia.

RAYES Ghazi al, b. 23 Aug 1935, Kuwait. Diplomat. Education: Univ Cairo, Egypt. Appointments: 3rd Sec, Min of Fgn Affairs, 1962; Kuwaiti Emb, Washing & Beirut, 1965-67; Chair, Intl Affairs Section, Min of Fgn Affairs, 1967-70; Cnslr, Kuwaiti Emb, Beirut, 1970-73; Amb to Bahrain, 1974-80, to UK, 1980-93, to China, 1993-97; Hd, Follow-up & Coord Off, Hd, Protocol Dept, Min of Fgn Affairs, 1997-. Address: Ministry of Foreign Affairs, PO Box 3, 13001 Safat Gulf Street, Kuwait City, Kuwait.

RAYMOND Oliver John, b. 7 Feb 1939, Melbourne, Vic, Aust. Retired Defence Scientist; Musician. m. Helen Dalrymple Hamilton, 12 May 1962, 2 s, 1 d. Education: BE (Elec), Univ of Melbourne, 1960; DPhil, Univ of York, Eng, 1968; AMusA, Austl Music Examinations Bd, 1990. Appointments: Sci Offr, Rsch Sci, Def Standards Labs, 1961-69; Snr Rsch Sci, Austl Army Ops Rsch Grp, 1969-72; Prin Rsch Sci (policy and analysis positions), Dept of Def, 1972-78; Cmmnr in ACT Br, Scout Assn of Aust, 1975-89, Br Cmmnr for Rsch, 1981-89; Asst Sec, Force Devl and Analysis Div, Dept Def, 1978-82; Chmn, ACT Br, Austl Inst of Phys, 1981, 1982; Air Force Sci Advsr, 1982-84; Snr Exec Positions, Def Sci and Technol Org, 1984-91 (1st Asst Sec, Sci Policy, 1988-91); Special Advsr, Intellectual Property, Dept of Def, 1991-92; Pres, Canberra Repertory Soc, 1990-93; Choirmaster, St Paul's Anglican Ch, Manuka, ACT, 1994-; Pres, Oriana Chorale, 1988-91, 1995-; Pres, ACT Lieder Soc, 1995-; Mbr, Judging Panel, Canberra Area Th Awds, 1995-. Honour: Medal of Merit, Scout Assn of Aust, 1984. Membership: FAIP. Hobbies: Music, especially singing; Theatre. Address: 91 Jansz Crescent, Griffith, ACT 2603, Australia.

RAYMONT Warwick Deane, b. 14 June 1941, Jamestown, S Aust. Research Scientist; Consultant. m. Sandra, 23 Oct 1988, 3 s, 1 d. Education: BSc, Dip Ed (ASOPA/UNSW); PhD, USM, London; DSc, Cty Univ Los Angeles; Dip Chem, ICS; Dip T Sec, Univ of SA. Appointments: Mngr, R&D Pharmalliance Pty Ltd, 1990-; Priv Prac, 1980-; Postdoct Fellshp, NY, 1977-79; Second Sci Tchng, 1972-77; Chem, Chf Chem, Dir, Dairy Analytical Labs, Tasmania, 1965-72; Sci Master, 1963-65. Publications: Num publs and invited participation in symposia. Honours: 20th Century Achievement Awds (US), 1995, 1997; Golf Record for Achievement (US), 1995; 20th Century Awd for Achievement (UK), 1996; Lifetime Dpty Gov, ABI Rsch Assn, 1995; Aust Patent 679162, 1997. Memberships: Amn Chem Soc, 1970; Chmn, Mordla Community Assn, 1985-87; NY Acady Scis, 1992. Hobbies: Aviation; Languages; Environment. Address: PO Box 963, Kent Town, SA 5071, Australia.

RAYNER Moira Emilie, b. 10 Nov 1948, Dunedin, NZ. Barrister; Solicitor. Education: Univ WA; Murdoch Univ. Appointments: Admitted to Bar & Solr Supreme Crt, WA, 1972, Vic, 1990, NSW, 1994; Chmn, Law Reform Commsn, WA, 1988-90; Commsnr, Equal Opportunity, Vic, 1990-94; Cmmsnr, C'wlth Human Rights & Equal Opportunity Commsn, 1994-; Adj Prof, Fac of Arts, Deakin Univ, 1994; Chair, Cl Complaints Resolution Scheme Fin Planning Assn, Aust, 1995-; Trustee, Stegley Fndn, Chair, Natl Children's & Youth Law Cntr, Intl Commsn Jurists Vic, Univ Melbourne Advsry Bds, Cl Law Inst, Vic, 1995-. Publications: The Commonwealth's Role in Preventing Child Abuse, 1995; Rooting Democracy: Growing the Society We Want, 1997. Hobbies: Music; Reading; Walking the Dog; Writing. Address: c/o Almost Managing Co, PO Box 1034, Carlton, Victoria 3053, Australia.

RAZAK Dato Sri Mohamad Najib bin tun Haj Abdul, b. 23 July 1954, Kuala Lipis, Pahang, Malaysia. Politician. m. Tengku Puteri Zainah bint Tengku Iskandar, 3 children. Education: Univ of Nottingham. Appointments: Exec, Patronas, 1974-78; MP, 1976-; Pengerusi Majuternak, 1977-78; Dpty Min of Energy, Telecoms & Posts, 1978-80, of Educn, 1980-81, of Fin, 1981-82; Mbr, UMNO Supreme Cncl, 1981-; VP, UMNO Youth, 1982-; Mbr, State Assembly for Pakan Constituency, 1982; Apptd Menteri Besar Pahang, 1982; Chair, Pahang Fndn, 1982-86; Min of Youth & Sports, 1986-90. Address: Ministry of Culture, Youth & Sports, 15th Floor, Wisma Keramat, Jalan Gurney, 50570 Kuala Lumpur, Malaysia.

READ Ian Gregory, b. 2 Oct 1950, Sydney, Australia. Author. Education: BA; Dip, Edcn. Publications: The Bush: A Guide to the Vegetated Landscapes of Australia, 1994; Australia's Outback, 4 vol guide, 1994-97; Continent of Extremes, 1998; Australia's Eastern Outback: The Eco-Touring Guide. Hobbies: Car Touring; Travelling; Photography; Camping. Address: The Dairy Cottage, Bamarang via Nowra, NSW 2540, Australia.

READ John Russell Lee, b. 9 June 1939. Geological Engineer. m. Valerie Thorp, 28 Aug 1968, 2 d. Education: BSc, Univ of NZ, 1962; MSc, Univ of Canterbury, 1965; Grad Dip Mngmt, Capricornia Inst Adv Educ, 1982; PhD, Purdue Univ, 1987. Appointments: Dpty Chf, CSIRO Exploration & Mining, 1994; Exec Mngr, Qld Cntr for Advd Technologies, 1994; Prin, John R Read Assocs Pty Ltd, 1990; Snr Engr Geol and Assoc, Golder Assocs Inc, 1987; Supt Engrng Geol, Bougainville Copper Ltd, 1980; Supt Geol, MMBW Melb, 1977; Snr Engr Geol & Assoc, Coffey & Ptnrs Pty Ltd, 1968; Engrng Geol, Aust Bur of Mineral Resources, 1964. Memberships: MIE Aust; CPEng; FAusIMM; Intl Soc of Rock Mechs; Intl Soc Engrng Geols; Austn Geomechanics Soc. Hobbies: Cricket; Rugby; Scuba Diving; Music; Ceramic Art. Address: 27 Adsett Street, Taringa, Qld 4068, Australia.

REDDING Paul Michael, b. 14 Oct 1948, Sydney, Australia. Philosopher. m. Vicki Varvaressos, 7 Dec 1972. Education: MBBS, hons, Univ NSW, 1972; BA, hons, 1976, PhD, 1984, Univ Sydney. Appointments: Lectr, Philos, 1985-87, 191-92, Snr Lectr, 1993-97, Assoc Prof, 1998-, Univ Sydney; Lectr, Philos, Macquarie Univ, 188-90. Publication: Hegel's Hermeneutics, 1996. Honour: Philos Fell, Sch of Adv Study, Univ London, 1996. Membership: VP, Sydney Sco of Lit & Aesthetics, 1997-. Hobby: Surfing. Address: Department of General Philosophy, University of Sydney, NSW 2006, Australia.

REDDY Krishna N, b. 15 July 1925, Chittoor, Andhra Pradesh, India. Artist; Teacher. m. Judith Blum, 27 July 1967, 1 d. Education: Dip in Fine Arts, Vishvabharti Univ, Santiniketan, India, 1947; Ctf, Fine Arts, Slade Sch of Art, London Univ, London, 1951. Career: Joined S W Hayter, 1952; Co-dir, Atelier 17, 1965-76; Prof, Artist-in-Res and Dir, Graphics and Printmaking Prog, NY Univ, NY, USA; Artist; Printmaker; Sculptor; Author; Educator; Lecturer; Over 50 one-man shows and participation in intl exhibns worldwide; Innovations in printmaking incl discovery of color viscosity. Honours: Padma Shree title awarded by Pres of India, 1972; Title of Kala Ratna, All India Fine Arts and Crafts Soc, New Delhi, 1997. Membership: Bd of Dirs, Intl Soc for Advmnt of Living Trads in Art, NY. Address: 80 Wooster Street, New York, NY 10012, USA.

REDFORD Amy, b. 19 May 1954, Petersburg, VA, USA. Teacher. Div. 1 d. Education: MEduc; BA. Appointments: Virginia Beach Pub Schs elem tchr, 1990-97; Nagoya Intl Sch, 1997-. Honours: Reading Tchr of Yr, 1995-96; Champion Cable in the Classroom Tchr, Cox Coms, 1996; Grt Rdr, Cox Comms, 1996. Memberships: VA Educ Assn, 1990-99; PTA, 1990-; VA Beach Symph Orch League; Japan Tchr Conf Repr, 1998-99. Hobbies: Travelling; Reading; Piano; Tennis; Sailing. Address: 1200 Yancey Circle, Virginia Beach, VA 23454, USA.

REDFORD Robert, b. 18 Aug 1937, Santa Monica, California, USA. Actor. m. Lola Van Wegenen (div), 3 children. Education: Univ CO. Creative Works: Films incl:

War Hunt, 1961; Situation Hopeless But Not Serious, 1965; Inside Daisy Clover, 1965; The Chase, 1965; This Property is Condemned, 1966; Barefoot in the Park, 1967; Tell Them Willie Boy is Here, 1969; Butch Cassidy and the Sundance Kid, 1969; Downhill Racer, 1969; Little Fauss and Big Halsy, 1970; Jeremiah Johnson, 1972; The Candidate, 1972; How to Steal a Diamond in Four Uneasy Lessons, 1972; The Way We Were, 1973; The Sting, 1973; The Great Gatsby, 1974; The Great Waldo Pepper, 1974; Three Days of the Condor, 1975; All the President's Men, 1976; A Bridge Too Far, 1977; The Electric Horseman, 1980; Brubaker, 1980; The Natural, 1984; Out of Africa, 1985; Legal Eagles, 1986; Havana, 1991; Sneakers, 1992; A River Runs Through It, 1992; Quiz Show, 1994; The River Wild, 1995; Up Close and Personal, 1996; The Horse Whisperer, 1997. Honours include: Acady Awd & Golden Globe Awd for Best Dir, 1981; Audubon Medal, 1989; Dartmouth Film Soc Awd, 1990. Address: c/o Wildwood Productions, 1101 Montana Avenue, Suite E, Santa Monica, CA 90403, USA.

REDMOND John Kyle, b. 27 June 1947, London, Eng. Faculty Dean; Professor. m. Helen Olivia Bondfield, 1 d. Education: BA, Hons, Cntrl Sch of Art and Des, London, 1970; MA, Roy Coll of Art, 1973. Appointments: Cnslt Des, 1970-75; Snr Lectr, Indl Des, 1975-, Dir, Grad Prog in Indl Des, 1983-, Unv of NSW, Aust; Cnslt Des in conjunction w Unisearch Ltd; Prof of Indl Des and Dean of Art and Des, Monash Univ; Visng Prof, Dept of Indl Des, Univ of NSW. Publications: Articles in profl jrnls. Honours: Yablon Awd for Des, 1968; Royal Soc of the Arts Bursary, 1969. Memberships: Mbr Austl Acady of Des; Fell, Royal Soc of Arts; Fell, Des Inst of Aust; Fell, Des Rsch Soc. Address: Faculty of Art & Design, Monash University, 900 Dandenong Road, Caulfield Gast, Vic 3145, Australia.

REECE Rodney Leon, b. 9 Jan 1949. Vet Pathologist. m. Janette Gladys Evelyn Mitchell, 1 s, 2 d. Education: BVSc, Sydney Univ, 1971; MSc, James Cook Univ, 1975; PhD, Bristol Univ, 1996; MACVSc, Avian Diseases, 1985; FACVSc, Avian Mngmt & Hlth, 1987; MRCVS, London, 1987; Dip, Bible Studies, Vision Coll, 1987; Regd Specialist in Avian Med (Poultry), 1997. Appointments: Vet prac at Wingham, NSW, 1971-72; Overseas aid expert w Austl Dev Assistance Bur in Solomon Is, 1974-77; Vet path specialising in avian diseases for Agric Vic at Vet Rsch Inst, Melbourne, 1977-87; Prin vet offr for Inst of Animal Hlth at Houghton Lab, UK, 1987-92; Vet Pathologist, Taronga Zoo, Sydney, 1992-94; Registrar, natl Registry Domestic Animal Path, Camden NSW, 1992-; Snr Vet Rsch Offr (poultry), NSW Agric EMAI, Camden, NSW, 1994-97; Vet Pathologist (diagnostic path), NSW Agric, Camden, NSW, 1997-. Publication: Color Atlas of Avian Histopathology (w Randall C J), 1996; Regularly reviews and referees article submitted to sci jrnls for publication. Memberships: Treas, Pathobiology Chapt Austl Coll Vet Scientist, 1993-; Coord, Austl Soc Vet Pathologist, 1993-; Cand in Avian Hlth for Austl Coll Vet Scientists, 1994-; Austl Soc Vet Path; Austl Vet Poultry Assn; Wildlife Diseases Assn; World Poultry Sci Assn (NSW Div); C L Davis Fndn for Comparative Path; Postgrad Fndn Vet Sci, Univ Sydney; Austl Vet Christian Fellowship. Hobbies: Swimming; Guitar music. Address: NSW Agriculture Elizabeth MacArthur Agricultural Institute, Private Mailbag, 8 Camden, NSW 2570, Australia.

REED Kevin Francis Morland, b. 7 May 1942, Caulfield, Aust. Research Scientist. m. Rhonda Frances Moore, 31 Aug 1970, 1 s, 2 d. Education: BAgSci, 1964, MAgSci, 1972, Univ of Melbourne; PhD, Univ Dublin, 1976. Appointments: Dept of Agricl, Vic, 1965-; CSIRO, 1967. Publications: 7 chaps, 20 pprs in rsch jrnls, 84 conf pprs and tech rprts. Honours: Fell, Austl Inst of Agricl Sci, 1991. Memberships: Austl Agron Soc; Austl Inst of Agricl Sci. Hobbies: Reading; Swimming; Skiing. Address: Lucan, RMB 4580, Hamilton, Victoria 3300, Australia.

REEVE Thomas Smith, b. 23 Nov 1923, NSW, Aust. Emeritus Professor of Surgery. m. Mary J Bradley, 2 s, 1 d. Education: MBBS, Sydney Univ, 1947; Amn Bd of Surg, 1958; FACS, 1961; FRACS, 1967; FRACR, Hon,

1980. Appointments: Supt, Collinsville Dist Hosp, 1948-50; Surg Trng, Albany Med Coll and Hosp; Surg Rsch Fell, Roy N Shore Hosp, Sydney, Aust, to 1961; Snr Lectr, 1961, Assoc Prof, 1964, Prof, 1974, Chmn, Dept Surg 1982-88, Emer 1989, Univ of Sydney; Pres, Roy Australasian Coll of Surgs, 1989-91; Chair, N Sydney Area Hlth Serv, 1988-96; Exec Offr, Austl Cancer Netwrk, 1994. Publications: Num publs. Honours: CBE, 1973; MD (Hon), Univ of Sydney, 1991; Hon Fell, Coll of Surgs of S Afr, 1991; Fell, Roy Austl Coll of Med Admnstrs, 1991; Hon Fell, Philippine Coll of Surgs, 1993; Hon Fell, Roy Coll of Physns & Surgs of Can, 1992; AC, 1994. Memberships: Roy Austl Coll of Surgs; Amn Coll of Surgs; Coller Soc; Société Internationale de Chirugie; Intl Assn of Endocrine Surgs; FACS Hon, 1987; Amn Surg Assn, Hon, 1988. Hobbies: Travel; Reading; Gardening. Listed in: Who's Who in Australia; Who's Who in the World. Address: Room 34, Vindin House, Royal North Shore Hospital, St Leonards, NSW 2065, Australia.

REEVES Keanu, b. 2 Sept 1964, Beirut, Lebanon. Actor. Education: Toronto HS for Performing Arts; 2nd City Workshop, Toronto. Creative Works: TV Films: Letting Go, 1985; Act of Vengeance, 1986; Babes in Toyland, 1986; Under the Influence, 1986; Brotherhood of Justice, 1986; Save the Planet (TV specl), 1990. Films: Prodigal, Flying, 1986; Youngblood, 1986; River's Edge, 1987; Permanent Record, 1988; The Night Before, 1988; The Prince of Pennsylvania, 1988; Dangerous Liaisons, 1988; 18 Again, 1988; Bill and Ted's Excellent Adventure, 1988; Parenthood, 1989; I Love You to Death, 1990; Tune In Tomorrow, 1990; Bill and Ted's Bogus Journey, 1991; Point Break, 1991; My Own Private Idaho, 1991; Bram Stoker's Dracula, 1992; Much Ado About Nothing, 1993; Even Cowgirls Get the Blues, 1993; Little Buddha, 1993; Speed, 1994; Johnny Mnemonic, 1995; A Walk in the Clouds, 1995; Chain Reaction, 1996; Feeling Minnesota, 1996; The Devil's Advocate, 1996; The Last Time I Committed Suicide, 1997. Mbr, Rock Band, Dogstar, 1996-. Address: c/o Erwin Stoff, Jake Bloom Agency, 7920 West Sunset Boulevard, Suite 350, Los Angeles, CA 90064, USA.

REEVES Paul Alfred, b. 6 Dec 1932, Wellington, New Zealand. Ecclesiastic; Administrator. m. Beverley Watkins, 1959, 3 d. Education: Wellington Coll; Vic Univ of Wellington; St John's Theol Coll, Auckland; St Peter's Coll, Oxford. Appointments: Deacon, 1958; Curate, Tokorao, NZ, 1958-59, St Mary of the Virgin, Oxford, 1959-61, Kirkley St Peter, Lowestoft, 1961-63; Priest, 1960; Vicar, St Paul, Okato, NZ, 1964-66; Lectr, Ch Hist, St John's Coll, Auckland, 1966-69; Dir, Christian Educn, Diocese of Auckland, 1969-71; Bish of Waiapu, 1971-79, of Auckland, 1979; Primate & Archbish of NZ, 1980-85; Gov-Gen of NZ, 1985-90; Rep of Anglican Ch to UN, 1991-93; Vis Prof, Univ of Auckland, 1997. Honours include: Hon Fell, St Peter's Coll, Oxford, 1980; Hon DCL, Oxon, 1985; Hon LLD, Vic, NZ; Hon DD, NY; Dr.h.c. Edinburgh, 1994; Kt St John, 1986. Memberships: Sev. Hobbies: Swimming; Sailing; Jogging. Address: 16E Cathedral Place, Parnell, Auckland, New Zealand.

REFSHAUGE William Dudley, b. 3 Apr 1913, Vic, Aust. Retired Health Administrator. m. Helen Elizabeth Allwright, 29 Aug 1942, 4 s, 1 d. Education: MBBS, Melbourne Univ, 1938. Appointments: Med Supt, Womens Hosp, Melbourne, 1948-51; Dpty Dir Gen, Army Med Servs, 1951-55; Dir Gen, Army Med Servs, 1955-60; C'wlth Dept of Hlth, 1960-73; Sec-Gen, World Med Assn, 1973-76; War Serv, 1939-46; Hon Cnslt, Alcohol and Drug Fndn of Aust, 1979-88; Natl Tstee, Returned Servs League, 1962-; Chmn, Menzies Sch of Hlth Rsch, Darwin, 1983-87; Chmn, Ethics Cttee, Walter & Elizabeth Hall Inst of Med Rsch, 1983-88; Chmn, Rsch into Drugs Abuse Advsry Cttee, 1986-88; Hon VP, Intl Cncl on Alcohol & Addictions, 1988-. Honours: Mentioned in despatches 4 times; OBE, 1944; World War II; CBE, 1959; KB, 1966; AC, 1980; Efficiency Decoration, 1956; RSL Anzac Peace Prize, 1990; RSL Meritorious Serv Medal, 1993. Memberships: Patron, Field Ambulance Assn; Natl Tstee, RSL of Aust; Patron, 2/2 Field Regt Assn; Austl Sports Med Assn; Medl Assn for Prevention of War. Hobbies: Rug making; Gardening. Address: 26 Birdwood Street, Hughes, ACT 2605, Australia.

REGENVANU Dorothy Margaret, b. 28 Nov 1942. Pator; Teacher. m. Sethy Regenvanu, 3 Sept 1969, 5 s. Education: BA, Univ of Qld, Aust, 1963; BD, Hons, Melbourne Coll of Div, Ormond Coll, 1966. Appointments: Tchr, Pastor Trng, Tangoa, Vanuatu, 1968-69; Ed, Pacific Christian Educ Curric, Suva, Fiji, 1971-72; Dir, Christian Educ, Presby Ch of Vanuatu, 1980-81; Tchr, Malapoa Coll, Vila, Vanuatu, 1982-98; Ordained Pastor, Vila, Vanuatu, 1999. Honour: Vanuatu Disting Serv Medal, 1993. Membership: Treas, Vanuatu Natl Cncl of Women, 1980-83. Hobbies: Music (piano); Reading Theology; Swimming. Address: Box 1189, Vila, Vanuatu.

REGENVANU Ralph John, b. 20 Sept 1970, Suva, Fiji. Cultural Resource Manager. Education: BA, hons, Devel Studies. Appointments: Field Survey Offr, Vanuatu Cultural & Hist Sites Survey, 1992, 1995-; Curator, Natl Mus of Vanuatu, 1994-95; Acting Dir, 1995, Dir, 1995-, Vanuatu Cultural Cntr; Dir, Vanuatu Natl Cultural Cncl, 1995-. Publications: Sev articles in profl jrnls. Honours include: 1st Prize, Art '92 Art Exhbn, Port Vila, Vanuatu, 1992. Memberships include: Vanuatu Natl Cultural Cncl; Pacific Islands Mus Assn; Intl Advsry Cttee, Jean-Marie Tjibaou Cultural Cntr, Noumea, New Caledonia. Hobbies: Music; Painting. Address: c/o Vanuatu Cultural Centre, PO Box 184, Port Vila, Vanuatu.

REID Anthony John Stanhope, b. 19 June 1939, Wellington, NZ. Historian. m. Helen Margaret Gray, 31 Aug 1963, 1 s, 1 d. Education: BA 1960, MA 1st Class Hons 1961, Vic Univ of Wellington; PhD, Cambridge Univ, Eng, 1965. Appointments: Lectr in Hist, Univ of Malaya, Kuala Lumpur, 1965-70; Fell, 1970-74, Snr Fell 1974-, Austl Natl Univ; Prof, SE Asian Hist, Rsch Sch of Pacific and Asian Studies, Austl Natl Univ, 1988-; Prof of Hist and Dir of Cntr for Southeast Asian Stdies, Univ of CA, Los Angeles, 1999-. Publications: The Contest for North Sumatra, 1969; The Indonesian National Revolution, 1974; The Blood of the People: Revolution and the End of Traditional Rule in North Sumatra, 1979; Slavery, Bondage and Dependency in Southeast Asia, ed, 1983; Southeast Asia in the Age of Commerce, 1450-1680, 2 vols, 1988, 1993; Southeast Asia in the Early Modern Era, ed, 1993; Sojourners and Settlers, ed, 1996; The Last Stand of Asian Autonomies, ed, 1997; Essential Outsiders: Chinese and Jews in the Modern Transformation of Southeast Asia and Central Europe, co-ed, 1997; Asian Freedoms: The Idea of Freedom in East and Southeast Asia, co-ed, 1998. Honours: Visng Fell, All Souls Coll, 1996; Fell, Austl Acady of the Hums, 1987-. Memberships: Assn of Asian Studies; Asian Studies Assn of Aust, Initial Convenor 1975-76, Cncl Mbr 1975-78, 1984-86, VP 1995-96, Pres, 1996-98; Aust Acady of the Hums, Intl Sec 1987-; Malaysian Br, Roy Asiatic Soc; Corresp Fell, Roy Histl Soc. Listed in: Who's Who in Australia. Address: History Department, UCLA, Box 951473, Los Angeles, CA 90095, USA.

REID Ian William, b. 10 Sept 1943, Wellington, NZ. University Administrator. M. Gale MacLachlan, 29 Sept 1992, 2 d. Education: MA, Univ of Canterbury, 1965; PhD, Univ of Adelaide, 1970; Exec MBA, Monash Univ, 1995. Appointments: Jnr Lectr, Massey Univ, 1965-66; Tutor, 1967-69, Lectr, 1970-74, Snr Lectr, 1975-78, Adelaide Univ; Prof of Lit, 1978-91, Deakin Univ; Dpty Vice-Chan, Curtin Univ, 1991-. Publications: 10 books incl: The Shifting Shore (poems), 1997. Honours: Fell, Amn Cncl of Learned Socs, 1974; Fell, Austl Inst of Mngmt, 1995; Fell, Austl Coll of Educ, 1997. Memberships: Pres, Austl and S Pacific Assn for Comparative Lit Studies, 1986-91. Hobbies: Gardening; Walking; Cemetery conservation. Address: 38/240 Burke Drive, Attadale, WA 6156, Australia.

REID James Balfour, b. 19 Jan 1951. Botanist; Geneticist; Educator. m. Patricia Jane Frances Nally, 10 Jan 1976, 3 s. Education: BS, Univ of Tas, 1971; BS Hons, 1972; PhD, 1977; DSc, 1995. Appointments: Tutor, Univ of Tas, 1972-78; Lectr, Snr Lectr, 1978-87; Rdr in Botany, 1988-89; Prof Plant Dev and Genetics, 1989-; Chmn, Acad Senate, 1994-; Dir, Coop Rsch Cntr for Temperate Hardwood Forestry, 1992-97; Dir, Co-op Rsch Cntr for Sustainable Production Forestry, 1997-. Publications: 160 refreed rsch publs and invited reviews, 1974-. Honour: David Syme Rsch Medal, Univ of Melbourne, 1989. Memberships: Tstee, Tasmanian Mus and Art Gall, 1994-; Bd Mbr, The Friend's Sch, Hobart, 1994-; Cnclr, Roy Soc of Tas, 1994-; Cnclr, Pisum Genetics Assn; Austl Soc Plant Physiology. Address: 90 Forest Road, West Hobart, Tas 7000, Australia.

REID Margaret Elizabeth (Hon), b. 28 May 1935, Crystal Brook, SA, Aust. Senator. m. Thomas Reid, 2 s, 2 d. Education: LLB, Adelaide. Appointments include: Mbr, Advsry Cncl on Austl Archives, 1985-96; Dpty Pres of the Senate and Chair of Cttees, 1995-96; Pres of the Senate, 1996-. Address: Parliament House, Canberra, ACT 2600, Australia.

REINER Rob, b. 6 Mar 1947 NY. Actor; Writer; Director. m. (1) Penny Marshall, 1971, div, (2) Michele Singer, 1989. Education: Univ of CA at Los Angeles. Appointments: Has appeared with comic improvisation grps The Session and The Committee; Scriptwriter for Enter Laughing, 1967; Halls of Anger, 1970; Where's Poppa, 1970; Summertree, 1971; Fire Sale, 1977; How Come Nobody's On Our Side, 1977. TV appearances: All In The Family, 1971-78; Thursday's Game, 1974; Free Country, 1978; More Than Friends, 1979; Million Dollar Infield, 1982; Morton Hayes, 1991; Director: This is Spinal Tap, 1984; The Sure Thing, 1985; Stand By Me, 1986; The Princess Bride, 1987; Misery, 1990. Co-prodr and dir: When Harry Met Sally, 1989; A Few Good Men, 1992; North, 1994; The American President, 1995; Ghosts of Mississippi, 1996; The Story of Us, 1999. Address: c/o Castle Rock, Entertainment, 335 North Maple Drive, Suite 135, Beverly Hills, CA 90210, USA.

REINER Thomas Karl, b. 29 Dec 1931, Hungary (came to USA, 1959). Engineer; Businessman. m. Bonnie, 31 Dec 1995, 3 s, 2 d. Education: Dip, Optics Trade Sch, Budapest, 1952; MSME, Tech Univ, Budapest, 1955; Postgrad, London Coll, 1958, Univ Pitts, Carnegie Inst Tech. Appointments: Engr, Cntrl Power Generating Stn, Hungary, 1954-56; Cnslt Engr, test Engr, Blaw-Knox Co, London, 1956-57; Snr Engr, Eubank & Ptnrs, London, 1957-59; Rsch Engr, Pitts Plate Glass Co, 1959-60; Prod Mngr, Copes-Vulcan Div, 1960-62; Chf Engr, J W Fecker div Amn Optical Co, 1962-66; Prod Mngr, Carco Electrons, Menlo Pk, CA, 1966-68; Chf Engr, Fairchild Camera, El Segundo, CA, 1968-70; Dir, Engrng, Templeton, Kenly & Co, Los Angeles & Chgo, 1970-72; Gen Mngr, Foremark Corp, Gdns, 1972-74; Pres, Kinetron Inc, Long Beach, CA, 1974-76; Pres, Prin Owner, GRW Inc, Hawthorne, CA, 1977-. Publications: Sev pats. Memberships: Bd Pres, Peacock Ridge Homeowners Assn, Palos Verde, CA; Intl Soc Weighing & Measurements. Address: 14110 Valley Vista Boulevard, Sherman Oaks, CA 91423, USA.

REINKER Remy Achim, b. 13 Aug 1958, Soltau, Germany. Chartered Accountant. m. Sue, 18 July 1986, 1 s. Education: BCompt (hons), S Africa; Dip in Corp Mngmt, AGSM (Univ of NSW). Appointments: Snr Auditors Arthur Anderssen & Co, 1984-85; Mngr Ops Analysis BTR Dunlop (S Africa), 1985-88; Acct, 1988-91, Acct Mngr, 1991-95, Mngr Fin and Admin, 1995-, Toshiba Intl Grp. Memberships: Inst of Charterd Accts in Aust; Chartered Inst of Co Secs in Aust; S African Inst of Chartered Accts; Austl Inst of Co Dirs. Hobbies: Numismatics; Travel; Camping. Address: Toshiba International Corporation Pty Ltd, Locked Bag 5029, Parramatta, NSW 2124, Australia.

REITH Peter K, b. 15 July 1950. Member of Parliament. m. Julie, 4 children. Education: BEcon, 1972; LLB, 1974. Appointments include: Articled Clk, Keith Ness & Son, 1974; Sol, J A Wilmoth & Son, 1975-76; Self-employed Solicitor, 1976-82; Shadow Min for Indl Rels, Mngr of Opposition Bus in the House, 1995-96; Min for Indl Rels, Ldr of the House of Reps, Min Assisting the PM for the Pub Serv, 1996-; Min for Employment, Workplace Relations and Small Bus, Ldr, House of Reps, 1998. Publication: The Reith Papers. Hobbies: Reading; Family history. Listed in: Who's Who in Australia. Address: Shop 4, 184 Salmon Street, PO Box 274, Hastings, Vic 3915, Australia.

REMENGESAU Thomas Jr, b. 28 Feb 1956, Koror, Palau. Government Official. m. 3 children. Education: BS, Criminology, Grand Valley State Univ, 1979; Postgrad, MI State Univ, 1979-81. Appointments: Legal Rschr, Fed Dist Crt, Saipan, No Mariana Is, 1981; Hlth Planner, Admin Offr, Govt of Palau, 1982; Pub Info Offr, Palau Natl Cong, 1983; Senator, 2nd Oibiil Era Kelulau, 1984-92; Chmn, Ways and Means Commn; VP, Min Admin, Repub of Palau Natl Govt, 1992-. Memberships: Chmn, Palau/Micronesia Olympic Games Cttee, 1990; Compact of Free Assn Transition Commn, 1994; Presdtl Task Force on Polit Status Negotiations w USA Govt, 1991; Chmn, Palau Sports Commn, 1994-; Chmn, Disaster Plan Task Force, 1996-; Chmn, Coral Reef Plng Cncl, 1997-. Address: Office of the VP, PO Box 100, PW 96940, Palau.

REN Aiguo, b. 21 Jan 1957, Hebei, China. Epidemiologist. m. Xiuzhen, 29 Nov 1983, 1 s. Education: Mater, N China Coal Medl Coll; Bachelor; Dr, Univ of Occupational and Environl Hlth, Japan. Appointments: Chr, Dept of Epidemiology; Assoc Dean, Sch of pub hlth. Creative Works: Occupation and Cardiovascular Diseases, 1998. Honours: Natl Awd for Ex in Tchng. Memberships: Div of Occupational Epidemiology; Chinese Soc of Occupational Med. Hobbies: Internet; Reading; Pop Music. Address: 57 Jianshe Road, Tangshan 063000, Hebei, China.

REN Lin Seng, b. 26 Feb 1937, NanChong County, SiChuan Prov, China. Burns Specialist and Plastic Surgeon. m. Wang Yuan Fang, 1 Oct 1967, 2 d. Education: MD. Appointments: Resident and Asst, 1965-80; Attending Dr and Lectr, 1980-87; Assoc Prof, 1987-93; Dir of Dept of Burn and Plastic Surg, 1989-97; Prof, 1993-. Publications: Analysis of Operative Results on Late Deformities of Burnt Hands, 1985; The Effect of Magnetotherapy on Cerebral Edema in Rabbits, 1993; Some Problems Induced in Hand Reconstruction After Burn Injury, 1995; Assoc Ed, Transfer Flap with Vascular Pedicle, 1988. Honours: 2nd Grade Awd, ChengDu Sci and Technol Prize, 1975; 3rd Grade Awd, 1990, 1997, SiChuan Sci and Technologic Prize. Memberships: Chinese Reparative and Reconstructuve Assn; Cnsltng Ed, Chinese Jrnl of Reparative and Reconstructuve Surg, 1987; Vice Dir, SiChuan Reparative and Reconstructive Assn, 1993; Cnsltng Ed, Jrnl of Prac Aesthetic and Plastic Surg, 1994; Vice Dir, SiChuan Burn and Plastic Soc, Chinese Medl Soc, 1997. Hobbies: Music; Table tennis. Address: Department of Burns and Plastic Surgery, 1st University Hospital of West China University of Medical Sciences, Cheng Du, SiChuan 610041, China.

REN Jianxin, b. Aug 1925 Fencheng - now Xiangfen - Co Shanxi Prov. Chf Jus. Education: Engrng Coll Beijing Univ. Appointments: Joined CCP, 1948; Sec Sec N China People's Govt, 1948-49; Sec Gen Off Cntrl Commn for Polit Sci and Law Sec Cntrl Commn for Legis Affairs, 1949-54; Sec Legis Affairs Bur State Cncl, 1954-59; Sect Ldr Div Chf China Cncl for the Promotion of Intl Trade - CCPIT - 1959-71; Dir Legal Dept CCPIT lawyer, 1971-81; Vice-Chmn CCPIT, 1981-83; VP Supreme People's Crt, 1983-88; Pres Supreme People's Crt, 1988-; Sec-Gen Ldng Grp of Cntrl Cttee for Polit Sci and Law, 1989; Dep Sec and Sec Gen Cntrl Cttee, 1990; Sec Sec 14th CCP Cntrl Cttee, 1992; Sec CCP Cntrl Commn for Polit Sci and Law, 1992-; Dir Cntrl Cttee for Comprehensive Admin of Socl Security, 1992-; Chmn Soc of Chinese Judges, 1994-; Dir China Trng Cntr for Snr Judges; Prof - part time - Beijing Univ. Honours: Hon Chmn China Law Soc - fmr VP; Hon Chmn China For Econ Trade and Arbitration Cttee; Hon Chmn China Maritime Arbitration Cttee - fmr Chmn; Hon Pres China Intl Law Soc - fmr VP. Memberships: Mbr 13th CCP Cntrl Cttee, 1987-92; Mbr 14th CCP Cntrl Cttee, 1992-; Mbr Cntrl Grp for Co-ord of Tibetan Activities. Address: 27 Dongjiaomingxiang, Beijing, People's Republic of China.

RENDEL David George Aidan, b. 7 Feb 1918, London, Eng. Former Aeronautical Engineer; Scientist; Publisher. m. (1) Eve Spicer, 9 Nov 1940, 2 s, 2 d, (2) Barbara Stintion, 17 Jan 1971, (3) Ann Mallinson, 4 Jan 1982. Education: BA, New Coll, Oxford Univ, 1937-40. Appointments: Roy Aircraft Estab, Farnborough, 1940-48, 1953-63; Min of Supply, London, 1948-53; Aeronautical Cnslt to Publr, 1963-72; Aviation Cnslt and Publr, 1979-; Chmn, Mallinson Rendel Publrs Ltd, 1980. Publications: Reg radio talks on NZ Radio; Earthing and Hellene; Scene with Variations; The Eye of the Needle; Civil Aviation in New Zealand; Contbr of num sci rprts. Memberships: Retd Mbr, UK Inst of Mech Engrs; Roy Aeronautical Soc; Ex Pres, NZ Aviation Fedn. Hobbies: Countryside; Philosophy. Address: 4/248 Oriental Parade, Wellington, New Zealand.

RENNER John Martyn, b. 23 Apr 1931, Masterton, NZ. Emeritus Professor, International Projects. m. Jennifer Louise Henderson, 15 Dec 1956, 1 s, 1 d. Education: BSc, Univ of NZ, 1954; MSc, 1955, Dip of Educ, 1972, Univ of Canterbury, Eng; MPhil Massey Univ, 1978; PhD, Murdoch Univ, 1988. Appointments: HS Tchr 1956-63, Snr Lectr later Prin Lectr, Christchurch Tchrs Coll, 1964-73; Visng Prof, Univ of IA & State Univ of CA, USA, 1968-70; Cnslt to var Pacific Govts, 1970-75; Snr Fell, Massey Univ, 1974; Vice Prin, Palmerston N Tchr's Coll, NZ, 1975-79; Dir, Nedlands Coll of Advd Educ, Perth, WA, 1980-82; Dean, Arts and Applied Scis, WA Coll of Advd Educ, 1982-90; Dean, Sci and Engrng, 1990-96, Emer Prof, 1997-, Edith Cowan Univ. Publications: Source Book on South American Geography, 1976, 1978; Source Book on African Geography, 1976; Source Book on British Isles Geography, 1976, 1980; Source Book on South East Asian Geography, 1980; Articles and reviews. Honours: NZ Del, UNESCO-IGU Conf, Sydney, 1973; NZ Environmental Awd for Environmental Rsch. Memberships: Austl & NZ Assn for Advancment of Sci; Profl Assoc, E W Cntr, 1977; Fell, Austl Inst Mngmt; Companion, Instn of Engrs (Aust). Hobbies: Jogging; Gardening; Rotary International; Cricket. Address: 35 College Road, Claremont, WA 6010, Australia.

RENNIE Heughan Bassett, b. 7 Apr 1945, Wanganui. Barrister. m. (1) Caroline Harding, dec, Nov 1992, 3 s, (2) Penelope Ryder-Lewis, 1998. Education: BA, Vic, 1965; LLB, Vic, 1969. Appointments: Pt-time Law Clk, Wanganui, 1960-67; Legal Offr, NZ Elec, Wellington, 1967-70; Bar, Solicitor, Macalister Mazengarb Parkin and Rose, Wellington, 1970-91; Ptnr, 1972; Snr Litigation Ptnr, 1982; Chmn, 1989-91; Bar sole, Wellington, 1991-95; Queens Cnsl, 1995-. Honours: CBE, 1989; NZ Medal, 1990; Queen's Cnsl, 1995. Memberships: Chmn, Roy NZ Ballet; Chatham Is Enterprise Trust; Frmr Chmn, Brdcstng Corp of NZ; Dir, Bank of NZ; Fletcher Challenge Ltd, other co's. Hobbies: History; Travel; Writing; Cycling; Reading. Address: P O Box 10-242, Wellington, New Zealand.

RENNIE Sandra Joy, b. 25 Apr 1947. International Consultant. m. BA, Hons, MA, La Trobe Univ; MA, Comm Health, Liverpool Sch of Tropical Med, Eng, 1992; PhD, Austl Natl Univ, 1986; Dip, Freelance Jrnlsm, 1996. Appointments: Tchr, 3 univs, La Trobe, Melbourne, 1973-75; Univ of NSW, Canberra, 1975-78; The Austl Natl Univ, 1982; Evaluation Offr, AIDAB, 1983-89; Served in Bangladesh as Labour Welfare Advsr for Tea Estate Workers, 1989-90; Served in India as Snr Sociol, 1990; Tanzania, Survey in Children's Health, 1992; Snr Advsr on Gender, Population and Dev, UN, 1993-96; Intl Soc for Renal Sociol, 1982-; Gender Specialist, Vanuatu, 1997; Sales Evaluator, Fiji and Solomon Is, 1998; Indnesia Women in Dev Specialist, 1998. Publications: Num acad articles. Hobbies: Theatre; Yoga; Bushwalking; Journalism; Photography; Travel. Listed in: World Who's Who of Women; International Who's Who of Contemporary Achievement; Dictionary of International Biography. Address: 4 Magdalen Street, Pascoe Vale Sth, Melbourne, Vic 3044, Australia.

RENOUF Susan, b. 15 July 1942, Melbourne, Australia. Interior Decorator. m. Hon A S Peacock, 8 Feb 1964, 3 d. Hobbies: Interior Decorating; Gardening; Thoroughbred Racing. Address: Toorak, Melbourne, Australia.

REPPAS George Peter, b. 19 Nov 1964, Sydney, Aust. Veterinarian. Education: BVSc Hons, Sydney University, 1986; Dip Vet Path, 1989. Appointments : Fell, Aust Coll Vet Scientists, 1995; Reg Specialist Vet Pathol, NSW, 1995; Reg Specialist Vet Clinl Pathol, UK, 1996; Diplomate, Eurn Coll of Vet Pathologists, 1998. Creative Works: Many Pprs, Book Chpts in Intl Vet Jrnls and Textbooks. Memberships: Aust Vet Assn; Aust Coll Vet Scientists; Roy Coll of Vet Surgs; Eur Coll of Vet Pathols; Hellenic Vet Medl Assn. Hobbies: Byzantine Musicology; Study of Greek Orthodox Church History, Tradition. Address: 304-310 Horsley Road, Horsley Park, NSW 2164, Australia.

RETTER Catharine Josephine, b. 3 Nov 1946, Netherlands. Marketing and Communications. m. Peter Owen Retter, 9 Feb 1974. Education: BA studies, Macquarie Univ, NSW, Aust, 1982-99; Mktng, Univ of NSW, 1978. Appointments: Account Dir, Fountain Huie Fish Pty Ltd, 1979-82; Jt Owner, Retter Advtng Pty Ltd, 1982-85; Dir of Mktng, Austl Bicentennial Auth, 1985-89; Dir, Retter Advtng, Dir, The RH Factor, Dir, Retter Mktng & Comm Pty Ltd, 1989-; Dir, Rotary Club of Sydney, 1994-95; Dir, Tall Ships Aust 1998 Ltd, 1997; Mngng Dir, Driza-Bone Pty Ltd, 1998-. Publication: Legends, Lore and Lies; Letters to Ann: The love story of Matthew Flinders and Ann Chappelle. Memberships: Fell, Aust Mktng Inst; Fndng Exec of Women in Mktng; Look of the Cty Cttee, Sydney. Hobbies: Writing; Horseriding; Reading. Address: PO Box 135, Beenleigh, Qld 4207, Australia.

REYNOLDS Albert Gordon, b. 25 Jan 1926, Vashon Island, WA, USA. Physician. m. (2) Jonelle, 1 s, 2 d. Education: MD, Univ of Michigan, 1949; Ob/Gyn Residency, Univ of Michigan, 1950-55; Rsch Fell, Amn Cancer Soc, 1950-51. Appointments: Chm, Dept ObGyn, Redlands Community Hosp, 1955-80; Asst Clin Prof, UCLA, 1964-80; Asst Clin Prof, Lom Linda Univ Medl Cntr, 1966-80; Lacosta Spa Dir and Exec Dir Life Fitness and Longevity Cntr, 1984-92; Chf attending Staff ObGyn, San Bernardino Co Medl Cntr, 1995-80. Publication: The Lacosta Book of Nutrition, 1988. Honours: Galens Hon Medl Soc; Purple Heart; Meritorious Awds (Korean Battalion Surg). Memberships: Dipl, Amn Bd of Obstets and Gynae; Fell, Amn Coll of Surg; Amn Coll of Preventive Med; Amn Coll of Sports Med; Amn Geriatric Soc; (now retd status). Address: 6542 Avenuda Del Paraiso, Carlsbad, CA 92009, USA.

REYNOLDS Barrie Gordon Robert, b. 8 July 1932, London, Eng. Museum Professor. m. Ena Margaret Foster, 27 Dec 1953, 1 s, 1 d. Education: BA hons, Anthropology, 1954, MA, 1958, MSc, 1963, Cambridge Univ; DPhil, Oxford Univ, 1968. Appointments: Tchr, London Nautical Sch, 1954-55; Keeper of Ethnography, 1955-64, Dir, 1964-66, Livingstone Mus, Zambia, 1955-66; Curator, Open Air Crafts Mus, Zambia, 1961-64; Chf Curator, Vancouver Centennial Mus, Can, 1968-69; Chf Ethnologist, Natl Mus of Can, Ottawa, 1969-75; Fndn Prof of Material Culture, 1975-97, Dir, Material Culture Unit, 1975-96, Dean of Arts, 1985-87, James Cook Univ, Townsville, Aust; Adj Prof, Macquarie Univ, Sydney, 1998-; Adj Prof, Univ of Western Sydney, 1998-. Publications: Magic, Divination and Witchcraft Among the Barotse of Northern Rhodesia, 1963; The Material Culture of the Peoples of the Gwembe Valley, 1968; Material Anthropology: Contemporary Approaches to Material Culture (ed w Margaret Stott); Material Culture of Northeast Australia, ed; Co-auth, Cinderella Collections: University Museums and Collections in Australia, 1996; Co-auth, Transforming Cinderella Collections, 1998. Contbr to profl jrnls. Memberships: Fell, Mus Assn, London; Fell, Roy Anthropol Inst; Fell, Am Anthropol Assn; Pres, Cncl of Aust Univ, Mus & Collects, 1992-96. Hobbies: Walking; Chess; Reading. Address: Prospect Cottage, 40-44 Hume Avenue, Wentworth Falls, NSW 2782, Australia.

REYNOLDS Burt, b. 11 Feb 1936 Waycross GA. Actor. m. (1) Judy Carne, div 1965; (2) Loni Anderson, 1988, 1 adopted s. Education: FL State Univ. Stages appearances incl: Mister Roberts; Look We've Come Through; The Rainmaker. Films incl: Angel Baby, 1961; Operation CIA, 1965; Navajo Jose, 1967; Impasse, 1969; Skullduggery, 1970; Deliverance, 1972; Everything You've Always Wanted to Know about Sex But Were Afraid to Ask, 1972; The Man Who Loved Cat Dancing, 1973; Hustle, 1975; Silent Movie, 1976; Gator - also dir - 1976; Nickelodeon, 1976; Smokey and the Bandit, 1977; Starting Over, 1979; Cannonball Run, 1981; Sharky's Machine - also dir - 1981; City Heat, 1984; Stock - also dir - 1984; Rent A Cop, 1987; Breaking In, 1988; Switching Channels, 1988; Physical Evidence, 1989; B L Stryker, 1989; Modern Love, 1990; Alby's House of Bondage, 1990; Cop and a Half, 1993; Striptease, 1996; Mad Dog Time, 1996; Boogie Nights, 1997. Tv appearances incl: Riverboat; Pony Express; Gunsmoke; Hawk; Dan August; B L Stryker; Evening Shade, 1990-94. Publication: My Life - autobiog - 1994. Address: William Morris Agency, 151 El Camino, Beverly Hills, CA 90212, USA.

REYNOLDS Edward Francis, b. 29 Nov 1942, Coffeyville, KS, USA. Pharmacist. m. Beverly, 5 May 1973. Education: BSc, Pharm, Univ of WY, 1966. Appointments: Chf Pharm, Frank Wat King Weed Army Hosp, Ft Irwin, CA, 1967-69; Apptd to Pharm Supvsr, Loma Linda Univ, Medl Cntr. Honours: High Power Rifle Marksman of Denver, 1963; Expert, High Power Rifle Sharpshooter, 1967. Memberships: Treas, Santa Cruz Corvettes; & Amn Inst of Hist of Pharm, 1971-76. Hobbies: First Day Cver Collector. Address: 11617 Toplar Street, Loma Linda, CA 92354, USA.

REYNOLDS Jonathan Hall, b. 3 Feb 1948. Winemaker. m. Jane, 15 May 1976, 3 d. Education: Dip Oenology. Appointments: Winemaker, Chateau Reynella, SA; Chief Winemaker, Houghton Wines, WA; Grp Snr Winemaker, Wyndham Grp, NSW, Aust; Winemaker, Promoter, Co Dir, Reynolds Yarraman, NSW, Co Dir, Reynolds Wine Co Ltd, NSW. Publications: Wine. Membership: Austl Soc of Oenology and Viticulture. Hobbies: Snow Skiing; Tennis. Address: Reynolds Yarraman, Yarraman Road, Wybong, Upper Hunter Valley, NSW 2333, Australia.

REYNOLDS Margaret Ann Osborn, b. 9 Dec 1920, York, NE, USA. Teacher; Clergy. m. Reverend John M Reynolds, 2 s. Education: BA, Univ of NE, 1942; Columbia Univ, NYC, 1947; Union Theol Seminary, NYC, 1948. Appointments: Dir, Christian Educ, First Congregational Ch, Ft Wayne, IN; Natl Sec, Forerunners, NYC, 1943-45; Dir, Yth Campaign, Japan Intl Christian Univ; County Dir, Retarded Handicapped Cntr, San Bernardino, 1966-67; Tchr, Mckinley Sch, Colton, 1967-78; Assoc Min, UCC, Laguna Beach, 1979-83. Publications: Smiles for Miles '68, Handbook for Retarded and Handicapped, 1967. Honours: Life Mbr, McKinley PTA, 1978; Ch of the Good Shepherd; Min Emerita, Corina, CA; Min Emerita, Laguna Beach, CA Neighbourhood Congregational UCC, 1983. Memberships: Charter Mbr, Natl Mus of Women in the Arts; AAUW; Histn, East Assn UCC, S California. Hobbies: Painting; Swimming; Reading. Address: 729 Plymouth Road, Claremont, CA 91711, USA.

REYNOLDS Thomas Carter, b. 19 Dec 1936, Moe, Vic, Aust. Member of Parliament. m. Helen, 5 Aug 1961, 2 s. Appointments: Mbr for Gisborne, 1979-; Min for Sport, Recreation and Racing, 1992-96; Min for Sport, 1996-; Min for Rural Dev, 1996-. Hobbies: Racing and all sports. Address: 3/3 Hamilton Street, Gisborne, Vic (PO Box 39), Australia.

REZNIK Leonid, b. 18 Oct 1955, St Petersburg, Russia. Educator; Researcher. m. Olga Kuftova, 6 Dec 1982, 1 s. Education: Dip, Elec Engr, St Petersburg Aircraft Acady, 1978; PhD, Engrng, St Petersburg Univ of Technol, 1983. Appointments: Progmr, Jnr Sci, Snr Sci, Prin Sci, Rsch Inst of Shipbldng Technol, St Petersburg; Prin Sci, Interquadro, Moscow; Lectr, Snr Lectr, Vic Univ of Technol, Melbourne, Aust. Publications: Fuzzy Controllers, 1997; Co-ed, Fuzzy Systems Design: Social and Engineering Applications, 1998. Honour: Title of Snr Rschr, High Certifying Cmmn, Russia, 1986. Memberships: IEEE; NY Acady of Scis. Hobbies: Swimming; Detective Stories. Address: School of Communication & Informatics, Victoria University, PO Box 14428 MCMC, Melbourne 8001, Australia.

RI Jong Ok. Politician. Appointments: Min of Light Ind, 1951; Vice-Premier, 1960; Polit Commisar of WPK, 1960-70; Alt Polit Commissar, 1973; Vice-Premier, 1976; Premier, 1977; Deleg to Supreme People's Assn, 1986, 1990; Supreme Cmdr of Korean People's Army, 1991; Title of Marshal conferred, 1992; Chmn Natl Def Cttee, 1993-; VP Dem People's Repub of Korea. Memberships: Mbr Cntrl Cttee Wrker's Party - WPK - 1956; Mbr Polit Bur of Cntrl Cttee of WPK. Address: Office of the Vice-President, Pyongyang, Democratic Republic of Korea.

RIACH Alan Scott, b. 1 Aug 1957, Scotland. University Lecturer. m. Rae, 12 Sept 1992, 2 s. Education: BA, 1979; MA, 1986; PhD, 1986. Appointment: Assoc Prof, Univ Waikato. Publications: This Folding Map, 1990; An Open Return, 1991; Hugh MacDiarmid's Epic Poetry, 1991. Memberships: Assn for Scottish Lit Studies; Scottish Studies Assn, Univ Waikato. Address: c/o Department of English; University of Waikato, PB 3105, Hamilton, New Zealand.

RIANNE Patricia Elizabeth, b. 23 June 1943. Ballerina; Dance Tutor; Choreographer. m. 30 Dec 1976, Michael Zachary Lloyd, 1 s, 1 d. Education: St Mary's Convent, Naenae and Wanganui; Sacred Heart Coll, Wanganui; NZ Govt Bursary to study at Roy Ballet Sch, London, 1962. Appointments: Soloist, Ballet de l'Opera de Marseilles, France, 1963-64; NZ Ballet, NZ, 1964-65; Ballet Mediterranée, France, 1965; Prin Artist, New Ballet Rambert, London, 1965-69; Fndr Mbr, Prin Dancer, Scottish Ballet, 1970-77; Guest Artist: Giselle, NZ Ballet, Auckland Fest, 1973; London Cty Ballet, 1976-80; Sleeping Beauty, NZ Ballet, 1979; La Sylphide, NZ Ballet, 1980; Giselle, Sir Anton Dolin Prodn, UK Tour, 1982; Dowager Princess, Swan Lake, Royal NZ Ballet, 1985; Choreography includes: Bliss, NZ Ballet, 1987; Poems, Southern Ballet, NZ, 1989; Summers Day, NZ Sch of Dance, 1990; Snow Maiden, NZ Sch of Dance, 1992; Summers End, Royal NZ Ballet, 1992; Guest Tutor: City Contemp Dance Co, Hong Kong Ballet, The Acady of Performing Arts Ballet Grp, Jean Wong Acady, Hong Kong, 1980-85; GOH Ballet & Acady, EXPO-Marathon Dance, Vancouver, Can, 1985, 1986; Urdang Studios, London Sch of Contemp Dance, London Coll of Dance, London, Eng, 1987; Beijing Acady, Beijing, China, 1987; NZ Sch of Dance, Summer Sch Adelaide, Aust, 1988; Edinburgh Workshop, Dance Base, Scotland, 1989, 1993; Guest Tutor, Ballet Rambert, London, 1997-98; Summer Sch, Rimini, Italy, 1997, 1998; Res Snr Tutor in Ballet, London Contemp Dance Sch, 1996-. Honours: Critical Aclaim for The Title Role in Giselle, 1976. Memberships: Scottish Arts Advsry Cncl, 1974-77; Trust Mbr, A H Australasia Awds Trust, 1991-94; Caretaker Artistic Dir, NZ Ballet, 1980-81. Hobbies: Gardening; Restoring Antiques; Painting; Knitting. Listed in: Who's Who in New Zealand. Address: 7 Cleveland Avenue, Chiswick, London W4 1SN, England.

RICHARDS James Harray (Ray), b. 1 Feb 1921. Literary Agent; Publisher. m. Barbara Jeanne Pryke, 10 Dec 1949, 3 d. Appointments: Naval Aviator, 1942-46; Book Publr, AH & AW Reed, MD, 1946-76; Self-employed, 1977-. Publication: Ed, NZ Holiday mag. Honour: DSC, 1945. Membership: Pres 4 yrs, 1965-7, 1975-76, Hon Life Mbr, 1977, Book Publrs Assn of NZ. Address: 49e Aberdeen Rd, Castor Bay, Auckland, New Zealand.

RICHARDSON Donald Knowles, b. 11 Feb 1929, Burnie, Tasmania. Artist; Educator; Writer. Education: Dip Art and Tchrs Dip Art, 1956; BA, 1965, Univ of Tasmania; MA, Studies, Fine Arts, Melbourne Univ and Flinders Univ. Appointments: Art Tchr, Tasmanian Schs, 1956-65;

Lectr in Comms, Gordon Inst of Technol, Geelong, 1966-67; Supt of Studies, Visual Arts, Educ Dept of SA, 1968-88; Lectr, Art Theory, Univ of SA, 1989-99; Profl Painter, Sculptor, Art and Des Theory Study and Writing. Publications: Books: Introducing Art (for jnr second students), 1983; Art in Australia (for snr second students), 1988; Teaching Art, Craft and Design (a univ level text), 1992; Art and Design in Australia (for snr second students), 1995; Many articles in Educ, Media and Art-Educ jrnls. Memberships: Contemporary Art Soc (Tas Branch), 1960-65; SA Visual Arts Educ Assn, 1985-88; SA Pub Serv Assn, 1969-89; Mt Barker Residents Assn, Chairperson, 1995-99. Address: 21 Druids Avenue, Mount Barker, SA 5251, Australia.

RICHARDSON Gordon John Dalyell, b. 16 Feb 1947. Barrister (Senior Counsel). m. 23 Dec 1970, 1 s, 1 d. Education: BA, UNSW; MA, UNSW. Appointments: Sch Master, The Scots Sch, Bathurst, 1968; Newington Coll, Stanmore, 1970-71; Legal Clk, Legal Offr, Instructing Offr for the Crown in Crt of Criminal Appeal, Off of Clk of Peace, NSW, 1973-75; Pt Commnr, Legal Aid Commn, Nom of Bar Assn, 1982, 1984-86; Hon Mbr, Legal Aid Cttee, 1980-81; Visng Lectr, Austl Natl Univ, Fac of Law, Legal Wrkshp in Pleading, 1989-95, in Civ Prac, 1996-; Cmndr RANR, Mbr of Austl Def Force Panel of Judge Advocates, 1985-; Def For Magistrate, 1996-; Hd, ACT Reserve Legal Panel, 1996-; Pres, ACT Bar Assn, 1994-96, VP 1992-94; Snr Cnsl for ACT and NSW, 1994-; Barrister, Sup Crt of NSW, High Crt of Aust, Austl Fed Crts, 1975-, Supreme Crt of ACT, 1976-. Honours: Snr Cnsl for the ACT, 1994; Snr Cnsl for NSW, 1994. Hobbies: Painting; Motorcycles; Golf. Address: Blackburn Chambers, GPO Box 789, Canberra, ACT 2601, Australia.

RICHARDSON Graham, b. 27 Sept 1949 Kogarah Sydney. Politician; Brdcstr; Jrnlst. m. Cheryl Gardener, 1973, 1 s, 1 d. Education: Marist Brothers Coll Kogarah. Appointments: State Organiser Austl Labor Party NSW, 1971-76; Gen Sec, 1976-94; State Campaign Dir, 1976; VP Natl Labor Party, 1978; Deleg to Natl Conf, 1977-94; Convenor Natl Indl Platform Cttee; Sen for NSW, Mar 1983-94; Fmr Chmn Senate Estimates Cttee, 1986; Min for the Environment and the Arts, 1987-90; Min for Sports Tourism and Territories, 1988-90; Min for Socl Security, 1990; Min of Transp and Comms, 1991-92; Min of Hlth, 1993-94; Polit commentator on election coverage and jrnlst The Nine Network, 1994-; Jrnlst The Bulletin, 1994-; Fmr chmn Senate Select Cttee on tv Equalisation. Memberships: Mbr sev senate cttees and three ministerial cttees; Mbr Bd Sydney Organizing Cttee for the Olympic Games, 1996-. Hobbies: Golf; Reading; Skiing. Address: 24 Artarmon Road, Willoughby, NSW 2028, Australia.

RICHARDSON James Longden, b. 1 Dec 1933. Professor Emeritus. m. 21 Aug 1976. Education: BA, Sydney, 1954; BA, Oxford, 1958. Appointments: Rsch Assoc, Harvard Cntr for Intl Affairs, 1961-63; Balliol Coll, Oxford, 1964-65; Lectr, Snr Lectr, Univ of Sydney, 1967-74; Prof, Pol Sc, Austl Natl Univ, 1975-85; Professorial Fell, Prof, Intl Rels, Austl Natl Univ, 1986-, Prof Emer, 1998-. Publications: Germany and the Atlantic Alliance, 1966; Charting the Post-Cold War Order, 1993; Crisis Diplomacy, 1994. Memberships: Intl Studies Assn; Austl Pol Studies Assn; Brit Intl Stdies Assn. Address: c/o Department of International Relations, RSPAS, Australian National University, Canberra, ACT 0200, Australia.

RICHENS Muriel Whittaker, b. Princeville, OR, USA. AIDS Therapist; Counselor; Educator. 1 s, 4 d. Education: BS, OR State Univ; MA, San Fran State Univ, 1962; Postgrad, Univ CA, Berkeley, 1967-69; Univ Birmingham, Eng, 1973; Univ Soria, Spain, 1981; Lic sch admnstr; Tchr 7-12; Pupil personnel specialist; CA marriage & family therapist. Appointments: Instr, Springfield (OR) hs; San Fran State Univ; Instr, Cnslr Coll, San Mateo, CA; San Mateo hs Dist, 1963-86; Therapist, AIDS Hlth Proj, Univ CA, San Fran, 1988-; Priv prac, MFI, San Mateo. Honours: Pi Lambda Theta; Delta Pi Epsilon; Univ CA Berkeley Alumni Assn; Postgrad Student Cntr for Hum Comms, Los Gatos, CA, 1974, Univ PR, 1977; Univ

Guadalajara, Mexico, 1982. Memberships: Amn Contract Bridge League (Diamond Life Master, Cert Instr, Tournament Dir); Women in Comm; Computer-Using Educrs; Commonwealth Club. Address: 847 N Humboldt St Apt 309, San Mateo, CA 94401-1451, USA.

RICHEY Everett Eldon, b. 1 Nov 1923, Claremont, IL, USA. Religious Educator. m. Mary 9 Apr 1944, 3 s, 1 d. Education: ThB; MDiv; ThD. Appointments: Profl Min, 1946-; Theol Ref Libn, Azusa Pacific Univ, 1985-93; Coll Prof, 1961-93 (retired). Publications: The Gospel of Luke, 1971-72; The Gospel of Matthew, 1975-76; From Slavery to Nationhood, 1977; The New Convenant in Christ, 1980; God Redeems His People, 1983; The Church: Its Message and Mission, 1984; Christian Stewardship: Love in Action, 1997. Memberships: Christian Commn on Christian Higher Educ; Ch of God, 1982-93; Pres, Ch Growth Investors Inc, 1981-93. Hobby: Gardening. Address: 413 N Valencia Street, Glendora, CA 91741-2418, USA.

RICHTER PRADA Pedro. Politician; Army Offr. Appointments: Fmr Chf of Staff of the Army; Fmr Min of the Interior; Chmn Jnt Chfs of Staff, Jan 1978-81; PM Min of War and Cmdr in Chf of Armed Forces of Peru, 1978-80; Pres Mokichi Okada Fndn Peru, 1981-. Address: c.o Oficina del Primer Ministro, Lima, Peru.

RIDLEY Ronald Thomas, b. 27 Dec 1940, Sydney, NSW, Aust. University Professor. m. Therese Dominguez, 1 Mar 1965. Education: Univ of Sydney, 1958-61; MA, Sydney, 1966; LittD, Melbourne, 1992. Appointments: Tchng Fell, Univ of Sydney, NSW, 1962-64; Lectr, Snr Lectr, Rdr, Prof, Univ of Melbourne, Vic, 1965-. Publications: The Unification of Egypt, 1973; Zosimus, New History, translation w commentary, 1983; Gibbon's complement: Louis de Beaufort, 1986; History of Rome, 1988; Perizonius, Animadversiones historicae, 1988; The Eagle and the Spade, 1992; Jessie Webb, a memoir, 1994; Melbourne's Monuments, 1996; Napoleon's Proconsul in Egypt: The Life and Times of Bernardino Drovetti, 1998; Articles in all ldng Eurn classical jrnls. Honours: FSA, 1991; FRHistS, 1998. Hobbies: Music; Literature. Listed in: Who's Who in Australia; Who's Who in the World. Address: Department of History, University of Melbourne, Parkville, Vic 3052, Australia.

RIEK Edgar Frederick, b. 1 May 1920. Winemaker. m. 6 Jan 1947, 3 d. Education: DSc, Univ of Qld. Appointments: Rsch Sci, CSIRO, Div of Entomology, 1945-78; Visng Prof, Univ CA, 1964; Visng Prof, Univ FL, 1973; Viticulteur, Owner, Winemaker, Lake George Winery, 1979-. Publications: The Canberra Gardener, 1959; Insects of Australia, 1st ed, 1963, 3rd ed, 1975. Honour: OAM. Hobbies: Trout (fly) Fishing; Wines of the world. Address: 19 Duffy Street, Ainslie, ACT 2602, Australia.

RIESENHUBER Klaus, b. 29 July 1938, Frankfurt am Main, Germany. Professor of Philosophy; Jesuit Priest. Education: Lic, Philos, Berchmanskolleg Pullach; DPhil, Univ München; DTheol, Sophia Univ. Appointments: Lectr, Sophia Univ, 1969; Asst Prof, 1974, Dir, Inst of Medieval Thought, 1974-, Prof, 1981-. Publications: Die Transzendenz der Freiheit zum Guten; Existenzerfahrung und Religion; 4 Japanese books on medieval philos; Ed and co-auth of 36 books, num articles in profl jrnls. Memberships: Dir of Zen-Hall, Akikawa Shinmeikutsu, Tokyo, 1990-; Standing Cttee, Japan Soc of Medieval Philos. Hobbies: Interreligious Dialogue; Zazen; Art. Address: S J House, Sophia University, 7-1 Kioicho, Chiyoda-ku, Tokyo 102-8571, Japan.

RIESS Gordon Sanderson, b. 25 Feb 1928, Thessaloniki, Greece. Consultant; Trainer. m. Priscilla, 2 June 1951, 2 s, 1 d. Education: AB, Highest Hons, Econs and Bus Admin, Whitman Coll; MBA, cum laude, Harv Bus Sch. Appointments: Infantry Platoon Ldr, Admin NCO, Off of Chf Cheml Offr, US Army Far East Cmd, 1946-47; Div Gen Mngr, Eurn Tractor Ops, Ford Motor Co, Brussels, Belgium, 1965-68; VP, Eur Reg, Intl Ppr Co, Zurich, Switz, 1968-71; Exec VP, Cinema Intl Corp,

London, Eng, 1972-75; Chmn and Pres, Stewart-Riess Labs Inc, Los Angeles, 1976-83; Pres, CEO, Intercontinental Enterprises Ltd, CA, 1983-. Publications: Num articles in var prof and trade mags. Honours: Alumnus of Merit, Whitman Coll, 1983; R H Macy Schlshp, Retailing, Harv Bus Sch. Memberships include: Inst of Mngmt Cnslts; Amn Cnslts League; Amn Assn of Profl Cnslts; Licensing Execs Soc; Hollywood Radio and TV Soc; Vice Chair, Bd of Overseers, Whitman Coll; Beverly Fndn; Czech Mngmt Cntr. Hobbies: Skiing; SCUBA diving; Travel. Listed in: Who's Who in California; Who's Who in Business. Address: 256 South Robertson Boulevard, PMB 3194, Beverly Hills, CA 90211, USA.

RIGHTER Rhonda Lee, b. 11 Sept 1959, Washington, DC. Professor. m. E A Lee, 20 Sept 1982, 1 d. Education: BS, Carnegie Mellon Univ; MS; PhD, Univ of CA, Berkeley. Appointments: Asst Prof, Assoc Prof, Prof Santa Clara Univ, 1987-. Creative Works: More than 30 articles in profl jrnls. Honours: Dean's Awd for Rsch, 1990, 1997, 1998; Winkler and Lund awd, 1993; Arthur Viring Davis Jnr Fac Fellshp. Memberships: Pres, Applied Probability Soc. Hobbies: Hiking; Political Theory; French. Address: Operations and MIS Dept, Santa Clara Univ, Santa Clara, CA 95053, USA.

RIGNEY Harry (Henry) Maxwell, b. 2 Apr 1948, Burnie, Tasmania. Lawyer (Tax and Revenue). m. Susan Denny, 16 Aug 1996, 3 s, 3 d. Education: LLB (Hons First), Tasmania, 1979; LLM, Harvard, 1980; Grad Dip Ed, Adelaide, 1982. Appointments: Prin Lectr, Capricornia Inst, 1987; Natl Tax Dir, Pannell Kerr Forster, 1989; Dir, Austl Tax Systems, 1992. Publication: Australian Business Taxation, 1990. Memberships: Fell, Tax Inst of Aust, 1983; Queensland Law Soc, 1991. Hobbies: Sailing; Music. Address: 65 Coast Road, Macleay Island, Qld 9184, Australia.

RILEY Murdoch Byron, b. 14 May 1927, Auckland, New Zealand. Director. m. Eldbjorg, 11 Oct 1954, 2 s. Appointment: Dir, Viking Sevenseas NZ Ltd. Publications include: Jade Treasures of the Maori, 1986; Maori Vegetable Cooking, 1987; Maori Sayings & Proverbs, 1990; Maori Healing & Herbal, 1994; Know Your South Island Places, 1995; Neuseelands Maori ABC, 1995; Maori Bird Law: An Introduction, 2000. Honour: 2nd Prize, NZ Montana Book Awds, 1995. Membership: Pres, Record Ind of NZ, 1973-79. Hobby: New Zealand Natural History. Address: 201a Rosetta Road, Raumati, New Zealand.

RILEY Tracy Lipscomb, b. 5 May 1966, Memphis, USA. Lecturer. 2 s. Education: BS, Delta State Univ; MEd, PhD, Univ of S MS. Appointments: Lectr, Gifted Educn, Dept of Learning & Tchng, Massey Univ, 1996-. Publications: Competitions: Maximizing Students Abilities. Memberships: Ed, Apex, NZ Jrnl of Gifted Educn; NZ Assn for Gifted Children; Natl Assn for Gifted Children. Hobbies: Reading; Travel; Entertaining Family & Friends. Address: Department of Learning & Teaching, Massey University, Hokowhitu Campus, Private Bag 11222, Palmerston North, New Zealand.

RIMMER Sheila Mary, b. 4 Mar 1944, Glasgow, Scotland. Economist; Writer. m. R Rimmer, 29 Nov 1986. Education: PhD; B Econs, Hons; Dip of Arts, Profl Writing and Editing. Appointments: Tchr, Dpty Prin, Victorian Educ Dept, 1961-75; Cnslt Economist; Advsr, num Govt, Pvte Sector, Union and Non-Profit Orgs; Speaker, 47 Intl and Austl Confs; Dpty Master, Ormond Coll, The Univ of Melbourne, 1995-96; Acad Economist, La Trobe Univ; Melbourne Univ; Deakin Univ; Austl Cath Univ; Stirling Univ; Glasgow Univ; Caledonian Univ, 1978-95; Advsr, Queen Vic Women's Cntr; Cnslt Ed, Natl Cncl of Women, Aust; Cnslt Ed, Writer, Melbourne Cath Socl Servs; Publns Asst, Austl Econ Review; Lit Rsch Agent, Searching Questions. Publications: Opportunities Lost; A Workbook to Introduce Macroeconomics; Australian Labor Market and Microeconomic Reform; More Brilliant Careers; 46 Articles publshd in Aust and Intl. Honours: Medal, La Trobe Univ, D M Myer Univ, 1976; Best Ppr Prize, Econ Soc of Aust, 1991. Memberships: Inst of Applied Econ and Socl Rsch, 1984-86. Hobbies: Music;

Reading; Walking. Address: 55 The Righi, Eaglemont 3084, Australia.

RIMOIN David L, b. 9 Nov 1936, Montreal, Quebec, Can. Chairman of Paediatrics. m. Ann Piilani Garber, 1 s, 2 d. Education: BSc, 1st Class Hons, Genetics, 1957, MD, CM, 1961, MSc, Genetics, 1961, McGill Univ, Montreal, Can; PhD, Human Genetics, Johns Hopkins Univ Sch of Med, Baltimore, MD, USA, 1967. Appointments include: Assoc Prof, Paediats and Med, UCLA Sch of Med, Los Angeles, 1970-73; Assoc Dir, Clinl Rsch Cntr, Harbor Gen Hosp, 1970-73; Chf, Div of Medl Genetics, Harbor-UCLA Medl Cntr, 1970-86; Vice Chmn, Dept of Paediats, 1986-, Prof of Paediats and Med, 1973-, UCLA Sch of Med; Chmn, Dept of Paediats and Dir of Medl Genetics-Birth Defects Cntr, Cedars-Sinai Medl Cntr, Los Angeles, 1986-. Publications: Mbr, Editl Bds of num projs medl jrnls. Honours include: Rosenfeld Prize, Microbio, 1959, Drake Prize in Pathology, 1960, Frederick Smith Meml Fellshp, 1961, Holmes Gold Medal for Highest Acad Stndng, 1961, Forsyth Prize in Surgery, 1961, McGill Univ; Ross Outstndng Young Investigator Awd, Western Soc for Paediat Rsch, 1976; E Mead Johnson Awd for Rsch in Paediats, Amn Acady of Paediats, 1976; March of Dimes Col Harland Sanders Awd, Lifetime Achmnt in Genetic Scis, 1997; Hon Doct Humane Letters, Finch Univ of Hlth Scis, 1997. Memberships include: Amn Acady of Paediats; Fell, Amn Assn for Advmnt of Sci; Fndg Fell, Amn Coll of Medl Genetics, Pres 1991-96; Fell, Amn Coll of Physns; Amn Fedn for Clinl Rsch; Amn Paediat Soc; Soc for Paediat Rsch; Endocrine Soc; Mbr, Stndng Cttee on Genetic Servs, Pres, 1984, Amn Soc of Human Genetics; Grievance Cttee, Amn Bd Medl Genetics; Bd Dirs, Pschological Trauma Cntr; Pres, Amn Coll of Medl Genetics Fndn. Address: Cedars Sinai Medical Center, 8700 Beverly Boulevard, Ste 4310, Los Angeles, CA 90048, USA.

RINEHART Francis E, b. 6 Jan 1927, USA. Attorney. m. Georgina Hope Rinehart, 13 Jan 1983, 3 s, 3 d. Education: Harvard Coll; Harvard Engrng Sch; Harvard Law Sch. Appointments: State Dept, USA; Army Air Corps; Davis Polk, USA; Newmont Mining Co; Consulted to Exton, Arco, Standard Oil and Mobil; Own Law Firm, NY. Publications: Past Ed, Boston Newspaper. Honours: 1st Place, Harvard Coll; 1st Place, Harvard Law Sch; Kentucky Col and Hall of Fame, Louisville, Kentucky. Hobbies: Education; Horse Racing; Scouts. Address: 150 Victoria Avenue, Dalkeith, WA 6009, Australia.

RINKEVICH Baruch, b. 25 Feb 1948, Tel Aviv, Israel. Scientist. m. Sofnat, 1973, 2 s, 1 d. Education: PhD, Tel Aviv Univ, 1982. Appointments: Prof, 1994, Hd, 1995, Minerva Cntr for Marine Invertebrates Immunology and Dev Bio. Publications: Over 120 sci articles; Ed, book; Chapts in sev sci books. Honours: Career Awd Cancer Inst, 1993; Minerva Cntr, 1995; Tobias Londau Awd, 1998. Memberships: Israel Acady in 5 sci assns. Hobby: Diving. Address: National Institute of Oceanography, Tel Shikmona, PO Box 8030, Haifa 31080, Israel.

RIPPON Lesley Margaret, b. 10 Mar 1936, Merrylands, NSW, Aust. Artist. m. 9 Feb 1960, 1 s, 1 d. Education: Art Cert, Meadowbank Coll, TAFE, 1979-80; Study tours to Eng and France, 1985; Yugoslavia, Greece and Greek Islands, Italy, 1986; Italy, Germany, Switz, Austria, Can, 1988; Austria, Italy, 1996. Appointments: Tchr, Epping, YMMCA, 1977; Tchr, RMAS Willandra Art Cntr, 1981-86; Tchr, Castle Hill Art Soc, 1982-83; Tchr, Castle Hill Evening Coll, 1982-83; Workshops all over Aust for many yrs. Creative works: 2-woman art exhibns, 1976-78, Sydney; 1-woman show, Sydney, 1989; Broken Hill, 1995; Num other exhibns in Aust; Article in Austl Art mag, 1985; Demonstrator for 19 yrs for leading art wholesaler; Organised Amns Christopher Schink and Maxine Masterfield workshops, Aust, 1990; Accredited Embroidery Tutor, tchng designing embroidery and painted background. Honours: 1st Prize, Meadowbank Coll of TAFE, 1979-80; Recip of other awds. Memberships: Assoc Mbr, Roy Art Soc of NSW; Peninsular Art Soc; Trinity Delmar Soc of The Arts; Art Gall Soc of NSW; Embroiderer's Guild of NSW.

Hobbies: Photography; Gardening; Embroidery. Listed in: Who's Who in Australasia and Southeast Asia; Who's Who of Women of the World; Who's Who of Australasia and the South Pacific; Dictionary of Women Artists of Australia. Address: PO Box 139, Epping 1710, NSW, Australia.

RITCHIE Alastair Ian Maxwell, b. 16 Nov 1936. Physicist. 2 d. Education: BS, Glasgow; PhD, UNSW. Appointments: Proj Mngr, Environmental Phys, 1978; Proj Mngr, Mngng Mine Wastes, Austl Nuclear Sci & Technol Orgns, 1996. Publications: Over 120 jrnl articles, book chpts and techl reports covering aspects of phys transport phenomena. Honour: Lucas Heights Sci Soc Medal, 1989. Memberships: Austl Nuclear Assn; Amn Soil Soc; Internal Assn of Hydrogeologists. Hobbies: Bush walking; Skiing; Paleoanthropology. Address: 22 Boronia Parade, Lugarno, NSW 2210, Australia.

RITCHIE Ian Mackay, b. 18 Mar 1936. Research Scientist. m. Maureen Ann McMahon, 6 June 1959, 2 s, 1 d. Education: BA, MA, MEng, ScD, Cambridge Univ, Eng; PhD, Melbourne Univ, Aust. Appointments: Engr, Transitron Elec Corp, Wakefield, MA, USA, 1959-62; Snr Demonstrator, Lectr, Snr Lectr, Univ of Melbourne, 1962-71; Assoc Prof, Univ of West Aust, 1972-83; Prof of Chem, Murdoch Univ, 1984-92; Dir, A J Parker CRC for Hydrometallurgy, 1992-. Publications: Over 130 pprs in sci jrnls on corrosion, electrochem and hydrometall. Honours: Australasian Corrosion Medal, 1979; Stokes Medal for Electrchem, Roy Austl Chem Inst, 1997; Applied Rsch Awd, Roy Austl Chem Inst, 1997; WA Citizen of Yr (Professions) Awd, 1997. Memberships: Fell, Austl Acady of Technol Scis and Engrng; Fell, Roy Austl Chem Inst; Fell, Australasian Inst of Mining and Metall. Hobbies: Badminton; Family history; Woodworking. Address: 11 Beatrice Road, Dalkeith, WA, Australia.

RITHAUDDEEN AL-HAJ BIN TENGKU ISMAIL Y M Tengku Ahmad, b. 24 Jan 1932 Kota Bharu. Politician; Bar. m. Y M Tengku Puan Sri Datin Noor Aini, 1957, 3 s, 2 d; Mbr Roy family of Kelantan. Education: Nottingham Univ; Lincoln's Inn UK. Appointments: Ciruit Magistrate in Ipoh, 1956-58; Pres of Sess Crt, 1958-60; Dep Pub Prosecutor and Fed Cnsl, 1960-62; Chmn E Coast Bar Cttee of Malaya; Chmn Sri Nilam Co-op Soc Malaysia; Sponsor Adabi Fndn; Sponsor Kelantan Yth; Advsr Kesatria; Chmn Farmer's Org Authy; Min with Spec Functions Asstng PM on For Affairs, 1973-75; Min for For Affairs, 1975-81, 1984-86; Min for Trade and Ind, 1981-83; Min for Info, 1986; Min of Def, 1986-90; Jnt Chmn Malaysia-Thailand Dev Authy - Gas and Oil; Chmn Kinta Kellas Invmnts PLC, 1990-; Chmn Idris Hydraulic - Malaysia - Holdings Berhad; Advsr KPMG Peat Marwick Malaysia; Pro-Chan Natl Univ of Malaysia; Dep Pres Football Assn of Malaysia. Memberships: Mbr Cncl of Advsrs to Ruler of State of Kelantan - MPR - resigned to enter priv prac; Mbr Malayan Cncl, 1967, 1968, 1969, 1970. Hobbies: Golf. Address: Road Builder - M - Holdings Bhd, 5th Floor, 38 Jalan Dang Wangi, Kuala Lumpur, Malaysia.

RIVAS Daniel E, b. 11 Dec 1945, Camaguey, Cuba. College Professor. Education: BA (Hons), Marist Coll; AM, PhD, Univ of IL. Appointments: Asst Prof, 1977-82, Assoc Prof, 1982-85, Auburn Univ; Dean, Liberal Arts, Saddleback Coll, 1985-97; Dean, Hum and Langs, Irvine Valley Coll, 1997-98; Prof of French, Irvine Valley Coll, 1998-. Publications: Articles and reviews in French jrnls. Honours: Undergrad Awd in French, Marist Coll, 1967; Univ Fell, French, Univ of IL, 1971-73. Memberships: Amn Assn of Tchrs of French; Amn Transls Assn. Address: Humanities and Languages, Irvine Valley College, 5500 Irvine Center Drive, Irvine, CA 92620, USA.

RIX Alan Gordon, b. 12 Dec 1949, Sydney, Aust. University Professor. m. Judith McGuigan, 12 Mar 1977, 2 s. Education: BA, 1972; PhD, 1977, Austl Natl Univ. Appointments: Rsch Fell, Austl Natl Univ, 1977-79; Rsch Offr, Dept of For Affairs, 1979-81; Snr Lectr, Sch of Modern Asian Studies, Griffith Univ, 1982-84; Prof of

Japanese Studies, Univ of Qld, 1985-; Pro-Vice-Chan (External Affairs), 1994-96; Exec Dean, Fac of Arts, 1997. Publications include: Japans Economic Aid, 1980; Quantity vs Quality: Japans Aid Programme, 1987; Intermittent Diplomat: The Diaries of W MacMahon Ball, 1988; Japans Foreign Aid Challenge, 1993. Memberships: Asian Studies Assn of Aust. Hobbies: Reading; Gardening; Natural history. Address: Faculty of Arts, University of Queensland, St Lucia, Qld 4072, Australia.

ROACHE June Ruby, b. 19 Aug 1948, Australia. Chief Executive Officer. m. George, 21 Mar 1969, 1 d. Education: BAcc; Grad Cert in Mngmt. Appointments: Chief Exec Off, SA Lotteries, 1994-; former Chief of Staff to Hon Diana Laidlaw, MLC; former Snr Exec w SA TAB; JP, S Aust. Memberships: Fell, Austl Inst of Co Dirs; Fell, Austl Inst of Mngmt; Assoc, Austl Soc of Certified Practising Accts; Fndn Mbr, Univ of S Aust Alumni Assn, Bus and Mngmt Chapt. Hobbies: Walking; Swimming; Reading. Address: 9 Classic Court, West Lakes, SA 5021, Australia.

ROBBINS Jack Howard, b. 16 May 1957, Los Angeles, CA, USA. Lawyer; Mediator; Arbitrator. m. Cindy Robbins, 1 July 1990. Education: JD, 1982. Appointments: Atty, Assoc, Wilson, Kenna & Borys, Los Angeles, 1985-88; Bottum & Feliton, Los Angeles, 1988-90; Pvte Law Practice, Sacramento, 1991-; Judge, Pro Tempore, Sacramento Co, Superior Crt, 1994-; Early Neutral Evaluator, US Dist Crt, Eastern Dist of CA, 1996-. Memberships: Arbitration Panel, Sacramento & Placer Counties Superior Crt; Amn Bar Assn; State Bar of CA; Sacramento County Bar Assn; CA Dispute Resolution Cncl. Hobbies: Skiing; Tennis. Address: Robbins, & Robbins, 24681 La Plaza, Suite 220, Dana Point, CA 92629, USA.

ROBERTS Barney (Bernhard Knyvet), b. 31 Jan 1920. Writer. m. Jean (Elizabeth J) Weatherhead, 1 Mar 1947, 3 s, 1 d. Publications: Flowerdale to 63, 1963; The Phantom Boy, 1976; Stones in the Cephissus, 1979; The Penalty of Adam, 1980; A Kind of Cattle, 1985, 1986; Where's Morning Gone, 1987-88; The Poetry of Earth, 1989; Tales I Carry With Me, 1988; Gods and Neighbours, 1992; Gone Bush with Horrie and Me (poetry), 1998; Anthologies. Honour: NSW Premiers Lit Awd, Spec Peace Prize Intl Year of Peace, 1986; Tas Premier's Lit Awd Bicentennial Awd, 1988; Rolf Boldrewood Awd, for short stories. Memberships: TFAW, State Sec, 3 yrs; TWU; ASA, 20 yrs. Hobbies: Appreciation and preservation of natural and beautiful ideas, things, people, environments. Listed in: International Register of Profiles. Address: Bush House, Flowerdale, Tas 7325, Australia.

ROBERTS Cedric Kenelm, b. 19 Apr 1918, Birmingham, Eng. Retired Naval Officer. m. Audrey Elias, 11 Nov 1940, 4 s. Education: Naval Staff Coll, 1949. Appointments: Naval Airman 2nd Class, RN, 1940; Cmnd Temp Sub-Lt (A); RNVR, 1940; Sunk in HMS Manchester, Malta Convoy, 1942; Interned in Laghouat, Sahara, 1942; Personal Pilot to Vice-Admiral Sir Lumley Lyster, 1943; HMS Trumpeter, Russian Convoys, 1944; Perm Commnto Lt RN, HMS Vindex, Pacific, 1945; Cmndg Offr, 813 Sqdn, 1948; Cmndg Offr, 767 Sqdn, 1950-51; Cmndg Offr, 825 Sqdn, 1951-52; Cmndr, 1952; Served Korean War, shot down, rescued by US Forces; On loan as Dpty Dir of Air Warfare, Roy Austl Navy, 1953-55; Capt, 1958; Cmndg Offr, RNAS Eglinton, 1958-59; Chf Staff Offr, Flag Offr, Naval Flying Trng, 1959-61; Chf Staff Offr: Flag Offr, Aircraft Carriers, 1961-62; Cmndg Offr, HMS Osprey, 1962-64; Cmndg Offr, RNAS Culdrose, 1964-65; Chf Staff Offr (Ops), Far East Fleet, 1966-67; Rear-Admiral, 1968; Flag Offr, Naval Flying Trng, 1968-71; Retd, 1971; Farming, Somerset, Eng, 1971-79; Emigrated to Aust, 1979. Honours: Awd'd Companion of the DSO, 1953; Awd'd Companion of the Most Hon Order of the Bath, 1970; Hobbies: Sitting in the sun, drinking plonk, and watching the sheilas go by. Address: 11 Collins Street, Merimbula, NSW 2548, Australia.

ROBERTS Charles Morgan, b. 13 June 1932, Roswell, NM, USA. Optometric Physician; Professor. m. Gloria, 20 Feb 1962, 1 s. 1 d. Education: BS Electronic Engrg; BA, MS, Org Chem; BS Ocular Physiol; OD (Doctor of Optometry). Appointments: Electronic Des Engr, Atron Div of Aerojet Gen, 1956-66; Rsch Chem, Sunkist Growers Inc, Orange Prods Div, 1966-70; Cnsltng Dr in Eye Clinic, US Pub Hlth Serv Hosp, 1974-77; Assoc Prof, S CA Coll of Optometry, 1974-; Rschr, 1973-; Pvt Practice, 1975-. Publications: 15 articles in field of optometry. Honours: Diplomate of the Corneal and Contact Lens, Amn Acady Optometry; Cert'd in Contact Lenses, Nat Eye Rsch Fndn; Bausch and Lom Rsch Fellshp, Bausch & Lomb Outstndng Achievement Awd; SCCO Instr of Yr; Rotarian of Yr; Optometric Recog Awd; Capistrano Valley HS Sports Appreciation Awd; Nat Sci Fndn Schlshp in Org Chem. Memberships: FAAO; Amn Optometric Assn; CA Optometric Assn; Orange Co Optometric Soc; Omega Epsilon Phi; Omega Delta; CA Profl Hypnosis Assn. Hobbies: Writing; Electronics and computers. Address: 32282 Camino Capistrano B, San Juan Capistrano, CA 92675, USA.

ROBERTS Denys Tudor Emil, b. 19 Jan 1923, London, Eng. Judge. m. Fiona Alexander, 10 Feb 1985, 1 s. Education: MA; BCL. Appointments: AG, Hong Kong, 1966-73; Chf Sec, Hong Kong, 1973-79; CJ, Hong Kong, 1979-88; C J, Brunei, 1979-. Creative Works: 8 Books, 1954-. Honours: OBE, 1960; CBE, 1970; KBE, 1975; SPMB, 1984. Memberships: MCC. Hobbies: Writing; Cricket; Walking. Address: Supreme Court, Bandar Seri Bedawan, Darussalam, Brunei.

ROBERTS John Heath, b. 5 Sept 1949, Adelaide, S Aust, Aust. Academic; Company Director. m. Pamela, 2 Oct 1976, 2 d. Education: BA (Hons); MComm, Melbourne; MSc; PhD, MIT. Appointments: Snr Rsch Ofr, Austl Bur of Stats, 1970-72; Mngr, Forecasting, Postmaster Gens Dept, 1972-75; NSW Mktng Mngr, Telstra, 1975-84; Prof, UNSW, 1984-. Publications: In profl jrnls. Honours: Amn Mktng Inst John Howard Dissertation Awd, 1985; Runner Up, INFORMS John DC Little Awd, 1988, 1990; AGSM Distinguished Tchr Awd, 1994; Amn Mktng Assn O'Dell Awd, 1996; ANZ Distinguished Acad Awd, 1997; Alpha Mu Alpha. Memberships: Fell, Austl Inst of Mngmt; Fell, Austl Mktng Inst; Fell, Advtng Inst of Aust; US Harkness Fell; Fell, UK 21st Century Trust; Amn Mktng Assn. Hobbies: Tennis; Bushwalking; Wine. Address: National Australia Bank Professor of Marketing, Australian Graduate School of Management, University of New South Wales, Sydney, NSW 2052, Australia.

ROBERTS Kevin Laurence, b. 1 Dec 1952, Wellington, NZ. Writer. Career: Freelance. Publications: Plays: Step, Walk and Tumble, 1981; The Marriage Stakes, 1982; Forgive and Forget, 1985; TV: Heartbreak High, 1995-98; Something in the Air, 1999; Film: Dear Claudia, 1999. Memberships: NSW State Chair, Austl Writers' Guild, 1992-98. Hobbies: Sport; Arts. Address: GPO Box 4536, Sydney, NSW 2001, Australia.

ROBERTS Richard John, b. 21 June 1945, Sydney, Aust. Senior Lecturer. Education: BA, DipEd, New Eng; BSocStud, Sydney; PhD, NSW; MAASW. Appointments: NSw Dept of Hlth, 1972-73; Lectr, Tech and Further Educ, 1973-75, Snr Lectr, 1975-77, Darwin Community Coll; Snr Lectr, Univ of NSW, 1978-91, 1993-; Assoc Prof, Charles Sturt Univ, 1991-93. Publications: Lessons from the Past: Issues for Social Work Theory, 1990. Honour: Medal for Serv, AASW. Memberships: Austl Assn of Socl Workers; Soc for the Sci Stdy of Sex; Amn Bd of Sexology. Hobbies: Classical music; Classical ballet; Weightlifting; Fitness. Address: School of Social Work, University of New South Wales, Sydney, NSW, 2052, Australia.

ROBERTS Robert Walter, b. 27 Nov 1923, London, Eng (Austl citizen). Chartered Quantity Surveyor. m. Winifred May Ager, 2 Apr 1955, 3 s. Education: Polytechnic, London, 1948-51; Assoc, 1953, Fell, 1956, Roy Inst of Chartered Surveyors. Appointments: Assoc, S W Appleyard & Ptnrs, London, 1951; Ptnr, John

Rawlinson & Ptnrs, 1956; Mngng Dir, Rawlinson, Roberts & Ptnrs, 1970; Chmn, John Rawlinson Co-Partnership, 1977; Cost Planner, Aust's New Parl House, 1980. Publications: Foundation Correspondent, The Building Economist; Ed, Spons Australian Architects and Builders Price Book. Membership: Fell, Austl Inst of Quantity Surveyors. Hobbies: Distance running; Golf; Woodwork; Clubs: The Weld, Lake Karrinyup County Club, WA. Address: 3 Stewart Place, 6 Bellvue Terrace, West Perth, WA 6005, Australia.

ROBERTS William Kerry, b. 12 June 1937, Sydney, NSW, Aust. Deputy Managing Director. m. Maureen Mary Queale, 12 Aug 1959, 2 s, 3 d. Education: Fellshp, Inst of Actuaries, London, Eng, 1961. Appointments: Austl Mutual Provident Soc, Brisbane, 1964; Hd Off, Sydney 1968, served in London, Sydney, Melbourne, Wellington; Dpty Mngr for NZ 1975, Chf Actuary 1984-86, Gen Mngr and Chf Actuary 1987-88; Chf Gen Mngr, Aust, 1988-91; Chf Gen Mngr, Fin and Chf Actuary, 1991-97; Dpty Mngng Dir, 1997-; Dir, AMP Ltd, G10 Aust Holdings Ltd, United Energy Ltd; Ret'd, 1998. Publications: Contbr of var pprs for profl bodies. Honours: Pres, Inst of Actuaries of Aust, 1982, Mbr of Cncl 1980-83; Chmn, MacQuarie Univ Actuarial Fndn, 1989, Pres, Austl Ins Inst, 1991; Mbr, Cncl of Austl Ins Inst, 1986-92; Mbr, Cncl of Austl Mngmt Coll, Mt Eliza, 1990-92. Memberships: Inst of Actuaries, London; Intl Acturial Assn, Ins Inst of Aust. Hobbies: Reading; Current Affairs; Australian Football. Address: c/o Australian Mutual Provident Society, GPO Box 4134, Sydney, NSW, Australia.

ROBERTS-THOMSON Peter John, b. 28 Sept 1946, Devonport, Aust. Immunologist; Rheumatologist. m. 30 Mar 1972, 3 d. Education: MB, BS, Adelaide Univ, 1971; DPhil (Oxon), 1976; MRCP, Eng, 1976; FRACP, 1980; FRCPA, 1980; MD Adelaide, 1988; FRCP, 1995. Appointments: Roy Adelaide Hosp, 1971; Nuffield Dept of Med, 1972-75; Flinders Med Cntr, Adelaide, 1986-; Prof, Flinders Univ, 1997. Publications: Co-auth, Diagnostic Immunopathology, 1996; Num publs in med, immunology and rheumatology. Honours: Snr Hulme Schl, Brasenose Coll, Oxford, Eng, 1972-74; Fulbright Schlshp, 1980. Memberships: Fell, ARA Aust and USA; Fell, ASI, Aust. Hobbies: Bushwalking; Australian history. Address: Department of Clinical Immunology, Flinders Medical Centre, Bedford Park, Adelaide, SA 5042, Australia.

ROBERTSON John Fraser (Sir), b. 3 Aug 1925, Takaka, NZ. Public Sector Consultant. m. Phyllis Irene Walter, 5 Apr 1947, 2 s, 1 d. Education: ACA, Canterbury Univ & Vic Univ of Wellington, 1950; DPA, Vic Univ of Wellington, 1956; Harkness C'wlth Fund Fell, Cntr for Advd Stdy, Brookings Inst and Harvard, USA, 1961; Imperial Def Coll, London, 1968. Appointments: Sec & Asst Commnr, State Servs Commn, 1963-67; Dpty Sec of Def, 1967-69; Sec of Def, 1969-79; Sec for Jus, 1979-82; Co Dir & Mngmt Cnslt, 1982-84; Ombudsman, 1984-86; Chf Ombudsman, 1986-94; Pres, Intl Ombudsman Inst, 1992-94. Publications: Long-time contbr to learned jrnls on pub admin specialising in reorganisation and resistance to change . Honours: CBE, 1992; KCMG, 1994. Memberships: Life Mbr, Fell, NZ Inst of Pub Admin; Life Mbr, Intl Ombudsman Inst; One-time Cncl Mbr, long-time Topic Supvr, NZ Admnstrv Staff Coll. Hobbies: Bowls; Golf; Fishing; Grandchildren. Address: 5 Kabul Street, Khandallah, Wellington, New Zealand.

ROBERTSON Robert Peter, b. 27 Mar 1949, Melbourne, Australia. Physicist. m. Diane Elizabeth Stagoll, 9 July 1976, 2 d. Education: BSc, hons, 1971, MSc, 1973, Univ Melbourne. Appointments: Asst Ed, Nuclear Phys, Copenhagen, 1975-79; Rsch Fell, Univ Melbourne, 1979-80; Ed, Austl Jrnl of Phys, CSIRO, 1981-. Publications: History of the Niels Bohr Institute, 1979; Beyond Southern Skies - Radio Astronomy and the Parkes Telescope, 1992. Honour: Fell, Austl Inst of Phys, 1986. Memberships: Austl Inst of Phys; Astron Soc of Aust; Aust and NZ Assn for the Adv of Sci. Hobbies: Swimming; Football; Carpentry. Address: 21 Clark Road, Ivanhoe, Vic 3079, Australia.

ROBINS-BROWNE Roy Michael, b. 3 June 1947. Professor; Microbiologist; Educator. m. Gail Mary Dixon, 6 Dec 1970, 3 d. Education: MB.BCh; PhD; FCPath; FRCPath; FRCPA; FASM. Appointments: Intern, Johannesburg Hosp; Registrar, Microbiol, Snr Microbiol, Sch of Path, Johannesburg; Asst Prof, Univ MD; Prof, Univ of Natal, Durban; Rdr, Univ of Melbourne; Rsch Prof, Univ MD; Dir, Microbiol & Infectious Diseases, Roy Childrens Hosp, Melbourne; Prof, Dir, Microbiol Rsch, Roy Childrens Hosp & Univ of Melbourne. Publications: Auth and co-auth of sev book chapts, reviews, articles and over 100 original sci reports dealing w med microbiol and infectious diseases. Memberships: Am Soc for Microbiol; Austl Soc for Infectious Diseases; Austl Soc for Microbiol. Address: Department of Microbiology and Immunology, University of Melbourne, Parkville, Vic 3052, Australia.

ROBINSON Angus Muir, b. 15 June 1947, Melbourne, Aust. Geologist. m. Jeanette, 18 Jan 1974, 1 s. Education: BSc, Univ Melbourne. Appointments: Geol, Cundill Meyers & Assocs, 1969-70; Exploration Geol, Cyprus Mines Corp, 1971-75, Occidental Minerals Corp, 1975-76; Area Mngr, Mt Hotham Alpine Resort, 1977-80; Snr Geol, NSW Dept of Mineral Resources, 1980-82; Regl Mngr, N Coalfields, NSW Dept of Mineral Resources, 1982-87; Dir, The Earth Exchange Mus, 1988-90; Dir, Coml Servs, Zoological Parks Bd of NSW, 1990-94; Gen Mngr, The Warren Cntr for Adv Engrng, Univ Sydney, 1994-98; Gen Mngr, Austl Technol Park, 1998-. Memberships: Fell, Austl Inst of Mngt; Fell, Australasian Inst of Mining and Metallurgy, Austl Inst of Geoscientists; Environtl Inst of Aust; Geol Soc of Aust; Melbourne Cricket Club; Roy Prince Alfred Yacht Club; Rotary Club of Sydney; C'Wlth Club. Address: 43 The Chase Road, Turranurra, NSW 2074, Australia.

ROBINSON Barbara, b. 22 Nov 1936, Brisbane, Australia. Retired. widowed, 1 s, 1 d. Appointments: VP, 1991-92, Sec, 1995-96, Ed, Generation, 1997-98, Jrnl of Genealog Soc of Qld. Membership: Genealog Soc of Qld Inc. Hobbies: Genealogy; Reading; Music; Crafts; Travel. Address: 20/104 Dornoch Tce, Highgate Hill, Qld 4101, Australia.

ROBINSON Clint David, b. 27 July 1972, Brisbane, Australia. Athlete; News Presenter. Honours: OAM, 1990; Austl Jnr Sports Star of the Yr, 1992; Olympic Champion, 1994; World Champion, 1994; Bronze Medal, 1995; Silver Medal, 1996; Atlanta Olympics Bronze Medal; 26 times Natl Kayaking Gold Medalist; 24 times Natl Surf Life Saving Gold Medalist. Memberships include: Sunshine Coast Canoe Club; Austl Inst of Sport Kayaking; Qld Racing Drivers Assn; Confed of Aust Motor Sports. Hobbies: Surf Life Saving; Motorsport; Surfing; Movies; Friends. Address: Lot 4 Sanctury Drive, Forest Glen, Qld 4556, Australia.

ROBINSON Donald William Bradley, b. 9 Nov 1922, Sydney, Aust. Minister in Holy Orders. m. 1949, 3 s, 1 d. Education: BA, Sydney Univ, 1946; BA (Theol Trip. Part 1a, C1 II i) 1949, (Part III C1 II i) 1950, MA 1954, Queen's Coll, Cambridge; Deacon, 1950; Priest, Archbish of Sydney; Thd, honoris causa, Aust, 1979. Appointments: Curate, St Matthew's, Manly, 1950-51; Curate, St Philip's, Sydney, 1952-53; Lectr, 1952-53, Snr Lectr, 1954-59, Vice Prin, 1959-72, Acting Prin, 1968, Moore Theol coll; Lectr, Union Biblical Seminary, Yeotmal, India, 1969; Consecrated Asst Bish of Sydney in St Andrew's Cath, 1973; Bish in Parramatta, 1973-82; Archbish of Sydney, 1982-93. Honour: AO, 1984. Address: 1 Jubilee Avenue, Pymble, NSW 2073, Australia.

ROBINSON Raymond George, b. 8 July 1917, Sydney, Aust. Medical. m. Pamela, 26 Feb 1944, 3 s. 1 d. Education: MBBS; FRACP. Appointments: Retd, 1989-. Honours: OBE, 1979; R G Robinson Oration; Austl Rheumatism Assn; Hon Mbr, ILAR; VP Emeritus, Arthritis Fndn of Aust. Memberships: Austl Medl Assn, 1942; Austl Rheumatism assn, 1953, Sec, Pres; Pres, Intl League of Assn for Rheumatism. Hobbies: Sailing; Gardening. Address: 62A Lucretia Avenue, Longueville 2066, NSW, Australia.

ROBINSON Wayne Francis, b. 4 Mar 1944. Veterinary Scientist. m. Jennifer Jane Loughlin, 3 Jan 1967, 1 s. Education: BVSC, MVSc, Melbourne; PhD, OH State; Dipl, Amn Coll of Vet Pathologists, MACVS. Appointments: OH State Univ, 1976-77; Murdoch Univ, 1977-93; Prof & Hd of Dept of Vet Path, Univ of Queensland, 1993-. Publications: Over 100 pprs in sci jrnls; Co-ed, Clinicopathologic Principles for Veterinary Medicine; Co-auth, Cardiovascular System in Pathology of Domestic Animals. Honours: Meritorious Serv Awd: Austl Vet Assn, 1987; Disting Sci Awd: Austl Vet Assn, 1991. Memberships: Austl Vet Assn, Pres, WA Div, 1986; Amn Coll of Vet Pathologists; Austl Coll of Vet Scientists; Amn Royal Soc of Qld. Address: Department of Veterinary Pathology, School of Veterinary Science, University of Queensland, St Lucia, Qld 4072, Australia.

ROBINSON FLANNERY Nancy Elizabeth, b. 12 Aug 1929. Author; Editor. m. (1) David Robinson, 31 Mar 1951, (2) Alick Whittle, 8 Sept 1979, (3) Ian Flannery, 27 Apr 1990, 2 d. Appointment: JP, 1981-; Freelance Book Editor; Property Manager. Publications: Books: Change on Change, 1971; Bend Down & Listen, 1972; Stagg of Tarcowie, 1973; Coothidie, 1973; Sweet Breathes the Breast, 1974; Reluctant Harbour, 1976; Mastectomy, 1977; Net Result: Profiles of the Executive Women, 1992; Net Result II: Success Stories, 1993; This Everlasting Silence, 1999; Biography of Paquita, Lady Mawson, forthcoming. Honours: Shell Essay Awd, 1943; Lit Bd Grant, 1977. Memberships: Austl Soc of Auths; Histl Soc of S Aust. Hobbies: Gardening; Reading; Family; Natural Health. Address: Gongolope, 13 Hallett Road, Erindale 5066, SA, Australia.

ROBSON Brian Albert, b. 7 Sept 1934, Leeds, Eng. Theoretical Physicist. m. Joan Mena Freeman, 2 Jan 1961, 1 s, 2 d. Education: BSc 1955, MSc 1957, PhD 1960; DSc 1986, Univ of Melbourne, Aust. Appointments: Snr Demonstrator, Univ of Melbourne, 1956-60; Rsch Fell, 1960-62, Fell, 1963-68, Snr Fell, 1968-, Hd, Dept Theort Phys, 1987-95, Assoc Dir, Rsch Sch of Phys Scis and Engrng, Aust Natl Univ, 1995-97. Publications: Auth, Book: The Theory of Polarization Phenomena, 1974; Ed, Books: Nuclear Interactions, 1979; Nuclear and Particle Physics, 1990; Atomic and Molecular Physics and Quantum Optics, 1992; Cosmology: The Physics of the Universe, 1995; Num sci papers in jrnls. Honours: Exhib Schlsp, Queens Coll, 1952; Kernot Rsch Schlshp Prize 1957, Univ of Melbourne; Life Mbr, Box Hill Chess Club, Melbourne, 1960; Chmn, ACT Br, Aust Inst of Phys, 1987-88. Memberships: Fell, Aust Inst of Phys (FAIP); Aust Computer Soc; ANZAAS. Hobbies: Chess; Golf; Orienteering. Address: 12 Glasgow Street, Hughes, ACT 2605, Australia.

ROBSON Robert Alick, b. 5 Jan 1927, St Kilda, Vic, Aust. Company Director. m. Joan Elizabeth Murdoch, 12 Dec 1953, 3 s. Education: BCivEng, 1951, BA, 1960, Melbourne, Univ; MSc(Eng), Univ of the Witwatersrand, S Afr, 1963. Appointments: Civil Engr, Melbourne and Metrop Bd of Wrks, Vic, 1951-54; Var managerial posns, Rocla Pipes Ltd, 1954-75; Gen Mngr, Dir, Rocla Inds ltd, 1970-75; Mngng Dir, BMI Ltd, 1975-83; Mngng Dir, AGC Ltd, 1983-89; Directorships: Lanarka Pty Ltd, NSW, 1976-; Colonial Mutual Life Assurance Soc Ltd, Vic, 1990-96; Jardine Fleming China Region Ltd, Sydney, 1993-; Chmn, Ciba-Geigy Aust Ltd, NSW, 1986-96. Honour: CBE, 1980. Memberships: Hon Fell, Inst of Quarrying. Hobbies: Boating; Fishing. Address: Suite 363, 656 Military Road, Mosman, NSW 2088, Australia.

ROBSON Ross McKenzie, b. 20 July 1946, Hamilton, Vic, Aust. Barrister-at-Law; Queen's Counsel. m. (1) Kathryn Mary Symes, 14 Jan 1974, diss 1990, 1 s, 1 d, (2) Maureen Patricia Stockdale (Ryan), 15 Jan 1994, 2 d. Education: Hamilton Coll; Geelong Coll; Ormond Coll; BA, BCom, LLM Univ of Melbourne; MSc (Econs), London Sch of Econs; FCPA. Appointments: Pres, MUFS, 1969; Melbourne Film Fest Cttee, 1969-71; Tutor in Fin Acctng, Univ of Melbourne, 1971; Tutor in Property Law, RMIT, 1971; Auditor, Ormond Coll Studs Cncl, 1971-72; Treas, UNIFED Film Fndn, 1970-73; Articles Mallesons, 1971; Bar & Sol, Supreme Crt of Vic, 1972;

Assoc to Jus of the High Crt, 1972, Victorian Bar, 1973, pupil master Mr J D Merralls QC, Bar NSW, 1977; Tstee, Victorian Bar Superannuation Fund, 1980-94; Dir, Barfund Pty Ltd as Tstee of Victorian Bar Superannuation Fund, 1994-, Chmn, 1997-; Dir, Barristers Chmbrs Ltd, 1994-; Dir, Liquor Shop Promotions Ltd, 1998-; Bar and Sol: Tas and ACT, 1986, SA, 1987, NT, Qld and WA, 1990, QC: Vic, 1988, NSW, ACT, SA and Tas, 1990, WA and NT, 1991. Publication: Guide to Company Law, w A G Topp and A E Talbot, 1975. Memberships: Clubs: Hamilton; Melbourne; Australian; Athaeneum; Essoign; HRC; VRC; MCC; MUBC. Hobbies: Reading; Film; Rowing. Address: Owen Dixon Chambers West, 205 William Street, Melbourne, Vic 3000, Australia.

ROCHA VIEIRA Vasco Joaquim, b. 16 Aug 1939. Governor of Macau. m. Maria Leonor, 3 s. Education: MA, Civil Engrng, Tech Univ of Lisbon, Portugal, 1962; Army Staff Basic & Complementary Courses, 1969-72; Armed Forces Command and Dir Course, 1982-83; Natl Def Studies, 1984. Appointments include: Prof, Army War Coll, Lisbon, 1983-84; Dpty Dir, Natl Def Inst, Lisbon, 1984-86; Min in Charge, Portuguese Autonomous Reg of Azores, 1986-91; Gov of Macau, 1991-. Honours: Silver Medal, Exemplary Conduct of Mil Merit; Silver Medal, Gold Medal, Disting Serv; Kt Cmndr, Mil Order of Aviz; Grand Cross of Order of Prince Henry, Portugal; Cmndr of Order of Merit, USA; Cmndr of Legion d'Honneur, France; Kt Cmndr of Ordre de Leopold, Belgium; Grand Cross of Order of Rio Branco, Brazil. Hobbies: Tennis; Golf. Address: Palacio do Governo, Rua da Praia Grande, Macau, South China.

ROCHFORD Patricia Anne, b. Sydney, Aust. Psychologist. Education: BA, MA, Univ of Sydney. Appointments: Presently, Chmn, Rochford Intl Bd Dictatorships; Univ of NSW; UNSW Fndn; Sydney Tourism Advsry Cttee. Memberships: Chf Exec Women, mbr, 1989-, ex-cnclr, 1995-96; Tstee, Cttee for Econ Dev of Aust; var psychol socs. Hobbies: Music; Theatre; Opera; Ballet; Reading; Art. Address: GPO Box 2672, Sydney, NSW 2001, Australia.

RODERICK Colin, b. 27 July 1911, Qld, Aust. Author. m. Margaret Joyce Smith, 15 Oct 1954. Education: BA, 1935; MA, 1946, PhD, 1954, Qld; BEd, Melbourne, 1939; MEd, 1945; FRAHS, Sydney, 1959; DLitt h c Caen, 1978, James Cook, 1991. Appointments: Lectr, Engl, Qld Agricl Coll, 1935; Enlisted, Austl Light Horse 2/14 Regt, 1939; Seconded Censorship North Cmnd, 1940; Educ Ed, 1946; Dir, 1959; Angus & Robertson Ltd; Fndn Prof of Engl, 1966; Emer Prof, 1977, James Cook Univ. Publications include: Twenty Australian Novelists, 1947; In Mortal Bondage, 1948; The Lady and the Lawyer, 1955; Miles Franklin: Her Brilliant Career, 1982; Henry Lawson: A Life, 1991; Leichhardt the Dauntless Explorer, 1988; Banjo Paterson, Poet by Accident, 1993. Honours: CBE, 1966; Gold Medal Austl Lit Soc, 1974; Visng Prof, Eurn Univs, 1973, 1975, 1977; Elected Hon Sec, Movt to estab Chair of Austl Lit, Univ of Sydney, 1956-58. Memberships include: Life Mbr, Roy Austl Histl Soc; Vice-Patron, Fndn for Austl Lit Studies; Henry Lawson Lit & Mem Soc; Société des Anglicistes de l'Enseignement Supérieur, France. Hobby: Gardening. Address: 3 Armati Street, Townsville, Qld 4810, Australia.

RODRIGUEZ Judith, b. 13 Feb 1936, Perth, WA, Aust. Lecturer; Poet. m. Thomas Shapcott, 1982. Education: Univ of Qld; MA, Girton Coll, Cambridge, 1965; Cert Educ, Univ of London, 1968. Appointments include: Lectr, Colls and Univs in London, W Indies, Aust; Lectr, Victoria Coll, 198-92; Snr Lectr, Deakin Univ, 1993-; Poetry Series Ed, Penguin Books Aust, 1989-97. Publications: Nu-Plastik Fanfare Red and Other poems, 1973; Water Life, 1976; Shadow on Glass, 1978; Mudcrab at Gambaros, 1980; Witch Heart, 1982; Floridian Poems, 1986; New and Selected Poems, 1988; The Cold, 1992; Poor Johanna (play, written w Robyn Archer, produced Adelaide, 1994; publd in Heroines 1991); Lindy (Libretto, commissioned by Australian Opera), 1994; Editor, Mrs Noah and the Minoan Queen, 1983; Co-Editor, Poems from the Australians 20th Anniversary Competition, 1985; Editor, Collected Poems of Jennifer Rankin, 1990.

Honours include: AM, 1994; Austl Cncl Fellowships; Christopher Brennan Awd, Fellshp Austl Writers, 1994. Memberships: Cttee of Mngmt, Austl Soc of Auths; Pres, Austl Literary Translators Assn; Cttee of Mngmt, Assn of Austl Writing Progs; VP, Melbourne PEN Cntr. Address: PO Box 231, Mont Albert, Vic 3127, Australia.

RODRIGUEZ Placid, b. 5 Oct 1940, Quilon. Nuclear Scientist; Director, IGCAR-DAE. m. Blossom Rodriguez, 29 Apr 1972, 1 s, 1 d. Education: BS, Univ of Kerala, 1958; BE, Metallurgy, Indian Inst of Sci, Bangalore, 1960; MS, Univ of TN, 1965; PhD, Indian Inst of Sci, Bangalore, 1976. Appointments: Sci Offr, 1961-69, Grp Ldr, 1969-74, Mechl Properties (Metallurgy Div), BARC, Mumbai; Hd, Metallurgy and Materials Prog, 1974-92, 1992-, Dir, Indira Gandhi Cntr for Atomic Rsch, Kalpakkam. Tamil Nadu. Publications: 207 sci rsch pprs; 34 sci reviews; 136 publs; Ed, 4 books. Honours: Natl Metallurgists Day Awd, Min of Steel and Mines, 1978; HD Govindaraj Mem Rsch Awd, 1980, 1987, Keith Hartley Mem (Lect) Medal, 1986, LM Mirchandani Rsch Awd, 1988, Indian Inst of Welding; GD Birla Gold Medal, Indian Inst of Metals, 1987; Vividhlaxi Audyogik Samshodhan Vikas Kendra (VASVIK) Rsch Awd, 1990; MRSI Lect Medal 1991, MRSI-ICSC Awd, 1997, Materials Rsch Soc of India. Memberships include: Fell, Indian Natl Acady of Engrng; Fell, Indian Acady of Scis; Natl Acady of Scis; Tamil Nadu Acady of Scis; Fell, Indian Inst of Metals, Pres, 1996-97, Elected Hon Mbr, 1997; Fell, Indian Inst of Welding, Pres, 1992-95; Fell, Soc for Advmnt of Electrochemical Sci and Technol; Hon Fell, Non-Destructive Soc of India, 1986; Electron Microscope Soc of India; Electrochemical Soc of India; Materials Rsch Soc of India, VP, 1998-2001. Hobbies: Music (jazz music); Theatre; Swimming; Reading. Address: Indira Gandhi Centre for Atomic Research, Kalpakkam 603 102, TN, India.

ROGACHEV Igor A, b. 1 Mar 1932, Moscow, Russia. Diplomat. m. Diulbez Rogacheva, 1 d. Education: Cand of Histl Scis, Moscow Inst of For Rels under For Min, 1955; Appointments: Tranls, Min of Hlth, China, 1956; Translator, Interpreter, Attaché, USSR Emb to Cgina, 1956; 3rd, 2nd, 1st Sec, USSR Min For Affairs, 1961-65; Cnsllr, Emb in Peking, 1969-72; Mbr, Soviet Govt, deleg at Soviet-Sino negotiations on frontier questions, Asst Chf of Dept, 1st Far East Dept, 1972-75; Chf, S E Asian Dept, 1978-83, Hd, 1st Far East Dept, 1983-86, Chf of Dept for Socialist Countries of Asia, 1986-87; Dpty Min of For Affairs, 1986-91; Hd, USSR deleg, Intl talks on Cambodia, 1988-91; Amb to China, 1992-p/t. Publications: Numerous articles and essays on Asia-Pacific Region, Home and External. Honours: Order of Friendship of the Peoples, Badge of Hon Order; Order of Friendship; Sev decorations. Hobbies: Piano; Theatre. Address: Dongzhimeynei Beizhongjie, Beijing, 100600 China.

ROGERS Anthony Howard, b. 9 Nov 1936, Adelaide, S Aust. Academic. m. Dorothy, 6 Dec 1958, 3 s, 1 d. Education: BS (Adelaide); MSc (Adelaide); PhD; FASM. Appointments: Rothmans Postdoct Fell, 1968-69, Lectr, Oral Bio, 1970, Snr Lectr, Oral Bio, 1974, Rdr/Assoc Prof, Orch Microbiol, 1984-, Univ of Adelaide. Honours: Rothmans Postdoct Fellshp, 1968-69; Dist Serv Awd, Roy Austl Coll Dental Surg, 1987; Travel Awd Aust Acad Sci, Roy Soc (Lond). Memberships: Soc Gen Microbiology; Austl Soc for Microbio. Hobbies: Music; Tennis; Reading. Address: 2 Caulfield Avenue, Cumberland Park, SA 5041, Australia.

ROGERS Colin, b. 1 Dec 1940, Oxford, Eng. Professor. Education: BA, Oxon; MEd, Toronto; MSc, PhD, DSc, Nottingham; FIMA. Appointments: Lectr, Univ Nottingham, UK, 1968-71; Asst Prof, Univ W Ontario, Can, 1971-73; Assoc Prof, Old Dominion Univ, USA, 1973-74, Univ W Ontario, 1974-78, Univ Waterloo, Can, 1978-81; Snr Vstr, Univ Cambridge, UK, 1979; Prof, Univ Waterloo, Can, 1981-88; Chair, Mathl Eng Loughborough Univ Tech, UK, 1988-92; Prof, Appl Maths, Sch of Maths, Univ NSW, 1992-. Publications include: Backlund Transformations and Their Applications, 1982; Nonlinear Boundary Value Problems in Science and Engineering, 1989; Wave Phenomena: Modern Theory and Applications, 1986. Address: Department of Applied Mathematics, University of New South Wales, Sydney, NSW 2052, Australia.

ROGERS George Ernest, b. 27 Oct 1927, Melbourne, Vic, Aust. Professor of Biochemistry. m. (1) diss, (2) Racheline Rogers, 7 Oct 1972, 2 d. Education: BSc, 1949, MSc, 1951, Melbourne Univ; PhD, Trinity Coll, Cambridge, Eng, 1956; DSc, Adelaide Univ, 1976. Appointments: Snr Rsch Offr, CSIRO, 1951-54, 1957-62; Rdr, 1963-77, Prof, Biochem, 1977, Univ of Adelaide; Emer Prof, 1993-; Hon Visng Rsch Fell, Depts Biochem and Animal Sci, Univ of Adelaide. Publications: Book on Keratins (w R D B Fraser and T P Macrae), 1972; Many pprs in biol jrnls and chapts in monographs/books on biochem of skin and hair growth. Honours: CSIRO Postgrad Overseas Awd, 1954-56; Visng Fell, Clare Hall, Cambridge, Eng, 1970; Lemberg Medal, Austl Biochem Soc, 1976; Visng Rschr under French Govt Bourse Scientifique at Univ of Grenoble, 1977; Elected Fell, Austl Acady of Sci, 1977; Eleanor Roosevelt Cancer Fellshp, Amn Cancer Soc, at NIH, MD, USA, 1985. Memberships: Austl Soc of Biochem and Molecular Biol; NY Acady of Scis; Austl Hair and Wool Rsch Soc, Past Pres. Hobbies: Boating; Swimming; Reading; Walking. Listed in: Who's Who in Australia. Address: Department of Animal Science, Waite Campus, University of Adelaide, Glen Osmond, SA 5064, Australia.

ROGERS Jennifer Ann, b. 1 July 1946, Perth, West Aust, Aust. Journalist. m. John Rogers, 1973, 1 d. Education: BA, Engl, Univ of WA, 1967. Appointments: On staff of Hong Kong Standard, 1968-69; Evening Post, Reading, Eng, 1970; UN, 1970-72; Birmingham Post and Mail, 1973-78; Taught in Nigeria 1982-85; On the Sunday Times, Perth, WA, Aust, 1985-87; Salisbury Journal, Eng, 1988-89; PR, Natl Hlth Serv, 1989-99. Hobbies: Travel; Music. Address: PO Box 2287, Strawberry Hils, NSW 2012, Australia.

ROGERS Lesley Joy, b. 31 July 1943. Ethologist; Neorobiologist. Education: BSc (Hons), Adelaide; DPhil, DSc, Sussex, Eng. Appointments: Snr Tutor, Monash Univ, 1971-75; Snr Rsch Fell, Austl Natl Univ, 1976; Lectr, Monash Univ, 1977-85; Lectr, 1985-87, Snr Lectr, 1987, Assoc Prof, 1989-, Prof, 1992-, Univ of New Eng. Publications: The Evolution of Lateral Asymetrics, Language, Tool Use and Intellect, 1993; Orang-utans in Borneo, 1994; The Development of Brain and Behaviour in the Chicken, 1995; Minds of Their Own: Thinking and Awareness in Animals, 1997; Not only Roars and Rituals: Communication in Animals, 1998; The Orang-utans, 1999; Sexing the Brain, 1999. Honours: Academician, Womens Assn Achievement Awd; VC's Awd for Excellence in Rsch, 1997. Memberships: Pres, Austl Soc for the Stdy of Animal Behaviour; Pres, Intl Soc for Comp Psychol. Hobby: Gardening. Address: School of Biological Sciences, University of New England, Armidale, NSW 2351, Australia.

ROGERS Phyllis Nancy, b. 17 Sept 1920. m. 27 Dec 1947, 3 d. Education: SRN; SCM. Appointments: First Woman, Unley Cty Cncl, Salvation Army Prop Winchester Rehab Hosp; Co-Fndr, Priv Hosp Assn, 1962; First Women Pres, Priv Hosp Assn of Salvation Army, 1959. Publications: Co-Author, Traveller Brown, 1988; Birthing a Private Hospital, 1999; RAM the Man. The Legend, A Biography, 1999. Memberships: Life Mbr, Red Cross; First Woman Pres, Salvation Army Child Care Cntr. Hobbies: Collecting Antiques and Art Works; Music; Singing; Writing Novels. Address: 4 Poinsettia Avenue, Runaway Bay, Qld 4216, Australia.

ROHERA Parshottam, b. 22 Nov 1943, Karachi (Than-India). Executive. m. Maiden, 28 May 1967, 2 s, 1 d. Education: BA, Bombay Univ, India. Appointment: Mngr, 1980-87, Gen Mngr, 1987-96, VP, 1996. Hobbies: Free time with family; Music. Address: E8, Malinee Apartments, 42, Mahakali Caves Road, Andheri (East), Mumbai 400 093, India.

ROJAS DE MORENO DIAZ Maria Eugenia, b. 1934. Politician. m. Samuel Moreno Diaz, 2 s. Appointments: Majority Ldr Bogota Cty Cncl; Ldr Alianza Nacional Popular - ANAPO - 1975-. Memberships: Fmr mbr of the Senate. Address: Alianza Nacional Popular (ANAPO), Santa Fe de Bogota, DC, Colombia.

ROMERO Segundo Joaquin, b. 29 May 1950, Tarlac, Philippines. Professor. 3 s, 1 d. Education: AB, Pol Sci, 1970, MA, Pol Sci, 1981, PhD, Pol Sci, 1990, Univ of Philippines, Diliman. Appointments include: Pres, Civic Imagineers Inc; Assoc Prof, Univ of Philippines, Coll of Socl Sci, Dept of Pol Sci; Adj Prof, Natl Defense Coll of Philippines. Publications include: Philippine NGOs in the Asia-Pacific Context, 1996; Reconciliation for Development: The Philippine Experience, 1995; Transportation and Traffic Management Sector, 1995. Memberships: past Pres, CoCAP, 1997-98; Charter Pres, AGILA, 1992-93; Pres, C'Wealth Heights Homeowners Assn, 1992-94; Life Mbr, Philippine Pol Sci Assn, 1997-; Life Mbr, Philippine Statl Assn, 1997-. Address: Philippine Social Science Centre, Commonwealth Avenue, Room 311, Diliman, Quezon City 1101, Philippines.

RONG Yiren, b. 1 May 1916 Wuxi Jiangsu. Finl Co Exec; Govt Offic. m. Yang Jinaqing, 1936, 5 c. Education: St John's Univ Shanghai. Appointments: Mngr Mow Sing Flour Mills Wuxi, 1937-55; VP Foh Sing Flour Mills Shanghai, 1947-55; Pres Sung Sing Textile Printing and Dyeing Co Shanghai, 1950-55; Vice-Chmn then Chmn All-China Assn of Ind and Com, 1953-93; Vice-Mayor Shanghai, 1957-66; Vice-Min min of Textile Ind, 1959-66; Vice-chmn 7th Natl Cttee; Vice-Chmn Natl CPPCC, 1978-83; Vice-Chmn Standing Cttee 6th 7th NPC; Chmn and Pres China Intl Trust and Invmnt Corp - CITIC - Beijing, 1979-82 and Chmn, 1983-93; Vice-Chmn Soong Ching Ling Fndn Beijing, 1982-; Chmn Bd of Trustees Jinan Univ Guangzhou, 1985-; Chmn Bd of Dirs Jinan Univ, 1986-; A Pres China Cncl for Promoting Peaceful Reunification, 1988-; VP People's Repub of China, Mar 1993-. Publications: Articles and speeches on China's dev and related matters. Honours: Hon Chmn China Football Assn, 1984; Hon Chmn Bd CITIC Indl Bank, 1987; Hon Advsr China Confucius Fndn, 1992-. Memberships: Mbr 2nd 3rd 4th 5th 6th NPC. Hobbies: Walking; Rose-gardening; Spectator sports inclng soccer. Address: Office of the Vice-President, Great Hall of the People, Beijing, People's Republic of China.

ROSE Alan Douglas, b. 3 May 1944, Brisbane, Aust. President, Australian Law Reform Commission. m. Helen Elizabeth, 25 Nov 1966, 2 d. Education: Univ Qld; London Sch of Econs. Appointments: Lectr in Law, Univ Qld, 1971-73; Barrister, Supreme Crt Qld, 1973; Dept Liaison Off, PM's Off, 1975; Asst Sec, 1975-79, 1st Asst Sec, 1979-82, Dpty Sec, Dept PM & Cabinet, 1982-86; Sec, Dept of Cmty Servs, 1986-87; Assoc Sec, 1987-89, Sec, Atty-Gen's Dept Canberra, 1989-94. Publications: Sev articles in profl legal jrnls. Memberships include: Austl Law Soc; Austl Inst of Admin Law; Austl Inst of Pub Admin; Austl Inst of Polit Sci. Address: Australian Law Reform Commission, GPO Box 1995, Canberra City, ACT 2601, Australia.

ROSE Raymond James, b. 17 Nov 1942. Cell and Molecular Biologist. m. Joy Ellen Rose, 27 Feb 1965, 1 s, 1 d. Education: BScAgr, Sydney, 1964; PhD, Macquarie, 1970. Appointments: Postdoc Rsch Fell, Carleton Univ, Ottawa, Can, 1970-71; Lectr, Massey Univ Palmerston N, NZ, 1972-73; Rsch Sci, Snr Rsch Sci, CSIRO Adelaide, Aust, 1973-75; Lectr 1975, Snr Lectr 1978, Univ of Newcastle, Aust; Assoc Prof, 1987-; Hd, Dept of Bio Scis, 1990-96. Publications: Rsch publs. Honours: PL Goldacre Medal, Austl Soc Plant Physiologists, 1977; Ed, Plant Cell Reports, 1998-. Memberships: Austl Soc of Plant Physiol; Austl Soc of Biochem and Molecular Biol; Austl Inst of Agric Sci and Technol. Hobbies: Tennis; Theology. Address: Department of Biological Sciences, University of Newcastle, NSW 2308, Australia.

ROSEANNE, b. 3 Nov 1953 Salt Lake Cty. Actress. m. (2) Tom Arnold, div; (3) Ben Thomas, 1995, 3 c from previous marriage. Appointments: Fmr window dresser cocktail waitress; Wrked as comic in bars and ch coffeehouse Denver; Prod'd forum for women perfs Take

Back the Mike Univ of Boulder CO; Perf The Comedy Store Los Angeles; Featured on tv spec Funny and The Tonight Show; Tv spec On Location; The Roseanne Barr Show, 1987; Star of tv series Roseanne ABC, 1988-. Film: She Devil, 1989; Freddy's Dead, 1991; Even Cowgirls Get the Blues, 1994. Publications: My Life as a Woman, 1989; Roseanne: My Lives, 1994. Honours: Emmy Awd - Outstanding Ldng Act in a Comedy Series - 1993. Address: c/o ABC-TV 2040 Avenue of the Stars, Los Angeles, CA 90067, USA.

ROSEN Ronald, b. 27 May 1933. Health Physicist. m. Ruth Leah Cher, 1956, 1 s, 1 d. Education: MSc, NZ; PhD, Univ NSW; CPhys, FAIP; FInstP; FARPS; MACPSEM. Appointments: Jnr Lectr, Phys Dept, Vic Univ Coll, 1956; Physicist, Natl Radiation Lab, Christchurch, 1956-60; Radiation Protection Offr, 1961-82, Hd, Safety Unit, 1982-84, Snr Lectr, Nuc Engrng, 1984-86, Snr Lectr, Safety Sci, 1986-96, Visng Fell, Safety Sci, 1996-, Univ NSW. Publications: Auth or co-auth of 30 jrnl pprs and pub rprts. Honours: Merit Awds: Austl Radiation Protection Soc, 1989, Hlth Phys Soc, 1989, Intl Radiation Protection Assn, 1992, Univ NSW, 1999. Memberships: Austl Radiation Protection Soc; Hlth Phys Soc; Intl Radiation Protection Assn Hobbies: Music; Gardening. Address: 5 Aboud Avenue, Kingsford, NSW 2032, Australia

ROSENBERG David, b. 20 Nov 1946, Münchberg, Germany. Attorney; County Supervisor. m. Lea, 30 June 1968, 1 s, 1 d. Education: BS, Jrnlsm, California Polytechnic State Univ, 1968; JD, Law, Univ of California, Davis, USA, 1974. Appointments: Chmn, California Law Revision Commn; Mbr, California Cncl on Criminal Justice Planning. Publication: Endgame, full-length novel, 1986. Honours: Elected to Davis City Cncl, 3 times, 1984-96; Mayor, Davis, 2 times, 1986-88, 1994-96; Elected to Yolo Co Bd of Spvrs, 1996. Membership: Rotary Intl. Address: The Wild Rose House, 1112 Westfield Terrace, Davis, CA 95616, USA.

ROSENFELDT Franklin Lawrence, b. 15 May 1941, NSW, Aust. Head, Cardiac Surgical Research Unit. m. Anne Lewis, 12 June 1971, 1 s, 2 d. Education: MB, BS, 1963, MD, 1975, Univ of Adelaide; FRCS, Edinburgh, 1969; FRACS, 1983. Appointments: Res Med Offr, Queen Elizabeth Hosp, SA, 1964; Rsch Fell, Hon Lectr, St Thomas' Hosp, London, Eng, 1977; Prin Rsch Fell, NHMRC, Cardiovascular Surg Rsch Unit, Baker Inst; Visng Surgn, CJOB Cardiac Surg Unit, Alfred Hosp, Pahran; Assoc Prof, Dept of Surg, Monash Univ, 1993-. Publications: Pprs in sci and med jrnls. Memberships: Cardiac Soc of Australasia; Soc of Thoracic & Cardiovascular Surg of GB & N Ireland; Instl Soc of Heart Rsch; Ed, Asia Pacific Heart Jrnl. Hobbies: Music; Tennis; Gardening; Hiking. Address: 15 Dunstan Street, North Balwyn, Vic 3104, Australia.

ROSENTHAL Gert, b. 11 Sept 1935 Amsterdam. Economist. m. Margit Uhlmann Rosethal, 1959, 4 d. Education: Univ of CA Berkeley USA. Appointments: Economist Natl Plng Off Guatemala, 1960-65; Snr Offic min of Fin, 1966-67; Snr Economist Sec of the CntrlAm Common Market, 1967-68; Min of Plng Natl Plng Off, 1969-70; Fell Adlai Stevenson Inst for Intl Affairs Chgo USA, 1971; Proj Co-ord UNCTAD Geneva, 1972; Dir Mexico Off ECLAC Mexico Cty, 1975-85; Dep Exec Sec ECLAC Santiago Chile, 1986-87; Exec Sec, 1987-88; Intl Consultant, 1998; Permanent Representative of Guatemala to UN, 1999-. Publications: Num articles on dev econs especially relating to Cntrl Am from 1965 to the present. Address: 57 Park Avenue, New York, NY 10016, USA.

ROSOFF Elayne, b. New York, NY, USA. Clinical Psychologist. m. div. 1 s. Education: BA, 1977, UCLA; MA, 1979, Pepperdine Univ; PhD, 1984, CA Sch of Profl Psychol. Honours: Angel of the Yr, Mothers Against Drunk Driving, 1986; Caring Californian, 1987, May Co Stores; Commend LA County, 1991; CA Legislative Assembly Recog, 1987; Fndrs Awd, Mothers Against Drunk Driving, 1991. Memberships: Am Psychol Assn; LA County Psychol Assn; Natl Register of Psychol. Hobbies:

Films; Astronomy. Address: PO Box 1346, Santa Monica, CA 90406-1346, USA.

ROSS Desmond Glyn, b. 15 July 1928, Moonta, Aust. Grazier. m. Joyce Treloar, 7 Feb 1953, 1 d. Education: Scotch Coll, Adelaide, SA, 1941-45. Appointments: Mbr, Riverton Soldiers Mem Hosp Bd, 1966-76; Cnclr, Owen and Wakefield Plains Dist Cncls, 1966-87; Commnr, Animal and Plant Control Commn, 1979-96; Fed Pres, Austl Local Govt Assn, 1984-85; Pres, Local Govt Assn of SA, 1984-86; Mbr, Aust Day Cncl of SA Inc, 1984-89; Admnstr, Dist Cncl of Stirling, 1990; Mbr, SA Natl Football League Boundaries Commn, 1990-91; Chmn, Mngmt Cttee of Local Govt Servs Bur (SA), 1991-92; Mbr, Constl Centenary Fndn Bd, 1991-94; Chmn, Libs Bd of SA, 1987-95; Mbr, Balaklava Racing Club Cttee, 1993-; Chmn, Peter Lehmann Wines Ltd, 1993-. Honours: Mbr, Gen Div, Order of Aust, 1986; Sunday Mail Medal, 1950, 1951, 1952, 1955, 1957; Adelaide Plains Football Assn. Membership: Jus of the Peace, 1978-. Hobbies: Soil Conservation; Lions International, 1969-. Address: Erskine Park, Salter Springs, via Hamley Bridge, SA 5401, Australia.

ROSS James Robert Holland, b. 1 Sept 1940. Geologist; Company Director. m. (1) Adrienne Olive, 12 Sept 1971, 2 d, (2) Anna McDonell, 14 Dec 1996. Education: BSc, hons, Univ of WA, 1962; PhD, Univ CA, Berkeley, 1974. Appointments include: Cnsltng Geol and Mngr, Diamonds Exploration, Western Mining Corp, 1979-88; Mbr, Sci, Ind and Technol Cncl of WA, 1983-86; Mbr, CSIRO State Cttee for WA, 1984-86; Mbr, Advsry Cncl, Austl Geol Survey Org, 1985-87; Chmn, Cnsltative Cttee, CSIRO Div Min Minerals and Geochem, 1985-87; Mngng Dir, World Geosci Ltd, 1988-90; Exec Dir, Aerodata Holdings Ltd, 1988-90; Mbr, Cnsltative Cttee, CSIRO Div Exploration Geosci, 1988-92; Advsry Cttee for Key Cntr in Strategic Mineral Studies, 1989-96, Chmn, Advsry Bd, 1996-, Univ WA; Advsry Cttee, Rsch Sch of Earth Sci, Austl Natl Univ, 1992-96; Mngng Dir, Odin Mining & Investment Co Ltd, 1990-95; Tech Dir, Emperor Gold Mining Co Ltd, 1990-92; External Dir, Aerodata Holdings Ltd, 1990-98; Exec Dir, Chmn, Tanganika Gold, 1995-; Chmn, Bd of Dirs, Cntr of Excellence in Mass Spectrometry, Curtin Univ, 1999-; Chmn, Tanzania-Aust Bus Cncl Inc, 1999-. Publications: Auth or co-auth of 8 pprs on Economic Geology of Nickel Sulphide Deposits, published in intl sci jrnls, 1974-82; Mngng Ed, 2 vol proceedings of 4th Intl Kimberlite Conf, 1986-89. Honours: Visng Fell, Econ Geol, Rsch Sch of Earth Scis, Austl Natl Univ, 1977-78; Repd WA in 1st Grp Stdy Exch Team, Rotary Intl, 1967. Memberships: Fell, Australasian Inst of Mining & Metallurgy; Past Pres, WA Br, Geol Soc of Aust, 1982-84. Hobbies: Tennis; Walking; Football; Paleoanthropology; Pre-Columbian Archaeology. Listed in: Who's Who in Australian Business. Address: 260A Salvado Road, Floreat, WA 6014, Australia.

ROSS Ruth Winifred, b. 3 May 1924, Aust. Physiotherapist. Education: Dip, Sydney Univ, 1945; MAPA. Appointments: Physiotherapist, Pvte Prac, Wollongong, 1945-88; Pt-time Physiotherapist, Wollongong Hosp, 1948-77, Bulli Hosp, 1965-80. Honours: Life Mbr, Roy Inst for Deaf and Blind Children, 1975; Queen's Silver Jubilee Medal, 1977; MBE, 1978; JP, 1979; Life Mbr, Bus and Profl Womens Club of Wollongong. Memberships: Past Austl Pres and Intl VP, Bus and Profl Women; Pres, Illawarra Br, Assn of Indep Retirees. Hobbies: Photography; Classical Music; Reading; Travel. Address: 28 Railway Avenue, Austinmer, NSW 2515, Australia.

ROSSER Glenda Dawn, b. 27 Feb 1946, Brisbane, Aust. Missionary housewife. m. Allan, 18 Dec 1965, 1 s, 2 d. Education: Dip in Jrnlsm, Tafe Writing Course; Cert w Austl Writer's Profl Servs. Appointments: Missionary appointments, FINGAL Hd, NSW; Walgett, NSW; Toowoomba, Qld. Publications: Under the Shadow of His Wing, 1990; Here I am but Please Send my Sister!; Missus Bindi of Bunglegum; Bindi - the Girl from Wangaroo (reprint). Honours: 1st, 3rd place, short story comp; poems and articles in 3 books. Membership: Christian Writer's Fellowship, Aust. Hobbies: Craft

teaching; Machine knitting; Musical instruments. Address: PO Box 7022, Toowoomba Mail Centre, Qld 4352, Australia.

ROSTVOLD Gerhard, b. 15 Oct 1919, Minnesota, USA. Economist. 1 s, 3 d. Education: BA, Econs, Acctcy, 1948; MA, Econs, 1949; PhD, Econs, Stanford Univ, 1955. Appointments: Instr of Acctng, Stanford Univ, 1949-51; Prof, Econs & Acctng, Pomona Coll, 1952-66; Cnsltng Economist Urbanomics Rsch Assocs, 1965- Visng Prof, Stanford Univ, summer 1974; Econ Newscaster, KHJ-TV "10 O'Clock News", 1978-82; Adj Prof of Econs, Pepperdine Univ, 1984-94. Publications: In the fields of tax and fiscal policy incl: Financial Planning for Retirement in the 1980s, 1983; (co-auth) Report to Congress, New Perspectives in Grazing Fees and Public Land Management in the 1990s, 1992; Report to Congress and to the Secretaries of the Departments of the Interior and Agriculture: A Comparative Analysis of the Economic, Financial and Competitive Conditions of Montana Ranches Using Federal Forage and Montana Ranches Without Federal Grazing Allotments, 1993; Articles, book reviews, num monographs. Honours: Wig Distinguished Professorship Awd, Pomona Coll, 1962; Natl Sci Fndn Fell, Stanford Univ, 1965-66; Sec of Interior's Conservation Awd, 1975; Lambda Alpha Hon Frat, Pres, Los Angeles Chapt, 1976-77. Memberships: Amn Econ Assn; Natl Advsry Bd Cncl on Pub Lands, Pres Kennedy Appointee, 1962-75; Chmn, 1971-75; West Econ Assn, Pres, 1966-67. Listed in: Many including: Who's Who in the World; Who's Who in America; American Men of Science; Contemporary Authors. Address: 4 Montpellier, Laguna Niguel, CA 92677, USA.

ROTEM Arie, b. 8 May 1945. Academic. m. Wendy-Ann, 2 s. Education: BA, Psychol and Educ, Hebrew Univ, Jerusalem, 1971; MA, Educl Admin, Univ of CA, Santa Barbara, 1973; PhD, Educ, Univ of CA, Santa Barbara, CA, 1975. Appointments: Snr Lectr, Cnslt, 1980-88, Assoc Prof and Hd, 1989-93, Sch of Medl Educ; Dir, WHO, Regl Trng Cntr for Hlth Dev, 1988-; Dir, Cntr for Pub Hlth, UNSW, 1993-; Prof and Hd, Sch of Medl Educ, Fac of Med, UNSW, 1994-; Dir, Bd of War Mem Hosp, Waverley, NSW, 1997-; Chmn, Sydney Pub Hlth Consortium, UNSW, 1997-. Honour: Fred Katz Medal for Excellence in Intl Medl Educ, ANZAME, 1995. Address: School of Medical Education, UNSW, Sydney, NSW 2052, Australia.

ROTH Vanessa Jane, b. 23 Dec 1971, Hobart, Tasmania. Conservator. Education: BApplSc, Conservation of Cultural Materials, Univ of Canberra. Appointment: Conservator, Belau Natl Mus, Repub of Palau, 1997-98. Honour: Queen's Trust Awd, 1996. Memberships: Austl Inst for Conservation of Cultural Materials (AICCM); Austl Inst for Maritime Archaeology (AIMA). Hobby: Scuba diving. Address: 42 Bissenberger Crescent, Kambah, ACT 2902, Australia.

ROTHSCHILD Georg Heinrich Ludwig, b. 11 July 1936, Germany. Former Director General. m. (1) Jennifer M Jarmih, 15 Aug 1959, 3 s, 1 d, (2) Katelijne van Look, 13 Jan 1996. Education: BSc, hons, Univ Nottingham, 1959; PhD, 1962, DICC, 1962, Imperial Coll, London. Appointments: Govt Entomologist, Brit Colonial Serv, 1962-63, Malaysian Govt, 1964-68; Chf Rsch Sci, Asst Chf, CSIRO Aust, 1969-87; Dir, Bur of Rural Resources, 1987-89; Dir, Austl Cntr, Inst of Agricl Rsch, 1989-95; Dir Gen, Intl Rice Rsch Inst, Philippines, 1995-97. Publications: Over 80 in profl jrnls. Honour: Fell, Austl Acady of Technol Scis, 1991. Memberships: Austl Inst of Agricl Scis; Austl Ecol Soc; Austl Entomol Soc; Brit Ecol Soc; Roy Entomol Soc. Hobbies: Walking; Music; Reading. Address: PO Box 113, Gundaroo, NSW 2620, Australia.

ROUSSEAU Yvonne Margaret, b. 1 Aug 1945, Benalla, Victoria, Aust. Writer. div, 1 s dec'd, 1 d. Education: BA, hons, Melbourne Univ, 1967. Publications: The Murders at Hanging Rock, 1980; Minmers Marooned and Planet of the Marsupials: The Science Fiction Novels of Cherry Wilder, 1997. Address: PO Box 3086, Rundle Mall, Adelaide, SA 5000, Australia.

ROUSSELIN Yves, b. 25 Jan 1945, Meulan, France. General Manager of UBAF, Seoul Branch. m. Laure, 14 Oct 1972, 1 s, 1 d. Education: BA, Ecole de Com de Chmbr de Com et d'Inds de Paris (ECCIP). Appointments: Gen Mngr, UBAF Seoul Branch, 1 Aug 1996; Hd, Inspection Team, Credit Lyonnais, Paris, 1994. Hobbies: Golf; Judo; Sailing; Canadian private and commercial pilot licences. Address: Union de Banques Arabes et Francaise, UBAF Seoul Branch, 3rd Fl Samdo Bldg, 1-170 Soonhwa-dong, Chung-ku, Seoul, Korea.

ROWE James Babek, b. 2 Nov 1951, Johannesburg, S Africa. Academic. m. Sally, 25 Mar 1978, 2 s, 1 d. Education: Brural Sci; PhD. Appointments: Rsch Fell (FAO); Rsch Fell (ICI Pharms); Nutritionist, Agric, WA; Hd, Cattle Branch, Agric WA; Prof, Animal Sci, UNE, Honours: Moir Medal, 1988; Aust Soc Animal Prodn; Nutrition Soc of Aust. Hobbies: Sport; Reading. Address: Animal Science, University of New England, Armidale, NSW 2351, Australia.

ROWE Jennifer June, b. 2 Apr 948, Sydney, Aust. Writer. m. Bob Ryan, 3 s (from previous marriage), 1 d. Education: BA, MA (Hons), 1973, Sydney Univ, Aust. Appointments: Asst Ed, Book Ed, Paul Hamlyn Pty Ltd, 1968-70; Book Ed, Snr Ptnr, Publng Mngr, Dpty Publr, Angus & Robertson Publrs, 1974-87; Publr, Angus & Robertson Publrs, 1986-87; Ed, Austl Women's Weekly, 1988-92; Writer, mysteries, childrens books (as Emily Rodda), 1992-. Publications: adult novels incl: Grim Picking (made into TV mini-series), 1987; Murder by the Book, 1989; The Makeover Murders, 1992; Stanglehold, 1993; Lamb to the Slaughter, 1995; Deadline, 1997; Something Wicked, 1998; Short stories; Children's books: Something Special, 1985; Pigs Might Fly, 1987; The Best Kept Secret, 1989; Crumbs!, 1990; Finders Keepers, 1990 (made into TV series with The Timekeeper, 1992); Rowan of Rin, 1993; Rowan and the Travellers, 1994; Rowan and the Keeper of the Crystal, 1996; 27 books in The Teen Power Inc series, 1994-; Picture books, inclng: Power and Glory, 1994, Green Fingers, 1998; TV series, Murder Call, 1996-98; Screenplay for Blue Heelers episode, 1996. Honours: 5 times winner of Austl Chidren's Book Cnsl's Book of Yr Awd; Dromkeen Medal for servs to Austl Children's Lit, 1995; Austl Speech Comm Assn Awd for Excellence in Comm, 1996; Intl Bd on Books for Young People (IBBY) Hon Awd, 1996; Hon Book Austl Children's Book Cncl's Book of Yr, 1996. Address: Children's Books of Scholastic Australia, PO Box 579, Lindfield 2070, Australia.

ROWE John Seymour, b. 20 Mar 1936, Sydney, Aust. Writer. m. Marianne, 2 s. Education: Grad, Roy Mil Coll, Duntroon, 1957. Appointments: Army, 1958; Pl Comd 2 Rar, 1959; Pl Comd 3 Rar; Capt un Observer Kashmir, 1960-61; Intelligence Offr, Canberra, 1962-63; Intell Offr Borneo, 1964; Intelligence Major, Vietnam, 1965-66; Snr Instr, SMI, 1967; Intelligence Dir Washington, 1968. Publications: Count Your Dead, 1968; McCabe Am, 1972; Chocolate Crucifix, 1973; The Warlords, 1974; The Jewish Solution, 1978; Long Live the King, 1984; Vietnam, The Australian Experience, 1987. Hobbies: Surfing; Skiing; Skindiving. Address: 118 Bower Street, Manly, NSW, Australia.

ROWE Reginald George, b. 14 June 1918, Sydney, Aust. Artist; Author. m. (1) Betty Small, dec, 1 s, (2) Zadee Irene Frances Marcroft, 1989, 2 stepdaughters. Appointments: Served in AIF/Papua New Guinea, WWII, 1940-45; Assoc, Roy Art Soc of NSW, 1995. Creative Works include: The Art and Life of Reg Rowe; Aust Landscape Painting in Oils; Paintings in collections in UK, France, Switz, Spain, Greece, USA, Canada, Japan and many other countries. Honours: Highly Commended, Ryde Munic Art Exhib, 1968; 2nd Prize, Stanley Art Fest, 1975; Commended Berrima Dist Art Soc, 1979; 2nd Prize, 1979; 1st Prize, 1980, Mittagong Dahlia Fest; Highly Commended, Stonequarry Exhib, 1981; 1st Prize Bowral-Mittagong Rotary Art Prize, 1986; 1st Prize, Merriwa Art Prize, 1990. Membership: Roy Art Soc of NSW. Hobbies: Painting; Writing; Art history; Music; Cricket; Gardening; Reading. Address: 30 Philip St, Burrado, NSW 2576, Australia.

ROWLANDS Allison Claire, b. 25 Apr 1955, Ballarat, Aust. Social Worker. m. Thomas Fallon, 19 Nov 1982, 1 d. Education: BSW (UNSW); Grad Dip Soc Admin, Newcastle; AMusA, Sydney, Aust. Appointments: Child Protection Worker, 1985-89; Snr Socl Worker Hunter Rehab Serv, 1989; AVA, 1990-; Lectr, Univ of Newcastle, 1993-; Mngr, Brain Injury Rehab Prog, 1991-93. Honours: Acad Awd (Highest Aggregate Wrks) Grad Dip, Socl Admin, Newcastle, 1988; Duke of Edinburgh 7th C'wlth Stdy Conf, 1992. Memberships: Austl Assn of Socl Workers; Brain Injury Assn of NSW; Australasian Critical Incident Stress Assn. Hobbies: Choral singing; Voice training; Surfing; Travel; Politics. Address: Department of Social Work, University of Newcastle, Callaghan, NSW 2308, Australia.

ROWLANDS David, b. 23 Sept 1932. Mining Engineer. m. Patricia Elizabeth Clements, 19 Mar 1955, 3 s, 1 d. Education: BS (Hons), Dip Met Mining, Wales, 1953; Ctf, Mine Mngr, UK, 1956; MEng, NSW, Aust, 1969; PhD, Qld, Aust, 1974. Appointments: Mine Dpty and Overman, 1956-57; Mine Undermngr, 1957-62; Univ Lectr, NSW, 1962-68; Snr Lectr, Univ of Qld, 1968-79; Rdr and Prof Mining Engr, Univ of Qld, 1979-92; Hd of Dept, Mining and Metallurgical Engrng, 1976-86; Mining Cnslt, 1992-. Publications: 3 thes; 1 book chapt; Jt auth 1 book; Auth num publs and reports. Honours: Brit Ropes Prize, Univ of Wales Coll, Cardiff, 1953. Memberships: Fell, Inst of Engrs, Aust; Fell, Austl Inst of Mining and Metallurgy, Chartered Profl Engr. Hobbies: Lawn bowls; DIY: Home mechanic and handyman. Address: 158 Little Mountain Home Park, Mark Road, Caloundra, Qld 4551, Australia.

ROWNEY George Edward Penrose, b. 24 Dec 1920, Melbourne, Aust. Retired Secondary Principal. 1 s, 1 ss, 1 d , 1 sd. Education: BSc, DipEd, Melbourne. Publications: New General Science, 1953; Practical Science Manual, 1954; Pursuit of Science, 1964; Pursuit of Fly Tying, 1987. Membership: VP, Southern Fly Fishers Aust Inc; Roy Soc. Hobby: Fly fishing. Address: 4 Riddle Street, Bentleigh, Australia, 3204.

ROWSE Timothy Michael, b. 11 Feb 1951, Sydney, Aust. Academic. m. Jan Mackay, 1984, 1 d. Education: BA, Hons; MA; PhD. Appointments: Lectr, Sch of Behavioural Scis, Macquarie Univ, 1978-85; Rsch Offr, Menzies Sch of Hlth Rsch, 1989-94; Rsch Fell, Dept of Govt & Pub Admin, Univ Sydney, 1994-. Publications: Australian Liberalism and National Character, 1978; Arguing the Arts, 1985; Remote Possibilities, 1992; After Mabo, 1993; Traditions for Health, 1996; White Flour, White Power, 1998. Hobby: Family Life. Address: 15 Myall Street, O'Connor, Australian Capital Territory 2602, Australia.

ROY Avijit, b. 20 Dec 1948, Bishnupur, India. Engineer. m. Jhara Guha Neogi, 18 Jan 1974. Education: BEChem, hons, Jadavpur Univ, Calcutta, India, 1971. Appointments: Engr, W S Atkins, India, Priv Ltd, Calcutta, 1971-74; Proj Mngr, Tech Elec & Engrng Co Ltd, Calcutta, 1974-79; Snr Dpty Gen Mngr, 1997-; Supt Engr, Specialist Engr, M N Dastur & Co Ltd, Calcutta, 1979-86; Proj Mngr, Sys Specialist, 1992-96; Gen Mngr (Tech) Thermon Heat Tracers, India Ltd, Pune, 1982-92; Chf Tech Mngr, Bells Controls, Calcutta, 1996-97. Publications: Var articles in profl jrnls. Honours: Natl Stand Cttee, ED 63 (lubrication) Bur of Indian Stands, 1982-86; Natl Stand Cttee, ET 22/P4, Heat Tracing, Bur of Indian Stands, 1992-96; Natl Stand Cttee, HMD 22, Compressors, Bur of Indian Stands, 1996; IBC 20th Century Awd for Achievement. Memberships: Am Soc of Mech Engrs, USA; Natl Fire Protection Assn, USA; Indian Inst of Fire Engrs; Loss Prevention Assn of India. Hobbies: Reading; Light Music. Address: c/o Mr A B Roy, Flat No 11, 15/1 Ekdalia Place, Calcutta 700 019, India.

ROY Durga Prasad, b. 29 July 1941, Cuttack, India. Scientist. m. Manika, 27 July 1968, 2 d. Education: PhD, Phys. Appointments: Rutherford Lab, UK, 1970-74; Visva Bharati Univ, India, 1974-76; Tata Inst of Fundamental Rsch, India, 1976-. Publications: Monographs, review articles, rsch pprs (about 100) in particle phys. Honours:

Megh and Saha Awd for Rsch in Theort Scis, Univ Grants Commn, India, 1989. Memberships: Fell, Indian Acady of Sci; Fell, Indian Natl Sci Acady; Fell, Natl Acady of Scis, India. Hobbies: Listening to classical music; Playing tennis. Address: Theoretical Physics Department, Tata Institute of Fundamental Research, Homi Bhabha Road, Mumbai 400005, India.

ROYCHOWDHURY Anita, b. 18 July 1938, Calcutta, India. Painter. Education: Grad, Govt Coll of Arts & Crafts, Calcutta, 1980; Art Appreciation Course Calcutta Univ, 1960-. Appointment: Tchr, Appreciation of Art. Memberships: Soc of Contemp Artist, Calcutta, 1959-64; Calcutta Painters, 1966. Hobbies: Poetry; Music. Address:53/8 Dharmatala Lane, Shibpur, Howrah 711 102, India.

ROZZOLI Kevin Richard, b. 13 Sept 1939, Sydney, Aust. Member of Parliament. m. Carol Anne, 2 s, 1 d. Education: Dip of Law, Sydney Univ, 1985. Appointments: Mbr for Hawkesbury, NSW Parl, 1973-; Dpty Ldr of the Opposition, 1981-83; Speaker, NSW Parl, 1988-95; Chmn, Natl Drug and Alchol Rsch Cntr, 1989-; Chmn, Haymarket Fndn Ltd, 1984-; Gov, Law Fndn of NSW, 1999-. Publications: Num articles on parly prac and catchment mngmt. Honour: Top Apprentice, Watchmaking, 1960. Memberships: Union Club; City Tatterals. Address: Parliament House, Macquarie Street, Sydney, NSW 2000, Australia.

RUBENSTEIN Kim, b. 2 Oct 1965, Melbourne, Aust. Academic. m. Garry Ellis Sturgess, 28 Sept 1997, 1 d. Education: BA, LLB (Hons), Melbourne; LLM, Harvard. Appointment: Snr Lectr in Law; Barrister and Solicitor, Supreme Crt of Vic. Publications: Improving Criteria and Feedback in Student Assessment in Law, w R Johnstone and J Patterson, 1998; var articles on citizenship, constl law, admnstv law. Honours: Sir Robert Menzies Schl, Harvard, 1991; Fulbright Awd, 1991; Queens Trust Awd, 1991. Address: Law School, Univ of Melbourne, Parkville, 3052 Vic, Australia.

RUBINSTEIN Amnon, b. 5 Sept 1931 Tel Aviv. Polit; Auth; Prof of Law. m. Ronny Havatgeleth, 1959, 1 s, 1 d. Education: Hebrew Univ; London Sch of Econs. Appointments: Mil service Israeli Def Forces; Fmr Dean Fac of Law and Prof of Law Tel Aviv Univ; Min of Comms, 1984-87; Min of Energy and Infrastructure and Sci and Tech, 1992-93; Min of Educ and Culture, 1993-96; Fmr Chmn Shinui Party. Publications: Jurisdiction and Illegality, 1965; The Zionist Dream Revisited, 1985 - French transl Le Reve et l'histoire; The Constitutional Law of Israel - 4th edn - 1991. Memberships: Mbr Knesset - Parl - 1977-; Mbr Constitution Cttee. Hobbies; Music; Drama; Swimming. Address: Shinui, 19 Rehov Levontin, Tel Aviv 65112, Israel.

RUDOLPH Verna Pauline, b. 5 Mar 1946, Warracknabeal, Aust. Secretary. m. Andrew, 29 Apr 1972, 4 s. Books: Personal Moments; Personal Quiet Time. Hobbies: Writing; Craft. Address: PO Box 3, Horsham, Vic, Australia 3402.

RUDOWICZ Czeslaw Zygmunt, b. 20 July 1948, Poznan, Poland. Physicist. m. Elizabeth, 1 s, 1 d. Education: MS, Theort Phys, A Mickiewicz Univ, Poznan, 1970; PhD, Solid State Phys, 1974; DSc, Phys Scis, 1989. Appointments: Snr Rsch Asst, A Mickiewicz Univ, 1972-75; Lectr, 1975-84; Snr Lectr, Univ Port Harcourt, Nigeria, 1978-80; Humboldt Rsch Fell, Univ Erlangen, Nuremberg, Germany, 1980-82; Rsch Fell, Austl Natl Univ, Canberra, 1982-89; Rdr, 1989-95, Prof, 1995, Chair Prof, 1995-, Cty Univ, Hong Kong, Kowloon. Memberships: Catenian Assn, Hong Kong, 1991-; Fell, Austl Inst Phys; Alexander von Humboldt Fndn; Hong Kong Phys Soc; Intl Soc Magnetic Resonance; Intl Electron Paramagnetic Resonance Soc; Chmn, local and intl organising cttee, 1st Asia-Pacific Symposium, 1997; Pres, Asia-Pacific EPR/ESR Soc, 1997-. Address: City University of Hong Kong, Department of Physics and Materials Science, Kowloon, Hong Kong, SAR.

RUEBNER Boris Henry, b. 30 Aug 1923, Germany. Physician. m. Susan, 21 July 1957, 1 s, 1 d. Education: MD, Univ of Edinburgh; FRC Path; Fell, Amn Coll of Pathologists. Appointments: Asst Prof, Path, Halifax, Can; Assoc Prof, Johns Hopkins; Prof, UC Davis. Publications: US/Can Acady of Pathologists; Path Soc, GB. Hobbies: Swimming; History. Address: Department of Medicine, Pathology, University of California, Davis, CA 95616, USA.

RUIT Sanduk, b. 4 Sept 1954, Walung, Nepal. Eye Surgeon. m. Nanda, 26 Jan 1987, 1 s, 2 d. Education: MBBS; MD. Appointments: Fell Univ, NSW, Sydney, 1987-89; Medl Dir, Tilganga Eye Cntr; Medl Offr, Bir Hosp, 1978-82; Res, AIIMS, Delhi, 1982-84; Eye Surg, Eye Hosp, 1985-87; Medl Advsr, Fred Hollows Fndn. Publications: Surgical Operating Procedure - Cataract Surgery, 1996; Surg trng manual and videos. Honour: Fell, Roy Austl Coll of Opthamologist (FRACO), 1996. Memberships: Gen Sec, Nepal Opthalmic Soc, 1985-87; Gen Sec, Nepal Eye Prog, 1994-; Trainer in Vietnam, China, Tibet. Hobbies: Trekking; Games; Movies. Address: Medical Director, Tilganga Eye Centre, PO Box No 561, Gaushala, Bagmati Bridge, Kathmandu, Nepal.

RUNA Sultana Nasrin Jahan, b. 18 Dec 1979, Pabna, Bangladesh. Student. Education: HSC Womens Coll, Pabna, 1996; Student, Dept of Philos, Rajshahi Univ, Bangladesh. Appointment: Mbr, Bangladesh Cultural Assn. Publications: Bhalobasha Bhalo Noy (poetry) 1st ed, 1995; Poems; Story; Fairy tales. Honour: Title: Kabbo Conkkan, sponsored by Pabna District Cultural Acady, Bangladesh, 1998. Membership: Bangladesh Cultural Assn, Pabna, 1998. Hobbies: Reading; Writing; Drawing; Gardening. Address: Munu Manzil, House No C1, Block # E, Shibram Pur, Pabna 6600, Bangladesh.

RUNDLE Anthony Maxwell (Hon), b. 5 Mar 1939. Member of Parliament. m. Caroline Watt, 2 d. Appointments: Jrnlst, Austl Assoc Press, London, 1961-62; Eric White and Assocs Pub Rels, London, 1963-68; Jrnlst, Tasmanian TV, 1979; Govt Whip, Tas, 1986; Speaker, House of Assembly, 1988-89; Shadow Min for Tourism and Transp, 1989-92; Min for Forests and for Mines, 1992-93; Asst to Premier of Econ Dev, 1992-93, Pub Sect Mngmt, 1993-94, Fin, 1993-95, Employment and Racing and Gaming, 1993-95; Asst to Premier, State Dev and Rescs, 1993-96, Energy, 1995-96; Chmn, Port Devonport Authy, 1982-87. Membership: Roy Yacht of Tas. Hobbies: Yachting; Tennis; Fishing. Address: Department of Premier and Cabinet, GPO Box 123B, Hobart, Tasmania 7001, Australia.

RUSH Geoffrey, b. Toowoomba, Qld. Actor. Education: Studied at Jacques Lecoq Sch of Mime Paris. Appointments: Began profl career with Queensland Th Co. Films incl: The Wedding, 1980; Starstruck, 1982; Twelfth Night, 1986; Midday Crisis, 1994; Dad and Dave on our Selection, 1995; Shine; Children of the Revolution, 1996. Honours: Acady Awd; BAFTA Awd; Austl Film Inst Awd; Golden Globe Awd; Num other awds for Shine.

RUSSELL Allen Maurice, b. 4 May 1938, Tasmania, Aust. m. Wendy, 5 Jan 1963, 2 s. Education: BSc, Hons; Dip.Ed; MSc; PhD; FIMA. Appointments: Snr Tutor, 1960-62, Lectr, 1962-70, Snr Lectr, 1970-86, Rdr, 1986-94, Maths Dept, Mbr of Cncl, St Hilda's Coll, 1988-, Univ of Melbourne; Rsch Fell, Univ of Southampton, 1969. Publications: Num articles in profl jrnls. Honour: B H Neumann Awd, Ex in Maths Enrichment, 1996. Memberships: Fell, Inst of Maths and Its Applications, Chart Mathn. Hobbies: Sailing; Cycling; Walking; Gardening; Music. Address: 16 Dalvey Street, Heidelberg, Victoria, Australia.

RUSSELL David William Alan, b. 15 Mar 1942. Science Teacher. m. Jacqueline Sally Kennelson, 5 May 1962, 3 s, 1 d. Education: BEd, Grad Dip Computer Ed (QUT); MSc, Sci Ed, Curtin. Appointments: Sandgate Dist State hs, Banyo Secnd hs, Marlborough hs, Harare, Zimbabwe; Ferny Grove Secnd hs, Qld; Editl Staff, Austl Sci Tchrs Jrnl. Creative Works: Dev lab computer interface for sch sci experiments, Lab Mate, 1990-96; Microlab, 1998; Sci and maths software for 100 experiments and experiment simulations. Honours: Awd for Serv to Sci Tchng, 1990; Classroom Tchr Fellshp, 1991; UK/Aust Fellowship for Tchrs of Sci, 1991. Memberships: Austl Inst of Phys; Sci Tchrs Assn of Qld. Hobbies: Proficient in Bahasa Indonesia; Inservice teacher education; Electronics. Address: 12 Wivenhoe Avenue, Albany Creek, Qld 4035, Australia.

RUSSELL John McRae, b. 18 June 1949. Specialist Urologist. m. Lorraine, 2 s, 1 d. Education: MBBS, Melbourne Univ; FRACS (Urology); FACS. Appointments: Snr Urologist, Albury Base Hosp, 1981-; Snr Urologist, Wodonga Dist Hosp, 1981-; Urologist, Albury Wodonga Priv Hosp, 1981-; Austin Repatriation Medl Cntr, 1996-; Deniliquin Hosp, 1998-. Publications: Articles in profl jrnls. Memberships: AMA; Austl Urology Assn; Vic Exec AUA, 1997-; Eurn Urological Soc; Amn Urology Soc. Hobbies: Golf; Tennis; Fly fishing. Address: Border Urology Clinic, Suite 6, 2 Ramsay Place, Albury, NSW, Australia 2640.

RUSSELL (Eileen) Monica, b. 1 May 1938, Vic, Aust. Missionary Teacher; Administrator. Education: Primary Sch Tchr's Cert, 1958.Appointments: Tchng, Vic, 1959-63; Tchng, Miss Sch, Misima, Papua New Guinea, 1965-68; I/c, Expatriate Children's Corresp Sch, Salamo, 1969; Ch Educ Sec, 1970-73, Bish's Sec 1974-79, Regl Sec 1980-86, Utd Ch, Papuan Is Reg. Honour: Awd'd Papua New Guinea Medal to commemorate 10th Anniversary of Indep. Memberships: Accredited Local Preacher, Meth Ch of Australasia (now Uniting Ch in Aust). Hobbies: Sport; Dressmaking; Reading; Stamp Collecting; Photography; Gardening. Address: 143 Carpenter Street, North Brighton, Vic 3186, Australia.

RUTLAND Suzanne Dorothy, b. 3 July 1946, Sydney, Aust. Lecturer. div, 1 s, 1 d. Education: BA, hons; MA, hons; PhD; Dip, Educn. Appointments: Tchr, Canterbury Girls HS, 1970-74, Moriah Coll, 1976-78; Pt-time Adult Educn, London, Sydney, 1979-89; Tchr of Educn, Snr Lectr, Jewish Civilisation, Dept of Semitic Studies, Univ of Sydney, 1990-. Publications: Seventy-Five Years: The History of a Jewish Newspaper, 1970; Take Heart Again: The Story of a Fellowship of Jewish Doctors, 1983; Edge of the Diaspora: Two Centuries of Jewish Settlement in Australia, 1988, 2nd ed, 1997; Pages of History: A Century of the Australian Jewish Press, 1995; Opposite the Lion's Den: A Story of Hiding of Dutch Jews, 1996; With One Voice: A History of the New South Wales Jewish Board of Deputies, 1998. Memberships: Austl Jewish Histl Soc; Austl Assn of Jewish Studies; Roy Austl Histl Soc; Oral Hist Assn of Aust; Profl Histns Assn, NSW. Hobbies: Swimming; Bush Walking; Music; Theatre. Address: Department of Semitic Studies, University of Sydney, NSW 2006, Australia.

RUTLEDGE Cheryl Juanita, b. 18 May 1946, Chattanooga, TN, USA. Pianist; Music Educator. Education: BM, magna cum laude, Univ of Chattanooga, 1968; MA, Jacksonville State Univ, 1973; Grad study: Univ of AL, 1970; Peabody Conservatory of Music, 1974; Univ of MS, 1978-80; Memphis State Univ, 1980; PhD, LA State Univ, 1983. Appointments: Instr of Piano, Cadek Conservatory of Music, Univ of TN, Chattanooga, 1968-69, 1973-81; Grad Asst in Piano and Music Theory, LA State Univ, 1982-83; Dir of Piano, Suzuki Inst for Musical Trng, Little Rock, AR, 1984-85; Prof of Piano and Co-Chmn, Dept of Sacred Music, Sheng-te Christian Coll, Chungli, Taiwan, 1986-90; Adj Assoc Prof of Piano Pedagogy, Soochow Univ, Taipei, Taiwan, 1987-89; Adj Assoc Prof, Engl, Chung Yuan Christian Univ, Chungli, Taiwan, 1990-98; Adj Assoc Prof of Piano Pedagogy, Taiwan Theol Coll, Taipei, 1992; Adj Assoc Prof of Piano, Natl Chiao Tung Univ, Hsinchu, Taiwan, 1992-94; Ed, Off of Rsch and Dev, Chung Yuan Christian Univ, Chungli, 1993-98; Freelance Writer, Travel in Taiwan Monthly, 1994-; Assoc Prof of Engl, Da Yeh Univ, Changhua, Taiwan, 1998-. Publications: Cert Theory Workbooks and Tchr's Manual, 1978; Rote 'n' Read: A Piano Book for the Young Beginner, 1986; Chinese Opera Experience, Travel in Taiwan, 1995; Amazing Mazer, Travel in Taiwan, 1997. Honours: Phi Kappa Phi; Pi Kappa Lambda Natl Music Hon Soc; Alpha Soc; Profl Cert in Piano, Music Tchrs Natl Assn, 1978, 1979, 1984; Cert of Profl Advancement, TN Music Tchrs Assn, 1978, 1983, 1985; Tchr of Yr, Chattanooga Music Tchrs Assn, 1978; Profl Cert in Piano, Music Tchrs Natl Assoc, 1989, 1994 (Permanent); Cert of Profl Advancement, TN Music Tchrs Assoc, 1989, 1994 (Permanent). Memberships: Music Tchrs Natl Assn; Chattanooga and TN Music Tchrs Assns; Suzuki Assn of the Ams; Intl Computer Music Assn. Hobbies: Reading; Sewing; Musical composition. Listed in: International Who's Who in Music; World Who's Who of Women; International Directory of Distinguished Leadership; American Keyboard Artists; International Leaders in Achievement. Address: Da Yeh University, E 401, 112 Shan Jiau Road, Datsuen, Changhua, Taiwan 515, China.

RUVINSKY Anatoly, b. 24 July 1947, Berlin, Germany. Geneticist. m. Ilina L, 7 Mar 1968, 1 s, 1 d. Education: MSc, Novosibirsk Univ, Russia, 1969; PhD, 1974; DSc, 1985; Prof of Genetics, 1989. Appointments: Rschr, Inst Cytology and Genetics, 1974-85; Hd of Labor, 1986-92; Vice Dir, 1988-92; Jnt Appt Prof, Novosibirsk Univ, 1985-92; Currently Assoc Prof, Univ of New Eng, NSW. Creative Works: Biology (text book); Advanced Biology (text book); Problems on Genetics and Evolutionary Theory; The Genetics of Sheep; The Genetics of the Pig; The Genetics of Cattle. Honours: Var Medals. Memberships: Vavilov's Genetic Soc; NY Acady Scis; Genetic Soc of Aust; Genetic Soc of Am; Intl Mammalian Genome Soc. Hobbies: World Hist. Address: 31 The Avenue, Armidale, NSW 2350, Australia.

RYAN Donnell Michael, b. 3 June 1941, Melbourne, Vic, Aust. Federal Court Judge. m. Gabrielle Josephine Vandeleur, 26 Nov 1976, 1 s, 1 d. Education: BA, 1963; LLB (Hon), 1964. Appointments: Bar, Vic, 1965, NSW, 1978; QC, Vic and NSW, 1980; Pt-time Mbr, Austl Law Reform Commn; Judge, Fedl Crt of Aust, 1986-; Additional Judge of ACT Supreme Crt, 1989-; Judge of Indl Rels Crt of Aust, 1994-. Memberships: Maritime Law Assn of Aust and NZ; Austl Inst of Judicial Admin; Melbourne Savage Club; Melbourne Cricket Club. Hobbies: Tennis; Reading. Listed in: Who's Who in Australia; Who's Who in the World. Address: Judge's Chambers, Federal Court of Australia, 305 William Street, Melbourne, Vic 3000, Australia.

RYAN Judith Anne, b. 21 Jan 1949, Melbourne, Aust. Art Museum Curator. m. Kevin W, 16 Aug 1975, 1 s. Education: BA, hons, Univ Melbourne; Ctf, Educn, Oxon. Appointments: Secnd Art and Engl Tchr, sev schs, England and Vic, 1971-76; Circulations Offr, Natl Gallery of Vic, Melbourne, 1977-80; Curator of Pre-Columbian Art and Ed of Publns, Natl Gallery of Vic, 1981-87; Curator of Aboriginal and Oceanic Art, 1987-92, Snr Rsch Curator, Austl Art, 1993, Natl Gallery of Vic; Mbr Austl Inst of Aboriginal and Torres Strait Islander Stdies, 1995; Assoc, Fine Arts Dept Univ Melbourne, 1998; Snr Curator, Aboriginal and Torres Strait Islander Art, Natl Gall, Vic; Fell, Fine Arts Dept, Univ of Melbourne, 1999. Publications include: Mythscapes, 1989; Spirit in Land, 1990; Images of Power, 1993; Ginger Riley, 1997. Creative Works: Sev exhbns of Aboriginal Art. Hobbies: Classical Music; Films; Drama; Literature. Address: 1 Otterington Grove, East Ivanhoe, Victoria 3079, Australia.

RYAN Kevin William, b. 9 Sept 1925, Melbourne, Aust. Former Judge, Supreme Court of Queensland; Emeritus Professor of Law. m. Josephine Margaret Morrison, 22 May 1954, 1 d. Education: BA, 1948, LLB, 1956, Qld; PhD, Cambridge, 1960. Appointments: Sch Tchr, 1944-48; Bar, 1951-52, 1982-83; Univ Tchr of Law, 1953-64, 1969-83; Trade Cmmnr, 1964-69; Judge, 1984-94; Emer Prof of Law, 1995-; Judge, Crt of Appeal, Kiribati, 1996-. Publications: Introduction to the Civic Law; Manual of Income Tax Law in Australia; Co-auth, Constitution of Australia; Ed, International Trade Law; Ed, International Law in Australia; Co-auth, Qld Supreme Court Practice. Honours: QC, 1978; CBE, 1981; Hon Col, Austl Army Legal Corps, 1982-88; RFD, 1988 Hon LLD, Univ of Qld, 1988; DUniv, Qld Univ of Technol, 1995. Memberships: Fell, Acady of Socl Scis of Aust; Intl Acady of Comparative Law. Address: 15 Orkney Street, Kenmore, Qld 4069, Australia.

RYAN Matthew Morgan, b. 3 June 1964, Sydney, Aust. Horse Trnr; Competitor. m. Niki, 27 Nov 1993. Education: Level 1 EFA Instr. Appointments: Sports and Tour Amb, Aust, 1993. Honours: OAM; 2 Olympic Gold Medals; Sports Personality of the yr; Aust Sports Personality of NSW, 1992. Memberships: 5 Circles Club. Hobbies: Philately; Bird Watching; Sport. Address: 1 Kitford Cottage, East Lockinge, Wantage, Oxfordshire, OX12 8QN.

RYAN Meg, b. 19 Nov 1961 Fairfield CT. Actress. m. Dennis Quaid - qv - 1991, 1 s. Education: Bethel High Sch; NY Univ. Appointments: Fmrly appeared in tv comls; Tv appearances in As the World Turns; One of the Boys; Amy and the Angel; The Wild Side; Charles in Charge; Owner of Prufrock Pictures. Films: Rich and Famous, 1981; Amityville III-D; Top Gun; Armed and Dangerous; Innerspace; DOA; Promised Land; The Presidio; When Harry Met Sally; Jose Versus the Volcano; The Doors; Prelude to a Kiss; Sleepless in Seattle; Flesh and Bone; Significant Other; When a Man Loves a Woman; IQ; Paris Match; Restoration; French Kiss, 1995; Two for the Road, 1996; Courage Under Fire, 1996; Addicted to Love, 1997. Address: c/o ICM, 8942 Wilshire Boulevard, Beverly Hills, CA 90211, USA.

RYAN Michael Hugh Muvihille, b. 25 Aug 1912, Melbourne, Aust. Ophthalmic Surgeon. m. Beryl Elvira Donald, 16 May 1946, 3 d. Education: MB, BS, Melbourne Univ, 1936 MRCS, Eng; LRCP, London; DO, Melbourne, 1946; FRCS, Eng, 1947; DOMS, 1947; FRACS, 1948; FACS, 1949. Appointments: RMOS, 1937; Asst Pathologist, pt-time, St Vincents Hosp, Melbourne, 1941-43; Registrar, 1938, Demonstrator, Melbourne Univ; Clin Asst, St Vincents Hosp, 1945 Asst Ophthalmic Surgn, 1946-59, Ophthalmic Surgn, 1972-. Publications: Num articles in profl jrnls; Exhibited var art exhbns. Honours: KSCG CR, 1965; SB StJ, 1970. Memberships: BMA; AMA; OSUK; Roy Austl Coll of Ophthalmologists; Roy Australasian Coll of Surgns; Vic Artists Soc; Natl Gallery Soc. Hobbies: Golf; Painting; Fishing; Audio-Visual Electronics. Address: Mullion, 6 Stonehaven Court, Toorak, Vic 3142, Australia.

RYAN Peter Allen, b. 4 Sept 1923, Melbourne, Aust. Secretary. m. Gladys A Davidson, 23 May 1947, 1 s, 1 d. Education: BA Hons, Univ of Melbourne. Appointments: PR Mngr, ICI, Aust and NZ, 1958-62; Asst to Vice-Chan, Univ of Melbourne, 1962; Dir, Melbourne Univ Press, 1962-88; Mbr, Solicitors Disciplinary Tribunal, 1984-88; Sec, Bd of Examiners for Bars and Solicitors for Vic, 1988-. Publications include: Fear Drive My Feet, 1966; Redmond Barry, 1973; Black Bonanza, 1992. Honours: Mil Medal, MID, 1943; Hons Deg. Hobbies: Reading; Writing; Riding. Address: Supreme Court, Melbourne, Vic 3003, Australia.

RYAN Robert John Andrew, b. 17 June 1968, Sunderland, Eng. Investment banker. m. Renata, 26 Oct 1996, 1 s. Education: LLB, Law (Hons), Leicester Univ, 1989; Law Soc Solicitors Final exam, 1990; Japanese Min of Educ Proficiency Test (level 2), 1994; Participant in Eurn Union's 14th Exec Trng Prog in Japan, grad, 1995. Appointments: Allen & Overy, London, 1990-92; Allen & Overy, Tokyo, 1992-93, London, 1993-94; Snr Assoc, Allen & Overy, Tokyo, 1994-98; Exec Dir, Fin Prods, CIBC Wood Gundy Securities, Japan, 1998-99; Exec Dir, Int Asset Securitisation, Canad Imperial Bank of Commerce, Tokyo Branch, Japan, 1999-. Memberships: Law Soc Eng and Wales, 1988-; ETP Assn, 1994-. Hobbies: Rugby; Scuba diving; Travelling; Reading. Address: King Homes #24, 6-5-36 Miniami-Aoyama, Minato-ku, Tokyo 107-0062, Japan.

RYCKMANS Pierre, b. 28 Sept 1935, Brussels, Belgium. Scholar (Chinese Studies). m. Chang Hanfang, 1964, 3 s, 1 d. Publications: The Death of Napoleon, 1991, 1992; The Analects of Confucius, 1997; Essais Sur la Chine, 1998; L'Age et le Cachelot, 1998. Honour: Officier de l'Ordre de Léopold; Lit Prizes: Inst de Fin,

Stanislas Julien Prize; Académie Française, Jean Water Prize; The Indep (London) Best Foluyen Fiction Awd; Christina Stead Prize (Fiction), Sydney, NSW. Memberships: Académie Royale de Language et de Littérature Françaises (Brussels); Fell, Austl Acady of Hums. Address: 6 Bonwick Place, Garran, ACT 2605, Australia.

RYDER Paul Anthony, b. 18 Sept 1947. Academician. m. 12 Apr 1969, Mona Irene Ryder, 3 s. Education: BA (Hons), Psych; PhD, Univ of Qld. Appointments: Lectr and Snr Lectr, Univ of Qld, Dept of Com, 1974-87; Assoc Prof and Hd, Overseas Progs, Curtin Univ of Technol, 1987-90; Assoc Prof, Bond Univ, 1990-92; Fndn Prof of Bus and Strategic Mngmt and Dean, Fac of Bus and Hotel Mngmt, Griffith Univ, Gold Coast Campus, 1992-98; Exec Dean, Fac of Arts and Bus, James Cook Univ, Cairns Campus, 1998-. Publications: 40 Journal Articles and Conference Presentations. Honours: Fell, Austl Inst of Mngmt, 1994-. Memberships: Pres, Austl and NZ Acady of Mngmnt, 1995, 1996; Austl Psychol Soc. Hobbies: Art. Address: Faculty of Arts and Business, James Cook University, PO Box 6811, Cairns, Qld 4870, Australia.

RYE C Richard, b. 1935. Civ Servant. m. Blanca Luz Rye, 1963, 1 d. Education: Univ of Melbourne. Appointments: Joined Austl Bur of Statistics, 1953; Transferred to Treas, 1968; Asst Sec Econ Branch, 1970; Min for Finl Affairs Emb WA DC, 1975-76; First Asst Sec Gen Finl and Econ Policy Div Treas, 1976-79; Dep Sec for Econ Affairs, 1979-83; Dep Sec of the Treas, 1983-85; Exec Dir IMF, 1985-89; Chmn C'wlth Grants Commn, 1989-. Address: 59 Pandanus Street, Fisher, ACT 2611, Australia.

RYMILL Thomas Mark, b. 19 Feb 1950, Penola, SA. Aust. Solicitor. m. Catherine Margaret Walters, 10 May 1979, 1 s, 1 d. Education: LLB, Univ of Adelaide, 1974. Appointments: Prin, Thomas Rymill & Co, 1991-; Ptnr, Brown Aston & Hamilton, 1984-91; Residential Tenancies Tribunal (auxiliary), 1993-. Honour: Natl Medal, 1986. Memberships: Law Cncl of Aust; Life Mbr, Adelaide Zool Soc. Hobbies: Volunteer Fire Service; Conservation particularly arborculture. Address: 65 Bay Road, Mount Gambier, SA 5290, Australia.

S

SABA Elias, b. 1932 Lebanon. Politician; Economist. m. Hind Sabri Shurbagi, 1960, 5 d. Education: Am Univ of Beirut; Univ of Oxford. Appointments: Econ Advsr to min of Fin and Pet Kuwait and Kuwait Fund for Arab Econ Dev, 1961-62; Chmn Dept of Econs Am Univ of Beirut, 1963-67; Assoc Prof of Econs Am Univ of Beirut, 1967-69; Dep PM of the Lebanon Min of Fin and of Def, 1970-72; Econ and Finl Advsr to the Pres, 1972-73; Chmn Gen Mngr St Charles Cty Cntr SARL, 1974-; Vice-Chmn Banque du Credit Populaire, 1981-. Publications: Postwar Developments in the Foreign Exchange Systems of Lebanon and Syria, 1962. Memberships: Mbr Natl Dialogue Cttee, 1975. Hobbies: Hunting; Vintage and classic cars. Address: P O Box 5292, Ayoub Centre, Ashrafieh, Beirut, Lebanon.

SABA Shoichi, b. 28 Feb 1919. Bus Exec. m. Fujiko Saito, 1945, dec, 2 s - 1 dec - 1 d. Education: Tokyo Imperial Univ. Appointments: Pres Toshiba Corp, 1980-86; Chmn The Japan Inst of Indl Engrng, 1982-88; Dir ICI - UK - 1985-91 and num other bodies; Chmn Toshiba Corp, 1986-87; Vice-Chmn Keidanren, 1986-92; Chmn Electron Inds Assn of Japan, 1986-87; Advsr Toshiba Corp, 1987-; Chmn Japan Intl Dev Org Ltd - JAIDO - 1989-94; Vice-Chmn Bd of Cnclrs, 1992-94; Advsr Bd of Cnclrs, 1994-; Chmn Natl Bd of Govs Natl Assn Boy Scouts of Nippon, 1994-; Pres Japanese Ind Standards Cttee, 1994-. Honours: Progress Prize - Inst of Elecr Engrs of Japan - 1958; Blue Ribbon Medal - Govt of Japan - 1980; Cmdrs Cross Order of Merit - Fed Repub of Germany - 1988; Hon CBE - UK - 1989; Order of the Sacred Treas - 1st Class - 1990; Hon KBE - UK - 1993. Memberships: Mbr Pub Review Bd; Mbr Arthur Andersen and Co - USA, 1991-. Hobbies: Golf; Yachting. Address: c/o Toshiba Corp, 1-1 Shibaura 1-chome, Minator-ku, Tokyo 105, Japan.

SABAH Sheikh Jaber al-Ahmad al-Jaber al-, b. 1928 Kuwait. Amir of Kuwait. Education: Almubarakiyyah Sch Kuwait; Priv tutors. Appointments: Gov of Ahmadi and Oil areas, 1949-59; Pres Dept of Fin and Econ, 1959; Min of Fin Ind and Com, 1963, 1965; PM, 1965-67; Crown Prince, 1966-77; Amir, Dec 1977- succeeding his uncle. Address: Sief Palace, Amiry Diwan, Kuwait.

SABAH Sheikh Jaber al-Ali al-Salem al-, b. 20 Oct 1928. Politician. Appointments: Pres Dept of Electricity Water and Gas, 1952-63; Min of Info, 1964-71, 1975-81; Dep PM, 1975-81; Chmn Kuwait Intl Pet Invmnt Co, 1981. Memberships: Mbr High Exec Cttee to organize estabs and depts, 1954; Mbr Def High Cncl. Address: c/o Council of Ministers, Kuwait City, Kuwait.

SABAH Sheikh Saad al-Abdullah al-Salim al-, b. 1930 Kuwait. Kuwaiti Crown Prince; Politician. m. Sheikha Latifah Fahad al-Sabah, 1 s, 4 d. Education: Kuwait Govt Schs; Hendon Coll UK. Appointments: Ex-officio Chmn Supreme Def Cncl; Ex-officio Chmn Supreme Pet Cncl; Ex-officio Chmn Civ Serv Cncl; Ex-officio Chmn Supreme Housing Cncl; Dep Chf Police and Pub Security Dept, 1959; Chf, 1961; Min of Interior, 1961; Min of Def, 1965; Crown Prince, Jan 1978-; PM, Feb 1978-. Hobbies: Fishing; Gardening; Photog. Address: Diwan of HH The Crown Prince and Prime Minister, P O Box 4, Safat, 13001, Kuwait.

SABA Sheikh Sabah al-Ahmad al-Jaber al-, b. 1929. Politician. Education: Mubarakiyyah Natl Sch Kuwait; Privately. Appointments: Min of Pub Info and Guidance and of Socl Affairs, 1962-63; Min of For Affairs, 1963-91; Acting Min of Fin and Oil, 1965; Min of the Interior, 1978; Dep PM, 1978-91; Acting Min of Info, 1981-84; Now First Dep PM and Min of For Affairs. Memberships: Mbr Supreme Cttee, 1955-62. Address: c/o Ministry of Foreign Affairs, P O Box 3, Safat, Gulf Street, Kuwait.

SABAH Sheikh Salim al-Sabah al-Salim al-, b. 18 June 1937. Diplomatist. Education: Secondary Sch Kuwait; Gray's Inn London; Christ Ch Oxford.

Appointments: Joined For Serv, 1963; Fmr Hd Polit Dept min of For Affairs; Amb to the UK, 1965-70; Amb to Norway Denmark and Sweden, 1968-70; Amb to USA, 1970-75; Also accred to Canada; Min of Socl Affairs and Labour, 1975-78; Min of Def, 1978-87; Min of the Interior, 1987-91; Dep PM and Min of For Affairs, 1991. Address: Ministry of Foreign Affairs, P O Box 3, Safat, Kuwait.

SACHAR Rajindar, b. 22 Dec 1923, Lahore (fmr India now Pakistan). Retired Chief Justice, Delhi High Court. m. Raj, 23 Oct 1954, 1 s, 1 d. Education: BA (Hons); LLB. Appointments: Judge, Delhi High Crt, 1970; Chf Justice, 1985-1990; Mbr, UN Sub-Commn on Prevention of Discrimination and Protection of Minorities. Publication: UN Spec Rapportuer, Rigt to Adequate Housing, Publd by Cntr for Hum Rights, Geneva, 1996; Pres, Peoples Union for Civil Liberties (India). Honours: Sitar-e-Hind, All India Milli Cncl, 1997; Gulzari Lal Nanda Awd, pres of India, 1998. Membership: Pres, Peoples Union for Civil Liberties, India. Hobbies: Human Rights activist; Regular contributor to national newspapers. Address: A/19 New Friends Colony, New Delhi, India.

SACHDEV P Mohan, b. 1 Oct 1930, Daska Dist, Sialkot (now Pakistan). Advertising and Marketing Manager; Public Relations Executive. m. Raj, Feb 1956, 1 s, 1 d. Education: MA, ECO, Delhi Univ; Postgrad Prog, Indian Inst of Mngmt, Ahmedabad. Appointments: J Walter Thompson, New Delhi, 1956-64; Nestlé India, New Delhi, 1964-89; Branch Mngr, Advtng Mngr; Retd. Honours: Media India Awd, New Delhi. Memberships: All India Mngmt Assn; Delhi Mngmt Assn; Pub Rel Soc of India; Delhi Advtng Club; India Intl Cntr; Press Club of India, New Delhi. Hobbies: Professional Interactivity and Updates; Consulting; Writing. Address: 24 Mangla Apt G Block, Kalkaji, New Delhi 119910, Inida.

SACHDEV Perminder Singh, b. 27 July 1956, Ludhiana, India. Neuropsychiatrist. m. Jagdeep, 19 Mar 1986, 2 d. Education: MBBS, 1978, MD, 1981, AIIMS; FRANZCP, 1985; PhD, Univ NSW, 1991. Appointments: Dir, Neuropsych Inst, Prince Henry Hosp, Sydney, 1987-; Prof of Neuropsych, Univ NSW, 1999-. Publications: Sev articles in profl med jrnls. Honour: Snr Organon Rsch Awd, Roy Aust and NZ Coll of Psychs, 1995. Memberships: Intl Neuropsych Assn; Soc of Biol Psych; Tourette Syndrome Assn. Hobbies: Reading; Chess. Address: NPI, Prince of Wales Hospital, Randwick, NSW 2031, Australia.

SACK Karen Jean Svitavsky, b. 12 Sept 1955, Cleveland, OH, USA. Tree Farmer. m. Gary N, 2 Aug 1987, 1 s. 1 d. Education: BS Chem, Cleveland State Univ; MBA, Univ Wisconsin. Appointments: Sales Rep, Tech Sales, Sales Mgr. Creative Works: Painted satellite image of earth on 3 foot diameter globe, 1998; Report, The Impact of Technology on Human Behaviour, 1982; Tracked market prices for forestry newsletter, 1988-89. Honours: Volunteer of Yr, 1988, Redwood Discovery Mus. Memberships: TAPPI, conf moderator, coating additives, Portland; Sec Coating Additives Cttee, 1985-86, Vice Chmn, 1986-87, Chmn, 1987-88; Treas, Woodside Preschool, Humboldt Home Schoolers; Humboldt Beekeepers; Four Winds, West Winds, Coastal Winds; All Seasons Orchestra; Member of Div Cncl for Coating and Graphic Arts Div of TAPPI; Bd Dirs, Lion Chemicals Inc, 1986-88. Hobbies: Music; Gardening; Travel. Address: PO Box 6082, Eureka, CA 95502, USA.

SADDAM Hussein, b. 1937 Tikrit nr Baghdad. Politician. m. Sajida Khairalla, 1963, 2 s, 2 d. Education: Al-Karkh Secondary Sch Baghdad; Al-Qasr al-Aini Secondary Sch Cairo; Cairo Univ; Al-Mustanseriya Univ Baghdad. Appointments: Joined Arab Baath Socl Party, 1957; Sentenced to death for attempted execution of Gen Abdul Karim Qassim, 1959; Joined ldrship of Cairo branch of Baath Party, 1962; Returned to Iraq following revolution, 1963; Arrested for plotting overthrow of Abdul Salam Aref, 1964; Dep Sec Regl Ldrship of Baath Party, 1966-79; Sec Baath Party, 1979-; Played prominent role in revolution, Jul 1968; Dep Sec Regl Ldrship in 7th Regl Congress, 1968; Actng Dep Chmn Revolutionary Cmd Cncl, 1968-69; Dep Chmn Revolutionary Cmnd Cncl,

1969-79; Rank of Gen, 1976; Chmn Revolutionary Cmnd Cncl, 1979-; Forces invaded Iran, Sep 1980 initiating 1980-88 Iran-Iraq War; Pres of Iraq, Jul 1979-; Invaded and annexed Kuwait, Aug 1990; Forces defeated and forced to withdraw by UN-backed Allied Force under cmnd of Gen Norman Schwarzkopf - qv - Feb 1991; PM, May 1994-. Publications: One Trench or Two. Honours: Order of Rafidain 1st Class, 1976. Memberships: Mbr 4th Regl Congress and 6th Natl Congress of Baath Paryt, 1963; Mbr Regl Ldrship of Baath Party in Iraq following overthrow of Party rule, 1963; Mbr 7th Natl Congress Syria, 1964; Elected mbr Ldrship by 8th Natl Congress while still in prison, 1965; Mbr Natl Ldrship of Party in 10th Natl Congress, 1970. Address: Presidential Palace, Karradat Mariam, Baghdad, Iraq.

SADHAK Hira, b. 20 Nov 1950, Rongakathi, Bengal, India. Financial Economist; Fund Manager. m. Manjushree, 25 Nov 1977, 1 s, 1 d. Education: BA Hons, Econs; MA, Econs; PhD, Indl Fin. Appointments include: Lectr, Econs, Univ of Kalyani; Probationary Offr, Union Bank of India; Asst Sec, LI C of India; Asst Gen Mngr, Mktng, Dpty Gen Mngr, Fin, Joint Gen Mngr, Fin, Lic Mutual Fund/JBS AMC Ltd. Publications: Impact of Incentives on Industrial Development in Backward Regions, 1986; Role of Entrepreneur Backward Areas, 1989; Mutual Funds in India Marketing Strategies and Investment Practices, 1997; over 100 articles. Honours: Awds/Hons from: Maharashtra Chmbrs of Comm, 1984; Tourist Camp, New Dew Delhi, 1985; Parly Forum on Pub Enterprises & Cntr for Pub Sector Studies, 1986, 1987; Rotary Club of KANPUR, 1988; AMEX Bank Book Awd, 1990; Discount & Fin House of India, 1992; Govt of India, 1996; LIC of India. Memberships: Convenor, Working Grp on Rsch & Stats, Assn of Mutual Funds of India; Gov, Indian Inst of Merchant Banking, New Delhi, India; IMC Expert Cttee, Fin & Banking, Assn of Fin Servs, Bombay Mngmt Assn/ Indian Econometric Soc. Address: LIC Mutual Fund, Industrial Assurance Building, Churchgate, Mumbai 400020, India.

SADIK Nafis, b. 18 Aug 1929 Jaunpur India. Intl Offic; Physn. m. Azhar Sadik, 1954, 1 s, 2 d, 2 adopted d. Education: Loretto Coll Calcuttta; Calcutta Med Coll; Dow Med Coll Karachi; Johns Hopkins Univ. Appointments: Intern Gynae and Obstets Cty Hosp Baltimore MD, 1952-54; Civn medl offr in charge of women's and children's wards in var Pakistani armed forces hosps, 1954-63; Res Physiology Queens Univ Kingston Ont, 1958; Hd Hlth Sec Plng Commn on Hlth and Family Plng Pakistan, 1964; Dir of Plng and Trng Pakistan Cntrl Family Plng Cncl, 1966-68; Dep Dir-Gen, 1968-70; Dir Gen, 1970-71; Tech Advsr UN Population Fund - UNFPA - 1971-72; Chf Prog Div UN Population Fund, 1973-77; Asst Exec Dir, 1977-87; Exec Dir UNFPA, 1987-; Sec-Gen Intl Conf on Population and Dev, 1994; Pres Soc for Intl Dev, 1994-. Publications: Population: National Family Planning Programme in Pakistan, 1968; Population: the UNFPA Experience - ed - 1984; Population Policies and Programmes: Lessons learned from Two Decades of Experience, 1991; Making a Difference: Twenty-five Years of UNFPA Experience, 1994; Articles in profl jrnls. Honours: Hugh Moore Awd, 1976; Fell ad eundem Roy Coll of Obstrns and Gynaecologists; Hon DHum Litt - Johns Hopkins - 1989; Brown, 1993; Women's Global Ldrship Awd, 1994; Order of Merit First Class - Egypt - 1994; Peace Awd - UNA - 1994; Prince Mahidol Awd, 1995; Duke, 1995; Hon LLD - Wilfrid Laurier - 1995; Bruno H Schubert-Stiftung Prize, 1995; Hon DSc - MI - 1996; Claremont, 1996. Hobbies: Bridge; Reading; Th; Travel. Address: United Nations Population Fund, 220 East 42nd Street, 19th Floor, New York, NY 10017, USA.

SADLER David Royce, b. 31 Aug 1942, Brisbane, Aust. Educator. m. Merideth Boyce, 18 Dec 1965, 3 s. Education: BSc, 1965, DipEd, 1975, BEd, 1969, Univ Queensland; MLitt, Univ New Eng, 1992; PhD, Univ Queensland, 1985. Appointments: Tchr, Mt Morgan hs, 1965-67; Lectr, Maths, QIT Capricornia, Rockhampton, 1968-70; Lectr, Maths, Gordon Inst of Technol, Geelong, 1971-73; Lectr/Snr Lectr Educ, Univ of Queensland, Dir, Assessment & Evaluation Rsch Unit, 1973-91; Prof of

Educ, Griffith Univ, 1991-; Dean, Fac of Educ, Griffith Univ, 1992-95. Publications: Numerical Methods for Nonlinear Regression, 1976; Up the Publication Road, 1990; Managing Your Academic Career, 1999; Over 60 rsch reports and acad articles on educl asessment and policy. Memberships: Advsry Bd, Int Cntr for Rsch on Assessment, Univ of London; Editl Bds of jrnls; Assessment & Evaluation in Higher Educ, Assessment in Educ. Address: School of Curriculum, Teaching and Learning, Mt Gravatt Campus, Griffith University, Queensland 4111, Australia.

SAEKI Satoru, b. 21 Sept 1961, Hyogo, Japan. Medical Doctor. m. Masae Itoh, 30 Apr 1988, 2 s, 1 d. Education: DMS, Grad Sch of Med Sci, Univ of Occl and Environ Hlth, Japan. Appointments: Instr, Univ of Occl and Environ Hlth, 1994-95; Dir of Rehab Med, Moji Rosai Hosp, 1995-. Publications: Sev Articles in Profl Jrnls. Honours: Ramazzini Prize, 1988. Memberships: Amn Heart Assn. Hobbies: Tennis. Address: Moji Rosal Hosp Dept Rehab, 3-1 Higashiminato-machi, Moji-ku, Kitakyushu 801-0853, Japan.

SAEMALA Francis Joseph, b. 23 June 1944. Diplomatist; Civ Serant. m. Eve Mercy, 1974, 4 s, 1 d. Education: Vic Univ Wellington NZ. Appointments: Hd of Plng Cntrl Plng Off, 1976; Sec to Indepence Timetable Talks deleg and Jnt Sec to Constl Conf in London, 1977; Spec Sec to Chf Min, 1976; Spec Sec to PM, 1978-81; Sec to Ldr of the Opposition, 1981-82; Perm Rep to UN, 1983-90; MP, 1989-; Chmn Solomon Islands Ports Authy Bd, 1991-93; Chmn Parly For Rels Ctte, 1992-93, 1995; Dep PM Min of For Affairs, 1993-94. Publications: Our Independent Solomon Islands; Solomon Islands in Politics in Melanesia. Address: Auki, Malaita Province, Solomon Islands.

SAENGHIRUN VATTANA Sawang, b. 25 Jan 1955, Bangkok. Professor of Medicine. m. Rungsima, 3 Jan 1987, 2 s. 1 d. Education: Fell, Critical Care Med, Chicago, Illinois, 1988. Appointments: Asst Dean, 1998; Asst Ed, Rama Med Jrnl, 1999; Prof of Med, 1996. Publications: Update Internal Medicine, vol I-VI, 1997. Honours: Instr Awd, 1987; Roy Cypher Medal, 1995; Rschr Awd, 1996. Membership: Natl Rsch Inst. Hobbies: Tennis; Swimming; Table tennis; Badminton; Volleyball. Address: 1121 Praholyothin Road, Bangkok, Thailand 10400.

SAFFAR Salman Mohamed al-, b. 1931 Bahrain. Diplomatist. m. Education: Baghdad Univ Iraq; Sorbonne Paris. Appointments: Primary Sch tchr Bahrain, 1949-54; Secondary Sch tchr, 1959-60; With min of For Affairs, 1970-; Permanent Rep to UN, 1971-81; Amb to France, 1982-88; Dir of Econ Affairs min of For Affairs, 1988-91; Amb to Russia, 1992-94. Address: Ministry of Foreign Affairs, P O Box 547, Manama, Bahrain.

SAGIE Abraham, b. 9 Sept 1947, Jerusalem, Israel. Professor. m. Raaya Sagie, 1 s, 4 d. Education: BA, Sociol and Psychol, 1972, MA, Psychol, 1977, Hebrew Univ, Jerusalem; PhD, Psychol, Bar-Ilan Univ, 1987. Appointments:Psychol, Org Cnslt, Yaad Ltd, Jerusalem, 1987-; Snr Lectr, 1988-, Dpty Dir, 1995-97, Sch of Bus Admin, Bar-Ilan Univ; Sec, Treas, Intl Soc for the Stdy of Work and Organizational Values, 1996-; Book Review Ed, Intl Jrnl of Manpower, 1998. Publications include: Employee absenteeism, organizational commitment, and job satisfaction: Another look, 1998; Teachers' physical, mental and emotional burnout: Impact on intentions to quit; Achievement motive and entrepreneurial orientation: A structural analysis; Participation and empowerment in organizational settings: Modeling, effectiveness, and applications. Honours: Prize, Human Engrng of a Computer, IRA Fndn for Human Engrng in Israel, 1975; Prize, Rsch Worker Responses to Org Computing, System Analysts' Assn, Israel, 1984; Prize, Rsch in Computer-Based Selection of Programming Staff, System Analysts' Assn, Israel, 1990; Cand Studies Fac Enrichment Awd, Govt of Can, 1996; Grant, Japan Soc for the Promotion of Sci, 1996. Memberships: Acady of Mngmt; Intl Soc for the Stdy of Work and Org Values; Facets Theory Assn; Israeli Psychol Assn. Address: Bar-Ilan University, School of Business Administration, Ramat-Gan 52900, Israel.

SAH Bindeshwar Prasad, b. 3 Sept 1946, Shak Kusiyari, Bihar. College Teacher. m. Sumitra, 10 May 1965, 3 s. Education: BA (Hons), Engl; LLB; MA (Engl); MA (Hindi); BT; MEd; Dip in Distance Educ; PhD (Engl). Appointments: Postgrad Tchr; Lectr; Snr Lectr; Lectr (select grade); Rdr. Publications: Poems in Engl and Hindi, 1962-. Honours: Nehru Acad Awd, 1964; Merit Schlshp; Univ Topper in engl Hons Exam, 1967; Gold Medal in MA (Hindi) Exam, 1978. Memberships: Life Mbr, ASRC, Hyderabad; The Quest, Ranchi, 1997; Sec, Arunachal Pradesh Coll Tchrs Assn. Hobbies: All help for the distressed; Happy always with work. Address: Lecturer (SG), Department of English, Government College, Itanagar 791113, Arunachal Pradesh, India.

SAHABDEEN Abdul Majeed Mohamed, b. 19 May 1929, Gampola, Sri Lanka. Former Civil Servant. m. Ruchia Halida, 1959, 1 s, 1 d. Education: Univ Ceylon. Appointments: Civil Serv, 1950; Sec, Dir, Cmmnr, Chmn, Sev maj govt orgs until 1973; Vis Hd, Dept of Western Philos, Univ Sri Lanka, 1957-59; Chmn, Majeedsons Grp of Cos, 1973; Chmn, Muslim Law (Amendments) Cttee, 1990; Fndr, A.M.M. Sahabdeen Trust Fndn, 1991; Fndr, Desamanya Mohamed Sahabdeen Inst for Adv Studies and Rsch in Pahamune, 1997. Publications: Sev articles and books. Honours: Desamanya, 1992; Est'd Intl Awds, Sci, Lit and Human Devel. Address: A.M.M. Sahabdeen Trust Foundation, 10 Ward Place, Colombo 07, Sri Lanka.

SAHABDEEN Desamanya Abdul Majeed Mohamed Sahabdeen, b. 19 May 1926. Fndn Adminstr; Entrepreneur; Fmr Civ servant. m. Ruchia Halida, 1959, 1 s, 1 d. Education: Univ of Ceylon. Appointments: Joined Ceylon Civ Serv, 1950; Visng Hd Dept of West Philos Univ of Sri Lanka Vidyodaya - now Sri Jayawardanapura - 1957-59; Served as Sec Dir Commnr Chmn sev maj govt orgs until, 1973; Chmn Majeedsons Grp of Cos, 1973-; Chmn Muslim Law - Amendments - Cttee, 1990; Fndr AMM Sahabdeen Trust Fndn for Educ and Socl Dev, 1991; Fndr Mohamed Sahabdeen Intl Awds for sci lit and human devt est by Act of Parl, 1991; Fndr Mohamed Sahabdeen Inst for advd studies and rsch in Pahamune, 1997. Publications: Sev articles and books on philos and allied subjects inclng Sufi Doctrin in Tamil Literature, 1986; God and the Universe, 1995; The Circle of Life. Honours: Received Desamanya - highest Civl honour - 1992. Memberships: Mbr Presdtl Commns on Delimitation of Electoral Dists, 1988; Mbr Presdtl Commns on Taxation, 1989; Mbr Presdtl Commns on Fin and Banking, 1990; Mbr Presdtl Commns on Industrialization, 1990; Mbr Presdtl Commns on Pub Serv Commn, 1989. Hobbies: Philos; Classical music. Address: AMM Sahabdeen Trust Foundation, 10 Ward Place, Colombo 07, Sri Lanka.

SAHARI Wajid Rizvi, b. 1939, Rampur, India. Service. Education: ADEEB. Appointments: Sev positions in All India Radio & TV. Publications: Sunehri Aanch, 1984; Chalib-Ki-Rangular, 1990; Karavan e Adab, 1996. Honours: Ahabab-e-Rampur Intl Awd; Moulana Mohd Ali Jouhar Awd. Memberships: Ali Jauhar Acady; Bazm-e-Saal-o; Adab Sahitya Sangam, Delhi. Hobby: Poetry. Address: Educational Publication House, 3108 Gali Azizuddin Vakila Kucha Pandit, Delhi 110006, India.

SAHAY Prem Nath, b. 22 Jan 1929, Buxar, India. University Professor. m. Shanti Sahay, 5 May 1950, 1 s, 4 d. Education: BA, hons; MA; PhD. Appointments: Lectr, 1951; Rdr, 1975; Univ Prof, 1985-. Publictions: An Introduction to English Literature, 1963; Jawaharlal Nehru: A Literary Artist, 1983; Indian Writing in English - Nehru's Prose Style. Hobbies: Reading Books on Religion and Spiritualism. Address: White House Compound, Road No 5, Gaya, Bihar, India.

SAHE AL KAFAJE Galib Nahe, b. 1932 Emara. Artist. m. 1967, 3 d. Education: Inst of Fine Arts Baghdad; Acady Fine Arts Rome. Appointments: Instr Inst of Fine Arts Baghdad, 1966; Instr Acady of Fine Arts Baghdad, 1969; Wrk incls mural at Saddam Airport, 1987; 130 Graphics at Rashed Hotel Baghdad; Wrks collect at Saddam Art Cntr and have been widely exhib'd in Eurn cities New Delhi Cairo etc. Honours: Sev awds. Hobbies: Handicrafts in gold. Address: College of Fine Arts, University of Baghdad, P O Box 17635, Jadiriya, Baghdad, Iraq.

SAHGAL Nayantara, b. 10 May 1927 Allahabad. Writer. m. (1) Gautam Sahgal, 1949, div 1967, 1 s, 2 d; (2) E N Mangat Rai, 1979. Education: Wellesley Coll USA. Appointments: Schl-in-Resn holding creative writing seminar S Methodist Univ Dallas TX, 1973, 1977; Advsr Eng Lang Bd Sahitya Akademi - Natl Acady of Lets - New Delhi; Chmn Eurasia Reg, 1991. Publications: Prison and Chocolate Cake, 1954; A Time to be Happy, 1958; From Fear Set Free, 1962; This Time of Morning, 1965; Storm in Chandigarh, 1969; History of the Freedom Movement, 1970; The Day in Shadow, 1972; A Situation in New Delhi, 1977; A Voice for Freedom, 1977; Indira Gandhi's Emergence and Style, 1978; Indira Gandhi: Her Road to Power, 1982; Rich Like Us, 1985; Plans for Departure, 1985; Mistaken Identity, 1988; Relationship: Extracts from a Correspondence, 1994; Point of View, 1997. Honours: Fell Radcliffe Inst - Harvard Univ - 1976; Fell Wilson Intl Cntr for Schls WA DC, 1981-82; Fell Natl Humans Cntr NC, 1983-84; Sinclair Prize for Rich Like Us, 1985; Sahitya Akady Awd for Rich Like Us, 1987; C'wlth Writers' Prize for Plans for Departure, 1987; Annie Besant Memorial Lect - Banares Hindu Univ - 1992; Arthur Ravenscroft Memorial Lect - Univ of Leeds - 1993; Hon D Litt - Leeds - 1997. Memberships: Mbr Indian Deleg to UN Gen Ass, 1978; Mbr Natl Exec People's Union for Civ Liberties; Mbr Jury C'wlth Writers' Prize, 1990; Mbr Am Acady Arts and Scis, 1990. Hobbies: Walking; Reading; Music. Address: 181B Rajpur Road, Dehra Dun, 248009 Uttar Pradesh, India.

SAID Sayed Faisal bin Ali al-, b. 1927 Muscat. Diplomatist; Politician. Appointments: Attached to min of For Affairs Muscat, 1953-57; Lived abroad, 1957-70; Perm Under-Sec min of Educ, 1970-72; Min of Econ Affairs, 1972; Perm Rep to UN Amb to USA, 1972-73; Min of Educ, 1973-76; Min of Omani Heritage, 1976-; Min of Culture, 1979-. Address: Ministry of National Heritage and Culture, P O Box 668, Muscat 113, Oman.

SAID Walid Abdulrahman, b. 29 Oct 1947, Jenin, Jordan. Senior Financial Analyst. m. Fatema, 17 May 1974, 2 s, 5 d. Education: Bach Deg, Acctng, 1973, Bach Deg, Bus Admin, 1977, Arab Univ of Beirut, Lebanon; Ctf, Bokkeeping & Accts, 1984, Dip, Bookkeeping & Accts, 1985, Trans-World Tutorial Coll, England; Doct, Bus & Mngmt, Sussex Coll of Technol, England, 1988. Appointments: Acct, Pub Natl Co for Mills & Fodders, Tripoli, Libya, 1977-80; Chf Acct, Al Mimary Establishment, Amman, Jordan, 1981-82; Snr External Auditor, Saudi Acctng Bur, Riyadh, 1982-89; Snr Fin Analyst, Saudi Consolidated Elec Co, Riyadh, 1989-. Publications: Sev articles in profl jrnls. Honour: 20th Century Awd for Achievement, IBC, ABI Gold Record of Achievement, 1995. Memberships: Assn of Cost & Exec Accts, England; Inst of Internal Auditors, USA; Brit Inst of Mngmt. Hobbies: Swimming; Table Tennis; Reading. Address: PO Box 42886, Riyadh 11551, Saudi Arabia.

SAIKUMAR M L, b. 27 July 1954, Vijayawada, India. Professor. m. Mrs Vijayrani, 10 May 1985, 1 s. Education: MSc (Applied Stats), 1978; MSc (Agricl Stats), 1979; MTech (Computer Sci), 1993. Appointments: Rsch Assoc, 1979-80, Trainee Programmer, 1980-81, Systems Analyst, 1983-84, Fac Mbr, 1984-85, System Analyst, 1985-86, System Mngr, 1986-93, Snr Asst Prof, 1993-96, Assoc Prof, 1996-98, Prof, 1998-, Inst Pub Enterprise. Publications: (auth) Guide and work books: Lotus 1-2-3, 1989, WordStar, 1989, Dbase III Plus, 1989; (book) Computer Fundamentals and Applications, 1997; Ed, Tech Proceedings: Natl Seminar of Software Engrng and Its Application, 1995, 1997, Intl Conf on Software Engrng and Its Application, 1996, 1997. Honours: Fellshp, Indian Cncl of Agricl Rsch, 1978-79; 1991-93. Memberships: Snr Life Mbr, Computer Soc of India; Life Mbr, Indian Soc of Agricl Stats; Intl Soc for Technol in Educ, 1991-; Sec,

Computer Soc of India, Hyderabad Chapt, 1994-95. Hobbies: Participtaing in organizing of events related to Computer Science both at national and international levels; Delivering popular talks. Address: Professor and Head, Information Technology Division, Institute of Public Enterprise, Osmania University Campus, Hyderabad 500 007, India.

SAIKUMAR M L, b. 27 July 1954, Vijayawada, India. Professor. m. Mrs Vijayrani, 10 May 1985, 1 s. Education: MSc, Appl Stats, 1978; MSc, Agricl Scis, 1979; MTech, Computer Sic, 1993. Appointments: Rsch Assoc, 1979-80, Trainee Progmr, 1980-81, Systems Analyst, 1983-84, Fac Mbr, 1984-85, System Analyst, 1985-86, System Mngr, 1986-93, Snr Asst Prof, 1993-96, Assoc Prof, 1996-98, Prof, 1998-, Inst of Pub Enterprise. Publications include: LOTUS 1-2-3, A Guide and Work Book, 1989; WordStar, A Guide and Work Book, 1989; Dbase III Plus, Guide and Work Book, 1989; Computer Fundamentals and Applications, 1997. Honours: Fellshp, Indian Cncl of Agricl Rsch, 1978-79, 1991-93. Memberships: Computer Soc, India; Indian Soc of Agricl Scis; Intl Soc for Technol in Educn; Computer Soc of India, Hyderabad Chapt, sec, 1994-95. Hobbies: Organizing Computer Science Events; Public Speaking. Address: c/o Information Technology Division, Institute of Public Enterprise, Osmania University Campus, Hyderabad 500 007, India.

SAINI Balwant Singh, b. 6 Feb 1930, Simla, India. University Professor. Architect. m. 9 July 1978, 2 d. Education: BA, Univ of Punjab, 1948; BArch 1954, PhD 1967, Univ of Melbourne, Aust. Appointments: Snr Lectr, Rdr, Univ of Melbourne, 1959-72; Snr Rsch Fell, Austl Govt Dept of Housing and Constrn, 1963; Prof, 1973, Hd Dept of Arch, 1973-80, Univ of Qld. Publications include: Architecture in Tropical Australia, 1970; The Australian House, 1982. Honours: Book Awd, 1974; Austl Govt Habitat Awd, 1976. Memberships include: Life Fell, Roy Austl Inst of Archts; Fell, Roy Inst of Brit Archts; Austl Comm for UNESCO. Hobbies: Music; Writing; Golf; Swimming; Travel. Address: 11 Montrose Road, Taringa, Qld 4068, Australia.

SAINSBURY Maurice Joseph, b. 18 Nov 1927, Sydney, NSW, Aust. Registered Medical Practitioner (Psychiatrist). m. 22 Aug 1953, 1 s, 2 d. Education: MBBS, Univ of Sydney, 1952; DPM, Roy Coll of Physns and Surgs, Eng, 1960; MHP, Univ of NSW, 1980; FRANZCP, FRCPsych. Appointments: Gen Med Prac, Wollongong Area, 1953-57; Psych postings in Eng, 1957-62; Psych and Dpty Med Supt, Psych Cntr, N Ryde, Aust, 1962-68; Dir, NSW Inst of Psych, 1968-83; Snr Spec, Mental Hlth Servs, NSW Dept of Hlth, 1983-87; Col (retd), RAAMC; Cnslt Psych, Army Off Def Dept, 1976-86; Mbr, Guardianshp Trib, NSW, 1989-; Mbr, Mental Hlth Review Trib, NSW, 1990-. Publications: Key to Psychiatry (students textbook), 1973, 2nd ed 1976, 3rd ed 1980; Sainsbury's Key to Psychiatry, co-auth, 1980; Articles on psych topics in learned jrnls. Honours: Robin May Meml Prize, Sydney Univ, 1952; Reserve Force Decoration, 1985; AM, 1987. Memberships: Past Pres, Roy Aust and NZ Coll of Psychs; Fndn Mbr, Pres, After Care Assn of NSW, 1983-95; Fndn Mbr, Austl Acady of For Scis. Hobbies: Golf; Gardening; Welding; Music. Address: 3 Bimbil Place, Killara, NSW 2071, Australia.

SAINT-JACQUES Bernard, b. 26 April 1928, Montreal, Canada. Professor of Linguistics. m. Education: BA Classics and Philos, 1949, MA Philos, 1954, Montreal Univ; MA Japanese Culture and Relig, 1962, Sophia Univ, Tokyo; MS Ling, 1964, Georgetown Univ, Washington DC; Doct de Troisieme Cycle Ling and Asian Stdies, 1975, Doct d'Etat, Doct es Lettres et Sciences Humaines, 1975, Univ of Paris. Appointments: Instr in Classics, French and Soc Scis, 1954-62; Asst Prof in French and Ling, 1966-67; Asst Prof in Ling, 1967-69; Assoc Prof in Ling, 1969-78; Acting Hd Ling Dept, 1969-72, 1978-80, Prof in Ling, 1978-88, Grad Advr of Ling Dept, 1984-88, Univ BC; Cnslt, Inter Pacific Club, Vancouver, 1986-88; Prof in Ling and Intercultural Comms, 1988-, Dir, Inst of Lang and Culture, 1994-, Head, Grad Prog in Intercultural Comms, 1995-, Aichi

Shukutoku Univ. Publications: Language and Ethnic Interaction, 1979; Structural Analysis of Modern Japanese; and others. Memberships: 16 profl and learned socs including: The Roy Soc of Can; Ling Soc of Am; Canad Soc for Asian Stdies; Intl House of Japan; NY Acady Sci. Address: Aichi Shukutoku University, Katahira Nagakute, Aichi-gun, Aichi 480-1197, Japan.

SAIRAM T V, b. 7 Feb 1946, Tirupattur, India. Public Administration. 1 s, 1 d. Education: Doct of Philos; MA, MSc, MPhil, Dips in French, Pub Admin, Intl Mktng, Intl Econs, from India and France. Appointments: Commnr of Customs, 1990-; Mbr, Indian Revenue Serv, 1970-90. Publications: 4 books: Outlines of Cytology, 1970; Indian Temple: Forms & Foundations, 1982; Fiscal Policy & Environment, 1986; Home Remedies: A Handbook of Herbal Cures for Common Ailments, 1998; Over 100 articles on an assortment of subjs. Memberships: Auths Guild of India, New Delhi; Indian Inst of Pub Admin, New Delhi, India. Address: 199 RPS, Sheikh Sarai I, New Delhi, 110017, India.

SAITO Gunzi, b. 10 Mar 1945, Otaru, Hokkaido, Japan. University Professor of Chemistry. m. Atsuko NishikaWa, 25 May 1972, 3 s. Education: BS, 1967, MSc, 1969, DSc, 1972, Hokkaido Univ. Appointments: Rsch Assoc, Inst Molecular Sci, Obazaki, 1979-84; Assoc Prof, Inst Solid State Phys, Univ of Tokyo, 1984-89, Prof, Kyoto Univ, 1989-; Mbr, Sci Cncl, Min of Educ, Culture, 1996-. Publication: Organic Superconductors, 2nd ed, 1998. Honours: Inoue Awd, 1988; Nishima Awd, 1988; Japanese Surface Sci Article Awd, 1991. Memberships: Chem Soc of Japan; Applied Phys Soc of Japan; Material Rsch Soc. Address: Chemistry Division, Graduate School of Science, Kyoto University, Kitashirakawa, Oiwakecho, Sakyo-ku, Kyoto 606 8502, Japan.

SAITO Hitoshi, b. 30 June 1936, Osaka, Japan. Professor; Chairman. m. Hisayo, 9 Apr 1967, 1 d. Education: MD, PhD, Kyoto Prefectural Univ of Med. Appointments: Fukui Medl Univ, Dept of Otorhinolaryngology, 1983-. Publications: Encyclopedia o flaps, 2nd ed, Vol 1, p 685-687, 1998. Memberships: Assn for Rsch in Otolarygology, 1994-; Amn Hd and Neck Soc, 1996-. Hobbies: Golf; Travel. Address: Department of Otorhinolaryngology, Fukui Medical University, 23 Shimoaitsuki, Matsuoka-cho, Yoshida-gun, Fukui 910-1193, Japan.

SAITO Theodore Teruo, b. 9 Sept 1942, Poston, AZ, USA. Scientist. m. Diane G Signorino, 31 Aug 1968, 1 s, 1 d. Education: BS, USAF Acady; MS, Phys, MIT; PhD, Phys, Penn State Univ. Appointments: Cmdr, F J Seiler Rsch lab, AF Matl Lab, AF Weapons Lab, US Air Force, Lawrence Livermore Natl Lab. Publications: Over 100 in optics, lasers, precision engrng, technol transfer, laser spectroscopy and damage. Honours: R&D Awd, 1979; SPIE Gov's Awd, 1979; SPIE Techl Achievement; Meritorious Serv Medal w Oak Leaf. Hobby: Bible study. Address: Initiatives for Proliferation Prevention Leader, Lawrence Livermore National Laboratory, POB 808, L-175, CA 9455, USA.

SAKAI Hiroshi, b. 11 Aug 1946, Osaka, Japan. Professor of Gene Engineering. m. Tomoko, 23 Sept 1976, 2 s, 1 d. Education: PhD, Kyoto Univ, 1974. Appointments: Rsch Instr, 1974-85, Assoc Prof, 1985-99, Kyoto Univ; Prof, Okayama Univ, 1999-. Publications: 87 sci pprs in profl jrnls. Memberships: Am Soc for Microbiol; Japan Soc for Biosci, Biotechnol & Agrochem; Molecular Biol Soc of Japan; Japanese Biochem. Hobbies: Reading; Swimming; Art Appreciation; Skiing; Travel. Address: Department of Bioscience & Biotechnology, Faculty of Engineering, Okayama University, Tsushima-Naka 3-1-1, Okayama 700-8530, Japan.

SAKAMOTO Yoshikazu, b. 16 Sept 1927, Los Angeles, California, USA. Professor Emeritus. m. Kikuko Ono, 2 June 1956, 2 d. Education: Tokyo Univ. Appointments: Prof, Intl Politics, Univ Tokyo, 1964-88; Prof, Peace Studies, Meiji Gakuin Univ, 1988-93; Snr Rsch Fell, Intl Christian Univ, Tokyo, 1993-96. Publications: Global Transformation; Asia: Militarization

and Regional Conflict; Democratizing Japan. Honours: Fulbright Grant, 1955-56; Rockefeller Fellshp, 1956-57; Eisenhower Fellshp, 1964; Spec Fell, UN Inst for Trng and Rsch, 1972-74; Mainichi Press Natl Book Awd, 1976. Memberships: Intl Peace Rsch Assn, sec-gen, 1979-83; Sci Cncl, Stockholm Intl Peace Rsch Inst, 1983-97. Address: 8-29-19 Shakujii-machi, Nerimaku, Tokyo 177-0041, Japan.

SAKER Ahmad, b. 17 May 1938. Diplomatist. m. Layla Hassan, 3 s, 1 d. Education: Damascus Univ; Govt Univ of Moscow. Appointments: Postings in Czechoslovakia Iran India Turkey USSR, 1966-75; Min Plenipotentiary min of For Affairs Damascus; Lectr in Polit Econ Damascus Higher Plng Inst, 1976-79; Perm Mission to UN Geneva, 1980-85; Dir Ams Div min of For Affairs, 1985-88; Amb Plenipotentiary and Extraordinary to Poland, 1988-93; Dir Africa Dept then Asia Dept min of For Affairs, 1993-95; Dir Asia Aust Dept, 1995-. Publications: Num articles on econ and polit affairs and human rights. Hobbies: Reading; Sports - esp swimming; Painting. Address: Adawi Inshaat Building 101, Apt 10, Damascus, Syria.

SAKTHIVEL Marimuthu, 8 July 1972, Paraipatty Village. Teaching; Research. m. Lalitha, 20 Oct 1972, 3 d. Education: BSc, Zool, Alagappa Coll, Karaikudi, 1966; MSc, Amn Coll, Madurai, 1969; MPhil, Thiyagarajar Coll, Madurai, 1986; PhD, Madurai Kamaraj Univ, Fish Physiology, 1990. Appointments: Demonstrator in Zool, 1971-73; Lectr in Zool, 1973-74; Asst Prof, Zool, 1974-82; Prof, Zool, 1982-; Principal, Department of Zool, Kamaraj Coll, Tuticorin, India. Publications: Ultimate Manual of Aquarium Fishes, 1995; Proceedings of Aquameet (w focus on ornamental fishes), 1997. Honours: Best Natl Serv Scheme Offr Awd, Tamil Nadu Govt, 1992-93. Memberships: Exec Mbrs, Prin's Assn, Tamilnadu. Hobbies: Yoga; Aquarium fish keeping; Music; Reading poems. Address: Principal, Kamaraj College, Tuticorin, Tamil Nadu, India.

SAKYA Manju Ratna, b. 1 June 1946, Kathmandu, Nepal. Journalist. m. Subha Luxmi, 1965, 1 s, 1 d. Education: Master Deg, Commerce, 1967. Appointments: Pres, Nepal Jrnlsts Assn; Chmn, Soc for Human Rights and Socl Justice. Publications: Many books on jrnlsm. Honour: Gorkha Dashin Bahu Second Class, Coronation Medal Finland Medal. Memberships: Pres, Nepal Jrnlsts Assn, 1979-. Hobby: Newspaper Reading. Address: Post Box No 285, Maitighar, Kathmandu, Nepal.

SALAAM Salim A, b. 9 Aug 1922. Airline Exec. m. Maha Mohamad Salaam, 1947, 2 s, 1 d. Education: Am Univ of Beirut; Harvard Univ. Appointments: Insp-Gen Middle East Airlines - MEA - 1948; Asst Mngr Airport, 1950; Mngr Ops, 1952; Gen Sales Mngr, 1957; Snr VP Intl Affairs, 1963; Gen Mngr Intl and Govt Affairs, 1977; Mngng Dir, 1981; Chmn of Bd and Pres, 1982; Chmn IATA, 1986-87. Honours: Al Kawkab decoration - Jordan; Egyptian Order of Merit; Grand Offr Natl Order of Cedar; Etc. Memberships: Mbr Bd MEA, 1981; Mbr Exec Cttee IATA. Hobbies: Big game hunting; Swimming; Shooting; Golf; Flying; Firearms collect. Address: MEA Headquarters, Beirut International Airport, P O Box 206, Airport Boulevard, Beirut, Lebanon.

SALAM Isam Mohamed Abdel, b. 20 Feb 1948, Omdurman, Sudan. Doctor; Consultant Surgeon. m. Gamar, 28 Aug 1980, 1 s, 3 d. Education: FRCS; MBBS. Appointments: Snr Cnslt Surgn, Al Ain Hosp; Cnslt Surgn, Gastroenterologist, Khartoum Hosp. Publications: Sev articles in profl jrnls. Memberships: Sudan Assn of Surgns, sec, 1985-88; Intl Coll of Surgns; SLS. Hobbies: Reading; Music; Sports; Bridge. Address: PO Box 1006, Al Ain Hospital, Al Ain, United Arab Emirates.

SALAS Henry Joseph, b. 30 Jan 1947, New York City, USA. Environmental Engineer. m. Mirna, 22 Oct 1991, 1 s. Education: Bach Deg, Civil Engrng, 1969; MSc, Environ Engrng, 1970. Appointments: Hydro Sci Co Inc, Westwood, NJ, USA, 1970-79; Environ Quality Bd, San Juan, 1979-82; Regl Advsr, Pan Amn Hlth Org, Lima, Peru, 1982-. Publications: Manual for the Evaluation and

Management of Toxic Substances in Surface Waters, 1988. Memberships: Amn Soc of Civil Engrs; Water Environ Fedn; Chi Episilon. Address: Malecon de la Reserva, 457/1102 Miraflores, Lima 18, Peru.

SALAS Margaret Laurence (Dame), b. 8 Feb 1922, Wellington, NZ. m. John Reuben Salas, 27 June 1946, 2 s, 4 d. Education: BA, Univ of NZ, 1942. Appointments: Tchr, 1942-43; Pres, Wellington Br, NZ Fedn Univ Women, 1970-72; Natl Sec, VP, Natl Cncl of Women, 1976-84; Audiometrist, 1978-; Med Sec, 1985-; Mbr, Aid Advsry Cttee, 1985-87; Mbr, Pub Advsry Cttee Disarmament Arms Control, 1987-95; Natl Pres, UN Assn, 1988-92; VP, NZ Inst of Intl Affairs, 1994-. Publication: Disarmament, 1982. Honours: Queen's Silver Jubilee Medal, 1977; QSO, 1982; DBE, 1988; Commemoration Medal, NZ, 1990. Memberships: VP, World Fedn UN Assns, 1993-; NZ Cttee, Cncl for Security and Cooperation in Asia and Pacific. Hobbies: Choral and classical music. Address: 2 Raumati Terrace, Wellington 4, New Zealand.

SALAWATI Ahmed, b. 7 Apr 1943, Mecca, Saudi Arabia. Consultant. 3 s, 2 d. Education: FACH ARZT in Primary Care. Career: Consultant of Primary Care, Allergolist, King Fahd Armed Forces Hospital, Saudi Arabia. Address: King Fahd Armed Forces Hospital, Jeddah 21159, P B 9862, Saudi Arabia.

SALDANHA Arnold Joseph, b. 3 Dec 1939, Bombay, India. Teacher. m. 2 s, Education: Licentiate Performer's Exam, Pianoforte, Trinity Coll of Music, London, 1956; BA, St Xavier's Coll, Bombay, India, 1965. Appointments: Gen Mngr, Furtados, 1965-66; Advsr Gen, 1966-75; Tchr, Kenya Conservatoire of Music, 1975; Dean of Studies, Kenya Conservatoire of Music, 1984-; Advsr, Western Music Sect of Kala Acady, Goa; Many performances. Memberships: UNESCO; Intl Music Acady; Goan Cultural Soc; Nairobi Inst; Nairobi Toastmaster's Assn. Address: G7 St Britto's Apartments, Feira Alta, Mapusa Bardez, Goa-403507, India.

SALEH Ali Abdulla, b. 1942, Beit Al Ahmar, Sanhan Region, Governate of Sana'a. Education: Armed Forces of the Yemen, NCO Sch, 1960; Armor Sch, 1964. Appointments: NCO, Warrent Offr, 1960-63, 2nd Lt, 1963; Wounded in action, one of heroes of 70 day siege of Sana'a; Mil Cmdr in posts: Dir, Armor Corps Arsenal; Commandant, Armor Co; Armor Battalion Staff Offr; Commandant Armor Battalion; Commandant, Armor Brigade, Mil Govr, Bab El Mandeb Reg; Commandant Taiz Governorate; Mbr of Provisional Republican Presidency Cncl, Dpty-in-Chf and Chf of Staffs of Armed Forces; Elected Pres of Repub, Cmdr-in-Chf of Armed Forces, 1978; Promoted to Full Col in recog of his efforts in dev of armed forces and gen security forces; Sec-Gen, People's Gen Congress, 1982; Re-elected Pres of Repub and Cmdr-in-Chf of Armed Forces, 1983; Re-elected for 3rd term by consultative assembly (Majles al Showra), 1988; Elected Chmn of Presdtl Cncl after reunification of Yemen, 1990, re-elected, 1993; Promoted to Gen, 1993; Elcted Pres of Repub of Yemen by Parl after amendments to constn, 1994. Honours include: Repub Awd for efforts and sacrifices for the country, People's Constituent Assembly.

SALEH Ali Abdullah, b. 1942. Politician; Army Offr. Appointments: Participated in 1974 coup; Mil Gov Taiz Prov until Jun 1978; Dep Cmdr-in-Chf of Armed Forces, Jun-Jul 1978; Cmdr-in-Chf of Armed Forces, Jul 1978-90; Pres of Yemen Arab Repub, 1978-90, 1990-94; Pres of Presdtl Cncl of Repub of Yemen, 1990-94; Pres of Repub of Yemen, 1994-. Address: Office of the President, Sana'a, Republic of Yemen.

SALGANIK Rafael Lev, b. 19 Mar 1934, Odessa. Mathematician. m. Zhukov Svetlana, 14 Mar 1958, 1 s, 1 d. Education: ME, Oil Inst, Moscow, 1957; MS, 1962, PhD, 1965, State Univ, Moscow; DSc, Inst for Problems in Mechs, USSR Acady of Scis, Moscow, 1972; Prof, USSR Supreme Ctf Commn, Moscow, 1984. Appointments: Engr, Engrng Bur, Moscow, 1957-61; Snr Rsch Sci, Inst for Mechs, State Univ, Moscow, 1961-74;

Chf Sci, Inst for Problems in Mechs, USSR Acady of Sci, Moscow, 1974-92; Rsch Prof, Tel Aviv Univ, 1992-94; Snr Rsch Sci, Cntr for Technol Educn, Holon, Israel, 1994-. Publications: Rock Pressure, textbook (co-auth), 1992; Contr, articles in profl jrnls. Memberships: Presidium Mbr, Israel Assn of Immigrant Scis; Bd of Eds, Theoretical and Appl Fracture Mechs jrnl. Address: Centre for Technological Education Holon, 52 Golomb Street, PO Box 305, Holon 58102, Israel.

SALIBA Holem Mansour, b. 25 Jan 1967, Bteghrine, Lebanon. Teacher; Researcher. Education: Maitrise, Maths, Univ of Lebanon, 1992; PhD, Mathl Logic and Number Theory, Moscow State Univ, 1997. Appointments: Asst Prof, Notre Dame Univ, Zouk Mosbeh, Lebanon. Publications: On the Mean Value of Ternary Function of Divisors on Sparse Sequences, 1997; Mathematical Logic and Two Verses From the New Testament, 1998. Address: Bteghrine, Mtn, Lebanon.

SALINAS DE GORTARI Carlos, b. 1948 Mexico Cty. Politician. Education: Natl Univ of Mexico; Harvard Univ. Appointments: Asst Prof of Stats Natl Univ of Mexico, 1970; Asst Dir of Pub Fin min of Fin, 1971-74; Hd of Econ Studies, 1974-76; Rsch Asst Harvard Univ, 1974; Taught Pub Fin and Fiscal Policy in Mexico, 1976, 1978; Asst Dir of Finl Plng, 1978; Dir-Gen, 1978-79; Dir-Gen of Econ and Socl Policy min of Progng and Budget, 1979-81; Dir-Gen Inst of Polit Socl and Econ Studies, 1981-82; Min of Plng and Fed Budget, 1982-87; Named as Presdtl Candidate by Partido Revolucionario Institucional - PRI - 1987; Pres of Mexico, 1988-94. Publications: Num articles and essays. Address: c/o Office of the President, Los Pinos, Puerta 1, Col San Miguel, Chapultepec, 11850 Mexico, DF, Mexico.

SALJUKI Javed, b. 7 Feb 1946, Rawalpindi, Pakistan. Electrical Engineer. Education: BS, Elec Engrng, Intl Univ MO, USA, 1983; Engrng Cncl's Part 1 Exam, UK, 1988. Appointments: Trainee Engr, 1983; Engr, 1984-99. Memberships: IEEE Inc, USA. Hobbies: Reading books; Photography; Playing cricket. Address: Flat no 1606, 1st Floor, Block 16, Phase 1, Plot 87, Defence Gardens, Defence Housing Authority, Karachi 75500, Pakistan.

SALLOUM Nasir Muhammad, b. 4 Nov 1936 Medina Saudi Arabia. Engr. Appointments: Res engr min of Comms, 1965; Hd of Study Dept min of Comms, 1965-68; Dep Min of Comms, 1976-96; Min of Transp, Aug 1996-. Memberships: Mbr Bd of Saudi Arabian Railways Authy. Hobbies: Reading; Travel. Address: Ministry of Transport, Airport Road, Riyadh, Saudi Arabia.

SALMAN IBN ABDUL AZIZ (HRH Prince), b. 13 Dec 1936. Politician. m. Appointments: Gov of Riydah, 1962-; Chmn Bd Riyadh Water and Sanitary Drainage Authy; Chmn num other orgs; Active in Abdul Aziz Fndn. Hobbies: Reading. Address: Office of the Governor, Riyadh, Saudi Arabia.

SALMON John Tenison, b. 28 June 1910, Wellington, NZ. Emeritus Professor. m. Pamela Naomi Wilton, 7 Dec 1948, 4 s. Education: BSc 1932, DSc 1945, Wellington Coll, Vic Univ of Wellington. Appointments: Entomologist and Photographer, Natl Mus of NZ, 1934-48; Snr Lectr, Bio, 1948-58, Assoc Prof of Zool, 1959-64, Acting Hd, Zool Dept, 1964-65, Prof of Zool & Hd of Dept 1965-75, Dean of Sci, 1971-72, Vic Univ of Wellington. Publications include: Heritage Destroyed, 1960; New Zealand Flowers and Plants in Colour, 1963; Field Guide to the Alpine Plants of New Zealand, 1968; Butterflies of New Zealand, 1968; The Native Trees of New Zealand, 1980; Collins Guide to the Alpine Plants of New Zealand, 1985; Field Guide to Native Trees of New Zealand, 1986. Memberships include: Cncl Mbr, Roy Soc of NZ, 1948-65; Pres, Entomological Soc of NZ, 1955-57; Pres, NZ, Geographical Soc, 1948; VP, 1948-49, Pres, 1949-50, NZ Assn of Scis; Pres, Wellington Camera Club, 1936-39, 1955-64; Ed, Roy Soc of NZ, 1953-65; Chmn, Roy Soc of NZ Conserv Cttee, 1955-58, 1962-65; Mbr, Nga Manuu Trust, 1974-; Chmn, 1974-79; Chmn, Conserv NZ, 1975-81; Cnclr, Waikanae Comm Cncl, 1977-83; Hon Assoc, Natl Mus of NZ, 1982-. Honours: FRES, 1937;

FRSNZ, 1949; Hon Mbr, Amn Entomologist Soc, 1959; FRPS, 1966; Hon Lectr, WEA Summer Schs, Napier 1971, Oamaru, 1975; CB, 1981; Nature Conservation Cncl Citation, 1982; NZ, 1990; NZ Commemoration Medal, 1990. Address: 9 Astelia Way, Taupo, New Zealand.

SALMON Nathan, b. 2 January 1951, Los Angeles, CA, USA. University Professor. div, 1 d. Education: BA, 1973, MA, 1974, CPhil, 1977, PhD, 1979, Univ CA Los Angeles. Appointments: Instr, UCLA p-t, 1976, 1977; Instr, CA State Univ, p-t, 1976-77; Lectr, CA State Univ Northridge, 1977-78; Asst Prof, Princeton Univ, 1978-82; Visng Snr Rsch Philos, Princeton Univ, 1982; Assoc Prof, Univ CA, Riverside, 1982-84; Santa Barbara, 1984-85; Prof, Univ CA, Santa Barbara, 1985-. Publications: 2 books; Co-ed, Propositions and Attitudes, 1988; 43 articles; On 7 editl and advsry bds; 41 speaking engagements. Honours: Gustave O Arlt Awd in Humanities, 1984; Fullbright Disting Prof Lecturing Grant, Yugoslavia, 1986; Disting Guest Speaker, 1987, Alberta Philos Conf, Banff, Alberta; Aristotelian Soc Speaker, London, England, 1988; One-Year Rsch Fell, Cntr for Adv Stdy in Behavioural Scis, Stanford, CA, 1989; Sev Travel and Rsch grants. Memberships: Am Philosl Assn; Bertrand Russell Soc; Phi Beta Kappa; Soc for Ethics, Hon Mem; Royal Inst of Philos, Hon Life Mem. Address: 1105 Orchid Drive, Santa Barbara, CA 93111, USA.

SALOKHE Vilas Mahadeo, b. 4 May 1951, India. Educator. m. Shobha, 26 July 1975, 1 s, 1 d. Doctor of Engineering. Appointments: Asst Prof, MPAV, Rahwi, India, 1975-80; Assoc Prof, 1980-96, Prof, 1996-, AIT, Bangkok. Honours: 14. Memberships: AAAE; ASAE; CSAM; JSAM: ISAE; ISTVS; ISTRO. Hobbies: Jogging; Watching TV; Reading. Address: AFE Program, Asian Institute of Technology, PO Box 4, Klang Luang, Pathunthani 12120, Thailand.

SALUJA Harish Kumar, b. 23 July 1971, Gurgaon, India. Cad Consultant. m. Moromi, 14 Dec 199. Education: BE, Mech; PGDBA; PGDMM; PGDFM. Appointments: Engr, Punsumi (I) Ltd, 1991-92; Asst Mngr, D&G, Sona Steering Syst Ltd, 1992-97; Consultancy, MD, Saluja, 1997-. Honours: Matric, 1985; IAPT Awd, 1997. Hobbies: Stamp Collection; Swimming; Travelling. Address: 2 Civil Lines Enclave, Civil Lines, Gurgaon 122001, India.

SAMANT Kamalakar, b. 6 June 1935, Bombay, India. Company Director. m. Shaila, 23 Feb 1964, 1 s, 1 d. Education: BCom, Hons; LLB; Fell, Inst of Chart Accts, India; Assoc, Indian Inst of Bankers. Appointments: Chf Mngr, Bank of India; Dir, AMAS UK Ltd, London, 1986-. Publications: Sev articles in newspprs and mags in Bombay, Hong Kong, London. Honours: Bombay State Awd, 1971; Sev Prizes in Bridge, Badminton and Table Tennis. Memberships: MCC, London; Matunga Gymkhana; Dadar Club; Garware Stadium. Hobbies: Reading; Travel; Writing. Address: 30 Regency Lodge, Swiss Cottage, London NW3 5EE, England.

SAMANT Shaila, b. 10 Aug 1940, Bombay, India. Civil Servant. m. K L Samant, 23 Feb 1964, 1 s, 1 d. Education: BSc; LLB. Appointment: Exec Offr, Home Off, Brit Civil Serv. Publications: Sev articles in profl mags. Honours: Sev Prizes in Bridge Competitions, Bombay, Singapore, Hong Kong, Cyprus, London. Memberships: MCC, London; Garware Stadium, Bombay. Hobbies: Reading; Cooking; Travel; Bridge; Swimming. Address: 30 Regency Lodge, Swiss Cottage, London NW3 5EE, England.

SAMBATHKUMAR S A, b. 16 Mar 1958, India. College Librarian. m. Andal, 13 Sept 1982, 1 s. Education: BSc, MA, Sociol; MA, Tami; BLIS; MLIS. Appointment: Senate Mbr, 1981; Bharathidasan Univ, 1995-98. Publications: 14 articles in profl jrnls. Memberships: Indian Lib Assn; Indian Assn of Spec Libs & Info Cntrs; Nadu Lib Assn. Hobby: Reading. Address: S.K.S.S. Arts College, Tirudanandal, Tamil Nadu 612504, India.

SAMBROOK Paul John, b. 13 Dec 1961, Eng. Oral and Maxillofacial Surgeon. m. Heather, 24 Mar 1990, 3 s, 1 d. Education: BDS, 1985, MDS, 1990, MBBS, Adelaide, 1993; FRACDS (Oms), 1990. Appointments: Snr Visng Cnslt, Roy Adelaide Hosp, 1994-; Asst Dir, Maxillofacial Surg Servs, 1996-; Snr Lectr, Univ of Adelaide, 1997-. Memberships: Austl Medl Assn; Intl Assn OMFS; Austl Dental Assn; Asian Assn OMFS; Aust and NZ OMFS, Sec Eect, Bd Mbr, RACDS. Hobby: Computing. Address: 1 Hutt Street, Adelaide, SA 5000, Australia.

SAMETHANAHALLI Rama Rao, b. 24 Nov 1917, Samethanahalli. Retired Senior Health Inspector. m. Pankajakshamma, 11 June 1941, 2 s, 2 d. Appointments: Snr Hlth Inspector, Pub Hlth Servs, Govt of Karnataka, India. Publications: Plays, novels, opera, epic poems, short stories incl: (histl novel) Yaduvodeya, 1981; (rsch novel) Shri Krishnadarshana, 1987; (histl novel) Monegara, 1989; (autobiography) Kotename, 1991; (rsch novel) Shriparashurama, 1993; (collection of short stories) Eesabeku, 1993; (collection of poems) Udayodyana, 1993; (collection of plays) Shrikrishna Manasa, 1994; (socl novel), Vikasa, 1997; (histl novel) Attimabbe, 1998. Honours: Lit awds incl Kannada Sahitya Parishnath Bangalore, for Shrikrishnadarshana, 1987; Sir M Visweswaraaya Mem Fndn, Bangalore, 1994; Monthly honorarium for life, granted by Govt of Karnataka, recognition as Poet Laureate of Karnataka State, 1976. Memberships: Life Mbr, Kannada Sahitya Parisnath, Bangalore; Pres, Mandya Dt Kannada Sahitya Parishath. Hobbies: Reading; Writing. Address: 518, Kotemane, Fourth Main Road, Gokula Third Stage, Mysore 570002, India.

SAMPATHACHARY K, b. 3 Sept 1943. Documentation Officer. m. K Hari Priya, 27 Feb 1965, 2 s, 1 d. Education: BSc; MLISc; Pre PhD; Cert P French. Appointments: Asst Libn, 1966-69; Libn, 1969-75; Snr Libn, 1975-83; Documentation Offr, 1983-. Publications: Publ over 15 pprs in Lib Sci Jrnls and Proceedings of Lib Assns in India; Ed, sev Documentation Bulletins in Nutrition. Honours: Worked as Rapporteur-Gen, MLAI Confs, Ahmedabad, 1991, New Delhi, 1993; Man of the Awd, 1996; MLAI-S J Kulkarni Awd, 1997. Memberships: MLAI, New Delhi; NSI, Hyderabad; EC Member, MLAI, 1992-96; ALSD, 1989-90; Life Mbr, IATLIS, Hyderabad, SIS, New Delhi. Listed in: 500 Leaders of Influence. Hobbies: Playing Carroms; Gardening; Watching TV. Address: A-7 Quarter, NIN Campus, National Institute of Nutrition, Taranaka, Hyderabad 500 007, India.

SAMPATHKUMARAN E V, b. 6 Dec 1954, Kavanur, TN, India. Scientist. m. Sujatha, 4 Feb 1983, 2 s. Education: PhD. Appointments: Fell, Rdr, Assoc Prof, Prof, Tata Inst of Fundamental Rsch. Honours: INSA Medal for Young Scientist, 1986; MRST Medal, 1996; Fell, Indian Acady of Scis, 1998. Memberships: Fell, Indian Acady of Scis, Bangalore. Hobby: Music. Address: Department of Condensed Matter Physics & Materials Science, Tata Institute of Fundamental Research, Homi Bhabha Road, Mumbai 400 005, India.

SAMSON Stephen Rajan, b. 2 June 1951, Kackottumoola, Mayyanad, India. Free-Lance Writer. m. Annaamma, 27 Oct 1985, 1 s. 1 d. Education: BA Hons Econ, 1974, Univ Bombay. Appointments: Gandhi Peace Fndn, Delhi; Tech Aluminii Industries, Ajman; UAE, USSR Book Centre, New Delhi. Publications: Fettered Verse, 1995; My Mango Tree, 1995, 1996; Situations Vacant, 1997; On a Rainy Night, Poems '96, an anthology; One Word, Poems '97, an anthology; Deep and Dark, Wonderlust, an anthology, 1998; Father, Skylark Aligarh, 1983; Love Alighar, 1998; Various articles. Membership: Writers Forum, Ranchi. Hobbies: English cinema; Cricket; Travel. Address: Pavel Purayidom House, Kackottumoola, Mayyanad PO, Kollam, 691 303, Kerala India.

SAMUDIO Jeffrey B. Cultural Resource Planner; Architectural Historian; Educator. Education: BArch, MArch, Master Deg, Urban and Regl Planning, Univ S CA. Appointments include: VP, Acquisitions and Proj Dev, NE Des and Dev Grp Inc, 1989-90; Pres, 1993-96,

Chair, Advsry Bd, 1996-97, Soc of Arch Histn, S CA Chapt; Dir, Fndr, Cntr for Preservation Educ and Plng, 1994-; Ptnr, Des AID, Arch Plng Preservation, 1987-. Publications: Sev articles in profl jrnls. Honours include: Ctf of Appreciation, Cty of Los Angeles Richard Alatorre, 1989; Phi Kappa Phi Rsch Mentorship Awd, Univ S CA Grad Sch, 1991; Outstndng Serv to the Profession Awd, Pasadena and Foothill Chapt AIA, 1991; Los Angeles Conservancy Hist Preservation Awd, 1995; Awd of Hon, Amn Inst of Archts. Memberships: Amn Inst of Archts, Pasadena Chapt; Amn Plng Assn, Los Angeles Sect; Soc of Archl Histns; Los Angeles City Histl Soc; Intl Cttee on Monuments and Sites; Natl Preservation Forum of the Natl Trust for Historic Preservation; Los Angeles Conservancy; Assn for Preservation Technol. Address: Design Aid Architects, Whitley Court, 1722 North Whitley Avenue, Hollywood, CA 90028, USA.

SAMUEL Geoffrey Brian, b. 22 Nov 1946, Leeds, Eng. University Lecturer. Education: MA, Nat Sci, Oxford, Eng; PhD, Socl Anthropology, Cambridge, 1975; Conducted field rsch in Nepal, India, Tibet, 1971-. Appointments: Dept of Socl Anthropology, Univ of Manchester, Eng, 1972-73; Dept of Anthropology, Univ of Otago, NZ, 1973-76; Sch of Hums, Griffith Univ, Aust, 1977; Dept of Sociol, Univ of Newcastle, NSW, 1978-; Prof of Relig Studies, Lancaster Univ, Eng, 1995-97; Prof of Anthropology, Univ of Newcastle, NSW, 1998-. Publications: Songs of Lhasa, 1976; Mind, Body and Culture, 1990; Civilized Shamans, 1993; Nature Religions Today, 1998. Memberships: Soc for Ethnomusicology; AAA; RAI; Austl Anthropological Soc; Amn Acady of Religion; Asian Studies Assn of Aust. Address: Department of Sociology and Anthropology, University of Newcastle, NSW 2308, Australia.

SAMUELS Gordon (Jacob), b. 12 Aug 1923. Governor of New South Wales. m. Jacqueline Kott, 1957, 2 d. Education: Univ Coll, London; MA, Balliol Coll, Oxford, Eng. Appointments: Served in war, 1942-46; Capt, 96th Roy Devon Yeomanry, Field Regt, RA; Called to Bar, 1948; Tchng Fell, Jurisp, Sydney Univ Law Sch, 1952-56; QC, NSW, 1964, Vic, 1965; Challis Lectr in Pleading, Sydney Univ Law Sch, 1964-70; Judge, Supreme Crt of NSW, 1972-92; Crt of Appeal, 1974-92; Indep Arbitrator, Ref and Mediator, 1992-96; Gov of NSW, 1996-. Honours: AC, 1987; Hon LLD, Sydney, 1994; Hon DSc, NSW, 1994. Memberships: Pres, Austl Security Appeals Tribunal, 1980-90; NSW Migrant Employment and Qualifications Bd, 1989-95, Chmn, 1992-95; Chairman: Law Reform Commn of NSW, 1993-96, Mediator Accreditation Bd, Austl Coml Disputes Cntr, 1994-96; Snr Commnr, Commn of Inquiry into Austl Secret Intelligence Serv, 1994-94; Pres, NSW Bar Assoc, 1971-72, Acad of Forencic Scis, 1974-76, Austl Soc of Legal Phil, 1976-79; Chan, Univ of NSW, 1976-94; Bd of Govs, Law Fndn of NSW, 1992-94, Chmn, 1992-93. Hobbies: Reading; Music; Theatre. Address: Office of the Governor, Macquarie Street, Sydney, NSW 2000, Australia.

SAMUELS Leonard Ernest, b. 28 Feb 1922, Brisbane, Qld, Aust. Metallurgical Consultant. m. Patricia Mary Barry, 29 Nov 1947, 2 s. Education: Bach, Metall Engrng, 1942; DSc, 1959. Appointments: Jnr Metallurgist, 1942, Rsch Sci, 1943, Prin Rsch Sci, 1953, Supt, Metall Divsn, 1962, Chf Supt, 1981-83, Materials Rsch Labs, Austl Dept of Def; Currently Cnslt. Publications: Metallurgical Polishing by Mechanical Method, 1967, 3rd ed, 1981; Light Microscopy of Carbon Steels, 1980, 2nd ed, 1999; Metals Engineering: A Technical Guide, 1988; Over 80 pprs in tech and sci publns. Honours: David Syme Rsch Prize and Medal, 1958; Silver Medal, Austl Inst of Metals, 1972; Awd of Merit, Profl Offrs Assn, 1978; Sorby Awd, Intl Metallographic Soc, 1980; AM, 1982. Memberships: Fell, Austl Acady of Technol Scis and Engrng; Fell, Inst of Engrs of Aust; Fell ASM Intl, Intl Metallographic Soc. Hobbies: Gardening; Photography; Archaeometallurgy. Address: 30 Eildon Road, Ashwood, Vic 3147, Australia.

SAMUELS Stephen Edmund, b. 17 May 1949, Sydney, Australia. Research and Consulting Engineer. m.

Lyndell, 22 Mar 1997, 2 s, 1 d. Education: BE; MEngSci; PhD. Appointments: Rsch and Cnsltng Engr, Oslan Cnsltng; Snr Lectr, Univ of NSW; Acoustical and Environmental Cnslt; Prin Rsch Sci, Austl Rd Rsch Bd. Publications: Auth, over 100 publs, 1972-98; Conf and jrnl pprs, articles, rsch reports. Memberships: Fell, Inst of Engrs Aust, 1994; Austl Acoustical Soc, 1976; Acoustical Soc of Am, 1982. Hobbies: Playing tennis and golf; Surfing; Watching test cricket. Address: 2/85-87 Kurnell Road, Cronulla, NSW 2230, Australia.

SANBERK H E Ozdem, b. 1 Aug 1938 Istanbul. Diplomatist. m. Sumru Sanberk, 1 d. Education: Univ of Istanbul. Appointments: Fmrly at Embs in Bonn, Paris, Madrid, Amman; Fmr For Policy Advsr to PM Turgut Ozal; Fmr Perm Under-Sec to Min of For Affairs: Fmr Amb to EU; Amb to London, 1995-. Address: Turkish Embassy, 43 Belgrave Square, London, SW1X 8PA, England.

SANCAR M Sitki, b. 8 Oct 1941, Gemlik. Pet Exec. m. Ayse Sancar, 1968, 1 s, 1 d. Education: Univ of Istanbul; Univ Tulsa OK. Appointments: Well site geol Turkish Pet Co - TPAO - 1967-70; Rsch Geol and Dist Mngr, 1974-79; Gen Dir MTA-Mineral Rsch & Exploration Inst of Turkey, 1979-88; Dep Under-Sec min of Energy, 1988-93; Chmn and Gen Mngr TPAO, 1993-. Publications: Sev sci papers. Honours: Hon mbr Chamber of Pet Engrs of Turkey. Address: TPPAO, M Kemal Mah 2 Cad 86, 06520 Ankara, Turkey.

SANDS Donald Peter Andrew, b. 13 Aug 1937. Retired Research Scientist. m. Susan Ann Sands, 1 s, 1 d. Appointmemts: CSIRO, Div of Entomology, 1967-. Publications: Book: A Revision of the Genus Hypochrysops, C & R Felder, 1986. Honours: UNESCO sci prize (shared), 1985; AIDAB for Excellence in Overseas Dev (shared) 1988; Eureka Prize (shared pol prize), 1990. Memberships: Entomological Soc of Queensland, 1963-, pres, 1982-; Austl Entomological Soc, 1965-. Hobby: Entomology. Address: CSIRO, Divison of Entomology, Private Bag 3, Indooroopilly, Qld, Australia.

SANGMA Shri P A, b. 1 Sep 1947 Chapahati Village W Garo Hills Dist. Polit; Lawyer. m. Soradini K Sangma, 1973, 2 s, 2 d. Education: Dalu High Sch; St Anthony's Coll; Shillong and Dibrugarh Univ. Appointments: Dep Min min of Ind, 1980-82; Dep Min min of Com, 1982-85; Min of State for Com, 1985-86; Min for Home Affairs, 1986; Min of State - Indep Charge - for Labour, 1986-88; Chf Min Meghalaya State, 1988-90; Min of State - Indep Charge - for Coal, 1991-95; Also for Labour, 1993-95; Min of Info and Brdcstng, 1995-96; Speaker Lok Sabha, 1996-; Deleg to var intl confs. Memberships: Mbr Lok Sabha, 1977-79, 1980-84, 1985-89, 1991-; Mbr Congress. Hobbies: Reading; Discussion; Music; Indoor Games. Address: Lok Sabha, New Delhi 110001, India.

SANJEL Uma Nath, b. 18 July 1959, Nepal. Financial Controller. Education: BBA, MBA, BLL, Tribhuvan Univ, Nepal. Appointments: Admin cum Accts Offr, 1983-84; Pt-time Lectr, Acctcy and Tax Subjs, Ratna Jyoti Multiple Campus, 1985-89; Pt-time Lectr, Acctcy and Mngmt Subjs, Kavre Mulitple Campus, 1985-89; Internal Auditor, HMG/Nepal, Min of Ind, Bhaktapur B Factory Ltd, 1984-90; Finl Controller and Dpty Dir, HR/OD, Plng, Budgeting, Fin and Admin Depts, HMG/Nepal, Min of Educ, Cncl for Tech Educ and Vocational Trng, 1990-95; Finl Controller, Admin and Fin Dept, ActionAid, Nepal, 1996-; Worked in UK and Kenya in ActionAid's intl proj as team mbr, mid 1997, early 1998. Address: c/o ActionAid Nepal, PO Box No 6257, Kathmandu, Nepal.

SANKU Sarath Chandar Rao, b. 30 Mar 1960, Hyderabad, India. Firmware Engineer. m. Jeevarani Angelina, 21 Aug 1987, 2 s. Education: BS Engrng, REC Kurvkshetra, India; MTech & PhD, IIT Madras, India; Dip (Japanese), Osaka Univ For Studies, Japan. Appointments: Asst Mngr, Praga Tools Ltd, 1986; Firmware Dev Engr, Yokogawa Precision Corp, Tokyo, 1991-. Honours: Natl Govt Schlshp, India, 1975; Monbusho Schlshp, Japan, 1989-91. Memberships:

ASME, 1994-. Hobbies: Sketching; Reading; Computers, Travel. Address: 201, Kangin Mansion, 2-9-3, Seki-Mae, Musashino Shi, Tokyo 180-0014, Japan.

SANTEE Dale William, b. 28 Mar 1953, Washington, USA. Lawyer; Air Force Officer. m. 1 child. Education: BA, WA and Jefferson Coll, 1975; MA, Univ N AZ, 1982; JD, Univ Pitts, 1978. Appointments include: Floor Mngr, Commn Salesman, J C Penney Co, WA, 1971-76; Asst Mngr, Rach Enterprises, Charleroi, PA, 1977-78; Legal Intern, WA Cnty Pub Defender; Commd, 2nd Lt, USAF, 1979, Adv through grades to Lt Col, 1996; Asst Staff Judge Advocate to Area Def Cnsl, Luke Air Force Base, AZ, 1979-81; Claims Offr, 343 Combat Support Grp, Judge Advocate, Eielson AFB, Alaska, 1981-83; Snr Staff Legal Advsr, Dept of Vet Affairs, WA, 1983-89; Asst Staff Judge Advocate, Mil Justice Divsn, Air Force Judge Advocate Gen's Off, Wash DC, 1986-89; 63CSG/Judge Advocate, Norton Air Force Base, CA, 1989-91; Dpty Pub Defender, Juvenile Divsn, San Diego Cnty, 1990-93; Dpty Alt Pub Defender, 1993-98; Supervising AHY Conflict Parent-Child Office, Alt Pub Defende:, 1998-. Honours include: Air Force Commendation Medal, 1981, 1989; Air Force Meritorious Serv Medal, 1991, 1996, 1999; 4th Air Force Atty of the Yr, 1997; US Air Force Reserve Cmnd Atty of the Yr, 1997; Dale Ray Awd, 1998. Memberships: PA Bar Assn; CA Bar Assn; San Diego Bar Assn; San Diego Cnty Psych-Law Soc. Hobbies: Swimming; Softball; Stamp and Coin Collecting; Foreign Travel. Address: 1156 Corrales Lane, Chula Vista, CA 91910-7956, USA.

SANTOSO Budi, b. 16 Aug 1946, Yogyakarta, Indonesia. Expert Staff to the National Security and Defence Council. m. Princess Sri Kusaladewi Hamengkubuwono IX, 27 Feb 1982, 2 s. Education: Grad in Phys, Gajah Mada Univ, 1970; MSc, Phys, 1971, PhD, Theoretical Phys, 1973, Essex Univ, England. Appointments Hd of Atomic & Nuclear Phys, Yogyakarta Nuclear Rsch Cntr, 1974-86 Dir, Nuclear Technol Assessment Cntr, 1986-; Atomic Energy Agcy of Indonesia, 1986-; Proj Co-ord. Publications: Var in fields of atomic, nuclear and reactor phys and lasers, inclng: On the Born Series (w A R Holt), 1974; Some Observed Effects on the Nitrosil Ruthenium Complexes Irradiated by Laser, 1981; Technology of Carbon Dioxide Laser, 1985; Study on Isotope Separation Using the Laser Techniques, 1986 A Modified Second Born Approximation in Scattering by Spherically Symmetrical Central Potentials, 1986 Potential Models in Nuclear Scatterings, 1986; Early History of Reactor Physics Potential Interactions Between Water Microemulsions in Oil, 1987. Honours: Awd, Obtaining Highest Rank in hs Exam, Indonesian Inst of Scis; Awd, Phys Tchng, Indonesia Mil Acady, 1968; PhD Schlsp, Brit Cncl Colombo Plans Awd, 1970-73. Memberships: Indonesian Physl Soc; Am Physl Soc, 1979; Indonesian Nuc Med Soc; Assoc Mbr, Intl Cntr for Theort Phys, Trieste, 1983-90; Verification Bd for Rschrs in Atomic Energy Agcy, Indonesia, 1975-; Rsch Prof (APU) in Phys. Hobbies: Old Javanese Arts, such as Keris, Spear; Chess. Address: Atomic Energy Agency of Indonesia, PO Box 85 Kby, Jakarta 12710, Indonesia.

SANTRY Michel John, b. 21 May 1934. Artist; Designer. 2 adopted s. Appointments: Archtl Draughtsman, 2 yrs; Scenic Artist on 37 stage shows for Elizabethian Th J C Williamson, Borovansky Ballet and other grps; 2 feature films, 1 Treasure Island; 6 yrs w ABC Channel 2 in TV Design Dept. Creative Works: Over 300 artistic comms, 1957-: Sculptures, murals, mosaics, ceramics, tapestries, glass and kinetic works, located in art cntrs, chs, pub bldngs, shopping cntrs, univ; Selected Commissioned Works include: Barbican Arts and Conference Centre, London, 1980; Victorian Arts Centre, Melbourne, 1982; Xiyuan Hotel, Beijing, China, 1984; Peninsular Hotel Annex, 1986; Natl Aust Bank House, Sydney, 1985; The C & L Tower (Coopers & Lybrand), Sydney, 1986; Tapestries and Sculptures Wrk, Pacific Place, Swire Properties, Cntrl, Hong Kong, 1988; Devon House, Swire Properties, Quarry Bay, Hong Kong, 1993; Dorset House, Swire Properties, Quarry Bay, Hong Kong, 1995; 4 relief sculptures, Harbourfront Towers, Hong Kong, 1995; 2 large relief sculptures, J W Marriott Hotel, Hong Kong, 1996; 9-storey sculpture, Hong Kong Convention and Exhibn Cntr, 1997; Sculpture, Chek Lap Kok Airport, Hong Kong, 1998. Memberships: Chelsea Arts Club, London, Eng; Queens Club, Real Tennis, London, Eng. Hobbies: Chess; Squash; Tennis. Address: PO Box 41, Hunters Hill, NSW 2110, Australia.

SANYAL Nilanjana, b. 21 Sept 1954. Academician; Postgraduate Psychology Teacher. m. 14 May 1983, 2 s. Education: BA, Hons, Psychol; MA, Psychol; PhD, Psychol. Appointments: Snr Prof Asst, Indian Inst of Mngmt, Calcutta, 1982-83; Lectr, Dept of Psychol, Calcutta Univ, 1983-88; Snr Lectr, Dept of Psychol, CU, 1988-94; Rdr, Dept of Psychol, 1993, Hd of Dept, 1997, Calcutta Univ. Publications: 32 sci articles in different natl and intl jrnls of psychol; 18 popular articles in psychol publd in important newspprs and mags, Calcutta. Honours: Bhanu Dutta Mem Medal from Calcutta Univ, 1974; Jubilee Merit Prize, Indian Govt, 1974; Jawaharlal Nehru Awd from India Govt, 1974; N N Sengupta Mem Prize from Alumni Assn of Calcutta Univ, 1975; Gold Medal, Calcutta Univ, 1976; Suhashini Basu Meml Prize, Indian Psychoanalytical Soc, 1992. Hobbies: Academic research; Photography. Address: Greenview, 119 Dr Meghnad Saha Sarani, 8th Floor, North West Calcutta 70029, India.

SANYAL Pradosh, b. 8 Feb 1951, Kanpur, India. Researcher; Teacher. m. Deepannita, 27 Jan 1981, 1 s. Education: MS (Chem); PhD (Chem). Appointments: Technol Assistance to Govt of India in field of sugar and allied inds (in Natl Sugar Inst, Kanpur, India). Publications: Num rsch pprs in natl & intl jrnls. Honours: Many cash awds from natl and intl jrnls for publs. Memberships: Sugar Technol Assn of India. Hobby: Applied research in the field of sugar. Address: 186(1) 5A, Bairi, Bithoor Road, Kalyanpur, Kanpur, India, PIN 208017.

SAOUMA Edouard, b. 6 Nov 1926 Beirut. Intl Offic; Agricl Engr. m. Ines Forero, 1 s, 2 d. Education: St Joseph's Univ Sch of Engrng Beirut; Ecole natl Superieure d'Agronomic Montpellier France. Appointments: Dir Tel Amara Agricl Sch, 1952-53; Dir Natl Cntr for Farm Mechanization, 1954-55; Sec-Gen Natl Fed of Lebanese Agronomists, 1955; Dir-Gen Natl Inst for Agricl Rsch, 1957-62; Lebanese deleg to FAO, 1955-62; Dep Regl Rep for Asia and Far East, 1962-65; Dir Land and Water Devt Div, 1965-75; Dir-Gen of FAO, 1976-93; Min of Agric Fisheries and Forestry, Oct-Nov 1970. Publications: Tech publs in agric. Honours: Hon Prof of Agronomy Agricl Univ of Beijing; Accademico Corrispondente dell' Accademia Nazionale di Agricoltura - Italy; Dr hc from 16 univs; Order of the Cedar - Lebanon; Said Akl Prize - Lebanon; Chevalier du Merite agricole - France; Grand Croix Ordre natl du Tchad du Ghana de la Haute Volta - Burkina Faso; Gran Cruz al Merito Agricola - Spain; Kt Cmdr Order of Merit - Greece; Orden del Merito Agricola - Colombia; Gran Oficial del Orden de Vasco Nunez de Balboa - Panama; Orden al Merito Agricola - Peru; Order of Merit - Egypt Mauritania; Grand Offr Ordre de la Repub - Tunisia; Grand Offr Ordre Nal - Madagascar. Memberships: Mbr Govng Bd Natl Grains Off, 1960-62; Mbr of Sec, 1963-. Address: P O Box H0210, Baabda, Lebanon.

SARA Vicki R, b. 19 Sept 1946. Education: BA, (1st Class Hons), Univ Sydney, 1969; Grad, Fac of Sci - Physiology, Univ of Sydney, 1971; PhD, 1974; Docent in Expmntl Psychoendocrinology, Fac of Med, Karolinska Inst, Stockholm, 1981. Appointments: Snr Rsch Offr, Natl Hlth & Medl Rsch Cncl, Garvan Inst Medl Rsch, Sydney, 1973-76; Snr Rsch Offr, Gravan Inst Medl Rsch, St Vincent's Hosp, Sydney, 1976-77; IBRO/UNESCO Fell, Karolinska Inst Dept Psych, St Göran's Hosp, Stockholm, Sweden, 1977-79; Rsch Fell, Karolinska Inst's Dept of Psych, 1980; Assoc Prof, 1981, Acting Prof, 1982, Expmntl Psychoendocrinology, Karolinska Inst; Spec Rsch Position in Hormonal Regulation of Growth, Karolinska Hosp's Rsch Cntr, 1987; Hd, Endocrine Path Rsch Unit, Karolinska Inst's Dept Path, 1987-92; Prof and Hd, Sch Life Sci, Qld Univ of Technol, Brisbane, Aust, 1993-96; Dir, Co-op Rsch Cntr for Diagnostic Technols, Qld Univ Technol, 1995-; Adj Prof, Karolinska Inst, 1995-; Dean, Fac of Sci, Qld Univ of Technol, 1996-97; Austl Rsch Cncl, 1997-. Publications include: 4 patents; 150 pprs in med and sci jrnls; 72 abstracts. Honours: Num grants, awds incl: Swedish Cancer Soc, 1992-95; Dr Med Letten F Saugstad's Fund, 1993-95; Rolf Luft Medal, 1993; Sir John Eccles Awd, 1994; Austl Rsch Cncl Large Grant, 1994-96; Coop Rsch Cntr for Diagnostic Technols, Cwlth of Aust, 1995-2002. Memberships: NY Acady Sci; AAAS; Intl Brain Rsch Org; Endocrine Soc of Aust; Endocrine Soc of Am; Swedish Endocrine Soc; Cancer Soc in Stockholm (elected); Austl Soc for Medl Rsch. Hobby: Sailing. Address: Australian Research Council, GPO Box 9880, Canberra, ACT 2601, Australia.

SARABHAI Mrinalini, b. 11 May 1918 Madras. Dancer; Chgph. m. Dr Vikram A Sarabhai, 1 s, 1 d. Education: Studied under Meenakshi Sundaram Pillai. Appointments: Fndr-Dir Darpana Acady of Performing Arts Ahmedabad, 1949; Chmn Handicrafts & Handloom Devt Corp of Gujarat State; Chmn Friends of Trees Gujarat State; Pres Alliance Francaise; Pres Exec Cttee Intl Dance Cncl, 1990; Advsr to many arts and cultural insts in India. Publications: Staging a Sanskrit Classic - Bhasa's Vision of Vasavadatta - with John D Mitchell - 1992; One novel; Textbook on Bharata Natyam; A book on var classical dance-dramas; Children's books; Articles in newspapers and jrnls. Honours: Vishwa Gurjari Awd, 1984; Deshikothama Awd - Vishwa Bharati Univ Shantiniketan - Awd, 1987; Fell'ship Awd Kerala Acady of Arts, 1990; Hon Summus Awd - Watumull Fndn - 1991; First Hall of Fame Awd for lifelong service to dance, 1991; Vijay Shri Awd - Intl Friendship Soc of India - 1991; Pandi Omkarnath Thakur Awd - Gujarat Govt - 1991; Pres Awd of Padmabhushan, 1992; Raseshwaar Awd, 1992; Fell Sangeet Ntak Akademi, 1994; Kerala Kalamandalam Fell'ship, 1995; Scroll of Honour for wrk in dance and chgh, 1995; Kalidas Samman Awd, 1996. Address: Darpana Academy of Performing Arts, Usmanpura, Ahmedabad 380013, Gujarat, India.

SARAH Peter John, b. 7 Aug 1946, WA. Arts Administrator. Education: Scotch Coll Perth; Univ of WA; Univ of London, BA; MPhil; LRAM; ARCM; FRSA. Appointments: Asst Dir - Touring and Devt - WA Arts Cncl, 1977-81; Gen Mngr Arts Cncl of SA, 1981-85; Dir Arts and Entertainment Austl Bicentennial Authy, 1985-89; Chf Exec Contemporary Dance Trust, 1990-94; Chf Exec The Year of Opera and Music Theatre, 1995-97; Gen Mgnr, Theatre Royal, Newcastle upon Tyne, 1998-; Tstee Acady of Indian Dance. Hobbies: Sailing; Arch. Address: 10 Mall Chambers, Kensington Mall, London, W8 4DY, England.

SARALINOV Marat, b. 19 May 1941, Bishkek, Kyrgyz. Diplomat. m. Tinatin, 6 Feb 1964, 1 s, 1 d. Education: Grad, Kyrgyz State Univ; Grad, Dipl Acady of USSR. Appointments: Vice Consul, 1st Sec, Emb of USSR to Egypt, 1974-81; Consul of USSR in Nigeria, 1986-91; 1st Dpty Min, MFA of Kyrgyz Repub, 1991-93; Gen Consul, KR to Hong Kong, 1994; Amb Extraordinary and Plenipotentiary, KR to China, 1996-, & to Mongolia, 1997-. Honours: Govtl medals & decorations. Hobbies: Literature; Music. Address: Embassy of the Kyrgyz Republic.

SARANDON Susan Abigail, b. 4 Oct 1946 NY. Actress. m. (1) Chris Sarandon, 1967, div, 1 s, 1 d; 1 s with Tim Robbins - qv. Education: Catholic Univ of Am. Appointments: Stage appearances incl: A Coupla White Chicks Sittin' Around Talkin'; An Evening with Richard Nixon; A Stroll in the Air; Albert's Bridge; Private Ear; Public Eye; Extremities; Num tv appearances. Films incl: Joe, 1970; Lady Liberty, 1971; The Rocky Horror Picture Show, 1974; Lovin' Molly, 1974; The Great Waldo Pepper, 1975; The Front Page, 1976; Dragon Fly, 1976; Walk Away Madden; The Other Side of Midnight, 1977; The Last of the Cowboys, 1977; Pretty Baby, 1978; King of the Gypsies, 1978; Loving Couples, 1980; Atlantic City, 1981; Tempest, 1982; The Hunger, 1983; Buddy System, 1984; Compromising Positions, 1985; The Witches of Eastwick, 1987; Bull Durham, 1988; Sweet Hearts Dance,

1988; Married to the Mob; A Dry White season, 1989; The January Man, 1989; White Palace; Thelma and Louise, 1991; Light Sleeper, 1991; Lorenzo's Oil; The Client; Little Women, 1995; Safe Passage, 1995; Dead Man Walking,1996; James and the Giant Peach, 1996. Honours: Acady Awd for Best Actress for Dead Man Walking, 1996. Address: c/o ICM, Martha Luttrell, 8942 Wilshire Boulevard, Beverly Hills, CA 90211, USA.

SARANIN Alexander Peter, b. 9 Sept 1921, USSR. Chemical Engineer. m. Barbara Martin, 1 Mar 1980, 2 s. Education: BEng, Univ L'Aurore, Shanghai, China, 1944; Dip, Sugar Technol, 1953, MEng, 1963, PhD, 1986, Univ of Qld, Aust. Appointments: Chem Engr, Shanghai, China, 1946-51; Sugar Chem, 1952-53; Rsch Technologist, 1953-64; Chf Technologist, 1965-70; Technologist Mbr, CSCPB, 1970-86, Qld, Aust. Publications: Autobiog, Child of the Kulaks, 1997; 25 tech pprs on Sugar, Ethanol and Rum Technol. Honours: Austl Soc of Sugar Cane Technologists Pres Medal, 1955; Gertrude Kumm Awd, 1959. Memberships: Austl Soc of Sugar Cane Technologists; Intl Soc of Sugar Cane Technologists; Austl Inst of Food Sci Technol; Fell, Roy Austl Chem Inst; Fell, Inst of Engrs (Aust). Hobbies: Tennis; Swimming; Bushwalking; Oil Painting; Reading. Address: 10 Launceston Street, Salisbury, Qld 4107, Australia.

SARASIN Arsa, b. 1936. Diplomatist. Education: Boston Univ. Appointments: Perm Sec min of For Affairs until 1986; Amb to USA, 1986-88; Min of For Affairs, 1991-92; Fmr PM of Thailaind -qv. Address: c/o Ministry of Foreign Affairs, Saranrom Palace, Bangkok 10200, Thailand.

SAREL Sir Alexis Holyweek, b. 25 Mar 1934 Buka. Diplomatist; Ecclesiastic. m. Claire Dionne, 1972, 3 s, 3 d, - all adopted. Education: Univ. Appointments: Roman Catholic Priest, 1966-71; Priv Sec to Chf Min, 1972-73; Dist Commnr, 1973-75; Warden Univ of Papua New Guinea, 1972; Premier N Solomons Prov Govt, 1976-80; High Commnr in UK - also Amb to other Eurn and Middle Eastern Cos - 1980-83; Perm Rep to UN and Amb to USA, 1983-86; Succeeded uncle as Chf of Petisuun Clan. Publication: The Practice of Marriage Among the Solos, 1974. Honours: Papua New Guinea Independence Medal. Hobbies: Music; All sports; Writing letters; Swimming; Hunting. Address: 8039 Adoree Street, Downey, CA 90242, USA.

SARIG Yoav, b. 27 July 1937, T Aviv, Israel. Agricultural Engineer. m. Benjamin, 13 June 1961, 1 s, 1 d. Education: BSc, Agric Engrng; MSc, Agric Engrng; PhD, Agric Angrng. Appointments: Snr Rsch Scientist, 1965-83; Dpty Dir, ARO, 1983-85; Dr, Inst of Agric Engrng, 1985-88; Min, Colin Sellors, Israeli Emb, 1993-99. Creative Works: Ocer 150 publd pprs; Chapts in books. Honours: Hon Prof, China Agric Univ, 1997. Memberships: Israel Assn, Agric Engrng; Amn Soc Agric Engrs. Hobbies: Travelling; Fitness. Address: 65 David Elzar St, Raanana, 43204, Israel.

SARKAR Bipul Kumar, b. 3 Sept 1919, Maulmein, Burma. General Medical Practitioner. m. Monjusri, 3 May 1955, 1 s, 2 d. Education: MBBS. Appointments: World War II, 1941; Indian Natl Army, 1942-50; Indian Natl Army Assn, W Bengal, 1962; Dr, Natl Hlth Serv, 1974-80. Honours: Best Students Awd, 1948; Freedom Fighter's Pension. Memberships: Sec, Med Students Union, Calcutta; Chmn, Indian Natl Army Assn, W Bengal. Hobbies: Reading; Football; Tennis. Address: 5 Pearl Road, Park Circus, Calcutta 700017, India.

SARKAR Sabyasachi, b. 17 May 1947, W Bengal, India. m. Karabi, 6 July 1975, 1 d. Education: BSc, Hons; MSc; PhD. Appointment: Full Prof, Dept of Chem, IIT, Kanpur, India, 1988-. Honours: Alexander-von-Humboldt Fell, 1976-78; Indian Natl Sci Acady Rsch Fell, 1987-90. Memberships: Fell, Indian Chem Soc; Fell, Indian Acady of Scis. Hobbies: History and Philosophy of Science and Culture. Address: Department of Chemistry, Indian Institute of Technology-Kanpur, Kanpur 208016, India.

SARRE Warwick Turner, b. 25 July 1955, Adelaide, Aust. Barrister, Solicitor. Education: LLB, Adelaide Univ, 1977; MA, Univ of Toronto, Can, 1983. Appointments: Legal Practitioner, 1978-; Lectr in Law, 1984, Snr Lectr, 1992, SACAE; Assoc Prof, Hd of Sch of Law, Univ of SA, 1992-. Publications: Leisure Time and the Law, 1987; Uncertainties and Possibilities, 1994; Exploring Criminal Justice (w J Tomaino), 1999. Memberships: Law Soc of SA; VP, SA Jus Admin Fndn, 1995. Address: North Terrace, GPO Box 2471, Adelaide, SA 5001, Australia.

SARTORIS David John, b. 25 Nov 1955, Chgo, IL, USA. Professor. m. Education: BS, Bio, Stanford Univ, 1976; MD, Stanford Med Sch, 1980. Appointments: Asst Prof, Univ of CA, 1985-87; Chf, Musculoskeletal Imaging, UCSD Medl Cntr, 1985-91; Chf, Quantitative Bone Densitometry, Univ of CA, 1985-94; Assoc Prof, Univ of CA, 1987-94; Prof, Radiology, Univ of CA, 1994-. Creative Works: 480 Publs; 57 Book Chapts; 14 Text Books; 13 Abstracts; 215 Sci Presentations; 689 Lectrs; 26 Panel Discusions; 15 Exhibits. Honours: Silver Spoon; Pride O Gram; Third Place Article; Editors Recognition Awards. Memberships: Phi Beta Kappa; Amn Coll of Radiology; Amn Roentgen Ray Soc; Assn of Univ Radiologists; Radiological Soc of N Am; CA Radiologica Soc; Many or mbrshps. Address: 8585-24 Via Mallorca, La Jolla, CA 92037, USA.

SASAKI Motomasa, b. 7 Dec 1924, Fukuoka, Japan. Maxillo-Facial & Oral Surgeon. m. Hisako, 25 Mar 1951, 1 d. Education: MD, Kyushu Univ, 1949; DDS, Tokyo Med & Dental Univ, 1953; PhD, Physiol, Kyushu Univ, 1960. Appointments: Assoc Prof, Kyushu Univ, 1956-61; Prof, Maxillo-Facial Surg, Sapporo Med Coll, 1961-76, Nagasaki Univ, 1976-90; Pres, Seika Womens Jnr Coll, 1990-97; Prof Emer, Nagasaki Univ, 1990-. Publications: Sev articles in profl jrnls. Honour: Med Awd, Hokkaido Med Assn, Japan, 1965. Memberships: Japan Soc of Oral & Maxillo-Facial Surngs; Japanese Stomatol Soc; Japanese Cleft Palate Assn; Japanese Dental Soc. Hobby: Painting. Address: Yayoi-machi 680-6-803, Nagasaki 850-0823, Japan.

SASAKI Naosuke, b. 17 Jan 1921, Tokyo, Japan. Epidemiologist; Educator. m. Etsu Toyota, 26 May 1951, 3 s. Education: MD, Keio-Gijuku Univ, Tokyo, 1943; PhD, 1950. Appointments: Japanese Naval Surg, 1943-45; Asst Keio-Gijuku Univ, Tokyo, 1946-52; Instr, 1952-54; Assoc Prof, Hirosaki (Japan) Univ, 1955-56; Prof, Dept Hygiene, 1956-86; Prof Emer, 1986. Publications: Apple and Health, 1990; Salt and Health, 1993. Honour: Hoken-Bunka-Sho Awds, Japanese Welfare Min, 1986. Memberships: Emer Mbr, Cncl on Epidemiology and Prevention, ISFC. Address: 2-14-5 Jonan Hirosaki, 036-8232, Japan.

SASAKI Nobuaki, b. 25 Feb 1949, Hyogo Pref, Japan. Professor of Osaka City University. m. Makoto, 25 Feb 1979, 1 s, 3 d. Education: DEcon, Osaka Cty Univ. Publications: The Basic Structure of Multi National State China; The Marketization of Chinese Economy. Memberships: Exec Dir, Japan Assn for Asian Polit and Econ Studies; Dir, Japan Assn for Contemporary China Studies. Hobbies: Fishing; Golf; Mountain climbing. Address: Sanno 80-3, Shingucho Ibogun Hyogoken, Japan, 679-4325.

SASAO Tsutomu, b. 26 Jan 1950, Osaka, Japan. University Professor. Education: PhD, Osaka Univ, japan, 1977. Publications: Logic Synthesis and Optimisation, 1993; Representations of Discrete Functions, 1996. Honour: Fell, IEEE, 1994. Membership: IEEE. Address: Department of Computer Science & Electronics, Kyushu Institute of Technology, Iizuka 820-8502, Japan.

SASTRI P S, b. 22 Jan 1920, India. Professor. m. Janaki, 30 Jan 1947, 2 s, 4 d. Education: MA, Sanskrit; MA, Tehgar; MA, Engl; MA, Philos; Dip, German; DLitt, Philos. Appointments: Asst Prof, Prof of Engl & Philos, Segan Univ, 1947-60; Prof of Engl, Naghar, 1960-86. Publications: Sev articles in profl jrnls. Memberships include: Pres, Indo-German Cultural Soc, 1972-89.

Hobbies: Painting; Drama. Address: 1-35-41 Makedi Vari Street, Nazan, Tenali AP, India.

SATA Toshikatsu, b. 16 May 1933, Fukuoka Cty, Japan. Educator; Engineering Consultant. m. Takako Sata, 1 s, 2 d. Education: BS, Kysuhu Univ, 1963; DSc, 1975. Appointments: Hd Staff of Rsch, Tokuyama Soda Co Ltd, Tokuyama Cty, Yamaguchi Pref, Japan, 1963-92; Prof, Fac Engrng, Yamaguchi Univ, Ube Cty, Yamaguchi Pref, Japan, 1992-97; Japanese Govt Authorized Engrng Cnslt, 1992-. Publications: Num pprs to var jrnls. Honours: Hatsumei Sho (Invention Prize), Nippon Hatsumei Kyoukai, 1974; Person of Sci and Tech Merits Awd, Sci and Tech Agcy of Japanese Govt, 1979; Tanahashi Sho (Tech Prize), Electrochemical Soc of Japan, 1979; Gijitsu Sho (Tech Prize), Nippon Kagaku Kyokai, 1980; Gijitsu Sho (Tech Prize), Nippon Soda Kogyokai, 1982; Gakujutsu Sho (Sci Prize), Soc of Sea Water Sci of Japan, 1997. Memberships: Chem Soc Japan; Electrochemical Soc of Japan; Electrochemical Soc Inc (USA); Soc of Polymer Sci of Japan; Soc Sea Water of Japan; AAAS; Membrane Soc of Japan; Japan Assn of Ion Exchange. Address: Ohoshima Ohara 89-57, Tokuyama City, Yamaguchi Prefecture, 745-0803, Japan.

SATHYANARAYANA R, b. 9 May 1927, Mysore Cty, India. Musicologist; Danceologist. m. Gowri, 18 Aug 1976, 1 s, 1 d. Education: MSc; PhD; DLitt; DLitt Hons. Appointments: Prof, Chem; Prof, Musicology, Danceology. Creative Works: Sangeetharatnakara; Veenalakshana Vpma Rshe; Bharatanatya, A Critical Study; Poundarikamala. Honours: Mahamahopadhyaya Karnatakakalatilaka; Sangeetakalaratna; Sangeetashastra Saraswati. Memberships: Indian Music Congress; Kalasaravati. Hobbies: Theory and Practice of Shree Vidya Tantral Indological Studies; Yoga. Address: Trayeelakshmi CH 12, 9th Cross, Jayanagar, Mysore 570014, India.

SATIAWIHARDJA Budiatman, b. 15 Aug 1953, Tasikmalaya. Food Biotechnologist. m. IIS H, 17 Aug 1980, 1 s, 2 d. Education: Engr, Agric Prod Processing, 1978; Engr, Agric Prod Processing, 1978; MSc, Food Technol, Univ Mysore, India, 1982; PhD, Biotech, Univ NSW, Aust, 1991. Appointments: Jnr Lectr, 1983-92; Lectr, 1993-95; Snr Lectr, 1996-; Prof, Staff Food Technol Dev Cntr, 1979-85; Sec, FTDc, 1998-; Domestic Exptl IUC FN, 1991-93. Publications: Advances in Food Engineering; Dasar-Dasar Biosintesis Asam-Asam Amino. Honour: Piagam Tanda Kehormatan Pres Republik Indonesia; Satyalancana Karya Satya 10 Tahun, 1997. Memberships: Indonesian Food Technol Assn, Bogor, 1998; Indonesian Soc for Microbiology. Hobbies: Sports; Travel. Address: Melati II, Blok E6/5, Bogor 16610, Indonesia.

SATO Eunice, b. 8 June 1921, Livingstone, CA. Educator. m. Thomas T, 9 Dec 1950, 2 s, 1 d. Education: BA, Univ of Northern CO, 1944; MA, Tchrs Coll, Columbia Univ, NY, 1948. Appointments: Pub Sch Tchr, MI, 1944-47; Educl Miss, Japan, 1948-51; Long Beach Cty Cncl, 1975-86; Mayor, Long Beach, 1980-82. Publications: Monthly Article for Neighbourhood Newspaper. Honours: Humanitarian of the Yr Awd; Outstndng Lay Woman of the Yr; Woman of the Yr; Outstndng Service Awd; Natl Merit Awd; Mother of the Yr; William F Prisk Awd; Citizen of the Yr Awd; Many or Awds. Memberships: Natl Advsry Cncl; Gen Cncl, Fin and Admin; Meth Ch; S CA Edison Equal Oppys Advsry Cncl; Amn Red Cross; Natl Conf for Community Justice. Hobbies: Collecting Words of Wisdom; Collecting new recipes of healthy easy to prepare dishes. Address: 551-101 Pittsfield Court, Long Beach, CA 90803-6355, USA.

SATO Kazuo, b. 15 Mar 1932, Doshimura, Japan. University Professor; Inventor; Designer. m. 5 May 1961, 2 s. Education: BEng, 1957, MEng, 1959, DEng, 1983, Meiji Univ. Appointments: Engrng Educr, 1963-71; Lectr, Asst Prof, Prof, Chmn of Dr Course Cttee, Shibaura Inst of Technol, Minato, Tokyo. Publications: 500 pprs. Creative works: Invention of two-stroke engine, 1991. Honours: Prize from Kanagawa, 1991; Swedish Awd for

Rsch; Awd for High Technol in Mechl Devices from Fire Assn. Memberships: Soc of Automotive Engrs of Am; Soc of Automotive Engrs, Japan; Japan Soc of Mechl Engrs; Japan Soc for Des Engrng; Japan Soc for Agricl Machinery. Hobbies: Fishing; Reading; Japanese wrestling; Japanese board game of "Go". 3-11-21 Yabe, Sagamihara-shi, Kanagawa-ken 229, Japan.

SATO Megumu, b. 28 Feb 1924, Osaka Cty. Director General. m. Sadako, 26 Sept 1951, 1 s, 1 d. Education: Kyoto Univ. Appointments: Min, Postal Servs and Telecomms, 1984; Min, jus, 1990; Dir Gen, Natl Land Agcy, 1993. Publications: Memorandums in Europe, 1962; Travelling Around the World, 1973. Honours: The First Order of Merit, 1996. Hobbies: Reading; Play of Go. Address: 1-32-18 Hannan-cho, Abeno-ku, Osaka-City, Osaka, 545-0021, Japan.

SATO Mitsuo, b. 1 Feb 1933 Gunma. Banker. m. - wife dec - 2 s. Education: Univ of Tokyo; Harvard Law Sch. Appointments: Entered min of Fin, 1955; Snr Dep Dir Intl Taxation and Div Tax Bur min of Fin, 1968-70; Snr Economist Tax Policy Div Fiscal Affairs Dept IMF, 1970-73; Dir Rsch Div Tax Bur min of Fin, 1976-78; Dir Securities Cos Div Securities Bur min of Fin, 1978-79; Dir-Gen Fukuoka Regl Tax Bur Natl Tax Admin Agcy, 1980-81; Dep Dir-Gen Customs and Tariff Bur min of Fin, 1981-83; Dep Dir-Gen Intl Fin Bur, 1983-84; Dir-Gen Customs and Tariff Bur min of Fin, 1985-86; Mngng Dir Tokyo Stock Exchange, 1986-88; Snr Mngng Dir, 1988-91; Dep Pre, 1991-93; Pres and Chmn Bd of Dirs Asian Devt Bank, 1993-. Memberships: Mbr Plicy Bd Bank of Japan, 1984-85. Address: Asian Development Bank, 6 ADB Avenue, Mandaluyong City, 01401, Metro Manila, Philippines.

SATO Shinji. Politician. Appointments: Fmr Min of Transp; Min for Intl Trade and Ind, 1996. Memberships: Mbr HoR. Address: c/o Ministry of International Trade and Industry, 1-3-1, Kasumigaseki, Chiyoda-ku, Japan.

SATO Toshihide, b. 27 Jan 1936, Otarau, Hokkaido, Japan. University Professor. m. Kyoko, 20 Jan 1966, 1 s, 1 d. Education: BS, Hokkaido Univ, 1995; MSc, Hokkaido Univ Grad Sch; PhD, Hokkaido Univ Grad Sch, 1996. Appointments: Rsch Assoc, Tokyo Medl Dent Univ, 1966; Rsch Assoc, FL State Univ, 1970; Assoc Prof, Tokyo Medl Dent Univ, 1976; Prof, Nagasaki Univ, 1980. Publications: Olfaction & Taste XI, 1994; New Taste Science, 1997. Memberships: Physiological Soc of Japan, 1966; Japanese Soc of Oral Biol, 1966; Japanese Assn for the Stdy of Taste and Smell, 1966. Hobbies: Gardening; Sketching. Address: Department of Physiology, Nagasaki University School of Dentistry, 1-7-1 Sakamoto, Nagasaki 852-8588, Japan.

SATTAR Aldus, b. 3 Jan 1946, Bangladesh. Professor. m. Nasima, 24 Feb 1977, 1 d. Education: BA Hons; MA. Appointments: Lectr, Bengali Mugil Coll, Tangnil, 1975; Prof, Bengali Dept, 1980. Creative Works: Poems and Articles in different dailies, weeklies, jrnls. Honours: Shahitya Shekwar title, Pabna Dist Shahitya; Championship Lit, Cul Competition, Edward Coll; First Prize, E Pak Essay Competition. Memberships: Bangladesh Cultural Parishad Cntrl Offs; Poet Club. Hobbies: Song; Cricket. Address: Gobinda Nazim Uddin Road, Pabna, India.

SATTHERTHWAITE John Steven, b. 11 Aug 1928, Sydney, NSW, Aust. Catholic Bishop. Education: BE, Univ of Sydney; DD, Lateran Univ, Rome. Appointments: Asst Priest, Glen Innes, 1959-61; Bishop's Sec, Armidale, 1961-69; Co-adjutor Bishop Lismore, 1969-71; Bishop of Lismore, 1971-. Address: Bishop's House, PO Box 1, Lismore, NSW 2480, Australia.

SAUD HRH Prince Sultan Bin Abdulaziz Al, b. 1930. Politician. Education: At crt and abroad. Appointments: Gov of Riyadh, 1947; Min of Agric, 1954; Min of Transportation, 1955; VP Supreme Cttee for Educ Policy; Min of Def and Aviation and Insp Gen, 1963, 1982-; Chmn Bd Saudi Airlines, 1963; Chmn Bd Gen Enterprise of Mil Inds; Chmn Cncl of Manpower, 1980; Second Dep

PM, 1982-; Chmn Supreme Cncl for Islamic Affairs, 1994. Honours: Order of Merit - First class - from many cos. Address: Ministry of Defence and Aviation, Riyadh, Saudi Arabia.

SAUD Al-Faisal HRH Prince, b. 1941 Riyadh. Politician; Diplomatist. Education: Princeton Univ USA. Appointments: Fmr Dep Min of Pet and Mineral Rescs, 1971-74; Min of State for For Affairs, Mar-Oct 1975; Min of For Affairs, Oct 1975-; Ldr deleg to UN Gen Ass, 1976; Spec Envoy of HM King Khaled in dip efforts to resolve Algerian-Moroccan conflict over Western Sahara and the civ war in Lebanon. Memberships: Mbr Saudi Arabian deleg to Arab restricted Summit Riyadh, Oct 1976; Mbr to full Summit Conf of Arab League, Oct 1976; Fndng Mbr King Faisal's Intl Charity Soc. Hobbies: Reading. Address: Ministry of Foreign Affairs, Nasseriya Street, Riyadh 11124, Saudi Arabia.

SAUNDERS Cheryl Anne, b. 28 Aug 1944, India. Constitutional Lawyer. 1 s, 2 d. Education: BA; LLB; PhD. Appointments: Pers Chair in Law, 1989; Dir, Cntr for Comparative Constl Studies, 1989; Dpty Chair, Constl Centenary Fndn, 1991. Honours: AO, 1994; Acady of Soc Sci, 1994. Address: 157 Barry St, Carlton, VIC 3052, Australia.

SAUNDERS Kay Elizabeth Bass, b. 19 Aug 1947, Brisbane, Aust. Academic. m. Raymond Leslie Evans, 21 Dec 1968, div 1982, 1 d. Education: BA, 1st class hons, 1970, PhD, 1975, Univ of Qld. Appointments: Tutor in Hist, 1975-79, Snr Tutor, 1980-84, Snr Lectr, 1985-, Rdr in Hist, 1990-, Univ of Qld; Dir, Natl Aust Day Cncl, 1992-96; Dir, Cncl, Aust War Mem Cncl of Aust, 1994-97; Chair, Qld Cultural Advsry Cncl, 1997-; Mbr, Premier's Advsry Cncl on Women, 1999-2001. Publications: Exclusion, Exploitation and Extermination, 1975; Workers in Bondage, 1982; Indentured Labour in the British Empire, 1984; Gender Relations in Australia, 1992; Australia's Frontline, 1992; War on the Homefront, 1993; Aboriginal Writers, 1995; 1901: Our Future's Past, 1997; Australian Masculinities, 1998. Honours: C'wlth Undergrad Schlshp, 1967-69; C'wlth Postgrad Schl, 1970-73; Austl Rsch Grants Commn Awd, 1979-81; Order of Aust, 1999. Memberships: NY Acady of Scis; Austl Histl Assn; Assn of Univ Women; Fedn Univ Staff Assn; Order of Aust Assn. Hobbies: Reading; Cinema; Exotic Travel. Address: History Department, University of Queensland, Qld 4072, Australia.

SAUNDERS Sally, b. 15 Jan 1940, Bryn Mawr, PA, USA. Poet; Poetry Therapist; Lecturer; Freelance Writer; Workshop Leader. Education: BS, George Williams Coll, Downers Grove, IL, 1965; Poetry Writing Course, The New Sch, 1968-69; Sev or courses. Appointments: Poetry Therapist, Inst of PA Hosp, PA, Univ of Louisville, KY; Lects, Tchng at Schs and or venues; Appearances on TV and Radio; Num Poetry Writing Workshops; Poetry Readings. Publications: Past the Near Meadows, 1961; Pauses, 1978; Fresh Bread, 1982; Random Thoughts, 1992; Patchwork Quilt, 1993; Quiet Thoughts and Gentle Feelings, 1996; Word Pictures, 1998; Contbns to var jrnls. Honours: Hon Mention, New Amn Poetry Contest, 1988; Silver Poet Awd, World of Poetry, 1989; Nutmegger Book Awd. Memberships: Natl Writers Club; Press Club of San Fran; Poets and Writers Guild; Assn for Poetry Therapy; Poetry Society of Am; Ina Coolbrith Circle; Pen and Pencil Club; Acady of Amn Poets; Amn Poetry Cntr. Address: 2030 Vallejo Street #501, San Francisco, CA 94123, USA.

SAVSAR Mehmet, b. 10 Feb 1952, Kars, Turkey. Professor. m. Necmiye, 25 June 1978, 2 s, 1 d. Education: BSc, 1975; MSc, 1978; PhD, Indl Engrng & Ops Rsch, 1982. Appointments: Process Engr, 1975-76, Rsch Asst, 1980-82, Asst Prof, 1982-92, Assoc Prof, 1992-. Publications: 30 jrnl articles, 25 conf pprs. Honour: Schlsp, Turkish Min of Educn, 1976-82. Memberships: NY Acady of Scis; Inst for Ops Rsch & Mngmt Sci. Hobby: Travel. Address: Kuwait University, College of Engineering & Petroleum, PO Box 5969, Safat 13060, Kuwait.

SAWAI Atsuhiro, b. 9 Feb 1939, Osaka, Japan. University Professor. m. Yoko, 10 Oct 1963. Education: BD, Kyoto Univ. Publications: Devils of Adolescence (poetry collection), 1968; The Mirror (poetry collection); Collected Poems of Theodore Roethke (trans), 1985. Memberships: Western Hist Soc; NZ Rsch Soc. Hobbies: Spinning; Go. Address: 62 Semiga Kakiuchi-cho, Kamigamo, Kita-ku, Kyoto, Japan.

SAWARKAR Rajesh, b. 15 Nov 1968, Kawasa, India. Teacher. m. Pratibha, 1999. Education: MSc; BEd; BA. Appointments: Member, Varkari Vaishnao Mandal Akot; Mbr, Akot Jnr Chamber. Publications: Shri Vasudeo Dnyanamrut, 1998; many articles publs in var mags. Honour: Cert, Vedacharya Shri Vasudeo Maharaj, 1982. Memberships: Sec,Shri Bhaskar Maharaj Sansthan Adgaon, Telhara, Akola, 1992. Hobbies: Reading; Writing; Social Work. Address: Krishnarpan, Saraswati Nagar, Akot, Akola, 444101, MS, India.

SAWATARI Hajime, b. 1 Jan 1940, Tokyo, Japan. Photographer. m. 1968, 1 d. Education: Dept of Photography, Coll of Art, Nihon Univ. Appointments: Nihon Design Cntr, 1963-66; Freelance Photographer, 1966-. Publications: Nadia, 1973; Alice, 1973; Alice From the Sea, 1979; Showa, 1994. Honours: Japan Photography Assn Awd, 1973; Kodansha Publng Culture Awd, Photography, 1979. Address: 2-19 601 Tomihisa machi, Shiniuku-ku, Tokyo, Japan.

SAX Herbert, b. 15 Aug 1943, Switz. Artist Painter. m. K Inoue, 1982, 1 s, 1 d. Education: Swiss Matura, Univ Studies in Berne, Florence, Basle. Career: Freelance activities in performing arts until 1972; Artist painter, 1973-; Exhibns: French-Japanese Culture Inst, Kyoto, Japan, 1984; Goethe Inst (Kyoto); Yougen Gall (Tokyo), 1995; Kisshodo Gall (Kyoto), 1997. Creative works: Japanese ink paintings, 1977-; Tempera colour wrks, 1980-; Oil paintings, 1987-. Membership: Awanosuto Art Forum Fndng Mbr, Tokushima, Japan, 1992-95. Hobbies: Humanities; All arts and nature; Love and friendship. Address: Ijiri, Mizuho, 622-0323 Kyoto, Japan.

SAXENA Suresh Chandra, b. 5 July 1950. Information Scientist. m. Meera Saxena, 4 Mar 1972, 1 s, 1 d. Education: MSc, Chem, 1st, Kanpur Univ, 1969; Dip in Japanese Lang, Delhi Univ, 1975; Associateship in Info Sci, INSDOC, New Delhi, 1981. Appointments: JSA, 1971-76, SSA, 1976-83, JSO, 1983-91, Sci B, 1991-94, Sci C, 1994-99, Sci D, 1999-, DESIDOC, Delhi. Publications: 21 rsch pprs in Indian and for jrnls. Memberships: Life, IASLIC, Calcutta; AGLIS, New Delhi; Exec Mbr, Life Mbr, ISTA, New Delhi, 1992-94, 1994-96. Hobbies: Reading; New development in the information field. Address: c/o DESIDOC, Ministry of Defence, Metcalfe House, Delhi 110054, India.

SCAGLIONE Cecil Frank Joseph, b. 2 Dec 1934, North Bay, Ontario, Canada. Writer; Reporter. m. Beverly, 25 Mar 1983, 2 s, 1 d. Education: Herbert J Davenport Fellowship, Bus and Econ Reporting, Univ of Missouri, USA. Publications: Tomato Capital of Canada; 100's of freelance mag and newsppr articles. Honours: B F Goodrich of Can, San Diego Press Club; Airline Eds Forum, All Jrnlsm Awds; US Small Bus Admin Natl Media Adv of Yr. Memberships: Soc of Profl Jrnlsts; San Diego Press Club. Hobbies: Photography; Travel. Address: 3911 Kendall St, San Diego, CA 92109, USA.

SCANLAN Joseph Cooper, b. 10 Dec 1952. Environmental Scientist. m. Susan Joy Newton, 25 May 1974, 2 s, 1 d. Education: BAgrSc (Hons), Univ Qld; MAgric Sci, Univ of Qld; PhD, TX A&M. Appointments: Pasture Agronomist, 1974-84, Snr Pasture Agronomist, 1984-92, QDPI; Snr Environmental Sci, Prin Sci, Qld Dept Nat Resources. Publications: 25 refereed jrnl articles; 24 conf pprs; 6 books, thes; 10 other articles on pasture and weed ecology, and modelling. Hobbies: Woodwork; Golf. Address: PO Box 318, Toowoomba, Qld 4350, Australia.

SCARBOROUGH Vernon Marcus, b. 11 Feb 1940. Diplomat. m. Jennifer Bernadette Keane, 1966, 3 d.

Education: Passport Off, FO, 1958-61; CRO, 1961; Served Dacca, Karachi, Brussels, Bathurst, later Banjul, FCO, Muscat and Lagos, Kuala Lumpur, 1983-86, First Sec 1984; FCO, 1986; Chargé d'Affaires, San Salvador, 1987-90; Consul, Auckland, 1990-94; Brit Amb to Repub of Palau, Repub of Marshall Is and Federated States of Micronesia; Brit Dpty High Commnr to Fiji Is, Tuvalu, Kiribate, Nauru. Hobbies: Photography; Golf; Vintage Vehicles. Address: c/o Foreign and Commonwealth Office, London, SW1A 2AH, England.

SCARFE Allan John, b. 30 Mar 1931, Caulfield, Vic, Aust. Retired Teacher. m. Wendy E Scarfe, 6 Jan 1955, 1 s, 3 d. Education: BA; DipEd; TPTC. Publications: (w Wendy Scarfe) A Mouthful of Petals, 1967, 1972; Tiger on a Rein, 1969; People of India, 1972; The Black Australians, 1974; Victims or Bludgers? Case Studies of Poverty in Australia, 1974; JP, His Biography, 1975, 1998. Victims of Bludgers? A Poverty Inquiry for Schools, 1981; Labor's Titan. The Story of Percy Brookfield, 1878-1921 (eds), 1983; All That Grief. Migrant recollections of Greek resistance to facism 1941-1949, 994; Remembering Jayaprakash, 1997; No Taste for Carnage. Alex Sheppard: A Portrait 1913-1997, 1998. Honour: Austl Lit Bd Grants, 1980, 1988. Memberships: Community Aid Abroad; Amnesty Intl. Hobbies: Piano; Swimming; Walking; Gardening; Reading; Music. Address: 8 Bostock Street, Warrnambool, Vic 3280, Australia.

SCARFE Wendy Elizabeth, b. Adelaide, S Aust. Teacher (now retired). m. Allan J Scarfe, 6 Jan 1955, 1 s, 3 d. Education: BA; BLitt; ATTC. Publications: Shadow and Flowers (poetry), 1964 (2nd enlarged ed), 1984; The Lotus Throne, 1976; Neither Here Nor There, 1984; Laura: my alter ego, 1988; The Day They Shot Edward, 1991, 1992; Miranda, 1998; (w Allan J Scarfe) A Mouthful of Petals, 1967, 1972; Tiger on a Rein, 1969; People of India, 1972; The Black Australians, 1974; Victims or Bludgers? Case Studies of Poverty in Australia, 1974; JP His Biography, 1975, 1998; Victims or Bludgers? A Poverty Inquiry for Schools, 1981; Labor's Titan. The Story of Percy Brookfield, 1878-1921 (eds), 1983; All That Grief, Migrant recollections of Greek Resistance to Facism 1941-1949, 1994; Remembering Jayaprakash, 1997; No Taste for Carnage. Alex Sheppard: A Portrait 1913-1997, 1998. Honours: Austl Lit Bd Grants, 1980, 1988. Memberships: Fellshp of Austl Writers, Community and Abroad; Amnesty Intl. Address: Violin; Swimming; Classical studies; Theatre; Walking; Reading; Music. Address: 8 Bostock Street, Warrnambool, Vic 3280, Australia.

SCARR Deryck Anthony, b. 7 Sept 1939, Newbury, Berks, Eng. Historian. m. Marion, 23 Oct 1988, 1 d. Education: BA; PhD. Appointments: Rsch Fell, Fell, Snr Fell, Rsch Sch of Pacific and Asian Stdies, Austl Natl Univ. Publications include: Fragments of Empire, 1967; I, the Very Bayonet, 1973; Viceroy of the Pacific, 1980; Ratu Sukuna: soldier, statesman, man of two worlds, 1980; Fiji: a short history, 1984; Politics of Illusion: the military coups in Fiji, 1988; Kingdoms of the Reefs: the history of the Pacific Islands, 1990; Slaving and Slavery in the Mascareignes, 1998-; Seychelles since 1770 - a slave and post-slavery society, 1999-; Ed: A Cruise in a Queensland Labour Vessel to the South Seas, 1968; Pacific Islands Portraits, w J W Davidson, 1970, 1973; More Pacific Islands Portraits, 1978; Fiji: The Three Legged Stool - selected writings of Ratu Sir Lala Sukuna, 1982; France in the Pacific, 1991. Memberships: Bd Mbr, 1966-, Ed, 1972-94, Assim; Review Ed, The Jrnl of Pacific Hist, 1967-84. Hobby: Sailing. Address: 16 Richmond Street, Macquarie, ACT 2614, Australia.

SCHAIBLE Siegfried, b. 18 Aug 1940, Marburg, Germany. Professor. m. Ingrid, 14 May 1967, 1 s, 2 d. Education: Dip, Maths, Phys, Mainz, 1967; PhD, Appl Maths, Koeln, 1971; Habilitation, Ops Rsch, Koeln, 1978. Appointments: Prof, Univ Alberta, Can, 1979-87, Univ CA, Riverside, 1987-. Publications: Num articles in profl jrnls. Honours: McCalla Rsch Profshp, Univ Alberta, 1981-82; Fell, AAAS, 1998. Memberships: Inst for Ops Rsch and the Mngmt Scis; Math Prog Soc. Hobbies: Modern and Ancient Languages; Travel; Hiking; Classical Music. Address: A G Anderson Graduate School of Management, University of California, Riverside, CA 92521, USA.

SCHARP David Wingrove, b. 30 May 1943, Melbourne, Aust. Veterinarian. m. Ann, 22 Feb 1985, 1 s, 1 d. Education: BVSc, Univ of Queensland, Aust, 1966; MACVS (Cattle Med), 1981. Appointments: Lectr Univ of Queensland, Pastoral Vet Cntr, 1967; Vet Prac, Muswellbrook, NSW, 1967-81; Dir, Livestock Servs Intl, 1982-83; Rsch Univ of New Eng, NSW, 1983; Vet Offr, DPI, Papua New Guinea, 1984; Lectr, Univ of Queensland Pastoral Vet Cntr, 1984; Livestock Advsr, AusAID, Jiangsu Dairy Dev, Peoples Repub of China, 1985-86; Austl Trade Commnr Agric, Mid E (Riyadh), 1988-90; Mngr, India Mid E and Africa, Austl Trade Commn, Canberra, 1991; Austl Snr Trade Commnr, Sub Saharan Africa (excluding RSA) and Indian Ocean (Nairobi), 1992; Proj Mngr, Austl Ttade Commn/GRM Intl, Livestock Servs Dev Prog, State of Kuwait, 1993-99. Publications: 4 sci publs (ed jrnls). Honours: Commonwealth Vet Interchange Fund Grant, Ont Vet Coll, Can, 1976. Memberships: Aust's Vet Assn (AVA); Austl Coll of Vet Sci (ACS). Hobbies: Skiing; Tennis; Reading; Horse racing. Address: c/o GRM International, 244 Edward Street, Brisbane 4000, QLD, Australia.

SCHEDVIN Carl Boris, b. 23 May 1936, Sydney, Australia. Deputy Vice Chancellor. m. Bernardette Schedvin, 1 s, 1 d. Education: BEc, 1st class hons, 1960, PhD, 1964, Univ Sydney. Appointments: Lectr, Econ Hist, London Sch of Econs and Polit Sci, 1964-65; Lectr, Econs, 1966, Lectr, Econ Hist, 1967, Univ Sydney; Vis Fell, Dept of Econ Hist, Rsch Sch of Socl Scis, Austl Natl Univ, 1972, 1983; Snr Lectr, Econ Hist, Univ Sydney, 1968-73; Vis Lectr, Socl Sci, Univ Kent, Canterbury, 1973; Rdr, Econ Hist, Monash Univ, 1973-79; Vis Prof, Dept of Econs, Queens Univ, Kingston, Can, 1988; Chair, Econ Hist, 1979-91, Dpty Vice Chan (Acad), 1991-97, Dpty Vice Chan, 1998-, Univ Melbourne. Publications include: Australia and the Great Depression: A Study of Economic Development and Policy in the 1920s and 1930s, 1970; War Economy, 1942-1945, Vol IV in Series 4 (Civil), Australia in the War of 1939-45, 1977; Shaping Science and Industry: A History of Australia's Council for Scientific and Industrial Research 1926-49, 1987; In Reserve: Central Banking in Australia 1945-47, 1992. Honours include: Brit Cncl Travel Schlsp, 1964; Denison Miller Travel Schlsp and Herbert Johnson Travel Grant, Univ Sydney, 1964. Memberships: Edl Bd, Histl Stdies; Pres, Econ Hist Soc of Aust and NZ, 1988-94; Cnslt, Austl Wheat Bd, 1988-92. Hobby: Farming. Address: University of Melbourne, Parkville, Victoria 3052, Australia.

SCHEFF Thomas, b. 1 Aug 1929, Oklahoma, USA. Sociologist. m. Suzanne Retzinger, 1988, 1 s, 2 d. Education: PhD, Sociol, Univ CA, Berkeley. Appointments: Univ WI, Madison, 1959-64; Univ CA, Santa Barbara, 1965-. Publications: Being Mentally Ill, 1966, 1984; Microsociology, 1990. Address: Department of Sociology, University of California, Santa Barbara, CA 93106, USA.

SCHEIBER Harry N, b. 1935, USA. Educator; Historian. Education: AB, Columbia; MA & PhD, Cornell; D Jur Hon, Uppsala, Sweden. Appointments: Riesenfeld Prof of Law & Hist, Univ of California, Berkeley, USA, 1981-; Prof, Hist, Univ California San Diego, 1971-80; Dir, Sko Sato Prog in US & Japanese Law, Univ of California, Berkeley, 1992-. Publications: Articles on Pacific Ocean Resources in Law and soc sci jrnls, 1986-. Honours: Natl Endowment for Humanities Fell, 1984-; Guggenheim Fellowships, 1966, 1989; ACLS Fell, 1966. Memberships: Ocean Gov Study Grp, Dir, 1993-; Law & Soc Assn, Tstee, 1981-85, 1994-99. Address: Jurisprudence & Social Policy Program, School of Law, University of California, Berkeley, CA 94720, USA.

SCHEPISI Frederic Alan, b. 26 Dec 1939, Melbourne, Aust. Film Writer; Producer; Director. m. (1) Joan Mary Ford, 2 s, 2 d, (2) Rhonda Elizabeth Finlayson, 1973, 2 d, (3) Mary Rubin, 1984, 1 s. Appointments: TV Prodn Mngr, Paton Advsry Serv, Melbourne, 1961-64; Victorian Mngr, Cinesound Prodns, Melbourne, 1964-66; Mngng Dir, The Film House, Melbourne, 1964-66; Governing Chmn, 1979-. Creative Works: Films: The Devil's Playground, 1975; The Chant of Jimmie Blacksmith, 1978; Barbarosa, 1981; Iceman, 1983; Plenty, 1984-85; Roxanne, 1986; Evil Angels, 1987; The Russia House, 1989; Mr Baseball, 1991; Six Degrees of Separation, 1993; IQ, 1994. Honours: Best Film, Austl Film Awds, 1975, Best Film, Best Achmt in Direction, Best Screenplay Adapted from Another Source, AFI Mbrs Spec Awd, 1989. Address: PO Box 743, South Yarra, Vic 3141, Australia.

SCHERER Peter Julian, b. 15 Aug 1937 Stratford. Jrnlst. m. Gaelyn P Morgan, 1964, 1 s, 1 d. Education: Browns Bay Sch; Takapuna Grammar Sch. Appointments: Joined NZ Herald, 1955; Chf Wellington Bur, 1960-71; Chmn Parly Press Gall, 1965; Dir Community Newspapers Ltd, 1972-73; Ldr-writer Duty Ed Business News Ed, 1973-76; Editl Mngr, 1977-83; Asst Ed, 1977-85; Ed New Zealand Herald, 1985-96; Chmn NZ Assocd Press, 1985-90; Chmn NZ sec C'wlth Press Union - CPU - 1989-94; Cnclr CPU London, 1989-94; Dir Wilson & Horton Grp, 1989-96; Dir NZ Press Assn, 1991-96; Chmn plng cttee N Hlth med wrkforce, 1996-. Honours: Cowan Prize, 1959; CPU Fell'ship, 1963. Memberships: Mbr Wellington Bur, 1960-71; Mbr NZ Press Cncl, 1988-97; Mbr NZ Div Inst of Dirs, 1989-; Mbr Comms Advsry Cncl NZ Commn for UNESCO, 1989-94; Mbr Bd of Control Newspaper Pubs in Asia-Pacific, 1994-96; Mbr Comms and Media Law Assn, 1990-97; Mbr other profl appts. Hobbies: Rreading; Tennis; Gardening; Fishing. Address: 267 School Road, Tomarata, RD 4 Wellsford, New Zealand.

SCHINDHELM Klaus, b. 15 Sept 1952, Federal Republic of Germany. Professor. m. Anne Martinson, 15 Oct 1977, 2 s. Education: BE, 1975; PhD, 1978. Appointments: Rsch Fell, Medizinische Hochschule, Hanover, Germany, 1978-79; Lectr 1980-85, Snr Lectr 1985-88, Cntr for Biomed Engrng, Univ of NSW, Aust; Rsch Fell, Univ of Munich, Germany, 1986; Assoc Prof 1988-91, Prof & Dir 1992-94, Cntr for Biomed Engrng, Univ of NSW; Prof & Hd, Grad Sch of Biomed Engrng, Univ of NSW, 1994-. Honour: Alexander von Humboldt Fellshp, 1978-79. Memberships: Inst of Engrs, Aust; Australasian Soc of Nephrology; Intl Soc of Artifical Organs; Amn Soc of Artifical Internal Organs; Soc for Biomaterials; Chmn, Natl Cttee on Biomed Engrng, Inst of Engrs, Aust, 1989-92; Chmn, Coll of Biomed Engrs, Inst of Engrs, Aust, 1992-95. Hobbies: Squash; Sailing. Address: 72 Francis Greenway Drive, Cherrybrook, NSW 2120, Australia.

SCHLECHT Wolfgang E, b. 27 Apr 1950, Wemding, Germany. University Professor. m. 27 Dec, 1 s. Education: Univ of Munich; Univ of For Studies Tokyo; Tokyo Univ. Appointments: Assoc Prof, 1988, Prof, 1995, Waseda Univ, Tokyo, Japan. Publications: Var transl of pre-modern & modern lit wrks from Japanese into German. Membership: Pen Club of Japan. Hobbies: Literature; Translation Science; Computing. Address: 5-26-13 Inokashira, Mitaka-Shi, Tokyo 181-0001, Japan.

SCHLUETER Erika Manriquez, b. Santiago, Chile (came to USA, 1980). Civil Engineer Research Scientist. m. Ross Donald Schlueter, May 1981, 2 s. Education: B of Civil Constrn, Cath Univ, Santiago, 1980; Postgrad, MIT, 198-81, San Jose State Univ, 1983; MS, Civil Engrng, Univ WA, 1986; PhD, Engrng Sci, Univ CA, Berkeley, 1995. Appointments: Instr, Continuing Educ, 1975-77, Tchng Asst, 1976-77, Cath Univ, Santiago; Hydrogeologist, Celzec Co, Santiago, 1978; Med Asst, 1981, Fin Aids Analyst, 1981-82, Stanford, CA, Univ Medl Cntr; Homemaker, Pleasanton, 1986-88; Rsch Asst, Lawrence Berkeley Natl Lab, Univ CA, Berkeley, 1995-. Publications: Contbr num articles to profl jrnls. Honours: Fulbright Fell, 1980-81; Jane Lewis Fell, 1990-91. Memberships: ASCE; Soc Pet Engrs; Amn Geophysical Union; Soc Exploration Geophysicists, Awd of Merit, 1994-95. Address: Lawrence Berkeley Nat Lab MS 44B 1 Cyclotron Road, Berkeley, CA 94720, USA.

SCHMID Rudi (Rudolf), b. 2 May 1922, Switzerland. Professor of Medicine; Dean Emeritus, School of Medicine. m. Sonja Wild, 17 Sept 1949, 1 s, 1 d. Education: BS, Gymnasium Zürich, 1941; MD, Univ of Zürich, 1947; PhD, Univ of MN, 1954. Appointments: Asst Prof of Med, Harvard, 1959-62; Prof of Med, Univ of Chicago, 1962-66; Prof of Med, Univ of CA, San Fran, 1966-91; Dean, Sch of Med, 1983-89. Publications: Over 300 orig sci publs in the fields of: Porphyrins, bile pigments, liver and muscle diseases and hematology. Honours: Disting Lectr Awd, Assn Amn Physns, 1976; Aschoff Prize, Univ of Freiburg, 1979; Canad Liver Fndn Gold Medal, 1985; Mayo Soley Awd. Memberships: Amn Soc, Biol Chems and Molecular Biolsts, 1960; Leopoldina, German Acady of Scis, 1967 Natl Acady Sci, USA, 1974; Amn Acady of Arts and Scis, 1982; Swiss Acady Med Sci, 1982. Hobbies: Travelling; Reading; Tennis; Skiing; Hiking. Address: 211 Woodland Road, Kentfield, CA 94904, USA.

SCHMIDMAIER Dagmar Barbara, b. 10 Sept 1944. State Librarian. m. Horst Schmidmaier, 5 Oct 1969, 1 s, 1 d. Education: BA, Sydney; Dip Lib, MLib, Hon DLitt, Univ NSW; ALIA. Appointments: Libn, State Lib of NSW, 1967-70; Systems Libn, Moonee Valley Regl Lib, 1969-70; Systems Libn, ACI, 1971-73; Systs Libn, Univ of Sydney, 1974-75; Hd, Dept of Info Studies, Ku-ring-gai Coll of Advd Educ, 1975-84; Mngr, TAFE Lib Servs, NSW, 1984-90; Netwrk Mngr, Prin, Open Coll Netwrk, 1990-92; Dir, Open Trng and Educ Netwrk, 1993-95; State Libn, State Lib of NSW, 1995-. Memberships: Judge, Miles Franklin Lit Awd, 1995-; Chair, Cncl Austl State Libs, 1998-; Bd of Stdies NSW, 1998-; AARL Editl Bd, 1999-; Austl Libs Copyright Cttee, 1999- Austl Digital Alliance, 1999-. Hobbies: Ballet; Music; Skiing; Water Sports; Reading. Address: State Library of New South Wales, Macquarie Street, Sydney, NSW 2000, Australia.

SCHNAGL Roger Dieter, b. 10 Oct 1944, Reitendorf, Austria. Microbiology Educator; Researcher in Virology. m. Heather York Syme. Education: BS (Hons), 1969, PhD, 1975, Univ of Melbourne. Appointments: Postdoct Rsch Fell, Univ of Melbourne, 1975-78; Lectr, 1979-86, Snr Lectr, 1987-, Hd of Dept, 1993-95, Dpty Hd of Dept, 1996-, Dept of Microbiology, LaTrobe Univ, Melbourne. Publications: Over 50 articles in num intl sci jrnls. Honours: Num rsch grants and awds, 1979-. Memberships: Fell, Austl Soc for Microbiology; NY Acady of Scis. Hobbies: Squash; Tennis; Scuba diving; Philately. Address: Department of Microbiology, La Trobe University, Bundoora, Victoria 3083, Australia.

SCHNEIDER Richard C, b. 20 Sept 1927, Jefferson, Wisconsin, USA. Professor. m. BA; MDiv; MEd. Appointments: Organizer, Admin, Lutheran Ch; Admin, Carrhage Coll; Prof, Riverside Cmty Coll. Publication: Freedom and Lawful Behavior, 1970. Honours: Natl Sci Fndn, 1964; Riverside Cmty Coll Fac Lectr, 1970; US Dept of Educn, India, 1980; US Dept of Educn, Egypt, 1981; US Dept of Educn, Nigeria, 1982. Membership: Psychol, Psychotherapy Conservation. Hobbies: Mountaineering; Backpacking; Wilderness Travel. Address: 257 Arcturis Circle, Bishop, CA 93514-7053, USA.

SCHNEIDER Valerie Ann, b. 6 March 1963, Tacoma, WA. Physician. m. William Schneider, 7 July 1990. Education: BA Spanish, Univ AZ, 1985; MD, St George's Univ Sch of Med, 1991. Appointments: Fac Physician, ICU, Kaiser Permanente Hosp, Walnut Creek, CA. Memberships: Amn Medl Women's Assn; Amn Thoracic Soc; Amn Coll Physicians. Hobbies: Sewing; Crafts; Baking; Snowskiing. Address: 1425 South Main Street, Walnut Creek, CA 94596, USA.

SCHNITZER Moshe, b. 21 Jan 1921. Diamond Exporter. m. Varda Reich, 1946, 1 s, 2 d. Education: Balfour High Sch Tel-Aviv; Hebrew Univ of Jerusalem. Appointments: Chmn Assn of Diamond Instrs, 1943-46; VP Israel Diamond Exchange, 1951-66; Partner Export Enterprise, 1953-; Ed The Diamond; Pres Israel Diamond Exchange, 1966-93; Pres Israel Exporter's Assn of Diamonds, 1962-; World Pres Intl Fedn of Diamond

Exchanges, 1968-72. Publication: Diamond Book - in Hebrew - 1946. Honours: Most Distinguished Exporter of Israel, 1964; Hon Pres Israel Diamond Exchange, 1993-; Hon World Pres Fedn of Diamond Exchanges, 1993-. Memberships: Mbr Consulting Cttee to Min of Com and Ind, 1968-. Address: Israel Diamond Exchange, 1 Jabotinsky Road, Ramat Gan 52520, P O Box 3025, Israel.

SCHOLTENS James Henry, b. 12 June 1920, Moreland, Vic, Aust. Retired. m. Mary Maguire, 17 Mar 1945, 1 s, 5 d. Education: PMGS Dept, Melbourne, 1935; Cntrl Tax Off, Melbourne, 1936-38; Dept of Com, Melbourne & Canberra, 1938-49; Served RAAF, 1942-45; Acct Dept, PM&C, 1949-54; I/c of Govt Ceremonial and Hospitality, 1955-80; Dir, Visits by Mbrs of Roy Family, For Hds of State, Hds of Govt, etc, 1961-80; CEO, C'wlth Visits, 1963-70; Dir, Off of Govt Ceremonial and Hospitality, Dept of PM and Cabinet, 1973-80; Austl Dir, Roy Visits by HM The Queen and HRH The Duke of Edinburgh, 1973, 1974, 1977, 1980; App Extragentlemen Usher to HM The Queen, 1981. Honours: CVO, 1963; KCVO, 1977. Address: 34 Teague Street, Cook, ACT 2614, Australia.

SCHONFELD William Rost, b. 28 Aug 1942, NYC, USA. Dean; Professor. m. Elena Beortegui, 23 Jan 1964, 2 d. Education: BA (cum laude), Govt, NY Univ, 1964; MA, Pol, Princeton Unv, 1968; PhD, Pol, 1970. Appointments: Rsch Asst, Cntr of Intl Stdies, 1966-69, Rsch Assoc, 1969-70, Visng Lectr, 1970, Princeton Univ; Asst Prof Pol Sc, Univ CA, Irvine, 1970-75; Dir Grad Studies, Sch of Socl Scis, 1970-73, Assoc Prof, Pol Sc, 1975-81, UC Irvine; Co-dir, focused rsch prog in authy stdies, 1981-84, Acting Assoc Dean Grad Stdies, Sch of Socl Sci, 1985-86, 1991-98, Prof Pol Sc, 1981-, Dean, Sch of Socl Sci, 1982-; Visng Asst Prof UC Berkeley, Summer, 1972; Snr Lectr, Fndn Natl des Sciences Politiques, Paris, 1973-74; Rschr, Cntr de Sociologie des Orgns, Paris, 1976-78. Publications: Youth and Authority in France: A Study of Secondary Schools, 1971; Obedience and Revolt: French Behaviour Toward Authority, 1976; Ethnographie du PS et du RPR: Les elephants et l'aveugle, 1985; Contbr, num book/MS reviews and over 20 articles to profl jrnls. Honours: Phi Beta Kappa, 1964; Phi Sigma Alpha, 1964; Fulbright Fellshp, France 1964-65; Danforth Grad Fellshp, 1964-69; Summer Fac Fellshp, Univ of CA, 1971; Fulbright Snr Lectr, France, 1973-74; NSF-CNRS Exchange of Sci Prog Fell, France 1976-78; Ford Fndn grantee, 1978-79; Distingushed Tchg Awd UC Irvine, 1984; Prof of Yr Finalist, Cncl for Advmnt and Support of Educ, 1984; Outstndng Tchr Effectiveness Awd, Inter-Frat Cncl and Panhellenic Assn, 1987; Distinguished Fac Lectureship Awd for Tchng (Univ of CA, Irvine), 1998. Address: University of California, Irvine, School of Social Sciences, 3151 Social Science Plaza, Irvine, CA 92697-5100, USA.

SCHROEDER William John, b. 9 June 1944, Havre de Grace, MD. Electronics Executive. m. Lee, 28 May 1966, 3 d. Education: BEE, Marquette Univ, 1966; MSEE, Marquette Univ, 1968; MBA, Harvard Univ, 1972. Address: Diamond Multimedia Systems Inc, 2880 Junction Avenue, San Jose, CA 95134-1922, USA.

SCHUNTNER Lyle Thomas, b. 2 Dec 1936. Company Director. m. Valerie Shannon, 4 May 1959, 2 s, 1 d. Education: BA; AEd; Ctf in Educ, Univ Qld. Appointments: Tchr, 1956-77; Pres, Qld Tchrs Union, 1978-86; Chmn, Qld Tchrs Credit Union, 1985-; Mbr, State Parly, 1986-89; Mngr, Review Sect, Bd of Snr Second Sch Stdies, 1990-93. Honour: Life Mbr, Qld Tchrs Union, 1988. Memberships: FACE; FAICD. Hobby: Golf. Address: 34 Woonalee Street, Kenmore, Qld 4069, Australia.

SCHURMANN Edwin Adolf (Ted), b. 7 Aug 1917, Natimuk, Vic, Aust. Author. m. Victoria Riddles, 29 Apr 1944, 1 s, 1 d. Publications: No Trains on Sunday, 1967; Shop!, 1975; The Showie, 1978; Charlie up a Gum Tree, 1985; I'd Rather Dig Potatoes, 1987; The Moon is Shining, 1988; Boobook, 1991; The Big Horses, 1993; Bird Books: Every Australian Bird Illustrated, 1975;

Australian Waterbirds, 1982; Birdwatching in Australia, 1977; Australian Birdwatchers Diary, 1984; Columnist, Weekly Times, 1973-83. Honour: Shortlisted, Jnr Book of the Yr, 1983. Memherships: Quill Club, 1939-80, Pres, 1961-70; PEN; Austl Soc of Auths; Ringwood Field Naturalists, fndng mbr; Bird Observers Club. Hobbies: Birdwatching; Land for Wildlife; Conservation; Family history; Travel. Listed in: Australian Writers' Who's Who; Australian Children's Writers' Who's Who. Address: Inbarendi, RMB 610, Inglewood, Vic 3517, Australia.

SCHUSTER Danny Frank, b. 20 July 1949. Winemaker; Viticultural Consultant. m. Mari S Schuster, 15 July 1989, 1 s, 2 d. Education: Dip in Viticulture and Oenology. Appointments: Dir, Winemaker, Omihihills Vineyard NZ; Pt-time Lectr, Lincoln Univ and Poly Inst, NZ; Cslt, Stag's Leap Wine Cellars, USA, and Tenuta Ornellaia-Antinori, Italy; Wine Judge, Pacific Northwest Competition, USA; Top-100 Competition, NZ; Patron, Canterbury Chess Assn; Wine Columnist, Christchurch Press, NZ. Publications: Grape Growing, Winemaking in Cool Climates, 1981, 1985, 1995; Wine Service and Appreciation, 1983; Introduction to Cacti, 1983; World of Cacti, 1990. Memberships: NZ Wine Inst Inc; Austl Soc of Oenology/Viticulture; Canterbury Chess Assn; NZ Guild of Food/Wine Writers; Intl Wine and Food Soc. Hobbies: Wine appreciation; Chess; Travel; Wine education; Cacti; Tennis. Address: 192 Reeces Road, Omihi Valley, Waipara - Rd 3, Amberley, New Zealand.

SCHWARTZ Herb, b. 1 May 1940, Chicago, IL, USA. Mediation Lawyer. m. Karen Lawson, 1 Sept 1991, 1 s, 2 d. Education: JD; Tchng Cert. Appointments: Sec, SPIDR; Pres, East Bay League; Chairperson, Concord Naval Weapons Restoration Advsry Bd. Publication: Conservation Easements, 1999. Memberships: SPIDR; ABA; NLG. Address: PO Box 370, Garberville, CA 95542, USA.

SCHWARZ Mark Philip, b. 25 Dec 1953. Research Scientist. Education: BSc hons, Phys, Univ Qld, 1975; PhD, Phys, ANU, 1979. Appointments: J Willard Gibbs Instr, 1979-81, Lectr, 1981-82, Yale Univ; Monash Univ Fell, 1982-84; ICI Rsch Sci, 1984-85; Rsch Sci, 1985-87, Snr Rsch Sci, 1987-91, Proj Ldr, 1990-, Prin Rsch Sci, 1992-, CSIRO. Publications: Over 100 jrnl pprs and ind rprts. Honours: Univ Medal, Univ of Qld, 1975; J Willard Gibbs Instrshp, Yale Univ, 1979; Inaugural CSIRO Minerals Innovation Awd, 1996. Memberships: Amn Physl Soc; Iron and Steel Soc; Austl Inst of Mining and Metall. Hobbies: Reading; Gardening. Address: CSIRO Minerals, PO Box 312, Clayton North, Vic 3169, Australia.

SCORGIE Michael Edwin, b. 3 Feb 1936, Melbourne, Australia. University Professor. m. Kathleen, 19 Dec 1975, 1 s. Education: BCom, hons, Melbourne. Appointment: La Trobe Univ, 1973-. Publications: Sev articles in profl jrnls. Membership: Inst of Chart Accts in Aust. Hobby: Tennis. Address: 19 Hardwood Court, Micham, Victoria 3132, Australia.

SCOTT Brian Walter, b. 23 Apr 1935, Melbourne, Vic, Aust. Company Director. m. Dorothy Allen, 15 Aug 1959, 2 s, 2 d. Education: BEcon, Sydney Univ, 1955; MBA, Stanford Univ, USA, 1959; DBA, Harvard Univ, USA, 1963. Appointments: Mngt Dir, W D Scott & Co Pty Ltd, 1974-85; Chmn Mngmt Frontiers Pty Ltd, W D Scott Intl Dev Cnslts Pty Ltd, TV Makers Pty Ltd, ACI Intl Ltd (Chmn 1986-89), Fndn for Dev Corp Ltd; Chmn, ASEAN-Austl Bus Cncl, 1980-82; Dirshp, ANZ Banking Grp Ltd & Liquid Air (Aust) Ltd; Chmn, Austl Govts Trade Dev Cncl, 1984-90; Chmn, Aust Korea Fndn. Publication: Long-Range Planning in American Industry, 1965. Honours: AO, 1985 Austl Mftng Export Cncl Awd for Personal Contbn to Export, 1989. Memberships: Dir, Austl Grad Sch of Mngmt, 1974-84; Chmn, Knox Grammar Sch, Sydney, 1981-89; Fell, Inst of Dirs in Aust, Pres, 1982-86; Cttee to Review, Effectiveness and Efficiency in Higher Educ, 1985-86; Fell, Intl Acady of Mngmt; Fell, Inst of Mngmt Cnslts in Aust; Fell, Austl Inst of Mngmt; Dir, Mngmt Review of Educ Portfolio for NSW Govt, 1988-90; Chmn, External Cncl of Review, NSW Schs Renewal Prog, 1990-94; Fell of Senate, Univ of

Sydney, 1990-95; Bd of Govs, Asian Inst of Mngmt. Hobbies: Reading; Travel. Address: 47 Arabella Street, Longueville, NSW 2066, Australia.

SCOTT Catherine Margaret Mary (Dame), b. 26 Apr 1922, S Afr. Ballet Dancer; Ballet Director. m. Derek Ashworth Denton, 13 Mar 1953, 2 s. Education: Parktown Convent, Johannesburg, S Afr. Appointments: Sadlers Wells Ballet, London, Eng, 1941; Prin, 1943-48, Ballet Mistress, 1951-53, Ballet Rambert; Prin, Natl Th, Vic, Aust, 1949; Fndr, Dir, Austl Ballet Sch, 1963-90; Dance Panel, Austl Cncl, 1972-73; Mbr, Cncl, Vic Coll of Arts, 1973-87; Bd Dir, Austl Dance Th, 1980-83. Honours: OBE, 1977; DBE, 1981; Doct of Law honoris causa, Melbourne Univ, 1989. Memberships: Austl Ballet Soc Cttee, 1983-84; Hon Life Mbr, Austl Ballet Fndn, 1988-; Lifetime Achmt Awd, Green Room Awds, 1998; Lifetime Achmt in Dance, Austl Dance Awds, Sydney, 1998. Hobbies: Music; Gardening. Address: 816 Orrong Road, Toorak, Vic 3142, Australia.

SCOTT Keith Malcolm, b. 24 Oct 1948, Glenelg, South Australia. Geochemist; Mineralogist. m. Geochemist; Mineralogist. m. Lynette Sandra Hood Penn, 6 Jan 1973, 1 s, 2 d. Education: BSc, Adelaide Univ, 1970; MSc, Macquarie Univ, 1975. Appointments: CSIRO Div of Exploration and Mining, Scientist, 1969; Prin Rsch Sci, 1990; Cooperative Rsch Cntr for Landscape Evolution and Mineral Exploration, CRC LEME, 1995-. Membership: Fell, Assn Exploration Geochemists. Address: 1 David Avenue, North Ryde, NSW 2113, Australia.

SCOTT Kenneth John, b. 15 June 1933. Biochemist. m. Janet S D Graham, 24 May 1963, 2 s, 2 d. Education: BScAgr, 1st class hons; MScAgr; PhD; DSc.Agr. Appointments: Lectr, Snr Lectr, Univ of Sydney; Rdr, Prof, Univ Qld. Publications: 1 book and over 100 sci pubs in intl sci jrnls. Honours: Life Mbr, Clare Hall, Cambridge; Fell, Am Phytopathol Soc; Fell, Aust Inst of Biol; Mr, R & A Golf, St Andrews. Memberships: Am Soc of Plant Phytopathol; Am Phytopathol Soc; Austl Biochem Soc; Austl Plant Pathol Soc. Hobbies: Music; Golf; Farming. Address: Department of Biochemistry, University of Queensland, St Lucia, Qld 4072, Australia.

SCOTT Rosie, b. 22 Mar 1948, NZ. Writer. m. 28 Nov 1987, 2 d. Education: MA Hons, Engl, 1968; Grad Dip, Drama, 1984. Appointments: Mbr, Qld Lit Bd, Cttee Mbr Austl Soc of Auths, 1994-. Publications: Flesh and Blood, poetry, 1984; Queen of Love, stories, 1989; Novels: Glory Days, 1988; Nights with Grace, 1990; Feral City, 1992; Lives on Fire, 1993; Movie Dreams, 1995; The Red Heart (collec of non-fiction), 1999; Cntbtns to: Literary essays, poems, stories to: Rolling Stone; Metro; Island; Australian Book Review; 24 Hours; Australian Author. Honours: Sunday Times Bruce Mason Awd for play, Say Thankyou for the Lady, 1986; Glory Days, shortlisted, Natl Book Awd, 1988; Feral City, shortlisted, Austl Natl Book Awds; Movie Dreams Shortlisted, Natl Book Awd and NSW Book Awds; Austl Writers Fellowship, Category A, 1992; Shortlisted for Austl-Can Lit Awd, 1993. Memberships: PEN NZ; Austl Soc of Auths; Elected Chmn, Austl Soc of Auths, 1998; Greenpeace; ACF. Address: 21 Darghan Street, Glebe, NSW 2037, Australia.

SCOTT Tony, b. 21 Jun 1944. Film Dir. Education: Sunderland Coll of Art; Leeds Coll of Art; Roy Coll of Art Film and TV Dept. Appointments: Dir One of the Missing, 1989; Asst Dir Dream Weaver, 1967; The Movement Movement, 1967; Cameraman The Visit; Cameraman Untitled; Cameraman Compromise; Cameraman Milian; Cameraman Fat Man; Wrked for Derrick Knight & Alan King Assocs; Visual Dir and Cameraman pop promotional films Now Films Ltd; Tv Cameraman Seven Sisters, 1968; Co-prodr and actor Don't Walk - promotional film; Asst Cameraman Gulliver; Writer Dir Ed Loving Memory, 1969-70; Visual Dir and Cameraman publicity film for Joe Egg; Other films incl: Revenge; Top Gun; Beverly Hills Cop II; Days of Thunder; The Last Boy Scout; True Romance; Crimson Tide; The Fan; Dir Scott Free Enterprises Ltd; Dir of Tv and cinema comls for Ridley Scott and Assocs. Honours: Grand Prix; Mar Del Plata

Fest Argentina; Prix de la Tv Suisse; Nyon; Second Prize Equire Film Fest USA; Dip of Merit Melbourne for One of the Missing, 1989. Address: c/o Bill Unger, 752 26th Street, Santa Monica, CA 90402, USA.

SCOTT William John, b. 9 Sept 1916, Te Awamutu. Former MP and Minister of the Crown, now Company Director. m. Mary Royal Jackson, d. 1981. Appointments: MP, Rodney (natl), 1954-69 (retd); Snr Govt Whip, 1961-63; Mbr, Exec Cncl, 1963-69; Postmaster-Gen, responsible for 1st Earth Satellite Stn, 1963-66; Min of Brdcstng, introduced TV to NZ, 1963-66; Min of Marine, created 1st sci marine reserve (Goat Island), 1963-69; Min in Charge, Govt Printing Off, 1963-69; Ldr, NZ deleg CPA Conf, Malaysia, 1963; Trinidad, 1969; Dpty-Chmn CPA, 1962-63; Colombo Plan Conf, 1969; Dir, Seatrans (NZ), 1970-75; N Shore Ferries, Waiheke Shpping Co Ltd; Kawau Island Ferries Ltd, 1977-80; Governing Dir Lakewood Trading Co Ltd, WJ Scott Holdings Ltd, Mngng Dir Devonport, Glen Eden, Mangere Bridge and Ponsonby Travel Cntrs, 1976-84. Honours: Hon Col of KY; Freeman Cty of Louisville, KY, 1961; Chmn nd Life Mbr, NZ Historic Places Trust, 1970-73; Trustee and Life Mbr of Mus of Transport & Technol, 1970-78; Awd'd NZ Commemoration Medal, 1990 and QSO, 1995. Memberships: Auckland Club; Roy NZ Yacht Squadron. Hobbies: Fishing; Gardening. Address: 1201/45 Stanley Point Road, Devonport, Auckland 1309, New Zealand.

SCRIVEN Wilton Maxwell, b. 10 Dec 1924, SA, Aust. Engineer. m. 10 Jan 1948, 2 s, 2 d. Education: BSc, Univ of Adelaide, 1951. Appointments: Flying Offr, Mildenhall, Eng, 1942-45; Engr, P G Dept, 1952-65; Regl Dir, Dept of Trade, Adelaide, 1966-67; Chmn, I R & D Grants Bd, Canberra, 1967-69; Dir, Indl Dev, SA Govt, 1970-76; Agent-Gen, Dept of Premier and Cabinet, SA, 1981-83; Dir of Lands, SA, 1983-84; Present Appts: Dir, Cncl on the Ageing; Dir, Investigator Sci and Technol Cntr. Honour: AO, 1983. Membership: Fell, Inst of Engrs, Aust. Hobbies: Woodcarving; Flute; Tennis; Golf. Address: 7 Knightsbridge Road, Leabrook, SA 5068, Australia.

SCULTHORP Richard John, b. 6 May 1949. Teacher. m. (1) Peta Torpy, 8 May 1975, (2) Gretta O'Brien, 20 Oct 1980, 1 s, 1 d. Education: BSc, hons, Durham, 1973; Ctf in Educ, London, 1974. Appointments: Dickson Coll, ACT, 1976-85; Chmn, Phys Accreditation Panel, ACT, 1977-85; Chmn, Astron Accreditation Panel, ACT, 1980-85; Newington Coll, Sydney, 1986-; HS Ctf Phys Examiner, 1988-96; Pre-Puln Assessor, 1989, 1990; Snr Examiner, 1994-96. Publications: Apparent magnitude, absolute magnitude and the distance formula, 1989; Static Electricity and Electric Potential, 1990; The Teaching of Electro-Magnetism and the Speed of Light, 1991. Honour: CRA Fellshp, 1985. Memberships: MAIP; Fndr Mbr, Astronomy and Space Exploration Liaison Cttee. Hobbies: Chess; Golf; Live theatre; Literature. Address: PO Box 48, Balmain, NSW 2041, Australia.

SE-IL Sonn, b. 10 June 1935, Pusan. Politics. m. Hu-Suk Ko, 1 s, 1 d. Education: Bachelor of Pols, Seoul natl Univ. Creative Works: Human Right and Nationalism; Lee Sung Man and Kim Gu; The Study of Outbreak Korean War Backgroung. Memberships: Trade, Ind and Energy Cttee; Natl Assembly Rep of Korea. Hobbies: Reading. Address: 323 Assemblyman Hall, 1 Yoido-Dong, Youngdeungpo-Gru, Seoul, Korea.

SEAMAN Gerald Roberts, b. 2 Feb 1934, Leamington Spa, Eng. Musicologist. m. (1) Lorna Viven Johnston, 21 Dec 1964, dec 1993, 2 d, (2) Katherine Fairchild, 27 Apr 1995. Education: Birmingham Sch of Music, 1951-52; MA, DPhil, Keble Coll, Oxford, 1954-62; Leningrad Conservatory, 1960-61. Appointments include: 1st brdcst at age 15; Regular brdcstr in Eng, then Aust and NZ. Publications: History of Russian Music, 1968; Orchestral Scores: A Finding List, 1984; Rimsky-Korsakov, A Bibliography Research Guide, 1988; The Letters of Borodin, in Musical Quarterly, 1984. Honour: Snr Assoc Mbr, St Antony's Coll, Oxford, 1972-. Membership: Intl Assn of Music Lib, NZ Br, Pres, 1981-82. Hobbies: Languages; Travel. Address: St Antony's College, Oxford OX1 6JF, England.

SEAMAN Keith Douglas (Sir), b. 11 June 1920, McLaren Vale, SA, Aust. Former State Governor. m. Joan Isabel Birbeck, 17 Aug 1946, 1 s, 1 d. Education: BA 1953, LLB 1955, Adelaide Univ; DipHum 1985, MA 1987, Flinders Univ. Appointments: Pub Serv 1937-54; Served to Flt-Lt, RAAF, 1941-45; Meth Min, 1954-; Supt, Adelaide Cntrl Miss and Chmn, 5KA, 5AU, 5RM Brdcstng Socl Welfare Commn, 1973-76; Gov of SA, 1977-82; Visng Schl, Flinders Univ, 1987-. Honours: OBE, 1976; KStJ, 1978; KCVO, 1981. Hobbies: Gardening; Reading; Australian History. Address: 93 Rosetta Village, Maude Street, Victor Harbor, SA 5211, Australia.

SEAWA Isoa, b. 15 Oct 1956, Nadroga, Fiji Islands. Market Vendor. m. Naheni, 13 Apr 1987, 2 s. Appointment: Cttee Mbr, Cagimaira Devel Assn, Fiji. Hobbies: Television; Soccer. Address: c/o Cagimaira Development Association, PO Box 1038 BA, Fiji.

SECCOMBE Philip Kenneth, b. 19 Feb 1944. Geologist. m. Margaret Ann Godson, 23 Dec 1967, 2 s, 1 d. Education: BSc, 1966, MSc, 1968, Melbourne; PhD, Manitoba, 1973. Appointments: Mine Geol, Emperor Mines Ltd, Fiji, 1968-69; Geol, Selco Mining Corp, Toronto, Can, 1970; Postdoct Rsch Fell, Dept of Econ Geol, Univ of Adelaide, 1974-76; Lectr, Dept of Geol, Univ of Newcastle, 1976-83; Visng Rsch Fell, Dept of Geoscis, PA Univ, USA, 1981-82; Snr Lectr, Dept of Geol, Univ of Newcastle, 1984-92; Visng Prof, Dept of Geol Scis, Univ BC, Can, 1989-90; Assoc Prof, Geol, Univ of Newcastle, 1993-, Hd, Dept of Geol, 1994-95, 1998-. Publications include: Multiple sulphur sources for seafloor exhalative mineralisation: Sulphur isotopic distribution in the Buttle Lake polymetallic massive sulphide deposits, 1991; Lead isotopes as genetic indicators in the turbidite-hosted gold deposits of Hill End, NSW, 1993; Nature and evolution of metamorphic fluids associated with turbidite-hosted deposits: Hill End goldfield, NSW, 1993; Stable isotope systematics of Cu-Zn-Pb mineralisation in the Olary Block, SA, 1995. Memberships: Assn of Exploration Chems; Austl Inst of Geoscis; Geol Soc of Aust; Geol Assn of Can; Intl Assn for the Genesis of Ore Deposits; Mineralogical Assn of Can; Soc of Econ Geol; Soc for Geol Applied to Mineral Deposits. Hobbies: Skiing; Bushwalking; Music. Address: 124 Andrew Road, Valentine, NSW 2280, Australia.

SEDIVKA Jan Boleslav, b. 8 Sept 1917, Czechoslovakia. Concert Violinist. m. Beryl Thomas. Education: Pvte Stdy in violin; Masters Dip, Prague Conservatoire; French Govt Schlshp, Ecole Normale de Musique, Paris; Czech Govt Schlshp, London. Appointments: Hd, Instrumental Dept, Surrey Coll of Music, Eng; Dir, Chmbr Music Classic, Goldsmiths Coll, Univ London; Prof of Violin and Chmbr Music, Trinity Coll, London; Prin Violin Lectr, Qld Conservatorium, Brisbane, Aust; Dir, Tasmanian Conservatorium; Currently Master Musician-in-Res, Univ Tas; Visng Lectr, num univs and conservatoria; Ldr, London Czech trio; London Intl trio; Tasmanian Conservatorium Trio. Creative works include: Solo perfces w many orchs; recdngs; Sonata recitals w Beryl Sedivka. Honours: AM, 1987; Fell, Trinity Coll, London; Prof, Shanghai Conservatory; LLD, Univ Tasmania; Hon Prof, Univ Tas; Gold Medal, Prague Acady Musical Arts, 1992; Hon Citizen, Roy Cty of Slany, Czech Repub; Sir Bernard Heinze Mem Awd, 1996. Memberships: Rotary Clubs; Life Mbr, Austa. Address: 25 Browns Road, Kingston, Tas 7050, Australia.

SEFTON Ann Elizabeth, b. 8 July 1936. Professor. m. 9 Jan 1961, 1 s, 1 d. Education: BSc, Med; MB. Appointments: RMO, Prince Alfred Hosp, 1960; Rsch Fell, 1962-64; Lectr, Dept of Physiol, Univ of Sydney, 1965-79; Snr Lectr, 1980-84, Assoc Prof, 1985-91, Prof, 1992-, Assoc Dean, Fac of Med, 1994-; Assoc Dean, Facs of Med and Dentistry, 1999-; Chair, Acad Forum, Univ of Sydney, 1999-2000. Publications: 80 sci and educl pprs; 11 book chapts; 2 ed books; 17 misc publns; 85 abstracts for sci and educl meetings; 6 invited book reviews; 46 rprts and plcy docs. Honours: Ex in Tchng, Univ of Sydney, 1990; Achievement Awd, Aust NZ Assn of Med Educ, 1993; Lions Awd, 1995; Austl Awd, Univ Tchng, 1998. Memberships: Aust Neurosci Soc; Aust

Physiol and Pharm Assn; Aust NZ Med Educ Assn; Higher Educ Rsch and Devl Soc; NY Acady of Scis; Chair, Tchng Comms, Intl Union of Physiological Scis, 1997-2001. Hobbies: Music; Reading; Growing Austl Plants; Bushwalking. Address: Faculty of Medicine, University of Sydney, NSW, Australia.

SEGAL Helene Rose, b. 31 Jan 1955, Los Angeles, CA, USA. Managing Editor. Education: BA, Engl, Univ of CA, Santa Barbara, 1978. Appointments: Mngng Ed, ABC POI SCI, ABC-CLIO, 1983-; Asst Ed, ABC POL SCI, ABC-CLIO, 1980-83. Memberships: Advsry Bd Mbr, Current World Ldrs, 1989-; Amn Polit Sci Assn. Hobbies: Reading; Swimming; Arts. Address: 130 Cremona, Santa Barbara, CA 93117, USA.

SEGAR Ashok, b. 14 Feb 1962, Singapore. General Practitioner. Education: BMEdSci, Sri Lanka; MBChB, Aberdeen. Appointments: CEO, Segar Medl Servs Pte Ltd, 1996; CEO, House of Segar Pte Ltd, 1998. Hobbies: Philately; Reading; Movies. Address: 522, East Coast Road, #15-03, Singapore 458966, Republic of Singapore.

SEHGAL Amar Nath, b. 5 Feb 1922 Campbellpur W Pakistan. Sculptor. m. Shukla Dhawan, 1954, 2 s. Education: Punjab Univ; Govt Coll Lahore; NY Univ. Appointments: One-man exhibns NY, 1950-51; Paris, 1952; E Africa and India; Organized sculpture exhibns in Belgrade, 1964; Musee d'Art Etat Luxembourg, 1966; Wiener Secession Vienna, 1966; Participated in Sculpture Biennale Musee Rodin Paris, 1966; Flemish Acady Arts, 1967; Tokyo Intl Fair, 1973; Etc; Retrospective exhibn Natl Gall of Modern Art New Delhi, 1972; UNESCO Conf on role of art in contemporary soc, 1974; Retrospective exhibn Cty Hall Ottawa, 1975; Aerogolf Luxembourg, 1975; India House NY, 1976; Rathaus Fransheim Fed Repub of Germany, 1977; Frankfurt Airport, 1977; Neustadt, 1978; Brenners Park Baden-Baden, 1979; Org Intl Children Art Workshop UNESCO Paris, 1979; Luxembourg, 1980; Exhibns Dubai Abu Dhabi, 1980; Jeddah, 1981; Chaux de Fond - Switzerland - 1982; Cercle Munster Luxembourg, 1987; Berne, 1988; NY, 1991; London, 1991; New Delhi, 1992; Est The Creative Fund charitable org. Major Wrks: Voice of Africa - Ghana - 1959; A Cricketer, 1961; Mahtma Gandhi; Amritsar; To Space Unknown - bronze Moscow - 1963; Commissioned to decorate Vigyan Bhawan - India's Intl Confs Bldg - with bronze sculptural mural depicting rural life of India; Bronze wrk Conquest of the Moon; White House Collection, 1969; Anguished Cries - bronze - monument W Berlin, 1971; Gandhi monument Luxembourg, 1971; Monument to Aviation New Delhi Airport, 1972; Rising Spirit White House Collection, 1978; The Crushing Burden inaugurated 2nd World Population Conf Mexico, 1984; Victims of Torture designed for UN; Monument to Freedom Fighters of Namibia Vienna, 1986; Bust of Sam Nujoma - qv - Natl Gall of Modern Art New Delhi, 1993; Intl Year of Peace sculpture Head with Horns, 1986; Captive inaugurated at UN Conf on sanctions against S Africa Paris, 1986; Nari monument to Women Intl Women's Day, 1986; Flute Player - gift of children of India to UNICEF - 1986; Monument to Nehr, 1989; Exhibn of gold scultpures Luxembourg, 1990; Wrks in Jerusalem Vienna Paris W Berlin Antwerp Luxembourg CT New Delhi. Publications: Arts and Aesthetics; Organising Exhibitions in Rural Areas; Der Innere Rhythmus - poems - 1975; Folio of Graphics, 1981; Folios of graphics with poetry in English French Arabic, 1981-84; Folio on Ganesha, 1991; Lonesome Journey; A Collection of Poems, 1996; Awaiting a New Dawn, 1997. Honours: Hon Art Consultant to min of Community Dev Govt of India, 1955-66; Sculpture Awd Lalit Kala Acady, 1957; Pres's Awd Lalit Kala Acady, 1958 - donated to PM Nehru during Chinese invasion; UN Peace Medal, 1985; Fell Lalit Kala Acady, 1992. Hobbies: Writing poetry; Photog. Address: The Creative Fund, 1 Montee de Clausen, 1343 Luxembourg.

SEIDLER Harry, b. 25 June 1923, Vienna, Austria. Architect. m. Penelope Evatt, 15 Dec 1958, 1 s, 1 d. Education: BArch, 1st class hons, Univ of Manitoba, Can, 1944; MArch, Harvard Univ, USA, 1946; Black Mountain Coll, NC, USA, 1946. Appointments: Chf Asst Arch, Marcel Breuer, NY, USA, 1946-48; Worked w Oscar Niemeyer, Rio de Janeiro, Brazil, 1948; Pvte Prac, Sydney Aust, 1949-. Publications: Houses, Interiors & Projects, 1949-54, 1954; Harry Seidler, 1955-63, 1963; Architecture for the New World, 1973; Australian Embassy, 1979; Two Towers, 1980; Internment: The Diaries of Harry Seidler, 1986; Towers in the City, 1988; Riverside Centre, 1988; Harry Seidler: Four Decades of Architecture, 1992; Harry Seidler: Master Architect Series III, 1996. Honours: Sir John Sulman Medal, 1951, 1967, 1981, 1983, 1991; Wilkinson Awd, RAIA, 1965, 1966, 1967, 1999; Zelman Cowan Awd, 1987; Hon Dr, Univ Manitoba, 1988, Univ Technol, Sydney, 1991, Univ of NSW, 1999; Qld RAIA Triennial Robin Dods Medal, 1989; RAIA Natl Com Arch Awd, 1991, 1992; RAIA Natl Interior Arch Awd, 1991; Hon LLD, Univ of Technol, Sydney, 1991; Cross of Hons 1st Class, Arts and Scis, Repub of Austria, 1995; Roy Gold Medal, RIBA, 1996. Memberships: Hon Fell, RIBA, 1997; Hon Fell, Am Inst of Archs, 1966; Life Fell, RAIA (Aust), 1970; Acad D'Arch, Paris, 1982; Acad, Intl Acady of Archs, Sofia, 1987; Fell, Austl Acady of Technol Scis, 1989. Hobbies: Music; Skiing; Photography. Address 2 Glen Street, Milsons Point, NSW 2061, Australia.

SEILER Sylvia Lucy, b. 10 June 1922, Streatham, London, Eng. Writer; Ex-Occupational Therapist. m. JTS Seiler, 29 Aug 1950, dec, 5 s. Education: Dip in Occupational Therapy; Strategies for Lit Tutoring, Open Learning Inst. Appointments: Occupational Therapist, Natl Orthopaedic Hosp; Occupational Therapist in Post War Germany under Brit Red Cross; Occupational Therapist, Concord Repatriation Hosp, Sydney, Aust. Publications: Kettle of Little Fish, 1991; Feathered Frolics and Diverse Verses, 1996. Membership: Murgon Field Naturalists. Hobbies: Writing; Art and sculpture; Botanic Drawing; Social Work. Address: Killara, MS660 Proston, Queensland, 4613, Australia.

SEITZ Konrad, b. 18 Jan 1934, Munich, Germany. Diplomat. m. Eva, 30 Jan 1965. Education: DrPhil; MA, Fletcher Sch. Appointments: Hd, Policy Plng, German For Off, 1980; Amb to India, Italy, China. Publications: The Japanese-American Challenge to Europe, 1990; Race into the 21st Century - The Future of Europe Between America and Asia, 1998; The Global High-Tech War, 1998. Honour: Gropes Bundesverdienst Izrenz, 1998. Hobbies: Literature; Art. Address: Dahlienweg 4, 53343 Wachtlieng-Pech, Germany.

SEKO Miki, b. 26 Apr 1948, Japan. Professor. Education: MA, Keio Univ, 1974; MS, MIT, 1982; PhD, Keio Univ, 1990. Appointments: Asst Prof, Nihon Univ, Japan, 1981-85; Assoc Prof, 1985-90, Prof, 1990-98, Prof, 1998-, Keio Univ. Publication: An Econometric Analysis of Land and Housing in Japan, 1998. Honours: Swan Fndn Schlshp, MIT, 1981; Japanese Real Estate Sci Awd, 1996. Memberships: VP, Asian Real Estate Soc; Amn Econ Assn; Econometric Soc. Hobby: Tennis. Address: 1-2-32 Yukinoshita Kamakura, 248-0005, Japan.

SELANGOR HRH the Sultan of: Sultan Salahuddin Abdul Aziz Shah ibni Al-Marhum Sultan **Hisamuddin Alam Shah Haji,** b. 8 Mar 1926. Ruler. Education: Sekolah Melayu Pangkalan Batu Kelang Malay Coll Kuala Kangsar; London Univ; Tengku Laksamana Selangor, 1946. Appointments: Regent of Selangar during father's absence, 1960; Succeeded his late father as Ruler of Selangor, Sep 1960; Maj Roy Malay Regent; Chanc Univ of Agric. Honours: Hon Grp Capt Roy Malaysia Air Force. Address: Shah Alam, Selangor, Malaysia.

SELBY David Mayer, b. 13 May 1906, Melbourne, Aust. Retired Judge. m. Barbara Phillips, 29 Mar 1939, 1 s, 2 d. Education: BA 1927, LLB 1931, Sydney Univ. Appointments: War Serv, New Guinea, 1941-45; Queens Cnsl, 1960; Acting Judge, Sup Crt, Papua New Guinea, 1961-62; Jus, Sup Crt of NSW, 1962-76; Chf Judge, Family Law Div, 1976; Fell of Senate, Sydney Univ, 1964-89; Dpty Chan, Sydney Univ, 1971-86; Parly Remuneration Tribunal, 1977-80. Publications include: Hell and High Fever, 1956; Itambu, 1963; var articles in profl jrnls. Honours: Efficiency Decoration, 1962; Hon Gov, Austl Post Grad Fed of Med; AM, 1989; Hon Life Mbr, Austl Red Cross Soc, 1990; Hon Dr, Sydney Univ, 1991. Memberships: Life VP, Marriage Guidance Cncl of NSW; Chmn, Handcraft Cttee, Austl Red Cross Soc, 1971-; Med Ethics Cttee, 1981-; Past Pres, Sydney Univ Arts Assn; Medico-Legal Soc; Sydney Univ Law Grad Soc. Hobbies: Lawn Bowls; Reading; Foreign Travel. Address: 19 Pibrac Avenue, Warrawee, NSW 2074, Australia.

SELLECK Tom, b. 29 Jan 1945 Detroit MI. m. (1) Jackie Ray, div 1982, 1 step-s; (2) Julie Mack, 1987, 1 d. Education: Univ of SCa. Films incl: Myra Breckenridge; Midway; Coma; Seven Minutes; High Road to China; Runaway; Lassiter; Three Men and a Baby; Her Alibi, 1988; Quigley Down Under; An Innocent Man, 1989; Three Men and a Little Lady, 1991; Folks, 1991; Mr Baseball, 1991; Christopher Columbus: The Discovery, 1992; Mr Baseball In & Out. Tv incls: Returning Home; Bracken's World; The Young and the Restless; The Rockford Fils; The Sacketts; Played Thomas Mangum in Magnum PI; Divorce Wars; Countdown at the Super Bowl; Gypsy Warriors; Boston and Kilbridge; The Concrete Cowboys; Murder She Wrote; The Silver Fox. Honours: Hon Capt US Men's Volleyball Team, 1984. Hobbies: Volleyball; Outrigger canoe specialist.

SEN Bimal Kanti, b. 16 Apr 1941. Professor. m. Beauty, 17 June 1968, 2 s. Education: BSc, (distinction); BA, Dip in Libnshp; MLISc (gold medalist); Dip in Russian; PhD. Appointments: Offr i/c, Russian Sci Info Cntr, INSDOC, New Delhi, India, 1971-81; Dpty Hd, Educ & Trng Div, INSDOC, New Delhi, 1988-95; Co-ord, Natl Cntr on Bibliometrics, 1988-95; Hd, Natl Sci Lib, INSDOC, New Delhi, 1995; Vis Prof, Univ of Malaya, Malaysia, 1995-. Publications: On Bengali Scientific Terminology (in Bengali), 1985; Glossary of Lib & Info Sci Terms Engl-Bengali, 1988; In Search of Knowledge, 1988; Directory of Scientific Research Institutions in India, 1989; 35 rsch pprs; 6 reviews; 72 other pprs; 12 course materials for grad and master deg courses; 30 other publns; Contents List of Soviet Scientific Periodicals, 1971-80; Russian Scientific and Technical Publications: An Accession List, 1971-80; Annals of Library Science and Documentation, 1981-89; Malaysian Journal of Computer Science, 1995-; Malaysian Journal of Library & Information Science, 1996-. Honours: Prof S Dasgupta Meml Gold Medal, Univ of Delhi, 1983; Dr T M Das Fndn Awd for Popular Sci Writing in Bengali, 1994. Memberships: Life Mbr, Indian Lib Assn, Indian Assn of Spec Libs & Info Cntrs, Bengali Lib Assn, Delhi Lib Assn. Hobbies: Birdwatching; Sky Watching; Lexicographic Compilation; Popular Science Writing; Graphology; Palmistry. Address: c/o Faculty of Computer Science & Information Technology, University of Malaya, 50603 Kuala Lumpur, Malaysia.

SEN Gour Chand, b. 1 Mar 1930. Mining Consultant; Visiting Professor. m. Brigid, 3 Feb 1955, 2 s, 3 d. Education: BSc; MSc; PhD. Appointments: Mine Worker, Natl Coal Bd, 1956-58; Explosives Tech Serv Engr, ICI, India, 1962-65; Tech Serv Mngr, Rock Fall Co, 1966-81; Lectr, Snr Lectr, Assoc Prof, Hd of Dept, Mining Engrng Dept, Univ NSW, 1981-96; Fedl Univ of Rio Grande do Sul, Brazil, 1997-. Publication: Blasting Technology for Mining and Civil Engineers, (book), 1995. Honour: Fellshp, Inst of Explosive Engrs, 1993. Memberships: Fellshps: Inst of Engrs, Aust; Austl Inst of Mining and Metall; Inst of Mining Engrs. Hobbies: Rowing; Orchid growing. Address: 6/65 St Pauls Street, Randwick, NSW 2031, Australia.

SEN Mrinal, b. 14 May 1923 Faridpur - now Bangladesh. Film Dir. m. Gita Shome, 1953, 1 s. Appointments: Started making films, 1956; Dir'd 24 feature films; Vice-Chmn Fedn of Film Socs of India, 1980-92; Pres Padma Bhushan, 1981; Chmn Govt Cncl Film & Tv Inst of India, 1983-85; Chmn Indian People's Human Rights Commn, 1987-90; Pres Intl Fedn of Film Socs, 1991-; Vice-Chmn Cinema et Liberte - Paris - 1992.

Films incl: The Dawn, 1956; Wedding Day, 1960; Up in the Clouds, 1965; Calcutta, 71 and Guerrilla Fighter - Calcutta Trilogy, 1971-73; Royal Hunt, 1976; The Outsiders, 1977; Man with an Axe, 1978; And Quiet Rolls and Dawn, 1979; In Search of Famine, 1980; The Kaleidoscope, 1982; The Case is Closed, 1983; The Ruins, 1984; Genesis, 1986; Suddenly One Day, 1989; World Within World Without, 1991. Honours: Hon DLitt - Burdwan Univ - 1981; Cmdr Ordre des Arts et Lettres, 1985; Num awds. Memberships: Mbr Jury num intl film fests. Hobbies: Reading; Travelling; Loafing about. Address: 4E, Motilal Nehru Road, Calcutta 70029, India.

SEN Rabindra Nath, b. 1 Feb 1931, Calcutta, India. Professor of Ergonomics. m. Chhabi Sen, 3 Dec 1965, 1 s. Education: BSc, Hons, Psychol, 1952, MSc, 1st Class, 1954, DSc, 1963, Calcutta Univ. Appointments: Hd, Indl Psysiol Div, Asst Dir, Cntrl Labour Inst, Bombay, 1962-67; Visng Fac, Dept of Ergonomics and Cybernetics, Loughborough Univ of Technol, Eng, 1967-70; Rdr, Tchr in Charge, Ergonomics, 1970-83, Hd, Dept of Physiol, 1981-83, Prof and Tchr in Charge, 1983-97, Calcutta Univ; Visng Prof, Inst of Conservatorie Nationale des Arts et Metiers, Paris, 1990, Univ of WI, USA, Univ of Milwaukee, 1990, Nagoya Cty Univ Medl Sch, Japan, 1997; Prof, Fac of Mngmt, Univ Multimedia Telekom, Malaysia, 1998-. Publications: 275 rsch projs; 175 books and scientific pprs in peer reviewed natl and intl jrnls; Estab, 1st Postgrad tchng and rsch facility in Ergonomics in Indian subcontinent; Num pats. Honours: Firestone Awd, Soc of Indl Med, 1966; Ergonomics Soc Lectrshp, Roy Soc, UK, 1983; Disting For Scientist Awd, Human Factors Soc, USA, 1991; Hon Fellshp Awd, Ergonomics Soc, UK, 1997; Technol Transfer Awd, Ergonomics Assn, 1997. Memberships include: Mbr of Senate, Univ Multimedia Telekom, Malaysia; Cncl Mbr, Intl Ergonomics Assn; ILO Expert, 1976, 1978, 1982, 1983; Chmn, Scientific Subcttee, Regl Cntr of Occupational Hlth, Calcutta; Hon Fell, Ergonomics Soc, UK; Scientific Advsry Cttee, Indian Cncl of Medl Rsch; Inst of Instrumentation Scientists and Technolsts; Life Mbr, Indian Soc of Biomechanics; Life Mbr, Indian Sci Cong Assn. Address: HB-260, Sector 3, Salt Lake City, Calcutta 700091, India.

SEN-SARMA Parimal Kumar, b. 1 Apr 1929, Calcutta, India. Academician. m. Aparna, 7 Dec 1959, 1 s, 2 d. Education: BSc Hons, MSc, PhD, Calcutta Univ; Advd Training, Termites Culture, Inst für Angewandte Zoo, Univ Würzburg, Germany. Appointments: Rsch Asst, 1951-53, Rsch Offr, 1953-63, Snr Rsch Offr, 1963-73, Chief Rsch Offr, 1973-80, Dir, 1980-87, Forest Rsch Inst and Colls, Dehradun; Prof, Forestry and Dean, Fac of Forestry, Birsa Agricl Univ, Ranchi, 1987-92; Em Sci, Cntr for Afforestation and Ecodev, N East Hill Univ, Shillong, 1992-; Hon Sci, PG Dept of Zoo, Presidency Coll, Calcutta, 1993-. Publications: Systematics of Orental Termites, 1961; Wood Destroying Termites, 1975; Ecology of Insect Communities, 1982; Social Forestry and Environmental Management, 1990; Agroforestry - Indian Perspective, 1993; Forestry for the People, 1994; Forest Entomology, 1994; Manual of Forestry Extension Education, 1996. Honours: Jubilee Postgrad Schlsp of Calcutta Univ, 1949; Brahma Mohan Mullick Gold Medal, 1951; Univ Gold Medal, 1951; Sir Dietrisch Brandis Mem Plaque, 1984. Memberships include: Fell, Natl Acady of Scis, India; Indian Acady of Scis; Natl Acady of Agricl Scis; Indian Acady of Wood Scis; Mendelian Acady; Life Mbr, Indian Inst of Pub Admin; Zool Soc, Calcutta. Hobbies: Reading; Viewing Films; Listening to Music; Sports Viewing. Address: 334 NSC Bose Road, Debjan Apartment Complex, Flat B/4/3W, Calcutta, 700 047, India.

SENANAYAKE Y Don Ariyatilake, b. 22 Apr 1932, Colombo, Sri Lanka. Retired University Professor. m. Padma, 15 Sept 1966. Education: BS, Agric, Univ of Peradeniya, Sri Lanka, 1956; MS, Agronomy, LA State Univ, Baton Rouge, 1959; PhD, Genetics, Univ of CA at Davis, 1966; Trng Prog, Horticulture, TX A&M Univ, 1959-60; DSc, Honoris causa, Ruhuna Univ, Sri Lanka, 1996. Appointments: Tchr, Undergrad and Grad Courses on Plantation Crops, Principles of Horticulture, Crop Physiology, Horticultural Crops and Cropping Systems; Visng Prof, Agronomy, PA State Univ, 1982; Visng Prof, Horticulture, TX A&M Univ, 1983; Lectr, Div of Agronomy, 1969-73, Hd of Dept, Crop Sci, 1974-78, Dean, Fac of Agric, 1978-82, Dir, Postgrad Inst of Agric, 1986-97, Univ of Peradeniya, Sri Lanka. Publications: Over 90 articles and 40 sci commns; 1 monograph; Ed, proceedings of 1 intl conf, 2 wrkshops; Chapts for 4 books; Auth and Co-auth, 14 dev rprts; Editl Bds, num jrnls publd in Sri Lanka. Memberships: Pres, Natl Agricl Soc of Sri Lanka, 1998-99; Num plcy and advsry Cttees in the Univ, and 7 mins of gov in Sri Lanka; Cnslt, Intl Serv for Natl Agricl Rsch, the Hague, Netherlands; Assoc, external reviews of rsch instns in Sri Lanka. Address: Summerhill No 532/12, Siebel Place, Kandy, Sri Lanka.

SENARATNA Tissa, b. 15 Nov 1951, Pareigama, Sri Lanka. Research Scientist. Education: Dip, Engr Agronomist, Peoples Friendship Univ, 1975; MSc, 1975; MSc, 1981, PhD, 1985, Univ of Guelph, Can. Appointments: Tchng Asst, Univ of Guelph, Can, 1979-84; Post-doctoral Rsch Fell, 1985-86; Rsch Assoc, 1986-91; VP, Rsch, Dev, Somatica Plant Technol, 1991-93; Rsch Scientist, Adj Prof, Univ of Guelph, Can, 1993-96; Rsch Scientist, Kings Park and Botanic Garden, W Perth, Aust, 1997-. Creative Works: Inv, Process to Developm Artificial Seels, Method to Induce Multiple Stress Tolerance in Plants. Honours: Mclean's Hon Roll, 1990. Hobbies: Reading; Growing Flowers. Address: Kings Park and Botanic Garden, West Perth, WA 6005, Australia.

SENDA Kei, b. 17 Aug 1963, Shinminato, Toyama, Japan. Associate Professor. m. Yoko, 3 May 1991, 1 s. Education: PhD (Engrng). Appointments: Rsch Assoc, 1988, Lecr, 1994, Assoc Prof, 1994, Dept of Aerospace Engrng, Osaka Prefecture Univ; Visng Prof, MI State Univ, 1996-97. Publications: Introduction to Aerospace Engineering, 1998; Over 50 pprs. Honours: Best Presented Ppr Awd, AIAA Guidance, Navigation and Control Conf, 1992; Best Ppr Awd, Inst of Systems, Control and Info Engrs, 1994. Memberships: Snr Mbr, AIAA (Amn Inst of Aeronautics and Astronautics); Japan Soc for Aeronautical and Space Scis; JSME; RSJ; iSCIe; SICE. Hobbies: Playing soccer; Skiing. Address: Department of Aerospace Engineering, College of Engineering, Osaka Prefecture University, 1-1 Gakuen-cho, Sakai, Osaka 599-8531, Japan.

SENDO Takeshi, b. 5 Aug 1917, Japan. Educator; Researcher; Author. m. 16 Apr 1945, 2 s, 1 d. Education: BE, Tokyo Univ, Japan. Appointments: Prof, Mech Engrng, Meijo Univ, Nagoya, Japan, 1959-90; Hon Prof, Meijo Univ, 1990-; Curator of Lib, Meijo Univ, Nagoya, 1975-80. Publications: Treatise of High Speed Deformation of Metal, 1993, 2nd ED, 1994; Papers About Behaviour of AL Column by Drop Hammer Test, 1959-90; Over 60 collected pprs to profl jrnls. Memberships: Fell, Japan Soc Mech Engrng; Fell, Japan Soc Precision Engrng. Hobbies: Composing Haiku and Tanka; Writing; Jogging. Address: 21-8, Choei, Moriyama-ku, Nagoya 463, Japan.

SENEVIRATNA Peter, b. 30 Dec 1927, Colombo, Sri Lanka. Veterinarian. m. Kamanee, 15 Mar 1974, 2 s, 2 d. Education: DSc (hon causa); PhD, London; FRCVS, Eng; MACVS, Aust; BVSc, Madras. Appointments: Lectr, 1953-66; Prof of Vet Sci and Dean, Univ of Ceylon, 1966-74; Snr Vet Offr, Austl Govt; Snr Lectr, Murdoch Univ, 1985-90. Publications: Diseases of Poultry, 1969; (co-auth) Manual of Meat Inspection for Developing Countries, FAO, Rome, 1994. Honours: Fulbright-Hays Postdoct Rsch Awd, 1963-64; Visng Prof, Wayne State Univ, Detroit, MI, 1973. Memberships: Ceylon Vet Assn, Pres, 1963, 1968; Ceylon Assn Advmnt of Sci; Pres, Medl and Vet Sci Sects, 1961. Hobbies: Listening to classical music; Writing poetry; Reading. Address: 25, Broadbent Loop, Leeming, Perth, Australia, WA 6149.

SENFF Hans-Dieter, b. 16 Aug 1940, Germany. Author; Poet; Publisher. m. Patricia Jean Sawtell, 7 Nov 1964, 1 s, 1 d. Education: Real Estate Agt, Univ Sydney External Bd, 1968; Strata Mngr, 1983, Auctioneers Cert, 1983, TAFE, Newcastle; Grad Dip, Multicultural Stdies, Newcastle Univ, 1986; BA, Hums, Deakin and Qld Univs, 1991; Bachelor Lit, Comm, Murdoch Univ, incomplete; MA, Modern Langs, PhD, in progress, Newcastle Univ. Appointments: Chem Analyst, CSR Chems, 1971; Editl Bd, Impact, 1971-80; VP, 1972, Trade Union Sec, Assn Foremen and Supvsrs, Real Estate Agt, 1981; Auctioneer, 1983. Publications: Unheilbares Deutschland, documentation on the division of Berlin, 1983; Novel, Firestorm, 1984; Novel, West of the Wall, 1984; Australia's forgotten migrants, the Sorbs, 1984; Play, Tales from a strange land, 1985; Thesis, Setting the record straight; History of the Sorbs and their contribution to the settlement of Australia, 1986; Co-auth, The Sorbs/Wends of Lusatia, the unknown immigrants, 1988; Black Poetry with a Red Heart, 1989; Novel, Victims of the glittering Cross, 1992; Sorb Tales and Fairy Tales, 1993; Co-auth, Sorbian Folkdances, 1993; Poetry, Just another drop of Red Poison, 1995; Thes, The German Democratic Repub 1980-1995 as Reflected in German Literature, forthcoming. Honours: JP, 1971; Ernst Thaelmann Medal, VEB Ernst Thaelmann, Magdeburg, 1974; 25 Yrs German Demo Repub Medal, City Cncl Magdeburg; Kt Templars. Memberships: Full Mbr, Foremen and Supvsrs (State) Conciliation Cttee; Sch Bd, Newcastle Coll Advd; FIBA; Fell, Inst Real Estate Agts and Valuers; Multicultural Writers Assn NSW; Aust-German Demo Repub Friendship Soc, Newcastle Br Sec, Natl Cnclr; Exec Mbr, Ethnic Cmnty Cncl, Newcastle; Exec Mbr, Newcastle Progressive Alliance, 1995. Hobbies: Intl law; Multiculturalism; History; Anthropology; Writing; Art; Poetry; Austl Aborigines; Music; Working for peace and international understanding. Address: 2 Burke Street, Swansea, NSW 2281, Australia.

SENGUPTA Indra Narayan, b. 1 May 1931, Kotwalipara, Dighirpar, India. Scientist. m. Parijat, 8 Aug, 1964, 2 s. Education: MSc; AISc; PhD (Sc); PhD; FSIS; Dip in German Lang. Appointments: Snr Documentation Offr, 1968; Scientist B, 1969; Dpty Dir (documentation), 1973; Scientist C, 1975; Scientist EI, 1979; Scientist EII, 1984; Scientist F, 1989. Publications: Bibliometric Research, 1988; Scientific comms: Bibliometrics & Informetrics, 1988; 120 sci pprs inclng 1 in Nature, London. Honours: Dr Ranganathan, Kaula Gold Medal; Hon Prof of Sci, Inst of Sci, Beijing; Hon Lectr, Calcutta Univ; Cnslr, Indira Gandhi Natl Open Univ; Mbr, FID Cttee for Informetrics; Assoc Ed, Scientometrics, ILA Bulletin, Indian Jrnl of Info, Lib and Soc. Memberships: Life Mbr: Indian Lib Assn; Soc for Info Sci; Indian Medl Lib Assn; Indian Techno-Sci Libs and Info Scientists Assn. Hobbies: Stamp collecting; Gardening. Address: Indrajata A B - 277, Salt Lake City, Sector-1, Calcutta, 700064, India.

SENIBUA Aisea, b. 27 Apr 1939, Nadroga, Fiji Islands. Business Consultant. m. Salote, 6 June 1966. Appointment: Sec, Cagimaira Devel Assn, Fiji; Retd Bus Cnslt. Hobbies: Reading; Watching Soccer & Rugby. Address: c/o Cagimaira Development Association, PO Box 1038 BA, Fiji.

SENSARMA Priyadarsan, b. 1 Oct 1933, Dacca. Teacher; Researcher. m. Ira, 14 Feb 1962, 2 d. Education: MSc, 1st Class, Botany. Appointments: Lectr in Bot, 1954-72, Hd of Dept of Bot, 1972-93, Bangabasi Coll, Calcutta; Currently, Hon Coord for Classical Lit as Source of Indigenous Knowledge, Cntr for Indigenous Knowledge on Indian Bioresoureces (CIKIB), Inst of Ethnobiology, Lucknow; Currently, Hon Rsch Assoc, G C Bose Biol Rsch Unit, Bangabasi Coll, Calcutta. Publications: 35 in profl jrnls; Books include: Kurukshetra War: A Military Study, 1975; The Military Profile of Sher Shah Sur, 1976; The Military History of Bengal, 1977; Military Wisdom in the Puranas, 1979; Military Thoughts of Tiruvalluvar, 1981; Plants in the Indian Puranas: An Ethnobotanical Investigation, 1989; Ethnobiological Information in Kautiliya Arthasastra, 1998; A Lexicon of Medicinal Plants in India, 1999; Udbhider Anargathan (Plant Anatomy, in Bengali); Bharater Astra-Shastra: Pracheen theke Adhunik (in Bengali), 1998; 3 textbooks on mil sci. Honours include: Fellshp Soc of Living World

(FSLW) for outsndng contbns in Bot, 1994; Elected Fell, Soc of Ethnobotanists (FES) for important contbns in Ethnobotany, 1997. Memberships include: Mbr, Editl Bd, Jrnl of the Living World, Gorakhpur; Mbr, Exec Ctee, Natl Botl Soc, Dept of Bot, Univ Calcutta. Hobbies: Histrionics; Indology; Plants. Address: 8/P Chandra Mondal Lane, Calcutta, 700 026, India.

SEO Jung Uck, b. 14 Nov 1934. Businessman. m. 23 Oct 1963, Jung Sook Lee, 3 d. Education: BS, Elecl Engrng, Seoul Natl Univ, 1957; PhD, Elecl Engrng, TX A&M Univ, USA, 1969. Appointments: Fac Mbr, ROK Air Force Acady, 1957-70; Div Hd, VP, Pres, Agcy for Defense Dev, 1970-83; Snr Exec VP, Korea Telecom, 1984-90; Pres, Korea Inst of Telematics and Electrons, 1986-87; Vice Min of Sci & T, 1990-92; Pres, Korea Inst of Sci and Technol, 1992-93; Chmn, Commn for Radiocomms Dev, min of Info and Comms, Korea, 1993-95; Pres, SK Telecom, 1995-; Chmn, Commn for IMT-2000 System II Dev, 1998. Honours: Iron Tower Order of Indl Serv Merit, 1978; Camellia Order of Civ Merit, 1986; Yellow Stripes Order of Serv Merit, 1992; Gold Tower Order of Indl Serv Merit, 1996; Fell, IEEE, 1982. Memberships: IEEE; KITE. Hobby: Ham Radio. Address: 303 Mirabo Villa, 10-13 Yangjae 1-dong, Socho-gu, Seoul, Korea.

SEOL Woo Seok, b. 10 May 1961, Korea. Research. m. J Sohn, 16 June 1990, 2 d. Education: MSc, PhD, Univ of MN. Appointments: Postdoct, Univ of MN; Snr Rschr, Korea Aerospace Rsch Inst. Publications: Pprs in profl jrnls. Honours: Hon Soc of Phi Kappa Phi, 1990-; Excellent Rsch Awds of Kari, 1998. Memberships: ASME, 1994-; KSME, 1994-; KSAS, 1994-; KFMA, 1997-. Hobbies: Sports; Travel. Address: Korea Aerospace Research Institute, PO Box 113, Yusung, Taejon 305-600, Korea.

SEOW James Kim Chwee, b, 18 Feb 1964, Singapore. Economist. Education: MA, Econs, Univ of BC. Appointments: Econ Advsr, UOB Bank Grp w Dr Goh Keng Swee (former Dpty Prime Min of Singapore), Govt of Singapore. Honours: Funtronix Amusements Pte Ltd Bursary, 1987; 2 Univ Merit Awds, 1987, 1988. Hobby: Antiques. Address: 35 Jalan Kelempong, Singapore 509543.

SEPPI Edward J, b. 16 Dec 1930, Price, UT, USA. Physicist. m. Betty, 25 Aug 1953, 2 s, 1 d. Education: BS, Brigham Yng Univ, 1952; MS, Univ of ID, 1956; PhD, CA Inst of Technol, 1962; Postgrad, 1962. Appointments: Physicist, Hanford Labs, Gen Elec Co, WA, 1952-58; Rsch Asst, CA Inst of Technol, CA, 1958-60; Gen Elec Fell, 1960-62; Physicist, Inst of Def Analysis, DC, 1962-64; Lde, Rsch Area Phys Grp, Stanford Linear Accelerator Cntr, Stanford, CA, 1964-66; Cnslt, Inst for Def Analyses, Washington, DC, 1964-72; Mngr, Rsch Area Dept, 1966-68; Mngr, Expmtl Facilities Dept, 1968-74; Mngr, Medl Diagnostic Instrumentation, Varian, Palo Alto, CA, 1974-76; Engrng Mngr, Varian Radiation Div, 1976-77; Mngr, Varian Computer Tomography Div, 1977-78; Tech Dir, 1978-80; Snr Scientist, Varian Rsch Lab, 1980-93; Scientist, Superconducting Super Collider, Dallas, TX, 1990-91; Prin Scientist, Varian Ginston Rsch Cntr 1993-. Creative Works: Over 84 Sci publs and abstracts; Inv, 23 issued pats; Contbr, Basic Technology in Nuclear, Laser and Solid State Phys; Prin developer of electron accelerator and beam transport medl imaging instrumentation; Fast body CT system; Amorphous silicon imagers for radiology. Honors: Phi Eta Sigma, 1952; Sigma Pi Sigma; Phi Kappa Phi. Memberships: Amn Physl Soc; Cub Scout Chmn; Asst Scout Master; Ladera Comnty Assn; Genealogy Lib; LDS Ch. Hobbies: Computers; Photography; Genealogy. Address: 320 Dedalera Drive, Portola Valley, CA 94028, USA.

SEPULVEDA Bernardo, b. 14 Dec 1941 Mexico Cty. Politician. m. Ana Yturbe, 1970, 3 s. Education: Natl Univ of Mexico; Queens Coll Cambridge. Appointments: Fmrly taught intl law El Colegio de Mexico and Fac Polit Sci Univ of Mexico; Asst Dir of Juridical Affairs min of Presidency, 1968-70; Dir-Gen of Intl Fin Affairs min of Fin, 1976-81; Pres to UN Sixth Commn on Transnatl

Corps, 1977-80; Intl Advsr Min of Progng and Budget, 1981; Sec Intl Affairs Institutional Revolutionary Party - PRI - 1981-82; Amb to USA, Mar-Dec 1982; Sec of For Affairs, 1982-88; Amb to UK, 1989-93; For Affairs Advsr to Pres of Mexico, 1993-. Publications: Foreign Investment in Mexico, 1973; Transational Corporations in Mexico, 1974; A View of Contemporary Mexico, 1979; Planning for Development, 1981. Honours: Hon GCMG. Address: Rocas 195, Mexico, DF 01900, Mexico.

SERAVO Viviso, b. 3 MaR 1956, Hogotery Vill, Henganofi Dist, Eastern Highlands Prov, Papua New Guinea. Education: Goroka Techl Sch, 1970; Lae Techl Coll, Cert Plumber, 1977. Appointments: Plumber, var co's; Min for Lands.

SERIU Masafumi, b. 23 Sept 1964, Kyoto, Japan. Theoretical Physicist. Education: BS, 1987, MSc, 1989, DSc, 1992, Kyoto Univ. Appointments: Rsch Fell, Dept of Phys, Kyoto Univ, 1992-93; Postdoct Fell, Inter-Univ Cntr for Astron and Astrophys, Pune, 1993-95; Yukawa Mem Fell, Yukawa Inst for Theort Phys, Kyoto Univ, 1996; Rsch Fell, Japan Soc fr Promotion of Scis, 1996; Assoc Prof, Fukui Univ, 1996-. Publications: Sev articles in profl jrnls. Honours: Prize, Silver Jubilee Essay Comp, Indian Assn for Gen Relativity and Gravitation, 1993; Honda Heihachiro Mem Schlshp, Japan Assn for Math Scis, 1994, 1995; Yukuwa Mem Fellshp, 1995; Rsch Fellshp, Japan Soc for Promotion of Scis, 1996; Grant-in-Aid, Inamoni Fndn, 1998. Memberships: Japan Phys Soc; Japan Astron Soc; Seiwa Schls Soc. Address: Fukui University, Bunkyo 3-9-1, Fukui 910-8507, Japan.

SESSLER Andrew Marienhoff, b. 11 Dec 1928, Brooklyn, NY, USA. Physicist. m. Gladys Lerner, 23 Sept 1951, div 1994, 1 s, 1 d. Education: BA, Maths, cum laude, Harv Univ, 1949; MA, Theort Phys, Columbia Univ, 1951; PhD, Theort Phys, 1953. Appointments: Asst Prof, OH State Univ, Columbus, 1954, Assoc Prof, 1960; Visng Physicist, Lawrence Radiation Lab, 1959-60' Rschr, Theorts Phys, 1961-73, Rschr, Energy and Environ, 1971-73, Dir, 1973-80, Snr Scientist, Plasma Phys, 1980-94, Disting Snr Staff Scientist, 1994-, Univ CA Lawrence Berkeley Lab; Num advsry posns. Publications: Contbr articles in field to profl jrnls. Honours: E O Lawrence Awd, US Atomic Energy Commn, 1970; US Particle Accelerator Prize, 1988; Nicholson Medal, 1994; Robert R Wilson Prize, 1997. Memberships include: Advsry Bd, Inst Advd Phys Stdies; Amn Phys Soc; IEEE; NAS; Fedn Amn Scientists Cncl; NY Acady Sci; Assoc Univ Inc. Address: 225 Clifton Street, Apt 313, Oakland, CA 94618, USA.

SETCHELL Martin Philip, b. 16 Feb 1949, Blackpool, Lancs, Eng. Concert Organist; Lecturer; Conductor. m. Jenny Appleton Feltham, 8 May 1988, 2 d. Education: BA, French, Music, 1971, MA Music, 1973, Univ of Exeter, Eng; Dip of Educ, Music, Univ of Bristol, Eng, 1972; Fell, Roy Coll of Organists, 1979. Appointments: Asst Dir of Music, Rossall Sch, 1973; Snr Lectr in Music, Tutor in Organ, Univ of Canterbury, Christchurch, NZ, 1974-; Recd num talks and recitals for concert prog, Radio NZ; Dir of Music, Parish of Fendalton, 1988-; Music Critic, Christchurch Press, 1992-; Organist, Christchurch Town Hall, 1997-. Creative Works: Books: Aural Perception, 1979; Let the Pealing Organ Blow, 1997. Honours: Limpus and Shinn Prizes, Roy Coll of Organists, 1979. Memberships: Roy Coll of Organists; Assoc, Inst of Regd Music Tchrs. Hobbies: Cricket; Reading. Address: 235 Ilam Road, Christchurch, New Zealand.

SETH Vijendra Lal, b. 10 Nov 1945, Vitawa, Raki Raki, Fiji. Farmer. m. Pushpa Kumdri, 5 May 1985, 1 s, 1 d. Appointments: FSC Harvesting, Sang Sardor, 1989; Proprietor, Mngng Dir, Seth's Hldngs Farm and Shops; Chmn, Crime Prevention, 1995. Honours: Best Farmer of the Yr, 1996, 1997; Highest Cane Prodr, 1994-98. Memberships: Trade Union Cong, 1991; Pres, Fiji Labour Party, Raki Raki Br, 1995; Tstee, Wairuku Pub Sch; Fndn Mbr, Baily Meml Sch; Mngr, Maria Bhartiya Sch, 1997. Address: PO Box 330, Karowaqa, Raki Raki, Fiji.

SETHURAMAN Raju, b. 23 Mar 1963, Madurai. Teacher and Researcher. m. Vijayalakshmi, 19 May 1997, 1 d. Education: BE, Hons, Mech Engrng, Madurai Univ, India, 1984; PhD, Mech Engrng, Indian Inst of Technol, Bombay, India, 1990. Appointments: Asst Prof, Indian Inst of Technol, Kanpur, 1990-96; Assoc Prof, Indian Inst of Technol, Madras, 1996-. Hobby: Reading. Address: D1/111 Bonn Ave, IIT Campus, Madras, 600036, India.

SETT Smita, b. 8 Feb 1958, Calcutta, India. Teacher. m. Ranjan, 22 Apr 1990, 1 d. Education: BLISc; ADIS. Appointments: Asst Libn, S Point HS, 1982-86; Documentation Offr, Natl Inst for Enterpreneurship & Small Bus Devel, 1988-89; Ref Libn, Am Cntr Lib, 1989-95; Lectr, Vidyasagar Univ, 1995-. Memberships: Bengal Lib Assn; Indian Assn for Specl Libs & Info Cntrs. Hobbies: Reading; Music. Address: 49/8D Ballygunge Place, Calcutta 700019, India.

SEYA Tsukasa, b. 18 Oct 1950, Fukushima Prefecture, Japan. Director. m. Michiyo, 10 Nov 1990, 1 s, 1 d. Education: PhD, 1984; MD, 1987. Address: Department of Immunology, Osaka Medical Center for Cancer and Cardiovascular Diseases, Higashinari-ku, Osaka 537, Japan.

SEYMOUR Alan, b. 6 June 1927, Perth, WA. Writer. Appointments: Brdcstr; Film Critic, ABC Radio; Writer, Radio and TV Educl Drama; Opera Dir; Playwriter; TV Dramatist; BBC Commng Script Ed; Novelist. Creative Works: Swamp Creatures, 1957; The One Day of the Year, 1960; A Break in the Music, 1966. Honours: Spec Creative Awd, Roy TV Soc, 1978; BAFTA Awd; Best Children's Drama, 1984. Hobbies: Theatre; Opera; Reading; Swimming; Long Walks. Address: c/o Hilary Linstead Assoc, PO Box 1536 Strawberry Hills, NSW 5012, Australia.

SEYMOUR Tony, b. 22 Sept 1956, Hartlepool, Eng. Extension/ Community Developer. m. Lynn, 14 Apr 1982, 1 s, 2 d. Education: BSc, Hons, Agric Univ, Newcastle upon Tyne, Eng; M Applied Sci, Univ NSW, Hawkesbury. Hobbies: Dairy farming; My family's development and joy. Address: Lot 9, McIntyre Road, Yarragon, Vic 3823, Australia.

SEYPIDIN Aze, b. 1916 Artush Xinjiang. Politician. Education: Cntrl Asia Univ Moscow. Appointments: Ldr of Uighur Uprisings, 1933, 1944; Participant in armed rebellion and estab of E Turkestan Repub, 1944; Min of Educ E Turkistan Repub, 1945; Dep Chmn Xinjiang Uighur People's Govt, 1949-54; Chmn Xinjiang Uighur People's Govt, 1955-63; Dep Cmdr Xinjiang Uighur Mil Reg PLA, 1949; Second Sec CCP Xinjiang Uighur, 1956-58; Pres Xinjiang Uighur Univ, 1964; Vice-Chmn Xinjiang Uighur Revolutionary Cttee, 1968; Second Sec CCP Xinjiang Uighur, 1971; Chmn Xinjiang Uighur Revolutionary Cttee, 1972-78; First Sec CCP Xinjiang Uighur, 1973-78; First Polit Commissar Xinjiang Uighur Mil Reg PLA, 1974-78; Chmn Presidium Natl People's Congress, 1975; Exec Chmn Presidium 5th Natl People's Congress; Vice-Chmn Cttee 5th Natl People's Congress, 1978-83; Vice-Chmn Standing Cttee, 6th NPC, 1983-88; Vice-Chmn Standing Cttee 7th NPC, 1988; Exec Chmn Presidium 6th NPC, 1986-88; Exec Chmn Presidium 7th NPC, 1988; Pres China-Pakistan Friendship Assn; Vice-Chmn 8th Natl Cttee CPPCC, 1993-. Honours: Hon Chmn China Soc for Study of Yugur Hist and Culture; Hon Pres Minority Writers' Soc, 1985-; Hon Pres Minority Lit Fndn, Dec 1986. Memberships: Alt mbr 8th Cntrl Cttee of CCP, 1956; Mbr 9th Cntrl Cttee of CCP, 1969; Alt mbr Politburo 10th Cntrl Cttee of CCP, 1973, 1975-78; Alt mbr Politburo 11th Cntrl Cttee of CCP, 1976; Mbr 12th CCP Cntrl Cttee, 1982-87; Mbr 13th Cntrl Cttee, 1987-92; Mbr Presidium of 14th CCP Natl Congress, Oct 1992-. Address: 19 Xi Jiaomin Xiang Street, Xicheng District, People's Republic of China.

SEZGIN Ismet, b. 1928 Aydin. Politician. m. 2 c. Education: Izmir Sch of Econ and Trade; Dep from Aydin True Path Party - DYP - 1961-80; Fmr Min of Yth and Sports; Fmr Min of Fin; Min of the Interior, 1991-93; Min of Natl Def and Dep PM, Jun 1997-. Memberships: Fndr mbr True Path Party - DYP. Address: Milli Savunma Bakanligi, 06100 Ankara, Turkey.

SHAER Ali Hassan ash-, b. 1927 Medina. Politician. Education: Mil Acady King Saud Univ. Appointments: Chf Instr Mil Sch Taif; Dir Topography Div Mil Ops Dept; Cmdr Medina Mil Sch King Abdulaziz Mil Acady; Mil Attache Emb Pakistan; Amb to Lebanon, 1975-83; Min of Info, 1983-95. Honours: King Abdulaziz Medal - First Class; Sev for decorations. Address: c/o Ministry of Information, P O Box 570, Nasseriya Street, Riyady 11161, Saudi Arabia.

SHAFEEU Ismail, b. 15 May 1955, Malé, Maldives. Government Official. m. Aishath Nadira, 1 s, 1 d. Education: BA, Econs, Macquarie Univ, NSW, Aust, 1976; Hubert Humphrey Fell, Boston Univ, 1984-85. Appointments: Dir, Plng, Min of Plng and Environ, 1989, Dpty Min, 1989-90; Min, 1991-93; Min of Tourism, 1990-91; Min Plng, Human Rescs and Environ, 1993-. Memberships: Chmn, Natl Cncl for Protection and Preservation of Environ, Malé; Gov, Asian Dev Bank, Manila, Philippines; Active Vols for Environ and Socl Harmony and Improvement, Malé. Address: Ministry of Planning, Human Resources and Environment, Amir Ahmed Magu, Malé 20-05, Maldives.

SHAFFER John Ordie, b. 29 Aug 1920, MN, USA. Surgeon. m. Dorothea, 1 s, 1 d. Education: BS; MB; MD Surg. Appointments: Intern, Philadelphia Gen Hosp, 1943-44; Fell, Mayo Fndn, 1944-46; Chf of Surg, USS Hosp Ship Comfort, Mil Servs in Pacific Th, 1946-48; Instr, In Surg Univ of UT Med Sch; Pvt Surg Prac, Hayward CA, 1952-; Past Chf Surg, Eden Hosp, 1961; Surg Lectr, all six continents. Creative Works: Num Publs in Med Jrnls; Jama Surgery; Amn Surgeon; CA Med, Archives of Surg; Ors. Honours: San Fran Surgical Soc Awd; Dinner in his hon and citation for bravery, rescuing multiple injured sailors from pacific tanker and saving lives with emer surg at sea. Memberships: AMA; CMA; ACCMA; Amn Bd of Surg; Amn Coll of Surgs; Amn Medl Soc; Hayward C of C. Hobbies: Gardening; Photography. Address: 4584 Ewing Rd, Castro Valley, CA 94546, USA.

SHAH Aishwarya Rajya Laxmi Devi (HRH), b. 7 Nov 1949, Kathmandu, Nepa. Queen of Nepal. m. King Birendra Bir Bikram Shah Dev, 27 Feb 1970, 2 s, 1 d. Education: BA, Tribhuvan Univ, Kathmandu, 1967; Ctf in Music; Kalanidhi Sangeet Mahavidhyalaya, Kathmandu. Publications: Sev poems and lyrics under pseud Chandani Shah. Honours include: Grand Cordon of the Supreme Order of the Chrysanthemum, Japan, 1970; Order of Million Elephants and White Umbrella Grade of the Grand Cross, Laos, 1970; Grand Cordon of Yugoslav Star 1st Class, 1974; Kt Grand Cross of Most Illus Order of Chula Chom Klao, Thailand, 1979; Spec Level of the Grand Cross Order of Merit, Germany, 1986; Collar de Carlos III, Spain, 1987; Fellshp, Roy Coll of Surgeons of Edinburgh, UK, 1990; Order National du Merite, France, 1994. Memberships: Patron, Intl Women's Yr Cttee, 1975; Chair, Socl Serv Natl Co-ord Cncl, 1977-89; Chf Patron, Nepal Red Cross Soc. Hobbies: Literature; Gardening; Music. Address: Narayanhity Royal Palace, Kathmandu, Kingdom of Nepal.

SHAH Ali Mohamad, b. 27 May 1943, Srinagar, India. University Teacher (Professor). m. Wazira, 11 June 1970, 1 s, 1 d. Education: MSc; PhD. Appointments: Univ Lectr, 1971; Reader, 1980; Prof, 1988-. Publications: 2 books & rsch publs in diff sci fields. Membership: IPS, 1980-. Hobbies: Photography; Reading. Address: CORD, Kashmir University, Srinagar, J&K, India.

SHAH Ashokkumar Purshottamdas, 7 Sept 1955, Dabhoi, India. Service. m. Darshna, 9 Dec 1982, 2 d. Education: BE, Chem, 1976, Postgrad, Indl Mngmt, 1988, MS Univ, Baroda, India. Appointments: Snr Mngr, Design-Process, at pres, Gujarat State Fertilizers & Chems Ltd, 1976-. Publications: Many articles publs and presented at natl and intl levels. Honours: Awd for Safety, 1992-94; 1st Prize for Best Ppr, 1992. Memberships: Joint Sec, Offr's Club, GSFC, 1994-95; GRC - GSFC Ltd,

1990-95. Hobbies: Reading; Movies; Cricket; Writing articles. Address: Shreedhan, 50/1 Kadamnagar, Nizampura, Vadodara, 390002, Gujarat, India.

SHAH Indravadan S, b. 23 Dec 1944, Sankheda, India. Physician. m. Arvinda, 11 May 1971. Education: Grad, Baroda Med Coll, Baroda, India, 1970. Appointments include: Santa Ana Tustin Comm Hosp, Western Med Cntr, Santa Ana, CA, USA, 1978; Foothill Presbyterian Hosp, Glendora, CA, 1991-93; Santa Teresita Hosp, Duarte, CA, 1978-; Meth Hosp, Arcdadia, CA, 1979-. Memberships: Fell, Amn Coll of Physns; California Soc of Internal Med; Amn Soc of Internal Med; Fell, Amn Coll of Intl Physn; Amn Assn of Physns, India; Baroda Medl Coll Alumni Assn Inc, USA; Amn Diabetic Assn; Amn Soc of Hypertension; Indian Med Assn of Gtr Los Angeles. Hobbies: Photography; Travelling. Address: 931 Buena Vista St, #504, Duarte, CA 91010, USA.

SHAH Jayendra Arvindlal, b. 9 Jan 1937, Nadisar, India. Medical Doctor. m. Usha, 16 Feb 1963, 2 s. Education: BMedSc; MD; MBBS. Appointments: Neurol and Med Servs, Beach Neuro Electro Diagnostic Lab, Huntington Beach, 1979-86; Dir, Indl Pain Med Grp, Westminster, 1981-; Rehab Cnslt, State of CA Dept of Disability and Med, Utilization Reviewer, 1981-94; Med Dir, Inst of Rehab Med, S CA, Garden Grove, 1982-88; Spec Asst, Rehab Quality Care, Rancho LAHC, Downey DHS, LA Co, 1994-; Ptve Prac, Rehab Med and Pain, 24yrs. Publications: Sev articles in profl jrnls. Memberships: Indian Med Assn of S CA; CA Rehab Soc; CMA; Intl Rehab Med Soc; AMSUS; FAAPMR; FAAPM; FABS. Hobbies: Table Tennis; Travel; Yoga; International Festivals. Address: 1855 South West Street, Anaheim, CA 92802, USA.

SHAH Manubhai Dalsukhbhai, b. 25 Aug 1930, Wadhwan City, Gujarat. Social Services. m. Prabhavati Shah, 18 Feb 1949, 1 s, 2 d. Education: LLB. Appointments: Provident Fund Offr, The Arvind Mills Ltd, 1952-55; Labour Offr, 1955-56; Legal Offr, 1956-60; Factory Mngr, Asoka Mills Ltd, 1960-62; Gen Mngr, 1962-69; Gen Mngr, The Arvind Mills Ltd, 1969-82; Dir, Bd of Gen Ins Corp, India. Creative Works: A Fraud on Policyholders, 1978; Swallow Thy Tears; Women, A Risky Proposition; Plight of Policy Holders; A Tale of Torture; L I C and Consumer Interest; Light Fixtures or Crystal Chandeliers; Corporate Denies Life Insurance; Freedom of Expression Against L I C Vindicated; Life Insurance: A Consumer Handbook. Honours: Paul Harris Awd. Memberships: Cntrl Consumer Protection cncl; Gujarat State Consumer Protection cncl; NABL; Steering Cttee; USAEP; Many or mbrshps. Hobbies: Swimming; Boating; Reading. Address: Consumer Education and Research Centre, Suraksha Sankool, Thaltej, Ahmedabad 380054, India.

SHAH Rajesh Virendra, b. 12 June 1960, Pune, Maharashtra, India. Engineering Executive. m. Meena, 4 May 1984, 1 s, 1 d. Education: DME; BE (Mech); MDBA; MTech (Mech), IIT; Dip in Mech Engrng, 1980; BEng (Mech), 1983; MBA, 1986; MTech, Indian Inst of Technol, Bombay, 1989. Appointments: Snr Engr, Morris Electrics Ltd, Pune, 1983-87; Mngr, Tool-Room, Bajaj Tempo Ltd, Pune, 1989-; Trainee, Deckel GMBH, Munich, Germany, 1994. Honour: Spec Contbn Awd, 1997. Memberships: Soc Mfg Engrs Conf, Singapore, 1995; Visng Lectr, Cusrow Wadia Inst Technol, Pune; Jain Socl Grp, Pune, 1995-; Sec, Jain Dnyati Mandal, 1993-. Hobbies: Playing Chess, Badminton; Yoga; Music. Address: F73, Indraprastha Complex, 589 Rasta Peth, Pune 411011, India.

SHAH Shamim-ul-Sibtain, b. 10 Apr 1962, Jhang, Pakistan. Agricultural Engineer. m. 25 Dec 1995, 1 d. Education: BSc, Agric Engrng. Appointments: Water Mngmt Offr, 1985-86; Asst Agric Engr, 1986-. Publications: 3 articles in prog. Memberships: Pakistan Engrng Cncl; Jica Alumni Assn of Pakistan; Pakistan Soc of Agric Engrs. Hobbies: Reading; Music; Friendship. Address: National Agricultural Research Centre, Park Road, Islamabad, Pakistan.

SHAH Suresh Gialalchand, b. 29 Jan 1941, Ghatkoper, Manager. m. Vasanti, 17 Feb 1972, 1 s, 1 d. Education: BA. Appointments: Tstee, Bhuj Khartargachchh Jain Sangh; Tstee, Bhadreshwar Jain Dadawadi Trust; Tstee, Bhuj Jain Pathshala Trust; Tstee, Premji Bhavanji Charitable Trust; Tstee, Rashtra Bhasa Prachar Trust; VP, Bhuj Visa Oswal Jain Gyabi; Treas, Ku Kavita Sachade Smarak Trust; MD, Shah Natavarlal Magnlal Fndn Trust; Advsr, S B Gardi Blood Bank. Honours: Integrity by Chf Justice Mr Bhagavati, 1969-70; Awd, Employment with Deaf and Dumb Persons, 1985; Kutch-Shakti Awd; Fulshankar Patani. Memberships: Indian Newspapers Soc; Indian Lang Newspaper Assn; Audit bur of Circulation. Hobbies: Sports; Reading. Address: Kutchmitra (Daily) Kutchmitra Bhavan, Nerr-Indrabai Park, Bhuj-Kutch 370001, India.

SHAH DEV Birendra Bir Bikram, b. 28 Dec 1945, Kathmandu, Kingdom of Nepal. King of Nepal. m. HM Queen Aishwarya Rajya Laxmi Devi Shah, 2 s, 1 d. Education: Univ of Tokyo, Japan; Harv Univ, USA, 1967-68. Appointments: Heir-apparent to Throne of Kingdom of Nepal, 1955; Coming of Age, Grand Master of all Orders of Kingdom of Nepal and Col-in-Chf, Roy Nepalese Army, 1964; Ascended throne, 1972. Honours include: Sovereign of all orders, Kingdom of Nepal; Supreme Cmndr, Roy Nepalese Army; Hon Gen, Brit Army, 1973; Collar of the Nile, Egypt, 1974; Roy Victorian Chain, UK, 1975; Grand Cross of the Netherlands Lion, 1975; Field Marshall, UK, 1980; Grand Cross, Legion of Honour, France, 1983; Spec Level of the Grand Cross Order of Merit, Germany, 1986; Order of Repub Star 1st Class, Romania, 1987; Order of the Elephant, Denmark, 1989; Hd of State Medal, 1991; Num hon docts. Memberships: Patron, Roy Nepal acady of Sci and Technol; King Mahendra Trust for Nature Conservation; Chan, Tribhuvan Univ, Mahendra Sanskrit Acady. Hobbies: Nature conservation; Riding; Painting. Address: Narayanhity Royal Palace, Kathmandu, Kingdom of Nepal.

SHAH DEV Dipendra Bir Bikram (HRH), b. 27 June 1971, Kathmandu, Nepal. Education: BA, MA, Geog, Tri-Chandra Campus, Tribhuvan Univ. Appointments: Heir-apparent to Throne, Kingdom of Nepal, 1972; Coming of Age, Grand Master, all Orders of Kingdom of Nepal, Col-in-Chf, Roy Nepalese Army, 1990. Honours: Shubha Rajyabhisheka Padaka, 1975; Daivi Prakopa Piditoddhara Padaka, 1989; Grand Cross, Order of Dennebrog, Denmark, 1989; Grand Cross, Fed Repub of Germany, 1997; Commemorative Medal, Silver Jubilee of Accession to Throne, 1997; Vishista Seva Padaka, 1999. Memberships: Patron, Nepal Olympic Cttee, Natl Sports Cncl; Roy Nepal Golf Club. Hobbies: Geography; Information/communication technology; Nature conservation. Address: Narayanhity Royal Palace, Kathmandu, Kingdom of Nepal.

SHAHA Rishikesh, b. 16 May 1925, Tansen Palpa, Nepal. Educator; Diplomat; Elder Statesman. m. Siddhanta, 12 July 1946, 1 s. Education: MA, Engl, Patna Univ, 1945; MA, Pol, Allahabad Univ, 1954. Appointments: Lectr in Engl and Nepali, TC Coll, Kathmandu, 1945-48; Ldr of Opp, Nepal's 1st nom legislature, 1952-53; Gen Sec, Nepali Cong, 1954-55; Perm Rep, Amb to US, 1955-60; Min of Fin and For Affairs, 1960-62; Chmn Intl Commn of UN investigating death of Dag Hammarskjold, 1961; Chmn Stndng Cttee, Nepal Cncl of State, 1963-64; Snr Fell, East-West Cntre, Univ of HI, Honolulu, 1965-66; Visng Prof, Jawharlal Nehru Univ, New Delhi, 1971; Regent's Prof, Univ CA, Berkeley, 1971-71; Fell, Woodrow Wilson Intl Cntr for Schlrs, Washington DC, 1976-77; Alumni in Res, Fell, East-West Cntre, Univ of HI, Honolulu, 1984-85. Publications: Nepal and the World, 1954; Houses and Builders of Nepal, 1965; Nepali Politics: Retrospect and Prospect, 1974; Modern Nepal. A Political history, 1990; Ancient and Medieval Nepal, 1992; Politics in Nepal 1980-1991. Honours: 1st Class Order of the Right Hand of Gorkha, 1960; 1st Class Order of Trinity of Power, 1962; Honoured by the Hum Rights Watch, NY, 1989. Memberships: Fndr Chmbn, Assn of Profs and Coll Tchrs, 1961-71; Fndr, Pres, Hum Rights Org of Nepal. Hobbies:

Big game hunting; Swimming; Reading. Listed in: Who's Who in the World; International Who's Who; Men of Achievement. Address: 1/483 Chandol, Bishalagar, Kathmandu, Nepal.

SHAHA Rishikesh, b. 1925 Tansen Palpain Prov. Politician; Diplomatist. m. Siddhanta Rajyalakshmi, 1946, 1 s. Education: Patna Univ; Allahabad Univ India. Appointments: Lectr in Eng and Nepalese Lit Tri-Chandra Coll, 1945-48; Opposition Ldr First Advsry Assembly, 1952; Gen Sec Nepalese Congress, 1953-55; Perm Rep - with rank of Amb - to UN, 1956-60; Amb to USA, 1958-60; Chmn UN Intl Commn investigating death of Dag Hammarskjold, 1961; Min of Fin Plng and Econ Affairs, 1961-62; Min of For Affairs, Jul-Sep 1962; Amb-at-large, 1962-63; Chmn Standing Cttee Cncl of State, 1963-64; Vising Prof E-W Cntr Univ of HI, 1965-66; MP, 1967-70; Solitary confinement, 1969-70; Vising Prof Sch of Intl Studies of Jawaharlal Nehru Univ, 1971; Regent's Prof Univ of CA Berkeley, 1971-72; Returned to Nepal arrested, Dec 1974; Fell Woodrow Wilson Intl Cntr for Schls WA DC, 1976-77; Returned to Nepal arrested, May 1977 and Released, 1989; Campaigned for restoration of multi-party dem before 1980 referendum; Alumni Fell, 1984; Pres Human Rights Org of Nepal, 1988. Publications: Nepal and the World, 1954; Heroes and Builders of Nepal - in UK - 1965; An Introduction to Nepal, 1975; Nepali Politics - Retrospect and Prospect - in UK - 1975; Essays in the Practice of Government in Nepal - in India - 1982; Future of South Asia - in India - 1986; Modern Nepal: A Political History - 1769-1955 - 1990; Politics in Nepal 1980-1990, 1990; Ancient and Medieval Nepal, 1991. Honours: Hon'd by Human Rights Watch and Asia Watch for wrk as Human Rights Monitor, 1989. Hobbies: Reading; Writing; Big game hunting. Address: Shrio Nivas, Chandol, Kathmandu, Nepal.

SHAHAL Moshe, b. 1934 Iraq. Politician; Lawyer. m. 2 c. Education: Haifa Univ Tel Aviv. Appointments: Mil serv Israeli Def Forces; Dep Speaker Knesset Cttee; Min of Energy and Infrastructure, 1984-90, 1993-94; Min of Pol and Comms, 1992-93; Min of Internal Security, 1993-96; Fmr Chmn Israeli Consumers' Cncl; Fmr Perm Observer to Eurn Cncl; Fmr Perm Rep to Inter-Parly Union. Memberships: Mbr Seventh Knesset - Parl - 1974; Mbr Fin Cttee; Mbr Econ Cttee; Mbr Labour Cttee; Mbr Eighth Knesset, 1974-77; Mbr Constitution Law and Jus Cttee; Mbr Tenth Knesset, 1983-; Mbr Knesset Cttee; Mbr Labour Party. Address: c/o The Knesset, Jerusalem, Israel.

SHAHIDULLAH Mohammad, b. 1 Mar 1964, Pirojpur, Bangladesh. Research. m. Shaida Afroz, 27 Dec 1993, 1 s. Education: MSc, Phys; PhD, Biophys, Japan. Appointments: Asst Aerodrome Offr, Bangladesh Civil Aviation Authority. Rsch Fell, Japanese Min of Educ, Japan; Postdoct Fell, Thomas Jefferson Univ, Philadelphia, USA. Honours: Halem Ali Fndn, Barisal Bangladesh, 1977; Univ Grant Commn, Bangladesh, 1987. Memberships: Organised Sci Club in Bangladesh; NY Acady Sci, 1993-95; Neuroscience Soc, Wash DC, 1995-96; Biophys Soc, USA, 1997-98. Hobbies: Music; Drawing. Address: Thomas Jefferson University, 1020, Locust Street, JAH Rm # 245, Phildelphia, PA 19107, USA.

SHAIKH Mushtaq, b. 19 June 1971, Sangli, India. Executive Manager. m. Reshma, 28 Dec 1994, 1 d. Education: BCom. Appointment: Exec Mngr, Mapro Foods, Panchgani. Hobbies: Reading; Travel; Music. Address: Shivaji Chowk, Main Road, Panchgani 412805, India.

SHAILER Gregory E P, b. 21 June 1957, Gosford, NSW, Australia. Academic. m. Sandy Stevenson, 1 s. Education: BCom, 1979, MCom, 1987, Univ of Newcastle; PhD, Adelaide, 1996. Appointments: Tutor, Univ Newcastle, 1980-82; Lectr, Flinders, 1983-90; Visng Asst Prof, Univ of Arizona, 1989; Touche Ross Visng Fell, Univ of Bristol, 1990; Snr Lectr, The Austl Natl Univ, 1990-. Membership: Fell, Austl Soc of CPA. Address: Department of Commerce, ANU, Canberra, 0200, Australia.

SHAKAA Riyadh al, b. 1941 Nablllus. Politician; Lawyer. Education: Univ of Cairo. Appointments: Lawyer; Min of Jus, 1985-89 and currently. Memberships: Mbr Jordanian Bar Assn; Mbr Lower House of Parl for Nablus, 1985-. Address: Ministry of Justice, P OBox 6040, Amman, Jordan.

SHAKAR Karim Ebrahim al-, b. 23 Dec 1945 Manama. Diplomatist. m. 3 d. Education: Univ of New Delhi. Appointments: Joined min of For Affairs, 1970; 1st Sec Perm Miss to the UN, 1972-76; Apptd Chf For Affairs and Intl Org Bahrain, 1977; Consul-Gen Switzerland, 1982; Amb - non-res - to Fed Repub of Germany and Austria, 1984-; Perm Rep to the UN Off Vienna, 1982; Perm Rep - non-res - 1984; Perm Rep to the UN, 1987-90; Amb to UK, 1990-95; Amb - non-res - to Ireland Denmark and the Netherlands, 1992-95; Dir Intl Directorate at min of For Affairs Bahrain, 1995-. Membership: Mbr Perm Miss to UN. Hobbies: Readin; Travelling. Address: c/o Ministry of Foreign Affairs, P O Box 547, Government House, Government Road, Manama, Bahrain.

SHAKER Sharif Zaid ibn, b. 4 Sep 1934 Amman. Politician; Army Offr. m. 1 s, 1 d. Education Vic Coll Alexandria; Sandhurst Mil Coll UK; Long Armour Course and Staff Coll Leavenworth USA. Appointments: Asst Mil Attache Emb UK, 1957-58; Cmdr 1st Infantry Regt, 1963; Asst Chf of Staff for Ops, 1970; Chf of Staff, 1972; Cmdr in Chf Jordan Armed Forces, 1976-88; Min of State Chf of the Roy Crt Mil Advsr to King Hussein - qv - on Armed Forces Affairs, 1988-89, 1989-91; PM of Jordan, Apr-Dec 1989, 1991-93; Chf of Roy Crt, 1993, 1995-96. Honours: Num decorations inclng Order of the Star of Jordan - First Class. Address: c/o Office of the Prime Minister, P O Box 80, 35216 Amman, Jordan.

SHALINI Khosla, b. 24 Dec 1976, Kalka. Student. Education: Grad, Kurukshetra Univ; Postgrad, H P Univ; Computers Dip; First Aid Dip. Appointments: Owner of Handloom Items Shop. Creative Works: Articles Publd in Coll Mags. Honours: Books and Certs Awd on coming first in coll. Memberships: Rotaract Club; PAHAL; Ponds Inst. Hobbies: Collect of Cards; Reading Books; Socl Wrk. Address: Gansht Chowk, Kalka 133302, Haryana, India.

SHAMEEM Shaista, b. 1 Oct 1954, Suva, Fiji. University Lecturer. Education: BA, 1976; MA, 1983; DPhil, 1991; LLB Hons, 1997; Legal Practitioners Ctf, 1997; LLM, 1999. Appointments: Jrnlst, 1976-79; Tchr of Engl, 1979-82; Lectr, Univ of Waikato, Hamilton, NZ; Gates, Sols and Bars, 1998-. Publications: A Conference to Maximise the Interests of a Pressure Group: the 1975 Tourism Convention, 1976; The performance of an ancient Indian drama on the night before the firewalking ceremony at Howell Road Temple, Suva, 1978; The Art of Raymond Pillay, Subramani and Prem Banfal: A Feminist Critique of the Indo-Fijian Short Story, 1985; The Fiji Labour Party: What Gains for the Fijian Working Class - Indo-Fiji Women and Work, 1986; Gender, Class and Race Dynamics: Indian Women in Sugar production, 1987; The New Zealnd Media and the Fijian Coups: Who Decides What's Real, 1988; Girmitiya Women: Work Resistance and Survival, 1990; The New Zealand Justice System Under Scrutiny: Contemporary Critiques, 1994; Labour, Law, Information Technology and Value: Productivity Redefined in the 21st Century, 1996; Migration, Labour and Plantation Women, 1998. Creative works: Films: Fijian Praxis Series (documentary), 1990-95; Paintings: Twister, Irit the Rebel, 1998; Meridian, Millennium, 1999. Honours: Fijian Govt Schl, 1975-76; Vacation Schlshp, Fedn of Univ Women, 1986; Awd for Acad Excellence, Educ Fndn of NZ, 1990; Univ of Waikato, Staff Merit Awd, 1992. Memberships: Fedn of Univ Women; Young Women's Christian Assn, Fiji; NZ Sociological Assn; Intl Women's Anthropology Inc; Mbr, Fiji Law Soc. Hobbies: Fencing; Interior design; Golf. Address: PO Box 324, Lautoka, Fiji.

SHAMGAR Alex, b. 28 May 1945, Romania. Prosperity Planner. m. 1973, 2 s. Education: BSc.Agr; Dip.Ed; MSc.Agr; PhD. Appointments: Snr Tutor, Med,

Univ of Melbourne; Ind Devel Specialist, NSW Govt; Prosperity Planner, Parramatta Cncl. Address: c/o Parramatta Council, PO Box 32, Parramatta, NSW 2124, Australia.

SHAMIR Jacob, b. 7 June 1927, Berlin. Professor. m. Anka, 18 Dec 1951, 1 s, 2 d. Education: MSc, 1953; PhD, 1958. Appointments: Snr Lectr, 1966; Assoc Prof, 1971; Prof, 1977. Creative Works: Profl Jrnls. Honours: Snr For Scientists, Natl Sci Fndn, 1971; Snr Fellshp, Natl Rsch Cncl, 1985. Address: Dept of Inorganic Chemistry, The Hebrew University, Jerusalem 91904, Israel.

SHAMIR Joseph, b. 20 May 1936, Romania. University Professor. m. Tova, 3 Oct 1961, 2 s. Education: BSc, MSc, DSc, Phys, Technion-Israel Inst of Technol. Appointments: Lectr, Snr Lectr, Assoc Prof, Prof, Dept EE, Technion-Israel Inst Technol. Publications: Publs in sci jrnls and confs, 1963-. Honours: Dennis Gabor Awd, SPIE, 1996; Henry Taub Rsch Awd, Technion, 1997. Memberships: Israel Laser and Electro-Optics Soc, Pres, 1980-90; Fell, IEEE, OSA; SPIE. Address: Department of Electrical Engineering, Technion-Israel Institute of Technology, Haifa 32000, Israel.

SHAMKHANI Ali, b. 1955, Ahvaz, Khuzestan Prov, Iran. Minister of Defence and Logistic. Education: BS Deg, Agricl Engrng, Univ of Ahvaz; MS, Mil Affairs, MA, State Mngmt, Univ of State Mngmt Org. Appointments: Var Mil posts inclng Cmdr, IRGC Forces in Ahvaz, Khuzestan, Acting Cmdr, IRGC, Cmdr, IRGC Ground Forces, Dpty in Charge of Info and Ops of Armed Forces HQ, IRGC Min and Official in Charge of implementation of UN resolution to end Iran/Iraq war; Cmdr, Naval Forces of army, IRGC and Cmdr of Khatam Ul-Anbia Naval HQ in Persian Gulf; Elected, Min of Def and Logistic.

SHAMSHUDDIN Jusop, b. 16 July 1947. Professor of Soil Science. m. Salleh Fadzilah, 8 Apr 1977, 2 s, 2 d. Education: BS, Univ of Malaya; MS, Univ of Newcastle-upon-Tyne, Eng; PhD, Univ of Gent, Belgium. Appointments: Prof, 1993; Dir, Cntr for Tropical Soil Stdies; Chf Ed, Malaysian Jrnl of Soil Sci, 1997; Hd, Dept of Land Mngmt, 1999. Publications: Quantitative Relationship Between Mineralogy and Properties of Tropical Soils, 1993; Recent Developments in Land Evaluation, 1994. Honours: Professorial Chair Awd, SE Asia Univ Consortium, 1993-94; Belgian Roy Acady of Overseas Scis, 1996, Institute of Geology, Malaysia. Memberships: Pres, Malaysian Soc of Soil Sci, 1993-96; Pres, East and SE Asia Fedn of Soil Sci Soc, 1995-97; Tech Advsry Bd, Malaysian Cocoa Bd, 1995-97. Hobby: Golf. Address: Department of Land Management, Faculty of Agriculture, UPM, 43400 Serdang, Selangor, Malaysia.

SHAND David Hubert Warner, b. 6 Apr 1921, Qld, Aust. Anglican Bishop. m. 5 Jan 1946, 1 s, 3 d. Education: ThL, 2nd class hons, St Francis Theological Coll, Brisbane, 1946-48; BA, 2nd class hons, Mental and Moral Philos, Univ of Qld, 1946-51. Appointments: Lt, AIF, 1941-45; Deacon, 1948; Priest, 1949; Asst Curate, Lutwyche, Parishes of Moorooka, Inglewood, Nambour, Ipswich; Organizing Sec, Home Miss Fund; Diocese of Brisbane Chap CMF, 1950-57; Rural Dean of Ipswich, 1963-66; Vicar, S Yarra, 1966-69, Brighton, 1969-73; Rural Dean, St Kilda, 1972-73; Diocese of Melbourne, 1973; Consec Bish, St Pauls Cath, Melbourne, 1973; Bish of St Arnaud, 1973-76, Amalgamation Dioceses Bendico and St Arnaud; Vicar, St Stephens, Mt Waverley, 1976-78; Chair, Gen Bd, Relig Educn, 1974-84; Bish of Southern Region, 1978-85; Bish in Geelong, Archbish Prov Asst, Mbr, Cath Chapt, Vicar Gen, 1985-88; Retd, 1988. Address: 40 Volitans Avenue, Mount Eliza, Vic 3930, Australia.

SHANKARANARAYANA JOIS Kulapathi Asthana Jyotishya Vidwan Jyotisha Ratna, b. 30 Aug 1903, Sringeri Chikmagalur District, Karnataka State, India. Jyotisya Vidwan (Astrologer). m. Sharada, 1 s, 4 d. Education: Jyotishya Viwan, at Maharaja Sanskrit Coll, Mysore, India. Appointments: Lectr, S S Pathashala, Sringeri, 1926-59; Pres, S S Pathashala, 1954-64.

Honours: Kulapathi Jyotishyaratna, Asthan Ajyotisha Vidwan, Karnataka State Awd, 1964, 1978, 1988. Membership: Pres, Sadvidya Sanjivini Mahapathashala Sringeri. Hobbies: Teaching; Astrology; Study; Reading. Address: S Joshi Shivadatta No 780, 7th Cross, 10th Mian Banashankari 1st Stage, II Block, Bangalore 560050, Karnataka, India.

SHANNON Peter Clifford, b. 20 Feb 1953, Cheshire, Eng. Composer; Songwriter; Musician. m. Carol, 8 Feb 1987, 1 d. Appointment: NZQA, Music Advsry Grp. Publications: Love is the Hardest Thing of All; Scream - You're Dead. Memberships: Sec, NZ Musician's Union; Sec, Indep Music Prodrs and Perfs Assn. Address: Private bag, 68-914 Newton, Auckland, New Zeland.

SHAO Wei Wen, b. 1 Oct 1934, Huangyan, Zhejiang Prov, China. Senior Engineer. m. Zhang Xiu Wen, 2 s. Education: Bachelor degree, Fudan Univ. Snr Engr, CSSRC; Prof, Yunnan Univ; Chf Ed, Jrnl of Hydrodynamics. Publications: Chf Ed, An English-Chinese Dictionary of New and Developing Science and Technology, 1992. Honour: Natl Sci Meeting Awd, 1979. Memberships: China Shipbuilding Engrng Assn; Shanghai Maritime Exchange Assn. Hobbies: Golf; Bowling; Dancing; Reading. Address: China Ship Science Research Center, 185 Gaoxing Road, 200011 Shanghai, China.

SHAO Ziwen, b. 16 Apr 1938, Shanghai, China. Laser, Spectroscopy, Physics. m. Lian Cheng, Feb 1977, 1 s. Education: Grad, Dept of Phys, Peking Univ, Beijing. Appointments: Dir, Chf Ed, Jrnl Appl Laser, 1981-; Prof, 1987-. Publications: 30 sci pprs in profl jrnls. Honours: 3rd Awd, Shanghai Important Achievements in Sci & Technol, 1984; Silver-Ox Decoration, Chinese S&T Ed Assn. Memberships: Chinese Optical Soc; Sci Sec, Shanghai Laser Soc. Hobbies: Swimming; Chinese Classical Poems. Address: Shanghai Institute of Laser Technology, 770 Yishan Road, Shanghai 200233, China.

SHAPIRO Harvey Allan, b. 21 Apr 1941, Toledo, OH, USA. Environmental Planner. m. Fukiko N, 2 d. Education: BArch; Master Regl Plng; DAgric, Ecological Plng. Appointments: Lectr, Environ Plng (full-time), 1980; Prof, Environ Plng (tenured), 1987. Publications include: Ecological Planning in Japan, in, Hazard Waste Control, 1984. Memberships: Intl Geog Union; Pacific Sci Assn; World Conservation Union (IUCN); JEA; ACZS; JCZS; Sierra Club. Address: Department of Environmental Planning, Osaka Geijutsu University, Minami-Kawachi-Gun, Kanan-cho, Osaka Prefecture 585-8555, Japan.

SHAPLA Kamrunnahar, b. 23 Mar 1976, Gaibandha. Education: BA; Dips in Agric. Publications: Lit wrks in Poems and Poet, 1990-. Memberships: Gaibandha Shahitto Parishad Rajshahi Shahitto, Uttar Bangla Shahitto Parishad. Address: c/o MD Abul Kasam Prodhan Professor's Colony, Gaibandha 5700, Bangladesh.

SHARA' Farouk Al-, b. 1938, Dara'a, Syria. Minister of Foreign Affairs. m. 2 children. Education: BA, Engl Lit, Univ of Damascus, 1953; Intl Law, London Univ, 1972. Appointments: Sev major posts in Syrian Arab Airlines incl Regl Mngr in London; Coml Dir and Mbr, Bd of Dirs, Damascus; Amb to Italy, 1976-80; Min of State for For Affairs, 1980-84; Min of For Affairs, 1984-; Spec Envoy of Pres Hefez Assad to sev countris; Min of Jus and Min of Info. Address: Ministry of Foreign Affairs, Damascus, Syria.

SHARANSKY Natan (Anatoly), b. 20 Jan 1948 Donetsk Ukraine. Politician; Human Rights Activist. m. Natalya (now Avital) Stiglitz, 1974. Appointments: A ldng spokesman for Jewish emigration movement in USSR; Arrested by Soviet authys for dissident activities, 1977; Received 13 yr prison sentence on charges of treason, 1978; Following worldwide campaign Soviet authys released and he took up resn in Israel, Feb 1986; Visng Prof Brandeis Univ Waltham MA; Ldr Israel B'Aliyah Party; Min of Ind and Trade, 1996-99; Min of Interior,

1999-. Publication: Fear No Evil, 1988. Address: Ministry of Interior, 2 Kiryat Hamemshala, Jerusalem, Israel.

SHARIATMADARI Mohammad, b. 1957, Tehran, Iran. Minister of Commerce. Education: Higher Dip. Electrons, Tehran Techl and Electrons Trng Cntr; Studying Pol, Grad Level, Tehran Univ. Appointments: Mbr, Islamic Revolution Cntrl Cttee; Dpty Chf, Prime Min's Off i/c Info and Rsch; Dpty Info Min; Acting Com Min; Mbr, Ldr's Representative Off for Haji Affairs, 1991-; Elected, Min of Com.

SHARIF Mohammad Nowaz, b. 25 Dec 1948, Lahore, Pakistan. Prime Minister. Education: Stud, Govt Coll of Lahore; Grad in Law, Univ of Pubjab. Appointments: Min of Fin, Prov of Punjab, Pakistan; Prime Min, Islamic Repub of Pakistan, 1990-. Address: Office of the Prime Minister, Islamabad, Pakistan.

SHARIFF Mohamed, b. 14 Mar 1949. Lecturer. m. Sharifah Abudllah, 21 Dec 1971, 2 s, 1 d. Education: PhD 1985, MSc 1977, Univ of Stirling, Scotland; DVM, Univ of Agric, Lyallpur, 1975. Appointments: Tutor 1976-77, Lectr 1977-87, Assoc Prof 1988-92, Prof 1993-, Universiti Putra, Malaysia; Dpty Dean, Fac of Vet Med. Publications: More than 80 publs on fish diseases in natl and intl jrnls; Ed, 4 books related to fish disease. Honours: Fed Malaysian Schlsp for Masters, 1975-76, Doct, Univ of Stirling, Scotland, 1992; Awd, Intl Dev Rsch Cntr, Can, 1992. Memberships: Pres, Asian Fisheries Soc, 1995-98; Ed, Fish Hlth Sect, Asian Fisheries Soc, 1988-95; Pres, Malaysian Fisheries Soc, 1987, 1992-94. Hobby: Rearing aquarium fish. Listed in: Who's Who in Malaysia and Singapore; Who's Who in ASEAN. Address: No 9 Road 8, Taman Sungai Jelok, 43000 Kajang, Selangor, Malaysia.

SHARMA Balkrishna, b. 25 Nov 1947, Jaipur, India. Teaching. m. Dr Meenakshi Sharma, 8 July 1980, 2 d. Education: BSc, 1965, MSc, 1967, Univ of Rajasthan, Jaipur; Dip, Univ of Uppsala, Sweden, 1975. Appointments: Lectr in Phys, Univ of Rajasthan, Jaipur, 1970; Rdr in Phys, 1976; Prof of Phys, 1988; Hon Dir, Rajasthan Univ Lib, 1995; Hd, Phys, 1996-99; Dir Cntr for Dev Phys Educ, 1996. Publications: Positron Annihilation and Compton Scattering, 1990; Ed, Organised Sci and Technol Exhibn, 1994; Invited Speaker, Intl Conf, 1991; Convenor ISRP7 (Jaipur). Honours: Nom by INSA to IUC and Commn on Charge, Spin and Momentum Densities in 1993, 1996; Invited Speaker at Sagamore X, 1991; Chmn, Sessions at XI XII Sagamore Conf, 1997. Memberships: Life Mbr, IAPT; Life Mbr, INDO-ICTP Chapt; MRSI. Hobbies: Music; Sports (cricket, tennis); Physics teaching; Tourism. Address: F-182, Subhash Marg, Naval Niwas, C-Scheme, Jaipur 302001, India.

SHARMA Bishnu Prasad, Media Project Manager. m. 31 Jan 1979, 1 s, 1 d. Education: MA, Polit Sci, MEd, Engl, Tribhuvn Univ, Kathmandu, Nepal. Appointments: Libn, 1984; Offr, Audit Bur of Circulations, 1988; Admnstv Offr, 1993; Sec, ACC, 1993; Proj Mngr, Media Dev Fund, Press Cncl Nepal, 1996. Publications: Ed, Girls Child of Nepal, 1991; Compiler and Ed, Press Council: An Introduction, 1999. Memberships: Exec Dir, Rural Area Dev Prog, NGO, 1996; Advsr, Leisure World Tours and Travels. Hobbies: Trekking; Travel; Reading; Writing. Address: Press Cncl Nepal, PO Box 3077, Kathmandu, Nepal.

SHARMA Dev Raj, b. 9 Apr 1944, Saloh, India. Librarian. m. Shaiwal, 19 May 1967, 2 s, 1 d. Education: MA, Hindi; MA, Sanskrit; BLib.Sc; MLib.Sc. Appointments: Asst Libn, DAV Coll, Ambala Cty, 1971-72; Libn, DAV Coll, Sadhaura, 1972-73; Asst Univ Libn, 1973-92, Dpty Libn, 1992-98, Univ Libn, 1998-. Memberships: Indian Lib Assn, New Delhi; IASLIC, Calcutta; PU Alumni Assn. Hobby: Reading. Address: c/o University Library, Himachal Pradesh, Krishi Vishva Vidyalaya, Palampur 176062, India.

SHARMA Janak Raj, b. 7 Jan 1939. Librarian. m. Rama Sharma, 3 Aug 1964, 1 s, 1 d. Education: MA, Philos; MA, Lings; MLibSc; PhD, Lings; Cert in French.

Appointments: Libn, GGD Coll, Baijinath, 1962-63; Libn, Vaish Coll, Bhiwani, 1963-67; Asst Libn, Regl Engrng Coll, Kurukshetra, 1967-68; Officiating Libn 1968, Libn 1968-81; Dpty Libn, Univ of Kurukshetra, Kurukshetra, 1981-88; Pt Lectr in Lib & Info Sci, 1984-85, 1985-86; Univ Libn, Thapar Inst of Engrng and Technol, Deemed Univ, Patiala, 1988-. Publications include: Preparing Libraries for the 21st Century, 1995; Handbook of Libraries, Archives and Information Centres, 1996; Practical Aspects of Library Automation in the Indian Context, 1997; Internet and Subject Resource Guides, 1997. Honours: Inter-Sch Lajpat Rai Mem Declamation Contest, 1953; Sch Declamation Contest, 1954; Sch Declamation Contest, 1958-59; Local Coll Declamation Contest, 1959-60; Most Disciplined Cadet Awd, 1959-60; 2nd Best NCO, Awd for the Yr, 1959-60; Roll of Hon, 1959-60. Memberships include: Expert Mbr, Select Cttess of var insts; Pres, Haryana Lib Assn, 1986-88; VP, Indian Lib Assn, 1988-90, 1994-96; Punjab Lib Assn, 1992-94, 1996-98; Cncl of Indian Lib Assn, 1996-98. Hobbies: Reading; Spirituality; Culture; Library and Information Science. Listed in: International Directory of Distinguished Leadership. Address: University Librarian, Thapar Institute of Engineering and Technology, PO Box 32, Patiala 147 001, Punjab, India.

SHARMA Kamla Nath, b. 3 Mar 1946, Jaipur, India. Water Resources Professional. m. Chandrika, 13 May 1970, 1 s, 1 d. Education: ME, Water Rescs; BE, Civ Engrng. Appointments: Lectr, Civ Engrng, Univ of Rajasthan, 1969-81; Snr Mngr, Hd, Natl Hydro Elec Power Corp, 1981-89; Intl Commn on Irrigation and Drainage, New Delhi, 1989-. Creative Works: Water Power Engineering, 1979; Tech ppr for confs; Satires, short stories in Hindi mags. Honours: Fellshp, Univ Grants Commn, 1972-76; Ford Fndn Fellshp, 1976-77. Memberships: Inst of Engrs; Indian Assn of Hydrologists; Indian Water Resources Soc; Indian Assn for Desert Technol. Hobbies: Painting; Indian Classical Music; Lit Writing; Reading. Address: 8263, Sector B/XI, Vasant Kunj, New Delhi 110070, India.

SHARMA Ram Sanehi Lal, b. 5 July 1949, Ki-Tilokpur, Dist Firozabad. Lecturer (Hindi Department). m. Mrs Shauntla, Apr 1966, 1 s, 3 d. Education: MA; PhD. Appointment: SRK (PG) Coll Firozabad, UP, India, 1974. Publications: Man Palashoon Aur Dahakati Samothya (A Book of Songs); Gialiare Gandh Ke (A Book of Love Songs), 1998. Honours: Sahitya Wachaspati, Title given by Abhil Bhartiya Brij Sahitya Sangar; Guta Gandhroiva, Title given by Guta Gandhra. Memberships: Fndr Sec, Manisha (a lib Sanstha); All India Lib Parishad. Hobbies: Writing; Creative writing and study. Address: 86 Tuilak Nagar, Bypass Road, Firozabad, UP, India 283203.

SHARMA Ravi, b. 20 June 1974, Rajasthan, Jaipur, India. Study. Education: BFA, Rajasthan Sch of Art; Appearing for MFA, IKSVV (Univ), Khairagarh (MP). Career: Many large wrks w Dr Sumahendra Sharma (Hd of Sculpture Dept, RSA), Jaipur; Collected, Rajasthan Small Scale Inds, Jaipur; Portrait of Govinda film star collection in film ind, Mumbai; Exhibns incl: 14th & 15th Student Art Exhibns, organised by Jawahar Kala Kendr, Jaipur; Solo Exhibn, IKSVV KHairagarh (MP), 1998; Indira Kala Mea, Khairagarh, 1998. Publications: Rajasthan Traditional Marble Carving, Part I, 1998, Part II, 1999. Honour: Best Artist Awd, Clay Modelling (RSA), Jaipur, 997. Hobbies: Old songs; Visiting; Photography. Address: A-192 Indira Verma Colony, Shastri Nagar, Jaipur (Raj), India 302016.

SHARMA Sachida Nand, b. 15 July 1941, Naitasiri, Nausori, Fiji. Manager. m. Sarita, 30 Aug 1976, 3 s, 1 d. Education: Dip, Sale/Bus Mngmt, Sydney, Aust. Appointments: Exec Mbr, Treas, Indian Alliance Party (Suva Branch), 1980-87; VP, Suva Constituency Alliance Party, 1980-86; Cty Cnclr, Suva Cty Cncl, 1985-; Chmn, Traffic Cttee, Suva Cty Cncl, 1985-; Mbr, Rd Safety Cncl, 1988-93; Mbr, Suva Advsry Cncl, 1989-92; Mbr, Suva Rural Local Authy, Chmn, Taxi Base/Bldg Cttee (SRLA), 1992-; Chmn Fiji Labour Party (Suva Br), 1995-99; Natl VP, Fiji Labour Party, 1995-99; Chmn, Fin and Econ Dev

Cttee (Suva Cty Cncl), 1996- 99. Address: 23 Storck Street, Nasese, Suva, PO Box 12800, Suva, Fiji.

SHARMA Sangeeta, b. 12 Oct 1972, Lucknow, India. Artist. Education: Master Deg, Sculpture Art, Lucknow Univ, 1997. Appointment: Freelance Artist. Publications: Sev articles in newspprs and mags. Honours: Artist of the Yr, UP Artists Assn; Rsch Awd, Byuip Lalit Kala Akadmi. Membership: The UP Artists Assn, India. Hobbies: Games; Art Photography; Acting. Address: Rashtriya Lalit Kala, Kendra, Aliganj, Lucknow, India.

SHARMA Santosh, b. 15 Jan 1945, Karnal, India. Detective. m. 8 Nov 1979, 2 s. Education: PhD, DLitt; MBA; BEE. Appointments: Chmn; Mngng Dir. Creative Works: Economy Cook Book. Honours: Indian Gandhi Priyadarshini Awd; Best Citizen Awd; Vikas Ratna; Rashtriya Ratna; Bharat Samman; Gem of India; World Bus Growth Awd; World Econ Trade; Global Ex Awd; Intl Disting Ldrshp Awd; Pandit Jawaharlal Nehru Ex Awd; Natl Hlth Awd; Bus Ex Awd; Himachal Gaurav Awd; Man of the Year; Intl Status Awd; Many or Awds. Memberships: World Assn of Detectives; World Investigatiors Network; Assn of Security Orgs of india; Security Assn of India; Cncl of Indl Safety; Intl Chamber of Commerce; Natl Cncl for Snr Citizens of India; Natl Geo Soc; ABI; Utd Writers Assn; Many or mbrshps. Hobbies: Socl Work; Spiritual Thinking; Reading; Writing; Global Travng. Address: 110, Great Eastern Chambers, Sector 11, Plot 28, CBD, New Mumbai 400 614, India.

SHARMA Shalendra, b. 3 Apr 1958. University Professor. m. Vivian, 1 s. Education: PhD, Polit Sci, Univ of Toronto, Canada. Appointments: Assoc Prof, Univ of San Fran, 1993. Publications: Democracy and Development with Equity; India in Comparative Perspectives. Honours: Disting Tchng Awd, Univ of San Fran, 1997. Memberships: Am Polit Sci Assoc. Hobbies: Television; Soccer. Address: University of San Francisco, 2130 Fulton Street, San Francisco, CA 94117, USA.

SHARMA Shanker Dayal, b. 19 Aug 1919. Politician; Bar. m. Vimala Sharma, 2 s, 1 d. Education: Lucknow Univ; Cambridge Univ; Lincoln's Inn. Appointments: Lawyer, 1942-; Pres Bhopal State Congress Cttee, 1950-52; Chf Min of Bhopal, 1952-56; Min Madhya Pradesh Govt, 1956-57; Gen Sec Indian Natl Congress, 1968-72; Pres All India Congress Cttee, 1972-74; Min of Comms, 1974-77; Fmr Gov of Andhra Pradesh, - 1985; Gov of Punjab, 1985-86; Suspended from Congress - I - Party, 1986; VP of India, 1987-92; Pres of India, 1992-97; Ed-in-Chf Light and Learning Ilm-au-Noor; Ed Lucknow Law Jrnl; Served as Chmn of num parly cttees. Publication: Congress Approach to International Affairs. Honours: Hon DPA - London; LLD - Vikram and Bhopal Univs; LLD - Cambridge - 1993. Memberships: Mbr All India Congress Cttee, 1950-; Mbr Cntrl Advsry Bd of Educ, 1952-64; Mbr Consultative Cttees on Legislation Bhopal and Madhya Pradesh Legs Assemblies, 1952-64; Mbr Lok Sabha - Parl - 1971-77; Mbr of num parly cttees. Hobbies: Travel; Reading; Swimming. Address: Rashtrapati Bhavan, New Delhi 110 004, India.

SHARMAN William (Bill), b. 25 May 1926, Abilene, TX, USA. Professional Sportsman. m. (2)Joyce McLay, 2 s. 2 d. Education: BS, Univ SC. Appointments: Basketball Player, Washington Capitols, 1950-51; Boston Celtics, 1951-61; Coach LA/Utah Stars, 1968-71; Coach, LA Lakers, 1971-76; Gen Mngr, 1976-82, Pres, 1982-88, Spl Cons, 1991-. Publications: Author: Sharman on Basketball Shooting, 1965. Honours: Named to All Star 1st Team, NBA, 1956-59, 2nd Team, 1953, 55 (game MVP), 1960, All Laegue Team, 7 times; Named Coach of Yr, 1972; One of Top Players in NBA History, league 50th anniversary, 1997; League Leader free throw percentage, 7 times; Named to Basketball Hall of Fame, 1975; Naismith Basketball Hall of Fame, 1976; Named All-Am, twice; Inductee Univ SC Hall of Fame, 1994; Porterville HS gymnasium renamed in his honour, 1997. Address: 27996 Palos Verdes Dr E, Rancho Pls Vrd, CA 90275-5153, USA.

SHARON Ariel, b. 1928. Politician; Army Offr - retd. m. 2 s. Education: Studies at Hebrew Univ, 1952-53; Studies Staff Coll Camberley UK, 1957-58. Appointments: Active in Hagana since early yth; Instr Jewish Police units, 1947; Platoon Cmdr Alexandroni Brigade; Regimental Intell Offr, 1948; Co Cmdr, 1949; Cmdr Brigade Reconnaissance Unit, 1949-50; Intell Offr Cntrl Cmd and N Cmd, 1951-52; In charge of Unit 101 on num reprisal ops until 1957; Cmdr Paratroopers Brigade Sinai Campaign, 1956; Trng Cmdr Gen Staff, 1958; Cmdr Infantry Sch, 1958-69; Cmdr Armoured Brigade, 1962; Hd of Staff N Cmd, 1964; Hd Trng Dept of Def Forces, 1966; Hd Brigade Grp during Six-Day War, 1967; Resigned from Army, Jul 1973; Recalled as Cmdr Cntrl Sect of Sinai Front during Yom Kippur War, Oct 1973; Forged bridgehead across Suez Canal; Advsr to PM, 1975-77; Min of Agric in charge of Settlements, 1977-81; Min of Def, 1981-83; Min without Portfolio, 1990-92; Min of Trade and Ind, 1984-90; Min of Constrn and Housing, 1990-92; Min of Natl Infrastructure, 1996-; Chmn Cabinet Cttee to oversee Jewish immigration from USSR, 1991-96. Publication: Warrior - autobiog - 1989. Memberships: Fndr mbr Likud Front, Sep 1973; Mbr Knesset - Parl - 1973-74, 1977-; Mbr Ministerial Def Cttee, 1990-92. Address: Ministry of National Infrastructure, P O Box 13106, 234 Jaffa Street, Jerusalem 91130, Israel.

SHARON Nathan, b. 4 Nov 1925, Brisk, Poland, emigrated to Israel, 1934. Professor Emeritus. m. Rachel Izikson, 1948, 2 d. Education: MSc, Biochemistry, Hbrew Univ, Jerusalem, 1950 PhD, Biochemistry, Hebrew Univ, Jerusalem, 1953; Postdoct rsch, Biochem Rsch Lab, MA Gen Hosp & Harvard Medl Sch, Boston, MA, 1956-57; Lab for Carbohydrate Rsch, MGH & HMS, 1957-58; Dept Bio, Brookhaven Natl, Upton, NY, 1958. Appointments include: Rsch Asst, Agricl Rsch Stn, Dairy Rsch Lab, Rehovot 1949-53; Rsch Asst, 1954, Rsch Assoc, 1957, Snr Scientist, 1960, Assoc Prof, 1965, Prof, 1968, Hd, Dept Biophys, 1973-83, 1987-90, Dean, Fac of Biophys-Biochem, 1976-77, 1980-83, 1984-86, Prof Emer, 1995, Dept of Biophys, Weizmann Inst Sci, Rehovot; Disting Visng Scientist, NIADDK, NIH, Bethesda, MD, 1983-84; Greenberg Schl, OK Medl Rsch Fndn, Oklahoma Cty, OK, 1991; Visng Prof, Harv Medl Sch, 1992-93; Disting Visng Scientist, Roche Inst Molecular Bio, Nutley, NJ, 1993. Publications: Over 400 sci publs inclng review articles; 3 books in Hebrew on popular science; Other books incl: Complex Carbohydrates, Their Chemistry, Biosynthesis and Functions, 1975, Japanese transl, 1977; Lectins (co-auth), 1989, Japanese transl, 1990. Honours include: Landau Prize, Mifal Hapayis, 1973; Weizmann Prize in Exact Scis, Cty of Tel Aviv, 1977; Olitzki Prize, Israel Soc for Microbiology, 1989; Israel Prize in Biochem and Med, 1994; Visng Prof, Coll de France, Paris, 1994. Memberships include: Amn Chem Soc; The Biochem Soc; Intl Sci Writers Assn; Israel Biochem Soc, Pres, 1969-70; Intl Glycoconjugate Org, Pres, 989-91; Israel Soc for Chem and Biochem of Carbohydrates, Pres, 1997-.

SHARP John Randall, b. 15 Dec 1954, Sydney, Aust. Director. m. Victoria, 2 s, 1 d. Education: Assoc Dip, Farm Mngmt; FCIT. Appointments: Elected Parl of Aust, 1984-98; Fed Mbr for Hume, Min for Transp and Regl Dev, 1996. Hobbies: Skiing; Bushwalking; Reading; Jogging. Listed in: Who's Who in Australia. Address: 6 Greenaway Place, Goulburn, NSW 2580, Australia.

SHARPHAM John Raymond, b. 29 Nov 1940, Sydney, Aust. Academic; Director; CQU Fiji Camps. m. (1) 2 d, (2) Irene Jean Tirbutt. Education: BA (Hons) Sydney; Dip Ed, Sydney; MA, Univ of CO; PhD, Univ of CO. Appointments: Dpty Vice-Chancellor (Acad), Curtin Univ, 1983-87; Dir, Ballarat Univ Coll, 1987-93; Interim Vice-Chancellor, Univ of Ballarat, Vic, 1994; Dpty Vice-Chancellor (Resources & Plng), UNE, 1994-99; Dir, CQU Fiji Intl Campus. Publication: Australia's Future Universities (w Grant Harman), 1997. Honour: Fell, Univ of Ballarat, 1997. Hobbies: Rugby; Jogging; Theatre; Music. Address: 641 Boorolong Road, MSF 2007, Armidale, NSW 2350, Australia.

SHASTRI Ved Prakash, b. 15 Oct 1934, Kaul, India. Teacher. m. Darshan Devi, Feb 1950, 4 s, 3 d. Education: MA; PhD; DLitt; DSc. Appointments: Tchr, Agrawal HS, Hyderabad, 1950-52; Keshava Meml HS, Hyderabad, 1953-55; Lectr, Govt Arts & Sci Coll, Adilabad, 1957-59; Osmania Univ, Hyderabad, 1961-65, sev colls; Hindi Tchng Scheme, Govt of India, Min of Home Affairs, New Delhi, 1965-70; Rdr, Hd, Dept of Hindi & Skt, Sardar Patel Coll, 1970-93, Hindi Arts Coll, 1993-97. Publications: Over 700 articles in profl jrnls and mags. Honours: Hindi Pratishthan Awd, 1974; Hindi Acady Awd, 1978; Best Tchr Awd, 1991. Memberships: Pres, Students Lit Assn; Sec, Vaidio Vachnalaya; Book Selection Cttee, Ctrl Lib, Hyderabad; Fndr Mbr, Veerputra Hindi Vidyalaya; VP, Twin City Lib Assn, Hyderabad. Hobbies: Writing; Visiting New Places; Study. Address: No 21-1-198 Gandhi Bazar, Opp High Court, Hyderabad 500 002 AP, India.

SHATNER William, b. 22 Mar 1931 Montreal PQ Can. Actor. m. (1) Gloria Rand, 1956, div 1969; (2) Marcy Lafferty, 1973, 3 d. Education: McGill Univ. Appointments: Appeared Montreal Playhouse, 1952, 1953; Juvenile roles Canad Repertory Th Ottawa, 1952-53, 1953-54; Appeared Shakespeare Fest Stratford Ont, 1954-56; Broadway appearances incl: Tamburlaine the Great, 1956; The World of Suzie Wong, 1958; A Shot in the Dark, 1961; Num tv appearances. Films incl: The Brothers Karamazov, 1958; The Explosive Generation, 1961; Judgement at Nuremberg, 1961; The Intruder, 1962; The Outrage, 1964; Dead of Night, 1974; The Devil's Rain, 1975; Star Trek, 1979; The Kidnapping of the President, 1979; Star Trek: The Wrath of Khan, 1982; Star Trek III, The Search for Spock, 1984; Star Trek IV: The Voyage Home, 1986; Star Trek V: The Final Frontier, 1989; Star Trek VI: The Undiscovered Country, 1991; National Lampoon's Loaded Weapon, 1993; Star Trek: Generations, 1994; Ashes of Eden, 1995; Star Trek: Avenger, 1997; Tek Net, 1997. Address: c/o Lemli Productions, 760 North La Cienega Blvd, Los Angeles, CA 90069, USA.

SHAUKAT Tajwar, b. 18 Apr 1924. Housewife. m. 24 Feb 1946, 1 s, 2 d. Education: Grad, Punjab Univ. Appointments: Dir Fin, Shaukat & Raza Ltd. Memberships: VP: Pakistan Women's Assn, Fin & Admin; Gul-i-Rana Community Ctr; Area Pres, Assocd Country Women of the World, Ctrl & South Asia, India, Pakistan, Nepal, Sri Lanka; Pres: Zonta Intl, Karachi; Family Planning Assn, Karachi; Socl Sevs Co-ordng Cncl; Mbr, Govt Natl Population Cncl; Censor Board, Karachi; Banking Publicity Board, State Bank, Pakistan; Mbr of Hon, All Pakistan Women's Assn. Address: F-48, Block 8, KDA Scheme No 5, Kehkashan, Clifton, Karachi, Pakistan.

SHAW Alan George Lewers, b. 3 Feb 1916, Melbourne, Vic, Aust. Professor Emeritus. m. Peggy Perrins, 21 May 1956. Education: BA, Univ of Melbourne, 1938; Christchurch, Oxford, Eng; BA (Oxon), 1940; MA (Oxon), 1944. Appointments: Lectr, Econ Hist, 1941-45; Lectr, Mod Hist, 1946-50, Univ of Melbourne; Dean, Trinity Coll, 1946-51; Snr Lectr, Univ of Sydney, NSW, 1952-64; Prof of Hist, 1964-81, Prof Emer, 1982-, Monash Univ, Melbourne; Assoc Ed, Dictionary of Natl Biog, OUP, 1994-99. Publications: Economic Development of Australia, 1944; Story of Australia, 1956; Modern World History, 1959; Convicts and the Colonies, 1966; Sir George Arthur, Bart, 1785-1855, 1980; Gipps - La Trobe Correspondence, 1939-46 (ed), 1989; A History of the Post Phillip District: Victoria Before Separation, 1996. Honours: Nuffield Dominion Travelling Schlsp, 1950-51; Smuts Dominion Fellshp, Cambridge, 1967-68; Fell, Austl Acady of Hums, 1967; Fell, Roy Histl Soc of Vic, 1973; Fell, Roy Histl Soc of Aust, 1977; AO, 1982; DLitt, Newcastle, Aust, 1984; Fell, Federated Histl Socs of Aust, 1998. Memberships: Vic Hist Inst, Pres 1986-87; Austl Histl Assn, Pres, 1973-74; Pres, Roy Histl Soc of Vic; Roy Austl Histl Soc; Austl Inst of Intl Affairs. Hobbies: Golf; Bridge; Travel; Reading. Listed in: Who's Who in Australia. Address: 161 Domain Park, 193 Domain Road, South Yarra, Vic 3141, Australia.

SHAW John Hendry, b. 13 June 1922, Sydney, Aust. University Teacher. m. Gloria, 2 s. Education: MSc; MEd; FNGS; FAIEx; Dip, Educn. Appointments: Rsch Offr, Min of Post-War Reconstrn; Lectr, Tchrs Colls; Lectr, Univ New England and NSW. Publications: Man and His World, 1956; From Jungles to Snowlands, 1958; Cities and Industries, 1968; Growing Up in Gladesville, 1997. Honours: Macdonald Holmes Medal, 1981; Vis Prof, Univ GA, USA, 1968-69, 1972; OAM, 1997. Memberships: Hon Fell, Geog Soc of NSW, Austl Inst of Export, Geog Tchrs Assn. Hobbies: Photography; Stamp Collecting; Bowls. Address: 6 Lumsdaine Avenue, East Ryde, NSW 2113, Australia.

SHAW Keith M. Design Engineer, Mechanical Building Services. Education: BEng, Mech Engrng, Univ of Sydney, 1966; Postgrad Dip, Bldng Sci, Univ of Sydney, 1971. Appointments: Prod Engr, Elec Engrng Div, 1966-67, Des Engr, Site Engr, Air Condition and Indl Refrigeration Div, 1967-68, Email Ltd; Des Engr, Cnsltng Engrs, Rankine & Hill, 1968; Des Engr, Coml Equip Div, Email Ltd, 1969; C'wlth Dept of Works, NSW Reg, 1969-93; C'wlth Dept of Admin Servs, Natl Interest Grp, 1993-95; Self Employed, 1995-. Honours: Intl Cultural Dip of Hon, ABI, 1994; 20th Century Awd of Achievement, IBC, 1994. Address: PO Box 189 H, Australia Square, Sydney, NSW 1215, Australia.

SHAW Raymond Walter, b. 30 Jan 1950, Bendigo, Aust. Research Metallurgist. m. Alesia, 5 July 1975, 1 s, 1 d. Education: BSc, Hons; PhD. Appointments: Rsch Fell, Imperial Coll, 1976-78; Copper Proj Leader Bhas, 1978-84; Mngr, DCC Proj, Chief Scis, Rsch & Technol, 1984-96; Chief Technologist, Rio Tinto Rsch & Technol Dev. Membership: Fell, Austl Acady of Technol Sci & Engrng. Hobbies: Tennis; Golf; Music. Address: PO Box 230 New Gisborne, Victoria, 3438, Australia.

SHAW Russell Douglas, b. 4 May 1942. Geologist; Geophysicist. m. Prudence Margaret Packer, 9 Jan 1967, 1 s, 2 d. Education: BS (Hons), Univ of Sydney; MSc, Dip, Structural Geol and Rock Mechs, Imperial Coll, London; PhD, Geophys and Geodynamics, Rsch Sch of Earth Scis, Austrl Natl Univ. Appointments: Geol, Bur of Mineral Resources, Austl Govt, 1993; Currently, Prin Rsch Scientist, Austl Geol Survey Org, Dept Priary Ind and Energy. Publications: (w D J Forman) Deformation of Mineral Resources Bulletin 144, 1973; (w W J Collins) Time Limits on Tectonic Events and Caustal Evolution Using Geochronology, Some Australian Examples, Precambrian Research Elsevier, Amsterdam. Honours: Dux, Canberra Grammar Sch, 1958; Top of Yr, Geol and Geophys, Adv Univ of Sydney, 1962; Sheila Mitchell Swain Mem Prize for Fieldwork, Univ of Sydney, 1962; Pub Serv Bd Postgrad Schlshp Overseas Study, 1975-76; Stillwell Medal for Best Publ, Geol Soc of Aust, 1984. Memberships: Austl Soc of Exploration Geophysicists; Geol Soc of Aust; Amn Geophys Union; Amn Soc of Pet Geols. Hobbies: Travel; Music; Bushwalking. Address: c/o Australian Geological Survey Organisation, GPO Box 378, Canberra, ACT 2601, Australia.

SHEARER Ivan Anthony, b. 9 Dec 1938, Adelaide, Aust. Professor of Law. Education: LLB, LLM, Univ of Adelaide, 1956-60; SJD, NW Univ, Chgo, 1964-65. Appointments: Lectr, 1963-64, Snr Lectr, 1964-71, Rdr, 1971-74, Univ of Adelaide Law Sch; Prof of Law, 1975-, Dean, Fac of Law, 1984-90, Univ of NSW Law Sch, Sydney, Aust; Visng Fell, All Souls Coll, Oxford, Eng, 1978; Mbr, Perm Crt of Arbitration, The Hague, 1984; Cnslt in Intl Law, Dept of For Affairs & Trade, Canberra, 1991; Challis Prof of Intl Law, Univ of Sydney, 1993-. Publications: Extradition in International Law, 1971; Ed of D P O'Connell, International Law of the Sea, 1982, 1984; Articles in Legal Jrnls. Honours: Kt of Magistral Grace, Sov Mil Order of Malta, 1975; Reserve Forces Decoration, 1989; AM, 1995. Memberships: Amn Soc of Intl Law; Intl Law Assn; Austl Inst of Intl Affairs, Pres, NSW Br; Bar Assn of NSW; Intl Commn of Jurists; Law Asia. Hobbies: History; Music; Wine; Golf; Vintage Cars. Address: 76 Goodhope Street, Paddington, NSW 2021, Australia.

SHEEBA Jebaseeli Jasmine, b. 4 June 1972. Librarian. Education: BS, Phys, Lady Doak Coll, Madurai; BLISc, Maduria Kamaraj Univ; MLISc, Madurai Kamaraj Univ. Appointments: Libn, YWCAMH Sec Sch, Madurai; Lib Asst, Data Entry Operator, MS Univ, Tirunelveli; Trainee Libn, Equatorial Geophysical Rsch Lab, Tirunelveli; Lib Asst, St Christopher's Coll of Educ, Chennai. Honour: 2nd Rank, BLISc, Maduria Kamarai Univ, 1992-93. Membership: Life Mbr, Indian Assn of Spec Libs & Info Cntrs. Hobbies: Reading; Gardening. Address: No 4 Appar Street, Srinivasa Nagar, New Perungialathur, Chennai 600063, Tamilnadu, India.

SHEEN Martin, b. 3 Aug 1940 Dayton OH. Actor. m. Janet Sheen, 3 s, 1 d. Appointments: Wrked as shipping clerk Am Express Co NY. Stage Appearances: The Connection - debut NY and Eurn tour; Never Live Over A Pretzel Factory; The Subject Was Roses; The Crucible. Films: The Incident; Catch-22; Rage; Badlands; Apocalypse Now; Enigma; Gandhi; The King of Prussia; That Championship Season; Man Woman and Child; The Dead Zone; Final Countdown; Loophole; Wall Street; Nightbreaker; Da, 1988; Personal Choice, 1989; Cadence - also dir - 1990; Judgement in Berlin, 1990; Limited Time; The Maid, 1990; Hear No Evil; Hot Shots Part Deux - cameo; Gettysburg, 1993; Trigger Fast Hits!; Fortunes of War; Sacred Cargo; The Break; Dillinger & Capone; Captain Nuke and the Bomber Boys; Ghost Brigade; The Cradle Will Rock; Dead Presidents; Dorothy Day; Gospa; The American President; The War At Home; Spawn. Tv appearances incl: The Defenders; East Side/West Side; My Three Sons; Mod Squad; Cannon; That Certain Summer; Missiles of October; The Last Survivors; Blind Ambition; Shattered Spirits; Nightbreaker; The Last POW?; Roswell. Address: c/o Jeff Ballard, 4814 Lemona Avenue, Sherman Oaks, CA 91403, USA.

SHEIKH Abdulla bin Muhammad bin Ibrahim al-, b. 1949. Politician. Education: Shari'ah Coll; Imam Muhammad bin Saud Univ; Al-Azhar Univ Cairo. Appointments: Dean Imam Muhammad bin Saud Univ, 1975; Asst Prof, 1988; Min of Jus, 1992-. Address: Ministry of Justice, University Street, Riyadh 11127, Saudi Arabia.

SHEIKH Ehsanuddin, b. 15 July 1934. Senior Executive Vice-President. m. Mashkoor Fatima, 2 May 1964, 1 s, 3 d. Education: BCom; Fell, Inst Bankers, Karachi, Pakistan. Appointments: Habib Bank Ltd, Karachi, 1955-86, Zurich, 1986-. Membership: Inst of Bankers, Karachi. Hobbies: Photography; Reading. Address: Habib Bank AG Zurich, 149-151 Main Street, Colombo 11, Sri Lanka.

SHELTON James Norman, b. 23 Mar 1930. Veterinarian; Research Scientist. m. Pauline O'Neil, 24 June 1961, 4 s, 2 d. Education: BVSc, 1952, DVSc, 1994, Univ Qld, PhD, Univ Sydney, 1965; Fell, Aust Coll Vet Sc, 1981. Appointments: Qld Dept Agric: Vet Offr, 1953-58; Univ of Sydney, Rsch Fell, 1958-64; Snr Lectr, 1965-71; Sire Power P/L M/D, 1971-73; Vet Mngr, Austl Transplant Breeders, 1973-78; Austl Natl Univ: Snr Fell, 1978-93. Creative Works: Initiated Cattle Embryo Transfer, Aust, 1973. Publications: Over 100 on Controlled Breeding; Cryopreservation of Embryos; Embryo Transfer; Reproductive Biology and Immunology; Exchange Scientist, Japan, 1986; China, 1986; Consultancies in Africa, 1988; India, 1994-95. Memberships: Austl Vet Assn, Pres, ACT Div, 1983; Austl Soc Reproduction Bio, Sec, 1988-90; Intl Embryo Transfer Soc. Hobbies; Rugby League; Cricket; Fishing. Address: Unit 1 Oceanic Point, 185 Landsborough Avenue, Scarborough, Qld 4020, Australia.

SHEN Hong Xun, b. 13 Apr 1925, Shanghai, China. Researcher into Automation of Electric Drive. m. Zhou, 2 July 1952, 3 d. Education: BA, Fac of Elec Engrng, La Univsersitato Utopia, 1948. Appointments: Shift Engr in Power Plant, 1950; Designer of Elec Motors, 1952; Des Engr of Elec Drive, 1956; Snr Engr, 1980; Prof, 1987-. Publications: Principle of Electric Driving System, 1983; Theory of Synchronizing for Multi-Motor Driving System, 1987; General Concept of Mechatronics, 1993. Honours: Awd and Prize, Sci Tech Progress, Min of Textile Ind, 1987. Membership: Cttee, Low Voltage Elec Apparatus Grp, China Elec Soc, 1981-88. Hobby: Peking Opera. Address: 510-1-301 Jin Song, No 5 District, Chao Yang District, Beijing 100021, China.

SHEN Mason Ming-Sun. , Acupuncturist. Education: BSc, 1968; MSc, Chem, USA, 1971; Cert, Advd Acupuncturist, Hong Kong, 1972; Rsch Fell, Acupuncture Inst of NY, 1974-77; PhD, Biochemistry, Pharmacology Cornell Univ Medl Coll, NY, 1977; Postdoct Fell, Univ of CA, 1977-79; Rsch Assoc, Lawrence Livermore Natl Lab, CA, USA< 1979-80; Master Chinese Med, Inst Chinese Med, China Acady, Taiwan, 1982; Dr Oriental Med, San Fran Coll of Acupuncture & Oriental Med, San Fran, USA, 1984; MD (Medicina Alternativa) Intl Univ, Colombo, Sri Lanka, 1988. Appointments: Chf Acupuncturist, Acupuncture Cntr of Pleasanton, 2993-; Admnstr, Amn East medl Inst, Pleasanton, 1993-; Pres, Florescent Inst of Tradl Chinese Med, Oakland, CA, 1995-; Dir, Utd CA Practitioners of Chinese Med, San Fran, 1995-; Chf Acupuncturist, East Medl Cntr, Danville, CA, 1996-; Pres, Intl Congress of Chinese Med, Daniville, 997-; Exec Dir, Amn Assn of Tradl Chinese Med, Hayward, CA, 1997-; VP, Univ of Hlth Sci, Honolulu, HI, 1997-; Admnstv Offr, Rsch Inst of Chinese Med, San Fran, 1998-. Publications: Pprs to profl jrnls; Abstracts. Honours include: Presdtl Order of Merit, USA, 1991; Intl Man of Yr, IBC (Eng), 1991-92; Modern World Trad Med Hon Schl, Beijing, China, 1996; Acupuncturist of Yr, Amn Assn of Oriental Med, San Fran, 1998. Memberships include: Ny Acady Scis; Acupuncture Assn of Am; CA Cert Acupuncturists Assn; Amn Assn of Acupuncture & Oriental Med; Cntr for Chinese Med; Acupuncture Assn of Repub of China; Hong Kong and Kowloon Chinese Medal Assn. Address: 3240 Touriga Drive, Pleasanton, CA 94566, USA.

SHENG Ching Lai, b. 20 July 1919, Kahsing, China. Professor Emeritus. m. Josephine Yu-Ying, Dec 1981, 5 children by 1st m. Education: BSc, Natl Chiaotung Univ, 1941; PhD, Univ Edinburgh, 1948. Appointments: Prof, Natl Taiwan Univ, Univ Ottawa; Pres, Natl Chiaotung Univ; Prof, Univ of Windsor; Chair Prof, Tamkong Univ. Publications: Over 110 pprs and 8 monographs. Honours: Prize, Schl Publn, Sun Yat-Sen Cultural Fndn, 1972. Memberships: Roy Inst of Philos; Chinese Assn of Philos; Austl Philos Assn; Canad Philos Assn; N Amn Soc for Socl Philos; Intl Soc for Value Inquiry. Hobbies: Go; Table Tennis. Address: Tamkong University, Taipei Campus, 5 Lane 199, King Hwa Street, Taipei, Taiwan 106.

SHENG Lijun, b. 26 Jan 1958, China. Scholar; Political Scientist. m. Yang Xiaohua, 31 Jan 1984, 2 s. Education: BA, Beijing Fgn Lang Inst; MA, Austl Natl Univ; PhD, Univ Qld. Appointments: Fell, ISEAS, Singapore; Rsch Fell, ISEAS, Singapore; Vis Fell, SDSC, Austl Natl Univ, ADEA. Publications: China's Dilemma: The Taiwan Issue; Reinterpreting Chinese Foreign Policy. Hobbies: Swimming; Chinese Qigong. Address: Institute of Southeast Asian Studies, 30 Heng Mui Keng Terrace, Singapore 119614, Singapore.

SHENG Zheng-Mao, b. 14 Mar 1963, Zhejiang, China. Professor. m. Wu Hui-ping, 31 Dec 1987, 1 s. Education: MS, Hangzhou Univ, 1985-88; PhD, Zhejiang Univ, 1991-94. Appointments: Lectr, 1988-92, Asst Prof, 1992-96, Prof, 1996-98, Hangzhou Univ; Prof, Zhejiang Univ, 1998-. Publication: College Physics Experiments, 1994. Honour: Zhejiang Prov Sci Prize. Membership: ICTP. Hobby: Sports. Address: Department of Physics, Zhejiang University, 34 Tian Mushan Road, Hangzhou 310028, China.

SHEPHEARD Lois Anne, b. 27 Dec 1934, Lithgow, NSW, Aust. Teacher of Violin and Viola specialising in teaching blind students. m. Edmund Richard Shepheard, 10 Dec 1958, 1 s, 1 d. Education: Dip, State Conservatorium of NSW, 1956; Grad, Talent Educ Sch of Music, Matsumoto, Jap, 1981. Appointments: Res Music Mistress, Presby Ladies' Coll, Pymble, 1955-57; Sydney Symph Orch, 1958-60; Shelford Grammar Sch, 1965-71; Lectr, State Coll Vic Inst Early Childhood Dev, 1972-74; Introduced Suzuki Method to Vic, 1975; Studied and

Grad, Suzuki Method in Jap, 1980-81; Dir, Suzuki Prog, Prof of Viola, Western IL Univ, USA, 1989-91; Examiner, Austl Music Exams Bd, 1991-99. Publications: Contbr of article to an intl conf; Music for Flute and Strings, 1999. Memberships: Suzuki Talent Educ Assn of Aust, Vic; Suzuki Assn of the Ams Inc; Intl Suzuki Assn; Aust String Tchrs; Assn. Address: 2 Kennedy Street, Oakleigh S 3167, Australia.

SHEPHERD James Harcourt, b. 6 Dec 1927, York, WA, Aust. Merino Sheep Breeder. m. Lois Cross, 17 Feb 1962, 1 s, 2 d. Education: BSc, Forestry, BADSci, Univ of WA; Forestry Dip, Canberra, ACT. Appointments: Took over family property, 1953; Started Austl Merino Soc, 1967. Honours: Order of Aust, 1987; Fell, Austl Soc of Animal Production, 1982; Life Mbr, Austl Merino Soc. Memberships: Inst of Foresters of Aust; Austl Inst of Agricl Sci. Address: Box 63, Shackleton, WA 6386, Australia.

SHEPPARD Nancy Lee, b. 13 Sept 1933, Sydney, Aust. Teacher. m. 30 Sept 1967, 1 s, 1 d. Education: DipT; DipSociol. Appointments: Tchr, NSW state sch, 1953; Sch for Pitjantjatjara, 1955; Armidale Demonstration Sch, 1967. Publications: Pitjantjatjara Primer, 1962; Alitji in Dreamland Alitjinya Ngura Tjukurmankuntjala, 1992. Hobbies: The Pitjantjantjara Language; Travel. Address: 13 Salisbury Terrace, Collinswood, South Australia, 5071, Australia.

SHERA Geoffrey Paul, b. 16 Nov 1954, Ipswich, Australia. Writer; Library Worker. m. Nguyen Thi Thu Quyen, 30 Nov 1997. Education: BA, Canberra, 1975. Appointments: Educ Dept, Canberra, 1975; ANU Hist Dept Lib, 1983; Canberra Coll of Advd Educ Lib Cttee, 1982-84; Univ Qld Lib, 1991-97. Publications: Death on the Dole, 1979; Brizb'n Boy Canberra Girl, short stories, 1991; Citizen Queen, video, 1995. Memberships: Austl Film Inst; Brisbane Indep Filmmakers, Sec, 1985-89. Address: 39 Bangalee Street, Jindalee 4074, Qld, Australia.

SHERIDAN John Edmund, b. 1 Feb 1937, N Ireland. Plant Pathologist. m. Mary Witherford, 15 Aug 1964, 1 s, 3 d. Education: BSc 1960, BAgr 1961, Queens Univ, Belfast; DIC; PhD, Imperial Coll, Univ of London, 1964. Appointments: Demonstrator, Botany Imperial Coll, 1961-64; Lectr 1965-71, Snr Lectr 1971-83, Reader 1983-89, Hon Rsch Assoc 1989-90, Vic Univ, NZ; Dir, Plant Drs Ltd, 1988; Current research: cereal diseases, fungicide resistance. Publications: Over 100 sci articles in profl jrnls. Honour: Gibson Schlsp, 1958. Memberships: Inst of Bio; Brit Mycological Soc; NY Acady of Scis; Fell, Intl Biographical Assn; Fell, Roy Soc of Health. Hobbies: Gardening; Walking. Address: 108 Park Road, Carterton, New Zealand.

SHERIEF Hany H, b. 11 Dec 1949, Alexandria, Egypt. Professor of Mathematics. m. Tahany, 11 Dec 1974, 1 s, 1 d. Education: PhD, Univ of Calgary, Can. Appointments: Prof, Dept of Math, Univ of Qatar; Prof, Dept of Math, Univ of Alexandria, Egypt; Assoc Prof, Univ of Kuwait. Publications: 45 publ rsch pprs in intl jrnls in maths & engrng. Honour: Best Rsch ppr, Applied Math, Egypt, 1994. Memberships: NYAS; AAAS; Amn Math Soc. Hobby: Painting. Address: Department of Math, University of Qatar, PO Box 2713, Doha, Qatar.

SHERIF Osama El-, b. Jun 1960 Jerusalem. Publr. m. Ghada Yasser Amr, 1984, 1 s, 1 d. Education: Univ of MO. Appointments: Chf Ed The Jerusalem Star, 1985-88; Pres Info-Media Jordan, 1989-; Publr Chf Ed and weekly columnist The Star Jordan, 1990-; Publr Arabian Communications & Publishing - ACP - 1994-; Publr BYTE Middle East, 1994-; Publr Al Tiqaniyyah Wal 'Amal, 1995-. Hobbies: Novel and short-story writing; Travel; Photog; Horse riding. Address: P O Box 9313, Amman 11191, Jordan.

SHERIMKULOV Medethan, b. 17 Nov 1939, Jylamysh Village, around Bishkek. Politician. m. Chinara, 5 Sept 1964, 3 s. Education: BS, Histl sci, Kyrgyz State Univ; Postgrad educ, Dept of Philos, Moscow Lomonosov's State Univ. Appointments: Instr, Kyrgyx State Univ, 1970-71; Admnstv positions in Communist Party, 1971-90; Rector, Kyrgyz State Inst of phys culture and sport, 1980-86; Elected Dpty, Jogorku Kenesh (Parl), Kyrgyzstan, 1980-95; Speaker of Parl, Kyrgyz Repub, 1990-95; Prof of Pols, Kyrgyz State Natl Univ, 1995-98; Assigned by Pres of Kyrgyz Repub as Amb Extraordinary & Plenipotentiary of Kyrgyz Repub to Repub of Turkey, 1998. Publications: Over 100 essays on Pub Admin, Parliamentarianism, problems of intl and inter-ethnic conflicts; 4 books incl: Work of Parliament, 1994; Time and People Will Judge, 1998. Honours: Order of Hon, 1976; Order of Nations Friendship, 1982; Medals. Hobbies: Books; Horse riding. Address: Boyabat Sok No 11, Gaziosmanpasa, Asnkara, Turkey.

SHERMAN Barbara, b. 3 Aug 1922. Social Worker. m. William Alexander Sherman, 24 May 1947, 2 d. Education: Dip, Socl Work, Univ Sydney. Appointments: Snr Socl Worker, Gladesville Psych Hosp; Cnslt, Educr, Aged Care; Cnslt, Dementia Educ, C'wlth Dept, Hum Servs. Publications: Dementia With Dignity, 1991, 1994, 1999; Sex, Intimacy and Aged Care, 1998; Num articles on socl aspects of mental illness and Dementia. Memberships: Austl Assn Gerontology; Alzheimers Assn, NSW; Aust Soc of Auths; Cncl of the Ageing; Univ of the 3rd Age. Hobbies: People; Reading; History; Gardening; Swimming. Address: 4 Carawatha Street, Beecroft, NSW 2119, Australia.

SHERRY Ann Caroline, b. 2 Feb 1954, Gympie, Queensland, Aust. m. Michael Hogan, 25 Jan 1975, 1 s. Education: BA, Univ of Queensland, 1977; Grad Dip of Indl Rels, 1980; Grad Dip in Ergonomics, Lincoln Inst of Hlth Scis, 1986. Appointments include: Radiographer, Queensland Radium Inst, Roy Brisbane Hosp, 1972-74; Rsch and Educ Offr, Dept of Indl Rels, Queensland, 1979-81; Coord, London Team, Apex Trust (UK), 1981-83; Indl Rels Offr, Dept of Indl Rels, Vic Reg, 1982-83; Snr Orgnr, ACOA, Vic Branch, 1983-85; Occupational Hlth and Safety Offr, Admnstv and Clerical Offrs Assn (ACOA), Vic Branch, 1985-87; Asst Dir, Women's Policy Co-ord Unit, Dept of the Premier and Cabinet, 1987-88; Mngr, Women's Employment Branch, Dept of Labour, 1988-90; Gen Mngr, Off of Preschool and Child Care and Children's Servs Div, Community Servs Vic, 1990-92; Dir, Children and Family Servs, Dept of Hlth and Community Servs, 1992-93; 1st Asst Sec, Off of Status of Women, Dept of Prime Min and Cabinet, 1993-94; Gen Mngr, Hum Resources, Westpac Banking Corp, 1994-96; Gen Mngr, Hum Resources, IIBG, Westpac Banking Corp, 1996-; Gen Mngr, Hum Resources and Pub Affairs and policy, Bank of Melbourne, Westpac, 1997-. Publications: num pprs to jrnls and confs. Memberships: Chair, Austl Inst of Family Studies, 1995-; Austl Cncl of Businesswomen, 1996-; NSW Govt Remuneration Tribunal, 1997-.

SHERWIN Murray Allan, b. 4 Apr 1952, Te Awamutu, New Zealand. Bank Executive. m. Willemijntje Antonia Van der Vorm, 23 Nov 1974, 1 s, 1 d. Education: Bach Deg, Socl Scis, 1974, Master Deg, Socl Scis, 1976, Univ Waikato. Appointments: Econ Advsr, PM's Adv Grp, Wellington, NZ, 1982-83; Chf Mngr, Intl Res Bank, NZ, Wellington, 1984-87; Exec Dir, World Bak, WA, 1987-89; Chf Mngr, Fin Mkts, Chf Mngr, Banking Systems, Reserve Bank NZ, 1989-95, Dpty Gov, 1995-. Hobbies: Commercial Forestry; Skiing; Classic Automobiles. Address: Reserve Bank New Zealand, 2 The Terrace, PO Box 2498, Wellington, New Zealand.

SHETREET Shimon, b. 1946 Morocco. Politician. Education: Hebrew Univ; Chgo Univ. Appointments: Sec Cncl for Pub Jus; Chmn Cttee on Brdcstng Authy Law; Chmn Intl Conf on Legal Matters; Chmn Bd Dirs Afr-Asian Inst of the Histadrut; Served on the Landau Commn on the Israeli Crt System The Cncl for Admin Crts Plenum of the Israel Brdcstng Authy, 1984-87; Served on num cttees, 1988-92; Min of Econ Sci and Tech, 1992-95; Min of Rel Affairs, 1995-96; Dir Leumi Bank. Publications: Num books and articles on legal matters. Address: c/o Hebrew University of Jerusalem, Mount Scopus, Jerusalem 91905, Israel.

SHETTY A Chandra, b. 20 July 1958, Akkunje, India. Engineering Consultant. m. Sadhana, 28 May 1986, 1 s, 1 d. Education: BTech degree in Mech; P G Dip, Export Mktng Mngmt; P G Dip, Small Inds Mngmt; Dip in Refrigeration and Air-conditioning; Dip in Bus Admin. Appointments: Chf Exec, M/s Kohinoor Computers Servs; Dir, M/s Freight Links Priv Ltd. Honours: GMP Awd in Prodn Mngmt; Super Intellectual Awd; Vijaya Shree Awd; Best Citizen of India Awd; MSPI Outstndng Personality Awd. Memberships: Instn of Engrs; Indian Inst of Prodn Engrs; ISHRAE; Assoc Mbr, Fluid Power Soc of India; Inst of Law & Mngmt; Assn of Cnsltng Engrs; Fell, All India Mngmt Cncl; Fell, Mngmt Studies Promotion Inst. Hobbies: Technical writing; Attending seminars; Attending institutional activities. Address: 53, Kohinoor, S C Road, Opp Movieland/Royal Lodge, Bagalore 560009, India.

SHEU Wayne H H, b. 17 Nov 1957, Taiwan. Physician. m. Terry, 12 Nov 1983, 2 d. Education: MD; PhD. Publications: More than 60 original sci articles. Membership: Amn Diabetes Assn. Address: Endocrinology & Metabolism, Department of Medicine; Taichung Veterans General Hospital, No 160, Section 3, Chung Kang Road, Taiwan, 40705, Taiwan.

SHI Dao Yuan, b. 6 July 1935, Jiangshu Prov, China. Doctor. m. Wu Shuhong, 15 Aug 1962, 2 s. Education: Medl Bachelor Deg, W China Medl Univ. Appointments: Prof, W China Medl Univ, 1985; Dean, Friendship Hosp, 1997. Creative Works: Spinal Surgery Operation; Degenerative Spondylolisthesis; Clinical Features and Treatment of the Fracture of the Odontoid Process; Early Diagnosis of Atlanto-axial Tuberculosis; Treatment of the Posterior Longitudinal Ligament of the Cervical Spine; Myelopathy and Cervial Spino-stenosis; Protrusion of Lumber Inervertebrai Disk in the Adolescents. Memberships: Sichuan Orths Acady; SW China Spinal Trng Cntr; Sichuan Spinal and Spinal Cord Acady. Hobbies: Swimming; Reading; Music. Address: Friendship Hospital, Gao Sheng Qiao, Chengdu, Sichuan 610041, China.

SHI Guiying, b. 14 Oct 1933, China. Doctor. m. Xin Tian, 2 s. Education: MB, First Mil Medl Univ. Appointments: Hs Physn, 1957; Visng Physn, 1965; Vice Dir, 1975; Dir of Div of Rheumatology, 1984-96; Snr Prof, 1997-. Creative Works: 300 Questions and Answers of Arthritis, 1993; Chinese Version of Aches and Pains, Living with Arthritis and Rheumatism, 1994. Honours: Clinical Medl Prize in Rheumatology; Sci Prize in Rheumatology, 1998. Memberships: Asian Pacific League of Assn for Rheumatology; Chinese Rheumatology Assn. Hobbies: Music. Address: Division of Rheumatology, Chinese PLA General Hospital, 28 Fuxing Road, Beijing 100853, China.

SHI Hanmin, b. 28 Aug 1937, Hubei, China. Professor of Mechanical Engineering; Head of Department. m. Huiying Gao, 18 July 1968, 1 s, 1 d. Education: Grad Cert, Wuchang Secondary Sch of Trade, Hubei, China, 1951-54; Dept of Mech Engrng, Huazhong Univ of Sci and Technol (HUST), 1957-62; Postgrad Sch of Huazhong Univ of Sci and Technol (HUST), 1962-65. Appointments: Statn, Bur of Commerce of Hubei Prov, 1954-57; Lectr, Dept of Mech Engrng, Huazhong Univ of Sci and Technol (HUST), 1978-83; Hon Rsch Fell, Dept of Mech Engrng, The Univ of Birmingham, Eng, 1980-82; Prof, Dept of Mech Engrng, Huazhong Univ of Sci and Technol, 1983-; Visng Prof, Dept Mech Engrng and Applied Mechs, MI Univ, USA, 1992-93; Mbr, Acad Deg Cttee Cttee, HUST, 1995-98; Pres, Mngmt Inst of State Sci and Techol Comm of China, 1995-98; Vice Chmn of Bd, Kayu Soft Engrng Co Ltd, Beijing, China, 1995-98; Pres, Informatics Coll, Wuhan, 1996-98; Visng Prof, Hong Kong Univ of Sci and Tech, 1999. Creative Works: Theory of Fiite Amplitude Machine Tool Instability, 1984; The Systems of Mechanical Vibration, 1992; The Science of Manufacturing, 1994; The New Progress in Machine Tool Chatter and Control, 1994; A Study on Curved Edge Drills, 1994; A Model for Non-Free-Cutting, 1995; Multi-Functional Scanning Tunnelling Micropsope, 1995; Chip-ejection interference in cutting process of modern cutting tools, 1999; About 300 pprs publ in China and abroad. Honours: Rsch Work on Nonlinear Maching Tool Chatter Theory, Won State Prize of Nat Sci, 1987; State Prize of Ex Tchng Wrk, 1993; Sci and Technol Progress Prize, State Educ Commn, 1996. Memberships: Dir of Rsch Cntr for Mech Engrng, Huazhong Univ of Sci and Technol; Mbr of Cncl, Chinese Soc of Vibration Engrng; Cncl, Hubei Prov Soc of Mech Engrng; Stndng Prod Engrng Comm, Chinese Soc of Mech Engrng; VP, Chinese Soc of Scientific Indexes, 1995. Hobbies: Mathematics; Chinese Classical literature; Painting. Listed in: International Who's Who of Intellectuals. Address: School of Mechanical Science and Engineering, Huazhong University of Science and Technology, Wuhan, Hubei 430074, China.

SHI Haoxin, b. 24 Sept 1934. Professor. m. 1963, 1 s, 2 d. Education: BSc, Chem, Anhui Normal Univ, 1959. Appointments: Lectr, Dept of Chem, Anhui Normal Univ, 1978-85; Assoc Prof, Dept of Chem, Anhui Normal Univ, 1985-93; Prof, Dept of Chem, Anhui Normal Univ, 1993-. Publications include: Synthesis and Analytical Application of a New Fluorescent Reagent 3-p-Tolyl-5 (2'-Carboxyphenylazo) Rhodanine, 1995; Study of the Synthesis and Analytical Application of 3-Phenyl-5 (4'-Nitro-2'-Carboxylphenylazo) Rhodanine, 1995. Honours: Natl Natural Sci Fndn of China Grant for Rsch, 1992-94; Fndn of Anhui Sci and Technol Cttee, 1992-94; Anhui Prov Sci Congress Awd, 1978; Anhui Xinghuo Awd, 1993; Anhui Sci and Technol Developing Awd, 1997. Membership: Chinese Chem Soc. Hobbies: Chemistry Experiments; Reading Books. Address: Department of Chemistry, Anhui Normal University, Wuhu, Anhui 241000, China.

SHI Jian Yi, b. 31 Mar 1948, Zhejiang, China. Professor, Group Theory and Combinatorics. m. Xin-Xin Cao, 10 Feb 1981, 1 d. Education: Master Deg, E China Normal Univ, 1978-81; PhD, Warwick Univ, England, 1981-84. Appointments: Lectr, 1985-86, Assoc Prof, 1986-91, Prof, 1991-, Dept of Maths, E China Normal Univ; Mbr, IAS, NJ, USA, 1988-89; Vis Assoc Prof, Univ MN, USA, 1989-90, Osaka Univ, Japan, 1992-93; Guest Prof, Max Planck Inst fur Maths, Germany, 1996; Snr Rsch Assoc, Dept of Maths, Sydney Univ, Aust, 1997-98. Publications: The Kazhdan-Lusztig Cells in Certain Affine Weyl Groups, 1986; The Representation Theory of Finite Groups, 1992; The Enumeration of Coxeter Elements, 1997. Honours: Prize, Progress in Sci and Technol, Chinese Natl Educ Cttee, 1985; Prize of Ex Univ Tchrs, Huo Ying-dong Educn Fndn, 1987; Prize, Outstndng Schl, Qiu Shi Sci and Technol Fndn, 1995; Prize, Natl Nat Sci, Sci and Technol Dept of China, 1999. Hobbies: Chinese Chess; History. Address: Apt 301, No 220, Lane 3671, Zhongshan Northern Road, Shanghai 200062, China.

SHI Lei, b. 17 Nov 1935, Shanghai, China. Chief Doctor. m. Bi H Shen, 28 Aug 1960, 1 s, 1 d. Education: Dips, Shanghai Second Med Univ, 1959. Appointments: Vice Prof, 1986; Prof, Chf Dr, 1990. Publictions: Sev books and num articles in profl med jrnls. Memberships: NASPE; N Am Soc of Pacing and Electrophysiol. Hobby: Music. Address: c/o Rui Jin Hospital, 197 Rui Jin No 2 Road, Shanghai 200025, China.

SHI Peng, b. 2 Oct 1958, Harbin, China. Lecturer. m. Mei Sun, 23 May 1983, 1 s, 1 d. Education: PhD. Appointments: Lectr, Sch of Math, Univ of SA, 1998-; Postdoc, Univ of SA, 1995-97. Publications: Pprs publs in intl jrnls and confs. Honour: Sec Prize, Heilongjiang Prov Sci and Technol Cttee, 1987. Memberships: IEEE; SIAM. Hobbies: Bridge Cards; Tennis; Swimming. Address: School of Mathematics, University of South Australia, The Levels Campus, SA 5095, Australia.

SHI Renmin, b. 25 Mar 1957, Dalian, China. Researcher in Science. m. Sun Yan, 25 Sept 1985, 1 d. Education: MEng, Dalian Univ of Technol. Appointments: Engr, Dalian Inst of Soda Mfng, 1984; Rsch Assoc, Dalian Inst of Chem Phys, 1985; Visng Schl, Univ of Alberta, Can, 1990-92; Assoc Prof, DICP. Honours: Top Grade Awds of Advances in Scis & Technol, Chinese Acady of Scis, 1997. Memberships: Chinese Assn of Chem: Chinese Assn of Chem Engrng. Address: Dalian Institute of Chemical Physics, Chinese Academy of Sciences, 457 Zhongshan Road, PO Box 110, Dalian, China, 116023.

SHI Shilong, b. 31 Dec 1935. Teacher. m. 16 Feb 1954, 2 s, 1 d. Education: Grad, Dept of Hist of Chinese Communist Party, People's Univ of China, 1960. Appointments: Pols Prof, Yunnan Univ, China; Tutor, Postgrads for Master's Degree, Pols Dept, Yunnan Univ. Publications: Chinese Victory in the War of Resistance Against Japan and Historical Experience in the National Anti-Japan United Front, 1985; The Historical Research About the Struggle Line, 1988; Mao Tse-Tung and Marxism in China, 1993; On Perfection of System of People's Congress in China, 1994. Honours: Exemplary Tchr, Yunnan Colls & Univs, 1985; Exemplary Tchr in Yunnan Province, 1994; Exemplary Tchr, China, 1995. Memberships: Dirs of Inst Chinese Communist Party History; Vice Dir Inst of C P Yunnan; Dirs, China Natl Assn of CDC Hist Rsch; Vice Dir, Yunnan CPC Hist Inst. Hobbies: Reading; Music. Address: Department of Politcal Science, Yunnan University, Kunming 650091, China.

SHI Tiansheng, b. 9 Jan 1936, Jiangsu Prov, China. Scientist. m. Yunxia He, 1 Jan 1962, 2 d. Education: Moscow Inst of Steel, 1954-60; SUNY, Albany, USA, 1981-83. Appointments: Assoc Rsch Prof, 1986; Rsch Prof, 1988; Hd, Dept of Physl Characterization of Materials; Acting Vice Ed in Chf, Functional Materials and Devices, 1995-. Creative Works: State and Behavior of Hydrogen in Silicon Lattice; Hydrogen in Crystalline Semiconductors. Honours: Sci and Tech Awd, China Acady of Sci. Hobbies: Reading; Tour. Address: Shanghai Inst of Metallargy, Chinese Academy of Sciences; 865 Changning Road, Shanghai 200050, China.

SHI Xiao-chun, b. 20 Apr 1944, China. Associate Professor. m. Jin-biao Sun, 1 Oct 1970, 1 s. Education: MD, Zhejiang Medl Univ, 1966; Advd Stdy, New Drug Preclinl Safety, Ciba-Geigy, Basle, Switz, 1996. Appointments: Rsch Asst, 1966-70, Rsch Assoc, 1970-80, Snr Rsch Assoc, 1980-87, Assoc Prof, Tox, 1990-93, Inst Microbio and Epidemiology, Mil Acady Medl Scis, Beijing; NRC Rsch Assoc, NIOSH, Morgantown, WV, USA, 1987-89; Rschr, Dept Biochem, WV Univ, 1989-90; Assoc Prof, Tox, Inst Pharmaco-Tox, Mil Acady Med Scis, Beijing, 1993-. Publications include: Bone Marrow Toxicity Studies of Sodium Artesunate in Dogs, 1986; Studies on Combination of Artemether and Benflumetol in China, Summarized from Experiments of the Institute of Microbiology and Epidemiology, AMMS, A Presentation for the Ciba Pharma Overseas Delegation, Beijing, 1990; Induction of Micronuclei in Rat Bone Marrow by Four Model Compounds, 1992; The cytogenetic effects of benzene on rat bone marrow, 1993; Preclinical Studies of Artesunate Tablets for Malaria Research Center, Delhi, India, 1995. Honours: Awd, Sci Conf, Gen Logistic Min, Naonujia Stdys Grp, 1978; Citation, Outstndng Sci Wrk in Inst Microbio and Epidemiology, Mil Acady Med Sci, 1979; Chinese 1st Class Medl Inv Awd, Studies of New Anti-Malarial Drug Benflumetol resp for tox studies, 1988; 3rd Class Merit Awd, Toxicity Stdy of Benflumetal, Chinese People's Liberation Army, 1991. Memberships: Chinese Soc Pharmacology; Chinese Soc Tox; Chinese Soc Mutagens; Chinese Gonfu Soc. Hobbies: Tai-ji; Qi-gon; Acupuncture. Address: 27 Taiping Road, Beijing 100850, China.

SHI Dazhen, b. 1932 Wuxi Cty Jiangsu Prov. Govt Offic; Engr. Education: Shandong Inst of Tech, 1955; Joined CCP, 1978; Vice-Min of Energy and Rescs, 1988-93; Min of Power Ind, Mar 1993-. Memberships: Alt mbr 13th Cntrl Cttee CCP, 1988-93; Alt mbr 14th Cntrl Cttee CCP, 1993-. Address: Ministry of Electric Power, 3-5 Baiguang Road, Beijing 100761, Pepole's Republic of China.

SHI Yunshen, b. Jan 1940 Fushun Cty Liaoning Prov. Naval Offr. Education: PLA Air Force Aviation Sch; PLA Navy Acady. Appointments: Joined PLA, 1956; Pilot Squadron ldr dep grp Cmdr and dep regt Cmdr Naval Aviation, 1962-70; Dep Cmdr Naval Fleet Aviation, 1976-81; Div Cmdr Naval Aviation, 1981-83; Cmdr Naval Fleet Aviation, 1983-90; Rep 13th Natl Congress of CCP, 1987; Dep Cmdr PLA Naval Aviation Dept, 1990-92; Dep Cmdr PLA Navy, 1992-97; Cmdr, 1997-. Address: c/o Ministry of National Defence, Jingshanqian Jie, Beijing, People's Republic of China.

SHIBA Tetsuo, b. 17 June 1924, Onomichi, Japan. Professor Emeritus. m. Michiko, 15 Apr 1952, 1 s, 1 d. Education: PhD. Appointments: Visng Sci, Natl Inst of Hlth; Prof, Osaka Univ; Prof Emer, Osaka Univ; Dir Emer, Plant Prodn Cntr, Nishinomiya; Fmr Pres, Soc of Hist of Chem, Japan. Publications: Chemical Research on Bioactive Peptides; Immunoadjurant Active Peptide-glycan; Historical Research on Chemistry in Japan. Honours: Awd, Chem Soc, Japan; Hogarty Schl, Natl Inst of Hlth, USA; Awd of Culture, Nishinomiya. Memberships: Chem Soc, Japan; Soc of Chem Hist, Japan. Hobbies: History of Chemistry; Plants. Address: 1-2-28 Hattorihommachi, Toyonaka, Osaka 561-0852, Japan.

SHIBAMOTO Yuta, b. 13 Dec 1955, Kakogawa, Japan. Radiation Oncologist. m. Hiromi Yanagawa, 3 May 1980, 1 s, 2 d. Education: MD, 1980, DMedSc, 1987, Kyoto Univ. Appointments: Asst Prof, 1987, Lectr, 1992, Assoc Prof, 1992, Kyoto Univ; Guest Rschr, Univ of Essen, 1989-90. Creative work: Inventor, Fluorine-containing radiosensitizer, 1987. Honours: Hanns-Langendorff Prize, 1992; Sci Ppr of Yr 1995, Japan Radiological Soc, 1995. Memberships: Japan Radiological Soc, Tokyo, 1981-; Japanese Soc for Therapeutic Radiology and Oncology, 1988-; Japanese Cancer Assn. Hobbies: Classical music; Golf; Table tennis. Address: 72-23 Kyoto 603-8074, Japan.

SHIBAYAMA Hiroshi, b. 15 Dec 1919, Kyoto, Japan. Professor Emeritus of Osaka Institute of Technology. m. Chieko Kubo, 3 Nov 1949, dec'd Jan 1984. Education: BE, Electr Engin, Kyoto Univ, 1942; DEng, Kyoto Univ, Japan, 1962. Appointments: Rsch Engr, Mitsubishi Elec Corp, 1942-46; Tchr, Rakuyo hs, Kyoto, 1946-50; Lectr, Electr Engin, 1950-56, Asst Prof, 1956-62, Prof, Electr Engin, 1962-90, Prof Emeritus, 1992-, OIT. Publications: Pprs on Nonlinear Oscillations in profl jrnls. Honours: Commended in Pub for Servs to Indl Educ by min of Educ, Japan, 1984; Decorated w 4th Order of Sacred Treasure, by Emperor of Japan, 1993. Memberships: Inst of Elec Engrs of Japan, 1941-; Inst of Electrons, Info and Comm Engrs. Hobbies: Appreciation of Classical music and ancient arts of Japan. Address: Kouri Minamino-cho 28-24-806, Neyagawa, Osaka 572-0084, Japan.

SHIEH Samuel C. Banker; Academic. Education: Univ of MN. Appointments: Fmr Prof; Gov Cntrl Bank of China, 1989-94; Natl Policy Advsr to Pres, 1994-. Address: c/o Office of the Governor, Central Bank of China, 2 Roosevelt Road, Sec 1, Taipei 10757, Taiwan.

SHIELDS Margaret Kerslake b. 18 Dec 1941, Wellington, NZ. Politician; Social Scientist. m. Patrick John Shields, 25 Nov 1960, 2 d. Education: BA, Vic Univ, Wellington, 1973. Appointments: Fndr, Soc for Rsch on Women in NZ, 1966; Rschr, NZ Consumers' Inst, 1966-71; Snr Rsch Offr, Dept of Stats, 1973-81; MP for Kapiti, 1981-90; Min of the Crown, 1984-90; Dir, UN Intl Rsch and Trng Inst for the Advancement of Women, 1991-94; Mbr, Wellington Regl Cncl, 1995-; Mbr, NZ Human Rights Commn Complaints Review Tribunal, Mbr, Vic Univ Wellington Cncl, 1996- ; Dpty Chair, Welligton Regl Cncl. Honours: Winston Churchill Fellshp, 1970; Tressa Thomas Awd, NZ Fedn of Univ Women, 1973; Queen's Serv Order, 1996. Memberships: Life Mbr, Past Pres, Soc for Rsch on Women in NZ; Pres, NZ Natl Cttee for UNIFEM; Mbr, NZ Cncl for Intl Dev. Hobbies: Gardening; Walking; Reading; Music; Theatre. Address: 23 Haunui Road, Pukerua Bay, Porirua, New Zealand.

SHIGEHARA Kumiharu, b. 5 Feb 1939, Maebashi, Japan. Economist. m. Akiko, 14 Apr 1965, 1 s, 1 d.

Education: BL, Univ of Tokyo. Appointments: Dir Gen, Inst for Monetary and Economic Stdies, Bank of Japan, 1989-92; Hd, Econ Dept and Chf Economist, OECD, 1992-97; Dpty Sec-Gen, OECD, 1997-. Publications: Stable Economic Growth and Monetary Policy, 1991; New Trends in Monetary Theory and Policy, 1992; The Options Regarding the Concept of a Monetary Policy Strategy, 1996. Honour: Doct honoris causa, Univ of Liège, 1998. Address: 101 Avenue Henri Martin, 75116 Paris, France.

SHIH Chih-yu, b. 8 Aug 1958, Taipei, Taiwan. College Professor. m. Eva Ho, 26 June 1983, 1 s, 1 d. Education: MPP, Harvard Univ; PhD, Univ of Denver. Asst Prof, Winona State Univ; Asst Prof, Ramapu Coll of NJ; Assoc Prof, Prof, Natl Taiwan Univ. Publications: The Spirit of Chinese Foreign Policy, 1990; Contending Drama, 1992; Symbolic War, 1993; China's Just World, 1993; State and Society in China's Political Economy, 1995; Collective Democracy, 1999; Reform, Identity and Chinese Foreign Policy, 1999. Honours: Stanely Hornback Fell, 1986; Outstndng Fell, Natl Sci Cnl, 1994-98; CCK Fell, 1994; Fulbright Schl, 1997. Memberships: Amn Polit Sci Assn; Chinese Polit Sci Assn. Hobbies: Coaching intermural basketball. Address: Graduate Institute of Political Science, National Taiwan University, 21 Hsu Chow Road, Taipei, Taiwan, China.

SHIH Ming-Teh. Politician. m. Linda Gail Arrigo. Appointments: Fmr polit prisoner in Taiwan; Ldr Taiwan Dem Progressive Party - DPP - 1993-. Memberships: Mbr Taiwan Legis Cncl. Address: Room 601, 10 Tsingtao E Road, Taipei, Taiwan.

SHIKHMURADOV Boris Orazovich, b. 1949 Ashkhabad. Politician; Diplomatist. Education: Moscow State Univ; Diplomatic Acady. Appointments: Jrnlst; Diplomatist Press Agcy Novosti and USSR min of For Affairs, 1971-72; Resp positions in miss abroad then on staff USSR min of For Affairs, 1983-86; Wrked in USSR Embs to Pakistan India miss to Turkey Afghanistan USA China Singapore; Apptd Dep then First Dep Min of For Affairs of Turkmenistan, May 1992; Dep Chmn Cabinet of Mins of Turkmenistan, 1992-; Min of For Affairs, 1995-. Address: Ministry of Foreign Affairs, Ashgabat, Turkmenistan.

SHILLONY Ben-Ami, b. 28 Oct 1937, Tarnopol, Poland. Professor of Japanese History. m. Lena, 4 Apr 1962, 2 d. Education: PhD, Princeton Univ. Appointments: Chmn, The Truman Inst, 1987; Chmn, Dept of E Asian Stdies, Hebrew Univ of Jerusalem. Publications: Revolt in Japan, 1973; Politics and Culture in Wartime Japan, 1981; The Jews and the Japanese, 1991. Honour: Michael Milken Prize for Ex Tchng, 1996. Memberships: Assn of Asian Stdies; Eurn Assn of Japanese Stdies. Address: Department of East Asian Studies, The Hebrew University of Jerusalem, Jerusalem 91905, Israel.

SHIMOYAMA Hifumi, b. 21 June 1930, Hirosaki City, Japan. Music Composer. m. Yoko, 29 July 1959. Education: Grad, Hirosaki Univ. Appointment: Prof. Publications: Dialogue For Cello and Piano, 1962; Saikyo For Orchestra, 1979; Doubridge For String Orchestra, 1995. Honours: Prize of Ex, Art Fest, Min of Educn, 1979; Italy Prize, 1981. Memberships: Exec Cttee, Japanese Soc for Contemp music; Japan Fedn of Composers. Hobbies: Swimming; Gardening. Address: 4-11-9-307 Kami-Ikebukuro, Toshima-ku, Tokyo, Japan.

SHIN Dong-So, b. 7 Feb 1931, Korea. Professor Emeritus. m. 1 Apr 1968, 3 s. Education: PhD, Fac of Agricl, Kyushu Univ. Appointments: Asst Lectr, Asst Prof, Assoc Prof, Prof, Gyenogsan Natl Univ, 1960-73; Prof, Seoul Natl Univ, 1973-96; Vis Schl, Swedish Roy Inst of Technol, 1979; Advsry Cttee, Min of Trade, Ind & Energy, 1982-83; Chmn, Cttee on Ppr & Pulp, Korean Ind Standards Divsn, Natl Inst of Technol & Quality, Medium & Small Bus Admin, 1983-; Pres, Korea Tech Assn of Pulp & Ppr Ind, 1986-; Dir, Inst of Forestry & Product, Coll of Agricl & Life Sci, Seoul Natl Univ, 1991-93; Dir, Korea Packaging Rsch Inst, 1997-. Publications: Sev articles in

profl jrnls. Honours: Cultural Prize, Gyeongsangnam-do, Natural Scis Divsn, 1970; Grand Prize, Fndn of Agricl Acad & Rsch, Seoul Natl Univ, 1994; Awd, Natl Order (Seuk-reu), 1996. Memberships: Tech Assoc, Pulp & Ppr Ind; Cand Pulp & Assn; Pres, Korea Soc of Packaging Sci & Technol; Fell, Korean Acady of Scis & Technol. Address: 7-96 Sambu Apt, Yoido-dong, Youngdungpo-ku, Seoul 150-010, Korea.

SHINDE Anusayabai, b. 5 Oct 1927, Kalamnuri. Folk Artist (Singer); Social Work. m. Anandrao, 11 Nov 1948, 3 s, 2 d. Publications: Compositions: Ballado; Social Songs. Honours: Shahir Amar Sheikh Awd, Mumbai, Racian Tour, 1984; Hon, Stri Sanghatana, Mumbai, Freedom Fighter. Membership: Pres, Akhil Bharatiya Shahir Parishad, Marathwada Div. Hobbies: Singing; Social Work. Address: Malli Galli, Kalamnuri, Hangoli, MS, 431702, India.

SHING Shiu Ching Elizabeth, b. 30 June 1946, Educator; Management Consultant. m. 5 July 1986, 1 s, 2 d. Education: BA (Hons), Univ Hong Kong, 1970; MA Admin Sci, City Univ Bus Sch, London, 1975. Appointments: Community Rels Offr, SARDA, 1970; Mbrshp and Pub Rels Offr, Hong Kong Mngmt Assn, 1972; Mngr, External Affairs, 1973; Asst Sec (Admin, Mngmt Dev & Spokeswoman), 1974; Dir, Mngmt Servs (Admin, mktng of Mngmt Servs & Mngmt Dev), 1975; Jt Exec Dir, 1980; Dir Gen, 1990. Publications: 15 articles incl: Hong Kong's Civil Service and Public Policy During the Transition to 1997, HMKA Specialist Club Annual Report, 1993; Challenges of HR Planning in Hong Kong, Hong Kong Economic Report, 2 Jan 1995; The Role of the Hong Kong Management Association in the Territory's Economic Transition, Hong Kong Economic Report, 2 Jan 1996. Honours; BA (Hons), 1970; MSc FIM, 1975. Memberships: Advsry Cttee on Bus and Mngmt Studies, Hong Kong Poly Univ, 1979-; Course Advsry Cttee, BA (Hons) in Arts & Socl Scis, Hong Kong Bapt Univ, 1991-; Cncl Mbr, Hong Kong Liver Fndn, 1992-; Advsry Bd, Dept Mktng & Intl Bus, Lingnan Coll, 1993-. Hobbies: Chinese Antiques and Work of Art; Classical Music. Address: 14/F Fairmont House, 8 Cotton Tree Drive, Central, Hong Kong.

SHINKLE John Thomas (Jack), b. 9 May 1946, Albany, NY, USA. Attorney. m. Csilla Elizabeth Bekasy, 2 Sept 1967, 2 d. Education: JD, Harvard Law Sch; BA, Yale Coll. Appointments: Assoc Dir, 1981, Dpty Gen Cnsl, 1982, Div of Copr Fin, U S Securities & Exchange Commn, Wash DC, USA. Publications: Var articles in profl jrnls; Observations on Capital Market Regulation: Hong Kong and the People's Republic of China, Univ of PA, 1997. Memberships: Securities Ind Assn, Chmn, Fedl Regulation Cttee, 1989-91; Dir, Futures Ind Assn, 1989-97. Hobbies: Tennis; Swimming. Address: Saloman Smith Barney, 20th Floor, 3 Exchange Square, 8 Connaught Place, Central, Hong Kong, SAR China.

SHINOHARA Masaru, b. 20 Feb 1948, Tamano, Okayama, Japan. Physicist. m. Miyo, 3 June 1979, 2 d. Education: DSc, Univ Tokyo. Appointments: Rsch Assoc, Nagasaki Inst Appl Sci, 1978-79; Lectr, 1979-81, Assoc Prof, Prof, Gifu Natl Coll of Technol. Publication: Mechanical Engineering, 1987. Memberships: Physl Soc of Japan, 1972-; Japan Soc of Fluid Mechs, 1974-. Hobbies: Yachting; Fishing. Address: Kami Makuwa 2236-2, Sinsei-tyo, Gifu 501-0461, Japan.

SHINTANI Kazuhito, b. 28 Dec 1952, Hokkaido, Japan. Materials Scientist. m. 20 May 1979, 3 d. Education: BEng, Univ of Tokyo, 1977; MEng, 1979; PhD, 1982. Appointments: Postdoctoral Fell, Japan Soc for the Promotion of Sci, 1982-83; Rsch Assoc, 1983-90; Asst Prof, 1990-91; Assoc Prof, Univ of Electro Comms, 1992-. Publications: Jrnl Applied Phys, Vol 75, 78, 79. Memberships: The Materials Sci Soc of Japan; Materials Rsch Soc. Hobbies: Badminton; Jogging. Address: Department of Mechanical and Control Engineering, University of Electro Communications, 1-5-1 Chofugaoka, Chofu, Tokyo 182, Japan.

SHIPLEY Jennifer Mary (Right Hon), b. 4 Feb 1952, Gore, NZ. Prime Minister of New Zealand. m. Burton Ross Shipley, 1 s, 1 d. Education: Dip in Tchng. Appointments: Tutor Lincoln Coll, 1983-87; Malcolm County Cnclr, 1983-87; Min of Socl Welfare, 1990-93; Min of Women's Affairs, 1990-; Min of Hlth, 1993-96; Min of Transport, 1996-97; Min in charge of Accident Compensation, 1996-97; Min for State Owned Enterprises, 1996-97; Min of State Servs, 1996-97; Min Responsible for Radio NZ, 1996-97; PM, 1997-; Min in charge of NZ Security, Intell Serv, 1997-. Honour: 1990 Suffrage Medal, 1993. Hobbies: Family; Reading; Gardening. Address: Parliament Buildings, Wellington, New Zealand.

SHIPLEY Jenny, b. 1952. Politician. m. 2 c. Appointments: Fmr Primary sch tchr; Farmer, 1973-88; Joined Natl Party, 1975 Fmr Malvern Co Cnclr; MP for Ashburton - now Rakaia - 1987-; Min of Socl Welfare, 1990-93; Min of Women's Affairs, 1990-98; Min of Hlth, 1993-96; Min of State Servs, 1996-97; Also Min of State Owned Enterprises; Min of Transp; Min of Accident Rehabilitation and Compensation Ins; Min Resp for Radio NZ; Min in Charge of NZ Security Intell Serv, 1997-; PM of NZ, Dec 1997-. Address: Parliament Buildings, Wellington, New Zealand.

SHIPTON Warren Arthur, b. 4 Feb 1940, Cooranbong, NSW, Aust. Academic. m. Janet Hazel Bucknell, 23 June 1974, 2 s. Education: BSc Agr, hons 1, 1961, PhD, 1965, Univ of Sydney; Dip Ed, Univ of WA, 1972; MEd, James Cook Univ, 1975; Dip Bact, Univ of Manchester, Eng, 1976. Appointments: Plant Pathologist, Dept of Agric, WA, 1965-67; Natl Rsch Cncl Fell, Can Dept of Agric, 1976-79; Lectr, Snr Lectr, James Cook Univ, 1969-85; Rdr, 1985-, Dpty Dean, Dean of Scis, 1983-88, Hd, Div of Microbio and Immunol, 1993-95, Dept of Biomed and Tropical Vet Sci, Hd, Dept Microbiol and Immunol, 1997-, James Cook Univ; Rdr, 1985-87, Assoc Prof, 1988-. Publications: Over 70 rsch articles and book chapts. Honour: Fell, Austl Soc for Microbiol, 1992. Memberships: Plant Pathol Soc; Assoc, Brit Mycological Soc. Hobbies: Reading; Horticulture; Woodwork. Address: 6 Bendigo Court, Annandale, Qld 4814, Australia.

SHIRAI Hiroshi, b. 17 Mar 1958, Aichi, Japan. University Professor. 1 s. Education: BSEE, Shizuoka Univ, 1980; MSEE, 1982; PhD, Polytechnic Univ, NY, USA, 1986. Appointments: Asst Prof, Chuo Univ, 1987-88; Assoc Prof, Chuo Univ, 1988-98; Prof, Chuo Univ, 1998-; Lectr, Tokyo Denki Univ, 1988-91. Publications: Introduction to Applied Analysis; Complex Analysis; Fourier Analysis; Laplace Transformation. Honours: RWP King Awd; Shimohara Kinen Awd. Memberships: IEEE; IEICE; Sigma Xi; Acoustical Soc of Japan; Acoustical Soc of Am. Address: Chuo U Dept Elec and Electronic Engr, 1-13-27 Kasuga, Bunkyo-ku, Tokyo 112-8551, Japan.

SHIRAKAWA Katsuhiko. Politician. Appointments: Fmr Parly Vice-Min of Posts and Telecomms; Min of Home Affairs, 1996. Memberships: Mbr HoR. Address: Ministry of Home Affairs, 2-1-2, Kasumigaseki, Chiyoda-ku, Tokyo 100, Japan.

SHIRALKAR Anagha, b. 28 Mar 1951, Solapur, Maharashtra, India. Library; Information. m. Anant, 25 Dec 1975, 2 s. Education: MSc, 1973; MLibSci, 1988; PhD, 1997. Appointments: Natl Chem Lab, Pune, 1976-79; Indian Inst of Trop Meteorol, Pune, 1979-. Publications: Sev articles in profl jrnls and newspprs. Honours: Merit Schlsp, Shivaji Univ, 1971; Fellshp, 1993-94. Memberships: Indian Lib Assn; Indian Assn of Spec Libs & Info Cntrs. Hobbies: Reading; Drawing; Painting; Writing. Address: A-3 Hill Top Apts, S B Road, Pune 411 016, India.

SHIRILLA Robert Michael, b. 21 Mar 1949, Youngstown, OH, USA. Management Consultant. Education: BA, magna cum laude, Univ of California, Los Angeles, USA, 1967-71; MBA (Hons), Harvard Bus Sch, 1973-75. Appointments: First Lt, Mil Intelligence, US

Army/82d Airborne Div, Ft Bragg, NC, 1971-73; Cnslt, Boston Cnsltng Grp Inc, Boston, MA, 1974; Asst Prd, Mngr, 1975-76, Assoc Prod Mngr, 1977, Gen Foods Corp, 1975-77; Prod Mngr, 1977-78, Mktng Mngr, 1978-79, Snr Mktng Mngr, 1979-80, Grp Mktng Mngr, 1980-81, Hunt Wesson Foods Inc, Fullerton, CA; Dir of Mktng, 1981, VP, Mktng, 1982-84; Citicorp, NY, NY; VP, Mktng, 1984, Snr VP Mktng, 1984-86, Amn Savings Bank, Los Angeles, CA; Pres, Co-Fndr, Computerized Vehicle Registration, Los Angeles, CA, 1986-91; Gen Mngr and Mngng Dir, Inst of Mngmt Resources, Los Angeles, 1991-93; Prin, Stanton Chase Intl, Los Angeles, 1993-. Publications: Num articles on econs, banking, mktng, for policy. Honours: Pi Mu Epsilon; Beta Alpha Psi; Psi Chi; Pi Gamma Mu; Phi Eta Sigm; Omicron Delta Epsilon; Pi Sigma Alpha; Beta Gamma Sigma; Alpha Kappa Psi. Memberships include: Col, US Army Reserves; Pres' Commn on White House Fellshps; Mbr, Bd of Dirs, March of Dimes, Los Angeles Jnr Chmbr of Com; Charity Fndn; Golf Fndn; Amn Mngrmt Fndn; Los Angeles Rotary; World Affairs Cncl; Acady of Polit Sci. Address: 425 Sunbonnet Street, Simi Valley, CA 93065, USA.

SHIVANNA G K, b. 5 Aug 1959, Konigarahalli, Karnataka, India. Art Teacher. m. Parvathi, 24 May 1984, 1 s, 1 d. Education: Dip in Fine Art. Appointments: Illustrator in Newspprs, 1987-89; Art Dir, 1987-; Art Tchr, 1989-; Solo exhibns: ken Sch Fine Arts, Banglaore, 1983; Jilla Sahitya Sammelana, Challakere, 1984; Kannada Sangharsha Vedike, Rajainagar, Bangalore, 1990; Flood Relief Fund, 1993; Basavana Bagevadi, 1 Man Show on Vachanas, 1996; 100 Vachanas in Bijapur, 1997; Ruthu Painting Exhibn, Bangalore, 1998; Vachana, Dharwad, 1998; Grp Exhibns: Mass Exhibn, Bangarapet, Kolar Dist, 1983; Rajya Chitrakala Shikshakara Samavesha, 1991; Mass exhibn in Memory of Late B P Bayari, 1997; Introductory Prog in Bangalore DD, Introduction of Artist and his Wrks, 1997. Honour: For Spec Achievement, Art Tchrs Assn, Buijapur, Karnataka, 1998. Hobbies: Classical music; Acting and Direction; Yoga. Address: No 310, 5th Cross, 4th A Main Road, West of Chord Road, Bangalore 560 044, India.

SHKOLNIK Vladimir Sergeyevich, b. 17 Feb 1949 Serpukhov Moscow Reg. Politician; Sci. m. 2 c. Education: Moscow Inst of Physics and Math; Var posts from engr to Dep Dir Mangistauz Energy Complex, 1973-92; Dir-Gen Agcy of Atomic Energy Repub of Kazakhstan, 1992-94; Min of Sci and New Tech, 1994-96; Min of Sci, 1996-; Pres Kazakhstan Acady of Scis, Mar 1996-. Memberships: Kazakhstan Acady of Scis. Address: Shchevchenko str 28, Almaty, Kazakhstan.

SHOBHA H G, b. 16 Mar 1970, Shikaripura, India. Social Worker; Journalist. Education: MA; Dip in Jrnlsm. Appointments: Cnslr, Family and Self Employment. Publications: Sev articles in profl jrnls. Honours: State Yth Awd, Best Socl Worker; Dist Bangalore Youth Awd; Awds, Helen Keller Assn. Memberships: Pres, Anna Porna Mahila Credit Co and Soc; Sec, Samaja Seva Samithi; Pres, Anna Porna Yuvati Mandali. Hobbies: Writing; Speech making. Address: No 4 West Anjaneya Temple Street, Gandhibazar, Bangalore, Karnataka, India.

SHOBOKSHI Osama Ibn Abdul Majeed, b. 1943. Minister of Health. Education: PhD, Internal Med, Germany, 1976; Fell, Roy Irish Coll of Surgeons, 1993. Appointments: Assoc Prof, Fac of Med, VP, Fac of Med, Univ Hosp Affairs, 1979, Dean, Fac of Med, 1984-90, Pres, 1993, King Abdulaziz Univ; Min of Hlth, 1995-. Address: Ministry of Health, Airport Road, Riyadh 11176, Saudi Arabia.

SHOCHAT Avraham, b. 1936 Tel Aviv. Politician; Constrn Engr. Appointments: Paratrooper Israel Def Forces; Br Dir Solel Boneh - Histadrut constrn co; Co-Fndr cty of Arad; Mayor of Arad, 1967-89; Chmn Citizens' Cttee Arad; Chmn Devt Towns Cncl; Chmn Econ Cttee; Chmn Fin Cttee; Dep Chmn Union of Local Authys; Min of Fin, 1992-96; Also Min of Energy; Dir

Israel Aircraft Inds. Memberships: Mbr Knesset, 1988-; Labour. Address: c/o The Knesse, Jerusalem, Israel.

SHORLAND Francis Brian, b. 14 July 1909, Wellington, NZ. Scientist. Education: MSc, Vic Univ of Wellington, NZ, 1932; PhD, 1937, DSc, 1950, Univ of Liverpool, Eng, Dsc, Univ of Wellington, NZ, 1970. Appointments: Cadet then Chem, Agricl Chem Lab, Dept of Agric, Wellington, 1927-45; Offr in Charge, then Dir, DSIR Fats Rsch Lab, 1946-69 (renamed Food Chem Div in 1966); Hon Lectr, Hon Rsch Fell, Biochemistry Dept, Vic Univ of Wellington, 1969-; Visng Prof and Snr Fulbright Schl, MI State Univ, USA, 1974-76. Publications: Contbr of some 250 sci papers to profl jrnls. Honours: ICI Medal, 1951; Hector Medal and Awd, 1959; OBE, 1959; Liversidge Lect, 1955; Marsden Medal, 1970; Hudson Lect, 1986; IOM, 1994; IBC, 20th Century Awd for Achievement, 1994. Memberships: NZ Inst of Chem; Nutrition Soc of NZ; NZ Assn of Scis; Amn Oil Chems Soc; Fell, Roy Soc of NZ. Hobbies: Gardening; Fishing. Address: School of Biological Sciences, Victoria University of Wellington, PO Box 2447, Wellington, New Zealand.

SHORT Andrew Damien, b. 10 Oct 1946, Sydney, Aust. Geographer. m. Julia, 5 Nov 1982, 1 s, 2 d. Education: BA, Hons, Sydney, 1968; MA, Hawaii, 1969; PhD, Marine Scis, Louisiana State, 1973. Appointments: Asst Prof, Louisiana State, 1973-75; Queens Fell in Marine Sci, Macquarie Univ, 1975-77; Lectr, Snr Lectr, Assoc Prof, Univ of Sydney, 1977-. Publications: 3 books; 124 rsch pprs & reports. Honours: Snr Fulbright Fell, 1983; Belle van Zuylen Visng Prof, Univ of Utrecht, 1989; Commemorative Medal, Intl Life Saving, 1994. Hobby: Surfing. Address: Coastal Studies Unit, School of Geosciences, University of Sydney, Sydney, NSW 2006, Australia.

SHORT James Robert, b. 7 Dec 1936, Shepparton, Aust. Bank Director. m. Jan, 4 Nov 1961, 1 s, 1 d. Education: BArts, BComm, Melbourne. Appointments: Fedl Treas, 1963-75; MHR for Ballarat, 1975-80; Chf Economist, ACI Intl Ltd, 1981-84; Sen, Fedl Parl, 1984-97; Shadow Min of Fin, 1987, 1990-93; Shadow Min, Immigration and Multicultural Affairs, 1993-96; Asst Treas, 1996; Austl Dir, Eurn Bank for Reconstruction and Dev, 1997-. Honour: Queen's Silver Jubilee Medal, 1977. Hobbies: Reading; Touring; Golf. Address: EBRD, One Exchange Square, London EC2A 2JN, England.

SHORT Kenneth Herbert, b. 6 July 1927, Kenya. m. Gloria Noelle Funnell, 28 Jan 1950, 1 s, 2 d. Education: THL, Moore Coll; Dip, Moore Theol Coll. Appointments: Commissioned Austl Infantry Forces, 1946; Served w Brit Occupation Forces, Japan, 1946-48; Ordained Anglican Min, 1952; Min-i/c, Parish of Pittwater, Diocese of Sydney, 1952-54; Missionary, Tanganyika (now Tanzania), 1955; Chaplain, Mwanza and Lake Dist, 1955-59; Fndng Prin, Msalato Bible Sch, Dodoma, 1961-64; Gen Sec, Ch Missionary Soc, NSW Br, 1964-71; Sec, Ch Missionary Soc, work in S Am, 1964-71; Canon, St Andrews Cathedral, Sydney, 1970-75; Examining Chaplain, Archbishop of Sydney, 1971-82; Rector, St Michaels Vaucluse, Sydney, 1971-75; Consecrated Bish, 1975; Bish of Wollongong, 1975-82; Archdeacon of Wollongong and Camden, 1975-79; Chaplain Gen, Austl Army, 1979-81; Anglican Bish to Austl Def Force, 1979-89; Anglican Bish of Parramatta, Diocese of Sydney, 1982-89; Dean of Sydney, 1989-92; Asst, St Johns Shaughnessy Diocese, New Westminster, BC, Can, 1992-93; Bish of Wollongong, 1993; Acting Rector, Berry and Kangaroo Valley, 1994; Acting Dean, Geraldton, WA, 1995; Acting Rector, Holy Trinity Sandy Bay, Tas, 1995; Asst, St Johns Shaughnessy BC, Can, 1995-96; Acting Gen Sec, Ch Missionary Soc, Victoria, 1997, NSW, 1998; Acting Dean of Geraldton, WA, 1997; Acting Bish of Wollongong, 1999. Publications: Guidance, 1969; Evangelism and Preaching in Secular Australia, 1989. Honours: AO, 1988; ChStJ, 1989. Hobbies: Fishing; Reading; Woodturning. Address: 16 Chapman Street, Kiama, NSW 2533, Australia.

SHORTHOSE William Robin, b. 19 Apr 1936, Branston, Eng. Research Scientist. m. Virginia, 23 Feb 1963, 1 s, 2 d. Education: BSc; PhD. Appointments: Leverhulme Rsch Fell, Univ of Nottingham; Asst Lectr, Roy Vet Coll, Univ of London; CSIRO, Div of Food Rsch. Memberships: Austl Soc of Animal Prodn; Amn Meat Sci Assn. Hobbies: Reading; Fishing; Woodwork. Address: 608 Ford Road, Burbank, QLD 4156, Australia.

SHOUSHTARI Hojatoleslam Mohammad Esmail, b. 1949, Qouchan, Khorasan Prov, Iran, Minister of Justice. Appointments: Official, Cntrl Revolutionary Crt; Friday Prayer Ldr, Shriven; Khorasan Prov Dpty, 1st and 2nd Majlis; Mbr, Majlis Commn for Judicial Affairs.

SHROFF Ateet, b. 5 Mar 1976, Surat, India. Visualiser. Education: BFA, Appl Arts, MS, Univ Baroda. Appointments: La-Cardé (design shop); Mudra Adv, Bombay; Bates Clarion Adv, Bombay. Hobbies: Movies; Books; Travel. Address: Manisha, 76 Narmadnagar, Athwa Lines, Surat, India.

SHTRIKMAN Shmuel, b. 31 Oct 1930, Poland. Physicist. m. Rachel, 2 s, 1 d. Education: DSc, 1958, Dip Eng, 1954, BSc, 1953, Technion Israel Inst of Technol. Appointments: Prof, Weizmann Inst of Sci; Adj Prof, Univ of CA, San Diego, USA. Honours: 1st Prize, Application Electrics, Ben Gurion Univ, 1988; Rothschild Prize, Yad Hanadiv Fndn, 1984; Michael Landau Prize, Mifal Hapayis Fndn, 1975, 1992; R M Burton Awd, The Weizmann Inst Fndn, London, 1988; Armando Kaminitz Prize, The Weizmann Inst of Sci, 1985; Weizmann Prize, Sci-Tel Aviv Muni, 1968. Memberships: Fell, APS; Fell, IEEE; Israel Acady of Sci and Hums, 1994. Address: Department of Electronics, The Weizmann Institute of Science, Rehovot 76100, Israel.

SHU Zhangzhou, b. 9 Jun 1924. Mechanics Educator. m. 2 Feb 1951, Zhiju Zhang, 1 s, 3 d. Education: Grad, Tangshan Engrng Coll, 1950. Appointments: Asst, 1950-54; Lectr, 1954-79; Assoc Prof, 1979-81; Prof, 1981-. Publications: Stability of Motion, 1989; Stability of Comparison Equation, 1986; Motion Types and Chaos of Multi-Body Systems Vibrating with Impacts, 1991; General Criteria for the Asymptotical Stability of Large Scale Systems, 1990; Axiomatics of Newtonian Mechanics for Particle Systems and Special Relativistic Mechanics, 1991. Honours: Sci and Technol Awds of Sichuan Provl People's Govt, 1990 and Chinese Natl Educ Cttee, 1992, 1995. Memberships: Editl Bd, Acta Mechanica Sinica; Chinese Soc of Theort and Applied Mechs, 1989-. Hobbies: Reading; History. Listed in: Who's Who in the World; Dictionary of International Biography. Address: Department of Engineering Mechanics, Southwest Jiaotong University, Chengdu, Sichuan 610031, China.

SHU Shengyou, b. Dec 1936 Yushan Co Jiangxi Prov. Appointments: Joined CCP, 1959; Mayor Jingdezhen Cty; Vice-Gov Jiangxi Prov, 1991; Vice-Sec CCP Jiangxi Provincial Cttee, 1995-; Gov Jiangxi Prov, 1996-. Memberships: Mbr 15th CCP Cntrl Cttee, 1997-. Address: Jiangxi Provincial Government, Nanchang, Jiangxi Province, People's Republic of China.

SHUAI Zhen, b. 27 Aug 1931, Beijing, China. m. Jing Yu Zhen, 23 Feb 1958, 1 s, 2 d. Education: Grad, Ha Er Bin Medl Univ, China. Appointments: Physn, Vice Dir, Dir. Publications: About 30 pprs, 1 book. Honours: Tianjin Assn of Clin Pathol, 1987; Vice Dir, -1999. Honour: Awd for 8th Int Symposium on Quality Control, Japan. Hobby: Music. Address: No 122, Mu Nan Road, Tianjin, China 300050.

SHUANG George Kuo-ning, b. 18 Mar 1953, Taipei, Taiwan. Executive Editor, United Daily News. m. Gloria, 26 July 1980, 1 s, 1 d. Education: BA, Natl Chengchi Univ; MA, Univ of IA; PhD, Univ of MD. Memberships: Intl Press Inst; Assn for Educ in Jrnlsm and Mass Comm. Address: 555, Chunghsaio East Road, Sec 4, Taipei, Taiwan, China.

SHUKLA Chandra Shekhar, b. 15 July 1953, Sultanpur, UP, India. Industrial Research. m. Geeta, 13 May 1977, 1 s. Education: MSc, Chem; PhD, Chem. Appointment: Dpty Mngr, R&D, 1994. Memberships: Catalysis Soc of India; Catalysis Div, Pune, India. Address: R&D Division, Hindustan Organic Chemicals Ltd, PO Rasayani, Raigad, MS, 410207, India.

SHUKLA Kedar Nath, b. 8 July 1945, Mangurahi, Kushinagar. Research Scientist. m. Indira, 18 June 1967, 1 s, 2 d. Education: MSc, Gorakhpur Univ, Gorakhpur, 1966; PhD, Banaras Hindu Univ, Varanasi, 1973. Appointments: Lectr, SGS Coll, Hata, India, 1966-69; Buddha Coll, Kushinagar, 1969-71; Scientist, VSSC, Trivandrum, 1974-. Publications: Diffusion Processes During Drying of Solids, 1990; Mathematical Principles of Heat Transfer, 1999; Over 75 rsch articles on math modelling comp simulation and thermal scis. Honours: Humboldt Fell, Univ Stuttgart, 1978-79, 1997-98; Tech Univ, Munich, 1985. Membership: Fell, AIAA, Assoc. Hobby: Reading religious literature. Address: TC2/930 (1), Puthupally Lane, Medical College, Trivandrum, 69501, India.

SHUKSO Ootru Dorje, b. 1 July 1944, Shigatse, Tibet, China. Director of the Tibetan Song Conductor and Dance Ensemble. m. Dawa Drolgar, 18 Aug 1970, 1 d. Education: Bachelor's degree (Hons), Composition & Conducting, Shanghai Music Conservatory, 1980. Appointments: 1st Tibetan Conductor and Chf Conductr, Tibetan Song, Dance & Orch Ensemble, 1972-; Dpty Dir, Tibetan Song & Dance Ensemble, 1984-; Dir, Tibetan Song & Dance Ensemble, 1993. Creative work: Composer, A Grand Prayer Ceremony of the Snowland, 1988. Honours: Hoso-Bunka Fndn Radio Prize, ABU Gen Assembly, 990; Best Wrkr of China Awd, 1995. Memberships: Assn of Chinese Musicians, 1983-; Dpty Dir, Assn of Tibetan Musicians, 1983. Hobbies: Jogging; Snooker. Address: Director of Tibetan Song and Dance Ensemble, Lhasa, Tibet 850000, China.

SHUM Kui-Kwong, b. 12 Mar 1948, Hong Kong. Principal. m. Shui-Har, 27 July 1974, 1 s, 1 d. Education: BA (Hons), 1971, MPhil, 1973, Hong Kong; PhD, Canberra, 1979. Appointments: Lectr, 1978-86, Snr Lectr, 1986-94, Sch Hist, Univ NSW; Advsr, Advsry Cntr for Aust Educ; Registered Migration Agent, 1994-; Prin, Sydney Study Cntr, 1995-. Publications: The Chinese Communist Road To Power: The Anti-Japanese United Front, 1937-45, Hong Kong, 1988. Honours: Univ Hong Kong: Higher Degree Studentship, 1971-73; Swire Schl, 1971-73; Japanese Monbusho Schl, 1973-75; PhD Schl, Aust Natl Univ, 1975-78. Memberships: Chinese Acads Assn, NSW, Pres, 1982-83; Migration Inst of Aust, 1994-. Address: 12 Norton Street, Randwick, NSW 2031, Australia.

SHUM Ying Loon, b. 6 Sept 1965, Kuala Lumpur. Regional Business Manager. m. Christine Heng, 1 June 1997, BBA, Natl Univ Singapore, 1988. Appointments: Fin Exec, Matushita Refrigeration Inds (s) Pte Ltd, 1988; Lectr, Temasek Polytechnic, 1991; Fin Mngr, Matsuhita Refrigeration Inds (M) Sdn Bhd, 1992; Fin Controller, Assab Steels (M) Sdn Bhd, 1995; Regl Bus Plng Mngr, Gateway 2000 (M), San Bhd, 1998. Membership: Assoc Mbr, Malaysian Inst of Mngmt, 1992. Hobbies: Reading; Coin and notes collecting; Web-surfing. Address: C2-15-2, Vista Komanwel C2, Bukit Jalil 57000 Sri Petaling, Kuala Lumpur, Malaysia.

SI Li Geng, b. 8 June 1931, Huhehot, China. Teacher. m. Zhen Su Fang, 3 Feb 1962, 1 d. Education: Grad, Dept of Maths, HeBei Normal Coll, 1958; Postgrad Studies, Nan Kai Univ, 1960-62. Appointments: Asst 1958-78, Assoc Prof 1978, Dpty Dir 1981-83, Prof 1983-, Dept of Maths, Inner Mongolia Tchrs Univ. Publications: On the Boundedness and Stability of Solutions for Neutral Type Systems with Variable Delay, 1974; On the Stability of Control Systems with Delay, 1983; Behaviour of Solution of Nonlinear Delay Equations of Neutral Type, 1988. Honours: 3rd Awd, Sci and Technol in Inner Mongolia, 1981; 2nd Awd, 1988, 1st Awd, 1992, Inner Mongolia Sci Prog. Membership: VP, Inner Mongolia

Math Soc, 1990-. Hobbies: Reading history and novels. Address: Department of Mathematics, Inner Mongolia Teachers (Normal) University, Huhehot, China.

SIAZON Domingo L, b. 1939 Aparri Cagayan. Politician; Intl Civ Servant. m. Education: Ateneo de Manila Univ; Tokyo Univ Japan; Harvard Univ USA. Appointments: Interpreter and translator then Attache and Third Sec and Vice-Consul Emb in Tokyo, 1964-68; Acting Res Rep to IAEA; Alt Perm Rep to UNIDO; Third Second then First Sec Emb in Berne, 1968-73; First Sec and Consul-Gen Emb in Vienna then Amb to Austria Also Perm Rep to IAEA UNIDO and UN at Vienna, 1973-85; Dir-Gen UNIDO, 1985-93; Min of For Affairs, May 1995-. Address: Department of Foreign Affairs, 2330 Roxas Blvd, Pasay City, Metro Manila, Philippines.

SICKS Laurel Eileen Willis, b. 10 May 1947, Canada. Publisher; Author. Appointment: Publr, Abiko Quarterly. Publications: Growing Up In Canada; The Book of Life; White Trash; Going Home. Membership: James Joyce Fndn. Hobby: Japanese Language. Address: 8-1-8 Namiki, Abiko, Chiba 270-1165, Japan.

SIDDHI Savetsila, b. 7 Jan 1919 Bangkok. Politician; Air Force Offr. m. Khunying Thida Savetsila, 1952, 2 s, 2 d. Education: Chulalongkorn Univ; MIT. Appointments: Fmr pilot offr Roy Thai Air Force and Advsr to Roy Thai Air Force; Min PMs Off, 1979-80; Second Kriangsak Govt; Sec-Gen Natl Security Cncl, 1975-80; Min of For Affairs, 1980-90; MP, 1983-90; Ldr Socl Action Party, 1986-90; Dep PM, 1986; Spec ADC to HM the King, 1986. Honours: Hon LLD - Philipines - 1983; Natl Univ Singapore, 1985; Num decorations. Memberships: Mbr Natl Ass, 1973; Mbr Natl Reform Cncl, 1976. Hobbies: Reading; Exercise. Address: c/o Ministry of Foreign Affairs, Saranrom Palace, Bangkok 10200, Thailand.

SIDDIQUI Nadeem Parvaiz, b. 26 June 1947, Rotak, India. Mechanical Engineer. m. Fauzia, 12 June 1977, 3 s. Education: BSc, Mech Engrng, USA, 1981; MSc, Mech Engrng, USA, 1985; Dip of Assoc Engr, Air Conditioning & Refrigeration Technol, Pakistan, 1967. Appointments: Field Engr, 1967-72; Airconditioning Engr, 1972-73; Mech Engr, 1973-95; Snr Mech Engr, 1995-. Memberships: ASHRAE, USA, 1979-; ASME, USA, 1984-. Hobby: Reading English Literature. Address: Dubai Municipality, PO 67 Dubai, United Arab Emirates.

SIDDLE David Alan Tate, b. 27 July 1943. Educator. m. Lyndal Ann Blake, 18 Apr 1990, 1 s, 2 d. Education: BA, hons; PhD. Appointments: Lectr, Snr Lectr, Rdr, Univ Southampton, Eng, 1971-83; Assoc Prof, Macquarie Univ, 1983-88; Prof, Univ of Tas, 1989-90; Prof, 1991-93, Dean, Postgrad Studies, 1993-97, Univ of Qld; Pro-Vice Chan, Rsch, Univ of Sydney, 1997-. Publications: 2 books; 15 book chapts; 100 articles in sci jrnls. Memberships: Fell, Acady of Socl Scis, Aust; Fell, Austl Psychol Soc; Pres, Soc for Psychophysiol Rsch, 1989-90; Chair, Hum and Socl Scis Panel, Austl Rsch Cncl, 1993-94. Hobbies: Music; Films. Address: Main Quadrangle, A14, University of Sydney, NSW 2006, Australia.

SIDDONS John Royston, b. 5 Oct 1927, Melbourne, Vic, Aust. Company Chairman. m. Rosemary Anne Wallace, 15 May 1954, 4 s, 1 d. Education: Preston Tech Coll. Appointments: Fndr, Ramset Fasteners (Aust) Ltd, 1952; Chmn, Siddons Inds Ltd, 1963-; Sen, Vic, elected 1st Term, 1980-83, elected 2nd Term, 1984-87. Publications: Industrial Democracy: Impossible Dream or Practical Reality, presentation ppr for James N Kirby Awd; The Regeneration of Australian Politics; Who Will Own Australia, 1972; Industrial Democracy, Private Member's Bill passed by Senate, 1981. Honour: James N Kirby Awd, Austl Cncl, Inst Prodn Engrs, 1977. Membership: Fell, Austl Inst Mngmt. Hobbies: Yachting; Tennis. Address: Chandella, Rosehill Road, Lower Plenty, Vic 3093, Australia.

SIDERIDOU Niki Stella, b. 1915, Smyrna, Greece. General Inspectress of Secondary Education; Writer. Education: Studies, Philos, Lit and Pedagogics, Greece,

Uppsala, Sweden. Publications include: A Karkavitsas and His Era; Impressions From Ethiopia; Uncertain Wall (poems); The Song of Loneliness (short stories); Return (poems); Love in the Stars, poems; Before Dawn, short stories; ...and Peace on Earth, poems; Nini and Chrini, fairy tales; Contemporary Philological Problems; On the Border of Phantasy, poems; The Melody of Love, poems; Snowy Spring, poems; The Water Lilies of Farewell, poems; Open Horizons, articles, studies and reviews. Honours: Sev Prizes, Medals, Ctfs and Hon Distinctions by Spiritual Cntrs in Greece and Abroad; Prize, Athens Acady; Prize, Supreme Cncl of Natl Educ. Memberships: Greek Lit Soc; Hon Chmn, Greek Lit Intl Soc, Intl Writers and Artists Acady; Olympoetry Movement Cttee. Address: Galaxidiou St 17, 104 43 Athens, Greece.

SIDHU Gurmel, b. 23 May 1944, Jullundur, India. Professor; Scientist. 2 s, 1 d. Education: PhD, Genetics, UBC, Can, 1974. Appointments: Postdoctoral Fell, SFU, Bulnaby, Can; Asst Prof, Univ of Nebraska, US; Prof, CA State Univ, USA. Creative Works: Genetics of Plant Pathoganic Fungie; 6 Vols of Poetry; Criticism of Face Verse. Honours: Postdoctoral Fellshp; Summer Awd. Memberships: Amn Jrnl of Phytopathology; Amn Assn of Advmnt Sci. Hobbies: Creative Writing; Soccer. Address: 1637 Gettysburg, Clovis, CA 93611, USA.

SIEGEL Gilbert Byron, b. 19 Apr 1930, Los Angeles, CA, USA. Professor Emeritus; Consultant. m. Darby Day, 16 Oct 1954, 1 s, 1 d. Education: BS, Pub Admin, USC, 1952; MS, 1957, PhD, Polit Sci, Univ Pittsburgh, 1964. Appointments: Admnstv Analyst and Mngr, County of Los Angeles, 1954-57; Visng Asst Prof, USC, Tehran, Iran, 1957-59; Instr, Univ Pittsburgh, 1959-61; Visng Asst Prof, USC, in Rio de Janeiro, 1961-63; Asst Prf, Assoc Prof, Prof, Assoc Dean, Dean, Univ South CA, Los Angeles, 1966-95; Dir, USC Productivity Netwrk, 1985-; CC Crawford Disting Prof of Pub Productivity, 1994, Emer, 1996; Cnslt, Brazilian Govt, 1961, 1976, 1977, 1979; Evaluator, USN Demonstration Proj, China Lake & San Diego, 1979-81; Cnslt, UN in Bangkok, 1981, USAID in Panama, 1986; Cnslt, Amideast/Palestine Natl Auth, west Bank & Gaza, 1996. Pubications: The Vicissitudes of Government Reform in Brazil: A Study of the DASP, 1978; Employee Compensation and its Role in Public Sector Strategic Management, 1992: (co-auth) Public Personnel Administration, 1985, 1989; Management in Public Systems, 1986; Mass Interviewing and Marshalling of Ideas to Improve Performance: the Crawford Slip Method, 1996; (ed) Human Resource Management in Public Organisations: A Systems Approach, 1974; Breaking With Orthodoxy in Public Administration, 1980. Honours: Pi Sigma Alpha; Mosher Awd, Amn Soc for Pub Admin, 1967; Olson Awd, Personnel Mngmt Assn, 1984, Hon Life Mbr, 1998; Vargas Fndn Medal of Merit, 1975; Personnel Mngmt Assn, 1984. Memberships: S CA Personnel Mngmt Assn, BD; Intl Personnel Mngmt Assn; Amn Soc Pub Admin. Hobby: Classical music; Travel. Address: 208 N Poinsettia Avenue, Manhattan Beach 90266, USA.

SIERRA-ROMERO Norma, b. 24 Feb 1956, Mexico Cty. Biology. Education: MSc, Biol. Appointments: Rsch, Microbiol, Virus, Parasites and Leptospirosis. Creative Works: Mystery Swine Disease, 1992. Honours: Honorific Mention for the Isolation of PRRSV in Mexico, Memberships: CONASA; Fac of Vet Sci, UNAM. Hobbies: Metaphysics; Kabala; Reading; Music; Meditation. Address: California 19-A-403, Col Parque San Andres 04040, Mexico DF.

SIETSMA Maggi, b. 8 Aug 1951, Singapore. Artistic Director. m. Abel Valls, 1 d. Education: Dip of Dance, 1970; MA, Qld Univ of Technol, 1995. Appointments: Austl Ballet, 1970-73; London Festival Ballet, 1973-75; th du chenc Nair, France, 1978-; Asst Artistic Dir, res Chgph, Dancer, N QLD Ballet, Dance Soc, 1982-; Lectr, Qld Univ of Technol, 1983-86; Artistic Dir, Chgph, Fndr, Expressions Dance Co, 1984-. Creative Works: Chgph, Adam in Wonderland, 1996; Alone Together; Connections; Direct heat; Dream Hunters; Landscapes; Difficult Pleasures. Honours: Sydney Myer Perfng Arts Awd, Expressions Dance Co, 1997. Memberships: Qld

Arts cncl; Sch Touring Assessment Panel; Qld Govt Perfng Arts Panel; Qld Govt Arts Advsry Cttee. Hobbies: Dogs; Films; Reading. Address: Level 3, 99 Elizabeth St Brisbane, Australia.

SIEW Vincent C, b. 3 Jan 1939, Chiayi Cty, Taiwan. Premier of China. m. 3 d. Education: Master of Laws, Intl Law and Diplomacy, Natl Chengchi Univ, China, 1965; Ldrshp Seminar, Georgetown Univ, USA, 1982; Eisenhower Fell, USA, 1985. Appointments: Vice Cnsl, Consulate Gen, Kuala Lumpur, Maaysia, 1966-69, Cnsl, 1969-72; Sect Chf, E Asian and Pacific Affairs Dept, Min of For Affairs, 1972; Dpty Dir, 4th Dept, Bd of For Trade, Min of Econ Affairs, 1972-74; Dir, 4th Dept, Bd of For Trade, Min of Econ Affairs, 1974-77, Dpty Dir Gen, 1977-82, Dir Gen, 1982-88; Vice Chmn, Cncl for Econ Plng and Dev, Exec Yuan, 1988-89; Dir Gen, Dept of Organizaional Affairs, Cntrl Cttee, Kuomintang, 1989-90; Min of Econ Affairs, 1990-93; Min of State, Chmn, Cncl for Econ Plng and Dev, Exec Yuan, 1993-94; Min of State, Chmn, Mainland Affairs Cncl, Exec Yuan, 1994-95; Legislator, 1996-97; Premier, 1997-.

SIKKEMA Mildred, b. 19 Jan, USA. Social Worker. Education: BS, Univ Chgo, 1937; MSS, Smith Coll Sch for Socl Work, 1939; PhD, Univ Chgo, 1964. Appointments: Case Worker, Child Guidance Clin, Wilkes Barre, PA, 1939-40; Case Worker, 1940-42, Supvsr, 1942-44, Foster Home Dept, Childrens Aid Soc; Supvsr, Med Socl Serv, Queens Hosp, Instr, Sch of Nursing, Queens and Kuakini Hosps, 1944-45; Asst Dir, Dept of Pupil Guidance, Territorial Dept of Pub Instrn, HI, 1945-47; Exec Sec, Natl Assn of Sch Socl Workers, 1947-51; Cnslt, Divsn of Spec Servs, Baltimore City Schs, 1951-52; Prof, Sch of Scol Work, Univ of HI, 1952-54; Cncl on Socl Wrk Educ; Sec to Cmmn on Accreditation, 1954-68; Prof, Grad Students, Guam, 1972, 1973; Prof, Asst to Dean, Intl Progs, Univ HI, 1968-73; Socl Welfare Survey, Pacific Islands, S Pacific Cmmn, 1973; Cnslt, Intl Assn for Schs of Socl Work, Bangladesh, Indonesia, Malaysia, Pakistan, Philippines, Sri Lanka, 1973-79; Visng Prof, Univ Hong Kong, 1975; Volun, NASW Pac Steering Cttee, Civic Forum on Pub Schs, 1995-. Publications: Design for Crosscultural Learning, 1987; Challenging the Status Quo: Public Education in Hawaii 1840-1980, 1994. Honours: Sev; Socl Wrk Pioneer, NASW, 1993. Memberships: Natl Assn of Socl Work; Intl Assn of Schs of Scol Work; Intl Congress of Schs of Socl Work. Hobbies: Gardening; Reading; Improving Public Education. Address: 326 Halaki Street, Honolulu, HI 96821, USA.

SILAPA-ARCHA Banharn, b. 20 Jul 1932. Politician. Education: Ramkhamhaeng Univ. Appointments: Elected to Suphan Buri Municipal Cncl, 1973; Co-fndr Chart Thai Party, 1975; Sec-Gen Chart Thai Party, 1976; Dep Min of Ind, 1976; Min of Agric, 1980; Sen, 1986; Min of Comms, 1986; Min of Ind, 1989; Min of Fin, 1990; Min of Interior, 1990-91; Min of Comms, 1992; Ldr of Opposition, 1992-95; Party Ldr Chart Thai Party, 1994-; PM, 1995-96; Also Min of the Interior. Memberships: Mbr Legis Ass, 1973-. Address: c/o Office of the Prime Minister, Bangkok 10300, Thailand.

SILSBURY Elizabeth Alice, b. 13 Jan 1931, Adelaide, SA, Aust. Music Lecturer; Critic. m. James Henry Silsbury, 12 Jan 1957, 2 d. Education: BA, 1955; BMus, 1957; BMus hons, 1968. Appointments: Music Mistress, Adelaide Girls hs, 1956-60; Lectr in Music, Western Tchrs Coll, 1960-67; Lectr in Music, 1968-73, Snr Lectr, 1974-90, Sturt Coll of Adv Educ, Bedford Pk; Snr Lectr in Music, Flinders Univ, 1991-95; Visng Schl, 1995-; Prin Music Critic, The Advertiser, Adelaide, 1976-; Mbr, Bd of Dirs, Austl Opera, 1977-94; Mbr, Austl Opera natl Cncl, 1994-; Repetiteur, Choral Dir, Accompanist (Piano and Harpsichord) for opera and concerts. Publications: Tertiary Music Directory, 1976; The Arts in Post Secondary Education in South Australia, 1978; Num reviews, features, rprts for newspprs, music and music educ jrnls, radio and Eng. Honours: Churchill Fellshp, 1967; Life Mbrshp, Adelaide Univ Th Guild, 1967, Adelaide Choral Soc, 1970, Adelaide Chorus, 1984; OAM, 1985. Memberships: Austl Soc for Music Educ; Intl

Soc for Music Educ; MEAA. Hobbies: Music; Gardening; Cooking; Society for the Protection of Abused Words; Reading. Address: 44 Tusmore Avenue, Tusmore, SA 5065, Australia.

SILVER Lynette Ramsay, b. 23 Oct 1945, Brisbane, Aust. Investigative Historian; Writer. m. Neil, 20 Aug 1966, 1 s, 1 d. Education: Tchng Dip, 1965. Appointments: Cnslt, DVA, 1996, OAWG, 1996, Hoyts Ths, 1998; Offl Histn, 8th Austl Divsn Assn, 1996. Publications: A Fool's Gold?, 1986; Battle of Vinegar Hill, 1989; Heroes of Rimau, 1990; Krait, 1992; Var childrens books, 1992-95; Fabulous Furphies, 1997; Sandakan: A Conspiracy of Silence, 1998. Honour: Fell, FAIHA, 1989. Memberships: RUSI, NSW, 1994-; Austl and NZ Forensic Sci Soc, 1994-. Hobbies: Art; Literature; Australian History. Address: 15B Ada Avenue, Wahroonga, NSW 2076, Australia.

SILVERMAN Edward I, b. 5 May 1952, Chicago, IL, USA. Attourney. m. Sandra M, 22 Nov 1987, 1 s, 1 d. Education: AB, High Distinction, Maths, Univ of MI; JD, Univ of CA. Appointments: Law clk, Hon L C Nielson, US Dist Judge, 1977-79; Judge, Pro Tem, San Diego co crts, USA, 1983-. Honours: Phi Betta Kappa. Memberships: State Bar of CA; Bar of US Supreme Crt; Bar of US Crt of Appeals; Bar of US Dist. Hobbies: Skiing; Children. Address: 53- B Street, Suite 2100, San Diego, CA 92101, USA.

SILVESTER Richard, b. 21 June 1924, Perth, WA. Coastal Engineer. m. Marion, 11 Dec 1951, 4 s. Education: BE Hons, 1946; BA, 1948; PhD, 1958. Appointments: Snr Lectr Hydraulics, Univ of West Aust, 1949-77; Assoc Prof, Coastal Engr, 1977-89. Publications: Over 200 Profl Articles; 3 Books. Honours: Natl Sci Fdn Fell, Univ of CA, 1963-64; Carnegie Trav Fell, 1964; Guest Prof, Tianjin Univ, China, 1983. Memberships: FIEAust; MASCE; MICE. Address: University of Western Australia, Dept of Civil Engineering, 6907 Nedlands, West Australia.

SIM Lee-Ling, b. 29 Mar 1949, Penang, Malaysia. Liason Officer. m. 8 May 1976 (div), 2 d. Education: BS, BS (Hons in Botany), Effective Sci and Tech Comm. Appointments: Snr Rsch Offr, Sci Publs, Rubber Rsch Inst of Malaysia, 1973-91; Rsch Liason Offr, Sci Publs, NSW Agric Liason Offr, NSW Agric, 1992-. Memberships: Snr Offrs Assn, RRIM, Sec, 1977. Hobby: Travelling. Address: 13 Karimi Way, Orange, NSW 2800, Australia.

SIMANCAS ROBLES Antonio, b. 22 Nov 1945, Tepic, Nayarit, Mexico. Certified Public Accountant. m. Ileana, 23 July 1971, 1 s, 1 d. Education: MBA. Appointments: Snr Ptnr, Antonio Simancas & Assocs; Fin Advsr, var coms; Prof, Pub Fins & Taxes, Universidad Autonoma of Nayarit; Tax Advsr to sev cos. Publications: Freelance Writer, sev subjects inclng: pols, econ & socl problems for var newspapers. Memberships: Colegio de Contadores Publicos de Nayarit, Pres, 1983-89; Instituto Mexicano de Contadores Publicos. Hobbies: Reading; Music; Swimming. Address: San Luis 116 Sur, Tepic, Nayarit, Mexico ZC 63000.

SIMICH Clem R, b. 1939, Te Kipuru, New Zealand. Member of Parliament. m. 3 children. Appointments: Natl Party Exec Mbr; Property Dev Mngr; Bus Proprietor; Mbr NZ Police; Bar and Solicitor, High Crt of NZ; Elected to Parl, Tamaki, 1992; Min for Police, Corrections, Racing; Min in Charge, Audit Dept. Membership: Chair, Govt Admin Select Cttee. Address: 26 St Heliers Bay Road, PO Box 25-189, St Heliers, Auckland 1005, New Zealand.

SIMMONS David, b. 7 Nov 1947 Broken Hill NSW. Politician. m. Kaye Simmons, 1 s, 1 d. Education: Univ of New England NSW. Appointments: Hd Socl Sci Dept Bathurst High Sch NSW; Alderman Bathurst Cty Cncl, 1978-83; MP for Calare NSW, 1983-; Min for Def Sci and Personnel, 1989-90; Min for Arts Tourism and Territories, 1990-91; Min for Local Govt and Family Support, 1991-93; Chmn HoR Cttee on Banking Fin and Pub Admin, 1994; Exec Dir Hunter Regl Tourism Org,

1996-97; Gen Mngr Newcastle Regl Chamb of Com, 1997-. Memberships: Mbr HoR Cttee on Fin and Pub Admin, 1985-89. Hobbies: Golf; Stamp collecting. Address: Newcastle Regional Chamber of Commerce, 51 King Street, Newcastle, NSW 2300, Australia.

SIMONS Martin, b. 15 Mar 1930, Grindleford, Derbyshire, UK. Author. m. Jean, 2 d. Education: BS (1st Class Hons), London Univ; MEd, Univ of Durham, 1965; MA, Univ of London, 1974. Appointments include: RAF, 1948-50; Asst Tchr, 1953-59; Lectr, Snr Lectr, Newcastle upon Tyne, Kenton Lodge Tchrs Trng Coll, 1959-63; Lectr in Educ, London Univ Inst of Educ, 1963-68; Lectr in Educ, Snr Educ, Univ of Adelaide, 1968-1993, Retd, 1993. Publications: Windows on Geography, 1962-63; People of Britain: A Tyneside Shipyard, 1963; Deserts, The Problem of Water in Arid Lands, 1967; Poverty and Wealth, 1972; Three Giant Powers, USA, USSR, China, 1974; Model Aircraft Aerodynamics, 1978; Airflow, 1984; Model Flight, 1988, The World's Vintage Sailplanes 1909-1945, 1986; Slingsby Sailplanes, 1996; German Air Attaché, 1997; Gliding with Radio Control, 1998; Num articles (auth, co-auth, in refereed and unrefereed jrnls; Jt auth 4 wrks; Tech articles on aviation topics; Conf pprs; Transl, The Piedmont Flats of the Southern Black Forest, by Walter Penck. Address: 13 Loch Street, Stepney, SA 5069, Australia.

SIMPSON Dudley George, b. 4 Oct 1922, Melbourne, Vic, Aust. Composer; Conductor; Pianist. Education: Studied piano w Vera Porter and Victor Stephenson, Melbourne Univ; Orchestration w Elford Mack, Melbourne and Dr Gordon Jacob, England; Composition w John Ingram, Aust. Appointments: Debut, 1st and 2nd M D Borovansky Ballet, 1960-62; Roy Ballet, Covent Garden, London; Guest Conductor, Roy Ballet, 1960-62; Conducted own wrk Class/Ballet, Covent Garden, 1986; Record In a Covent Garden, Blakes 7 Theme and incidental music, Monsieur Quixote Suite; Prin Conductor, maj fests, UK and Eur, inclng Monte Carlo, Nice, Athens, also Mid E, 1961-63; World tours w Dame Margot Fonteyn and Rudolph Nureyev; Conducted Tokyo Philharmonic Orch, Ballet Fest, 1985. Creative Works: The Winter Play, ballet; Here We Come, ballet transcription; Num TV themes and incidental music; Shakespeare Canon; Oliver Twist; Sense and Sensibility, Diary of Anne Frank, Dr Who. Honour: Dip of Music, Melbourne Conservatorium, 1949. Hobbies: Gardening; Photography. Listed in: International Who's Who in Music; Men of Achievement. Address: 6 Tristania Grove, Menai, NSW 2234, Australia.

SIMPSON Frederic Olaf, b. 22 Oct 1924. Physn. m. Isobel Ann Oman, 28 Sept 1951, 1 s, 1 d. Education: MB; ChB; FRCP, Edinburgh; FRACP. Appointments: House Physn, Roy Infirmary, Edinburgh, 1950; Lieut to Capt, RAMC, 1951-53; Registrar, Roy Infirmary, Edinburgh, 1953; Edward Wilson Mem Fell, Baker Medl Rsch Inst, Melbourne, 1958; Snr Medl Rsch Offr, Otago Medl Sch, Dunedin, NZ, 1960; Assoc Prof, 1967; Prof, 1972; Emer Prof, Otago Medl Sch, 1990; Physn in Charge, Hypertension Clin, Dunedin Pub Hosp, 1968-89; Visng Prof, Shimane Medl Univ, Japan, 1992. Publications: 304 Pprs and Book-Chapts on: Hypertension (Clinical, Epidemiological and Experimental); Fine Structure of Myocardium and Blood Vessels; Salt Intake and Body Sodium. Honours: R T Hall Prize in Cardiology, 1971. Memberships: Roy Coll of Physn of Edinburgh; Roy Austl Coll of Physns; Cardiac Soc of Aust and NZ. Hobbies: Gardening; Trout Fishing; Joinery; Amnesty International. Address: 19 Brownville Crescent, Maori Hill, Dunedin, New Zealand.

SIMPSON John Ewen, b. 11 Apr 1933, Goulburn, NSW, Aust. Headmaster. m. Annette Laura Harvison, 4 Jan 1964, 2 s, 1 d. Education: BSc, Qld; Dip Ed, Sydney. Appointments: Rsch Chem, CSR Plastics Lab, 1955; Sci Tchr, Tenterfield hs and Mullumbimby hs, 1957-62; Sci Master, Liverpool Girls hs and Asquith Boys hs, 1963-75; Prepared, presented Secnd Sci Progs, ABC-TV Network, 1964-66; Represented NSW Dept Educ, Austl Sci Educ Proj and Film Appraisal Cttee, 1971-74; Dpty Hdmaster, N Ryde hs, 1976-82; Hdmaster, Conservatorium hs,

1983-92. Memberships: Austl Cncl Educl Admin; JP; Advsry Panel, Sch's Bldg and Dev Grp, 1971-73; Conservatorium Assn; Life Mbr, Conservatorium Assn; Life Mbr, Sydney Univ Union. Hobbies: Reading; Music; Squash. Address: 8 Amesbury Avenue, St Ives, NSW 2075, Australia.

SIMPSON Robert George, b. 27 Feb 1921, Loch, Vic, Aust. Engineer; Company Director. m. Rosemary, 18 June 1963, 1 s, 2 step s, 2 step d. Education: Dip Mechl Engrng, Sydney, NSW, Aust. Appointments: Chmn, Furnace Engrng Grp, fmrly Chmn, BTR Aust. Honour: Mention in Dispatches, 1945. Memberships: Fell, Austl Inst of Mining and Metallurgy; Instn of Engrs Aust. Hobbies: Skiing; Agro-forestry; Travel. Address: 61 Wattle Road, Hawthorn, Victoria, Australia 3122.

SIMS Francis Harding, b. 27 Jan 1913, Auckland, NZ. Pathologist (retired). 1 s, 1 d. Education: BSc, NZ, 1933; MSc, NZ, 1934; MBChB, NZ, 1941; PhD, Edinburgh, 1951; FRCPA, 1965; FAACB, 1968. Appointments: Res, Auckland Hosp, 1940-43; F/Lt RNZAF, 1943-45; Asst Pathol, Wellington Hosp, 1946-48; Postgrad Stud, Pathol, Univ of Edinburgh, 1948-51; Lectr, Clin Chem, Univ of Edinburgh, 1949-51; Chem Pathol, Auckland Hosp, 1951-64; Pathologist i/c, Greenland Hosp, 1964-70; Pathol, Clin Biochem, Women's Coll Hosp, Toronto, 1970-78 (Assoc Prof, Univ of Toronto in Clin Chem and Pathol); Tutor in Pathol, Fiji Sch of Med, 1979-81 (Voluntary WHO Honorarium); Hon Rsch Fell, Dept of Pathol, Univ of Auckland Sch of Med, NZ. Publications: The Mechanism of Intimal Thickening in Arteriosclerosis, 1978; The Arterial Wall in Malignant Disease, 1979; Discontinuities of the Internal Elastic Lamina, 1985; The Internal Mammary Artery as a Bypass Graft?, 1987; The Early Development of Intimal Thickening of Human Coronary Arteries, 1990; The Importance of a Substantial Elastic Lamina Subjacent to the Endothelium in Limiting the Progression of Atherosclerotic Changes, 1993; A Comparison of Intimal Thickening of Chinese and New Zealand Coronary Arteries, 1993. Memberships: Pathol Soc of GB & Ireland, Snr Mbr; Canad Soc of Clin Chem, Emer; NZ Assn of Clin Biochems, Hon; Australasian Coll of Pathols; Austl Assn of Clin Biochems; NY Acady of Scis; AAAS. Hobbies: Sailing; Woodwork and Building Construction. Address: 13 Endymion Place, Half Moon Bay, Bucklands Beach, Auckland, New Zealand.

SINANI Musaid bin Muhammad al-, b. 1946. Politician. Education: King Saud Univ; Univ of Ariz. Appointments: With the Gen Org for Socl Ins - GOSI - 1970; Dep Gov, 1980-81; Gov, 1982; Min of Labour and Socl Affairs, 1995-. Address: Ministry of Labour and Social Affairs, Omar bin al-Ghatab Street, Riyadh 11157, Saudi Arabia.

SINCLAIR Ian McMahon (Rt Hon), b. 10 June 1929. Politician; Grazier. m. Margaret Sinclair, 1956, dec 1967, 1 s, 2 d, (2) Rosemary Fenton, 14 Feb 1970, 1 s. Education: BA, LLB, Univ Sydney. Appointments: Pilot, No 22 Cty of Sydney (F) Sqdn, Citizens' Air Force, 1948-52; Admitted Bar, 1952; Grazier, 1953; Mngng Dir, Sinclair Pastoral Co, 1953-; Mbr Leg Cncl, NSW, 1960-63; Dir, Farmers and Graziers Co-op Ltd, 1962-65; Natl Party Mbr House Reps, for New Eng, NSW, 1963-98 (retd); Min Socl Servs, 1965-68; Min assisting Min Trade and Ind, 1966-71; Min Shipping and Transp, 1968-71; Dpty Ldr, Natl Coalition Party, 1971-84; Min Primary Ind, 1975-79; Mbr Opposition, House Bus Reps Caretaker Govt, 1975; Min Agric and Northern Aust, Caretaker Govt, 1975; Ldr, House Reps, 1975-79, 1980-82; Min Spec Trade Reps, Aug 1980; Min Comms, 1980-82; Min Def, 1982-83; Mngr, Opposition Bus in House, 1983-87; Shadow Min Trade and Resources, 1987-89; Ldr, Natl Party, 1984-89; Shadow Spec Min State, 1994; Chmn, Austl Parly Grps for UK, Papua New Guinea, Vietnam, 1996-98; Perm Rep on Exec, Inter-Parly Union, 1996-98; Chmn, Jnt Standing Cttee, For Affairs, Def, Trade; MHR, 1963-98; Chmn Austl Constitutional Convention, 1998; Speaker, House of Reps, 1998; Co-Chair, NSW Drugs Summit, 1999; Chair Austl Reg Summit, 1999. Honours: Mbr, Sydney Univ 1st XV Grade Premiers, 1951; Austl Univs XV vs NZ Univs, 1951; Rugby Blue, Univ Sydney; PC, 1977; Hon D Univ (NE), 1996. Hobbies: Squash; Swimming. Address: Glenclair, Bendemeer, NSW 2355, Australia.

SINCLAIR John Bowditch, b. 25 Aug 1926, Brisbane, Qld, Aust. District Court Judge. m. Joy Eva Palmer, 21 May 1946, 2 s, 1 d. Education: Roy Austl Naval Coll; LLB, Sydney Univ, 1954; Admitted Sol, 1954; Called to the Bar, 1955. Appointments: Served to Lt, Roy Austl Navy, 1940-50; Later Cmdr, Roy Austl Naval Reserve; Sol and Bar; Appointed QC, 1974; Appointed to Bench Dist Crt of NSW, 1977; Ret'd 1997 Currently Acting Judge, Dist Crt of NSW, Sydney. Hobbies: Golf; Swimming. Address: 20/69 Bradleys Head Road, Mosman, NSW 2088, Australia.

SINCLAIR Keith Val, b. 8 Nov 1926, Auckland, NZ. Retired Emeritus Professor. Education: MA, Lit D, (Univ of NZ); PhD (Paris and Oxford); DLitt (Oxford); hon DLitt (James Cook and Sydney). Appointments: Lectr, Snr Lectr, ANU Canberra, 1955-62; Snr Lectr, Assoc Prof, Univ of Sydney, 1962-71; Visng Prof, Northwestern Univ, 1971-; Full Prof, Univ CT, 1972-79; Prof & Hd of Dept, James Cook Univ, 1980-81. Publications: 14 scholarly monographs and books, 1961-95; 100 learned pprs, 1955-97; Num reviews. Honours: Offr in Natl Order of Merit (in Aust, France, Luxembourg); Cmdr, Natl Order of Merit (Italy); Cmdr, Acad Palms Order (France); Offr, Order of Crown (Belgium); Kt Cmdr, Order of St John & Jerusalem. Memberships: Fell, Soc Antiquaries London; Fndn Fell, Austl Acady of Hums, 1969; Hom mbr, num medieval assns. Hobbies: Swimming; Tennis. Address: 56 Bertel Crescent, Chapman ACT, Australia 2611.

SINCLAIR Robert Keith, b. 22 Aug 1927, Sydney, Aust. Associate Professor of History. m. Patricia Clyde Watkin, 14 May 1955, 4 d. Education: BA, hons, 1948, DipEduc, 1949, Univ of Sydney; MA, Univ of Cambridge, Eng, 1956. Appointments: Classics Master, Grafton hs and Liverpool hs, 1952-56; Lectr in Classics, Univ of Qld, 1957-58; Lectr in Classics, Newcastle Univ Coll, 1958-59; Lectr in Hist, 1959-63, Snr Lectr, 1964-70, Assoc Prof, 1971-89, Hd of Dept, 1977-79, Hon Assoc, 1990-99, Univ of Sydney. Publications: Democracy and Participation in Athens, 1988; Past, Present and Future: Ancient World Studies in Australia (ed), 1991; Num articles in profl jrnls. Honours: J B Watt Travelling Schlshp, 1949-51; Rsch Fellshp, Univ of Edinburgh, Scotland, 1964; Mbrshp, Inst for Adv Study, Princeton, USA, 1976; Visng Fellshp, Clare Hall, Cambridge, Eng, 1985. Memberships: Past Chmn, Hist Tchrs Assn of NSW; Past Pres, Austl Soc for Classical Stdies. Hobbies: Reading; Tennis. Address: 46 Nelson Road, Lindfield, NSW 2070, Australia.

SINDEL Brian Mark, b. 5 Sept 1959, Sydney, Australia. Weed Scientist; University Lecturer. m. Pauline, 5 May 1984, 2 s. Education: BSc.Agr, Hons; Dip, Educ; PhD. Appointments: HS Tchr, NSW Dept of Educ, 1983-84; Ex Sci, CSIRO Plant Ind, 1989-90; Rsch Sci, CSIRO Plant Ind, 1991-93; Lectr, 1994-97, Snr Lectr, 1998-, Univ New England. Publications: Ecology and Control of Fireweed, 1989; Ecology and Control of Thistles in Australia, 1991; Germination and Establishment of Themeda triandra, 1993; Restoration Issues in Lowland Native Grasslands, 1995; Integrated Weed Management, 1995; Outcrossing of Transgenes to Weedy Relatives, 1997. Memberships: Weed Soc of NSW; Austl Inst of Agricl Sci; Grassland Soc of NSW. Hobbies: Family; Sport. Address: Division of Agronomy and Soil Sciences, School of Rural Science and Natural Resources, University of New England, Armidale, NSW 2351, Australia.

SINGANAPALLI Balaram, b. 18 Nov 1943, Gunnathota Valasa, India. Principal Designer; Educator. m. Padmini, 7 Feb 1982, 2 s. Education: MPhil, Roy Coll of Art, Lodnon; Postgrad, Design, NID; Dip, Mech Engrng. Appointments: Vice Chmn, Indl Design, 1972; Chmn, Extension Progs, 1976; Chmn, Educ Progs, 1985; Hd, Des Fndn Stdies, 1998. Publications: Adalaj Village, 1992; Thinking Design, 1998. Honours: ICSID-Philip Awd for Des, 1979; Fell, Soc of Indl Designers of India, 1986. Memberships: VP, Fndr Mbr, Soc of Indl Designers of India; Edl Advry Bd, Design Issues. Hobbies: Writing; Film Criticism; Crafts; Ecology. Address: c/o National Institute of Design, Paldi, Ahmedabad 380007, India.

SINGAY Karma, b. 27 Oct 1962, Thimphu, Bhutan. Business. Div, 1 s, 1 d. Education: SGTB Khalsa Coll, Delhi; BA, Engl, Hons. Appointment: Mng Dir, Peljorkhang Enterprises, 1993. Hobbies: Golf; Baseball; Trekking. Address: 11 Chang Lam, Thimphu, Bhutan.

SINGER Alan Evan, b. 14 Feb 1954, London, Eng. Academic. m. Ming, May 1983, 1 s. Education: BSc, Hons, BA, Hons; PhD. Appointments: Univ Canterbury, Eng. Publications: Strategy as Rationality, 1996; Business Ethics (w P Werham), 1999. Memberships: NYAS. Hobbies: Tennis; Skiing. Address: Department Management, University Canterbury, Christchurch, New Zealand.

SINGER Peter Albert David, b. 6 July 1946, Melbourne, Aust. University Professor. m. Renata Diamond, 16 Dec 1968, 3 d. Education: BA, hons, 1967, MA, 1969, Univ of Melbourne; BPhil, Univ of Oxford, Eng, 1971. Appointments include: Radcliffe Lectr, Univ Coll, Oxford, 1971-73; Snr Lectr, La Trobe Univ, 1975-76; Fell, Woodrow Wilson Intl Cntr for Schls, USA, 1979; Disting Visng Humanist, Univ CO, USA, 1984; Var other visng appts o'seas; Prof, Monash Univ, Aust, 1977-; Dir, Cntr for Human Bioethics, 1983-91, Dpty Dir, 1991-; Disting Visng Prof, Univ CA, USA, 1987; Ira W DeCamp Chair, Bioethics, Princeton Univ, NJ, USA, 1999-. Publications include: Democracy and Disobedience, 1974; Animal Liberation, 1975, 2nd ed, 1990; How Are We To Live?, 1993; Rethinking Life and Death, 1994; Co-Ed, Bioethics, 1985-99; Ethics into Action, 1998. Honour: Natl Book Cncl Banjo Awd, 1994. Hobbies: Walking; Swimming. Address: University Center for Human Values, Princeton University, Princeton, NJ 08544, USA.

SINGH Amar Bahadur, b. 15 Mar 1965, Varanasi, India. Journalist. Education: BA; MA; BJ; MJ; PhD. Appointment: Special Corresp, Natl Hindi Daily, Janvarta, Newsppr. Publications: Pracheen Bharat Main Jansanchar Ka Itihas; Mahamana Madan Mohan Malvia Aur Hindi Patrakarita. Honours: Bhartendu Harish Chand Awd, Govt of India; Outstndng People of the 20th Century Awd, IBC, London; Disting Ldrshp Awd, ABI, USA. Membership: Rastriya Yuva Patrakar Sanghatan, Varanasi. Hobby: Creative Journalism. Address: H. No C.26/36 A-3 Ram Katora Crossing, Varanasi 1 UP, India.

SINGH Amar Nath, b. 28 Sept 1968, Varanasi, India. Advocate. Education: BA; MA; LLB; PhD. Appointment: Advocate. Publications: Prachin Bharat Main Nyaya Vyavastha Ka Itihas; Bharat Main Rashtriya Ekta Aur Sampradayiksadbhav. Honours: Outstndng People of the 20th Century Awd, IBC, London; Disting Ldrshp Awd, ABI, USA. Membership: Ctrl Bar Assn, Varanasi, India, life mbr. Hobbies: Reading; Social Activities. Address: H.No. C.26/36 A-3 Ram Katora Chowraha, Varanasi 1, UP, India.

SINGH Amarjit, b. 19 Nov 1924. Scientific Research. m. Surinder, 3 s. Education: MSc, Punjab; MEngg Sc, PhD, Harvard. Appointments: Lectr, Delhi Univ; Scientist, Natl Phys Lab; Dir, Cntrl Electrons Engrng Rsch Inst; Visng Scientist, Univ of MD. Publications: Ed: Microwave Integrated Circuits; About 100 rsch pprs on microwave tubes, millimeter waves and semiconductors. Honours: DSc (hon causa), Punjabi Univ, 1976; Padma Bhushan, Pres of India, 1985. Memberships: Life Fell, IEEE (NY); Distinguished Fell, Instn of Electrons and Telecomm Engrs. Hobbies: Making video documentaries; Music. Address: 5803, Cherrywood Terrace, Apt 301, Greenbelt, MD 20770, USA.

SINGH Buta, b. 21 Mar 1934 Jalandhar Punjab. Politician. Education: Lyallpur Khalsa Coll Jalandhar; Guru Nanak Khalsa Coll Bombay. Appointments: Elected for Lok Sabha, 1962, 1967, 1971, 1980, 1984; Union Dep Min for Railways, 1974-76; Pres Amateur Athletic Fedn of India, 1976-84; Union Dep Min for Com, 1976-77; Gen Sec Indian Natl Congress, 1978-80; Min of State in min of Shipping and Transp, 1980-81; Min of Supply and Rehabilitation, 1981-82; Min of Sport, 1982-83; Cabinet Min oin charge of sev mins, 1983-84; Min of Agric, 1984-86; Min of Home Affairs, 1986-89; Min of Civ Supplies Consumer Affairs and Pub Distribution, 1995-96; Min of Comms, Mar 1998-. Memberships: Mbr Plng Commn, 1985. Address: Ministry of Communications, Sanchar Bhavan, 20 Asoka Road, New Delhi 110 001, India.

SINGH Digvijai, b. 11 Dec 1934, Lucknow, India. Engineering Education. m. Usha Singh, 23 Apr 1966, 1 d. Education: BSc, Allahabad Univ; BE, Civil, BE, Mech, Univ of Roorkee; MS, PhD, Univ WI, USA. Appointments: Prof, Univ of Roorkee, 1967-90; Dir, Ctrl Road Rsch Inst, 1990-96; Vice Chmn, All India Cncl for Tech Educn, 1990-. Publications: 160 pprs in profl jrnls, 1 monograph. Honours: Shanti Swarup Bhatnagar Prize, Engrng Scis, 1978; Sev Instn of Engrs Prizes, 1970-90; India Silver Jubilee Awd, 1982. Memberships: Indian Natl Sci Acady; Indian Natl Acady of Engrng; Natl Acady of Scis; Indian Acady of Scis; Tribiol Soc of India; Intl Fndn for Sci. Hobbies: Photography; Sketching; Clay Sculpture. Address: All India Council for Technical Education, IG Sports Complex, IP Estate, New Delhi 110002, India.

SINGH Din Dayal, b. 8 Oct 1931, Hazaribagh, India. Surgeon. m. Prema, 1954, 2 s, 2 d. Education: MBBS, Hons; MS, Gen Surg, Patna; FRCS, Edinburgh. Appointments: Bihar Hlth Servs; Var tchng positions in med colls. Publication: Experimental Studies in Portal Hypertension, 1959. Memberships: IMA; Assn of Surgns of India. Hobbies: Teaching; Reading; Indoor games. Address: 214 A P Colony, Gaya 803001, India.

SINGH Jaipal, b. 24 Sept 1953, India. Librarianship. m. Usha, 8 Mar 1978, 2 s. Education: MA, Hist; MLi.Sc. Appointments: Asst Libn & Info, 1995-96; Snr Libn, 1998-. Publications: Sev conf pprs. Honour: IFLA-ALP Attachment Awd, 1995. Memberships: ICOM; ILA; IASLIC; GILA; AGLIS; IRT; ISI; IASC; MAI. Hobbies: Reading; Gardening. Address: Centre for Information Systems, Chanakyapuri, New Delhi 110021, India.

SINGH Joginder, b. 15 Oct 1962, Samtehan, Bilaspur, India. Teaching. m. Neelam, 1 s, 1 d. Education: BCom, (Hons); MBA, Fin; MPhil, Bus Admin; PhD, Mngmt Studies. Appointments: Econ Analyst, Himcon, Shimla, 1986; Asst Mngr, Dpty Mngr, Fin, P.F.C, Chandigarh, 1986-92; Hd, Dept of Tech Educn, 1992-. Publications: Working of Security Market in India, 1994; A Text Book on Environmental Education and Pollution Control, 1996. Honours: 3 Gold Medals; Roll of Hon; Univ Jnr Rsch Fellshp. Membership: Indian Soc for Tech Educn, New Delhi. Hobbies: Music; Reading. Address: Government Polytechnic for Women, Kandaghat, District Solan HP 173215, India.

SINGH Neena, b. 6 Mar 1969, Allahabad, India. Assistant Librarian and Incharge. Education: BHSc (Gold Medallist); BLibISc and Masters in Lib and Info Sci (MLibISc), N East Hill Univ. Appointments: Libn, Indian Inst of Hlth Mngmt, 1995; Asst Lib and Incharge, G B Pant Univ of Agril and Tech Hill Campus; Freelance writer. Honours: Gold Medal in BHsc; Fr CSA Univ of Agril and Tech, (Univ Merit Schlshp, Fr N East Hill Univ, Shillong). Memberships: Indian Lib Assn (ILA), New Delhi; Indian Assn of Spec Lib and Info Sci (IASLIC), Calcutta; Amn Stdies Rsch Cntr, Hyderabad, India. Hobbies: Reading; Philately; Interested mostly in library automation. Address: Asst Librarian Officer Incharge Library, G B Pant University of Agril & Technology, Hill Campus, Tehri Garwhal Pin 249199 (UP), India.

SINGH Nityanand, b. 14 Aug 1953, Varanasi, UP, India. Scientific Researcher. m. Urmila, 7 Mar 1974, 2 s, 1 d. Education: BS; MSc (Geophysics w Meteorology); PhD (Geophysics). Appointments: Rsch Schl, 1976-79; Jnr Hydrometeorologist, 1979-82; Snr Sci Offr II, 1982-89; Snr Sci Offr I, 1989-94; Asst Dir, 1994. Publications: 3 books; 45 sci rsch publs. Honours: Fellshp World Meteorological Orgn; 13th SAARC Young Scientist Awd in Meteorology and Environ, 1993-94. Memberships: Indian Meteorological Soc; Indian Agrometeorological Soc; Indian Hydrologist Soc. Listed in: Who's Who in the World, 1999. Hobbies: Reading; Tourism; Religious Fellowship; Listening to Music. Address: Indian Institute of Tropical Meteorology, Dr Homi Bhabha Road, Pashan, Pune 411008, India.

SINGH R B, b. 1 July 1943, Kakhawtoo, Auraiya, UP, India. Cardiologist; Physician. m. Sushav Singh, 26 Feb 1970, 1 s. Education: MDIDTNH. Appointments: Dir, Medl Hosp and Rsch Cntr, 1975-; Prof, Preventive Cardiology NKP Salve Inst of Med Scis, Nagpur. Publications: 6 books on Nutrition in Cardiovascular Disease; 250 rsch pprs. Honours: 8 intl awds, inclng Annual Sci Awd of Univ of Exeter, Eng, 1996. Memberships; Pres, Indian Soc of Hypertension, 1995; Intl Coll of Nutrition, 1997; Mbr, 10 other socs. Address: Civil Lines, Moradabad-10 (UP) 244001, India.

SINGH Rajendra Pal, b. 29 Nov 1941, Buland Shahr, India. Scientist. m. Rajesh Singh, 18 Jan 1966, 1 s, 3 d. Education: BSc, Agra Univ, 1961; MSc, Phys, Baroda Univ, 1964; PhD, Solid State Phys, SP Univ, 1970. Appointments: SSO, Forensic Sci Lab, New Delhi, 1972-80; Asst Dir, Forensic Sci Lab, Haryana, 1980-84; PSO, Min of Sci and Technol, New Delhi, 1984-88; Dir, Min of Sci and Technol, New Delhi, 1988-94; Jnt Advsr, Min of Sci and Technol, New Delhi, 1994-98; Scientist G, Min of Sci and Technol, New Dehli, 1999-. Publications include: Dislocations in MgO, 1973; Unusual Instrument Marks on Bones, 1977; Detection of Cement Adulteration, 1977; Short Gun Pellets - Analysis by Spectrograph, 1980; Light Bulb Filament Exam by SEM, 1983; Building Materials Analysis, 1983; Wires and Tools Exam by SEM, 1984; Tool Marks Exam by SEM, 1986; Burnt Electric Wires Exam by SEM, 1987. Memberships: Indian Acady Forensic Scis, Calcutta; IETE; EMSI. Hobbies: Gardening; Worship. Address: c/o Department of Science and Technology, Ministry of Science and Technology, Bhavan New Mehrouli Road, New Delhi 110016, India.

SINGH Rajkumar Prasad, b. 2 Juy 1947, Sheotar, Gaya, Bihar, India. Engineer. m. Chintamani, 21 Apr 1969, 1 s, 1 d. Education: MTech (Ferrous Process Metallurgy); IIT, Mumbai PhD (Met); IIT, Chennai. Appointments: Grad Engr, 1972; Sail, Foreman, Metallurgist, 1977; Asst Rsch Mngr, Prin Rsch Mngr, Asst Gen Mngr, RDCIS, Gen Mngr (QC, R&D), Lloyds Steel (India). Publications: 25 pprs in natl & intl jrnls. Honours: Life Fell, Indian Inst of Metals, Past Hon Sec, Bokaro Chapt, Indian Inst of Metals. Memberships: Life Fell, Indian Inst of Metals; Past Hon Sec, Bokaro Chapt, Indian Inst of Metals. Hobbies: Gardening; Homeopathy; Yoga. Address: M3(A1), Llloyds, Nagar, Wardha, 442 001 Maharashtra, India.

SINGH Ram Krishna, b. 31 Dec 1950, Varanasi, India. University Professor; Teaching. m. Durga, 1 Mar 1978, 1 s, 1 d. Education: BA, Harish Chandra Coll, Varanasi, 1970; Dip. Russian Lang, Varanaseya Sanscrit Vishwavidyalaya. 1970; MA, Engl Lit, Banaras Hindu Univ, 1972; PhD, Engl, Kashi Vidyapith, 1981. Appointments: Jrnlst, Press Trust of India, New Delhi, 1973-74; Lectr, Roy Bhutan Polytechnic Deothang, Bhutan, 1974-76; Lectr, 1976-83, Asst Prof, 1983-93, Prof, 1993-, Indian Sch of Mines, Dhanbad. Publications: 22 books inclng: Savitri: A Spiritual Epic, 1984; My Silence and Other Selected Poems, 1996; Above the Earth's Green, 1997; Anger in Action: Explorations of Anger in Indian English Writing (ed), 1997; Psychic Knot: Search for Tolerance in Indian English Fiction (ed), 1998; New Zealand Literature: Recent Trends (ed), 1998; Every Stone Drop Pebble, 1999. Honours: Hon LittD, World Acady Arts and Culture, Taipei, 1984; Fellshp, Intl Poets Acady, Madras, 1987; Cert Excellence and Mention, Directory Intl Writers, 1987; Michael Madhusudan Awd, Michael Mahusudan Acady, Calcutta, 1994; Poet of Yr Awd, Alumni of World Univ, Toronto, 1995. Memberships; Intl Writers and Artists Assn, USA; World Poetry Soc Intercontinental; Intl Poets Acady; PEN India; Soc for Intl Dev, Hon Sec, Dhanbad Dev Forum, 1992-. Hobbies: Writing poetry; Haiku; Yoga; Homeopathic medicines. Address: Type VI/4, Teachers Colony, Indian School of Mines, Dhanbad 826004, India.

SINGH Rishi Ram, b. 12 June 1939, Rampur, India. Teaching. m. Indu Singh, 14 June 1955, 1 s, 1 d. Education: BA; MA; PhD. Appointments: Lectr, 1960-70, Rdr, 1970-83, Prof, 1983-. Publictions: Social Work Perspectives on Poverty, 1980; Field Work in Social Work Education, 1985; Whither Social Development?, 1995. Memberships: Pres, Assn of Schs of Socl Work in India; Acad Cncls, 3 Univs; UGC Panel on Socl Work Educn & Expert Cttss. Hobbies: Gardening; Nature Study. Address: Department of Social Work, University of Delhi, 3 University Road, Delhi 110 007, India.

SINGH Sanjay Kumar, b. 26 Jan 1967. Librarian. Education: BSc, hons; MLISC; Ctf in French Lang; Ctf in Computing; MA, Sociol. Appointments: Rsch Assoc; Computer Operator; Libn; Lectr. Publications: Articles on computer application in lib and info servs. Memberships: Indian Lib Assn; Indian Assn of Spec Libs and Info Cntrs; Guwahati Lib Assn; Life Mbr, Indian Lib Assn; Indian Assn of Spec Libs and Info Cntrs; Exec Mbr, Assam Lib Assn, Hobbies: Touring; Reading; Attending Seminars and Conferences. Address: Department of Library and Information Science, Gauhati University, Guwahati 781014, Assam, India.

SINGH Sewa, b. 1 Jan 1946. Teacher. m. Narinder Kaur, 18 June 1967, 1 s, 2 d. Education: BA, hons, 1967; MA, 1969; LibSci, 1970; PhD, 1984. Appointments: Snr Li Asst, 1970-72; Lectr, 1972-84; Rdr, 1985-. Publications: 18 books, 95 articles, 20 popular articles, 28 book reviews, 8 rprts, 13 short stories and 4 biogs of painters. Honour: ABI Gold Record of Achievement, 1996. Memberships: Indian Assn of Special Lib and Info Cntrs; Indian Lib Assn; Indian Assn of Tchrs in Lib & Info Sci; ISKO; SIS; AGLIS. Hobbies: Reading books; Music; Touring. Listed in: Reference Asia; Who's Who in India; Indo-American Who's Who. Address: Department of Library and Information Sciences, Guru Nanak Development University, Amritsar 143 005, India.

SINGH Shri Nar, b. 21 Oct 1925, Ateli Begpur, Mahendergarh Dist, India. Member of Parliament. m. Surjit Kaur, 9 July 1954, 2 s, 1 d. Education: BA, LLB, Lucknow Univ. Appointments: Mbr, Punjab Legis Assembly, 1967-77, 1985-87; Min of Educ, Punjab, 1969-71; Elected 6th Lik Sabha, 1977; Union Cabinet Min, Agric, Food and Irrigation, 1977-79; Chf Min, Punjab, 1985-87; Gov, Tamil Nadu, 1990-91; Re-elected, 11th Lok Sabha, 2nd term, 1996; Mbr, Cttee on Urban and Rural Dev, 1996-98; Re-elected, 12th Lok Sabha, 1998; Union Cabinet Min, Chemicals and Fertilzers, Food, 1998-. Publication: Story of an Escape. Creative Works: 15 paintings. Membership: Chmn, Guru Nanak Fndn, 1969-73. Hobbies: Travelling; Agriculture; Painting; Reading; Writing; Indoor games; Mountaineering. Address: 23 Tughlak Road, New Delhi, India.

SINGH Sitasaran, b. 13 Apr 1937, Laheriasarai, India. Consultant. m. Urmila, 26 May 1966, 1 s, 1 d. Education: BSc Econs (LSE); MSc (Akron); MCP (Cincinnati); LLB; PhD; CMC. Appointments: Snr Planner, Commonwealth of KY, 1978-80; Dir, Cntr for Plng Dev & Sci, 980; Cnslt, Global Reach, 1995; Publications: Developing Training Manuals (report), 1995; Professional Competence for Multi Caste System (book), 1998; The Antelope (play for radio, TV, Film). Honours: Univ of Akron & Cincinnati Asstshps, 1977, 1978. Membership: Inst of Mngmt Cnslts of India. Hobbies: Screenplay writing; Conducting OD Assignments, media development. Address: Global Reach, Pustak Bhandar, Govind Mitra Road, Patna 800 004, India.

SINGH Yudhvir, b. 20 Dec 1952, Hamirpur, HP, India. Research. m. Sarita Singh, 4 Feb 1980, 1 s, 2 d. Education: PhD; MSc Agric (Agron); BSc Agric Hons; EAH. Appointments: Sci, 1978, Snr Sci, 1984, Cazri Jodhpur, India. Publication: Efficient Management of Resources for Sustainable and Production in Arid Regions, bulletin. Honour: Recip, Team Rsch Awd, Biennium, ICAR, New Delhi, India, 1983-84. Membership:

Arid Zone Assn of India, Jodhpur, India. Hobbies: Sports; Music; Reading. Address: Division of Soil Water Plant Sciences, Central Arid Zone Research Institute, Jodhpur, India.

SINGH CHARU SHEEL Devendra, b. 15 May 1955, Farrukhabad, UP, India. Teaching. m. Maya, 6 June 1987, 1 s. Education: BA Hons, Engl, 1974; MA, Engl, 1976; PhD, 1978. Appointments: Lectr, Engl, MBS Coll, Gangapur, Varanasi, 1977-79; Lectr, Engl, Kashi Vidyalith, 1979-86; Reader, Engl, MG Kashi Vidyapith, 1986-91; Prof, Engl, 1991-. Publications: 5 Collections of Poems in English, 1981, 1987, 1990, 1993, 1997; The Chariot of Fire, 1981; Auguries of Evocation, 1987; Self-Reflective Materality, 1997; Ed, 5 books on theory and criticism. Honours: Brit Cncl Fellowship, 1982-83; UGC Rsch Sci 'B' Awd, 1986-91; Rsch Assoc, Indian Inst of Advd Study, 1993; Fell, Indian Inst of Advd Study, 1996; UGC Maj Proj, 1997-2000. Memberships: Jrnl of Indian Writing in Engl; Lit Crit, Amn Stdies Rsch Cntr; Indian PEN. Address: 36-20A/36, Brahmanand Nagar Ext 1, Durga Kund, Varanasi 221005, India.

SINGSON Gabriel, b. 18 Mar 1929 Lingayen Pangasinan. Banker. m. Moonyeen Retizos, 2 s, 1 d. Education: Pangasinan Provincial High Sch Ateneo de Manila; Univ of MI Law Sch Ann Arbor. Appointments: Assoc Attorney Law Off of Jus Jose Bengzon, 1952-55; Prof of Com Law and Civ Law Ateneo de Manila Law Sch, 1956-72; Legal and Evaluation Offr Cntrl Bank, 1955-60; Tech Asst Monetary Bd, 1960-62; Asst to Dep Gov, 1963-66, 1968-70; Legal Offr Asian Devt Bank, 1967-68; Asst to Gov - with rank of Dir - Cntrl Bank, 1970-73; Spec Asst to Gov, 1973-74; Gen Cnsl, 1974-75; Dep Gov and Gen Cnsl, 1975-80; Snr Dep Gov, 1980-92; Pres Philippine Natl Bank, 1992-93; Chmn Monetary Bd and Gov Bangko Sentral ng Pilipinas, 1993-; Chmn PR Holdings Inc - holding co of Philippine Air Lines; Vice-Chmn Philippine Air Lines. Publications: Articles on Asian Devt Bank for loans for invmnts and for exchange regulations. Hobbies: Golf. Address: Bangko Sentral ng Pilipinas, A Mabini corner Vito Cruz Streets, Malate, 1004 Metro Manila, Philippines.

SINHA Anshu Kumar, b. 12 Jan 1942, Bihar, India. Director; Research scientist. m. Dr (Mrs) Meenakshi Sinha, 7 Mar 1975, 1 s, 1 d. Education: BS (Hons); MTech; PhD; DSc. Appointments: Scientific Offr, 1973, to Scientist "F", 1997; Wadia Inst of Himalayan Geol, Dehradun, India; Dir, BSIP, Lucknow. Publications: Geology of Higher Central Himalaya, 1989; Himalayan Orogeny and Global Tectonics, 1992; Geodynamic Domains in Alpine-Himalayan Tethys, 1997. Honour: Natl Mineral Awd, Govt of India, 1986. Memberships: Geol Soc, London; UNESCO-IGCP Sci Cttee, Paris, 1984-90. Hobbies: Trekking in high mountains; Western Classical music. Address: Director, BSIP, Government of India, Under Department of Science and Technology, 53, University Road, Lucknow 226007, India.

SINHA Asha, b. 28 Oct 1943, Gaya, India. Teacher. m. B N Sahay, 10 May 1955, 1 s. Education: MA; PhD. Appointments: Lectr, 1970, Rdr, 1986, Hd, Dept of Hindi, GBM Coll, Gaya. Publications include: Balmukund Gupt Ki Rajnitik Aur Samajic Chetna, 1986; Ratnakar Ki Den, 1993; Ratnakar Evam Hindi Ke Samtulya Prachin Navin Kavi, Tulnatmak Anushilan, 1996; Ed, Gaurav. Hobbies: Art; Knitting; Cooking. Address: MIG House No 38, Chanakya Puri, Gaya, India.

SINHA Manoj Kumar, b. 1 June 1965. Librarian; Researcher. Education: MSc Zoology; MLib and Info Sci, NET; BEd; PGDHE; PhD, Zool, T M Bhagalpur Univ. Appointments: JRF, 1988-90, SRF, 1990-93, CSIR Proj; Libn, JNV Gorakhpur, 1993-97; Asst Libn, Assam Univ, Silchar, 1997-. Publications: Publshd 10 rsch pprs in natl and intl jrnls. Memberships: ILA; IASLIC; AGLIS; UPLA; DBIT; Amnacet; ICS, Fellow; ISCA; FBAI; AEB; Natl Inst of Ecology; Intl Soc for Tropical Ecology; KELPRO; Soc of Info Sci. Hobbies: Reading; Gardening. Address: S/O Late Parmanand Prasad, Advocate, Basant Bahar, Ishakchak, Bhagalpur, Bihar 812001, India.

SINHA Ramanath, b. 9 Feb 1914, Mallickpur, Suri, Birbhum, India. Journalist; Editor. m. Jyotirmoyee Sinha, 1 s. Education: Matriculation, Calcutta Univ, 1931. Appointments: The Birbhum Barta, weekly, 1931, Viswakosh, Calcutta, 1933; Krishak, daily, Calcutta, 1944; Lokesebak, daily, Calcutta; The Bharat, daily, Calcutta; The Satyajug, daily, Calcutta; Mbr, Indian Jrnlsts Assn, 1946. Publications: Kaak Dake Kaka, short stories, 1978; Dur Gaganer Tara, novel, 1982; Jeeban Dar Pan, novel, 1984. Honours: Gold Medallist in Adya, Shantipur Puran Parishad, Bengal (India), 1939; Titled Puran Ratna, Parishad, 1940. Memberships: Indian Jrnlsts Assn, Calcutta, 1946; Chmn, St John Ambulance Assn, Birbhum Dist Cntr, 1976-96; Pres, Birbhum Press Club; Ex Mbr, Indian Red Cross Soc; VP, Birbhum Sahitya Parishad. Hobbies: Writing poems and articles. Address: Suri Dist Birbhum, 731 101 West Bengal, India.

SINHA Sushanta Kumar, b. 4 Oct 1948, Bhagalpur, India. Scientist. m. Tapasi, 7 May 1990, 1 d. Education: BS, 1966; MSc, 1968, PhD, Maths, 1975; PhD, Meteorology, 1993. Appointments: Sci Asst, 1976-81, Snr Sci Asst, 1981-86, Jnr Sci Offr, 1986-91, Snr Sci Offr, 1991-, Indian Inst of Tropical Meteorology, Pune, India. Publications: 15 in jrnls. Honours: Trng in Ltd Area Modelling, Italy, 1990; Attended Intl Conf in Japan, 1993. Memberships: Indian Meteorlogical Soc. Hobby: Indian classical music. Address: Indian Institute of Tropical Meteorology, NCL PO, Pashan, Pune 411008, India.

SINHA Yashwant, b. 6 Nov 1937, Patna, Bihar, India. Memher of Parliament. m. Nilima Sinha, 17 Feb 1961, 2 s, 1 d. Education: MA, Patna Univ. Appointments: Lectr, Pol Sci, Patna Univ, 1958-60; Mbr, IAS, 1960; Dpty Commnr, Santhal Paraganas; Chmn, DTC, Delhi; Chmn, Drafting Cttee, UNCTAD Conf on Shipping, Geneva; Consul-Gen of India, Frankfurt; Prin Sec to Chf Min, Bihar; Jt Sec, Gov of India in Min of Shipping and Transp; Joined Janata Pty, 1984; Gen Sec, Janata Pty, 1986-88; Mbr, Rajya Sabha, 1988; Mbr Cttee of Petitions, 1989; Joined Janata Dal (Samajwadi), 1990; Union Min of Fin, 1990-91; Elected, 12th Lok Sabha, 1998; Union Min, Fin, 1998-; Mbr, Parly Pay Cttee, 1998-99. Memberships: Delhi Gymkhana Club; Bankipur Club, Patna. Hobbies: Reading; Travelling. Address: 6 Kushak Road, New Delhi, India.

SINNATHURAI Sothirachagan, b. 12 Aug 1946, Batugajah, Perak, Malaysia. Professor and Dean. m. S Jayaranee, 1983, 2 d. Education: BA, Univ of Malaya, 1968; Postgrad Dip of Arts, Univ of Otago, NZ, 1971; MA, Univ of Otago, NZ, 1972; PhD, SOAS, Univ of London, 1978; Dip in Law, Polytechnic of Cntrl London, 1978; Barrister at Law, Lincoln's Inn, 1984; LLM, Univ of Bristol, 1990. Appointments: Tchr, 1968-69, Tchng Asst, Univ of Otago, NZ, 1971-72; Lectr, 1972-81, Assoc Prof, 1982-92, Dept of Geog, Fac of Arts & Socl Scis, Univ of Malaya; Assoc Prof, 1992-94, Prof & Dean, Fac of Law, Univ of Malaya, 1994-. Publication: Law and the Electoral Process in Malaysia, 1993. Honours: Tokoh Pengguna (Consumer Ldr of Yr, Govt of Malaysia Awd, 1995; Darjah Dato Paduka Mahkota Perak (Hon Awd, carries title Dato) conferred by his Roy Highness, Sultan of Perak), 1998. Memberships include: Ins Mediation Bur, Cncl Mbr, 1991-, Dpty Chmn of Cncl, 1994-; Bar Cncl of Malaya, Investigation Tribunal Panel, 1994-, Disciplinary Cttee Panel, 1998-; LAWASIA, Chmn, Standing Cttee on Consumer Law, 1993-; Intl Assn for Consumer Law, VP, 1995-; ASEAN Law Schs Assn, VP, 1995-; IUCN, World Conservation Union, Commn on Environ Law, 1996-; Govt cttees; Editl Boards of sev profl jrnls. Hobby: Badminton. Address: 76 Jalan Terasek 1, Bangsar Baru 59100 Kuala Lumpur, Malaysia.

SINNOTT Donald Hugh, b. 17 Mar 1944, Melbourne, Aust. Engineer. m. Wendy, 13 Aug 1966, 2 s, 2 d. Education: BE, Elect, 1966; MEngSc, 1967; PhD, 1972; FAICD (Diplomate), 1990. Appointments: Sci Offr, Dept Supply, 1967; Adelaide Aust; Rsch Sci, Defence Sci and Technol Org, Adelaide, 1972; Snr Prin Rsch Sci, 1983; Chief Microwave Radar Div, 1987; Chf, IT Div, 1993; First Asst Sec, Dept of Defence, Canberra Aust, 1995; Chf Surveillance Systs Div, Adelaide, 1998. Publications: Over the Horizon Radar, book chapt, 1989; Radar Technology, book chapt, 1991; Contbr, articles in profl jrnls. Memberships: FIEAust, 1989; FIREE Aust, 1987; FIEEE, 1996. Hobbies: Reading; Music. Address: 37 Janlyn Road, Vista, SA 5091, Australia.

SIRAJ Sirajul Islam, b. 3 Dec 1940. Teaching (Professor). m. Tahera, 2 s, 1 d. Education: MA. Appointments: Lectr, Palashbari Coll, Rangpur, Bangladesh; Asst Prof, Shah Niamatullah Coll, Nawabganj. Publications: Bengali Grammar & Essays. Membership: Dist Coord, Bangladesh Open Univ. Honour: Divisional & Provincial Awd for Music. Hobbies: Reading; Composing Song. Address: Sirajul Islam, Head of the Department Bengali, Shah Niamatullah College, PO Chapainawaganj, Bangladesh.

SIRIVEDHIN Tanya, b. 19 Feb 1946. Central Bank Official. m. Anumongkol Sirivedhin, 7 May 1968, 2 d. Education: BA Econs, VUW; MA Econs, UW. Appointments: Economist, Bank of Thailand, 1972; Chf, For Ops, 1980; Advsr to Ed, IMF, 1984-85; Dpty Dir, Intl Dept, 1985; Exec Dir, IMF, 1989-92; Dir, Econ Rsch Dept, 1992; Asst Gov, 1996, Dpty Gov, 1998. Memberships: Securities Analysts Assn; Siam Soc; NZ Alumni Assn; Triam Udomsuksa Alumni. Hobbies: Reading; Tennis; Golf. Address: 88-73 Paholyotin 7, Bangkok 10400, Thailand.

SIRIWARDHANA Sita Eileen, b. 6 Apr 1928, Matara. Prinicpal. m. DBIPS, 22 Aug 1953, 2 s, 1 d. Education: BA, Gen, Sinhala Eng Pali, Univ of Colombo. Appointments: Asst Tchr, Princess of Wales Coll, 1950; Asst Tchr, St Joseph's Convent, 1961; Asst Tchr, 1951; Dpty Prin, 1973; Prin, Samudra Devi Balika Vidyalaya, 1978; Offr of Class 1, Sri Lanka Educl Admin Serv, 1983; Prin, Visakha Vidyalaya, Colombo, 1983-88; Dir, Sahanaya, Colombo, 1989-90; Prin, Shinyo-En-Lanka, Kohuwela, Colombo, 1991-92; Prin, Buddhist Ladies Coll, Colombo, 1995-. Creative Works: 24 Publs. Honours: Awd for Best Film of the Third World; D R Wijewardena Awd; Natl Presl Hon, Kala Keerthi; Many or Hons. Memberships: Cttee to Compilation of Code of Ethics for Tchrs; Cttee of Natl Cncl for Mental Hlth; Intl Assn of Writers; All Ceylon Women's Congress; Min of Women Affairs; Many ors. Hobbies: Music; Bird Watching; Reading; Meditation. Address: 57 Railway Avenue, Nugegoda, Sri Lanka.

SIRIWEERA Wathuge Indrakeerti, b. 26 Apr 1942, Sri Lanka. Professor. m. Lalitha, 26 Sept 1968, 1 s, 1 d. Education: BA (Hons), Univ of Ceylon, 1964; PhD, London, Sch of Oriental and African Studies, 1969. Appointments: Prof, Univ of Peradeniya, 1991-; Chmn, Univ Grants Commn, Sri Lanka, 1994-95; Vice Chancellor, Rajarata Univ, 1995-. Publications: The Warden (short stories), 1977; The Craving (novel), 1979; The Artist, Beauty and the Woman (short stories), 1998. Memberships: Ed, Sri Lanka Histl Assn, 1991-92; Mbr Governing Bd, Kotelawala Def Acady, Natl Educ Commn, Human Rescs Dev Cncl, Inst of Socl Dev, 1994-95; Pres, Rajarata Profls' Assn, 1996-97. Hobbies: Music; Drama; Table tennis; Bridge. Address: Rajarata University, Mihintale, Sri Lanka.

SISELY Lorna Verdun, b. 14 Mar 1916, Aust. Surgeon. Education: MB BS, Melbourne Univ; Janet Clark Hall, 1939-42; Jnr and Snr Res Med Offr, St Vincents Hosp, Melbourne, 1942-44; Demonstrator, Anatomy and Pathol Depts, 1947-49. Appointments: Surgn, Snr Staff, Queen Vic Med Cntr, 1947-81; Snr Surgn, 1958-81; Surg Tutor, Monash Univ, 1967-81; Mbr, Bd Examiners, Monash Univ, 1972, 1973, 1979; Mbr, Med and Sci Cttee, Anti-Cancer Cncl of Vic, 1964-81; Mr, Exec Cncl, 1970-81; Demonstrator, Melbourne Univ, 1950's, Assoc Surg, Roy Childrens Hosp, 1950's; Fndr Cnslt Surg, Breast Clin, Monash Med Cntr, 1980. Publications include: Granular Cell Tumour in a Male Breast, 1973. Honours: Exhbn and 1st Class Hons, Pathol, Melbourne Univ, 1940; Michael Ryan Prize in Surg, 1942; Gordon Craig Travelling Schlshp, 1949; OBE, 1980; MB; BS; MS; FRACS; FACS. Memberships: Assn of Surgs; Austl Med Assn; Pan-Pacific Surg Assn.

Hobbies: Music; Gardening. Address: 18/740 Orrong Road, Toorak, Vic 3142, Australia.

SITSKY Larry, b. 19 Sept 1934, China. Composer; Pianist; Musicologist; Broadcaster. m. 8 Feb 1961, 1 s, 1 d. Education: Grad 1956, Postgrad studies 1956-58, NSW State Conserv, Sydney; Studied w Egon Petri, San Fran Conserv of Music. Appointments: 1st recital at 11; Many recitals, comms, recdngs; Piano Tchr, Qld State Conserv of Music, Guest Lectr, Qld Univ, 1961-65; Hd, Keyboard Studies, 1966-78, Dept Hd, Comp Elect Music, 1978-81; Dept Hd, Comp, Musicology, 1981-, Canberra Sch of Music, ACT; Examiner, Comp, Piano Perf, Austl Univs/Colls of Advd Educ; Artistic Dir, Bicentennial Recdng Proj; Dir, Austl Contemporary Music Ensemble; Reader, 1993; Prof, 1994; Resident Composer, Intl String Sch, Melbourne, 1996, 1997; Resident Composer, Austl Acady of Music, 1998. Creative Works: Num wrks for orch, solo instruments, ensembles, orch/ensemble, vocal wrks inclng: Sonata, Solo Violin, 1959; Dimensions, Piano, 2 Tape Recorders, 1964; Fall of the House of Usher, opera, 1965; Apparitions, orch, 1966; Prelude, orch, 1968; Narayana, piano trio, 1969; Concerto No 1, 1971; Sonata, Solo Guitar, 1974; The Ten Sephiroth of the Kabbalah, choral, 1974; Music in Mirabell Garden, soprano, instruments, 1977; Arch, piano, 1980; De Profundis, opera, 1982; Gurdjieff, Concerto No 2, 1983; Khavar, Solo Trombone, 1984; Armenia Suite, Solo Saxophone, 1984; Dagh, Solo Trumpet, 1984; Sayat-Nova, Solo Oboe, 1984; Tetragrammation, violin, piano, 1987; Incidental Music to Faust, 1996; Grande Variations Brillante on Waltzing Matilda for double-bass solo, 1997; Sonette for Jazz Singer, 1997; Concerto No 4 for Violin and Orch, 1998; Concerto No 5 for Violin and Orch, 1998; Bone of My Bones, 5 love lyrics for voice and piano, 1998; Zohar, Sephardic Concerto for mandolin and small orch, 1998; Publications include: The Reproducing Piano Roll: A Treasure Trove of 19th Century Practice, 1982; Busoni and the Piano: The Music, the Writings, the Recordings: A Complete Survey, 1986; Book of Russian Romantic Miniatures, transcribed for oboe and piano, 1997; Anton Rubinstein, 1998; Contrb to Companion to Music in Australia, 1988 and sev jrnls. Honours include: Many grants, prizes, fellshps; 1st Austl Travelling Fell, USSR, 1988; Adv Aust Awd, 1989; Critics Circle Awd, 1994; Fndn Awd, Higher Doct in Arts, Aust Natl Univ, 1997; Elected Fell, Austl Acady of the Hums, 1998. Memberships: Fndn Chair, Guild of Composers; ACT Rep, Fellshp of Composers; Music Bd of Aust Cncl; Austl Soc for Music Educ. Address: 29 Threlfall Street, Chifley, ACT 2606, Australia.

SIVAKUGAN Nagaratnam, b. 26 July 1956, Sri Lanka. Senior Lecturer. m. Rohini, 9 Feb 1986. Education: BSc, Eng, Hons; MSCE, Purdue; PhD, Purdue; RPEQ; CPEng; MASCE. Appointments: Site Mngr, State Engrng Corp; Asst Prof, Oman; Snr Lectr, Aust. Memberships: Amn Soc of Civil Engrs; Inst of Engrs, Aust. Hobbies: Bridge; Share Market; Reading; Movies. Address: 15 Chatsworth Crescent, Annandale 24814, Australia.

SIVAKUMAR Bhattiprolu, b. 25 Sept 1945. Research Scientist. m. B Suryakumari, 3 s. Education: MSc; PhD. Appointments: Demonstrator, Rsch Asst, Asst Rsch Offr, Rsch Offr, Snr Rsch Offr, Asst Dir & Dpty Dir. Publications: Carbohydrates, chapt, 1996. Honours: Brit Cncl, TCTP Awd to visit insts in Engl, 1990; Visng Fell, Baylor Coll of Med, Houston, TX, USA, 1992-94. Memberships: Nutr Soc of India; Soc of Biologica Chemists, India. Hobby: Filming with video camera. Address: Head of Biophysics Division, National Institute of Nutrition, Jamai-Osmania, Hyderabad, 50007, India.

SIVUA Epeli, b. 24 Oct 1949, Nadroga, Fiji Islands. Driver. m. Vika III, 21 July 1986, 3 s, 1 d. Appointment: Asst Sec, Cagimaira Devel Assn, Fiji. Hobbies: Reading; Playing Soccer; Rugby. Address: c/o Cagimaira Development Association, PO Box 1038 BA, Fiji.

SIYAL Mohammed Yaloob, b. 1 June 1961, Sinoh, Pakistan. Assistant Professor. m. G J Siyal, 20 Jan 1996. Education: BE; MSc; PhD. Appointments: Research Assoc; Lectr; Asst Prof. Memberships: MPEC 1985; MIEE, 1988; SMIEEE, 1991. Hobbies: Playing squash; Swimming. Address: School of EEE, Block 52, NTU, Nanyang Avenue, Singapore, 639798.

SKATE William Jack, b. 1953 Baimuru Dist Gulf Prov. Politician. m. 3 c. Education: Univ of Tech Lae. Appointments: Fmr Gen Mngr PSA Savings and Loans Soc; Fmr Gen Mngr Natl Capital Dist Commn; Fmr Govt advsr; MP, 1992-95; Speaker of Parl, 1992-94; Dep Ldr of Oppositin, 1994-95; Gov Natl Capital Dist, 1995-97; PM of Papua New Guinea, Jul 1997-. Address: Office of the Prime Minister, P O Box 6605, Boroko, NCD, Papua New Guinea.

SKERRITT John Howard, b. 8 Mar 1959. Scientist. m. Amanda Hill, 23 Apr 1988, 2 d. Education: BSc, 1st class Hons, PhD, Univ of Sydney. Appointments: Postdoct Fell, Univ MI, USA, 1983; Rsch Sci, Snr Prin Rsch Sci, CSIRO Plant Ind, 1983-99; Rsch Prog Mngr, Quality Wheat CRC Ltd, Sydney, 1996-99; Dpty Dir, Rsch and Dev, Austl Cntr for Intl Agricl Rsch, 1999-. Publications: 200 rsch articles in scholarly jrnls; 8 pats; 2 books. Honours: Univ Medal, 1980; Percy Pharmacol Prize, 1981; Rotary Fndn Fellshp, 1983; Roy Soc of NSW Edgeworth David Prize, 1993; Murex Diagnostics Awd, 1994. Memberships: Soc for Food and Agricl Immunol; AOAC Internatl; Amn Assn of Cereal Chems. Hobbies: Bushwalking; Gardening; Carpentry. Address: 38 Booth Crescent, Cook, ACT 2614, Australia.

SKULLY Michael Thomas, b. 19 June 1947, USA. Academic. m. Dian, 10 Feb 1977. Education: BS Bus Admin, 1968, Univ Arizona; MBA, 1972, Univ Utah; Grad Dip Econ, 1973, Univ Stockholm. Appointments: Asst Acct, Fin Dept, General Electric Company, AZ, 1968; Armour Offr, US Army, Fort Knox, Frankfurt and Helsinki, 1969-71; Asst Mgr, Universal Underwriting Services, UT, 1972; Seconded Lectr, Dept Intl Bus Mgmt, Nanyang Univ, Singapore, 1978-79; Visng Fell, Prin Lectr, Dept Econ and Fin, City Polytech of Hong Kong, 1989-90; Assoc Prof, Snr Lectr in Fin, Univ NSW, Aust, 1973-92; Prof Banking, Monash Univ, Aust, 1992-. Publications: Co-ed, Handbook of Australian Corporate Finance, 1997; Co-ed, ASEAN Business, Trade and Development: an Australian Perspective, 1996; Ed, Financial Institutions and Markets in Southeast Asia: a study of Brunei, Indonesia, The South Pacific: finance, development and the private sector, 1997. Memberships: Aust Soc of CPA, FCPA; Inst of Corp Mgrs, ACIM; Aust Inst Banking and Fin, AAIB, Snr; Securities Inst of Aust, ASIA; Chartered Inst Chartered Secs, ACIS. Hobby: Family history. Address: Monash University-Accounting Dept, PO Box 197, Caulfield East, Melbourne VIC 3145, Australia.

SLAPE Norman Edward, b. 4 Feb 1928, Cairns, Queensland, Aust. Company Executive, Mineral & Oil Exploration. m. 8 Dec 1951, 1 d. Membership: Centenary Inst, Cancer Med & Cell Biol. Hobby: Parapsychology. Address: 40 Urben Street, Urbenville, NSW 2475, Australia.

SLATER Christian, b. 18 Aug 1969 NY. Actor. Appointments: Appeared at age of seven in tv series One Life to Live; Profl stage debut at age of nine in touring prodn of The Music Man; Sentenced to 90 days imprisonment, 1998. Stage appearances incl: Macbeth; David Copperfield; Merlin; Landscape of the Body. Films incl: The Name of the Rose; Tucker: The Man and his Dream; Heathers; The Legend of Billie Jean; Cry Wolf; Tales from the Darkside: The Movie; Gleaming the Cube; The Wizard; Pump up the Volume; Young Guns II; Robin Hood: Prince of Thieves; Kuffs; Mobsters; Where the Day Takes You; Untamed Heart; True Romance; Murder in the First; Untitled; Jimmy Hollywood; Interview with a Vampire; Bed of Roses; Hard Rain. Address: c/o CAA, 9830 Wilshire Boulevard, Beverly Hills, CA 90212, USA.

SLIPPER Peter Neil, b. 14 Feb 1950, Ipswich, Eng. Federal Member of Parliament. m. Lyn Margaret, 14 Dec 1985, 1 s, 1 d. Education: BA, LLB (Qld); Barrister at Law (NSW); Solicitor (Qld); Barrister & Solicitor (Vic). Appointments: Mbr, House of Reprs Standing Cttee, Expenditure,, 1985-87; Sec, Govt Mbrs Atty Gen & Justice Cttee; Chmn, W Moreton Regl Community Corrections Bd (Parole Bd), 1989-90; Mbr, House of Reprs Standing Cttee on Legal & Constl Affairs, 1993-96; Mbr, House of Reprs Standing Cttee on Publs, 1993-96; Govt Whip; Chmn, House of Reprs Standing Cttee on Family & Community Affairs, 1996-. Chmn, Aust/Japan, Aust/Slovenia & Aust/Slovakia, Parly Grp of Inter Parly Union; Mbr Jt Parly Standing Cttee on For Affairs, Def & Trade.

SLOAN Lionel Eric George, b. 17 Mar 1924, Vic, Aust. Paediatrician. m. Mardi Newton, 26 Mar 1980. Education: MB, BS, Trinity Coll, Univ of Melbourne, 1952; FRACP, 1959; FRACMA, 1966. Appointments: Ord Seaman to Lt, Roy Austl & Roy Navy, 1942-46; Chf Res, Roy Children's Hosp, Melbourne, 1955-56; Paediatn, Alfred Hosp, Melbourne, 1961-65; Med Dir, 1965-81, Snr Physn, 1981-90, Hon Cnsltng Physn, 1990-, Roy Children's Hosp, Melbourne; Registrar, Cnclr, Austl Coll of Paediats, 1986-90. Memberships: Roy Austl Coll of Paediats; Roy Austl Coll of Physns; Melbourne Club; Melbourne Cricket Club; Metro Golf Club; Roy S Yarra Tennis Club; Sorrento Golf Club. Hobbies: Golf; Tennis; Swimming; Painting. Address: Kingstoun, 181/461 St Kilda Road, Melbourne, Vic 3004, Australia.

SLOGGETT Robyn Joyce, b. 2 Oct 1955, Melbourne, Aust. Art Conservator. m. Willem Snoek, 4 July 1981, 2 s, 1 d. Education: Asst Dip, Applied Sci (Materials Conservation), Univ of Canberra, Aust, 1981; BA, Hons, Univ of Melbourne, Aust. Appointment: Chf Conservator, Univ of Melbourne, 1989. Memberships: Pres, Austl Inst for the Conservation of Cultural Material Ltd, AICCM. Hobbies: Gardening; Reading; Music. Address: The Ian Potter Art Conservation Centre, The University of Melbourne, Parkville, Victoria, Australia 3052.

SLOMP Andrew John, b. 8 Nov 1968, Australia. Resort Manager. m. Sheryle, 10 Mar 1996. Hobbies: Golf; Outdoors; Family. Address: 68 Southside Drive, Hillarys, WA 6025, Australia.

SLYNKO Basil, b. 19 Aug 1951, Australia. Educator. m. Susan Margaret Sherwell, 9 May 1998. Education: Dip in Tchng; Bach of Educl Studies; MA. Appointments: Tchr, 1973-75, 1977-80; Lectr, 1976; Hd, Dept, 1981-82, 1984-89, 1991-92, 1996-. Grad Tchng Asst, 1983-84; Educ Offr, 1990-91, 1994-96. Publications include: Graphics 8, 1983, Tcher's Edition, 1983; Technology Activity Book 1, 1986, 2nd edition, 1994, Tchr's Edition, 1986, 2nd Tchr's Edition, 1994; Introducing Technology: A Text for Australian Secondary Schools, 1991; Technology Activity Book 2, 1992, Tcher's Ed, 1992; Contributing auth, Queensland Cement: Project and Activity Folder, 1995; Co-auth, Graphics Booklets and Work Sheets, 1994-96. Honours: Postgrad Schlsp, 1983-84; Epsilon Pi Tau, 1984. Memberships: Intl Technol Educ Assn, 1983-; Design in Educ Cncl Aust, 1991-. Hobbies: Bush Walking; Cycling; Furniture Restoration. Address: 37 Fairy Street, Moorooka, Qld 4105, Australia.

SMALL Arthur Francis, b. 26 Feb 1946. Managing Director, Transport Company. m. Sandra Dianne Collins, 25 Mar 1972, 3 s. Education: BE Hons, Civ, 1968; ME, Civ, 1969; PhD, Engrng, 1972; MIPENZ, 1972; FIPENZ, 1988; CEng MICE, Eng, 1976; CEng FICE, Eng, 1993; FIE, Aust, 1993; FCIT, 1986. Appointments: NZ Railways, Auckland, 1964; Railway Civ Engr, 1972-76; Permanent Way Engrng, 1976-78; Plng Engr, 1979-81; Dir of Plng and Dev Unit, 1982; Dpty Chf Traffic Mngr, 1982-83; Chf Traffic Mngr, 1983-85; Grp Mngr, Freight Bus Grp, 1985-88; Grp Gen Mngr, NZ Railways Corp, 1988-90; Mng Dir, NZ Rail Ltd, Tranz Rail Ltd, 1990-; Dir'shps: WI Cntrl Transportation, 1996-, Austl Transport Netwrk, 1997-, Tasrail, 1997; Mbr, Austl Natl Transportation Cttee, 1997-, Treas, Austl Railway Assn, 1997-, Meridian Energy Ltd, 1998-. Publications: Hydroelastic Excitation of Cylinders, Thesis, 1972; A View of Management Practice Within Freight Transport, 1985; Overview of NIMT Electrification, 1987; Another International Conference Learns From NZ Rail, 1991; Building a Model Railway, 1996. Honour: BP Transp Awd, 1986.

Memberships include: Chmn, Wellington Br, IPENZ, 1983-84; Chmn, IPENZ Continuing Educ Cttee, 1980-83; Cncl of IPENZ, 1983-90; Pres, IPENZ, 1996; Natl Trng Cmmn, 1984-95, Natl Pres, 1997-; Scout Assn of NZ; Warden, All Saints Ch, Ngaio, 1983-93; Dir, Rehabilism Trust, 1990-; NZ Quality Awds Fndn, 1992-; Engrs Registration Bd, 1994-98; Standards Assn of NZ, 1998-. Hobbies: Walking; Golf; Travel; Music. Address: Tranz Rail, Private Bag, Wellington, New Zealand.

SMALL David Henry, b. 12 Apr 1956, Hobart, Australia. Research Scientist. m. Agnes-Marie, 19 Oct 1991, 1 s, 1 d. Education: BSc, Hons; PhD. Appointments: Hd, Lab of Molecular Neurobio, 1991-; Rsch Fell, 1993; Snr Rsch Fell, 1995. Publications: More than 80 publs in intl jrnls; Ed, Jrnl of Neurochem. Hobby: Chess. Address: Department of Pathology, University of Melbourne, Parkville, Vic 3052, Australia.

SMALL Michael Ronald, b. 3 Jan 1943, Croydon, Surrey, Eng. Teacher; Writer. Education: BA (London); BEduc (LaTrobe) Aust; MA, (Windsor), Can; Postgrad Cert of Educ (London); TESL Roy Soc of Arts (London). Publications: Her Natural Life and Other Stories, 1988; Films: A Resource Book for Studying Film as a Text (co-auth), 1994; Unleashed: A History of Footscray Football Club (co-auth), 1996; Urangeline: Voices of Carey 1923-1997, 1997. Membership: Victorian Fellshp of Austl Writers. Hobbies: Reading; Writing; Travelling. Address: 71 Strabane Avenue, Box Hill North, Victoria 3129, Australia.

SMATHERS James, b. 26 Aug 1935, Prairie du Chien, Wisconsin, USA. Medical Physicist. m. Sylvia R, 20 Apr 1957, 2 s, 2 d. Education: BNE Nuclear Engrng, NC State Coll; MS Nuclear Engrng, NC State Coll; PhD Nuclear Engrng, Univ Maryland. Appointments: Asst Prof Nuclear Engrng, 1967, Assoc Prof, 1971, Prof Nuclear Engrng, 1973, Texas A&M Univ; Hd, Bio Engrg Prog, 1976, Prof Radiation Oncol, 1980, UCLA. Publications: Over 100 publd pprs. Honours: Gen Dynamics Tchg Awd, TAMU, 1971; ASEE Nuclear Engrng Div Tchg Awd, 1972; Fac Dist'd Awd, TAMU, 1976. Memberships: Am Assoc Physicists Med, Treas 1992-97; Am Coll Medl Phys, V Chmn 1998, Chmn 1999; ACR; HPS; ANS; NSPE. Hobbies: Photography; Gardening. Address: Dept Radiation Oncology, B265 200 UCLA Medical Plaza, Los Angeles, CA 90095-6951, USA.

SMEAL Malcolm George, b. 31 Aug 1938, Sydney, Aust. Veterinary Scientist. m. Deanna, 27 Aug 1965, 1 s, 1 d. Education: BVSc, MVSc, PhD, Univ of Sydney. Appointments: Vet Offr, NSW Dept of Agric, 1962; Vet Rsch Offr, 1965, Snr Rsch Scientist, 1976, Dir, Cntrl Vet lab, Glenfield, 1983; Dir, Animal Hlth Rsch, 1985; Inst Supvsr, Biol and Chem Rsch Inst, Rydalmere, 1993; Vet Cnslt, Beef Prodn from Pastures, Estab prac, South Beef Advsry, 1998. Publications: Parasites of Cattle, 1995; 20 sci pprs in intl jrnls. Honours: Govt NSW Serv Awd, for Meritorious Serv, 1998. Pastures, Estab prac, South Beef Advsry, 1998. Memberships: Austl Vet Assn; Austl Soc for Parasitology. Address: 19 Elouera Road, Westleigh, NSW 2120, Australia.

SMITH A Lockwood, b. 1948. Government Minister. Education: Masters Deg, Agricl Sci; Massey and Brit C'Wlth Schlshp; PhD, Animal Sci, Adelaide Univ, 1980. Appointments: Mngr, family beef property, Matakohe; Lectr, Agricl Sci, Univ Massey, 1971-72; Mktng Mngr, Cntrl and SE Asia, NZ Dairy Bd; Elected to Parl, 1984; Natl Party Spokesperson, Educ, 1987-90; Min of Educ, 1990-96; Min responsible for Educ Review Off, 1990-96; Min responsible for Natl Lib, 1990-96; Dpty Min of Fin, 1996; Min of Agric, 1996-98, and Forestry, 1996-98; Min for Intl Trade, Assoc Min of Fin, Min responsible for Contact Energy Ltd. Address: PO Box 573, Warkworth, New Zealand.

SMITH Arabella, b. 10 Jan 1938, Prague, Czechoslovakia. Medicine. m. Robert Smith, 8 Mar 1966, 4 d. Education: MBBS (Hons), Sydney Univ; Dip RCPath; RCDA; HGSACC. Appointments: Res, Roy Prince Alfred Hosp; Medl Offr, Dept of Hlth, NSW. Memberships: Hum

Genetics Soc of Australasia; Aust Assn of Cytogenics (ASOC); Fndr, Past Pres, Medl Womens Soc, Past Pres. Hobbies: Literature Discussion Group. Address: 245 The Promenade, Sans Souci 2219, Australia.

SMITH Bernard William, b. 3 Oct 1916, Aust. Senior Associate. Education: Univ Sydney, Warburg Inst, London Univ, ANU. Appointments: Sch Tchr, 1935-44; Educ Off, Art Gall, NSW, 1944-52; Mbr, Aust Hum Rsch Cncl, 1956-68; Lectr, Snr Lectr, 1955-63, Rdr, Fine Arts, Univ Melbourne, 1964-66; Art Critic, The Age, Melbourne, 1963-66; Power Prof, Contemporary Art and Dir, Power Inst, Fine Arts Univ Sydney, 1967-77; Pres, Aust Acady Humanities, 1977-80; Snr Assoc, Dept of Fine Arts, Univ Melbourne, 1977-. Publications: Place, Taste and Tradition, 1945; European Vision and the South Pacific, 1960; Australian Painting, 1962; Architectural Character of Glebe Sydney, 1973; Documents on Art and Taste in Australia, 1975; The Antipodean Manifesto, 1976; The Boy Adeodatus, 1985; The Art of Captain Cook's Voyages, 1985-87; The Death of the Artist as Hero, 1988; The Critic as Advocate, 1989; Imagining the Pacific, 1992; Noel Counihan, 1993; Poems: 1938-1993, 1996; Modernisms' History, 1998. Honours: Chevalier dans l'Ordre des Arts et Lettres; Henry Lawson Fest Awd Prize for Poetry; Ernest Scott Prize for Aust Hist, Univ Melbourne; Hon LittD, Sydney. Hobbies: Swimming; Walking. Address: Jeansville, 168 Nicholson Street, Fitzroy, Victoria 3065, Australia.

SMITH Brenda Margaret, b. 15 Sept 1951, Eng. Chemical Engineer. Education: BS (Hons), Chem Engrng, ACGI. Memberships: Inst of Petroleum. Hobbies: Field hockey; Sailing. Address: Block F, Lot 231, DD 229, Clear Water Bay, Kowloon, Hong Kong.

SMITH Damien Patrick, b. 26 June 1945, Melbourne, Vic, Aust. Optometrist. m. Helen Elizabeth Dickinson, 18 May 1968, 3 s, 1 d. Education: BAppSc, 1967, MSc, 1970, PhD, 1974, Univ of Melbourne; Licentiate Dip of Optometric Sci, 1968; Fellshp, Amn Acady of Optometry, 1974; Vic Coll of Optometry. Appointments: Natl Dir, Austl Optometrical Assn, 1972-80; Sec-Gen, Intl Fedn of Asian and Pacific Assn of Optometrists, 1978-95; Pvte Clin Prac, 1980-; Dir, 20/20 Laser Vision, 1998-. Publications: Contr of 51 pprs in sci and profl jrnls. Honours: Inaugural Ivor G Lewis Mem Medal; Inaugural Disting Intl Serv Awd, Samahan NG Optometrist SA Pilipinas, 1988; Disting Serv Awds, Japan Optometric Assn, Indonesian Optical Assn, Malaysian Optical Assn; Disting Person Mbr Inaugural Awd, Asia-Pacific Cncl of Optometry, 1995; Intl Optometrist of the Yr, World Cncl of Optometry, 1995; Disting Practitioner and Mbr, Natl Acady of Practice in Optometry, 1995; AM, 1995; DOS, honoris causa, New Eng Coll of Optometry, 1996; Prestl Awd and Citation for Meritorious Serv, Asia-Pacific Cncl of Optometry, Seoul, S Korea, 1997; 4th K B Woo Meml Oration, Manila, 1999. Memberships: Austl Hlth Assn; Austl Optometric Panel; Dir, Austl Refractive Surg Grp; Natl Vision Rsch Inst of Aust; Fell, Am Acady of Optometry; Austl Optometrical Assn; Contact Lens Soc of Aust; Governing Bd, World Cncl of Optometry, 1998-. Hobbies: Skiing; Golf; Scuba Diving. Address: Davies Building, 7 Cookson Street, Camberwell, Vic 3124, Australia.

SMITH (Ernest) Ross, b. 24 Jan 1938, Southport, Qld. Member of Parliament. m. Sarah, 2 ss, 4 d. Education: Tchrs Cert, Balmain Tchrs Coll, 1956; JP, NSW, 1965. Appointments: Primary Tchr, NSW Educ Dept, 1957-59; Immigration Dept, Aust House, London, 1960; Jrnlst, Daily Telegraph and Sydney Sun, 1961-64; Regular Army Offr, 1964-84; Elected MLA, Glen Waverley, 1985, re-elected 1988, 1992, 1996; Socl Dev Cttee and Legal and Constl Cttee, 1988-92; Pub Acts and Estimates Cttee, 1992-96; LA Privilege Cttee, 1992-; Govt Whip, LA, 1996-. Memberships: Brentwood Second Coll Cncls; People Against Child Exploitation; Barracks Offrs Mess; Waverley RSL; Aust Family Assn; Hon Mbr, Mulgrave Rotary Club. Address: 73 Railway Parade, Glen Waverley, Vic 3150, Australia.

SMITH Edgar Roderick, b. 17 Sept 1944. Mathematician; Professor. m. Sian Scott Jones, 21 Apr

1979, 2 s, 3 d. Education: BSc, Melbourne; PhD, London. Appointments: Assoc Prof, Maths, Univ of Newcastle, 1973-76; Reader, Univ of Melbourne, Aust, 1976-85; Prof, La Trobe Univ, 1985-; Dean, Fac of Sci and Technol, LTU, 1996-; Pro Vice Chan, Info Technol, LTU, 1995-. Membership: Melbourne Cricket Club. Hobbies: Watching cricket; Cabinet making. Address: Faculty Office, Faculty of Science and Technology, La Trobe University, Bundoora, Vic 3083, Australia.

SMITH Edward Durham, b. 27 May 1992, Sunderland, Eng. Paediatric Surgeon. m. Dorothy Lois, 28 Dec 1948, 4 s. Education: MCEGS, MBBS, 1948; MD 1967, MS 1972, Melbourne Univ; Fell, Roy Australasian Coll of Surgs, 1956; Fell, Amn Coll of Surgs, 1963. Appointments: Res, then Registrar, 1948-49 and 1953-56, Alfred Hosp, Melbourne, Postgrad trng in Gen Surg, Neurosurgery & Paediat Surg, 1953-58, Alfred and Roy Children's Hosps, Melbourne; Fell, Boston Children's Hosp, USA, Hosp for Sick Children London, 1959; Paediat Surg, Alfred Hosp, 1960-65; Surg Rsch Fell, 1957-75; Snr Paediat Surg, 1965-87; Hon Cnslt, 1987-, Roy Children's Hosp, Melbourne; Snr Paediat Surg, 1971-87, Mercy Hosp for Women, Melbourne; Snr Paediat Surg, 1982-87, St George's Hosp, Melbourne; Chmn, Bd of Paediat Surg, 1980-86, Examiner, 1972-83 and Chmn of Crt of Examiners, 1983-87; Snr VP 1985-87, Pres 1987-89, Exex Dir Surg Affairs 1989-92, Roy Australasian Coll of Surgs, Snr Assoc in Surg, 1965-86, Univ of Melbourne. Publications: 4 books on Paediatric Surgery: Spina Bifida and the Total Care of Myelomeningocele, 1963; Ano-Rectal Malformations in Children, 1971; The Care of an Ileal Conduit and Urinary Appliances in Children, 1976; Ano-Rectal Malformations: Update, 1988; Num papers on paediatric urology and hypospadias and chapts in 11 books. Honours: Simpson-Smith Prize, London Univ, Eng, 1959; Hon Mbr, Amn Paediat Surg Assn, 1986; Gold Medal for Paediat Surg, Roy Children's Hosp, Melbourne, 1987; Hon Mbr, Brit Assn Paediat Surgs, 1988; Hon Fell, Roy Coll of Surgs: In Ireland 1987 Eng 1988, Edinburgh 1988, Glasgow 1990, Coll of Surgs S Afr 1990, Jap 1995; Devine Medal, Roy Australasian Coll of Surgs, 1990; AO, 1991; Denis Browne Gold Medal, Brit Assn Paediat Surgeons, 1996. Memberships: Australasian Assn of Paediat Surgs, Pres 1985-87; Pacific Assn of Paediat Surgs, Pres 1984-85; World Fedn of Paediat Surg Assns, VP 1974-80; Intl Fedn of Surg Colls, Hon Sec 1991-95; Urological Soc of Australasia; Austl Med Assn; Austl Assn of Surgs. Hobbies: Music; Tennis; Golf; Gardening; Carpentry; Clubs: Melbourne Club, Melbourne Cricket Club, Kew Golf Club. Listed in: Who's Who in Australia. Address: Unit 3, 42 Severn Street, North Balwyn, Vic 3104, Australia.

SMITH Gordon Keys, b. 9 Nov 1915, Colac, Vic, Aust. Surgeon. m. Rosa Catherine Baker, 22 Nov 1941, 1 s, 1 d. Education: MMBS, 1940, BA, 1983, Univ of Melbourne; FRACS; FACRM; BD, Melbourne Coll of Divinity, 1991. Appointments: Lectr in Anatomy, Univ of Melbourne, 1946-48; Chf Med Offr, St Andrew's Hosp for Children, Singapore, 1948-60; Med Supt, Orth Sect, 1960-70, Dir, Handicapped Children's Cntr, 1970-78, Roy Children's Hosp, Melbourne, Vic. Publications: 33 jrnl articles and chapts in books on med subjs, esp rehab. Honour: OBE, 1982. Memberships: Austl Coll of Paediats; Med Cnslt, Epilepsy Fndn, 1979-90; Natl Advsry Cncl for Handicapped, 1980-83; Pres, Yooralla Soc, 1980-83; Vic Consultative Cncl on Rehab, 1981-86. Hobbies: Classical studies; Theology; Natural history. Listed in: Who's Who in Australia. Address: 3 Berwick Street, Camberwell, Vic 3124, Australia.

SMITH L Ann, b. 4 Aug 1942, Leicester, Eng. Musician; Teacher. m. 1 d. Education: Roy Acady of Music, London, 1960-62; LRAM, Tchr Dip. Appointments: Tchr, Overstone Sch, Northampton, 1963-66, Ladies Coll, Ballarat, Aust, 1967-68; Bushey, Herts, Eng, 1970, Ballarat High, Aust, 1970-87; Presently i/c of String Prog, Conductor of String Orch and Chmbr Orch, Ballarat and Clarendon Coll; Vocal Soloist; Mngr, Ballarat Symph Orch. Creative Works: Performances incl: Gall String Quartet; Player, Cttee Mbr, Ballarat Symph Orch.

Membership: Austl String Tchrs Assn. Hobby: Philately. Address: 340 Spencer Street, Ballarat East, Vic 3350, Australia.

SMITH Lawrence Ralph, b. 6 Jan 1928, Melbourne, Aust. Managing Director. m. Betty Catherine Feehan, 25 Nov 1950, 1 s. Education: Assoc, Roy Melbourne Inst of Technol, 1950. Appointments: Tech Offr, Materials Rsch Labs, 1951-55; Rsch Chem, Olympic Tyre & Rubber Co Ltd, 1956-58; Tech Mngr, Ormiston Rubber Co, 1959-64 Gen Mngr, Ormiston Roer Co, 1965-75; Mktng & Tech Dir, 1975-87, Mngng Dir, 1987-, Continental Carbon Aust Ltd. Honours: George Milne Mem Medal, 1975; Fell, Plastic & Rubber Ind, England, 1983; Fell, Soc of Snr Execs, 1987. Memberships: Plastics & Rubber Ind Assn; Soc of Snr Execs; Cttee, Econ Devel of Aust; Austl Indonesian Bus Cncl. Hobbies: Boating; Yachting; Walking; Photography. Address: Essington Crescent, Sylvania, NSW 2224, Australia.

SMITH Leo, b. 21 Mar 1938. Education: Victoria Univ, NZ. Appointments: Prime Min's nominee, Senate, 1985-91; Mbr of Parl, Northern Eastern Gen Constituency, 1987; Fndr Mbr and Natl Gen Sec, Gen Voters' Party, 1990; Elected to Parl, 1991; Min for Hlth, 1992; Min for Infrastructure and Pub Wrks, 1993; Min for Hlth, 1996-98. Address: PO Box 2223, Government Buildings, Suva, Fiji.

SMITH Lincoln Cain, b. 8 Oct 1971, Taree, Aust. Bank Manager. m. Helen Grace Richardson, 12 Oct 1996. Education: Higher Sch Cert, 1989. Appointments: Bank Offr, 1989; Supvsr, 1993; Mngr Personal Lending, 1995; Rel Mngr, 1997; Mngr, Sales and Serv, Commonwealth Bank of Aust, 1999; Composer and keyboard performer for pop groups Boxy Smith and Necrophilia. Membership: Austl Inst of Bankers. Hobbies: Stock Trading; Travelling; Snow skiing. Address: PO Box 917 Maroubra 2035, NSW, Aust.

SMITH Michael Kevin, b. 8 Nov 1955, Portsmouth, OH, USA. Research Scientist. m. Judy Hillhouse, 11 Dec 1976, 3 s. Education: BS, 1977; BS (Hons), 1978; PhD, 1982. Appointments: Postdoct Rsch Assoc, ARCO, Plant Cell Rsch Inst (USA), 1982-83; Scientist ARCO Seed Co (USA), 1983-84; Rsch Fell, Univ of Queensland (Aust), 1984-85; Biotechnologist, Queensland Dept of Primary Inds (Aust), 1985-90; Snr Biotechnologist, QDPI, 1990-97; Prin Biochemist, QDPI, 1997-; Chf Sci Investigator, FAO/IAEA, 1989-93. Publications: 25 articles in intl sci jrnls; Over 140 publs in conf proceedings, workshops and tech newsletters. Honours: Eagle Scout, Boy Scout Assn of Am, 1971; Queen's Scout, Boy Scout Assn of Aust, 1974; Commonwealth Postgrad Rsch Awd, Austl Govt, 1978-81. Memberships: Intl Assn for Plant Tissue Culture, 1978-, Natl Corresp, 1990-94; Austl Soc of Plant Physiologists, 1984-; Austl Soc of Horticultural Sci, 1991-; Intl Soc of Horticultural Sci, 1997-. Hobbies: Bushwalking; Camping; Birdwatching. Address: Queensland Horticulture Institute, Maroochy, QDPI, Box 5083, SCMC, Nambour, Qld, Australia.

SMITH Nick R, b. 1964. Government Minister. m. Cyndy, 1 d. Education: 1st Class Hons Deg, PhD, Engrng, Canterbury Univ. Appointments: Elected to Parl, Nelson, 1990; Min responsible for Educ Review Off, Min of Conservation. Memberships: VP, NZ Young Nationals; Rangiora Dist Cnclr. Address: 544 Waimea Road, Annesbrook, Nelson, New Zealand.

SMITH Richard John, b. 14 Dec 1934 Tamworth NSW. Diplomatist. m. Janet Campbell, 1958, 2 s, 2 d. Education: Sydney High Sch; Sydney Univ. Appointments: Tchr London, 1958-59; Solicitor NSW, 1959-61; For Affairs trainee, 1961; First Sec WA, 1967-70; Dep Perm Rep Austl Miss to the UN Geneva, 1972-74; Asst Sec Intl Legal Branch, 1974-75; Amb to Israel, 1975-77; First Asst Sec Legal and Treaties Div, 1977-81; First Asst Sec Mngmnt and For Serv Div, 1981-83; Acting Dep Sec Dept of For Affairs, 1983-85; Amb to Thailand, 1985-88; Dep Sec Dept of For Affairs and Trade Canberra, 1988-90; High Commnr in UK,

1991-94; Amb to the Philippines, 1994-96; Dir Gen Off of Natl Assessments Canberra, 1996-. Hobbies: Walking; Reading; Travel. Address: Office of National Assessments, P O Box E436, Queen Victoria Terrace, Canberra, ACT 2600, Australia.

SMITH Ross, b. 27 Nov 1950, Melbourne, Aust. University Lecturer. m. Helen Yvonne Prentice, 1 d. Education: BS (Hons); PhD, Melbourne Univ; Grad Dip, Computer Studies, Canberra Univ. Appointments: Melbourne Univ, 1977; Austl Natl Univ, 1978-84; Def Sci and Technol Org, 1984-89; Swinburne Univ of Technol, 1989-99; Deakin Univ, 1999-. Publications: Over 75 jrnl articles, conf pprs, book chapts on info technol, computational phys and def sci. Honours: Wyselaski Prize, Melbourne Univ, 1972; Dunlop Schlshp, Melbourne Univ, 1973; Kernot Rsch Schlshp, 1973. Memberships; Austl Computer Soc; UK Systems Soc; Intl Soc for the Systems Scis; ACM. Hobbies: Reading; Gardening; Watching cricket. Address: 7 Dickinson Street, Belgrave, Vic 3160, Australia.

SMITH Russell Hugh, b. 10 Mar 1930, Warracknabeal, Vic, Aust. Senior Lecturer; Freelance Opera and Concert Singer. m. Anje Kristin Marten, 30 Oct 1964, 1 s, 1 d. Education: Assoc, Austl Soc of Accts, 1954; Assoc, Guildhall Sch of Music, London, Eng, 1962; BA Music 1979, MMus 1987, Tas; Mbr, Austl Coll of Educ, 1984; PhD, Tas, 1997. Appointments include: Acct, Melbourne and London, 1950-60; Student, London and Germany, 1960-64; Bass-Buffo, var German Theatres, 1963-70; Lectr, Snr Lectr, Music Fac, Univ of Tas, Aust, 1970; Snr Lectr, Resigned 1993; Intl Opera Dir, Singer and Concert Artist. Performances include: Sung over 70 operatic roles, directed over 35 operas; Natl concert artist & broadcaster; Unpubls dissertations; Elements of Opera Seria in Mozart Arias; Lortzing's Der Wildschütz; Biography: Peter Dawson (1882-1961). Honours: May Cattel Schlsp, singing, Guildhall Sch, 1960-62; Silver Jubilee Cup, best stud, ibid, 1961; Deutscher Akademischer Austauschdienst Schlshp, DAAD, 1962-64; DAAD Wiedereinladung, 1982-83; Italian Govt Schlshp, 1992; OAM, 1993. Memberships: Austl Soc of Accts; Austl Coll of Educ, Pres 1980-84; Rosny Children's Choir, Exec Dir, Tas Opera Co, 1971-75. Hobbies: Horse Riding; Bushwalking. Listed in: Who's Who in Australia. Address: 428 Nelson Road, Mount Nelson, Tas 7007, Australia.

SMITH Stephen Francis, b. 12 Dec 1955. Member of Parliament. m. Jane Seymour, 1 s, 1 d. Education: BA, Univ of WA; BLaw, Univ of WA; MLaw, London Univ, Eng. Appointments: Articled Law Clk, Bar and Sol, Law Lectr and Tutor, 1978-83; Prin Pvte Sec, Atty Gen of WA, 1983-87; State Sec, WA Br of Austl Labor Party, 1987-91; Snr Advsr to Dpty PM/Treas and Min for Sci and Technol, 1991; Spec Advsr to PM of Aust, 1992; Fed Mbr for Perth, 1993; Shadow Min for Trade, 1996-97; Shadow Min for Resources and Energy, 1997-98; Shadow Min for Comms, 1998-. Address: 43 Old Perth Road, Bassendean, WA 6054, Australia.

SMITH Sydney Thomas, b. 15 Nov 1941. Educationalist; Manager, Environmental Education Unit. m. Marilyn Moreen Smith, 19 May 1981, 3 s. Education: MEd, Univ Sydney; BA, Univ of New Eng. Appointments: Tchr Primary and Secnd; NSW Dept Educ, 1961-77; Curric Cnslt, 1978-87; Insp of Schs, 1988-89; Dir of Schs, 1990-94; Mngr Quality Ass, 1995; Mngr, Environmental Educ, NSW Dept Educ and Trng, 1996-99. Publications: Jacaranda Atlas Program, 1983; Conflict at Kurnell, 1976; Accent on Work, 1988; Heinmann Primary Atlas, 1995; Pathways to Geography, 1996. Honours: Aust Bookpubrs Awd for Best Sch Educl Publ, 1995 for Heinemann Atlas and Skills Book. Memberships: Aust Coll of Educ; Inst of Snr Educl Admnstrs; Austl Assn of Environl Educators; Austl Rep, OECD proj, Environ and Sch Initiatives. Hobbies: Gardening; Photography; Stamps; Bushwalking. Address: 25A Finlay Road, Turramurra, NSW 2074, Australia.

SMITH Trevor William, b. 16 Feb 1951, Portsmouth, UK. Trade Union Official. 1 s. Appointments: Natl Pres,

Constrn, Forestry, Mining and Energy union (CFMEU); Natl Sec, Forestry and Forest Bldg Prods Mgng Div (Forestry div - formally the Austl Timber Workers Union (ATWU) of the CFMEU; Chairperson, Forest and Forest Prods Employment Skills Co (FAFPESC); Co-Chair Timber Ind Superannuation Scheme (TISS); Dir, IFS; Govt Wood and Ppr Ind Forum Mbr; Dir, ACTU Organising Wrks; Wages Cttee, Austl Cncl of Trade Unions (ACTU); Intl Cttee, ACTU; VP, Intl Fedn of Bldg and Wood Workers (IFBWW); Mbr, Mngmt Cttee, Exec Cttee, Chairperson Asia-Pacific Reg, Wood and Forestry Hlth Cttee Mbr, IFBWW. Hobbies: Golf; Cricket; Football; Soccer. Address: Level 3, Trades Hall, South Toe, Adelaide 5000, Australia.

SMITH Vivian Brian, b. 3 June 1933, Hobart, Tasmania. Writer. m. Sybille Gottwald, 15 Feb 1960, 1 s, 2 d. Education: BA; MA, Tasmania; PhD, Sydney. Appointments: Rdr in Engl, Univ of Sydney, 1985-1995 (retd, 1995). Publications: 21 books, Most Recent New Selected Poems, 1995. Honours: Grace Leven Prize, 1985; NSW Premier's Prize for Poetry, 1985; The Patrick White Lit Awd, 1997. Membership: Austl Soc of Authors. Address: 19 McLeod Street, Mosman, NSW 2088, Australia.

SMITH Warren Morrison, b. 15 Mar 1945, New Zealand. Cardiologist. m. 2 Mar 1974, 2 s, 1 d. Education: Stud, 1963-68, MB ChB, 1968, Otago Univ; MRACP, 1973; FRACP, 1976. Appointments: House Staff Trng, Auckland Hosps, 1969-70; Volun Serv, Malaysia, 1971, 1972-73; Medl Tutor, Auckland Hosp, 1974-75; Cardiology Fell, 1975-79; Assoc Dir, Electrophysiology Lab, Duke, 1979-80; Cardiologist, Greenlane Hosp, 1981-97; Personal Physn to PM, 1988. Publications: Contbr of chapts in books; Over 50 articles in medl jrnls. Honours: RMH Mem Prize, Med, Auckland, 1968; Heart Fndn Overseas Fellshp, 1978. Memberships: Roy Australasian Coll Physns; Cardiac Soc Aust and NZ; Medico-Legal Soc; Intl Physns Against Nuc War; Sci Cttee, Natl Heart Fndn; Scientific Cttee, Natl Heart Fndn, 1992-98; NASPE, 1996-98. Hobbies: Tramping; Ancient Roman and Greek history; Films. Listed in: Who's Who in the World. Address: 1A Lurline Avenue, Epsom, Auckland, New Zealand.

SMITH Wendy Irene, b. 6 June 1950, Adelaide, Australia. Member of Parliament. m. Michael, 3 s, 1 d. Education: BA, Melbourne Univ. Appointment: Min Advsr, Maj Projects, 1993-96. Hobbies: Archaeology; Music; Swimming. Address: 13A Civic Place, Ringwood, Victoria, Australia.

SMUTS-KENNEDY Olive Evelyn, b. 23 Mar 1925, Wellington, NZ. Retired Lawyer; Mediator. m. Arthur Edward Smuts-Kennedy, 14 Apr 1945, 1 s, 2 d. Education: BA, 1954; LLB, 1955; Dip Bus Studies (Dispute Resolution), 1997. Appointments: Practised Law, 1955-93; Hon Sol, Natl Cncl of Women, 1958-66; Chairperson, Cncl for Equal Pay and Opportunity, 1960-65; Wellington City Cnclr, 1965-74; Chmn for Cultural, Libs & Pub Rels Cttee, 1968-74; Chf Legal Advsr, Health Dept, 1976-85. Publication: Ed, A Tree Evaluation Method for New Zealand, Royal New Zealand Institute of Horticulture, 1988. Honour: Queens Serv Order, 1990. Memberships: Assoc Mbr, NZ Law Soc; Fell, Arbitrators and Mediators Inst of NZ. Listed in: New Zealand Aotearoa Who's Who. Hobbies: Gardening; Visual Arts. Address: PO Box 333, Waikanae, 6454, New Zealand.

SMYTH Dacre Henry Deudraeth, b. 5 May 1923, London, Eng. Retired Naval Officer; Artist. m. Jennifer Haggard, 11 Jan 1952, 1 s, 4 d. Appointments: Roy Aust Navy (retd as Commodore), 1940-78; Dir, David Syme Co, Publishers, 1982-94; Dpty Chmn, Tstees Of The Shrine Of Remembrance. Creative Works: 23 one-man painting exhibns held; 11 books of paintings publshd: The Bridges of the Yarra, 1979; The Lighthouses Of Victoria, 1980; Historic Ships Of Australia, 1982; Old Riverboats Of The Murray, 1982; Views Of Victoria, 1984; The Bridges of Kananook Creek, 1986; Waterfalls Of Victoria, 1988; Gallipoli Pilgrimage, 1990; Immigrant Ships To

Australia, 1992; Pictures In My Life, 1994; Images of Melbourne, 1998. Honours: AO, 1977; Intl Order of Merit, 1992; Off, Order of Merit Of France, 1994. Memberships: Victorian Artists Soc; Aust Guild of Realist Artists; Tstee, Victorian Shrine Of Remembrance, Overseas Studs Assistance Fund; Cncl Aust Maritime Trust; Past Pres, Bayside Area, Scout Assn. Hobbies: Painting; Writing; Creating stained glass windows. Address: 22 Douglas Street, Toorak, Vic 3142, Australia.

SNAPE Leslie, b. 27 Jan 1947, Chesterfield, Eng. Maxillofacial Surgeon. m. Ruth, 14 Apr 1979, 2 children. Education: MBChB, hons, Univ Bristol; FRCS, Edinburgh; BDS, hons, Univ Bristol; FFDRCS, Ireland; FRACDS. Appointments: Cnslt, Oral & Maxillofacial Surgn, Canterbury Hlth Ltd, Christchurch Hosp, 1987-; Clin Snr Lectr, Oral and Maxillofacial Surg, Univ of Otago, 1993-, Dept of Surg, Christchurch Clin Sch of Med, 1998-. Publications: 10 articles in profl jrnls. Memberships: Austl and NZ Assn of Oral and Maxillofacial Surngs; Brit Assn of Oral and Maxillofacial Surgns; Examiner, Oral and Maxillofacial Surg, RACDS. Hobbies: Tramping; Skiing; Travel. Address: Oral and Maxillofacial Surgery, Christchurch School of Medicine, PO Box 4345, Christchurch, New Zealand.

SNELLING Michael, b. 29 Dec 1950, Sydney, Aust. m. Suhanya Raffel, 2 s. Appointments: Dir, Experimental Art Fndn, 1987-89; Prog Mngr, Aust Cncl, 1989-94; Dir, Inst of Modern Art, Brisbane, Aust, 1994-. Publications: Artistic Dir, IMA, 1994-; Mngng Ed, IMA Publng; Curator (w Clare Williamson) Above & Beyond, 1996. Honours: Aust Japan Arts Network Residency, 1999. Memberships: Pres, Contemporary Art Orgns, Aust; Chair, Asialink Visual Arts Panel. Hobbies: Talking and listening; Parenting; Swimming; Arts. Address: IMA GPO Box 1897, Brisbane, 2001 Australia.

SNOOKS Graeme Donald, b. 22 July 1944, Perth, Aust. Research Professor of Economics. m. Loma Rae Graham, 24 Jan 1970, 2 s. Education: BEc, hons, 1966, MEc, 1968, Univ of WA; PhD, Austl Natl Univ, 1972. Appointments: Lectr, Univ of Qld, 1971-72; Lectr, 1973-74, Snr Lectr, 1975-83, Rdr, 1984-89, Flinders Univ; Coghlan Rsch Prof, Austl Natl Univ, 1989-; Hd, Dept of Econ Hist, Rsch Sch of Socl Scis, Austl Natl Univ, 1989-97. Publications include: Depression and Recovery, 1974; Domesday Economy, 1986; Economics Without Time, 1993; Historical Analysis in Economics, 1993; Economic Policy in Australia Since the Great Depression, 1993; Portrait of the Family, 1994; Was the Industrial Revolution Necessary?, 1994; The Dynamic Society, 1996; The Ephemeral Civilization, 1997; The Laws of History, 1998; Longrun Dynamics, 1998; Global Transition, 1999; The Global Crisis Makers, 1999; Over 70 articles in acad jrnls; Ed, MacMillan Econ Hist of SE Asia (20 vols), 1990-; Ed, Austl Econ Hist Review, 1988-1996. Honours: Fell, Roy Histl Soc, 1989; Fell, Austl Socl Sci Acady, 1991. Memberships include: Cliometric Soc; Econ Hist Soc, UK; Econ Hist Assn, USA; NY Acady of Scis, 1995. Hobbies: Ecology; Fishing; Gardening; Literature; Art. Listed in: Who's Who in the World; Who's Who in Australia. Address: Department of Economics, Research School of Social Sciences, Australian National University, Canberra, ACT 0200, Australia.

SNOW Philip Albert, b. 7 Aug 1915. Author; Bibliographer; Administrator. m. Anne Harris, 1940, 1 d. Education: MA (Hons) Cambridge; FRAI, 1952. Appointments include: HM Colonial Admnstv Serv: Procl Commnr, Magistrate, Estab and Protocol Offr, Asst Colonial Sec, Fiji and West Pacific, 1937-52; ADC to Gov and C-in-C, Fiji, 1939; Dpty Sheriff, Fiji, 1940-52; Tstee, Fiji Mus, 1950-52; Offic Mbr, Legis Cncl, Fiji, 1951; Fiji Govt Liaison Offr, US and NZ Forces, 1942-44; Bursar, Rugby Sch, 1952-76. Publications include: Cricket in the Fiji Islands, 1949; Rock Carvings in Fiji, 1950; Report on the Visit of Three Bursars to the United States of America and Canada in 1964, 1965; Best Stories of the South Seas, 1967; Bibliography of Fiji, Tonga and Rotuma, vol 1, 1969; (co auth) The People From the Horizon: An Illustrated History of the Europeans among the South Sea Islanders, 1979; Stranger and Brother. A Portrait of C P

Snow, 1982; The Years of Hope: Cambridge, Colonial Administration in the South Seas, Cricket, 1997; A Time of Renewal: Clusters of Characters, C P Snow, Coups, 1998; Contbr, newspprs, mags, jrnls; Reviews, introductions to books. Honours include: JP; For Ldr Specialist Awd, US Govt, 1964; Orgnr, Rugby Sch 400th anniversary celebrations, 1967; Hon Life Mbr, MCC, 1970; Des, Fiji Govt stamps for centenary of Fiji cricket, 1974; MBE, 1979; OBE, 1985; Indep Silver Jubilee Medal, Fiji, 1995. Memberships include: FRSA; FRAI; Fndr, 1946, Vice-Patron, 1952-, Fiji Cricket Assn; Capt, Fiji Cricket Team, NZ 1st-Class Tour, 1948; Perm Repr, Fiji, Intl Cricket Confs, 1964-90; Liaison Offr and Acting Mngr first Fiji Cricket Team in Eng, 1979; Perm Repr, Fiji Intl Cricket Cncl, 1990-94. Hobbies: Taming robins; Formerly cricket; Chess (half-Blue); Table-tennis (half-Blue and Cambs); Deck-tennis; Tennis. Address: Gables, Station Road, Angmering, West Sussex, BN16 4HY, England.

SNOW Rodney James, b. 5 Oct 1959, Melbourne. Academic; Exercise Biochemist. m. Andrea, 9 Nov 1986, 1 s, 1 d. Education: BA, Applied Sci; MA, Applied Sci; PhD. Appointments: Snr Lectr, Dept of Chem and Biol, 1993; Lectr, 1989; Lectr, Sch of Hum Movement, Deakin Univ, 1997. Publications: 17 Rfrd Sci Jrnl Articles. Memberships: Sports Med Aust. Address: Sch of Human Movement, Deaking University, 221 Burwood Hwy, Burwood 3125, Australia.

SNOWDON John Ambler, b. 30 Apr 1940, Warlingham, England. Psychiatrist. m. Elizabeth, 16 June 1979, 2 s, 1 d. Education: MA, MB, BChir, Cambridge Univ, Eng; MPhil, London Univ, Eng; MD, Univ of NSW; FRACP; FRCPsych; FRANZCP. Appointments: Snr Spec, Prince of Wales and Prince Henry Hosp, 1977-92; Dir, Psychogeriatric Servs, Cntrl Sydney Health Serv, Assoc Prof, Univ of Sydney, Aust, 1992-. Publications: Pprs in jrnls on psych. Memberships: Chair, Fac of Psych of Old Age, 1995-; Vice Chmn, Psych Rehab Assn, 1995-. Hobbies: Tennis; Theatre. Address: Rozelle Hospital, PO Box 1, Rozelle, NSW 2039, Australia.

SNUGGS Olive, b. 26 Nov 1924, Coventry, Eng. Retired Freelance Writer. m. Eric, 29 Jan 1944, 1 s, 4 d. Publications: (poetry books) Ollies Overtures, vols 1 & 2, 1985; Reflections in Cameo, 1986; (prose) I Came a Migrant, 1990; Striped Caps and Saturday Serials, 1996. Memberships: Fellshp Austl Writers; Writers Profl Servs; S Aust Writers Cntr; World Poetry Soc; Enfield Writers Club. Hobbies: Reading; Writing poetry; Children's stories; Short stories; Reading poetry (performance). Address: 6 Jacaranda Drive, Salisbury East, South Australia 5109, Australia.

SOEHARTONO Irawan, b. 22 Dec 1940, Magelang, Indonesia. Lecturer. m. Ramlah, 25 June 1964, 1 s, 2 d. Education: Dr of Socl Welfare, Columbia Univ Sch of Socl Work. Appointments: Lectr, Bandung Coll of Socl Welfare; Snr Lectr, Sch of Socl & Polit Scis, Pasundan Univ, Indonesia; Lectr, Sch of Socl Scis, Univ of Sci, Malaysia. Membership: Malaysia Assn of Socl Workers. Hobbies: Reading; Music. Address: Taman Desa Permai Indah, M-11-2 Jalan Helang, Sungai Dua 11700, Penang, Malaysia.

SOETANTO Melinda, b. 10 Oct 1964, Indonesia. Director. Education: BSc, Computer Application and Systems; MBA, Intl Bus. Hobbies: Travel; Skiing; Tennis; Music; Reading. Address: Orchard Post Office, PO Box 224, Singapore 912308, Singapore.

SOEYA Yoshihide, b. 1 May 1955, Ibaraki, Japan. Professor. m. Kazuko. Education: PhD, Polit Sci, Univ MI, USA. Appointment: Rsch Assoc, Rsch Inst for Peace & Security, Tokyo. Publications: Japan's Economic Diplomacy with China, 1945-1978, 1998. Memberships: Assn for Asian Studies, USA; IISS, London; Japan Assn for Intl Studies. Address: 2-15-45 Mita, Minato-ku, Tokyo 108-8345, Japan.

SOGIURA Nobuaki, b. 1 Feb 1956, Aichi, Prefecture, Japan. Electronic Mechanic. m. 7 Oct 1984, 3 s.

Education: BS, Nagoya Inst of Technol, 1979; MS, Nagoya Univ, 1981; Dr, 1997. Memberships: IEEE; IEICEI IMAPS. Address: 1458-9 Kitairiso, Sayama 350-1315, Japan.

SOH Chin Thack, b. 30 Jan 1921, Korea. Doctor; Professor. m. Moon-Ae Roh, 12 Sept 1942, 2 s, 4 d. Education: Yonsei Univ Medl Coll; DMS, Yonsei Univ Grad Sch. Appointments: Prof, Parasitology, 1957-86, Dir, Yonsei Univ, Inst of Tropical Med, 1969-86; Prof of Parasitology, Wonkwang Univ, 1987-98; Advsr, Mbr, World Hlth Org, 1984-88. Publications: Parasitic Diseases, 1975; Amoebiasis in Korea, 1981; Contbr of num articles. Honour: Natl Prize, Magnolia, 1986. Memberships: Korean Soc of Parasitology; Korean Soc of Electromicroscopy; Hon Mbr, Amn Soc of Tropical Med & Hygiene. Address: Department of Parasitology, Wonkwang University Medical College, Sinyong-dong, Dksan Jeonra-buk-do, Korea.

SOHAIL H Masood, b. 2 Apr 1933, Khanpur, Pakistan. Business Executive. m. Nadira, 7 July 1962, 1 , 2 d. Education: BS (Hons) Phys, Univ of Karachi; BSE (Mech), MSE (Mech), Univ of MI, USA. Appointments: Worked w cnsltng engrs in Ann Arbor, MI, 1957-58; Joined Pakistan Pet Ltd (PPL), Sept 1958-; Var tech and managerial positions, 1958-1990; CEO and MD, 1990-97; Chmn, PPL's Bd, 1997-. Publications: pprs in natl and intl symposia on var subjs. Memberships: Soc of Pet Engrs; Inst of Engrs (Pak); Pakistan Engrng Cncl; Dir, Sui South Gas Co; Bd of Govs, Indus Valley Sch of Art and Arch; Bd Dirs, Oil and Gas Dev Co. Hobby: Social work. Address: Pakistan Petroleum Limited, PIDC House, 4th Floor, Dr Ziauddin Ahmed Road, PO Box 3942, Karachi 75530, Pakistan.

SOLIDUM Estrella D, b. 23 Nov 1927, Manila, Philippines. Professor of Political Science. m. Ifor B Solidum, 23 Nov 1954, 3 d. Education: AB, Polit Sci, 1951; MA, Polit Sci, 1955; MA, Polit Sci, 1968; PhD, Polit Sci, 1970. Appointments: Instr, 1962-70, Asst Prof, 1970-74, Assoc Prof, 1974-81, Full Prof, 1981-97, Univ of Philippines, Quezon Cty; Visng Prof: USA, 1976-77, 1981, German Dem Repub, 1978, Chulalonkorn Univ, Thailand, 1983, Free Univ, Berlin, 1984, Griffith Univ, Aust, 1987, Moscow State Univ, 1996. Publications: Towards a SE Asian Community, 1974; Security in a New Perspective, 1987; The Small State: Security and World Peace, 1991; About 45 articles in intl publs on Asean, security, regionalism. Honours: Rockefeller Fndn, 1965-70; Asian Schl in Res, Fulbright, 1976-77; Japan Fndn Fell, 1980; German Acad Exchange Serv, DAAD, 1984; Friedrich Ebert Stiftling Awd, 1986; Professorial Chairs, UP, 1982-93; Most Outstndng Fac Awd of Univ of the Philippines, 1992; Phi Kappa Phi; Pi Gamma Mu. Memberships: Trustee, Philippine Cncl for For Rels, 1989-; Philippine Soc of Intl Law; Natl Rsch Cncl of Philippines for Life; Philippine Polit Sci Assn; Pres, Univ of Philippines Fac Choral Ensemble, 1996-97. Hobbies: Music; Singing; Dancing; Travelling; Bible study. Address: 25 Road 4, Project 6, Quezon City, Philippines.

SOLIMAN Hani, b. 3 Sept 1938, Egypt. Geneticist; Higher Education Consultant. m. Izabel Soliman, 5 Aug 1970. Education: BSc, hons; MSc; MSc; PhD. Appointments: Grad Tchng Asst; Tchng Fell; Lectr; Assoc Prof; Prof; Mngng Dir, HI-Educonsult. Publications: Sev articles in profl jrnls. Honours: Num. Memberships: Am Assn for the Adv of Sci; NY Acady of Sci; Am Human Biol Cncl; Intl Soc for the Study of Evolution; Genetics Soc of Am. Hobbies: Travel; Stamp Collecting. Address: PO Box 1182, Armidale, NSW 2350, Australia.

SOLINGER Dorothy J, b. 20 Sept 1945, Cincinnati, Ohio, USA. Professor. m. Thomas P Bernstein, 23 Dec 1990. Education: BA, hons, Univ Chgo; MA, PhD, Stanford Univ. Appointment: Univ of Pitts; Univ of CA at Irvine. Publications include: Regional Government and Political Integration in Southwest China 1949-1954: A Case Study, 1977; Chinese Business Under Socialism: The Politics of Domestic Commerce 1949-1980, 1984; From Lathes to Looms: China's Industrial Policy in Comparative Perspective 1979-1982, 1991; China's

Transition From Socialism: Statist Legacies and Market Reforms 1980-1990, 1993; Contesting Citizenship in Urban China: Peasant Migrants, the State and the Logic of the Market, 1999; Three Visions of Chinese Socialism (ed), 1984; States and Sovereignty in the Global Economy (co-ed), 1999. Memberships: Assn for Asian Stdies; Amn Polit Sci Assn. Hobbies: Piano Playing; Swimming; Biking. Address: School of Social Sciences, University of California, Irvine, CA 92697, USA.

SOLIS PALMA Manuel. Politician. Appointments: Min of Educ, 1984-88; PM of Panama, 1988-89; First VP of Panama, 1988-89; Min in charge of the Presidency of the Repub, 1988-89. Address: c/o Office of the Prime Minister, Panama City, Panama.

SOLOMON David Henry, b. 19 Nov 1929, Adelaide, SA, Aust. Scientist. m. Valerie Dawn Newport, 28 Jan 1954, 3 d. Education: Assoc, Sydney Tech Coll, 1950; BSc Hons, NSW, Univ of Technol, 1952; PhD 1960, DSc 1969, Univ of NSW. Appointments: Balm Paints Pty Ltd, 1946-53; Demonstrator Tchr Fell, NSW Univ of Technol, 1953-55; Balm Paints Pty Ltd, 1955-63; Ldr, Resin and Polymer Rsch, 1959-63; Rsch Sci, CSIRO Div of Applied Mineralogy, 1963-70; CSIRO Div of Applied Organic Chem, 1970-86; Chief of Div, 1974-86; Acting Dir, CSIRO Inst of Indl Technologies, 1986-87; Chf of Div, CSIRO Div of Chems and Polymers, 1988-; Dpty Dir, CSIRO Inst of Indl Technologies, 1989-90; Prof of Chem, Univ of Melbourne, 1990-94; Professorial Fell, Dept of Chem Engrng, Univ of Melbourne, 1995-. Creative Works: 6 books, over 184 sci publs, 23 patents, books: The Chemistry of Organic Film Formers, 1967; Step-Growth Polymerizations - Kinetics and Mechanisms Polyesterification, 1972; The Chemistry of Organic Film Former, 2nd ed, 1977; The Catalytic Properties of Pigments, 1977; The Chemistry of Pigments and Fillers, 1983; Free Radical Polymerization, 1995. Honours: Archibald D Olle Prize of NSW Br, 1967; H G Smith Mem Medal of RACI (shared w CCJ Culvenor), 1971; David Syme Rsch Prize, 1976; Polymer Medal, 1977; Liversidge Lectr, 1977; Applied Rsch Medal, 1980; Hartung Youth Lectr, 1982; Leighton Mem Medal, 1985; TGH Jones Lectr, 1986; Austl Bicentennial Sci Achievement Awd, 1989; CSIRO Medal (shared w Mr D Addison), 1987; Ian Wark Medal and Lectr, 1989-; AM, 1990; Clunies Ross Sci and Technol Awd, 1994. Memberships: Fell, Roy Austl Chem Inst; Austl Acady of Sci; Austl Acady of Technological Scis and Engrng. Hobbies: Farming; Interests: Government/Industry interactions with Particular Emphasis on Establishing a Viable Manufacturing Industry. Address: Department of Chemical Engineering, The University of Melbourne, Parkville, Vic 3052, Australia.

SOLOMON Robert John, b. 2 Nov 1931, NSW, Aust. Writer. m. (1) Gillian Kirkland, 1957, 2 d, (2) 1971, 1 s. Education: BA Hons, Dip Ed, Sydney Univ, 1954; MA, Oxford Univ, Eng, 1957; PhD, Univ Tas, Aust, 1969; Dip Law, Bars Admission Bd, NSW, 1983. Appointments: Secnd Sch Tchr, 1955; Lectr, Snr Lectr, 1957-69; Mbr, Austl House Reps, 1969-72; Dir, Mngng Dir, Plant Location Int, 1973-75, 1981-84; Exec Dir, Advtng Fedn, Aust, 1975-77; Prin, R J Solomon Cnslts, 1978-84; Bar-at-Law, NSW, 1983-86; Dir Dev, Univ NSW, 1987-91; Writer, Cnslt, 1992-. Publications include: Tasmania, 1972; Urbanisation: The Evolution of an Australian Capital, 1976; Ed, Urban Strategies for Australia, 1980; The Richest Lode, Broken Hill 1883-1988, 1988; Dreyfus in Australia, 1996; Contbr, num papers and reports. Honours: NSW Rhodes Schl, 1955; Hon Fell, Austl Inst Urban Studies, 1986. Memberships: Austl Inst Urban Studies; Inst Austl Geogs; NSW Geogl Soc; NSW Bar Assn; Assn Fmr Mbrs Parl Aust, Pres, NSW Chapt, 1993-95, Natl Commn, 1995-, Ed, Fed Gall, 1997-; Pres, NSW Veterans Athletics Club, 1995-. Hobbies: Photography; Gardening; Veteran athletics; Swimming. Address: 171 Rochford Street, Erskineville, NSW 2043, Australia.

SOMARE Michael Thomas (Rt Hon Sir), b. 9 Apr 1936, Rabual E New Brit Prov, Papua New Guinea. Politician. m. Veronica Bula Kaiap, 1965, 3 s, 2 d. Appointments: Tchr, 1957-64; Jrnlst and Radio Brdcstr, 1964-68; Mbr of House of Assembly, 1968-72; First Chf Min of Self-governing Papua New Guinea, First PM at Independence, 1975-80; Re-elected PM at Second Gen Elections, 1982-85; Min of For Affairs and Trade, 1988-92; Gov of East Sepik Prov. Honours: Hon Degs: Hon Doctorate of Hum, Philippines, 1976, Hon LLD honoris causa, Austl Natl Univ, 1978, Doctorate of South Pacific, Univ of South Pacific Suva, Fiji, 1978, Hon Doctorate of Technol, Univ of Technol, Lae, Papua New Guinea, 1982, Hon LLD honoris causa, Univ of Papua New Guinea, Port Moresby, 1986, Doctorate of Letters, honoris causa, Univ of Woolongong, NSW, Aust, 1986, Diplomatic Order of Merit, Pres of S Korea, 1990; Ancient Order of Sikatuna Philippines, 1976; Privy Cnclr, 1977; Companion of Hon, 1978; Grand Cross of St Michael and St George, 1990; Pontifical Order Equestrian Order of Grand Cross of St Gregory the Great, 1991. Publication: Sana (autobiog). Membership: Rotarian Paul Harris Fell. Address: Karao, Murik Lakes, East Sepik, Papua New Guinea.

SONG Guangwen, b. 28 Jan 1960, Tengzhou, China. Professor of Psychology. m. Zhangyong, 1 May 1983, 1 s. Education: BA, 1981; MEduc, 1984. Appointments: Dir, Psychol Rsch Cntr, Qufu Tchrs Univ; Dpty Pres, Sangdong Psychl Soc. Publications: Modern Mental Health, 1991; An Introduction to Psychology, 1994; Selected Works of S Freud, 1998. Honours: Cert of Excellent Rsch in Psychol of Sangdong Socl Sci Assn, 1996, 1997. Memberships: Chinese Psychol Soc, 1983; Cttee Mbr, Theort Study of Chinese Psychol Soc. Hobby: Playing basketball. Address: Department of Education, Qufu Teachers' University, Sangdong, China, 273165.

SONG Hong-zhao, b. 13 Aug 1915, Suzhou, China. Physician; Professor. m. 15 Jan 1945, 3 s, 1 d. Education: BS, Soochow Univ, 1938; MD, Peiping Union Med Coll, 1943. Appointments: Res Physn, 1943-48; Chf Res, 1948-50; Attending Physn, Asst, 1950-53; Instr, 1953-56; Asst Prof, 1956-58; Assoc Prof, 1958-65; Prof, 1965-; Visng Prof, Univ of Hong Kong, 1984, 1994; Mbr, Natl Standing Cttee, Chinese Peoples Polit Consultation Conf (Vice Chmn of Subcttee of Scis, Educn, Culture, Hygiene and Athletics); Mbr, Chinese Acady of Engrng (Divsn of Med Sci). Publications: 3 books on Trophoblastic Dieseases, 1981, 1988, 1989; 120 pprs. Honours: 1st Grade Awd, Sci Achievement, Min of Pub Hlth, 1981; 1st Grade Awd, Promotion of Sci and Technol, State Cmmn of Sci and Technol, 1985; Hon of Adv Sci Investigator, State Commn of Educn and State Commn of Sci and Technol, 1990; Prize of Chen Jia-Keng Sci Fndn, 1990; Prize of Ho-Leung-Ho-Lee Fndn, 1995; Fell ad enudem, Roy Coll of Obstetricians and Gynaecologists, London, 1996. Memberships: Hon Chmn, Chinese Soc of Obs & Gyn; Advsr, Chinese Jrnl of Obs & Gyn; Exec Cttee, Intl Soc on the Study of Trophoblastic Disease (Pres Elect, IV Congress); Intl Soc of Gynecol Oncol. Listed in: Who's Who in the World. Address: Department of Obstetrics & Gynaecology, Peking Union Medical College Hospital, Beijing 100730, China.

SONG Jian, b. 29 Dec 1931, Rongcheng Co, Shangdong Prov, China. State Official. m. Wang Yusheng, 1961,1 s, 1 d. Education: DSc. Appointments: Hd, Lab of Cybernetics, Inst of Maths, Acad Sinica, 1960-70; Dir, Guided Missile Control Lab, 7th Ministry of Machine Bldg Ind, 1962-70; Hd, Chf Scientist, Space Sci Div, Acad of Space Technol, 1971-78, VP, Dpty Sci Dir; Vice Min and Chf Engr Scientist, Min of Astronautics, 1981-84; Rsch Prof, Beijing Inst of Info and Control, 1983-; Chair, State Sci and Technol Commn, 1984-98; Mbr, Chinese Acady of Scism 1991-, State Cnclr, 1986-98; Visng Prof, MIT, Harv Univ of MN, 1980; VP, China Soc of Demographic Sci, 1982-86; Assoc Chf Ed, System and Control Letters, 1983-85; Chf Ed, Automatic Control and System Engring, Encyclopaedia of China, 1983-, Mbr, Editl Bd, 1984-. Publications: Reference Frames in Space Flight, 1963; Engineering Cybernetics (co-auth), 1980; China's Population: Problems and Prospects, 1981; Recent Development in Control Theory and its Applications, 1984; Population Projections and Control, 1981; Population Control Theory, 1985; Population Control in China: Theory and Applications, 1985; Population System Control, 1988; Science and Technology and Social System, 1988; Num articles. Honours: Hon DHum Litt, Houston, 1996; Num natl and intl awds. Memberships: Cncl Mbr, Intl Fed of Automatic Control, 1984-87; VP, China System Engrng Soc, 1985-87; Chinese Acady of Engrng, 1994; For Mbr, Russian Acady of Scis, 1994, Roy Swedish Acady of Engrng Scis, 1994; Corresp Mbr, Natl Acady of Engrng of Mexico, 1985; Prof, Qinghua Univ, Fudan Univ, Harbin Univ of Technol, 1986-. Address: c/o State Science and Technology Commission, 15B Fuxing Road, Beijing 100862, China.

SONG Ruixiang, b. 1939, Jintan Co, Jiangsu Prov, China. Politician. Appointments: Gov, Qinghai Prov, 1988-93; Min of Geol and Mineral Rescs, 1993-98, Party Grp Sec; Chair, Natl Min Reserves Commn, 1995-96; Vice Chair, Natl Mineral Rescs Cttee, 1996-98. Membership: 15th CCP Cntrl Cttee, 1997-. Address: c/o Ministry of Geology and Mineral Resources, 62 Funxi Street, Xicheng District, Beijing 100812, China.

SONG Tao, b. 31 Aug 1932, Wuhan City, China. Teacher of Cello. m. Tian Liantao, 7 July 1957, 1 d. Education: Grad, Cntrl Music Conservatory (Dept of String & Wind). Appointments: Dpty Dir, Sect of Cello, 1973-84, Dir of Cello Sect, 1984-94. Publications: Course: The Course of Cello Playing (including 3 series, 7 vols), 1985. Honours: Hon Title, Outstndng Tchr of Beijing Cty, 1991; Spec Subsidy for Outstndng Achievement, State Cncl of China, 1994. Membership: Assn of Chinese Cellists. Hobby: Movies. Address: Central Music Conservatory, Xicheng Dist, #43 Baojia Street, Beijing, China.

SONG Wencong, b. 26 Mar 1930, Kunming, Yunnan Prov, China. Aircraft Designer. m. Zhang Yi, 18 June 1965, 1 d. Education: Grad, Aircraft Des Dept, Mil Engrng Acady, PLA, 1959. Appointments: Early 60s, Ldr of China's 1st Aerodynamic Layout Grp for fighter aircraft des, led grp, tactical technol demonstration, des of aerodynamic layout and gen layout for China's 1st self-des fighter aircraft; Chf Designer, natl major proj J-7III, -1987; Chf Designer, Chengdu Aircraft Des and Rsch, 1980-; Chf Designer, new major proj, 1986-. Honours: Prof, 1987; Natl Excellent Sci and Technological Workfellow, 1988; Hon Cert, Cttee of Sci and Technol for Natl Def Ind; Natl 2nd Class Awd for Sci and Technol Prog, 1991; Prominent Contbn Expert, Min of Aerospace Ind. Memberships: Sci and Technol Cttee, AVIC; Hon Mbr, Sichuan Aerospace Assn Soc; Concurrent Prof, Beijing Univ of Aeronautical and Astronautical; Nanjing Univ of Aeronautical and Astronautical, NW Polytechnical Univ. Hobbies: Swimming; Tennis. Address: 89, Wuhouci Street, Chengdu 610041, Sichuan, China.

SONG Xin-Qi, b. 7 Aug 1928, Jiangshu, China. Education. m. Chen Qi-Ai, 8 July 1948, 1 s, 2 d. Education: BS, Chem. Appointments: Prof, Tsinghua Univ; Adj Prof, Beijing Chem Engrng Univ; Adj Prof, Qing Dao Univ; Adj Prof, Inst of Chem, Chinese Acady of Sci. Creative Works: Lasers in Future Chem; The Tomorrow of Chem; Photochemistry, Principles, Techniques and Applications. Honours: Educ Rsch Awd; Mei Ye-Qi Rsch Awd; Outstndng Grad Stud Spvsr Awd. Memberships: Chinese Chem Soc. Hobbies: Travelling; Playing Go; Reading Novels. Address: Deptartment of Chemistry, Tsinghua Univ, Beijing 100084, China.

SONG Yeng Wook, b. 13 Feb 1956, Taejeon, Korea. Physician; Researcher. m. Hee Jeong Kwon, 20 Dec 1980, 1 s, 2 d. Education: MD, 1980, PhD, 1988, Seoul Natl Univ. Appointments: Clin Fell, UCLA Medl Cntr, 1990-92; Asst Prof of Med, Seoul Natl Univ, 1992-95; Assoc Prof of Med, Seoul Natl Univ, 1995-. Honours: Ellis Dressner Awd, S CA Chapt, Arthritis Fndn, 1992; Memberships: Fell, Amn Coll of Rheumatology; Korean Assn of Internal Med; Korean Rheumatism Assn. Hobby: Playing golf. Address: Department of Internal Medicine,

Seoul National University Hospital, 28 Yungun-dong, Chongno-ku, Seoul 110-744, Korea.

SONG Baorui, b. Dec 1937 Shunyi Co Beijing. Politician. Education: Qinghua Univ. Appointments: Joined CCP, 1958; Fmr Dep Dir Chf Engr China Welding Rod Plant; Dir China Welding Rod Plant Inst, 1975-82; Mngr China Welding Materials Manufacture Co, 1982-83; Dep Sec then Sec CCP Zingong Cty Cttee, 1983-86; Chmn Sichuan Prov Commn for Restructuring the Economy, 1986-89; Exec Dep Sec CCP Sichuan Prov Cttee, 1989-; Gov of Sichuan Prov, 1996-; Dep 8th NPC. Memberships: Fmr mbr Standing Cttee CCP Sichuan Prov Cttee; Alt mbr 14th CCP Cntrl Cttee; Mbr 15th CCP Cntrl Cttee, 1997-. Address: c/o People's Government of Sichuan, Chengdu, Sichuan Province, People's Republic of China.

SONG Defu, b. 1946 Yanshan Co Hebei Prov. Party and Govt Offic. Appointments: Joined PLA and CCP, 1965; First Sec of Sec Communist Yth League of China, 1985-93; Min of Personnel, 1993-98; Party Grp Sec min of Personnel; Hd Natl Ldng Grp for Placement of Demobilised Army Offrs; Dep Hd Org Dept. Memberships: Mbr 13th CCP Cntrl Cttee, 1987-92; Mbr 14th CCP Cntrl Cttee, 1992-97; Mbr 8th NPC, 1993-; Mbr 15th CCP Cntrl Cttee, 1997-; Mbr Org Cttee. Address: 12 Hepingli Zhongjie Street, East District, Beijing 100716, People's Republic of China.

SONTHALIA Navin, b. 31 July 1969, Calcutta, India. International Trader. m. Shewta Sonthalia, 24 June 1997. Education: BComm. Appointments: Pratap Company Ptnr; Pratap Cold Storage Ptnr; Dir, Star Commercial Co Pvt Ltd, 1989-. Hobbies: Gardening; Relaxing to Indian music. Address: 43 Zakaria Street, 700 073 Calcutta, India.

SOOD Ajay Kumar, b. 26 June 1951, Gwalior, India. Teaching and Research. m. Anita, 12 Oct 1980, 1 s, 1 d. Education: Bs, 1971, MSc, 1972, Phys, Punjab Univ; PhD, Phys, Indian Inst of Sci, Bangalore, 1982. Appointments: Sci Offr, Dept of Atomic Energy, 1972-88; Assoc Prof, 1988-94, Prof, 1994-, Indian Inst of Sci, Bangalore; Chmn, Div of Phys & Math Scis, Indian Inst of Sci, Banglaore, 1998-. Publications: 107 + 4, rsch pprs in jrnls; 5 sci reviews; 5 chapts in books; 74 pprs in seminars, symposia & conf; Pprs incl (as co-auth) Vacuum Squeezing of Solids: Macroscopic Quantum States Driven by Light Pulses, 1997; X-Ray fluorescence correation spectroscopy: A method for studying particle dynamics in condensed matter, 1998. Honours: Shanti Swarup Bhatnagar Awd in Phys Scis, 1990; Fell, Indian Acady of Scis, 1990; Fell, Natl Sci Acady, 1995; Fell, Natl Acady Scis, India, 1995; Assoc Mbr, Intl Cntr for Theort Phys, Trieste, Italy, 1995-2000; Mbr, Intl Steering Cttee of Raman Spectroscopy, 1994-99; Mbr, Sci & Engrng Rsch Cncl (SERC), Dept of Sci & Technol, Govt of India, 1995-97, 1997-2000, 1997-2000. Hobbies: Hindustani; Classical music; Long walks. Address: Department of Physics, Indian Institute of Science, Bangalore 560 012, India.

SOONG James Chu-yul, b. 16 Mar 1942 Hunan. Politician. m. Viola Chen, 1 s, 1 d. Education: Natl Chengchi Univ Taipei; Univ of CA Berkeley; Cath Univ of Am; Georgetown Univ WA DC. Appointments: Sec Exec Yuan Taiwan, 1974-77; Dep Dir-Gen Govt Info Off, 1977-79; Assoc Prof Natl Taiwan Univ, 1975-79; Rsch Fell Inst of Intl Rels Natl Chengchi Univ, 1974; Personal Sec to the Pres, 1978-89; Dir-Gen Govt Info Off Govt Spokesman, 1979-84; Mngng Dir China tv co, 1984-93; Mngng Dir Taiwan tv Enterprise, 1984-93; Dir-Gen Dept of Cultural Affairs Kuomintang, 1984-87; Dep Sec-Gen Cntrl Cttee Kuomintang, 1987-98; Sec-Gen Cntrl Cttee Kuomintang, 1989-93; Gov Taiwan Provincial Govt, 1993-; Chmn Hua-hsia Invmnt Corp. Publications: A Manual for Academic Writers; How to Write Academic Papers; Politics and Public Opinions in the United States; Keep Free China Free. Honours: Eisenhower Fell'ship, 1982; Sev decorations. Memberships: Mbr Cntrl Cttee Kuomintang, 1981-; Mbr Cntrl Standing Cttee, 1988-.

Address: 1 Sheng-Fu Road, Chung-Hsin New Village, Nantou, Taiwan.

SOONS Jane Margaret, b. 18 June 1931, Grantham, Eng. University Professor. Education: BA, hons II, 1952, Dip in Educ, 1953, Sheffield Univ, Eng; PhD, Glasgow Univ, Scotland, 1958. Appointments: Asst in Geog, Glasgow Univ, Scotland, 1953-56; Brit Cncl Schl, Institut de Geomorphologie Appliquee, Strasbourg, France, 1957; Tutor, Bedford Coll, London Univ, Eng, 1957-59; Lectr, 1960-70, Prof, 1971-92, Prof Emer, 1992-, Dept of Geog, Canterbury Univ, Christchurch, NZ. Publications: Landforms of New Zealand (ed w M S Selby), 1982, 2nd ed, 1992; 47 pprs in var jrnls. Honours: Pres, Intl Union for Quaternary Rsch, 1977-82; Amn Geog Soc David Livingstone Medal for Southern Hemisphere Rsch, 1988. Memberships: Intl Union for Quaternary Rsch; Roy Soc of NZ; NZ Geog Soc; Geol Soc of NZ. Hobbies: Sailing; Gardening. Address: Department of Geography, University of Canterbury, Private Bag 4800, Christchurch, New Zealand.

SOPIAN Kamaruzzaman, b. 4 Apr 1962, Batu Gajah, Malaysia. Associate Professor. m. Saniah, 3 s, 1 d. Education: BS, WI; MSc, Pittsburgh; PhD, Miami. Appointments: Tutor, 1986; Lectr, 1989; Assoc Prof, 1997. Publications: 10 Intl Jrnls, 1993-98; 60 Intl Prongs, 1989-98; Chapt in a book, 1989. Honours: Acady Merit Awd, Univ of Miami, 1997; Grad Excellence Awd, Univ of Miami, 1997. Memberships: Malaysian Inst of Energy; Intl Solar Energy Soc. Hobbies: Fishing; Cycling; Art. Address: U Kebangasan Dept Mech Engr, 43600 Bangi, Selangor, Malaysia.

SORAI Michio, b. 4 Aug 1939, Ryojun. Professor. m. Noriko Kida, 15 Jan 1966, 2 s, 1 d. Education: BSc, Osaka Univ, 1962; MSc, 1964; DSc, 1968. Appointments: Rsch Assoc, Osaka Univ, 1964-81; Assoc Prof, 1981-87; Prof, 1987-; Dir, Microcalorimetry Rsch Cntr, Osaka Univ, 1993-99; Dir, Rsch Cntr for Molecular Thermodynamics, Osaka Univ, 1999-. Memberships: The Chem Soc of Japan; The Phys Soc of Japan; The Japan Soc for Calorimetry and Thermal Analysis; The Japanese Liquid Crystal Soc. Hobbies: Wood Prints; Gardening; Art. Address: Research center for Molecular Thermodynamics, Graduate School of Science, Osaka University, Toyonaka, Osaka 560-0043, Japan.

SORESI Stephen, b. 3 Apr 1968, Washington, DC, USA. Broadcaster. Education: Master Deg, Waseda Univ, Tokyo, Japan. Appointments: Fellowship, Waseda Univ Pol Sci Dept, 1995-98; Host, Let's Start Talking, NHK Network, 1999. Publications: English Communication Text; Mastering Japan and Japanese Essay Column, 1998-99. Honours: RTNDA Regl Awd, 1994; For Min's Awd, 1995. Hobbies: Karaoke; Sports; Politics. Address: 1-27-16 Takaido higashi, Suginami-ku, F168-0072, Tokyo, Japan.

SOTHI RACHAGAN Sinnathurai, b. 12 Aug 1946, Batugajah, Perak, Malaysia. Professor; Dean. m. S Jayaranee, 1983, 2 d. Education: BA, Univ of Malaya, 1968; Postgrad Dip of Arts, Univ of Otago, NZ, 1971; MA, Univ of Otago, 1972; PhD, SOAS, Univ of London, 1978; Dip in Law, Polytechnic of Cntrl London, 1978; Barrister-at-Law, Lincoln's Inn, 1984; LLM, Univ of Bristol, 1990. Appointments: Tchr, 1968-69; Tchng Asst, Univ of Otago, NZ, 1971-72; Lectr, 1972-81; Asoc Prof, Dept of Geog, Fac of Arts & Socl Scis, Univ of Malaya, 1982-92; Assoc Prof, 1992-94; Prof & Dean, fac of Law, Univ of Malaya, 1994-. Publication: Law and the Electoral Process in Malaysia, 1993. Honours: Tokoh Pengguna (Consumer Leader of the Yr) Govt of Malasia Awd, 1995; Darjah Dato Paduka Mahkota Perak (Hon Awd, which carries title Dato), conferred by His Roy Highness, the Sultan of Perak, 1998. Memberships include: Natl Advsry Cncl for Consumer Protection, 1990-; Cttee on Consumer Lww, Redress and Codes of Prac, Chmn, 1990-; Current Affairs Cttee, 1994-; Min of Trade and Consumer Affairs; Cttees on Stands for Consumer Prods (SRIM), 1991-; and Review of Environ Laws, 1992-; Min of Sci, Technol & Environ; Cttee Mbr, Min of Energy, Posts & Telecomms; Bar Cncl of Malaya; Ins Mediation Bur; Legal

Advsr: Fedn of Malasian Consumers Assns; Hlth Action Intl; Consumers Intl; Chmn, Standing Cttee on Consumer Law, 1993-; VP, Intl Assn for Consumer Law, 1995-; VP, ASEAN Law Schs Assn, 1995-. Hobby: Badminton. Address: 76 Jalan Terasek 1, Bangsar Baru, 59100 Kuala Lumpur, Malasia.

SOUTER Gavin Geoffrey, b. 2 May 1929, Sydney, New South Wales, Australia. Author. m. Ngaire, 30 Sept 1952, 2 d. Education: BA, Univ Sydney. Appointments: Jrnlst, 1947-87, Asst Ed, 1981-82, Sydney Morning Herald. Publications: New Guinea: The Least Unknown, 1963; Lion and Kangaroo, 1976; Company of Heralds, 1981; Bicentennial Narrative History of Federal Parliament, 1983-87; Acts of Parliament, 1988; Mosman: A History, 1994; A Torrent of Words, 1996. Honours: AM, 1988; AO, 1995. Membership: VP, Austl Soc of Auths, 1975-78. Hobby: Kayaking. Address: 21 Everview Avenue, Mosman, NSW 2088, Australia.

SOUTHALL Ivan Francis, b. 8 June 1921, Melbourne, Aust. Writer. m. (1) Joy Blackburn, 1945, 1 s, 3 d, (2) Susan Westerlund Stanton, 1976. Appointments: Roy Austl AF, 1942-47; Self-employed Writer, 1947-; Lectd widely on childrens lit in many pts of world. Publications include: 60 books, var titles in 23 langs. Honours: DFC, 1944; Austl Childrens Book of the Yr, 1966, 1968, 1971, 1976; Children's Welfare and Culture Encouragement Awd, Japan, 1969; Carnegie Medal, 1971; AM, 1981; Natl Children's Book Awd, 1986; Aust Cncl Emer Awd, 1993; Retrospective Exhibn, Southall A-Z, State Lib of Vic, 1998; Var others. Hobby: Gardening. Listed in: Who's Who in the World; Who's Who in Australia; Who's Who in the USA. Address: PO Box 25, Healesville, Vic 3777, Australia.

SOUTHALL Susan Westerlund, b. 1 Oct 1942, Long Beach, CA, USA. Painter. m. (1) Frank Anthony Stanton, (2) Ivan Francis Southall, 1976. Education: BA, Art Hist, Pomona Coll; MLS, Univ CA, Berkeley; Dip, Visual Arts, Box Hill Inst. Creative Works: Solo Exhbns: Fifty Years After the War, 1995; Studies for the Annunciation, 1996; Doctor Faustus, 1996; Embarkation, 1997; House of Gold, 1998; Awareness, 1999. Honour: Hugh Ramsay Art Awd, 1995. Hobby: Photography. Address: 32 Crowley Road, Healesville, Victoria, Australia.

SOUTHCOTT Andrew John, b. 15 Oct 1967. Medical Practitioner; Member of Parliament. Education: MB, BS, Univ of Adelaide, Aust. Appointments: Intern, 1991, Res Med Offr, 1992-93, Roy Adelaide Hosp; Res Med Offr, Flinders Med Cntr, 1994-96; Elect Mbr, House of Reps, 1996. Hobbies: Running; Rowing; Cycling. Listed in: Who's Who in Australia. Address: 760 Marion Road, Marion, SA 5043, Australia.

SOVE Emosi, b. 8 Nov 1930, Nadroga, Fiji Islands. Retired Chief. m. Laite, 17 Mar 1950, 2 s, 1 d. Appointments: Retd Chf, Ilami Soc; Patron, Cagimaira Devel Assn, Fiji. Hobbies: Reading; Television. Address: c/o Cagimaira Development Association, PO Box 1038 BA, Fiji.

SOWRY Roger M, b. 1958, Palmerston North, NZ. Government Minister. m. 4 children. Education: Dip, Bus Admin, Victoria Univ, Wellington. Appointments: Distbn Mngr, R Hannah and Co; Elected to Parl, Kapiti, 1990; Jnr Whip, Snr Govt Whip, 1993-96; Min for Socl Welfare, 1996; Additional portfolios, Min in Charge of War Pensions and Assoc Min for Hlth, 1997; Min of Socl Services, Work and Income, Ldr of House, Min responsible for Minority Govt Mngmt, 1998-. Memberships: Dpty Divl Chmn, Wellington Young Nationals, 1979-80; Electorate Chmn, Pencarrow, 1982-86; Divl Cnclr, 1985-96; Dpty Chmn, Wellington Div, 1988-90; Wellington Rep on NZ Natl Exec, 1989-90. Address: 16 Seaview Road, PO Box 1524, Paraparaumu Beach, New Zealand.

SPAIN Alister Vincent, b. 21 Apr 1941, Dunedin, New Zealand. Research Scientist. m. Christine, 1 s, 1 d. Education: MAgr Sci; PhD. Appointments: Lectr, Zool, James Cook Univ of N Qld, 1971-74; Rsch Sci, CSIRO,

1974-. Memberships: Austl Entomol Soc; Austl Inst of Bio; Austl Soc of Soil Sci Ecological Soc of Aust. Hobbies: Natural science; Soil science; Minesite Rehabilitation. Address: Davies Laboratory, CSIRO, Private Mail Bag, Aitkenvale, Qld 4814, Australia.

SPALVINS Janis (John) Gunars, b. 26 May 1936, Riga. Company Director. Widowed, 16 Dec 1961, 2 s. Education: BEcon; FCPA; FCA; FCIS; FAICD; FAIM. Appointments: Grp Sec/Dir subsidiary cos, Camelec Grp of Cos, 1955-73; Asst Gen Mngr, 1973, Gen Mngr, 1977, Chf Gen Mngr and Dir, 1979, Mngng Dir, 1981-91, Adelaide Steamship Co; Dir and Chf Exec, David Jones Ltd, 1980-91; Memberships: Bus Cncl of Aust, 1986-91; FAIM; MIstD, Aust, 1981; Crusing Yacht Club of SA; Roy SA Yacht Squadron (Adelaide). Hobbies: Snow skiing; Water skiing; Tennis; Sailing. Address: Galufo Pty, 2 Brookside Road, Springfield, SA 5062, Australia.

SPARKES Alonzo Clive William, b. 6 Dec 1935, Brisbane, Aust. Lecturer. m. Veronika Zakany, 10 Jan 1970, 1 s, 2 d. Education: BA, Univ of Qld, 1959; BA, Univ of London, England, 1962; MA, Univ of NSW, Aust, 1970; PhD, Univ of Newcastle, 1985. Appointments: Lib Asst, Parl House, Brisbane, 1955-60; Lectr in Philos, Univ of NSW, 1965-69; Tutor, Snr Tutor, Philos, Univ of Newcastle, 1970; Lectr in Polit Philos, Univ of Papua New Guinea, 1971-73; Lectr, 1974-85, Snr Lectr in Philos, 1985-96, Hon Assoc in Philos, 1996-, Univ of Newcastle, Aust. Publications: Words Words Words: A Guide to Philosophical Technology and the Language of Argument; Talking Philosophy: A Wordbook, 1991; Talking Politics: A Wordbook, 1994. Hobbies: Observing Politics; Miscellaneous Reading. Address: Department of Philosophy, University of Newcastle, NSW 2308, Australia.

SPARROW David Hereward Burnaby, b. 11 Dec 1927, Bournemouth, Eng. Research Scientist, Plant Breeding. m. Gwyneth Mae Bode, 5 Sept 1959, 1 s, 1 d. Education: BS (hons), Reading, 1952; PhD, Adelaide, 1972. Appointments: Sci Offr, Plant Breeding Inst, Cambridge, 1953-60; Lectr, 1960-65, Snr Lectr, 1965-80, Asst Prof, 1980-92, Visng Rsch Fell, 1992-, Dept Plant Sci, Univ of Adelaide. Publications: Approximately 60 sci pprs over 40 yrs, 1952-92. Honours: Urrbrae Awd, 1979; Farrer Medal, 1990; Fell, Univ of Tas, 1997. Memberships: Inst of Brewing; Fell, Austl Acady of Technol Scis and Engrng. Hobbies: Bushwalking; Swimming; Croquet; French cuisine. Address: 6 Aerial Road, Belair, South Australia 5052, Australia.

SPARROW John Maxwell, b. 9 June 1940, Aust. Medical Administrator. m. Helen Rae Taylor, 5 Apr 1969, 1 s, 1 d. Education: MBBS, Melbourne Univ, 1964; MHA, NSW Univ, 1973; FRACMA, 1976. Appointments: Res Med Offr 1965-67, Dpty Supt 1968-72, Gen Supt 1972-75, Roy Hobart Hosp; Dir of Hosp and Medl Servs for Tas, 1975-89; Dir of Ambulance Servs for Tas, 1983-89; Dir of Statewide Hlth Servs and Chf Hlth Offr for Tas, 1989-93; Chf Med Offr for Tas, 1993-; AM, 1999. Memberships: Fell, Roy Austl Coll of Medl Admnstrs; Fell, Austl Coll of Hlth Serv Execs; Fell, Austl Fac of Pub Hlth Med. Hobbies: Sports; Running; Tennis; Swimming; Gardening; Travel; Wine; Food; Antique Furniture. Address: 14 Chessington Court, Sandy Bay, Tas 7005, Australia.

SPEIRS Victor Cecil, b. 6 Apr 1943, Charlton, Victoria, Australia. Veterinary Surgeon. m. Jennifer Kaye Coffield, 22 Jan 1966, 2 d. Education: BVSc, MVSc, PhD, Melbourne; Dr.med.vet. Habil, Switz; FACVSc; Dipl, Amn Coll of Vet Surgs, Eurn Coll of Vet Surgs. Appointments: Gen Vet Pract, Vic, Aust, 1968; Lectr, Dept of Med, Univ Saskatchewan, Can, 1969; Snr Lectr, Fac of Vet Sci, Univ Melbourne, 1969-87; Visng Prof, Univ Bern, Switz, 1976-77; Prof, Chf, Large Animal Surg, Auburn Univ, USA 1987-91; Prof, Chf, Equine Surg, Univ Bern, Switz, 1991-94; Reg Spec Equine Surg, Melbourne, 1994-. Publication: Clinical Examination of Horses, 1998; Other book chapts and num jrnl publs. Memberships: Austl Coll of Vet Scis, Cncl, 1984-87; Amn Coll of Vet Surgs; Eurn Coll of Vet Surgs; Austl Vet Assn. Hobbies: Running; Bird watching; Classical guitar; Eucalypt taxonomy. Address: 17 Jessamine Avenue, East Prahran, Melbourne, Victoria 3181, Australia.

SPENCER Hamish Gordon, b. 18 July 1960, Gisborne, NZ. Senior Lecturer. m. Abigail Marion Smith, 22 Feb 1986, 2 s. Education: BS Hons, Maths, 1982; MSc, Zool, Univ of Auckland, 1983; PhD, Bio, Harvard Univ, 1988. Appointments: Lectr, Maths, Univ of Waikato, 1989; Lectr, Zool, Univ of Otago, 1992; Snr Lectr, Zool, 1997. Creative Works: Speciation and the Recognition Concept, Theory and Application; The Marine Fauna of New Zealand, Index to the Fauna; 45 Sci Articles. Honours: Fulbright Trav Awd, 1983-88. Memberships: Genetics Soc of Am; Genetics Soc Aust; Soc for the Stdy of Evolution; Amn Soc of Naturalists. Hobbies: Bird Watching. Address: Department of Zoology, University of Otago, PO Box 56, Dunedin, New Zealand.

SPIELBERG Steven, b. 18 Dec 1947 Cincinnati OH. Film Dir. m. (1) Amy Irving, 1985, div 1989, 2 s; (2) Kate Capshaw, 2 d - 1 adopted. Education: CA State Coll Long Beach. Appointments: Dir episodes of tv series inclng Night Gallery; Marcus Welby MD; Columbo; Dir'd 20 minute short Amblin'; Dir tv films Duel, 1971; Something Evil, 1972; Fndr Starbright Fndn; Co-fndr Dreamworks SKG, 1995-. Films dir'd: The Sugarland Express, 1974; Jaws, 1975; Close Encounters of the Third Kind, 1977; I Wanna Hold Your Hand - prod'd - 1978; 1941, 1979; Raiders of the Lost Ark, 1981; ET - The Extra Terrestrial - 1982; Poltergeist - co-wrote and prod'd - 1982; Gremlins - prod'd - 1984; Indiana Jones and the Temple of Doom, 1984; Young Sherlock Holmes - exec prod - 1985; The Color Purple - also prod'd - 1985; Back to the Future - co-exec prodr; The Goonies - writer and exec prodr - 1986; Batteries Not Included - exec prodr - 1986; The Money Pit - co-prodr - 1986; An American Tale - co-exec prodr - 1986; Empire of the Sun, 1988; Always, 1989; Gremlins II - exec prodr; Dad - exec prodr; Joe versus the Volcano - exec prodr; Hook, 1991; Cape Fear - co-exec prodr - 1992; Jurassic Park, 1992; Schindler's List, 1993; Casper - prodr - 1995; Some Mother's Son, 1996; Twister - exec prodr - 1996; The Lost World: Jurassic Park, 1997; Amistad, 1997. Publication: Close Encounters of the Third Kind - with Patrick Mann. Honours: Won film contest with war film Escape to Nowhere, 1961; Dirs Guild of Am Awd Fell'ship, 1986; Irving G Thalberg Awd, 1987; Golden Lion Awd - Venice Film Fest - 1993; BAFTA Awd, 1994; Acady Awd for Schindler's List, 1994; Dr hc - Univ of S Ca - 1994; David Lean - BAFTA; John Huston Awd for Artist Rights, 1995; John Huston Awd, 1995; Hon D Litt - Sussex - 1997. Address: CAA, 9830 Wilshire Boulevard, Beverly Hills, CA 90212, USA.

SPITZ Robert John, b. 26 May 1947, NYC, NY, USA. Attorney. m. Suzie, 9 Dec 1979, 1 s. Education: BS, Purdue Univ, 1969; JD, USC, 1975; MA, Unification Theol Sem, 1985. Honours: Golden Star Awd, Golden Star Club, 1984; Natl Security Affairs Symp, 1988. Memberships: Amn Bar Assn, Gen Prac Sect, Chmn Corp Cnsl Cttee, 1986-87; Chmn, Annual Meeting, 1986; NY State Bar Assn, Vice Chmn, 1982; Corp Cnsl Cttee; State Bar of CA, Toastmasters Intl, Club Pres, 1991, VP, 1992; Family Fedn for World Peace, 1993-99; Amn Inns of Crt, Mt Baldy Chapt, 1995-99; Amn Leadership Conf, CA Dir, 1998. Hobbies: Racquetball; Golf; Travel. Address: 204 North San Antonio, Ontario, CA 91762, USA.

SPOLTER Pari, b. 30 Jan 1930, Tehran, Iran. Writer of scientific books. m. Herbert Spolter, MD, 16 Aug 1958, 1 s, 1 d. Education: Licence es Science Chimique mention Biologique, Univ of Geneva of Switz, 1952; MS, 1959, PhD, 1961, Biochemistry, Univ of WI, Madison. Appointments: Postdoct Fell and Instr, Temple Univ, PA, 1961-65; Rsch Biochemist, US Pub Hlth Serv, San Fran, CA, 1966-68; Writer and Publr, 1988-. Publication: Gravitational Force of the Sun, 1994. Memberships: AAAS; Amn Math Soc; NY Acady of Sci; WI Alumni Assn. Address: Orb Publishing Company, 11862 Ballsa Boulevard # 182, Granada Hills, CA 91344-2753, USA.

SPRING Dryden Thomas (Sir), b. 6 Oct 1939. Chairman of New Zealand Dairy Board. m. 13 Aug 1960, 3 s, 3 d. Appointments: Pres, NZ Sharemilker's Assn, 1966; VP, 1969, Pres, 1972-76, Life Mbr, Waikato Federated Farmers; Dir, 1973, Dpty Chmn, 1979, Chmn of the Dirs, 1982-89, NZ Co-op Dairy Co Ltd; Fndg Dir, Rural Bank, 1974-88; Dir, 1983, Chmn, 1989, NZ Dairy Bd; Tstee, Waikato Medl Rsch Fndn Ltd, 1986-91; NZ's Rep on the APEC Eminent Persons Grp, 1994-95; Currently: Hon Chmn of NZ Philippines Bus Cncl; Patron, Thailand/NZ Bus Cncl; Dir, NZ Co-Op Dairy Co Ltd, Fernz Corp Ltd, Natl Bank of NZ Ltd & Goodman Fielder Ltd. Honours: NZ's Outstndng Young Man of the Yr, 1973; NZ 1990 Commemoration Medal, 1990; KB, 1994; Fell, Inst of Dirs in NZ. Memberships: Tstee, NZ Bus and Parl Trust and Asia 2000 Fndn; Wellington Club; Te Aroha Club; Coll Old Boys Rugby Club. Hobbies: Farming; Reading; Sport especially rugby and cricket; Jogging; Golf. Address: RD 3, Te Aroha, New Zealand.

SPRINGER Robert L, b. 8 Sept 1945. Radio Station Engineer. m.Jeannette A Miller, 20 Dec 1975, 1 d. Education: Dip, Moody Bible Inst. Appointments: Audio Engr, Far E Brdcstng Co, Manila, 1979; Audio Engr, 1982, Chf Engr, 1986, Field Dir, 1996, Saipan, C'wlth of Northern Mariana Islands. Memberships: Audio Engrng Soc; Soc of Brdcst Engrs; SBE Cert Profl Brdcst Engr; Cert Comms Technician, Personal Comms Ind Assn. Hobbies: Ham Radio; Computing; Photography. Listed in: Who's Who in Entertainment. Address: c/o Far East Broadcasting Company, Box 209, Saipan, MP 96950, USA.

SPRINGS Alice, (June Brown),b. June 1923 Melbourne. Photogr. m. Helmut Newton - qv - 1948. Appointments: Fmrly profl actress; Profl photogr, 1970-; Clients have incld Jean-Louis David; Fashion Mag Depeche Mode; Elle; Marie-Claire; Vogue; Vogue Homme; Nova; Mode Intl; Absolu; London Cosmoplitan; Contbnsto Egoiste; Vanity Fair; Interview; Passion; Stern; Decoration Internationale; Tatler; Photo; Les Cahiers de L'Energumene. Solo exhibns: Canon Gall Amsterdam, 1978; Canon Gall Geneva, 1980; Duc et Camroux Paris, 1980; David Heath Gall Atlanta, 1982; Yuen Lui Gall Seattle, 1982; Olympus Gall London, 1983; Galerie de France Paris, 1983; Musee Cheret Nice, 1984; Musee de Sainte Croix Poitier, 1985; Documenta Gall Turin, 1985; Centre Culturel Orlean, 1985; Centre Culturel et Artistique Arbusson, 1986; Espace Photographie de la Ville de Paris Paris Audiovisuel, 1986; Fotoform Frankfurt Main, 1987; Gerfiollet Amsterdam, 1988; Olympus Galerie Hamburg, 1988; Natl Portrait Gall London, 1988; Musee d'Art Moderne Paris, 1988; Museo Contemporaneo Mexico Cty, 1990; Rheinishces Landesmuseum Bonn, 1991-92; 'Arret sur l'image' Bordeaux, 1993; Galerie im alten Rathaus am Markt Wittlich, 1993; Hochshule fur Graphik und Buchkunst Leipzig, 1993; Forum Bremen, 1993. Grp exhibns incl: Photokina Cologne, 1976; Photogrs Gall London, 1979; G Ray Hawkins LA, 1981; Grey Art Gall NY, 1981; Paris Audiovisuel French Photogrs Mus of Modern Art Bratislava, 1991; Teatro Circo - courtesy of Paris Audiovisuel - Braga, 1992. Catalogues: Alice Springs Portraits; Musee Saint Croix Poitiers, 1985; Espace Photo Paris, 1986; Musee d'Art Moderne de la Ville de Paris, 1988; Centro Cultural Arte Contemporaneo Mexico Cty, 1991; Rheinishces Landesmuseum Bonn, 1991-92. Publications: Alice Springs Portraits, 1983, 1986, 1991. Film: TV documentary 'Helmut by June' for Canal Plus, 1995.

SQUIBB Geoffrey Bruce (Geoff) (Hon), b. 27 Oct 1946, Devonport, Tas, Aust. Member of Parliament; Mayor. m. Helen Squibb, 8 Feb 1969, 1 s, 1 d. Education: Studied, Austl Dip Recreation, 1970-75; Spec Recreation Admin Course, Springfield Coll, USA, 1975-76. Appointments: Family Orchard, 1963-65; Field Offr, Glaxo-Allenbury's, Aust, 1965-68; Recreation Offr, Tasmanian Govt, 1968-84; Liaison Offr, Dept of Premier and Cabinet, 1984-90; JP, 1984; Mayor of Devonport, Tas, 1984-99; Elected Mbr for Mersey, Tasmanian Legis Cncl, 1990, 1996, 1997. Honours: Rural Yth Stdy Tour Exch to Vic, 1967; Rotary Yth Ldrship Awd, 1972; Rotary

Fndn Fellshp, Stdy in USA, 1975-76; Travelling Schlshp, Tas Educ Dept, 1975-76; Austl Dip Recreation, 1977; 1 of 5 Outstndng Young Austls, Tasmanian Jaycees, 1980. Membership: Roy Austl Inst Pks and Recreation; Rotary Club, Devonport, 1977. Hobbies: Jogging; Sport; Gardening; Reading; Tourism. Address: 68 Rooke, Devonport, Tas 7310, Australia.

SQUIRES Dale Edward, b. 28 Aug 1950, San Diego, California, USA. Economist. m. Virginia Shaizifzadeh, 31 Jan 1986, 1 s, 1 d. Education: BSc, MSc, Univ CA, Berkeley; PhD, Cornell Univ. Appointments: Univ Putra, Malaysia, 1974-76; Natl Marine Fisheries Serv, La Jolla, CA, 1984-; Adj Assoc Prof, Dept of Econs and Grad Sch of Intl Rels and Pacific Studies, Univ CA, San Diego, 1990-. Publications: Over 50 sci pprs in profl jrnls. Memberships: Am Econ Assn; Am Agricl Econ Assn. Hobbies: Surfing; Jogging; Hiking; Camping; Nordic Skiing; Music. Address: Southwest Fisheries Science Center, National Marine Fisheries Service, PO Box 271, La Jolla, CA 92038-0271, USA.

SQUIRES Victor Roy, b. 18 Dec 1937, Wollongong, NSW, Australia. Professor. m. Coralie, 30 Jan 1990, 3 s. Education: MA, Hons; PhD. Appointments: Snr Rsch Sci, CSIRO; Prin Lectr, Univ of Adelaide; Adj Prof, Univ Arizona, USA. Publications: Livestock Management in the Arid Zone, 1981; Dryland Agriculture: A Systems Approach, jointly, 1991; Halophytes as a Resource for Livestock and for Rehabilitation of Degraded Lands, jointly, 1994; Combating Global Climate Change by Combating Desertification, jointly, 1997; Drylands: Sustainable Use of Rangelands into the Twenty-First Century, jointly; num pprs on rangeland management and sustainable agriculture. Hobbies: Travel; Antiques. Address: 497 Kensington Road, Wattle Park, SA 5066, Australia.

SRIDHAR M K, b. 10 Feb 1956, Bangalore, India. Professor. m. Veena H S, 6 May 1988, 1 s. Education: BSc, Natural Scis, 1977, MA, Sanskrit, 1979, PhD, Sanskrit, 1995, Bangalore Univ; MA, Engl, Venkateshwara Univ, 1988. Appointments: Lectr, Sanskrit, 1979-92, Prof, 1997-, Natl Coll, Bangalore. Publications: 5 books in Kannada Lang, 2 books in Engl. Honours: Prof M Hiriyanna Gold Medal. Memberships: Bangalore Sci Forum; Gandhi Cntr of Sci and Human Values; Bharatiya Vidya Bhavan; Press and Publicity Cttee Mbr, Xth World Sanskrit Conf, Bangalore, 1997; Visng Prof, Indian Inst of Ayurvedic Med, Bangalore, 1999; Hon Dir, Indological Rsch Fndn. Hobbies: Trekking; Writing; Meeting People. Address: No 125 Srividya, 7th Main, 5th Cross, Bikasipura Layout, Subramanyapura Post, Bangalore 560061, Karnataka State, India.

SRIVASTAVA Deepak Chandra, b. 10 Jan 1956, Barabanki, India. Teaching and Research. m. Amita, 4 June 1985, 1 s, 1 d. Education: PhD, Structural Geol, Indian Sch of Mines, Dhanbad, 1982. Appointments: Lectr, Rdr, Univ of Roorkee, 1982-; Assoc Prof, Univ of Roorkee, 1997-. Publication: Rsch in structural geol; Role of fluids in deformation. Honours: Sir Henry Hayden Medal, 1977; ISM Medal, 1977; Marie Curie Awd, Eurn Community, 1993. Memberships: Life Mbr, Indian Geol Congress; Life Mbr, Geol Soc of India; Life Mbr, Indian Inst Pub Admin. Hobbies: Cricket; Badminton; Music. Address: Department of Earth Sciences, University of Roorkee, Roorkee 247667 (UP), India.

SRIVASTAVA Shailesh Kumar, b. 1 July 1969, Gorakhpur, India. Insurance; Computer Professional. m. Anshu, 26 Nov 1996, 1 d. Education: PGDHRM, MBA, Ignou, New Delhi; DCA DDU Gorakhpur Univ, CMM (USA). Appointments: Ins Profl, LIC of India, Jubilee Coml, Promotor, LIC(P) Ltd, Gorakhpur. Creative work: Talk/th show on air, Doordarshan Students as "Sec", Student Union, MGPG Coll, Gorakhpur. Honour: Fellshp, Living World Soc, Gorakhpur; Fuwai, Chennai. Memberships: Leo Club; Cultural Sec, Chitranshi Kalyan Samiti; Rotract Club and Natl Yth Proj (India); Exec Mbr, The Living World Soc, Gorakhpur; Gmus, Nepal. Hobbies: Music; Social work; Tourism; Cricket. Address: Shailesh Kumar Sriyastava, HN 416, Alinagar (North), Gorakhpur, PIN 273001, India.

SRIVASTAVA Shubha Rani, b. 27 June 1963, Kanpur, India. Scientist. m. Dr V Kumar, 17 Feb 1990, 1 d. Education: MSc, Stats, IIT, Kanpur; PhD, Stats, IIT, Kanpur. Appointments: Lectr, PPN Coll Kanpur; Sci, Dept of Biostats and Computers. Memberships: Life Mbr, Indian Stat Soc; Life Mbr, Gujarat Stat Assn; Indian Pharm Assn. Hobbies: Reading; Drawing; Painting. Address: B V Patel Pharmaceutical Education and Research Development Centre, Thaltej Gandhinagar, Thaltej, Ahmedabad 380054, India.

ST JOHN Donald James Bourne, 12 June 1936, Melbourne, Aust. Clinical Gastroenterologist; Researcher. m. Margaret Anne Watson, 10 Mar 1962, 2 s, 2 d. Eduaction: MBBS, Melbourne; FRCP, London; FRACP. Appointments: Medl Registrar, Guys Hosp, London, 1965-66; Rsch Registrar, W Middlessex Hosp, London, 1966-67; Asst Physn, Clin Rsch Unit, Alfred Hosp, Melbourne, 1967-69; Lectr in Med, Monash Univ, Melbourne, 1969-71; Snr Lectr in Med, 1971-77; Dir of Gastroenterology, Roy Melbourne Hosp, 1977-; Snr Assoc, Med, Univ of Melbourne, 1977-; Cnslt Gastroenterologist, Fairfield Hosp for Infectious Diseases, Melbourne, 1979-91. Publications: Num articles to intl profl jrnls. Memberships: Gastroenterological Soc of Aust, Pres, 1987-89; Sci Advsry Bd, WHO Cntr for Prevention of Colorectal Cancer, NYC, 1988-; Chmn, Austl Gastroenterology Inst, 1993-95; Austl Medl Assn; Amn Gastroenterological Assn; Clin Oncological Soc of Aust; Hum Genetics Soc of Australasia; Intl Mbr, Italian Soc of Gastroenterology; Pres, 7th World Congress of Digective Endoscopy, Sydney, 1990. Hobbies: Gardening; History; Music; Tennis; Canoeing. Address: Department of Gastroenterology, The Royal Melbourne Hospital, RMH Post Office, Vic 3050, Australia.

STA MARIA Felice Prudente, b. 7 May 1950, San Fran, CA, USA. Writer; Museologue; Culture Worker. m. Andres B Sta Maria. Education: BA, Univ of Philippines (Diliman). Appointments include: Columnist, Manila Times, 1986-89; Pres, Metrop Mus of Manila, 1986-93; Vice-Chair, Natl Commn for Culture and the Arts (NCCA) Cttee for Museums, 1987-92; Opinion Page Columnist, Philippine Star, 1989-96; Chair, Intl Cncl of Mus (ICOM), Philippines, 1992-95; Chair, NCCA Cttee f Mus, 1992-95; Chair, NCCA Subcommn for Cultural Heritage, 1992-95; Commnr, Philippine Centennial Commn, 1993-99; Vice-Chair, Metrop Mus of Manila, 1993-; Commnr, UNESCO Natl Commn of the Philippines, 1993-; Pres, Atocha Alternatives, 1993-. Publications: Contbng Auth, Culinary Culture of the Philippines, 1976; Contbng Auth, Turn of the Century, 1978; Auth, Household Heirlooms and Antiques, 1979; Co-auth, Values Education Through History, 1996; Auth, In Excelcis: The Mission of Jose P Rizal, Humanist and Philippine National Hero, 1996; Ed, Contbng Auth, Discovering Philippine Art in Spain, 1998; Auth, Visions of the Possible: Legacies of Philippine Freedom, 1998. Honours include: Repub of France, Rank of Chevalier (Kt), le Grand Ordre des Artes des Lettres, 1990; Manila Critics Circle Natl Book Awd, Best Biography of Yr, 1997; Best Art Book of Yr, 1980 Book Dev Assn of Philippines, Gintong Aklat Awd, 1998; Ceres Alabado Awd for Outstndng Lit for Children, 1998; UP Sigma Delta Phi Alumnae Assn, Mariang Maya Awd for Lit (Hist and Culture), 1998; Pub Rels Soc of Philippines, Anvil Awd for Excellence, 1999; Philippine Centennial Commn, Gawad Sentenaryo, 1998; Univ of Philippines Alumni Assn, Outstndng Profl Awd for Arts and Letters, 1999. Memberships: Asia-Pacific Network for Intl Educ and Values Educ; Camera Club of Philippines; PEN; Sigma Delta Phi.

STACE Francis Nigel, b. 10 Oct 1915, Hamilton, NZ. Semi-retired Technical Editor. m. 16 Dec 1939, 1 s, 4 d. Education: BE, Elec Mech, 1937, BE, Mech, 1938, Cert of Proficiency in Prins and Prac of Jrnlsm, 1937, Univ of Canterbury, NZ. Appointments: Mngng Ed, Dir, Tech Publns Ltd, 1947-81; Sec, Elec Supply Authy Engrs Inst of NZ, 1946-81; Dir, Tech Books Ltd, 1948-78; Cnsltng Ed, 1980-. Publications: Technical Exposition Principles and Practice, 1940; Learning Service Achievement: 50 Years of Engineering in New Zealand (w W L Newnham), 1971; The Engineering History of Electric Supply in New Zealand, Vols 1, 2 and 3, (w L B Hutton), 1975; The Lineman's Handbook, 1985; 100 Years of Electricity Supply in New Zealand: The Contribution of the Electricity Supply Authorities, 1988; Mowats From Marlborough (w S Clarke and K H Mowat), 1993; Contbr of articles to confs. Memberships: Assn of Sci and Tech Commnrs (NZ); Inst of Elec Engrs, London; Inst of Elec and Electronic Engrs, NY, USA; Electricity Engrs Assn of NZ; Amn Soc for Engrng Educ; Inst of Profl Engrs, NZ. Hobbies: Engineering History; Rotary. Address: 58 Cecil Road, Wellington 6001, New Zealand.

STACK Barbara, b. 4 June 1929, Johannesburg, S Afr. Author. m. George Patrick, 22 May 1952, 4 s. Education: Postgrad Dip, Occupational Hazard Mngmt, Ballarat Univ Coll. Publications: Handbook of Mining and Tunnelling Machinery; RSI: The Practical Solution; Encyclopaedia of Tunnelling, Mining and Drilling Equipment. Honours: Ctf of Merit by Tasmanian Br of Inst of Engrs; Cert of Commendation, Natl Body of Inst of Engrs. Memberships: Austl Soc of Writers; Tasmanian Writers Assn. Hobbies: Aikido; Gardening; Painting; Cake decorating; Table tennis. Address: GPO Box 516E, Hobart, Tasmania, Australia.

STALEY Anthony Allan, b. 15 May 1939. Company Director; Federal President, Liberal Party of Australia. m. (1) Elsa (diss), 3 s, 1 d, (2) Maggie, 2 Dec 1989, 1 d. Education: University of Melbourne. Appointments: Pres, Students Rep C1, 1961-62; Ldr, Aust Univs Students Deleg to USSR & USA, 1962; Tutor, 1965, Lectr, 1966, Snr Lectr, Polit Sci, 1969, Univ Melbourne; Mbr, Vic Exec Lib Party, 1968-70; MHR (lib) Chisolm Vic, 1970-80; Parly Sec to Ldr Opposition, 1973-75; Min, Capital Territory and Asstng PM Arts, 1976-77; Ldr, Parly DDeleg Mid E, 1977; Min, Post & Telecomms, 1977-80; Mbr, Bd of Advice AON, Chmbn Austl Bus Access; Mbr, Taxation Concession Cttee of the Ind Rsch & Dev Bd; Chmn, Elec Ind Ombudsman VIC; Chmn, Coop Rsch Cntrs Assn; Dir, RAMS Home Loans Pty Ltd, 1994-; Chmn, Cl Telecomms Ind, Ombudsman Ltd, 1996-. Membership: Melbourne MCC. Hobbies: Reading; Tennis; Sports; Poetry; Theatre. Address: Feeneys lane, Lancefield, Vic 3435, Australia.

STALLON Sylvester Enzio, b. 6 Jul 1946 NY. Actor; Film Dir. m. (1) Sasha Czach, 1974, div, 2 s; (2) Brigitte Nielsen, 1985, div 1987; 1 d by Jennifer Flavin. Education: Am Coll of Switzerland; Univ of Miami. Appointments: Has had many jobs inclng usher bouncer horse trainer store detective physical educ tchr; Now actor and prodr and dir of own films; Fndr White Eagle Co. Film appearances incl: Lords of Flatbush, 1973; Capone, 1974; Rocky, 1976; FIST, 1978; Paradise Alley, 1978; Rocky II, 1979; Nighthawks, 1980; Escape to Victory, 1980; Rocky III, 1981; Prodr dir film Staying Alive, 1983; First Blood Rambo, 1984; Rocky IV, 1985; Cobra, 1986; Over the Top, 1986; Rambo II, 1986; Dir Carolco Pictures Inc, 1987-; Rambo III, 1988; Lock Up, 1989; Set Up, 1990; Tango and Cash, 1990; Rocky V, 1990; Isobar, 1991; Stop or My Mom Will Shoot, 1991; Oscar, 1991; Cliffhanger, 1992; Demolition Man, 1993; Judge Dredd, 1994; The Specialist, 1994; Assassins, 1995; Firestorm, 1996; Daylight, 1996; Cop Land. Honours: Oscar for best film, 1976; Golden Circle Awd for best film 1976; Donatello Awd, 1976; Christopher Relig Awd, 1976; Hon mbr Stuntmans' Assn; Officier Ordre des Arts et des Lettres. Memberships: Mbr Screen Actors Guild; Mbr Writers Guild; Mbr Dirs Guild. Address: William Morris Agency, 151 El Camino Drive, Beverly Hills, CA 90212, USA.

STAMM Walter John, b. 12 May 1926, Bowral, NSW, Aust. Director of Engineering Consultancy. m. Helen Elizabeth Van Scyoc, 21 Feb 1953, 2 s, 2 d. Education: BE, Sydney Univ, 1944-47; Advd Mngmt Prog, Harvard Bus Sch, 1976. Appointments: Cadet Engr rising to Wrks Mngr, Fans and Motors Div, Email-Orange, 1948-60; Chf Prodn Engr, Prod Dev Mngr, Coml Prods Sales Mngr, Grp Gen Mngr, Coml Prods, Simpson Pope, 1961-79; Mngng Dir, John Shearer, 1979-85; Chmn of Dirs, Hlth &

Life Care, 1986-87; Engrng Cnlts Dir, Bishop Stamm Assocs, 1986-. Honours: Jack Finlay Awd, Inst of Prodn Engrs, 1982; AM, 1986. Memberships: Fell, Inst of Engrs, Aust, Pres 1986; Fell, Austl Acady of Technological Sci. Hobbies: Golf; His small farm; Metal working; Woodworking. Address: Box 456, Morphett Vale, SA 5162, Australia.

STANBRIDGE Beverley Anne, b. 6 July 1946, Oxford, Eng. Teacher. m. Frank Stanbridge, 9 Oct 1977, 1 d. Education: BS (Hons); MSc; DipEd; MEd; Currently completing PhD. Appointments: Sci Coord, St Mary's Coll, Woree, Cousins, Queensland 4868, 1978. Publications: Num pprs, some in sci educ jrnls. Honours: Inaugural Fell, UK Aust Exchange for Tchrs of Sci, 1990. Memberships: Austl Sci Tchrs Assn; Assn for Sci Educ (UK). Hobbies: Bushwalking; Horse trekking; Environmental conservation. Address: 51, Sheehy Road, Whiterock, Cairns, Queensland, Australia 4868.

STANBURY Peter John, b. 28 Sept 1934, Exeter, Devon, England. Museum Director. 1 s, 1 d. Education: PhD. Appointments: Snr Lectr in Zoology, Dir of News & Pub Rels, Univ of Sydney; Dir of Mus, Natl Trust of NSW; Advsr, Mus & Collections, Macquarie Univ. Publications include: Looking at Mammals, 1970; Reproduction, 1971; 100 Years of Australian Scientific Exploration, 1975; Man and Life, 1975; Household and Garden Pests, 1976; The Mechanical Eye, 1977; Australia's Animals Discovered, 1979; Conserving Historic Photographs, 1982; Discovwer Australia's Museums, 1983; Rediscovering Historic Photographs, 1983; Toys to Remember, 1987; A Field Guide to Aboriginal Rock Engravings, 1990; Cinderella Collections: The Management and Conservation of Australian University Museums and Herbaria, 1998. Honour: OAM. Hobbies: Objects; Outdoors. Address: c/o Vice Chancellors Office, Macquarie University, Sydney, NSW 2109, Australia.

STANDEN David Herbert, b. 8 May 1929, Denman, NSW, Aust. Architect; Lecturer; Commercial Arbitrator. m. Janice Patricia Standen, 26 July 1969. Education: BArch, Univ of Sydney, 1951. Appointments: Govt Archt, Port Moresby, Papua New Guinea, 1952-55; In local govt, NZ, 1955-61; Archt in priv prac, Perth, WA, 1962-73; Lectr, Snr Lectr, Assoc Prof, Dept of Archt, Curtin Univ, Perth, 1974-93; Bldng Dispute Cnslt & Coml Arbitrator, 1994-. Publications: Construction Industry Terminology, 3 eds; Construction Industry Specifications; If You Practise Architecture. Honour: Mbr, Order of Aust, 1985. Memberships: Life Fell, Roy Austl Inst of Archts; Hon Fell, NZ Inst of Archts; Fell, Inst of Arbitrators, Aust. Hobbies: Cryptic Crosswords; Marron Fishing. Address: 17 Gemsarna Crescent, Kelmscott, WA 6111, Australia.

STANFORD Peter Seymour Bedel, b. 17 Aug 1947, Singapore. Diplomate. m. Janni, 1 s. Education: BA, LLB, ANU; Hon Dip, Cmty Med, John A Burns Sch of Med, Univ HI. Appointments: Dpty High Cmmnr, Suvca Fiji, 1986-88; Austl Amb to Fed States of Micronesia, Repub of the Marshall Islands, Repub of Palau, 1991-95. Memberships: Rotary Club VP; Roy Selawgur Club, Malaysia; C'wlth & Roy Canberra Golf Clubs. Hobbies: Farming; Fishing; Gardening; Skiing. Address: c/o Department of Foreign Affairs & Trade, Kingston, ACT 2604, Australia.

STANFORD-SMITH Jonathan Kim Roylance, b. 4 Nov 1951, Aylesbury, Eng. Lawyer. m. Susan Beverley Fullick, 1970, div, 2 s. Education: LLB, hons, Univ London, 1976. Appointments: Snr Crt Clk, W Sussex Magistrates Crt Cttee, 1977-80; Litigation Solicitor, Pvte Prac, 1980-83; Chf Magistrate, Solomon Islands, 1983-87; Reg of the High Crt, Chf Magistrate, Reg of the Crt of Appeal, Sheriff, Cmmnr of the High Crt of the Solomon Islands, 1987-90; Snr Lectr, Univ of the S Pacific, Pacific Law Unit, 1990-93; Regl Legal Advsr, Oceania, ODA-Pacific Regl Advsry Grp, 1990-93; Regl Legal Advsr, ODA Pacific/Judicial, Legal & Rights Educn Prog, 1993-95; Dir, Resource Trainer, Regl Legal Advsr, DFID Pacific-Pacific Regl Human Rights Educn Resource Team, 1995-98. Publication: Benchbooks for a number of Pacific Is Cntrs, Fiji, Samoa, Niue, Cook Is. Honours:

Edis Conveyancing and Real Property Prize, Worthing Law Soc, 1980; UNICEF Maurice Pate Awd, 1998. Hobbies: Squash; Diving; Music. Address: 40 St Francis Close, Haywards Heath, West Sussex RH16 4JP, England.

STANLEY Madan Kumar, b. 24 Mar 1947, Kolar, India. Librarian. m. Padma, 9 Feb 1995. Education: BSc, Mysore Univ: BLibSc, MA, MLibSc, PhD, Karnatak Univ. Appointments: Tchr, Libn, Sainik Sch, Bijapur, 1966-69; Lib Asst, Asst Libn, Dpty Libn, Univ of Agricl Scis, Bangalore, 1969-87; Libn, Univ of Agricl Scis, Dharwad, 1987-. Publications: Sev chapts in books. Honour: State Awd. Memberships: IASLIC; ILA; AALDI; SIS. Hobbies: Reading; Travel. Address: University of Agricultural Sciences, Dharwad 580005, India.

STANNARD Robert William, b. 16 Sept 1926. Director. m. Shirley Mavis Sparkes, 11 Dec 1956, 1 son, dec, 2 d. Education: BCom; FCA. Appointments: Ptnr, Peat Marwick (now KPMG), Chart Accts, 1954-87; Statutory Mngr, Pu Serv Invest Soc, 1979-87; Chmn, Milburn NZ, 1987-97; Fruitfed Supplies Ltd, 1992-97, Bank of NZ, 1992-96, Tstees Executors, 1991-. Honours: CMG, 1982; NZ Medal, 1990. Memberships: NZ Inst of Dirs; NZ Soc of Accts. Hobbies: Tramping; Lawn bowls; Reading. Listed in: Who's Who in New Zealand; International Who's Who. Address: 36 Spencer Street, Crofton Downs, Wellington, New Zealand.

STANTON Harry Edward, b. 28 Apr 1932, Melbourne, Aust. Clinical Psychologist. m. Valerie Joy, 1 Feb 1956, 1 s, 1 d. Education: BA; BEd; MA; PhD. Appointments: Tchrs Colls, 1964-68, Lectr to Snr Lectr in Educ, Flinders Univ, S Aust, 1969-74; Dir, HERAC, Univ of Tasmania, 1974-92. Publications: Over 200 articles; 8 books inclng: Help Students Learn: The Improvement of Higher Education, 1978; The Plus Factor: A Guide to Positive Living, 1979; The Healing Factor: A Guide to Positive Health, 1981; The Stress Factor: A Guide to More Relaxed Living, 1983; The Fantasy Factor: Using the Imagination to Solve Everyday Problems, 1985; The Success Factor: Succeeding in Business and later in Life, 1988; Study Skills, 1991; The Winning Factor: Using Psychology to Achieve Sporting Sucess, 1994; Let the Trade Winds Flow: Psychology for Supertraders, 1997. Honour: Fell, Amn Soc of Clin Hypnosis. Memberships: Aust Psychol Soc; Austl Soc of Hypnosis; Intl Soc of Hypnosis; Intl Inst of Psychosomatics; Intl Soc of Eclectic Psychologists. Hobbies: Swimming; Dancing; Reading; Music; Tennis. Address: 12 Sonning Crescent, Sandy Bay, Tasmania 7005, Australia.

STANTON John Edward, b. 4 Oct 1950, Howick, NZ. Anthropologist. Education: BA, MA, Auckland; PhD, W Aust. Appointments: Snr Tutor Anthropol, 1978, Curator, Berndt Mus of Anthropol, 1980, Univ W Aust. Publications: Aboriginal Australian Art, 1982-98; Images of Aboriginal Australia, 1988; Nyungar Landscapes, 1992. Memberships: Austl Inst Aboriginal Stdies; Pres, Anthropol Soc of WA. Hobbies: Photography; Landscape architecture. Address: Berndt Museum of Anthropology, University of Western Australia, Nedlands, WA 6907, Australia.

STANWIX Justin Thomas. Lawyer. m. 29 Dec 1965, 2 s, 2 d. Education: Bachelor Laws. Appointments: Ptnr, Mallesons Stephen Jaques, Canberra, ACT; Natl Hd, Govt Grp; Mbr, ACT Bars and Sols Admission Bd, Law Cncl Legal Aid Admnstv Law Cttee. Memberships: Law Cncl Aust; Law Socs NSW, Vic, ACT, WA. Hobbies: Reading; Travel; Bush walking. Address: 60 Marcus Clark Street, Canberra, ACT 2601, Australia.

STAPLES Robert Eugene, b. 28 June 1942, Roanoke, VA, USA. University Professor. Div. Education: AA; AB; MA; PhD. Publications: 13 books. Honours: Distinguished Achievement Awds, Harvard Univ and the Natl Cncl of Family Rels. Memberships: Amn Sociology Assn; Natl Cncl on Family Rels. Hobbies: Reading; Tennis; Movies; Travel. Address: Box 0612, University of California, San Francisco, CA 94143, USA.

STARK Richard James, b. 6 Oct 1950, Melbourne, Aust. Medical Practitioner (Neurologist). m. Janet Keys-Brown, 15 Dec 1972, 1 s, 1 d. Education: C'wlth Schlsp, Gen Exhbn, Snr Govt Schlsp, 1967; MB, BS, 1st class hons, 1973, Monash Univ, 1968-73; FRACP, 1980. Appointments: Res Med Staff, Alfred Hosp, 1974-78, Neurol Registrar, 1977-78; London Hosp, 1979-81, Natl Hosps for Nervous Disease, 1981; Visng Asst Neurologist, Alfred Hosp, 1982-84; Visng Neurologist, Caulfield Hosp, 1982-, Peter MacCallum Hosp, 1982-, Alfred Hosp, 1984-. Publications: Var sci pprs on neurol. Honours: Sophie Davis Mem Prize, 1973; Robert Power Schlsp in Surg, 1973; AHRG Assn Prize, 1973; PHH Prize in Clin Med, 1973; Bushell Fellshp in Med of the Allied Scis, 1977; AAN Appointee to NHQS, 1981. Memberships: Austl Med Assn; Fell, Roy Austl Coll of Physns; Austl Assn of Neurologists, Cncl Mbr, 1983-, Hon Sec, 1983-86, Hon Treas, 1997-; Sec, SAC, Neurol of RACP, 1983-; Melbourne Cricket Club; XXIX Club; S Hampstead Cricket Club; Roy Melbourne Tennis Club. Hobbies: Cricket; Real tennis. Address: 15 Collins Street, Melbourne, Vic, Australia.

STAUBUS George Joseph, b. 26 Apr 1926, Brunswick, Mo, USA. Accounting Educator. m. Sarah Mayer, 11 Apr 1949, 2 s. 2 d. Education: BS, Univ Mo; MBA, PhD, Univ Chicago; Cert'd Pub Acct, Ill. Appointments: Instr, Univ Chicago; Visng Prof, London Bus Sch; Visng Prof, NYU; Erskine Fellow, Univ Canterbury; Asst, Assoc Prof, Haas Sch of Bus, Univ CA at Berkeley. Publications: A Theory of Accounting to Investors, 1961; Activity Costing and Input-Output Accounting, 1971; Making Accounting Decisions, 1977; Economic Influences on the Development of Accounting in Firms, 1996. Honours: Amn Acctng Assn Disting Intl Lectr, 1982; CA Soc of CPAs Outstndng Acctng Educr, 1981. Memberships: Amn Acctng Assn; Amn Inst CPAs; Fin Exec Inst. Address: El Cerrito, CA, USA.

STCHIN Gowa, b. 2 Nov 1949 Guangzhou Cty. Actress. Appointments: With Inner Mongolia Song and Dance Ensemble, 1965-79; Film actress First August Film Studio, 1981-. Films incl: Luotuo Xiangzi, 1981; Fleeting Time, 1984; Xianghun Girl, 1992. Honours: Winner Golden Rooster Awd Hundred Flowers; Best Actress Awd in China for Luotuo Xiangzi, 1982; Best Actress Awd in Hong Kong for Fleeting Time; Best Film in Berlin Film Fest for Xianghun Girl. Address: Room 307, Building 2, Panjiapo Hutong, Beijing 100020, People's Republic of China.

STEANE David Frank Athol, b. 22 May 1927, Kashmir, India. Consultant. m. Adrienne Beatrice Mary Hadden, 10 Feb 1956, 4 s. Education: BSc, 1951, BForestry, 1951, Tas Univ; Dip Forestry, Austl Forestry Sch, Canberra, 1951; MSc, Conserv, Univ Coll, London, Eng, 1967; Dip of Gemmology. Appointments: Sand Dune Reclamation Offr, Conserv Offr, Chief Land Mngmt Offr, Lands Dept, Tas, 1954-86; Cnslt, Coastal Protection and Land Mngmt, 1987-. Honours: Churchill Fellshp, 1966, 12 mnths to study conserv and land use w MSc in Conserv, Univ Coll, London, Eng; Hon Rsch Assoc, Dept of Agricl Sci, Univ of Tas, 1987-. Memberships: Inst of Foresters of Aust; Environl Inst of Aust; Assoc, Austl Inst of Landscape Archts. Hobbies: Bushwalking; Skiing; Landcare; Natural History; Gemmology; Lapidary. Address: 7 Montagu Street, New Town, Tas 7008, Australia.

STEANE Dorothy Anne, b. 7 Oct 1966, Hobart, Tasmania. Plant Scientist. m. G J Davidson, 2 d. Appointments: Post-doct Rsch Fell, Coop Rsch Cntr for Temperate Hardwood Forestry, 1995-. Honours: Rhodes Schlshp, Tasmania, 1991; TAsTV-Temco Young Achiever Awd for Sci and Technol, 1991; Irene Manton Prize, Linnaean Soc, London, 1995. Memberships: Soc of Systematic Biologists; Botl Soc of Am; Amn Soc of Plant Taxonomists; Soc of Austl Systematic Biologists. Hobbies: Cycling; Walking; Underwater hockey; Scuba diving; Cross-country skiing, Yoga. Address: PO Box 592, Sandy Bay, Tasmania 7006, Australia.

STEEDMAN David MacGregor, b. 8 Dec 1919. Presbyterian Minister. m. Elaine Mayfield Cooper, 22 Jan 1947, 1 s, 2 d. Education: MA, NZ; BD, Melbourne; PhD, Vic, Univ of Wellington, NZ. Appointments: Presby Parish Min: Ashburton, 1945-49, Geraldine, 1949-54, Anderson's Bay, Dunedin, 1954-62, Cashmere Hills, Christchurch, 1962-67; Tchr, Presby Trng Inst, Tangoa, Vanuatu, 1967-68; St Andrew's Christchurch, 1969-76; St John's Wellington, 1976-85; Retd; Convenor, publ cttee, The Outlook, 1963-66. Honour: Moderator, Presby Ch of NZ 1982-83. Memberships: Allan McLean Trust, 1969-75; Bd of Govs Ch Schs, inclg Columba Coll, Dunedin, 1955-62; Convener, Presby Ch Schs Cttee, 1981-88; Hon Pres, Wellington Boy's and Girl's Inst, 1976-84; Sec Seafarer's Welfare Bd for NZ, 1981-96; Padre Wellington Toc H, 1976-95; Bible Soc, NZ, 1983-94, Pres 1982. Hobbies: Seafarers Welfare; NZ History; Reading. Address: 4 Laurent Place, Wellington, 6002, New Zealand.

STEELE Henry Charles, b. 21 Dec 1944, Eng. Lecturer. m. Bunyen, 9 Nov 1994. Education: BSc Econ, London; MA Mktg, Lancaster. Appointments: Stats (MR) Ltd, Middlesex Poly, Wolverhampton Poly, Hong Kong Poly, Lingnan Coll. Memberships: Pres, HK Inst of Mktg, Chmn, Dir of Educ, Educl Plcy; MCIM; MILOG; MMRSHK; FRGS; AIB; ACR; AMI; FHKIM. Hobbies: Music; Travel; Natural history. Address: Dept of Marketing & International Business, Lingnan College, Fu Tei, Tuen Mun, NT, Hong Kong, SAR.

STEELE John Gladstone, b. 20 July 1935, Brisbane, Aust. Anglican Priest. Education: BSc, 1960, PhD, 1964, Univ of Queensland; ThL, Austl Coll of Theol, 1958. Appointments: Lectr in Phys, Univ of Queensland, 1967-95; Anglican Priest, 1959-; Priest in Charge, Parish of Stradbroke Island, 1993-. Publications: The Explorers of the Moreton Bay District, 1770-1830, 1972; Brisbane Town in Convict Days, 1824-1842, 1975; The Brisbane River, 1976; Conrad Martens in Queensland, 1978; Aboriginal Pathways in Southeast Queensland and the Richmond River, 1984. Honours: J P Thomson Medal, Roy Geogl Soc of Australasia, 1985; Hon Canon, St John's Cath, Brisbane, 1995. Memberships: Fmrly Mbr of Austl Inst of Phys; Austl Marine Scis Assn; Austl Meteorological and Oceanographic Soc. Hobbies: History; Religion; Travel. Address: 7/48 Dunmore Terrace, Auchenflower, Qld 4066, Australia.

STEGGALL Barry Edward Hector, b. 19 Aug 1943, Swan Hill, Vic, Aust. Member of the National Party of Victorian Parliament. m. Sue, 29 Jan 1972, 1 s, 2 d. Education: Swan Hill Sch; Gordon Inst of Technol, Geelong, Vic. Appointments: Sec, Coalition since its inception; Convenor Food Vic, 1992-; Parly Sec for State Dev, 1996-. Hobby: Golf. Address: 274 Campbell Street, Swan Hill, Vic, Australia 3585.

STEHBENS Ian Robert, b. 25 July 1946, Gympie, Aust. Minister of Religion. m. Margaret Baker, 14 Dec 1968, 1 s, 2 d. Education: Cert of Tchng, Kelvin Grove, 1966; BA, Qld Univ, 1974; MSc, Griffith Univ, 1983; BTh, Brisbane Coll of Theol, 1990. Appointments: Second Tchrm Clifton, 1967-71, Camp Hill, 1972, Oxley, 1973-74; Hd, Geog Dept, Holland Park hs, 1975-77; Visng Tchr, C'wlth Inst, London and Edinburgh, UK, 1978; Hd, Socl Scis Dept, Holland Park hs, 1979-82; Hd, Geog/Econs Dept, Toowoomba hs, 1983-88; Chf Examiner, Geog, Bd of Snr Second Sch Studies, Qld, 1982-90; Ordained Min, Uniting Ch in Aust, 1990; Min, Laidley Parish, 1991-95; Prin, Alan Walker Coll of Evangelism, 1995-; Dir, Indonesian Miss Inst, 1998-. Publications: The Changing Surface of the Earth, 4th ed, 1985 (w C R Twidale); Settlement Patterns and Processes, 4th ed, 1987 (w D D Harris); Human and Environmental Hazards, 1986 Macmillan Australian Atlas, 1983 (co-auth); Nile: Simulation of Human Responses to River Behaviour, 1987; Body of Christ, 1990. Honours: C'wlth Inst Awd, 1978; Thompson Medal, Roy Geog Soc, 1985. Memberships Fell, Roy Geog Soc, London; Roy Geog Soc of Australasia; Geog Tchrs Assn of Qld; Qld Family Hist Soc; Natl Goals and Directions Inc. Hobbies: Family History; Social Geography. Address: 6 Lincluden Place, Oatlands, NSW 2117, Australia.

STEHBENS William Ellis, b. 6 Aug 1926, Sydney, Aust. Professor of Pathology. m. Jean S Raeside, 25 Mar 1961, 2 s, 3 d. Education: MBBS, Univ of Sydney, 1951; DPhil, Univ of Oxford, Eng, 1960; MD, Univ of Sydney, 1962; FRCPath; FRCPA. Appointments: Lectr, Snr Lectr, Univ of Sydney, 1952-62; Deptl Demonstrator, Univ of Oxford, 1958-60; Snr Rsch Fell, Snr Fell, Austl Natl Univ, 1962-66; Assoc Prof, Prof, Wash Univ of St Louis Sch of Med, USA, 1966-68; Prof, Union Univ, NY, 1968-74; Prof, Chmn, Wellington Sch of Med, Univ of Otago, NZ, 1974-92; Dir, Malaghan Inst of Med Rsch, 1974-93; Emer Prof of Path, 1992-. Publications: 4 books and 272 sci pprs. Honours include: Schlshps and Fellshps; Agnes Guthrie Prize for Rsch, 1959; Peter Bancroft Prize for Rsch, 1965; RT Hall Rsch Prize, 1965; Alexander von Humboldt Rsch Prize, 1993. Memberships: Fell, Roy Coll of Pathols, Eng; Fell, Intl Col of Angiologists; Life Mbr, Soc for Biomed Rsch. Hobby: Raising sheep. Address: Department of Pathology, Wellington School of Medicine, PO Box 7343, Wellington South, New Zealand.

STEICKE Lance Graham, b. 19 Feb 1933, Murray Bridge, Sth Aust. Clergyman. m. Leah, 13 Dec 1955, 2 s, 2 d. Education: Concordia Coll, Adelaide; Concordia Seminary, Adelaide, S Aust. Appointments: Pres, Ev Luth Ch, NZ, 1964-79; 2nd VP Luth Ch of Aust, 1981-87; Dir, Luth Radio and TV, 1979-87; Pres, Luth Ch of Aust, 1987-. Honour: DD, Luth Ch, MO Synod, USA, 1989. Memberships: Natl Hds of Chs, Aust. Hobbies: Love for the Gospel of Christ; Gardening; Walking. Address: 197 Archer Street, North Adelaide 50006, South Australia, Australia.

STEIN Clarissa Ingeborg, b. 3 Sept 1948. Editor; Publisher. m. Herbert, 1 d. Education: Dip, Finanzwirt (FH). Appointment: Ed, w Papyrus Publng, 1991-. Creative works: New Melodies - Neue Melodien; Notes of My Land; Billy Tea and Sand Ballet. Membership: Soc of Women Writers (Aust). Hobbies: Philosophy; Reading. Address: PO Box 7144, Upper Ferntree Gully, Vic 3156, Australia.

STEIN Eduardo, Minister of Foreign Affairs. Education: Univ of St Louis, MO, USA; Northwestern Univ, IL, USA. Appointments: Pres Advsr, Interior Affairs, Panama, 1980-82; Dir, Cntrl Amn Prog, Univ Commns; Reg Devs, Latin Amn Econ System and Techl Co-ordinator, Latin Amn Agy of Spec Info Servs, 1982-93; Regl Proj Cnslr for Cntrl Am, Intl Org for Migration, 1993-95; Mbr, Assn for Rsch and Socl Stdies, 1993-95. Address: Ministry of Foreign Affairs, Palacio Nacional, 6a Calle y 7a Avda, Zona 1, Guatemala City, Guatemala.

STENZEL David Bentheim, b. 5 Jan 1927, NY, USA. Professor of History. m. Muriel Powers, 12 Sept 1958, 2 s, 1 d. Education: MA, 1954, PhD, 1957, Univ of CA at Berkeley. Appointments: Asst Prof, Stanford Univ, 1957-61, Univ of CA at Berkeley, 1957; Prof of Hist, CA State Univ, 1961-91. Publications: Book, The Russians: Victims of History, 1991; Num articles in learned jrnls, 1961-91. Honours: Phi Beta Kappa, 1957; Paul Harris Fell, Rotary, 1972. Memberships: Amn Histl Assn 1954-98; Enrichment Lectr, Roy Viking Line, 1982-91; Crystal Cruises, 1991-. Hobbies: Philately; Numismatics; Travel. Address: 761 East Tuolumne Road, Turlock, CA 95382, USA.

STEPHAN John J, b. 8 Mar 1941, Chgo, USA. Historian. m. Barbara Brooks, 22 June 1963. Education: BA, MA, Harvard Univ; PhD, London Univ. Appointments: Asst Prof, 1970-72, Assoc Prof, 1972-77, Prof of Hist, 1977-, Univ of HI. Publications: Sakhalin, 1971; The Kuril Islands, 1974; The Russian Facists, 1978; Hawaii Under the Rising Sun, 1984; The Russian Far East, 1994. Honours: Japan Culture Translation Prize, 1973; Kenneth W Baldridge Prize, 1996. Memberships: Life Mbr: Assn for Asian Studies; Amn Histl Assn; Canad Histl Assn. Address: Department of History, University of Hawaii, 2530 Dole Street, Honolulu, HI 96822-2383, USA.

STEPHENS Frank Douglas, b. 10 Oct 1913, Melbourne, Vic, Aust. Paediatric Surgeon. m. (1) Rosalie Wood Tyler, 21 Oct 1943, dec 1994, 2 s, 1 d, (2) Victoria Gladys Cook, 4 Mar 1995. Education: MB, BS, 1936, MS, 1942, Univ of Melbourne; FRACS, 1942. Appointments: Served in World War II, Mid E and SWPA, 1939-45; Rsch Fell, Hosp for Sick Children, London, Eng, 1948-50; Dir of Surgl Rsch, 1957-75, currently Hon Rsch Fell, Roy Childrens Hosp, Melbourne, Vic; Emer Prof of Surg and Urology, Northwestern Univ, Chgo, IL, USA; Urologist, Childrens Mem Hosp, Chgo, USA. Publications: Auth of 5 books on Congenital Anormalities; 150 orig articles in medl jrnls. Honours: DSO, AIF, 1942; OA, 1987; Denis Browne Medal, Brit Assn of Paediat Surgns, 1976; Urology Medal, 1986, W E Ladd Medal (Surg), 1989, Amn Acady Pediats; Disting Serv Awd, Roy Childrens Hosp, 1995. Memberships: Austl Med Assn; Brit Assn of Paediat Surgns; Amn Acady of Pediats. Hobbies: Watercolour painting; Tennis; Golf; Trout fishing. Listed in: Who's Who in Australia. Address: 26 Grange Road, Toorak, Vic 3142, Australia.

STEPHENS Tainui, b. 26 Apr 1958, Christchurch, NZ. Televison Producer. m. 1 s, dec, 1 d. Education: Tribal affiliation - Te Rarawa. Creative works include: Dir/Reporter, KOHA, weekly Maori mag series, 1985; OB Dir, New Zealand Polynesian Fest, cultural perf event, 1986; Prodr/Dir, Te Kohanga Reo, 100 episode maori lang childrens series, 1987; Prodr/Dir, KOHA, weekly Maori mag series, 1988; Prodr/Dir/Writer, Maori Battalion March to Victory, documentary, 1990; Prodr/Dir, Marae, a 38 part two-hour maori mag and archive series, 1991; Prodr/Dir, When the Haka Became Boogie, a four part musical series for Marae, 1992; Prodr/Dir, 1993 MDC Maori Sports Awards, a sporting awards highlights package, 1993; Prodr/Dir, Storytellers of the Pacific, a four part documentary series, an intl co-prodn, 1995; Prodr/Dir, Writer, Icon in B Minor, an arts documentary featuring New Zealand's leading concert pianist, 1996; Exec Prodr, Mai Time, 35 part maori bilingual yth entertainment series, Prodr, Waka Huia, 38 part maori lang histl series, Dir, The New Zealand Wars, 5 part histl documentary series, Exec Prodr, Maori Progs Dept, TVNZ (admin, trng, network liason w indeps, cnslt, 1998. Hobbies: Te Ao Maori; Music; Literature; People. Address: 1/11 William Street, Takapuna, Auckland.

STEVENS Graeme Roy, b. 17 July 1932, Lower Hutt, NZ. Palaeontologist. m. Diane Louise Morton Olivier, 20 Oct 1962, 2 s, 1 d. Education: BSc, MSc, 1st class hons, Geol, Vic Univ of Wellington, 1951-55; PhD, Geol, Cambridge Univ, Eng, 1956-59. Appointments: Lectr, Vic Univ of Wellington, 1954-55; Chf Palaeontologist, Dpty Dir, NZ Geol Survey, 1956-92; Demonstrator in Geol, Cambridge Univ, 1956-59; Snr Rsch Assoc, Inst of Geol and Nuclear Scis. Publications: 171 publd sci wrks inclng the books: Rugged Landscape, 1974; A Trampers Geology of the Tararuas, 1974; New Zealand Adrift, 1980; Lands in Collision, 1985; Prehistoric New Zealand, 1988; The Great New Zealand Fossil Book, 1990; On Shaky Ground, 1991. Honours: McKay Hammer Awd, Geol Soc of NZ, 1959; Wattie Book of the Yr Awd, 1974, 1980; Fellshp, Roy Soc of NZ, 1976; DSc, Vic Univ, 1988; QSO, Serv to NZ Sci, 1994. Memberships: Roy Soc of NZ; NZ Assn of Scis; Geol Soc of NZ; Systematics Soc; Palaeontol Assn. Hobbies: Cross Country Running; Walking; Swimming; Reading; Local History; Presenter of Science to the Public; Museum Display Techniques. Address: Institute of Geological & Nuclear Sciences, PO Box 30368, Lower Hutt, New Zealand.

STEVENS Thomas Granville, b. 9 Jan 1942, Los Angeles, CA, USA. Psychologist, Professor. m. Sherry Bene, 23 June 1991, 2 s, 1 d. Education: BA, Sch of Theo Clarement, 1964; MA, 1967, MTh, 1968; PhD, Psychol, Univ of HI, 1973. Appointments: Utd Methodist Min, 1967-68; Phys Instr, Univ of HI, 1970-71; Psychol, CA State Univ, 1973-. Publications: A Guide to Better Self Management and Career Planning, 1975; Our Journey to Self Actualization, 1993; You Can Choose to Be Happy, 1998. Honours: Lic MFT and Psychol; 5 Grants. Memberships: APA; WPA; AABT; CFA. Hobbies: Tennis; Skiing; Hiking; Music; Travel. Address: 481-102 Medford Court, Long Beach, CA 90803, USA.

STEVENSON Eric Houston, b. 19 Sept 1923, UK (Edinburgh). Company Director. Education: BCom, 1947; CA (Chartered Acct), 1948; ACMA (Cost & Mngmt Acct), 1949. Appointments: Mngng Dir, Cottage Rusks Ltd, 1948-65; Affined Foods Ltd, 1965-67; Cerebos Asia Ltd, 1969-72; Highland Flies (s) Pte Ltd, 1972-. Honour: Ford Fndn Bus Grant, 1958. Memberships: Pres, Edinburgh Jnr Chmbr of Com, 1955; Jnr Chmbr, Scot, 1958; Jnr Chmbr Intl, 1963. Hobbies: Snooker; Bridge; Sailing. Address: 7-B Jalan Berjaya, Singapore 578603.

STEVENSON Graeme Tyson, b. 22 June 1945, Melbourne, Aust. Agricultural Consultant; Educator. m. Janice, 13 Mar 1973, 1 s, 2 d. Education: HDA, Hawkesbury Dip of Agric; Bachelor Rural Sci (1st Class Honours), PhD, Animal Sci, Univ of New Eng. Honours: 1st Class Hons, Univ of New Eng, 1984; Gowrie Schlshp, 1986. Memberships: Austl Inst of Agricl Sci and Technol; Indep Organic Inspectors Assn (Intl). Hobbies: Modern History; Organic Gardening; Farming. Address: 13 Guy Crescent, Somerset, Tasmania, Australia 7320.

STEWART Alfred Neil, b. 19 Aug 1930, Fremantle, WA, Aust. Educational Consultant. m. Patricia Kori Kavenagh, 7 May 1985, 3 s, 2 d. Education: Tchrs Cert, 1951; Tchrs Higher Ctf, 1962; Dip in Educ, 1961, BA, 1969, Univ of WA; Med, 1966, PhD, 1968, Univ of Alberta. Appointments: Prin, Primary & Secnd Schs, WA, 1952-69; Supt, Educ Dept of WA, 1969-73; Dir, Spec Servs, 1973-76, Asst Dir Gen, 1976-79, Educ Dept of WA; Dir, Mt Lawley Coll of Adv Educ, 1979-81; Cmnr, NT Tchng Serv, 1981-85; Educl Cnslt. Publications: Rsch pprs publd and unpubld over many yrs. Honours: WA Educ Dept Stdy Fellshp, 1965 Prov of Alta Grad Fellshp, 1967. Memberships: Fell, Austl Coll of Educn Fell, Austl Inst of Mngmt; Fell, WA Inst of Educl Admin; Phi Delta Kappa; Austl Inst of Tertiary Admnstrs. Hobbies: Fishing; Bushwalking; Tennis; Canoeing; Music. Address Unit 4, 219 Mill Point Road, South Perth, WA 6151, Australia.

STEWART James Ross, b. 3 Oct 1932, Kempsey, NSW, Aust. Geologist. m. 7 Jan 1956, 3 d. Education: BSc, Hons 1, Univ of Sydney, 1953; MSc, Univ of New Eng, 1959. Appointments: Geol, Bur of Mineral Resources; Hd, Mngng Dir, Raw Materials Sect, Austl Atomic Energy Commn Kratos Uranium NL and other pub and pvte cos, 1970-93; Geol Ed, NSW Dept of Mineral Resources, 1994-. Publications: Num tech publs in fields of geol and mining. Memberships: Fell, A/Asian Inst of Mining and Metallurgy; Geol Soc Aust, Chmn NSW Div 1966-67. Hobby: Home improvements. Address: c/o Department of Mineral Resources, 29-57 Christie Street, St Leonards, NSW, Australia.

STIMSON John Alan, b. 16 June 1963, Orange, NSW, Aust. Urban and Regional Planner. m. Wendy, 19 Dec 1987, 2 s. Education: BA, Flinders Univ, 1985; Grad Dip in Regl and Urban Plng, S Austl Inst of Technol, 1987; MAppSc (Proj Mngmt), Univ of S Aust, 1994. Memberships: Roy Austl Plng Inst; Philippine Inst of Environ Planners; Urban Land Inst; Cttee Mbr HIA (SA), 1995-97; Exec Cttee Mbr, AIUS (SA), 1995-97. Hobbies: Cricket; Football; Golf; Travel; Collecting Phantom Comics. Address: C/o Hassell U2101 Antel 2000, 121 Valero Street, Salcedo Village, Makati City, Philippines.

STOCKDALE Alan Robert, b. 21 Apr 1945, Melbourne, Aust. Barrister; Member of Parliament. m. Doreen Kiely, 23 July 1975, 3 s. Education: LLB, 1966, BA 1969, Melbourne. Appointments: Indl Offr, Vic Employers Fedn, 1967; Indl Rels Advsr, Austl Wool Selling Brokers Employers Fedn, 1968; Personnel and Indl Rels Mngr, Leighton Contractors, 1969; Indl Rels Cnslt, Austl Wool Selling Brokers Employers Fedn, 1975; Articled Law Clk to Sols, 1976; Bar, 1977; Elected to Victorian Parl, 1985; Shadow Treas, 1985; Dpty Leader of Opposition, 1990; Victorian Treas, 1992; Victorian Min for Multimedia, 1996. Memberships: CPA; Melbourne Football Club; Melbourne Cricket Club; Roy Melbourne Golf Club. Hobbies: Golf; Fishing; Australian Rules Football; Reading. Address: 4 Male Street, Brighton, Vic 3186, Australia.

STOLTZFUS Ben Frank, b. 15 Sept 1927, Sofia, Bulgaria. Professor Emeritus. m. Judith, 8 Nov 1975, 2 s, 1 d. Education: PhD. Appointments: Tchng Asst, Univ WI, Madison, 1956-58; French Instr, Smith Coll, Northampton, MA, 1958-60; Prof of French, Comparative Lit and Creative Writing, Univ CA, Riverside, 1960-93. Publications include: Novels: The Eye of the Needle, 1967; Black Lazarus, 1972; Red White & Blue, 1989; Literary Criticism: Alain Robbe Grillet and the New French Novel, 1964; Gide and Hemingway: Rebels Against God, 1978; Alain Robbe-Grillet: Life Work and Criticism, 1987; Lacan and Literature: Purloined Pretexts, 1996. Honours: Fulbright-Hays Rsch Grants to Paris, France, 1955-56, 1963-64; Univ CA Creative Arts Inst Awds, 1967, 1975; Univ CA Humanities Inst Awds, 1969-72; DLitt, Amherst Coll, 1974; Camargo Fndn Grants, 1983, 1985; NAAP Gradiva Awd, 1997. Memberships: Mod Lang Assn; Am Comparative Lit Assn; S Comparative Lit Assn; Hemingway Soc; Camus Soc; Amn Lit Assn; New Novel Assn. Hobbies: Skiing; Tennis; Scuba Diving. Address: 2040 Arroyo Drive, Riverside, CA 92506, USA.

STONE Dulcie May, b. 29 May 1924, Preston, Australia. Teacher; Writer. m. David, 28 Mar 1945, 1 s, 3 d. Education: Cert of Educ of Intellectually Disabled. Appointments include: Fndn Coord of Vols, Options Residential Servs, Melbourne, 1987-88; Tutor, Creative Writing, Spring Dale Comm Cottage, Drysdale, Vic, 1992-; Tutor, Creative Writing for people w intellectual disability, Geelong area, 1996-. Publications include: Non Fiction: What's Volunteering & What's Not, 1993; Parent Power '94, 1994; Creative Writing for People with Intellectual Disability, 1996; Fiction: I Laugh I Cry I Feel, 1978; Jonny Love, 1982; Hullo Fay, 1991; Ask Me About Saturdays, 1995. Honours: Hon Life Gov, Roy Children's Hosp, Melbourne, 1962; Life Mbr, W J Christie Cntr, 1979; MBE, 1981; Finalist, Upper Yarra Citizen of the Century Awd, 1988-98; Apostolic Blessing, 1989; Life Mbr, Upper Yarra Comm House Inc, 1990; Intl Woman of Yr, 1996-97. Hobbies: Reading; Music (Trained Pianist; Concert Singer). Address: Cifton Springs, 5 Central Road, Australia.

STONE John Owen, b. 31 Jan 1929, Perth, West Aust, Aust. Finance; Politics. m. Nancy Enid Hardwick, 14 July 1954, 4 s, 1 d. Education: BS (Hons I), Univ of WA; BA (Hons I), Univ of Oxford. Appointments: Austl Treasury, 1954-66; Exec Dir for Aust, NZ, S Africa, Intl Monetary Fund and World Bank, 1967-70; Sec, Austl Loan Cncl and Sec, Natl Debt Commn, 1971; Dpty Sec, Austl Treasury, 1971-79; Sec to Treasury, 1979-84; Senator for Queensland, 1987-90. Publications: Weekly newsppr columnist, 1985-89, 1990-98; Ed, Proceedings of the Samuel Griffith Soc, 1992-. Honours: Rhodes Schl for West Aust, 1951; James Webb Medly Schl, Oxford Univ, 1953. Hobbies: Reading; Promoting debate about public affairs. Address: 70 Gipps Street, East Melbourne, Victoria 3002, Australia.

STONE Jonathan, b. 10 Apr 1942. Professor of Anatomy. m. Margaret Ackary, 3 d. Education: BMedSci, 1963, PhD, 1963, DSc, 1977, Sydney. Appointments: Rsch Fell, ANU, 1970; Snr Lectr, Assoc Prof, Prof, Univ NSW, 1976-86; Challis Prof of Anatomy, Univ of Sydney, 1987-. Publications: Over l00 articles in sci lit; 3 books. Membership: Fell, Austl Acady of Sci, 1984. Hobby: Sailing. Address: Department of Anatomy & Histology, University of Sydney, NSW 2006, Australia.

STONE Shane Leslie (Hon), b. 1950, Bendigo, Vic, Aust. Member of Parliament. m. Josephine, 1977, 1 s, 1 d. Education: LLB, Melbourne; BA, Austl Natl Univ; GradDipEdAdmin, Adelaide; DipTchng, RCAE; TPTC; FAIM; MACE; MRIPAA; FAICD; QC. Appointments: Tchr, Children w Learning Difficulties, Vic, 1972-74; Admin Off, State Coll, Vic; Dpty Warden, Intl House, Univ Melbourne; Bar-at-Law, NSW, Tas; Assoc, Hon Sir Edward Woodward; Law Prac, Alice Springs and Darwin; LCDR, Roy Austl Naval Reserve; Responsible, Menzies Sch, Hlth Res; Responsible, NTU Off PS Commnr and Equal Opportunities, 1990-; Min Educ and Trng, Pub Employment; Ldr Govt Bus, Responsible, Trade Dev Zone; NT Atty Gen, 1992-93; Min,NT Rsch and Dev Adv Cncl, Inds and Dev, Asian Rels and Trade, the Arts, 1992-95, Ethnic Affairs, 1993-95, Ethnic Affairs, the Arts and Mus, 1995-96, Police, Fire and Emergency Servs, 1995-97, Constl Dev, 1996-97, Pub Employment, 1997; Mbr of Parl, Port Darwin, NT, 1990-; Min, Def and Support, 1997-, Statehood, 1997-, Women's Plcy, 1997-, Young Territorians, 1997-, Tourism, 1998-; Atty Gen, 1997-; NT Chf Min; QC, 1997-. Hobbies: Gardening; Diving; Alpine Skiing. Address: GPO Box 559, Darwin, NT 0801, Australia.

STONIER Kenneth Brian, b. 24 July 1932, Prospect, Aust. Publisher. m. Noel Jeanette Lidgett, 11 Dec 1954, 1 s, 2 d. Education: LLB, Melbourne Univ, 1953; Kent Brierly & Barraclough, Chartered Accts, 1954-56; FCA, 1956. Appointments: Ptnr, Kent Brierly & Barraclough, 1960-65; Mngng Dir, Penguin Books Aust, 1964-65; Co-Fndr, Sun Books, 1965; Sun Books acquired by Macmillan Co Aust, 1971; Chmn, Mng Dir, 1971-86; Exec Chmn, 1986-99, Macmillan Aust. Honour: Order of Aust, 1980. Memberships: Austin Hosp Bd of Mngmt, 1965-75; VP 1972-75; Natl Gall Soc of Vic, 1971-91; Dpty Pres 1984-91; Vic Arts Cntr Trust, 1980-83; Aust Cncl Mbr, Natl Lib of Aust; Dir, GRE Holdings Ltd, 1990-93. Hobbies: Reading; Viticulture; Farming. Address: Apt 9, 21 Park Lane, South Yarra, Vic 3141, Australia.

STOPP Eric John Chancellor, b. 10 June 1933, Norfolk Is. Member of Legislative Council. m. Alison Duncan, 19 Sept 1957, 2 d. Appointments: Dir, Tas Perm Bldg Soc, 1965; Mngng Dir, Chancellors P/L, 1982; Mbr, Legis Cncl, 1983-95; Pres, Legis Cncl, 1992-95. Membership: Pres, Hobart Chmbr of Com, 1988. Hobbies: Golf; Sailing; Tennis; Bushwalking. Address: 3 Ethelmont Road, Sandy Bay, Hobart, Tas, Australia.

STOREY David Maxwell, b. 3 Sept 1919, Sydney, NSW, Aust. Health Commissioner (Retired). m. Gwendolyn Ethel Wickham, 4 Jan 1944, dec 5 Oct 1992, 1 s, 2 d. Education: MBBS, Univ of Sydney, 1942; Res Med Offr, Roy Prince Alfred Hosp, 1942-44; Dip in Hosp Admin, 1957. Appointments: Served Austl Army Med Corps, 1944-46; Asst Med Supt, 1946-49, Med Supt 1949-65, St George Hosp; Dpty Chmn, Hosps Commn of NSW, 1965-73; Commnr, Health Commn of NSW, 1973-77; Chmn, Parramatte Hosps Bd, 1978-85; Chmn, NSW Div, Austl Red Cross Soc, 1981-88. Honour: AM, 1987. Memberships: Fell, Austl Coll of Health Serv Execs, 1958; Fell, Roy Austl Coll of Med Admnstrs. Hobbies: Fishing; Lawn bowls. Address: 50 Barker Road, Strathfield, NSW 2135, Australia.

STOTT DESPOJA Natasha Jessica, b. 9 Sept 1969. Senator. Education: BA, Univ Adelaide. Appointments: Centenary of Womens Suffrage Cttee, SA, 1992-94; Co-Chair, SA Repub Movement, 1995-; Dpty Ldr, Austl Democrats, 1997. Publications: Contbr: Living Generously, 1996; DIY Feminism, 1996; Saving Our ABC, 1996. Honour: Finalist, Young Austl of the Yr, 1996. Hobbies: Constitutional Change; Reading; Writing. Address: Parliament House, Canberra, ACT 2600, Australia.

STOWASSER Helen Margaret, b. 16 Mar 1933, Sheffield, Eng. Associate Professor of Music Education. m. 10 July 1954, 3 s. Education: BA, hons, Music Tripos, 1954, MA, 1974, Cambridge Univ; Dip in Tchng, Kelvin Grove Tchrs Coll, Brisbane, Aust, 1971; PhD, Univ of Qld, 1983. Appointments: Tchr of Clarinet, Peninsula Ch of Eng Sch, Mt Eliza, Vic, Aust, 1967-68; Tchr i/c of Music, The Gap State HS, Brisbane, Qld, 1972-77; Tutor in Music, Univ Qld, 1977-81; Lectr, Snr Lectr, Qld Conservatorium of Music, 1982-88; Assoc Prof of Music Educn, Univ of WA, Nedlands, 1989-97. Publications: Discover Music 1-3, tchrs and students eds, 1979, 1983; Discover Music-Making, tchrs and students eds, cassetts, 1989; Num compositions and arrangements for vocal and instrumental ensembles, inclng Valse Volante for flute, clarinet & piano, 1988; String Quartet in D, 1988; Swingsongs, Flutesongs and Aussie Jam, 1990. Honour: Music Prize, Newnham Coll, Cambridge, 1953. Memberships: Austl Soc for Music Educ; Sounds Austl;

Intl Soc Music Educ; Chmn, Callaway Intl Resource Cntr Music Educ, 1989-97. Hobby: Bushwalking. Listed in: Debrett's People of Today. Address: PO Box 256, Mapleton, Qld 4560, Australia.

STRAEDE (née Howard) Truda Mary, b. 9 Dec 1944, Queenstown, Tasmania. Plant Ecologist; Cat Breeder. Education: BSc, PhD, Ecology, (Melbourne), 1971. Appointments: Rsch Offr, Austl Forest Inds, 1971-73; Bot, UNSW, 1973-75; Lectr, Landscape Archt, UNSW, 1975-77; Casual Lectr, West Sydney, 1978-90; Ecological Cnslt, 1978-98; Developed pedigree cat breed "Austl Mist". Publications: Breeding Cats - a practical guide, 1997; Ed: Cats in the Mist, 1998. Memberships: Ecological Inst of Aust, from fndn to 1996; NSW Govt Companion Animals Bd, 1998-; Mbr of Working party on this act and Animal Trades Regulations under POCTA. Hobbies: Gardening; Writing poetry; Reading; Showing Cats. Address: Vale Ridge, Days Rd, South Maroota, NSW 2756, Australia.

STRANSKY Santina, b. 18 May 1938, Italy. Author; Painter. m. Carlo, 25 June 1955, 2 s. Education: Dip, Italian Lyceum. Appointments: Roving Amb for Save the Children Fund. Publications: 3 books; Co-auth, 1 book; Sev personal exhibns in Aust and overseas. Honours: Adv Aust Awd, 1993; AO, 1994. Hobbies: Cooking; Sewing; Crochet. Address: 73 Vincent St, Nedlands, WA 6009, Australia.

STRATFORD Stephen Paul, b. 25 Aug 1953, Tauranga. Journalist. m. Sarah Fraser, 22 Aug 1998. Appointments: Ed, New Outlook, Dpty Ed, Metro; Ed, Quote Unquote; Ed, Arch NZ; Judge Wattie Book Awd; Convenor, Montana Book Awds. Publications: First Aid for NZ PC Users, 1997; Safe Sex: An Email Romance, 1997; Readers Digest Motoring Guide to NZ, 1998; The Jafa Joke Book, 1998. Honours: Qantas Awd for Travel Writing, 1988, 1991-; Book Page of the Yr, 1994. Memberships: NZ Soc of Auths; Sargeson Trust. Hobbies: Music; Gossip. Address: 14 St Alban Avenue, Balmoral, Auckland, New Zealand.

STREET Anthony Austin, b. 8 Feb 1926, Melbourne, Aust. Manager; Company Director. m. Valerie Erica Rickard, 6 July 1951, 3 s. Appointments: Prim Prodr, Lismore, Vic, 1946; Mbr of Fed Parl for Corangamite, Vic, 1966-84; Chmn, Fed Rural Cttee of the Liberal Party, 1970-74; Mbr, Fed Exec Cncl, 1971; Asst Min for Labour and Natl Serv, 1971-72; Mbr of Opposition Exec, 1973-75; Spec Asst to Ldr of the Opposition & Shadow Min for Labour, 1975; Min for Labour and Immigration in Caretaker Min, 1975; Min for Employment and Indl Rels, also Min Asstng PM in Pub Serv Matters, 1975-77; Min for Employment and Indl Rels, 1977-78; Min for Indl Rels, 1978-80; Min for For Affairs, 1980-83, resigned from Parl, 1984; Mngr, Co dir. Publications: Alfred Deakin Memorial Lecture, 1979-; Industrial Relations: Class Conflict or Common Goals; Roy Milne Memorial Lecture, 1982-; Alliances and Foreign Policy Today. Hobbies: Cricket; Golf; Flying. Address: 153 The Terrace, Ocean Grove, Vic 3226, Australia.

STREET Laurence (Sir), b. 3 July 1926, Sydney, Australia. m. (1) Susan Gai, (2) Penelope Patricia, 3 d, 2 s. Education: LLB Hons, Sydney, 1951. Appointments include: QC, 1963-; Fmr Judge, NSW Supreme Crt, 1965 -74;Fmr Chf Jus, 1974-88; Fmr Lt Gov of NSW, I974-89; Intl Law Assn, World Pres 1990-92, Life VP 1992-, Pres Aust Br 1990-94; Chmn, Aust Govt Intl Legal Servs Advsry Cncl, 1990-; John Fairfax Holdings Ltd, Dir 1991-94, Chmn, 1994-97; Chmn, Sch Law Advis Cncl, New Eng Univ, 1992-; Chmn, Advsry Bd, UTS Cntr for Dispute Resol, 1994-97. Honours: KStJ, 1976; KCMG, 1976; Grand Off of Merit of Order of Malta, 1977; Hon LLD, Sydney, 1984; Hon Col 1/15 Roy NSW Lancers, 1986-96; AC, 1989; Hon Fell, Inst Arb Aust, Gr 1 Arb, 1989; Hon LLD, Macquarie, 1989; Fell, UTS, 1990; Hon DEc, New Eng, 1996; Hon LLD, UTS, 1998. Memberships: Crt Mbr, LCIA, 1988-; Fell, CInstArb, Eng, 1992; Austl Mbr, World Intellectual Property Org; Arbit Cnsltv Comm, Geneva, 1994-; Austl Govt Designated Conciliator Intl Cntr for Settlement of Investment Disputes, Wash, 1994-. Address: 121 Macquarie Street, Sydney, NSW 2000, Australia.

STREET Robert, b. 16 Dec 1920. Research Physicist. m. Joan Marjorie Bere, 26 June 1943, 1 s, 1 d. Education: BSc, MSc, PhD, DSc, Univ of London, Eng. Appointments: Tchng Appts in Dept of Phys at the Univs of Nottingham and Sheffield; Fndn Prof of Phys, Monash Univ, Vic, Aust, 1960-74; Dir of Rsch, Sch of Physl Scis, Austl Natl Univ, Canberra, 1974-78; Vice Chan, Univ WA, 1978-86; Snr, Rsch Fell, Univ WA, 1986-. Publications: Rsch pubs in learned jrnls. Honours: AO; Hon DSc, Univ of Sheffield and Univ WA. Membership: FAA. Hobby: Research in Magnetism. Address: Department of Physics, University of Western Australia, Nedlands, WA 6907, Australia.

STREET Ross Howard, b. 29 Sept 1945, Sydney, Aust. Mathematician. m. Margery, 30 May 1970, 2 s. Education: Hurlstone Agricl hs, Glenfield, 1956-61; Univ of Sydney, 1962-68; BS, 1st Class Hons, 1966; PhD, 1969. Appointments: Pt-time Tutor of Maths, Univ of Sydney, 1964-68; Post-Doct Fellshp, Univ of IL (Champaign-Urbana), 1968-69; Asst Prof, Tulane Univ, New Orleans, 1969-70; Lectr, 1970-71, Snr Lectr, 1972-74, Assoc Prof, 1975-90, Macquarie Univ; Rsch Assoc, Wesleyan Univ, CT, 1976-77; Visng Prof, Univ de Milano, Italy, 1981; Rsch Affiliate, 1983-95, Hon Rsch Assoc, 1997-, Univ of Sydney; Visng Prof, McGill Univ, Montreal, SUNY at Buffalo, NY State, 1985; Occasional Visng Prof, Univ of Quebec, Montreal, 1987-93; Prof, Maths Personal Chair, Macquarie Univ; dir, Macquarie Univ Rsch Cntr of Austl Category Theor, 1999-. Publications: 70 in profl jrnls. Honours: C'wlth Schlshp, 1962-65; George Allen Schlshp for Maths, 1965; Sydney Univ Math Soc Problem Competition, 1st prize for 4th Yr Studs, 1965; CSIRO Postgrad Schlshp, 1966-68; Num grants. Memberships: Dir, Cntr of Austl Category Theor (CoACT); Amn Math Soc; Austl Math Soc; Austl Acady of Sci; NY Acady of Scis. Listed in: Who's Who in Australia; Who's Who in the World. Address: Maths Dept, Macquarie University, NSW 2109, Australia.

STREHLE Ute Claudia, b. 19 Aug 1965, Bad Liebenwerda, Germany. Conservator. Education: B Applied Sci, Univ Canberra, Australia. Appointments: Conservator Works of Art on Paper, Auckland Art Gall, 1998-. Memberships: NZPCG; AICCM for ACT and VIC Div. Hobbies: Fine art; Science. Address: 2-16 Stack Street, Herne Bay, Auckland, New Zealand.

STREISAND Barbra Joan, b. 24 Apr 1942 Brooklyn NY. Actress; Singer. m. Elliot Gould, 1963, div 19971, 1 s. Education: Erasmus Hall High Sch. Appointments: Nightclub debut at Bon Soir, 1961; Appeared in off-Broadway revue Another Evening with Harry Stoones, 1961; Appeared at Caucus Club Detroit and Blue Angel NY, 1961; Played in musical comedy I Can Get It for You Wholesale, 1962; Began recording career with Columbia records, 1963; Appeared in musical play Funny Girl NY, 1964; London, 1966; Tv prog My Name is Barbra shown in Eng Holland Aust Sweden Bermuda and the Philippines; Second prog Color Me Barbra also shown abroad; Num concert and nightclub appearances. Films incl: Funny Girl, 1968; Hello Dolly, 1969; On a Clear Day you can see Forever, 1969; The Owl and the Pussycat, 1971; What's up Doc?, 1972; Up the Sandbox, 1973; The Way We Were, 1973; For Pete's Sake, 1974; Funny Lady, 1975; A Star is Born, 1977; Yentl - also dir and prod'd - 1983; Nuts, 1987; Sing, 1989; Prince of Tides - also dir co-prodr - 1990; The Mirror Has Two Faces - also dir - 1996. Honours: Five Emmy Awds for My Name is Barbra; NY Critics Best Supporting Actress Awd, 1962; Grammy awds for Best Female Pop Vocalist, 1963, 1964, 1965, 1977, 1986; London Critics' Musical Awd, 1966; Acady Awd - Oscar - for film Funny Girl, 1968; Am Guild of Variety Artists' Entertainer of the Yr Awd, 1970; Cmdr des Arts et Lettres, 1984. Address: c/o ICM, 8942 Wilshire Boulevard, Beverly Hills, CA 90211, USA.

STREMSKI Richard, b. 15 Aug 1941, Chgo, Il, USA. General Manager. m. Karen, 20 Aug 1966, 3 s, 1 d. Education: BS, Hist, Loyola Univ, Chgo, USA, 1962; MS, 1963, PhD, 1968, Univ of Wisconsin, Madison. Appointments: Asst Prof, Socl Sci, KS State Coll, 1967-68; Asst Prof, Univ of AL, 1968-72; Snr Lectr, Hist, La Trobe Univ, Melbourne, 1972-92. Publications: Britain's China Policy During the Nationalist Revolution, 1925-28; Kill for Collingwood, 1986; The Greatest Game, 1988; Oxford Companion to Australian Sport (Selections), 1992. Honours: Outstndng Tchr, Univ of AL, 1991; Sub-Dean, Hums, La Trobe Univ, 1981-83. Memberships: Austl Soc for Sports Hist, Fndn Sec, 1983-87, Pres, 1990-91; Austl Histl Assn, Exec Cttee, 1986-87; LTU Credit Union, Chmn of Bd, 1987-89. Hobbies: Dir, Collingood Football Club, 1997-98. Address: 56 Lawanna Dr, Templestowe, Vic, Australia, 3106.

STRIZIC Mark, b. 9 Apr 1928, Berlin, Germany. Visual Artist. m. Suzanna Zador, 6 July 1952. Education: BA (Fin Art) Victorian Coll of the Arts, 1985. Appointments: Lectr in Charge of Photog, Melbourne Coll of Advd Educ, 1977-81. Creative works: Photog illustrator of books; Melbourne; A Portrait, 1960; Involvement, 1968; Living in Australia, 1970; Krimper, 1988; Inge King, 1996; Major corp murals: Woodside Petroleum, Perth, 1986; The Austl Wheat Bd, Melbourne, 1987; ICI Rsch Grp, Ascot Vale, Vic, 1988; Roy Children's Hosp, Melbourne, 1990; Xavier Coll, Kew, Vic, 1993; Austl Postal Corp, 1993; Metromedia Tech Intl, Brisbane, 1994; Epworth Hosp, Richmond, Vic, 13mx3.25m, 1995. Honours: 1st Prize Photo Competition, 1955; 1st Prize Photog Competition, 1969; Austl Cncl Emeritus Fellshp Awd, 1994. Memberships: Natl Assn for the Visual Arts Ltd (NAVA). Hobbies: Music; General Reading. Address: PO Box 119 Wallan, 3756, Australia.

STROJNIK Marija, b. 13 July 1950, Ljubliana, Slovenia. Optical Scientist. Education: BS, Phys, 1972, MSc, Optical Scis, 1977, MSC, Engrng Exec Prog, 1981, Univ CA, Los Angeles; PhD, Univ of AZ, 1979; CA Inst of Technol, 1987-93. Appointments: Mngr, Optics Tech, Rockwell Intl, 1978-81; Staff Scientist, Honeywell Tech Cntr, 1982-87; Snr, Optical Scientist, CA Inst of Technol, 1987-93; Prof, Centro de Investigaciones en Optica, México, 1994-. Publications: Ed (w Bjorn Anderson) Infrared Technology and Applications (book, yearly), 1990-; Infrared Spacebourne Remote Sensing (book, yearly), 1993-. Honours: Fell, Intl Soc for Optical Engrng, 1994; Infrared Phys & Technol Editl Bd, 1994; George W Goddar Awd, SPIE, 1996; Topical Ed, Applied Optics, 1992-98. Memberships: Optical Soc of Am, 1971; Intl Soc for Optical Engrng, 1972; Sigmaxi, 1980; AAAS, 1982.

STUBBINGS Leon George, b. 17 May 1923, Melbourne, Aust. Former Secretary General, Australian Red Cross Society, 1955-88. m. Elvina Eva Dickson, 15 May 1948, 3 d. Education: BA, Univ of Melbourne, 1946-49. Appointments: Pres, 3 Div Signals Ass 13/66 Club, 1946-; Sec Gen, Austl Red Cross Soc, 1955-88; Chmn, Intl Jnr Red Cross Cttee, 1964-72; Mbr, Austl Fndn Prevention of Blindness, 1968-76; Dpty Chmn, Austl Cncl of Socl Serv, 1970-71; Pres, Child Accident Prevention Fndn, Aust, 1988-89. Publications: Look What You Started Henry - A History of Australian Red Cross 1914-1991, 1992; Command Wisely, 1996; Mercury's Mate (autobiog), 1998. Honours: OAM, 1984; AM, 1986; CStJ, 1988; Henry Dunant Medal (Highest Intl Red Cross Awd), 1989; Medal of Hon, Austl Red Cross. Hobbies: Philately; Gardening; Theatre. Listed in: Who's Who in Australia. Address: 12 Olive Street, East Malvern, Vic 3145, Australia.

STUDEMEISTER Paul A, b. 20 Mar 1954, Caracas. Environmental Scientist. Education: BA, Geol, Univ CA, Berkeley, 1973-77; PhD, Geol, Geochem, Univ Western Ontario, London, Can, 1977-82. Appointments: Asst Prof, Ottawa Univ, 1982-83; Project Geol, Dunraine Mines Ltd, Toronto, 1983-85; Rsch Petrographer, Portland Cement Assn, Skokie, IL, 1985-90; Project Mngr, EVAX Technols, Scotts Valley, CA, 1990-93, The Bentley Co, San Fran, CA, 1993-94, LEE Inc, San Jose, CA, 1994-. Publications include: Greenschist Metamorphism of Archaean Synvolcanic Stocks Near Wawa, Ontario, Canada, 1985; Gold-Bearing Quartz Veins Around a Felsic Stock Near

Wawa, Ontario: Implications for Gold Exploration, 1985; Distribution of Gold Occurrences on the Dunraine Property Near Wawa, Ontario, Canada, 1986; Alteration Pattern and Fluid Inclusions of Gold-Bearing Quartz Veins in Archean Trondhjemite Near Wawa, Ontario, Canada, 1987. Memberships: Groundwater Resources Assn of CA; Assn of Engrng Geols. Address: 2140 Santa Cruz Avenue, Suite D-105, Menlo Park, CA 94025, USA.

STURMA Michael Thomas, b. 9 July 1950, Philadephia, PA, USA. Historian. m. Ying, 5 July 1990. Education: BA (Cntr); MA (UNC Chapel Hill); PhD, Austl Natl Univ. Appointments: Tutor, Austl Natl Univ; Lectr, Univ of New Eng; Snr Lectr, Murdoch Univ. Publications: Vice in a Vicious Society, 1983; Australian Rock'n'Roll: The First Wave, 1991. Honours: Phi Beta Kappa, 1972; Phi Alpha Theta, 1971; ANU Schlshp, 1976. Memberships: Austl Histl Assn; Pacific Histl Assn; Inst of Commonwealth Studies. Address: Social Inquiry, Murdoch University, Perth, WA, Australia 6150.

STYLES Lawrence Edgar, b. 5 May 1919, London, Eng. Research Director. m. Norah Patricia Mitchell, 11 Mar 1942, 3 s, 3 d. Education: MA, Cambridge Univ, Eng; Dip Theol. Appointments: Offr Cadet, Metro Police, 1938-41; Pilot, Fleet Air Arm, RN; Ordained in the Anglican Ch, 1951; Asst Priest, St Michael & Angels, Bishops Stortford, Herts, Eng, 1951-53; Parish Priest, St George's Tydesley, Lancs, Eng, 1953-60; Mbr, Manchester Indl Miss; Fed Chmn 1960-87, Rsch Dir 1987-89, Cnslt 1989-; Interch Trade & Hist Miss, 1960-87; Canon of St Paul's Cath, 1981-. Publications: Direction Signs to an Achievable Future, 1982; Planning with People; Industrial Mission in the UK; Industrial Mission in the 80's; Industrial Relations in the Essential Services; A Guide to London Census Returns, 1995; Five Augarde Sailed to Australia, 1995; A History of Industrial Mission, 1998. Honours: Advance Aust Awd, 1987; AM, 1988. Memberships: Cambridge Soc of Aust; Fleet Air Arm Assn; Naval and Mil Club. Address: 25 Carson Street, Kew, Vic 3101, Australia.

SU Chi, b. 1 Oct 1949 Taichung. Govt Offic. m. Grace Chen, 1 s, 1 d. Education: Natl Chengchi Univ; Johns Hopkins Univ; Columbia Univ. Appointments: Assoc Prof Dept of Diplomacy Natl Chengchi Univ, 1984-90, Prof, 1990-; Sec Off of the Univ Pres, 1989-90; Sec-Gen China Polit Sci Assn, 1990-91; Dep Dir Inst of Intl Rels, 1990-93; Dep Dir Kuomintang Cntrl Cttee Dept of Mainland Affairs, 1992-93; Vice-Chmn Exec Yuan Mainland Affairs Cncl, 1993-96; Dir-Gen Govt Info Off, 1996-97; Exec Yuan Min of State, 1997; Natl Advsr to Pres of Repub, 1997; Dep Sec-Gen to Pres, 1997-. Publications: The Normalization of Sino-Soviet Relations; Over 20 papers and articles. Memberships: Mbr Exec Yuan Rsch Devt and Evaluation Commn, 1990-94. Address: Office of the President, 122 Chung-Ching S Road, Sec 1, Taipei, Taiwan.

SU Hongye, b. 10 Nov 1969, Jiangsu, China. Automation. m. Jiangxin Ge, 19 May 1995. Education: PhD, Zhejiang Univ, China, 1995. Appointment: Lectr, 1995-97, Prof, 1997-. Publication: Robust Control Theory and Application. Honours: The Kezheng Zha Schlshp, 1994, The Excellent PhD Cand Awd, 1995, Zhejiang Univ. Hobbies: Music; Table tennis; Touring. Address: Institute of Industrial Process Control, Zhejiang University, Hangzhou 310027, China.

SU Xing, b. 15 Feb 1926, Chifeng Cty, Inner Mongolia, China. m. Shuying Jin, 2 s, 2 d. Education: Grad, Polit Dept, Huabei Utd Univ, 1948. Appointments: Tchr, Lectr, Assoc Prof, Dir, Polit Econ Tchng and Rsch Sect, China People's Univ, Beijing, 1950-58; Dpty-Dir, Editl Dept, Front, Beijing, 1959-61; Grp-Gen, Econ Grp, 1961-66; Dir, Econ Sect, 1979-82, Dpty-Gen-Ed, 1982-88, Red Flag, Beijing; Gen-Ed, Seeking Truth, Beijing, 1988-89; VP, Party Sch, CPCCC, Beijing, 1988-98; Mbr, 5th, 6th, 7th CPCCC Natl Cttee, Standing Cttee, 8th CPPCC Natl Cttee. Publications: Co-ed, Political Economy (Capitalism Section), 1961; Socialist Transformation of Agriculture in China, 1980; Theory and Practice of Socialist Reproduction, 1987; Housing Problems in Urban China,

1987; Selected Works of Su Xing, 1987; A Study on Socialist Economy With Chinese Characteristics, 1992; On Socialist Market Economy, 1994. Honours: Sun Yefang Econs Prize ofr Acad Ppr, 1985; Best Book Awd, Dept of Publicity of CPCCC, 1995. Memberships: Natl Urban Housing Assn; Natl Price Soc; Chinese Natl Conditions Soc. Address: Party School of CPCCC, Beijing 100091, China.

SU Ya-Xin, b. 22 July 1972, Gaoyang, Hebei Province, China. PhD student of Zhejiang University. Education: BEng, Exploring Engrng, China Univ of Geoscis, 1994; Mechl Engrng in Heat & Mass Transfer and their Enhancement from Natl Huaqiao Univ, 1997; Working for PhD degree of Engrng Thermophysics in Zhejiang Univ. Publications: Extended Surfaces Heat Transfer (co-auth), 1997. Hobbies: Music; Opera; Travelling; Collecting stamps; Horticulture. Address: Institute of Thermal Power Engineering, Zhejiang University, Hangzhou 310027, China.

SUBANOV Murzakan. Appointments: Minister of Defence, Kyrgyzstan. Address: Ministry of Defence, 720001 Bishkek, Logvinenko 26, Kyrgyzstan.

SUBRAHMANYAM P V, b. 11 June 1950, Chennai, India. Teaching and Research in Mathematics. m. Dr S Alamelubai, 8 Feb 1981, 2 d. Education: MSc, Maths, PhD, Maths, Indian Inst of Technol, Madras, India. Appointments: Lectr, Hyderabad Cntrl Univ, 1979-81; Lectr, IIT, Madras, 1981-88; Asst Prof, 1988-93, Assoc Prof, 1993-95, Prof, IIT, Madras, 1995-. Publications: 50 incl rsch pprs in maths in Fuzzy Functional and Integral Equations; Contractor Theory and Nonmetrizable Topological Fixed Joint Theory. Memberships: Life Mbr, Indian Maths Soc Fell, Forum d'Analystes; Ed, Jrnl of Analysis, Madras. Hobbies: Indian classical music; Tamil literature; Philosophy. Address: Department of Mathematics, Indian Institute of Technology, Madras, Chennai 600036, India.

SUBRAMANIAM Chidambaram, b. 30 Jan 1910 Pollachi Coimbatore Dist of Tamil Nadu. Politician. Education: Madras Univ. Appointments: Joined Satyagraha Movement and imprisoned, 1932; Started legal prac Coimbatore, 1936; Polit imprisonment, 1941, 1942; Pres Coimbatore Dist Congress Cttee; Min of Fin Educ and Law Madras State, 1952-62; Min of Steel, 1962-63; Min of Steel Mines and Heavy Engrng, 1963-64; Min of Food and Agric, 1964-66; Min of Food Agric Community Devt and Co-op, 1966-67; Chmn Natl Commn on Agric, 1970; Dep Chmn Natl Plng Commn, 1971; Min of Plng Sci and Tech, 1971-72; Min of Indl Devt Sci and Tech, 1972-74; Min of Fin, 1974-77; Min of Def, 1979-80; Chmn Rajaji Intl Inst of Pub Affairs and Admin, 1980-; Pres Madras Voluntary Hlth Servs, 1987-; Pres Bharatiya Vidya Bhavan, Feb 1990-; Gov of Maharashtra, 1990-93; Pres All India Tennis Assn. Publications: Travelogues in Tamil; Countries I Visited; Around the World; India of my Dreams; War on Poverty; New Agricultural Strategy. Honours: Hon Pres Intl Cntr for Pub Enterprises in Developing Cos Ljubljana Yugoslavia, 1985-87. Memberships: Mbr Wrkng Cttee of All India Congress Cttee; Mbr Constituent Assn of India, 1946-51; Mbr Madras Legis Ass, 1952-62; Mbr Lok Sabha, 1962-67; Mbr Govng Cncl of Intl Wheat and Maize Improvmnt Cntr Mexico; Mbr Bd of Govs Intl Rice Rsch Inst Manila. Address: River View, Kotturpuram, Madras 600085, India.

SUBRAMANIAN Ramachandran, b. 15 Sept 1937, Tiruchirapalli, India. Teaching Research. m. 6 Sept 1962, 1 s, 1 d. Education: MA, 1959; MSc, 1960; PhD, 1965. Appointments: Jnr Tech Asst, 1960-61; Snr Tech Asst, 1961-65; Lectr, 1965-71; Asst Prof, 1971-80; Prof, 1980-98. Honours: Snr Humboldt Fellshp, Univ of Bonn, 1971-72, 1976-76; Tech Univ of Munich, 1988; Visng Univ of Bielefeld, 1988. Memberships: Opl Rsch Soc of India; Indian Maths Soc; Assn of Maths Tchrs of India; Indian Soc for Probability and Stats; Amn Math Soc. Address: A1 & A1 Sri Sakthi Flats, Plot 5A, III Cross Street, Dhandeeswarar Nagar, Velachery, Chennai 600 042, India.

SUDOMO, b. 20 Sep 1926 Malang E Java. Politician. Education: Navigation High Sch Cilacap Cntrl Java; Artillerie Sch Koninklijke Marine Den Helder Netherlands; Inst for Natl Def - LEMHANAS; Sch for Marine Cmdrs Surabaya; Naval Staff and Cmd Coll Jakarta. Appointments: Battalion III Base IX, 1945-40; Cmdr Flores and First Offr Gajah Madah, 1950-56; Hd Directorate of Ops and Trng Credits Naval Hq; Cmdr Spec Fighting Unit; Promoted Vice-Admiral, 1956-62; Th Naval Cmdr for liberation of W Irian, 1962-64; Asst to Min of Sea Comms, 1964-66; Insp-Gen of Navy, 1966-68; Cmdr Cntrl Maritime Territory, 1968-69; Chf of Staff of Indonesian Navy promoted Admiral, 1969-73; Dep Chf of Cmd for Restoration of Security and Order, 1973-74; Chf of Staff, 1974-78; Dep Cmdr in charge of Armed Forces, 1978-83; Min of Manpower, 1983-88; Co-ordng Min of Polit Affairs and Security, 1988-93; Chmn Supreme Advsry Cncl, 1993-98. Address: Supreme Advisory Council, Jalan Merdeka Utara 15, Jakarta Pusat 10110, Indonesia.

SUDRADJAT Edi, b. 22 Apr 1938, Jambi, Sumatra. Education: Mil Acady. Appointments: Platoon Cmdr, Infantry Battalion 515, Brawidjaja Div, Malang, E Java; Army Chf of Staff, Jakarta, 1988-93; Cmdr-in-Chf, Armed Forces, 1993. Address: Ministry of Defence and Security, Jalan Merdeka Barat 13-14, Jakarta 10110, Indonesia.

SUENAGA Shigeru, b. 27 May 1953, Yamagata, Japan. Economist. m. Miyako, 9 Mar 1980. Education: MA (Master of Econs) Takushoku Univ. Publications: Rice Price Cycles of Super Longterm: AD 407-1993, 1997. Memberships: Intl Assn of Agricl Economists (IAAE), IL, USA. Hobby: Natural gardening. Address: 1-15 Yasuura-cho, Yokosuka City, Kanagawa, 238-0012, Japan.

SUFIAN Abu Jafar Mohammad, b. 15 Apr 1949, Barisal, Bangladesh. University Teacher. m. Jahanara Begum, 4 Aug 1966, 2 s, 1 d. Education: PhD, MI Univ, USA, 1984. Appointments: Lectr, Assoc Prof, Jahangir Nagar Univ, Dhaka, 1974-86; Asst Prof, Prof, King Faisal Univ, Saudi Arabia, 1986-. Publications: Methods & Techniques of Social Research, 1998. Honours: Colombo Plan Awd, Aust, 1979; Thoman Fellshp, USA, 1983. Memberships: PAA; IUSSP; AMSS; ISI; ISOSS; JSA. Hobby: Reading. Address: King Faisal University, PO Box 2397, Damman 31451, Saudi Arabia.

SUGANO Takuo, b. 25 Aug 1931, Tokyo, Japan. President. m. Nobuko, 24 Sept 1960, 2 d. Education: PhD, Elec Engrng, Univ of Tokyo. Appointments: Prof, Dept of Elec Engrng, 1971, Dean, Fac of Engrng, 1991, Pres, 1994, Univ of Tokyo. Publication: Semiconductor Integrated Circuits, 1995. Honours: Disting Sci Awd, 1988; Jack A Morton Awd, 1992; Purple Ribbon Prize, 1995. Memberships: Life Fell, Inst of Elec & Electron Engrs; Hon Mbr, Japan Soc of Appl Phys. Hobby: Golfing. Address: 2-2-3 Sakura Setagaya-ku, Tokyo 156-0053, Japan.

SUGISAKI Shigemitsu, b. 7 Feb 1941, Tokyo, Japan. Economist. m. Michiko Sugisaki, 2 Dec 1971, 1 s, 2 d. Education: Master of Intl Affairs. Appointment: Dpty Mngng Dir, Intl Monetary Fund, 1997-. Hobbies: Outdoor sports. Address: 4200 Massachusetts Ave 802, Washington, DC 20016, USA.

SUGISAKI Shigemitsu, b. 1941. Intl Offic; Fmr Civ servant. Education: Univ of Tokyo; Columbia Univ. Appointments: Positions with min of Fin, 1964-76, 1979-94; Personal Asst to Pres Asian Devt Bank, 1976-79; Dep Vice-Min of Fin for Intl Affairs, 1990-91; Dep Dir-Gen Intl Fin Bur, 1991-92; Commnr Tokyo Regl Taxation Bur, 1992-93; Sec-Gen Exec Bur Securities and Exchange Surveillance Commn, 1993-94; Spec Advsr to Mngng Dir IMF, 1994-97; Dep Mngng Dir, Feb 1997-. Memberships: Mbr Mins Sec for Intl Affairs, 1990-91. Address: IMF, 700 19th Street, NW, Washington, DC 20431, USA.

SUGITA Nobud, b. 8 Sept 1921, Osaka, Japan. Publisher. m. 23 Jan 1948, 1 s, 1 d. Education: BA,

Doshisha Univ. Appointments: Pres, Minerva Shobo, 1948-; Bd Dir, Japan Publrs Assn. Publication: WSatashi No Tabiji, 1998. Membership: Rotary Club of Kyoto-Yamashina. Hobby: Travel. Address: c/o Minerva Shobo Co Ltd, 1 Tsutsumidani Cho Hinooka, Yamashina-ku, Kyoto 607-8494, Japan.

SUGIURA Akihiko, b. 16 Oct 1965, Aiohi, Japan. Associate Professor (Engineering). m. Yasuko H, 17 oct 1 d. Education: PhD, Univ of Tokyo. Appointments: Rsch Assoc, Toyota Technol Inst, 1990-; Assoc Prof, Toyohashi Univ of Technol, 1998-. Honours: Grantee, The Telecomm Advmnt Fndn, 1994; Hoso-Bunka Fndn, 1995; Tokai Sci Acady, 1995; Hari Info Sci Promotion Fndn, 1995; The Grant-in-Aid, 1996. Membership: IEEE. Hobbies: Travel; Skiing; Cabin cruisers. Address: Tempaku-cho, Toyohashi, 441-8580, Japan.

SUH Dae-Sook, b. 22 Nov 1931, Korea. Professor. m. Yun-Ok, 29 Oct 1960, 2 s. Education: PhD, Columbia Univ, NY, USA. Appointments: Prof, Pol Sc, Univ of HI at Manoa, Honolulu, HI, 1972-. Publications: Kim Il Sung, The North Korean Leader. Honours: Korea Fndn Prof of Polit Studies, Univ of HI. Memberships: Assn for Asian Studies; Amn Pol Sc Assn. Hobbies: Tennis; Golf. Address: University of Hawaii - Manoa, Honolulu of Hawaii - Manoa, Honolulu, HI 96822, USA.

SUH Sang-Mok, b. 11 July 1947, Hongsung, Korea. Member of Parliament. m. 3 July 1972, 1 s. Education: Clark Univ, USA, 1965-67; BA, Econs & Maths, Amherst Coll, 1967-69; PhD, Econs, Stanford Univ, 1969-73. Appointments: Econ, World Bank, 1973-78; Snr Fell, 1978-83, VP, 1983-88, Korea Devel Inst; Snr Cnslr to Dpty PM & Min for Econ Planning Bd, Korea, 1983; Mbr, Pacific Bd of Econs, Time Mag, 1983-87; Mbr, Natl Assembly, 1988-98; Min, Min of Hlth & Welfare, 1993-95; Pres, Inst for Pub Policy Studies, 1990-97; Chmn, Campaign Planning Bur of 15th Presl Election, 1997. Publications include: Patterns of Poverty and Anti-Poverty Program, 1981; Nationwide Old-Age Pension Program and its Socio-Economic Impact, 1986; Response, 1987; The Crisis of Capitalism in Korea: How to Overcome It, 1989; There is No Free Lunch: Suh, Sang-Mok's Economic Essay, 1994; Why Just Argue! Let's Work!: Stories Behind the Policy Making Process, 1996. Honours: Phi Beta Kappa, 1969; Order of Natl Serv Merit, Korean Govt, 1983, 1996; Sequoia, Stanford Univ, 1995; Citation, World Hlth Org, 1996; Citation, UN Environ Prog, 1997. Memberships: Intl Rotary Club; Christian Bus Mens Cttee of Korea; Gangnam Forum; Educl & Cultural Forum for the 21st Century. Hobby: Golf. Address: #24-1001 Hyundai Apt, Apgujeong-Dong, Gangnam-Gu, Seoul, Korea.

SUHARTA Herliyani, b. 8 Aug 1952, Surabaya, Indonesia. Senior Researcher. m. N Suharta, 2 s, 1 d. Education: Engr (Phys), MPhil, Sheffield Univ; Doct stud, Hertfordshire Univ, UK. Appointments: Conversion and Conservation of Energy and Renewable Energy, 1979-; Transfer of a New Technol, 1989-; Solarthermal Pump, 1989-93; Solar Oven, 1995-; RUT-DRN, 1994-97; TCFR, USA, 1995-. Publications: Sci pprs in var jrnls and congresses. Honour: Cand from Indonesia UNESCO Sci Prize, Paris, 1995. Memberships: CMDC, 1991-92; Indonesian Soc of Engrs and Techns, 1992-; Indonesia Phys Soc, 1994-; ISES, 1995-96; Earthwatch, USA, 1995. Hobbies: Reading; Travelling; Swimming.

SUHARTO Mohamed, b. 8 Jun 1921 Kemusu Yogjakarta. Politician; Army Offr. Education: Mil schs; Indonesian Army Staff and Cmd Coll. Appointments: Offr in Japanese sponsored Indonesian Army, 1943; Battalion later Regimental Cmdr Yogjakarta, 1945-50; Regimental Cntrl Java, 1953; Brig-Gen, 1960; Maj-Gen, 1962; Dep Chf of Army Staff, 1960-65; Chf of Army Staff, 1965-68; Supreme Cmdr, 1968-73; Min of Army, 1965; Assumed emergency exec powers, Mar 1966; Dep PM for Def and Security, 1966; Chmn of Presidium of Cabinet in charge of Def and Security also Min of Army, 1966-67; Full Gen, 1966; Acting Pres of Indonesia, 1967-68; PM, 1967; Concurrently Min for Def and Security, 1967-73; Pres of Indonesia, Mar 1969-98. Publications: Suharto: My

Thoughts Words and Deeds, 1989. Honours: UN Population Awd, 1989. Address: 8 Jalan Cendana, Jakarta, Indonesia.

SUISSA Eli, b. 1955 Afula. Politician. m. 4 c. Appointments: Joined min of Interior firstly in charge of Jerusalem Dist then as Dep Dir-Gen; Min of the Interior and of Relig Affairs, 1996-. Memberships: MbrShas - Sephardic Torah Guardians. Address: Ministry of the Interior, P OBox 6158, 2 Rehov Kaplan, Kiryat Ben-Gurion, Jerusalem 91061, Israel.

SULAIM Suliman Abd al aziz as-, b. 1941. Politician. Education: Cairo Univ; Univ of S Ca; Johns Hopkins Univ. Appointments: Dir Dept of For Rels and Confs; Min of Labour; Asst Dir-Gen Gen Org of Socl Ins; Prof Polit Sci Riyadh Univ, 1972-74; Dep Min of Com and Ind for Trade and Provisions, 1974-75; Min of Com, 1975-95; Chmn Bd Saudi Arabian Specifs and Standardizaiton Org; Chmn Bd Wheat Silos and Flour Mills Org. Address: c/o Ministry of Commerce, P O Box 1774, Airport Road, 1162 Riyadh, Saudi Arabia.

SULEIMENOV Olzhas Omarovich, b. 1936. Politician; Writer. Education: Kazak State Univ; Maxim Gorky Inst of Lit in Moscow. Appointments: Debut as writer, 1960; Ed-in-Chf Studio Kazakh film, 1962-71; Hd of div Prostor - mag - 1971-; Sec Bd Kazakh Writers' Union, 1971-; Chmn Kazakh Cttee on rels with writers of Asia and Africa, 1980-; Actively participates in ecological movement; Actions of protest against nuclear tests in Semipalatinsk since late 1980s; Dep to USSR Supreme Soviet, 1984-89; People's Dep USSR Supreme Soviet, 1989-91; Fndr and ldr of People's Progress Party of Kazakhstan, 1992-95; Amb to Italy, 1995-. Publications: Collects of poetry inclng: Argamaki, 1961; Sunny Nights, 1962; The Night of Paris, 1963; The Kind Time of the Sunrise, 1964; The Year of Monkey, 1967; Above White Rivers, 1970; Each Day - Morning, 1973; Repeating in the Noon, 1973; A Round Star, 1975; Definition of a Bank, 1976; And others. Honours: USSR Komsomol Prize; State Abai Prize of Kazakh SSR. Memberships: Mbr CPSU, 1989-90; Mbr USSR Supreme Soviet, 1989-91. Address: Via Cassia 185, Rome, Italy.

SULEIMENOV Tuleutai Skakovich, b. 1941 Semipalatinsk. Diplomatist. Education: karaganda Polytech Inst; Dip Acady of USSR; Min of For Affairs. Appointments: Foreman Karaganda Metallurgic factory, 1969; Foreman Comsomol and CP functionary, 1969-80; Cnslr USSR Emb to Iran, 1988-91; Kazakhstan Min of For Affairs, 1991-94; Amb to USA, 1994-95; Amb to Hungary, 1995-. Memberships: Mbr USSR Min of For Affairs, 1980-. Address: 1025 Budapest, III ker, Kapi ut 59, Hungary.

SULLIVAN Kenneth Milton, b. 27 July 1927. Engineer. m. Joyce C Sullivan. Education: BE, hons, Sydney; PhD. Appointments: Engr, AGL Co; Engr, BORAL; Mngr, ACIRL; Mngng Dir, K M Sullivan & Assocs Pty Ltd. Publications: Over 100 pprs and tech publns. Honour: AM for serv to sci, 1984; Clean Air Medal, CASANZ, 1994. Memberships: FIE Aust; FAIE; F Inst E. Hobby: Golf. Address: 67 Eurobin Avenue, Manly, NSW 2095, Australia.

SULLIVAN Martin Roy, b. 26 Oct 1960, Sydney, Aust. Adult Foot & Ankle Surgeon. m. Allison, 29 Aug 1989, 2 s, 2 d. Education: MBBS (Hons); FRACS. Appointments: Cnslt Surg, St Vincent's Clin, 1994; Chf Foot & Ankle Serv, St George, 1996; Cnslt Sports Clin, Univ of Sydney, Cumberland. Memberships: Amn Orth Foot & Ankle Soc; West Pacific Orth Assn; Tattersall's Club; AJC. Hobbies: Golf; Cigars; Australian watercolours. Address: Ste 901E, St Vincent's Private Clinic, 438 Victoria Street, Darlington 2010, Sydney, Australia.

SULLIVAN Patrick Alexander, b. 16 Mar 1942, Dunedin, NZ. Professor of Biochemistry. m. Mary, 11 Dec 1967, 3 d. Education: BSc, 1963, MSc, 1965, PhD, 1968, Univ of Otago. Appointments: Hd, Dept of Biochem, 1996-98, Hd, Inst of Molecular Bioscis, 1998-, Massey Univ. Honours: Nuffield Fellshp, 1977; Fell, NZ Inst of

Chem, 1980; Fulbright Fellshp, 1984; Watson Victor Prize, 1993. Memberships: Intl Biol Network for Asia and Pacific Rim; Fell, Roy Soc of NZ; NZ Soc for Biochem and Molecular Biol. Hobbies: Hiking; Music. Address: c/o Institute of Molecular Biosciences, Massey University, Private Bag 11222, Palmerston North, New Zealand.

SHEIKH Mohammad Sultan, b. 5 Mar 1965, Hari Pari Gam, Tral, India. Lecturer. Education: Doct; PhD, Botany. Appointments: Lectr, Dept of Botany, Kashmir Univ. Publications: About 12 Pprs on Cut Flower Senessence. Memberships: Guest Lctr, Div of PHT, SKUAST, Srinagar. Hobbies: Listening to music; Watching movies; Reading. Address: Dept of Botany, University of Kashmir, Srinagar, Kashmir, India.

SULTANOV Outkir Tukhtamuradovich, b. 14 Jul 1939. Politician. m. 1 d. Education: Tomsk state Polytech Inst. Appointments: Electn Tomsk plant of cutting metals, 1963; Master Hd of lab Hd of prodn automatization Dep Chf Engr Dep Dir-Gen Tashkent Aviation Prodn Union, 1964-85; Hd Sci Prodn Unit Vostok, 1985-91; Chmn State Cttee for For Trade and Intl Rels, 1991-92; Min of External Econ Rels Dep PM, 1992-95; PM of Uzbekistan, Dec 1995-; People's Dep of Uzbekistan. Honours: Awd'd Mekhnat Shukhradi; Merited Engr Repub of Uzbekistan. Address: Government House, Mustarilik 5, 700008 Tashkent, Uzbekistan.

SUMMER Donna, b. 31 Dec 1948 Boston. Singer; Actress. m. (1) Helmut Sommer, div, 1 d; (2) Bruce Sudano, 1 s, 1 d. Appointments: Singer, 1967-; Appeared in German stage prodn Hair; In Eur, 1967-75; Appearing in Vienna Folk prodns of Porgy and Bess; German prodns of The Me Nobody Knows; Has sold over 20 million records. Albums: The Wanderer; Star Collection; Love to Love You Baby; Love Trilogy; Four Seasons of Love; I Remember Yesterday; The Deep; Shut Out; Once upon a Time; Bad Girls; On the Radio; Walk Away; She Works Hard for the Money; Cats without Claws; All Systems Go, 1988; Another Time and Place, 1989. Honours: Best Rhythm and Blues Female Vocalist Natl Acady of Recording Arts and Scis, 1978; Best Female Rock Vocalist, 1979; Favourite Female Pop Vocalist Am Music Awds, 1979; Favourite Female Vocalist of Soul Music, 1979; Ampex Golden Reel Awd for single and album On the Radio, 1979; Ampex Golden Reel Awd for Album Bad Girls, 1979; Soul Artist of Yr Rolling Stone Mag, 1979; Best Rock Performance; Best of Las Vegas Jimmy Awd, 1980; Grammy Awd for Best Inspirational Performance, 1984; Sev awds for best-selling records. Address: 2401 Main Street, Santa Monica, CA 90405, USA.

SUMMERHAYES Geoffrey Edwin, b. 15 Sept 1928, Perth, Aust. Architect. m. (1), 1 s, 1 d, (2), Elizabeth Ann O'Neil, 1993. Education: Assoc Archt, Perth Tech Coll, 1946-50; BArch, Princeton Univ, USA, 1952. Appointments: Micklewright & Mountford, NJ, 1952; Kump & Assoc, San Fran, 1952; Pthr, 1953; Snr Ptnr, 1965; Summerhayes Assns: Dir, 1979; Summerhayes Way & Assocs Pty Ltd, 1979; Geoffrey E Summerhayes, 1991. Honours: Loweel M Palmer Fell, 1951; Home of Yr Awd, 1960, 1960; Bronze Medal Awd Citation, 1969, 1970; Clay Brick Awd, 1973; Queens Silver Jubilee Medal, 1977; Archts Bd Awd, 1983; New Club Awd, 1984; RAIA Bronze Medal Awd, Art Gall WA, 1958; Austl Roll of Hon. Memberships: Life Fell, Roy Aust Inst Archts; Assoc, Des Inst Aust: Fell, Roy Inst Brit Archts. Hobbies include: Rotary Club; Swimming. Address: 25A Osborne PDE, Claremont, WA 6010, USA.

SUMMERS Gregory Robin, b. 16 Apr 1955, NC, USA. Engineer; Researcher. m. Alison, 28 Dec 1984, 3 s. Education: BSCE, MSCE, NC State Univ, Raleigh, NC, USA. Appointments include: From Staff Engr to Corp Snr Engr, Law Cos Grp (now merged w Gibb Ltd), Mid E (Saudi Arabia), USA (FL); Hd, Archtl and Engrng Servs, Coastal Cnstrn Prods Inc, USA (FL), 1987-89; Mngrng Dir and Fndr, Engrng Materials Cnslts Ltd, UK (Wales), 1989-93; Hd of Advsry Servs Rsch and Testing, Pub Wrks Affairs, Bahrain, 1993-. Publications: Over 40 publs or presentations. Honours; Chi Epsilon Hon Soc, 1978;

Outsndng Grad Tchng Cert, 1981; Apptd Natl Chmn, Materials Evaluation Cttee, ACSE. Memberships: Lic Profl Engr, NC, USA, 1984; Lic Profl Engr, FL, USA, 1986; Lic Profl Engr, GA, USA, 1986; Amn Soc of Civil Engrs; Amn Concrete Inst, Chapt Dir, Chapt Pres, 1986-88; Constrn Specifications Inst, Chapt Dir, 1988; Bahrain Soc of Engrs, 1998. Hobbies: Writing; Travelling; Exercise. Address: PO Box 25081, Awali, Bahrain.

SUMMERS Justine Rae, b. 17 July 1970, Sydney, Aust. Principal Artist. Education: Victorian Coll of Arts, 1984-86; Austl Ballet Sch, 1987-88. Appointments: Contract, Austl Ballet, 1989-99; Soloist, 1992; Snr Artist, 1994; Prin Artist, 1996. Creative Works: Prin Roles in the Ballet; Sleeping Beauty; Giselle; Swan Lake; Manon; Onegin; Romeo and Juliet; Madame Butterfly; The Nutcracker; La Sylphide le Concours; Fall River Legend; Apollo; Catalyst; Divergence; Gemini; Voluntaries; Afternoon of A Faun; Symphony in C; The Merry Widow. Honors: Green Room Awd; Victorian Sector, Yng Austl of the Yr Awd. Hobbies: Extenside Reading; Attending th; Films; Music; Trav; Exploring Art galls. Address: c/o The Australian Ballet, 2 Kavanagh Street, Southbank, Vic 3006, Australia.

SUMNER Christopher John, b. 17 Apr 1943, Melbourne, Aust. Member, National Native Title Tribunal. m. Suzanne Roux, 13 May 1978, 1 s, 1 d. Education: BA, LLB, Grad Dip A (Community Langs), Adelaide Univ. Appointments: Bar and Solicitor, 1967; Atty Gen, Min of Prices and Consumer Affairs, Min Asstng the Premier on Ethnic Affairs, 1979; Ldr of Opposition Legis Cl, 1979-82; Atty Gen, Min of Corp Affairs, Min of Consumer Affairs, Min of Ethnic Affairs, 1982-89; Atty Gen, Min of Corp Affairs, Min for Crime Prevention, 1989-92; Atty Gen, Min for Crime Prevention, Min of Pub Sector Reform, 1992-93; Atty Gen, Min of Jus, Min for Crime Prevention, Min of Correctional Servs, Min of Pub Sector Reform, 1993; Mbr, Natl Native Title Tribunal, 1995-. Honour: Italian Hon of Commendatore, Pres of the Italian Repub, Francesco Cossiga, 1989. Memberships: Pres, Australasian Soc of Victimology, 1988-; Pres, World Soc of Victimology, 1991-94. Address: 194 Childers Street, North Adelaide, SA 5006, Australia.

SUN Bi, b. 24 Jan 1943, Xingcheng, China. Teacher Researcher. m. Sun Furong, 12 Nov 1967, 1 s, 1 d. Education: Grad, Xian Jiaotong Univ. Appointment: Pres, Coll of Vocational and Tech Educ, 1997-. Publication: Steam Turbine, coord, wrote, 1988. Membership: Machinery and Engrng Assn, 1981. Hobby: Literature. Address: 3-34-141 Xian Jiaotong University, Xian, Shaanxi, 710049, China.

SUN Qian, b. 14 Apr 1935, Fushun, China. Professor of Mathematics. m. Madam Duan Yong, 1959, 1 s, 2 d. Education: BS, Dept of Maths & Mechanics, Peking Univ, 1954-59. Appointments: Maths Lectr, Maths Dept of the Univ of Heilongjiang, 1959-72; Maths Prof, Fushun Indl Cll of Mine Bur, 1973-95. Publications: 4 pprs in mathl jrnls, 1988-. Honours: Model Tchr, Inst for Decades; Model Tchr, Fushun Cty for Annuals; Model Tchr, Liaoning Prov for Annuals; Repr, Hua, Luogeng (Chinese Mathn) to popularise the Optimum Seeking Method and Critical Path Method in Cty of Fushun, Heilongjiang Prov and NorthEast China, 1973-75. Memberships: Dir, Fushun Math Inst; Dir, China Coal Higher Learning Math Inst; In chf charge of the Unitary Exam of Advd Maths of China Northeastern Coal Cttee and China Coal Higher Learning System annually for over 10 yrs. Hobbies: Swimming; Singing; Music. Address: Fushun Industrial College of Mine Bureau, Fushun, Province Liaoning 113008, China.

SUN Shiwen, b. 14 Aug 1963, Shanghai, China. Professor in Urban Planning. m. Liya Zhou, 7 Oct 1987, 1 d. Education: BEng, Tongji Univ, 1985; Master of Urban Plng, 1990; Dr Urban Plng, Tongji Univ, 1994. Appointments: Shanghai Cty Plng Mngmt Bur, 1985; Tongji Univ, 1994. Publications: Philosophy of Urban Planning, 1997; The Reader in the Law of Urban Planning, 1998. Membership: Urban Plng Soc of China,

1995. Hobby: Art. Address: Department of Urban Planning, Tongji University, Shanghai 200092, China.

SUN Shiying, b. 11 Mar 1933, Shanghai, China. Professor. m. Han-Yang Zhang, 23 Mar 1965, 1 d. Education: Grad, Dept of Electron Engnrg, Shanghai, 1953; Grad, Dept of Russian, Harbin For Lang Inst, 1955; Grad student, Univ of Electron Scis and Technol of China, Chengdu, 1956-58. Appointments: Lectr, Univ of Electron Sci and Technol of China (VESTC), Chengdu, 1961; Assoc Prof, 1982; Prof, 1988-, Shanghai Jiaotong Univ; Co-chmn, MMIC Session of APMC '88, 1988; Snr Mbr, IEEE, 1995. Publications: (book) Measurement of Microwave Devices, 1961; Co-auth, Microwave Techniques, Microwave Electronic Devices, vols I and II, 1961. Honours: Natl Advd Grp and Dip of Hon, 1960; 1st Class Prize, SJTU, 1986; IEEE, MTTS Centennial Medal, 1989; 5 Ctfs of Natl Sci and Technol Achmnts, SSTCC, 1992; 3rd Prize and Dip, Pei-yuan Zhou Fndn, 1998. Memberships: Snr Mbr, IEEE; Snr Mbr, Chinese Inst of Electrons; Microwave Cttee of Shanghai Inst of Electrons. Address: Department of Electronic Engineering, Shanghai Jiaotong University, No 535 Fa Hua Zhen Road, Shanghai 200052, China.

SUN Xing Qun, b. 18 Apr 1938, Fuzhoum Fujian, China. Professor. Appointments: Prof, Fujian Arts Rsch Inst; Mngng Dir, Soc for Chinese Minority Natly Music; Dir, Trad Musical Soc of China; Dir, Cntr for Intercultural Music Arts; Mbr, Intl Advsry Cncl, London. Publications: A Study of Fujian Nayin Music; History of Music in Xixia, Liao and Jin; The Primitive Ancestors of the Classic on Aesthetics of Music Record of Music and peri Poietikes; Num articles in profl jrnls. Membership: Chinese Musicians Assn. Address: 183 Yang Qian Road, Fuzhou, Fujian, China.

SUN Yuxia, b. 7 Nov 1962, Shaanxi, China. Teacher; Doctor. m. Zhang Bin, 25 May 987, 1 s. Education: BMed, Shaanxi Coll of Tradl Chinese Med. Appointment: Acupuncture Lectr, 1993. Publication: Annotation of A-B Classic Acupuncture and Moxibustion. Honours: Hlth Min of Sdan, Omdurman Friendship Hosp, Hon Cert for Oustndng Medl Serv, 1997. Membership: Acupuncture & Moxibustion. Hobby: Playing basketball. Address: Shaanxi College of Traditional Chinese Medicine, Acupuncture Section, XianYang, Shaanxi, China.

SUN Zhongcai, b. 21 Mar 1950, Liaoning. Professor. m. Lanfen Liu, 1 Mar 1977, 1 d. Education: Undergrad, 1971; MEcon, 1987; PhD Econ, 1994. Appointments: Assoc Prof, 1993-97; Prof, 1997-, Dept of Agric Econs, Renmin Univ of China; Advsr, The World Bank. Creative Works: Agricultural Economics, A Theoretical Inquiry; Introduction to Agricultural Information Systems; Agriculture and Economics Growth. Honours: Folkswagen Awd; Outstndng People of the 20th Century Awd, IBC, 1999. Memberships: NY Acady of Sci. Hobby: Literature. Address: Inst for Rural Development, Renmin Univ of China, 175 Haidian Road, 100872 Beijing, China.

SUN Chen. Politician. Appointments: Fmrly Min of Def. Memberships: Mbr Kuomintang Cntrl Standing Cttee, 1994-. Address: c/o Ministry of National Defence, P O Box 9001, Taipei, Taiwan.

SUN Dao Lin, b. 18 Dec 1921. Actor; Film Dir. m. Wang Wenjuan, 1962, 1 d. Education: Yanjing Univ. Films incl: Reconnaissance Over Yangtze River, 1954; The Family, 1956; Constant Beam, 1958; Early Spring in February, 1963; Go Master, 1982; Thunderstorm, 1983; Special President, 1986; Stepmother, 1992. Publication: Anthology of Sun Daolin's Poems and Prose, 1994. Honours: Grand Prix Montreal Film Fest for Go Master, 1984; Best Film Actor - Lian-Ho Daily Singapore - 1987; Outstanding Film Artist Prize - Wen-Hui Daily Shanghai - 1989; One of Ten Most Popular Film Stars - China Film Weekly - 1990; Hon mbr China Fedn of Lit and Art Circles, 1996-. Hobbies: Lit; Music - especially singing. Address: Shanghai Film Studio, 595 Tsao Hsi North Road, Shanghai 200030, People's Republic of China.

SUN Fuling, b. 1921 Shaoxing Cty Zhejiang Prov. Offic; Bus Exec. Appointments: Vice-Chmn Beijing Mun Cttee 8th CPPCC, 1988-92; Vice-Chmn 8th Natl Cttee CPPCC, 1993-. Memberships: Mbr 5th Natl Cttee CPPCC, 1978-82; Perm mbr 6th Natl Cttee, 1983-87; Perm mbr 7th Natl Cttee, 1988-92. Address: National Committee of Chinese People's Political Consultative Council, 23 Taiping Qiao Sstreet, Beijing, People's Republic of China.

SUN Jiazheng, b. 1944 Siyang Co Jiangsu Prov. Politician. Educaiton: Nanjing Univ. Appointments: Joined CCP, 1966; Min of Radio Film and TV, 1994-98. Honours: Hon Chmn Bd of Dirs Beijing Film Coll. Memberships: Mbr 14th CCP Cntrl Cttee, 1992-97; Mbr 15th CCP Cntrl Cttee, 1997-. Address: c/o Ministry of Radio, Film and Television, 2 Fuxing Menwai Dajie Street, Beijing 1000866, People's Republic of China.

SUNADA John, b. 17 Sept 1946, Fresno, CA, USA. Fisheries Biologist. m. Mary, 13 Dec 1980, 2 s. Education: BA, CSU Fresno; MS, Humboldt State Univ. Appointments: Fishery Biologist, Bur of Land Mngmt, Portland, OR, 1970; Jnr Aquatic Biologist, CA Dept Fish and Game, Long Beach, 1970-72; Asst Marine Biologist, 1972-80; Assoc, Marine Biologist, 1980-92; Assoc Fishery Bio, 1992-. Publications: Sci publs to Fish and Game Quarterly Jrnl, 1974-86; Sci articles in CA Coop Oceanic Fisheries Investigation Reports, 1979-81. Honour: Awd of Hon. Memberships: Amn Fisheries Soc; Amn Inst of Fishery Rsch Biologists; South CA Acady of Scis. Hobbies: Fishing; Hiking; Investing; Art; Coin collecting. Address: State of California, 4775 Bird Farm Road, China, CA 91709, USA.

SUNAKAWA Megumi, b. 1 Jan 1928, Japan. Professor Emeritus. m. Terue, 26 May 1957, 2 s, 2 d. Education: BS, 1954; PhD, Univ of Tokyo, 1962. Appointments: Prof, Univ of Tokyo, 1973; Yokohama Natl Univ, 1988; Nihon Univ, 1993. Creative Works: Over 100 Pprs in profl jrnls. Honours: Fellow, JSASS; Assoc Fell, AIAA; Silver medal, JSME. Memberships: ISASS; JSME; AIAA; JRS. Address: 4-9-8-607 Motonakayayama Funabashi, Chiba 273-0035, Japan.

SUNDER Ramasubhu, b. 8 Aug 1953, Poona, India. Research and Development. m. Kala, 1 July 1976, 1 d. Education: PhD, Aeroengineering, 1978. Appointments: Scientist, Natl Aeronautical Lab, Bangalore, 1978-86; Vsing Scientist, Wright Aero Labs (USAF), 1986-88; Hd, Sructural Integrity, NAL, Bangalore, 1988-94; Dir, Bangalore Intl System Solutions (P) Ltd, 1994-. Publications: About 35 pprs. Honour: US Natl Rsch Cncl Associateship, 1986-88. Membership: Amn Soc for Testing & Materials, 1984-. Hobbies: Computer applications in the laboratory. Address: 41A, 1st A Cross, AECS 2nd Stage, RMV Extn, Bangalore 560 094, India.

SUNDERLAL Aruna, b. 4 Feb 1939, Delhi, India. Singer (Mezzo-Soprano); Music Educator; Social Worker. m. Rajinder P Sunderlal, 7 Mar 1959, 1s, 1d. Education: Isabella Thoburn Coll, Lucknow Univ; Medl Coll, Punjab Univ; Voice Trng, Private Tchrs, India, UK, Germany; LTCL, Singing; Dip, Cnslng, Bombay. Appointments: Fndr Mbr, Indus Intl, Bombay; Chairperson, Activities, YWCA, Bombay, 1968; Artist, All India Radio, 1970-; Chairperson, Home for Aged, Bombay, 1970, Calcutta, 1977; Dir, Stewardship St Paul's Cath and Diocese of Calcutta, 1980; Chairperson Woman's Welfore Soc, Calcutta, 1984; Convenor Christian Musicians Conf, India, 1986; Mbr, Org Cttee for visit of His Grace, the Archbish of Canterbury and Mrs Runcie to W Bengal, 1986; Fndr, Dir, Mngng Tstee, Bangalore Sch of Music, 1987; Artistic Dir, Intl Fest, The East West Music and Dance Encounters, 1990-. Creative Works: Recitals India, Far E, UK, illustrated talks, radio brdcsts, 1970-; An East West Choral, Dance Ballet, Song of India, 1990; Conceived East West Fusion Concerts for Intl Encounters, 1990-; Presented pprs at India Intl Fest, 1993, intl seminars, 1990-; Dir, TV series, East West Music Encounters, 1994. Honours: Hon Life Mbr, Calcutta Dicesan Stewardship, 1985; Hon by Karnataka Gov to release Mozart Stamp, India, 1991; Awd, British Cncl

Schl, 1993; Indian Cncl for Cultural Rels Grantee, 1993; Assoc, Natl Inst Adv Stdies, India, 1994; Exceptional Serv to Music Awd, Musicians Karnataka, 1997; Interviewed for TV, 1998; Awd Hon Life Mbrshp, Cancercare, Karnataka. Memberships include: Mbr Bd, YWCA, Bombay, 1967, Calcutta, 1974; Mbr Bd, Samaritans Intl, 1982; Mbr Intl Soc Music Educ, 1994; Fndr Mbr, Fedn of W Music Socs in India, 1994, AMAMIKA, 1995, Assn of Western Music Schs in India, 1997. Hobbies: Gardening: Horticulture; Environment; Youth welfare; Collecting antiques. Address: Sunder-Grih, 32 Netaji Road, Fraser Town, Bangalore 560005, India.

SUNGURLU Mahmut Oltan, b. 1936 Gumushane. Politician. m. 1 c. Education: Bursa Lycee Istanbul Univ. Appointments: Prac'd law in Gumushane; Fndr Motherland Party prov org in Gumushane; Dep for Gumushane, 1983-; Min of Jus, 1986-87, 1987-88, 1989-92; Dep Chmn Motherland Party, Jun 1988. Address: c/o Ministry of Justice, Adalet Bakaligi, Bakanliklar, Ankara, Turkey.

SUNITHA Prithviraj, b. 8 July 1974, Madras, India. Teacher. Education: BA, Engl; BEd; MA, Hindi. Appointment: Tchr, Engl, Alan Feldman Pub Sch. Publications: Mother - A Painting, 1992; Poems, short stories. Memberships: Quest India Publs; Young Poet; Poesie India, Orissa. Hobbies: Writing poems and articles; Music (singing & listening) Stitching; Antiques. Address: No-14 Sree Rengam, Mamtha Nagar, Kazhakuttom, Trivandrum 695582, India.

SUPOYO, b. 30 July 1924, Solo, Indonesia. Certified Public Accountant. m. Miryani, 28 Oct 1951, 2 s, 1 d. Education: Econ Dept, State Univ of Airlangga, Surabaya, Indonesia. Appointments: Dean, Econ Fac; Chmn, E Java Chmbr of Com and Ind; Pres, E Java Dev Bank; Pres, SCTV. Publications: Article on acctng issues in the Netherlands, 1972-77. Memberships: Indonesian Acctng Inst; Indonesian Econ Assn. Hobbies: Moral principles. Address: JL Imam Bonjol 40, Surabaya, Indonesia.

SURESH MOONA, b. 13 Jan 1951, Tumkar, India. Teacher; NCG Officer. m. V Ramadevi, 11 Oct 1978, 1 s, 1 d. Education: BS, BEd, Postgrad Dip in Engl Lit, MA, Engl, Mysore Univ. Appointments: Tchr, APS Boy's hs, Bangalore; Chf Offr, Natl Cadet Corps (NCC), India. Publications: About 100 articles on the important histl monuments publd. Honors: Spirit in Workmanship Awd, Rotary Intl, Bangalore, 1998. Memberships: Fndr Dir, An Assn for Reviving Awareness about Monuments. Hobby: Conservation of historical monuments. Address: No 85/86, 2nd Cross, Gavipuram, Bangalore, 19, Karnataka, India.

SURIYAMOORTHY S Kasthuri, b. 26 May 1973, Chennai, India. Education: MA; MPhil. Honours: Many in coll. Membership: Indrakarnan Unique Art Gall Trust. Address: Kadaikadu, Neidayasal Post, Sirkali TK, Namai; Tamil, India.

SURYOHADIKUSUMO Jamaludin, b. 11 Oct 1934. Government Official. Education: Deg in Forestry, Gadjah Mada Univ, 1961. Appointments: Asst, Gadjay Mada Univ, 1958-61; Snr Asst, 1961-63; Admnstr, Randublatung Forest Dist, 1963-66, Cepu Forest Dist, 1966-71; Hd, Mktng Div, Perum Paerhutani, 1973-81; Dir, Prodn, Directorate Gen of Forestry, Min of Agric, 1981-83; Pres, PT Inhutani II, 1983-88; Dir Gen, Forest Utilization, Min of Forestry, 1988-93; Min of Forestry, Govt of Indonesia, 1993-. Address: Ministry of Forestry, Jalan Jenderal Gatot Sutroto, Jakarta 10270, Indonesia.

SUSANTO Harta, b. 6 Aug 1931, Medan, Indonesia. Publisher; Journalist. m. Widijawanti Susanto, 1 June 1958, 1 s, 3 d. Education: Meth Engl Snr hs Dip. Appointments: Chmn/Fndr, Harian Analisa (Indonesian Lang Newspaper), 1972-; Exec Dir, Harian Garuda (Indonesian Lang Newspaper), 1976-. Honours: Best publr in Indonesia (Anugerah Jurnalistik), 1994; Best Publr in Indonesia, 1995. Memberships: Indonesian Jrnlsts Assn; Indonesian Publrs Assn; Bd Chmn, Gen Sudiman sch of Bus and Acady Fndn. Hobbies: Sports

(especially basketball); Collecting antiques. Address: 414 Bell Fork Road, Jacksonville, NC 28541, USA.

SUSHEELAMMA S G, b. 24 May 1939. Founder, Sumangali Seva Ashrama. Appointments: Employed at REMCO Factory (now Bharat Heavy Electricals Ltd), 1959-73; Joined spiritual instn under guidance of Mathe Mahadevi, 1973-74; Warden, Bhuvaneswari Mahila Samaj, 1974-78; Regd Sumangali Seva Ashrama, 1975; Projs incl: Basvananda Nursery Sch, Audugodi slum, 1976; Orphanage for girls and boys 5-18 yrs, 1979; Working Women's Hostel, 1979; Dairy Unit, 1980; Vocational Trng, 1981; Cheshire Homes for the Aged, Trng for Rural Women, 1982; Home for Physically Handicapped, 1983; Micro-credit Facilities, 1986; Formation of Mahila Vokkoota, Cmnty Dev, 1986; Sch at Guddadahalli, 1987; Non-Formal Educ in rural areas, Creche Workers Trng, 1988; Twisting of Dupion Silk Vocational Trng Cum Prodn Prog for benefit of Rural Women, 1997; Other positions incl: Fndr, Pres, Sumangali Multi Purpose Co-op Soc. Honours incl: Natl Awd for Child Welfare, 1985; Kanataka State Awd for Child Welfare, and for Sports & Yth Servs, Sumangali Yuvathi Madali, 1985; Natl Awd for Handloom Unit for excellence, 1991; Best Citizen Awd, Bangalore Cty Corp Awd for Outstndng Socl Wrk, 1992; Janaki Devi Bajaj Purskar, for Outstndng Contbn to Rural Entrepeneurship, 1994; Mysore Dasara Awd for Rural and Women Dev, Dept of Women and Child, Govt of Karnataka, 1994; Lakshmi N Menon Literacy Awd, Deena Seva Ratna Awd, Veera Yogini Awd, Karnataka Kalpavalli Awd, 1995; Samaja Seva Bhushan Awd, 1996; Margadarshi Awd, Best Mother Teresa Awd, 1997; Pragathi Ratna Awd, 1998; Rani Kittur Chennamma Awd, 1999. Memberships: Fndr Pres, Sumangali Seva Ashrama, 1975; Pres, Taluk Level Kaveri Mahila Mandal Vokkoota, Bangalore N Taluk, 1987; Exec Dir, Samuha Socl Instn, Jalahalli, 1987; Pres, Bangalore Cty Dist Mahila Maha Mandala, 1992; Sec, Cncl for Coord Voluntary Agcies, 1993; Pres, Bangalore Cty Dist Multipurpose Coop Soc, 1993; Pres, Samuha, 1996; Exec Mbr, Dist Inst for Educl Trng, 1997. Address: Sumangali Seva Ashrama, Cholanayakahalli, Nr Hebbal, R T Nagar Post, Banglaore, 560 032.

SUSHIL KUMAR Kesavan Chandrika, b. 9 Apr 1960, Tiruvalla, India. Director. Education: Postgrad, Econs, Sch of Socl Scis, India, 1983; Appointments: Offr, State Bank of Travancore, India, 1984-90; Mngr, Patels Wall St, Hong Kong, 1991-96; Dir, City for exch, 1996-. Honours: Gold Medal, Ranking 1st, Masters deg in Econ, 1983. Hobbies: Reading; Music; Tennis; Surfing The Net. Address: No 88-B G/F, Chungking Mansions, 36-44 Nathan Road, Kowloon, Hong Kong.

SUSRAMA I Putu, b. 8 Feb 1953, Waikabubak, Sumba. Managing Director. m. Ariani, 5 June 1984, 2 s, 2 d. Education: MBA. Honour: Presidency Awd, 1996. Memberships: ASITA; ASEPHI; API; GAFESKI; AMA; Kadin Bali; ASPINDO. Hobbies: Tennis; Boxing.

SUTCLIFFE John Foster, b. 2 Nov 1946, Halifax, UK. Medical Physicist. Education: BSc, Newcastle Univ, 1965-68; Dip Educ, Leeds Univ, 1968-69; MSc, Salford Univ, 1969-70; PhD, Dundee Univ, 1970-74. Appointments: Physicist, 1975-80; Snr Physicist, 1980-83; Rsch Fell, 1983-86; Rsch Physicist, 1986-88; Clinl Scientist, Leeds Gen Infirm NHS Tr, 1988-94; Radiotherapy Physicist, Palmerston N Hosp, 1996-. Publications: 26 Publs. Memberships; Inst of Physicists and Engrs in Med. Hobbies: Classical Music; Electrons; World Affairs; Cycling; Walking. Address: 114 Kelvin Grove Road, Palmerston North, New Zealand.

SUTHERLAND Joan (Dame), b. 7 Nov 1926, Sydney, NSW, Aust. Singer (Soprano). m. Richard Bonynge, 1954. Education: Roy Coll of Music, London, Eng, 1951. Appointments: Richard Bonynge became her accompanist & musical advsr; Mbr of Covent Garden Opera Co, w first role as First Lady in The Magic Flute, 1952; In early yrs sang Amelia in A Masked Ball, Aida, Eva in the Mastersingers, Gilda in Rigoletto, Desdemona in Othello, Agathe in Der Freischütz, Olympia, Giuletta, Antonia and Stella in Tales of Hoffman; Sang Jennifer in

the premiere of Tippett's The Midsummer Marriage, 1955; Became intl star w Covent Garden perf of Lucia di Lammermoor, 1959; Sang at Covent Garden in operas inclng: I Puritani, Dialogues of the Carmelites, Lucia di Lammermoor, Norma; Sang in world's major opera houses inclng Paris, Vienna, La Scala, Hamburg, Buenos Aires, Metrop NY, Chgo Lyric, San Fran, Austl Opera in Sydney, Glyndebourne, & in Edinburgh, Leeds & Florence Fests; Specialised in bel canto operas, particularly of Rossini, Donizetti and Bellini, and operas of Handel, as well as in 19th century French repertoire; W husband was resp for bringing back into stand repertoire previously more obscure works such as Esclarmonde, Le Roi de Lahore, Semiramide, Les Huguenots, of French & Italian composers; Retd in 1990; Last operatic role as Marguerite de Valois in Les Huguenots for Austl Opera, 1990; Sang as guest in Die Fledermaus at Covent Garden. Creative works: Recordings: Lucia di Lammermoor, Alcina, La Sonnambula, Faust, Semiramide, I Puritani, Les Huguenots, Turandot, La Traviata, Les Contes d'Hoffman, Don Giovanni, Don Pasquale, Adriana Lecouvreur, Le Roi de Lahore, Rodelinda, Athalia, Norma, Anna Bolena, La Fille du Régiment and num recital discs. Publication: A Prima Donna's Progress (autobiog), 1997. Honours: AC, 1975; Dame Cmndr of Brit Empire, 1979 & Order of Merit from HM The Queen; Cmndr, Ordre Natl du Mérit, France. Address: c/o Ingpen and Williams, 14 Kensington Court, London W8, England.

SUTHERLAND Margaret, b. 16 Sept 1941, Auckland, NZ. Author; Nurse; Music Teacher. m. 2 s, 2 d. Education: Regd Comprehensive Nurse, 1979; ATCL (Piano Perf), 1995. Appointments: Lit Career extends from 1974-; Publshd in Brit, USA, NZ. Publications: 5 novels; 2 short story collections; Childrens book. Honours: Lit fellshps in Aust, 1991, 1994; NZ Schlshp in Letters, Katherine Mansfield Awd, NZ. Memberships: Austl Soc of Auths; Music Tchrs Assn of NSW. Hobbies: Literature; Piano and guitar stdies; Gardening; Health and healing. Address: 10 Council Street, Speers Point, NSW 2284, Australia.

SUTHERLAND Robert Lyndsay, b. 18 July 1947. Director. m. 3 July 1982, 2 s, 2 d. Education: BAgrSci, 1965-68, MAgrSci, 1969-70, Lincoln Coll, Univ of Canterbury, NZ; PhD, Austl Natl Univ, 1971-74. Appointments: Prof, Sch of Med, Univ of NSW, 1991-; Snr Prin Rsch Fell, Natl Hlth and Med Rsch Cncl, Garvan Inst of Med Rsch, 1991-; Dir, Cancer Rsch Prog, Garvan Inst of Med Rsch, 1996-. Publications: 175 sci publns in boimed rsch jrnls. Honours: John Bell Mem Schlsp, 1965-68; NZ Wool Bd Schlsp, 1969-70; Austl Natl Univ Rsch Schlsp, 1971-74; C'wlth Sci and Indl Rsch Org Postdoct Fellshp, 1974-75; Searle Travelling Fellshp in Endocrinol, 1974-75; World Hlth Org Rsch Trng Fellshp, 1975-76; Snr Rsch Fell, Natl Hlth and Med Rsch Cncl, 1985, Prin Rsch Fell, 1988, Snr Prin Rsch Fell, 1991; DSc honoris causa, Lincoln Univ, Canterbury, 1994. Memberships include: Natl Hlth and Med Rsch Cncl Quinquennial Review Cttee of the Walter and Eliza Hall Inst, Melbourne; Natl Hlth and Med Rsch Cncl Rep on the Austl Cancer Network; Dept of Hlth and Cmnty Servs Cttee to Evaluate Natl Hlth and Med Rsch Cncl. Hobbies: Cricket; Rugby; Reading; Gardening. Address: 20 Northcote Road, Lindfield, NSW 2070, Australia.

SUTHERLAND Wallace Charles, b. 13 June 1928, Albury, NSW, Aust. Regular Army Personnel (retired); RSLA Secretary (retired). m. June Valerie Howard, 1 July 1950, 5 s. Education: Merit Ctf, NSW; Army, 1st Class Cert of Educ. Appointments: Served Austl Army, 1946-49; Hosp Attendant, 1950-51; Served Austl Regular Army, 1951-78; State Sec (Tas); Returned Servs League, 1980-87; Retd 1987 (totally and permanently incapacitated war pensioner); Mbr, Bd of Dirs, RSL, Windermere Hostel, 1994-; Dpty State Pres, RandSLA Tas, 1994-97; State Pres, R&SLA, 1997-. Honours: MBE (Mil Div), 1978; Appointed JP, 1981; OAM, 1998. Memberships: Pres, Glenorchy RSLA; State Exec, RSLA; Treas, OBE Assn; RSL Pensions Offr/Advocate; Regl Cttee, Vietnam Veterans War Trust Fund; Tstee, Austl Forces Overseas Fund; Elected State Pres, R&SLA Tas,

1997-; Elected State Pres, Korean Veterans Assn, Tas, 1997-98. Address: 1/4 Whitbread Court, Glenorchy, Tas 7010, Australia.

SUTHERLAND SMITH Beverley Margaret, b. 1 July 1935, Melbourne, Australia. Food Writer. div, 2 s, 2 d. Publications: A Taste For All Seasons, 1975; A Taste of Class, 1980; A Taste in Time, 1981; Gormet Gifts, 1985; Chocolates & Petit Fours, 1987; Delicious Desserts, 1989; Oriental Cookbook, 1990; Simple Cuisine, 1992; Vegetables, 1994; Decadent Desserts. Memberships: Intl Wine & Food Soc; Zonta. Hobbies: Painting; Ceramics; Gardening; Charity Work. Address: 29 Regent Street, Mount Waverley, Victoria 3149, Australia.

SUTRESNA Nana S, b. 21 Oct 1933 Ciamis. Diplomatist. m. 1973, 2 s, 1 d. Education: Univ of Wales Aberystwyth; Acady for the For Serv. Appointments: For news ed for the Indonesian News Agcy ANTARA, 1955-57; Joined Dept of For Affairs, 1957; Hd of Pub Rels and Spokesman, 1972-76; Dir for Eurn Affairs, 1979-81; Dir-Gen for Polit Affairs, 1984-88; Served at Indonesian Emb in WA DC and in Mexico Cty as Min Cnslr then Min in Vienna, 1976-79; Hd of Indonesian Deleg to Disarmament Conf Geneva, 1981-83; Dep Perm Rep to the UN Geneva, 1981-84; Perm Rep to the UN - also accred to Bahamas Jamaica and Nicaragua - 1988-92; Now Amb at large Hd Exec to Pres of Indonesia in his capacity as Chmn Non-Aligned Movt. Hobbies: Golf. Address: c/o Ministry of Foreign Affairs, Jalan Taman Pejambon 6, Jakarta, Pusat, Indonesia.

SUTTON Richard John, b. 23 Sept 1938, London, Eng. Lawyer. m. 2 s, 1 d. Education: BA, LLM, Auckland; LLM, Harv. Appointments: Lectr, Snr Lectr, Assoc Prof, Auckland Univ, 1963-79; Prof of Law, 1980-, Dean, 1981-85, 1998-, Law Commnr, 1992-97, Univ of Otago. Memberships: Treas, Otago Dist Law Soc, 1981-86; Pres, Law Econ Assn of NZ, 1995-96. Hobbies: Chess; Golf; Music. Address: 351 Highgate, Roslyn, Dunedin, New Zealand.

SUZUKI Isao, b. 6 Jan 1945, Akiruno, Tokyo. Scientist. m. Chikako, 21 May 1972, 3 d. Education: DSc, Univ of Tokyo. Appointments: Rschr, 1970, Snr Rschr, 1977, Section Chf, 1990, Electrotech Lab. Publications: Synchrotron Radiation Technique (book), 1990; Sci pprs in profl jrnls. Honours: Awd, Electrotech Lab, 1989; Awd, Outstndng Invention, Min of STA, 1998. Memberships: Chem Soc, Japan; Phys Soc, Japan; Japan Soc of Appl Phys. Hobbies: Table Tennis; Travel. Address: Umezono, Tsukuba, Ibaraki 305-8568, Japan.

SUZUKI Jiro, b. 11 Feb 1936. Medical Doctor; Professor. m. Hiroko, 17 Nov 1964. Education: MD; PhD; Postgrad Course, Toyko Univ. Appointments: Tohu Univ Sch of Med, 1987. Publication: Art and Science of Epilepsy. Honour: Awd of JSPN, 1967. Membership: Pres, Japanese Soc of Psych and Neurol. Hobbies: Tennis; Golf. Address: 2-12-1, Narita-nishi, Suginamiku, Tokyo 166-0016, Japan.

SUZUKI Osamu, b. 30 Jan 1930, Gero, Gifu, Japan. Business Executive. m. Shoko Suzuki, 1958, 2 s, 1 d. Education: Chuo Univ. Appointments: Joined Suzuki Motor Co Ltd, 1958; Dir, 1963-66, Jnr Mngng Dir, 1967-72, Snr Mngng Dir, 1973-77, Pres, 1978-. Honours: Awd Sitara-i-Pakistan, 1985; Medal of Hon w Blue Ribbon, 1987; Mid Cross of Order of Repub of Hungary, 1993. Hobby: Golf. Address: Suzuki Motor Corporation, 300 Takatsuka, Hamamatsu, Shizuoka-ken, Japan.

SUZUKI Seijun, b. 24 May 1923, Tokyo, Japan. Movie Director. m. Shizuka Suzuki, 1951, (dec). Education: Hirosaki Hight Sch (in old system). Publications: Tokyo Drifters, 1966; Branded to Kill, 1967; Zigeunerweisen, 1980. Honours: Prize of Critical and of arts at Berlin Film Fest for Zigeinerweizen zu 1980; Other prizes from Japanese Film Fest. Hobby: Go (Japanese chess). Address: 1-5-9-504 Komatsugawa, Edogawa-ku, Tokyo, Japan 132-0034.

SVEC Richard S, b. 16 Oct 1942, Los Angeles, CA, USA. Insurance Broker. m. Barbara, 24 Sept 1966, 1 s. Education: BA, St Mary's Coll of CA. Appointments: Pres, Bd of Dirs, Second Harvest Food Bank of Santa Clara, & San Mateo Counties, 1998-; Chmn, Build Amn Awds Cttee, Assoc Gen Contractors of Am, 998-. Publications: Num articles in ins and constrn trade jrnls. Memberships: Constrn Finl Mngmt Assn; Bd Dirs, Silicon Valley Chapt, 1995-; Assoc Gen Contractors of CA. Hobbies: Golf; Tennis; Running. Address: 7007 Quail Cliff Way, San Jose, CA 95120, USA.

SWAMI Medhasananda, b. 30 Mar 1946, Baduria, West Bengal, India. Monk. Appointments: Prin, Ramakrishna Mission, Vidyamandira, India, 1980-93; Pres, Nippon Vedanta Kyokai, 1993. Publications: Ascharyo Vakta, 1993. Memberships: Cttee, Ramakrishna Mission, 1986-90. Hobbies: Reading; Autobiography; Music. Address: c/o Nippon Vedanta Kyokai, 4-18-1 Hisagi, Zushi 249, Kanagawa, Japan.

SWAMINATHAN Monkompu Sambasivan, b. 7 Aug 1925, Kumbakonam, India. Agricultural Scientist. m. Mina, 11 Apr 1955, 3 d. Education: BSc, Travancore Univ, 1944; BSc, Agricl, Coimbatore Agricl Coll, Madras Univ, 1947; Assocshp, Indian Agricl Rsch Inst, New Delhi, 1949; UNESCO Fell, Genetics, Agricl Univ, Wageningen, Netherlands, 1949-50; PhD, Sch of Agricl, Univ Cambridge, Eng, 1952; Rsch Assoc, Genetics, Univ WI, USA, 1952-53; Num non degs. Appointments: Tchr, Rschr, Rsch Admnstr, Ctrl Rice Rsch Inst, Cuttack and Indian Agricl Rsch Inst, New Delhi, 1954-72; Dir-Gen, Indian Cncl of Agricl Rsch, Sec, Govt of India, Dept of Agricl Rsch and Educ, 1972-80; Sec, Govt of India, Min of Agricl and Irrigation, 1979-80; Acting Dpty Chmn, 1980, Mbr, Agricl, Rural Devel, Sci and Educn, 1980-82, Planning Cmmn, Govt of India; Dir-Gen, Intl Rice Rsch Inst, Los Banos, Philippines, 1982-88; Hon Dir, Cntr for Rsch on Sustainable Agricl and Rural Devel, Madras, 1989-. Publications: Num articles in profl jrnls. Honours include: World Food Prize, Ramm Mansaysay Awd; Dr B.P. Pal Medal, Natl Acady of Agricl Scis, India, 1997; V Gangadharan Awd, 1997; B.P. Pal Meml Awd, Indian Sci Congress Assn, 1998. Menberships include: Intl Bee Rsch Assn, Pres, 1978-90; Sci and Tech Advsry Cttee, Tropical Diseases Rsch, World Hlth Org, 1983-85; Chmn, Gov Bd, CAB Intl, 1991-94; Tstee, Ford Fndn, 1989-97. Address: 11 Rathna Nagar, Teynampet, Madras 600 018, India.

SWAMY Narayana, b. 20 May 1963, Bangalore. Assistant Superintendent. m. Darvathamma, 24 Feb 1982, 2 s, 1 d. Education: BA, Govt Coll, Kolar Town, India. Appointments: Non Tchng Staff, Karnataka State Pub Educ Dept; Org Sec; Gen Sec, Karnataka State Culture Cttee; Org Sec, Karnataka State Yth Forum; Chf Co-ord; Spec Police Offr. Hobbies: Singing; Drama Artist; Dancer. Address: Girisha Nilaya V D Chandru Layout, Devasandra, K R Puram, Bangalore 365, India.

SWAN Norman, b. 26 Mar 1953, Glasgow, Scotland. Broadcaster; Physician. m. Lee Sutton, 16 Aug 1981, 1 s, 2 d. Education: MBChB; MRCP, UK; DCH; RCP; SEng. Appointments: Ho Offr, Aberdeen Roy Infirm, W Mody Hosp; SHO, Hillingdon Hosp, Middx; Registrar, Roy Alexandra Hosp for Children. Prodr, Presenter, ABC Radio Natl, 1982-90; Gen Mngr, Radio Natl, 1996-. Creative Works: Life Matters; Invisible Enemies. Honours: Austl Radio Prodr of the Yr, 1984; Gold Walkley Awd for Jrnlsm, 1988; Walkley Awd, 1997; Daily Awd Sci Jrnlsm, 1989; Peter Grieve Awd Medl Jrnlsm, 1996. Hobbies: Reading; Sailing; Bushwalking; Th; Film. Address: ABC Radio, GPO Box 9994, Sydney 2001, Australia.

SWAN Ralph Alexander, b. 22 Aug 1936, Brisbane, Australia. Veterinary Surgeon. m. Diana, 3 s. 1 d. Education: BVSc, PhD, Qld; MPVM, Calif; MACVSc; MRCVS. Appointments: Wool Rsch Fell, Univ Qld, 1960-64; Dir, Pastoral Vet Cntr, Goondiwindi, Univ Qld, 1964-76; Fndng Prof Clin Stdies, Murdoch Univ, 1976-. Publications: Num sci pubs in clinl vet med on wide var domestic animal and wild life topics. Honours: Kesteven Medal, Aust Vet Assoc, Aust Col Vet Scientists, 1994.

Memberships: Austl Vet Assn; Sheep Vet Assn; Cattle Vet Assn; Vet Conservation Biol Assn; Aust/Asian Primatol Assn. Hobbies: Emu farming; Marron farming; Fishing; House renovations; Hobby farming. Address: Division of Veterinary & Biomedical Sciences, Murdoch University, South St, Murdoch 6150, Western Australia.

SWAN Robert Arthur, b. 2 Oct 1917. Retired Civil Servant. m. 14 Oct 1949, Marie Kathleen McClelland, dec, 1 d. Education: BA, Univ of Melbourne, 1950. Publications: Argonauts Returned and Other Poems, 1946; Australia In The Antartic: Interest, Activity and Endeavour, 1961; To Botany Bay: If Policy Warrants The Measure, 1973; 13 Collections of Poems, 1982-96; Of Myths and Mariners: A Study of Doubtful Island... In High Southern Latitudes As Reported by Sealers, Whalers, et al. Honours: FRGS, London, 1978. Memberships: Utd Servs Inst, Sydney; Commando Assn, Aust; Z Spec Unit Assn, Aust. Listed in: International Authors and Writers Who's Who; Who's Who of Australian Writers. Hobbies: Book Collecting; Historial Research. Address: 64 Beach Drive, Woonona, NSW 2517, Australia.

SWAN Rothesay Cathcart, b. 1 June 1926, Orange, NSW, Aust. Retired Naval Officer. m. Margaret Bretton, 6 Apr 1953, 1 s, 2 d. Education: Corowa HS; Roy Austl Naval Coll. Appointments: Served to Rear Admiral, Roy Austl Navy: Midshipman, HMAS Shropshire, 1943-45; Minesweeping & Palestine Ops, 1946; Qual'd Commns, UK, 1951; Fleet Commns Offr, 1959; Exec Offr & Second-in-Cmnd, HMAS Voyager, 1960-61; Planner, SEATO HQ, Bangkok, Thailand, 1961-63; Cmdr, HMAS Derwent, 1964-65; Serv Projs Offr, Dept of Def, 1965-66; Dir of Manning & Trng, Roy Austl Navy, 1967-69; Cmdr, HMAS Hobart, 1969-70 Dir, Naval Commns, 1971; Dir, Jnt Servs Commns, 1971-74; Chf of Staff, Fleet HQ, 1976; Cmdr, HMAS Melbourne, 1977-78; dir Gen, Natural Disaster Org, 1978-81; Controller of Estabs in Def Ctrl, 1981-83; Dir of Tallships, Austl Bicentennial Authy, 1984-88; Admor Opera Fndn of Aust, 1988-96. Honours: CBE, 1971; AO, 1982. Memberships: Pres, NSW Br, Order of Aust Assn, 1988-92; Pres, NSW Aust-Brit Soc, 1993-95; Natl VP, Aust-Brit Soc, 1995-; Pres, Austl Sail Trng Assn, 1996-. Address: 1 Montah Avenue, Killara, NSW 2071, Australia.

SWARD Robert Stuart, b. 23 June 1933, Chicago, IL, USA. Professor; Writer. 2 s, 3 d. Education: BA Hons, Univ Illinois, USA, 1956; MA, Univ Iowa, USA, 1958; Postgrad, Univ Bristol, Eng, 1960-61; Middlebury Coll, VT, USA, 1956-60. Appointments include: Radio Broadcaster, Can Broadcasting Corp, Toronto, Ont, Can, 1979-84; Tech Writer, Santa Cruz Op (SCO), Santa Cruz, CA, USA, 1987-89; Writer-in-Residence, extension prog, Univ California, Santa Cruz, 1988-; Writer-in-Residence, Cabrillo Coll, Aptos, CA, 1988-; Visng Poet Creative Writing Prog, Univ California, Santa Cruz, 1992-; Writer in schs, Ont Arts Cncl, Toronto, 1979-84; Cultural Cncl, Santa Cruz, 1984-. Publications include: Uncle Dog and Other Poems, auth, 1962; Autobiography, CAAS, 1991; Poems: New and Selected, 1983; Four Incarnations: New and Selected Poems, 1957-91; A Much-Married Man, novel, 1996; Uncivilizing, 1997; Blue Penny Quar, 1996. Honours include: Fulbright Grantee, 1961; Guggenheim Fell, 1964-65; D H Lawrence Fell, Univ N Mexico, 1966-67; Yaddo MacDowell Colony Grantee, 1959-82; Djerassi Fndn Grantee, 1990-; Villa Montalvo Lit Arts Awd, 1989-90. Memberships: League of Can Poets; Writers Union of Can, Newsletter Ed, 1983-84; Natl Writers Union. Hobbies: Yoga; Macintosh Computers; Photography; Swimming; Book Design. Address: 435 Meder Street, Santa Cruz, CA 95060-2307, USA.

SWAROOP Neeraj, b. 15 July 1958, Lucknow, India. Business Executive. m. Reena, 8 Dec 1985, 2 s. Education: BTech, Mech; MBA; Grad, Sch of Retail Bank Mngmt. Appointment: Dir, Sales & Mktng, Retail Banking, Bank of Am, India. Memberships: Indian Mngmt Assn; Indian Soc of Advtrs. Hobbies: Sports; Travel; Reading; Music. Address: Bank of America, DCM Building, 6th Floor, Barakhamba Road, New Delhi 110001, India.

SWARTZ Reginald William Colin (Hon Sir), b. 14 Apr 1911, Brisbane, Aust. Retired Federal Parliamentarian; Company Director. m. (1) Hilda Robinson, 24 Apr 1936, dec 18 Dec 1995, 2 s, 1 d, (2) Muriel Elizabeth McKinstry, 18 July 1998. Education: 3 courses, Shell Co, 1934, 1935, 1947; Biet Ctf, Petroleum Technol, 1979; Austl Army Exams to Lt Col, 1934-60. Appointments: Coml and Tech Appts: Shell Co, 1927-49; Parly Sec, 9 yrs, Min for 11 yrs; Austl Fed Parl, 1949-72; Ldr, House of Reps, 2 yrs; Co Dir, 1972-84, retd, 1984; Mil Serv: CMF, 1928-; Lt, 1934; Cap AIF, 1940-46; Prisoner of War, Singapore, Malaya, Thailand; CMF, 1947-61; AQMG, Col. Publications include: Parliamentary Institutions in Australia; Australias Natural Resources Green Paper; Contbr of num pprs. Honours: ED, 1948; MBE (Mil), 1948; KBE (Civil), 1972. Memberships: Fell, Brit Inst of Mngmt; Fell, Austl Inst of Mngmt; Fell, Inst of Dirs in Aust. Hobbies: Bowls; Numerous Boards, Committees of Charitable, Community and Ex-Service Organizations. Address: 56 Immanuel Gardens, 10 Magnetic Drive, Buderim, Qld 4556, Australia.

SWAYZE Patrick, b. 18 Aug 1954. Actor; Dancer. m. Lisa Niemi, 1976. Education: Harkness and Joffrey Ballet Schs. Appointments: Began as dancer in Disney on Parade on tour as Prince Charming; Appeared on Broadway as dancer in Goodtime Charley Grease; Tv appearances in North and South: Books I and II; The New Season; Pigs vs Freaks; The Combeack Kid; The Return of the Rebels; The Renegades. Films incl: Skatetown USA, 1979; The Outsiders; Uncommon Valor; Red Dawn; Grandview USA - also choreographer; Dirty Dancing - co-wrote song and sings She's Like the Wind; Steel Dawn; Tiger Warsaw; Road House; Next of Kin; Ghost; Point Break; City of Joy; Father Hood; Tall Tales; To Wong Foo - Thanks for Everything - Julie Newmar; Three Wishes. Address: c/o William Morris Agency, 151 El Camino, Beverly Hills, CA 90212, USA.

SWE Than, b. 30 Mar 1938. Medical Doctor. m. Daw, 3 s, 2 d. Education: MB; BS; DBact; DS; FRCP. Appointments: Cnslt Virol; Dir of Rsch; Dpty Dir Gen; Dir Gen; Mbr, ACHR. Honours: Pub Serv Medal; Med for Ex Performance in Admin Field, 1998. Memberships: Myanmar Med Assn, 1962; Roy Coll of Physns, Edinburgh, 1995. Hobbies: Sports; Reading. Address: 5 Ziwaka Road, Dagon PO, 11191 Yangon, Myanmar.

SWINBOURNE Ellice Simmons, b. 18 July 1925, Sydney, Aust. Scientist; Educationist. m. Valmai Drummond, 27 Aug 1949, 2 s, 1 d. Education: Dip in Chem w Hons (ASTC) Sydney Tech Coll, 1948; BSc Hons, 1952, PhD 1960, Univ of NSW. Appointments: Lectr in Chem, 1951-60, Snr Lectr, 1960-65, Assoc Prof, 1966-68, Univ of NSW; Dean of Sci, 1969-74, VP, 1977-80, NSW Inst of Technol (now Univ of Technol, Sydney); Chmn, Austl Fedn Comm on Advd Educ, 1975-77; Prin, Nepean Coll of Advd Educ (now Univ of West Sydney-Nepean), 1980-85 (retired); Dpty Chmn, 1988, Chmn, 1989-91, NSW Bd of Adult Educ. Publications: Textbook Analysis of Kinetic Data, auth, 1971; Book: Government Roles in Adult Education: International Perspectives, ed in conjunction w John Wellings, 1989; Sev sci and educl pprs, book chapts. Honours: Sydney Tech Coll Medal for Highest Hons in Chem Dip Course, 1948; First ICIANZ Overseas Travelling Fellshp, 1958 (2 yrs rsch in chem at Univ Coll, London, 1958-60); AM, 1993; DUniv, Univ of Technol, Sydney, 1994. Memberships: Fell, Roy Austl Chem Inst; Roy Soc of NSW. Hobbies: Swimming; Hiking. Address: 30 Ellalong Road, Cremorne, NSW 2090, Australia.

SWINDON Val Gregory, b. 12 Mar 1933, Rushworth, Australia. Director. m. Doris, 12 Nov 1960, 3 d. Education: BSc, 1953, Hons Geol, 1955, Univ of Qld. Appointments: Gen Mngr, Oil & Gas Div, CSR Ltd, 1982-85; Exec Gen Mngr, Oil & Gas, CSR Ltd, 1985-87; Pres, Jindavik Petroleum Inc, 1987-; Chmn, Petrol NL, 1993-. Honours: Pres, Qld Chmbr of Mines, 1985-87; Vice Chmn, Austl Petroleum Prodn & Exploration Assn, 1985-87. Memberships: VP, Qld div, Austl Inst of Co Dirs, 1996-. Hobbies: Fishing; Gardening; Reading. Address:

Dirleton, 59 Hunter Street, Indooroopilly, Qld 4068, Australia.

SWOKIN Kala, b. 22 Nov 1948, Drimgas Vill, Western Prov, Papua New Guinea. Minister for Transport and Civil Aviation. m. 12 children. Education: Vanadidir; ASOPA; Local Gov course, Admin Coll. Appointments: Intl Trng Inst, Mosman, 1974; Exec Offr, Tariu Local Gov Cncl, 1970-1975; Exec Offr, Fly River Area Authy, 1975-76; Co-ord, East Awin Forestry Proj; Min for Transport and Civ Aviation.

SY Yinchow (Chua Kee), b. 16 Mar 1919, China. Journalist; Writer. m. Jade Co, 3 s, 3 d. Appointments: Ed in Chief, Manila New Day, 1945; The Chiang Kai Shek Daily News, 1946-48; Gt China Daily News, 1949-72; Pres, Philippine Chinese Writers Assn, 1950-72; Ed in Chief, United Daily News, 1972-. Publications: The World's Best Poems: Selected Modem Poems; The World's Great Poems; Shakespeare's Sonnets; The First Three Volumes Complete The Poet's translation of Anthology of World Poetry. Contributions to: All major Chinese newspapers and magazines. Honours: Chiang Kai Shek Prize; Best Writer Prize; Pres, Marcos Prize. Memberships: Fil Chinese Lit Assn; Asia Chinese Writers Assn. Address: PO Box 1747, Manila, Philippines.

SYDDALL Thomas Harold, b. 23 Dec 1938, Auckland, NZ. Patent Atty. m. Ann, 24 Dec 1983. BSc, 1960; LLB, 1966; Regd Patent Atty, 1963; Bar and Sol, High Crt of NZ, 1966. Appointments: Ptnr, A J Park & Son, Intellectual Ppty Lawyers, 1966-; Notary Pub, 1995. Publications: Contbns to profl jrnls. Honour: IOM, 1997. Memberships: Fell, NZ Inst Pat Attys, Pres, 1980-82, Exam Board, 1991-; Wellingtn Dist Law Soc; NZ Grp, Asian Pat Attys Assn, Exec 1985-; NZ Inst Chem; NZ Assn Scientists, Cncl Mbr, 1992-; NZ Grp, Intl Assn Protection of Indl ppty; NZ Sect, Intl Fedn Indl Ppty Attys; Brit Oversea Mbr, Chartered Inst Pat Agts. Hobbies: Performing arts, supporter Royal NZ Ballet; Walking. Address: A J Park & Son, Huddart Parker Building, Post Office Square, Wellington, New Zealand.

SYDOR Marcia Alice, b. 11 June 1933, Antioch, CA, USA. Teacher. m. Richard, 24 Aug 1984. Education: BA, Univ of California, Berkeley, USA; MA, California State Univ, Sacramento, CA, USA; Cert, Shandong Univ, China. Appointments: Sec, Tchrs Coll, Columbia Univ, NYC, USA, 1963-64; Tchr, Spec Educ Spec, Resource Spec Prog, Sacramento City Unified Schs, 1967-. Honours include: DTM 5t, ATM 5t, ATM Bronze 5t, ATM Silver 5t; Alumnae Cert of Merit, 1997; Den Mother Tchng Awd, 1967; Den Ldr Coach's Tchng Awd, 1969. Memberships include: Youth Band Parent's Assn; Colonial Daughters of Indian Wars. Address: 1092 Salmon Drive, Roseville, CA 95661, USA.

SYED Mubin Akhtar, b. 2 Jan 1933, Lahore, Pakistan. Psychiatrist. m. Kauser, 10 March 1986, 2 s. Education: MBBS, 1956, King Edward Med Coll; Am Bd Psych, USA. Appointments: MD, Karachi Psych Hosp. Publications: Book, Psychosexual disorders in Pakistan; Book, URDU, The special problems of youngsters. Memberships: Islamic Med Assn; Fedn of Islamic Med Assns, Chmn, Pres; Jamaat-e-Islami Pakistan. Address: Karachi Psychiatric Hospital, Nazimabad No 3, Karachi, Pakistan.

SYMONS Jack Gilroy, b. 6 Sept 1915, Aust. Mining Engineer. m. Helen Alison Dobbyn, 3 Apr 1940, 1 s, 1 d. Education: BEng, Adelaide, SA, 1936; Fell, SA Sch of Mines, 1936. Appointments: Stoping Engr, 1945-46, Underground Mngr, 1947-54, N Broken Hill Ltd; Dir of Mines, Govt of Tas, 1954-80, Dir of Mines, Mt Lyell Mining and Railway Co Ltd, 1980-81; Dir, Chmn, Indl and Mining Investigations Pty Ltd, 1981; Chmn, Savage Resources Ltd, 1984-89; Dir, Savage Resources Ltd, 1984-93; Dir, KTM Gold Ltd, 1986-93; Dir, Tas Chmbr of Mines, 1986-93. Publications: Var for Tas Dept and Austl Inst of Mining and Metall. Honours: Hon Fell, Inst of Quarrying, Eng; Hon Fell, Australasian Inst of Mining and Metall, 1993; Hon Life Mbr, Tas Chmbr of Mines, 1993. Membership: Austl Inst of Mining and Metall, Pres, 1977, Cnclr, Rep for Tas, 1973-88. Hobbies: Yachting; Tennis;

Skeet shooting. Address: 2/14 Lincoln Street, Lindisfarne, Tas 7015, Australia.

SZEPS Henri, b. 2 Oct 1943. Actor. m. Mary Ann Severne, 28 June 1969, 2 s. Education: BSc, Maths and Phys, Univ Sydney, 1964; BE, Elec Engrng, Hon 2, 1966. Appointments: Studied acting, w Hayes Gordon, Sydney, 1962-66; Th incl: The Boys In The Band, Aust, 1968-70; London: I Claudius, Queens Th, 1972; Pericles, Royal Hunt Of The Sun, Twelfth Night, Prospect Th Co, 1973-74; Returned to Aust, 1974; The Good Doctor, Ensemble Th, Sydney, 1975; Saul, in Travelling North, Nimrod Theatre, 1979; Sexual Perversity In Chicago, Nimrod Th, 1980; Oklahoma, Sydney, Melbourne, Brisbane, 1982; Glengarry Glen Ross, Sydney Opera House, 1986; (Co-transl), The Double Bass, Ensemble Th, natl tour, 1990-91; Sky, Ensemble Th, natl tour, 1992-93; World premières of David Williamson's Dead White Males, 1994, and Heretic, 1995, Sydney Th Co; (Auth), I'm Not A Dentist (autobiog 1-man show), 1995; Première, Ensemble Th, 1997 and 18 week natl tour, 1998; Willy Clarke in The Sunshine Boys, Ensemble Th, 1998; Aust TV incl: Homicide, Division 4, Woodbinda, Riptide, Skippy, Spyforce, 1967-71; Eng: Misleading Cases; Colditz, The Rivals Of Sherlock Holmes, Dixon Of Dock Green, Spyders Web, Strauss Family, 1971-74; Hannay, 1988; Continuing roles in Aust TV Ser, Ride On Stranger (ABC), 1979; Daily At Dawn (sit-com), 1980; City West, 1984; Robert in Mother And Son, 1983-93; Mick Mendel in Palace Of Dreams (Drama, ABC TV), 1984-85; Harold Holt, in Vietnam, 1986; Mission Impossible, 1990; Man From Snowy River, 1994; Films incl: You Can't See Round Corners, 1967; Tully, 1974; The Plumber, 1978; Run Rebecca Run, 1981; Warming Up, 1983; Travelling North, 1986; Les Patterson Saves The World, 1986; Book: All In Good Timing (a book on acting), 1996. Honours include: Penguin Awd, Best Actor in mini-ser, 1985; Norman Kessel Awd, Outstndng Perf, 1997. Hobbies: Tai-chi; Swimming; Astronomy; Writing; Reading. Address: Cameron's Management, Suite 5, 2 New McLean Street, Edgecliff, NSW 2027, Australia.

T

TABAI Ieremia T, b. 1950 Nonouti. Politician. m. 2 c. Education: King George V Sch Tarawa; St Andrew's Coll Christchurch NZ; Vic Univ Wellington NZ. Appointments: Fmr Ldr of the Opposition; Chf Min of the Gilbert Islands, 1978-79; Also Min of Local Govt; Pres of Kiribati and Min of For Affairs - fmrly Gilbert Islands - 1979-91; Sec-Gen S Pacific Forum, 1991-. Honours: Hon LLD - Vic Univ of Wellington. Memberships: Mbr Gilbert Islands - later Kiribati - House of Ass, 1974-91. Address: South Pacific Forum Secretariat, GPO Box 856, Suva, Fiji.

TABARA BAHIJ, B. 1929, Beirut, Lebanon. Government Official. m. Huda Saad, 3 children. Education: St Joseph Univ, Beirut; D Laws and Polit Econ, Paris Univ. Appointments: Prac Law, 1954-; Prof, Lebanese Univ, St Joseph Univ; Min, Trade and Econ, Govt of Lebanon, Beirut, 1973; Min Jus, 1992-; Prof Law, St Joseph Univ, Lebanese Univ. Address: Ministry of Justice, Rue Sami Solh, Beirut, Lebanon.

TABER Patricia Elizabeth, b. 22 Feb 1926, NSW, Aust. Artist. m. 12 Dec 1946, 2 s, 1 d. Education: E Techl Coll, Sydney. Education: Aircraft Mechanic, Womens Austl Air Force, 1944-46. Creative works: Exhibns incl Merrylands, Royal Art Soc, many others. Honours: Many awds inclng 1st Austl Sect, Merrylands Hall, 1978; Annual Awd, Macquarie Towns Hawkesbury Shire Awd, 1982; 1st Animal Study Awd, Cty of Parrmatta Art Soc, 1983; 1st Tradl Painting, Gold Coast Show, 1989. Memberships: Roy Art Soc, Sydney; Royal Arts Coast, Qld. Hobbies: Painting; Lapidary. Address: 12 The Grange, Nerang Gardens 4211, Gold Coast Hinterlands, Qld, Australia.

TACHIKI Dennis, b. 10 Mar 1952. Researcher; Consultant. Education: BA, UCLA, 1974; MA, Univ of MI, 1985. Appointments: Univ of MN, 1974; Univ of MI, 1980; Sophia Univ, 1988; Sakura Inst of Rsch, 1988; Asian Productivity Orgn, 1998. Publications: Going Transnation: Japanese Subsidiaries in the Asia-Pacific Region, 1990; Developing Human Resources for Sustainable Economic Growth, 1994; Total Quality Control, 1995. Honours: Amn Sociological Assn Fellshp, 1980; Ford Fndn Grant, 1982. Memberships: Amn Sociological Assn; Indl Rels Rsch Assn; Assn for Asian Stdies. Address: 540-16 Kamoshida-Cho, Aoba-Ku, Yokohama 227-0033, Japan.

TADAYON Mohammad Kazem, b. 22 May 1963, Abadeh, Iran. Metallurgical Specialist. m. Zohreh, 23 Sept 1993, 1 d. Education: MSc, Metallurgical Engrng. Appointments: Chf Engr, Isfahan Steel Plant, 1989-90; Metalurgical Specialist, Mobarakeh Steel Co, 1990-97; Rschr, Auditor of Quality, 1997-. Publications: Sev pprs in profl jrnls. Honour: Disting Rschr, Iranian Steel Works, 1998. Memberships: Am Soc of Metals; Materials Soc; Iranian Metallurgical Engrng Assn; Corrosion Assn; Surface Engrng Assn. Hobbies: Music; Research; Tourism; Movies; Study. Address: Mobarakeh Steel Co, Research & Development Department, Esfahan 84885, Iran.

TAGAEV Abdujapar A, b. 20 Feb 1953, Barpy Village, Kyrgyzstan. Government Official. 3 children. Education: Deg, Electr Engrng, Radioelectrons Inst, Harkov, Ukraine, 1976. Appointments: Chmn, State Property Fund, Gov of Kyrgyzstan, 1992-93; Gov, Talal-Abad Reg, 1993-95; Chmn, Natl Commn Securities Mkt, Gov of Kyrgyzstan, Bishkek, 1995-. Address: Office of the Prime Minister DP, ul Pravitelstva 57, Bishkek 720040, Prospect Chui 114, Kyrgyzstan.

TAHER Mohamed, b. 14 Mar 1955, Mysore, India. Information Scientist. m. Ameena, 26 Apr 1981, 1 s, 2 d. Education: MA, Islamic Studies; MA, Hist; MLibSc; PhD, Lib Sci; DLitt (thesis submitted). Appointments: King Abdulaziz Cty, Riyadh, Saudi Arabia, 1997-; Amn Studies Rsch Cntr, Hyderabad, India, 1983-97. P u b l i c a t i o n :   W e b p a g e www.geocitoes.com/research#triangle/thinktank/8596.

Honours: Fulbright Schlshp, 1990-91; Advsr, Info Rsch Mngmt Assn, 1998-. Address: ASRC, Hyderabad 500007, India.

TAHER Tarmizi, b. 7 Oct 1936, Padang, Indonesia. Government Official. Education: Grad in Med, Airlanagga Univ, Surabaya, Indonesia, 1964; Postgrad Sch. Appointments: Cmnd Staff, 1976; Cmnd Off, Indonesian Navy, Medl Offr, 1964-79; Div Hd, Navy Cntr for Medl Guidance, 1979; Chf, Dept, 1980-84; Lectr, Sch Mil Staff Cmnd, 1984-87; Sec Gen, Min Relig Affairs, Jakarta; Min Relig Affairs, 1992-. Address: Embassy of Indonesia, 202 Massachusetts Avenue NW, Washington, DC 20036, USA.

TAHIR-UL-QADRI Muhammad, b. 19 Feb 1951, Jhang, Sadar, Pakistan. Education: FSc, Govt Deg Coll Faisal Abad, 1968; BA, Punjab Univ Lahore, 1970; MA, 1970-72; LLB, 1974; PhD, Islamic Law, 1986. Appointments: Chan, Minhaj-ul-Quran Intl Islamic Univ, Pakistan; Fdr, Ldr, Minhaj-ul-Quran Intl Movement; Patron in Chf, Minhaj-ul-Quran Model Schs; Patron in Chf, Minhaj-ul-Quaran Dawah Centres; Patron in Chf, Mass Educ Centres; Chmn, Minhaj-ul-Quaran Ulama Cncl; Fdr, Chmn, Pakistan Awami Tehreek; Fdr, Chmn, Minhaj Intl Welfare and Cultural Soc; Pres, Pakistan Awami Ittehad; VP, Mohtamar Alam-e-Islami. Creative Works: More than 270 Publshd Books; About 800 Un-Publshd Books. Honours: Quaide-e-Azam Gold Medal, 1971; Univ Gold Medal, 1972; Pakistan Cultural Gold Medal, 1972; Qarshi Gold Medal, 1984. Memberships: Syndicate Punjab Univ; Senate Punjab Univ; Acad Cncl Punjab Univ; Natl Cttee of Islamic Curricula, Min of Educ; Fed Shariat Crt of Pakistan. Address: Tehreek e Minhaj ul Quran, 365 M Model Town, Lahore, Pakistan.

TAIT Robin Margaret, b. 21 Aug 1958, Brisbane, Qld, Aust. Book Conservator. m. David, 17 Dec 1983, 1 s, 1 d. Education: Cert in Hand Book Binding and Book Restoration; BScApp, Conservation of Cultural Material. Appointments: Conservator, Austl War Mem; Hd, Paper Conservation (AWM); Dir, The Tait Bindery; Snr Conservator, State Lib of Qld; Mngr, Conservation Serv (SLQ). Creative works: Des bindings in pvte and pub collects. Honour: Rotary Fndn Schl, 1981. Memberships: AICCM (Aust); Inst of Ppr Conservation, Des Bookbinders (UK). Hobbies: Drawing; Bushwalking; Printmaking. Address: 60, Currey Avenue, Mooroka, Queensland 4105, Australia.

TAK Shaukat Ara, b. 25 May 1965, Srinigar, Kashmir, India. Researcher; Trainer. Education: DPhil. Appointments: Rsch Asst, CSIR Proj, Univ of Kashmir; Asst Prof, Jnr Sci, Div of Environmental Scis, SKUAST, Srinigar. Publications: 20 rsch publs. Memberships: Bombay Natl Hist Soc; JK Acady of Scis, Srinigar. Hobbies: Research; Book reading; Gardening.

TAKAGI Isao, b. 6 June 1956, Fukui, Japan. Associate Professor. m. Akiko, 18 May 1986, 2 s, 1 d. Education: MA, Econs, Soka Univ. Appointments: Assoc Prof, Dept of Econs, 1992-; Vice Dir, Intl Affairs Offr, Soka Univ. Creative Works: ASEAN Integration Policy Towards the Formation of South East Asian Community. Memberships: Japan Soc of Intl Econs; Japan Assn for Asian Pols and Econs Studies. Hobbies: Travelling around Asian countries; Folk art; Music. Address: Soka University, 1-236 Tangi-cho, Hachioji-shi, Tokyo 192-8577, Japan.

TAKAGI Ryosuke, b. 10 Feb 1947, Kobe, Japan. Professor. m. 2 Aug 1973, 1 s. Education: BS; MSc; DPharmSc. Appointments: Rschr, C Uyemura Co Ltd, 1972-77; Lectr, Shukugawa Gakuin Coll, 1977-83; Assoc Prof, 1983-96; Prof, 1996-. Publications: Membranes and Membrane Processes, 1986; Seitai Koroido, 1990; Contbr, articles to profl jrnls. Memberships: Chem Soc Japan; Phys Soc Japan; Membrane Soc Japan; Pharm Soc Japan. Hobbies: Yachting; Skiing. Address: Shukugawa Gakuin College, 6-58 Koshikiiwa-cho, Nishinomiya 662-8555, Japan.

TAKAHASHI Hachiro, b. 18 Oct 1919, Gunma, Japan. Emeritus Professor. m. Asako, 11 May 1956, 2 d. Education: Tokyo Phys Sch, 1939-41; BSc 1951, DSc 1961, Tohoku Univ. Appointments: Asst Prof, 1958-64, Prof, 1964-85, Dept of Phys, Iwate Univ; Emer Prof of Phys, 1985-, Pres, 1986-90, Iwate Univ; Dean, Educ Fac, Iwate Univ, 1977-81, 1982-83; Visng Assoc Prof, Univ of West Ontario, Can, 1965-66; Prof and Libn, Morioka Coll, 1960-61. Publications: About 100 sci pprs, mainly on cosmic ray physics. Honour: Order of Rising Sun, 2nd Class, Jap Emperor, 1993. Memberships: Amn Geophys Union; Phys Soc of Jap; Soc of Geomagnetism and Earth; Planetary and Space Scis; Intl Mbr of AAAS; NY Acady of Scis; Planetary Sci. Hobbies: Golf; Music; Driving. Address: 13-18 Takamatsu 2-chome, Morioka 020-01, Japan.

TAKAMATSU Shin, b. 5 Aug 1948, Shimane, Japan. Architect Professor. 2 s. Education: PhD, Kyoto Univ. Publications: Origin, 1981; Kirin Plaza Osaka, 1987; Syntax, 1990; Kunibiki Messe, 1993; Shoji Ueda Mus of Photog, 1995; Meteor Plaza, 1996; Myokn-Zan Buddhist Hall, 1998. Honours: Intl Interior Des Awd, 1987; Annual Prize, Archtl Inst of Japan, 1989; Educ Min's Art Encouragement Prize, 1996. Memberships: Hon Mbr, Amn Inst of Archts, 1995. Address: Shin Takamatsu Architect & Assocs, 195 Jyobodain-cho Takeda Fushimi-ku, Kyoto 612-8445, Japan.

TAKASHIMA Susumu, b. 11 Feb 1933, Tokyo, Japan. Professor, Nihon Fukushi University. m. Hisako Yokoi, 2 Apr 1963, 2 s, 1 d. Education: BA, Fac of Lit, Tokyo Univ. Appointments: Lectr, 1959, Assoc Prof, 1970, Prof, 1975-, Dean of Fac of Socl Welfare and Grad Prog of Socl Welfare, 1993-95, Dean of Grad Prog, 1995-97, Nihon Fukushi University, Japan. Publications: (in Japanese) Treatise of the English History of Social Welfare, 1979; Theory and Policy of Social Welfare, 1986; Welfare of the Super-aged Society, 1990; History of Social Welfare, 1995; Articles in profl jrnls (in Engl). Honours: 8th Prize for Important Contbn on Histl Study of Socl Welfare, by Rsch Assn for Histl Study of Socl Welfare, 1989. Memberships: Japanese Soc for Study of Socl Welfare (Mbr of Board), 1971-. Hobby: Reading detective stories. Address: 4-61-1 Nakaji, Tsushima Cty, Aichi 496-0847, Japan.

TAKATSUJI Masamoto, b. 22 Feb 1940, Tokyo, Japan. Professor of Tokai University. m. Reiko, 3 Nov 1967, 2 s, 1 d. Education: BEng, Univ of Tokyo; PhD, Phys, Univ of Tokyo. Appointments: Snr Rschr, Hitachi Ltd, 1976; Lectr, Kyoto Univ, 1976; Lectr, Univ of Tokyo, 1981; Prof, Tokai Unv, 1991. Publications: Plant Factory, 1979; Do Earth and Mankind Sustain?, 1994; Introduction to the Synergy of Various Sciences, 1998. Honour: Prize, SHITA, 1989. Memberships: Japanese Soc of High Technol in Agric, 1989; Inst of Synergy of Arts and Scis, 1996. Hobby: Japanese chess (Shôgi). Address: 4-16-9, Seijo, Setagaya-ku, Tokyo, Japan.

TAKEDA Hiroshi, b. 12 Sept 1934, Okayama Cty, Japan. Mineralogist; Meteoriticist; Educator. m. Chizuko Matsunaga, 4 Jan 1960, 2 children. Education: BS, Okayama (Japan) Univ, 1957; MSc, Univ Tokyo, 1959; PhD, 1962. Appointments: Cert Tchr, Second Sch Rsch and Instrn Assoc, Univ Tokyo, 1962-70; Lectr, 1970-74, Assoc Prof, 1974-84, Prof, 1984-95, Prof Emer, 1995-, Prof, Chiba Inst Tech, Narashino Cty, Japan, 1996-; Rsch Assoc, Johns Hopkins Univ, Baltimore, 1962-65; Guest Investigator, US Geol Survey, WA, 1965; Snr Rsch Assoc, NRC/NASA Manned Spacecraft Cntr, Houston, 1970-72; Vis Prof, Natl Inst of Polar Rsch, Tokyo, 1979-86; Visng Scientist, The Roy Soc, London, 1987; Exchange Prof, Univ Louis Pasteur, Strasbourg, France, 1994; Visng Prof, CA Inst Tech, Pasadena, 1997. Publications: Material Sciences of Planets, 1982; A Lost Protoplanet, 1991; Contbr, 148 articles to profl jrnls. Honours: Spec Recog on 10th anniversary of Apollo 11, NASA, Wash, 1979; NASA Pub Serv Medal, , 1996; Grantee: Mitsubishi Fndn, 1988, The Tokyo Club, 1994. Memberships: Fell, Meteoritical Soc, Cnclr, 1981-85; Mineralogy Soc, Japan; Japan Soc for Planetary Sci, VP, 1992-96. Hobbies: Vineyard visiting; Italian opera;

Photography. Address: 6-11 Takinoi 1-chome, Funabashi Chiba 274-0073, Japan.

TAKEMURA Masayoshi, b. 26 Aug 1934, Yokkaichi Cty, Japan. Member of the House of Representatives. m. Chizuru, 7 Nov 1959, 1 s, 1 d. Education: Fac of Econs, Univ of Tokyo, 1962. Appointments: Mayor, Yokkaichi City, 1971; Gov, Shiga Pref, 1974; Chf Cabinet Sec, 1993; Fin Min, 1994. Publications: Mizu no Ningen-Biwa-Ko Kara no Houkou (Water and People - A Report From Lake Biwa. Hobbies: Swimming; Cycling; Reading. Address: 238, 2-1-2 Magatacho, Chiyodaku, Tokyo, Japan.

TAKEMURA Yousuke, b. 27 Dec 1961, Tokyo, Japan. Physician. Education: MD, Natl Def Med Coll; PhD, Juntendo Univ Sch of Med; Am Bd of Family Practice. Appointments: Dept of Gen Med, Natl Def Med Coll, Japan. Publications: Sev med rsch pprs. Honour: Ex of Rsch, AAFP, 1994. Address: c/o Department of General Medicine, National Defense Medical College, 3-2 Namiki, Tokorozawa, Saitama 359-8513, Japan.

TAKESHITA Noboru, b. 26 Feb 1924. Politician. m. 3 d. Education: Sch of Com Waseda Univ. Appointments: Jnr High Sch Tchr; Elected to Shimane Pref Ass - two terms - 1951; Parly Vice-Min For Intl Trade and Ind, 1963-64; Dep Chf Cabinet Sec, 1964-65; Chf Cabinet Sec, 1971-72, Nov-Dec 1974; Min of Constrn, 1976, 1982-86; Chmn Diet Policy Cttee Natl Org Cttee of Liberal Dem Party - LDP; Chmn Standing Cttee on Budget HoR, 1978; Chmn Bd of Govs IMF and World Bank, 1984; Chmn Grp of Ten, 1985; Sec-Gen LDP, 1986-87; Pres, 1987-89; PM of Japan, 1987-89. Publications: Six books inclng Waga michi o yuku - Seeking after the path - 1979;Magokoro no seiji - Honest Politics - 1983; Subarashi kuni Nihon - Wonderful Japan - 1987. Honours: Hon LLD - Columbia - 1986. Memberships: Mbr HoR, 1958-. Hobbies: Judo - holds 5th dan; Golf; Reading; Fine arts - esp Japanese-style painting; yachting. Address: 955 Oaza-Kakeai, Iishi-gun, Shimane 690-27, Japan.

TAKESHITA Toru, b. 16 Dec 1931, Nishinomiya Cty, Japan. University Professor. m. Yumiko, 20 Oct 1963, 1 s, 1 d. Education: PhD, Computer Sci, Univ of Beverley Hills, USA. Appointments: Mngr, IBM Tokyo Olympic Systems, 1960; IBM World Trade Corp Prod Mngr, 1972; IBM Japan Prod Mngmt Dept Mngr, 1975; IBM Corp Cnslt, Software Tech, 1983; IBM Snr Tech Staff Mbr, 1984; IBM Tokyo Rsch Lab Computer Sci Inst Mngr, 1990; Prof, Chubu Univ, 1991; Dir, Inst for Info Sci, 1997. Publications: 30 books in programming and other software subjs and num pprs and articles. Honours: Yamanouchi Outstndng Achmnt Awd, IPSJ, 1988. Memberships: Info Proc Soc of Japan, Dir, 1971-73, 1992-94; Japan Artificial Intelligence Soc, Dir, 1990-92; IEEE Computer Soc; ACM; Japan Soc for Software Sci and Technol. Hobbies: Photography; Reading; Travelling. Address: 3-11-1-410 Soshigaya, Setagaya-ku, Tokyo 157-0072, Japan.

TAKEUCHI Keiko, b. 27 July 1934, Tokyo, Japan. University Professor of English. Education: MA, Lingustics, Univ of Hawaii; MA, Lang Arts, San Fran State Univ. Appointments: Def Lang Inst (USA), Japanese Lang Instr, 1965-66; Univ of Hawaii (USA), Japanese Lang Instr, 1966-71, 1973-80; Prof of Engl, Kyoto Univ of For Studies (Japan), 1980-. Publications: Acad pprs incl: Diffusion of English worldwide, 1992; Sexism in the English Language, 1993; Language Variation and Linguistic Theory, 1993; The Models of English: Some terminological problems and the referent entity, 1995; In Search of Ideal Language Education (co-auth) in a series of 4, 1994-98. Memberships: Japan Assn for Coll Engl Tchrs (cnclr), 1993-; Linguistic Soc of Japan; Amn Assn for Applied Linguistics; Engl Linguistic Soc of Japan; Intl Assn for World Englishes. Hobby: Classical music. Address: c/o Kyoto University of Foreign Studies, Saiin, Ukyo-ku, Kyoto Japan 615.

TAKEUCHI Nobuo, b. 30 Mar 1941, Tokyo, Japan. Professor. m. Yoshiko, 3 s. Education: BSc, 1963, MSc,

1965, DSc, 1968, Univ of Tokyo. Appointments: Rsch Assoc, ISSP, Univ of Tokyo, 1968-73; Rsch Assoc, Columbia Univ, NYC, 1971-75; Rsch Assoc, NRCT, Can, 1973-75; Sect Hd, Natl Inst Env Studies, Env Agcy, Japan, 1975-91; Prof, Chiba Univ, 1992-; Rsch into laser spectroscopy; atmospheric remote sensing. Publications: Patents: Random Modulation CW Lidar; High Repetition Low Energy Lidar, 1997. Memberships: OSA; JAPS. Hobby: Trip. Address: CERES, Chiba University, 1-33 Yayoi-cho, Inage-ku, Chiba 263-8522, Japan.

TAKUMA Tadasu, b. 30 Sept 1938, Ise-shi, Mie-Pref, Japan. University Professor. m. Choko, 25 Oct 1967, 1 s, 1 d. Education: PhD, Engrng, Univ of Tokyo, Japan. Appointments: Lectr, Univ of Tokyo; Rschr, CRIEPI; Visng Prof, Kyushu Univ; Prof, Kyoto Univ. Publications: Numerical Calculation Methods of Electric Fields, 1981; High Voltage-High Current Engineering, 1991. Honours: Maxwell Premium, IEE, GB, 1975; Fell Grade IEEE, 1991; Commendation by Min of State for Sci and Technol, Japan, 1992; Outsndng Achievement Awd, IEE, Japan, 1992. Memberships: Editl Dir, IEE, Japan, 1989-91; Chmn, Mbrshp Cttee, IEEE Tokyo Chapt, 1995-97. Hobbies: Playing go; Playing shogi (Japanese chess); Reading detective novels. Address: Department of Electrical Engineering, Kyoto University, Yoshida-Honmachi, Sakyo-ku, Kyoto 606-8501, Japan.

TALAIE Afshad, b. 2 Sept 1961, Tehran, Iran. Scientist. Education: BE, Chem Engrng, 1985; ME, Polymer Engrng, 1988; MSc, Info Technol, 1991; PhD, Chem, 1994; MER, Artificial Intelligence. Appointments: Postdoctoral, Sydney Univ, Aust, 1994-97; Selected Sci Fell, Osaka Natl Rsch Inst, Japan, 1997-99. Publications: Over 80 pprs. Honours: 4 schlshps for degs; 2 fellshps, Austl Acady of Sci, 1996, 1998; OPRA Awd, Austl Govt, 1992. Memberships: Material Rsch Soc; Japan Polymer Soc; Solid State Ionics; NYAS; AAAS; Soc for Advmnt of Material and Process Engrng. Hobbies: Soccer; Volleyball; Bushwalking. Address: 20 Murranar Road, Towradgi, NSW 2518, Australia.

TALAIE Farhad, b. 24 Aug 1964, Tehran, Iran. Academic. Education: LLB, Judicial Scis; BS, Applied Chem; LLM, Intl Law; PhD, Intl Law. Appointment: Univ Tchr and Rschr, Shiraz Univ, Shiraz, Iran. Publications: Over 20 pprs since 1995, in intl conf proceedings and jrnls in fields of intl law of the sea, intl law of outer space, intl environ law, intl telecomms law. Honours: 2 schlshps, Iranian Min of Culture and Higher Educ, 1989, 1992. Memberships: Austl Branch Intl Law Assn; Austl Inst of Intl Affairs; Knowledge Soc UK; Cntr for Nat Resources Law and Policy (Fac of Law, Univ of Wollongong, Aust). Hobbies: Martial Arts (holder of Black Belt in Tae Kwon Do); Soccer; Bushwalking. Address: 20 Murranar Road, Towradgi 2518, NSW, Australia.

TALALLA Richard, b. 8 Sept 1930. Retired High Court Judge; Arbitrator; Company Director. m. 14 Jan 1961, 4 s. Education: LLB, hons. Appointments: Bar, Solicitor, Supreme Crt of WA; Fell, Chartered Inst of Arbitrators, London; Advocate, Solicitor, High Crt of Malaysia; Retd Judge, High Crt of Malaysia, 1995. Hobby: Walking. Address: 1037 Bukit Rasah, 70300 Seremban, Negeri Sembilan, Malaysia.

TALBOT Norman Clare, b. 14 Sept 1936, Suffolk, Eng. Poet; Author; Scholar; Editor. m. Jean, 17 Aug 1960, 1 s, 2 d. Education: BA, Hons, Durham Univ, 1959; PhD, Amn Lit, 1962. Appointments: Lectr in Engl, 1962; Snr Lectr, 1969, Asst Prof, 1972, Newcastle Univ Coll, NSW Univ, Retd, 1993. Publications include: The Major Poems of John Keats (criticism), 1967; Poems for a Female Universe (poetry), 1968; Son of a Female Universe (poetry), 1972; The Fishing Boy (poetry), 1975; Weaving the Heterocosm: An Anthology of British Narrative Poetry, 1989; Four Zoas in Australia (poetry), 1992; Australian Skin, Suffolk Bones (poetry), 1997; Myths and Stories, Lies and Truth, 1999. Honours: E C Gregory Awd for Poetry, 1965; Amn Cncl of Learned Scos Fellshp, 1967-68; Visng Profshp, Yale, 1967-68, E Anglia, 1975-76, Aarhus, 1976, OR, 1983, Leicester, 1984, Linacre Coll, Oxford, 1987-88, Exeter, 1992.

Memberships: Soc of Friends (Quakers); William Morris Soc; Mythopoeic Soc; Mythopoeic Lit Assn of Aust; Pres, Newcastle Poetry at the Pub; Newcastle Writers' Cntr; Friends of the Univ of Newcastle; Ed-in-Chf, Mngr, Nimrod Publns and Lit Cnslty; Ed, Babel Handbooks; VP, Catchfire Press. Hobbies: Poetry; Fantasy and Science Fiction writing; Cricket; Croquet; Wine; The Hunter Valley environment. Address: PO Box 170, New Lambton 2305, Australia.

TALLBOYS Richard Gilbert, b. 25 Apr 1931, Eng. International Trade Advisor; Writer; Lecturer. m. Margaret Evelyn Strutt, 27 Mar 1954, 2 s, 2 d. Education: BComm, Univ of Tas, 1960; LLB, Univ of London, 1968. Appointments: Apprentice and Deck Offr, Brit and Austl Merchant Ships, 1947-55; Accounting Profession, Tas, Aust, 1955-62; Austl Govt Trade Commnr, 1962-68; Brit Diplomatic Serv, 1968-88; Consul-Gen, Houston, USA, 1980-85; Amb to Vietnam, 1985-87; Chf Exec, World Coal Inst, 1988-93Ed, Developing Vietnam, 1995; Co-auth: 50 Years of Business in Indonesia: 1945-1995, 1995. Publications: var articles and speeches, on world coal industry. Honours: OBE, 1974; CMG, 1981; Freeman, Cty of London, 1985. Memberships include: Fell, Inst of Chartered Accts in Aust; Fell, Austl Soc of Cert Practicing Accts; Cncl of Royal Inst of Intl Affairs. Listed in: Who's Who; Who's Who in the World. Hobbies: Skiing; Speaking. Address: 5/362 Sandy Bay Road, Hobart, Tasmania 7005, Australia.

TALLEY Nicholas Joseph, b. 9 Jan 1956, Perth, Aust. Physician. m. Penelope Ann Steele, 9 Feb 1985, 2 s. Education: MBBS (Hons), Univ NSW, 1979; PhD, Univ Sydney, 1987; MD, Univ NSW, 1993; FRACP, 1985; FACG, 1988; FACP, 1989; FAFPHM, 1991; MRACMA, 1994; FRCP (ED), 1995. Appointments: Asst Prof, Mayo Medl Sch, 1988-91; Assoc Prof of Med, Mayo Medl Sch, 1991-93; Fndn Prof of Med, Nepean Hosp, 1993-. Publications: Clinical Examination, 1988, 3rd ed, 1996; Exam Medicine, 1985, 3rd ed, 1996; Internal Medicine - The Essential Facts, 1991. Honours: NH and MRC Postgrad Schl, 1984, 1985; Travelling Schl, Roy Australasian Coll of Physns, 1987; Sharron Awd NIH, 1991; Cottrell Fellshp, 1993. Memberships: Fellshp, Roy Australasian Coll of Physns; Amn Gastroenterological Assn; Brit Soc of Gastrenterology. Hobbies: Writing; History; Tennis; Chess. Address: 25 Verdelho Way, Orchard Hills, NSW 2748, Australia.

TALUKDAR Mohammad Mahiuddin, b. 20 Nov 1962, Bangladesh. Pharmaceutical Scientist. m. Naila Akhter. Education: MPharm, 1984, BPharm, hons, 1989, Univ Dhaka; Med and Pharm Rsch, Brussels, Belgium, 1991; PhD, Pharm Scis, Cath Univ, Leuven, Belgium, 1997. Appointments: Rschr, Lab of Clin Pharm, VUB Brussels, 1989-92; Rschr, Lab of Pharmtech and Biopharm, KUL, Belgium, 1992-98; Asst Prof, Univ of Asia Pacific, Dhaka, 1998-. Publications: Sev rsch articles in profl jrnls. Memberships: Fndr Mbr, Galachipa Up-Zila Samitee; Am Assn of Pharm Scis. Hobbies: Travel; Reading; Sports. Address: Galachipa Sador Road, Galachipa Patuakhali, Bangladesh.

TAM Alfred, b. 28 Aug 1953, Hong Kong. Medical Doctor. m. Rosanna, 31 Mar 1996, 2 s, 1 d. Education: MBBS, Hong Kong; MRCP, UK; FRCP, Edinburgh; FHKCPaed; FHKAM, Pediats; FCCP. Appointments: Medl Offr, 1978-84; Lectr, Pediats, 1984-89; Cnslt Pediatrician, Grantham Hospital, 1989-92; Cnslt, Pediatrician, Canossa Hosp, 1992-. Honours: C'wlth Schl, 1982-83. Memberships: Roy Coll of Physns; ACCP; ERS; APSR. Hobbies: Golf; Badminton. Address: 1106 Melbourne Plaza, 33 Queens Road, Hong Kong, China.

TAM Man Kwan, b. 10 Oct 1944, China. Education. m. Yung Lai Chun, 15 July 1968, 2 s. Education: BA (hons), Univ of Hong Kong, 1967; Dip Ed, Chinese Univ of Hong Kong, 1972; MA (Ed), Chinese Univ of Hong Kong, 1979; PhD, London Inst of Educ, 1993; Hon Fell, London Inst of Educ, 1997. Appointments: Pak Kau Coll, 1969-; Pak Kau Girls' Sch, 1974-; Pak U Mid Sch, 1986-; RTC Alumni Assn Sch, 1991-. Publications: Book-Cert Econs, 1983; Video-Money and Banking, 1985. Honours: Badge of

Hon, Hong Kong Govt, Hong Kong, 1983; Non-Offl JP, Hong Kong Govt, Hong Kong, 1992. Memberships: Amn Educl Rsch Assn (Wash); Hong Kong Educl Rsch Assn (Hong Kong). Hobby: Reading. Address: c/o Pak Kau Coll, 20 Nam Pak Road, Ping Shan, Yuen Long, NT, Hong Kong.

TAM Sheung Wai, b. 29 July 1934, Hong Kong. Professor; University President. m. Arleta Y Chang, 30 Mar 1963, 1 s, 1 d. Education: BS, 1958; MSc, 1961; PhD, 1964. Appointments: Lectr, Snr Lectr, Rdr abd Prof, Chinese Univ; Pres, Chung Chi Coll; Dean, Grad Sch; Pro-Vice Chan, Chinese Univ of Hong Kong; Pres, The Open Univ of Hong Kong. Honours: JP; OBE, 1992. Membership: FRSC. Hobbies: Swimming; Classical music. Address: The Open University of Hong Kong, 30 Good Shepherd Street, Homantin, Kowloon, Hong Kong.

TAM Suk-Ching, b. 3 Apr 1955, Hong Kong. Assistant Professor. m. Daniel Wong, 6 Aug 1994. Education: PhD. Appointment: Hong Kong Poly Univ. Publications: Biographical Disruptions and Their Implications for Counselling: A Study of Persons with AIDS in Hong Kong, 1998. Hobbies: Swimming; Meditation. Address: Department of Applied Social Studies, Hong Kong Polytechnic University, Hung Hom, Kowloon, Hong Kong.

TAM Yiu-Chung, b. 15 Dec 1949, Hong Kong. Trade Union Officer. m. Xiang-ming Lai, 24 Mar 1974, 2 s. Education: Aust Natl Univ, Cntr for Continuing Educn; Trade Union Studies, London Sch of Econs & Polit Sci, Univ of London. Appointments: Mbr, Exec Cncl, HKSAR, China; Mbr, Legislative Cncl, HKSAR, China; Vice Chmn, Hong Kong Fedn of Trade Unions, HKSAR, China. Honour: JP, 1997. Membership: Inst of Coml Mngmt, Eng, Hon Life Fell. Address: 12/F Sup Tower, 83 King's Road, North Point, Hong Kong.

TAM Yiu Chung, b. 15 Dec 1949 Hong Kong. Trade Unionist; Govt Offic. m. Lai Xiang Ming, 2 c. Education: Austl Natl Univ LSE. Appointments: Trade union offr; Vice-Chmn Hong Kong Fedn of Trade Unions; Employees' Retrng Bd. Honours: Hon Life Fell Inst of Coml Mngment UK. Memberships: Fmr mbr Preparatory Cttee for Hong Kong Spec Admin Reg; Mbr Exec Cncl Hong Kong Spec Admin Reg; Mbr Vocational Trng Bd; Mbr Standing Commn on Civ Serv Salaries and Conditions of Serv; Mbr Ind Commn Against Corruption Complaints Cttee; Mbr Servs Promotion Strategy Unit; Mbr Dem Alliance for Betterment of Hong Kong. Address: Executive Council Secretariat, 1st Floor, Main Wing, Central Government Offices, Central, Hong Kong Special Administrative Region, People's Republic of China.

TAMAI Hiroshi, b. 3 May 1953, Kochi, Japan. Medical Doctor (Pediatrics). m. Ruka, 10 June 1984, 1 s, 3 d. Education: Postgrad Sch of Osaka Medl Coll; Prof, Dept of Pediats, Osaka Medl Coll; MD; PhD. Appointments: Rsch Fell; Asst Prof; Prof. Creative works: Rsch in Vitamin E. Memberships: NY Acady of Sci; Japan Pediat Soc; Vitamin Soc of Japan. Hobby: Tennis. Address: 1-1-31-509 Kitanaburi, Hirakata, Osaka 573-0064.

TAMARI Moshe, b. 20 May 1910. Editor of Books and Periodicals. m. Miriam Gefel, 31 Dec 1937, 1 s, 1 d. Education: Cultural Doct, DLitt, World Univ Roundtable, USA; Life Fell, World Lit Acady, Cambridge, Eng. Appointments: Parly Sec, 2nd Knesset, 1952; Rep WZO, Rio de Janeiro, Brazil, 1963-65; Fndr Chmn, Israel-Aust Cultural Exch and Friendship Assn, 1978-; Mbr, Control Cttee, PEN-Israel, 1996. Publications: Voice of Life; In Vain; From Scene to Scene; Bible Miniatures - Days Gone By; Two Brazilian Books; Blossoming Orange Groves; Ancient Foundations of Middle Eastern Culture; The Life/Death Experience: Around the Sea of Galilee. Honours: ABI, Plaque for Serv Cultural Exch, Israel-Aust; Histl Preservations of Am, Serv to the Arts and World Comm; Notable Mbr Israel Assn Periodic, 1996; Decree of Letters, Golden Medal 2000, ABI, USA, 1999. Membership: Hebrew Writers' Assn; PEN Israel; Intl Writers Assn, OH, USA; Intl Platform Assn, USA. Address: PO Box 21488, Tel Aviv 62265, Israel.

TAN Charlie Keah Lock, b. 1 Apr 1932, Malaysia. Engineer. m. Sally, 1968, 1 s, 1 d. Education: Grad, Univ; Dip, Polytechnic. Appointments: NCO Roy Air Force, 1956-61; Snr Offr, Singapore Airlines, 1961-92; Mngng Dir, Alltrade Aerospace/Ground Support Servs, 1992-; Writing 2 books: "365's Management" and "Management in Perfection". Memberships: People's Action Party, 1981-; Life Cttee, SIA Grp Retd Staff Assn; SIA-Minds Proj Cttee; Invited guest. New Millenium Cttee, Planetary Soc, attended Planetfest, 1997. Hobbies: Games; Reading; Attending lectures and seminars. Address: Mananging Director, Alltrade Aerospace/Ground Support Services, Blk 3 Haig Road, #02-519, Singapore 430003.

TAN Han-Thor, b. 10 Oct 1944, Kuala Lumpur. Stock and Shares Broker. m. Yau Kit-Ching, 24 Sept 1977, 1 d. Education: Dip, Sales a Mktndng; Dip Computer Systems Analysis; Dip, Fin; Dip, Intl Trade. Appointments: Commodity Trader, Cargill, 1980-87; Gen Mngr, Itrafi, 1989-91; Bus Dev Mngr, Ace Com Ent, 1991-92; Cnslt - Innotech Mngmt Cntr, 1993; Dealer - Klce, 1994-; Presently Dealer, Rep-KLSE. Honours: Cert of Merit, Ace Japan, 1978; 2000 Outstndng People of 20th Century Awd. Memberships: Malaysian Inst of Mngmt, 1978; Amn Inst of Mgmt Exec Cncl Mbr, 1982-83; Malaysian Chinese Assn, Vice-Chmn, 1992-; Oxford Club Mbr, 1994-. Hobbies: Chess; Swimming. Address: c/o TA Securities BHD, 17th Floor Room 32, Menera Ta One, 22, Jalan Ramlee, 50250 Kuala Lumpur, Malaysia.

TAN Weikang, b. 30 June 1932, Kiangsu Prov, China. Professor. m. Shufang Sung, 10 June 1960, 1 s, 1 d. Education: Dip, Dept of Elecr Engrng, 1955-72, Assoc Prof and Sub-Dean, Electron Engrng Dept, 1972-81, Taiyuan Polytech Univ; Prof, Chf of Tchng and Rsch Grp and Dean, Dept of Computer Sci and Technol, N Jiaotong Univ, Beijing, 1982-. Creative works: Perfd the rsch wrk of new magnetic distributor exhib at 1960 Natl Telemechs 1st Annual Symposium, Beijing, China; Relevant pprs took pt in exch at IFAC No 1 in 1960, Moscow, USSR; 6 pprs publd on Reliability Optimum Link Allocation at intl symposia, 1980-. Honour: Awd of Natl Educ Cttee of China, 1989; Specialist of Govt Allowance of China, 1994. Memberships: Chinese Inst of Automation; Chinese Inst of Electrics; IEEE: Cttee Mbr, Reliability Maths Cttee, Ops Rsch Soc of China. Hobbies: Travel; Swimming. Address: Department of Computer Science and Technology, Northern Jiaotong University, West Gate, Beijing, China.

TAN Yonghong, b. 2 July 1958, Guilin, China. Professor. m. Rong Wang, 20 Aug 1985, 1 s. Education: PhD, Electr Engin, Univ of Ghent, Belgium, 22 Apr 1996. Appointments: Assoc Prof, Control Engrng, 1992; Prof, Computer Engrng & Control Engrng, 1998. Publications: Over 70 pprs in jrnls & confs. Honours: Awd for Outstndng Young Scientists Sponsored by Min of Electron Ind, China, 1991; Awd for Outstndng Young Scientist, sponsored by Guangxi Yth Union, 1998. Memberships: NY Acady of Scis, 1998; Natl Yth Assn of China, 1998. Hobbies: Reading; Travelling; Swimming. Address: School of Computer Science, Guilin Institute of Electronic Technology, 541004 Guilin, China.

TAN KENG YAM Tony, b. 7 Feb 1940 Singapore. Politician; Banker. m. Mary Chee Bee Kiang, 1964, 4 c. Education: St Patrick's Sch; St Joseph's Inst; Univ of Singapore; MA Inst of Tech; Univ of Adelaide. Appointments: Lectr in Maths Univ of Singapore, 1967-69; Sub-Mngr Overseas Chinese Banking Corp, 1969; Gen Mngr, 1978; MP, 1979-; Snr Min of State - Educ - 1979; Min of Educ, 1980; Concurrently Vice-Chan Natl Univ of Singapore; Min for Trade and Ind concurrently Min in charge of Natl Univ of Singapore and Nanyang Tech Inst, 1981-83; Min of Fin, 1983-85; Min of Educ and Hlth, Jan-Apr 1985; Min for Trade and Ind, 1985-86; Min of Educ, 1985-91; Chmn People's Action Party Cntrl Exec Cttee, 1993; Chmn and CEO Oversea-Chinese Banking Corp Ltd, 1992; Dep PM and Min of Def, Aug 1995-. Hobbies: Swimming; Golf; Walking. Address: Ministry of Defence, Gombak Drive, Singapore.

TAN-BOURDILLON Ningxia, b. 18 June 1966, Sichuan, China. Principal Engineer. m. Antony Bourdillon, 22 Dec 1989, 1 s, 1 d. Education: BS, Chongqing Inst of Arch and Engrng, 1985; PhD, Univ of NSW, 1991. Appointments: Rsch Fell, State Univ of NY, 1991-92; Prin Engr, Hewlett-Packard (Singapore), 1994-. Publications: High Temperature Superconductor: Progress and Science, 1995; Over 750 sci pprs. Hobbies: Reading; Swimming. Address: Kent Ridge Post Office, PO Box 1039, Singapore 911102.

TANABE Kozo, b. 7 May 1926, Hyogo Prefecture, Japan. Professor of Chemistry. 2 d. Education: BS, Chem, 1951; DSc, 1956, Hokkaido Univ. Appointments: Rsch Asst, 1951, Asst Prof, 1956, Prof, 1960, Rsch Inst for Catalysis, Hokkaido Univ; Prof, Dept of Chem, Hokkaido Univ, 1965-90, Prof Emer, 1990-, Hon Prof of Jilin Univ, 1988-; Rsch and Dev Cnslt, Nippon Shokubai Co Ltd, 1990-. Publications: Solids Acids and Bases, 1970; Function of Catalysts, 1974; Super Acids and Super Bases, 1980; New Solid Acids and Bases, 1989; 410 sci pprs; 16 pats. Honours: Matsunaga Prize, 1966; Chem Soc of Japan Awd, 1979; Toray Sci and Technol Prize, 1987; Catlysis Soc of Japan Awd, 1987; Purple Ribbon Medal, 1988; Japan Pet Inst Awd, 1989; Hon Awd, Catalysis Soc of Japan, 1990. Memberships: Japan Pet Inst; VP, Chem Soc of Japan, 1988; Pres, Catalysis Soc of Japan, 1988. Address: 14-11 Sonomachi, Oasa, Ebetsu-shi, Hokkaido 069-0851, Japan.

TANABE Makoto, b. 25 Feb 1922 Maebashi Cty Gunma Pref. Politician. Appointments: Chmn All Japan Postal Wrkrs Union Gunma Dist, 1949; Pres Wrkrs Unions Cncl Gunma Dist, 1951-60; Vice-Chmn Cntrl Exec Cttee Socl Party of Japan - SPJ - 1982-83; Gen Sec, 1983-86; Vice-Chmn, 1990-91; Chmn Cntrl Exec Cttee Socl Dem Party of Japan - SDPJ - 1991-. Memberships: Mbr Gunma Pref Ass, 1955-60; Mbr HoR, 1960-. Address: Social Democratice Party of Japan, 1-8-1 Nagata-cho, Chiyoda-ku, Tokyo, Japan.

TANAKA Kouichi R, b. 15 Dec 1926, Fresno, CA, USA. Medical Educator. m. Grace, 23 Oct 1965, 1 s, 2 d. Education: BS, MD, Wayne State Univ. Appointments: Instr, 1957-59, Asst Prof, 1959-61, Assoc Prof, 1961-68, Prof of Med, 1968-97, Prof Emer, 1998-, Univ CA, Los Angeles Sch of Med. Publications: 134 sci publns. Honours: Alpha Omega Alpha, 1950; Sigma Xi, 1950; Amn Coll of Physns Laureate Awd, 1991; Mastership, 1998. Memberships: Amn Soc of Hematol; Assn of Amn Physns; Amn Soc for Clin Investigation; Amn Coll of Physns. Hobby: Horticulture. Address: Department of Medicine, Box 400, Harbor University of California at Los Angeles Medical Center, Torrance, CA 90509-2910, USA.

TANDBERG Ronald Peter, b. 31 Dec 1943, Melbourne, Aust. Cartoonist; Political Cartoonist. m. Glenys, 31 Oct 1987, 1 s, 4 d. Education: Dip of Art. Creative Works: The Age of Tandberg; Tandberg Draws the Line; Tandberg's Age of Consensus; The Ageless Tandberg. Honours: Goldwalkley; Walkley for Best Cartoon. Hobbies: Swimming; Beach; Cooking. Address: P O Box 72, Queenscliff, Vic, Australia.

TANDON Rakesh K, b. 1 Apr 1941, Allahabad, India. Physician. m. Manjula, 22 May 1966, 1 s, 1 d. Education: MBBS; MD (Med); PhD (Gastro). Appointments: Asst Prof, Med, AIIMS, 1972; Prof and Hd, AIIMS, 1991-. Publication: How to Live Healthy. Honours: Shakuntala Amir Chand Awd, Indian Cncl of Medl Rsch, 1982; Boots Gastroenterology Oration, ISG, 1983. Memberships: Indian Soc of Gastro, Hon Sec, 1984-91; Pres, 1990-91; Amn Gastro Assn, 1990-. Hobbies: Photography; Tennis. Address: Department of Gastroenterology, All-India Institute of Medical Sciences, Ansari Nagar, New Delhi 10029, India.

TANDON Sampat Kumar, b. 13 Aug 1945, Delhi, India. University Teacher. m. Anita, 1 June 1972, 2 s. Education: MSc (Hons) Panjab; PhD, Delhi. Appointments: Assoc Lectr, Indian Inst of Tech, 1966-68; Sci Offr, Wadia Inst of Himalayan Geol, 1971-76; Rdr,

Univ of Delhi, 1976-86; Prof, Univ of Delhi, 1986-. Publication: Sedimentary Basins of India: Tectonic Context, 1991. Honours: INSA Young Scientist Medal, 1974; Krishnan Gold Medal, 1985; Fell, Indian Acad of Scis, 1987; SS Bhatnagar Prize, 1988; Fell, Indian Natl Sci Acady, 1999. Memberships: Fell, Geol Soc of India, Sec, 1986-92, 1998-; VP, Indian Assn of Sedimentologists; Fell, Indian Geophys Union. Hobbies: Reading; Travel. Address: Department of Geology, University of Delhi, Delhi 110007, India.

TANENBAUM Robert, b. 31 July 1936, USA. Artist. m. Trish, 7 Sept 1959, 1 s, 1 d. Education: BFA. Appointments: Bd, Brandise Art Cntr, Juvenile Diabetes Fndn. Creative Works: Life Size Portrait of Howard Hughes, 1979; 3 Past CEO's of United Parcel Serv, 1991, 1992, 1999. Memberships: Soc of Illustrations of LA; Am Portrait Soc; Portrait Soc; Natl Water Soc; Natl Water Color Soc. Hobbies: Skiing; Photography; Shooting; Pool; Reading; Exercise. Address: 5505 Corbin Avenue, Tarzana, CA 91356, USA.

TANG Caixian, b. 16 Jan 1963, Zhejiang, China. Soil Scientist. m. C Zhu, 30 Dec 1988, 1 s, 1 d. Education: BS Agric, Zhejiang Agric Univ, 1982; PhD, Univ West Aust, 1991. Appointments: Assoc Lectr, Zhejiang Agric Univ, 1982-86; Visng Fell, Univ West Aust, 1987; Postdoct, Univ West Aust, 1991-95; Rsch Fell, Univ West Aust, 1995-. Publications: Over 40 jrnl articles. Honours: Rsch Schlshp, Univ West Aust, 1988; Guest Prof, Zhejiang Univ; Hon Rsch Fell, Huazhong Agric Univ; Hon Rsch Fell, Anhui Agric Univ. Hobbies: Table tennis; Running; Fishing. Address: Centre for Legumes in Mediterranean Agriculture, University of Western Australia, Nedlands, WA 6907, Australia.

TANG Fei, b. 15 Mar 1932, Taitsang Co, Chiangsu, China. Minister of National Defence. m. 1 s, 2 d. Education: Air Force Acady, 1952; Air Cmnd and Gen Staff Coll, 1971; War Coll, Armed Forces Univ, 1979. Appointments: Wing Cmndr, Air Force, 1983-84; Dpty Chf of Staff and Plng, Air Force Gen HQ, 1984-85; Supt, Air Force Acady, 1985-86; Dir, Pol Warfare Dept, Air Force Gen HQ, 1986-89' Cmndr, Combat Air Cmnd, 1989; Dpty Cmdr in Chf, Air Force, 1989-91; Dir, Jt Ops Trng Dept, Min of Natl Def, 1991-91; Cmdr in Chf, Air Force, 1991-95; Vice Chf, Gen Staff (Exec), Min of Natl Def, 1995-98; Chf of Gen Staff, Min of Natl Dec, 1998-99.

TANG Hongqing, b. 1 Dec 1937, Hunan Prov, China. Nuclear Physicist. m. Wang Yayi, 7 Dec 1973, 1 d. Education: Dip, China Univ of Sci and Technol, 1963. Appointments: Rsch Asst, CIAE, Beijing, 1963-78; RSch Assoc, 1978-87; Assoc Rsch Prof, 1987-92; Rsch Prof, 1993-. Publications: Abnormal Fast Neutron Time of Flight Spectrometer, 1991. Memberships: Nuc Data Cttee of China, 1995-. Address: China Institute of Atomic Energy, P O Box 275-46, Beijing 102413, China.

TANG Ian S K, b. 18 Jan 1959, Kuala Lumpur, Malaysia. Engineer. m. Esther Lo, 18 Aug 1980, 1 s, 1 d. Education: BS, Chem Engrng. Appointments: Shift Supt, 1986-94; Snr Engr (process), 1994-97; Mngr (process), 1997-. Memberships: Instn of Chem Engrs, 1993; Instn of Gas Engrs, 1995; Hong Kong Instn of Engrs, 1995. Hobbies: Reading; Popular music. Address: Hong Kong China Gas Co Ltd, 17-19 Dai Fat Street, Tai Po Industrial Estate, Tai Po, NT, Hong Kong.

TANG Jia-Yong, b. 6 Nov 1935, Shanghai, China. Professor of Physics; Director, Institute of Modern Physics. m. Shi-wen Li, 15 July 1967, 1 d. Education: Grad, Dept of Phys, Peking Univ, 1957. Appointments: Assoc Prof, 1980-85, Prof, 1985-, Dept Chmn, 1986-89, Lab Dir, 1990-97, Inst Dir, 1997-, Fudan Univ, Visng Prof, Caltech, Pasadena, CA, USA, 1984-85; Visng Schl, Aarhus Univ, Denmark, 1979-81. Publications: Auth of 10 books,transls and 100 pprs, inclng: Study of the Polarization Mechanism of Beam-Foil Interaction Using the Channeling Effect, 1986; Stopping, Range and Channeling Effect of Ions in Solids (book), 1988; Interface Adhesion Enhanced by MeV Ions, 1991; Comments on the Classical Approach to Non-Rutherford Cross Section

Calculations, 1993; Advances of Nuclear Microprobes and Their Applications, 1995; Development from Rutherford Backscattering to High Energy Backscattering Spectrometry, 1996. Honours: Achievement Awd, 1985, Adv Awd, 1992, 1997, State Commn of Educ. Memberships: Vice-Chmn, Learned Soc of Nuc Sci and Technol, Shangahi, 1987-91; Dpty-Dir, Natl Lab of Material Modification by Ion, Electron and Laser Beams, 1988-98. Listed in: Who's Who in the World. Hobbies: Classic music; Bridge; Swimming. Address: Institute of Modern Physics, Fudan University, Shanghai 200433, China.

TANG Xiao-Xuan, b. 25 July 1925, Jiangsu Prov, China. Professor; Senior Engineer. m. Yun-Rong Shen, 1 May 1958, 3 s. Education: Freshman, Chem Dept, Utopia Univ, Shanghai, China, 1945-46; Sophomore, Chem Dept, Univ of Shanghai, Shanghai, China, 1946-47; BS, Chem Dept, Beloit Coll, Beloit, WI, USA, 1949; MS, Chem Dept, Grad Sch, Univ of WI, USA, 1950. Appointments: Chf Engr, N China Pharmaceutical Corp, Shi Jia Zhuang, Hebei, China, 1955-81; Chf Engr, Pharmaceutical Admin of Hebei Prov, China, 1981-83; Gen Dir, Pharmaceutical Co of Hebei Prov, China, 1983-85; Hon Dir, Rsch Inst of Biochemical Engrng, E China Univ of Chem Technol, Shanghai, China, 1985-. Publications: Development of High Fructose Syrup Technology in Starch and Sugars from Starch, China, 1983; Prevention of Non-sterilness in Antibiotic Fermentation in Journal of Antibiotics, China, 1981; Advances in Antibiotic Fermentation in Journal of Industrial Micro-organisms, China, 1987; Recent Development of Protoplast Fusion of Micro-organisms in Journal of Industrial Micro-organisms, China, 1987; Chf Compiler, Biotechnology, 1991. Honour: Awd, as Chf Ed of Biotechnology, Shanghai, 1998. Memberships: Chmn, Chinese Indl Biochemical Soc; Pharmaceutical Grp, China Natl Cttee of Sci and Technol; Vice Chf Ed, Jrnl of Antibiotics, China. Address: College of Biotechnology, East China University of Science and Technology, Mei Long Road, Shanghai 200237, China.

TANG Zhao Lian, b. 25 Feb 1934, Guangzhou, China. Educator. m. Zheng Peiyu, 31 Jan 1961, 1 d. Education: BEcon, Nankai Univ, 1960. Appointments: People's Repr, Guangzhou People's Congress, 1952; Lectr, 1960-79, Asst and Lectr, Econs Dept, Nankai Univ; Dept Vice Dean and Dept Dean, Econs Dept, Zhongshan Univ, 1979-89; Prof, Vice Coll Dir, Lingnan Coll of Zhongshan Univ, 1989-. Publications: (co-auth) History of Modern Chinese Economic Thoughts, 1980; China's Merchandise Bureau and China's Modernization, 1994; Vice Chf-Ed, History of Chinese Economic Thoughts in Management and Economy; Chf Ed, Studies on Lingnan Economic Thoughts, 1996; Chf-Ed, Deng Xiaoping's Thought on Economic Development, 1998. Honours: Ist Class Excellent Textbook Awd, Min of Educ, 1988; State Spec Subsidy for Outsndng Contbn to Dev of China's Higher Educ, Min of Educ, 1993; Excellent Staff in Guangdong Higher-Educ Line, Guangdong Provcl Higher Edic Bur, 1995; Excellence Awd, Publishing House of Central S China Univs, 1996. Memberships: Cttee Mbr, Evaluation Cttee of Profl Titles for Zhongshan Tchng Staff, Degree Evaluation Cttee in Zhonshan Univ; VP, Soc of Chinese Econ Thoughts Hist, 1988-; Team Ldr, Econs Evaluation Team, Evaluation Cttee of Guangdong Higher Educ Tchrs Advd Profl Titles. Hobbies: Chinese chess; Weiqi; Peking opera; Canton music; Basketball. Address: Lingnan College, Zhongshan University, 510275, Xingangxi Road, GZ, China.

TANG Zhongming, b. 5 Apr 1963, Jiangsu, China. Professor. m. Dongmei Teng, 18 July 1987, 1 s. Education: PhD. Appointment: Dean of the Dept. Membership: Math Assn of China. Hobby: Chinese chess. Address: Department of Mathematics, Suzhou University, Jiangsu 215006, China.

TAN Shubei, b. Jan 1931 Shanghai. Govt Offic. m. Liang Wenfeng, 1 s, 1 d. Appointments: Joined CCP, 1949; Fmrly offic Shanghai Fedn of Trade Unions; Ed Hd of Reporters Cntr Fujian Daily; Chf Editl Dir China News Serv, 1957-69; Dep Div Chf Dept of Consular Affairs,

1971-78; First Sec Tokyo Emb, 1978-82; Div Chf Dept of Consular Affairs, 1982-83; Consul-Gen San Francisco, 1983-86; Envoy of Emb USA, 1986-88; Dir Off for Taiwan Affairs of For Min, 1988-89; Dep Dir for Taiwan Affairs of State Cncl, 1989-; Dep Dir CCP Cntrl Cttee Taiwan Affairs Off, 1991-; Exec Vice-Chmn Assn for Rels Across the Taiwan Straits, 1991-; Dep Dir CCP Cntrl Cttee Co-ordng Cttee for Reunification of the Motherland, 1993-. Memberships: Mbr Standing Cttee 8th Natl Cttee CCP Cntrl Cttee. Address: Central Office for Taiwanese Affairs, c/o State Council, Beijing, China.

TANG Tianbiao, b. Oct 1940 Shimen Co Hunan Prov. Army Offr. Education: Harbin Inst of Mil Engring; Inst of PLA Engr Corps; Propaganda and Theort Cadre Trng Course of CCP Cntrl Cttee Party Sch; Univ of Natl Def. Appointments: Var posts in Guangzhou Mil Reg; Dep Dir Propaganda Dept Guangzhou Mil Reg, 1983; Dep Off Hd and Dep Dir Cadre Dept of PLA Gen Polit Dept; Dep Dir Ldng Grp for the Placement of Demobilized Army Offrs, 1993-; Asst Dir PLA Gen Polit Dept, 1993-95; Dep Dir, 1995-; Rank of Lt Gen, 1994-; Dep to 8th NPC, 1993. Memberships: Mbr CCP, 1961-; Mbr 15th CCP Cntrl Cttee, 1997-. Address: c/o Ministry of National Defence, Jingshanqian Jie, Beijing, People's Republic of China.

TANIGAKI Masataka, b. 2 Oct 1942, Kobe, Japan. Professor. m. Tomoyo, 29 Apr 1973, 2 d. Education: PhD, Univ of WI, USA, 1972. Appointments: Rsch Assoc, Inst of Atomic Energy, 1972-83; Assoc Prof, Dept of Chem Engrng, Kyoto Univ, 1983-94; Prof, 1994-. Memberships: AIChE; Soc of Chem Engrng, Japan; Japan Membrane Soc. Hobbies: Fishing; Music. Address: Department of Chemical Engineering, Kyoto University, Honmachi, Yoshida, Sakyo-ku, Kyoto 606-8501, Japan.

TANIGUCHI Makoto, b. 31 Mar 1930, Osaka, Japan. Professor. m. Hiroko, 1 s. Education: BA, MA, St John's Coll, Cambridge Univ; BA, MA, Hitotsubashi Univ, Tokyo. Appointments: Prof, Inst of Asia-Pacific Studies, Waseda Univ; Intl Christian Univ; Toyo Eiwa Women's Univ; Dpty Sec Gen, OECD, Paris; Amb of Japan, UN. Creative Works: North South Issues: A Path to Global Solutions, 1993. Memberships: The Tokyo Club. Hobbies: Sports; Music. Address: 901 Azabu House 1-7-13, Roppongi, Minato-ku, Tokyo, Japan.

TANNER Douglas Alan, b. 30 Aug 1953. m. 28 May 1977, 3 d. Education: AB, Hist, 1974, MBA, 1978, JD, 1978, Stanford Univ. Appointments: Law Clk, Judge Joseph T Sneed, US 9th Circuit Crt of Appeals, 1978-79; Orrick, Herrington & Sutcliffe, San Fran, 1979-84; Ptnr, San Jose, 1984-86; Ptnr, NY Cty, 1986-89; Milbank, Tweed, Hadley & McCloy, Ptnr, LA, 1989-92, Hong Kong, 1992-. Memberships: NY Bar Assocs, Amn Bar Assn; CA Bar Assn. Address: 3007 Alexandra House, 16 Chater Road, Hong Kong SAR, PR China.

TANNER Paul D, b. 8 Dec 1958, Bay City, MI, USA. English Professor. Education: BA, Michigan State Univ; MA, California State Univ. Appointments: Engl Prof, Meiji Univ, 1992-; Sugiyama Univ, 1993-; Nanzan Univ, 1994-. Memberships: Assn of Asian Stdies; Japan Assn of Language Tchrs; Comp Educ Assn. Hobbies: Travel and travel literature; Japanese and Chinese history. Address: Grandeur Motoyama 3-D, 3-26 Hashimoto-cho, Chikusa-ku, Nagoya, 464-0035, Japan.

TANNER Peter Anthony, b. 6 Jan 1945, Birmingham, Eng. Professor. m. Stella, 24 Dec 1984, 3 s. Education: DSc, MSc, Univ Surrey; PhD, BSc, Univ of London; Cert Educ, Univ Birmingham. Appointment: Prof, Cty Univ of Hong Kong, 1997. Memberships: CChem; FRSC; MCIWEM. Hobbies: Travel; Distance-running. Address: 13A Dragon Court, 28 Caine Road, Hong Kong.

TANNOCK Gregory Austin, b. 17 Feb 1939, Perth, WA, Aust. Virologist. m. Jessica, 1 Feb 1964, 1 s, 5 d, 1 dec). Education: BS; MSc; PhD; DSc. Appointments: Virologist, CSI, Melbourne, 1960-61, 1973-79; Virologist Natl Biolst (Stands Lab, 1961-73); Univ of Newcastle, 1979-93; RMIT Roy Melbourne Inst Technol, 1993-. Publications: Over 70 pprs on refereed jrnls; 17 reviews or book chapts. Honours: US Pub Hlth Serv Post-Doct Fellship, CDC, Atlanta, 1975; DSc, Univ of Newcastle, 1996. Memberships: Austl Soc of Microbiology; Austl Vet Poultry Assn. Hobbies: Reading; Gardening. Address: C/o Department of Applied Biology, RMIT, GPO Box 2476V, Melbourne, Vi Australia.

TAO Ji Kan, b. 28 Nov 1913, Zhejiang, China. Professor of Economics. m. J Y Zuo, 10 Apr 1945, 2 s, 2 d. Education: BA, Univ of Beijing, 1935; MA, Nankai Inst of Econs, Nankai Univ, 1937; Advd Studies, Univ of Denver and Univ of WI, USA, 1947-48. Appointments: Rsch Fell, Nanakai Inst of Econs, Chongqing, 1938-41; Adj Prof, Univ of Chongqing, 1942-45; Prof of Econs, Nankai Univ, 1949-. Creative works: Lectures on Economic Crisis, 1975; An Introduction to World Economy, 1984; State Monopoly Capitalism and its Effect on the Capitalistic Economy, in Essays in Economic History and Economic Theory, 1982; Handbook of International Economy, 1991; Contemporary Public Finance in Western Countries, 1992; Contemporary Tax Systems in Western Countries, 1997. Memberships: Cncl Mbr, All China Assn for World Econ Rsch; Cnslt, All China Assn for Oceanian Econ Rsch; Cnslt, Tianjin Assn for Pub Fin Rsch. Address: Department of International Economics, Nankai University, Tianjin, China.

TAO Long-Xiang, b. 14 Sept 1933, Peking. Chemist; Senior Researcher; Professor. m. Zou Duo-Xiu, 22 Oct 1960, 1 s, 1 d. Education: Tsinghua Univ, 1952-53; Peking Inst of Petroleum, 1954-56; ND Zelinsky Inst of Org Chem, Russian Acady of Scis, Moscow, 1962-66; DSc, 1966. Appointments: Hd, Sci Rsch Grp, 1966-92; Ldr, 2 Projects, Fndn of China Petro-Chem Technol Co, 1986-89, 1987-89, 3 Projects, Natl Natural Sci Fndn, China, 1985-87, 1990-92, 1992-94; Advsr, Sci Rsch Grp, 1993-. Publications include: Pillared Interlayered Clay Catalyst, 1986-93; Catalytic Oxidative Dehydrogenation - Cracking of Light Alkane, 1991-96; Catalytic Synthesis of Benzene From Methane on Mo/ZSM-5 Catalyst, 1992-97. Honours: Adv Worker, 1959; Hon Ctf of Merit, Sci Rsch, 1977; Achievement Awd, Sci and Technol, 1980; Ex Worker, 1986; Govt Specl Subsidy, State Cncl of China, 1992-. Memberships: Chinese Chem Soc; Chinese Petroleum Soc. Address: Dalian Institute of Chemical Physics, Chinese Academy of Sciences, PO Box 100, Dalian 116012, China.

TAO Siju, b. 1935, Jingjiang Co, Jiangsu Prov, China. Chinese Party Official. Appointments: Vice Min of Pub Security, 1984-90; Min, 1990-98; Accompanied Pres Li Ziannian on sev visits abroad; Mbr, 14th CCP Cntrl Cttee, 1992-97, 15th CCP Cntrl Cttee, 1997-; Chair, Natl Narcotics Control Commn, 1993-; 1st Pol Commissar, Chinese People's Armed Police Force, 1991-; Mbr, Cntrl Commn of Pol Sci and Law. Address: Ministry of Public Security, 14 Dongchangan Jie, Beijing 100741, China.

TAO Xueliang, b. 15 Sept 1930. Teacher. m. Cheng Siqing, Feb 1964, 1 s, 1 d. Education: Chinese Lang and Lit, Bach Deg. Appointments: Yi Nationality Area, Yunnan, 1949-55; St Yunnan Univ, Yunnan Coll of Nationalities, 1955-96. Publications include: Happiness of Waxi, 1979; Cha Mu, 1981; Literature of Yi Nationality, 1983; On Bimo (Yi Shaman) Culture, 1993; Poems Collection of Dashan, 1994. Honours: Selected Works of Yi Nationality Folk Stories, 1983; Third Class Prize, Nation Nationality Ctte, 1989; Ex Writing Prize by Rsch Inst of Minority Lit, Chinese Acady of Socl Sci, 1990. Memberships: China Folklore Artist Assn; China Auth Assn, Yunnan Br. Hobbies: Reading; Writing; Chinese chess; Bridge. Address: Yunnan College of Nationalities.

TAO Bojun. Army Offr. Appointments: Fmrly with 43rd Army aide to Gens Wuhan and Chengdu Mil Regs; Chf of Staff Guangzhou Mil Reg, 1992; Promoted to Lt Gen, 1993; First Dep Cmdr Guangzhou Mil Reg, 1994-96; Cmdr Guangdong Mil Reg, 1996-. Memberships: Mbr CCP Standing Cttee Guangzhou Mil Reg, 1993; Mbr 15th CCP Cntrl Cttee, 1997. Address: Peopl'es Liberation Army, c/o Ministry of National Defence, Jingshanqian Jie, Beijing, China.

TARANTINO Quentin, b. 27 Mar 1963 Knoxville TN. Film Dir. Appointments: Wrked in Video Archives Manhattan Beach; Brief acting career; Prodr Killing Zoe; Wrote screenplay for True Romance; Natural Born Killers. Films Dir'd: Reservoir Dogs; Pulp Fiction, 1994; Appearances incl: Sleep with Me, 1994; Destiny Tunes on the Radio, 1995; Desperado, 1995; Girl 6, 1996; From Dusk Till Dawn, 1996. Films Prod'd: Red Rain, 1995; Four Rooms, 1995; From Dusk Till Dawn, 1996; Curdled, 1996. Publications: True Romance, 1995; Natural Born Killers, 1995; Jackie Brown, 1998. Honours: Golden Palm Cannes Film Fest for Pulp Fiction. Address: 6201 Sunset Boulevard, Suite 35, Los Angeles, CA 90028, USA.

TARANUPI Muki, b. 25 July 1957, Bika Vill, Gadsup, Kainantu Dist, Eastern Highlands Prov, Papua New Guinea. Minister for Education, Culture and Science. m. 6 children. Education: Grad w Dip, course in Secondary Tchng, UPNG Goroka Tchrs Coll, 1978. Appointments: Secondary Sch Tchr; Dpty Ldr, Christian Democratic Party; Headmaster, Kainantu hs; Min for Educ, Culture and Sci. Membership: Evangelical Brotherhook Ch.

TARAR Muhammad Rafiq, b. 2 Nov 1929 Pir Kot Ghakkar Mandi. Politician; Lawyer. Education: Govt Islamia High Sch Gujranwala; Guru Nanak Khalsa Coll Gujranwala; Punjab Univ Law Coll. Appointments: Legal Prac Gujranwala; Additional Sess Judge Gujranwala Bahawalnagar Sargodha; Chf Jus, 1989; Sen Pakistan Muslim League, Mar-Dec 1997; Pres of Pakistan, Jan 1998-. Memberships: Mbr Lahore High Crt, 1974; Mbr Electoral Commn of Pakistn, 1980-89; Mbr Supreme Crt, 1991-94. Address: Office of the President, Aiwan-e-Sadr, Islamabad, Pakistan.

TARCZYNSKA Halinka Cecylia Anna de, b. 9 July 1923, Melbourne, Aust. Musician. m. Ian Paull Fiddian, 25 May 1963. Education: Life Schlshp, Piano w Edward Goll, 1935-46 Singing w Thea Phillips, 1941-42, Dominique Modesti, 1948, Elizabeth Forini, London, 1951-55; Piano Interpretation w Ignace Friedman, 1945; Theory, Harmony, Counterpoint w Dr von Keussler, 1935, May Richards, 1937-40. Appointments: Num appearances as Pianist, Singer and Accompanist at brdcsts and concerts, 1944-50; Prin Roles w Natl Opera, 1947-50; Singer, BBC TV, Opera and Childrens Progs, Eng, 1950-55; Num appearances at Edinburgh Fest, Glyndebourne Opera; Recitals in UK, Melbourne, Bermuda; Tchr; Adjudicator, Accompanist; Organised and performed in Rossini Centenary Concert for Italian Cultural Inst, Melbourne, 1968; Illustrated lectr entitled Exploring the Polish Song, 1986; Workshop on Essential Basics for Accurate Sight Singing, 1987; Examiner, Piano and Singing, Austl Music Examinations Bd, 1979-97. Honours: Pianist, Radio Discovery Broadcast Station 3UZ Melbourne, 1942; Finalist, ABC Vocal and Concerto Fest, 1944; 3rd Prize, Melbourne Sun Aria Competition, 1949; Austl Medal, Overseas League Fest of C'wlth Youth, 1953. Memberships: Fndn and Cttee Mbr, Austl Musicians Guild, London, 1952; Fndn Mbr, Austl Musicians Guild, Melbourne, 1969; Fndn Mbr, Lieder Soc of Vic, 1976, VP, 1987, Artistic Dir, 1988-93; Vic Music Tchrs Assn, 1972- Inst of Music Tchrs, 1978-; Austl Natl Assn Tchrs of Singing, 1989-; 5 perfs in Beethoven's 1 Act Opera The Ruins of Athens. Hobbies: Art; Theatre; Languages; Tennis; Self-improvement. Address: 107 Leopold Street, South Yarra, Vic 3141, Australia.

TARLINTON Rachel Frances (Sister), b. 27 June 1925, Cobargo, NSW, Aust. Microbiologist. Education: Technologists, 1959; Fellshp, AIMLT, 1969; Fellshp, Australasian Coll of Biomed Scientists in Biomed Arts and Scis, 1976; Cert in Gen Nursing, 1950. Appointments: Nursing 1950-52, Dept of Path, Lewisham Hosp, West St Petersham, 1953-86, Med Technologist 1959-62, MT Microbiology, 1952-66, Chief Technologist, 1967-68, Microbiologist-in-Charge, 1966-80; Prin Microbiologist, 1980-86; Superior, Little Company of Mary, Calvary Hosp, ACT. Publications: Identity of a Disputed Haemophilus-like Organism in Non-specific Vaginalis (w D'Abrera), 1967; A Study of Haemophilus Vaginalis (thesis), 1969; Haemophilus Vaginalis - further investigations into its identity (w D'Abrera), 1974.

Honours: ABI Commemorative Medal of Hon, 1988; Hall of Fame, Amn Biographical Inst, 1989; Woman of the Yr 1990, ABI, 1990. Memberships: Fell, Austl Inst of Med Lab Scis; Fell, Australasian Coll of Biomed Scis. Hobbies: Reading; Music; Sport; Care of the aged and dying. Address: Little Company of Mary Sisters, 100/678 Victoria Road, Ryde, NSW 2112, Australia.

TATEMATSU Masae, b. 15 July 1946, Nagoya, Japan. Pathology. m. Keiko, 2 s, 1 d. Education: DMedSc, Nagoya Cty Univ, 1975. Appointments: Asst Prof, Nagoya Cty Univ Medl Sch, 1979; Chf, Dept of Pathol, Nagoya Cty, Higashi Gen Hosp, 1982; Chf, Lab of Pathol, Aichi Cancer Cntr Rsch Inst, 1990-. Publications: Atlas of Tumors Pathology of the Fischer Rat, 1990; Pathology of Neoplasia and Preneoplasia in Rodents, 1997. Honours: 1st Prize, 2nd Annual Residents and Fells Competition of Univ of Toronto, 1982; 5th Incitement Awd, Japan Cancer Assn, 1986. Memberships: Editl Bd Mbr: Japanese Jrnl of Cancer Rsch; Jrnl of Cancer Rsch and Clin Oncology; Gastric Cancer; Pathology Intl. Hobby: Trilobites collection. Address: Takemi-Cho 4-26-2, Mizuho-ku, Nagoya 467-0043, Japan.

TATSUOKA Yoshihisa, b. 7 Aug 1949, Kagoshima, Japan. Neurologist. m. Kyoko Morimune, 27 Mar 1977, 2 s. Education: Md, Osaka Medl Coll, 1976; PhD, Medl Sci, Kyoto Univ, 1985. Appointments: Kitano Hosp, 1976-79; Rsch Assoc, Fac of Med, Kyoto Univ, 1979-84; Kyoto Cty Rehab Cntr, 1984-85; Rsch Fell, Harvard Medl Sch, Massachusetts Gen Hosp, 1985-87; Chf, Dep Neur, Kyoto Cty Hosp, 1987-; Lectr, Fac of Med, Kyoto Univ, 1987-. Memberships: Japanese Soc of Neur; Japanese Soc of Internal Med; Japanese Diabetes Soc; Japanese Assn of Rehab Med. Hobbies: Photography; Golf; Amateur radio. Address: 289-5 Miyakecho Iwakura Sakyoku, Kyoto 600-0022, Japan.

TATTAMANGALAM   RAMACHANDRAN Padmanabhan, b. 26 Sept 1941. Engineer. m. Parvati, 1 s, 1 d. Education: MTech; PhD. Appointments: Asst Lectr, Lectr, Asst Prof, IIT Kharagpur, India; Asst Supt, Electrics Div, Tisco, India; Dpty GM (Rsch and Dev), Crompton Greaves, India; GM (Rsch and Dev), Premier Polytronics, India. Publication: Microprocessors and Digital Systems, 1983. Membership: Snr Mbr, IEEE; Fell, IE, India. Hobbies: Homeopathy; Indian classical music; Classical literature. Address: S-8 Mithila, Sathyamurthy Road, Ramnagar, Coimbatore 641009, India.

TAUCHI Hisashi, b. 13 Oct 1913, Gifu, Japan. President; Professor. m. Shinako Tanaka, 13 Oct 1942, 1 s. Education: MD, Nagoya Medl Coll; DMS, Nagoya Imperial Univ. Appointments: Asst Prof of Path, Nagoya Imperial Univ Sch of Med, 1943-44; Prof, Path, Nagoya Women's Med Coll, 1944-50; Prof, Path, Nagoya Cty Univ Med Sch, 1950-58; Prof, Path, Nagoya Univ Sch of Med, 1958-77; Dean, 1974-76; Prof Emer, 1977-, Nagoya Univ; Prof, Path, Aichi Med Univ, 1977-83; Prof, Inst for Med Sci of Aging, 1983-87, Chf, 1983-85; Pres, 1977-82, 1985-91, Aichi Med Univ; VP, Bd of Dirs, Aichi Ika Daigaku, 1982-89; Prof Emer, Guest Prof, Aichi Med Univ, 1991-. Publications: The Morphology of Ageing, 1980; Ageing of the Cells (w Y Kuroda), 1981; Contbr to about 40 books on gerontology and path and about 130 orig pprs in the medl field. Honours: Chunichi Prize, 1970; Baelz Prize w T Sato, 1973; Japan Med Assn Med Prize, 1983. Memberships: Hon Pres, Japan Lung Cancer Soc, 1992-, Pres, 1967-68; Hon Mbr, Japanese Pathol Soc, Pres, 1974-; Hon Mbr, Japan Geriatrics Soc, Pres, 1976-77; Hon Mbr, Japan Soc of Biomed Gerontology, Chmn, 1981; Japan Gerontological Soc, Pres, 1987-89; Chmn, Bd of Dirs, Assn Against Lung Cancer in Aichi Prefecture, 1979-; Editl Bd, Mechanisms of Ageing and Devel, 1972-82. Listed in: Who's Who in the World Address: 2-9 Yukimi-cho, Showa-ku, Nagoya, Japan.

TAUFA'AHAU Tupou IV (HM King of Tonga), b. 4 July 1918. m. HRH Princess Halaevalu Mata'aho, 1947, 3 s, 1 d. Education: Newington Coll; Sydney Univ; BA; LLB. Appointments: Min of Educ, 1943; Min of Hlth, 1944-49; Premier of Tonga, also Min of For Affairs and Agric, 1949-65; King of Tonga, 1965-; Estab Tchrs' Trng

Coll and revised Tonga alphabet, 1944; Chan, Univ S Pacific. Honours: Hon LLD; Kt Cmdr, Order of Merit, Germany, 1978; GCVO; GCMG; KBE; Num citations and awds. Address: The Palace, PO Box 6, Nuku'alofa, Tonga.

TAVAI Etuate Vugakoto, b. 20 Feb 1958, Lautoka, Fiji. Legal Practitioner. m. Iva, 30 Aug 1984, 2 d. Education: BL, Auckland Univ, NZ, 1981. Appointments: Min of State, PM's Off, 1992; Min for Info, Telecomms, 1995; Attourney Gen, 1996-99. Honours: Fiji Independence Medal. Memberships: Fiji Law Soc; Fiji Parly Assn. Address: Attourney Generals Office, Governement Buildings, Suva, Fiji Islands.

TAY Alice Erh-Soon, b. 2 Feb 1934, Singapore. Professor. m. Eugene Kamenka, 18 Dec 1964. Education: Bar-at-Law, Lincoln's Inn, London, Eng, 1956; Advocate, Sol, Supreme Crt of Singapore, 1957; PhD, Austl Natl Univ, 1965; Bar, Supreme Crt of NSW, Aust, 1966; Bar, Sol, Supreme Crt of Aust and ACT, 1971. Appointments: Advocate, Sol, David Marshall Law Firm, Singapore, 1957-58; Asst Lectr, Law, Univ of Malaya, Singapore, 1958-60; Rsch Schl, Law, Rsch Sch of Socl Scis, 1961-64; Snr Tutor, Lectr, Snr Lectr, Rdr, Fac of Law, Austl Natl Univ, 1966-75; Prof of Jurisprudence, Fac of Law, Univ of Sydney, 1975-; Pres, Human Rights and Equal Opportunities Commn, 1998-2003. Publications: Human Rights, 1978; Law and Society: The Crisis in Legal Ideals, 1978; Law and the Future of Society, 1978; Law Making in Australia, 1980; Justice, 1980; Law and Social Control, 1980, (all ed w Eugene Kamenka); Teaching Human Rights; An Australian Symposium, ed Human Rights for Australia, survey of lit and devels/selected and annotated bibliography of recent lit, Australia and Abroad, 1986; Law and Australian Legal Thinking in the 1980's, ed 1986; Law in China - Imperial, Republican, Communist, 1986; The Role of Law in the Twentieth Century: From Law to Laws to Social Science, 1990; Australian Law and Legal Thinking Between the Decades, ed 1990; Constitution-Making in the Former Communist World, 1992; Legal Persons and Legal Personality, 1994; Australian Law and Legal Thinking in the 1990's, 1994; Greater China - Law, Society and Trade, 1995. Honours: AM, 1985; Fell, Acady of Socl Scis in Aust, 1986; LLD h c, Univ of Edinburgh, 1989. Memberships: Acad, Intl Acady of Comparative Law, Paris; Pres, Intl Assn of Philos of Law & Socl Philos, 1987-. Address: Human Rights and Equal Opportunities Commission, 133 Castlereagh Street, Sydney, NSW 2000, Australia.

TAYAMA Yoshio, b. 16 July 1926. Chairman; Director. m. 18 Jan 1959, 1 s, 1 d. Education: BL, Univ of Tokyo. Appointments: Dir and Mngr of Fin, 1968, Mngng Dir, 1974, Snr Mngng Dir, 1980, Exec VP, 1983, Pres and Dir of the Bd, 1986, Chmn and Dir of the Bd, 1994-, Snr Advsr, 1998- Kyoei Life Ins Co Ltd; Dir, Oriental Life Ins Cultural Dev Cntr, 1991-; Mbr of Intl Bd, Bank Austria Aktiengesellschaft, 1992-. Publications: Auth of essays in sev mags and books. Honour: Blue Ribbon Medal, Japanese Govt, 1991. Memberships: Dir, Rsch Inst of Software Engrng Fndn, 1988-; Mbr, Intl Cncl, 1992-; Auditor, Japan Inst of Life Ins, 1994-; Vice Chmn, Life Ins Assn, 1991-94; Dir from Japan, Pacific Ins Conf, 1994-. Hobbies: Literature; Drama; Art. Address: 4-4-1 Hongoku-cho, Nihonbashi, Chuo-ku, Tokyo 103-0021, Japan.

TAYLOR Alan, b. 26 Nov 1938, Newcastle upon Tyne, Eng. Metallurgist. m. Joan, 25 May 1964, 5 d. Education: BSc Hons, Chem Engrng, Durham Univ, Eng, 1960. Publication: Technical Manuals for Extraction of Metals. Memberships: Austl Inst of Mining and Metall, Fell, 1980; Minerals Ind Cnslts Assn, 1985. Hobbies: Sport; Gardening; Films; Railway history/preservation. Address: 8 Rosen Street, Blackburn South, Vic, 3130, Australia.

TAYLOR Andrew McDonald, b. 19 Mar 1940, Warnambool, Aust. Professor; Writer. m. (1) 1 s, (2) Beate Josephi, 1980, 1 d. Education: BA, Hons, MA, Hons, LittD, Melbourne Univ. Appointments: Lectr, Snr Lectr, Assoc Prof, Engl, Univ of Adelaide, 1971-92; Prof of Engl, Edith Cowan Univ, WA, 1992. Publications: Reading Australian Poetry (crit), 1987; Selected Poems 1960-85, 1988; Folds in the Map (poems), 1991; Sandstone (poems), 1995; Honours: Regl Winner, C'wlth Poetry Prize, 1987; AM, 1990. Memberships: PEN Intl; Aust Soc of Auths. Hobbies: Travel; Gardening; Music. Address: Edith Cowan Univeristy, Mount Lawley, WA 6050, Australia.

TAYLOR David Kent, b. 25 May 1941, Malvern, Vic, Aust. Landscape Painter specializing in watercolour; Teacher. m. Brenda Marjorie Taylor, 29 Feb 1964, 1 s, 1 d. Education: Jnr Techl Cert, Caulfield Inst of Technol, 1956; Colour Etching Apprentice, 5 yrs; Cert of Proficiency, Photoengraving, Half-Tone Etching, 1965; Studied watercolour painting; Oil and Figure Drawing w Ian Armstrong, Natl Gall Art Sch, 1970. Appointments: Tchng; Lecturing, Waverley and Victorian Art Socs, 1970-; 15 solo shows, 1975-; incl: Adelaide, Canberra, Sydney, Melbourne, and Newcastle Aqueous Open w Pittsburgh Watercolour Soc, 1982, Watercolour Today, Aust, USA, 1983; Num grp exhibns incl: 10 Watercolourists Salute Victoria in London, 1985; Grp Exhibn, Adelaide, 1985; Austl Watercolour Inst Manyung, Melbourne, 1986; 14 Austl Painters, Canberra, Major Watercolour Exhibn, Canberra Playhouse Gall, 1986; Collectors Choice Exhibn, Von Bertouch Gall, Newcastle, NSW, 1986; 27 solo exhibns, 1975-; Further tours to Eng and Eur; Intl exhibns in Taiwan and UK; Represented, Repco Calendar, 1974, 1975, Austl Maritime Arts Calendar, 1988; Radio interviews; Tutor study tour, Greece, Egypt, 1988. Creative works include: Works in pub and priv collections, Aust, Eng, Singapore, Italy, S Africa, USA, Switz, Japan. Honours: Over 50 major awds in painting, 1975-; Artist of the Yr Bronze Medallion, Victorian Artists Soc, 1976, 1980; Watecolour Prize, Camberwell Rotary, 1977; Overseas Travel Study Grant, 1979; Camberwell Rotary Club; Vic Watercolour Prize, Royal Agricl Soc, NSW, 1982; Watercolour Prize, Vic Harbour, S Aust, 1986, 1988; Bollard Awd, 1 of 6 finalists, Austl Maritime Art Competition, 1987; Fell. Victorian Artists Soc, 1989; Disting Ldrshp Awdfor Outstndng Servs to Watercolour and Tchng; Cert of Merit, Community Serv. Memberships: Austl Watercolour Inst; Victorian Artists Soc; Twenty Melbourne Painters; Austl Guild of Realist Arstist; Austl branch, Old Engl Water Colour Soc Club, London. Hobbies: Communicating with fellow artists; Music; Singing; Reading; Outdoor activites; Travel; Challenging tasks; Painting in all media; Golf; Kayaking; Walking; Table-tennis; Swiming. Address: 170, One Tree Hill Road, Smith's Gully, Victoria 3760, Australia.

TAYLOR Gail, b. 21 June 1953, Eng. Education. Education: BA, Hons, Textile Des, Leeds Univ, Eng, 1974. Appointments: Full Time Rsch, 1974-77; Pt-time Postgrad Demonstrator, 1974-77; Pt-time Asst, 1974-79; Contbr to Textile Asia, 1974-82; Contbr to Textile Inst and Ind, 1975-79; Pt-time Lectr, 1977-78; Mngng Dir, 1977-79; Pt-time Lectr, 1978-79; Visng Prof, 1979-81; Contbr, Bobbin (SC), USA, 1979-82; Mkt Rschr, 1981-82; Fashion Ed, Textile Asia, 1982-; Lectr, 1982-84; Snr Lectr, 1984-90; Prin Lectr, 1990-93; Snr Lectr, 1993-95; Assoc Hd, Inst of Textiles and Clothing, Honk Kong Polytechnic, 1994-; Assoc Prof, 1995-; Cnsltng Prof, Beijing Inst of Clothing Techol, China, 1996-. Publications: Pprs on Fashion and Textiles, 1975-. Honours: Serv Medal, The Textile Inst, UK, 1998. Memberships: Hon Sect, Textile Inst, UK; Exec Cttee Mbr, Asst Hon Sect, Clothing and Footwear Inst, Hong Kong; Exect Cttee Mbr, Textile Inst Hong Kong Sect; Mbr, Hong Kong Instn of Textile and Apparel; Mbr, Textile Cttee, Amn Chmbr of Com, Hong Kong; Sect Gen, Fed of Asian Profl Textile Assocs; Chmn, Organising Cttee; Ed, Jrnl of Fed of Asian Profl Textile Assocs. Hobbies: Writing; Cycling; Squash; Travel. Address: Institute of Textile and Clothing, The Hong Kong Polytechnic, University of Huyng Hom Kowloon, Hong Kong.

TAYLOR Geoffrey Ian, b. 25 Sept 1938, Melbourne, Aust. Plastic Surgeon. m. Claudette, 21 Dec 1963, 2 s, 1 d. Education: MBBS, 1963, MD, 1991, Melbourne Univ; FRACS, 1968; FRCS(Eng), 1970; Hon Dr Causa, 1991; FRCS(Ed), 1993; FACS(Hon), 1997. Appointments: Assoc Plastic Surg, Univ of Melbourne, 1975-; Snr, Cnslt Plastic Surg, Preston and Northcote Cmnty Hosp, 1975-; Hon Cnsltng Plastic Surg, Roy Children's Hosp, 1986-; Professorial Assoc, Univ of Melbourne, 1989-; Hd, Plastic Surg Unit, Roy Melbourne Hosp, 1992-; Snr Assoc, Dept of Anatomy, Univ of Melbourne, 1992-; Prof, Plastic Surg, Dept of Surg, Roy Melbourne Hosp, Univ of Melbourne, 1996-. Publications: 107, as auth, co-auth, in profl jrnls, book chapts. Honours include: Mowlem Awd of 1986, James Barrett Brown Prize, 1989, 1995; Hon Awd, Amn Assn Plastic Surgs, 1990; Johann Friedrich Dieffenbach Awd, 1992; Chinese/Japanese Cong of Plastic Surg, 1996; 5 1st Prizes in Snr Div, Basic Sci Category of Educl Fndn, Amn Soc of Plastic and Reconstructive Surgeons, Schlshp Essay Contest, the most recent in 1997. Memberships: Pres, Melburnia Rowing Club, 1988-93; Pres, Intl Soc of Reconstructive Microsurgery, 1988-91; Snr Corresp Mbr, Amn Soc of Plastic and Reconstructive Surgeons; Amn Assn of Plastic Surgeons; Brit Assn of Plastic Surgeons; Hon Mbr, Canad Soc of Plastic and Reconstructive Surgeons; Hon Mbr, NZ Soc of Plastic and Reconstructive Surgeons; Corresp Mbr, Japanese Soc of Plastic and Reconstructive Surgeons; Soc of Hd and Neck Surgeons of Am; Assn of Plastic Surgeons of S Africa. Hobbies: Photography (wildlife); Fly fishing; Rowing. Address: 7th Floor, 766 Elizabeth Street, Melbourne, Australia.

TAYLOR Gregory Lawton, b. 19 Oct 1926, Culcairn, NSW, Aust. Teacher. m. Patricia Anne Williams, 18 Mar 1989, 2 s, 3 d. Education: Tchng Ctf, Sydney Tchrs Coll, 1945; BA, Sydney Univ, 1951; Elected Mbr, Austl Coll of Educ, 1980. Appointments: Maths/Sci Tchng, Randwick, Ashfield, Bondi, S Sydney and Paddington hs, 1946-60; Prin, Bondi-Waverley Evening Coll, 1954-89; Hdmaster: Botany Sch, 1961-65, Randwick Sch, 1966-86; Mbr, 1979-84, Literacy Cnslt, 1989, NSW Bd of Adult Educ; Mbr Austl Delegation UNICEF Exec Bd, Manila, Philippines, 1977, UN, NY, 1980, 1981; Represented Aust at many intl confs, fetivals and seminars; UNICEF Educ Cnslt, Phnom Phen Kampuchea, 1982. Publications: Auth/Ed/Publr, Australian International Year of the Child-Newsletter, 1977-80; Compiler/Publr, A Reference History - Presbyterian Church - Mittagong, Bowral-Mittagong, 1868-93; Auth/Ed/Publr, The Taylors - A Directory, 1996; The Lawtons - A Directory, 1997. Honours: Appointed JP, 1952; Queen's Jubilee Medal, 1977; Intl Yr of the Child Medal, 1979; Medal, OAM, 1980, Mbr, AM, 1987, AM; Kt, Polish Order of Smile, 1981. Memberships: NSW Tchrs Fedn, 1944-; Fndn Mbr, NSW Chapt, Austl Cncl of Educl Admin; Evening Coll Prins Assn; Mbr, NSW Cncl on Christian Educ in Schs, 1953-1978; Fndng Mbr and Treas, NSW Primary Prin's Cncl; Past Pres, Rotary Club of Randwick, 1975-76; Presbytery of Sydney, Presby Ch, NSW, Moderator, 1978-79, 1987-88; Cmnty Welfare Advsry Cncl, 1974-94; Life Mbr, UNICEF Cttee of Aust, Pres, 1973-77; Cnclr Austl Cncl for Overseas Aid, 1971-94; AUSTCARE Mngmt Cttee, 1972-92; Chmn, Austl Intl Disaster Cttee, 1978-95; Dist Gov, Rotary Intl Dist, 975, 1983-84; Chmn, Austl Intl Yr of the Child NGO Cttee, 1978-82; Chmn, Bot Cemetary and East Suburbs Crematorium Trusts, 1989-; Dpty Chmn, Bd of the Scottish Hosp, 1989-95; Session Clk, Randwick Presby Ch, 1962-67, Bowral Mittagong Presby Ch, 1991-; Offl Visitor, Juv Jus Cntrs, 1989-93, Goulburn Correctional Cntr, 1993-. Hobbies: Long distance walking; Swimming. Address: Tree Haven, 10 Badgery Street, Willow Vale, NSW 2575, Australia.

TAYLOR Jennifer Evelyn, b. 12 Apr 1935, Sydney, Aust. University Lecturer in Architecture. Education: BArch, 1967, MArch, 1969, Univ of Wash. Appointments include: Lectr, 1972-79, Snr Lectr, 1980-82, Assoc Prof, 1983-98, Dept of Arch, Univ of Sydney; Adj Prof, Qld Univ of Technol, 1998-; Visng Fac, Visng Schl, Univ of Fine Arts, Univ of PA, Phila, Feb-May, 1990; Visng Prof, Dept of Arch, Coll of Environ Des, Univ CA, Berkeley Campus, Spring, 1991; Visng Prof, Dept of Arch, Univ of Washington, Fall, 1993; Visng Prof, Univ of Arch, Ho Chi Minh Cty, Vietnam, 1994; Visng Prof, UNITEC, Auckland, NZ, 1997; Visng Prof, Queensland Univ of Technol, 1997. Publications: Books incl: Appropriate Architecture: Ken

Wolley, RA, IA, 1985; Australian Architecture Since 1960, 1986, 1990; Contbns to archtl wrks incl: Oceania: Australia, New Zealand, Papua New Guinea and the smaller islands of the South Pacific, in Banister Fletcher, History of Architecture, 1987, 1995; "Australia" Encyclopaedia of Twentieth Century Architecture. Creative works: Archtl des: The Bungalow, Hunters Hill, 1978-80; Beach House at Palm Beach, 1983-87; House at Stradbroke Island, 1997-98. Honours: Japan Fndn Profl Fellshp, 1975; Visual Arts Bd, Aust Cncl Grant, 1980-81; Univ of VA, Pan Pcific Exchange Fellshp, 1991; Univ of Sydney Rsch Grant, 1993; Japan Fndn Fellshp, 1994-95; CHASA Archtl Des Citation, House at Palm Beach, 1994; Inaugural Marion Mahony Griffin Awd, 1998; Hon Mention via Jean Tschumi Prize, 1999. Grants, 1995, 1996. Memberships include: Fell, Roy Austl Inst of Archts; Fell, Rsch Inst for Asia and the Pacific; Fndng Mbr, Asian Arts Soc of Aust; Regd, Bd of Archts of NSW; Intl Cttee, Archtl Critics; Intl Cncl on Monuments and Sites; Art Assn of Aust; Arch Soc. Address: School of Architecture, Interior and Industrial Design, Queensland University of Technology, Gardens Point Campus, Brisbane, Queensland 4000, Australia.

TAYLOR Jillian Annette, b. 10 Mar 1952, Sydney, NSW, Aust. Teacher; Educational Consultant; Managing Director. 2 d. Education: BA Dip Ed. Appointment: MD, Intext Book Co, 1982. Memberships: AFMLTA; MLTAV; JLTAV; VECCI; APA; ABA; AGTV; AFTV; VILTA; VATI; Ed, Japanese Lang Tchrs Assn Vic Inc Newsletter. Hobbies: Singing; Scuba; Gardening; Wine. Address: 825 Glenferrie Road, Hawthorn, Vic 3122, Australia.

TAYLOR Keith Francis, b. 11 May 1932, Ilford, Eng. University Teacher; Occupational Psychologist. m. Susan Mary Swift, 10 Aug 1963, 1 s, 1 d. Education: Dip, Socl Studies, Leicester Univ, 1952; BA, Hons, Psychol, Manchester Univ, 1957; MA, Psychol, London Univ, 1960; PhD, Psychol, Melbourne Univ, Aust, 1975. Appointments: Rsch Wrkr, Univ of Leicester, 1960-63; Snr Lectr Psychol, Univ of Melbourne, 1964-90; Visng Rsch Assoc, Johns Hopkins Univ, USA, 1970; Prin Psychol, Civ Serv Dept, London, 1971, 1975; Natl Dir, Austrl Psychol Soc, 1979-82; Assoc Prof, Mngt, Natl Univ of Singapore, 1984-87; Rdr, Bus and Mngmt, Cty Polytech of Hong Kong, 1991-94; Prof, Bus and Mgt, Cty Univ of Hong Kong, 1995-97. Publications: Holland in Australia; A Vocational Choice Theory in Research and Practice, 1986; Co-ed, 40 articles in profl jrnls; book chapts, 1961-. Memberships: Fell, Brit Psychol Soc; Fell, Austl Psychol Soc. Hobbies: Reading; Collecting and drinking Australian wines; Gardening; Watching cricket and football. Address: 1 Torrington Place, Canterbury, Victoria, 3126, Australia.

TAYLOR Luke, b. 11 Mar 1958, Sydney, Aust. Museum Curator. m. Maureen, 2 s. Education: BA, Hons, 1st Class Anthropology, Austl Natl Univ, 1979; PhD, Anthropology, Austl Natl Univ, 1987. Appointments: Visng Rsch Fell, Austl Inst of Aboriginal Studies, Canberra, 1987-89; Curator, Natl Mus of Aust, Canberra, 1990-92; Snr Curator, NMA, 1992-. Publications: Marketing Aboriginal Art in the 1990s. Address: Main Street, Michelago, NSW 2620, Australia.

TAYLOR Michael Robert, b. 26 May 1946, Epsom, Surrey, Eng. Banker. m. Lucille, 6 July 1968, 1 d. Education: LLB, Univ Coll, London, Eng. Appointments: Barton Mayhew & Co, 1968-72; Charterhouse Japhet, 1972-75; Chase Manhattan Bank, 1975-. Memberships: FCA (Fell, Inst of Chartered Accts in Eng and Wales). Hobbies: Current affairs; Reading; Golf; Skiing; Tennis. Address: Chase Manhattan Bank, Seoul Branch, 34-35 Chung-Dong, Choong-Ku, Seoul, Korea.

TAYLOR Richard Edward, b. 2 Nov 1929, Medicine Hat, Alberta, Can. Physicist; Educator. m. Rita Jean Bonneau, 25 Aug 1951, 1 s. Education: BS, Univ of Alta, 1950; MA, 1952; PhD, Stanford Univ, 1962; Docteur Honoris Causa, Univ of Paris, 1980; DSc, Univ Alta, 1991; LLD, Univ Calgary, Alta, 1993; DSc, Univ Lethbridge, Alta, 1993; Univ of Vic, BC, Canada, 1994; Docteur H C, Univ of Blaise Pascal, 1997. Hons: WKH Panofsky Prize Div; Nobel Prize in Phys, 1990. Memberships: Fell, Guggenheim Fndn, 1971-72; vonHumboldt Fndn, 1982; AAAS; Amn Acady Arts and Scis; Amn Phys Soc; Roy Soc Canada; Roy Soc of London; Canadia Assn Physicists; Natl Acady Scis. Address: SLAC, PO Box 4349, MS 96, Stanford, CA 94309, USA.

TAYLOR Roger Ralph, b. 27 May 1935, Tenterfield, NSW, Aust. Cardiologist. m. Lorraine, 29 July 1961, 2 s, 1 d. Education: MB; BS; FRACP. Appointments: Rsch Fell, Natl Heart Fndn Aust in Lab of Cardiovascular Physiol, Natl Heart Inst, Bethseda, MD, USA, 1965-67; Noel Bevan Rdr (Assoc Prof), Cardiol and Cardiovascular Rsch Univ of WA), 1968-74; Prof of Cardiol, Univ of West Aust and Roy Perth Hosp, 1974-; Hd and Chmn, Dept of Cardiol, Roy Perth Hosp, 1993-96. Publications: On Cardiovascular Physiology, Pathophysiology and Clinical Cardiology. Honour: RT Hall Prize, Cardiac Soc of Aust and NZ, 1974. Memberships: Roy Austl Coll of Physns; Cardiac Soc of Aust and NZ; Intl Soc for Heart Rsch; Austl Arteriosclerosis Soc. Hobbies: Fishing; Swimming; Gardening. Address: 40 Buntine Road, Wembley Downs, Western Australia 6014, Australia.

TAYLOR Roy Frances Le Cappelaine, b. 28 Nov 1931, Aust. Ophthalmic Surgeon. m. 21 Jan 1959, 2 s, 2 d. Education: MB, BS, Sydney, 1957; FRCS, 1965; FRACS, 1967; FRACO, 1978. Appointment: Hd, Ophthalmology, Roy Prince Alfred Hosp, Sydney; Currently, Area Dir of Ophthalmology, Central Sydney Hlth Serv. Publications: Var articles in profl jrnls, inclng, Austl Med Jrnl, Brit Jrnl of Ophthalmology. Memberships: Fell, Roy Coll of Surgeons; Roy Austl Coll of Ophthalmologists; Chmn, Med Bd, Roy Prince Alfred Hosp, 1991-93. Hobbies: Cattle breeding; Tennis; Reading. Address: 82 Elizabeth Street, Sydney, NSW 2000, Australia.

TAYLOR Susan Virginia, b. 18 Sept 1946, Perth, Aust. Paralegal; Business Proprietor; Sports Administrator. Education: Dip of Legal Stdies; Master degree, Intl Sports Law, in progress. Appointments: Lectr, Sports Law and Sports Admin, 1993-. Honour: AM, 1999. Memberships: VP, Austl C'Wealth Games Assn, 1998-; Pres, All Aust Netball Assn, 1995-; Chmn, Bd of Dirs, AANA, 1995-; Chmn, Bd of Natl Netball League Pty Ltd, 1995-; Deleg, Intl Fedn of Netball Assns, 1989-; Exec Mbr, Asian Fedn of Netball Assns, 1995-; Serv Awd Holder, AANA; Life Mbr, Westn Austl Netball Assn; Bd Mbr, Austl Sports Cntr Trust, 1993-; Austl and NZ Sports Law Assn, 1991-; Natl Sports Law Assn, 1999. Hobbies: Gardening; Reading; Craftwork; Lecturing in sports law. Address: PO Box 91, South Perth, WA 6151, Australia.

TE HEUHEU Georgina M. Government Minister. m. 2 s. Appointments: Served, Waitangi Tribunal and sev other statutory bds; Dir, Midland Regl Hlth Authy; Maori Dev Corp; Mus of NZ; Lawyer; Elected to Parl, 1996; Min of Crts, Min of Women's Affairs, Assoc Min in Charge of Treaty of Waitangi Negotiations, Assoc Min of Hlth, Chair, Maori Affairs Select Cttee. Address: PO Box 949, Taupo, New Zealand.

TE KANAWA Kiri (Dame), b. 6 Mar 1944, Gisborne, NZ. Singer (Soprano). m. Desmond Park, 1967, div, 1997, 2 children. Education: St Mary's Coll, Auckland; London Opera Cntr. Appointments: Debut, Roy Opera Covent Garden, 1970; La Scala, Milan, debut 1978; Sang at Salzburg Fest in 1979, w San Fran Opera Co in 1980, and at Edinburgh and Helsinki Fests, 1980; Operas incl: Boris Godunov; Parsifal; The Marriage of Figaro; Otello; Simon Boccanegra; Carmen; Don Giovanni (also film vern 1979); Faust; The Magic Flute; La Bohème (5 times); Eugene Onegin; Cosi Fan Tutte; Arabella; Die Fledermaus; La Traviata; Der Rosenkavalier; Manon Lescaut; Sang at the wedding of HRH The Prince of Wales, London, 1981; Sang the Countess in Capriccio at San Fran, 1990, and Covent Garden; Sang the premiere of Paul McCartney's Liverpool Oratorio, at Liverpool Cath and in London, 1991; Sang Amelia in new prodn of Simon Boccanegra at Covent Garden, 1991; Season 1992 w Mozart's Countess at Metrop, and Desdemona at Covent Garden. Creative works: Recordings incl: Elvira in Don Giovanni; Fiordiligi in Cosi Fan Tutte; Otello; Micaela in Carmen; Mozart Vespers and C Minor Mass; Pamina in The Magic Flute; The Marriage of Figaro; Hansel and Gretel; Strauss' Songs with Orchestra; Die Fledermaus; Woodbird in Siegfried; Recitals records. Honours: OBE; DBE; ONZ, 1995; Hon Degs, Oxford, Cambridge, Dundee, Nottingham, Auckland, Durham Univs and Post Univ in USA. Address: c/o Jules Haefliger, Impressario AG, Postfach 3320, CH-6002 Lucerne, Switzerland.

TEAGUE Bernard George, b. 16 Feb 1938, Melbourne. Judge. m. Patrice Connolly, 19 Jan 1963, 4 s, 3 d. Education: BA; Univ of Melbourne, 1956-60; LLB, 1956-60. Appointments: Ptnr, Corr and Corr, 1963-87; Chmn, Austl Legal Conv, 1985; Judge, Supreme Crt of Vic, Melbourne, 1987-; Dpty Chmn, Vic Parole Bd, 1991-; Chairperson, Vic Forensic Leave Panel, 1998-. Memberships: Law Inst of Vic; C'wlth Lawyers Assn; Vic Law Fndn; Law Cncl; Austl Inst Jud Admin; Intl Bar Assn; Law Soc NSW. Hobbies: Tennis; Computers. Address: 14 Callantina Rd, Hawthorn, VIC 3122, Australia.

TEAKLE David Sydney, b. 1 Feb 1932. Plant Pathologist. m. Kathryn Yarwood, 29 Jan 1961, 3 s, 1 d. Education: MAgrSc; PhD. Appointments: Qld Dept of Primary Inds, 1954-66; Univ Qld, 1966-94. Publications: Over l00 rsch pprs in sci jrnls. Honours: Fulbright Awd, 1959; Miller Fellshp, 1962-63; Humboldt Fellshp, 1972-73. Memberships: Australasian Plant Pathol Soc; Amn Phytopathol Soc; Austl Soc for Microbiol. Hobby: Music. Address: 42 Clarence Road, Indooroopilly, Qld 4068, Australia.

TEANNAKI Teatao. Politician. Appointments: Fmr VP of Kiribati; Pres of Kiribati, 1991-94. Memberships: Mbr Parl for Abiang. Address: c/o Office of the President, Tarawa, Kiribati.

TEDESCHI Mark, b. 31 Mar 1952, Sydney, Aust. Education: LLB, 1974; MA, Bus Law, 1975. Appointments: Lectr, Law, Cty London Polytech, Eng, 1974-75; Lectr, Law, Kuring-Gai Coll Advd Educ, Aust, 1975-77; Bar -at-Law, 1977-83; Crown Prosecutor, 1983-; QC, 1988-; Snr Crown Prosecutor for NSW, 1997-; Pres Austl Assn of Crown Prosecutors. Publications; The Law of International Business in Australia, 1980; Var articles on bus law, environ law, photog. Hobbies: Photography; Bushwalking; Gardening. Address: 265 Castlereagh Street, Sydney, New South Wales, 2000 Australia.

TEH Hong Piow, b. 14 Mar 1930, Singapore. Banker. m. Puan Sri Datin Tay Sock Noy, 8 Feb 1956, 1 s, 3 d. Appointments; Bank Offr, Overseas-Chinese Banking Corp Ltd, Singapore, 1950-60; Mngr, 1960-64, Gen Mngr, 1964-66, Malayan Banking Berhad; Mng Dir, Grp Chf Exec Offr, Public Bank, Berhad, 1966-78; Chmn/Grp Chf Exec Offr, Pub Bank Berhad, 1978-86; Pres/Grp Chf Exec Offr, Pub Bank Berhad, 1986-; Pres Chf Exec Offr, Pub Bank Berhad Malaysia Grp; Chmn: Pub Fndn, Malaysia; London & Pacific Insurance Co, Berhad; Dir, Asean Fin Corp Ltd, Singapore; Chmn, Tong Meng Inds Ltd, Singapore; Chmn, Pub Securities Ltd, Singapore (Grp); Cncl Mbr, Inst Bank-Bank, Malaysia. Honours: From the Sultan of Pahang: Datuk Kurnia Sentosa, 1966; JP, 1967; Darjah Sultan Ahmad Shah Pahang, 1978; Sri Indera Mahkota Pahang 1st Class Awd, 1983; From the Sultan of Johore: Dato Paduka Mahkota Johore, 1973; Dato Sri Paduka Mahkota Johore, 1974; Dato Seri Setia Sultan Ismail Johore, 1978; From His Majesty, the Yang DiPertuan Agung: Panglima Setia Mahkota, 1983; Hon LLD (Mal), Univ Malaya, 1989. Memberships: Fndr Mbr, Bankers Club; Life Mbr, Royal Selangor Club; Kelab Golf DiRaja Selangor; Kelab Taman Perdana DiRaja; Kelab Shah Alam Selangor; Penang Turf Club; Selangor Shooting Assn; Individual Mbr, Ayer Keroh Country Club; Appointed Cttee, The Selangor and Kuala Lumpur Teo Chew Assn; Hon Pres: Eng Yong Tong Tay Si Assn Muar, Johore; Teh Si Eong Tong, Penang; Tung Shin Hosp; Cncl Mbr, Assn Banks, Malaysia, 1986-; Mbr Natl Trust Fund Panel, Malaysia, 1988-; Cncl Mbr, Inst of Bankers, Malaysia, 1990. Hobbies: Photography; Reading. Address: Menara Public Bank, 146 Jalan

Ampang, 50450 Kuala Lumpur, Malaysia.

TEHRANIAN Majid, b. 22 Mar 1937, Iran. Director, Toda Institute. m. Katherine Kia, 2 s, 2 d. Education: BA, Govt, Dartmouth Coll, 1959; MA, Mid East Studies, 1961, PhD, Polit Econ & Govt, 1969, Harvard Univ. Appointments include: Asst Prof, Econs, Lesley Coll, 1964-69; Assoc Prof, Pol Sci, New Coll, Univ S FL, 1969-71; Snr Analyst & Dir of Rsch, Indl Mngmt Inst, 1972-74; Prof, Fndng Dir, Iran Comms & Dev Inst, 1976-78; Visng Fell, St Antony's Coll, Oxford Univ, 1978-79; Prog Spec, Comm, Plng & Studies, UNESCO, Paris, 1979-80; Visng Schl, Cntr for Intl Affairs, MIT, 1980-81; Fell, Comm Inst, E-W Cntr, 1981-82, 1988-89; Visng Prof, Dept of Govt, Summer Sch, Harvard Univ; Rsch Fell, Socl Sci Rsch Inst, 1982-83, 1984-86, Chair, Dept of Comms, 1986-88, Dir, Spark M Matsunaga Inst for Peace, 1990-92, UHM; Exchange Prof, Div of Mass Comms, Emerson Coll, 1994-96; Snr Fell, Cntr for study of world religions, Harvard Univ, 1994-95; Adj Prof, Intl Pols, Fletcher Sch of Law & Diplomacy, Tufts Univ, 1994-96; Rsch Affiliate, Cntr for Intl Affairs, Harvard Univ, 1994-96; Visng Prof, Imam Sadeq Univ, Tehran, Iran, 1996-. Publications: 19 books & monographs; Over 30 chapts in books & yearbooks; Over 50 jrnls; Over 15 op-ed articles; Over 20 book reviews; Wrk translated into 13 langs. Honours: Fellshps, grants and awds incl: Rsch Affiliate, Cntr for Intl Affairs & Prog on Info Resources Policy, Harvard Univ, 1994-. Memberships include: Intl Inst of Comms; Intl Comm Assn; Intl Peace Rsch Assn. Hobbies: Swimming; Tennis; Running; Chess; Poetry. Address: 2627 Manoa Road, Honolulu, HI 96822, USA.

TELFER Barbara Jane, b. 13 Aug 1945, Wellington, NZ. Author. m. Maxwell, 14 Mar 1970, 2 d. Education: NZ Sch Dental Nurse Cert, 1965. Publications: The Great New Zealand Puzzle Book, 1987; The Great International Puzzle Book, 1988; The Great Crafty Ideas Book, 1988; A Book of Australian Puzzles, 1988; A Great Number Puzzle Book, 1990; Summertime Puzzles, 1992; Astro Puzzles, 1992; World of Puzzles, 1992; Mystery Word Puzzles (3), 1993; The Windsor St Mystery, 1993; The Great Christmas Activity Book, 1993; The Great Junior Puzzle Book, 1994; The 2nd Great Number Puzzle Book, 1994; The Zoo Mystery, 1994; The Greenhouse Mystery, 1994; Barbara Telfer's Paper Fun, 1995; Craft pages in Jabberwocky Magazine, Kiwi Kids. Hobbies: Bridge; Bowls; Embroidery; Reading. Address: 4/96 Elliot Street, Howick, Auckland, New Zealand.

TELFER Josephine Margaret, b. 28 Nov 1940, Kangaroo Is, S Aust, Aust. Painter; Sculptor. m. 1 s, 1 d. Education: Dip in Art and Des (painting, sculpture), Chisholm Inst of Technol; Stdy visits, schs and galls, USA, 1978, 1980; Holmsglen Coll of TAFE 1984, Austl Print Wrkshp, 1994, NY Drawing Marathon, Adelaide, 1995; Electric Des and Multimedia. Western Coll of TAFE, 1997; La Trobe St Gall Sch of Arts and Des. Appointments: Artist-in-Res, Caulfield Grammar Sch, 1982; Artist-in-Res, Korowa Anglican Girls Sch, Aust, 1985; Exhibited in grp shows, Melbourne, Adelaide and Sydney; Developed Austl bus and represented in Dept of Tourism, Osaka, Jpan, 1986-87; Key merchandise in Victorian Pavilion Expo 88 Brisbane 1988; Solo exhibns at Caulfield Arts Cntr, Melbourne, 1995; St John's Southgate, Melbourne, 1997; Melbourne Arts Club, 1998; Band Hall Gall, Kyneton, 1999; Young Artists Schs, 1995; Org, Travellers' Aid Exhbn for People w Disabilities, 1997. Creative works incl: Stage sets for Born Lucky theat prodn, 1982; Community sculpture from Broome (WA) Centenary, 1983; Mural for Potters House Restaurant, Melbourne, 1984. Publications: Australian Religious Diary, 1994, 1995, 1997; 1999; The Islander, 1996; Headway Victoria, 1997. Memberships: Women's Art Register, Vic; Natl Assn for the Visual Arts. Hobbies: Bushwalking; Camping; Concerts. Address: 108 Danks Street, Albert Park, Vic 3206, Australia.

TELFER Ross Alexander, b. 17 Sept 1937, Newcastle, NSW, Aust. University Professor. m. Bronwyn Edwards, 9 Jan 1960, 3 d. Education: Tchr's Cert, Newcastle Tchrs' Coll, NSW, 1956; BA, Univ of NSW, 1964; Dip in Educl Admin, 1968, Master Educl Admin

(Hons), Univ of New Eng, 1972; PhD, Univ of Newcastle, 1977. Appointments: Tchr and Subj Hd, NSW Dept of Educ, 1957-70; Lectr, Newcastle Coll of Advd Educ, 1972-75; Lectr in Educ, 1976-78, Snr Lectr in Educ, 1978-84, Prof and Hd, Dept of Educ, 1985-93, Dir, Inst of Aviation, 1987-93, Mngng Dir, Instrnl Rsch and Dev, 1994-, Univ of Newcastle. Publications: Auth/co-auth of 7 books inclng How to Sail Small Boats, 1968, 3rd ed, 1976; Teacher Tactics, 1975; Process of Learning, 1981, 2nd ed, 1987; Australian Sailing, 1984; Psychology and Flight Training, 1987; Aviation Instruction and Training, 1993; Aviation Training, 1997; Over 70 published profl articles. Honours: NSW Pub Serv Bd Fell, 1971; Emer Prof, 1994. Membership: Austl Aviation Psych Assn; Austl Cncl for Educl Admnstrs. Hobbies: Sailing; Golf; Jogging and fun runs. Address: 3/105 Brighton Avenue, Toronto, NSW 2238, Australia.

TEMIZEL Zekeriya. Government Official. Appointment: Min Fin, Govt of Turkey, Ankara, 1997-. Address: Maliye Bakanlige, Dikmen Cad Ankara, Turkey.

TEMKO Florence. Author. Appointments: Writer. Creative Works: Tradl Crafts Series of Six Books; Origami Favorites Series; Paper Magic Series; Origami Magic; Paper Pandas and Jumping Frogs; Ors. Memberships: Auths Guild; Amn Soc of Jrnlsts and Auths; San Diego Press Club; Origami USA. Address: 5050 La Jolla Blvd, Ste P-C, San Diego, CA 92109, USA.

TENNANT Brian George, b. 10 Apr 1935. Retired. Career: Human rights and social law reform campaigner; Through extensive lobbying of State and Fedl Govts has assisted in achieving spec benefits for those in custody awaiting trial, postal votes for remand prisoners, defendents costs in magistrate's crts, improvements in conditions in State prisons for remand prisoners, improvements in East Perth lock-up for prisoners and visitors, video and audio tapes of record of interview for suspects of serious crime, Freedom of Info Act, Spot Fines under the Dog Act, Optional photograph and five yr driving licences, concessional fares for unemployed, the wiping out of old criminal convictions after 10 yrs, all yr sittings of District and Supreme Crts, JPs listed in Yellow Pages for easy ref; Defender of rights of accused in criminal cases. Honour: JP. Memberships: Life Mbr, Cncl for Civil Liberties WA; Fedl Life Mbr, Austl Liquor Hospitality and Misc Worker Union; Mbr, Austl Crime Prevention Cncl (WA Branch). Address: Subiaco.

TENORIO Froilan. Government Official. Gov, 1994-. Government Headquarters, Caller Box 10007, Capitol Hill, Saipan MP 96950, Northern Mariana Islands.

TENORIO Norman, b. 28 July 1951. Business Executive. m. Keli Aiken, 14 Feb 1981, 2 s, 3 d. Education: BSc, Bus Admin; Profl Real Estate Appraiser (PRRA). Appointment: Vice Chmn, Mariana Is Housing Authy. Honour: Cert for Precision Truck Selling Course II, Truck Mktng Inst, 1997. Memberships: Senator, 5th Northern Mariana Is Dist Legislature, 1977; Pres, Saipan Chmbr of Comm, 1985; Rep, Intl Game Fish Assn; Amn Soc of Profl Appraisers. Hobbies: Golf; Fishing; Water sports. Address: PO Box 168 Saipan, Commonwealth of the Northern Mariana Islands 96950, Pacific Islands.

TENTOA Tewardka. Government Official. Appointment: VP, Govt of Kiribati, Tawara Atoll. Address: Ministry of Home Affairs and Rural Development, PO Box 75, Bairiki Tarawa Atoll, Kiribati.

TEPLIZKY Benjamin, b. 1933, Santiago, Chile. Minister of Mining. m. 3 children, Education: Deg in Law, Univ of Chile; Postgrad, Univ Salamanca Cumpultense, Madrid, Spain. Address: Lawyer, Prof, Univ Chile, 1961-73; Visng Prof, Hebrew Univ, Israel, 1976; Pres, Polit Commn, Exile in Italy, 1982-90; Supt, Socl Security, Govt of Chile, 1990; Min, Mining, 1994-. Memberships: Fndng Dir, Natl Ind Cement, 1970-73; Dir, Natl TV, 1971; Advsr, Natl Org Hydrocarbons, Intl Free Univ Socl Scis, Rome, 1986-89; Prof, Law Jrnlsm, Republic Univ, 1988-; Hd, Socl Div, Inst Provisional Normalization, 1991-93; Regl Advsr, Met Reg, 1993-94; Coll Lawyers, Madrid.

Address: Teatinos 120 Piso 9, Casilla 54 Correo 21, Santiago, Chile.

TERESHCHENKO Sergey Alexandrovich, b. 30 Mar 1961 Chimkent Reg. Politician. Education: Alma-Ata Inst of Agric. Appointments: Held offs in state power orgs of Chimkent Reg, 1986-89; Chmn of the Exec Cttee of Chimkent Reg, 1990-91; First Dep-Chmn Cncl of Mins of Kazakh Soviet Repub, 1989-90; VP of Kazakhstan, Apr-May 1991; PM of Kazakhstan, 1991-94; Amb at large min of For Affairs, 1994-95; Wrks as bus consultant. Address: Parliament Building, pl Respubliki, 1480091 Almaty, Kazakhstan.

TERRILL Ross, b. Melbourne, Aust. Research Associate. Education: BA, 1st class hons, Univ Melbourne, 1962; PhD, Polit Sci, Harv Univ, 1970. Appointments: Austl Army, 1957-58; Tutor, Polit Sci, Univ of Melbourne, 1962-63; Staff Sec, Austl Stud Christian Movement, 1962, 1964-65; Tchng Fell, 1968-70, Lectr on Govt, 1970-74, Harv Univ; Contbng Ed, Atlantic Monthly, 1970-84; Rsch Fell, Asia Soc, 1978-79; Dir, Stud Progs in Intl Affairs, 1974-77, Assoc Prof of Govt, 1974-78, Harv Univ; Visng Prof, Monash Univ, 1996, 1997, 1998; Visng Prof, Univ of TX at Austin, 1998, 1999; Rsch Assoc, Fairbank Cntr for E Asian Rsch, Harvard Univ, 1970-. Publications include: Mao: A Biography, 1980, 1999; The White-Boned Demon: A Biography of Madame Mao Zedong, 1984, 1999; The Australians, 1987; China in Our Time, 1992. Honours: Frank Knox Meml Fellshp, Harvard Univ, 1965, 1966; Natl Mag Awd, Reporting Ex, 1972; George Polk Meml Awd, Outstndng Mag Reporting, 1972. Address: 200 Saint Botolph Street, Boston, MA 02115, USA.

TERUTUNG Hendra, b. 28 July 1960, Jakarta. Entrepeneur. m. Gwenda, 8 Nov 1992, 1 d. Education: BSME (Bachelor of Sci in Mechl Engr, 1986, MSME, 1989, Tuskegee Univ, AL, USA. Appointments: Rsch Asst, Material Sci Lab, Sch of Engrng, Tuskagee Univ, 1983-87; Rsch Assoc, Carver Rsch Fndn, Tuskgee, AL, 1987-90; Sales Mngr, Atlas Asia Pacific, Indonesia, 1990-96; Pres Dir, Mekanik Automotive Mag, Jakarta, 1994-96; Pres Dir, PT Bima Terensa Perkasa, Jakarta, 1994-. Honours: Sigma Xi; Pi Tau Sigma; Beta Kappa Chi; Natl Soc of Black Engrs; Tuskegee Univ's Hon Roll, nom for Natl Dean's List & Engrng Repr Cncl (Grad Repr, 1988-89). Address: JL Tanjung Duren Timur 2A, Jakarta 11470, Indonesia.

TESHABAEV Fatikh, b. 18 Oct 1939 Tashkent. Diplomatist. m. Mauludfa Teshabaev, 1966, 2 s, 1 d. Education: Univs of Tashkent and Delhi. Appointments: First Dep Min for For Affairs, 1991-93; Amb to USA and Perm Rep of Repub of Uzbekistan at UN, 1993-95; Amb at large, 1995-. Publications: Articles on polit thought in oriental cos. Honours: Nehru Awd. Hobbies: Tennis. Address: c/o Ministry of Foreign Affairs, ul Gogolya 87, 700047, Tashkent, Uzbekistan.

TEWARI Satya Prakash, b. 2 Aug 1954, Lucknow, India. Teaching. m. Mamata Tewari, 16 May 1989, 1 d. Education: BE (Mech Engrng); ME, Mech Engrng (Prodn Engrng); PhD, Mechl Engrng (Welding). Appointments: Lectr, 1981-89, Snr Lectr, 1989-, Dept of Mech Engrng, IT, BHU, Varanasi, India. Honours: Merit Schlsp Holder Schl, from Sch to Univ. Memberships: Instn of Engrs (India). Hobbies: Reading books; Newspapers; Viewing good and scientific TV programmes. Address: Mechanical Engineering Department, Institute of Technology, Banaras Hindu University, Varanasi 221005, India.

THAIVANAYAGAM A, b. 10 Feb 1949. Librarian. m. 27 May 1979, 1 d. Education: MA; MLIS; MPhil. Appointments: Asst Libn, 1975-88; Libn, 1988-. Publications: A Concise Bibliography on Psychiatry: An Annotated Guide to Journal Articles, 1992. Memberships: VP, Tamil Nadu Med Lib Assn; Exec Cncl Mbr, Med Lib Assn; IASLIC; Life Mbr, Madras Lib Assn; Indian Lib Assn. Hobbies: Reading; Writing articles to library science; Travelling. Address: 14 Harris Road, Madras 600 002, Tamil Nadu, India.

THAKUR Ramesh C, b. 23 Nov 1948, Sitamarhi, India. University Administrator. m. Bernadette, 31 May 1974, 2 s. Education: BA (Hons), 1969; MA, 1972; PhD, 1978. Appointments: Lectr, Univ of the S Pacific, Fiji, 1978-79; Lectr/Prof, Univ of Otago, NZ, 1980-95; Prof and Hd, Peace Rsch Cntr, Aust, 1995-98; Vice Rector, UN Univ, Japan, 1998-. Publications: 13 books; Over 100 articles. Address: United Nations University, 53-70 Jingumae 5-chome, Shibuya-ku, Tokyo 150-8925, Japan.

THAKUR Vijay, b. 1 July 1959, Jabalpur, India. Teaching. Education: MA, Engl Lit; Postgrad Dip, Tchng of Engl. Appointments: Ceat Ltd, 1979-91; Cnsltncy, Engl for Adult Learners, 1991-94; Dept of Engl, St Aloysius Coll, 1994-. Publications: Publ peoms in Engl & Hindi in newspprs, periodicals, jrnls and anthologies; A Collection of Hindi Poems, Patton Ki Goad Mei. Memberships|: Writers' Forum; Ranchi; India. Hobbies: Teaching; Cooking; Meaningful relationships; Gardening. Address: 78 Apr Colony, Bilehri, Jabalpur, 482020, MP, India.

THALBEN-BALL Evelyn Pamela, b. 3 Oct 1927, London, Eng. Painter. Education: Heatherley Art Sch, 1946-50. Appointments: Sec, Chelsea Art Soc, 1964-68. Creative works: Exhibns: Walkers Galls, London; Chenil Galls, London; Sladmore Gall, London; Grads Cub, Sydney; MacDonald Galls, Sydney and Queensland; Galerie Tapande, Canberra; Tininburra Gall, Tamworth; Austl War Mem, Canberra, Aust House, London and sev other collects in Aust and overseas. Honours: Painting Awds: Currabubula, 1980, 1981, 1989, 1995, Royal Agricl Soc, 1981, Goulburn, 1981, Singleton, 1996, 1998, Newcastle, 1997, Grenfell, 1998; Taree, 1998; Judge, Doug Moran Natl Portrait Prize, 1990, 1992. Memberships: Roy Art Soc, NSW; Peninsula Art Soc; Fell Roy Art Soc. Listed in: Artists and Galleries of Australia; Women Artists of Australia. Address: 35 Riviera Avenue, Avalon Heights, NSW 2107, Australia.

THAMAN Konai Helu, b. 6 Feb 1946, Tonga. Academic. m. Randolph, 1 s, 1 d. Education: BA, Auckland Univ; MA, Univ CA, Santa Barbara; PhD, Univ of S Pacific. Appointments: Prof, Pacific Educn & Culture, USP; UNESCO Chair in Tchr Educn & Culture. Publications: Poetry: You the Choice, 1974; Langakali, 1981; Inselfes, 1986; Hingano, 1987; Kakala, 1993. Memberships: CEART; SEAPREAMS. Hobbies: Writing; Travel; Wine tasting. Address: University of the South Pacific, Suva, Fiji.

THAMBIRATHAM David Pathmaseelan, b. 12 Aug 1943, Sri Lanka. University Professor. m. Sulogini, 3 Feb 1973, 2 s, 1 d. Education: BS, Engrng, 1st Class Hons, Univ of Ceylon; MSc, PhD, Structural Engrng, Univ of Manitoba, Canada. Appointments: Dist Constrn Engr, 1968-73; Canadian C'wlth Schl, 1973-78; Chf Constrn Engr, 1978-79; Snr Structural Engr, 1979-80; Lectr, 1980-81; Visng Fell, Visng Schl, 1987-88, 1988; Snr Lectr, 1988-90; Lectr, Sch of Civ Engrng, 1990-91; Snr Lectr, 1991-93; Assoc Prof, 1993-96; Prof, 1996-. Publications: Over 150 inclng: Monographs; Sers; Chapts in Books; Intl Rfrd Jrnl Articles; Rfrd Intl Conf Pprs; Rsch and High Level Const Rprts. Honours: Canadian C'wlth Schl; Univ of Manitoba Grad Fellshp; Chartered Profl Engr, UK and Aust; Commendation, PM, Sri Lanka; Intl Man of the Yr, 1996-97, IBC. Memberships: Inst of Civ Engrs; Inst of Engrs. Hobbies: Music; Travelling; Stamps; Video filming. Address: 19 Manmarra Crescent, Eight Mile Plains, QLD 4113, Australia.

THAMMAIAH Keekira Annaiah, b. 10 Feb 1935. Teacher. m. Naila, 26 Dec 1971, 1 s. Education: BA, St Joseph's Coll, Bangalore; MA, Univ Coll, Bombay; LLB, Law Coll, Bombay. Appointments: Adv, High Crt, Bangalore, 1960-64; Tchr, St Pauls Way Sch, London, 1964-85; Lectr, Cty of Westminster Coll, London, 1985-. Honours: Cnclr, 1994-; Dpty Mayor, 1999-, London Borough of Harrow, 1994-. Memberships: Natl Union of Tchrs; Univ Coll Lectrs Union; Labour Party Mbr. Hobbies: Reading; Travelling; Community work. Address: 26 Longcroft Road, Edgeware, Middlesex HA8 6RR, England.

THAMPU Valson, b. 1 Mar 1951, Kerala, India. Teaching. m. Grace Valson, 5 Jan 1978, 2 d. Education: MA, Engl Lit. Appointments: Rdr in Engl, 1973. Publications: AIDS: Heresy and Prophecy, 1993; The Dream and the Dragon, 1994; Cross-Cultural Issues in AIDS, 1995; Rediscovering Mission; The Word and the World; Be Thou My Vision. Membership: Exec Cttee, CMC, Vellore, Dir, TRACI, New Delhi. Hobbies: Research; Writing; Public speaking. Address: Valson Thampu, St Stephen's College, University of Delhi, Delhi 110007, India.

THAN Shwe. Politician; Army Offr. Appointments: PM and Min of Def, Apr 1992-; Chmn State Law and Order Restoration Cncl - SLORC - 1992-97; Chmn State Peace and Dev Cncl - SDP - 1997-. Address: Office of the Prime Minister, Yangon, Myanmar.

THAPA Surya Bahadur, b. 20 Mar 1928 Muga E Nepal. Politician. m. 1953, 1 s, 2 d. Education: Allahabad Univ India. Appointments: House Speaker Advsry Ass to King of Nepal, 1958; Min of Forests Agric Com and Ind, 1960; Min of Fin and Econ Affairs, 1962; Vice-Chmn Cncl of Mins Min of Fin Econ Plng Law and Jus, 1963; Vice-Chmn Cncl of Mins Min of Fin Law and Gen Admin, 1964-65; Chmn Cncl of Mins Min of Palace Affairs, 1965-69; Arrested, 1972, 1975; PM of Nepal and Min of Palace Affairs, 1979-83; Min of Fin, 1979-80; Min of Def, 1980-81, 1982-83; Min of For Affirs, 1982; PM of Nepal, Oct 1997-. Honours: Tri-Shahkti-Patta, 1963; Gorkha Dakshinbahu I, 1965; Om Rama Patta, 1980; Sev Nepalese and for awds. Memberships: Mbr Upper House of Parl, 1959; Mbr Roy Advsry Cttee, 1969-72. Address: Tangal, Kathmandu, Nepal.

THAPPA Devinder Mohan, b. 9 Mar 1961, Jammu, India. Physician. m. Nirmal Kumari, 9 Dec 1990, 1 s. Education: MBBS; MD, Dermatology; DHA. Appointments: Dermatologists, 1992-94; Asst Prof, 1994-96; Assoc Prof, Hd, Dermatology and STD Dept, JIPMER, Pondicherry, 1996-. Honours: Sardarilal Mem Oration Awd, 1998; Intl Man of Millennium CBC, 1999. Memberships: IADVL; IAL; IASSTD; Alumni Assn of NTTC; Sec, IADVL Pondicherry Br, 1995-98; VP, CHS Welfare Assn, 1997-99. Hobbies: Watching TV; Reading journals. Address: Dermatology and STD Department, JIPMER, Pondicherry 605006, India.

THATHACHAR Mandayam A L, b. 20 May 1939, Mysore, India. Professor of Electrical Engineering. m. Yadugiri, 5 July 1968, 1 s, 1 d. Education: BE; ME; PhD. Appointment: Prof, Dept of Elec Engrng, Indian Inst of Sci, Bangalore, 1978-. Publications: Learning Automata, 1989; Over 100 rsch pprs. Honours: Alumni Awd, Ex in Rsch, 1992; Jawaharlal Nehru Natl Awd, Engrng Technol, 1993. Memberships: Fell, IAS, 1987, INSA, 1989, INAE, 1991, IEEE, 1991. Hobbies: Chess; Philosophical discussions. Address: Department of Electrical Engineering, Indian Institute of Science, Bangalore 560012, India.

THAUGSUBAN Suthep, b. 7 July 1949, Suratthani, Thailand. Minister of Transport and Communications. Education: Bach, Pol Sci, Chiang-Mai Univ; Master, Pol Sci, Middle Tennessee State Univ, USA. Appointments: Sec to Min, Min of Com, 1980; Sec to Min of Agric and Co-ops, 1981; Sec to Attached Min, Min to Prime Min's Off, 1983; Dpty Min of Agric and Co-ops, 1986-88, 1992-94; Min of Transp and Comms. Honour: Kt Grand Cordon, Spec Class, Most Exalted Order of the White Elephant. Address: Ministry of Transport and Communications, Thanon Ratchadamnoen Nok, Bangkok 10100, Thailand.

THAYER Carlyle Alan. Professor. Appointments: Tchr, Intl Voluntary Servs, An Loc Town, Binh Long Prov, Vietnam, 1967-68; Tchr, Swaneng Hill Sch, Serowe, Botswana, 1968-69; Tutor, Dept of Asian Civilisations, Austl Natl Univ, 1973; Lectr, Bendigo Coll of Adv Educn, 1975-78; Lectr, 1979-83, Snr Lectr, 1983-85, Roy Mil Coll, Duntroon; Snr Lectr, 1986-89, Assoc Prof, 1990-97, Prof, 1998-, Sch of Polit, Austl Def Force Acady; Visng Fell on Secondmnt, Rsch Sch of Pacific and Asian Studies, Austl Natl Univ, 1991-94; Rsch Assoc, Intl Inst for Strategic Studies, London, 1993; Hd, Dept of Polits, Austl Def Force Acady, 1995-97. Visng Fell, Strategic and Defence Stdies Cntr, The Austl Natl Univ, 1998. Publications: War By Other Means: National Liberation and Revolution in Vietnam, 1954-1960, 1989; Soviet Relations with India and Vietnam, 1992; Vietnam, 1992 Soviet Relations with India and Vietnam, 1945-1992, 1993; The Vietnam People's Army Under Doi Moi, 1994; Beyond Indochina, 1995; Num other profl publns. Honours: US Natl Def For Lang Fellshp, Yale Univ, 1969-71, Cornell Univ, 1970; Cntr for Vietnamese Studies Fellshp, S IL Univ, USA, 1971; PhD Rsch Schl, Austl Natl Univ, 1971-74; Austl Rsch Cncl Rsch Awd, 1990. Memberships: Natl Sec, Austl Soccer Refs Fedn, 1985-95; Natl Sec, Vietnam Studies Assn of Aust, 1989-; Life Mbr, Bendigo CAE Soccer Club, Austl Soccer Refs Fedn (ACT Div); Natl Sec, Asian Stdies Assn of Aust, 1996-. Listed in: Many including: Who's Who in America, Who's Who in the World; Dictionary of International Biography. Address: 11 Ambara Place, Aranda, ACT 2614, Australia.

THEILE David Egmont, b. 17 Jan 1938. Professor of Surgury. m. 3 May 1963, 2 s. Education: MB BS (Hons), MS; FRACS; FRCS(Eng); FRCS (Ed); FAMS; FANZCA. Appointments: RMO, Surg Reg, Roy Brisbane Hosp, 1963-67; Lectr, Dept of Surg, The London Hosp, 1968; Snr Surg Reg, Whittington Hosp, London, 1969-70; Visng Surg, Redcliffe Hosp, Qld, 1971-74; Visng Surg, Princess Alexandra Hosp, Brisbane, 1974-; Clin Prof of Surg, Univ Qld, 1994-. Publications: Num sci pprs in profl jrnls. Honours: Olympic Gold Medal, 100m Backstroke, Melbourne, 1956, Rome, 1960; Olympic Silver Medal, Relay, Rome, 1960; AO. Membership: Roy Austl Coll of Surgs, Pres, 1993-95; Chmn, Pacific Is Proj, 1995-. Hobby: Swimming. Address: 201 Wickham Terrace, Brisbane, Queensland 4000, Australia.

THEW Joanne, b. Sydney, Aust. Artist. m. John Hunter, 8 Nov 1976, 1 s, 2 d. Education: Natl Art Sch, Sydney, 1969-73. Honours: Over 100 Awds, Latest 1st Prizes in Art Competitions incl: Coffs Harbour, 1985, 1986, 1987; Young, 1985; Portland, 1985; Condobolin, 1985; Boggabri, 1985, 1986, 1988; Narrabri, 1986; Adelong, 1986; Raymond Terrace, 1986; Narrandera, 1986; Penrith, 1987, 1989; Macquarie Towns, 1988; Macquarie Awd 1,000, 1989; Port Macquarie, 1989 (twice); Roy Easter Show, Sydney, 1985, 1986, 1987, 1989, 1992, 1993. Membership: Fell, Roy Art Soc, NSW, 1987. Listed in: The World Who's Who of Women. Address: 55 Fairlawn Avenue, Turramurra, NSW 2074, Australia.

THIELE Albert Neville, b. 4 Dec 1920, Brisbane, Qld, Aust. Engineer. m. Lexie Elizabeth Anderson, 12 Dec 1953, 1 s, 1 d. Education: Queensland Univ, 1938-41; Aust Army, 1941-46; BEng (Mech and Elec), Sydney Univ, 1952. Appointments: Adv Dev Engr, Elec and Musical Inds (Aust), 1952-61; Aust Brdcstng Corp, 1962-85; Dir, Engrng Dev, 1980-85; Cnsltng Engr, 1986-; Hon Visng Fell, Univ NSW, 1991-93; Hon Profl Assoc, Sydney Univ, 1995-. Publications: Contbr of 36 publications to profl jrnls, inclng origination of Thiele-Small parameters for measuring and designing loudspeakers, 1961; Total Difference Frequency Distortion measurement of transmission channels, 1975; Honour: Norman W V Hayes Awd, IREE, 1968, 1992; Silver Medal, AES, 1994. Memberships: Pres, Inst Radio and Electronic Engrs, Aust, 1986-88; Inst Engrs, Aust; Audio Engrng Soc; VP, Intl Reg, Audio Engrng Soc, 1991-93; Soc Motion Picture and TV Engrs. Listed in: Dictionary of International Biography. Hobbies: Music; Theatre; Bushwalking. Address: 10 Wycombe St, Epping, NSW 2121, Australia.

THIELE Colin Milton, b. 16 Nov 1920, Eudunda, S Aust. Author. m. Rhonda Gill, 17 Mar 1945, 2 d. Education: BA; Dip Ed; Dip Tchng. Appointments: RAAF; Sch Tchr; Coll Lectr; Prin; Dir. Publications: More than 100 Books; Sun on the Stubble, 1958; The Shadow on the Hills; The Valley Between; Uncle Gustav's Ghosts; Emma Keppler; Labourers in the Vineyard; The Seed's

Inheritance; Storm Boy; Blue Fin; Fire in the Stone; The Water Trolley; Jodie's Journey; Martin's Mountain; Many other books. Honours: Book of the Yr Awd, Children's Book Cncl of Aust; Austrian State Prize for Children's Books; Silver Pencil Awd; Cert of Hon, IBBY; Grace Leven Poetry Prize; W J Miles Poetry Prize; Dromkeen Medal; Companion of the Order of Aust; Many other hons and awds. Memberships: Austl Soc of Auths; Austl Coll of Educ. Hobbies: Travelling; Reading. Address: Endeavour Lane, King Scrub, Via Dayboro, QLD 4521, Australia.

THOMAS Adrian Peter, b. 19 Feb 1945, Devon, Eng. British Council Officer. m. Robyn Alycon Malcolm, 21 Aug 1977, 2 s, 1 d. Education: BA, Philos, Pol and Econ, 1967, MA, 1974, Univ of Oxford. Appointments: Tchr, Tanzania, 1967-68; Acct, Cooper Bros, 1969-70; Brit Cncl Serv, Sierra Leone, London, Iran, Malaysia, Dpty Dir, Nigeria, Dir, Sudan, Dir, East India. Honour: OBE, 1995; Hon PhD, Univ of Gezira, Sudan, 1995. Hobbies: Hill walking; Running; History; Poetry; Wildlife. Listed in: People of Today. Address: The British Council, 5 Shakespeare Sarani, Calcutta 700 071, India.

THOMAS Edmund Barrington, b. 11 Oct 1929, Vic, Aust. m. Elizabeth Ann Robinson, 11 Jan 1958, 2 s, 1 d. Education: Primary Tchrs Cert, Victorian Educ Dept, 1948; BCom, 1952; BEd, 1960, Univ of Melbourne; MEd, Univ of Alta, Can, 1969; PhD, Univ of Papua New Guinea, 1978. Appointments: HS Tchr, Victorian Educ Dept, 1952-65; Prin, Charlton hs, Vic, 1966-67; Prin, Heywood hs, Vic, 1968-70; Lectr, Snr Lectr, Educl Admin, Univ of Papua New Guinea, 1971-76, Dean, 1973-74; Snr Lectr, Univ of New Eng, Armidale, NSW, 1976-84; Master, Earle Page Coll, 1976-79; Snr Lectr in Educl Admin, Deakin Univ, Geelong, Vic, 1984-86; Currently, Dir, Educl and Staff Dev Servs, Educl Cnslts; Ed and Publr, The Profl Reading Guide for Educl Admnstrs. Publications include: Lets Talk of Many Things, 1966; Papua New Guinea Education, 1976; Principal and Task: an Australian Perspective (co-auth), 1982l Principal and Change: The Australian Experience (co-auth), 1987; The School Principal's Handbook Series (ed), 1992-. Honour: Austl Cncl for Educl Admin Ansett Travel Awd, 1983. Memberships include: Fell, Austl Coll of Educ; Assoc Fell, Austl Inst of Mngmt; Chairperson, Victorian Chapt; Austl Coll of Educ, 1988-90. Listed in: Who's Who in Australia. Hobbies: Reading; Farming; Food and wine. Address: The Lagoon, 395 Shell Road (PO Box 104), Point Lonsdale, Vic 3225, Australia.

THOMAS Michael David, b. 8 Sept 1933, London, Eng. Queen's Counsel. m. Baroness Lydia Dunn, 2 Apr 1988, 2 s, 2 d. Education: LLB, London Sch of Econs, 1954. Appointments: Called to the Bar by Middle Temple, 1955; Natl Serv w RN, 1955-57; Prac at the Bar of Eng and Wales, 1958-83; Treasury Counsel for Admiralty Matters, 1966-73; Appt QC, 1973; Bencher of Middle Temple, 1981; Mbr, Lloyd's Panel of Salvage Arbitrators, 1973-83; Wreck Commnr, 1973-83; Atty Gen of Hong Kong and Mbr of Exec and Legis Cncls of Hong Kong, 1983-88; Called to the Bar in Hong Kong, 1983; Prac at the Bar in Hong Kong, 1988. Honours: CMG, 1985; JP, 1989. Memberships: China Intl Econ and Trade Arbitration Commn, China Maritime Arbitration Commn; Assoc Mbr, Chartered Inst of Arbitrators. Listed in: Who's Who, 1996. Address: Essex Court Chambers, 24 Lincoln's Inn Fields, London WC2A 3ED, England.

THOMAS Nihal, b. 23 June 1964, Bangalore, India. Medical Doctor. m. Maya Thomas, 1 June 1991, 1 s. Education: MBBS; MD (Int Med). Appointments: Tutor in Endocrinology; Lectr in Endocrinology. Publications: 18 in field of endocrinology. Honour: Best Ppr, Assn of Physns meeting "33 Cases of Cushing's Syndrome", 1995. Hobbies: Poetry; Pianoforte; Choreography; Long distance running. Address: Diabetes Centre, Adnmin Bldg 2, Prince of Wales Hospital, Randwick 2031, NSW, Australia.

THOMAS Shirley, Education: Bus Coll. Appointment: Asst to Admin Mngr, T & G Life Assurance Soc. Publications: Auth, Pub in lit mags and newspprs, Aust and abroad; Books, Commissioned histories T & G Life Assurance Soc, 1976; Fed Insurance Ltd, 1977; Victorian Employers' Fed, 1985; Poetry - In Common, 1970; Chameleon, 1978; Two Summers, 1983; Solstice, 1992; A Different Perspective, 1995. Honours: Charles Thatcher Poetry Awd, 1975; Jessie Litchfield Poetry Awd, Ola Cohn Plaque, 1975; Geelong Autumn Arts Fest, 1st Prize, Poetry, 1976; Lit Bd, Aust Cncl Grant, 1983. Memberships: Fellshp of Aust Writers, Vic; Soc of Women Writers, Aust, Vic br. Hobbies: Travel; Golf; Opera; Ballet; Art shows; Reading. Address: 96 Fischer Street, Torquay, Vic, Australia.

THOMAS Trang Ngoc, b. 14 Aug 1946, Vietnam. Professor of Psychology. m. David T, 2 d. Education: BA; MA; PhD. Appointment: Prof of Psychol, 1991-. Honour: AM. Memberships: Rotary Club of Melbourne; Fell, Aust Psychol Soc. Address: Department of Psychology, RMIT, GPO Box 2476V, Melbourne, VIC 3001, Australia.

THOMAS V K, b. 15 June 1950. Research Officer. m. Molly Thomas, 27 May 1979, 1 s, 1 d. Education: PhD, Lib and Info Sci; MA, Econs; Dip, Mktng; Course for Publng Profls; Ctf, Info Storage & Retrieval Syst; Ctf, Application of Computer in Lib and Info Activities. Appointments: Rsch Assoc, Small Enterprises Natl Documentation Cntr, Hyderabad, 1978-87; Rsch Offr, Raja Rammohun Roy Lib Fndn, Calcutta, 1987-. Publications: Co-Ed, Public Libraries in Developing Countries: Status and Trends, 1996; Public Libraries in India: Development and Finance, 1997. Membership: Indian Assn of Spec Libs and Info Cntrs, Calcutta. Hobbies: Reading; Trekking. Address: 15 Neelkamal Apartments, BD43 Rabindrapally, Prafullakanan PO, Calcutta 700059, India.

THOMAS Vadaketh Abraham, b. 15 Aug 1912. Chartered Engineer. m. Ruth Thomas, 2 Nov 1978, dec, 5 s. Education: Tech Coll, Kuala Lumpar, 1936-40; Brighton Tech Coll, Eng, 1953-54; PhD, World Univ, USA. Appointments: Asst Controller, 1955-60, Controller, Regs, 1960-66, Dir, 1967-69, Telecoms, Malaysia; Hd of Electl and Electric, Fedl Inst of Technol, KL, 1971-75; Fndr Prin and Dir, Inst Technol Jaya, KL, 1975-85; Tech Advsr to FIT and other tech insts, 1986-90. Publications: Autobiography, 1990; History of the Early Mar Thoma Immigrants and Mar Thoma Churches in Malaysia, 1999. Honours: Johore State Schlshp to K L Techl Coll, 1936-40; Fed Schlshp to UK, 1952-55; FSE Fell, Soc of Engrs, UK, London; DDG, Intl Biographical Assn, Cambridge, Eng; LFIBA, Life Fell; LFABI, Life Fell. Memberships: Rotarian, Johore Bahru Rotary Club; PEng LFIEM Profl Engr, Life Fell of Inst of Engrs, Malaysia; Chartered Engr, Life Fell, Inst of EE, London. Listed in: Who's Who in Malaya and Singapore; Who's Who in the Commonwealth; The First Five Hundred. Hobbies: Reading; Writing; Hiking; Watching TV. Address: 22 Jalan 8/1A, 46050 Petaling Jaya, Selangor, Malaysia.

THOMPSON Allan Norman John, b. 6 May 1931, The Rock, NSW, Australia. School Teacher. m. Lotus, 24 Aug 1957, 2 s. Education: BA, Univ of New Eng, Armidale, NSW, Aust. Appointments: Hd Tchr, Maths, Smiths Hill HS, Wollongong, NSW, 1971-86; Retd 1994. Publications: Developmental Mathematics Book, 1, 2, 3, 4, 1973, 1981, 1988; Mathsworld 7, 1986; Mathsworlds, 1987. Hobbies: Playing and administration of lawn books; Pilot of light aircraft. Address: 33a Pass Avenue, Thirroul, NSW, Australia.

THOMPSON Clifford Harry, b. 1 Apr 1926. Soil Scientist. m. Bethea Brown Kennedy, 15 Apr 1950, 1 s, 1 d. Education: QDH (Qld Dip of Horticulture), Qld Agricl Coll. Appointments: Horticultural Cadet, 1945; Techl Offr, CSIR, Div Soils, 1945; Experimental Offr, CSIRO Div Soils, 1958; Snr Rsch Scientist, CSIRO Div Soils, 1980; Prin Rsch Scientist, CSIRO Div Soils, 1982; Hon Rsch Fell, CSIRO Div Tropical Crops and Pastures, 1989-97; CSIRO Div Trop Agric, 1998- Publications: Over 70 pprs, bulletins, book chapts; Over 40 conf abstracts or posters. Honour: FAIAS, for outstndng contbn in field of agricl sci, 1990. Memberships: Aust Inst of Agricl Sci, Mbr, 1963, Fell, 1990; Aust Soil Sci Soc, fndn mbr, 1956, Qld Branch Pres 1965, Intl Soc Soil Sci, 1958; Fell Roy Geogl Soc, London, 1963; Geol Soc Aust, 1963; Ecol Soc Aust, 1974; Roy Soc Qld, 1974. Hobby: Enjoying good red wine. Address: 85 Savages Road, Brookfield, Queensland, Australia.

THOMPSON Maxwell Mostyn Henry, b. 18 Jan 1927, Mittagong, NSW, Aust. Chartered accountant. m. Joy, 8 Dec 1956, 1 s, 1 d. Education: FCA; MA Syd. Publications: William Wolls: A Man of Parramatta, 1986; The First Election: the New South Wales Legislative Council Election of 1843, 1996. Memberships: Fell, Inst Chartered Accts in Aust. Hobbies: Painting; Reading; Listening to music; Gardening. Address: PO Box 485, Mittagong, NSW 2575, Australia.

THOMPSON Roy Harold, b. 23 July 1947, Cairns, Aust. Music Educator. m. Julianne, 16 Dec 1979, 1 s, 1 d. Education: LTCL(Tchrs-Saxophone), 1974; LTCL (Performers-Clarinet), 1975; FTCL, 1975; BA Mus (QCM), 1976; Grad Dip of Educ (Tertiary) (DDIAE), 1980; Grad Dip of Educl Admin (BCAE), 1986; MME (USC), 1982; DMA, USC, 1983; M Coml Law, 1998. Appointments: Profl Musician, 1968-72; North Command Army Band, 1972-73; Music Instr, Dept of Educ, 1976-80; Examiner for the Austl Music Exams Bd, 1980-87; Pt time Lectr, Qld Conserv of Music, Darling Downs Inst of Advd Educ, Univ of Qld, 1983-87; State Coordr of Instrumental Music, Qld Dept of Educ, 1984-87; Adjudicator, Pacific Basin Band Fest, Hawaii, 1987; Qld Fest of Music, 1985-1987; Yamaha Woodwind/Brass Prizes, 1986; Pine Rivers Music Fest, 1984-87; Young Performers Comp, 1984-1987; Fanfare, 1985; Woodwind Clinician and/or Conductor/Musical Dir, MacGregor Summer Sch, 1985-1988; Musically Oustndng Stud Prog, 1983, 1985, 1987; Music Camps in Cairns, Townsville, Gold Coast, Brisbane, 1976-87; Rockhampton Chamber Music Soc Music Camps, 1973-1975; Hc Sch Fine Arts, John Paul Coll, 1993-94; Assoc Dir, Gold Coast Inst of TAFE, 1995-97; Assoc Dir, TAFE, Qld, 1997-99. Creative Works: Saxophone Composition Premiere-Prose (Hultgren 1987); Scherzo and Air, Hultgren, 1986; Rhapsodette, Hammer, 1986; Extracts, Wade, 1985; Sonata, Spiers, 1980; Performed Glazunauv, Concerto, 1987; Claude T Smith Fantasia, 1987; Natl Band and Orch Dirs Clinics, Melbourne, 1986. Honours: Jaycees Natl and State Awd, Five Outstndng Young Austls Awds, 1984; Music Educ Deptl Hons Awd, USC, 1982; Awd of Merit (Los Angeles Rotary Club), 1982; Dean's List (USC), 1981; Postgrad Schlsp, Qld Dept of Educ, 1981-83. Memberships: Austl Band and Orch Dirs'Assn; Pi Kappa Lambda, Natl Music Hon Soc. Hobbies: Surfing; Martial Arts (past Australian and Queensland Champion); Tennis; Furniture Restoration; Computers. Address: 26 Birkin Road, Bellbowrie, Brisbane, Qld 4070, Australia.

THOMS Albie, b. 28 July 1941, Sydney, Aust. Film & TV Producer, Director, Writer. m. Linda, 1 s, 1 d. Education: BA, Postgrad Studies, Sydney Univ. Appointments: Prodr, Dir, Writer, Contemporary Th Co, 1963-64; Prodr, Dir, Writer, Austl Brdcstng Cmmn, 1965-68; Freelance, 1968-. Publications: Polemics for a New Cinema, 1978; Bohemians in the Bush, 1991; Stage: Review of the Absurd, 1963; Theatre of Cruelty; Film: Bolero, 1967; Marinetti, 1969; Sunshine City, 1973; Palm Beach, 1979; TV: Contrabandits, 1967-68; Skippy, 1969; GTK, 1974-75. Honours: Agfa-Gevaert Awd, 1967; Intl Cinema Prize, 1968; Best Film, Adelaide Film Fest, 1980; Expmntl Film Fund Grant, Creative Devel Fund Grant; Power Inst Fellshp; Austl Film & TV Sch Stdy Grant. Memberships: Austl Screen Dirs Assn; Austl Writers Guild; Screen Prodrs Assn of Aust; Austl Film Inst. Address: PO Box 409, Spit Junction, NSW 2088, Australia.

THOMSON Elizabeth L, b. Can. Lawyer; Entrepeneur. m. K Sakhrani, 1 s, 1 d. Education: BA (Hons), Univ of West Ont; LLB and BCL, McGill Univ, Can. Appointments: Dir, Hong Kong Bus and Profl Women; Dir, Hong Kong Can Bus Assn (Toronto Chapt); Dir, Can Bus Assn, Hong Kong (now Canad Chmbr of Com); VP, Canad Club of Hong; Fndr and Chairwoman of Women Bus Owners Club. Memberships: Law Socs of Upper Can

(Ont), Eng, Wales, Hong Kong, Aust. Address: Nine Queen's Road, Suite 605-6, Central, Hong Kong.

THOMSON John Dugald, b. 20 Feb 1950, Brisbane, Aust. Aquaculture Consultant. m. Bethlyn Jan Blackwood, 8 Dec 1984, 2 s. Education: BAgrSc, 1973; MAgrSc, 1982, Sydney Univ, Aust. Appointments: Demonstrator, Dept Agric Chem, Sydney Univ, 1972-74; Marine Chemist, Tasmanian Dept Agric, 1974-85; Snr Fish Mngr Sci, Tasmanian Dept Sea Fish, 1986; Snr Mngmt, Bio, 1986-88; Dir, Scall Enhancement Proj, 1988-93; Mngng Dir, Aquaculture Cnslt, 1994-98. Memberships: Aust Soc Biochem and Molecular Bio; Roy Soc Tasmania, Cnclr, 1977-80; Aust Mar Sci Assn, Cnclr, 1979-82, 1984-85; Stud Merino Assn of Tasmania; Sydney University Agric Grad Assn; Wellington Ski Club; Roy Yacht Club of Tasmania. Hobbies: Skiing; Sailing. Address: 32 McNeil Street, Peppermint Grove, Western Australia 6011, Australia.

THOMSON Kelvin John, b. 1 May 1955. Member of Parliament. m. Marsha Rose Thomson, 29 Nov 1981, 1 s, 1 d. Education: BA, hons, 1977, BLL, hons, 1988, Univ of Melbourne. Appointments: Cnclr, Cty of Coburg, 1981; Mr, Vic Legislative Assembly for Pascoe Vale, 1988; Mbr, C'wlth House of Reps, 1996. Publications: Co-ed, Labor Essays, 1983. Honour: Supreme Crt Prize, Univ of Melbourne, 1987. Memberships: Moonee Ponds Creek Assn; Austl Labor Pty. Address: 3 Munro Street, Coburg, Vic 3058, Australia.

THOMSON Peter William, b. 23 Aug 1929 Melbourne. Golfer. m. Stella Mary, 1960, 1 s, 3 d. Appointments: Turned profl, 1949; Brit Open Champion, 1954, 1955, 1956, 1958, 1965 - only player to win three successively since Open became 72 hole event since 1892; Won Brit PGA Match-Play Championship four times and 16 major tournaments in Brit; Austl Open Champion, 1951, 1967, 1972; NZ Open Champion nine times; Won open titles of Italy Spain Hong Kong Philippines India and Germany; Played 11 times for Aust in World Cup - won twice; Won World Snrs Championship, 1984; PGA Snrs Championship of Am, 1984; Fmr Pres Profl Golf Assn of Aust; Dir Thomson Wolveridge Perrett. Memberships: Mbr James McGrath Fndn Vic. Hobbies: Classical music; Lit. Address: Carmel House, 44 Mathoura Road, Toorak, Vic 3142, Australia.

THOMSON Warren Milton, b. 2 Aug 1935, Parramatta, NSW, Aust. Educator; Musician; Administrator. Education: BMus; DipEd, Univ of Melbourne; MACE. Appointments: Dir of Music, Trinity Grammar Sch, Kew, Vic, 1960-72; Dir of Studies, Austl Music Exams Bd, 1973-74; Hd, Sch of Extension Studies, Sydney Conservatorium, NSW, 1974-95; Num radio brdcsts on piano, Aust, USSR; Num perfs as soloist and accompanist, Aust; Fedl Examiner, Austl Music Exams Bd, 1972, 1973, 1974, 1992, 1993. Creative works: Piano Tutor, Vols 1-3, (composer etc w Miriam Hyde), 1975-76; about 50 other publications inclng Bach Inventions, Sinfonias, Well Tempered Clavier and Mozart Sonatas; Recdngs for AMEB Pianoforte Course Preliminary Grade (w Larry Sitsky), AMEB Nos 10 and 11 12 and 13 Grade Books and comprehensive lists, Preliminary 1st, 2nd and 3rd Grades; Articles in var profl jrnls, Aust, USA, Hungary. Honours include: OAM; Appt to Aust Opera Auditions Cttee; Hon Life Mbr, Victorian Music Tchrs Assn. Memberships: Music Tchrs Assn of NSW, Pres, 1978-84; Fedn of Austl Music Tchrs Assn; Fedl and State Chmn, Austl Music Exams Bd; Dir, Cty of Sydney Cultural Cncl; Artistic Dir and Friend of Sydney Intl Piano Competition. Hobbies include: Swimming; Travel. Address: 1 Woodward Place, St Ives, NSW 2075, Australia.

THORNE John Gilroy, b. 24 July 1937, Launceston, Tas, Aust. Education Consultant. m. Shirley Andrews, 7 Jan 1961, 1 s, 2 d. Education: Ctf of Educ, Hobart, 1958; Tchr of the Deaf, Melbourne, 1960; BEd, Hobart, 1978; MA, CA, USA, 1979; PhD, Tas, 1989. Appointments: Tchr, Sch Prin, Spec Primary and Dist HS, 1959-93; Assoc, Jane Franklin Hall, Univ of Tas Coll; Natl Pres, Aust and NZ Coll for Snrs, 1997-2000. Publications

include: An Examination of Hearing Impaired Children's Needs; Employment Opportunities for Developmentally Delayed Young Adults; Sev pamphlets on learning trails in Tasmania; Reports on disability issues in Tasmania; Ed writing w Bryce Courtnay, 1995, 1997, 1998. Honours: Medal of Merit, Scout Assn of Aust, 1977; Rotary Fndn Amb Schlshp, 1978; Educ Dept Traveling Schl, 1979; Paul Harris Fell, 1979; Aust-Japan Visng Educ Fell, 1983; JP, 1983; Dist Gov D 9830, 1989-90; Fell, Austl Cncl for Educl Admin, 1993; Past Fell, Jane Franklin Hall, Univ of Tas, 1994; Disting Serv Awd, Rotary Fndn, 1995; Disting Schl Alumni, Rotary Fndn, 1998. Memberships: Austl Cncl for Educl Admin; Austl Deafness Cncl; Rotary Intl; Roy Soc of Tas, VP, 1996-98; Friends of the Tasmanian Mus and Art Gall. Hobbies: Photography; Bush Walking; Computers; Family History; Rotary Service. Address: PO Box 170, South Hobart, Tas 7004, Australia.

THORNLEY Jennifer, b. 27 Sept 1948, Tasmania, Australia. Filmmaker; Writer. m. S Ginsborg, 3 Oct 1985, 1 s, 1 sd. Education: BA, Monash Univ, 1969; Dip in Libnship, UNSW, 1972; MFA, UNSW, 1997. Appointments: Coord, Intl Women's Film Fest, 1975; Mngr, Women's Film Fund, Austl Film Commn, 1984-85; Reader, Documentary Film, Austl Film Commn, NSW Film & Off. Publications: Maidens, 16mm film, 1978; For Love or Money: a pictorial history of women & work in Australia, 16mm feature documentary & penguin book; To the Other Shore, 16mm film, 1996. Honours: First Prize, Maidens' 78, Sydney Film Fest; Best Feature, For Love or Money. Memberships: Austl Film Inst; Women in Film & TV; ASDA. Hobbies: Yoga; Psychoanalysis; Environmental Issues; Landrights. Address: PO Box 320, Newport Beach, NSW 2156, Australia.

THORNTON Caroline Rouse, b. 29 Oct 1937, NSW, Aust. Freelance writer; Teacher. m. E B C Thornton. Education: BA (UNE), 1970; MEd (UWA), 1982; FTCL, 1962; PGCE (Southampton), 1972. Appointments: Tchr, Engl, Hist, Th, Drama, Speech inclng Engl as a for lang (9-18 age range). Publications: Rouse Hill House and the Rouses, 1988. Memberships: Pres, Grad Dramatic Soc; Past Pres, Univ of West Aust Choral Soc; Roy Assn Histl Soc; Karrakatta Club. Hobbies: Drama; History; Music. Address: 18 Doonen Road, Nedlands, Western Australia 6009.

THORNTON William Henry, b. 25 Feb 1950, Pensacola, FL, USA. Professor. m. Songok Han, 10 Feb 1988. Education: BA, Econs, Univ of W FLA, 1972; MA, Hist, 1974; MLS, Lib Sci, FSU, 1979; PhD, Hum, FLA State Univ, 1985. Appointments:Asst Prof, Korea Inst of Technol, 1987-89; Assoc Prof, Providence Univ, 1989-91; Prof, Natl Cheng Kung Univ, 1991-; Publications: Cultural Prosaics: The Second Postmodern Turn; Approximately 50 Articles in Acad Jrnls. Honours: 3 Rsch Grants; Korea Fndn Fellshp. Memberships: Mod Lang Assn; Amn Pop Culture Assn; Fax W Amn Culture Assn. Hobbies: Skydiving; Oil Painting. Address: National Cheng Kung University, Tainan, Taiwan, China.

THORPE Adrian Charles, b. 29 July 1942. Ambassador. m. Miyoko Kosugi, 26 Oct 1968. Education: BA, 1964, MA, 1970, Christ's Coll, Cambridge. Appointments: Entered HM Dipl Serv, 1965; 3rd/2nd Sec, Brit Emb Tokyo, 1965-70, FCO, 1970-73, 1st Sec, Brit Emb Beirut, 1973-76, 1st Sec, Brit Emb Tokyo, 1976-81, FCO 1981-85; Hd of Info Technol Dept, 1982-85, Econ Cnslr, Brit Emb Bonn, 1985-89, Dpty High Cmmnr, Coml Cnslr, HM High Cmmn Kuala Lumpur, 1989-91, Min, Brit Emb Tokyo, 1991-95, Amb, Brit Emb Manila, 1995. Honour: CMG, 1995; Membership: FRSA. Hobbies: Opera; Books. Address: c/o FCO (Manila), King Charles Street, London SW1A 2AH, England.

THURGOOD Nevil, b. 29 Dec 1919, Stansted, Essex, Eng. Writer; Director; Actor. m. Eva Mary Hopper, 23 Aug 1941, 4 children. Education: Nat Cert Mech E. Appointments: Creator, Fndr, Mountview Th and the Mount Players, 1972. Publications: The Magnificent Melodrama, 1984; Good Eveneing Ladies & Gentlemen, 1988; Sleeping Beauty Panto; Mr Plinges Magnificent Melodramas; Thurgood, a family history. Honours: Best

Actor, South Street, Ballarat, 1982; Top Music Hall Awds, Ballarat, 1982-83. Memberships: Life Mbr, Actors' Equity, State Pres, 1966-84; Austl Writers Guild; Brit Music Hall Soc. Hobbies: Genealogy (President, Gisborne, 1998); GDCA Umpires Association (President, 1995). Address: The Croft, 329 Mount Road, Mount Macedon, Victoria 3441, Australia.

THURMAN Uma, b. 29 Apr 1970. Actress. m. Gary Oldman, 1991. Appointments: Wrkd as model dishwasher. Films: The Adventures of Baron Munchhausen, 1988; Dangerous Liaisons, 1988; Even Cowgirls Get the Blues; Final Analysis; Where the Heart Is; Henry and June; Mad Dog and Glory; Pulp Fiction; Robin Hood; Dylan; A Month by the Lake; The Truth About Cats and Dogs; Batman and Robin; Gattaca. Address: c/o CAA, 9830 Wilshire Boulevard, Beverly Hills, CA 90212, USA.

THWAITES Des, b. 15 Sept 1938, Sydney, Aust. Managing Director. m. Janice Grover, 20 Jan 1959, 3 s. Education: Sydney Techl Coll, RMIT, Melbourne; Univ of New Eng. Appointments: Engr, govt serv in broadcasting and Dept of Trade promoting secondary ind exports; Civil Serv, 11yrs; Mngr, Import Export Orgs; Joined 2 trans-natls and worked w intl mngmt consultancy; Mngng Dir, Des Thwaites and Assocs Pty Ltd, 1975-. Publications include: Contbr of articles to profl jrnls; Speaker at bus and mngmt confs; Guest Lectr in Mngmt, Univ of NSW Inst of Admin. Honour: JP. Memberships: CMIMC; MIME; Fell Inst of Co Dirs (FICD); Chartered Mbr Inst of Mngmt Cnslts (CMIMC); Assoc, Inst of Credit Unions. Hobbies: Opera; Ballet; Restoring old motor vehicles; Tennis; Swimming; Cricket; Travel. Address: Oliver Street, Harbord, NSW 2096, Australia.

TIAN Bo, b. 12 Dec 1963, Tianjin, China. Applied Mathematician. Education: BS, Nankai Univ, China, 1985; MA, Univ of CA, Santa Barbara, USA, 1990. Appointments: Assoc Prof, Computer Sci & Dir of Computer Theory Div, Lanzhou Univ, China, 1993-96; Assoc Prof of Applied Maths, Beijing of Aeronautics & Astronautics, China, 1996-. Honours: The 4th-ranked most productive auth of China for the SCI jrnl pprs, 1996; Winner, 1st Rate, Sci Tech Prog Awd, Beijing Univ of Aeronautics & Astronautics, China. Address: Department of Applied Mathematics, Beijing University of Aeronautics & Astronautics, Beijing 100083, China.

TIAN Enrui, b. 3 Dec 1937, Yu Tian Co, Hebei Prov, China. Teacher. m. Xu Xiulan, 18 Jan 1963, 1 s, 1 d. Education: Grad, Harbin Inst of Technol. Appointments: Vice Chmn, Applied Phys, Harbin Inst of Technol, 1985; Pres, Harbin Univ, 1985-88; Pres, Harbin Tchrs Coll, 1988-. Publications: Chf Ed, Collegiate Physical Experiments, 1989; Research on the Quality and Efficiency of Teacher's Colleges in the New Century, 1997; Research on the Educational Reform and Development of Teachers' Colleges in the 21st Century, 1998; Over 30 acad pprs. Honours: 3rd Prize, Natl Min Level Sci Achievement Awd, 1983; 3rd Prize, Natl Min Level Sci Prog Awd, 1986; State Cncl Spec Subsidy Awd, 1992; Provcl Educl Rsch Awd, 1996, 1997, 1998. Memberships: Exec Dir, Natl Tchrs Colls Phys Rsch Assn, 1991-; Chmn, Heilongjiang Provincial Tchr's Colls Rsch Assn, 1991-; Chmn, Natl Tchrs Colls Assn, 1994-1998, 1998-. Hobbies: Photography; Strolling. Address: No 9, Xue Fu Si Doa Jie, Nangang District, Harbin, Heilongjiang Province, 150086 China.

TIAN Keqin, b. 26 Dec 1945, Joutai, Jilin, China. Teacher. m. Gao Fengying, 28 Dec 1969, 2 s. Education: BA, NE Normal Univ, 1979. Appointments: Asst Prof, 1979-88, Assoc Prof, 1988-92, Prof, 1992-. Publications: On the Essentials of the Relationship between the Communist Party of China and the Kuomindang, 1992; A Study of Deng Xiaoping's Theoretical System, 1997. Honours: Ex Awd for Tchrs, Jilin Prov, 1993; Specl Subsidy, Chinese Govt, 1993. Memberships: Bd Dir, Rsch Cntr for Deng Xiaoping's Theories, Min of Educn, China, 1995; Chmn, Bd of Dirs, CPC's Hist Assn, Jilin Prof, 1998. Hobby: Literature. Address: Theory Research Center, Northeast Normal University, Changchun 130024, China.

TIAN Lian-Tao, b. 23 Jan 1930, Tianjin Cty, China. Education; Researching; Composing. m. Song Tao, 7 July 1932, 1 d. Education: Nanking Univ Coll of Engrng, 1948-49; Grad, Cntrl Consrvatory of Music, Beijing, Dept of Composition, 1955-60. Appointments: Dir, composition sect, Art Dept, Cntrl Inst Chinese Minorities, 1979-84; Dpty Dir, Music Rsch Inst Cntrl Conservatory, 1986-94. Publications: The Essence of Tibetan Traditional Music; Movie music, Princess Peacock. Honours: Spec subsidy for outstndng achievement, State Cncl of China. Memberships: Dpty Pres, Chinese Minorities Music Soc; Mbr, Standing Cttee, Chinese Tradl Music Soc. Hobbies: Football (Soccer) Movies. Address: Central Conservatory, Xicheng District #43, Baojia Street, Beijing, China.

TIAN Zaiyi, b. 6 Dec 1919, Shaanxi, China. Petroleum Geologist. m. Hu Jingxin, 1 Mar 1953, 3 s, 1 d. Education: BSc, Ctrl Univ, 1945. Appointments: Geol, Yumen Oilfield and Xian Geol Bur, 1945-54; Chf Geol, Xinjiang Oilfield, 1955-59; VP, Gen geol, Daqing Oilfield, 1960-63, Dagang Oilfield, 1964-66, Jianghan Oilfield, 1967-73, Jilin Oilfield, 1974-79, Rsch Inst of Petroleum Exploration and Devel, Beijing, 1980-84; Rsch Prof, Advsr of Grads, 1985-; Mbr, CAS, 1997-. Publications: The Mesozoic-Cenozoic East China Rift System, 1992; Petroliferous Sedimentary Basins in China and Basin Analysis, 1996; Lithofacies Paleogeography of Petroliferous Basins in China and Oil and Gas Distribution, 1997. Honours: 1st Prize, China Natl Awd, 1982; Li Siguang Awd, Geosci Rschrs, 1989; Spec Govt Subsidy, 1991-. Memberships: Geol Soc of China, standing mbr, 1983-92; Petroleum Soc of China, standing mbr, 1979-95. Hobby: Sports. Address: c/o Research Institute of Petroleum Exploration & Development, PO Box 910, Beijing 100083, China.

TIAN Zhaobin, b. 10 July 1938, Yanchen, Jiangsu, China. Physicist. m. Daolian Xia, 1 Oct 1966, 1 s, 1 d. Education: Grad, Nankai Univ, 1962; Postgrad, 1966. Appointments: Rschr, Shanghai Inst Optics and Fine Mechs, 1966-76; Engr, Taizhou Municpial Com Sci & Tech, 1976-89; Prof, Yangzhou Inst Tech, 1984-. Publications: Introduction to Medical Laser, 1992; Modern Physics and Its Application, 1995. Honours: Recip, Sci Prize, Govt Jiangsu Prov, 1981-. Memberships: Jiangsu Inst Lasers, 1978-; Chinese Inst Optics, 1981-. Hobbies: Literature; Chinese chess; Qigong. Address: Yingxin Road #36, Yangzhou 225009, China.

TIAN Chengping, b. 1940. Admnstr. Appointments: A Dep Sec CPC 8th Qinghai Prov Cttee, 1988-; Gov of Qinghai Prov, 1993-; Sec CCP Qinghai Prov Cttee, 1997-. Memberships: Alt mbr 13th Cntrl Cttee CCP, 1987-91; Mbr 14th CCP Cntrl Cttee, 1992-97; Mbr 15th CCP Cntrl Cttee, 1997-. Address: Office of the Governor, Qinghai Provincial Government, Xining City, Qinghai Province, People's Republic of China.

TIAN Fengshan, b. Oct 1940. Admnstr. Appointments: Joined CCP, 1970; Dep Commnr Prov Admin Off, 1985-88; Sec CCP Mudanjiang Municipal Cttee, 1988-89; Vice-Gov Heilongjiang Prov, 1989-94; Acting Gov, 1994-95; Gov, 1995-; Sec CCP Harbin Municipal Cttee, 1992; Dep to 8th NPC from Heilongjiang Prov, 1996; Dep Sec CCP Heilongjiang Prov Cttee. Memberships: Mbr CCP Suihua Prefectural Cttee Heilongjiang Prov, 1985-88; Alt mbr 13th CCP Cntrl Cttee, 1987-91; Alt mbr 14th CCP Cntrl Cttee, 1992-97; Mbr 15th CCP Cntrl Cttee, 1997-. Address: Office of the Governor, Heilongjiang Provincial Government, Harbin City, People's Republic of China.

TIAN Jiyun, b. Jun 1929 Feicheng Co Shandong. Politician. Appointments: Joined CCP, 1945; Dep Sec-Gen State Cncl, 1981-83; Sec-Gen, 1983-85; Vice-Premier, 1983-93; Sec-Gen State Cncl, 1983-88; Hd Commodity Prices Grp State Cncl, 1984-93; Hd State Flood Control Hq, 1988-93; Hd Cntrl Forest Fire Prevention Hq, 1987-93; Vice-Chmn Standing Cttee 8th NPC, 1993-; NPC Dep Guizhou Prov; Chmn Inst of Dip, 1995-. Memberships: Mbr 12th CCP Cntrl Cttee, 1982-87; Mbr Politburo, 1985-; Mbr Secr CCP Centrl Cttee, 1985-87; Mbr 13th CCP Cntrl Cttee, 1987-92; Mbr 14th CCP Cntrl Cttee, 1992-97; Mbr 15th CCP Cntrl Cttee,

1997-. Address: State Council, Beijing, People's Republic of China.

TIFFIN John Weightman, b. 10 Sept 1932, Leeds, UK. Academic. m. Jean Tiff, 16 Jan 1959, 1 s, 2 d. Education: BA (Hons) Leeds Univ, 1953; MA, Liverpool Univ, 1968; PhD, Florida State Univ, 1976. Appointments: Snr Specialist in Educ, Tech of Multinational Proj in Ed Tech of Org of Div Armenian States, 1976-80; Dir, Aries Intl Wash Dc, 1980-83; Mngr, Rsch, Progeni Ltd, NZ, 1983-85; The Beattie Prof of Comms, Vic Univ of Wellington, NZ, 1985-98. Publications: Co-auth: In Search of Virtual Class, 1995; Num books and articles in profl jrnls. Honour: Prof Emeritus.

TILLEKERATNE Herbert Walter, b. 5 Mar 1932, Kadugannawa, Sri Lanka. Education. m. Elizabeth, 30 Dec 1965, 2 s. Education: BS; Dip, Bus Mmgmt and Admin; Sci Trained Certs (CTC, GTC); YMCA Sec Trng (Hong Kong). Appointments: Sci Tchr, 1959, Sci Lectr, 1972, Nat Trng Sec, 1984, Sri Lanka Educ Serv, 1984, VP, 1986, Snr Educ Cnslt, Tertiary and Vocl Educ Commn (Si Lanka), 1992. Publications: Books: Towards the Challenge of YMCA Mission; Women in Society - A Report. Memberships: Hon Sec, SLTCTSU (Sri Lanka Trng Colls Tutorial Staff Union), 1971, VP, 1973; VP, CDSFA (Colombo Dist Schs Football Assn), 1987; VP, JASS (Jathika Adyapana Sevaka Sangamaya) (GTC), 1983; Chmn, Ldrshp Dev, Natl Cncl YMCAs, 189; Ed, news bulletin, Concern, 1996; Pres, Sri Lanka Fellshp YMCA Retirees, 1998; Sec-Treas, S Asia Fellshp of YMCA Retirees, 1998. Hobbies: Agriculture; Collecting snaps; Environmental concerns; Rebirth/reincarnation; Astrology; Evolution; Religion. Address: 72/6, Chakkindarama Road, Ratmalana, Sri Lanka.

TILLEY Raymond Francis, b. 21 Feb 1923. Managing Director; Businessman. m. Yvonne Grace Charlton, 4 s. Education: Fell, Austl Inst Mngmt; Fell, Retail Mgmnt Inst Aust; Licensed Pilot and Radio Opr. Appointments include: Employer Rep, Tas Wages Bd, 1960-73; Mbr, Consumer Affairs Cncl Tas, 1970-86; Alderman, Launceston City Cncl, 1973-76; Cttee, Tas Orch Advsry ABC, 1973-76; Mngng Dir, A W Birchall and Sons Pty Ltd and Assocd Cos, Launceston and Hobart, Tas; JP; Natl Pks Advsry Cttee, Ben Lomond. Honour: OAM, 1992. Memberships include: Life Mbr, Past Pres, Austl Booksellers Assn; Life Mbr, Past Pres, Tas Booksellers Assn; Past Pres, Life Mbr, Retail Traders Assn Tas; Past Chmn, Past Registrar, Cncl Hon Justices Assns; Life Mbr, Past Pres, Hon Justices Assn Tas; Life Mbr, Past Pres, Tas Aero Club; Life Mbr, Roy Flying Dr Serv; Life Mbr, Past Pres, Patron, Northern Tas Alpine Club; Past Pres, Paul Harris Fell, Rotary Club Launceston. Hobbies: Skiing; Trout fishing; Wind surfing; Music; Woodworking; Outdoor pursuits. Address: 56 Bald Hill Road, Launceston, Tas 7250, Australia.

TIMM Robert Merle, b. 7 Oct 1949, Pomona, CA, USA. Superintendent; Extension Wildlife Specialist. m. Janice Howard Hawthorne, 31 May 1986, 1 s, 2 d. Education: BS, Biol, Univ of Redlands, CA, 1971; MS, Univ of CA Davis, Ecology, 1973; PhD, Ecology, 1977. Appointments: Extension Vertebrate Pest Specialist, Assoc Prof, Univ of NE, Lincoln, 1978-87; Supt, Ext, Wildlife Specialist, UC Hopland Rsch and Extension Cntr, 1987-. Publications: Co-Ed, Co-Auth, Prevention and Control of Wildlife Damage, 1983, 1994. Honours: Outstndng Book, Natural Rescs Cncl of Am, 1983; Keynote Speaker, 5th Eastern Wildlife Damage Conf, 1991; Magna Cum Laude. Memberships: The Wildlife Soc; Amn Soc of Mammalogists; Natl Animal Damage Control Assoc; Soc for Range Mngmnt; Sigma Xi; Vertebrate Pest Cncl. Hobbies: Choral Music; Photography; Travel. Address: University of California Research and Extension Center, 4070 University Road, Hopland, CA 95449, USA.

TIMNAT Yaakov M, b. 22 June 1923, Trieste, Italy. Professor of Aerospace Engineering. m. Shoshand, 30 July 1947, 1 s, 1 d. Education: MSc, 1947, PhD, 1951, Hebrew Univ. Appointments: Rsch Scientist, Rafael, 1959; Snr Rsch Scientists, Rafael, 1956; Fac Mbr,

Techion, 1962-. Publications: 3 books: Advanced Chemical Rocket Propulsion, 1987; Advanced Air Breathing Propulsion, 1991; Rocket propulsion. Memberships: MAA; AE; ASME; Inst of Energy (London); Israel Soc of Aeronautics and Astron, Pres, 1970, 1994. Address: Department of Aerospace Engineering, Techion, Israel Institute of Technology, Haifa 32000, Israel.

TIMONEY JENKIN Ann, b. 6 July 1933, London, England. Writer. div, 2 s, 1 d. Publication: Midwinter Light (poetry collection), 1995. Honour: Individual Project Grant, SA Dept of the Arts & Cultural Heritage, 1990. Membership: Austl Soc of Auths. Hobbies: Writing; Reading; Gardening. Address: 10 Margaret Street, Norwood, South Australia 5067, Australia.

TIMPSON Thomas Henry, b. 3 Sept 1913, Manchester, Eng (Austl citizen). Retired Educator. m. Norma Brahe Percival, 10 Mar 1940, 2 s, 2 d. Education: Univ of Melbourne, Trinity Coll, 1932, BA, 1936, MA, 1938, BEd, 1952. Appointments: Pt-time Lectr in Philos, Canberra Univ Coll; Tchr, Canberra Grammar Sch, 2 yrs; Uppingham Sch, Eng, 1946-54; Headmaster, Camberwell Grammar Sch, Vic, 1955-65; Exams Bd, 1966-75; Registrar, Austl Coll of Educ, 1976-81, retd 1981. Honours: AO, 1978; Hon Fell, Austl Coll of Educ. Hobbies: Gardening; Lecturing for University of the Third Age; Listening to music. Address: 13 Albany Crescent, Surrey Hills, Victoria 3127, Australia.

TIN Shwe, b. 13 Aug 1936, Maw La Myine, Myanmar. Physician. m. Aye Thant, 23 Oct 1960, 1 s, 2 d. Education: MBBS; DPTM; DCMT; DLSHTM; MSc, London; FACTM, Aust; FRCP, Edinburgh, Scotland. Appointments: Township Medl Offr, var locations; Rsch Scientist, Dept of Medl Rsch, Yangon. Publications: Over 220 books on hlth educ and buddhism. Honours: 2 Natl Awds on Myanmar Lit and 1 Natl Awd on Medl Rsch. Membership: Cntrl Cttee Mbr, Writers and Auths Assn, 1988-. Hobby: Writing books. Listed in: Who's Who in the World; Dictionary of International Biography. Address: 39 Oo Kywe Hoe Street, Yangon, Kyimyindine, Myanmar.

TINAYE-TEHRANI Alireza, b. 29 Jan 1969, Tehran, Iran. Mechanical Engineer; Designer; Consultant; Computer Programmer. Education: BS, Mechl Engrng, Sharif Univ of Technol, 1992; MS, Mechl Engrng, Amirkabir Univ of Technol, 1995. Appointments: Numerical Simulation of Local Scour at the Downstream end of Hydraulics Structures, Power Min, 1995-97; Tchr, Aerospace Dept, Fac of Airforce Univ 1996-98; Mechl Designer, Cnslt, Numerical Simulation; Computer Programmer, Testing Apparatus to Control Via a Computer, 1998-. Creative Works: Ppr, Numerical Simulation of Fluid Flow in a Channel with Step; Ppr, Numerical Simulation of Supersonic Jet Injection in a wind tunnel. Hobbies: Astronomy; Space Sci; Sci Studies; Rsch; Football; Tab Tennis. Address: #23 Northern 123 st Western 212 St, Tehranpars Avenue, 16537 Tehran, Iran.

TING Wai, b. 30 Mar 1954, Hong Kong. Associate Professor. m. Charlotte Kwok See Wai, 21 Sept 1992, 1 s, 1 d. Education: BS (Hons), Chinese Univ of Hong Kong, 1976; DPol Sci, Univ of Paris X, 1984. Appointments: Rsch Fell, Inst of S E Asian Studies, Singapore, 1985-86; Lectr, Dept of Comm Studies, 1986-94; Lectr, Dept of Govt and Intl Studies, 1994-95; Assoc Prof, Dept of Govt and Intl Studies, Hong Kong Bapt Univ, 1995-. Publications: Num articles to acad jrnls, books, mags and newspprs. Honours: Robert Schuman Schlshp, Eurn Parl, 1984; Intl Visitors Prog, Dept of State, USA; Eurn Union Vis Prog, Eurn Commn, 1996. Memberships: Asian Studies Assn (USA); Intl Studies Assn (USA); Amn Pol Sci Assn. Hobbies: Hiking; Music; Fine arts; Opera. Address: Department of Government and International Studies, Hong Kong Baptist University, Kowloon Tong, Hong Kong.

TINGA Beniamina, Government Official. Appointments: Min, Fin and Econ Plng, Govt Kiribati, Tarawa Atoll; Mbr Parl, Nikunau; Chmn, Pub Accts Com;

Auditor, Gen Sec, Fin and Econ Plnt, Controller, Customs and Excise. Address: Ministry for Finance and Economic Planning, PO Box 67, Bairiki, Tarawa, Kiribati.

TINGSANCHALI Tawatchai, b. 2 Feb 1947, Bangkok, Thailand. Professor. m. Nuasom, 1976, 1 s, 1 d. Education: BEng, Chulalongkorn, Hon, 1968; MEng, Asian Inst of Technol, 1970; DEng, Asian Inst of Technol, 1974. Appointments: Asst Prof, 1975-78; Assoc Prof, 1978-88; Full Prof, 1988-; Major Admin, Chmn, Div of Water Resc Eng, 1985-87; Forum Chmn, Sch of Civil Engrng; Asian Inst of Technol, 1998-. Publications: More than 100 pprs in intl jrnls and conf proceedings. Honours: Outstndng Rsch Awd, Thailand Natl Rsch Cncl, 1981; Rsch Fell Awd, Alexander von Humboldt Stiftung, 1983, 1984; Lectr Awd, Natl Taiwan Univ; Top Hon Rsch Awd, Indian Inst of Hydrologist, Roorkee, 1995. Memberships: Fell, Instl Water Resc Assn, USA; Fell, Indian Inst of Hydrologist; Fell, Eng Inst of Thailand; Amn Soc Civil Engrng; Intl Assn for Hydraulic Rsch. Hobbies: Jogging; Swimming; Reading; Amateur radio. Address: School of Civil Engineering, Institute of Technology, PO Box 4, Klong Luang, Pathom Thani, 12120, Thailand.

TIRKEL Anatol Zygmunt, b. 30 Aug 1949, Krakow, Poland. Scientist; Engineer. Education: BSc (1st Hon), 1970; PhD, 1975. Appointments: PI w Varian, 1975-76, Martin Marietta, 1977, Hughes Aircraft, 1978-80, TRW, 1980-82; Snr Lectr, RMIT, 1982-86; Dir, Sci Technol, 1986-; Visng Prof, Monash Univ, 1991-. Publications: Over 50 pprs (tech and sci) in diverse jrnls, 1972-. Memberships: IEEE, 1977, Snr Mbr, 1984; APS, 1977-. Hobbies: Travel; Sports. Address: PO Box 3032, Dendy Brighton 3186, Australia.

TISCH Johannes Hermann, b. 11 Dec 1929, Austria. (Swiss and Australian citizen). University Professor; Educator; Honorable Justice of the Peace; Consul for Switzerland. m. Regula B C Wackernagel, 12 Apr 1957, 2 s, 2 d. Education: Univ of Basle, Switz, 1949-53; Univ of Oxford, Eng, 1953-54; Univ Göttingen, 1954-55; PhD, Univ of Basle, 1961. Appointments include: Lectr, German, Univ of Oxford, Eng, 1957-60; Lectr, Austl Natl Univ, 1961-63; Snr Lectr, Univ of Sydney, 1964-65; Fedn Prof, Jt Hd, Mod Langs Dept, Univ of Tas, 1966-92; Visng Prof, Univ of Pitts, USA, 1970; Comparative Lit Sch, La Nouvelle Sorbonne, Paris, France, 1973-74; Prof Emer, Hon Rsch Assoc, 1993-98. Publications include: Over 100 articles in profl jrnls; Books incl: Andrean Gryphius: Leo Arminius, 1968; Renaissance and Rococo, 1973; The Italian Novella and German Humanism, 1984; Samson Agonistes and Milton's Ideas of Worldly and Religious Immortality, 1984; The Red Cross and Modern Switzerland, 1987; Hrafnkels Saga - A Reappraisal, 1995. Honours include: Cmdr of Order of St Lazarus; PhD, Marquis Giuseppe Scicluna Intl Univ Fndn, USA; DSc (HC), Peace Stdies, Albert Einstein Acady Bronze Medal for Peace; Amb at Large, Hon Dpty Gov, ABI; Hon Dir-Gen, IBC, Cambridge; G Marconi Medal, Civic Merit; Cmdr of Merit (Companion of Merit); Order of St Lazarus of Jerusalem. Memberships include: Austl Coll of Educ; Life Patron, IBA; LFWIA; Roy C'wlth Soc; Bd, Hutchins Fndn; Austl Inst of Dirs; Inaugural Mbr of TACMEA Tasmanian (Ministerial) Advsry Cncl on Multicultural and Ethnic Affairs, 1992-95. Address: Swiss Consulate, 1 Cedar Court, Sandy Bay, Hobart, Tas 7005, Australia.

TISDELL Clement Allan, b. 18 Nov 1939, Taree, New South Wales, Australia. Lecturer; Economist. m. Marie-Elisabeth, 1 s, 1 d. Education: BCom, Econs, Univ NSW, 1961; PhD, Austl Natl Univ, 1964. Appointments include: Temp Lectr, Econs, Austl Natl Univ, 1964; Visng Fell, Princetown Univ, 1965; Vis Schl, Stanford Univ, 1965; Lectr, Econs, Austl Natl Univ, 1966-67; Snr Lectr, 1967, Rdr in Econs, 1967-72, Prof of Econs, 1972-89, Dean, Fac of Econs and Com, 1977-78, 1985-86, Univ Newcastle, NSW; Prof of Econs, 1989-, Hd of Dept, 1989-98, Dept Dir, Sch of Marine Sci, 1993-98, Univ Qld. Publications: Economics in Canadian Society, 1986; Weed Control Economics, 1987; Economics of Environmental Conservation, 1993; Economic Development in the Context of China, 1993; Economics of Giant Clam Mariculture, 1994; Economic Development

and Women, 1996; Bounded Rationality and Economic Evolution, 1996; The Environment and Economic Development in South Asia, 1998. Memberships: Fell, Japan Soc for Promotion of Sci, 1991; Acady of Socl Sci, Aust; Econs Soc; Intl Soc of Agri Econs. Address: 319 Cliveden Avenue, Corinda, 4075 Brisbane, Queensland, Australia.

TITO Teburoro, b. 25 Aug 1953, Tabiteuea N, Kiribati. Politician. m. Nei Keina, 1 child. Education: Univ of S Pacific, Suva; Papua New Guinea Admin Coll. Appointments: Pres, Univ of the S Pacific Studs Assn, 1976-77; Stud Co-ord, Univ of S Pacific Studs' Assn, 1977-79; Schlshp Offr, Min of Educ, 1980-82; Snr Educ Offr, 1983-87; Mbr, Maneaba ni Maungatabu (Parl), and Ldr of Opposition, 1987-94; Mbr, parly Pub Accts Cttee, 1987-90; Pres of Kiribati, 1994-; Mbr, CPA Exec Cttee for Pacific Reg, 1989-90. Membership: Chair, Kiribati Football Assn, 1980-94. Hobby: Sport. Address: Office of the President, PO Box 67, Hairiki, Tarawa, Kiribati.

TIVER Newton Stanley, b. 10 Aug 1920, Adelaide, Aust. Retired Agricultural Scientist, Consultant. m. Joan Adelaide Cavell Kneebone, 6 Oct 1943, dec 1989, 1 s, 1 d. Education BAgSc, 1940, BAgrSc, 1st class hons, 1942, MSc, 1946. Appointments: War Serv, Lt, Roy Austl Navy, 1942-45; Asst Agronomist, Grassland Ecologist, Waite Agric Rsch Inst, 1945-50; Asst Mngr, Agrostologist, Koniak Seeds Ltd, 1950-51; Snr Rsch Offr, later Snr Agronomist, SA Dept of Agric, 1951-60; Chf Agricl Advsr, 1960-65; Agric Cnslt Dir, Hugh Robinson & Co, 1965-71; Austl Agric Cnsltng and Mngnt Co, Dir, Snr Cnslt, 1971-84. Publications: Articles in profl jrnls. Honours: Agricl Technologist of Aust, 1980; Fell, Aust Inst of Agric Sci, 1980; AM, 1981. Memberships: Fell, Austl Inst of Agricl Sci and Technol. Hobbies: Farming; Bowls. Address: Unit 2, 412 Fullerton Road, Myrtle Bank, SA 5064, Australia.

TIZARD Catherine Anne, b. 4 Apr 1931, Auckland, NZ. Lecturer; Mayor. m. James Tizard, 1951, div 1983, 1 s, 3 d. Education: BA, Univ Auckland. Appointments: Tutor, Zoology, Univ Auckland, 1963-83; Mayor of Auckland, 1983-90; Govt Gen of NZ, 1990-96; Chair, NZ Hist Places Trust, 1996-; Bd, NZ Symph Orch, 1996-. Honours: OBE, 1985; GCMG, 1990; NZ Medal, 1990; Freedom of the City of London, 1990; Hon LLD, Univ Auckland, 1992; Suffrage Centennial Medal, 1993; GCVO, 1995; QSO, 1996. Memberships: Num. Hobbies: Music; Drama; Scuba Diving; Cryptic Crosswords. Address: c/o New Zealand Historic Places Trust, PO Box 2629, Wellington, New Zealand.

TIZARD Robert James (Rt Hon), b. 7 June 1924, Auckland, NZ. Teacher; Politician. m. (1) Catherine Anne Maclean, 1951, 1 s 3 d, (2) Mary Nacey, 1983, 1 s. Education: MA, Auckland Univ. Appointments: Served in Roy NZ Air Force, Can and UK, 1943-46; Jnr Lectr in Hist, Auckland Univ, 1949-53; Tchng posts, 1955-57, 1961-62; MP, 1957-60, 1963-90; Min of Hlth and State Servs, 1972-74; Min of Fin, Dpty PM, 1974-75; Dpty Ldr of Opposition, 1975-79; Min of Energy Stats, Sci and Technol, Min in Charge of Audit Dept, 1984-87; Min of Sci and Technol and Def, 1987-90; Privy Cncl, 1986. Hobby: Golf. Address: 8 Glendowie Road, Auckland 5, New Zealand.

TJIPTOHERIJANTO Prijono, b. 3 Apr 1948, Malang, Indonesia. Professor. m. Yumiko, 29 Dec 1978, 1 s, 1 d. Education: PhD, Econs, Univ of HI, USA. Appointments: Asst, State Sec, Rep of Indonesia, 1993-98. Creative Works: Writing Poems. Honours: Outstndng Lectr, 1983; Outstndng Scientist in Indonesia, 1990. Memberships: Amn Econs Assn; Phillipines Econ Soc. Hobbies: Swimming; Reading. Address: Kompleks Perumahan Dosen, UI No 60,Ciputat 15419, Jakarta Selatan, Indonesia.

TLASS Mustapha el-, b. 11 May 1932 Rastan Cty Mouhafazat Homs. Politician; Army Offr. m. Lamyaa al-Jabri, 1958, 2 s, 2 d. Education: Mil and Law Colls; Voroshilov Acady Moscow. Appointments: Sec of Rastan Sect, 1951; Sports tchr Al-Kraya Sch Mouhafazat

al-Soueda, 1950-52; Deputed to Egyptian army, 1959-61; Insp min of Supply, 1962; Detained, 1962-63; Cmdr Tank Bat and Chf of Cntrl Reg of Natl Security Crt, 1963; Chf of Staff 5th Armoured Brig, 1964-66; Participated in movement of 23 Feb promoted to Cmdr of Cntrl Reg and of 5th Armoured Brig rank of Maj-Gen, 1968; Chf of Staff of Armed Forces, 1968-70; First Dep Min of Def, 1968-72; Participated in coup installing Pres Hafez Al-Assad, Nov 1970; First Dep Cmdr in Chf Armed Forces, 1970-72; Dep Cmdr in Chf, 1972-; Min of Def, 1972-; Now also Dep PM; Dep Chf of Joint Supreme Mil Cncl of Syrian and Egyptian Armed Forces, 1973; Rank of Lt-Gen, 1978. Publications: Guerilla War; Military Studies; An Introduction to Zionist Strategy; The Arab Prophet; Memories in the Military Prison of Mezzah; The Fourth War between Arabs and Israel; The Second Chapter of the October Liberation War; Selections of Arab Poetry; The Steadfastness Front in confrontation with Camp David; The Algerian Revolution; Art of Soviet War; American Policy under the Carter Regime; The Technological Revolution; Development of the Armed Forces. Honours: 33 Orders and Medals. Memberships: Mbr Baath Arab Socl Party, 1947-; Mbr Free Offrs Movement, 1962-63; Mbr Regl Cmd Regl Congress of Baath Arab Socl Party, 1965, 1968, 1969, 1975; Mbr of Politbureau, 1969-; Mbr of Natl Cncl of Revolution, 1965-71; Mbr People's Cncl, 1971-. Hobbies: Reading; Writing books; Mil and histl studies; Photog. Address: Ministry of Defence, Damascus, Syria.

TOBIAS Murray Herbert, b. 27 Mar 1939, Sydney, Aust. Barrister (QC). m. Colleen, 2 s, 2 d. Education: LLB (Hons Class I), Sydney Univ; Bch (Hons Class II) Oxfod Univ. Appointment: Casino Control Authority of NSW, 1993-96. Honour: AM, 1998. Memberships: Pres, NSW Bar Assn, 1993-95; Snr VP, Austl Bar Assn, 1999. Hobbies: Golf; Music (classical); Reading; Walking. Address: 26 Kardinia Road, Clifton Gardens 2088, Australia.

TOBIN Meryl Elaine (Writing name: Meryl Brown Tobin), b. 26 Aug 1940, SW Brunswick, Vic, Aust. m. Hartley Tobin, 6 Jan 1962, 2 s, 1 d. Education: BA, Melbourne Univ, 1961; Dip Educ, Melbourne Univ, 1962. Publications: 11 books inclng: Puzzles Galore!, 1978, 1993; More Puzzles Galore!, 1980, 1994; Exploring Outback Australia, 1988 Puzzleways: Grammar and Spelling, 1990; Animal Puzzle Parade, 1991; Puzzle Round Australia, 1992; Puzzling Cats!, 1994; Puzzles Ahoy!, 1995; Pets to Puzzle, 1995; Play With Words, 1996; 52 short stories; hundreds of articles; 91 poems; 4 cartoons; 4 comic strips. Honours: Winner 1st Lit Competition (poetry), Redoubt, 1993; Winner Haiku Competition, The Lyrebird Monthly, 1993; 3rd, Best Children's Story, 1994; Highly Commended, Best Presentation, 1995, 3rd, Best Children's Story, 1997, 2nd, Best 50 Word Novel, 3rd Prize Best memories, 1998, 1st, Best Childrens Story, 1998, 2nd Best 50 Word Novel, 1998, Soc of Women Writers (Aust) Vic Branch, Christmas Luncheon Awds. Memberships: Austl Soc of Auths Ltd; Fellshp of Austl Writers (Vic Branch) Inc; Soc of Women Writers Aust (Vic Branch); Vic Writers Cntr. Hobbies: Bushwalking; Conservation; Travel; Social Issues. Address: Ningan, Bass Highway, The Gurdies, Victoria, 3984, Australia.

TOBIN Roderick Charles, b. 10 Sept 1933. Lecturer. m. 7 Aug 1964, 2 s, 1 d. Education: BSc, hons, 1960; PhD, 1980. Appointments: Sci Offr, Aeronautical Rsch Lab, 1960-63; Lectr, 1964-69, Snr Lectr, 1970-95, Rdr, 1996-98 (ret'd), Snr Hon Rsch Fell, 1999- Monash Univ. Publications: Sev articles in jrnls and confs; 2 US Patents. Memberships: Fell, Austl Inst of Phys; Austl Optical Soc; IEEE, USA. Hobbies: Golf; Bridge. Address: Department of Physics, Monash University, Clayton, Vic 3168, Australia.

TODA Kunio, b. 11 Aug 1915, Tokyo, Japan. Composer; Music Educator. m. 21 Nov 1963. Education: Grad, Law and Polit Scis, Tokyo Univ, 1938; Class of Prof Poppen, Heidelberg Univ, Germany, 1938; Studied Composition w Prof Saburo Moroi, Tokyo, 1941-43. Appointments: Debut w Overtura Sinfonica, Tokyo, 1943;

Prof of Composition, Harmony, Counterpoint, etc, Toho Gakuen Sch of Music, 1955-96; Perm Delegate of Japan for UNESCO, Paris, 1959-63; Dir, then Guest Prof, Senzoku Gakuen Music Acady, 1977-88. Creative Works: Sonatina per Pianoforte; Quattro pezzi deformati per Pianoforte; Fantaisie sur les sons de koto (Pour piano seul); Message for Soprano, Clarinet and Harp; Concerto grosso per sei strumenti ed orchestra; Setti canti dall'antologia Mannyosyu; San Paulo, Oratorio-misterio nella forma di no; Takase-bhune, Recitativo per voce d'uomo e violoncello solo; Sonata per violino e pianoforte; 2 operas; Sev ballets; Cantata for solo voices and orch, based on ancient Chinese poems; Var chamber and vocal works inclng mono-and duodrams. Publications: Rosia Ongaku (History of Russian Music), 1953; Prokofiev, 1957; Kindai to Gendai no Ongaku (Modern and Contemporary Music), 1959; Ongaku to Minzokusei (National Traits in Music), 1967; Num transl and articles in Japanese Music Mags, Newspprs and Jrnls. Honours: Japan Victor Prize for Debut, 1943; NHK-Jiji Press Music Prize, 1944, 1948, 1949; Odaka Prize, 1953; Offr, Legion d'Honneur, France, 1958; 4rd Order Rising Sun Decoration, 1988. Memberships: Sec Gen, Japanese Natl Cttee, Intl Music Cncl, 1965-95; Hon Mbr, Japanese Soc for Contemporary Music; Japan Composers Fedn. Address: 4-16-13 Seijo, Setagaya-ku, Tokyo 157-0066, Japan.

TODD Trevor Roy, b. 11 Dec 1947, Eng. Writer. 2 d. Education: BA, Western Austl Inst of Technol. Publications: 7 books for children. Honours: Austl Writers Guild AWGIE, Best Children's TV Drama, 1994. Membership: Austl Writers Guild. Address: c/o Curtis Brown (Aust) Pty Ltd, 27 Union Street, Paddington, NSW 2021, Australia.

TOH Chooi Gait, b. 30 Dec 1950, Taiping, Perak, Malaysia. m. Alex Chan Heng Wye, 1 s, 1 d. Education: BDS Hons, Univ of Singapore, 1970-74; MSc, Conserv Dentistry, Inst of Dental Surg, Univ of London, Eng, 1977-78; DRDRCS, Roy Coll of Surgs of Edinburgh, 1980; FDSRCPS, Roy Coll of Physns & Surgs of Glasgow, 1980. Appointments: Asst Lectr 1974, Lectr 1975, Assoc Prof 1984, Prof 1995, Dept of Conserv Dentistry, Fac of Dentistry, Univ of Malaya, Kuala Lumpur; Acting Dpty Dean, 1986-87, Dpty Dean 1987-92, Hd of Dept of Conserv Dentistry 1994-. Publications include: Surface Microhardness of Glass-ionomers Used for Restorations, 1994; Porcelain Laminate Veneers - Considerations for a Successful Approach in the Conservative Treatment of Aesthetic Problems, 1994; A Comparison of Plaque Control Between A Conventional Toothbrush and a Unique Design Toothbrush, 1995; An Evaluation of Debris Accumulation and Fraying of Bristles of a Unique Design Toothbrush, 1995. Honours: Univ Silver Medal, 1971, 1972, 1974; Malaysian Dental Assn Medal, 1974; Tratman Medal, 1974; C'wlth Med Schlshp, 1977-80; Acad Staff Trng Scheme, 1977-80; Fell, Acady Dentistry Intl, 1987; Fell, Intl Coll of Dentists, 1993; Excellent Serv Awd, Univ of Malaya, 1995; FDSRCS, 1996. Memberships: Malaysian Dental Assn; Brit Endodontic Soc; Intl Assn for Dental Rsch, Pres, 1997-99; SE Asian Assn for Dental Educ, Pres Elect, 1998-2000. Listed in: Who's Who in the World. Hobbies: Gardening; Listening to Music; Reading. Address: Department of Conservative Dentistry, Faculty of Dentistry, University of Malaya, 50603 Kuala Lumpur, Malaysia.

TOH Kok-Aun, b. 24 Aug 1943, Malaysia. University Lecturer. m. Swee-Har, 8 Dec 1968, 1 d. Education: DPhil, Oxford; AM, Stanford; BSc Hons, Dip Ed, Malaya. Appointment: Dpty Hd, Cntr for Educl Rsch, Natl Inst of Educ, Nanyang Technol Univ, Singapore. Publications: More than 100 publs and presentations on rsch, sci tchng, tchr educ. Honours: Fulbright Schlr, 1982-83; St Cross Schlr, 1989. Membership: Pres, Educl Rsch Assn, Singapore, 1997-99. Address: c/o National Institute of Education, Nanyang Technological University, Singapore.

TOKAYEV Kasymzhomart Kemelevich, b. 17 Mary 1953 Almaty Kazakhstan. Diplomatist. m. Nadeyda Poznanskaya, 1983, 1 s. Education: Moscow Inst of Intl

Rels; Dip Acady USSR Min of For Affairs. Appointments: With USSR min of For Affairs, 1975; Emb Singapore, 1975-79; Attache Third Sec min of For Affairs, 1979-83; Second Sec of Dept, 1984-85; Second First Sec Emb People's Repub of China, 1985-91; Rank of Amb of Kazakhstan, 1994; Dep First Dep Min of For Affairs Repub of Kazakhstan, 1992-94; Min, Oct 1994-. Honours: Parasat - Natl Awd - 1996. Hobbies: Reading; Playing tennis. Address: Ministry of Foreign Affairs, Aiteke-bi str 65, Almaty, Kazakhstan.

TOKOMBAYEVA Aysulu Asanbekovna, b. 22 Sep 1947 Frunze - now Bishkek. Ballerina. Education: Vaganova Dancing Sch Leningrad. Appointments: Soloist with Th of Kirghizia, 1966-. Major roles incl: Odette-Odile - Swan Lake; Aurore - Sleeping Beauty; Giselle; Bayadere: Frigia - Spartacus; Lady Macbeth - by K Molchanov. Honours: USSR State Prize, 1976; People's Artist of Kirghizia, 1976; USSR People's Artist, 1981. Memberships: Mbr CPSU, 1973-91. Address: Kyrgyz Opera Theatre, Bishkek, Kyrgystan.

TOKUDA Yoshihito, b. 22 Nov 1925, Yokohama, Japan. Psychiatric Artist. m. Mrs Hidoko, 12 Dec 1972, 1 s. Education: MD. Publications: Art Therapy; Dictionary of Psychiatry and Behavioral Sciences; Pathography of Artists; Clinical Psychiatry. Honours: Prinzhorn Medal, 1982; Ernst Kris Medal, 1984; IAWA Bridgebuilder Awd, 1992. Memberships: Pres, Assn of Psychopathology of Expression and Arts Therapy; Dir, Neuropsychiatric Rsch Inst; Pres, Hasegawa Hosp. Hobbies: Painting (oil, water, color pencil). Address: 6 8-2 Asahigaola, Hiho, Tokyo 1010065, Japan.

TOKUMARU Hiroshi, b. 5 Feb 1953, Tokyo, Japan. Businessman. m. Naomi, 4 May 1985, div 1993. Education: BS, St Sophia Univ, 1976; MS, Stanford Univ, 1982. Appointments: Asst Mngr, Mitsubishi Heavy Ind Nagoya Aircraft Works, 1982-89; Dpty Dir, Nippon POP Rivets, Black & Decker, 1989-91; Engrng Mngr, Tenjin Seiki Co Ltd, 1991-93; Engrng Sales Mngr, Feintool Japan, 1995-96; Pres, Global Co Ltd, 1993-. Publications: Multi Layered Missile Launcher; AP-Dynamics Gust, Take-off, Landing Analysis; Patents applied for: Elderly Home-Care Syst; Load Alleviating-Energy Efficient Clutch. Honour: Pride in Ex Awd, Boeing Coml Airplane Grp, 1986. Memberships: SAE; AIAA; NY Acady of Scis; TFOS. Hobbies: Jogging; Swimming; Tennis; Reading; Gardening; Travel. Address: 2-6-18 Takamoridai Isehara, Kanagawa 259-1115, Japan.

TOLCHER Helen Mary Forbes, b. 28 Dec 1928, Werrimul, Victoria, Aust. Author. m. V A Tolcher, 1 Dec 1948, 5 s. Publications: Drought or Deluge, 1986; Innamincka - Town With Two Lives, 1990; Conrick of Nappa Merrie, 1997; Rogues and Heroes, 1999. Honours: Canning Lit Awd, 1984; Jessie Litchfield Prize, 1974; Rolf Boldrewood Awd, 1987; Amstrad Awd, 1988. Memberships: Austl Soc of Auths; Stockman's Hall of Fame. Hobbies: Outback Travel; Arid Zone Botany; Archaeology; Anthropology; History; Reading. Address: 6 Warrego Crescent, Linden Park, South Australia 5065, Australia.

TOLIVER Raymond Frederick, b. 16 Nov 1914, Ft Collins, CO, USA. Aviator; Author; Historian. m. Jennie S, 28 Apr 1935, 3 d. Education: CO State Univ, Ft Collins, CO, USA, 3 yrs; Air Command & Staff Coll, 1947-48; Air War Coll, 1951. Appointments: Air Corps, 1937-40; TWA Pilot, 1940; RAF Ferry Command, 1941; US Air Force, 1942-66; Lockheed, 1967-76; Retired to Full time Writing, 1977-. Publications: Blond Knight of Germany, 1968; Fighter Aces of USA, 1980; Fighter Aces of the Luftwaffe, 1980; Holt Hartmann Vom Himmel, 1980-; The Interrogator, 1998. Honour: Var Aviation Writing Awds. Memberships: Daedalians; Intl Order of Characters; Hon Mbr, Amn Fighter Aces Assn. Hobbies: Golf; Writing. Address: 4116 Rhodes Way, Oceanside, California, 92056-7412, USA.

TOMASETTI Glen, b. 21 May 1929, Melbourne, Aust. Writer; Musician. m. (1) P Balmford, 1 Sept 1950, (2) A S Jorgensen, 2 Apr 1961, 1 s, 2 d. Education: BA Hons,

Melbourne Univ, 1950. Publications: The Future is in Your Hands; Labels for Ladies; The Ballad of Bill White (discs); Songs from a Seat in the Carriage, 1970; Thoroughly Decent People; Man of Letters, novel. Memberships: Janet Clarke Hall Soc; The Catalysts; Austl Soc of Auths. Hobbies: Conversation; Meditation; The Sea. Address: c/o Janet Clarke Hall Society, Janet Clarke Hall, Parkville 3052, Vic, Australia.

TOMBLESON Esme Irene, b. 1 Aug 1917. Retired Politician; Community Worker. m. Thomas Tombleson MM JP. Education: MISTD, London (Cecchetti). Appointments include: Assoc, Austl Examination Music Bd; Mbr Italian Opera Co, Sydney Visit, 1932; Mbr Fullers Eng Grand Opera Co, Sydney, 1934; Mbr Monte Carlo Ballet Co, Sydney Visit, 1939; War Serv, Mbr Women's Auxiliary Signalling Corps, Sydney; Sec, Manpower Advsry Cttee, NSW, 1942-47; Section Hd, C'wlth Employment Serv, Sydney 1947-50; Exec Cncl, NZ Neurological Fndn, 1975-91; Cnclr, NZ Comm Welfare Disabled Persons Bd, 1976-88; Intl Patient Servs Cttee IFMSS, 1976-88; Intl Patient Servs Cttee IFMSS, 1976-97; Hon Patron IFMSS, 1977-; Exec Cncl, IFMSS, 1979-97; Mngmt Cttee NZ M S Soc Inc, 1982-; Fndr Sec, DPA Gisborne; Fndr Pres, MS Soc Inc, Gisborne, E Coast, 1988; Pres, DPA Gisborne, 1989-93; Dir, Vanessa Lowndes (Abilities) Gisborne, 1990-97; Fndr Tstee, Esmé and Tom Tombleson Trust for disabled and disadvantaged persons - Gisborne/E Coast, 1993; Dir, Vanessa Lowndes Centre, 1997-; Tstee, Esmé Tombleson Educ Schl, 1998-. Honours: USA Vis Study Awd, 1970; QSO, 1977; Life V Pres and Life Mbr, NZ Multiple Sclerosis Soc Inc, 1983; Insignia Medal of Hon IBI, 1985; Gold Medal of Hon ABI, 1988; Cert of Merit IBC, 1988; Ex Medal, ABI, 1989; NZ Medal, 1990; Woman of the Yr, ABI, 1991; CBE, 1992; DPA Cup Awd, 1992; Suffrage Medal, 1993; Intl Woman of the Yr, ABI, 1993; Commemorative Medal, ABI, 1996. Memberships: C'wlth Parly Union, 1960; VP, Assoc Former MPs, 1972-; VP, Gisborne Cycling Club, 1962; VP, Gisborne Athletic Club, 1962; Gisborne Mus and Art Gall, 1963; Gisborne Music Soc, 1980; Overseas League, 1995; Disabled Persons Assembly, NZ, 1988; Gisborne Cncl of Socl Servs, 1990; Women and Children's Rep, NZ Road Safety Cncl, 1963-66; Tree, Winston Churchill Men Trust Bd, 1966-76; Exec Cncl, Assn Former MPs NZ, 1990-; VP, Assn Former MPs NZ, 1993-96; Pres, Assn Former MPs, 1996-. Listed in: New Zealand Who's Who; Australian Who's Who Hobbies: Music; Gardening; Travel; Charities. Address: 61 Harris St, Gisborne, New Zealand.

TOMITA Ken-ichi, b. 5 June 1928, Nagasaki, Japan. Emeritus Professor, Osaka University. m. Namie Tokuhisa, 20 May 1961, 1 s, 1 d. Education: BS, Phys, Hiroshima Univ, 1953; MSc, Phys, Hiroshima Univ, 1955; DSc, Phys Chem, Osaka Univ, 1959. Appointments: Rsch Assoc, MIT, 1959-64, Rsch Assoc, Inst for Protein Rsch, Osaka Univ 1965; Assoc Prof, fac Pharm Sci, Osaka Univ, 1966-75; Prof, Fac Pharm Sci, Osaka Univ, 1976-93. Publications: Nucleic Acid Structure (transl into Japanese); X-Ray Crystal Structure Analysis; Structural Information of Nucleic Acids and Protein (co-auth). Honour: Sci Awd, Pharm Soc of Japan. Memberships: Pharm Soc of Japan; Crystallographic Soc of Japan. Hobbies: Fishing; Painting; Gardening. Address: 1-82 Hagiwaradai-higashi, Kawanishi-City, Hyogo 666-0005, Japan.

TOMITA Masaru, b. 28 Dec 1957, Tokyo, Japan. Professr. m. Yuko, 28 Mar 1981, 1 s, 1 d. Education: BS, Maths, Keio Univ; PhD, Computer Sci, Carnegie Mellon Univ; PhD, Electr Engin, Kyoto Univ, 1994; PhD, Molecular Bio, Keio Univ, 1998. Honour: Natl Sci Fndn, Presditl Young Investigators Awd, 1988. Address: 5322 Endo Fujisawa 252, Japan.

TOMKINS James Bruce, b. 19 Aug 1965, Sydney, Aust. Education: Bachelor of Bus, Econs and Fin. Honours: Olympic Gold Medallist, Mens Coxless Fours, 1992, 1996. Hobbies: Surfing; Golf. Address: Australian Rowing Cncl Inc, GPO Box 4372QQ, Melbourne, Vic 3001, Australia.

TOMLIN Robert, b. 20 Jan 1945, Norwich, Eng. Investment Banker. m. Monica Villegas, 22 Mar 1980, 2 s. Education: BA; MBA. Appointments: Schroder Grp, London, NY, Singapore, 1969-98; Mngng Dir, Dane Crt, Singapore, 1998-. Memberships: Chmn, Singapore Repertory Th; Former Chmn, Singapore Merchant Bankers Assn; Former Cncl Mbr, Singapore Stock Exchange, 1986-87. Address: 22 Saunders Road, Singapore 228266, Singapore.

TOMLINSON John, b. 18 Nov 1942, Warwick, QLD, Aust. Lecturer. Education: BSoc St, QLD; BA Hons, QLD; MSW, QLD; PhD, Murdoch. Appointments: Socl wrkr, c'wlth, 1965-77; Lectr, Community Coll, 1977-85; Dir, ACTCOSS, 1986-93; Snr Lectr, 1993-. Creative Works: Is Band-Aid Social Work Enough; Social Work: Community Work. Hobbies: Fishing. Address: School of Human Sciences, QUT, Australia.

TOMPKINS Joanne Elizabeth, b. 9 Sept 1961, Oxford, Eng. University Lecture. m. Alan Lawson, 25 Nov 1995. Education: PhD, York, Can; MA, Waterloo; BA Hons, Toronto. Appointments: Lectr, La Trobe Univ, 1991-94; Snr Lectr, Hd of Dept, 1994-95; Lectr, Univ QLD, 1996-98; Snr Lectr, Univ Qld, 1999-. Creative Works: Post-Colonial Drama; Performing Feminisms-Performing Women. Memberships: Australasian Drama Stdies Assn. Address: Department of English, Univ of Queensland, Q 4072, Australia.

TOMUR Dawamat, b. 1927 Toksun Xinjiang. Party Offic. m. Gulzirahan, 1944, 5 s, 2 d. Education: Cntrl Nationalities Coll Beijing. Appointments: Village Chf, 1950; Joined CCP, 1952; Sec CCP Cttee Toksun Cttee Tunpan Basin, 1956; First Sec, 1960; Vice-Chmn Xinjiang Autonomous Reg, 1964; Dep for Xinjiang 3rd NPC; Disappeared until 1976; Dep for Xinjiang 5th NPC, 1978; Dep Sec CCP Cttee Xinjiang, 1978-; Vice-Min of State Nationalities Affairs Commn State Cncl, 1979; Chmn Autonomous Regl People's Congress Xinjiang, 1979-85; Gov Xinjiang Autonomous Reg, 1986-93; Vice-Sec Xinjiang Autonomous Reg CCP Cttee, 1985; A Vice-Chmn Standing Cttee 8th NPC, 1993-. Memberships: Mbr Standing Cttee Autonomous Regl Revolutionary Cttee Xinjiang, 1968; Mbr Standing Cttee 5th NPC, 1978; Mbr 12th Cntrl Cttee CCP, 1982; Mbr 13th Cntrl Cttee CCP, 1987-92; Mbr 14th Cntrl Cttee CCP, 1992-. Hobbies: Writing poetry; Playing Chinese Checkers. Address: The Great Hall, Beijing, People's Republic of China.

TONG Wai Kwok Aaron, b. 25 Feb 1958, Hong Kong. Managing Director. m. Patricia Cheung, 1986, 2 s. Education: BSc. Appointments: Quality Dir, Computer Products Asia Pacific Ltd, 1989-93; Mngng Dir, TQM Cnslts Co Ltd, 1994-. Honour: Gov Awd, Quality Grand Awd, 1992. Memberships: Pres, Inst of Indl Engrs, 1998-99; Chmn, Hong Kong Univ Indl Engrs Assn; Vice Chmn, Hong Kong Soc of Quality. Address: 12C Eastern Commercial Centre, 83 Nam On Street, Shau Kei Wan Road, Hong Kong.

TONG Wenting, b. 29 Oct 1939, Xuzhou, China. Professor of Mathematics. m. Yang Yirong, 29 Dec 1969, 1 d. Education: BS, Maths, Nanjing Univ, 1962. Appointments: Tchr of Maths, Nanjing Univ, 1962-84, 1985-; Visng Prof, Dept of Maths, Brown Univ, USA, 1984-85. Publications include: prin papers: A spectrum on the tensor product of matrices, Acta Math Sinica, 1980; Clifford algebra over a ring, Journal of Mathematical Research Exp, 1981; On IBN rings, Journal of Nanking Univeristy Mathematics Biquarterly 1, 1986; On the spectral radius of matrices, Linear and Multilinear Algebra, vol 20, 1987; Connected PT rings, Alg Colloq, 1994; IBN rings and orderings on Grothendieck groups, Acta Math Sinica, 1994; Finitely generated projective modules over exchange rings, Manuscripta Math, 1995. Honours: Sci and Technol Prize of Jiansu, China, Oct 1980; Sci and Technol Prize of Jiansu, China, 1990; Sci and Technol Prize of State Educl Commn of China, 1995. Memberships: Ed, Algebra Colloquium; Ed, Jrnl of Nanjing Univ Math Biquarterly; Ed, Jrnl of Maths Rsch exp; Reviewer of Zent fur Math (Zbl); Mbr, People's

Repub of China Soc for Maths. Hobbies: Stamp collecting; Music; Fiction; Photography. Address: Department of Mathematics, Nanjing University, Nanjing, China.

TONG Yin Chu, b. 1915 Hefei Cty Anhui Prov. Politician. Education: Shanghai Jiaotong Univ. Appointments: Living in Indonesia, 1938-47; Joined China Dem Constrn Assn, 1948; Chmn Cntrl Cttee of China Zhi Gong Dang, 1988-97; Vice-Chmn 8th Natl Cttee CPPCC, 1993-; Chmn CPPCC Overseas Chinese Cttee; Advsr China Cncl for Promotion of Peaceful Natl Reunification; Advsr All China Fedn of Returned Overseas Chinese. Honours: Hon Chmn Cntrl Cttee of China Zhi Gong Dang, 1997-. Address: National Committee of Chinese People's Political Consultative Congress, 23 Taiping Qiao Street, Beijing, People's Republic of China.

TONGLAGE Bu He, b. Nov 1933, Kulun County, Inner Mongolia. Teacher in College. m. Yao Sumei, Jan 1962, 1 s, 1 d. Education: Bachelor degree. Appointments: Sec of Animal Husbandry Dept; Dean of Animal Husbandry Dept. Publications: Study on Animal Genetics and Breeding; Lects and books about Animal Husbandry Using Chinese and Mongolian. Honours: Scientific & Technological Prize of Inner Mongolia, 1990, 1992, 1997; Educational Achievements Prize, 1997. Hobbies: Playing tennis; Horseriding. Address: Animal Science Department of Inner Mongolia, Agricultural University.

TONKIN James Anthony, b. 5 Apr 1935, Balmain, NSW, Aust. Managing Director. m. Adelaide Mary Bartle, 9 Nov 1961, 2 s, 1 d. Education: Dip, Advertising; Fell, Advertising Inst of Aust; Assoc Fell, Austl Inst of Mngmt. Appointments: Features Mngr, Mirror Newspapers, 1959; Advertising Mngr, TV Times, 1963; Sales Mngr, 3AK, 1967; Advertising Mngr, Austl Home Jrnl, 1971; Sales Dir, Macquarie Brdcstng Serv, 1974; Dir, Tonkin Media Pty Ltd, 1982-. Publications: Radio Journalists Handbook, 1975, reprinted 1977. Memberships: Tattersals Club; Advertising Inst of Aust; Life Mbr, Justices of the Peace Assn; Past VP, Advertising Club; Past Pres, Austl Sporting Car Club. Hobbies: Royal Surf Life Saving Assn; Motor Sport. Address: Thirston Cottage Farm, Scenic Highway, Avoca, NSW 2260, Australia.

TOOHEY John Leslie, b. 4 Mar 1930, Perth, Aust. m. 11 Apr 1953, 2 s, 5 d. Education: LLB First Class Hons, 1950; BA, 1956. Appointments: Legal Practitioner, 1952; West Aust Bar, 1967; QC, 1968; Judge, Fedl Crt of Aust, 1977-87; Judge, Supr Crt of NT, 1977-87; Aboriginal Land Commnr, 1977-82; Jus, High Crt of Aust, 1987-98; Visng Prof, Law Sch, Univ of W Aust, Mar-Apr, 1998, Mar-Aug, 1999. Honours: AO, 1986; AC, 1988; Hon LLD, Murdoch Univ, 1998. Memberships: Pres, Bar Assn of WA, 1970; Pres, Law Soc of WA, 1972-73; Mbr, Constl Commn, 1985-86. Address: 13A Rosser Street, Cottesloe, Western Australia 6011.

TOOULI James, b. 29 Nov 1945. Professor of Surgery. m. Helen Olga, 3 Jan 1970, 1 s, 1 d. Education: BMedSci, hons; MBBS, hons; PhD. Appointments: Surg Registrar, 1974-78; Snr Registrar, 1978; NHMRC Fellshp, USA and Aust, 1979-81; Lectr, Dept of Surg, 1982; Snr Lectr, Dept of Surg, Flinders Univ, 1984-86; Assoc Prof, 1987-89; Prof of Surg, 1990-, Flinders Univ; Hd, Gastrointestinal Surg Unit, Flinders Med Cntr, 1984-; Prof, Univ of Nice, France, 1995. Publications: Num profl articles in sci jrnls. Honours: Lectrshps and Profshps. Membership: Gastrointest Soc of Aust. Hobby: Tennis. Address: Department of General and Digestive Surgery, Flinders Medical Centre, Bedford Park, SA 5042, Australia.

TOPLEY John, b. 8 Feb 1938, Brisbane, Aust. Research Consultant. m. Jane Margaret Stephenson, 26 Aug 1967, 1 s, 1 d. Education: Cert in Tchng, Qld Tchrs Coll, 1956; BEd, Univ of Qld, 1965. Appointments: Tchr, Primary and Secnd Schs, 1957-63; Roy Austl Air Force, Directing Staff, Offrs Trng Sch, 1964-67; Admnstr, Austl Natl Univ, 1967-68; Asst to Vice-Chan, Univ of Qld, 1968-71; Sec to Plng Cncl and Actng Registrar, 1971-74; Registrar, 1974-93; Griffith Univ; Rsch Cnslt, Serv Orgs, 1996-. Honour: Reserve Forces Decoration, 1986.

Memberships: RANR, LCDR, 1970-; Fell, Austl Coll of Educ, Prog Chair, 1995-; Fell, Austl Assn of Tertiary Educl Mngrs, Natl Pres, 1983-86; Fell, Austl Inst of Mngmt; Bd, Flying Arts Inc, 1992-96, Spec Advsr, 1997-99; Bd, Canterbury Coll, 1993-97. Hobbies: Reading; Fishing; Walking; Music; Theatre. Address: 4 Roedean Street, Fig Tree Pocket, Qld 4069, Australia.

TOPP Alphonso Axel Emil Jr, b. 15 Oct 1920, Indpls, USA. Scientist. 2 s, 8 d. Education: BS, Chem Engrng, Purdue Univ, 1942; MS, Appl Phys, Univ CA, Los Angeles, 1948. Appointments: 2nd Lt to Col, US Army, 1942-66; Environ Sci, State of NM, 1970-80; Chf, Radiation Protection Bur, State of NM, 1980-83. Publication: Radiation Protection Regulations, State of New Mexico, 1973. Honours: Bronze Star, 1945; 1st Oak Leaf Cluster Bronze Star, 1950; 2nd Oak Leaf Cluster Bronze Star, 1951; Joint Servs Commendation Medal, 1968; Legion of Merit, 1971. Memberships: Triangle Fraternity, 1939; Sigma Xi, 1948; Hlth Phys Soc, 1974-89; Rotary Intl, 1976-. Hobbies: Boy scouts; Photography; Recreation vehicles. Address: 872 Highland Drive, Los Osos, CA 93402-3902, USA.

TOROBERT Sir Henry Thomas, b. 1942 Kokopo. Banker. Education: Univ of Sydney. Appointments: Asst Rsch Offr Reserve Bank of Aust Port Moresby, 1965; Dep Mngr Reserve Bank of Aust Port Moresby, 1971; Mngr Reserve Bank of Aust Port Moresby, 1972; Gov and Chmn of Bd Bank of Papua New Guinea, 1973-93; Chmn Mngr Bd Bankers' Coll, 1973-; Chmn Papua New Guinea Inst of Applied Soc and Econ Rsch, 1975-82; Pres Amateur Sports Fedn and PNG Olympic and C'Wlth Games Cttee, 1980-; Partner Deloitte Touche Tohmatsu, 1993-; Chmn Credit Corp - PNG - Ltd, 1993-; Govt Super Task Force on Proj Implementation, 1994-. Address: P O Box 898, Port Moresby, Papua New Guinea.

TORRES DEL CASTILLO Gerardo Francisco, b. 3 Oct 1956, Guadalajara, Jalisco, Mexico. Theoretical Physicist. m. Cecilia Uribe, 4 July 1989. Education: MS. Phys, 1979; PhD, Phys, 1982. Appointments: Rschr, Universidad Autónoma de Puebla. Publications: 90 pprs in profl jrnls. Honours: Acad Medal, Mexican Soc of Phys, 1991; Rsch prize, Mexican Acady of Scis, 1996; Clavijero Medal, Univ Autónoma de Puebla, 1996. Memberships: Mexican Soc of Phys; Mexican Acady of Scis; NY Acady of Scis; Amn Phys Soc. Address: 7 Sur 5911, Villa Encantada, 72440 Puebla, Pue, Mexico.

TORRES Y TORRES LARA Carlos. Politician. Appointments: Fmr Min of Labour; PM and Min of For Affairs, 1991-92. Address: c/o Office of the Prime Minister, Ucayali 363, Lima, Peru.

TORY Ethel Elizabeth, b. 27 July 1912, Subiaco, WA, Aust. University Lecturer (retired). Education: St Mary's Ch of Eng Sch for Girls, W Perth, WA, 1922-30; BA Hons in French, 1936; BA Hons in Latin, 1938, Dip Ed, 1939, Univ of WA; DU (Paris), Univ of Paris, 1961. Appointments: Secnd Sch Tchr, West Aust, 1933-46; Tutor in French, 1946-47; Lectr in Latin, 1947, Univ of WA; Lectr in French, 1961-65, Snr Lectr in French, 1965-77, Austl Natl Univ; Tutor, French, Univ of the Third Age, Batemans Bay, NSW, 1997-. Creative works: Introduction and Notes to Intermezzo by Jean Giraudoux (Harrap), 1970; Articles in Cahiers, Jean Giraudoux (Grasset) Paris; Reviews in French Studies, Cambridge; Article in Christian Science Sentinal, 1989. Honours: Hackett Rsch Schlshp, 1941; French Govt Schlshp, 1947-49; Palmes académiques, 1992. Memberships: Alliance Francaise, Perth, 1933-47, Canberra, 1961-; Eurobodalia, 1984-; AULLA, 1961-; FILLM, 1975-; Soc for French Studies of GB, 1967-; Amis Jean Giraudoux, 1973-; Univ of the Third Age, 1982. Listed in: Who's Who of Australian Women, 1982. Hobbies: Language and literature, especially Drama; Stamp collecting; Gardening; Bird watching. Address: 34/41 David Street, O'Connor, ACT 2601, Australia.

TOTLANI Manohar, b. 14 Oct 1941, Karachi. Materials Scientist; Engineer. m. Neeta, 9 Nov 1968, 1 s, 3 d. Education: Masters in Chem and Metallurgical Engrng;

Doct in Metallurgy Engrng, Indian Inst of Technol, Bombay, Mumbai. Appointment: Scientist in Metallurgy Div, Bhabha Atomic Rschh Cntr, Mumbai, 1964-; Sci Hd, Surface Engrng Activity. Publications: Co-ed, books: Corrosion and its Control; Metallic Corrosion - Principles and Control; Applied Electrochemistry; Electro-Plating and Metal Finishing; Coating Technology, Chemical Metallurgy. Honours: Natl Awd for contbn to advmnt in Plating Technol in India; 3 Best Ppr Awds; Chf Ed, Trans of the MFAI, 1993-; On panel of experts of Natl Aerospace Lab, Space Appl Cntr, Ahmedabad; Natl Bd of Accreditation; All India Cncl of Tech Educ, New Delhi; Visng Prof of many engrng colls and univs in India. Memberships: Indian Inst of Metals; Powder Metallurgy Assn of India; Indian Phys Assn; Indian Nuclear Soc; Metal Finishers Assn of India; Soc for Advmnt Electrochem Sci and Technol. Hobbies: Philately; Writing; Table tennis. Address: 43, Shri Niketan, Anushaktinagar, Mumbai 400094, India.

TOYAMA Hideo, b. 22 Nov 1954, Miyazaki Cty, Miyazaki Pref. Assistant Professor. m. Akiko, 4 Aug 1985, 2 s. Education: PhD, Osaka Univ. Appointments: Engr, Chf Engr, Lectr, Asst Prof. Publications: Construction of Cellulose Hyper-producers in Fungus, 1996; Construction of Rapidly Strains of Lentinus Edodes, 1998. Memberships: Soc for Bioscience and Bioengineering, Japan; Japan Soc for Bioscience, Biotechnology and Agrochemistry; NY Acady of Sci. Hobbies: Reading books; Netsurfing (Internet). Address: Maruyama 2-235, Miyazaki 880-0052, Japan.

TOYNE Albert Howard, b. 10 Nov 1920, Dandenong, Aust. Orthopaedic Surgeon (Retired). m. (2) 15 June 1979, 3 s. Education: MBBS, Melbourne Univ, 1944. Appointments: RMO, Prince Henry's Hosp, 1944; Gen Prac, Cooroy, Qld, 1949-52; Registrar, Rowley Bristow Orthopaedic Hosp, 1953-54 Orthopaedic Surg, 1954; Pvte Prac, Melbourne, 1982-. Publication: St John Amulance Manual, 1969. Honours: CBE, 1975; K St J; FRACS; FRCS. Memberships: Former Pres, Vic Civil Ambulance Assn; Cnslt Surg, RAAF, Wing Cmdr (ret) MO, 1945-49; Pres, Roy Flying Dr Serv, Vic, 1971-74; Treas, Fedn Intl de Med Sportive, 1972-82; Dir, St John Ambulance Assn, 1974-84; Hon Life Mbr, Austl Sports Med Fedn; Exec Mbr, St John Priory in Aust; Med Mbr, Repatriation Review Tribunal, 1980-85. Hobbies: Cycling; Golf; Swimming. Address: 5 Lake Court, Tewantin, Queensland 4565, Australia.

TOYODA Tetsuya, b. 2 Feb 1958, Toyokawa, Japan. Virologist. m. Michiko, 29 Mar 1987, 2 s. Education: MD, Nagoya Univ Sch of Med; PhD, Grad Sch of Nagoya. Appointments: Asst Prof, Nagoya Univ; Asst Prof, Natl Inst of Genetics; Prof, Dept of Virology, Kurume Univ, 1995-. Interest: Molecular biology of influenza virus. Address: Department of Virology, Kurume University School of Medicine, 67 Asahimachi, Kurume, Fukuoka 830-0011, Japan.

TRACHTENBERG Shlomo, b. 31 Aug 1950. Structural Biology. m. Bella, Jan 1977, 1 s, 1 d. Education: BSc, 1974; MSc, 1976; PhD, 1982. Appointment: Snr Lectr, 1988; Prof, 1992.

TRAN Van Hoa, b. 10 Nov 1939, Vietnam. University Professor. m. Souraya, 5 Jan 1965, 2 d. Education: BEcon (Hons); MEcon; PhD. Appointments: Tutor, 1965, Prog, 1966, Fell, 1972, Snr Rsch Fell, 1981, Snr Lectr, 1987, Prof, 1988. Publications: Regression Analysis, 1971; Economic Development, 1997; Vietnam's Reform, 1997; Sectoral Analysis, 1999; Prospects in Trade, 1999; The Asia Crisis, 1999; Causes and Impact, 1999. Honours: Colombo Plan Schlshp, 1960; DAAD Fellshp, 1979; Austl Acad of Socl Scis Fellshp, 1993. Memberships: Econometric Soc; Econ Soc; Dir, T & M Enterprises, 1985. Hobbies: Tennis; Music; Painting; Photography; Gardening; Fishing. Address: Department of Economics, Wollongong Univ, Wollongong, NSW 2522, Australia.

TRAN DUC LONG, B. 1937. Politician; Mining Engineer. Appointments: Vice Prime Min, 1992; Mbr,

Dang Cong san Vietnam, Politburo, 1996-. Address: c/o Dang Cong san Vietnam, 1 Hoang Van Thu, Hanoi, Vietnam.

TRAVERS Desmond Benedict, b. 28 Aug 1924, Sydney, Aust. Medical Practitioner. m. Yvonne, 8 Jan 1949, 2 s, 3 d. Education: MS BS, Univ of Sydney, 1954; DPH, 1967; FRSH, 1976. Appointments: RMO, Roy Prince Alfred Hosp, Sydney, 1954; Bombala, NSW, 1958-63; CMO, Canberra, 1963-64; SMO, Pub Hlth Bd, 1965-67; Dir, Natl Persons Bd, 1967-70; Asst Dir, Gen Pub Hlth, 1970-72; Dir, NT Med Serv, 1972-74; Dir, QLD, 1974-78; Asst Dir Gen, Natl Hlth, 1975-83; CMO, Canberra, 1984; Mbr, Admin Appeals, 1985-94; Med Practitioner, 1995-. Creative Works: num publs on pub hlth. Memberships: Natl Hlth and Medl Rsch Cncl; Natl Pathology Adv Cttee; Natl Tech Advsry Panel. Hobbies: Writing; Gardening. Address: 6 Rosson Place, Isaacs, ACT 2607, Australia.

TREADGOLD Malcolm Lloyd, b. 10 May 1942, Perth, Australia. Economist. m. Elaine, 30 Nov 1967, 1 s, 1 d. Education: BEc, W Aust; BPhil, Oxon; PhD, ANU. Appointments: Rsch Fell, ANU, 1969-73; Snr Rsch Fell, ANU, 1973-75; Prof of Econs, Univ of New Eng, 1975-. Publications: Bounteous Bestowal: The Economic History of Norfolk Island, 1988; The Economy of Fiji: Performance, Management and Prospects, 1992; A Guide to the Australian Economy, 1994. Honours: Rhodes Schlshp, 1963; C'wlth Fell, St John's Coll, Cambridge, 1981. Hobbies: Swimming; Rowing; Reading. Address: 22 Curtis Street, Armidale, NSW 2351, Australia.

TREMBATH Owen Thomas, b. 5 Apr 1958, Wollongong, NSW, Aust. Solicitor. Education: BA, Univ of Sydney, 1980; BLL, Univ of Sydney, 1982. Appointments: Supreme Crt of NSW, Aust, 1982; Law Soc of NSW, 1982. Publications: Stay Out of Trouble, 1996. Honours: Best Austl Music Bus Lawyer, 1990, 1991. Membership: Pres, NSW Young Lawyers, 1992. Address: 1 Stanley Street, East Sydney, NSW 2010, Australia.

TRENGGANU Mahmud Al Muktafi Billah Shah (HRH The Sultan of), b. 29 Apr 1930. Malaysian Ruler of Trengganu State. m. Tengku Bariah, 1951. Education: Grammar Crown Eng Sch; Mil trng, 1955. Appointments: Offr Territorial Army; Yang di-Pertuan Muda, 1951; Regent of Trengganu, 1954, 1965; Sultan, Sep 1979-. Honours: Num hon degress. Hobbies: Golf. Address: Istana Badariah, 20500 Kuala Trengganu, Malaysia.

TRENT Faith, b. 30 May 1941, Sydney, Aust. Professor. 2 s. Education: BSc, Dip Teach; MA; MA Hons. Appointments: Hd, Fac of Educ, Hums, Law and Theol, Flinders Univ, 1997-; Dean, Sch of Educ, Flinders Univ, 1994-97; Dean Sturt Coll, 1988-91. Publications: Var articles on higher educ, 1991-97. Memberships: HERDGA; AARE; ACE; SA Multicultural Forum. Hobby: Reading. Address: 32 Deepdene Avenue, Bellevue Heights, SA 5050, Australia.

TRESS Brian Maxwell, b. 4 Mar 1944, Melbourne, Aust. Radiologist. m. Marijke, 2 Feb 1970, 2 d. Education: MBBS, Melbourne Univ, 1967; FRACR, 1974; FRCR, 1975; MD, Melbourne Univ, 1989. Appointments: 1st Asst, 1976-88, Prof, Hd, Dept of Radiol, 1989-, Univ Melbourne. Memberships: Cnclr, RACR, 1988-96; Snr Mbr, WFITN, 1988-; Pres, ANZSNR, 1997-. Hobbies: Golf; Fitness Activities; Jazz; Theatre; Hiking. Address: University of Melbourne, Department of Radiology, c/o The Royal Melbourne Hospital, Vic 3050, Australia.

TRIBE David Harold, b. 17 Dec 1931, Sydney, Australia. Writer. Education: Univ Qld, 1950-54. Appointments: Writer; Lectr; Broadcaster; Ed; Publr; Pub Rels and Sci Advsr. Publications: Why Are We Here?, 1965; 100 Years of Freethought, 1967; President Charles Bradlaugh, MP, 1971; Nucleoethics, 1972; Questions of Censorship, 1973; The Rise of the Mediocracy, 1976. Honours: Hon Assoc, Rationalist Press Assn, 1996, NZ Assn of Rationalists and Humanists, 1997. Memberships:

Sev. Address: 12/2B Wallaringa Avenue, Neutral Bay, NSW 2089, Australia.

TRICKETT Joyce, b. Uralla, NSW, Aust. Broadcaster; Writer; Poet; Teacher of Speech and Drama; Artist. Education: Pvte stdy in Singing and Pianoforte. Appointments: Full-time Brdcstr, women's and childen's Sessions in coml radio, 1940-47; Freelance ABC Radio and TV compere, devotional brdcstr, feature writer, 1950-80, Stage entertainer, poet, auth, songwriter, playwright, tche, adjudicator of singing, speech and drama and artist, 1970-87. Creative works: Books (poems and essays): I Found Driftwood; The Light Shines; Pool of Quiet; Bless This House; An Australian Vision; Christmas is Forever; The Cattitudes of Chairman Miaow (illus by auth); Children's poetry: Seven to Ten and Back Again; Up to Six and Over; Songs: The Wooden Madonna; Dearer Than Yesterday; Bridge Blues (in film); City in Cellophane; Quittin Time; You'll Remember Sydney; Prize Musical plays: Jenolan Adventure; The Bold Endeavour; Exhibns: 7 one-woman art shows (paintings). Honour: Prize for Jenolan Adventure, 1952; Order of Aust Medal, 1992. Memberships: Austl Soc of Auths; Intl PEN. Address: 23 Lavender Crescent, Lavender Bay, North Sydney, NSW 2060, Australia.

TRIMMER Joshua, b. 31 July 1923, Sydney, Aust. Company Director. m. 7 July 1945, 1 s, 1 d. Education: BEc, Sydney, 1950. Appointments: Var positions held in Pub Serv Bd, Dept of Tourism, Treasury Dept, Dept of Railways, -1966; Pres, State Superannuation Bd, 1967-72; Comnr, Pub Transport Commn, 1972-79; Chf Exec, GIO, 1979-83; Co Dir, 1983-; Dir, GIO (UK) Ltd, Chmn; GIFC; TIO; CDF Minerals; GIO Blg Soc. Hobbies: Golf; Woodturning. Address: 140 Lorraine Street, Peakhurst, NSW 2210, Australia.

TRINCA Gordon Walgrave, b. 7 Jan 1921, Melbourne, Vic, Aust. Specialist General Surgeon. m. Elizabeth Harvey Robertson, 4 Dec 1946, 2 s, 1 d. Education: MBBS, Univ of Melbourne, 1945; Dip Fellshp, FRACS, 1958; Res, Roy Melbourne Hosp, 1945-46. Appointments: Served as Lt, AMF; Gen Surg, 1962-74; Snr Gen Surg, 1974-86, Preston and Northcote Cmnty Hosp, Natl Chmn, Rd Trauma Cttee, Roy Australasian Coll of Surgs, 1975-93; Pres, Bd of Mngmt, Ambulance Serv of Melbourne, 1977-82; Sometime Cnslt, WHO, on traffic injury prevention and mngmt; Fndr, Global Traffic Safety Trust. Honours: Gerin Medal, Intl Assn for Accident and Traffic Med, 1978; OBE, 1980; Awd for Merit Amn Assn for Automotive Med, 1981; Adv Aust Awd, 1985; Victorian Rd Traffic Authy Awd, 1985; Roy Australasian Coll of Surgs Medal, 1988; Co-winner, Volvo Traffic Safety Awd, 1988; AO, 1991. Memberships: VP, Intl Assn for Accident and Traffic Med; Austl Medl Assn; Hon Fell, Austl Inst of Ambulance Offrs; Assn for the Adv of Automotive Med. Hobbies: Literature; Music; Tropical rainforest ecology. Address: 29 Tintern Avenue, Toorak, Vic 3142, Australia.

TROMPF Garry Winston, b. 27 Nov 1940, Melbourne, Aust. History and Religious Studies Educator. m. Robyn Rowena Brewster, 1 s, 4 d. Education: BA (Hons), Melbourne; MA, Monash; MA, Oxon; PhD, ANU; DipEd (Hons), Melbourne. Appointments: Prof of Hist, Univ of Papua New Guinea, 1985-85; Assoc Prof, Relig Stdies, Univ Sydney, 1986-94; Prof, Hist of Ideas, Univ of Sydney, 1995-. Publications: The Idea of Historical Recurrence in Western Thought, 1979; Melanesian Religion, 1991; Payback, 1994. Memberships: Chmn, Human Rights Assn, Papua New Guinea, 1985; Austl Assn for Stdy of Religious; Assn for Jrnl of Relig Hist, Chmn, 1997-. Hobby: Tennis. Address: 58. Boundary Rd, Wahroonga, Australia 2076.

TRUSS Warren Errol, b. 8 Oct 1948, Qld, Aust. Farmer; Federal Member of Parliament. Appointments include: Farmer, Kumbia, 1964-; Var Presdtl posns inclng: Pres, Luth Yth Qld and Mbr, Luth Ch Aust Bd of Min, 1970-73; Pres, Burnett Local Govt Assn, 1989-90; Pres, S Burnett Local Authys Assn, 1989-90; Chmn, sev orgs inclng: Austl Cncl Rural Yth; Burnett Dist Cncl Qld Graingrowers, 1984-90; Dpty Chmn, Qld Grain Handling

Authy, 1984-90; Fed MP for Wide Bay, 1990-; Dpty Chmn Cttees, House of Reps, 1991-95; Shadow Min Consumer Affairs, 1994-96; Chmn, House of Rps Cttee on Environment, Recreation and the Arts, 1996-97; Min for Customs and Consumer Affairs and Dpty Ldr of the House of Reps, 1997-98; Min for Cmnty Servs, 1998-. Honours: Rural Yth Golden Plough Awd, 1975; Hon Amb, Expo 88, 1987-88. Listed in: Who's Who in Australia. Hobbies: Sport; Budgerigars; Debating. Address: PO Box 283, Maryborough, Queensland 4650, Australia.

TSAGAN Puntsag, b. 1959, Bulgan, Mongolia. Minister of Finance. m. Education: Mongolian State Univ; Inst of External Rels, Moscow; Mongolian Inst of Mngmt and Dev; Acady of Intl Customs and Laws; Univ of WA, USA. Appointments: Lawyer, Intl Law; Offr, Organizer and Sect Dir, Cntrl Cncl of Trade Union, 1985; Asst Sec, Great Hural State, 1990-92; Dpty Min of Labour, 1992; Asst to Cnslr on Law and 1st Asst to Pres, 1992; Gen Dir, Golamt Bank, 1995. Address: Ministry of Finance, Ulan Bator, Mongolia.

TSAI Chong-Shien, b. 23 Dec 1953, Taiwan, China. Professor. m. Min-Whei, 26 Apr 1980, 1 d. Education: PhD. Appointments: Rsch Asst Prof, Dept of Civil Engrng, State Univ of NY at Buffalo, 1991-96; Assoc Prof, Dept of Civil Engrng, 1996-. Publications: Nonlinear Stress Analysis, User's Manual, 1996. Honours: 1st Prize for ppr competition, Intl Bridge Conf, 1986; Utd Univ Professions Excellent Awd, 1990. Memberships: Amn Soc of Civil Engrs; Intl Soc for Computational Mechs. Hobbies: Football; Music; Swimming; Reading; Basketball. Address: 76 Summerview Road, Williamsville, NY 14221, USA.

TSAI Hsung-Hsiung, b. 23 June 1941, Changhwa, Taiwan. Government Officer. m. Shu-yung Wang, 1 s, 1 d. Education: LLB, Natl Taiwan Univ; Master Deg, Urban Planning, MA Inst of Technol, USA; PhD, Princeton Univ, USA. Appointments: Snr Specl, Cncl for Econ Plng and Dev, Exec Yuan, 1979-80; Dpty Dir, 1980-83, Dir, 1983-92; Urban and Housing Dev Dept, Cncl Vice Chmn, 1992-96, Cncl Mbr, 1996-; Admnstr, Environ Protection Admin, Exec Yuan, 1996-. Publications: Many articles publd. Memberships: Pres, Chinese Inst of Urban Plng, 1981-82; Cttee Mbr, Cty Plng Cttee, Min of Interior, Exec Yuan, 1983-92; Pres and Bd Dir, Chinese Inst of Reg Sci, 1986-87; Dpty Exec Sec, Environ Protection Cttee, Exec Yuan, 1986-88, Exec Sec, 1988-90; Cncl Mbr, Natl Sci Cncl, 1996-; Atomic Energy Cncl, Exec Yuan, 1996-. Address: Environmental Protection Admnstration, Executive Yuan, 10th Floor, 41 Chung-Hwa Road, Section 1, Taipei, Taiwan.

TSAKHILGAAN Dagva, b. 25 Oct 1942, Gobi-Altai Prov, Mongolia. Diplomat. m. M Gapilmaa, 8 Dec 1968, 1 s, 2 d. Education: Mongolian State Univ, Ulaan Baatar; PhD, Higher Party Sch & Acady of Socl Scis, Moscow. Appointments: Tchr, Gobi-Altai Prov, 1963; Functioner, Friendship Soc, 1968; VP, Fedn of Mongolian Peace & Friendship Orgn, 1976; Dpty Hd of the Ideological Dept of the CC, MPRP, 1982; Pres, Fedn of the Mongolian Peace & Friendship Orgn, 1986; Hd, Ideological Dept, CC, MPRP, 1989; Dir, Cultural Affairs Dept, Min of External Rels, 1990; Sec-Gen, Mongolian Natl Commn for UNESCO, 1992; Amb of Mongolia, to China, 1994 and concurrently to Aust & NZ, 1995. Publications: PhD dissertation; Sev books on hist, archeology, ethnology, for rels; Many popular & sci articles. Honours: Silver Star of Peace, 1998; Envoy Extraordinary & Plenipotentiary, 1999. Hobbies: Poetry; Painting; Music. Address: No 2, Xiu Shui Beljie, Jian Guo Men Wai, Beijing, China.

TSALOUMAS Dimitris, b. 13 Oct 1921, Leros, Greece. Teacher. m. 2 s, 2 d. Education: BA; DipEd. Appointments: Var Secnd Schs; Writer in Resn, Univ of QLD; Melbourne Univ; La Trone Univ. Creative Works: To Taxidi; Falcon Drinking; Portrait of a Dog; The Barge. Honours: Natl Book Cncl Awd; Wesley M Wright Prize for Poetry; Patrick White Awd. Memberships: NAtl Assn of Greek Writers. Hobbies: Music; Painting; Hist; Art. Address: 72 Glenhuntly Road, Elwood, Vic 3184, Australia.

TSE Edmund Sze-Wing, b. 2 Jan 1938, Hong Kong. Insurance Executive. m. Peggy Pik Kin Wai, 2 d. Eucation: BA, Univ of Hong Kong, 1960; Dip, Mktng Mngmt, Stanford Univ Grad Sch of Bus, 1980. Appointments: Directorships include: (USA) Dir, 1966, Vice-Chmn Life Ins, 1997, Amn Intl Grp Inc; Dir, Vice Chmn, Amn Life Ins Co, Wilmington DE, 1992; Dir, 1994, Snr VP, 1998, C V Starr & Co Inc; (Can) Dir, 1994, Chmn, 1997, AIG Life Ins Co of Can; (Bermuda) Dir, 1983, Pres, 1992, Amn Intl Assurance Co (Bermuda) Ltd; (Hong Kong), Dir, Pres and Chf Exec Offr, Amn Intl Assurance Co Ltd, 1983; Dir, Chmn, Asia Pacific Assistance Servs Ltd, 1991; Dir, Chmn, AIG Taiwan Fund Ltd, 1992; Dir, 1996, Chmn, 1997, SPC Credi Ltd; Dir and Pres, AIA Fndn, 1995; Dir, 1984, Chmn, 1997, Amn Intl Data Cntr Data Ltd; (Panama) Dir, Chmn and Pres, Green Heights Inc (The "Lookout"), 1986; (Taiwan) Mngng Dir, 1975, Chmn, 1990, Nan Shan Life Ins Co Ltd; Dir, Chmn, Universal Fin Co, 1991; Dir, Chmn, The Philippine Amn Life & Gen Ins Co, 1992; (Malaysia, Singapore, Thailand), Dir, Pres and CEO, Amn Intl Assurance Co Ltd, 1983; (Thailand) Dir, Chmn, AIG Fin (Thailand) PLC, 1998; (Indonesia) Pres Komisaris, PT Asuransi AIA Indonesia, 1997; Chmn bd of Komisaris, Dana Pensiun Lembaga Keunangan AIA Indonesia, 1997; (Australia) Dir, 1985, Chmn, 1997, Amn Intl Assurance Co (Aust) Ltd; Dir, 1986, Chmn, 1997, AIA Superannuation Co Ltd. Honour: Hon Fellshp, Univ of Hong Kong, 1998. Memberships include: Exec Cttee, Bus and Profls Fedn of Hong Kong; Natl and Area Chmn of Hong Kong, Pacific Ins Conf; Appts Bd, Chinese Univ of Hong Kong; Hong Kong Forum; Chf Execs Org Inc, USA; 1st Exec Cttee, China Overseas Friendship Assn; Chmn Asia Advsry Bd, Proj HOPE, USA; Tstee, The Harvard Club Fndn of Hong Kong. Hobbies: Tennis; Bridge. Address: AIA Building, 19th Foor, 1 Stubbs Road, Hong Kong.

TSE Kam Keung, b. 12 Dec 1959, Hong Kong, China. Banking. m. Wendy Lai, 11 Jan 1992, 2 s. Education: BA, Lawrence Univ of WI, 1981; MBA, Chinese Univ of Hong Kong, 1985; MPA, Univ of Hong Kong, 1988. Appointment: Mbr, Hong Kong Govt MPF Specialists Panel. Memberships: Hong Kong Investment Funds Assn; Hong Kong Trustee Assn; Asia Soc. Hobbies: Golf; Soccer. Address: 32/F, Two Exchange Square, Central, Hong Kong.

TSERENPILYN Gombosuren, b. 5 Jan 1943, Uvurhangai, Mongolia. m. Surenkhorloo Demberelin, 20 Feb 1970, 3 s. Education: Dip in Printing Engrng, 1966; Higher Polit Educ, 1976. Appointments: Engr, Technolst, State Printing House, Ulaanbatar, Mongolia, 1967-70; Chf of Sect, Min of For Affair, 1970-74; Higher Party Sch, Moscow, 1974-76; Hd of Dept, Min of For Afairs, 1982-84; Min-Cnslr, Mongolian Emb in Moscow, 1987-87; Mbr, Cntrl Cttee, Mongolian People's Revolutionary Party (MPRP), 1986; Hd, For Rels Dept of Cntrl Cttee, 1987-88; Min for For Affairs, 1988-90; min for External Rels, 1989-96; Mbr, Politburo, MPRP, 1990-91; Mbr, State Grt Hural (Mongolian Parl), 1992-96; Ldrshp Cncl, MPRP, 1996-97; Chmn, Bd of Dirs, Natl Security Printing Co, 1997-. Publications: Lit transl from Russian. Honours: Order of Poalr Star, 1991, Sukhbaatar Order, 1996, Mongolian Govt; Order of Gwanghwa, Repub of Korea, 1991; Title of Amb Extraordinary & Plenipotentiary, 1991. Memberships: Rsch Bd of Advsrs, ABI; Advsr, Tech Univ of Mongolia. Hobbies: Reading; Walking. Address: Po Box 44/310 Ulaanbator 13, Mongolia.

TSHERING Dago, b. 17 July 1941, Paro, Bhutan. Government Official. m. 3 children. Education: Deg, Univ Bombay, Idia, 1961; Indian Admnstrn Serv Trng; Indian Audit and Acct Serv Trng; Deg, Pub Admin, Univ Manchester, Eng; Deg in Natl Admin, Univ Tokyo. Appointments: Asst, Min of Dev, Bhutan, 1961-65, Sec, 1965-68; Mbr, Natl Assembly, Bhutan, 1968-70; Roy Advsry Cncl, Bhutan, 1968-71; 1st Sec, Emb of Bhutan, New Delhi, 1971-73; Dpty Perm Rep, Govt of Bhutan UN, NYC, 1973-74; Amb and Perm Rep, Govt of Bhutan to UN; Amb to Bangladesh, 1980-84; Dpty Min, Home Affairs, 1991-; Chmn, Roy Monetary Authy, Govt of

Bhutan, 1994-. Address: Ministry of Home Affairs, Tashichhodzong, Thimphu, Bhutan.

TSO Chih-Ping, b. 6 Feb 1944, Malysia. Lecturer. m. S L Fung, 2 s, 1 d. Education: B Tech, Loughborough Univ of Technol, 1986; SM, MA Inst of Technol, 1970; PhD, Univ of CA, 1979. Appointments: Assoc Prof, Dept Hed, Univ of Malaysia, 1984-86, 1988-90; Assoc Prof, Nanyang Technol Univ, Singapore, 1990-. Creative Works: Over 100 Tech Pprs, Termal Sci and Engrng. Honours: Exchange Scientist, Power Reactor, Nuclear Fuel Corp, Inst of Engrng, 1988; Fulbright Schlshp; Natl Elec Bd Schlshp. Memberships: Inst of Mechl Engng; Inst of Phys; Inst of Engrs. Hobbies: Travel; Gardening; Table Tennis. Address: c/o School of MPE, NTU, Nanyang Avenue, Singapore 639798.

TSOI Ah Chung, b. 30 Aug 1947, Hong Kong. Professor of Electrical Engineering. m. Tuula Tuovinen, 14 May 1974, 3 s. Education: Higher Dip in Electrons Engrng; Msc; PhD; BD. Appointments: Dean, Univ of Wollongong, 1996-; Prof, Univ of Qld, 1990-96; Univ of NSW, 1985-90. Publications: Over 60 jrnl pprs; Over 100 conf pprs. Memberships: Fell, Inst of Engr, Aust; Fell, Inst of Elec Engrs. Address: Dean, Faculty of Informatics, University of Wollongong, Northfields Avenue, Wollongong, NSW 2522, Australia.

TSUDA Hiroshi, b. 15 Mar 1961, Osaka, Japan. Medical Doctor. m. Keiko, 12 Dec 1991, 2 s. Education: MD; PhD. Appointment: Chief, Gynaecology. Memberships: Amn Soc of Clinl Oncology; Amn Assn of Cancer Rsch; Amn Inst of Ultrasound in Med. Hobbies: Golf; Ski. Address: 2-13-22 Miyakojimahondori, Miyakojima, Osaka, Japan.

TSUI Bing-Yue, b. 29 Aug 1963, Taiwan, China. Engineer. m. Yuh-Shyan Shih, 2 Sept 1995, 1 s. Education: PhD, Inst of Electronics, Natl Chiao Tung Univ. Appointments: Process Intergration Engr, 1992-94, proj Mngr of Device Technol, 1995-96, Sect Mngr, Device Technol, 1995-96, Sect Mngr, Etching Technol, 1997, Proj Mngr of Etching Technol, 1997-, Assoc Prof, natl Chiao Tung Univ, 1996-; ERSO/ITRI; Dept Mngr, Etching and Integration Technol, 1998-. Publications: 17 jrnls pprs; 26 Conf pprs; 11 patents. Honours: Best Serv Awd, Indl Technol Rsch Inst, China, 1996; Outstndng Young People, Hsinchu, China, 1997; Outstndng Young Electr Engnr, 1998. Memberships: IEEE; Material Sci Assn; Phi Tau Phi. Hobbies: Badminton; Classic music; Bridge card; Reading. Address: 14-2, No 56, Ta-Hsieh Rd, Hsinchu, Taiwan, China.

TSUJI Yoshifuma, b. 6 Feb 1928, Japan. Business Executive. Education: Univ Tokyo. Appointments: Joined Nissan Motor Co Ltd, 1954; Gen Mgr, Tochigi Plant, 1984; Dir, Mbr Bd, Gen Mgr, Tochigi Plant, 1985; Mngng Dir i/c Prod Plng, 1987; Exec Mngng i/c Plant Ops, Eng Dept, 1989; Exec VP i/c Prod Op Grp, Purchasing Grp, Non-Auto Ops Grp, 1990; Exec VP i/c Prodn Op Grp, Non-auto Ops Grp, 1991; Pres, 1992-96; Chair, 1996-. Memberships: Chmn, Japan Automobile Manufacturers Assn Inc, 1996; Vice-Chmn, KEIDANREN, 1997. Honours: Order of Queen Isabel la Catolica, King of Spain, 1995; Blue Ribbon Medal, Emperor of Japan, 1995. Address: Nissan Motor Co Ltd, 17-1 Ginza 6-chome, Chuo-ku, Tokyo 104-23, Japan.

TSUJI Yutaka, b. 20 June 1943, Osaka, Japan. Professor. m. Megumi, 11 Feb 1972. Education: Dr of Engrng, Osaka Univ. Appointments: Rsch Assoc, Osaka Univ, 1970-72; Assoc Prof, 1972-89; Prof, 1989-. Publications: Multiphase Flows with Droplets and Particles. Honours: JSME Medal; Jetaki Awd. Memberships: JSME, Tokyo; ASME, NY. Hobbies: Mountaining. Address: 5-11-14 Toyosato, Higashi-yodogawa, Osaka 533, Japan.

TSUJITA Yoshiharu, b. 29 Oct 1942, Saga, Japan. Professor. m. Mariko, 2 s, 1 d. Education: BEng, Agric and Engr, Tokyo Univ of Agric & Engr, Tokyo, 1966; MEng, 1968, DEng, 1971, Tokyo Inst Tech, Tokyo, Japan. Appointments: Asst Prof, Tokyo Inst Tech,

1971-75; Assoc Prof, 1975-89, Prof, 1989-, Dir of Instrument & Analysis Cntr, 1977-99, Nagoya Inst Tech. Publications: Membrane Science and Technology, 1992; Polymer and Water (in Japanese), 1995; New Polymer Experimentals (in Japanese), 1995; Ppr in jrnl, 1998. Memberships: The Soc of Fiber Sci & Technol, Japan, 1975-; Soc of Polymer Sci, Japan, 1975-, Sci Cncl of Japan, 1994-.

TSUNO Katsushige, b. 23 July 1945, Niigata, Japan. Electron Optics Researcher. m. Shoko, 6 May 1973, 2 s, 1 d. Education: Master degree, Tohoku University Engineering Department. Appointments: JZOL Ltd. Publications: Magnetic Lenses for Electron Microsopy in Charged Particle Optics, ed, J Orloff. Honour: Seto Awd, Japan Electron Microscopial Soc, 1988. Memberships: Roy Microscopial Soc; Microscopial Soc Am; Japan Electron Microscopial Soc. Hobby: Computer programming. Address: 10-11 Mihori 2-chome, Akishima, Tokyo 196-0001, Japan.

TU Guo-shi, b. 21 June 1919, Beijing, China. Professor of Pharmaceutical Chemistry. m. Wu Zhong-shu, 29 May 1951, 1 s, 1 d. Education: Pharmacist's Dip, Natl Coll Pharm, 1942; BPharm, London, Univ Coll, Nottingham, Eng, 1947; BSc Spec, Chem, London, 1949. Appointments: Chf, Dept Chem, Natl Inst Control Food and Drugs, 1951-61; Mbr, 1952-, Vice-Chmn, 1986-, Chinese Pharmacopeia Commn; Chf, Div Pharm Chem, 1962-85, Supvsr, Advd Deg Studs, 1982-, Prof, Pharm Chem, 1981-, Natl Inst Control Pharm and Biol Products, Beijing; Mbr, WHO Expert Advsry Panel Intl Pharmacopoeia and Pharm Preparations, 1974-; Participated, Expert Cttee Meeting, Geneva WHO HQ, many times, 1974-88; Mbr, Vice-Chmn, Expert Commn Natl Agricl Analysis and Specifs, 1979-92; Dir, WHO Collaborative Cntr Drug Qlty Assurance, Beijing, 1986-; Profl visits, Algeria, Tanzania, 1973, Egypt, 1974, USA, Japan, 1981, Thailand, 1986. Publications: Ed in Ch, Pharmacopoeia of the People's Republic of China, Engl Ed, 1988, 1992, 1997,(ed-in-chief Vol II), 1st time published in Engl in Natl Stands; Over 40 published papers, China and abroad, on chem investigation of Nat and synth Drugs and Chinese tradl med such as musk, bezoar, Corydalis spp, Cadonopsis spp and others, w interest in alkaloids and steroids; Ed in Ch, Chinese Journal of Pharmaceutical Analysis. Honour Brit Cncl Schlshp, 1945-49. Memberships: Editl Bd, Acta Pharmaceutica Sinica; Chinese Pharm Assn. Hobbies: Photography; Reading; Swimming. Address: National Institute for the Control of Pharmaceutical and Biological Products, Temple of Heaven, Beijing 100050, China.

TU King-Ning, b. 30 Dec 1937, Canton, China. Professor. m. Ching Chaio, 25 Sept 1967, 1 s, 1 d. Education: BSc, Natl Taiwan Univ; MSc, Brown Univ; PhD, Applied Phys, Harv Univ, 1968. Appointments: Snr Mngr, Materials Sci Dept, IBM, T J West Rsch Cntr; Full Prof, Dept of Materials Sci and Engrng, UCLA. Honours: Application to Prac Awd, Metallurgical Soc, 1988; Humboldt Awd for Snr US Scis, 1996. Memberships: Fell, Amn Phys Soc; Fell, Metallurgical Soc; Overseas Fell, Churchill Coll. Hobby: Chinese Calligraphy. Address: 11500 Sunset Boulevard Los, Angeles, CA 90049, USA.

TU Yaqing, b. 18 June 1963, Chongqing, China. Scientist. m. Wei Wang, 22 June 1988, 1 s. Education: Bsc, Chengdu Univ of Sci & Technol, 1984; MS, 1991, PhD, 1994, Chongqing Univ, China. Appointments: Prof, 1995; Dir, Automatic Rsch Off, 1998. Publications: Distributed Control System - Design and Applications, 1997; Basis of Fiberoptic Smart Structures, 1998; Many pprs about control and instruments. Honours: China Instrument Soc Spec Prize, 1994; Outstndng Youth Prize; China Assn for Sci & Technol, 1998. Memberships: SPIE; AAAS. Hobbies: Photography; Watching TV.

TU'IPELAHAKE HRH Prince Fatafehi, b. 7 Jan 1922. Politician. m. HRH Princess Melenaite Topou Moheofo, 1947, 2 s, 4 d. Education: Newington Coll Sydney NSW; Gatton Agricl Coll Queensland. Appointments: Fmr Min for Agric and Marine Affairs; Fmr Min for Forestry and Fisheries; Gov of Vava'u, 1952-65; PM of Tonga,

1965-91; Chmn Commodities Bd. Honours: 'Uluafi Medal, 1982. Address: c/o Office of the Prime Minister, Nuku'alofa, Tonga.

TUCKER Kerrie Robyn, b. 15 Sept 1948, Darwin, Australia. ACT Greens Member of ACT Legislative Assembly. m. John Tucker, 1 s, 2 d. Education: Karitane Nurse. Appointments: Chair, Socl Plcy Cttee, ACT Legislative Assembly, 1995-98; Chair, Educ Cttee ACT Legislative Assembly, 1999. Hobbies: Bush Walking; Gardening; Arts. Address: Member for Molonglo, GPO Box 1020, London Circuit, Canberra, ACT 2601, Australia.

TUCKER Michael Trevor Graham, b. 11 Oct 1934, Epsom, Surrey, Eng. Professional Dog Trainer. m. Valerie, 2 d. Publications: Dog Training Made Easy; The Eyes That Lead; Solving Your Dog Problems; Dog Training Step By Step; Dog Training for Children & Parents, 1998. Memberships: Pres, Profl Dog Trainers Assn of Vic; Chmn, Roy Air Forces Assn (Melbourne); Life Mbr, Doncaster & Templestowe Histl Soc. Hobbies: Carpentry; Playing chess; Community work. Address: 12, Ashford Street, Lower Templestowe, 3107 Victoria, Australia.

TUDEV Lodongiyn, b. 8 Feb 1935. m. Naidangiin Tsagaach, 17 Oct 1968, 1 s, 2 d. Education: BS, Pedagogical Inst, Ulan Bator, Mongolia, 1956; MS, Lings, Acady Socl Scis, Moscow, 1967; PhD, Lings, 1984. Appointments: Tchr, Secnd Sch, altai, Mongolia, 1956-59; Meth Tchrs Inst, Ulan Bator, 1959-60; Lit Sec, Unen, Ulan Bator, 1960-63; Ed-in-Chf, 1984-; Ed-in-Chf, Soyol Utga Zohiol, 1963-64; Vice Chmn, Chmn, Mongolian Writers Union, 1969-75; Gen Sec, Mongolian Yth Union, 1975-84; Prof, 1996-; Fndr, Owner, Ed-in-Chf, Scapula, newspaper, 1996-. Publications: Mountain Stream, 1960; Nomadism and Urbanism, 1964; First Year of Republic, 1981; Roofless Temple, 1985; Spiral, 1988; Problem, 1990; Bluie Sky Above, Brown Earth Below, 1994; Three Doors to Sin, 1996. Honours include: Order of Sukhhaatar, 1981; Order of People's Friendship, Govt of Russia, 1979; Order of Kirill and Mephodil, Govt of Bulgaria, 1980; Labor Hero of Mongolia, Highest Hon of Mongolia, by decree of the Pres of Mongolia, 1998. Memberships include: MP, People's Grt Khural, 1963-91; Hd, Parly Union, 1984-90; Hd, Peace Commn, 1973-76; Cand for Pres of Mongolia, 1993; Chmn, Jrnlsts Union. Listed in: Who's Who; Men of Achievement. Hobbies: Table tennis; Folk collecting. Address: Central Post Office, CPO Box 5, Ulaan Bataar, Mongolia.

TUDOR Edward Richard, b. 29 Dec 1947. Secondary School Teacher. m. Elizabeth, 21 Dec 1974, 1 s, 3 d. Education: BSc, Monash Univ; MSc, Dip Educ, Melb Univ. Appointments: Dpty Hdmaster, Peninsula Sch, Mt Eliza, Vic, 1984-88; Hdmaster, Beaconhills Christian Coll, Pakenham, Vic, 1989-97; Dpty Hdmaster, Hd of Snr Sch, Melbourne Grammar Sch, 1997-98; HdMaster, Trinity Grammar Sch, Kew, 1999-. Publications: Understanding the Human Body, 1981, 2nd ed, 1985; Resource Manual, 1983, 2nd ed, 1987. Membership: Austl Coll Educ. Hobbies: Bushwalking; Painting. Address: 49 Wellington Street, Kew Victoria 3101, Australia.

TUIVAGA Hon Sir Timoci, b. 21 Oct 1931. Judge. m. Vilimaina Leba Parrott Tuivaga, 1958, 3 s, 1 d. Education: Univ of Auckland. Appointments: Native magistrate, 1958-61; Called to the Bar Gray's Inn, 1964; Called to Bar NSW, 1968; Crown Cnsl, 1965-68; Prin Legal Offr, 1968-70; Puisne Judge, 1972; Acting Chf Jus, 1974; Chf Jus of Fiji, 1980-87; Sometime Acting Gov Gen, 1983-87. Hobbies: Golf; Gdng. Address: 228 Ratu Sukuna Road, Suva, Fiji.

TULLOH Norman McCall, b. 22 Apr 1922, Horsham, Vic, Aust. Agricultural Scientist. m. Ailsa, 31 Dec 1954, 2 s, 1 d. Education: BAgrSc, 1947, MAgr, 1952, PhD, 1963, DAgrSc, 1975, Univ of Melbourne, Vic, Aust. Appointments: CSIRO Div, Animal Hlth Prodn, 1949-56; Snr Lectr, Rdr, Prof, Animal Prodn (Personal Chair), 1974-; Dean Fac of Agric and Forestry, Univ of Melbourne, 1976-78; Acad Dir, Austl-Asian Univs Co-op

Scheme, 1978-80; Retd, 1987. Publications: Auth (jt) and/or Ed, 5 books, 80 sci publs. Honours: Silver Medal, Austl Inst of Agric Sci, 1975; Medallion for Disting Serv to Meat Scis, Intl Meat Sci and Technol, 1988. Memberships: Fell, Austl Inst of Agricl Sci and Technol, 1971; Fell, Austl Acady of Technol Sci and Engrng, 1981 Fell, Austl Soc of Animal Prodn, 1982. Hobbies: Walking; Gardening; Golf. Address: 955 Riversdale Road, Surrey Hills, Vic 3127, Australia.

TUN-PE, b. 8 Aug 1942, Rangoon, Burma. Immunologist. m. Sann Mya, 23 Oct 1976, 2 d. Education: MBBS, Inst of Med, Rangoon, 1964; DCP, 1971, PhD, 1975, Univ London. Appointments: Postgrad Fell, Hammersmith Hosp, London, 1970-71; Rsch Fell, St Mary's Hosp, London, 1971-75; Asst Lectr, Lectr, Inst of Med, Rangoon, 1971-81; Hd, Immunol, Dir of Rsch, Dept of Med Rsch, 1981-. Honour: Hertford Fell Schlsp, 1993, 1995. Memberships: Intl Soc on Toxicol; Roy Coll of Trop Med and Hygiene; Fell, Roy Coll of Physns, Edinburgh. Hobbies: Reading; Music. Address: 25 Pyithayar Road, 11082 Rangoon, Burma.

TUNG Chee-Hwa, b. 29 May 1937, China. Business Executive. m. Betty H P Tung, 2 s, 1 d. Education: Univ of Liverpool. Appointments: Chair, Island Navigation Corp Ltd; Chair, Orient Overseas (Holdings) Ltd; Dir, Sing Tao Newspprs Ltd, Sun Hung Kai Bank Ltd, Hsin Ching Properties Ltd, Mass Transit Railway Corp; Vice Chair, Preparatory Cttee for Hong Kong Spec Admin Region; Mbr, Exec Cncl, Hong Kong Govt, 1992-96; Chief Exec, Hong Kong Spec Admin Reg, 1997-. Memberships: 8th NPC, 1993-; Num civic appts; Hon Cnsl of Monaco, Hong Kong. Address: Suite 705-708 Asia Pacific Finance Tower, Citibank Plaza, 3 Garden Road, Hong Kong Special Administrative Region, China.

TUNKU IMRAN Tuanku Ja'afar, b. 21 Mar 1948. Holding Company Director. m. 18 Feb 1987, 2 s. Education: LLB (Hons), Nottingham Univ, 1967-70; Called to Bar, Gray's Inn, 1971. Appointments: Joined the Malaysian Natl Corp, PERNAS, 1971; Rep for PERNAS in Indonesia, later Grp Co Sec; Joined the Haw Par Grp, 1973; Mngmg Dir, Haw Par Malaysia, -1976. Chf Exec Offr, Antah Grp Cos, 1976-; Bd Mbr, sev pub listed cos in Malaysia and abroad incl: Chmn, Aluminium Co of Malaysia Berhad and Minho (M) Berhad; Austral Enterprises Berhad; Island and Peninsular Berhad; Malayan Cement Berhad. Memberships: Dir, Inst of Strategic and Intl Studies (ISIS) Malaysia; Mbr, Malaysian Bus Cncl; Immediate Past Pres, Badan Warisan Malaysia (Heritage of Malaysia Trust); Bd Mbr, Sukom Ninety Eight Berhad; Natl Sports Cncl of Malaysia; Pres, Malaysian Cricket Assn; Fndng Chmn of the Fndn for Malaysian Sporting Excellence; Pres, Olympic Cncl, Malaysia; Emer Pres, World Squash Fedn. Honours: Malaysia's 1st Natl Squash Champion, 1973; PJK Negeri Sembilan, 1978; DKYR Negeri Sembilan, 1979; AMN Malaysia, 1980; Chef-de-Mission to Olympic Games in Seoul, 1988; Natl Sports Leadership Awd by King of Malaysia, 1991; PSM Malaysia. Hobbies: Squash; Tennis; Cricket; Rugby; Golf. Address: 33 Jalan Semantan Dua, Damansara Heights, Kuala Lumpur, Malaysia.

TUNLEY David Evatt, b. 3 May 1930, Sydney, Aust. University Emeritus Professor of Music. m. Paula Patricia Laurantus, 26 May 1959, 1 s, 2 d. Education: DSCM, State Conservatorium of Music, 1950; BMus, 1958, MMus, 1963, Univ of Durham, Eng; DLitt, Univ of WA, 1970. Appointments: Music Master, HS, Sydney, 1954-58; Acad Staff, Univ of WA, 1959-; Personal Chair in Music, 1976-; Hd of Dept, 1985-89; Emer Prof, 1994-. Publications include: Ed, sev books inclng, The 18th Century French Cantata, 1974, 2nd revised ed, 1996; Couperin, 1982; Harmony in Action, 1984; Studies in Music (annual periodical), 1976- The French Cantata in Facsimile (17 vols), 1991; Romantic French Song in Facsimile (6 vols), 194-95; The Bel Canto Violin: The Life and Times of Alfredo Campoli 1906-91, 1999; Contr to var music publns. Honours: French Govt Schlsp, 1964-65; Chevalier dans l'ordre des Palmes Academiques; AM; Rockefeller Fndn Res Schl, Italy, 1987; Fowler Hamilton Visng Rsch Fell, Christchurch,

Oxford, 1993; Visng, Schl, Wolfson Coll, Oxford, 1996. Memberships: Austl Acady of the Humanities, Fell; Past Natl Pres, Musicol Soc of Aust. Listed in: Who's Who in Australia; Oxford Companion to Australian Music. Hobbies: Theatre; Travel; Reading. Address: 100 Dalkeith Road, Nedlands, WA 6009, Australia.

TUNNEY John V, b. 26 Jun 1934 NYC. Politician. m. (2) Kathinka Osborne, 1977, 2 s, 2 d. Education: Westminster Sch Simbury CT; Yale Univ; Univ of VA Sch of Law; Acady of Intl Law The Hague. Appointments: Practised law NYC, 1959-60; Judge Advocate US Air Force, 1960-63; Practised law Riverside, 1963-; Taught Bus Law at Univ of CA Riverside; Sen from CA, 1971-77; Chmn Bd of Dirs Cloverleaf Grp Inc Los Angeles, 1986; Democrat. Memberships: Mbr US HoR, 1964-70; Mbr Manatt Phelps Rothenberg and Tunney Los Angeles, 1977-86. Hobbies: Tennis; Sailing; Skiing; Handball. Address: 1819 Ocean Ave, Santa Monica, CA 90401, USA.

TUNSTALL Arthur, b. 22 Feb 1922, Adamstown, NSW, Aust. Sports Administrator. m. Peggy Irene Craven, 30 Mar 1946, 1 s. Career: Life Mbr, 1970-, NSW Amateur Boxing Assn, 59 yrs, Hon Sec, 47 yrs, attended hundreds of boxing tournaments acting as referee, judge, coach and arena mngr; Hon Sec Treas, Amateur Boxing Union of Aust, 46 yrs; Hon Sec, 22 yrs, Pres, 1989-, Oceania Amateur Boxing Assn, Noumea; Elected VP, Oceania Bur, Intl Amateur Boxing Assn, 1989; Apptd Hon Sec, Commonwealth Amateur Boxing Assn, Edmonton, Can (w 56 mbr countries), 1978-98; Fully Qualified Austl and Oceania Referee and Judge and Intl Judge, conducts Olympic Solidarity courses and exams for Referees and Judges at both Oceania and Intl levels; As Mngr took teams to intl competitions, 1960-; Tech Deleg, Seoul Olympics, 1988, Barcelona Olympics, 1992, Atlanta Olympics, 1996; Deleg for Boxing on NSW Div of Ausl Commonwealth Games Assn, Hon Sec Treas, 1965-90, Pres, 1990-; Hon Sec, Austl Commonwealth Games Assn, 1969-98, Life Mbr, 1979-; Austl deleg, Commonwealth Games Fedn, 1972-98; VP, Oceania Reg (only Austl in this position), 1994-98. Publications: Australia at the Commonwealth Games, 6th - 13th eds, 1970-90 (4 yearly). Honour: OBE, 1979. Hobbies: Swimming; Amateur boxing events; Olympic & Commonwealth Games. Address: 27 South Avenue, Double Bay, NSW 2028, Australia.

TUPOU Tevita Poasi, b. 27 July 1941, Nukualofa, Tonga. Attorney General & Minster of Justice. m. Ilaisaane, 28 Sept 1968, 2 s, 2 d. Education: LLB, Auckland Univ, NZ, 1965; Pupillage in Barrister's Chmbrs in the Middle Temple and Lincoln's Inn, London, 1965-67; Dip in Law Study, Oxford (Univ Coll), 1967-68. Appointments: Asst Crown Solicitor, 1968-69; First Sec, Tonga High Commn, London, 1969-72; Crown Solicitor, 1972-84; Solicitor Gen, 1984-88; Atty Gn Admnstr, 1988. Memberships: Barrister, Solicitor of the High Ct of NZ, 1965-; Mbr of Cabinet, Privy Cncl & Legis Assembly, 1988-; Snr VP, Tonga Olympic Cttee, 1988-. Hobbies; Fishing; Watching sports (cricket, tennis, rugby, motor games); Reading. Address: Ministry of Justice, PO Box 130, Nukualofa, Salote Rd, Fasi-Moe-Afi, Nukualofa, Tonga.

TURBOTT Ian Graham (Sir), b. 9 Mar 1922, NZ. Company Director. m. Nancy Hall Lantz, Aug 1950, 3 d. Education: Auckland Univ, NZ; Auckland Tchr Trng Coll; Colonial Serv Course, Jesus Coll, Cambridge, Eng, 1946-47; London Sch of Econs, 1947; London Cert Coastal Navigation, 1947. Appointments include: Mil Serv, NZEF, 1941-46; HMOCS, 1948-86; duties included: Secretarial Offr, Suva, Fiji, Tarawa, Gilbert & Ellice Islands, 1949-50; Deleg, S Pacific Comn, 1950; Prin, Overseas Serv Div, Colonial Off, London, Eng, 1956-58; Admnstr, Antigua, 1958-64; Admnstr, Grenada, W Indies, 1964-67; Gov, Associated State of Grenada, retiring voluntarily on appointment of local Gov, 1967-68; Chf, Armed and Civil Forces; Coml experience w Spencer Stuart and Assocs, established co in Pacific; Chmn, Austl Hong Kong, Singapore, 1968-82; Dir, Capita Fin Grp, 1978-90; Stand Chartered Bank Aust Ltd, 1980-82; Chmn, Hoyts Grp, Chmn Penrth Lakes Dev Corp, 1980-, TNT Securities P/Ltd, 1976-93; Chmn 2MMM Radio Grp, 1980-93; Chmn, Chloride Patteries Aust Ltd, 1974-86; Chmn, Duke of Edinburgh Awd Scheme, NSW, 1984-85; Chancellor, Univ of West Sydney, 1989-; Num other involvements pub/community wrk, W Indies, Pacific, UK, Aust; Hon Consul, Cook Islands, Aust, 1995-. Publications: Var publs on tech and sci aspects of the Pacific Is 1950's; Lands of Sun and Spice, 1996. Honours include: CMG, 1962; Cmdr, Order of St John, 1964; CVO, 1966; KB, 1968; Silver Jubilee Medal, 1977; AO, 1997. var awds, W Indian Govts; Hon DLitt (UWS), Univ of West Sydney; var mil decorations inclng The Solomon Islands Govt Guadalcanal Medal. Memberships: FRSA, 1959-; Fell, Inst of Dirs, 1971; Hon Mbr, Diet of Japan, 1977; Chmn, NSW Trade Miss, Yugoslavia, 1986, Japan, 1987. Listed in: Who's Who. Address 8/8 Lauderdale Avenue, Fairlight, NSW 2094, Australia.

TURCHI Patrice E A, b. 23 June 1952, Lorient (56), France. Senior Research Scientist. m. Michèle Boyle, 1 d. Education: Dip of Engr, Ecole Natl Supérieure de Chimie de Paris, 1975; Thèse de Docteur Ingénieur, Univ of Paris VI, 1982; Thèse de Doctorat d'Etat es Sciences Physiques, Univ of Paris VI, 1984. Appointments: Asst Prof, Univ of Paris VI, 1975-85; Visng Rsch Asst, Univ of Berkeley, CA, USA, 1985-86; Visng Rsch Scientist, Lawrence Livermore Natl Lab, 1986-89; Snr Rsch Scientist, Lawrence Livermore Natl Lab, 1989-. Publications: Over 150 sci publs; 4 book chapts; Co-ed, 8 tech proceedings; over 100 presentations and 60 invited talks at sci meetings and rsch instns. Honours: Medal for highest ranking Alumni, Ecole Natl Supérieure de Chimie de Paris, 1975; DOE Awd, Outstndng Rsch Accomplishments, DOE-OBES, 1987; Invited Prof, Univ Joseph Fourier, Grenoble, France, 1994. Memberships: Soc des Ingénieurs et Scientifiques de France, 1986-; Amn Phys Soc, 1986-; Materials Rsch Soc, 1989-; Minerals, Metals and Materials Soc, TMS, 1989-; Elected Mbr, Tech Cttee on Alloy Phases (CAP), TMS, 1991-; Chair of Hume-Rothery and Acta Metallurgica Awd Cttee, 1998-99, TMS; Chair, Programming and Cncl Mbr, Electron, Magnetic and Photonic Materials Div, TMS, 1999-; Reviewer, num sci jrnls; US Ed, Rsch Jrnl, Metals Physics and Advd Technol, 1995-. Hobbies: Bonsai; Painting; Reading; History of science; Hiking; Skiing; Sailing; Tennis. Address: Lawrence Livermore National Laboratory, Chemistry and Materials Science Department (L-353), PO Box 808, Livermore, CA 94551, USA.

TURKI Abdul Aziz Al-Abdullah Al-, b. 12 Aug 1936 Jeddah. Oil Offic. m. 2 d. Education: Univ of Cairo; Appointments: US Emb Jeddah, 1953-54; ARAMCO, 1954-66; Dir Off of Min of Pet and Mineral Rescs, 1966-68; Dir of Gen Affairs Directorate of Mineral Rescs, 1968-70; Asst Sec-Gen OAPEC, 1970-75; Sec-Gen Supreme Advsry Cncl for Pet and Mineral Affairs Saudi Arabia, 1975-90; Sadir Gov for OPEC, 1975-90; Dep Min min of Pet and Mineral Rescs, 1975-; Chmn Arab Maritime Pet Transp Co Kuwait, 1981-87; Pemref, 1982-89; Sec-Gen OAPEC, 1990-. Memberships: Mbr Bd of Dirs Petromin, 1975-89; Mbr Bd of Dirs ARAMCO, 1980-89. Hobbies: Tennis; Swimming. Address: Organization of Arab Petroleum Exporting Countries, P O Box 20501, Safat 13066, Kuwait.

TURLAPATY Kutumba Rao, b. 10 Aug 1933. Journalist. m. Krishnakumari, 12 June 1959, 1 s, 1 d. Education: Natl Citizen Awardee in Jrnlsm, Arts, Culture. Appointments: Mbr, Bharatidasan Univ, Tamil Nadu, 1995; Mbr, Central Film Censor Bd of India, 1996. Publications: Andhra Kesari Jeevitamio Konni Adbhuta Ghattalu, 1954; Jataka Kathalu, 1958; Lal Bahadur Shastri, 1966; Jaati Nirmatalu, 1968; Vartalaloni Vyaktulu, 1969; Mahanayakulu, 1971; Andhra Kesari, 1971; 1857; Viplava Veerulu, 1975; Upanyasakala, 1988; Tenneti Viswanatham, 1989; Tholi Telugu Pradhani PV Narasimha Rao, 1992; Kotla Vijaya Bhaskara Reddy, 1993. Honours: Best Biographer Awd, 1990; Mutnuri Krishna Rao Best Ed Awd, 1989; Natl Citizen Awd, 1991; Kasinathuni Nageswara Rao Best Jrnlst Awd, 1994; Made intl recd by delivering over 12,000 pub speeches during 50 yrs; HonD, Andhra Univ, 1997; Spec Hon, All India Newsppr Eds Conf, 1997; Life Time Achievement Awd, Govt Andhra Pradesh, 1997. Memberships: Acads Review Cttee; Bd of Govs, Intl Telugu Inst; Natl Film Advsry Cttee, 1990; Natl Films Awds Cttee, Govt of India, 1969. Hobbies: Cinemas; Music; Public Speaking. Address: Turlapaty Kutumba Rao Street, Labbipet, Vijayavada-520 010, South India.

TURNER Cameron Archer, b. 29 Aug 1915, Wanganui, NZ. Air Vice-Marshal (retired), Royal NZ Air Force. m. Josephine Mary Richardson, 25 Jan 1941, 2 s. Education: Vic Univ, Wellington, 1932-33; RAF, Elecl and Wireless Sch, Cranwell, Eng, 1938-39; RAF Staff Coll, Bracknell, 1947; Imperial Def Coll, London, 1960; Massey Univ, Palmerston N, 1983-92; Appointments: Commnd, RAF, 1936, Transferred, Roy NZ Air Force, 1938, served Eur, 1939, Pacific, 1940-45, Chf of Air Staff, 1966-69, retd, 1969; Dir, ZN Inventions Dev Authority, 1969-76. Memberships: Fell, Instn of Elecl Engrs (London); Fell, Roy Aeronautical Soc (London). Honours; OBE, 1947; CBE, 1960; CB, 1968. Hobbies: Angling; Polynesian studies; Religious studies; Wellington Club. Address: 37A Parkvale Road, Karori, Wellington 5, New Zealand.

TURNER Geoffrey Bernard, b. 10 Jan 1934, Tas, Aust. Company Secretary, Executive Officer (Retired). m. Patricia Francis Turner, 21 Dec 1957. Appointments: Mngr, Elec Retail, 1958-81; St Giles Soc (Charitable Inst for disabled children & adults), 1981-94; retd. Honour: Senator, J C Intl. Hobby: Trout Fishing. Address: Riverside, 21 Penrith Street, Launceston, Tas 7250, Australia.

TURNER Graeme Murray, b. 22 Apr 1957, Melbourne, Aust. Communications Officer; Writer. m. Elaine, 28 Sept 1991. Education: BA, Hons, 1979; Dip Arts, 1981; Cert Justice Studies, 1995. Appointments: Advtng Copywriter, 1981; Jrnlst w comm newsppr, 1984; Descripitive Cataloguer, 1986; Communications Offr, Vic Legal Aid, 1990-; Freelance Writer. Publications: Books: Touch of the Twaddles, 1980; Nobbles the Troll, 1987; Plays: Not Just a Cog, 1983; Canvas Town, 1983; Barbecued History of Australia, 1983; Love With the Lights Out, 1985; Gum Deal, 1988; Super Cool, 1990; Bridesmaids & Undertakers, 1991; Amazing Doughnut Strike, 1993; Radio: Inspection, 1992; Blinkered, 1996; Contributor to: Age; Advertiser; Reveille; Melbourne Update; Anthologies: Stuff & Nonsense; More Stuff & Nonsense; Puffinalia; Exploring Relationships, 1990. Honour: Ford Young Playwrights Comp, 1979. Memberships: Austl Writers Guild; Fellowship of Austl Writers; Melbourne Writers' Theatre. Hobbies: Theatre; Fantasy and Science Fiction; Poetry; Music. Address: 225 Ross St Port Melbourne, Vic 3207, Australia.

TURNER John Harcourt, b. 22 Apr 1949, Sydney, Aust. Member of Parliament. m. Ann, 27 July 1975, 1 s, 2 d. Education: Dip of law; BA; BLitt. Appointments: Chmn, Parly Cttee, The Ombudsman, 1991-93; Dpty Speaker, NSW Parl, 1993-95; Shadow Min, Local Govt, 1996; Shadow Min, Hunter Dev, 1996; Shadow Min, Fisheries, 1996-98; Shadow Min, Fairtrading, 1996-99; Shadow Min, Mineral Rescs, 1996-98; Dpty Ldr Natl Party NSW, 1999-; Shadow Min, Roads, Tourism, Hunter Dev and Hunter Water, 1999-. Hobbies: Reading; Surfing; Cricket; Rugby Union. Address: Suite 1-5 Manning St, Tuncurry, NSW, Australia.

TURNER John Neville, b. 17 Apr 1936, Bury, Eng. Law Teacher; Barrister; Solicitor. m. Brigitte, 19 Apr 1936, 2 s. Education: LLB, Hons, Manchester; BA, Music, Monash Univ. Appointments: Instr, Univ of Michigan, USA, 1963-64; Assoc Prof, Snr Lectr in Law, Monash Univ, 1973-97; Visng Lectr, Univ of Birmingham, 1972-73, Visng Lectr, Northern Territory Univ, Darwin, 1997. Publications include: The Family Law Case Book, 1986; Lawyers, Families and Social Workers, 1990; International Encyclopaedia, 1996; Australian Family Law in The International Encyclopaedia of Laws. Memberships: Pres, Austl Cricket Soc, 1997-; Hon Legal Advsr, Austl Soc of Sports Hist, 1987-; Founder Mbr, Law and Lit Assn of Aust, 1990-. Hobbies: Cricket; Music;

Literature. Address: The Gingerbread House; Donna Buang Road, Warburton, Victoria, Australia.

TURNER Neil Clifford, b. 13 Mar 1940, Preston, UK. Research Scientist. m. Jennifer Ruth Gibson, 2 Mar 1968, 3 s. Education: BS (Hons), Agrcl Sci, 1962; PhD, Agronomy, Crop Physiol, 1968; DSc, Agric, 1983. Appointments: Plant Physiologist, CT Agricl Expmt Stn, New Haven, CT, USA, 1967; Crop Physiologist, CSIRO Plant Ind, Canberra, ACT, Aust, 1974; Rsch Ldr, CSIRO Plant Ind, Perth, West Aust, 1984. Publications: Adaption of Plants to Water and High Temperature Stress, 1980; Plant Growth, Drought and Salinity, 1986; Crop Production on Duplex Soils, 1992. Honours: Fell, Amn Soc Agronomy, 1982; Fell, Crop Sci Soc Am, 1985; Fell, Austl Acady Technological Scis & Engring, 1922; Medallist, 1993, Fell, 1995, Austl Inst Agricl Sci & Technol; Adj Prof, Univ of West Aust. Memberships: Austl Acady Technological Scis & Engrng; Austl Inst Agricl Sci & Technol, ACT Pres, 1978-79, Fed Cnclr, 1979-80; Bd, Trustees, ICRAF, Chmn Prog Cttee, 1996-; Amn Soc Agronomy; Crop Sci Soc Am; Amn Soc Plant Physiologists; Austl Soc Plant Physiologists; Austl Soc Agronomy; Continuing Cttee, Intl Crops Sci Congress; Crawford Fund Intl Agricl Rsch, WA Sect Cttee; Fac Agric & Higher Degrees Cttee, Univ WA. Hobbies: Gardening; Swimming; Hiking. Address: CSIRO Plant Industry, Private Bag, PO, Wembley (Perth), WA 6014, Australia.

TURNER Tina - Annie Mae Bullock, b. 26 Nov 1939 Brownsville TN. Singer. m. Ike Turner, 1956, div 1978, 4 s. Appointments: Singer with Ike Turner Kings of Rhythm; Ike and Tina Turner Revue; Concert tours of Eur, 1966, 1983-84; Japan and Africa, 1971. Films: Gimme Shelter, 1970; Soul to Soul, 1971; Tommy, 1975; Mad Max Beyond Thunderdome, 1985; What's Love Got to Do with It - vocals - 1993; Last Action Hero, 1993. Recordings incl: River Deep Mountain High, 1966; Proud Mary, 1970; Blues Roots, 1972; Nutbush City Limits, 1973; The Gospel According to Ike and Tina, 1974; Solo albums: Let Me Touch Your Mind, 1972; Tina Turns the Country On, 1974; Acid Queen, 1975; Rough, 1978; Private Dancer, 1984; Break Every Rule, 1986; Foreign Affair, 1989; Simply the Best, 1991; The Collected Recordings: Sixties to Nineties - with others - 1994; Wildest Dreams, 1996. Honours: Grammy Awd, 1972, 1985 - three -, 1986; Chevalier des Arts et des Lettres. Address: c/o CAA, 9830 Wilshire Boulevard, Beverly Hills, CA 90212, USA.

TWENTYMAN Leslie Jack, b. 3 Feb 1948, Carlton, Vic, Aust. Youth Worker. Honours: OAM (Order Aust Medal); Adv Aust Awd; Tatersall's Enterprise and Achievement Awd; Save the Children's White Flame Awd; Cttee of Melbourne Awd. Memberships: Pres, 20th Man Homeless Young People Fund; VP, Westadd Daug Treatment; Western Bulldogs Football Club. Address: 3 Myamyn St, Braybook, Victoria, Australia 3019.

TYAGI Krishana Gopal, b. 5 Aug 1942. Social Science Researcher. Education: PhD Polit Sci; MA Polit Sci; MLib and Info Sci. Appointments: Dpty Dir, Natl Socl Sci Documentation Cntr, 1977-88; Dir, Indian Cncl of Socl Sci Rsch, New Delhi, 1988-. Publications: Education Index, 1980; Samyukta Socialist Party of India, 1984; Party and Politics in India, 1994. Honour: Man of the Yr, 1993. Memberships: Chmn, Intl Cttee of Socl Sci Info and Documentation, Paris; Pres, Asia Pacific Info Netwrk in Socl Sci, Bangkok. Hobbies: Reading; Writing; Gardening; Yoga. Address: Indian Council of Social Science Research, 35 Ferozshah Road, New Delhi 110001, India.

TYLER Ewen William John, b. 24 Aug 1928. Consulting Geologist; Company Director. Aldyth Dorothy Watts, 3 Mar 1951, 2 s, 1 d. Education: BSc (Hons), FAus IMM; MIMM, CEng. Appointments: Exploration Geol, Geita Gold Mining Co Ltd, Tanzania, 1950-55; Asst Mngr, Geita, 1955-59; Exploration Geol, Tanganyika Holdings Ltd, London, 1959-65; Dir Tanganyika Holdings Ltd, 1965-69; Dir, Gen Mngr, Rhodesia Katanga Ltd, London, 1965-69; Gen Mngr, Tanganyika Holdings Ltd, Aust, 1969-75; Mngng Dir, Tanaust Proprietory Ltd, Aust, 1975-81; Exec Dir, Ashton Mining Ltd, 1981-90; Chmn,

Austl Diamond Exploration, NL, 1989-97; Chmn, Helix Resources, NL, 1996-; Dir, Ashton Mining Ltd, 1996-; Chmn Lion Selection Grp, 1997-. Publication: Australia's New Diamond Search, 1983. Honours: AM, 1991; Recip, Clunies Ross Awd for Sci and Technol, 1992. Memberships: Educ and Accreditation Cttee of Australasian Inst of Mining and Metallurgy, 1991-; Chmn, Victorian Cttee, United World Colls (Aust) Trust, 1989-; Dpty Chmn, Mission to Streets and Lanes and Cnclr, 1973-97. Hobbies: Walking; Reading; Spiritual development of Homo Sapiens. Address: c/o Ashton Mining Ltd; Level 4, 441 St Kilda Road, Melbourne 3004, Australia.

TYLER Michael James, b. 27 Mar 1937, Surbiton, Eng. Zoologist. m. Ella Patricia Edwards, 29 Dec 1962, 1 s, 2 d. Education: MSc. Appointments: Lectr, 1975-78; Snr Lectr, 1979-83; Assoc Prof, 1984-. Publications: Frogs of South Australia, 1966; Frogs, 1976, 1982; Australian Frogs, 1989; Australian Frogs, A Natural History, 1994, 1998. Honours: Sir Joseph Verco Medal, 1980; Austl Nat Hist Medallion, 1980; City of Adelaide, Aust Day Citizen of Yr, 1993; Offr, Order of Aust, 1995; Michael Daley Eureka Prize for Sci Comm, 1997; Riversleigh Medal, 1998. Memberships: Sec Gen, World Congress of Herpetology, 1997-; Chmn, S Austl Mus, 1982-92; Pres, Roy Zool Soc of S Aust, 1994-. Hobbies: Antiquarian books; Gardening. Address: Department of Environmental Biology, University of Adelaide, Adelaide, SA 5005, Australia.

TYREE (Alfred) William, b. 4 Nov 1921, Auckland, NZ. Electrical Engineer; Chief Executive; Chairman. m. Joyce Lyndon, 3 Jan 1946, 2 s, 1 d. Education: Dip, Elec Engrng, 1949; Mbr, 1966, Fell, 1968, Inst of Engrs, Aust; Fell, Inst of Elec Engrs, 1983. Appointments: Fndr, Tyree Inds and Westralian Transformers and Subsids, 1956; Chmn, Fndr, Alpha Air (Sydney) Pty Ltd; Tech Components Pty Ltd; Tycan Aust Pty Ltd; Tyree Holdings Pty Ltd; A W Tyree Transformers Pty Ltd; Wirex Pty Ltd; A W Tyree Fndn. Honours: OBE, 1971; KB, 1975; James N Kirby Gold Medal, Inst of Prod Engrs, Aust, 1980; Hon Fell, Univ of Sydney, 1985; Hon Life Gov, Austl Postgrad Fedn of Med, 1985; Hon Med, Inst of Elec and Electron Engrs, NY, USA, 1984; Peter Nicol Russell Mem Medal, Inst of Engrs, Aust, 1984; DSc, Honoris Causa, Univ NSW, 1986. Memberships: Cncl and Natl Exec, Austl Ind Grp; Austl Inst of Co Dirs; Amn Club; Austl Golf Club; Kosiusko Alpine Club; Roy Prince Alfred Yacht Club; Cruising Yacht Club of Aust; Roy Motor Yacht Club; Roy Automobile Club. Hobbies: Skiing; Yachting; Tennis; Music; Golf; Sail boarding; Photography; Computers. Address: 60 Martin Place, Sydney, NSW 2000, Australia.

TYSON Matthews Stanley, b. 22 June 1954, Launceston, Aust. Self-employed Music Teacher and Administrator. Education: Lic Trinty Coll Music, London, 1975. Appointments: Tchr, Hobart, 1973-78; Pvte Tchr, Launceston, 1978-; Chmn, Aust Natl Cttee, Trinity Coll, London Exec Cttee, Launceston Chmbr Music Soc; Tasmanian Rep for Trinity Coll, London, 1974. Honours: Fell, Aust Guild Music, 1978; Hon Mbr, St Cecilia Sch Musical Nom Young Aust of Yr, 1981; Hon Membership, Trinity Coll Music, London, 1984. Memberships: United Music and Speech Tchrs, Tasmania; Aust String Tchrs Assn; Amn String Tchrs Assn. Hobbies: Furthering the development of music in Tasmania; Travel; Antique and art collecting; Local history; The History of theatre and cinema buildings. Address: 59 Bourke Street, Launceston, Tas 7250, Australia.

TZUOO Keh-Lih (Steve), b. 21 July 1956, Taipei, Taiwan. General Manager. m. Wen-Chuen, 30 Dec 1979, 2 s. Education: BS, Mech Engrng, Taiwan Univ; MS, Mech Engrng, Univ of Missouri-Rolla, USA; PhD, Mech Engrng, Stanford Univ, USA. Appointments: Gen Mngr, Shanghai Tetra Pak Hoyer; Gen Mngr, SJZ Guoxiang Refrigeration Co; Mngr, ITRI, Taiwan. Publications: 12 tech pprs in Heat Transfer, Fluid Mechanics and Turbomachinery. Honour: Gen Motors Fellship, 1983-86. Memberships: Sigma Xi, sci rsch soc; Connecticut State Licensed Profl Engr. Hobbies: Travel; Music; Fishing.

Address: #43 Long Dong Garden, Lane 2255, Long Dong Road, Pudong, Shanghai 201203, China.

U

U OHN GYAW, B. 3 Mar 1932, Myanmar. Minister of Foreign Affairs. Education: Univ of Yangon. Appointments: For Serv, missions in Yugoslavia, USA, Singapore, Aust, USSR; Min of For Affairs, 1956-85; Dir, S and SE Asia Div, 1985-86; Dir Gen, Pol Dept, 1986; Dpty Min and Dir Gen, 1988. Address: Ministry of Foreign Affairs, Prome Court, Prome Road, Yangon, Myanmar.

U SEIN WIN. Politician. Appointments: Ldr, New Democratic Party; Pres, Natl Coalition Govt, Union of Burma, 1990.

UCHIDA Kengo, b. 5 May 1934, Aomori, Japan. Professor, Hirosaki University. m. Atsuko, 2 s, 1 d. Education: BS, Hirosaki Univ; DSc, MSc, Tohoko University. Appointments: Rsch Assoc, Tohoku Univ, 1962; Assoc Prof, 1965, Prof, Chem, 1981, Hirosaki Univ. Memberships: Chem Soc of Japan. Hobbies: Philately; Japanese chess. Address: 13-12 Matsubara Higashi, 1-chome, Hirosaki-shi, 036-8141, Japan.

UCHIJIMA Zenbei, b. 27 Aug 1929, Nagasaki, Shimahara, Japan. President of Miyazaki, Municipal University. m. Tomoko Miyake, 22 Dec 1957, 1 s, 1 d. Education: Miyazaki Univ, Miyazaki Agricl Coll. Appointments: Natl Inst of Agricl Scis, 1950; Kyushu Agricl Experimental Stn, 1981; Natl Inst Agricl Sci, 1983; Ochanomizu Univ, 1987; Miyazaki Municipal Univ, 1995. Publications: Vegetation and Atmosphere II, 1976; Agricultural Meteorology in Japan, 1973; Agricultural Meteorology, 1990; Degradation of Earth Environment, 1990; Global Warming and Its Effects, 1996. Honours: Prize of Agricl Meteorology Soc of Japan, 1965; Prize of Min of Agric, Forestry and Fisheries, 1986; Prize of Miyazaki Prefecture (Sci), 1996. Memberships: Agricl Meteorological Soc of Japan, 1950; Meteorological Soc of Japan, 1985; Japanese Biometeorology Soc, 1995; Hon mbr, Est Naturalist Soc, 1993. Hobby: Tennis. Address: T880-0805 Miyazaki, Tachibanatori-higashi 5-6-3, Flower-Mansion 702, Japan.

UDAY Hussein, b. 1964. Militia Ldr; Bus Exec. Education: Baghdad Univ. Appointments: Ed Babil - pro govt newspaper; Owner tv and radio station; Hd Fedaycen of Saddam - militia. Address: c/o Presidential Palace, Kawadaf Mariam, Baghdad, Iraq.

UEDA Yoko, b. 4 Mar 1958, Nigata. Associate Professor. Education: PhD, Econs, Kyoto Univ, 1997. Appointments: Rsch Assoc, Kyoto Univ, 1990-95; Lectr, 1995-98, Assoc Prof, 1998, Univ of Mktng and Distribution Scis. Publication: Local Economy and Entrepreneurship in Thailand, 1995. Address: Faculty of Commerce, University of Marketing and Distribution Sciences, Nishi-ku, Kobe 651-2188, Japan.

UELMEN Gerald, b. 8 Oct 1940, Greendale, WI, USA. Law Professor. m. Martha, 30 Apr 1966, 1 s. 2 d. Education: BA, Loyola Mary Mount Univ, Los Angeles; JD, LLM, Georgetown Univ Sch of Law. Appointments: Prof of Law, 1986-, Dean, Sch of Law, 1986-94, Santa Clara Univ. Publications: Books: Lessons From the Trial, 1996; Drug Abuse & the Law, 1998. Honours: Ross Essay Prize, Am Bar Assn, 1982. Memberships: CA Acady Appellate Lawyers, Pres 1990; Markkula Ctr for Applied Ethics, Schl 1992. Hobbies: Collecting Political Americana; Music. Address: Santa Clara University School of Law, Santa Clara, CA 95053, USA.

UGAJIN Ryuichi, b. 17 June 1963, Tokyo, Japan. Physicist. Education: PhB, 1988, MSci, 1990, PhD, 1997, Univ of Tokyo. Appointment: Rsch Sci, Rsch Cntr, Sony Corp, 1990-. Publications: Applied Physics Letters, 1996; Physical Review Letters, 1998; Physical Review B, 1999. Membership: Phys Soc of Japan. Hobbies: Music; Brain Science. Address: Frontier Science Laboratories, Sony Corporation, 134 Goudo-cho, Hodogaya-ku, Yokohama 240-0005, Japan.

UHERBELAU Andres. Government Official. Appointment: Min of State, Govt of Palau, Koror. Address: Ministry of State, PO Box 100, Koror, PW 96940, Palau.

UHERBELAU Andres, b. 21 Aug 1934, Angaur, Republic of Palau. Former Minister of State. m. Roania, 24 Aug 1963, 1 s, 3 d. Education: BA in Bus Admin & Mngmt, Univ of Guam; Univ of HI. Appointments: Min of State, Dir of Fin, Admnstr of Congress of Micronesia (FSM). Publications: Procedures for Collection, Recording and Reporting Revenue Taxes, 1980; Co-auth: Constitution of Angaur. Honours: Congressional Resolution Expressing Appreciation, 1979; 25Yr Awd for Govt Serv, 1993. Memberships: Pub Land Authority, 1980-85; Chmn, Angaur Constitutional Commn, 1982; Chmn of Cttee of Angaur Mining Trust Fund, 1983-94. Hobbies: Reading; Fishing. Address: Dngeronger Hamlet, Koro, Republic of Palau 96940.

ULIKI - Wu Liji -, b. 1940 Inner Mongolia. Politician. Appointments: Chmn Govt of the Inner Mongolia Autonomous Reg, 1993-97. Address: c/o Office of the Government for Inner Mongolia, Hohhot City, Inner Mongolia Autonomous Region, People's Republic of China.

ULUFA'ALU Bartholomew. Politician. Appointments: Ldr Solomon Islands Liberal Party; PM of Solomon Islands, Aug 1997-. Address: Office of the Prime Minister, P O Box G1, Honiara, Solomon Islands.

ULUSU Bulent, b. 7 May 1923 Istanbul. Politician; Naval Offr. m. Mizat Erensoy, 1951, 1 d. Education: Naval Acady; Var cmd posts in navy; Rank of Rear Adm, 1967; Vice-Adm, 1970; Adm, 1974; Fmr Cmdr of War Fleet; Cmdr of Turkish Naval Forces until 1980; Fmr Under Sec min of Def; PM of Turkey, 1980-83; MP, 1983-87. Address: Ciftehavuzlar Yesilbahar 50K.8/27, Kadikoy/Istanbul, Turkey.

UM Chung-In, b. 22 June 1940, Seoul, Korea. Physicist (Statistical Physics). m. Agnes Chung, 20 Dec 1969, 2 s. Education: BS, Phys, 1964, MS, 1966, Seoul Natl Univ, Korea; MS, Phys, Univ of Notre Dame, S Bend, IN, USA, 1972; PhD, Phys, State Univ of NY, Buffalo, NY, USA, 1978. Appointments: Lt, Korean Naval Acady, 1967-69; Asst Prof, Phys Dept, Assoc Prof, Phys Dept, 1978-79, Prof, Phys Dept, 1979-, Korea Univ; Chmn, Dept of Phys, 1982-84; Adj Rsch Prof, SUNY, Buffalo, 1985-90; Vice Dean, Coll of Sci, 1990-92; Visng Prof, Lebedev Phys Inst, Moscow, 1991; Dir, Cntr for Thermal & Statistical Phys, designated by Korean Sci and Engrng Fndn (KOSEF), 1991-94; Adj Rsch Professorship, Wash State Univ, 1994-97; Dir, Rsch Inst of Basic Sci, Korea Univ, 1994-96; Visng Prof, Korea Inst for Advd Study, 1999; Adj Rsch Professorship, Univ WI at Stevens Pt, 1999-2001. Publications: Over 180 articles inclng: The Quantum Damped Harmonic Oscillator, J Phys A: Math, 1987; 10 books incl: Many Body Problems, 1991; Quantum Liquid 4H, 1998. Honours: Korean Phys Soc Awd, Most Productive and Disting Scientist of Yr, 1982; Natl Awd for contbng to dev of basic sci, Korean Govt, 1983; Acad Awd, Outsndng Rsch and Tchng, Korea Univ, 1989. Memberships: Cttee Mbr, Nat Sci Sect, UNESCO Off, Korea, 1991-95; Life Mbr, Korean Acady of Sci and Technol, 1995-; Steering Cttee, Phys Div, Korea Inst for Advd Study. 1997-; Korean Cttee, Asia Pacific Cntr for Theort Phys, 1997-. Hobbies: Tennis; Jogging.

UMA SHREE BHARATI Sadhvi, b. 3 May 1959, Dunda, Tikamgarh Dist, India. Member of Parliament. Appointments: VP, Bharatiya Janata Pty, Madhya Pradesh, 1988-; Elected, 9th Lok Sabha, 1989; Mbr, Consultative Cttee, Min of Agric, 1990; Mbr, Pub Accounts Cttee, 1991-92; Mbr, Consultative Cttee, 1990-92; Re-elected, 10th Lok Sabha, 1991; Mbr, Pub Accounts Cttee, 1992-93; Pres, BJP, Yth Wing, 1993-; Re-elected, 11th Lok Sabha, 1996; Mbr, Cttee on Sci and Technol, Environ and Forests, 1996-97; Re-elected, 12th Lok Sabha, 1998; Union Min of State, Human Resc Dev, 1998-. Publications: Swami Vivekananda, 1972; Peace of Mind, 1978; Manav ek Bhakti ka Naata, 1983.

Memberships: Mata Betibai Charitable Trust; Manav Jagriti Sangh; Ram Janam Bhoomi Trust; Vishwa Hindu Parishad. Hobbies: Reading and writing; Watching movies; Travelling; Driving; Badminton; Composing Hindi poems. Address: 9 Tyag Raj Marg, New Delhi 110001, India.

UNDERWOOD Barney Alan, b. 3 Apr 1943. Academic. m. Annette Hannan, 25 July 1969, 2 s, 1 d. Education: BBus (QIT); Ms (MIS) TX Tech; MBA (Queensland); PhD (QUT). Appointments: Engrng Draftsman, Dept of Local Govt, Queensland, 1961-66; Programmer, Systems Analyst, Applications Mngr, Ops Mngr, Main Rds Dept, Queensland, 1967-75; Lectr, Snr Lectr, Assoc Prof, QUT, 1975-. Honours: Fell, Austl Computer Soc, 1992; Hon Life Mbr, ACS, 1994. Memberships: VP ACS, 1988-89; Techl Bd Gov, 1989; Pres, ACS, 1990-91; Dir, ACS Profl Dev Bd, 1995-96; Asst Sec Gen, SE Asian Regl Computer Confedn, 1992-99. Hobbies: Golf; Surf lifesaving. Address: 68-70 Springlands Drive, Slacks Creek Qld 4127, Australia.

UNGER Jonathan, b. 3 May 1946, NY City, USA. University Researcher. m. Dr Anita Chan, 29 Nov 1976, 1 d. Education: PhD, Sussex Univ. Appointments: Dir, Contemporary China Cntr, Australian Natl Univ; Ed, The China Journal. Publications: 13 books including: Education Under Mao; Chen Village. Address: Contemporary China Centre, RSPAS, ANU, Canberra 0200, Australia.

UNNIKRISHNAN Seema, b. 3 May 1967, Kerala, India. Assistant Professor. m. 18 Jan 1993, 1 d. Education: BSc, Zool; MSc, Environmental Tox, Madras Univ; Environmental Law Dip, Madwai Kamraj Univ; Fell, Hazardous Waste Mgmnt, NITIE. Appointments: Trnee Sci, Cntrl Pollution Control Bd; Asst Prof, NITIE, 1994-. Creative Works: Book for AICTE, Environmental Legislation, 1997. Honours: Gold Medalist, Madras Univ, 1989; Jawahailal Nehru Awd, Proficiency, 1989. Memberships: Natl Safety Cncl, 1996; Indian Environmental Assn; Natl Solid Waste Assn. Hobbies: Gardening; Reading; Music. Address: Type IV, No 8, NITIE, Vihar Lake, Mumbai 400087, India.

UNSWORTH Barrie John, b. 16 Apr 1934, Dubbo, NSW, Australia. Company Director. m. Pauline, 13 Aug 1955, 3 s, 1 d. Education: Harvard Univ TUP. Appointments: Sec Lab Cncl of NSW, 1979-84; NSW Min for Transport, 1984-86; NSW Min for Health, 1986; Premier of NSW, 1986-88; Gen Mngr, 2KY Broadcasters Pty Ltd, 1992-. Memberships: Chmn, Aust Day Cncl of NSW, 1995-; Chmn, NSW Centenary of Fedn Cttee, 1997-. Hobbies: Gardening; Golf; Bushwalking. Address: 7 Northwood Close, Mona Vale, NSW 2103, Australia.

UPADHYA Padma Vasudev, b. 15 July 1963. Librarian. m. 21 Apr 1988, 2 d. Education: MLISc; PhD. Appointment: Joined as Additional Libn, now Libn, Manipal Inst Technol, 1986-; Presented pprs at Natl Confs and workshops; Currently wrkng with Prof Neelameghan on a multiling thesaurus. Honour: Karnataka State Awd, 1987. Memberships: Indian Lib Assn; Indian Assn of Spec Libs and Info Cntrs; Soc of Info Sci; Dakshina Kannada and Kodagu Lib Assns; Sec, Dak Kannada and Kodagu Lib Assn. Hobbies: Reading; Writing; Teaching; Community/rural information services; Library automation; Information technology applications in library and information services. Address: Manipal Institute of Technology, Manipal 576119, India.

UPADHYAYA Abhishek, b. 1 Feb 1979, Allahabad, India. Student. Education: ICSE, 1994; ISC, 1996; BA, Allahabad Univ, current. Publications: Sev poems, short stories and articles in newsppprs, anthologies and mags. Hobby: Creative Writing. Address: 136 Rajapur, Allahabad, Uttar Pradesh, India.

UPTON Simon D, b. 1958. Government Minister. m. 2 children. Education: Degs in Engl and Law, Auckland Univ; Rhodes Schl; MLitt, Pol Philos, Oxford Univ, Eng. Appointments: Natl Party Cand, Waikato, 1981; Elected MP for Raglan, 1984; Min of Hlth, Min for Environt and

Min of Rsch, Sci and Technol, 1990; Min for Crown Rsch Insts, 1991; Assoc Min of Fin, 1993; Min of Enviromt, Crown Rsch Insts, Rsch, Sci and Technol, 1993; Min of Biosecurity, Cultural Affairs, 1996; Min of State Servs, Enviromt, Crown Rsch Insts, Assoc Min of For Affairs and Trade. Address: 1st Floor, 71 Seddon Road, PO Box 1399, Hamilton, New Zealand.

URANO Yasuoki. Politician. Appointments: Fmr Parly Vice-Min of For Affairs; Fmr Parly Vice-Min of Intl Trade and Ind; Chmn Cttee on Com and Ind; Min of State; Dir-Gen Sci and Technol Agcy, 1995-96. Membershps: Mbr HoR. Address: c/o Science and Technology Agency, 2-2-1 Kasumigaseki, Chiyoda-ku, Tokyo 100, Japan.

UREN Judith Olive Ann, b. 30 Apr 1943. Nurse. m. 30 Apr 1965, David W Uren, 2 s, 2 d. Education: Cert, Gen Nursing; Cert, Reg'd Midwife; Grad Dip, Applied Sci. Appointments: Elected Asst Sec, Austl Nursing Fedn, 1989; Re-Elected to Position, 1993; Elected as Fed Sec of Austl Nursing Fedn, 1995. Memberships: Austl Nursing Fedn; Fell, Royal Coll of Nursing, Aust; Fell, Coll Nursing NSW; Victorian Womens Trust. Hobbies: Reading; Travel; Gardening; Cycling. Address: 373-375 St Georges Road, North Fitzroy, Melbourne, Vic 3068, Australia.

UREN Nicholas Charles, b. 23 Feb 1940. Soil Scientist. m. Marian Lynette Fraser, 20 Feb 1965, 2 d. Education: BAgrSc, Univ of Melbourne, Aust, 1962; PhD, Univ of Melbourne, Aust, 1969; Dip of Educ, Monash Univ, Aust, 1974. Appointments: Snr Demonstrator in Agricl Chem, 1965-66; Lectr, Soil Sci, La Trobe Univ, 1969-77; Snr Lectr, Soil Sci, 1977-91, 1991-; Assoc Prof and Rdr in Soil Sci, La Trobe Univ, Aust. Publications: Manganese in Soil and Plants (co-ed), 1988; Soil Science: An Introduction, co-auth, 5th ed, 1993; Publs in sci jrnls on soil chem of trace elements. Honour: G W Leeper Mem Lectr, 1994; C S Piper Awd, RACI, 1997. Memberships: Fell, Royal Austl Che Inst; Austl Soc of Soil Sci; Intl Soc of Soil Sci. Hobbies: Sport (golf, tennis, skiing); Gardening; Fishing; Theatre. Address: 58 Devon Street, Eaglemont, Vic 3084, Australia.

UREN Norman Frederick, b. 11 Aug 1939, Perth, WA, Aust. Geophysicist. m. 6 Jan 1987, 2 s, 1 d. Education: BS; DipEd; PGDApp Phys; MAPP Sci; PhD. Appointments: WA Educ Dept, 1961; WA Inst of Technol, 1966; Curtin Univ of Technol. Honours: WAIT Sportsman of the yr, 1972. Memberships: ASEG; SEG; EAGE; Aus IMM; AIP; GSA; AGU. Hobbies: Fishing; Woodwork; Gardening. Address: Department of Exploration Geophysics, Curtin University of Technology, Kent St, Bentley 6102, Western Australia, Australia.

URUSHIHARA Asako, b. 5 Sept 1966, Chiba, Japan. Violinist. m. Toshio Hosokawa, 5 Sept 1996. Education: BM, Juillard Sch, NY, USA. Recordings: CDs: Mendelssohn and Tchaikovsky concertos w Royal Liverpool Philharmonic under Vernon Handley, 1991; Camerata, 1993; Bartok and Janacek sonatas, 1994; Ave Maria, 1995. Honours: First Prize, Prize for Best Perf, 2nd Intl Music Comp of Japan, 1983; Walker Fund Prize, Young Concert Artists Instl Auditions, 1988; Arion Prize, Arion-Edo Fndn, 1987; Mobil Music Awd, 1990. Address: 1-9-45-106 Sekimachi-minami, Nerima-ku, Tokyo, 777-0053, Japan.

USAGAWA Tsuyoshi, b. 7 Mar 1959, Shimonoseki, Japan. Associate Professor. m. Kuniko, 1980, 3 s. Education: MEng, Tohoku Univ, 1983; DEng, Tohoku Univ, 1988. Publications: 25 jrnl pprs; over 100 pprs to intl confs on acoustics & signal processing. Honour: Awaya Awd, Acoustical Soc of Japan, 1992. Memberships: Acoustical Soc of Japan; Inst Elec Com Info Eng; Inst EE Eng; Acoustical Soc Am; INCE, Japan. Hobbies: Drive; Travel; Listening to Music. Address: Department Computer Science, Kumamoto University, 2-39-1 Kurokami, Kumamoto 860-8555, Japan.

USUI Hideo. Politician. Appointments: Fmr Parly Vice-Min Econ Plng Agcy; Min of State and Dir Gen Def Agcy, Jan-Nov 1996. Memberships: Mbr HoR; Mbr LDP.

Address: c/o Defence Agency, 9-7-45, Akasaka, Minato-ku, Tokyo 107, Japan.

UTTARAVICHIEN Thongueb, b. 5 July 1935. Medical Practitioner. m. Orapin Pathomvanich, 25 Dec 1960, 2 s, 2 d. Education: MB; BS, Melb; FRCSE; FRCST; FICS; Specialty Bd, Gen Surg, Sp Bd Orths. Appointment: Hd Dept Surg, Snr Cnslt, Dept Surg, Srinagarind Hosp, Fac Med, Khon Kaen Univ. Publication: Experience Of Non-Jaundiced Cholangio Carcinoma, 1990. Honours: Fac Tchr of Yr, Fac Med, Khon Kaen, 1989; Kt Grand Cross (1st Class) of Most Noble Order of the Crown of Thailand, 1990; Univ Tchr Yr, Khon Kaen Univ, 1991; Kt Grand Cross (1st Class) Most Exalted Order of the White Elephant, 1993; Disting Surg of the Yr, Intl Coll of Surgs, Thailand Sect, 1998. Memberships: Intl Gastro-Surg Club; Soc Minimally Invasive Surg. Hobbies: Reading; Fishing. Address: Department of Surgery, Faculty of Medicine, Khon Kaen University, Thailand.

V

VACCARO Pablo Oscar, b. 6 Jan 1964, Buenos Aires, Argentina. Scientific Researcher. Education: MSc, Phys, Univ Nac Cuyo, Argentina, 1986; PhD, Phys, Univ Nac Cuyo, Argentina, 1991. Appointments: Post Doct Rschr, Kyoto Univ, Japan, 1991-93; Rschr, ATR Opt and Radio Comm Rsch Labs, Kyoto, 1993-96; Rschr, ATR, Adaptive Commun Rsch Labs, 1996-. Publications: Over 50 pprs in jrnls; Presentations in intl confs. Honours: Schlshps, Argentine Natl Atomic Energy Commn (CNEA), 1983-86; Fellshp from CNEA, 1986-91; Fellshp, Min of Educ, Japan, 1991-93. Address: ATR Adaptive Commun Research Labs, 2-2 Hikaridai, Seika-cho, Kyoto 619-0288, Japan.

VAEA Hon Baron, b. 15 May 1921, Tonga. Prime Minister of Tonga. m. Baroness Tuputupu Vaea, 3 s, 3 d. Education: Tupuo Coll, Tonga, 1933-37; Wesley Coll, NZ, 1938-41; Oxford Admin Course, Air Trng Sch, Oxford, 1967-68. Appointments: Roy NZ Air Force, 1942-45; Tongan Civ Serv, 1945-53; ADC to HM Queen Salote Tupou III, 1954-59; Acting Gov, Vava'u, 1958-59; Gov of Ha'apai, 1960-68; 1st High Commnr and Consul of Tonga to London, 1969-72; Min for Lab, Com and Inds, Mbr, Cabinet, Privy Cncl, Legis Assembly, Acting Dpty PM, Acting Min of Educ and Civ Aviation, Acting Min of Fin, In Charge, Tonga Visitor's Bur and Coop Socs, 1973-91; PM, Min of Agric and Forestry, Min of Fisheries, Marine and Ports, 1991-. Honours: Baron Vaea of Houma, HM King Taufa'ahau Tupou IV, 1969; Recip, NZ Commemorative Medal, 1990; Recip, HM the King's Silver Jubilee Medal, 1996. Memberships include: Dir, Tonga Commodities Bd; Registrar, Incorporated Socs; Registrar of Co'c; Chmn, Tonga Natl Reserve Bank; Tonga Investment Ltd; Natl Reserve Bank of Tonga; Tonga Brdcstng Commn; Tonga Def Bd. Address: Office of the Prime Minister, POB 62, Nuku'alofa, Tonga.

VAHIA Mayank, b. 24 Sept 1956, Kutch, Gujarat, India. Scientist. m. Neeta, 22 Feb 1985, 2 d. Education: MSc, 1979; PhD, 1984. Appointments: Rsch Schlr, TIFR, 1979; Rsch Assoc, 1984, Fell, 1990, TIFR; Reader, 1994; Assoc Prof, 1998. Publications: 150 sci publs in jrnls; International Conferences in High Energy Astrophysics, book. Honour: Pub Serv Grp Achmnt Awd, NASA, 1986. Memberships: Intl Astronomical Union; Astronomical Soc of India; Bombay Assn in Sci Educ, 1990, Chmn, 1995-. Hobbies: Science education; Philosophy of science. Address: Department of Astronomy and Astrophysics, Tata Institute of Fundamental Research; Homi Dhabha Road, Colaba, Mumbai 400 005, India.

VAHLQUIST Magnus, b. 24 May 1938. Ambassador. m. Christina Trana. Education: BA, Uppsala Univ. Appointments: Min for For Affairs, 1962; Embassies in Moscow and Beijing, 1963-67; Permanent Mission, Geneva, 1972; Dpty Sec-Gen, EFTA, 1976; Dir Gen, Min for For Affairs, 1982; Exec VP, Swedish Trade Cncl, 1986; Amb, Tokyo, 1992; Amb, Oslo, 1998. Hobbies: Skiing; Hiking; Books. Address: Embassy of Sweden, Nobelsgate 16, NO-0244 Oslo, Norway.

VAIDYANATHA IYER Kamala, b. 24 Sept 1945, Hyderabad, India. Engineer. Education: BE, Mechl Engrng, Osmania Univ Coll of Engrng, Hyderabad, 1966; MTech, Mechl Engrng, Machine Des, 1970, PhD, Mechl Engrng, 1977, Inst of Technol, Madras; PG Dip, Mktng Mngmt, 1993, MBA Human Resource Mngmt, 1997, Indira Gandhi Natl Open Univ, New Delhi. Appointments include: Pt-time Fac, Jawaharlal Nehru Technological Univ, 1979-95; Rsch Assoc, CASCADE, Dept of M and AE, Carleton Univ, Ottawa, can, 1986-87; Visng Rsch Scientist, Dept of Mechl Engrng, Concordia Univ, Montreal, 1987-89; Snr Engr, Dpty Mngr, Mngr, BHEL Corp Rsch and Dev Div, 1978-95; Snr Mngr, Bharat Heavy Electricals Ltd, Corp Rsch and Dev Div, Hyederabad, 1995-. Honours: Best Des Orientated Ppr Awd, All India Machine Tool Des and Rsch Conf, Chennai, India, 1984; Best Citizens of India Awd, 1998; 20th Century Awd for Achievement, 1999, Intl Woman of

the Yr, 1999-2000, IBC; Num merit schlshps. Memberships: Amn Soc of Mechl Engrs, 1980; Life Fell, Inst of Engrs, India, 1982; Soc of Indl Tribology, India, 1989; Forum of Women in Pub Sector, 1990. Hobbies: Music; Travel. Listed in: Who's Who in the World; Who's Who in Science and Engineering; The Hundred Best Honoured Citizens of India; Who's Who of Fellows of Institution of Engineers; Who is Who of ASME International Members. Address: 1.3 RTLIGH, Barkatpura, Hyderabad 500027, India.

VAISHNAVI Motilal Anand, b. 30 June 1939. Teacher; Researcher. m. 5 Oct 1965, Krishna Dhar, 2 s. Education: MS; MD; PhD; MSc; Envtl Hlth, Sch of Plng and Environment; Envt Hlth, Sch of Arch; Envtl Hlth, Univ Gujarat; Creative Des and Prod Des, Natl Inst Des, Ahmedabad and NIMID, Bombay; Mental Hlth, Sch of Socl Scis, Univ Gujarat. Appointments: Vet Offr and Farm Supvsr, Aaray Milk Colony, Bombay, 1962-63; Insp, Vet Pub Hlth, Govt of Maharashtra, Bombay Cty Port and Harbour, 1964-66; Lectr, Biol and Vet Med, Bombay Vet Coll, 1964-66; Rsch Offr, Environmental Hlth and Med, Govt of India, New Delhi, 1970-72; Rsch Offr, Divs of Hlth Phys, Instrumentation and Biomedl Engrng, Ergonomics and Wrk Des, Govt of India, Ahmedabad, 1972-73; Proj Ldr, Mental Hlth Psychosomatic Aberrations, Govt of India, Ahmedabad, 1974-80; Div Hd, Biophys and Instrumentation, Govt of India, Bombay, 1980-84; Snr Rsch Offr, 1985-94, Asst Dir, 1994, Inst for Rsch in Reprodn, Govt of India; Exec Dir, Reproductive Hlth Care Delivery Systs Tech Rsch Cntr, Civ Hosp, Gandhinagar, 1984-. Publications: 14 orig contrbs to medl and applied hlth rsch. Honours: Global Man of Yr, 1995; Ldr of Influence; Intl cultural Dip of Hon, 1995. Hobbies: Singing; Writing Poetry; Romance; Perseverance. Address: Vaishnavasa Matkuj, Bungalow 200, Sector 29, Gandhinagar-Gujarat 382029, India.

VAJPAYEE Atal Bihari, b. 25 Dec 1926 Gwalior Madhya Pradesh. Politician. Education: Victoria - now Laxmibai - Coll Gwalior; DAV Col Kanpur. Appointments: Parly Ldr, 1957-77; Chmn Pub Accounts Cttee Lok Sabha, 1969-70, 1991-93; Detained during emergency, 1975-77; Min of External Affairs, 1977-79; Pres Bharatiya Janata Party, 1980-86; Parly Ldr, 1980-84, 1986; Ldr Opposition Lok Sabha, 1993-98; Chmn Standing Committee on External Affairs, 1993-95; PM of India, 15-28 May 1996, Mar 1998-; Min of External Affairs and Agric, Mar 1998-. Publications: New Dimensions of India's Foreign Policy; Jan Sangh Aur Musalmans; Three Decades in Parliament; Collects of poems and num articles. Honours: Hon PhD - Kanpur Univ - 1993; Bharat Ratna Pt Govind Ballabh Pant Awd, 1994; Padma Vibhushan; Lokmanya Tilak Pururskar. Memberships: Mbr Rashtriya Swayamsewak Sangh, 1941; Mbr Indian Natl Congress, 1942-46; Fndr mbr Bharatiya Jana Sangh, 1951; Mbr Lok Sabha, 1957-62, 1967-84; Mbr Natl Integraton Cncl, 1961-; Mbr Rajya Sabha, 1962-67; Fndr Janata Party, 1977; Mbr Lok Sabha - for New Delhi Mar 1977-84 - 1991-. Hobbies: Reading; Writing; Travelling; Cooking. Address: Office of the Prime Minister, S Block, New Delhi 110001, India.

VAKATALE Taufa. Government Minister; Deputy Prime Minister. Education: Tchr's Ctf, Advd, Nasinu Trng Coll, 1956; Bach of Arts. Auckland Univ, NZ, 1962; Dip Ed Amin, Leeds Univ, Eng, 1972. Appointments: Tchr, Prin, Secnd Sch, 1958-79; Dpty High Commnr, London, 1980-82; Chf Educ Offr, Min of Educ, 1983-85; Dpty Sec for Educ, 1986-87; Perm Sec, var Ministries, 1987-92; Contested Gen Elections, 1992; Portfolio enlarged to incl Sci and Technol, Min for Educ, Women and Culture, Sci and Technol, Min for Educ, 1993; Dpty Prim Min, Min for Educ and Technol, 1997. Address: Private Mail Bag, Suva, Fiji.

VALDEZ Ernesto Venegas, b. 18 Nov 1927, Dagupan, The Philippines. Physician. m. Resurreccion Jamias Valdez, 16 Apr 1958, 2 s, 3 d. Education: AA, Univ Phillipines, 1948; MD, Univ Philippines, 1953; Pharm Fell, UCSF, 1960; Cardiovascular Fell, Georgia Med, 1960; Admin, Kanasash, 1968; Pop Mngmt, Govt Al, 1971; Mngmt, Louis Allen, 1977; Basic Mngmt, AIM,

1979. Appointments include: Prof, Pharm, 1969-92, Chmn, Dept of Pharm, 1973-75, Univ of Philippines, Coll of Med, Manila; Corp Med Dir, Johnson & Johnson Phil Inc, 1974-87; Chmn, Dept of Pharm, Univ of Philippines, Coll of Med, 1988-91; Med Cnslt, Johnson & Johnson Phil Inc, 1987-95; Prof Emer, Univ of Philippines, Coll of Med, 1992-. Honours include: Meritorious Serv Awd, 1974; Most Outstndng Tchr, 1992; Disting Serv Awd, 1992; Meritorious Serv Awd, 1994. Memberships include: Philippine Med Assn; Manila Med Soc; Pain Soc of Philippines; Philippine Soc of Exptl and Clinl Pharm; Philippine Assn for Advancement of Sci; Philippine Soc of Microbiology and Infectious Dis; Natl Rsch Cncl of Philippine; NYAS. Hobbies: Tennis; Bowling; Classical Music. Address: 82 Guiho, Monte Vista SUB, Marikina City, Philippines.

VALENTE Sharon, b. 25 July 1945, San Francisco, California, USA. Assistant Professor of Nursing; Psychologist. m. Mario, 27 Oct 1973. Education: BSN, Mt St Mary's Coll, Los Angeles, 1972; MN, Univ CA, Los Angeles, 1974; PhD, Univ of S CA, Los Angeles, 1990. Appointments: Clin Instr, Mt St Mary's Coll, Pediats, Los Angeles, 1975-77; Nurse Practitioner, Santa Fe Meml Hosp, Los Angeles, 1977-79; Clin Specialist, Crisis Therapist, Los Angeles Suicide Prevention Cntr, Dir, Sch & Coll Nurse Practitioner Prog, UNEX, Univ CA, Los Angeles, 1979-81; Asst Prof, Fellshp in Psychosocl Oncol, Univ CA, Los Angeles, 1981-83; Clin Specialist, Mental Hlth, Pvte Prac, Los Angeles, 1978-; Adj Asst Prof, 1983-93, Asst Prof, Dept of Nursing, 1993-, Univ of S CA, Los Angeles. Publications include: Suicide: Assessment and Intervention. Honours include: Shneidman Awd, 1996; Phi Kappa Phi Disting Lectr, 1997; Bullough Awd, USC Nursing, 1998. Memberships: Amn Assn of Suicidology; Profl Advsr, Bd Dir, Death w Dignity; Sigma Theta Tau; Iota Lambda; Chi Eta Phi; Amn Acady of Nursing; Amn Psychol Assn. Hobbies: Calligraphy; French; Gardening; Camping. Address: 346 N Bowling Green Way, Los Angeles, CA 90049, USA.

VALENTINE Roger Stuart James, b. 5 July 1932, Hobart, Tas, Aust. Retired Barrister; Solicitor. m. Barbara, 12 Jan 1955, 1 s, 2 d. Education: LLB. Appointments: Ptnr, Hodgman & Valentine, 1956-77; Snr Solicitor, Pub Trust Off, Tas, 1977-84; Chmn, Child Protection Assessment Bd, 1977-85; Chmn, Liquor Licensing Bd, 1980-85; The Pub Serv Arbitrator, 1984-85; The Tasmanian State Serv Inaugural Commnr for Review, 1985-87; The Pub Tstee, Tas, 1987-93; Mbr, Tasmanian State Serv Appeal Bd, 1993-97; The Natl Chmn, C'Wlth Aged Care Complaints Resolution Scheme, 1998-. Honour: OAM, 1997. Memberships include: VP, Associated Chmbrs of Comm, Aust, 1970-71; Dpty Chmn, Univ of Tas Alumni, 1995-96; Pres, Probus Club of S Launceston, 1998-99; VP, Launceston Legacy and Tstee; Fell, Chartered Inst of Secs and Administrators. Hobbies: Motor sports; Water skiing. Address: 72 New World Avenue, Trevallyn, Tas 7250, Australia.

VALLER Rachel, b. 14 Sept 1929, Sydney, NSW, Aust. Pianist. m. Walter Travers, 28 Feb 1965. Education: LTCL, 1947; BA, 1952; DipEd, 1960; Conservatorium of Music, Sydney; University of Sydney; Pupil of Ignaz Friedman. Appointment: Soloist, Assoc Artist Chmbr Ensembles, ABC Radio, TV; Appearances w Sydney, Melbourne and Queensland Symph Orchs; Toured w cellist Andre Navarra, violinists Wanda Wilkormirska, Stoika Milanova, Zvi Zeitlin, Erick Friedman, Erich Gruenberg and bassoonist George Zuckerman; Recorded some lesser known Beethoven piano wrks for composer's bicentenary, ABC and World Record Club, 1970; Recorded Schubert's sonatinas w violinist Susanne Lautenbacher for 150th anniversary of composer's death, Germany, 1978. Publications: Contbr to: Eastern Suburbs Newspaper and to 2MBS FM, Music Broadcasting Society of New South Wales Coop Ltd. Honours: NSW Finalist, ABC Concerto and Vocal Competition; Harriet Cohen C'wlth Medal, 1956; OAM, 1995. Membership: Cultural Grants Advsry Cncl to NSW Min of Arts, 1986-87. Listed in: Who's Who in Music. Address: 22 Allen's Parade, Bondi Junction, NSW 2022, Australia.

VALLIAPPAN Kannappan, b. 31 Dec 1956, Devakottai, India. Pharmacy Teacher. m. V Dhanalakshmi, 27 May 1979, 1 s, 1 d. Education: BSc; BPharm; MPharm. Appointments: JKKN Coll of Pharm, 1986-88; Inst of Pharm Technol, Annamalai, 1989-. Honour: PG Fellshp, Univ Grants Cmmn, 1983-85. Memberships: Indian Soc of Tech Educn; Assn of Pharm Tchrs of India; Indian Pharm Assn. Hobbies: Tennis; Television; Reading Books. Address: Institute of Pharmacology Technology, Annamalai University, 608002 India.

VALSALA Kizhakkae Valappil, b. 6 June 1944, Guruvayoor, India. Professor. m. Arajan, 12 Sept 1965, 3 s. Education: BVSc; MSc, Pathol; PhD; FRVCS. Appointments: Asst Prof, Instr, Vet Surg, 1965; Assoc Prof, Prof, 1986. Publications: 62 rsch pprs. Honour: Govt Awd, Outstndng Rsch, 1981. Memberships: IVA; IAVP. Hobbies: Reading; Gardening. Address: Department of Pathology, Veterinary College, Kerala Agricultural University, Mannuthy Thrissur, Kerala, India.

VAMUZO, b. 17 Oct 1936, Yoruba, Nagaland. Public Leader, Cabinet of the State. m. Dec 1967, 4 s, 3 d. Education: Inter Arts, St Edmunds Coll, Shillong; BA, Wilson Coll, Bombay; LLB, Govt Law Coll in Bombay, India. Appointments: Naga Army, Naga Natl Movement for Freedom; Brig, Naga Army, Fed Govt of Nagaland; First Gen Sec, Utd Front, Nagaland, 1968; Contested in the Second Nagaland State Gen Elections, 1969; Third Gen Elections, 1974; Cabinet Min, 1974; Elected Min, 1977-82; Ldr of Opposition, 1982, 1987; Ldr Utd Legis Party of NCP, 1990. Address: East Circular Road, Kohima 797001, Nagaland, India.

VAN DE PAS Leonardus Franciscus Maria, b. 28 Oct 1942, De Bilt, The Netherlands. Genealogist. Education: St Bonifacius Lyceum, Utrecht, The Netherlands. Appointments include: Netherlands Dept of Customs, 1964-68; Asst to Auth, GM Glaskin, 1968-73; MacRobertson Miller/Ansett Airlines, 1973-95; Genealogy, full time, 1995-. Publications include: Sarah Ferguson, 1986; Clifton Ancestry, 1987; Van De Pas: A Genealogy, 1987; Grosvenors, Dukes of Westminster, 3 vols, 1989; Assisted, Cupid and the King by HRH Princess Michael of Kent, 1991; Diana, Princess of Wales, 1997; Fraser of Saltoun, 1997; Bonnie Prince Charlie, 1998; Crommelin, 1998; Giscard, 1998. Memberships: Dutch Genealogical Soc, The Hague; Friend of Cntrl Bur for Genealogy, The Hague; Austl Genealogy Soc, Sydney; WA Genealogical Soc, Perth. Hobbies: History; Reading. Address: PO Box 79, Mosman Park, WA, 6012, Australia.

VAN DER BURGHT Gregorius, b. 27 Mar 1944. Professor. m. Aline, 1967. Education: Masters deg, Law Sch Univ of Amsterdam, 1969; Doct, Univ of Amsterdam, 1973. Appointments: Prof, Priv and Notarial Tax Law, Vrije Univ Amsterdam, 1978-; Hd, Intl Rels Fac of Law, 1978-; Visng Prof, Cath Univ, Leuven, 1983-; Instr, Acady Pensionright and Life Ins Consultants, The Netherlands, 1987-; Cnclr, Law Firm Russel Advocation, Amsterdam, 1988-; Fndr, Sec, Fndn for Legal Educ and Rsch in Indonesia, 1992-; Intl Consultant, Law Spec, Asian Devel Bank, Higher Educ Proj of Indonesia, 1998-. Publications: Aspects of Law of Obligation; Handbook on Inheritance Law; Family Law; Legal and Practical effects of registration and publications of legal facts; Law of Cohabitation; Case Law, Inheritance Tax and Transfer Tax; Family Law Matrimonial Property Law; Corporate Law in Practice with H Burgers Publ; On Donations, Private and Tax; Many or pubis. Memberships: Intl Acady of Estate and Trust Law; Intl Rels Fac of Law; Intl Acady of Estate and Trust Law, San Fran; Roy Assn of Civil Law; Many or mbrshps. Address: Bispincklaan 13, 2061 EM Bloemendaal, The Netherlands.

VAN DER LELY Matthijs, b. 2 Jan 1959, Voorburg, The Netherlands. President Director. m. M A R Hezemans, 31 Aug 1985, 2 s. Education: Higher Inst of Hospitality Mngmnt, The Hague, Netherlands. Appointments: Gen Mngr, Vroom and Dreesmann, 1985; Snr Buyer, Makro, Netherlands, 1987; Grp Operations

Dir, Siam Makro PC Ltd, 1990; Tech Advsr, Makro Indonesia, 1994; Pres, Dir, 1998-. Hobbies: Golf; Travel. Address: c/o Makro Indonesia, Jl Lingkar Luar Selatan, Kav 6 Ciracas, Jakarta 13750, Indonesia.

VAN HEYST Jocelyn, b. 17 Feb 1936, Perth, Aust. Speech Pathologist. m. Cyrille, 10 Apr 1957, 2 s, 1 d. Education: Dip, Appl Sci, Maj, Speech Pathol, Melbourne. Appointments: Supvsr, Clin Stdies, 1970; Specl, Rehab Speech Pathol, 1998. Publication: Gamekeeper Cookbook, 1980. Memberships: Speech Pathol, Aust; Univ Club, Sydney. Hobbies: Tennis; Skiing; Cinema; Music; Theatre. Address: 86 Brougham Street, Potts, NSW, Australia.

VAN LIEROP Robert F, b. 17 Mar 1939. Diplomatist; Tv jrnlst; Univ lectr; Lawyer. m. 1 s. Education: NY Univ USA. Appointments: Practised law; Subsequently wrkd as jrnlst writer and univ lectr NY; VP 43rd UN Gen Ass Sess; Vanuatu's Rep to Preparatory Commn for the Intl Sea-Bed Authy and Intl Tribunal for Law of the Sea; Perm Rep of Vanuatu to UN, 1988-93; Elected Chmn Gen Ass Fourth Cttee - Decolonization - 1989. Memberships: Mbr Vanuatu delegs to meetings of Non-Aligned Movement inclng summits New Delhi, 1983; Harare, 1986; Belgrade, 1989; Mbr sev UN Gen Ass sess. Address: c/o Department of Foreign Affairs, PMB 51, Port Vila, Vanuatu.

VAN SCHAIK Leon H R, b. 25 Oct 1944. Architect; Dean. Div, 1 s, 1 d. Education: BArch Stud (NCLE); AA Dip (SADG); M Arch (UCT); PhD (Ports). Appointments: Unit Master, Archtl Assn, London, 1971-76; Chf Archt, Urban Fndn Johannesburg, 1978-81; Archt, Funda Cntr, 1981-86; Hd Arch, RMIT, 1986; Dean, Fac of the Constructed Environment, RMIT, 1993. Creative Works: Buildings: Ian Hamilton Findlay Gallery (w Kate Heron), 1971; The Funda Centre, Soweto, 1981-86; RMIT Technol Estate Master Plan; Books: Fin De Siecle: Architecture Of Melbourne, 1993; Transfiguring The Ordinary, 1995; Building 8 - Edmund and Corrigan at RMIT, 1997; Tom Kovac AD Monograph, 1998; Ushida Findlay, 1998; The Life Work of Guilford Bell, Architect, 1912-1992, 1999. Memberships: Royal Inst of Brit Archts; Archtl Assn; Royal Aust Inst Archts. Honours: RAIA Bates Smart McCutcheon Awd For Archtl Jrnlsm, 1990; AA Yr Prize, SADG, 1971; RIBA Design Prize, 1968. Hobbies: Landscapes, urban and rural; Literature; Collecting contemporary art. Address: c/o RMIT, 124 La Trobe St, Melbourne, Vic 3001, Australia.

VAN TOORN Penelope, b. 19 Dec 1952, Sydney, Australia. University Lecturer. Education: BA, Hons, 1980; MA, Hons, 1984; PhD, 1991. Appointments: Asst Prof, Engl, Univ BC, 1992-93; ARC Rsch Fell, Lectr, Univ Sydney, 1993-. Publications: Rudy Wiebe and the Historicity of the Word, 1995; Speaking Positions. Honour: ARC Postdoct Fellshp, 1993-96. Address: c/o Department of English, University of Sydney, NSW 2006, Australia.

VAN ZAK David B, b. 5 Nov 1950, Santa Monica, CA, USA. Psychologist; Neuropsychologist. m. Nina Weinstein, 14 Feb 1981, 1 s. Education: Psychodrama, 1976; MFCC, 1977; Biofeedback, 1983; PsyD, USIU, 1984; Psychol, 1988; Stress Mgmnt, 1992; QME, 1996. Appointments: Clinl Instr, USIU, 1984; Adj Prof, 1987; Core Fac, PSPS, 1983; Clinl Instr, Sch of Dental Med, USC, 1989. Creative Works: 26 Psychol Rsch Pprs, 1974-98; Book Chapt; 1 Article on Psychol and Culture. Honours: Sci Rsch Awd; Competition Awd; Winner BCA, 1989, 1990, 1991, 1992; Prof of the Yr Awd; Outstndng Rsch Awd Recognition Cert. Memberships: Biofeedback Soc of CA; AAPB; Intl Psychols Inst and Soc; APA; ISPA. Hobbies: Tae Kwan Do; Weight lifting; Peopl; Science Fiction. Address: 6733 S Sepulveda Blvd, Ste 275, LA, CA 90045, USA.

VANAHALLI Shivaram Mahadevappa, b. 6 Oct 1937, Doddwad, India. Rural Development Worker. m. Shakuntal, Dec 1960, 2 s, 1 d. Education: Matriculation. Fndr, Pres, Sec, Kalaposhak Sangh, Ribyadagi, Haveri, Karantaka, India. Honour: Kanakdas 400 Yrs Received

Awd, 15 Apr 1965. Memberships: Awd No5, (FF) DD U Marg, New Delhi; Icurd No 16, Bhai Veer Shigh Marg, Gole Mkt, New Delhi. Hobbies: Rural development activities. Address: Founder President, Kalaposhak Sangh, (R) Byadagi 581106, Haveri, Karnataka, India.

VANCLAY Francis Martin (Frank), b. 17 Sept 1960, Brisbane, Austl. Academic. m. Jacqueline, 3 s. Education: BSc, Griffith Univ; MSoc Sci, QLD Univ; PhD, Wageningen Agric Univ, The Netherlands. Appointments: Rsch Asst, Inst of Applied Environl Rsch, Griffith Univ, 1982-85; Lectr, Sch Austl Environl Studies, 1987-87; Snr Rsch Fell, Sch of Agric and Forestry, Univ of Melbourne, 1988; Snr Rsch Offr, Dept of Psych, Univ of QLD, 1989. Sub Dean, Rsch, Fac of Arts; Univ Key Rschr; Assoc Dir, Cntr for Rural Socl Rsch, Charles Stuart Univm 1990. Creative Works: The Environmental Imperative; Critical Landcare; Sustainability and Social Research ; Environmental and Social Impact Assessment; Agriculture, Environment and Society. Honours: Land and Water Resources and Devel Corp Trav Fellshp; Inaugural Rsch Ex Awd; Pres Cncl Awd; Visng Schl Rsch Fellshp. Memberships: Intl Rural Sociological Assn; Intl Assn for Impact Assessment; Austl Assn for Socl Rsch; X World Congress of Rural Sociology. Hobbies: Bushwalking; Camping; Outdoor Activities. Address: Centre for Rural Social Research, Charles Sturt University, Locked Bag 678, Wagga Wagga, NSW 2678, Australia.

VANDERHEEG Johannes, b. 21 Sept 1919, Amsterdam, Netherlands. Executive Chairman. m. Joan May Wood, 24 Feb 1943, 1 s, 1 d. Education: Coml Coll Amsterdam, 1936; Acctcy, Bus Mngmt, 1938. Appointments: Acctcy, Publicity, Warner Brothers, Amsterdam Off, 1936-39; Conscripted Dutch Coastguard Serv, 1939; Voly Serv, Roy Dutch Navy, Active Serv, UK, Spec Reserve Bch, 1940-47; Publicity Mngr, Holland-Am Filmbooking Off, Amsterdam, 1947-52; Pub Acct, Bus Mngmt Advsr, C P Bird and Assoc, Perth, WA, Aust, 1952-62; Dir, Co Sec, 1962, Chmn, Bd Dirs, 1972-89; Austl Agricl Mach Grp; Hilversea Intl Cnslts, 1989-. Publications include: Discovering the West: 300 years of maps and sea-charts from 1550-1850, 1979. Honours: Dutch War Cross w Bars, 1940; JP, 1963; Queen's Silver Jubilee Medal, 1977. Memberships: FRSA, London; Inst Sworn Valuers; Rotary Intl; Past Pres, Ascot Club. Hobbies: Collection of antique maps; Sailing. Address: 49 Marapana Road, City Beach, WA 6015, Australia.

VANGARI Vishwa Mohan, b. 23 Jan 1958. E Shashikala, 1 s, 1 d. Education: BCom, 1978; MLISc, 1982; MA, 1985; PhD Lib and Info Sci, 1995. Appointments: Libn, Govt Poly, Masab Tank, Hyd, 1982-84; Lectr, Dept of Lib and Info Sci, Osmania Univ, Hyd, 1984-94; Assoc Prof, Dept of Lib and Info Sci, Osmania Univ, Hyd, 1994-; Chmn, Bd of Stdies in Lib and Info Sci, 1997-99, Hd Dept of Lib and Info Sci, 1999-, OU. Publications: 30 articles publs; Books: Do You Want a Better Life?; Be Happy!. Honours: Sri K Raghava Reddy Gold Medal for having secured 1st rank in MLISc, 1982; ICSSR Fellshp, 1992. Memberships: ILA; IASLIC; IATLIS, VP, 1998-2000; ALSD, Mngn Cttee Mbr: 1997-99; ASRC; Cncl Mbr ILA 1992-94; IATLIS, 1996-98; Life Mbr, APLA; Hobby: Light Music. Address: Department of Library and Information Science, Osmania University, Hyderabad 500 007, India.

VANSTONE Amanda Eloise, b. 7 Dec 1952, Adelaide, S Aust, Aust. Commonwealth Parliamentarian (Senator for South Australia). m. Tony, 16 June 1978. Education: Mktng Stdies Cert, 1972, SAIT (now Univ of S Aust); BA, 1981, LLB, 1983, Univ of Adelaide; Grad Dip, Legal Prac, SAIT, 1983. Appointments: Retailer, Wholesaler, admitted to prac as a Barrister and Solicitor, 1970-84; Elected to Sen, 1984-. Min for Employment, Educ, Trng and Yth Affairs, 1996-97; Employment, Educ, Trng and Yth Affairs Cttee, 1996-97; Min for Justice, 1997-98; Atty-Gen and Justice Cttee, 1997-98; Min for Justice and Customs, 1998-; Att-Gen, Justice and Customs Cttee, 1998; Mbr of Liberal Pty State Cncl, Women's Cncl, Women's Network. Memberships: Law Soc S Aust; Life Mbr, Roy Zool soc; Animal Sponsor, Adelaide Zoo (Indian Porcupine and Disky Langur); RSPCA; Alumni Assn of the Univ of Adelaide; Flinders Fndn; Friend of the Art Gall of SA; Austl War Mem Fndn; Patron, Univ of Adelaide Liberal Club. Hobbies: Reading; Trying to instil some sense into her husband's Weimeraner dog, Freddy. Address: 100 Pirie Street, Adelaide, South Australia 5000, Australia.

VARGAS LLOSA Mario, b. 28 Mar 1936, Arequipa, Peru. Writer. m. Patricia, May 1965, 2 s, 1 d. Education: BLitt, Univ Natl Mayor de San Marcos, 1953-58; PhD, Univ of Complutense de Madrid, 1971. Appointments: Jrnlst, Local Newspapers, Piura, 1952; Jrnlst, Mag, Turismo, Cultural Peruana, El Comercio, 1955; Tchr, Spanish, Berlitz Sch, 1959; Mbr of the Jury, Premios Casa de las Americas, 1965; Tchr, Queen Mary Coll, Univ of London, 1967; Visng Prof, WA Univ, 1968; Prof, King's Coll, Univ of London, 1969; Visng Prof, Univ de Puerto Rico, 1969; Visng Prof, Columbia Univ, USA, 1975; Pres, PEN Club Intl, 1976; Prof, Univ of Cambridge, ENg, 1977; Res Writer, Woodrow Wilson Intl Cntr for Schls, 1980; Dir, La Torre de babel, 1981; Conf, Scottish arts cncl, 1986; Presdtl Candidate, 1990 Elections; Post-grad stud Sem, FL Intl Univ of Miami, 1991; Visng Prof, Harv Univ, 1992; Visng Prof, Princeton Univ, 1993; Visng Prof, Georgetown Univ, 1994; Pres of the Jury, Iberoamerican Film fest of Huelva, 1995; Fell, Deutscher Akademischer Austauschdienst, Berling, Germany, 1997-98. Creative Works: Many Publs. Honours: Second Place, Prix Formentor; Critica Espanola Prize; Jrnlsm Prize; Freedom Prize; Many or prizes. Memberships: Acady Peruana de la Lengua; Real Academia Espanola; Amn Acady and Insts of Arts and Letters; Many or mbrshps. Address: Las Magnolias 295, 6 Piso, Barranco, Lima 4, Peru.

VARMA Amar Nath, b. 25 Sept 1936. Publisher and Distributor. m. Suman Varma, 15 Feb 1958, 3 s. Education: BCom, Delhi Univ. Appointments: Involved in publng and bookselling, 1950-; Mngng Dir, Star Publs Ltd, New Delhi; Mngng Dir, Hindi Book Centre, New Delhi and Star Publishers Distributors, London. Publications: Compiler and fmr ed. Honours: Sev awds for Export Promotion. Memberships: Treas in Fedn of Publrs, Exec Cttee Mbr, Fedn of Indian Publrs, 1985-. Address: Star Publications Pvt Ltd, 4/5 Asaf Ali Road, New Delhi 110001, India.

VARMA Chandra Shekher, b. 25 Dec 1941, Jodhpur, Rajasthan, India. Import and Export Consultant. m. Mrs Rajesh Varma, 1 s, 1 d. Education: Dip in Elec Engin, 1962; Dip in Automobile Engrng, 1968; BA, 1976; Postgrad Dip, Int Mktng, 1978; Fellshp, ITC Geneva, SIDA, 1980. Appointments: Mngr, Exports, Kirloskar Tractors Ltd, 1977-84; Gen Mngr, Int Trade Alkyl Aines Chem, Ltd, 1987-88; Gitanji Ecports, 1988-91; Church Gate Grp, Bombay, 1991-93; VP, AI Rama Intl Traders Grp, Bombay, 1993; Kalyani Intl, 1994; Cnslt (Import and Export), Proprietor of Durgesh Cnslts, 1995-. Honours: Indian Air Force, 1958-66; Decorated, War Medal, 1965; Capt, Indian Army, 967-76; War Medal, 1971; 9 Yrs Long Serv Medal, Indian Army, 1975; Fellshps, Intl Trade Cntr, Geneva and Swedish Intl Dev Authority, 1980. Memberships: Fell, Indian Inst of For Trade, New Delhi; Aeronautical Soc of India; Bombay Productivity Cncl; Rotary Intl Yth Exchange Cttee Dist 3140 YEP Prog, 1996-97, 1997-98; Chmn, Rotaractors Club, 1996; Rotary Coub of Thane N End. Hobbies: Power flying; Gliding. Address: Durgesh Cnsultants (Import and Export Consultants), 23/304 Ananat, Vasant Vihar, 2nd Pokharan Road, Thane (West) 400601, India.

VARTAK Padmakar, b. 25 Feb 1933, Pune, Maharashtra, India. Surgeon. m. Shobhana, 1 Jan 1962, 2 s, 1 d. Education: MBBS. Appointments: Hs Surg, STR Hosp; Tutor; Lectr; Hon Surg; Pres, Adhyatma Samshodhan mandir and Veda Vidnyan Mandal. Creative Works: 12 Books, Swayambhu, 1971; Vastava Ramayan, 1978; Scientific Interpretation of Upanishands, 1981; Patanjala Yoga, 1986; Goeta, 1989; Rebirth, 1997; Aurobiography, 1995; Scientific Knowledge in Vadas, 1998. Many ors. Honours: Hon as Brahmarshi, 1993; Samaja Bhushan, 1996; Awd, Hinduja Fndn. Membership: Adhyatma Samshodhan Mandir and Veda

Vidyan Mandal; Pune City Lib, Parapsycology Rsch Cntr. Hobbies: Yoga; Spiritual Science; Astral Travel. Address: 521 Shaniwar Peth, Pune, Maharashtra, India.

VASANADU Mohan Rao, b. 1 July 1936, Kuppam, India. Businessman. m. Nirmala, 23 Apr 1961, 1 s, 1 d. Appointments: Mngng Ptnr, Mysore Fertilizer Co, Madras, 1959-65; Mngng Dir, MFC Inds, Madras, 1965-74; Chmn, Mngng Dir, MFC Inds, Madras, 1974-; Mngng Dir, MICO Farm Chems, Madras, 1971-89; Chmn, Lotos Roofings, Madras, 1986-, Hassan (India) Coffee Curing Works, 1974-; Dir, India Potash, New Delhi, 1975-81, Sanco Trans, Madras, 1984-; Chmn, Devashola Tea Estates, Nilgiris, India, 1974-; Regl Advsr, Small Inds Devel Bank of India, Bombay, 1994-96; Rep, Govt of India, Intl Labour Org, Geneva, 1994-96,. Honours: Shironmani Awd, Shironmani Inst, 1993; Vikas Rattan Awd, Intl Friendship Soc, India, 1991, 1992. Memberships: Fertilizer Assn of India; All-India Mfrs Assn; Indo-Am Soc. Hobbies: Photography; Social Service. Address: Mysore Fertiliser Co, Lotus Court, 165 Thambu Chetty Street, Chennai 1, India.

VASCONCELLOS John, b. 5 Nov 1932, San Jose, California, USA. Legislator. Education: BS; LLB. Appointments: Chair, Assembly Ways & Means; Fndr, CA Tast Force to Promote Self-Esteem; Chair, Assembly Democratic Econ Prosperity Team; Chair, Senate Pub Safety Cttee. Publications: A Liberating Vision, 1979; Toward a Healthier State. Honours: Legislator of the Decade, 1980s; Fac Assn, CA Comm Colls; Over 100 other awds. Memberships: State Bar, 1959-; Bd Dir, CA Ldrshp, 1987-95. Hobbies: Racquetball; Friends; Reading; Writing; Jazz. Address: 100 Paseo de San Antonio, Suite 209, San Jose, CA 95113, USA.

VAUGHAN Gerard Marshall, b. 1 Dec 1946, Melbourne, Aust. Consultant. m. Teresa, 9 Nov 1974, 3 s, 2 d. Education: ARMIT; BE(Hons); MEngSc; DipEd; PhD. Appointments: Rsch Scientist, CSIRO, 1977-79; MLA, Parl of Vic, 1979-96; Cnslt, 1996-. Address: 13 Clyde Street, Oakleigh, Victoria 3166, Australia.

VAUGHAN Rodney Grant. Electrical Engineer; Communications Scientist. m. Helen, 16 Apr 1977, 2 s, 1 d. Education: BE, Elect; ME, Elect; PhD. Appointments: Asst Engr, NZ Post Off, 1977-78; Sci, DSIR, 1978-92; Team Leader, Comms Grp, Indl Rsch Ltd, 1994-96; Prog Leader, 1994-. Publications: Num conf & sci jrnl publs, book chapts. Honours: Ministerial Awd for Sci Achievement, NZ, 1989; URSI Young Sci Awds, 1983, 1984; NZ Govt Sci Study Awd, 1982-85. Memberships: IEEE; Union of Radio Scis Corresp. Hobbies: Piano; Classical Guitar. Address: 12 Junction Street, Lower Hutt, New Zealand.

VEDAVATHY Sanagavarapu, b. 1 Aug 1942, Kovur, Nellore, AP, India. Reader and Head of Department of Botany. m. V V Sivaiah, 31 Nov 1965, 1 s, 2 d. Education: MSc; PhD. Appointments: Lectr, Rdr, Hd of Dept of Bot; Dir, Herbal Folklore Rsch Cntr. Publications: Tribal Medicine of Chittoor (Dt), 1977; Gardens - Ethno Medico Gardens (2). Honours: Talented Scientist Awd, SV University, Tirpati, India, 1997. Memberships: ISMAP; IUCN; IDRC; Ethnobotanical Assn; MFP. Address: B-23 Vaikuntapuram, Tirupati 517502, India.

VEERAKYATHIAH V D, b. 25 May 1926, Vaddagere Village, India. IAS (retd). m. V Rajamma, 25 June 1955, 2 s. Education: BSc, Agric; Indian Admnstv Serv by Selection. Appointments: Vill Level Worker; Extension Offr; Block Dev Offr; Dpty Dev Comnr; Dir. Publications: 3 pprs presented in 3 Indian Sci Congress; Active involvement of var agencies in rural dev. Honours: 6 x felicitations, from 6 different orgns on different occaisions. Memberships: Advsr, Ganga Charitable Trust for Rural Dev; Hon Pres for 2 orgns. Hobbies: Social work both in urban and rural areas. Address: 596 II Stage, I E Block, Rajajinagar, Bangalore 560 010, India.

VEJJAJIVA Abhisit, b. 3 Aug 1964. Minister to the Prime Minister's Office. m. Mrs Pimpen. Education: BA, Philos, Pol and Econs, MA, Econs, Oxford Univ; LLB,

Ramkhumhaeng Univ. Appointments: Lectr, Fac of Econs, Thammasat Univ; Mbr of Parl, Spokesman Democratic Party; Dpty Sec-Gen to Prime Min; Min to Prime Min's Off. Honour: Kt Grand Cross, 1st Class, Most Exalted Order of the White Elephant. Address: 32 Sukhumvit 31 Road, Klongtan, Klongtoey, Bangkok, Thailand.

VEMULPAD Subramanyam, b. 11 Feb 1956, Anantapur, India. Microbiologist. m. Chandrika, 15 Aug 1986, 1 s. Education: BSc, 1973; MSc, 1976; PhD, 1982. Appointments: Demonstrator, Microbiol, Maulana Azad Med Coll, Delhi, 1977-82; Hd, Divsn of Microbiol, Indian Cncl of Med Rsch, Bhubaneswar, 1984-94; Hd, Dept of Microbiol, Univ Coll of Med, Blantyre, Malawi, 1994-96; Pub Hlth Offr, Western Sydney Pub Hlth Unit, Parramatta, 1996-. Memberships: Austl Soc for Microbiol; Assn of Microbiols of India; Indian Assn of Med Microbiols. Hobbies: Classical Music; Travel; Alternate Medicine. Address: Western Sydney Public Health Unit, Locked Bag 7118, Parramatta, NSW 2150, Australia.

VENKATA RAMANA Vepachadu, b. 21 June 1963, Khammam, India. Teacher and Researcher. m. Renuka Devi, 4 Oct 1995, 1 s. Education: PhD, Biochemistry. Appointments: Rsch Assoc at Biocehmistry Dept, Indian Inst of Sci, Bangalore, India; Asst Prof, Biochemistry Dept, Acaharya N G Ranga Agricl Univ (formerly Andhra Pradesh Agricl Univ). Publications: Stories; Popular sci articles; Des and participated in Experiment-based Sci Progs on TV. Memberships: Soc of Biol Chems, India. Hobbies: Writing poetry; Stories; Watching TV; Playing table tennis. Address: Assistant Professor, Biochemistry Department, Acahrya NG Ranga, Agricultural University at Agricultural College, PO Aswaraopet 507301, Dist Kahmman (AP), India.

VENKATARAMANI Kaniyur Sundaram, b. 17 Jan 1924, Madras. Scientist. m. S Kan Khamani, 29 May 1966. Education: MSc; PhD. Appointments: Botst, 1948-65; Dir, Tea Rsch, 1965-75. Creative Works: Sev Sci Publs, Tea Clonal Selection, All Aspects of Tea Culture. Honours: FASc, For the Sake of Hon Awd; Lifetime Achievement in Tea Rsch Awd. Memberships: Indian Acady of Scis; Indian Botl Soc. Hobbies: Photography; Gardening. Address: B1, Premier Grihalakshmi Apts, Fourth Seaward Road, Valmikinagar, Thiruvanmiyur, Chennai 600 041, India.

VENNING Robert Stanley, b. 24 July 1943, Boise, ID, USA. Lawyer. m. Laura Siegel, 24 Mar 1979, 1 s. Education: AB, Harv Univ; MA, Univ of Chicago; LLB, Yale Univ. Appointments: Ed, Yale Law Jrnl; Early Neutral Educr, US Dist Ct. Memberships: Amn Bar Fndn. Hobbies: Travel; Golf. Address: Heller Ehrman, White and McAuliffe, 333 Bush Street, San Francisco, CA 94104, USA.

VERNON Janet Dianne, b. 9 Feb, Adelaide, Aust. Dancer; Associate Artistic Director. Appointments: Dancer, The Austl Ballet; Sydney Dance Co; Ballets Felix Blaska. Honours: AM, Servs to Dance. Address: Sydney Dance Co, The Wharf, Pier 4/5 Hickson Road, Walsh Bay, NSW 2000, Australia.

VERRALL Leigh Ernest, b. 30 May 1937, Medindie, S Aust. Organic Vigneron and Director, Glenara Wines Pty Ltd; Director, Bay Wine Distributors Pty Ltd. m. Janet Lauren Rayner, 5 Feb 1966, 2 s, 1 d. Appointments: Organic Fedn of Aust, 1997-98; Organic Prodrs Advsry Cttee, 1997-98. Memberships: Life Mbr, NE Hills Table Tennis Assn; Life Mbr, Country Fire Serv, Hermitage Brigade; Houghton Primary Sch Cncl, Mbr, 1973-76, Chmn, 1977-83; Cty of Tea Gully Flora and Fauna Advsry Cttee; Cty of Tea Gully Community Dev Bd; Organic Vigenrons Assn of Aust, Mbr, 1992-94, Chmn, 1995-98. Hobbies: Gardening; Fishing; Camping; Bushwalking; Flora and Fauna; Environment; Endangered species. Address: 126 Range Road North, Upper Hermitage, South Australia 5131, Australia.

VERTZBERGER Yaacov, b. 13 Oct 1947, Romania. Professor. Education: PhD, summa cum laude, Intl Rels.

Appointment: Prof, Dept of Intl Rels, Hebrew Univ, 1997-. Publications: China's Southwestern Strategy, 1985; The World in Their Minds, 1990; Risk Taking and Decision Making, 1998. Honours: Karmon Awd, 1972, 1973; Herzog Awd, 1975; Fulbright Fellshp, 1978-79. Memberships: Intl Studies Assn; Intl Soc of Polit Psychol; Am Polit Sci Assn. Hobbies: Travel; Jazz Music; Cinema. Address: Department of International Relations, Hebrew University, Jerusalem 91905, Israel.

VESIKULA Ratu Timoci, b. 30 July 1947. Government Minister. Appointments: Mbr, House of Representatives, 1983-87; Mbr for Tailevu Prov, Elected to Parl, 1992; Min of State for Rural Dev, Relief and Rehab and Rural Housing, incl Women's Affairs, 1985; Mbr, Econ Strategy; Chmn, Disaster Mngmt Cncl; Dpty Prime Min and Min for Fijian Affairs and Regl Dev, 1992. Address: PO Box 2222, Government Buildings, Suva, Fiji.

VICKERS David Whitman, b. 28 Oct 1940, Perth, Aust. Medical Orthopaedic Surgeon. m. Jennifer, 7 Dec 1968. Education: MB BS, Qld, 1964; FRACS, Orth Surg, 1973. Appointments: RMO, Bundeberg Gen Hosp, 1965-66; Surg Registrar, Princess Alexandra Hosp, 1970-71; Orth Registrar, Roy Brisbane and Childrens Hosps, 1972-74; Supvsr, RBH, RCH, 1975-76; Visng Orth Surg, RBH, 1976-90; Snr Specialist, RBH, RCH, 1990. Publications: Sev articles for medl and sci jrnl; Chapts in medl books. Honours: Brit Des Cncl Awd for Excellence in Des, 1981; Best ppr presented at annual Sci Meeting, Austl Hand Club, 1983, 1991, 1992; Prof (Clin) Fac of Med, Univ of Qld, 1994. Memberships include: Roy Austl Coll of Surgs; Austl Medl Assn; Austl Hand Club; Pres, Austl Hand Surg Soc, 1995-96. Hobbies: Photography; Inventions; Horticulture. Address: Watkins Medical Centre, 225 Wickham Terrace, Brisbane, Qld 4000, Australia.

VICKERS Douglas, b. 17 Feb 1940, Tidworth, Wilts, Eng. Associate Professor of Psychology. m. Yvonne Victoria Jouty, 1 May 1965, 1 s, 1 d. Education: MA, Edinburgh, 1961; BA, 1963, PhD, 1967, ScD, 1994, Cambridge. Appointments: Lectr in Psychol, Univ of Adelaide, 1967; Rdr in Psychol, Univ of Adelaide, 1980; Assoc Prof, Univ of Adelaide, 1987. Publications: Book: Decision Processes in Visual Perception, London, 1979; Num articles in rsch jrnls. Honour: French Govt Sci and Profl Schl, 1980. Memberships: Cncl Mbr, Intl Assn of Attention and Perf; Founding Mbr, Editl Bd of Jrnl: Nonlinear Dynamics, Psychol and Life Scis. Listed in Who's Who in the World; International Directory of Psychologists. Hobbies: Literature; Theatre; Film; Dance; Visual arts. Address: 113 Young Street, Young Street, Parkside, Adelaide, SA 5063, Australia.

VIDLER Valda Marie, b. 24 Jan 1932, Sydney, NSW, Aust. Cellist. m. John St George, 18 May 1965, 1 s, 1 d. Education: Dip, Sydney Conservatorium of Music, 1952. Appointments: Cellist, ABC Orchs, 5 yrs; Prin Cellist, Tivoli Th, Sydney, 5 yrs; ABC Dance Band, 3 yrs; Played in backing orchs for visng Amn artists, sev yrs; TV and radio wrk; Now mainly tchng. Membership: Musicians Union. Hobbies: Ballroom dancing; Bridge. 112 Beaconsfield Road, Chatswood, NSW, Australia.

VIJAYA MAHANTESH MATH CHITTARAGI Mahanta Swamiji, b, 1 Aug 1932, Malali in Karnataka, India. Religious and Social Reformer. Education: Higher stdies, Sankrit, Varanasi, UP, India; Vachana Lit, Shivayoga Mandir, Karnataka. Appointments: Fifth pontiff, Sanganabasava Math, Savadi, 1961-; Nineteenth pontiff, Vijaya Mahantesh Math Chittaragi-Ilkal, 1970-. Publications: bio of Hanagal Kumara Swamiji; sev articles on relig; More than 100 books on Basava philos. Honours: Kayaka Yogi. Memberships: Pres, Basava Intl Fndn, London; Hon Pres, 5 educl and relig insts; Fndr, Sharana Siddhanta Vidyapeeth, Ilkal. Hobby: Delivering religious discourses. Address: Ilkal-587125, Karnataka, India.

VILLA Jose Garcia, b. 5 Aug 1914 Manila. Poet; Critic. 2 s. Education: Univ of the Philippines; Univ of New Mexico; Columbia Univ. Appointments: Guggenheim

Fell'shp, 1943; Assoc Ed New Directions Books, 1949; Bollingen Fell'shp, 1951; Dir NY Cty Coll Poetry Workshop, 1952-63; Cultural Attache Philippine Miss to UN, 1953-63; Rockefeller Grant, 1964; Prof of Poetry New Sch for Socl Rsch, 1964-73; Philippines Presdl Advsr on Cultural Affairs, 1968-. Publications: Footnote to Youth - stories - 1933; Many Voices, 1939; Poems by Doveglion, 1941; Have Come, Am Here, 1942; Volume Two, 1949; Selected Poems and New, 1958; Poems Fifty-five, 1962; Poems in Praise of Love, 1962; Selected Stories, 1962; The Portable Villa, 1963; The Essential Villa, 1965; Appassionata, 1979; Ed: A Celebration for Edith Sitwell, 1948; Doveglion Book of Philippine Poetry, 1975; Bravo: the Poet's Magazine, 1981; New Doveglion Book of Philippine Poetry, 1993. Honours: Am Acady of Arts and Letters Awd, 1942; Shelley Memorial Awd, 1959; Hon DLitt - Far East Univ - 1959; Pro Patria Awd, 1961; Philippines Cultural Heritage Awd, 1962; Natl Artist in Lit, 1973; Hon LHD - Philippines - 1973. Hobbies: Dogs; Plants; Cooking. Address: 780 Greenwich Street, New York, NY 10014, USA.

VILLAR Florita, b. 11 Mar 1955, Valguiman, Samal, Bataan. Social Worker. m. Agerico Acosta Villar, 2 Dec 1979, 1 d. Education: BS, Socl Wrk, 1976; MA, Socl Wrk (in prog). Appointments: Socl Welfare Spec, 1980; Asst Regl Dir, 1994; Regl Dir, 1994. Publications: Disater in Emergency management publd in Re Phil Encyclopedia of Socl Work, 1998. Honours: Summa cum laude, 1976; Women of the Yr (region III), 1997; Most Outstndng Profl (SW), 1998. Memberships: Sec of Bd of Cntrl Assn of Regl Offrs; Bd of Dirs of the ISSEC Fndn. Hobbies: Reading; Gardening; Playing bowls; Chess. Address: PSP Building, Gapan Olongapo Road, San Fernando, Pompanga.

VIMPANI Graham Vernon, b. 12 Feb 1944, Adelaide, Australia. Professor of Community, Child and Family Health; Director, Child, Adolescent and family Health Service. m. Anne Stachan, 24 Jan 1970, 2 s. Education: Prince Alfred Coll; Univs of Adelaide and Edinburgh. Appointments: RMO Queen Elizabeth Hosp, 1967, Roy Children's Hosp, Melbourne, 1968; Registrar Adelaide Children's Hosp, 1969-71; Lectr, Dept of Paediats, Univ of Adelaide, 1972; Heinz Fell, 1973; Rsch Fell, Dept of Child Life and Hlth, Univ Edinburgh, 1974-77; Coord, Maternal and Child Hlth Servs, SA Hlth Commsn, 1977-81; Dir, Ctrl Sector, Child Adolescent and Family Hlth Serv, 1983-85; Res and Evaluation, 1981-83; Staff Paediatn, Snr Lectr, Flinders Med Cntr, Flinders Univ, 1985-89; Natl Project Dir, Natl Injury Surveillance and Prevention Project, 1987-89; Mbr, NSW Child Protection Cncl, 1997-; Mbr, NSW Child Death Review Team, 1997- Prof, Cmnty, Child and Family Hlth, 1990-, Hd, Discipline of Paediats and Child Hlth, 1999-, Univ of Newcastle. Publications: 70 articles in profl jrnls. Memberships include: NHMRC Child Hlth Cttee, 1985-93; Sci Prog Cttee, Austl Coll of Paediats, 1991-95; Hon Life Mbr, Child Accident Prevention Fndn, Aust, 1996-. Hobbies: Running; Bushwalking; Early Music; Reading; Spirituality. Address: Locked Bag 1014, Wallsend, NSW 2287, Australia.

VINCENT Paul Craig, b. 18 July 1935, Sydney. Physician; Medical Researcher. m. Kerry, 12 Dec 1958, 1 s, 3 d. Education: BSc, Med; MB BS, Hons; MD; FRACP; FRCPA. Appointments: Dir, Kanematsu mem Inst, Sydney Hosp, 1980-82; Dir, Kanematsu Labs, Roy Prince Alfred Hosp, 1982-. Creative Works: 179 Publd Works; Chapts in Books; Orig Articles; Reviews. Honours: C J Martin Fellow of NHMRC, 1966-68; Visng Prof, Ulm, Germany. Memberships: Roy Australasian Coll of Phys; Roy Coll of Pathol of Australasia. Hobbies: Golf; Skiing; Sail Boarding. Address: 46 Finlay Road, Turramurra, NSW 2074, Australia.

VINE David, b. 1943, London, Eng. Conductor; Harpsichordist. Education: Roy Coll of Music, London, 1961-65; Studied piano w Cornelius Fischer, Bernard Roberts, Eric Harrison, piano accompaniment w Joan Trimble, harpsichord w Millicent Silver, baroque ensemble playing w Hubert Dawkes, conducting w Sir Adrian Boult, ARCM; MusB 1st Class Hons, Harpsichord

Perf, Canterbury Univ. Appointments: Cellist, local yth orch, Northampton; Specialist Music Tchr, Inner London Educ Authy; Tutored in Baroque Music, Guildhall Sch of Music and Cty Lit Inst, London; Fndr, London Telemann Ensemble; Settled in NZ, 1974; Conductor, NZ Natl Yth Orch, Wellington Polytech Orch, Dunedin Sinfonia and Schola Catorum, Amici Chmbr Orch, Christchurch Symph Orch; Musical Dir, Gisborne Choral Soc, Christchurch Operatic Soc, Jubilate Singers, Perkel Opera; Orchl Pianist, NZ Symph Orch; Reg harpsichord recitals and perfs on Radio NZ's Concert Prog; Currently Musical Dir, Acady Opera, conducting NZ premiéres of operas by Handel, Mozart and Puccini; Lectrs, Univs of Canterbury, Auckland, Waikato, Massey, 1988, Correspondence Sch, Wellington, 1993; Lecturer, Wellington Poly, 1997. Publications: Early Music Publns, USA, 1993, Austria, 1996. Honours: 1st Prize, 3 times, Northampton Eisteddfod Piano Sect; Acknowledged as one of NZ's finest harpsichordists and conductors. Address: PO Box 2815, Wellington, New Zealand.

VINE Peter Alan Lee, b. 2 Dec 1921, Weymouth, England. Solicitor; Notary Public. m. Aida, 17 Aug 1970, 2 s, 2 d. Education: LLB, London; LLD, Hon, Univ of Hong Kong, 1986. Appointment: Cnslt, Hobson & Ma. Memberships: Law Soc of Eng and Wales, 1947; Law Soc of Hong Kong, 1947; Pres, 1962-64; Hong Kong Soc of Notaries, Pres 1977-79, 1996-98. Honours: VRD, 1962; OBE, 1965. Address: Suite 1005, World Wide House, 19 Des Voeus Road Centra, Hong Kong.

VINE HALL Nick, b. 17 Aug 1944. Genealogist; Radio Broadcaster. m. (1) Patricia Pryor, 1966, 1 s, 1 d, (2) Patricia Esther Barth, 5 Jan 1991, div. Education: Sydney Tech Coll. Appointments: Asst Sugar Sales Mngr, NSW CSR Ltd, 1972-78; Dir, Soc Austl Genealogists, 1978-88; Brdcst Coml and ABC Radio - Metro and Rural Stns throughout Aust, 1979-; Genealogist, Radio 2 CBA-FM, Sydney, 1981-, Radio 2CN Canberra, 1983-95, Radio 2GB, Sydney, 1986-92, Radio 7NT, Launceston, 1989-97, Radio 6WF, Perth, 1989-91, Radio 3AW, Melbourne, 1990-94, Radio 7ZR, Hobart, 1990-, Radio 3LO, Melbourne, 1994-. Publications: Buxton Forbes Laurie of Southcote, 1976; Gore Hill Cemetery Transcripts, 1976, 1977; English Parish Register Transcripts, 1980, 1981, 1983, 1985; My Name is Blacket, 1983; Tracing Your Family History in Australia, 1985, 1994; Parish Registers in Australia, 1989, 1990; Gissing Monumental Inscription 1376-1976, 1991; Authors, Publishers, Mariners and Clergy, 1992; Manly Cemetery Transcripts 1845-1993, 1993; Ships Pictures Index 1491-1991, 1995. Honours: 1st Prize, Excellence in Writing Competition, Genealogy Columnists, USA, 1991; Book Awd, Inst Heraldic and Genealogical Stdies, Kent, Eng, 1988; First Neil T Hansen Awd, Austl Fed Family Hist Organs, 1988; Fell, Soc Austl Genealogists, 1984-; UT Genealogical Assn, 1986-; Fell, Huguenot Soc, GB and Ireland, 1983-. Memberships: Chmn, Austl Assn Genealogists and Record Agts, 1993-; Tstee, Assn Profl Genealogists, USA, 1995-; Tree, Intl Soc Brit Genealogy and Family Hist, USA, 1987-90; Patron, Eurobodalla Family Hist Soc, 1989-; Dubbo Macquarie Family Hist Soc, 1984-; Friends Gore Hill Cemetery, 1979-. Hobbies: Linguistics; Surname etymology; Collecting dictionaries. Address: PO Box 725, Mt Eliza, NSW 3930, Australia.

VINER Robert Ian, b. 21 Jan 1933, Claremont, WA, Aust. Barrister. m. Ngaire, 19 May 1956, 3 s, 4 d. Education: LLB Hons, Univ of WA; Pil Course, Advd Negotiation, Harv L S; Ldr Accreditation in Meditation. Appointments: MP, Stirling, C'wlth Parl, 1972-83; Min, Asstng the Treas; Min, Aboriginal Affairs, 1975-78; Min, Asstng PM, 1978-81; Min, Employment, Yth Affairs, 1978-81; Ldr of the House, 1979-80; Min, Indl Rels, 1981-82; Min, Def Spt, Min, Asstng Min for Def, 1982-83; Past Pres, Aust, Indonesia Bus Cncl, 1990-92; Past Pres, Liberal Party, WA, 1992-93; Dpty Chairperson, Bd of Govs, St Mary's Anglican Girls Sch, 1987-; Dir, Anzoil NL, 1995-; Chairperson, Bd of Mngmnt, Austls for Reconciliation, 1997-. Honour: Hons in Law, 1958; Memberships: Natl Native Title Tribunal, 1995-96; W Austl Bar Assn; Law Soc of WA. Hobbies: Hockey;

Swimming. Address: 23rd Floor Allendale Sq, 77 St Georges Terrace, Perth, WA 6000, Australia.

VINES William Joshua (Sir), b. 27 May 1916, Vic, Aust. Retired; Grazier. Education: Haileybury Coll, 1928. Appointments: Austl Estates Co Ltd, 1932-38; Sec, Alexander Fergusson Pty Ltd, 1938-40; Mil Serv, 1940-45; Sales Dir, Goodlass Wall Ltd, 1945-48; Mngng Dir, Lewis Berger Ltd, Vic, 1948-55; Grp Mngng Dir, Lewis Berger Ltd, London, 1955-61; Mngng Dir, Intl Wool Secretariat, London, 1961-69; Chmn, Thorn Elec Inds Ltd, 1964-74; Wiggins Teape Ltd, Aust, 1969-72; Dir, Coml Union Assurance Co Ltd, 1969-78; P & O Aust Holdings Pty Ltd, 1969-71; Chmn, Dalgety Aust Ltd, 1969-80; Fndr, Chmn, Aust Wool Cmmn, 1970-72; Dir, 1970, Dpty Chmn, 1973-86, Tubemakers of Aust Ltd; Dir, 1976, Dpty Chmn, 1981, ANZ Banking Grp Ltd; Chmn 1982-89, Dir, Conzinc Riotinto of Aust, 1977-84; Chmn of Dirs, Natl Priorities Proj Ltd, 1987-. Honours: KB, 1977; CMG, 1969; AC, 1987. Memberships include: Pt-time Mbr, Exec, C'wlth Sci and Indl Rsch Org, 1973-78; Chmn, Cncl, Hawkesbury Agricl Coll, 1975-85; Chmn, Sir Robert Menzies Mem Trust. Address 1/10 West Street, Balgowlah. NSW 2093, Australia.

VINSON Tony, b. 11 Nov 1935, Sydney, NSW, Aust. Professor. m. Diana Whitechurch, 9 Aug 1958, 1 s, 1 d. Education: BA, Dip Socl Stdys, Sydney, 1956; Dip, Sociol, 1962, MA, 1965, PhD, 1972, NSW. Appointments: Asst Psychol, Parole Offr, NSW Dept Prisons, 1957-62; Tutor, Lectr, Univ NSW, 1962-69; Snr Lectr, Univ Sydney, 1969-71; Fndn Dir, Bur Crime Stats and Rsch, NSW Dept Atty-Gen and Justice, 1971-76; Fndn Prof, Behavioural Sci in Med, Univ Newcastle, NSW, 1976-79; Chmn, NSW Corrective Servs Commn, 1979-81; Prof, 1981, Hd, Sch Socl Wrk, 1983-88, Dean, Fac Profl Stdys, 1988-92, Hd, Sch Soc Wrk, 1996-97, Emer Prof, 1997, Univ NSW; Dir of Rsch, Uniya Jesuit Soc Justice Cntr. Publications include: Wilful Obstruction, 1982. Honours: ECAFE Fell'ship, Bangkok, 1966; Austl Socl Welfare Commn Fell'ship, 1976. Hobbies: Films; Jazz; Making Pavlovas. Address: Uniya Jesuit Social Justice Centre, PO Box 522, Kings Cross, NSW 2011, Australia.

VIRATA Cesar Enrique Aguinaldo, b. 12 Dec 1930, Manila, Philippines. Managment Consultant; Banker. m. Joy Gamboa, 1956, 2 s, 1 d. Education: BS Bus Admin; BS Mechl Engrng; MBA; Univ Philippines; Univ PA. Appointments: Dean, Coll Bus Admin, Univ Philippines, 1961-69; Chair, Bd, Philippines Natl Bank, 1967-69; Dpty Dir-Gen, Presdtl Econ Staff, 1967-68; Under-Sec of Ind, 1967-69; Chair, Bd Invmnts, 1968-70; Min of Fin, 1970-86; PM of the Philippines, 1981-86; Chair, Land Bank of the Philippines, 1973-86; Mbr, Natl Assembly, 1978-86; Monetary Bd, Natl Econ and Dev Authy, 1972-86; Commn on the Future of Bretton Woods Insts, 1992-94; Advsr to Coord Cncl for the Philippines Aid Plan, 1989-90; Chair, IMF and IBRD Dev Cttee, 1976-80; Prin, C Virata and Assocs, Mngmt Cnslts, 1986-; Chair, Bd Govs, Asian Dev Bank, 1979-80; Dir, Philippine Stock Exch Inc, 1992-94; Dir, 1994-, Chmn, 1995-98, Rizal Coml Banking Corp; Vice-Chmn Phil Centennial Com, 1994-99. Honours: LHD hc; DPA hc; Dr hc, Philippines. Address: B1101 Alexandra, 29 Meralco Ave, Pasig City, Philippines 1601.

VNUKOV Konstantin, b. 9 May 1951, Moscow, Russia. Diplomat. m. Yulia, 16 Mar 1979, 2 s. Education: Dip of Higher Educ, 1973; Moscow State Inst of Intl Rels; PhD (Hist), Inst of Far E, Acady of Sci, Russian Fedn, 1991. Appointments: Attaché, 3rd Sec, 2nd Sec, USSR Emb in Beijing, 1974-77, 1980-85; Cnslr, Russian Emb in Beijing, 1991-95; Hd of Sect, 1st Asian Dept, MFA, 1995-98; Russian Consul-Gen to Hong Kong, SAR, PRC, Macau, 1998-. Memberships: Russo-Chinese Friendship Soc, 1973-; Russian Assn of Sinologists, 1980-. Hobbies: History, culture and music of China; Fishing. Address: 2932, 29/FL, Sun Hung Kai Centre, 30 Harbour Road, Wanchai, Hong Kong.

VO Van Kiet, b. 1922 S Viet Nam. Politician. Appointments: Joined CP of Indo-China, 1930s; Vice-Chmn Cncl of Mins, 1982-91; Chmn State Plng Cttee, 1982-88; Chmn Cncl of Mins, 1991; Chmn party Cttee in Ho Chi Minh Cty; PM of Viet Nam, 1992-97. Memberships: Mbr Lao Dong Party - renamed Communist Party of Vie Nam, 1976 - Mbr Cntrl Cttee, 1958-; Mbr Cntrl Off for S Viet Nam during war; Alt mbr Politburo CP of Viet Nam, 1976; Mbr Politburo CP of Viet Nam. Address: c/o Council of Ministers, Hanoi, Viet Nam.

VOLKMAN John Kingston, b. 22 Apr 1952. Research Scientist. m. Kaye Price, 23 Aug 1975, 2 s. Education: BSc, hons, PhD, Univ of Melbourne. Appointments: Postdoct Fell, Univ of Bristol, Eng, 1978-80; Postdoct Schl, Woods Hole Oceanographic Inst, USA, 1980-81; Rsch Fell, WA Inst of Technol, 1981-82; Rsch Scientist, CSIRO Div of Oceanography, 1982-96; Snr Prin Rsch Scientist, 1992-97; Chf Rsch Sci, 1997-; Visng Rsch Sci, Netherlands Inst for Sea Rsch, 1996; Fell Hansewissenschaftskolleg, Germany, 1998. Publications: 120 sci pprs and book chapts; Many invited lectrs at intl confs; Assoc Ed, Organic Geochemistry, 1989-. Honours include: Liversidge Lect, ANZAAS, 1994. Memberships include: Fell, Roy Austl Chem Inst; Austl Marine Scis Assn; Eurn Assn of Organic Geochem. Hobbies: Photography; Travel. Address: CSIRO Division of Marine Research, GPO Box 1538, Hobart, Tas 7001, Australia.

VOLLER Claus, b. 22 June 1935, Neustrelitz, Germany. Diplomat. Education: Law Exam, Univ of Freiburg, Germany; Bologna Cntr of Advd Intl Stdies of Johns Hopkins. Appointments: German For Serv, 1962-; Chf of Miss, Phnom Penh, 1975; Amb in Laos, 1976, in Vietnam, 1981, in Albania, 1991, in Korea, 1995. Address: 308-5 Dongbinggo-Dong, Yongsan-GU, Seoul 140-230, Korea.

VON DOUSSA John William, b. 17 Sept 1940, Aust. Justice of the Federal Court of Australia. m. (1) Joanna Grierson Howard, dec, 7 Nov 1964, 4 s, 1 d, (2) Julie Alexandra Bissland, 1 Feb, 1997, 1 s. Education: LLB, Univ of Adelaide, 1961. Appointments: Admitted Bar and Sol, Supreme Crt of SA, 1963; Admitted Practitioner of High Crt of Aust, 1963, QC, 1978-86; Judge of the Supreme Crt of S Aust, 1986-88; Justice of Fedl Crt of Aust, 1988-; Additional Judge, Supreme Crt of the Austl Capital Territory, 1989-; Commnr (pt-time) Austl Law Reform Commn, 1992-; Presdtl Mbr of the Admnstv Appeals Tribunal, 1993-; Justice of the Indl Rels Crt of Aust, 1994-; Dpty Pres, 1996-98, Acting Pres, 1998- Austl Competition Tribunal; Mbr, Crt of Appeal of Vanuatu, 1998. Honour: Hon DUniv (SA), 1996. Memberships: Law Soc of S Aust, 1963-86, Pres, 1982-83; Law Cncl of Aust, 1983-86, VP, 1984-86. Address: c/o Federal Court of Australia, 25 Grenfell Street, Adelaide, SA 5152, Australia.

VON LEVEN Elizabeth, b. 2 Feb 1931, Glen Iris, Melbourne, Australia. Religious Sister; Writer. Education: Tchrs' Cert. Appointments: Prin, Sacred Heart, 1973-80; Prin, St Anne's Seaford, 1981-94. Publications: Children's Books: The Search, 1990; Dawning Point, 1991; Adult Books: Before the Leaves Wither, 1993; Time Inside Out, 1994. Memberships: Vic Writers' Cntr; Fellship of Austl Writers. Address: 190 Arthur Street, Fairfield, Melbourne 3078, Australia.

VON SCHRAMEK Edith Antonia (Lady), Interior Designer. m. Eric, 21 Feb 1948, 1 s, 2 d. Education: SA Inst of Technol; FDIA. Appointments: Pvte Prac, 1969-; Pt-time Lectr, SA Inst of Technol Sch of Arch and Bldng, 1979-89; Former Dir, von Schramek & Dawes Pty Ltd; Pres, Des Inst of Aust, SA Chapt, 1979-81. Membership: Bd Mbr, S Austl Housing Trust, 1979-84. Address: The Olives, Yankalilla, SA 5203, Australia.

VON SCHRAMEK Eric Emil (Sir), b. 4 Apr 1921, Prague, Czech. m. Edith Popper, 21 Feb 1948, 1 s, 2 d. Education: Dip Ing-Arch, Tech Univ of Prague; Life Fell, Roy Austl Inst of Archts; Life Fell, Inst of Arbitrator, Mediators, Aust. Appointments include: Town Planner, Bavaria, Germany, 1946-48; Snr Supvsng Arch, NT, Aust, 1948-51; Chmn, von Schramek & Dawes Pty Ltd, 1963-91; Cnslt, Hames Sharley Aust, 1989-97. Creative Works include: Multi Storey Off Bldngs, Adelaide Wesley House, Melbourne; Westpac House, Hobart; AMP Bldng, Darwin and Chs in Aust and Papua New Guinea. Publications: Contbrns to var jrnls. Honours: Kt, 1982, KSJ, 1995; Hon Assoc (Archl), SA Inst of Technol, 1989. Memberships: Natl Pres, 1970-72, Bldng Sci Forum of Aust; Pres, SA Capt, Roy Austl Inst of Archs, 1974-76; Past Natl Dpty Chmn, Austcare; Past Cnclr, Cncl of Professions; Pres, SA Chapt of Inst of Arbitrators, Aust, 1977-79. Hobbies: Music; Reading; Golf. Address: The Olives, Yankalilla, SA 5203, Australia.

VON WILPERT Gero, b. 13 Mar 1933, Estonia. (Austl citizen). Emeritus Professor. m. Margrit Laskowski, 25 July 1953, 3 s. Education: Univ of Heidelberg, 1953-57; PhD, Univ of NSW, 1977. Appointments: Ed-in-Chf, Lit Dir, Alfred Kröner Publrs, Germany, 1957-72; Snr Lectr, 1973-78; Assoc Prof, 1979-81, Univ of NSW; Prof, Univ of Sydney, 1982-94; Emeritus Prof, 1994-. Publications: sev books and papers. Memberships: Austl Acady of Hums; Internationale Vereinigung für Germanistik; PEN. Hobbies: 18th Century French art and antiques. Address: Werrington House, Werrington, NSW 2747, Australia.

VONGSAY Kithong, b. 17 May 1937 Vientiane. Diplomatist. m. 3 c. Education: Toulouse Univ. Appointments: Cnslr Paris, 1970-73; Dep Min for For Affairs of Prov Govt, 1975; Hd Press and Info Dept min of For Affairs, 1975-78; Amb to India Burma Sri Lanka and Nepal, 1978-83; Perm Rep to UN NY, 1983-88. Address: c/o Ministry of Foreign Affairs, Vientiane, Laos.

VOSE Godfrey Noel, b. 23 Dec 1921, Perth, Aust. Minister of Religion. m. 24 Jan 1953, 1 s, 1 d. Education: LTh, Melbourne Coll of Divinity, 1949; BA, 1955; BEd, 1958, Univ of WA; ThM, N Bapt Theol Sem, 1960; PhD, Univ of IA, USA, 1963. Appointments: C'wlth Pub Serv, 1937-46; Min w Pastoral Charges, 1948-63; Fndng Prin, Bapt Theol Coll of WA, 1963-90, Prin Emer, 1991-; Mbr Austl Bd, World Vision, 1979-95; Min, Parkerville Bapt Ch, 1992-98. Publications include: Profile of a Puritan: John Owen (1616-1683); If God So Loved; Num articles in relig jrnls. Honours: Univ of IA Fellshp, 1962; Jubilee Medal, 1977; Hon DD, N Bapt Theol Sem, 1988; AM, 1989; Hon DD: E Bapt Theol sem, 1989; Hon DD, McMaster Univ Can, 1990. Memberships: Pres-Gen, Bapt Union of Aust,1975-78; Gen Cncl, Bapt World Alliance; VP, Austl Fellshp of Evang Studs; VP, Asia-Pacific Reg, Utd Bible Socs, 1990-. Hobbies: Music; Reading. Address: Mt Annan, 17 Padbury Road, Darlington, WA 6070, Australia.

VUNIBOBO Berenado. Government Minister. Education: Imperial Col of Tropical Agric, Trinidad; DP Horti, Qld Univ, Aust; BA Sc, Qld Agricl Coll. Appointments: Var Govt posts, Dept of Agric, 1951-76; Perm Rep of Fiji to UN, 1976-80; Chmn, UN Missions to Cayman Is, US Virgin Is and Vanuatu, VP Govng Cncl, UN, High Commnr to Can, 1980-81; Res Rep, UN Dev Prog, Korea, 1981-86, Pakistan, 1986-88; Min for Trade and Com, 1988-92; Chmn, var bds, 1992-94; Min for Home Affairs, Immigration, Labour and Indl Rels, 1994; Min for Fin and Econ Dev, 1994-97; Min for For Affairs and External Trade, 1997. Honours: CBE; Gold Medal, HM the Queen, Eng, 1989. Address: PO Box 2220, Government Buildings, Suva, Fiji.

VUTUKURI Venkata Satyanarayana, b. 22 Sept 1937, Vetapalem, AP, India. Teacher and Researcher. m. Venkata Kotiratnamma, 30 June 1961, 2 s, 1 d. Education: BS, Banaras Hindu Univ, 1960; MS, Univ Wisconsin, 1965; Dr Tech Sci, Polish Cntl Mining Inst, 1992. Appointments: Lectr, 1960-65; Reader, Banaras Hindu Univ, 1966-70; Lectr, 1970-77; Snr Lectr, 1978-97; Hon Visng Fell, 1997-, Univ NSW; Adj Prof, Curtin Univ Technol, 1997-. Publications: Handbook on Mechanical Properties of Rocks, 4 vols, 1974-78; Environmental Engineering in Mines, 1986; Introduction to Rock Mechanics, 1994. Memberships: Fell, Australasian Inst Mining andMetall; Austl Geomechs Soc; Instl Soc Rock Mech; Mining, Geol and Metall Inst, India. Hobbies: Reading religious books; Writing technical books. Address: 4 White Avenue, Mardubra, NSW 2035, Australia.

VYAS Ramesh Chandra, b. 10 Jan 1948, Dhar. Teacher (Government Service). m. Manju Vyas, 24 Feb 1976, 1 s. Education: BA, 1980, MA, 1982, Vikram Univ, Ujjain. Appointments: Lower Div Tchr, Gardawad, Dhar Dist, 1973; Dir (Hon) Vyas Computers, Indore, 1995; Upper Div Tchr, Rampura, Dhar Dist, 1997-; Participated in num seminars, radio progs on All India Indore (Malwa House), 1974, 1979. Honours: Merit Schlshps, Higher Second Techl Bd Bhopal, 1968, Polytechnic Bd of MP Govt, 1969; Natl Schlshp, Vikram Univ, Ujjain, 1980-81; Natl Level Cert of Sanskrit Lang, Natl Sanskrit Exam Bd, Surat, Gujrat. Membership: Life Mbr, Cancer Care Trust, 1993-. Hobbies: Reading books based on different literature; Listening to classical music (vocal & recital); Writing poetry in regional language; Travelling to natural places; Specially devoted to Meditation. Address: 925, Sudama Nagar, Indore 452 009, India.

VYAS Ved Prakash, b. 10 July 1961, India. Pediatrician. m. Vibha, 27 Feb 1990, 1 s, 1 d. Education: MD; BSc, Biol; BMus. Appointments: Lectr, Dept of Pediats; HOD Incharge, Pediats, Hosp Incharge, Dean Incharge, Dir, Herbal Garden Project, Chitrakoot. Publications: Sev articles in profl jrnls. Honour: Gold Medal, Grad Med Deg, 1988. Memberships: Radio & TV Artists Soc; Sev tchng & med assns. Hobbies: Hindi Poetry; Singing. Address: Department of Pediatrics, 27 University Campus, Sphatik Shila, Chitrakoot MP 485 331, India.

W

WADA Juro (Jerry), b. 11 Mar 1922, Tokyo, Japan. Emeritus Professor of Surgery. m. Shuko Christina Shimizu, 24 Oct 1958. Education: MD, Hikkaido Imperial Univ Med Sch, 1944; PhD, Surg, 1949; Postdoc, Univ of MN, USA, 1950; NY Ray Brook TBC Hosp, 1951; OH State Univ, 1952; Peter Brent Brigham and Boston City Hosp, 1953-54. Appointments: Fndr Chmn, Prof, Sapporo Med Coll, Prof Em, 1958; Dept of Thoracic and Cardiovascular Surg, Tokyo and Chmn, Heart Inst of Jap; Prof, Womens Med Coll, 1972; Hon Prof, Heineman Med Rsch Cntr, North Carolina; China Geriatric Cntr of Beijing; Chonnan Univ Med Sch, Korea; Dir, Wada J Commemorative Heart & Lung Inst; Adjunct Staff, Cleveland Clinic Fndn; Pioneer in Heart Surg, Jap. Publications: Ed, Jrnls in Jap, USA, Finland, Italy, Nigeria and Eng. Honours include: World Assn of Mil Surgs; DACCVS Disting Awd; Intl Hyperbaris Med Coerema Awd; Many Jap Med and Surg Socs. Memberships include: Soc of Thoracic Surgs; Amn Trauma Soc; Corresp Mbr, UK, Ireland and Scandinavian Soc of Cardio Thoracic Surg; Chan, Intl Soc of Cardio Thoracic Surgs; Pres, World Soc for Artificial Organs, Immunol and Transplantation; Pres, Intl Symp on Thoracic Deformity. Hobbies: Golf; Rotarian. Address: 5-21-6-602 Nishi-Ikebukuro, Toshima-ku, Tokyo 171, Japan.

WADA Koji, b. 7 Nov 1928, Tokyo, Japan. Professor Emeritus of Kyushu University. m. Sachie Ishibashi, 21 Mar 1957, 2 d. Education: BA, Agricl Chem, 1951, Dr Agric, 1960, Kyushu Univ. Appointments: Assoc Prof, 1954-75, Prof, 1975-91, Dept of Agricl Chem, Kyushu Univ; Dean, Fac of Agric, Kyushu Univ, 1987-91; Pres, Kyushu Univ, 1991-95; Prof Emer, Kyushu Univ, 1995-. Creative works: Amorphous Clay Constituents of Soils, 1974; Allophane and Imogolite, 1977, 2nd ed, 1989; Mineralogical Characteristics of Andisols, 1981; Distinctive Properties of Andosols, 1985. Honours: Japanese Soc of Soil Sci and Plant Nutrition Awd, 1961; Japan Agronomy Awd, 1981; Canad Soil Sci Visng Scientist Travel Awd, 1992; Pioneer in Clay Sci Awd, Clay Minerals Soc, 1997. Memberships: Intl Soc of Soil Sci, Hon Mbr, 1998; Japanese Soc of Soil Sci and Plant Nutrition; Soil Sci Soc of Am; Assn Intl pour l'Etude des Argiles; Clay Minerals Soc; Clay Sci Soc of Japan. Hobbies: Reading; Tennis. Address: Aoba 7-48-2, Fukuoka 813-0025, Japan.

WADDELL James Lewis, b. 19 Nov 1946, Tennessee, USA. Businessmab; Actor. Education: Bus Admin, Acctng, Cleveland State Univ, 1966; Real Estate, Univ San Fran, 1976. Appointments: Actor, 1966-; Broker, Owner, JLW Realty, 1986-; Brewmaster, Miller Brewing Co, 1989-. Honours include: Souverain Noble Relig Order of St Tatjana; Grand Inspector Gen, 33rd Deg Scottish Rite F and A M; Order of the Eastern Star. Memberships: Screen Actors Guild; Amn Fedn of TV and Radio Artists; Amn Soc of Composers, Auths and Publrs; SAG Conservatory at Amn Film Inst; SAG Film Soc; CA and Natl Assn of Realtors. Address: 11684 Ventura Boulevard, Ste 10, Studio City, CA 91604, USA.

WADE Jan Louise Murray, b. 8 July 1937, Sydney, Aust. Attorney General; Minister. m. (1) Francis, 1960, (2) Peter, 23 Mar 1978, 3 s, 1 stepd. Education: LLB, 1959; BA, Hist, 1970. Appointments: Parly Cnsl, 1967-79; Former Cmmnr of Corporate Affairs, 1979-85; Former Pres, Equal Opportunity Bd, 1985-88; Shadow Atty Gen, 1988-89; Shadow Min for Consumer Affairs, 1989-90; Shadow Atty Gen, Shadow Min for Women's Affairs, 1990-92; Atty Gen, Min for Fair Trading, Min for Women's Affairs, 1992-. Memberships: Vic Bar; Inst of Pub Admin of Aust; Lyceum Club. Hobbies: Family; Art; Reading; Gardening. Address: Suite 1, 400 High Street, Kew, Victoria 3101, Australia.

WADE John Harington, b. 4 Jan 1948, Brisbane, Aust. Meditator; Teacher; Lawyer. m. Susan, 12 June 1971, 1 s, 2 d. Education: LLB, Sydney; Dip Jur; LLM Hons, UBC. Appointments: Law Schs, Osgoode Hall, 1971; Manitoba, 1972-74; Sydney, 1974-89; Calgary, 1980-81; Pepperdine, 1993-99; Bond, 1990-99; Family Law Cncl of Aust, 1988-90; Dean, Law Sch, Bond Univ, 1991-93. Creative Works: Over 90 Publd articles and books, Legal Educ, Family Law, Conflict Mngmnt. Honours: Univ Tchng Awds. Hobbies: Family; Guitar; Tennis. Address: c/o School of Law, Bond University, Gold Coast, 4229 QLD, Australia.

WADE Robert Albert William, b, 29 July 1930, Melbourne, Aust. Artist. m. (1) 1 s, 2 d, (2) Ann Callander, 2 June 1979. Education: Scotch Coll, Melbourne, 1949. Appointments: Mng Dir, own Advtng Co, 1949-89; Natl Pres, Screen Printers Assn, 1972-76; Pres, Old Watercolour Soc, 1982-86. Publications include: Num articles for jrnls and mags; Painting More Than the Eye Can See; Exhib w worlds maj watercolour socs and other prestigious exhibs; Paintings reproduced, Australian Aerogramme, 1985; Australia's Bi-Centenary Bible, 1988; Painting Your Vision in Watercolour, 1993; Watercolour Wade's Way; Simply Watercolour, video, 1998. Honours: 109 Awds for Watercolours; Vic's Artist of Yr, 1985, 1986; Gold Medal, Camberwell Rotary, 1981, 1985, 1987; Cornelissen Awd, London, 1983; Clay Kent Medal, 1985; Paul Bransom Medal, 1984; Gwynne-Lennon Awd, 1987; Macowin Tuttle Awd, 1988, 1989; Adv Aust Medal, 1986. Memberships include: Life Mbr, Old Watercolour Soc Club; Life Mbr, Screen Printers Assn of Aust; Hon Mbr, Mexican Watercolour; Fell, Roy Soc of Arts, London; Salmagundi Club (NYC). Listed in: Who's Who of Visual Artists; Who's Who in the Commonwealth. Hobbies: Golf; Travel. Address: Dunoon, 524 Burke Road, Camberwell, Vic 3124, Australia.

WADE Robert Hunter, b. 14 June 1916, Balclutha, NZ. Diplomat (Retired). m. Avelda Grace Petersen, 16 Aug 1941, dec 1990, 2 s, 1 dec, 2 d. Education: BA, Otago Univ, 1937; MA, Vic Univ, 1940. Appointments: Offic Sec, NZ Deleg, East Grp Supply Cncl, Delhi, India, 1941-43; NZ Govt Offs, Sydney, 1943-46; Interim Secretariat, S Pacific Commn, 1947; NZ High Commn, Canberra, 1947-49; Hd, East Polit Div, Min of For Affairs, Wellington, 1949-51; First Sec, NZ Embassy, Washington, USA, 1951-56; NZ High Commn, Ottawa, Can, 1956-57; Dir, Colombo Plan Bur, Colombo, 1957-59; Dir of External Aid, MFA Wellington, NZ, 1959-62; NZ Commnr in Singapore, 1962-63; NZ High Commnr to Malaya/Malaysia, 1963-67; Dpty High Commnr, London, Eng, 1967-69; NZ Amb to Japan and Korea, 1969-71; Dpty Sec Gen of the C'wlth, London, Eng, 1972-74; NZ Amb, Fedl Repub of Germany and Switz, 1975-78. Memberships: Fell, Roy C'wlth Soc; Roy Asiatic Soc; Roy Soc of Arts. Address: 12 Pleasant Place, Howick, Auckland, New Zealand.

WADIA Maneck S, b. 22 Oct 1931, Mumbai, India. Professor; Author; Management Consultant. m. Harriet, 1 s, 1 d. Education: BA, hons, 1952; MA, 1955; PhD, 1957; MBA, 1958. Appointments: Fac, IN Univ, 1958-60, Stanford Univ, 1961-65; Mngmt Cnslt, 1965-. Publications: Num books and articles in profl jrnls. Honours: Awd, Acady of Mngmt, 1963; Red Hot Prof, Stanford Univ, 1964-65. Memberships: Sigma Xi; Sigma Iota Epsilon; Acady of Sci; Soc for the Adv of Mngmt; Acady of Mngmt. Hobbies: Travel; Cooking; Gardening; Reading; Painting. Address: 1660 Luneta Drive, Del Mar, CA 92014, USA.

WAGHMARE Nishikant, b. 2 June 1948. Crew Member, Air India. m. 11 May 1975, Nishat Rane, 1 s, 1 d. Education: Hist and Pol Sc, Univ of Mumbai. Appointments: CDA (Navy) Mumbai, 1969-72; Indian Airlines, 1972-76; Air-India, Mumbai, 1976; Sec-Gen, World Philos Meeting, Pune, 1996; NGO Observer, UN Econ and Soc Commn on Asia and the Pacific; 1997; Convenor, Forum against Comunalism and Terrorism, NGO India; Attended many seminars and natl and intl peace confs. Honours: Peace Rep Plaque, World Peace Prayer Soc, NY, USA, 1993; Attended Hum Rights Convention against Torture and other Cruel Punishment held at the UN, Geneva, 1994; Intl Rep, Fedn of Ambedkarite and Buddhist Org, UK; Bhim Ratna Awd, London, 1992; Fndr Pres, Life Worldwide, NGO Promoting movement for socl awakening through Educ; Civic Awd and Citation, London Borough of Ealing; Met His Holiness The Dalai Lama and the Late Mother Theresa. Memberships: Intl Rep, Fedn of Ambedkarite and Buddhist Org, UK; Special Exec Magistrate; Intl Peace Rep to the World Peace Prayer Soc, USA; Gen Sec, Buddha's Light Intl Assn USA, Chapt Pune, Nagpur, Kalyan, Ahmedabad; Mbr, Airlines Ambs, USA. Hobbies: Social Activist; Public Relations; Music; Travel. Address: 22 Rajnigandha, Juhu-Parle Scheme, 11 Gulmohar Road, Juhu, Mumbai 400 049, Maharashtra State, India.

WAHID Mohd Basri Bin, b. 18 Oct 1952, Malaysia. Scientist. m. Mislamah A B, 19 Mar 1979, 1 s, 1 d. Education: BHortSci, Lincoln, NZ; MHortSci, Lincoln, NZ; PhD, Guelph, Can. Appointments: Agricl Offr, 1978-82, Rsch Offr, 1982-95, Rsch Unit Hd, 1995-. Publications: 35 tech pprs in profl jrnls. Honour: Ex Serv and Best Publn Awd, PORIM, 1996. Memberships: Malaysian Plant Protection Soc, life mbr; Entomol Soc of Malaysia. Hobby: Reading. Address: PORIM, PO Box 10620, 50720 Kuala Lumpur, Malaysia.

WAHLQVIST Mark L, b. 5 Feb 1942, Adelaide, Aust. Physician. m. Soo Sien Huang, 25 Nov 1967, 1 s, 1 d. Education: BMedSc, 1962, MB BS, 1966, MD, 1970, Adelaide Univ; MD, Uppsala Univ, 1972; MRACP (Roy Australsian Coll of Physns), 1975; FRACP, 1978; FAINST (Fell, Austl Inst of Food Sci and Technol, 1982; FACN (Fell, Amn Coll of Nutrition), 1988; FAFPHM (Fell, Australasian Fac of Pub Hlth Med), 1991. Appointments: Apptd to Prince Henry's Hosp, 1976-; Cnslt Physn in Endocrinology and Diabetes; Cnslt Gen Physn; Dir, Clin Nutrition and Metabolism Unit, Prince Henry's Hosp; Fndn Prof, Hum Nutrition, Deakin Univ, 1978-87; Cnslt Physn, Geellong Hosp, 1978-87; Prof and Hd of Med, Monash Univ, 1987-98; Prof of Med, Monash Univ, 1987-; Chmn, Div of Med, Prince Henry's Hosp, 1987-91, Monash Medl Cntr, 1987-96; Fndn Ed-in-Chf, Asia Pacific Jrnl of Clin Nutrition, 1992-; Assoc Dean, Intl Hlth and Dev, Fac of Med, 1999-, Chair, Asia Pacific Hlth and Nutrition Cntr, Monash Asia Inst, 1999-, Monash Univ. Publications: Over 350 pprs in sci jrnls on food, nutrition and metabolic problems; 17 books (as co-auth) incl: Preventive Nutrition in Medical Practice, 1994; Exercise and Obesity, 1994; Nutrition in a sustainable environment, 1994; Food and Nutrition: Australasia, Asia and Pacific, 1997. Honour: Charlotta Medal, Sweden, 1994. Memberships include: Chmn, Weight Loss Mngmt Code of Prac Cncl, 1997-; Pres-Elect, Intl Union of Nutritional Scis, 1997-; Chmn, Food Safety Cncl of Vic, 1997-. Hobbies: Music; Farming; Involved in migrant genealogy as member of Emigrants Research Institute, Sweden; International relations.

WAITE Allan George, b. 18 Mar 1924, Goulburn, NSW, Aust. Artist. m. (1) Marjorie Mary Chapman, 1948, div, 1 d, (2) Daphne Joan. Appointments: Entered Austl Army, 1942; Transferred to AIF serving in New Guinea and Japan; Mngr and Dir of Studio, 1951; Own studio, Coml Graphics Studio Pty Ltd, 1976-81; Retd to paint, 1981-. Publications: Australian Artist magazine, Co-fndr and Cnslt; How to Paint Portraits, 1987; Artists and Galleries of Australia; Australian Painters Series; 10 books; Contbr of articles in art mags and jrnls; Num commns inclng portrait of Sir Roden Cutler, VC, AK, KCMG, KCVO, CBE, fmr Gov of NSW. Honours: Num maj awds in oils and watercolours; Recip of many commendations. Honour: Combined Art Socs Artist of the Yr, 1992. Memberships: Fell Mbr, Roy Art Soc, NSW; Austl Watercolour Inst; Exhibiting Mbr, Drummoyne Art Soc; Exhibiting Mbr, Ryde Art Soc; Exhibiting Mbr, N Shore Art Soc; Fell Mbr, Advd Motorists Inst. Hobbies: Golf; Reading; Natural study; Travel. Address: 5/32 Undercliff Road, Harbord, NSW 2096, Australia.

WAKED Maher, b. 3 July 1941, Salt, Jordan. Commissioner. m. Layla, 24 Aug 1972, 2 s, 2 d. Education: BS; MPA; MBA; PhD. Appointments: Commnr, Jordan Securities Commn; Asst Gen Mngr, Bank; Dpty Hd, Cntrl Bank. Publications: Auditing practical perceptions, thesis-dissertation; Num articles and publd pprs. Hobbies: Reading; Travel; Social activities. Address: Commissioner, Jordan Securities

Commision, Amman, Jordan, Box 8802.

WALDBY David Walter, b. 21 Sept 1930. Civil Engineer; Arbitrator. m. Valerie Marie Dews, 26 May 1956, 1 s, 1 d. Education: BEng(Civil), Univ of Queensland, 1953; Registered Arbitrator w Inst of Arbitrator Aust. Appointments: Wrks Dept, Brisbane Cty Cncl, 1953-57; Entered pvte ind in field of des and construction, 1957-76; Entered cnsltng engrng w E W Karamisheff and Assocs, 1976-81; Joined CMPS and F Engrs and Proj Mngrs, involved projs inclng: Gateway Arterial Rd proj, Logan Motorway proj (Brisbane); Sunshine Motorway proj Stage II, Sunshine Coast, Queensland, 1981-95; Currently cnslt in areas of dispute resolution (Arbitration and Mediation). Publications: Papers to Natl and Intl Engrng Confs, 1974-94. Memberships: Instn of Engrs, Aust; Fell; Pres, Queensland Div and Mbr of Natl Cncl, 1989; Other positions 1982-92; Civil Coll Bd; Natl Cttee on Structures; Chmn of judges Natl Civil Engrng Excellence Awds, Cttee on Colls Structure; Cttee on Registration and Continuing Profl Dev; Inst of Arbitrators, Aust; Chmn of Queensland Chapt, 1995, Cnclr, 1997-98, 1999-2000. Hobbies: Reading widely; Music; Gardening. Address: 8 Avocado Lane, Maleny, Qld 4552, Australia.

WALDEN Graham Howard (Rt Rev), b. 19 Mar 1931, Brisbane, Aust. m. Margaret Ann, 13 Jan 1964, 2 s, 1 d. Education: BA; MA (Qld); ThL (Bris); BLitt; MLitt (Oxon). Appointments: Asst, Bishop Ballarat Vic, 1981-89; Archdeacon and Vicar, Gen Diocese Ballarat, 1970-89; Rector and Bishop Hamilton, 1981-84; Archdeacon Barker Diocese Bathurst, NSW, 1968-70; Rector Mudgee, 1965-70, Vice Prin, Torres Strait Miss Theo Coll Moa Island, 1963-65. Publications: Publ pprs on Christian Doctrine and Liturgy. Honours: Douglas Price Mem Prize Univ Qld, 1952. Memberships: VP, Anglican Men's Soc Nat, 1993-, Chmn, 1983-93; Gen Synod Commn on Doctrine, 1989, Chmn, 1992. Hobbies: Walking; Swimming; Reading; History. Address: PO Box 269, Murray Bridge, SA 5253, Australia.

WALDRAFF Tilmann, b. 30 Dec 1937, Germany. m. Janaki Narkar-w, 22 June 1983, 3 d. Education: MA, Engl Lit, German Lit, Philos. Appointments: Dir, Goethe Institut (G I), Achenmühle; Hd Lang Dept, G I, Rio de Janeiro; Hd, Trng Dept, G I, Münich; Dir, G I, Pune, India; Dir, G I, Mexico City; Dir, G I, Münich; Dir, G I, New Delhi. Hobbies: Horse Riding; Photography; Music; History; Travel. Address: c/o Max Mueller Bhavan, 3 Kasturba Gandhi Marg, New Delhi 110001, India.

WALES Raymond George, b. 24 Aug 1931, Melbourne, Aust. Physiologist. m. Margaret Anne, 15 Aug 1959, 1 s, 2 d. Education: BVSc, 1954, PhD, 1960, DVSc, 1972, Sydney Univ. Appointments: Acad Staff Mbr, Vet Physiol, Sydney Univ, 1960-74; Fndn Prof of Physiol, Murdoch Univ, WA, 1975; Retd, 1996; Now Prof Emer, Murdoch Univ. Publications: 150 articles in sci jrnls. Honours: Population Cncl Fell, 1966; Snr Hays Fulbright Fell, 1973; Roy Soc Bursary, 1984; Visng Prof, Univ of York, 1993. Memberships: Life Mbr, Austl Soc for Reproductive Biol; Life Mbr, Natl Tertiary Educ Union. Hobbies: Art; Music; Gardening. Address: 19 Strome Road, Applecross, WA 6153, Australia.

WALFORD Reginald Neil, b. 3 Apr 1922, Melbourne, Aust. Company Director. m. Patricia, 23 Feb 1949, dec, 2 s, 2 d. Education: BCom, Melbourne; FCA. Appointments: Chmn, Track N Field Pty Ltd; Chmn, Electrolux Pty Ltd, 1977-92; REPCO Ltd, 1980-86, Actrol Ltd, 1956-82, Costain Aust Ltd, 1965-71, Wilkinson Match Aust Sunbeam Corp, Penguin Books Aust Ltd, Longman Aust, Grosby Footwear, PE Cnsltng Grp (Aust), Hawker Richardson & Co, Dunlop Domestic Textile Grp, Candy Footwear, Hollandia Footwear, Dpty Chmn, David Syme and Co Ltd, 1970-77, former Dpty Chmn, H C Sleigh Ltd, Power Corp Aust Ltd, former Dir, Alliance Oil Dev, Weeks Petroleum, A and K Cement, City Mutual Life (Vic Bd), Wreckair, Kauri Holdings, Holderbank (Aust), East Asiatic Co (Aust), Woodall-Duckham, Hambros Aust, Richard Allen and Sons, Ord B-T, Commnr, State Bank of Vic, 1972-75, Snr Ptnr, R H Walford and Co, 1945-55, Co-Founder and Hd Gen, Shoe Grp, 1955-64, Mbr, Sydney Stock Exchange and Ptnr Ord Minnett, 1964-72, Hon Fed and Vic Sec, Navy League, 1951-57, Pres, MU Comm Grad Assoc, 1957, Chmn, Murdoch Inst Rsch into Birth Defects Ltd, 1986-93, Chmn, Vic Clinl Genetic Servs Ltd, 1986-93, Chmn, RSL War Veterans Homes Trust Vic, 1993-94, Tstee, 1957-, Life Mbr, RSL, 1987, Life Govr, Free Kindergarten Assn Vic, Life Govr, Assn for Blind, former Cl Mbr, Clyde Sch Woodend (Vic), Latrobe Univ (Vic), Chmn, Adv Cl Noosa Fedn of the Arts; Personal Asst to Chief Acct UNRRA Europe, 1946, Acct, UNRRA 30 Corps Dist Brit Zone Germany, 1945, Navigating and ASDIC Off, HMS Woodruff Atlantic, 1944-45, RANVR Lt, 1942-45, AMF, 1941-42.

WALKER Alan, b. 4 June 1911, Sydney, Aust. Minister of Religion. m. Winifred Walker, 3 s, 1 d. Education: Leigh Theol Coll, Enfield, Sydney, 1929-32; BA, Sydney Univ, 1936; MA, 1943; Hon DD, Bethany Biblical Sem, Chgo, USA, 1956. Appointments: Assoc Dir, 1936-38; Min, 1939-44; Supt Waverley Meth miss, 1944-54; Dir, miss to the Nation for the Meth Ch of Australasia, 1953-55; Visng Prof of Evang, Boston Sch of Theo, 1956-57; Supt Cntrl Meth miss, 1958-78; Dir of World Evang for the World Meth Cncl, 1978-87; Prin, Pacific Coll for Evang, 1988-95; Prin Emer, Alan Walker Coll of Evang, 1995-. Publications: Auth of over 30 books; There is Always a God; Everybody's Calvary; Coal Town; Heritage Without End; The Whole Gospel for the Whole World; The Many Sides of Jesus. Honours: OBE, Ldrshp of the miss to the Nation; Upper Room Cit; Inst de la Vie Awd; Kt Batchelor, Queen Elizabeth II; World Meth Peace Awd. Memberships: Sydney Life Line tel cnclng cntr; World Cncl of Chs; NSW Meth Conf. Hobbies: Swimming; Tennis. Address: 14 Owen Stanley Ave, Beacon Hill, NSW 2100, Australia.

WALKER Campbell John, b. 29 June 1963, Australia. Environmentalist. Education: BEd, Environ Scis. Appointments: Coord, Friends of the Earth, Melbourne, 1989-; Natl Liaison Offr, Friends of the Earth, Aust, 1991-. Address: 46 Helen Street, Northcote, Victoria 3070, Australia.

WALKER Constance Hannah, b. 22 July 1924, Red Cliffe, Vic, Aust. Artist. m. Ronald Arthur Walker, 21 Jan 1950, 2 s, 1 d. Education: Water-colour tuition w David Taylor, 1970-75; Oil Painting tuition w Carol Boothman, 1970-75, w Ken McFadyen, 1977. Appointments: Austl Army Medl Women's Serv, 1942-47; Freelance Artist, Oils and Water-colour. Creative Works: Water-colours and oil paintings exhibited in num solo and grp exhibns; 6 commissioned wrks for Little Am's Cup, 1976. Honours: Over 40 1st Awds inclng: Roy Agricl Shows, 1971-84; Sir John Monash Awd, 1975, 1976; Ringwood Rotary, 1979; Waverley Arts Soc Awd, 1980, 1987, 1990; Springvale City Cncl, 1986; Clayton Cncl, 1986; Glen Waverley Rotary, 1988; Mazenod Coll Awd, 1988; Included in perm collects, Cty of Waverley, Kerang Cncl, Clayton Arts Cncl, Victorian Artists Soc; Elected Fell, Victorian Artists Soc, 3 Apr 1990; Roy Overseas League Mountbatten Awd, 1992. Memberships: Pres, Victorian Artists Soc, 1989, 1990, 1991; Old Water-Colour Soc's Club, Aust; Waverley Arts Soc, Fndn Sec, 1970-72, Pres, 1980-81; Melbourne Soc Women Painters and Sculptors; Waverley Cty Cncl Art Acquisition Cttee; Sorrento Sailing Club; Hon Life Mbr, Victorian Artists Soc. Hobbies: Tennis; Theatre; Sailing; Travel. Address: 18 Wilson Road, Glen Waverley, Vic 3150, Australia.

WALKER Donald Murray, b. 5 July 1939, Cardiff, Wales. Professor of Oral Pathology. m. Susan, 6 Sept 1966, 1 s, 1 d. Education: BDs, Univ Bristol, 1962; MB BCL, Univ Wales, 1969; FDS RCS (Eng), 1971; MD, Univ of Wales, 1976; FRCPA, 1992; FRCPath, 1995; FFOP, 1996. Appointments: Lectr, 1971, Snr Lectr, 1976, Rdr, 1984, Oral Med, Dental Sch, Univ of Wales; Prof of Oral Path, Sydney Univ, 1992. Publications: Texbook chapts in: The Oral Mucosa in Health and Disease, 1975; Co-auth: Introduction to Oral Immunology, 1981; Principles and Practice of Geriatric Medicine, 1998; Over 100 pprs in jrnls. Memberships: Pres, Brit Soc for Oral Med, 1988-91; Pres, Aust and NZ Assn for Oral Path, 1994-; Sec, Fac of Oral Path Cttee, Roy Coll of Pathologists of Australasia, 1996-. Hobbies: English literature; Music; Theatre. Address: Department of Oral Pathology, Westmead Hospital, Dental Clinical School, Westmead, NSw 2145, Australia.

WALKER Frank Bartley, b. 21 May 1919. Author. 2 s. Education: BA, Sydney Univ. Membership: Austl Soc for Auths. Address: 117 Sunrise Avenue, Budgewoi, NSW 2262, Australia.

WALKER Ian Kenneth, b. 19 Feb 1917, Birkenhead, NZ (Brit citizen). Physical Chemist. m. Ann Teresa Earley, 11 Dec 1948, 2 s, 1 d. Education: BS, 1937, MSc, 1939, DSc, 1962, Univ of NZ. Appointments: Asst Chemist, Westfield Freezing Co, 1933-35; Chem, Dominion Lab, NZ DSIR, 1936-40; Radar Rsch, 1940-46; Atomic Energy of Can, 1946; Atomic Energy Rsch Estab, Harwell, Eng, 1946-49; Chem Div, DSIR, NZ, 1949-72; Asst Dir-Gen, Dept of Sci and Indl Rsch, 1972-77; Snr Rsch Fell, Univ of Leeds (UK), 1978-79. Publications: Contbr of over 70 pprs in sci jrnls. Honours: Morcomb Green and Edwards Prize of NZ Inst of Chem, 1950; Imperial Chem Inds (NZ) Prize for Chem Rsch, 1965; Queen Elizabeth II Silver Jubilee Medal. Membership: Fell, NZ Inst of Chem, 1977. Address: 19 Cresswell Avenue, Governors Bay, Lyttelton RD1, New Zealand.

WALKER James Christopher, b. 4 Dec 1944, Sydney, Aust. Academic. m. Pauline Leila Newport, 1 Feb 1998. Education: BA; DipEd; MEduc; PhD (Sydney). Appointments: Lectr, Snr Lectr, Assoc Prof in Educ, Univ of Sydney, 1972-89; Rsch Fell, Inst of Educ, London Univ, Visng Schl, Tvind Coll, Ulfborg, Denmark, 1977; Visng Rschr, German Yth Inst, Munich, 1979; Rsch Fell, Cntr for Philos and Hist of Sci, Boston Univ, 1982; Disting Visng Schl, King's Coll, London Univ, 1984; Prof and Dean of Educ, Dir, Cntr for Rsch in Profl Educ, Univ of Canberra, 1990-94; Prof and Dean of Educ, Univ of West Sydney, Nepean, 1995-97; Adj Prof of Educ, Univ of Technol, Sydney, 1998-; Visng Prof, Ont Inst for Studies in Educ, Univ of Toronto, 1998, Visng Prof, Sch of Educ, Univ of CO, Boulder, 1998; Visng Schl, Grad Sch of Educ, Harv Univ, 1998. Publication: Louts and Legends: Male Youth Culture in an Inner City School, 1988. Honour: Fell, Austl Coll of Educ, 1993. Memberships: Pres, Philos of Educ Soc of Australasia, 1987-90; Pres, Austl Assn for Rsch in Educ, 1991; Fndn Pres, Austl Cncl of Deans of Educ, 1991-93. Address: School of Teaching and Educational Studies, University of Western Sydney, Nepean, PO Box 10, Kingswood, NSW 2747, Australia.

WALKER Jinnie, b. 31 Aug 1922, Colac, Victoria, Aust. Teacher; Writer; Artist. m. Ralph, 2 s, 1 d. Education: Tchrs Dip, Art Dip, Melbourne Univ. 2 Schlshps. Appointments: Art Tchr, J H Boyd Domestic Coll, S Melbourne; Melbourne Ch of Eng Girls Grammar, Queenswood, Sydney. Publications: Co-auth w sister, Designing Aust Bush Gardens; More About Bush Gardens. Honours: Book of Yr, 1967; Inaugural opening, Women's Art Mus, Washington; Video of Ceramic Wicked Ladies, Beijing. Memberships: Soc of Auths; Cttee Bradley Friends. Hobbies: Puppetry; Environment. Address: 86 Woodland St, Balgowlah Heights, NSW 2093, Australia.

WALKER Sally Ann, b. 6 July 1955, Melbourne. Lawyer. m. Brendan Murphy, 31 Mar 1979, 2 s. Education: LLB Hons; LLM. Appointments: Prof, Law, Univ of Melbourne, 1993; VP, Acad Bd, Univ of Melbourne, 1996; Pro Vice Chan, Univ of Melbourne, 1997. Creative Works: The Law of Journalism in Aust, 1989; The Law of Securities, 1993; Communications Laws of Australia, 1996. Address: Law School, University of Melbourne, Parkville 3052, VIC, Australia.

WALKER Thomas William, b. 17 July 1923, Wesley Vale, Tas. Retired. m. Leonore, 3 Jan 1951, dec 1989. Education: BSc, Tas; DipEd, Melbourne. Appointments: Prin, Devonport Tech Coll; Prin, Launceston Tech Coll. Honour: OBE, 1982. Memberships: Launceston Legacy; Pres, Tas Br, 1977-91, Returned and Servs League of

Aust. Hobbies: Reading; Gardening. Address: 3 Fairthorne Road, Trevallyn, Tasmania 7250, Australia.

WALKER Timothy Alexander, b. 23 Nov 1954. Arts Administrator. Education: BA, hons; Dip, Ed; Dip, Fin Mngmt; AMus. Appointments: Concert Mngr, Canberra Sch of Music, 1981; Mktng and Dev Mngr, Austl Chmbr Orch, 1987; Gen Mngr, Austl Chmbr Orch, 1989. Memberships: Intl Soc of the Performing Arts, Dir, 1995-; Music Cncl of Aust, Dpty Chair, 1996-; Austl Inst of Arts Admin: Advsry Cncl, Sydney Conservatorium of Music, 1996-; Austl Intl Cultural Cncl, 1998-. Listed in: Who's Who in Australia; Who's Who in Business in Australia. Hobbies: Arts; Architecture; Environment. Address: 2 East Circular Quay, Sydney, NSW 2000, Australia.

WALKER Warren E, b. 7 Apr 1942, NY City, USA. Policy Analyst. m. div. 1 s. 2 d. Education: BA, 1963, MS, 1964, PhD, 1968, Cornell Univ. Appointments: Policy Analyst, The NY City-Rand Inst, 1970-75; Asst VP, Chemical Bank, 1975-77; Snr Policy Analyst, The Rand Corp, 1977-88, 1989-, Snr Policy Analyst, Rand Europe, 1992-; Visng Prof, Delft Univ of Technol, 1988-89. Publications: Book: Fire Department Deployment Analysis, 1979; Building Organizational Decision Support Systems, 1992. Honours: Lanchester Prize, Ops Rsch Soc of Am, 1974; NATO System Sci Prize, 1976; Pres's Awd, Informs, 1997. Membership: Inst for Ops Rsch and Mngmt Sci (Informs). Hobbies: Photography; Bicycling; Travel. Address: The Rand Corporation, 1700 Main Street, Santa Monica, CA 90407-2138, USA.

WALKLEY Gavin, b. 8 July 1911, Adelaide, SA, Aust. Architect. m. Barbara Esther Burton, 8 July 1944, dec 1955, 1 s, 1 d. Education: BE, St Marks Coll, Univ of Adelaide, 1934; MLitt, 1939, MA, 1941, Clare Coll, Univ of Cambridge. Appointments: Archt, Sir John Burnet, Tait & Lorne, London, 1939; Archt, Woods Bagot Laybourne Smith & Irwin, Adelaide, 1940; War Serv, Roy Austl Engrs, Middle E, Major, 1940-45; Archt, SA Housing Trust, Adelaide, 1945-49; Priv Prac, Overall & Walkley, then Walkley & Welbourn, 1949-70; Hd of Sch of Arch, SA Inst of Technol, 1951-76. Publications: William Wilkins 1778-1839, Dissertation for Cambridge degree of MLitt, 1939; Bibliography of Urban Studies in Australia, Vol 1, 1966-68 (ed); School of Architecture, South Australia Institute of Technology, 1906-76; Louis Laybourne Smith: A Memoir, Adelaide, 1977; St Marks College: The Buildings and Grounds, 1985; La Confrerie des Chevaliers du Tastevin in Australia, 1987. Honours include: CBE, 1968; Sidney Luker Medal for Plng, Roy Austl Plng Inst, 1962; Hon Fell, St Marks Coll, Univ of Adelaide, 1977; Dr of the Univ of SA, 1995. Memberships include: Fell, 1951, Pres, 1964-66, Roy Austl Plng Inst; Fell, 1954, Pres, 1965-66, Roy Austl Inst of Archts; Pres, 1971-73, Fell, 1976, Austl Inst of Landscape Archts. Hobbies: Writing; Cooking; Heraldry; Genealogy; Conservation (Pres, Natl Trust of SA, 1988-90); Wine; Travel (around the world 7 times). Address: 22/52 Brougham Place, North Adelaide, SA 5006, Australia.

WALKOWSKI Marjory Alice Hamlet Taylor, b. 3 July 1920, Corowa, NSW, Aust. Retired Nursing Administrator. m. Franciszek Walkowski, 13 Dec 1968, dec, 1987. Education: RN, Geelong Hosp, 1943; Dip Nursing Admin, Coll Nursing Aust, 1959; Fell, Roy Coll Nursing Aust, 1962. Appointments: RAAF Nursing Serv, 1944-46; Voly Snr Nursing Offr, Girl Guide Intl Serv, w Intl Refugee Org, W Germany, 1947-50; Midwifery Supvsr, 1951-56, Dir Nursing, 1956-81, Geelong Hosp, Geelong, Vic. Publications: Co-auth, History of Geelong Hospital Nurses League; Co-auth, Wihout a Blaze of Trumpets (history of Geelong YWCA); From Matron to Director of Nursing, 1991; The Gift of Time, History of Geelong Hospice, 1992. Honours: AM, 1980; Hon MA, Deakin Univ, 1991. Hobbies: Reading; University of Third Age studies; Church affairs. Address: 17 Villamanta Street, Geelong Street, Geelong West, Vic 3218, Australia.

WALL Clive Frederick, b. 4 Oct 1946, Melbourne, Aust. Judge. m. Angeline, 3 Jan 1981, 2 s, 1 d. Education: LLB, Melbourne, 1968. Appointments: Mbr, currently Grp Capt, RAAF Spec Reserve (Legal), 1972-; Judge Advocate, Austl Def Force, 1987-; Def Force Magistrate, Austl Def Force; Pt-time Dpty Chmn, Land Tribunal, estab under Aboriginal Land Act (Qld), 1992-96; Pt-time Mbr, Land Crt, Qld, 1992-96; Judge, Dist Crt of Qld, Judge of Childrens Crt of Qld, Judge of Plng and Environl Crt of Qld, 1996-; Reviewing Judge Advocate, Austl Def Force, 1997-. Honours: QC, Qld, 1986; QC, North Territory of Aust, 1989; Reserve Force Decoration, 1990; First Clasp to Reserve Force Decoration, 1995; Second Clasp to Reserve Force Decoration, 1997. Memberships: Roster Experts, UN Transnatl Corps; North Supreme Crt Lib Cttee, Townsville; Pres, N Qld Bar Assn, 1992-96; Fmr, Mbr of Cttee of Bar Assn of Qld. Hobbies: Tennis; Squash; Lawn bowls; Skiing; Reading. Address: Judge's Chambers, District Court, 31 Walker Street, Townsville, QLD, Australia.

WALLACE Henry Robert, b. 12 Sept 1924. Retired Professor. m. 10 Aug 1950, 2 d. Education: PhD; DSc. Appointments: Rsch Scientist, Univ of Cambridge, 1952-55; Prin Rsch Scientist, 1955-63; Chf Rsch Scientist, CSIRO, 1963-71; Prof, Plant Pathol, Waite Inst, Univ of Adelaide, 1971-89. Publications: Num profl articles in sci jrnls. Honour: Hon Life Fell, Amn Nematol Soc, 1965. Memberships: Pres, Aust Parasitol Soc, 1971; FAA, 1975. Hobbies: Running; Natural History; Conservation. Address: PO Box 84, Meningie, SA 5264, Australia.

WALLACE John Macdonald, b. 23 July 1926, Aust. Civil Engineer. m. Heather Stewart Smith, 31 Mar 1951, 2 s, 1 d. Education: Dip, Civ Engrng, Sydney Techl Coll, 1949. Appointments: Snr Constrn Engr, 1956-64; Prin Engr, 1964-66; Engr-i/c, 1966-75; Pres of Bd, 1975-84; Maritime Servs Bd of NSW; Chmn, Westham Dredging Co Pty Ltd, 1985-99; Chmn, NZ Dredging and Gen Wrks Pty Ltd, 1992-99. Honour: Efficiency Decoration, Austl Mil Forces, 1970. Memberships: Fell, Instn of Engrs; Fell, Chartered Inst of Transp; Hon Mbr, Intl Assn of Ports and Harbours. Hobbies: Surfing; Tennis; Fishing; Gardening. Address: 46 Greendale Avenue, Pymble, NSW 2073, Australia.

WALLER Louis, b. 10 Feb 1935, Siedlce, Poland. Professor of Law. m. Wendy, 11 Jan 1959, 2 s, 1 d. Education: LLB, Hons, Melbourne; BCL, Oxford; FASSA. Appointments: Tutor, 1956; Snr Lectr, Law Univ of Melbourne, 1959-65; Dean, Fac of Law, Monash Univ, 1968-70; Visng Prof, Univ of Kent, 1971; Fndng Pres, Vic Aboriginal Legal Servs, 1972-74; Cnsltnt, Law Reform Commn of Canada, 1974-75; Commnr, 1982-84; Visng Prof, Univ of Vic BC, 1981; Chmn, Law Reform Vic, 1984-85; Chmn, Stndng Review and Adv, Cttee on Infertility, 1985-93; Pt-time Commnr Law Reform Commn, Vic, 1986-91; Chair, Vic Infertility Treatment, 1995-. Publications: An Introduction to Law. Memberships: Mortimer and Raymond Sackler Inst of Adv Studies Univ, Tel Aviv, 1985-86; Austl Natl Fell, Inst for Adv Studies in the Hum Univ, 1990; Inst Advd Studies Hebrew Univ; Intl Hum Law Cttee, Aust; Red Cross Soc. Hobbies: Reading; Theatre; Cinema. Address: 2 Hartley Avenue, Caulfield, Vic 3162, Australia.

WALSH John Richard, b. 21 July 1941, Sydney, Australia. Publisher. m. Susan, 18 Aug 1966, 1 d. Education: BA, MB, BS, Univ Sydney. Appointments: Ed, OZ; Ed, Pol; Publr, Nation Review; Mngng Dir, Angus & Robertson Publrs; MD, Aust Consol Press. Publication: Ferretabilia, 1994. Memberships: Lit Bd of Aust Cncl, 1973-76; Pres, Art Book Publrs Assn, 1986; Aust Soc of Auths. Hobbies: Reading; Theatre; Music. Address: c/o 54 Park Street, Sydney, New South Wales, Australia.

WALTER Geoffrey William, b. 8 July 1941. Research Scientist. m. Bette Palfry Willis, 6 Apr 1968, 2 s. Education: BS, Applied Chem, Univ NSW, 1964; MPhil Chem, Univ Surrey, Eng, 1968; PhD, Mat Eng, Univ of Wollongong, NSW, 1989. Appointments: Lab Chem, N Shore Gas Co, 1962-64; Rsch Asst, Thermochem Lab, Battersea Coll, UK, 1964-68; Snr Rsch Offr, John Lysaght (Aust), Rsch and Technol Cntr, 1968-79; Snr Prin Rsch Scientist, BHP Rsch Port Kembla Labs, 1980-95; Sci Leadership Team (Corrosion), BHP Rsch Port Kembla Labs, 1995-97; Prin Fell, Materials Engrng Dept, Univ Woolangong, 1997-; Corrosion Cnslt, Walter Corrosion Servs Pty Ltd, 1997-. Publications: 28 pprs pubd in intl jrnls, 31 conf pprs in the field of electrocheml lab techniques for corrosion of painted and unpainted metals. Honours: George Wright Prize for Chem 1, 1960. Memberships: Sec, Newcastle Branch, Austl Corrosion Assn, 1976-78; Australasian Pres, Australasian Corrosion Assn, 1978; Mbr, Sydney Br, Australasian Corrosion Assn, 1995-; Stands Aust (MT14 Corrosion, MT14/2 Corrosion Protection of Steelwork, and MT14-6 Dissimilar Metals in Contact) cttee mbr. Hobbies: Classical music; French horn; Hi-fi; Tennis; Jogging; Bushwalking. Address: 9 Highcrest Avenue, Balgownie, NSW 2519, Australia.

WALTER James Arnot, b. 13 Oct 1949, Hamilton, Vic, Aust. Academic. m. Robyn, 9 Dec 1972, 1 s, 3 d. Education: BA, Hons; MA, 1st Class Hons; PhD. Appointments: Prof, Austl Studies, Griffith Univ, 1987-; Prof, Hd, Sir Robert Menzies Cntr for Austl Stdies, Univ of London, 1990-93; Pro-Vice-Chan, Arts, Griffith Univ, 1996-. Publications: The Leader, 1980; The Ministers' Minders, 1986; Tunnel Vision, 1996. Honours: Fell, Roy Soc of Art and Mfrs, 1991; Fell, Acady Socl Scis in Aust, 1996. Memberships: Aust-China Cncl, 1994-; Mbr of Bd, Austl Natl Archives, 1997-. Address: Vice-Chancellors Office, Griffith University, Nathan, Queensland, Australia 4111.

WAMA Jacob, b. 25 May 1952, Yangoru, East Sepik, Papua New Guinea. Minister for Finance and Internal Revenue. m. 5 children. Education: Para Medl Coll, Madan, 1973-75. Appointments: Pastor, Four Square Gospel Ch; Bank Offl, Papua New Guinea Banking Corp, 8 yrs; Cnclr, Madang Town Cncl, 1977-85; Pres, Madang Town Cncl (later Town interim Commn); Local vill magistrate, chmn, 1981-97; Min for Fin and Internal Revenue.

WAN Guang, b. 5 Nov 1929. Research Fellow; Professor. m. Chen Peiming, 30 Jan 1957, 1 d. Education: Grad, Nanjing Cntrl Univ, 1949. Appointments: Ed, Corresp, Commentator, Chf Ed, Intl News Dept, Xinhua News Agcy, 1950-77; Xinhua Corresp, Cairo, 1979-83; Rsch Fell, Exec Bd, China Cntr for Intl Studies, 1984-; Prof, Cntr for Chinese & Amn Studies, Nanjing Univ and Johns Hopkins Univ, 1985-; Prof, Dept of Intl Polits, People's Univ of China, 1986-. Publications: Challenges to US Foreign Policy, 1957; The Crux of Middle East Problem, 1984; Egypt in Transition, 1985; Trends of World Multipolarization, 1987; China's Foreign Policy Goals: Peace and Development, 1989; 1990s - A Decade of Transformation of World Pattern, 1990; North-South Relations in 1990s, 1992; The Evolution of Asia-Pacific Situation in 1990s, 1992; Relations Between Powers in Asia-Pacific, 1994; The Rise of Asian Developing Nations, 1996; The US in Transition, 1997. Honour: Awd for Outstndng to Socl Scis, Chinese Govt, 1992. Memberships: Vice Chmn, China Soc of Mid East Studies, Beijing, 1985-; Exec Cncl Mbr, China Soc of Asian and African Studies, Beijing, 1986-. Listed in: Five Hundred Leaders of Influence. Hobby: Music. Address: China Center for International Studies, 22 Xi An Men Street, PO Box 1744, Beijing 100017, China.

WAN Hiu (Ven Shig), b. 21 Aug 1913, Nan Hai, Kuangtung, China. Buddhist Nun; Professor; Founder of Huafan University. Education: BA, Kuangfung Coll of Hum and Nat Sci; MA, Tagore Univ of India. Appointments: Fndr, Lotus Buddhist Ashram, 1970; Inst of Sino Indian Buddhist Stdies, 1979; Huafan Univ, 1990. Publications: 86 Book, Buddhist Educ. Honours: Culture Prize, Exec Yuan of the Repub of China, 1997. Address: Hua Fan University, 2 Hua Fan Road, Shihting Hsiang, Taipei Hsian, Taiwan.

WAN Lee, b. 9 Feb 1961, Seoul, Korea. Professor. m. Lee, 9 June 1990, 1 s, 1 d. Education: PhD. Appointment: Rsch Fell, Natl Hist Compilation Cttee. Publication: The Korean History Before & After the Liberation, 1989. Membership: AKSE. Hobby: Mountain Climbing. Address:

Academy of Korean Studies, 50 Unjoong-Dong, Sungnam City, Korea.

WAN ABDULLAH Wan Ahmad Tajuddin, b. 8 June 1960, Malaysia. Academic. m. Nur Azian, 13 June 1987, 1 s, 4 d. Education: PhD, Phys, Univ of London. Appointments: Lectr, Phys Dept, 1985, Assoc Prof, 1992, Hd of Dept, 1998, Univ of Malaya. Publications: Book: Lawatan Lain, 1995; Var pprs and articles in jrnls and mags. Honours: ARCS, 1982; DIC, 1985; Natl Young Scientist Awd, 1995. Memberships: Malaysian Inst of Phys; NY Acady of Sci, 1991; Artificial Intelligence Soc; Intl Neural Networks Soc. Hobby: Poetry. Address: Physics Department, University of Malaya, 50603 Kuala Lumpur, Malaysia.

WAN Shaofen, b. 1930 Nanchang. Party Offic; Economist; Lawyer. Education: Zhongzheng Univ. Appointments: Joined CCP, 1952; Ldng Sec CCP Cttee Jiangxi, 1985-87; Chmn Prov Women's Fedn Jiangxi, 1983-85; Dep Hd Utd Front World Dept of CCP Cntrl Cttee, 1988-; Vice-Chmn Overseas Chinese Affairs Cttee; Advsr Women Entrepreneurs' Assn; NPC Dep Tibet Autonomous Reg. Memberships: Mbr CCP Cntrl Cttee, 1985-; Mbr CCP Cntrl Discipline Inspection Commn, 1992-; Mbr 8th NPC Standing Cttee, 1993-; Mbr Preliminary Wrkng Cttee of the Preparatory Cttee of the Hong Kong Specl Admin Reg, 1993-96. Address: The Uniterd Front Work Department of the CCP Central Committee, Beijing, People's Republic of China.

WANG Ao Ge, b. 7 Mar 1928, Dandong. Professor. m. Wei Sin Wang, 1 May 1956, 1 s, 1 d. Education: Grad Cert, Univ. Appointment: Dir, Dept of Path, 1979-95. Publications: Malakoplakia, 1982; Effect of cridium monier, 1990. Honours: Advd Worker, Tech Innovation Awd, 1958, 1960; Advd Worker Awd, 1973. Memberships: Chinese Medl Assn; Chinese Pharm Soc. Hobbies: Western classical music; Playing piano and flute. Address: Jinzhou Medical College, Jinzhou City, Liaoning Province, China 121000,

WANG Bao-Ping, b. 9 Jan 1952, Tengzhou Cty, Shandong, China. Doctor. m. Chen Jie, 8 June 1980, 1 d. Education: Bachelor degree, Jining Medl Coll, Clin Med Dept. Appointment: Dir, Jining Blood Vessel Hosp of the Old Pres Hemodilution Rsch Inst under Jining Medl Coll. Publications: Bsic & Clinical Hemorrheology, 1994; Hemorrheology, 1989; Blood Life Balance Medicine - Medical Developing Direction of 21st Century, Outstndng Article Prize, Hong Kong, 1997. Honours: Rsch Fell, China Confucius Inst; Hon Dir, 97 Hong Kong Intl Tradl Medl Acady. Membership: Dir, Blood Balance Rsch Cntr under China Hlth Protection Sci & Technol Inst, 1999. Hobbies: Sports; Music; Literature. Address: Jining Blood Vessel Hospital of the Old North of Non Dai Village of 327 RD, Jining, Shandong, China.

WANG Bu Xuan, b. 5 Feb 1922, Jiangsu, China. Teacher; Researcher. m. Bao-Ci Gu, 4 July 1948, 2 s, 1 d. Education: BS, Mechl Engrng, Tsinghua Univ, 1943; MSME, Pardue Univ, 1949. Appointments: Assoc Prof, Peking Univ, 1950; Prof, Chmn, Grp of Thermodynamics and Heat Transfer, 1961; Dir, Rsch Inst of Therm Sci and Engrng, Tsinghua Univ, 1984. Publications: 10 Textbooks; 2 Monographs; Over 500 Refereed Pprs, Therm Sci and Engrng. Honours: Academician of China Acady of Sci, 1980-; Rsch Fellshp Awd. Memberships: China Solar Energy Soc; China Sect of ISES; Chinese Soc of Engrng Thermophysics. Hobbies: Heat transfer; Thermophysical properties of matter; Energy planning. Address: Thermal Engineering Dept, Tsinghua University, Beijing 100084, China.

WANG Chen-Ya, b. 26 Mar 1922, He-Nan Provcl, Zhen-Ping Country. Composer. m. Wen-Xian, 1948, 1 s, 3 d. Education: Grad, Natl Conservatory of Music Composition Dept. Appointments: Chf of Composition Dept, 1972; Asst Chf of Cntrl Conservatory of Music, 1986. Publications: Compositions: Three Couplets on Yang Kuan (choral); Movements for Jire-Zhai Valley (orch); Book: Pentatonic Scale and Its harmony. Honour: Lifelong Allowance Awarded by the Govt to Those Who

Made a Spec Contbn. Membership: Perm Mbr, Assn of Chinese Musicians. Hobby: Travel. Address: Central Conservatory of Music, Beijing 100031, China.

WANG Cheng Huan, b. 23 May 1937, Yongian of Hebei, China. Senior Engineer, Port Construction. m. Wang Gui Yun, 18 Jan 1961, 2 s. Education: Dip, Tianjin, China. Appointments: Engr, 1978-88; Vice Dir, Chf Engr, Jingtang Harbor Bur, Snr Engr, Prof Snr Engr, 1991-96. Silty Sand Movement for Port Engineering, 1996. Honours: Four first level of provincial level in technol adv, 1992; State Level Expert, 1993; State Level Labour Model, 1996. Hobbies: Reading books; Watching TV. Address: Jingtang Harbor Bureau, Tangshan 063611, Hebei, China.

WANG Cheng Zu, b. 20 Sept 1934, Guizhou, China. Musician. m. Wei Qi Hua, 1954, 2 s, 2 d. Education: BA. Appointments: Chmn, Musicians Assn, Qiandongnan, 1984-95; Dean, Music Theory Cttee, Guizhou Musicians Assn, 1995-98. Publications include: Collection of Lusheng Music in Leshan County, 1981; To Music Teachers in High and Primary Schools, 1982; Composing Songs, 1988; Kam Minority Songs in Paris, 1990. Honours: Tour State Prizes. Memberships: Chinese Musicians Assn, 1985-98; Soc for Chinese Minority Natl Music, 1986-98; Standing Dir, Guizou Musicians Assn. Hobbies: Music; Literature; Writing. Address: The Culture Association, Kaili City, Qiandongnan Autonomous Prefecture, Guizhou 556000, China.

WANG Chien-Shien, b. 7 Aug 1938 Anhwei. Politician. m. Fa-jau Su. Education: Harvard Univ USA. Appointments: Snr Specialist Taxation and Tariff Commn min of Fin, 1971-73; Dir 1st Div Dept of Taxation, 1973-76; Dir 4th Dept Exec Yuan, 1976-80; Dir-Gen Dept of Customs Admin min of Fin, 1980-82; Dir-Gen Pub Fin Trng Inst, 1982-84; Admin Vice-Min of Econ Affairs, 1984-89; Polit Vice-Min, 1989-90; Min of Fin, 1990-92; Sec-Gen New Party, 1994-. Publications: Sev wrks on income tax and bus. Honours: Asian Fin Min of the Yr, 1992. Memberships: Mbr Legis Yuan, 1993-. Address: New Party, 4th Floor, 65 Guang Fuh S Road, Taipei, Taiwan.

WANG Chunlin, b. 23 Mar 1960, Leshan Cty, Sichuan Prov, China. Administrator. m. Huang Youling, 26 Sept 1985, 1 s, 1 d. Education: BSc, SW Agric Univ. Appointments: Div of Plant Quarantine, Bur of Plant Protection, Natl Plant Protection Stn, MOA, 1982-87; Agronomist, Natl Plant Protection Stn, MOSA, 1987-92; Dpty Dir, Div of Plant Quarantine, NPQS, MOA, 1992-95; Dir, Div of Plant Quarantine, Natl Agro-Tech Extension and Serv Cntr, MOA, 1995; Asst Gov, Liaocheng Admin Off, Shandong Prov; Vice Gv, Yanggu Co Govt, Sec, Yanggu Cttee of Chinese Communist Party, 1996-97; Dir, Plant Quaratine Div, NATESC, MOA, 1998. Publications include: Breach of Vitalizing Economy in Less Developed Area, 1996; Discussion on Township Enterprise Reform, 1996; Seed Engineering, Plant Quarantine and Development of China's Agriculture, 1997; Agriculture Industrialization Is the Only Way to Realize the Second Leap of Rural Areas, 1998; Occurrence and Control of Liriomyza sativae Blanchard, 1998. Honours include: 3rd Level Awd, Seed World, 1987; Excellent Wrks, Chinese Agric Press, 1993; Invention and Innovation Sci-Tech Star, Natl Bur in China Technol Info Promotion System, UN, 1995; Excellent Cadre for concurrent post in grassroot of MOA, 1998. Memberships include: Cncl, Sci and Technol cttee of Chinese Grass Assn, 1995; Ed, Plant Protection Technol and Extension, 1997; Vice-Chf, Chinese Plant Quarantine Assn, 1998. Hobby: Fine arts. Address: 20 Mai Zi Dian Street, Natl Agro-Tech Extension & Serv Cntr, Beijing 100026, China.

WANG Cun-Xin, b. 7 Nov 1943, Jiangsu, China. Biophysicist; Educator. m. Chen Wei-Zu, 20 Feb 1970, 1 s, 1 d. Education: BS, Univ of Sci and Technol of China, Beijing, 1968; Grad, Univ of Sci and Technol, Hefei, 1980; Postdoct, Rutgers Univ, 1985-86. Appointments: Asst, Univ of Sci and Technol, Hefei, 1980-82; Lectr, 1982-90, Assoc Prof, 1990-96, Prof, Biophys, 1996-98, 1998-, Beijing Polytech Univ. Publications: Over 40

articles in profl jrnls. Honour: 2nd Awd, Natural Sci, Chinese Acady of Scis, 1996. Memberships: Biophys Soc of China; Assoc Mbr, Intl Cntr for Theoretical Phys. Hobby: Theoretical studies of structure. Address: Center for Biomedical Engineering, Beijing Polytechnic University, Beijing 100022, China.

WANG Da Peng, b. 28 Aug 1946, Nanjing, China. Professor of Chinese Traditional Medicine. m. Xu Meizi, 2 Sept 1973, 2 d. Education: MD Deg; Dr Deg. Appointments: Dr, Tianjin Metallurgy Hosp, 1970-78; Prof, Tianjin Trad Med Univ, 1978-. Publications: Thinking Mode and Basic Viewpoints of Traditional Medicine, 1991; 14 books, 170 articles, 130 compositions. Honours include: Grand Prizes, Best Pprs on World Trad Med, 1996. Memberships: Countrywide Cttee Mbr, Trad Med Learned Soc; Dir of 9 assns. Hobbies: Art; Literature. Address: 3-104 Building 4, Linxiangli Lane, Qijing Lu Road, Hedong District, Tianjin 300012, China.

WANG Daqi, b. 11 Nov 1935. University Teacher. m. Li Huatian 15 July 1967, 2 d. Education: Grad, Wuhan Univ, 1961. Appointments: Asst Instr, Wuhan Univ, 1961-73; Asst Instr, Lectr, Assoc Prof, Prof, Zhongshan Univ, 1973-. Publications: Algorithms with Automatically Adjustable Properties; Some of Problems in Non-Linear Functional Analysis. Honours: Awd of Sci and Technol Achievement, Zhongshan Univ, 1977; Awd, Meeting of Sci of Guangdong, 1978; 3 Awd, Ex Ppr, Guangzhou Assn for Sci and Technol, 1988, 1989, 1991; Awd of Nat Sci of Guangdong Govt, 1989; Spec Allowance for Outstndng Contbn, Govt, PRC, 1992; Cert of Sci and Technological Achievement of SSTCC, 1993; Awd of Inv and Innovation Sci-Tech Star, UN TIPS Natl Bur, China, 1996; Cert of Imp Sci Achievement of World Chinese, Intl Econ Estimate (HK) Cntr, 1999. Memberships: China Assn for Maths; A Routine Bd Dir and Assoc Bd Chair, Systs Engrng Soc of Guangzhou, 1987-. Hobby: Mathematics and Its Application. Address: Department of Mathematics, Zhonghsan University, Guangzhou, China.

WANG Dashou, b. 30 Nov 1944, Kunming, Yunnan, China. Professor. m. Jun Ma, 1 May 1976, 1 d. Education: MS. Appointments: Network Grp Dir, Elec Engrng Dept, Testing Cntr Dir, Elec Equipment, Dalian Maritime Univ. Publications: A Method of Passive Filter Designing by Optimization, 1993. Honours: 1st Class Awd, Tech Innovation, Dalian City, 1996; 2nd Class Awd, Superior Achievement in Computer Application, Dalian, 1996. Memberships: Chf Sec, CAS Comm; Liaoning Elec Assn & Graph Theory Br; Dir, China Elec Assn. Hobby: Sport. Address: Information Engineering College, Dalian Maritime University, Dalian, Liaoning 116026, China.

WANG Dexiao, b. 11 Apr 1934, Shanghai, China. Professor. m. Zhu Huixia, 27 July 1957, 1 s, 1 d. Education: PhD, Russian. Appointments: Tutor, Russian, Shanghai Intl Stdies Univ, 1979-; Prin, Universal Pt-time Sch of For Langs and Sci Technol, 1984-; Dpty Dean, Acad Affairs, 1986-89, Dpty Dir, Divsn of Grad Studies, 1989-92, Shanghai Intl Stdies Univ. Publications: History of WWII, vol 1, 1978; Usage of Russian Verb Tenses, 1979; Russian Language Grammar Rhetoric, 1981; Collection of Theses on Modern Russian Language Syntex Published in the Soviet Union, 1983; Annotated Concise Russian-Chinese Dictionary, 1985; Theoretical Aspects of the Russian Language - A Teaching Program, 1989; Grammar of the Russian Language, 1990; Book of Russian Synonyms, 1991. Honour: Spec Welfare of Chinese Govt Awd. Memberships: Shanghai CPPCC; Shanghai Municipal Cttee, Dir, Cttee on Liaison Work, Jiu San Acad Soc; Vice Dir, Cttee on Acad Affairs, SISU; Dir, Shanghai Univs Overseas Cmmn Fedn. Hobby: Travel. Address: 3/13 You Yi Yi Cun, Guang Lin Yi Road, Shanghai 200083, China.

WANG Dezi, b. 27 June 1927, Tai-Xing City, Jiang-Su Prov. Professor. m. Hong Feng-Qing, Nov 1953, 2 d. Education: Grad, Dept of Geol, Nanjing Univ, 1950. Appointment: Prof, Nanjing University. Publications: Optical Mineralogy, 1974; Petrology of Volcanic Rocks, 1982; The Mesozoic Volcanic - Intrusive Complexes and Their Metallogenic Relations in East China, 1996.

Honours: Natl Nat Sci Awd (2 Class), 1982; Sci Progress Awd (1st Class), 1991; Mbr Chinese Acady of Scis, 1997. Hobbies: Beijing Opera; Travelling. Address: Department of Geology, Nanjing University, Nanjing City, China.

WANG Eric Min-Yang, b. 13 Feb 1953, Kaohsiung, Taiwan. Educator. m. Mu-Mei Hsia, 22 Dec 1983, 2 s. Education: BS, Dept Indl Mngmt, Natl Cheng Kung Univ, Tainan, Taiwan, 1975; ME, Hum Factors, Dept of Indl Engrng, TX A&M Univ, Coll Stn, TX, USA, 1983; PhD, Indl Ergonomics, Dept of Hum Wrk Scis, Lulea Univ, Sweden, 1992. Appointments: Indl Engr, San-Fu Motor Co Ltd, Taichung, 1977-78; Prodn Planner, Timex (Taiwan) Co Ltd, Chung-Li, Taiwan, 1978-79; Exec Admnstr, Tjing-Ling Indl Rsch Inst, Taipei, 1979-80; Lectr, Ming-Chi Inst of Technol, Taipei, 1983-84; Mngng Dir, Chuan-Wei Cnsltng Engrs Co Ltd, Taipei, 1983-85; Lectr, Natl Tsing Hua Univ, Hsinchu, 1983-92; Cnsltng Ergonomist, Indl Technol Rsch Inst, Hsinchu, 1991-92; Assoc Prof, Ming-Hsin Inst of Technol, Hsinchu, 1992-93; Assoc Prof, Chung Yuan Christian Univ, Chung-Li, 1993-94; Assoc Prof, 1992-, Dir, Off of Engrng and Maintenance Servs, 1998, Dean of Gen Affairs, 1998-, Natl Tsing Hua Univ, Hsinchu. Publications: Books incl: Industrial Pollution Prevention by Management, 1987; (ed) Industrial Ergonomics Application Handbook, 1998; Searching System for Computerized Anthropometric Database, 1998; Tech reports, jrnl and conf pprs. Honour: Phi Tau Phi Hon Soc. Memberships: Hum Factors and Ergonomics Soc; Ergonomics Soc of Taiwan, exec cncl, 1993-97; Pan Pacific Cncl on Occupational Ergonomics, 1997-. Address: Department of Industrial and Engineering Management, National Tsing Hua University, 101, Sec 2, Kuang Fu Road, Hsinchu 30043, Taiwan.

WANG Erqi, b. 28 Apr 1938, Chengdu, Sichuan. Construction Engineer. m. Zhongsu Liao, 1963, 1 s. Education: Bachelor degree. Appointments: Dir, Dept of Tech of SW Arch Inst; Pres, China SW Arch Coll. Publications: Matrix solution for multi free dimension vibration and frequency; Analysis for constructional stress of random loading various in time and space; Optimized design of factory; Optimized design of cultivated land schedule; General method of constructional optimzation; How to prevent continuous landslip. Honour: Sichuan important sci result. Memberships: China Arch; China Optimzation Construction. Address: China Southwest Architecture Design Institute, Chengdu, Sichuan, China 610000.

WANG Guangying, b. 1919 Beijing. Bus Exec. m. 1943. Education: Cath Fudan Univ. Appointments: Set up own bus in Tianjin, 1943; Vice-Chmn China Dem Natl Constrn Assn, 1954; Gaoled for eight yrs during cultural revolution, 1967-75; Vice-Chmn All China Fedn of Ind and Com, 1982; Fndr Chmn and Pres China Everbright Co - China's first trans-natl corp - Hong Kong, 1983-90; Exec Chmn Presidium CPPCC, 1983-; Vice-Chmn 6th CPPCC, 1983-87; Vice-Chmn 7th CPPCC, 1988-; Vice-Chmn Standing Cttee of 8th NPC, 1993-; NPC Dep Tianjin Municipality; A Pres China Cncl for Promoting Peaceful Reunification, 1990-. Honours: Hon Chmn All China Fedn of Ind and Com, 1993-; Hon Vice-Chmn Red Cross Soc of China, 1994-. Address: All China Federation of Industry and Commerce, 93 Beiheyan Dajie, Beijing, People's Republic of China.

WANG Guiming, b. 7 Oct 1932, Tianjin, China. Chief Engineer of China Automotive Technology and Research Center. m. Fan Shujuan, 2 d. Education: BEng, major in Internal Combustion (IC) Engine, Mechl Dept, Tianjin Univ, 1953. Appointments: Engine Plant of First Auto Wrks (FAW), Changchun, Jilin prov, 1954-60; Des & Rsch Inst, China Natl Automotive Ind Corp, 1960-63; Process Engr, 1963-83, Snr Engr, 1983-88, Professorship Snr Engr, 1988: Dpty-Chf Engr, China Automotive Technol & Rsch Cntr, Tianjin, 1985-92; During career, in charge of over 30 plant-des projs inclng Tianjin Mini Vehicle Mfrng Plant, Guangzhou Auto Wrks, Nanjing Auto Wrks, Hunan Auto Wrks, Changchun Automotive Rsch Insts "Red Flag" car plant of FAW; Also employed by Guangzhou Peugeot Auto Corp (Sino-French Jv), Fosti Motorcyle Corp (Sino Am Jv), Tianjin Desiging & Rsch Inst as tech cnslt for sev yrs, travelling to Japan, Germany, Italy, France, Spain for tech investigation.

WANG Gungwu, b. 9 Oct 1930, Indonesia. Historian. m. Margaret Lim, 1955, 1 s, 2 d. Education: Natl Cntrl Univ, Nanking, China; BA, Hons, MA, Univ of Malaya; PhD, Univ of London, 1957. Appointments: Asst Lectr, 1957-59, Lectr, 1959, Univ of Malaya, Singapore; Lectr, 1959-61, Snr Lectr, 1961-63, Dean of Arts, 1962-63, Prof of Hist and Hd of Dept, 1963-68, Univ of Malaya, Kuala Lumpur; Rockefeller Fell, Univ of London, 1961-62; Prof of Far East Hist, 1968-86, Hd of Dept, 1968-75, 1980-86, Dir, Rsch Sch of Pacific Studies, 1975-80, Austl Natl Univ; Snr Visng Fell, Univ of London, 1972; Visng Fell, Univ of Oxford, All Souls Coll, 1974-75; John A Burns Disting Visng Prof of Hist, Univ of HI, 1979; Rose Morgan Visng Prof of Hist, Univ of KS, 1983; Vice Chancellor, Univ of Hong Kong, 1986-95; Exec Chmn, Inst of Esian Polit Econ, Singapore, 1996-97; Dir, E Asian Inst Natl Univ of Singapore, 1997-. Publications include: Community and Nation: Essays on Southeast Asia and the Chinese, 1981; Society and the Writer: Essays on Literature in Modern Asia (ed M Guerrero and D Marr), 1981; Dongnanya yu Huaren (Southeast Asia and the Chinese), 1987; Nanhai Maoyi yu nanyang Huaren (Chinese Trade and Sputheast Asia), 1988; Changing Identities of Southeast Asian Chinese since World War II (ed w J Cushman), 1988; Lishi di gongneng (The Function of History), 1990; The Chineseness of China, 1991; China and the Chinese Overseas, 1991; Zhonguo yu Haiwai Huaren, 1994; The Chinese Way: China's Position in International Relations, 1995; Global History and Migrations (ed), 1997; The Nanhai Trade, 1998; China and South East Asia: Myths, Threats and Culture, 1999; General Editor of East Asian Historical Monographs Series for Oxford University Press, 30 vols published since 1968; Articles on Chinese and Southeast Asian History in intl jrnls; Contbr to collected vols on Asian History. Honours: Emer Prof, Austl Natl Univ; FAHA; CBE, 1990; Mbe, Academica Sinica, 1992; For Hon Mbr, Amn Acady of Arts and Sci, 1995; Hon DLitt, Univ of Sydney, 1991, Univ of Hull, 1998; Hon LLD Monash Univ, 1993, Austl Natl Univ, 1996, Univ of Melbourne, 1997. Memberships include: Dir, E Asian Hist of Science Foundation Ltd, Hong Kong, 1987-; Fell, Hon Corresp Mbr for Hong Kong, Royal Soc of Arts, London; Exec Cncl, Hong Kong, 1990-92. Hobbies: Music; Reading; Walking. Address: #08-02, 7 Ardmore Park, Singapore 9954.

WANG Guozhi, b. 15 Sept 1936, Yiu Lin, Shann'xi, China. Professor. m. Li Lijuan, 1 Feb 1961, 2 d. Education: BSc. Appointments: Asst Prof, Univ, 1958-77; Asst Prof, 1977-86; Prof, Xian Inst of Opt and Prcs, 1986-. Honours: 2nd Class Awd, Dev of Sci and Technique; 1st Class Awd, Dev of Sci and Technique; 2nd Class Awd, Dev of Sci and Technique. Memberships: China Optical Soc; China Physl Soc. Hobby: Sport. Address: 234 Friend W Rd, 710068 Xian, China.

WANG Hai, b. 1925 Weihai City, Shandong Prov. Army Officer. Education: China's NE Aviation Acady. Appointments: Joined PLA, 1945; Grp Cmdr air force brig and sent to Korean battlefield, 1950; Promoted Col PLA, 1964; Cmdr Air Force of Guangzhou Mil Reg, 1975-83; Dep Cmdr PLA Air Force, 1983-85; Cmdr PLA Air Force, 1985; Promoted Gen PLA, 1988. Memberships: Mbr CCP 12th Cntrl Cttee, 1985-87; Mbr 13th Cntrl Cttee, 1987-92; Mbr 14th Cntrl Cttee, 1992-. Address: Ministry of Defence, Beijing, People's Republic of China.

WANG Han Gong, b. 16 Oct 1940, Jiyuan Prov, China. Vice-Director. m. Zhang Hui Qing, 18 Sept 1967, 1 s, 1 d. Education: Grad. Appointments: Vice-Dir, Fac off dir, Fac Off; Vice Dir, 2nd Artillery Logistic Sci and Technol Inst. Publications: Optics Apparatus Basics, 1983; Operation & Maintenance Engineering of Missiles, 1987; Maintenance Management of Equipment, 1996. Honours: Army Sci and technol Prog Awd Grade I, 1996, 1997; Natl Sci and Technol Prog Awd, Grade I, 1998. Memberships: Technol Cttee, Chinese Equipment Assn; Cncl Mbr, Surface Engrng Branch; Chinese Mechanism Engrng Assn. Hobbies: Basketball; Volleyball; Middle-distance races. Address: 203 Second Artilery Engineering Institute, 710025 Xian, China.

WANG Hanbin, b. 28 Aug 1925 Fujian Prov. State and Party Official. m. Peng Peiyun, 2 s, 2 d. Appointments: Joined CCP in Burma, 1941; Dep Sec-Gen NPC Legal Commn, 1979-80; Vice-Chmn and Sec-Gen NPC Legal Commn, 1980-83 Dep Sec-Gen Polit and Legal Commn of CCP Cntrl Cttee, 1980-82; Dep Sec-Gen Constitution Revision Cttee of PRC, 1980-82; VP Chinese Law Soc, 1982-91; Dep Sec-Gen 5th NPC Standing Cttee, 1982-83; Dep Sec-Gen of Presidium of NPC, 1982-87; Chmn Legis Affairs Commn, 1983-; Dep for Beijing to 6th NPC, 1983-88; Sec-Gen NPC Standing Cttee, 1983-87; Vice-Chmn Cttee for Drafting Basic Law of Hong Kong Specl Admin Zone of People's Repub of China, 1988-; Dep for Fujian to 7th NPC, 1986, 1987; Standing Chmn Presidium of All the Sess 7th 8th NPC; Vice-Chmn NPC 7th Standing Cttee, 1988-93; Vice-Chmn Standing Cttee 8th NPC, 1993-; Vice-Chmn Preparatory Cttee Hong Kong Specl Admin Reg, 1995-. Honours: Hon Pres Chinese Law Soc, 1991-. Memberships: Mbr 12th CCP Cntrl Cttee, 1982-86; Mbr Presidium of All the Sess 7th 8th NPC; Mbr 13th Cntrl Cttee, 1987-92; Mbr 14th Cntrl Cttee, 1992-; Alt mbr Politburo, 1992-. Hobby: Bridge. Address: c/o National People's Congress Standing Committee, Beijing, People's Republic of China.

WANG Hao, b. 14 May 1931, Jiangsu, China. Educator; Researcher. m. Lin Rongzhen, 14 June 1952, 1 s, 2 d. Education: Dip, Dept of Bio, Nanjing Univ. Appointments: Assoc Prof, 1982, Prof, 1987, Dept of Bio, Nanjing Univ. Publication: Sev articles in profl jrnls. Honour: Invention Prize in Sci, China, 1992. Membership: Vice Chmn, Zoology Soc, Jiangsu, 1985-94. Hobby: Research. Address: Department of Biology, Nanjing University, Nanjing 210093, China.

WANG Hongxun, b. 10 Nov 1939, Pingyi County, Shandong Prov, China. College Teacher. m. Liu Ruizhi, 8 Aug 1962, 2 d. Education: Bachelor degree, Shandong Tchr's Univ. Appointments: Lectr, 1980; Assoc Prof, 1986; Hd of Tchng and Rsch Sect, 1988-; Prof, 1993. Publications: Practical Care of Traditional Chinese Medicine, 1989; Traditional Chinese Medicine Care, 1993; Observation on Improvement of Sports Ability and Intelligence Through Regular Vital Point Attacking and Brain Care Massage, 1998. Honour: 2nd Prize, Tchng, Shandong Phys Educ Inst, 1986. Memberships: Chmn, All-China Higher Colls Sports Med Tchng Rsch Bd, 1981; Mngng Dir, Shandong Manipulation Inst, 1982. Hobbies: Music; Dancing. Address: Sports Medicine Teaching and Research Section, Shandong Physical Education Institute, Jinan, China.

WANG Ji Zu, b. 24 Oct 1924, Hebei, China. Professor of Finance. m. Xi Ru Guo, 1958, 1 s, 1 d. Education: PhD, Econs, Univ of Il, Champaign, IL, USA. Appointments: Rsch Assoc, Inst of Intl Rels, Beijing; Prof, Fin Dept, fmr chmn, Nankai Univ. Publications: About 8 books on trade & fin; About 100 articles on fin, econs, trade. Honours: Acad Awd, book, World Economy; 2 articles. Memberships: Vice Chmn, Fin Assn; Fin Trade Assn of Tianjin, China. Hobbies: Table tennis; Chess. Address: Finance Department, Nankai University, Tianjin, China.

WANG Jian, b. 13 Oct 1958, Beijing, China. University Educator. m. Zheng Xuejun, 1 s. Education: Grad Study in Can, Univ Laval, UQAM; BEng, China; Undergrad study in Agric, Univ of Hebei, 1978-82; 3 terms grad courses study, VXian, 1983; Dalian, 1984; Beijing, 1985; PhD student, Laval, 1989-92. Publications: Occidental Economics, 1998; Information Energy and Management, 1997, 30 compositions. Honours: Sn Agric Advsr, TC Union Trade Co Ltd, 1997-98; Acad ppr awds, 2 in Hebei Prov, 2 in Beijing Cty, 2 in Agric Univ of Hebei. Memberships: RSS Mbr of Amn, 1996-98; Agricl Techeconomics Assn, 1994-2001; VP, Price Assn of Baoding; MME System Engrng Soc. Hobbies: Table tennis; Swimming; Natural science reading. Address:

Economic Management College, Agricultural University of Hebei, Baoding City, Hebei Province, China, 071001.

WANG Jian Guo, b. 1 July 1938, Nan Pin, Fujian, China. Science Researcher. m. Wang Bi Sheng, 16 July 1966, 1 s. 1 d. Education: BSc, Beijng Agricl Mechanization Coll. Appointments: Engr, Dir, Rsch Dept, 1980; Dpty Chief Engr, Fujian Acady of Mech Scis, 1985; Snr Engr, 1987; Prof Snr Engr. Publications: Many pprs about agricl machinery rsch & mech & elec info. Honours: Achievement Prize, Natl Sci Meeting; Second Class Sci Tech Achievement Prize, Machinery Min; Third Class Sci Tech Progress Prize, Machinery Min; Ex Expert, Fujian Prov, Fujian Provl Govt; Elect Advd Worker, Natl Sci Tech Info Syst, Natl Sci Tech Cttee, Chinese Acady of Scis. Address: 115 Liuiyi Road, Fuzhou, Fujian, China.

WANG Jianli, b. 23 May 1955, Beijing, China. Medicine. Appointments: Licenced Acupuncturist, 1997; Dr Naturopathic Med, 1999. Publication: Acupuncture Treat Mariuana Withdrawal Syndrome on Oriental Medicine Journal, 1996. Honour: Received by Pope John Paul II in Vatican, 8 June 1988. Membership: West Returned Schl Assn, Beijing, China. Hobbies: Music; Politics; Poetry; Movies; Travel; Sports, Dance. Address: 10735 Ross Road, #317 Bothell, WA 98011, USA.

WANG Jilun, b. 3 Dec 1930, Shenyang, China. Director, Geophysical Exploration Bureau; Senior Geophysicist; Professor. m. Zhang Hongyu, 1 Jan 1955, 1 s, 2 d. Education: Degree in Applied Phys, Dalian Indl Coll, 1952. Appointments: Field Geophysicist, gravity and ground EM survey, 1962-70; Rsch Geophysicist, magnetic and gravity data processing w linear filtering and IP dev, 1970-83; Dir, Geophysical Exploration Bur, Min of Metallurgical Ind, Visng Prof, NE Univ of Technol, tchr, doct studs, 1983-; In charge, Natl Gold Sci and Techl Proj for Geophysl and Geocheml Exploration; Involved in IP theory and intergrated airborne geophysics dev; Dir, GEB, MII, 1983-90; Cnslt Geophysicist, GEB, MII, 1991. Publications: Fundamental characteristics of an approximate correction method for EM coupling in frequency-domain induced polarization; Designing principles of a two-dimensional optimum linear digital filter; Intrinsic Relationship Between Surface and Volume Polarizations in frequency domain IP Method, 1989; Geophysical and Geochemical Exploration for Gold in China - Research and Applications, 1997. Honours: Advd Sci and Techl Worker, 1978, 3 Sci and Techl Rsch Awds, 1981, 1983, 1997, Min of Metallurgical Ind; Excellent Profl Rschr, Baoding Cty Govt, 1987; Expert w Outstndng Contbn and Spec Govt Subsidy, 1992. Memberships: Bd of Dirs, Chinese Geophysical Soc; VP, Hebei Provincial Geophysical Soc; VP, Inst of Geol, Chinese Soc of Metals; Bd of Dirs, Enterprisers Soc of Baoding Cty, Hebei; Mbr Specialists Cttee, Natl Modern Geoexploration Technol Rsch Cntr, 1995. Hobbies: Classical music; Chinese calligraphy. Address: Geophysical Exploration Bureau, Ministry of Metallurgical Industry, No 38 Hancun North Road, Baoding City, Hebei Province, China.

WANG Jing-hu, b. 9 Jan 1936, Ning-Po, China. Senior Engineer; Chief Engineer. m. Cao Yu-fang, 1 Oct 1979, 2 s. Education: Grad, Tianjin Univ, 1960. Appointments: Techn, Shanghai Hu-Dong Shipyard, 1960-62 and Shanghai No 4 Machine Tool Works, Aug-Sept, 1962; Joined, 1962, Engr, 1979, Vice-Dir, 1983, Chf Engr, 1983-86, Dir, 1986-90, Snr Engr, 1988-90, Shanghai Automobile Engines Works; Chf Engr, Snr Engr, Shanghai Tractor & ICE Corp, 1990-95; Dir, RDC of Shanghai Tractor & ICE Corp, 1992-95; Retd, 1996; Tech Cnslt, Shanghai Benz Co, 1996-98; Chf Engnr, Automobile Engine Co, WC Investments Grp, Ltd, 1998-. Publications: The Calculation Method for the Disc of Turbine Machinery, 1963; The Piston Ring, 1978; Gas Flow in the Internal Combustion Engine, 1981; The Internal Combusion Engine, 1982; The Unusual Engines, 1990; Theory of Quantitative Analysis, 1991; The Unusual Engine in Theory and Practice, 1998. Honours: 1st Prize, Ex Organiser for Tech Coop, 1987; 2nd Prize for Enterprise Mngmt, 1988; 3rd Prize, Voice of Men of

Enterprise, Chinese daily Newsppr Bright, 1989; 3rd Prize for Enterprise Mngmt, 1989. Memberships: Soc of Automotive Engrs (Intl); Stndng Cttee, Shanghai Soc of Internal Combustion Engrs; Stndng Cttee, Shanghai Soc for Automotive Engrs; Stndng Cttee, Chinese Soc for Internal Combustion Engrs. Hobbies: Enterprise Management; Writing and Translating Technical Papers; Writing Novels, Poems and Comments. Address: Room 2206, Building 3/2021, Chang-yang Road, Shanghai 200090, China.

WANG Jiuling, b. 26 Apr 1932, Gao Yang County, Hebei Prov, China. Teacher. m. Li Yingxiu, 1 Oct 1960, 1 s, 1 d. Education: PhD, Leningrad Forestry Univ, USSR. Appointment: Ldr, Silviculture Lab, 1980-87. Publications: Silviculture, 1987; Collection of Forestry Technology in North China, 1992; Forestry Division, Chinese Agricultural Encyclopedia, 1993. Honours: 1st Awd, Natl Sci and Tech Dev, 1988; The 1st awds of Sci and Tech Min of Forestry, 1994; 3rd Awd, Natl Sci and Tech Dev. Memberships: Chinese Forestry Soc, 1960-; Cnslt Grp of Beijing Municipality, 1978-; Nat Sci Fndn Convention. Hobbies: Reading; Sports. Address: PO Box 116, College of Forestry Resource and Environment, Beijing Forestry University 100083, China.

WANG Ke Qian, b. 9 Apr 1930. Philosopher. Div, 1 s, 1 d. Education: Dip, Sverdlov Law Sch, USSR, 1953-57. Appointments: Dir of Rsch Sect. Publications: Books: Comments on Existentialism, 1982; On Jean Paul Sartre, 1985; What is Value, 1992. Honours: Awd for Outstndng Papers in Shanghai Acady of Socl Sci for Achievements in Philosl Stdy in Shanghai, 1993. Memberships: Cncl Mbr, Chinese Assn of Mod Western Philos; Exec Dir, Shanghai Philos Assn. Hobby: Reading. Address: Philosophy Institute, 7 Lane, 622 Huai Hai Zhong Road, Shanghai, China.

WANG Liankui, b. 3 Sept 1929, Shangdong, China. Geologist. Education: Univ of Chinghua, Beijing, 1951; Beijing Coll of Geol, 1952-55; Postgrad as PhD, Acad USSR, Moscow, 1960. Appointments: Trainee Rschr, Inst of Geol, Academia Sinica, 1956; Rsch Asst of Geol, Inst of Geol and Inst of Geochem, Academia Sinica, 1962-78; Assoc Rsch Prof, Geochem, 1978, Rsch Prof, Guangzhou Inst of Geochem 1986-99. Publications: Geochemistry of Granite in South China, book, 1979; On Skernoid, 1960; Evolution of Granite of Two Series, 1982; Liquid Segregation of Granite and Mineralization, 1983; Relationship Between Zonal Distribution of Granite and Plate, 1984; Three in One Evolution-Model for Granite Type U-Ore Deposits in South China; Double Differentiations of Rare-Metal Mineralized Granites, 1995. Honours: 2nd Deg Nation Prize of Nature Sci, 1980; 2nd Deg Prize of Sci and Technol, Academia Sinica, 1984; 2nd Deg Prize, Nat Sci in GD prov, 1994; 2nd Deg Prize, Sci and Technol in GD Prov, 1996. Memberships: Standing Cttee Mbr, Cttee of Petrology, Chinese Soc of Geol, 1975-95; Cnclr, Cttee of Petrology, Geochem Soc, 1978-95. Hobbies: Drama; Reading. Address: Guangzhou Institute of Geochemistry, Chinese Academy of Sciences, Guangzhou, Wushan 510640, China.

WANG Lin-Fa, b. 31 May 1960, Shanghai, China. Scientist. m. Meng Yu, 4 Aug 1984, 1 s, 1 d. Education: BSc, 1982; PhD, 1986. Appointments: Undergrad Stud, Dept of Biol, E China Normal Univ, 1981-82; Postgrad, 1982-86, Postdoct, 1986-89, Dept of Biochem, Univ CA, Davis; Adj Assoc Prof, Molecular Biol Lab, E China Normal Univ, 1989-; Snr Tutor, Dept of Biochem, 1989-90, Snr Rsch Offr, Cntr for Molecular Biol and Med, 1990, Monash Univ; Rsch Sci, 1990-92, Snr Rsch Sci, Project Ldr, 1992-96, Prin Rsch Sci, Project Ldr, 1996-, CSIRO Austl Animal Hlth Lab, Geelong, Vic. Publications: over 60 sci articles in profl jrnls. Honours: Outstndng Undergrad Awd, E China Normal Univ, 1981-82; Chinese Govt Schlshp, Min of Educ, China, 1982-83; Peter J Shields Fellshp, Univ CA, Davis, 1984-85; Jastro-Shields Grad Rsch Schlshp, Univ CA, Davis, 1984-85; Earle C Anthony Fellshp, Univ CA, Davis, 1985-86; UCD Grad Rsch Awd, 1985-86; Rsch Awd, Outstndng Young Scientist, Natl Sci Fndn of China, 1988-90; Rsch Awd, Outstndng Young Univ Tchrs, Huo-Ying-Dong Educ

Fndn, 1992-95; Nominee, Participant, CEO's Workshop for CSIRO Outstndng Yng Staff, 1994. Memberships: Amn Soc of Microbio; Austl Soc for Biochem and Molecular Bio; Austl Soc for Microbio. Hobbies: Reading; Gardening; Tennis. Address: Private Mail Bag 24, CSIRO DAH AAHL, Geelong 3720, Australia.

WANG Ming-Rong, b. 30 Nov 1956, Anhui, China. Professor. m. Xiao-Ming Wu, 11 Feb 1984, 1 s. Education: PhD, Faculté de Médécine, Clermont I, France, 1993. Memberships: HUGO, 1997; Chinese Medl Assn, 1995; Genetics Soc of China, 1995. Address: National Laboratory of Molecular Oncology, Cancer Institute, CAMS, PUMC, Panjiayuan, Chaoyang Qu, P O Box 2258, Beijing 100021, China.

WANG Pei-Yen, b. 1 Feb 1926. Thoracic Surgeon. m. Shu-Mei Chu, 24 Oct 1954, 2 s, 1 d. Education: MB, Natl Def Med Cntr, 1952. Appointments: Surg Res, 1952-57; Thoracic Surg, First Army Gen Hosp, 1957-65; Fellshp, Sloan Kettering Mem Hosp, 1965-67; Chf of Thoracic Surg, 1968-74; Chf of Exp Surg, Taipei Veterans Gen Hosp, 1974-82; Chmn, Dept of Surg, Taichung Veterans Gen Hosp, 1982-94. Memberships include: Intl Coll of Surgs; Cncl Mbr, Assn of Surgs SE Asia; Assn of Thoracic and Cardiovascular Surgs of Asia. Hobbies: Tennis; Go-Go; Chess; Golf. Address: 160 Taichung Kang Road, Section III, Taichung 407, Taiwan.

WANG Quixin, b. 16 Apr 1953, Shangdong, China. University teacher. m. Wang Lianhua, 1 Dec 1985, 1 d. Education: Bachelor of Geog, 1982; Master, Hum Geog, 1985; Dr Human Geog, 1996. Appointments: Vice-Dir, Population Rsch Inst. Publication: China's Population Distribution and Regional Economic Development, 1997. Honour: 1st Rank Prize, for Wrks of Philos & Socl Sci in Shanghai, 1998. Membership: Sec, Shanghai Population Assn, 1994. Hobby: Reading. Address: Population Research Institute, E China Normal University, North Zhang Shan Road, Shanghai, China 200062.

WANG Qi-Zhi, b. 25 Apr 1964, Beijing, China. Associate Professor. m. Zhang Qing-Chun, 27 Sept 1993, 1 d. Education: BE, ME, PhD, Beijing Univ of Aerons & Astrons. Publications: 1 book and 18 pprs. Honours: Natl Awd, 3rd Class, Progress of Sci & Technol, 1988; Awd of 2nd Class, Progress of Sci & Technol, Natl Educn Cttee of China, 1992. Address: Mail Box 508, Department of Flight Vehicle Design & Applied Mechanics, Beijing University of Aeronautics & Astronautics, Beijing 100083, China.

WANG Qun, b. 1926 Xinzhou Hubei. Party Official. Appointments: Sec Hubei Br Communist Yth League, 1978; Dep Sec CCP Cttee Hubei Prov, 1978-82; Sec CCP Cttee Hubei Prov, 1982-83; First Sec CCP Cttee Wuhan Municipality, 1982-87; NPC Dep Inner Mongolia Autonomous Reg Henan Prov; Sec Inner Mongolia Autonomous Regl Cttee, 1987-94; Party Cttee First Sec Inner Mongolia Mil Cmd Area, 1989-94; Chmn Inner Mongolia Autonomous Reg 8th People's Congress, 1993-. Memberships: Alt mbr 12th CCP Cntrl Ctrtee, 1982-87; Mbr 13th Cntrl Cttee, 1987-92; Standing Cttee mbr Inner Mongolian Autonomous Regl Cttee, 1987-94; Mbr 14th Cntrl Cttee, 1992-. Address: Inner Mongolia Autonomous Regional Committee, People's Republic of China.

WANG Run-Wen, b. 1 Mar 1936, Shanghai, China. Head of Basic Research in High Power Lasers. m. 1 Sept 1966, 2 d. Education: Doctor's degree, Zhejiang Univ, China. Appointment: Prof, 1987-. Publication: Laser Physics, 1974. Honours: 1st Class Awd, Sci and Tech, Shanghi, 1988; 2nd Class Awd, Sci and Tech in China, 1990, 1996. Memberships: Optics Soc of China, 1975; Optics Soc of Am, 1985; SPIE Soc of Am, 1990. Hobbies: Optical Physics; Laser Physics. Address: Shanghai Institute of Optics and Fine Mechanics, PO Box 800-211, Shanghai 201800, China.

WANG RuZhu, b. 22 Dec 1964, Jiangsu, China. Professor. m. Chen Zhihong, 1 May 1990, 1 s. Education: B Eng, 1984; M Eng, 1987; PhD Eng, 1990.

Appointments: Asst, 1987; Lectr, 1990; Assoc Prof, 1992; Prof, 1994. Publications: Over 100 peer reviewed pprs 1987-98. Honours: 2nd Prize of Advancement of Sci and Tech, State Educ Comm, 1996; 6th Young Scientist Awd of China, 1998; 3rd Prize of Advancement of Sci and Tech of Shanghai, 1998. Memberships: Standing Dir, Shanghai Soc of Refrigeration; ASHARE; New York Acad of Scis. Address: School of Power and Energy Engineering, Shanghai Jiao Tong University, 1954 Huashan Road, Shanghai 200030, China.

WANG Sen, b. 25 Aug 1932, Beijing, China. Professor. m. Huang Jing, 1 Oct 1956, 1 s, 1 d. Education: BEng, 1953, MEng, 1966, Dept of Electr Engin, Tsinghua Univ. Appointments: Asst, Lectr, Dir of Power Syst Grp, Vice-Chmn, Dept of Electr Engin, 1953-70, Hd of Automation Dept, 1970-75, Assoc Prof, Dir of Tchng Affairs, 1975-83, Prof, Hd of Automation Dept, 1983-, Tsinghua Univ, Beijng. Publications: On The Structure of Knowledge and Ability of Undergraduates in Engineering Institutes; A Simple Discussion on the Development of Persons of Ability in the New Era; Researches in High Education of Engineering. Memberships: Cncl Mbr, Beijing Soc of Higher Educ; 1st Sec-Gen, Higher Engrng, Educ Soc, State Educ Commn. Hobbies: Music; Tennis; Fishing. Address: Department of Automation, Tsinghua University, Beijing, China.

WANG Senhao, b. 1932 Cixi Zhejiang. Govt Official. 2 s. Appointments: Dep to 6th NPC, 1983; Dep Sec CCP Cttee Shaanxi, 1983-93; Gov of Shaanxi Prov, 1983-93; Min of Coal Ind, 1993-98. Memberships: Mbr CPC 4th Prov Cttee Shaanxi, 1983-88; Mbr CCP 12th Cntrl Cttee, 1985-87; Mbr 13th Cntrl Cttee, 1987-92; Mbr 14th Cntrl Cttee, 1992-; Mbr 8th NPC, 1993.

WANG Shaojun, b. 23 Sept 1966, Shanghai, China. Researcher. m. Li Bo, 16 Jan 1997. Education: LLB, 1990, BA, 1992, LLM, 1997, E China Normal Univ; DSc, Shanghai Jiaotong Univ, 1998. Appointments: Shanghai Jiaotong Univ, 1987-98; Visng Schl, Technische Universität, Berlin, 1998. Publications include: The Study on the Thought of Running a State, 1997; Understanding Total Quality Management (transl); Sam Walton, Made in America, My Story (transl). Address: 12-2-805ON Cao Xi Bei Road, Shanghai 200030, China.

WANG Shi Ru, b. 30 Aug 1936, Hebei, China. Teacher. m. Cui Suru, 8 Mar 1962, 2 d. Education: BA, Dept of Lib Study, Peking Univ. Appointments: Chf, Index Ed Rsch Sect, Dept of Lib Study, Beijing Univ. Publications: 42 articles in profl jrnls. Honours: Nations Rsch Work Ex Prize, 1990; Nations Index Study Contbrn Prize, 1994. Memberships: China Inst of Lib Rsch; Sec-Gen, China Cai Yuanpei Study Assn. Hobbies: Music; Reading; Chess. Address: Room 207, Building 313, Yan Bei Garden, Beijing University, Haidian, Beijing 100091, China.

WANG Shi-Hua, b. 10 Aug 1936, Shaanxi, China. Professor; Senior Researcher. m. Wu Qiu-Xia, 6 Aug 1962, 2 s. Education: NW Univ, Xian, 1955-59; Nanjing Univ, 1960-61; Inst of Elem Soedin, Acady of Scis, Moscow, 1965-66. Appointment: Dir of Lab, Dalian Inst of Chem Phys. Publications: Over 60 pprs in profl jrnls. Honours: 2nd State Class Awd, Progress in Sci & Technol, 1992; Govt Specl Subsidy, State Cncl. Memberships: Chinese Chem Soc; Acad Cttee, Dalian Inst of Chem Phys. Address: Dalian Institute of Chemical Physics, Chinese Academy of Sciences, 457 Zhongshan Road, PO Box 110, Dalian 116023, China.

WANG Shi-Liang, b. 2 Apr 1935, Shanghai, China. Doctor. m. Dr Jie-Fang Xu, 8 Mar 1960, 2 d. Education: Grad, Shanghai Second Mil Medl Univ, 1956; Fell to Dr J W Alexander, Shriners Burn Inst, Cincinnati, OH, USA, 1984-85. Appointments: Res, SW Hosp (SP), 3rd Mil Medl Univ (3MMU), 1957-; Attending, SP, 3MMU, 1970-; Vice Prof, SP, 3MMU, 1983-; Prof, SP, 3MMU, 1987-; Dir, Burn Rsch Inst, SP, 3MMU, 1988-. Publications: Over 100 pprs, 1961-98; Jt creator of 20 books (2 as ed-in-chf), 1974-98. Honours: Army Prize of Sci and Technol, 2nd Awd, 1993, 1st Awd, 1996; Natl Prize of Sci and Technol,

2nd Awd, 1997. Memberships: ISBI, 1984; ESPEN, 1992; Chmn, SW Area of Chinese Burn and Plastic Surg Assn, 1996. Address: Burn Research Institute, Southwestern Hospital, Chongging, China 400038.

WANG Shou Chang, b. 15 Nov 1936, Wuchu, Anhui, China. Teacher. m. Dai Xu, 1 Jan 1963, 1 s, 1 d. Education: Dept of Philos, Fudan Univ, 1956-61. Appointments: Tchr, Shandong Univ, 1961-78; Prof, Xiangfan Univ, 1978-88; Prof, S China Normal Univ, 1988-. Publications: Introduction to Western Philosophy; Contemporary American Philosophy; Western Social Philosophy. Honour: Intl Cultural Dip of Hon, ABI, 1995. Memberships: VP, Natl Exec, Chinese Soc for Contem Fgn Philos. Hobby: Swimming. Address: Institute of Philosophy, South China Normal University, Guangzhou 510631, China.

WANG Shou Chun, b. 26 Dec 1930, Jiangyin, Jiangsu, China. Professor. m. Guo Juan Fen, 1 Aug 1959, 1 s, 1 d. Education: Master, Univ of Intl Bus & Econs (cert No 1), 1955. Appointments: Asst, 1955; Lectr, 1963; Assoc Prof, 1981; Prof, 1987. Publications: China's Foreign Ecnomic Relations, 1988; A Complete Work on Foreign Trade and Economic Cooperation System Reform in China, 1995. Honours: Theory & Policy of China's For Trade, Univ Textbook Awd, 1992; China's For Trade Econs, Univ Textbook Awd, 1995. Membership: Cncl Mbr, China Assn of Intl Trade, 1988-. Hobbies: Literature; Music; Photography; Film; TV. Address: University of International Business and Economics, Hepingjie Beikou, Huixindongjie, Beijing 100029, China.

WANG Shouming, b. 9 Oct 1940, Shanghai, China. Professor. m. Ying Liu, 21 Apr 1969, 1 d. Education: BA, E China Normal Univ. Appointments: Lectr, 1968-86, Vice Dean, 1986-94, Assoc Prof, 1986-92, Prof, 1992-94, Chinese Langs Dept, E China Normal Univ; Prof, Intl Chinese Stdies Dept, E China Normal Univ, 1994-. Publications: (co-auth) Grammar, 1978; Rhetoric, 1978; Logic, 1978; (auth) Historical Chinese Phonology, 1986; (co-auth) Shanghai Dictionary, 1989; Chf Ed, Instruction on Self-Study of Historical Chinese, 1991; (auth) About China Dialect, 1992; Responsible for main chapts of: Introduction of Historical Chinese Phonology, 1992; How to Express in Chinese, 1994. Memberships: Assn of Chinese Lang; Inst of Intl Chinese Stdies; Inst of Worldwide Chinese Stdies; Dir, Assn of Histl Chinese Phonology. Hobbies: Calligraphy; Pekin Opera; Music. Address: First Village of East China Normal University, No 622 Rm 1505, Shanghai 200062, China.

WANG Sing-Wu, b. 24 Dec 1920, China. Retired Librarian. m. Chan-Mei (May) Lou, 20 Nov 1957, 3 d. Educations: BA, Natl Univ, Zhejiang, 1944; MA, Aust Natl Univ, 1969; Grad Studies, Sch of Lib Sci, OH, USA, 1960. Appointments: Chf Cataloguer, Chinese Books, Natl Cntrl Lib, China, 1945-49; Chf Libn, Yangmingshan Inst Lib, Taiwan, 1949-55; Dir, Taiwan Provl Lib in Taipei, 1955-64; Chf Libn, Spec Libn, Oriental Sect, Natl Lib of Aust, 1964-85. Publications include: Introduction to Classification of Books, in Chinese, Taipei, 1955; On the Development of Library Services in Taiwan, in Chinese, Taipei, 1963; The Organization of Chinese Emigration, 1948-88, with special reference to Chinese Emigration to Australia, San Francisco, 1978; Recent Development of Library & Information Services in China, 1982; Survey of East Asian Language Collections in Australian Libraries, 1979, 1983; Life of Chinese Gold-Miners in Australian in the Latter Half of the 19th Century, in Chinese, 1987; Chinese Emigration 1840s-1890s; Reactions of Chinese Residents and Chinese Official Representatives in Australia to the White Australia Policy, in Chinese, 1992; and others. Honours: For Libn Prog Awd, US, 1959-60; AM, 1986. Memberships include: Assn for Asian Studies; Asian Studies Assn of Aust; E Asian Libs Resources Grp of Aust, Chmn 1978-79, 1982-84, Newsletter Ed, 1980-81, 1985-86; Libns Grp of Aust, Newsletter Ed, 1980-82, 1985-86, Chmn, 1982-85. Listed in: Many including: Men of Achievement; Who's Who in the World. Address: 123 Namatjira Drive, Fisher, ACT 2611, Australia.

WANG Songjiang, b. 24 Mar 1960, Heilong, Jiang Prov, China. University Teacher; Researcher. m. Ning Ping, 4 Apr 1985, 1 s. Education: Postgrad Dip, Spatial Plng, Univ of Dortmund, Germany; MSc, Spatial Plng, Asian Inst of Technol, Thailand. Memberships: Books: Pilot Community Forestry in Yunnan, 1992; Spatial Planning for Regions of Economic Growth, 1994; Sustainable Management of Forests in Lam Thk Khung Watershed, Thailand, 1995. Memberships: Chinese Soc of Ecology; Chinese Soc of Ecological Econs; Eurn Spatial Plng Assn; Asian-Pacific Community Forestry Assn. Hobbies: Reading; Playing Chess. Address: School of Business Administration, Yunnan Polytechnic University, Kunming 650051, Yunnan, China.

WANG Sujuan, b. 1 May 1928, Yidu County, Shandong Prov, China. Teacher. m. Yu Benkai, 15 Aug 1953, 2 s. Education: BSc, Shandong Univ, 1953. Appointment: Prof of Psychol, Shanghai Fisheries Univ, 1953-. Publications: Cultivation of Seaweeds, 1963; Study on Ultrastructure of Economic Seaweeds in China, 1991; Seaweed Biotechnology, 1994. Honours: 2nd Awd on Sci & Tech Prog of the Min of Agric in China, 1986, 1997; 3rd Awd on Natl Sci & Tech; 1st Shanghai Sci & Technol Fair, Outstndng Prize, for "Application of cell engrng to breeding of Porphyra", 1991; Advd Sci & Technol Wrkr of the Colls & Univs of China, 1991. Memberships: Psychol Assn of China. Hobbies: Football; Music; Ping Pong; Peking Opera. Address: College of Fishery Sciences, Shanghai Fisheries University, 334, Jungong Road, Shanghai, 200090, China.

WANG Tao, b. 1931 Leting Hebei. Politician; Geologist. Appointments: Chf Geol Dagang Oil Field; Chf Geol Liaohe Pet Prospecting Bur; Gen Mngr S China Sea East Br of China Natl Offshore Oil Corp; Min of Pet Ind, 1985-88; Pres China Natl Pet Corp, 1988-97. Memberships: Mbr CCP 12th Cntrl Cttee, 1985-87; Mbr 13th C ntrl Cttee, 1987-92; Mbr 14th Cntrl Cttee, 1992-; Mbr Environmental and Rescs Protection Cttee NPC Dep Shandong Prov. Address: China National Petroleum Corporation, P O Box 766, Liupukang, Beijing 100724, People's Republic of China.

WANG Tian-Ren, b. 26 Jul 1939 Henan. Sculptor; Artist; Calligrapher. m. Zhang Pei, 1969, 1 s. Education: Xi'an Acady of Fine Arts. Appointments: Wrkd as art des and sculp at Shaanxi Exhibn Hall, 1963-79; Wrkd on constrn, 1964-65; Created sculps for Yanan Revolution Memorial Hall, 1968-71; Dir Grp sculps for Shaanxi Exhibn Hall, 1972-75; Participated in grp sculp for Chmn Mao Memorial Hall, 1976-78; Pres Shaanxi Sculp Inst, 1995-; Vice-Dir of Sculp Art Cttee; Shaanxi Br Natl Assn of Artists; Art Dir Dir of Creation Off Shaanxi Sculp Inst. Wrks incl: Hou Ji, 1980-81; Flower; The Morning Rooster; Qin Ox; Zebra; Tang Dynasty Musicians in Nishang and Yuyi; Letter Carrier Goose; Biaoqi General of Han Dynasty Huo Qu'bing; Rising to the Sky, 1985; Qin Unification, 1992; Unification of Qin Dynasty, 1994; Yu Youren, 1994; Sign sculp for Xijiang Chem Fertilizer Factory, 1995; Civic scenery sculp for Hejin Shaanxi Prov, 1995; Soar Aloft, 1996; Zhao Hongzhang, 1996; Hou Ji, 1996; Large cty sign sculp for Shanxi, 1996; Calligraphy wrks exhibd in Chinese and Japanese ctys. Honours: Copper Medal Natl Cty Sculp Desng Exhibn for Nishang and Yuyi, 1983; Copper Medal Natl Cty Sculp Desng Exhibn for Letter Carrier Goose, 1983; Excellent Prize 6th Natl Art Wrks Exhibn for Biaoqi Gen of Han Dynasty Ho Qu'bing, 1984; First Prize Shaanxi Art Wrks Exhibn for Biaoqi Gen of Han Dynasty Huo Qu-bing, 1984; Prize for Excellence Natl min of Urban Constrn Natl Assn of Artists for Rising to the Sky, 1987; Selected for 2nd Natl Cty Sculp Natl Prize from Natl Constrn min min of Culture and Assn of Natl Artists for Unification of Qin Dynasty; Selected for 8th Natl Arts Exhibn for Yu Youren. Hobbies: Chinese classical lit; Poetry; Music. Address: Shaanxi Sculpure Institute, Longshoucun, Xi'an, Shaanxi 710016, People's Republic of China.

WANG Wei, b. 9 Oct 1966, Shaanxi, China. Engineer. Education: BS, 1988, MS, 1991, BUAA, PhD, CALT, 1998. Appointments: Autocontrol Snr Engr, Beijing Inst of Control Devices, 1998-. Publications: Pat of oxymeter;

Pprs on inertial tech & autocontrol. Memberships: Chinese Soc of Inertial Technol; Chinese Space Soc. Address: Beijing Institute of Control Devices, PO Box 3913, Beijing 100039, China.

WANG Weiqiang, b. 22 Aug 1959, Qingdao, Tsingtao, China. Professor. m. Aiju Li, 30 July 1984, 1 s. Education: PhD, E China Univ of Sci & Technol, 1990. Appointments: Lectr Asst, Lectr, Assoc Prof, Prof, Vice Hd of Dept, Dept Mech Engrng, Qingdao Inst Chem Technol, 1984-86, 1990-92, 1992-95, 1995-97; Prof, Dept Chem Engrng, Shandong Univ Technol, 1997-. Publications: Num articles to profl jrnls. Honours: Sci Dev Awds of Educ Cttee of China; Young Sci Awds of Govt of Shandong Prov. Memberships: Chinese Soc Mechs, Beijing, China; Chinese Mech Engrng Soc, Beijing; Shandong Mech Engrng Soc, Jinan, China. Hobbies: Swimming; Badminton; Classical Music; Touring; Fishing. Address: Department Chemical Engineering, Shandong University of Technology, 73 Jingshi Road, Jinan 250061, China.

WANG Wenfu, b. 28 Oct 1943, Nanchong, Sichuan, China. Professor of Physics. m. Dexiu Xian, 1 Oct 1973, 1 s, 1 d. Education: BS, 1967, MS, 1981, Lanzhou Univ. Appointments: Assoc Prof, 1988-93, Prof of Phys, 1994-. Publications: General Physics, 1997; Sev articles in profl jrnls. Honours: Ex in Sci Rsch Awd, Sichuan Govt, 1996; Ex in Sci Rsch Awd, SW Petroleum Inst, 1995. Memberships: Soc of Chinese Physicists; Chinese Petroleum Inst. Hobbies: Fishing; Table Tennis. Address: SW Petroleum Institute, Nanchong 637001, China.

WANG Xiaofeng, b. Oct 1944 Cili Co Hunan Prov. Politician. Education: Beijing Mining Inst. Appointments: Joined CCP, 1973; Vice-Sec CCP Changde Prefectural Cttee Cmdr Changde Prefectural Admin Commn, 1983; Dir Hunan Provincial Plng Commn, 1986; Vice-Gov Hunan, 1990; Vice-Sec CCP Hunan Prov Cttee, 1992; Vice-Sec CCP Hainan Provincial Cttee; Vice-Gov Hainan Prov, 1993-. Memberships: Alt mbr 14th CCP Cntrl Cttee, 1992; Mbr 15th CCP Cntrl Cttee, 1997-. Address: Office of the Governor, Haikou City, Hainan Province, People's Republic of China.

WANG Xiaojing, b. 12 Feb 1955, Suzhou, China. Plant Biologist. m. Zhong MJ, 18 June 1984, 1 s. Education: BS, Shanxi Tchrs Univ, 1981; MSc, Northwestern Univ, China, 1984; PhD, S China Normal Univ, 1990. Appointments: Asst Prof, Lectr, 1984-87; Lectr and Assoc Prof, S China Normal Univ, 1990-95; Postdoct Fell, Osaka Cty Univ, Japan, 1995-97; Prof, S China Normal Univ, 1998-. Publications: Pprs in profl jrnls. Honours: Sci and Tech Prize, Guang Dong Educ Min, 1987. Memberships: Chinese Soc Plant Physiol, 1982-; Chinese Soc of Bot, 1982-; Japan Soc of Plant Physiol, 1995-97; Japan Soc of Bot, 1995-97. Hobbies: Travel; Reading. Address: Department of Biology, South China Normal University, 510631, Guangzhou, China.

WANG Xingzhi, b. 10 Aug 1944, Jilin, China. Scientist in Genetics. m. Xiru Sun, 20 Feb 1970, 1 s, 1 d. Education: PhD, Genetics, Copenhagen Univ, Denmark, 1988. Appointments: Inst of Genetics, Chinese Acady of Scis, 1978-84; Carlsberg Lab, Copenhagen, Denmark, 1985-95; Sch of Life Sci, NE Normal Univ, 1995-. Hobby: Tennis. Address: c/o School of Life Science, Northeast Normal University, 138 Renmin Street, Changchun 130024, China.

WANG Xiuzhang, b. 25 Dec 1931, Dazhu, Sichuan Prov, China. Geochemist; Geologist (Economic Geologist). m. Liu Xing, 27 Dec 1959, 2 s. Education: Grad, Fac of Geol, Univ of Chongqing, 1953; Grad, Postgrad Sch of Beijing Coll of Geol, 1956. Appointments: Asst Prof, Inst of Geol, Chinese Acady Scis (Asst Rsch Fell), 1956-66; Asst Prof, 1967-78, Assoc Prof, 1979-85, Prof, 1986-89, Inst of Geochem, Chinese Acady Scis; Prof, Guangzhou Inst of Geochem, Chinese Acady of Scis, 1990-. Publications: Written and compiled over 10 books and 100 acad theses in total; Geochemistry and Mineralogy of PGE in PGE-Bearing Geological Bodies of China (w Zhou Lingdi), 1981;

Handbook of Identification of PGE Minerals (w Zhou Lingdi), 1981; Geochemistry of Stratabound Deposits of China, vols 1-3 (w Tu Guangzhi), 1984, 1987, 1988 respectively; Geochemistry of Reworking Gold Deposits in China, (w Cheng Jingping), 1992. Honours: 2nd Awd, Sci and Technol Achievement, Chinese Acady of Scis, 1982; 1st Awd, Natl Scis of China, 1987; 3rd Awd, Scis, Guangdong Prov, 1994; Spec Awd, Sci and Technol Progress, Chinese Acady of Scis, 1997. Hobbies: Reading; Walking. Address: Guangzhou Institute of Geochemistry, Chinese Academy of Sciences, Wushan, Guangzhou 510640, China.

WANG Ya-Guang, b. 1 Oct 1965, Jiangsu, China. Professor. m. Hui-Hong Zhu, 3 Sept 1990, 1 s. Education: Bach Deg, 1985, Master Deg, 1988, Dr Deg, 1992, Fudan Univ. Appointments: Assoc Prof, Shanghai Jiaotong Univ, 1995; Lise Meitner Postdoct Fellshp, Aust Sci Fndn, Innsbruck Univ, 1995. Publications: Sev articles in profl jrnls. Honour: Youth Ex Sci Work Prize, Shanghai Sci & Technol Cttee, 1993. Address: Department of Applied Mathematics, Shanghai Jiaotong University, Shanghai 200240, China.

WANG Ying-Luo, b. 21 May 1930, Anhui, China. University Professor and Vice-President. m. 19 July 1955, 1 s, 1 d. Education: Bach, Mechl Engrng Dept, Jiaotong Univ, Shanghai, 1952; Postgrad, Mngmt Engrng Dept, Harbin Technol Inst, Harbin, 1955. Appointments: Lectr, Jiaotong Univ, Shanghai, 1955-58; Assoc Chmn, Mechl Engrng Dept, 1958-80, Assoc Prof, Chmn, Mngmt Engrng Dept, 1980-84, Prof, Dean, Mngmt Sch, 1984-, VP, 1984-, Xian Jiaotong Univ. Publications: Systems Engineering Guidance, 1982; Systems Engineering, 1986; The development planning model of Shanxi Provincial energy resource base. Honours: 1st Prize, Sci Technol Advmnt, Comprehensive Evaluation and Analysis of 3 Gorges Proj of Yangtze River, State Commn Educ, 1986; 2nd Prize, Sci Technol Advmnt, Syst Analysis Method for Natl Educ Plng, SCEC, 1986; Dev Plng Model of Shanxi Provl Energy Res Base listed as Nationally Imp Achmnt in Sci Rsch, SCSTC. Memberships: VP, Systs Engrng Soc China; Dpty Chf Mbr, Cttee Systs Engrng, Chinese Assn Automation; Systs Engrng Cttee, Intl Fedn Auto Control; Dpty Sec-Gen, Econs Rsch Cntr, Shaanxi Provincial Govt. Hobbies: Listening to classical music; Travelling. Address: Management School, Xian Jiaotong University, Xian, Shaanxi, China.

WANG You-Tsao, b. 2 Jul 1925 Chinchiang Co Fukien. Politician. m. Jean Eng-ling, 1954, 2 s, 1 d. Education: Natl Taiwan Univ; IA State Univ USA. Appointments: Asst Instr Assoc Prof Dept of Agric Econs Natl Taiwan Univ, 1954-60; Prof Dept of Agric Econs Natl Taiwan Univ, 1960-73; Specialist in Rural Econs Div Jnt Commn on Rural Reconstrn - JCCR - 1960-63; Snr Specialist, 1965-66; Chf Rural Econs Div, 1966-71; Chf Off of Plng and Progng, 1971-72; Dep Sec Gen JCCR, 1972-73; Sec-Gen, 1973-79; Sec-Gen Cncl for Agric Plng and Devt Exec Yuan, 1979; Vice-Chmn, 1979-84; Chmn, 1984; Chmn and Chf Opng Admin, 1984-88; Min of State, 1988-90; Natl Policy Advsr to Pres, 1990-. Publications: Sev wrks on agricl econs. Address: 14-6 Alley 1, Lane 194, Chung Hsiao East Road, Sect 4, Taipei, Taiwan.

WANG Yu He, b, 12 June 1929, Suzhou, Jiangsu Prov, China. Research Fellow in CCM; Teacher of PhD Graduates. m. Pu Yi Mu, 3 July 1955, 1 s, 1 d. Education: Grad, Dept of Composition in CCM, 1955. Appointments: Lectr, Assoc Prof, CCM, 1959-84; Vice-Dir, Dept of Musicology, 1980-84; Dir, Rsch Inst of Music, Rsch Fell, Musicology, CCM, 1985-. Publications include: The History of Chinese Modern Music, 1984, revised ed, 1994; An Outline of the Chinese Contemporary Music (1949-86), 1991; The Critical Biography of Nie-Er, 1987; The Critical Biography of Chinese Modern Musicians, vol 1, 1992; vol 2, 1998; A New Selection Thesis of the Theory and History of Music, 1996; The Music and Musicians, 1996; Chf Ed, The History of The Central Conservatory of Music, 1990. Memberships: Chinese Musicians Assn, 1961-; Dir, Theort and Compositional Dept, Beijing Musicians Assn, 1980-; Vice Ed-in-Chf, Jrnl

of Cntrl Conservatory of Music, 1980-87; VP, Pres, Soc for the Study of Ma Si-Cong, 1990-. Address: Central Conservatory of Music, 43 Baojia Street, Beijing 100031, China.

WANG Yuanmei, b. 7 Oct 1945, Lepin, Jiangxi, China. Professor. m. 1988, 1 s, 1 d. Education: BA, 1968; MS, 1982; PhD, 1989. Publication: Vector Entropy Optimization Based Neural Network Approach to Image Reconstruction from Projections, 1997. Honour: Advd Prof, 1996. Membership: NYAS, 1997. Hobbies: Walking; Reading. Address: Zhejiang University, Department of Life Science and Biomedical Engineering, Hangzhou, 310027, China.

WANG Yumiao, b. 10 May 1945, Nantong, Jiangsu, China. Teacher. m. Mingzhi She, 1 Jan 1975, 1 s. Education: Bachelor's deg, For Lang Dept, Nanjing Normal Univ, 1967. Appointments: Vice Dean, 1988; Dean, 1988-90, Nantong No 9 Mid Sch; Vice Prin, Nantong No25 Mid Sch, 1990-94; Vice Prin, Nantong Mid Sch, attached to Nantong Tchrs Coll, 1994-95; Vice Prin, Nantong Experimental Mid Sch, 1995-. Publications: Articles in profl jrnls. Creative works: (calligraphy) Following the Army by Changling Wang, a poet in Tang Dynasty, selected on the show of calligraphy, drawing, photog by tchrs in Jiangsu prov, Sept, 1987. Honours: Excellent Awd, Nantong Pen Calligraphy Competition, 1987; Outstndng Individual for hard wrk in popularizing sci knowledge, 1989, 1997; Merit, Nantong Educ Bur, 1990; Hon Top Spec, Young and Mid Aged in Depts of Educ, 1993; Commendation by Nantong Educ Bur, 1995; Outstndng Individual, Jiangsu Red Cross, 1996; Hon ex model tchr for wrk in PE affairs, Nantong Educ Bur, PE Bur, Bd of Hlth, 1997. Memberships: Mid Sch Chinese Tchng Seminar, Nantong Educ Assn, 1987; Mid Sch Hist Tchng Seminar, Nantong Educ Assn, 1990; Cnslt, Nantong Self-Study Coaching and Tchng Assn, 1990-; Nantong Workers Calligraphy Assn. Hobbies: Calligraphy; Music; Art; Reading. Address: Huan Cheng Dong Lu No 153, Nantong, Jiangsu, China.

WANG Yuming, b. 15 Mar 1932, Shanghai, China. Professor. m. Peiyau Hu, 2 Feb 1962, 1 s. Education: Dip, 1954, Dip, PhD equiv, 1958, Jilin Univ; Trng, Moscow Inst Steels, USSR, 1960-62. Appointments: Asst, 1958-60, Assoc Prof, Prof, 1962-, Jilin Univ, Changchun; Visng Schl, Moscow Inst Steels, USSR, 1960-62; Visng Schl, 1979, Guest Prof, 1983, Tech Univ, Vienna, Austria. Publications: Contbr, over 150 tech pprs in profl jrnls; Monographs: X-ray Diffraction of Amorphous Materials and Crystal Defects, 1988; An Introduction to Physics and Technology of Thin Films, 1994. Honours: Awd, Outstndng Pprs, local Soc Mechl Engrng, 1984; Awd, Outstndng Tech Pprs, local Soc Metals, 1986; Awds, Sci and Tech Progress, China Educ Min, 1987, 1988, 1990, 1994, 1995, 1998. Memberships: Vice Chmn, Cttee X-Ray Diffraction, Chinese Soc Phys, 1988-; China Materials Rsch Soc, 1988-; Chinese Soc Metals; China Soc Crystallography, 1992-; Materials Soc; Chinese Soc Mechl Engrng. Hobbies: Science; Teaching; Computer graphics; Music; Table tennis. Address: Department of Materials Science, Jilin University, 79 Jie Fan Road, Changchun 130023, China.

WANG Yunhong, b. 30 Aug 1952. Professor; Senior Engineer; Supervisor of Doctoral Students. m. Yan Muxian, 18 Oct 1980, 1 d. Education: DEng; MSc. Appointment: Dir, Communication Dept, Tianjin Water Conservancy Bur. Publication: Numerical Modeling of Hydrodynamic Sediment, 1994; Lake Current of Yu-Qiao Reservoir, 1996. Honours: Prize of Promoting Sci and Technol Dev, Min of Water Resources; Prize of Promoting Sci and Technol Dev, Tianjin Munic. Memberships: Amn Soc Civ Engrs, 1994; Jap Soc Civ Engrs, 1986; Dir, Tianjin Hydraulic Computer Application Speciality Commn, 1987. Listed in: Dictionary of International Biography; International Who's Who of Intellectuals. Hobbies: Swimming; Horseriding; Golf. Address: Tianjin Water Conservancy Bureau, 210 Wei-Di Road, Tianjin 300074, China.

WANG Yunkun, b. Dec 1942 Liyang Co Jiangsu Prov. Politician. Education: Tianjin Univ. Appointments: Joined CCP, 1966; Mayor of Jilin Cty and Vice-Sec CCP Jilin Cty Cttee; Vice-Gov Jilin Prov; Sec CCP Changchun Cty Cttee; Acting Gov Jilin Prov, 1995; Gov, 1996-. Memberships: Mbr 15th CCP Cntrl Cttee, 1997-. Address: Jilin Provincial Government, Changchun City, Jilin Province, People's Republic of China.

WANG Zemin, b. 2 Feb 1936, Fujian, China. Professor. m. Aug 1963, 2 s. Education: Xian Jiaotong Unv, 1954-58. Appointments: Vice Dean, Dept of Energy and Power Engrng, Xian Jiotong Univ, 1958-1990; Dir, Naut Sci and Technol Rsch Inst, Jimei Univ, 1990-. Creative Works: More than 50 Jrnl, Natl, Intl Conf Pprs, 1982-98. Honours: 4 Sci Rsch Awds. Hobbies: Swimming; Chinese Chess. Address: Nautical Sciences and Technology, Research Institute, Jimei Navigation Institute, Jimei University, Xiamen 361021, China.

WANG Zhen, b. 8 Mar 1933, Yanggu County, Shangdong Prov. Editor; Art Researcher. m. Wu Xiaming, 18 Dec 1966, 1 d. Education: BLL, Dept of Pols and Law, Shanghai Socl Sci Acady, 1960. Appointments: High Level Lib, Shanghai Lexicographical Publng hs, 1992; Rsch Fell, Shanghai Rschng Assn. Creative Works: The Great Artist - Xu Beihong; Achromicle of Xu Beihongs Life; The Art Worls of Xu Beihong. Memberships: Shanghai Lexicographical Assn; Shanghai Rsch Assn of Xu Bingshons Art. Hobby: Hist of Art. Address: Room 302, No 21, Lane 937, Juxi Street, Shanghai 200023, China.

WANG Zhen Gang, b. 2 June 1923, China. Professor of Pharmacology. m. X Z Qui, 8 Oct 1949, 3 s, 1 d. Education: BS, Chengtu Cheeloo Univ, 1944-48; Postdoct Fell, Beijing PUMC (Peking Union Medl Coll), 1950-53. Appointments: Asst, 1953-56, Lectr, 1956-78, Assoc Prof, 1978-80, Chmn and Prof, 1981-, Dept of Pharmacology, Peking Union Medl Coll; Hon Pres, Advsry Editl Bd TiPS; Corresp Ed, BJP; Mbr, CMA New Drug Evaluation Cttee. Publications: Advances in Natural Products in China, 1985; The biological effects of Astragalus, 1982; Recent advances on the calcium channel, 1985; Ginseng research of China during the past twenty years, plenary lecture at Ginseng day Ceremony meeting, Nov 10th, 1995; Seoul Olympic Parktoul, Seoul, Korea, 1996. Honours: Model Tchr, Peking Union Medl Coll, 1987; Model Wrkr, China Assn of Sci and Technol, 1987; Model Ed, Acta Acad Med Sn, 1987. Memberships: Pres, Chinese Pharm Soc, 1958-88; Pres, 1989-93, Hon Pres, 1994-2001, CNPHARS; Mbr Edmonton Snrs Club, Canada, 1993-. Address: Yong Ding Men Dong Jie, D-9-4-303, Dong Lee, Beijing 100050, China.

WANG Zhi-Gong, b. 6 May 1954, Henan, China. Electronic Engineer. m. Xiaoying Lu, 2 s. Education: D-Ing, Germany. Appointments: Dir of Inst RFandOEICS, SE Univ, 1997; Vice-Dir, Natl Key Lab of MMWs, 1998. Publications: 80 pprs in intl and natl jrnls and confs; 10 German and intl patents; 1 book. Honours: Best Ppr Awd of Intl Conf on GaAs Mfng Technol, 1997; Chinese Outstndng Young Scientist, 1998. Memberships: Snr Mbr, IEEE, 1993-; NY Acady of Scis, 1996-. Hobbies: Garden work; Swimming. Address: Department of Radio-Engineering, SE Univ, Sipailou 2, 210096 Nanjing, China.

WANG Zhibao, b. 30 Jan 1938, Tianjin, China. Professor. m. Qu Wenying, 23 Dec 1967, 1 s, 1 d. Education: Dip in Maths, Nankai Univ, 1964. Appointments: Mbr of Fac, 1964-, Lectr in Maths, 1980-83, Lectr, Computer and System Sci, 1983-86, Assn Prof of Computer and System sci, 1986-90, Prof, Computer and System Sci, 1990-, Nankai Univ. Publications include: ICS Language and LANMIP Software package, 1982; The Design of a Software Package for CAD of Control System-Overall Structure Design, 1984; A General Expert System and its Application in Diagnostics and Treatment of Chinese Traditional Medicine, 1984; Expert System of Computer Dispatch for Road Transportation, 1985; The Design of

CAD Language in Control System: The Text of CSCADL and its Implementation, 1985; The Implementation of Robot Control System Language RCL and its Application, 1987; Problems on Expression's Inputting and Evaluating in CADCS, 1989; CADCS Software System, 1992; Distribution Control System (DCS) and its Application in Metallurgical Industry, 1993; The Survey on the Development of CADCS in the World, 1994; M-Turbo C Development environment and its Application, 1996. Honours: 2nd Awd, Min of Electrons Ind, 1985; Awd of Excellence of Tianjin Cty Govt, 1985; Medal for Contbns to 7th 5-Yr Plan, 1989; 2nd Awd of Adv in Sci and Technol in Natl Educ Cttee, 1993; 3rd Awd of Adv in Sci and Technol in China, 1995; Natl Spec Allowance; HUAYE Tchng PRize, Nankai Univ, 1998. Memberships: Dir, Chinese Assn of System Simulation, 1989-; Vice Chmn, Assn of System Simulation and CADCS, 1992-; VP, Tianjin Assn of Computers, 1988-; Stndng Dir, Tianjin Assn of Automatin, 1994-; Chmn, Assn of CADCS; Dpty Chf Ed, Micro Minicomputer Dev and Application. Address: Department of Computer and System Science, Nankai University, Balitai Tianjin, 300071 China.

WANG Zhicheng, b. 1 Sept 1929, Jiangsu, China. Medical Professor. m. Zhou Sumei, 12 Jan 1963, 2 s. Education: Grad, Shanghai Med Univ, 1952-58. Appointments: Internist, 1958-72; Lectr, 1973-85; Assoc Prof, 1986-88; Prof, 1988-. Publications: Sev articles in profl jrnls. Honours: 1st Prize Awd, 1988; Hon, 1989, 1990; 3rd Inventive Awd, 1995. Hobby: Photography. Address: Nanking Road 288, Institute of Hematology, Chinese Academy of Medical Sciences, Tianjin 30020, China.

WANG Zhong Han, b. 2 Aug 1913, Dung-an, Hunan, China. Professor. m. Tu Yen-Sung, 14 Sept 1949, 1 s, 2 d. Education: BA, 1938, Yenching Univ, Peking; MA, Grad Sch, Yenching Univ, Peking, 1940. Appointments: Instr, Yenching Univ Hist Dept, Peking, 1940; Lectr, Yenching Univ, Chengdu, 1943-45; Asst Prof, Yenching Univ, Beijing; Prof, Cntrl Univ of Nationalities, Beijing, 1952-. Publications: Miscellaneous on the History of Qing; A Brief History of the Manchu People; New Studies on the History of Qing, 1990; Continued Studies, 1993; A History of the Nationalities of China (ed-in-chf), 1994. Memberships: Soc of Hist of Nationalities, 1978-; Soc of Chinese Hist, 1981-. Hobbies: Walking; Reading. Address: 5 Unit 34, Faculty Apartment, The Central University of Nationalities, 27 Bai Shi Chao Road, beijing 100081, China.

WANGCHUK Jigme Singye King, b. 11 Nov 1955. Education: N Point Darjeeling; Ugyuen Wangchuk Acady Paro also in Eng. Appointments:Chmn Plng Commn of Bhutan, Mar 1972-; Cmdr in Chf of Armed Forces; Chmn Cncl of Mins, 1972-; Crown Prince, Mar 1972; Succeeded to throne 24 Jul 1972; Crowned 2 Jun 1974. Address: Royal Palace, Thimphu, Bhutan.

WANGCHUCK Sonam Chhoden (Princess), b. 26 July 1953, Zurich, Switz. Government Official. m. Tsewang Jurmed Rixin, 15 Oct 1979, 2 children. Appointments: Chmn, Roy Ins Corp of Bhutan, 1975-; Druk Air Corp, 1981; Roy Civil Serv Commn, 1982-; Roy Monetary Authy, 1982-; Min of Fin, 1985-. Membership: Pres, Natl Womens Assn of Bhutan, 1981-. Address: Ministry of Finance, Tashichho Dzong, Thimphu, Bhutan.

WANNAN Lynette Mary, b. 10 June 1951, Australia. Managing Director, Retail. m. 31 July 1989, 1 s. Education BA; Dip of Educ, Monash Univ. Appointment: Mng Dir, Hop Step & Jump. Publications: Columnist, Quality Time, 1990-. Memberships: Pres, Indep Toy Specialists of Aust; Convenor, Natl Assn of Comm Based Childrens Servs; Chair, Comm Child Care. Hobbies: Gardening; Reading. Address: 300 Bridge Road, Richmond, Victoria, Australia.

WAQAR Younis, b. 16 Nov 1971 Vehari. Cricketer. Education: Pakistani Coll Sharjah; Govt Coll Vehari. Appointments: Right-hand lower-order batsman; Right-arm fast bowler; Played for Multan, 1987-88 to 1990-91; United Bank, 1988-89 to date; Surrey, 1990-91

and 1993; Glamorgan, 1997; Played in 48 Tests for Pakistan, 1989-90 to 31 Dec 1997; 1 as Cap taking 238 wickets - average 21.6; Has taken 699 wickets in first-class cricket to 31 Dec 1997; Toured Eng, 1992 and 1996; 163 limited-overs intls to 31 Dec 1997. Hobbies: Football; Badminton; Squash. Address: c/o Glamorgan County Cricket Club, Sophia Gardens, Cardiff, CF1 9XR, Wales.

WARD Colin Rex, b. 31 Dec 1945. Geologist. m. Kathleen May Reeks, 12 Oct 1968, 1 s, 1 d. Education: BSc, hons, 1967, PhD, 1971, Univ NSW. Appointments: Lectr, 1971-80, Snr Lectr, 1980-84, NSW Inst of Technol; Lectr, 1984, Snr Lectr, 1985-91, Assoc Prof, 1992-, Univ NSW; Hd, Dept of Applied Geol, Univ NSW, 1993-97; Hd, Sch of Geol, Univ NSW, 1999-. Publications: Coal Geology and Coal Technology, 1984; Geology of Australian Coal Basins, 1995; Geology in Longwall Mining, 1996; Over 60 sci pprs in profl jrnls. Honour: Univ Medal in Applied Geol, Univ NSW, 1967; Awd for Excellence, Coalfield Geol Cncl of NSW, 1998. Memberships: Fell, Austl Inst of Geoscis; Fell, Australasian Inst of Mining & Metallurgy. Hobbies: Geology; Computing. Address: School of Geology, University of New South Wales, Sydney, NSW 2052, Australia.

WARD David Harvey, b. 23 Dec 1956, Ashford, Kent, Eng. Manager. m. Jeanette, 1 s, 1 d. Education: BSc (Hons), 1st Class, Univ of Canterbury, NZ. Appointments: Diplomat, NZ For Serv, 1979-86; Gen Mngr, ANZ Banking Grp, 1987-97; Gen Mngr, Off of Chf Exec, 1997-. Hobbies: Golf; Snow skiing; Sailing. Address: Level 32, 100 Queen Street, Melbourne, VIC 3000, Australia.

WARD Gordon (Hon Mr Justice), b. 18 Aug 1938, Kuching, Sarawak. Judge. m. Margaret, 1 June 1963, 2 s. 1 d. Education: BSc Hons, Reading Univ; Bar, 1964, Middle Temple. Appointments: Biol Tchr, Foyle Col, Londonderry, 1963-67; Bar, Temple, London, 1967-79; Res Magistrate, 1979-80, Chf Magistrate, 1980-85, Judge of Appeal, 1992-, Fiji; Snr Magistrate, 1981-85, Chf Justice, 1985-86, Tuvalu; Chf Justice, Solomon Islands, 1985-92; Supreme Crt Judge, Vanuatu, 1986-92; Chf Justice and Pres of Crt of Appeal, Tonga, 1992-95, 1998-; Judge of Appeal, Western Samoa, 1992-93; Res Judge, Sovereign Base Areas, Cyprus, 1995-98. Honour: OBE, 1996. Hobbies: Sailing; Gardening; Music. Address: Chief Justices Chambers, Supreme Court, Nuku'Alofa, Tonga, South Pacific.

WARD Lionel Edward, b. 5 Feb 1936, WA, Aust. Marketing Consultant. m. (1) Robin Gribble, 16 May 1962, 2 d, (2) Pamela Crabtree, 25 Apr 1986, 1 d. Education: BAgSci, 1956, BA, 1962, Univ WA; MS, Univ CA, USA, 1964; PhD, Univ CA at Davis, 1969. Appointments: Self-employed Orchardist, 1957-63; Rsch Fell, 1964-66, Lectr, 1969-71, Monash Univ, Melbourne, Vic; Var posns inclng Gen Mngr, Mktng, Austl Wool Corp, 1971-88; Dir, own strategic mktng consultancy Mktng and Plng Pty Ltd, 1988-. Publications: Contrb, num acad articles; Co-ed, monthly mkt intell mag for wool. Memberships: Austl Agricl Econs Soc; Cttee Econ Dev Aust. Hobbies: Gardening; Theatre; Sport. Address: 2 Riverhill Drive, Lower Plenty, Vic 3093, Australia.

WARD Marion Wybourn, b. 18 June 1930, Johnsonville, NZ. Economic Consultant. m. Ralph Gerard Ward, 7 Aug 1959, 1 s, 2 d. Education: BSc, 1955; MSc, 1956; PhD, 1960; MSc, Bus Admin, 1981. Appointments: Lectr, Univ of Auckland, NZ, 1960-61; Lectr, Univ of Reading, Eng, 1964-67; Snr Rsch Fell, Austl Natl Univ, 1967-73; Assoc, Gavan McDonell & Co, 1973-84; Independent Cnslt, 1985-90; Prin, Ward Cnsltng Pty Ltd, 1991-. Publications: Malaya and Singapore, 1963; The Rigo Road, 1970; Roads and Development in Southwest Bougainville, 1975; The Role of Women in the Australian National University, 1976; Ed of sev vols and serial publns; Auth of num acad pprs. Honours: Fulbright Travel Grant, 1956; Carnegie Fellshp, 1958; Brit Cncl Younger Rsch Workers Awd, 1967. Memberships: Fell, Chart Inst of Transp; Bd Mbr, Austl Cntr for Maritime Studies. Hobbies: Bird Watching; Flower Arranging; Gardening;

Travel; Badminton. Address: 8 Booth Crescent, Cook, ACT 2614, Australia.

WARD Ralph Gerard, b. 20 May 1933, NZ. Geographer. m. Marion Wybourn, 7 Aug 1959, 1 s, 2 d. Education: BA, MA, NZ; PhD, London, Eng. Appointments: Jnr Lectr, Lectr, Univ of Auckland, 1956-61; Lectr in Geog, Univ Coll, London, Eng, 1961-67; Prof of Geog, Univ of Papua New Guinea, 1967-71; Prof of Hum Geog, 1971-98, Dir, Rsch Sch of Pacific Studies, 1980-93, Emer Prof, 1999-, Austl Natl Univ. Publications: New Zealand's Industrial Potential (w M W Ward), 1961; Islands of the South Pacific, 1961; Land Use and Population in Fiji, 1965; American Activities in the Central Pacific 1790-1870, 1966-69; An Atlas of Papua New Guinea (w D A M Lea), 1970; Man in the Pacific Islands, 1972; The Settlement of Polynesia: A Computer Simulation (w M Levison and J W Webb), 1973; South Pacific Agriculture: Choices and Constraints (w A Proctor), 1980; Land, Cane and Coconuts (in) Fiji (w H C Brookfield and F E Ellis), 1985; Land Custom and Practice in the South Pacific (w E Kingdon), 1995; Samoa: Mapping the Diversity (w P Ashcroft), 1998. Memberships: Fell, Roy Geogl Soc; Inst of Austl Geogs; Fell, Acady of Socl Scis in Aust. Address: 8 Booth Crescent, Canberra, ACT 2614, Australia.

WARD Ronald Bentley, b. 6 Oct 1928, Sydney, NSW, Aust. Academic and Consultant. m. Brenda, 7 Jan 1955, 1 s, 1 d. Education: Associateship, Syd Tech Coll; BEng, Univ of NSW; MBA, Macquarie Univ; Dir of Phil, Univ of NSW. Appointments include: Plant Mngr, Pacific Chem Inds Pty Ltd, 1972-73; Engrng Mngr, A C Hatrick Chems Pty Ltd, 1973-79; Dir and Cnslt, Proj ACTION Pty Ltd, 1979-90; Proj Engr, The Austl Gas Light Co, 1984-85; Lectr, Sch of Mech Engrng, NSW Inst of Technol (now Univ of Technol, Sydney), 1984-. Publications include: The Relationship Between Quality and Safety, w A Ajdinovic, 1996; From Engineer to Manager - A Final Step Along the Path, 1996; Some Conclusions from Student Reactions to Small-e Ethical Dilemmas, 1996; Engineers' Dreams and Folklore, 1996; Management Risks as Perceived by Engineering Students, 1997. Memberships: Fell, Inst of Engrs in Aust; Austl Inst of Mngmt. Hobbies: Writing; Consulting on accidents; Teaching. Address: 13 Landscape Avenue, Forestville, NSW 2087, Australia.

WARD Vincent, b. 1956 Greytown. Film Dir. Education: Elam Sch of Fine Art Christchurch - graduated in film. Films incl: A State of Siege, 1977; In Spring one Plants Alone, 1979; Vigil, 1984; The Navigator, 1988; Map of the Human Heart. Honours: Grand Prix co-winner in 1982 and Cinema du Reel Silver Hugo at Chgo Film Fest for In Spring on Plants Alone; Grand Prix at Madrid and Prades Film Fests for Vigil. Address: P O Box 423, Kings Cross, Sydney, NSW 2011, Australia.

WARNE James Neil, b. 21 June 1943, Southern Cross, Western Aust. Local Government Official. m. Elsie, 31 Aug 1974, 2 s, 2 d. Education: Dip.LG (WA TAFE); Grad Ctf, Local Govt Mngmt, Deakin; FIMM. Appointments: Asst Shire Clk, Shire Gomalling, 1965-70, Shire of Moora, 1970-79; Shire Clk, CEO, Shire Moora, 1979-. Honour: Serving Brother, OStJ. Membership: Fell, Inst of Municipal Mngmt, Aust. Hobbies: Politics; Gardening; Travel; Sport on television. Address: Lot 19, Broad Way, Moora, Western Australia 6510, Australia.

WARNER Denis Ashton, b. 12 Dec 1917, Hobart, Tasmania. Writer. m. P S Hick, 12 June 1945, 1 s, 2 d. Appointments: Reuter-AAP Bureau Chief, Tokyo; Roving Far Eastern Correspondent, London, Daily Telegraph, East Asian Correspondent Reporter, magazine, Look. Publications: The Tide at Sunrise, 1974; The Last Confucian, 1964; The Sacred Warriors, 1986; Disaster in the Pacific, 1992; Wake Me If There's Trouble, 1995; Not Always on Horseback, 1997. Honour: OBE, 1971; CMG, 1981. Address: Ramslade, Nepean Highway, Mt Eliza, Victoria, Australia.

WARREN Bruce Albert, b. 2 Nov 1934, Sydney, Aust. Pathologist. m. Diana Mary King, 14 Aug 1964, diss, 1990 1 s, 1 d. Education: BS, Medl 1st Class Hons, 1957; MBBS, Sydney Univ, 1959; DPhil, 1964, MA, 1967, DSc, 1984, Oxford Univ, Eng. Appointments include: Intern, RMO, Sydney Hosp, 1959-61; Brit C'wlth Schl, Oxford Univ, Eng, 1962-64; Rsch Fell, Oncology, Chgo Medl Sch, Inst for Medl Rsch, USA, 1964-65; Lectr, Oxford Univ, Eng, 1966-68; Pt-time Tutor in Path, Oxford Medl Sch, 1967-68; Asst prof, 1968-69; Assoc Prof, 1969-74; Prof, 1974-80, Univ of West Ont, Can; Dir, Cytopathology, Univ Hosp, London, Can, 1976-80; Clin Prof, 1980-83; Prof, Univ of NSW, 1983-97; Hd, Anatomical Path, Prince Henry Hosp, Sydney, 1980-97. Publications include: Histology (jointly w B J Jeynes), 1983; Atheroembolism, 1986; Ed, Pathology, jrnl of Roy Coll of Pathologists of Aust, 1988-95; chapts in var books; over 80 articles in profl jrnls; Assoc Ed, Integrated Medicine, 1981. Honours: Pub Exhibn and Austl C'wlth Schlshp, 1952-58; Prosector in Anatomy, Sydney Univ, 1953-54; G S Caird Schlshp, 1955; Brit C'wlth Schlshp, UK, 1962-64. Memberships include: Fell, Roy Coll of Pathologists of Australasia; Life Fell, Roy Microscopical Soc; AAAS. Hobbies: Swimming; Gardening; Reading.

WARREN David Ronald, b. 20 Mar 1925, Aust. Research Scientist. m. Ruth Meadows, 3 Jan 1948, 2 s, 2 d. Education: BSc Hons, Sydney; PhD, London; Dip Imperial Coll; Dip Ed, Melbourne. Appointments: Tchr, Geelong Grammar, 1946-7; Lectr, Sydney Univ, 1948-49; Scientist, Woomera Rocket Range, 1949-51; Aero Rsch Labs, 1951-83; Sci Advsr, 1981-82. Publications: Basic Combustion Reactions; Conception, Production and Demonstration of Black Box. Memberships: Combustion Inst, 1958-; Austl Inst of Energy, 1978-. Hobbies: Communal Activities; Adult Educ. Address: 31 Olive St, Caulfield South, Vic 3162, Australia.

WARREN John Robin, b. 11 June 1937, Adelaide, SA, Aust. Medical Practitioner. m. Winifred Teresa Willliams, 5 May 1962, 4 s, 2 d. Education: MB BS, Univ of Adelaide, 1961. Appointments: Lectr in Path, Univ of Adelaide, 1963; Registrar of Path, Melbourne Hosp, 1964-67; Cnslt Pathologist 1968-98, Emer Cnslt Pathologist, 1998-, Roy Perth Hosp. Publication: Discovery of Campylobacter pylori (now Helicobacter pylori), the Bacteria Causing Gastritis and Peptic Ulcer. Honours: Sixth Workshop Campylobacter, Helicobacter and related organisms, Guest of Hon, 1991; Warren Alpert Fndn Prize, Harv Medl Sch (w Dr B J Marshall), for rsch that has lead to improved understanding and trtmnt of a specific disease: identifying Helicobacter pylori as a cause of peptic ulceration, 1991; Awd, Austl Medl Assn, WA Branch, 1995; Disting Fells Awd, Roy Coll of Pathologists of Australasia, for Disting Serv to the Sci and Prac of Path, 1995; Inaugural Awd, 1st Western Pacific Helicobacter Congress, 1996; Medal of Univ of Hiroshima, 1996; Disting Alumni Awd, Univ Adelaide Alumni Assn, 1996; Paul Ehrlich and Ludwig Darmstaedter Awd, 1997; Guest Speaker, Centenary Meeting, German Soc Path, 1997; Hon MD, Univ of WA, 1997; Faulding Florey Centenery Medal, 1998. Memberships: Fell, Coll of Pathologists of Aust; Brit Medl Assn; Intl Acady of Path; Austl Medl Assn. Hobbies: Photography; Rifle shooting. Address: 26 Lacey Street, Perth, WA 6000, Australia.

WARRENDER Simon George, b. 11 Aug 1922, London, England. Aviation Consultant. m. Pamela Myer, 2 s, 2 d. Appointments: Fndr, Chmn, Aust World Airways. Publication: Score of Years, biography, 1972. Honours: Distinguished Serv Cross, 1943; Russian Star, 1996. Hobbies: Flying; Swimming; Fencing; Space Science. Address: 3/5 Woorigoleen Road Toorak, Melbourne 3142, Australia.

WARRIER S S, b. 7 Dec 1946, Poothrikka, India. Teacher. m. Rema P M, 10 Dec 1979, 1 s, 1 d. Education: BA, 1st class, 1st Rank; MA 1st Class, 1st Rank; MPhil, Hist. Appointments: Lecturer in Hist, Snr Lectr, Prof, Hd of Dept, Govt Arts Coll. Honour: K P Gopalamenon Prize for Hist, 1968. Membership: Indian Hist Congress. Hobby: Reading. Address: Anaswara (XV-63), Island Avenue, Punkunnu, Thrissur, Kerala 680002, India.

WASHINGTON Denzel, b. 28 Dec 1954 Mt Vernon NY. Actor. m. Pauletta Pearson, 2 s, 2 d. Education: Fordham Univ; Am Conservatory Th San Fran. Appointments: Wrkd at NY Shakespeare Fest and Am Place Th; Off-Broadway appearances incl: Ceremonies in Dark Old Men; When the Chickens Come Home to Roost; A Solier's Play - Negro Ensemble Co; Played young Dr in tv series St Elsewhere. Films incl: A Soldier's Story, 1984; The Mighty Quinn; Cry Freedom; Heart Condition, 1989; Glory, 1990; Love Supreme, 1990; Mo' Better Blues, 1990; Ricochet, 1992; Mississippi Masala, 1991; Much Ado About Nothing; Malcolm X, 1992; The Pelican Brief, 1993; Philadelphia, 1993; Devil in a Blue Dress, 1995; Courage Under Fire, 1996; The Preacher's Wife, 1996; Fallen, 1997. Honours: Acady Awd for Best Supporting Actor for Glory. Address: c/o ICM, 8942 Wilshire Boulevard, Beverly Hills, CA 90211, USA.

WASHINGTON Patrick John, b. 25 Aug 1943, Melbourne. Managing Director. m. Joan, 4 July 1969, 2 s. Appointments: Chmn of Bd, Austl Natl Univ, Trng Cntr. Chmn of Bd, Victorian Recreational Fishing Peak Body; Dir, Oceaneering Aust p/l. Honours: OAM, 1994. Hobbies: Fly Fishing; Golf. Address: 141 Patten Street, Sale, Vic, Australia.

WASIM Akram, b. 3 Jun 1966 Lahore. Cricketer. Education: Islamia Coll. Appointments: Left-hand middle-order batsman; Left-arm fast bowler; Played for PACO, 1984-85; Lahore, 1985-86; Lancashire, 1988 to date - Cap for 1998; Played in 77 Tests for Pakistan, 1984-85 to 31 Dec 1997; 17 as Cap; Scoring 1971 runs - average 21.4 - inclng 2 hundreds and taking 334 wickets - average 22.3; Has scored 5407 runs - 5 hundreds - and taken 852 wickets infirst-class cricket to 31 Dec 1997; Toured Eng 1987, 1992, 1996 - Cap; 238 limited-overs intls taking record 341 wickets to 31 Dec 1997. Address: c/o Lancashire County Cricket Club, Old Trafford, Manchester, M16 0PX, England.

WATABE Tomiji, b. 26 Oct 1927, Tokyo, Japan. Mechanical Engineer. m. 26 Oct 1927, Tokyo, Japan. Education: Mechl Engrng Dept, Tokyo Techl Coll, 1950; DEng, Tokyo Univ, 1970. Appointments: Machine Des, Kameari Wrks, Hitachi Co Ltd, 1950-71; Rschr, Mechl Engrng Lab, Hitachi Co Ltd, 1972-77; Pt-time Lectr, Elec Techl Univ of Tokyo, 1971-77; Prof, Muroran Inst of Tech, 1978-93; Vol (Rsch & Engrng Cnslt of T-Wave), 1994-; Cnslt: Muroran Inst of Tech; Narasaki Machine Mfrng Co Ltd; Hitachi Co Ltd; Hokkaido Dev Bur; Ocean Eng Inst of Teanjin, China; Haiyou Machine Mfrng Co, China. Publications: 11 books; 15 jrnl pprs; 14 proceedings; 150 patents. Honours: Hon Mention Prize, Hyd & Pneu Prize Ppr Contest, 1977, 1978; Invention Prize, Japan Soc of Invention, 1978; Awd for Superior Ppr, Fndn for promotion of Hyd & Pneu Tech, 1990. Address: 5-23-3, Misono, Norboribetsu, 059-0036, Japan.

WATERHOUSE Douglas Frew, b. 3 June 1916, Sydney, Aust. Entomologist. m. Dawn, 4 Mar 1944, 3 s, 1 d. Education: BSc (Hons); MSc; DSc, Sydney Univ; DSc (Hon), Aust Natl Univ. Appointments: Rsch Staff, CSIRO, Div of Entomology, 1938, Chf, 1960-81, Hon Rsch Fell, 1981-; Cnslt in Plant Protection to ACIAR (Austl Cntr for Intl Agricl Rsch), 1983-. Publications: Over 150 sci pprs; 15 books, many dealing w pest problems and biol control in the Pacific, SE Asia and South China. Honours: FRACI, 1951; FAA, 1954; FRS, 1967; Hon FRES, 1972; For Fell: Brazilian Acady Sci, 1974, USSR Acady Scis, 1982, US Natl Acady Scis, 1983; AO, 1980; Hon Mbr, Aust, Ent Sci, 1996; FTSE, 1998. Memberships: Pres, Austl Entomol Soc, 1967-72; 14 Intl Congress of Entomol, 1972; Co-fndr, Chan, 1968-84, Canberra Univ. Hobbies: Gardening; Fishing; Gyotaku (fish printing). Address: 60 National Circuit, Deakin, Canberra, ACT 2600, Australia.

WATERS Donald Mathew, b. 13 Mar 1929, Caithness, Scotland (Austl citizen). Rector (Retired). m. Margaret Elizabeth Angus, 31 Aug 1957, 2 s, 1 d. Education: Leith Nautical Coll, Scot; Royal Coll of Sci and Technol, Glasgow; MSc, Univ of Wales, 1970. Appointments: Ships Offr and Shipmaster, Merchant Navy, 1944-59;

Lectr in Maritime Studies; Plymouth Polytechnic, Eng, 1959-60; Univ of Strathclyde, Scot, 1960-66; Maritime Safety Admin/Gen Maritime Admin, C'wlth Pub Serv, Aust, 1966-78; Fndn Prin, Austl Maritime Coll, 1978-90; Rector, World Maritime Univ, Sweden, 1990-96. Publications: Var papers and articles on maritime educ and trng. Honour: AM, 1992. Hobbies: Fishing; Sailing. Address: 68 Salamanca Square, Hobart, Tasmania 7000, Australia.

WATERS Richard Hugh, b. 3 July 1923, SA, Aust. Former Chief Executive. m. Pauline Gertrude Pryor, 4 Oct 1945, 1 s. Education: Scotch Coll; Fell, Austl Inst of Mngmt. Appointments: RAAF Air Crew, Can, Eng, 1942-46; Renmark Irrigation Trust, 1946-60; Roy Auto Assn of SA, 1960-88. Memberships: JP; Austl Admin Staff Coll Assn; Premiums Cttee, SA, 1975-; Roy Soc of SA, Hon Treas, 1989, 1994; Adelaide Club; Roy Adelaide Golf Club. Hobbies: Golf; Tennis; Motoring. Address: 28 Pitcairn Avenue, Urrbrae, SA 5064, Australia.

WATKINS Richard, b. 13 Sept 1950, Eng. Chief Executive. Education: BA, Curtin; MA, Essex; PDESL, Leeds; PhD, Leeds; MPA, Tas. Appointments: Dpty Sec, Dept of Vocational Educ and Trng, 1993-99; Chf Exec, NZ Cncl of Educl Rsch, 1999-. Memberships: Austl Coll of Educ, 1987-; Inst of Pub Admin, 1996. Hobbies: Reading; Travel. Address: New Zealand Council for Educational Research, PO Box 3237, Wellington, New Zealand.

WATKINS Rodney Dennis, b. 9 Aug 1942, Warragul, Victoria, Aust. Company Director. 1 s, 1 d. Education: PhD; MApp.Sci; DIC. Appointments: Chf Exec, Scan Optics Pty Ltd, 1987-; Bd, Natl Vision Rsch Inst of Aust, 1972-. Address: c/o Scan Optics Pty Ltd, 35 Stirling Street, Thebarton, SA 5031, Adelaide, Australia.

WATSON Bruce Dunstan (Sir), b. 1 Aug 1928, Stanthorpe, Aust. Company Chairman. m. 30 Dec 1952, 1 s, 2 d. Education: BEng (Elec), 1949, BCom, 1957, Univ of Qld. Appointments: Engr, Tasmanian Hydro Elec Commn, 1950-54; Engr, Townsville Regl Elec Bd, 1954-56; MIM Holdings Grp Cos: Engr, Copper Refineries Pty Ltd, Townsville, 1956-69; Mt Isa Mines Ltd, Mt Isa, 1970-73; Grp Indl Rels Mngr, MIM Grp, Brisbane, 1974-75; 1st Gen Mngr, Agnew Mining Co, West Aust, 1975-77; Dir, 1977-80, Mngng Dir, 1980-83, CEO, 1981-90, Chmn, 1983-91, MIM Holdings Ltd, Brisbane; Dir, Boral Ltd, 1991-; Dir, Natl Aust Bank Ltd, 1987-91, 1992-98; Pres, Australsian Inst of Mining and Metall, 1992; Pres, Australian Inst of Co Dirs, 1992-95. Honours: KB, Queens Birthday Hons, 1985; Hon Doct Engrng, 1989; Cmdr's Cross of the Order of Merit of Fed Repub Germany, 1991; Hon D Uni, Griffiths Univ, 1992. Hobby: Golf. Address: 272 Jesmond Road, Figtree Pocket, Qld 4000, Australia.

WATSON Donald, b. 6 Mar 1949, Warragul, Vic, Aust. Writer. m. Hilary McPhee, 21 Aug 1986, 1 d. Education: BA Hons; PhD. Appointments: Lectr, Hist, Footscray Inst of Technol, 1977-83; Speechwriter-Advsr Prime Min of Asst, 1992-96. Publications: Brian Fitzpatrick, book, 1978; A Story of Australia, book, 1984; Caledonia Australis, book, 1984. Membership: Austl Soc of Auths. Address: PO Box 1751, Collingwood, Vic 3066, Australia.

WATSON Eric George, b. 16 Feb 1926, Newtown, Sydney, NSW, Aust. Record Label Proprietor; Freelance Writer; Musician. Appointments: Record Label Proprietor; Composed country songs. Creative works: When Snowy Sings of Home; Roses in the Rain; The Last of the Bushman; Queen of Ice; The Light of Country Stars; Fireball Dan; Our Country was Stolen; Click Go The Gears; Over 50 other country songs; Country Music in Australia, vol 1, 1975, vol 2, 1983; Num articles in Country and Western Spotlight, Capital News, Country Music Express. Honour: Tamworth Capital Country Awd (Gold Guitar) for servs to Austl Country Music Ind, 1977. Memberships: Pres, Tamworth Songwriters Assn, 1981-87; Austl Soc of Auths. Hobbies: Farming; Cricket. Address: Theresa Creek, Via Casino, NSW 2470, Australia.

WATSON Frederick Vernon (Hon), b. 2 May 1921, Bundeberg, Qld, Aust. Judge. m. Marjorie Ethel Fowles, 23 Sept 1944, 2 s, 1 d. Education: BA, 1947, LLB, 1950, Sydney Univ. Appointments: Bar-at-Law, 1950; QC, 1971; Presdtl Mbr, Austl Conciliation and Arbitration Commn, 1972; Judicial Mbr, Indl Commn. NSW, 1973-89. Publication: Long Service Leave, 1958. Honours: Shared Sydney Univ Medal, Law; Class I Hons Law. Hobby: Golf. Address: 20 Bonner Avenue, North Steyne, NSW 2095, Australia.

WATSON Graeme Ross, b. 21 Dec 1955, Sydney, Aust. Lawyer. m. Roslyn Williamson, 23 Apr 1983, 1 s, 3 d. Education: BA; LLB; Grad Dip IR. Appointment: Ptnr, Frehill Hollingdale & Page. Publications: Guide to Victoria's Employee Relations Laws, 1993; The Workplace Relations Handbook (co-ed), 1998. Hobbies: Music; Cricket; Tennis; Reading. Address: Level 43, 101 Collins Street, Melbourne, Australia.

WATSON Ian Robert, b. 9 Feb 1955, Ballarat, Australia. Australian Industrial Relations Commission. m. Pippy Sakellaridis, 4 Sept 1981, 2 s. Education: Bach Commerce, Hons, Univ of Melbourne. Appointments: Dpty Pres, Austl Indl Rels Commn, 1991; Snr Dpty Pres, ARC, 1997. Membership: Austl Inst of Judicial Admin. Hobbies: Australian Rules Football; Wine; Family. Address: Australian Industrial Relations Commission, 80 Collins St, Melbourne, 3000, Australia.

WATSON John Odin Wentworth, b. 25 Jan 1937, Tas, Aust. Senator. m. Jocelyn Yvonne, 11 Mar 1963, 2 s, 2 d. Education: BEc, 1960, BCom, 1962, Univ of Tas. Appointments: Price Waterhouse & Co, Chartered Accts, Melbourne, 1962-63; Bennell & Bennell, Launceston, 1963-66; Co Sec, Kelsall & Kemp Pty Ltd, 1966-78; Pt-time Lectr; Launceston Techl Coll, 1964-78, TCAE, Launceston, 1974-78; Sen (Liberal) State of Tas, 1978-; Vice-Chmn, Pub Accounts Cttee, 1986-93; Parly Sec to the Dpty Ldr of the Opposition, 1990-94; Chmn, Sen Select Cttee for Superannuation, 1993-; Tstee, Parly Retiring Allowances Trust, 1994-; Dir, Accts Superannuation Fund, Alexander Cnsltng Grp, 1995-. Memberships: Fell, Inst of Chartered Accts; Fell, Chartered Inst of Secs and Admnstrs; Fell, Austl Inst of Mngmt; Fell, Austl Soc of Accts; Fell, Austl Soc of Certified Practising Accts. Hobbies: Primary Producer; Tennis; Cattle breeding; Family; Yachting. Address: 6 Junction Street, Launceston, Tas 7250, Australia.

WATSON Nigel Mott, b. 28 Sept 1928, Wellington, New Zealand. Minister of Religion. m. Stella Milnes, 25 Nov 1961, 1 s, 2 d. Education: BA, NZ, 1949; MA, 1950; BA, Cantab, 1953; MA, 1957; PhD, Princeton, 1958. Appointments: Min, Palmerston N & Riversdale, 1959-64; Prof of New Testament, Ormond Coll, Melbourne, 1965-93. Publications: Striking Home, 1987; Easter Faith and Witness, 1990; Commentary on I Corinthians, 1992; Commentary on 2 Corinthians, 1993. Membership: Soc for New Testament Studies, 1974-. Hobbies: Tramping; Drama. Address: 10 Chatham Street, Flemington, 3031, Australia.

WATSON Reginald Andrew Wentworth, b. 5 Sept 1949. Writer. m. Rosalie Newborn, 9 Nov 1974, 4 d. Publications: Heroes All: Tasmania's Involvement in the Boer War; Thomas Francis Meagher: Irish Exile; Those Who Served: Tasmanian WW2 Fatalities; The Scandalous Adventures of Capt Frederick Watson; Tasmanian Historical Parliamentarians. Memberships: Dir, Anglo Saxon Keltic Soc; Chmn, Austl Natl Flag Assn; Convener, Tas Heritage Cncl. Listed in: Who's Who in Australian Writers. Hobbies: Racquet Sports. Address: Rockingham Cottage, 8 View Street, Blackmans Bay, Tas 7052, Australia.

WATT Lindsay J, b. New Zealand. Administrator, Tokelau. Appointments: Amb to China; Administrator, Tokelau, 1993-. Address: Tokelau Apia Liaison Office, POB 865, Apia, Samoa.

WATTERS Roger Allan, b. 25 July 1938. Geochemist. m (1) Heather Gatt, 18 Jan 1963, 1 s, 1 d, (2) Jeanette Wong, 14 Nov 1993. Education: BSc, Univ of Adelaide, 1962; Dip Mineral Technol in Applied Geochemistry, Camborne Sch of Mines, 1966; DipEd, SACAE, 1983. Appointments: Rsch Chem, FIRA, Stevenage, 1963-64; Chem, Mufulira, Zambia, 1964-65; Geochemist, Cominco, Adelaide, 1966-68; Agric Chem, DASF, PNG, 1968-69; Snr Geochemist, Ethiopian Govt, 1969-70; Cnslt Geochemist, Brisbane, 1970-72; Snr Geochemist/Geol, Alcoa, Brisbane, 1972-74; UN Expert Geochemist/Geol, Morocco-UNDP, Indonesia & Sri Lanka-IAEA, 1974-79; Cnslt Geochemist, Cairns, 1979-84, 1987-90; Nuclear Uranium Advisor, NT Govt, 1984-87, 1990-95; Cnslt Geochemist, Darwin, specialising in Indonesia, 1995-. Publications: The Nuclear Power Industry: A Responsible Approach (w Subash Chandra), 1985. Memberships: Assn of Exploration Geochemists; Fell, Australasian Inst of Mining and Metall; Mineral Ind Cnslts Assn; Austl Nuclear Assn. Hobbies: Golden Oldies Rugby Union; Masters Athletics. Address: 12 Achernar Court, Woodroffe, NT 0830, Australia.

WATTISON Meredith, b. 5 Feb 1963. Poet. m. 23 Dec 1989, Alexander Gillon, 2 s. Publications: Psyche's Circus, 1989; Judith's Do, 1996. Memberships: Poets Union; NSW Writers Cntr. Address: c/o Penguin Books Australia, PO Box 257, Ringwood, Vic 3134, Australia.

WATTS Donald Walter, b. 1 Apr 1934, WA, Aust. President; Vice-Chancellor. m. Michelle Rose Yeomans, 30 July 1960, 2 s. Education: BS, Hons, 1954; PhD, 1959, Univ of WA; Univ Coll, London, Eng, 1959-61. Appointments: Personal Chair, Physical and Inorganic Chem, Univ of WA, 1977-79; Dir, WA Inst of Technol, 1987; Pres, Vice-Chancellor, Bond Univ, 1987-90; Chf Exec Offr, Trade Dev Zone Authority, 1990-91; Chmn, NT Employment and Trng Authority, 1991-93; Exec Chmn, Trade Dev Zone Authority, Darwin, NT, 1993-95; Chmn, Austl Space Cncl, Canberra (C'wlth Govt Appts), 1993; Non-Exec Chmn, Advd Energy Systems, Perth, WA, 1994-; Dean, Rsch and Postgrad Stdies, Prof, Sci and Educ, Univ of Notre Dame, Fremantle; Dir, Vasse Newtown Ltd, 1997-98; Cnclr Austl Acady of Technological Scis and Engrng, 1996-. Publications include: The School Chemistry Project, a Secondary School Chemistry Syllabus for Comment, 1978; Higher Education in Australia: A Way Forward, 1986; A Private Approach to Higher Education, 1987. Honours: Hackett Schl, 1953; Gleddon Fell, 1957; CSIRO Postdoct Fell, 1959; DSIR Postdoct Fell, 1961; Rennie Medallist Royal Austl Chem Inst, 1967; Fulbright Schl, 1967; Hon Life Mbr, Currie Hall, Univ WA, 1974; Japan Fndn Visitation Fell, 1984; Hon Fell, Mktng Inst of Singapore, 1988; Leighton Medalist, Royal Austl Chem Inst, 1987; Hon Dr, Technol, Curtin Univ of Technol; Emeritus Prof, Bond Univ, 1990; AM, 1998; ANZAAS Medallist, 1999; Fell, Roy Austl Chem Inst. Memberships include: Fell, Austl Coll of Educ; Fell, Austl Acady of Technol Scis and Engrng; Amn Chem Soc; Sci and Ind Forum Austl Acady of Scis; Austl Inst of Mngmt. Hobbies: Squash; Tennis; Golf. Address: The University of Notre Dame Australia, 13-19 Mouat Street, Fremantle, WA 6160, Australia.

WATTS Robert Oliver, b. 23 Sept 1940. Professor. m. 1 s, 3 d. Education: BSc, Univ of London, 1965; PhD, Austl Natl Univ, 1968. Appointments: Lab Techn, Animal Hlth Trust, UK, 1958; Snr Rsch Asst, A Wander Ltd, UK, 1960; Postdoct Fell, Univ of Waterloo, Can, 1968; Rsch Fell, 1970, Snr Rsch Fell, 1973, Fell (tenured), 1973, Snr Fell, 1976, Dir of Computing, 1977, Snr Fell, 1978, Austl Natl Univ; Prof, Univ of WA, 1986; Chmn of Chem, Univ of WA, 1990; ICI-Masson Prof and Hd of Chem Sch, Univ of Melbourne, 1995; Chf Scientist, BHP, 1997. Honours: Snr Fulbright Fell, 1972; CP Cross Lectr, Univ of WA, 1985; Snr Humboldt Fell, 1990; Cnsltng Scientist, Biosym Technols, San Diego, 1990-94; Battelle Profshp in Chem, 1991-95; Disting Scientist, Pacific N W Labs, 1991-; Chair, External Advsry Cttee, Environmental and Molecular Scis Labs, Battelle Pacific N W Labs, Hanford, 1991-95. Memberships: Fell, Royal Austl Chem Soc; Amn Chem Soc; Amn Physl Soc. Hobbies: Music; Outdoor Activities. Address: BHP, 245-273 Wellington Road, Mulgrave, Vic 3170, Australia.

WAUGH Russell F, b. Sydney, Aust. Senior Lecturer, Edith Cowan University. m. Bernadette, 3 s. Education: BSc, BEduc, Univ West Aust; MSc, Macquarie Univ; MEduc, PhD, Univ West Aust. Honour: Fulbright Schlshp, 1981. Hobbies: Special interest in research management (education, social sciences and psychology). Address: Edith Cowan Univ, Pearson Street, Churchlands, Western Australia 6018, Australia.

WAUGH Stephen Rodger, b. 2 Jun 1965 Canterbury Sydney. Cricketer. Education: East Hills High Sch. Appointments: Right-hand batsman and right-arm medium-fast bowler; Teams - NSW, 1984-85 to date; Somerset, 1987-88; 100 Tests for Aust, 19085-86 to 6 Jan 1998 scoring 6288 runs - average - 49.5 - inclng 14 hundreds and taking 85 wickets - average 34.8; Has scored 16238 first-class runs - average 52.2 - with 46 hundreds to 6 Jan 1998; Shared world record 5th wicket stand of 464 - unbroken - with M E Waugh for NSW v WAust Perth, 1990-91; Toured Eng, 1989, 19883, 1997; 225 limited-overs intls to 31 Dec 1997. Publications: South African Tour Diary, 1995; Steve Waugh's West Indies Tour Diary, 1996; Steve Waugh's World Cup Diary, 1997.

WAVISH William Paul Renton, b. 4 Feb 1948, Auckland, NZ. Chartered Accountant. m. Yvonne, 13 Sept 1991. Education: ACA (NZ); CMANZ; ACIS; ANZIM. Appointments: Mngng Dir, Dairy Farm Intl, Hongkong & N Asia, 1970-81; Grp Gen Mngr, Intl, Hongkong Land Ltd, 1981-85; Grp Ops Mngr, Indl Equity Ltd, 1985-86; Mngng Dir, Chase Corp Ltd, Aust, 1986-89; CFO Asia Pacific, Campbell Soup Co, 1996-; Apptd by HK Govt to Indep Commn Against Corruption. Hobbies: Basketball; Golf; Horse racing. Address: 11 Magazine Gap Road, Hong Kong, China.

WAWRZYNIAK Andrzej Michal, b. 3 Dec 1931, Warsaw, Poland. Sailor; Oriental Studies Scholar; Diplomat. 2 s, 2 d. Education: MA, Intl Law, Sch of For Serv, Warsaw, 1955; PhD stdies, Sch of Socl and Polit Scis, 1969. Appointments: Sailor and then Offr, Polish Merchant Navy, 1948-55; Polish For Serv, Over 25 yrs in Asia, Vietnam, Indonesia, Laos, Nepal, Afghanistan, 1956-93; Min plenipotentiary dipl rank; Fndr, dir, curator-i/c, The Asia and Pacific Mus of Warsaw, 1973-; Hon Consul-Gen or Sri Lanka in Poland, 1997-. Publications: Hundreds of publs, radio and TV progs and exhibns on Asian and Pacific problematics; Lectd as Visng Prof in sev Asian countries. Honours: Kt's Cross, Polonia Restituta Order, 1967; Min of Culture and Arts Awd for contbn to culture, 1976; Cty of Warsaw awd for contbn to culture, 1987; Trybuna Ludu awd for promoting friendship w Asian countries, 1989; Disting Offr of Polish Dip Serv, 1978; Recip, Offr's Cross, 1992; Cmdr's Cross, Polonia Restituta Order; Indonesian Order of Serv w Star (Bintang Jasa Pratama), 1999; Sev other Polish and for citations. Memberships: Mbr, Polish Acady of Scis Cttee for Oriental Stdies; Mbr, Polish Acady of Scis Cttee for Rsch on Asian Countries; Intl Assn of Friends of the Khmer Culture; Mbr, Polish Natl Cttee of UNESCO. Hobbies: Collecting Asian and Pacific wrks of art; Bridge. Address: The Asia and Pacific Museum, 24 Solec Street, 00-403 Warsaw, Poland.

WAY E Leong, b. 10 July 1916, USA. Pharmacology. m. Madeline Li, 11 Aug 1944, 1 s, 1 d. Education: BS, Univ of CA, 1938; MS, 1940; PhD, 1942. Appointments: Pharm Chem, Merck Co, 1942-43; Instr, Pharmacology, 1943-46, Asst Prof, 1946-48, George Washington Univ; Asst Prof, Pharmacology, 1949-52, Assoc Prof, 1952-57, Prof, 1957-87, Chmn, 1973-78, Prof Emer, 1987-, Univ of CA, San Fran; Visng Prof, Univ of Hong Kong, 1962-63; Hon Prof, Guangzhou Medl Coll, 1986; Tsumura Prof, Neuropsychopharmacology, Gunma Univ Medl Sch, Japan, 1989-90; Snr Staff Fell, Natl Inst on Drug Abuse, 1990-91. Creative Works: About 400 Publs; Books, Endogenous and Exogenous Opiate Agonist, Antagonist. Honours: USPHS Spcl Rsch Fellshp, Univ of Berne; China Medl Bd Fellshp, Univ of Hong Kong; Amn Pharmacology Fndn, Achvmnt Awd; Elected Academician, Acady Sinica; Fac Rsch Lectr Awd; San Fran Chinese Hosp Awd; Gold Medal and Cultural Citation; Nathan B Eddy mem Awd; Sterling Sullivan Disting Prof Awd; Chans Awd for pub Serv; Disting Alumnus of the Yr; Torald Sollman Awd. Address: Dept of Pharmacology, University of California, San Francisco, CA 94143-0450, USA.

WEAVER Geoffey Alexander, b. 28 Apr 1949, Adelaide, Aust. Winemaker. m. Judith, 20 Aug 1979, 1 s, 1 d. Education: BAgrSc; RDOcn. Appointments: Winemaker, Orlando, 1974; Winemaker, Thomas Hardy, 1975; Chf Winemaker, Hardy Grp, 1988; Estab Stafford Ridge Vineyards, 1982. Memberships: Dir, Aust Wine Rsch Inst, 1988-; Bdmbr, GWRDC (Grape and Wine Rsch and Dev Corp, 1994-. Hobby: Landscape painting. Address: 2 Gilpin Lane, Mitcham, South Australia 5062, Australia.

WEAVER Sigourney, b. 1949 NY. Actress. m. James Simpson, 1984, 1 d. Films incl: Annie Hall, 1977; Tribute to a Madman, 1977; Camp 708, 1978; Alien, 1979; Eyewitness, 1981; The Year of Living Dangerously, 1982; Deal of the Century, 1983; Ghostbusters, 1984; Une Femme ou Deux, 1985; Half Moon Street, 1986; Aliens, 1986; Gorillas in the Mist, 1988; Working Girl, 1988; Ghostbusters II, 1989; Aliens 3, 1992; 1492 Conquest of Paradise, 1993; Dave, 1993; Death and the Maiden, 1994; Jeffrey, 1995; Copycat, 1996; Snow White in the Black Forest, 1996; Ice Storm, 1996; Alien Resurrection, 1997. Honours: Golden Globe Best Actress Awd for Gorillas in the Mist; Best Supporting Actress Awd Golden Globe for Working Girl. Address: c/o ICM, 8942 Wilshire Boulevard, Beverly Hills, CA 90211, USA.

WEBB Charles Joseph, b. 1 Jan 1951. Professor. m. 16 Apr 1983. Education: BSc, hons, PhD, Cert Ed, Bristol Univ, Eng. Appointments: Lectr, Snr Lectr, Zoology, Univ of S Pacific; Snr Lectr, Assoc Prof, Assoc Dean, Biol Scis, Dean of Sci, Prov Chan, Rsch and Intl, NT Univ, Aust; Chf Exec Offr and Chmn of the Bd, Strehlow Rsch Cntr, Alice Springs, NT, 1997. Publications: Contrb to sci lit. Memberships: Fell, Linnean Soc; Bd Mbr, Mus and Art Galls of NT; Bd Mbr, Coop Rsch Cntr for Sustainable Devl of Tropical Savannas; Mbr Bd, Co-op Rsch Cntr for Aboriginal and Tropical Hlth. Address: Research & International, Northern Territory University, Darwin, NT 0909, Australia.

WEBB Geoffrey Ian, b. 6 Oct 1960, Melbourne, Australia. Professor. m. Janine Carol McGuinness Webb, 13 Apr 1985, 1 s. Education: BA, hons, 1982, PhD, 1987, LaTrobe Univ. Appointments: Lectr, Griffith Univ, 1986-88; Lectr, Snr Lectr, Rdr, 1988-98, Personal Chair, 1998-, Deakin Univ. Publications include: Integrating machine learning with knowledge acquisition through direct interaction with domain experts, 1996; Comparative evaluation of alternative induction engines for Feature Based Modelling, 1998; Using decision trees for agent modelling: Improving prediction performance, 1998; An experimental evaluation of integrating machine learning with knowledge acquisition, 1999. Memberships: Pres, Austl Soc for Computers in Learning in Tertiary Educ, 1988-91. Hobbies: Reading; Sailing; Computing. Address: School of Computing & Mathematics, Deakin University, Geelong, Victoria 3217, Australia.

WEBB Leonard James, b. 28 Oct 1920, Qld, Aust. Rainforest Ecologist; Eco-Philosopher. m. Doris Mary Browning, 8 Oct 1942, 1 s, 1 d. Education: BS Hons; MSc; PhD, Univ of Qld. Appointments: Field Botanist, Ecologist, CSIRO Div of Plant Ind, Brisbane; Austl Phytochemical Survey, 1944-52; Rainforest Ecology, 1953-80, retd; Hon Prof, Austl Environmental Studies, Griffith Univ, 1981-; Mbr, var Austl govt and intl cttees for heritage and nat conservation. Publications include: Over 100 articles; auth 2 books; co-ed, contbr, sev ecology books. Honours: Inaugural Gold Medal, Ecological Soc of Aust, 1983; ANZAAS Mueller Medal, 1983; BHP Pursuit of Excellence, 1984; AO, 1987; DUniv (Griffith), 1991. Memberships include: Austl Conservation Fndn; Wildlife Preservation Soc of Qld; Inst Foresters of Aust; Austl Inst for Aboriginal and Torres Srait Islander Studies. Hobbies: Gardening; Classical music; Poetry. Address: 15 Prospect Street, Wilston, Brisbane, Qld 4051, Australia.

WEBB Philippa Janet, b. 14 Nov 1933, Melbourne, Aust. Artist. m. Donald, 2 June 1956, 2 d. Education: ALAA. Publications: The Wombat and the Snail, book, 1992; Tidalik's Tale, book, 1994; Solo painting exhibs, 1986-99. Honours: Austl Bicentennial Commn, 1988; Pine Rivers Heritage Awd, Brisbane, Aust, 1997. Memberships: Assoc Lib Assn Aust; Roy Qld Art Soc. Hobbies: Painting; Printmaking; Calligraphy. Address: PO Box 441, New Farm, 4005, Australia.

WEBB Ronald Campbell, b, 5 Mar 1925, Melbourne, Aust. Medical Practitioner; Medical Administrator. m. Denise Victoria Clarke, 16 Dec 1948, 3 s, 3 d. Education: MB BS, Melbourne Univ, 1951; DTM&H, Sydney Univ, 1957; FRACP, 1976; FRACMA, 1968; FAIM, 1970; FAMA, 1976. Appointments: Flying Dr, Alice Springs, 1956; NT, Medl Serv, 1953-61; MOH, NT, 1958-61; NT CQO, General and Plants, 1958-61; CMO, Aust House, London, Eng (Mbr of Diplomatic Corps), 1962-65; C'wlth Dir of Hlth, WA, 1966-67; C'wlth Dir of Hlth, Vic, 1968-83. Honours: AM, 1980; Mbr, Legis Cncl, NT (MLC, 1958-60). Memberships: Austl Medl Assn, Branch Cncl, WA, 1966-67, Br Cncl, Vic, 1968-88; Roy Austl Coll of Medl Admnstrs, Fedl Cncl, 1975-83, Pres, 1980-82; Fac Med, Monash Univ, 1975-, Mbr, Bd Acady of Gen Prac, 1985-96; Fac Med, Melbourne Univ, 1976-83. Hobbies: Chess; Oil Painting; Photography; Family history; Tennis. Address: Inveraray, 137 Holm Park Road, Beaconsfield, Vic 3807, Australia.

WEBER Stephen L, b. 17 Mar 1942, Boston, MA, USA. University President. m. Susan K, 27 June 1965, 2 s. Education: BA, Philos, Bowling Green Univ, OH, 1964; Grad Studies in Philos & Classics, Univ of CO, Boulder, CO, 19064-66; PhD, Philos, Univ Notre Dame, IN, 1969. Appointments: Grad Asst in Hons, Univ CO, 1965-66; Tchng Asst, Dept of Philos, Univ Notre Dame, 1966-69; Asst Prof, 1969-74, Assoc Prof, 1974-79, Philos, Univ of ME; Assoc Prof, Philos, Dean of Arts & Scis, Fairfield Univ, 1979-84; VP, Acad Affairs, St Cloud State Univ, MN, 1984-88; Prof, Philos, Pres, State Univ, NY at Oswego, 1988-96; Prof of Philos, Pres, San Diego State Univ, 1996-. Publications: Reviews, articles, in profl jrnls; Exec Prodr, Paul Cadmus: Enfant Terrible at 80 (dir, David Sutherland), winner of var natl & intl awds, 1984. Honours: Rsch Fellshp, Univ Notre Dame, 1968-69; Outstndng Humanities Tchr, Univ of ME, Oronno, 1975; Invited to 1981 Sloan Fndn Conf on New Liberal Arts, 1981; Participant, Harvard Inst for Educl Mngmt, 1985; Mentor, Amn Cncl on Educ Fellshp Prog, 1985-86, 1996-97; Hon Degree, Beijing Capital Normal Univ, Beijing, 1994; Headliner of Yr, San Diego Press Club, 1997; Peacemaker Awd, San Diego Mediation Cntr, 1997. Memberships include: Amn Philosophic Assn; Amn Assn of Higher Educ; Amn Assn of State Colls & Univs; Amn Cncl on Educ, Commns on Intl Educ and on Govtl Rels. Hobbies: Art; Woodworking; Swimming; Boating. Address: San Diego University, 5500 Campanile Drive, San Diego, CA 92182-8000, USA.

WEBSTER John Alexander, b. 12 Feb 1943, Aberdeen, Scotland. Chief Executive. m. Mary, 29 Dec 1965, 3 d. Education: BSc, 1st class hons, 1964, MSc, 1965, PhD, 1968, Aberdeen Univ. Appointments: Asst Lectr, Engrng, 1965-66, Lectr, Engrng Maths, 1966-69, Univ of Aberdeen; Rsch Sci, CSIRO Divsn of Computing Rsch, Canberra, 1969-72; Snr Engr, Min of Works & Devel, Wellington, NZ, 1972-75; Snr Lectr, Rdr, Sch of Arch, 1975-85, Dean, Fac of Arch, 1982-85, Vic Univ of Wellington, NZ; Dean, Acad Servs, Tas State Inst of Technol, 1986-88; Prin, Pro-Vice-Chan, La Trobe Univ Coll of Northern Vic, 1989-92; Chf Exec, Instn of Engrs, Aust, 1992-99; Pres, United Inst of Technol, Auckland, NZ, 1999-. Publications: 5 textbooks, 25 jrnl articles, 60 monographs and tech reports, 50 conf pprs. Memberships: Fell, Inst of Profl Engrs, NZ, Inst of Engrs, Aust, Inst of Engrs, Ireland. Hobbies: Aviation; Computing; History; Reading. Address: 63 Victory Road, Laingholm, Auckland, New Zealand.

WEBSTER Ross Wharton, b. 5 Jan 1924, Melbourne, Aust. Physician. m. Jill, 2 s, 1 d. Education: MBBS; FRACP; FRACGP; FAFPHM. Appointments: Dpty Medl

Dir, Peter MacCallum Cancer Inst, 1972-75; Prof, Community Med, Univ of Melbourne, 1975-89. Honour: Queens Jubilee Medal, 1977. Memberships: Pres, AMA, Vic, 1977; Chmn, Fedl Assembly, AMA, 1979-85. Hobbies: Medical Idemnity; Athletics; Gardening. Address: 807 Park Street, Brunswick 3056, Victoria, Australia.

WEE Chong Jin, b. 28 Sep 1917 Penang Malay. Judge. m. Cecilia Mary Henderson, 1955, 3 s, 1 d. Education: Penang Free Sch; St John's Coll Cambridge. Appointments: Called to Bar Middle Temple London, 1938; Admitted Advocate and Solicitor of Straits Settlements, 1940; Practised in Penang and Singapore, 1940-57; Puisne Judge Singapore, 1957; Chf Jus, 1963-90; Acting Pres of Singapore, Mar-Aug 1985; Hd Predl Cncl for Relig Harmony, 1992-. Honours: Hon DCL - Oxford - 1987. Hobby: Golf. Address: 1 Colombo Court, # 09-05, Singapore 0617.

WEE Wee Kim, b. 4 Nov 1915, Singapore. Diplomat. m. Koh Sok Hiong, 1936, 1 s, 6 d. Education: Raffles Inst. Appointments include: Dpty Ed, Ed Mngr, Straits Times, Singapore, 1959-73; Covered civ war in Belgian Congo (now Zaire); First Singapore Jrnlst to enter Jakarta during Confrontation, 1966; Joined Utd Press Assn, 1941, rejoined, 1945-59; High Commnr to Malaysia, 1973-80; Dean, Diplomatic Corps, Kuala Lumpur, 1978-80; Mbr, Singapore Del to UN Gen Assembly, 1977; Amb to Japan, 1980-84; Amb to Repub of Korea, 1981-84; Chair, Singapore Brdcstng Corp, 1984-85; Pres, Repub of Singapore, 1985-93. Honours: Pub Serv Star, 1963; JP, 1966; Meritorious Serv Medal, 1979; Hon GCB, 1989; Laila Utama, Brunei, 1990; Order of Temasek 1st Class, 1993; Hon DLitt, Natl Univ Singapore, 1994. Hobbies: Golf; Walking; Writing. Address: 25 Siglap Plain, Singapore 456014.

WEI Baowen, b. 22 Nov 1935, Henan, China. Professor of Physics. m. G Z Xu, 15 Aug 1961, 1 s, 1 d. Education: Grad, Peking Univ, 1957. Appointments: Dir, Natl Lab of Heavy Iron Accelerator, Lanzhou, 1992-. Publications: Cross Section Measurement for Light Ion Induced Nuclear Reactions, 1989; Heavy Ion Cooling Storage Ring, 1994. Honour: Natl Prize, Sci and Technol Progress, 1992. Membership: Mbr, Chinese Acady of Scis, 1995-. Address: Institute of Modern Physics, Chinese Academy of Sciences, PO Box 31, Lanzhou 73000, China.

WEI Cheng Lian, b. 2 June 1938, Guangdong Prov, China. Fellow. m. 11 Dec 1969, 1 s. Education: Univ man, Fudan Univ, Shanghai, 1959-60; BS, Shanghai Univ of Sci and Technol, Shanghai, 1961-63. Publications: A new phenomenon about the (111) Planar Particles blocking dip in single crystal Si, 1980; Measurement of the K value in gold jewelry by XRF method, 1992; X-ray fluorescence analysis of the silver content of ancient Chinese silverware, 1996. Honour: Sci and Inventor in Modern China, Editl Cttee, Sci and Inventor in Modern China, 1995. Memberships: Chinese Nuc Phys Soc, Beijing, 1982; High Energy Phys Soc of China, 1983; Profl Mbrshp, AAAS, 1987. Hobbies: Watching football; Music; Going for walks. Address: Institute of High Energy Physics, Academia Sinica, PO Box 2732, 10080 Peijing, China.

WEI Fengsi, b. 5 Nov 1941, Chendu, China. Space Physicist. m. Zheying Ren, 24 Apr 1968, 1 s, 1 d. Education: Deg in Geophys, Univ of Sci & Technol, Beijing, China, 1963. Appointments: Visng Schlr, Cath Univ Am, Washington, 1980-82; Prof, 1998-; Supr, 1990-; Mbr, SOLTIP/SCOSTEP, 1990-; Dir, Lab for Heliosphys, Acad Sinia, 1988-; Mbr, Expert Cttee for Tech Sci, 1994-; Prin Investigator, maj progs Natl NSF, Beijing, 1995-99. Honours: Nat Sci Prize, Sec Class, Scientia Sinica, 1987, 1989; Nat Sci Prized, Third Class, China, 1993. Memberships: Lab of Numerical Study for Heliospheric Phys; Chinese Acady of Scis; AGU, 1980-. Address: Center for Space Science and Applied Research, Academia Sinica, PO Box 8701, Beijing 100080, China.

WEI Lai Lin, b. 30 Mar 1963, Linqing, Shandong, China. Doctor. m. Zhang yan, 30 Mar 1986, 1 s. Education: Undergrad Course. Appointment: Dir, Med Matters Dept. Publications: Clinical Medicine Handbook; Intervenient Treat Therapeutics of Congenital Cardiovascular Disease. Membership: Intervenient Assn, Shandong. Hobbies: Music; Football. Address: c/o 2nd Affiliated Hospital, Shandong Medical University, Jinan, Shandong 250017, China.

WEI Wei, b. 4 Apr 1947, Tianjin, China. Entrepreneur. m. Liu Bao Zhen, 1 May 1977, 1 s. Education: Econ Mngmnt spec, Beijing Econ Corresp Univ. Appointment: Dir, Tianjin Arts Printing Factory. Publication: Practical Color Standard, 1993. Honours: Advd Worker, Natl Book Printing, 1980; Tianjin Model Worker, 1986-95; Natl Model Worker, Tianjin Spec-Class Model Worker, 1995; Morisama Nobuo Printing, 1st Awd, 1995. Memberships: Enterprise Mngmt Cttee, Printing Technol Assn, China, 1991-; Standing Dir, Tianjing Printing Technol Assn. Hobbies: Music; Painting. Address: No 12, Binxi Road, Hexi District, Tianjin, 300061, China.

WEI Wei. Singer. m. Michael Smith, 1 s. Appointments: Singer at 11th Asian Games Beijing, 1990; Performed a duet with Julio Iglesias - qv - at E Asian Games Shanghai, 1993; Tour of China, 1995. Albums incl: Twilight.

WEI Xianyong, b. 14 Apr 1958, Xuzhou City, China. Teacher. m. Zong Zhimin, 24 July 1984, 1 s. Education: Grad, DEng, Univ Tokyo, 1992. Publications: Energy & Fuels, 1989; Fuel Processing Technology, 1990. Honours: Ex Worker of Sci and Technol, Jiangsu Prov, 1995; 3rd Awd, Progress in Sci and Technol, Natl Educ Cttee, 1996; Nom Winner of Jiangsu Yth Scientist. Memberships: Coal Chem Cttee, Coal Inst of China, 1995; Acad Cttee, Open Lab for Comprehensive Utilization of Carbon Resources, Dalian Univ. Hobbies: Badminton; Table Tennis. Address: Department of Energy Utilization and Chemical Engineering, China University of Mining and Technology, Xuzhou, Jiangsu 221008, China.

WEI Xiyun, b. 3 Oct 1940, Nanjing, China. Professor of Anatomy. m. Zhang Jinkun, 23 Jan 1971, 1 s. Education: BS, Nanjing Railway Med Coll, 1964. Appointments: Lectr, Dept of Anatomy, Nanjing Railway Med Coll, 1964-87; Vice Prof, Dept of Anatomy, China Pharm Univ, 1987-92; Prof, Hd, Dept of Anatomy, Shantou Univ Med Coll, 1992-. Publications include: Observations of the dorsal scapular nerve and its clinical application, 1987; Anatomical study on compression syndrome of common peroneal nerve, 1987; Morphological observation of thymic changes of aged mice after excising sex glands, 1992; Morphological quantitave study of protective effect of tonic traditional Chinese medicines on thymus in mice, 1996. Honour: 2nd Prize, Sci and Technol Progress, Railway Dept, 1987. Memberships: Chinese Soc of Anatomical Scis; Chinese Soc for Stereology. Address: Department of Anatomy, Shantou University Medical College, Xingling Road, Shantou 515031, China.

WEINBERG William Henry, b. 5 Dec 1944, Columbia, SC, USA. Technologist; Educator. m. Ann Muir, 25 Mar 1989. Education: BS, Univ S Carolina, 1966; PhD, Chem Engrng, Univ California, Berkeley, 1970; NATOA Postdoc Fell, Phys Chem, Cambridge Univ, Eng, 1971. Appointments: Asst Prof, Chem Engrng, California Inst Technol, 1972-74; Assoc Prof, 1974-77; Prof Chem Engrng & Chem, Univ California, Santa Barbara, 1989-; Assoc Dean, Coll Engrng, 1992-96; Chief Tech Offr, Symyx Techs, Santa Clara, CA, 1995-; Visng Prof, Chem, Harvard Univ, 1980; Univ Pitts, 1987-88; Oxford Univ, 1991. Publications include: Low-Energy Electron Diffraction, auth w Van Hove and Chan, 1986; ed, 4 book sin field; Handbook Surfaces and Interfaces, 1978-80; Contbr, articles to profl jrnls, chapts to books. Honours include: Giuseppe Parravano Awd, 1989; Disting Tchng Awd, 1995; Arthur W Adamson Awd, 1995. Memberships include: Amn Chem Soc; N Amn Catalysis Soc; Natl Acady Engrng; Phi Beta Kappa. Address: Symyx

Technologies 3100 Central Expy Santa Clara, CA 95051-0801, USA.

WEINSTOCK Wolfowicz, b. 17 Dec 1931, San José, Costa Rica. Minister of Public Health. m. 3 children. Education: Deg in Medl Surg, Univ Buenos Aires, Argentina, 1956; Grad, Inst Cardiology, Mexico, 1959, Harv Univ, 1962. Appointments: Kidney Surg, Calderon Guardia Hosp; Chf Kidney Surg, Mexico Hosp, Costa Rica, 1982-86; Majority Whip; Min, Pub Hlth, Govt Costa Rica, 1994-. Memberships: Bd Govs, Mortgage Housing Bank; Exec Pres, Costa Rican Inst Aquaducts Sewers; Pres, Renal Surg Assn; Liberacion Nacional. Address: Ministry of Public Health, Apartado 10123, 1000 San José, Costa Rica.

WEIR James Harrison, b. 6 June 1922, Christchurch, NZ. Diplomat (Retired). m. Mary Helen De Muth, 1 Nov 1947, 1 s, 3 d. Education: MA, NZ. Appointments: Dept of External Affairs (now Min of For Affairs),Wellington, NZ, 1947-49, 1952-56, 1961-62; Third Sec, NZ Mission to UN, NY, USA, 1949-51; Second Sec, NZ High Cmmn, Ottawa, Can, 1951-52; First Sec, Cnslr, NZ High Cmmn, Canberra, Aust, 1956-61; Cnslr, Min, NZ Emb, Wash DC, USA, 1963-65; NZ High Cmmnr, Singapore, 1966-70; Asst Sec, Min of For Affairs, Wellington, NZ, 1970-73 High Cmmnr, Kuala Lumpur, Malaysia; Amb, Burma; Cmmnr, Brunei, 1973-76; Amb, Moscow, Russia, Finland, Mongolia, 1977-80; Amb, Rome, Italy, Egypt, Malta, Saudi Arabia, Yugosalvia, 1980-83; Chmn, Wellington Civ Trust, 1986-89; Book Reviewer, Evening Post, 1988-. Publications: Letters from Moscow, 1988; Russia Through New Zealand Eyes - to 1944, 1996; New Zealand Wit and Wisdom, 1998. Address: 20A Lancaster Street, Karori, Wellington, New Zealand.

WEIR Peter Lindsay, b. 21 Aug 1944. Film Director. m. Wendy Stites, 1 s, 1 d. Education: Univ Sydney. Appointments: Stagehand, Channel 7, 1967-68; C'wlth Film Unit, 1969-70, 1972-73; Ind Feature Films, 1974-79; Dir: The Cars That Ate Paris, 1974; Picnic at Hanging Rock, 1975; Last Wave, 1977; The Plumber, 1978; Gallipoli, 1981; The Year of Living Dangerously 1983; Witness, 1985; The Mosquito Coast, 1986; Dead Poets Society, 1989; Green Card, 1990; Fearless, 1992; The Truman Show, 1997. Honours: AM, 1982; DLitt honoris causa, Macquarie Univ. Address: c/o C.A.A., 9830 Wilshire Bvd, Beverly Hills, CA 90212, USA.

WEISS Anthony Steven, b. 16 June 1957, Sydney, Aust. Scientist. m. Jacqueline, 6 Feb 1983, 2 s, 1 d. Education: BSc, hons, 1979; PhD, 1984; ARC Rsch Fell, 1984; Stanford Univ Postdoct Schl, 1984-86; Fogarty Intl Fell, NIH; Fulbright Schl; CSIRO Postdoct Fell. Appointments: Lectr, 1987, Snr Lectr, 1992, Univ Sydney; Roy Soc Exchange Fell, 1995. Publications: Num sci pprs in profl jrnls. Honours: Hon Visng Sci, Molecular Genetics, RPAH; Num schlshps and fellshps; Hd, Molecular Bio Biotech Lab; Amersham Pharmacia Biotech Medal, 1999. Memberships: Sev. Hobbies: Handyman; Parenting. Address: Department of Biochemistry, University of Sydney, NSW 2006, Australia.

WEIZMAN Ezer, b. 15 Jun 1924 Tel Aviv. Politician; Air Force Offr. m. 2 c. Education: RAF Staff Coll. Appointments: Offr Israel Air Force, 1948-66; Fmr CO IAF; Chf Gen Staff Branch, 1966-69; Min of Transp, 1969-70; Chmn Exec Cttee Herut Party, 1971-73; Min of Def, 1977-80; In priv bus, 1980-84; Min of Comms, 1984-88; Min without Portfolio in Cabinet Hd of Yahad Party in Natl Unity Govt, 1984-89; Min of Sci, 1988-92; PM of Israel, May 1993-. Publications: On Eagles Wings, 1978; The Battle for Peace, 1981. Address: Beit Hanassi, Jerusalem, Israel.

WELCH Anthony Rogers, b. 22 Sept 1949, Adelaide, Aust. Associate Professor (Reader). Div, 1 s, 1 d. Education: HDT(S), Melbourne CAE; DipEd 1975, MA (distinction) 1976, PhD, 1988, Univ of London. Appointments: Subject Master, Glenroy Tech Sch, 1972-73; Supply Tchr, London, 1974-75; Lectr 1977-85; Snr Lectr 1985-, Univ New England; Visng Schl, Univ London, 1982. Publications include: Contemporary

Perspectives in Comparative Education, 1992; A Knowledge, Culture and Power, 1993; Australian Education: Reform or Crisis?, 1996; Quality and Equality in Third World Education, 1999. Honours: Visng Schl, Univ London, 1982; Vising Schl, Carnegie Fndn for the Adv of Tchng, USA, 1993; Visng Prof, Humboldt Universität zu Berlin, 1994, 1997; Visng Schl, Waseda Univ, Tokyo, 1997. DAAD Schl, 1994. Memberships: Pres, ANZCIES, 1986; Exec Mbr, 1985, 1996, VP, 1996-98, WCCES. Hobbies: Music; Reading; Sport. Address: Social & Policy Studies in Education, University of Sydney, NSW 2006, Australia.

WELCH Bruce Everest, b. 10 Oct 1928, Melbourne, Aust. Retired Newspaper Executive. m. Beatrice Nancy Lyons, 11 Dec 1953, 2 s, 1 d. Appointments: Jrnlst, Brdcstr, Sportswriter, 1946-60; Reporter, Olympic Games, Helsinki, Finland, 1952; Mbr, Olympic Press Cttee, Melbourne, 1951-56; Sales Promotion Mngr, The Age Newspaper, 1960-63; Circulation Mngr, 1964-84; Mngr, Sunday Press, 1974-89, Corp Plng Mngr, 1984-89; Asst to the Mngng Dir, 1989-92. Publications include: Num articles in newspprs, mags. Honours: Runner-up, Walkley Awd, 1957; VP and Serv Awd, Swimming Vic; Life Mbr, Malvern Swimming Club. Memberships: Chmn, Newsppr Publrs Assn of Melbourne, 1986-92; Intl Circulation Mngrs Assn, 1964-84; Hon Mbr, 1984-. Hobbies: Travel; Swimming. Address: 92 Doubleview Drive, Elanora, Qld 4221, Australia.

WELFORD Rodney Jon, b. 30 Sept 1958, Brisbane, Aust. Shadow Minister; Lawyer. BA Hons; LLB; Grad Dip, Legal Prac; Grad Dip, Ind Rel. Appointments: Lifeguard, 1977-81; Sol, Supreme Ct of QLD, 1982-; Bar, High Ct of Aust, 1987-; State Mbr for Stafford, 1989-92; State Mbr, Everton, 1992-; Shadow Min, Environ, 1996-98. Memberships: Environ Inst of Aust; Natl Environl Law Assn; Permaculture Intl; Austl Conserv Fndn; Whitham Inst for Soc and Econ Rsch. Hobbies: Polit Sci; Philos; Surfing; Music. Address: 510 South Pine Road, Everton Park, Qld 4053, Australia.

WELLBY Maurice Lindsay, b. 27 Feb 1929, Adelaide, Aust. Chemical Pathologist. m. Marjorie Rasch, 14 Sept, 1970, 1 d. Education: MSc, 1954, MBBS, 1958, BSc, 1959, MD, 1962, Univ of Adelaide; MRCPA, 1963; FRCPA, 1971; Fell, Austl of Clin Biochemists, 1968; MRACP, 1974; FRACP, 1977. Appointments: Grad Rsch Asst, Dept of Path, 1951, Clin Asst, 1951-61, Medl Rsch Fell, 1959-61, Tutor, 1962-66, Lectr, 1967-80, Clin Snr Lectr, 1980-83, Clin Rdr, 1984-89, Assoc Prof, 1989-; Dir, Clin Chem, 1962-93; Hon Visng Cnclt, 1994-. Publications: 3 book chapts and approx 80 pprs mainly in thyroid pathophysiology in medl jrnls. Honours: Roman Mem Travelling Lectr, 1981, Life Fell, 1996, Austl Assn of Clin Biochemists. Memberships: S Austl Cttee, Roy Coll Pathologists of Australasia, 1971-73; Chmn, Bd of Examiners, 1974-80; Pres, Austl Assn of Clin Biochemists, 1981-83; Mbr of Cncl, 1978-82; Chmn, Prog Organising Cttee, 1980-82, Endocrine Soc of Aust. Address: Department of Clinical Chemistry, Queen Elizabeth Hospital, Woodville Road, Woodville, Adelaide, SA 5011, Australia.

WELLER Robert Francis, b. 11 Apr 1955, Melbourne, Aust. Consultant Physician in Rehabilitation Medicine. m. Carolina, 4 Oct 1981, 2 s. Education: MBBS (Melb), 1978; FACRM; FAFRM (RACP). Appointments: Medl Dir, IMO Hosp Grp; Dir, Medl Servs, Victorian Rehab Cntr; Currently Clin Servs Dir, Roy Talbot Rehab Cntr. Memberships: Pres, AACRM; Fedl Cnclr, AFRM; Immediate Past Pres, AFRM Vic Branch; AMA; VAMMI; UMMS. Hobbies: Painting; Fly fishing; Music. Address: c/o ARMC, Heidelberg 3084, Australia.

WELLINGS Paul William, b. 1 Nov 1953, Nottingham, England. Research Manager. m. Annette, 22 Dec 1990. Education: BSc, Hons, Kings Coll, London Univ; MSc, Durham Univ; PhD, Univ of E Anglia. Appointments: Rschr, CSIRO Entomol, 1981-95; Chf of Divsn, 1995-97; Hd, Sci & Technol Divsn, 1997-99. Publications: Over 40 n profl jrnls. Memberships: Bd, Trop Pest Mngmt, 1991-97; Bd, ANSTO, 1997-99; Vice Chair, Cttee for Sci

& Technol Policy, 1997-99. Hobbies: Bushwalking; Cricket; Visual Arts. Address: c/o CSIRO, GPO Box 1700, Canberra, ACT 2601, Australia.

WELLS Carol, b. 7 Mar 1942, NY, NY, USA. Consultant. Appointment: Fedl, State Cnslt, Cnslt to Fortune 20 cos. Publications: Articles, publs, Amn Mngmt Inst. Honours: Dana Schl, Fully Funded Grants, inclng Stocker Fndn Grant. Address: PO 3854, Fullerton, CA 92634, USA.

WELLS Dean, b. 13 Jan 1949, Australian Army Base, Hiroshima, Japan. Member of Parliament. Education: BA, Hons 1, 1972, MA, 1976, LLB, 1980, Monash Univ, Aust. Appointments: Lectr, Philos, Univ Qld, 1978-81; Visng Lectr, Univ Wales, UK, 1981; Fed MP for Petrie, Austl Parl, 1983-84; State Mbr for Murrumba, Qld Parl, 1986-; Att Gen of Qld, 1989-95; Atty-Gen, Min for Justice and Min for the Arts, 1992-95; Shadow Min for Emergency Servs and Pub Serv Matters, 1996-98; Min for Educ, 1998-. Publications: Books: The Wit of Whitlam, 1977; Power Without Theory, 1978; The Deep North, 1981; The Reproduction Revolution, 1984, US edition as Making Babies, 1985; Short stories; Many articles in profl jrnls. Hobbies: Family; Reading; Scuba diving; Films; Chess. Address: Electorate Office, Suite 6, Professional Centre, Kippa Ring Village, Boardman Road, Kippa Ring, Qld 4021, Australia.

WELLS Peter Frederick, b. 28 Feb 1918, Cardiff, Wales. Retired University Professor. m. (1) Jeanne Chiles, 17 Feb 1945, (2) Rita Davenport, 26 Mar 1994, 3 children. Education: MA; Dip.Ed; DPhil. Appointments: Lt, (exec), RNVR, 1939-45; Asst to Chair of Engl, Geneva Univ, 1947; Lectr, Mod Langs, Auckland Second Tchrs Coll; Lectr, French, Univ of Auckland; Snr Lectr, Rdr, Assoc Prof, Hd of Lang Studies, Univ of Waikato, NZ, 1962-63; Prof of French, Dir, Inst of Mod Langs, James Cook Univ, Aust; Tutor in Watercolour Painting, Waikato Art Sch, 1975-. Publications include: Confrontation, 1985; Three Loves and a Minesweeper, 1998; Myra Migrating, 1999. Honours: Order of the Sacred Treas, Rosette & Gold Rays, Japan, 1991; Offr of the NZ Order of Merit, 1998. Memberships: Fndr, Pres, Japan Friendship Soc; RSA; Waikato Art Soc. Hobbies: Painting; Writing; Linguistics. Address: 249 Bankwood Road, Chartwell, Hamilton 2001, New Zealand.

WELLS Richard Charles, b. 23 Nov 1954, Singapore. Executive Director. m. Julie-anne, 30 May 1982, 2 s, 1 d. Education: BS, ANU. Honour: Hon Life Mbr, APPEA. Hobbies: Farming; Sport; Reading. Address: Mining Industry House, 216 Northbourne Avenue, Canberra, ACT 2602 (PO Box 363, Dickson, ACT 2602) Australia.

WELLS Roger, b. 1 June 1945, Hampshire, Eng. Chartered Engineer. Education: Univ of S Hampton, Eng. Appointments: Pres, Intl Consultation Corp; Pres, AAI Inc. Publications: Patents in Automatic Ind; Expert in Automotive Safety and Prog Mngmt. Honours: Pat Awds. Membership: Automotive Expert Witnesses. Address: PO 3854 Fullerton, CA 92634, USA.

WELLS Ronald, b. 5 Feb 1926, Saffron Walden, Essex, Eng. Medical Administrator. m. Betty, 5 Feb 1948, 2 s, 1 d. Education: BSc; MB; BS Lond; DTM&H, Eng; OTM&H, London Univ; MD Lond; MRCP Lond; FRACP; FAM Singapore; FRIPH. Appointments: Dpty Dir Gen of Health, 1973; Chmn, ACT Health Commn, 1974; Chmn, Natl Hosps in Hlth Servs Commn, 1976. Publications: Human Sex Determination, 1990; Sexual Odds, 1990; A Conceipt of Ancestors, 1996; Ancient Ancestors with Modern Descendants, 1999. Honour: AM, 1981. Hobbies: Medieval History; Genealogy. Address: Unit 1, Shackleton Park, Mawson, ACT 2607, Australia.

WELLS William Andrew Noye, b. 6 Mar 1919, N Adelaide, SA, Aust. Retired Supreme Court Judge. m. Eleanor Caroline Jacobs, 14 July 1948, 4 s. Education: LLB, Univ of Adelaide, 1938-39, 1944-45; MA, BCL, Univ of Oxford, Eng 1946-49. Appointments: MEF (8th Army), New Guinea (Signals), 1940-44; State Crown Law, 1950-70; QC, 1962; Crown Solicitor, 1968; Solicitor Gen,

1969; Justice of Supreme Crt of S Aust, 1970-84. Publications: An Introduction to the Law of Evidence, 1963; Evidence and Advocacy, 1988; Evidence: Its History and Principles; Law Judges and Justice (for the Community); Natural Logic, Judicial Proof and Objective Facts. Honours: Stow Schl, 1945; Davis Murray Schl, Adelaide, 1945; Rhodes Schl, 1940; Eldon Schl, Oxford, 1949; Offr of the Order of Aust (AO). Memberships: Life Mbr, Law Soc of S Aust, 1981; Hon Fell, Austl Inst of Valuers, 1985; Fell, Hatfield Coll, Univ of Durham, 1985. Hobbies: Music; Literature; Boat building; Ornithology. Address: 1 Hillside Avenue, Glen Osmond, South Australia 5064, Australia.

WELTON Michael P, b. 19 Apr 1957, Milwaukee, WI, USA. Dentistry. m. Lucia, 2 d. Education: DDS, 1983; BS, Bio, 1979; Gen Proc Res, 1984. Appointments include: US Navy Dental Corps, 1983-90; Periodontocs Dept, Naval Dental Clin Yokosuka, Japan, 1984-85; Clin Dir, Negishi Dental Annex, Yokhama, 1985-87; Branch Dental Clin Mare Island, 1987-90; Gateway Dental off, 1990-91; Napa Valley Community Dental Clin, 1991-92; Paul R Thomasson & Assocs, 1993-94; Priv prac, 1994-. Publications include: Presidents Message, monthly column for the Oracle, 1997. Honours: Delta Sigma Delta, 1979-, Treas, Theta Chapt, 1982-83; Oustndng Dental Sig, 1983; Paul Harris Fell, Rotary, 1997; Fell, Acady of Dentistry Instl, 1998. Memberships: Napa/Solano Dental Soc, 1988-, Pres, 1997; CA Dental Assn, 1987-, deleg, Annual CDA House of Delegs, 1996-98, Cttee on Rules and Order mbr, 1998; Amn Dental Assn, 1980-, Alternate Deleg to ADA Hose of Dlegs, 1997; Vacaville Chmbr of Com, 1994-; North CA Golf Assn; Art Deco Soc of CA; Ducks Unlimited; Pheasants Forever. Hobbies: Golf; Skiing (snow); Reading. Address: 3000 Alamo Drive, Suite 103, Vacaville, CA 95687, USA.

WEN Carson, b. 16 Apr 1953 Hong Kong. Lawyer. m. Julia Fung Yuet Shan, 1983, 1 c. Education: Diocesan Boys' Sch Hong Kong; Natl Jnr Coll Singapore; Columbia Univ NY; Univ of Oxford. Appointments: Singapore Govt Schl, 1971-72; Partner Siao Wen and Leung - Solicitors - Hong Kong, 1982-; Dir and Sec-Gen Hong Kong Kwun Tong Inds and Com Assn, 1982-; Pres Emer, 1989-; Dir Banco Delta Asia SARL Macau, 1992-; Attesting Offr apptd by min of Jus of China, 1992-; Spec Advsr to China Snr Prosecutors Educ Fndn under the auspices of the Supreme People's Procurate of People's Repub of China, 1993-; Deleg People's Congress of Guangdong Prov China, 1993-; Hong Kong Affairs Advsr to Govt of China, 1993-; Vice-Chmn The Hong Kong Progressive Alliance, 1994-. Publications: Contbns to 13 lects on Hong Kong Law; Articles in jrnls mags and newspapers. Honours: Hon Life Pres Hong Kong Sze Yap Ind and Com Assn, 1983-; Hon Pres Hong Kong Indl Dists Ind and Com Assn Ltd, 1993-. Memberships: Mbr Kwun Tong Dist Bd, 1983-85; Mbr Standing Cttee Fedn of Yth of Shenzhen China, 1992-; Mbr Selection Cttee for First Govt of Hong Kong Spec Admin Reg, 1996. Hobbies: Reading; Golf. Address: 15th Floor, Hang Seng Building, 77 Des Voeux Road, Central, Hong Kong Special Administrative Region, People's Republic of China.

WEN Jiabao, b. Sep 1942 Tianjin. Party and State Official. Education: Beijing Geogl Coll. Appointments: Joined CCP, 1965; Geogl Rsch wrkr in Gansu Prov, 196882; Dir Reform Rsch Off of the Geogl and Mining Bur of the State Cncl, 1982-83; Dep Min of Geol and Mining, 1983-85; Dir Cntrl Gen Off of CCP Cntrl Cttee, 1986; Sec CCP Cntrl Organs Wrkng Cttee, 1988; Sec Secr of Cntrl Cttee, 1992; Fmr Vice-Dir CCP Agricl Ldng Grp; Sec Gen Cntrl Finl and Econ Ldng Grp, 1993-; Dep Hd Natl Ldng Grp for Sci and Tech. Memberships: Alt mbr Secr of Cntrl Cttee, 1987; Mbr 14th CCP Cntrl Cttee, 1992; Alt mbr CCP Politburo, 1992-97; Mbr Politburo, 1997-; Mbr 15th CCP Cntrl Cttee, 1997-. Address: Zhong Nan Hai, Beijing, People's Republic of China.

WEN Kung-Chen, b. 10 Mar 1956, Taoyun, Taiwan. Businessman. m. Wei Chun-Fang, 1 s, 1 d. Education: Grad, Dept of Educl Media Sci, Tamkang Univ, Taiwan. Appointments: Shareholder, N Taoyuan Cable TV Co Ltd; pres, Yow Sheng Enterpose Co Ltd; Holder, Description

Photo Studio Taoyuan; Vice Chf, New Horizon Off, 1994; Joined UN 50th Celebration, Took part in Pres Clinton's Speech, 1995; Personal Asst and Cameraman to Sen Hsiu-Len Annette's Personal Asst, took part in Gen Sec's Lunch Party, 1995. Creative works: 21st Century Paradise, Taoyuan. Honours: Photochem Spec Awd (Can), 1998. Hobbies: Farming; Sport. Address: No 9 Shinn Yang Street, Taoyuan City, Taoyuan County, Taiwan.

WEN Lipen, b. 5 Oct 1931, Xishui County, Hubei Pov, China. Head of Oil Painting Department, Central Academy of Fine Arts; Professor. m. Tungxia Zhang, Feb 1952, 2 s. Education: Grad, 1958, Post-grad, 1963, Oil Painting Dept, Cntrl Acady of Fine Arts. Creative works: Major oil painting works exhibited in: Beijing, Hong Kong, Japan, France, Soviet Union, Kuwait; Works include: Daughter of the Land (Chinese National Gallery), 1984; Moonlight, Blue Night (Fukuyama Museum of Fine Arts, Japan); Major writings: Exploration of Fine Arts, 1981; Passion, Idea, Formation in Painting, published in Art, 1980; Gain New Insights Through Restudying Old Material, published in Art, 1984. Honours: Ode to Red Candle, Oil Painting, won Golden Prize in Natl Painting Show, 1984; Rock of Snow Colour, Oil Painting, won Honourable Prize, 1991. Memberships: Mbr of Cttee, China Artist Assn; Vice-Chmn of Oil Painting Art Cncl, China Artist Assn; Mbr Acad Cttee, Cntrl Acady of Fine Arts. Address: No 3 Lane, Shuai Fuyuan Street, Wangfujing, Beijing, China.

WEN Senfar, b. 29 July 1961, Fengyuan, Taiwan. Electro-Optics Educator; Researcher. m. Shieh Yi-Ling, 18 Jan 1989, 2 s, 1 d. Education: BS, 1983, MS, 1985, PhD, 1989, Natl Chiao Tung Univ, Taiwan. Appointments: Assoc Prof, Chung-Hua Polytech Inst, Hsinchu, 1991-97; Assoc Prof, Chung Hua Univ, Hsinchu, 1997-. Publications: Over 30 tech pprs in profl jrnls. Honour: Jia-Biing Tyan Youth Acad Awd, Optical Engrng Soc, China, 1994. Memberships: Optical Soc of Am; Taipei Dan Tao Culture Rsch Soc. Hobbies: Meditation; Reading; Music; Swimming; Jogging. Address: Electrical Engineering Department, Chung Hua University, 30 Tung Shiang, Hsinchu 30067, Taiwan, China.

WEN Yong, b. 29 Sept 1928, Shandong Prov, China. Professor. m. Yu-rong Yang, 1 s. Education: Grad, Qilu Theol Coll, Jinan, 1952; Grad, Haerbin Inst of For Langs, 1956. Appointments: Visng Prof, Dept of For Langs, Hebei Normal Univ; Assoc Rschr, Ricci Inst, Univ of San Fran, USA. Publications: The Christian Occupation of China (chf translator); The History of Christianity (co-auth); An Introduction to Christianity (co-auth); A Biograph of Jesus Christ in the Bible (auth); A Short History of the Holy Bible (auth); A Dictionary of World Religions (auth); A Dictionary of Christianity (co-auth); The Ocean in a Seashell: An Introduction to the Bible (auth); An Introduction to Christianity: A Thousand Questions and Answers (co-auth); Jesus Among Men (auth). Membership: Fndr Mbr and Dir, Beijing Assn for Comparative Stdies in Chinese-Western Cultural Hist, 1996-; Hobby: Calligraphy. Address: Department of Eastern European Languages, Beijing Foreign Studies University, Beijing 100081, China.

WENDT Albert, b. 1939 Apia. Auth. 3 c. Appointments: Prof Hd of Eng Dept Auckland Univ. Publications incl: Pouliuli - novel; Leaves of the Banyan Tree - novel; Flying Fox in a Freedom Tree - novel; Sons for the Return Home - novel; Ola - novel; Black Rainbow - novel. Honours: Hon PhD - Univ de Bourgogne France, 1993; Order of Merit - W Samoa. Address: Department of English, University of Auckland, Private Bag 92019, Auckland 1, New Zealand.

WENG Chung-Nan, b. 19 Aug 1942, Jiayi, Taiwan. Researcher. m. Su-Ping Sung, 1 d. Education: PhD, Dept of Clin Vet Med, Univ Cambridge, England, 1985. Appointments: Rsch Asst, Dept of Pathol, 1975-77, 1978-81, Snr Sci, Chmn, 1986-94, Vice Dir, 1994-95, Dir, 1995-, Pig Rsch Inst, Taiwan; Visng Sci, Vet Med Rsch Inst, IA Univ, 1977-78; Vis Sci, Lab Animal Rsch Cntr, Rockefeller Univ, 1989; Assoc Prof, Dept of Natl Taiwan

Vet Med Univ, 1986-; Pres, Chinese Soc of Vet Sci, 1994-. Publications include: Clinical and pathological observation of experimentally induced swine dysentery, 1975; Serotype and drug susceptibility of E Coli isolated from healthy and scouring piglets, 1975; Study on humoral and cellular responses of Latent infection of toxoplasma in swine, 1977; Protective effects of an oral microencapsulated M. hypeniumoniae vaccine against experimental infection in pigs, 1992. Honours: Prize of Acad Thesis, Chinese Acady of Vet Sci, 1976; Prize, Outstndng Rsch, Natl Sci Cncl, 1992; Acad Prize, Agricl Sci, Min of Educ, 1993. Hobbies: Table tennis; Golf; Bridge. Address: c/o Pig Research Institute, PO Box 23, Chunan 350099, Miaoli, Taiwan.

WENG Maidong, b. 18 Jan 1928. Teacher. m. Wei Dauqing, 11 Nov 1953, 3 s, 1 d. Education: Univ Grad. Appointments: Assoc Prof 1983, Prin of Agricl Sch 1984; Hon Prin of Agricl Sch, 1987; Natl Agricl-Educ Insp, 1995; Professor, 1997. Publications: Citriculture, 1985; Genetics and Breeding for Horticultural Plant, 1989; Citrus Growing in Coastal Mud Flat, 1985. Honours: Natl Outstndng Personnel in Tech-Sci, 1993; Natl Adv Tchr in Agricl, 1994; Winner, China Agric Sci and Educ Prize, 1998 Memberships: Intl Soc of Citriculture, 1988; Staff of Chinese Soc of Citriculture, 1993. Hobby: Music. Address: Taizhou Agricultural School, Huangyan, Zhejiang Prov 318020, China.

WENG Sihao, b. 25 Mar 1939, Zhoushan Cty, Zhejiang Prov, China. Researcher; Educator. m. 1 May 1975, 1 s. Education: Grad w hons, Beijing Univ of Aeronautics and Astronautics, Beijing, 1962. Appointments: Worker, Engr, Shanghai Brdcstng Apparatus Factory, Shanghai, 1962-78; Prof, Dir of Rsch, E China Normal Univ, Shanghai, 1979-. Publications: In profl jrnls. Honours: Awd for dev of Sci and Technol; State Educ Commn, China, 1991, 1992; Awd for Modern Phys Tchng, Cty Educ Commn, Shanghai, 1990. Memberships: NY Acady of Scis, 1997-; China Cntr of Advd Sci and Technol; China Soc of Nuclear Phys. Hobbies: Literature; Music; Works of calligraphy and painting. Address: Department of Physics, East China Normal University, 3663 North Zhong Shan Road, 20062 Shanghai, China.

WENG Yueh-Sheng, b. 1 July 1932, Chai-Yi, Taiwan. President; Chairman. m. Chuan Shu-Chen, 3 d. Education: LLB, Natl Taiwan Univ; DJur, Heidlberg Univ, Germany. Appointments: Assoc Prof, 1966-70; Prof, NTU, 1970-72; Commnr, Legal Com Exec, Yuan, 1971-72; Visng Prof, Sch of Law, Univ of WA, 1991; Grand Jus, Judicial Yuan, 1972-99; Pres, Judicial Yuan, 1999-; Chmn, Cncl of Grand Jus, 1999-. Creative Works: Die Stellung der Justiz im Verfassungsrecht der Republik China; Administrative Law and Rule of Law; Administrative Law and Judicatory in a State Under the Principal of the Rule of Law; Administrative Law I and II. Memberships: Admin Law Assn; Intl Assn of Constl Law. Hobbies: Reading; Hiking. Address: 19 Alley 9, Lane 143, Jiung Gong Road, Taipei, Taiwan.

WENSLEY Penelope Anne, b. 18 Oct 1946, Toowoomba, Aust. Diplomat. m. Stuart McCosker, 31 Aug 1974, 2 d. Education: BA, Hons First Class; Hon DPhil, Univ of Qld. Appointments: Austl Consul-Gen, Hong Kong, 1986-88; Amb for the Environment, 1992-95; Amb to UN, Geneva, 1993-96; Amb to UN, NY, 1997-. Hobbies: Music; Reading. Address: Australian Mission to the United Nations, New York, 150 East 42nd Street, New York, NY 10017, USA.

WENTRUP Curt, b. 11 July 1942, Holtug, Denmark. Professor. m. Edeline, 1975, 3 s. Education: Cand Scient, Univ Copenhagen, 1966; PhD, Austl Natl Univ, 1969; DSc, Univ of Copenhagen, 1977. Appointments: Asst Prof, Univ Lausanne, Switz, 1969; Prof, Univ of Marburg, Germany, 1976; Prof, Univ of QLD, Aust, 1985. Publications: Reaktive Zwischenstufen, 1979; Reactive Molecules, 1984; Over 200 Publs. Honours: P & E Thomsen's Schlshp, 1963-66; Alexander von Humboldt Fellshp, 1969; Von't Hoff Awd, 1974. Memberships: Fell Roy Soc of Chem, London; Fell, Roy Aust Chem Inst.

Hobbies: Skiing; Sailing; Ancient History. Address: 33 Blackstone St, Indooroopilly, Qld 4068, Australia.

WERDER Felix, b. 24 Feb 1922, Berlin, Germany. Composer; Lecturer. m. Vera, 29 Aug 1976. Appointments: Lectr in Adult Educ, 1952-; Music Critic, Melbourne Age, 1960-79; Freq Broadcaster, formed ensemble, Australia Felix; toured overseas, 1976-. Publications: 7 symphonies; 13 string quartets; 8 operas; 7 concerti; chamber music; More than Music, 1991; More or Less Music, 1993. Honours: Order of Aust, 1976; STAMITZ Perf Prize, 1984; Aust Cncl Fellowship, 1986; Arts Guild of Germany Comp Prize, 1988. Membership: Guild of German Artists. Hobby: Chess. Address: 3/374 Auburn Road, Hawthorn, Vic 3122, Australia.

WERNER Alfred Emil Anthony, b. 18 June 1911, Dublin, Eire. Chemist. m. M Davies, 25 Sept 1939, 2 d. Education: MA, MSc, DPhil, Freiburg and Breisgaug; ScD (hc) Dublin Univ. Appointments: Dir, Pacific Regl Conservation Cntr, 1975-83; Rdr, Chem, Dublin Univ, 1937-46; Rsch Chem, Natl Gall, London, 1948-56; Rdr, Brit Mus Rsch Lab, 1959-75. Publications: Sci Exam of Paintings, 1952. Memberships: FSA, 1958; MRIA, 1963; Pres, FMA, 1967; Pres, FIIC, 1971. Hobbies: Chess; Travel; Bridge; Croquet. Address: 11/73 South Street, Bellerive, Tasmania 7018, Australia.

WERNER Roger, b. 11 Nov 1950, NYC, USA. Geographer; Archaeologist; Computer Specialist. m. Kathleen, 20 Feb, 1982, 1 s, 3 d. Education: BA; MA; PhD. Appointments: Cnslt, Pvt Sector, 1979-. Creative Works: Over 1000 Tech Rpts. Memberships: Soc of Amn Archs; Amn Sch of Oriental Rsch; Geol Soc of Am. Hobbies: Reading; Travel; Wood Working; Writing. Address: 1117 Aberdeen Am, Stockton, CA 95209, USA.

WESLEY-SMITH Peter, b. 10 June 1945, Adelaide, Aust. Freelance Author. Education: LLB, Univ of Adelaide, 1969; BA, Hons, Univ of Adelaide, 1970; PhD, Univ of Hong Kong, 1976. Appointments: Tutor, Hist, Univ of Adelaide, 1970; Lectr, Law, 1973-79, Snr Lectr, 1979-87, Prof, 1987-99, Univ of Hong Kong. Publications: Ombley-Gombley, 1969; Boojum! (opera), 1986; QUITO, 1994; Foul Fowl, 1995; The Hunting of the Snark: Second Expedition, 1996; Unequal Treaty 1989-1997, 1998. Hobbies: Cricket; Lewis Carroll; Noel Coward. Address: PO Box 144, Kangaroo Valley, NSW 2577, Australia.

WEST Morris Langlo, b. 26 Apr 1916, Melbourne, Aust. Writer. m. Joyce Lawford. Career: Over 60 million copies of wrks sold; Translated into over 27 langs. Publications: Gallows on the Sand, 1955; Kundu, 1956; Children of the Sun, 1957; The Crooked Road, 1957; The Concubine, 1958; Backlash, 1958; The Devil's Advocate (Natl Brotherhood Awd, Natl Cncl Christians and Jews, 1960, James Tait Black Mem Awd, 1960, William Heinemann Awd Roy Soc, 1960), 1959, filmed 1977; The Naked Country, 1960; Daughter of Silence, 1961, play, 1961; The Shoes of the Fisherman, 1963; The Ambassador, 1965; Tower of Babel, 1968; Scandal in the Assembly (w R Francis) 1970; Summer of the Red Wolf, 1971; The Salamander, 1973; The Harlequin, 1974; The Navigator, 1976; Proteus, 1979; The Clowns of God, 1981; The World is Made of Glass, Cassidy, 1986; Member of the Order of Australia, 1985; Masterclass, 1988; Lazarus, 1990; The Ringmaster, 1991; The Lovers, 1993; Vanishing Point, 1996; A View From the Ridge, 1996; Images and Inscription, 1997; Eminence, 1998. Honours: Intl Dag Hammarskjold Prize (Grand Collar of Merit), 1978; Fell, Roy Soc Lit, World Acady Arts and Sci, Hon D Litt, Santa Clara Univ, 1968; Hon D Litt mercy Coll, NY, 1982; Hon D Litt Univ of West Sydney, 1993; Hon D Litt, The Austl Natl Univ, Canberra, 1995; Offr in the Order of Aust, 1997; Lloyd O'Neill Awd (Austl publng ind accolade), 1997. Address: PO Box 102, Avalon, NSW 2107, Australia.

WESTBURY Harvey Arthur, b. 27 Nov 1941, Melbourne, Vic, Aust. Veterinarian. m. Joan, 2 s. Education: BVScC (Hons); MVSc; PhD. Appointments: Prog Mngr, CSIRO Animal Hlth, 1990-. Publications: Over 100 sci publs. Honours: CSIRO Chmn's Golf Medal, Austl

Poultry Ind Awd, 1997. Memberships: Austl Vet Assn; Gafia Co-op. Hobbies: Orchestral Recitals; Snow skiing; Surfing. Address: 5 Portarlington Road, Geelong, Vic, Australia 3220.

WESTE Gretna Margaret, b. 5 Sept 1917, Scotland, England. Botanist. m. Geoffrey Weste, 20 Dec 1941, 1 s, 2 d. Education: BSc; MSc; PhD; DSc. Appointment: Rdr in Botany, Univ Melbourne. Publications: Num sci pprs, 10 book chaps. Honour: AM, 1989. Memberships: Austl Plant Pathol Soc; Field Naturalists Club of Vic; Roy Soc of Vic. Hobbies: Bush Walking; Reading; Gardening; Music. Address: 605 Park Road, Park Orchards, Victoria 3114, Australia.

WESTLY Steve, b. 27 Aug 1956, Los Angeles, USA. Internet Executive. m. Anita, 13 Sept 1997. Education: BA, 1978, MBA, 1983, Stanford. Appointment: Lectr, Stanford Univ, Grad Sch of Bus, 1991-95. Publications: Ed, Energy Eficiency & Utilities; The Future of Utilities: The Next Ten Years. Memberships: Vice Chmn, CA Democratic Party, 1987-89; Democratic Natl Cttee. Address: 2120 Camino De Los Robles, Menlo Park, CA 94025, USA.

WESTON Peter Henry, b. 22 Oct 1956, Lower Hutt, NZ. Research Scientist (Botany). m. Bridget Susan O'Donoghue, 2 s, 1 d. Education: BS (Hons), Univ of Sydney, 1979; PhD, Univ of Sydney, 1984. Appointments: Sci Offr, Roy Bot Gdns, Sydney, 1982; Rsch scientist, RBG, Sydney, 1989. Publications include: Indirect and Direct Methods in Systematics, pp 27-56 in C J Humphries (ed) Ontogeny and Systematics, 1988. Memberships: Soc of Systematic Biologists, 1980-, editl bd, 1993-95; Willi Hennig Soc, 1985-, Cnclr, 1997-. Hobbies: Guitar; Orchids; Soccer; Philosophy. Address: Plant Sciences Branch, Royal Botanic Gardens, Sydney, Mrs Macquarie's Road, Sydney 2000, Australia.

WESTPHALEN John Brock, b. 10 July 1925, Aust. Medical Practitioner. m. Marie McCowage, 5 May 1951, 3 d. Education: MB BS, Sydney Univ, 1950; BHA, Univ of NSW, Priv Prac, 1953-64; Asst Sec-Gen, Austl Medl Assn, 1965-66; Medl Supt/Chf Exec Offr, Mater Misericordiae Hosp, N Sydney, 1966-82; Medl Supt, Newcastle Mater Misericordiae Hosp, 1983-87; Area Dir of Medl Servs, Hunter Area Hlth Serv, 1987-90. Honours: AM, 1980; Reserve Force Decoration, 1984; Efficiency Decoration, 1964. Memberships include: Past Pres, Medl Supts Assn; Fell, Roy Austl Coll of Gen Practitioners; Roy Austl Coll of Medl Admin; Austl Geriatric Soc; Pub Serv Assn. Hobbies: Golf; Fishing; Sailing; Bridge; Music. Address: 58 Barnhill Road, Terrigal, NSW 2260, Australia.

WESTWOOD Peter Stuart, b. 29 Dec 1936, Clacton, England. University Lecturer. div, 2 s, 1 d. Education: MEd; LCP; DipSpec Ed; Dip Outdoor Ed; TCert. Appointments: Snr Lectr, Spec Educ, Manchester Coll of Educ, 1968-73; Snr Lectr, Torrens Coll of Advd Educ, S Aust, 1974-76; Prin Educ Offr, Educ Dept, S Aust, 1976-79; Lectr, Educl Psychol, Adelaide, 1980-87; Assoc Prof, Flinders Univ, S Aust, 1990-98. Publications: The Remedial Teachers Handbook, auth, 1975; Helping Children with Spelling Difficulties and Commonsense Methods for Children with Special Needs, 1997. Honour: Ex in Tchng Awd, Flinders Univ, 1995. Hobbies: Bushwalking; Sailing; Theatre. Address: School of Special Education, Flinders University, Bedford Park, South Australia 5042.

WETTENHALL Roger Llewellyn, b. 4 Feb 1931. Public Administration Teacher; Reseacher; Editor. 1 s, 2 d. Education: MA, Dip Pub Admin, Univ Tas, 1956; PhD, Austl Natl Univ, 1962. Appointments: Austl C'wlth Pub Serv, 1948-59; Rsch Schl, Austl Natl Univ, 1959-62; Lectr, Snr Lectr, Rdr in Pub Admin, Univ Tas, 1962-71; Hd of Sch, Prof, Univ of Canberra, 1971-94; Prof Emer of Pub Admin, Univ of Canberra, 1994-. Publications: Ed, Austl Jrnl of Pub Admin, 1989-95; Over 100 books, chapts, articles and reports. Honours: Haldane Silver Medal, Roy Inst of Pub Admin, 1966; Natl Fell, Inst of Pub Admin, Aust, 1983; Disting Serv Awd, Eastern Reg Org

for Pub Admin, Manila, 1995. Memberships: Inst of Pub Admin, Aust; Intl Assn of Schs and Insts of Admin. Address: 12 Carmichael Street, Deakin, ACT 2600, Australia.

WHAN Bryan Richard, b. 30 July 1945, Melbourne, Aust. Director. m. Margaret Allison, 17 Aug 1970, 1 s, 2 d. Education: Dip in Agric, 1964; BAgSc, 1969, MAgSc, 1974, Univ of Melbourne; PhD, Univ of Adelaide, 1979. Appointments: Wheat Breeder, Dept of Agric, Vic, 1969-82; Study Leave, Waite Agricl Rsch Inst, Univ of Adelaide, 1975-78; Wheat Breeder, Dept of Agric, WA, 1982-91; Dir, Qld Wheat Rsch Inst, 1991-94; Cnslt, 1994-98; Dir, Co-op Rsch Cntr for molecular Plant Breeding, 1998-. Publications: Bred a number of wheat cultivars; Presentations at var confs and workshops associated w plant breeding; Sev sci pprs, articles and items in profl sci jrnls; Dept of Agric Publns and Newsletters. Memberships: Austl Inst of Agricl Sci; Pres, S Qld Br, Austl Inst of Agric Sci, 1993-94; Cttee Mbr, S Qld Br, Austl Inst of Agricl Sci, 1994-; Past Pres and Cttee Mbr, Wheat Breeding Soc of Aust. Hobbies: Sports (Football, Cricket); Sports Administration. Address: 26 The Boulevard, Bellevue Heights, SA 5050, Australia.

WHEATLEY Glenn Dawson, b. 23 Jan 1948, Nambour, Queensland, Australia. Executive Director. m. Gaynor Cherie Martin, 14 July 1982, 1 s. Appointments: Bass Guitarist, The Masters Apprentices, 1967-72; Bay City Union, 1966-67, Purple Hearts, 1966; Mngr, Little River Band, 1975-85, Aust Crawl, 1978-83, Pseudo Echo, 1980-83; Fndr, Mngng Dir, The Wheatley Orgn (TWO Aust Ltd), 1975-92; Fndng Dir, ECON FM, 1980; Mngr, Glenn Shorrock, 1975-, John Farnham, 1980-, John Farnham Band, 1985-, Ian Baker-Finch, 1997-; Dir, Advantage Intl (formerly Wheatley Sport Pty Ltd), 1985-88, Syd Hard Rock Cafe, 1988-89; Mngng Dir, Hoyts Media (formerly Wheatley Commns Pty Ltd 1986-87) 1987-89, Radio 2BE Bega NSW, 1987-89, Radio 3CV Vic, 1987-89; Co-Owner, Dir, Syd Swans Football Club, 1988-90; Mngng Dir, Emerald City Records, 1991-; Dir, 1997, Exec Dir, 1998-; Intl Media Mngmt. Honours include: Outstndng Contbrn in the Entertainment Ind Awd, Adv Aust, 1987; Mktng Awd, Bus Review Weekly, 1988. Memberships: AUSMUSIC, bd mbr, 1993; Tourism Task Force; Austrade (Music); Trustee, AIDS Trust Aust, 1990-93. Address: c/o Talent Works, Suite 1, 663 Victoria Street, Abbotsford, Victoria 3067, Australia.

WHEELER Christine Ann, b. 16 Jan 1954, Sydney, NSW, Aust. Judge. m. G Gorman, 31 Aug 1991, 1 s. Education: BJuris (Hons); LLB (WA); LLM (London). Appointments: QC, 1994; Judge, Supreme Crt of West Aust, 1996. Address: Supreme Court, Stirling Gardens, Perth, Western Australia, Australia.

WHELAN Daniel J, b. 1940. Research Scientist. Education: BS, PhD, Melbourne. Appointments: Prin Rsch Scientist, Def Sci and Technol Orgn, 1989-; Rsch Scientist, Materials Rsch Lab, Melbourne, Aust. Publication: Velocity of Detonation. Memberships: Fell, Roy Austl Chem Inst; Fell, Roy Soc of Chem (GB); Editl Bd: Jrnl of Energetic Materials. Address: DSTO Weapons Systems Division, Aeronautical and Maritime Research Laboratory, PO Box 4331, Melbourne, Vic 3001, Australia.

WHILLANS Francis David, b. 4 Feb 1942. Chemist. m. Susan Theresa Eklund, 7 Jan 1967, 1 s, 1 d. Education: BS, Dip Ed, PhD, Univ of Melbourne. Appointments: Snr Lectr in Analytical Chem, 1985-92, Assoc Prof of Indl Chem, 1992-96, Roy Melbourne Inst of Technol, Melbourne, Aust. Publications: X-Ray Crystallography (11); Chemical Hazards (4); Microparticle Protection (4); Indoor Air Quality (7); Research Evaluation (1). Memberships: Roy Austl Chem Inst, Fell, 1988-; Victorian Br Pres, 1990; Intl Soc Indoor Air Qlty, 1992-. Hobbies: Genealogy; Lawn bowling. Adddress: Coranderk, 47 The Righi, Eaglemont, Melbourne, Vic 3084, Australia.

WHITE Gary R, b. 15 Nov 1962, Detroit, MI, USA. Electrical Engineer, Plant Operations. Education: BSEE, Wayne State Univ, Detroit, MI, USA, 1986; Grade 2 Wastewater Treatment Plant Operators Lic, State of HI, 1998. Appointments: Electrons Engr, US Army Info Systems Engrng Command, Ft Belvoir, VA, 1987-88; Electrons Engr, US Army Infosystems Engrng Command - Pacific, Ft Shaffer Plant Operator, 1988-92; Elec Worker, US Navy Pub Wrks Cntr, Pearl Harbor, HI, 1992-96; US Navy Pub Wrks Cntr, Pearl Harbor, HI, 1996-. Publication: Tech ppr on Corporate Networking, 1988. Honours: 20th Century Awd for Achievement (IBC), 1998; Advsry Cncl (IBC) Awd, 1998; Disting Ldrshp Awd. Memberships: IEEE; NSPE; AMA. Hobbies: Bodybuilding; Bike riding; Beautiful women; Aerobics; Rock n Roll music; Cooking; Movies; Hardware/software. Address: 555 North King Street, Apt 215, Honolulu, HI 96817, USA.

WHITE Guy Kendall, b. 31 May 1925. Scientist. m. Judith Kelly McAuliffe, 15 July 1955, 1 s, 2 d. Education: BSc (Hons), Sydney; MSc, Sydney; DPhil, Oxon. Appointments: Rsch Offr, CSIRO, 1950-55, Post Doct Fell and Assoc Rsch Offr, NRC, Ottawa, 1953-58; Prin Rsch Offr, CSIRO, 1958-62; Snr Prin Rsch Offr, CSIRO, 1962-69; Chf Rsch Scientist, CSIRO, 1969-90; Hon Fell, CSIRO, 1990-; Also Visng Mbr, Techl Staff Bell Labs, NJ, 1964-65. Publications: Experimental Techniques in Low Temperature Physics, 1959, 1968, 1979; Heat Capacity and Thermal Expansion at Low Temperatures (w T H K Barron), 1999; 200 rsch papers, reviews. Honours: Syme Medal, 1966; Armco Iron Awd, 1983; Touloukian Medal, 1994; Hon DSc, U Woll, 1994. Memberships: Fell, Aust Acady Sci, 1970-; VP, AAS, 1979-80; Fell, Brit and Aust Inst of Phys. Hobbies: Golf; Tennis; Swimming. Address: c/o CSIRO, PO Box 218, Lindfield, NSW 2070, Australia.

WHITE Halbert Lynn Jr, b. 19 Nov 1950, Kansas City, Mo, USA. Professor of Economics. m. Kim A Titensor, 25 Oct 1986, 1 s. 1 d. Education: AB, 1972, Princeton Univ; PhD, 1976, MIT. Appointments: Asst Prof, Univ Rochester, NY, 1976-80; Assoc Prof, Univ CA at San Diego, 1980-84; Prof, 1984-95, Prof above scale, 1995-. Publications: Asymptotic Theory for Econometricians, 1984; A Unified Theory of Estimation and Inference for Nonlinear Dynamic Models, 1988; Artificial Neural Networks, 1992; Estimation, Inference and Specification Analysis, 1994; Advances in Econometric Theory, 1998. Honours: Guggenheim Fell, 1988; Fell, Econometric Soc, 1983; Jrnl of Econometrics Fell, 1995; Best Article Awd, Intl Jrnl of Forecasting, 1996-97; Multa Scripsit Awd, Econometric Theory Jrnl, 1997; Fell Amn Acady of Arts and Scis, 1999. Memberships: Econometric Soc; IEEE; AMS; Amn Statist Assn; Neural Network Soc; Natl Future Assn; Big Band and Jazz Hall of Fame. Hobbies: Music; Art; Antiques. Address: Dept of Economics 0508, UCSD, La Jolla, CA 92093-0508, USA.

WHITE Harvey Douglas, b. 19 Nov 1947, Te Awamutu, NZ. Cardiologist. m. Janette Frances Venus, 3 Feb 1973, 1 s, 1 d. Education: MB, ChB, Otago Univ Med Sch, 1973; FRACP, 1980; DSc, Otago Univ, 1995. Appointments: Clin Fell, Natl Heart Fndn of NZ, Harvard Med Sch, Brigham and Women's Hosp, Boston, MA, USA, 1981-82; Rsch Fell, Med, Harvard Med Sch, 1981-84; Rsch, Clin Fell, Med, Brigham and Women's Hosp, 1981-84; Odlin Rsch Fell, Roy Austl Coll of Physns, 1982-83; Snr Fell, Natl Heart Fndn of NZ, 1984-87; Cardiologist, Green Lane Hosp, Auckland, 1984-; Dir, Cardiovascular Rsch, 1990-, Dir of Coronary Care, 1992-; Prof of Med, Auckland Univ, 1997. Publications: Auth or co-auth, contbrns to var profl jrnls inclng, Circulation, Am Jrnl of Cardiol, Am Jrnl of Med. Honours: Am Field Serv Schlsp, NJ, USA, 1965; Overseas Clin Fell, NZ Heart Fndn, 1980; Odlin Rsch Fellshp, 1981; Snr Heart Fndn Fellshp, 1984; Matai, W Samoa, 1994; Prince Mahidol Awd in Med, Thailand, 1999. Memberships: NZ Med Assn; Fell, Roy Austl Coll of Physns; Cardiac Soc of Aust and NZ; Am Coll of Cardiol; Fell, Eurn Soc of Cardiol. Hobbies: Skiing; Farming. Address: Cardiology Department, Green Lane Hospital, Private Bag 92 189, Auckland 1030, New Zealand.

WHITE John William, b. 25 Apr 1937, Newcastle, NSW, Aust. Professor and Head of Physical and Theoretical Chemistry, 1 s, 3 d. Education: Hons 1st Class, Frank Dixon Prize, 1957. MSc, 1959, Univ of Sydney; 1851 Schl to Oxford, 1959, Oxford Univ, 1959-62; ICI Fell, 1961, Rsch Fell, 1961, Lincoln Coll; MA, DPhil, 1962. Appointments: Univ Lectr, 1963-85, Assessor, 1981-82, Oxford Univ, 1963-85; Fell, St John's Coll, 1963-85; Neutron Beam Co-ord, (Exec Cnslt), AERA Harwell, 1973-74; Ajoint Dir, 1974-77, Dir, 1977-80, Institut Laue-Langevin, Grenoble, 1974-77; Prof, Physl and Theort Chem, 1985-, Dean, Rsch Sch of Chem, Pro Vice Chan, 1992-94 ANU; Sec for Sci Policy, Austl Acady of Sci, 1997-; Pres Elect, Roy Austl Chem Inst, 2001. Publications include: Neutron Scattering in Biology, Chemistry and Physics (co-ed w R Mason, E W J Mitchell), 1980; Auth of over 200 pprs in sci jrnls. Honours: Marlow Medal and Prize, Faraday Soc, 1968; Tilden Lectr, Roy Soc of Chem, 1976; Companion of St Michael and St George, 1981; Argonne Fellshp and Prize, Univ of Chgo, 1985-90; Hinshelwood Lectr, Oxford Univ, 1991; Fndn Lectr, Fedn of Asian Chem Socs, 1991; Fell, Austl Acady of Sci, 1991; Roy Soc, London, 1993. Memberships: Fell, Roy Austl Chem Inst, 1986; Fell, Austl Inst of Phys, 1986. Hobbies: Skiing; Squash; Family. Address: Research School of Chemistry, Australian National University, PO Box 4, Canberra, ACT 2601, Australia.

WHITE Leslie, b. 7 Nov 1911, Gympie, Queensland, Australia. Public Servant (retired). m. Thelma, 26 Aug 1949, 1 s, 3 d. Education: BA Hons. Appointment: Pt time Lectr, Econs, ANU, 1945-50. Publications: Wool in Wartime, 1981. Honour: Best Econ of Yr, Qld Univ, 1940. Hobbies: Football; Swimming; Gardening. Address: 23 Chermside St, Deakin, Canberra, 2600, Australia.

WHITE Robert Lee, b. 14 Feb 1927, Plainfield, New Jersey, USA. Professor. m. Phylis Arlt, 14 June 1952, 2 s, 2 d. Education: BA, Phys and Maths, Columbia, 1949; MA, Phys, 1951; PhD, Phys, 1954. Appointments: Sci, Hughes Rsch Labs, 1954-61; Sci, Gen Tel and Electrons Labs, 1961-62; Assoc Prof, Stanford Univ, 1963-66; Prof, 1966-. Publications: Over 150 articles in profl jrnls, 3 books. Honours: Guggenheim Fell, Oxford Univ, 1969-70; ETH Zurich, 1977-78; Japan Soc for Promotion of Sci Vis Prof, Tokyo Univ, 1975; Christeusen Fell, Oxford, 1986; SONY Sabbatical Fell, 1994; IEEE Disting Lectr, 1998-99. Memberships: Am Physl Soc; IEEE; Materials Rsch Soc; Am Optical Soc; Phi Beta Kappa; Sigma Xi. Hobbies: Gardening; Hiking. Address: Department of Materials Science & Engineering, Stanford University, CA 94305-2205, USA.

WHITE Robert Stephen, b. 28 Dec 1920, Ellsworth, KS. Physics Educator. m. Freda Marie Bridgewater, 30 Aug 1942, 2 s, 2 d. Education: AB, SWest Coll, 1942, Winfield, KS; DSc hon, 1871; MS, Univ of IL, 1943; PhD, Univ CA, Berkley 1951. Appointments: Physicist, Lawrence Radiation Labs, Berkeley and Livermore, CA, 1948-61; Lectr, Univ CA, 1953-54, 1957-59; Hd, Dept Particles, Fields Space Phys Lab, Aerospace Corp, El Segundo, CA, 1962-67; Phys Prof, Univ CA, Riverside, 1967-92; Dir, Inst Geophys and Planetary Phys, 1967-92; Chmn, Dept Phys, 1970-73; Prof Emer, Phys Dept, Phys, Inst Geophys and Planetary Phys 1992-. Publications: Space Physics, 1970; Why Science?, 1998; Contbr, articles to profl jrnls. Honours: Offr USNR; Snr Postdoctoral Fell NSF; Grantee, NASA, NSF, USAF; num others. Memberships: AAAS; Amn Phys Assn; Amn Geophys Union; Amn Astron Soc. Address: 5225 Austin Rd, Santa Barbara, CA 93111-2905, USA.

WHITE Saxon William, b. 9 Mar 1934. Professor of Human Physiology. m. Julie Ann Mountain, 1 s, 2 d. Education: MB; BS; MD: FRACS. Appointmemts: Snr Tutor, Det Surg Unv, NSW; Overseas Fell Life Ins Fund Aust and NZ; Chapman Fell in Cardiology, Univ Sydney; Snr Lectr Physiology, Fac Med, Flinders Univ, SA; Fndn Prof of Hum Physiology, Fac Med, Univ of Newcastle, Aust, 1976-. Publications: Co-ed, The Drug Controversy in Sport; num rsch papers and book chapts on control of circulation. Honours: Blues in Cricket and Rugby, Univ Sydney, 1955, 1957; Life Gov Aust Postgrad Fed Med; Represented Aust Rugby in 7 Tests. Memberships: Austl Physiological and Pharmacological Soc (past cncl mbr); Cardiac Soc Aust NZ; Intl Soc Hypertension; Amn Physiol Soc; Da Vinci Soc for Study of Bronchial Circulation; Past Chmn Hunter Academy of Sport. Hobbies: Cartooning; Running. Address: 114 Henry Street, Merewether, NSW 2291, Australia.

WHITE Sheila Patricia Mary, b. 12 Oct 1927, Cardiff, Wales. Artist. m. Clifford Alan White, 1 s, 1 d. Career: Wrkshops at Royal Art Soc of NSW; 3 one-man exhibs, Beechworth; 2 one man exhibs Newcastle, NSW; 2 solo exhibns, Q Gall, Sydney; 5 major paintings in municipal collections; 1 wrk in ANZ Bank collection, 2 purchased by Artbank, 2 wrks in Newcastle Univ collection; Exhibited in: Portia Geach Mem prize for Portraits, 1973, 1974; Wynne Prize for Landscape, 1974; Blake Prize, 1986, 1997. Honours: Over 60 awds and prizes incl Wyong Contemporary Art Awd, 1998. Memberships: Assoc, Roy Arts Soc of NSW; Fell, Roy Art Soc, NSW; Elected Mbr of Contemporary Art Soc of Victoria, 1997. Hobby: Bird watching. Address: RMB 5465, The Ridgeway, Holgate, NSW 2250, Australia.

WHITE Stephen Harold, b. 15 Oct 1957. Winemaker. Div, 1 s. Education: Dip in Hort, Lincoln Coll, Univ of Canterbury. Publications: Winemaking: Stonyridge La Rose Cabernet Blend. Honours: Num Gold Medals and top awds for LaRose. Hobbies: Marathon Running; Aerobics; Yacht Racing (Whitbread). Address: PO Box 265, Ostend, New Zealand.

WHITEHEAD Charles William, b. 14 Dec 1944, Australia. Farmer; Agricultural Politician. m. Roz, 24 Feb 1968, 2 s, 1 d. Appointments: Dpty Pres, Vic Farmers Fedn; Bd Mbr, Vic Meat Authy. Hobbies: Golf; Horse Racing. Address: "Cairnlea", PO Box 168, Mortlake 3272, Australia.

WHITEHEAD Daniel, b. 26 May 1934, Brisbane, Aust. Company Director. m. 12 Nov 1956, 3 d. Appointments: Joined Robinsons Sports Store Grp Co, 1960, Grp Merchandising Mngr, 1968, Mngng Dir, 1971, Chmn 1976; Fndr, Intersport (Aust) Pty Ltd, 1975; Appt Gen Mngr and Dir of the XII C'wlth Games, 1981; Appt Gen Mngr to secure the right to hold a specialised Expo in Brisbane, 1983. Honour: CBE, 1983. Membership: Volun Chmn, Playground-Recreation Assn of Qld, 1972-. Hobbies: Tennis; Golf; Boating; Stamp collecting; Gardening. Address: Villa 118, The Cascades, Noosa Springs Drive, Noose Wead, Qld 4567, Australia.

WHITELAW John, b. 11 June 1921, Hawthorn, Vic, Aust. Business Consultant. m. Nancy Lockhart Bogle, 27 Dec 1947, 3 d. Education: Wesley Coll, Melbourne; Cand Army Staff Coll (PSC). Appointments: Served to Maj-Gen, Austl Army to 1978, inclng: Chf of Ops, 1974-75; Chf of Personnel, 1975-77; Dpty Chf of Gen Staff, 1977-78; Exec Dir, Natl Farmers Fedn, 1979-86; Bus Cnslt, particularly w Greening Aust Ltd, 1986-. Honours: MID, 1945; CBE, 1971; AO, 1977; Bronze Star, USA, 1997. Memberships: United Serv Institution of ACT, Pres, 1977-80; Regular Def Force Welfare Assn, Natl Pres, 1978-90; Austl Veterans & Def Serv Cncl, Natl VP, 1990-99. Address: 91 Mugga Way, Red Hill, ACT 2603, Australia.

WHITESIDE Carol, b. 15 Dec 1942, USA. President Great Valley Centre. m. John, 15 Aug 1964, 2 s. Education: BA Psychol, Univ Calif, Davis. Appointments: Dir, Intl Govt Affairs, Gov Pete Wilson, 1991-97. Honours: Elected, Sch Bd, 1983, Modesto City Council, 1987, Mayor City of Modesto, 1987; Outstanding Woman, 1988; Woman of the Yr, 45 Assm DLST, 1991. Memberships: Sutter Memorial Hosp Bd Dirs, 1998; P/Lincoln Inst of Land Policy Bd, 1991-98. Address: Great Valley Centre, 911 13th Street, Modesto, CA 95354, USA.

WHITMORE Raymond L. Professor Emeritus. m. Ruth H Franklin, 23 Oct 1947, 2 s. Education: BS (Hons) Phys, London, 1942; PhD, Birmingham, 1959; DSc, Birmingham, 1969. Appointments include: Flying Offr, Roy Air Force Vol Reserve, 1942-46; Proj Engr, Simon-Carves Ltd, Cheadle Heath, Cheshire, 1946-48; 1st Overseas Visng Fell, Anglo-Amn Corp's S Africa, 1956; Hd, Mechl Scis Div, Ferdodo Ltd, 1951-53; Rdr, Mining Engrng, Univ of Nottingham, 1953-67; Prof, Mining and Metallurgical Engrng, Univ of Queensland, 1967-85; Worked extensively in Brit and USA on behaviour of biol fluids, particularly blood, also lectured in Brit, Germany, Sweden, Japan, Can, USA, 1960s; Established the Julius Kruttschnitt Mineral Rsch Cntr, Univ of Queensland, and Dept of Mining Engrng, Univ of Technol, Lae, PNG. Publications: Books: Rheology of the Circulation, 1968; Riding the Minerals Boom, 1969; Coal in Queensland, 1981, 1985, 1991; Queensland's Early Waterworks, 1997; 140 pprs; Ed, 4 wrks; 10 contbns. Honours: Overseas Awd, Instn of Mining Engrs, 1981; Monash Medal, Instn of Engrs Aust, 1990; AM, 1994. Memberships include: Hon Fell, Inst of Engrs Aust; Snr Fell, Inst of Energy (London); Fell, Instn of Mining Engrs (London); Fell, Instn of Mining and Metall (London); Fell, Australasian Inst of Mining and Metall; Chartered Engr, GB; Chartered Profl Engr, Aust; Chartered Physicist, GB; Brisbane Hist Grp (Past Pres); Austl Soc of Histl Archaeology. Hobbies: Mountaineering; Travel. Address: R4/356 Blunder Road, Durack, Brisbane, Qld 4077, Australia.

WHITNEY Jayne Ann, b. 1 May 1967, Germany. Business Development Manager. m. Timothy Whitney, 23 Mar 1998, 2 d. Education: BSc, Econs, Hons, Univ Coll of Swansea, 1989; MBA, Warwick Bus Sch, Warwick Univ, 1997. Appointments: Mktng Mngr, Hytork Grp, 1989-91; Intl Mktng Mngr, Matcon Grop, 1992-97; Bus Devel Mngr, Transfield Pty Ltd, 1997-. Hobbies: Windsurfing; Swimming; Farming.

WHITTAKER Cameron James Gavin, b. 3 Oct 1966, Sydney, Aust. Veterinary Ophthalmologist. Education: BVetSci; Dip Vet Clin Stdies; Mbr, Roy Coll of Vet Scientists (MRCVS); Diplomate Amn Coll Vet Scientists (Dip ACVO). Appointments: Internship, Vet Clin Stdies, Univ of Sydney, 1992; Res, Vet and Comparative Ophthalmology, Univ of FL, USA, 1993-96; Visng Asst Prof, OH State Univ, USA, 1996-97; Pt-time Lectr, Univ of Sydney, 1998-. Publications: Contbng Auth to 3 books inclng: Veterinary Clinics of North America, 1998; Manual of Equine Practice, 2nd Ed, 1999; Veterinary Ophthalmology, 3rd Ed, 1999; Pprs to num intl jrnls. Honour: Sybill Greenwell Bequest Schlshp, 1992. Memberships: Roy Coll Vet Surgeons, 1992; Cttee, NSW Div, Austl Vet Assn, 1998-. Hobbies: Various outdoor sports; The arts; Environmental preservation. Address: 122 Franklin Road, West Pennant Hills, Sydney 2126, Australia.

WHITTAKER John, b. 6 Feb 1963, New Zealand. Manager. m. 17 Oct 1992, 1 s, 1 d. Education: BCom; ACA. Appointments: Mktng Mngr, 1995, Mngr, 1997-, Mount Cook Airline. Membership: NZ Soc of Accts, 1985. Address: PO Box 14020, Christchurch, New Zealand.

WHITTEN Wesley Kingston, b. 1 Aug 1918. Scientist. m. Enid Elsbeth Meredith, 13 Dec 1941, 2 s, 2 d. Education: BVSc, Hons; BS; DSc. Appointments: Hall Fell, Vet Sci, 1940; Capt Austl Army, 1941-45; Rsch Offr, CSIRO, 1946-50; Fell, Austl Natl Univ, 1950-61; Assoc Dir, Nat Bio Scis Lab, 1961-66; Scientist, Asst Dir, Jackson Lab, ME, USA, 1966-80; Rsch Assoc, Univ Tas, 1980-89; Dir, Invitro Fertilisation Lab, Univ of Tas, 1983-86; Disting Visng Prof, Mem UnivNfld, 1984; Visng Fell, Austl Natl Univ, 1980, 1989; Visng Prof, Dalhousie Univ, Can, 1993-94; Assoc Scientist, Co-op Rsch Cntr, CSIRO, 1992-97; Visng Schl, John Curtin Medl Sch, Austl Natl Univ, 1997-99; Publications: Over 100 rsch papers, 1940-96; Mammalian Embryos InVitro Mammalian Pheronomes, Gonadotrophins. Honours: Elected Austl Acady of Sci, 1982; Awd Marshall Medal, Soc Study Fertil, 1993; Pioneer Awd, Intl Emb Trans Soc, 1996. Memberships: Soc for Study of Reproduction; Austl Soc Reprod Bio; Intl Embryo Transfer Soc; Aust Inst Bio. Hobbies: Swimming; Science; Forests. Address: 24 Somerville Street, Spence, ACT 2615, Australia.

WICKEN Anthony John, b. 1 July 1934, Shoreham by Sea, Eng. Academic. Education: BS, 1954; BS Hons, 1955; PhD, Cape Town, 1958; BA, 1961; MA, Cambridge, 1965. Appointments: Snr Lectr, Biochem, Univ of Canterbury, NZ, 1963-67; Snr Lectr, Univ of NSW, 1967-71; Assoc Prof, 1972-78; Pers Chair, Microbiology, 1979-; Dean Fac, Bio Sci, 1986-90; Dpty Vice Chan 1996-. Publications: Over 100 Rsch Articles. Honours: Schl, St John's Coll, Cambridge; Wright Prize; Fulbright Schl Awd, 1975. Memberships: Austl Soc of Microbiology; Fedn of Austl Sci and Technol. Hobbies: Music; Cooking; Gdnng. Address: 1 Kangaroo Point Road, Sylvania, NSW 2224, Australia.

WICKHAM Jonathan Anthony, b. 12 Apr 1943, Perth, Aust. Farmer; Headmaster. m. Sally Jane Bird, 18 Dec 1970, 2 s. Education: BA; DipEd, Univ of WA; BEd, Univ of New Eng. Appointments: Asst Master, Kings Sch, Parramatta, 1968; Asst Master, Larchfield Sch, Scot, 1971; Asst Master, Kings Sch, Ely, Eng, 1972; Housemaster, Kings Sch, Parramatta, Aust, 1974; Exchange Master, Tonbridge Sch, Eng, 1980; Snr Master, 1982; Hdmaster, Kings Sch, Parramatta, Aust, 1984-97. Honours: Mbr, West Austl Kings Cup Rowing VIII, 1964-66. Memberships: Austl Coll of Educ. Listed in Who's Who in Australia. Hobbies: Reading; Genealogy; Walking; Inland fishing; Farming. Address: Edenburn, Essington, Via Bathurst, NSW 2795, Australia.

WICKREMESINGHE Ranil, b. 24 Mar 1949 Colombo. Politician; Banker. m. Maithree Wickremesinghe, 1995. Education: Roy Coll Colombo; Univ of Colombo; Sri Lanka Law Coll. Appointments: Attorney at Law Supreme Crt; Dep Min of For Affairs, 1977-79; Min of Yth Affairs and Employment, 1978-89; Min of Educ, 1980-89; Min of Inds, 1989-90; Ldr of House, 1989-93; Min of Inds Sci and Tech, 1990-94; PM, 1993-94; Ldr Opposition Ldr Utd Natl Party, 1994-. Memberships: Elected mbr Parl, 1977, 1989. Address: Parliament Building, Sri Jayewardanapura, Kotte, Sri Lanka.

WIERZBICKA Anna, b. 10 Mar 1998, Warsaw, Poland. Linguist (Academic). m. John Besemeres, 8 Aug 1970, 2 d. Education: MA, Warsaw Univ; PhD, Habilitation, Polish Acady of Scis. Appointments: Rsch Fell, Snr Rsch Fell, Polish Acady of Scis, 1960-73; Lectr, Snr Lectr, ANU, 1973-87; Prof of Linguistics, Austl Natl Univ, 1987-. Publications: 20 books inclng: Semantic Primitives, 1972; Ligua Mentalis, 1980-; Semantics, Culture and Cognition, 1992; Semantics: Primes and Universals, 1996; Understanding Cultures through their Key Words, 1997. Honour: Humboldt Prize for For Schls in the Hums, 1995. Memberships: Fell Austl Acady of the Hums; Fell, Socl Scis Acady of Aust. Hobbies: Interests; Research; Teaching; Family; Religion; Theology. Address: Department of Linguistics, Arts, Australian National University, Canberra, ACT 0200, Australia.

WIGGLESWORTH David C, b. 23 Sept 1927, Passaic, NJ, USA. Management Consultant. m. (1) Rita Dominguez, 15 Mar 1956; (2) Gayle Coates, 1 Aug 1981, 3 s, 1 d. Education: BA, 1950, MA, 1953, Occidental Coll; Universidad de las Amorica, 1954-56; PhD, Univ of G FL, 1957. Appointments: Dir, Spoken Engl Inst, Lectr, Mexico City Coll, 1954-56; Headmaster, Harding Acady, 1956-58; Dir, Burma Am Inst, 1958-60; Lectr, Univ of Libya, 1960-64; Mngng Ed, T Y Crowell Publrs, 1964-66; Dir of Studies, Behavioral Rsch Labs, 1966-67; DCW Rsch Assocs Intl, 1967-. Publications: ASTD in China, 1981; Bibliography of International Resources, 1990; Bibliography of Intercultural Resources, 1994. Honours: Intl Practitioner of Yr, 1988; ASTD Clubs; Orient Club, Rangoon; Benghazi Sailing Club. Memberships: Intl Div, Mbr of Bd; ASTD; Sietar; OD Network. Hobbies: Travel; Cult anthropology. Address: PO Box 5469, Kingwood, TX 77325-5469, USA.

WIGNELL Edel. Publications include: Fiction: Spider in the Toilet, 1988; You'll Turn into a Rabbit!, 1988; Escape By Deluge, 1989; My Special Place, 1996; The Ghost Wagon Mystery, 1966; We Wrote to Grandma, 1997; The Mighty Sparrow; The Look-Alikes; Hands Up; Non-Fiction: A Bogy Will Get You!; Saving Wildlife; Battlers of the Great Depression; The Portland Fairy Penguins; A Boggle of Bunyips, 1981; A Bluey of Swaggies, 1985; Scripts: The Hobyahs and Other Plays from Around the World, 1995; The Raven's Magic Gem: Five Plays based on Asian Folk Tales; Children's Magazines: Comet; Explore; Challenge; Pursuit; Jabberwocky; The Friend; Raining Cats and Dogs, 1987; I Wonder Who Lives Upstairs, 1993. Honours include: Mary Grant Bruce Short Story Awd, 1983, 1985; Clever Juice, Sec Prize, 1986; Hon Awd, 1989; Holiday Fantasia Lit Awds, 1997 x 2. Address: PO Box 2484, Rowville, Vic 3178, Australia.

WIJETUNGA Dingiri Banda, b. 15 Feb 1922 Polgahanga Kandy. Politician. m. 1 d. Appointments: Offic in Co-op Dept, 1942-47; Joined Utd Natl Party, 1946; Apptd Min of Info and Brdcstng, 1977; Min of Power and Highways, 1978; Min of Power and Energy, 1979; Min of Agricl Devt and Rsch and Min of Food, 1987; Gov Northwestern Prov, 1988; PM of Sri Lanka and Min of Fin, 1989-93; Elected Exec Pres of Sri Lanka, 1993-94. Memberships: MP for Udunuwra, 1965-. Address: c/o Office of the President, Republic Square, Colombo 1, Sri Lanka.

WIKRAMANAYAKE Thomas Walter, b. 9 Apr 1918, Sri Lanka. Professor Emeritus. m. Eugene R Wikramanayake, 23 Jan 1959, 3 s. Education: MB.BS, Ceylon; PhD, Glasgow; DSc, Honoris Causa, Univ of Perademiya and Ruhuna. Appointments: Med Offr, Min of Hlth; Lectr in Physiol, Snr Lectr in Biochem, Prof of Biochem, Univ of Peradeniya. Publication: Food and Nutrition, 3rd ed, 1997; Over 80 publs in Sci jrnls; Over 70 scientific pprs in jrnls. Memberships: Fell, Natl Acady of Scis; Hon Fell, Sri Lanka Coll of Pedatrns; Mbr, Ed of Jrnl Roy Asiatic Soc of Sri Lanka; Ed, Ceylon Jrnl of Medl Sci; Pres, Nutrition Soc of Sri Lanka, 1974-76; Sri Lanka Med Assn; Atomic Energy Authy, 1972-82. Hobbies: Wild Life; Music; Stamp Collecting. Address: 40 Welikadawatte, Rajagiriya, Sri Lanka.

WILAIRAT Nibbon, b. 13 Apr 1916, Thailand. Former Ambassador. m. Sadappin Chandhanasiri, 21 Nov 1940, 4 s. Education: LLB, Thamasart Univ, Bangkok, Thailand, 1935; London Inst of World Affairs, Eng, 1953; Grad Sch of Pub Law, Geo Wash Univ, Wash DC, USA, 1965. Appointments: Entered Diplomatic Serv, Min of For Affairs, 1954-55; Consul-Gen to Singapore, 1956-64; Cnslr, Roy Thai Wash DC, USA, 1965-66; Amb, Singapore, 1967-72; Amb Egypt and Lebanon, 1973-74; Amb, Italy, Greece and Israel, 1975-76; Advsr, Universal Mining Co Ltd, Bangkok, Thailand, 1977-. Honours: Kt Grand Cross of the Order of the Crown of Thailand; Coronation Medal and Ratanaporn Medal (3rd Class) of HM King Bhumibel Aduldej of Thailand; 1st Class of the Order of El Gamhoria of Egypt; Kt Cross of the Order of Merit of Italy; Coronation Medal of HM Queen Elizabeth II, Eng. Membership: Life Mbr, Bar Assn of Thailand. Hobby: Golf. Address: 252 Soi Wat Rakhang, Arun Amarin Road, Bangkok 10700, Thailand.

WILDER Gene (Jerry Silberman), b. 11 Jun 1935 Milwaukee WI. Film Actor; Dir; Prodr. m. (1) Mary Joan Schutz, 1967, div 1974, 1 d; (2) Gilda Radner, 1984, dec; (3) Karen Boyer, 1991. Education: Univ of IA; Bristol Old Vic Th Sch. Appointments: Served with US Army, 1956-58; Broadway play: The Complaisant Lover, 1962; W End play Laughter on the 23rd Floor, 1996. Films incl: Bonnie and Clyde, 1966; The Producers, 1967; Start the Revolution Without Me, 1968; Quackser Fortune Has a Cousin in the Bronx, 1969; Willy Wonka and the Chocolate Factory, 1970; The Scarecrow, 1972; Everything You Always Wanted to Know About Sex But Were Afraid To Ask, 1971; Young Frankenstein, 1974; The Little Prince, 1974; Rhinoceros, 1972; Blazing Saddles, 1973; Thursday's Game, 1974; The Adventure of Sherlock Holmes's Smarter Brother, 1975; Silver Streak, 1976; The World's Greatest Lover, 1977; The Frisco Kid, 1979; Stir Crazy, 1980; Sunday Lovers, 1980; Hanky Panky, 1982; The Woman in Red, 1984; Haunted Honeymoon, 1986; See No Evil Hear No Evil, 1989; Funny About Love, 1990; Another You, 1991. Tv appearances incl: The Scarecrow, 1972; The Trouble With People, 1973; Marlo Thomas Special, 1973; Thursday's Games, 1973; Something Wilder, 1994-. Address: William Morris Agency, 151 S Camino Drive, Beverly Hills, CA 90212, USA.

WILDING Michael, b. 1942, Worcester, England. Writer. Education: BA, 1st Class Hons, Engl Lang and Lit, 1963, MA, 1968, Oxford Univ; DLitt, Univ of Sydney, Aust, 1996. Appointments: Lectr, Engl, Univ of Sydney, 1963-66; Asst Lectr, Engl, 1967, Lectr, Engl, 1968, Univ of Birmingham, Eng; Snr Lectr, Engl, 1969-72, Reader, Engl, 1973-92, Prof, Engl and Austl Lit, 1993-, Univ of Sydney. Publications include: The Man of Slow Feeling: Selected Short Stories, 1986; Under Saturn, 1988; Great Climate, 1990; Her Most Bizarre Sexual Experience, 1991; This is For You, 1994; Somewhere New: New and Selected Stories, 1996; Wildest Dreams, 1998; Raising Spirits, Making Gold and Swapping Wives: The True Adventures of Dr John Dee and Sir Edward Kelly, 1999. Memberships include: Advsry Bd, Intl Milton Symp, 1992, 1995; Austl Ed, Stand Mag, UK, 1972-; Gen Ed, Asian and Pacific Writing, 20 vols, 1972-82. Address: Department of English, University of Sydney, Sydney, NSW 2006, Australia.

WILKINSON Gordon Thomas, b. 12 June 1940. Chemical Engineer. m. Nereda Patricia Milne, 14 Aug 1965, 2 s. Education: BE, Chem; PhD, Chem Engrng. Appointments: Tchng Fell, Univ NSW, 1963-67; Proj Engr, Mt Lyell M & R Co Ltd, 1967-69, SAIT, 1970-75; Snr Lectr, 1976-89; Prin Lectr, Univ SA, 1990-96; Cnslt, 1997-. Publications: Over 40 profl articles in sci jrnls. Honour: Paul Harris Fell, Rotary Intl, 1995. Memberships: Fell, Roy Austl Chem Inst; Fell, Inst of Chem Engrs; Chair, Indl Chem Divsn, Exec Cncl, 1997-99, RACI. Hobbies: Golf; Travel; Rotary International; Music. Address: 4 Barker Grove, Toorak Gardens, SA 5065, Australia.

WILKINSON Ralph, b. 15 Nov 1953, Ashby de la Zouch, Eng. Economist. m. Yuko Susannah, 20 Apr 1996. Education: MA, Trinity Coll, Cambridge, 1972-75; MSc, Univ Coll, London, 1975-76. Appointments: UK Civil Servant, 1976-84; Nomura Rsch Inst, Toyko, 1984-86; Eurn Commn, 1987-; Cnslr, Econ & Fin, Tokyo Deleg, 1993-. Membership: Roy Econ Soc. Hobby: Walking. Address: Kureru JHakusan No 3, 21-7 Hakusan 2-chome, Bunkyo-ku, Tokyo 112-0001, Japan.

WILKS Christopher David, b. 14 Sept 1958, Melbourne, Australia. Finance Director. Education: BCom, Melbourne Univ. Appointments: Dir, Sonic Hlthcare Ltd, Silex Systems Ltd. Memberships: FCIM; FAICD; FCIS; ASA. Hobbies: Art; Sport; Investment. Address: 707-127 Kent Street, Sydney, Australia.

WILLEE Paul Andrew, b. 20 Nov 1941, Brighton, Sussex, Eng. Queen's Counsel. m. Alice Sadler, 27 July 1968, 2 s. Education: LLB; LLM, Univ Melbourne; Grad Dip, Com Data Prcsng, Roy Melbourne Inst Technol. Appointments: RANR, 1960-; OIC Diving Team 6; Seconded Min for Def, 1978-79; Appointed Mbr, Judge Advocates Panel, 1985; Def Forces Magistrates, 1996; Cmdr (RANR), Priv Prac, 1967-75; Prosecutor for Queen, 1975-85; Snr Prosecutor, Com Crime Grp, 1981-84; Mbr, AUst Deleg OECD Conf, W Berlin, Info Technol, 1984, and Beyond, Aust Deleg OECD-ICCP Conf on Compterrelated criminality, Paris, 1984, 1985; First Gen Counsel Natl Crime Authy, 1984-86; Resumed Priv Prac, 1986-; QC, 1991-. Publications: Var Articles in Profl Jrnls and confs on subjects inclng: Diving Safety; Legal Status of Oil Rigs; Duty of Prosecutors to Reveal Evidence; A Review of 1910 Salvage Convention; Government Action on Computer Crime; Computer Systems in the National Crime Authority; Chapt 8 of Preparation of Criminal Trials in Victoria (VSPS). Honours: Datec Prize (First) Info Systems Des, 1984; Reserve Forces Decoration; Reserve Forces Decoration (Clasp); 2nd Clasp, 1994. Memberships: Victorian Bar; Maritime Law Assn of Aust Inst Judicial Admin; Inst Arbitrators Cnslt Advocacy Leo Cussen Inst Continuing Educ, 1983-; Pres, Univ hs Alumni Assn, 1986-96; Victorian VP, Ran Ski Club, 1989-95; Pres, Naval and Mil Club, Pres, 1995-98; Mbr

C'wlth Assn of Armed Forces Lawyers, 1995-. Hobbies: Reading; Computers; Systems Design and Implementation; Swimming; Squash; Skiing. Address: Owen Dixon Chambers, 205 William Street, Melbourne, Vic 3000, Australia.

WILLETTS Neil Stanley, b. 4 Oct 1939. Biotechnologist. m. Ruth Linda, 3 d. Education: BA, Hons, 1961, MA, 1965, PhD, 1965, Cambridge Univ, Eng. Appointments: Lectr, 1974-77, Rdr, 1977-82, Prof, 1980-82, Dept of Molecular Biol, Univ of Edinburgh; Dir, R&D, Biotech Aust, 1982-97. Publications: Over 100 in intl sci jrnls. Honours: Vis Prof, Univ of Sydney, 1985-97; Fell, Austl Acady Technological Scis and Engrng. Memberships: Soc for Microbiol, England, 1982-97, USA, 1986-87, Aust, 1989-97; Austl Biotechnol Assn, Dir, 1988-94, 1998-, Pres, 1992-93. Hobbies: Scubadiving; Bush Walking; Music. Address: 113 Bent Street, Lindfield, NSW 2070, Australia.

WILLIAMS Bruce Rodda (Sir), b. 10 Jan 1919, Vic, Aust. Economist. m. Roma Olive Hotten 27 July 1942, 5 d. Education: BA Hons, 1939, MA, 1944, Melbourne. Appointments: Lectr, Econs, Univ Adelaide, SA, 1939-46; Lectr, Econs, Queen's Univ, Belfast, N Ireland, 1946-50; Prof, Econs, Univ Coll N Staffs, Eng, 1950-59; Sec, Jnt Dir, Rsch, Sci and Ind Cttee, 1952-59; Ed, Sociolgcl Review, 1953-59; Prof, Econs, Univ Manchester, 1959-67; Ed, Manchester Sch, 1960-67; Natl Bd Prices and Incomes, 1966-67; Econ Advsr to Min Technol, 1966-67; Vice Chan, Univ Sydney, NSW, Aust, 1967-81; Chmn, NSW Cancer Cncl, 1967-81; Bd, Reserve Bank Aust, 1969-81; Chair, Cttee Inquiry into Educ and Trng, 1976-79; Dir, Tech Change Cntr, UK, Visng Prof, Imperial Coll, London, 1981-86; Chair, Aust, Review Discipline and Engrng, 1987-88; Visng Fell, Austl Natl Univ, 1987, 1988, 1990, 1993-96; Chair, Exec, Intl Piano Competition Aust, 1988-; Fell, Univ Sydney, Chair of Fin and Invmnt Cttees, 1994-98. Publications: The Socialist Order and Freedom, 1942; Co-auth, Industry and Technical Progress, 1957; Investment in Innovation, 1958; Science in Industry, 1959; Investment Behaviour, 1962; Investment Proposals and Decisions, 1965; Investment, Technology and Growth, 1967; Ed, Science and Technology in Economic Growth, 1973; System of Higher Education: Australia, 1978; Education Training and Employment, vol 1, 1979; Living with Technology, 1982; Attitudes to New Technologies and Economic Growth, 1986; Review of the Discipline of Engineering, vol 1, 1988; Ed, Overseas Students in Australia, 1989; Academic Status and Leadership, 1990; The Effects of New Funding Methods on British Universities, 1991. Honours: KBE, 1980; Hon DLitt: Keele, 1973, Sydney, 1982; Hon DEcon, Qld, 1980; Hon LLD: Melbourne, 1981, Manchester, 1982; Hon DSc, Aston, 1982; Kirby Mem Awd, Inst Prodn Engrs, 1988; Hon Fell, Instn Engrs, Aust, 1989. Membership: Fell, Austl Soc Sci Acady. Address: 106 Grange Road, London W5 3PJ, England.

WILLIAMS Geoffrey John, b. 22 Feb 1940, Cessnock, NSW, Aust. Secretary-Treasurer. m. Sandra, 1 s, 1 d. Appointments: SAWEFA Orgnr, 1965; SDA Natl Cnclr, 1966; SAWEFA Indl Offr, 1968; SDA Branch Sec, 1978; SAWEFA Sec-Treas, 1978; SDA Natl Exec, 1978; SDA Natl VP, 1995. Address: 17, William Street, Hamilton, NSW 2303, Australia.

WILLIAMS Gerald, b. 17 Sept 1930, Sydney, NSW, Aust. Conductor; Pianist; Composer. Education: Dip, Sydney Conservatorium of Music, 1951; Dip, Akademie der Musik, Vienna, Austria, 1967; Master Course for Conductors, Hilversum, Netherlands, 1967-68. Appointments: Conductor, Roy Philhamonic Soc of Sydney, 1959-63; Fndr, Conductor, Sydney Baroque Ensemble, 1959; Kapellmeister, var German Theatres, 1967-81; Guest Conductor, Aust Broadcasting Corp, 1982-86; Appeared as Pianist, country tours, 1983, 1985, 1986; Formed Mountain Opera Co, 1987; Fndr, Conductor, Hildesheimer Kammerorchestra, LP Disc, Georg Philipp Telemann. Publications: Var incidental music, Germany, 1970-78; Sinfonietta for Strings, 1983; Three Songs, 1986; Rhapsody for Orchestra and Mezzosoprano (unpubld). Memberships: Tchrs' Fedn, NSW; Fndr, West Philharmonic Soc, Sydney, (now Penrith Symph Orch), 1988. Hobbies: Philosophy; History; Teaching. Address: 11 Davies Avenue, Springwood, NSW 2777, Australia.

WILLIAMS Ian Stuart, b. 1 May 1952. Isotope Geochemist. m. Janet Elizabeth Hadley, 23 Apr 1976. Education: BSc, 1974, PhD, 1978, Austl Natl Univ. Appointments: Rsch Fell, CA Inst of Technol, 1978-80; Visng Fell, Austl Natl Univ, 1981; Rsch Offr, Austl Natl Univ, 1982-92; Fell, Austl Natl Univ, 1992-. Publications: 95 sci pprs in profl jrnls. Honours: D A Brown Medal, 1989; Stillwell Awd, 1990. Memberships: Geol Soc of Am, 1979-88; Geol Soc of Aust, 1979-; Fell, Geol Soc of Am, 1988-. Hobby: Woodwork. Address: Research School of Earth Sciences, Australian National University, Canberra, ACT 0200, Australia.

WILLIAMS James Francis, b. 24 Nov 1935, Newcastle, NSW, Aust. University Professor. m. Barbara Woods, 9 Jan 1960, 2 s, 2 d. Education: PhD, 1965; DSc, 1982; ANU. Appointments: Snr Demonstrator, ANU, 1960-65; Rsch Scientist, ANSTO, 1965; Canad Natl Rsch Cncl Fell, Laval Univ, San Diego, CA, USA, 1967-70; Lectr, 1970-73, Snr Lectr, 1973-76, Rdr, 1976-80, Queen's Univ, Belfast, 1976-80; Prf, Phys, Univ of West Aust, 1980-; Dean, Fac of Sci, UWA, 1992; Hd, Div of Agric and Sci, UWA, 1993. Honour: Boas Medal, Austl Inst of Phys, 1989; Elected Fell, Austl Acadys of Scis, 1998. Memberships: FlInst Phys, 1974; FAmn Inst Phys, 1977; FAust Inst Phys, 1980; NY Aacdy Sci, 1988; S M IEEE, 1992. Hobbies: Family; Gardening; Travelling; Swimming. Address: Physics Department, Centre for Atmic Molecular and Surface Physics, University of Western Australia, Nedlands, Perth, WA 6907, Australia.

WILLIAMS John Christopher, b. 24 Apr 1941, Melbourne, Vic, Aust. Guitarist. Education: Taught guitar by father from age 4; Studied w Segovia, London, 1952; Later study at Accademia Musicale, Chigiana, Siena and Roy Coll of Music, London. Appointments: Toured Russia, 1962, Japan, USA, 1963; Regular tours to USA, Aust, Far E, S Am, Eur; Frequent TV appearances; Mbr of grp, SKY; Many concerts w grp John Williams and Friends inclng Italian tour, 1987; Has appeared at Ronnie Scotts Club; Performed w: Acady of St Martin-in-the-Fields, City of Birmingham Symph Orch, Engl Chmbr Orch, London Symph Orch and others; Performed w Natl Yth Jazz Orch, 1988 Proms; Composers written for him incl: Takemitsu, Leo Brouwer, Stephen Dodgson, André Prévin, Peter Sculthorpe (concerto) and Nigel Westlake (concerto); Artistic Dir, S Bank Summer Music Fest, 2 yrs, Melbourne Arts Fest, 1987; Premiered Brouwer's 4th Concerto in Toronto, 1987; US tour, 1989, and recital at S Bank Latin Am Fest; Premiered Sculthorpe's works in Aust, 1989, Nigel Westlake's Antarctica w London Symph, 1992; Attacca tour, UK, Aust, 1992; Solo tours, UK, 1992, 1993; Documentary film, The Seville Concert for Sony/LWT S Bank Show, 1993; Wigmore Hall series, US tour, Barcelona, Prague Spring Fest, 1994; Japan, Aust & Eurn recitals, 1995; USA, Austl and Eurn recitals, 1996. Creative works: Recdngs of classical and pop wrks; Vivaldi Concertos; Australian Album; Music of Agustin Barrios Mangoré. Honours: OBE; AO. Hobbies: Tennis; Chess; Table Tennis; Politics. Address: c/o Askonas Holt Ltd, 27 Chancery Lane, London WC2A 1PF, England.

WILLIAMS Keith Leslie, b. 16 Mar 1948, Melbourne, Aust. Biotechnologist. Life Ptnr, Brynnie Goodwill, 3 s, 1 d. Education: B of Agric, Melbourne Univ, 1969; PhD, Biochem, Aust Natl Univ, 1972. Appointments: Demonstrator, Biochem Dept, Oxford Univ, Eng, 1972-75; Rsch Fell, Genetics, RSBS, Austl Natl Univ, 1975-80; Nachwuchsgruppenleiter, Max Planck Inst, Biochemie Munich, Germany, 1980-83; Prof, Bio, Macquerie Univ, Sydney, Aust, 1984-; Dir, Cntr for Analytical Biotech, 1992-; Bd Dirs, Austl Technol Innovation Corp Pty Ltd, Sydney; Austl Proteome Analyss Facility; Cnslt to Austl & Intl Biotech cos. Publications: Num articles to profl jrnls; Ed of book, Proteome Research: New Frontiers in Functional Geno, 1997. Honours: Recip, Samuel Wadham Univ Medal of Agric, Melbourne Univ, 1969; Wolfson Coll, Jnr Rsch Fell, Univ Oxford, 1973-75; Austl Biotech Assn; Aust & NZ Soc for Cell Bio. Hobbies: Gardening; Reading; Movies. Address: Biological Sciences, Macquarie University, Sydney 2109, Australia.

WILLIAMS Mack Geoffrey, b. 16 July 1939. Ambassador. m. Carla Michalin, Jan 1966, 1 s, 3 d. Education: BA Hons, Univ of Sydney, Sydney, Aust. Appointments: High Commnr, Bangladesh, 1980-82; Amb, Phillipines, 1989-93; Amb, Repub of Korea, 1994-98; Ret'd from For Serv, 1998; Asian Bus Cnslt, 1998-. Honours: Hon Doctorate, Univ of San Carlos, Philippines, 1991; Hon Fell, Senate Univ of Sydney, 1996; Korean Pres Order of Merit for Diplomatic Serv, 1998. Memberships: Bd Austl-Korean Fndn, 1998; Mbr Exec Austl-Korean Bus Cncl, 1998. Hobbies: Sport; Maps; Reading. Address: 87 Ferry Road, Glebe, NSW 2037, Australia.

WILLIAMS Martin John, b. 3 Nov 1941. British High Commissioner to New Zealand and Samoa; Governor, Pitcairn, Henderson, Oeno and Ducie Islands. m. Susan Dent, 2 s. Education: BA, Corpus Christi Coll, Oxford. Appointments: C'wlth Rels Off, 1963; Private Sec to Permanent Under Sec, 1964; Third, later Second Sec, Manila, 1966; Vice Consul (Commercial), Milan, 1970; Civil Service Coll, 1972; FCO, 1973; First Sec (Commercial), Tehran, 1977; FCO, 1980; Cllr and Hd of Chancery, New Delhi, 1982; Cllr and Hd of Chancery, Rome, 1986; Cllr and Hd of South Asia Dept, FCO, 1990; NIO, 1993; HC, Harare, 1996. Honours: OBE, 1979; CVO, 1983. Hobbies: Music; Gardening. Adddress: c/o Foreign and Commonwealth Office (Wellington), King Charles Street, London, SW1A 2AH, England.

WILLIAMS Paul Colin, b. 14 Mar 1946, Brisbane, Queensland, Australia. Writer; Film Maker. div, 20 Apr 1968, 2 s. Education: Grad Dip, Applied Film and TV, Swinburne Coll, 1976. Publications: The Shenandoah Affair, novel; The Adventures of Black Ned; A Kids Guide to Cubbies Houses. Memberships: Austl Writers Guild; Austl Dirs Guild. Hobbies: History; Classic Sports Cars; Historic Building Preservation. Address: 3 Eileen Close, Warrendyte, Vic 3113, Australia.

WILLIAMS Peter Owen, b. 13 May 1937, Albury, Aust. Medical Practitioner; Cardiologist. Education: MB BS, Melbourne, 1961; MRCP, Glasgow, 1968; MRCP, London, 1968; FRACP, Aust, 1970. Appointments Sessional Cardiologist, Natl Heart Fndn Rehab Cntr, (Vic Div), 1971-83; Med Dir, Natl Heart Fndn Rehab Cntr (Vic Div), 1976-83; Visng Physn, 1975-91, Sessional Cardiologist, 1983-91, Prince Henry's Hosp, Melbourne, 1975-91; Sessional Cardiologist, Cardiac Rehab Unit, Caulfield Hosp, Melbourne, 1990-96; Hon Cnslt to Monash Med Cntr, 1992. Memberships: Cardiac Soc of Aust and NZ; Roy Austl Coll of Physns. Hobbies: Tennis; Music. Address: Epworth Medical Centre, 62 Erin Street, Richmond, Vic 3121, Australia.

WILLIAMS Philip Gladstone, b. 31 Mar 1932, Sydney, NSW, Aust. Experimental Mycologist. m. Maria Paula Wilma Kappenstein, 17 Dec 1963, 1 s, 1 d. Education: BSc Agr, 1954, MSc Agr, 1959, Univ of Sydney; PhD, Univ of WI, USA, 1960. Appointments: Tas Dept of Agric, 1955-57; Univ of WI, USA, 1957-60; NRC Prairie Regl Lab, 1960-62; Univ of Sask, 1962-64; Univ of Sydney, 1965-76; NSW Dept of Agricl, 1977-85; Univ of NSW, 1985-. Publications: 39 rsch pprs in intl sci jrnls and 3 book chapts. Honours: Sch Cap, 1949; Natl Rsch Cncl of Can Postdoct Fellshp, 1960-62; Alexander von Humboldt Fellshp, 1972-73; US-Aust Sci and Technol Collaboration Prog, Rsch Fellshp, Univ of RI, 1990; Mycological Soc of Japan Invited Lectr, Tokyo, 1991. Membership: Australasian Mycological Soc. Hobbies: Voluntary Work for the environment; Music; Gardening; Fishing; Home brewing. Address: School of Biological Sciences, University of New South Wales, Sydney, NSW 2052, Australia.

WILLIAMS Philip Laurence, b. 11 Nov 1949, Melbourne, Aust. Economist. m. Elizabeth Anne Huwie, 12 Jan 1972, 4 s. Education: MEcon (Monash); PhD

(London). Appointments: Tchng Fell, 1971-72, Snr Tchng Fell, 1973-74, Monash Univ; Lectr, 1978-82, Snr Lectr, 1983-87, Univ of Melbourne, Dept of Econs; Rdr, 1988-94, Asst Dir, 1990-, Prof, 1994-, Melbourne Bus Sch. Publication: The Emergence of the Theory of the Firm, 1978; The Cost of Civil Litigation Before Intermediate Courts in Australia, 1992; Review of Scales of Legal Professional Fees in Federal Jurisdictions, 1998. Memberships: Cncl of Austl Ballet Sch, 1983-89, Chmn, 1985-89; Law Reform Commn of Vic, 1986-92; Bd, Inner and East Hlth Network, 1997-. Hobbies: Visual and performing arts. Address: 2000 Leicester Street, Carlton, Vic 3053, Australia.

WILLIAMS S Linn, b. 7 Jan 1946, St Louis, MO, USA. Attorney. m. Noriko. 13 Sept 1975, 1 s, 1 d. Education: BA, Princeton, 1968; JD, Harvard Law Sch, 1971; Study, Intl Law, Cambridge Univ, 1972-74. Appointments: Clrk for Judge Irving L Goldberg, US Crt of Appeals, 5th Cicuit, 1971-72; Practiced corp law, Ptnr, Leva Hawes Symington, Martin & Oppenheimer, Wash DC, Gibson, Dunn & Crutcher, Wash DC & Tokyo, Jones Day Reavis & Pogue, Wash DC, 1974-81, 1985-89, 1992-94; Apptd by Pres Reagan as VP & Gen Cnsl, Overseas Priv Investment Corp, 1981-84; Dpty US Trade Repr, apptd by Pres Bush, w Rank of Amb, 1989-91; Snr VP & Gen Cnsl of Edison Mission Energy, 1994-. Publications: Developing an Export Trading Business, 1989; Chapts on countertrade and investment protection in Doing Business in China, 1993; Num articles on corp & trade matters. Honours: Fulbright Schlshp; Natl Endowment for Humanities Fellshp; Ford Fndn Fellshp. Memberships include: US Prin of Inter-Pacific Bar Assn; Snr Assoc, Cntr for Strategic & Intl Studies, Wash DC; Bd Trustees: Japan-Am Soc of South CA; Inst of Intl Coml Law, NYC; US Natl Cttee of Pacific Econ Coop Cncl, Wash DC. Address: Lansdowne House, Berkeley Square, London, W1X 5DH, England.

WILLIAMS Thomas Stafford, b. 20 Mar 1930, Wellington, NZ. Archbishop. Education: STL, Pontifical Urban Coll de Propaganda Fide, Rome, Italy; BSocSc, Univ Coll, Dublin, Ireland. Appointments: Ordained Priest, Rome, 1959; Chap, Dublin, 1960-62; Asst Priest, Palmerston N, NZ, 1963-64; Dir of Studies, Cath Enquiry Cntr, Wellington, NZ, 1965-70; Parish Priest, Leulumoega, Western Samoa, 1971-75; Parish Priest, Porirua E, 1976-79; Appointed Archbish of Wellington and Metrop of NZ, 1979; Ordained Bish, 1979; Appointed Cardinal, 1983. Address: Catholic Centre, PO Box 1937, Wellington 6015, New Zealand.

WILLIAMS William David, b. 21 Aug 1936, Liverpool, Eng. Limnologist. m. Anne, 16 Jan 1961, 2 s. Education: BSc; PhD; DSc, Liverpool, Eng; DipEduc, Monash Univ, Aust. Appointments: Lectr, Monash Univ, Aust, 1961; Prof, Adelaide Univ, 1975. Publications: Sev books on limnological topics; 250 sci pprs. Honours: Fell, Austl Inst for Bio, 1974; For Fell, Russian Acady of Nat Scis, 1994. Membership: Intl Assn for Limnology, 1961. Hobbies: Classical music; Gardening. Address: Department Environmental Biology, University of Adelaide, Adelaide, 5005, Australia.

WILLIAMSON Ian Philip, b. 29 Sept 1947, Sydney, Australia. Professor of Surveying and Land Information. m. Munlika, 29 Sept 1973, 1 s, 1 d. Education: Bach Hons, Surveying, NSW, 1970; Master, Surveying Sci, NSW, 1974; DPhil, NSW, 1983. Appointments: Fndn Prof, Surveying and Land Info, Univ of Melbourne, 1986-93; Hd, Dept of Geomatics, Univ of Melbourne, 1998-; Dir, UN Liaison, Intl Fedn of Surveyors, 1998-2002. Honours: Eminent Individual Awd, Australasian Urban and Reg Info Systs Assn, 1996; Medal, Inst of Surveyors, Aust, 1997; Acknowledgement from Pres, World Bank, 1997; Awd for Ex, 1997. Hobbies: Fly-Fishing; Hiking; Swimming. Address: Department of Geomatics, University of Melbourne, Parkville, Victoria 3052, Australia.

WILLIAMSON John Charles, b. 23 Jan 1947, Melbourne, Aust. University Professor. m. Marion, 28 June 1980, 2 d. Education: BA, DipEd, Univ NSW; MEd,

Univ Sydney; MA(Ed), PhD, Univ Leicester; Grad Dip Pub Sect Mngmt (Distinction), Curtin Univ. Appointments: Hd, Sch of Tchng Studies, Curtin Univ, Perth, 1982-93; Prof of Educ, Hd, Sch of Second and Post Compulsory Educ, Univ of Tasmania, 1993-. Publications: Groupwork in the Primary School, 1992; Interactive Multimedia: Progress and Promise (ed), 1993; Teacher Education in the Asia-Pacific Region: Practice, Promise and Tensions. Honours: Fell, Austl Tchr Educ Assn, 1992; FRSA. Memberships: Amn Educl Rsch Assn; Austl Assn for Rsch in Educ; Austl CColl of Educ; Austl Psychol Assn; Austl Tchr Educ Assn; Brit Educl Rsch Assn; Higher Educl Rsch and Dev Soc of Australasia. Hobbies: Reading; Australian Rules Football; Church architecture. Address: University of Tasmania, Launceston 7200, Tasmania, Australia.

WILLIAMSON Maurice D, b. 1951, Auckland, NZ. Government Minister. m. 3 children. Education: BSc, Auckland Univ; Postgrad Stdies, Computer Sci and Applied Maths. Appointments: Plng Analyst, Air NZ, 12 yrs; Joined Natl Party, 1978; Elected to Parl, 1987; Retained seat, 1993, 1996; Min of Comms, Min of Brdcstng, Assoc Min of Hlth, Assoc Min of Sci and Technol, 1990; Min of Transp, Min of Rsch, Sci and Technol, Min of Local Govt, Min of Statistics, Min of Comms, Min of Info Technol, Assoc Min of Tertiary Educ, Assoc Min of State Servs. Honour: Serv to the Citizen Awd, Amn Intl Summit on Serv to the Citizen Prog Cttee, 1997. Membership: Fell, NZ Computer Soc. Address: Suite 6, Pakuranga Professional Centre, 267 Pakuranga Highway, PO Box 51-158, Pakuranga, Auckland, New Zealand.

WILLMOT Eric Paul, b. 31 Jan 1936, Australia. Consulting Engineer; Managing Director. m. Sue, 20 Jan 1976, 1 child. Education: BSc; DipEd (ANU); MEd (Canb); DLitt (Newcastle); LLB (Melbourne). Appointments include: Chief Educ Offr, ACT Sch Auth, 1987; Sec, ACT Dept Educ & Arts, 1991-92; Dir Gen, Educ Dept, SA, 1992; CEO, Dept Arts & Cultural Heritage, SA, 1992-94; Visng Fell, Univ Canb, 1994; Prin Ptnr, Vision 2 Pty Ltd, 1994; Ptnr Aimbridge Pty Ltd, Melbourne, 1995-. Publications: Australia The Last Experiment, 1986; Pemulwuy the Rainbow Warrior, 1987; Below the Line, 1991. Honours include: Advance Aust Awd Mech Engrng; Medale D'Orr Geneva Salon Technologie; Austl Inventor of Yr; Holder 71 Intl Patents. Memberships include: Austl Natl Comm UNESCO, 1984; Dir Rsch, Rsch Sch Soc Scs, 1979-80; Austl Inst Aboriginal Affairs, 1983; Inventors' Assn Aust Ltd Sydney. Address: 169 Kingsford Smith Drive, Melba, ACT 2615, Australia.

WILLS Dean Robert, b. 10 Jul 1933 Aust. Bus Exec. m. Margaret F Williams, 1955, 1 s, 2 d. Education: Sacred Heart Coll SA; SA Inst of Tech. Appointments: Dir W D & H O Wills - Aust - 1974-86; Dir AMATIL Ltd, 1975; Mngng Dir W D & H O Wills - Aust - 1977-86; Chmn W D & H O Wills - Aust - 1983-89; Dep Chmn AMATIL Ltd, 1983; Chmn Mngng Dir Coca-Cola AMATIL Ltd, 1984-; Chmn Austl Eagle Ins Co, 1986-; Trustee Mus of Applied Arts and Scis, 1986-90; VP Bus Cncl of Aust, 1987-88; Pres Bus Cncl of Aust, 1988-90; Pres Medl Fndn - Univ of Sydney - 1990; Vice-Chmn Natl Mutual, 1992-97; Chmn Natl Mutual, 1997-; Dir Microsurgery Fndn Melbourne, 1992-; Dir John Fairfax Holdings Ltd, 1994-; Dir Westfield Holdings Ltd, 1994-. Memberships: Bus Cncl of Aust, 1984-94; Mbr Bd Austl Grad Sch of Mngmnt - Univ of NSW - 1985-92. Hobbies: Tennis; Vintage Cars. Address: Coca-Cola AMATIL Ltd, GPO Box 145, Sydney, NSW 2001, Australia.

WILLWEBER Martin, b. 15 Dec 1951, Ashiya, Japan. Marketing Consultant. m. Kazuko, 7 Apr 1992. Education: BA, Polit Sci, Sophia Univ, Tokyo; MA, Polit Sci, Sophia Univ. Appointments: Artist Endorsee, Cnslt, Yamaha Corp; Advsr, Koyo Kanri Co Ltd. Memberships: Dir, Intl Hosp and Medl Servs Assn, Kobe, Japan; Cnclr, Kobe Kaisei Hosp; Dir, Socl Welfare Fndn Kaiseikai and Nursing Home Umi No Hoshi; Intl House of Japan (Tokyo); Tokyo Club; Yokohama Country and Athletic Club, Kobe Club; Century Club (Osaka); WA Athletic Club

(Seattle); Suma Yacht Club (Kobe). Hobby: Sailing. Address: 9-96 Koyoen Higashiyama-Cho, Nishinomiya 662-0012, Japan.

WILMOTH Geoffrey David, b. 4 Nov 1946, Bundaberg, Aust. City and Regional Planner. m. Vivian Lin, 1 s, 2 d. Education: PhD, Univ CA, Berkeley; Master Deg, Town and Country Plng, Univ Sydney; BEcon, Hons, Univ Qld. Appointments: Dir, Dept of Urban and Regl Devel, Aust Govt, 1973-78; Hd, Plcy and Plng Divs, NSW Dept of Plng and Environ; Dean, Fac of Environ Design, Roy Melbourne Inst of Technol, 1988-89; Dpty Vice Chan, RMIT, 1989-. Memberships: Fell, Austl Inst of Mngmt, 1990-; Austl Inst of Co Dirs; Austl Inst of Urban Stdies. Address: 23 Kendall Street, Elwood, Victoria 3184, Australia.

WILSON (Thomas) Douglas, b. 18 July 1955, Kirkcaldy, Scot. Veterinary Surgeon and Homeopath. m. Martina, 26 July 1984, 1 s, 1 d. Education: BVM&S; MRCVS; PhD; MACVSc; DipHom. Dir, Holistic Vet Clin, 1998. Membership: Fndr Mbr, Austl Assn of Holistic Veterinarians, 1995. Hobbies: Permaculture; Family activities. Address: The Holistic Veterinary Clinic, 308 Glen Osmond Road, Fullarton, South Australia 5251.

WILSON Andrew Bray Cameron (The Hon Mr Justice), b. 3 June 1936, Adelaide, S Aust. Justice of the Supreme Court of Samoa. m. Julie Elizabeth Pearce, 11 Apr 1987. 2 s, 6 d. Education: LLB, Univ of Adelaide, 1959. Appointments: Bar and Sol, 1960-72; Judge Adelaide Juvenile Crt, 1972-76; Judge Dist Crt of S Aust, 1972-99; Acting Justice of the Supreme Crt of Papua New Guinea, 1973; Lectr, Criminology, Univ Adelaide, 1973; Justice of the Natl and Supreme Crts, Papua New Guinea, 1978-80; Justice of the Supreme Crt of Samoa, 1999-. Honours: Churchill Fellshp, 1972; AM, 1998. Memberships: Mbr, Cncl, Law Soc, S Aust, 1961-72; Chmn, Prisoners Aid Assn, S Aust, 1966-73; Mbr, Socl Welfare Advsry Cncl, 1970-72; Mbr, Aust and NZ Soc Criminology, 1971-; Mbr, Law Reform Cttee, S Aust, 1972; Mbr Coalition Against Crime, 1990-94; VP, 1973-77, 1991-93, Pres, 1993-95, Aust Crime Prevention Cncl; Chmn, McDouall Stuart Brd, Burra Art Gall, S Aust, 1995-97; Pres, Offenders Aid and Rehab Servs, S Aust, 1997-99. Listed In: Who's Who in Australia. Hobbies: Swimming; Gardening; Criminology. Address: c/o Supreme Court, Box 49, Apia, Samoa.

WILSON Brian Thomas, b. 17 May 1941. National Chairman of Law Firm. m. Sharyn Margaret Hall, 29 Sept 1978, 3 s, 1 d. Education: BLaw; MLaw; Licentiate of Theol. Appointments: Joined Clayton Utz, 1969; Ptnr, 1974-; Hd, Sydney Litigation Sect, 1974-90; Mng Ptnr, Sydney/Melbourne, 1981-83, 1990-96; Natl Chmn, 1992-; Hd, Intl Servs Grp, 1990-; Hd of Govt Servs Grp, 1997. Publications: Var articles and papers on legal issues. Memberships: Intl Bar Assn; Inter Pacific Bar Assn; Austl Inst of Co Dirs. Hobbies: Golf; Cricket; Skiing; Farming. Address: Clayton Utz, Levels 27-35 No 1 O'Connell Street, Sydney, NSW 2000, Australia.

WILSON David Clive (Lord Wilson of Tillyorn), b. 14 Feb 1935, Alloa, Scot. m. Natasha (Helen Mary) Alexander, 1 Apr 1967, 2 s. Education: Keble Coll, Oxford; PhD, London Univ, London, 1973. Appointments: For Serv, 1958; Third Sec, Vientiane, 1959-60; Second then First Sec, Peking, 1963-65; For and C'wlth Off, 1965-68; Ed, China Quarterly, 1968-74; Diplomatic Serv: Cabinet Off, 1974-77; Polit Advsr, Hong Kong, 1977-81; Hd, S Eurn Dept, For and Cwlth Off, 1981-84; Asst Under-Sec of State, 1984-87; Gov of Hong Kong, 1987-92; Chmn, Scottish and Southern Energy plc (Scottish Hydro-Elec plc, 1993-98) 1998-; Chmn, Scottish Cttee Brit Cncl, 1993-; Brit Cncl Bd, 1993-; Chan, Univ of Aberdeen, 1997-; Pres, Bhutan Soc of the UK, 1993-; VP, Roy Scottish Geogl Soc, 1996-; Tstee, Mus of Scotland, 1999-. Honour: KCMG, 1987; GCMG, 1991; Life Peer, 1992. Memberships: Pres, Hong Kong Soc and Hong Kong Assoc, 1994-. Hobbies: Mountaineering; Reading. Address: House of Lords, London SW1A 0PW, England.

WILSON Edwin James, b. 27 Oct 1942. Poet. m. Cheryl Lillian Turnham, 1 Sept 1975, 2 s, 1 d. Education: BSc, UNSW. Appointments: Sci Tchr, Lectr Armidale Tchr's Coll; Educ Offr, Aust Mus, Comm Relations Roy Botanic Gardens, Sydney. Publications: Banyan, 1982; Royal Botanic Gardens Sydney, 1982; Liberty, Egality Fraternity, 1984; The Dragon Tree, 1985; Discovering the Domain, 1986; Wild Tamarind, 1987; Falling up Into Verse, 1989; Songs of the Forest, 1990; The Rose Garden, 1991; The Wishing Tree, 1992; The Botanic Verses, 1993; Chaos Theory, 1997; Cosmos Seven: Selected Poems, 1967-1997, 1998. Hobbies: Gardening, Orchids. Address: c/o Woodbine Press, PO Box 32, Lane Cove, NSW 2066, Australia.

WILSON Geoff, b. 23 Sept 1938, Melbourne, Victoria, Australia. Vice Chancellor; President. m. Beverley, 2 s, 2 d. Education: BSc, 1958, MSc, 1960, DSc, 1977, Melbourne Univ; PhD, Monash Univ, 1964. Appointments: Vice Chan, Pres, Deakin Univ; Vice Chan, Qld Univ; Rector, Univ Coll NSW; Dean, Fac of Mil Studies. Honours: AM, 1997. Memberships: Aust Vice Chans Cttee, 1990-97; Chair of Bd, Thailand-Aust Fndn; Intl Bus Exchange; Austl Educn Off. Address: c/o Deakin University, Woolstores Campus, Geelong, Victoria 3217, Australia.

WILSON Ian Bonython Cameron (Hon), b. 2 May 1932, Adelaide, SA, Aust. Former Federal Member of Parliament. m. Mary Roubel Scales, 7 May 1960, 4 s. Education: LLB, Adelaide Univ, 1951-55; SA Rhodes Schl, 1955 BCL, Oxford Univ, 1956. Appointments: Bar (Gray's Inn), Bar and Solicitor, Supreme Crt of SA, 1958-; Elected to House of Reps as Mbr for Sturt, 1966-69, 1972-93; Parly Sec to PM, 1980-81; Min for Home Affairs and Environ, 1981-82; Min for Aboriginal Afffairs and Assisting Min for Socl Security, 1982-83. Memberships: Former VP, Good Neighbour Cncl, SA; Former Chmn, St Matthews Aged Homes Inc; Dpty Chmn, Nutlote Trust Pty Ltd; Cmmnr, Charitable Funds, SA; Former Mbr of the Cncls or Bds of Kathleen Lumley Coll, The Bible Soc (SA), Aged Cottage Homes and other community orgs. Address: 2 Ringmer Drive, Burnside, SA 5066, Australia.

WILSON John Henry Bruce, b. 26 July 1956, Rostrup, Germany. Securities Analyst. m. Akiko, 6 Jan 1996, 1 d. Education: MA Hons, Cambridge; Japan Fndn Proficiency Exam, Top Level. Appointments: Snr Analyst, HSBS Securities. Creative Works: Japanese Pharmaceutical Industry Spreading Wings Overseas, 1998. Honours: MA Hons, Eng Lit, Land Economy, Cambridge. Memberships: Philippine Self Help Fndn. Hobbies: Wind Surfing; Kayaking; Skiing; Sailing. Address: Komachi 2-22-13, Kamakura, Kanagawa-Ken, Japan.

WILSON John Leslie, b. 7 Apr 1946. Occupational Physician; Winemaker. m. Patricia Anne Burgess, 7 Jan 1969, 1 s, 1 d. Education: MBBS, Adel, 1970; FACOM, 1985; FAFOM (RACP), 1994. Appointments: Proprietor and Winemaker, Wilson Vineyard, 1974-; Pvte Occupational Hlth Pract, 1978-; Cnslt Occupational Physn, McWork Rehab, 1989-98; Snr Visng Med Spec, Occupational Hlth Unit, Roy Adelaide Hosp, 1993-. Publications: Wine Columnist for Medical Observer mag, 1987-98. Honours: Champion Cabernet Sauvignon in Winewise, small vigneron awds, 1996. Memberships: Profl Mbr, Austl Soc Viticulture and Oenology, Aust; NZ Soc Occupational Med Treas 1982-88, 1993-96. Hobbies: Pichi Richi Railway Preservation Society. Address: The Wilson Vineyard, Box 11, Sevenhill, SA 5453, Australia.

WILSON John Spencer, b. 15 Nov 1949, Melbourne, Aust. Union Secretary. m. Helen, 31 Mar 1990. Memberships: Bd Dir, Western Region Hlth Cntr, 1992-; Natl Trust; Geelong Austl Rules Football Club; Austl Labor Party; Fin Sector Union; Save Albert Park. Hobbies: Football; Travel; Reading. Address: 56 Regent Street, Elsternwick 3185, Australia.

WILSON Linda, b. 17 Nov 1945, Rochester, MN, USA. Librarian. Education: BA, MA, Univ MN. Appointments: Libn, Univ CA at Riverside, 1968-71; Cty Libn, Belle

Glade Fl, 1972-74; Adult Ext, Hd, Kern Co Lib, Bakersfield, CA, 1974-80; District Lib Dir, Lake Agassiz Regl Lib, Crookston, MN, 1980-85; Supervising Libn, San Diego Co (CA) Lib, 1985-87; County Libn, Merced Co (CA), 1987-93; Learning Network Dir, Merced Coll, 1993-95; City Libn, Monterey Park, CA, 1995-. Honours: Pub Lib Assoc's Leonard Wertheimer Awd, 1998; Libn of Yr, 1990, CA Lib Tstees and Commnrs; Educ Awd, Merced Co Comm on the Status of Women. Memberships: Amn Lib Assn; CA Lib Assn; Ldrshp Merced; Monterey Park Chamber of Commerce; E LA Bus and Profl Women; Rotary Intl of Monterey Park. Hobbies: Travel; Walking; Reading; Stamp collecting. Address: 1000 E Newmark Ave #22, Monterey Park, CA 91755, USA.

WILSON Lionel Leopold, b. 29 Sept 1926, Sydney, NSW, Aust. Medical Practioner (Health Consultant). m. Margaret Lillian, 18 Jan 1956, 1 s, 2 d. Education: MB BS; FRACGP. Appointments: Invitation to join fac of Lincoln Sch of Hlth Systems Scis, La Trobe Univ to lect in 1st postgrad dip course on quality mngmt and quality assurance in hlth care. Publication: Quality Management in Healthcare, 1995. Honours: Fell, Roy Austl Medl Assn, 1969; Gold Medal, Austl Medl Assn, 1982; Medal of Achievement, Austl Cncl of Healthcare Stands, 1984; Mbr, Gen Div of Order of Aust, 1986; Life Gov, Austl Postgrad Fedn in Med, 1987; DSC Honoris Causa, la Trobe Univ, 1999. Memberships include: Mbr, Treas, VP, Pres, Austl Cncl of Healthcare Stands, 1974-84; Mbr, Vice-Chmn, Chmn, Cncl of Wrld Medl Assn, 1976-85; Advsr, Hosp Corp, Aust, 1981-85; Life Gov, Austl Postgrad Fedn in Med, 1987; Mbr, Natl Bd, Chmn, NSW Bd, Austl MedicAlert Fndn, 1989-91. Hobby: Gardening. Address: 134 Queens Road, Connell's Point, NSW 2221, Australia.

WILSON Lorraine Margaret, b. 18 May 1939, Echuca, Vic, Aust. Education Consultant. Education: Trained Infant Tchr's Cert, 1956-58; Cert A Vic Educ Dept, 1974. Appointments: Tchr w Vic Educ Dept, 1959-77, in cl Vice Prin, Helen St Northcote Primary Sch, 1973-77; Lectr (Pt-time), Lang and Lit, Dept, Coburg Tchrs Coll, 1978; Lectr (pt-time), Curric Studies Dept, Melbourne State Coll, 1979-82; Educl Consultancy, 1978-98; Cnslt to schs in CO, USA, Apr 1989; Cnslt to schs, Wash DC, USA, May 1992; Cnslt to schs in VA, USA, Jan 1993. Publications: Num pprs at intl, natl and state confs; Jrnl articles; Ref books inclng: Getting Started, series of titles, 1978-83; (co-auth) An Integrated Approach To Learning, 1991; (auth) Write Me a Poem, 1994; Children's books: City Kids (60 titles), 1978, 1979, 1980, 1981, 1986; Country Kids (48 titles), 1982, 1983, 1985, 1987; Footy Kids (24 titles), 1982, 1984; Champions (6 titles), 1984; Firefighters (6 titles), 1986; Police (10 titles), 1989; My Mum has False Teeth and Other Stories, 1990; The Lift-Off Kids (4 titles), 1992; I Have Two Dads, 1995; I Speak Two Languages, 1995; Footy Kids, 1995; James and Jessie Books, 1995, 1996; The Best of City Kids (20 titles), 1997; New City Kids (10 titles), 1997. Honours: ALEA Medal, Austl Literacy Edurs Fndn Assn, 1996. Memberships: Auth Repr, Fedl Govt Pub Lending Right Cttee, 1995-98; Pub Lending Right Cttee repr, Steering Cttee for Evaluation of the Pub Lending Right Scheme, 1998; Austl Literacy Educrs Assn; Intl Reading Assn; Austl Educ Network; Austl Soc Auths; Cntr for Pub Educ. Address: 81 Amess St North Carlton, Victoria, Australia, 3054.

WILSON Paul Richard, b. 9 Mar 1941, Chirstchurch, NZ. Criminologist. Education: PhD; MA. Appointments: Dir Resch, Austl Inst of Criminology, 1989-93; Dean of Arts, QLD Univ of Technol, 1993-94; Dean of Hum and Socl Scis, Bond Univ, 1994-. Creative Works: 25 Books; Black Death White Hands; The Last Woman Hanged in Australia. Honours: Fulbright Schl, 1983. Memberships: Austl Criminology Assn. Hobbies: Tennis; Swimming; Travelling. Address: 2/104 Hedges Avenue, Mermaid Beach, QLD, Australia.

WILSON Peter John, b. 24 Apr 1944, Sydney, NSW, Australia. Mathematics Tutor. m. Sau Ching Au, 27 Apr 1988. Education: Bach of Sci, 1964, MA, 1989, Univ of

Sydney. Appointments: Self employed Writer/Photographer, 1967-; Lab Techn, Austl Natl Univ, Canberra, 1969; Examiner of Patents, Patent Off, Canberra, 1973-81; Self-employed Maths Tutor, 1987-. Publications: Books: Australia's Insect Life, 1970; The Living Bush: A Naturalist's Guide, 1977; Australia's Butterflies, 1987; Articles: Modelling the SR 71A, 1976; Darkness, no darkness, 1978; The Convair F106 Delta Dart, 1978; World of Insects, 1979; Depth of Field, 1980; Extreme Close-up Photography, 1981; Insect Photography, 1985; Butterflies of the Rainforest, 1986; Going it Alone, 1989. Memberships: Austl Entomological Soc, 1981-; Austl Math Soc, 1987-. Hobbies: Nature photography; Oil painting and drawing; Surfing; Distance running; Designing, building and flying model aircraft. Address: 49 Despointes Street, Marrickville, NSW 2204, Australia.

WILSON Robin Ernest, b. 22 May 1950, Mt Gambier, SA, Aust. Plant Breeder (Wheat). m. Colleen Glenyse Jackson, 19 Jan 1974, 2 s. Education: BAgSc, Adelaide Univ, 1971; Regd Secnd Sch Tchr. Appointments: Secnd Sch Tchr, 1972-74; Rsch Assoc, Roseworthy Agricl Coll, S Aust, 1975-85; Wheat Breeder, West Austl Dept of Agric, 1985-. Publications: Conbr of var articles to confs. Memberships: Austl Grain Inst; Austl Wheat Breeding Soc; Australasian Plant Path Soc. Hobbies: Botany (native flora); Collecting Australian Stamps and Coins. Address: Department of Agriculture, Plant Industry Division, 3 Baron-Hay Court, South Perth, WA 6151, Australia.

WILSON Ronald Darling, b. 23 Aug 1922, WA, Aust. Retired. m. Leila Amy Gibson Smith, 29 Apr 1950, 3 s, 2 d. Education: LLB, hons; Hon LLD, Univ Western Aust, 1980; LLM, Univ PA, USA, 1957; Hon DED, Keimyung Univ, Korea, 1989. Appointments: Queens Counsel, 1963; Sol-Gen, WA, 1969-79; Justice, High Crt of Aust, 1979-89; Chan, Murdoch Univ, 1980-95; Moderator, WA Synod, 1977-79; Pres, Assembly, Uniting Ch in Aust, 1988-91; Pres, Human Rights & Equal Opportunity Commn, 1990-97; Dpty Chmn, Cncl for Aboriginal Reconciliation, 1991-94. Honours: CMG, 1978; KBE, 1979; AC, 1988; Hon Deg, Dr of the Univ, Murdoch Univ, 1995. Address: 6B Atkins Road, Applecross, WA 6153, Australia.

WILSON Stanley, b. 2 Feb 1947, Los Angeles, CA, USA. Visual Artist, Educator. m. Jacquelyn Bellard, 1978, 1 s, 1 d. Education: BFA, Visual Art Inst, 1969; MFA, Otis Art Inst, 1971. Appointments: Asst Prof, Southwestern Coll, Chula Vista, 1972-73; Prof, Art CA State Polytechnic Univ, Pomona, 1973-; Acting Dir, Univ Art Gall, 1988-89; Dir, 1989-; Instr, Otis Parsons Watts Towers, Los Angeles, 1981-; Bd Dirs, Watts Tower Art Centre; Artist, LACTC, Metro Rail, Green Line, Avalon Stn, 1993-96; Artist in Resn, Studio Mus, Harlem, NY, 1987; Visual Artist, Univ NV, Las Vegas; Visual Artist, Spokane Coll, River Falls Coll, Spokane, WA; Artist in Resn, Spokane Coll, 1997; Advy Bd, Los Angeles Pub Art Cttee; Advy Bd, Pasadena Arts Cttee, 1991-; Chmn, 1997-. Honours: Brody Fellshp, CA Cmnty Fndn; Natl Endowment of the Arts, Sculp; Res, NY. Memberships: Natl Advy Bd, Art Fac Cons, Natl Advy Placement Prog, Princeton, NJ; Dev Cttee, Advmnt Placement, Coll Bds, Princeton, NJ; Bd Advsrs, Armory Centre for the Arts, Pasadena, Desauble Mus, Chicago; CA Mus of Afro Amn Art and Cutlture; NAACP. Hobbies: Sports; Sculpture; Landscape; Gardening; Travelling. Address: Art Department, c/o California State Polytechnic University, Pomena, CA 91768, USA.

WILSON Trevor Gordon, b. 24 Dec 1928, Auckland, NZ. Historian; Professor of History. m. Jane Verney, 5 Sept 1957, 2 d. Education: MA, 1st Class Hons, Univ of Auckland, 1952; DPhil, Univ of Oxford, 1959. Appointments: Asst Lectr in Hist; Canterbury Univ, 1952; Auckland Univ, 1953-55; Rsch Asst, Univ of Manchester, 1957-59; Lectr, Snr Lectr, 1960-67, Prof of Hist, 1968-, Univ of Adelaide; C'wlth Fell, St Johns Coll, Cambridge Univ, Eng, 1972; Visng Fell, Magdalen Coll, Oxford Univ, 1987; Disting Drinko Prof, History, Marshall Univ WV, USA, 1989. Publications: The Downfall of the Liberal

Party 1914-1935, 1966, 1968; The Political Diaries of C P Scott 1911-1928, 1970; The Myriad Faces of War: Britain 1914-1918, 1986; Command on the Western Front 1914-1918 (w Robin Prior), 1992; Passchendale the Untold Story (w Robin Prior), 1996, 1997. Honours: Univ of NZ Overseas Travelling Schlshp, 1953; Gilbert Campion Prize, 1960; Nuffield Dominion Travelling Fellshp, 1964-65; Higby Prize Amn Histl Assn, 1965; Adelaide Fest of Arts Lit Awd, 1988. Memberships: Fell, Roy Histl Soc; Fell, Austl Acady of the Hums, Cncl Mbr, 1984-86; Cncl Mbr, Historiale de la Grande Guerre, Peronne, France. Hobbies: Collecting jazz records; Table tennis. Address: Department of History, University of Adelaide, SA 5001, Australia.

WILSON Warwick Raymond, b. 1 Aug 1941, Sydney, Aust. Academic. Education: Tchng Cert, 1961; BA, 1971; MEd, 1980; MA (Hons), 1987. Appointments: Primary Sch Tchr, 1962-69; Secnd Sch Tch, 1970-72; Secnd Sch Subj Master, 1973-75; Lectr, Milperra Coll of Adv Educ, 1975-80; Snr Lectr, 1980-86, Macarthur Inst of Higher Educ; Prin Lectr, 1987-88; Assoc Prof, 1989-, Hd, Div of Socl Scis, 1992-94, Dir (Acad), Fac of Arts and Socl Scis, 1994-, Dir, Cntr for Canad Studies, 1994-; Chmn, Acad Senate, 1994-98, Dean, Intl Inst, 1998-, Univ of W Sydney, Macarthur. Honours: FABINYI Awd, Best Book, Austl Book Publrs Assn; Category Awd Winner, 1985, 1986, Austl Geog Tchrs Assn; Excellence in Cartography Awd, Austl Inst of Cartographers; Fell, Geog tchrs Assn, NSW. Memberships: Past Pres, Austl Geog Tchrs Assn; Fell, Roy Geog Soc. Hobbies: Travel; Reading; Jogging. Address: 9 Moolanda Avenue, West Pennant Hills, NSW, Australia.

WILTSHIRE Kenneth William, b. 11 Dec 1944, Brisbane, Aust. University Academic. m. Gail Jocelyn Raymond, 27 Apr 1968, 1 s. Education: BEcon, 1967; BECon, Hons, 1970; PhD, 1985, Univ of Queensland; MSCEcon, London Sch of Econs, 1972. Appointments: Rsch Economist, Queensland Govt, 1962-70; Lectr, Snr Lectr, Assoc Prof, Univ of Queensland, 1972-87; JD Story Prof of Pub Admin, Univ of Queensland, 1988-; Visng Prof, Univ of Toronto, Can, 1981; Chmn, Austl Heritage Commn, 1982-85; Exec Mbr, 1984; Dpty Chmn, 1988-, UNESCO Natl Commn; Chmn, UNESCO Natl Commn, 1992-; Mbr, C'wlth Grants Commn, 1995-. Publications include: An Introduction to Australian Public Administration, 1974; Privatisation: The British Experience, 1987; and many other books. Honours: Prize in Pub Admin, UK; Canad Govt Spec Vis to Can, 1979; Natl Fell, Austl Inst of Pub Adin, 1984; Communicator of the Yr, 1984; Can Fac Enrichment Awd, 1989; UNESCO Medal, 1995; AO. Memberships include: Roy Inst of Pub Admin, UK; Inst of Pub Admin of Can; Intl Inst Admin Scis; Intl Polit Sci Assn; Roy Histl Soc. Hobbies: Broadcasting; Jazz; Theatre. Address: Centre for Public Administration, University of Queensland, St Lucia, Brisbane, Qld 4072, Australia.

WIN TIN, b. 5 July 1935, Mawlamyaing, Myanmar. Politician. m. 2 children. Appointment: Minister of Finance and Revenue, Myanmar, 1992-. Address: Ministry of Finance and Revenue, Theinphyu Street, Botahtaung Township, Yangon, Myanmar.

WINDHEIM Lee Stephen, b. 3 Mar 1926, Omaha, NE. Architect. m. Devah Hansen, 2 Aug 1950, 2 s. Education: BArch, IA State Univ. Appointments: Snr VP, Leo A Daly Co, 1949; Rtd, 1988; Prin Investigator for Energy Conserv AIA Rsch Fndn. Creative Works: Article and Pprs in Tech Jrnls. Honours: Delta Sigma Roe; Tau Sigma Delta; Tau Beta Pi. Memberships: AAAS; Intl Solar Energy Soc; World Future Soc; Intl Soc Gen Semantics; Soc Arch Historians; C'wlth Club. Hobbies: RV'6; Photography. Address: 375 Crown Road, Kentfield, CA 94904, USA.

WINER Conrad Edward Robert, b. 11 Jan 1931, Essex, Eng. Physician. m. Marguerita Ann Dutton, 13 Apr 1957, 3 s. Education: LLB, Univ Coll, London, 1953; MRCS (Eng), 1959; LRCP, London, 1959; MB BS, Univ Coll, London, 1960; DRCOG, Eng, 1961; MLCOM (Mbr, London Coll of Osteopath Med), London, 1964; Mbr, Fac

of Homeopathy, 1965; DPRM (Dip, Phys and Rehabilitation Med), Univ of Sydney, 1969; FACRM (Fell, Austl Coll of Rehab Med, 1979; FAFRM, RACP (Fell, Austl Fac of Rehab Med, RACP), 1993. Appointments: Capt, Roy Army Medl Corps (Obstetrician), 1960-63; Visng Specialist: Clin of London Coll of Osteopathy (UK), Roy London Homeopathic Hosp, Nature Cure Clin (London), 1964-67; Visng Snr Spec, Dept Rehab Med, Roy Prince Alfred Hosp, Sydney, Aust, 1967-79; Clin Dir, 1980-97, Cnslt, 1998-, Dept Rehab Med, RPA Hosp, Sydney, Aust. Publications: (co-auth) Manual Medicine 1984; Book chapts; Profl jrnls; Pprs in proceedings of confs in Aust, NZ, Eng, France, Switz, Germany, Denmark, Russia. Honours: RSPCA Medal, 1949; Thomas Skurray Prize, W London Hosp Sch, 1958; BMA Essay Competition Winner, 1959, 1960; Travel Fellshp, L'Inst Natl de la Rsch Medl and Ciba Fndn, 1965; Travel Grant, Post-grad Cttee, Medl Univ of Sydney, 1969; Hon Life Mbr, Austl Assn Musculo-Skeletal Med, 1983; Hon Life Mbr, Osteopathic and Naturopathic Rsch Soc, UK, 1984; Hon Life Mbr, Childbirth Educ Assn, Sydney, 1974; Hon Mbr, Vetebro-Neurol Assn of Russia, Kazan, 1994. Memberships include: Pres, Austl Assn Phys Med and Rehab Med, 1979-81; Pres, Austl Assn Musculo-skeletal Med, 1984-86; Pres, Austl Coll of Rehab Med, 1983-85; Austl Fac of Rehab Med (Roy Austl Coll of Physns); Intl Fed Manual Med; Brit Osteopathic Assn; Osteopathic and Naturopathic Rsch Soc, UK; Austl Rheumatism Assn; Austl Medl Assn; Spine Soc; Stroke Soc; Medico-Legal Soc, NSW (Aust) and UK. Hobbies: Horseriding; Snowskiing; Bushwalking. Address: Royal Prince Alfred Hospital Medical Centre, Carillon Avenue, Newtown, Sydney 2042, Australia.

WINGTI Paias, b. 2 Feb 1951 Moika Village. Politician. 5 s. Education: Univ of Papua New Guinea. Appointments: Apptd Asst Speaker Pub Accounts Cttee; Elected Govt Whip; Min for Transp and Civ Aviation, 1978-80; Dep PM and Min for Natl Plng and Devt, 1982-84; Min for Educ, 1984-85; Resigned from Govt and co-fndr People's Democratic Movement, 1985; Ldr of Opposition, Mar-Nov 1985, 1988-92, 1994; PM, 1985-88, 1992-94. Memberships: MP, 1977-97; Mbr Pub Accounts Cttee. Hobbies: Playing Golf; Watching Rugby League. Address: People's Democratic Movement, P O Box 972, Boroko, Papua New Guinea.

WINKLER Nicholas Gary, b. 24 June 1948, Sydney, Aust. Solicitor; Management Consultant. m. 1 s, 2 d. Education: BA; LLM(Hons). Publications: Jrnl articles, on mngng change, improving productivity, measuring bd perf. Memberships: Cttee for Econ Dev of Aust; Austl Inst of Co Dirs; Amn Chmbr of Com in Aust. Hobby: Sailing. Address: 26/10 Ray Street, Turramurra, NSW 2074, Australia.

WINTERTON George Graham, b. 15 Dec 1946, Hong Kong. University Teacher. m. Rosalind Julian, 18 Aug 1979, 2 s, 2 d. Education: LLB, Hons, LLM, Univ of W Aust; JSD, Columbia; Bar, NSW; Bar and Solicitor, Vic & WA. Appointments: Assoc in Law, Columbia Univ, 1973-75; Snr Lectr, Assoc Prof, Prof of Law, Univ of NSW, 1975-; Exec Govt Advsry Cttee, Austl Constitutional Commn, 1985-87; Repub Advsry Cttee, 1993. Publications: Parliament, the Executive and the Governor-General, 1983; Monarchy to Republic, 1986; Judicial Remuneration in Australia, 1995; We, the People: Australian Republic Government (ed), 1994; Australian Federal Constitutional Law: Commentary and Materials (co-auth), 1999. Hobbies: Reading; Music. Address: Faculty of Law, University of New South Wales, Sydney, NSW 2052, Australia.

WIRYONO Sastrohandoyo, b. 31 May 1934, Jogyakarta, Java, Indonesia. Ambassador of Indonesia to Australia. m. Retno Rahayu Wiryono, 20 May 1962, 1 s, 2 d. Education: DRS, Gajah Mada Univ; BA, Univ of Indonesia. Appointments: Rsch Bur of For Min, 1962; Third Sec, Indonesian Emb in Buenos Aires, Argentina, 1964-68; Offr in Charge, Amn Desk, 1968-71; First Sec, Cnslr, Washington, 1971-74; Sub-Dir, N Amn Affairs, For Min until 1978; Min-Cnslr, Emb in Paris, 1978-80; Perm Mission, UN in New York, 1980-82; Dpty Chief of Mission,

Emb in Washington, 1982-84; Dir, Amn Affairs; Dpty Perm Rep, Indonesian Perm Mission to UN in New York; Indonesia's Amb Extraordinary & Plenipotentiary, Repub of Austria, 1988-89; Rep, UN Off in Vienna, UN INdl Dev Org & Intl Atomic Energy Agcy; Dir Gen, Pol Affairs, For Min, Jakarta, 1990-93; Amb to France, 1993-96. Honours: Order of Merit, 4th Class, Egypt, 1977; Order of Merit, 4th Class, Kuwait, 1977; Satya Lencana Karya, Satya Kelas II, Indonesia, 1989; Bintang Jasa Utama, Indonesia, 1995; Grand Officier de l'Ordre Natl du Merite, France, 1996. Membership: Patron, Asia Educ Fndn, Aust, 1997-. Hobbies: Reading; Tennis; Golf. Address: Embassy of the Republic of Indonesia, 8 Darwin Avenue, Yarralumla, ACT 2600, Australia.

WITHERS Glenn Alexander, b. 27 Aug 1946, Melbourne, Australia. Economist. m. Marion H Powall, 17 Aug 1974, 2 s. Education: BEcon, hons, Monash; AM, PhD, Harvard. Appointments: Prof of Econs, LaTrobe Univ, 1986; Dir, Econ Plng Advsry Cncl, 1991; Prof of Pub Policy, Austl Natl Univ, 1997. Publications: Conscription, 1972; Economics of the Performing Arts, 1979; Financing the Courts, 1989; Australia and Immigration, 1997. Honours: Fulbright, Knox & Menzies Schl, 1970; Offr, Order of Aust, 1991. Membership: Fell, Acady of Socl Scis of Aust. Address: Public Policy Program, Australian National University, ACT 0200, Australia.

WITHERS Robert Thomas, b. 26 Aug 1938, Birmingham, Eng. Exercise Physiologist; Educator. m. Pamela Sue Peridier, 5 July 1974. Education: Ctf in Educ, Alsager Coll of Educ, Eng, 1961; Dip in Phys, Educ, St Luke's Coll, Eng, 1962; MSc, WA Univ, 1967; PhD, Univ of MD, 1974. Appointments: Rdr Phys Educ, Flinders Univ, Bedford Park, Aust; Mbr, Natl Lab Accreditation; Aust Sports Commns, 1990-96; Chmn, 1997-. Publications: Contbr over 70 articles to profl jrnls. Memberships: Assoc Ed, Austl Jrnl of Sci and Med in Sport, 1985-; Editl bd, Intl Jrnl Sports Med, 1994-; Fell, Austl Sports Med Fedn; Amn Coll of Sports Med. Hobbies: Reading; Weight training; Jogging; Spectator sports. Address: Flinders U, Exerc Phys Lab, Bedford Park, South Australia 5042, Australia.

WITT Howell Arthur John, b. 12 July 1920, Newport, Gwent, Wales. Retired Bishop. m. Gertrude Doreen Edwards, 16 June 1949, dec, 3 s, 2 d. Education: BA, Univ Leeds, Eng, 1942; Coll Resurrection, Mirfield, Yorkshire, 1942-44. Appointments: Asst Curate, Usk, Gwent, 1944-47; Asst Curate, St George's, Camberwell, London, 1948-49; Chap, Long Range Weapons Expmtl Range, Woomera, SA, Aust, 1949-54; Rector, St Mary Magdalene's, Adelaide, SA, 1954-57; Priest i/c, Elizabeth, 1957-65; Bish, NW Aust, 1965-81; Bish, Bathurst, 1981-89; Retd, 1989. Publications: Bush Bishop; Verily, Verily; Witts End; More Witts End. Hobbies: Writing; Golf. Address: U20, DGV, 99 McCabe Street, Mosman Park, WA 6012, Australia.

WIZINOWICH Peter Lindsay, b. 2 June 1956, Winnipeg, Can. Optics Engineer. m. Janice, 3 Aug 1995, 1 s. Education: BS, Phys & Astronomy, Univ of Toronto; MASc, Inst of Aerospace Studies, Univ of Toronto; PhD, Optical Scis Cntr, Univ of AZ. Appointments: Univ of Toronto South Observatory, 1980-81; Instrument Techn, Can-France-HI Telescope, 1982-85; Staff Scientist, Steward Observatory, 1989-91; Optics Engrng Mngr, W M Keck Observatory, 1991-. Publications: Sci & technol pprs on adaptive optics, interferometry, astron; Fabrication of the Keck Observatory Adaptive Optics Facility. Honour: Soc of Photo-Optical Instrument Engrs (SPIE) Schlshp, 1987. Memberships: SPIE; OSA (Optical Soc of Am).

WOLANSKI Eric JA, b. 19 Oct 1946, Bukavu, Belgian Congo. Civil Engineer; Oceanographer. m. Therese, 18 Nov 1978, 2 s. Education: BS Eng; MSc Eng, Princeton; PHD, Env Engrng, Johns Hopkins. Appointments: Hydrologist, SPCC and SMEC, 1974-78; Aust Inst Marine Sci, 1978-. Publications: Over 220 publs, 3 books. Honours: IBM Environmental Model Awd, 1994; Qld IT&T Awd, 1996; SCOR Working Grp, Muddy Coast; Ed and

Asst Ed, 6 Intl Jrnls on Marine Sci. Memberships: Inst Engrs (Aust); Sigma Xi; Rotary Club; Coral Reef Assn. Hobbies: Tennis; Wildlife. Address: c/o AIMS PMB No 3 Townsville MC, Qld 4810, Australia

WOLFENSOHN James David, b. 1 Dec 1933, Sydney, Aust. President. m. Elaine Ruth, 26 Nov 1961, 1 s, 2 d. Education: BA, Univ of Sydney; LLB, Univ of Sydney; MBA, Harvard Grad Sch of Bus. Appointments: Lawyer, Austl Law Firm, Allen Allen and Hemsley; Offr, Roy Austl Air Force; Olympic Fencing Team, 1956; NY Carnegie Hall, 1970; Chmn of the Bd, 1980-91; Chmn Emer, Carnegie Hall; Chmn of Bd of Tstees, John F Kennedy Cntr, Perfng Arts, Washington, 1990; Chmn Emer, 1996-; Pres, World Bank Grp; Chmn Bd of Inst for Advd Stdy, Princeton Univ. Honours: Hon Kthood, Queen Elizabeth II; David Rockefeller Prize. Memberships: Amn Acady of Arts and Scis; Amn Philos Soc. Address: The World Bank Group, 1818 H Street NW, Washington, DC 20433, USA.

WOLFF Rodney Carl, b. 13 Apr 1966, Melbourne, Aust. University Lecturer. Education: BSc (Qld); DPhil (Oxon). Appointments: Lectr, Univ of Glasgow, 1991-95; Snr Lectr, Queensland Univ of Technol, 1995-. Honours: Natl Shell Uk Schl, 1988; Snell Fell, Balliol Coll, Oxford, 1994. Memberships: Roy Statistical Soc, 1989-; Cnclr, Statistical Soc of Aust Inc, 1989-. Hobbies: Music; Acting. Address: School of Mathematical Sciences, Queensland University of Technology, GPO Box 2434, Brisbane, Qld 4001, Australia.

WOLKOV Harvey Brian, b. 8 Feb 1953, Cleveland, OH, USA. Physician. m. Lauren, 9 Jan 1993. Education: BS; MS; MD. Appointments: Med Dir, Radiation Oncology Cancer Cntr, 1990-; Assoc Clinl Prof of Radiation Oncology, Univ of California Davis, 1997-; Assoc Clinl Prof Surg, Univ of California, Davis, 1992-. Publications: 20 sci publs; 8 book chapts in med textbooks, 1989-98. Honours: Eta Sigma Gamma Hon Soc, 1976; Fell, Amn Coll of Radiology, 1986; Amn/Eurn Soc of Therapeutic Radiology and Oncology Travel Awd, 1987; Amn Cancer Soc Classical Fell, 1982, 1983. Memberships: Cncl, Affiliated Regl Radiation Oncology Socs, Pres-Elect, 1998; Pediat Oncology Grp, Co-Prin Investigator, 1989-; Natl Graves Fndn, Bd of Advsrs, 1989-; Northern Radiation Oncology Soc, Pres, 1999. Hobbies: Sculpture; Oil Painting; Art Collector. Address: 4810 Winding Ridge Court, Sacramento, CA 95841, USA.

WOMACK Thomas Houston, b. 22 June 1940, Gallatin, TN, USA. Executive. m. Pamela Reed, 23 Apr 1991, 1 s, 1 d. Education: BSME. Memberships: Soc of Mfng Engrs; Amn Soc of Mechl Engrs; Amn Filtration Soc. Address: 700 Walnut Avenue, Mare Island, CA 94592, USA.

WONDER Stevie, b. 13 May 1950 Saginaw MI. Singer; Musician; Composer. m. (1) Syreeta Wright, 1971, div 1972; (2) Yolanda Simmons, 3 c. Education: MI Sch for the Blind. Appointments: First appeared as solo singer at Whitestone Baptist Ch Detroit, 1959; Recdng artist with Motown Detroit, 1963-70; Fndr and Pres Black Bull Music Inc, 1970-; Fndr and Pres Wondirection Records, 1982-; Owner KJLH Los Angeles. Num recdngs incl: Singles incl: Fingertips, 1963; Uptight/Purple Raindrops, 1965; Someday At Christmas/The Miracles of Christmas; I'm Wondering/Everytime I See You I Go Wild, 1966; I Was Made To Love Her/Hold Me, 1967; Shoo-Be-Doo-Be-Doo-Da-Day/Why Don't You Lead Me To Love; You Met Your Match/My Girl, 1968; For Once in My Life; I Don't Know Why; My Cherie Amour; Yester-Me Yester-You Yesterday; Never Had A Dream Come True; Signed Sealed Delivered I'm Yours; Heaven Help Us All; Superstition; You are the Sunshine of My Life; Higher Ground; Living For the City; Boogie on Reggae Women; Don't You Worry About a Thing; I Wish; Sir Duke; Another Star; Lately; Jammin'; We Are the World - with others; I Just Called to Say I Love You; Albums incl: Little Stevie Wonder: The Twelve-Year-Old Genius; Tribute to Uncle Ray; Jazz Soul; With A Song In My Heart; At The Beach; Uptight, 1966; Down To Earth, 1966; I Was Made To Love Her, 1967; Someday At Christmas, 1967; Stevie

Wonder: Greatest Hits, 1968; Music of My Mind, 1972; Innervisions, 1973; Fulfillingness' First Finale, 1975; Songs in the Key of Life, 1976; Journey Through the Secret Life of Plants, 1979; Hotter than July, 1980; Original Musiquarium, 1981; Woman in Red, 1984; In Square Circle, 1986; Characters, 1987; Jungle Fever, 1991; Inner Peace, 1995; Motown Legends, 1995. Honours: Named Best Selling Male Soul Artist of Yr - Natl Assn of Rec Merchandisers - 1974; Grammy Awds - You Are the Sunshine of My Life, Innervisions, Superstition - 1974; Grammy Awds - Fulfillingness' First Finale, Boogie on Reggae Woman, Living for the City - 1975; Grammy Awds - Songs in the Key of Life, I Wish - 1977; Acady and Golden Globe Awds for song I Just Called to Say I Love You, 1985. Address: c/o Steveland Morris Music, 4616 W Magnolia Boulevard, Burbank, CA 91505, USA.

WONG Felix, b. 28 Apr 1951, Hong Kong. Medical. m. Angela, 1983, 2 s. Education: MMED; MD; FRCS; FRCOG; FRACOG; FHKCOG; FHKAM. Appointments: Medl Offr, 1976-83; Lectr, 1983-87; Snr Lectr, 1987-93; Prof, 1993-. Publications: 3 Medl Books, 1990-96. Honours: Croucher Fndn Fellshp, 1986. Memberships: Many Medl Assns and Adac Insts. Hobbies: Fishing; Swimming; Stamp Collectng. Address: 7 Governor Phillip Place, West Permanant Hills, NSW 2125, Australia.

WONG Lawrence T, b. 1 Sept 1939, Fukien Prov, China. Businessman; Chief Executive. m. Agnes Lai Wong, 27 Nov 1965. Education: BS, Natl Cheng Kung Univ, Taiwan, 1961; MSc, Univ of Toledo, USA, 1964; PhD, Michigan State Univ, USA, 1970. Appointments: Ford Motor Co in USA, Aust, Taiwan, 1964-95; Var tech and managerial posns; Pres and CEO, Ford Lio Ho Co, Taiwan, 1993-95; Chf Exec, Hong Kong Jockey Club, 1996-. Honours: Outsndng Rsch Awd, Michigan State Univ, 1970; Businessman of Yr, Taiwan, 1994. Memberships: Soc of Automotive Engrs, USA, Mbr, 1964-95; Hong Kong Mngmt Assn (Fell), 1996-. Hobbies: Tennis; Music. Address: The Hong Kong Jockey Club 16/f, Jockey Club Headquarters, 1 Sports Road, Happy Valley, Hong Kong.

WONG Mun Hoong, b. 2 Mar 1966, Singapore. Investment Banker. m. Gerk Kuan Ang, 22 July 1994. Education: BAcctncy (Hons); Chartered Finl Analyst. Appointments: Staff Acct, Arthur Andersen & Co, 1990-91; Corp Fin Exec, Schroder Intl Merchant Bank, 1991-92; VP, Merrill Lynch Pte Ltd, 1992-. Memberships: Inst of Cert Pub Accts of Singapore, 1992-; Inst of Chartered Finl Analysts, 1994-; Singapore Soc of Finl Analysts, 1994-; Mensa, Singapore, 1995-. Hobbies: Tennis; Reading. Address: 57 Telok Kurau Lor H, #03-03, Telok Kurau Lodge, Singapore 426065.

WONG Nelson L, b. 13 Nov 1964, Singapore. Regional Manager. m. Yao Yi Ju, 22 July 1995, 1 s. Education: BBA; Dip of Advtng. Appointments: Br Mngr, Parlson Systs; Cnslt; MMS Consultancy (Asia) Plc; Regl Mngr. Memberships: Singapore Inst of Mngmnt. Hobbies: Reading; Water Sports. Address: 30 Mayflower Way, Singapore 568520.

WONG Poh Poh, b. 1945, Singapore. Associate Professor. m. 3 s. Education: BA(Hons), 1966, MA, 1969, Singapore Univ; PhD, McGill Univ, 1971. Appointments: Asst Lectr, 1966-69, Lectr, 1969-77, Snr Lectr, 1977-87. Publications: Coastal Tourism in Southeast Asia, 1991; Tourism vs Environment: The Case for Coastal Areas, ed, 1993. Honour: Univ of Singapore Geog Soc Medal, 1966. Membership: Geol Soc of Malaysia. Address: Department of Geography, National University of Singapore, 10 Kent Ridge Crescent, Singapore 119260.

WONG Soak-Koon, b. 30 Mar 1948. Lecturer. Education: BA Hons, 1968-70; DipEd, 1973; MA, 1975; PhD, Univ of CA, Berkeley, 1986. Appointments: Tutor, Dept of Engl, Univ of Malaya, 1971-72; Tchr, La Salle Secondary Sch, Malaya, 1973-74; Lectr, Univ of Sci, Malaya, 1975-93; Assoc Prof, 1994-. Publications: Co-Ed: Feminism - Malaysian Critique and Experience, 1994; Guest Ed: Representations of Women in SE Asia, 1995; Num articles on Feminist Lit Theory, and SE Asian

Women Writers. Honour: Harvard-Yenching Doctoral Fellowship, Harvard, 1978-83; Fulbright Fell, Dept of Engl and Women's Stdies, Univ CA, Santa Barbara, 1999. Memberships: Rsch Assoc, Unit for Study of Women and Human Resources, 1992-; Malaysian Assn of C'wlth Lang and Lit Studies; Modern Lang Assn of Am; Mbr Panel, Natl Lit Awds, Malaysia, 1980-92. Address: School of Humanities, University Sains Malaysia, Penang, Malaysia.

WONG Tok Chai, b. 21 Mar 1918. Company Director. m. Chen Yu, 2 s, 1 d. Education: BS, Agric, St Joseph's Coll, Hong Kong; Lingnan Univ, Canton. Appointments: Bus Advsr, Stand Chartered Bank, 1968-87; Exco Chmn, Unico Holdings Bd, 1984-92; Chmn. Mngng Dir, Amoy Canning Corp Grp of Cos, 1954-; Dir, Univ Tstee (Malaysia Bd), 1969-96; Pres, Sato Amoy Constrn (M) Sdn Bd, 1971-; Dir, Perbadnan Natl Ins Sdn Bd, 1983-; Dpty Chmn, Cypress Lakes Grp, Aust, 1995-. Honours: KMN (Kesatria Mangku Negara), conferred by DYMM Yang Dipertuan Agung, 1966; JMN, Johan Mangku Negara conferred by DYMM Yang DiPertuan Agung, 1976; DJMK, Dato Paduka Jiwa Mahkota Kelantan (Al Ismaili II), conferred by DYMM Sultan of Kelantan (on his 58th birthday), 1976; PSM, Panglima Setia Mahkota, conferred by DYMM Yang DiPertuan Agung, 1987; Order of Rising Sun Gold Rays w Neck Ribbon, conferred by His Majesty, Emperor of Japan, 1987. Memberships: VP, Fedn of Malaysian Mfrs, 1968-82; Chmn, Kwang Hua hs Bd Govs, 1968-82; VP, Malaysia Leprosy Relief Assn, 1971-86; Treas, Malaysia-Japan Econ Assn, 1978-89; Pres, KL/Selangor Chinese Chmbr of Comm and Ind, 1981-87; Dpty Pres, Assoc Chinese Chmbr of Comm and Inds, 1981-87; VP, Malaysia/Aust Bus Cncl, 1986-87; Chmn, Kuen Cheng Girl's hs, 1989-98. Listed in: Reference Asia. Address: Amoy Canning Corp (Malaya) Bhd, 7 km Jalan Kelang Lama, 58000 Kuala Lumpur, Malaysia.

WONG Wui Min, b. Sept 1950, Singapore. Consultant Cardiologist. m. Dr Chan Hsiu Mei, 1984, 2 s, 1 d. Education: MB BS, Univ of Singapore, 1974; MMed Internal Med, 1980; MRCP (UK), 1980; FRCP (Edinburgh), 1995. Honour: Datukship conferred by Sultan of Brunei, 1986; Memberships: Fell, Acady of Med (Singapore), 1986; Fell, Soc Coronary Angiography and Intervention (USA), 1996. Hobbies: Singing; Playing the piano; Assembling computers. Address: 6 Napier Road, #10-10 Gleneagles Medical Centre, Singapore 258499.

WONG YICK MING Rosanna, b. 15 Aug 1952 Hong Kong. Administrator; Official. Education: Univ of Hong Kong; Univ of Toronto; LSE; Chinese Univ of Hong Kong; Univ of CA Davis. Appointments: Exec Dir Hong Kong Fedn of Yth Grps; Chmn Hong Kong Housing Authy; Chmn Complaints Cttee of Hong Kong Ind Commn Against Corruption; Chmn Children's Thalassaemia Fndn; Chmn Socl Welfare Advsry Cttee, 1988-91; Chmn Commn on Yth, 1990-91; Chmn Police Complaints Cttee, 1993; Patron Mother's Choice; Patron Children's Kidney Trust Fund. Honours: Hon Fell Hong Kong Inst of Housing, 1994; Hon Mbr Chartered Inst of Housing, 1994. Memberships: Mbr Legis Cncl, 1985-91; Mbr Exec Cncl, 1988-91, 1992-97; Mbr Exec Cncl of Hong Kong Specl Admin Reg, Jul 1997-; Mbr Co-ordng Cttee for Children and Yth at Risk; Mbr Exec Cttee Hong Kong Cncl of Socl Service; Mbr Bd World Vision Hong Kong. Address: Executive Council Secretariat, First Floor, Main Wing, Central Government Offices, Central, Hong Kong, Special Administrative Region, People's Republic of China.

WOO John, b. 1948 Guangzhou. Film Dir. Education: Matteo Ricci Coll Hong Kong. Appointments: Started making experimental 16 mm films in 1967; Entered film ind, 1969; Prodn Asst Cathay Film Co Asst Dir, 1971; Later joined Shaw Bros as Asst Dir to Zhang Che. Films: The Young Dragons - debut - 1973; The Dragon Tamers; Countdown in Kung Fu; Princess Chang Ping; From Riches to Rags; Money Crazy; Follow the Star; Last Hurrah for Chivalry; To Hell with the Devil; Laughing Times; Plain Jane to the Rescue; Sunset Warriors - Heroes Shed No Tears; The Time You Need a Friend; Run Tiger Run; A Better Tomorrow; A Better Tomorrow

II; JustHeroes; The Killer; Bullet in the Head; Once a Thief; Hard Boiled; Hard Target; Broken Arrow.

WOO Peter K C, b. 1946 Shanghai. Bus Exec. Education: Univ of Cincinnati; Columbia Bus Sch USA. Appointments: Chmn Wheelock & Co Ltd, 1986-96; Dir Standard Chartered Bank PLC, 1986-89; Chmn Wharf - Holdings - Ltd, 1986-94; Dep Chmn Prince of Wales Bus Ldrs Forum, 1991-; Fndng Chmn The Wharf - Holdings - Ltd, 1992-; Hong Kong - now Hong Kong Specl Admin Reg - Affairs Advsr to People's Repub of China, 1993-; Chmn Hong Kong - now Hong Kong Specl Admin Reg - Environment and Conserv Fund Cttee, 1994-; Chmn Hosp Authy, 1995-; Fndng Chmn Wheelock NatWest Ltd, 1995-. Publication: The Challenge of Hong Kong Plus, 1991. Honours: Hon Chmn Wharf - Holdings - Ltd, 1994-; Ldr of the Yr - Hong Kong Standard - 1995; Cross of Offr Order of Leopold - Belgium; Hon Chmn Wheelock & Co Ltd, 1996-. Memberships: Mbr Intl Advsry Bd Chem Banking Corp, 1981-; Mbr Hong Kong - now Hong Kong Specl Admin Reg - USA Econ Co-opn Cttee, 1989-95; Mbr Nat West Bank PLC, 1992-; Mbr Hong Kong Govs Bus Cncl, 1993-97; Mbr Gen Electric, 1994; Mbr Elf Aquitaine, 1994-. Hobbies: Golf; Tennis. Address: Penthouse, Wheelock House, 20 Pedder Street, Central, Hong Kong Special Administrative Region, People's Republic of China.

WOOD Alexander Sandford, b. 9 July 1927. Urologist. m. Jennifer Maddern, 2 June 1956, 2 s, 1 d. Education: MBBS, Melbourne, 1951; FRCS, Eng, 1956; FRACS, 1959. Appointments: Fell, Asst Urologist, Alfred Hosp, Melbourne, 1959-76; Asst Surg, Austin Hosp, Melbourne, 1959-63; Urologist, Bethlehem Hosp, Caulfield, Melbourne, 1965-93; Urologist, Mental Hlth Dept, Vic, 1969-73, 1988-91; Asst Surg, Nephrology, Roy Melbourne Hosp, 1976-78; Urologist, Roy Southern Mem Hosp, Caulfield, Vic, 1978-85; Chmn of Staff, Roy Southern Mem Hosp, Caulfield, Vic, 1983; Chmn of Staff, Bethlehem Hosp, Caulfield, 1989-93; Dir, Continence Serv, Maroondah Hosp, Ringwood, Vic, 1992-95; Hon Snr Lectr, Surg, Monash Univ, 1994-96. Publications: 3 pprs in med jrnls. Honours: Vic Logistic and Support Medal, 1995. Memberships: Austl Med Assn; Austl Assn of Surgs; Hlth Ins Commn. Hobbies: Birdwatching; Plants and trees; Gardening; Bushwalking; Music; Theatre; Reading; Religion; Food; Wine. Address: 108 Burke Road, East Malvern, Vic 3145, Australia.

WOOD Beverley, b. Sydney, Aust. Dietitian. Education: PhD; FAIH; MDAA. Appointments: Snr Proj Offr, Dietitians Assoc Aust, Vic, 1999; Snr Rsch Fell, Melbourne, Unv; Chf Dietitian - Nutritionist, St Vincent's Hosp, Melbourne. Publication: Tucker in Australia (Ed), 1977. Membership: Dietitians Assn of Aust. Hobbies: Art and creative expression; Outdoor activities and conservation. Address: PO Box 1264, Carlton, Vic 3053, Australia.

WOOD Clyde Maurice, b. 7 Jan 1936, Melbourne, Aust. Anglican Bishop. m. Margaret, 13 Apr 1957, 2 s, 1 d. Education: CSandJ; ThL; BA. Appointments: Armadale/Hawksburn, 1970-72; Rector and Canon Res, 1974 i c; Dean, Christ Ch Cath, Darwin, 1978-83; Bishop Diocese NT, 1983-92; Bishop West Reg, Anglican Diocese (Brisbane), 1992-96; Bish, N Qld, 1996. Hobbies: Golf; Gardening. Address: PO Box 1244, Townsville, Queensland 4812, Australia.

WOOD Graham Raymond, b. 24 Oct 1947. Statistician; Mathematician. m. Stephanie Frances Gardiner, 2 May 1975, 1 s, 2 d. Education: BSc, Hons, Otago, 1969; PhD, ANU, 1973. Appointments: Lectr, Univ Canterbury, 1974; Prof, Ctrl Qld Univ, 1994; Prof, Massey Univ, NZ, 1998. Publication: Statistical Methods: The Geometric Approach, 1991. Honour: Fulbright Snr Schl, 1982-83. Membership: NZ Stats Assn. Hobbies: Music; Sailing; Tramping. Address: Massey University, Institute of Information Sciences and Technology, College of Sciences, Private Bag 11 222, Palmerston North, New Zealand.

WOOD John, b. 31 Mar 1944, Kaikoura, NZ. Ambassador. m. 1 child. Education: MA, 1st class hons, Canterbury Univ, 1965; BA, hons, Balliol Coll, Oxford, 1968. Appointments: Joined Min of For Affairs, 1969; Seconded to the Treasury, 1971-72; Econ Div, Min of For Affairs, 1972-73; Second, later First Sec, NZ Emb, Tokyo, 1973-76; Seconded to the PM Dept, Intl Affairs, Advsr to the PM, 1976-78; First Sec, later Cnslr and Consul-Gen, NZ Emb, Bonn, 1978-82; Hd, Eurn Div, Min of For Affairs, 1982; Hd, Econ Div, Min of For Affairs, 1983; Min, Dpty Chf of Mission, NZ Emb, Wash, 1984-87; Amb, NZ Emb, Tehran, 1987-90; Dir, N Asia Div, Min of External Rels and Trade, 1990-91; Dpty Sec, Econ and Trade Rels, Min of External Rels and Trade, 1991-94; NZ Amb to the USA, Wash DC, 1994. Address: New Zealand Embassy, 37 Observatory Circle, NW, Washington DC 20008, USA.

WOOD Lynette Eva, b. 11 Jan 1951, Sydney, Australia. Company Director. m. Maxwell Berghase, 8 Sept 1989, 1 s, 1 d. Education: MA; MBA. Appointments: Fgn Investment Review Bd; NSW Batteries Corp; Sedgwick (Holdings) Pty Ltd. Membership: Fell, Austl Inst of Co Dirs. Hobbies: Gym; Tennis. Address: 20 Mears Avenue, Randwick, NSW 2031, Australia.

WOOD Robert Warren, b. 5 July 1955, Des Moines, IA, USA. Attorney. m. Beatrice, 4 Aug 1979, 1 d. Education: AB, Humboldt State Univ; Further Educ, Univ of Sheffield, Eng; JD, Univ of Chgo. Appointments: Steefel Levitt & Weiss, 1985-91; Ptnr, Bancroft & McAlister, 1992-93; Prin, Robert W Wood Profl Corp, 1993-. Publications: 25 books on taxation and business topics incl: Taxation of Corporate Liquidations, 2nd ed, 1994, w 1998 supplement; Taxation of Damage Awards and Settlement Payments, 2nd ed, 1998. Editl Consultant, CA Small Business Guide, Volumes 1-4, 1998; Num articles in legal, acctng and bus publs. Honour: AV-Rated by Martindale-Hubell. Memberships: Editl Bds, num profl jrnls; Sects on Tax, CA, NY, DC, MT, AZ Bars; Qualified Solicitor, Supre Crt of Eng and Wales; Law Soc of Eng and Wales; US Tax Crt, North Dist of CA, 9th Circuit, Cntrl Dist of CA, Dist of AZ Bars; Cert Tax Spec, CA Bd of Legal Specialization; Fell, Amn Coll of Tax Counsel; Tax Law Advsry Commn, CA Bd of Legal Spec, Chair, 1991-92. Address: 477 Pacific Avenue, Suite 300, San Francisco, CA 94109, USA.

WOODBRIDGE Todd Andrew, b. 2 Apr 1971. Professional Tennis Player; Athlete. m. Natasha Provis, 8 Apr 1995. Appointments include: Champion, Mixed Doubles, Austl Open, Melbourne, 1993; Champion, Doubles, US Open, Flushing Meadow, NY, 1996, Wimbledon, London, Eng, 1996; Semi-finalist, Doubles, French Open, Paris, France, 1996; Finalist, du Maurier Ltd Open, Toronto, Canada, 1996; Semi-finalist, Comcast US Indoor, Phila, PA, 1996; Champion, Doubles, 1996 Olympic Games, Atlanta, GA; Champion, Doubles, Lipton Championships, Key Biscayne, FL, 1996; Champion, Doubles, Newsweek Champion Cup, Indian Wells, CA, 1996; Champion, Doubles, Japan Open, Tokyo, 1996. Honours: Mbr, Austl Davis Cup Team, 1991-96; Winner, 7 Grand Slam Jnr Titles; Olympic Gold Medal, Atlanta, GA, 1996; Champion, Doubles, Wimbledon, Eng, 1997; AOM, 1997. Address: 2 Chapel Street, Richmond 3121, Victoria, Australia.

WOODFIELD David Graeme, b. 9 May 1935, NZ. Medical Director. m. Annabell, 18 Dec 1962, 1 s, 3 d. Education: MBChB, 1960; MRCPE, 1965; FRCPE, 1965; PhD, 1968; FRCPA, 1975. Appointments: Dir, Red Cross Blood Transfusion Servs, Papua New Guinea, 1970-76; Medl Dir, Auckland Regl Blood Serv, 1976-98; Assoc Prof, Transfusion Med, Auckland Medl Sch, 1999-. Publications: Approximately 250 sci pprs on most aspects of Transfusion Med. Memberships: Cnclr, Exec Mbr, Intl Soc of Blood Transfusion, 1978-92; Pres, Australasian Soc of Blood Transfusion, 1992-94. Hobbies: Chestnut farming; Social support activities. Address: Dept of Molecular Medicine, Auckland University School of Medicine Private Bag 92019, Auckland, New Zealand.

WOODLAND Alan Donald, b. 4 Oct 1943, Dorrigo, NSW, Aust. Economics Educator. m. Narelle, 9 Dec 1966, 1 s, 2 d. Education: BA (Hons), UNE, Armidale, Aust, 1965; PhD, 1970. Appointments: Lectr, Econs, Univ of New Eng, 1967-69; Asst Prof, Econs, UBC, Vancouver, 1969-74; Assoc Prof, Econs, UBC, Vancouver, 1974-77; Prof, Econs, UBC, Vancouver, 1978-81; Prof, Econometrics, Univ of Sydney, 1982-. Publications: International Trade and Resource Allocation, 1982; Jrnl articles. Honours: Fell, Econometric Soc; Fell, Acady of Socl Scis in Aust. Membership: Exec Cttee, Intl Econs Assn, 1992-. Hobbies: Tennis; Bridge. Address: Department of Econometrics, Universty of Sydney, NSW 2006, Australia.

WOODS Elizabeth Jean, b. 18 Oct 1955, Brisbane, Aust. University Professor. m. Michael Grundy, 22 Sept 1979, 2 s. Education: BAgr Sci, 1st Hons; DPhil, Agr Econs, Oxon. Appointments: Chmn, Rural Inds Rsch and Dev Corp, 1998; Suncorp Metway Prof in Agribus, Univ of Qld, 1997; Acting Gen Mngr, Hort, Qld, Dept of Primary Inds; Dir, Rural Extn Cntr, Univ of Qld. Honour: OAM, 1991. Memberships: CSIRO Bd, 1995-98; ACIAR Plcy Advsry Cncl, 1991-97; Rural Adjustment Scheme Advsry Cncl, 1996-97; AIAST, 1977-; Austl Agribus Assn, 1997-; Aust-Pacific Extn Network, 1994-. Hobbies: Gardening; Reading; Walking. Address: School of Natural and Rural Systems Management, University of Queensland, Gatton, Qld 4345, Australia.

WOODS Jack Tunstall, b. 10 Dec 1925, Ipswich, Qld, Aust. Company Director. m. Nell Estelle Stephenson, 10 Dec 1948, 2 s, 1 d. Education: BSc, 1946, MSc, 1953, Univ of Qld. Appointments: Dir, Qld Mus, 1964-67; Chf Govt Geol, 1968-75, Under Sec, 1976-82, Qld Dept of Mines; Dir-Gen, 1982-85; Co Dir (var), 1986-. Publications: Num articles and pprs in the fields of Geol, Mining and Energy. Honour: Companion of the Imperial Serv Order, 1985. Memberships: Fell, Australasian Inst of Mining and Metall; Fell, Austl Inst of Energy. Hobbies: Art Collecting; Surfing; Reading. Address: 88 Crescent Road, Hamilton, Qld 4007, Australia.

WOODS Peter Robert, b. 29 Mar 1943, NZ. Mayor of Concord; President, Local Government Association of NSW. m. Joyce Lorraine Grant, 14 Jan 1967, 1 d. Education: Trained Tchrs Ctf, Christchurch Tchrs Coll, NZ, 1960-61; Diagnostic Trng & Remedial Tchng, Balmain Tchrs Coll, NSW, 1970; BA, 1972, MLitt, 1975, Univ of New England, NSW. Appointments: Tchr, NZ, 1962-67; HS Tchr, NSW, 1967-70; Itinerant Remedial Tchr, NSW, 1971-72; Asst Dir, Educn, NSW Dept of Corrective Servs, 1973-76; Lectr, Sociol, Sydney Tchrs Coll, 1976-77; Dpty Prin, Relieving Prin, NSW Dept of Educn, 1977-79; State Organiser for Lectrs, NSW Tchrs Fedn, 1979-; Mbr, var Govt Working Parties; Local Govt: Elected to Concord Municipal Cncl as Alderman, 1977, Dpty Mayor, 1985-86, Mayor, 1986-87, 1991-99, Mbr of States Exec of Local Govt Assn of NSW, 1983, VP, 1987, Pres, 1991-96; Pres, Austl Local Govt Assn, 1993-94; Exec VP, 1993-96, Pres, 1998-99, Asia-Pacific Region, Intl Union of Local Authys; World Exec Mbr, 1993-96, World VP, 1998-99, IULA; Bd Mbr, C'wlth Local Govt Forum, 1995-. Publications: Dissertation: Women Unliberated: A Study of Social Class Values and Education of Women Prisoners in New South Wales, 1975. Honours: JP, 1971; OAM, 1995. Memberships: Austl Coll of Educn; Life Mbr, NSW Tchrs Fedn. Hobbies: Environment; Public Speaking; Debating Politics. Address: 17 Jones Street, Concord, NSW 2137, Australia.

WOODS Robin George, b. 13 Nov 1932, Sydney, Aust. Dental Surgeon. m. Judith, 27 Jan 1958, 2 d. Education: BDS, Sydney Univ; FRACDS; FICD. Appointments: Therapeutics Advsr, Austl Dental Assn; Mbr, Editl Bd, The Austl Prescriber; Mbr, Poisons Advsry Cttee, NSW; Mbr, ADS Assoc Prof, 1997-, Fac of Dentistry, Sydney Univ. Publications: A Guide to the Use of Drugs in Dentistry, 12 ed, 1996; An Australian Glossary of Dental Teams, 4th ed, 1994; rsch pprs in var jrnls, 1996-97; 6 pprs on infection control (in 6 langs). Honours: AM, 1982; Hon Life Mbr, Aust Dental Assn, 1991; World Dental Fedn Merit Awd, 1996. Memberships: Austl Dental Assn; World Dental Assn; Intl Assn for

Dental Rsch. Hobbies: Classical Music; Writing. Address: 77 Lead St, Yass, NSW 2582, Australia.

WOODWARD (Albert) Edward (Sir), b. 6 Aug 1928, Ballarat, Vic, Aust. Chancellor of Univ of Melbourne. m. Lois Thorpe, 20 Sept 1950, 1 s, 6 d. Education: LLB, 1949, LLM, 1950, Univ of Melbourne. Appointments: Practising Bar, 1953-72; Chmn, Victorian Dried Fruits Bd, 1963-72; Chmn, Natl Stevedoring Ind Conf and Stevedoring Ind Cncl, 1965-72; Pres, Victorian Assn of Yth Clubs, 1966-72; Judge, C'wlth Indl Crt and Supreme Crts of ACT, 1972-90, also of NT, 1972-79; Chmn, Armed Servs Pay Enquiry, 1972; Roy Commnr, Aboriginal Land Rights, 1973-75; Mbr, Cncl of Melbourne Univ, 1973-76 and 1986-; Pres, Trade Pracs Tribunal, 1974-76; Dir-Gen of Security, 1976-81; Judge, Fedl Crt of Aust, 1977-90; Roy Commnr, Austl Meat Ind, 1981-82; Chmn, Austl Def Force Acady Cncl, 1982-; Chmn, Camberwell Ch of Eng Grammar Sch, 1983-87; Chmn, Schizophrenia Aust Fndn, 1985-97; Pres, Def Force Discipline Appeal Tribunal, 1988-90; Chan, Univ of Melbourne, 1990-; Mbr, Judicial Remuneration Tribunal (Vic), 1995; Chmn Austl Banking Ind Ombudsman Cncl, 1997-. Honours: QC, 1965; OBE, 1969; Kt, 1982; Hon LLD, Univ of NSW, 1986; Hon D Litt, Univ of Ballarat, 1998. Hobbies: Birdwatching; Walking; Reading. Address: 63 Tivoli Road, South Yarra, Vic 3141, Australia.

WOODWARD Roger Robert, b. 20 Dec 1942 Sydney. Pianist; Conductor; Composer. 1 s, 1 d. Educaiton: Conservatorium of Music Sydney; PWSH Warsaw. Appointments: Debut at Roy Fest Hall London, 1970; Subseqently appeared with the five London Orchs; Has performed throughout East and West Eur Japan and the USA; Has appeared at intl fests and with the maj orchs throughout world; Extensive repertoire and is noted for interpretation of Chopin Beethoven Bach and Twentieth Century Music; Artistic Dir Natl Chamber Orch for Contemporary Music in Aust 'Alpha Centaure', 1989; Artistic Dir for fests in London; Performs each season at ldng intl fests wrks by contemporary composers. Honours: Fell Chopin Inst Warsaw; Kt - Breffini. Hobbies: Cooking; Chess; Swimming; Grdng; Painting; Design. Address: LH Productions, 2/37 Hendy Avenue, Coogee, NSW 2034, Australia.

WOOLCOTT Richard Arthur, b. 11 June 1927, Sydney, Aust. Company Director; Consultant. m. Birgit, 11 July 1952, 2 s, 1 d. Education: BA, Univ of Melbourne; Sch of Slavonic Stdies, London Univ. Appointments: Austl Amb to Indonesia, 1975-78, Philippines, 1978-82, UN, 1982-88; Repr, Aust, Security Cncl, 1995-96; Sec, Dept of For Affairs and Trade, 1988-92; Fndng Dir, Australasia Cntr, Asia Soc, 1997-; Dir, Bonlac Foods Ltd, 1996-. Publications: Contbns to num publs. Honours: AO, 1985; AC, 1993. Memberships: Chmn, Aust-Indonesia Inst, 1992-98; Chmn, Offic Estabs Trust, 1992-. Hobbies: Writing; Photography; Cricket. Address: PO Box 3926, Manuka, Canberra, ACT, Australia 2603.

WOOLDRIDGE Micahel Richard Lewis, b. 7 Nov 1956, Melbourne, Aust. Federal Member of Parliament. m. Michele Marion Colman, 17 Dec 1988, 2 s. Education: Scotch Coll; MBBS, BS, Melbourne and Monash Univs; MBA, Monash. Appointments: Resident Medl Staff to Surgical Registrar, Alfred Hosp, 1982-85; Tutor, Univ of Melbourne, 1985-86; Medl Practitioner, Priv Prac, 1985-87; Elected Fedl Mbr of Parl for Chisholm (Liberal), 1987; Shadow Min for Aboriginal Affairs, 1990; Shadow Asstng Ldr of Opposition on Yth Affairs, 1992-93; Dpty Ldr of the Opposition, Shadow Min on Educ Employment & Trng, 1993-94; Shadow Min for Community Servs, Snr Citizens and Aged Care, 1994-95; Shadow Min for Hlth and Hum Servs, 1995-96; Min for Hlth and Family Servs, 1996; Min of Health and Aged Care, 1998; Mbr, Cabinet Expenditure Review Cttee. Honours: Natl Heart Fndn Rsch Schlshp, 1979; C'wlth Postgrad Schlshp, 1986. Hobbies: Real tennis; Skiing; Reading. Address: Parliament House, Canberra, ACT 2600, Australia.

WOOLLER Harry Owen, b. 3 Aug 1932, Toronto, Ont, Can. Physician; Medical Director. m. Deborah Hardman, 3 s, 1 d. Education: MB, ChB, Univ Birmingham, Eng, 1951-56; DCH, London, 1960; MRCP, London, 1969. Appointments: House Offr, Med, Surg, 1956-58; Registrar, Children's Hosp, Birmingham, 1958-60; Prin, Gen Prac, Newcastle, NSW, Aust, 1961-67; Registrar, Exminster Hosp, Exeter, Eng, 1967-68; Hon Clinl Registrar, Physn, Wallsend Hosp, NSW, 1969-72; Medl Dir, Lilly Inds, Aust and NZ, 1972-85; Clinl Asst, R PAH, Sydney, 1972-; Medl Dir, Roussel Pharms, Sydney, 1985-87; Clinl Rsch Dir, Pfizer Pharms Pty Ltd, W Ryde, NSW, 1987-89; Snr Medl Dir, Aust and NZ, Pfizer Pharms, 1989-94; Cnslt to Pharm Ind, Sydney, Aust, 1995-. Publications: Contbr, sci articles in medl jrnls. Honours: FFPM, London, 1990. Memberships: AMA; BMA; Austl Pharm Physns Assn. Hobbies: Tennis; Squash; Riding; Photography; Jogging. Address: 1 Glenrock Avenue, Wahroonga, NSW 2076, Australia.

WOOLLERTON Maxim, b. 21 Apr 1963, London, Eng. Teacher. Education: BA, Hons, Engl Hist, Engl Lit, Univ E Anglia, 1981-84. Appointments: VP, 1989-91, 1992, Gen Sec, 1994-, Tokyo Fgn Lang Coll Tchrs Union; Gen Sec, 1990-93, Pres, 1993-, Kanto Fgn Lang Tchrs Union Fedn; S Exec Mbr, Natl Union of Gen Workers, Tokyo. Hobbies: History; Geneology; Videography; Extra Terrestial Intelligence. Address: c/o National Union of General Workers Tokyo South, 5F, 3-21-7 Shimbashi, Minato-ku, Tokyo 105, Japan.

WOOLLIAMS Anne Hawker, b. 3 Aug 1926, Folkstone, Eng. Ballet Director. m. Jan Stripling, 23 Dec 1976. Education: ARAD, Engl Pvte Schs. Appointments: Dozentin, Cl Ballet, Folkwangschule Essen; Asst Dir, John Cranko Stutgart Ballet; Art Dir, Austl Ballet; First Dean, Dance Victorian Coll of the Arts; Art Dir, Ballett Der Wiener Staatsoper. Creative Works: Ballettsaal, Ballet Studio, 1973, 1976; Num Choreographies, Articles. Honours: John Cranko Medal; Natl Critics Circle Dance Awd; Adams Awd; Green Room Th Awd. Memberships: Ehrenmitglied Des Deutschen; Roy Acady of Dance Grand Cncl. Hobbies: Painting; Trav. Address: 17 Best Lane, Canterbury, Kent, CT1 2JB, UK.

WORDSWORTH David John, b. 9 June 1930, Kashmir, India. Retired Member of Parliament; Vigneron. m. Marie-Louise Johnston, 17 May 1958, 1 s, 3 d. Education: Agricl Dip, Lincoln Univ, NZ; Bus Exec course, Stanford Univ, USA. Appointments: Farmer, Tas, Aust, 1953-67; Pastoralist, WA, 1964-; MP, WA, 1971-93; Min Transp, 1977, 1978; Min Lands and Forests, 1978-82; Dpty Pres, Chmn Cttees, Legis Cncl, WA, 1983-89; WA Rep, Inter-Parly Conf, 1974; Ldr, Austl Delegation to World Forestry Conf, Jakarta, 1978; Murdoch Univ Senate, 1993-97; Vigneron, Harvey, WA. Memberships: Weld Club, Perth; Patron, Esperance Bay Yacht Club; Stanford Univ Alumni. Hobbies: Fishing; Sailing; Photography; Bowling; Restoration of historic buildings and furniture. Address: 8 The Esplanade, Peppermint Grove, WA 6011, Australia.

WORKMAN Barbara Skeete, b. 17 Apr 1954, Melbourne, Australia. Geriatrician. m. Michael, 21 May 1983, 3 d. Education: MBBS; MD; FRACP. Appointments: Prof, Geriatric Med, Monash Univ and Southern Hlth Care Network. Memberships: Chmn, SAC, 1997-; Federal Cnslr, ASGM, 1994, 1997-; IASP; Austl Pain Soc; ASCEPT; UMMS; Chmn, Educ and Trng Subcttee, ASGM, 1997-. Hobbies: Gardening; Sewing. Address: Academic Unit of Geriatric Medicine, Kingston Centre, Warrigal Road, Cheltenham 3192, Melbourne, Australia.

WORNER Howard Knox, b. 3 Aug 1913, Vic, Aust. Professor; Metallurgical Scientist; Engineer. m. Rilda Beryl Muller, 11 Dec 1937, 2 s, 1 dec, 1 d. Education: Dip, Applied Chem, 1932; BS, Hons, 1934; MSc, Hons, 1936; DSc, 1942, Melbourne. Appointments: Lectr, Univ of Melbourne, 1936-38; Rsch Fell, Natl Hlth and Medl Rsch Cncl, 1939-46; Prof, 1946-55; Dean Engrng, Univ of Melbourne, 1952-55; Dir Rsch, BHP Co Ltd, 1956-62; Intl Cnslt, 1963; Rsch Dir, CRA Ltd, 1964-75; Chmn, Brown Coal Cncl, 1976-82; Sci Cnslt, 1982-85; Hon Prof, Dir, Microwave and Rsch Inst of Univ of Wollongong, 1986-. Publications: 200 sci pprs and monographs; Prin Ed, Minerals of Broken Hill, 1982. Honours include: CBE, 1978; Var medals, awds from profl and acad instns, inclng, Fellshp, Austl Acady of Sci (FAA); Fell, Austl Acady of Technol Scis and Engrng (FTS); Hon DSc, Univ of Newcastle, 1966; Kernot Medal, Univ of Melbourne, 1976; Hon DEng, Melbourne, 1983; Hon DSc, Wollongong, 1988; Hon DSc, La Trobe, 1994; Johnson Medal, Mineralogical Soc of SA, 1986. Memberships include: Hon Fell, Instn of Engrs (Aust); Hon Fell, Australasian Inst of Mining and Metallurgy; Hon Fell, Australasian Inst of Energy; Fell, Instn of Metals and Materials; Fell, Inst of Metals, London. Hobbies: Mineral collecting; oil painting. Address: 16/10 Smith Street, Wollongong, NSW 2500, Australia.

WORTH Trish. Parliamentary Secretary. Education: Cabra Coll. Appointments: Nurse, Pvt Pathol Co; Hlth Profl; Patients Servs Mngr; Defeated Bob Catley for seat of Adelaide, 1993; Retained Seat of Adlaide, 1996; Govt Whip, Hs of Repr, 1996-97; Parly Sec, Min for Hlth and Family Servs, 1997-98; Re-elected Mbr for Adelaide, 1998; Parly Sec, Min of Educ, Trng, Yth Affairs, 1998-. Honours: Calvary Hosp Nurse of the Yr; State Gold Medalist, 1967. Memberships: Jus for Cyprus Co-ordng Cttee; Amnesty Intl; Inter-Parly Union; Autsl Reproductive Hlth Alliance; Parly UNICEF. Address: 93 Frome Street, Adelaide 5000, Australia.

WORTHINGTON CLARK Janet Robyn, b. 12 Aug 1941, Waverley, NZ. Genealogist. m. Donald John Clark, 14 Dec 1963, 1 s, 1 d. Education: NZRN; Dip FHS; FSAG. Appointments: Nurse Educr, Wellington Pub Hosp, NZ; Roy N Shore Hosp, Sydney, MSR Computer Ind, self-employed. Publications: (auth) The Dalby Years, 1989; Eds 1-5, Computers for Genealogy, 1985-92; Coopers and Customs Cutters, 1997. Honour: Fell, Soc of Austl Genealogists, 1994. Memberships: Assn of Profl Genealogists, Regl VP, 1988-94; Cnclr, 1984-, VP, 1992-95, Soc of Aust Genealogists. Hobbies: Swimming; Gardening; Reading; Painting. Address: PO Box 161, Lane Cove, NSW 2066, Australia.

WOTTON David Charles, b. 14 Aug 1942. Member of the House Assembly (MHA), Liberal Party State Government. m. (1) 1969, (2) 24 May 1982, 3 s, 1 d. Appointments: Prior to entering Parl, involved in family bus/primary prodn; Mbr for Heysen, 1975; Mbr for Murray; Liberal Opposition Shadow Portfolios Community Welfare and Environ, later Plng and Environ; Min for Environment and Plng, 1979; Shadow Chf Sec, Shadow Min for Environment and Plng, 1982; Shadow Min for Environment and Plng, Water Resources, Aboriginal Affairs, 1990; Min for Environment and Natural Resources, Family and Community Servs, Ageing, 1993; Dpty Speaker and Chmn of Ctees, 1997. Hobbies: Music; Theatre; Travelling. Address: PO Box 755, Stirling, SA 5152, Australia.

WRAN Neville Kenneth (The Hon), b. Sydney, Aust. Company Director. m. (1) 1s, 1 d, (2) Jill Hickson, 1 s, 1 d. Education: Sydney Univ. Appointments: QC; Solicitor; Hon DL (Sydney); Mbr, NSW Legis Cncl, 1970-73; Dpty Ldr of Opposition, 1971-72; Ldr, Legis Cncl, 1972-73; Mbr, NSW Legis Assembly for Bass Hill, 1973-86; Ldr of the Opposition, 1973-76; Premier and Min for Arts, 1976-86; inclng var other mins; Natl Pres, Austl Labor Party, 1980-86; Exec Chmn, Wran Partners; Chmn, CSIRO, 1986-91; Chmn, Lionel Murphy Fndn, 1986-; Dir, FTR Ltd, Brit Aerospace Aust Pty Ltd; Hopetown Sch, Gov of Aust-Israel Chmbr of Com, Aust's Repr on the Em Person's Grp (EPG) of APEC (Asia-Pacific Econ Community), 1993-95; Pres, Austl Soccer Fndn; Fndn Mbr, Austl Republican Movement; Fell, Powerhouse Mus; Life Gov, Art Gall of NSW; Chmn, Victor Chang Cardiac Rsch Inst. Honours: AC, 1988. Hobbies: Reading; Tennis; Walking. Address: GPO Box 4545, Sydney, NSW 2001, Australia.

WRIEDT Paula, b. 11 Dec 1968, Hobart, Tasmania, Australia. Minister for Education. m. Dale Rahmanovic, 17 Jan 1998. Education: BA (undergrad). Appointments: Shadow Min for Educ, 1996-98; Min for Educ, 1998-. Hobbies: Netball; Snow Skiing; Travel; Cooking. Address: Level 8, 10 Murray Street, Hobart, Tas 7002, Australia.

WRIGHT Anthony Thomas, b. 21 Apr 1959, Adelaide, Australia. m. Chantal, 1 s, 1 d. Appointments: Owner, Synchronized Direction, 1984-; Logistics Mngr, Protech Aust, 1988-93; Distbrn Mngr, Intercel, 1994; Acct Mngr, Ericsson, 1995. Memberships: MRAA; KSC. Hobbies: Motorcycling; Agriculture; Travel; Gardening; Herbalism. Address: PO Box 4075, McKinnon, Victoria 3204, Australia.

WRIGHT Donald Ian, b. 22 Oct 1934, SA, Aust. Academic Historian. m. Janice Melva Gambling, 9 Jan 1960, 3 s. Education: BA, 1956, BA, hons, 1965, Adelaide Univ; PhD, Austl Natl Univ, 1968. Appointments: Tchr, SA Educ Dept, 1956-62; Hist Master, Westminster Sch, 1963-65; Acad, Fmr Assoc Prof (retd), Univ of Newcastle; Mbr, Univ of Newcastle Cncl, 1982-88. Publications include: Shadow of Dispute, 1970; Federalism in Canada and Australia: The Early Years, 1978; The French Revolution, 1980; Mantle of Christ, A History of the Sydney Central Methodist Mission, 1984; Looking Back, A History of the University of Newcastle, 1992; The Methodists, A History of Methodism in New South Wales 1812-1977; Dalmar, A Century of Caring for Children and Families; Alan Walker: Conscience of the Nation, 1997; Also over 50 articles in var learned jrnls. Memberships include: Austl Histl Assn; Ch Hist Assn of India; S Asian Studies Assn. Listed in: Who's Who in Australia; Who's Who in the World. Hobbies: Walking; Lay preacher. Address: Department of History, University of Newcastle, Callaghan, NSW 2308, Australia.

WRIGHT Elizabeth Jane, b. 19 Jan 1953. Science Teacher. Education: BSc, hons; PhD; Dip Ed. Appointments: Tutor, Zool, Univ of Adelaide, 1975-80; Postdoct Fell, Zool Dept, Univ of Adelaide, 1983; Tchr, Loreto Coll, Adelaide, 1985-. Memberships: Aust Inst of Biol, Dpty VP, 1996-; Pres, Aust Sci Tchrs Assn, 1998, 1999; Immed Past Pres, S Aust Sci Tchrs Assn. Hobbies: Squash; Tennis. Address: Loreto College, Marryatville, SA 5068, Australia.

WRIGHT John Kevin, b. 22 Aug 1944, Sydney. Research Manager. Education: BS, Metall, Univ of NSW 1966; PhD, Metall, 1970. Appointments: Sci Offr, Amdel, 1970; Prin Scientist, CSIRO, 1973; Chf Engr, Hatch Assocs, 1980; Asst Chf, CSIRO, 1984; Chf, CSIRO, Div of Energy Technol, 1994-. Memberships: Austl I M M ; Austl Cncl of Energy; CRC for Black Coal Utilization; Energy Mngrs Assn. Hobbies: Amateur Radio; Radio Restoration. Address: CSIRO, Division of Energy Technology, PO Box 136, North Ryde, NSW 1670, Australia.

WRIGHT John MacNair Jr, b. 14 Apr 1916, Los Angeles, CA, USA. US Army Officer. m. Helene Tribit, 28 June 1940, 2 s. Education: BS, US Mil Acady, 1940; MBA, Univ of S CA, 1956; MS, Intl Affairs, George Washington Univ, 1973. Appointments: Battery Cmdr, 91st Coast Artillery, Philippine Is, 1940-41; POW of Japan, 1942-45; Gen Staff, War Dept, WA, 1946-48; Mil Att, US Emb, Asuncion, Paraguay, 1948-50; Exec Offr, 30th Infantry Regt, Fort Benning, GA, 1950; Stud, Advd Course, Infantry Sch, 1950-51; Cmdr, 3rd bat, 508th Airborne Regtl Combat Team, 1951-52; Stud, Cmnd and Gen Staff Coll, Fort Levenworth, KA, 1952-53; Asst Chf of Staff, Pers, Logistics, 7th Infantry Div, Korea, 1953-54; Off of Dpty Chf of Staff, Logistics, Dept of the Army, DC, 1956-58; Off of Chf of Staff, US Army, 1958-60; Stud, Natl War Coll, DC, 1960-61; Chf of Staff, 8th Infantry Div, Germany, 1961-62; Asst Chf of Staff, Plans and Operations, VII Corps, Germany, 1962-63; Asst Chf of Staff, Plays and Ops, 7th Army, Germany, 1963; Asst Div Cmdr, 11th Air Assault Div, Fort Benning, GA, 1963-65; Asst Div Cmdr, 1st Cavalry Div, Vietnam, 1965-66; Off of Asst Chf of Staff, Force Dev, Dept of the Army, DC, 1966-67; cmdng Gen, US Army Infantry Cntr; Cmdt, The Infantry Sch, 1967-69; Cmdng Gen, 101st Airborne Div, Vietnam, 1969-70; Comptroller of the Army, DC, 1970-72; Retd from US Army, 1972; Natl Dir of Rsch and Dev; Natl Dir of prog; Natl Dir of Exploring, Boy Scouts of Am, NJ, TX, 1973-81; Retd from Boy Scouts, 1981. Honours: George Washington Hon Medal; Silver Beaver; Silver Antelope; Disting Eagle Scout Awd; Many Mil Decorations; Many other awds. Memberships: Natl Eagle Scout Assn; Amns of Armorial Ancestry; NAtl Gavel Soc; Phi Kappa Phi; Many or mbrshps. Hobbies: Genealogy; Stamp Collecting. Address: 21227 George Brown Ave, Riverside, CA 92518-2881, USA.

WRIGHT Judith (Arundell), b. 31 May 1915, Armidale, NSW, Aust. Auth; Poet; Critic; Ed. m. J P McKinney, 1 d. Education: Univ of Sydney. Appointments: Dir, C'wlth Lit Fund, 1952; Lectr in Austl Lit at var univs. Publications: Poetry: The Moving Image, 1946; Woman to Man, 1950; The Gateway, 1953; A Book of Australian Verse (anthology), 1956; The Two Fires, 1955; Biography: The Generations of Men, 1955, new ed, 1995; New Land, New Language (anthology), 1956; A Book of Birds, 1962; Five Senses - Selected Poems, 1963; The Other Half, 1966; The Oxford Book of Australian Verse (anthology), 1968; Poetry from Australian Pergamon Poets (anthology), 1969; Collected Poems 1942-1970, 1971; Alive: Poems 1971-1972, 1972; Fourth Quarter and Other Poems, 1976; The Double Tree: Selected Poems 1942-1976, 1978; Phantom Dwelling, 1985; A Human Pattern, 1990; Collected Poems 1942-1985, 1994; Criticism: Charles Harpur, 1963; Preoccupations in Australian Poetry, 1964; Because I Was Invited, 1975; The Cry for the Dead, 1981; Short Stories: The Nature of Love, 1966; The Coral Battleground, 1977; We Call for a Treaty, 1985; Born of the Conquerors, 1991; Going on Talking, 1992; Other: Four books for children; Critical essays and monographs. Honours: C'wlth Lit Fund Schlshp, 1949, 1962; Many Hon DLitt degs; Ency Britannica Writers' Awd, 1964; Robert Frost Mem Medallion, Fellowship of Austl Writers, 1975; Alice Awd, 1980; Asan World Prize, Asan Mem Assn, 1984; Queen's Gold Medal for Poetry, 1991; Spec Premier's Prize for Poetry, 1991. Memberships: Fell, Austl Acady of Hum, 1970; Creative Art Fell, Aust Natl Univ, 1974; Snr Writers Fellowship, 1977-79, Emer Fellowship, 1981-93, Aust Cncl. Hobbies: Gardening; Walking. Address: 1/17 Devonport Street, Lyons, ACT 2606, Australia.

WRIGHT Matthew, b. 27 Oct 1959, Eng. Artistic Director, Choreographer. m. Celia Chun, 24 Feb 1993, 1 d. Education: Roy Ballet Sch, 1971-79; ISTD Advd. Appointments: Dancer: Hamburg Ballet, Ballet de Tours, Atlanta Ballet, Ballet HI; Choreographer: Hamburg Ballet, Ballet de Tours, Atlanta Ballet, Joffrey Ballet II, Ballet HI; HI Opera Th; Honlulu Symph; Honolulu Dance Th; Artistic Dir: Honolulu Dance Th. Creative works: Choreographed: Overture, 1983; The Transfigured Night, 1984; Femmes Silencieuses, 1985; Visitations, 1985; Dialogues, 1987; Gustav Farewell, 1987; Song of Remembrance, 1987; The Nutcracker, 1988; Urashima Taro, 1989; Strike Up the Band, 1989; Evolution, 1990; Peter and the Wolf, 1992; Puss in Boots, 1992; A Christmas Carol, 1993; Apparition, 1994; Almost Like Being in Love, 1994; Billy the Kid, 1996; Gotta Dance!, 1997; Frankenstein, 1998. Honours: Ceccetti Schlshp Awd, 1978; SERBA Choreographic Awd (USA), 1978; HSDC Choreographic Awd (USA), 1994, 1995; Fndn Awds: NEA, SFCA, HI Community Fndn, Cooke Fndn, Freer Eleemosynary Trust, Hawaiian Elec Inds Charitable Fndn, Fin Factors Charitable Fndn. Memberships: HI State Dance Cncl; HI Alliance for Arts and Educ. Hobbies: Piano; Electric guitar; Woodwork; Travel. Address: 3041 Manoa Road, Honolulu, HI 96822, USA.

WRIGHT ST-CLAIR Rex, b. 3 Sept 1922, Medical Historian. m. Elizabeth Lindsay, 4 May 1950, 1 s, 2 d. Education: MB ChB, 1947; MD, 1971; FRNZCGP, 1990; FAFPHM, 1994. Appointments: Gen Prac, 1949-69; Asst Medl Supt, Waikato Hosp, 1969-77; Medl Supt, Community Hlth Serv, 1977-88; Medl Offr Hlth, 1989-90. Publications: Doctors Monro, 1964; Biography Of Sir David Monro, 1972; History Of The NZ Medical Association, 1987; St John In NZ, 1985; History Of General Practice, 1989. Honours: KStJ, 1977. Memberships: Order Of St John; Prin Medl Offr, Waikato Reg, 1961-81; Libr, 1984-93. Hobbies: Reading; Writing History. Address: 479 River Road, Hamilton, NZ.

WRIGLEY Colin Walter, b. 25 Dec 1937, Sydney, Australia. Cereal Chemist. m. Janice, 4 d. Education: BSc, Hons, 1959, MSc, 1961, PhD, 1967, Univ of Sydney. Appointments: Tchng Fell, Rsch Fell, Univ of Sydney; Offr, Rsch Sci, CSIRO Sydney. Publications: Over 370 rsch pprs. Honours: Sev, incl 4 intl rsch awds. Memberships: Fell, Roy Austl Chem Inst; Life Mbr, Am Assn of Chem. Address: c/o CSIRO Plant Industry, PO Box 7, North Ryde, Sydney, NSW 1670, Australia.

WRONSKI Ian, b. 10 Apr 1951, Flavin. Medical Practitioner. m. Maggie, 28 Nov 1982, 1 s, 1 d. Education: MBBS, DTM&H, Liverpool; MPH, Harv; SM, Harv; DipRalog, FRACGP; FAFPHM; FACTM; FACRRM. Appointments: Exec Dean, Fac Health Life & Molecular Sci, JIU, 1997-; Prof, Pub Health, 1994; Dir, Anton Breinc Cntr, 1992-98; Dir, Health Servs, KAMSC. Memberships: Roy Soc Tropical Med, 1984-; AMA. Address: 33 Stanton Terrace, Northward, Qld 4810, Australia.

WU Ai-Ru, b. 10 Feb 1931. Gynaecological Oncologist. m. Liu Ke-Jun, 20 Nov 1956, 1 s, 1 d. Education: Grad, Beijing Medl Univ, 1955; Postgrad, First Moscow Medl Coll, Russia, 1956-58. Appointments: Dr, 1958-82, Hd & Prof, 1985-, Gynaecol Oncology Dept, Assoc Prof, 1982, Vice Dir, 1984-85, Cancer Inst Hosp, Chinese Acady of Medl Scis; Visng Schl, Ludwig Inst for Cancer Rsch, Sydney Univ, Aust, 1982-83. Publications: Flow Cytometric Analysis of DNA Content in Cancer of the Cervix; Epidemiological Characteristics of Cancer in the Cervix and Prevention in China; The Application of Monoclonal Antibody OC125 in Gynaecologic Cancer; Multidisciplinary Approach to the Treatment of Ovarian Carcinoma; Management of Primary Carcinoma of Fallopian Tubes; A Study of Genital HPV Infection and Cervical Cancer in a High Rate Area of Cervical Cancer in China, 1991; Etiology and Prevention of Cervical, Corpus and Ovarian Cancer, 1993; Combined Treatment with Surgery and Radiotherapy for Cervical Cancer, 1994. Honour: CAMS Awd for Rsch Achievement in Prevention and Treatment of Cancer of the Cervix, 1993. Memberships: Ldng Grp, Chinese Cancer Control Cttee; Stndng Cttee, Chinese Cancer Rsch Fndn; Vice Chmn, Chmn, 1995, Rsch Cttee of Cancer of the Cervix, Chinese Anticancer Soc; Chinese Assn of Scis. Listed in: Who's Who in Australia and the Fae East; International Who's Who in Medicine. Hobbies: Music; Travel; Cooking. Address: Cancer Institute Hospital, Chinese Acady of Medl Scis, Zuonmenwai Panjiayao, Beijing 100021, China.

WU Allen C-H, b. 23 Aug 1957, Taipei, Taiwan. Professor. Education: PhD, Univ of CA, Irvine, 1992. Appointment: Prof, CS Dept, Tsing Hua Univ, Taiwan, 1998. Publication: High Level Synthesis: Introduction to Chip and System Design. Memberships: IEEE; ACM. Hobbies: Travel; Music. Address: Computer Science Department, Tsing Hua University, Hsinchu, Taiwan 30043.

WU Bangguo, b. Jul 1941 Feidong Anhui Prov. Party Official; Engineer. Education: Radio Electrons Dept Qinghua Univ Beijing. Appointments: Joined CCP, 1964; Wrkd at Shanghai No 3 Electron Tube Factory progressing from freight wrkr to Factory Dir - 1978; Dep Mngr Shanghai Municiapl Electrons Components Ind Co; Dep Mngr Shanghai Municipal Elecl Vacuum Device Co, 1979-81; Dep Sec Parly Cttee Shanghai Municipal Instruments Bur, 1981-83; VP Assn for Intl Understanding, 1986-; Dep Sec Shanghai Municiapl CCP Cttee, 1986-89; Sec Shanghai Municipal CCP Cttee, 1991-; A Shanghai deleg to 8th NPC, 1993; VP State Cncl - Vice-Premier - resp for indl econ and enterprise reform, 1995-; Dep Hd Cntrl Finl and Econ Ldng Grp; NPC Dep Shanghai Municipality. Memberships: Mbr Standing Cttee Shanghai Municipal CCP Cttee, 1983-85; Alt mbr CCP Cntrl Cttee, 1985-92; Mbr 14th Cntrl Cttee, 1992-; Mbr Politburo CCP, 1992-; Mbr CCP Secr, 1994-; Mbr 15th CCP Cntrl Cttee, 1997-. Address: State Council, Beijing, People's Republic of China.

WU Cheng-Wen, b. 19 June 1938, Taipei, Taiwan, China. Founding President. m. Felicia Y-H, 10 Nov 1963, 2 s, 1 d. Education: MD, Natl Taiwan Univ, 1964; PhD, Biochemistry, Case West Res Univ, 1969. Appointments:

Fndng Pres and Disting Investigator, Natl Hlth Rsch Inst, China, 1996-. Honours: Fell, NIH Spec Fellshp, USA, 1972; Mbr, Academia Sinica, 1984; Fell, Amn Inst of Chemists, USA, 1986. Memberships: Trustee, Chinese Oncology Soc; Chinese Soc of Cell and Molecular Bio, 1992-. Hobbies: Reading; Hiking. Address: National Health Research Institute, No 128 Sec 2, Yen-Chiu-Yuan, Road, Taipei, Taiwan, China.

WU Chun Xuan, b. 18 Mar 1917, Anxiang, China. Politician. m. Jiang Ping, 18 Mar 1951, 1 s, 1 d. Education: LLB, Wuhan Univ. Appointments: Mngr, Democracy Daily, 1946; Vice Dir, Org Dept, 1979, Dir, Socl Serv Dept, Cntr Cttee of the Democratic Alliance of China; Mbr, 7th Chinese Peoples Polit Consolative Conf, 1986-92. Publications: How to Scientifically Understand the Contemporary Chinese Marxism, 1996; How to Strengthen Democratic Parties Self-Building, Raise the Level of Participating in and Discussing on Political Affairs, 1997. Honours: 1st Class Achievement Prize, Beijing, 1996; Two 2nd Class Achievement Prizes, 1995, 1997. Hobbies: Walking; Reading. Address: 1 Dongchang Lane N Dongchang Alley, Dongchang District, Beijing 100006, China.

WU Delong, b. 5 Nov 1935, Anhui, China. Professor, Adviser of Doctorate Degrees. m. Zhenni Liu, 19 June 1965, 2 s. Education: Grad, Shanghai Jiaotong Univ, 1960; Schlshp, Athens Natl Tech Univ, Greece, 1982-83; PhD, World Open Univ, NV, USA, 1997. Snr Rsch Scientist, Beijing Inst of Astronautical Systems Engrng, 1986-; Vice Sec-Gen, Degree Cttee, China Natl Space Admin, 1994. Publications: Research and Design of Astro-Structures, 1960-; Nonlinear Buckling of Shells, 1991; 3 Cell Model of Braided Composites, 1996; Multibody Dynamics, 1997. Honours: Scientist and Returned Stud of Disting Achmnt of Aero-Astronautic Min, 1991; Natl Spec Allowance for Outstndng Contbn, 1992. Memberships: Spec Cttee of Chinese Soc of Mechs and Chinese Soc of Composites, 1995-. Hobbies: Painting; Literature. Address: PO Box 9200-10-13, Beijing 100076, China.

WU Enboa, b. 7 Feb 1956, Pingtong, Taiwan, China. Mechanical and Packaging Engineer; Educator. m. Jenny Chii-Wei Tai, 8 Aug 1980, 1 s, 1 d. Education: BSCE, Matl Cheng-Kung Univ, Taiwan, 1978; MSCE, Univ IA, 1981; PhD, Univ CA, Berkeley, 1988. Appointments: Regd Profl Engr, CA, Taiwan; Staff Engr, Nutech Engrs, Inc, San Jose, CA, 1982-83; Snr Engr, Bechtel Power Co, San Fran, 1983; Impell Corp, Walnut Creek, CA, 1988-89; Assoc Prof, 1989-95, Prof, 1995-, Inst Applied Mechs, Natl Taiwan Univ, Taipei; Cnslt, Inst Astron & Astrophys, Academia Sinica, Taiwan, 1995-; On leave from Natl Taiwan Univ to Electrons Rsch & Serv Orgn (ERSO), Indl Technol Rsch Inst (ITRI) as Dir for Electron Packaging, 1998-; R&D on IC packaging, precision measurements, impact dynamics, composite materials. Publications: Over 100 rsch pprs and tech reports, 1989-. Honours: Recip Outstndng Tchn Awd, Min of Educ, Taiwan, 1991; Excellent Rsch Awd, Natl Sci Cncl, Taiwan, 1991, 1994; Best Ppr Awd, Chinese Inst Engrs, 1994; Conf Ppr Awd, Soc Orth Rsch, Taiwan, 1994. Memberships: Intl Advsry Bd Mbr, Polymers & Polymer Composites, 1997-2000; Sec-Gen, Copper IC Packaging Consortium, 1998-; IMAPS; ASME; SAMPE, Bd Dirs, Taiwan Chapt, 1991-; Chinese Soc Theort & Applied Mechs; Chinese Inst Engrs. Address: 28 Lane 60, Chou-San Road, Taipei 106, Taiwan, China.

WU Felicia Y H, b. 27 Feb 1939, Taipei, Taiwan. Research Fellow; Special Medical Research Chair. m. Cheng-Wen, 10 Nov 1963, 2 s, 1 d. Education: BS, Chem, Natl Taiwan Univ, 1957-61; MS, Organic Chem, Univ of MN, 1961-63; PhD, Organic Chem, Case West Reserve Univ, 1965-69. Appointments: Rsch Asst, Tchng Asst, 1961-63; Medl Techn, Spec Asst to Chmn, 1963-65; Rsch Asst, 1965-69; Rsch Assoc, 1969-71,1971-72; Instr, 1972-78; Asst Prof, 1978-79; Visng Prof, 1979-80; Assoc Prof, Prof, SUNY, 1980-90; Rsch Fell, Div of Cancer Rsch, 1989-; Spec Medl Rsch Chair, 1989-; Adj Prof, Univ of CA, 1991-96; Adj Prof, Inst of Life Sci, 1992-; Jnt Prof, Inst of Tox, 1998-. Publications: Many Publs,

Reviewed in Jrnls; Book Chapts. Honours: First Gold Medal, Model Youth Awd; Natl Taiwan Univ Pres Schlshp; Tchng Assistantship, Univ Fellshp, Univ of MN; Many Rsch Grants; Many or honours, Awds. Memberships: ASBMB; ASPET; AACR; WICR; ABS; AIC; ACS; SCBA; Sigma Xi Soc; Assn for Women in Sci; Intl Assn for Women Bioscientists; APSB; Many other mbrshps. Hobbies: Piano playing; Various sports; Hiking; Flower arrangement; Coin and stamp collections. Address: Institute of Biomedical Sciences, Academia Sinica, 128 Yen Chiu Yuan Rd, Sec 2, Taipei 11529, Taiwan, China.

WU Guang Lie, b. 27 Nov 1925, Nanan, Fujian, China. Doctor. m. Chen Yue Mei, 11 Feb 1951, 4 s, 1 d. Appointments: Dr, Clin in Shisan, 1949-53; Dir, Rsch Cntr of Trad Chinese Med, Nanan, 1953-60; Dir, Trad Chinese Med Section, Dir, Trad Med Hosp, Nanan. Publications: Works of Clinical Experience by Wu Guang Lie, 1996; Formula for Gynaecological Treatment by Wu Guang Lie, 1999. Honours: Specl Govt Allowance, State Cncl, 1992; Prof of Outstndng Contbrn, Personnel Dept, Sanitary Dept & Trad Med Mngmt Bur, 1996. Memberships: Trad Med Assn ofChina; VP, Trad Med Assn of Quan Zhou, 1980; Pres, Trad Med Assn of Nanan. Hobbies: Literature; Medicine. Address: Traditional Medical Hospital, Nanan City, China.

WU Guanzheng, b. 25 Aug 1938 Yugan Co Jiangxi Prov. Government Official. m. Zhang Jinshang, 1959, 3 s. Education: Power Dept Winghua Univ Beijing. Appointments: Joined CCP, 1962; Dep Dir Revolutionary Cttee of Wuhan Gedian Chem Plant, 1968-75; Dep Dir Wuhan Sci and Tech Cttee; Vice-Chmn Wuhan Cty Assn of Sci and Tech; Dep Cmdr and Dir of Gen Off Wuhan Cty Tech Innovation hq; Dir Sec CCP Cttee of Wuhan Cty Engrng Sci and Tech Rsch Cntr, 1975-82; Sec CCP Cttee and Mayor of Wuhan Cty, 1983-86; Dep 6th NPC, 1983-87; Dep Sec Jiangxi Prov CCP Cttee Acting Gov Gov Jiangxi Prov, 1986-95; Dep 7th NPC, 1988-92; Dep 8th NPC, 1993-98; Sec CCP Cttee Jiangxi Prov; First Sec CCP Cttee Jiangxi Prov Mil Cmd, 1995-97; Sec CCP Cttee Shandong Prov and Princ of Sch for CCP Shandogn Cttee; First Sec CCP Cttee of Pronvincial Mil Cmd; Dep 9th NPC, 1998-. Memberships: Standing mbr CCP Cttee of Wuhan Cty, 1982-83; Alt mbr 12th CCP Cntrl Cttee, 1982-87; Mbr 13th CCP Cntrl Cttee, 1987-92; Mbr 14th CCP Cntrl Cttee, 1992-97; Mbr Polit Bur of 15th CCP Cntrl Cttee; Mbr 15th CCP Cntrl Cttee, 1997-. Hobbies: Reading; Sports. Address: 482 Weiyi Road, Jinan City, Shandong, People's Republic of China.

WU Guhua, b. 12 July 1937, Shanghai, China. University Academic. Education: BA, Majoring in Engl, 1955-59; MA, Engl and Engl Lit, 1959-62. Appointments: Instr, TEFL, Tsinghua Univ, 1962-84; Rsch Studies, Sydney Univ, Aust, 1984-86; Dean, Dept of For Langs, 1986-90; Dean, Dept of For Langs, 1990-93. Publications: A series of pprs on Application of Integrated Approach to Non-English Majors, 1990-93; Academic Paper Writing 1998; Breakthrough (Spoken English Textbook), in progress, 1999; Translator and co-translator of books and papers in subjects in var fields; Papers on language teaching and Australian literature published or presented in anthologies or confs. Honours: Natl Awd for Outstndng Achievement in Higher Educ (China); 1989; Natl Awd for Outstndng Achievement in Higher Educ (China), 1993; Fulbright Schl, 1994-95. Memberships: VP, China Coll For Langs Tchng Assn; Mbr of TESOL (Tchng Engl to Speakers of Other Langs); VP, China Coll For Langs Tchng Assn, 1987-94; Pres, Beijing Coll Engl Tchng Assn, 1990-93; Present mbr, Natl Strategy Cttee for For Langs Major Progs, 1990-; Spec invited ed, Engl Stdy, Shanghai For Lang Press.. Hobbies: Reading; Sports; Films. Address: c/o Foreign Languages Department, Tsinghua University, Beijing, China.

WU Guo-Xiong, b. 20 Mar 1943, Chao-yang, Guangdong, China. Scientific Researcher. m. Liu Huan-Zhu, June 1972, 1 s, 1 d. Education: PhD, Phys, London Univ; Dip, Imperial Coll. Appointments: Vis Sci, Eurn Cntr for Medium-Range Weather Forecast, 1983-84; Snr Rsch Prof, GFDL, Princeton Univ, 1989-91; Snr Prof,

IAP, 1985. Publications: Time-Mean Statistics of the General Circulation of the Atmosphere, 1987. Honours: Ex Mid-Age Sci of China, 1988; Acad, Chinese Acady of Scis, 1997. Memberships: Ex Mbr, Intl Assn of Meteorol and Atmospheric Scis; Roy Meteorol Soc, UK; Amn Meteorol Soc; China Meteorol Soc. Address: Laboratory of Atmospheric Sciences and Geophysical Fluid Dynamics, Institute of Atmospheric Physics, Chinese Academy of Sciences, Beijing 100029, China.

WU Hsin-Hsing, b. 26 Dec 1953, Kaohsiung, Taiwan, China. Professor. m. Dimyi Chow, 1 July 1993, 2 s, 1 d. Education: PhD, Polit Sci, Univ of Melbourne, Aust. Appointments: Prof, Dir, Grad of Polit Econ, Natl Chang-Kung Univ, Tainan, Taiwan, 1991-98; Dpty Sec-Gen, Strait Exchange Fndn, Taiwan. Publications: 3 books incl: Bridging the Strait, 1994; 24 articles. Hobbies: Sports; Movies. Address: F6, No 30-1, Lane 133, Chung-hsin Street, Yung Ho City, Taopei County, Taiwan.

WU Huanjia, b. 18 Nov 1929, Suzhou, Jiangsu, China. Professor. m. Luo Binsu, 2 d. Education: Bachelor degree. Appointments: Asst Prof, Instr to Doct Cand. Publications: On Modern Architecture, 1996; A History of Western Architecture in 20th Century, 1998. Membership: Chinese Assn of Archts. Hobby: Painting. Address: School of Architecture, Tsinghua University, Beijing, China 100084.

WU Jiann-Kuo, b. 25 Feb 1950, Taipei, Taiwan. Professor. m. Li-Hwa Kuo, 14 Dec 1973, 1 s, 2 d. Education: PhD, Univ of NE, USA. Appointments: Prof, 1989-, Dean of Acad Affairs, 1993-97, Pres, 1997-, Natl Taiwan Ocean Univ. Publications: Over 200 jrnl and conf pprs in materials sci and 4 US patents. Membership: Minerals, Metals and Materials Soc. Address: 2, Pei-Ning Rd, Keelung, Taiwan 20224, China.

WU Jichuan, b. 1937 Changning Co Hunan Prov. Party and Government Official. Appointments: Joined CCP, 1960; Vice-Min of Posts and Telecomms, 1984-90; Dep Sec Henan Prov CCP Cttee, 1990-93; NPC Dep Henan Prov; Vice-Chmn State Radio Regulatory Cttee; Min of Posts and Telecomms, 1993-98. Memberships: Alt Mbr 14th Cntrl Cttee, 1992-97; Alt mbr 8th NPC, 1993; Mbr 15th CCP Cntrl Cttee, 1997-. Address: c/o Ministry of Posts and Telecommunications, Beijing, People's Republic of China.

WU Jin, b. 9 Apr 1934. Professor. m. Tzu-Chen Chang, 9 Sept 1961, 3 s. Education: PhD, MS, Univ IA; BS, Natl Cheng Kung Univ. Appointments include: Dir, Air-Sea Interaction Lab, 1979-; H Fletcher Brown Prof of Marine Studies and Civil Engrng, Univ DE, 1980-; Advsry Cttee Mbr, Rsch Inst for Applied Mechs, Natl Taiwan Univ, 1988-; Pres, 1994-, Prof, 1994-95, Disting Prof, 1996-96, 1998- Hydraulic and Ocean Engrng, Natl Cheng Kung Univ; Min of Educ, 1996-98. Publications include: An Air-Sea Interaction Process at Light Wind Observed From a Coastal Tower, 1995; Laboratory Measurements of Spume Drop Production, 1995; A Light Sheet for Studying Air-Sea Interaction Process, 1995; The Conception and Implementation of General Education: The National Cheng Kung University's Experience, 1995; Air-Sea Interaction - Environmental and National Interests, 1995. Honours include: Off of Naval Rsch, Ocean Sci Educr Awd, 1991-94; Chinese Am Oceanic and Atmospheric Assn, Fndr 1993, Prin Mbr, Bd Dir, 1993-95; Asian Pacific Amn of the Yr, Fed Asian Pacific Am Cncl, 1995; Pres, Chinese Soc of Marine Sci and Technol, 1995-; Natl Acad of Engrng, Mbr, 1995-; Cncl Mbr, Academia Sinica, 1996; Disting Intl Serv Awd, Univ of IA, 1997; Medal of Disting Serv, Repub of China, 1998; HonD, Natl Taiwan Univ of Sci and Technol, 1998; Disting Engrng Alumni Acady Mbr, Univ of IA, 1999. Memberships: Amn Geophysl Union; Amn Meteorological Soc; Amn Soc of Civil Engrs; Chinese Soc of Civil Engrs; Chinese Soc of Marine Sci and Technol; Chinese Soc of Theoretical and Applied Mechs. Address: President's Office, National Cheng Kung University, Tainan, Taiwan, China.

WU Jinsheng, b. 14 Mar 1965, Heilongjiang Prov, China. Senior Engineer. m. Wu Wei, 19 Jan 1998. Education: MSc, Polymeric Phys and Chem, Chinese Acady of Sci, 1998. Appointments: Dpty Dir, Li-initiated Polymer R and D Dept, RIBYPEC, 1994-97; Dpty Dir, Polymer Analysis and Test Dept, RPNERC, 1997-. Creative Works: Stdy on Characterization of Compositional Dist of Styrene-Butadiene Copolymer; GPC-FTIR On-Line Technology; SBS Papering Adhesive R and D; SIS Pilot Technique Development; FTIR Quantitative Software of Styrene-Butadiene/Isoproprene Copolymers; Many other publs. Honours: Disting Techn Awd, Beijing, 1995; Sic and Tech Progress 2nd Prize Awd, BYPEC, 1998; World Cultural Celebrity Achievement Prize Awd, CIBC, 1999; Major Sci and Acad Achievements Awd, HK, 1999; Profession Expert Awd, RIBYPEC, 1999. Memberships: Chinese Sci and Technol Assn; Chinese Computer Enthusiast Assn. Hobbies: Photography; Football; Travelling; Computer; Music. Address: 15 Yanshan Fenghuangting Road, Fangshan Dist, Beijing 102500, China.

WU Kunjun, b. 5 Apr 1938, Shanghai, China. Scientist. m. Ding Cui, 8 Jan 1968, 1 s. Education: BS, Zoology, Fudan Univ, 1963; MS, Insect Physiol, Inst of Zoology, Chinese Acady of Scis, 1966. Appointments: Rsch Asst, Inst of Zoology, CAS, 1966-68, Jiangxi Prov Acady of Agricl Scis, 1968; Manual Labour, 1969-71; Staff Mbr, Plant Protection and Quarantine Station, Jiangxi, 1972-73, In Charge, 1974-75; Rsch Asst, 1976-77, Rsch Assoc, 1978-85, Assoc Prof, 1986-90, Prof, 1991-, Inst of Zoology, CAS; Cncl, Entomol Soc of Beijing, 1992-97, Entomol Soc of China, 1997-; Assoc Ed-in-Chf, Acta Entomologia Sinica, 1998-. Publications include: Life tables of experimental population of the cotton bollworm, Heliothis armigera (Hübner), at different temperatures, 1978; The age-stage specific life table of the armyworm, M. separata, 1994; A new and practical artificial diet for the cotton bollworm Helicoverpa (Heliothis) armigera, 1997; The diapause in pupae of the cotton bollworm, H. armigera, induced by high temperature, 1997. Memberships: Ecol Soc of China; Entomol Soc of China. Address: c/o Institute of Zoology, Chinese Academy of Sciences, 19 Zhongguancun Lu, Beijing 100080, China.

WU Peide, b. 13 Sept 1932, Chengdu, Sichuan, China. Professor. m. Chen Shufen, 27 Jan 1976, 1 s, 1 d. Education: Chinese Dept, Sichuan Univ. Appointments: Ed, Broadcasting Fan, Broadcasting Bur, Ctrl Cttee of China, 1955-57; Tchng Asst, 1957, Lectr, 1978, Assoc Prof, 1985, Prof, 1991-. Publications: A History of Chinese Literature, 1980; A Symposium on the Book of Songs, 1993; Ed of 4 books, written and publ over 100 essays and thesis. Honours: 2nd Awd, Tchng Achievement, Educn Dept of Yunnan, 1985; Sci Rsch Awds, KM Normal Coll & KM Normal Univ; Awd, Outstndng Thesis, Yunnan Socl Scis. Memberships: Yunnan Rsch Sco of Confucianism; Consultative Ed, Confucianism Study, 1997. Hobbies: Reading; Travel; Cooking. Address: Department of Chinese, Yunnan Normal University, Kunming 650092, Yunnan, China.

WU Poh-Hsiung, b. 19 Jun 1939 Taoyuan Co. Politician. m. Dai Mei-yu, 2 s, 1 d. Education: Natl Cheng Kung Univ; Sun Yatsen Inst of Policy and Rsch and Dev. Appointments: Sch-tchr, 1963-65; Assoc Prof Nan Ya Jnr Coll of Tech, 1972-73; Magistrate Taoyun Co, 1973-76; Dir Inst of Ind for Wrkmen and Friends of Labour Assn; Dir-Gen Taiwan Tobacco and Wine Monopoly Bur, 1976-80; Dir Inst of Indl and Vocational Trng for Wrkmen, 1976-80; Chmn Repub of China Amateur Boxing Assn, 1981-82; Dir Secr Cntrl Cttee Kuomintang, 1982-84; Chmn Cntrl Exec Cttee; Min of Interior, 1984-88, 1991-94; Mayor of Taipei, 1988-90; Min of State, 1990-91; Chmn Cntrl Election Commn, 1991-94; Chmn Polit Party Review Cttee, 1991-94; Sec-Gen Off of the Pres, 1994-. Memberships: Mbr Taiwan Prov Ass, 1968-72. Address: Office of the President, 122 Chungking South Road, Sec 1, Taipei, Taiwan.

WU Qing Yu, b. 27 Jan 1952. (Doctor) Cardiovascular Surgeon. m. Wang Weiqing, 1 d. Education: MD. Appointment: Dir, Cardiovascular Surg, Fu Wai Hosp.

Publication: Guidance of Cardiovascular Surg. Membership: Intl Eurasian Acady of Scis. Address: Department of Cardiovascular Surg, Fu Wai Hospital, Beijing, China.

WU Shaozu, b. 1929, Laiyang Co, Hunan Prov, China. Politician. 2 s. Education: Qinghua Univ, Beijing. Appointments: Dpty, 3rd NPC, 1964-66; Vice Min, State Commn of Sci, Technol and Ind for Natl Def, 1982-88; Promoted, Maj-Gen, PLA, 1988; Min of State, Physl Culture and Sports Commn, 1988-98. Memberships: 14th Cntrl Cttee, CCP, 1992-; Pres, Chinese Olympic Cttee. Address: c/o Commission for Physical Culture and Sports, 9 Tiyuguan Road, Chongwen Dist, Beijing 100763, China.

WU Shi Qiu, b. 5 July 1942, Shaoyang, Hunan, China. Doctor. m. Binhong Yu, 5 Aug 1964, 4 s. Education: Bach Deg. Appointment: Dir. Publications: Therapy of 100 Cases of Acute CUD by Combining Traditional Chinese and Western Medicines; Qiu Ye Chun Longevity Water; Before the Hospital of the Emergency Medicine System and Vitality. Memberships: China Continuing Educ Commn; China Emergency Med Assn; Ed, Theory and Prac of China Emergency Med. Hobby: Reading. Address: No 3 Futian Temple, Shijingshan, Beijing, China.

WU Shisi, b. 7 May 1929, Zhejiang, China. Professor; Research Worker. m. 1 Oct 1960, 1 s, 1 d. Education: Grad, Agric Dept, Zhejiang Univ, 1955; Advd studies in Agricl Mechanization, 1955-57. Appointments: Primary Sch Tchng, 1949-51, Tchng, 1957-, currently Hd, Dept of Agricl Engrng, Zhejiang Agricl Univ, Hangzhou. Publications: The Programme of Agrcultural Mechanisation for Zhejiang Prov; The Comprehensive Effect of Tillage or Non-Tillage in the Paddy Field; The Ecological Engineering of Rural Production Structure; Farm Power and Machinery Management in Southern China. Honours: 2nd Awd for Ex Thes, 1985; 2nd Awd for Prog in Sci & Technol, 1987. Memberships: Hobbies: Handwriting in Chinese characters; Planting and working in the field during his vacation; Visiting historical sites. Address: Department of Agricultural Engineering, Zhejiang Agricultural University, Hangzhou, China.

WU Shun-Hua, b. 12 Nov 1952, Mao-Gi Zhangze Yixing. Ceramic Artist. m. 20 Nov 1979, 1 s. Education: Undergrad, Trng Acady of Qi Bei-shi. Appointments: Tchr at Sch, 1976; Ceramics, 1982. Creative works: Painting, 1980; Ceramic Arts and Crafts, 1988. Honour: Awd, Contemporary Ceramic Artists in Yixing. Memberships: Inst of Qi Bei-shi Arts Rsch, 1988. Hobbies: Drawing; Ceramic arts. Address: Mao-gi Zhang-ze Town, Yixing, Jiangsu, China.

WU Tai Tsun, b. 1 Dec 1933, Shanghai, China. Physicist; Educator. Education: BS, Univ MN, 1953; SM, Harvard Univ, 1954; PhD, Harvard Univ, 1956. Appointments: Jnr Fell, Soc of Fells, Harvard Univ, 1956-59; Asst Prof, 1959-63, Assoc Prof, 1963-66, Gordon McKay Prof Applied Phys, 1966-, Prof of Phys, 1994-, Harvard Univ; Visng Prof: Rockefeller Univ, NY, 1966-67; Kramers Prof, Riksuniversiteit, Utrecht, The Netherlands, 1977-78. Publications: (co-auth) Scattering and Diffraction of Waves, 1959, in Russian, 1962; The Two-Dimensional Ising Model, 1973; Antennas in Matter: Fundamentals, Theory and Applications, 1981; Expanding Protons: Scattering at High Energies, 1987; The Ubiquitous Photon: Helicity Method for QED and QCD, 1990; Lateral Electromagnetic Waves: Theory and Applications to Communications, Geophysical Exploration and Remote Sensing, 1992. Honours: NSF Snr Postdoct Fell, 1966-67; Guggenheim Fell, 1970-71; Alexander von Humboldt US Sen Sci Awd, Germany, 1985; Dannie Heineman Prize for Math Phys, Amn Phys Soc, 1999. Memberships: Inst Adv Study, Princeton, NJ, 1958-59, 1960-61, 1962-63; Fell, Amn Acady Arts & Sci, 1977-. Address: 35 Robinson Street, Cambridge, MA 02138, USA.

WU Ting, b. 1 Nov 1935, Yiwu, Zhejian, China. Public Health Official. m. Qian Jinyu, 1 Feb 1964, 1 s, 1 d.

Education: Grad, Shanghai Med Univ, 1961. Appointments: Asst, 1952-56; Dr, 1956-80, Dr in Charge, 1980-86; Vice Chief Dr, 1986-92; Chief Dr, 1992-. Publications include: A Study on Epidemiological Characteristics of Vaccinated Group of Measles, 1989; The Policy About Control of Measles, 1998; Epidemiology, 1996; Planning Immunology, ed, 1997. Honours: Second Prize, Zhejiang Prov Sci & Technol Achievement, 1983; Third Prize, Natl Sci & Technol Achievement, 1993. Memberships: Sec, Planning Immunization Joint Cttee, Huadong Dist, 1983-99; Chmn, Br Cttee of Planning Immunization, Zhejiang Preventive Med Assn, 1996-99. Hobbies: Reading; Climbing mountains. Address: Zhejiang Health and Anti-epidemic Station, No 17 Lao Zhe Da Zhi Road, Hangzhou, Zhejiang 310009, China.

WU Wei, b. 11 Oct 1957, Guangzhou, China. Cardiologist. Education: BM, Med, 1982; MD, Cardiol, Sun Yat-sen Univ of Medl Scis (SUMS), Guangzhou, China, 1991. Appointments: Res, 1982-91, Lectr, Attending Cardiologist, 1991-93, Assoc Prof, 1993-97, Prof, 1997-, Sun Yat-sen Mem Hosp, SUMS; Vice Dir, Div of Cardiol, 1996-. Publications: Articles to profl jrnls. Honours: China Guangdong Prov, 3rd Awd for Prog in Scis and Tech, 1994, 1996; China Min of Educ, 3rd Awd for Prog in Sci and Tech, 1998. Memberships: Cttee Mbr, Guangdong Branch of Cardiovascular Cttee; Chinese Medl Assn. Address: Sun Yat-sen Memorial Hospital/University, 107 W Yan Jiang Road, 510120 Guangzhou, China.

WU Wei-Ran, b. 14 Oct 1920, China. Professor of Surgery. m. Huang Wu-Chiung, 17 May 1952, 3 d. Education: BSc, Yenching Univ, Peking, 1942; MD, Western China Med Coll, Chengdu, 1946. Appointments: Asst Res in Surg, 1947-51, Chf Res, Asst in Surg, 1951-52, Instr in Surg, 1953-79, Prof in Surg, 1979-, Peking Union Med Coll Hosp. Publications: Contbr to chapts on gen surg in textbooks and pprs in gastrointestinal surg. Memberships: Chinese Surgl Sco; Societe Internationale de Chirurgie. Hobby: Handicraft with Chinese Arts. Address: Beijing Hospital, 1 Dahua Lu, Beijing, China.

WU Wei-xian, b. 14 Dec 1928, Xiamen (Amoy), China. Professor. m. Chao-zheng Chen, 11 Nov 1956, 2 s, 2 d. Education: Grad, Fumin Primary Sch, Xiamen (Amoy), China, 1941; Grad, Yinghua Secnd Sch, Xiamen, 1947; Grad, For Langs Dept, Xiamen (Amoy) Univ, 1952. Appointments: Sec, Pres Off, 1952-54; Lectr of For Langs Dept, tchng Engl & Transl, 1961; Assoc Prof of For Langs Dept, tchng Transl & Jrnl Engl, 1983; Prof of For Langs Dept, 1987; Dean of For Lang Dept, 1984-90; Admin Cttee Mbr, 1985-89; Mbr, Snr Transl, Promotion Cttee of Fujian Prov, 1986-93. Publications: Chf Compiler & Transl: A Comprehensive Dictionary of English Idioms and Phrases, 1985; A Dictionary of Current English Idioms, 1990; Collins Gem English Learner's Dictionary, 1993. Transl: Room At The Top by John Braine (E-C), 1985; The Island by Ronald Lockler (E-C), 1985; Theses: On Translation of Figurative Expressions in English Idioms, 1981; On Translation of Certain English Expressions Affirmative in Form But Negative in Meaning, 1985. Honours: Winner, Tan Kah Kee Schslp, Amoy Univ, 1948; Entitled Adv Tchr, Xiamen Univ, 1961; Winner, w others, Ed Prize of Ex Books and Dictionaries publd in E China, 1986; 1st Prize Winner, w others, Fujian Ex Books and Articles of Socl Scis and Lang (1978-88); Lifelong Winner Spec Allowance for Contbns to Educ, Central Govt, 1992-. Memberships: Dir, Transl Assn of China, 1986-; Pres, S Fujian For Langs Soc, 1986-90; Pres, Transl Assn of Xiamen, 1988-; Exec Dir, Transl Assn of Fujian Prov, 1985-92; Dir of For Langs Serv, Dept of Xiamen Snr Profs Assn, 1995-. Hobbies: Volley Ball; Mountaineering; Chinese Chess. Address: Foreign Languages Department, Xiamen University, Xiamen, China.

WU Wen, b. 7 Oct 1963, Qingdao. Vice Professor. m. Zhou Shangyi, 29 July 1994, 1 d. Education: BEng, Qingdao Inst of Arch Engrng; BA, Nanjing Univ. Appointments: Dir, Info Cntr. Creative Works: Information

Retrieval for Scientific Technological Literature; Dispose of Oil Spilled at Sea; Article, How to Develope the Information Service in High College Library. Honours: Third Awd, Qingdao Fifth Natural Sci Ex Acad Thesis; Ex Awd, Article. Memberships: Qingdao Lib Assn; Qingdao Info Assn. Hobbies: Playing the Piano; Lit; Dancing. Address: 11 Fushan Road, Qingdao 266033, China.

WU Xing Yan, b. 16 Dec 1929, Zhejiang, China. Teacher. m. Cai Xun Yuan, 15 Apr 1958, 2 d. Education: BEng, Dept of Chem Engrng, Zhejiang Univ, 1951. Appointments: Assoc Prof, 1980; Hd, Biochemical Engrng Lab, 1985; Prof, 1987; Chf Engr, 1993. Publications: Technology of Antibiotic Production (ed), 1982; Biotechnology (assoc ed), 1991; Sorption and Chromatology of Antibiotics (transl from Russian), 1965. Memberships: AAAS; Editl Bd, Ion Exchange and Adsorption. Address: Department of Biochemical Engineering, East China University of Science and Technology, Shanghai 200237, China.

WU Xuangang, b. 23 May 1927, Shuangcheng City, Heilongjiang Prov, China. Professor. 3 s. Education: Undergrad, Norman Bethune Univ of Medl Scis; Trng Cntr for Higher Tchrs in Latin, 2nd Shanghai Medl Coll; Trng Course in Russian, 3rd Mil Coll. Appointments: Hd of Dept Japanese Lang, NBUMS and Sasagawa Med Schlshp, Japanese Lang Trng Cntr of Chinese Min of Hlth, 1987-93. Publications: 9 dictionaries and textboks and over 60 pprs inclng: Japanese (for Higher Medical and Pharmaceutical School); Elementary Course in Medical Japanese; Medical Japanese Grammar; Read Elementariness for Medical Japanese; Idioms and Phrases of Medical Japanese; A Concise Dictionary of Japanese-Chinese Medicine, Russian (for Higher Medical and Pharmaceutical School); Latin Textbook; Latin-Chinese Scientific and Technical Dictionary. Honours include: Excellent Textbook Prize, Min of Hlth for "Japanese". Memberships: Asst Chf Ed, jrnl, Introduction to Japanese Medicine; Hd, Japanese-Chinese Acad Branch of Japan Intl Nat Med Soc; Higher Medl Textbooks Compiling Cttee, China Min of Hlth, Hd of Japanese Grp; Vice Chmn, For Langs Proposition Cttee of Natl Medl Test Cntr of China Min of Hlth and hd of Japanese Grp. Address: Department of Japanese Language, Norman Bethune University of Medical Sciences, Changchun, China.

WU Yang Jie, b. 1 Jan 1928. Researcher. m. Zhi Xian Zhou, 20 Oct 1959, 1 s. Education: BS, Fudan Univ, Shanghai, China, 1951; PhD, Moscow State Univ, 1958. Appointments: Vice Chmn, Chem Dept, Zhengzhou Univ, 1965; Dean, Chem Dept, Zhengzhou Univ, 1987; Hon Chmn, Chem Dept, Zhengzhou Univ, 1990-. Creative Works: New Synthetic Method of Crown Ethers (invention), 1984; Synthetic Method of Benzocrown Ethers (patent), 1986; New Synthetic Method of Pestiside Intermediate (sci rsch), 1976. Honours: Ex Rschr Awd, State Educ Commn of China, 1990; Ex Tchr Awd, Natl Labor Union, 1991; Ex Worker Awd, State Dept, 1995. Memberships: Chinese Chem Soc, 1951-; Natl Educ Labour Union of China, 1958-; AAAS, 1995; NY Acady of Sci, 1997. Listed in: Who's Who in the World, 14th ed, 1997. Hobby: Natural Science. Address: Department of Chemistry, Zhengzhou University, 75 Daxue Road, Zhengzhou 450052, China.

WU Yang-Chang, b. 24 Jan 1951, Taiwan, China. Professor of Pharmacognosy. m. 17 Jan 1978, 2 s. Education: BS, Pharm, 1971-75, MSc, 1979-82, PhD, 1982-86, Kaohsiung Medl Coll, Taiwan; Postdoct Fell, Sch of Pharm, Univ of NC. Chapel Hill, USA, 1986-87. Appointments: Tchng Asst, 1977-82, Instr, 1982-86, Assoc Prof, 1986-90, Prof, 1990-, Sch of Pharm (KMC); Prof and Dir, Grad Inst of Nat Prods (KMC), 1992-. Publications: Over 100 pprs; Over 100 invited and confs lects. Honours: Excellent Rsch Awd, Natl Sci Cncl, Taiwan, 1992; Excellent Tchng Prize, Min of Educ, Taiwan, 1992; Exam Cttee, Min of Educ, Taiwan, 1994; Cnslt, Cttee, Chinese Med and Pharm, Dept of Hlth, Exec Yuan, Taiwan, 1995. Memberships: Pharm Soc of Taiwan; Chinese Chem Soc of Taiwan; Nat Medicinal Prods Soc of Taiwan; Soc of Chinese Bioscientists in Am (SCBA). Hobbies: Tennis; Sport. Address: Graduate Institute of Natural Products, Kaosiung Medical College, 100 Shih Chuan 1st Road, Kaosiung 807, Taiwan.

WU Yigong, b. 1 Dec 1938, Chongqing, Sichuan Prov, China. Film Director. m. Zhang Wen Rong, 1967, 1 s. Appointments: Dir, Shanghai Film Bur; Gen Mngr, Shanhai Film Corp; VP, China Film Artists' Assn, 1985-; Alt Mbr, 14th CCP Cntrl Cttee, 1992-97, 15th Cttee, 1997-; Vice Chair, China Fed of Lit and Art Circles, 1996. Creative Works: Films: My Memories of Old Beijing; A Man Aged 18; University in Exile; The Tribulations of a Chinese Gentleman; Bitter Sea. Honours: Golden Rooster Awd, 1984; Magnolia Prize, 1988. Hobbies: Music; Sports. Address: 52 Yong Fu Road, Shanghai, China.

WU Yong Zhang, b. 20 Nov 1936, Mei County, China. Educationist; Writer. m. Xie Kei-Rong, 1 Jan 1962, 2 d. Education: Grad, Hist Dept, Beijing Univ, 1960. Appointments: Tchr, Hist Dept, Beijing Univ, 1960; Prof, Ethnol Dept, S-Ctrl Coll for Nationalities, Hubei. Publications include: Origin and Development of the System of China Local Tyrants, 1988; The History of Hubei Nationalities, 1990; Explanations for the Chief Historic Works Related to the Nationalities in South China, 1991; The History of Yao Nationality, 1993; The Culture of Kejia Branch of Han Nationality, 1998. Honours: Awd, Outstndng Thesis of Socl Sci, 1989; Bright-Cup Awd, Outstndng Works of Socl Sci, 1991; Awd, Outstndng Works Related to S-W China, 1992; Awd, Outstndng Works Related to China Nationalities, 1993; Awd, Outstndng Works of Humanities & Socl Sci, 1995. Memberships: Dir, China Bai-Yue Study Inst, China Nationality-Hist Study Inst; Exec Bd, Intl Yao-Nationality Study Inst; Perm Dir, Tai-Wan Minor-Nationalities Study Inst. Hobbies: Reading; Writing; Calligraphy. Address: c/o Ethnology Department, South-Central College for Nationalities, Wuhan, Hubei 430074, China.

WU Zheng-Yi, b. 13 June 1916, Yangzhou, Jiang-su Prov, China. Director Emeritus, Kunming Institute of Botany. Education: Tsinhua Univ, 1933-37; Completed grad studies, 1942. Appointments: Tchr, Qinghua Univ, 1938-40; Lectr, Qinghua Univ and SW China Utd Univ, 1946-48; Appointed Prof and Duty Dir, Inst of Botany, Academia Sinica, 1950; Elected a mbr of the Biol Dept, Academia Sinica, 1958-68; Dir, Kunming Branch of Academia Sinica, 1979-84; Currently, Dir of Kunming Inst of Botany, Academia Sinica; Hon dir, Kunming Inst of Botany, Academia Sinica, 1984-. Publications: Chf Ed, Flora Xizangica; Ed, 1958-, Chf Ed, 1987, Flora Yunnica, 1979; Ed, Flora of China, jt proj by Chinese and Amn botanists, 1989-; Auth, preliminary report about Flora of tropic and subtropic of Yunnan, Acta Phytot 6(2-3), 1956, 7(2), 1957; On the tropical affinity of the Chinese flora, Science News, Jan 1965; On the division of Chinese floristic areas, Acta Botanica Yunnan 1(1), 1979; Mbr, Editl Cttee of the National Geography of China, The Natural Geography of China Vol 1 Phytogeography, Science Press, Beijing, 1983; Chf ed, Chinese Vegetation, Science Press, Beijing, 1980; On the Significance of Pacific Intercontinental Discontinuity, Annals of Missouri Botanical Gardens 70:577-590, 1983; (ed) Wild Flowers of Yunnan (in Japanese), I Alpine, II Temperate and Subtropical, III Tropical Japan, 1986; (ed), Outline of New China Herbals, Tom I-III, 1988-91. Honours: Natl Model of Wrkrs of China, 1979; 1st Class Awd of Natl Invention of China, 1982; 1st Class Awd of Nat Scis of China, 1987. Memberships: Vice-Chmn, Chinese Bot Soc; Chmn, Sci & Techl Assn of Yunnan Prov; For Fell, Amn Bot Soc; Hon Fell, Swedish Bot Soc. Address: Kunming Institute of Botany, Academia Sinica, Kunming, Yunnan 650204, China.

WU Zhenglai, b. 26 June 1941, Shanghai, China. Professor. m. Xin Yin, 16 Sept 1971, 2 s. Education: MD, Beijing Medl Univ, 1959-65; Msc, Peking Union Medl Coll, 1979-82; Spec studies, Johns Hopkins Sch of Hygiene & Pub Hlth, 1985-86. Appointments: Chf Epidemiologist & Dpty Dir, Tacheng Prefecture Disease Prevention Cntr, 1965-78; Assoc Prof & Chm, Dept of Epidemiology, Xinjiang Medl Coll, 1982-89; Chf Epidemiologist, Shanghai Inst for Occupational Hlth in Chem Ind, 1989-92; Chmn, Fac of Pub Hlth, Peking Union Medl Coll, 1993-; Dir, Off for Tchng Affairs, Peking Union Medl Coll, 1997-. Publication: Modern Research Methods in Epidemiology, 1994. Honours: Outstndng Tchr Citation, Xinjiang Govt, 1983; 3rd Prize of Prog in Scis & Technol, Min of Hlth, 1996. Memberships: Chinese Medl Assn & Chinese Preventive Medl Assn, 1984-; Standing Mbr, Chinese Soc of Hygiene, CMA; Sec, Chinese Soc of Gen Prac, CMA, 1997-. Hobbies: Reading; Music. Address: 5 Dong Dan San Tiao, Beijing 100005, China.

WU Zhi Sheng, b. 3 May 1941, Beijing, China. Engineer. m. Guifang Qiao, 10 July 1971, 1 s, 1 d. Education: Bach Deg, Hydrogeol & Engrng Geol, China Geol Univ, Beijing Geol Inst. Publications: Comprehensive Improvement Technology of Bursting Water and Spring Mud of Nanling Tunnel, 1990; Research on Hydrogeological Features and Priction of Spring Water Quantity of Nanling Tunnel, 1991; Karst Engineering Geology Features of Nanling Tunnel on Hengyang-Guangzhou Double-track Line, 1996; Spring Mud of Karst Pipeline and Experences of Treatment of Naling Tunnel, 1998. Honours: Pacesetter of Pathbreaker & Adv Individual Awds, Natl Comp, 1987; Hubei Prov Model Worker, 1989; Title, Ex Intellectual of Railway Dept, 1991; Prize, Sci & Technol Adv, Railway Dept, 1991; Natl Prize, Sci & Technol Adv, 1993; Natl Adv Worker. Memberships: China Railway Soc; Hubei Prov Geol Soc; 30th Intl Geol Congress, 1996. Address: Department of the 4th Survey & Design Institute of MOR, Wuhan, Hubei 430063, China.

WU Zhong-Xiang, b. 31 Oct 1929. Physicist. m. 12 Aug 1956, Wang Wan-Yi, 2 s, 1 d. Education: Grad, Wuhan Univ, 1952. Appointments: Asst, Phys Dept, Wuhan Univ, 1952-60; Rsch Asst, Theory Dept, 9th Acady, 2nd Machinery Ind Dept, 1960-72; Rsch Asst, Inst of Mechanics, Academia Sinica, 1972-79; Assoc Rsch Prof, 1979-89; Rsch Prof, 1989-96. Publications: More than 30 Papers published, including: Expression of Huygen's Principle for Active Gases, 1982; The Behaviour of Non-Equilibrium Flow Gas in Laser Cavity, 1990; The Basic Property Comparison Analysis of Flow Laser Oscillator and Amplifier, 1993; Deductive 4-D Space Time Generalized Covariant Mechanics and some Applications on Gravity, 1988; The Electrodynamic Equations Generalised in Arbitrary Reference Systems, 1991; 4-D Space Time Multi-Linear Vectorial Generalized Covariant Physics, 1995. Honours: 1st Reward of Natl Nat Sci, 1982; 3rd Reward of Sc & T Results, 1986; The Important Sc & T Results, 1990, 1992. Address: Institute of Mechanics, Academia Sinica, Beijing 100080, China.

WU Zuqiang, b. 24 July 1927, Peking, China. Professor. m. Zheng Liqin, 29 Jan 1953, 1 s, 1 d. Education: Grad in Composition, China's Cntrl Conservatory of Music, 1952; Grad, Tchaikovsky Music Conservatory, Moscow, 1958. Appointments: Tchr, 1952, Snr Lectr, 1962, Assoc Prof, 1978, Dpty Pres, 1978-81, Pres, 1982-88, Prof, 1983-, Supvsr of Doct Wrk, 1986-, Hon Pres, 1998- Cntrl Conservatory of Music; Hd of Composition Sect, China's Cntrl Phil Orch, 1972-75; Vice-Exec Chmn, 1988-, Vice-Chmn, 1996-, China Fedn of Lit and Art Circles, 1988-; Bd of Dirs, China's Copyright Agcy Corp, 1988-; Advsr, 1993, Hon Pres, 1999-, Chinese Music Copyright Assn; Advsr, China Natl Symph Orch, 1996-; Adjudicator of many Chinese and for music competitions. Publications: Analysis of Music Form and Composition, textbook; Selected Writings of Wu Zuqiang - Morning Splendour and Evening Glow, 1997. Creative works: Compositions: String Quartet, 1957; The Mermaid, dance drama, 1959; Red Woman's Detachment, ballet, 1964; Moon Refected in the Erquan Pool for String Orchestra, 1976; Young Sisters of the Grassland, pipa concerto, 1973-76. Honour: Ex Textbook Prize, Natl Univs and Colls, 1987. Memberships: VP, Chinese Musicians Assn, 1985-; Exec Vice Chmn, China Symph Dev Fndn, 1994-. Hobbies: Literature; Fine Arts; Travel. Address: Central Conservatory of Music, 43 Baojia Street, Beijing 100031, China.

WURM Stephen Adolphe, b. 19 Aug 1922, Budapest, Hungary. Linguist. m. Helen, 21 July 1946. Education: PhD, Vienna Univ, 1944. Appointments: Lectr, Vienna Univ, 1946-50; Cntrl Asian Rsch Inst, London/Oxford, 1950-54; Rsch Fell, Sydney Univ, 1954-56; Snr Fell, Austl Natl Univ, 1957-67; Prof of Linguistics, Austl Natl Univ, 1968-87; Prof, Rsch Dir, Austl Natl Univ, 1988-. Publications: Languages, Australia, 1972; Papuan Languages, New Guinea, 1982; Language Alas, Pacific, 1981-83; Language Atlas, China, 1987-90; Atlas Languages, Intercultural Communications (3 vols), 1996-97; Atlas World's Endangered Languages, 1996. Honours: AO, 1987; Hon Pres, Intl Cncl Hum Studies, 1997-. Memberships: Pres Ling Soc Aust, 1967-70, 1976-78; Fell, Austl Acady Soc Scis, 1978; Fell, Austl Acad Hums, 1977, Pres, 1986-89; Pres, Union Académique Intl, 1986-89; Pres, Intl Cncl Hum Studies, 1988-96; Pres, Perm Intl Cncl of Linguists, 1997-. Hobbies: Languages; Language endangerment; Language in culture; Photography. Address: 5 Patey St, Canberra, Australia 2612.

WYETT John William Cardwell, b. 22 July 1908, Beaconsfield, Tas, Aust. Director (retired). 1 s. Education: Dip Pharm, 1927; ARACI; FAIA; C Chem; BSc, Univ of Tas, 1930. Appointments: Maj Gen, Staff 8th Austl Div, 1941-45; Grad Cmnd and Staff Coll, Quetta, 1941; Chmn, Hob Techl Coll Cncl; Dir, Vol Hlth Assn, Aust, 1966-86; Fndng Mbr, Stand Commn of Convocation, Univ of Tas, 1970-; Chmn, Utd World Colls, Tas, 1973-; Chmn, Medl Benefits Assn; Cnclr, Austl Photographic Bird Index, 1975-80; Gov Dir, Blue Cross Assn, Aust, 1977-86; Fndr Mbr, Consumer Affairs Cncl; Tstee, Blinded Ex-Servicemen's Assn. Publication: Staff Wallah at the Fall of Singapore. Honour: AM, 1988. Memberships: VP, Roy Soc of Tas, 1956-58; Fell, Adv Inst, Aust; Assoc, Roy Austl Chem Inst, Tas; Roy Utd Servs Inst; Bio Club of Hobart; Tas Naval and Mil Club; RACV, Hobart; RYCT, Hobart; Tasmanian Club. Hobbies: Farming; Qenology. Address: 40 Marieville Esplanade, Sandy Bay, Tas 7005, Australia.

WYNDHAM Edmund, b. 8 Sept 1943, Narrabri, NSW, Aust. Grazier. m. Frances Catherine McInherny, 5 Dec 1970, 1 s, 1 d. Education: BS, 1964, PhD, 1978, Univ of New Eng, NSW. Appointments: Bio Tchr, Rutlish Grammar Sch, London, Eng, 1966-68; Rsch Asst, Zool Dept, 1969-72, Hon Fell, Dept of Ecosyst Mngmt, 1979-, Univ of New Eng, Armidale, NSW, Aust; Tchng Fell, Sch of Austl Environmental Stdies, Griffith Univ, 1975-78; Mngng Dir, Wyndham Pastoral Co, 1979-; Hon Ed, The Emu, 1985-. Publications: Environment and Food of the Budgerigar; Total Body Lipids of the Budgerigar; Moult of Budgerigars; Gonadal Cycles of Wild Budgerigars; Movements and Breeding Seasons. Memberships: Royal Australasian Ornithological Union; Ecological Soc of Aust; Brit Ornithological Union; Austl Soc for Animal Prodn. Hobby: Ornithology. Address: Karuah Wollomombi, NSW 2350, Australia.

WYNTER Michael Rodney, b. 8 May 1943, Hamilton, New South Wales, Australia. Lawyer. m. Jane, 10 Apr 1982, 3 s, 1 d. Education: BA, Univ NSW; LLB, Univ Sydney. Appointments: Chmn, Austl Chem Holdings Ltd, 1995-98; Dir, Nuplex Ind Ltd, 1998-. Address: Level 4, Gold Fields House, 1 Alfred Street, Sydney, NSW 2000, Australia.

X

XI A Xing, b, 28 Jan 1944, Shanghai, China. Artist. m. 1 May 1976, 1 s. Education: Self taught. Appointments: Contemporary Asian Art Show, Fukuoka, Japan, 1980; 7th Norwegian Intl Print Biennale, 1984; 9th Norwegian Intl Print Triennale, 1989. Creative works: Premio internazionale Biella Per L'incisione Italia; Contemporary Fine Art Exhibition, Reno, USA, 1990; The International Art Exhibition on Motif: ou l'utopie ... sans illusion, Fribourg, Switzerland, 1991. Memberships: China Artists Assn; China Engravers Assn; Dpty Dir of Art Acadys Rsch Div of Shanghai Engraving Assn. Hobbies: Photography; Cooking; Archaeology; Chinese folk art. Address: Juvenile and Children's Books Publishing House, 1538 Yan-An West Road, Shanghai, China.

XI DanLi, b. 9 Feb 1939, Shanghai. Teacher. m. Zhang WeiYan, 2 s. Education: Univ. Appointments: Dean, Environment Sci and Engrng Dept. Publication: Handbook of Environmental Engineering, Ed. Honours: 1st Prize, Shanghai Sci Progress, 1992; 3rd Prize, Natl Inv, 1992; 3rd Prize, City Progress, 1998. Memberships: Dir, China Environment Assn. Hobbies: Music; Sports. Address: Environment Engineering Dept, China Textile University, 1882 Yanan (West) Rd, Shanghai 200051, China.

XI Guang-Kang, b. 26 Feb 1928, Hunan, China. Teacher; Researcher. m. Er-Ti Xu, 6 Feb 1959, 2 d. Education: BS, Fudan Univ, Shanghai, China, 1953. Appointments: Asst, Nankai University, Tianjin, China, 1953-60; Lectr, 1961-80; Assoc Prof, 1981-84; Prof, 1986-; Visng Prof, Hamburg Univ, Hamburg, Germany, 1985-86. Creative Works: Inv, Mass Spectrometer, 1964; Inv, Surface Analysis Apparatus, 1985; 50 Contbr Articles to Profl Jrnls, 1964-97; Solid Surface and Interfaces, 1996. Honours: Sci Prize, Tianjin Govt, 1986; Sci Prize, Natl Educl Commn, 1991. Memberships: NY Acady Scis; Chinese Vcm Soc; Tianjin Vcm Soc. Hobbies: Swimming; Table Tennis. Address: Department of Electronic Science, Nankai University, Tianjin 300071, China.

XI Xu, b. 16 Jan 1921, China. Senior Professor. m. Qi Guangmei, 9 Feb 1947, 2 s, 1 d. Education: BS, Natl Chekiang Univ, 1944; MS, Lehigh Univ, USA, 1948. Appointments: Acad, Chinese Acady of Scis; Prof, Dir, Polymer Rsch Inst, Chengdu Univ of Sci and Technol; Chmn, Acad Cttee, State Key Lab of Polymer Materials Engrng, Chengdu Univ of Sci and Technol and State Rsch Lab of Flame Retarding Materials, Beijing Inst of Technol; Dir, Polymer Materials Rsch Inst, Shanghai Jiaotong Univ; Pt-time Prof, Tsinghua Univ, Zhejiang Univ, Xian Jiaotong Univ, Beijing Univ of Chem Technol. Publications: Auth of 4 books and over 200 articles concerning polymer structure and properties, polybends, and polymer stress reactions; 16 pats. Honours: Creative Invention Prize, Natl Cttee of Sci, 1983; Sci and Technol Achievement Prize, State Educn Cmmn, 1985, 1992; Natural Sci Achievement Prize, Natl Cttee of Natural Sci Achievement, 1987; Tchng Awd, Chinese Chem Soc and State Educ Commn, 1989; Technological Sci Prize, Ho Leung Ho Lee Fndn, 1996; Title, Sci and Technol Forerunner, State Educ and State Sci and Technol Commn, 1990 Hon Title, Nation-wide Model Worker for Serv to Educ, Min of Labour and Personnel and State Educ Commn, 1993. Memberships: Chinese Chem Soc; Stndng Cnclr, Chinese Chem Ind and Engrng Soc; Chinese Petro-Chem Ind Soc; Chinese Composite Materials Soc; Chinese Materials Rsch Soc; Am Chem Soc; Intl Polymer Processing Soc. Address: Polymer Research Institute, Chengdu University of Science and Technology, Sichuan 610065, China.

XIA Chunlin, b. 3 Dec 1963, Nanjing, China. Teacher; Researcher. m. Ihau Qing, 25 Jan 1990, 1 s. Education: Dr, Tsinghua Univ, Beijing, China. Appointments: Tchr, SE Univ, Nanjing, 1987; Assoc Prof, 1992, Prof, 1995, Nanjing Univ of Aero and Astro. Publications: Natural Convections; Boiling in Narrow Channels; Heat Transfer; Combustion in Supersonic Flow; Price Analysis. Honours: One of Ten Outstndng Yths in Jiansu Prov, 1998; Young Scientist Awd; Outstndng Dr in China; Nat Sci Prize (1st Grade twice, 2nd grade, 3 x). Memberships: ASME; AIAA; Eng Thermophysics Assn; Mech Eng Assn of China; Dir, China E Sci-Tech Assn; Chinese Soc of Aero and Astro. Hobbies: Riding; Computer games; Cooking. Address: Department of Power Engineering, Nanjing University of Aeronautics and Astronautics, Nanjing 210016, China.

XIA De Qin, b. 8 Nov 1941, Qinchun Co, Hubei Prov. Director. m. Wu Suyue, 1 Oct 1972, 2 s, 1 d. Education: Middle China Tchrs Univ Schl. Appointments: Middle China Tchrs Univ; China Cntrl Educ Rsch Inst; Shenzhen Educ Rsch Inst; Presently Dean and High Rschr, Shenzhen Educ Rsch Inst. Publications: Chf ed: (book) Asia Four Dragons Economy and Education; (periodical) Shenzhen Zhuzi Learning Journal; (book) Tao Xingzhi Completed Collection (6 vols as chf ed, 10 vols as ed); Many wrks in intl jrnls. Honours: 1st Prize for article, Li Shiguan Educ Idea; 2nd Prize for book, China Educ Instn and Background Rsch; 3rd Prize for book, Asia Four Dragons Econ and Educ. Memberships: China Document Info Assn; Zhuzi Learning Assn; China Old Profs Assn; Tao Xingzhi Rsch Assn; China Educ Specialist Assn; Li Shiguang Rsch Assn. Hobbies: Music; Sports; Handwriting. Address: Department of Education, University of Hong Kong, China.

XIA Daiguang, b. 26 Aug 1926, Sichuan Prov, China. Medical Scientist. m. Chen Yu, 1953, 3s. Education: MD. Appointments: Asst Prof, Medl Sch, Yunnan Univ; Asst prof, Assoc Prof, Prof, Kunming Medl Coll, Yunnan. Publications: Chinese Animal Fauna, Plate Helminthes, Trematoda, Digenea I, 1985; Zoonosisology of China 9, 1988, 1st Ed, 6, 1996, 2nd Ed. Memberships: Chinese Medl Assn; Soc of Medl Parasitology; Chinese Preventative Med Assn. Hobbies: Basketball; Soccer; Music. Address: Department of Parasitology, Kunming Medical College, Yunnan 650031, China.

XIA Guang, b. 5 Sept 1944, Liaoyang, China. Editor. m. Lu Fengzhu, 19 Apr 1969, 2 s. Education: BA, Inst of For Langs, China. Appointments: Dir, Edl Off, ECOM, 1987, Dir, Sci Technol Serv Dept, 1993. Publications: Sev pprs in profl jrnls. Memberships: NY Acady of Scis; FIT. Hobbies: Reading; Fishing; Music; Translation. Address: c/o Institute of Chemical Metallurgy, Chinese Academy of Sciences, PO Box 353, Beijing 100080, China.

XIA Jianxin, b. 6 July 1928, Shanghai, China. Professor of Mechanical Engineering; Institute President. m. Shunhua Chen, 8 Apr 1956, 2 d. Education: Grad, Mechl Engrng Dept, Shanghai Jiao Tung Univ, 1950. Appointments: Asst, then Lectr, Mechl Engrng Dept, Tangshan Engrng Coll; Lectr, Vice-Chmn, Locomotive and Car Dept, Shanghai Jiao Tung Univ; Lectr, Assoc Prof, Chmn, 1973-83, Prof, 1984, Mechl Engrng Dept, VP, 1981-83, Pres, 1984-88, Shanghai Inst Railway Technol; Visng Schl, Mechl Engrng and AM Dept, Univ MI, USA, 1983-84. Publications: Fundamentals of Power Machinery, 1956; Diesel Locomotive Manufacture and Repair Technology, 1960; Analytical Calculation of Serrated Joint Strength on Obliquely Split Connecting Rod of Diesel Engine, 1982; The Experimental Investigation on the Dynamic Strength of the Spiral Bevel Gear for Diesel Hydraulic Locomotive, 1983; The Hydrodynamic Lubrication Analysis on the Oil Film Load Carrying Capacity of the Internal Combustion Engine Honed Cylinder Bore Surface, 1987; Engine Blowby and Oil Consumption, 1988; The Measurement of Oil Film Thickness and Journal Centre Orbit for Diesel Engine Main Bearing, 1988; Computer Simulation of Piston Secondary Movement for Internal Combustion Engine, 1989; Design and Development of Articulated Piston for Diesel Engine, 1991; Development of Model 495AZD Turbocharged Diesel Engine, 1995; An Experimental Investigation on the Distortion of Connecting Rod Bearing for 16V280ZL Locomotive Diesel Engine under Statical Loading, 1997. Honours: 3rd Prize, Shanghai Munic Sci and Techl Progress, 1987; Gold Medal, Shanghai Sci and Technol Fair, 1995. Memberships: Shanghai Soc Mechl Engrng; Shanghai Soc Internal Combustion Engine Engrng; Dir, Stndng Cttee, Shanghai Soc Railway; Soc Auto Engrs Intl USA; Shanghai Soc Auto Engrng. Hobbies: Reading; Music. Address: Shanghai Tie Dao University, 450 Zhennan Road, Shanghai 200331, China.

XIA Jisong, b. 15 May 1925. Professor in Modern Philosophy. m. 1 Apr 1956, 1 s, 1 d. Education: Bachelor in Pols, Natl Cntrl Univ, Nanjing, 1943-48; MPhil, People's Univ of China, Beijing, 1952-54. Appointments: Asst Lectr, Dept Pols, Natl Cntrl Univ, 1948-52; Lectr, Dept Pols, Nanjing Univ, 1954-78; Assoc Prof and Dpty Hd of Dept, Dept Philos, Nanjing Univ, 1978-82; Prof and Head of Dept, Dept Philos, Nanjing Univ, 1982-90; Prof, Dept Philos, Hangzhou Univ and Zhejiang Univ, Hangzhou, 1990-. Publications: Course of the Modern Philosophy in the West, 1985; Mathematics Philosphy in the West, 1986; Review on Existentialism, 1987; Philosphy of Science in the West. Honours: Hon Hd of Philos Dept, Nanjing Univ. Memberships: Philos Div of the State Cncl's Acad Deg Cttee in China; Vice Chmn, Soc of Mod For Philos Stdy in China; Chmn of Soc of For Philos Stdy in China. Hobbies: Chinese Painting; Chinese Poetry. Address: Department of Philosophy, Zhejiang University, Hangzhou 310028, China.

XIA You Wei, b. 1 Oct 1933. Teacher. m. 1 July 1957, 2 d. Education: Grad, Mech Engrng Dept, Shanghai Jiao Tong Univ. Appointments: Dir, Solid Mechs Lab, 1958-86; Lectr 1978, Assoc Prof 1982, Dir of Lab Div of SJTU 1986-93; Prof, 1990; Exec Ed in Chief, 1991, Chf Ed, 1996, Jrnl of Lab Rsch and Exploration. Publications: Engineering Mechanics, 1978; The Handbook of Mechanical Engineering, vol 1, part 5, 1982; The Handbook of Mech Engineers, part 4, 1989; The Practical Handbook of Lab, 1994; 40 rsch papers in Pressure Vessel and Lab Management, 1958-96; Annals of Shanghai Jiaotong University, 1996; Handbook of Mechanical Engineering, Vol 1, Part 5, 1997. Honours: 2nd-Class State Sci and Technol Progress Prize of China, 1985; Commend of State Sci Technol Commn, 1985; The Ex Lab Dir of SJTU. Memberships: Assn of Mechs in Shanghai, 1963; Cnclr, 1985, VP 1989-96, PV Inst of Shanghai; Snr Fell, Chinese Mech Engrng Soc, 1990; Cnclr, Lab Rsch Inst of China's Univ, 1986; VP, LM Inst of Univs in Shanghai, 1990. Hobby: Recitation of Poems. Address: Department of Engineering Mechanics, Shanghai Jiao Tong University, 1954 Huashan Road, Shanghai 200030, China.

XIAN Baiqi, b. 25 Dec 1940, Guangdong, China. Official. m. 10 July 1967, 3 s. Education: Grad, Mining Univ. Appointments: Geol Exploration, 15 yrs; Geol Rsch, 15 yrs; Admnstrn, 9 yrs. Publications: Geology of non-ferrous metal and rare metal deposits associated with Mesozoic granite in Nanling Region; On metallogenic condition and distribution pattern of Sn-deposits in Guangxi; On Metalogenic characteristics of Sn and other metals in Guangxi; Development and construction accordant with environment protection in Hainan. Honours: 2nd Prizxe, State Sci Adv Awd; 1st Prize, Two 2nd Prizes, Four 3rd and 4th Prizes of Prov Awd. Memberships: Geol Soc of China; Geol Soc of Guangxi Zhuang-Autonomous Region; Geol Soc of Hainan Prov. Hobby: Scientific research. Address: 12 South Longkun Road, Haikou City, Hainan 570206, China.

XIANG Huaicheng, b. 1939 Wujiang Co Jiangsu Prov. Politician. Education: Shandong Univ. Appointments: Joined CCP, 1983; Vice-Min of Fin; Vice-Min State Admin of Taxation, 1994. Memberships: Mbr 15th CCP Cntrl Cttee, 1997-. Address: State Administration of Taxation, Beijing, People's Republic of China.

XIANG Zhenlong, b. 24 June 1937, Nanjing, Jiangsu province, China. Professor of Clarinet. m. Zhang Meiling, 28 Oct 1967, 1 d. Education: BA, Sichuan Conservatory of Music; Cert of Advd Stdies, Shanghai Conservatory of Music. Appointments: Asst to Pres of Sichuan Conservatory, 1986; Assoc Prof, 1990, Dir of Orch Dept, Sichuan Conservatory; Full Prof of Clarinet, 1992. Creative works: Clarinet solo works: Guishan Festival; Cappricio; Morning Song at a Village; Lishu Dance Music; Books: A course of Clarinet, I, II, III; Scale Etudes of

Clarinet. Honours: 2nd Prize in Chengdu for an essay; Prize of Min of Culture for solo works, Guishan Festival; and others. Memberships: Chinese Musicians Assn; Permanent Mbr, Chinese Clarinet Soc; Dir, Sichuan Wind and Percussion Soc; Intl Clarinet Soc. Hobbies: Collecting Chinese minority instruments; Research; Fishing. Address: Sichuan Conservatory of Music, 6 Xinsheng Rd, Chengdu, Sichuan, China.

XIAO Feng, b. 11 Feb 1932, Jiangsu, China. Artist (Oil Paintings). m. Song Ren, 1 Oct 1959, 2 d. Education: E China Br, Ctrl Acady, 1950; Langs Inst, Beijing, 1953; Lepin Acady of Fine Arts, China, 1960. Appointments include: Young Performer, 4th Route Army, 1943; Actor, Artist, Xin-an Troupe, 1944-50; Shanghai Oil Painting and Sculpture Studio, 1973-82; Pres, 1983-96, Prof, 1983-, China Acady of Art (formerly Zhejiang Acady of Fine Arts), Hangzhou; Grp exhbns in USA, Can, Japan, Aust, Austria, Xingapo. Publications: Selected Oil Paintings (w Song Ren); Goodbye to South China; Dawn; Call of Victory; The June 3rd Strike; Exhibition of Xiao Feng and Quan Shanshi. Honours: 3rd Prize, Natl Exhbn, 1979; Hon Mention, Shanghai Fine Arts Exhbn. Memberships: VP, Chinese Artists Assn; VP, Zhejiang Lit and Arts Assn; Pres of Art Weekly. Hobby: Hunting. Address: 218 Nanshan Road, Hangzhou, China.

XIAO Han Liang, b. 8 Mar 1935, Shanghai, China. Teacher. m. Jie Yuan, 7 Sept 1958, 2 s. Education: Dalian Maritime Univ, China, 1958. Appointments: Assoc Prof, 1987; Hd of Dept of Marine Mechl Engrng, 1987-95; Prof, 1991-; Supvsr for doct cand, 1996-. Publications: Ferrography and its Application in Machine Failure Diagnosis (book), 1993; Machine Condition Monitoring and Fault Diagnosis (book), 1994. Honours: Outstndng Tchr: Min of Comm, China, 1986, Govt of Hubei Prov, China, 1989; Spec Govt Allowance for Outsndng Higher Educ, China, 1992; 2nd Class Achievement Awd, 1990, 3rd Class Achievement Awd, 1996, of Sci and Technol, Min of Comm, China. Memberships: Chinese Soc of Nav Arch and Marine Engrng; Chinese Mechl Engrng Soc; Chinese Vibration Engrng Soc; Soc of Tribologist and Lubrication Engrs, USA. Hobbies: Swimming; Stamp collecting. Address: Department of Marine Mechanical Engineering, Wuhan Transportation University, Yu Jia Tou, Wuhan 430063, China.

XIAO Yang, b. 1929 Langzhong Co Sichuan Prov. Administrator. Education: Qinghua Univ Beijing; GDR. Appointments: Joined CCP, 1947; Vice-Mayor of Chongqing, 1983-85; Mayor of Chongqing, 1986; Party Cttee Sec Chongqing, 1988; Dep Sec CPC 6th Sichuan Prov Cttee, 1989-; Gov Sichuan Prov People's Govt, 1993-96; Min of Jus, 1993-98; NPC Dep Sichuan Prov. Memberships: Alt mbr 14th CCP Cntrl Cttee, 1992-97; Mbr 8th NPC, 1993-96. Address: Office of Provincial Government, Chengdu City 610016, Sichuan Province, People's Republic of China.

XIAO Young, b. Aug 1938 Heyuan Co Guangdong Prov. Party and Government Official. Education: People's Univ of China. Appointments: Joined CCP, 1966; Imprisoned during 'Cultural Revolution', 1968-71; Dep Dir Qujiang Co CCP Cttee Off then var party posts, 1971-81; Sec CCP Cttee of Wujiang Reg Shaoguan Cty Guangdong Prov, 1981-83; Dep Sec Qinguyang Prefectural CCP Cttee Guangdong, 1983; Dep Chf Guangdong Prov Procurator's Off Dep Sec CCP Ldrshp Grp, 1983-86; Procurator-Gen Guangdong Prov Procurator's Off, 1986-90; Dep Procurator-Gen Supreme Procurator's Off Dep Sec CCP Ldrshp Grp, 1990-92; Min of Jus, 1993-; Dep Sec CCP 6th Sichuan Prov Cttee; Chmn People's Armament Cttee; Vice-Chmn Three Gorges Project Constrn Cttee; VP China Culture Promotion Assn. Memberships: Alt mbr 14th CCP Cntrl Cttee, 1992-97; Mbr 15th CCP Cntrl Cttee, 1997-. Address: Ministry of Justice, 11 Xianguanli, Sanyuanqiao, Chaoyang District, Beijing 100016, People's Republic of China.

XIE Chu, b. 6 Aug 1935, Zhejiang, China. Editor. m. Li Jian, 7 July 1959, 1 d. Education: Bachelor degree, Beijing Univ of Aeronautics and Astronautics, 1958.

Appointments: Ed-in-Chf, Aerospace Knowledge Mag, 1984-; Prof, Beijing Univ Aero and Astro, 1987-; Sec-Gen, Chinese Soc of Aero and Astro, 1992-96. Publications: The Chronological History of Aviation and Space, 1987; The Pilots, 1961; Air Battles Over Gulf, 1992; Spaceflight, 1995. Honours: Brilliant Contbn Awd, Chinese Natl Sci Conf, 1978; One of Chinese Best Publrs Awd, 1997. Memberships: Vice Chmn, Aero Sports Fedn of China, 1996-; Pres, Chinese Aerospace Sci Writers's Assn, 1991-. Hobbies: Reading; Photographing. Address: Aerospace Knowledge, 37 Xueyuan Road, 100083, China.

XIE Dao-Zhen, b. 8 Aug 1961. Medical Doctor. m. Y Qiu, 2 d. Education: BS, He Bei Medl Coll (now He Bei Univ). Appointments: Physn, Tchr, Neur Dept, Hosp affiliated to Tian Jing Medl Coll (now Univ), 1959-70; Physn, Neur Dept, Second Cntrl Hosp, Tian Jing, 1970-74; Physn-in-charge, Neurosurgical Dept, Xuan Wu Hosp, Beijing, 1974-79; Assoc Physn, 1985, Chf Physn, 1990, Supvsr of Cand Drs, 1991, Neur Dept, Beijing Xi Yuan Hosp, China Acady, Tradl Chinese Med, 1979-. Publications: Over 20 pprs and 3 books in collaboration w others; Rsch wrk on hypertensive cerebral hemorrhage (HCH) for 20 yrs. Honours: Awds for Nao Xue-Kang oral liquor, China Acady Tradl Chinese Med, Sci Technol Prog, Natl Admin of Tradl Chinese Med, 1987; Awds for Nao Xue Shu-tong oral liquor, 1st Working Conf of Sci and Technol, Xi Yuan Hosp, China Acady of Tradl Chinese Med, 1996. Spec Allowance, Govt People's Repub of China, 1993-. Memberships: China Neur Assn of Integrated Tradl Chinese and West Med; Chf Mbr, Beijing Neur Assn, Integrated Tradl Chinese and West Med, 1995-99; Exec Cncl, Intl Hua Xia Medl Assn, 1997. Hobby: Likes fishing. Address: Department of Neurology, Xi Yuan Hospital, China Academy of Traditional Chinese Medicine, Xi Yuan, Beijing 100091, China.

XIE Guozhang, b. 18 June 1929, Feng Cheng, Jiangxi, China. Researcher and Educator of Solid Physics. m. Wu He Zheng, 25 Jan 1960, 2 d. Education: Bach Deg, Phys Dept, Tsing Hua Univ, 1951. Appointments: Rschr, Inst of Appl Phys, Acady of Sci, China, 1951-58; Rschr, Inst of Chem, 1958-65; Snr Engr, Semi Conductor Factory, 1965-85; Prof, Hehai Univ, 1985-. Publications: Translation Skill on Science and Technology English, 1987; The Fabrication and Application of Micromechanism, 1991; Over 100 pprs in profl jrnls. Honours: Ldr Awd, Min, 1987; 1st Prize, Cty Govt, 1988; 20th Century Awd for Achmnt, IBC, 1997. Memberships: China Phys Assn; China Electron Assn; Dir, Changzhou Br, Tsing Hua Alumni Assn; Dpty Dir Gen, IBC. Hobbies: Chess; Physical training. Address: 85-2-301 South Lao Don Xin Cun, Changzhou, Jiangsu 213001, China.

XIE Harhuu, b. 27 July 1938, Maohao Village, Baicheng Pref, Jilin Prov. Teacher. m. Qimuge, 1 May 1964, 3 s. Education: Grad, Dept of Chinese, Inner Mongolia Normal Univ. Appointment: Vice-Chmn, Mongolian Dept, Inner Mongolia Normal Univ, 1975-81. Publications: Theoretic Basis on Literature; Selected Review by Harhuu; Study on Aesthetic Characteristics of Mongolian Literature. Honours: 2nd Prize of Second Outstndng Achievements in Philos and Socl Scis of Inner Mongolia Autonomous, for Theoretic Basis on Literature, 1987. Memberships: Bd of Rsch Assn of Mongolian Lit, China; Vice-Chmn, Rsch Assn of Mongolian Lit. Hobbies: Listening to music; Dancing; Writing a form of pre-Tang poetry. Address: Institute of Mongolian Langauge and Literature of Inner Mongolia Normal University, Huhehote 010022, China.

XIE Hong-Quan, b. 16 Jan 1931, Shanghai, China. Researcher; Educator. m. J S Guo, Feb 1959, 2 s. Education: BSc, Chem Dept, Univ of Shanghai, 1952. Appointments: Asst Rschr, Changchun Inst of Applied Chem, Academia Sinica, 1952-72; Assoc Rschr, Hubei Rsch Inst of Chem, 1973-97; Prof, Dept of Chem, Huazhong Univ of Sci and Technol, 1987-. Publications: 260 pprs inclng 65 publd in intl jrnls; 70 pprs cited by SCI d 65 by EI. Honours: 2 second grade Sci and Tech Prog Awds, Natl Educ Cttee of China, 1991, 1997; 3 second grade Awds, Hubei Prov., 1985, 1987, 1993.

Memberships: Cncl Mbr, Chinese Chem Soc; Chinese Polymer Cttee. Hobbies: Music; Football. Address: Department of Chemistry, Huazhong University of Science and Technology, Wuhan 430074, China.

XIE Hua-An, b. 16 Aug 1941, Longyan, Fujian, China. Agricultural Researcher; Crop Breeder. m. Fengying Lu, 2 Nov 1965, 2 s, 1 d. Education: Grad, Coll of Agricl. Appointments: Sch Tchr; Techn; Asst Rschr; Dir of Off; Dpty Dir of Inst; Dir of Inst; Pres of Acady. Publications: Fine Variety "Shan you 63" The Largest Area of Rice Planted in China, 1997. Honours: Natl Expert of Prominent Contbrns of Mid-Yng Aged, 1988; Specl Allowance, 1991; Adv Person at Natl 8th-5 Target, 1996. Memberships include: Prov Genetic Assn; Prov Seeds Assn. Hobbies: Music; Sports. Address: Fujian Academy of Agricultural Sciences, 247 Wusi Road, Fuzhou, Fujian, China.

XIE Qinan, b. Dec 1934, Meixian Cty, Guangdong Prov, China. Teacher. m. 1 s, 1 d. Education: Bachelor, Dept of Stats, Hubei Univ, China, 1960. Appointments: Tchr, Hubei Univ, 1960-1970; Tchr, Wuhan Univ, 1970-72; Tchr, Hubei Coll of Fin and Econs, 1972-80; Prof, Jinan Univ, 1980-; Vice-Hd, 1984-88, Hd, 1988-95, Dept of Stats, Jinan Univ. Publications: 49 pprs in profl jrnls. Honours include: 1st Prize, Stats, Guangdong Prov, 1989; 2nd Prize, Ex Publ in Stats of Guangdong Prov, 1991; 2nd Prize, Ex Achievements in Socl Sci of Guangzhou Cty, 1996; 1st Prize Ex Publ in Statistical Achievements of Guangzhou Cty, 1996; 3rd Prize, Ex Achievements in Socl Sci of Guangdong Prov, 1998; 2nd Prize Ex Publ in Statistical Achievements of China, 1999. Memberships: Mngng Dir, Statistical Soc of China; Vice-Chmn, Statistical Socs of Guangdong Prov and Guangzhou Cty; Mngng Dir, Rsch Assn, intl macreconomics of Guangdong Prov; Mngng Dir, Theort Rsch Assn of Marxistic Stats of China. Address: Department of Statistics, Jinan Univ, 510632 Guangzhou, China.

XIE Yi-Min, b. 23 Dec 1963, Jiangsu, China. Engineering Educator. m. Grace, 1 s, 1 d. Education: BSc, Jiaotong Univ, China, 1984; PhD, Univ Wales, UK, 1991. Appointments: Rsch Fell, Univ Sydney, Aust, 1992-93; Lectr, 1993-95; Snr Lectr, 1995-97, Assoc Prof, 1998-, Vic Univ of Technol, Melbourne. Publication: Evolutionary Structural Optimisation, 1997. Honour: Best Student Awd, K C Wong Educ Fndn, Hong Kong, 1985. Address: Victoria University of Technology, PO Box 14428 MCMC, Victoria 8001, Australia.

XIE Jin, b. 1923 Shangyu Co Zhenjiang Prov. Education: Sichuan Natl Drama Sch. Appointments: Film Dir Datong Film Studio Shanghai, 1948-50; Film Shanghai Film Studio, 1953-88; A VP Chinese Fed for the Disabled, 1988-; Exec Vice-Chmn 5th Nal Cttee Chinese Fedn of Lit and Art Circles, 1988-96; Vice-Chmn, 1996-. Films incl: Red Girl's Army, 1960; Legend of Tian Yun, 19981; Lotus Town, 1987. Honours: Hundred Flavers Awd or Red Girl's Army; 1st Golden Rooster Best Fillm Awd for Legend of Tian Yun; Golden Rooster Best Film Dir Awd for Lotus Town; May 1 Labour Medal, 1987. Memberships: Mbr 8th Natl Standing Standing Cttee CPPCC, 1994-. Address: c/o Shanghai Film Studio, 595 Caoxi Beilu, Shanghai, People's Republic of China.

XIE Shijie, b. 1934 Liangping Co Sichuan Prov. Admnstr. Education: S W Agricl Coll. Appointments: Joined CCP, 1954; Vice-Gov of Sichuan Prov, 1986; Sec 6th CCP Sichuan Prov Cttee, 1993-. Memberships: Mbr 14th CCP Cntrl Cttee, 1992-97; Mbr 15th CCP Cntrl Cttee, 1997-. Address: Sichuan Provincial Government, Chengdu City, Sichuan Province, People's Republic of China.

XIN Dianfeng, b. Dec 1933 Shuangliao Co Jilin Prov. Air Force Offr. Education: Air Force Aviation sch. Appointments: Joined CCP, 1951; Joined NE Dem Utd Army, 1947; Took part in Liaoxi-Shenyang and Marching SW campaigns; Served as team ldr of cultural troop of Polit Dept of Chinese People's Volunteers in Korean War; Served as pilot Sqdn Ldr dep Grp Cmdr Cmdr of ind grp regt Dir then Dir Mil Trng Dept PLA Air Force, 1978-83; Dir of a mil regl Air Force cmd post, 19983-84; Dep Chf of Staff PLA Air Force, 1984-90; Dep Cmdr of Air Force of Ji'nan Mil Reg, 1990-93; Dep Cmdr and Air Force Cmdr of Shenyang Mil Reg, 1993; Chf of Staff PLA Air Force, 1993; Rank of Air Force Lt Gen, 1993; Dep Cmdr PLA Air Force, 1995-. Address: Ministry of National Defence, Beijing, People's Republic of China.

XING Chongzhi, b. 1927 Shexian Hebei Prov. Party Offic. Appointments: Joined CCP, 1943; Vice-Chmn Preparatory Cttee 10th Congress of Communist Yth League, 1978; Vice-Min of Agric, 1979-82; Sec CCP Cttee Hebei, 1985-92. Memberships: Mbr Cntrl Cttee Communist Yth League, 1964; Alt mbr 12th CCP Cntrl Cttee, 1982; Mbr 12th CCP Cntrl Cttee, 1985; Mbr 13th CCP Cntrl Cttee, 1987-92; Mbr Presidium 14th CCP Natl Congress, 1992; Mbr 8th CPPCC Natl Cttee, 1993-. Address: Hebei Provincial Chinese Communist Party, Shijiazhung, Hebei, People's Republic of China.

XIONG Guangchu, b. 9 Jan 1927, Nanchang, China. Geophysicist. m. Chen Zhisun, 30 Apr 1954, 2 s, 1 d. Education: Qing Hua Univ, Beijing, China. Appointments: Hd, Geophysical Exploration Team, 1954-58; Eng, Geophysical Exploation, Beijing Rsch Inst of Geol, Min of Metallurgical Ind, 1959-62; Snr Engr, Geophysical Exploration, Beijing Rsch Inst of Mineral Resources and Geol, 1983-; Adj Prof of Geophysics, Chendou Geol Coll, 1985-88. Publications: Some Problems of Mining Geophysics, 1959; Interpretation of Magnetic Anomaly of Iron Ore Deposits, 1964; Lecture on Magnetic Exploration, 1976; Introduction to Mining Geophysics, 1980; Interpretation of Magnetic Anomaly of Ore Deposits, 1981; Prediction of Mineral Deposits by Geophysical Method, 1987; Filtering and Transforming of Magnetic and Gravity Anomalies, 1990; Case history of discovery of main Au and Cu deposits in Xinjiang, 1996; A rapid exploration system of metallic deposits in Xinjiang, 1997; Information theory, system theory and exploration, 1998. Honours: Natl Conf of Sci and Technol of China, 1978; Min of Metallurgical Ind, People's Repub of China, 1982; China Natl Non-Ferrous Metals Ind Corp, 1983, 1986; Lee Siguang Prize Committee, 1997. Memberships: Geophysical Soc of China. Hobby: Music. Address: Beijing Research Institute of Mineral Resources and Geology, Beiyuan, Andinmenwai, Beijing, China.

XIONG Xiyuan, b. 6 Mar 1918. University Tutor. m. 8 Jan 1945, 1 s, 2 d. Education: Dept Pols, Yunnan Univ, 1942; Postgrad Studies in State Law, Dept of Law, Chinese People's Univ, 1952-55. Appointments: Tchng Asst, Dept of Pols, 1942, Lectr, 1948; Assoc Prof, Dept of Hist, 1985, Full Prof, Dept of Hist, 1987, Yunnan Univ. Publications: A Collection of Essays on Ethnic Features of Various Nationalities, 1987; A Primer to Theories of Ethnology, 1989; National Psyche and National Consciousness, 1995. Honours: Univ Awds and Academia Awds by Yunnan Univ and Yunnan Acady of Socl Scis, for pprs written on natl psyche of var ethnic grps, 1985-87; Feature Rprt by Yunnan Univ Jrnl (Sixiang Zhanxian) under heading Xiong Xiyuan - Ethnology Theorist, 1991; Seven essays, On National Psyche and National Consciousness (in Chinese and transl), 1997. Memberships: China Soc of Ethnology Theorists, Mbr and Advsr, 1992-; China Soc of World Ethnologists; Yunnan Assn of Ethnologists; Acad Cttee Mbr, 1989-; Hon Ed, Yunnan Univ Press, 1993-95. Hobbies: Classical music; Folk music; Walking. Address: Dept of Hist, Yunnan Univ, Kunming, Yunnan, China 650091.

XIONG Guangkai, b. Mar 1939 Nanchang Cty Jiangxi Prov. Diplomatist; Army Offr. Education: August 1st Middle Sch Beijing; PLA Trng Sch for For Langs. Appointments: Joined PLA, 1956; Joined CCP, 1959; Translator secl asst Off of Mil Attache Chinese Emb German Dem Repub, 1960-72; Asst Mil Attache Chinese Emb Fed Repub of Germany, 1972-80; Student PLA Mil Acady, 1981-83; Asst Div Chf Intell Dept Gen Staff Hq, 1983-85; Dep Dir, 1985-87; Dir, 1987-88; Rank of Maj, 1988; Asst to Chf of Gen Staff, 1988; Rank of Lt Gen, 1993; Hd of mil deleg to USA, 1995; Dep Chf of Gen Staff, 1996-. Memberships: Alt mbr 14th CCP Cntrl Cttee,

1992-97; Mbr 15th CCP Cntrl Cttee, 1997-; Mbr Cntrl Cttee Ldng Grp on Taiwan, 1993-.

XIONG Qingquan, b. 1927 Shuangfeng Hunan Prov. Party and State Offic. Appointments: Mayor of Changsha, 1982; Sec CCP Cttee Hunan Prov, 1983-85; Gov of Hunan, 1985-89; Dep Sec CCP Cttee Hunan Prov, 1985-88; Sec CCP Cttee Hunan Prov, 1988-93; Fmr Party Cttee First Sec PLA Hunan Prov Cmd; NPC Dep Hunan Prov. Memberships: Alt mbr 12th CCP Cntrl Cttee, 1982; Mbr, 1985-87; Mbr 13th Cntrl Cttee CCP, 1987-92; Mbr Presidium 14th CCP Natl Congress, 1992; Mbr 8th NPC, 1993-. Address: Hunan Provincial People's Government, Changsha, Hunan, People's Republic of China.

XONGERIN Badai, b. 5 Jun 1930 Bayinguoltng Prefecture Hejin Co Xinjiang. Writer; Poet. Admnstr. m. 1952, 2 s, 2 d. Appointments: Pres Xinjiang Brdcstng and TV Univ, 1982-; Chmn Cttee of Xinjiang Uygur Autonomous Reg of CPPCC, 1989. Publications: Sev books of prose and poetry and hist in Mongol lang and Chinese. Memberships: Mbr Standing Cttee CPPCC, 1991. Hobbies: Hist of poetry; Writing plays; Mongol Hist. Address: 15 South Beijing Road, Urumqi, Xinjiang, People's Republic of China.

XU Caidong, b. 1919 Fengxin Co Jiangxi Prov. Admnstr; Engr. Education: Tangshan Inst Jiaotong Univ Hebei; Grenoble Inst France. Appointments: Returned to China, 1955; Prof Guizhou Engrng Inst, 1958-; Pres Sci Acady of Guizhou Prov, 1978; Vice-Gov Guizhou Prov, 1983; Vice-Chmn Jiu San Soc, 1983-; NPC Dep Guizhou Prov. Publication: The Physical Chemistry of Zinc. Memberships: Mbr Dept of Tech Scis Academia Sinica, 1985-; Mbr 7th Natl People's Congress 8th NPC, 1993-; Mbr Educ Sci Culture and Pub Hlth Cttee. Address: Guizhou Provincial People's Government, Guiyang Province, People's Republic of China.

XU Deming, b. 8 July 1939, Shanghai. Educator. m. Wu Suzheng, 1 Jan 1967, 1 d. Education: Undergrad, Dept of Phys, Shanghai Norm Univ. Appointments: Hd, Phys Branch Tchng; Dpty Dir of Tchng, Rschng Sect; Dir, Audio, Visual Educ Center, Educ Coll. Publications: Equilibrium of Force; Force and Motion; On Demonstartion in Physics Experiment; SCR Light Modulated Projects. Honours: State Model Tchr; Tchr of a Spec Grade; Top Notch of Zhabei Dist; Awd for Educ Outstndng Achmnts. Memberships: China Assoc of Phys Tchng and Rschng; Assoc of Audio-Visual Educ; Soc of Phys. Hobbies: Reading. Address: The Education College of Zhabei District, 249 Zhijiang Rd W, Shanghai 200070, China.

XU Guoqing, b. 10 Feb 1932, Chekiang Prov, China. Geologist. m. Dingsheng Ding, 26 July 1962, 3d. Education: Grad, Beijing Coll of Geol, 1956; Doct, Moscow State Univ, USSR, 1963. Appointments: Tchr, Beijing Coll of Geol, 1956-59; Prof, Beijing Uranium Geol Rsch Inst, 1987-. Publications: 30 pprs on fluid inclusion rsch and geneses of ore deposits inclng: Visual Fixation of Inclusion Decrepitation and Statistic Investigation of their Results at Ore Deposit Karasuk, in Russian, 1965; Some Characteristics of Uranium Oxudes in China (co-auth), in Engl, 1981; In Chinese: Current Situtation of the Study on Inclusion Compounds, 1981; Some Characteristics of Formation Temperatures of Uranium Ore Deposits in China, 1982; Present Situation of Application abd Development Tendency of Decrepitation Method, 1983; Genetic Model for a Certain Uranium Ore Field in the South of China and its Significance for Prospecting (co-auth), 1983; A Study on Metallogenetic Model of Uranium Ore Field No 1220; Origin of Granite and Mineralization of Uranium Ore Field No 6210, 1987; 40 pprs on geological disposal of radwastes including: Use of Inorg Hanic Repositories as Backfill Material for Underground Repositories in English, 1992; Study on Migration Properties of U, 90Sr, 137 Cs on Zeolites, in English, 1992. Honours: Prizes, 1979, 2 prizes, 1982, prize 1986, prize, 1997, from relevent authorities. Memberships: Standing Mbr, China Mineralogy, Petrology and Geochemistry Assn; Hd, Rsch Coord Grp

on Deep Geol Disposal of HLW, China Natl Nuclear Corp. Address: Beijing Uranium Geology Institute, PO Box 9818, 100029 Beijing, China.

XU Huizi, b. 9 Dec 1932 Penglai Co Shandong Prov. Army Offr; Party Offic. Appointments: Joined PLC, 1948; Joined CCP, 1950; Dep Chf of Gen Staff, 1985-95; Rank of Lt Gen, 1988; Vice-Chmn People's Air Def Cttee, 1988-; Dep Sec for Discipline Insp, 1994-; Rank of Gen, 1994; Pres Acady of Mil Scis, 1995-97. Memberships: Mbr 14th CCP Cntrl Cttee; Mbr Preliminary Wrkng Cttee of the Preparatory Cttee of the Hong Kong Spec Admin Reg, 1993-. Address: Academy of Military Sciences, P O Box 998, Beijing 100091, People's Republic of China.

XU Jian Bin, b. 27 Aug 1961, Zhejiang, China. Professor. m. Chow Kit Shui, 17 Dec 1991, 2 d. Education: BS, 1983; MSc, 1986; Dr rer nat, 1993. Appointments: Rsch Assoc, 1986-87; Rsch Asst, 1988-93; Rsch Assoc, 1993-94; Asst Prof, 1994-. Creative Works: More than 40 Intl Jrnl Pprs, 1988-. Honours: Compative Ermarked Rsch Grants, Rsch Grant Cncl, Hong Kong, 1995, 1996, 1997. Memberships: Amn Physl Soc; Amn Vcm Soc; Inst of Elecl and Electron Engrng; Materials Rsch Soc. Hobbies: Swimming; Chinese Gong Fu; Tab Tennis. Address: Dept of Electronic Engineering, The Chinese University of Hong Kong, Shatin, NT, Hong Kong.

XU Jian-Ping, b. 29 Oct 1936, Shanghai, China. Professor and Chief Doctor of Neurosurgery. m. Chiu Yin-Ping, 1 s, 1 d. Education: Au Hui Medl Univ and Moscow Neurosurgical Rschng Inst. Appointments: Asst Prof, Dr, Hosp of Au Hui Medl Univ, 1956-83; Prof, Pres, Au Hui Medl Univ, Rschr and the Hd of Auhui Stereotactic and Functional Neurosurgical (SFN) Inst, 1983-99; Pres, China SFN Soc; Chf, China SFN Mag; Mbr, China Surg Mag editl cttee; Chmn, Hong Kong Mbrs Fedn of CMA. Publications: 4 books of Stereotactico and Functional Neurosurgery (SFN); Over 150 articles; 4 patents. Honours: The Whole Nation Outstndng Medl, 1978; Whole Nation Lab Model, 1980; Winner, state sci and technol advd prize, 1985; Outstndng expert enjoying spec subsidy from State Dept, 1992. Address: 1/12E, Biyunge, Zhonglu Plaza Huaqiao Cheng, Shen Zhen 518053, China.

XU Jiatun, b. 1916 Jiangsu. Politician. Appointments: Sec Nanjing Municipal Cttee CCP in Jiangsu, 1954; Sec Secr Standing Cttee Jiangsu Provincial Cttee CCP: Dep Gov of Jiangsu, 1956; Vice-Chmn Jiangsu Prov Revolutionary Cttee, 1970, 1974; Chmn Jiangsu Prov Revolutionary Cttee, 1977-79; Sec then First Sec Jiangsu Prov Cttee CCP; Chmn Standing Cttee of Fifth People's Congress of Jiangsu; First Polit Commissar of PLA of Jiangsu Prov Mil Dist, 1977-90; First Sec of Party Cttee, 1977-83; Chmn Jiangsu Prov People's Congress, 1979-83; Dir Xinhua News Agcy Hong Kong, 1983-90; Vice-Chmn Cttee for Drafting Basic Law of Hong Kong Spec Admin Reg, 1985-91; Stripped of all CCP posts, 1991; Living in Buddhist retreat, 1991. Publication: Hong Kong Memoirs, 1994. Memberships: Mbr of CCP Dep Sec Sec Fuzhou Municipal Cttee in Fujian, 1950; Mbr Standing Cttee Jiangsu Provincial Cttee CCP; Mbr 11th Cntrl Cttee of CCP, 1977-82; Mbr 12th Cntrl Cttee CCP, 1982-85; Mbr Cntrl Advsry Cttee, 1985-90; Mbr Presidium 6th NPC, 1986-90; Mbr Standing Cttee CCP, 1988.

XU Jingjun, b. 21 Nov 1935, Anhui, China. Professor; Dean. m. Zhoujuan Xu, 1 Jan 1967, 1 s, 1 d. Education: Undergraduate and postgraduate studies in Econs, Fu Dan Univ, 1955-64; Title of Econs Prof, 1987. Appointments: Rsch on Natl Minorities Econ, Yunann Hist Rsch Inst, 1964-71; Tchng and Rsch, Econs (Capital and Theory and Prac of Socialistic Econ Reform), 1971, currently Prof, Dean of Dept of Econs and Mngmt, Yunnan Inst of Nationalities, Kunming, Yunnan; Invited Rsch Worker, Econ Rsch Cntr, Yunnan Rural Dev Cntr. Publications: Economy of Mountainous Areas of Yunnan, 1983; From Nationalization to Enterprisation - Discussion on the Theory and Practice of the Reform of State-Owned Economy; The Allocation and Use of Urban Lands, 1993; Research of Chinese Economic Development Strategies, with an Emphasis on the Western Minorities, 1995; 100 thes on economic problems such as reformation of the pricing system, regional economic development; A New Course on Capital, 1992. Honours: Yunnan Socl Scis Rsch Awd for Econ of Mountainous Areas of Yunnan, 1986; Socl Scis Rsch Awd, for thesis Probe on Problems Concerning the Situation of Finance Revenue in Yunnan and Ways to Seek after New Sources of Revenue, Acady of Socl Scis, Yunnan, 1987; Natl Awd for Prominent Contrb, 1992. Memberships: China Natl Minorities Econ Assn; VP, Econ Soc of Yunnan Prov; Advsr, Kunming Municipality's People's Govt. Hobby: European classical music. Address: 112-161 North Court of Yunnan Institute of Nationalities, Yunnan Institute of Nationalities, Kunming, Yunnan, China.

XU Kuangdi, b. 1937 Tongxiang Co Zhenjiang Prov. Politician; Educationist. Education: Beijing Metallurgy Inst. Appointments: Joined CCP, 1983; Prof VP Shanghai Indl Univ; Dir Shanghai Higher Educ Bur; Dir Shanghai Plng Commn; Vice-Mayor Shanghai Municipality, 1992-; Vice-Sec CCP Shanghai Municipal Cttee, 1994; Mayor Shanghai Municipality, 1995-. Memberships: Alt mbr 14th CCP Cntrl Cttee, 1992; Mbr 15th CCP Cntrl Cttee, 1997-. Address: Shanghai Municipal Government, Shanghai, People's Republic of China.

XU Liejiong, b. 28 Oct 1937, Shanghai, China. Professor of Linguistics. m. Yiyi Wang, 13 Oct 1967, 2 d. Education: Beijing Univ, 1955-60; Shanghai For Langs Inst, 1962-64. Appointments: Asst Prof, Shanghai For Langs Inst, 1964-72; Asst Prof, 1972-78, Lectr, 1978-85, Prof, 1985-, Fudan Univ, Shanghai; Prof, City Univ of Hong Kong, 1993-. Publications: Topic Structures in Chinese (co-auth), D Terence Langendoen Language; Free Empty Category, Linguistic Inquiry; Theory of Generative Grammar; Semantics, Beijing, 1996; Topics: Structural and Functional Analysis, 1998. Memberships: Ling Soc of Am; Ling Soc of Hong Kong. Honours: Shanghai Philos and Socl Scis Awd, 1979-85. Address: Department of Chinese Translations and Linguistics, City University of Hong Kong, 83, Tat Chee Ave, Kowloon, Hong Kong.

XU Meili, b. 28 May 1928, Shandong, China. Physiologist. m. Xianhua Gao, 15 Aug 1953, 2 s. Education: Grad, Sch of Med, Natl Univ of Chongqing, 1952; Advd Trng at Dept of Physiology, First Medl Coll of Shanghai, 1955-57. Appointments: Asst in Phsysiology, Sch of Med, Natl Univ of Chongqing, 1952; Asst, Dept of Physiology, Sichuan Medl Coll, 1952-78; Lectr, 1978-80, Assoc Prof, 1980-87, Prof of Physiology, 1987-, Dept of Physiology, W China Univ of Medl Scis (WCUMS); Hd of Rsch Grp of control of breathing, Dept of Physiology, WCUMS, 1983. Publications: One of the contbrs to Textbook of Physiology, 1st ed, 1978, 3rd ed, 1989, 4th ed, 1996; pprs and review articles. Honours: Ex Sci Article Cert, Sichuan Provl Sci and Technol Assn, 1986; Ex Sci Article Cert, Sichuan Assn of Physiological Scis, 1987; 3rd Awd for Sci-Technol Prog, Sichuan Prov, 1991, 1994. Memberships: Chinese Assn of Physiological Scis (CAPS); Int; Brain Rsch Org; Chinese Soc for Neurosci; Editl Bd, CAPS News Commn, 1984-95. Hobby: Music. Address: Department of Physiology, W China Univ of Medl Scis, Chengdu, Sichuan 610044, China.

XU Ningzhi, b. 12 June 1954, Hunan, China. Research Scientist. m. Ping Liao, 5 Aug 1983, 1 s. Education: MD, Suzhou Medl Coll, 1983. Appointments: Rsch Assoc, 1986; Assoc Rsch Fell, 1997; Rsch Fell, 1997; Chf, Lab of Cell and Molecular Bio, 1998. Publications: Sev articles in profl med jrnls. Honour: Young Scientist Awd, Min of Pub Hlth, China, 1986. Memberships: Chinese Assn of Biochem; Chinese Assn of Med; Acady Cttee, Cancer Inst, CAMS. Hobbies: Reading; Sports. Address: c/o Cancer Institute, Chinese Academy of Medical Sciences, PO Box 2258, Beijing 100021, China.

XU Qinghua, b. 28 Sept 1952, Beijing, China. Environmental Engineering and Management. m. J Y Zhou, 9 Feb 1980, 1 d. Education: MSc. Appointments: Dpty Dir, Plng Dept for NEPA, 1985; Dir, Env Stands Dept for NEPA, 1988; VP, Chinese Rsch Acady, 1991; Dpty Permanant Repr of China to UNED, 1993; Sec-Gen of CEPF, 1996. Memberships: Sec-Gen, Chinese Water Quality Cttee, 1989; Snr fEll for Environ and Population Cttee of China; Prof (pt-time) Geog Univ of China, 1997. Hobbies: Bowling; Table tennis. Address: No 19-6-7, Dongjing RD, Xuanwu District, Beijing 100050, China.

XU Qinquan, b. 24 Jan 1933, Taixing, Jiangsu, China. Professor of Mechatronics. m. Yuhua Duan, 25 Oct 1958, 1 s. Education: Grad, Beijing Univ of Aeronautics and Astronautics (BUAA). Appointments: Asst, Lectr, BUAA, 1953-63; Lectr at the Beijing Inst of Machinery (BIM), 1963-80; Assoc Prof, First Branch of Beijing Polytechnic Univ, 1980-85; Assoc Prof, Full prof, Beijing Union Univ, 1985-; Auth of Mechatronics special field of study. Publications: Over 30 rsch pprs and books inclng: The Kinetic Misalignment of Gera and Its Compensation; The Mechatronics and Mechatronics Education. Honours: Cert of Commendation for Educ Outstndng by Beijing Munic Higher Educ Bur, 1984; Ctf of Commendation for Educ Contbn by min of Machinery Ind of China, 1986. Memberships: Mbr of Cncl, Chinese Univ and Coll Soc for Interchangeability and Measurement Technol, 1984, 1989, 1994-99; Expert of Experts' Commn of China Sci and Technol Assembly Hall, 1994-99. Hobby: Making model airplanes. Address: College of Mechanical Engineering of Beijing Union University, Beijing 100020, China.

XU Ren-sheng, b. 11 Aug 1931, Jiangsu, China. Professor, Natural Products Chemist. m. Hai-lan Zhang, 19 May 1959, 2 d. Education: BS, hons, Leningrad Inst of Pharm Chem, Russia, 1959; PhD, Dept of Natural Prod Chem, All-Union Rsch Inst of Pharm Chem, Mosocw, 1963. Appointments: Rsch Assoc, 1963-79, Assoc Prof, 1979-85, Prof, 1985-, Shanghai Inst of Materia Medica, Academia Sinica; Chmn, Dept of Phytochem, Vice Chmn, Sci Cncl, Shanghai Inst of Materia Medica, Academia Sinica, 1978-; Sabbatical leave to Suntory Inst for Bio-org Rsch, Japan & Dept of Chem, Columbia Univ, USA, 1981-83. Publications: Natural Products Chemistry, 1993, and three other books in Chinese; Over 100 sci pprs published in Chinese and other intl jrnls. Honours: 2nd Prize of Natural Scis, Natl Cttee of Sci & Technol, China, 1982; 3rd Prize of Natural Scis, 1990. Memberships: Chinese Pharm Assn; Chem Soc of China; Soc of Medicinal Plant Rsch (Eurn); VP, Shanghai Pharm Assn; Co-opted Mbr, Sec of Medicinal Chem, IUPAC. Address: Shanghai Institute of Materia Medica, Academia Sinica, 319 Yue-yang Road, Shanghai 200031, China.

XU Rongchu. Govt Offic. Appointments: Dir Dept of Fixed Assets Invmnt State Plng Commn, 1988-93; Pres State Comms Invmnt Corp, 1993-. Address: State Communications Corporation, Beijing, People's Republic of China.

XU Shu Yun, b. Jiangchuan, Yunnan, China. Researcher. Education: Yuxi Agricl Sch. Appointment: Rschr, Yunnan Tobacco Rsch Inst. Publications: Over 30 rsch pprs in profl jrnls. Membership: Entomol Assn of China. Address: Institute of Yunnan, Yu Xi, Yunnan 653100, China.

XU Xiao-zhong, b. 7 Oct 1928, Nanjing, China. Director; President; Vice President. m. Huang Ui-lin, July 1957, 2 s. Education: Nanjing Natl Drama Trng Sch, 1948; Ctrl Acady of Drama, 1949-51; Dept of Directing, Lunacharsky Natl Acady of Drama, Russia, 1955-60. Appointments: Students Drama Movement, Wuhan City, 1955; Ldr, Tchng & Rsch Section of Directing Dept, 1960, Vice Dir, Dir, Dept of Directing, 1972-82, Pres, 1983-, Ctrl Acady of Drama, Beijing. Creative Works include: Directed: Macbeth (Shakespeare), 1981, Peer Gynt (Ibsen), 1983, Chronicle of Sang Shu Ping, 1988, The Cherry Orchard (Anton Chekhov), 1995, Qu Yuan (Chinese Play), 1995; Opera: Turandot. Publication: Introduction to Stage Directing, 1983. Honours: 1st Prize, Natl Fest, 1980; Ex Prize, Beijing Dramatic Criticism, 1987. Memberships: 2nd Session Acad Commenting Grp; Deg Cttee of State Cncl; Art Educn Cttee, China Natl Educn Cttee; Educn Cttee, Intl Th Inst, UNESCO; VP, Study Assn of Chinese Drama Art; VP, Soc of Chinese Trad Opera. Hobbies: Chinese Classical Opera; Music; Fiddle (Jing Hu). Address: Central Academy of Drama, 39 Mianhua Hutong, Beijing, China.

XU Xue Ji, b. 8 Aug 1934, Shanghai, China. Professor. m. Liu Bi Ying, Feb 1963, 1 s, 1 d. Education: Grad, Phys, Fudan Univ, Shanghai, 1952-56. Appointments: Tchng Asst, Phys Dept, 1958-60, Lectr, Dir, Rsch Lab for Plasma Phys, Phys II Dept, 1960-69, Lectr, Optics Dept, 1970-77, Assoc Prof, Inst for Elec Light Sources, 1978-85, Prof, Chmn, Dept of Light Sources and Illuminating Engrng, 1985-, Fudan Univ; Visng Schl, Natl Bur of Stands, USA, 1981-82; Guest Prof, Ruhr Univ, Bochum, Germany and Orleans Univ, France, 1988-89; Guest Prof, Tokyo Denki Univ, Japan, 1994. Publications: 60 pprs publd in sci jrnls, inclng: Lidar for Smoke Pollution Detection; 125, 250 and 400 watt Metal Halide Lamps; Radiance Meter for Nuclear Explosion. Honours: Shanghai Sci and Tech Awd, 1982, 1987; Sci and Tech Awd, Natl Agricl, Animal Husbandry and Fishery, 1987. Memberships: Cnclr, Chinese Illuminating Soc; Cnclr, Chinese Soc of Luminescence; Chinese Physl Soc. Address: Department of Light Sources & Illuminating Engineering, Fudan University, 220 Handan Road, Shanghai 200433, China.

XU Xurong, b. 23 Apr 1922, Jinan, Shandong, China. Physics Researcher. m. Yuying Liu, 13 Feb 1950, 2 s, 1 d. Education: Cand, Soviet Union Acady of Scis, Lebedev Inst of Phys. Appointments: Dir, Hon Dir, Changchun Inst of Phys; VP, Changchun Branch, Chinese Acady of Scis, 1980-85. Publications: Unification of Contradicted Theory of Mechanism of Recombination Luminescence; Discovery of Hot Electrons; Direct Proof of Impact Ionization in Electroluminescence. Honours: Model Worker, Prov Jilin, 1983; Excellent Rschr, Tianjin; 2nd Class Sci and Technol Prize of Chinese Acady of Scis, 1989. Membership: Chmn, Chinese Luminescence Soc, 1980-. Hobbies: Sport; Different ball games. Address: Optoelectronics Institute, Northern Jiaotong University, Sizhimenwai Shangyuancun, Beijing 100044, China.

XU Ya-Bo, b. 11 Mar 1931, Hangzhou, China. Professor. m. Bi-ru Wu, 1 Jan 1957, 2 s. Education: Grad, Phys Dept, Zhejiang Univ, 1951. Appointments: Asst, 1951-56, Lectr, 1956-78, Assoc Prof, 1978-85, Chmn, Phys Dept, 1981-88, Prof, 1985-, Zhejiang Univ; Visng Sci, Fitz-Haber Inst of Max-Planck-Gesellschaft, W Berlin, Germany, 1979-81. Publications: Adsorption on Ni(110) at 20K, 1982; UPS Study of GaAs(100)(4x1) Surface, 1984; Step-related surface states on vicinal surfaces of Si (100), 1987; Metallic surface states on Si (100)-(2x1), 1987; Introduction to surface physics (in Chinese), 1992; Oscillations in the Photoionization cross sections of C60, 1996. Memberships: Chinese Physl Soc; VP, Zhejiang Prov Br Soc of Chinese Physl Soc. Listed in: Who's Who in Australasia and the Far East. Address: Physics Department, Zhejiang University, Hangzhou, China.

XU Yinsheng, b. 12 Jun 1938. Govt Offic. m. Chen Liwen, 1 s. Appointments: World table tennis champion three times; Vice-Min State Physl Culture and Sport Commn, 1977-; Pres Chinese Table Tennis Assn, 1979-; Pres Chinese Boxing Assn, 1987-; Exec Vice-Chmn Preparatory Cttee for 6th Natl games, 1985; VP Chinese Olympic Cttee, 1986-89, 1994-; VP All-China Sports Fedn, 1989-; Exec VP XIth Asian Games Organizing Cttee, 1990-; Pres Intl Table Tennis Fedn, 1997-; NPC Dep Shangdong Prov. Publication: How to Play Table Tennis by Dialectics. Hobbies: Tennis; Fishing. Address: 9 Tiyuguan Road, Beijing, People's Republic of China.

XU Youfang, b. 1939, Guangde Co, Anhui Prov, China. Politician. Education: Anhui Agricl Coll. Appointments: Dir, Forestry Ind Bur, Min of Forestry, 1985; Vice Min for Forestry, 1986-93, Min, 1993-; Dpty Dir, State Cncl, Environt Protection Commn; Dir, China Forestry Sci and Techl Commn; Vice-Chair, Natl Afforestation Commn, 1993-; Chair, Beijing Univ of Forestry, 1994-; Pres, China Wildlife Conservation Assn, 1993-; Sec, CCP Heilongjiang Prov Cttee, 1997-; Mbr, 15th CCP Cntrl Cttee, 1997-. Address: Office of the

Governor, Heilongjiang Provincial Government, Harbin City, China.

XU Zhenci, b. 25 Oct 1951, Ding Zhou, Hebei Prov, China. Researcher, Water Resources Science. m. Li Yanxue, 2 Feb 1977, 1 s. Education: Spec postgrad Dip, Intl Cntr for Advd Mediterranean Agronomic Studies. Appointments: Assoc Prof, 1987-94; Dir, Water Resources Dev Cntr of Hebei, 1994-98; Dir, Hebei Inst of Water Resources Rsch, 1998-. Honours: Expert, winner of the State Spec Bonus, 1996; Leading Rschr, Water Resources Mngmt, 1998. Memberships: Assn of Water Conservancy; Soc of Agricl Ecology. Hobbies: Reading; Sport; Music. Address: No 310, Taihua Street, Shijiazhuang 050051, China.

XU Zhiwei, b. 16 May 1952, Shanghai, China. Pediatric Cardiovascular Surgeon. m. Yang Fumei, 5 Nov 1981, 1 s. Education: MD, Shanghai Second Med Univ, 1976; Clin Rsch Fell, Hosp for Sick Children, Toronto, Can, 1986-87. Appointment: Vice Chf, Dept of Pediat Thoracic and Cardiovascular Surg, Xinhua Hosp, Shanghai. Publications: Surgical Repair of Venticulon Septal Defect on 2085 Pediatric Patients; Effect of Deep Hypothermia and Low-Flow Cardiopulmonary Bypass on Cerebral Function: An Experimental Study. Membership: Thoracic and Cardiovascular Surg Assn, China. Hobbies: Sports; Music. Address: Department of Cardiovascular and Thoracic Surgery, Shanghai Childrens Medical Center, 1678 Dongfang Road, Shanghai 200127, China.

XUE Ju, b. 1922 Yuncheng Shanxi. Politician. Education: Datong Univ Shanghai. Appointments: Joined CCP, 1938; Dep Sec CCP Cttee Zhejiang, 1978-79; Vice-Chmn Prov CPPCC Cttee Zhejiang, 1979-83; Gov of Zhejiang, 1983-87; Sec Zhejiang CCP Cttee, 1987-88; Chmn CCP Zhejiang Provincial Advsry Cttee, 1988-92; Exec VP Cntrl Party Sch, 1989; NPC Dep Zhejiang Prov; Chmn Law Cttee. Memberships: Mbr 12th Cntrl Cttee, 1982-87; Mbr Presidium 6th NPC, 1986; Mbr Presidium 14th CCP Natl Cnogress, 1992; Mbr 8th NPC, 1993-; Mbr Cntrl Ldng Grp for Party Bldg Wrk. Address: Zhejiang Provincial People's Government, Hangzhou, Zhejiang Province, People's Republic of China.

XUE Lan, b. 25 June 1959, Beijing, China. Professor. m. Xiaoping Li, 1985, 1 s. Education: BEng, Changchu Inst of O&M, 1982; MSc, SUNY, 1986, 1987; PhD, Carnegie Mellon, 1991. Appointments: Instr, Changchun Inst, 1982-85; Rsch and Trng Asst, SUNY and CMU, 1985-91; Asst Prof, Geo Wash Univ, 1991-96; Prof, Dpty Dir, Tsinghua Univ. Publications: Ed, writer of books, book chapts, jrnl articles, over 40, 1991-98. Honours: Stephen Lee Awd, 1991; Dithy Fellshp, 1993; PRIDE Awd, 1994. Memberships: Chinese Economist Soc; Tech Transfer Soc, Wash Chapt, BdDir and VP; CAST, Wash, Pres, 1996-96. Hobbies: Reading; Table tennis; Tai-Chi; Travel. Address: Development Research Academy for the 21st Century, Tsinghua University, Beijing 100084, China.

XUE Qi-ming, b. 28 Dec 1928, Jiangsu, China. Doctor; Medical Scientist. m. Wu Zhong-xuan, 31 Jan 1959, 1 s. Education: Medl Coll, Natl Chekiang Univ, 1952; MD, Hsiang-Ya Medl Coll, 1953. Appointments: Asst Res to Visng Physn, Beijing Medl Coll, 1953-60; Chf, Assoc Prof, Prof, Beijing Friendship Hosp, 1961-91. Publications: 5 books; 130 pprs; 17 reviews. Honours: Testimonials and Medals: Tohoku Univ, Kitasato Univ, Japan, 1980, 1983; Montreal Neurol Inst, 1987; Johns Hopkins Univ, USA, 1987. Memberships: Intl Soc Neurochem (ISN); Intl Brain Rsch Orgn (IBRO); Intl Soc Dev Neurosci (ISDN). Address: New Apt 1-3-1, Beijing Friendship Hospital (affiliate of Capital University of Medical Sciences), 95 Yong-an Road, Beijing 100050, China.

XUE Yongbiao, b. 2 Jan 1963, Taiyuan, China. Geneticist. m. Junqing Wang, 24 Jan 1987, 1 s. Education: BS, Lanzhou Univ, China, 1983; MSc, Inst Dev Bio, Acady Sinica, Beijing, 1986; PhD, Univ E Anglia, Norwich, UK, 1989. Appointments: Postdoct Fell, Univ of Oxford and John Innes Scientist, John Innes Cntr, Norwich, Eng, 1995-97; Prof of Dev Bio, 1996-.

Publications: Num rsch pprs to sci jrnls. Honours: ORS Awd, UK, 1986-89; K C Wong (Hong Kong) Fell, 1995, 1996. Memberships: Dpty Dir, Acad Sinica Plant Biotechnology Lab; Vice-Chmn, Acad Advsry Cttee of Inst Dev Bio, Beijing. Address: Institute of of Devel Biology, Chinese Academy of Sciences, PO Box 2707, Beijing 10080, China.

Y

YABUKI Nobuyoshi, b. 21 July 1959, Tokyo, Japan. Educator; Associate Professor. m. Tomoko, 15 Mar 1986, 2 s. Education: BE, Univ Tokyo, 1982; MS, 1989, PhD, 1992, Stanford Univ. Appointments: Des Off, Elec Power Dev Co Ltd, 1982-86; Kumaushi Hydropower Constrn Off, 1986-88; Des Off, 1992-94, Engrng Rsch Inst, 1994-97; Intl Activities Dept, 1997-99; Muroran Inst of Technol, Dept of Civ Engrng and Architecture, 1999-. Publication: An Integration Framework for Design Standard Processing, 1992. Honour: Fulbright Schl, 1988. Memberships: ASCE; IEEE; AAAI; ACM; Japan Soc of Civil Engrs. Hobbies: Piano; Igo; Astronomy; Music. Address: 2-35-12 Takasago-cho, Muroran-shi 050-8585, Japan.

YABUSHITA Shin, b. 4 Feb 1936, Osaka, Japan. Educator. m. Eiko, 1 Oct 1966, 2 d. Education: BEng, 1958, MEng, Kyoto Univ; PhD, Theort Astron, Cambridge, UK. Appointments: Univ MD; Yale Univ; Lectr, 1969, Assoc Prof, 1971, Prof, 1996, Prof Emer, 1999, Kyoto Univ, Japan. Publications: In profl jrnls. Memberships: Roy Astron Soc (London); Intl Astronomical Union. Hobby: Classic cars. Address: 8 babawakicho, Shuakuin, Sakyoku, Kyoto 606, Japan.

YACOOB Shaista, b. 9 Feb 1975, Bangalore, India. m. Zahir Ammed, 6 Jan 1997, 1 d. Education: BA, Mount Carnel Coll, Bangalore. Creative Works: Poets Intl; The Quest; Asian Age; Skylark; ors. Honours: Poet of the Month, SCORIA. Hobbies: Yoga; Painting; Music; Socl services. Address: 8 Benson Cross Road, Benson Town, Bangalore 560046, India.

YADAV Suryadeen, b. 15 July 1952, Dhaha, India. Lecturer. m. Sarita, 2 s, 2 d. Education: BEd; MA; PhD. Appointment: Lectr, MS Patel, Vidyalaya, Alindra. Publications: Books, short stories, novels, reviews, play, poems and sev articles in profl jrnls. Honours include: 1st Awd, Hindi Shahitya Acady; Padavi, Jamini Sahitya Acady. Hobbies: Reading; Writing. Address: 3 Puneet, Coloney Near Parag Society, Pavan Chakki Road, Nadiad Gujarat 387002, India.

YAGABO Dibara, b. 1959. Minister for Provincial and Local-Level Government. Appointments: Owner, Dibsy Landscape Gardening Pty Ltd, 1980-; Self-Employed; Elected to Parl, 1992; Shadow Min, Pub Serv and Labour and Employment, 1994; Shadow Min for Fisheries, 1995; Min for Fin; Min for Provincial and Local-level Gov. Membership: Peoples Natl Cong Party.

YAGUCHI Koichi, b. 20 Feb 1920. Former Chief Justice of the Supreme Court of Japan. m. Kazuko Sakamoto, 16 Dec 1946, dec, 2 s. Education: Passed the Higher Civ Serv (Judicial) Exam, 1943; LLB, Fac of Law, Kyoto Imperial Univ, 1943. Appointments: Chf Judge, Tokyo Family Crt, 1978; Sec Gen of the Supreme Crt, 1980; Pres, Tokyo High Ct, 1982; Jus of the Supreme Crt, 1984; Chf Jus of the Supreme Crt, 1985; Retd, 1990. Honours: La Orden del Libertador San Martin Gran Cruz, Argentina, 1986; Order du Mérite du Niger Grand-Croix, Niger, 1986; Order of the White Rose of Finland Grand Cross, Finland, 1986; La Condecoración del Aguila Azteca en Grado de Banda, Mexico, 1986; La Orden del Libertador en el Grado de Gran Cordón, Venezuela, 1988; Ordre du Mérite Grand-Croix, Senegal, 1988; Grand Cordon of the Order of the Rising Sun, Paulownia Flowers, Japan, 1993. Hobby: Golf.

YAKOVER Yosef, b. 21 Dec 1950, Moscow, USSR. Physicist. m. Diana, 4 Apr 1981, 2 s. Education: MSc, Univ Vilnius, 1973; PhD, Univ Minsk, USSR, 1984. Appointments: Engr, Snr Engr, Rschr, Sci Rsch Inst of Radio, Vilnius, 1973-89; Snr Rschr, Zondas Co, 1990; Snr Rschr, Dept of Phys Elec, Univ of Tel-Aviv, 1991-. Publications: About 60 Pprs in Sci Jrnls. Honours: USSR Inv Medal, 1989. Hobbies: Travelling; Music; Photography. Address: Tel Aviv University, Dept of Phys Elec, P O B 39040, 69978 Ramat Aviv, Tel Aviv, Israel.

YAMADA Shichi, b. 16 Sept 1930, Aichi, Japan. Electronic and Computer Engineering. m. Kuni Ko, 24 Nov 1959, 1 s. Education: DEng, Nagoyu Univ. Appointments: BS, Electr Engin, Nagoya Inst of Technol, Japan, 1953; Asst of Nagoya Univ, 1953-56; Chf Rschr, Hitachi Rsch Lab, 1956-79; Prof of Electr Engin, 1979-97. Publication: System Engineering. m. Honours: Kantodenki Kyokai Prize, 1965; No 19 OHM Prize, Elec Soc Engrng Cttee, 1971; Invention Cttee of Japan Prize, 1977. Memberships: SCIE; Electron Comm Engrng of Japan; Electr Engin of Japan; Info Processing Soc of Japan; Soc of Fuzzy Theory and Systems; Acady of Sci, Am. Address: Musashi Institute of Technology, 1-28-1 Tamazutsumi Setagaya Tokyo 158-8557, Japan.

YAMAGUCHI Akira, b. 15 Oct 1940, Ayabe, Kyoto, Japan. Professor of Nagoya Institute of Technology. m. Shunko, 11 June 1972, 2 s, 1 d. Education: Doctor. Appointments: Assoc Prof, NIT, 1978-89; Prof, NIT, 1989-. Publications: Books: 12 vols incl How to Use Phase Diagram, 1997; 74 pprs. Honours: Ceramic Soc of Japan Awd, Advd Achievement in Ceramic Sci and Technol, 1972; New Technol Dev Fndn Awd for Technol Contbn, 1981; Tech Assm of Refractories of Japan: Awd for Excellent Pprs, 1984, Awd for Disting Contbn, 1993; Japanese Soc for Engrng Educ Awd for Excellent Writings, 1994; Ceramic Soc of Japan Awd for Acad Achievement in Ceramic Sci and Technol, 1995. Memberships: Ceramic Soc of Japan; Amn Ceramic Soc; Tech Assn of Refractories; Japan; Iron and Steel Inst of Japan. Hobbies: Music; Travel; Address: 5-5-3, Iwanaridai, Kasugai, Aichi, 487-0033, Japan.

YAMAGUCHI Kenji, b. 19 July 1933, Japan. m. Mamoe Matsumoto, 18 May 1962, 1 s, 1 d. Education: BEcon, Tokyo Univ, 1956; Equiv MA, Acady of Theort Econs, 1962; Diplomat Trng Inst, Min of For Affairs, 1971-72; Exec Cncl for Dev, USA. Appointments: Cnsl for Japan, Sydney, Aust, 1972-75; Cnslr, Personel Bur, PM Off, 1975-77; Dir, Natl Property Div, Min of Fin, 1977-81; Dir Gen, NE Fin Bur, Min of Fin, 1981-82; Spec Asst, For Mins, 1982-87; Exec Dir, IBRD, IDA, IFC, 1982-87; Dean, Bd, 1985-87; Snr Exec Dir, Water Resources Dev Pub Corp, 1988; Coordinating Mngr, OISCA, Tokyo, 1993-97; Exec Advsr to Mitsui Trust Bank, Tokyo; Chmn for Mitsui Trust Intl (London) and Mitsui Trust Bank (Switz), Zurich; Exec Advsr, Chiyoda Life Ins, 1997-. Publications include: Japan-Aust Relations, 1977; Dean of the Bd, 1985; The World Bank, 1995; Land is Public Property, 1997. Honours: Life Rescue Awd, 1954; Min for Fin Awd, 1956; Hon 25 yr serv, Min of Fin, 1981. Memberships: Intl Toastmasters Club, USA; Inst of Pub Affairs, Aust; World Econ Cncl, USA; Rep of World Econ and Land Lab, 1995. Hobbies: Swimming; Skiing; Golf; Reading; Music; International affairs. Listed in: International Who's Who; Who's Who in India. Address: 3-16-43, Utsukushiga-oka, AOBA-KU, Yokohama City, 225-0002, Japan.

YAMAGUCHI Shigeru, b. 4 Nov 1932, Chiba, Japan. Education: Grad, Fac of Law, Kyoto Univ, 1955. Appointments: Asst Judge, Okayama Dist Crt, Family crt, 1957; Judge, Hakodate Dist Crt, 1967; Dir of the Sec, Rsch and Trng Inst for Crt Clks, 1969; Judge, Tokyo Dist Crt, 1976; Dir of the Sec, Tokyo High Crt, 1980; Dir, Gen Affairs, Bur of the Gen Sec of the Supreme Crt, 1983; Pres, Kofu Dist Crt, Family Crt, 1988; Judge, Tokyo High Crt, 1989; Pres, Legal Trng, Rsch Inst, 1991; Pres, Fukuoka High crt, 1994; Jus, Supreme Crt, 1997; Chf Jus, Supreme Crt, 1997. Address: Supreme Court of Japan, 4-2 Hayabusa-cho, Chiyoda-ku, Tokyo 102-8651, Japan.

YAMAGUCHI Tsuruo. Politician. Appointments: Chmn Socl Dem Party of Japan - SDPJ - Diet Affairs Cttee; Gen-Sec SDPJ; Min of state Dir Gen Mngmnt and Co-ord Agcy, 1994-95; Chmn Budget Cttee. Memberships: Mbr HoR for Guma. Address: c/o Management and Co-ordintion Agency, 3-1-1, Kasumigaseki, Chiyoda-ku, Tokyo, Japan.

YAMAMOTO Masahiro, b. 22 Nov 1933, Wakayama, Japan. Physician; Researcher; Hospital Director. m. Kazuko Mio, 26 July 1963, 3 s. Education: MD, Sch of Med, 1959; PhD, Grad Sch, Osaka Univ, Japan, 1965. Appointments: Rsch Assoc in Biochem, Pitts Univ, USA, MI State Univ, 1966-68; Lectr, 1971-74, Assoc Prof, 1975-79, Internal Med, Lectr, 1979-, Chiba Univ, Japan; Hd, 3rd Dept, Internal Med, 1979-90, Assoc Dir, 1988-90, Dir, 1990-, Nissei Hosp, Osaka; Lectr, Osaka Univ, 1979-; VP, Local Med Assn, 1994-. Publications: 12 talks on Ginseng Research, 1987; Many books and pprs on Internal Med, Pharmacology and Biochem. Honour: Soc Awd, Med Pharm Soc Wakan-Yaku, 1995. Memberships: Japanese Endocrinology Soc; Japanese Soc Internal Med; Fmr Mbr, NY Acady of Sci, USA. Address: Director, Nissei Hospital, Nishi-ku, Osaka 550-0012, Japan.

YAMAMOTO Takuma, b. 11 Sep 1925 Kumamoto. Businessman. Appointments: Joined Fujitsu Ltd, 1949; Bd Dir, 1975-; Mngng Dir, 1976-79; Exec Dir, 1979-81; Pres and Rep Dir, 1981-90; Vice-Chmn Comm Inds Assn of Japan, 1986; Chmn Japan Electron Ind Dev Assn, 1987-89; Vice-Chmn Japan Electron Ind Devt Assn, 1989-; Chmn Cttee on Intl Co-ord of Econ Policies - KEIDANREN - 1988-; Chmn and Rep Dir Fujitsu Ltd, 1990-. Honours: Blue Ribbon with Medal of Honour, 1984; Hon Dr Hum Litt - Chaminade Univ of Honolulu. Hobbies: River-fishing; Golf; Gardening. Address: Fujitsu Ltd, 1-6-1 Marunouchi, Chiyoda-ku, Tokyo 100, Japan.

YAMANAKA Nobuhiko, b. 26 Nov 1960, Warabi, Saitama, Japan. Linguist. Education: BA, Tokyo Univ, 1983; MA, Grad Sch, Tokyo Univ, 1986. Appointments: Asst Prof, 1987-90, Assoc Prof, 1990-, Saitama Univ. Publications: Sev articles in profl jrnls. Memberships: Intl Pragmatics Assn; Ling Soc of Japan; Soc for the Study of Japanese Lang. Address: Saitama University, 255 Simo-ookubo, Urawa 338 8570, Japan.

YAMANE Linus, b. 19 Apr 1959, Los Angeles, CA, USA. Professor of Economics. 1 s. Education: PhD, Yale Univ. Appointments: Wellesley Coll, 1994-96; Pitzer Coll, 1996-. Memberships: Amn Econ Assn; Phi Beta Kappa, 1981. Hobby: Tae Kwon Do. Address: 1050 North Mills Avenue, Claremont, CA 91711, USA.

YAMANI Hashim bin Abdullah bin Hashim al. Politician. Education: Harvard Univ. Appointments: Prof and later Chmn Physics Dept King Fahd Univ of Pet and Minerals; VP King Abdul Aziz Cty for Sci and Tech; Dir Dept of Energy Rescs Rsch Inst King Fahd Univ of Pet and Minerals; Min of Ind and Electricity, 1995-. Address: Ministry of Industry and Electricity, P O Box 5729, Omar bin al-Khatab Street, Riyadh 11432, Saudi Arabia.

YAMANOUCHI Shuichiro, b. 10 July 1933, Tokyo. Chairman. m. Misako Y, 21 May 1960, 1 s, 1 d. Education: Grad, Tokyo Univ, 1956. Creative Works: If there were no Shinkansen Train; Railway and Information Systems; others. Honours: Min of Transp Prize; Offr de l'Ordre Natl du Merit. Memberships: Union Intl de Chemins de fer; World Exec Cncl. Hobbies: Music; Travel; Art. Address: 2-2-2 Yoyogi, Shibuya-ku, Tokyo 151-8578, Japan.

YAMASHITA Yasuhiro, b. 1 June 1957, Kumamoto, Japan. Judo Player and Coach. m. Midori Ono, 1986, 2 s, 1 d. Education: MA, Tokai Univ. Appointments: Prof, Dept Sports, Tokai Univ, 1986-; Team Mgr, Univ Judo Team, 1988-; Mgr, Japanese Natl Judo Team, 1990-. Publications include: Young Days with Black Belt; Enjoyable Judo; The Moment of Fight; Osoto-Gari; Judo with Fighting Spirits. Honours include: Winner, 9 consecutive times, All Japan Judo Tournament; World Judo Champion, 1979, 1981, 1983; Unbroken record of 203 consecutive wins before retd, 1977; Sev awds. Address: 1117 Kitakaname, Hitatsuka Kanagawa, 259-12 Japan.

YAN Chengzhong, b. 15 Apr 1946, Shanghai, China. Researcher; Teacher; Consultant. m. Q Y Wang, 28 Sept 1970, 1 d. Education: BA equiv, Engl, Shanghai Normal Univ, 1967; MA, Econs, Shanghai Acady of Socl Scis, 1982; MA student, Indl Rels, Univ of Warwick, 1988-90. Appointments: Rsch Fell, SASS, 1988; Visng Prof, York Univ, Can, 1990; Dean, Dept of Engl for Bus, 1990; Dpty

Chmn, Bus Sch, E China Univ of Sci and Technol (ECUST), 1991. Publications: China's Township Enterprises, 1988; MBO Practice in China, 1991; An Oral English Course for Chinese Interpeters, 1996; International Economic Cooperation, 1998. Honours: Shanghai Govt Awd, 1986; Sino-Brit Friendship Schlshp Scheme, 1988; Dpty Chmn, Coventry-Jinan Friendship Assn, 1989; ECUST Awd, 1993. Memberships: Shanghai Econs Assn; Shanghai Behavioral Scis Assn; Dpty Pres, Shanghai Qian Jin Coll; WGA Warwick Univ, Eng. Hobbies: Swimming; Bridge; Reading; Tourism. Address: College of Business and Economics, ECUST, 130 Meilong Road, Shanghai 200237, China.

YAN Ming, b. 18 Mar 1945. Teacher. m. 9 Dec 1972, 2 s. Education: Master, Shanghai Jiao Tong Univ, 1982. Appointments: Assoc Prof 1988, Prof 1992, Shanghai Jiao Tong Univ. Publications: Aircraft Dynamic Response to Variable Wing Sweep Geometry, 1988; Aerodynamic-Guidance-Trajectory Simulation of Tactical Missile, 1989; The Numerical Simulation of Unsteady Multi-Nozzle Exhaust in the Chamber During Missile Separation, 1997. Honours: 1st Awd, Shanghai Sci and Tech Achmnts, 1992; 3rd Awd, Natl Sci and Tech Achmnt, 1993; Reward for Nominees, Talent in Shanghai Sci and Tech Circles, 1995. Memberships: Snr Mbr, AIAA; Fell, China Soc of Computational Fluid Dynamics. Hobbies: Travel; Basketball. Address: Department of Engineering Mechanics, Shanghai Jiao Tong University, 1954 Hua Shan Road, Shanghai 200030, China.

YAN Pengfei, b. Oct 1946, Yiyan, Hunan, China. Professor. Education: Bach Deg, Econs, Beijing Univ, China, 1969; Master Deg, Econs, Wuhan Univ, China, 1981. Appointments: Prof, PhD Advsr, Dean of Econ Dept, Wuhan Univ, China. Publications: The School of Radical Political Economics; Free Market or State Intervention; The Evolution of Two Basic Economic Thought Trends of the West; History of Marxist Economics; The History of Western Economics; The Insurance History of China. Honours: Awd'd Spec Govt Subsidies. Memberships: VP, For Econs Theory Rsch Soc, China; Pres, For Econs Theory Rsch Soc; Dir, China On Capital Rsch Soc; Stndng Dir, China Marxist Econ Doctrine Assn. Address: College of Economics, Wuhan University, Wuhan, Hubei, China.

YAN Shaoyi, b. 7 Feb 1932, Jiangsu Prov, China. m. Youhua Fa, 2 s. Education: Grad, Dept of Zool, Shandong Univ, China, 1953; Dr of Sci, Hokkaido Univ, Japan, 1992. Appointments: Res Asst, Inst of Oceanology, 1953, Inst of Zool, 1960, Assoc Prof, 1978, Assoc Prof, Dpty Dir IDB, 1980, Prof, Dir, Inst of Developmental Bio, 1986, Chinese Acady of Scis. Publication: Cloning in Fish: Nucleocytophosmic Hybrids, 1998. Honours: 1st Place, Awd of Sci Rsch, CAS Inst Marine Bio, 1955; Awd of Impt and Great Achmnt in Sci Rsch, 1978; 1st Place, Guangzi Zhuang Autonomous Reg Agri Husbandry and Fisheries Bur, 1986; 2nd Place, 1987, 3rd Place, 1990, Min of Agric, China. Membership: Inst of Dev Bio, 1980-. Hobby: Reading. Address: Rm 504, Building 811, Zhong Guan Cun, Haidian District, Beijing 100080, China.

YAN Zhen Guo, b. 18 July 1933, Shanghai, China. Teacher. m. Mi Jing-hua, Aug 1960. Education: Bach Deg, Shandong Normal Univ, 1956. Appointments: Dpty Dir, Dir, Dept of Anatomy, Shanghai Univ of Trad Med, 1984-. Publications: Hanging Atlas of Acupoints, 1976; Dissective Atlas for Acupoints, 1980; Practical Analomical Charts of Acupuncture and Moxibustion, 1992; Normal Gross Anatomy; Local Anatomy. Honours: 15 awds. Memberships: Guest Rsch Fell, Med Dept, Osaka Univ, Japan; Hon Dir, Nippoxinlingai Tokyo Med Rsch Inst; Cttee, Assoc Dir, Shanghai Anatomy Sub-Assn, China Anatomy Assn; Edl Bd, Shanghai Jrnl of Acupuncture and Moxibustion. Hobbies: Music; Reading. Address: 530 Lingling Road, Shanghai University of Traditional Chinese Medicine, Shanghai 200032, China.

YAN Zongda, b. 5 May 1926, Shenyang, China. Professor of Solid Mechanics. m. Wang Hong, 1 Feb 1953, 1 s, 2 d. Education: Bachelor's degree, Dept of Civil Engrng, Peiyang Univ, Tianjin, 1948. Appointments: Asst, Peiyang Univ, 1948-51, Asst, 1951-52, Lectr, 1952-62, Assoc Prof, 1962-80, Prof, 1980-, Libn, 1985-92, Tianjin Univ. Publications: in Chinese: Theory of Plasticity, textbook, 1988; Fourier Series Solutions in Strutural Mechanics, monograph, 1989; Thermal Stresses (textbook), 1993. Memberships: Dir, Chinese Soc of Teort and Applied Mechanics; ASCE (Amn Soc of Civil Engrs). Hobbies: Bridge; 'Go'. Address: Deaprtment of Mechanics, Tianjin University, Tianjin 300072, China.

YAN Haiwang, b. Sept 1939 Zhengzhou Cty Henan Prov. Politician. Education: Harbin Archtl Engrng Inst. Appointments: Joined CCP, 1966; Vice-Gov Gansu Prov, 1987; Vice-Sec CCP Gansu Provincial Cttee, 1988; Gov Hansu Prov, 1993-; Sec CCP Gansu Provincial Cttee, 1993-. Memberships: Alt mbr 14th CCP Cntrl Cttee, 1992; Mbr 15th CCP Cntrl Cttee, 1997-. Address: Office of the Governor, Lanzhou City, Gansu Province, People's Republic of China.

YANAGISAWA Renzo, b. 21 Jan 1919, Togura, Nagano, Japan. Advisor, Democratic Socialist Association. m. Hideko Asahara, 12 May 1947, 1 s, 1 d. Appointments: Ishikawajima Shipyard, 1933; Japanese Imperial Navy (Air Patrol Squadron), 1940; Maintenance Offr High Class, 1945; Chmn, Ishikawajima Workers Union, 1949; Chmn, All Japan Shipbldg Workers Fedn, 1974; Elected as Mbr of House of Cnclrs (The Diet), 1977-89. Publications: Japan - A Part of the World, 1973; Strange Happenings in the Diet, 1982; Challenge to Reforms, 1987; Seeking a New Path, 1989. Honour: 2nd Class Order of the Sacred Treas, 1989. Memberships: Ctrl Labour Cttee, 1963; Dir, Japan Productivity Cntr, 1974; Vice Chmn, Domei (Japanese Confed of Labour), 1975; Exec Cttee, Democratic Socialist Party, 1979; Vice Chmn, Intl MRA Assn of Japan, 1984. Hobbies: Reading; Photography; Mountain climbing. Address: 4-18-6 Takaido-Higashi, Suginami-ku, Tokyo 168, Japan.

YANG Ao, b. 25 Nov 1929. Professor. m. Chang Guihua, 25 July 1957, 1 s, 1 d. Education: Dept of Mine & Metallurgy, Yunnan Univ, Kunming, 1948-52; Cntrl S Mine & Metallurgy Inst, Changsha, Hunan, 1954-56. Appointments: Vice Dean, Dean, Dept of Metallurgy and Mineral Processing, Kunming Inst of Technol, 1957-59; Gen Engr, Yao An Lead Mine, Yao An, Yunnan, 1959-60; Mngr, Sci and Rsch Dept, Kunming Inst of Technol, 1958-62; Dir, Higher Educ Rsch Off, Kunming Inst of Technol, 1989-92; Assoc Prof 1978-87, Prof 1987-, Kunming Inst of Technol; Higher Educ Insp, Yunnan Prov Educ Cttee, 1995-. Publications: Flotation, co-auth, 1983; Laboratory Administration, 1989; Flotation of Oxidized Lead and Zinc Ores, 1996; Co-transl, Principles of Flotation, 1966. Honours: Prizes, Yunnan Prov, 1989, 1995; Prize, Natl Educ Cttee, 1992; Prize, Yunnan Prov, 1992; Awd, Outstndng Contrbn, State Cncl, China, 1992. Memberships: Vice Sec-Gen, Yunnan Higher Educ Assn, 1987-92; Vice-Chmn, Bai Natl Assn, 1990-93. Hobbies: Swimming; Music; MTV; Tennis. Address: 121 Street, Kunming, Kunming University of Science and Technology, Kunming 650093, China.

YANG Chang Shu, b. 27 Jan 1947, Shanghai. Consultant Geologist. m. Qianhui Huang, 2 Oct 1974, 1 s. Education: PhD, Nanjing Univ, China, 1989. Appointments: Geol, Min of Geol, China, 1976-81; Snr Geol, 1984-87; Snr geol, SedCon, Netherlands, 1987-89; Snr Geol, InterGeos, Netherlands, 1989-94; Snr Geol, IGC, Netherlands, 1994-96; Cnslt Geol, YGC, Netherlands, 1997-; Geol Advsr, Aker Geo, Norway, 1997-. Creative Works: Application of High Frequency Cycle Analysis in High Resolution Sequence Stratigraphy; Applications of High Resolution Sequence Stratigraphy to the Upper Rotliegend in the Netherlands Offshore; Milankovitch Cyclicity in the Upper Rotliegend Group of the Netherlands; Tidal Sand Ridges on the East China Sea Shelf; The Estimation of Palaeohydrodynamics Processes from Subtidal Deposits Using Tim Series Analysis Methods. Memberships: Amn Assn of Petroleum Geols; SEPM; Petroleum Geol Circle of the Netherlands. Hobbies: Reading; Swimming; Sightseeing. Address: Torenwacht 5, 2353 DB Leiderdorp, The Netherlands.

YANG Chen-Chung, b. 15 July 1927, Taiwan. Professor. m. Yang Yeh-Hsiang, 18 Dec 1951, 2 s, 3 d. Education: MD, Natl Taiwan Univ, 1950; DMedSc, Tokyo Jikei Univ, Japan, 1956; Rsch Assoc, Univ WI, USA, 1961-62. Appointments: Prof, Biochem, 1958-73, Pres, 1967-73, Kaohsiung Medl Coll; Natl Rsch Chair Prof, Natl Sci Cncl, 1964-67; Dir, Inst Molecular Bio, Natl Tsing Hua Univ, 1973-85; Prof, Inst Life Scis, 1985-94; Disting Chair Prof, Natl Tsing Hua Univ, 1994-; Chmn, Advsry Cttee, Inst Biol Chem, Academia Sinica, 1994-; Mbr, Exec Bd, Cntrl Advsry Cttee, Academia Sinica, 1995-. Publications: Over 150 rsch articles in intl jrnls. Honours: 1 of 10 Outstndng Young Men, 1965; Chuang Shou-Keng Sci Awd, 1974; Premier's Awd, Outstndng Scientist, 1983; Outstndng Rsch Awd, Natl Sci Cncl, 1985-95; Javits Neurosci Investigator Awd, Natl Inst Hlth, 1987-94; Elected Mbr, Life Mbr, Academia Sinica, Taipei, 1990. Memberships include: Cncl Mbr, Intl Soc Toxicology; Amn Chem Soc; The Protein Soc;; NY Acady Scis; Life Mbr, AAAS; Japanese Biochem Soc; Life Mbr, Chinese Biochem Soc; Life Mbr, Chinese Chem Soc; Formosan Medl Assn. Hobbies: Stamp collecting; Reading. Listed in: Who's Who in the World; International Who's Who of Intellectuals; International Book of Honor; Who's Who in Science and Engineering. Address: 61-5F West Compound, National Tsing Hua University, Hsinchu, Taiwan 300042.

YANG Chunghai, b. 4 Nov 1928, Shanghai, China. Chemist; Researcher. m. Wenyou Sha, 10 Feb 1959, 1 s. Education: BSc, Tangshan Jiaotung Univ, 1952. Appointments: Lectr, Anshan Inst of Iron and Steel, 1952-56; S E Univ, 1957-58; Snr Rschr, Inst of Atomic Energy, Chinese Acady of Sci, Beijing, 1958-61; Nanjing, 1961-73; Prof, Physl Chem, Nanjing Inst of Chem Technol, 1973-. Creative Works: Articles to Jrnl, Golloid and Interface Sci; Jrnl of Physl Chem; Chinese Jrnl of Chem Phys; Jrnl of Chinese Soc of Corrosion and Protection. Memberships: Amn Assn for the Advancement of Sci; NY Acady of Sci; Chinese Chem Soc. Hobby: Stamp collecting. Address: Department of Applied Chemistry, Nanjing Institute of Chemical Technology, 5 New Model Road, Nanjing Jiangsu 210009, China.

YANG Dah-Jung, b. 28 Feb 1931, Shanghai, China. Orthopedic Surgeon. m. D H Hsia, 30 Apr 1961, 1 s, 1 d. Education: MD, Natl Def Medl Cntr. Appointments: Prof in Surg, NDMC and Natl Yang-Min Univ; Cnslt, Orthopedic Surg, Taipei and Taichung Veteran Gen Hosp. Publications: Over 50 pprs in related medl jrnls. Honours: 6 medals from the govt; Over 10 var medl assns and hosps or medl cntrs. Memberships: Chinese Surg Assn; Chinese Orthopedic Assn; Chinese Jt Reconstruction Assn; Intl Coll of Surgs. Hobbies: Classical music; Chinese opera; Golf. Address: 29-3, Sec 4 Jen-ai Road, Taipei, Taiwan, China.

YANG Disheng, b. 17 Mar 1931. Professor. m. Cui Kunying, 1 Aug 1962, 2 d. Education: BPhil, Tsinghua Univ. Appointments: VP, HS, Tsinghua Univ, 1977-83; VP, Inst of Hums, 1985-93; Prof, Inst of Hums, Tsinghua Univ. Publications include: A Preliminary study of cultural synthesis and Innovation, 1988; The Traditional Ideas of the Value in China and Science, 1989; Chinese Traditional Thinking Way and Sciences - On Chinese Traditional Thinking Being Primitive Thinking, 1989; Inherit the May Fourth New Culture Movement, 1990; A Brief study about the Ancient Chinese Dialectic Thought and its Contribution to the Whole World, 1991; History of the development of materialism of China, 1994. Memberships: VP, China Confucianism Soc; VP, Jin Yuelin Acad Fndn; VP, Soc for Civilization of Chinese Spec Zone; Perm Mbr, Soc for Hist of Mod Chinese Philos. Hobbies: Poetry; Music. Address: Institute of Humanities, Tsinghua University, Beijing 100084, China.

YANG Henry T, b. 29 Nov 1940, Chungking, China. University Chancellor; Engineering Professor. m. Dilling, 2 Sept 1966, 2 d. Education: BSCE Natl Taiwan Univ, 1962; MSCE, W VA Univ, 1965; PhD, Cornell Univ, 1968.

Appointments: Asst Prof, 1969, Assoc Prof, 1972, Prof, 1976-94, Sch Hd, 1979-84, Dean Schs of Engrng, 1984-94, Neil A Armstrong Distinguished Prof of Aeronautics and Astronautics, 1988-94, Purdue Univ, Sch of Aeronautics and Astronautics; Chan, Univ of CA, Santa Barbara, 1994-. Pubications: 1 book; 160 jrnl articles on engrng. Honours: Fell, Amn Inst Of Aeronautics and Astronautics, 1985; Mbr, Natl Acady of Engrng, 1991; Mbr, Academia Sinica, 1992; Fell, Amn Soc Engrng Educ, 1993; Centennial Medal, Amn Soc of Engrng Educ, 1993; Recip, 12 outstndng tchng awds, Purdue Univ, 1970-94; Hon Doct, hc, Purdue Univ, 1996; Benjamin Garver Lamme Awd, Gold Medal, Amn Soc of Engrng Educ, 1998; Tau Beta Pi. Memberships: AIAA; ASME; ASCE; ASEE; Allied Signal Bd of Dirs, 1996-. Hobbies: Aerospace engineering; Aircraft structures; Structural dynamics and control; Transonic aeroelasticity; Finite elements; Composite materials; Seismic-and wind-structural control; Intelligent manufacturing systems; Engineering education. Address: University House, UC Santa Barbara, Santa Barbara, CA 93106, USA.

YANG Jae-Soo, b. 8 Apr 1959, Korea. Managing Director. m. Hyun-Ju Lim, 11 Jan 1986, 1 s, 1 d. Education: PhD, Elec and Computer Engrng Dept, NJ Inst of Technol, USA. Appointments: Plant Chf, Telegraph and Telephone Off, Min of Commns, 1981-82; Commn Offr, Air Force, 1982-85; Dir, Mngng Dir, Korea Telecom, 1985-. Publications: Wire Communication Engineering, 1987; Hello Internet, 1995; Peep Into Korea Internet, 1997; Computer Networks, 1999. Honours: Min of Info and Commns. Memberships: Cttee, Korean Inst of Commn Sci; Cttee, Korean Info Processing Inst. Hobbies: Golf; Mountain climbing; Tennis. Address: 407-1403 Sindong A Apt, Sadang 105, Tongjak, Seoul 156-090, Korea.

YANG Ji-yun, b. 14 Apr 1932, Beijing, China. Professor of Pediatrics. m. Cheng Bin Xu, 15 Sept 1957, 1 s, 1 d. Education: Grad, Beijing Med Univ, 1955; Visng Schl, Dept of Pediat Nephrol, Univ MN, USA, 1979-81. Appointments: Res, 1955-62, Attending Dr, 1962-82, Assoc Prof, 1983-85, Prof, 1985-, Chf, Nephrol Div, Pediat Dept, 1985-, 1st Tchng Hosp, Beijing Med Univ. Publications: 2 books, sev chapts in books, 5 pprs in Engl, sev in Chinese. Honours: Ex Contbrn to Med Sci, 1992; Prize, Achmnt of Sci and Technol, 1994. Memberships: Chinese Soc of Pediat Nephrol; Intl Pediat Nephrol Assn. Hobbies: Reading short stories; Travel. Address: Pediatric Department, First Teaching Hospital, Beijing Medical University, Beijing 100034, China.

YANG Jian Min, b. 21 June 1956, Linhai City, China. Doctor. m. Li Na, 14 Sept 1983, 1 s. Education: Bach Deg, 1978-83, Master Deg, 1985-88, Dr Deg, 1990-93, 3rd Mil Med Univ. Appointments: Res Physn, 1983, Chf Res, 1988, Vis Physn, 1989, Assoc Prof, Vice Chf Physn, 1994, Vice Deam of the Dept, 1998. Publications: Progress in Infectious Diseases, 1995; Modern Gastroenterology, 1997; Modern Diagnosis and Treatment of Gastrointernal Tumours, 1998. Honours: 2nd Prize, 1992, 3rd Prize, 1996, Sci & Technol Progress, PLA. Memberships: Chinese Med Assn, 1992. Hobby: Touring. Address: c/o Southwest Hospital, Chongqing 400038, China.

YANG Jin, b. 22 June 1925, Taiyuan, Shanxi, China. Teacher. m. Jin-xin Zhang, 20 Jan 1951, 2 s, 2 d. Education: MD, Sch of Med, Peking Univ, 1950. Appointments: Asst, Dept of Histol and Embryol, 1950-56, Lectr, 1956-60, Beijing Med Coll; Lectr, Dept of Histol and Embryol, 1960-79, Assoc Prof, 1979-86, Prof, 1986-, Capital Univ of Med Scis. Publications: Histology, 1981; Anatomy of Giant Panda, 1987; Chinese Encyclopaedia of Medical Sciences: Histology and Enbryology Volume, 1988; Neuroanatomy, 1988, 1993; Textbook of Histology and Embryology, 4th ed, 1994. Honour: Ex Scientist w Outstndng Achievements, Natl Cncl, China, 1991. Memberships: Mbr, 1954-, Stndng Cncl, 1978-94, Chinese Soc for Anatomical Scis; Chinese Soc of Zool, 1979-; Vice-Ed, Acta Anatomica Sinica, 1982-90, Ed-in-Chf, 1990-94; Vice-Ed, Acta Zoologica Sinica, 1995-; Intl Anatomical Nomenclature Cttee, London. Hobby: Music. Address: Dormitory of Beijing Medical University, #443 Unit 21 Building 8, Haidian District, Beijing 100083, China.

YANG Jing-Hao, b. 5 Feb 1926, Hangzhou, China. Professor of Composition; Chorus Conductor. m. 26 Dec 1949, 4 d. Education: Studied Composition, Shanghai Conservatory of Music, 1942-44; BEng, Hangzhou University, 1943-47. Appointments: Communist Yth League of China, Beijing, 1949; Chinese Musicians Assn, 1950; Tchr, Music Dept, Hebei Tchrs Coll, Tianjin, 1953; Tianjin Conservatory of Music, 1959-. Creative works: Composition incl: Over 100 songs and chorus wrks inclng: The New Song of The Countryside; The New Sixth Door; The Overture of Harvest; Music for chinese instruments orchestra. Publications: Harmonics; Method of Playing and Impromptu Accompaniment; Translator, Mackay's The Techniques of Modern Harmony. Memberships: Vice-Chmn, Tianjin Musicians Assn; Dir, Tianjin Lit and Art Union; Dir, Tianjin Aesthetics Assn; Dir, Beijing Chorus Soc. Address: No 15 Yong Xing Lane, Zheng Zhou Road, Heping District, Tianjin, China.

YANG Kun, b. 8 Oct 1901. Research Fellow; Professor. m. Zhang Ruoming, 31 May 1930, 2 s, 1 d. Education: MSc, 1923-26, PhD, 1927-30, Lyon Univ. Appointments: Prof, Univs, Beijing, 1931-47, Yun Nan Univ, 1948-77; Rsch Fell, PhD Dir, Inst of Ethnology, Chinese Acady of Socl Scis, 1978-96. Publications: Ethnos and Ethnology, 1983; Manual of Ethnology, 1984; Development History of Primitive Society, 1986; Yang Kun Works About Ethnology, 1991. Memberships: Fndr, 2nd Pres, Chinese Folklore Soc; Fndr, Advsr of Chinese Primitive Ethnology, Sociology, Anthropology Socs. Hobby: Study of Religion. Address: Building No 12, 1-2 Zao Jun Dong Li, Xue Yuan Nan Lu, Beijing 100081, China.

YANG Li Guo, b. 29 Aug 1962, Hunan, China. Teacher. m. Guo Aizhen, 28 Dec 1989, 1 d. Education: BAgr; MAgr; PhD. Appointments: Coll of Animal Sci and Technol, Nanjing Agricl Univ, 1985-. Publications: Animal Reproduction, 1997; Techniques and Theory of ELISA, 1998; Pig Reproduction, 1999. Honours: Outstndng Sci in China, 1998; Awd, Sci Achmnts, 1993, 1998. Memberships: Stndng Cttee, Intl Cong on Animal Reproduction; Stndng Cttee, Chinese Assn on Animal Reproduction. Address: College of Animal Science and Technology, Nanjing Agricultural University, Nanjing 210095, China.

YANG Li Qing, b. 30 Apr 1942, Sichuan, China. Composer; Pianist. Div, 1 d. Education: BA, 1970, MA, 1980, Shanghai Conservatory; Dip of Soloists Class, Music Coll, Hanover, Germany, 1983. Appointments: Asst, 1970-78, Lectr in Composition, 1983-86, Asst Prof, 1986-89, Prof, Dean, Dept of Composition, 1991-96, Vice-Pres, 1996-, Shanghai Conservatory; Guest Prof, Music Coll, Salzburg, Aust, 1990; Vis Prof, Cornell Univ, 1995. Publications: Book: The Compositional Techniques of Olivier Messiaen, 1989. Compositions: Suicide by the Wujiang, 1986; Elegy, 1991; Red Cherry, 1995; Si, 1996. Honours: Chinese Record Prize, 1986; DAAD Schlsp, 1990; Lit and Arts Prize, Shanghai, 1991; Dist Achmnt Awd, Classic Arts, 1994; ACC Grant, USA, 1995; CSCC Grant, USA, 1995. Memberships: Chinese Musicians Assn; Shanghai Musicians Assn; Mod Music Soc, Shanghai. Hobbies: Literary; Photography; Records; CD and VCD Collecting; Hi-Fi Equipment. Address: 1855 Tianshan Road, Apt 1710, Shanghai 200051, China.

YANG Lixin, b. 13 Apr 1929, Shanghai, China. Translator; Senior Editor. m. Wan Mingyu, 12 Oct 1958, 2 children. Education: BA, Jrnlsm, St Johns Univ, Shanghai. Appointments: Dpty Ed-in-Chf, Shanghai Trans Publng House, 1985; Advsr, STPH, 1993; Snr Cnslt, Shanghai Far East Publrs, 1999. Publications: Chinese trans of: A Son of the Middle Border, 1958; The Bosses, 1960; Hotel, 1981; Blithedale Romance, 1996. Memberships: Cncl, Shanghai Fgn Langs Soc, 1981-84; SORSA, 1987-; Shanghai Lit Trans Assn, 1987-. Hobby: Light music. Address: 14/955 Yanan Road Central, Shanghai 200040, China.

YANG Mansu, b. 3 Nov 1948. Professor of International Relations. m. An Ping, 6 Dec 1976, 1 d. Education: MA, Hist, Yunnan Univ, 1985. Appointments: Lectr, 1987, Hd of Middle E Studies, 1987, Assoc Prof, 1992, Prof, 1994-, Dir, 1998, Southwest Asia Inst. Publications: Books incl: Israel a Mysterious Country, 1992; Israeli Premier Rabin, 1994; Holocaust, 1995; The Biography of Rabin, 1997. Honours: Awd in Socl Scis Studies, Yunnan Provl Govt, 1994; Awd'd Socl Sci Stdies, Educl Cttee of Yunnan Prov, 1997. Memberships: Cncl, China Middle E Assn, 1995; China Asia Afr Assn. Listed in: American Biographical Institute. Hobby: Playing tennis. Address: The Southwest Asia Institute, Yunnan University, Kunming 650091, Yunnan, China.

YANG Qidong, b. 19 July 1935, Beijing, China. Educator; Librarian; Researcher. m. Li Fuquan, 30 Jan 1962, 2 s, 1 d. Education: Bach, Telecomm Engrng, Telecomm Engrng Inst, 1958. Appointments: Tchr, Lectr, Northwest Telecomm Engrng Inst, 1958-79; Visng Engr, MA Inst of Technol, Cambridge, MA, USA, 1979-81; Assoc Prof, NTEI, 1983-90, Xidian Univ, 1990-93; Chf Libn, NTEI, 1984-90, Xidian Univ, 1990-96; Estimation Expert, Shaanxi Prov Univ Libs, 1989-93; Snr Rschr, 1993-99; Hd, Shaanxi Prov Univ Lib Automation Expert Grp Cnltng Expert, 1995-96; Lib of Xidian Univ, 1996-99. PUblications: Co-auth, Transistor Amplifier Circuits, 1974; Co-auth, Fundamentals of Electronic Circuits, 1985. Honours: Ex Tchr, NTEI, 1985; Ex Textbook of XTEI, 1987; Outstndng Lib Administrator, Higher Educ Bur of Shaanxi Prov, 1989; gov Spec Subsidy, State Cncl of China, 1992. Memberships: Electron Assn of Shaanxi Prov, 1964-67; Assn of Sci and Technol of China, 1983-99; IEEE, 1992-99. Hobbies: Sports; Reading novels; Watching TV; Music appreciation. Listed in: Who's Who in the World. Address: Library, Xidian University, 2 Tai Bai Road, Xi'an 710071, Shaanxi, China.

YANG Ru-Huai, b. 13 Aug 1925, Beijing, China. Professor, Central Conservatory of Music in China. m. Hu Yu-Tong, 12 July 1954, 1 s, 1 d. Education: BLitt, Cath Univ of Peking, 1948; BMus, Yanjing Univ of Beijing, 1950. Appointments: Tchr, Cntrl Conservatory of Music of China, Beijing, 1952-. Publications: (book) Music Analysis and Composition; Over 15 articles; Some transl wrks; Other compositions. Honours: Many citations, awds, medals, Govt, Min of Culture or Conservatory, 1984-. Memberships: Chinese Musician Assn; Beijing Musician Assn; Acad Cttee of Cntrl Conservatory of Music; Fmr Dir, Tchng Grp of Music Analysis of Composition Dept; 7th and 8th sessions of Beijing People's Polit Consultation Conf. Hobbies: Travel; Photography. Address: 43 Bao-jia-jie, Xi-Cheng District, Beijing, China 100031.

YANG Shan-Rang, b. 7 Nov 1938, Huaining Co, Anhui Prov, China. m. Wang Ying-guan, 9 Nov 1968, 1 s, 1 d. Education: Zhejiang Univ of China, 1957-62; Univ of NC at Charlotte, 1983-85; UNCC and Stan, 1994-95. Appointments: Lectr, 1978, Assoc Prof, 1983, Prof, 1988; Hd of Tchng Grp, 1978, Vice-Dean of Thermal Power Engrng Dept, NorthEast China Inst of Elec Power Engrng (NEIEP), 1982; Dean of Thermal Power Engrng Dept, 1986; VP, NEIEP, 1992. Publications: Power Condenser and its Management, 1993; Fouling of Heat Exchanger and Countermeasures, 1995; English-Chinese Dictionary of Electric Power Technology, 1999. Honours: Excellent Tchr of Jilin Prov, 1987; Excellent Sci and Technol Wrkr of CSEE (Chinese Soc of Elecl Engrng), 1993; 1st Class Prize of Technol Prog of Elec Power Engrng Min of China, 1995. Memberships: Snr Mbr, ISA, 1985; Snr Mbr, CSEE, 1989; Pres, Jilin Soc of Engrng Thermophysics, 1992; Visng Prof, N China Univ of Elec Power Engrng. Hobbies: Light music appreciation; Chinese classical literature appreciation. Address: 18-1-7 Diannan Lane, Changchun Road, Jilin City 132012, China.

YANG Shi-O, b. 9 Aug 1931, Tianjin, China. Professor. m. Amy Hsieh, 15 Dec 1956, 3 s. Education: Grad, Qinghua Univ, 1951. Appointments: Asst, Navy Coll Cmdng, 1951-52; Lectr, Acady Mil Engrng, 1953-57; Visng Mbr, Acoustic Inst, USSR, 1958-59; Assoc Prof, Harbin Shipbldg Engrng Inst, now Harbin Engrng Univ,

1960-; prof, 1979-. Publications: Theory of Acoustics; Theory of Underwater Noise; Theory of Underwater Sound Propagation; Acoustic Positioning System. Membership: Chinese Acady Engrng, Beijing, 1995-. Hobby: Literature. Address: Harbin Engineering University, Harbin, China.

YANG Shiruo, b. 2 Jan 1928, Chongqing, China. Physiologist. m. Li Guangfu, 30 July 1953, 1 s, 1 d. Education: Grad, Sch of Med, Natl Univ of Chongqing, 1952; Advd Trng, Dept of Physiology, Beijing Medl Coll, 1954-55; Electrophysiological Technique Wrkshp, Second Medl Coll of Shanghai, 1964-66. Appointments: Asst on Physiology, Sch of Med, Natl Univ of Chongqing, 1952; Asst, Dept of Physiology, Sichuan Medl Coll, 1952-78; Mbr, Grp on prevention and cure of mountain sickness in Sichuan Prov, 1960; Lectr, 1979-80, Assoc Prof, 1980-86, Chmn, Dept of Physiology, 1984-87, Prof of Physiology, 1986-, Hd, Rsch Unit of Neurophysiology, 1986-97, W China Univ of Medl Scis, Chengdu, Sichuan; Visng Assoc Prof of Pharmacology, Sch of Med, Univ of PA, Phila, USA, 1983-84. Publications: Co-auth of some 30 pprs mainly on neural mechanisms of acupuncture analgesia; The effects of active components from certain Chinese herbs on sleep and on epileptic activity; Calcium channels; Glutamate- and acetylcholine- activated single channels; Effects of seasons and hormones on neuromuscular transmission; Co-auth of 3 med textbooks: The Applied Occlusion, 1990; Physiology in Anaesthesia, 1990; The Procedures of Physiolgical Experiments, 1991, 1996; Ed and Dir of a tchng film: Phenomena of Bioelectricity in Cells, w permission and publ of Natl Bur of Hlth, 1993. Honours: Won w 3 colleagues, the 1991 Sichuan Prov Sci-Technol Prog 3rd Awd for wrks on Mechanisms of Effects of Elecl Stimulation of Renzhong (Du 26) on Phrenic Discharge in Rabbits. Memberships: Chinese Assn of Physiological Scis, 1954; Chinese Biophysl Soc, 1981; Chinese Soc of Neuroscis, 1994; IBRO, 1995; Editl Bd, Chinese Jrnl for Applied Physiology, 1984-89; Basic Medl Scis and Clins, 1991-94. Hobbies: Collecting stamps; Playing table-tennis. Listed in: High-ranking Specialists in Sichuan Province. Address: Department of Physiology, West China University of Medical Sciences, Chengdu, Sichuan 610041, China.

YANG Si-Ze, b. 4 Feb 1947, Taipei, Taiwan, China. Scientific Research. m. Li Hong-mei, 1 July 1992, 1 s. Education: PhD, Nuclear Engrng, Univ of CA at Berkeley, CA, USA, 1978. Appointments: Rsch Scientist, Inst of Phys, Acady of Scis, Beijing. Publications: Over 90 pprs in jrnls and conf proceedings. Honour: ECRH experiment on HL-I Tokamak, Progressive Awd in Sci and Technol by Min of Nuclear Ind. Memberships: Natl Energy Cttee, 863 Hi-tech Rsch and Dev Prog of China, 1997-2000; Deleg, 9th Natl Cttee pf People's Polit Consultative Conf. Hobbies: Swimming; Music. Address: Institute of Physics, Academy of Sciences, Beijing, 100080, China.

YANG Song Song, b. 1 Jan 1937, Shanghai, China. Professor. m. Baoqin Ren. Education: BD, 1961, MD, 1964, Med Univ, Shanghai; Vis Schl, Univ TX, Austin, USA, 1986-88. Appointments: Assoc Prof, 1982, Prof, 1985-, Liaoning Coll of TCM. Publications: Flavonoids of Lotus Creticus, 1989; Flavonoids of Ononis Vaginalis, 1989; Flavonoids of Critonis Daleoids, 1989; Flavonoids of Centanrea Alexandria Ibid, 1989; The Chemistry of Chinese Material Medica, 1997. Memberships: Chmn, Dept of Chinese Material Medica, Liaoning Coll of TCM, 1992-96; Pres, Liaoning Prov Chinese Material Medica Assn, 1996-; Cncl, Chinese Pharm Assn, 1997-. Address: Research Center of Chinese Material Medica, Liaoning College of Traditional Chinese Medicine, Liaoning, China.

YANG Sung Chul, b. 20 Nov 1939, Koksung, South Cholla, Korea. Member, National Assembly. m. Lee Jung Jin, 1 s, 1 d. Education: BA, Pol Sci, Seoul Natl Univ; MA, Pol Sci, Univ of HI, Honolulu, HI, E-W Cntr Schlshp; PhD, Pol Sci, Univ of KY, Lexington. Appointments include: Grad Fac, Grad Sch, Univ of KY, Lexington, 1982-86; Prof, Pol Sci, Grad Inst of Peace Stdies, Kyunghee Univ, 1986-96; Mbr, Korean Natl Assembly, Cttee for Unification and For Affairs, 1996-; Chmn, Intl Coop Cttee, Natl Congress for New Politics, 1998-. Honours: Presdtl Awd, April 19th Revolution Leaders; State of KY Col Awd; Socl Sci Rsch Cncl Rsch Awd. Memberships: VP, Univ of HI, E-W Cntr Schlsp Assn, 1965-66; Sec-Gen, Assn of Korean Pol Sci in N Am, 1979-86; Pres, Korean Assn of Intl Studies, 1994-95; Korea Intl Coop Agcy, Advsr, 1998-; Reunification Specialist, 300 Liberal Intellectuals, 1986-; Dir, Korean Pol Sci Assn, 1986-. Hobbies: Mountain climbing; Tennis; Reading. Address: Suite 534, Office Building, National Assembly Yoido, Seoul, Korea.

YANG Tong Li, b. 11 Dec 1933, Jianette Co, Juizhou Prov, China. Traditional Chinese Medicine Scientist. m. Ye Ju Yeng, 18 Feb 1958, 1 s, 2 d. Education: Undergrad. Appointments: Fmr Dir, Shenyang Tradl Chinese Med Rsch Inst. Publications: Outline of Prevention and Cure of Tumour in Chinese Medicine; Comprehensive Summary of Special Techniques to Prevent and Cure Tumours in Chinese Medicine; Collection of Sores; Dietary Disease and Health. Honours: Spec Finl Aid, State Cncl of China, 1992; 2 Champions on Acupuncture and Moxibustion and Med Rsch at Intl Symposium of Tradl Chinese and West Med Coop, Los Angeles, USA, 1994; Hon of Liaoning Excellent Expert, 1996. Memberships: Dir, Tradl Chinese Med Assn of China; Dpty Dir, Tradl Chinese Med Assn; Mngng Dir, World Tradl Chinese Med Assn; Mngng Dir, Intl Tradl Chinese Med Anticancer Assn; Mngng Dir, Laio Ming Tradl Chinese Med Assn. Hobbies: Reading; Writing; Flowers and plants. Address: No 1-8, Lianette Road, Dadong District 6, ShenYoung, China.

YANG Xiuming, b. 23 Sept 1942, Xingping, Shaanxi Prov, China. Doctor. m. Zhang Xiuju, 1 Oct 1970, 2 s. Education: Xian Medl Univ, 1963-67. Appointments: Dean of Orth Dept, Xing Ping People's Hosp, Shaanxi, China, 1967-97; VP, Disabled Mbrs Assn, Xian Yang Cty, 1991-97; Dir, Shaanxi Cervicodyni and Lumbodynia rsch Inst, 1994-97; VP, Shaanxi Massage Assn, Chinese Medl Sci Soc, 1995-97; Polit Consultative Conf, Xing Ping Cty, Shaanxi Prov, 1997; Mbr, World Fedn Chinese Orthopedics, 1998. Publications: 3 patents; 15 pprs in profl jrnls. Honours include: Model Worker, Xian Yang Cty, 1989; Chinese Model of Being Self-Reliant, 1991; A Intervertebral Discs Restitution Machine, Invention Prize of Chinese Invention Assn rcd by Chinese Gen Sec, Jiang Zemin Premier Li Peng, 1991; Chinese Sci and Technol Star, 1994; Most Outstndng in Shaanxi Prov, 1996; Adv Worker, Shaanxi Disabled Mbrs Assn; Adv Worker, Xian Yang Cty; Adv Worker, Xing Ping Cty (5 x). Hobbies: Music; Opera. Address: Cericodynia and Lumbodynia Research Institute, Xing Ping, Shaanxi Province, China.

YANG Xun, b. 5 Jan 1968, Chengdu, China. Physician. Education: BMed, 1990; Doct degree postgrad of Opth, 1997-2000. Appointments: Intern, 1990-91, Jnr Res, 1991-94, Snr Res, 1994-96, Attending Dr, 1996-97. Publication: The Tensile Strength of the Anterior and Posterior Capsules in Eye-Bank Eye, 1998. Honour: Awd for Prog in Sci and Technol in Beijing, 1995. Hobbies: Table tennis; Photography. Address: #35 Bld, Guangming Road, West China University of Medical Sciences 610041, Chengdu, China.

YANG Yi, b. 20 Apr 1938, Shanghai, China. Teacher. m. Shaolan Hu, 12 Feb 1968, 1 s, 1 d. Education: China Univ of Mining and Technol. Appointments: Dpty Dean, Coal Comprehensive Utilization Dept, China Univ of Mining and Technol, 1982-91. Creative Works: Parameter Testing Technique of Mineral Processing Flowsheet, 1991; Particle Size Study of Mineral Processing, 1995. Honours: Natl Awd for Inv, 1996; First Prize of State Educ Commn for the Progress of Sci and Technol, 1997. Memberships: China Soc of Coal; China Assn for Coal Processing and Utilization. Address: Center of Minerals Processing, China University of Mining and Technology, Xuzhou Tinagsu 221008, China.

YANG Yu Hua, b. 23 Mar 1952, Nanjing, China. Medical Doctor. m. Jixin Wang, 27 Aug 1987, 1 s. Education: Grad, Jining Med Acady, 1981. Appointments: Physn, 1981, Visng Physn, 1987, Assoc Chf Physn, 1992-. Publications include: An Experimental Study on the Endurance of Immunologic Memory of Intradermal Micro-Injection with Rabies Vaccine and Boosting Immune Effect. Honours: Achievement Awds, Min and Prov Level, Sci and Technol, 1986, 1988. Memberships: IEA; ISID. Hobbies: Music; Radio communication technology. Address: 72 Jingshi Road, Jinan, Shandong, China.

YANG Yue Qin, b. 28 July 1941, County Yas Xian, Shanxi, China. Scholar. Cheng Xueren, 27 Sept 1964, 1 s, 2 d. Education: Grad, Medl Sch, Yong Chuan Cty, Shanxi, China, 1959-62. Appointments: Medl Rschr, Xian Pharmaceutical Factory; Gen Directory, Pres, Xian Shenchungwang Hlth Prods Co Ltd. Publications: Yang Yuegin poetry anthology and film script. Honours: Gold Medal for hlth liquid "Shenchunwang", Beijing Invention Exhibn, 1996; Memberships: Snr Mbr, Chinese Pharmaceutical Assn; China Sexology Assn. Hobbies: Poetry; Literature; Playwriting. Address: Xian Yang Yue Qin Health Products Research Institute, 56 Diaoqiao Western Street, Xian 710014, China.

YANG Zhi Yong, b. 31 Oct 1925, Mandalay, Burma. Professor, Head of Institute's Library, Yunnan Institute of the Nationalities. M. Ping Chen, 10 Apr 1953, 3 s. Education: Grad in Pols, Yunnan Univ, 1949. Appointments: Asst Hd, Wulong County, Yunnan Prov, 1949; Asst Hd, Yunnan Prov Arts Grp, Yunnan Prov, 1950; Hd, Dongchuan Cultural Bur, Yunnan Prov, 1956; Asst Dir, Chinese Dept, 1980, Hd of Inst's Lib, 1983, Yunnan Inst of the Nationalities. Creative works: Ashma (Yi People's Narrative Poetry); Religion, Myth and Folk Ways (Selected Theses); Witchcraft and Poetry; 32 other theses on all Religion and Folk Ways; Yunnan Minority Nationalities Marriage Customs, China Myth (ed); Value Selection and Re-integration of Ethnic Culture; People's Outlook of Life and Death in Southwest China, 1992; Folk Ways of Yunnan Minority Nationalities Production (chf ed); Folk Ways of Yunnan Minority Nationalities Daily Life (chf ed); Dictionary of All Nationalities' Religion and Mythology-Yunnan (chf ed); Student Movements in Yunnan University: 1937-1949 (chf ed), 1995. Honours: Top-grade Prize in Yunnan Folk Lit Thesis Contest, 1982; Flying Eagle Awd of Folk Lit and Art Quarterly. Memberships: Mbr of Cncl, China Folk Lit and Arts Rsch Soc; China Writers Union, Yunnan Chapt; Mbr of Cncl, China Folklore Soc, 1993; Mbr of China Writers Union, Yunnan Chapt. Hobbies: Reading literature; Beijing Opera; Flower growing; Taijiquan (kind of traditional Chinese shadow boxing). Address: Yunnan Institute of the Nationalities, Kunming, Yunnan, China.

YANG Zhixin, b. 14 Mar 1933, Linhai, Zhejiang, China. Research Worker. m. Liu Lingling, 2 s. Education; Dip, Taichow Agricl Jnr Coll. Appointments: Vice Dir, Citrus Inst of Linhai Cty, Zhejiang Prov, China; Snr Agronomist. Publications: Parasitic Wasps of Citrus Insect Pests in Zhejiang Province; Over 90 pprs, some listed in World Acad Lib, Sel Pprs of Chinese Contemporary Schls. Honours: 5 citrus items and rsch pprs awd'd 1st to 3rd Prizes, Cntrl Min of Agric and Zhejiang Provcl Govt. Memberships: China Agricl Soc; China Horticultural Soc. Listed in: Chinese Experts Dictionary; World Cultural Dictionary. Hobbies: Reading; Fishing. Address: Citrus Research Institute of Linhai City, Linhai, Zhejiang, China.

YANG Zunyi, b. 7 Oct 1908, Jiyang, Guangdong, China. Professor. m. (1) Esther Z Xu, 22 Aug 1939, (2) Xiaozhen Li, 1 s, 3 d. Education: BS, Tsinghua Univ, 1933; PhD, Yale Univ, 1939. Appointments: Asst, Tsinghua Univ, 933-35; Prof and Hd, Dept Geol, Sunzhong-shan Univ, also Dir, Geol Survey Kwangtung and Kwangsi, 1939-42; Joined army, 1942-45; Prof, Tsinghua Univ, 1946-52; Beijing Coll Of Geol (Wuhang Coll of Geol and the present China Univ of Geosci), 1952-. Publications: (Ed) Permo-Triassic Events in the Eastern Tethys, 1991; The Jurassic Brachiopod Sequences of the Qinghai-Tibetan Plateau, in Brachiopods Through Time, 1991; (Ed) Late Palaeozoic and Early Mesozoic Circum-Pacofic Events and Their Global Correlation, 1997. Honours: Wilbur Cross Medallist, 1994; Awdee, HLHL Fndn for Earth Scis Prize,

1997; Hon Fell, Geol Soc Am. Memberships: Geol Soc China; Geol Soc Beijing; Palaeontology Soc China. Hobbies: Bicycling; Swimming. Address: China University of Geosciences, Beijing 100083, China.

YANG Di, b. 1924 Qingpu Co Shanghai. Politician. Appointments: Joined New 4th Army, 1938; Joined CCP, 1939; Dep Dir Shanghai Bur of For Trade, 1960-76; Dir Shanghai Post and Telecomms Bur; Dir Shanghai Pub Security Bur; Vice-Mayor Shanghai, 1977-83; Deleg 12th and 13th CCP Congresses; Sec CCP Cttee Shanghai, 1983; Dep Sec CCP Cttee Shanghai, 1983-89. Memberships: Mbr 12th CCP Cntrl Cttee, 1982-87; Mbr Standing Cttee 7th CPPCC, 1989; Mbr Standing Cttee 8th CPPCC, 1993-98. Address: Shanghai Municipal Chinese Communist Party, Shanghai, People's Republic of China.

YANG Guoliang, b. Mar 1938 Zunhua Cty Hebei Prov. Army Offr. Education: Beijing Aeronautics Inst. Appointments: Joined CCP, 1961; Vice-Cmdr PLA Second Artillery Force, 1985; Rank of Maj Gen, 1988; Rank of Lt Gen, 1990; Cmdr PLA Second Artillery Force, 1992-. Memberships: Alt mbr 12th CCP Cntrl Cttee, 1985; Alt mbr 13th CCP Cntrl Cttee, 1992; Mbr 14th CCP Cntrl Cttee, 1992; Mbr 15th CCP Cntrl Cttee, 1997-. Address: People's Liberation Army Second Artillery Force Hq, Beijing, People's Republic of China.

YANG Zhenhuai, b. Jan 1928 Anhui. Govt Offic. m. Yang Duanyi, 1960, 1 s, 1 d. Appointments: Vice-Min for Water Rescs and Electric Power, 1983-88; Sec Gen State Flood Control Hq, 1986-88; Dep Hd State Flood Control Hq, 1988; Min for Water Rescs, 1988-93; Dep Hd State Ldng Grp for Comprehensive Agric Dev, 1990-; Vice-Chmn Environmental and Rescs Protection Cttee; NPC Dep Anhui Prov. Memberships: Alt mbr 14th CCP Cntrl Cttee, 1992-; Mbr 8th NPC, 1993-. Hobbies: Reading; Hist; Geol; Humane Studie. Address: c/o Ministry of Water Resources, 3-5 Baiguang Road, Beijing 100761, People's Republic of China.

YANG-KANG Lin (Chih-Hung), b. 10 June 1927 Nantou Co Taiwan Prov. Politician. m. Chen Ho, 1945, 1 s, 3 d. Education: Dept of Polit Sci Natl Taiwan Univ; Chf Admin Civ Affairs Sect Nantou Co Govt, 1952-61; Sec Civ Affairs Sect Nantou Co Govt, 1962-64; Sec Taiwan Prov Govt, 1964; Chmn Yunlin Co Hq Kuomintang, 1964-67; Magistrate Nantou Co, 1967-72; Commnr Dept of Reconstrn, 1972-76; Mayor Taipei Spec Municipality, 1976-78; Gov of Taiwan Prov Govt, 1978-81; Min of Interior, 1981-84; Vice-Premier of Exec Yuan Govt, 1984-87; Premier of Judicial Yuan, 1987-94; Vice-Chmn Kuomintang, 1993-; Snr Advsr to Pres, 1994-. Honours: Order of Dip Service Merit Korea, 1977. Hobbies: Hiking; Reading; Studying; Music. Address: 5 Chao-Chou Street, Taipei, Taiwan.

YAO Bi Yun, b. 13 June 1935. Maths Educator. m. Si Zhong Shao, 20 Aug 1963, 2 s, 1 d. Education: Grad Dip, E China Norm Univ, Shanghai, China. Appointments: Asst, 1957-78, Lectr, 1978-81, Assoc, 1981-88, Dean of Dept of Maths, 1987-89, Prof of Maths, 1988-98, Hangzhou Univ; Prof of Maths, 1998-, Zhejiang Univ. Publications: Math articles to profl jrnls, 1963-98; Books on Complex Analysis, 1983, 1991. Memberships: Chinese Math Soc; Amn Math Soc, 1990-. Hobby: Music. Listed in: Who's Who in the World. Address: Renmin Road 35, Hangzhou 310001, China.

YAO Tai, b. 31 Jan 1938, Zhejiang, China. Professor of Physiology. m. Wen-Ying Cheng, 28 Jan 1963, 1 s, 1 d. Education: Dip, Fac of Med, Shanghai First Med Coll, 1954-59; Postgrad Dip, Dept of Physiol, Shanghai First Med Coll, 1959-62; Mbr, Chinese Neurophysiol Stdy Grp Visng Can, 1974; Visng Schl, Dept of Physiol Univ of Goteborg, Sweden, 1979-81. Appointments: Asst, Lectr, Assoc Prof, Shanghai Med Univ (SMU), 1962-86; Dpty Dir, Shanghai Med Team travelling to Tibet, 1975-77; Prof, Dean of Sch of Basic Med Scis, SMU, 1986-88; VP, SMU, Dean of Grad Sch, SMU, 1988-93; Pres, SMU, 1994-; Assoc Ed in Chief, Acta Physiologica Sinica, 1985-; Edl Bd, Chinese Jrnl of Physiological Scis, 1985-;

Editl Bd, Blood Pressure, 1993-. Publications include: Respiratory Rhythm of Sympathetic Discharges, 1963; Long-Lasting Cardiovascular Depression by Acupuncture-like Sciatic Stimulation in Spontaneously Hypertensive Rats, 1982; Baroreceptors with Non-Medullated Afferents, 1983; Somatosympathetic Responses, 1985; Baroreflex Resetting During Somatic Stimulation, 1985-89. Honours: Rsch Awd, State Educ Comn of China, 1987; Rsch Awd, Chinese Min of Health, 1989, 1993; Symposium Chmn, Recent advs in basic rsch of acupuncture, XXXI Intl Congress of Physiological Scis, Helsinki, Finland, 1989; Fndn Visitor, Univ of Auckland Fndn, NZ, 1990; Dr Hon causa, Univ of Göteborg, Sweden, 1997. Memberships: Intl Brain Rsch Org; Chinese Assn of Physiological Scis; Shanghai Brain Rsch Soc; Chinese Med Assn; Chinese Acupuncture Soc; Chinese Soc for Acad Deg and Postgrad Educ; Assoc Dir, Chinese Association of Physiological Scis, 1998-. Hobbies: Music; Cycling; Photography. Address: President's Office, Shanghai Medical University, 138 Yixueyuan Road, Shanghai 200032, China.

YAO Zukang, b. 6 July 1934, Suzhou, Jiangsu, China. Professor. m. Gongyu Fan, 22 July 1962, 1 s, 1 d. Education: Grad Dip, Tongji Univ, China, 1951-55; Postgrad Dip, 1955-59. Appointments: Asst, Tongji Univ, China, 1959-60; Lectr, 1960-80; Assoc Prof, 1980-86; Prof, 1986-. Publications: Pavement Management Systems, 1993; Highway Subgrade and Pavement Engineering, 1994; Planning and Design of Airport, 1994; Introduction to Transportation Engineering, 1994; Concrete Pavement Design, 1998. Honours: Sci and Technol Prize, 1996; 3rd Grade; 2nd Grade; 1st Grade. Memberships: China Civ Engrng Soc; China Hwy and Transp Soc. Address: Tongji University, Department of Road and Traffic Engineering, 1239 Siping Road, Shanghai 200092, China.

YASASSI THERO Ven Diviyagaha, b. 2 Jan 1935, Matara. Monk. Education: BA, 1959; Dip in Educ, 1980. Appointments: Vice Prin, Ananda Coll, Colombo; Chf Sangha Nayaka. Creative Works: Lankawa ha Asanna Rajjyayo. Honours: Saddharma Kirthi Sri Tripitakaicariya. Memberships: Sri Lanka Buddhist Congress; Asian Buddhist for Peace. Hobbies: Reading; Preaching; Listening to others. Address: Bauddhayatanaya, Watarappola Road, Mt Lavinia, Sri Lanka.

YASSIN Salim, b. 10 Oct 1937, Lattakia, Syria. Professor of Economics. m. Najwa, 1962, 2 s, 3 d. Education: BCom, Syria, 1960; MA, Econs, USA, 1963; PhD, Econs, USA, 1965. Appointments: Pres of Univ, 1972-78; Min, 1978-85; Vice Prime Min for Econ Affairs, 1985-. Publications: International Economics: The Theory of Correlation. Honours: EI, Boulder, CO, USA. Memberships: AEA; SEA. Address: Board of Ministers Building, Damascus, Syria.

YASUDA Keigo, b. 10 Nov 1939, Sendai, Japan. Professor. m. Kieko Marumori, 26 Apr 1969, 1 d. Education: MD; PhD. Appointments: Asst Prof, 1976, Assoc Prof, 1986, Prof, Chf, Dept of Intern Med, 1993, Dir, Hlth Mngmt Cntr, 1994, Gifu Univ; Rsch Fell, Univ TN, 1986. Publications: Insulin Secretion in Hypoparathyrndism, 1975; Secondary Diabetes, 1980. Memberships: Am Endocrine Soc; Am Diabetes Assn; Japan Diabetes Assn; Japan Endocrine Soc; Japan Intern Med Assn. Hobby: Classical music. Address: 3-25-106 Sakaeshin-machi, Gifu, Japan.

YASUHARA Michiru, b. 22 Mar 1928, Taiwan, China. Education. m. Yumiko Shinohara, 30 Mar 1959, 1 s. Education: BEng, 1951, DEng, 1962, Univ of Tokyo, Japan. Appointments: Tahara Mfg Tokyo, 1951-54; Rsch Assoc, Univ of Tokyo, 1954-58; Assoc Prof, Nagoya Univ, 1958-67; Prof, 1967-91; Prof, Aichi Inst Technol, 1991-; Rsch Assoc, Cornel Univ, 1963-65; Assoc Prof, USC, 1965. Publications: The Day Japanese Space Shuttle Flies, 1984; Numerical Fluid Dynamics (co-ed), 1992. Honours: Ppr Awds, 1993; Hon Mbr, JSASS, 1997. Memberships: Japan Soc Aeronautical and Space Scis (JSASS), Bd Dirs, 1984-85, Dir Cntrl Br Japan, 1987.

Hobbies: Driving; Go game; Golf. Address: 34-18 Neura Iwasaki Nissin, Aichi, 470-0131, Japan.

YASUMURA Seiji, b. 25 Sept 1958, Tokyo, Japan. Associate Professor. m. Misako, 21 May 1988, 1 d. Education: Dr of Med Sci, Yamagata Univ, Grad Sch of Med. Appointments: Chief Rschr, Tokyo Metropolitan Inst of gerontology, 1989; Asst Prof, Yamagata Univ Sch of Med, 1993; Assoc Prof, Yamagata Univ Sch of Med, 1994. Publications: Facts Research Gerontology, 1996, 1997. Honour: Young Investigator Awd, Japanese Soc of Pub Hlth, 1996. Memberships: Japan Soc Pub Hlth; Intl Epidemiological Assn; Amn Geriatric Soc; Japan Soc Hyg; Japan Epidemiological Assn; Japan Geriatric Soc; Japan Soc Gerontological Soc. Hobbies: Tennis; Ski. Address: Department of Public Health, Yamagata University, School of Medicine, 2-2-2 Iida-nishi, Yamagata, 990-9585, Japan.

YATES Deborah Helwen, b. 11 Jan 1957, London. Doctor. m. Paul Thomas. Education: MAMB; BClair; MRCP; FRACP; MSc; AFom. Appointments: Respiratory Physn, Roy N Shore Hosp; Dir, Dept of Res Trng, RNSH. Memberships: Brit Thoracic Soc; Austl and NZ Thoracic Soc; Soc of Occupational Med. Address: Department of Respiratory Medicine, Royal North Shore Hospital, St Leonard's, NSW 2065, Australia.

YATES Renate Maria, b. Vienna, Austria. Writer; Dental Surgeon. m. Timothy C Yates, 1 s, 1 d. Education: BDS, Sydney. Publications: Fine Bones, short stories, 1985; Social Death, novel, 1984; Rural Pursuits, novel, 1988; The Narcissus Conspiracy, novel, 1991. Membership: Austl Soc of Auths. Address: Warabina, Cobbitty, NSW 2570, Australia.

YATIM Dato Rais, b. 1942 Jelebu Negeri Sembilan. Politician. m. Datin Masnah Mohamat, 3 s, 1 d. Education: Univ of N IL; Univ of Singapore. Appointments: Lectr at ITM Sch of Law and also mngd own law firm in Kuala Lumpur, 1973; Parly Sec min of Yth Sport and Culture, 1974; Dep Min of Law, 1976; Dep Min of Home Affairs, 1978; Elected to State Ass Negeri Sembilan, 1978; Menteri Besar Negeri Sembilan, 1978; Min of Land Regl Devt, 1982; Min of Info, 1984-86; Min of For Affairs, 1986-87; Advocate and Solicitor High Crt of Malaysia, 1988-; Returned to Law pract Kuala Lumpur, 1988-; Dep Pres Semangat, 1989-. Memberships: Mbr Utd Malays Natl Org - UMNO - Supreme Cncl of Malaysia, 1982-; Mbr Civ Liberty Cttee Bar Cncl Kuala Lumpur, 1996-. Address: 41 Road 12, Taman Grandview, Ampang Jaya, 68000 Ampang, Selangor Darul Ehsan, Malaysia.

YAZAKI Yoshikazu, b. 22 Jan 1942, Kofu, Japan. Research Scientist. m. Chieko Nire, 4 Apr 1969, 1 s, 2 d. Education: BS, Tokyo, Kyoiku Univ, 1964; MSc, Tokyo Kyoiku Univ, 1966; PhD, Tokyo Kyoiku Unv, 1969. Appointments: Rsch Scientist, Soc for Promotion Sci, Tokyo, 1969; Rsch Scientist, CSIRO, Melbourne, Aust, 1969-71; Snr Rsch Scientist, 1976-85, Prin Rsch Scientist, 1985-95, Snr Prin Rsch Scientist, 1995-, Proj Ldr, 1988-, Sub-Proj Ldr, ACIAR, Canberra, 1986-93; Mbr, Advsry Bd, Holzforschung, Berlin, 1992-; Intl Prog Cttee, Huan, China, 1994-95; Intl Prog Cttee, Kyoto, Japan, 1995-96; Mbr, Intl Advsry Bd, Jrnl of Wood Science, 1998-. Publications: Pats for Tannin Extraction, 1980, Adhesives, 1989, Adhesive Composition, Aust, USA, Can, Japan. Honours: Siemens Schlshp, Hamburg Univ, Germany, 1982; Hon Fell, The Chinese Soc of Chem and Chem Engrng of Forest Prods, 1989; Rsch Schl, Natl Inst for Resources and Environment, AIST, MITI, Tsukumba/Japan, 1995, 1996. Memberships: NY Acady of Scis, NY, 1994-; AAAS, Wash, 1995-; Visng Prof, Inst of Wood Technol, AIKITA, Japan, 1995, 1996, 1997. Hobbies: Arts; Music; Table tennis. Address: CSIRO Forestry and Forest Products, Bayview Avenue, Clayton, Vic 3168, Australia.

YE Liansong, b. 1935 Shanghai. Politician; Engr. Education: Jiaotong Univ Shanghai. Appointments: Engr Shijiazhuang Municipal Diesel Plant, 1960-80; Vice-Mayor Shijiazhuang, 1982-85; Dep Sec Standing

Cttee Hebei Prov CCP Cttee; Vice-Gov Hebei Prov, 1985-93; Gov Hebei Prov, 1993-; Dep to 8th NPC. Memberships: Mbr Standing Cttee Hebei Prov CCP Cttee, 1983-; Alt mbr 13th Cntrl Cttee CCP, 1987-92; Mbr 14th Cntrl Cttee, 1992-97; Mbr 15th CCP Cntrl Cttee, 1997-. Address: Office of the Governor, Hubei Provincial Government, 1 Weiming Jie Street, Shijiazhuang City, People's Republic of China.

YE Ming-Lu, b. 13 Apr 1936. Professor of Chemistry. m. 30 Dec 1961, 1 s, 1 d. Education: Grad, Chem Dept, Fudan Univ, 1958. Appointments: Dir, Radiochem Sect, Dept of Nuc Sci, Fudan Univ. Publications: Radiochemistry Experiments, textbook, 1991; Introduction to Environmental Chemistry, 1997; Over 60 sci pprs, 1980-97. Honours: 5 Sci and Technique Prizes, Shanghai Sci Commn and Min of Nuc Ind of China, 1984-92. Memberships: Cncl Mbr, Isotope Soc of China, 1985-96; Cncl Mbr, Radiochem Soc of China, 1991-96. Hobby: Music. Address: Department of Environmental Science and Engineering, Fudan University, Shanghai 200433, China.

YE Weichun, b. 10 May 1945, Shanghai, China. Researcher. m. Meiping Wu, 4 Feb 1970, 1 d. Education: BSc, Fu-Dan Univ, Shanghai, China, 1967; MSc, Shanghai Jiao Tong Univ, Shanghai, China, 1982. Appointments: Engr, Co, Shanghai, China, 1967-82; Assoc Prof, Jiao Tong Univ, Shanghai, China, 1982-; Mbr, Tech Staff, NUS, Singapore, 1994-. Honour: Inventor, High Capacity Disk Drive Science and Technology Progress Awd, Shanghai, China, 1992. Address: 10 Kent Ridge Crescent, Data Storage Institute, Singapore 119260, Singapore.

YE Xuanping, b. Nov 1924 Meixian Co Guangdong Prof. State Offic. Education: Yan'an Coll of Nat Scis Qinghua Univ; Studies in USSR, 1950-54. Appointments: Dir Beijing No 1 Machine-tool Factory, 1963; Vice-Gov Guangdong Prov, 1980-83; Chmn Guangdong Prov Sci and Tech Cttee, 1981; Dep Sec CCP Cttee Guangzhou Municipality, 1983-; Acting Mayor Guangzhou, 1983; Mayor Guangzhou, 1983-85; Dep for Guangdong Prov to 6th NPC, 1983; Exec Chmn Preparatory Cttee for 6th NPC Games, 1985-89; Gov of Guangdong, 1985; Chmn Zhongkai Inst of Agricl Tech, 1987-; Vice-Chmn 7th CPPCC Natl Commn, 1991-; Vice-Chmn 8th Natl Cttee CPPCC, 1993-. Honours: Hon Chmn Beijing Sci and Engrng Univ, 1995-. Memberships: Alt mbr 12th CCP Cntrl Cttee, 1982; Mbr 12th CCP Cntrl Cttee, 1985; Mbr 13th CCP Cntrl Cttee, 1987-92; Mbr 14th Cntrl Cttee, 1992-. Address: Office of the Governor, Guangdong Province, People's Republic of China.

YEATS Christopher Jon, b. 6 Apr 1968, Newcastle Upon Tyne, Eng. Ore Deposit Geologist. m. Kelley, 3 Jan 1998. Education: BS, Univ of Tas, Hobart, Aust, 1989; BS, Hons, Geol, 1990; PhD, Ore Deposit Geol, Univ of West Aust, Perth, 1996. Appointments: Exploration Geol, CRA Exploration, 1990-92; Tchng, Rsch Fell, UWA, 1996-98; Rsch Geol, CSIRO Exploration and Mining, 1998-. Publications: Var Publs in Profl jrnls, 1996-. Memberships: Mbr, Soc of Econ Geol. Hobbies: Swimming; Water polo; Wine. Address: CSIRO, P O Box 136, North Ryde, NSW 1670, Australia.

YEGNESWARAN Ariyur Halasyam, b. 20 Apr 1949, Ariyur, Tamilnadu, India. Research Scientist. m. Revathi, 19 Jan 1979, 1 s, 1 d. Education: BE, Metallurgy; ME, Metallurgy; PhD, Metallurgical Engineering. Appointments: Asst Prof, PSG Coll of Tech, Coimbatore, India; Postdoct Fell, Univ of Manitoba, Winnipeg, Can; Scientist, Regl Rsch Labs, Bhopal, MP, India, 1983-. Publications: 85 rsch pprs in intl and natl jrnls publd. Address: Scientist, Regional Research Laboratory, Bhopal 462026, India.

YELDHAM Peter. Writer. m. Marjorie Crane, 27 Oct 1948, 1 s, 1 d. Creative works include: Brit TV: Armchair Th, Play of the Week, 1959-63, 1963-70; Feature Films: The Comedy Man; The Liquidator; The Long Duel; Age of Consent; Exec Prodr and writer of 10 maj Austl mini series inclng Tusitala; 1915; The Alien Years; Captain

James Cook; Naked Under Capricorn; The Heroes; The Private War of Lucinda Smith, 1978-90. Publications: Novels: Reprisal, 1994; Without Warning, 1995; Two Sides of a Triangle, 1996; A Bitter Harvest, 1997; The Currency Lads, 1998; Against the Tide, 1999. Honours: Brit Writers Guild Awd, 1963; Austl Writers Guild Awds, 1980, 1983, 1986, 1989; Sammy Awd (Best Script); 1979; Penguin Awd, 1982; AM, 1991. Membership: VP, Austl Writers Guild. Address: 1102 Yarramalong Road, Yarramalong, NSW 2259, Australia.

YEN Chen-Hsing, b. 10 July 1912 Junan Co Honan. Govt Office. m. Sou-lien Yen, 2 s, 1 d. Education: Natl Tsinghua Univ; Univ of IA. Appointments: Prof Natl Tsinghua Univ, 1941-46; Dean Coll of Engrng Natl Honan Univ, 1947-48; Chf Engr Kaohsiung Habor Bur, 1949-57; Dean Coll of Engrng Natl Taiwan Univ, 1953-55; Commnr Dept of Educ Taiwan Provincial Govt, 1962-63; Pres Natl Chengkung Univ, 1957-65; Min of Educ, 1965-69; Chmn Natl Yth Commn Exec Yuan, 1966-70; Pres Chunghsan Inst, 1969-75; Pres Natl Tsinghua Univ, 1969-70; Pres Natl Taiwan Univ, 1970-81; Chmn Atomic Energy Cncl Exec Yuan, 1981-. Honours: Hon Prof, 1981-. Memberships: Mbr Acady Sinica. Publications: Num publs on constrn. Address: Atomic Energy Council, 67 Lane 144, Keelung Road, Sec 4, Taipai, Taiwan.

YEN Kai, b. 10 Aug 1912, Fujian, China. University Professor and Honorary President. m. Chen Fangzh, July 1940, 2 s, 1 d. Education: BS, Civ Engrng, Tangshan Coll of Engrng, Chiao Tung Univ, 1933; Dip of Civ Engrng, Delft Univ of Technol, Netherlands, 1938. Appointments: Asst Engr, Pub Wrks Bur, Wuchang Municipality, 1933-35; Engr, Irrigation Serv, Yunnan Prov, 1938-40; Prof and Chmn of Hydraulic Engrng, Natl Cntrl Univ, 1940-43; Chf Des Engr, Yellow River Commn, 1943-48; Prof of Hydraulic Engrng, Chiao Tung Univ, 1948-52; Prof and Pres E China Tech Univ of Water Resources (now Hohai Univ), 1952-84; now Hon Pres; Dir, Nanjing Hydraulic Rsch Inst, 1956-84, Hon Dir, 1984-. Creative works: Articles on River and Coastal Engineering, published var periodicals and proceedings; Cnslt to a number of important engrng projs. Honours: Mbr, Chinese Acady of Scis, 1955-; Hon Pres, Hohai Univ, 1984-; Hon Dir, Nanjing Hydraulic Rsch Inst, 1984-; Hon Prof, Chengdu Univ of Sci and Technol, 1985-; Hon Prof, E China Normal Univ, 1986-; Academician, Chinese Acady of Engrng, 1995; 1st Class Prize Winner, Advmt of Sci and Technol, 1992; China Sci and Technol Prize in Engrng, 1996; Technological Sci Prize, Ho Leung Ho Lee Fndn, 1997. Memberships: Pres, Chinese Hydraulic Engrng Soc, Hon Pres, 1989-; Pres, Chinese Ocean Engrng Soc, Hon Pres, 1999-; Mbr, Bd of Dirs, China Assn for Sci and Technol; Chmn, Chinese Natl Cttee on Large Dams; Hon Mbr, Intl Asn for Hydraulic Rsch. Hobbies: Reading; Watching games. Address: Hohai University, Xikang Road 1, Nanjing 210024, China.

YEN Wen-Hsiung, b. 26 June 1934, Tainan, Taiwan. Musician. m. Yuan Yuan, 6 Jan 1961, 3 s. Education: BA, Natl Taiwan Normal Univ, 1960; MA, UCLA, 1971; Deg, Cand, Philos, Ethnomusicology, the Cultural Doctorate in Philos of Music, World Univ, 1988; Postgrad, 1995. Appointments; Instr, Natl Taichung Tchr Coll, 1961-62; Fndr, Wen Yen Piano Studio, 1972-; Fndr, Dir, Chinese Mus Orch S CA, 1974-; Fndr, Chinese Culture Sch, Los Angeles, 1976-; Prof, Chinese Culture Univ, Taipei, 1964-69; Lectr, W LA CC, 1978-82; Grad Tchng Asst, Univ MD, 1982-83; Instr, Los Angeles Cty Coll, 1983-, CA Sate Univ, Los Angeles, 1984-, Prof, Chinese Santa Monica (CA) Coll, 1986-, Pasadena Cty Coll, 1989-. Creative works: Compositions incl: Collection of Wrks by Mr Yen, 1969; Recordings: Art Songs and Chinese Folk Songs, 1982. Publications: (Auth) Taiwan Folk Songs, 1967, vol 2, 1969; A Dictionary of Chinese Music and Musicians, 1967; A Collection of Wen-hsiung Yen's Song, 1968, vol 2, 1987; Achievement and Methodology for Comparative Musicology, 1968; (transl) Chinese Musical Culture and Folk Songs, 1989; Contbr to profl jrnls. Honours: Outstndng Tchr Confucius Commemorate Day, 1984; Outstndng Tchr of 22 Yrs Serv; Chinese Overseas Affairs Commn. Memberships: Soc for Ethnmusicology; Intl Cncl for Tradl Music, Chinese-Amn Musician Assn;

Chair, Exec Cttee S CA Cncl of Chinese Sch, 1998. Hobbies: Taichi; Chuan; Table tennis; Music appreciation. Address: 482, Los Altos Avenue, Arcadia, CA 91007, USA.

YEO Cheow Tong, b. 1947. Government Minister. m. 3 d. Education: Bach of Engrng (Mechl), Univ of Western Aust. Appointments: Econ Dev Bd, 1972-75; Staff Engr, 1975, Engring Mngr, Operations Dir, Mngng Dir, 1981, LeBlond Making Asia Pte Ltd; Elected to Parl, 1984; Min of State for Hlth, Min of State for For Affairs, 1985; Returned to Parl, 1988; Snr Min of State, Acting Min for Hlth, 1988; Min for Hlth, 1990; Re-elected, 1991; Min for Hlth, Min for Cmnty Dev, 1991; Min of Trade and Ind, 1994; Re-elected, 1997; Min for Hlth, Min for Environt, 1997-.

YEO Ek-Khuan, b. 19 Dec 1947. Chartered Accountant. m. Lim Puay Chay Dora, 6 June 1978, 1 s. Education: Inst of Chart Accts, Aust. Appointments: Hon Treas, 1988-90, 1994-96, 1997-98, 2nd VP, Assn of Small and Medium Enterprises; Chmn, Granton Thornton Asia Pacific Acctng and Auditing Cttee, 1986-89; d Mbr, Singapore Natl Heart Assn, 1992, 1996, Hon Treas, 1979-92, 1993-96; Cttee Mbr, Fin and Establishment Cttee, Chinese Devel Assistance Cncl, 1996; Chmn, Audit Cttee, Singapore Natl Kidney Fndn, 1996. Membership: Kiwans Club of Singapore. Hobbies: Stamp collecting; Reading. Address: 47 Hill Street #05-01, Chinese Chamber of Commerce and Industry Building, Singapore 179365, Singapore.

YEO George Yong-Boon, b. 13 Sept 1954, Singapore. Minister. m. Leong Lai Peng, 17 June 1984, 3 s, 1 d. Education: BA, Engrng, Cambridge; MBA, Harv Univ. Appointments: MP, Aljunied GRC; Min for Trade and Ind. Hobbies: Travel; Jogging; Reading; Swimming; Golf. Address: Ministry of Trade and Industry, 100 High Street, #90-01, The Treasury, Singapore 179434, Republic of Singapore.

YEO Ning Hong, b. 3 Nov 1943. Chairman. m. Janny Hong Shien Zee, 12 Aug 1967, 2 d. Education: BSc, hons, MSc, Singapore, 1968; MA, PhD, Cambridge, 1970; Exec Prog, London Bus Sch, 1977. Appointments: Rsch Assoc, Stanford Univ, 1970-71; Lectr, Univ of Singapore, 1971-74; Mngmt Appts, Intl Pharm Co, 1974-80; Min of State for Def, Singapore, 1981-83; Min for Commns and Info, 1983-91; Min for Def, 1991-94; Chmn, Port of Singapore Authy, 1994-; Chmn, Keppel Golf Club, 1994-; Exec Chmn, Singapore Technols Grp of Cos, 1995-97; Hon Fell, Christ's Coll, Cambridge, 1998-; Pres, Singapore Natl Olympic Cncl, 1991-98. Publications: 25 rsch pprs on chem in num intl jrnls. Honours: Charles Darwin Mem Prize, Christ's Coll, Cambridge, England, 1970; Intl Olympic Cttee Centennial Trophy, 1994. Hobbies: Sailing; Golfing; Reading. Address: PSA Corporation Ltd, 460 Alexandra Road, Singapore 119963, Singapore.

YEOH Barbara May, b. 13 Oct 1948, Melbourne, Aust. Director. 2 d. Education: BSc, hons, Melbourne. Appointments: Cncl Mbr, LaTrobe Univ, 1987-97; Bd Mbr, Rural Fin Corp, 1988-, Credit Union Servs Corp, 1992-, Natl Rail Corp Ltd, 1993-, Housing Guarantee Fund Ltd, 1996-; Mbr, Vic Atty-Gen's Law Reform Advsry Cncl, 1997-. Memberships: Fin Execs Inst of Aust; Fell, Austl Inst of Co Dirs. Hobbies: Gardening; Reading; The Arts; Cooking. Address: 4 Elgin Street, Hawthorn, Victoria 3122, Australia.

YEOMANS Neville David, b. 4 Mar 1943, Melbourne, Aust. Physician. m. Margot, 22 Feb 1968, 1 s, 1 d. Education: MBBS (Melb); MD (Mon); FRACP; FACG. Appointments: Snr Lectr, 1977, Assoc Prof, 1980, Prof, 1988-, Med, Univ of Melbourne. Publications: Approximately 150 scientific papers, 1970-. Memberships: Pres, Gastroenterological Soc of Aust, 1997-99; Cnclr, Roy Austl Coll Physns, 1995-97. Address: University of Melbourne Department of Medicine, Western Hospital, Footseray, Vic 3011, Australia.

YEUNG Chap Yung, b. 29 Dec 1936, Hong Kong, China. Paediatrician. m. Helen Chiu, 1963, 2 s. Education: MBBS (Hong Kong); DCH (London); MRCP (UK); FRCP (Edin); FRCP (C); FRCP (Lond); FRCP (Glasg); FRCP (Ireland); Amn Bd Pediatns. Appointments: Cnslt i/c Pediat Unit, QEH (Hong Kong), 1970-72; Asst Prof, McMasters Univ, 1972-76; Cnclt, Toronto, 1977-80; Prof & Hd, Dept Pediats, Univ Hong Kong, 1980-. Publications: 2 books: 20 chapts in books; 176 pprs in intl sci jrnls; 150 abstracts in var sci meetings. Honours: Hon Prof of 7 univs in China; Hon Mbr, Amn Pediat Soc, 1990; Hon Fell, Philippines Pediat Assn, 1997; Hon Life Mbr, HK Pediat Soc, 1990-. Memberships: Pres, Fedn China Can Profls, 1979-80; Pres, Hong Kong Maternal and Neonatal Hlth, 1984-97; Pres, HK Coll Pediatns, 1990-97. Hobbies: Reading; Cross-country. Address: Department of Pediatrics, University of Hong Kong, Queen Mary Hospital, Hong Kong, China.

YI Kyongsu, b. 12 Nov 1962, 1 s, 1 d. Education: PhD, Univ of CA, Berkeley, CA, USA, 1992. Appointments: UC Berkeley ITS, USA, 1992-93; Assoc Prof, Hanyang Univ, Seoul, Korea, 1993-. Honour: KSME Ppr Awd, 1997. Memberships: ASME; KSME; KSAE; ICASE. Hobbies: Tennis; Soccer. Address: Mido Apt #201-903, Daechi-dong 544 Kangnam-ku, Seoul 135-280, Korea.

YILMAZ A Mesut, b. 6 Nov 1947 Istanbul. Politician. m. Berna Muren, 2 s. Education: Istanbul High Sch for Boys; Fac of Polit Studies Ankara; London and Cologne. Appointments: Fmr co dir in priv bus sector; Dep for Rize, 1983-; Fmr Min of State; Min of Culture and Tourism, 1986-87; Min of For Affairs, 1987-90; PM of Turkey, Jun-Nov 1991, 1996, Jun 1997-. Ldr Motherland Party; Vice-Chmn EDU. Address: Basbakanlik, Bakanliklar, Ankara, Turkey.

YIM Wyss Wai-Shu, b. 14 Oct 1947, Hong Kong. Academic. m. Fiona, 10 Aug 1976, 2 s. Education: DSc (London); PhD (Tasmania); Dip of Imperial Coll DIC; BS, MPhil (London); Dip in Mineral Technol (Camborne). Appointments: Asst Prof to Assoc Prof, 1974-. Publications: Geol of Surficial Deposits in Hong Kong, 1984. Memberships: Pres, W Pacific Subcommn on Quatenary Shorelines; Intl Union for Quatenary Rsch, 1995-99; Co-Ldr IGCP (Intl Geol Correlation Prog, Proj 396, "Continental Shelves in the Quatenary"), 1996-2000; Fell, Geol Soc; Chartered Engr; Chartered Geolst. Hobbies: Scuba; Golf. Address: Department of Earth Sciences, The University of Hong Kong, Pokfulam Road, Hong Kong SAR, China.

YIN Guoming, b. 16 Dec 1956, Yining Cty, Xinjiang Prov, China. Professor. m. Josephine Chao, 4 Sept 1986, 1 s. Education: Masters degree, Chinese Lit, East China Normal Univ of Shanghai, 1984. Appointments: Prof, Guangzhou Jinan Univ, 1993-; Prof, Dr-Dir, Shanghai East China Normal Univ, 1995-. Publications: Forms of Art Are Not the Only Forms, 1988; Artists and Death, 1990; Thinking at Night, 1990; To Look at USA by Third Eye, 1995. Hobbies: Chinese chess; Swimming; Travel. Address: Chinese Language and Literature Department, Eastern China Normal University, Shanghai 200062, China.

YIN Hongfu, b. 15 Mar 1935, China. Professor. m. Hu Yong, Apr 1964, 1 s, 1 d. Education: Undergrad, BA, Dept Geol, Beijing Coll of Geol, 1952-56; Rsch Student, MA, Grad Sch of Beijing Coll of Geol, 1956-61. Appointments: Asst Prof, 1961-78, Lectr, 1978-80, Assoc Prof, 1980-86, Prof, 1986-, China Univ of Geosciences, formerly Beijing, 1952-75, Wuhan Coll of Geol, 1975-87; Pres, China Univ of Geoscis (Wuhan); State Level Specialist nominated by State Cncl, 1990-. Publications: 170 acad pprs; 18 books. Memberships: Acady of China, 1993-; Chinese People's Polit Consultative Conf, 1998-. Address: Office of the President, China University of Geosciences, Wuhan, Hubei 430074, China.

YIN Jun, b. Sept 1932. Politician. Appointments: Chmn and Gov Dali Bai Autonomous Pref Yunnan Prov, 1982-84; Sec Discipline Insp Cttee Yunnan CCP Prov Cttee, 1985; Dep Sec Yunnan Prov Cttee, 1989; Chmn Yunnan Prov 8th People's Congress, 1993-. Memberships: Alt mbr 12th CCP Cntrl Cttee, 1982; Alt mbr 13th CCP Cntrl Cttee, 1987. Address: Dali Bai Autonomous Prefectural People's Government, Yunnan, People's Republic of China.

YIN Kesheng, b. 1932. Politician. Education: Beijing Pet Inst. Appointments: Vice-Gov Qinghai, 1983; Sec CCP Cttee Qinghai, 1985. Memberships: Mbr 12th CCP Cntrl Cttee, 1985-87; Mbr 13th CCP Cntrl Cttee, 1987-92; Mbr 14th Cntrl Cttee, 1992-. Address: Qinghai Provincial Chinese Communist Party, Xining, Qinghai, People's Republic of China.

YIN Weihong, b. 19 Nov 1936, Zhejiang Prov, China. Profesor. m. Shen, 7 Feb 1969, 2 s. Education: NE Univ, 1957-62; Tech Univ of Vienna, Aust, 1979-82; DTech, 1982. Appointments: VP, NW Inst for Nonferrous Metal Rsch, 1985-95; Ed-in-Chf, J Rare Metal Materials and Engrng, 1986-. Publications: 60 pprs on rare metal materials, 1971-; Ed, Proceedings of Refractory Metals, Sci and Technol, 1993, 1998. Honours: Awds of Sci and Technol Achmnts of Min and Prov in China, 1980, 1988, 1995; Prizes of China Natl Outsndng Sci and Technol periodical, 1993, 1997. Memberships: Cncl Nonferrous Metals Soc of China, 1984-; Intl Liason Bd of Intl Plansee Seminar, 1993-. Hobby: Table tennis. Address: Northwest Institute for Nonferrous Metal Research (NIN), Po Box 51, Xi'an, Shaanxi 710016, China.

YIN Xing, b. 14 Feb 1933, Shanghai, China. Consultant. m. Chen Ding-Hua, 4 Nov 1962. Education: Grad, Shanghai Second Medl Univ, 1956. Appointments: Hd, Dept of Diagnostic Reagents, 1979; Hd, Dept of Bacterial Vaccines, 1980; Hd, Dept of Bacterial Diagnostic Reagents, 1986; Hd, Dept of Bacterial and Immune Diagnostic Reagents, 1989; Cnslt, Shanghai Inst of Biol Prods, 1991; Cnslt, Bacteriology Rsch Lab, 1996-; Cnslt, Dept of Bacterial Rsch, 1999-. Publications: Manual of Practical Pharmacology (co-auth), 1991; Manual of Medical Laboratory Diagnostics (co-auth), 1992; Preparation and Application of Medical Laboratory Diagnostic Reagents (co-auth), 1996. Honour: Professorship, 1987. Memberships: cnsl Mbr, Shanghai Assn for Anti-Tuberculosis, 1986-97; Editl bd, Jrnl of Microbiological Vol of Medl Abroad, 1990-. Hobbies: Watching television; Sightseeing. Address: 1262 Yan An Road (Western) Shanghai 200052, China.

YING Mingde, b. 26 Feb 1929, Wuxi, Jiangsu, China. Medical Teaching, Practice and Scientific Research. m. Jiangming Bei, 27 Mar 1958, 1 s. Education: BM, Natl Jiangsu Med Coll, 1946-52; Postgrad, Beijing Univ Med Coll, 1953. Appointments: Asst, Res Dr, 1953, Visng Lectr, 1956, Vice Chf Assoc Prof, 1981, Chf Prof, 1986. Publications: Emergency Otolaryngology; Dizziness; Fundamentals of Otolaryngology; Otolaryngology - Head and Neck Surgery; Chaps in 10 books and 100 medl articles in profl jrnls. Honours: 3rd Municipal and 4th Prov Sci and Technol Awds, Ctrl Peoples Govt Allowance. Memberships include: Soc of Otolaryngol CMA; Chinese Assn of the Integration of TCM and Western Med; Am Acady of Otolaryngol, Hd and Neck Surg; Amn Rhinol Soc; Amn Coll of Allergy Asthma and Immunology; Intl Soc of Otorhinolaryngolgic Allergy and Immunol. Hobbies: Music; Poetry; Literature; Arts. Address: 1st Affiliated Hospital, Nanjing Medical University, 300 Guangzhou Road, Nanjing 210029, China.

YISHAI Eliyahu, b. 1963 Jerusalem. Politician. m. 4 c. Appointments: Fmr hd of Interior Mins bur; Acting Sec Gen Shas - Sephardic Torah Guardians - 1991-; Dir Gen Shas-affiliated El ha-Ma'ayan movement; Min of Labour and Socl Welfare, 1996-. Address: Ministry of Labour and Social Welfar, P O Box 915, Rehov Kaplan, Kiryat Ben-Gurion, Jerusalem 91008, Israel.

YIXI Zeren, b. 26 May 1952, Kangding, Sichuan, China. Writer; Editor. m. Gao Lanling, 28 Dec 1980, 1 d. Education: Grad, Inst of Lit, Chinese Writers Union, 1981. Appointments: Reporter, Seda Grassland, 1971-; Newsppr Reporter, 1973-; Ed, Lit Mag, 1983-. Publications: The Hometown of the Wild Goose, 1983; The Necklace of Turquoise, 1987; The Polar Region, 1991; Long for the Balkan (prose), 1996; The Selected Fictions of Yixi Zeren, 1998. Honours: Prize, Ex Works, 1985; Prize, Lit Creation, Chinese Minoirty Natl, 1985, 1990; Highest Prize, Sichuan Lit of Guo Moruo, 1988. Memberships: Chinese Writers Union; Vice Chmn, Chinese Acady of Arts and Letters, Sichuan, Chinese Writers Union, Sichuan. Hobbies: Football; Singing; Collecting books; Drawing. Address; Sichuan Literature Monthly, 85 2nd Sect, Red Star Avenue, Chengdu 610012, China.

YOCKLUNN John Soong Chung (Sir), b. 5 May 1933, Canton, China. Retired Librarian. m. Patricia Ann Mehegan, 29 Jan 1981. Education: BA, Univ of WA, 1960; BA, Austl Natl Univ, 1963; MA, Univ of Sheffield, 1974. Appointments include: Natl Lib of Aust, 1964-67; Exec Offr, Pub Serv Bd of Papua New Guinea, 1969-70; Advsr on Hons to PM of PNG, Chmn, Hons and Awds Advsry Cttee, 1975-83; Dir, Roy Visits to PNG, 1975, 1977, 1982; Polit Advsr, Pangu Pati, 1968-83; Natl Libn of PNG, 1978-83; Chf Libn, Monash Univ Coll, Gippsland, Vic, 1983-93; Assoc Univ Libn, Monash Univ, 1994-98; Retired. Honours: KB, 1975; KCVO, 1977; James Cook Bicentenary Schl, 1972. Memberships include: Assoc, Lib Assn, UK; Assoc, Lib Assn of Aust; Orders and Medals Rsch Soc, UK; Heraldry Soc, UK; Heraldry Aust Inc; Rockhampton Chinese Assn, VP, 1999-; Univ Lib Soc of Rockhampton, VP, 1999; Mus of Chinese Austl Hist, Life Mbr and VP, 1992-98. Hobbies: Heraldry; Orders and medal research; History of the Chinese in Australia. Listed in: Who's Who; Who's Who in Australia. Address: 11 Melbourne Street, Rockhampton, Qld 4700, Australia.

YOKOSAKA Yasuhiko, b. 5 Feb 1956, Aomori, Japan. Associate Professor of Music History and Musicology. m. 10 July 1983, 1 s, 2 d. Education: BA, Baker Univ, 1978; MM, Yale Inst of Sacred Music, 1981; DEd, Columbia Univ, 1985. Appointments: Assoc Prof of Music History and Musicology, Fac of Educ, Univ of Niigata. Publications: Developing Guidelines for the Revision of the Hymnal, 1954, 1985; Stylistic Development of the Choral Preludes by J S Bach, 1986; Music Critiques, in the Niigata Nippoh, 1988-; Introduction to Church Music and Hymnody, 1993. Honour: Hugh Porter Schl Awd, Yale Inst of Sacred Music, 1981. Memberships: Hymn Soc, US, Can; Hymn Soc of GB and Ireland; Musicological Soc of Japan. Hobbies: Swimming; Travel. Address: Faculty of Education, The University of Niigata, 8050 Ikarashhi Ni-No-cho, Niigata-shi, 950-21, Japan.

YOKOYAMA Shoichi, b. 9 Nov 1945, Japan. Managing Director; General Manager. m. Emi Hirase, 26 Mar 1970, 1 s, 1 d. Education: BA, Keio Univ; Dip, Inst for Intl Stdies and Trng. Publication: Asagiri, co-auth, book. Memberships: Abu Dhabi Mitakai, Chmn, 1997; Roy Automobile Club; Intl House of Japan. Hobbies: Tennis; Golf; Skiing; Classical music. Address: PO Box 2374, Abu Dhabi, United Arab Emirates.

YOMA Edmundo J Pérez. b. 10 Jan 1939, Antofagasta, Chile. Minister of National Defence. m. 6 children. Education: BA, Univ WA, USA. Appointments: Mbr, Christian Democratic Party, 1957-; Mbr, Natl Cncl, 1988-91; Pres, Def Commn 1991-94; Natl VP, 1993-94; Mngr, Empresa Pesquera Guanaye, 1963-71; Dir, Labour Bank, 1965-71; Pres, Dir, Co-op Radio, 1972-94; Pres, Metropolitan Petrox and Chilectra, 1990-92; Min of Natl Def, 1994-. Address: Ministry of National Defence, Villavicencio 364, 22 Edif Diego Portales, Santiago, Chile.

YOMTOV Michelle, b. 24 Mar 1948, Galveston, TX, USA. Writer; Investigative Journalist. m. Joseph Yomtov. Education: MA, Spec Educ. Appointment: Advsr, Los Angeles Metro Transit Authy, 1997. Publications: Year Book of Modern Poetry, 1975; Burbank: The Fourth Reich, 1986; Something Strange Called Depression, 1996. Honour: Educr of the Yr, CA Cncl on Depression, 1992. Memberships: Fndr, Legal Assistant for Mental Patients; Investigator for Citizen Cmmn on Human Rights. Hobbies: Classical music; Child advocacy; Mental health advocacy; Hiking. Address: 3361 Perlita Avenue, Los Angeles, CA 90039, USA.

YON Hyong-Muk, b. 3 Nov 1931 N Hamgyong Prov. Politician. Education: Univ. Appointments: Wrkd as farm labourer then techn; Dep to Supreme People's Ass, 1967-; Vice-Dir then Dir of Dept Cntrl Cttee Wrkrs Party of Korea - KWP; Vice-Premier then First Vice-Premier Admin Cncl; Sec to Party Ctr; Premier Admin Cncl, 1988-92. Honours: Kim Il-Sung Medal; Order of the Natl Flag - First Class; Order of Freedom and Indep - First Class. Memberships: Mbr KWP Cntrl Cttee, Nov 1970-; Mbr Polit Bur, 1973-. Address: c/o Office of the Premier, Pyongyang, Democratic People's Republic of Korea.

YONG Pung How, b. 11 Apr 1926. Chief Justice of Supreme Court. m. Cheang Wei-woo, 1955, 1 d. Education: Vic Instn, Kuala Lumpur; Dwoning Coll, Cambridge; Harvard Bus Sch; Called to Engl Bar, Inner Temple, 1951, Hon Bencher, 1997. Appointments include: Ptnr, Shook Lin & Bok, 1952-70; Gov of Singapore, 1953; Chmn, Malayan Pub Serv Arbitration Tribunal, 1955-60; Chmns Panel, Malayan Indl Crt, 1961-67; Chmn, Malayan Airways Ltd, Malaysia-Singapore Airlines Ltd, 1964-69; Dpty Chmn, Malayan Banking Bhd, 1966-70; Chmn, Mngng Dir, Singapore Intl Merchant Bankers Ltd, 1971-81; Dir, Overseas-Chinese Banking Corp Ltd, 1972; Vice Chmn, 1977-80; Mbr, Securities Ind Cncl, 1974-81; Fell, Malaysian Inst of Mngmt, 1975-; Mngng Dir, Govt of Singapore Investment Corp, 1981-83, Dir, 1983-89; Mngng Dir, Nonetary Authy of Singapore, 1982-83; Dpty Chmn, Bd of Cmmnrs of Currency, 1982-83; Alternate Gov for Singapore Intl Monetary Fund, 1982-83; Mbr, Prov Mass Rapid Tansit Authy; Judge, Supreme Crt, 1989-90; Chf Justice, 1990-; Chmn, Pres Cncl for Minority Rights, 1990-; Pres, Legal Serv Cmmn, 1990-; Pres, Singapore Acady of Law, 1990-; Acting Pres, Singapore, 1991. Memberships: Pyramid Club; Singapore Cricket Club; Warren Golf Club. Address: c/o Supreme Court, 1 St Andrews Road, Singapore 178957, Singapore.

YOO Changsik, b. 15 Dec 1969, Daejon, Korea. Research Staff. Education: PhD, Electron Engrng, Seoul Natl Univ. Appointment: Rsch Staff, Swiss Fed Inst of Technol, Zurich, 1998-. Publications: Sev articles in profl jrnls. Honours: Highest Hon, Seoul Natl Univ, 1992; Silver Prize, LG IC Design Contest, 1996. Memberships: IEEE; KITE. Hobbies: Reading; Swimming. Address: Gloriastrasse 35, IIS, ETH Zentrum, 8092 Zurich, Switzerland.

YOO Chong-Ha, B. 28 July 1936. Minister of Foreign Affairs. m. 3 s. Education: Seoul Natl Univ; Univ of Bonn. Appointments: Joined Min of For Affairs, 1959; 3rd Sec, Emb, Germany, 1963-68; Cnsl, Chgo, USA, 1968, Islamabad, 1968-71; Dir, S E Asia Div, Min of For Affairs, 1971-74; Cnlr, Emb, USA, 1974-77; Dpty Dir-Gen, Amn Affairs Bur, Min of For Affairs, 1977-78; Dir-Gen, 1978-80; Min, Emb, UK, 1980-83; Amb to Sudan, 1983-85, Belgium, 1987-89, EC (now EU), 1989; Asst Min for Econ Affairs, Min of For Affairs, 1985-87; Vice Min of For Affairs, 1989-92; Perm Rep to UN, 1992-94; Snr Advsr to Pres, For Plcy and Natl Security, 1994-96, Honours: Order of Serv Merit w Red Stripes, Yellow Stripes and Blue Stripes. Address: Min of For Affairs, 77 Sejong-no, Chongno-ku, Seoul, Republic of Korea.

YOO Chong Ha, b. 28 July 1936. Politician; Diplomatist. m. 3 s. Education: Seoul Natl Univ; Bonn Univ. Appointments: Joined Min of For Affairs, 1959; Third Sec Bonn Emb, 1963-68; Consul Chgo, May-Oct 1968; Cnsl, Islamabad, 1968-71; Dir SE Asia Div Min of For Affairs, 1971-74; Cnslr WA Emb, 1974-77; Dep Dir-Gen Amn, Affair Bur min of For Affairs, 1977-78; Dir-Gen Am Affairs Bur min of For Affairs, 1978-80; Min Emb London, 1980-83; Amb to Sudan 1983-85; Amb to Belgium, 1987-89; Min to EC, Feb-Dec 1989; Asst Min for Econ Affairs, Min of For Affairs, 1985-87; Vice-Min of For Affairs, 1989-92; Perm Rep to UN, 1992-94; Snr Advsr to Pres for For Policy and Natl Security, 1994-96; Min of For Affairs, 1996-98. Honours: Order of Service Merit w Red Stripes. Address: c/o Ministry of Foreign Affairs, 77 Sejong-no, Chongno-ku, Seoul, Republic of Korea.

YOO Vak Yeong, b. Seoul, Korea. Physician. Education: MA; MD. Appointments: Dir of Clin, 1982-92; Hd of Medl Exam Cntr, 1982-; Dir of Hosp, 1992; Pres, Support grp for Menoosteoporosis; Ed, Jrnl Meno/Osteoporosis; Assoc Ed, Jrnl Korean Soc of Menopause. Publications: Phytoestrogen, 1995; Quality of Mid-Beyond Women's Life, 1996; Aging and Gender Specific, 1997. Memberships: Inter Menopause Society, Belgium, 1994; NAMS, Cleveland, 1995; The Endocrine Society, Bethseda; NOF, Wash DC. Hobbies: Computers; Singing; Listening to music. Address: Ceongvak Primebeyond Hospital, 582 Shinsa Dong Kangnam Ku Seoul 135-120, Korea.

YOON Hoil, b. 22 Nov 1943, Japan. Lawyer. m. Giyun Yoon, 1 June 1968, 1 s, 3 d. Education: LLB, magna cum laude, Seoul Natl Univ Law Sch, 1965; LLM, summa cum laude, Seoul Natl Univ Grad Sch of Justice, 1967; JD, magna cum laude, Univ of Notre Dame Law Sch, 1973. Appointments: Judge, Seoul Civil Dist Crt, 1970; Cmmnr, Korea Fair Trade Commn, 1996-98. Publications: Taxation of Foreign Investment and Trade, 1977; Legal Aspects of Doing Business in and with the Republic of Korea, 1978; Relief for Wrongful Conduct in Futures Trading, 1993. Honour: Presl Citation, Decoration, Korean Govt, 1984. Memberships: Korean Bar Assn; Am Bar Assn; NY, IL and WA DC Bar Assns. Hobbies: Hiking; Golf. Address: Suite 831, Korea Chamber of Commerce and Industry Building, 45 Namdaemoonro-4-ka, Chung-ku, Seoul 100 743, Korea.

YORK Michael DeDutton, b. 7 Oct 1926, Sydney, Aust. Retired Company Director. m. Jeannette Dorothy Davey, 25 Mar 1955, 2 s, 1 d. Education: Cranebrook Sch, Sydney. Appointments: Marine Engr, Shaw Savill, 1948-50; Co-Fndr, Dir, Barlow Winch Co, 1962-80; Fndr, Borg-Warner, (Aust), Ltd, Mech Seal Div, Aust and S E Asia, 1966; Appointed Mngng Dir, subsequently Gen Mngr; Retired Memberships: Innovation Cncl NSW, Dir, 1986-; Cttee for Econ Dev Aust, Mbr Bd Trees; Inst Dirs; Roy Sydney Yacht Sqdn; Cruising Yacht Club Aust, Fndr Mbr and Rear Commodore, 1965; Inst Navig, 1969-; Natl Trust Aust, NSW; Sydney Maritime Mus, Pres, 1980-82; Life Gov, 1982; Yachting Fedn, NSW, Mbr Rules Cttee, 1987-. Hobby: Yachting; Sailed in Sydney to Hobart Races, sailed aboard Kialoa II, Record Race Holder, 1975. Address: 18A Drummoyne Ave, Drummoyne, NSW 2047, Aust.

YOSANO Kaoru, b. 22 Aug 1938. Politician. Education: Tokyo Univ. Appointments: Fmr Parly Vice-Min of Intl Trade and Ind; Min of Educ, 1994-95; Dep Chmn LDP Diet Affairs Cttee; Chmn LDP Pub Rels Cttee. Memberships: Mbr HoR. Address: c/o Jiyu-Minshuto, 1-11-23 Nagata-cho, Chiyoda-ku, Tokyo 100, Japan.

YOSHIDA Yoichi, b. 19 Jan 1938, Akita, Japan. President. m. Sachiko Sakurai, 29 Mar 1971, 3 s. Education: Fac of Com, Takushoku Univ. Appointments: Sec, Tokyo Hamamatsucho Lions Club, 1983-84; VP, THLC, 1988-90; Chmn, PTA, Akasaka Primary Sch, 1986-88; Chmn, PTA, Akasaka Jnr HS and Fedn of PTAs, Minato-Ward, 1990-91. Memberships: Med Instrument Soc of Japan; Japan Med Products Intl Trade Assn. Hobbies: Music; Camping; Hiking; Travel. Address: Villurage Nogizaka 203, No 5 28 Akasaka 9-chome, Minato-ku, Tokyo 107-0052, Japan.

YOSHIDA Yutaka, b. 28 Aug 1930, Japan. University President. m. Toshiko, 30 Sept 1957, 2 d. Education: PhD, Hirosaki Univ Sch of Med, 1964. Appointments: Instr, 1st Dept of Internal Med, 1961-64, Asst Prof, 1964-65, Assoc Prof, 1965-75, Prof, Chmn, 1975-96, Dean of Sch, 1988-96, Pres, 1996-, Hirosaki Univ Sch of Med. Publications: Studies on CPSF, 1964; Gastroenterology, 1997. Honours: Too (Newsppr Co) Awd, 1991; Aomori Prefectural Awd, 1992; Kahoku Culture Awd, 1996. Memberships: Amn Gastroenterol Assn; Bd of Govs, Japan Soc of Gastroenterol. Hobby: Golf. Address: Office of the President, Hirosaki University, 1 Bunkyo-cho, Hirosaki, Aomori-ken 036-8560, Japan.

YOSHIHARA Hideki, b. 2 Apr 1941, Osaka, Japan. University Professor. m. Fusaka, 15 Jan 1969, 1 s, 1 d. Education: BA, Dept of Bus Admin, 1964, MBA, Grad Sch of Bus Admin, 1966, PhD, Grad Sch of Bus Admin, 1988, Kobe Univ. Appointments: Asst, 1966-71, Assoc Prof, 1971-83, Prof, 1984, Dir, Prof, 1992-96, Prof-, 1996-, Research Institute for Economics and Business Administration (RIEB), Kobe Univ. Publications; Business History of General Trading Companies (co-ed), 1987; Strategy and Performance of Foreign Companies in Japan, (co-auth), 1994. Membership: Acady of Intl Bus. Hobby: Gardening. Address: The Research Institute for Economics and Business Administration, (RIEB), Kobe University, 2-1 Rokko-dai Nada-ku, Kobe City, Japan.

YOSHIKAWA Masanosuke, b. 19 Dec 1934, Osaka, Japan. Professor of Microbiology. 2 s. Education: CMD, Univ Tokyo; DMS. Appointments: Prof, Univ Tokyo, 1982; Prof, Nipon Dental Univ, 1995; Emer Prof, Univ Tokyo. Publications: Over 150 sci articles in profl jrnls. Honour: Asakawa Awd, Japanese Soc for Bacteriol. Memberships include: Am Soc for Microbiol. Address: 2-13-36 Edakita, Aoba-ku, Yokohama Kanagawa-ken 225-0015, Japan.

YOSHIMURA Toshio, b. 30 Jan 1934, Tokyo, Japan. Journalist. m. Eiko Watanabe, 27 Sept 1959, 1 s. Education: BEcon, Kanto Gakuin Univ, Yokohama, 1956; Postgrad Studies, Cornell Univ, Ithaca, NY, USA, 1957. Appointments: Editl Asst, Tokyo Bur, Intl News Serv, 1958; Reporter, Japan News Ed, Far E Bur, Fairchild News Serv, 1959-65; Corresp, Far E Bur, McGraw-Hill World News, 1965-69; Chf, Tokyo Bur, Far Eastern Econ Review, 1970-72; Ed, Publr, Asia Pacific Forum, 1974-80; Ed, Publr, Tokyo Report, 1979-. Publications: The Long March: The Untold Story, Harrison E Salisbury (trans), 1985; Chosei: Katararezaru Shinjitsu, 1988; Num news and commentaries published in newspprs and mags at home and abroad. Honours: Grand Prize, Fiarchild News and Reporting Contest, 1959, for the coverage of devl of tunnel diode by Dr Leo Esaki; Grand Prize, Daily News Record, News and Reporting Contest, 1962, for the coverage of the Japan-US textile negotiations. Hobby: Hiking. Address: 1-14-8 bubai-cho, Fuchu, Tokyo 183-0033, Japan.

YOSHINO Fumio, b. 7 Aug 1925, Tokyo, Japan. Physician; Nursing Educator. m. Hisayo Niwa, 15 Nov 1955, 1 s, 1 d. Education: MD, Yokohama Medl Coll, 1951; DMedSc, Kyoto Univ, 1959. Appointments: Prof, Medl Technol, Kanagawa Prefectural Coll of Nursing and Medl Technol, 1968-91; Prof Emer, 1991-. Publications: Textbooks of Medical Technology; Handbook for Diagnosis Using Laboratory Data; S1 Units in medicine. Honour: Mbr Emeritus, Amn Assn for Clin Chem. Memberships: Japanese Soc of Clin Path; Japanese Soc of Path; Japanese Soc of Clin Chem. Address: 174-44, Ooba-cho, Aoba-ku, Yokohama 225-0023, Japan.

YOSHIO Sugimoto, b. 7 Dec 1939, Japan. Professor of Sociology. m. Machiko Sato, 16 July 1966, 1 s, 2 d. Education: BA, Kyoto Univ, 1964; PhD, Univ Pitts, 1973. Appointments: Staff Writer, The Nainichi Newspprs, Tokyo, 1964-67; Tchng Fell, Dept of Sociol, Univ Pitts, USA, 1967-72; Lectr, 1973-74, Snr Lectr, 1975-82, Rdr, 1983-87, Dept of Sociol, Prof, Sch of Sociol, Politics and Anthropol, 1988-, La Trobe Univ. Publications include: Popular Disturbance in Postwar Japan, 1981; Democracy in Contemporary Japan, 1986; The Japanese Trajectory: Modernization and Beyond, 1988; The MFP Debate: A Background Reader, 1990; An Introduction to Japanese Society, 1997. Honours: Japan Intercultural Publns Awd, Japan Soc of Trans, 1987; FAHA, 1988-. Memberships: Sev. Address: School of Scoiology, Politics and Anthropology, La Trobe University, Bundoora, Melbourne, Victoria 3083, Australia.

YOU Jian Qi, b. 9 Apr 1936, Fuzhou, China. Astronomer; Researcher. m. Wang Chuan jin, 20 Jan 1960, 1 d. Appointments: Rsch Asst, 1958-64, Asst Rschr, 1964-83, Assoc Rschr, 1983-86, Rschr, Hd of Solar Div, 1986-96, Purple Mountain Observatory. Creative Works: Has been working on the Solar Physics and Solar Instrumentation since 1958, including design and installation of the multi-channel solar spectrograph, four successful observations of solar total eclipses in 1968, 1980, 1983 and 1991, investigations on the infrared 10830Å spectra of the quiet and active sun with solid state detectors; Contbrns to var mags and jrnls. Honour: 1st Class Prize, Sci and Technique Achievement, Chinese Acady of Scis, 1981. Memberships: Intl Astronomical Union; Chinese Astronomical Soc. Listed in: Worlds Who's Who of Women. Hobbies: Literature appreciation; Gardening; Stone collecting. Address: Purple Mountain Observatory, Nanjing 210008, China.

YOU Xigui. Army Officer. Appointments: Personal bodyguard to Pres Jiang Zemin, 1994-; Fmr acting Dir Bodyguards Bur PLA; Dir Bodyguards Bur PLA, 1996-. Memberships: Alt mbr 15th CCP Cntrl Cttee, 1997-. Address: People's Liberation Army, c/o Ministry of National Defence, Jingshanqian Jie, Beijing, People's Republic of China.

YOUNG Gloria Frances, b. 12 Aug 1941. Potter. Education: NZ Cert in Ceramics. Honours: McSkimmings Awd of Merit in Ceramics, 1979; GEC Awd for Raku, 1982; Judges Commendation Awd, 1992. Memberships: NZ Acady of Fine Arts; NZ Soc of Potters; Wellington Potters Assn. Hobby: Skiing. Address: c/o Bloomsbury, 16 Majoribanks St, Mt Victoria, Wellington, New Zealand.

YOUNG Gregory Cyril, b. 24 Oct 1947, Hobart, Tas, Aust. Historian; Planner. Education: BA Hons, Univ Tas, 1971; Dip Urban Studies, Macquarie Univ, Sydney, NSW, 1980; MA, Univ Sydney, 1988. Appointments: Histn, NSW Min Plng, 1976-78; Histn, NSW Plng and Environment Commn, 1978-80; Histn, Planner, NSW Dept Environment and Plng, 1980-86; Plcy Advsr, NSW Dept Plng, 1986-90; Mngr, Plng, Tourism-NSW, 1990-91; Chair, Sydney Harbour Natl Pk Advsry Cttee, 1990; Mbr, NSW Govt Patrick White Nurse Wrkng Party, 1996; Dir, Pac Rim Plng Pty Ltd, 1991-97; Young Cnslts Pty Ltd, 1997-. Publications: Environmental Conservation - Towards A Philosophy, 1984; Conservation, History and Development, 1988; NSW Cultural Tourism Strategy, 1991; Mapping Culture - A Guide for Cultural and Economic Development in Communities, 1995. Honours: Max Kelly Schlshp, NSW Govt Inaugural Sydney-Venice Exch Schl, 1997. Memberships: Roy Austl Plng Inst; ICOMOS, Aust; Austl Rep, Intl ICOMOS Cultural Tourism Cttee, 1998-. Hobbies: New writing; Music; Global culture; Travel. Address: 211 Underwood Street, Paddington, Sydney, NSW 2021, Australia.

YOUNG John Atherton, b. Brisbane, Aust. Professor of Physiology; Pro Vice Chancellor (Health Sciences). Education: BSc Hons, 1958; MBBS Hons, 1960; MD, 1965; DSc, 1975; Univ of Qld; FRACP, 1973; FAA, 1986. Appointments: JRMO, Roy Brisbane Hosp, 1961; NH & MRC Snr Rsch Offr, Sydney Hosp, Kanematsu Inst, 1962-64; C J Martin Rsch Fell, Physiology Inst, Free Univ of Berlin, 1965-66; Snr Lectr, 1967-70; Assoc Prof 1971-75, Prof 1976-, Dean of Fac of Med, 1989-97, Pro Vice Chan, Hlth Scis, 1994-, Sydney Univ; Pres, Austl Physiological and Pharmacological Soc, 1995-99; Chair, Menzies Sch of Hlth Rsch, Darwin, 1992-96, Dpty Chair, 1996-; Cncl, Intl Union of Physiological Scis, 1993-2001; Fedn of Asian and Oceanic Physiological Socs; VP, Biol Sec, Austl Acady of Sci, 1998-2001; Pres, Fed of Asian and Oceanian Physiological Socs, 1998-; Chair, Anzac Hlth and Medl Rsch Fndn, 1995-. Publications include: 150 sci articles, 5 books. Honours: AO; Rsch Prize, Humboldt Fndn, Germany. Memberships: Physiological Soc; Austl Physiol and Pharmacological Socs; Amn Physiological Soc; Deutsche Physiologische Gesellschaft (Korrespondierendes Mitglied), 1991-; Cntrl Sydney Area Hlth Serv; Bd, Alexandra Hosp for Children, Sydney. Address: Pro Vice Chancellor (Health Sciences), Edward Ford Building, University of Sydney, NSW 2006, Australia.

YOUNG John McIntosh (Hon Sir), b. 17 Dec 1919, Melbourne, Aust. Lawyer. m. Elisabeth Twining, 25 Oct 1951, 1 s, 2 d. Education: MA (Oxon); LLB (Melb). Appointments: QC, 1961; Chf Justice Supreme Crt of Vic, 1974-91; Lt Gov of Vic, 1974-95; Chmn, Police Bd of Vic,

1992-98. Publication: Australian Company Law and Practice, jointly, 1965. Honours: KCMG, 1975; AC, 1989; Hon LLD, Monash, 1986; Hon LLD, Melb, 1989. Memberships: Chan, Order of St John in Aust, 1982-91; Chief Scout of Aust, 1989-96. Address: 17 Sorrett Avenue, Malvern, Vic 3144, Australia.

YOUNG Nicholas Henry, b. 14 Sept 1960, Keith, S Aust. Stockbroker. m. Emma, 17 Feb 1989, 2 s, 2 d. Education: Dip Securities Inst; BEcons; MBA. Mngng Dir, Johnson Taylor Ltd. Assoc Securitues Inst of Aust. Address: C/o Level 12, 4 O'Connell Street, Sydney, Australia.

YOUNG Norman James, b. 31 July 1930, Geelong, Aust. Professor of Theology. m. Barbara, 28 Aug 1954, 2 s. Education: BA, Hons; BD, Hons; PhD. Appointments: Dpty Master, King's Coll, Univ of Qld, Aust, 1960-63; Prof, Theo, Queen's Coll, Univ of Melbourne, 1964-95; Prof Emer, 1996-. Publications: History and Existential Theology, 1969; Creator, Creation and Faith, 1976. Memberships: Fell, Queen's Coll, Univ of Melbourne, 1994-; Fell, Melbourne Coll of Divinity, 1995. Hobbies: Golf; Gardening. Address: 31 Seymour Grove, Camberwell, Vic 3124, Australia.

YOUNG Paul Tze-Kong, b. 5 Jan 1942. Executive Company Director. Education: St Paul's Convent, St Joseph's Coll, Hong Kong; Waverley Coll, Indl Engrng and Sci, Univ NSW, Aust; BS, Bus Admin, NY Univ, USA. Appointments include: Exec Dir, Ppty Dev, Trade and Ind, Sze Kuen Invmnts Ltd; Gen Mngr and Exec Dir, Plastics Material Distbr and Gen Import/Export, Yuen Hing Hong & Co Ltd; Pt-time Lectr, Dept of Mngmt, Lingnan Coll, Hong Kong, 1975-96; Chmn, Advsry Bd, Dept of Mngmt, Lingnan Coll; Bd, Lingnan Educ Org Ltd; Chmn, Prisoners' Educ Trust Fund Cttee; Mbr, Econ Servs Bch, Air Transp Licensing Authy; Mbr Antiquities Advsry Bd, Hone Affairs Bch; Bd, Cheshire Home, Chung Hom Kok; Cncl, Bd Mbr, and Fell, Hong Kong Mngmt Assn. Honours: Badge of Hon, 1982; JP, 1992. Memberships: Dist Bds, 1982-89; Urban Cncl 1987-95; Amn Econ Assn; Hong Kong Econ Assn; Hong Kong Computer Soc; Austl Chmbr of Comm; Chinese Chmbr of Comm; Past Pres, Rotary Club of Hong Kong S. Address: Yuen Hing Hong & Co Ltd, 1001 On Lok Yuen Building, 25 Des Voeux Road Central, Hong Kong.

YOUNG Robert Bruce, b. 30 June 1944, Sydney, Aust. University Lecturer. m. Helen, 12 Aug 1967, 1 s, 1 d. Education: BEcon; BA, Sydney; PhD, Flinders Univ of S Aust; FAHA. Appointments: Lectr, 1974-76, Snr Lectr, 1977-81; Rdr, La Trobe Univ, 1982-. Publications: Freedom, Responsibility and God, 1975; Personal Autonomy, 1986; Over 50 articles in books and profl jrnls. Honours: Fulbright Snr Schl-in-Res, GA, USA, 1989. Memberships: Fell, Acady of Hums (FAHA). Hobbies: Sports of all kinds. Address: School of Philosophy, La Trobe University, Bundoora, Vic 3083, Australia.

YOUNG William, b. 16 Jan 1949, Scotland. Civil Engineer. m. Marianne, 10 May 1975, 1 s, 2 d. Education: PhD; BE; MBA; Grad Dip Mngmt; MSc. Appointments: Student to Prof, Monash, 1975-. Honours: FIE Aust; FITE; FCIT. Address: Department of Civil Engineering, Monash University, Wellington Road, Clayton, Vic 3168, Australia.

YOUNGBLOOD Ronald Fred, b. 10 Aug 1931, Chgo, IL, USA. Professor of Old Testament and Hebrew. m. Carolyn, 16 Aug 1952, 1 s, 1 d. Education: BA, Valparaiso Univ, 1952; BD, Fuller Theol Seminary, 1955; PhD, Dropsie Coll for Hebrew and Cognate Learning, 1961; Postdoct Fellshp, NY Univ, 1966. Appointments: Asst Prof, 1961-65, Assoc Prof, 1965-70, Prof, 1970-78, Old Testament and Hebrew, Bethel Theol Seminary, S Paul, MN; Assoc Dean, 1978-80, Dean, 1980-81, Wheaton Coll Grad Sch; Prof of Old Testament and Semitic Langs, Trinity Evangelical Divinity Sch, 1981-82; Prof of Old Testament and Hebrew, Bethel Seminary San Diego, 1982-. Publications: Great Themes of the Old Testament, 1968; Special Day Sermons, 1973; Exodus, 1983; New International Version Study Bible (assoc ed),

1985; Themes from Isaiah, 1983; The Genesis Debate, ed, 1986; Genesis: A Commentary, 1991; 1,2 Samuel, 1992. Honours: Owen Young Fellowships, Gen Elec Corp, 1959-61; NYU Student Fellshp, 1966; Christian Booksellers Assn, Golden Book Awd, 1997. Memberships: Evangelical Theol Soc, Jrnl Ed, 1976-98; Near E Archaeological Soc, Sec, 1980-; Cttee on Bible Translation, Mbr, 1980-; Intl Bible Soc, Mbr of Bd of Dirs, 1988-. Hobbies: Reading; Walking; Swimming. Address: Bethel Seminary San Diego, 6116 Arosa St, San Diego, CA 92115, USA.

YOUNIS Waqar, b. 16 Nov 1971 Burewala. Cricketer. Education: Pakistani Coll Sharjah; Sadiq Pub Sch Burewala. Appointments: Right-hand batsman right-arm fast bowler; Test match debut, 1989-90; Co - Surrey - debut, 1990; Has played in 20 Test matches 71 one-day intls overseas tours; India Aust and Sharjah, 1989-90; Eng, 1992. Hobbies: Football; Badminton; Squash. Address: c/o Surrey County Cricket Club, Kennington Oval, London, SE11 5SS, England.

YOVICH John Lui, b. 31 July 1945. Consultant in Gynaecology, Andrology and Reproductive Technology. m. Jeanne Marie Conceicao, 26 Jan 1968, 1 s, 1 d. Education: MBBS; MD; MRCOG; FRACOG; FRCOG; CREI. Appointments: Snr Lectr, Univ of London (Roy Free Hosp), 1976-80; Snr Lectr, Rsch Fell, Univ of Western Aust (King Edward Mem Hosp), 1980-90; Med Dir, PIVET Med Cntr, 1981-; Med Dir, Hallam Med Cntr, London, 1990-91. Publications: The Management of Infertility (co-auth), 1990; IVF and Assisted Reproduction (co-auth), 1992; Gametes - The Oocyte (ed), 1995; Gametes - The Spermatozoon (ed), 1995. Honours: C'wlth Schlshp, 1963-69; Duff-Freeman Mem Awd, 1977-78; Rsch Fellshp, Univ of London, 1978-79; Bank of NSW Fellshp, King Edward Mem Hosp Rsch Fndn, 1980-81. Memberships: AMA, 1970-; Fertility Soc of Aust, Pres, 1987-88; Austl Gynae Endoscopy Soc; Eurn Soc of Human Reproduction & Embryology. Hobbies: Long distance running; Triathlon; Surfing; Skiing; Sailboarding. Address: PIVET Medical Centre, 166-8 Cambridge Street, Leederville 6007, Perth, Western Australia.

YU Aibing, b. 18 Jan 1963, Kaiping, China. University Professor. m. Ruiping Zou, 25 Jan 1988, 1 s, 1 d. Education: BEng, 1982; MEng, 1985; PhD, 1990. Appointments: Rsch Assoc, Univ Wollongong, 1989; Postdoc Fell, CSIRO, Melbourne, 1990-91; Lectr, Univ NSW, 1992-94, Snr Lectr, 1995-97, Assoc Prof, 1998-. Honours: CSIRO Postdoc Fellowship Awd, 1990; ARC Queen Elizabeth II Fellowship Awd, 1993. Memberships: AIChE, 1993-; Amn Ceramic Soc, 1992-; Minerals, Metals and Materials Soc, 1992-. Hobbies: Reading; Sightseeing; Table tennis; Swimming. Address: 24c Linden Street, Mascot, NSW 2020, Australia.

YU Chengyang, b. 4 Aug 1928, Ninbo, Zhejiang, China. Professor. m. Kao Chan, 16 Feb 1962, 1 d. Education: Bach, Shanghai Jiao Tong Univ, 1951. Appointment: Tchng, Shanghai Univ of Fin and Econs, 1952-. Publications: Economic Statistics of Western Countries, 1983, 1989, 1994; Professional English on Statistics, 1991; The World Industrial Census of the United Nations, 1984; Probability and Statistics, 1986; Compositions include: The Standard Classification of Statistics of UN and Western Countries, 1988; On the Compilation of the Employment Cost Index of the United States, 1991; A Brief Introduction of the Statistical Abstract of the United States, 1991. Membership: Dir, Shanghai Statistical Soc. Hobby: Reading. Address: House 6-602, 274 Xiangde Road, Shanghai 200081, China.

YU Chien-Chih, b. 2 Apr 1953, Keelung, Taiwan. Educator. m. Hsiu-Yuan Hsu, 25 Dec 1978, 1 s, 2 d. Education: BA, Natl Cheng Chi Univ, Taiwan, 1975; MS, Univ of Toledo, OH, USA, 1980; MA, 1983, PhD, 1985, Univ TX, Austin, USA. Appointments: Asst Instr, Univ TX, Austin, 1983-85; Assoc Prof, 1985-91, Chairperson, 1986-90, Prof, 1991-, Dept of MIS, Natl Cheng Chi Univ, Taiwan. Publications: Integrated Expert Decision Support Systems: Architecture, Development and Applications,

1991; Handbook of Electronic Commerce: Technology, Management and Applications, 1999. Honours include: Intl Man of the Yr, IBC, 1993-94; Ex Rsch Awd, Natl Cheng Chi Univ, 1995; Intl Rsch Fell, Intl Cntr for Electron Com, 1997. Memberships: ACM; IEEE CS; IEEE COMM; Chinese Soc of Info Mngmt; Phi Kappa Phi. Hobbies: Travel; Mountain climbing; Painting; Writing. Address: Department of MIS, National Cheng Chi University, Taipei, Taiwan.

YU De-Quan, b. 22 Oct 1932, Yan-Tai, Shandong, China. Scientific Researcher; Teacher. m. Hui-Lan Zhang, 31 Dec 1956, 1 s, 1 d. Education: BA, Coll of Pharm, Beijing Med Univ, 1956. Appointments: Assoc Prof, 1981, Prof, 1985-; Vice Ed-in-Chf, Jrnl Asian Natl Prod Rsch, 1998-. Publications: 4 books, 170 pprs, 7 pats. Honours: 1st Class Awd, Progress of Sci and Technol, Natl Bur of Chinese Trad Med, 1997; 1st Class Awd, Progress of Scis and Technol of China, 1998. Memberships: Cnclr, China Chem Soc, 1990-; China Pharm Assn; Amn Soc of Pharmacognosy. Hobbies: Music; Penmanship; Reading; Table tennis. Address: 1 Xian Nong Tan Street, Beijing 100050, China.

YU Jin-sheng, b. 4 Dec 1933, Tianjin, China. Professor. m. 11 Feb 1956, 1 s, 2 d. Education: Beijing Geol Coll, 1952-56; Beijing For Lang Coll, 1960-61; Dept of Nuclear Phys, Chinese Univ of Sci and Technol, 1961-62. Appointments: Rsch Fell, Geochem, Inst of Geol, Academia Sinica, 1956-65; Asst Prof, Isotope Geochem, 1966-79, Assoc Prof, 1979-86, Prof, 1986-, Inst of Geochem, Academia Sinica, Guiyang, Guizhou; Prof, Guangzhou Inst of Geochem, Chinese Acady of Sci, 1989-. Publications: Nuclear-Transferred Energy and the Evolution of Terrestrial Materials in the Earth; Stable Isotope Compositional Characteristics of Strata-Bound Ore Deposits; The Altitude and Latitude Effect of H-O Isotopic System in Granitoid Rocks; Correlation Between d+D and H20 in Some Granitoids; Oxygen and hydrogen isotopic compositions of meteoric waters in the eastern part of Xizang (Tibet); Sr-O isotope system of some granitoids in China; Isotope Geochemistry Researches in China, 1998. Honour: Ex Tchr of Postgrads, Chinese Acady of Sci. Memberships: Dir, Div of Isotope Geochem, 1979-88; Cnclr, Chinese Soc of Mineral, Petrol and Geochem, 1983-88. Hobbies: Vocal music; Opera. Address: Division of Isotope Geochemistry, Guangzhou Institute of Geochemistry, Chinese Academy of Science, PO Box 1131, Wushan, Guangzhou 510640, China.

YU Julian Jing-Jun, b. 2 Sept 1957, Beijing, China. Composer. m. 9 Nov 1984. Education: Cntrl Conservatory of Music, Beijing; Tokyo Coll of Music; Queensland Conservatorium of Music; MA, La Trobe Univ, Melbourne. Appointments: Emigrated to Aust, 1985; Tanglewood Fell, 1988; Victorian Min for the Arts Music Advsry panel, 1991-96; Wrk Commissioned by Hans Werner Henze, BBC Proms; Jury Mbr for BMW Music th Prize at 3rd Munich Biennale, 1992; Wrks performed at ISCM World Music Days in Zurich, 1991, New Mexico, 1993. Creative Works: Num compositions; Recordings: Wrks recorded by ABC and BBC; Work perf by London Sinfonietta and Ensemble Intercontemporain. Publications include: Wu-Yu; Hsiang-Chi; Great Ornamented Fuga Canonica; Scintillation I, II, III; Reclaimed Prefu I and II; The White Snake; Medium Ornamented Fuga Canonica; In the Sunshine of Bach; Impromptu; First Australian Suite; Philopentatonia; Sinfonia Passacaglissima. Honours: 56th Japan Music Concours Awd, 1987; Intl New Music Composer's Awd, 1988, 1989-90; 35th Premio Musicale, Citta d Trieste, 1988; Koussevitzky Composition Prize, Tanglewood, 1988; 10th Irino Prize, 1989; Inaugural and 2nd Paul Lowin Orchestral Awds, 1991, 1994; Vienna Modern Masters Recording Awd, 1992; Spivakovsky Composition Awd, 1992; Jean Bogan Mem Prize for Piano Composition, 1993. Memberships include: Austl Music Cntr. Hobbies: Photography; Drawing; Audio. Address: c/o Australian Music Centre, PO Box N690, Grosvenor Place, Sydney, NSW 2000, Australia.

YU Kuo-Hwa, b. 10 Jan 1914, Chekiang, China. Politician; Banker. m. Yu Toong Metsung, 1946, 2 s. Education: BA; Tsinghua Univ; Harvard Univ Grad Sch. Appointments: Sec to Pres, Natl Mil Cncl, 1936-44; Alt Exec Dir, Intl Bank for Reconstrn and Dev, 1947-50; IMF, 1951-55; Pres, Cntrl Trust of China, 1955-61; Chair, Bd Dirs, Bank of China, 1961-67; Alt Gov, IBRD, 1964-67; Gov for Repub of China, 1967-69; Min of Fin, 1967-69; Gov, Cntrl Bank of China, 1969-84; Min of State, 1969-84; Gov, IMF, 1969-80; Asian Dev Bank, 1969-84; PM of Taiwan, 1984-89; Snr Advsr to Pres of Taiwan, 1989-; Chair, Cncl for Econ Plng and Dev, 1977-84. Honour: Hon Dr, St John's Univ, Jamaica, NY. Membership: Vice Chmn, Cntrl Standing Cttee, Kuomintang, 1997-. Address: 135 Sze-wei Road, Taipei, Taiwan, China.

YU Kwang-chung, b. 9 Sept 1928, Nanking, China. Poet; Translator; Professor. m. Fan Wo-chun, 2 Sept 1956, 4 d. Education: BA, Natl Taiwan Univ, 1952; MFA, State Univ IA, USA, 1959. Appointments: Fulbright Visng Prof, USA, 1964-66, 1969-71; Prof, Natl Taiwan Normal Univ, 1966-72; Prof, Natl Chengchi Univ, Taiwan, 1972-74; Rdr, Chinese Univ Hong Kong, 1974-85; Prof, Dean, Coll Liberal Arts, Natl Sun Yat-sen Univ, Kaohsiung, 1985-. Publications: The White Jade Bitter Gourd, 1974; The Selected Poetry of Yu Kwang-chung, 1981; All by a Map, 1988; Dream and Geography, 1990; Calling for Ferry, 1990; The Chinese Knot, 1993; From Hsu Hsia-Ke to Van Gogh, 1994; Gen Ed, A Comprehensive Anthology of Contemporary Chinese Literature in Taiwan, 1970-89. Honours: 10 Outstndng Young Men in Repub China, 1966; Austl Cultural Awd, 1972; Golden Tripod Awd, Lyrics, 1981, 1984; Wu San-lien Awd, Prose, 1984; China Times Poetry Awd, 1985; Golden Tripod Awd, Edshp, 1989; Natl Lit Awd, Poetry, 1990; Best Book Awd, Utd Daily News, 1994, 1996; Chair Profshp, Natl Sun Yat-sen Univ, 1994-97. Membership: Pres, Taipei Chinese Cntr, PEN Intl. Hobbies: Travel; Hiking; Movies; Astronomy. Address: National Sun Yat-sen University, Kaohsiung, Taiwan, China.

YU Long, b. 21 Jan 1957, Beijing, China. Scientist. m. Di Pei, 1 Oct 1983, 1 s. Education: PhD. Appointments: Rsch Fell, 1988-90; Rsch and Dev Mngr, 1992-93; Proj Ldr, 1994-96; Sci, 1996-. Publications: 67 pprs in jrnls and confs; 2 chapts in books. Honours: OPRA, 1990; Best Lect, in antic, 1996. Membership: RACI, 1989. Hobby; Reading books. Address: CSIRO, MST, Private Bag 33, Clayton, Vic 3169, Australia.

YU Ming Xia, b. 16 Sept 1925. Professor. Education: LLB, Nanjing Ctrl Univ, 1947. Appointments: Lectr, Dept of Hist and Chinese Lang and Lit, Jiangsu Tchr Coll, 1956-74; Chmn, Dept of Hist, Xuzhou Tchr Coll, 1975-78; Assoc Prof, 1978-86, Prof, 1986-98, Chmn, Acad Cttee, 1992-94, Xuzhou Normal Univ. Publications: The History of Xuzhou Coal Industry; The History of Legal System in the Republic of China; A Criticial Biography of Zhu Ge Liang; Contemporary History of China. Honours: Outstndng Socl Sci Rschr Awd, Chinese Govt, 1990, 1992, 1994, 1996; Outstndng Educr Awd, Cen Xian Zi Educl Fndn, 1992; Hist Specialist Awd, Chinese Govt, 1992. Memberships: Chmn, Hist Soc of Xuzhou, 1980-98; Advsr, Tai Ping Tian Guo Rsch Soc of China, 1986-98; Vice Chmn, Hist Soc of Jiangsu Prov, 1988-97. Hobbies: Chinese go; Bridge; Jogging. Address: Xuzhou Normal University, Xuzhou, Jiangsu 221009, China.

YU Naimei, b. 21 May 1924, Fujian, China. Professor. m. Lin Zhaochen, 15 Sept 1950, 2 s, 2 d. Education: BSc, Zhejian Univ, 1948. Appointments: Tchr, Mid Sch, 1948-50; Asst Tchr, Chem Dept, Nankai Univ, 1950-51; Asst Tchr, Asst Prof, Visng Prof, Prof, Chem Dept, Xiamen Univ, 1951-. Publications: Collected Works About Teaching on Physical Chemistry, 1986; Over 50 sci articles, 1 patent. Honour: 1st Prize, Sci Progress, 1986. Memberships: Chmn, Polymer Cttee, 1981-93, Hon Advsr, 1994-, Fujian Chem Engrng Soc; Chinese Chem Soc. Hobby: Music. Address: c/o Chemistry Department, Xiamen University, Xiamen, Fujian, China.

YU Peter Kien-Hong, b. 26 July 1953, Taiwan. University Professor. m. Tan Lee Suang, 25 Dec 1989, 1 s, 1 d. Education: PhD, Politics. Appointments: Sun Yat-Sen Inst, Natl Sun Yat-Sen Univ, 1983-99; E Asian Inst, Natl Univ of Singapore, 1997-. Publications: Some 40 articles in profl jrnls and sev books. Address: East Asian Institute, National University of Singapore, Singapore 119260, Singapore.

YU Peter Kwan-Ngok, b. 25 July 1963, Hong Kong (Singapore citizen). Associate Professor. m. Rebecca Ching-Wa Kwok, 26 Aug 1989. Education: BSc Hons, 1985; PhD, 1988. Appointments: Lectr, 1988-95; Assoc Prof, Dept Phys and Materials Sci, Cty Univ Hong Kong, 1995-. Publications: 3 books; Num papers in sci jrnls and conf proceedings. Memberships include: Chartered Physicist, Inst Phys, UK; Fell, Roy Astronomical Soc; Fell, Roy Statistical Soc, UK; Fell, Roy Soc Hlth, UK; Fell, Roy Inst Pub Hlth and Hyg, UK; Chartered Mathn, Inst Maths and its Applications, UK. Listed in: International Directory of Distinguished Leadership; Who's Who in the World. Hobbies: Computers: Astronomy. Listed in: Who's Who in the World; International Directory of Distinguished Leadership. Address: Department of Physics and Materials Science, City University of Hong Kong, Tat Chee Avenue, Kowloon Tong, Kowloon, Hong Kong.

YU Qing, b. 13 Oct 1962, Beijing, China. Doctor. Education: Master, Peking Union Medl Coll, 1988; 8th Study Class of Learning Tradl Chinese Med, 1993. Appointment: Dr, Peking Union Med Coll Hosp, 1988. Publications: A Hypothesis on the Effect of Coriolis Force on the Development of Right-left Asymetry of Mammals. Memberships: Chinese Assn of the Integration of Tradl and West Med, 1989. Hobbies: Research on Traditional Chinese Medicine. Address: Department of Traditional Medicine, Peking Union Medical College Hospital, Beijing 10073, China.

YU Shu-wen, b. 26 Nov 1925, Chekiang, China. Research Professor of Plant Physiology and Environmental Biology. m. Kai-ling Ho, 9 June 1928, 4 s. Education: BS, Dept of Bio, Chekiang Univ, Hangchow, 1948. Appointments: Rsch Assoc, 1953-60, Assoc Prof, 1961-85, Prof, 1985-; Shanghai Inst Plant Physiol, Academica Sinica; Visng Schl, Japanese Natl Inst for Environmental Stdies, 1983-84; Prof, Inst of Hydrobio, Academica Sinica, 1988-92. Publications: 142 sci pprs on plant environmental physiology, drought and salt tolerance, air pollution effects on plants and allelopathy. Honours: Shanghai Municipal Awd for Gt Achievement in Sci and Technol, 1980; Academia Sinica Awd in Promotion of Sci and Technol, 1987; Academica Sinica Awd in Nat Sci, 1989; Sci and Technol Prog Prize, Natl Educ Cttee, 1989. Memberships: Chinese Soc for Plant Physiology; Chinese Soc for Environmental Scis; Environmental Sci Cttee, Academica Sinica; IUBS Intl Commn on Bioindicators; Intl Cttee on Air Pollution and Plant Effects, ISPP; Dpty Ed-in-Chf, Acta Phytophysiologia Sinica; Ed, Acta Scientiae Circumstantiae; Editl Bd, Intl Jrnl Environmental Pollution. Hobbies: Reading; Travel. Address: 300 Fenglin Road, Shanghai Institute of Plant Physiology, Shanghai 200032, China.

YU Sile, b. 10 Aug 1930, Suzhou Cty, China. University Professor; Director, Institute of TV and Image Information. m. Yan Hua, 1 Jan 1955, 1 s, 1 d. Education: Dip, Elec Engrng, Nankai Univ, 1952. Appointments: Asst, Telecomms Dept, Elec Engrng Dept and Electronic Engrng Dept, 1952-62; Lectr, Electronic Engrng Dept, Dpty Dir, Div of Circuits and Signals, 1962-79, Assoc Prof, Elec Engrng Dept, Dir, Image Info Lab, 1979-83, Prof, Chmn, electronic Engrng Dept, 1983-91, Dir, Inst of TV and Image Info, 1991-, Tianjin Univ. Publications: Nationwide textook, Fundamentals of TV, 1981, 1984, 1988, 1994; Advances in Research and Development of HDTV Systems, 1993; Research on the Bit-Rate Control Algorithm based on the Frequency Domain Activity, 1996; Noises Analysis and Optimal Bit Allocation in Image Coding based on Wavelet Transformation, 1997. Honours: Title, Adv Sci and Technol Worker in Tianjin City, 1977; Advd Individual for Key Sci and Technol Projs of the Natl 8th 5-Yr Plan, 1996; Proj Dev of a Chinese Teletex, won Awd for Adv of Sci and Technol, State Educ Commn, 1987; Measurement on Colour TV Receivers;

Awd for Superior Achievement, NBS and Electronic Ind Min, 1981; Video Wall System, won Awd for Adv of Sci and Technol, Electronic Ind Min, 1990. Memberships: China SMPTE; Exec Cnclr, Broadcast Technol Soc of CIE; Editl Bd, Electronica Sinica (jrnl of CIE). Listed in: Who's Who in the World. Address: Institute of TV and Image Information, Tianjin University, 92 Weijin Road, Tianjin, China.

YU Tianren, b. 4 Feb 1920, Shandong, China. Professor. m. Baohua Li, 28 Sept 1951, 2 s. Education: BS, N W Agricl Coll, China, 1945. Appointments: Rsch Asst, Natl Geological Surv, 1945; Rsch Assoc, Inst of Soil Sci, 1951; Assoc Prof, 1956; Prof, 1978. Creative Works: Physical Chemistry of Paddy Soils, 1985; Electrochemical Methods in Soil and Water Research, 1993; Chemistry of Variable Charge Soils, 1997. Honours: NAtl Prize, 1978, 1987, 1991; First Grade Prize, Academia Sinica, 1987, 1996; Academician, Academia Sinica, 1995-. Memberships: Soil Sci Soc of China; Chem Soc of China; Intl Soc of Soil Sci. Hobbies: Classical music; Photography. Address: Institute of Soil Science, Academia Sinica, P O Box 821, Nanjing, China.

YU Tiejie, b. 20 June 1941, Ning Xiang, Haunan, China. Geology & Mineral Research. m. Chen, 1 s. Education: Univ. Appointments: Geol Exhbn Hall Dir; Jewellery Sci Vice Ed. Publications: Material Analysis of Geology and Geochemistry, 1993. Honour: Hon Ctf, 2nd, 3rd and 4th Grades, 1983-95. Memberships: Cttee, Geochem Assn, Geol Assn of China. Hobby: Chinese chess. Address: Research Institute of Geology for Mineral Resources, CNNC Fuxing Road No 2, Guilin, Guangxi, China.

YU Tsan Jung, b. 1 Oct 1953, Taiwan. Urologist. m. Wen-Hsueh, 21 Jan 1983, 3 d. Education: China Med Coll, 1973-80; Fell, Brown Univ, USA, 1990, Harvard Med Sch, USA, 1990, Cancer Genetics Lab, Otago Univ, NZ, 1998. Appointments: Chief, Dept of Pediat Urology, Assoc Prof, Chang Gung Mem Hosp, Chang Gung Univ, Taiwan. Publications: Surgical Management of Vesicoureteral Reflux in Children, 1997; Early Vs Late Surgical Management of Fetal Reflux Nephropathy, 1997. Honour: Outstndng articles of Urological Assn, China, 1996. Memberships: Urological Assn of USA; Urological Assn of China. Hobbies: Swimming; Cricket; Golf. Address: 123-3, Niao Sung, Ta Pei Road, Kaohsiung, Taiwan.

YU Winnie, b. 16 Apr 1954, Hong Kong. Appointments: DJ, Hong Kong Coml Brdcstng Co Ltd, 1971-82; Creative Dir; Progng Dir; Dir, Mes Amis Prodns Ltd, 1982-88; Gen Mngr, Hong Kong Comml Brdcstng Co Ltd, 1988-94; Mngng Dir, 1994-97; Chf Exec Offr, 1997-. Address: Hong Kong Commercial Broadcasting, 3 Broadcast Dr, Kowloon, Hong Kong.

YU Xiling, b. 1938. Professor. Education: Grad, Shandong Univ, 1962. Appointments: Tchng and Rsch Work on Crystallography, Functional Crystal Materials and Crystal Growth Kinetics, Shandong Univ; Prof and Tchr of MD Studs, Shandong Univ; Assoc Prof, 1986-93, Prof, 1994-. Publications: More than 70 pprs in natl and intl acad jrnls inclng: Mass Transport Effect within the Boundary Layers in Solution Crystal Growth, 1994; Some New Optical Measurements Techniques for the Study of Crystal Growth and Electrode Process, 1996; Growth Kinetics of the Metastable Tetragonal Phase of DKDP Crystals, 1996; Interface Kinetics and Crystal Growth Mechanism of a New Organometallic Coordination Compound, 1997. Honours: ADP Crystal Growth won the 2nd Awd of Natl New Prods, 1964; DKDP Single Crystal Growth won prize of Natl Congress of Sci, 1978; DTGS Crystal Growth won prize of Shandong Congress of Sci, 1978; New Method of Metastable Phase Growth of DKDP Crystal won 1st Awd of Sci and Technique of Shandong, 1981; Holographic Phase-Contrast Microphotography for Crystal Growth Rsch won 3rd Awd of Advd Sci and Technol of Shandong, 1988; Study of Kinetics for Crystal-Liquid Interface Boundary Layer won 2nd Awd of Adv'd Sci and Technol of Chinese Educ Commn, 1998 and won an Inv Pat of China, 1999 Elected Top-Notch

Expert in special Sci and Technique of Shandong Prov, 1993; Won Spec Allowance of the State Cnclof China, 1997. Memberships: Chinese Optics Soc; Chinese Citieate Assn; Chinese Crystallography Assn; Amn Assn for Advmt of Sci. Address: Institute of Crystal Materials, Shandong University, Jinan 250100, China.

YU Xiping, b. 26 Dec 1962, Anhui, China. Professor of Engineering Mechanics. m. Zhi Jun Chen, 7 Dec 1993, 1 s. Education: BEng, Tsinghua Univ, 1984; MEng, Tsinghua University, 1986; DEng, Univ of Tokyo, 1990. Appointments: Snr Rsch Asst, Univ of Hong Kong, 1992; Assoc Prof, Nagasaki Univ, Japan, 1993; Assoc Prof, Univ of Tokyo, Japan, 1997; Prof, Shanghai Jiao Tong Univ, China, 1999. Publication: Numerical Solution of Coastal Water Wave Equations in Coastal Engineering Handbook. Membership: Japan Soc of Civil Engrs. Hobby: Reading newspapers. Address: Department of Engineering Mechanics, Shanghai Jiao Tong University, 1954 Hua Shan Road, Shanghai, 200030, China.

YU Zhengsheng, b. Apr 1945 Shaoxin Cty Zhejiang Prov. Politician. Education: Harbin Mil Engrng Inst. Appointments: Vice-Chmn Exec Cncl of Welfare Fund for the Handicapped, 1984; Vice-Sec CCP Yantai Cty Cttee and Vice Mayor Yantai Cty, 1985; Mayor Yantai Cty, 1987; Sec CCP Qingdao Cty Cttee and Mayor Qingdao Cty, 1992; Vice-Min of Constrn, 1997-. Memberships: Alt mbr 14th CCP Cntrl Cttee, 1992; Mbr 15th CCP Cntrl Cttee, 1997-. Address: Ministry of Construction, Baiwanzhuang, Western Suburb, Beijing 100835, People's Republic of China.

YUAN Fa-Huan, b. 1 Feb 1957, Hubei Prov, China. Education: Physician. Appointments: Vice-Chmn, Nephrological Soc, Chongqing, 1992-; Asst Prof, Vice Chf, Dept of Nephrology, Xingqiao Hospital. Publications: 59 pprs to medl jrnls. Honours: 2nd Grade Medl Prize, 3rd Mil Medl Univ, 1990, 1994, 1996; 4th Grade Sci and Techl Prize, PLA, 1991; 3rd Grade Sci and Techl Prize, PLA, 1994; 3rd Grade Sci and Techl Prize, Sichuan Prov, 1995; 2nd Grade Sci and Techl Prize, PLA, 1998. Membership: Chinese Soc of Medl Sci, 1985-. Hobbies: Photography; Swimming (including in cold water in winter). Address: Department of Nephrology, Xingqiao Hospital, Third Military Medical University, Chongqing 400037, China.

YUAN Jiu Rong, b. 5 Nov 1935, Shandong, China. Teacher. m. Li Yan, 7 Feb 1959, 1 s, 2 d. Education: Dip, Chem Dept, Shandong Univ. Appointments: Assoc Dir, Vice Rschr, Shandong Inst of TCM & Materia Medica, 1961-85; Dir, Prof, Dept of Trad Chinese Materia, Shandong Coll of TCM, 1985-93; Hd, Tutor of DS Lab of Natural Durgs, Shandong Univ of TCM, 1993-. Publications: Studies on Group of Ultraviolet Absorption Spectra Lines for Identification of Chinese Materia Medica; Gossypol Formic Acid: An Antifertility Agent for Males; Studies on the Chemical Constituents of Chinese Sealavender (Limonium sinense); Commonly Used Chinese Patent Medicines. Honours: Prizes, Invention and Significant Results. Memberships: Dir, Chinese Pharm Assn. Address: No 53 Jingshi Road, Jinan, China.

YUAN Juxiang, b. 29 Mar 1956, Xingtai, Hebei, China. Professor of Epidemiology, Vice President. m. Guirong Li, 10 Dec 1982, 1 d. Education: Dip of Occupational Hlth and Safety, Mc Master, Can; MD, Peking Union Medl Coll; VP, College. Appointments: VP, Coll, 1995; Prof, Epidemiology, 1996. Publications: Occupational Epidemiology, 1993; Handbook of Epidemiology, 1996. Memberships: Vice-Chmn, Chinese Soc of Occupational Epidemiology (off in coll), 1997. Hobbies: Winter swimming; Fishing. Address: No 57, Jianshe Lu, Tangshan City, Hebei, China.

YUAN Luke C L, b. 5 Apr 1912, Changtefu, Henan, China. Senior Scientist (Retired). m. Chien Shiung Wu, 1 s. Education: BS, Yenching Univ, 1932; MS, 1934; PhD, CA Inst of Technol, 1940; Grad, Yenching Univ, 1932-34; Grad Asst, CA Inst of Technol, 1937-40. Appointments: Rsch Fell, CA Inst of Technol, 1940-42; Rsch Physicist, RCA Labs, 1942-46; Rsch Assoc, Princeton Univ,

1946-49; Physicist, Snr Physicist, Brookhaven Natl Lab, 1949-82; Cnslt, 1982-87. Honours: Hon Prof, Chinese Univ of Sci and Technol; Achmnt Awd, Chinese Acady of Sci. Memberships: Honan Acady of Sci; NY Acady of Sci. Address: 15 Claremont Avenue, New York, NY 10027, USA.

YUAN Wang Shan, b. 5 Aug 1941, Nanjing, China. Researcher. m. Yang, 24 Apr 1970, 2 d. Education: Grad, Beijing Sci Technol Univ, 1963. Appointments: Dir of the Rsch Off, 1983-86, Vice Gen Engr, 44th Inst of CASC, 1986-89; Vice Gen Econ Engr, Acady of CASC, 1989-93. Publications: Over 20 pprs in profl jrnls. Honours: 3rd Class Prize, Sci & Technol Progress, CASC, 1985, 1987. Memberships: Edl Bd, Aerospace Ind Mngmt. Hobbies: Reading; Table tennis; Music. Address: PO Box 120, Xian 710025, China.

YUAN Xiao-ying, b. 2 Apr 1950, Harbin, China. Teacher. m. Wang Ye, 10 June 1984, 1 d. Education: Master Deg; Dip. Appointments: Asst, Natural Resources Inst, Heilongjiang, 1979-81; Ed, 1984-86; Lectr, 1987-93; Asst Prof, 1994-98. Publication: Flora Heilonjiangensis, vol XL, 1993, Vol IX, 1997. Address: Northeast Forestry Univ, Hexing Road, 26, Harbin 150040, China.

YUAN Xiugan, b. 23 Mar 1934. University Professor. m. Fenghua Han, 30 Sept 1960, 1 d. Education: Dr-Ing, RWTH Aachen, Germany. Appointments: Hd Dept, 1988-93; Hd Inst of "Man" Machine-Environment Engrng; Hd Inst Air Conditioning & Refrigeration Technique, BUAA (Current). Publications: 10 books: 1977-99; 2 pats, 1989, 1993; 90 rsch publs, 1980-97. Honours: 13 awds, Sci and Technol, Nation and Min, 1989-99. Memberships: Chinese Soc Aeronautics and Astronautics; Chinese Soc System Engrng. Hobbies: Ergonomics; Flight vehicle environment control and life support system; Air conditioning and refrigeration engineering, heat transfer. Address: No 505, Beijing Univ of Aeronautics And Astronomics, Beijing, 100083, China.

YUAN Yi Quan, b. 27 July 1938, Wu Xi, China. Physician. m. Liu Xuefen, 1 d. Education: SE Univ, Nanjing, China. Appointments: Communist Party, China, 1961; Lectr, Dept Radio, SE Univ, Nanjing, China, 1987-91, 1992-. Publications: Auth, ppr, IEEE Transactions on UFFC, 1991, 1992, 1995, 1997; Auth, Sensors and Actuators, Auth, 1993; Auth, Ultrasonic Transducer, book; Lately Acoustic arry Principle and Its Application; Lately Ultrasonic Principle and Application, 1992, 1994, 1996. Honours: Second Rate Awd, Sci and Technol, China State Shipbuilding Corp, 1992; Second Rate Awd, Sci and Technol, State Educ Cttee, 1996; Invitation, NYAS, 1996. Memberships: Visng Rsch Fell, Shanghai Inst Ceramics Chinese Acady Sci, 1984-90; Modern Acoustics Lab, Nanjing, 1994-96; Glacier Frozen Sand Rsch Inst, SAC, Lan Zhon, 1997-99; Chinese Assn Technol. Hobbies: Basketball; Shooting; Swimming; Erhu; Opera. Address: Southeast University Si Pai Lou #2, Nanjing 210018, China.

YUAN Zhenhuan, b. 14 Feb 1947, Qidong Cty, Jiangsu, China. Painter. m. Gao Yuechun, 28 Dec 1971, 1 s. Education: Dip, Painting, Art Sch, Zhongquo Acady of Fine Arts. Appointments: Mngng Vice Chmn, Wenling Fedn of Lit and Arts Circles, 1994-. Creative Works: 2 Woodcuts: Dring Kelps in the Sun; Fishing Village in Spring; Watercolor Block Painting: Dancing in Dunhuang. Honours: To-Notch Artist, Taizhou City, won twice. Memberships: Vice Chmn, Taizhou Assn of Artists; Cncl, Assn of Artists in Zhejiang; China's Assn of Artists. Hobby: Gardening. Address: No 7-7 Lane 160 Zhonglou Road, Taiping, Wenling City, Zhejiang, China.

YUE Biao, b. 30 Oct 1926, Changchun, Jilin, China. Professor; Research Fellow; Senior Lawyer. m. Zhao Gong Fang, 15 Dec 1932, 3 s, 1 d. Education: Harbin Univ and Beiping NE Univ, 1947-49; BA, Law, Peoples Univ of China, Beijing, 1950. Appointments: Rschr, Criminal Law Regulation Cttee, Ctrl Govt, China, 1950-54; Lectr, Chinese Ctrl Cadres's Polit and Law Inst, then Hubei Univ, 1954-60; Rschr, Section Chf, Higher Peoples Crt, Harbin, VP, Law Inst, Hei Long Jiang Univ,

1960-86; Dean of Law Dept, Snr Lawyer Postgrad tutor, Nankai Univ, Tianjin; Tutor of Postgrad Studs, 1960-86; Standing VP, Dir, Rsch Cntr, Tianjin Democratic Legal System Construction; Snr Cnslt, Legal System Cttee of the Standing Cttee, Tianjin Peoples Congress, 1986-; Hon Dir, Standing Cnslt-Gen, Snr Lawyer, Dalian Lawyers' Off, Tianjin, 1991-. Publications: Basic theories on the Relationship Between State and Law; Answering Questions About Constitution; The Third Side in Civil Lawsuits; Regulations Regarding the Punishment of Venality; How to Improve Law Education; Encyclopaedical Book About Law; The Research on Crime and Legal System Construction; The Perspective and the Method and Tactics of Tackling China's Social Problems in the New Period. Memberships: Sec-in-Charge, Criminal Law Branch of Chinese Law Inst and Criminal Inst; Cttee Mbr, Chinese Behaviourism Inst and Behaviourist Law Inst; Sec-in-Charge, S China External Law Rsch Cntr; Sec-in-Charge, Tianjin Procurators' Assn and other 4 socs. Hobbies: Hunting; Camping in Prairies. Address: Room 304, 42nd Building, Southwest Village, Nankai University, Balitai, Tianjin 300071, China.

YUE Fenglin, b. 3 Sept 1929. Professor of Russian Language and Literature. m. Yu Zhonglian, 18 Aug 1954, 1 s. Education: BA, Dept of Russian Lang and Lit, Peking Univ. Appointments: Asst, 1952-62, Lectr, 1962-83, Assoc Prof and Hd of Tchng and Rsch Sect, 1983-89, Prof, 1989-, Russian Dept, Peking Univ. Publications: An Anthology on Majakovski (ed), 1987; A Collection of Critical Essays on Yesenin (eds), 1987; A Bouquet of White Flowers in Remembrance of Cao Jinghua (eds), 1988; Books: A History of Russian Literature (eds), 1989; A History of Russian and Soviet Literature (eds), 3 vols, 1992-93; A Collection of Patriotic Poems of the World (ed),1996-97; Essays and reviews incl: Splendid Verses and Monumental Work: on Majakovski Depiction of a Revolutionary Leader in His Long Poem Lenin,1979; An Exotic Flower in the World of Poetry: On Mayakovski's Long Poem Good, A Special Collection of Mayakovski Studies, pp 220-230, 1980; Past and Present of Mayakovski Studies in the Soviet Union, 1985; Two Great Pastoral Poets: Tao Yuanming and Yesenin, 1993. Honour: Prize of Spec Excellence for Fine Tchng Material awd'd by State Educ Commn, 2nd Natl Prize Awdng Conf, 1992. Memberships: Dir, China Inst of Russian Lit; Dir, Beijing Transls Assn. Address: 204 Bldg, 47 Zhongguanyuan, Peking Univ, Beijing 100871, China.

YULO Jose Luis U Jnr, b. 22 Dec 1947, Manila, Philippines. Business Executive; President. m. Kathleen L Velayo, Nov 1977, 2 s, 1 d. Education: BA, Univ of the Philippines, 1971; Master in Bus Mngmt, Asian Inst of Mngmt, 1974. Appointments: Family bus mfng and mktng Philippine furniture, handicrafts, 1965-71; Gen Diesel Power Corp, Gen Motors, 1974-76; Estab and pioneered Philippine Trade Fairs and Indl Exhibs, 1976-; Pres, Phil Intl Trading Corp; Pres, Centrex Corp; Pres, Philippine Stock Exchange, 1997-. Publications: Trade Fairs and Exhibitions - How to Participate and Get Maximum Benefits; Countertrade and Offsets in the Philippines, 1993-94. Honours: Gold Medals for 1st Hon, Declamation and Conduct, HS, 1964; Coll Entrance Schl, 1965; Agora Awd for Mktng Ex, 1985; Outstndng Profl Awd, 1985. Memberships: Philippine Chmbr of Comm & Ind; Employers Confed of the Philippines; Trade Show Bur; Fairs, Exhibns and Related Inds Assn; Pres, Philippine Chmbr of Comm and Inds, 1995; Sec-Gen, Chmbr of Comm and Ind, 1989-90; Chmn, Intl Assn of State Trading Orgs, 1991-. Hobbies: Reading; Travel; Swimming. Address: CentrexHouse, 208 Pilar Street, Corner Shaw Boulevard, Mandaluyong, Metro Manila, Philippines.

YUN Sock-Sung, b. 14 Dec 1943, Kunson, Korea. Professor of Chemistry. m. 23 June 1973, 2 s. Education: BS, Yonsei Univ, Seoul, Korea, 1966; PhD, Univ of Houston, Houston, TX, USA, 1973. Appointments: Asst Prof, 1977-81, Assoc Prof, 1981-86, Prof, 1986-, Chem Dept, Chungnam Natl Univ; Dean, Coll of Natl Scis, Chungnam Natl Univ, 1997-99. Publications: Contbr, about 80 original pprs to profl jrnls. Memberships: Amn Chem Soc, 1973-; Korean Chem Soc, 1976-; Phi Kappa Phi, 1971-. Hobby: Tennis. Address: 106-208 Durea Apt, Shinsung-Veng, Yusung-Gu, Taeion 305-764, Korea.

Z

ZABLAH TOUCHÉ Eduardo. Minister of the Economy. Education: Cntrl Amb Univ José Simeón Cuñas, San Salvador; Duke Univ, NC, USA. Appointments: Pres and Exec Dir, Socl Fund for Housing, 1994. Address: Ministry of the Economy, 1A Calle Poniente 2310, Col Escalón, San Salvador, El Salvador.

ZACKHRAS Ruben. Government Official. Appointments: Min of Fin, Govt of Marshall Is, Majuro. Address: Ministry of Finance, PO Box D, Cabinet Building, Majoro, MH 96960, Marshall Islands.

ZAENTZ Saul. Film Producer. b. Passaic NJ. Appointments: Prod'd: One Flew Over the Cuckoo's Nest, 1975; Three Warriors, 1977; Lord of the Rings, 1978; Amadeus, 1984; Exec Prodr The Mosquito Coast, 1986; The Unbearable Lightness of Being, 1988; A Play in the Fields of the Lord, 1991; The English Patient, 1996. Honours: Acady Awd for Best Picture for One Flew Over the Cuckoo's Nest; Acady Awd for Best Picture for The English Patient; Irving G Thalberg Memorial Awd, 1996. Address: Saul Zaentz & Co, Film Cnter, 2600 10th Street, Berkeley, CA 94710, USA.

ZAGAR Cilka, b. 26 Aug 1939, Slovenia. Teacher. m. Joe, 2 s. Education: BEduc, Justice Studies. Publications: Growing up Walgett, 1990, 1995; Barbara (novel in Slovenian), 1995; Magdalena (novel), 1999. Hobbies: Talking; Listening; Politics.

ZAHALKA Anne Monica, b. 14 May 1957, Sydney, Aust. Artist. m. Ian Collie, 1 d. Education: BVA, PGD, Sydney Coll of the Arts; MFA, Coll of Fine Arts, Univ NSW. Appointments: Artist Residencies: Künstlerhaus Bethanien, 1986, Bondi Pavilion Cmty Cntr, 1989, Gertrude St Artist Studios, 1990. Creative Works: Resemblance, 1987; Bondi: Playground of the Pacific, 1989; Artists, 1990; Open House, 1995; Num solo and grp exhbns. Honours: Aust Cncl of Visual Arts Crafts Bd Dev Grant, 1993, Proj Grant, 1996. Memberships: Artspace; Mus of Contemporary Art; Austl Cntr for Photography. Hobby: Collecting postcards. Address: 146 Australia Street, Newtown, NSW 2042, Australia.

ZAIDI Zafar Hasnain, b. 4 Mar 1939, Buland Shaher, UP, India. Teacher and Researcher. m. Dr Shalinda Zaidi, 12 May 1972, 3 d. Education: BS; MSc; PhD; DSc. Appointments: Lectr, 1963-65; Instr, 1973-76; Assoc Prof, 1978-82; Prof, 1982-, Vice-Chan, 1997-. Hobbies: Reading; Travelling; Chemistry. Address: Vice-Chancellor, University of Karachi, Karachi, 75270, Pakistan.

ZAIN MAJID Mohamed, b. 15 Nov 1938, Negri Sembilan, Malaysia. Director. m. Datin Amna Zain, 13 Jan 1967, 2 s, 1 d. Education: MA, Univ of Glasgow; LLB, Univ of London. Appointments: MSC Offr; Dir Gen, Malaysian Ind Dev Auth; Exec Chmn, Urban Dev Auth; Grp Exec Dir, SPTI Bhd; CEO Malaysian Employers Fedn. Honours: Fed awds, JMN, 1977, PSD, 1997; NS State awd, DSN, 1979. Hobbies: Quiet reading (especially biographies); Family travels; Golf. Address: 4 Lorong 5/13G, 46000 Petaling Jaya, Malaysia.

ZAINU'DDIN Ailsa Gwennyth Thomson, b. 8 Apr 1927, Melbourne, Aust. Historian. m. Zainu'ddin, 10 Dec 1954, 2 d. Education: BA, Hons I, Hist and Engl, Melbourne Univ, 1948; MA, Melbourne Univ, 1954; BEd, Melbourne Univ, 1964; PhD, Monash Univ, 1983. Appointments: Tutor, Hist, Melbourne Univ, 1948-51; Rsch Asst to Prof CMH Clark, Canberra Univ Coll, 1952-54; Vol Grad for Indonesia, 1954-56; Tutor/Asst Lectr, Melbourne Univ Law Sch, 1960-64; Lectr, Snr Lectr, Monash Univ Educ Fac, 1965-92. Publications include: Books: A Short History of Indonesia, 1968, revised edn, 1980; They Dreamt of a School: A Centenary History of Methodist Ladies' College, Kew, 1882-1982, 1982; Articles: Building the Future: The Life and Work of Kurnianingrat Ali Sastroamidjoyo, 1997;

Education in the Netherlands East Indies and the Republic of Indonesia, 1970; Admission of Women to Melbourne University 1869-1903, 1973. Honours: E J Roberts Residential Schlsp, Govt Schlsp, 1945-48; Myer Fndn Travel Grant, 1966-67. Memberships: Austl Indonesian Assn Ed, 1960; Meth Ladies' Coll Cncl, 1972-97. Hobbies: Reading; Writing; Photography; Knitting; Travel; Conversation. Address: 27 Stableford Avenue, Glen Waverley, Vic 3150, Australia.

ZAINUDDIN Daim, b. 1938 Alor Star Kedah State. Politician; Lawyer; Bus Exec. Education: London; Univ of CA. Appointments: Called to the Bar Lincoln's Inn; Magistrate then Dep Pub Prosecutor; Later set up own law firm; Hd Peremba, 1979-; Min of Fin, 1984-91; Chmn Fleet Grp; Treas UMNO; Exec Dir Natl Econ Action Cncl, 1998-; Econ Advsr to PM Mahathir bin Mohammad - qv; Chmn and Dir num cos. Memberships: Mbr Dewan Negara - Senate - 1980-82; Mbr Dewan Rakat - HoR - 1982-. Address: c/o Ministry of Finance, Block 9, Jalan Duta, Kuala Lumpur, Malaysia.

ZAKARIA Bin Datij Mahawangsa Haji Awang Sulaiman. Government Official. Appointments: Perm Sec, Min of For Affairs; Dept Min, For Affairs, Govt of Brunei; Min Comm, 1988-. Address: Ministry of Communications, Old Airport Berakas, Bandar Seri Begawan 1-150, Brunei.

ZAMBONI DI SALERANO Mario Vittorio, b. 29 Aug 1938, Rome, Italy. Diplomat. 2 s. Education: Econs Univ of Rome. Appointments: UN New York Italian Mission, Consul in S Afr, Italian Emb in Belgium. Address: 9 Le Phung Hieu, Hanoi, Vietnam, Italian Embassy.

ZANG Shao Xian, b. 28 Nov 1938, Shandong, China. Professor. m. 1 Oct 1969, 1 d. Education: BA, Peking Univ, 1964. Appointments: Asst Prof, Assoc Prof, Prof, Geophys, Peking Univ, 1964-; Hon Rsch Fell, Univ Coll, London, 1977-79. Publications: Sev articles in profl jrnls. Memberships include: Geophysl Soc of China. Hobbies: Swimming; Climbing. Address: No 104 Bl 47, Zhong Guan Yuan, Peking University, Beijing 100871, China.

ZANG Yan, b. 12 Sept 1962, Changchun, China. m. Yuxun Zhang, 20 July 1987, 1 s. Education: Master Deg, Med. Appointments: Asst Rschr; Lectr. Publications: The Roles of Mesothelial Cells in Peritoneal Antibacterial Defence. Honours: ALMGEN Outstndng Jnr Nephrologist Awd, Nephrol Soc of China and ALMGEN Great China. Memberships: Chinese Soc of Immunol; Chinese Med Assn; Chinese Soc of Nephrol. Hobby: Basketball. Address: c/o Department of Nephrology, Nanfang Hospital, Guangzhou 510515, China.

ZAOUI David, b. 16 May 1971, Versailles, France. Import/Export Agent. Education: BEcons. Memberships: Austl Inst of Mngmt; Young Bus Forum. Hobbies: Record producing; Mountaineering; Meditation; Yoga; Sailing. Address: 35/87 McLachlan Avenue, Rushcutters Bay, NSW 2011, Australia.

ZECHA Alexander William Lauw Roberts, b. 18 July 1963, Kuala Lumpur, Malaysia. Distribution Manager. 1 d. Education: "Thunderbird", MBA/MIM Amn Grad Sch of Intl Mngmt. Honours: Corp Cnsltng Prog, Thunderbird. Memberships: Amn Mktng Assn. Hobbies: Golf; Scuba diving; Tennis; Sailing; Arts. Address: 9 Leonie Hill, #11-11 Hilton Towers, Singapore 239220.

ZEDILLO PONCE DE LEON Ernesto, b. 27 Apr 1951 Mexico Cty. Politcian; Economist. m. Nilda Nunez, 5 c. Education: Instituto Nacional Politecnico; Bradford Univ; CO Univ; Yale Univ. Appointments: Joined Partido Revolucionario Institucional - PRI - 1971; With Instituto de Estudios Politicos Economicos y Sociales - Ipese affil to PRI; Econ rschr Direccion Gen de Programacion Economica y Social; Dep Mngr of Fin and Econ Rsch Banco de Mexico - BANXICO; A Dir in charge of the bank's Ficorca scheme; Advsr to Bd of Dirs; Tchr Colegio de Mexico; Dep Sec for Plng and the Budget, 1987-88; Fndr Programa Nacional de Solidaridad; Sec for Plng and the Budget, 1988-92; Sec of Pub Educ, 1992-93;

Campaign mngr for the late Luis Donaldo Colosio - fmr presdl cand - 1993; Pres of Mexico, 1994-. Address: Partido Revolucionario Institucional Insurges Norte 61, 06350 Mexico DF, Mexico.

ZEHEB Ezra, b. 2 March 1937, Haifa, Israel. Professor. m. Ruth, dec, 7 June 1960, 3 s. Education: BSc EE, 1958; MSc EE, 1962; DSc EE, 1966. Appointments: Prof Electr Engrng, Tel-Aviv Univ, 1985-88; Prof Electr Engrng, Technion-Israel Inst of Tech, 1989-. Publications: 109 in refereed jrnls and conf proceedings. Honours: Elected Fell, IEEE; 2000 Millennium Medal of Hon. Memberships: Chmn, IEEE Israel Sect, 1986-88, 1990-92; Sigma Xi. Hobbies: Hiking; Reading. Address: Technion, Electrical Engineering Department, Haifa 32000, Israel.

ZELLING Howard Edgar, b. 14 Aug 1916, Adelaide, Aust. Judge. m. Sesca Ross Anderson, 21 Jan 1950. Education: Scotch Coll, Adelaide; LLB, 1938; Hons LLB, 1941; DUni, 1983, Univ of Adelaide. Appointments: Called, 1938; Procurator, Presby Ch of SA, 1945-69; Lectr, Constitutional Law, 1949-62; Queens Cnsl, 1962; Pres, Law Cncl of Aust, 1966-68; Chmn, Law Reform Cttee of SA, 1968-; Grand Master, Grand Lodge of SA, 1972-76; Judge, SA Supreme Crt, 1969-86; Acting Judge Supreme Crt, 1988-93. Publications: Australian Maritime Law, co-auth, 1991; Many articles in learned periodicals. Honours: CBE, 1969; AO, 1986. Hobby: Numismatics. Address: 43 Edwards Street, South Brighton, SA 5048, Australia.

ZELON Laurie D, b. 15 Nov 1952, Durham, NC, USA. Attorney. m. David George, 30 Dec 1979, 2 s. Education: BA (Engl major, distinction in all subjs), Cornell Univ, 1974; JD, Harv Law Sch, 1977. Publications: Equal Credit: Promise or Reality?, 1976; West's CA Litigation Forms: Civil Procedure Before Trial (contbng ed), 1996. Honours: Winner, Williston Competition, 1975; Recip, The William Reece Smith Jr Spec Servs to Pro Bono Awd, 1993. Memberships: Los Angeles County Bar Assn, 1977-; Pres, 1995-96; State Bar of CA, 1977-; Amn Bar Assn, 1978-; Women Lawyers Assn of LA, 1977-; CA Women Lawyers Assn, 1978-. Address: Morrison & Foerster, LLP, 555 W Fifth Street, Suite 3500, Los Angeles, CA 90013, USA.

ZEMECKIS Robert, b. 1952 Chgo. Film Dir; Writer. m. Mary Ellen Trainor. Films incl: I Wanna Hold Your hand - co-screen play writer - 1978; Romancing the Stone; Back to the Future - co-screen play writer - II, III; Death Becomes Her - also co-prodr; Trespass - co-screen play writer; Forrest Gump; Who Framed Roger Rabbit?; Contact; Sev tv films. Address: c/o CAA, 9830 Wilshire Boulevard, Beverly Hills, CA 90212, USA.

ZEMING Mao, b. 11 Nov 1963, Madang. Minister for Housing. m. 4 children. Education: PETT Course as Motor Mechanic, Goroka Techl Coll, 1981; Officer Cadet, Def Acady, Lae, 1983-85. Appointments: Self-Employed; Salesman, Arnott's PNG Pty, 1989-93; Won By-election for Tewae/Siassi, 1995; Min for Housing. Hobbies: Bush walking; Enjoying and listening to nature.

ZENG Ding, b. 3 Mar 1930, Fuzhou, China. Professor of Biochemistry; Director of Tumour Cell Engineering Laboratory. m. Jue-min Qiu, 1 Oct 1962, 2 s. Education: Grad, Dept Bio, Xiamen Univ, 1954; Visng Schl, Dept Biochem, Univ WI-Madison, USA, 1981-82. Appointments: Asst, 1954-61, Lectr, 1961-81, Assoc Prof, 1981-87, Chmn, 1984-92, Prof, 1987-, Dept Bio, Xiamen Univ; Dir, State Lab Tumour Cell Engrng, Xiamen Univ; Dpty Ed in Chf, Nat Sci, Jrnl Xiamen Univ. Publications: Books: Methods of Biological Chemistry, 1978; Biology of Nitrogen Fixation, 1987; Ed, auth, Biotechnology, The Encyclopaedia of High Technology sub-vol, 1995; More than 50 rsch pprs about biochem, molecular bio, plant chem and bio of nitrogen fixation. Honours: Nat Sci Meeting Awd, 1978, Sci and Technological Achievement Awd, 1979, Ex Nat Sci Pprs Awd, 1986, 1996, 1990, Fujian Prov Govt; Outstndng Tchng and Rsch Awd, Xiamen Univ, 1978; Scis and Tecnol Progress Awd, Natl Educ Commn, 1996. Memberships: Pres, Xiamen Soc

Bio; VP, Fujian Soc Biochem; FIBA; Soc Chinese Bioscientists Am; Chinese Soc Botany; Chinese Soc Biochem. Hobbies: Classical music; Photography; Volleyball. Address: Department of Biology, Xiamen University, Xiamen, Fujian 361005, China.

ZENG Junwen, b. 25 Dec 1961, Guangzhou, China. Ophthalmologist. m. Min Lu, 22 July 1986, 1 d. Education: MD, 1984, Sun Yat-sen Univ of Medl Scis, China; PhD, 1993, Meharry Medl Col, USA. Appointments: Ophth Res, 1984; Rsch Asst, 1988; Rsch Assoc, 1993; Asst Prof, 1998; Prof, 1999. Memberships: Amn Acady Ophth; Assn for Rsch in Vision and Ophth; Chinese Ophth Soc. Hobbies: Sports; Travel; Arts. Address: Zhongshen Ophthalmic Centre, 54 S Xie lei Rd, Guangzhou 510060, China.

ZENG Peiyan, b. Dec 1938 Shaoxing Cty Zhejiang Prov. Politician. Education: Tsinghua Univ. Appointments: Joined CCP, 1978; Second then First Sec Coml Cnslrs Off Emb USA; Dir Gen Off then Dir Plng Dept of min of Electrons Ind; Vice-Min of Electrons Ind, 1988; Vice-Min State Plng Commn and Vice Sec-Gen Cntrl Fin Ldng Grp, 1993-. Memberships: Alt mbr 14th CCP Cntrl Cttee, 1992; Mbr 15th CCP Cntrl Cttee, 1997-. Address: State Planning Commission, Beijing, People's Republic of China.

ZENG Shilin, b. 30 Sept 1928, Nan Chang, Jiangxi, China. Scientific Inventor. Appointments: Clerk; Technician; Worker; Engineer; Senior Engineer; Chf of Research; Chf of Factory. Publications: The Model AYH-1 Pressure-Wind Respirator, 1993; The Model AYH Pressure-Wind Respirator, 1998. Address: Kunming Pressure-Wind Respirator Factory, N 21 Minhang Road, Kunming 650041, Yunnan, China.

ZENG Tao, b. 18 July 1944, Liaoyang Cty, Liaoning Prov, China. Professor. m. Chenfeng Qin, 1 s, 1 d. Education: BA. Appointments: VP, Shenyang Sci and Technol Cadres Coll, 1987; Pres, Shenyang TV and Brdcstng Univ, 1994. Publications: On How to Write Business Applying Essays, 1988; On How to Write Economy Applying Essays, 1997. Honours: First Prize, Liaoning Writing Assm , 1997; Memberships: VP, China TV and Brdcstng Further Educ Assn, 1995; Pres, Shenyang TV and Brdcstng Educ Assn. Hobbies: Russian; Music. Address: No 7, 14th Weilu, Heping District, Shenyang 110003, Liaoning, China.

ZENG Xi Yuan, b. 18 July 1933, Beijing, China. Chairman. m. Jing Wu Yang, 1 Aug 1961, 1 s, 1 d. Education: BN, Grad, Nursing Dept, Capital Medl Univ. Appointments: Mngng Dir, Chinese Nursing Assn, 1987-91; Dir, Nursing Dept, Beijing Hosp, 1981-94; Vice Chmn, CNA, 1991-95; Chmn, CNA, 1995-. Creative Works: Aging Nursing, Nursing Psychology; Theory and Practice of Entirety Nursing; Home Nursing Techniques and General Dis Care. Honours: Ex Nurse of the Hosp; Hlth and Educ Advd Worker of Nation. Memberships: Surg Cttee, CNA; 5tr Chinese Sci and Technol Assn. Hobbies: Music. Address: No 7 Dong Jiao Min Xiang, Beijing 100730, China.

ZENG Xian Zhang, b. 7 Nov 1955, Ningxiang, Hunan, China. Teacher. m. Xiao Ling Huang, 1 s. Education: BEng, Mech Engrng Dept, Hunan Univ, 1981. Appointments: Tchr, Longtian HS, Ningxiang, 1975-77; Asst Lectr, Hunan Coal Ind Coll, 1982-85; Lectr, Hd, Mech Engrng Tchng & Rsch Off, Hunan Coll of Bldng Materials Ind, 1986-91; Snr Lectr, VP, Hunan Coll of Mech & Elec Engrng, 1992-. Publications include: How to Strengthen the Teaching Supervision of Producing Practice Under the Situation of Opening and Reform, 1992; A Thermodynamic Calculation of the Ni-No Phase Diagram, 1992; Rules of Cement Plant's Equipments. Honour: Adv Tchng Worker, Hunan Agricl Machinery System, 1994-95, 1997-98. Memberships: China Agricl Engrng Insts; China Mech Engrng Inst; Vice Bd Chmn, Hunan Vocational Educn Engrng Mech Drafting Rsch Inst; Dir, Vocational Educn Tchng & Rsch Assns of China Vocational Educn Inst. Address: Hunan College of Mechanical & Electrical Engineering, Hunan 410126,

China.

ZENG Xiang Qiu, b. 21 Aug 1933, Wenzhou, Zhejiang, China. Automatic Control. m. Zhu Ping, 5 Jan 1965, 3 d. Education: Grad, Shanghai Liao Tong Univ, 1955; MSc, Moscowskii Energeticheckii Inst, 1960. Appointments: Visng Schl, John Hopkins Univ; Chmn, Auto Control Dept, Nanjing Univ of Sci and Technol; Dpty Hd, Interpreteur, Tech Inspection miss to Russia. Creative Works: Spectral Methods for Analysis of Time Varying Linear Systems and Synthesis of Optimal Control, 1990; On Identification of Systems; Proceedings of the Conf on Info Sci and Sys. Memberships: Assn of Automation of Jiangsu Prov. Hobbies: Russian Lang; Chinese Calligraphy; Eng Lang. Address: Nanjing University of Sci and Technol #15-3, Nanjing 210094, China.

ZENG Xianlin, b. 1929 Anyue Sichuan. Govt Offic. Appointments: Vice-Min for Sci and Tech, 1985-87; Vice-Min for State Plng Commn, 1986-87; Min for Light Ind, 1987-93; Vice-Chmn Finl and Econ Cttee; NPC Dep Sichuan Prov. Memberships: Alt mbr 13th CCP Cntrl Cttee, 1987-92; Alt mbr 14th CCP Cntrl Cttee, 1992-; Mbr 8th NPC, 1993-. Address: c/o State Planning Commission, People's Republic of China.

ZHA Zi Zhong, b. 28 Oct 1936, China. Teacher; Researcher. m. Rui Liu, 2 Apr 1968, 1 s, 1 d. Education: Dip, Nuclear Phys, Harbin Inst of Technol, 1964. Appointments: Asst, 1964, Lectr, 1976, Assoc Prof, 1986, Prof, 1996. Publication: Realization of Laser Protection Using Nonlinear Optics Principles, 1994. Honours: 3rd Class Awd, Natural Sci, Acady of Sci, China, 1992; Ex Ppr Awds, Harbin Inst of Technol. Memberships: Assn of Phys and Optics, Heilongjiang. Hobbies: Travel; Music. Address: Harbin Institute of Technology, PO Box 309, Harbin 150001, China.

ZHA Zixiu, b. 29 Nov 1929, Anhui, China. Scientific Researcher. m. Fangding Wang, 1 Feb 1959, 1 s, 1 d. Education: Grad, Jin Ling Univ, Nanking, China. Appointments: Dir, Dept of Devl Psychol, Inst of Psychol, Chinese Acady of Scis, 1974-87; Dir, Rsch Cntr of Gifted Children, Inst of Psychol, CAS, 1993-; Leader, Supernormal Children Cooperative Rsch Grp of China, 1978-99. Publications: Research Methods in Child Psychology, 1989; Gifted Child Psychology, 1993; Exploration The Secrets of the Development of Gifted and Talented Children, 1999. Honours: Third Prize, Acad Rsch, Chinese Acady of Scis, 1981; First Prize, Educl Rsch, Educl Cttee of Beijing, 1992; Outstndng Contbn Awd, World Cncl for Gifted and Talented Children, 1995. Memberships: Cncl of Chinese Psychol Soc, 1984-93; Stndng Cttee, Devl Spec Cttee Chinese Psychol Soc, 1984-93. Hobby: Reading. Address: 58/18/1 Hiaidan Lu, Beijing 100086, China.

ZHAI Taifeng, b. May 1933 Tangshan Cty Hebei Prov. Party Offic. Education: Chinese People's Univ, 1955-57. Appointments: Joined CCP, 1949; Vice-Chmn Beijing Fedn of Trade Unions, 1981; Dep Sec-Gen Propaganda Dep of CCP Cntrl Cttee, 1986; Sec-Gen and Vice-Dir Propaganda Dept of CCP Cntrl Cttee, 1991-; Vice-Chmn Chinese Writers' Assn. Memberships: Mbr 14th CCP Cntrl Commn for Discipline Insp, 1992-97. Address: Propaganda Department, Chinese Communist Party Central Committee, Beijing, People's Republic of China.

ZHANG Baifa, b. 1934 Xianghe Co Hebei Prov. Admnstr. Appointments: Joined CCP, 1954; Vice-Min of State Capital Constrn Commn, 1976-82; Vice-Mayor of Beijing Municipality, 1982-97; Deleg 13th Cntrl Cttee CCP, 1987-91; Deleg 14th Cntrl Cttee CCP, 1992; Vice-Chmn Capital Plng and Constrn Commn. Memberships: Standing Cttee mbr CPC 7th Beijing Municipal Cttee, 1992-97. Address: Office of Vice-Mayor, Beijing Municipal Government, Beijing City, People's Republic of China.

ZHANG Bangwei, b. 20 Apr 1940, Jiangan, Sichuan, China. Teacher. m. Jinhua Zhang, 31 Jan 1968, 1 s, 1 d. Education: MA, Northwest Normal Univ. Appointment: Chinese People's Polit Consultative Conf, Sichuan Prov,

China, 1992-97, 1998-. Publications: Marriage and Society, 1989; The Royal Family and Politics, 1993; The Rise and Fall of the Chinese Dynasties (Sung Dynasty), 1996. Honour: Receiver of Spec Allowance from Govt, 1992-. Membership: Assn of Hist Rsch, Sung Dynasty. Hobby: Football. Address: Department of History, Sichuan Normal University, Chengdu, China.

ZHANG Baoning, b. 18 July 1946, Beijing, China. Surgeon. m. Lingyuan Zhang, 31 Jan 1980, 1 d. Education: Beijing Med Coll. Appointments: Assoc Prof, 1991, Prof, 1996. Publications: 4 wrks; 25 pprs; 7 trans works; 27 popular sci articles. Memberships: CMA; Cancer Inst; Peking Med Coll; Chinese Acady of Med Scis. Hobbies: Sport; Music; Painting. Address: c/o Cancer Hospital, Peking Union Medical College, Chinese Academy of Medical Sciences, Zuo An Men Wai Pan Jia Yuan, Beijing 100021, China.

ZHANG Bin, b. 15 Jan 1962, Shaanxi, China. Repairing Medical Equipment. m. Sun Yuxia, 25 May 1987, 1 s. Education: Bachelor of Ind, Xi Bei Indl Univ. Appointments: Engr, 1992; Higher Engr, 1998. Publication: Pat, Machines of ion's improving looks. Membership: Assn of Preparing of Medl Equipment of China. Address: Teaching Hosp of Shaanxi College of Traditional Chinese Medicine, Xian Yang, Shaanxi, China.

ZHANG Binggen, b. 22 Jan 1934, Shanghai, China. m. 2 children. Education: Grad, Dept of Maths, Shandong Univ, 1957. Appointments: Asst, Shandong Univ, 1957-59; Asst Lectr 1962, Assoc Prof 1978, Full Prof 1985, Shandong Coll of Oceanology; Full Prof, Ocean Univ of Qingdao, 1987; Invited talks at Univ of Graz, Austria, Univ of Paderborn, Germany, Sticting Mathematisch Centrum, Netherlands, Applied Maths Div, Willington, NZ, Univ of Auckland, NZ, 1987; Rsch Fell, Flinders Univ of SA, 1987; Visng Prof, Univ of NSW, Aust, 1987; Var talks at Univ of Alberta, Can, Univ of Sask, Can, Univ of BC, Can, Univ of Hong Kong Math Soc, 1988; Visng Prof, Sask Univ, Can, 1990. Publications: Over 150 pprs including: On Stability of a System of Two Differential Equations, 1959; The Solution of Automatic Central System, 1961; Random Differential Equations in Science and Engineering, 1980; Oscillation Theory of Differential Equations with Deviating Arguments, 1987; Mathematical Model of Ecology, 1990; On the Oscillation of Solutions of Reduced Wave Equations, 1990; Theory of Differential Equations with Unbounded Delay, 1994; Oscillation Theory for Functional Differential Equations, 1995. Honours: Awd for Achievement of Sci and Technol, Govt of Shandong, 1991, 1993 and State Educ Commn, China, 1993, 1996. Memberships: Soc of Maths, China; Cncl of Maths of Shandong Provs; Amn Math Soc. Listed in: Who's Who in the World. Address: Dept of Applied Maths, Ocean Univ of Qingdao, Qingdao, Shandong 266003, China.

ZHANG Bo Long, b. 6 Nov 1945, Beijing, China. Doctor. m. Xian Ping Kang, 8 Apr 1972, 1 d. Education: MD; PhD. Appointments: Prof, Dept of Hematol, Peking Union Med Coll Hosp; Prof, Dept of Hematol, Chinese PLA Gen Hosp. Publications: 15 books in med. Honour: ORS Awd, London, 1983. Membership: Chinese Med Assn. Hobbies: Reading; Swimming; Football. Address: Department of Hematology, Chinese PLA General Hospital, Beijing 100853, China.

ZHANG Chunting, b. 30 Aug 1934, Shantung Prov, China. Senior Editor; Reporter. m. Zhang Yuee, 30 June 1962, 2 d. Education: Bachelor, Shandong Tchr's Univ. Appointments: Reporter in Xinhua News Agcy, China, 1960-85; Mbr, Compiler, Cttee and Dir, Chf Ed Off, 1988; Dir, Outlook Weekly, Hong Kong. Publications: (book) People Who Perform Miracles; Collection of Prose; Poem: Ode for Solar Deity. Memberships: China Reporter Assn, 1996; China Old Professor Assn, 1998. Hobbies: Writing poems; Horticulture. Address: HuaYanLi 33, Apartment 808, Deshengmenwai Dajie, Beijing, China 100029.

ZHANG Dao Hua, b. 29 Apr 1956, Zhang Zhuang, Gaotang, China. Teaching and Research. m. Liping Ye, 1 d. Education: BS; MSc; PhD. Appointments: Lectr, 1991-94, Snr Lectr, 1995-, Assoc Prof, 1999-, NTU, Singapore; Rsch Assoc, UNSW, Aust, 1989-91. Publications: Profl pubs in intl jrnls. Honour: 2000 Outstndng People in 20th Century, 1997; Life Achievement Awd, 1997. Memberships: Snr Mbr, IEEE. Hobbies: Music; Singing; Sport. Address: School of Electrical and Electronic Engineering, Nanyang Technological University, Singapore.

ZHANG De, b. 13 Oct 1932, Hebei Prov, China. College Professor. m. He Wen-Yan, 9 July 1961, 2 s, 1 d. Education: Bachelor, Grad from NE Norm Univ, Dept of Educ, 1956. Appointments: Asst Prof, Dept of Educ, NE Norm Univ, 1956; Lectr, 1978; Assoc Prof, 1983; Prof, 1992. Publications: Social Psychol, 1990; Psychol, 1993; Some Problems About Social Psychol, 1987; Improve Family Interpersonal Relation, 1998. Honours: Jilin Prov Ex Tchr, 1989; State Cncl Spec Allowance, 1993. Memberships: Chinese Assn of Social Psychol. Address: No 404 Gate 2 Bld 5, First Resid Quarter, North East Normal Univ, Changchun 130022, China.

ZHANG Dejiang, b. Nov 1946 Taian Co Liaoning Prov. Politician. Education: Yanbian Univ; Kim Il Sung Univ N Korea. Appointments: VP Yanbian Univ, 1980-83; Dep Sec CCP Yanji Cty Cttee, 1983-85; Dep Sec CCP Yanbian Korean Autonomous Prefectural Cttee, 1985-86; Vice-Min of Civ Affairs, 1986; Sec CCP Jilin Provincial Cttee, 1995-. Memberships: Mbr CCP, 1971-; Alt mbr 14th CCP Cntrl Cttee, 1992-97; Mbr 15th CCP Cntrl Cttee, 1997-. Address: Jilin Provincial Committee of Chinese Communist Party, Jilin, People's Republic of China.

ZHANG Fugi, b. 22 Feb 1937. Senior Teacher of Mathematics. m. Yue Zhe Sun, 1 Jan 1962, 1 s, 2 d. Education: Bachelor, Dept of Maths, Capital Normal Univ. Appointments: Exec Dir, Natl Assn of Sci Rsch of Key Mid Schs; Dpty Dir, Management Inst of China and Educl Mngmt Cttee. Publications: Co-auth: Series of Letures On Middle School Mathematics; Analysis On Senior High School Maths Subjects; Ed-in-Chf: Behavior (tchng material). Honours: Num Socialist Constrn Activist Awds; Outstndng Tchr, Advd Worker, 1990s. Exec Dir, Natl Assn of Sci Rsch of Key Mid Schs (Dir, China Snr Sch Profs Assn). Hobbies: Sports. Address: No 46 Enji Zhuang, Haidan District, Beijing 10036, China.

ZHANG Guogang, b. 21 June 1956. Professor of History. m. 6 Oct 1984, 1 s. Education: MS; PhD. Appointments: Lectr, 1983; Assoc Prof, 1986; Prof, 1994; Dean, Dept of Hist, Nankei Univ, 1998-2001. Publications: The Civil Service System of the Tang China, 1987; Studies on the Tang Dynasty Military Governor, 1987; Studies on the Political System of the Tang China, 1994; The Civilization Collision between China and the West, 1996; Ed, Survey of the Studies of Sui, Tang and Five Dynasty, 1996. Memberships: Dpty Chmn, Tang Soc of China; China and For Rels Assn. Hobby: Chess. Address: Nankai University, Department of History, Tianjin 300071, China.

ZHANG Guoguang, b. Apr 1945 Suizhong Co Liaoning Prov. Politician. Education: Beijing Aeronautics Inst. Appointments: Joined CCP, 1966; Sec CCP Shenyang Cty Cttee, 1990; Vice Sec CCP Liaoning Provincial Cttee, 1993-. Memberships: Mbr 15th CCP Cntrl Cttee, 1997-. Address: Chinese Communist Party Liaoning Provincial Committee, Shenyang. Liaoning Province, People's Republic of China.

ZHANG Heng, b. 21 May 1961, Changchun, Jilin, China. Scientist. m. 1 d. Education: BA, 1982; MB, 1984; PhD, 1989. Appointments: Asst Prof, 1989; Assoc Prof, 1992; Prof, 1996. Creative Works: Telescience Technology for Space Experiments; Non-Modelistic Method for Robust Control; Analytic Approach State Feedback. Memberships: Bd Mbr, Mag Computer Simulation. Hobbies: Swimming. Address: Inst of Mechanics, Chinese Academy of Sciences, Beijing

100080, China.

ZHANG Hongqiang, b. Oct 1934, Zhejian Prov, China. Senior Engineer. m. Ji Ying Fang, 18 Oct 1964, 1 s, 1 d. Education: Grad, Fu Dan Univ, 1955. Appointment: Exec VP, Shanghai Maritime Exchange Assn, 1993. Publications: Ed-in-Chf: An English-Chinese Dictionary of New and Developing Sciences and Technologies. Memberships: Shanghai Maritime Exchange Assn, 1993; Shanghai Scis and Technols Info Inst, 1980. Hobbies: Literature; Music. Address: Room 717, 3 Wuzhong Road, Shanghai 200233, China.

ZHANG Huan-zong, b. 4 Oct 1939, Tianjin, China. Faculty. m. Sun Shao-qi, 7 Sept 1976, 1 s. Education: BA. Appointments: Ref Rm, Hist Dept, 1977-92, Lib, 1992, Ref Rm, Hist Dept, 1993-, Nankai Univ. Publications: Mystery About Chinese and World History, 1987; Tang Shao-yi and the Republic of China in the Late Qing Dynasty, 1998. Honours: Outstndng Contbrn Medal, 1995; Outstndng Tchr, Tianjin City, 1997. Membership: Dir, Natl Liberal Arts Stdy Info Inst. Hobbies: Peking Opera; Music. Address: Department of History, Nankai University, Tianjin 300071, China.

ZHANG Jia-Xun, b. 6 Jan 1934, Zhongshan, Guangdong, China. Professor. Education: Sun yat-Sen, Univ of Medl Sci, 1956; Trng Course in Malariology, 1957; Trng Course in Parasitology, 1958. Appointments: Prof, Chf, Dept of Parasite Bio, Inst of Parasitic Diseases, Chinese Acady of Preventive Med; Supvsr, Epid Sit of Hlth Min, China. Publications: Malaria in the Medical Encyclopaedia of China; The Large Encyclopaedia of China; Chemical Cure of Parasitosis; Improve the Diagnosis and Treatment of the Cerebral Malaria; Appeal to Prevent Spread of AIDS, Chinese Jrnl of Intl Med. Honour: Prize, Hlth Min of China. Membership: Medl Inst of China. Hobbies: Literature; Music. Address: Institute of Parasitic Disease, Chinese Academy of Preventive Medicine, 207 Rui Jin Er Lu, Shanghai 200025, China.

ZHANG Jiacheng, b. 13 July 1927, Supu, Hunan, China. Scientist. m. Wang Li, 1 Feb 1959, 1 s, 2 d. Education: Grad, Qinghua Univ, 1951; Doct, after postgrad stdy in fmr Hydrometeorological Inst of Leningrad in Soviet Union. Appointments: Weather Forecaster, Hd of Lang weather forecast; Dir, Weather and Climate Rsch Inst; Vice Dir, AMS. Publications: Climate Change and its Causes, 1976; Climate of China, 1985, English version, 1992; Climate and Man, 1988. Honours: Prize of All China Conf of Sci and Technol, 1978; Natl Prize, 1982. Memberships: Commn for Climatology in WMO, 1982-96; Chmn, Climate Comn in China Meteorological Soc. Hobbies: Thinking; Writing. Address: The Chinese Academy of Meteorological Science, Beijing 100081, China.

ZHANG Jialong, b. 6 June 1938, Jiangsu, China. Logician; Philosopher. m. Jiang Rongdi, 13 Nov 1973, 1 d. Education: Grad Dip, Philos, Peking Univ, 1961; Postgrad Dip, Math Logic, Peking Univ, 1965. Appointments: Rsch Prof, Inst of Philos, Chinese Acady of Socl Scis, 1990-; Dir, Logic Sect, Inst of Philos, CASS, 1994-. Publications: Axiomatics, Mathematics and Philosophy, 1983; The Development of Mathematical Logic, 1993; On A J Ayer, 1995; On F H Bradley, 1997. Honours: Sci Achmnts Prize of Chinese Acady of Socl Scis, 1993, 1997. Memberships: VP, Sec Gen, Chinese Assn of Logic. Hobby: Literature. Address: Institute of Philosophy, Chinese Academy of Social Sciences, Beijing 100732, China.

ZHANG Jian, b. 15 Jan 1963, Hunan, China. Thermal Engineer. m. Liu Hui, 1 Oct 1990, 1 s. Education: Univ Dips, Thermal Engrng. Honours: Gold Prize, 22nd Salon Geneva Invention; Sci and Technol Progress Awd, Natl S & T Cttee, 1996. Membership: Congressman, China. Hobbies: Golf; Reading; Tennis. Address: Broad Air Conditioning, Broad Town, Changsha City, Hunan, China.

ZHANG Jianhua, b. 8 Nov 1940, Honghe, Yunnan, China. Professor; Vice-Dean. m. July 1969, 3 s. Education: BA, Philos, Pols Dept, Yunnan Univ.

Appointments: Kunming Medl Coll, 1964-71; Socl Wrker; Assoc Prof, Prof, Yunnan Inst of Nationalities, 1971-. Publications: Contrb of 38 articles in field of philos in newspprs and mags; Ed of 9 books. Honours: Best Tchr Awd, 3 times, 1970-87; 2nd prize for articles, 1982; 2nd prize for tchng achievement, 1987. Memberships: Dir, China Ethnic Theor Assn, Yunnan Br; Vice-Chmn, Yunnan Yi Assn; Dir, Ed-in-Chf of mag, Yunnan Philos Tchr Assn. Listed in: Dictionary of Chinese Minority Nationality Experts. Hobbies: Reading; Music; Swimming; Fishing; Badminton. Address: Cadre Training Department, Yunnan Institute of the Nationalities, Kunming, Yunnan, China.

ZHANG Jinkun, b. 7 Mar 1943, Shanghai, China. Professor of Histology and Embryology. m. Wei Xiyun, 23 Jan 1971, 1 s. Education: BS, Nanjing Railway Med Coll, 1965. Appointments: Lectr, 1965-87, Vice Prof, Grad Advsr, Hd, Dept of Histology and Embryology, Nanjing Railway Med Coll, 1987-92; Prof, Grad Advsr, Hd, Dept of Histology and Embryology, Hd, Cancer Cell Biol Lab, Shantou Univ Med Coll, 1992-. Publications include: Comparative Observation of Phagocylic Capacities of Dendritic Cells and Macrophages in Rat Spleen, 1992; Morphological Quantitative Analysis of Interdigitating Cells and Macrophages in Rat Splenic White Pulp, 1996; Observation on Capacity of Human Blood Dendritic Cells to Form Cell Clusters in Vitro, 1997; Ultrastructural Comparison of Apoptosis of Human Hepatoma Cells and LAK Cells, 1998. Honours: 3rd Prize, Sci and Technol Progress, Jiangsu, 1992; 2nd Prize, Sci and Technol Progress, Railway Dept, 1993; Govt Specl Allowance, 1993. Memberships: Chinese Soc of Anatomical Scis; Cnclr, Guangdong Soc of Anatomical Scis; Chinese Soc of Cell Biol; Chinese Soc for Stereology. Address: Department of Histology and Embryology, Shantou University Medical College, Xingling Road, Shantou 515031, China.

ZHANG Kangda, b. 18 June 1935, Hangzhou, China. Teaching. m. Bitian Hu, 17 Jan 1971, 1 s. Education: BEng, Dalian Inst of Technol, China, 1956. Appointments: Lectr 1956-78, Assoc Prof, 1978-83, Prof, 1983-, Zhejiang Univ of Technol Hangzhou. Publications: The Equipment of Chemical Engineering, auth, book, 1961; Project Head Research into Fatigue and Fracture of Pressure Vessels. Honours: Awd, Min Mech Engrng, 1986; Awd, Natl Educ Comm, 1993. Memberships: Ed, Zhejiang Gongxueyuan Xuebao, 1993-97; Chinese Mech Engrng Soc; Chinese Soc Pres Ves, Bd Dirs, 1983-98. Hobbies: Football; Swimming. Address: 6 Dist Zhaohui 72#2-502, Hangzhou, Zhejiang, 310014, China.

ZHANG Li, b. 5 May 1963, Jilin, China. Teacher. m. Hongyu Chen, 12 May 1988, 1 s. Education: BA, Peking Univ, 1985; Dip, Postgrad Study, 1987. Appointments: Lectr, Beijing Lang Inst, 1987-94; Assoc Prof, Moscow State Inst of Intl Rels, 1994-97; Assoc Prof, Beijing Lang & Culture Univ, 1997-. Publications: Foreign Trade Chinese: 30 Lessons, 1991; Qingxilanxi (poems), 1994; A Dictionary of Semastic Variation in Current Chinese, 1998. Hobby: Sport. Address: c/o College of Chinese Language, Beijing Language and Culture University, Beijing 100083, China.

ZHANG Liang Shun, b. 12 Mar 1944, Wuhan, Hubei, China. Official. m. Yin, Jan 1974, 1 s, 1 d. Education: Bachelor's degree. Appointments: Sect Chf, 1983; Dpty Div Dir, 1989; Div Dir, 1996; Visng Prof, Zhong Nan Univ of Fin and Econs, 1993; Visng Prof, Hubei Provcl For Trade Sch, 1998. Publications: Over 30 creative wrks inclng books, pprs and compositions. Honours: 3rd Awd of Ex Ppr, 1987; 2nd Awd, Ex Ppr, 1991. Memberships: Hubei Procl Trans' Union; Hubei Popular Sci Writers Assn; China Intl Chmbr of Com, Hubei Branch; Sanding Dir, Hubei Intellectual Prop Rsch Acady, 1993; Dir, Hubei Intl Econ & Trade Inst, 1993; Standing Dir, Hubei Intl Sci and Technol Coop Assn, 1997. Hobbies: Stamp collection; Basketball; Swimming. Address: 9F Jinmao Building, North Jianghan Roar 8, Wuhan, Hubei, China.

ZHANG Lichang, 1939 Nanpi Co Hebei Prov. Admnstr. Appointments: Joined CCP, 1966; Vice-Mayor of Tianjin Municipality, 1985; NPC Dep Dep Sec CPC 6th Tianjin Municipal Cttee, 1989-92; Sec CPC 7th Tianjin Municipal Cttee, 1992-; Mayor of Tianjin municipality, 1993-; Sec CCP Tianjin Municipal Cttee, 1997-; Fmr Sec-Gen CCP Cntrl Cttee Intl Liaison Dept; VP China Mayors' Assn. Memberships: Alt mbr 13th CCP Cntrl Cttee, 1987-92; Alt mbr 14th CCP Cttee, 1992-; Mbr 15th CCP Cntrl Cttee, 1997-. Address: Mayor's Office, Tianjin Municipality, People's Republic of China.

ZHANG Lining, b. 26 Aug 1935, Nanjing, China. Professor. m. Ruilian Ding, 1 Oct 1959, 1 d. Education: Grad, Nanjing Inst of Technol, 1956. Appointments: Lectr, Nanjing Inst of Technol, 1960-79; Visng Rschr, Oxford Univ, 1980-82; Assoc Prof, Nanjing Inst of Technol, 1983-86; Prof, SE Univ, 1987-. Publications: Advanced Materials Technique, 1992; Over 70 rsch pprs. Honours: Named Outstndng Supvsr of Rsch Students, Educ Commn, Jiangsu Prov, 1993; 3rd Prize, Natl Educn Cttee, China, 1995; 3rd Prize, Natl Sci and Technol Progress, China, 1996. Memberships: Dir, Chinese Soc of Composite Materials; Hon Dir, Metal Soc of Jiangsu. Hobbies: Music; Photography. Address: Department of Materials Science & Engineering, Southeast University, Nanjing 210018, China.

ZHANG Man-da, b. 6 Sept 1937, Wuxi, China. Doctor. m. Zhang Huinan, 1 Oct 1961, 2 d. Education: BMed. Appointments: Dir, Jiangsu Inst of Nuclear Med, 1985-97; Dir, State Key Lab of Nuclear Med, 1993-; Rsch Prof, Inst. 1990-. Creative works: An English-Chinese Dictionary of Nuclear Medicine, 1986; Applied Clinical Nuclear Medicine, 1990; Study of Dopamine Receptor Imaging, 1990. Honour: Govt Prominent Achievements for Middle-Aged Specialists, 1988. Memberships: Dpty Chmn, Chinese Nuclear Med Soc, 1984-93. Hobby: Traditional Chinese Painting. Address: 20 Qian Rong Road, Wuxi, 214063, Jiangsu, China.

ZHANG Ping, b. 24 Sept 1937, Wuxi, China. Scientist, Combustion Diagnostics and Solid Rocket Propulsion. m. Kexian Hu, 26 Jan 1962, 1 s, 1 d. Education: Undergrad, Mechl Engrng, Beijing Inst of Technol, 1954-59; Grad, Mechl Engrng, BIT, 1960-62. Appointments: Instr, Dept of Flt Engrng, BIT, 1963-77; Asst Prof, 1978-79; Assoc Hd, 1981-86; Assoc Prof, 1986-90; Prof, 1991-. Publications: Combustion Diagnostics, 1988; Soild Rocket Propulsion, 1993. Honours: 3rd Awd, Progress in Sci and Technol, 1992; 2nd Awd, 1993; 1st Awd, Ex text book; Outstndng Articles to Profl Publs; Natl Pat. Memberships: Jrnl of Propulsion; Aerospace Inds Grp Corp; Solid Rocket Propulsion; China Aerospace Propulsion. Hobbies: Collecting stamps; Music. Address: Dept of Flight Vehicle and Control, Beijing Inst of Technology, P O Box 327, Beijing 100081, China.

ZHANG Pu Sheng, b. Apr 1934, Shanghai, China. Research Professor. m. Wang Lin, 1 Dec 1964, 1 s. Education: BA, Fudan Univ. Appointment: Rsch Prof, Nanjing Mus. Publications: Scientific Study of Sacrificial Red, 1992; An Excavation on Rongxian Kiln, 1992; Authentication of Ancient Chinese Ceramics, 1995. Honour: Perm Vis Prof, Dept of Hist, Fudan Univ, 1990-. Memberships: VP, Rsch Instn of Chinese Porceilain & Pottery; Natl Cttee, Authentication of Cultural Relics. Hobby: Antiques. Address: 321 East Zhongshan Road, Nanjing 210016, China.

ZHANG Qingguo, b. 4 Oct 1959, Wuhu, Anhui, China. Teacher; Researcher. m. Li Xu, 12 June 1983, 1 d. Education: BS, Maths, Anhui Labor Univ; PhD, Ecology, Zhejiang Agricl Univ. Appointments: Lectr, 1987; Assoc Prof, 1993; Prof, 1998. Publications: Num publs in jrnls. Honours: Awds, fin support as Visng Schlr, China Schlp Cncl, 1998. Memberships: Ecol Prof, Coll of Letter and Sci, Anhui Agricl Univ, 1990-99. Hobbies: Football; Music. Address: College of Letter and Science, Anhui Agricultural University, Hefei, Anhui 230036, China.

ZHANG Qingying, b. 19 Mar 1932. Professor. m. Ouyang Zhihui, 18 Jan 1975, 1 d. Education: Grad, Dept of Phys, Beijing Univ, 1957-61. Appointments: Mbr, Ed Bd of Phys Bulletin, 1982-; Cttee Mbr, Hunan Polit Consultative Conf, 1983-; Chmn, Dept of Phys, Hunan Sci and Technol Univ, 1984-85; Investigator, Dept of Phys, Univ PA, USA, 1985-86; Mbr, Consultative Cttee of Sci and Technol Expert of Hunan Prov Gov, 1987-. Publications: Estimation of the Nuclear Moment of Inertia and the gR-Factor, 1960; The Theory of Collective Hamiltonian, 1982; Closed Analytic Boson Realization for Sp(4), 1986; Some Recent Results on Boson Mappings of Symplectic Shell Model Algebras, 1987; Boson Realization of Shell Model Algebras Sp(2), 1994. Honours: 3 Hunan Sci Congress Awd's, 1978; 1st Class Awd, Ex Acad Thesis of Hunan Prov, 1987, 1994; Hon Title, Exemplary Worker of Sci and Technol of Hunan Prov, 1992. Vice Chmn, Hunan Physl Soc, 1984-; Advsr, Hunan Nuclear Soc, 1984-; Dir, Chinese Physl Soc, 1991-95; Nuclear Structure Specialty Commn of Chinese Nuclear Physl Soc, 1992-. Listed in: Who's Who in the World. Hobbies: Walking; Music; Fiction; Travel; Chess; Go. Address: Department of Physics, Hunan University, Hunan Province, Changsha 410082, China.

ZHANG Qunqun. Economist. Education: BEcon, 1991, MEcon, 1994, Grad Sch, Dongbei Univ of Fin and Econs, Dalian; PhDEcon, Grad Sch, CASS, Beijing, 1997. Appointments: Lectr, Dept of Pub Fin, Dongbei Univ of Fin and Econs, Dalian, 1994; Asst Rsch Fell, Inst of Fin and Trade Econs, CASS, 1997. Publications: The Reconstruction of Economics: Is There Still a Place for Neoclassical Theory?, transl, 1993; Futures Market: Mechanism or Institution?, 1993; An Empirical Summation of the Developing Practice of Futures Market in China, 1994; Games with Imcomplete Information (translation), 1995; The Development and Creation of Game Theory, 1995; Inflation: The Symptom of the Disequilibrium of Institutional Transition, 1995; A Research on the subjects in the Evolution of Futures Market, 1995; The Functions of Local Government and the Transformation of the Models of Institutional Change, 1995; On Excessive Speculation and Its Influence on the Futures Market, 1996; The Different Theoretical Traditions of the Concept of Transaction and Their Comparison, 1997; Financial Service Act of England (co-transl), 1998; On Transaction Organisation and Its Emergence and Evolution, 1999; Antitrust Economics: Merger, Contracting and Stategic Behaviour (co-transl), 1999. Honours: Awd'd Golden Time Prize Schlshp, Grad Sch, CASS, 1995-97; Awd'd the Qualified Yth Rschr of Socl Scis Prize by CASS, 1995-97; Hon by Dalian Municipal Govt as Excellent Grad, 1991 and Excellent Student, 1990; Wrote Prize-winning Economic Article for the Cntrl People's Brdcstng Stn of China, 1992. Hobbies: Reading; Writing. Address: Institute of Finance and Trade Economics, Chinese Academy of Social Sciences, No 2 Yuetan Beixiaojie Street, Beijing 100836, China.

ZHANG Rende, b. 24 Nov 1938. University Professor. m. Wu Guocun, May 1966, 2 d. Education: BEcons, Nankai Univ, Tianjin, China, 1962; MEcon, People's Univ, Beijing, China, 1983; PhD, Econs, Zagreb Univ, Yugoslavia, 1983. Appointments: Tchng Asst, Jinan Univ, Guangdong, China, 1965-78; Lectr, Dept of Econ, Nankai Univ, Tianjin, China, 1978-85; Assoc Prof, Vice-Dean, Dept of Econ, Nankai Univ, 1986-97; Prof, Dir of PhD studs, Dept of Econ, Nankai Univ, 1988-. Publications: Comparative Researches of Ecnomic Systems, Shaanxi Commonwealth of Independent State Transferring to Market Economy, 1994; General Review on Modern Corporation Economy, 1995. Honours: Prize Rsch on Philos & Socl Sci, 1984, 1988, 1990; The Exemplary Tchr, Nankai Univ, 1994. Memberships: Vice-Chmn, Chinese Soc of Hist of Econ Theories, 1994; Cncl of Chinese Rsch Assn of Cncl of Chinese Rsch Assn of East Eur and Mid-Asia Econ, 1996; Acad Supvsr, Rsch Inst, Chinese West Area's Econ, 1996. Hobbies: Music and sports. Address: Department of Economy, Nanakai University, Tianjin, China.

ZHANG Shi-Ying, b. 20 May 1921, Wuhan, China. Professor of Philosophy. m. Peng Lan, 22 July 1945, 2 s, 1 d. Education: Grad, BA, Philos Dept, SW United Univ, China, 1946. Appointments: Asst Instr in Philos, Nankai Univ, 1946-51; Lectr in Philos, Wuhan Univ, 1951-52; Lectr, Assoc Prof, Prof in Philos, Inst of For Philos, Peking Univ, 1952-. Publications: On Hegel's Philosophy, 1956, 1973; On Hegel's Phenomenology of Spirit, 1962; On Hegel's Logic, 1981; Japanese transl, 1975; A History of Western Philosophy (w Wang Zisong, Ren Hua), 1972; A Commentary on Hegel's Logic in Encyclopaedia, 1982; On Hegel's Philosophy of Spirit, 1986; Kant's Critique of Pure Reason, 1987; Hegel-Lexicon, 1991; Between Heaven and Man, 1995; The New Orientation of Philosophy, 1999; Auth, 110 articles. Honours: Hon Dir, Inst of Philos, Hubei Univ, Wuhan, 1989-95; Chinese Culture Awd, 1996. Memberships: Pres, Acad Cttee, Inst of For Philos, Peking Univ; Pres, Soc for the Stdy of Chinese and West Philos and Culture; Advsr, Chinese Assn Stdy of Hist of For Philos; Advsr, Acad Cttee, Jin Yue-Lin Fndn; Conductor, Cntr of Domain of Hist of West Philos in all Chinese Univs; Intl Gesellschaft; Hon Advsr, Rsch Bd of Advrs, ABI; Ed in Chf, German Philos Jrnl; Ed in Chf, Chinese and West Philos and Culture Jrnl. Hobbies: Reading; Writing Chinese Classical Poems. Address: Institute of Foreign Philsophy, Peking University, Beijing, China.

ZHANG Shizheng, b. 10 Jun 1938. Professor of Thermophysics. m. 28 Jan 1968, 2 d. Education: BS, Tsinghua Univ, Beijing, China, 1962. Publications: Books: Nomenclature of Energy Fundamentals, 1991; Total Energy System of Gas Turbine, 1989; Journals: Journal of Engineering Thermophysics, 1980-95. Honours: Sci and Technol Awd of Academia Sinica, Grade 1, 1985 and Grade 3, 1980, 1989; Nat Sci Awd of Academia Sinica, Grade 2, 1991. Memberships: Fell, Chinese Soc of Thermophys, Beijing, 1980-; Fell, Chinese Soc of Aero-Astronautics, Beijing, 1983-; ASME, NY, 1993-. Hobbies: Swimming; Poetry. Address: Institute of Engineering Thermophysics, Academia Sinica, P O Box 2706, Beijing 100080, China.

ZHANG Shunian, b. 29 Aug 1940, Shanghai, China. Professor of Mathematics. m. Xinglin Zhang, 1 May 1964, 2 s. Education: Dept Maths, Anhui Univ, Hefei, 1958-62. Appointments: Asst, 1962-78, Lectr, 1978-79, 1982-84, Prof, 1986-90, 1993-94, Dept Maths, Anhui Univ, Hefei; Rsch Assoc, Dept Maths, Univ Toronto, Can, 1980-81; Visng Assoc Prof, Dept Maths, Southern IL Univ, Carbondale, USA, 1984-86; Visng Prof, Dept Maths, Univ RI, Kingston, USA, 1991-92; Prof, Dept Applied Maths, Shanghai Jiaotong Univ, 1994-. Publications: Asymptotic Behaviour of Solutions of Periodic Delay Differential Equations, 1984; Fundamental Theory of Extended Functional Differential Equations, 1985; Comparison Theorems on Boundedness, 1988; Razumikhin Techniques in Infinite Delay Equations, 1989; Unified Stability Theorems in RFDE and NFDE, 1989; Limiting Equations and Stability for FDE, 1991; The Basic Theory of Topological Dynamics in FDE, 1993; Stability of Infinite Delay Differential Systems, 1994; Boundedness of Infinite Delay Differential Systems, 1994; Invariance Principle for Autonomous Delay Differential Systems, 1995; The Unique Existence of Periodic Solutions of Linear Volterra Differential Equations, 1995; Stability Analysis of Delay Difference Systems, 1997; Quantitative Result on Stability for Delay Difference Systems, 1997; An Improvement in Stability of Delay Difference Systems, 1998; Almost Periodic Solutions of Difference Systems, 1998. Honours: Hon Citizen of OK, USA, 1985; Natl Ex Tchr China, Min Educ China, 1989; Spec Reward, Outstndng Achievements, State Cncl China, 1993-. Memberships: Math Soc China; Intl Fedn Nonlinear Analysis; Amn Math Soc; Academician, Acady of Non-Linear Scis, 1997-; Mbr, NY Acady of Scis, 1998-. Hobbies: Stamp collecting; Playing bridge. Address: Dept of Applied Mathematics, Shanghai Jiaotong University, Shanghai 200240, China.

ZHANG Wanxin, b. 5 May 1930, Harbin, China. Vice President; Senior Engineer; Professor; Research Fellow. m. Deng Yinyin, 15 May 1958, 1 s, 1 d. Education: Peking Tsinghua Univ, 1948, 1952; Rsch and Dev, Prodn Trng, Russia, 1956-70. Appointments: Lanzhou Petro-Chem Corp, 1970-80; Beijing Yanshan Petro-Chem Corp, 1981-83; Beijing Munic Plng Cttee, 1983-88; Prof, Shenzhen Univ, 1984-88; China Petro-Chem Corp, 1988-; Prof (pt-time), Tsinghua Univ, Advsr of Doct Deg studs, 1989-93; Current: Dev Rsch Cntr (DRC) State Cncl of China, Chmn, Intl Multi-Petrochem Enterprise Ltd, Exec Chmn, Himont-Impel Ltd (USA), 1989-97, Vice Chmn and Pres, Create Grp Inc, 1990-; Vice Chmn, Pres, China Natl Soc of Taiwan Stdies, Vice Chmn, NW Econ Assn, 1995-. Publications: The Development of Petro-Chemical Industry and Energy Prob; The Study of Multinational Corporations; Num Rsch and Dev wrks. Honours: Prov and Munic Adv Sci and Technol Awds, 1962, 1963, 1964; Beijing Adv Sci and Technol Awd, 1977; Natl Spec Awd, Top Grade, 1985. Memberships: Vice Chmn, China Chem Ind and Energy Soc; Chmn Bd, Petro-chem Inst; Advsry Bd, China MBA Prog of Bus Mngmt Sch, NY State Univ, Buffalo, USA; Vice Chmn, China Charity Assn. Address: 22 Xianmen Street, Beijing 100017, China.

ZHANG Wei, b. 22 May 1913, Beijing, China. University Professor. m. Shi-Jia Lu dec, 1 s, 1 d. Education: BSc; DIC; Dr.Ing. Appointments: Asst, Tangshan Chiao-Tung Univ, 1934-37; Asst, Mechs, Tech Hochschule, Berlin, 1942-44; Res Engr, Escher-Wyss, Zurich, 1945-46; Prof of Mechs, Tung-Ji Beiyang Univ, 1946-; Provost, VP, Tsinghua Univ, 1959-66, 1977-84; Pres, Shenzhen Univ, 1963-66. Publication: Introduction in Shell-Theory, 1964. Honours include: Medal, Alex von Humboldt. Memberships: MVDI; IABSE; MAIAA. Hobbies: Tennis; Classical Music; Chinese Opera. Address: Tsinghua University, Beijing, China.

ZHANG Wen Xun, b. 15 Dec 1937. Educator; Researcher. m. Zhi Rui Shen, 1 May 1965, 1 s, 1 d. Education: Grad, Nanjing Inst of Technol, 1958. Appointments: Tchng Asst 1958, Lectr 1965, Assoc Prof 1981, Prof 1985, Advsr of Doctoral Cands 1986, Mbr of Natl Advsry Cttee for EE 1991-95, Dean of Div 1992, Dpty Chmn of Steering Cttee 1993, State Key Lab of Millimeter Waves; Mbr Awd Ctee for Achievement in Sci and Technol, State Educ Commn of China, 1996-; Mbr Steering Cttee, Natl Lab of Antenna and Microwave Technol, China, 1997-. Publications: Differential Equations in Radio Engineering, 1982; Functional Methods in Electromagnetic Engineering, 1985; Engineering Electromagnetism: Functional Methods, 1991; Technical Papers, 300. Honours: Highest Awd of Achievements in Sci and Technol, State Educ Commn of China. Memberships: Chinese Inst of Elects, Mbr 1964-, Fell 1987-, Cncl Mbr 1992-; VP, Antennas Soc, 1991-; IEEE, Snr Mbr 1988-; Chair, Shanghai Sub Sect, 1991-92; Chair, Nanjing Chapt, 1995-; IEE, Fell, 1992-; Hon Sec, Beijing Cntr, 1993-; URSI, Official Mbr 1994-; Chinese Math Soc, 1988-; Mbr Transnatl Cttee, IEEE Antennas and Propagation Soc, 1996. Listed in: Dictionary of International Biography; Who's Who in the World. Hobbies: Classical music; Photography; Philosophy; Poetry. Address: 22-1001, 2nd Suo-Jin-Cun, Nanjing 210042, China.

ZHANG Wenpeng, b. 20 Aug 1958, Shaanxi, China. Teacher. m. Zhang Cuncao, 8 Jan 1984, 1 s, 1 d. Education: BSc, Shaanxi Normal Univ, 1983; MS, 1985, PhD, 1988, Shandong Univ. Appointments: Maths Prof, NW Univ, Xian, 1988-95; Rsch Schl, Univ GA, USA, 1995-96. Publications: Dirichlet Divisor Problem, 1988; The Mean Value of Number Theory Function, 1990. Honour: Huo Yindong Awd, 1993. Memberships: AMS; MS, China. Hobby: Table Tennis. Address: Department of Mathematics, Northwest University, Xian, Shaanxi, China.

ZHANG Wu-Cheng, b. 3 Mar 1933, Qingdao, China. Professor of Human Parasitology. m. Chen Cui-E, 15 Sept 1956, 1 s. Education: Grad, Shanghai 1st Medl Coll, 1956. Appointments: Lectr, Assoc Prof, Dir of Rsch Lab, Hunan Medl Coll, 1963-87; Prof, Dir, Rsch Cntr, Zhejiang Medl Univ, 1988-. Publications: Immunology of Schistosmiasis Japonica, 1983, 1994; Development and application of Plastic Strip-ELISA for diagnosis of schistosomiasis japonica, 1966. Honours: Awd, Sci and Technol Prog, Hunan Prov, 1986, 1987, Zhejian Prov, 1992, 1996; Spec Allowance of the State Cncl, 1993-. Memberships: Fell, Roy Soc of Tropical Med & Hygiene; Pub Hlth Serv Intl Rsch Fell, NIH, USA. Hobbies: Music; Sports. Address: Department of Parasitology, Zhejiang Medical University, Hangzhou, Zhejiang 310031, China.

ZHANG Xiang-dong, b. 11 Dec 1936, Gao Cheng, Hebei Prov, China. Teacher. m. Wang Xiu Zhen, 27 Sept 1959, 1 s, 1 d. Education: Master's degree, Phillos Dept, Chinese People's Univ, 1963. Appointments: Professor, Philos & Sociol, 1991-; Dir, Tianjin Inst of Pan-Asia Econ and Technological Dev; Dir, Sect of Sociol Theories, Sociol Dept, Nankai Univ. Publications: 14 major publs incl: An Introduction to Social Development Strategies, 1991; A Study of Marxist Sociological Theories, 1996; Entries concerning social systems and social changes in the Volume of Sociology of the Encyclopedia China; New Ideas in Interpersonal and Social Communication; An Introduction to Social Development Strategies; A Study of the Social Foundations of China's Regional Economic Development; A Strategic Study of the Opening and Development of Tianjin's New Coastal Area. Honours: 1st Prize, Tianjin's 2nd Awd of Excellent Rsch Achievement, 1992; Medal for Achievement, 8th 5-Yr Plan period, Tianjin Municipal Govt. Membership: Chinese Sociol Soc. Hobbies: Literature; Sports. Address: Apt 12-1-301, South-West Village, Nankai University, Tianjin 300071, China.

ZHANG Xianke, b. 29 Feb 1944, Ling-Bi, China. Professor and Researcher on Mathematics. m. Fuhua Xu, 16 Feb 1972, 1 s, 1 d. Education: BS, 1969, MSc, 1981, PhD, 1985, Univ Sci & Technol of China. Appointments: Instr, Prof, 1973-93, Prof, Chmn of Cttee of Acad Degrees, 1993-, Univ of Sci & Technol, Tsinghua Univ. Publications: 70 rsch pprs in USA and China on Number Theory, 1981-; Books: Intro. Algebraic Number Theory, 1998; Algebra, 1998. Honours: Prize of Sci Treatise, 1986; Sci Prog Prize, 1988; Natl Nat Sci Prize, 1990; PhD having Outstndng Merit of China, 1991. Memberships: Regular Assoc Mbr, Intl Cntr of Theort Phys (Italy); Standing Dir, Beijing Maths Soc; Amn Math Soc. Hobbies: Likes music; Literature; Philosophy; History; Poem. Address: Department of Mathematics, Tsinghua University, Beijing 100084, China.

ZHANG Xiao-Shan, b. 14 Oct 1950, Jiangyin, China. Doctor; Research Fellow. m. Yao Pei-Qin, 6 Jan 1979, 1 d. Education: Med, Tangshen Medl Coll, 1975; Med, Tianjin Univ of Brdcstng and TV, 1982; Medl Biochemistry, Flinders Univ, Sch of Med, Aust, 1993. Appointments: Snr Phys, 1986; Hd of Dept of Lab Med, 1989; Chf Physn, 1994; Rsch Fell, 1998. Publications: Enzymatic Determinations of Na+, K+ and Mg+ in Serum, 1996, 1997, 1998; The Study of the Cysteine in Prevention of Isolated Rat Hepatocytes from FCCP, 1996. Honours: Study of the Cysteine in Prevention of Isolated Rat Hepatocytes from FCCP, selected into WWW of Internet by CICSC, USA, 1997; Medl of Who's Who in Sci, by AASB, USA, 1998. Memberships: Chinese Medl Assn, 1987; China Assn of Biochemistry and Molecular Bio, 1993; Intl Fedn of Clin Chem, 1996. Hobbies: Reading; Raising pets. Address: Laboratory of Medical Biochemistry, Tianjin Institute of Medical & Pharmaceutical Sciences, 96 Guizhou Road,Tianjin 300070, China.

ZHANG Xiaoling, b. 13 Jan 1972, Wuxi, Jiangsu Prov, China. Economist. Education: BA, Engl, Nanjing Normal University. Appointments: Dir, EMS Dept of Wuxi Post Off, 1990-; Mbr, Provcl Cttee, Jiangsu Prov, under Natl Post and Telecomm Trade Union of China, 1997; Mbr, Provcl Cttee, Communist Yth League, China, 1997; Mbr, Wuxi Municipal Cncl, Chinese People's Polit Consultative Conf (CPPCC), 1998. Publications: Chinese-English Dictionary of Posts and Telecommunications Economy and Management, 1994; World Briefs of Post and Telecommunications, 1995; 200 Questions of Common Knowledge on Telephone, 1995; Source Exploration of Post and Telecommunications, 1996; Titbits of Posts and Telecommunications, 1998; Mini-Encyclopedia of Telecommunications, 1999; Over 100 essays in newspprs and mags. Honours: Natl Awd for Self-taught Success, 1998; Gold Medal, 20th Century Success, 1999. Memberships: China Success Rsch Inst; Chinese Soc of Future Search (CSFS). Hobbies: Stamp collection; Coin collection. Address: EMS Department of Wuxi Post Office, Wuxi, Jiangsu Prov, 214001, China.

ZHANG Xing, b. 20 Jan 1934. Medical Doctor; Hepatologist. m. Dahe Zhang, 28 Sept 1982, 1 d. Education: Grad in Med, Mil Med Coll of SW Area Command of PLA, China, 1955. Appointments: Surg, Chengdu Hosp of PLA Air Force, 1955; Physn and Instr, Xuzhou Hosp for Infectious Diseases, Res 1956, Dept Hd 1960, Visng 1972, Asst Chf Physn 1987, Prof and Chf Physn 1993-. Publications: Over 50 original articles on clin and epidemiological stdies of viral hepatitis and other infectious diseases publd and/or presented on natl and intl confs. Honours: Model Worker, Jiangsu Prov, 1973, 1978; Winner, Sci and Technol Progress Awd of Xuzhou, 1994; Merit Citation, Class III of Xuzhou, 1995. Memberships: Chinese Med Assn, 1966-; Co Chmn, Soc Inf Dis of CMA Xuzhou Br, 1972-; Chf Ed, Chinese Med Symposium, 1993; Res Prof, Chinese Qigong Inst, 1993; Supvsr, Jiangsu Team for Control of Epidemic Hemorrhagic Fever, 1995. Hobbies: Sports; Music. Address: Xuzhou Hospital for Infectious Diseases, Xuzhou, Jiangsu 221004, China.

ZHANG Yanchun, b. 1 Feb 1958, Hebei, China. Lecturer. m. Jinli, 28 June 1982, 1 d. Education: PhD, Computer Sci. Appointments: Rsch Fell, 1992-93; Lectr, 1994-. Publications: Over 70 referred pprs in intl jrnls and conf proceedings or databases, inclng ACM transactions and conf proceedings. Honours: PhD, Computer Sci, Univ of Qld, 1991; Inviation Fellshp, Japan Soc for Promotion of Sci, 1997. Memberships: AZM; IEEE. Hobbies: Travelling; Fishing. Address: Department of Mathematics and Computing, University of Southern Queensland, Toowoomba, Qld 4350, Australia.

ZHANG Yebai, b. 10 July 1936, Shanghai, China. Political Scientist. m. Zhang Jiemin, 5 June 1963, 1 s, 1 d. Education: Engl Dept, Luoyang Fgn Lang Inst. Appointments: Policy Analyst, Gen Staff Dept, PLA, 1957-70; Rsch Fell, Shanghai Inst for Intl Studies, 1977-80; Snr Fell, Inst of Am Studies, CASS, 1981-. Publications: American Diplomatic History Since WWII - From Truman to Reagan, 1994; Sino-US Relations Toward the 21st Century, 1996. Honour: Fulbright Schl, 1982-83. Memberships: Cncl, Chinese Natl Assn for Am Studies, China Assn for Intl Friendly Contact. Hobbies: Basketball; Badminton; Ballroom dancing. Address: Dongyuan, 3 Zhangzizhong Lu, Beijing 100007, China.

ZHANG Yong, b. 1 Feb 1939, Rongjiang, Guizhou, China. Professor of Music. m. Li Chang-lian, 8 Mar 1970, 1 s, 2 d. Education: Grad, Spec Second Sch. Appointments: Tchr, Lu-shan Primary Sch and Wang-you Mid Sch, 1958-62; Clk, Centremaster, Prof, Rongjian Co Cultural Cntr, 1962-. Publications: Sing of Guizhou Mountains, 1959; Be Good Vocalists When Grown-Up (songbook), 1986; Dong Nationality Traditional Opera, Arts and Music, 1997; China Dong Nationality Opera and Music, 1997; History of Dong Nationality Music, 1998. Honours: Sev. Memberships: China Folk Lit and Art Assn; Cnclr, China Minority Musical Inst, 1985. Hobbies: Reading; Writing. Address: No 2, 2nd Floor, Cultural Bureaus' Domicile, Guzhou, Rongjiang, China.

ZHANG Yongmin, b. 19 Feb 1932, Ningbo, China. Professor. m. Youyu Zhu, 1 Oct 1956. Education: Dip Chem, Grad, Dept of Chem, St John's Univ, Shanghai. Appointments: Instr, Lectr, Organic Chem, Henan Norm Univ, 1952-64; Lectr, Assoc Prof, Prof, Hangzhou Univ, China, 1965-; Visng Prof, Univ of Florida, FL, USA, 1988-89. Creative Works: CP2TICL2 Catalyzed Reaction of Grignard Reagents; The Synthesis of Allyl Selenides by Organosamarium Reagent; 160 Pprs; 3 Books. Honours: 2nd Awd, Sci Progress; 3rd Awd, Sci Progress; 1st Awd, Sci Progress. Memberships: Chinese Chem Soc; Zhejiang Chem Soc. Hobbies: Classical Music; Volleyball; Soccer; Base Ball. Address: Department of Chemistry, Zhejiang University, at Xixi Campus, 34 Tian Mu Shan Road, Hangzhou, Zhejiang 310028, China.

ZHANG Youxin, b. 24 July 1932, Haining, Zhejiang, China. Architect; Professor; Artist. m. Yunxuan Tian, 10

Aug 1956, 2 s, 1 d. Education: MSc, Qinghua Univ, 1956. Appointments: Asst, 1956-61, Lectr, 1961-81, Assoc Prof, 1981-86, Prof, 1986-, Dept of Arch, Tianjin Univ. Publications include: Ancient Building of Chende; Watercolor Rendering and Rendering Technics by Youxin Zhang. Honours include: 1st Prize, Sci Book Awd, 1983; 2nd Prize, Sci Book Awd, 1993. Memberships: China Interior Archs Inst; China Ind Design Inst. Hobbies: Painting; Music; Travel. Address: School of Architecture, Tianjing University, Tianjing 300023, China.

ZHANG Yu, b. Oct 1957 Shanghai Cty. Film Actress. m. Zhang Jianya. Education: Advd studies USA, 1985-90. Appointments: Amb to Guyana, 1994-. Honours: Hundred Flowers Best Actress Awd for Evening Rain, 1981; Golden Rooster Best Actress Awd for Love at Lushan, 1981. Memberships: Mbr 8th NPC, 1993-. Address: Shanghai Film Studio, 595 Caoxi Beilu Street, Shanghai Cty, People's Republic of China.

ZHANG Yuan Yuan, b. 19 July 1926, Zhejiang, China. Professor. m. Wu Jing Fang, 12 Dec 1950, 1 s, 1 d. Education: BA, Bus Coll, Shanghai, 1950. Appointments: Dir, Fin Dept, 1982, Dean of Econs Coll, 1984, Jinan Univ. Publication: The Financial System Reform in Guangdong Province, 1991. Honour: Govt Prize, Guangdong Prov, 1992. Membership: Vice Chmn, Guangdong Econs Assn, 1983-. Hobby: Reading. Address: c/o College of Economics, Jinan University, Guangzhou, China.

ZHANG Yusheng, b. 15 Jan 1939, Xiong Co, Hebei, China. Teacher. m. Zhou Jianmin, 1 Oct 1972, 1 s, 1 d. Eduction: Dips, Northwest China Univ, Dept of Chinese Lang and Lit. Appointments: Tchr, No 1 Normal Coll, Xinjiang, 1963; Sec, Revolutionary Cttee of Urumchi, 1975; Tchr, Xinjiang Normal Univ, 1979. Publication: Compilation and Narration of Guan Yunshi's Works. Honours: Silver Medal, Outstndng Behavior in Tchng, 1991; Awd of Ex Works, 1994. Memberships: Book of Song Soc, dir; Soc for the Study of Si Maqian; Chinese Tour Lit Soc; Chinese Sanqu Soc. Hobby: Sport. Address: c/o Xinjiang Normal University, Urumchi, Xinjiang, China.

ZHANG Zhenxiang, b. 30 Aug 1947, Jiangsu, China. m. Chen Xinzhen, 1 s. Education: Bach, Dept Automation, Tsinghua Univ, 1970; Master, Math Dept, Anhui Normal Univ, 1981; PhD, Math Dept, Univ of Limoges, France, 1993. Appointment: Prof, Math Dept, Anhui Normal Univ. Publications include: On a Problem of Erdos Concerning Primitive Sequences, 1993. Honours: Anhui Prov Higher Learning Insts Sci and Technique Prog Awds, 1997; Anhui Prov Nat Sci Awds, 1998. Membership: Amn Math Soc. Address: Anhui Normal University, Math Department, 241000 Wuhu Anhui, China.

ZHANG Zhijian, b. 1934 Wenxi Co Shanxi Prov. Army Offr; Politician. Appointments: Joined PLA, 1951; Tchr Speeded-Up Educ Sch Chahar Mil Dist Hubei - N China - Mil Reg; Lit Tchr in div hosp of Chinese People's Voluns Korea, 1953-56; Staff Offr, 1957-69; Chf Ops and Trng Div PLA Jinan MI Reg Hq, 1971-78; Div Chf of Staff, 1978-79; Army Dep Chf of Staff, 1979-880; Div Cmdr, 1980-83; Army Cmdr, 1983-85; Dep Cmdr Jinan Mil Reg, 1985; Polit Commissar Chengdu Mil Reg, 1994-; Vice Min of Personnel Dir Sci and Tech Dept mn of Radio Film and tv. Memberships: Mbr CCP, 1956-. Address: Office of the Political Commissar,Chengdu Military Region, People's Republic of China.

ZHANG Zhongxian, b. Jan 1926 Weishan Co Shandong Prov. Army Offr. m. Yufen Yang, 1953, 3 s, 1 d. Appointments: Polit Commissar Canton Mil Reg PLA, 1985; Polit Commissar, 1986-; Sec Party Cttee Canton Mil Reg, 1987; Rank of Lt Gen, 1988; NPC Dep PLA. Memberships: Alt mbr 12th CCP Cntrl Cttee, 1985-87; Mbr 13th Cntrl Cttee, 1987-92; Standing mbr Party Cttee Canton Mil Reg, 1986-; Mbr Presidium 14th CCP Natl Congress, 1992; Mbr 8th NPC, 1993-. Address: Canton Military Region Hq, Guangzhou, Guangdong, People's Republic of China.

ZHANG Zhu Guo, b. 3 Apr 1938, Shanghai, China. Artist. m. Xia Qin Gao, 1 Apr 1966, 2 s. Education: BA, Fine Arts, Lian Zhou Coll. Publications: Mother's Heart (drama), 1963; Well (drama), 1981; National Explanation (short novel), 1990; Five Thousand Years Brilliance (classic drama), 1991; Red Mansion Dream (fashion drama), 1997. Memberships: Chinese Drama Master Assn; Chinese Writers Assn. Address: No 4, 31 Lane, Shi Men Road (First), Shanghai 200041, China.

ZHAO Han-Yang, b. 10 Dec 1954, Jiang-Su Prov, China. Music Education and Performance. m. Wang Xiao-Yong, 31 Jan 1983, 1 d. Education: Bachelor, Cntrl Conservatory of Music, 1982. Appointment: Assoc Prof, Cntrl Conservatory of Music, Beijing, China. Publications: The Exercise of Intervals and Arpeggios of Ehru (Chinese String Instrument), 1996; The Technique of Ehru, 1999. Honour: Awd'd in Chinese Competition of Ehru, 1985. Membership; Assn of Chinese Musicians. Hobby: Computer. Address: Central Conservatory of Music, 43 Baoja Street, Xicheng District, 100031 Beijing, China.

ZHAO Hongbin, b. 15 Aug 1952, Shanghai, China. Artist. m. Mei-Jun Gu, 1 child. Education: Studies, Fine Arts Rsch, Shanghai Jiaotong Univ. Appointments: Art Ed, Desig, Sci Life Mag, Sci and Tech Assn, Shanghai, 1979-85; Chf Ed, Mod New Prods Pictorial, Shanghai Univ of Technol, 1985-88; Freelance Artist, Mulgrave, Aust, 1988-. Creative Works: Art works published in natl and intl newspprs, mags and books; Sev one man and grp shows. Honours: Ctf of Hon, Shanghai Govt, 1986; Dick Ovenden Mem Art Show 1st Prize, 1991; Victoria Harbor Art Exhibn 1st Prize, 1991; Mulcahy Mazda Awd, 1991; Omega Contemporary Art Awd, Roy Overseas League, 1992; Ernest Henry Mem Art Show 1st Prize, 1992-94; Bronze Medal, China Famous Figures Works Exhibn of Arts Circles, 1994. Memberships: Chinese Celebrity's Assn; Life Fell, IBA; Advsr, Chinese Poetry, Calligraphy and Painting Inst. Hobbies: Dancing; Writing Poetry; Chinese calligraphy. Address: 36 Fernbank Crescent, Mulgrave, Vic 3170, Australia.

ZHAO Shaorong, b. 14 Oct 1962, Zhejiang, China. Researcher. m. Yi Li, 20 Apr 1990, 1 s. Appointments: Assoc Prof, 1994-95, Prof, 1996-. Membership: NY Acady of Scis, 1995-98. Hobby: Computer Games. Address: School of Geosciences, Building F05, University of Sydney, Sydney 2006, Australia.

ZHAO Shujiang, b. 21 Nov 1936, Tsinan, Shandong, China. Teacher. m. Liu, 19 July 1963, 2 s. Education: Dip, Theoretical Phys, Wuhan Univ, 1958. Appointments: Lectr, 1978, Assoc Prof, 1987, Prof, 1994-, Wuhan Yejin Univ of Sci and Technol. Publications: Designing OTA-C Filters by SFG Approach, 1993; A Novel Approach for Designing CT Filters Based on CCT, 1994. Memberships: CIE Circuits and Systems Soc, 1987-. Hobbies: Football; Swimming. Address: c/o Wuhan Yejin University of Science & Technology, Campus Box 164, Wuhan 430081, China.

ZHAO Wei-Xin, b. 27 Nov 1937, Jiangsu, China. Professor. m. Jiang, 1 Nov 1965, 1 s, 1 d. Education: Zoological Dept, Nanjing Univ, 1956-60. Appointments: Lectr, 1976, Assoc Prof, 1986, Prof, 1990. Publication: Fish Physiology, 1993. Memberships: Cncl, Chinese Soc for Comparative Endocrinol; Cncl, Chinese Ichthyol Soc; Asian Fisheries Soc. Hobbies: Swimming; Reading. Address: 334 Jun Gong Road, Shanghai 200090, China.

ZHAO Weijiang, b. 13 Sept 1938, Shanghai, China. Teacher. m. Zhang Jiping, 20 Feb 1968, 2 s. Education: Dept of Phys, Fudan Univ, Shanghai, China, 1955-58; Dept of Tech Phys, Peking Univ, Beijing, China, 1958-59. Appointments: Peking Univ, 1959-; JINR, Dubna, USSR, 1962-65; State Jian Zhong Machinery Factory, Beijing, China, 1969-79; GSI Darmstadt, Germany, 1981-82, 1989-91. Publications: Ion Implantation in Semiconductors, 1979; Industrial Electron Accelerators and Applications, 1996; Ion Beam Equipments, 1997; 60 acad pprs. Memberships: Vice Chmn, Dept of Tech Phys, Peking Univ, Beijing, China, 1986-89; Vice Chmn, Stndng Mbr, Particle Accelerator Soc of China, 1996-. Address:

Institute of Heavy Ion Physics, Peking University, Beijing 100871, China.

ZHAO Yufang, b. 21 Jan 1941, Peking Cty, China. Associate Professor of Biophysics. m. Beibei Ling, 19 Nov 1966, 2 s. Education: BS, Phys, Peking Univ, 1964. Asst, Lectr, Assoc Prof, Harbin Engrng Univ, 1964-1989; Assoc Prof, Zhejiang Agricl Univ, (now Zhejiang Univ, Hua Jia Chi Campus); Assoc Prof, Zhejiang Univ; Dirm Applied Biophys Rsch Lab, Inst of Nuclear Agricl Sci; Mbr, Acad Cttee of INAS, 1989. Publications: Books incl: Fundamentals of Acoustic Theory; Basic Radiobiology; Applications of Radiotracer Technique to Molecular Biology; Num pprs to profl jrnls. Honours: 1st Prize, Min No 6, 1987; 3rd Prize of Sci and Technol Min No 6, 1987; Natl Outstndng Prize of Outstndng Tchng Materials, 1988. Memberships: Dir, Nuclear Agricl Sci Soc of Zhejiang Prov; Acad Cttee, INAS. Address: Institute of Nuclear Agricultural Science, Zhejiang University, Hua Jia Chi Campus, Kai Xuan Road, Hangzhou 310029, China.

ZHAO Zhihao, b. 1931 Longkou Cty Haungxian Co Shandong Prov. Govt Offic. Appointments: Joined CCP, 1947; Sec CCP Teng and Wenshang Co Cttee, 1958-82; Sec CCP Qufu Normal Coll Cttee, 1982-83; Dep Sec CCP Shandong Prov Cttee Dir Gen Off, 1983-85; Sec CCP Zibo Municipal Cttee, 1985-88; Vice-Gov Shangong Prov, 1988-89; Gov Shangong Prov, 1989; NPC Dep Shandong Prov; Dep Sec CCP Shandong Prov Cttee, 1988-94; Sec CCP Shandong Prov Cttee, 1994-. Memberships: Mbr 14th CCP Cntrl Cttee. Address: c/o Office of Provincial Governor, Jinan City, Shandong Province, People's Republic of China.

ZHEN Haixia, b. 1967 Shandong. Basketball Player. Appointments: Started playing basketball aged 12; Joined natl team aged 15 now Cap; Cap of Chinese basketball team which won Silver Medal at Barcelona Olympic Games, 1992; Cap of team which won Gold Medal at World Univ Games, 1993; Cap of team which won Silver Medal at Women's World Basketball Championships Sydney, 1994. Memberships: Mbr PLA team. Hobbies: Music; Poetry.

ZHEN Xian En,b. 4 July 1925, Wuhan, China. Professor of Music. m. X Zhu, 5 Oct 1948, 1s, 2d. Education: BA, Music, Former Natl Cntral Univ, Nanking, China, 1949. Appointments: Soloist and Vocal Lectr, Central Opera Th, Beijing and Gansu Provincial Song and Dance Ensemble, 1950-62; Dir, later Prof, Vocal Tchng and Rsch Div, Dept of Music, N W Normal Univ, Langzhou and Hangzhou Normal Coll, 1962-89; Retired but tchng in Coll, 1989-96; Tchng studs at home, 1996-. Creative Works: Perfd in La Traviata, Beijing, 1950's; Sev solo singing perfces of var Chinese and Western classical songs, Beijing, Langzhou, Hangzhou, 1950's and 1960's. Honours: Spec Prog, The Ever Young Soloist with her Booming Students, prepared by Gansu People's Broadcasting Station and broadcast with high acclaim, 1982-89; Spec Concert, For Professor Zhen Xian En and Her Students, sponsored by Zhejiang Provincial Music Assn, Zhejiang Provincial Vocal Inst and Hangzhou Normal Coll, 1989. Memberships: Mbr, China Musicians Assn; Hon Pres, Zhejiang Vocal Assn. Listed in: China Musicians Biography. Hobbies: Music; Travelling; Shopping. Address: Department of Music, Hangzhou Normal College, Jiao Gong Yi Road, Hangzhou 310012, China.

ZHENG Du, b. 26 Aug 1936, Jiexi, Guangdong, China. Geographer. m. Guilin Wang, 20 Jan 1966, 1 d. Education: Grad, Dept of Geog, Sun Yat-Sen Univ, Guangzhou, 1958. Appointments: Hd, Dept of Physl Geog, 1984-91, Prof, 1989-, Dir, Inst of Geog, 1991-95, Chinese Acady of Scis. Publications include: Physical Geography of Xizang (Tibet), 1982; The Qinghei-Xiang Plateau of China, 1985; A Study on the Physico-Geographical Regional System, 1997. Honours: Sci and Technol Progress Spec Awd, Chinese Acady of Scis, 1986; 1st Awd, Natl Nat Sci Awd of China, 1987; Mid-Aged Expert for Disting Contbns in Natl Level. Memberships: Stndng Cncl, Geog Soc of China; VP, China Soc for Qinghai-Tibet Plateau. Hobbies: Travel;

Stamp Collecting. Address: Institute of Geography, Chinese Academy of Sciences, Building 917 Datun Road, Beijing 100101, China.

ZHENG Guoqi, b. 25 Oct 1935, Fujian, China. Economics. m. Huang Zonghan, 2 d. Education: China People's Univ; Grad, Beijing For Lang Univ, 1958. Appointments: Inst of Econs, Chinese Acady of Socl Scis (CASS); Dir, Editl Dept, Econs Info, for over 10 yrs; Mbr, Snr Ed Title Ratification Cttee of CASS; Dir, China East & Mid Asian Soc; Russian Translator & Ed, over 30 yrs; Rsch wrk, participated in proj supported by State Socl Scis Fund and proj supported by Ford Fund; Visited India & USA for investigation and acad comm. Publications: China's Labor and Wage System: History, Present Condition and Reform Ways; Some Basic Theoretical Problems of Current Wage Reform; A Survey of Xiamen Special Economic Zone; An Investigation Report on US Labor and Ways; The Evolution of the Theory of the Relationship between Commodity and Money in Recent 60 Years in Soviet Union; The Evolution of Soviet Agricultural Policy and Management System; The Utilization of Economic Lever in Foreign Countries and its Experience and Lessons; Ed and translator of 5 books. Honour: Spec Allowance, State Cncl, for outstndng contbns in socl servs, 1992-. Address: Building A13 Unit C-6, 83 Fuxing Road, Beijing 100865, China.

ZHENG Han Chen, b. 14 Mar 1939, Wu Xi Cty, Jiang Su prov, China. Professor of Pharmacognosy. m. Wang Xiang Qiong, 30 Sept 1967, 1 s, 1 d. Education: Grad, Dept of Bio, E-China Normal Univ, 1962. Appointments: Asst, 1963; Lectr, 1978; Assoc Prof, 1987; Prof, 1990. Publications: Rsch into 60 species of medicinal plants and animals publd in 98 acad pprs and 41 books (co-auth) in Chinese; Books incl: A Colored Atlas of the Chinese Materia Medica Specified in Pharmacopoeia of the People's Republic of China, 1991, 1995; Resource Science of Chinese Medicinal Materials, 1993; Color Pictorial Handbook of Toxic Chinese Herbs, 1994; Pharmaceutical Botany, 1995; A Coloured Atlas Compilation of Chinese Traditional and Herbal Drugs, 1996; A Coloured Atlas of Medicinal Plants in Chang-Bai Mountain of China, 1997. Honours: About 30, 1979-98. Memberships: VP, Shanghai Botanical Soc, 1996; VP, China Soc of Nat Medicinal Material Resources, 1992; Bd Mbr, China Soc of Nat Resources (CSNR), 1998; Commnr, 7th Chinese Pharmacopoeia Commn, 1996; Bd Mbr, Shanghai Pharm Assn, 1996; Pres, Mil Soc of TCM, 1993. Hobbies: Painting; Photography; Calligraphy; Classical music. Address: College of Pharmacy, Second Military Medical University, 325 Guohe Road, Shanghai 200433, China.

ZHENG Mao, b. 25 Jan 1959, Shaanxi, China. System Control Engineer. m. Qu Xiao Jun, 27 Sept 1987, 1 s. Education: BS, Engrng, #1 Beijing Inst of Technol, 1982, BS Engnrg, #2 Beijing Inst of Technol, 1987. Appointments: Asst Engr, 1982-89, Engr, 1989-94, Snr Engr, 1994-98, Snr Engr (Prof), 1998-, Shaanxi Mechl & Elecl Inst, Xianyang; Vice Dir, Technol Dept of Shaanxi Mechl & Elecl Inst, Xianyang; Pres, Sci & Technol Assn for Yth, Xianyang, 1996-. Publications: (auth) Self Adaptive Control for Blood Pressure, 1994; Self Adaptive Control Approach to Blood Pressure Control, 1994. Honours: Sci & Technol Adv Awd, NORINCO, 1st Class, 1996, 2nd Class, 1996. Memberships: China Ordnance Soc, 1990-; Shaanxi Computer Soc, 1992-. Address: #5 Eastern Biyuan Road, Xianyang, Shaanxi, China 712099.

ZHENG Peiyu, b. 26 Mar 1937, Guangzhou, China. Educator. m. Tang Zhaolian, 1 d. Education: BEcon, Jilin Univ, 1960. Appointments: Lectr, 1980-85, Assoc Prof, 1985-92, Econs Dept, Dir, 1991-, Prof, 1992-, Hong Kong and Macao Rsch Inst, Dpty Chf, 1991-, Cntr for Hong Kong and Macao Rsch, Zhongshan Univ. Publications: Survey of Hong Kong Economy, 1985; A Precise Course on Modern Capitalist Economy, 1987; The Mabamen are on the Way of Growth, 1989; Contemporary Capitalist Economy, 1993; Stategic Research on Cooperation Between Mainland China and Hong Kong in Biotechnological Medicine (a jt proj), 1997; Research on Hong Kong's Development in Science, Technology and

High-Tech Sectors (a jt proj), 1997; Development and Prospects of Hong Kong Foreign Economic Relations, 1998. Honours: 2nd Prize, Outstndng Wrks, 1988, 3rd Prize, Outstndng Textbooks, 1989, Guangdong Higher Educ Commn; 2nd Prize, Outstndng Textbooks, Higher Educ Commn of Cntrl-S China, 1995; State Spec Subsidy for Outstndng Contbn to Dev of China's Higher Educ, Min of Educ, 1995; Hon for Sci and Technol Adv of Guangdong Prov, 1998. Memberships: Acad Cttee, Admnstv Affairs Cttee, Admnstv Affairs Cttee, Zhongshan Univ; VP, Guangdong Hong Kong and Macao Econ Rsch Assn; Cncl Cntr for Taiwan-Hong Kong-Macao Econ Studies, For Econs and Trade Univ; Advsry Cttee, Hum Socl Scis to State Min of Educ; Apptd Rschr, Hong Kong and Macao Rsch Cntr of Guangdong Socl Sci Acady; Apptd Rschr, Rsch Cntr of Socl and Econ Dev of Guangdong Govt; Fellow Rschr, Hong Kong Cty Univ, 1998-. Address: Research Institute for HK-Macao Studies,Zhongshan University, Guangzhou, Guangdong Province, China 510275.

ZHENG Silin, b. May 1940 Wu Co Jiangsu Prov. Admnstr. Appointments: Joined CCP, 1965; Wrkd at Dandong Autombile Repair Plant Liaoning Prov, 1965-81; Dir Dandong Tv Parts Factory, 1982-83; Vice-Mayor Dandong Cty, 1983-84; Dir Commn for For Econ Rels and Trade and Asst Gov Liaoning Prov, 1984-85; Vice-Gov Shaanxi Prov People's Govt, 1989-93; Vice-Min of For Trade and Econ Co-op, 1993-94; Dep Sec 9th CCP Jiangsu Prov Cttee; Acting Gov of Jiangsu Prov, 1994-95; Gov Jiangsu Prov, 1995-. Memberships: Mbr Standing Cttee CCP Shaanxi Prov Cttee People's Govt, 1989-93; Mbr Standing Cttee CCP Shaanxi Prov Cttee; Alt mbr 13th Cntrl Cttee CCP, 1987-91; Alt mbr 14th Cntrl CCP, 1992-; Mbr 15th CCP Cntrl Cttee, 1997-. Address: Office of the Governor, Jiangsu Provincial Government, Nanjing City, People's Republic of China.

ZHENG Siming, b. 11 Oct 1939, Shanghai, China. Physicist. m. Qiaoai Zhang, 27 Dec 1968, 1 s, 1 d. Education: Fudan Univ, Shanghai, China, 1956-61. Appointments: Asst, 1961; Lectr, Luoyang Inst of Technol, 1979; Visng Schl, Univ of Newcastle Upon Tyne, Eng, 1981-83; Assoc Prof, Luoyang Inst of Technol, 1986; Visng Prof, Portland State Univ, USA, 1987; Prof, 1991. Creative Works: College Physics, 1997. Honours: Spec Subs of State Cncl, 1992; Ex Tchr Awd; Ex Tchng Achmnt Awd; Ex Rsch Ppr Awd. Memberships: Chinese Phys Soc; Henan Phys Soc. Hobbies: Computer; Music. Address: Physics, Luoyang Inst of Technology, Xi Yuan Road, Henan 471039, China.

ZHENG Wenlin, b. 1936. Publisher. m. Zhu Yufen, 1 Oct 1961, 1 d. Education: BA. Appointments: Asst Prof, 1960; Rschr, 1965; Dpty Sect Chf, 1976; Sect Chf, 1980; Ed-in-Chf, 1988; Pres, 1991. Publications: The Comment on the Responsibility of Ethics, 1964; The Discussion of Profession Morality and Its Education, 1982; The Review to Chinese Publication Reform, 1993. Honours: Awd'd Spec Subsidy, Chinese Govt, 1992. Memberships: China Ethics Assn, 1980; The Publrs Assn of China, 1990; Eds Assn of China, 1991. Hobbies: Reading; Strolling. Address: China Social Sciences Publishing House, Jia 158 Gulou Xidajie, 100720, Beijing, China.

ZHENG Xiangmin, b. 24 Apr 1954, China. Teacher. m. Wei Lihua, 1 July 1980, 1 s. Education: PhD, Hist. Appointments: Dean, Yangen Coll; Vice Dean, Tourism Dept, Dean of Tourism Dept, Hua Qiao Univ. Publications: The Maintenance and Management of Modern Hotel; Tourism Nutrictogy. Honours: Best Tchr Title, Off of Overseas Chinese Affairs, State Cncl. Membership: Dir, Fujian Tourism Soc, 1989-. Hobbies: Literature; Basketball. Address: Tourism Department, Hua Qiao University, Quanzhou, Fujian 362011, China.

ZHENG Xinsheng, b. 8 Feb 1951, Jiangsu, China. Executive. m. Xiang Guang, 25 Jan 1979, 1 s. Education: MDA, Birmingham Univ, UK. Appointments: Dpty Dir, Dept of Cultural and Educl Experts, State Admin of For Experts Affairs. Publication: (ed) Selected Articles on Foreign Experts Work, 1993. Honours: Awds, Distinguished Work for For Experts Affairs, 1995.

Memberships: Cncl Mbr, China Assn for Intl Experts Exchange & Dev; Dpty Sec-Gen of China Cntr for Intl Legal Study. Hobbies: Music; Sports. Address: State Administration of Foreign Experts Affairs, 61634, Friendship Hotel, Beijing 100873, China.

ZHENG Yu Yan, b. 19 May 1928. Doctor. m. Yu Jing Fen, 1 s, 1 d. Education: Grad of Med Coll, 6 yrs; Grad of Coll of Tradl Med, 4 yrs. Appointments: Cttee Man of Intl Assn for Radiated Rsch; Edng Cttee of Chinese Radiation & Tumor Mag. Publications: Observation of Radio Therapy NSCL for 100 Examples, 1987. Honour: Third Gr Prize in Sci Rsch in Beijing, 1978. Hobby: Reading. Address: No 403, Gate 1, Jiao Yu Ju Xu She, 171 Middle School, He Ping Li, Beijing 100013, China.

ZHONG Chongxin, b. 22 May 1908. Professor of Plant Ecology. m. 28 July 1935, Ze Rong Xu, 3 s. Education: AB, Univ of Southern CA, 1931; MS, 1932, PhD, 1935, OH State Univ. Appointments: Beijing Normal Univ, 1935; Sichuan Univ, 1936-42; Tongji Univ, 1942-46; Zhejiang Univ, 1944-52; Nanjing Univ, 1952-; Visng Prof, Grinnell Coll, Grinnell, IA, USA, 1994. Publications: Ecological Engineering, 1989; Thirty Years of Ecological Engineering with Spartina Plantations in China, 1993. Honours: Many Awd's in China; Hon 100 Sch of Nat Resources, OH State Univ, 1992; Intl fell Awd and Lifetime Mbrshp, Soc Wetland Scientists, USA, 1996; Intl Ecological Engrng Soc Awd, 1996; Hon Doct of Science, OH State Univ, 1999. Memberships: Advsr, Chinese Soc of Ecol, 1991-; Intl Ecological Engrng Soc, 1993-. Hobbies: Reading; Radio and Television Programmes; Music Appreciation.

ZHONG Di Sheng, b. 27 Dec 1942, Shenyang, Liaoning, China. Physicist; Researcher. m. Gui Yun Li, 26 Sept 1978, 1 child. Education: Grad, Liaoning Univ, 1967. Appointments: Rsch Fell, Shenyang Inst, Instrumentation Technol, 1976-85; Rsch Fell, Min Machine Building Ind, Zhejiang Univ, Hangzhou, China, 1977-78; Rsch Fell, Hefe (China) Poly Univ, 1982-83; Prof, Liaoning Univ, 1985-; Cnslt, Inst Bur Liaoning Prov Geo Minerals, 1980-81, Geo Inst, Cheng Du, China, 1984-85; Inventor in field. Memberships: Phys Inst Liaoning Prov; Optical Inst China; Calculation Inst, Liaoning Prov, 1996. Hobbies: Music; Games; Walking. Address: Liaoning University Department Physics, Huang Gu Dist Chong Shan 66, 110036 Shenyang, China.

ZHONG Jian Jiang, b. 6 Apr 1965, Zheijiang Province, China. Education. Education: PhD, Osaka Univ, Japan, 1993. Appointments: Dir, State Key Lab of Bioreactor Engrng, min of Educ, 1998-. Creative Works: Cell and Tissue Cultures and Prilla; Biorechual Bioeng. Honours: State Educ Commns, Outstndng Yng Investigatiors; Fell, Japan OSc for Promotion of Sci. Memberships: NY Acad of Sci; Soc for Fermentation and Bioenginering; Intl Assoc of Plant Tissue Culture. Address: East China Unive of Science and Tech, State Key Lab Bioreactor, 120 Meilong Road, 200237 Shanghai, China.

ZHONG Ziran, b. 3 Aug 1962, Anhui, China. Deputy Director General, Ministry of Land and Resources. m. Education: BEng, Dept of Geol, Hefei Univ of Technol, 1979-83; MSc, Grad Sch, Chinese Acady of Geoscis, 1985-88; PhD, Grad Sch, Chinese Acady of Geoscis, 1988-91. Appointments: Inst of Planning and Design for Chem Mines, Min of Chem Ind, 1983-85; Bur of Mineral Devel Mngmt, 1991-94; Dpty Chf, Divsn of Mining Law Affairs, 1994-96; Chf, Divsn of Mining Law Affairs, 1996-97; Dpty Dir Gen, 1997-, Bur of Mineral Devel Mngmt, Min of Geol and Mineral Rescs; Dpty Dir Gen, Oil and Gas Admin, Natl Cmmn of Mineral Rescs, 1997-98, 1998-; Dpty Dir Gen Min of Land and Rescs; Mbr Editl Bd of Rescs Policy. Publications: Economic Evaluation on Tungsten Resources in China, 1993; International Mineral Investment Climate, Legislation and Policy, 1994; Sev articles in profl jrnls. Address: c/o Ministry of Land and Resources, 37 Guanyingyuan West Area, Xicheng District, Beijing 100035, China

ZHONGDI Zhu, b. 29 May 1941, Shanghai, China. Professor. m. Yang Aizhen, 20 Apr 1974, 1 d. Education:

MA, Econs, Fudan Univ, 1983. Appointments: Chmn, Prof, Dept of Intl Econs, Shanghai Univ of Fin & Econs. Publications: The Theory and Practice of Open Economics, 1992; International Marketing, 1997; Studies on Multinational Enterprises, 1997. Honours: Univ Awds, 1992, 1995; Ex Tchr Awd, 1994. Membership: Acad Cttee, Shanghai Educl Bur. Hobbies: Classical Music; Sports. Address: Shanghai University of Finance & Economics, 777 Guoding Road, Shanghai 200433, China.

ZHOU Chixing, b. 16 Mar 1943, Ningbo, Zhejiang, China. Professor. m. Guangyu Feng, Jan 1973, 1 s, 1 d. Education: BS, Plastics Engrng, Zhejiang Univ, 1965; MS, Polymer Materials, Chengdu Univ of Sci and Technol, 1968. Appointments: Engr, 1968-84, Snr Engr, Depty Chf Engr, 1986-89, Chongqing Synthetic Chem Factory; Vis Schl, Univ MA, Lowell, USA, 1984-86; Assoc Prof, 1989-92, Prof, 1993-, Shanghai Jiaotong Univ; Vis Prof, Laual Univ, Can, 1994-95. Publications: Over 80 pprs in profl jrnls. Address: Department of Polymer Science and Engineering, Shanghai Jiaotong University, Shanghai 200240, China.

ZHOU Fa Xiu, b. 17 Apr 1937, Qingdao, China. Teaching in University. m. Yu Shen Yu, 19 Jan 1963, 3 d. Education: Grad from univ. Appointments: Vice Chmn, Oceanography, 1989-93; Chmn, Marine Meteorology, 1993-95. Publication: Fog, 1981; Introduction to Atmospheric Sciences, 1990. Honour: Model Tchr, 1993, 1995, 1997; Spec subsidy of govt. Memberships: Chinese Meteorological Soc; Duty Mbr, Shandong Meteorological Soc, 1994-. Hobby: Reading. Address: Ocean University of Qingdao, 5 Yushan Road, Qingdao, China 266003.

ZHOU Guobiao, b. 27 Aug 1946, Shanghai, China. Foreign Language Teacher and Researcher. m. Tao Zheng, 18 July 1974, 1 s. Education: Grad, La Havana Univ, Cuba; Grad, Shanghai Intl Stdies Univ. Appointment: Chf, For Langs, Sect of Beijing No 171 hs. Publications: How to Learn English in High School; Middle School English Grammar; Senior English Teaching Methods and Practice. Honours: Nationwide Outsndng Tchr, 1995; Best Model Tchr in Beijing, 1996. Memberships: Dir, Beijing For Lang Tchng Rsch Inst; West Returned Students Assn in China. Hobbies: Literature; Music; Tennis; Stamp-collection; Computer. Address: Apartment Bldg 2-402, He Pingli, Beijing No 171 High School, Beijing, China 100013.

ZHOU Hong Fei, b. 17 Sept 1946, Tianjin, China. Executive Editor. m. Liwen Yan, 1 Mar 1988, 1 s, 1 d. Education: Coll. Appointments: Sec, Bur of Raise Poultry, Xinjiang, 1964; Sec, Bur of Agricl, Xinjiang, 1969; Jrnlst, Ed, Vice Exec Ed, Exec Ed, Publng House of Rural China Periodical, 1979. Publications: Shock Waves From Xinzheng, 1992; Random Thoughts After Editing, 1995; Civilization's Collection, 1996; Civilization's Step, 1997. Honours: Chinese Govt Allowance, 1994; Outstndng Middle Age & Yng Specl, Min of Agricl, China, 1994. Memberships: Mngr, Reporters Cncl of China, 1996; Routine Mngr, Agricl Reporters Cncl of China, 1996; Routine Mngr, Periodical's Cncl of China, 1997. Hobbies: Reading; Writing; Chinese Opera; Football. Address: Publishing House of Rural China Periodical, Fuxing Road 61, Beijing 100036, China.

ZHOU Hongyu, b. 10 May 1945, Haian County, Jiangsu Prov, China. Teacher; Researcher. m. Tingyu Ma, 10 July 1976, 1 d. Education: Master's degree, Tsinghua Univ, 1981. Appointments: Hd, Rsch Grp, 1975-84, Dir of Nuclear Phys Lab, 1985-92, Dir, 1997-, Inst of Low Energy Nuclear Phys. Publications: Over 60 rsch pprs in mags & jrnls. Honour: 2nd Awd, Sci & Technol, Natl Educ Commn of China, 1989. Memberships: Chinese Nuclear Phys Soc; AAAS; NY Acady of Sci (NYAS). Hobbies: Reading novels and biographies; Listening to music; Playing bridge. Address: Institute of Low Energy Nuclear Physics, Beijing Normal University, Beijing 100875, China.

ZHOU Jihua, b. 20 July 1933, Jiangsu, China. Research Professor. m. Huixuan Jia, 3 Mar 1997, 2 s, 1

d. Education: Grad, Peking Univ. Appointments: Rsch Prof, Chinese Acady of Socl Scis, 1981-; Guest Prof, Inst of Asia-African Studies, Peking Univ, 1996-. Publications: Japan Towards Political Power, 1994; Australia's Options in External Affairs, 1997; Thinking of Sino-Japanese Relations in the Multipolarizational Century, 1999. Honours: Gov's Awd, Fukuoka Pref, Japan, 1988; Spec Contbn Awd, State Cncl, China, 1992-. Memberships: Exec Cttee Mbr, Vice Sec Gen, Chinese Assn for Japanese Studies; Cttee Mbr, Chinese Assn for Asia-Pacific Studies. Hobbies: Swimming; Reading; Sightseeing. Address: Japanese Research Centre of Peking University, Beijing 1000871, China.

ZHOU Jing, b. 1942, Anshan, Liaoning, China. Editor; Publisher. m. Shuzhen Zhang, 1968, 2 d. Appointments: Dpty Dir, Ed Off, Dir of Ed Off, Chf Ed. Publications: New Book of Dupian; Two Kinds of Xiao Lin Guang Ji. Memberships: Cmmnr, Chinese Inst of Jin Ping Mei; Cmmnr, Inst of Chinese Classical Lit. Hobby: Chinese Classical Literature. Address: No 39 Shengli Avenue, Jingjiu Road, Jinan, Shandong, China.

ZHOU Jun Yan, b. 23 Oct 1942, Gui Lin, China. Professor. m. Linlin Fu, 30 Dec 1964, 1 s, 1 d. Education: Degree, Coll of Natl Arts. Appointments: Vice Chmn, Prof, Art Inst, Dept of Arch, Tong-Ji Univ; VP, Environ Art Dept, Shanda Univ. Publications: How to Paint in Ink, 1983; How to Paint Scenary in Ink, 1986; The Technique of Painting in Ink, 1990; The Technique of Painting Ink-Colour, 1988; Historical Architecture of China, 1996; The Selection of Wooden Handicraft from the Ming Qing Dynasty. Honours: Awds for water colour paintings: Moon, 1982, Port, Water Village, 1983, Step by Step, 1985, Ancient Customs, 1990, Ancient Customs No2, 1991. Memberships: Chmn, Art Tchng Assn, Shanghai; China's Art Assn, Shanghai Branch. Hobby: Photography. Address: Zhang Wu Road, 120 Long, No 1, 1808, 200092, Shanghai, China.

ZHOU Lanxian, b. 22 May 1931, Hubei, China. Professor of Anatomy. m. G Zhang, Apr 1954, 2 s. Education: Dr, Hubei Medl Univ, Wuhan, 1959. Appointments: Assoc Prof, 1986; Prof, 1991. Publications: Books, 1990, 1993; 64 compositions on neuroanatomy, 1978-98. Honours: Prize in Sci Congress, Hubei, 1978; Prog Prize in Sci & Technol, Hubei, 1987, 1997. Memberships: Chinese Soc for Anatomical Scis; Intl Assn for the Study of Pain. Address: Department of Anatomy, Hubei Medical University, 39 Doug Hu Road, 430071, Wuhan, China.

ZHOU Meng-Sheng, b. 9 July 1932, Zhejiang Prov, China. Biochemist. m. Chen Yin Hui, 25 Aug 1957, 2 s, 1 d. Education: Dalian Medl Coll, 1951-56. Appointments: Asst, Dept of Biochem, Dalian Medl Coll, 1956-59; Asst, Dept of Biochem, Lianing Coll of tradl Chinese Med, 1959-78; Lectr, 1978-93; Assoc Prof, 1983-85; Prof, 1985-. Creative Works: From History of Chienese Medicine to Know Recognition of Ancients Regarding Food Nutrition, 1960; Study of Catharsis Treatment on Poisoning Nephritis in Rabbit, 1978; Study of Replication of Mimicked Qi Deficiency in Animal Models, 1989; Textbook of Biochemistry Experiments, 1988, 1996; Biochemistry, 1988, 1996. Memberships: Biochem Sci Grp of trad Chinese med; Chinese Biochem Soc; Liaoning Jrnl of TCM; Soc of Geriatric nutr and hlth. Address: 79 Chongshan East Road, Huang-qu District, Shenyang, China.

ZHOU Nan, b. 1927 Qufu Cty Shandong. Government Official. m. Huang Guo. Appointments: Cnslr Chinese Miss to UN and Dep Rep of People's Repub of China, rank of Amb, 1971-81; Vice-For Min Pres Coll of For Affairs, 1984-90; Hd of deleg to Sino-Brit talks on Hong Kong Question,1 894; Hd of deleg to Sino-Portuguese talks on Macau Question, 1986; Dir Xinhua News Agcy Hong Kong, 1990-; Dep Hd Preliminary Wrkng Cttee of the Preparatory Cttee of the Hong Kong Spec Admin Reg, 1993-95; Vice-Chmn Preparatory Cttee, 1995-. Memberships: Mbr CCP Congress, 1991; Mbr 7th Standing Cttee NPC, 1991; Mbr 14th CCP Cntrl Cttee, 1992; Mbr 8th NPC, 1993-. Address: Hong Kong Bureau

of Xinhua News Agency, 387 Queen's Road, East Hong Kong, Hong Kong Special Administration Region, People's Republic of China.

ZHOU Qiang-Tai, b. 1 Feb 1935. Teacher. m. Xue-Yuan Qian, 1 Feb 1963, 2 s. Education: BSc, Cntrl China Univ of Sci and Technol, 1956; MSc, SE Univ, 1960. Appointments: Assoc Prof, SE Univ, 1983; Prof, SE Univ, 1987-90; PhD Stud Supvsr, SE Univ, 1990-. Publications: 5 books, 100 pprs, 3 Chinese patents, 3 patents. Honours: 3rd Class Adv Awd, Sci and Technol, Natl Educ Commn, 1991; 1st Class Adv Awd, Sci and Technol, Cntrl China Bur of Elec Power Syst, 1993; 2nd Class Adv Awd, Sci and Technol, Elec Min, 1993. Memberships: VP, Nanjing Soc for Labour Protection, 1986-95; VP, Nanjing Soc for Boilers, 1990-; Ctteeman, Energy Utilisation Cttee of Chinese Soc for Engrng Thermophys, 1993-; Ctteeman, Sci and Technol Cttee of Jiang-su Branch of Chinese Soc for Elecl Engrng, 1996-. Hobbies: Chinese chess; Watching TV. Address: Department of Power Engineering, Southeast University, Nanjing 210018, China.

ZHOU Qicheng, b. 31 Mar 1923, City Ningbo, prov Zhejiang, China. Professor. m. Wu Xiuyu, 20 Feb 1960, 1 s, 1 d. Education: Bachelor, Jiaotung Univ, Shanghai, China, 1950; PhD, Moscow Textile Inst, Moscow, 1959. Appointments: Lectr, 1959; Assoc Prof, 1978; Hd of Textile Rsch Inst, China Textile Univ, 1981; Prof, 1986; Cnslt Coll of Textiles, CTU, 1994. Publications: History of Textile Technology of Ancient China, 1984; General Conceptions of Textile Technology, 1985; Principles of Yarn Manufacturing, 1995; Stories of Woollen and Worsted, 1997; History of Textile Industry of China, 1997. Honours: 2nd State Awd for Sci Popularization, 1996; 1st Grade Awd of Prog, Sci and Technol in Textile Ind, 1998. Memberships: VP, Cttee of Wool Textile Ind, Shanghai Assn of Textile Engrng, 1985. Hobby: Taiji Boxing (Chinese traditional physical exercise for old men and women). Address: 240-19-402 An Shun Road, Shanghai 200051, China.

ZHOU Qing Qing, b. 16 Oct 1954, Shanghai, China. Professor. Education: MA, The Cntrl Conserv of Music, 1978-83. Appointments: Tchr, Cntrl Conserv of Music, 1983-, Asst Instr, 1983-87, Lectr, 1987-92, Assoc Prof, 1992-96, Prof, 1996-. Publications: Chinese Folk Songs, 1993; Chinese Folk Music, 1993; The Artistic Appreciation of the Chinese Folk Songs, 1996. Memberships: Chinese Musicians Assn, 1991; Tradl Chinese Soc, 1986. Address: Central Conservatory of Music, 43 Baojia Street, Xicheng District, 100031 Beijing, China.

ZHOU Shaopeng, b. 30 Nov 1946, Henan, China. Professor. m. Chang Rifang, 27 Jan 1973, 1 d. Education: PhD, Ind Econ, Chinese Acady of Socl Scis. Appointments: Dir, Rsch Off, Chinese Acady of Socl Scis, 1993; Vice Mayor, Hulun Bei Er League, Inner Mongolia, 1994; Dir, Econ Mngmt Dept, Natl Sch of Admin, 1995. Publications: Introduction of Enterprise Economics, 1991; Management Research on Industrial Enterprise in China, 1993; Investigation of Operation and Management in Capital Steel and Iron Company; Research on China Business System Reform; Introduction of China Government Economics. Honours: Awds, Ex Articles, 10 times. Hobby: Industry Economy. Address: National School of Administration, China Economic Management Department, 11 Changwa Street, Haidian, Beijing 100089, China.

ZHOU Xian, b. 19 Sept 1954, Nanjing, China. Teacher. m. Sa Xinyan, 20 Sept 1983, 1 s. Education: BA; MA; PhD. Appointments: Lectr, 1988-92, Assoc Prof, 1992-98, Prof, 1998-. Publications: Toward Creativity, 1992; Beyond Literature, 1998; Chinese Contemporary Culture in Aesthetic Perspective, 1998. Honours: Fellshp, Natl Philos & Socl Sci, 1996; Fellshp, Global Fndn (Japan), 1997. Memberships: Natl Aesthetics Assn; Comparative Lit Assn; Bd Dirs, Chinese & For Lit Theory. Hobbies: Painting; Music; Chinese calligraphy and writing. Address: Chinese Department, Nanjing University, Nanjing 210093, China.

ZHOU Xian-Bin, b. 5 June 1938. Professor; Director. m. Ai-Ya Chen, 8 Mar 1967, 2 d. Education: BSc, Beijing Univ of Aeronautics and Astronautics, (BUAA), 1956-61; MSc, BUAA, 1964-67; Dr.Ing, ISMCM, France, 1979-82. Appointments: Aero Dept, Harbin Inst of Technol, 1961-64; Seaplane Rsch Inst, 1967-73; Beijing Aero Mfng Technol Rsch Inst, 1973-78; Dept of Mfng Engrng, BUAA, 1978-; Visng Prof, ISMCM, 1986-87, 1995. Publications: Plasticité Appliquée, 1987; Backward Extrusion of Steels, 1987; Handbook of Stamping Technology, 1989; Stretch Forming of Aircraft Complex Skin, 1991; Analysis on Wrinkling, 1993; High Pressure Hydro-flexforming Technique and Application, 1997; Denting Resistance of Autobody Panels, 1998; Precision Forming of Large Reflector Panels, 1998. Honours: Sci and Technol Adv Prize, AVIC, 1990, 1991, 1998; Merit Citation, Class II, AVIC, 1992; Guanghua Sci and Technol Prize, 1992; Natl Prize, Class II of Ex Educl Achievement. Memberships: CSAA, 1984-; CDDRG, 1986-; VP, Forging and Stamping Inst of CMES, 1995-; Cncl of Mfng Technol Cttee of CSA, 1993-; Sci and Technol Cttee of Aviation Ind of China, 1994-; Editl Ctte, Chinese Jrnl of Aeronautics and Jrnl of Plasticity Engrng. Hobby: Music. Address: Sheet Metal Forming Research Centre, Department of Aerocraft Manufacturing Engineering, Beijing University of Aeronautics & Astronautics, 37 Xueyuan Road, Beijing 100083, China.

ZHOU Xiaohong, b. 3 Mar 1957, Hangzhou Cty, China. Teacher. m. Dr Zhouyi, 10 Oct 1983. Education: BM, Nanjing Medl Coll, 1982; MA of Law, Nankai Univ, Tianjing, 1987; PhD, Socl Hist, Nanjing Univ, 1997. Appointments: Lectr, 1988; Asst Prof, 1991; Prof, 1994; Hd, Inst for Socl Psychol, Nanjing Univ, 1993; Dpty Chmn, Dept of Sociol. Creative Works: Tradition and Changes, Social Mentality of Jiangsu and Zhejiang Farmers and Its Changes Since Modern Times; Modern Social Psychology; The History of Modern Social Psychology; Cultural Feedback, Culture Transmit Between Parent-Children in Changing Society; The Social Psychology of Rural Chinese During the Present Period of Social Transformation, A Comparison of ZhouZhuang Township and Beijing's Zhejiang Village. Honours: Spec Prize, State Dept of China, 1993. Memberships: China Socl Psychol Assn; China Advtng Assn; Socl Psychol Assn of Jiangsu Prov. Hobbies: Tennis; Table tennis; Swimming; Chitchat. Address: Dept of Sociology, Nanjing University, 23 Hankou Road, Nanjing 210093, China.

ZHOU Xiyuan, b. 24 May 1938, Wuxi, China. Research Professor of Civil Engineering. m. Yixian Ling, 15 Nov 1969, 2 d. Education: Grad, Coll of Bldg Engrng, Suzhou, China, 1956. Appointments: Rsch Fell, 1956-78, Rsch Engr, 1978-83, Snr Engr, Dpty Dir, 1983-97, Rsch Prof, 1988-. Publications: An Introduction to Earthquake Engineering, 1977, (2nd ed) 1985; Site-Foundation-Design Earthquake (in Chinese), 1990. Honours: Citation of Natl Sci Conf, 1978; 2nd prizes and 3rd Prize, Natl Sci and Technol Prog, 1988, 1998, 1995. Membership: Chinese Acady of Scis, 1997. Hobby: Reading. Address: 30 Beishanhuandonglu, Beijing 10013, China.

ZHOU Yaoqi, b. 24 Oct 1963, Yueyang Hunan Prov, China. Geoscientist. m. Xia Changlan, 30 June 1986, 1 s. Education: BA, China Univ of Geosciences, 1983; MA, 1989; PhD, 1993. Appointments: Asst Engr, Geol Surv of Heilongiiang, 1985-87; Visng Rschr, Inst of High Energy Phys, Academia Sinica, Beijing, 1993-95; Postdoctoral Rschr, China Univ of Geosci, Beijing, 1995-; Prof, Dir of Inst, Pet Resources and Environl Geol Rsch Inst, Univ of Pet, Dongying, Shandong. Creative Works: 63 Sci Pprs, Congress Abstracts Publs Natl and Intl; 8 Eng Pprs; 9 Chinese Pprs. Honours: Intl Meteoritics Acady, Geol Soc of China; Intl Meteoritics Congress Praise Awd; First Class Awd of Natural Sci; Ex Awd of Fellshp, Academia Sinica, 1992; Golden Hammer Awd; Many or Honours. Memberships: Intl Meteoritics Acady; Geol Soc; Space Scis Soc of China and Nature Dialectics Acady of China. Hobbies: Play Go; Ping pong. Address: Inst of Petroleum Resources and Environmental Geology, China Univ of Petroleum, Dongying 257062, Shandong, China.

ZHOU Yong Qi, b. 29 Jan 1939, Yulin Cty, Guangxi, China. Doctor, Teacher. m. Ke Minghua, 20 Jan 1971, 1 s. Education: University postgraduate. Publications: Experiment and study of the siegebeckia orientalis I for affct intraveular pressure of the rabbits, 1996; Measurement of the trabecular width by the slit-lamp and micrometer eyepiece, 1998. Honours: Awd of excellent treatise, 1988; Awd of exemplary tchr, 1996; Awd of achievement in sci, 1996. Memberships: Chinese Medl Assn of Opth; Vice-Chmn, Nanning. Hobby: Stamp collecting. Address: Department of Opthalmology, Guangxi Medical University of Hospital, 6 Binhu Road, Nanning, Guangxi, China

ZHOU Yongkang, b. Dec 1942, Wuxi Cty, Jiangsu Prov. Politician. Education: Beijing Pet Inst. Appointments: Joined CCP, 1964; Dir and Vice-Sec CCP Cttee of Liaohe Pet Exploration Bur; Mayor Panjin Cty, 1983; Vice Sec CCP Panjin Cty Cttee, 1983-85; Vice-Min of Pet Ind, 1985; Vice-Gen Mngmnt Hd Off of China Pet and Nat Gas Co, 1988; Gen Mngr Hd Off of China Pet and Nat Gas Co, 1997-. Memberships: Alt mbr 14th CCP Cntrl Cttee, 1992; Mbr 15th CCP Cntrl Cttee, 1997-. Address: China Petroleum and Natural Gas Company, Beijing, People's Republic of China.

ZHOU Zhi-Gang, b. 22 Aug 1931, Shanghai, China. Professor. m. Cui Wen-Jun, Feb 1961, 1 s, 1 d. Education: BE, Tongji Univ, Shanghai, China, 1953; ME, Tsinghua Univ, Beijing, China, 1956. Appointments: Lectr, Dept of Civil Engrng and Chem Engrng, Tsinghua Univ, 1956-78; Assoc Prof, Dept Chem Engrng, Tsinghua Univ, 1979-88; Prof, Dept of Mat Sci and Engrng, Tsinghua Unv, 1988-99; Expert, Cnslt, UN Ind Dev Org, 1988-91; Dir, Natl Nat Sci Fndn of China, 1991-95; Pres, Dielectrics Phys Cttee, Chinese Phys Soc; VP, Sensor Technol of Chinese Electronics Inst, 1989-99. Publications: Ferrite, 1981; Elemental Theory of Piezoelectric Physics, 1984; Physics of Ferroelectrics, 1989; Pats: 1 from USA, 1989, 1 from Eur, 1986, 2 from China, 1985, 1993; Over 150 pprs. Honours: Fell Awds, CIE, 1987, IEEE, 1994, Chinese Electron Components Soc Sci Awds, 1981, 1983, 1985, 1987, 1989, 1992; Chmn, 7th Intl Meeting on Chem Scis, Beijing, 1998; Chmn, Intl Steering Cttee, 8th Intl Meeting on Chem Sensors, 1998-2000. Memberships: CSS, 1982; Fell, IEEE, 1994l Fell, CIE, 1987; Snr Mbr, IEE, 1989; NY Acady of Sci, 1995. Listed in: Five Hundred Leaders of Influence of 20th Century. Hobbies: Reading; Touring; Watching TV. Address: Department of Materials Science & Engineering, Tsinghua University, Hai-Dian District, Beijing 100084, China.

ZHOU Zhide, b. 20 Oct 1933, Beijing, China. Civil Engineering. m. Feng Wanzhi, 22 Nov 1963, 1 s. Education: DEng, Hokkaido Univ, Japan. Appointments: Snr Engr, Intl Rsch and Trng Cntr on Erosion and Sedimentation. Publications: Fluvial Processes; Estuarine Processes of Chinese Estuaries. Memberships: IAHR; Chinese Hydraulic Engrng Soc; NY Acady of Scis. Hobby: History. Address: 20 Chegongzhuang Xilu, Beijing 100044, China.

ZHOU Zhongfei, b. 12 Nov 1954, Nanking, China. Professor of Politics. m. Riquan Zhong, 14 Apr 1982, 1 s. Education: PhD, Socl Sci. Appointment: Vice Prof. Publications: Clinton Administration's China Policy, 1993; Sino-American Normalization & Taiwan Issue, 1994. Membership: Inst of World Economy, Shanghai Acady of Socl Scis, 1992-. Hobbies: Sports; Literature. Address: c/o Institute of World Economy, Shanghai Academy of Social Sciences, 622/7 Huaihai Zhong Lu, Shanghai, China.

ZHOU Zonglu, b. 5 May 1935, Nanxi, Sichuan, China. Telecommunication Interference Engineer. m. X G Huang, 14 Mar 1963, 1 d. Education: Bach Deg, Chongying Univ. Appointments: Project Chf Engr, T/L Design, 1958-. Publications: Compositions of Code for Design of Telecommunication Lines Against Danger Effects From Electric Power Lines, 1997. Honours: 2nd Grade Awd, Sci and Technol Progress, Min of Elec Power, 1996; 1st Grade Awd, Sci and Technol Progress, Min of Elec Power. Memberships: Elec-Magnetic Interference Cttee; China Proj Constrn Standardization Assn. Hobby: Paintings. Address: Retirement Department, Southwest Electric Power Design Institute, 18 Dongfeng Road, Chengdu, China.

ZHU Deming, b. 23 Mar 1947, Shanghai, China. Professor. m. L Zhang, 26 Sept 1973, 1 s, 1 d. Education: BSc, Daqing Petroleum Coll, 1982; MSc, 1984, PhD, 1987, Nanjing Univ. Appointments: Chmn, Dept of Maths, E China Normal Univ, 1995-. Publications: Smooth Dynamical Systems, 1993; Bifurcation Theory in Differential Equations, 1994; Bifurcation Theory and Methods of Dynamical Systems, 1997. Honours: 3rd Class Awd, Progress in Sci & Technol, State Educn Cncl of China, 1990, 1996. Memberships: Exec Dir, Shanghai Maths Soc; Dir, Shanghai Nonlinear Rsch Cntr. Hobby: Reading. Address: c/o Department of Mathematics, East China Normal University, Shanghai 200062, China.

ZHU Ge-lin, b. 28 Oct 1934, Yan-Liang, Shaanxi, China. Botany. m. Shao-Zhen Zhang, 2 s, 1 d. Education: Bio, Northwest Normal Univ, 1952-56. Appointments: Lectr, Assc Prof, Prof, rschr on plant taxonomy, in Inst of Botany, 1956-; Visng Schl, Inst of Bot, Aademia Sinica, 1961-66, 1972-73; Mercer Fell, Arn Arb, Harvard Univ, 1982-83; Visng Prof, Dept of Bot, Brigham Young Univ. Publications: Rsch findings & pprs in var jrnls; Publd 3 new genera and some new species of Chenopodiaceae from Asia & N Am, in which most are endangered species; Treated Chenopodiceae & Boraginacae for Flora Republicae Popularis Sinicae and Engl ed of Flora of China. Honours: Outstdng Achievement Medal, IBC, Eng; 20th Century Awd & World Lifetime Achievement Awd, ABI, USA; Title, Profls of Outstndng Contbn, Peoples Repub of China. Memberships: NY Acady of Scis; VP, Botanical Soc of Gansu, 1980-. Hobbies: Photography; Reading; Swimming. Address: Institute of Botany, Northwest Normal University, Lanzhou, Ganshu, China 730070.

ZHU Jiahua, b. 12 Nov 1953, Sichuan, China. Professor of Chemical Engineering. m. Sulan Xia, 1 Jan 1983, 1 s. Education: BEng, Dalian Inst of Technol, 1982; MEng, 1985, DEng, 1991, Chengdu Univ of Sci & Technol. Appointments: Hon Rsch Fell, Univ of Birmingham, England, 1993; Prof, Hd, Dept of Chem Engrng, Chengdu Univ of Sci & Technol, 1994; Prof, Dean, Sch of Chem Engrng, Sichuan Union Univ. Publication: A Practical Dictionary for English-Chinese Translation with Classification, 1997. Membership: Fell, Chem Engrng Inst of China. Hobbies: Collecting Stamps; Classical Music. Address: School of Chemical Engineering, Sichuan Union University, Chengdu 610065, China.

ZHU Jian-er, b. 18 Oct 1922, Tianjin, China. Composer; Professor of Composition. m. Qun Shu, 1949, 2 s, 1 d. Education: Grad, Moscow State Conservatory; Studies w Prof Sergey Balasanian. Appointments: Composer, Art Troupe, New 4th Army, 1945-49; Conductor, Brass Band, 1946-49; Composer, Shanghai and Peking Film Studios, 1949-63; Shanghai Opera House, 1963-73; Shanghai Symph Orch, 1973-; Prof of Composition, Shanghai Conservatory of Music; Num recordings. Creative Works include: Orchl works: Festival Overture, 1958; In Memorium, for strings, 1978; Symphony Fantasia, 1980; Sketches in Mountains of Guizhou, 1982; A Wonder of Naxi, 1984; Symphony No 1, 1986, No 2, 1987, No 3 Tibet, 1988; Concerto for so-na and orch, 1989; Symphony No 4, 1990, No 5, 1991, No 6, 1994, No 7, 1994, No 8, 1994; No 9, 1999;, No 10, 1998; Sinfonietta, 1994; Hundred Year Vicissitudes, 1996. Choral works: Salute 1946, 1945; Gada-meilin, 1958; Heroic Poems, symph-cantata, 1960; The Green, Green Water Village, a cappella cycle, 1981; Day of Liberation, folk instrumental ensemble, 1953; Song of the Spring, for oboe and piano, 1956; String Quartet, 1957; Trio, 1958; Quintet, 1992; Piano Works: Preludes, 1955; Theme and Variations, 1956; Ballade, 1958; Five Yunnan Folk Songs, 1962; Num songs; Over 50 articles in profl jrnls. Honours: China State Prize for Songs, 1951, 1952, 1982-83, for symph works, 1981, 1992, 1994, 1997,

1998; Prizes, Musical Spring Fest, Shanghai; Musical Prize, Shanghai Fedn of Culture and Arts, 1984-85; Queen Marie-Jose Intl Prize, Musical Composition Contest, Switz, 1990; Golden Prize, Contest for the return of Hong Kong. Memberships: Bd Dir, Standing Cttee, China Fedn of Culture and Arts; Chair, Shanghai Musicians Assn; Chair, Shanghai Fedn of Culture and Art. Address: Shanghai Symphony Orchestra, 105 Hu Nan Road, Shanghai 200031, China.

ZHU Jianhua, b. 23 Dec 1963, Henan, China. Professor. m. Hou Xuejun, 2 June 1987, 1 d. Education: PhD, Chem Engrng, Tianjin Univ, China. Appointments: Dpty Dean of Sch of Chem Engrng, Univ of Pet, 1993; Dean of Sch of Chem, 1995. Publications: Over 50 pprs in jrnls & conf proceedings, 1983-; 2 pats, 1996, 1997. Honours: Young Scientist Awd, Suns Sci & Technol Dev Fndn, 1998; Excellent Young Scientist Awd, CNPC, 1995; Young Tchr Awd of Beijing, 1995. Memberships: Cncl of Pet Processing & Chem Engrng, CPS, 1994; Cncl of Chem Engrng, CIESC, 1996. Hobbies: Fishing; Listening to music. Address: School of Chemical Engineering, University of Petroleum, Changping, Beijing 10220, China.

ZHU Kaixuan, b. 1932, Shanghai Cty, China. Engineer; Administrator. Education: Beijing Aeronautical Inst. Appointments: Vic-Min in Charge of State Educ Commn, 1985-92; Vice-Chair, Acad Degrees Cttee, State Cncl, 1988; Head, Natl Co-ord Grp for Anti-Illiteracy Wrk, 1994-; Alt Mbr, 14th CCP Cntrl Cttee, 1992-; Party Grp Sec, State Educ Commn, 1993-. Address: State Education Commission, 35 Damucang Hutong Road, Beijing 100816, China.

ZHU Liang, b. 1924, Chaoyang Co, Guangdong Prov. Party and Government Official. Education: Shanghai St John Univ; Appointments: Joined CCP, 1945; Hd Intl Liaison Dept CCP, 1985; A VP Chinese People's Assn for Peace and Disarmament, 1985-; Chmn For Affairs Cttee Repub of Korea Friendship Grp. Memberships: Mbr 13th Cntrl Cttee CCP, 1987-91; Mbr 14th Cntrl Cttee CCP, 1992-; Mbr 8th NPC, 1993-. Address: International Liaison Department, Zhonggong Zhongyang, Beijing 100001, People's Republic of China.

ZHU Li-Xia, b. 2 Feb 1931, Shanghai, China. Professor of Physiology. m. Deng Ci-Xian, 4 Aug 1956, 2 d. Education: MD, Medl Coll, Dai-Lian Univ, 1954; Peking Coll of Tradl Chinese Med, 1976-77. Appointments: Dept of Physiology, Natl Inst of Hlth, Beijing, 1954-58; Dept of Physiology, Inst of Experimental Med, Chinese Acady of Medl Scis, 1958-64; Dept of Physiology, Inst of Acupuncture and Moxibustion, China Acady of Tradl Chinese Med, 1964-. Publications: Over 70 pprs on Neurophysiology, mainly on Acupuncture Analgesia. Honours: Prize of Sci and Technol awarded her grp, China Acady of Tradl Chinese Med, 1978, 1980, 1982, 1986, 1988, 1990, 1993, 1993, 1995; Prize for her grp, PLA, 1988; Prize of Sci Progress awd'd her grp by State Admin of Tradl Chinese Med, 1988, 1991, 1994, 1996. Memberships: IBRO, Commnr of Chinese Assn for Neurosciences, Comnr of Beijing Assn for Neural Scis; IASP, Chinese Assn for Study of Pain; IUPS, Commnr of Beijing Assn for Physiolagial Sciences, 1985-97. Address: Department of Physiology, Institute of Acupuncture and Moxibustion, China Academy of Traditional Chinese Medicine, Beijing 100700, China.

ZHU Lin, b. 22 May 1923, Lianyungang Cty, Jiangsu Prov. Actress. m. Diao Guangtan, 1943, 3 s, 1 d. Education: Huaying Tchrs' Coll; Wuchang Art Trng Sch. Appointments: Actress Anti-Japanese Performing Grp, 1938-45; Actress Datong Film Studio, 1948-50; Actress China Yth Art Th, 1950-52; Actress Beijing People's Art Th, 1953-. Films: Weakling Your Name is Woman, 1948; Trials and Hardships, 1949; Waiting, 1950; The Last Emperor, 1989; Su Wu Graze Sheep, 1996. Th incls: Put Down Your Whip, 1937; Beautiful Women, 1947; Thunderstorm, 1953; Three Sisters, 1959; Cai Wenji, 1959, 1962, 1978; Wu Zetian, 1962-64; Death of a Salesman, 1983; Win Game, 1987; Candied Haws on a Stick, 1996; Thunderstorm, 1997. Honours: Awd for

Promoting China's Drama, 1988; Golden Eagle Prize for Best Supporting Actress for role of Dowager Empress in film The Last Emperor, 1989. Address: Room 601, Unit 2, Building 38, Dongzhi Menwai Street, Beijing 100027, People's Republic of China.

ZHU Min, b. 4 Apr 1956, Beijing, China. Pharmacy Education and Pharmaceutical Research. m. Rong Li, 27 Sept 1983, 1 d. Education: BS, Peking Univ, 1982; MPhil, Peking Union Medl Coll, 1988; PhD, Univ of London (Sch of Pharm), 1994. Appointments: Rsch Asst, Inst of Material Medica, Chinese Acady of Medl Scis, 1982-85; Rsch Assoc, Inst of Medicinal Plant Dev, 1988-91; Asst Prof, Dept of Pharm, Chinese Univ of Hong Kong. Publications: over 50 sci rsch pprs in intl jrnls, 1984-98. Honours: Pfizer Studentship (London), 1991-94; Hon Prof, Inst of Medicinal Plant Dev, Chinese Acady of Medl Scis, Beijing, 1995-99. Memberships: Amn Assn of Pharm Scientists, 1996-99; Amn Soc of Pharmacognosy, 1997-99; Eyrn Soc of Phytochemistry, 1992-96; Cncl Mbr, Hong Kong Soc of Tradl Med and Nat Prod Rsch, 1996-99; Snr Mbr, China Pharm Soc. Hobbies: Swimming; Travelling; Many aspects of physical exercise. Address: Department of Pharmacy, the Chinese University of Hong Kong, Shatin, NT, Hong Kong, China.

ZHU Mingshan, b. May 1937 Jiutai Co Jilin Prov. Jurist. 2 s. Education: People's Univ Beijing. Appointments: Joined CCP, 1961; Judge Criminal Crt Supreme People's Crt, 1978-82; VP, 1982-83; VP Supreme People's Crt, 1983-. Address: Supreme People's Court, Beijing, People's Republic of China.

ZHU Muzhi, b. 25 Dec 1916, Jiangyin Cty, Jiangsu. Government Official. m. Zhou Luo, 1945, 1 s, 2 d. Appointments: Joined CCP, 1938; Dep Ed in Chf Xinhua News Agcy, 1950; Dep Dir Xinhua News Agcy, 1952; Dep Dir New China News Agcy - NCNA - State Cncl, 1952-72; Dep for Jiangsu 2nd NPC, 1958; Dep for Jiangsu 3rd NPC, 1964; Disappeared during Cultural Revolution; Dir NCNA, 1972-77; Dep Dir Propaganda Dept CCP Cntrl Cttee, 1977; Advsr Beijing Jrnlsm Studies Soc, 1980; Min of Culture, 1982-86; Pres Assn for Cultrual Exchanges with For Cos, 1986-; Dir Off of News under State Cncl, 1992; Pres China Soc for the Study of Human Rights, 1994-. Memberships: Mbr 10th Cntrl Cttee CCP, 1973; Mbr 11th Cntrl Cttee, 1977; Mbr Standing Cttee Natl Cttee 5th CPPCC, 1978; Mbr Commn for Inspng Discipline CCP Cntrl Cttee, 1978; Mbr Fedn of Lit and Art Circles, 1982; Mbr 12th Cntrl Cttee CCP, 1982-85; Mbr Advsry Cntrl Cttee CCP, 1985; Mbr 13th Cntrl Cttee, 1987. Address: State Council, Beijing, People's Republic of China.

ZHU Ning, b. 18 Aug 1935, Hangzhou, China. Professor. m. Zhang Xiaofang, 18 Aug 1963, 2 d. Education: Bachelor, NE Forestry Univ. Appointments: Prof, NE Forestry Univ, Harbin, China, 1957. Publications: The Heterogenous Habitat Influence on the Seed Germination of Acanthopunax Senticosus and its Seed Pool Dynamic, 1996. Honours: 2nd Sci Prog Prize, 1987; 3rd Sci Prog Prize, Forestry Min, 1996. Membership: Chinese Soc of Ecology. Hobby: Ecology. Address: PO Box 333, Northeast Forestry University, Harbin 150040, China.

ZHU Qizhen, b. 19 Dec 1927, Jiangsu. Government Official. m. Wang Yude, 1955, 1 d. Appointments: Gen Off min of For Affairs, 1949-62; Second Sec First Sec Chinese Emb UAR, 1963-68; Div Chf African Affairs Dept min of For Affairs, 1969-71; Dep Dir W Asian and N African Affairs Dept, 1972-73; Cnslr Chinese Emb Aust, 1973-76; Dep Dir Am and Oceanic Dept min of For Affairs, 1977-81; Dir Am and Oceanic Dept min of For Affairs, 1982; Asst Min min of For Affairs, 1982-84; Vice-Min min of For Affairs, 1984-89; Amb to USA, 1989-93; Vice-Chmn For Affairs Cttee 8th NPC, 1993-; NPC Dep Henan Prov. Memberships: Mbr Standing Cttee 8th NPC, 1993. Address: 23 Xi Jiao Min Xiang, Beijing 100805, People's Republic of China.

ZHU Rongji, b. 20 Oct 1928, Changsha Cty, Hunan Prov. Engineer; Government Official. Education: Qinghua

Univ. Appointments: Joined CCP, 1949; Dir Tech Transformation Bur under State Econ Commn, 1982-83; Vice-Min of State Econ Commn, 1983-88; Dep Sec Shanghai Municipal Cttee, 1987-; Sec Shanghai Municipal Cttee, 1989; Mayor Shanghai Municipal People's Govt, 1988-91; A Vice-Premier State Cncl, Apr 1991-; Gov Cntrl Bank of PRC, 1993-95; Dep Hd Cntrl Finl and Econ Ldng Grp, 1992-; Fmr Chmn State Radio Regulatory Cttee; Pres Bus Mngmnt Inst, 1994-. Memberships: Mbr 8th NPC, 1993; Alt mbr 13th CCP Cntrl Cttee, 1987-92; Mbr CCP Politburo, 1992-; Mbr 14th CCP Cntrl Cttee, 1992-97; Mbr 15th CCP Cntrl Cttee, 1997-. Address: State Council, Xi Changan Jie, Beijing, People's Republic of China.

ZHU Senlin, b. 1930 Chuansha Co Shanghai. Governor. Education: Qinghua Univ. Appointments: Dep Sec Gen Guangzhou Cty Parly Cttee and Dir Gen Off, 1981; Later Dep Sec Guangzhou Cty Party Cttee and Mayor Guangzhou Cty; Sec Guangzhou Cty Party Cttee; Dep Sec CPC 7th Guangdong Prov Cttee, 1991; Dep Sec Provincial Vice-Gov and Acting Provincial Gov, 1991-93; Gov of Guangdong Prov, 1992-96; Dep 7th Natl People's Congress; Dep 8th NPC, 1993-; Chmn Guangdong People's Congress Standing Cttee, 1996. Memberships: Mbr Provincial Party Cttee; Mbr Guangzhou Cty Party Cttee; Alt mbr 13th CCP Cntrl Cttee; Mbr 14th CCP Cntrl Cttee, 1992-97. Address: 305 Central Dongpeng Road, Guangzhou, People's Republic of China.

ZHU Shanli, b. 26 Sept 1953. Professor of Economics. m. Suping Fang, 13 Jan 1982, 1 daughter. Education: BA, Econs, 1982; MA, Econs, 1984; PhD, Econs, 1992. Appointments: Asst Dean, Econ Mngmt Dept, 1985-87; Dean of the Econ Mngmt Dept, 1992-; Dpty Dir of the Cntr for Mngmt Sci, 1995-97; Dean of Applied Econs, 1997-99, Assoc Dean of Guanghua Sch of Mngmt, 1999-, Peking Univ. Publications: The Road to Prosperity of Economy-Efficient Allocation of Resources and Property Right, 1994. Honours: Winner, First Class Prize for Yth Tchrs of Colls and Univs, awd'd by Fok Ying Tung Educ Fndn, 1993; 2nd Class Prize of 4th Beijing Philos and Socl Sci Prize, 1996. Memberships: Dir, Spec Cttee of Overseas Mkt Econ, Rsch Inst of Mkt Econ of China. Hobbies: Swimming; Music. Address: Guanghua School of Management, Peking University, Beijing 100871, China.

ZHU Shengxiu, b. 27 Jan 1930, Macheng Cty, China. Orthopedic Surgeon. m. Chen Xiugui, 1 May 957, 2 s. Education: Bachelor degree, Ha'erbin Medl Univ, 1956. Appointments: Vice-Dir, Dept of Orthopedics, Gen Hosp of Chinese PLA, 1977-90. Publications: Modern Microsurgery, 1994. Honours: 42 Awds in Sci & Technol, 1978-; Natl Excellent Scientist, 1997. Memberships: Chmn, Microsurgical Cttee of Chinese Medl Assn, 1984-92, 1995-. Address: Orthopedic Department, General Hospital of Chinese PLA, 28 Fuxing Road, Beijing 100853, China.

ZHU Weishen, b. 19 Dec 1932. Scientist. m. 24 Sept 1967, 1 d. Appointments: Asst Prof, Hd of Div, Assoc Prof, Vice-dir, Hd of Educ Dept, Prof. Publications: 1 book, 1995; Co-auth or ed, 5 books, 1982-96. Memberships: Adv Bd, Intl Jrnl Rock Mech and Rock Engrng, 1983; Intl Bur of Strata Mech, World Min Congress, 1987; Ed-in-Chf, Chinese Jrnl of Rock Mechs and Engrng, 1994. Hobby: Classical music. Address: Institute of Rock and Soil Mechanics, The China Academy of Sciences, Wuhan, Xiao Hongshan 430071, China.

ZHU Yanfu, b. 6 July 1933, Zhangjiaquan Vill, Yiyuan County, Shandong, China. Special-class Disabled Soldier. m. Chen Xirong, 12 Sept 1951, 1 s, 5 d. Appointments: Joined PLA in 1947; Crippled in Korean War, losing both hands, 1 foot and 1 eye, 1950; Overcame disabilities to serv as CPC Sec of Zhangjiaquan Vill Branch, 1955-80. Publication: Autobiography: The Limit of Human Life, 1996. Honours: CPC Outstndng Mbr of China, 1997; Self-Improvement Model of China, 1997. Membership: Chinese Writer Assn of Shandong Branch, 1996. Hobbies: To be warm-hearted in the causes of public good and charities; Reading; Sports. Address: Honor Soldier Sanatorium, Yiyuan County, Shandong, China.

ZHU Yilin, b. 17 Aug 1934, Shanghai, China. Research Professor. m. Ye Bihua, 1 Oct 1959, 1 s, 1 d. Education: BS, Civil Engrng, Nanjing Inst of Technol; MS, Mechs, Tsinghua Univ. Appointments: Vice-Dir, Sci and Technol Commn, Beijing Inst of Spacecraft System Engrng, 1983-89; Sec-Gen, Sci and Tech Cttee, CAST, 1989-. Publications: 7 booklets and over 500 articles on Space Science and Technology, 1964-97; Elementary Space Technology, 1986; An Introduction to Chinese Space Endeavour (in Engl), 1995. Honours: 2nd Class State Prize, State Cncl of China, 1985; Govt Spec Subsidiary, 1992-; Merit Citation Class II, Min of Aerospace of China. Memberships: Cncl, Cinese Soc of Space Sci; Chinese Soc of Sci Writers; Chinese Soc of Astronautics. Hobbies: Reading; Tourism; Seeing films; Climbing mountains. Address: 31 Baishigiao Road, Haidian District, PO Box 2417, Beijing 100081, China.

ZHU Yinghuang, b. 28 Dec 1943, Shanghai, China. Editor-in-Chief; Journalist. m. Yao Xiang, 12 Feb 1972, 1 d. Education: BA, Engl, Fudan Univ, Shanghai, 1967; MA, Jrnlsm, Stanford Univ, USA, 1983. Appointments: Chf Ed, Opinion Dept, 1983-83, Dpty Ed-in-Chf, 1986-93, Ed-in-Chf, 1993-, China Daily. Honour: Outstndng Jrnlst of China, 1984. Memberships: China Natl Newsppr Assn, vice chmn; All-China Jrnlsts Assn & Transl Assn of China, standing cttee. Address: c/o China Daily, 15 Huixin Dongjie, Chaoyang, Beijing 100029, China.

ZHU Yinghuang. Journalist. Appointments: Ed in Chf China Daily. Address: China Daily, 15 Huixin Dongjie, Chao Yang Qu, Beijing 10029, People's Republic of China.

ZHUANG Tian Shan, b. 1 Oct 1934, Quanzhou, Fujian, China. Professor. m. Shu Yan Wang, 1 July 1972, 1 s. Education: Bachelor degree. Appointments: Rsch Fell, Astron, Chinese Acady of Scis, 1958; Techn, Meteorological Observ of Nan Ling, 1961; Phys Lectr, Medl Inst of Guang Xi, 1982; Vice-Prof, Socl Sci, Chinese Overseas Univ, 1987; Prof, Socl Sci, Chinese Overseas Univ, 1993. Publications: Ancient Chinese Historical Records on Meteor Showers, 1966; Assemblage of Ancient Chinese Astronomical Records/Meteor Section, 1988; Comet and Meteor, 1993; Series of research on Leo shower, 1991-1994. Honours: Oustndng Sportsman, 1957; Oustndng Tchng Achievements, 1989; Oustndng Rsch Pprs, 1991, 1994. Memberships: Dpty Sec-Gen, Inst of Sci and Tech Hist in Fu Jian, 1989; Perm Mbr Cncl, Nat Dialectics Rsch Assn in Fu Jian; VP, 1992, Pres, 1999 Inst of Astron in Fu Jian. Hobbies: Ancient Chinese literature; Football; Ping-pong. Address: Department of International Economy, Chinese Overseas University, Quanzhou 362011 Fu Jian, China.

ZHUANG Zhuo, b. 22 June 1952, Liaoning, China. Professor. m. Ling Ju, 8 Feb 1983, 1 d. Education: PhD, Univ Coll, Dublin, Ireland, 1995. Publications: Engineering Mechanics, 1998; Getting Started with ABAQUS/Standard, 1998. Membership: Chinese Soc of Theoretical & Appl Mechs. Hobbies: Sports; Travel. Address: Department of Engineering Mechanics, Tsinghua University, Beijing 100084, China.

ZIA Begum Khaleda, b. 15 Aug 1945. Politician. m. Cap Ziaur Rahman - later Pres of Bangladesh - 1960, dec, 2 s. Education: Surendranath Coll Dinajpur. Appointments: Held captive during Bangladesh war of indep; Vice-Chmn Natl Party - BNP - 1982-84; Chmn Natl Party, 1984-; Helped to form seven party alliance ldng to ousting Pres Ersha from power, 1990; Elected PM of Bangladesh, 1991-96; Chmn SAARC, 1993-94. Hobbies: Reading; Listening to music; Gdng. Address: c/o Office of the Prime Minister, Tejgaon, Dhaka, Bangladesh.

ZIFCAK Michael Gejza, b. 28 Sept 1918. Executive Chairman. m. Ludmilla Matos, 31 Dec 1944, 2 s. Education: Comenius Univ, Bratislava; BCom; FAIM; FRMIA. Appointments: Mngr, 1950-61; Gen Mngr,

1961-63; Mng Dir, World Books Pty Ltd, 1957-68; Hill of Content Pub Co Pty Ltd, 1965-; Griffith Bookstore Pty Ltd, 1976-; Chmn and Mngng Dir, Collins Booksellers Investments Pty Ltd, 1986-. Honours: OBE, 1981; Lloyd O'Neil Awd for Servs to Austl Book Ind, 1992; Hon Consul of Slovak Repub, 1995. Memberships: Pres, Austl Booksellers Assn, 1968-79; Austl Booksellers Assn Fedn, 1973-75; Vice Chmn, Austl Lib Promotion Cl, 1973-78; VP, Intl Booksellers Fedn, 1977-81, Pres 1981-85; Aust Cncl Lit Bd, 1978-83; Aust Natl Commn for UNESCO, 1980-83; Chmn, Intl Book Cttee, 1989-94. Hobbies: Tennis; Clubs: RACV; Melbourne Club. Address: 109 Grange Road, Toorak, Vic 3142, Australia.

ZINES Leslie Ronald, b. 12 Dec 1930, Sydney, Australia. Lawyer. Education: LLB, Sydney, 1952; LLM, Harvard, 1956; Hon LLD, Austl Natl Univ, 1994. Appointments: Barrister, NSW, 1952; Legal Positions in Atty-Gens Dept, Canberra, 1952-61; Sec, Copyright Law Review Cttee, 1958-59; Snr Lectr, Law, 1962-65, Rdr, Law, 1965-67, Prof, Law, 1967-77, Robert Garran Prof of Law, 1977-92, Univ Fell, 1994-96, Austl Natl Univ; Mbr, Roy Cmmn on Tas Constitution, 1981-82; Mbr, Constitutional Cmmn, 1985-88; Arthur Goodhart Prof of Legal Sci, Cambridge Univ, 1992-93; Hon Fell, Wolfson Coll, Cambridge, 1995-; Visng Fell, Law Prog, RSSS, 1997-. Publications: Commentaries on the Australian Constitution, 1977; Federal Jurisdiction in Australia (joint), 1978; The High Court and the Constitution, 1st ed, 1981, 4th ed, 1997; Sawer's Australian Constitutional Cases, (joint), 4th ed, 1982; Constitutional Change in the Commonwealth, 1991. Honour: AO. Membership: FASSA, 1987-. Address: Law Program, RSSS Australian National University, Canberra, ACT 0200, Australia.

ZIPFINGER Frank Peter, b. 27 Feb 1953, Sydney, Australia. Solicitor. m. Susan, 5 Jan 1979, 2 s, 1 d. Education: BA, Macquarie Univ; LLB, Sydney Univ; LIM. Appointments: Ptnr, Mallesons Stephen Jaques, 1983-. Publications: Australian Stamp Duties law, 1982; Stamp Duty Aspects of Trusts Settlements and Gifts in Australia, 1984; The Stamp Duty Book, 1994. Memberships: Law Soc, NSW; Amn Bar Assn. Hobbies: Tennis; Philately. Address: C/- Mallesons Stephen Jacques, 50 Bridge St, Sydney, NSW 2000, Australia.

ZIV-AV Itzhak, b. 4 June 1907 Russia. Admin Offic; Jrnlst. m. Debora Kobrinsky, 1934, 2 s. Education: Inst of Pedagogy Smolensk. Appointments: Farmer and Mngr Local Cncl of Magdiel settlement Israel, 1926-34; Mngng Ed Haboker - daily - 1935-48; Dir Pub Rels Div min of Def and GHQ Israel Def Force, 1948-52; Dir-Gen Israel Farmers' Union, 1952-75; Chmn Bd Land Dev Authy, 1960-98; Ed Farmers of Israel monthly, 1962-87; Chmn Exec Cttee Co-ordng Bur Israeli Econ Orgs, 1967-86; Chmn Cncl, 1975-86; Pres Hon Crt, 1986-90. Publications: The Unknown Land; I Seek My Brethren; The Price of Freedom; Forever Ours; From Frontier to Frontier; A World to Live in; Another World; There is a Land; All the Hopes are Reborn; Beautiful Are the Nights in Canaan; The People of 1948; There is No Other Homeland for Me; Poetry for Children. Memberships: Mbr Bd of Dirs Jewish Natl Fund; Mbr Exec Bd Intl Fed Agricl Prodrs - IFAP - 1960-80; Mbr Cncl State Land Authy, 1962-97. Address: Ramat-Qan 52587, Sh'mueli Street 3, Israel.

ZMOOD Ronald Barry, b. 15 Aug 1942. Engineer. m. 6 Dec 1966, 2 s, 1 d. Education: MEngSc, 1963, BE (Electrical), 1967, Univ of Melbourne; PhD, Univ of MI, 1971. Appointments: Engr, PMG Rsch Labs, 1965-67; Lectr, Univ of Queensland, 1971-74; Lohning Brothers, Cnsltng Engrs, 1974-76; Expmntl Offr, Aeronautical Rsch Labs, Dept of Def, 1976-80; Prin Lectr, Dept of Elec Enrng, Roy Melbourne Inst of Technol, 1980-; Visng Prof, Dept of Mechl Engrng, Univ of MD, 1989-90. Publications: Introduction to Control Systems, 1994; 48 refereed jrnl and conf publs. Membership: MIEEE. Listed in: Many including: Who's Who in the World; Who's Who in Finance and Industry. Hobbies: Photography; Bushwalking. Address: Department of Electrical Engineering, Royal Melbourne Institute of Technology, Melbourne, Vic, Australia.

ZONG Bo, b. 6 Feb 1933, Shanghai. Professor. m. Hu Jun Chi, 10 Jan 1961, 2 s. Education: Grad, Liszt Conservatory of Music, Hungary. Appointments: Exec Dir, Chinese Violoncello Soc, 1986-; Vice Chmn, Beijing Musicians' Assn, 1987-97; Pres, Kodaly Acady, 1988-; Advsr, Beijing Musicians' Anns, 1997-. Creative Works: The Art of Violoncello Playing; The Explanation of Playing Nine Famous Violoncello Concerts. Honours: Liszt Medal, Hungarian Govt, 1986. Memberships: China Musicians' Soc. Hobbies: Music. Address: Central Conservatory of Music, Beijing 100031, China.

ZORIG Lhagvajav, b. 1958, Huvsgul animag, Mongolia. Government Executive. m. Education: Grad, Medl Univ, Mongolia, 1982; Surgery Course, 1986; Grad, Hosp Mngmt Sch, India, 1992-94. Appointments: Dr, Ulaan Uul sum, Huvsgul aimag, 1983; Surg, Mil Cntrl Hosp, 1985; Rsch Fell, Cntr for Medl Sci, 1987; Spec, Exec Cncl for People's Hural Parl, 1992; Employee, Ardyn Erh Newsppr, 1994; Gen Dir, Monsei Friendshp Hosp, 1994; Min of Hlth and Socl Safety, Ulan Bator, Mongolia, 1996-. Address: Ministry of Health, Karl Marx St 4, Ulan Bator, Mongolia.

ZOU Dayan, b. 13 Dec 1935, Hunan, China. Professor of Psychology. m. Yang Huiming, 23 Mar 1973, 2 s. Education: Grad, Dept of Philos, Peking Univ, 1961. Appointments: Tutor of Postgrads, 1987, Vice Dir, 1990, Prof of Psychol, 1992-, Hebei Normal Univ. Publications: Review of Fanzhen's Psychological Ideas, 1983; Review of Gong Zizhen's Psychological Ideas, 1984; History of Chinese Psychology, 1986; Initial Study of the Literary Psychological Ideas in The Book of Songs, 1987; Initial Study of Yan Yuan's Educational Psychological Ideas, 1992. Honour: Ctf, China Natl News Press Org, 1993. Memberships: Spec Cttee, Theoretical Psychol & Psychol Hist, Chinese Psychol Soc, 1985. Hobby: Peking Opera. Address: c/o Department of Pedagogy, Hebei Normal University, Shijiazhuang, Hebei 050016, China.

ZOU Wei Jun, b. 26 Jan 1943, Wuxi, Jiangsu, China. Doctor. m. Gu Kehui, 26 Dec 1968, 2 s. Education: Grad, Chinese Linguistics & Lit Dept, Nanjing Univ, China, 1966. Appointments: Tchr, Wujiang Mid Sch, Huangchi Mid Sch of Dantu County, Anhui prov, Study w Prof Zon Yun Xiang (old & famous dr of tradl Chinese med); Dr, Tradl Chinese Med: Hexian People's Hosp, Anhui Prov, 971-78; Jiangpu People's Hosp, Nanjing, 1978-88; Jiangpu People's Hosp, Nanjing, 1988-93; Pres, Phenomenal Tradl Chinese Med Soc, 1993-98. Publications include: An Introduction to Phenomenal Traditional Chinese Medicine; New Trend of Thoughts of Contemporary Traditional Chinese Medicine; Be Healthy With Entertainment; Researches on Multiple Branches of Traditional Chinese Medicine; Methods About the Development of Traditional Chinese Medicine. Honours: Hon title, Advd Sci & Tech Worker, Nanjing Municipal Govt, 1983, 1991; Best thesis: Researches on Phenomenal Traditional Chinese Medicine, Acad Cttee, 1st Session Intl Acad Discussion, 1995. Memberships: Jiangsu Psychol Soc, 1985; China Soc Somatic Sci; Pres, Phenomenal Tradl Chinese Med Soc, 1989; Hon Advsr, Singapore's Tradl Chinese Med Fedn, 1992; Protestor, Hong Kong Tradl Chinese Med, 1993; Prof, Hong Kong Tradl Chinese Med Coll, 1994; Advsr, Taiwan Nat Hlth-Care monthly, Oct 1994; Hon Advsr, Hong Kong Phenomenal Tradl Chinese Med Soc, 1996. Hobbies: Literary creation; Chinese folk music; Chinese painting and calligraphy; Travel. Address: Outpatient Department of Jiangpu Traditional Chinese Medicine Hospital, 211800, Nanjing, China.

ZOU Jiahua, b. Oct 1926 Shanghai. Engineer; State Official. Education: Moscow. Appointments: Joined CCP, 1945; Fmr Dir Shenyang No 2 Mach Tool Plant; Dir Mach Tool Inst First min of Mach Bldg; Dep Dir Comms of Sci Tech and Ind for Natl Def; Min of Ordnance Ind, 1985-86; Min of State Mach-Bldg Ind Commn, 1986-88; Min of Mach Bldg and Electrons Ind, 1988-93; State Cnclr, 1988-91; Min in charge of State Plng Commn, 1992-93; Vice-Premier, 1991-; Vice-Premier State Cncl, 1993-; Chmn State Radio Regulatory Cttee, 1994-. Memberships: Alt mbr 12th CCP Cntrl Cttee, 1982-87;

Mbr 12th CCP Cntrl Cttee, 1985; Mbr 13th CCP Cntrl Cttee, 1987-92; Mbr Ldng Grp for Nuclear Power Plants, 1988-; Mbr Distribution System Reform Cttee, 1991-; Mbr 14th Cntrl Cttee, 1992; Mbr CCP Politburo, 1992; Mbr 8th NPC, 1993; Mbr Ldng Grp for Beijing-Kowloon Railway Constrn, 1993-; Mbr Cntrl Finl and Econ Ldng Grp, 1994-. Address: c/o Office of the Prime Minister, Beijing, People's Republic of China.

ZOUBI Mahmoud al-, b. 1938 Khirbet Ghazaleh Dar'a Governate. Politician. m. 3 c. Appointments: Fmr Chmn Agricl Cntr al-Ghab; Chmn Agricl Produce Dept, 1963-64; Dir of Agric and Agrarian Reform al-Ghab Dist, 1964-68; Dir of Agric and Agrarian Reform Hama, 1969-71; Sec Bath Party Peasants' Bur, 1972-73; Gen Dir Euphrates Basin Invmnt Estab, 1973-76; Speaker People's Ass, 1981-87; PM of Syria, 1987-. Memberships: Mbr al-Ghab Dist Baath Party ldrshp; Mbr Admin Cncl Agronomists's Union; Mbr People's Ass, 1971; Reserve mbr Baath Party's Regl Ldrshp, 1975-80; Mbr Baath Party's Regl Ldrshp, 1980. Address: Office of the Prime Minister, Damascus, Syria.

ZUBEIDI Mohammed Hamzah al-. Politician. Appointments: Dep PM, Mar-Sep 1991; PM of Iraq, 1992-93. Address: c/o Office of the Prime Minister, Baghdad, Iraq.

ZULFAQAR Ghulam Hussain, b. 15 Aug 1924, Batala. Professor. m. Anka, 1957, 2 s, 6 d. Education: MA; PhD. Appointments: Rsch Schl, 1956; Lectr, 1959; Rdr, Assoc Prof, 1970; Prof, 1982; Visng Prof, Istanbul Univ, 1985-90; Dir, 1994-. Publication: Ed, Qtly Iqbal; Many or Publs. Memberships: Var Univ Bodies. Hobby: Travel. Address: Bazmi Iqbal, 2 Club Road, Lahore, Pakistan.

Appendices

Appendices

APPENDIX A
ORGANIZATIONS and ASSOCIATIONS

While not comprehensive, this listing contains over 450 organizations, associations and societies based in the Australasia and Asia-Pacific region, many of which have contributed to the production of this directory. We have taken every care to ensure accuracy. If however there have been any changes, we would be most grateful for new details supplied to the International Biographical Centre care of "The Editor".

AUSTRALIA

Better Hearing Australia
10 Gordons Rd
Lower Templestowe
Vic 3107

ACT Association of Occupational Therapists
PO Box E171
Queen Victoria Terrace
ACT 2600

Accordion Society of Australia
579 Prince Highway
Rockdale
NSW 2216

Accounting Association of Australia and New Zealand
Department of Commerce
University of Queensland
QLD 4067

African Research Institute
La Trobe University
Bundoora
Victoria 3083

Anthony A Williams Management Pty Ltd.
1st Floor, 50 Oxford Street
Paddington
NSW 2021

Architects' Board of South Australia
1 King William Road
Unley
SA 5061

Art Craft Teachers Association
217 Church St
Richmond
Vic 3121

Asian-Australasian Society of Neurological Surgeons
201 Wickham Terrace
Brisbane
QLD 4000

Asian Pacific Confederation of Chemical Engineering
Institute of Engineers
11 National Circuit
Barton
ACT 2600

Association of Consulting Engineers, Australia
75 Miller Street, PO Box 1002
North Sydney
NSW 2060

Association of Medical Women in Western Australia
PO Box 133
Nedlands
WA 6009

Association of Professional Engineers Australia
360 King Street
West Melbourne
VIC 3003

Association of Taxation and Management Accountants
Level 3, 31 Burwood Rd
Burwood
NSW 2134

Association of Wall and Ceiling Contractors of South Australia
219 Henley Beach Rd
Torrensville
SA 5031

Australian Association of Genealogists and Record Agents
PO Box 268
Oakleigh
Victoria 3166

Australasian Association of Philosophy
Philosophy Department
La Trobe University
VIC 3083

Australian Hotels Association
24 Brisbane Avenue
Canberra
ACT 2600

Australasian Society of Engineers
2nd Floor, 422-424 Kent Street
Sydney
NSW 2000

Australasian Universities Language and Literature Association
University of Queensland
St Lucia
QLD 4072

Australia Indonesian Chamber of Commerce
PO Box 96
North Sydney
NSW 2059

Australian Institute for the Conservation of Cultural Materials
GPO Box 1638
Canberra
ACT 2601

Australian Academy of the Humanities
GPO Box 93
Canberra
ACT 2601

Australian Academy of Science
GPO Box 783
Canberra
ACT 2601

Australian Airline Flight Engineers Association
1st Floor, 197 Dryburgh Street
North Melbourne
VIC 3051

Australian Book Publishers' Association
59/889 Jones Street
Ultimo
NSW 2007

Australian Business Aircraft Association
Main Terminal, Essendon Airport
Essendon
VIC 3041

Australian Collaborative Land Evaluation Program
CSIRO Land and Water
Bruce E Butler Laboratory
GPO Box 1666
Canberra
ACT 2601

Australian Council / Council for Arts
PO Box 788
Strawberry Hills
NSW 2012

Australian Council for Educational Research
Private Bag 55
Camberwell
VIC 3124

Australian Council for Overseas Aid
Private Bag 3
Deakin
ACT 2600

Australian Council of Professional Associations
360 King Street
West Melbourne
VIC 3003

Australian Electric Traction Association NSW Division
PO Box 112
Eastwood
NSW 2122

Australian Federation of Business and Professional Women
PO Box 617
Belconnen
ACT 2616

Australian Fellowship of Evangelical Students
PO Box 684
Kingsford
NSW 2032

Australian Journalists' Association
405 Elizabeth Street
Surry Hills
NSW 2010

Australian Mineral Foundation
63 Conyngham Street
Glenside
SA 5065

Australian Music Therapy Association
18 Collins Street
Box Hill
VIC 3128

Australian Nuclear Association
PO Box 445
Sutherland
NSW 2232

Australian Railway Historical Society
Box 5177 AA
GPO Melbourne
VIC 3001

Australian Science Teacher's Association
4 Juwin Street
Aranda
ACT 2614

Australian Society of Legal Philosophy
University of Sydney
Department of Jurisprudence
173 Phillip Street
Sydney
NSW 2000

Australian Society for Limnology
Museum of Victoria
71 Victoria Cresent
Abbotsford
VIC 3067

Australian Society for Music Education
5H Parkhill Street
Pearce
ACT 2607

Australian Society of Travel Writers
PO Box 37
Rozelle
NSW 2039

Australian Sound Recording Association
1 Lloyd Place
Kambah
ACT 2902

Australian String Teachers' Association
16 Clapham Street
Balwyn
VIC 3103

Australian Veterinary Association
PO Box 371
Artarmon
NSW 2064

Australian Wine Foundation
Wine Ind Hse
555 The Parade
Magill
SA 5072

Australian Wine and Brandy Producers Association
Wine Ind Hse
555 The Parade
Magill
SA 5072

Australian Women Pilots' Association
4/7 Meredith Street
Redcliffe
QLD 4020

British Dancing Association
14 Sterling Court
Castle Hill
NSW 2154

British Working Mens Club
11-15 Davis Street
Wingfield
SA 5013

Camberwell Music Society Incorporated
10 Grosvenor Road
Glen Iris
VIC 3146

Canberra Gem Society
Griffin Ctr 19 Bunda St
Canberra City
ACT 2601

Chamber of Commerce and Industry South Australia
136 Greenhill Road
Unley
SA 5061

Christian Dance Fellowship of Australia
PO Box 210
Broadway
NSW 2007

City of Whitehorse
Locked Bag 2
Eastern Mail Centre
VIC 3110

Ecological Society of Australia
GPO Box 1564
Canberra
ACT 2601

Exhibition and Event Association of Australia
Level 1, 21 Burwood Rd
Hawthorn
VIC 3122

Federal Council Military Historical Society of Australia
PO Box 30
Garran
ACT 2605

Festival of Perth
The University of Western Australia
Nedlands
WA 6907

Food Retailers Association
263 Wardell Rd
Dulwich Hill
NSW 2203

Filipino Cultural Association Incorporated
PO Box 2309
Whyalla Norrie
SA 5608

Genealogical Society of Victoria
Lvl 6 179 Queen St
Melbourne
Vic 3000

Geography Teachers Association of South Australia
163a Greenhill Road
Parkside
SA 5063

History Trust of South Australia
Edmund Wright House
59 King William St
Adelaide
SA 5000

Holstein Friesian Association of Australia
504 Racecourse Rd
PR. Bag 14
Flemington
VIC 3031

Hotel Motel and Accomodation Association of Queensland
6th Floor Alexandra House
201 Wickham Terrace
Brisbane
QLD 4001

Historic Commercial Vehicle Association Coop Ltd
IB Gannon St
Tempe
NSW 2044

Institute of Patent Attorneys of Australia
207 Riversdale Road
Hawthorn
VIC 3122

Institute of Chartered Accountants
GPO Box 3921
Sydney
NSW 2001

Institute of Legal Executives
PO Box 17
Collins St West
Melbourne
VIC 8007

Institute of Strata Title Management Ltd
Ste 107 284 Victoria Ave
Chatswood
NSW 2067

International Association of Botanic Gardens
Botanic Gardens, North Terrace
Adelaide
SA 5000

International Christian Dance Fellowship
11 Amaroo Crescent
Mosman
NSW 2088

International Commission for Uniform Methods of Sugar Analysis
c/o CSR Central Laboratory
70 John Street
Pyrmont
NSW 2009

International Social Service
260 Church Street
Richmond
VIC 3121

Journalists' Club
36 Chalmers Street
Sydney
NSW 2000

Law Asia (Law Association of Asia and the Pacific)
11th Floor, NT House
22 Mitchell Street
Darwin
NT 0800

MIAA
PO Box 1477
Neutral Bay
NSW 2089

Mortgage Industry Association of Australia
GPO Box 4060
Sydney
NSW 2001

Museums Australia
24 Queen's Parade
North Fitzroy
VIC 3068

Musicological Society of Australia
GPO Box 2404
Canberra
ACT 2601

National Association of Medical Specialists
229 Macquire Street
Sydney
NSW 2000

National Council of Jewish Women of Australia
PO Box 57
Woollahra
NSW 2025

Organic Gardening and Farming Society of Tasmania
PO Box 228
Ulverstone 7315
TAS

Performers' Management
120 Johnston Street
Fitzroy
VIC 3065

Poets' Union of NSW
Box 166, Wentworth Building
University of Sydney
NSW 2006

Queensland Produce Seed and Grain Merchants Association Incorporated
MS 664B
East Greenmount
QLD 4359

Regional Airlines Association of Australia Plc
15/255 Elizabeth St
Sydney
NSW 2000

Resturant and Catering Queensland
PO Box 101
Royal Brisbane Hospital
QLD 4029

Royal Australian Historical Society
History House, 133 Macquarie Street
Sydney
NSW 2000

Royal District Nursing Service
31 Alma Rd
St Kilda
VIC 3182

Share Holder Action Group
40 Carinish Rd
Huntingdale 3167

Society of Women Writers (Australia)
GPO Box 2621
Sydney
NSW 2001

Statistical Society of Australia
GPO Box 85
Ainslie
ACT 2602

Sydney Journalists' Club
36 Chalmers Street
Surry Hills
NSW 2010

Sydney Theatrical Centre
1st Floor, 2-8 Ennis Road
Milsons Point
NSW

TASDEC - Global Learning Centre
International House
4 Battery Square
Battery Point
Hobart
TAS 7000

Tweedshire Council
PO Box 816
Murwillumbah
NSW 2484

United Nations Association of Australia
1 O'Sullivan Street
Higgins
ACT 2615

Uniting Church Historical Society
28 Page Street
Mitcham
VIC 3132

Victorian Scottish Union Incorporated
6 Union Street
Lower Templestowe
VIC 3107

Woolpackers Association of Australia
Box 1855
Ballarat Mail Centre 3354
VIC

Women in Education
37 Cavendish Street
Stanmore
NSW 2048

Women Lawyers Association of New South Wales
170 Phillip Street
Sydney
NSW 2000

BANGLADESH

Young Womens Christian Movement of Bangladesh
3/23 Iqbal Road
Mohammadpur
Dhaka-1207

BRUNEI

Brunei Bumputra Chamber of Commerce and Industry
PO Box 203
Gadong Post Office
Bandar Seri Degawan 3102

Women Graduates' Association
PO Box 2282
Bandar Seri Begawan 1922

CHINA

Accounting Society of China
2 Nanhengjie
Sanlihe
Fuxingmenwai
Beijing

China Agricultural Film and Television Association
28 Baishiqiao Road
Beijing 100081

China Association of Industrial Economics
9 Xihuangchenggen Nanjie
Xicheng District
Beijing 1000321

China Association of Inventions
PO Box 8020
Beijing 100088

China Association of Railway Engineering Construction
1 Jinjiacun
South Wanshou Road
Beijing 100036

China Association for Science and Technology
Chen Hong
Sanlihe
Beijing

China Civil Aviation Association
155 Dongsi Xidajie
Beijing 100710

China Electronics Chamber of Commerce
49 Fuxing Road
Beijing 100036

China Entomological Society
c/o Institute of Zoology
Zhongguancun
Beijing 100080

China Environmental Science Press
8 Beigangzi Lane
Chongwen District
Beijing 10062

China Film Association
22 Beisanhuan East Road
Beijing 100013

China Film Editing Association
15 Beisanhuan West Road
Beijing 100088

China Musical Instrument Association
6 East Chang'an Avenue
Beijing 100005

China Photojournalist Society
57 Xuanwumen Xidajie
Beijing 100803

China Senior Professors Association
41 Xue Yuan Rd. Bldg 7
Beijing 100088

China Society for International Professionals Exchange and Development
61721 The Friendship Hotel
Unit 17
Beijing 100820

China Society of Toponymy
147 Berheyan Street
Dongcheng District
Beijing 100032

China Sound Engineers' Association
4 Zhenwumiao Second Lane
Xicheng District
Beijing 100866

China Surface Engineering Association
182 Baofeng Second Road
Wuhan 430030

China Textile Engineering Society
3 Yanjingli Zhjongjie
Chaoyang District
Beijing 1000025

Chinese Association of Agricultural Science
11 Nongzhanguan Nanli
Chaoyang District
Beijing 100026

Chinese Association for Cultural Relics Preservation Technology
29 Wusi Dajie
Dongcheng District

Chinese Chemical Society
PO Box 2709
Beijing 100080

Chinese Dancers' Association
10 Nongzhanguan Nanli
Beijing 100026

Chinese Folk Literature and Art Society
10 Nonmgzhanguan Nanli
Beijing 100026

Chinese Institute of Technology
Nongzhanguan Nanlu No 12
Room 2310
Beijing 100026

Chinese Law History Society
15 Shatan Beijie
Beijing 100720

Chinese Pharmaceutical Association
A38 North Lishi Road
Beijing 100810

Chinese Pharmacological Society
1 Xian Nong Tan Street
Beijing 100050

Chinese Photographers' Association
61 Hongxing Lane
Dongcheng District
Beijing 100005

Chinese Quyi Artists' Association
10 Nomgzhanguan Hanli
Beijing 100026

Chinese Radio and Television Society
2 Fuxingingmenwai Street
Beijing 100866

Chinese Society of Naval Architecture and Marine Engineering
5 Yeutan Beijie Street
Beijing 100861

Chinese Society of Theoretical and Applied Mechanics
15 Zhongguancun Road
Beijing 100080

Technological Information Promotion System National Bureau in China
PO Box 3811
No 15 Fuxing Road
Beijing 100038

COOK ISLANDS

Cook Islands Association of Non-Governmental-Organisations
PO Box 733
Ragotonga

FIJI

Textile, Clothing and Footwear Council of Fiji
PO Box 10015
Nabua

Cagimara Development Association
PO Box 1038
Yalalevu BA

GUATEMALA

Desalt Desarrollo Alternativo
Ed. El Centro 14-10
7a ar. y 9a calle Z. 1
Ciudad Guatemala
Guatemala

HAWAII

Association of Rehabilitation Nurses
226 N. Kuakini St
Honolulu
HI 96817

Hawaii Geographic Society
49 S Hotel St
PO Box 1698
Honolulu 96806-1698

HONG KONG

Asian Students' Association
353 Shanghai Street 4/F
Kowloon

Asian Surgical Association
Department of Surgery
Queen Mary Hospital
University of Hong Kong
Pokfulam Road
Hong Kong

Association of Accredited Advertising Agents of Hong Kong
604 McDonnell Building
48 Yee Wo Street
Hong Kong

Association of Consulting Engineers of Hong Kong
56/F Hopwell Center
183 Queen's Road East
Hong Kong

Association of International Accountants
GPO Box 6778
Hong Kong

Business and Professionals' Federation of Hong Kong
Suite 2112
2 Pacific Place
88 Queen'sway

Chartered Association of Certified Accountants - Hong Kong
1401 Century Square
1 D'Aguilar Street
Hong Kong

Chartered Institute of Management Accountants - Hong Kong
13/F Cindic Tower
Unit A
128 Gloucester Road
Hong Kong

Chinese Manufacturers' Association of Hong Kong
5/F CMA Building
64-66 Connaught Road
Central

Federation of Asian and Oceania Pest Managers Associations
15-A Kam Chung Commercial Building
19-21 Hennessy Road
Wanchai

Federation of Hong Kong Industries
Hankow Centre 4th Floor
5-15 Hankow Road
Tsim Sha Tsui
Kowloon

Gemological Association of Hong Kong
PO Box 97711
TST
Kowloon

Hong Kong Amateur Athletic Association
Room 1017
Sports House
1 Stadium Path
So Kon Po
Causeway Bay

Hong Kong Anti-Cancer Society
30 Nam Long Shan Road
Wong Chuk Hang
Aberdeen

Hong Kong Association of Banks
Prince's Building, Room 525
GPO Box 11391
Hong Kong

Hong Kong Association of Freight Forwarding Agents Ltd.
Room 318 3/F, Hactl Terminal II
Hong Kong International Airport
Kowloon

Hong Kong Association of Property Management Companies Ltd.
PO Box 47160
Morrison Hill Post Office HR
Hong Kong

Hong Kong Bar Association
LG/2 The Supreme Court
38 Queensway
Hong Kong

Hong Kong Construction Association
180 Hennessy Road 3/F
Hong Kong

Hong Kong Chefs Association
PO Box No. 91614
Tsimshatsui Post Office
Kowloon

Hong Kong Christian Institute
10/F 11 Mongkok Road
Kowloon

Hong Kong Dental Association Ltd.
Duke of Windsor Social Service
8/F 15 Hennessy Road
Hong Kong

Hong Kong Educational Publishers Assocaition Ltd
18/F Warwick House East
Taikoo Place
979 King's Rd
Quarry Bay

Hong Kong Ethnomusicology Society
Centre of Asian Studies
University of Hong Kong
Pokfulam Road

Hong Kong Exporters' Association
Star House, Room 825
3 Salisbury Road
Tsimshatsui
Kowloon

Hong Kong Federation of Women's Centres
58-9 2/F Lai Kwai House
Lai Kwok Estate
Kowloon

Hong Kong Film Awards Association
8/ Floor Lockville Commercial Building
25-27 Lock Road
Tsimshatsui
Kowloon

Hong Kong General Chamber of Commerce
United Centre
22nd Floor
95 Queensway
Hong Kong

Hong Kong General Chamber of Pharmacy
401 Winning House
14 Cochrane Street
Hong Kong

Hong Kong Institute of Company Secretaries
22/F Prosperous Commerce Building
54 Jardine's Bazaar
Hong Kong

Hong Kong Institution of Engineers
9/F Island Centre
1 Great George Street
Hong Kong

Hong Kong Jockey Club
1 Sports Road
Happy Valley

Hong Kong Kennel Club Ltd.
28B Stanley Street, 3 rd Floor
Hong Kong

Hong Kong and Kowloon Electrical Contractors' Association
Kwong Ah Building 8/F
195 Johnston Road
Hong Kong

Hong Kong Library Association
GPO Box 10095
Hong Kong

Hong Kong News Executives' Association
GPO Box 11682
Hong Kong

Hong Kong Psychological Society
Department of Psychology
University of Hong Kong
Pokfulam Road
Hong Kong

Hong Kong Quality Management Association Ltd
PO Box No. 90952
Tsimshatsui Post Office, Kowloon

Hong Kong Schools of Music and Speech Association
7 Carmel Village Street, 2nd Floor
Homatin
Kowloon

Hong Kong Ship Owners' Association
12th Floor
Queen's Centre
58 Queen's Road East
Wanchai

Hong Kong Society of Accountants
17/F Belgian House
77 Gloucester Road
Hong Kong

Hong Kong Society of Professional Optometrists
PO Box 98603
Tsimshatsui Post Office
Kowloon

Hong Kong Venture Capital Association
Room 1503 15/F, Wanchai Commercial Centre
194-204 Johnston Road
Wanchai

Hong Kong Youth Hostels Association
Room 225, Block 19
Shek Kip Mei Estate
Kowloon

Institute of Incorporated Engineers
PO Box 91214
Tsimshatsui Post Office
Kowloon

Institute of Industrial Engineers
GPO Box 6635
Hong Kong

Institution of Electrical Engineers Hong Kong
PO Box 10007
Hong Kong

Institution of Fire Engineers
1 Hong Chong Road
Kowloon

Newspaper Society of Hong Kong
7/F Culturecom Centre
No 47 Hung To Road
Kwun Tong
Kowloon

Radio Association of Hong Kong
2/F Wyndham Mansion
32 Wyndham Street
Hong Kong

Raja Yoga Centre Ltd
17 Dragon Rd
Hong Kong

Tobacco Institute of Hong Kong Ltd.
Room 1807, Harbour Centre
25 Harbour Road
Wanchai

University of Hong Kong
Department of Paediatrics, Queen Mary Hospital
Room 112, New Clinical Building
Pokfulam Rd

YMCA of Hong Kong
PO Box 95096
TST
Kowloon

Young Presidents' Organization
Room 1103
World Trade Centre
280 Gloucester Road
Causeway Bay

INDIA

Anthropological Survey of India
27 Jawaharlal Nehru Road
Calcutta 700 016

Association of Indian Universities
AIU House
16 Kotla Marg
New Delhi 110002

Centre for Application of Science and Technology for Rural Development
6 Koyna Apartments
Survey No.133
Kothrud
Pune 411029
Maharashtra

Indian Pest Control Association
Flat No.11 1st Floor
40 D.L.F Industrial Area
Kirti Nagar
New Delhi 110015

Indian Society of Advetisers
Army and Navy Building
148 Mahatma Ghandhi Rd
Mumbai 400 001

International Society for Krishna Conciousness
PO Box 10279
Ballygani
Calcutta 700 019

Ryan Foundation International
8 West Mada St
Srinagar Colony
Madras 600015

Social Education and Environmentalist Development
101-D Kaliamman Pandal Street
Annthanapatty
Salem 636 002
Tamil Nadu

Sulabh International Institute of Technical Research and Training
Sulabh Bhawan
Mahavir Enclave
New Delhi 110045

Silk and Silk Mills Association Ltd
3rd Floor Sasmira Bldg
Sasmira Marg
Worli
Mumbai 400025

Society for Enviromental Pollution Control
17/423 New Hyderabad
Lucknow-226007
U.P.

INDONESIA

American Chamber of Commerce in Indonesia
The Landmark Centre
22/F Suite 2204
Jin Jendral Sudirman 1
Tromol Pos 3060
10002 Jakarta

Asian Agricultural Journalists' and Writers' Association (AAJWA)
Gedung Dewan Pers, 4th Floor
Jalan Kebun Sirih 34
10110 Jakarta

Asian and Pacific Coconut Community
Lina Building
J.L Rasuna Said
Kuningan
Jakarta

Care Indonesia
PO Box 4123
Jalan Kemang Utara No 34
12041 Jakarta

Indonesia Veterinary Drug Association
Jalan Raya Pasar Minggu
No 97A
12510 Jakarta

Indonesian Association of Oceanologists
Jalan Pasir Putih 1
Ancol Timur
Jakarta 1100 1

Indonesian Consumers' Association
Jalan Pacoran Barat VII
No 1 Duren, Tiga
Pasar Minggu
12760 Jakarta
Selaton

Indonesian Environmental Forum
J L Penjernihan I
Complex Keuangan No 15
Penjompongan
10210 Jakarta

Indonesian Geologist Association
Jalan Diponegoro 57
Bandung

Indonesian Historians' Community
Puslitbang Kemasyarakatan LIPI
Jalan Gatot Subroto 10
Jakarta

Indonesian Librarians' Association
Jalan Merdeka Selatan 11
Jakarta

Indonesian Medical Association
J1 Dr Samratulangi No 29
Jakarta Pusat 10350

Indonesian Nutritionist Association
FIDC-IPB
Kampus Dermaga
Bogor

Indonesian Phytopathology Association
Facultas Pertanian UNBRAW
Jalan Mayjen Haryono
Malang

Psychology Association
c/o Fakultas Psiologi UI
Komplek UI
Depok 16424
Jakarta

Institute for Philosophy and the Future of Humanity
Universitas Nasional
J1 Sawomanila
Pejatan
Jakarta

National Association of Indonesian Engineering Consultants
J1 Bendungan Hilir Raya 29
10210 Jakarta

World Trade Centre Jakarta
Jalan Jend
Sudirman Kav 29-31
PO Box 8395
12920 Jakarta

IRAN

Institute for the Intellectual Development of Children and Young Adults
22-24 Khaled Eslamboli Ave
Tehran 15116

ISRAEL

Israeli Society for the Abolition of Vivisection
PB 519
Givataim 53104

JAPAN

Asian Club
World Trade Center Building, Suite 23022
2-4-1 Hamamatsu-cho
Minato-ku
Tokyo 105

Asian Electronics Union (AEU)
Kyodo Building 5F
2-4-10 Iwamoto-cho
Chiyoda-ku
Tokyo 101

Asian Pacific Cultural Centre for UNESCO
Nihon Shuppam Kaikan
6 Fukuromachi
Shinjuku-ku
Tokyo 162

Asiatic Society of Japan
OAG House , 4th Floor
7-5-56 Akasaka
Minato-ku
Tokyo 107

Association of Japanese Consulting Engineers
3-16-4 Veno
Taito-ku
Tokyo 110

Care Japan
2-3-2 Zoshigaya
Toshima-ku
Tokyo 171

Earth Day Japan
Tokyo Office
Nishikawa Building 3F
2-7-3 Kojimachi
Chiyoda-ku
Tokyo 102

Engineering Consulting Firms Association
Kasumigaseki Building, 32nd Floor
3-2-5-Kasumigaseki,
Chiyoda-ku
Tokyo 100

Federation of Bankers' Associations of Japan
3-1 Maruniuchi 1-chome
Chiyoda-ku
Tokyo 100

Glaucoma Society of International Congress of Ophthalmology
c/o Department of Ophthalmology
Gifu University School of Medicine
40 Tsukasamachi
Gifu-shi 500

Industry Club of Japan
1-4-6 Marunouchi
Chiyoda-ku
Tokyo

Institute of Cultural Affairs - Japan
2-38-4-102 Seijo
Setagaya-ku
Tokyo 157

Institute of Eastern Culture
2-4-1 Nishi Kanda
Chiyoda-ku
Tokyo 101

International Women's Education Association of Japan
Shiba-Koen 2-6-8
Minato-ku
Tokyo 105

Japan Arab Association
Toshiba Building 7th Floor
1-1-1 Shibaura
Minato-ku
Tokyo

Japan Association of Corporate Executives
1-4-6 Marunouchi
Chiyoda-ku
Tokyo 100

Japan Automobile Importers' (JAIA)
Akiyama Building No 7
5-3 Koji-machi
Chiyoda-ku
Tokyo 102

Japan Database Industry Association
3-2 Nishishinjuku 2-chome
Shinjuku-ku
Tokyo 163-03

Japan Dredging and Reclamation Engineering Association
Toranomon
Minato-ku
Tokyo 105

Japan Electric Measuring Instruments Manufacturers' Association
1-9-10 Toranomon
Minato-ku
Tokyo 105-0001

Japan Foundation
Park Building
3-6 Kioi-cho
Chiyoda-ku
Tokyo 102

Japan Foundation for the Earth
1-13-17-809 Tanimachi
Chuo-ku
Osaka 540

Japan Industrial Design Promotion Organization
World Trade Centre Building, Annex 4th Floor
2-4-1 Hamamatsu-cho
Minato-cho
Tokyo 105

Japan International Volunteer Center
Maruku Building, 6th Floor
1-20-6 Higash-Ueno
Taito-ku
Tokyo 110

Japan Machine Tool Importers Association
Toranomon Kogyo Bldg 4F
2-18 Toranomon 1-chrome
Minato-Ku
Tokyo 105-0001

Japan Medical Library Association
Gakkai Center Building 5 F
2-4-16 Yayoi
Bunkyo-ku
Tokyo 113

Japan Medical Products International Trade Association (JAMPITA)
Ninjin Building 7-1
Nihonbashi-Honcho 4-chome
Chuo-ku
Tokyo 103

Japan Medical Women's Association
Aoyama-Miyano Building, 3rd Floor
Shibuya 2-8-7
Shibuya-ku
Tokyo 150

Japan Microphotography Association (JMA)
Okochi Building No 2
1-9-15 Kaji-cho
Chiyoda-ku
Tokyo 101

Japan Newspaper Publishers' and Editors' Association
Nihon Press Center Building
2-2-1 Uchisaiwai-cho
Chiyoda-ku
Tokyo 100

Japan Singapore Association
Asia Kaikan Bekkan, 3rd Floor
8-10-32 Akasaka
Minato-ku
Tokyo 107

Japan Sugar Import and Export Council
9-15 Ginza 7-chome
Chuo-ku
Tokyo 244

Japanese Association of University Women
Toyama Mansion, No 24
7-17-18 Shinjuku
Shinjuku-ku
Tokyo 160

Maruzen Company Ltd.
Book Division
PO Box 5050
Tokyo 100-31

Membrane Society of Japan
4-14-9 Hongo
Bunkyo-ku
Tokyo 113

Mining and Materials Processing Institute of Japan
Nogizaka Building
9-6-41 Akasaka
Minato-ku
Tokyo 107

Society of Materials Science
Yoshina-Izumidono-cho 1-401
Sakyo-ka
Kyoto 606

World Trade Center of Japan
World Trade Center Building, 37th Floor
PO Box 57, 2-4-1 Hamamatsu-cho
Minato-ku
Tokyo 105

WSAA Japan Atami Office
Atami Daiichi Building 8F
Tawarahon-cho 9-1
Atami
Shizuoka 413

KOREA

Cho Patent and Trademarks
C. P. O. Box 7254
Seoul

Foreign Patent Center Chang Sun Lee's Office
Rm. 1102, Woonam Bldg. 7
1-KA Bongnae-Dong, Chung-Ku, Seoul

International Patent and Trademark Law Office
Hwain B/D 824-29
Yeoksam-Dong
KangNam-ku 135-080

Institute of Cultural Affairs - Korea
KPO Box 1052
Seoul

Korea Foreign Trade Association
159-1 Samsung-Dong
Kangnam-ku
Seoul

Korea Foundation
CPO Box 2147
Seoul 100-095

Korea Industrial Technology Association
KOTEF Building, 7th Floor
35-3 Yoido-dong
Youngdeungpo-ku
Seoul 150-010

Korea Meterological Society
c/o Department of Astronomy and Meteorology
Seoul

Korean Academy of Psychotherapists
178-23 Song-buk dong
Song-buk-ku
Seoul 136-020

Korean Council of Consulting Engineers
302 Jungang MS and F Building
61-5 Nonhyong-dong
Kangnam-gu
Seoul

Korean Nurses' Academic Society
Ewha Women's University
College of Nursing
Seoul 120-750

Korean Society of Agricultural Chemistry and Biotechnology
c/o Department of Agricultural Chemistry
College of Agriculture and Life Science
Seoul National University
SuWon 441-N44

Korean Society of Electron Microscopy
Korea University
Anatomy Lab
12-6-1 Anam-dong
Sung-bouls-ku
Seoul 136-701

Korean Society of Pharmacology
Yonsei University
Department of Pharmacology
Seoul 120-752

Origin International Patent and Law Firm
SL, Kangnam
PO Box 1584
Seoul 135-615

World League for Freedom and Democracy
CPO Box 7173
Seoul

Wonjon Intellectual Property Law Firm
8th Floor
Poonglim Building 823-1
Yeoksam-dong
Kangnam-ku
Seoul 135-784

Y.S. Chang and Associates
K. P. O Box 136
Seoul 110

MALAYSIA

All Women's Action Society
11 Jalan Bukit
Mentri Selatan 7/2
46050 Petaling Jaya
Selangor

Asean Valuers' Association
c/o Institution of Surveyors Malaysia
Bangunan Juruukur, 3rd Floor
64-66 Jalan 52/4
Petaling Jaya
46200 Selangor

Asia-Pacific Broadcasting Union
PO Box 1164
59700 Kuala Lumpur

Asia-Pacific Institute for Broadcasting Development
PO Box 1137
Jalan Pantai Baru
597 Kuala Lumpur

Asia-Pacific People's Environment Network
c/o Sahabat Alam Malaysia
49 Salween Road
10050 Penang

Association of Consulting Engineers Malaysia
63-2 and 65-2 Medan Setia 1
Damansara Heights
50490 Kuala Lumpur

Confederation of Asian and Pacific Accountants
c/o Malaysian Institute of Accountants
Dewan Akautan No 2
Jalan Tun Sambanthan 3
Brickfields
50470 Kuala Lumpur

Federation of Malaysian Manufacturers
17th Floor
Wisma Sime Derby
Jalan Raja Laut
50359 Kuala Lumpur

Federation of National Writers' Associations of Malaysia
PO Box 540
46760 Petaling Jaya

Geological Society of Malaysia
c/o US Department of Geology
University of Malaysia
59100 Kuala Lumpur

Institute of Cultural Affairs - Malaysia
Lorong Awan
Taman Yari
58200 Kuala Lumpur

Institution of Engineers Malaysia
Lots 60 and 62
Jalan 52/4
Peti Surat 223
Jalan Sultan
46720 Petaling Jaya

International Council for the Education of People with Visual Impairment
37 Jesselton Crescent
10450 Penang

Malaysian Association of Certified Public Accounts
No 15 Jalan Medan Tuanku
50300 Kuala Lumpur

Malaysian Book Publishers' Association
10 Jalan 217
46050 Petaling Jaya

Malaysia International Chamber of Commerce and Industry
10th Floor, Wisma Damansara
Jalan Semantan
50490 Kuala Lumpur

Malaysian National Committee of the International Association on Water Pollution Research and Control
c/o ENSEARCH
38A Jalan SS 21/58
Damansara Utama
Petaling Jaya
47400 Selangor

Malaysian Paediatric Association
PO Box 10153
59100 Kuala Lumpur

Malaysian Society of Radiographers
General Hospital
Department of Radiology
50586 Jalan Pahang
Kuala Lumpur

Malaysian Trade Union Congress
112 Jalan Gasing
46000 Petaling Jaya

National Union of the Teaching Profession
13B Jalan Murai Dua
Complex Batu
51100 Kuala Lumpur

Northern Malaya Rubber Millers' and Packers'
Association
3rd Floor, Rooms 301-303
No 22 Lebuh Pitt
10200 Penang

Nutrition Society of Malaysia
Division of Human Nutrition
Institute for Medical Research
Jalan Pahang
50588 Kuala Lumpur

Sahabat Alam Malaysia (Friends of the Earth)
27 Lorong Maktab
10250 Penang

MONGOLIA

Institute of Geology and Mineral Resources
PO Box 118
Peace Avenue 63
Ulaanbaatar 210351

MYANMAR (BURMA)

Myanma Oil and Gas Enterprise
No.74-80 Minye Kyaw Zwa Rd
Lanmadaw Township
Yangon

NEPAL

WEAN
PO Box 129
Lalitpur

NEW ZEALAND

Australasian Performing Right Association
92 Parnell Road
PO Box 6315
Auckland

Craft Aotearoa
32 Butley Dr
Pakuranga

Girl's Brigade
PO Box 68547
Newton
Auckland

Labour Women's Council
PO Box 784
Wellington

League of Mothers and Homemakers New
Zealand
Kern Road
RD 3 Drury
Auckland

New Zealand Airwomen's Association
118B Wairau Road
Oakura
Taranaki

New Zealand Association of Women in Aviation
17B Wiremu Street
Christchurch 8005

New Zealand Geographical Society Inc.
Department of Geography
University of Canterbury
Private Bag
Christchurch

New Zealand Heavy Engineering Research
Association
HERA House
Gladding Place
PO Box 76134
Manukau City

New Zealand Journalists and Graphic Process
Union
Central Chambers, 3 Eva Street
PO Box 6545
Wellington 1

New Zealand Pain Society
4 Hollyhock Place
Browns Bay
Auckland

New Zealand Playcentre Federation
236 The Parade
Island Bay
Wellington

New Zealand Psychological Society
PO Box 4092
Wellington

New Zealand Society of Accountants
Willbank House
57 Willis Street
PO Box 11342
Wellington

New Zealand UFO Studies Centre
168 Brooklands Road
New Plymouth

New Zealand Veterinary Association
PO Box 27499
Wellington

New Zealand Women's Studies Association
PO Box 5067
Wellington

Pan Pacific South-East Asia Womens Association
CF-8 Hutchison Cres
Wanganui

Perinatal Society of New Zealand
Department of Obstetrics and Gynaecology
Wellington Hospital
Wellington

Queen Elizabeth II Arts Council of New Zealand
PO Box 3806
Wellington

Society for Research on Women in New Zealand
PO Box 13-078
Johnsonvillle
Wellington

University Business Directories
360 Dominion Road
Mount Eden
Auckland 3

Women's Golf Victoria Inc
PO Box 608
Elsternwick
Victoria 3185

Women's Soccer Association N.Z. Inc
PO Box 2606
Christchurch
New Zealand

PAKISTAN

Rural Development Foundation
RDF Centre (I&T) Mauve Area
G-9/1
PO Box 1170
Islamabad

PERU

Latin American Civil Aviation Organization
Apartado 4127
Lima 100

PHILIPPINES

Asean Federation of Cement Manufacturers (AFCM)
Philippine Cement Center Building
No 4 EDSA Cor Connecticut Street
Greenshills
San Juan
Metro Manila

Asian Women's Human Rights Council
PO Box 190
1099 Manila

Asian Women's Research and Action Network
PO Box 208
Davao City 9501

Care Philippines
PO Box 2052
Manila

Filipino Inventors' Society
Hall 5 CITEM
Roxas Boulevard
Corner Puyat Avenue
Pasay 1300

Malacological Society of the Philippines
c/o Natural Sciences Research Institute
University of the Philippines
Diliman
Quezon City 1101

Maternal and Child Health Association of the Philippines
NFP Building
107 E Rodriguez Senior Boulevard
Quezon
Metro Manila 1102

National Academy of Science and Technology
Mezzanine Floor, TAPI Building
DOST Compound
Bicutan, Tagig
Metro Manila

National Research Council of the Philippines
Patrocinio Valenzuela Hall
General Santos Avenue
Bicutan, Tagig
Metro Manila

Nutrition Foundation of the Philippines
107 E Rodriquez Senior Boulevard
Quezon City

Philippine Convention and Visitors Corporation
Legaspi Towers 300
Units 5 7 10-17, 4th Floor
Roxas Boulevard
Manila

Philippine Educational Publishers' Association
Phoenix Publishing House
937 Quezon Avenue
Quezon City
Metro Manila

Philippine Science and Mathematics Council
De La Salle University, LS 135
PO Box 3819
Manila

Women for Women Foundation
Development Academy of the Philippines
Building, Lower 2nd Floor
San Miguel Avenue
Paisg
Metro Manila

Women Lawyers' Association of the Philippines
4 New Jersey
New Manila
Quezon City
Metro Manila

World Trade Center
Solid Bank Building, 15th Floor
Paseo de Roxas Street
Makati
Metro Manila

SINGAPORE

Asean Bankers' Association
180 Cecil Street, 17-00
Singapore 0106

Asian Mass Communication Research and Information Centre
39 Newton Road
Singapore 1130

Asia-Pacific Academy of Ophthalmology
Mount Elizabeth Medical Centre
3 Mount Elizabeth, 06-05108
Singapore 0922

Association of Women for Action and Research
PO Box 244
Tanglin 9124

Dermatological Society of Singapore
1 Mandalay Road
Singapore 308205

Environmental Engineering Society of Singapore
Department of Civil Engineering
National University of Singapore
Kent Ridge
Singapore 119260

International Business Women's Association
PO Box 23, Orchard Point Post Office
Singapore 9123

Library Association of Singapore
c/o National Library
Stamford Road
Singapore 0617

Musicians' and Singers' Association Of Singapore
c/o SMMWU, No 3-6-28 Rochore Centre
1 Rochore Road
Singapore 0718

National Book Development Council of Singapore
c/o Bukit Merah Branch Library
Bukit Merah Central
Singapore 0315

Pharmaceutical Society of Singapore
Alumni Medical Centre
2 College Road
Singapore 0316

Singapore Association of Women Lawyers
14 Robinson Road
No 09-02 Far East Finance Building
Singapore 0104

Singapore Book Publishers' Association
Chopmen Publishers
865 Mountbatten Road, 05-28/29
Katong Shopping Centre
Singapore 1543

Singapore Computer Society
131 C/D Tanglin Road
Tudor Court
Singapore 247924

Singapore Indian Chamber of Commerce
101 Cecil Street
No 23-01 Tong Eng Building 0106
Singapore 0106

Singapore Industrial Automation Association
151 Chin Swee Road
03-13 Manhattan House
Singapore 0316

Singapore Manufacturers' Association
SMA House
20 Orchard Road
Singapore 0923

Singapore Merchant Bankers' Association
24 Raffles Place
No 16-02 Clifford Centre
Singapore 0104

Singapore National Employers' Federation
19 Tanglin Road
10-01/04 Tanglin Shopping Centre
Singapore 1024

Singapore Paediatric Society
Alumni Medical Centre
2 College Road
Singapore 0316

South East Asian Computer Confederation
c/o Singapore Arts Centre Company Ltd.
2 Raffles Link
No 01-04 Marina Bayfront
Singapore 0103

Susan Wakeford Literary Agency
11 Malcom Road
Singapore 308254

SRI LANKA

All- Ceylon Union of Government English Teachers
Acuget Secretariat
No. 6/4 Ananda Mawatha
Beddegana
Kotte

Buddist Publication Society
PO Box 61
54 Sangharaja Mawatha
Kandy
Sri Lanka

Ceylon Tourist Board
78 Steuart Place
PO Box 1504
Colombo 3

Sri Lanka Importers, Exporters and Manufacturers Association
PO Box 12
Colombo

Samasevaya-Peace Through Development
Anuradhapura Road
Talawa
N. C. P 50280

TAIWAN

American Chamber of Commerce in Taipei
PO Box 17-277
Taipei 104

Asia Ecology Society
Biology Department
Tanghai University
Box 843
Taichung 400

Asia-Pacific Council of American Chamber of Commerce
PO Box 22048
Taipei 10099

Chinese Association for Human Rights
102 Kuang Fu South Road, 8th Floor
Taipei 10553

Chinese Taipei Pediatric Association
11 Ching-Tao West Road 4?-4
Taipei 10022

Confederation of Asian-Pacific Chamber of Commerce and Industry
122 Tunhua North Road, 10 F
Taipei 105

National Federation of Certified Public Accountants Associations of the Republic of China
1 Nanhei Road, 9th Floor
Taipei
Taiwan

THAILAND

American Chamber of Commerce in Thailand
7/F Kian Gwan Building 1
140 Wireless Road
Bangkok 10330

Asean Federation of Accountants (AFA)
c/o Institute of Certified Accountants and Auditors of Thailand
ITF - Silom Palace Building
160/31-3 9th Floor
Bangrug
Bangkok 10500

Asia-Pacific Telecommmunity
12/49 Chaegwattana Road
Bangkhen
Bangkok 10210

Asian Institute of Technology
PO Box 2754
Bangkok 10501

Business and Professional Women's Association of Thailand
Phrakaruna Nivas Building
6/2 Pichai Road
Dusit
Bangkok 10300

Care Thailand
GPO Box 19
Bangkok 10501

Dental Association of Thailand
7I SOI Prangthip
Lardprao 95
Bangkapi
Bangkok 10310

Federation of Thai Industries
Queen Sirikit National Convention Center
Zone C, 4th Floor
60 New Ratchadapisek Road
Klongtoey
Bangkok 10110

Lawyers' Association of Thailand
5th Mansion
26 Rajdamnoen Avenue
Bangkok 10200

Medical Association of Thailand
105/4 Soi Theveevorayart
Luang Road
Bangkok 10100

Press Association of Thailand
299 Rajchasima Road
Bangkok 10300

Public Relations Society of Thailand
117/10 Sukhothi Road
Bangkok 10300

Rice Exporters' Association of Thailand
37 Soi Ngamdupli
Thanon Phra Ram IV
Bangkok 10120

Seameo Regional Centre for Archaeology and Fine Arts
SPAFA Headquarters Building
81/1 Si-Ayutthaya Road
Sam-sen
Theves
Bangkok 30300

South East Asia Geotechnical Society
Asian Institute of Technology
PO Box 2754
Bangkok 10501

Southeast Asian Ministers of Education Organization
Darakarn Building
920 Sukhumvit Road
Bangkok 10110

Sports Writers' Association of Thailand
National Stadium
Rama 1 Road
Pathumwan
Bangkok 10330

Thai Astronomical Society
928 Sukhumvit Road
Bangkok 10110

Thai Bankers' Association
Sathorn Thani Building
14th Floor
90 North Sathorn Road
Bangrak
Bangkok 10500

Thai Chamber of Commerce
150 Rajabopit Road
Bangkok 10200

Thai Rubber Traders' Association
57 Thanon Rongmuang
Pathumwan Bangkok 10500

Tourism Authority of Thailand
372 Thanon Bamrung Muang
Bangkok 10100

Tourist Association of Northern Thailand
Old Chiang Mai Cultural Centre
185/3 Thanon Wualai
Chiang Mai 50000

Women Lawyers' Association of Thailand
6 Sukhothai Road
Dusit
Bangkok 10300

TURKEY

South West Anatolia Forest Research Institute
PK 264 07002
Antalya

VANATU

CUSO
PO Box 158
Port Vila

Foundation for the Peoples of the South Pacific
PO Box 951
Port Vila

APPENDIX B
CHAMBERS OF COMMERCE AND INDUSTRY

AFGHANISTAN
Afgan Chamber of Commerce and Industry
Mohd Jan Khan Wat
Kabul

AUSTRALIA
Australian Chamber of Commerce and Industry
POB E14
Queen Victoria Terrace
Canberra
ACT 2600

Australian Indonesian Chamber of Commerce
PO Box 96
North Sydney
NSW 2059

BAHRAIN
Bahrain Chamber of Commerce and Industry
PO Box 248
Manama

BANGLADESH
Federation of Bangladesh Chambers of Commerce and Industry
Federation Bhaban
60 Motijheel C/A
4th Floor
POB 2079
Dhaka 1000

BHUTAN
Bhutan Chamber of Commerce
POB 147
Thimphu

BRUNEI
Brunei Darussalam International Chamber of Commerce and Industry
POB 2246
Bandar Seri Begawan 1922

Brunei Bumputra Chamber of Commerce and Industry
PO Box 203
Gadong Post Office
Bandar Seri Degawan 3102

CAMBODIA
Cambodian Chamber of Commerce
Phnom Penh

CHILE
AmCham Chile
Americo Vespucio Sur 80
Piso 90
Las Condes

CHINA
All-China Federation of Industry and Commerce
93 Beiheyan Dajie
Beijing 100006

China Electronics Chamber of Commerce
49 Fuxing Road
Beijing 100036

COOK ISLANDS
Cook Islands Chamber of Commerce and Industry
POB 242, Rarotonga

COSTA RICA
Camara de Industyries de Costa Rica
Apdo 10003-1000
San Jose

FIJI
Suva Chamber of Commerce
29 Acland St
Vatuwara
POB 337
Suva

FRENCH POLYNESIA
Chambre de Commerce Polynésie d'Industrie, des Services et des Métiers de Française
BP 118, Paptee

GUAM
Guam Chamber of Commerce
Suite 102
Ada Plaza Center
173 Aspinall Ave
POB 283
Agaña GU 96910

HONG KONG
Hong Kong General Chamber of Commerce
United Centre
22nd Floor
95 Queensway
Hong Kong

INDIA
Associated Chambers of Commerce and Industry of India
2nd Floor Allahabad Bank Bldg
17 Parliament St
New Delhi 110 001

The Council of the EU Chambers of Commerce in India
Y.B. Chavan Centre 3rd Floor
Gen. J. Bhosale Marg
Mumbai 400 021

Indian Chamber of Commerce
India Exchange 4
India Exchange Place
Calcutta 700001

INDONESIA

Kamar Dagang dan Industri Indonesia
Chandra Bldg 3rd-5th Floor
Jalan M. H. Thamrin 20
Jakarta

IRAN

The Joint Chambers of Commerce of Iran
4th Floor Suite 404
254 Taleghani Ave
Tehran 15814

IRAQ

Federation of Iraqui Chambers of Commerce
PO Box 11348
Mustansir St
Baghdad

ISRAEL

Chamber of Commerce and Industry of Haifa and the North
Haifa

JAPAN

The Japan Chamber of Commerce and Industry
3-2-2 Marunouchi
Chiyoda-ku
Tokyo 100

Japan Chamber of Commerce and Industry, Sydney Inc.
7th Floor, 83 Clarence Street
Sydney
NSW 2000

JORDAN

Federation of Jordanian Chambers of Commerce
PO Box 7029
Amman 11118

KAZAKHSTAN

Chamber of Commerce and Industry
480091
Kazakhstan
Almatz
Mananchi 26

KIRIBATI

Kiribati Chamber of Commerce
POB 550
Betio
Tarawa

KOREA REP OF (SOUTH)

Korea Chamber of Commerce and Industry
45 4-ka Namdaemun-no
Chung-ku CPOB 25
Seoul 100-743

KOREA DPR (NORTH)

Committee for the Promotion of International Trade
Pyongyang City

KUWAIT

Kuwait Chamber of Commerce and Industry
Chambers Building
PO Box 775
Safat

KYRGYZSTAN

Kyrgyzstan Chamber of Commerce and Industry
Abdumamunowa St 205
720080 Bishkee

LAOS

Lao National Chamber of Commerce and Industry
rue Phonsay
BP 4596
Vientiane

LEBANON

Chamber of Commerce and Industry
Beirut

MACAU

Associação Comercial de Macau
Rua de Xangai 175
Edif. ACM, 5/F

MALAYSIA

Associated Chinese Chambers of Commerce and Industry of Malaysia
Office Tower Plaza Berjaya (Kompleks Nagaria)
8th Floor 12 Jalan Imbi 55100
Kuala Lumper

MALDIVES / MICRONESIA

Maldives National Chamber of Commerce and Industry
G Viyafaari Hiyaa
Ameenee Magu
POB 92
Malé 20-04

MARSHALL ISLANDS

Majuro Chamber of Commerce
Majuro
MH 96960

MONGOLIA

Mongolian Chamber of Commerce and Industry
Huv'sgalchdyn Gudamj 11
Ulan Bator 38

MYANMAR (BURMA)

Chamber of Commerce and Industry
Ruby House
74-86 Bo Sun Pat St
Yangon 11141

NEPAL

Federation of Nepalese Chambers of Commerce and Industry
Shahid Shukra Milan Marg
Teku POB 269
Kathmandu

NEW CALEDONIA

Chambre de Commerce and d' Industrie
BP M3 98849
Nouméa Cédex

NEW ZEALAND

New Zealand Chambers of Commerce and Industry
POB 11-043
Wellington

NORFOLK ISLAND

Norfolk Island Chamber of Commerce
POB 370
Norfolk Island 2899

NORTHERN MARIANA ISLANDS

Saipan Chamber of Commerce
Chanlan Kanoa
POB 806
Saipan MP 96950

OMAN

Oman Chamber of Commerce and Industry
Ruwi

PAKISTAN

The Federation of Pakistan Chambers of Commerce and Industry
St 28 Block 5
Sharea Firdousi Main Clifton
Karachi 75600

PANAMA

Panamanian Chamber of Commerce and Industry
Apartado 74
Panama 1

PAPUA NEW GUINEA

Papua New Guinea Chamber of Commerce and Industry
POB 1621
Port Moresby

PHILIPPINES

Federation of Filipino- Chinese Chambers of Commerce and Industry Inc,
Federation Center,
6th Floor Muelle de Binondo St
POB 23
Metro Manila

QATAR

Qatar Chamber of Commerce and Industry
PO Box 402
Doha

SAMOA (AMERICAN)

Department of Commerce
Goverment of American Samoa
Pago Pago
AS 96799

SAMOA (FORMERLY WESTERN SAMOA)

Chamber of Commerce and Industry
C/O Pacific Forum Line
Matautu-tai
POB 655
Apia

SAUDI ARABIA

Abu Dhabi Chamber of Commerce and Industry
Abu Dhabi
PO Box 662

SINGAPORE

Singapore Federation of Chambers of Commerce and Industry
47 Hill St
03-01 Chinese Chamber of Commerce Bldg
Singapore 179365

Singapore Indian Chamber of Commerce
101 Cecil Street
No 23-01 Tong Eng Building 0106
Singapore 0106

SOLOMON ISLANDS

Soloman Islands Chamber of Commerce
POB 64
Honiara

SRI LANKA

Federation of Chambers of Commerce and Industry of Sri Lanka
29 Gregory's Rd
Colombo 7

SYRIA

Federation of Syrian Chamber of Commerce
PO Box 5909
Damascus

TAIWAN

General Chamber of Commerce of the Republic of China
6th Floor 390 Fu Hsing South Rd
Sec. 1, Taipei

Asia-Pacific Council of American Chamber of Commerce
PO Box 22048
Taipei 10099

THAILAND

Thai Chamber of Commerce
150 Thanon Rajbopit
Bangkok 10200

TONGA

Tongan Chamber of Commerce and Industry
Muka Alofa

TURKEY

Turkish Chamber of Commerce and Industry
Ataturk Cad. No. 126
Pasaport/ Yzmir

TUVALU
Tuvalu Chamber of Commerce
POB 17
Funafuti

UNITED ARAB EMIRATES
Federation of U.A.E Chambers of Commerce and Industry
PO Box 3014
Abu Dhabi
UAE

VANUATU
Vanatu Chamber of Commerce
POB 189,
Port Vila

VIETNAM
Chamber of Commerce and Industry of Vietnam (VCCI)
9 Dao Duy Anh Str
Hanoi
Vietnam

YEMEN
Sana'a Chamber of Commerce and Industry
Sana'a

APPENDIX C
CAPITAL CITIES AND CURRENCIES

AFGHANISTAN

Kabul
Afghani (Af) of 100 Puls

AUSTRALIA

Canberra
Australian Dollar ($A) of 100 Cents

BAHRAIN

Manama
Bahrain Dinar (BD) of 1000 Fils

BANGALDESH

Dhaka
Taka (Tk) of 100 poisha

BHUTAN

Thimphu
Ngultrum of 100 chetrum (Indian currency is also legal tender)

BRUNEI

Bandar Seri Begawan
Brunei dollar (B$) of 100 sen

CAMBODIA

Phnom Pehn
Riel of 100 sen

CHILE

Santiago
Chilean peso of 100 centavos

CHINA

Beijing (Peking)
Renminbi Yuan of 10 jiao or 100 fen

COLOMBIA

Bogotá
Colombian peso of 100 centavos

COOK ISLANDS

Avarua
New Zealand dollar (NZ$) of 100 cents

COSTA RICA

San José
Costa Rican colón (¢)of 100 céntimos

ECUADOR

Quito
Sucre of 100 centavos

EL SALVADOR

San Salvador
El Salvador colón (¢) of 100 centavos

FIJI

Suva
Fiji Dollar($) of 100 cents

FRENCH POLYNESIA

Papeete
CFP franc (CFPT) of 100 centimes

GUAM

Agaña
USA currency

GUATEMALA

Guatemala City
Quetzal (Q) of 100 centavos

HONG KONG

Victoria
Hong Kong dollar (HK$) dollar of 100 cents

INDIA

New Delhi
Indian rupee (Rs) of 100 paisa

INDONESIA

Jakarta
Rupiah (Rp) of 100 sen

IRAN

Tehran
Rial

IRAQ

Baghdad
Iraqui dinar (ID) of 1000 fils

ISRAEL

Jerusalem (Although the UN and International law considers Tel-Aviv as Israel's capital)
Shekel of 100 agora

JAPAN

Tokyo
Yen of 100 sen

JORDAN

Amman
Jordanian dinar (JD) of 1000 fils

KAZAKHSTAN

Alma-Ata (Almaty)
Tenge

KIRIBATI

Tarawa
Australian dollar ($A) of 100 cents

KOREA REP OF (SOUTH)

Seoul
Won of 100 jeon

KOREA DPR (NORTH)

Pyongyang
Won of 100 chon

KUWAIT

Kuwait City
Kuwaiti dinar (KD) of 1000 fils

KYRGYSTAN

Bishkek
Som

LAOS

Vientiane
Kip (K) of 100 at

LEBANON

Beirut
Lebanese pound (L£)

MACAU

Macau
Pataca (P) of 100 avos

MALAYSIA

Kuala Lumpur
Malaysian dollar (ringgit) (M$) of 100 sen

MALDIVES

Malé
Rufiyaa of 100 laaris

MARSHALL ISLANDS

Dalap-Uliga-Darrit
USA currency

MEXICO

Mexico City
Peso of 100 centavos

MICRONESIA (FEDERATED STATES OF)

Palikir, on Pohnpei
USA currency

MONGOLIA

Ulan Bator
Tugrik of 100 möngö

MYANMAR (BURMA)

Yangon (Ragoon)
Kyat (K) of 100 pyas

NAURU

Nauru
Australian dollar ($A) of 100 cents

NEPAL

Kathmandu
Nepalese rupee of 100 paisa

NEW ZEALAND

Wellington
New Zealand dollar (NZ$) of 100 cents

NEW CALEDONIA

Nouméa
CFP franc (CFPF) of 100 centimes

NICARAGUA

Managua
Córdoba (C$) of 100 centavos

NIUE

Alofi
New Zealand dollar (NZ$) of 100 cents

NORFOLK ISLAND

Kingston is the administration centre and Burnt Pine is the commercial centre
Australian dollar (A$) of 100 cents

NORTHERN MARIANA ISLANDS

Saipan (Seat of Government)
USA currency

OMAN

Muscat
Rial Omani (OR) of 1000 baiza

PAKISTAN

Islamabad
Pakistan rupee of 100 paisa

PALAU

Koror
USA currency

PANAMA

Panama City
Balboa of 100 centésimos

PAPUA NEW GUINEA

Port Moresby
Kina (K) of 100 toea

PERU

Lima
New Sol of 100 cénts

PHILIPPINES

Manila
Philippine peso (P) of 100 centavos

PITCAIRN ISLANDS

Adamstown
Pitcairn dollar of 100 cents

QATAR

Doha
Qatar riyal of 100 dirhams

SAMOA, AMERICA

Pago Pago
USA currency

SAMOA, (FORMERLY WESTERN SAMOA)

Apia
Western Samoan dollar - tala (WS$) of 100 cents (sene)

SAUDI ARABIA

Riyadh
Saudi riyal (SR) of 20 qursh or 100 halala

SINGAPORE

Singapore
Singapore dollar (S$) of 100 cents

SOLOMAN ISLANDS

Honiara
Soloman Islands dollar (SI$) of 100 cents

SRI LANKA

Sri Jayawardenapura (Columbo is the commercial capital)
Sri Lankan rupee of 100 cents

SYRIA

Damascus
Syrian Pound (S$) of 100 piastres

TAIWAN

Taipei
New Taiwan dollar (NT$) of 100 cents

TAJIKSTAN

Dushanbe
Tajik rouble (TJR) of 100 tanga

THAILAND

Bangkok
Baht of 100 satang

TOKELAU

No national capital as each atoll has its own administration centre
New Zealand dollar (NZ$) of 100 cents

TONGA

Nuku'alofa
Pa'anga (T$) of 100 seniti

TURKEY

Ankara
Turkish lira (TL) of 100 kurus

TURKMENISTAN

Ashkhabad
Manat

TUVALU

Funafuti
Australian dollar ($A) and Tuvalu dollar and cents

UNITED ARAB EMIRATES

Abu Dhabi
UAE dirham of 100 fils

UZBEKISTAN

Tashkent
Sum (Som) of 100 tiyin

VANATU

Port Vila
Vatu of 100 centimes

VIETNAM

Hanoi
Dông of 10 hào or 100 xu

WALLIS AND FORTUNA ISLANDS

Mata-Utu
Pacific Franc of 100 centimes

YEMEN

Sana'a
Riyal of 100 fils

APPENDIX D
EMBASSIES AND CONSULATES

AFGHANISTAN

China, People's Republic
Sahah Mahmud Wat, Shar-i-Nau, Kabul
India
Malalai Wat, Shar-i-Nau, Kabul
Iraq
POB 523,Wazir Akbar Khan Mena, Kabul
Japan
POB 80, Wazir Akbar Khan Mena, Kabul
Korea, Democratic People's Republic
Wazir Akbar Khan Mena, House 28, Sarak 'H' House 103, Kabul
Mongolia
Wazir Akbar Khan Mena, Sarak 'T' House 8714, Kabul
Turkey
Shar-i-Nau, Kabul
Vietnam
3 Nijat St, Wazir Akbar Khan Mena, Kabul

AUSTRALIA

Bangladesh
POB5 Red Hill, ACT 2603
Brunei
16 Bulwarra Close O'Malley, ACT 2606
Cambodia
5 Cantebury Cres, Deakin, ACT 2600
Chile
POB 69, Monaro Cres, ACT 2603
China People's Republic
15 Coronation Drive, Yarralumla, ACT 2600
Colombia
GPOB 2892, Canberra, ACT 2601
Fiji
POB 159, Queen Victoria Terrace, ACT 2600
India
3-5 Moonah Place, Yarralumla, ACT 2600
Indonesia
8 Darwin Ave, Yarralumla, ACT 2600
Iran
POB 3219, Manuka, ACT 2603
Iraq
48 Culgoa Circuit, O'Malley, ACT 2606
Israel
6 Turrana St, Yarralumla, ACT 2600
Japan
112 Empire Circuit, Yarralumla, ACT 2600
Jordan
20 Roebuck St, Red Hill, ACT 2603
Korea Republic
113 Empire Circuit, Yarralumula, ACT 2600
Laos
1 Dalman Cres, O'Malley, ACT 2606
Lebanon
27 Endeavour St, Red Hill, ACT 2603
Malaysia
7 Perth Ave, Yarralumla, ACT 2600
Mexico
14 Perth Ave, Yarralumla, ACT 2600
Myanmar
22 Arkana St, Yarralumla, ACT 2600
New Zealand
Commonwealth Ave, Canberra, ACT 2600
Pakistan
POB 684, Mawson, ACT 2607

Papua New Guinea
POB E432, Queen Victoria Terrace, Parkes, ACT 2600
Peru
POB 106, Red Hill, ACT 2606
Philippines
POB 3297, Manuka, ACT 2603
Samoa
POB 3274, Manuka, ACT 2603
Saudi Arabia
POB 63, Garran ACT 2605
Singapore
17 Forster Cresent, Yarralumla, ACT 2600
Soloman Islands
Unit 4, JAA House, 19 Napier Close, Deakin, ACT 2600
Sri Lanka
35 Empire Circuit, Forrest, ACT 2603
Thailand
111 Empire Circuit, Yarralumla, ACT 2600
Turkey
60 Mugga Way, Red Hill, ACT 2603
Vietnam
6 Timbarra Cresent, O'Malley, ACT 2606

BANGLADESH

Afganistan
House CWN(C)-2a Gulshan Ave, Gilshan Model Town, Dhaka 12
Australia
184 Gulshan Ave, Gulshan Model Town, Dhaka 12
Bhutan
House No. F5 (SE), Gulshan Ave, Dhaka 1221
China, People's Republic
Plot NE (L) 6, Rd 83, Gulshan Model Town, Dhaka 12
India
House 120, Rd 2, Dhanmandi R/A, Dhaka 1205
Indonesia
75 Gulshan Ave, Gulshan Model Town, Dhaka 1212
Iran
CWN(A)-12 Kamal Ataturk Ave, Gulshan Model Town, Dhaka 12
Iraq
112 Gulshan Ave, Gulshan Model Town, Dhaka 12
Japan
5&6, Dutabash Rd, Baridhara, Dhaka
Korea, Democratic People's Republic
House 6, Rd 7, Baridhara Model Town, Dhaka
Korea, Republic
House NW(E)17, Rd 55, Gulshan Model Town, Dhaka 12
Kuwait
Plot 39, Rd 23, Block J, Banani, Dhaka 13
Malaysia
House 4, Rd 118, Gulshan Model Town, Dhaka 1212
Myanmar
89 (B), Rd 4, Banani, Dhaka
Nepal
United Nations Rd 2, Baridhara Model Town, Dhaka
Pakistan
House NEC-2, Rd 71, Gulshan Model Town, Dhaka 12
Philippines
House NE(L) 5, Rd 83, Gulshan Model Town, Dhaka 1212
Qatar
House 23, Rd 108, Gulshan Model Town, Dhaka 12
Saudi Arabia
House 12, Rd 92, Gulshan (North), Dhaka 1212

Sri Lanka
House 15, Rd 50, Gulshan 2, Dhaka
Thailand
House NW (E) 12, Rd 59, Gulshan Model Town, Dhaka
Turkey
House 7, Rd 62, Gulshan Model Town, Dhaka 12
United Arab Emirates
House CEN (H) 41, Rd 113, Gulshan Model Town, Dhaka 1212

BHUTAN

Bangladesh
POB 178, Upper Choubachu, Thimpu
India
India House, Lungtenzampa, Thimpu

BRUNEI

Australia
Teck Guan Plaza, 4th Floor, Jalan Sultan, Bandar Seri Begawan 2085
China, People's Republic
Lot 23966, Simpang 612, Kampong Salambigar, Jalan Muara, Bandar Seri Begawan 3895
India
Lot 14034, Simpang 337, Kampong Manggis, Jalan Muara, Bandar Seri Begawan
Indonesia
Jalan Sungai Hanching Baru, simpang 528, off Jalan Muara, Bandar seri Begawan 3890
Iran
Bandar Seri Begawan
Japan
1-3 Jalan Jawatan Dalam, Kampong Mabohai, Bandar Seri Begawan 2092
Korea, Republic
No.9, Lot 21652, Kampong Beribi, Jalan Gadong, Bander Seri Begawan 3188
Malaysia
473 Kampong Pelambayan, Jalan Kota Batu, Bandar Seri Begawan 2282
Oman
35, Simpang 100, Kampong Pengkalan, Jalan Tungku Link, Gadong, Bandar Seri Begawan
Pakistan
No.5, Simpang 396/128, Kampong Sungai Akar, Jalan Kebangsaan, Bandar Seri Begawan 3026
Philippines
Badiah Bldg, 4th-5th floors, Mile 1, Jalan Tutong, Bandar Seri Begawan 1930
Singapore
RBA Plaza 5th Floor, Jalan Sultan, Bandar Seri Begawan 2085
Thailand
No.13, Simpang 29, Jalan Elia Fatimah, Kampong Kiarong, Bandar Seri Begawan
Vietnam
Lot 13489, Jlan Manggis Dua, off Jalan Muara, Bandar Seri Begawan

CAMBODIA

Australia
Villa 11, rue 254, Chartaumuk, Daun Penh, Phnom-Penh
China People's Republic
256 blvd Mao Tse Toung, Phnom-Penh
India
Villa 777, blvd Monivong, Phnom-Penh
Indonesia
179 rue 51, Phnom-Penh
Japan
75 blvd Noordom, Phnom-Penh
Korea, Democratic People's Republic
39 rue 268, Phnom-Penh

Laos
15-17 blvd Mao Tse Toung, Phnom-Penh
Malaysia
Villa 161, rue 51, Beng Rang Precinct, Daun Penh, Phnom-Penh
Philippines
33 rue 294, Phnom-Penh
Singapore
313 blvd Sisowath, Phnom-Penh
Thailand
4 blvd Monivong, Sangkat Srass Chork, Khan Daun Penh, Phnom-Penh
Vietnam
436 blvd Monivong, Phnom-Penh

CHINA

Afganistan
8 Dong Zhi Men Wai Dajie, Chao Yang Qu, Beijing
Australia
21 Dong Zhi Men Wai Dajie, San Li Tun, Beijing 100600
Bahrain
2-9-1 Tayuan Diplomatic Office Bldg, Beijing 100600
Bangladesh
42 Guang Hua Lu, Beijing
Cambodia
9 Dong Zhi Men Wai Dajie, Beijing 100600
Colombia
34 Guang Hua Lu, Beijing 100600
Ecuador
2-41 San Li Tun, Beijing
India
1 Ri Tan Dong Lu, Beijing
Indonesia
San Li Tun, Diplomatic Office, Bldg B, Beijing 100004
Iran
Dong Liu Ji, San Li Tun, Beijing
Iraq
3 Ri Tan Dong Lu, Chao Yang Qu, Beijing
Israel
1 Jian Guo Men Wai Dajie, Beijing 100004
Japan
7 Ri Tan Lu, Jian Guo Men Wai, Beijing 100600
Jordan
5 Dong Liu Jie, San Li Tun, Beijing 100600
Kazakhstan
9 Dong 6 Jie, San Li Tun, Beijing 100600
Korea, Democratic People's Republic
Ri Tan Bei Lu, Jian Guo Men Wai, Beijing
Korea, Republic
3rd-4th Floor, China World Trade Centre, 1 Jian Guo Men Wai Dajie, Beijing
Kuwait
23 Guang Hua Lu, Beijing 100600
Kyrgyzstan
2-4-1 Tayuan Office Bldg, Beijing
Laos
11 Dong Si Jie, San Li Tun, Chao Yang Qu, Beijing 100600
Lebanon
51 Dong Liu Jie, san Li Tun, Beijing
Malaysia
13 Dong Zhi Men Wai Dajie, San Li Tun, Beijing
Marshall Islands
2-14-1 Tayuan Diplomatic Bldg, Beijing 100600
Mexico
5 Dong Wu Jie, San Li Tun, Beijing 100600
Mongolia
2 Xiu Shui Bei Jie, Jian Guo Men Wai, Beijing
Myanmar
6 Dong Zhi Men Wai Dajie, Chao Yang Qu, Beijing

Nepal
1 Xi Liu, San Li Tun Lu, Beijing
New Zealand
1 Ri Tan, Dong Er Jie, Chao Yang Qu, Beijing 100600
Oman
6 Liang Ma He Nan Lu, San Li Tun, Beijing
Pakistan
1 Dong Zhi Men Wai Dajie, Beijing 100600
Peru
2-82 San Li Tun, Bangonglou, Beijing 100600
Philippines
23 Xiu Shui Bei Jie, Jian Guo, Men Wai, Beijing
Qatar
2-9-2 Tayuan Diplomatic Office Bldg, 14 Liang Ma He Nan Lu,
Beijing 100600
Saudi Arabia
1 Beixiaojie, san Li Tun, Beijing 100600
Singapore
1 Xiu Shui Bei Jie, Jian Guo Men Wai, Beijing 100600
Sri Lanka
3 Jian Hua Lu, Jian Guo Men Wai, Beijing 100600
Syria
6 Dong Si Jie, SanLi Tun, Beijing 100600
Thailand
40 Guang Hua Lu, Beijing 100600
Turkey
9 Dong Wu Jie, San Li Tun, Beijing 100600
United Arab Emirates
1-9-1 Tayuan Diplomatic Office Bldg, Beijing 100600
Vietnam
32 Guang Hua Lu, Jian Guo Men Wai, Beijing
Yemen
5 Dong San Jie, San Li Tun, Beijing 100600

COSTA RICA

Chile
Los Yoses, Zera Entrada, 300 sur 50 Este, San Jose

FIJI

Australia
37 Princes Rd, POB 214, Suva
China, People's Republic
147 Queen Elizabeth Drive, PMB, Nasese, Suva
Japan
Dominion House, 2nd Floor, POB 13045, Suva
Korea, Republic
Vanua House, 8th Floor, PMB, Suva
Malaysia
Air Pacific House, 5th Floor, POB 356, Suva
Marshall Islands
41 Borron Rd, government Bldgs, POB 2038, Suva
Micronesia, Federated States
37 Loftus St, POB 15493, Suva
New Zealand
Reserve Bank of Fiji Bldg, 10th Floor, Pratt St, POB 1378, Suva
Papua New Guinea
Credit House, Govt Bldgs, POB 2447, Suva
Tuvalu
16 Gorrie St, POB 14449, Suva

HONGKONG

Australia
Consulate General of The Harbour Centre, 21-24 Floors, 25
Harbour Rd, Wanchai
India
Indian consular Office, 26-A United Centre, 95 Queensway

Israel
Rm 701, Amiralty Centre, Tower 2

INDIA

Afghanistan
5/50F Shanti Path, Chanakyapuri, New Delhi 110 021
Australia
1/50-G Shanti Path, Chanakyapuri, New Delhi 110-021
Bangladesh
56 Ring Rd, Lajpat Nagar-111, New Delhi 110 024
Bhutan
Chandragupta Marg, Chanakyapuri, New Delhi 110 021
Cambodia
B-47 Soami Nagar, New Delhi 110 017
Chile
R/7 Hauz Khas, New Delhi 110 016
China, People's Republic
50D Shanti Path, Chanakyapuri, New Delhi 110 021
Colombia
82D Malcha Marg, Chanakyapuri, New Delhi 110 021
Indonesia
50a Chanakyapuri, New Delhi 110 021
Iran
5 Barakhamba Road, New Delhi 110 001
Iraq
169-171 Jor Bagh, New Delhi 110 001
Israel
3 Aurangzeb Road, New Delhi 110 011
Japan
Plots 4-5, 50g Shanti Path, Chanakyapuri, New Delhi 110 021
Jordan
1/21 Shanti Niketan, New Delhi 110 021
Kazakhstan
EP 16-17 Chandragupta Marg, Chanakyapuri, New Delhi 110 021
Korea, Democratic People's Republic
42/44 Sundar Nager, New Delhi 110 003
Korea, Republic
9 Chandragupta Marg, Chanakyapuri, POB 5416, New Delhi 110
021
Kuwait
5a Shanti Path, Chanakyapuri, New Delhi 110 021
Laos
E53 Panchshila Park, New Delhi 110 017
Lebanon
10 Sardar Patel Marg, Chanakyapuri, New Deli 110 021
Malaysia
50m Satya Marg, Chanakyapuri, New Delhi 110 021
Mexico
B-33 Friends Colony (west), New Delhi 110 065
Mongolia
34 Archbishop Makarios Marg, New Delhi 110 003
Myanmar
3/50f Nyaya Marg, Chanakyapuri, New Delhi 110 021
Nepal
Barakhamba Rd, New Delhi 110 001
New Zealand
50n Nyaya Marg, Chanakyapuri, New Delhi
110 021
Oman
16 Olaf Palme Marg, New Delhi 110 057
Pakistan
2/50g Shanti Path, Chanakyapuri, New Delhi
110 021
Peru
D-6/13c, Vasant Vihar, New Delhi 110 057
Philippines
50n Nyaya Marg, Chanakyapuri, New Delhi 110 021

Qatar
G-5 Anand Niketan, New Delhi 110 021
Saudi Arabia
D-12, New Delhi South Extension Part II, New Delhi 110 049
Singapore
E-6 Chandragupta Marg, Chanakyapuri, New Deli 110 021
Sri Lanka
27 Kautilya Marg, Chanakyapuri, New Delhi 110 021
Thailand
56n Nyaya Marg, Chanakyapuri, New Delhi 110 021
Turkey
50n Nyaya Marg, Chanakyapuri, New Delhi 110 021
United Arab Emirates
EP-12 Chandragupt, New Delhi 110 021
Vietnam
17 Kautilya Marg, Chanakyapuri, New Delhi 110 021
Yemen
B-70 Greater Kailash-I, New Delhi 110 048

INDONESIA

Afganistan
Jalan Dr Kusuma Atmaja 15, Jakarta
Australia
Jalen H. R. Rasuna Said, Kav. C15-16, Jakarta 12940
Bangladesh
Jalan Situbondo 12, Menteng, Jakarta Puset
Brunei
Wisma BCA, 8th floor, Jalen Jenderal Sudirman, Kav. 22-23, Jarkarta Selatan 12920
Chile
Bina Mulia Bldg, 7th Floor, Jalen H. R. Rasuna Said, Kav 10, Kuningan, Jarkarta 12950
China, People's Republic
Jalan Jenderal Sudirman 69, Jarkarta
Colombia
Central Plaza Bldg, 16th Floor, Jalan Jenderal Sudirman, Kav. 48, Jakarta
India
Jalan H. R. Rasuna Said, Kav. S/1, Kuningan, Jakarta 12950
Iran
Jalan Hos Cokroaminoto 110, Menteng, Jakarta Pusat
Iraq
Jalan Teuka Umar 38, Jakarta 10350
Japan
Jalan M.H. Thamrin 24, Jakarta 10350
Jordan
Jalan Denpasar Raya, Blok A XIII, Kav. 1-2, Jakarta 12950
Korea, Democratic People's Republic
Jalen H. R. Rasuna Said, Kav X.5, Jakarta
Korea, Republic
Jalan Jenderal Gotat Subroto 57, Jakarta Selaton
Kuwait
Jalen Denaspar Raya, Blok A XII, Kuningin, Jakarta 12950
Laos
Jalan Kintimani Raya C-15, 33 Kuningan Timur, Jakarta 12950
Malaysia
Jalan H. R. Rasuna Said, Kav. X/6, Kuningan, Jakarta 12950
Mexico
Wisma Nusantara, 4th Floor, Jalan M. H. Thamrin 59, Jakarta 10310
Myanmar
Jalan Haji Agus Salim 109, Jakarta Salatan
New Zealand
Jalan Diponegro 41, Menteng, POB 2439, Jakarta 10310
Pakistan
Jalan Teuku Umar 50, Jakarta 10350
Papua New Guinea
Panin Bank Centre, 6th Floor, Jalan Jenderal Sudirman 1, Jakarta 10270

Peru
Bina Mulia Bldg 2, 3rd Floor, Janan H. R. Rasuna Said, Kav. 11, Kuningan, Jakarta 12950
Philippines
Jalan Imam Bonjol 6-8, Jarkarta 10310
Saudi Arabia
Jalan Teuka Cik Ditiro 42a, Menteng, Jakarta 10310
Singapore
Jalan H. R. Rasuna Said, Blok X/4, Kav.2, Kuningan, jakarta 12950
Sri Lanka
Jalan Diponegoro 70, Jakarta 10320
Syria
Jalan Karong Asem I/8, Jakarta 12950
Thailand
Jalan Imam Bonjol 74, Jakarta 10310
Turkey
Jalan H.R. Rasuna Said, Kav. 1 Kuningan, Jarkarta 12950
United Arab Emirates
Jalan Singaraja Blok C-4 Kav. 16-17, Jakarta Selatan
Vietnam
Jalan Teuku Umar 25, Jakarta
Yemen
Jalan Yosuf Adiwinata 29, Jakarta.

IRAN

Australia
No.11, 23rd St, Khalid Islamabuli Ave, ORP O Box 15875-4334 Abbasabad, Tehran 151387
New Zealand
Avenue Mizra-ye-ShiraziShahid Ali-ye- MizraHassani Street, No.29 (PO Box 11365-436), Tehran

ISRAEL

Australia
Beit Europa 37 Shaul Hamelech Blvd Tel-Aviv 64928
China
222 Rehov Ben Yehuda Tel-Aviv 64928
Colombia
52 Rehov Pinkas, 6th Floor Apt. 26
Tel-Aviv
Costa Rica
13 Rehov Diskin Apt 1
Kiryat Wolfson
Ecuador
Asia House, 4 Rehov Weizman, Tel-Aviv
El Salvador
34 Rehov Rahel Imeinu, Jerusalem 93228
Guatemala
74 Rehov He Be'lyar, Apt 6, Kikar HeMedina, Tel-Aviv 62198
India
Sharbat House 4 Rehov Kaufman, Tel-Aviv
68012
Japan
4 Rehov Weizman Tel-Aviv 64239
Jordan
12 Abba Hillel Silver, Ramat-Gan 52506
Korea
38 Chen Blvd 64166, Tel-Aviv
Mexico
3 Rehov Bograshov, Tel-Aviv 63808
Myanmar
26 Hayarkon, Tel-Aviv
Nepal
21 Komemiyuth Street 46683, Herelia
Panama
10 Rehov He Be'lyar Kikar HaMedina, Tel-Aviv
Peru
37 Rehov Hamarganit Ramat-Gan 52584

Philippines
Merkaz Hatextile 2 Rehov Kaufman Tel-Aviv 68012
Thailand
144 Sderot Shaul Hamelech Tel-Aviv 64367
Turkey
202 Rehov Hayarkon, Tel-Aviv 63405

JAPAN

Afghanistan
Olympia Annex Apt 503, 6-31-21, Jingumae, Shibuya-ku, Tokyo 150
Australia
2-1-14, Mita, Minato-ku, Tokyo 108
Bangladesh
4-15-15, Meguro, Meguro-ku, Tokyo153
Brunei
6-5-2, Kita Shingagawa-ku, Tokyo 141
Cambodia
8-6-9 Akasaka, Minato-ku, Tokyo 107
Chile
Nihon Seimai Akabanebashi Bldg, 8th Floor, 3-1-14, Shiba, Minato-ku, Tokyo
China, People's Republic
3-4-33, Moto Azabu, Minato-ku, Tokyo 106
Colombia
3-10-53, Kami Osaki, Shinagawa-ku, Tokyo 141
Costa Rica
Kowa Bldg, No. 38, Room 901, 4-12-24, Nishi Azabu, Minato-ku, Tokyo 106
Ecuador
Kowa Bldg, No. 38, Room 806, 4-12-24, Nishi Azabu, Minato-ku, Tokyo 106
El Salvador
Kowa Bldg, No. 38, 8th Floor, 4-12-24, Nishi Azabu, Minato-ku, Tokyo 106
Fiji
Noa Bldg, 14th Floor, 2-3-5, Azabudai, Minato-ku, Tokyo 106
Guatemala
Kowa Bldg, No. 38, Room 905, 4-12-24, Nishi Azabu, Minato-ku, Tokyo 106
India
2-2-11, Kudan Minami, Chiyoda-ku,Tokyo 102
Indonesia
5-2-9, Higashi Gotanda, Shinagawa-ku, Tokyo 141
Iran
3-10-32, Minami Azabu, Minato-ku, Tokyo 106
Iraq
8-4-7, Akasaka, Minato-ku, Tokyo 107
Israel
3, Niban-cho, Chiyoda-ku, Tokyo 102
Jordan
Chiyoda House, 4th Floor, 2-17-8, Nagata-cho, Chiyoda-ku, Tokyo 100
Korea, Republic
1-2-5, Minami Azabu, Minato-ku, Tokyo 106
Kuwait
4-13-12, Mita, Minato-ku, Tokyo 108
Laos
3-3-22, Nishi Azabu, Minato-ku, Tokyo 106
Lebanon
Chiyoda House, 5th Floor, 2-17-8, Nagata-cho, Chiyoda-ku, Tokyo 100
Malaysia
20-16, Nanpeidai-cho, Shibuya-ku, Toyko 150
Marshall Islands
Meiji Park Heights 101, 9-9, Minamimoto-machi, Shinjuku-ku, Tokyo 106
Mexico
2-15-1, Nagata-cho, Chiyoda-ku, Tokyo 100

Micronesia
Reinanzaka Bldg, 2nd Floor, 1-14-2, Akasaka, Minato-ku, Tokyo 107
Mongolia
Pine Crest Mansion, 21-4, Kamiyama-cho, Shibuya-ku, Tokyo 150
Myanmar
4-8-26, Kita Shinagawa, Shinagawa-ku, Tokyo 140
Nepal
7-14-9, Todoroki, Setagaya-ku, Tokyo 158
New Zealand
20-40, Kamiyama-cho, Shibuya-ku, Tokyo 150
Nicaragua
Kowa Bldg, No. 38, Room 903, 9th Floor, 4-12-24, Nishi Azabu, Minato-ku, Tokyo 106
Oman
Silva Kingdom Bldg, 3rd Floor, 2-28-11, Sendagaya, Shi-buya-ku, Tokyo 151
Pakistan
2-14-9, Moto Azabu, Minato-ku, Tokyo 106
Panama
Kowa Bldg, No. 38, Room 902, 4-12-24, Nishi Azabu, Minato-ku, Tokyo 106
Papua New Guinea
Mita Kokusai Bldg, Room 313, 3rd Floor, 1-4-28, Mita, Minato-ku, Tokyo 108
Peru
4-4-27, Higashi, Shibuya-ku, Tokyo 150
Philippines
11-24, Nampeidai-machi, Shibuya-ku, Tokyo
Qatar
6-8-7, Akasaka, Minato-ku, Tokyo 107
Saudi Arabia
1-53, Azubu Nagasaka-cho, Minato-ku, Tokyo 106
Singapore
5-12-3, Roppongi, Minato-ku, Tokyo 106
Sri Lanka
1-14-1, Akasaka, Minato-ku, Tokyo 107
Thailand
4-21-9, Kami Osaki, Shinagawa-ku, Tokyo 141
Turkey
2-33-6, Jingumae, Shibuya-ku, Tokyo 150
United Arab Emirates
9-10, Nanpeidai-cho, Shibuya-ku, Tokyo 150
Vietnam
50-11, Moto Yoyogi-cho, Shibuya-ku, Tokyo 151
Yemen
Kowa Bldg, No. 38, Room 807, 4-12-24, Nishi Azabu, Minato-ku, Tokyo 106

JORDAN

Australia
Between 4th and 5th Circles, Zahran Street, Jabel, Amman, ORPO Box 35201, Amman, Jordan
Israeli
Forte Grand Hotel, Amman, Jordan
New Zealand
4th Floor, Khalaf Building 99, King Hussein Street, PO Box 586, Amman, Jordan

KAZAKSTAN

Afganistan
Micr.8, 52 Shaliapin St, Corner Mate Zalka, Hotel Molodezhnaya, Kazakstan
Australia
20-a Kazybek St, Kazakstan
China
137 Furmanov St, Corner Kabanbai batyr St, Kazakstan
India
71 Maulenov St, Kazakstan
Iran
119 Kabanbai batyr St, Corner Michurin St, Kazakstan

Israel
87 Zheltoksan St, corner Kazybek bi St, Kazakstan
Japan
36 Micr. Samal-1, 4 floor, Kazakstan
Korea, Rep
Micr. Ainabulak-3, 58 Voronezhskaya St, Kazakstan
Kyrghystan
68-a Amangeldy St, Corner Kabanbai batyr St, Kazakstan

KIRIBATI

Australia
POB 77, Bairiki, Tarawa
China, People's Republic
Bairiki, Tarawa
New Zealand
POB 53, Bairiki, Tarawa

KOREA, REP OF (SOUTH)

Australia
Kyobo Bldg, 11th Floor, 1, 1-ka, Chongno, Chongno-ku, Seoul 110-714
Bangladesh
7-3, Hannam 1-dong, Yongsan-ku, Seoul
Brunei
1-94, Dongbinggo-dong, Yongsan-ku, Seoul 140-230
Chile
Youngpoong Bldg, 9th Floor, 142, Nonhyun-dong, Kangnam-ku, Seoul
China, People's Republic
83, 2-ka, Myong-dong, Chung-ku, Seoul
Colombia
Kyobo Bldg, 13th Floor, 1-ka, Chongno, Chongno-ku, Seoul
Costa Rica
101, Riverside Village, Dongbuichon-dong, Yongsan-ku, Seoul
Ecuador
262-58, Itaewon-dong, Yongsan-ku, Seoul
El Salvador
Graden Tower Bldg, Rm 1002, 98-78, Wooni-dong, Chongno-ku, Seoul 110-350
Guatemala
602, Garden Tower Bldg, 98-78 Wooni-dong, Chongno-ku, Seoul 110-350
India
37-3, Hannam-dong, Yongsan-ku, Seoul 140-210
Indonesia
55, Yoido-dong, Yongdeungpo-ku, Seoul 150-010
Iran
726-126, Hannam-dong, Yongsan-ku, Seoul
Israel
Dae-kong Bldg, 15th Floor, 823-21, Yoksam-dong, Kangnam-ku, Seoul
Japan
18-11, Chunghak-dong, Chongno-ku, Seoul
Kazakhstan
32-15, Nonhyun-dong, Kangnam-ku, Seoul
Kuwait
309-15, Dongbinggo-dong, Yongsan-ku, Seoul
Lebanon
1-48, Dongbinggo-dong, Yongsan-ku, Seoul
Malaysia
4-1, Hannam-dong, Yongsan-ku, Seoul 140-210
Mexico
33-6, Hannam-dong, Yongsan-ku, Seoul 140-210
Mongolia
1-104, Riverside Village, 300-24, Dongbuichon-dong, Yongsan-ku, Seoul
Myanmar
723-1, Hannam-dong, Yongsan-ku, seoul 140-210

New Zealand
Kyobo Bldg, Rooms 1802-1805, 1, 1-ka, Chongno, Chongno-ku, CPOB 1059, Seoul
Nicaragua
547-8, Kuui-dong, Kwangjin-ku, Seoul
Oman
309-3, Dongbinggo-dong, Yongsan-ku, Seoul
Pakistan
310-49, Dongbinggo-dong, Yongsan-ku, Seoul 140-230
Panama
1101, Garden Tower Building, 98-78, Wooni-dong, Chongno-ku, Seoul
Papua New Guinea
36-1, Hannam 1-dong, Yongsan-ku, Seoul
Peru
Namhan Bldg, 6th Floor, 76-42, Hannam-dong, Yongsan-ku, Seoul
Philippines
641-11, Yeoksam-dong, Kangnam-ku, Seoul
Qatar
1-77, Dongbinggo-dong, Yongsan-ku, Seoul
Saudi Arabia
1-112, 2-ka, Shinmun-no, Chongno-ku, Seoul
Singapore
Citicorp Center Bldg, 89-29, 2-ka, Shinmum-no, Chongno-ku, Seoul 110-062
Sri Lanka
Kyobo Bldg, Rm 2004, 1-1, 1-ka, Chongo, Chongno-ku, Seoul
Thailand
653-7, Hannam-dong, Yongsan-ku, Seoul
Turkey
726-116, Hannam-dong, Yongsan-ku, Seoul
United Arab Emirates
5-5, Hannam-dong, Yongsan-ku, Seoul
Vietnam
28-58, Samchong-dong, Chongno-ku, Seoul 140-210
Yemen
657-40, Hannam-dong, Yongsan-ku, Seoul 140-210

KOREA DPR (NORTH)

India
Taedongkang district, 6 Munsudong, Pyongyang
Indonesia
5 Foreigners' Bldg, Taedongkang District, Munsudong, POB 178 Pyongyang
Iran
Taedongkang District, Munnhongdong, Monsu St, Pyongyang
Pakistan
Taedongkang District, Munsudong, Pyongyang
Syria
Taedongkang District, Munsudong, Pyongyang.

KUWAIT

Afganistan
PO Box 22944, Safat 13090
Bahrain
PO Box 196, Safat 13002
Bangladesh
PO Box 22344, Safat 13084
Bhutan
PO Box 1510, Safat 13016
China
PO Box 2346, Safat 13024
India
PO Box 1450, Safat 13015
Indonesia
PO Box 21560, Safat 13076

Iran
PO Box 4686, Safat 13047
Japan
PO Box 2304, Safat 13024
Korea
PO Box 4272, Safat 13043
Lebanon
PO Box 253, Safat 13003
Malaysia
PO Box 4105, Safat 13042
Oman
PO Box 21975, Safat 13080
Pakistan
PO Box 988, Safat 13010
Philippines
PO Box 26288, Safat 13123
Qatar
PO Box 1825, Safat 13019
Saudi Arabia
PO Box 20498, Safat 13065
Sri Lanka
PO Box 13212, Kaifan 71952
Syria
PO box 25600, Safat 13116
Thailand
PO Box 66647, Bayan
Turkey
PO Box 20627, Safat 13067
United Arab Emirates
PO Box 1828, Safat 13019

LAOS

Australia
rue Pandit J. Nehru, quartier Phone Xay, BP 292, Vientiane
Brunei
No.333, Unit 25, Ban Phonxay, Xaysettha District, Vientiane
China, People's Republic
ruelle Uat Nak, Muang Sisattanak, BP 898, Vientiane
India
rue That Luang, BP 225 Vientiane
Indonesia
ave Phone Keng, BP 277, Vientiane
Japan
rue Sisangvone, Vientiane
Korea, Democratic People's Republic
quartier Wawt Nak, Vientiane
Malaysia
place That Luang, quartier Nongbone, POB 789, Vientiane
Mongolia
rue Thadeua, BP 370, Vientiane
Myanmar
rue Sok Paluang, Vientiane
Thailand
ave Phone Keng, Vientiane
Vietnam
85 rue That Luang, Vientiane

LEBANON

Australia
Farra Bldg, Bliss Street, Beirut

MALAYSIA

Australia
6 Jalen Yap Kwan Seng, 50450 Kuala Lumpur
Bangladesh
204-1 Jalen Ampang, 50450 Kuala Lumpar

Brunei
Wisma Sin Heap Lee, 8th Floor, Jalen Tun Razak, 50400 Kuala Lumpar
China, People's Republic
229 Jalan Ampang, 50450 Kuala Lumpar
India
Wisma Selangor Dredging, 20th Floor, West Block, 142c Jalan Ampang, 50450 Kuala Lumpar
Indonesia
233 Jalan Tun Razak, POB 10889, 50400 Kuala Lumpar
Iran
1 Lorong U Thant Satu, 55000 Kuala Lumpar
Iraq
2 Jalan Langgak Golf, off Jalan Tun Razak, 55000 Kuala Lumpar
Japan
11 Pesiaran Stonor, off Jalan Tun Razak, 50450 Kuala Lumpar
Kazakhstan
Menara Haw Par, 28th Floor, Jalan Sultan Ismail, 50250 Kuala Lumpar
Korea, Democratic People's Republic
203 Jalan Ampang, Kuala Lumpar
Korea, Republic
Wisma MCA, 22nd Floor, 163 Jalan Ampang, Kuala Lumpar
Laos
108 Jalan Damai, off Jalan Ampang, Kuala Lumpar
Myanmar
7 Jalan U Thant, 55000 Kuala Lumpar
New Zealand
Menara IMC, 21st Floor, 8 Jalan Sultan Ismail, 50250 Kuala Lumpar
Pakistan
132 Jalan Ampang, 50450 Kuala Lumpar
Philippines
1 Changkat Kia Peng, 50450 Kuala Lumpar
Saudi Arabia
11 Jalan Ampang, 55000 Kuala Lumpar
Singapore
209 Jalan Tun Razak, 50400 Kuala Lumpar
Sri Lanka
8 Jalan Murni, off Jalan Damai, 55000 Kuala Lumpar
Thailand
206 Jalan Ampang, Kuala Lumpar
Turkey
118 Jalan U Thant, 55000 Kuala Lumpar
Vietnam
4 Pesiaran Stonor, 50450
Kuala Lumpar

MALDIVES

India
H. Athireege-Aage, Ameeru Ahmed Magu, Malé
Pakistan
Penta Green, Majeedhee Magu, Malé
Sri Lanka
Sakeena Manzil, Medhuziyaaraiyh Magu, Malé

MEXICO

Australia
Plaza Polanco, Jaime Balmes No.11, B-Tower 10 Floor, Col. Polanco, México D.F 11510
Colombia
Paseo de la Reforma No. 1620, Col, Cuauhtémoc, México D.F 11000
Costa Rica
Rio Poo No.113, Col. Cuauhtémoc, México D.F 06500
Chile
Monte Urales No.460 1st Floor, Col Lomas Chapultepec, México D.F 11000

China, People's Republic
Rio Magdalena No.172, Col. Tizapan san Angel, México D.F 0109
Ecuador
Tennyson No.217, Col. Chapultepec Polanco, México D.F. 11560
Guatemala
Explanada No. 1025, Col. Lomas de Chapultepec, México D.F. 11000
Indonesia
Julio Verne No.27, Col. Chapultepec Polanco, México D.F. 11560
Iran
Paseo de la Reforma No. 2350, Col. Lomas Altas, México D.F. 11950
Iraq
Paseo de la Reforma No. 1875, Col. Lomas de Chapultepec, México D.F. 11000
Israel
Sierra Madre No.215, Col. Lomas de Chapultepec, México D.F. 11000
Japan
Paseo de la Reforma No. 395, Col. Cuauhtémoc, México D.F. 06500
Korea
Lope de Armendáriz No. 110, Col. Lomas Virreyes, México D.F. 11000
Lebanon
Julio Verne No. 8, Col. Chapultepec Polanc, México D.F. 11560
New Zealand
J.L Lagrange No. 103 10th Floor, Col. Los Morales Polanco, México D.F. 11510
Nicaragua
Valle de Riveria No.120, Col. Lomas de Chapultepec, México D.F. 11000
Pakistan
Hegel No.512, Col. Chapultepec Morales, México D.F. 11570
Panama
Schiller No. 326, Col. Chapultepec Morales, México D.F.
Peru
Paseo de la Reforma No.2601, Col. Lomas Reforma, México D.F. 11550
Philippines
Calderón de la Barca No. 240, Col. Polanco, México D.F. 11550
Saudi Arabia
Paseo de la Reforma No. 607, Col. Lomas Reforma, México D.F. 11020
Vietnam
Sierra Ventura No.255, Col. Lomas de Chapultepec, México D.F. 11000
Thailand
Sierra Vertientes No. 1030, Col Lomas de Chapultepec, México D.F. 11000
Turkey
Paseo de las Palmas No. 1525, Col. Lomas de Chapultepec, México D.F. 11000

FEDERATED STATES OF MICRONESIA

Australia
POB S, Kolonia, Pohnpei, Eastern Caroline Islands, FM 96941
China, People's Republic
Kolonia, Pohnpei, Eastern Caroline Islands FM 96941
Japan
Pami Bldg, 3rd Floor, POB 1837, Kolonia, Pohnpei, Eastern Caroline Islands, FM 96941

MONGOLIA

China People's Republic
Dzaluuchuudyn Orgon Choloo 5, Ulan Bator (CPO Box 627)
India
Enh Tayvny Gudamj 26, Ulan Bator (CPO Box 691

Japan
Zaluuchuudyn Gudamj 12, Ulan Bator 13 (CPO Box 1011)
Korea, Democratic People's Republic
Negdsen Undestniy Gudamj 12, Ulan Bator (CPO Box 671)
Korea, Republic
Karl Marksyn Gudamj 10, Ulan Bator (CPO Box 1039)
Laos
Ih Toy ruu 59, Ulan Bator (CPO Box 1030)
Vietnam
Enh Tayvny Orgon Choloo 47, Ulan Bator

MYANMAR (BURMA)

Bangladesh
56 Kaba Aye Pagoda Rd, Yangon
China People's, Republic
1 Pyidaungsu Yeiktha Rd, Yangon
India
545-547 Merchant St, Yangon
Indonesia
100 Pyidaungsu Yeiktha Rd, Yangon
Israel
49 Pyay Rd, Dagon PO, Yangon
Japan
100 Natmauk Rd, Yangon
Korea, Republic
97 University Ave, Yangon
Laos
POB 1550; A1 Diplomatic Headquarters, Taw Win Rd, Yangon
Malaysia
82 Pyidaungsu Yeiktha Rd, Yangon
Nepal
16 Natmauk Yeiktha Rd, Yangon
Pakistan
A4 Diplomatic Quarters, Pyi Rd, Yangon
Philippines
50 Pyay Rd, 6½ Mile, Yangon
Singapore
287 Pyi Rd, Yangon
Sri Lanka
34 Taw Win Rd, POB 1150, Yangon
Thailand
45 Pyay Rd, 6½ Mile, Yangdon
Vietnam
36 Wingaba Rd, Yangdon

NAURU

China (Taiwan)
POB 294, Nauru

NEPAL

Australia
Bansbari, Kathmandu
Bangladesh
Maharajgunj, Ring Rd, Municipality Ward No.22, Shanti Ashram, Kitta 9, POB 789, Kathmandu
China, People's Republic
Baluwatar, Kathmandu
India
Lainchaur, Kathmandu
Israel
Lazimpat, POB 371, Kathmandu
Japan
Durbar Marg, POB 264, Kathmandu
Korea, Democratic People's Republic
Lalitpur, Kathmandu
Korea, Republic
Himshah, Red Cross Marg, Tahachal, Kathmandu

Myanmar
Chakupat, Patan Gate, Lalitpur, Kathmandu
Pakistan
Panipokhari, POB 202, Kathmandu
Thailand
Bansbari, Ward No.3, POB 3333, Kathmandu

NEW ZEALAND

Australia
72-78 Hobson St, Thorndon, POB 4036, Wellington
Chile
Willis Corroon House, 7th Floor, 1-3 Willeston St, POB 3861, Wellington
China, People's Republic
2-6 Glenmore St, Wellington
Colombia
Wool House, Level 11, 10 Brandon St, POB 798, Wellington
Fiji
31 Pipitea St, Thorndon, POB 3940, Wellington
India
FAI House, 10th Floor, 180 Molesworth St, POB 4045, Wellington
Indonesia
70 Glen Rd, Kelburn, POB 3543, Wellington
Iran
POB 10-249, The Terrace, Wellington
Israel
DB Tower, 15th Floor, 111 The Terrace, POB 2171, Welllington
Japan
Norwich Insurance House, 7th and 8th Floors, 3-11 Hunter St, POB 6340, Wellington 1
Korea, Republic
ASB Bank Tower, Level 11, 2 Hunter St, POB 11-143, Wellington
Malaysia
10 Washington Ave, Brooklyn, POB 9422, Wellington
Mexico
GRE House, Level 8, 111-115 Customhouse Quay, POB 11-510, Manners St, Wellington
Papua New Guinea
279 Willis St, POB 197, Wellington
Peru
Cigna house, Level 8, 40 Mercer St, POB 2566, Wellington
Philippines
50 Hobson St, Thorndon, POB 12-042, Wellington
Samoa
1a Wesley Rd, Kelburn, POB 1430, Wellington
Singapore
17 Kabul St, Khandallah, POB 13140, Wellington
Thailand
2 Cook St Karori, POB 17-226, Wellington
Turkey
15-17 Murphy St, POB 12-248, Wellington

OMAN

New Zealand
PO Box 520, Muscat

PAKISTAN

Afganistan
176 Shalimar 7/3, Islamabad
Australia
Diplomatic Enclave 2, Plot 17, Sector G4/4, POB 1046, Islamabad
Bangladesh
24, St 28, F-6/1, Islamabad
Chile
Islamabad
China, People's Republic
Ramna 4, Diplomatic Enclave, Islamabad

India
G-5, Diplomatic Enclave, Islamabad
Indonesia
Diplomatic Enclave, Ramna 5/4, POB 1019, Islamabad
Iran
222-238, St.2, G-5/1, Diplomatic Enclave, Islamabad
Iraq
1, St 15, F-7/2, Islamabad
Japan
Plot No.53-70, Ramna 5/4, Diplomatic Enclave 1, Islamabad
Jordan
131, St 14, E-7, Islamabad
Kazakhstan
House No.2, St 4, Sector F-8/3, Islamabad
Korea, Democratic People's Republic
9, St 89, Ramna 6/3, Islamabad
Korea, Republic
St 29, Block 13, Diplomatic Enclave-II, POB 1087, Islamabad
Kuwait
University Rd, Diplomatic Enclave, Islamabad
Lebanon
24, Khayaban-e-Iqual, Shalimar F-6/3, Islamabad
Malaysia
224, Shalimar 7/4, Islamabad
Myanmar
12/1, St 13, F-7/2, Islamabad
Nepal
H. No.11, St 84, Atatürk Ave, G-6/4, Islamabad
New Zealand
Diplomatic Enclave, Islamabad
Oman
440 Bazar Rd, Ramna 6/4, Islamabad
Philippines
19, St 1, Shalimar 6/3, POB 1052, Islamabad
Qatar
201 Masjid Rd, Shalimar 6/4, Islamabad
Saudi Arabia
1, St 4, F-6/3, Islamabad
Singapore
Islamabad
Sri Lanka
315c, Khayaban-e-Iqbal, F-7/2, Islamabad
Syria
30 Hill Rd, Shalimar 6/3, Islamabad
Thailand
10, St 33, Shalimar 8/1, Islamabad
Turkey
58 Atatürk Ave, G-6/3, Islamabad
Turkmenistan
H 22a, Nazim-Ud-Din Rd, Sector F-7/1, Islamabad
United Arab Emirates
Plot No. 1-22, Diplomatic Enclave, Islamabad
Yemen
16, St 17, F-7/2, POB 1523, Islamabad 44000

PANAMA

Colombia
Piso 6 Calle Manuel M Icaza, 12 Panamá
Costa Rica
Embajada de Cuba Avenidas Cuba y Ecuador, Panamá
Chile
Embajada de Chile Calle E Méndez y Via Espanã, Panama
Ecuador
Embajada del Ecuador Calle Manuel Icaza, 12 Panamá
El Salvador
Embajada de El Salvador Avenida Manuel Espinosa Batista, Panamá

Japan
Embajada del Japon Edificio Sede Propia Calles 50 y 60-E Obarrio, Panamá
Mexico
Embajada de Mexico Edificio Bancomer, Piso 5 Calle 50 y 53, Panamá
Nicaragua
Embajada de Nicaragua Calle José de san martin, 31 Panamá
Peru
Embajada del Perú Calles Elvira Méndez y 52, Panamá

PAPUA NEW GUINEA

Australia
POB 129, Waigani, NCD
China, People's Republic
POB 1351, Boroko, NCD
India
Port Moresby
Indonesia
POB 7165, Boroko, NCD
Japan
ANG House, Hunter St, POB 1040, Port Moresby
Korea, Republic
POB 381, Port Moresby
Malaysia
POB 1400, Port Moresby
New Zealand
Embassy Drive, POB 1051, Waigani, NCD
Philippines
POB 5916, Boroko, NCD

PHILIPPINES

Australia
Doña Salustiana Dee Ty Bldg, Ground-5th Floors, 104 Paseo de Roxas, cnr Perea St, Makati, 1200 Metro Manila
Bangladesh
UniversalRe Bldg, 2nd Floor, 106 Paseo de Roxas, Legaspi Village, Makati, Metro Manila
Brunei
Bank of the Philippine Islands Bldg, 11th Floor, Ayala Ave, cnr Paseo de Roxas, Makati, 1226 Metro Manila
Chile
Doña Salustiana Dee Ty Bldg, 6th Floor, 104 Paseo de Roxas, Legaspi Village, Makati, Metro Manila
China, People's Republic
4896 pasay Rd, Dasmariñas Village, Makati, Metro Manila
Colombia
Aurora Tower, 18th Floor, Araneta Center, Quezon City, Metro Manila
India
2190 Paraiso St, Dasmariñas Village, Makati, Metro Manila
Indonesia
Indonesia Embassy Bldg, 185 Salcedo St, Legaspi Village, Makati, Metro Manila
Iran
Don Jacinto Bldg, 4th Floor, cnr Salcedo and de la Rosa Sts, Legaspi Village, Makati, Metro Manila
Iraq
2261 Avocado St, Dasmariñas Village, Makati, Metro Manila
Israel
Trafalgar Plaza, 23rd Floor, H.V. dela Costa St, Salcedo Village, Makati, 1200 Metro Manila
Japan
2627 Roxas Blvd, Pasay City, 1300 Metro Manila
Jordan
Golden Rock Bldg, 3rd Floor, Suite 502, 168 Salcedo St, Legaspi Village, Makati, Metro Manila
Korea, Republic
ALPAP 1 Bldg, 3rd Floor, 140 Alfaro St, Salcedo Village, Makati, Metro Manila

Malaysia
107 Tordesillas St, Salcedo Village, Makati, 1200 Metro Manila
Mexico
Adamson Center Bldg, 2nd Floor, 1221 Alfaro St, Salcedo Village, Makati, Metro Manila
Myanmar
Basic Petroleum Bldg, 4th Floor, 104 carlos Palanca Jr St, Legaspi Village, Makati, Metro Manila
New Zealand
Far East Bank Centre, 23rd Floor, Sen. Gil J. Puyat Ave, POB 3228, Makati, Metro Manila
Pakistan
Alexander House, 6th Floor, 132 Amorsolo St, Legaspi Village, Makati, Metro Manila
Panama
Victoria Bldg, 5th Floor, 429 United Nations Ave, Ermita, Metro Manila
Papua New Guinea
2280 Magnolia St, Dasmariñas Village, Makati, Metro Manila
Peru
F.M Lopez Bldg, cnr Legaspi and Herrera Sts, Legaspi Village, Makati, Metro Manila
Qatar
1346 Palm Avenue, Dasmariñas Village, Makati, Metro Manila
Saudi Arabia
Saudi Embassy Bldg, 389 Sen. Gil J. Puyat Ave Ext., Makati, Metro Manila
Singapore
ODC International Plaza Bldg, 6th Floor, 219 Salcedo St, Legaspi Village, Makati, Metro Manila
Thailand
107 Rada St, Legaspi Village, Makati, 1229 Metro Manila
Turkey
2268 Paraiso St, Dasmariñas Village, Makati, Metro Manila
United Arab Emirates
Renaissance Bldg, 2nd Floor, Sakedo St, Legaspi Village, Makati, Metro Manila
Vietnam
554 Vito Cruz, Malate, Metro Manila

SAMOA, (FORMERLY WESTERN SAMOA)

Australia
Beach Rd, POB 704, Apia
China, People's Republic
Vailima, Apia
New Zealand
Beach Rd, Apia

SINGAPORE

Australia
25 Napier St, Singapore 258507
Bangladesh
101 Thomson Rd, 06-07 United Sq, Singapore 307591
Brunei
325 Tanglin Rd, Singapore 247955
Chile
105 Cecil St, 25-00 The Octagon, Singapore 069534
China, People's Republic
70-76 Dalvey Rd, Singapore 1025
India
31 Grange Rd, India House, Singapore 239702
Indonesia
7 Chatsworth Rd, Singapore 1024
Israel
58 Dalvey Rd, Singapore 259463
Japan
16 Nassim Rd, Singapore 258390

Korea, Democratic People's Republic
133 Cecil St, 06-01A Keck Seng Tower, Singapore 0106
Korea, Republic
101 Thomson Rd, 10-02/04 United Sq, Singapore 1130
Malaysia
301 Jervois Rd, Singapore 249077
Myanmar
15 St Martin's Drive, Singapore 1025
New Zealand
391a Orchard Rd, 15-06/10 Ngee Ann City, Singapore 238873
Pakistan
20a Nassim Rd, Singapore 1025
Panama
16 raffles Quay, 41-06 Hong Leong Bldg, Singapore 0104
Philippines
20 Nassim Rd, Singapore 258395
Saudi Arabia
10 Nassim Rd, Singapore 258377
Sri Lanka
Newton Rd, 13-07 Goldhill Plaza, Singpore 1130
Thailand
370 Orchard Rd, Singapore 238870
Turkey
20b Nassim Rd, Singapore 258397

SOLOMON ISLANDS

Australia
Mud Alley, POB 589, Honiara
China (Taiwan)
Lengakiki Ridge, POB 586, Honiara
Japan
National Provident Fund Bldg, Mendana Ave, POB 560, Honiara
New Zealand
Mendana Ave, POB 697, Honiara
Papua New Guinea
POB 1109, Honiara

SRI LANKA

Australia
3 Cambridge Place, POB 742, Colombo 7
Bangladesh
47 Sir Ernest de Silva Mawatha, Colombo 7
China, People's Republic
191 Dharmapala Mawatha, Colombo 7
India
36-38 Galle Rd, Colombo 3
Indonesia
1 Police Park Terrace, Colombo 5
Iraq
19 Barnes Rd, POB 79, Colombo 7
Japan
20 Gergory's Rd, POB 822, Colombo 7
Korea, Republic
98 Dharmapala Mawatha, Colombo 7
Maldives
25 Melbourne Ave, Colombo 4
Myanmar
65 Ward Place, Colombo 7
Pakistan
211 De Saram Place, Colombo 10
Thailand
43 Dr C. W. W. Kannangara Mawatha, Colombo 7

TAIWAN

Costa Rica
6th Floor 1-1, 16 Lane 189
Sec. 1 Cheng Tai Rd, Wu Ku Rural Tapei

El Salvador
15 Lane 34, Ku Kang Rd, Shih Lin, Taipei 11102
Guatemala
12 Lane 88, Chein Kuo North Rd, Sec. 1, Taipei
Nicaragua
3rd Floor, 222-6 Jyi Shyan Rd, Lu Chow, Taipei
Panama
6th Floor, 111 Sung Chiang Rd, Taipei

THAILAND

Australia
37 Tahnon Sathorn Tai, Bangkok 10120
Bangladesh
6-8 Charoenmitr, Soi 63 Thanon Sukhumvit, Bangkok
Brunei
154 Soi 14, Ekamai, Sukhumvit 63, Bangkok 10110
Cambodia
185 Thanon Ratchadamri, Lumpini, Bangkok 10330
Chile
15 Soi 61 Thanon Sukhumvit, Prakanong, Bangkok 10110
China, People's Republic
57 Thanon Ratchadapiesk, Bangkok 10310
India
46 Soi Prasarnmitr, 23 Thanon Sukhumvit, Bangkok 10110
Indonesia
600-602 Thanon Phetchburi, Bangkok 10400
Iran
602 Thanon Sukhumvit, Bangkok 10110
Iraq
47 Thanon Pradpit, Samsen Nai, Phya Thai, Bangkok 10400
Israel
Ocean Tower II, 25th Floor, 75 Sukhumvit Soi 19, Thanon Asoke, Bangkok 10110
Japan
1674 Thanon Phetchburi Tadmai, Bangkok 10130
Korea, Democratic People's Republic
314/1 Soi Viraya, Thanon Sri Ayuthaya, Bangkok 10400
Korea, Republic
23 Thiam Ruammit, Huay Kwang, Thanon Samsen, Bangkok 10310
Laos
193 Thanon Sathorn Tai, Bangkok 10120
Malaysia
Regent House, 15th Floor, 183 Thanon Rajdamri, Pathumwan, Bangkok 10330
Myanmar
132 Thanon Sathorn Nua, Bangkok 10500
Nepal
189 Soi 71, Thanon Sukhumvit, Bangkok 10110
New Zealand
93 Thanon Witthayu, POB 2719, Bangkok 10500
Pakistan
31 Soi Nana Nua (3), Thanon Sukhumvit, Bangkok 10110
Philippines
760 Thanon Sukhumvit, Bangkok 10110
Saudi Arabia
Sathorn Thani Bldg, 10th Floor, 90 Thanon Sathorn Nua, Bangkok 10500
Singapore
129 Thanon Sathorn Tai, Bangkok 10120
Sri Lanka
48/3 Soi 1, Thanon Sukhumvit, Bangkok 10500
Turkey
61/1 Soi Chatsan, Thanon Suthisarn, Bangkok 10310
Vietnam
83/1 Thanon Witthayu, Bangkok 10330

TONGA

Australia
Salote Rd, Nuku'alofa
China (Taiwan)
Holomui Rd, POB 842, Nuku'alofa
New Zealand
cnr Taufa'ahau and Salote Rds, POB 830,
Nuku'alofa

Singapore
41-43 Tran Phu, Hanoi
Thailand
63-65 Hoang Dieu, Hanoi

UNITED ARAB EMIRATES

India
PO Box 4090
Abu Dhabi
Philippines
Villa No 1
Naida Street
PO Box 3215
Abu Dhabi

VANUATU

Australia
KPMG House, POB 111, Port Vila
China, People's Republic
PMB 071, Port Vila
New Zealand
POB 161, Port Vila

VIETNAM

Australia
Van Phuc Compound, Ba Dinh District, Hanoi
Cambodia
71 Tran Hung Doa, Hanoi
China, People's Republic
46 Hoang Dieu, Hanoi
India
58-60 Tran Hung Dao, Hanoi
Indonesia
50 Ngo Quyen, Hanoi
Iran
54 Tran Phu St, Ba Dinh District, Hanoi
Iraq
66 Tran Hung Dao, Hanoi
Israel
68 Nguyen Thai Hoc, Hanoi
Japan
61 Trung Chinh, Hanoi
Korea, Democratic People's Republic
25 Cao Ba Quat, Hanoi
Korea, Republic
29 Ngyuen Dinh Chieu, Hanoi
Laos
22 Tran Binh Trong, Hanoi
Malaysia
A3 Van Phuc Residential Quarter, Hanoi
Mongolia
39 Tran Phu, Hanoi
Myanmar
A3 Van Phuc Diplomatic Quarter, Hanoi
New Zealand
32 Hang Bai, Hanoi
Philippines
27a Tran Hung Dao, Hanoi